Crockford's Clerical Directory
1991/92

15020

2

London's own Mission needs your help

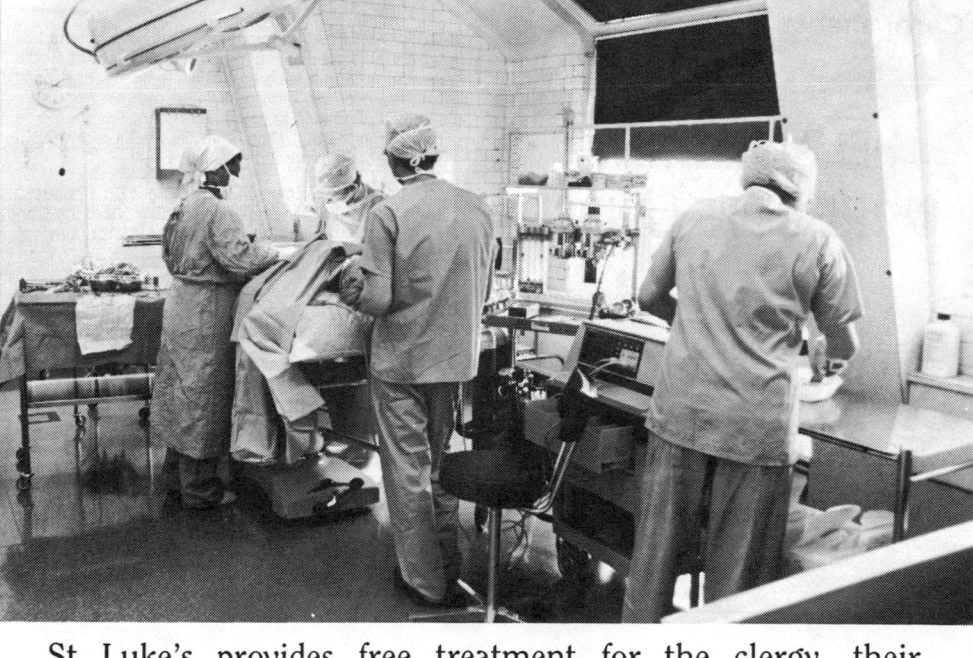
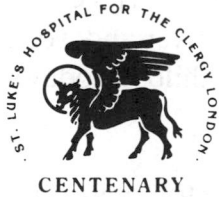

THE MOTHERS' UNION

(Incorporated by Royal Charter)

★ **THE M.U.** has a branch in most parishes. Behind each one are the resources of the largest voluntary body in the Anglican Communion. With over 490,000 members we are at work in every diocese in the British Isles and in 195 dioceses overseas.

★ **THE M.U.'s** purpose is to strengthen and preserve marriage and Christian family life. We care and share through prayer and work in both the joys and problems of being a parent or child in today's world.

★ **THE M.U.** exists to love and serve. If you would like to know more about us, please contact the Central Secretary, Mrs Margaret Chapman, MA, at The Mary Sumner House, 24 Tufton Street, London SW1P 3RB (telephone 071-222 5533).

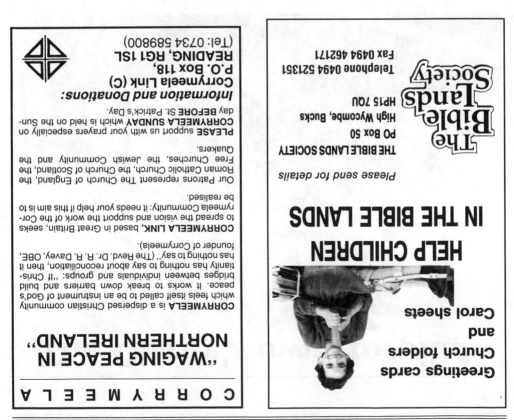

CORPORATION OF THE

SONS OF THE CLERGY

Founded A.D. 1655   Incorporated by Royal Charter 1678

For assisting Clergymen of the Anglican Church and their Widows and Dependants, and for providing Grants for Education, Maintenance or Apprenticeship of Children of the Clergy of the Dioceses of the United Kingdom, Ireland and the Mission Field

Office: 1 DEAN TRENCH STREET, WESTMINSTER LONDON, SW1P 3HB

Telephone: 071-799 3696 & 071-222 5887
(Charity registration number = 207736)

THE COURT OF ASSISTANTS

President:

THE ARCHBISHOP OF CANTERBURY

Vice-President:

The Right Honourable The LORD TEMPLEMAN, M.B.E.

TREASURERS:
THE VISCOUNT CHURCHILL
REAR ADMIRAL D. W. BAZALGETTE CB
CANON J. ROBINSON, BD, FKC

ASSISTANTS

THE BISHOP OF ARGYLL & THE ISLES and PRIMUS
THE BISHOP OF ARMAGH
R. J. ASKWITH, Esq., B.A., FRGS
C. F. BADCOCK, Esq., M.A.
T. D. BAXENDALE, ESQ.
P. W. BOORMAN, Esq., M.A.
C. B. BYFORD, Esq., O.B.E., A.T.I.
C. P. G. CHAVASSE, Esq. M.A.
MAJOR P. C. CLARKE, C.V.O.
H. C. COTTERILL, Esq., K.St.J., F.I.A.
BRIGADIER G. B. CURTIS, O.B.E., M.C.
R. H. N. DASHWOOD, Esq.
J. C. DAUKES, Esq.
THE VENERABLE K. GIBBONS, B.Sc.
A. P. H. GILLET, Esq., M.A., F.R.I.C.S.

PAUL GRIFFIN, Esq., M.B.E., M.A.
THE VENERABLE J. D. R. HAYWARD, M.A.
N. J. R. JAMES, Esq., M.A., J.P.
ALDERMAN, B. G. JENKINS, M.A., F.C.A.
THE VENERABLE W. F. JOHNSTON, C.B.
COLONEL R. S. LANGTON, L.V.O., M.C.
THE HONOURABLE A. LAWSON JOHNSTON, B.A., F.R.S.A., DL
P. LOCKE, Esq.
I. S. LOCKHART, Esq., M.A.
THE BISHOP OF LONDON
THE RIGHT REVEREND L. E. LUSCOMBE, LLD, CA
M. L. J. MARSHALL, Esq., M.A., F.R.I.C.S.

THE VENERABLE J. MORRISON
MAJOR GENERAL J. I. H. OWEN, O.B.E.
CANON C. G. H. RODGERS
PREBENDARY J. A. ROGERS, B.A.
PREBENDARY A. R. ROYALL, M.A.
MRS D. M. STANESBY, B.A., M.Ed., M.Sc.
CANON J. STEWART
L. H. G. TRIMM, Esq., B.Sc., A.C.I.I., F.R.E.cons
THE ARCHBISHOP OF WALES
ALDERMAN C. R. WALFORD
DOCTOR E. M. WEBB, M.B., B.S., M.R.C.G.P.
A. F. WOODALL, Esq.
THE ARCHBISHOP OF YORK

The Corporation distributed over £1,168,000 in 1990 by way of grants to 2000 clergymen, their widows and dependants. Education and maintenance help was given to 300 ordinands and 800 boys and girls.

The ANNUAL FESTIVAL SERVICE in St Paul's Cathedral is held in May and tickets may be obtained from the Registrar at the address given above.

Donors of not less than £50 may be elected to be Governors of the Corporation.

SUBSCRIPTIONS, DONATIONS, CHURCH and SCHOOL COLLECTIONS, and LEGACIES, in aid of funds or towards the extension of any of the above branches of work, are requested, and will be gratefully acknowledged by the Registrar, who will provide any information required.

1 DEAN TRENCH STREET, WESTMINSTER, LONDON SW1P 3HB   R. C. F. LEACH, Registrar.

The Leprosy Mission

*Reaching out in the Name of Christ to bring healing and hope
to the world's 12,000,000 leprosy victims.*

ROOM 41, GOLDHAY WAY, ORTON GOLDHAY, PETERBOROUGH, PE2 0GZ, CAMBRIDGESHIRE

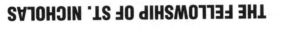

THE FELLOWSHIP OF ST. NICHOLAS
ST. LEONARDS-ON-SEA
EAST SUSSEX

Our services to young people include: support and accommodation for teenagers, a Housing Scheme for single parents and their babies, and family support schemes including Day-Care, Home-Start, and Afterschool Clubs and Holiday Playschemes.

Further details from: Tony Cox, Director, The Fellowship of St. Nicholas, 24 Stockleigh Road, St. Leonards-on-Sea, East Sussex TN38 0JP. Tel: 0424 423683/443358.

We try to give them that start in life that their fathers would have wished if they had lived.

In 1991 we gave £211,000 to 200 fatherless children of ordained clergymen of the Church of England and the Church in Wales to help with their education and general maintenance. Please send donations, or requests for further information to the Secretary.

CLERGY ORPHAN CORPORATION

57b Tufton Street, Westminster, London SW1P 3QL

OUR WORK IS CARING . . .

The Church of England Pensions Board offers support to retired clergy and their spouses, or the widow(er)s of clergy, and church workers retired from full time ministry.

Our greatest concern is for the welfare of our older pensioners, who because of age or infirmity need sheltered accommodation and some special care. The Pensions Board runs nine residential and nursing homes offering security and peace of mind to those who have given their lives towards helping others in the name of Christ. Plans for a further residential home are at an advanced stage.

We rely on support from donations, deeds of covenant, and legacies in order to continue this much needed work. Please help us in any way you can.

For further information about ways to help, forms of words for inclusion in a Will, or more details about our work, write to:

The Secretary, Department CD,
The Church of England Pensions Board
7 LITTLE COLLEGE STREET
WESTMINSTER, LONDON SW1P 3SF

Cliff Richard

Brigade Honorary Vice-President

says:

'Why Vice-President of The Boys' Brigade? Because I've seen it at work and been impressed. It stands for important values and challenging activities and is upfront and unashamed in commending Jesus.'

108 years of Christian Service

THE Boys' Brigade

Charity Regn. No: 305969

There are many ways in which you could help us financially, especially by making a donation to our general expenses or training appeals.

PLEASE send your donation to, or request further information about our work from:

THE BOYS' BRIGADE, 1, Galena Road, Hammersmith, London W6 0LT.
Telephone: 081-741 4001.

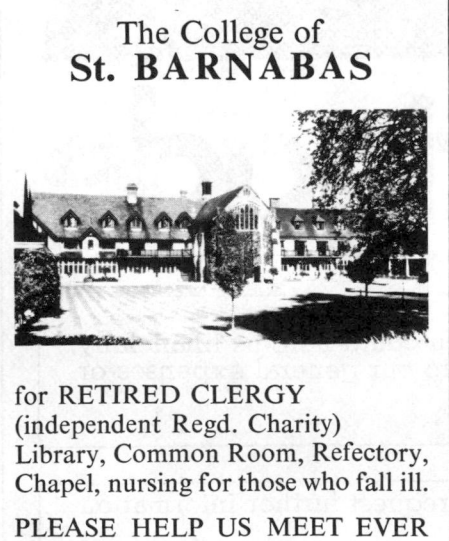
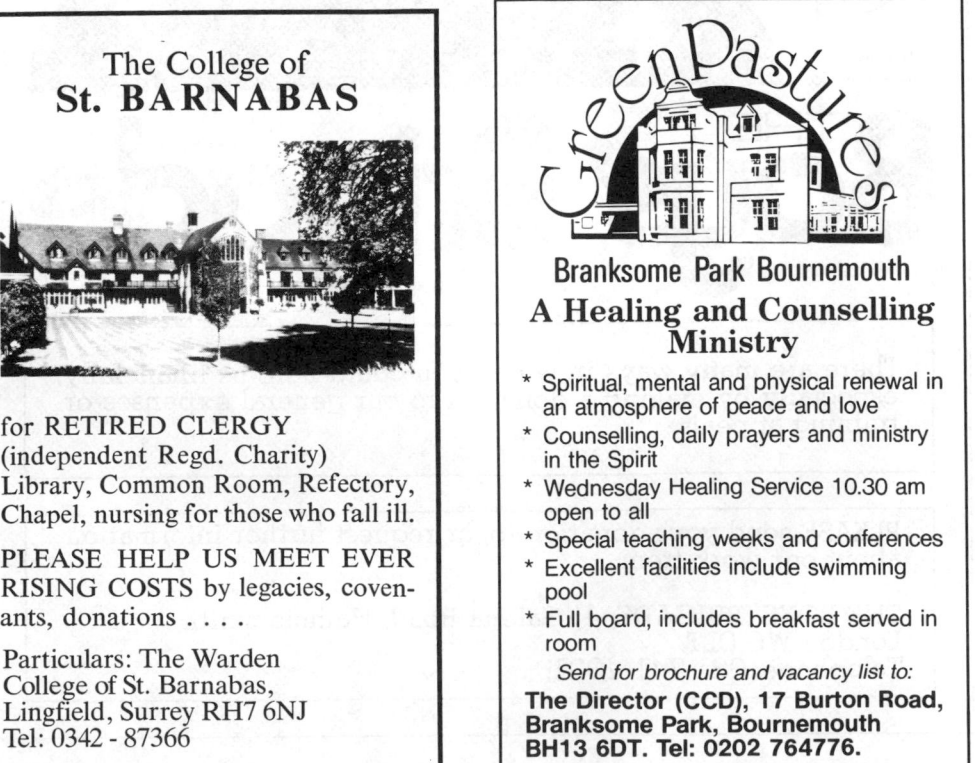

CHURCH PULPIT YEAR BOOK

Published every November

A complete set of expository sermon outlines for all Sundays of the year, plus Saints' Days and special occasions.

Two outlines are given for each Sunday. Usually based on the ASB readings for the day – but in many cases they suit also, or can be adapted to, the BCP readings. Can be taken as they stand, or adapted to suit your congregation's particular needs.

Invaluable aid to the hard-pressed parish priest, curate or reader.

CHANSITOR PUBLICATIONS

Subscription Office:
16 Blyburgate, Beccles,
Suffolk, NR34 9TB.
Tel: (0502) 711231.

BLOXHAM SCHOOL

Nr. Banbury, Oxon

Bloxham is an H.M.C. boarding school and a member of the Woodard Corporation. It has 365 pupils aged 13-18, with a co-educational academic Sixth Form of 170.

Generous scholarships and awards are available, including the Roger Raymond Scholarship. This offers full fees to a candidate who without such a Scholarship would not be able to afford a Bloxham education, and specifically mentions sons of clergy as likely beneficiaries. Other awards are also available for sons of clergy.

Sixth Form Entrance Scholarship exams are held in March, and 13+ Scholarships in May. For further details please apply to the **Headmaster, Bloxham School, Near Banbury, Oxon, OX15 4PE. Telephone Banbury (0295) 720206.**

AN INEXPENSIVE HOTEL
IN LONDON SW1

🛎 ELIZABETH HOTEL

37 ECCLESTON SQUARE,
VICTORIA,
LONDON SW1V 1PB.
Telephone: 071-828 6812

Intimate, friendly, private Hotel in ideal, central, quiet location overlooking attractive gardens of stately residential square (*circa* 1835), close to Belgravia, within walking distance of Westminster and yet only 750 yards from Victoria Station/Coach Station Air Terminals.

Comfortable Single, Double, Twin and Family Rooms.

Well furnished Lounge and pleasant Breakfast Room. Lift.

Good ENGLISH BREAKFAST or Continental Breakfast at any time for EARLY DEPARTURES.

MODERATE PRICES

EGON RONAY Recommended
RAC Listed
COLOUR BROCHURE AVAILABLE

HURSTPIERPOINT COLLEGE

A Woodward School. Founded 1849

There are Bursaries for sons of the Clergy. Awards are subject to good Common Entrance Examination results and a means test.

Government Assisted Places available at 13+ and at 11+, the latter in our Junior School.

Academic and Music Scholarships are offered on a percentage of fees basis, the top awards being to the value of one half fees.

Art and Sports Scholarships available up to one-third fees.

Senior School fees £9,555 (boarding), £4,800 (day) per annum

Particulars from the Registrar, Hurstpierpoint College, Hassocks, West Sussex, BN6 9JS.
Tel: (0273) 833636

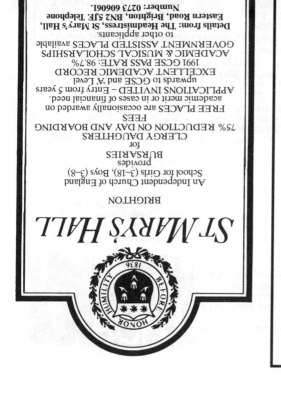

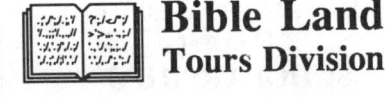

CHRIST'S HOSPITAL
Co-educational Boarding School
Horsham, West Sussex

Christ's Hospital aims to provide educational excellence in an ethos of care for children of families in need aged 11–18. Fee contributions are related to the family income and range from Nil for families whose gross income is less than £9000 to £8345 p.a. for families whose gross income is over £36,000.

Admission at 11 years only and all applicants sit an entrance examination which is held in January preceding September entry.

Five Government Assisted Places available annually.

Further information from: Mrs Jill Wilkinson, Admissions Officer, Christ's Hospital, Horsham, West Sussex, RH13 7YP. Tel: 0403 211293.

ST. ELPHIN'S SCHOOL
DARLEY DALE, MATLOCK, DERBYSHIRE, DE4 2HA
Est. 1844
Headmaster A. P. C. Pollard, B.A.
In Association with the Woodard Corporation

Church of England, Independent School, for up to 365 girls.
Beautiful setting.
Dedicated staff.
Excellent facilities for full curriculum. A happy, well disciplined, caring community.
Reduced fees and scholarships for clergy daughters.
For prospectus and full details please telephone 0629 732687.

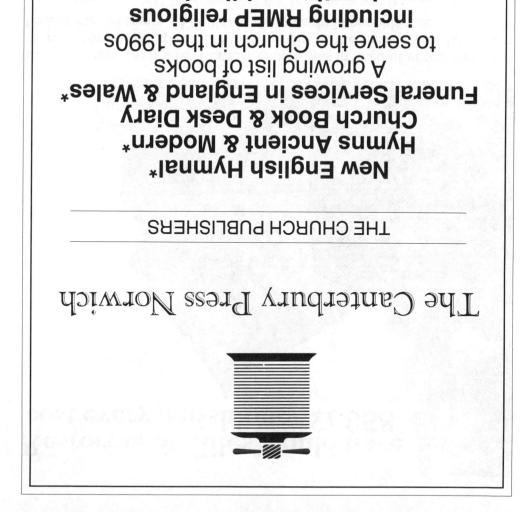

Restoring St Giles' could have cost every parishioner £1,058

Last year, this lovely 11th Century church was in need of urgent repairs to its roof, tower and spire. The 120 people in the Parish were faced with finding the necessary £127,000 – a seemingly impossible task.

Yet, with the aid of a grant and a loan from the Historic Churches Preservation Trust, together with assistance from English Heritage and some inspired fundraising in the Parish, this enormous sum was raised, and work begun.

There are many beautiful churches like St Giles'. Time, weather, dry rot and water ingress all take their toll, so that nearly all our irreplaceable churches are in continual need of renovation and repair. And costs are so high that few congregations nowadays can shoulder them unaided.

Let your donation or legacy to the Trust be a lasting memorial to your faith in the future of our unique heritage.

Historic Churches Preservation Trust

Fulham Palace, London SW6 6EA   *Tel: 071–736 3054.   Reg Charity 207402.*

INTRODUCTION

More than ten years have now passed since the Oxford University Press sought the help of the central bodies of the Church of England in securing the long-term future of Crockford. The last OUP edition (1980/82) was published in February 1983 with financial assistance from the Church. The selling price was £40, equivalent to £64 of to-day's money.

This is the fourth edition to appear, on the established biennial pattern, under the new ownership. The sale of the Directory has risen to over 8000 from a starting point of 3000 copies. Computer technology enables final compilation to be delayed until four months before publication, so that we are able to include changes up to 31 July.

With each edition the process of compilation has been refined so as to provide fuller coverage and greater variety of detail. The 1991/92 edition contains biographies of 24,596 clergy and 96 deaconesses. The Index of English Benefices and Churches covers 16,563 churches in 8,964 benefices. Wales, Scotland and Ireland bring the total number of benefices to 10,361.

Newly introduced in this edition are outline maps of England and Wales, Scotland and Ireland, showing diocesan and civil boundaries (these last appeared in 1979), and listings of European chaplaincies, of the staff of theological colleges and part-time courses, and of Assistant Bishops in each English diocese.

Many of those who make regular use of Crockford seem to be unaware of additional features which have been incorporated in successive editions. Those who consult it only occasionally may need help in using what is far more than an alphabetical clergy list. With such occasional users in mind we have provided a simple User's Guide which follows this Introduction. We have also reviewed and at points expanded our advice on How to Address the Clergy.

To provide a full record of service for all clergy, active and retired, would still extend the Directory beyond economic limits. The 1991/92 edition makes 1152 pages, compared with 1056 pages in 1989/90 and 1000 pages in 1987/88. The increase reflects the fact that we have pushed back to 1970 the date from which past appointments are recorded for retired clergy, mostly drawing pension. We have also been able to dispense with the concept of a qualifying appointment so that all clergy, parochial or non-parochial, whose names are on the Commissioners' database are in Crockford unless specifically excluded. For coverage of service overseas the reader is referred to the paragraphs on Overseas Information in the User's Guide.

In the preparation of this edition we have attempted to make contact with every member of the clergy, as a once for all operation, inviting them to verify their biographical record. We are grateful to the many who wrote to supply necessary details, and no less to those who gave tacit approval to their 'proof of entry'. We would make the particular request that clergy outside the parochial ministry inform us of new appointments and changes of address, and that all clergy let us know of additional degrees, honours or distinctions.

A list of clergy whose addresses were unknown appeared in the 1989/90 edition. Information has been received from our correspondents about many of them but the list in the current edition is no shorter, consisting largely of new names. Biographies are included for the clergy on this list, with 'address temporarily unknown'.

Comments and enquiries about information contained in the Directory, together with corrections of detail, should be sent to Crockford. The Church Commissioners (for address see below).

Curiosity surfaces from time to time about the man whose name has been associated with this Directory since its first issue in 1858. Little is known of John Crockford and we had accepted our predecessors' statement that he was clerk to Edward Cox, to whom the credit for founding the Directory properly belonged. A request for an article on John Crockford for the forthcoming supplement to the *Dictionary of National Biography* has prompted a fuller investigation and we hope to include the results in a future issue.

September 1991

Church Commissioners,
1 Millbank,
London SW1P 3JZ

Central Board of Finance,
Church House,
Great Smith Street,
London SW1P 3NZ

A USER'S GUIDE TO CROCKFORD

Appointment details	In general these reflect the legal pastoral situation prevailing at the time. Conventional Districts and Local Ecumenical Projects are also recorded. *Crockford does not record the following:* Group ministries Informal local arrangements Areas of special responsibility Emeritus appointments (except as reflected in style of address) Licence or permission to officiate, when held in conjunction with another appointment from the same diocese. Commissary appointments Examining chaplaincies Secular appointments (except educational or charitable posts)
Appointments before ordination	These are not included (apart from service as a deaconess) unless they straddle the date of ordination. Service in other denominations (when known) is indicated.
Archdeacons	Look up place name in Biographies, which is cross-referenced to personal name.
Archdeaconries	See Deaneries and Rural Deans in England, p 1028.
Benefice names in biographies	These are recorded only once when they apply to successive appointments.
Benefice vacant	A telephone number enables contact to be made with a new incumbent or priest-in-charge. The deanery reference (e.g. *Guildf 7*) following the benefice name cross-refers to Deaneries and Rural Deans in England, p 1028.
Bishops, Assistant	See p 1027.
Bishops, Diocesan, Area, Suffragan	Look up place name in Biographies, which is cross-referenced to personal name.
Bishops in the House of Lords	See *Church of England Year Book*, issued annually by Church House Publishing and covering most aspects of the life of the Church of England. See pp 1037ff.
Bishops overseas	See Succession of Archbishops and Bishops, pp 1051ff.
Cathedral clergy	See Cathedrals, p 1017.
Chapel Royal, Chaplains to the Queen	No separate listing. See *Church of England Year Book*.
Christian names in parentheses	These are names (often names 'in religion') by which a person is known in preference to his or her legal name.
Church Commissioners	For names see *Church of England Year Book*.
Clergy not in Crockford	See Clergy who have died since the Last Edition, p 1083. A small number of clergy are omitted for personal reasons. See also Overseas Information.
Clergy responsible for a particular church	Look up place name in the appropriate Benefice Index. In the Index of English Benefices and Churches there is a cross-reference to the benefice entry (bold type), if different, where the names of the clergy will be found.

College Chaplains

No separate listing. See biographies under personal name. For Chaplains in Higher Education see *Church of England Year Book*.

Crockford or Crockford's?

The full title is *Crockford's Clerical Directory*. Crockford (no 's') is the accepted shorter form.

Cross-references (e.g. from previous surname or name 'in religion')

When there has been a change of surname, for example on marriage, a cross-reference may be inserted from the previous name.

For members of religious orders where the Christian name alone is commonly used (e.g. Brother Aidan) a cross-reference is provided to the surname.

Deaconesses

See separate section, p 813.

Deacons (men and women)

See Biographies.

Deaneries

To find the deanery (or Rural Dean), look up the church or benefice name in the Index of English Benefices and Churches. A reference (e.g. *Guildf 7*) following the benefice name cross-refers to Deaneries and Rural Deans in England, p 1028.

Deans of Cathedrals and Collegiate Churches, of Peculiars, of Scottish dioceses

Look up place name in biographies, which is cross-referenced to personal name. See also Cathedrals, p 1017.

Dr

Inserted before Christian name when clergy with appropriate qualifications request this.

Europe, Chaplains in

See Anglican Chaplains in Europe, p 1035.
See *Church of England Year Book*.

General Synod membership

Honours and Education

The order of these items in a biography is normally as follows:
Honours
Professional qualifications and membership of learned societies
Education, i.e. academic qualifications including theological degrees from universities, normally in date order
Ministerial training: college or course (with qualification if any) and year of entry

Hospital Chaplains

For whole-time Hospital Chaplains at their base hospitals as defined by the Hospital Chaplaincies Council see p 1023.

How to Address the Clergy

See p 51.

Lay Workers, Accredited

Not included in Crockford; consult Diocesan Directories.

Married or Single?

Crockford does not provide this information, but see Mrs, Miss, Ms.

Mrs, Miss, Ms

Optionally inserted for women deacons and deaconesses.

Ordination Courses

See Theological Colleges and Part-Time Courses, p 1019.

Overseas Information

Current service overseas does not qualify as such for inclusion in Crockford. However, a number of clergy are included who have worked in one of the four 'home' Churches but are at present serving overseas or have retired overseas.

Service overseas is recorded by country, but higher office held (e.g. as Bishop or Archdeacon) is noted additionally.

The address and telephone information given is that required by a user in the UK. International dialling codes may need to be added to the area code.

Patronage	See Index of English Benefices and Churches.
Prison Chaplains	See p 1022.
Private Chapels	School, College, Hospital Chapels are not included in the Index of English Benefices and Churches unless they are centres of public worship under the control of an incumbent.
Proprietary Chapels	Included in Index of English Benefices and Churches.
Provosts of Cathedrals	Look up place name in biographies, which is cross-referenced to personal name. See also Cathedrals, p 1017.
Readers	Not included in Crockford; consult Diocesan Directories.
Religious Communities	See *Church of England Year Book*. See also Cross-references.
Retired clergy	Appointments are recorded from 1970 onwards.
Rev, Rt Rev, Very Rev	See How to Address the Clergy, p 51.
Rural Deans	See Deaneries and Rural Deans in England, p 1028.
School Chaplains	No separate listing. See Biographies under personal name.
Service Chaplains	See p 1020.
Theological Colleges	See Theological Colleges and Part-Time Courses, p 1019.

HOW TO ADDRESS THE CLERGY

In offering the advice below, we do not intend to imply that practices not referred to here are necessarily to be discouraged. Personal preferences will vary, and a good deal depends on circumstances. Where there are existing personal links it is natural to be less formal, while on occasions a greater degree of formality may be appropriate.

The following notes show customary current usage

A on an envelope or formal listing
B in starting a letter or in speech
C when referring to a member of the clergy

Category A is not open to much variation, but categories B and C will often be varied in practice when addressing or referring to a person one already knows well.

It is always acceptable to use a Christian name — provided it is the right name — in place of initials. A preference for using Christian names on their own wherever possible is reflected in such usages as Father David and Bishop Michael, though an existing relationship of some kind usually implied.

In the absence of any style or title conferred by a post, all deacons and priests are styled 'The Reverend' and all who have been consecrated bishop are styled 'The Right Reverend'.

For abbreviations see 13 below.

1 Deacons and Priests (male)

A The Reverend A B Smith or The Reverend Alan Smith
B Mr Smith (Father Smith, if a priest prefers this)
C The Reverend A B Smith, Mr Smith (Father Smith), Alan Smith
NOTE 'Reverend Smith' and 'The Reverend Smith' should not be used. If the Christian name or initials are not known, the correct forms are
A The Reverend — Smith   B Mr Smith   C the Reverend Mr Smith, Mr Smith.

2 Women Deacons

A The Reverend A B Smith or The Reverend Alice Smith
B Mrs Smith, Miss Smith, Ms Smith
The form applicable, where this is known, is given in each woman deacon's biography.
C the Reverend A B Smith, Mrs (Miss, Ms) Smith, Alice Smith
NOTE For women as for men, 'Reverend Smith' and 'The Reverend Smith' should not be used. If the Christian name or initials are not known, the correct forms are
A The Reverend — Smith   B Mrs (Miss, Ms) Smith   C (the Reverend) Mrs (Miss, Ms) Smith

3 Prebendaries

A The Reverend Prebendary A B Smith
B Prebendary Smith
C Prebendary Smith

4 Canons (both Residentiary and Honorary)

A The Reverend Canon A B Smith
B Canon Smith
C Canon Smith

5 Archdeacons

A The Venerable the Archdeacon of X, occasionally The Venerable A B Smith, Archdeacon of X
B Archdeacon; more formally Mr Archdeacon
C the Archdeacon of X; the Archdeacon; Archdeacon Smith
NOTES 1 In the case of an Archdeacon (or Dean or Provost, Bishop or Archbishop) in office, the territorial title is to be preferred. The personal name is to be used only for the purpose of identification.
2 For an Archdeacon Emeritus, the correct forms are A The Venerable A B Smith   B Archdeacon   C Archdeacon Smith. The form 'The Venerable Archdeacon A B Smith' should not be used.

6 Dean and Provosts

A The Very Reverend the Dean (the Provost) of X
B Dean (Provost); more formally Mr Dean (Mr Provost)
C the Dean (Provost) of X; the Dean (the Provost); Dean Smith (Provost Smith): see note at 5 above

7 Bishops, Diocesan and Suffragan

A The Right Reverend the Bishop of X *or* The Right Reverend the Lord Bishop of X
B Bishop; more formally My Lord
C the Bishop of X; the Bishop; Bishop Smith: see note at 5 above

NOTES 1 The use of 'Lord' before 'Bishop' is diminishing; it is a matter of individual preference whether it is retained.
2 The Bishop of London is a Privy Councillor and has the style 'The Right Reverend and Right Honourable the Lord Bishop of London'.
3 The Bishop of Meath and Kildare has the style 'Most Reverend'.

8 Assistant and Retired Bishops

A The Right Reverend A B Smith
B Bishop
C Bishop

9 Archbishops

A The Most Reverend (and Right Honourable) the Lord Archbishop of X
B Archbishop; more formally Your Grace
C the Archbishop of X; the Archbishop; Archbishop Smith: see note at 5 above

NOTES 1 The Archbishops of Canterbury and York, being Privy Councillors, have 'Right Honourable' included in their style.
2 The presiding bishop of the Scottish Episcopal Church is the Primus, and the correct forms are
A The Most Reverend the Primus   B Primus   C the Primus.
3 Retired Archbishops properly go back to the status of a Bishop but may be given as a courtesy the style of an Archbishop.

10 Chaplains to the Armed Forces

A The Reverend A B Smith RN (or CF or RAF)
B Padre or Padre Smith
C the Padre or Padre Smith

NOTE The Senior Chaplain in each of the three services (the Chaplain of the Fleet, the Chaplain General to the Forces, the Chaplain in Chief, RAF) has the status of Archdeacon and is styled 'The Venerable'.

11 Ordained Members of Religious Orders

A The Reverend Alan Smith XYZ; Brother Alan XYZ
B Father or Father Smith; Brother Alan
C the Reverend Alan Smith XYZ; Father Alan Smith (XYZ); Father Smith; Brother Alan (XYZ)

NOTES 1 A name 'in religion', shown in parentheses in the biographical entry, is used in preference to the baptismal name or initials.
2 Some orders use 'Brother' for lay and ordained members without distinction, along with Christian name. This Directory provides a cross-reference to the surname.

12 Clergy with several titles

When a member of the clergy has two or more titles it is correct to use the higher title or the one appropriate to the context.

Professor	A Professor the Reverend A B Smith *or* The Reverend Professor A B Smith
	B Professor Smith
	C Professor Smith
Professor also Canon	A Professor the Reverend Canon A B Smith *or* The Reverend Canon Professor A B Smith
	B Professor Smith, Canon Smith
	C Professor Smith, Canon Smith
Canon also Doctor	A The Reverend Canon A B Smith (degree)
	B Canon Smith, Dr Smith
	C Canon Smith, Dr Smith

13 Abbreviations

The following abbreviations are in common use

Reverend: Rev or Revd   Father: Fr
Right Reverend: Rt Rev or Rt Revd
Prebendary: Preb   Venerable: Ven

The Abbreviations for Reverend, Right Reverend and Venerable should be preceded by 'the'.

A

AAAI . . . Associate of the Institute of Administrative Accountants

AACCA . . Associate of the Association of Certified and Corporate Accountants (now see ACCA)

AB . . . . Bachelor of Arts (USA)

Ab. . . . . (Diocese of) Aberdeen and Orkney

ABAF . . . Associate of the British Academy of Fencing

Aber . . . . Aberdeen

ABIST . . . Associate of the British Institute of Surgical Technology

ABM . . . . Advisory Board of Ministry (formerly ACCM and CECD)

Abp . . . . Archbishop

ABPsS . . . Associate of the British Psychological Society (now see AFBPsS)

ABSM . . . Associate of the Birmingham and Midland Institute School of Music

Abth . . . . Aberystwyth

ACA . . . . Associate of the Institute of Chartered Accountants

ACC . . . Anglican Consultative Council

ACCA . . . Associate of the Chartered Association of Certified Accountants (formerly AACCA)

ACCM . . . Advisory Council for the Church's Ministry (formerly CACTM; now see ABM)

ACCS . . . Associate of the Corporation of Secretaries

AcDipEd. . Academic Diploma in Education

ACertCM . Archbishop of Canterbury's Certificate in Church Music

ACertEd . . Advanced Certificate of Education

ACF . . . . Army Cadet Force

ACGI. . . . Associate of the City and Guilds of London

ACIArb . . Associate of the Chartered Institute of Arbitrators

ACIB . . . . Associate of the Chartered Institute of Bankers (formerly AIB)

ACII . . . . Associate of the Chartered Insurance Institute

ACIS . . . . Associate of the Institute of Chartered Secretaries and Administrators

ACIT . . . . Associate of the Chartered Institute of Transport

ACMA . . . Associate of the Institute of Cost and Management Accountants (formerly ACWA)

ACP . . . . Associate of the College of Preceptors

ACS . . . . Additional Curates Society

ACSM . . . Associate of Camborne School of Mines

ACT . . . . Australian College of Theology

ACTVR . . Advanced Certificate in Television and Radio

ACUPA . . Archbishops' Commission on Urban Priority Areas

ACWA . . . Associate of the Institute of Cost and Works Accountants (now see ACMA)

AD . . . . Area Dean

ADB . . . . Associate of the Drama Board

ADC . . . . Advanced Diploma in Counselling

ADCM . . . Archbishop of Canterbury's Diploma in Church Music

ADipR . . . Archbishop's Diploma for Readers

ADipTh . . Advanced Diploma in Theology

ADME . . . Advanced Diploma in Maths Education

Admin . . . Administration Administrative Administrator

Adn . . . . Archdeacon

Adnry . . . Archdeaconry

ADPS . . . Advanced Diploma in Pastoral Studies

Adv . . . . Adviser Advisory

AFAIM . . . Associate Fellow of the Australian Institute of Management

AFBPsS . . Associate Fellow of the British Psychological Society (formerly ABPsS)

AFC . . . . Air Force Cross

AFIMA . . . Associate Fellow of the Institute of Mathematics and its Applications

Agric . . . . Agricultural Agriculture

AGSM . . . Associate of the Guildhall School of Music and Drama

AHSM or AHA . . . Associate of the Institute of Health Service Management (formerly Administrators)

AIA . . . . Associate of the Institute of Actuaries

AIAS . . . Associate of the Incorporated Association of Architects and Surveyors

AIAT . . . . Associate of the Institute of Animal Technicians

AIB . . . . Associate of the Institute of Bankers (now see ACIB)

Aid . . . . Aidan Aidan's

AIDS . . . . Acquired Immunity Deficiency Syndrome (also see HIV)

AIFST . . . Associate of the Institute of Food Science and Technology

AIGCM . . . Associate of the Incorporated Guild of Church Musicians

AIL . . . . Associate of the Institute of Linguists

AIMLS . . . Associate of the Institute of Medical Laboratory Sciences

AKC . . . . Associate of King's College, London

ALA . . . . Associate of the Library Association

ALAM . . . Associate of the London Academy of Music

ALCD . . . Associate of the London College of Divinity

ALCM . . . Associate of the London College of Music

ALSM . . . Associate of the Lancashire School of Music

alt . . . . . alternate

AM . . . . Albert Medal Master of Arts (USA)

AMBIM . . Associate Member of the British Institute of Management (later MBIM; now see FBIM)

AMCST . . Associate of the Manchester College of Science and Technology

AMCT . . . Associate of the Manchester College of Technology

AMGAS . . Associate Member of the Group-Analytic Society

AMIBF . . . Associate Member of the Institute of British Foundrymen

AMIC . . . Associate Member of the Institute of Counselling

AMICE . . . Associate Member of the Institution of Civil Engineers (now see MICE)

AMIDHE . . Associate Member of the Institute of Domestic Heating Engineers

AMIEE . . . Associate Member of the Institution of Electrical Engineers (now see MIEE)

AMIEHO . . Associate Member of the Institution of Environmental Health Officers

AMIM . . . Associate Member of the Institute of Metals

AMIMechE . Associate of the Institution of Mechanical Engineers (now see MIMechE)

AMInstTA . Associate Member of the Institute of Transport Administration

AMIWO . . Associate Member of the Institute of Welfare Officers

AMP . . . . Advanced Management Program

AMSIA . . . Associate Member of the Society of Investment Analysts

AMusTCL . Associate in Music of Trinity College of Music, London

Andr . . . . Andrew Andrew's Andrews

Angl . . . . Anglican Anglicans

Ant . . . . Anthony Anthony's

AP . . . . Assistant Priest

APhS . . . . Associate of the Philosophical Society of England

APM . . . . Auxiliary Pastoral Minister (or Ministry)

Appt . . . . Appointment

ARAM . . . Associate of the Royal Academy of Music

ARCA . . . Associate of the Royal College of Art

ARCIC . . . Anglican-Roman Catholic International Commission

ARCM . . . Associate of the Royal College of Music

ARCO . . . Associate of the Royal College of Organists

ARCS . . . Associate of the Royal College of Science

ARCST . . . Associate of the Royal College of Science and Technology (Glasgow)

Arg . . . . (Diocese of) Argyll and The Isles

ARHistS . . Associate of the Royal Historical Society

ARIBA . . . Associate of the Royal Institute of British Architects (now see RIBA)

ARIC. . . . Associate of the Royal Institute of Chemistry (later MRIC; now see MRSC)
ARICS . . . Associate of the Royal Institute of Chartered Surveyors
Arm . . . . (Diocese of) Armagh
ARMCM. . . Associate of the Royal Manchester College of Music
ARSM . . . Associate of the Royal School of Mines
AS. . . . . Associate in Science (USA)
ASCA . . . Associate of the Society of Company and Commercial Accountants
ASCAT . . . All Souls' College of Applied Theology
ASEEDip . . Association of Supervising Electrical Engineers Diploma
ASGM . . . Albert Schweitzer Gold Medal
Assn . . . . Association
Assoc . . . . Associate
Asst . . . . Assistant
ATC . . . . Air Training Corps
ATCL . . . Associate of Trinity College of Music, London
ATD . . . . Art Teacher's Diploma
ATh(SA). . . Associate in Theology (South Africa)
ATI . . . . Associate of the Textile Institute
ATII . . . . Associate Member of the Institute of Taxation
ATPL. . . . Airline Transport Pilot's Licence
ATV . . . . Associated Television
Aug . . . . Augustine Augustine's
Aus . . . . Australia Australian
Aux . . . . Auxiliary
AV . . . . Associate Vicar

B

b . . . . . Born
B & W . . . (Diocese of) Bath and Wells
B or Bapt . . Baptist Baptist's
BA . . . . Bachelor of Arts
BA(Econ) . . Bachelor of Arts in Economics
BA(Ed) . . . Bachelor of Arts in Education
BA(Theol) . . Bachelor of Arts in Theology
BAC Accred . British Accreditation Council Accredit
BAdmin . . . Bachelor of Administration
BAgr . . . . Bachelor of Agriculture
BAI . . . . Bachelor of Engineering (also see BE and BEng)
Ball . . . . Balliol
Ban . . . . (Diocese of) Bangor
BAO . . . . Bachelor of Obstetrics
BAOR . . . British Army of (formerly on) the Rhine
BArch . . . Bachelor of Architecture
Barn . . . . Barnabas Barnabas's
Bart . . . . Bartholomew Bartholomew's
BASc . . . . Bachelor of Applied Science
BBA . . . . Bachelor of Business Administration
BBC . . . . British Broadcasting Corporation
BBS . . . . Bachelor of Business Studies
BC . . . . British Columbia (Canada)
BCC . . . . British Council of Churches (now see CCBI)

BCh or BChir . Bachelor of Surgery (also see BS and ChB)
BCL . . . . Bachelor of Civil Law
BCMS . . . Bible Churchmen's Missionary Society
BCom . . . Bachelor of Commerce
BCombStuds . Bachelor of Combined Studies
BD . . . . Bachelor of Divinity
Bd . . . . . Board
BDip . . . . Bible Diploma
BDQ . . . . Bachelor of Divinity Qualifying Examination
BDS . . . . Bachelor of Dental Surgery
BE . . . . Bachelor of Engineering (also see BAI and BEng)
BEcon . . . Bachelor of Economics (USA)
BEd . . . . Bachelor of Education
Bedf . . . . Bedford
Beds . . . . Bedfordshire
Belf . . . . Belfast
BEM . . . . British Empire Medal
BEng . . . . Bachelor of Engineering (also see BAI and BE)
Berks . . . . Berkshire
BesL . . . . Bachelier es Lettres
BFBS . . . . British and Foreign Bible Society
BFPO. . . . British Forces Post Office
Bibl . . . . Biblical
BIE . . . . Bachelor of Industrial Engineering (USA)
Birkb . . . . Birkbeck
Birm . . . . (Diocese of) Birmingham
BL. . . . . Bachelor of Law
Blackb . . . (Diocese of) Blackburn
BLitt . . . . Bachelor of Letters
BM . . . . Bachelor of Medicine (also see MB)
BMet . . . . Bachelor of Metallurgy
BMin . . . . Bachelor of Ministry
BMMF . . . Bible and Medical Missionary Fellowship (now Intersave)
BMU . . . . Board for Mission and Unity
BMus . . . . Bachelor of Music (also see MusB or MusBac)
BMusEd . . . Bachelor of Music Education
BN . . . . Bachelor of Nursing
BNC . . . . Brasenose College
Boro . . . . Borough
Bp . . . . . Bishop
BPaed . . . . Bachelor of Paediatrics
BPh or BPhil . Bachelor of Philosophy
BPharm . . . Bachelor of Pharmacy
BPhil(Ed) . . Bachelor of Philosophy (Education)
Br . . . . . British
Bradf . . . . (Diocese of) Bradford
BRE . . . . Bachelor of Religious Education (USA)
Bre . . . . . (Diocese of) Brechin
BRF . . . . Bible Reading Fellowship
Brig . . . . Brigadier
Bris . . . . (Diocese of) Bristol
BS. . . . . Bachelor of Science (also see BSc) Bachelor of Surgery (also see BCh or BChir and ChB)
BSA . . . . Bachelor of Scientific Agriculture
BSB . . . . Brotherhood of St Barnabas
BSc . . . . Bachelor of Science (also see BS)
BSc(Econ) . . Bachelor of Science in Economics
BSc(Soc) . . . Bachelor of Science (Sociology)
BScAgr . . . Bachelor of Science in Agriculture
BScEng . . . Bachelor of Science in Engineering (also see BSE)
BScFor . . . Bachelor of Science in Forestry
BScTech . . . Bachelor of Technical Science

BSE . . . . Bachelor of Science in Engineering (also see BScEng)
BSEd . . . . Bachelor of Science in Education (USA)
BSocSc . . . Bachelor of Social Science (also see BSSc)
BSocStuds . . Bachelor of Social Studies
BSP . . . . Brotherhood of St Paul
BSSc . . . . Bachelor of Social Science (also see BSocSc)
BSW . . . . Bachelor of Social Work
BT. . . . . Bachelor of Teaching
Bt . . . . . Baronet
BTA . . . . British Tuberculosis Association Certificate
BTEC ND . . Business and Technican Education Council National Diploma
BTech . . . Bachelor of Technology
BTh . . . . Bachelor of Theology (also see STB)
BTS . . . . Bachelor of Theological Studies
Buckm . . . Buckingham
Bucks . . . . Buckinghamshire
BVetMed . . Bachelor of Veterinary Medicine (also see VetMB)
BVSc . . . . Bachelor of Veterinary Science

C

C . . . . . Curate
c . . . . . Consecrated
C & O . . . (Diocese of) Cashel and Ossory (united dioceses of Cashel, Waterford, Lismore, Ossory, Ferns and Leighlin)
C of E . . . Church of England
C, C & R. . . (Diocese of) Cork, Cloyne and Ross
C-in-c . . . . Curate-in-charge
c/o . . . . . Care of
CA . . . . Church Army Member of the Institute of Chartered Accountants of Scotland
CACTM . . . Central Advisory Council for the Ministry (later ACCM; now see ABM)
Cam . . . . Cambridge
Cambs . . . . Cambridgeshire
Can . . . . Canon
Cand . . . . Candidate Candidate's Candidates'
CANDL . . . Church and Neighbourhood Development in London
Cant . . . . (Diocese of) Canterbury
Capt . . . . Captain
CARA . . . Care and Resources for people affected by AIDS/HIV
CARE . . . Christian Action Research and Education
Carl . . . . (Diocese of) Carlisle
CASA . . . Anglican Church of the Southern Cone of America
CASS . . . Certificate in Applied Social Studies
Cath . . . . Catharine/Catherine Catharine's/Catherine's
Cathl . . . . Cathedral
CB . . . . Companion of the Bath
CBE . . . . Commander of the Order of the British Empire
CBIM. . . . Companion of the British Institute of Management
CBiol . . . . Chartered Biologist
CCBI . . . . Council of Churches for Britain and Ireland (formerly BCC)
CCC . . . . Corpus Christi College Council for the Care of Churches
CCCS. . . . Commonwealth and Continental Church Society
CChem . . . Chartered Chemist

54

CCouns	Certificate in Counselling
CCSk	Certificate in Counselling Skills
CCT	Certificate in Clinical Teaching
CD	Canadian Forces Decoration Conventional District (also see ED)
CD (US Air)	Commercial Diver (US Air Force)
CDipAF	Certified Diploma in Accounting and Finance
Cdre	Commodore
CECD	Church of England Council for the Deaf (now see ABM)
CECS	Church of England Children's Society (now known as the Children's Society)
CEIR	Certificate in Economics and Industrial Relations
CEMS	Church of England Men's Society
Cen	Centre Center Central
CEng	Chartered Engineer
Cert	Certificate
CertAnPsych	Certificate in Analytical Psychology
CertBS	Certificate in Bible Studies
CertCC	Certificate of Child Care
CertComp	Certificate in Computing
CertCS	Certificate in Christian Studies
CertCT	Certificate in Ceramic Technology
CertDiv	Certificate in Divinity
CertEd	Certificate of Education
CertEdD	Certificate in the Education of the Deaf
CertFAI	Certificate in French, Arabic and Islamic Studies
CertFT	Certificate in Family Therapy
CertHist	Certificate in History
CertJourn	Certificate in Journalism
CertMBiol	Certificate of Microbiology
CertMS	Certificate in Management Studies
CertPsych	Certificate in Psychology
CertRE	Certificate in Religious Education
CertRK	Certificate in Religious Knowledge
CertRS	Certificate in Religious Studies
CertTESOL	Certificate in Teaching English to Speakers of Other Languages
CertTS	Certificate in Timber Surveying
CertYS	Certificate in Youth Service
CES	Certificate in Ecumenical Studies
CEurStuds	Certificate in European Studies
CF	Chaplain to the Forces
CFTV	Certificate in Film and Television
CGA	Community of the Glorious Ascension
Ch	Christ Christ's Church
Ch Ch	Christ Church
Chan	Chancellor
Chapl	Chaplain Chaplaincy
Chas	Charles Charles's
ChB	Bachelor of Surgery (also see BCh or BChir and BS)
Chelmsf	(Diocese of) Chelmsford
Ches	(Diocese of) Chester
Chich	(Diocese of) Chichester
Chmn	Chairman Chairwoman
Chpl	Chapel

Chr	Christian
Chris	Christopher Christopher's
Chrys	Chrysostom Chrysostom's
ChStJ	Chaplain of the Most Venerable Order of the Hospital of St John of Jerusalem
Chu	Churchill
CIO	Church Information Office
CIPFA	Chartered Institute of Public Finance and Accountancy
CITC	Church of Ireland Theological College
Cl-in-c	Cleric-in-charge
Clem	Clement Clement's
CLHist	Certificate in Local History
CLJ	Commander of the Order of St Lazarus of Jerusalem
Cllr	Councillor
Clogh	(Diocese of) Clogher
CLRHist	Certificate in Local and Regional History
CM	Carnegie Medal
CMBHI	Craft Member of the British Horological Institute
CMD	Cambridge Mission to Delhi (now see USPG)
CME	Continuing Ministerial Education
CMG	Companion of St Michael and St George
CMJ	Church's Ministry among the Jews
CMM	Certificate in Ministry and Mission
CMS	Church Missionary Society
CNAA	Council for National Academic Awards
Co	Company County Counties
Co-ord	Co-ordinator Co-ordinating
Col	Colonel
Coll	College
Colleg	Collegiate
Comdr	Commander
Commn	Commission
Commr	Commissioner
Comp	Comprehensive
Conf	Confederation Conference
Congr	Congregation Congregational
Conn	(Diocese of) Connor
COPEC	Conference on Politics, Economics and Community
CORAT	Christian Organizations Research and Advisory Trust
Corp	Corporation
Coun	Council
Cov	(Diocese of) Coventry
CP	Community Priest
CPA	Chartered Patent Agent
CPAS	Church Pastoral Aid Society
CPC	Certificate of Professional Competence (Road Transport)
CPhys	Chartered Physicist of the Institute of Physics
CPM	Colonial Police Medal
CPPS	Certificate of Proficiency in Pastoral Studies
CPS	Certificate in Pastoral Studies
CPsychol	Chartered Psychologist
CPTS	Certificate in Pastoral and Theological Studies
CQSW	Certificate of Qualification in Social Work

CR	Community of the Resurrection (Mirfield)
CSA	Community of St Andrew
CSD	Co-operative Societies' Diploma
CSF	Community of St Francis
CSG	Company of the Servants of God
CSocSc	Certificate in Social Science
CSocStuds	Certificate in Social Studies
CSS	Certificate in Social Service
CSSM	Children's Special Service Mission
CStJ	Commander of the Most Venerable Order of the Hospital of St John of Jerusalem
CSWG	Community of the Servants of the Will of God
CTOSc	Certificate in the Teaching of Science
CTPS	Certificate in Theological and Pastoral Studies
Cttee	Committee
CTUS	Certificate in Trades Union Studies
CUF	Church Urban Fund
Cust	Custodian Custody
Cuth	Cuthbert Cuthbert's
CV	Clerical Vicar
CVO	Commander of the Royal Victorian Order
CWME	Commission on World Mission and Evangelism
CWWCh	Certificate of Women's Work in the Church
CYCW	Certificate in Youth and Community Work
CYFA	Church Youth Fellowships Association
CYPECS	Christian Youth Fellowship, Pathfinders, Explorers, Climbers and Scramblers
Cypr	Cyprian Cyprian's

D

d	Ordained Deacon
D & D	(Diocese of) Down and Dromore
D & G	(Diocese of) Dublin and Glendalough
D & R	(Diocese of) Derry and Raphoe
D&C	Dean and Chapter
DA	Diploma in Anaesthetics
DAA	Diploma in Archive Administration
DAC	Diploma in Adult Counselling
DAES	Diploma in Advanced Educational Studies
DAPC	Diploma in Advanced Psychological Counselling
Darw	Darwin
DASAE	Diploma of Advanced Study in Adult Education
DASE	Diploma in the Advanced Study of Education
DASS	Diploma in Applied Social Studies
DASSc	Diploma in Applied Social Science
DATh	Diploma of the Arts in Theology
Dav	David David's
DAVM	Diploma in Audio Visual Media
DB	Bachelor of Divinity (USA)
DBF	Diocesan Board of Finance
DBMS	Diploma in Biblical and Mission Studies

DBO . . . . Diploma of the British Orthoptic Society
DBP . . . . Diocesan Board of Patronage
DBRS . . . Diploma in Biblical and Religious Studies
DBS . . . . Diploma in Biblical Studies
DC . . . . Diocesan Certificate District of Columbia (USA)
DCAe . . . Diploma of the College of Aeronautics
DCE . . . . Diploma in Careers Education
DCEd . . . Diploma in Community Education
DCG . . . . Diploma in Careers Guidance
DCH . . . . Diploma in Child Health
DChCD . . . Diploma in Church Community Development
DChemEng . . Diploma in Chemical Engineering
DCHospC . . Diploma in Counselling and Hospital Chaplaincy
DCL . . . . Doctor of Civil Law
DCnL . . . Doctor of Canon Law
DCouns . . . Diploma in Counselling
DCR . . . . Diploma of the College of Radiographers
DCR, MU . . Diploma of the College of Radiographers in Medical Ultra Sound
DCYW . . . Diploma in Community and Youth Work
DD . . . . Doctor of Divinity
DDEd . . . Diploma in Distance Education
DDW . . . . Diploma in Deaf Welfare
DEdin Cert . . Duke of Edinburgh's Awards Certificate of Recognition
Dep . . . . Deputy
Dept . . . . Department
DesL . . . . Docteur es Lettres
Det . . . . Detention
DFC . . . . Distinguished Flying Cross
DFM . . . . Distinguished Flying Medal (Canada)
DGA . . . . Diploma in Government Administration
DHA . . . . District Health Authority
DHistA . . . Diploma in the History of Art
DHL . . . . Doctor of Humane Letters
DHRK . . . Diploma in Humanities and Religious Knowledge
DHSA . . . Diploma in Health Services Administration
DIC . . . . Diploma of Imperial College
DIH . . . . Diploma in Industrial Health
DIL . . . . Diploma of the Institute of Linguists
DIM . . . . Diploma in Industrial Management
Dio . . . . Diocese
Dioc . . . . Diocesan
Dip . . . . Diploma
DipAct . . . Diploma in Acting
DipAD . . . Diploma in Art and Design
DipAdEd . . Diploma in Advanced Education
DipAE . . . Diploma in Adult Education
DipAgr . . . Diploma in Agriculture
DipAI . . . Diploma in Artificial Insemination
DipAnPsych . . Diploma in Analytical Psychology
DipAnth . . . Diploma in Anthropology
DipApTh . . . Diploma in Applied Theology
DipArch . . . Diploma in Architecture
DipBS . . . Diploma in Business Studies
DipC&G . . Diploma in Counselling and Guidance

DipC&S . . . Diploma in Counselling and Supervision
DipCD . . . Diploma in Church Development
DipChD . . . Diploma of Chaplains to the Deaf
DipCM . . . Diploma in Church Music
DipCombStuds . Diploma in Combined Studies
DipContEd . . Diploma in Continuing Education
DipCOT . . . Diploma of the College of Occupational Therapists
DipCSM . . . Diploma of the Cork School of Music
DipDA . . . Diploma in Dramatic Art
DipDiet . . . Diploma in Dietetics
DipEcon . . . Diploma in Economics
DipEcum . . . Diploma in Ecumenicalism
DipEd . . . Diploma in Education
DipEdG . . . Diploma in Educational Guidance
DipEdHChild . Diploma in the Education of Handicapped Children
DipEdMan . . Diploma in Educational Management
DipFD . . . Diploma in Funeral Directing
DipFE . . . Diploma in Further Education
DipFL . . . Diploma in Foreign Languages
DipG&C . . . Diploma in Guidance and Counselling
DipGeochem . . Diploma in Geochemistry
DipHE . . . Diploma in Higher Education
DipHort . . . Diploma in Horticulture
DipHP . . . Diploma in Human Purposes
DipHums . . . Diploma in Humanities
DipHyp . . . Diploma in Hypnotherapy
DipInstAM . . Diploma of the Institute of Administrative Management
DipInstM . . . Diploma of the Institute of Marketing
DipL&A . . . Diploma in Liturgy and Architecture
Dipl-Reg . . . Diplom-Regiesseur fuer Musiktheater
DipLib . . . Diploma of Librarianship
DipLit . . . Diploma in Liturgy
DipMan . . . Diploma for Management
DipMaths . . . Postgraduate Diploma in Mathematics
DipMechEng . . Diploma in Mechanical Engineering
DipMentH . . Diploma in Mental Health
DipMin . . . Diploma in Ministry
DipMiss . . . Diploma in Mission
DipOAS . . . Diploma in Oriental and African Studies
DipOT . . . Diploma in Occupational Therapy
DipP&C . . . Diploma in Psychology and Counselling
DipPC . . . Diploma in Pastoral Counselling
DipPE . . . Diploma in Physical Education
DipPh . . . Diploma in Physiotherapy
DipPhil . . . Diploma in Philosophy
DipPM . . . Diploma in Personnel Management
DipPs . . . Diploma in Psychotherapy
DipPSA . . . Diploma in Public and Social Administration
DipPSE . . . Diploma in Personal and Social Education
DipPsych . . . Diploma in Psychology
DipRCM . . . Diploma of the Royal College of Music
DipRE . . . Diploma in Religious Education
DipREM . . . Diploma in Rural Estate Management

DipRIPH&H . Diploma of the Royal Institute of Public Health and Hygiene
DipRJ . . . Diploma of Retail Jewellery
DipRK . . . Diploma in Religious Knowledge
DipRS . . . Diploma in Religious Studies
DipRSAMDA . Diploma of the Royal Scottish Academy of Music and Dramatic Art
DipSC . . . Diploma in Student Counselling
DipSMan . . . Diploma in School Management
DipSoc . . . Diploma in Sociology
DipSocAnth . . Diploma in Social Anthropology
DipSocSc . . . Diploma in Social Sciences
DipSocWork . . Diploma in Social Work
DipSurg . . . Diploma in Surgery
DipT . . . . Diploma in Teaching
DipTE . . . Diploma in Transportation Engineering
DipTh . . . Diploma in Theology
DipTHPsych . . Diploma in Therapeutic Hypnosis and Psychology
DipTM . . . Diploma in Training Management
DipTP . . . Diploma in Town Planning
DipTS . . . Diploma in Transport Studies
DipVG . . . Diploma in Vocational Guidance
DipYL . . . Diploma in Youth Leadership
DipYW . . . Diploma in Youth Work
Dir . . . . Director
DIS . . . . Diploma in Industrial Studies
Distr . . . . District
DIT . . . . Diploma in Interpreting and Translating
Div . . . . Divinity
Div Test . . . Divinity Testimonium
DL . . . . Deputy Lieutenant
DLC . . . . Diploma of Loughborough College
DLIS . . . . Diploma in Library and Information Studies
DLitt . . . . Doctor of Letters (also see LittD)
DLitt et Phil . . Doctor of Letters and Philosophy
DLO . . . . Diploma in Laryngology and Otology
DLSc . . . . Doctor of Legal Science
DM . . . . Diploma in Management
DMA . . . . Diploma in Municipal Administration
DMEd . . . Diploma of Management in Education
DMin . . . . Doctor of Ministry
DMinlStuds . . Diploma in Ministerial Studies
DMS . . . . Diploma in Management Studies
DMSchM . . . Diploma of the Mission School of Medicine, London
DMusEd . . . Diploma in Music Education
DN . . . . Diploma in Nursing
Dn . . . . Deacon
Dn-in-c . . . Deacon-in-charge
DNEd . . . Diploma in Nursery Education
DNM . . . . Diploma in Nuclear Medicine
Dom . . . . Domestic
DOMS . . . Diploma in Ophthalmic Medicine and Surgery
DON . . . . Diploma in Ophthalmic Nursing
Down . . . . Downing
DPA . . . . Diploma in Public Administration
DPEd . . . Diploma in Primary Education
DPH . . . . Diploma in Public Health

DPhil . . . . Doctor of Philosophy (also see PhD)
DPM . . . . Diploma in Psychological Medicine
DPMSA . . . Diploma in Philosophy of Medicine, Society of Apothecaries
DPS . . . . Diploma in Pastoral Studies
DPSE. . . . Diploma in Professional Studies in Education
DPST. . . . Diploma in Pastoral and Social Theology
DPT . . . . Diploma in Pastoral Theology
Dr . . . . . Doctor
DRCOG . . . Diploma of the Royal College of Obstetricians and Gynaecologists
DRI . . . . Diploma in Radionuclide Imaging
DRS . . . . Diploma in Rural Studies
DRSS. . . . Diploma in Religious and Social Studies
DSA . . . . Diploma in Social Administration
DSC . . . . Distinguished Service Cross
DSc . . . . Doctor of Science (also see ScD)
DSCE . . . Diploma in Social and Community Education
DSM . . . . Distinguished Service Medal
DSMS . . . Diploma in Sales Management Studies
DSO . . . . Companion of the Distinguished Service Order
DSocSc . . . Doctor of Social Science
DSocStuds . . Diploma in Social Studies
DSpEd . . . Diploma in Special Education
DSPT. . . . Diploma in Social and Pastoral Theology
DSRS. . . . Diploma in Social and Religious Studies
Dss . . . . Deaconess
dss. . . . . Admitted Deaconess
DST . . . . Doctor of Sacred Theology (also see STD)
DTechM . . . Diploma in Technical Mining
DTEd. . . . Diploma in Tertiary Education
DTh . . . . Doctor of Theology (also see ThD)
DTI . . . . Department of Trade and Industry
DTM&H . . . Diploma in Tropical Medicine and Hygiene
DTPH . . . . Diploma in Tropical Public Health
DTPS . . . . Diploma in Theological and Pastoral Studies
DTS . . . . Diploma in Theological Studies
Dub . . . . Dublin
DUP . . . . Docteur de l'Universite de Paris
Dur . . . . (Diocese of) Durham

E

E . . . . . East
Eastern
EC . . . . Emergency Commission
Ecum . . . . Ecumenical
Ecumenics
ED . . . . Ecclesiastical District (also see CD)
Efficiency Decoration
Ed. . . . . Editor
Editorial
EdD . . . . Doctor of Education
Edin . . . . (Diocese of) Edinburgh
Edm . . . . Edmund
Edmund's
Educn . . . Education
Educational
Edw . . . . Edward
Edward's
EKD . . . . Evangelische Kirche Deutschland
Eliz . . . . Elizabeth
Elizabeth's

Em . . . . Emmanuel
Emb . . . . Embassy
EN(M) . . . Enrolled Nurse (Mental)
EngTech . . . Engineering Technician
Episc . . . . Episcopal
Episcopalian
ERD . . . . Emergency Reserve Decoration
ESC . . . . Ecole Superievre de Commerce
ESMI . . . . Elderley, Sick and Mentally Infirm
Esq . . . . Esquire
etc. . . . . et cetera
Eur . . . . (Diocese of) Gibralter in Europe Europe European
Ev. . . . . Evangelist Evangelists Evangelist's
Evang. . . . Evangelical Evangelism
Ex . . . . . (Diocese of) Exeter
Ex-paroch . . Extra-parochial
Exam . . . . Examining
Exec . . . . Executive
Exors . . . . Executors
Exper . . . . Experimental
Ext . . . . . Extension

F

FACC . . . Fellow of the American College of Cardiology
FACCA . . . Fellow of the Association of Certified and Corporate Accountants (now see FCCA)
FACOG . . . Fellow of the American College of Obstetricians and Gynaecologists
FAEB . . . Fellow of the Academy of Environmental Biology (India)
FAIW . . . Fellow of the Australian Institute of Welfare and Community Workers
FASI . . . . Fellow of the Architects' and Surveyors' Institute
FBA . . . . Fellow of the British Academy
FBCO . . . Fellow of the British College of Ophthalmic Opticians (Optometrists)
FBCS . . . . Fellow of the British Computer Society
FBIM . . . . Fellow of the British Institute of Management (formerly MBIM)
FBOA . . . Fellow of the British Optical Association
FBPsS . . . Fellow of the British Psychological Society
FCA . . . . Fellow of the Institute of Chartered Accountants
FCCA . . . Fellow of the Chartered Association of Certified Accountants (formerly FACCA)
FCFI . . . . Fellow of the Clothing and Footwear Institute
FCIArb . . . Fellow of the Chartered Institute of Arbitrators
FCIB . . . . Fellow of the Corporation of Insurance Brokers
FCII . . . . Fellow of the Chartered Insurance Institute
FCILA . . . Fellow of the Chartered Institute of Loss Adjusters
FCIS . . . . Fellow of the Institute of Chartered Secretaries and Administrators
FCIT . . . . Fellow of the Chartered Institute of Transport
FCMA . . . Fellow of the Institute of Cost and Management Accountants
FCO . . . . Foreign and Commonwealth Office
FCollP . . . Ordinary Fellow of the College of Preceptors

FCP . . . . Fellow of the College of Preceptors
FDS . . . . Fellow in Dental Surgery
FDSRCS . . . Fellow in Dental Surgery of the Royal College of Surgeons of England
FE. . . . . Further Education
Fell . . . . Fellow
FEng . . . . Fellow of the Fellowship of Engineering
FEPA. . . . Fellow of the Evangelical Preachers' Association
FETC. . . . Further Education Teacher's Certificate
FFARCS . . . Fellow of the Faculty of Anaesthetists, Royal College of Surgeons of England
FFChM . . . Fellow of the Faculty of Church Music
FFPHM . . . Fellow of the Faculty of Public Health Medicine
FGA . . . . Fellow of the Gemmological Association
FGS . . . . Fellow of the Geological Society of London
FHSM or FHA . Fellow of the Institute of Health Service Management (formerly Administrators)
FIA . . . . Fellow of the Institute of Actuaries
FIBD . . . . Fellow of the Institute of British Decorators
FIBiol . . . Fellow of the Institute of Biology
FICE . . . . Fellow of the Institution of Civil Engineers
FIChemE . . . Fellow of the Institution of Chemical Engineers
FIED . . . . Fellow of the Institution of Engineering Designers
FIEE . . . . Fellow of the Institution of Electrical Engineers (formerly FIERE)
FIEEE . . . Fellow of the Institute of Electrical and Electronics Engineers (New York)
FIERE . . . Fellow of the Institution of Electronic and Radio Engineers (now see FIEE)
FIFireE . . . Fellow of the Institution of Fire Engineers
FIHospE . . . Fellow of the Institute of Hospital Engineering
FIIM . . . . Fellow of the Institution of Industrial Managers (formerly FIPlantE)
FIL . . . . Fellow of the Institute of Linguists
FIMA. . . . Fellow of the Institute of Mathematics and its Applications
FIMarE . . . Fellow of the Institute of Marine Engineers
FIMechE. . . Fellow of the Institution of Mechanical Engineers
FIMEMME . . Fellow of the Institution of Mining Electrical & Mining Mechanical Engineers
FIMLS . . . Fellow of the Institute of Medical Laboratory Sciences
FIMM . . . Fellow of the Institution of Mining and Metallurgy
FIMS . . . . Fellow of the Institute of Management Specialists
FInstE . . . Fellow of the Institute of Energy
FInstFF . . . Fellow of the Institute of Freight Forwarders Limited
FInstP . . . Fellow of the Institute of Physics
FInstSMM . . Fellow of the Institute of Sales and Marketing Management
FIPlantE . . . Fellow of the Institution of Plant Engineers (now see FIIM)
FIPM . . . . Fellow of the Institute of Personnel Management

FIQA . . . . Fellow of the Institute of Quality Assurance
FIST . . . . Fellow of the Institute of Science and Technology
FIStructE . . Fellow of the Institution of Structural Engineers
FITD . . . . Fellow of the Institute of Training and Development
Fitzw . . . . Fitzwilliam
FIWSc . . . Fellow of the Institute of Wood Science
FKC . . . . Fellow of King's College, London
FLA . . . . Fellow of the Library Association
FLAME . . . Family Life and Marriage Education
FLAS . . . . Fellow of the Chartered Land Agents' Society (now see FRICS)
FLCM . . . . Fellow of the London College of Music
FLIA . . . . Fellow of the Life Insurance Association
FLS . . . . Fellow of the Linnean Society
FMA . . . . Fellow of the Museums Association
Foundn . . . Foundation
FPACert . . . Family Planning Association Certificate
FPhS . . . . Fellow of the Philosophical Society of England
FPWI . . . . Fellow of the Permanent Way Institute
FRAeS . . . Fellow of the Royal Aeronautical Society
FRAI . . . . Fellow of the Royal Anthropological Institute
FRAM . . . Fellow of the Royal Academy of Music
Fran . . . . Francis Francis's
FRAS . . . . Fellow of the Royal Asiatic Society Fellow of the Royal Astronomical Society
FRCGP . . . Fellow of the Royal College of General Practitioners
FRCO . . . . Fellow of the Royal College of Organists
FRCOG . . . Fellow of the Royal College of Obstetricians and Gynaecologists
FRCP . . . . Fellow of the Royal College of Physicians, London
FRCPath . . . Fellow of the Royal College of Pathologists
FRCPGlas . . Fellow of the Royal College of Physicians and Surgeons, Glasgow (also see FRCSGlas)
FRCPsych . . Fellow of the Royal College of Psychiatrists
FRCR . . . . Fellow of the Royal College of Radiologists
FRCS . . . . Fellow of the Royal College of Physicians and Surgeons of England
FRCSE or FRCSEd . . Fellow of the Royal College of Surgeons of Edinburgh
FRCSGlas . . Fellow of the Royal College of Physicians and Surgeons, Glasgow (also see FRCPGlas)
FRCVS . . . Fellow of the Royal College of Veterinary Surgeons
FRGS . . . . Fellow of the Royal Geographical Society
FRHistS . . . Fellow of the Royal Historical Society
FRIAS . . . . Fellow of the Royal Incorporation of Architects of Scotland
FRIBA . . . Fellow of the Royal Institute of British Architects

FRIC . . . . Fellow of the Royal Institute of Chemistry (now see FRSC)
FRICS . . . Fellow of the Royal Institute of Chartered Surveyors (formerly FLAS and FSI)
FRMetS . . . Fellow of the Royal Meteorological Society
FRS . . . . Fellow of the Royal Society
FRSA . . . . Fellow of the Royal Society of Arts
FRSC . . . . Fellow of the Royal Society of Canada Fellow of the Royal Society of Chemistry (formerly FRIC)
FRSE . . . . Fellow of the Royal Society of Edinburgh
FRSH . . . . Fellow of the Royal Society for the Promotion of Health
FRSL . . . . Fellow of the Royal Society of Literature
FRSM . . . . Fellow of the Royal Society of Medicine
FRTPI . . . . Fellow of the Royal Town Planning Institute
FSA . . . . Fellow of the Society of Antiquaries
FSAScot . . . Fellow of the Royal Society of Antiquaries of Scotland
FSCA . . . . Fellow of the Royal Society of Company and Commercial Accountants
FSI . . . . Fellow of the Chartered Surveyors' Institution (now see FRICS)
FSJ . . . . Fellowship of St John the Evangelist
FSMC . . . . Freeman of the Spectacle-Makers' Company
FSR . . . . Fellowship Diploma of the Society of Radiographers
FSS . . . . Fellow of the Royal Statistical Society
FTC . . . . Flying Training Command
FTCD . . . . Fellow of Trinity College, Dublin
FTCL . . . . Fellow of Trinity College of Music, London
FTSC . . . . Fellow of the Tonic sol-fa College
FWeldI . . . Fellow of the Institute of Welding

G

G&C . . . . Gonville and Caius
Gabr . . . . Gabriel Gabriel's
GB . . . . Great Britain
GBSM . . . Graduate of the Birmingham School of Music
Gd. . . . . Good
GDip . . . . Gemmology Diploma
GDipP . . . Graduate Diploma in Physiotherapy
Gen . . . . General
Geo . . . . George George's
GFS . . . . Girls' Friendly Society
GGSM . . . Graduate Diploma of the Guildhall School of Music and Drama
Gib . . . . Gibraltar
GIFireE . . . Graduate of the Institute of Fire Engineers
GIMechE . . Graduate of the Institution of Mechanical Engineers
GIPE . . . . Graduate of the Institution of Production Engineers
Glam . . . . Glamorgan
Glas . . . . (Diocese of) Glasgow and Galloway Glasgow

GLCM . . . Graduate Diploma of the London College of Music
Glos . . . . Gloucestershire
Glouc . . . . (Diocese of) Gloucester
GM . . . . George Medal
GNSM . . . Graduate of the Northern School of Music
Golds . . . . Goldsmiths'
Gov . . . . Governor
Gp. . . . . Group
Gr . . . . Grammar
Grad LI . . . Graduate of the Landscape Institute
GradIEE . . . Graduate of the Institution of Electrical Engineers
GradIPM . . Graduate of the Institute of Personnel Management
GradIT . . . Graduate of the Institute of Transport
Greg . . . . Gregory Gregory's
GRIC . . . . Graduate Membership of the Royal Institute of Chemistry
GRNCM . . Graduate of the Royal Northern College of Music
GRSC . . . . Graduate of the Royal School of Chemistry
GRSM . . . Graduate of the Royal Schools of Music
GSM . . . . (Member of) the Guildhall School of Music and Drama
Gt . . . . Great
GTCL . . . . Graduate Diploma of Trinity College of Music, London
Gtr . . . . Greater
Guildf . . . . (Diocese of) Guildford

H

H . . . . Holy
H&FE . . . . Higher and Further Education
HA . . . . Health Authority
Hants . . . . Hampshire
Hatf . . . . Hatfield
Hd. . . . . Head
HDipEd . . . Higher Diploma in Education
HDipRE . . . Higher Diploma in Religious Education
HE . . . . Higher Education
Heref . . . . (Diocese of) Hereford
Hertf . . . . Hertford
Herts . . . . Hertfordshire
Hist . . . . Historical History
HIV . . . . Human Immunodeficiency Virus (also see AIDS)
HM . . . . Her (or His) Majesty
HMI . . . . Her (or His) Majesty's Inspector (or Inspectorate)
HMS . . . . Her (or His) Majesty's Ship
HNC . . . . Higher National Certificate
HND . . . . Higher National Diploma
HND(IMechE) . Higher National Diploma, Institution of Mechanical Engineers
Ho. . . . . House
Hon . . . . Honorary Honourable
Hosp . . . . Hospital
HospCC . . . Hospital Chaplaincy Certificate
HQ . . . . Headquarters
HTV . . . . Harlech Television
Hunts . . . . Huntingdonshire
HVCert . . . Health Visitor's Certificate

I

I . . . . . Incumbent

IAAP . . . . . International Association for Analytical Psychology
IBA . . . . . Independent Broadcasting Authority
ICM . . . . Irish Church Missions
ICS . . . . Intercontinental Church Society
IDC . . . . . Inter-Diocesan Certificate
IDWAL . . . Inter-Diocesan West African Link
IEng . . . . . Incorporated Engineer (formerly TEng(CEI))
IGAP . . . . Independent Group of Analytical Psychology
ILEA . . . . Inner London Education Authority
IMinE . . . Institution of Mining Engineers
Imp . . . . Imperial
Inc. . . . . Incorporated
Ind . . . . Industrial
Info . . . . Information
Insp . . . . Inspector
Inst . . . . Institute Institution
Intercon . . . Intercontinental
Internat . . . International
Interpr . . . Interpretation
IPFA . . . . Member of the Chartered Institute of Public Finance and Accountancy
Is . . . . . Island Isle
ISO . . . . Imperial Service Order
ITV . . . . Independent Television
IVF . . . . Inter-Varsity Fellowship of Evangelical Unions (now see UCCF)
IVS . . . . International Voluntary Service

J

Jas. . . . . . James James's
JCL . . . . Licentiate in Canon Law
JD . . . . Doctor of Jurisprudence
JEM . . . . Jerusalem and the East Mission (now see JMECA)
Jes. . . . . Jesus
JMECA . . . Jerusalem and Middle East Church Association (formerly JEM)
Jo . . . . . John John's
Jos. . . . . Joseph Joseph's
JP . . . . . Justice of the Peace
Jt or jt . . . Joint
Jun . . . . Junior

K

K . . . . . King King's
K, E & A . . . (Diocese of) Kilmore, Elphin and Ardagh
Kath . . . . Katharine/Katherine Katharine's/Katherine's
KBE . . . . Knight Commander of the Order of the British Empire
KCB . . . . Knight Commander of the Order of the Bath
KCMG . . . Knight Commander of the Order of St Michael and St George
KCT . . . . Knight Commander of the Order of the Templars
KCVO . . . Knight Commander of the Royal Victorian Order
KIAD . . . Kent Institute of Art and Design
KLJ . . . . Knight of the Order of St Lazarus of Jerusalem
KPM . . . . King's Police Medal
Kt . . . . . Knight

L

L & K . . . . (Diocese of) Limerick and Killaloe (united dioceses of Limerick, Ardfert, Aghadoe, Killaloe, Kilfenora, Clonfert, Kilmacduagh and Emly)
Lamp . . . . Lampeter
Lanc . . . . Lancaster
Lancs . . . . Lancashire
LASI . . . . Licentiate of the Ambulance Service Institute
Laur . . . . Laurence Laurence's
Lawr . . . . Lawrence Lawrence's
LCC . . . . London County Council
LCP . . . . Licentiate of the College of Preceptors
LCST . . . . Licentiate of the College of Speech Therapists
Ld . . . . . Lord
LDA . . . . Louis Dublin Award of the American Association of Suicidology
LDiv . . . . Licentiate in Divinity
Ldr . . . . Leader
LDS . . . . Licentiate in Dental Surgery
LDSRCSEng . Licentiate in Dental Surgery of the Royal College of Surgeons of England
LEA . . . . Local Education Authority
Lect . . . . Lecturer
Leic . . . . (Diocese of) Leicester
Leics . . . . Leicestershire
Leon . . . . Leonard Leonard's
LEP . . . . Local Ecumenical Project
LesL . . . . Licencie es Lettres
LGCM . . . Lesbian and Gay Christian Movement
LGSM . . . Licentiate of the Guildhall School of Music and Drama
LHSM . . . Licentiate of the Institute of Health Services Management
Lib . . . . Librarian Library
Lic. . . . . Licensed Licentiate
LICeram . . . Licentiate of the Institute of Ceramics
Lich . . . . (Diocese of) Lichfield
LicScCat . . . Licence en Sciences Catechetiques
Linc . . . . (Diocese of) Lincoln
Lincs . . . . Lincolnshire
Lit . . . . . Literature
LittD . . . . Doctor of Letters (also see DLitt)
Liturg . . . . Liturgical
Liv . . . . . (Diocese of) Liverpool
LLA . . . . Lady Literate in Arts
LLAM . . . Licentiate of the London Academy of Music and Dramatic Art
Llan . . . . (Diocese of) Llandaff
LLB . . . . Bachelor of Laws
LLCM . . . Licentiate of the London College of Music
LLD . . . . Doctor of Laws
LLM . . . . Master of Laws
LMH . . . . Lady Margaret Hall
LNSM . . . Local Non-stipendiary Minister (or Ministry)
Lon . . . . (Diocese of) London
Loughb . . . Loughborough
LRAM . . . Licentiate of the Royal Academy of Music
LRCP . . . . Licentiate of the Royal College of Physicians
LRCPI . . . Licentiate of the Royal College of Physicians of Ireland
LRSC . . . . Licentiate of the Royal Society of Chemistry

LSE . . . . London School of Economics and Political Science
LSHTM . . . London School of Hygiene and Tropical Medicine
LSIAD . . . Licentiate of the Society of Industrial Artists and Designers
LSMF . . . . Licentiate of the State Medical Faculty
LST . . . . Licentiate in Theology (also see LTh)
Lt . . . . . Lieutenant Little
LTCL . . . . Licentiate of the Trinity College of Music, London
Ltd . . . . Limited
LTh . . . . Licentiate in Theology (also see LST)
Luth . . . . Lutheran
LVCM . . . Licentiate of the Victoria College of Music
LVO . . . . Lieutenant of the Royal Victorian Order
LWCMD . . . Licentiate of the Welsh College of Music and Drama

M

M . . . . . Mid
M & K . . . (Diocese of) Meath and Kildare
MA . . . . Master of Arts
MA(Ed) . . . Master of Arts in Education
MA(Theol) . . Master of Arts in Theology
MACC . . . Member of the Australian College of Chaplains
MACE . . . Member of the Australian College of Education
Magd . . . . Magdalen/Magdalene Magdalen's/Magdalene's
MAJA . . . Member of the Association of Jungian Analysts
MAMIT . . . Member of the Associate of Meat Inspectors Trust
Man . . . . (Diocese of) Manchester
Man Dir . . . Managing Director
Mansf. . . . Mansfield
MAOT . . . Member of the Association of Occupational Therapists
MAPCC . . . Member of the Association for Pastoral Care and Counselling
MArch . . . Master of Architecture
Marg . . . . Margaret Margaret's
Mass . . . . Massachusetts (USA)
Matt . . . . Matthew Matthew's
MB . . . . Bachelor of Medicine (also see BM)
MB, BS or MB, ChB . . Conjoint degree of Bachelor of Medicine, Bachelor of Surgery
MBA . . . . Master of Business Administration
MBAC . . . Member of the British Association for Counselling
MBAP . . . Member of the British Association of Psychotherapists
MBASW . . . Member of the British Association of Social Workers
MBC . . . . Metropolitan (or Municipal) Borough Council
MBCS . . . Member of the British Computer Society
MBE . . . . Member of the Order of the British Empire
MBHI . . . Member of the British Horological Institute

MBIM . . . Member of the British Institute of Management (formerly AMBIM; now see FBIM)

MBPsS . . . Member of the British Psychological Society

MBTI . . . Licensed Administrator of the Myers Briggs Type Indicator

MC . . . Military Cross

MCB . . . Master in Clinical Biochemistry

MCBiblAA . Member of the Catholic Biblical Association of America

MCCEd . . Member of the Craft College of Education

MCE . . . Master of Civil Engineering

MChemA . Master in Chemical Analysis

MChS . . . Member of the Society of Chiropodists

MCIBSE . . Member of the Chartered Institute of Building Service Engineers

MCIM . . . Member of the Chartered Institute of Marketing (formerly MInstM)

MCIMA . . Member of the Chartered Institute of Management Accountants

MCIOB . . Member of the Chartered Institute of Building

MCIT . . . Member of the Chartered Institute of Transport

MCollP . . Member of the College of Preceptors

MCom . . . Master of Commerce

MCSD . . . Member of the Chartered Society of Designers

MCSP . . . Member of the Chartered Society of Physiotherapy

MCThA . . Member of the Clinical Theology Association

MD . . . Doctor of Medicine

MDCT . . . Manager's Diploma in Ceramic Technology

MDiv . . . Master of Divinity

MEd . . . Master of Education

MEHS . . . Member of the Ecclesiastical History Society

MEng . . . Master of Engineering

Mert . . . Merton

MesL . . . Lettres Modernes

Meth . . . Methodist

Metrop . . Metropolitan

MFA . . . Master of Fine Art

MFBA . . . Member of the Freshwater Biological Association

MFCM . . Member of the Faculty of Community Medicine

MHCIMA . Member of the Hotel, Catering and Institutional Management Association

MHSA . . . Member of the Hymn Society of America

MHSGBI . Member of the Hymn Society of Great Britain and Ireland

MHums . . Master of Humanities

MIAAP . . Member of the International Association for Analytical Psychology

MIAAS . . Member of the Incorporated Association of Architects and Surveyors

MIBCO . . Member of the Institution of Building Control Officers

MIBF . . . Member of the Institute of British Foundrymen

MIBiol . . Member of the Institute of Biology

MICE . . . Member of the Institution of Civil Engineers (formerly AMICE)

MICFor . . Member of the Institute of Chartered Foresters

MICFRM . Member of the Institute of Charity Fund Raising Managers

Mich . . . Michael / Michael's

Michael and All Angels

MIChemE . Member of the Institution of Chemical Engineers

MICS . . . Member of the Institute of Chartered Shipbrokers

Middlesb . Middlesborough

Middx . . Middlesex

Midl . . . Midlands

MIDPM . . Member of the Institute of Data Processing Management

MIE . . . Member of the Institute of Engineers and Technicians

MIEE . . . Member of the Institution of Electrical Engineers (formerly AMIEE and MIERE)

MIEEE . . Member of the Institute of Electrical and Electronics Engineers (New York)

MIEH . . . Member of the Institute of Environmental Health

MIEleclE . Corporate Member of the Institution of Electrical and Electronics Incorporated Engineers

MIERE . . Member of the Institution of Electronic and Radio Engineers (now see MIEE)

MIEx . . . Member of the Institute of Export

MIGasE . . Member of the Institution of Gas Engineers

MIH . . . Member of the Institute of Housing

MIHospE . Member of the Institute of Hospital Engineers

MIHT . . . Member of the Institute of Highway Engineers

MIIExE . . Member of the Institute of Incorporated Executive Engineers

MIIM . . . Member of the Institute of Industrial Managers

MIL . . . Member of the Institute of Linguists

Mil . . . Military

MIM . . . Member of the Institute of Metals (formerly Institution of Metallurgists)

MIMarE . . Member of the Institute of Marine Engineers

MIMC . . . Member of the Institute of Management Consultants

MIMechE . Member of the Institution of Mechanical Engineers (formerly AMIMechE)

MIMI . . . Member of the Institute of the Motor Industry

MIMM . . Member of the Institute of Mining and Metallurgy

MIMunE . Member of the Institution of Municipal Engineers

Min . . . Minister / Ministry / Minor

Minl . . . Ministerial

MInstAM . Member of the Institute of Administrative Management

MInstC(Glas) . Member of the Institute of Counselling (Glasgow)

MInstE . . Member of the Institute of Energy

MInstGA . Member of the Institute of Group Analysis

MInstM . . Member of the Institute of Marketing (now see MCIM)

MInstP . . Member of the Institute of Physics

MInstPC . . Member of the Institute of Psychotherapy and Counselling

MInstPkg . Member of the Institute of Packaging

MInstPS . . Corporate Member of the Institute of Purchasing and Supply

MIOT . . . Member of the Institute of Operating Theatre Technicians

MIPM . . . Member of the Institute of Personnel Management

MIPR . . . Member of the Institute of Public Relations

MIProdE . . Member of the Institution of Production Engineers

MIQA . . . Member of the Institute of Quality Assurance

MISM . . . Member of the Institute of Supervisory Management

Miss . . . Mission / Missions / Missionary

Missr . . . Missioner

MIStructE . Member of the Institute of Structural Engineers

MISW . . . Member of the Institute of Social Welfare

MITD . . . Member of the Institute of Training and Development

MITE . . . Member of the Institution of Electrical and Electronics Technician Engineers

MITSA . . Member of the Institute of Trading Standards Administration

MIWEM . . Member of the Institution of Water and Environmental Management

MLawSoc . Member of the Law Society

MLitt . . . Master of Letters

MLS . . . Master of Library Studies

MM . . . Military Medal

MMCET . . Martyrs' Memorial and Church of England Trust

MMS . . . Member of the Institute of Management Services

MMus . . . Master of Music (also see MusM)

MNAAL . . Member of the North American Academy of Liturgy

MNACH . . Member of the National Association of Clergy Hypnotherapists

MNFSH . . Member of the National Federation of Spiritual Healers

MOD . . . Ministry of Defence

Mon . . . (Diocese of) Monmouth

Mor . . . (Diocese of) Moray, Ross and Caithness

MPhil . . . Master of Philosophy

MPS . . . Member of the Pharmaceutical Society (now see MRPharmS)

MPsychSc . Master of Psychological Science

MRAC . . . Member of the Royal Agricultural College

MRAeS . . Member of the Royal Aeronautical Society

MRCGP . . Member of the Royal College of General Practitioners

MRCO . . Member of the Royal College of Organists

MRCOG . . Member of the Royal College of Obstetricians and Gynaecologists

MRCP . . Member of the Royal College of Physicians

MRCPsych . Member of the Royal College of Psychiatrists

MRCS . . . Member of the Royal College of Surgeons

MRCSE . . Member of the Royal College of Surgeons of Edinburgh

MRCVS . . . . Member of the Royal College of Veterinary Surgeons
MRHS . . . Member of the Royal Horticultural Society
MRIA . . . Member of the Royal Irish Academy
MRIC . . . Member of the Royal Institute of Chemistry (formerly ARIC; now see MRSC)
MRIN . . . Member of the Royal Institute of Navigation
MRINA . . . Member of the Royal Institution of Naval Architects
MRIPHH . . Member of the Royal Institute of Public Health and Hygiene
MRPharmS . Member of the Royal Pharmaceutical Society (formerly MPS)
MRSC . . . Member of the Royal Society of Chemistry (formerly MRIC)
MRSH . . . Member of the Royal Society for the Promotion of Health
MRST . . . Member of the Royal Society of Teachers
MRTPI . . . Member of the Royal Town Planning Institute
MRTS . . . Member of the Royal Television Society
MS . . . Master of Science (USA) Master of Surgery
MSacMus . . Master of Sacred Music
MSAnPsych . Member of the Society of Analytical Psychology
MSAPP . . . Member of the Society of Advanced Psychotherapy Practitioners
MSBiblLit . . Member of the Society of Biblical Literature
MSc . . . Master of Science
MSc(Econ) . . Master of Science in Economics
MSE . . . . Minister in Secular Employment
MSERT . . . Member of the Society of Electronic and Radio Technicians
MSHAA . . . Member of the Society of Hearing Aid Audiologists
MSIAD . . . Member of the Society of Industrial Artists and Designers
MSLS . . . . Member of the Society of Liturgical Study
MSocSc . . . Master of Social Sciences
MSocWork . Master of Social Work (USA)
MSOSc . . . Member of the Society of Ordained Scientists
MSOTS . . . Member of the Society for Old Testament Study
MSR . . . . Member of the Society of Radiographers
MSSCh . . . Member of the School of Surgical Chiropody
MSSCLE . . Member of the Society for the Study of the Crusades and the Latin East
MSSTh . . . Member of the Society for the Study of Theology
MSW . . . . Master of Social Work
Mt . . . . . Mount
MTD . . . . Master of Transport Design Midwife Teacher's Diploma
MTech . . . Master of Technology
MTh or Master of Theology (also
MTheol . . . see STM and ThM)
MTS . . . . Master of Theological Studies
MU . . . . . Mothers' Union
MusB or Bachelor of Music (also
MusBac . . . see BMus)
MusD or
MusDoc . . . Doctor of Music
MusM . . . . Master of Music (also see MMus)

MVI . . . . . Member of the Victoria Institute
MVO . . . . Member of the Royal Victorian Order
MYPS . . . Member of the Yorkshire Philosophical Society

N

N . . . . . North Northern
Nat . . . . National
Nath . . . . Nathanael/Nathaniel Nathanael's/Nathaniel's
NCA . . . . National Certificate in Agriculture
NDA . . . . National Diploma in Agriculture
NDAD . . . National Diploma in Art and Design
NDD . . . . National Diploma in Design
NDH . . . . National Diploma in Horticulture
NDN . . . . National District Nurse Certificate
nee . . . . . Maiden name
Newc . . . . (Diocese of) Newcastle
NHS . . . . National Health Service
Nic . . . . . Nicholas/Nicolas Nicholas's/Nicolas's
NNEB . . . National Nursery Examination Board
Nor . . . . . (Diocese of) Norwich
Northants . . Northamptonshire
Northd . . . Northumberland
Northn . . . Northampton
Nottm . . . Nottingham
Notts . . . . Nottinghamshire
NRD . . . . National Registered Designer
NS . . . . . Nova Scotia (Canada)
NSM . . . . Non-stipendiary Minister (or Ministry)
NSPCC . . . National Society for the Prevention of Cruelty to Children
NSW . . . . New South Wales (Australia)
NT . . . . . New Testament
Nuff . . . . Nuffield
NUI . . . . National University of Ireland
NUU . . . . New University of Ulster
NWT . . . . North West Territories (Canada)
NY . . . . . New York (USA)
NZ . . . . . New Zealand

O

OBE . . . . (Officer of) the Order of the British Empire
OBI . . . . . Order of British India
OCF . . . . Officiating Chaplain to the Forces
Offic . . . . Officiate
OGS . . . . Oratory of the Good Shepherd
OHP . . . . Order of the Holy Paraclete
OM(Ger) . . Order of Merit of Germany
OMF . . . . Overseas Missionary Fellowship
ONC . . . . Ordinary National Certificate
OND . . . . Ordinary National Diploma
Or . . . . . Oriel
Ord . . . . . Ordained Ordinands Ordination
Org . . . . . Organizer Organizing
OSB . . . . Order of St Benedict
OSJM . . . (Prelate of) the Order of St John of Malta
OSP . . . . Order of St Paul
OStJ . . . . (Officer of) the Most Venerable Order of the Hospital of St John of Jerusalem
OT . . . . . Old Testament

Ox . . . . . (Diocese of) Oxford
Oxon . . . . Oxfordshire

P

p . . . . . Ordained Priest
P-in-c . . . . Priest-in-charge
P-in-O . . . Priest-in-Ordinary
Par . . . . . Parish Parishes
Paroch . . . Parochial
Past . . . . . Pastoral
Patr . . . . . Patrick Patrick's Patronage
Pb . . . . . Presbyterian
PBS . . . . Pengeran Bintang Sarawak (Companion of the Order of the Star, Sarawak)
PC . . . . . Perpetual Curate Privy Counsellor
PCC . . . . Parochial Church Council
Pemb . . . . Pembroke
Penn . . . . Pennsylvania (USA)
Perm . . . . Permission
Pet . . . . . (Diocese of) Peterborough Peter Peter's
Peterho . . . Peterhouse
PGCE . . . Postgraduate Certificate in Education
PhC . . . . Pharmaceutical Chemist
PhD . . . . Doctor of Philosophy (also see DPhil)
Phil . . . . . Philip Philip's
PhL . . . . . Licentiate of Philosophy
plc . . . . . public limited company
PM . . . . . Priest Missioner
PO . . . . . Post Office
Poly . . . . Polytechnic
Portsm . . . (Diocese of) Portsmouth
Preb . . . . Prebendary
Prec . . . . Precentor
Prep . . . . Preparatory
Pres . . . . President
Prin . . . . Principal
Pris . . . . . Prison Prisons
Prof . . . . Professor
Progr . . . . Programme Programmes
Prop . . . . Proprietary
Prov . . . . Provincial
Pt . . . . . Point
PV . . . . . Priest Vicar

Q

QC . . . . . Queen's Counsel
QFSM . . . Queen's Fire Service Medal for Distinguished Service
QGM . . . . Queen's Gallantry Medal
QHC . . . . Queen's Honorary Chaplain
QPM . . . . Queen's Police Medal
QSM . . . . Queen's Service Medal
Qu . . . . . Queen Queen's Queens'
QUB . . . . The Queen's University of Belfast

R

R . . . . . Rector Royal
R of O . . . Reserve of Officers
R&SChTrust . Rochester and Southwark Church Trust
RAChD . . . Royal Army Chaplains' Department
RAD or Royal Association in Aid
RADD . . . of Deaf People (formerly Deaf and Dumb)
RAEC . . . Royal Army Educational Corps
RAF . . . . Royal Air Force
RAFVR . . . Royal Air Force Volunteer Reserve

RAM	(Member of) the Royal Academy of Music
RC	Roman Catholic
RCA	Royal College of Art
RCAF . .	Royal Canadian Air Force
RCM . . .	Royal College of Music
RCN . . .	Royal Canadian Navy
	Royal College of Nursing
RCS	Royal College of Surgeons of England
RCSE. . .	Royal College of Surgeons of Edinburgh
RD . . .	Royal Navy Reserve Decoration
	Rural Dean
RE	Religious Education
Relig . . .	Religious
Relns . . .	Relations
Rem . . .	Remand
Rep . . .	Representative
Res . . .	Residence
	Resident
	Residential
	Residentiary
Resp . . .	Responsibility
Resurr . . .	Resurrection
Rev . . .	Reverend
RGN . . .	Registered General Nurse
RHV . . .	Registered Health Visitor
RIA . . .	Royal Irish Academy
RIBA . . .	(Member of) the Royal Institute of British Architects (formerly ARIBA)
Rich . . .	Richard
	Richard's
RM . . .	Registered Midwife
RMA or RMC	Royal Military Academy (formerly College), Sandhurst
RMCM . .	Royal Manchester College of Music
RMCS . .	Royal Military College of Science, Shrivenham
RMN . . .	Registered Mental Nurse
RN . . .	Registered Nurse (Canada)
	Royal Navy
RNIB . . .	Royal National Institute for the Blind
RNR . . .	Royal Naval Reserve
RNT . . .	Registered Nurse Tutor
RNVR . .	Royal Naval Volunteer Reserve
Rob . . .	Robinson
Roch . . .	(Diocese of) Rochester
RPC . . .	Romanian Patriarchal Cross
RSCM . .	Royal School of Church Music
RSCN . .	Registered Sick Children's Nurse
Rt	Right
RTC . . .	Religious Teaching Certificate
Rtd or rtd .	Retired
RTE . . .	Radio Telefis Eireann
RVC . . .	Royal Veterinary College
'RVO . . .	Royal Victorian Order

S

S	South
	Southern
S & B . .	(Diocese of) Swansea and Brecon
S & M . .	(Diocese of) Sodor and Man
S'wark . .	(Diocese of) Southwark
S'well . . .	(Diocese of) Southwell
SACert . .	Social Administration Certificate
Sacr . . .	Sacrist
	Sacristan
SAMS . .	South American Missionary Society
Sarum . .	(Diocese of) Salisbury
Sav . . .	Saviour
	Saviour's

SBStJ . . .	Serving Brother of the Most Venerable Order of the Hospital of St John of Jerusalem
ScD . . .	Doctor of Science (also see DSc)
Sch . . .	School
SCM . . .	State Certified Midwife
	Student Christian Movement
SDES . . .	Special Diploma in Educational Studies
Sec . . .	Secretary
Selw . . .	Selwyn
Sem . . .	Seminary
SEN . . .	State Enrolled Nurse
Sen . . .	Senior
SHARE .	Shelter Housing and Renewal Experiment
Sheff . . .	(Diocese of) Sheffield
Shep . . .	Shepherd
SMF . . .	Society for the Maintenance of the Faith
So	Souls
	Souls'
SOAS . . .	School of Oriental and African Studies
Soc . . .	Social
	Society
SOMA . .	Sharing of Ministries Abroad
SOSc . . .	Society of Ordained Scientists
Southn . .	Southampton
SPCK . . .	Society for Promoting Christian Knowledge
SPG . . .	Society for the Propogation of the Gospel (now see USPG)
Sqn Ldr . .	Squadron Leader
SRD . . .	State Registered Dietician
SRN . . .	State Registered Nurse
SRP . . .	State Registered Physiotherapist
SS	Saints
	Saints'
	Sidney Sussex
SSC . . .	Secretarial Studies Certificate
	Societas Sanctae Crucis (Society of the Holy Cross)
	Solicitor before the Supreme Court (Scotland)
SSF . . .	Society of St Francis
SSJ . . .	Society of St John of Jerusalem
SSJE . . .	Society of St John the Evangelist
SSM . . .	Society of the Sacred Mission
St	Saint
St Alb. . .	(Diocese of) St Albans
	St Alban
	St Alban's
St And . .	(Diocese of) St Andrews, Dunkeld and Dunblane
St As . . .	(Diocese of) St Asaph
St D . . .	(Diocese of) St Davids
St E . . .	(Diocese of) St Edmundsbury and Ipswich
Staffs . . .	Staffordshire
STB . . .	Bachelor of Theology (also see BTh)
STD . . .	Doctor of Sacred Theology (also see DST)
STDip . . .	Sister-Tutor's Diploma
Ste. . . .	Sainte
Steph . . .	Stephen
	Stephen's
STh . . .	Scholar in Theology (also see ThSchol)
STL . . .	Reader (or Professor) of Theology
STM . . .	Master of Theology (also see MTh or MTheol and ThM)
STV . . .	Scottish Television
Sub . . .	Substitute
Succ . . .	Succentor
Suff . . .	Suffragan
Supt . . .	Superintendent

Switz . . .	Switzerland
SWJ . . .	Servants with Jesus
Syn . . .	Synod

T

T, K & A . .	(Diocese of) Tuam, Killala and Achonry
TA . . .	Territorial Army
TAVR . .	Territorial and Army Volunteer Reserve
TC	Technician Certificate
TCD . . .	Trinity College, Dublin
TCert . . .	Teacher's Certificate
TD . . .	Territorial Efficiency Decoration
TDDSc . .	Technical Diploma in Domestic Science
TDip . . .	Teacher's Diploma
TEAR . .	The Evangelical Alliance Relief
Tech . . .	Technical
	Technology
TEM . . .	Territorial Efficiency Medal
temp . . .	temporarily
TEng . . .	Senior Technician Engineer
TEng(CEI) .	Technician Engineer (now see IEng)
Th	Theologian
	Theological
	Theology
ThA . . .	Associate of Theology
ThB . . .	Bachelor of Theology (USA)
ThD . . .	Doctorate in Theology (also see DTh)
ThDip . . .	Theology Diploma (Australia)
ThL . . .	Theological Licentiate
ThM . . .	Master of Theology (also see MTh or MTheol and STM)
Thos . . .	Thomas
	Thomas's
ThSchol . .	Scholar in Theology (also see STh)
Tim . . .	Timothy
	Timothy's
TM . . .	Team Minister (or Ministry)
TNC . . .	Thoracic Nursing Certificate
TP. . . .	Team Priest
TR . . .	Team Rector
Tr	Trainer
	Training
TransDip . .	Translator's Diploma
Treas . . .	Treasurer
Trin . . .	Trinity
TS	Training Ship
TSB . . .	Trustee Savings Bank
TV . . .	Team Vicar
	Television
TVS . . .	Television South

U

UAE . . .	United Arab Emirates
UCCF . .	Universities and Colleges Christian Fellowship of Evangelical Unions (formerly IVF)
UCD . . .	University College, Dublin
UEA . . .	University of East Anglia
UK . . .	United Kingdom
UMCA . .	Universities' Mission to Central Africa (now see USPG)
UMIST . .	University of Manchester Institute of Science and Technology
UPA . . .	Urban Priority Area (or Areas)
URC . . .	United Reformed Church
US or USA .	United States (of America)
USCL. . .	United Society for Christian Literature

USPG . . . United Society for the Propagation of the Gospel (formerly SPG, UMCA, and CMD)

UWIST . . . University of Wales Institute of Science and Technology

V

V . . . . . Vicar
          Virgin
          Virgin's
VC . . . . Vicar Choral
Ven . . . . Venerable
VetMB . . . Bachelor of Veterinary Medicine (also see BVetMed)

Vin . . . . Vincent
          Vincent's
Voc . . . . Vocational Vocations
VRD . . . . Royal Naval Volunteer Reserve Officers' Decoration

W

W . . . . . West
          Western
w . . . . . with
Wadh . . . Wadham
Wakef . . . (Diocese of) Wakefield
Warks . . . Warwickshire
Warw . . . Warwick

WCC . . . World Council of Churches
WEC . . . Worldwide Evangelism Crusade
Westf . . . Westfield
Westmr . . Westminster
Wg Comdr . Wing Commander
Wilts . . . Wiltshire
Win . . . . (Diocese of) Winchester
Wm . . . . William
Wolfs . . . Wolfson
Wolv . . . Wolverhampton
Worc . . . (Diocese of) Worcester
Worcs. . . Worcestershire
WRAF . . Women's Royal Air Force

Y

YMCA . . . Young Men's Christian Association

Supplement
your parish magazine
with
THE SIGN
—the inset worth looking into
and
Monthly Picture Covers

Send for samples and full details, to:

CHANSITOR PUBLICATIONS LTD
A wholly owned subsidiary of Hymns Ancient & Modern Limited, a Registered Charity

Subscription Office, 16 Blyburgate, Beccles
Suffolk, NR34 9TB. Tel: (0502) 711231

Also publishers of General Synod Digest — details on request

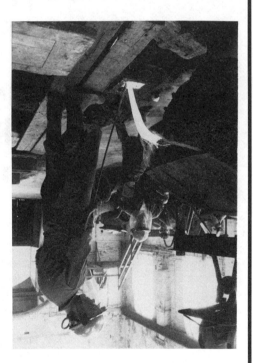

A

ABBEY, Canon Anthony James. b 36. ARCO61 Selw Coll Cam BA59 MA63. Ely Th Coll 59. **d** 61 **p** 62. C Wanstead St Mary *Chelmsf* 61-63; C Laindon w Basildon 63-67; R Sandon 67-76; V Epping St Jo from 76; Hon Can Chelmsf Cathl from 85. *The Vicarage, Hartland Road, Epping, Essex CM16 4PD* Epping (0378) 72906

ABBOTT, Barry Ingle. b 31. Sarum Th Coll 65. **d** 67 **p** 68. C Wilton w Netherhampton *Sarum* 69-71; V Warminster Ch Ch 71-76; Lic to Offic 76-77; P-in-c Figheldean w Milston 77-79; P-in-c Bulford 77-79; Lic to Offic B & W 79-88; Ex 80-88; Perm to Offic from 88; rtd 91. *Fern Cottage, Berwick Lane, Steeple Langford, Salisbury SP3 4NB* Salisbury (0722) 790348

ABBOTT, Charles Peter. b 25. Maryland Univ 60. Pecusa Ord Course. **d** 62 **p** 62. C Oxhey St Matt *St Alb* 66-70; Asst Chapl Alleyn's Foundn Dulwich 70-72; C Dulwich St Barn *S'wark* 70-72; V Southway *Ex* 72-78; V Whitgift w Adlingfleet and Eastoft *Sheff* 78-79; rtd 86. *Downs Cottage, Mutton Hall Hill, Heathfield, E Sussex TN21 8NB*

ABBOTT, Christopher Ralph. b 38. Univ of Wales (Lamp) BA59. Wells Th Coll 59. **d** 61 **p** 62. C Camberwell St Giles *S'wark* 61-67; C Portsea St Mary *Portsm* 67-70; V Portsea St Cuth 70-87; P-in-c Gt Milton *Ox* 87-88; P-in-c Lt Milton 87-88; R Gt w Lt Milton and Gt Haseley from 88. *The Rectory, Great Milton, Oxford OX9 7PN* Great Milton (0844) 279498

ABBOTT, David John. b 52. CertEd. St Jo Coll Nottm LTh. **d** 87 **p** 88. C Biddulph *Lich* 87-90; C Tunbridge Wells St Jas *Roch* from 90. *St Philip's House, Birken Road, Tunbridge Wells* Tunbridge Wells (0892) 31031

ABBOTT, David Robert. b 49. Edin Univ BD72 Birm Univ DipTh73. Qu Coll Birm 72. **d** 74 **p** 75. C Kirkby *Liv* 74-78; C Ditton St Mich 78-80; R Ashton-in-Makerfield H Trin from 80. *The Rectory, North Ashton, Wigan, Lancs WN4 0QF* Ashton-in-Makerfield (0942) 727241

ABBOTT, Miss Geraldine Mary. b 33. SRN55 SCM58 Open Univ BA77 Lon Univ MTh85. Oak Hill Th Coll BA82. **dss** 86 **d** 87. Tutor Oak Hill Th Coll from 86; St Alb St Paul *St Alb* 86-87; Hon Par Dn from 87. *2 Wheatleys, St Albans, Herts AL4 9UE* St Albans (0727) 860869

ABBOTT, Leslie Leonard. b 24. ARICS47 FRICS83. Wycliffe Hall Ox 55. **d** 56 **p** 56. V Attenborough w Chilwell *S'well* 67-73; Perm to Offic *Chich* 73-83; C Patcham from 83; rtd 89. *42 Heston Avenue, Brighton BN1 8UP* Brighton (0273) 553864

ABBOTT, Michael Reginald. b 40. Hull Univ BSc64. Cuddesdon Coll 64. **d** 66 **p** 67. C Workington St Jo *Carl* 66-68; C Ambleside w Rydal and Brathay 68-70; Hong Kong 70-71; Chapl RN 71-72; C Dalton-in-Furness *Carl* 72-73; V Stanbridge w Tilsworth *St Alb* 73-78; TV Dunstable 78-83; TR Chambersbury (Hemel Hempstead) from 83. *The Rectory, 14 Pancake Lane, Hemel Hempstead, Herts HP2 4NB* Hemel Hempstead (0442) 64860

ABBOTT, Nigel Douglas Blayney. b 37. Open Univ BA87. Bps' Coll Cheshunt 58. **d** 61 **p** 62. C Northn St Mich *Pet* 61-64; C Wanstead St Mary *Chelmsf* 64-66; Chapl St Jo Sch Tiffield Northants 66-69; V Earls Barton *Pet* 69-73; V Cov H Trin *Cov* 73-80; Provost St Jo Cathl Oban *Arg* 80-86; R Oban St Jo 80-86; TR Hemel Hempstead *St Alb* from 86. *The Rectory, 40 High Street, Hemel Hempstead, Herts HP1 3AE* Hemel Hempstead (0442) 213838

ABBOTT, Stephen Anthony. b 43. K Coll Cam BA65 MA69 Edin Univ BD68 Harvard Univ ThM69. Edin Th Coll 65. **d** 69 **p** 70. C Deal St Leon *Cant* 69-72; Chapl K Coll Cam 72-75; C Cam St Matt *Ely* 75-76; Asst Chapl Bris Univ *Bris* 77-80; Hon C Clifton St Paul 77-80; Perm to Offic from 81. *29 Withleigh Road, Knowle, Bristol BS4 2LG* Bristol (0272) 779270

ABDY, John Channing. b 38. Nottm Univ BA63. Cuddesdon Coll 63. **d** 65 **p** 66. C Leagrave *St Alb* 65-69; C N Mymms 69-72; V Kings Walden 72-79; V S Woodham Ferrers *Chelmsf* 79-85; V Walthamstow St Pet 85-91; V Burrington and Churchill *B & W* from 91. *The Parsonage, Bristol Road, Langford, Bristol BS18 7JE* Churchill (0934) 852295

ABEL, David John. b 31. S'wark Ord Course 71. **d** 74 **p** 75. NSM Crowhurst *S'wark* 74-85; NSM Lingfield and Crowhurst from 85. *Arden Green, Bowerland Lane, Lingfield, Surrey RH7 6DF* Lingfield (0342) 832714

ABELL, Brian. b 37. Nottm Univ BA61 DipEd. Cuddesdon Coll 61. **d** 63 **p** 64. C Lightcliffe *Wakef* 63-66; C-in-c Mixenden CD 66-68; Lect Linc Coll of Tech 68-69; Chapl Trent Coll Nottm 70-74; V Thorner *Ripon* 74-82; V Far Headingley St Chad 82-86; Deputation Appeals Org CECS 86-89; V Masham and Healey *Ripon* from 89. *The Vicarage, Masham, Ripon, N Yorkshire HG4 4JA* Ripon (0765) 89255

ABELL, George Derek. b 31. Selw Coll Cam BA54 MA68. Qu Coll Birm 54. **d** 56 **p** 57. R Bridgnorth St Mary *Heref* 64-70; P-in-c Oldbury 64-70; Australia 70-73; R Withington w Westhide and Weston Beggard *Heref* 73-81; R Withington w Westhide 81-83; P-in-c Sutton St Nicholas w Sutton St Michael 76-81; R 81-83; Preb Heref Cathl 82-83; V Basing *Win* 83-88; rtd 88. *51 Buckfield Road, Leominster, Herefordshire HR6 8SF* Leominster (0568) 4564

ABELL, Peter John. b 45. Chich Th Coll 67. **d** 70 **p** 71. C Churchdown St Jo *Glouc* 70-74; Chapl RAF from 74. *c/o MOD, Adastral House, Theobald's Road, London WC1X 8RU* 071-430 7268

ABERDEEN AND ORKNEY, Bishop of. See DARWENT, Rt Rev Frederick Charles

ABERDEEN AND ORKNEY, Dean of. See STRANRAER-MULL, Very Rev Gerald Hugh

ABERDEEN, Provost of. See WIGHTMAN, Very Rev William David

ABERNETHY, Alan Francis. b 57. QUB BA78. CITC 81. **d** 81 **p** 82. C Dundonald *D & D* 81-84; C Lecale Gp 84-86; I Helen's Bay 86-90; I Ballyholme from 90. *Ballyholme Rectory, 3 Ward Avenue, Bangor, Co Down BT20 5JW* Bangor (0247) 454836

ABERNETHY, David Terence Phillips. b 42. St D Coll Lamp 61. **d** 65 **p** 66. C Abergele *St As* 65-72; Bermuda 72-84; V Beaulieu and Exbury and E Boldre *Win* from 84. *The Vicarage, Palace Lane, Beaulieu, Hants SO4 7YG* Beaulieu (0590) 612242

ABLETT, Edwin John. b 37. Clifton Th Coll 64. **d** 67 **p** 68. C Sneinton St Chris w St Phil *S'well* 67-70; R High and Gd Easter w Margaret Roding *Chelmsf* 70-73; Chile 73-75; C Gt Baddow *Chelmsf* 75-78; V Newchapel *Lich* 78-82; V S Westoe *Dur* 82-86; V Tibshelf *Derby* from 86. *The Vicarage, 67 High Street, Tibshelf, Derby DE5 5NU* Ripley (0773) 872243

ABLEWHITE, John Leslie Charles. b 43. K Coll Lon BA66. Coll of Resurr Mirfield 84. **d** 86 **p** 87. C E Dereham *Nor* 86-88; C E Dereham and Scarning 89; P-in-c S Lynn from 89. *29 Goodwins Road, King's Lynn, Norfolk PE30 5QX* King's Lynn (0553) 771779

ABLEWHITE, Stanley Edward. b 30. Birm Univ BSocSc59 LSE CASS60. Tyndale Hall Bris 64 Wycliffe Hall Ox 73. **d** 73 **p** 74. C Much Woolton *Liv* 73-77; V Brough w Stainmore *Carl* 77-84; Min Aldridge *Lich* 84-90; P-in-c Swindon from 90; P-in-c Himley from 90. *12 St John's Close, Swindon, Dudley, W Midlands DY3 4PG* Kingswinford (0384) 278532

ABRAHAM, David Alexander. b 37. AKC61. **d** 62 **p** 63. C Oswestry St Oswald *Lich* 62-63; C Gt Wyrley 63-65; C Sprowston *Nor* 65-67; V Ormesby w Scratby 67-81; R Oxborough w Foulden and Caldecote 81-87; R Cockley Cley w Gooderstone 81-87; V Didlington 81-87; R Gt and Lt Cressingham w Threxton 81-87; R Hilborough w

1

Bodney 81-87; P-in-c Nor St Giles from 87; Chapl Asst Norfolk and Nor Hosp 87-91. *St Giles's Vicarage, Heigham Road, Norwich NR2 3AU*   Norwich (0603) 623724

ABRAHAM, Richard James. b 42. Liv Univ BA63. Ridley Hall Cam 64. **d** 66 **p** 67. C Warrington St Ann *Liv* 66-70; C Golborne 70-73; V Bickersham 73-78; V Ewerby w Evedon *Linc* 78-82; R Kirkby Laythorpe w Asgarby 78-82; R Kirkby Laythorpe from 82. *The Rectory, Kirkby Laythorpe, Sleaford, Lincs NG34 9NY*   Sleaford (0529) 304804

ABRAHAMS, Peter William. b 42. Southn Univ BA77. Sarum Th Coll 77. **d** 78 **p** 79. C Bitterne Park *Win* 78-82; C Old Brumby *Linc* 82-84; V Mitcham Ascension *S'wark* 84-91; TV Riverside *Ox* from 91. *The Vicarage, Mill Street, Colnbrook, Slough SL3 0JJ*   Slough (0753) 682156

ABRAM, Paul Robert Carrington. b 36. Keble Coll Ox BA62 MA65. Chich Th Coll 60. **d** 62 **p** 63. C Redcar *York* 62-65; CF 65-89; V Salcombe *Ex* from 89; Miss to Seamen from 89. *The Vicarage, Devon Road, Salcombe, Devon TQ8 8HJ*   Salcombe (054884) 2626

ABRAM, Steven James. b 50. Lon Univ DipTh74 BD76. Oak Hill Th Coll 71. **d** 76 **p** 77. C Biddulph *Lich* 76-79; C Heatherlands St Jo *Sarum* 79-83; Libya 83-84; C Stratford w Bishopton *Cov* 84; V Alderholt *Sarum* 84-90; V Daubhill *Man* from 90. *St George's Vicarage, Roseberry Street, Bolton BL3 4AR*   Bolton (0204) 61067

ABREY, Philip James. b 51. N Ord Course 82. **d** 85 **p** 86. NSM Hindley All SS *Liv* 85-90; C Caversham and Mapledurham *Ox* from 90; Min Caversham Park LEP from 90. *51 Galsworthy Drive, Caversham Park, Reading RG4 0PR*   Reading (0734) 475152

ABSALOM, Hugh Pryse. b 10. Fitzw Ho Cam BA31 MA36. Lon Univ BD56. **d** 36 **p** 37. Chapl and Sen Lect St Hild's Tr Coll Dur 61-73; R Walton W w Talbenny and Haroldston W *St D* 73-77; rtd 77. *34 Ruther Park, Haverfordwest, Dyfed*   Haverfordwest (0437) 765950

ABSOLON, Canon Peter Chambers. b 27. St Jo Coll Cam BA50 MA55. Linc Th Coll 50. **d** 53 **p** 54. TV Strood *Roch* 67-80; Hon Can Roch Cathl from 79; C Strood St Nic w St Mary 80-81; V Gillingham H Trin 81-91; RD Gillingham 90-91; rtd 91. *Holly Tree Cottage, 1 Itlay, Daglingworth, Cirencester, Glos GL7 7HZ*   Cirencester (0285) 654225

ACHESON, James Malcolm. b 48. BNC Ox BA70 MA73. Sarum & Wells Th Coll 83. **d** 85 **p** 86. C Highgate St Mich *Lon* 85-88; TV Tisbury *Sarum* from 88; OCF RAF from 88. *The Vicarage, The Street, Chilmark, Salisbury, Wilts SP3 5AU*   Teffont (072276) 307

ACHESON, Canon Russell Robert. b 16. Univ Coll Ox BA39 MA45 DipTh47. Wells Th Coll 45. **d** 47 **p** 48. V Much Wenlock w Bourton *Heref* 66-79; P-in-c Hughley w Church Preen 69-79; RD Condover 72-78; P-in-c Harley w Kenley 73-75; Preb Heref Cathl 74-79; Can Res 79-83; P-in-c Shipton 76-79; P-in-c Easthope w Long Stanton 76-79; rtd 83; Perm to Offic *Heref* from 83. *1 Penras, Newborough, Anglesey, Gwynedd LL61 6RS*   Newborough (024879) 325

ACHONRY, Dean of. See NEILL, Rt Rev John Robert Winder

ACKERLEY, Glyn James. b 57. HNC83. Cranmer Hall Dur 84. **d** 87 **p** 88. C Tonbridge SS Pet and Paul *Roch* 87-90; R Willingham *Ely* from 90. *The Rectory, Willingham, Cambridge CB4 5ES*   Willingham (0954) 61225

ACKERLEY, Herbert. b 20. St Deiniol's Hawarden 60. **d** 61 **p** 63. R Longsight St Matt w St Clem *Man* 68-71; R Longsight St Luke 71-85; rtd 85; Perm to Offic *Man* from 85; Ches from 86. *42 Newboult Road, Cheadle, Cheshire SK8 2AH*   061-428 5801

ACKLAM, Leslie Charles. b 46. Birm Univ BEd71. Ripon Coll Cuddesdon 78. **d** 80 **p** 81. C Chingford St Anne *Chelmsf* 80-83; C Spalding *Linc* 83-85; V Spalding St Paul from 85. *St Paul's Vicarage, 65 Holbeach Road, Spalding, Lincs PE11 2HY*   Spalding (0775) 722532

ACKLAND, John Robert Warwick. b 47. **d** 82 **p** 83. Lic to Offic *S'wark* 82-88; Hon C Mottingham St Andr from 88. *Priory Cottage, 39 Upton Road, Bexleyheath, Kent DA6 8LW*   081-301 0718

ACKROYD, Dennis. b 36. Cranmer Hall Dur 67. **d** 70 **p** 71. C Newc w Butterton *Lich* 70-73; C Horsell *Guildf* 73-77; P-in-c Moreton and Woodsford w Tincleton *Sarum* 77-82; R Dorchester 79-85; R Ewhurst *Guildf* from 86. *The Rectory, Ewhurst, Cranleigh, Surrey GU6 7PX*   Cranleigh (0483) 277584

ACKROYD, Eric. b 29. Leeds Univ BA51 Liv Univ MA71 Leic Univ MA(Ed)86. St Jo Coll Dur DipTh54. **d** 55 **p** 56. C Newland St Jo *York* 55-58; Succ Birm Cathl

Birm 58-60; Chapl K Sch Bruton 61-66; Lect Kirkby Fields Tr Coll Liv 67-72; Sen Lect Nene Coll of HE Northn 72-85. *247 Abington Avenue, Northampton NN3 2BU*   Northampton (0604) 717848

ACKROYD, John Michael. b 32. Lon Univ BSc53. Ripon Hall Ox 71. **d** 73 **p** 74. C Keighley *Bradf* 73-76; TV 76-81; V Keighley All SS 81; V Whalley *Blackb* from 81; Chapl Calderstones Hosp Blackb from 81. *The Vicarage, The Sands, Whalley, Blackburn BB6 9TL*   Whalley (0254) 823249

ACKROYD, Prof Peter Runham. b 17. Down Coll Cam BA38 Trin Coll Cam MA42 PhD45 Lon Univ MTh42 DD70 St Andr Univ Hon DD70. Westcott Ho Cam 57. **d** 57 **p** 58. Prof OT Studies Lon Univ 61-82; FKC from 69; rtd 82; Perm to Offic *St E* from 86. *Lavender Cottage, Middleton, Saxmundham, Suffolk IP17 3NQ*   Westleton (072873) 458

ACKROYD, William Lancelot. b 1900. Egerton Hall Man 31. **d** 33 **p** 34. V Eastleach w Southrop *Glouc* 64-68; rtd 68; C Stokenham w Sherford *Ex* 69-71; Perm to Offic Truro from 72. *2 Trelawney Road, Callington, Cornwall PL17 7EE*   Liskeard (0579) 83150

ACLAND, Simon Henry Harper. b 41. Westcott Ho Cam 65. **d** 67 **p** 68. C Prestwich St Marg *Man* 67-69; New Zealand 69-71 and 75-85; Singapore 71-74; C Kensington St Mary Abbots w St Geo *Lon* 85-87; C Chelsea Ch Ch 87; C Chelsea St Luke and Ch Ch from 87; Dir Post-Ord Tr from 87. *64A Flood Street, London SW3 5TE*   071-376 5492

ACOTT, David. b 32. Clifton Th Coll 54. **d** 58 **p** 59. C Streatham Park St Alb *S'wark* 58-60; C Maidstone St Faith *Cant* 60-64; R Pettaugh and Winston *St E* 64-76; R Pettaugh and Winston w Framsden 76-77; Area Sec (Dios Cant and Roch) CMS 77-85; C-in-c Hove H Trin CD *Chich* from 86. *Holy Trinity Parsonage, Blatchington Road, Hove, E Sussex BN3 3TA*   Brighton (0273) 739870

ACREMAN, John. b 53. Oak Hill Th Coll 86. **d** 88 **p** 89. C Iver *Ox* from 88. *St Leonard's House, St Leonard's Walk, Iver, Bucks SL0 9DD*   Iver (0753) 653532

ACWORTH, Oswald Roney. b 10. SS Coll Cam BA33 MA37. Westcott Ho Cam. **d** 46 **p** 47. V Chobham w Valley End *Guildf* 56-79; rtd 79; Perm to Offic B & W & Sarum from 82. *Farrs, Chapel Lane, Zeals, Warminster, Wilts BA12 6NP*   Bourton (0747) 840128

ACWORTH, Preb Richard Foote. b 36. SS Coll Cam BA62 MA65. Cuddesdon Coll 61. **d** 63 **p** 64. C Fulham St Etheldreda *Lon* 63-64; C Langley All SS and Martyrs *Man* 64-66; C Bridgwater St Mary w Chilton Trinity B & W 66-69; V Yatton 69-81; V Yatton Moor 81; P-in-c Taunton St Jo 81-85; P-in-c Taunton St Mary 81-85; V from 85; Preb Wells Cathl from 87. *St Mary's Vicarage, Church Square, Taunton, Somerset TA1 1SA*   Taunton (0823) 272441

ACWORTH, Richard John Philip. b 30. Ch Ch Ox BA52 MA56 Paris Univ DesL70. **d** 63 **p** 63. In RC Ch 63-67; C Walthamstow St Mary w St Steph *Chelmsf* 68-70; P-in-c Lt Sampford 70-76; P-in-c Gt Sampford 74-76; Lect Bath Coll of HE 76-77; Lect Th Derby Lonsdale Coll *Derby* 77-83; Derbyshire Coll of HE 83-88; P-in-c Newton Tracey, Alverdiscott, Huntshaw etc *Ex* from 88. *The Rectory, Newton Tracey, Barnstaple, Devon EX31 3PL*   Newton Tracey (027185) 292

ADAIR, Raymond. b 33. Ripon Hall Ox 70. **d** 72 **p** 73. C Knottingley *Wakef* 72-75; C Sandal St Helen 75-77; V Sandal St Cath 77-87; V Brownhill from 87. *The Vicarage, 24 Intake Lane, Batley, W Yorkshire WF17 0QQ*   Batley (0924) 471999

ADAIR, William Matthew. b 52. CITC 77. **d** 77 **p** 78. C Portadown St Mark *Arm* 77-78; Asst Chapl Miss to Seamen 78-80; C Lisburn Ch Ch Cathl *Conn* 80-84; I Kildress w Altedesert *Arm* from 84. *Kildress Rectory, 6 Rectory Road, Cookstown, Co Tyrone BT80 9RX*   Cookstown (06487) 51215

ADAM, Canon David. b 36. Kelham Th Coll 54. **d** 59 **p** 60. C Auckland St Helen *Dur* 59-63; C Owton Manor CD 63-67; V Danby *York* 67-90; Can and Preb York Minster 89-90; V Holy Is *Newc* from 90. *The Vicarage, Holy Island, Berwick-upon-Tweed TD15 2RX*   Berwick-upon-Tweed (0289) 89216

ADAM, Canon John Marshall William. b 09. Or Coll Ox BA31 MA36. Wycliffe Hall Ox 31. **d** 33 **p** 34. Hon Can Blackb Cathl *Blackb* 64-74; RD Preston 67-70; V Broughton 69-74; rtd 74; Lic to Offic *Blackb* from 74. *7 Caton Green Road, Brookhouse, Lancaster LA2 9JL*   Caton (0524) 770030

ADAM, Lawrence. b 38. N Ord Course 82. **d** 82 **p** 83. C Thornton-le-Fylde *Blackb* 82-86; Dioc Video Production Co-ord from 85; P-in-c Scorton 86-91; C W Burnley from 91. *Cranleigh House, 242A Burnley Road, Padiham, Burnley, Lancs BB12 8SS* Padiham (0282) 79291

ADAM, Michael MacIntosh. b 48. Sarum & Wells Th Coll. **d** 84 **p** 85. C Stamford Hill St Thos *Lon* 84-87; rtd 88. *Flat 1, 112 Millfields Road, London E5*

✠**ADAMS, Rt Rev Albert James.** b 15. K Coll Lon 39. St Andr Whittlesford 41. **d** 42 **p** 43 **c** 75. C Walkley *Sheff* 42-44; Succ Sheff Cathl 44; Prec 45-47; Chapl Bermondsey Medical Miss 47-55; R Bermondsey St Mary w St Olave and St Jo *S'wark* 47-55; RD Bermondsey 55; R Stoke Damerel *Ex* 55-63; R Wanstead St Mary *Chelmsf* 63-71; Adn W Ham 71-75; Suff Bp Barking 75-83; rtd 83; C Ridgeway *Sarum* 84-87. *89 Hardens Mead, Chippenham, Wilts* Chippenham (0249) 660728

ADAMS, Anthony John. b 42. St Jo Coll Nottm 83. **d** 85. C Wellesbourne *Cov* 85-89; R Weddington and Caldecote from 89. *The Rectory, Weddington, Nuneaton, Warks CV10 0EX* Nuneaton (0203) 386028

ADAMS, Arthur White. b 12. Sheff Univ BA35 MA36 Ox Univ MA49 BD50 DD67. Ripon Hall Ox 35. **d** 36 **p** 37. Fell and Dean of Div Magd Coll Ox 49-79; rtd 79. *30 Frenchay Road, Oxford OX2 6TG* Oxford (0865) 515092

ADAMS, Brian Hugh. b 32. Pemb Coll Ox BA54 MA57 Lon Univ DipTh56. Sarum & Wells Th Coll 77. **d** 79 **p** 80. Hon C Crediton *Ex* 79-81; Chapl St Brandon's Sch Clevedon 81-85; C Street w Walton *B & W* 86-88; RD Glastonbury from 86; V Baltonsborough w Butleigh and W Bradley from 88. *The Vicarage, Church Close, Butleigh, Glastonbury, Somerset BA6 8SH* Baltonsborough (0458) 50409

ADAMS, Celia. b 39. R Holloway Coll Lon BSc60 Cam Univ CertEd61. Sarum & Wells Th Coll 86. **d** 88. NSM Canley *Cov* 88-91; NSM Cov Caludon from 91. *Holy Cross Vicarage, 14 St Austell Road, Wyken, Coventry CV2 5AE* Coventry (0203) 635734

ADAMS, Ven Charles Alexander. b 29. MBE73 CBE82 JP. AKC59. **d** 60 **p** 61. C Bishopwearmouth St Mich w St Hilda *Dur* 60-63; C Ox SS Phil and Jas *Ox* 63-66; C Tunbridge Wells St Barn *Roch* 66-68; St Vincent from 68; Miss to Seamen from 68; Can Kingstown Cathl from 73; Adn St Vincent & The Grenadines from 76. *St Mary's Rectory, Bequia, Northern Grenadines, Windward Islands* St Vincent (1809) 458-3234

ADAMS, David John Anthony. b 46. BSc. Bris Sch of Min. **d** 84 **p** 85. NSM Sea Mills *Bris* from 84. *31 Elberton Road, Bristol BS9 2PZ* Bristol (0272) 684625

ADAMS, Denis Leslie. b 23. Ox NSM Course 78. **d** 81 **p** 82. NSM Reading All SS *Ox* 81-82; C Wargrave 82-83; C Skegness and Winthorpe *Linc* 83-85; V Gainsborough St Jo 85-89; rtd 89; Perm to Offic *Linc* from 89. *4 Collum Gardens, Ashby, Scunthorpe, S Humberside* Scunthorpe (0724) 842554

ADAMS, Donald John. b 46. St Jo Coll Nottm 86. **d** 88 **p** 89. C Byfleet *Guildf* from 88. *118 Rectory Lane, Byfleet, Weybridge, Surrey KT14 7NF* Byfleet (0932) 354627

ADAMS, Douglas George. b 39. Ex Univ MEd87. Lon Bible Coll 65 SW Minl Tr Course 86. **d** 89 **p** 90. NSM Bude Haven *Truro* 89; NSM Bude Haven and Marhamchurch from 89. *9 Arundel Terrace, Bude, Cornwall EX23 8LS* Bude (0288) 353842

ADAMS, Canon Douglass Arthur. b 04. Dur Univ LTh33. Bp Wilson Coll 29. **d** 32 **p** 33. V Market Harborough *Leic* 54-73; Hon Can Leic Cathl 59-73; RD Gartree I (Harborough) 69-73; rtd 73; Lic to Offic *Leic* 73-81; Perm to Offic from 81. *32 The Hawthorns, Holly Drive, Lutterworth, Leics LE17 4UL* Lutterworth (0455) 554709

ADAMS, George Ernest. b 12. Sarum Th Coll 37. **d** 39 **p** 40. V Arlesey w Astwick *St Alb* 66-70; R Gillingham w Geldeston and Stockton *Nor* 70-80; rtd 80; Perm to Offic Nor from 82; St E from 87. *4 Malthouse Court, London Road, Harleston, Norfolk IP20 9BU* Harleston (0379) 853445

ADAMS, Miss Gillian. b 57. SRN79 SCM81. Trin Coll Bris DipHE84 DPS85. **dss** 85 **d** 87. Easton H Trin w St Gabr and St Lawr and St Jude *Bris* 85-87; Par Dn 87-91. *23 Turner Way, Clevedon, Avon BS21 7YN*

ADAMS, James Michael. b 49. LLB. St Jo Coll Nottm DipTh CertEd. **d** 82 **p** 83. C Luton St Mary *St Alb* 82-85; TV Cove St Jo *Guildf* from 85. *66 Southwood Road, Farnborough, Hants GU14 0JJ* Farnborough (0252) 513422

ADAMS, John. b 38. Lon Univ DipEd66 Open Univ BA79. Linc Th Coll 68. **d** 70 **p** 71. C Skipton H Trin *Bradf* 70-72; C Bassingham *Linc* 72-73; Chapl Lingfield Hosp Sch 73-74; Hon C Keighley *Bradf* 76-79; P-in-c Bredenbury and Wacton w Grendon Bishop *Heref* 79-84;

P-in-c Edwyn Ralph and Collington w Thornbury 79-84; P-in-c Pencombe w Marston Stannett and Lt Cowarne 79-84; V Macclesfield St Jo *Ches* 84-87; R Wimblington *Ely* 87-90; V Manea 87-90; R Hallaton w Horninghold, Allexton, Tugby etc *Leic* from 90. *The Rectory, Churchgate, Hallaton, Market Harborough, Leics LE16 8TY* Hallaton (085889) 363

ADAMS, John David Andrew. b 37. TCD BA60 Div Test61 MA64 BD69 Reading Univ MEd74. **d** 62 **p** 63. C Belf St Steph *Conn* 62-65; Teacher 65-74; Hd Master St Paul's Secondary Sch Addlestone 74-82; NSM Bourne *Guildf* from 80; Weydon Secondary Sch Farnham from 82. *Brookside Farm, Oast House Crescent, Farnham, Surrey GU9 0NP* Farnham (0252) 726888

ADAMS, John Peregrine. b 25. Magd Coll Ox BA46 MA50. Wells Th Coll 48. **d** 49 **p** 50. V Stapleford w Berwick St James *Sarum* 57-91; RD Wylye and Wilton 77-85; rtd 91. *12 Harcourt Terrace, Salisbury* Salisbury (0722) 336061

ADAMS, John Peter. b 42. Lon Univ BD69. Oak Hill Th Coll 65. **d** 70 **p** 71. C Whitnash *Cov* 70-74; Chapl Davos *Eur* 74-75; Chapl Dusseldorf 75-76; C Gt Baddow *Chelmsf* 77-80; Asst Chapl Zurich *Eur* from 91. *Erlaufstrasse 43/2, A-2344 MA, Enzersdorf, Austria*

ADAMS, John Richard. b 38. St D Coll Lamp BA62 Lich Th Coll 62. **d** 64 **p** 65. C Falmouth K Chas *Truro* 64-68; C Bath Twerton-on-Avon *B & W* 68-72; C Milton *Win* 72-79; P-in-c Weymouth St Edm *Sarum* 79-90; V from 90. *The Vicarage, Lynch Road, Weymouth, Dorset DT4 0SJ* Weymouth (0305) 782408

ADAMS, Canon John Wrigley. b 07. St Chad's Coll Dur BA31 DipTh32 MA34. **d** 32 **p** 33. V Bentham St Marg *Bradf* 64-72; Hon Can Bradf Cathl 64-72; RD Ewecross 64-72; rtd 72. *46 Wollaston Road, Cleethorpes, S Humberside DN35 8DX* Cleethorpes (0472) 699616

ADAMS, Jonathan Henry. b 48. St Andr Univ MA73. Cranmer Hall Dur 73. **d** 76 **p** 77. C Upperby St Jo *Carl* 76-78; C Sunderland St Chad *Dur* 78-82; Soc Resp Officer from 83. *9 Brookside Terrace, Sunderland SR2 7RN* 091-565 6060

ADAMS, Martin Peter. b 57. Sarum & Wells Th Coll 88. **d** 90 **p** 91. C Sandringham w W Newton *Nor* from 90. *66 Church Road, Flitcham, King's Lynn, Norfolk PE31 6BU* Hillington (0485) 601147

ADAMS, Michael John. b 48. St Jo Coll Dur BA77. Ripon Coll Cuddesdon 77. **d** 79 **p** 80. C Falmouth K Chas *Truro* 79-81; C St Buryan, St Levan and Sennen 81-83; P-in-c Lanlivery w Luxulyan 83-84; V 84-88; V St Agnes from 88; RD Powder from 90. *The Vicarage, St Agnes, Cornwall TR5 0SE* St Agnes (087255) 2328

ADAMS, Miss Margaret Anne. *See* FREEMAN, Mrs Margaret Anne

ADAMS, Nigel David. b 40. Sarum & Wells Th Coll 86. **d** 88 **p** 89. C Tile Hill *Cov* 88-91; C Cov Caludon from 91. *Holy Cross Vicarage, 14 St Austell Road, Coventry CV2 5AE* Coventry (0203) 635734

ADAMS, Peter. **d** 91. NSM Towcester w Easton Neston *Pet* from 91. *Swandon, The Green, Thornborough, Buckingham MK18 2DT* Winslow (029671) 3491

ADAMS, Peter. b 37. AKC65 Trin Coll Cam MA70. **d** 66 **p** 67. C Clapham H Trin *S'wark* 66-70; Chapl Trin Coll Cam 70-75; Warden Trin Coll Cen Camberwell 75-83; V Camberwell St Geo *S'wark* 75-83; RD Camberwell 80-83; V W Dulwich All SS and Em from 83. *All Saints' Vicarage, 165 Rosendale Road, London SE21 8LN* 081-670 0826

ADAMS, Peter Anthony. b 48. K Coll Lon BD70 AKC70 MTh72. **d** 72 **p** 74. Lic to Offic *Eur* 72-73; C Ashford *Cant* 73-79; P-in-c Ramsgate H Trin 79-86; P-in-c Ramsgate St Geo 84-86; R Ramsgate H Trin and St Geo from 86. *Holy Trinity Rectory, Winterstoke Way, Ramsgate, Kent CT11 8AG* Thanet (0843) 53593

ADAMS, Peter Harrison. b 41. Tyndale Hall Bris 63. **d** 68 **p** 69. C Kendal St Thos *Carl* 68-71; C W Bromwich Gd Shep w St Jo *Lich* 71-75; R Aldham *Chelmsf* 76-81; R Marks Tey 76-81; R Marks Tey w Aldham and Lt Tey 81-85; Dioc Missr from 85. *4 St Jude's Gardens, St John's Estate, Colchester CO4 4PP* Colchester (0206) 854041

ADAMS, Canon Raymond Michael. b 41. Lon Univ BD67. ALCD66. **d** 67 **p** 68. C Old Hill H Trin *Worc* 67-73; TR Ipsley from 73; Hon Can Worc Cathl from 84. *The Rectory, Icknield Street, Ipsley, Redditch, Worcs B98 0AN* Redditch (0527) 23307

ADAMS, Raymond William. b 58. Reading Univ BA79. Oak Hill Th Coll BA85. **d** 85 **p** 86. C Blackpool St Thos *Blackb* 85-88; C Padiham 88-90; TV Rodbourne Cheney *Bris* from 90. *54 Furlong Close, Haydon Wick, Swindon, Wilts SN2 3QP* Swindon (0793) 726378

ADAMS, Richard. b 10. TCD BA32 MA35 BD44 PhD46. d 33 p 34. Dean Conn 63-75; rtd 75. *100 Newtownbreda Road, Belfast BT8* Belfast (0232) 691962

ADAMS, Robin Thomas. b 54. QUB BSc76. Oak Hill Th Coll BA79. d 79 p 80. C Magheralin *D & D* 79-82; C Coleraine *Conn* 82-86; I Belf St Aid 86-89; USA from 89. *332 North Union Street, Tecumseh, Michigan 49286, USA* Tecumseh (517) 423-3233

ADAMS, Roger Charles. b 36. Em Coll Cam BA60 MA64. Tyndale Hall Bris 60. d 62 p 63. C Longfleet *Sarum* 62-65; C Uphill *B & W* 66-71; R Ramsden Crays w Ramsden Bellhouse *Chelmsf* 71-78; SW Area Sec BFBS 78-84; P-in-c Plymouth St Aug *Ex* 84-85; TV Plymouth Em w Efford 85-90; V Paignton Ch Ch from 90. *Christ Church Vicarage, 133 Torquay Road, Paignton, Devon TQ3 2AG* Paignton (0803) 556311

ADAMS, Stephen Paul. b 56. Ex Univ BSc78. Sarum & Wells Th Coll 85. d 87 p 88. C Swansea St Nic *S & B* 87-88; C Llwynderw 88-91; V Badby w Newnham *Pet* from 91; R Charwelton w Fawsley and Preston Capes from 91. *The Vicarage, Vicarage Hill, Badby, Daventry, Northants NN11 6AP* Daventry (0327) 310239

ADAMSON, Anthony Scott. b 49. Newc Univ BA70. St Jo Coll Dur 75. d 78 p 79. C High Elswick St Paul *Newc* 78-86; C Benwell Team from 86. *53 Pipetruck Lane, Benwell, Newcastle upon Tyne NE4 8JQ* 091-273 1523

ADAMSON, Arthur John. b 38. Keble Coll Ox BA61 MA65. Tyndale Hall Bris 61. d 63 p 64. C Redhill H Trin *S'wark* 63-66; Chapl Trent Park Coll of Educn 66-69; C Enfield Ch Ch Trent Park *Lon* 66-70; Ind Chapl *S'wark* 70-74; V Battersea St Geo w St Andr 70-74; R Reedham *Nor* 74-80; Min Beighton and Moulton 75-80; P-in-c Cantley w Limpenhoe and Southwood 77-80; R Oulton St Mich 80-90; Chapl Lothingland Hosp 80-90; R Laceby *Linc* from 90. *3 Butterfield Close, Laceby, Grimsby, S Humberside DN37 7BG* Grimsby (0472) 70884

ADAMSON, Paul. b 35. Leeds Univ BA58. Coll of Resurr Mirfield. d 60 p 61. C Southwick St Columba *Dur* 60-63; Br Guiana 63-66; Guyana 66-75; C Benwell St Jas *Newc* 75-77; V Cowgate 77-83; V Prudhoe from 83. *The Vicarage, 5 Kepwell Court, Prudhoe, Northd NE42 5PE* Prudhoe (0661) 36059

ADAMSON, Richard Edwin Aidan. b 56. Pepperdine Univ BA76 Hamburg Univ Dipl-Reg86. Coll of Resurr Mirfield 89 Sarum & Wells Th Coll 90. d 91. C Reddish *Man* from 91. *24 Ainsdale Grove, Stockport, Cheshire SK5 6UF* 061-432 0147

ADAMSON, Warren Joseph. b 43. St Jo Coll Nottm. d 82 p 83. C S Croydon Em *Cant* 82-85; TV Folkestone H Trin and St Geo w Ch Ch 85-90; R Folkestone St Geo from 90. *St George's Parsonage, 133 Shorncliffe Road, Folkestone, Kent CT20 3PB* Folkestone (0303) 55907

ADDENBROOKE, Frank Gordon. b 06. Trin Coll Cam BA27 MA31. Westcott Ho Cam 28. d 29 p 31. R E and W Hendred *Ox* 63-74; rtd 74. *The Vicarage, Colgate, Horsham, W Sussex RH12 4SZ* Faygate (029383) 362

ADDENBROOKE, Peter Homfray. b 38. Trin Coll Cam BA59 MA. Lich Th Coll 61. d 63 p 64. C Bakewell *Derby* 63-67; C Horsham *Chich* 67-73; P-in-c Colgate from 73; Adv for Past Care and Counselling from 73. *The Vicarage, Colgate, Horsham, W Sussex RH12 4SZ* Faygate (029383) 362

ADDINGTON HALL, Gerald Richard. b 38. Qu Coll Ox BA62 MA67 Birm Univ MA69. Qu Coll Birm 62. d 65 p 66. C Leeds St Sav *Ripon* 65-69; Tanzania 69-75; V Ipswich St Fran *St E* 75-81; V Pakenham w Norton and Tostock 81-91; V Charsfield w Debach, Monewden, Hoo etc from 91; Warden of Readers from 91. *The Vicarage, Charsfield, Woodbridge, Suffolk IP13 7PY* Charsfield (047337) 618

ADDIS, Arthur Lewis. b 11. TD. Worc Ord Coll 62. d 64 p 65. R W Dean w E Grimstead *Sarum* 66-70; V Stratford sub Castle 70-79; rtd 79. *78 Park Street, Salisbury SP1 3AU* Salisbury (0722) 335476

ADDISON, Bernard Michael Bruce. b 31. Cam Univ MA73. St Steph Ho Ox 58. d 61 p 62. C Paddington St Sav *Lon* 61-64; C Primrose Hill St Mary w Avenue Road St Paul 64-66; S Africa 66-72; Australia 70-72; C Catford St Andr *S'wark* 72-73; Chapl Cam Coll Cam 73-78; Chapl Bonn w Cologne *Eur* 79-82; R Kegworth *Leic* 82-89; V Market Harborough from 89. *The Vicarage, 49 Burnmill Road, Market Harborough LE16 7JF* Market Harborough (0858) 63441

ADDISON, David John Frederick. b 37. Dur Univ BA60 Birm Univ MA79 DipEd. Wells Th Coll 64. d 66 p 71. C Rastrick St Matt *Wakef* 66-67; Perm to Offic Bradf 67-71; Glouc 77-79; Hon C Manningham St Luke *Bradf* 71-73; Hon C Bisley w Oakridge *Glouc* 79-81;

P-in-c Clearwell 81; P-in-c Newland w Redbrook 81; V Newland and Redbrook w Clearwell from 81. *The Vicarage, Newland, Coleford, Glos GL16 8NP* Dean (0594) 33777

ADDISON, Philip Ives. b 29. Dur Univ BA49. Ely Th Coll 59. d 61 p 62. C Waltham Cross *St Alb* 61-64; C Bedf St Paul 64-66; Chapl RN 66-70; V Foleshill St Laur *Cov* 70-74; P-in-c Halsham *York* 74-78; V Owthorne and Rimswell w Withernsea from 74. *The Vicarage, 28 Park Avenue, Withernsea, N Humberside HU19 2JU* Withernsea (0964) 613598

ADDISON KOJO, Samuel. b 63. St Nic Th Coll Ghana LTh87. d 87 p 87. Ghana 87-90; C S Moor *Dur* 90-91. *St George's Clergy House, Stanley, Co Durham DH9 7EN* Stanley (0207) 232564

ADDISON SMITH, Canon Anthony Cecil. b 18. Keble Coll Ox BA48 MA53. Linc Th Coll 48. d 49 p 50. V Easingwold w Raskelfe *York* 66-78; RD Easingwold 70-77; Can York Minster from 76; V Selby Abbey 78-83; rtd 83; Perm to Offic *Ox* 83-85 and from 87; C Cookham 85-86; C Hambleden Valley 87. *5 Tierney Court, Marlow, Bucks SL7 2BL* Marlow (06284) 3288

ADENEY, Arthur Webster. b 06. Clare Coll Cam BA27 MA32. Ridley Hall Cam 27. d 29 p 31. V Foxton w Gumley and Laughton *Leic* 67-74; rtd 74; Perm to Offic *Win* from 75. *c/o M Adeney Esq, 16 Southwood Lawn Road, Highgate, London N6 5SF* 081-340 9002

ADENEY, Dr Harold Walter. b 14. OBE76. Qu Coll Cam BA35 MB, BChir38 MA53. Trin Coll Bris. d 75 p 76. Burundi 75-82; Perm to Offic *St Alb* from 83. *24 Red Lion Close, Cranfield, Bedford MK43 0JA* Bedford (0234) 751609

ADENEY, Canon Ronald Edward. b 19. OBE79. Qu Coll Cam BA40 MA44 Birm Univ PGCE71. Ridley Hall Cam 41. d 42 p 43. Jerusalem 47-73 and 75-80; Perm to Offic *Birm* 73-75; Hon Can Jerusalem 77-80; P-in-c Fulmer *Ox* 81-85; rtd 85; Perm to Offic *Ox* 85-87; Jerusalem from 86. *c/o P R Webb Esq, 5 Silver Birches, Staunton St John, Oxford OX9 1HH*

ADEY, John Douglas. b 33. Man Univ BSc54. Coll of Resurr Mirfield 56. d 58 p 59. C Forton *Portsm* 58-64; C Northolt St Mary *Lon* 64-67; V Snibston *Leic* 67-72; V Outwood *Wakef* 72-78; V Clifton 78; V Upton Priory *Ches* 79-81; V Hyde St Thos 81-82; V Newton in Mottram 82-89; R Roos and Garton in Holderness w Tunstall etc *York* from 89. *The Rectory, Roos, Hull HU12 0LD* Withernsea (0964) 670362

ADFIELD, Richard Ernest. b 31. Oak Hill Th Coll 62. d 64 p 65. C Bedworth *Cov* 64-67; V Whitehall Park St Andr Hornsey Lane *Lon* 67-77; V Kensington St Helen w H Trin 77-86; V Turnham Green Ch Ch from 86. *The Vicarage, 2 Wellesey Road, London W4 4BL* 081-994 1617

✠ADIE, Rt Rev Michael Edgar. b 29. St Jo Coll Ox BA52 MA56. Westcott Ho Cam 52. d 54 p 55 c 83. C Pallion *Dur* 54-57; Abp's Dom Chapl *Cant* 57-60; V Sheff Broomhall St Mark *Sheff* 60-69; RD Hallam 66-69; P-in-c N w S Elkington *Linc* 70-75; TR Louth 75-76; V Morton w Hacconby 76-83; Can and Preb Linc Cathl 77-83; Adn Linc 77-83; Bp Guildf from 83. *Willow Grange, Woking Road, Guildford, Surrey GU4 7QS* Guildford (0483) 573922

ADKINS, Canon Harold. b 20. Lon Univ BA41. Wycliffe Hall Ox. d 43 p 44. Jerusalem 54-73; Can Res 65-70; Dean 70-73; V Barkby *Leic* 74-83; RD Goscote II 82-84; V Barkby and Queniborough 83-85; rtd 85; Perm to Offic *Leic* from 85. *14 Spinney Drive, Quorn, Loughborough, Leics LE12 8HB* Quorn (0509) 416080

ADKINS, Peter Vincent Alexander. b 44. Lanc Univ BA71 CertEd78. Kelham Th Coll 63. d 69 p 70. SSM 67-73; Tutor Kelham Th Coll 71-73; Jerusalem 74-75; Hon C Cam St Giles w St Pet *Ely* 76-78; Perm to Offic Lon 81; Ox from 89; Hon C Northolt St Mary *Lon* 81-83; P-in-c Hanworth St Geo 83-86; R 86-88; OSB from 89. *Priory of Our Lady, Burford, Oxford OX8 4SQ* Burford (099382) 3605

ADKINS, Ronald Charles Rutherford. b 14. St Cath Coll Cam BA35 MA47. Chich Th Coll 37. d 38 p 39. R S Pool w Chivelstone *Ex* 48-74; rtd 74. *Top Tops, The Orchard, Gunnislake, Cornwall* Tavistock (0822) 832934

ADLER, Thomas Payne. b 07. Selw Coll Cam BA29 MA36. Wells Th Coll 29. d 30 p 31. R Castor *Pet* 47-74; R Marholm 47-74; rtd 74; Perm to Offic Glouc from 75; Worc from 85. *Hill Cottage, Cottons Lane, Ashton-under-Hill, Evesham, Worcs WR11 6SS* Evesham (0386) 881431

ADLEY, Ernest George. b 38. Leeds Univ BA61. Wells Th Coll 62. d 64 p 65. C Bideford *Ex* 64-67; C Yeovil St

Mich *B & W* 67-70; V Taunton Lyngford 70-79; R Skegness and Winthorpe *Linc* from 79. *St Matthew's Rectory, Lumley Avenue, Skegness, Lincs PE25 2AT* Skegness (0754) 3875

ADLINGTON, David John. b 51. AKC73. **d** 74 **p** 75. C Clapham St Paul *S'wark* 74-77; C Bethnal Green St Matt *Lon* 77-80; P-in-c Stepney St Pet w St Benet 80-84; Succ S'wark Cathl *S'wark* 84-87; Min Llan w Capel Llanilterne *Llan* 88-91; PV and Succ Llan Cathl 88-91; Dioc Dir of Educn from 91; V St Hilary from 91. *Margam House, St Hilary, Cowbridge, S Glam CF7 7DP* Cowbridge (0446) 772460

ADLINGTON, Kenneth Leonard. b 27. Launde Abbey. **d** 74 **p** 75. C Braunstone *Leic* 74-76; C Eyres Monsell 76-78; V Whetstone 78-83; V Old Dalby and Nether Broughton 83-85; R Waltham on the Wolds, Stonesby, Saxby etc 85-89; rtd 89; Perm to Offic *Linc* from 89. *La Casita, Trusthorpe, Mablethorpe, Lincs LN1 2PG* Mablethorpe (0521) 477713

ADNETT, Roy Gumley. b 14. Tyndale Hall Bris 39. **d** 42 **p** 43. V Chilcompton *B & W* 55-80; RD Midsomer Norton 78-81; R Chilcompton w Downside and Stratton on the Fosse 80-81; rtd 81; Perm to Offic *Leic* from 81. *129 Harrowgate Drive, Birstall, Leicester LE4 3GS* Leicester (0533) 675315

AEGEAN, Archdeacon of the. *See* EVANS, Ven Geoffrey Bainbridge

AELRED, Brother. *See* STUBBS, Anthony Richard Peter

AFFLECK, John. b 20. Liv Univ LLB48. K Coll Lon 68 St Aug Coll Cant 71. **d** 71 **p** 72. C Hutton *Chelmsf* 71-74; P-in-c Hawkchurch, Fishpond, Bettiscombe, Marshwood etc *Sarum* 74-80; R Marshwood Vale 80-86; rtd 86. *3 St George's Close, Lower Street, Harnham, Salisbury SP2 8HA* Salisbury (0722) 334659

AFFLECK, Stuart John. b 47. AKC69. St Aug Coll Cant. **d** 70 **p** 71. C Prittlewell St Mary *Chelmsf* 70-75; Asst Chapl Charterhouse Godalming 75-78; Chapl 78-80; Warden Pilsdon Community Salisbury from 80. *Pilsdon Community, Pilsdon, Bridport, Dorset DT6 5NZ* Broadwindsor (0308) 68308

AGAR, Edward Walter Finlay. b 37. Lon Univ BD68 AKC68. Ripon Hall Ox 68. **d** 70 **p** 71. C Putney St Mary *S'wark* 70-73; Asst Sec C of E Nat Coun for Soc Aid 73-75; Gen Sec from 76. *38 Ebury Street, London SW1W 0LU* 071-730 6175

AGASSIZ, Canon David John Lawrence. b 42. St Pet Hall Ox BA64 MA68. Ripon Hall Ox 64. **d** 66 **p** 67. C Southn St Mary Extra *Win* 66-71; V Enfield St Jas *Lon* 71-80; P-in-c Grays Thurrock *Chelmsf* 80-83; P-in-c Grays All SS 81-84; P-in-c Lt Thurrock St Mary 81-84; P-in-c W Thurrock 81-83; P-in-c Grays SS Pet and Paul, S Stifford and W Thurrock 83-84; TR Grays Thurrock 84-90; Hon Can Chelmsf Cathl from 90; Dioc Development Rep from 90. *Glebe House, Brewer's End, Takeley, Bishop's Stortford, Herts CM22 6QH* Bishop's Stortford (0279) 870434

AGGETT, Vivienne Cecilia. b 33. Sarum & Wells Th Coll 86. **d** 88. C Binley *Cov* 88-91; C Hednesford *Lich* from 91. *76 Highmount Street, Cannock, Staffs WS12 9BN*

AGGREY, Solomon Samuel. b 49. BSc76. Immanuel Coll Ibadan MA84 Internat Bibl Inst Florida DMin86. **d** 80 **p** 82. Nigeria 80-88; Miss Partner CMS (Salford Deanery) from 88. *87 Littleton Road, Salford M6 6FB* 061-737 0584

AGLEN, Miss Elizabeth Senga. b 15. Cam Univ MA. Lambeth STh49. dss 87. Oxton *Ches* 72-76; rtd 76; Perm to Offic *Sarum* from 76. *23 High Street, Upavon, Pewsey, Wilts SN9 6EA* Stonehenge (0980) 630444

AGNEW, Kenneth David. b 33. Jes Coll Cam BA58 MA62. Clifton Th Coll 58. **d** 60 **p** 61. C Lozells St Silas *Birm* 60-63; C Skellingthorpe *Linc* 63-68; C Birchwood 68-72; R Willand *Ex* from 72; RD Cullompton from 89. *The Rectory, Willand, Cullompton, Devon EX15 2RH* Cullompton (0884) 32247

AGNEW, Stephen Mark. b 54. Univ of Wales BSc76 Southn Univ BTh81. Sarum & Wells Th Coll 76. **d** 79 **p** 80. C Wilmslow *Ches* 79-84; V Crewe St Jo 84-90; Chapl Bromsgrove Sch Worcs from 90. *97 Worcester Road, Bromsgrove, Worcs B61 7HN* Bromsgrove (0527) 575048

AIDAN, Brother. *See* THOMPSON, Barry

AIDAN, Brother. *See* MAYOSS, Anthony

AIKEN, Nicholas John. b 58. Sheff Univ BA. Wycliffe Hall Ox 80. **d** 82 **p** 83. C Ashtead *Guildf* 82-86; Dioc Youth Officer from 86. *2 South Hill, Godalming, Surrey GU7 1JT* Godalming (04868) 6539

AIKEN, Simon Mark. b 62. St Andr Univ MTh85. Ripon Coll Cuddesdon 86. **d** 88 **p** 89. C Burnley (Habergham Eaves) St Matt w H Trin *Blackb* from 88. *Trinity House,* *19 Durban Grove, Burnley, Lancs BB11 4JP* Burnley (0282) 21199

AINGE, David Stanley. b 47. Brasted Place Coll 68 Lon Univ DipTh74. Oak Hill Th Coll 70. **d** 73 **p** 74. C Bitterne *Win* 73-77; C Castle Church *Lich* 77-79; P-in-c Becontree St Alb *Chelmsf* 79-89; P-in-c Becontree St Jo 85-89; RD Barking and Dagenham from 86; TR Becontree S from 89. *St Alban's Vicarage, Vincent Road, Dagenham, Essex RM9 6AL* 081-592 5410

AINGER, John Allen. b 18. St Chad's Coll Dur BA39 MA42. Ripon Hall Ox 39. **d** 41 **p** 42. Asst Master Bedf High Sch for Girls 61-79; Lic to Offic *St Alb* from 61; rtd 83. *80 Falcon Avenue, Bedford MK41 7DX* Bedford (0234) 54683

AINSCOUGH, Malcolm Ralph. b 52. Liv Univ BEd76 Liv Inst of Educn DASE85 Univ of Wales (Cardiff) DipTh87. St Mich Coll Llan 85. **d** 87 **p** 88. C Fleur-de-Lis *Mon* 87-90; C Chepstow 90-91; TV Cwmbran from 91. *St Peter's Vicarage, Fairhill, Fairwater, Cwmbran, Gwent NP44 4QZ* Cwmbran (0633) 35229

AINSLEY, Canon Anthony Dixon. b 29. Or Coll Ox BA52 MA57 Univ of S Africa BA74. St Steph Ho Ox 53. **d** 55 **p** 56. C Burnley St Cath *Blackb* 55-60; S Africa 60-80; Adn All SS 73-80; Can St Jo Cathl Umtata 73-80; Hon Can from 81; Chapl Bordeaux w Riberac, Cahors, Duras etc *Eur* 81; V Blackpool St Steph *Blackb* from 81. *The Vicarage, St Stephen's Avenue, Blackpool FY2 9RB* Blackpool (0253) 51484

AINSLEY, Peter Dixon. b 32. OBE87. St Steph Ho Ox 58. **d** 60 **p** 61. C Bury St Thos *Man* 60-62; Chapl RN 62-87; Chapl HM Pris Liv 87-88; Chapl HM Pris Garth from 88. *HM Prison, Garth, Ulnes Walton Lane, Leyland, Preston PR5 3NE* Preston (0772) 622722

AINSWORTH, David Lawrence. b 28. AKC54. **d** 55 **p** 56. C Friern Barnet St Jas *Lon* 55-58; C Harrow Weald All SS 58-63; R Northrepps *Nor* from 63; R Sidestrand from 63; P-in-c Roughton 75-79. *The Rectory, Northrepps, Cromer, Norfolk NR27 0LH* Overstrand (026378) 444

AINSWORTH, Mark John. b 64. Wycliffe Hall Ox 86. **d** 89 **p** 90. C Chipping Barnet w Arkley *St Alb* from 89. *13 Cedar Lawn Avenue, Barnet, Herts EN5 2LW* 081-449 4797

AINSWORTH, Michael Ronald. b 50. K Coll Lon LLB71 LLM72 Trin Hall Cam BA74 MA79. Westcott Ho Cam 72. **d** 75 **p** 76. C Scotforth *Blackb* 75-78; Chapl St Martin's Coll of Educn 78-82; Chapl N Ord Course 82-89; Lic to Offic *Man* 82-89; R Withington St Chris from 89. *St Christopher's Rectory, Moorgate Avenue, Withington, Manchester M20 8HE* 061-445 2008

AINSWORTH, Peter. b 34. Lon Univ BD57. Coll of Resurr Mirfield 69. **d** 70 **p** 71. C Leeds St Wilfrid *Ripon* 70-74; TV Tong *Bradf* 74-77; V Fairweather Green from 77. *St Saviour's Vicarage, Ings Way, Bradford, W Yorkshire BD8 0LU* Bradford (0274) 544807

AINSWORTH-SMITH, Ian Martin. b 41. Selw Coll Cam BA64 MA68. Westcott Ho Cam 64. **d** 66 **p** 67. C Mill Hill Jo Keble Ch *Lon* 66-69; USA 69-71; C Purley St Mark Woodcote *S'wark* 71-73; Chapl St Geo Hosp Gp Lon from 73; Chapl Atkinson Morley Hosp Lon from 73. *107 West Side, London SW4 9AZ* 071-223 5302

AIRD, Donald Allan Ross. b 33. BSc84. AKC55. **d** 56 **p** 57. C N Wembley St Cuth *Lon* 56-59; C Sidmouth, Woolbrook and Salcombe Regis *Ex* 59-62; Youth Chapl *Ely* 62-68; V Swaffham Bulbeck 62-69; V Preston Ascension *Lon* 69-79; V St Marylebone St Mark Hamilton Terrace from 79. *St Mark's Vicarage, 114 Hamilton Terrace, London NW8 9UT* 071-328 4373

AIRD, Robert Malcolm. b 31. Lon Univ BSc54. Westcott Ho Cam 75. **d** 77 **p** 78. C Burnham *B & W* 77-79; P-in-c Taunton Lyngford 79-84; V 84-87; R Dulverton and Brushford from 87. *The Vicarage, Dulverton, Somerset TA22 9DW* Dulverton (0398) 23425

AIREY, Simon Christopher. b 60. Trin Coll Bris BA87. **d** 87 **p** 88. C Wilton *B & W* 87-90; Chapl Scargill Ho from 90. *Scargill House, Kettlewell, Skipton, N Yorkshire BD23 5HU* Kettlewell (075676) 234 or 315

AIRNE, Canon Charles Clement Wallace. b 17. Selw Coll Cam BA47 MA52. Qu Coll Birm 47. **d** 49 **p** 50. V Lydgate St Anne *Man* 58-84; Hon Can Man Cathl 80-84; rtd 84; Perm to Offic *Man* from 84. *Lydgate, 53 Ivygreen Drive, Lees, Oldham OL4 4PR* 061-626 0787

AISBITT, Michael. b 60. St Pet Coll Ox BA81 MA84. Westcott Ho Cam 81. **d** 84 **p** 85. C Norton St Mary *Dur* 84-87; C Kirkleatham *York* 87-90; V S Bank from 90. *The Vicarage, Normanby Road, South Bank, Middlesbrough, Cleveland TS6 6TB* Middlesbrough (0642) 453679

AISBITT, Osmond John. b 35. St Chad's Coll Dur BA57 DipTh61. **d** 61 **p** 62. C Ashington Newc 61-64; C Blyth St Mary 64-68; V Cleckheaton St Jo *Wakef* 68-75;

V Horbury 75-78; V Horbury w Horbury Bridge from 78. *St Peter's Vicarage, Horbury, Wakefield, W Yorkshire WF4 6AS* Wakefield (0924) 273477

AISH, Canon Norman Cyril Roslyn. b 20. St Steph Ho Ox 52. **d** 54 **p** 55. V Hyde Common *Win* 62-73; Adv Soc Resp 73-85; Hon Can Win Cathl 83-85; rtd 85; Perm to Offic *Win* 85-90. *51 Pearce Avenue, Poole, Dorset BH14 8EL* Parkstone (0202) 742077

AITCHISON, John Frederick. b 13. Ripon Hall Ox 66. **d** 67 **p** 68. C Boldmere *Birm* 67-70; C Pembury *Roch* 70-73; V Bassingbourn *Ely* from 73; V Whaddon from 74. *The Vicarage, Bassingbourn, Royston, Herts SG8 5NZ* Royston (0763) 43119

AITKEN, Christopher William Mark. b 53. Dur Univ BA75. Westcott Ho Cam 76. **d** 79 **p** 80. C Finchley St Mary *Lon* 79-82; C Radlett *St Alb* 82-85; V Sprowston *Nor* 85-90; R Beeston St Andr 85-90; R Sprowston w Beeston from 90. *The Vicarage, 2 Wroxham Road, Norwich NR7 8TZ* Norwich (0603) 426492

AITKEN, Leslie Robert. b 19. MBE76. St Aid Coll Dur. **d** 46 **p** 47. R Alvechurch *Worc* 68-84; rtd 84; Perm to Offic *Cant* from 84. *36 Ethelbert Road, Birchington, Kent CT7 9PY* Thanet (0843) 41877

AITKEN, Leslie St John Robert. b 41. Open Univ BA75. Cranmer Hall Dur 62. **d** 65 **p** 66. C Worc St Barn w Ch Ch *Worc* 65-69; C Halesowen 69-73; P-in-c Wyche 73-80; R Blackley St Pet *Man* from 80; Chapl Booth Hall Hosp Man from 80. *St Peter's Vicarage, 1161 Rochdale Road, Manchester M9 2FP* 061-740 2124

AITKEN, William Stuart. b 35. FCFI MSIAD CertEd. Cant Sch of Min 79. **d** 82 **p** 83. NSM Roch 82-86; C Orpington All SS 86-88; R Burham and Wouldham from 88; Dioc Info Officer from 88. *The Rectory, Rochester Road, Burham, Rochester, Kent ME1 3RJ* Medway (0634) 666862

AITON, Robert Neilson. b 36. Univ of Wales BA59 DipEd60. Chich Th Coll 74. **d** 76 **p** 77. C E Grinstead St Swithun *Chich* 76-83; R Lavant 83-90; V Durrington from 90. *The Vicarage, Bramble Lane, Worthing, W Sussex BN13 3JE* Worthing (0903) 60816

AIZLEWOOD, Geoffrey Rymer. b 27. St Aid Birkenhead. **d** 61 **p** 62. V Liv St Mark Edge Lane *Liv* 69-75; rtd 75. *21 Stratton Road, Liverpool L13 4BE* 051-228 5728

AJETUNMOBI, Jacob Ademola. b 48. Lon Bible Coll BA(Theol)80. Igbaja Sem Nigeria BTh73. **d** 83 **p** 83. Nigeria 83-89; Chapl to Nigerian Students in UK (CMS) from 89; Miss Partner CMS from 89. *82 Keslake Road, London NW6 6DG* 081-969 2379

AKEHURST, Peter Russell. b 16. Reading Univ BSc38 Trin Hall Cam. Wycliffe Hall Ox. **d** 48 **p** 49. S Africa 51-70; R Didsbury St Jas *Man* 70-74; V Totland Bay *Portsm* 75-81; rtd 81; Perm to Offic Bris from 86; Ox from 89. *Flat 4, Ellesborough Manor, Butlers Cross, Aylesbury, Bucks HP17 0XF* Aylesbury (0296) 696018

AKERMAN, Roy. b 37. ALCD63. **d** 63 **p** 64. C E Ham St Paul *Chelmsf* 63-67; C Hornchurch St Andr 67-69; Area Sec (Dios Ox and Win) CMS 69-75; V Ollerton *S'well* 75-79; V Boughton 76-79; V N and S Leverton from 79. *The Vicarage, South Gore Lane, North Leverton, Retford, Notts DN22 0AA* Gainsborough (0427) 880882

AKIN-FLENLEY, Kenneth Bernard. b 17. TD62 and Bar 69. St Pet Hall Ox BA41 MA43. Wycliffe Hall Ox 44. **d** 45 **p** 46. CF (TA) 49-80; V Bathford *B & W* 50-79; rtd 82. *Mudros, 85 Dovers Park, Bathford, Bath BA1 7UE* Bath (0225) 858763

AKKER, Derek Alexander. b 46. Bradf Univ MA83. N Ord Course 85. **d** 88 **p** 89. C Mossley *Man* 88-90; C Bury St Pet from 90. *424 Manchester Road, Bury, Lancs BL9 9NS* 061-761 7605

ALBAN-JONES, Timothy Morris. b 64. Warw Univ BA85. Ripon Coll Cuddesdon 85. **d** 88 **p** 89. C Tupsley *Heref* from 88. *4 Kentchurch Avenue, Hereford HR1 1QS* Hereford (0432) 267651

ALBANY, Edric George. b 06. **d** 39 **p** 41. C Ipswich St Mary Stoke *St E* 39-42; CF 42-45; V Wareside *St Alb* 45-50; C Felixstowe St Jo *St E* 50-51; R Holton w Blyford 51-56; V Goff's Oak St Jas *St Alb* 56-59; Australia from 59. *Moline House, Karrinyup, W Australia 6018* Perth (9) 341-3099

ALBANY, John Brian. b 10. ALCD40. **d** 40 **p** 41. C Forest Gate St Jas *Chelmsf* 40-42; P-in-c 42-44; R Farnham 44-49; Dioc Insp of RE 47-49; Australia from 49; Hon Can Perth 76-78. *48 Parry House, Lesmurdie, W Australia 6076* Perth (9) 291-7177

ALBIN, Colin Leslie. b 51. Cov Poly BA75 DCG78. Cranmer Hall Dur 89. **d** 91. C Chadderton Ch Ch *Man* from 91. *23 Lindale Avenue, Chadderton, Oldham OL9 9DW* 061-624 0278

ALBIN, Hugh Oliver. b 21. TCD BA41 MA44 BD46. **d** 44 **p** 45. V Bethersden *Cant* 57-70; V Cant St Dunstan w H Cross 70-88; rtd 88; Perm to Offic *Ex* from 89. *Panorama, Bovey Tracey, Newton Abbot, Devon TQ13 9EP* Bovey Tracey (0626) 833751

ALBON, Lionel Frederick Shapland. b 31. MIMechE60 CEng. St Alb Minl Tr Scheme 80. **d** 83 **p** 84. NSM Bromham w Oakley *St Alb* 83-88; NSM Bromham w Oakley and Stagsden 88-89; Ind Chapl from 89. *10 Turnberry Walk, Bedford MK41 8AZ* Bedford (0234) 46668

ALBUTT, Alfred Victor. b 22. Cuddesdon Coll 70. **d** 71 **p** 72. C Bournville *Birm* 71-74; C Tettenhall Regis *Lich* 74-77; R Ashley 77-85; Chapl Costa Blanca *Eur* 85-87; rtd 88; Chapl Gozo *Eur* from 88. *8 Qbajjar Bay, Qbajjar, Marsalforn, Gozo, Malta* Malta (356) 554692

ALBY, Harold Oriel. b 45. Witwatersrand Univ BA68 MA77. Sarum Th Coll 68. **d** 71 **p** 72. S Africa 71-89; P-in-c Forton *Portsm* from 89. *The Vicarage, 10 Spring Garden Lane, Gosport, Hants PO12 1HY* Gosport (0705) 581965

ALCOCK, Edwin James. b 31. AKC57. **d** 58 **p** 59. C Old St Pancras w Bedf New Town St Matt *Lon* 58-62; C Hillingdon St Andr 62-81; V N Acton St Gabr from 81. *The Vicarage, 15 Balfour Road, London W3 0DG* 081-992 5938

ALDCROFT, Malcolm Charles. b 44. Lon Univ DipSocSc68 Liv Univ DASS71. N Ord Course 79. **d** 82 **p** 83. NSM Alverthorpe *Wakef* 82-85; NSM Horbury Junction from 85. *47 Stannardwell Lane, Horbury, Wakefield, W Yorkshire WF4 6BL* Wakefield (0924) 261977

ALDER, Allen Edward. b 20. Univ of Wales BA46. Coll of Resurr Mirfield 46. **d** 48 **p** 49. V Trealaw *Llan* 66-77; V Cardiff St Andr and St Teilo 77-88; rtd 88. *St Teilo's Court, Sturminster Road, Cardiff CF2 5AW* Cardiff (0222) 488992

ALDER, Eric Reginald Alfred. b 23. St Luke's Coll Ex 47 Lon Univ BA55 Cam Inst of Educn 64. Chich Th Coll 70. **d** 71 **p** 72. C Deal St Leon w Sholden *Cant* 71-80; P-in-c Woodnesborough 80-83; P-in-c Worth 80-83; P-in-c Staple 80-83; V Woodnesborough w Worth and Staple 83-90; rtd 90. *3 Hackington Terrace, Canterbury, Kent CT2 7HE* Canterbury (0227) 766783

ALDER, William. b 09. Ripon Hall Ox. **d** 55 **p** 56. R Silchester *Win* 59-81; rtd 81; Perm to Offic *Ox* from 81. *17 Isis Close, Long Hanborough, Oxford OX7 2JN* Freeland (0993) 882198

ALDERMAN, John David. b 49. Man Univ BA71 Selw Coll Cam BA79. Ridley Hall Cam 77. **d** 80 **p** 81. C Hartley Wintney, Elvetham, Winchfield etc *Win* 80-83; V Bursledon from 83. *The Vicarage, School Road, Bursledon, Southampton SO3 8BW* Bursledon (042121) 2821

ALDERSLEY, Ian. b 42. AIMLS65 FIMLS68. Wycliffe Hall Ox 89. **d** 91. C Allestree *Derby* from 91. *39 Portreath Drive, Darley Abbey, Derby DE3 2BJ* Derby (0332) 556547

ALDERSON, Albert George. b 22. K Coll Lon 46. **d** 50 **p** 51. C Whitworth w Spennymoor *Dur* 50-54; V S Shields St Fran 54-69; P-in-c 69-72; V S Shields St Jude 69-72; R Penshaw 72-79; P-in-c Bilsdale Midcable *York* 79-80; P-in-c Hawnby w Old Byland 79-80; P-in-c Scawton w Cold Kirby 79-80; R Upper Ryedale from 80. *The Rectory, Old Byland, York YO6 5LG* Bilsdale (04396) 355

ALDERSON, Christopher Derek. b 21. AKC55. **d** 55 **p** 56. V Dunster *B & W* 67-82; P-in-c Brompton Regis w Upton and Skilgate 82-83; R 83-86; rtd 86; Perm to Offic *B & W* from 86. *377 Old Commercial Road, Portsmouth PO1 4QL* Portsmouth (0705) 821032

ALDERSON, Roger James. b 47. Lon Univ BD70 AKC71. **d** 71 **p** 72. C Lawton Moor *Man* 71-75; C Barton w Peel Green 75-76; R Heaton Norris St Thos 76-85; V Bedf Leigh from 85. *St Thomas's Vicarage, 121 Green Lane, Leigh, Lancs WN7 2TW* Leigh (0942) 673519

ALDERTON-FORD, Jonathan Laurence. b 57. Nottm Univ BTh85. St Jo Coll Nottm 82. **d** 85 **p** 86. C Gaywood, Bawsey and Mintlyn *Nor* 85-87; C Herne Bay Ch Ch *Cant* 87-90; Min Bury St Edmunds St Mary *St E* 90-91; Min Moreton Hall Estate St Edm CD from 91. *18 Heldhaw Road, Moreton Hall Estate, Bury St Edmunds IP32 7ER* Bury St Edmunds (0284) 769956

ALDIS, Canon Brian Cyril. b 14. St Pet Hall Ox BA36 MSc38. Lon Coll of Div 39. **d** 40 **p** 41. R Hamworthy *Sarum* 51-83; RD Poole 68-75; Can and Preb Sarum Cathl from 68; rtd 83. *4 Cotton Close, Broadstone, Dorset BH18 9AJ* Broadstone (0202) 693874

ALDIS, Canon John Arnold. b 43. Univ of Wales BA65 Lon Univ BD67. Clifton Th Coll 68. **d** 69 **p** 70. C Tonbridge SS Pet and Paul *Roch* 69-72; C St Marylebone All So w SS Pet and Jo *Lon* 72-77; Overseas Service Adv and Under Sec CMS 77-80; C Welling *Roch* 77-80; V Leic H Trin w St Jo *Leic* 80-89; Hon Can Leic Cathl from 88; Hong Kong from 89. *St Andrew's Church, 138 Nathan Road, Tsim Sha Tsui, Kowloon, Hong Kong* Hong Kong (852) 367-1478

ALDIS, Preb John Steadman. b 07. Magd Coll Cam BA28 MA42. Cuddesdon Coll 42. **d** 43 **p** 44. Preb St Paul's Cathl *Lon* 63-75; Chapl to Bp Edmonton 71-75; Hon C Edmonton St Mary w St Jo from 72; rtd 75. *College of St Barnabas, Blackberry Lane, Lingfield, Surrey RH7 6NJ* Dormans Park (034287) 648

ALDRED, Donald Bottomley. b 30. AKC55. **d** 56 **p** 57. C Cudworth *Wakef* 56-59; C Heckmondwike 59-62; V Gomersal 62-69; Chapl Scalebor Park Hosp W Yorkshire 69-84; V Burley in Wharfedale *Bradf* 69-84; R Skipton H Trin from 84; RD Skipton from 90. *The Rectory, Rectory Lane, Skipton, N Yorkshire BD23 1ER* Skipton (0756) 793622

ALDRIDGE, Christopher John. b 35. Trin Hall Cam BA57 MA61. Ripon Hall Ox 59. **d** 60 **p** 61. C Coalville *Leic* 60-64; P-in-c Clifton St Fran *S'well* 64-72; V Gospel Lane St Mich *Birm* 72-90; V Selly Oak St Mary from 90. *St Mary's Vicarage, Bristol Road, Birmingham B29 6ND* 021-472 0250

ALDRIDGE, Harold. b 35. Keble Coll Ox BA61 MA71. Chich Th Coll 60. **d** 62 **p** 63. C Notting Hill All SS w St Columb *Lon* 62-65; C Kensington St Mary Abbots w St Geo 65-69; Chapl Beech Hill Sch Macclesfield 69-82; TV Staveley and Barrow Hill *Derby* 82-86; P-in-c Longford 86-89; P-in-c Radbourne 86-89; P-in-c Dalbury, Long Lane and Trusley 86-89; V Braddan *S & M* from 89. *The Vicarage, Saddle Road, Bradden, Douglas, Isle of Man* Douglas (0624) 75523

ALDRIDGE, Harold John. b 42. Lon Univ DipTh67. Oak Hill Th Coll 65. **d** 69 **p** 70. C Rawtenstall St Mary *Man* 69-76; CMJ 72-76; C Woodford Wells *Chelmsf* 76-79; TV Washfield, Stoodleigh, Withleigh etc *Ex* 79-86; V Burton *Ches* 86-90; Chapl Clatterbridge Hosp Wirral from 86; P-in-c Shotwick *Ches* 90; V Burton and Shotwick from 91. *The Vicarage, Vicarage Lane, Burton, South Wirral L64 5TJ* 051-336 4070

ALDRIDGE, Mark Richard. b 58. Oak Hill Th Coll BA89. **d** 89 **p** 90. C Combe Down w Monkton Combe and S Stoke *B & W* 89-90; C Woodside Park St Barn *Lon* from 90. *12 Courthouse Road, London N12 7PH* 081-444 3404

ALEXANDER, David Graham. b 61. Ridley Hall Cam 87. **d** 89 **p** 90. C New Barnet St Jas *St Alb* from 89. *159 Victoria Road, New Barnet, Herts EN4 9PB* 081-449 2306

ALEXANDER, Douglas Keith. b 45. Ripon Coll Cuddesdon 87. **d** 89 **p** 90. C Thorpe St Matt *Nor* from 89. *15 Stanley Avenue, Norwich NR7 0BE* Norwich (0603) 33870

ALEXANDER, Ernest William. b 08. AKC34. **d** 34 **p** 36. R Acle *Nor* 57-75; R Beighton and Moulton 60-75; rtd 75; Perm to Offic *Guildf* from 75. *1 Glebe Cottages, Newdigate, Dorking, Surrey RH5 5AA* Newdigate (030677) 587

ALEXANDER, Hugh Crighton. b 03. Qu Coll Cam BA24 MA30. Ridley Hall Cam 29. **d** 30 **p** 31. R Hazelbury Bryan w Stoke Wake etc *Sarum* 64-71; rtd 71. *The Vicarage Flat, 99 Water Lane, Oakington, Cambridge CB4 5AL* Histon (022023) 2396

ALEXANDER, James Crighton. b 43. Qu Coll Cam BA65 MA69. Cuddesdon Coll 68. **d** 68 **p** 69. C Much Wenlock w Bourton *Heref* 68-72; V Oakington *Ely* from 72; P-in-c Dry Drayton 85-89. *The Vicarage, 99 Water Lane, Oakington, Cambridge CB4 5AL* Histon (022023) 2396

ALEXANDER, Canon James Douglas. b 27. Linc Th Coll 57. **d** 58 **p** 59. C Frodingham *Linc* 58-61; V Alvingham w N and S Cockerington 61-65; V Keddington 61-65; R Gunhouse w Burringham 65-70; R Peterhead *Ab* 70-76; R Aber St Mary from 76; Miss to Seamen from 76; Can St Andr Cathl *Ab* from 79; Chapl HM Pris Aber from 82; P-in-c Cove Bay *Ab* 85-90. *28 Stanley Street, Aberdeen AB1 6UR* Aberdeen (0224) 584123

ALEXANDER, Michael George. b 47. Sarum & Wells Th Coll 74. **d** 77 **p** 78. C Wednesfield *Lich* 77-80; C Tettenhall Wood 80-83; Distr Min Tettenhall Wood (Ecum Ch) 83-85; Dioc Adv in Adult and Youth Educn *Derby* 85-89; V Hazelwood 85-89; V Turnditch 85-89; Par Educn Adv (Laity Development) from 89. *14 Chevin Road, Duffield, Derby DE6 4DS* Derby (0332) 840817

ALEXANDER, Norman William. b 27. Chich Th Coll 54. **d** 56 **p** 57. R Mutford w Rushmere w Gisleham w N Cove w Barnby *Nor* 69-74; R W Winch 74-81; V Frensham *Guildf* 81-84; V Hemsby *Nor* 84-89; RD Flegg 87-89; rtd 89. *12 Planters Grove, Oulton Broad, Lowestoft, Suffolk NR33 9QL* Lowestoft (0502) 562144

ALEXANDER, Robert. b 37. Lon Univ LLB60 St Cath Coll Ox BA62. St Steph Ho Ox 60. **d** 63 **p** 64. C Kensington St Mary Abbots w St Geo *Lon* 63-68; C Notting Hill 71-74; TV 74-79; Australia from 79. *5/31 Alexandra Street, Drummoyne, NSW, Australia 2047* Sydney (2) 232-3592

ALEXANDER, Wilfred Robert Donald. b 35. TCD BA58 MA80. **d** 63 **p** 63. C Raheny w Coolock *D & G* 63-67; Min Can St Patr Cathl Dub 65-67; Hon C Herne Hill St Paul *S'wark* 68-70; Asst Master Gosforth Gr Sch 71-76; Hon C Long Benton St Mary *Newc* 74-76; Chapl SS Mary and Anne's Sch Abbots Bromley 76-80; V Cauldon *Lich* 80-83; V Waterfall 80-83; P-in-c Calton 80-83; P-in-c Grindon 80-83; V Blackb St Luke w St Phil *Blackb* 83-89; V Rainhill *Liv* from 89. *St Ann's Vicarage, View Road, Rainhill, Liverpool L35 0LE* 051-426 4666

ALFLATT, Malcolm Edward. b 35. FBA68 Bp's Univ Lennoxville BA64 Lon Univ BD69 Univ of New Brunswick MA74. Wells Th Coll 64. **d** 66 **p** 68. C Leeds St Marg *Ripon* 66-67; Canada 67-81; C Sheff St Oswald *Sheff* 81-83; V Sheff Abbeydale St Pet from 83. *St Peter's Vicarage, 21 Ashland Road, Sheffield S7 1RH* Sheffield (0742) 550719

ALFORD, John. b 35. Nottm Univ BSc58 NDA59 DipEd76. Qu Coll Birm 74. **d** 77 **p** 78. NSM Edgmond *Lich* 77-87; C Cheadle 87-88; C Cheadle w Freehay 88-89; Chapl to RD Alcester from 89; P-in-c Wootton Wawen *Cov* from 89. *The Vicarage, Wootton Wawen, Solihull, W Midlands B95 6BD* Henley-in-Arden (05642) 2659

ALFORD, Ven John Richard. b 19. Fitzw Ho Cam BA41 MA47. Cuddesdon Coll 41. **d** 43 **p** 44. V Shotwick *Ches* 67-72; Hon Can Ches Cathl 69-72; Adn Halifax *Wakef* 72-84; Can Res Wakef Cathl 72-84; rtd 85; Perm to Offic *Ripon* from 85. *College of St Barnabas, Blackberry Lane, Lingfield, Surrey RH7 6NJ* Dormans Park (034287) 260

ALGAR, John Herbert. b 29. Tyndale Hall Bris 54. **d** 57 **p** 58. C Stapenhill w Cauldwell *Derby* 57-61; C Willesborough w Hinxhill *Cant* 61-69; V Tipton St Martin *Lich* 69-89; P-in-c Tipton St Paul 86-89; V Tipton St Martin and St Paul from 89. *St Martin's Vicarage, Tipton, W Midlands DY4 7PR* 021-557 1902

ALKER, Adrian. b 49. Wadh Coll Ox BA70 Lanc Univ MA71. Ripon Coll Cuddesdon 77. **d** 79 **p** 80. C W Derby St Mary *Liv* 79-83; Dioc Youth Officer *Carl* 83-88; V Sheff Broomhall St Mark *Sheff* from 88; Dioc Dir of In-Service Tr from 90. *St Mark's Vicarage, 4 St Mark's Crescent, Sheffield S10 2SG* Sheffield (0742) 670362

ALLABY, Simon Arnold Kenworthy. b 65. St Chad's Coll Dur BA88. Trin Coll Bris 88. **d** 90 **p** 91. C Preston on Tees *Dur* from 90. *18 Elmwood Road, Eaglescliffe, Stockton-on-Tees, Cleveland* Eaglescliffe (0642) 782665

ALLAN, Andrew John. b 47. Westcott Ho Cam 76. **d** 79 **p** 80. C Whitstable All SS w St Pet *Cant* 79-84; C Whitstable 84-86; P-in-c Littlebourne 86-87; P-in-c Ickham w Wickhambreaux and Stodmarsh 86-87; R Littlebourne and Ickham w Wickhambreaux etc from 87. *The Vicarage, Littlebourne, Canterbury, Kent CT3 1UA* Canterbury (0227) 721233

ALLAN, Canon Archibald Blackie. b 35. Edin Th Coll 57. **d** 60 **p** 61. C Aber St Jo *Ab* 60-63; R from 82; Chapl St Paul's Cathl Dundee *Bre* 63-68; P-in-c Aber St Clem *Ab* 68-76; Vice-Provost St Andr Cathl 76-82; Can St Andr Cathl from 88. *15 Ashley Road, Aberdeen AB1 6RU* Aberdeen (0224) 591527

ALLAN, Arthur Ashford. b 18. Kelham Th Coll. **d** 44 **p** 45. V Brislington St Luke *Bris* 66-76; P-in-c Coalpit Heath 76-80; rtd 80; Perm to Offic *Ex* from 83. *4 Homer Close, Bratton Fleming, Barnstaple, Devon EX31 4TD* Brayford (0598) 710556

ALLAN, Donald James. b 35. Sarum & Wells Th Coll 63. **d** 65 **p** 66. C Royton St Paul *Man* 65-71; V Middleton Junction 71-78; P-in-c Finmere w Mixbury *Ox* 78-83; R Finmere w Mixbury, Cottisford, Hardwick etc 83; Chapl Westcliff Hosp 83-87; V Westcliff St Andr *Chelmsf* 83-87; R Goldhanger w Lt Totham from 87. *The Rectory, Church Street, Goldhanger, Maldon, Essex CM9 8AR* Maldon (0621) 88235

ALLAN, Jeanette Winifred. b 40. ALA63. **dss** 81 **d** 86. Hillfoot's Team Min from 81; NSM Bridge of Allan *St And* 86-88; NSM Dunblane from 88. *Pernettya,*

Sinclairs Street, Dunblane, Perthshire FK15 0AH Dunblane (0786) 822037

ALLAN, John William. b 58. St Olaf Coll Minnesota BA80 Bris Univ PhD90. Trin Luth Sem Ohio MDiv84 Qu Coll Birm 90. **d** 91. In Luth Ch (USA) 84-86; C Newport w Longford and Chetwynd *Lich* from 91. *9 Mere Close, Newport, Shropshire TF10 7SL* Newport (0952) 825209

ALLAN, Peter Burnaby. b 52. Clare Coll Cam BA74 MA78 St Jo Coll Dur BA82. Cranmer Hall Dur 80. **d** 83 **p** 84. C Chaddesden St Mary *Derby* 83-86; C Brampton St Thos 86-89; TV Halesworth w Linstead, Chediston, Holton etc *St E* from 89. *The Vicarage, Beccles Road, Holton, Halesworth, Suffolk IP19 8NG* Halesworth (0986) 874548

ALLAN, Peter George. b 50. Wadh Coll Ox BA72 MA76 Leeds Univ DipTh74. Coll of Resurr Mirfield 72. **d** 75 **p** 76. C Stevenage St Geo *St Alb* 75-78; Chapl Wadh Coll Ox 78-82; C Ox St Mary V w St Cross and St Pet Ox 78-82; CR from 85. *House of the Resurrection, Mirfield, W Yorkshire WF14 0BN* Mirfield (0924) 494318

ALLANDER, William Edward Morgell Kidd. b 15. TCD BA37 MA40. CITC 37. **d** 38 **p** 39. V Atherstone *Cov* 64-73; I Rathcooney Union *C, C & R* 73-88; rtd 88. *12 Richmond Park, Blackrock Road, Cork, Irish Republic* Cork (21) 293352

ALLARD, John Ambrose. b 30. Bps' Coll Cheshunt 63. **d** 65 **p** 66. C Leigh-on-Sea St Marg *Chelmsf* 65-69; P-in-c Rawreth w Rettendon 69-70; R 70-72; V Barkingside St Fran 73-84; V E Ham St Geo 84-86; V St Osyth from 86. *The Vicarage, The Bury, St Osyth, Clacton-on-Sea, Essex CO16 8NX* St Osyth (0255) 820348

ALLARD, Roy Frank. b 38. E Anglian Minl Tr Course 86. **d** 89 **p** 90. NSM Ipswich All Hallows *St E* from 89. *6 Mandy Close, Ipswich IP4 5JE* Ipswich (0473) 724470

ALLARD, Victor James. b 13. S'wark Ord Course 65. **d** 68 **p** 69. Hd Master Isleworth C of E Primary Sch 59-73; C Isleworth All SS *Lon* 68-73; C Stansted Mountfitchet *Chelmsf* 73-80; C Mayfield *Chich* 80-83; rtd 83; Perm to Offic *Leic* from 83. *1 Oakley Close, Shepshed, Loughborough, Leics LE12 9AS* Shepshed (0509) 502745

ALLARDICE, Alexander Edwin. b 49. SRN. Chich Th Coll 73. **d** 76 **p** 77. C Rugeley *Lich* 76-79; C Felixstowe St Jo *St E* 79-81; TV Ipswich St Fran 81-87; C Lostwithiel *Truro* 87-90; C Boconnoc w Bradoc 87-90; C St Veep 87-90; C St Winnow 87-90; R Lostwithiel, St Winnow w St Nectan's Chpl etc from 90. *The Rectory, 3 Springfield Close, Lostwithiel, Cornwall PL22 0ER* Bodmin (0208) 873448

ALLBERRY, William Alan John. b 49. Ch Coll Cam BA70 MA71. Ripon Coll Cuddesdon 84. **d** 86 **p** 87. C Brixton St Matt *S'wark* 86-90; V Wandsworth St Paul from 90. *St Paul's Vicarage, Augustus Road, London SW19 6EW* 081-788 2024

ALLCHIN, Canon Arthur Macdonald. b 30. Ch Ch Ox BA51 MA55 BLitt56. Bucharest Th Inst Hon DD77 Cuddesdon Coll 54. **d** 56 **p** 57. C Kensington St Mary Abbots w St Geo *Lon* 56-60; Lib Pusey Ho 60-69; Warden Community of Sisters of the Love of God Ox from 68; Can Res and Lib Cant Cathl *Cant* 73-87; Dir St Theosevia Cen for Chr Spirituality from 87; Hon Can Cant Cathl from 88. *2 Canterbury Road, Oxford OX2 6LU* Oxford (0865) 57905

ALLCHIN, Miss Maureen Ann. b 50. S Dios Minl Tr Scheme 88. **d** 91. NSM Southwick *Chich* from 91; Hd Sixth Form Steyning Gr Sch from 91. *73 Meadway Court, Southwick, W Sussex BN42 4SN* Brighton (0273) 596447

ALLCOCK, Arthur Charles Horace. b 12. AKC36. **d** 36 **p** 37. R Bickleigh (Tiverton) *Ex* 68-76; R Cadeleigh 68-76; rtd 77; Perm to Offic *Ex* from 87. *56 Exeter Road, Dawlish, Devon EX7 9PS* Dawlish (0626) 865877

ALLCOCK, David. b 28. Coll of Resurr Mirfield. **d** 66 **p** 67. C Shrewsbury St Chad *Lich* 66-70; Chapl K Coll Taunton 70-78; Chapl Shrewsbury Sch from 78. *The Schools, Shrewsbury SY3 7AP* Shrewsbury (0743) 3203

ALLCOCK, Peter Michael. b 37. Oak Hill Th Coll 65. **d** 68 **p** 69. C Upper Tulse Hill St Matthias *S'wark* 68-71; C Dunkeswell and Dunkeswell Abbey *Ex* 71-72; P-in-c Luppitt 72-75; P-in-c Monkton 72-75; V Okehampton w Inwardleigh 75-80; TV Solihull *Birm* 80-85; V Highbury New Park St Aug *Lon* from 85. *St Augustine's Vicarage, 108 Highbury New Park, London N5 2DR* 071-226 6870

ALLDRED, Kenneth. b 42. N Ord Course 82. **d** 85 **p** 86. NSM Goose Green *Liv* 85-87; C Padgate 87-89; R Lowton St Luke from 89. *The Rectory, 246 Slag Lane,*

Lowton, Warrington WA3 2ED Ashton-in-Makerfield (0942) 728434

ALLDRIT, Nicolas Sebastian Fitz-Ansculf. b 41. St Edm Hall Ox BA63 MA69 DPhil69. Cuddesdon Coll 72. **d** 72 **p** 73. C Limpsfield and Titsey *S'wark* 72-81; Tutor Linc Th Coll from 81; Sub-Warden from 88. *The Theological College, Drury Lane, Lincoln LN1 3BP* Lincoln (0522) 537339

ALLEN, Andrew Stephen. b 55. MPS Nottm Univ BPharm77. St Steph Ho Ox 78. **d** 81 **p** 82. C Gt Ilford St Mary *Chelmsf* 81-83; C Luton All SS w St Pet *St Alb* 83-86; TV Chambersbury (Hemel Hempstead) from 86. *The Vicarage, 31 Chipperfield Road, Hemel Hempstead HP3 0AJ* Hemel Hempstead (0442) 61610

ALLEN, Brian Stanley. b 24. Roch Th Coll 65. **d** 67 **p** 68. C Roch 67-74; P-in-c Drypool St Jo *York* 74-80; TV Drypool 80; V Marlpool *Derby* 80-87; rtd 87. *22 Sycamore Terrace, York YO3 7DN* York (0904) 653418

ALLEN, Bruce Owen. b 14. Lon Univ BA37. Clifton Th Coll 37. **d** 39 **p** 40. V Topcliffe w Dalton and Dishforth *York* 65-81; rtd 81; Perm to Offic *Linc* from 81. *Minerva, Bormans Lane, North Thoresby, Grimsby, S Humberside DN36 5RQ* Grimsby (0472) 840425

ALLEN, Christopher Dennis. b 50. Fitzw Coll Cam BA73 MA77. Cuddesdon Coll 74. **d** 76 **p** 77. C Kettering St Andr *Pet* 76-79; C Pet H Spirit Bretton 79-82; R Bardney *Linc* 82-87; V Knighton St Mary Magd *Leic* from 87. *The Vicarage, Church Lane, Knighton, Leicester LE2 3WG* Leicester (0533) 705730

ALLEN, Christopher Leslie. b 56. Leeds Univ BA78. St Jo Coll Nottm 79. **d** 80 **p** 81. C Birm St Martin *Birm* 80-85; Tr and Ed Pathfinders 85-89; Hd from 89; Midl Youth Dept Co-ord CPAS 85-89; Hon C Selly Park St Steph and St Wulstan *Birm* from 86. *18 High Heath Close, Bournville, Birmingham B30 1HU* 021-459 6530

ALLEN, David. b 38. Llan Dioc Tr Scheme. **d** 76 **p** 77. C Fairwater *Llan* 76-84; Lic to Offic from 84; Chapl The Bp of Llan High Sch from 84. *16 Restways Close, Llandaff, Cardiff CF5 2SB* Cardiff (0222) 554334

ALLEN, David Newall. b 37. **d** 65. C Allerton *Bradf* 65; Canada 74-75; Hon C Man Victoria Park *Man* 76-83. *Address temp unknown*

ALLEN, Derek Milton. b 45. Bradf Univ BTech67 Man Univ BD80. Oak Hill Th Coll 80. **d** 81 **p** 82. C Chadderton Ch Ch *Man* 81-84; V Roundthorn from 84. *Roundthorn Vicarage, 57 Melling Road, Oldham OL4 1PN* 061-624 1007

ALLEN, Preb Donovan Bawden. b 14. Keble Coll Ox BA36 MA40. Westcott Ho Cam 36. **d** 38 **p** 39. Chapl Cross Ho Hosp Shropshire 68-80; R Berrington and Betton Strange *Heref* 68-80; Preb Heref Cathl 73-80; rtd 80; Perm to Offic *Lich* from 80; Heref from 81. *26 Porthill Gardens, Shrewsbury SY3 8SQ* Shrewsbury (0743) 52412

ALLEN, Edward Charles. b 16. Bps' Coll Cheshunt 47. **d** 50 **p** 51. V E Molesey St Mary *Guildf* 60-87; rtd 87. *11 Cootham Green, Storrington, Pulborough, W Sussex RH20 4JW* Storrington (0903) 745932

ALLEN, Frank Brian. b 47. K Coll Lon BD AKC71. **d** 71 **p** 72. C Leam Lane *Dur* 71-74; C Tynemouth Ch Ch *Newc* 74-78; Chapl Newc Poly 78-84; V Newc St Hilda 84-88; Chapl Nottm Mental Illness & Psychiatric Unit 88-89; Chapl Newc Mental Health Unit from 89; Chapl St Nic Hosp Newc from 89. *43 Cherryburn Gardens, Newcastle upon Tyne NE4 9UQ* 091-274 9335

ALLEN, Frank John. b 17. FRIC58 Aston Univ BSc66 Birm Univ DipTh75. Qu Coll Birm 75. **d** 76 **p** 76. NSM Hobs Moat *Birm* 76-79; Perm to Offic *Heref* from 79. *Haresfield, Luston, Leominster, Hereford HR6 0EB* Leominster (0568) 5735

ALLEN, Canon Geoffrey Gordon. b 39. Sarum Th Coll 64. **d** 66 **p** 67. C Langley Marish *Ox* 67-70; Miss to Seamen from 70; Chapl Rotterdam w Schiedam *Eur* 78-82; Asst Chapl The Hague from 84; Chapl Voorschoten from 84; Can Brussels Cathl from 89. *Chopinlaan 17, 2253 BS Voorschoten, The Netherlands* Leiden (71) 612762

ALLEN, Gordon Richard. b 29. St Jo Coll Dur BA54 DipTh55 MA58. **d** 55 **p** 56. C N Meols *Liv* 55-58; Uganda 58-63; V Lathom *Liv* 64-68; USA from 68. *101 Chapel, Portsmouth, New Hampshire 03801, USA*

ALLEN, Hugh Edward. b 47. Sarum & Wells Th Coll 79. **d** 81 **p** 82. C Frome St Jo *B & W* 81-85; R Old Cleeve, Leighland and Treborough from 85. *The Rectory, Old Cleeve, Minehead, Somerset TA24 6HN* Washford (0984) 576

ALLEN, John Catling. b 25. Leeds Univ BA50. Coll of Resurr Mirfield 50. **d** 52 **p** 53. V Linc St Jo *Linc* 66-84;

C Tynemouth Ch Ch w H Trin *Newc* 85-87; C N Shields 87-89; rtd 89. *St Giles's House, Little Torrington, Devon EX38 8PS* Torrington (0805) 22497

ALLEN, John Clement. b 32. K Coll Lon 54. **d** 58 **p** 59. C Middlesb St Martin *York* 58-60; C Northallerton w Kirby Sigston 60-64; V Larkfield *Roch* 64-70; R Ash 70-79; R Ridley 70-79; RD Cobham 76-79; R Chislehurst St Nic from 79. *The Rectory, The Glebe, Chislehurst, Kent BR7 5PX* 081-467 0196

ALLEN, Very Rev John Edward. b 32. Univ Coll Ox BA56 MA63 Fitzw Coll Cam BA68. Westcott Ho Cam 66. **d** 68 **p** 69. C Deal St Leon *Cant* 68-71; P-in-c Clifton St Paul *Bris* 71-78; Chapl Bris Univ 71-78; P-in-c Chippenham St Andr w Tytherton Lucas 78-82; Provost Wakef from 82. *1 Cathedral Close, Margaret Street, Wakefield, W Yorkshire WF1 2DQ* Wakefield (0924) 372402

ALLEN, John Michael. b 27. Cuddesdon Coll 71. **d** 72 **p** 73. C Shrewsbury St Giles *Lich* 72-75; V Hengoed w Gobowen 75-82; V Burghill *Heref* 82-85; RD Heref Rural 83-85; TV Bracknell *Ox* from 85. *St Andrew's Vicarage, Stoney Road, Bracknell, Berks RG12 1XY* Bracknell (0344) 425229

ALLEN, John Ord. b 29. Wells Th Coll 64. **d** 66 **p** 67. C Honiton, Gittisham and Combe Raleigh *Ex* 66-71; R Sidbury 71-90; rtd 90. *5 Monkton Road, Honiton, Devon EX14 8PZ* Honiton (0404) 43291

ALLEN, Mrs Kathleen. b 46. N Ord Course 88. **d** 91. NSM Colne H Trin *Blackb* from 91. *St Mary's Vicarage, Burnley Road, Trawden, Colne, Lancs BB8 8PN* Colne (0282) 864046

ALLEN, Michael Edward Gerald. b 26. Selw Coll Cam BA50 MA53. Chich Th Coll 50. **d** 52 **p** 53. V Baswich (or Berkswich) *Lich* 60-75; V Highbrook and W Hoathly *Chich* 75-91; RD Cuckfield 77-88; rtd 91. *Michell House, 6 Chatsworth Gardens, Eastbourne, E Sussex BN20 7JP* Eastbourne (0323) 638688

ALLEN, Michael Stephen. b 37. Nottm Univ BA60. Cranmer Hall Dur 60. **d** 62 **p** 63. C Sandal St Helen *Wakef* 62-66; Hon C Tile Cross *Birm* 66-70; V 72-84; Hon C Bletchley *Ox* 70-72; Vice-Prin Aston Tr Scheme 84-91; Hon C Boldmere *Birm* 85-91; P-in-c Easton w Colton and Marlingford *Nor* from 91; Local Min Officer from 91. *The Vicarage, Dereham Road, Easton, Norwich NR9 5ES* Norwich (0603) 880235

ALLEN, Michael Tarrant. b 30. St Cath Coll Cam BA56 MA61. Ely Th Coll 56. **d** 58 **p** 59. C Portslade St Nic *Chich* 58-64; C Folkestone St Sav *Cant* 64-65; V Harston w Hauxton *Ely* from 65. *The Vicarage, Harston, Cambridge CB2 5NP* Cambridge (0223) 870201

ALLEN, Noel Stephen (Brother Noel). b 38. Kelham Th Coll. **d** 63 **p** 64. C Nuneaton St Mary *Cov* 63-67; Australia from 67. *23 Scott Avenue, Flinders Park, S Australia 5025* Adelaide (8) 450222 or 340-3231

ALLEN, Patrick Charles Benedict. b 55. St Steph Ho Ox 83. **d** 86 **p** 87. C Bethnal Green St Matt w St Jas the Gt *Lon* 86-90; C Kenton from 90. *St Leonard's House, 268A Kenton Road, Harrow, Middx HA3 8DB* 081-907 5993

ALLEN, Peter Henry. b 34. Nottm Univ BA66. Kelham Th Coll 58. **d** 66 **p** 67. C Salisbury St Martin *Sarum* 66-70; C Melksham 70-73; C Paignton Ch Ch *Ex* 73-76; P-in-c w Holl St Dav *Lon* 76-77; V Barnsbury St Dav w St Clem 77-84; P-in-c Brentford St Faith 84-87; TV Brentford 87-91; TV Catford (Southend) and Downham *S'wark* from 91. *St Luke's House, Northover, Bromley BR1 5JR* 081-698 1354

ALLEN, Peter John Douglas. b 35. Jes Coll Cam BA61 MA64. Westcott Ho Cam 60. **d** 62 **p** 63. C Wyken *Cov* 62-65; USA 65-66; Chapl Jes Coll Cam 66-72; Chapl K Sch Cant 72-87; Hon Min Can Cant Cathl *Cant* from 73; Second Master and Sen Chapl Sedbergh Sch Cumbria from 87. *Sedbergh School, Sedbergh, Cumbria LA10 5HG* Sedbergh (05396) 20535

ALLEN, Philip Gerald. b 48. Lon Univ DipTh71. Trin Coll Bris 71. **d** 73 **p** 74. C Portsea St Luke *Portsm* 73-75; C-in-c 75-79; C Southsea St Jude 75-79; P-in-c Gatten St Paul 79-85; V from 85. *St Paul's Vicarage, St Paul's Crescent, Shanklin, Isle of Wight PO37 7AW* Isle of Wight (0983) 862027

ALLEN, Richard James. b 46. Wells Th Coll 69. **d** 71 **p** 72. C Upholland *Liv* 71-75; TV 76-79; TV Padgate 79-85; V Weston-super-Mare St Andr Bournville *B & W* from 85. *St Andrew's Vicarage, Coniston Crescent, Weston-super-Mare, Avon BS23 3RX* Weston-super-Mare (0934) 627818

ALLEN, Richard Lee. b 41. Liv Inst of Educn TCert67. N Ord Course 80. **d** 83 **p** 84. NSM Colne Ch Ch *Blackb* 83-90; NSM Trawden from 90. *St Mary's Vicarage,*

Burnley Road, Trawden, Colne, Lancs BB8 8PN Colne (0282) 864046

ALLEN, Richard Walter Hugh. b 48. Linc Th Coll 75. **d** 77 **p** 78. C Plymstock *Ex* 77-80; C Leckhampton SS Phil and Jas w Cheltenham St Jas *Glouc* 80; C Shepton Mallet *B & W* 80-81; C Shepton Mallet w Doulting 81-83; V Newport St Matt *Mon* 83-91; P-in-c Telford Park St Thos *S'wark* from 91. *St Thomas's Vicarage, 39 Telford Avenue, London SW2 4XL* 081-674 4343

ALLEN, Roy Vernon. b 43. Open Univ BA81 Birm Univ MA84. Sarum Th Coll 67. **d** 70 **p** 71. C Hall Green Ascension *Birm* 70-74; V Temple Balsall 74-78; P-in-c Smethwick St Steph 78-81; V Smethwick St Mich 78-81; V Smethwick SS Steph and Mich 81-86; V Marston Green from 86. *The Vicarage, Elmdon Road, Birmingham B37 7BT* 021-779 2492

ALLEN, Samuel Joseph. b 25. CITC. **d** 65 **p** 66. C Bray *D & G* 65-75; P-in-c Carbury *M & K* 75-84; rtd 84. *2 Coastguard Terrace, Putland Road, Bray, Co Wicklow, Irish Republic* Dublin (1) 828476

ALLEN, Canon Stanley Leonard Sidney. b 26. K Coll Lon BD52 AKC52. **d** 53 **p** 54. C Friern Barnet St Jas *Lon* 53-55; Canada 55-58; Chapl K Coll Newcastle-upon-Tyne 58-61; P-in-c Woburn Square Ch Ch *Lon* 61-66; Chapl Gt Ormond Street Hosp for Sick Children Lon 61-66; Warden Roch Th Coll 66-70; Can Res Roch Cathl *Roch* 66-70; Hon Can from 70; V Sidcup St Jo from 70; Chapl Qu Mary's Hosp Sidcup from 70; RD Sidcup *Roch* from 75. *The Vicarage, 13 Church Avenue, Sidcup, Kent DA14 6BU* 081-300 0383

ALLEN, Steven. b 49. Nottm Univ BA73. St Jo Coll Nottm 73. **d** 75 **p** 76. C Gt Horton *Bradf* 75-80; V from 89; V Upper Armley *Ripon* 80-89. *The Vicarage, 30 Bartle Close, Bradford, W Yorkshire BD7 4QH* Bradford (0274) 521456

ALLEN, Thomas Davidson. b 49. DipTh. **d** 84 **p** 85. C Magheralin w Dollingstown *D & D* 84-86; I Kilwarlin Upper w Kilwarlin Lower from 86. *The Rectory, 9 St John's Road, Hillsborough, Co Down BT26 6ED* Hillsborough (0846) 683299

ALLEN, Thomas Henry (Tom). b 42. N Ord Course 87. **d** 90 **p** 91. C Upholland *Liv* from 90. *90 Cornbrook, Skelmersdale, Lancs WN8 9AQ* Skelmersdale (0695) 26869

ALLEN, William Charles Ralph. b 09. Clifton Th Coll 46. **d** 47 **p** 48. V Bris St Leon Redfield *Bris* 53-74; rtd 74; Perm to Offic *Bris* from 74. *17 Creswicke Avenue, Bristol BS15 3HD* Bristol (0272) 670955

ALLEN, Zachary Edward. b 52. Warw Univ BA74. Ripon Coll Cuddesdon 78. **d** 81 **p** 82. C Bognor *Chich* 81-84; C Rusper 84-86; C Roughey (or Roffey) 84-86; TV Carl H Trin and St Barn *Carl* 86-90; Chapl Strathclyde Ho Hosp Carl 86-90; V Findon w Clapham and Patching *Chich* from 90. *The Vicarage, School Hill, Findon, Worthing, W Sussex BN14 0TR* Findon (0903) 873601

✠**ALLENBY, Rt Rev David Howard Nicholas.** b 09. Lambeth MA57 Kelham Th Coll 28. **d** 34 **p** 35 **c** 62. SSM from 33; Tutor Kelham Th Coll 36-44; R Averham w Kelham *S'well* 44-57; Hon Can S'well Minster 53-57; RD Newark 55-57; Australia 57-62; Malaya 62-63; Malaysia 63-68; Bp Kuching 62-68; Asst Bp Worc from 68; rtd 74. *16 Woodbine Road, Worcester WR1 3JB* Worcester (0905) 27980

ALLEYNE, Sir John Olpherts Campbell, Bt. b 28. Jes Coll Cam BA50 MA55. **d** 55 **p** 56. C Southn St Mary w H Trin *Win* 55-58; Chapl Cov Cathl *Cov* 58-62; Chapl Clare Hall Cam 62-66; Chapl Bris Cathl *Bris* 66-68; Area Sec (SW England) Toc H 68-71; V Speke All SS *Liv* 71-73; TR Speke St Aid 73-76; R Win St Matt *Win* from 76. *The Rectory, 44 Cheriton Road, Winchester, Hants SO22 5AY* Winchester (0962) 854849

ALLFORD, Judith Mary. b 55. Sheff Univ BA Lon Univ BD. Trin Coll Bris 77. dss 86 **d** 87. Par Dn Deptford St Jo w H Trin *S'wark* 87-91; Asst Chapl Dulwich Hosp from 91; Asst Chapl K Coll Hosp Lon from 91. *Dulwich Hospital, South Wing, East Dulwich Grove, London SE22 8PT* 081-693 3377

ALLIN, Philip Ronald. b 43. Lich Th Coll 71. **d** 71 **p** 72. C Sutton in Ashfield St Mary *S'well* 71-74; Chapl to Sutton Cen 74-76; Lic to Offic 74-76; P-in-c Grove 76-77; R Ordsall 76-80; V Mansf St Mark 81-83; TR Hermitage and Hampstead Norreys, Cold Ash etc *Ox* from 83; CF from 83. *The Rectory, High Street, Hermitage, Newbury, Berks RG16 9ST* Hermitage (0635) 200448

ALLINGTON-SMITH, Canon Richard. b 28. Lon Univ BA49 MA52. Wells Th Coll 54. **d** 56 **p** 57. V Rainham *Roch* 67-79; V Gt Yarmouth *Nor* 79-89; TR 89-91; Hon Can Nor Cathl from 86; rtd 91; P-in-c Nor St Andr *Nor*

9

from 91. *14 Yare Court, Yarmouth Road, Norwich NR7 0EJ* Norwich (0603) 37185

ALLINSON, Capt Paul Timothy. b 63. Edin Th Coll 89. **d** 91. C Peterlee *Dur* from 91. *197 Hatfield Place, Manor Way, Peterlee, Co Durham SR8 5TA* 091-518 1775

ALLISON, Elliott Desmond. b 36. Univ of S Africa BA64 K Coll Lon MTh74. S Africa Federal Th Coll. **d** 69 **p** 70. S Africa 70-72; C Mottingham St Edw *S'wark* 73-76; P-in-c 76-80; V Ferry Fryston *Wakef* 80-84; Huddersfield St Jo 84-86; TV N Huddersfield from 86. *8 Oakdean, The Fairway, Fixby, Huddersfield HD2 2FA* Huddersfield (0484) 537959

ALLISON, James Timothy. b 61. Man Univ BSc83. Oak Hill Th Coll BA89. **d** 89 **p** 90. C Walkden Moor *Man* from 89. *37 Park Road, Worsley, Manchester M28 5DU* 061-799 1412

ALLISON, Keith. b 34. Dur Univ BA59. Ely Th Coll 59. **d** 61 **p** 62. C Sculcoates *York* 61-64; C Stainton-in-Cleveland 64-65; C Leeds St Pet *Ripon* 65-70; V Micklefield *York* 70-74; V Appleton-le-Street w Amotherby 74-78; P-in-c Barton le Street 77-78; P-in-c Salton 77-80; R Amotherby w Appleton and Barton-le-Street 78-82; Chapl Lister Hosp Stevenage 82-90; P-in-c St Ippolyts *St Alb* 82-85; V 85-90; Chapl Hitchen Hosp 86-90; Chapl Dur HA from 90; Chapl Shotley Bridge Hosp from 90. *c/o Shotley Bridge Hospital, Consett, Co Durham DH8 0NB* Consett (0207) 503456 or 503863

ALLISON, Canon Roger Grant. b 10. MBE54. Jes Coll Cam BA33 MA36. Ridley Hall Cam 32. **d** 34 **p** 35. Jerusalem 41-75; rtd 75; Perm to Offic *Chich* from 76. *Shalom, 11 Gloucester Avenue, Bexhill-on-Sea, E Sussex TN40 2LA* Bexhill-on-Sea (0424) 218786

✠ALLISON, Rt Rev Sherard Falkner. b 07. Jes Coll Cam BA29 MA33. Lambeth DD51. Ridley Hall Cam 29. **d** 31 **p** 32 **c** 51. C Tunbridge Wells St Jas *Roch* 31-34; Chapl Ridley Hall Cam 34-36; Prin 45-51; C Cam St Mark *Ely* 34-36; Lic to Offic *Bradf* 34-36; V Redbourne Cheney *Bris* 36-40; V Erith *Roch* 40-45; Bp Chelmsf 51-61; Bp Win 61-74; rtd 74; Perm to Offic *St E* from 79. *Winton Lodge, 27 Alde Lane, Aldeburgh, Suffolk* Aldeburgh (0728) 852485

ALLISON, William Gordon. b 12. Qu Coll Cam MA31. Ridley Hall Cam 34. **d** 38 **p** 39. R Inkpen *Ox* 67-74; R Inkpen and Combe 74-78; rtd 78; Perm to Offic *Chich* from 78. *1 Gloucester Avenue, Bexhill-on-Sea, E Sussex TN40 2LA* Bexhill-on-Sea (0424) 217462

ALLISTER, Donald Spargo. b 52. Peterho Cam BA74 MA77. Trin Coll Bris 74. **d** 76 **p** 77. C Hyde St Geo *Ches* 76-79; C Sevenoaks St Nic *Roch* 79-83; V Birkenhead Ch Ch *Ches* 83-89; R Cheadle from 89. *The Rectory, 1 Depleach Road, Cheadle, Cheshire SK8 1DZ* 061-428 3440

ALLISTON, Cyril John. b 11. Fitzw Ho Cam BA33 MA37. Cuddesdon Coll 33. **d** 35 **p** 36. V Penponds *Truro* 63-70; S Africa from 71; rtd 76. *14 Three Sisters, Sixth Street, Kleinmond, 7195 South Africa*

ALLON-SMITH, Roderick David. b 51. Leic Univ BA PhD Cam Univ MA. Ridley Hall Cam 79. **d** 82 **p** 83. C Kinson *Sarum* 82-86; V Westwood *Cov* from 86. *St John's Vicarage, Westwood Heath Road, Coventry CV4 7DD* Coventry (0203) 466227

ALLPORT, David Jack. b 55. Ox Univ BA Birm Univ DPS. Qu Coll Birm 78. **d** 80 **p** 81. C Abingdon w Shippon *Ox* 80-83; C-in-c Woodgate Valley CD *Birm* 83-91; Perm to Offic *Lich* from 91. *122 Cherry Tree Avenue, Walsall, W Midlands WS5 4JL* Walsall (0922) 640059

ALLRED, Frank. b 23. Tyndale Hall Bris 62. **d** 64 **p** 65. V Ravenhead *Liv* 67-75; R Chadwell *Chelmsf* 75-82; TV Heworth *York* 82-86; rtd 87. *12 Viking Road, Bridlington, N Humberside YO16 5TW* Bridlington (0262) 677321

ALLSO, Sydney Ernest. b 10. Qu Coll Birm 32. **d** 34 **p** 35. V Radley *Ox* 66-71; Perm to Offic *Sarum* 71-73; C Bawtry w Austerfield *S'well* 73-75; V Kirkby Woodhouse 75-79; rtd 79; Perm to Offic *Linc* from 79. *27 Witham Place, Boston, Lincs PE21 6LG* Boston (0205) 366425

ALLSOP, Anthony James. b 37. AKC62. **d** 63 **p** 64. C Leytonstone St Marg w St Columba *Chelmsf* 63-68; V Gt Ilford St Alb 68-80; V Gainsborough St Jo *Linc* 80-85; V Hockerill *St Alb* from 85; Chapl Herts and Essex Gen Hosp Bishop's Stortford from 85. *Hockerill Vicarage, All Saints' Close, Bishop's Stortford, Herts CM23 2EA* Bishop's Stortford (0279) 654930

ALLSOP, Patrick Leslie Fewtrell. b 52. Fitzw Coll Cam BA74 MA78. Ripon Coll Cuddesdon BA78 MA83. **d** 79 **p** 80. C Barrow St Matt *Carl* 79-82; Chapl Eton Coll Windsor 82-88; Chapl K Sch Roch from 89. *49 Holcombe*

Road, Rochester, Kent ME1 2HX Medway (0634) 400184

ALLSOP, Peter William. b 33. Kelham Th Coll 58. **d** 58 **p** 59. C Woodford St Barn *Chelmsf* 58-61; C Upholland *Liv* 61-65; V Wigan St Geo 65-71; P-in-c Marham *Ely* 71-72; TV Fincham 72-76; V Trawden *Blackb* 76-90; C Marton from 90. *31 Lomond Avenue, Blackpool FY3 9QL* Blackpool (0253) 62679

ALLSOPP, Mrs Christine. b 47. Aston Univ BSc68. S Dioc Minl Tr Scheme 86. **d** 89. C Caversham and Mapledurham *Ox* from 89. *25 Ilkley Road, Reading RG4 7BD* Reading (0734) 472070

ALLSOPP, Edmund Gibson. b 16. Dur Univ LTh41. St Pet Coll Jamaica 38. **d** 41 **p** 42. Jamaica 41-73; R Lansallos *Truro* 73-80; V Talland 73-80; V St Neot 80-88; RD W Wivelshire 81-87; rtd 89. *4 Mews Court, Menheniot, Liskeard, Cornwall PL14 3QW* Liskeard (0579) 47729

ALLSOPP, Stephen Robert. b 50. BSc71 MSc72 PhD75. Mon Dioc Tr Scheme 81. **d** 84 **p** 85. NSM Trevethin *Mon* 84-88; Asst Chapl K Sch Roch from 88; Hon PV Roch Cathl *Roch* from 89. *41 St Margaret Street, Rochester, Kent ME1 1UF* Medway (0634) 828804

ALLTON, Canon Paul Irving. b 38. Man Univ BA60 Dur Univ DipTh62. **d** 63 **p** 64. C Kibworth Beauchamp *Leic* 63-66; C Reading St Mary V *Ox* 66-70; R Caston *Nor* 70-75; R Caston w Griston, Mert and Thompson 70-75; P-in-c Sturston w Thompson and Tottington 70-75; V Holme-next-the-Sea 75-80; V Hunstanton St Mary w Lt Ringstead 75-80; V Hunstanton St Mary w Ringstead Parva, Holme etc 80-85; RD Heacham and Rising 81-85; Hon Can Nor Cathl from 85; TR Lowestoft and Kirkley from 85. *The Rectory, 16 Corton Road, Lowestoft, Suffolk NR32 4PL* Lowestoft (0502) 573046

ALLUM, Jeremy Warner. b 32. Wycliffe Hall Ox 60. **d** 62 **p** 63. C Hornchurch St Andr *Chelmsf* 62-67; P-in-c W Derby St Luke *Liv* 67-69; V 69-75; P-in-c Boulton *Derby* 75-90; RD Melbourne 86-90; V Hathersage from 90. *The Vicarage, Hathersage, Sheffield S30 1AB* Hope Valley (0433) 50215

ALLUM, Peter Drage. b 11. Univ Coll Dur LTh35 BA36 MA42. Sarum Th Coll 32. **d** 36 **p** 37. V Sheepscombe *Glouc* 51-77; rtd 77; Perm to Offic *Glouc* from 78; Heref from 82. *Rose Cottage, Kempley, Dymock, Glos GL18 2BN* Dymock (053185) 571

ALLWRIGHT, Mrs Janet Margaret. b 40. NNEB58. Oak Hill Th Coll 87. **d** 90. NSM Galleywood Common *Chelmsf* from 90. *26 Chaplin Close, Chelmsford, Essex CM2 8QW* Chelmsford (0245) 265499

ALMOND, Kenneth Alfred. b 36. E Midl Min Tr Course 76 Linc Th Coll 78. **d** 79 **p** 80. C Boston *Linc* 79-82; V Surfleet 82-87; RD Elloe W from 86; V Spalding St Jo w Deeping St Nicholas from 87. *St John's Vicarage, Hawthorn Bank, Spalding, Lincs PE11 1JQ* Spalding (0775) 2816

ALSBURY, Colin. b 56. Ch Ch Ox BA77 MA81. Ripon Coll Cuddesdon 77. **d** 80 **p** 81. C Oxton *Ches* 80-84; V Crewe All SS and St Paul from 84. *All Saints' Vicarage, Stewart Street, Crewe CW2 8LX* Crewe (0270) 60310

ALSOP, Eric George. b 12. Dorchester Miss Coll 34. **d** 37 **p** 38. P-in-c Bodiam *Chich* 69-72; V Burwash Weald 72-77; rtd 77; Perm to Offic *Chich* from 77. *Jacob's Well Farm House, 125 London Road, Hurst Green, Etchingham, E Sussex TN19 7PN* Hurst Green (058 086) 591

ALTHAM, Donald. b 40. Liv Univ BA62. N Ord Course 87. **d** 90 **p** 91. NSM Ramsbottom St Jo and St Paul *Man* from 90. *387 Whalley Road, Ramsbottom, Bury, Lancs BL0 0ER* Ramsbottom (0706) 822025

ALWAY, Cecil William. b 24. Glouc Th Course 67. **d** 69 **p** 70. C Wotton-under-Edge *Glouc* 69-73; P-in-c Pauntley w Upleadon 74-76; V Quinton w Marston Sicca 76-82; P-in-c Lower Cam 82-83; V Lower Cam w Coaley 83-90; rtd 90; Lic to Offic *Glouc* from 90. *Middlecot, 116A Parklands, Wotton-under-Edge, Glos GL12 7NR* Dursley (0453) 844346

AMBROSE, Edgar. b 22. N Ord Course 80. **d** 81 **p** 82. NSM Broughton *Blackb* from 81. *76 Conway Drive, Fulwood, Preston PR2 3EQ* Preston (0772) 717530

AMBROSE, Frederick Lee Giles. b 12. Kelham Th Coll 28. **d** 36 **p** 37. C Nottm St Geo w St Jo *S'well* 36-39; S Africa 39-63 and from 70; Lic to Offic *S'well* 63-70. *PO Box 1032, Pretoria, 0001 South Africa* Pretoria (12) 434787

AMBROSE, James Field. b 51. Newc Univ BA73. Cranmer Hall Dur DipTh80. **d** 80 **p** 81. C Barrow St Geo w St Luke *Carl* 80-83; C Workington St Jo 83-85; Ch Radio Officer BBC Radio Shropshire 85-88; R Montford w Shrawardine and Fitz *Lich* 85-88; Chapl RAF from 88.

c/o MOD, Adastral House, Theobald's Road, London WC1X 8RU 071-430 7268

AMBROSE, John George. b 30. Ox Univ PGCE Lon Univ BD. **d** 74 **p** 75. C Rayleigh *Chelmsf* 74-79; V Hadleigh St Barn from 79. *St Barnabas' Vicarage, 169 Church Road, Hadleigh, Essex SS7 2EJ* Southend-on-Sea (0702) 558591

AMBROSE, Thomas. b 47. Sheff Univ BSc69 PhD73 Em Coll Cam BA77. Westcott Ho Cam 75. **d** 78 **p** 79. C Morpeth *Newc* 78-81; C N Gosforth 81-84; R March St Jo *Ely* from 84; RD March from 89. *St John's Rectory, Station Road, March, Cambs PE15 8NG* March (0354) 53525

AMES, Henry George. b 33. Em Coll Cam BA56 MA60 Lon Univ BD58. Tyndale Hall Bris 56. **d** 59 **p** 60. Chapl Highbury Coll of Tech Portsm 66-88; Lic to Offic *Portsm* from 66; rtd 88. *49 Carmarthen Avenue, Cosham, Portsmouth PO6 2AG*

AMES, Jeremy Peter. b 49. K Coll Lon BD71 AKC71. **d** 72 **p** 73. C Kennington St Jo *S'wark* 72-75; Chapl RN from 75; RN Engineering Coll from 86; RN Dir of Studies RAF Chapl Sch from 89. *c/o MOD, Lacon House, Theobald's Road, London WC1X 8RY* 071-430 6847

AMES, Reginald John. b 27. Bps' Coll Cheshunt 51. **d** 54 **p** 55. C Edmonton St Alphege *Lon* 54-58; C Mill Hill Jo Keble Ch 58-60; P-in-c Northwood Hills St Edm 61-64; V from 64. *St Edmund's Vicarage, 2 Pinner Road, Northwood, Middx HA6 1QS* 081-866 9230

AMES-LEWIS, Richard. b 45. Em Coll Cam BA66 MA70. Westcott Ho Cam 76. **d** 78 **p** 79. C Bromley St Mark *Roch* 78-81; C Edenbridge 81-84; V 84-91; P-in-c Crockham Hill H Trin 84-91; P-in-c Barnes St Mary *S'wark* from 91. *The Rectory, 25 Glebe Road, London SW13 0DZ* 081-878 6982

AMEY, Graham George. b 44. Lon Univ BD70. Tyndale Hall Bris 67. **d** 71 **p** 72. C Hornsey Rise St Mary *Lon* 71-74; C St Helens St Helen *Liv* 74-79; V Liv All So Springwood from 79. *Springwood Vicarage, Mather Avenue, Liverpool L19 4TF* 051-427 5699

AMIS, Ronald. b 37. Linc Th Coll 74. **d** 76 **p** 77. C Grantham w Manthorpe *Linc* 76-78; C Grantham 78-79; P-in-c Holbeach Hurn 79-81; V Long Bennington w Foston from 81; RD Grantham from 90. *The Vicarage, Long Bennington, Newark, Notts NG23 5ES* Loveden (0400) 81025

✠**AMOORE, Rt Rev Frederick Andrew.** b 13. Leeds Univ BA34. Coll of Resurr Mirfield 34. **d** 36 **p** 37 **c** 67. C Clapham H Trin *S'wark* 36-39; S Africa from 39; Dean Pretoria 50-61; Adn 60-61; Can 62-67; Hon Can from 67; Bp Bloemfontein 67-82. *503 Salwood Court, Arbor Road, Rondebosch, 7700 South Africa* Cape Town (21) 685-7259

AMOR, Peter David Card. b 28. AKC53. **d** 54 **p** 55. C St Margarets on Thames *Lon* 54; C Leighton Buzzard *St Alb* 54-58; C Toxteth Park St Agnes *Liv* 58-62; C-in-c Aldershot Ascension CD *Guildf* 62-65; V Bishley H Trin *Bradf* 65-72; V The Collingbournes *Sarum* 72-75; R The Collingbournes and Everleigh 75-77; V Thorpe *Guildf* 77-85; P-in-c Monks Risborough *Ox* 85-89; R from 89. *The Rectory, Mill Lane, Monks Risborough, Aylesbury, Bucks HP17 9JE* Princes Risborough (08444) 3162

AMOS, Alan John. b 44. OBE79. K Coll Lon BD66 AKC67 MTh67. St Steph Ho Ox 68. **d** 69 **p** 70. C Hoxton H Trin w St Mary *Lon* 69-72; Lebanon 73-82; Lect Liturg Studies Westcott Ho Cam 82-85; Vice-Prin 85-89; Prin Cant Sch of Min from 89. *St Martin's Glebe House, North Holmes Road, Canterbury, Kent CT1 1QJ* Canterbury (0227) 459401 or 766719

AMOS, Gerald. b 31. St Mich Coll Llan. **d** 58 **p** 62. C Rhosymedre *St As* 58-59; C Peckham St Andr w All SS *S'wark* 62-65; C Walworth 65-72; C S Wimbledon H Trin 72-74; C S Wimbledon H Trin and St Pet 74-75; C Warlingham w Chelsham and Farleigh 75-78; V Speke St Aid *Liv* 78-88; P-in-c Fazakerley St Nath from 88. *St Nathanael's Vicarage, 65 Fazakerley Road, Liverpool L9 2AJ* 051-525 7720

AMOS, Patrick Henry. b 31. Roch Th Coll 63. **d** 65 **p** 66. C Strood St Nic *Roch* 65-68; C Polegate *Chich* 68-71; V Horam 71-83; R Chiddingly w E Hoathly from 83. *The Rectory, East Hoathly, Lewes, E Sussex BN8 6EG* Halland (082584) 270

AMYS, Richard James Rutherford. b 58. Trin Coll Bris 87. **d** 90 **p** 91. C Whitnash *Cov* from 90. *13 Palmer Road, Whitnash, Leamington Spa, Warks CV31 2MP* Leamington Spa (0926) 425366

ANCRUM, John. b 28. Clifton Th Coll 55. **d** 58 **p** 59. V Tibshelf *Derby* 63-70; Canada 70-74; P-in-c Salwarpe

Worc 74-75; P-in-c Tibberton w Bredicot and Warndon 75-76; P-in-c Hadzor w Oddingley 76-78; Lic to Offic *Chelmsf* 78-81; Chapl HM Pris Stafford 81-82; Dartmoor 82-89; Lic to Offic *Ex* from 88; rtd 89. *14 Merrivale View Road, Dousland, Yelverton, Devon PL20 6NS* Yelverton (0822) 853909

ANDERS, Jonathan Cyril. b 36. Wycliffe Hall Ox 69. **d** 71 **p** 72. C Prescot *Liv* 71-74; C-in-c 74-76; R Wavertree St Mary 76-81; V Aigburth from 81. *St Anne's Vicarage, 389 Aigburth Road, Liverpool L17 6BN* 051-727 1101

ANDERS-RICHARDS, Dr Donald. b 28. Dur Univ BA60 MA62 Leic Univ MEd72 Sheff Univ PhD76. Coll of Resurr Mirfield 60. **d** 62 **p** 63. Lic to Offic *Derby* from 68; Sen Lect Sheff Poly 75-88; rtd 88; Perm to Offic *Lich* from 88. *Laburnum Cottage, Gwern-y-Brenin, Oswestry, Shropshire SY10 8AS*

ANDERSON, Albert Geoffrey. b 42. Ex Univ BA65 MA67. Qu Coll Birm DipTh75. **d** 75 **p** 76. C Helsby and Ince *Ches* 75-77; C Helsby and Dunham-on-the-Hill 77-78; TV Gleadless *Sheff* 78-85; V Thorpe Hesley from 85. *The Vicarage, 30 Barnsley Road, Thorpe Hesley, Rotherham, S Yorkshire S61 2RR* Sheffield (0742) 463487

ANDERSON, Brian Arthur. b 42. Sarum Th Coll 75. **d** 78 **p** 79. C Plymouth St Jas Ham *Ex* 78-80; Org Sec (Dios B & W, Ex and Truro) CECS 80-89; Perm to Offic *B & W* from 86; TV Saltash *Truro* from 89; RD E Wivelshire from 91. *The Vicarage, 35 Lower Port View, Saltash, Cornwall PL12 4BY* Saltash (0752) 848691

ANDERSON, Brian Glaister (Jeremy). b 35. SSF. K Coll Lon 57. **d** 79 **p** 79. Chapl St Fran Sch Hooke 79; C Croydon *Cant* 80-83; Asst Chapl HM Youth Cust Cen Glen Parva 83-84; Chapl HM Young Offender Inst Hewell Grange 84-89; HM Rem Cen Brockhill 84-89; Chapl HM Pris Parkhurst from 89. *HM Prison Parkhurst, Newport, Isle of Wight PO30 5NX* Isle of Wight (0983) 523855

ANDERSON, David. b 19. Selw Coll Cam BA41 MA45. Wycliffe Hall Ox 47. **d** 49 **p** 50. Lic to Offic *St Alb* from 71; Prin Lect Wall Hall Coll Aldenham 74-84; rtd 84. *6 Flassburn Road, Durham DH1 4LX* 091-384 3063

ANDERSON, David Graham. b 33. MICE MIStructE. St Mich Coll Llan 85. **d** 88 **p** 89. C Llanishen and Lisvane *Llan* 88-90; C Fazeley *Lich* from 90. *59 Manor Road, Mile Oak, Tamworth, Staffs B78 3NB* Tamworth (0827) 285908

ANDERSON, Digby Carter. b 44. PhD. **d** 85 **p** 86. NSM Luton St Sav *St Alb* from 85. *17 Hardwick Place, Woburn Sands, Milton Keynes MK17 8QQ* Milton Keynes (0908) 584526

ANDERSON, Donald Whimbey. b 31. Trin Coll Toronto BA54 LTh57 STB57 MA58 ThD71. **d** 56 **p** 57. Canada 57-59 and 75-88; Japan 59-74; Philippines 74-75; Assoc Sec Ecum Affairs ACC from 88. *c/o ACC, Partnership House, 157 Waterloo Road, London SE1 8UT* 071-620 1110

ANDERSON, Francis Hindley. b 20. Ch Coll Cam BA43 MA47. Wycliffe Hall Ox. **d** 44 **p** 45. C Surbiton St Matt *S'wark* 44-48; C Loughb All SS *Leic* 48-50; C Pimlico St Pet w Westmr Ch Ch *Lon* 50-59; V Upper Chelsea St Sav from 59. *71 Cadogan Place, London SW1X 9RP* 071-235 3468

ANDERSON, Canon Gordon Fleming. b 19. TCD BA41 MA46. **d** 42 **p** 43. C Drumholm *D & R* 42-46; C Clooney 46-47; I Termonamongan 47-57; P-in-c Cumber Lower 57-61; I 61-72; I Cumber Lower w Banagher from 72; Can Derry Cathl from 76; Preb Howth St Patr Cathl Dub from 86. *Holy Trinity Vicarage, 291 Glenshane Road, Killaloo, Londonderry BT47 3SW* Claudy (0504) 338224

ANDERSON, Gordon Roy. b 30. FCA58. Ox NSM Course 83. **d** 86 **p** 87. NSM Beaconsfield *Ox* from 86. *9 Mynchen Road, Beaconsfield, Bucks HP9 2AS* Beaconsfield (0494) 676617

ANDERSON, Gordon Stuart. b 49. St Jo Coll Nottm. **d** 82 **p** 83. C Hattersley *Ches* 82-86; C Dagenham *Chelmsf* 86-91; TV Mildenhall *St E* from 91. *The Vicarage, 103 Melbourne Road, Mildenhall, Bury St Edmunds, Suffolk IP28 7BP* Mildenhall (0638) 718840

ANDERSON, Hugh Richard Oswald. b 35. Roch Th Coll 68. **d** 70 **p** 71. C Minehead *B & W* 70-76; C Darley w S Darley *Derby* 76-80; R Hasland from 80; V Temple Normanton from 80. *The Rectory, 49 Churchside, Chesterfield, Derbyshire S41 0JX* Chesterfield (0246) 232486

ANDERSON, James Frederick Wale. b 34. G&C Coll Cam BA58 MA62. Cuddesdon Coll 60. **d** 62 **p** 63. C Leagrave *St Alb* 62-65; C Eastleigh *Win* 65-70; R Sherfield-on-Loddon 70-86; P-in-c Stratfield Saye w Hartley Wespall

75-86; R Sherfield-on-Loddon and Stratfield Saye etc 86-87; R Newton Valence, Selborne and E Tisted w Colemore from 87. *The Vicarage, The Plestor, Selborne, Alton, Hants GU34 3JQ* Selborne (042050) 342

ANDERSON, Canon James Raffan. b 33. FRSA90 Edin Univ MA54. Edin Th Coll 56. **d** 58 **p** 59. Chapl St Andr Cathl *Ab* 58-59; Prec 59-62; CF (TA) 59-77; Chapl Aber Univ *Ab* 60-62; Chapl Glas Univ *Glas* 62-69; Chapl Lucton Sch Herefordshire 69-71; Chapl Barnard Castle Sch 71-74; Asst Dir of Educn *Blackb* 74-78; P-in-c Whitechapel 74-78; Bp's Officer for Min *Cov* 78-87; Hon Can Cov Cathl 83-87; Miss Sec Gen Syn Bd for Miss and Unity 87-91; Bd of Miss from 91. *15 Cotswold Drive, Coventry CV3 6EZ* Coventry (0203) 411985

ANDERSON, Jeremy Dudgeon. b 41. Edin Univ BSc63. Trin Coll Bris 75. **d** 77 **p** 78. C Bitterne *Win* 77-81; TV Wexcombe *Sarum* 81-91; Evang Enabler (Reading Deanery) *Ox* from 91. *6 Scholars Close, Reading, Berks RG4 7DN* Reading (0734) 48396

ANDERSON, Joanna Elisabeth. b 53. St Andr Univ MTh75. E Midl Min Tr Course 85. **d** 88. Par Dn Crosby *Linc* from 88. *14 Normanby Road, Scunthorpe DN15 6AL* Scunthorpe (0724) 850845

ANDERSON, John Michael. b 17. Madras Univ BA38. St Aug Coll Cant 59. **d** 60 **p** 61. Trinidad and Tobago 69-73; V Leic St Sav *Leic* 74-82; rtd 82; Perm to Offic *Leic* from 82. *4 Cooden Avenue, West End, Leicester LE3 0JS* Leicester (0533) 557112

ANDERSON, Canon Keith Bernard. b 36. Qu Coll Cam BA60 MA64. Tyndale Hall Bris 60. **d** 62 **p** 63. C Bootle St Leon *Liv* 62-65; Burundi 66-74; Kenya 74-83; Hon Can Mt Kenya E from 82; P-in-c Doddington w Wychling *Cant* 83-88; P-in-c Newnham 83-88; Chapl Cannes w Grasse *Eur* from 88. *Holy Trinity Church, 2-4 rue de General Ferrie, 06400 Cannes, France* France (33) 93 94 54 61

ANDERSON, Keith Edward. b 42. MRCS83 Fitzw Coll Cam BA77 MA83. Ridley Hall Cam 74. **d** 77 **p** 78. C Goodmayes All SS *Chelmsf* 77-80; Lic to Offic *Truro* 80-87; Chapl Coll of St Mark and St Jo Plymouth *Ex* 80-87; RD Plymouth Moorside 83-86; V Northn H Sepulchre w St Andr and St Lawr *Pet* from 87. *The Vicarage, Campbell Square, Northampton NN1 3EB* Northampton (0604) 230563

ANDERSON, Kenneth. b 38. G&C Coll Cam BA62 MA66. Westcott Ho Cam 63. **d** 65 **p** 66. C Nor St Steph *Nor* 65-68; C Wareham w Arne *Sarum* 68-71; Chapl Sherborne Sch Dorset 71-83; Zimbabwe from 83. *The Rectory, 27 Fourth Street, Marondera, Zimbabwe*

ANDERSON, Mark Jonathan David. b 59. Ruskin Coll Ox 81 Univ of Wales (Cardiff) BSc(Econ)86. St Steph Ho Ox 86. **d** 89 **p** 90. C Deptford St Paul *S'wark* from 89. *St Paul's Rectory, Deptford High Street, London SE8 3PQ* 081-692 1419

ANDERSON, Michael Garland. b 42. Clifton Th Coll 62. **d** 66 **p** 67. C Fareham St Jo *Portsm* 66-69; C Worting *Win* 69-74; V Hordle from 74; RD Lyndhurst from 82. *The Vicarage, Hordle, Lymington, Hants SO41 0HX* New Milton (0425) 614428

ANDERSON, Michael John Austen. b 35. AKC60. **d** 66 **p** 67. C Southall Ch Redeemer *Lon* 66-69; C Hampstead Garden Suburb 69-73; V S Mimms St Giles 73-80; V S Mymms *St Alb* 80; V The Brents and Davington w Oare and Luddenham *Cant* 80-86; V Margate All SS from 86. *All Saints' Vicarage, All Saints' Avenue, Margate, Kent CT9 5QL* Thanet (0843) 220795

ANDERSON, Nicholas Patrick. b 53. BA. **d** 81 **p** 82. In RC Ch 81-89; C Gt Crosby St Faith *Liv* from 89. *Clamaw, Sandringham Road, Liverpool L22 1RW* 051-480 3778

ANDERSON, Peter John. b 44. Nottm Univ BA65 BA73. St Jo Coll Nottm BA71 DPS. **d** 74 **p** 75. C Otley *Bradf* 74-77; TV Marfleet *York* 77-84; V Greasbrough *Sheff* from 84. *The Vicarage, 16 Church Street, Greasbrough, Rotherham, S Yorkshire S61 4DX* Rotherham (0709) 551288

ANDERSON, Peter Scott. b 49. Nottm Univ BTh72 CertEd. Kelham Th Coll 68. **d** 74 **p** 75. C Sheff Parson Cross St Cecilia *Sheff* 74-77; C Leytonstone St Marg w St Columba *Chelmsf* 77-81; P-in-c Forest Gate St Edm 81-89; V 89-90; P-in-c Plaistow from 90. *The Rectory, Abbey Street, London E13 8DT* 071-476 9920

ANDERSON, Robert Edwin. See MORTIMER-ANDERSON, Robert Edwin

ANDERSON, Roderick Stephen. b 43. Cant Univ (NZ) BSc63 PhD67 New Coll Ox BA72. Wycliffe Hall Ox 70. **d** 73 **p** 74. C Bradf Cathl *Bradf* 73-75; C Allerton 76-78; V Cottingley from 78; RD Airedale from 88. *St Michael's Vicarage, Littlelands, Cottingley, W Yorkshire BD16 1RR* Bradford (0274) 562278

ANDERSON, Mrs Rosemary Ann. b 36. Ex Univ BA59. N Ord Course 83. **dss** 86 **d** 87. Oldham St Paul *Man* 86-87; Hon Par Dn 87-89; Bp's Adv for Women's Min from 88. *Lydgate Vicarage, Stockport Road, Oldham OL4 4JJ* Saddleworth (0457) 872117

ANDERSON, Stuart. b 31. Dur Univ BA52. Linc Th Coll 52. **d** 54 **p** 55. C Billingham St Cuth *Dur* 54-57; C Fulham St Etheldreda *Lon* 57-61; New Zealand from 61. *61 McHardy Street, Havelock North, Hawkes Bay, New Zealand* Hastings (6) 877-8567

ANDERSON, Thomas. b 07. Dorchester Miss Coll 32. **d** 36 **p** 37. V Appleton-le-Street w Amotherby *York* 57-70; rtd 72. *Hillside Cottage, Appleton-le-Street, Malton, N Yorkshire YO17 0PG* Malton (0653) 693681

ANDERSON, Timothy George. b 59. Ealing Coll of HE BA82. Wycliffe Hall Ox 83. **d** 86 **p** 87. C Harold Wood *Chelmsf* 86-90; C Whitfield *Derby* from 90. *1 Cedar Close, Spire Hollin, Glossop, Derbyshire SK13 9BP* Glossop (0457) 855896

ANDERTON, Frederic Michael. b 31. IAAP IGAP Pemb Coll Cam MA57 Jung Institut Zurich DipAnPsych86. Westcott Ho Cam 64. **d** 66 **p** 67. C St Jo Wood *Lon* 66-69; C All Hallows by the Tower etc 70-77; C St Giles Cripplegate w St Bart Moor Lane etc 77-82; C Zurich *Eur* 82-86. *100 Harvist Road, London NW6 6HZ* 071-960 4780

ANDERTON, Peter. b 45. Sarum & Wells Th Coll 80. **d** 82 **p** 83. C Adel *Ripon* 82-86; P-in-c Dacre w Hartwith 86-90; P-in-c Thornthwaite w Thruscross and Darley 88-90; V Dacre w Hartwith and Darley w Thornthwaite 90-91; V Owton Manor *Dur* from 91. *The Vicarage, 18 Rossmere Way, Hartlepool, Cleveland TS25 5EF* Hartlepool (0429) 273938

ANDREW, Brian. b 31. Oak Hill Th Coll 75. **d** 77 **p** 78. C Broadwater St Mary *Chich* 77-81; R Nettlebed w Bix and Highmore *Ox* 81-87; V Shenstone *Lich* from 87. *The Vicarage, Shenstone, Lichfield, Staffs WS14 0JB* Shenstone (0543) 480286

ANDREW, Brother. See NORTON, John Colin

ANDREW, Donald. b 35. Tyndale Hall Bris 63. **d** 66 **p** 67. C Croydon Ch Ch Broad Green *Cant* 66-69; C Ravenhead *Liv* 69-72; Scripture Union 72-77; V Rushen *S & M* 77-82; TR Heworth *York* from 82. *Heworth Rectory, Melrosegate, York YO3 0RP* York (0904) 422958

ANDREW, Frank. b 17. St D Coll Lamp BA49 Ely Th Coll 50. **d** 51 **p** 52. R March St Jo *Ely* 69-77; R March St Mary 71-77; RD March 73-77; R Catworth Magna 77-83; R Covington 77-83; R Tilbrook 77-83; rtd 83; Perm to Offic *Chich* from 83. *11 Romney Close, Seaford, E Sussex BN25 3TR* Seaford (0323) 897352

ANDREW, John. b 07. AKC38. **d** 38 **p** 39. V Kniveton w Hognaston *Derby* 69-73; rtd 73. *57 Cherry Tree Road, Blackpool, Lancs FY4 4NS* Blackpool (0253) 64154

ANDREW, Michael Paul. b 51. Leic Univ CertEd83. Chich Th Coll 80. **d** 83 **p** 84. C Par *Truro* 83-86; Hon Chapl Miss to Seamen 86; P-in-c Salford Ordsall St Clem *Man* 86-91; P-in-c Hammersmith St Jo *Lon* from 91. *St John's Vicarage, Iffley Road, London W6 0LS* 081-748 3928

ANDREW, Richard Paul. b 53. Keble Coll Ox BA75 MA. St Steph Ho Ox 75. **d** 77 **p** 78. C Streatham St Pet *S'wark* 77-80; C Kenton *Lon* 80-86; V Hayes St Anselm from 86. *St Anselm's Vicarage, 101 Nield Road, Hayes, Middx UB3 1SQ* 081-573 0958

ANDREW, Ronald Arthur. b 27. Sarum Th Coll 64. **d** 65 **p** 66. C Darwen St Cuth *Blackb* 65-69; C Padiham 69-71; V Colne H Trin 71-76; V Adlington 76-85; V Goosnargh w Whittingham from 85. *The Vicarage, Goosnargh, Preston, Lancs PR3 2BN* Preston (0772) 865274

ANDREW, Sydney William. b 55. Cranmer Hall Dur 82. **d** 85 **p** 86. C Horncastle w Low Toynton *Linc* 85-88; V Worlaby from 88; V Bonby from 88; V Elsham from 88. *The Vicarage, Worlaby, Brigg, S Humberside DN20 0NE* Saxby-all-Saints (065261) 708

ANDREW, Canon William Hugh. b 32. Selw Coll Cam BA56 MA60. Ridley Hall Cam 56. **d** 58 **p** 59. C Woking St Mary *Guildf* 58-61; C Farnborough 61-64; V Gatten St Paul *Portsm* 64-71; R Weymouth St Mary *Sarum* 71-76; V Heatherlands St Jo 76-82; Can and Preb Sarum Cathl 81-86; R Alderbury and W Grimstead 82-86; Perm to Offic *Bris* 86-88; Communications Dir Bible Soc from 86; Hon C The Lydiards *Bris* from 88. *20 Chudleigh, Freshbrook, Swindon SN5 8NQ* Swindon (0793) 695313 or 513713

ANDREWES UTHWATT, Henry. b 25. Jes Coll Cam BA49 MA51. Wells Th Coll 49. **d** 51 **p** 52. V W Wimbledon Ch Ch *S'wark* 61-73; V Yeovil St Jo w Preston Plucknett *B & W* 73-76; TR Yeovil 76-82; V Burrington and Churchill 82-90; RD Locking 87-90; rtd 90. *71 Mount Road, Bath BA2 1LJ* Bath (0225) 482220

ANDREWS, Canon Alan Robert Williams. b 14. AKC37. **d** 37 **p** 38. V Quarndon *Derby* 58-79; Hon Can Derby Cathl 77-79; rtd 79; Perm to Offic *Derby* from 79. *4 Orchard Court, Hawthorn Close, Doveridge, Derbyshire DE6 5ND*

ANDREWS, Alfred Vincent. b 14. St D Coll Lamp 54. **d** 56 **p** 57. C Westmr St Sav and St Jas Less *Lon* 58-79; rtd 79. *3 Coast View, Bude, Cornwall* Bude (0288) 352609

ANDREWS, Anthony Brian. b 33. Lon Univ BA54 AKC58. Coll of Resurr Mirfield 56. **d** 58 **p** 59. C Haggerston St Columba *Lon* 58-60; C N Hammersmith St Kath 60-63; V Goldthorpe *Sheff* 63-74; V Notting Hill St Mich and Ch Ch *Lon* from 74. *St Michael's Vicarage, 35 St Lawrence Terrace, London W10 5SR* 081-969 0776

ANDREWS, Anthony Bryan de Tabley. b 20. K Coll Lon BA42. Linc Th Coll 42. **d** 44 **p** 45. V Babbacombe *Ex* 59-75; R Worth *Chich* 75-82; RD E Grinstead 77-82; P-in-c Exton and Winsford and Cutcombe w Luxborough *B & W* 82-83; R 83-85; rtd 85; Perm to Offic *Ex* from 86. *Cordwainers, Iddesleigh, Winkleigh, Devon EX19 8BG* Winkleigh (0837) 810116

ANDREWS, Anthony Frederick. b 25. K Coll Lon 54. **d** 55 **p** 56. C Bridgwater St Mary w Chilton Trinity *B & W* 69-70; R Cossington 70-73; C Highworth w Sevenhampton and Inglesham etc *Bris* 75-84; P-in-c Bishopstone w Hinton Parva 84-88; rtd 88. *Burford House, Highworth, Swindon SN6 7AD* Swindon (0793) 762796

ANDREWS, Anthony John. b 35. S'wark Ord Course 75. **d** 80 **p** 81. NSM Cheam *S'wark* 80-83; C Epsom St Martin *Guildf* 83-86; V Barton *Portsm* 86-89; Chapl Northwick Park Hosp Harrow from 90. *39 Eastcote Lane, Harrow, Middx HA2 8DE* 081-426 8236

ANDREWS, Brian Keith. b 39. Keble Coll Ox BA62 MA69. Coll of Resurr Mirfield 62. **d** 64 **p** 65. C Is of Dogs Ch Ch and St Jo w St Luke *Lon* 64-68; C Hemel Hempstead *St Alb* 68-71; TV 71-79; V Abbots Langley from 79; RD Watford from 88. *The Vicarage, High Street, Abbots Langley, Herts WD5 0AS* Kings Langley (0923) 263013

ANDREWS, Christopher Paul. b 47. Fitzw Coll Cam BA70 MA73. Westcott Ho Cam 69. **d** 72 **p** 73. C Croydon *Cant* 72-75; C Gosforth All SS *Newc* 75-79; TV Newc Epiphany 80-87; RD Newc Cen 82-87; V Alnwick St Mich and St Paul from 87. *The Vicarage, Alnwick, Northd NE66 1LT* Alnwick (0665) 602184

ANDREWS, Clive Francis. b 50. K Coll Lon BD72 AKC72. **d** 73 **p** 74. C Clapham H Trin *S'wark* 73-75; C Kidbrooke St Jas 76-78; Youth Officer 79-84; V Forest Hill St Aug 84-89; Perm to Offic *Sarum* from 89. *Cross River Cottage, Donhead St Andrew, Shaftesbury, Dorset SP7 9EQ* Donhead (0747) 828126

ANDREWS, Clive Frederick. b 43. St Jo Coll Nottm 81. **d** 83 **p** 84. C Leic St Jas *Leic* 83-86; Ind Chapl 86-90; Hon TV Melton Gt Framland 89-90; TV Clifton *S'well* from 90. *1 South Church Drive, Clifton, Nottingham NG11 8SN* Nottingham (0602) 212446

ANDREWS, Edward Robert. b 33. St Mich Coll Llan 62. **d** 64 **p** 65. C Kingswinford St Mary *Lich* 64-69; Chapl RAF 69-88; R St Just in Roseland w Philleigh *Truro* from 88. *The Rectory, St Just in Roseland, Truro, Cornwall TR2 5JD* St Mawes (0326) 270248

ANDREWS, Eric Charles. b 17. AKC41. **d** 41 **p** 42. V Eastbourne St Andr *Chich* 63-73; R E Blatchington 73-83; rtd 83; Perm to Offic *Chich* from 83. *3 The Spinney, Bexhill-on-Sea, E Sussex TN39 3SW* Cooden (04243) 3864

ANDREWS, Eric Keith. b 11. Tyndale Hall Bris 36. **d** 38 **p** 39. R Stanton *St E* 70-76; rtd 76; Perm to Offic *Heref* from 76. *79 Bearcroft, Weobley, Hereford HR4 8TD* Weobley (0544) 318114

ANDREWS, Frances. b 24. E Midl Min Tr Course 73. **dss** 78 **d** 87. Porchester *S'well* 78-86; Asst Chapl Nottm City Hosp 86-88; Hon C Gedling *S'well* from 88. *1 Cromford Avenue, Nottingham NG4 3RU* Nottingham (0602) 613857

ANDREWS, John Colin. b 47. Sarum & Wells Th Coll 78. **d** 80 **p** 81. C Burnham *B & W* 80-84; V Williton from 84. *St Peter's Vicarage, 30 Priest Street, Williton, Taunton, Somerset TA4 4NJ* Williton (0984) 32560

ANDREWS, Preb John Douglas. b 19. Keble Coll Ox BA39 MA44. Chich Th Coll 40. **d** 42 **p** 43. V Penkhull *Lich* 68-80; P-in-c Ellenhall w Ranton 80-86; P-in-c Chebsey 80-86; Preb Lich Cathl 81-86; rtd 86; Perm to Offic *Lich* from 86. *The Bungalow, 1 Belgrave Place, Shrewsbury SY2 5LT* Shrewsbury (0743) 240270

ANDREWS, John Elfric. b 35. Ex Coll Ox BA59 MA63. Wycliffe Hall Ox. **d** 61 **p** 62. C Pittville *Glouc* 61-66; Lic to Offic *S'wark* from 66; Cand Sec Lon City Miss

from 66. *27 Woodbourne Avenue, London SW16 1UP* 081-769 7569

ANDREWS, John Francis. b 34. Jes Coll Cam BA58 MA62. S'wark Ord Course 78. **d** 81 **p** 82. NSM Norwood All SS *Cant* 81-82; NSM Upper Norwood All SS w St Marg 82-85; NSM Upper Norwood All SS *S'wark* 85-87; NSM Dulwich St Barn 89-91; NSM S Dulwich St Steph from 91. *46 Cypress Road, London SE25 4AU* 081-653 5620

ANDREWS, John George William. b 42. Qu Coll Birm 65. **d** 68 **p** 69. C Smethwick St Matt w St Chad *Birm* 68-71; CF from 71. *c/o MOD (Army), Bagshot Park, Bagshot, Surrey GU19 5PL* Bagshot (0276) 71717

ANDREWS, John Vicars. b 31. St Edm Hall Ox BA55. St Steph Ho Ox 55. **d** 58 **p** 59. C Clerkenwell H Redeemer w St Phil *Lon* 58-63; C Tilehurst St Mich *Ox* 63-69; P-in-c Abingdon w Shippon 69-76; R Cranwich *Nor* 76-86; R Ickburgh w Langford 76-86; R Mundford w Lynford 76-86; R Seaton Ross Gp of Par *York* from 86; RD S Wold from 90. *The Rectory, Everingham, York YO4 4JA* Market Weighton (0430) 860602

ANDREWS, Keith. b 47. St Mich Coll Llan 79. **d** 81 **p** 82. C Penarth w Lavernock *Llan* 81-85; V Nantymoel w Wyndham 85-91; RD Bridgend from 89; R Coychurch w Llangan and St Mary Hill from 91. *The Rectory, Coychurch, Bridgend, M Glam CF35 5HF* Bridgend (0656) 860785

ANDREWS, Major Paul Rodney Gwyther. b 16. GM41. Mon Dioc Tr Scheme 74. **d** 77 **p** 78. NSM Goetre w Llanover and Llanfair Kilgeddin *Mon* 77-80; Lic to Offic *S & B* from 81. *Bromelys, Llangorse, Brecon, Powys LD3 7UG* Brecon (0874) 84296

ANDREWS, Peter Alwyne. b 44. Lon Univ BSc67. Westcott Ho Cam 70. **d** 73 **p** 74. C Barnoldswick w Bracewell *Bradf* 73-76; C Maltby *Sheff* 76-78; V Bradf St Oswald Chapel Green *Bradf* 78-85; V Hanwell St Thos *Lon* from 85. *St Thomas's Vicarage, 182 Boston Road, London W7 2AD* 081-567 5280

ANDREWS, Peter Douglas. b 52. SEN72 SRN78. St Steph Ho Ox 86. **d** 88 **p** 89. C Perry Barr *Birm* from 88. *16 Arden Court, Church Road, Birmingham B42 2LB* 021-356 2374

ANDREWS, Richard John. b 57. Bris Univ BA78 CertEd79. Ripon Coll Cuddesdon 82. **d** 84 **p** 85. C Kidderminster St Mary and All SS etc *Worc* 84-87; Hon C Derby Cathl *Derby* 87-89; Chapl Derbyshire Coll of HE 87-89; V Chellaston *Derby* from 89. *The Vicarage, St Peter's Road, Chellaston, Derby DE7 1UT* Derby (0332) 704835

ANDREWS, Thomas George Desmond. b 31. **d** 63 **p** 64. C Ballymacarrett St Patr *D & D* 63-66; C Ballynafeigh St Jude 66-70; I Scarva 70-81; I Newry St Mary from 81. *St Mary's Vicarage, Windsor Avenue, Newry, Co Down BT34 1EG* Newry (0693) 62621

ANDREWS, Walford Brian. b 34. Univ of Wales (Lamp) BA54. St Mich Coll Llan 54. **d** 57 **p** 58. C Canton St Jo *Llan* 57-62; Miss to Seamen from 62; India 62-65; Chapl Rotterdam 65-66 and 70-77; Australia 66-69; Chapl Hull 77-83; Regional Chapl Hong Kong from 83. *c/o The Mission to Seamen, Mariners' Club, 11 Middle Road, Kowloon, Hong Kong* Hong Kong (852) 368-8261

ANDREWS, Wilfrid Seymour. b 12. Trin Coll Ox BA34 MA38 Lon Univ PhD53. Ely Th Coll 34. **d** 35 **p** 36. Asst Master Gresham's Sch Holt 50-72; Chapl 50-60; Perm to Offic *Nor* from 50; rtd 72. *Hill House, Cley, Holt, Norfolk* Cley (0263) 740737

ANGEL, Gervais Thomas David. b 36. Ch Ch Ox BA59 MA62 Bris Univ MEd78. **d** 61 **p** 62. C Abth St Mich *St D* 61-65; Tutor Clifton Th Coll 65-72; Dean of Studies Trin Coll Bris 72-81; Dir of Studies 81-90; Hon C Clifton H Trin, St Andr and St Pet *Bris* 82-90; SAMS from 90; Perm to Offic *Ex* from 90. *24 Stoke Hill, Bristol BS9 1JW* Bristol (0272) 683996

ANGEL, Robin Alan. b 41. St Mich Coll Llan. **d** 89 **p** 90. C Whitchurch *Llan* from 89. *10 Keynsham Road, Whitchurch, Cardiff CF4 1TS* Cardiff (0222) 611388

ANGELO, Brother. *See* DEACON, Donald

ANGUS, Edward. b 39. Man Univ BA60. Qu Coll Birm DipTh61. **d** 62 **p** 63. C Chorley St Geo *Blackb* 62-65; C S Shore H Trin 65-68; R Bretherton 68-76; V Altham w Clayton le Moors 76-90; V Preesall from 90. *St Oswald's Vicarage, Lancaster Road, Fleetwood, Lancs FY6 0DU* Knott End (0253) 810297

ANGWIN, Richard Paul. b 25. ACA49 FCA60 AKC56. **d** 56 **p** 57. V Wanstead H Trin Hermon Hill *Chelmsf* 69-75; Chapl Wanstead Hosp Lon 69-75; Chapl Halstead Hosp 75-87; V Halstead St Andr *Chelmsf* 75-78; P-in-c Greenstead Green 75-78; V Halstead St Andr w H Trin 78-79; V Halstead St Andr w H Trin and Greenstead Green 79-87; RD Halstead and Coggeshall 84-87;

rtd 87. *2 Seckham Road, Lichfield, Staffs WS13 7AN* Lichfield (0543) 250848

ANIDO, John David Forsdyke. b 16. Ox Univ BA38 MA41 McGill Univ Montreal PhD75. Westcott Ho Cam 39. **d** 40 **p** 41. Canada 47-51 and 57-76; V Auckland St Andr and St Anne *Dur* 76-83; rtd 83; Perm to Offic *York* from 83. *The Spinney, 2 Park Road, Norton, Malton, N Yorkshire YO17 9EA* Malton (0653) 696338

ANKER, George William. b 10. AKC51. **d** 51 **p** 52. V Brockley Hill St Sav *S'wark* 68-72; C Sanderstead All SS 72-76; rtd 76; Perm to Offic *S'wark* from 76. *College of St Barnabas, Blackberry Lane, Lingfield, Surrey RH7 6NJ* Dormans Park (034287) 706

ANKER, Malcolm. b 39. Univ of Wales BA61. Bps' Coll Cheshunt 61. **d** 63 **p** 64. C Marfleet *York* 63-66; C Cottingham 66-69; V Skirlaugh w Long Riston 69-74; V Elloughton and Brough w Brantingham 74-84; V Tadcaster 84-86; V Tadcaster w Newton Kyme from 86. *The Vicarage, 78 Station Road, Tadcaster, N Yorkshire LS24 9JR* Tadcaster (0937) 833394

ANKETELL, Jeyarajan. b 41. MInstP Lon Univ BSc62 PhD67. Coll of Resurr Mirfield 69. **d** 73 **p** 74. Asst Chapl Newc Univ *Newc* 73-75; Asst Chapl Lon Univ *Lon* 75-77; Teacher from 78; Lic to Offic *S'wark* 81-83; Chasetown High Sch from 85; NSM Lich St Mary w St Mich *Lich* from 86. *7 Wissage Lane, Lichfield, Staffs WS13 6DQ* Lichfield (0543) 262032

ANNACEY, Felix. b 62. Hull Univ DipTh87. **d** 87 **p** 88. C Fenton *Lich* 87-88; Ghana from 88. *PO Box 248, Koforidva, Ghana*

ANNAKIN, William. b 15. Worc Ord Coll 63. **d** 65 **p** 66. P-in-c Wigtoft *Linc* 69-72; V 72-77; P-in-c Kirston Holme 75-79; P-in-c Wildmore 76-79; V Brothertoft 76-82; rtd 82. *Lovelle, School Lane, Mareham-le-Fen, Boston, Lincs PE22 7QB* Mareham-le-Fen (065886) 303

ANNAS, Geoffrey Peter. b 53. Sarum & Wells Th Coll. **d** 83 **p** 84. C S'wark H Trin w St Matt *S'wark* 83-87; TV Walworth from 87; Warden Pemb Coll Miss Walworth from 87. *78 Tatum Street, London SE17 1QR* 071-701 4162

ANNEAR, Hubert Tours. b 24. Dur Univ BA49 Leeds Univ MA58. Linc Th Coll 49. **d** 51 **p** 52. USPG 65-71; V Bierley *Bradf* 71-76; V Morley St Paul *Wakef* 76-87; rtd 88. *112 Asquith Avenue, Morley, Leeds LS27 9QN* Morley (0532) 537880

ANNELY, Maurice James Leonard. b 22. Qu Coll Birm 77. **d** 80 **p** 82. NSM Tettenhall Regis *Lich* 81-83; NSM Midsomer Norton w Clandown *B & W* 83-86; NSM Selworthy and Timberscombe and Wootton Courtenay 86-88; NSM Luccombe 86-88; rtd 88. *26 Jay Park Crescent, Kidderminster, Worcs DY10 4JP* Kidderminster (0562) 69821

ANNET, John Thomas. b 20. TD66. Selw Coll Cam BA49 MA53. Westcott Ho Cam 49. **d** 51 **p** 52. R Didsbury Ch Ch *Man* 66-75; V Gt Budworth *Ches* 75-86; rtd 86; Perm to Offic *Ex* from 86. *58 Lydgates Road, Seaton, Devon EX12 2BX* Seaton (0297) 23495

ANNIS, Herman North. b 28. Lich Th Coll 62. **d** 64 **p** 65. C Kilburn St Aug *Lon* 64-67; C Toxteth Park St Agnes *Liv* 67-70; V 70-82; V Hempton and Pudding Norton *Nor* 82-84; P-in-c Sculthorpe w Dunton and Doughton 82-84; V Northn H Trin *Pet* from 84. *Holy Trinity Vicarage, 24 Edinburgh Road, Northampton NN2 6PH* Northampton (0604) 711468

ANNIS, Rodney James. b 43. Ex Univ BA75 MA79 PhD86. Ripon Coll Cuddesdon 75. **d** 76 **p** 77. C Brixham *Ex* 76-77; Asst Chapl Ex Univ 77-80; Chapl Ex Sch 77-80; C Boston *Linc* 80-84; Chapl Trin Hall Cam 84-87; V Bush Hill Park St Steph *Lon* from 87. *St Stephen's Vicarage, Village Road, Bush Hill Park, Enfield, Middx EN1 2ET* 081-360 1407

ANNS, Miss Pauline Mary. See HIGHAM, Mrs Pauline Mary

ANSCOMBE, John Thomas. b 51. Ex Univ BA72. Cranmer Hall Dur DipTh73. **d** 74 **p** 75. C Upper Armley *Ripon* 74-77; C Leeds St Geo 78-81; Scripture Union from 81; Hon C Beckenham Ch Ch *Roch* from 82. *26 Wimborne Way, Beckenham, Kent BR3 4DJ* 081-658 4037

ANSCOMBE, Canon Thomas. b 15. Qu Coll Cam BA37 MA41. Ridley Hall Cam 37. **d** 39 **p** 40. R Kirkheaton *Wakef* 64-80; Hon Can Wakef Cathl 77-80; rtd 80; Perm to Offic Bradf and Wakef from 80. *28 South Street, Gargrave, Skipton, N Yorkshire BD23 3RT* Skipton (0756) 749289

ANSDELL-EVANS, Peter. b 25. Liv Univ BArch51. S'wark Ord Course 89. **d** 91. NSM Kennington St Jo w St Jas *S'wark* from 91. *9 Dalmore Road, London SE21 8HD* 081-670 8046

ANSELL, Antony Michael. b 40. St Jo Coll Nottm 78. **d** 80 **p** 81. C Harrow Weald St Mich *Lon* 80-84; C Harrow H Trin St Mich 84; Hon C Ches Square St Mich w St Phil 86-88; Hon C Mayfair Ch Ch from 88. *10 Durand Gardens, London SW9 0PP* 071-587 0997

ANSELL, Howard. b 36. St Jo Coll Cam BA59 MA62. NW Ord Course 73. **d** 76 **p** 77. C Chapeltown *Sheff* 76-79; V Worsbrough St Thos and St Jas 79-83; R Lt Waltham *Chelmsf* from 83. *The Rectory, Brook Hill, Little Waltham, Chelmsford CM3 3LJ* Chelmsford (0245) 360241

ANSELL, John Christopher. b 49. DipAD. Sarum & Wells Th Coll 79. **d** 81 **p** 82. C Dartford St Alb *Roch* 81-84; C Leybourne 84-88; C Larkfield 84-88; TV Mortlake w E Sheen *S'wark* from 88. *17 Sheen Gate Gardens, London SW14 7PD* 081-876 5002

ANSELM, Brother. See GENDERS, Rt Rev Roger Alban Marson

ANSLEM, Brother. See SMYTH, Robert Andrew Laine

ANSON, Harry. b 35. FInstFF79. St Jo Coll Nottm 83. **d** 88. NSM Ayr *Glas* from 88. *Fairview, Hollybush, Ayr KA6 7ED* Patna (0292) 531238

ANSTEY, Canon Christopher Robin Paul. b 25. Trin Coll Ox BA49 MA50. St Steph Ho Ox 49. **d** 51 **p** 52. V Headington Ox 64-71; Lic to Offic Ches 72-75; Worc 76-79; Hon Min Can Pet Cathl *Pet* from 79; Chapl Westwood Ho Sch Pet 79-83; V Gretton w Rockingham and Caldecote *Pet* 83-90; rtd 90; Hon C Warton St Oswald w Yealand Conyers *Blackb* from 91. *The Parsonage, Upphall Lane, Priest Hutton, Carnforth, Lancs LA6 1JL*

ANSTEY, Nigel John. b 55. Cranmer Hall Dur 84. **d** 87 **p** 88. C Plumstead St Jo w St Jas and St Paul *S'wark* from 87. *34 Earl Rise, London SE18 7NH* 081-855 1311

ANSTICE, John Neville. b 39. Lon Univ BSc63. Cuddesdon Coll 69. **d** 71 **p** 72. C Stonebridge St Mich *Lon* 71-74; Chapl Woodbridge Sch Suffolk 74-76; TV Droitwich *Worc* 76-80; P-in-c Salwarpe 76-79; Perm to Offic *Chich* from 80. *2 Fernhurst Close, Ifield, Crawley, W Sussex RH11 0AW* Crawley (0293) 35654

ANTHONY, Brother. See WILLIAMS, Howard Graham

ANTHONY, Brother. See MITCHELL, Keith Adrian

ANTHONY, Charles William. b 15. St Cath Coll Cam BA38 MA42 Leeds Univ DipEd. Ely Th Coll 38. **d** 39 **p** 40. P-in-c Airmyn *Sheff* 59-78; V Hook 60-78; V Hook w Airmyn 78-86; rtd 86; Perm to Offic Sheff from 86; S'well from 87. *The Old Rectory, Top Street, North Wheatley, Retford, Notts DN22 9OA* Gainsborough (0427) 880959

ANTHONY, Canon David Ivor Morgan. b 04. Dur Univ LTh32. St Aug Coll Cant 26. **d** 31 **p** 32. C Leic St Matt *Leic* 31-34; Australia from 34; Hon Can Bendigo 74-75. *52 Redford Street, Kingston, Queensland, Australia 4114* Kingston (7) 208-9869

ANTHONY, Gerald Caldecott. b 18. Down Coll Cam BA41 MA44. Wycliffe Hall Ox 41. **d** 43 **p** 44. R Bulmer *York* 66-72; V Broughton-in-Furness w Woodland *Carl* 72-75; P-in-c Seathwaite w Ulpha 73-75; V Broughton and Duddon 75-83; rtd 83; Perm to Offic *Worc* from 83. *2 Coppice Close, Malvern, Worcs WR14 1LE* Leigh Sinton (0886) 32930

ANTHONY, Ian Charles. b 47. NW Ord Course 76. **d** 79 **p** 80. NSM Lt Lever *Man* from 79. *36 Meadow Close, Little Lever, Bolton BL3 1LG* Farnworth (0204) 791437

ANTHONY-ROBERTS, Gelert Roderick. b 43. Southn Univ BEd78 Reading Univ MA84. Sarum & Wells Th Coll. **d** 90 **p** 91. C Alton St Lawr *Win* from 90. *13 Walnut Close, Alton, Hants GU34 2BA* Alton (0420) 88226

ap GWILYM, Gwynn. b 50. Univ of Wales (Ban) BA71 MA76. Wycliffe Hall Ox BA84 MA89. **d** 84 **p** 85. C Ynyscyhaiarn w Penmorfa and Porthmadog *Ban* 84-86; R Penegoes and Darowen w Llanbrynmair from 86. *The Rectory, Penegoes, Machynlleth, Powys SY20 8LW* Machynlleth (0654) 703214

ap IORWERTH, Geraint. b 50. Univ of Wales (Lamp) DipTh72 Univ of Wales (Cardiff) DPS73 MPhil90 Open Univ BA78. Burgess Hall Lamp 69 Westmr Past Foundn 73 St Mich Coll Llan 73. **d** 74 **p** 75. C Holyhead w Rhoscolyn *Ban* 74-78; R Pennal w Corris and Esgaergeiliog from 78; Founder and Ldr Order of Sancta Sophia from 87. *The Rectory, Pennal, Machynlleth, Powys SY20 9JS* Pennal (0654) 791216

ap IVOR, Canon Cyril Bernard Gwynne. b 17. St Chad's Coll Dur BA38 MA44. Bps' Coll Cheshunt 39. **d** 40 **p** 41. R Stockport St Thos *Ches* 59-75; V Macclesfield St Jo 75-84; RD Macclesfield 80-84; rtd 84; Hon Can Ches Cathl *Ches* from 84. *81 Newland Avenue, Cheadle Hulme, Cheshire SK8 6NE* 061-485 5571

APPELBE, Frederick Charles. b 52. TCD DipTh87. CITC 87. **d** 87 **p** 88. C Waterford w Killea, Drumcannon and Dunhill *C & O* 87-90; C Taney w St Nahi *D & G* from 90. *48 Wesley Lawns, Sandyford Road, Dublin 16, Irish Republic* Dublin (1) 952087

APPLEBY, Anthony Robert Nightingale. b 40. AKC62. **d** 63 **p** 64. C Cov St Mark *Cov* 63-67; CF from 67. *c/o MOD (Army), Bagshot Park, Bagshot, Surrey GU19 5PL* Bagshot (0276) 71717

APPLEBY, Miss Janet Mohr (Jan). b 32. Lon Univ TCert53 BA79 Sussex Univ MA(Ed)74. Chich Th Coll 90. **d** 91. NSM Rottingdean *Chich* from 91. *25 Eley Drive, Rottingdean, Brighton, E Sussex BN2 7FH* Brighton (0273) 304308

APPLEFORD, Canon Patrick Robert. b 25. Trin Coll Cam BA49 MA54. Chich Th Coll 50. **d** 52 **p** 53. Dean Lusaka Cath 66-72; P-in-c Sutton St Nicholas w Sutton St Michael *Heref* 73-75; Dir of Educn *Chelmsf* 75-90; Dioc Can Chelmsf Cathl 78-90; rtd 90. *6 Chestnut Walk, Chelmsford CM1 4JU* Chelmsford (0245) 265907

APPLEGARTH, Anthony Edgar. b 44. Chich Th Coll 82. **d** 84 **p** 85. C Cannington, Otterhampton, Combwich and Stockland *B & W* 84-86; C Bridgwater St Mary, Chilton Trinity and Durleigh 86-89; R Stogursey w Fiddington from 89. *The Rectory, High Street, Stogursey, Bridgwater, Somerset TA5 1PL* Nether Stowey (0278) 732884

APPLEGATE, John. b 56. Bris Univ BSc75. Trin Coll Bris DipHE PhD. **d** 84 **p** 85. C Collyhurst *Man* 84-87; C Higher Broughton from 87; C Broughton from 87; C Lower Broughton St Clem w St Matthias from 87. *237 Great Clowes Street, Higher Broughton, Salford M7 9DZ* 061-792 9161

✠**APPLETON, Most Rev George.** b 02. CMG72 MBE46. Selw Coll Cam BA24 MA29. St Aug Coll Cant 21. **d** 25 **p** 26 **c** 63. C Stepney St Dunstan and All SS *Lon* 25-27; Burma 27-47; Adn Rangoon 43-46; V Headstone St Geo *Lon* 47-50; Sec Conf Br Miss Socs 50-57; P-in-c Cricklewood St Mich 50-57; V St Botolph Aldgate w H Trin Minories 57-62; Adn Lon and Can Res St Paul's Cathl 62-63; Abp Perth 63-69; Abp Jerusalem 69-74; rtd 74; C St Mich Cornhill w St Pet le Poer etc *Lon* 74-80; Lic to Offic from 81; Perm to Offic *Ox* from 81. *112A St Mary's Road, Oxford OX4 1QF* Oxford (0865) 248272

APPLETON, John Bearby. b 42. Linc Th Coll 74. **d** 76 **p** 77. C Selby Abbey *York* 76-79; C Epsom St Barn *Guildf* 79-82; V Linc All SS *Linc* from 82. *All Saints' Vicarage, 173 Monks Road, Lincoln LN2 5JL* Lincoln (0522) 528695

APPLETON, Canon Paul Valentine. b 19. LRAM ARCM K Coll Cam BA42 MA46. Lich Th Coll 42. **d** 44 **p** 45. Hd Master Linc Cathl Sch 60-70; Succ Linc Cathl *Linc* 60-85; Can and Preb 77-90; V Owmby w Normanby 70-75; P-in-c Spridlington w Saxby and Firsby 73-90; R Owmby and Normanby w Glentham 75-90; rtd 90. *2 Eastfield Lane, Welton, Lincoln LN2 3NA* Welton (0673) 60667

APPLETON, Canon Ronald Percival. b 15. St Pet Hall Ox BA36 MA40. Ridley Hall Cam 36. **d** 38 **p** 39. V Winchcombe, Gretton, Sudeley Manor etc *Glouc* 62-86; RD Winchcombe 63-86; Hon Can Glouc Cathl 80-86; rtd 86. *1 Abbey Croft, Pershore, Worcs WR10 1JQ* Pershore (0386) 553023

APPLETON, Stanley Basil. b 04. Wycliffe Hall Ox 66. **d** 66 **p** 66. Lic to Offic *Ox* 66-74; Hon C Welford w Wickham and Gt Shefford 74-86; Hon C Welford w Wickham and Gt Shefford, Boxford etc from 86. *Leigh Cottage, Wickham, Newbury, Berks RG16 8HD* Boxford (048838) 239

APPLETON, Timothy Charles. b 36. Selw Coll Cam BA60 MA65 K Coll Lon PhD67 Cam Univ DSc81. S'wark Ord Course 69. **d** 72 **p** 73. NSM Harston w Hauxton *Ely* 72-76; Lect Cam Univ 73-88; Lic to Offic *Ely* 76-79 and from 84; P-in-c Gt w Lt Eversden 79-84; Chapl and Counsellor Bourn Hall Clinic from 88. *44 Eversden Road, Harlton, Cambridge CB3 7ET* Cambridge (0223) 262226

APPLEYARD, Edward. b 19. OBE75 RD68. Kelham Th Coll 37. **d** 43 **p** 44. V Gt Ayton w Easby and Newton in Cleveland *York* 68-78; RD Stokesley 70-77; P-in-c Middlesb St Columba w St Paul 78-84; rtd 84; Dioc Rtd Clergy and Widows Officer *York* from 87. *16 Linden Road, Great Ayton, Middlesbrough, Cleveland TS9 6AN* Middlesbrough (0642) 722488

APPLIN, David Edward. b 39. Oak Hill Th Coll 63. **d** 65 **p** 66. C Ox St Clem *Ox* 65-69; C Felixstowe SS Pet and Paul *St E* 69-71; Lic to Offic *Win* 71-91; Travelling Sec Rwanda Miss 71-74; Home Sec 74-77; Gen Sec 77-81; Dir Overseas Personnel Dept Tear Fund 82-88; Overseas Dir from 88; Hon C Kempshott *Win* from 91. *4 Norwich Close, Basingstoke, Hants RG22 4PL* Basingstoke (0256) 462592

APPS, Anthony Howard. b 22. Ch Coll Cam BA47 MA51. **d** 49 **p** 50. V Myddleton Square St Mark *Lon* 66-82; rtd 82. *18 Longworth Way, Guisborough, Cleveland TS14 6DG* Guisborough (0287) 37939

APPS, Bryan Gerald. b 37. Univ of Wales (Lamp) BA59 St Cath Coll Ox BA61 MA65. Wycliffe Hall Ox 59. **d** 61 **p** 62. C Southn St Alb *Win* 61-65; C Andover w Foxcott 65-69; P-in-c Freemantle 69-72; R 73-78; V Pokesdown All SS from 78. *All Saints' Vicarage, 14 Stourwood Road, Bournemouth BH6 3QP* Bournemouth (0202) 423747

APPS, David Ronald. b 34. Univ of Wales (Lamp) BA57. Sarum Th Coll 57. **d** 59 **p** 60. C Southbourne St Chris *Win* 59-62; C Weeke 62-67; V Alton All SS 67-80; V Charlestown *Truro* from 80; Miss to Seamen from 80. *The Vicarage, Charlestown, St Austell, Cornwall PL25 3PG* Par (072681) 2824

APPS, Canon Michael John (Brother Bernard). b 28. Pemb Coll Cam BA52 MA56. Cuddesdon Coll 53. **d** 55 **p** 56. C Spalding *Linc* 55-58; SSF from 58; Perm to Offic *Chelmsf* 59-63 and 67-69; P-in-c Plaistow 63-67; Australia 69-75; Guardian St Nic Friary Harbledown 77-78; Hilfield Friary Dorchester 78-89; Can and Preb Sarum Cathl *Sarum* 81-89. *10 Halcrow Street, London E1 2EP* 071-247 6233

APTHORP, Ven Arthur Norman. b 24. Pemb Coll Cam BA47 MA50. Chich Th Coll 48. **d** 50 **p** 51. C Henfield *Chich* 50-52; C Hove All SS 52-56; Australia from 56; Hon Can Perth 73-77 and from 79; Adn of the Country (Perth) 82-89. *2 Brookton Highway, Brookton, W Australia 6306* Brookton (96) 421046

ARBER, Gerald Kenneth. b 37. Open Univ BA87. Oak Hill NSM Course. **d** 84 **p** 85. NSM Romford St Edw *Chelmsf* from 84. *5 Hill Grove, Romford RM1 4JP* Romford (0708) 750070

ARBERY, Canon Richard Neil. b 25. AKC49. **d** 50 **p** 51. C Pemberton St Jo *Liv* 50-55; V Roundthorn *Man* 55-59; V Hindley All SS *Liv* 59-78; RD Wigan 75-89; Hon Can Liv Cathl from 77; V Wigan St Andr from 78. *St Andrew's Vicarage, 3A Mort Street, Wigan, Lancs WN6 7AU* Wigan (0942) 43514

ARBUCKLE, Canon James Hugh. b 19. AKC49. **d** 49 **p** 50. V Barnetby le Wold *Linc* 54-76; P-in-c Bigby 64-76; Can and Preb Linc Cathl from 70; RD Yarborough 70-76; P-in-c Somerby w Humby 74-76; Sec Linc Dioc Syn and Past Cttee 76-84; rtd 85. *The Burghersh Chantry, 17 St James Street, Lincoln LN2 1QE* Lincoln (0522) 29666

ARBUTHNOT, Andy. b 26. S'wark Ord Course 71. **d** 74 **p** 75. NSM Mortlake w E Sheen *S'wark* 74-77; Lic to Offic *Guildf* from 77; Missr Lon Healing Miss from 83. *20 Dawson Place, London W2 4TJ* 071-229 3641

ARBUTHNOT, Canon James. b 19. QUB BA42. CITC 44. **d** 44 **p** 45. I Belf St Phil *Conn* 60-70; I Belf St Paul 70-87; Can Conn Cathl 83-87; rtd 87. *6 St Elizabeth's Court, Ballyregan Road, Dundonald, Belfast BT16 0HX* Belfast (0232) 487951

ARCHER, Alan Robert. b 38. AKC56. Lich Th Coll 65. **d** 68 **p** 69. C Lower Mitton *Worc* 68-71; C Foley Park 71-74; V Warndon 74-79; P-in-c Clifton upon Teme 79-81; P-in-c Lower Sapey 79-81; P-in-c The Shelsleys 79-81; P-in-c Malvern Wells and Wyche 81; V 81-83; TV Braunstone *Leic* from 83. *498 Braunstone Road, Leicester LE3 3DG* Leicester (0533) 893262

ARCHER, Frederick John. b 06. Clifton Th Coll 29. **d** 33 **p** 38. V Corse and Staunton *Glouc* 61-73; rtd 73; Perm to Offic *Glouc* from 75. *The School House, Staunton, Gloucester GL19 3QF* Staunton Court (045284) 259

ARCHER, Graham John. b 58. Lanc Univ BSc79. St Jo Coll Nottm DipTh. **d** 85 **p** 86. C Ipswich St Matt *St E* 85-89; C Walton from 89. *2 Blyford Way, Felixstowe, Suffolk* Felixstowe (0394) 274284

ARCHER, John Thomas. b 28. Birm Coll of Commerce GIMechE68 Birm Poly CQSW83. E Midl Min Tr Course 79. **d** 80 **p** 81. NSM Derby St Thos *Derby* 80-86; V Edlington *Sheff* from 87. *The Vicarage, Broomhouse Lane, Edlington, Doncaster, S Yorkshire DN12 1LN* Rotherham (0709) 863148

ARCHER, Keith Malcolm. b 40. Man Univ BA61 MA80 Magd Coll Cam BA67 MA72. Ridley Hall Cam 66. **d** 68 **p** 69. C Newland St Jo *York* 68-72; Hon C Kersal Moor *Man* 72-79; Ind Chapl from 72. *67 Woodward Road, Prestwich, Manchester M25 8TX* 061-773 2249

ARCHER, Kenneth Daniel. b 23. Edin Th Coll 50. **d** 53 **p** 54. R Inverurie *Ab* 62-72; R Kemnay 63-72; R Cranham *Chelmsf* 72-82; V Gt Ilford St Clem 82-87; rtd 87. *22 Cherrywood, Penwortham, Preston PR1 0PJ*

ARCHER, Michael John. b 37. Trin Coll Bris 76. **d** 78 **p** 79. C Kinson *Sarum* 78-81; C Harpenden St Nic *St Alb* 81-88; P-in-c Rashcliffe and Lockwood *Wakef* from 88. *42 Beaumont Park Road, Huddersfield HD4 5JS* Huddersfield (0484) 653258

ARCHER, Stanley Edwin. b 21. St Jo Coll Dur 80. **d** 81 **p** 82. C Upper Nidderdale *Ripon* 81-83; P-in-c Wensley 83-89; P-in-c W Witton 83-89; rtd 89. *40 The Oaks, Masham, Ripon, N Yorkshire HG4 4DT* Ripon (0765) 89685

ARCHIBALD, George Stirling. b 12. Kelham Th Coll 30. **d** 36 **p** 37. V Chertsey *Guildf* 50-82; rtd 82; Perm to Offic *Guildf* from 82. *29 Masonic Hall Road, Chertsey, Surrey KT16 9DH* Chertsey (0932) 63078

ARCUS, Jeffrey. b 40. NW Ord Course 72. **d** 75 **p** 76. C Halliwell St Thos *Man* 75-78; C Walmsley 78-81; P-in-c Bury Ch King 81-82; TV Bury Ch King w H Trin from 82. *St Thomas's Vicarage, Pimhole Road, Bury, Lancs BL9 7EY* 061-764 1157

ARDAGH-WALTER, Christopher Richard. b 35. Univ of Wales (Lamp) BA58. Chich Th Coll 58. **d** 60 **p** 61. C Heavitree *Ex* 60-64; C Redcar *York* 64-67; C King's Worthy *Win* 67-69; C-in-c Four Marks CD 69-73; V Four Marks 73-75; P-in-c Eling, Testwood and Marchwood 76-78; TR Totton 78-83; R The Sherbornes w Pamber 83-88; V Froyle and Holybourne from 88. *The Vicarage, Holybourne, Alton, Hants GU34 4HD* Alton (0420) 83240

✠**ARDEN, Rt Rev Donald Seymour.** b 16. CBE81. Leeds Univ BA37. Coll of Resurr Mirfield 37. **d** 39 **p** 40 **c** 61. C Hatcham St Cath *S'wark* 39-40; C Potten End w Nettleden *St Alb* 41-43; S Africa 44-61; Can Zululand 59-61; Bp Nyasaland 61-64; Bp Malawi 64-71; Bp S Malawi & Abp Cen Africa 71-80; Asst Bp Willesden *Lon* from 81; P-in-c Uxbridge St Marg 81-86; rtd 86; Hon C N Harrow St Alb *Lon* from 86. *6 Frobisher Close, Pinner, Middx HA5 1NN* 081-866 6009

ARDFERT AND AGHADOE, Archdeacon of. *See* SHANNON, Ven Malcolm James Douglas

ARDIS, Very Rev Edward George. b 54. Dur Univ BA76. CITC 76. **d** 78 **p** 79. C Dub Drumcondra w N Strand and St Barn *D & G* 78-81; C Dub St Bart w Ch Ch Leeson Park 81-84; I Ardamine w Kiltennel, Glascarrig etc *C & O* 84-89; Can Tuam Cathl *T, K & A* from 89; Dean Killala from 89; I Killala w Dunfeeny, Crossmolina etc from 89. *The Rectory, Crossmolina, Co Mayo, Irish Republic* Ballina (96) 31384

ARDLEY, John Owen. b 39. Lon Univ BD70. S'wark Ord Course 70. **d** 72 **p** 73. C Caterham Valley *S'wark* 72-76; V Abbey Wood 76-84; Sub-Dean of Woolwich 77-84; P-in-c Lower Sydenham St Mich from 84; P-in-c Sydenham All SS from 84; RD W Lewisham from 87. *41 Trewsbury Road, London SE26 5DP* 081-778 3065

ARGUILE, Roger Henry William. b 43. Dur Univ LLB64 Keble Coll Ox BA70 MA75. Ripon Hall Ox 70. **d** 71 **p** 72. C Walsall *Lich* 71-76; TV Blakenall Heath 76-83; TV Stafford from 83. *St Bertelin's Vicarage, Holmcroft Road, Stafford ST16 1JG* Stafford (0785) 52874

ARGYLE, Douglas Causer. b 17. St Jo Coll Cam BA39 MA43. Ridley Hall Cam 39. **d** 41 **p** 42. Chapl Gresham's Sch Holt 59-74; P-in-c Eastleach w Southrop *Glouc* 74-82; rtd 82; Perm to Offic *Glouc* from 82. *East Lynn, London Road, Fairford, Glos GL7 4AR* Cirencester (0285) 713235

ARGYLE, Canon Edward Charles. b 55. ACT DipTh80. **d** 80 **p** 80. Australia 80-83; C Gt Yarmouth *Nor* 83-85; I Kilcooley w Littleon, Crohane and Fertagh *C & O* from 85; Preb Ossory and Leighlin Cathls from 91. *The Rectory, Grange Barna, Thurles, Co Tipperary, Irish Republic* Thurles (56) 34147

ARGYLE, Frank Martin. b 12. Clare Coll Cam BA33 MA38. Bps' Coll Cheshunt 38. **d** 38 **p** 39. Warden St Columba's Coll Dublin 49-74; V Newbottle *Pet* 74-76; R Aynho w Newbottle and Charlton 76-81; rtd 81; Perm to Offic *Ex* from 81. *31 Castle Gardens, Bath BA2 2AN* Bath (0225) 314774

ARGYLL AND THE ISLES, Bishop of. *See* HENDERSON, Most Rev George Kennedy Buchanan

ARGYLL AND THE ISLES, Dean of. *See* MACLEAY, Very Rev John Henry James

ARIES, William Albert. b 28. ACT ThL61 Bps' Coll Cheshunt 59. **d** 60 **p** 61. C Nuneaton St Mary *Cov* 60-63; C Chandler's Ford *Win* 63-66; C-in-c Ringwood St Ive and St Leon CD 66-70; V St Leonards and St Ives 70-75; V Bournemouth St Clem from 75. *The Vicarage, St Clement's Road, Bournemouth BH1 4DZ* Bournemouth (0202) 33151

ARKELL, Kevin Paul. b 53. Preston Poly DipSocWork81 BTh86. Sarum & Wells Th Coll 84. **d** 86 **p** 87. C S Petherton w The Seavingtons *B & W* 86-88; P-in-c Gt Harwood St Bart *Blackb* 88-90; V from 90. *St Bartholomew's Vicarage, 1 Church Lane, Great Harwood, Blackburn BB6 7PU* Great Harwood (0254) 884039

ARLOW, Canon William James. b 26. Edin Th Coll 59. **d** 59 **p** 60. I Newry St Patr *D & D* 66-70; I Belf St Donard 70-74; Dep Sec Irish Coun of Chs 74-75; Sec 75-79; Can for Ecum Affairs Belf Cathl from 79; Treas 85-89; P-in-c Ballyphilip w Ardquin 86-89; rtd 89; Lic to Offic *D & D* from 90. *13 Ashford Park, Bangor, Co Down BT19 2DD* Bangor (0247) 469758

ARMAGH, Archbishop of. *See* EAMES, Most Rev Robert Henry Alexander

ARMAGH, Archdeacon of. *See* COLTHURST, Ven Reginald William Richard

ARMAGH, Dean of. *See* CASSIDY, Very Rev Herbert

ARMAN, Brian Robert. b 54. St Jo Coll Dur BA77 LTh78. Cranmer Hall Dur 74. **d** 78 **p** 79. C Lawrence Weston *Bris* 78-82; C Bishopston 82-88; R Filton from 88. *The Rectory, Station Road, Bristol BS12 7BX* Bristol (0272) 791128

ARMES, John Andrew. b 55. SS Coll Cam BA77 MA81. Sarum & Wells Th Coll 77. **d** 79 **p** 80. C Walney Is *Carl* 79-82; Chapl to Agric 82-86; TV Greystoke, Matterdale and Mungrisdale 82-86; TV Watermillock 84-86; Chapl Man Univ *Man* from 86; TV Man Whitworth 86-88; TR from 88. *24 Darley Avenue, Manchester M20 8YD* 061-445 4994 or 273 1465

ARMFELT, Julian Roger. b 31. K Coll Cam BA53. Wells Th Coll 54. **d** 56 **p** 58. C Corringham *Linc* 69-73; TV Fincham *Ely* 73-75; V Freckleton *Blackb* 75-79; P-in-c Sherburn *York* 79-80; P-in-c W and E Heslerton w Knapton 79-80; P-in-c Yedingham 79-80; R Sherburn and W and E Heslerton w Yedingham 80-83; TV York All SS Pavement w St Crux and St Martin etc 83-84; P-in-c York St Mary Bishophill Junior w All SS 83-84; C Howden Team Min 84-86; P-in-c Laughton w Throapham *Sheff* 86-88; rtd 88. *Meadow Haven Cottage, Pier Road, Berwick-upon-Tweed TD15 1JB* Berwick-upon-Tweed (0289) 307241

ARMITAGE, Bryan Ambrose. b 28. K Coll Lon AKC55 BD57. **d** 56 **p** 57. C High Harrogate St Pet *Ripon* 56-59; S Africa 59-61; Uganda 61-74; Chapl Sutton Valence Sch Kent 74-75; Chapl Qu Ethelburga's Sch Harrogate from 76. *5 York Road, Harrogate, N Yorkshire HG1 2QA* Harrogate (0423) 504410

ARMITAGE, Michael Stanley. b 45. Jes Coll Cam BA67 MA71. Cuddesdon Coll 67. **d** 69 **p** 70. C Sanderstead All SS *S'wark* 69-70; C Battersea St Mary 70-71; Hon C Kingston St Jo 72-73; Chapl Kingston Poly 72-73; V Angell Town St Jo from 73. *St John's Vicarage, Wiltshire Road, London SW9 7NF* 071-733 0585

ARMITAGE, Richard Norris. b 51. AKC. St Aug Coll Cant 73. **d** 74 **p** 75. C Chapelthorpe *Wakef* 74-77; C W Bromwich All SS *Lich* 77-82; P-in-c Ketley 82-83; V Oakengates 82-83; V Ketley and Oakengates 83-89; V Evesham *Worc* from 89. *The Vicarage, 5 Croft Road, Evesham, Worcs WR11 4NE* Evesham (0386) 446219

ARMITSTEAD, Geoffrey Arthur Dymoke. b 02. Keble Coll Ox BA24 MA34. Cuddesdon Coll 26. **d** 26 **p** 27. V Hastings All So *Chich* 63-78; rtd 78; Perm to Offic *Chich* from 78. *43 First Avenue, Bexhill-on-Sea, Sussex TN40 2PL* Bexhill-on-Sea (0424) 215566

ARMSON, Canon John Moss. b 39. Selw Coll Cam BA61 MA64 St Andr Univ PhD65. Coll of Resurr Mirfield 64. **d** 66 **p** 67. C Notting Hill St Jo *Lon* 66-69; Chapl Down Coll Cam 69-73; Fell 70-73; Chapl Westcott Ho Cam 73-76; Vice-Prin 76-82; Prin Edin Th Coll 82-89; Can St Mary's Cathl *Edin* 82-89; Can Res Roch Cathl *Roch* from 89. *Easter Garth, King's Orchard, Rochester, Kent ME1 1SX* Medway (0634) 406992

ARMSTEAD, Geoffrey Malcolm. b 32. K Coll Lon AKC56 BD63. **d** 57 **p** 58. C Weymouth H Trin *Sarum* 57-60; C Mortlake w E Sheen *S'wark* 60-63; Chapl Em Sch Wandsworth 63-74; Dep Hd Master Harriet Costello Sch from 75; Perm to Offic *Win* from 75. *Polecat Cottage, Polecat Corner, Tunworth, Basingstoke, Hants RG25 2LA* Basingstoke (0256) 471650

ARMSTEAD, Gordon. b 33. Oak Hill Th Coll 73. **d** 74 **p** 75. C Woodside *Ripon* 74-76; C Heaton Ch Ch *Man* 76-79; Australia 79-81; R Levenshulme St Mark *Man* 81-86; V Borth and Eglwysfach w Llangynfelin *St D* from 86. *The Vicarage, Swn y Mor, The Cliff, Borth, Dyfed SY24 5NG* Borth (0970) 871594

ARMSTRONG, Adrian Christopher. b 48. LSE BSc70 K Coll Lon PhD80. E Anglian Minl Tr Course 84. **d** 87 **p** 88. NSM Linton *Ely* from 87. *17A Brinkley Road,*

Weston Colville, Cambridge CB1 5PA Cambridge (0223) 290755

ARMSTRONG, Christopher John. b 47. Nottm Univ BTh75. Kelham Th Coll 72. **d** 76 **p** 76. C Maidstone All SS w St Phil and H Trin *Cant* 76-79; Chapl St Hild and St Bede Coll Dur 79-84; Dir of Ords *York* from 85; Abp's Dom Chapl from 85. *Brew House Cottage, Bishopthorpe, York YO2 1QE* York (0904) 705822 or 707021

ARMSTRONG, Christopher John Richard. b 35. Fribourg Univ LTh60 Ch Coll Cam BA64 MA68 PhD79. Edin Th Coll 74. **d** 59 **p** 59. In RC Ch 59-71; Lect Aber Univ 68-74; C Ledbury *Heref* 74-76; P-in-c Bredenbury and Wacton w Grendon Bishop 76-79; P-in-c Edwyn Ralph and Collington w Thornbury 76-79; P-in-c Pencombe w Marston Stannett and Lt Cowarne 76-79; R Cherry Burton *York* 79-80; Tutor Westcott Ho Cam 80-85; V Bottisham *Ely* 85-89; P-in-c Lode and Longmeadow 85-89; P-in-c Cropthorne w Charlton *Worc* from 89; Dioc Local Min Sec from 89. *The Vicarage, Cropthorne, Pershore, Worcester WR10 3NB* Evesham (0386) 860279

ARMSTRONG, Colin John. b 32. St Cath Soc Ox BA59 MA65. Wells Th Coll 59. **d** 61 **p** 62. C Acomb St Steph *York* 61-64; C Newland St Jo 64-67; Chapl and Tutor All SS Coll Tottenham 67-78; Chapl and Tutor Middx Poly 78-85. *Address temp unknown*

ARMSTRONG, Edwin. b 23. TCD BA45 MA69. **d** 46 **p** 47. I Gilford *D & D* 57-85; rtd 85. *3 St Elizabeth's Court, Ballyregan Road, Dundonald, Belfast BT16 0HX* Belfast (0232) 487629

ARMSTRONG, Canon George. b 09. Clifton Th Coll 29. **d** 32 **p** 33. R Layer Marney *Chelmsf* 46-82; R Gt w Lt Birch and Layer Breton 47-82; RD Coggeshall and Tey 68-79; Hon Can Chelmsf Cathl 77-82; Perm to Offic Chelmsf & St E from 82. *11 The Westerings, Nayland, Colchester CO6 4LJ* Colchester (0206) 262952

ARMSTRONG, Guy Lionel Walter. b 18. Wycliffe Hall Ox 60. **d** 61 **p** 62. V Bagshot *Guildf* 65-73; V Ripley 73-77; rtd 77; Perm to Offic *Portsm* from 81. *The Briary, 3 Wood Street, Ryde, Isle of Wight PO33 2DH* Isle of Wight (0983) 62454

ARMSTRONG, Canon James Irwin. St Aid Birkenhead 57. **d** 59 **p** 60. I Badoney Upper *D & R* 65-75; I Camusjuxta-Bann 75-85; I Drumragh w Mountfield 85-89; Can Derry Cathl 87-89; RD Drumragh 87-89; rtd 89. *Drumragh, 9 Glenvale Crescent, Portrush, Co Antrim BT56 8EB* Portrush (0265) 822140

✠**ARMSTRONG, Rt Rev John.** b 05. CB62 OBE42. St Fran Coll Nundah ACT ThL32. **d** 32 **p** 33 **c** 63. Australia 32-33; C Scarborough St Martin *York* 33-35; Chapl RN 35-60; Chapl of the Fleet and Adn for the RN 60-63; QHC 58-63; Bp Bermuda 63-68; V Yarcombe *Ex* 69-73; Asst Bp *Ex* 69-73; rtd 73. *c/o Lady Riches, 34 Cheriton Road, Winchester SO22 5AY* Winchester (0962) 54067

ARMSTRONG, Canon John Hammond. b 24. Dur Univ BA47 DipTh49. **d** 49 **p** 50. R Sutton upon Derwent *York* 63-71; Dioc Stewardship Adv 63-75; P-in-c York All SS and St Crux w St Sav etc 71-72; R 72-76; Can and Preb York Minster 72-91; P-in-c York St Denys 74-76; RD City of York 76-86; TR York All SS Pavement w St Crux and St Denys 76-77; TR York All SS Pavement w St Crux and St Martin etc 77-91; rtd 91. *20 Hempland Avenue, Stockton Lane, York YO3 0DE* York (0904) 421312

ARMSTRONG, John James. b 15. TCD BA38 MA42 Div Test40. **d** 40 **p** 41. Miss to Seamen 58-77; Sudan 58-59; Dunkirk 60-62; Belf 75-77; C Derriaghy Conn 62-71; C Seagoe *D & D* 71-73; Hd of S Ch Miss Belf 73-75; C Belf St Simon w St Phil *Conn* 77-80; rtd 80. *60 The Green, Dunmurry, Belfast BT17 0QA* Belfast (0232) 623032

ARMSTRONG, Maurice Alexander. b 62. Ulster Poly BA84 TCD DipTh87. CITC 84. **d** 87 **p** 88. C Portadown St Mark *Arm* 87-90; I Sixmilecross w Termonmaguirke from 90. *104 Cooley Road, Sixmilecross, Co Tyrone BT79 9DH* Beragh (06627) 58218

ARMSTRONG, Canon Robert Charles. b 24. TCD BA46 HDipEd52 MA57. CITC 47. **d** 47 **p** 48. C Belf St Luke *Conn* 48-50; Warden Gr Sch Dub 50-59; Succ St Patr Cathl Dub 50-59; I Dub Finglas *D & G* 59-67; I Dun Laoghaire from 67; RD Newc 71-76; Dir of Ords (Dub) 74-84; USPG Area Sec from 77; Can Ch Ch Cathl Dub 84-88; Treas from 88. *The Vicarage, 2 Park Road, Dun Laoghaire, Co Dublin, Irish Republic* Dublin (1) 280-9537

ARMSTRONG, Ronald. b 09. St Jo Coll Dur BA38 MA42. **d** 38 **p** 39. Chapl Whipps Cross Hosp Lon 65-79; rtd 79.

Nether Barr, Newton Stewart, Wigtownshire DG8 6AU Newton Stewart (0671) 2236

ARMSTRONG, Samuel David. b 48. BD MTh. **d** 86 **p** 87. C Cam H Trin w St Andr Gt *Ely* 86-89; V Cam St Martin from 89. *33 Rustat Road, Cambridge* Cambridge (0223) 248648

ARMSTRONG, William. b 29. Sarum Th Coll 52. **d** 54 **p** 55. Australia 66-81 and from 90; Asst Dir of Educn *Liv* 81-90; V Aintree St Pet 81-88; TV Speke St Aid 88-90; rtd 90. *PO Box 151, Burwood, NSW, Australia 2134*

ARMSTRONG-MacDONNELL (nee Brooks), Mrs Vivienne Christine. b 42. Open Univ BA89. Ripon Coll Cuddesdon 88. **d** 90. C Crediton and Shobrooke *Ex* from 90. *Church House, Park Road, Crediton, Devon EX17 3ET* Crediton (03632) 3749

ARNAUD, John Charles Stanley. b 23. Aber Univ MA48 DipEd49. **d** 78 **p** 79. Hon C Huntly *Mor* 78-91; Hon C Aberchirder from 78; Hon C Keith from 78. *Rosemount, 10 Kynoch Terrace, Keith, Banffshire AB5 3EX* Keith (05422) 2240

ARNESEN, Christopher Paul. b 48. Lon Univ BA70. Sarum & Wells Th Coll 78. **d** 80 **p** 81. C Dalton-in-Furness *Carl* 80-83; C Ranmoor *Sheff* 83-86; R Distington *Carl* from 86. *The Rectory, Church Road, Distington, Workington, Cumbria CA14 5TE* Harrington (0946) 830384

ARNESEN, Raymond Halfdan. b 25. Qu Coll Cam BA49 MA54. Linc Th Coll 50. **d** 52 **p** 53. C Newc St Fran *Newc* 52-55; SSF 55-66; Cistercian from 66. *Ewell Monastery, West Malling, Maidstone, Kent ME19 6HH* West Malling (0732) 843089

ARNOLD, Alan Roy. b 33. Lon Univ BD79. S'wark Ord Course 75. **d** 78 **p** 79. C Fleet *Guildf* 78-81; V Hinchley Wood 81-84; C Cobham 84-89; C Addlestone from 89. *7 Lewis Close, Crouch Oak Green, Addlestone, Weybridge, Surrey KT15 2XG* Weybridge (0932) 845122

ARNOLD, Arthur Philip. b 46. Em Coll Cam BA67 MA71. Qu Coll Birm DipTh69. **d** 70 **p** 71. C Failsworth H Family CD *Man* 70-74; Asst Chapl Hurstpierpoint Coll Hassocks 74-77; Chapl K Coll Cam 77-80; Chapl St Chad's Coll Dur 80-82; Chapl Plymouth Coll from 83. *Mannamead Flat, Ford Park, Plymouth PL4 6RE* Plymouth (0752) 228239

ARNOLD, Brother. See NODDER, Thomas Arthur

ARNOLD, George Innes. b 22. Roch Th Coll. **d** 61 **p** 62. C Cullercoats St Geo *Newc* 61-64; C Benwell St Jas 64-68; Egypt 68-70; V Croydon St Jas *Cant* 71-80; P-in-c Dullingham *Ely* from 80; P-in-c Stetchworth from 80; RD Linton 81-88. *The Vicarage, Eagle Lane, Dullingham, Newmarket, Suffolk CB8 9UZ* Stetchworth (063876) 225

ARNOLD, Very Rev John Robert. b 33. SS Coll Cam BA57 MA61. Westcott Ho Cam 58. **d** 60 **p** 61. C Millhouses H Trin *Sheff* 60-63; Chapl and Lect Southn Univ *Win* 63-72; Sec Gen Syn Bd for Miss and Unity 72-78; Hon Can Win Cathl *Win* 74-78; Dean Roch 78-89; Dean Dur from 89. *The Deanery, The College, Durham DH1 3EQ* 091-384 7500

✠**ARNOLD, Rt Rev Keith Appleby.** b 26. Trin Coll Cam BA50 MA55. Westcott Ho Cam 50. **d** 52 **p** 53 **c** 80. C Haltwhistle *Newc* 52-55; C Edin St Jo *Edin* 55-61; R 61-69; CF (TA) 58-62; V Kirkby Lonsdale w Mansergh *Carl* 69-73; TR Hemel Hempstead *St Alb* 73-80; RD Berkhamsted 73-80; Suff Bp Warw *Cov* 80-90; Hon Can Cov Cathl from 80; rtd 90. *White Lodge, Dunstan, Alnwick, Northd NE66 3TB* Alnwick (0665) 76485

ARNOLD, Paul Maxwell. b 53. Or Coll Ox BA74 MA78. Ripon Coll Cuddesdon 79. **d** 82 **p** 83. C Kensington St Mary Abbots w St Geo *Lon* 82-86; C Wokingham St Paul *Ox* 86-90; C Fingringhoe w E Donyland *Chelmsf* from 90. *St Lawrence House, Rectory Road, Rowhedge, Colchester CO5 7HR* Colchester (0206) 728071

ARNOLD, Richard Nicholas. b 54. AKC76. S'wark Ord Course 76. **d** 77 **p** 78. C Nunhead St Antony *S'wark* 77-80; C Walworth 80-82; P-in-c Streatham Hill St Marg 82-84; V 84-89; P-in-c Kentish Town St Jo *Lon* from 89; P-in-c Kentish Town St Benet and All SS from 89; P-in-c Oseney Crescent St Luke from 89. *43 Lady Margaret Road, London NW5 2NH* 071-485 4231

ARNOLD, Roy. b 36. St D Coll Lamp BA62 DipTh63. **d** 63 **p** 64. C Brislington St Luke *Bris* 63-66; C Ches St Mary *Ches* 67-70; C Brinnington w Portwood 71-75; V Sale St Paul 75-82; R Dodleston 82-84; V Sheff St Oswald *Sheff* 84-90; Dioc Communications Officer from 84; Chapl to the Deaf from 90. *10 Devonshire Road, Sheffield S17 3NT* Doncaster (0302) 361972

ARNOTT, Arthur Frederick. b 14. S'wark Ord Course 66. **d** 70 **p** 71. C Reigate St Mary *S'wark* 70-74; Hon C Chislehurst Ch Ch *Roch* 74-90; rtd 90. *4 St Austins, Crossways Road, Grayshott, Surrey GU26 6HD* Hindhead (0428) 607894

ARNOTT, David. b 44. Em Coll Cam BA66. Qu Coll Birm 68. **d** 69 **p** 70. C Old Charlton *S'wark* 69-73; C S Beddington St Mich 73-78; Chapl Liv Poly *Liv* 78-82; V Bridgwater St Fran *B & W* from 86. *The Vicarage, Saxon Green, Bridgwater, Somerset TA6 4HZ* Bridgwater (0278) 422744

ARNOTT, Eric William. b 12. Cranmer Hall Dur 67. **d** 68 **p** 69. C Gosforth St Nic *Newc* 68-71; C Wooler 71-74; TV Wooler Gp 74-78; rtd 78. *Forge Cottage, Hoopers Lane, Puncknowle, Dorchester, Dorset DT2 9BE* Burton Bradstock (0308) 897768

ARNOTT, Thomas Grenfell. b 11. Solicitor. NE Ord Course 61 Cranmer Hall Dur 68. **d** 68 **p** 69. C Ryton *Dur* 68-71; V Weston-super-Mare Em *B & W* 71-73; R Brandesburton *York* 73-78; RD N Holderness 76-78; rtd 78. *The Birches, Westow, York YO6 7NE* Whitwell-on-the-Hill (065381) 543

ARRAND, Very Rev Geoffrey William. b 44. K Coll Lon BD66 AKC66. **d** 67 **p** 68. C Washington *Dur* 67-70; C S Ormsby w Ketsby, Calceby and Driby *Linc* 70-73; TV Gt Grimsby St Mary and St Jas 73-79; TR Halesworth w Linstead and Chediston *St E* 79-80; TR Halesworth w Linstead, Chediston, Holton etc 80-85; R Hadleigh w Layham and Shelley from 85; Dean Bocking from 85; RD Hadleigh from 86; Hon Can St E Cathl from 91. *The Deanery, Hadleigh, Ipswich IP7 5DT* Hadleigh (0473) 822218

ARRANDALE, Richard Paul Matthew. b 63. BA87. Chich Th Coll 87. **d** 90 **p** 91. C E Grinstead St Swithun *Chich* from 90. *11 Garden House Lane, East Grinstead, W Sussex RH19 4JT* East Grinstead (0342) 328306

ARRANTASH, Canon Reginald Thomas. b 12. Linc Th Coll 33. **d** 36 **p** 37. C Kennington St Jo *S'wark* 36-37; Australia 37-48 and from 52; R Kenchester and Bridge Sollers *Heref* 48-52; R Bishopstone 48-52. *Unit 15, Sundowner Centre, 416 Stirling Highway, Cottesloe, W Australia 6011* Perth (9) 385-2318

ARRIDGE, Leonard Owen. b 22. Univ of Wales (Ban) BA51. St Deiniol's Hawarden 64. **d** 67 **p** 68. Tutor Ches Coll of FE 67-79; Hon C Wrexham *St As* 69-79; Min Can Ban Cathl *Ban* 79-87; C Ban Cathl Par 79-87; rtd 87. *8 Ffordd Islwyn, Bangor, Gwynedd LL57 1AR* Bangor (0248) 362233

ARROWSMITH, Frederick John. b 39. Pemb Coll Ox BA61 MA66. St Steph Ho Ox 61. **d** 64 **p** 65. C Heref St Martin *Heref* 64-68; C Wilton Place St Paul *Lon* 68-73; P-in-c Kingsway H Trin and St Jo Drury Lane 73-85; Chapl Actor's Ch Union 75-85; P-in-c Covent Garden St Paul 75-85; V Hove St Barn and St Agnes *Chich* from 85; RD Hove from 91. *St Barnabas' Vicarage, 88 Sackville Road, Hove, E Sussex BN3 3HE* Brighton (0273) 732427

ARSCOTT, Barry James. b 36. AKC59. **d** 60 **p** 61. C Walthamstow St Andr *Chelmsf* 60-65; P-in-c Leyton St Luke 65-67; V 67-77; P-in-c Lt Ilford St Barn 77-86; R from 86. *St Barnabas' Vicarage, Browning Road, London E12 6PB* 081-472 2777

ARTHINGTON, Sister Muriel. b 23. dss 67 **d** 87. St Etheldreda's Children's Home 64-84; rtd 84; Hon Par Dn Bedf St Paul *St Alb* from 87. *St Etheldreda, 2 Conduit Road, Bedford MK40 1EQ* Bedford (0234) 52299

ARTHUR, Ian Willoughby. b 40. Lon Univ BA63 BA66 PGCE64. Ripon Coll Cuddesdon 78. **d** 80 **p** 81. C Kempston Transfiguration *St Alb* 80-83; R Potton w Sutton and Cockayne Hatley from 83. *The Rectory, Hatley Road, Potton, Sandy, Beds SG19 2DX* Potton (0767) 260782

✠**ARTHUR, Rt Rev Robert Gordon.** b 09. Melbourne Univ BA30 MA34. **d** 49 **p** 49 **c** 56. Australia 49-74; Adn Canberra 53-60; Asst Bp Canberra and Goulburn 56-61; Adn Wagga Wagga 60-61; Bp Grafton 61-73; P-in-c Bratton *Sarum* 75-78; RD Heytesbury 76-77; Asst Bp Sheff 78-80; rtd 80. *4 Berry Street, Downer, ACT, Australia 2602*

ARTISS, Joseph Sturge. b 28. Dur Univ BSc52. Cranmer Hall Dur DipTh67. **d** 67 **p** 68. C Dur St Cuth *Dur* 67-68; C Ches le Street 68-70; V Walsall St Pet *Lich* from 71. *St Peter's Vicarage, 22 Bloxwich Road, Walsall WS2 8DB* Walsall (0922) 23995

ARTLEY, Clive Mansell. b 30. St Jo Coll Dur BA56 DipTh58 LTCL75. **d** 58 **p** 59. C Eston *York* 58-61; R Burythorpe w E Acklam and Leavening 61-64; CF 64-73; Perm to Offic *York* from 73. *56 High Street,*

Castleton, Whitby YO21 2DA Guisborough (0287) 660470

ARTLEY, Harold Leslie. b 37. N Ord Course 79. **d** 82 **p** 83. NSM Flamborough *York* 82-89; R Bainton w N Dalton, Middleton-on-the-Wolds etc from 89. *The New Rectory, West End, Bainton, Driffield, N Humberside YO25 9NR* Middleton-on-the-Wolds (037781) 622

ARUNDEL, Canon Michael. b 36. Qu Coll Ox BA60 MA64. Linc Th Coll 60. **d** 62 **p** 63. C Hollinwood *Man* 62-65; C Leesfield 65-69; R Newton Heath All SS 69-80; RD N Man 75-80; P-in-c Eccles St Mary 80-81; TR Eccles from 81; Hon Can Man Cathl from 82. *The Vicarage, 12B Westminster Road, Eccles, Manchester M30 9EB* 061-789 1034

ASBRIDGE, Preb John Hawell. b 26. Dur Univ BA47. Bps' Coll Cheshunt 47. **d** 49 **p** 50. C Barrow St Geo *Carl* 49-52; C Fort William *Arg* 52-54; C Lon Docks St Pet w Wapping St Jo *Lon* 54-55; C Kilburn St Aug 55-59; V Northolt Park St Barn 59-66; V Shepherd's Bush St Steph w St Thos from 66; Preb St Paul's Cathl from 89. *St Stephen's Vicarage, Coverdale Road, London W12 8JJ* 081-743 3166

ASBRIDGE, Nigel Henry. b 58. Bris Univ BA80. Chich Th Coll 87. **d** 89 **p** 90. C Tottenham St Paul *Lon* 89; C W Hampstead St Jas from 89. *42 Birchington Road, London NW6 4LJ* 071-372 1050

ASH, Arthur Edwin. b 44. St Jo Coll Nottm 85. **d** 87 **p** 88. C Attleborough *Cov* 87-91; V Garretts Green *Birm* from 91. *The Vicarage, 112 Rotherfield Road, Birmingham B26 2SH* 021-743 2971

ASH, Brian John. b 32. ALCD62. **d** 62 **p** 63. C Plymouth St Andr *Ex* 62-66; Area Sec (Dios Cant and Roch) CMS 66-73; V Bromley Common St Aug *Roch* from 73. *St Augustine's Vicarage, Southborough Lane, Bromley BR2 8AT* 081-467 1351

ASH, Joseph Raymond. b 17. Tyndale Hall Bris. **d** 47 **p** 48. C Dagenham *Chelmsf* 47-50; Chapl RAF 50-72. *Address temp unknown*

ASH, Nicholas John. b 59. Bath Univ BSc81 Nottm Univ BTh88. Linc Th Coll 85. **d** 88 **p** 89. C Hersham *Guildf* from 88. *3 Burwood Road, Walton-on-Thames, Surrey KT12 4AA* Walton-on-Thames (0932) 247868

ASHBURNER, David Barrington. b 26. Ch Coll Cam BA51 MA55. Wycliffe Hall Ox 51. **d** 53 **p** 54. V Bucklebury w Marlston *Ox* 58-70; V Belton *Leic* 70-75; P-in-c Osgathorpe 73-75; R Belton and Osgathorpe 75-79; V Frisby-on-the-Wreake w Kirby Bellars 79-82; V Uffington w Woolstone and Baulking *Ox* 82-91; P-in-c Shellingford 83-91; RD Vale of White Horse 87-91; rtd 91; Perm to Offic Glouc and Ox from 91. *Rose Cottage, Bourton on the Hill, Moreton-in-Marsh, Glos GL56 9AE* Evesham (0386) 700682

ASHBY, Eric. b 37. E Midl Min Tr Course 78. **d** 81 **p** 82. C Hucknall Torkard *S'well* 81-85; V Lowdham from 85. *The Vicarage, Lowdham, Notts NG14 7BU* Nottingham (0602) 663069

✠**ASHBY, Rt Rev Godfrey William Ernest Candler.** b 30. Lon Univ AKC53 BD54 PhD69. **d** 55 **p** 56 **c** 80. C St Helier *S'wark* 55-57; S Africa 57-88; Can Grahamstown Cathl 69-75; Dean and Adn 75-80; Bp St John's 80-85; Asst Bp Leic from 88. *554 Bradgate Road, Leicester LE6 0HB* Markfield (0530) 242955

ASHBY, John Robert Patrick. b 36. Lon Univ BSc57. Coll of Resurr Mirfield 58. **d** 60 **p** 61. C Northolt St Mary *Lon* 60-64; Tanzania 64-66; C W Brompton St Mary *Lon* 66-68; V N Acton St Gabr 68-80; R Arlington, Folkington and Wilmington *Chich* 80-88; V Willingdon from 88. *The Vicarage, 3A Church Street, Willingdon, Eastbourne, E Sussex BN20 9HR* Eastbourne (0323) 502079

ASHBY, Kevin Patrick. b 53. Jes Coll Ox BA76 MA80. Wycliffe Hall Ox 76. **d** 78 **p** 79. C Market Harborough *Leic* 78-82; C Horwich H Trin *Man* 82-84; C Horwich 84; TV 84-90; R Gt w Lt Billing *Pet* from 90. *The Rectory, 25 Church Walk, Great Billing, Northampton NN3 4ED* Northampton (0604) 784870

ASHBY, Norman. b 13. Man Egerton Hall. **d** 39 **p** 40. Warden Ripon Dioc Retreat Ho 62-70; P-in-c Pickhill *Ripon* 70-72; V 72-84; R Kirkby Wiske 77-84; rtd 84. *8 Southolme Drive, York YO3 6RL* York (0904) 638422

ASHBY, Peter George. b 49. Univ of Wales (Cardiff) BSc(Econ)70 Nottm Univ DipTh71. Linc Th Coll 70. **d** 73 **p** 74. C Bengeo *St Alb* 73-75; Chapl Hatf Poly 76-79; C Apsley End 80; TV Chambersbury (Hemel Hempstead) 80-82; Zimbabwe 82-87; Adn N Harare 84-87; V Eskdale, Irton, Muncaster and Waberthwaite *Carl* from 87. *Eskdale Vicarage, Boot, Holmrook, Cumbria CA19 1TF* Eskdale (09403) 242

ASHCROFT, Ann Christine. N Ord Course. **dss** 86 **d** 87. Chapl Trin High Sch Man 86-89; Burnage St Nic *Man* 86-87; Hon Par Dn from 87. *Shalom, 37 Ainess Road, Whalley Range, Manchester M16 8HJ* 061-226 8512

ASHCROFT, Ven Lawrence. b 01. Univ Coll Dur 22. Lich Th Coll 24. **d** 26 **p** 27. Adn Stow *Linc* 54-62; V Flixborogh w Burton upon Stather 54-62; rtd 62. *44 George Street, St Catherines, Ontario L2R 5N6, Canada*

ASHCROFT, Mark David. b 54. Worc Coll Ox BA77 MA82 Fitzw Coll Cam BA81. Ridley Hall Cam 79. **d** 82 **p** 83. C Burnage St Marg *Man* 82-85; CMS from 86; Kenya from 86. *St Paul's School of Divinity, PO Box 18, Kapsabet, Kenya*

ASHDOWN, Andrew William Harvey. b 64. K Coll Lon BD88 AKC88. Sarum & Wells Th Coll 88. **d** 90 **p** 91. C Cranleigh *Guildf* from 90. *22 Orchard Gardens, Cranleigh, Surrey GU6 7LG* Guildford (0483) 272573

ASHDOWN, Anthony Hughes. b 37. AKC63. **d** 64 **p** 65. C Tettenhall Regis *Lich* 64-67; P-in-c Bassaleg *Mon* 67-70; Rhodesia 70-77; P-in-c Longton St Jas *Lich* 77-78; P-in-c Longton St Jo 77-78; R Longton 78-80; TR Cove St Jo *Guildf* 80-87; Chapl Lisbon *Eur* 87-90; V Wanstead H Trin Hermon Hill *Chelmsf* from 90. *Holy Trinity Vicarage, Hermon Hill, London E18 1QQ* 081-989 0912

ASHDOWN, Barry Frederick. b 42. St Pet Coll Ox BA65 MA69. Ridley Hall Cam 66. **d** 68 **p** 69. C Shipley St Pet *Bradf* 68-71; C Rushden w Newton Bromswold *Pet* 71-74; R Haworth *Bradf* 74-82; V Ore Ch Ch *Chich* 82-87; C Southwick from 91. *1 Church House Close, Southwick, Brighton BN42 4WQ* Brighton (0273) 594084

ASHE, Francis John. b 53. Sheff Univ BMet74. Ridley Hall Cam 77. **d** 79 **p** 80. C Ashtead *Guildf* 79-82; S Africa 82-87; R Wisley w Pyrford *Guildf* from 87. *The Rectory, Aviary Road, Woking, Surrey GU22 8TH* Byfleet (0932) 352914

ASHE, Francis Patrick Bellesme. b 15. St Jo Coll Cam BA37 MA41. Westcott Ho Cam 37. **d** 40 **p** 41. V Leamington Priors St Mary *Cov* 64-72; R Church Stretton *Heref* 72-74; rtd 80; Perm to Offic *Guildf* from 81. *62 Busbridge Lane, Godalming, Surrey GU7 1QQ* Godalming (04868) 22435

ASHENDEN, Gavin Roy Pelham. b 54. Bris Univ LLB76 Heythrop Coll Lon MTh89. Oak Hill Th Coll BA80. **d** 80 **p** 81. C Bermondsey St Jas w Ch Ch *S'wark* 80-83; TV Sanderstead All SS 83-89; Chapl and Lect Sussex Univ from 89. *The Meeting House, University of Sussex, Falmer, Brighton BN1 9QN* Brighton (0273) 678217

ASHFOLD, Sidney Sayer. b 10. St Jo Coll Morpeth. **d** 42 **p** 43. V Henlow St Alb 68-77; rtd 77. *Flamstead, 27 Boanyo Avenue, Kiama, NSW 2533, Australia*

ASHFORD, Ven Percival Leonard. b 27. Tyndale Hall Bris 49. **d** 54 **p** 55. Chapl HM Rem Cen Risley 66-69; HM Pris Dur 69-71; Wandsworth 71-75; Win 75-85; SW Regional Chapl of Pris and Borstals 77-81; Chapl Gen of Pris 81-85; Chapl to HM The Queen from 82; V Hambledon *Portsm* 85-87; rtd 87; Chmn Selectors ACCM 87-88. *Applewood, 14 South Hill, Alderholt, Fordingbridge, Hants SP6 3AS* Fordingbridge (0425) 54379

ASHFORTH, David Edward. b 37. ARCS59 Lon Univ BSc Birm Univ DipTh61. Qu Coll Birm. **d** 61 **p** 62. C Scarborough St Columba *York* 61-65; C Northallerton w Kirby Sigston 65-67; V Keyingham 67-73; Chapl Imp Coll *Lon* 73-89; V Balderstone *Blackb* from 89; Dir of Post-Ord Tr from 89. *The Vicarage, Commons Lane, Balderstone, Blackburn BB2 7LL* Mellor (025481) 2232

ASHLEY, Brian. b 36. S'wark Ord Course 75. **d** 77 **p** 78. NSM Horsell *Guildf* from 77. *Starston, Church Hill, Horsell, Woking, Surrey GU21 4QE* Woking (0483) 61232

ASHLEY, Brian Christenson. b 33. Roch Th Coll 68. **d** 70 **p** 71. C New Sleaford *Linc* 70-72; Min Basegreen CD 72-74; TV Gleadless *Sheff* 74-77; R Dinnington 77-85; RD Laughton 82-85; V Mosborough 85-88; P-in-c Curbar and Stoney Middleton *Derby* 88-91; rtd 91. *80 Old Hay Close, Sheffield S17 3GQ* Sheffield (0742) 362850

ASHLEY, Clive Ashley. b 54. SRN80 Croydon Coll of Art and Design LSIAD75 FETC81 NE Lon Poly NDN82. Cranmer Hall Dur 84. **d** 86 **p** 87. C Withington St Paul *Man* 86-89; Asst Chapl Freeman Hosp Newc from 89. *11 Countess Avenue, Whitley Bay, Tyne & Wear NE26 3PN* 091-251 2976

ASHLEY, John Michael. b 28. Worc Coll Ox BA51 MA54. Linc Th Coll 50. **d** 54 **p** 55. Australia 54-60; C Anderby w Cumberworth *Linc* 60-66; P-in-c Huttoft 60-61; V 61-66; R Woolsthorpe from 66; R W w E Allington and Sedgebrook from 66; CF (TAVR) from 79. *The Rectory,*

Woolsthorpe, Grantham, Lincs NG32 1NF Grantham (0476) 870206

ASHLEY, Reginald Clifford. b 16. Lon Univ BD63. Kelham Th Coll 34. **d** 39 **p** 40. SSM from 39; Chapl Ho of the Sacred Miss Kelham 56-71; C Ratby w Groby *Leic* 71-78; C Braunstone 78-81; TV 81-86; rtd 86; Perm to Offic *Leic* from 86. *23 Woodcote Road, Braunstone, Leicester LE3 2WE* Leicester (0533) 897126

ASHLEY-ROBERTS, James. b 53. Lon Univ BD77. Oak Hill Th Coll 75 Wycliffe Hall Ox 79. **d** 80 **p** 81. C Gt Warley Ch Ch *Chelmsf* 80-83; C E Ham St Paul 83-85; TV Holyhead w Rhoscolyn w Llanfair-yn-Neubwll *Ban* 85-88; R from 88. *The Rectory, Newry Street, Holyhead, Gwynedd LL65 1HS* Holyhead (0407) 763001

ASHLING, Raymond Charles. b 32. Dur Univ BA58. Linc Th Coll 58. **d** 60 **p** 61. C Halifax St Aug *Wakef* 60-63; C Farlington *Portsm* 63-65; Rhodesia 65-71; Chapl Rishworth Sch Ripponden 71-75; Lesotho 75-85; V Somercotes *Linc* 85-88; Ethiopia 88-89; R Gt w Lt Snoring w Kettlestone and Pensthorpe *Nor* from 89. *The Rectory, 118A The Street, Kettlestone, Fakenham, Norfolk NR21 0AU* Thursford (0328) 878213

ASHMAN, John Edmund George. b 47. Chich Th Coll 79. **d** 81 **p** 82. C Honicknowle *Ex* 81-85; P-in-c Barnsley St Pet and St Jo *Wakef* 85-89; V from 89. *St Peter's Vicarage, Osborne Street, Barnsley, S Yorkshire S70 1UJ* Barnsley (0226) 282220

ASHMAN, Peter Nicholas. b 52. CSS81 SEN73. Sarum & Wells Th Coll 87. **d** 89 **p** 90. C Stafford *Lich* from 89. *9 Brunswick Terrace, Stafford ST16 1BB* Stafford (0785) 43995

ASHTON, Anthony Joseph. b 37. Oak Hill Th Coll 62. **d** 65 **p** 66. C Crookes St Thos *Sheff* 65-68; C Heeley 68-73; V Bowling St Steph *Bradf* 73-78; R Chesterfield H Trin *Derby* from 78. *Holy Trinity Rectory, 31 Newbold Road, Chesterfield S41 7PG* Chesterfield (0246) 232048

ASHTON, Cyril Guy. b 42. Lanc Univ MA86. Oak Hill Th Coll 64. **d** 67 **p** 68. C Blackpool St Thos *Blackb* 67-70; Voc Sec CPAS 70-74; V Lanc St Thos 74-91; Lanc Almshouses 76-90; Dioc Dir of Tr *Blackb* from 91. *1 Piccadilly Grove, Scotforth, Lancaster LA1 4PP* Lancaster (0524) 841495

ASHTON, David William. b 51. Reading Univ BA CertEd. Wycliffe Hall Ox 79. **d** 82 **p** 83. C Shipley St Pet *Bradf* 82-85; C Tadley St Pet *Win* 85-88; V Sinfin *Derby* 88-91; Chapl Sophia Antipolis *Eur* from 91. *6 Traverse de Tourdres, Haut Sartoux, Valbonne 06560, France*

✠**ASHTON, Rt Rev Jeremy Claude.** b 30. Trin Coll Cam BA53 MA57. Westcott Ho Cam 53. **d** 55 **p** 56 **c** 76. C Bury St Mary *Man* 55-60; CF (TA) 57-60; CF (TA-R of O) 60-70; Papua New Guinea 60-86; Asst Bp Papua 76-77; Bp Aipo Rongo 77-86; rtd 86. *47 Naroo Street, Balwyn, Victoria, Australia 3103* Balwyn (3) 859-6625

ASHTON, Joseph Patrick Bankes. b 27. Jes Coll Cam BA49 MA52. Wells Th Coll 53. **d** 55 **p** 56. C Cheadle *Lich* 55-59; C Caverswall 59-61; C-in-c Werrington CD 61-66; R Eyke w Bromeswell and Rendlesham *St E* 66-76; R Eyke w Bromeswell, Rendlesham, Tunstall etc 76-86; Chapl Seckford Foundn from 86; Hon C Woodbridge St Mary from 86. *Drift Cottage, Church Lane, Rendlesham, Woodbridge, Suffolk* Eyke (0394) 461511

✠**ASHTON, Rt Rev Leonard James.** b 15. CB70. Tyndale Hall Bris 40. **d** 42 **p** 43 **c** 74. C Cheadle *Ches* 42-45; Chapl RAF 45-62; Asst Chapl-in-Chief RAF 62-65; Chapl St Clem Danes (RAF Ch) 65-69; Chapl-in-Chief RAF 69-73; QHC 67-83; Can and Preb Linc Cathl *Linc* 69-73; Asst Bp Jerusalem 74-76; Can from 76; Bp Cyprus and the Gulf 76-83; rtd 83; Asst Bp Ox from 84; Can Cyprus from 89. *60 Lowndes Avenue, Chesham, Bucks HP5 2HJ* Chesham (0494) 782952

ASHTON, Mrs Margaret Lucie. b 40. St Jo Coll Nottm DPS79. **dss** 83 **d** 87. Billericay and Lt Burstead *Chelmsf* 83-87; Hon Par Dn from 87. *The Rectory, 40 Laindon Road, Billericay, Essex CM12 9LD* Billericay (0277) 622837

ASHTON, Mark Hewett. b 48. Ch Ch Ox BA70 MA74 Trin Coll Cam BA72. Ridley Hall Cam 71. **d** 73 **p** 74. C Beckenham Ch Ch *Roch* 73-77; Win Coll 78-81; Lic to Offic *S'wark* 81-87; Sec of CYFA (CPAS) 81-87; V Cam H Sepulchre w All SS *Ely* from 87. *The Parsonage, Manor Street, Cambridge CB1 1LK* Cambridge (0223) 327331

ASHTON, Neville Anthony. b 45. Sarum & Wells Th Coll 78. **d** 80 **p** 81. C Hattersley *Ches* 80-82; C Lanc Ch Ch w St Jo and St Anne *Blackb* 82-84; R Church Kirk from 84. *Church Kirk Rectory, 434 Blackburn Road, Accrington, Lancs BB5 0DE* Accrington (0254) 236946

ASHTON, Nigel Charles. b 49. SW Minl Tr Course. **d** 78 **p** 79. NSM St Stephen by Saltash *Truro* 78-85; NSM Saltash from 85. *1 Summerfields, Saltash, Cornwall PL12 4AB* Saltash (0752) 846621

ASHTON, Canon Patrick Thomas. b 16. LVO. Ch Ch Ox BA46 MA46. Westcott Ho Cam 46. **d** 47 **p** 48. Chapl to HM The Queen from 55; TR Upper Kennett *Sarum* 75-77; rtd 77. *Field Cottage, Bottlesford, Pewsey, Wilts SN9 6LU* Woodborough (067285) 340

ASHTON, Peter Donald. b 34. Lon Univ BD62. ALCD61. **d** 62 **p** 63. C Walthamstow St Mary *Chelmsf* 62-68; V Girlington *Bradf* 68-73; Dir Past Studies St Jo Coll Nottm 73-80; TR Billericay and Lt Burstead *Chelmsf* from 80; Chapl Mayflower and St Andr Hosp from 80; RD Basildon *Chelmsf* from 89. *The Rectory, 40 Laindon Road, Billericay, Essex CM12 9LD* Billericay (0277) 622837

ASHTON, Samuel Rupert. b 42. Sarum & Wells Th Coll. **d** 83 **p** 84. C Ledbury w Eastnor *Heref* 83-86; R St Weonards w Orcop, Garway, Tretire etc from 86; RD Ross and Archenfield from 91. *The Vicarage, St Weonards, Hereford HR2 8NU* St Weonards (09818) 307

ASHTON, Stephen Robert. b 55. BA BPhil. Sarum & Wells Th Coll. **d** 84 **p** 85. C Penzance St Mary w St Paul *Truro* 84-86; C Tewkesbury w Walton Cardiff *Glouc* 86-89; P-in-c Newton Heath St Wilfrid and St Anne *Man* from 89. *St Wilfrid's Rectory, 929 Oldham Road, Newton Heath, Manchester M10 6EF* 061-205 1235

ASHTON, Thomas Eyre Maunsell. b 13. St Edm Hall Ox BA36 MA39. Wycliffe Hall Ox 36. **d** 38 **p** 39. R Lee St Marg *S'wark* 67-75; Chapl Morden Coll Blackheath 75-83; rtd 83; Perm to Offic *S'wark* from 83. *33 Kidbrooke Grove, London SE3 0LE* 081-853 1576

ASHTON, William Grant. b 57. St Chad's Coll Dur BA79. Oak Hill Th Coll BA85. **d** 85 **p** 86. C Lanc St Thos *Blackb* 85-89; CF from 89. *c/o MOD (Army), Bagshot Park, Bagshot, Surrey GU19 5PL* Bagshot (0276) 71717

ASHWELL, Anthony John. b 42. CChem74 MRSC74 St Andr Univ BSc65. Sarum & Wells Th Coll 86. **d** 88 **p** 89. C Plymstock *Ex* 88-91; C Axminster, Chardstock, Combe Pyne and Rousdon from 91. *The Vicarage, Chardstock, Axminster, Devon EX13 7BY* South Chard (0460) 20005

ASHWIN, Vincent George. b 42. Worc Coll Ox BA65. Coll of Resurr Mirfield 65. **d** 67 **p** 68. C Shildon *Dur* 67-70; V 79-85; C Newc St Fran *Newc* 70-72; Swaziland 72-79; V Fenham St Jas and St Basil *Newc* from 85; RD Newc W from 89. *The Vicarage, Wingrove Road, Newcastle upon Tyne NE4 9EJ* 091-274 5078

ASHWORTH, David. b 40. Nottm Univ BPharm62. Linc Th Coll 63. **d** 65 **p** 66. C Halliwell St Thos *Man* 65-69; C Heywood St Jas 69-72; C-in-c Heywood St Marg CD 72-78; V Hale *Ches* 78-87; RD Bowdon from 87; V Hale and Ashley from 87. *1 Harrop Road, Hale, Altrincham, Cheshire WA15 9BU* 061-928 4182

ASHWORTH, Edward James. b 33. Clifton Th Coll 60. **d** 63 **p** 64. C Spitalfields Ch Ch w All SS *Lon* 63-65; C Pennycross *Ex* 65-69; C Blackb Ch Ch *Blackb* 69-72; V Camerton H Trin w Seaton *Carl* 72-79; V Tunstead *Man* from 79. *The Vicarage, 33 Booth Road, Bacup, Lancs OL13 0QP* Bacup (0706) 874508

ASHWORTH, Canon James George Brooks. b 10. Hatf Coll Dur LTh33 BA34. Edin Th Coll 30. **d** 34 **p** 35. Can Res Ripon Cathl *Ripon* 66-79; rtd 79. *17 Bromley College, London Road, Bromley, Kent BR1 1PE* 081-460 6848

ASHWORTH, John Russell. b 33. Lich Th Coll 57. **d** 60 **p** 61. C Castleford All SS *Wakef* 60-62; C Luton St Sav *St Alb* 63-67; V Clipstone *S'well* 67-70; V Bolton-upon-Dearne *Sheff* 70-82; V Thornhill Lees *Wakef* from 82. *The Vicarage, Thornhill Lees, Dewsbury, W Yorkshire WF12 9PD* Dewsbury (0924) 461269

ASHWORTH, Keith Benjamin. b 33. NW Ord Course 76. **d** 79 **p** 80. C Pennington *Man* 79-83; P-in-c Bolton St Bede 83-88; V from 88. *St Bede's Vicarage, 92 Normanby Street, Bolton BL3 3QR* Bolton (0204) 61496

ASHWORTH, Martin. b 41. AKC63. **d** 64 **p** 65. C-in-c Wythenshawe Wm Temple Ch CD *Man* 64-71; R Haughton St Anne 71-83; V Prestwich St Marg from 83. *St Margaret's Vicarage, Prestwich, Manchester M25 5QB* 061-773 2698

ASHWORTH, Timothy. b 52. Worc Coll of Educn CertEd73. Trin Coll Bris DipHE79 Oak Hill Th Coll BA81. **d** 82 **p** 83. C Tonbridge St Steph *Roch* 82-85; C Whittle-le-Woods *Blackb* 85-90; Chapl Scargill Ho from 90. *Scargill House, Kettlewell, Skipton, N Yorkshire BD23 5HU* Kettlewell (075676) 234

ASHWORTH, Mrs Vivien. b 52. Worc Coll of Educn CertEd73. Trin Coll Bris 79 Oak Hill Th Coll BA82. **dss** 82 **d** 87. Tonbridge St Steph *Roch* 82-85; Whittle-le-Woods *Blackb* 85-87; Hon Par Dn 87-90; Chapl Scargill Ho from 90. *Scargill House, Kettlewell, Skipton, N Yorkshire BD23 5HU* Kettlewell (075676) 234

ASKE, Sir Conan, Bt. b 12. Ball Coll Ox BA33 MA39. Wycliffe Hall Ox 69. **d** 70 **p** 71. C Hagley *Worc* 70-72; C St Jo in Bedwardine 72-80; rtd 80; Perm to Offic *Worc* from 80. *167 Malvern Road, Worcester WR2 4NN* Worcester (0905) 422817

ASKEW, Canon Dennis. b 30. Open Univ BA76. Kelham Th Coll 45 Lich Th Coll 55. **d** 58 **p** 59. C Garforth *Ripon* 58-61; C Seacroft 61-64; V Holland Fen *Linc* 64-69; R Folkingham w Laughton 69-77; R Aswarby w Swarby 69-77; R Osbournby w Scott Willoughby 69-77; R Pickworth w Walcot 69-77; V Threckingham 69-77; P-in-c Newton w Haceby 72-77; P-in-c Aunsby w Dembleby 72-77; R S Lafford 77-87; Hon Can Linc Cathl from 86; R Ruskington from 87. *The Rectory, Ruskington, Sleaford, Lincs NG34 9AE* Ruskington (0526) 832463

ASKEW, Canon Reginald James Albert. b 28. CCC Cam BA51 MA55. Linc Th Coll 55. **d** 57 **p** 58. C Highgate St Mich *Lon* 57-61; Tutor Wells Th Coll 61-63; Chapl 63-65; PV Wells Cathl *B & W* 61-69; Vice-Prin 66-69; V Paddington Ch Ch *Lon* 69-73; Prin Sarum & Wells Th Coll 73-88; Can and Preb Sarum Cathl *Sarum* from 75; Dean K Coll Lon from 88. *King's College, The Strand, London WC2R 2LS* 071-873 2028

ASKEW, Canon Richard George. b 35. BNC Ox BA59 MA63. Ridley Hall Cam 62. **d** 64 **p** 65. C Chesham St Mary *Ox* 64-66; C Mossley Hill St Matt and St Jas *Liv* 66-67; Chapl Ox Pastorate 67-72; Asst Chapl BNC Ox 67-71; R Ashtead *Guildf* 72-83; RD Leatherhead 80-83; Can Res and Treas Sarum Cathl *Sarum* 83-90; Dioc Adv on Miss and Min *B & W* 83-90; R Bath Abbey w St Jas from 90. *Redwood House, Trossachs Drive, Bath, Avon BA2 6RP* Bath (0225) 464930

ASKEW, Sydney Derek. b 29. Roch Th Coll 66. **d** 68 **p** 69. C Kirkstall *Ripon* 68-73; V Markington w S Stainley and Bishop Thornton from 73. *The Vicarage, Markington, Harrogate, N Yorkshire HG3 3PB* Ripon (0765) 87282

ASKEY, Gary Simon (Brother Gary). b 64. St Steph Ho Ox 88. **d** 91. SSM from 87; C Middlesb All SS *York* from 91. *All Saints' Vicarage, Grange Road, Middlesbrough, Cleveland TS1 2LR* Middlesbrough (0642) 245035

ASKEY, John Stuart. b 39. Chich Th Coll 63. **d** 66 **p** 67. C Feltham *Lon* 66-69; C Epsom Common Ch Ch *Guildf* 69-72; C Chesterton Gd Shep *Ely* 72-74; R Stretham w Thetford from 74; Dioc Youth Officer from 80. *Field House, Watsons Lane, Little Thetford, Ely, Cambs CB6 3HE* Ely (0353) 649233

ASLACHSEN, Grosvenor Trevelyan. b 03. Dur Univ 25. Lich Th Coll 24. **d** 28 **p** 29. R Halstead *Roch* 40-68; rtd 68. *Bishopsdown Corner, 4 Manor Park, Tunbridge Wells, Kent* Tunbridge Wells (0892) 31535

ASPDEN, Peter George. b 28. Univ of Wales (Lamp) BA50. Ely Th Coll 52. **d** 53 **p** 54. C Morecambe St Barn *Blackb* 53-55; C Marton 55-58; V Tockholes 58-63; C St Annes 63-66; V St Annes St Marg 66-75; V Lanc Ch Ch 75-79; R Eccleston from 79. *The Rectory, Eccleston, Chorley, Lancs PR7 6NA* Eccleston (0257) 451206

ASPDEN, Richard William. b 49. Chich Th Coll 75. **d** 78 **p** 79. C Bedf Leigh *Man* 78-81; C Leeds All So *Ripon* 81-83; R Droylsden St Andr *Man* 83-86; Priest/Community Worker Oldham 86-87; C Tonge Moor 87-91; C Redruth w Lanner and Treleigh *Truro* from 91. *Pencoys Vicarage, Four Lanes, Redruth, Cornwall TR16 6LR* Redruth (0209) 215035

ASPINALL, Philip Norman. b 51. Cam Univ MA ATI. W Midl Minl Tr Course 86. **d** 89 **p** 90. NSM Cov E *Cov* from 89. *139 Wiltshire Court, Nod Rise, Mount Nod, Coventry CV5 7JP* Coventry (0203) 467509

ASQUITH, Eric Lees. b 24. St Aid Birkenhead 55. **d** 56 **p** 57. V Netherthong *Wakef* 59-68; rtd 68. *15 Heycroft Way, Nayland, Colchester CO6 4LN* Nayland (0206) 262593

ASSON, Geoffrey Ormrod. b 34. Univ of Wales BA54 St Cath Coll Ox BA56 MA61. St Steph Ho Ox 54. **d** 57 **p** 58. C Aberdare *Llan* 57-59; C Roath St Marg 59-61; R Hagworthingham w Asgarby and Lusby *Linc* 61-65; P-in-c Mavis Enderby w Raithby 62-65; V Friskney 65-69; R S Ormsby w Ketsby, Calceby and Driby 69-74; R Harrington w Brinkhill 69-74; R Oxcombe 69-74; R Ruckland w Farforth and Maidenwell 69-74; R Somersby w Bag Enderby 69-74; R Tetford and Salmonby 69-74; P-in-c Belchford 71-74; P-in-c W Ashby 71-74; V Riverhead w Dunton Green *Roch* 75-80; R Kington w

Huntington *Heref* 80-82; RD Kington and Weobley 80-86; P-in-c Almeley 81-82; P-in-c Knill 81-82; P-in-c Old Radnor 81-82; R Kington w Huntington, Old Radnor, Kinnerton etc 82-86; V Mathry w St Edren's and Grandston etc *St D* from 86. *The Rectory, St Nicholas, Goodwick, Dyfed SA64 0LG*   St Nicholas (03485) 230

ASTILL, Cyril John. b 33. Lon Univ DipTh64. Oak Hill Th Coll 62. **d** 65 **p** 66. C Carl St Jo *Carl* 65-68; C St Helens St Helen *Liv* 68-71; V Blackb Sav *Blackb* 71-85; P-in-c Blackb Ch Ch w St Matt 81-83; TR N Ferriby *York* from 85. *The Rectory, 20 Aston Hall Drive, North Ferriby, N Humberside HU14 3EB*   Hull (0482) 631306

ASTIN, Alfred Ronald. b 18. St Pet Hall Ox BA43 MA45. Ridley Hall Cam. **d** 47 **p** 48. V Earlham St Anne *Nor* 57-70; V Sheringham 70-84; rtd 84; Perm to Offic *Nor* from 84. *9 Cromer Road, Overstrand, Cromer, Norfolk NR27 0NU*   Overstrand (026378) 201

ASTIN, Howard Keith. b 51. Warw Univ LLB DipHE. Trin Coll Bris 83. **d** 83 **p** 84. C Kirkheaton *Wakef* 83-88; V Bowling St Jo *Bradf* from 88. *St John's Vicarage, 96 Lister Avenue, Bradford, W Yorkshire BD4 7QS*   Bradford (0274) 720660

ASTLEY, Jeffrey. b 47. Down Coll Cam BA68 MA72 Birm Univ DipTh69 Dur Univ PhD79. Qu Coll Birm 68. **d** 70 **p** 71. C Cannock *Lich* 70-73; Lect and Chapl St Hild Coll Dur 73-75; Sen Lect and Chapl SS Hild & Bede Coll Dur 75-77; Prin Lect & Hd Relig Studies Bp Grosseteste Coll 77-81; Lic to Offic *Linc* from 78; Dur from 81; Dir N England Inst for Chr Educn from 81. *Carter House, Pelaw Leazes Place, Durham DH1 1TB*   091-384 1034 or 386 4466

ASTON, Denys Gallen. b 19. **d** 41 **p** 42. V Basford *Lich* 62-67; rtd 84. *23 St Clement's Court, St Clement's Gardens, Worcester*   Worcester (0905) 428655

ASTON, Glyn. b 29. Univ of Wales (Abth) BA54. **d** 79 **p** 80. Hon C Newport Maindee St Jo Ev *Mon* 79-85; C 85-86; P-in-c Llangwm Uchaf w Llangwm Isaf w Gwernesney etc 86; V from 86. *The Rectory, Gwernesney, Usk, Gwent NP5 1HF*   Usk (02913) 2518

ASTON, John Bernard. b 34. Leeds Univ BA55 PGCE56. Qu Coll Birm 72. **d** 75 **p** 76. NSM Shenstone *Lich* from 75; Chapl HM Young Offender Inst Swinfen Hall from 90. *21 Wordsworth Close, Lichfield, Staffs WS14 9BY*   Lichfield (0543) 264960

ASTON, John Leslie. b 47. Oak Hill Th Coll 77. **d** 80 **p** 81. C Trentham *Lich* 80-83; C Meir Heath 83-85; V Upper Tean from 85. *The Vicarage, Vicarage Road, Tean, Stoke-on-Trent ST10 4LE*   Tean (0538) 722227

ASTON, Archdeacon of. See BARTON, Ven Charles John Greenwood

ASTON, Suffragan Bishop of. *Vacant*

ATACK, John Philip. b 49. Linc Th Coll 86. **d** 88 **p** 89. C Cleveleys *Blackb* from 88. *58 Stockdove Way, Thornton Cleveleys, Blackpool FY5 2AR*   Cleveleys (0253) 827744

ATCHESON, David Andrew Gregory. b 14. TCD BA36. **d** 37 **p** 38. V Studley *Cov* 54-86; rtd 86. *108 Station Road, Knowle, Solihull, W Midlands B93 0HJ*   Knowle (0564) 777082

ATFIELD, Gladys. Univ Coll Lon BSc53 DipTh76. Gilmore Course. **dss** 79 **d** 87. Bexley St Mary *Roch* 79-87; Hon Par Dn from 87. *72 Rochester Drive, Bexley, Kent DA5 1QD*   Crayford (0322) 551741

ATHERLEY, Keith Philip. b 56. St Steph Ho Ox 77. **d** 80 **p** 81. C St Bart Armley w St Mary New Wortley *Ripon* 80-82; C Harrogate St Wilfrid and St Luke 82-85; V Forcett and Stanwick w Aldbrough 85-89; CF from 89. *c/o MOD (Army), Bagshot Park, Bagshot, Surrey GU19 5PL*   Bagshot (0276) 71717

ATHERSTONE, Castell Hugh. b 45. Natal Univ BA67 St Chad's Coll Dur DipTh69 MA79. **d** 70 **p** 70. S Africa 70-83; Dioc Stewardship Adv *Ely* 83-87; P-in-c Doddington w Benwick 83-87; R Frant w Eridge *Chich* from 87; RD Rotherfield from 90. *The Rectory, Frant, Tunbridge Wells, Kent TN3 9DX*   Frant (089275) 638

ATHERTON, Albert. b 26. CQSW71. St Aid Birkenhead 60. **d** 62 **p** 63. C Northenden *Man* 62-64; C Newall Green CD 64-66; V Patricroft 66-70; Lic to Offic 71-72; V Mossley 77-83; V Ockbrook *Derby* 83-86; P-in-c Newall Green *Man* 86-91; V from 91. *St Francis's Vicarage, Chalford Road, Manchester M23 8RD*   061-437 4605

ATHERTON, Graham Bryson. b 47. GRSM69 FTCL69. Edin Th Coll 77. **d** 79 **p** 80. C Orford St Marg *Liv* 79-82; V Warrington St Barn 82-88; V Leeds Halton St Wilfrid *Ripon* from 88. *Halton Vicarage, Selby Road, Leeds LS15 7NP*   Leeds (0532) 647000

ATHERTON, Henry Anthony. b 44. FGS68 Univ of Wales BSc67 DipEd68 Fitzw Coll Cam BA72 MA75. Westcott Ho Cam 70. **d** 72 **p** 73. C Leamington Priors All SS *Cov*

72-75; C Orpington All SS *Roch* 75-78; V Gravesend St Mary 78-87; Chapl St Jas Hosp Gravesend 82-87; V Bromley St Andr *Roch* from 87. *The Vicarage, 1 Lake Avenue, Bromley, Kent BR1 4EN*   081-460 0481

ATHERTON, Canon John Robert. b 39. Lon Univ BA60 Man Univ MA74 PhD79. Coll of Resurr Mirfield 60. **d** 62 **p** 63. C Aber St Marg *Ab* 62-64; C Bury St Mark *Man* 64-67; P-in-c Glas St Marg *Glas* 67-68; R Hulme St Geo *Man* 68-74; Ind Chapl 68-74; Asst Dir Wm Temple Foundn 74-79; Dir from 79; Lic to Offic *Man* 74-84; Can Res Man Cathl from 84. *Latham, Myrtle Grove, Whitefield, Manchester M25 7RR*   061-766 9296

ATHERTON, Lionel Thomas. b 45. Univ of Wales (Ban) BA74 St Luke's Coll Ex. St Steph Ho Ox 74. **d** 76 **p** 77. C Chenies and Lt Chalfont *Ox* 76-79; C Fleet *Guildf* 79-84; V S Farnborough 84-89; TR Alston Team *Newc* from 89. *The Vicarage, Front Street, Alston, Cumbria CA9 3RE*   Alston (0434) 381317

ATHERTON, Paul Christopher. b 56. Chich Th Coll. **d** 82 **p** 83. C Orford St Marg *Liv* 82-86; Chapl Univ of Wales (Cardiff) *Llan* 88-89; TV Walton St Mary *Liv* from 89. *138 Queens Drive, Liverpool L4 6XD*   051-521 5276

ATHERTON, Percy Francis. b 22. Man Univ BA47 PGCE48 Univ of Minnesota MA56. Seabury-Western Th Sem 52. **d** 52 **p** 53. Lic to Offic *Ex* 66-75; HMI of Schs 70-75; Peru 75-76; Singapore 76-77; P-in-c Zeal Monachorum *Ex* 78-79; R Bow w Broad Nymet 78-79; V Colebrooke 78-79; Perm to Offic from 79; Algeria 80-81; rtd 89. *The Old Dame's Cottage, Cove, Tiverton, Devon EX16 7RX*   Bampton (0398) 31489

ATHERTON, Philip Andrew. b 51. BA. Wycliffe Hall Ox. **d** 84 **p** 85. C Ox St Clem *Ox* 84-87; Ind Missr *Man* from 87. *192 Windsor Road, Oldham OL8 1RG*   061-652 2684

ATHERTON, Timothy Edward John. b 60. Middx Poly DipHE83. Cranmer Hall Dur 83. **d** 86 **p** 87. C S Molton w Nymet St George, High Bray etc *Ex* 86-89; Canada from 89. *St John's Anglican Mission, PO Box 240, Tuktoyaktuk, NWT, Canada, X0E 1CO*   Tuktoyaktuk (403) 977-2216

ATKIN, Arthur Courtney Qu'appelle. b 19. Dur Univ BA44. Lich Th Coll 59. **d** 59 **p** 60. Chapl R Hosp Sch Holbrook 69-72; P-in-c Brixham *Ex* 72-74; Chapl Colston's Sch Bris 74-79; P-in-c Pitcombe w Shepton Montague and Bratton St Maur *B & W* 79-85; rtd 86; Perm to Offic *B & W* from 86. *Newlands Court, Victoria Road, Ledbury, Herefordshire HR8 2DD*   Ledbury (0531) 4526

ATKIN, John Anthony. b 33. Glouc Th Course 70. **d** 72 **p** 73. NSM Leamington Priors All SS *Cov* 72-77; NSM Barford 77-78; NSM Barford w Wasperton and Sherbourne 78-80; P-in-c Exford w Exmoor *B & W* 80-82; P-in-c Hawkridge w Withypool 80-82; P-in-c Exford, Exmoor, Hawkridge and Withypool 82-83; R from 83; RD Exmoor from 86. *Halsgrove Farm, Withypool, Minehead, Somerset TA24 7RX*   Exford (064383) 388

ATKIN, Stephanie. b 23. **d** 87. Boreham Wood St Mich *St Alb* 78-79; Borehamwood 79-81; Dunstable 81-87; Par Dn 87-90; rtd 90. *11 Mount Street, Lincoln*   Lincoln (0522) 560428

ATKINS, Anthony John. b 58. Nottm Univ BSc80 SS Paul & Mary Coll Cheltenham PGCE82. Cranmer Hall Dur 87. **d** 90 **p** 91. C Shipley St Paul and Frizinghall *Bradf* from 90. *14 Birklands Road, Shipley, W Yorkshire BD18 3BY*   Bradford (0274) 597601

ATKINS, Austen Shaun. b 55. St Pet Coll Ox MA82 Selw Coll Cam MA85. Ridley Hall Cam 79. **d** 82 **p** 83. C S Mimms Ch Ch *Lon* 82-86; C Fulham St Matt 86-91; P-in-c Fulham St Dionis Parson's Green from 91. *St Dionis' Vicarage, 18 Parson's Green, London SW6 4UH*   071-736 2585

ATKINS, Christopher Leigh. b 33. Keble Coll Ox BA55 MA58. Wells Th Coll 57. **d** 59 **p** 60. C Foley Park *Worc* 59-62; C Eastleigh *Win* 62-69; TV Lord's Hill 69-81; V 81-85; R Church Oakley and Wootton St Lawrence from 85. *The Rectory, 9 The Drive, Oakley, Basingstoke, Hants RG23 7DA*   Basingstoke (0256) 780825

ATKINS, David John. b 43. Lon Univ DipTh68. Kelham Th Coll 64. **d** 68 **p** 69. C Lewisham St Mary *S'wark* 68-72; Min Motspur Park 72-77; P-in-c Mitcham Ascension 77-82; V 82-83; P-in-c Downham w S Hanningfield *Chelmsf* 83-88; R from 88; Asst RD Chelmsford from 88; P-in-c W Hanningfield from 90. *The Rectory, Castledon Road, Billericay, Essex CM11 1LD*   Basildon (0268) 710370

ATKINS, Mrs Diana. b 31. K Coll Lon BD54 DipEd55. Qu Coll Birm 81. **dss** 83 **d** 87. De Beauvoir Town St Pet *Lon* 83-85; Gleadless *Sheff* 85-87; Par Dn from 87. *St*

Peter's Vicarage, 51 White Lane, Sheffield S12 3GD Sheffield (0742) 396132

ATKINS, Forrest William. b 59. Ch Coll Cam MA85 Lon Univ BD84. Ridley Hall Cam 83. **d** 86 **p** 87. C Normanton Derby 86-90; C Stratford St Jo and Ch Ch w Forest Gate St Jas Chelmsf from 90. 2 St James's Road, London E15 1RL 081-503 1476

ATKINS, Francis John. b 47. CEng MIStructE. S Dios Minl Tr Scheme. **d** 89 **p** 90. NSM Studley Sarum from 89. Church Cottage, 344 Frome Road, Trowbridge, Wilts BA14 0EF Trowbridge (0225) 761757

ATKINS, Graham Anthony Hazlewood. b 28. Selw Coll Cam BA52 MA57. Coll of Resurr Mirfield 52. **d** 54 **p** 55. C St Marychurch Ex 54-57; Chapl Prestfelde Sch Shrewsbury 58-76; P-in-c Ash Lich 76-77; P-in-c Tenbury St Mich Heref 77-84; R Hinstock and Sambrook Lich from 85. The Rectory, Ellerton Road, Hinstock, Market Drayton, Shropshire TF9 0NH Sambrook (095279) 532

ATKINS, Canon John Hamilton. b 15. AKC42. **d** 42 **p** 43. V Cuddington Guildf 63-72; Hon Can Guildf Cathl 71-80; R Walton-on-the-Hill 72-80; rtd 80; Perm to Offic Sarum from 81; B & W from 86. 2 Thames Close, Warminster, Wilts BA12 9QB Warminster (0985) 213035

ATKINS, Nicholas Steven. b 60. Oak Hill Th Coll BA88. **d** 88 **p** 89. C Shepton Mallet w Doulting B & W 88-91; C Combe Down w Monkton Combe and S Stoke from 91. 13A Foxhill, Combe Down, Bath, Somerset BA2 5QL Combe Down (0225) 836092

ATKINS, Canon Paul Henry. b 38. Univ of Wales DipTh65. St Mich Coll Llan 62. **d** 65 **p** 66. C Sheringham Nor 65-68; V Southtown 68-84; RD Flegg 78-84; R Aylmerton w Runton from 84; RD Repps from 86; Hon Can Nor Cathl from 88. The Rectory, West Runton, Cromer, Norfolk NR27 9QT West Runton (026375) 279

ATKINS, Peter. b 29. Edin Univ MA52. Edin Th Coll 52. **d** 54 **p** 55. C Edin Old St Paul Edin 54-59; P-in-c Edin St Dav 59-64; Chapl Fulbourn Hosp Cam 64-66; R Galashiels Edin 66-69; Perm to Offic 69-72; Divisional Dir Soc Services Brighton 72-83; Asst Dir Soc Services E Sussex from 83. 11 South Street, Lewes, E Sussex Lewes (0273) 476230

ATKINS, Roger Francis. b 30. AKC54. **d** 55 **p** 56. C Bromley All Hallows Lon 55-58; C Eastleigh Win 58-62; Australia 62-71; V Wolverley Worc 71-76; V S Hackney St Mich w Haggerston St Paul Lon 76-85; TV Gleadless Sheff from 85. St Peter's Vicarage, 51 White Lane, Sheffield S12 3GD Sheffield (0742) 396132

ATKINS, Timothy David. b 45. Ridley Hall Cam 71. **d** 74 **p** 75. C Stoughton Guildf 74-79; C Chilwell S'well 79-84; R Eastwood from 84. The Rectory, 5A Woodland Way, Eastwood, Nottingham NG16 3BU Langley Mill (0773) 712395

ATKINS, Timothy James. b 38. Worc Coll Ox BA62. Cuddesdon Coll 62. **d** 64 **p** 65. C Stafford St Mary Lich 64-67; C Loughb St Pet Leic 67-69; C Usworth Dur 69-71; Lic to Offic Newc 71-76; P-in-c Slaley 76-87; P-in-c Shotley from 87. St John's Vicarage, Snods Edge, Consett, Co Durham DH8 9TL Consett (0207) 55665

ATKINS, Timothy Samuel. b 22. DSC44. Em Coll Cam BA46 MA52. Ridley Hall Cam 47. **d** 49 **p** 50. V Bunbury Ches 53-87; RD Malpas 85-87; rtd 87; Perm to Offic Ches from 87. Lime Tree Cottage, Barton Road, Farndon, Chester CH3 6NL Farndon (0829) 270183

ATKINS, William Maynard. b 11. FSA TCD BA33 MA41. **d** 35 **p** 36. C Dundalk Arm 35-40; I Clonfeacle 40-46; Dep Min Can St Paul's Cathl Lon 46-49; Min Can 49-55; Hon Min Can from 55; C St Sepulchre w Ch Ch Greyfriars etc 49-55; Chapl Mercers' Sch Holborn 54-59; R Hanover Square St Geo 55-74; Chapl City of Lon Sch 62-67; P-in-c N Audley Street St Mark Lon 68-74; R Hanover Square St Geo w St Mark from 74. St George's Vestry, 2A Mill Street, London W1R 9LB 071-629 0874

ATKINSON, Albert Edward. b 35. St Deiniol's Hawarden 79. **d** 79 **p** 80. C Ellesmere Port Ches 79-81; TV 81-84; P-in-c Kirkby Malzeard w Grewelthorpe and Mickley etc Ripon 84-88; P-in-c Fountains 88-90; R Fountains Gp from 90. Fountains Rectory, Winksley, N Yorkshire HG4 3NR Kirkby Malzeard (076583) 260

ATKINSON, Brian Colin. b 49. Sarum & Wells Th Coll 85. **d** 87 **p** 88. C Up Hatherley Glouc 87-90; R Upper Stour Sarum from 90. The Rectory, Zeals, Warminster, Wilts BA12 6PG Warminster (0985) 840221

ATKINSON, Christopher John. b 57. Man Univ BA80 DipTh84. Qu Coll Birm 82. **d** 85 **p** 86. C Stalybridge Man 85-88; P-in-c Westhall w Brampton and Stoven St E 88-89; P-in-c Sotterley, Willingham, Shadingfield, Ellough etc 88-90; P-in-c Hundred River

Gp of Par from 90. The Rectory, Moll's Lane, Brampton, Beccles, Suffolk NR34 8DB Brampton (050279) 615

ATKINSON, Christopher Lionel Varley. b 39. K Coll Lon 63. Chich Th Coll 65. **d** 67 **p** 68. C Sowerby Bridge w Norland Wakef 67-70; P-in-c Flushing Truro 70-73; Dioc Adv in RE 70-73; Perm to Offic Worc 74-78; TR Halesowen 78-88; RD Dudley 79-87; Hon Can Worc Cathl 83-88; V Cartmel Carl from 88. Priory Vicarage, Cartmel, Grange-over-Sands, Cumbria LA11 6PU Cartmel (05395) 36261

ATKINSON, Canon David James. b 41. Lon Univ BD AKC63 Selw Coll Cam BA65 MA72. Linc Th Coll 65. **d** 66 **p** 67. C Linc St Giles Linc 66-70; Asst Chapl Newc Univ Newc 70-73; Adult Educn Officer Lich 73-75; P-in-c Adbaston 73-80; Dir of Educn 75-82; Preb Lich Cathl 79-82; Chapl Hull Univ York 82-87; Dir of Educn Linc from 87; Hon Can Linc Cathl from 89. 1 St Giles Avenue, Lincoln LN2 4PE Lincoln (0522) 28199

ATKINSON, Dr David John. b 43. K Coll Lon BSc65 PhD69 Bris Univ DipTh70 MLitt73 Ox Univ MA85. Trin Coll Bris 69. **d** 72 **p** 73. C Halliwell St Pet Man 72-74; C Harborne Heath Birm 74-77; Lib Latimer Ho Ox 77-80; Chapl CCC Ox from 80; Fell from 84. Corpus Christi College, Oxford OX1 4JF or, 51 Templar Road, Oxford OX2 8LS Oxford (0865) 276722 or 53720

ATKINSON, Derek Arthur. b 31. K Coll Lon BD59 AKC59. **d** 60 **p** 61. R E w W Ogwell Ex 68-81; Asst Dir of RE 68-78; Dep Dir and Children's Adv 78-88; R Ogwell and Denbury 81-84; R Kenton w Mamhead and Powderham 84-88; rtd 88; Perm to Offic Ex from 88. 13 Cypress Drive, Exeter EX4 2DP Exeter (0392) 75901

ATKINSON, Ian. b 33. BNC Ox BA58 MA63. Coll of Resurr Mirfield 56. **d** 58 **p** 59. C Welling S'wark 58-62; C Camberwell St Giles 62-63; V Wandsworth Common St Mary 63-67; S Africa 67-68; C Oxted S'wark 68-69; Asst Chapl Ch Hosp Horsham 70-85; NSM Dunkeld St And from 75; NSM Dalmahoy Edin 85-91; Asst Master Clifton Hall Sch 85-91. Dalbeathie House, Dunkeld, Perthshire PH8 0JA

ATKINSON, Canon Prof James. b 14. St Jo Coll Dur BA36 MA39 MLitt50 Univ of Munster DTh55. **d** 37 **p** 38. Prof Bibl Studies Sheff Univ 67-79; Lic to Offic Sheff 68-70; Can Th Sheff Cathl from 70; rtd 79; Latimer Ho Ox 81-84. Leach House, Hathersage, Sheffield S30 1BA Hope Valley (0433) 50570

ATKINSON, John Dudley. b 38. ACA60 FCA71. Qu Coll Birm 63. **d** 66 **p** 67. C Bishop's Stortford St Mich St Alb 66-70; C Norton 70-73; V Markyate Street 73-80; R Baldock w Bygrave from 80; RD Stevenage 83-89. The Rectory, 9 Pond Lane, Baldock, Herts SG7 5AS Baldock (0462) 894398

ATKINSON, Kenneth. b 16. Lon Univ BA37. Ox NSM Course. **d** 77 **p** 78. NSM Steventon w Milton Ox 77-91; NSM Denchworth 82-91; rtd 86. 21 Tatlings Road, Steventon, Abingdon, Oxon OX13 6AT Abingdon (0235) 831342

ATKINSON, Kenneth. b 24. Qu Coll Birm 74. **d** 77 **p** 77. C Olton Birm 77-82; Perm to Offic York from 83. 34 Scalby Mills Road, Scarborough, N Yorkshire YO12 6RW Scarborough (0723) 373676

ATKINSON, Lewis Malcolm. b 34. St Jo Coll Dur. **d** 82 **p** 83. C Chapeltown Sheff 82-85; V Sheff St Paul Wordsworth Avenue from 85; Ind Chapl from 85; RD Ecclesfield from 90. St Paul's Vicarage, Wheata Road, Sheffield S5 9FP Sheffield (0742) 468137

ATKINSON, Marianne Rose. b 39. Girton Coll Cam BA61 CertEd62 MA64. Linc Th Coll 86. **d** 88. C S w N Hayling Portsm from 88. 70 Saltmarsh Lane, Hayling Island, Hants PO11 0JT Hayling Island (0705) 461783

ATKINSON, Michael Hubert. b 33. Qu Coll Ox BA57 MA60. Ripon Hall Ox 56. **d** 58 **p** 59. C Attercliffe w Carbrook Sheff 58-60; Ind Chapl 60-66; C Sheff Sharrow 60-66; Ind Chapl Pet 66-71; Ind Chapl Cant 71-79; Research Officer Gen Syn Bd for Soc Resp 79-87; Representation Sec USPG from 88. 160 Markfield, Courtwood Lane, Croydon, Surrey CR0 9HQ 081-657 0859

ATKINSON, Michael James. b 38. AKC62. **d** 63 **p** 64. C Leeds Halton St Wilfrid Ripon 63-65; C Luton St Hugh Lewsey CD St Alb 65-67; V Luton Lewsey St Hugh 67-71; C Caversham Ox 71-73; P-in-c N Woolwich Chelmsf 73-74; V N Woolwich w Silvertown 74-78; V Clavering w Langley and Arkesden 78-89; V Chelmsf All SS from 89. The Vicarage, King's Road, Chelmsford CM1 4HP Chelmsford (0245) 352005

ATKINSON, Nigel Terence. b 60. Sheff Univ BA82. Westmr Th Sem (USA) MDiv87 Cranmer Hall Dur 87. **d** 89 **p** 90. C Oakwood St Thos Lon from 89.

22 Curthwaite Gardens, Enfield, Middx EN2 7LN 081-363 4396

ATKINSON, Mrs Patricia Anne. b 47. d 89. NSM Nor St Steph *Nor* from 89. *32 Berryfields, Brundall, Norwich NR13 5QE* Norwich (0603) 714720

ATKINSON, Peter Duncan. b 41. Univ Coll Dur BA62. Linc Th Coll 63. d 65 p 66. C Beckenham St Geo *Roch* 65-69; C Caversham *Ox* 69-75; P-in-c Millfield St Mark *Dur* 76-86; V Dedworth *Ox* from 86. *3 Pierson Road, Windsor, Berks SL4 5RJ* Windsor (0753) 864591

ATKINSON, Peter Geoffrey. b 50. Sarum & Wells Th Coll 81. d 83 p 84. C Aylesbury *Ox* 83-86; C Dorchester 86-87; TV 87-91; V Cropredy w Gt Bourton and Wardington from 91. *The Vicarage, High Street, Cropredy, Banbury, Oxon OX17 1NG* Cropredy (029575) 799

ATKINSON, Preb Peter Gordon. b 52. St Jo Coll Ox BA74 MA78. Westcott Ho Cam 77. d 79 p 80. C Clapham Old Town *S'wark* 79-83; P-in-c Tatsfield 83-90; R Bath H Trin *B & W* 90-91; Prin Chich Th Coll from 91; Preb Chich Cathl *Chich* from 91. *The Theological College, Chichester, W Sussex PO19 1SG* Chichester (0243) 783369

ATKINSON, Philip Charles. b 50. Hull Univ BA71 PhD76 Chorley Coll of Educn CertEd77. N Ord Course 81. d 84 p 85. NSM Bolton SS Simon and Jude *Man* 84-87; Chapl R Wolv Sch from 87. *9 Marlbrook Drive, Wolverhampton* Wolverhampton (0902) 330706

ATKINSON, Philip Stephen. b 58. K Coll Lon BD80 AKC80. Ridley Hall Cam. d 83 p 84. C Barrow St Matt *Carl* 83-86; C Kirkby Lonsdale 86-89; R Redmarshall *Dur* from 89; V Bishopton w Gt Stainton from 89. *The Rectory, Redmarshall, Stockton-on-Tees, Cleveland TS21 1EP* Sedgefield (0740) 30810

ATKINSON, Richard William Bryant. b 58. Magd Coll Cam MA. Ripon Coll Cuddesdon. d 84 p 85. C Abingdon w Shippon *Ox* 84-87; TV Sheff Manor *Sheff* from 87. *The Vicarage, Cary Road, Sheffield S2 1JP* Sheffield (0742) 398360

ATKINSON, Canon Samuel Charles Donald. b 30. TCD BA54. d 55 p 56. C Belf St Simon *Conn* 55-62; I Ballynaclough *L & K* 62-68; I Cloughjordan w Modreeny 68-87; Dioc Youth Adv (Killaloe) 75-83; Dioc Info Officer (Limerick and Killaloe) 76-88; Can Killaloe Cathl 76-82; Chan from 82; I Cloughjordan w Borrisokane etc from 87. *The Rectory, Cloughjordan, Co Tipperary, Irish Republic* Cloughjordan (505) 42183

ATKINSON, Terence Harry. b 52. Coll of Resurr Mirfield 88. d 90 p 91. C Bottesford w Ashby *Linc* from 90. *111 Ashby High Street, Scunthorpe, S Humberside DN16 2JX* Scunthorpe (0724) 860573

ATTERBURY, Ernest Harold. b 17. Oak Hill Th Coll. d 61 p 62. C Broadwater St Mary *Chich* 64-72; V Glentworth *Linc* 72-80; rtd 80. *Flat 7, Manormead, Tilford Road, Hindhead, Surrey GU26 6RA* Hindhead (0428) 604905

ATTFIELD, David George. b 31. Magd Coll Ox BA54 MA58 BD61 K Coll Lon MPhil72 Dur Univ MA81. Westcott Ho Cam 57. d 58 p 59. C Edgbaston St Aug *Birm* 58-61; C Ward End 61-62; Lect Div St Kath Coll Tottenham 62-64; All SS Coll Tottenham 64-68; Sen Lect St Bede Coll Dur 68-75; St Hild and St Bede Coll 75-80; TV Drypool *York* 80-86; R Newton Heath All SS *Man* from 86. *All Saints' Rectory, Culcheth Lane, Newton Heath, Manchester M10 6LR* 061-681 3102

ATTFIELD, James Andrew. b 07. Codrington Coll Barbados. d 55 p 56. Chapl Newington Lodge 62-72; Perm to Offic *S'wark* from 72; rtd 77. *26 East Road, Melsonby, Richmond, N Yorkshire DL10 5NF* Darlington (0325) 718297

ATTLEY, Ronald. b 46. Open Univ BA87. Chich Th Coll 68. d 70 p 71. C Heworth St Mary *Dur* 70-73; C Hulme Ascension *Man* 73-75; Belize 76-79; V Leadgate *Dur* 79-84; Chapl HM Rem Cen Ashford 84-87; Chapl HM Pris Ashwell and Stocken 87-89; Chapl HM Pris Frankland from 89. *HM Prison Frankland, PO Box 40, Durham DH1 5YF* 091-384 5544

ATTOE, Walter Thomas Davenport. b 16. St Aid Birkenhead 41. d 43 p 44. V Wolv St Paul *Lich* 56-73; V Wolv St Jo 62-73; V Wolv St Jo 73-83; rtd 83; Perm to Offic *Heref* from 83; Lich from 87. *3 Priory Close, St James's Drive, Bridgnorth, Shropshire WV15 6BL* Bridgnorth (0746) 763418

ATTRILL, Norman Edmund Charles. b 16. K Coll Lon BA37. Wm Temple Coll Rugby 65 Ripon Hall Ox 67. d 68 p 69. C Portsea St Mary *Portsm* 68-72; V Sea View 72-80; rtd 81; Perm to Offic *Ox* from 83. *27 Church Street, Henley-on-Thames, Oxon RG9 1SE* Henley-on-Thames (0491) 574268

ATTWATER, Stephen Philip. b 47. ALCM67. Linc Th Coll 85. d 87 p 88. C Warrington St Elphin *Liv* 87-90; P-in-c Eccleston St Thos from 90. *21 St George's Road, St Helens, Merseyside WA10 4LH* St Helens (0744) 22295

ATTWOOD, Anthony Norman. b 47. Univ of Wales (Abth) BSc(Econ)69 Birm Univ DipTh71 Hull Univ MA82. Qu Coll Birm 69. d 72 p 73. C Greenhill *Sheff* 72-75; V Elsecar 76-81; Ind Missr from 81; TV Maltby 81-86; Ind Chapl from 86; RD Adwick from 89. *5 Daw Wood, Bentley, Doncaster, S Yorkshire DN5 0PU* Doncaster (0302) 875904

ATTWOOD, Carl Norman Harry. b 53. Bris Univ BA74 Ox Univ BA76 MA80. Cuddesdon Coll 74. d 77 p 78. C Tupsley *Heref* 77-82; R Colwall w Upper Colwall and Coddington from 82; Bp's Voc Officer 83-89; Chapl St Jas and the Abbey Sch W Malvern from 85; RD Ledbury *Heref* from 90. *The Rectory, Colwall, Malvern, Worcs WR13 6EG* Colwall (0684) 40330

ATTWOOD, David John Edwin. b 51. Dur Univ BA76 Em Coll Cam BA73 MA74. Cranmer Hall Dur 74. d 77 p 78. C Rodbourne Cheney *Bris* 77-79; C Lydiard Millicent w Lydiard Tregoz 79-85; Lect Trin Coll Bris from 85. *24 Little Stoke Road, Bristol BS9 1HQ* Bristol (0272) 681943

ATTY, Canon Norman Hughes. b 40. Dur Univ BA62. Cranmer Hall Dur 62. d 65 p 66. C Blackb St Gabr *Blackb* 65-67; Asst Master Billinge Sch Blackb 67-71; City of Leic Boys' Sch 71-73; P-in-c Elmley Lovett w Hampton Lovett *Worc* 73-78; P-in-c Elmbridge w Rushock 74-78; R Elmley Lovett w Hampton Lovett and Elmbridge etc 78-85; Hon Can Worc Cathl 81-85. *3 Gilbertstone Road, Redditch, Worcs*

ATWELL, James Edgar. b 46. Ex Coll Ox BA68 MA73 Harvard Univ ThM70. Cuddesdon Coll 68. d 70 p 71. C E Dulwich St Jo *S'wark* 70-74; C Cam Gt St Mary w St Mich *Ely* 74-77; Chapl Jes Coll Cam 77-81; V Towcester w Easton Neston *Pet* from 81; RD Towcester from 83. *The Vicarage, Towcester, Northants NN12 7AB* Towcester (0327) 50459

ATWELL, Robert Ronald. b 54. St Jo Coll Dur BA75 Dur Univ MLitt79. Westcott Ho Cam 76. d 78 p 79. C Mill Hill Jo Keble Ch *Lon* 78-81; Chapl Trin Coll Cam 81-87; OSB from 87; Lic to Offic *Ox* from 87. *Priory of Our Lady, Burford, Oxford OX8 4SQ* Burford (099382) 3605

AUBREY, Canon John Watkin. b 17. Ch Coll Cam BA39 MA43. Westcott Ho Cam 39. d 40 p 41. S Africa 48-76; R Collyweston w Duddington and Tixover *Pet* 76-82; rtd 82. *The Beauchamp Community, Newland, Malvern, Worcs WR13 5AX* Malvern (0684) 892187

AUCKLAND, Canon Allan Frank. b 13. K Coll Lon 49. d 49 p 50. V Hatcham St Cath *S'wark* 56-74; RD Lewisham 65-70; Hon Can S'wark Cathl 67-81; R Burstow 74-81; rtd 81; Perm to Offic *Cant* from 81. *14 The Pavement, Front Road, Woodchurch, Ashford, Kent TN26 3QE* Woodchurch (0233) 861231

AUCKLAND, Canon Clifford Aubrey. b 14. Lon Univ BD41. ALCD41. d 41 p 42. R Maltby *Sheff* 50-80; rtd 80; Hon Can Sheff Cathl *Sheff* from 80; Ind Chapl from 80. *141 Trap Lane, Sheffield S11 7RF* Sheffield (0742) 308120

AUCKLAND, Archdeacon of. See HODGSON, Ven John Derek

AUDEN, Lawson Philip. b 45. Qu Coll Birm 73. d 78 p 81. C Spalding *Linc* 78-81; TV Wordsley *Lich* 81-82; TV Kidderminster St Mary and All SS etc *Worc* 82-87; Ind Chapl 82-87; Perm to Offic Cov and Worc from 87; Birm from 90. *Little Court, Radford Road, Rous Lench, Evesham, Worcs WR11 4UL* Evesham (0386) 793245

AUGUSTINE, Brother. See MORRIS, David Freestone

AUGUSTINE, Brother. See HOEY, Thomas Kenneth

AUST, Arthur John. b 14. St Aug Coll Cant 62. d 63 p 64. R Theddlethorpe w Mablethorpe *Linc* 67-71; Nigeria 71-74; S Africa 74-77; TV Clyst St George, Aylesbeare, Clyst Honiton etc *Ex* 79-81; rtd 81; Perm to Offic *Cant* from 81. *Overhill House, Upper Street, Kingsdown, Deal, Kent CT14 8DR* Deal (0304) 361583

AUSTEN, Glyn. b 54. UEA BA MPhil Ox Univ MA. Ripon Coll Cuddesdon 79. d 82 p 83. C Newport w Longford and Chetwynd *Lich* 82-85; C Hawley H Trin *Guildf* 85-87; R Barnack w Ufford and Bainton *Pet* from 87. *The Rectory, Barnack, Stamford, Lincs PE9 3ET* Stamford (0780) 740234

AUSTEN, John. b 46. St Cath Coll Cam BA69 MA72. Qu Coll Birm DipTh70. d 71 p 72. C Thornaby on Tees *York* 71-74; C Aston St Jas *Birm* 74-82; Chapl Aston Univ 82-88; C Handsworth St Andr from 88. *151 Church Lane, Birmingham B20 2RU* 021-554 8882

AUSTER, Neville Walter Lucas. b 12. Or Coll Ox BA34 MA38. Wells Th Coll 36. **d** 37 **p** 38. V Dullingham *Ely* 69-79; rtd 79; Perm to Offic *Ex* from 79. *9 Land Park, Chulmleigh, Devon EX18 7BH* Chulmleigh (0769) 80610

AUSTERBERRY, David Naylor. b 35. Birm Univ BA58. Wells Th Coll 58. **d** 60 **p** 61. C Leek St Edw *Lich* 60-63; Iran 64-70; Chapl CMS Foxbury 70-73; V Walsall Pleck and Bescot *Lich* 73-82; R Brierley Hill 82-88; R Kinnerley w Melverley and Knockin w Maesbrook from 88. *The Rectory, Kinnerley, Oswestry, Shropshire SY10 8DE* Knockin (069185) 233

AUSTERBERRY, John Maurice. b 62. Birm Univ BA83. Sarum & Wells Th Coll 84. **d** 86 **p** 87. C Clayton *Lich* 86-90; Asst Chapl Withington Univ Hosp Man from 89. *The Chaplain's Office, Withington Hospital, West Didsbury, Manchester M20 8LR* 061-445 8111

AUSTERBERRY, Ven Sidney Denham. b 08. Man Univ 27. Man Egerton Hall 30. **d** 31 **p** 33. Adn Salop *Lich* 59-79; V Gt Ness 59-77; V Lt Ness 73-77; rtd 80. *6 Honeysuckle Row, Shrewsbury SY3 7TW* Shrewsbury (0743) 68080

AUSTIN, Ven George Bernard. b 31. St D Coll Lamp BA53 Chich Th Coll 53. **d** 55 **p** 56. C Chorley St Pet *Blackb* 55-57; C Notting Hill St Clem *Lon* 57-60; Asst Chapl Lon Univ 60-61; C Dunstable *St Alb* 61-64; V Eaton Bray 64-70; V Bushey Heath 70-88; Hon Can St Alb from 78; Adn York from 88. *7 Lang Road, Bishopthorpe, York YO2 1QJ* York (0904) 709541

AUSTIN, Miss Jane. b 43. SRN64 SCM66. Trin Coll Bris DipTh81. dss 81 **d** 87. Tonbridge SS Pet and Paul *Roch* 81-87; Par Dn from 87. *6 London Road, Tonbridge, Kent TN10 3AH* Tonbridge (0732) 358892

AUSTIN, Preb John Michael. b 39. St Edm Hall Ox BA63. St Steph Ho Ox 62. **d** 64 **p** 65. C E Dulwich St Jo *S'wark* 64-68; USA 68-69; Warden Pem Ho and Missr Walworth St Chris CD *S'wark* 69-76; TV Walworth 75-76; Soc Resp Adv *St Alb* 76-84; Dir Dioc Bd for Soc Resp *Lon* from 84; Preb St Paul's Cathl from 89. *65 Burghley Road, London NW5 1UH* 071-821 0950

AUSTIN, Leslie Ernest. b 46. Trin Coll Bris 72. **d** 74 **p** 75. C Paddock Wood *Roch* 74-79; C Upper Armley *Ripon* 79-81; V Horton *Bradf* 81-85; V Long Preston w Tosside from 85. *The Vicarage, Long Preston, Skipton, N Yorkshire BD23 4NH* Long Preston (07294) 513

AUSTIN, Dr Michael John Lester. b 33. Ox Univ MA DPhil. Ox NSM Course. **d** 84 **p** 84. Asst Chapl Athens St Paul w Kyfissia *Eur* 84-85; NSM Coln St Aldwyn, Hatherop, Quenington etc *Glouc* 86-89; P-in-c Burwash Weald *Chich* from 89. *The Vicarage, Burwash Common, Etchingham, E Sussex TN17 7NA* Burwash (0435) 883287

AUSTIN, Canon Michael Ridgwell. b 33. FRHistS Lon Univ BD57 PhD69 Birm Univ MA66. Lon Coll of Div ALCD56 LTh. **d** 57 **p** 58. C Ward End *Birm* 57-60; V Derby St Andr *Derby* 60-66; Lect Th Derbyshire Coll of HE 66-73; Chapl Derby Cathl *Derby* 66-81; Prin Lect 73-85; Can Res Derby Cathl 81-85; Bp's Tr Adv *S'well* 85-88; Dir of Post-Ord Tr from 86; Can Res S'well Minster from 88; Dioc Dir of Tr from 88. *22 Marlock Close, Fiskerton, Southwell, Notts NG25 0UB* Southwell (0636) 830074

AUSTIN, Raymond Charles. b 23. St Edm Hall Ox BA48 MA53 Lon Univ BD70 DipEd74. Linc Th Coll 48. **d** 50 **p** 51. V Chapel-en-le-Frith *Derby* 57-66; Perm to Offic *Mon* 66-84; V Llantilio Crossenny w Penrhos, Llanvetherine etc 84-91; rtd 88. *Glanmor, Hardwick Hill, Chepstow, Gwent NP6 5PN* Chepstow (02912) 6828

AUSTIN, Ronald Glyn. b 52. **d** 90 **p** 91. C Llangynwyd w Maesteg *Llan* from 90. *The Old Vicarage, Llangynwyd, Maesteg, Bridgend, M Glam CF34 9SB* Maesteg (0656) 732472

AUTTON, Canon Norman William James. b 20. Selw Coll Cam BA42 MA46. St Mich Coll Llan 42. **d** 44 **p** 45. Dir of Tr Gen Syn Hosp Chapl Coun 67-72; Chapl Univ Hosp of Wales Cardiff from 72; Can Llan Cathl *Llan* from 77; rtd 85; Chan Llan Cathl *Llan* from 85. *112 St Anthony Road, Cardiff CF4 4DJ* Cardiff (0222) 625788

AVANN, Miss Penelope Joyce. b 46. Trin Coll Bris DipTh71. dss 83 **d** 87. Southborough St Pet w Ch Ch and St Matt *Roch* 83-87; Par Dn 87-89; Warden Past Assts from 89; Par Dn Beckenham St Jo from 89. *21 Glanfield Road, Beckenham, Kent BR3 3JS* 081-650 4061

AVELING, John Cedric. b 17. **d** 40 **p** 41. C Yaxley *St E* 69-71; rtd 82. *14 Weycrofts, Bracknell, Berks RG12 1TD*

AVENT, Raymond John. b 28. St D Coll Lamp BA55 Coll of Resurr Mirfield 55. **d** 57 **p** 58. C Bury H Trin *Man*

57-60; C Holborn St Alb w Saffron Hill St Pet *Lon* 60-66; C Munster Square St Mary Magd 66-67; V Tottenham St Paul 67-77; RD E Haringey 73-77; V Kilburn St Aug w St Jo 77-87; AD Westmr Paddington 79-84; R St Vedast w St Mich-le-Querne etc from 87. *St Vedast's Rectory, 4 Foster Lane, London EC2V 6HH* 071-606 3998

AVERY, Richard Julian. b 52. Keble Coll Ox BA73. St Jo Coll Nottm 74. **d** 77 **p** 78. C Macclesfield St Mich *Ches* 77-80; Canada 82-83 and from 87; C Becontree St Mary *Chelmsf* 84-87. *5984 Rothwell Place, Duncan, British Columbia, Canada, V9L 3B7* Duncan (604) 748-5729

AVERY, Russell Harrold. b 46. JP74. ACT ThDip75 Moore Th Coll Sydney 66. **d** 77 **p** 77. Australia 77-78 and from 88; C Prenton *Ches* 78-79; Egypt 79-82; Chapl Maisons-Lafitte *Eur* 82-88. *The Rectory, 6 Finlayson Street, Lane Cove, NSW, Australia 2066* Sydney (2) 427-6569 or 427-1163

AVES, John Albert. b 51. K Coll Lon AKC73 BD74 CertEd79 MA82. **d** 75 **p** 76. C Plaistow St Andr *Chelmsf* 75-77; Perm to Offic *Lon* 77-79; C Nor St Pet Mancroft *Nor* 79-82; R Attleborough w Besthorpe from 82. *The Rectory, Attleborough, Norfolk NR17 2AW* Attleborough (0953) 453185

AVES, Peter Colin. b 57. Qu Mary Coll Lon BSc79 CertEd80. Wycliffe Hall Ox 85. **d** 88 **p** 89. C Thames Ditton *Guildf* 88-90; C Chertsey from 90. *4 North Grove, Chertsey, Surrey KT16 9DU* Chertsey (0932) 567944

AVEYARD, Ian. b 46. Liv Univ BSc68. ALCD72 St Jo Coll Nottm 72. **d** 72 **p** 73. C Bradley *Wakef* 71-74; C Knowle *Birm* 74-79; P-in-c Cofton Hackett 79; P-in-c Barnt Green 79; V Cofton Hackett w Barnt Green from 80; Dioc Dir of Reader Tr from 85. *8 Cofton Church Lane, Barnt Green, Birmingham B45 8PT* 021-445 1269

AVIS, Paul David Loup. b 47. Lon Univ BD70 PhD76. Westcott Ho Cam 73. **d** 75 **p** 76. C S Molton, Nymet St George, High Bray etc *Ex* 75-80; V Stoke Canon, Poltimore w Huxham and Rewe etc from 80. *The Vicarage, Stoke Canon, Exeter EX5 4AS* Exeter (0392) 841583

AWDRY, Wilbert Vere. b 11. St Pet Hall Ox BA32 MA36. Wycliffe Hall Ox 32. **d** 36 **p** 37. V Emneth *Ely* 53-65; Perm to Offic *Glouc* 65-89; rtd 76. *Sodor, 30 Rodborough Avenue, Stroud, Glos GL5 3RS* Stroud (0453) 762321

AWRE, Edward Francis Wintour. b 11. St Jo Coll Dur BA37 DipTh38 MA40. **d** 38 **p** 39. V Nether Stowey *B & W* 56-70; P-in-c Over Stowey w Aisholt 69-70; rtd 71; Hon C Burnham *B & W* 72-81; Perm to Offic from 81. *3 Seaview Road, Burnham-on-Sea, Somerset TA8 2AJ* Burnham-on-Sea (0278) 782493

AWRE, Richard William Esgar. b 56. Univ of Wales BA78. Wycliffe Hall Ox 78. **d** 81 **p** 82. C Blackpool St Jo *Blackb* 81-84; Asst Dir of Ords and Voc Adv 84-89; C Altham w Clayton le Moors 84-89; V Longridge from 89. *The Vicarage, Church Street, Longridge, Preston PR3 3WA* Longridge (077478) 3281

AXFORD, Robert Henry. b 50. CEng85 Univ of Wales BEng72. Sarum & Wells Th Coll 89. **d** 91. C Castle Cary w Ansford *B & W* from 91. *35 Hallett Road, Castle Cary, Somerset BA7 7LG* Castle Cary (0963) 51286

AXTELL, Ronaid Arthur John. b 33. Lon Univ BSc54 St Cath Soc Ox BA58 MA62. Wycliffe Hall Ox 56. **d** 58 **p** 59. C Walton Breck *Liv* 58-61; Iran 63-78; Chr Witness to Israel Miss in Man 78-82; Perm to Offic *Man* 79-82; TV Man Resurr 82; TV Man Gd Shep 82-88; R Levenshulme St Pet from 88. *29A Ardwick Green North, Manchester M12 6FZ* 061-273 5020

AYAD, Karl. b 25. Cairo Univ BSc48 Lon Univ MSc53 PhD55. St Steph Ho Ox 80. **d** 81 **p** 82. C Allerton *Liv* 81-83; V Knowsley 83-90; rtd 90. *2 Stanley House, 46 Stanley Road, Hoylake, Wirral L47 1HY* 051-632 5519

AYERS, John. b 40. FCollP Bris Univ BEd75 Newton Park Coll Bath MEd89. **d** 77 **p** 78. NSM Corsham *Bris* 77-79; NSM Gtr Corsham 79-88; NSM Ditteridge from 88. *Toad Hall, Middlehill, Box, Corsham, Wilts SN14 9QP* Box (0225) 742123

AYERS, Paul Nicholas. b 61. St Pet Coll Ox BA82 MA86. Trin Coll Bris 83. **d** 85 **p** 86. C Clayton *Bradf* 85-88; C Keighley St Andr 88-91; V Wrose from 91. *St Cuthbert's Vicarage, 71 Wrose Road, Bradford, W Yorkshire BD2 1LN* Bradford (0274) 611631

AYERST, Edward Richard. b 25. Leeds Univ BA51. Coll of Resurr Mirfield 51. **d** 53 **p** 54. R Whippingham w E Cowes *Portsm* 66-77; V Bridgwater St Mary w Chilton Trinity *B & W* 77-84; V Durleigh 77-84; V Bridgwater St Mary, Chilton Trinity and Durleigh 84-90; Chapl to HM The Queen from 87; rtd 90. *56 Maple Drive,*

Burnham-on-Sea, Somerset TA8 1DH Burnham-on-Sea (0278) 780701

AYKROYD, Harold Allan. b 22. DFC. Man Univ BA48. Qu Coll Birm 73. **d** 76 **p** 76. NSM Moseley St Agnes *Birm* 76-82; NSM Bournville from 82. *108 Middleton Hall Road, Birmingham B30 1DG* 021-451 1365

AYLEN, George Richard. b 24. Chich Th Coll 48. **d** 52 **p** 53. V Whitstable St Pet *Cant* 67-75; R Petham w Waltham and Lower Hardres w Nackington 75-78; rtd 78; Perm to Offic *Cant* from 80. *20 Seymour Place, Canterbury, Kent CT1 3SF* Canterbury (0227) 456243

AYLETT, Graham Peter. b 59. Qu Coll Cam BA81 MA84 PhD85 St Jo Coll Dur BA88. Cranmer Hall Dur 86. **d** 90. C Wilton *B & W* from 90. *5 Wiltshire Close, Taunton, Somerset TA1 4JR* Taunton (0823) 283484

AYLETT, Mrs Nicola Jane. b 63. St Anne's Coll Ox BA84 St Jo Coll Dur BA89. Cranmer Hall Dur 87. **d** 90. C Wilton *B & W* from 90. *5 Wiltshire Close, Taunton, Somerset TA1 4JR* Taunton (0823) 283484

AYLING, Arnold Paul. b 38. Ball Coll Ox BA61. Wells Th Coll 65. **d** 67 **p** 68. C Weymouth H Trin *Sarum* 67-70; Chapl K Alfred Coll *Win* 70-73; Miss to Seamen 73-84; Dunkirk *Eur* 73; Nigeria 74-82; S Africa 82-84; Perm to Offic *Sarum* 85-86; Chich from 85; Chapl Leybourne Grange Hosp W Malling, Pembury Hosp Tunbridge Wells and Kent and Sussex Hosp Tunbridge Wells from 86; Distr Chapl Tunbridge Wells HA from 86. *Pembury Hospital, Pembury, Tunbridge Wells, Kent TN2 4QJ* Pembury (089282) 4954

AYLING, Preb John Charles. b 02. St Jo Coll Dur BA29. **d** 29 **p** 30. R Myddle *Lich* 59-70; V Broughton 59-70; P-in-c Grinshill 59-65; Dioc Dir RE 59-75; Preb Lich Cathl 61-75; rtd 70. *10 Church Close, Bicton, Shrewsbury SY3 8EN* Shrewsbury (0743) 850491

AYLING, John Michael. b 37. St Cath Coll Cam BA60 MA64. Linc Th Coll 60. **d** 62 **p** 63. C Stoke upon Trent *Lich* 62-66; C Codsall 66-67; Australia 67-71; Solomon Is 71-72; Lic to Offic *St Alb* 72-91; TR Boscastle w Davidstow *Truro* from 91. *The Rectory, Boscastle, Cornwall PL35 0DJ* Boscastle (08405) 359

AYNSLEY, Ernest Edgar. b 02. FRIC Dur Univ BSc23 MSc24 PhD34 DSc62. Westcott Ho Cam 42. **d** 42 **p** 43. Lic to Offic *Newc* from 63; Prof Chemistry Newc Univ 63-67; rtd 67. *7 Manor Court, Ulgham, Morpeth, Northd NE61 3BG* Morpeth (0670) 790197

AYRE, Henry George. b 08. AKC38. **d** 38 **p** 39. R Kentisbury *Ex* 46-72; R Trentishoe 60-72; R Kentisbury, Trentishoe, E Down and Arlington 72-87; rtd 88. *Beachborough, Kentisbury, Barnstaple, Devon EX31 4NH* Combe Martin (027188) 2487

AYRE, Canon James. b 15. Tyndale Hall Bris 46 Clifton Th Coll 48. **d** 49 **p** 49. R Cheadle *Ches* 61-88; Hon Can Ches Cathl from 74; rtd 88. *Flat 5, Moseley Grange, Cheadle Road, Cheadle Hulme, Cheshire SK8 5EZ*

AYRES, Anthony Lawrence. b 47. Trin Coll Bris 69. **d** 73 **p** 74. C Plumstead All SS *S'wark* 73-77; Hon C from 77; Member of Counselling Team CA from 83. *37 Donaldson Road, London SE18* 081-856 1542

B

BAAR, Canon William Henry. b 19. Yale Univ BA42 BD45 MA48 PhD53 STM55 DD77. Seabury-Western Th Sem. **d** 54 **p** 54. USA 54-86; Chapl Venice w Trieste *Eur* from 86; Can Malta Cathl from 89. *253 Dorsoduro, San Gregorio, 30123 Venice, Italy* Venice (41) 520-0571

BABB, Charles Thomas. b 47. Newfoundland Univ BA70. Qu Coll Newfoundland 64. **d** 70 **p** 72. Canada 70-80; Chapl Antwerp Seafarers' Cen *Eur* from 80; Miss to Seamen from 80. *Seafarers' Centre, Italielei 72, 2000 Antwerp, Belgium* Antwerp (3) 233-3475 or 665-1122

BABB, Canon Geoffrey. b 42. Man Univ BSc64 MA74 Linacre Coll Ox BA67. Ripon Hall Ox 65. **d** 68 **p** 69. C Heywood St Luke *Man* 68-71; P-in-c Loundsley Green Ascension CD *Derby* 71-76; TV Old Brampton and Loundsley Green 76-77; TV Stafford St Mary and St Chad *Lich* 77-79; Soc Resp Officer 77-88; TV Stafford 79-88; Preb Lich Cathl 87-88; P-in-c Salford Sacred Trin *Man* from 88; Dir of Continuing Min Educn from 88; Hon Can Man Cathl from 89. *197A Lancaster Road, Salford M6 8NB* 061-788 7077

BABER, Leslie Civil. b 02. ACII25 St Edm Hall Ox BA29 MA33. Westcott Ho Cam 29. **d** 30 **p** 31. Sec DBF

Ely 46-55; Perm to Offic *Win* 67-72 and from 85; rtd 70; Perm to Offic *Portsm* from 71; C Brockenhurst *Win* 72-83. *Bonham, Church Lane, Sway, Lymington, Hants SO41 6AD* Lymington (0590) 682776

BABINGTON, Canon Gervase Hamilton. b 30. Keble Coll Ox BA57 MA57. Wells Th Coll 55. **d** 57 **p** 58. C Sheff St Geo and St Steph *Sheff* 57-60; P-in-c Manor Park CD 60-65; R Waddington *Linc* 65-81; RD Graffoe 74-81; Can and Preb Linc Cathl from 77; V Gainsborough All SS 81-90; RD Corringham 82-87; R Walesby from 90. *The Rectory, Walesby, Market Rasen, Lincs LN8 3UT* Tealby (067383) 513

BABINGTON, Canon Richard Andrew. b 27. Keble Coll Ox BA49. Wells Th Coll. **d** 51 **p** 52. C Newmarket All SS *St E* 51-54; V Elton All SS *Man* 54-63; R Honiton, Gittisham and Combe Raleigh *Ex* 63-72; R Gittisham 63-72; R Combe Raleigh 66-72; R Blandford Forum and Langton Long etc *Sarum* 72-88; RD Milton and Blandford 86-91; Can and Preb Sarum Cathl from 88; R Blandford Forum and Langton Long from 89. *The Rectory, Blandford Forum, Dorset DT11 7DW* Blandford (0258) 453294

BACH, John Edward Goulden. b 40. JP. Dur Univ BA66 DipTh69. Cranmer Hall Dur 66. **d** 69 **p** 70. C Bradf Cathl *Bradf* 69-72; Chapl and Lect NUU 73-84; Ulster Univ from 84. *The Anglican Chaplaincy, 70 Hopefield Avenue, Portrush, Co Antrim BT56 8HE* Portrush (0265) 823348

BACHE, Edward Cyril Forbes. b 07. Dur Univ BA33 MA56. **d** 34 **p** 35. Chapl St Felix Sch Southwold 71-74; Lic to Offic *St E* 71-75; TV Halesworth w Linstead and Chediston 76-77; rtd 77; C Hardwick w Tusmore Ox 77-80; C Cottisford 77-80; Perm to Offic *St E* from 81. *Brook Cottage, Newbourn, Woodbridge, Suffolk IP12 4NY* Waldringfield (047336) 702

BACHELL, Kenneth George. b 22. Lon Univ BD49. K Coll Lon 55. **d** 56 **p** 57. V Southn St Alb *Win* 68-76; Warden Dioc Conf Ho Crawshawbooth *Man* 76-79; P-in-c Crawshawbooth 76-79; V Holdenhurst *Win* 79-83; V Froyle and Holybourne 83-87; rtd 87; Perm to Offic *Blackb* from 88. *8 Hazelwood, Silverdale, Carnforth, Lancs LA5 0TQ* Silverdale (0524) 701181

BACK, Christopher George. b 46. St Chad's Coll Dur BA69 Linacre Coll Ox BA71 MA. St Steph Ho Ox 69. **d** 72 **p** 73. C Hoxton H Trin w St Mary *Lon* 72-75; C Kenton 75-83; V Noel Park St Mark from 83. *St Mark's Vicarage, Ashley Crescent, London N22 6LJ* 081-888 3442

BACK, Esther Elaine. b 52. Saffron Walden Coll CertEd74. Trin Coll Bris 79 Oak Hill Th Coll BA81. **dss** 81 **d** 87. Collyhurst *Man* 81-84; Upton (or Overchurch) *Ches* 84-87; Par Dn 87-88; Par Dn Upper Holloway St Pet w St Jo *Lon* from 88. *4 Anatola Road, London N19 5HN* 071-263 8473

BACKHOUSE, Alan Eric. b 37. Keble Coll Ox BA61 MA67. Tyndale Hall Bris 61. **d** 64 **p** 65. C Burnage St Marg *Man* 64-67; C Cheadle Hulme St Andr *Ches* 67-70; V Buglawton 70-80; V New Ferry 80-87; V Tarvin from 87. *St Andrew's Vicarage, Tarvin, Chester CH3 8EB* Tarvin (0829) 40354

BACKHOUSE, Colin. b 41. MCSD82 Birm Poly BA67. Oak Hill Th Coll DipHE87. **d** 87 **p** 88. C Branksome St Clem *Sarum* 87-91; P-in-c Bluntisham cum Earith w Colne and Woodhurst *Ely* from 91. *The Rectory, Bluntisham, Huntingdon, Cambs PE17 3LN* Ramsey (0487) 740456

BACKHOUSE, John. b 30. Univ Coll Southn BA50. Wycliffe Hall Ox 51. **d** 53 **p** 54. C Eccleston St Luke *Liv* 53-55; C Maghull 55-58; V Lathom 58-64; Area Sec CMS 64-78; Dios Linc and Ely 64-71; Leic 72-78; Pet 72-75; Cov 75-78; V Dishley and Thorpe Acre *Leic* 78-83; R Ab Kettleby Gp 83-89; P-in-c Bitteswell from 89; RD Guthlaxton II (Lutterworth) from 90. *The Vicarage, Lutterworth Road, Bitteswell, Lutterworth, Leics LE17 4RX* Lutterworth (0455) 556367

BACKHOUSE, Robert. b 45. ALCD70. **d** 70 **p** 71. C Harold Wood *Chelmsf* 70-74; Publicity Sec CPAS 74-78. *Address temp unknown*

BACON, David Gary. b 62. Leic Univ BA83 Southn Univ BTh88. Sarum & Wells Th Coll 85. **d** 88 **p** 89. C Bromley St Mark *Roch* from 88. *25 Matfield Close, Bromley, Kent BR2 9DY* 081-466 5827

BACON, Derek Robert Alexander. b 44. TCD 69. **d** 71 **p** 72. C Templemore *D & R* 71-73; VC Derry Cathl 72-73; C Heeley *Sheff* 74-76; V Sheff Abbeydale St Pet 76-82; Chapl Gt Ormond Street Hosp for Sick Children Lon from 82. *Hospital for Sick Children, Great Ormond Street, London WC1N 3JH* 071-405 9200

BACON, Eric Arthur. b 23. Qu Coll Birm 68. **d** 69 **p** 70. C Linc St Pet-at-Gowts and St Andr *Linc* 69-71; C Asterby Gp 71-74; V Anwick 74-78; V S Kyme 74-78; P-in-c Kirkby Laythorpe w Asgarby 76-78; P-in-c Ewerby w Evedon 76-78; P-in-c Burton Pedwardine 76-78; V Messingham 78-89; rtd 89; Perm to Offic *Linc* from 89. *23 Londesborough Way, Metheringham, Lincoln* Metheringham (0526) 20418

BACON, Geoffrey Williams Anthony. b 28. AKC54. **d** 56 **p** 61. C Tottenham Ch Ch W Green *Lon* 56-57; C Finchley St Mary 61-64; C Haywards Heath St Wilfrid *Chich* 64-66; R Snailwell *Ely* 66-69; V Chippenham 67-69; Lic to Offic *Lon* 69-75; TV Thornaby on Tees *York* 81-87; P-in-c Beeford w Frodingham and Foston 87-89; R Dalbeattie *Glas* from 89. *319 High Street, Dalbeattie, Kirkcudbrightshire DG5 4DT* Dalbeattie (0556) 610671

BACON, Mrs Joan Winifred. b 25. NE Ord Course 84. **dss** 87 **d** 90. Beeford w Frodingham and Foston *York* 87-89; Dalbeattie *Glas* 89-90; Hon Par Dn from 90. *319 High Street, Dalbeattie, Kirkcudbrightshire DG5 4DT* Dalbeattie (0556) 610671

BACON, John Martindale. b 22. St Aid Birkenhead 54. **d** 57 **p** 58. C-in-c Clifton Green St Thos CD *Man* 59-71; V Astley Bridge 71-87; rtd 87. *21 Lichen Close, Charnock Richard, Chorley, Lancs PR7 5TT* Chorley (0257) 792535

BACON, Lionel William Rupert. b 06. Univ Coll Dur LTh31 BA32 MA40. St Paul's Coll Burgh 27. **d** 33 **p** 34. V Ancaster *Linc* 59-73; V Honington 59-73; rtd 73; Perm to Offic *Chich* from 73. *Nettlestead, 12 West Avenue, Worthing, W Sussex BN11 5LY* Worthing (0903) 48930

BADDELEY, Canon Martin James. b 36. Keble Coll Ox BA60 MA64. Linc Th Coll 60. **d** 62 **p** 63. C Stretford St Matt *Man* 62-64; Lic to Offic *Linc* 65-69; Lect Linc Th Coll 65-66; Tutor 66-69; Chapl 68-69; Chapl Fitzw Coll and New Hall Cam 69-74; Can Res Roch Cathl *Roch* 74-80; Hon Can from 80; Prin S'wark Ord Course from 80. *27 Blackfriars Road, London SE1 8NY* 071-928 4793

BADDELEY, Very Rev William Pye. b 14. St Chad's Coll Dur BA40. Cuddesdon Coll 40. **d** 41 **p** 42. R Westmr St Jas *Lon* 67-80; ChStJ from 70; RD Westmr St Marg *Lon* 74-80; Visiting Chapl Westmr Abbey from 80; rtd 80; Perm to Offic *St E* from 81. *Cumberland House, 17 Cumberland Street, Woodbridge, Suffolk IP12 4AH* Woodbridge (03943) 4104

BADEN, Peter Michael. b 35. CCC Cam BA59 MA62. Cuddesdon Coll 58. **d** 60 **p** 61. C Hunslet St Mary and Stourton *Ripon* 60-63; Lic to Offic *Wakef* 63-64; C E Grinstead St Swithun *Chich* 65-68; V Brighton St Martin 68-74; TR Brighton Resurr 74-76; R Westbourne 76-84; V Stansted 76-84; V Copthorne 84-91; V Clifton *Carl* from 91; R Dean from 91. *The Vicarage, 1 Clifton Gardens, Great Clifton, Workington, Cumbria CA14 1TT* Workington (0900) 603886

BADGER, Canon Bernard. b 16. Jes Coll Ox BA39 MA46. Cuddesdon Coll 46. **d** 48 **p** 49. V Leic St Andr *Leic* 53-82; Chapl Leic R Infirmary 71; Hon Can Leic Cathl *Leic* from 76; TV Leic H Spirit 82-87; rtd 87. *65 Saltersford Road, Leicester LE5 4DF* Leicester (0533) 742483

BADGER, Canon Edwin. b 09. Bris Univ BA32 MA86 Lon Univ BD57. St Boniface Warminster 28. **d** 34 **p** 35. C Kidderminster St Jo *Worc* 34-36; Australia from 36; Hon Can Wangaratta 69-76. *6 Malcolm Street, Bacchus Marsh, Victoria, Australia 3340* Bacchus Marsh (6153) 672316

BADHAM, Canon Herbert William. b 09. Hatf Coll Dur LTh30 BA31. St Boniface Warminster 27. **d** 32 **p** 33. V Bournemouth St Clem w St Mary *Win* 68-75; rtd 75; Perm to Offic *Win* from 75. *2 Northover, Dunbar Road, Bournemouth BH3 7AZ* Bournemouth (0202) 295781

BADHAM, Paul Brian Leslie. b 42. Jes Coll Ox BA65 MA69 Jes Coll Cam BA68 MA72 Birm Univ PhD73. Westcott Ho Cam 66. **d** 68 **p** 69. C Edgbaston St Bart *Birm* 68-69; C Rubery 69-73; Lic to Offic *St D* from 73; Lect Th Univ of Wales (Lamp) 73-83; Sen Lect 83-88; Reader from 88. *St David's College, Lampeter, Dyfed SA48 7ED* Lampeter (0570) 422351

BAELZ, Very Rev Peter Richard. b 23. Ch Coll Cam BA44 MA48 BD71 Ox Univ DD79. Westcott Ho Cam 44. **d** 47 **p** 50. Dean Jes Coll Cam 60-72; Lic to Offic *Ely* 61-72; Lect Th Cam Univ 66-72; Can Res Ch Ch *Ox* 72-79; Regius Prof Moral and Past Th Ox Univ 72-79; Dean Dur 80-88; rtd 88; Perm to Offic *S & B* from 88. *36 Brynteg, Llandrindod Wells, Powys LD1 5NB* Llandrindod Wells (0597) 825404

BAGGALEY, Canon Dennis. b 31. Dur Univ BA53 Liv Univ MA79 St Jo Coll Dur DipTh56. **d** 56 **p** 57. C Pennington *Man* 56-59; C N Meols *Liv* 59-60; V Bacup Ch Ch *Man* 60-65; R Burnage St Nic 65-71; V Onchan *S & M* from 71; Can St German's Cathl 80-91; RD Douglas 82-86. *The Vicarage, Onchan, Douglas, Isle of Man* Douglas (0624) 675797

BAGGALEY, John Roger Pocklington. b 14. MC45. Keble Coll Ox BA36 MA45. Westcott Ho Cam. **d** 47 **p** 48. R Badger *Lich* 69-83; R Ryton 69-83; R Beckbury 69-83; rtd 83. *21 Swanston Drive, Fairmilehead, Edinburgh EH10 7BP* 031-445 1331

BAGGLEY, John Samuel. b 40. Dur Univ BA62. Kelham Th Coll 62. **d** 66 **p** 67. C Poplar *Lon* 66-71; TV 71-72; V De Beauvoir Town St Pet 72-82; TR Bicester w Bucknell, Caversfield and Launton *Ox* from 82. *St Edburg's Vicarage, Victoria Road, Bicester, Oxon OX6 7PQ* Bicester (0869) 253222

BAGLEY, Canon John Marmaduke Erskine. b 08. G&C Coll Cam BA30 MA36. Ely Th Coll 30. **d** 32 **p** 33. V Ely 63-74; Chapl Ely Cathl 63-74; Hon Can 68-74; P-in-c Chettisham 68-74; rtd 74; Perm to Offic *St E* 74-77; Ely from 77. *19 Park Street, Dry Drayton, Cambridge CB3 8DA* Crafts Hill (0954) 780619

BAGLEY, Richard Alexander. b 25. New Coll Ox BA51 MA55 K Coll Cam MA57. Cuddesdon Coll 51. **d** 53 **p** 54. C Cam St Mary Less *Ely* 53-58; Malta from 58. *Address temp unknown*

BAGNALL, Harry. b 30. OBE82. S'wark Ord Course 64. **d** 67 **p** 68. C Goole *Sheff* 67-70; C Doncaster St Leon and St Jude 70-72; C-in-c New Cantley CD 72-79; Falkland Is 79-86; V Hook w Airmyn *Sheff* from 86. *The Vicarage, Church Lane, Hook, Goole, N Humberside DN14 5PN* Goole (0405) 3654

BAGNALL, Canon John Thomas. b 12. Leeds Univ BA34. Coll of Resurr Mirfield 34. **d** 36 **p** 37. V Bournemouth St Luke *Win* 71-79; rtd 79; Perm to Offic *Win* from 80. *57A Wentworth Avenue, Bournemouth BH5 2EH* Bournemouth (0202) 422356

BAGNALL, Roger. b 15. St Edm Hall Ox BA37 MA41. Linc Th Coll 37. **d** 39 **p** 40. V Ticknall *Derby* 66-84; RD Melbourne 68-78; P-in-c Stanton-by-Bridge and Swarkestone 80-84; V Ticknall, Smisby and Stanton by Bridge 84-86; rtd 86. *4 Westfield Rise, Withernsea, N Humberside HU19 2NS* Withernsea (0964) 613305

BAGOTT, Paul Andrew. b 61. Leeds Univ BA85. Westcott Ho Cam 86. **d** 88 **p** 89. C Chingford SS Pet and Paul *Chelmsf* 88-91; C Westmr St Sav and St Jas Less *Lon* from 91. *4 Brunswick Court, Regency Street, London*

BAGOTT, Robert Blakeway. b 25. St Aid Birkenhead 51. **d** 54 **p** 55. R Luton Ch Ch *Roch* 66-77; Chapl All SS Hosp Chatham 70-77; R Dowlishwake w Chaffcombe, Knowle St Giles etc *B & W* 77-82; R E w W Harptree and Hinton Blewett 82-90; Co-ord Retirement Officer from 89; rtd 90. *12 Hawkers Lane, Wells, Somerset BA5 3JL* Wells (0749) 74086

BAGSHAW, Paul Stanley. b 55. Selw Coll Cam BA78. N Ord Course 85. **d** 88 **p** 89. Ind Missr *Sheff* 86-90; C Handsworth Woodhouse 88-90; NSM from 91. *63 Station Road, Woodhouse, Sheffield S13 7RA* Sheffield (0742) 696878

BAGSHAWE, John Allen. b 45. Dur Univ BA70 DipTh71. Cranmer Hall Dur 67. **d** 71 **p** 72. C Bridlington Priory *York* 71-75; C N Ferriby 75-79; V Kingston upon Hull St Matt w St Barn from 79. *St Matthew's Vicarage, Boulevard, Hull HU3 2TA* Hull (0482) 26573

BAGULEY, Henry. b 23. Qu Coll Birm 55. **d** 58 **p** 59. V Kelsall *Ches* 61-75; V New Brighton St Jas 75-88; rtd 88. *The Meadows, Nantwich Road, Whitchurch, Shropshire SY13 4AA* Whitchurch (0948) 2692

BAILES, Kenneth. b 35. Dur Univ BA69 DipTh71 DPhil. **d** 71 **p** 72. C Redcar *York* 71-73; TV Redcar w Kirkleatham 73-74; P-in-c Appleton Roebuck w Acaster Selby 74-80; P-in-c Sutton on the Forest 80-82; R Stamford Bridge Gp of Par 82-90; V Healaugh w Wighill, Bilbrough and Askham Richard from 90. *The Rectory, Back Lane, Bilbrough, York YO23 PL* Tadcaster (0937) 833527

BAILEY, Adrian Richard. b 57. St Jo Coll Dur 89. **d** 91. C Oswestry St Oswald *Lich* from 91. *5 High Lea Close, Oswestry, Shropshire SY11 1SX* Oswestry (0691) 662125

BAILEY, Alan George. b 09. Qu Coll Cam BA39 MA43. Linc Th Coll 39. **d** 40 **p** 41. R Gt Mongeham *Cant* 55-60; R Ripple 56-60; rtd 61. *3 Glitter Bay Terrace, St James, Barbados*

BAILEY, Alan George. b 40. Ripon Hall Ox 62. **d** 64 **p** 65. C Formby H Trin *Liv* 64-67; C Upholland 67-70; P-in-c Edge Hill St Dunstan 70-74; V 74-81; RD Toxteth 78-81;

Perm to Offic 81-83; Asst Chapl Liv Cathl 83-85; C Liv Our Lady and St Nic w St Anne 85-89; V Waddington *Bradf* from 89. *The Vicarage, Waddington, Clitheroe, Lancs BB7 3JQ* Clitheroe (0200) 23589

BAILEY, Andrew Henley. b 57. AKC78. Sarum & Wells Th Coll 79. **d** 80 **p** 81. C Romsey *Win* 80-83; V Bournemouth St Alb from 83. *St Alban's Vicarage, 17 Linwood Road, Bournemouth BH9 1DW* Bournemouth (0202) 534193

BAILEY, Andrew John. b 37. Trin Coll Cam BA61 MA. Ridley Hall Cam 60. **d** 63 **p** 64. C Drypool *York* 63-66; C Melton Mowbray w Thorpe Arnold *Leic* 66-69; C-in-c Skelmersdale Ecum Cen *Liv* 69-79; V Langley Mill *Derby* 79-90; V Gt Faringdon w Lt Coxwell *Ox* from 90. *The Vicarage, Coach Lane, Faringdon, Oxon SN7 8AB* Faringdon (0367) 240106

BAILEY, Ms Angela. b 61. Kent Univ BA82. Qu Coll Birm 83. **dss** 85 **d** 87. Reculver and Herne Bay St Bart *Cant* 85-87; Par Dn 87-88; Asst Chapl Hull Univ *York* from 88. *39 Welbeck Street, Princes Avenue, Hull HU5 3SA* Hull (0482) 472677

BAILEY, Anthony. b 27. Univ of Wales (Lamp) BA51. Ely Th Coll 51. **d** 53 **p** 54. C Barkingside H Trin *Chelmsf* 53-55; Chapl W Buckland Sch Barnstaple 55-59; R Machen *Mon* 59-66; Min Can Bris Cathl *Bris* 66-84; Chapl Bris Cathl Sch 66-84; Succ Bris Cathl *Bris* 68-82; P-in-c Maenclochog w Henry's Moat and Mynachlogddu etc *St D* 83-90; V from 90. *The Village Stores, Charing Cross, Llangolman, Clunderwen, Dyfed SA66 7XN* Maenclochog (09913) 430

BAILEY, Bertram Arthur. b 20. Tyndale Hall Bris 65. **d** 67 **p** 68. C Bath St Luke *B & W* 67-72; C Bickenhill w Elmdon *Birm* 72-73; R N Tawton *Ex* 73-79; R N Tawton and Bondleigh 79-87; rtd 87; Perm to Offic *B & W* 87-89; Clergy Retirement and Widows' Officer from 89. *4 Uphill Road South, Uphill, Weston-super-Mare, Avon BS23 4SD* Weston-super-Mare (0934) 33552

BAILEY, Brian Constable. b 36. AKC62. **d** 63 **p** 64. C Mill Hill Jo Keble Ch *Lon* 63-66; C Gt Stanmore 66-69; C Gt Marlow *Ox* 69-72; R Burghfield 72-81; R Wokingham All SS from 81. *All Saints' Rectory, Wiltshire Road, Wokingham, Berks RG11 1TP* Wokingham (0734) 792999

BAILEY, David Charles. b 52. Linc Coll Ox BA75 MA78 MSc77. St Jo Coll Nottm BA79. **d** 80 **p** 81. C Worksop St Jo *S'well* 80-83; C Edgware *Lon* 83-87; V S Cave and Ellerker w Broomfleet *York* from 87; RD Howden from 91. *The Vicarage, 10 Station Road, South Cave, Brough, N Humberside HU15 2AA* Howden (0430) 423693

BAILEY, Dennis. b 53. Man Univ BEd74 BMus74. St Jo Coll Nottm BTh79. **d** 79 **p** 80. C Netherley Ch Ch CD *Liv* 79-83; S Africa from 83. *PO Box 11469, Dorpspruit, 3206 South Africa* Pietermaritzburg (331) 34479

BAILEY, Derek Gilbert. b 42. Div Hostel Dub 65. **d** 68 **p** 69. C Cork St Luke w St Ann *C, C & R* 68-72; CF from 72. *c/o MOD (Army), Bagshot Park, Bagshot, Surrey GU19 5PL* Bagshot (0276) 71717

BAILEY, Derek William. b 39. Lon Univ DipTh64. Cranmer Hall Dur 64. **d** 67 **p** 68. C Sutton *Liv* 67-69; C Chapel-en-le-Frith *Derby* 69-73; V Hadfield 73-90; R Collyhurst *Man* from 90. *The Rectory, Eggington Street, Collyhurst, Manchester M10 7RN* 061-205 2808

BAILEY, Canon Dr Edward Ian. b 35. CCC Cam BA59 MA63 Bris Univ MA69 PhD77. United Th Coll Bangalore 59 Westcott Ho Cam 61. **d** 63 **p** 64. C Newc St Jo *Newc* 63-65; Asst Chapl Marlborough Coll Wilts 65-68; Perm to Offic *Bris* 69-70; R Winterbourne from 70; P-in-c Winterbourne Down 75-81; RD Stapleton 77-83; Hon Can Bris Cathl from 84. *The Rectory, 58 High Street, Winterbourne, Bristol BS17 1JQ* Winterbourne (0454) 772131

BAILEY, Edward Peter. b 35. Qu Coll Birm. **d** 62 **p** 63. C Ordsall *S'well* 62-66; C Clifton w Glapton 66-71; V Lady Bay 71-83; Relig Affairs Adv to Radio Trent 83-85; C Gedling 86-89; C Bilborough St Jo from 89. *48 Longridge Road, Nottingham NG5 4LA* Nottingham (0602) 200580

BAILEY, Eric Arthur. b 14. AKC37. **d** 37 **p** 38. V Stonegate *Chich* 65-79; rtd 79; Perm to Offic *St E* 81-88. *Hill End, Sapiston, Bury St Edmunds, Suffolk IP31 1RR* Honington (03596) 638

BAILEY, Frederick Hugh. b 18. Keble Coll Ox BA40. Linc Th Coll 40. **d** 42 **p** 43. Chapl Rauceby Hosp Lincs from 49; R Quarrington w Old Sleaford Linc 49-84; R Silk Willoughby 57-84; rtd 84. *1 Willow Close, Scopwick, Lincoln LN4 3PJ* Lincoln (0522) 21127

BAILEY, Harold Edward. b 07. ARICS29 FRICS43. Bps' Coll Cheshunt 65. **d** 66 **p** 67. C Hazlemere *Ox* 67-71; rtd 71; Hon C Friern Barnet St Jas *Lon* 71-74; Perm to

Offic *Win* from 75. *11 Seaway, Milford Road, New Milton, Hants* New Milton (0425) 617015

BAILEY, Canon Ivan John. b 33. Keble Coll Ox BA57 DipTh58 MA65. St Steph Ho Ox. **d** 59 **p** 60. C Ipswich All Hallows *St E* 59-62; Clerical Sec CEMS 62-66; V Cringleford *Nor* 66-81; RD Humbleyard 73-81; R Colney 80-81; Relig Adv Anglia TV 81-91; Bp's Chapl for TV and Broadcasting *Nor* from 81; P-in-c Kirby Bedon w Bixley and Whitlingham from 81; Hon Can Nor Cathl from 84. *21 Cranleigh Rise, Norwich NR4 6PQ* Norwich (0603) 53565

BAILEY, John Ernest. b 32. Leeds Univ BA57. Coll of Resurr Mirfield. **d** 59 **p** 60. C Newbury St Nic *Ox* 59-62; Australia 62-63; V Uffington w Woolstone and Baulking *Ox* 63-70; P-in-c Gt w Lt Oakley *Pet* 70-72; Chapl Cen Hosp Warw from 72; Chapl Cen, Weston Hosp from 82; Abbeyfields Hosp 82-90. *Warwick Central Hospital, Hatton, Warwick CV35 7EE* Warwick (0926) 496241

BAILEY, John Robert. b 40. St Jo Coll Cam BA62 MA66 Nottm Univ MEd77. S'wark Ord Course 68. **d** 69 **p** 70. NSM Plumstead Wm Temple Ch Abbey Wood CD *S'wark* 69-70; Lon Sec Chr Educn Movement 69-71; NSM Markyate Street *St Alb* 70-71; RE Adv *Linc* 72-80; Perm to Offic Man 80-83; St Alb from 84. *12 Farrell Road, Wootton, Bedford MK43 9DU*

BAILEY, Ven Jonathan Sansbury. b 40. Trin Coll Cam BA61 MA65. Ridley Hall Cam 62. **d** 65 **p** 66. C Sutton *Liv* 65-68; C Warrington St Paul 68-71; Warden Marrick Priory *Ripon* 71-76; V Wetherby 76-82; Adn Southend *Chelmsf* from 82. *136 Broomfield Road, Chelmsford CM1 1RN* Chelmsford (0245) 258257

BAILEY, Joyce Mary Josephine. b 33. St Gabr Coll Lon CertEd69 DipRS83. S'wark Ord Course 80. **dss** 83 **d** 87. Par Dn Woolwich St Mary w St Mich *S'wark* 87-89; Par Dn Rusthall *Roch* from 89. *6 Ashley Gardens, Rusthall, Tunbridge Wells, Kent TN4 8TY* Tunbridge Wells (0892) 512587

BAILEY, Mark David. b 62. Ripon Coll Cuddesdon 87. **d** 90 **p** 91. C Leigh Park *Portsm* from 90. *13 Rider's Lane, Leigh Park, Havant, Hants PO9 4QS* Portsmouth (0705) 475746

BAILEY, Mark Robert. b 60. Trin Coll Bris BA89. **d** 89 **p** 90. C Heigham H Trin *Nor* from 89. *14 Trinity Street, Norwich NR2 2BQ* Norwich (0603) 614231

BAILEY, Martin Tristram. b 57. BA79. Oak Hill Th Coll DipHE91. **d** 91. C Brundall w Braydeston and Postwick *Nor* from 91. *8 Greenacre Close, Brundall, Norwich NR13 5QF* Norwich (0603) 714570

BAILEY, Nicholas Andrew. b 55. Nottm Univ CertEd80 Open Univ BA84. Ripon Coll Cuddesdon. **d** 90 **p** 91. C Guisborough *York* from 90. *16 Lealholm Way, Guisborough, Cleveland TS14 8LN* Guisborough (0287) 635873

BAILEY, Norman Gerald. b 25. **d** 83 **p** 84. Hon C Kingswood *Bris* 83-90; Hon C E Bris from 90. *71 Lincombe Road, Bristol BS16 5LL* Bristol (0272) 572822

BAILEY, Peter Robin. b 43. St Jo Coll Dur BA64. Trin Coll Bris 74. **d** 74 **p** 75. C Corby St Columba *Pet* 74-77; C Bishopsworth *Bris* 77-82; V Sea Mills from 82; RD Westbury and Severnside from 91. *St Edyth's Vicarage, Avon Leaze, Bristol BS9 2HV* Bristol (0272) 681912

BAILEY, Richard William. b 38. Man Univ BSc59. Ripon Hall Ox 63. **d** 65 **p** 66. C Tonge *Man* 65-68; C Stretford St Matt 68-71; R Abbey Hey 71-80; V E Crompton 80-86; V Chadderton St Matt from 86. *St Matthew's Vicarage, Mill Brow, Chadderton, Oldham OL1 2RT* 061-624 8600

BAILEY, Richard William. b 47. All Nations Chr Coll DBMS75 Oak Hill Th Coll BA84. **d** 84 **p** 85. C Huyton St Geo *Liv* 84-87; V Wombridge *Lich* from 87. *Wombridge Vicarage, Wombridge Road, Telford, Shropshire TF2 6HT* Telford (0952) 613334

BAILEY, Robert William. b 49. Lich Th Coll 69. **d** 72 **p** 73. C Stoke *Cov* 72-75; Chapl RAF from 75. *c/o MOD, Adastral House, Theobald's Road, London WC1X 8RU* 071-430 7268

BAILEY, Canon Ronald George Bainton. b 07. Trin Coll Cam BA28 MA37. Wycliffe Hall Ox 30. **d** 32 **p** 33. V Wray w Tatham Fells *Blackb* 69-73; rtd 73; Perm to Offic Guildf from 81; Portsm from 86. *Flat 20, Manormead, Tilford Road, Hindhead, Surrey GU26 6RA* Hindhead (0428) 607151

BAILEY, Ronald William. b 12. Linc Coll Ox BA35 BSc36 MA45. Ripon Hall Ox 57. **d** 58 **p** 59. V Lamberhurst *Roch* 61-77; rtd 77. *Tamarisk, Wagg Drove, Huish Episcopi, Langport, Somerset TA10 9ER* Langport (0458) 250103

BAILEY, Simon. b 56. Man Univ MusB Nottm Univ BCombStuds. Linc Th Coll. **d** 83 **p** 84. C St Bart Armley w St Mary New Wortley *Ripon* 83-86; C Harrogate St Wilfrid and St Luke 86-90; R Harby, Long Clawson and Hose *Leic* from 90. *The Rectory, Harby, Melton Mowbray, Leics LE14 4BA* Harby (0949) 60269

BAILEY, Simon Paul. b 55. Ox Univ BA77 MA81 Em Coll Cam BA80 MA. Westcott Ho Cam 78. **d** 81 **p** 82. C Norton *Sheff* 81-85; R Dinnington from 85. *The Rectory, 217 Nursery Road, Dinnington, Sheffield S31 7QU* Dinnington (0909) 562335

BAILEY, Stephen. b 39. Leic Univ BA61. Clifton Th Coll 61. **d** 62 **p** 63. C Wellington w Eyton *Lich* 62-66; C Rainham *Chelmsf* 66-69; V Ercall Magna *Lich* 69-75; V Rowton 69-75; RD Wrockwardine 72-75; V W Bromwich Gd Shep w St Jo 75-83; P-in-c W Bromwich St Phil 80-81; V 81-83; R Chadwell *Chelmsf* from 83; Area Warden Ords Brentwood, Basildon & Thurrock from 91. *The Rectory, Rigby Gardens, Grays, Essex RM16 4JJ* Tilbury (0375) 2176

BAILEY, Stephen John. b 57. NE Surrey Coll of Tech HNC78. Sarum & Wells Th Coll 88. **d** 90 **p** 91. C Redhill H Trin *S'wark* from 90. *3 Ringwood Avenue, Redhill, Surrey RH1 2DY* Redhill (0737) 762593

BAILLIE, Alistair Hope Pattison. b 50. Loughb Univ BSc73 Ox Univ DipTh. Ripon Coll Cuddesdon 73. **d** 76 **p** 77. C Aylestone *Leic* 76-79; C Leic All SS 79-82; C Leic H Spirit 82-83; TV Heavitree w Ex St Paul *Ex* 83-84; C 84-86; Asst Chapl N Gen Hosp Sheff 86-88; C Sheff St Cuth *Sheff* 86-88; Chapl Broadgreen Hosp Liv from 88. *Broadgreen Hospital, Thomas Drive, Liverpool L14 3LB* 051-228 4878

BAILLIE, Canon Frederick Alexander. b 21. FRGS Open Univ BA75 QUB MA86 PhD87. CITC 53. **d** 55 **p** 56. I Belf Whiterock *Conn* 69-74; Hd of S Ch Miss Ballymacarrett 74-79; I Magheraculmoney *Clogh* 79-87; Dioc Info Officer 80-86; RD Kesh 85-87; Can Clogh Cathl 85-87; rtd 87. *2 St Elizabeth's Court, Ballyregan Road, Dundonald, Belfast BT16 0HX* Belfast (0232) 487642

BAILLIE, Iain Robert Cullen. b 28. St Pet Hall Ox BA54 MA58. Wycliffe Hall Ox 54. **d** 56 **p** 57. C Penge Lane H Trin *Roch* 56-58; CF 58-83. *8 The Precincts, Canterbury, Kent CT1 2EE* Canterbury (0227) 768206

BAILLIE, John Launcelot. b 16. AKC47. **d** 47 **p** 48. V Milborne St Andrew w Dewlish *Sarum* 59-70; Peru 70-74; V Felkirk w Brierley *Wakef* 75-79; R Orford w Sudbourne, Chillesford, Butley and Iken *St E* 79-82; rtd 82; Perm to Offic *St E* from 82. *Long Walk, 99 Abbey Road, Leiston, Suffolk IP16 4TA* Leiston (0728) 830365

BAILLIE, Terence John. b 46. New Coll Ox BA69 MA78 Man Univ MSc72. St Jo Coll Nottm 74. **d** 77 **p** 78. C Chadwell *Chelmsf* 77-80; C Bickenhill w Elmdon *Birm* 80-84; V Bedminster St Mich *Bris* from 84. *St Michael's Vicarage, 153 St John's Lane, Bedminster, Bristol BS3 5AE* Bristol (0272) 776132

BAILY, Canon Robert Spencer Canning. b 21. G&C Coll Cam BA42 MA46. Westcott Ho Cam 42. **d** 44 **p** 45. P-in-c Perlethorpe *S'well* 69-87; Dir of Educn 69-87; Hon Can S'well Minster from 80; rtd 87. *17 Ravendale Close, Grantham, Lincs NG31 8BS* Grantham (0476) 68614

BAILY, Rodney Alexander. b 39. Bris Univ LLB61. Westcott Ho Cam 76. **d** 78 **p** 79. C Monkseaton St Mary *Newc* 78-81; C Hexham 81-83; TV Cullercoats St Geo from 83. *The Vicarage, Billy Mill Lane, North Shields, Tyne & Wear NE29 8BZ* 091-257 3616

BAIN, Alan. b 48. Thames Poly BSc72. St Jo Coll Nottm DipTh75. **d** 77 **p** 78. C Wakef St Andr and St Mary *Wakef* 77-81; V Bath Odd Down *B & W* 81-82; P-in-c Combe Hay 81-82; V Bath Odd Down w Combe Hay from 82. *The Vicarage, 39 Frome Road, Bath BA2 2QF* Combe Down (0225) 832838

BAIN, Andrew John. b 55. Newc Poly BA77 Edin Univ MTh. Edin Th Coll 86. **d** 88 **p** 89. Chapl St Mary's Cathl *Edin* from 88; C Edin St Mary from 88. *9 Torphichen Street, Edinburgh EH3 8HX* 031-229 2303

BAIN, David Roualeyn Findlater. b 54. Bris Univ BA75. Ripon Coll Cuddesdon 76. **d** 78 **p** 79. C Perry Hill St Geo *S'wark* 78-81; Chapl Asst Guy's Hosp Lon 81-84; Succ S'wark Cathl *S'wark* 81-84; V Streatham St Paul 84-90. *285 North Street, Bedminster, Bristol BS3 1JP* Bristol (0272) 636490

BAIN, John Stuart. b 55. Van Mildert Coll Dur BA77. Westcott Ho Cam 78. **d** 80 **p** 81. C Washington *Dur* 80-84; C Dunston 84-86; V Shiney Row from 86; V Herrington from 86. *The Vicarage, Shiney Row, Houghton le Spring, Tyne & Wear DH4 4JU* 091-385 7271

BAINBRIDGE, David George. b 42. Wadh Coll Ox BA63 MA67 Lon Univ CertEd67. Ridley Hall Cam 84. **d** 86 **p** 87. C Downend *Bris* 86-90; TV Yate New Town from 90. *The Vicarage, 57 Brockworth, Yate, Bristol BS17 4SJ* Chipping Sodbury (0454) 322921

BAINBRIDGE, Mrs Jean Waite. b 29. ALA54 Birm Univ BA77 DipL&A79. Qu Coll Birm 78. **dss** 79 **d** 87. Worc St Barn w Ch Ch *Worc* 79-82; Catshill and Dodford 82-87; Par Dn 87-90; rtd 90; Hon Par Dn Hallow *Worc* from 90. *18 Beaconshill Drive, Worcester WR2 6DR* Worcester (0905) 748593

BAINBRIDGE, John Richard. b 35. Pemb Coll Cam BA59 MA63. Clifton Th Coll 65. **d** 67 **p** 68. C Ex St Leon w H Trin *Ex* 67-70; P-in-c Penge St Paul *Roch* 70-73; Chapl Uppingham Sch Leics 73-87; Lic to Offic *Pet* 73-87; V Stevenage St Nic *St Alb* from 87. *St Nicholas House, 2A North Road, Stevenage, Herts SG1 4AT* Stevenage (0438) 354355

BAINBRIDGE, Norman Harold. b 15. St Jo Coll Dur LTh38. ALCD38. **d** 38 **p** 39. V Boscombe St Jo *Win* 66-80; rtd 80; Perm to Offic *Sarum & Win* from 81. *Churchmead, Chapel Street, Milborne St Andrew, Blandford Forum, Dorset DT11 0JP* Milborne St Andrew (025887) 601

BAINES, Bernard Frederick. b 20. JP. ACP BA. St Jo Coll Nottm 83. **d** 84 **p** 85. NSM Nottm All SS *S'well* 84-90; rtd 90; Perm to Offic *S'well* from 90. *18 Forest Road East, Nottingham NG1 4HH* Nottingham (0602) 784191

BAINES, John Edmund. b 22. Down Coll Cam BA47 MA50 Lon Univ BD51. New Coll Lon. **d** 58 **p** 59. V Cawthorne *Wakef* 69-89; rtd 89. *3 Huskar Close, Silkstone, Barnsley, S Yorkshire S75 4SX* Barnsley (0226) 791088

BAINES, Nicholas. b 57. Bradf Univ BA80. Trin Coll Bris BA87. **d** 87 **p** 88. C Kendal St Thos *Carl* 87-91; C Leic H Trin w St Jo *Leic* from 91. *15 Northcote Road, Leicester LE2 3FH* Leicester (0533) 703135

BAINES, Noel Edward. b 29. St Jo Coll Dur BSc52 DipTh54 MA62. **d** 54 **p** 55. C Rainham *Chelmsf* 54-58; C Surbiton Hill Ch Ch *S'wark* 58-61; V Southborough St Matt *Roch* 61-67; V Beckenham St Jo 67-74; Hd RE Taunton Manor High Sch Caterham 74-83; Perm to Offic *Roch* 74-90; Keston Coll 85-91; Hon C Bromley Ch Ch *Roch* from 90. *10 Bromley Avenue, Bromley BR1 4BQ* 081-460 8256

BAINES, Canon Roger Holford. b 07. St Jo Coll Cam BA29 MA32. Westcott Ho Cam 29. **d** 30 **p** 31. V High Harrogate St Pet *Ripon* 47-66; Lic to Offic *Heref* from 68; rtd 72. *Barn House, Ashford Bowdler, Ludlow, Shropshire SY8 4DJ* Richards Castle (058474) 602

BAIRD, Dr Edward Simpson. b 17. Lon Univ BD58 MLitt65 DLitt68 Newc Univ 62. Yorkshire United Th Coll 42 Selly Oak Coll 47 Sarum Th Coll 54. **d** 55 **p** 56. R Harrington *Carl* 66-75; V Barton w Peel Green *Man* 75-80; R Jarrow Grange *Dur* 80-83; rtd 83. *5 Hemsley Road, South Shields, Tyne & Wear N34 6HW* 091-456 1389

BAIRD, Paul Drummond. b 48. Newc Univ CertEd71 Open Univ BA85. Ripon Coll Cuddesdon 88. **d** 90 **p** 91. C Chandler's Ford *Win* from 90. *Belmont House, 105 Belmont Road, Chandler's Ford, Hants SO5 3FL* Chandler's Ford (0703) 261420

BAIRD, Robert Douglas. b 21. ERD56. Cam Univ MA64. Ripon Coll Cuddesdon. **d** 85 **p** 86. NSM Charlbury w Shorthampton *Ox* 85-87; Asst Chapl HM Pris Grendon and Spring Hill 85; Lic to Offic *Ox* from 87. *Glebe House, Ibstone, High Wycombe, Bucks HP14 3XZ* Turville Heath (049163) 642

BAIRD, Canon William Stanley. b 33. TCD BA54 Div Test. **d** 56 **p** 57. C Carlow *C & O* 56-59; I Dunganstown *D & G* 59-64; C Knock *D & D* 64-69; P-in-c Kilwarlin Upper w Kilwarlin Lower 69-71; I 71-72; Warden Ch Min of Healing (Ireland) 72-79; I Dub Drumcondra w N Strand *D & G* 79-91; Dir of Ords (Dub) from 84; Can Ch Ch Cathl Dub from 88; I Swords w Donabate and Kilsallaghan from 91. *The Rectory, Swords, Co Dublin, Irish Republic* Dublin (1) 402308

BAISLEY, Mrs Barbara Pauline. b 47. DipAD69. S Dios Minl Tr Scheme 79. **dss** 82 **d** 87. Glouc St Geo w Whaddon *Glouc* 82-83; Welford w Weston and Clifford Chambers 83-87; Chapl Warw Univ *Cov* from 87; Dioc Adv for Women's Min from 90. *92 De Monfort Way, Coventry CV4 7DT* Coventry (0203) 411854 or 523523

BAISLEY, George. b 45. Sarum & Wells Th Coll 78. **d** 80 **p** 81. C Glouc St Geo w Whaddon *Glouc* 80-83; R Welford w Weston and Clifford Chambers 83-87; Chapl Myton Hamlet Hospice from 87; Chapl Warw Univ *Cov* from 87. *92 De Montfort Way, Coventry CV4 7DT* Coventry (0203) 411854

BAKER, Albert George. b 30. Qu Coll Birm. **d** 61 **p** 62. C Mert St Mary *S'wark* 61-64; C Limpsfield and Titsey 64-65; C Chapel-en-le-Frith *Derby* 65-68; R Odd Rode *Ches* 68-76; V Holme Cultram St Mary *Carl* 76-78; R Blofield w Hemblington *Nor* from 78. *The Rectory, Oak Wood, Blofield, Norwich NR13 4JQ* Norwich (0603) 713160

BAKER, Angela. b 42. **d** 91. Par Dn Battersea St Sav and St Geo w St Andr *S'wark* from 91. *St George's Vicarage, Patmore Street, London SW8 4JD* 071-622 4244

BAKER, Miss Anne-Marie Clare. b 56. Wye Coll Lon BSc78 Glas Univ MSc80. St Jo Coll Nottm 88. **d** 90. Par Dn Levenshulme St Pet *Man* from 90. *5 Preston Road, Levenshulme, Manchester M19 2ER* 061-224 9800

BAKER, Anthony Peter. b 38. Hertf Coll Ox BA59 MA63. Clifton Th Coll 60. **d** 63 **p** 64. C Ox St Ebbe w St Pet *Ox* 63-66; C Welling *Roch* 66-70; V Redland *Bris* 70-79; Lect Tyndale Hall *Bris* 70-71; Trin Coll Bris 71-77; V Beckenham Ch Ch *Roch* from 79; Chapl Beckenham Hosp from 79. *Christ Church Vicarage, 18 Court Downs Road, Beckenham, Kent BR3 2LR* 081-650 3847

BAKER, Miss Barbara Ann. b 36. Linc Th Coll 85. **d** 87. Par Dn Hornchurch St Andr *Chelmsf* from 87. *St Matthew's Bungalow, 55A Chelmsford Drive, Upminster, Essex RM14 2PH* Hornchurch (04024) 52705

BAKER, Canon Bernard George Coleman. b 36. Lon Univ BD61. Oak Hill Th Coll 61. **d** 63 **p** 64. C Broadwater St Mary *Chich* 63-66; Tanzania 66-84; Hon Can Morogoro from 77; C-in-c Ryde St Jas Prop Chpl *Portsm* from 84. *77 Argyll Street, Ryde, Isle of Wight PO33 3BY* Isle of Wight (0983) 64893

BAKER, Brian Ernest Harry. b 38. Sarum & Wells Th Coll 74. **d** 76 **p** 77. C Cannock *Lich* 76-79; C Penkridge w Stretton 79-80; C Dunston w Coppenhall 79-80; P-in-c Earl Stonham w Stonham Parva and Creeting St Pet *St E* 80-89; V Staincliffe *Wakef* from 89. *The Vicarage, Staincliffe Hall Road, Batley, W Yorkshire WF17 7QX* Batley (0924) 473343

BAKER, Charles Edward. b 47. **d** 87 **p** 88. NSM Dub Clontarf *D & G* 87-90; NSM Delgany from 90. *12 Aranleigh Vale, Rathfarnham, Dublin 14, Irish Republic* Dublin (1) 946465

BAKER, Christopher James. b 54. MRAeS83 MICE83 CEng83 St Cath Coll Cam BA75 MA78 PhD78. E Midl Min Tr Course 85. **d** 88 **p** 89. NSM Matlock Bath *Derby* from 88. *31 Clifton Road, Matlock Bath, Derbyshire DE4 3PW* Matlock (0629) 582500

BAKER, Christopher Richard. b 61. Man Univ BA83. Sarum & Wells Th Coll 86. **d** 89. C Dulwich St Barn *S'wark* from 89. *11 Hinckley Road, London SE15 4HZ* 071-732 8983

BAKER, David Clive. b 47. Sarum & Wells Th Coll 76. **d** 78 **p** 79. C Shirley *Birm* 78-82; P-in-c Croft *Linc* 82-83; R Wainfleet All SS w St Thos 82-83; P-in-c Wainfleet St Mary 82-83; R The Wainfleets and Croft 83-86; V Stirchley *Birm* from 86. *The Vicarage, 95 Cartland Road, Birmingham B30 2SD* 021-458 3082

BAKER, David Frederick. b 32. Clifton Th Coll 67. **d** 69 **p** 70. C Bilton *Ripon* 69-71; C Heworth w Peasholme St Cuth *York* 71-75; V Sand Hutton w Gate and Upper Helmsley 75-77; P-in-c Bossall w Buttercrambe 75-77; V Sand Hutton 77-80; R Preston in Holderness 80; P-in-c Sproatley 80; R Preston and Sproatley in Holderness 80-89; C Topcliffe w Dalton and Dishforth 89; V Baldersby w Dalton, Dishforth etc from 89. *The New Vicarage, Baldersby St James, Thirsk, N Yorkshire YO7 4PT* Melmerby (076584) 471

BAKER, David James. b 40. Univ of Wales (Lamp) BA62 Linacre Coll Ox BA64 MA68. St Steph Ho Ox 62. **d** 65 **p** 66. C Newc St Jo *Newc* 65-69; C Leigh St Clem *Chelmsf* 69-73; Lic to Offic *Nor* 73-78; V Kingston upon Hull St Alb *York* 78-86; V Goodmayes St Paul *Chelmsf* from 87. *St Paul's Vicarage, 20 Eastwood Road, Goodmayes, Ilford, Essex IG3 8XA* 081-590 6596

BAKER, David John. b 27. LRAM50 GRSM51. Ely Th Coll 53. **d** 55 **p** 56. C Swanley St Mary *Roch* 55-58; C Guildf St Nic *Guildf* 58-63; Prec St Alb Abbey *St Alb* 63-67; P-in-c Colney St Pet 67-68; V 68-73; V Tattenham Corner and Burgh Heath *Guildf* 73-84; R Fetcham from 84. *Fetcham Rectory, 10A The Ridgeway, Leatherhead, Surrey KT22 9AZ* Leatherhead (0372) 372598

BAKER, David Jordan. b 35. Univ of Wales (Lamp) BA59. Ely Th Coll 59. **d** 61 **p** 62. C Spalding *Linc* 61-66; C Gainsborough All SS 66-69; V Wrawby 69-78; V Melton Ross w New Barnetby 70-78; V Linc St Pet-at-Gowts and St Andr from 78. *St Peter-at-Gowts' Vicarage,*

Sibthorp Street, Lincoln LN5 7SP Lincoln (0522) 530256

BAKER, Donald Alex. b 08. K Coll Lon 54. **d** 59 **p** 59. R Burstow *S'wark* 62-73; rtd 73; Perm to Offic *S'wark* from 83. *1 Westview, Peeks Brook Lane, Horley, Surrey RH6 9ST* Horley (0293) 771109

BAKER, Donald Shearsmith. b 09. TD46. St Aug Coll Cant 57. **d** 59 **p** 60. R Emley *Wakef* 63-75; rtd 75; Chapl Shoreham Coll 80-85 and from 90. *8 Montague Court, Rectory Road, Shoreham-by-Sea, W Sussex BN43 6EL* Brighton (0273) 595979

BAKER, Douglas Arthur. b 17. Lon Univ DipTh42. St Andr Coll Pampisford 49. **d** 49 **p** 50. V Hooton Pagnell *Sheff* 67-72; P-in-c Hickleton 71-72; R Kirby Underdale w Bugthorpe *York* 72-80; RD Pocklington 76-80; R Normanby w Edston and Salton 80-82; Perm to Offic Roch 82-90; Chich from 90. *21 Lychgates Close, Bexhill-on-Sea, E Sussex TN40 2EW* Bexhill-on-Sea (0424) 215124

BAKER, Elsie. b 13. dss 38 **d** 87. Blackheath Ascension *S'wark* 68-83; Hon Par Dn Lewisham St Swithun from 87. *24 Princes Rise, London SE13 7PP* 081-852 2169

BAKER, Frank Thomas. b 36. Selw Coll Cam BA61. Coll of Resurr Mirfield. **d** 63 **p** 64. C Leeds St Pet *Ripon* 66-73; P-in-c Stanley *Dur* 73-74; R Crook 73-74; Chapl Bucharest *Eur* 74-75; C Tewkesbury w Walton Cardiff *Glouc* 75-81; Min Can Windsor 81-86; rtd 86; Perm to Offic *Ox* from 86. *4 Riverway, Barry Avenue, Windsor, Berks* Newton Abbot (0626) 5444

BAKER, Frederick Leonard. b 06. K Coll Lon 58. **d** 59 **p** 60. R Heyford Warren and Lower Heyford w Rousham *Ox* 69-75; rtd 75; Perm to Offic *Ex* from 76. *42 Ridgeway Road, Aller Park, Newton Abbot, Devon TQ12 4LS* Newton Abbot (0626) 5444

BAKER, Frederick Peter. b 24. Bps' Coll Cheshunt 58. **d** 60 **p** 61. P-in-c Northn St Lawr *Pet* 69-71; V Northn St Edm 71-78; V Spratton 78-83; R Walgrave w Hannington and Wold 83-89; rtd 89. *1A Malvern Close, Bournemouth BH9 3BN* Bournemouth (0202) 512862

BAKER, Geoffrey Gorton. b 26. Chich Th Coll 63. **d** 65 **p** 66. C Jersey St Mark *Win* 65-66; V 66-73; Lic to Offic from 73; Chapl HM Pris Jersey from 80. *Roselle, rue de Haut, St Lawrence, Jersey, Channel Islands* Jersey (0534) 54735

BAKER, Canon Gerald Stothert. b 30. Univ of NZ MA54. St Jo Coll Auckland LTh56. **d** 56 **p** 57. New Zealand 56-87; Hon Can Wellington from 80; TV Kidderminster St Mary and All SS etc *Worc* 87-90; TV Kidderminster St Mary and All SS w Trimpley etc from 90. *St Barnabas's Vicarage, 50 Nursery Grove, Kidderminster, Worcs DY11 5BG* Kidderminster (0562) 748016

BAKER, Very Rev Graham Brinkworth. b 26. AKC54. **d** 55 **p** 56. C Wandsworth St Anne *S'wark* 55-58; Canada from 58. *PO Box 475, Kingston, Ontario, Canada, K7L 4W5*

BAKER, Harry Hallas. b 16. Bps' Coll Cheshunt 51. **d** 53 **p** 54. V Howdon Panns *Newc* 63-73; C Alnwick St Mich 73-74; C Alnwick St Mich and St Paul 74-84; rtd 84. *16 Canongate, Alnwick, Northd NE66 1NE* Alnwick (0665) 604716

BAKER, Henry Blandford Benedict. b 26. Univ of NZ BA49 MA50. Coll of Resurr Mirfield 51. **d** 53 **p** 54. C New Mills *Derby* 53-56; New Zealand 56-57; CSWG 57-66; Father Superior 65-66; Perm to Offic *Chich* 81-86; R Beckington w Standerwick, Berkley, Rodden etc *B & W* from 86. *8 Church Street, Beckington, Bath BA3 6TG* Frome (0373) 830314

BAKER, Henry Edward. b 09. Bris Univ BA31. Sarum Th Coll 31. **d** 32 **p** 33. C Kingswood *Bris* 69-74; rtd 74. *26 Henley Court, Buckingham Gardens, Lichfield, Staffs*

BAKER, Mrs Hilary Mary. b 61. Man Univ BA83 Univ of Wales (Cardiff) CQSW86. Sarum & Wells Th Coll 86. **d** 89. Par Dn E Dulwich St Jo *S'wark* from 89. *11 Hinckley Road, London SE15 4HZ* 071-732 8983

BAKER, Hugh John. b 46. Birm Univ BSocSc68 Nottm Univ DipTh69. Cuddesdon Coll 69. **d** 71 **p** 72. C Binley *Cov* 71-74; C Pemberton St Mark Newtown *Liv* 74-78; TV Sutton 78-90; V Fazeley *Lich* from 90; R Drayton Bassett from 90; V Canwell from 90. *St Paul's Vicarage, 9 West Drive, Bonehill, Tamworth, Staffs B78 3HR* Tamworth (0827) 287701

BAKER, Ivon Robert. b 28. St Aug Coll Cant 59. **d** 60 **p** 61. C Sutton in Ashfield St Mary *S'well* 60-62; V Gringley-on-the-Hill from 62; Chapl HM Young Offender Inst Gringley from 82; RD Bawtry *S'well* 85-90. *The Vicarage, Gringley-on-the-Hill, Doncaster, S Yorkshire DN10 4QP* Retford (0777) 817237

BAKER, James Henry. b 39. Lon Univ DipTh66. Kelham Th Coll 62. **d** 67 **p** 68. C Sheff Arbourthorne *Sheff* 67-70;

C Pemberton St Jo *Liv* 70-71; Chapl and Prec St Mary's Cathl *Edin* 71-74; R Lochgelly *St And* 74-84; P-in-c Rosyth 76-84; P-in-c Inverkeithing 76-84; Can St Ninian's Cathl Perth 83-84; V Whitehaven *Carl* from 84. *The Vicarage, Oakbank, Whitehaven, Cumbria CA28 6HY* Whitehaven (0946) 692630 or 62572

BAKER, Jean Margaret. b 47. Sheff Univ BSc70 DipEd71 Lon Univ DipTh75 BD78. Gilmore Course 81. **dss** 82 **d** 87. Liv Our Lady and St Nic w St Anne *Liv* 82-87; Dn St Mary & St Anne's Sch Abbots Bromley from 87. *St Mary and St Anne's School, Abbots Bromley, Rugeley, Staffs* Burton-on-Trent (0283) 840024

BAKER, John Albert. b 29. St Edm Hall Ox BA52 MA56 Lon Univ BSc68 MSc76. Cuddesdon Coll 52. **d** 54 **p** 55. C Battersea St Luke *S'wark* 54-58; Hon C from 84; C Richmond St Mary 58-62; V Battersea Park All SS 62-83. *44 Wroughton Road, London SW11 6BG* 071-585 2492

✠**BAKER, Rt Rev John Austin.** b 28. Or Coll Ox BA52 MA55 BLitt55 MLitt. Lambeth DD91 Cuddesdon Coll 52. **d** 54 **p** 55 **c** 82. C Cuddesdon *Ox* 54-57; Tutor Cuddesdon Coll 54-57; C Hatch End St Anselm *Lon* 57-59; Lect K Coll Lon 57-59; Chapl CCC Ox 59-73; Lect Th Ox Univ 59-73; Can Westmr Abbey 73-82; Sub-Dean Westmr 78-82; R Westmr St Marg 78-82; Chapl to Speaker of Ho of Commons 78-82; Bp Sarum from 82; Can and Preb Sarum Cathl from 82. *South Canonry, 71 The Close, Salisbury SP1 2ER* Salisbury (0722) 334031

BAKER, John Carl. b 55. Chich Th Coll 77. **d** 80 **p** 81. C Wigan St Andr *Liv* 80-83; V Hollinfare 83-85; TV Seacroft *Ripon* 85-89; TV Bottesford w Ashby *Linc* from 89. *The Vicarage, Bottesford, Scunthorpe DN16 3OL* Scunthorpe (0724) 867256

BAKER, John Reginald. b 62. Hatf Coll Dur BSc83. Wycliffe Hall Ox 86. **d** 89 **p** 90. C Amersham *Ox* from 89. *31 Pigotts End, Amersham, Bucks HP7 0JF* Amersham (0494) 726089

BAKER, Canon Michael Robert Henry. b 39. Keele Univ MA88. Lich Th Coll 63. **d** 66 **p** 67. C Wellingborough All SS *Pet* 66-68; C Pet All SS 68-73; V Earls Barton 73-87; RD Wellingborough 76-87; P-in-c Gt Doddington 77-82; Can Pet Cathl from 85; TR Kingsthorpe w Northn St Dav from 87. *The Rectory, Green End, Kingsthorpe, Northampton NN2 6RD* Northampton (0604) 717133

BAKER, Michael William. b 38. Roch Th Coll 68. **d** 70 **p** 71. C Woodmansterne *S'wark* 70-75; TV Danbury *Chelmsf* 75-78; P-in-c Barrington *Ely* 78-90; V from 90; P-in-c Shepreth 78-90; V from 90. *The Vicarage, 4 Church Road, Shepreth, Royston, Herts SG8 6RG* Royston (0763) 260172

BAKER, Canon Neville Duff. b 35. St Aid Birkenhead 60. **d** 63 **p** 64. C Stranton *Dur* 63-66; C Houghton le Spring 66-68; V Tudhoe Grange from 68; RD Auckland from 83; Hon Can Dur Cathl from 90. *St Andrew's Vicarage, Tudhoe Grange, Spennymoor, Co Durham DL16 6NE* Spennymoor (0388) 814817

BAKER, Noel Edward Lloyd. b 37. Sarum & Wells Th Coll 73. **d** 75 **p** 76. C Charlton Kings St Mary *Glouc* 75-79; V Clearwell 79-81; R Eastington and Frocester from 81; RD Stonehouse from 90. *The Rectory, Mill End Lane, Eastington, Stonehouse, Glos GL10 3SG* Stonehouse (0453) 822437

BAKER, Paul Anthony. b 64. St Chad's Coll Dur BA85. St Steph Ho Ox BA88. **d** 89 **p** 90. C Hartlepool St Aid *Dur* from 89. *St Aidan's Clergy House, St Aidan's Street, Hartlepool, Cleveland TS25 1SN* Hartlepool (0429) 273539

BAKER, Peter Colin. b 43. Sarum & Wells Th Coll. **d** 82 **p** 83. C Bridgemary *Portsm* 82-86; V Ash Vale *Guildf* from 86. *The Vicarage, 203 Vale Road, Ash Vale, Aldershot, Hants GU12 5JE* Aldershot (0252) 25295

BAKER, Peter Graham. b 55. MA PhD. St Steph Ho Ox. **d** 82 **p** 83. C Ches H Trin *Ches* 82-86; C Holborn St Alb w Saffron Hill St Pet *Lon* 86-91; V Golders Green from 91. *The Vicarage, 3 St Alban's Close, North End Road, London NW11 7RA* 081-455 4526

BAKER, Canon Peter Malcolm. b 21. Lich Th Coll 40. **d** 43 **p** 45. CF (TA) 53-75; V Inkberrow *Worc* 67-75; P-in-c Kington w Dormston 74-75; R Inkberrow w Cookhill and Kington w Dormston 75-77; P-in-c Wilden 77-80; R Mamble w Bayton 80-82; RD Stourport 80-88; R Teme Valley N 82-88; Hon Can Worc Cathl 84-88; rtd 88. *The Ryelands, Menith Wood, Worcester WR6 6UG* Eardiston (058470) 227

BAKER, Robert John Kenneth. b 50. MICE79 Southn Univ BSc71. Oak Hill Th Coll 88. **d** 90 **p** 91. C Cromer *Nor* from 90. *18 Vicarage Road, Cromer, Norfolk NR27 9DQ* Cromer (0263) 514352

BAKER, Robert Mark. b 50. Bris Univ BA73. St Jo Coll Nottm 74. **d** 76 **p** 77. C Portswood Ch Ch *Win* 76-80; R Witton w Brundall and Braydeston *Nor* 80-89; P-in-c Buckenham w Hassingham and Strumpshaw 80-86; R Brundall w Braydeston and Postwick from 89; RD Blofield from 89. *The Rectory, 73 The Street, Brundall, Norwich NR13 5LZ* Norwich (0603) 715136

BAKER, Canon Robin Henry. b 31. Man Univ BA52. Cuddesdon Coll 54. **d** 56 **p** 57. C Swinton St Pet *Man* 56-59; C Birch St Jas 59-61; R Stretford All SS 61-66; Chapl High Royds Hosp Menston 66-72; P-in-c Simpson w Woughton on the Green *Ox* 72-73; P-in-c Woughton 74; TR 74-79; RD Milton Keynes 78-86; C-in-c Milton Keynes City Cen 79-80; V Milton Keynes 80-86; Hon Can Ch Ch from 84; TR Banbury 86-91; P-in-c Scorton *Blackb* from 91; Bp's Adv on Healing from 91. *St Peter's Vicarage, Scorton, Preston PR3 1AY* Forton (0524) 791229

BAKER, Ronald Harry. b 21. Ely Th Coll 62. **d** 64 **p** 65. R Thornbury *Ex* 66-73; R Bradf 67-73; R Black Torrington, Bradf and Thornbury 73-77; P-in-c Broadhempston and Woodland 77-78; P-in-c Lt Hempston 77-78; P-in-c Berry Pomeroy 77-78; V Broadhempston, Woodland, Berry Pomeroy etc 78-86; rtd 86; Chapl Marseille w St Raphael Aix-en-Provence etc *Eur* 87-88; Perm to Offic *Ex* from 88. *2 West Park Cottages, Staverton, Totnes, Devon TQ9 6NY* Staverton (080426) 493

BAKER, Ronald Kenneth. b 43. Open Univ BA80 LTh. St Jo Coll Nottm 85. **d** 87 **p** 88. C Paddock Wood *Roch* 87-90; V Ramsgate St Mark *Cant* from 90. *St Mark's Vicarage, 198 Margate Road, Ramsgate, Kent CT12 6AQ* Thanet (0843) 581042

BAKER, Roy David. b 36. Lon Univ DipTh61. St Aid Birkenhead 59. **d** 62 **p** 63. C Garston *Liv* 62-64; C N Meols 64-68; V Newton-le-Willows 68-73; V Crossens 73-82; V Blundellsands St Nic from 82. *St Nicholas' Vicarage, Nicholas Road, Blundellsands, Liverpool L23 6TS* 051-924 3551

BAKER, Simon Nicholas Hartland. b 57. K Coll Lon BD78 Trin Hall Cam DipTh79. Qu Coll Birm 79. **d** 81 **p** 82. C Tupsley *Heref* 81-85; V Shinfield *Ox* from 85. *The Vicarage, Church Lane, Shinfield, Reading RG2 9BY* Reading (0734) 883363

BAKER, Stephen Anthony. b 55. St Luke's Coll Ex BEd80. Sarum & Wells Th Coll 88. **d** 91. C Guildf H Trin w St Mary *Guildf* from 91. *27 Pewley Way, Guildford, Surrey GU1 3PX* Guildford (0483) 68477

BAKER, Very Rev Thomas George Adames. b 20. Ex Coll Ox BA43 MA50. Linc Th Coll 43. **d** 44 **p** 45. Preb Wells Cathl *B & W* 60-71; Prin Wells Th Coll 60-71; Adn Bath and Preb Wells Cathl *B & W* 71-75; Dean Worc 75-86; rtd 86; Perm to Offic *B & W* from 86. *21 Brooklyn Road, Larkhall, Bath BA1 6TE* Bath (0225) 337243

BAKER, Thomas James William. b 35. St Edm Hall Ox BA59 MA64. St Steph Ho Ox 59. **d** 61 **p** 62. C Bitterne Park *Win* 61-64; C Pokesdown All SS 64-68; Asst Chapl Lancing Coll Sussex 68-70; Chapl 70-79; V Thatcham *Ox* 79-84. *Address temp unknown*

BAKER, Walter Donald. b 06. FRSA LTCL. St Aid Birkenhead 42. **d** 44 **p** 45. V Upper Holloway St Pet *Lon* 69-80; rtd 80; Hon C St Jas Garlickhythe w St Mich Queenhithe etc *Lon* from 80. *8 Bishop Street, London N1 8PH* 071-359 3498

BAKER, William Alfred Douglas. b 21. Lon Univ BSc52 MSc56. Qu Coll Birm 72. **d** 75 **p** 76. Hon C Bridgnorth w Tasley *Heref* 75-78; Hon C Bridgnorth, Tasley, Astley Abbotts, Oldbury etc from 78. *Oaklea, Astley Abbotts, Bridgnorth, Shropshire* Bridgnorth (07462) 2980

BAKER, William Douglas Willson. b 19. Linc Th Coll 79. **d** 80 **p** 81. NSM Mablethorpe w Trusthorpe *Linc* 80-84; NSM Sutton le Marsh 84-90; NSM Sutton, Huttoft and Anderby from 90. *7 Grove Road, Sutton-on-Sea, Mablethorpe, Lincs LN12 2LP* Mablethorpe (0521) 41506

BAKER, William George. b 07. St Cath Coll Cam BTh. **d** 38 **p** 42. V Moreton *Lich* 53-76; rtd 76. *Fidelis, 39 Lime Tree Road, Matlock, Derbyshire DE4 3EJ* Matlock (0629) 582717

BAKER, William John. b 45. FCII80. Cranmer Hall Dur 87. **d** 89 **p** 90. C Sale St Anne *Ches* from 89. *3 Windermere Avenue, Sale, Cheshire M33 3FP* 061-962 9608

BAKERE, Ronald Duncan. b 35. TCD BA58 HDipEd60 MA61 BD62 Ch Ch Ox MA66. **d** 59 **p** 60. C Knockbreda *D & D* 59-61; C Dub Zion Ch *D & G* 61-63; Min Can St Patr Cathl Dub 62-64; CF (TA) 65-67; CF (TA - R of O) 67-86; P-in-c Chew Magna w Dundry *B & W* 86-87; Perm to Offic *Lon* from 88. *404 Marlyn Lodge, 2 Portsoken Street, London E1 4RB* 071-265 0296

BALCH, John Robin. b 37. Lon Univ BSc61 Bris Univ CertEd62. ALCD68. **d** 68 **p** 69. C Bath Walcot *B & W* 68-71; C Fulwood *Sheff* 71-76; V Erith St Paul *Roch* from 76; RD Erith from 90. *The Vicarage, 44A Colyers Lane, Erith, Kent DA8 3NP* Dartford (0322) 332809

BALCHIN, Michael John. b 38. Selw Coll Cam BA60 MA64. Wells Th Coll 60. **d** 62 **p** 63. C Bournemouth H Epiphany *Win* 62-65; C Bris St Mary Redcliffe w Temple etc *Bris* 65-69; R Norton sub Hamdon *B & W* 69-70; P-in-c Chiselborough w W Chinnock 69-70; R Norton sub Hamdon w Chiselborough 70-77; P-in-c Chipstable w Huish Champflower and Clatworthy 77-82; R 82-88; Rural Affairs Officer 87-88. *Glyntwymyn, Commins Coch, Machynlleth, Powys SY20 8LS* Cemmaes Road (06502) 659

BALDOCK, Charles William Martin. b 52. Nottm Univ BPharm73. St Jo Coll Nottm LTh. **d** 85 **p** 86. C Nailsea Ch Ch *B & W* 85-89; V Brampton Bierlow *Sheff* from 89. *The Vicarage, Christchurch Road, Wath-upon-Dearne, Rotherham, S Yorkshire S63 6NW* Rotherham (0709) 873210

BALDOCK, Canon Norman. b 29. K Coll Lon BD52 AKC52. **d** 53 **p** 54. C Cant St Pet w H Cross *Cant* 53-54; C Thornton Heath St Jude 54-58; V Ash w W Marsh 58-67; V Sheerness H Trin w St Paul 67-75; V Margate St Jo from 75; RD Thanet 80-86; Hon Can Cant Cathl from 82; Chapl Margate Gen Hosp from 82. *The Vicarage, 24 St Peters Road, Margate, Kent CT9 1TH* Thanet (0843) 221300

BALDOCK, Reginald David. b 48. Oak Hill Th Coll 72. **d** 75 **p** 76. C Plymouth St Jude *Ex* 75-79; C Ardsley *Sheff* 79-85; V Rawthorpe *Wakef* from 85. *The Vicarage, 138 Rawthorpe Lane, Huddersfield HD5 9PB* Huddersfield (0484) 428045

BALDRY, John Netherway. b 19. Lon Univ BA53. **d** 79 **p** 80. Hon C Brighton St Paul *Chich* from 79. *26 Braybon Avenue, Brighton BN1 8HG* Brighton (0273) 501268

BALDRY, Ralph Yorke. b 18. St Jo Coll Ox BA40 MA44. Wycliffe Hall Ox 40. **d** 41 **p** 42. V Finchley St Luke *Lon* 64-72; V Golders Green St Alb 72-80; P-in-c Golders Green St Mich 77-80; V Golders Green 80-83; rtd 84. *159 Falloden Way, London NW11 6LG* 081-455 6926

BALDWICK, Frank Eric. b 24. Ripon Hall Ox 54. **d** 55 **p** 56. R Gt Lever *Man* 65-78; V Hindsford 78-81; TV Clifton *S'well* 81-89; rtd 89. *35 Ladybay Road, Nottingham NG2 5BJ* Nottingham (0602) 821273

BALDWIN, Derek Wilfred Walter. b 23. Lon Univ LTh74. ALCD56. **d** 52 **p** 53. Org Sec (Dios B & W, Ex and Truro) CECS 66-72; Lic to Offic *Ex* 67-72; R Morchard Bishop 72-73; Org Sec (Dios St Alb and Ox) CECS 73-77; C Portishead *B & W* 77-79; R Wymondham w Edmondthorpe *Leic* 79-80; P-in-c St Mewan *Truro* 80-81; V Crowan w Godolphin 81-83; C Cockington *Ex* 83-87; rtd 87; Perm to Offic *Ex* from 90. *5 Rushlade Close, Paignton, Devon TQ4 7BZ* Paignton (0803) 559643

BALDWIN, John Charles. b 39. FBCS CEng Bris Univ BSc61 Sussex Univ DPhil65. St Steph Ho Ox 82. **d** 83 **p** 84. C Llan w Capel Llanilterne *Llan* 83-90; R Ewenny w St Bride's Major from 90. *The Vicarage, St Brides Major, Bridgend, M Glam CF32 0SD* Southerndown (0656) 880108

BALDWIN, Miss Joyce Gertrude. See CAINE, Mrs Joyce Gertrude

BALDWIN, Peter Alan. b 48. Bede Coll Dur BA70 Birm Univ DipTh72. Qu Coll Birm 72. **d** 73 **p** 74. C Hartlepool St Oswald *Dur* 73-75; C Darlington H Trin 75-78; OGS from 77; C-in-c Bishop Auckland Woodhouse Close CD *Dur* 78-82; V Ferryhill 82-88; P-in-c Charlestown *Man* 88-89; V Pendleton St Thos 88-89; TR Pendleton St Thos w Charlestown 89-90; TR Newton Aycliffe *Dur* from 90. *St Clare's Rectory, St Cuthbert's Way, Newton Aycliffe, Co Durham DL5 5NT* Aycliffe (0325) 313613

BALDWIN, William. b 48. RMN73 FRSH83. NW Ord Course 75. **d** 78 **p** 79. C Royton St Anne *Man* 78-82; V Halliwell St Thos 82-87; TR Atherton from 87; OStJ from 88. *Atherton Rectory, Bee Fold Lane, Atherton, Manchester M29 0BL* Atherton (0942) 874666

BALE, Edward William Carre. b 22. ABAF74 AKC55 Leic Univ DSRS67. **d** 55 **p** 56. V Wollaston and Strixton *Pet* 69-87; rtd 88; Perm to Offic Ox from 88; Pet from 89. *49 Kilpin Green, North Crawley, Newport Pagnell MK16 9LZ* North Crawley (023065) 443

BALE, James Henry. b 30. St Pet Hall Ox BA53 DipEd54 MA57 CQSW81. Oak Hill Th Coll 56. **d** 58 **p** 59. C Walcot St Sav *B & W* 58-61; C Kinson *Sarum* 61-64; Sudan 64-69; Hon C Prestwick *Glas* 75-89; Brazil from 89. *CxP 2024, 30161 Belo Horizinti, MG Brazil*

BALE, Kenneth John. b 34. Univ of Wales (Lamp) BA58. Qu Coll Birm DipTh60. **d** 60 **p** 61. C Mitcham St Olave

S'wark 60-63; C Warlingham w Chelsham and Farleigh 63-67; V Battersea Rise St Mark 67-85; Perm to Offic 85-88; Hon C Balham St Mary and St Jo 88-90; V S Wimbledon All SS from 90. *All Saints' Vicarage, De Burgh Road, London SW19 1DX* 081-542 5514

BALES, Charles Noel. b 07. Dorchester Miss Coll 31. **d** 35 **p** 36. V Marshland St James *Ely* 42-84; rtd 84; P-in-c Marshland St James *Ely* from 84. *The Vicarage, Marshland St James, Middle Drove, Wisbech, Cambs PE14 8JS* Marshland Smeeth (094573) 240

BALFOUR, Hugh Rowlatt. b 54. SS Coll Cam BA76. Ridley Hall Cam 78. **d** 81 **p** 82. C Bedf Ch Ch *St Alb* 81-86; P-in-c Camberwell Ch Ch *S'wark* 86-90; V from 90. *Christ Church Vicarage, 79 Asylum Road, London SE15 2RJ* 071-639 5662

BALFOUR, Mrs Penelope Mary. b 47. St Andr Univ MA69 St Jo Coll York DipEd72. Coates Hall Edin 89 St Jo Coll Nottm 84. **d** 88. C Dundee St Marg *Bre* from 88. *10 Strathaird Place, Dundee DD2 4TN* Dundee (0382) 643114

BALKWILL, Michael Robert. b 67. **d** 91. C Llanrhos *St As* from 91. *All Saints' Parsonage, Tymwr Road, Deganwy, Conwy, Gwynedd LL31 9DŽ* Deganwy (0492) 583260

BALKWILL, Roger Bruce. b 41. Univ of Wales DipTh64 DPS66. St Mich Coll Llan 61. **d** 64 **p** 65. C Llantrisant *Llan* 64-68; C Caerphilly 68-73; Rhodesia 73-76; P-in-c Ilam w Blore Ray and Okeover *Lich* 76-81; P-in-c Albrighton 81-82; V from 82; P-in-c Beckbury 89-90; P-in-c Badger 89-90; P-in-c Ryton 89-90; P-in-c Kemberton, Sutton Maddock and Stockton 89-90; RD Shifnal from 89. *The Vicarage, High Street, Albrighton, Wolverhampton WV7 3EQ* Albrighton (0902) 372701

BALL, Alan. b 26. Qu Coll Birm 72. **d** 75 **p** 75. NSM Hamstead St Paul *Birm* from 75. *4 Kingshayes Road, Aldridge, Walsall WS9 8RU* Aldridge (0922) 54458

BALL, Albert Bernard. b 15. Coll of Resurr Mirfield. **d** 62 **p** 63. V Oldham St Jo *Man* 71-80; rtd 80. *4 Holly Mount, Seymour Grove, Stretford, Manchester M16 0ET* 061-860 7289

BALL, Andrew Thomas. b 54. K Coll Lon BD75 AKC75. Sarum & Wells Th Coll 76. **d** 77 **p** 78. C Ribbleton *Blackb* 77-80; C Sedgley All SS *Lich* 80-84; V Pheasey 84-90; Chapl Gd Hope Hosp Sutton Coldfield from 90. *c/o The Chaplain's Office, Good Hope Hospital, Sutton Coldfield, W Midlands* 021-378 2211

BALL, Anthony Charles. b 46. Lon Univ BD71. Chich Th Coll 72. **d** 73 **p** 74. C Heref St Martin *Heref* 73-76; C Ealing St Pet Mt Park *Lon* 76-82; V Ruislip Manor St Paul from 82. *St Paul's Vicarage, Thurlstone Road, Ruislip, Middx HA4 0BP* Ruislip (0895) 633499

BALL, Anthony Michael. b 46. Kelham Th Coll 66. **d** 70 **p** 71. C Kingswinford St Mary *Lich* 70-74; C W Bromwich All SS 74-76; P-in-c Priorslee 76-80; V 80-82; Asst Chapl HM Pris Liv 82-83; Chapl from 88; Chapl HM Pris Lewes 83-88. *The Chaplain's Office, HM Prison, 68 Hornby Road, Liverpool L9 3DP* 051-525 5971

BALL, Christopher Rowland. b 40. Wycliffe Hall Ox. **d** 82 **p** 83. C Heysham *Blackb* 82-86; TV Swanborough *Sarum* 86-90; R Llanyblodwel and Trefonen *Lich* from 90. *The Rectory, School Lane, Trefonen, Oswestry, Shropshire SY10 9DY* Oswestry (0691) 654184

BALL, Canon Frank. b 21. Leeds Univ BA47. Coll of Resurr Mirfield 46. **d** 48 **p** 49. V Sheff Norwood St Leon *Sheff* 61-87; RD Ecclesfield 80-87; Hon Can Sheff Cathl from 85; rtd 87; Gov and Chapl Shrewsbury Hosp Sheff from 87. *The Chaplain's House, Shrewsbury Hospital, Norfolk Road, Sheffield S2 2SU* Sheffield (0742) 720574

BALL, Geoffrey Williams. b 32. FLIA80 FInstSMM81. SW Minl Tr Course 82. **d** 85 **p** 86. NSM Sampford Spiney w Horrabridge *Ex* 85-87; TV Yelverton, Meavy, Sheepstor and Walkhampton 87-91; V Marystowe, Coryton, Stowford, Lewtrenchard etc from 91. *The Vicarage, Chillaton, Lifton, Devon PL16 0JB* Chillaton (082286) 279

BALL, George Raymond. b 15. Univ of Wales (Lamp) BA40. St Mich Coll Llan 40. **d** 42 **p** 43. R Bosherston w St Twynells *St D* 50-85; rtd 85. *1 Meadowbank, St Twynnells, Pembroke, Dyfed SA71 5HZ* Castlemartin (0646) 661432

BALL, Glynne Howell James. b 47. ACIS DMA. Llan Dioc Tr Scheme. **d** 90 **p** 91. NSM Llangynwyd w Maesteg *Llan* from 90. *7 Bridgend Road, Llangynwyd, Maesteg, Bridgend, M Glam CF34 9NW* Maesteg (0656) 734805

BALL, Harold Francis Noel. b 19. Leeds Univ BA41. Coll of Resurr Mirfield 41. **d** 43 **p** 44. CF 46-74; QHC 74; R W Grinstead *Chich* 74-85; RD Horsham 82-85; rtd 85; Perm to Offic *Win* from 85. *13 Abbey Hill Road, Winchester, Hants SO23 7AT* Winchester (0962) 861295

BALL, Ian Raymond. b 45. CertEd. Glouc Th Course 81. **d** 85 **p** 87. NSM Churchstoke w Hyssington and Sarn *Heref* from 85; Lic to Bp Ludlow from 87. *Bacheathlon, Sarn, Newtown, Powys SY16 4HH* Kerry (068688) 505

BALL, John Kenneth. b 42. Lon Univ BSc64 AKC64. Linc Th Coll 69. **d** 71 **p** 72. C Garston *Liv* 71-74; C Eastham *Ches* 74-75; C Barnston 75-77; V Over St Jo 77-82; V Helsby and Dunham-on-the-Hill from 82; RD Frodsham from 88. *St Paul's Vicarage, Vicarage Lane, Helsby, Warrington WA6 9AB* Helsby (0928) 722151

BALL, Canon John Martin. b 34. Univ of Wales BA55. Tyndale Hall Bris. **d** 59 **p** 60. C Blackb St Jude *Blackb* 59-63; Kenya 63-79; Dep Gen Sec BCMS 79-81; Gen Sec from 81; Hon C Sidcup Ch Ch *Roch* from 81; Hon Can Karamoja from 88. *12 Sandhurst Road, Sidcup, Kent* 081-300 5213 or 691 6111

BALL, John Roy. b 47. Fitzw Coll Cam MA71. Wycliffe Hall Ox 83. **d** 85 **p** 86. C Stockport St Mary *Ches* 85-88; C Fazeley *Lich* from 88; Res Min Drayton Bassett from 89. *1 Rectory Close, Drayton Bassett, Tamworth, Staffs B78 3UH* Tamworth (0827) 289164

BALL, Jonathan. b 63. BNC Ox BA85 Leeds Univ BA87. Coll of Resurr Mirfield 85. **d** 88 **p** 89. C Blakenall Heath *Lich* from 88. *27 Smithfield Road, Walsall WS3 1ND* Walsall (0922) 477015

BALL, Michael Gordon. b 12. St Aid Birkenhead 45. **d** 48 **p** 49. R Newington Bagpath w Kingscote and Ozleworth *Glouc* 70-74; P-in-c Boxwell w Leighterton 71-72; R Withington and Compton Abdale w Haselton 75-77; rtd 77; Perm to Offic *Ex* from 77. *5 Instow House, Marine Parade, Instow, Bideford, Devon EX39 4JJ* Instow (0271) 860593

✠**BALL, Rt Rev Michael Thomas.** b 32. Qu Coll Cam BA55 MA59. **d** 71 **p** c 80. CGA from 60; Prior Stroud Priory 64-76; C Whiteshill *Glouc* 71-76; Lic to Offic 76; P-in-c Stanmer w Falmer *Chich* 76-80; Chapl Sussex Univ 76-80; Suff Bp Jarrow *Dur* 80-90; Angl Adv Tyne Tees TV 84-90; Bp Truro from 90. *Lis Escop, Feock, Truro, Cornwall TR3 6QQ* Truro (0872) 862657

BALL, Nicholas Edward. b 54. Man Univ BA75 Ox Univ MA85. Ripon Coll Cuddesdon 79. **d** 80 **p** 81. C Yardley Wood *Birm* 80-83; C Moseley St Mary 83-86; Chapl Cen 13 83-85; V Bartley Green from 86. *The Vicarage, 96 Romsley Road, Birmingham B32 3PS* 021-475 1508

BALL, Norman. b 41. Liv Univ BA63. Cuddesdon Coll 67. **d** 68 **p** 69. C Broseley w Benthall *Heref* 68-72; Lic to Offic *Ches* 72-75; V Plemstall w Guilden Sutton 75-79; Perm to Offic 79-88; NSM Dodleston from 88. *White Cottage, Lower Mountain Road, Penyfford, Chester* Kinnerton (0244) 661132

BALL, Peter Edwin. b 44. Lon Univ BD65 DipEd. Wycliffe Hall Ox 75. **d** 77 **p** 78. C Prescot *Liv* 77-80; R Lawford *Chelmsf* from 80; RD Harwich from 91. *The Rectory, Church Hill, Lawford, Manningtree, Essex CO11 2JX* Colchester (0206) 392659

✠**BALL, Rt Rev Peter John.** b 32. Qu Coll Cam BA54 MA58. Wells Th Coll 54. **d** 56 **p** 57 **c** 77. C Rottingdean *Chich* 56-58; Novice SSM 58-60; CGA from 60; Prior 60-77; Lic to Offic Birm 65-66; B & W 69-77; P-in-c Hoar Cross *Lich* 66-69; Suff Bp Lewes *Chich* from 77; Can and Preb Chich Cathl from 78. *Beacon House, Berwick, Polegate, E Sussex BN26 6ST* Alfriston (0323) 870387

BALL, Canon Peter Prior. b 25. St Jo Coll Ox BA50 MA55. Ridley Hall Cam 51. **d** 53 **p** 54. Chapl RN 60-76; Chapl Cannes *Eur* 76-80; Visiting Chapl (Eur & N Africa) Intercon Ch Soc 80-86; Eur Rep Sharing of Min Abroad from 86; rtd 90; Hon Can Malta Cathl *Eur* from 91. *Chateau d'Azur, 44 Boulevard d'Italie, Monte Carlo MC98000, Monaco* Monaco (3393) 303079

BALL, Canon Peter William. b 30. Worc Coll Ox BA53 MA57. Cuddesdon Coll 53. **d** 55 **p** 56. R Shepperton *Lon* 68-84; RD Staines 72-74; RD Spelthorne 74-84; Preb St Paul's Cathl 76-84; Can Res and Chan 84-90; rtd 90; Perm to Offic *Sarum* from 90. *Whittonedge, Ramsbury, Marlborough, Wilts SN8 2PX* Marlborough (0672) 20259

BALL, Philip John. b 52. Bris Univ BEd75. Ripon Coll Cuddesdon 79. **d** 82 **p** 83. C Norton St Mich *Dur* 82-84; C Greenford H Cross *Lon* 84-88; V Hayes St Edm from 88. *St Edmund's Vicarage, 1 Edmund's Close, Hayes, Middx UB4 0HA* 081-573 6913

BALL, Richard. b 10. Dur Univ 32. St Paul's Coll Burgh. **d** 36 **p** 37. V Flitwick *St Alb* 47-78; rtd 78. *34 Lancaster Drive, Broadstone, Dorset BH18 9EL* Broadstone (0202) 604955

BALL, Canon Robert George. b 14. Pemb Coll Cam BA36 MA40. Ely Th Coll 36. **d** 37 **p** 38. V Ipswich St Thos *St E* 63-81; Hon Can St E Cathl 70-81; RD Ipswich 72-78; rtd 81; Perm to Offic *St E* 81-88. *481 Hawthorne Drive, Ipswich* Ipswich (0473) 687230

BALL, Vernon. b 34. Ox Min Course 87. **d** 90. NSM Banbury *Ox* from 90. *15 Crouch Street, Banbury, Oxon OX16 9PP* Banbury (0295) 259839

BALLANTINE, Peter Sinclair. b 46. Nottm Univ MTh85. K Coll Lon BA68 AKC68 St Jo Coll Nottm 70 Lon Coll of Div ALCD71 BD73 LTh74. **d** 73 **p** 74. C Rainham *Chelmsf* 73-77; C Wennington 73-77; TV Barton Mills *St E* 77-80; TV Barton Mills, Beck Row w Kenny Hill etc 80-82; Chapl Liv Poly *Liv* 83-86; Tr Officer Rugby Deanery *Cov* from 86; P-in-c Churchover w Willey from 86; P-in-c Clifton upon Dunsmore and Newton from 86. *The Rectory, Churchover, Rugby, Warks CV23 0EH* Rugby (0788) 832420

BALLANTINE, Roderic Keith. b 44. Chich Th Coll 66. **d** 69 **p** 70. C Nunhead St Antony *S'wark* 69-72; C S Hackney St Jo w Ch Ch *Lon* 72-75; P-in-c Kensal Town St Thos w St Andr and St Phil 75-79; V Stoke Newington St Andr from 79. *St Andrew's Vicarage, 106 Bethune Road, London N16 5DU* 081-800 2900

BALLANTYNE, John Ivan Terence. b 32. SS Coll Cam BA54. Ely Th Coll 55. **d** 57 **p** 58. C Poplar All SS w St Frideswide *Lon* 57-61; Asst Chapl Lon Univ 61-63; C Is of Dogs Ch Ch and St Jo w St Luke 63-64; S Africa from 64. *Address temp unknown*

BALLANTYNE, Miss Jane Elizabeth. *See* KENCHINGTON, Mrs Jane Elizabeth Ballantyne

BALLARD, Andrew Edgar. b 44. Dur Univ BA66. Westcott Ho Cam 66. **d** 68 **p** 69. C St Marylebone St Mary *Lon* 68-72; C Portsea St Mary *Portsm* 72-76; V Haslingden w Haslingden Grane *Blackb* 76-82; V Walkden Moor *Man* from 82; AD Farnworth from 90. *St Paul's Vicarage, Manchester Road, Walkden, Worsley, Manchester M28 5LN* 061-790 2483

BALLARD, Miss Anne Christina. b 54. LRAM76. Wycliffe Hall Ox 82. **dss** 85 **d** 87. Hove Bp Hannington Memorial Ch *Chich* 85-87; Chapl St Pet Sch Petworth 87-89; RCM *Lon* from 89; Imp Coll from 89. *13A Cranley Gardens, London SW7 3DB* 071-370 2270

BALLARD, Anthony James. E Midl Min Tr Course 86. **d** 89 **p** 90. Hon Chapl Woodbank Gr Sch Leic from 89; Hon C Clarendon Park St Jo w Knighton St Mich *Leic* from 89. *Flat 7, 51 Evington Road, Leicester LE2 1QG* Leicester (0533) 558086

BALLARD, Canon Michael Arthur. b 44. Lon Univ BA66. Westcott Ho Cam 68. **d** 70 **p** 71. C Harrow Weald All SS *Lon* 70-73; C Aylesbury *Ox* 73-78; V Eastwood *Chelmsf* 78-90; RD Hadleigh 83-90; Hon Can Chelmsf Cathl from 89; R Southchurch H Trin from 90. *The Rectory, 8 Pilgrims Close, Southend-on-Sea SS2 4XF*

BALLARD, Peter James. b 55. SS Hild & Bede Coll Dur BEd78 Lon Univ DipTh85. Sarum & Wells Th Coll 85. **d** 87 **p** 88. C Grantham *Linc* 87-90 and 91; Australia 90-91; V Lanc Ch Ch w St Jo and St Anne *Blackb* from 91. *Christ Church Vicarage, 1 East Road, Lancaster LA1 3EE* Lancaster (0524) 34430

BALLARD, Richard Ernest. b 37. Linc Coll Ox BA60 MA66 Lon Univ BD68. Wells Th Coll 60. **d** 62 **p** 63. C Farnham *Guildf* 62-67; Chapl Pierrepont Sch Frensham 67-69; Asst Chapl Eton Coll Windsor 69-74; P-in-c Fiddington *B & W* 74-76; P-in-c Stogursey 74-76; R Stogursey w Fiddington 76-78; V Trull 78; R Trull w Angersleigh 78-80; Chapl Qu Coll Taunton 78-80; Chapl Wells Cathl Sch 81-86; Chapl Haileybury Coll Herts from 86. *Heathgate, College Road, Hertford Heath, Hertford SG13 7PU* Hoddesdon (0992) 462000

BALLARD, Steven Peter. b 52. Man Univ BA73 MA74. St Steph Ho Ox 76. **d** 78 **p** 79. C Lanc St Mary *Blackb* 78-81; C Blackpool St Mich 81-84; V Brierfield from 84. *The Vicarage, 22 Reedley Road, Reedley, Burnley, Lancs BB10 2LU* Nelson (0282) 63235

BALLENTINE, Ian Clarke. b 46. Aston Univ BSc71. **d** 91. C Lurgan St Jo *D & D* from 91. *136 Lough Road, Lurgan, Craigavon, Co Armagh BT66 6JL* Lurgan (0762) 325962

BALLEY, John Frederick. b 05. ALCD41. **d** 41 **p** 42. Lic to Offic *Ex* 65-70; Chapl Torbay Hosp Torquay 65-70; rtd 70. *Hornsey Rise Memorial Home, Wellsborough, Nuneaton, Warks CV13 6PA*

BALLINGER, Francis James. b 43. AKC70. **d** 71 **p** 85. C Weston-super-Mare St Saw *B & W* 71-72; Dir Bd of Soc Resp *Leic* 85-88; Hon C Bringhurst w Gt Easton 85-88; TV Melksham *Sarum* from 88. *St Andrew's Vicarage, 33 Church Lane, Melksham, Wilts SN12 7EF* Melksham (0225) 702310

BALMER, Walter Owen. b 30. N Ord Course 83. **d** 86 **p** 87. NSM Gateacre *Liv* from 86. *38 Grangemeadow Road, Liverpool L25 4SU* 051-428 5594

BALMFORTH, Ven Anthony James. b 26. BNC Ox BA50 MA51. Linc Th Coll 50. **d** 52 **p** 53. V Kings Norton *Birm* 65-72; TR 73-79; RD Kings Norton 73-79; Hon Can Birm Cathl 75-79; Hon Can Bris Cathl *Bris* from 79; Adn Bris 79-90; rtd 90. *Slipper Cottage, Stag Hill, Yorkley, Lydney, Glos GL15 4TB* Dean (0594) 564016

BAMBER, David Beverley. b 51. Univ of Wales (Lamp) BA75. St Steph Ho Ox 75. **d** 77 **p** 78. C Altrincham St Geo *Ches* 77-80; C Oxton 80-81; Perm to Offic *Derby* 85-87; C Staveley and Barrow Hill 87-88; C W Retford *S'well* 89-90; C E Retford 89-90 and from 91. *The Vicarage, 1 Chapelgate, Retford, Notts DN22 6PL* Retford (0777) 702696

BAMFORD, Anthony. b 54. Sussex Univ BSc75 Ox Univ BA87 MA91. St Steph Ho Ox 85. **d** 88 **p** 89. C Uckfield *Chich* from 88. *School House, Belmont Road, Uckfield, E Sussex TN22 1BP* Uckfield (0825) 761373

BAMFORD, Mrs Marion. b 35. K Coll Lon BA56 AKC56. N Ord Course 81. dss 84 **d** 90. Baildon *Bradf* 84-85; S Kirkby *Wakef* 85-90; Chapl Pontefract Gen Infirmary Wakef from 89; Dn-in-c Brotherton *Wakef* from 90. *Brotherton Vicarage, North Road, Byram, Knottingley, W Yorkshire WF11 9ED* Knottingley (0977) 672370

BAMFORTH, Marvin John. b 48. N Ord Course 78. **d** 81 **p** 82. C Barnoldswick w Bracewell *Bradf* 81-84; V Cullingworth 84-88; New Zealand 88-89; V Thornton in Lonsdale w Burton in Lonsdale *Bradf* from 89. *The Vicarage, Low Street, Burton in Lonsdale, Carnforth, Lancs LA6 3LF* Bentham (05242) 61579

BAMFORTH, Stuart Michael. b 35. Hertf Coll Ox BA58 MA61. Sarum Th Coll 60. **d** 62 **p** 63. C Adel *Ripon* 62-67; V Hempton and Pudding Norton *Nor* 67-71; V Toftrees w Shereford 67-71; P-in-c Pensthorpe 67-71; P-in-c Colkirk 69-70; Lic to Offic *Derby* 72-77; Ripon from 77. *36 Gainsborough Avenue, Leeds LS16 7PQ*

BANBURY, David Paul. b 62. Coll of Ripon & York St Jo BA84. Ridley Hall Cam 85. **d** 88 **p** 89. C Blackb St Jas *Blackb* 88-90; C Preston St Cuth from 90. *46 Banksfield Avenue, Fulwood, Preston PR2 3RN* Preston (0772) 724730

BANFIELD, Andrew Henry. b 48. AKC71. St Aug Coll Cant 72. **d** 73 **p** 74. C Crayford *Roch* 73-76; Youth Chapl *Glouc* 77-89; Soc Services Development Officer Glos Co Coun from 89. *Rosemary Cottage, Oakwood Close, Bream, Lydney, Glos*

BANFIELD, Ven David John. b 33. ALCD56. **d** 57 **p** 58. C Middleton *Man* 57-62; Chapl Scargill Ho N Yorkshire 62-65; Asst Warden 65-67; V Addiscombe St Mary *Cant* 67-80; V Luton St Mary *St Alb* 80-90; Hon Can St Alb 89-90; RD Luton 89-90; Adn Bris from 90. *10 Great Brockeridge, Westbury-on-Trym, Bristol BS9 3TY* Bristol (0272) 622438

BANGERT, Henry Alfred. b 07. ALCD33. **d** 33 **p** 34. Chapl Knowle Hosp Fareham 67-75; rtd 76; Hon C E Preston w Kingston *Chich* 76-80. *8 Oaktree House, 153 Oaktree Lane, Birmingham B30 1TU* 021-472 5675

BANGOR, Archdeacon of. *See* ROBERTS, Ven Elwyn

BANGOR, Bishop of. *See* MEARS, Rt Rev John Cledan

BANGOR, Dean of. *See* EDWARDS, Very Rev Thomas Erwyd Pryse

BANISTER, Martin John. b 39. Worc Coll Ox BA62 MA68. Chich Th Coll 62. **d** 64 **p** 65. C Wellingborough All Hallows *Pet* 64-67; C Heene *Chich* 67-70; V Denford w Ringstead *Pet* 70-78; P-in-c Wilshamstead *St Alb* 78-80; P-in-c Houghton Conquest 78-80; V Wilshamstead and Houghton Conquest 80-89; RD Elstow 86-89; V Waltham Cross from 89. *The Vicarage, 5 Longlands Close, Waltham Cross, Herts EN8 8LW* Waltham Cross (0992) 33243

BANKS, Aleck George. b 18. Lon Univ BD42 AKC42. **d** 42 **p** 43. V S Benfleet *Chelmsf* 61-83; rtd 83; Perm to Offic Chelmsf from 83; St E from 85. *5 Gosford Close, Clare, Sudbury, Suffolk CO10 8PT* Clare (0787) 277088

BANKS, Brian William Eric. b 35. Lon Univ DipTh65 BD69 Birm Univ DPS70. Wycliffe Hall Ox 63. **d** 65 **p** 66. C Swindon Ch Ch *Bris* 65-68; C Halesowen *Worc* 68-71; R Wychbold and Upton Warren 71-77; V Bengeworth 77-87; RD Evesham 81-86; R Freshwater *Portsm* from 87. *The Rectory, Afton Road, Freshwater, Isle of Wight PO40 9TS* Isle of Wight (0983) 752010

BANKS, Ernest Leslie. b 10. Oak Hill Th Coll 53. **d** 55 **p** 56. R Kimberley w Gospel *S'well* 60-83; rtd 83; Perm to Offic *Derby* from 83. *32 King's Drive, Littleover, Derby DE3 6EY* Derby (0332) 360706

BANKS, Geoffrey Alan. b 43. St Andr Univ MA66. N Ord Course 84. **d** 87 **p** 88. NSM Shelley and Shepley *Wakef* 87-89; C Halifax 89-91; V Holmfield from 91. *St Andrew's*

Vicarage, Beechwood Road, Holmfield, Halifax, W Yorkshire HX2 9AR Halifax (0422) 244586

BANKS, John Alan. b 32. Hertf Coll Ox BA54 MA58. Westcott Ho Cam 56. **d** 58 **p** 59. V Ollerton *S'well* 64-75; V Boughton 64-75; R Wollaton 75-83; RD Beeston 77-81; rtd 83; Lic to Offic *S'well* 83-85; C Bramcote 85-86; C Arnold from 86. *247 Oxclose Lane, Arnold, Nottingham NG5 6FB* Nottingham (0602) 266814

BANKS, Joseph. b 23. CEng65 MIMechE65 FBIM70. **d** 80 **p** 81. NSM Bollington St Jo *Ches* 80-84; NSM New Galloway *Glas* from 84. *The Rectory, New Galloway, Castle Douglas, Kircudbrightshire DG7 3RP* New Galloway (06442) 235

BANKS, Michael Lawrence. b 40. Open Univ BA72 Brunel Univ MA82. Westcott Ho Cam 84. **d** 86 **p** 87. C Cheshunt *St Alb* 86-89; Chapl HM Pris Blundeston 89-90; V Leagrave *St Alb* from 90. *St Luke's Vicarage, High Street, Leagrave, Luton LU4 9JY* Luton (0582) 572737

BANKS, Canon Michael Thomas Harvey. b 35. Ushaw Coll Dur 58 Open Univ BA75. **d** 63 **p** 64. In RC Ch 63-69; C Winlaton *Dur* 69-71; P-in-c Bishopwearmouth Gd Shep 71-75; TV Melton Mowbray w Thorpe Arnold *Leic* 75-80; R Loughb Em 80-88; Dir of Ords from 83; Hon Can Leic Cathl 83-88; Can Res and Chan from 88. *Chancellor's House, 3 Morland Avenue, Leicester LE2 2PF* Leicester (0533) 708078

BANKS, Norman. b 54. Or Coll Ox BA76 MA80. St Steph Ho Ox 79. **d** 82 **p** 83. C Newc Ch Ch w St Ann *Newc* 82-87; P-in-c 87-90; V Tynemouth Cullercoats St Paul from 90. *The Vicarage, 53 Grosvenor Drive, Whitley Bay, Tyne & Wear NE26 2JR* 091-252 4916

BANNARD-SMITH, Dennis Ronald. b 22. Birm Univ BSc42. St Alb Minl Tr Scheme. **d** 83 **p** 84. NSM Pavenham *St Alb* 83-88; NSM Odell and Pavenham from 88. *Goodly Heritage, 10 The Bury, Pavenham, Bedford MK43 7PX* Oakley (02302) 2992

BANNER, John William. b 36. Open Univ BA78. Tyndale Hall Bris 61. **d** 64 **p** 65. C Bootle St Leon *Liv* 64-66; C Wigan St Jas 66-69; C Stapleton *Bris* 69-70; Australia 70-72; V Liv Ch Ch Norris Green *Liv* 72-82; V Tunbridge Wells H Trin w Ch Ch *Roch* from 82. *The Vicarage, Claremont Road, Tunbridge Wells, Kent TN1 1TE* Tunbridge Wells (0892) 26644

BANNER, Michael Charles. b 61. Ball Coll Ox BA83 MA86 DPhil87. **d** 86 **p** 87. Fell St Pet Coll Ox 85-88; Dean Peterho Cam from 88. *Peterhouse, Cambridge CB2 1RD* Cambridge (0223) 338200

BANNISTER, Anthony Peter. b 40. Ex Univ BA62. Clifton Th Coll 63. **d** 65 **p** 66. C Uphill *B & W* 65-69; C Hove Bp Hannington Memorial Ch *Chich* 69-74; V Wembdon *B & W* 74-91; Youth Chapl 80-83; RD Bridgwater 80-89; V Taunton St Jas from 91. *St James's Vicarage, 3 Richmond Road, Taunton, Somerset TA1 1EN* Taunton (0823) 333194

BANNISTER, Clifford John. b 53. Hatf Coll Dur BA76. Ripon Coll Cuddesdon 84. **d** 86 **p** 87. C Weymouth H Trin *Sarum* 86-89; TV Basingstoke *Win* from 89. *219 Paddock Road, Basingstoke, Hants RG22 6QP* Basingstoke (0256) 464393

BANNISTER, Edward. b 06. Lich Th Coll 27. **d** 29 **p** 30. V Sparsholt w Lainston *Win* 56-73; rtd 73; Warden Morley Coll from 76. *8 Morley College, Winchester, Hants SO23 9LF* Winchester (0962) 869834

BANNISTER, Grattan Eric McGillycuddy Colm Brendon. b 01. TCD BA50 MA53. **d** 52 **p** 57. P-in-c Schull *C, C & R* 63-75; rtd 75. *Schull, Co Cork, Irish Republic*

BANNISTER, John. b 24. Westcott Ho Cam 68. **d** 69 **p** 70. Hon C Rye *Chich* 69-73; Hon C Playden w E Guldeford 69-73; Hon C Rye w Rye Harbour and Playden 73-79; Hon C Rye, Rye Harbour and Playden and Iden 79-80; Hon C Rye from 80. *Wynfields, Grove Lane, Iden, Rye, E Sussex TN31 7PX* Iden (07978) 229

BANNISTER, Peter Edward. b 38. Leeds Univ BSc60. Linc Th Coll 72. **d** 74 **p** 75. C Norbury St Steph *Cant* 74-77; C Allington and Maidstone St Pet 77-80; R Temple Ewell w Lydden 80-86; TV Bracknell *Ox* from 86. *St Paul's Vicarage, 58 Harman's Water Road, Bracknell, Berks RG12 3PT* Bracknell (0344) 422819

BANNISTER, Canon Simon Monro. b 38. St Jo Coll Ox BA62 MA69. Linc Th Coll 61. **d** 63 **p** 64. C Prestwich St Marg *Man* 63-66; C Farnborough *Roch* 66-70; V Bury St Mark *Man* 70-78; V Oldham St Mary w St Pet 78; TR Oldham 78-87; Hon Can Man Cathl 81-87; V Hatf Hyde St Mary *St Alb* from 87. *The Vicarage, Ludwick Way, Welwyn Garden City, Herts AL7 3QW* Welwyn Garden (0707) 322313

BANNOCKS, David George. b 64. Trin Coll Bris DipHE84 Lon Bible Coll BA85 Cranmer Hall Dur 88. **d** 90 **p** 91. C Stapleford *S'well* from 90. *22 Shanklin Drive,*

Stapleford, Nottingham NG9 8EZ Sandiacre (0602) 392643

BANNON, Canon Richard Babington. b 20. TCD BA42 MA47. CITC 48. **d** 48 **p** 49. I Ardclinis w Tickmacrevan *Conn* 55-86; Can Belf Cathl 85-86; rtd 86. *Dean's Cottage, 7 Whin Road, Ballygally, Larne, Co Antrim BT40 2QJ* Ballygally (0574) 583230

BANTING, David Percy. b 51. Magd Coll Cam MA74. Wycliffe Hall Ox MA79. **d** 80 **p** 81. C Ox St Ebbe w H Trin and St Pet *Ox* 80-83; Min St Jos Merry Hill CD *Lich* 83-90; V Chadderton Ch Ch *Man* from 90. *Christ Church Vicarage, Block Lane, Chadderton, Oldham OL9 7QB* 061-624 2326

BANTING, Kenneth Mervyn Lancelot Hadfield. b 37. Pemb Coll Cam BA61 MA65. Cuddesdon Coll 64. **d** 65 **p** 66. Asst Chapl Win Coll 65-70; C Leigh Park *Portsm* 70-72; TV Hemel Hempstead *St Alb* 73-79; V Goldington 79-88; P-in-c Renhold 80-82; RD Bedf 84-87; V Portsea St Cuth *Portsm* from 88. *St Cuthbert's Vicarage, 2 Lichfield Road, Portsmouth PO3 6DE* Portsmouth (0705) 827071

BANYARD, Douglas Edward. b 21. S'wark Ord Course 69. **d** 71 **p** 72. NSM Selsdon St Jo w St Fran *Cant* 71-77; Perm to Offic *Portsm* from 77. *22 Lower Wardown, Petersfield, Hants GU31 4NY* Petersfield (0730) 61004

BANYARD, Peter Vernon. b 35. Sarum Th Coll 57. **d** 59 **p** 60. V Chesterfield St Aug *Derby* 68-74; TV Grantham w Manthorpe *Linc* 74-78; TV Grantham 78-79; Chapl Warminster Sch Wilts 79-85; V Hykeham *Linc* 85-88; rtd 88; Perm to Offic *Linc* from 88. *56 Western Avenue, Lincoln LN6 7SY*

BARBER, Charles William Walters. b 60. Pemb Coll Cam BA81 MA85. Wycliffe Hall Ox 83. **d** 86 **p** 87. C Wolv St Matt *Lich* 86-90; C Hornsey St Mary w St Geo *Lon* from 90; C Hornsey Rise Whitehall Park Team from 90. *94 Mowatt Close, London N19 3XZ* 071-272 3160

BARBER, Canon Christopher Albert. b 33. Ch Coll Cam BA53 MA57. Coll of Resurr Mirfield 56. **d** 58 **p** 59. C Cov St Pet *Cov* 58-61; C Stokenchurch and Cadmore End *Ox* 61-64; V Royton St Paul *Man* 64-70; V Stapleford *Ely* 70-80; RD Shelford 76-80; V Cherry Hinton St Andr 80-88; Hon Can Ely Cathl from 88; R Cottenham from 88; RD N Stowe from 90. *The Rectory, 6 High Street, Cottenham, Cambridge CB4 4SA* Cottenham (0954) 50454

BARBER, David. b 45. **d** 72 **p** 73. C Muswell Hill St Matt *Lon* 72-75; C St Pancras w St Jas and Ch Ch 75-77; Chapl Brook Gen Hosp & Greenwich Distr Hosp *Lon* 77-80. *Address temp unknown*

BARBER, Garth Antony. b 48. FRAS Southn Univ BSc69 Lon Univ MSc79. St Jo Coll Nottm LTh76. **d** 76 **p** 77. C Hounslow H Trin *Lon* 76-79; Chapl City of Lon Poly 79-86; P-in-c Twickenham All Hallows from 86. *All Hallows' Vicarage, 138 Chertsey Road, Twickenham TW1 1EW* 081-892 1322

BARBER, Geoffrey Thomas. b 23. Univ of Wales (Lamp) BA51. Ridley Hall Cam 51. **d** 53 **p** 54. V Rushden St Pet 66-75; V Leyton Em *Chelmsf* 75-81; rtd 81. *22 Longacre Drive, Ferndown, Wimborne, Dorset BH22 9EE* Ferndown (0202) 873626

BARBER, John Eric Michael. b 30. Wycliffe Hall Ox 63. **d** 65 **p** 66. C Lupset *Wakef* 65-68; C Halifax St Jo Bapt 68-70; V Dewsbury St Matt and St Jo 70-80; V Perry Common *Birm* from 80. *St Martin's Vicarage, 148 Witton Lodge Road, Birmingham B23 5AP* 021-382 7666

BARBER, Mrs Margaret Ann. b 31. GTCL52. Dalton Ho Bris 55 Sarum & Wells Th Coll 82. **dss** 83 **d** 87. Wimborne Minster and Holt *Sarum* 83-87; Par Dn 87-90; rtd 90; Hon Par Dn Hampreston *Sarum* from 90. *22 Longacre Drive, Ferndown, Wimborne, Dorset BH22 9EE* Ferndown (0202) 873626

BARBER, Martin John. b 35. Lon Univ BA61. Linc Th Coll 61. **d** 63 **p** 64. C Stepney St Dunstan and All SS *Lon* 63-67; Chapl K Sch Bruton from 67. *King's School, Bruton, Somerset BA10 0EF* Bruton (0749) 2290

BARBER, Michael. b 40. Open Univ BA83. Oak Hill Th Coll 69. **d** 71 **p** 72. C Rothley *Leic* 71-74; C Leic Martyrs 74-76; V Queniborough 76-82; V Monkwearmouth All SS *Dur* from 82. *All Saints' Vicarage, 3 Fulwell Road, Sunderland SR6 0JD* 091-565 6606

✠**BARBER, Rt Rev Paul Everard.** b 35. St Jo Coll Cam BA58 MA66. Wells Th Coll 58. **d** 60 **p** 61 **c** 89. C Westborough *Guildf* 60-66; V York Town 66-73; V Bourne 73-80; RD Farnham 74-79; Hon Can Guildf Cathl 80-89; Adn Surrey 80-89; Suff Bp Brixworth *Pet* from 89. *4 The Avenue, Dallington, Northampton NN5 7AN* Northampton (0604) 759423

BARBER, Philip Kenneth. b 43. St Jo Coll Dur BA65. NW Ord Course 74. **d** 76 **p** 77. NSM Burscough Bridge *Liv* 76-84; P-in-c Brigham *Carl* 84-85; V 85-89; P-in-c

Mosser 84-85; V 85-89; P-in-c Borrowdale from 89; Chapl Keswick Sch from 89. *The Vicarage, Borrowdale, Keswick, Cumbria CA12 5XQ* Borrowdale (07687) 77238

BARBER, Royston Henry. b 38. Univ of Wales (Abth) BD86. United Th Coll Abth 83. **d** 86 **p** 87. NSM Towyn w Aberdovey *Ban* from 86. *66 Faenol Isaf, Tywyn, Gwynedd LL36 0DW* Tywyn (0654) 710364

BARBER, William Ewart Worsley. b 15. Leeds Univ BA38. Coll of Resurr Mirfield 38. **d** 40 **p** 41. V Tuffley *Glouc* 67-74; R Huntley 74-79; rtd 79; Hon C Bromsberrow 79-90; Hon C Redmarley D'Abitot, Bromesberrow w Pauntley etc *Glouc* from 79. *37 St Mary's Square, Gloucester GL1 2QT* Gloucester (0452) 330842

BARBOUR, Mrs Jennifer Louise. b 32. JP67. Barrister-at-Law 55 St Hugh's Coll Ox BA54 MA57. Gilmore Course 80. **dss** 81 **d** 87. Bray and Braywood *Ox* 81-84; Hermitage and Hampstead Norreys, Cold Ash etc 84-87; Chapl Leeds Poly *Ripon* from 87. *St Stephen's Church House, Cranmer Road, Leeds LS17 5DR* Leeds (0532) 687338

BARBOUR, Walter Iain. b 28. FICE65 Pemb Coll Cam BA48 MA53. Ox NSM Course 78. **d** 81 **p** 82. NSM Bray and Braywood *Ox* 81-84; NSM Thatcham 84-87; TV Moor Allerton *Ripon* from 87. *St Stephen's Vicarage, Cranmer Road, Leeds LS17 5DR* Leeds (0532) 687338

BARBY, Mrs Sheana Braidwood. b 38. Bedf Coll Lon BA59. E Midl Min Tr Course 81. **dss** 84 **d** 87. Derby St Paul *Derby* 84-87; Hon Par Dn Derby Cathl from 87; Dioc Dir of Female Ords from 90. *2 Margaret Street, Derby DE1 3FE* Derby (0332) 383301

BARCLAY, Ian Newton. b 33. Clifton Th Coll 58. **d** 61 **p** 62. C Cullompton *Ex* 61-63; C Ashill w Broadway *B & W* 63-66; V Chatham St Phil and St Jas *Roch* 66-69; C St Helen Bishopsgate w St Martin Outwich *Lon* 70-73; V Prestonville St Luke *Chich* 73-81; Lic to Offic from 82. *35 Marine Avenue, Hove, E Sussex BN3 4LH* Brighton (0273) 421628

BARCLAY, Susan Molly. **d** 87. Hon Par Dn March St Wendreda *Ely* from 87. *6 Cavalry Drive, March, Cambs* March (0354) 56289

BARCROFT, Ambrose William Edgar. b 17. TCD BA40 MA46. **d** 41 **p** 42. Chapl RN 46-70; R Pitlochry *St And* 70-82; rtd 82. *The Old School House, Calvine, Pitlochry, Perthshire PH18 5UD* Calvine (079683) 224

BARCROFT, Ian David. b 60. UMIST BSc83 Edin Univ BD88. Edin Th Coll 85. **d** 88 **p** 89. Prec St Ninian's Cathl Perth *St And* from 88; Min Perth St Ninian from 88. *28B Balhousie Street, Perth PH1 5HJ* Perth (0738) 22140

BARD, Christopher Frederick Jesse. b 52. AKC75 Open Univ BA88. St Aug Coll Cant 75. **d** 76 **p** 77. C Billingham St Cuth *Dur* 76-79; Chapl to Arts and Recreation 79-81; C Egglescliffe 79-81; P-in-c Epping Upland *Chelmsf* from 81; Dioc Communications Officer 81-91; BBC Essex Relig Producer from 89; Bp's Adv on Satellite Broadcasting from 91. *The Vicarage, Epping Green, Epping, Essex CM16 6PN* Epping (0378) 72949

BARDELL, Frank Stanley. b 04. ARIBA38 Lon Univ BA24. Oak Hill Th Coll 54. **d** 55 **p** 56. R Maresfield *Chich* 59-73; rtd 73; Perm to Offic *Win* from 73. *Sanctuary Cottage, 13 Orchard Way, Dibden Purlieu, Southampton SO4 5AP* Hythe (0703) 845612

BARDSLEY, Cyril Booth. b 08. Dur Univ LTh32. St Aid Birkenhead 30. **d** 32 **p** 33. V Melbecks and Muker *Ripon* 65-73; rtd 73. *Abbotside, Burtersett Road, Hawes, N Yorkshire DL8 3NT* Hawes (09697) 417

BARDSLEY, Edwin Roy. b 24. St Jo Coll Cam BA47 MA52. Wells Th Coll 48. **d** 49 **p** 50. V Moulsham St Jo *Chelmsf* 58-74; Chapl Chelmsf and Essex Hosp 58-74; V Bittadon *Ex* 74-77; R Marwood 74-77; P-in-c Littleham 77-80; P-in-c Monkleigh 77-80; P-in-c Weare Giffard w Landcross 77-80; RD Hartland 79-80; V Tiverton St Andr 80-86; rtd 86; Perm to Offic *Ex* 87-90; Blackb from 90. *24 Knowlys Road, Morecambe, Lancs LA3 2PE* Heysham (0524) 52020

BARDSLEY, Warren Nigel Antony. b 52. AKC74. St Aug Coll Cant 74. **d** 75 **p** 76. C Leeds St Aid *Ripon* 75-78; C Cov St Jo *Cov* 78-80; P-in-c Stoke Golding w Dadlington *Leic* 80-89; TV Swinton and Pendlebury *Man* from 90. *St Augustine's Vicarage, Hospital Road, Swinton, Manchester M27 1EY* 061-794 1808

BARDWELL, Edward Mercer. b 12. ALCD41 LTh74. **d** 41 **p** 43. R Cranworth w Letton and Southbergh *Nor* 59-78; rtd 79; Perm to Offic *Ely* from 79; St E from 89. *6 Cromwell Road, Weeting, Brandon, Suffolk IP27 0QT* Thetford (0842) 810582

BARDWELL, Mrs Elaine Barbara. b 60. K Coll Lon BA81 AKC81. St Steph Ho Ox BA85 MA90. **dss** 86 **d** 87. Heref H Trin *Heref* 86-87; C 87-89; Dir Past

Studies St Steph Ho Ox from 89. *1 Moberly Close, 134C Cowley Road, Oxford OX4 1HX* Oxford (0865) 251500

BARDWELL, John Edward. b 53. Jes Coll Cam BA75 MA79 Ox Univ BA85 MA90. St Steph Ho Ox 83. **d** 86 **p** 87. C Heref H Trin *Heref* 86-89; Perm to Offic *Ox* from 90. *1 Moberly Close, 134C Cowley Road, Oxford OX4 1HX* Oxford (0865) 251500

BAREHAM, Miss Sylvia Alice. b 36. Hockerill Coll Cam CertEd59 Open Univ BA83 Ox Univ SDES84. Ox NSM Course 86. **d** 89. NSM N Leigh *Ox* from 89. *St Edmund's, East End, North Leigh, Witney, Oxon OX8 6PX* Freeland (0993) 881383

BARFETT, Ven Thomas. b 16. Keble Coll Ox BA38 MA42. Wells Th Coll 38. **d** 39 **p** 40. R Falmouth K Chas *Truro* 55-77; Asst ChStJ 63-71; Sub ChStJ from 71; Chapl to HM The Queen 75-86; Adn Heref 77-82; Can Res and Treas Heref Cathl 77-82; rtd 82; Bermuda 84; Chapl Menton w San Remo *Eur* 86. *Treberveth, 57 Falmouth Road, Truro, Cornwall TR1 2HL* Truro (0872) 73726

BARFF, John Robert. b 43. Ch Coll Cam BA66 MA70 K Coll Lon MTh69. ALCD68. **d** 69 **p** 70. C Fulham St Mary N End *Lon* 69-73; CMS 73-83; Sudan 75-83; P-in-c Compton Greenfield *Bris* 83-85; P-in-c Pilning 83-85; V Pilning w Compton Greenfield from 85. *The Vicarage, The Glebe, Pilning, Bristol BS12 3LE* Pilning (04545) 3409

BARFORD, Mrs Valerie Anne. b 43. Man Univ BSc64 MPS65. St Alb Minl Tr Scheme 80. **d** 87. Par Dn Weston Favell *Pet* 87-90; Lic to RD Northn from 90. *27 Elmhurst Avenue, Northampton NN3 2LD* Northampton (0604) 405743

BARGH, George Edward Norman. b 25. St Jo Coll Cam BA48 MA53 Leeds Univ LLB51. Carl Dioc Tr Course 80. **d** 83 **p** 84. NSM Ulverston St Mary w H Trin *Carl* 83-86; P-in-c Egton w Newland 86-87; P-in-c Blawith w Lowick 86-87; P-in-c Egton-cum-Newland and Lowick 87-89; rtd 90. *2 Woodheads, Grange Fell Road, Grange-over-Sands, Cumbria LA11 6AF* Grange-over-Sands (05395) 35151

BARHAM, Ian Harold. b 40. Clifton Th Coll 64. **d** 66 **p** 67. C Broadwater St Mary *Chich* 66-69 and 72-76; Burundi 71-72; R Beyton and Hessett *St E* 76-79; Perm to Offic 79-81; Hon C Bury St Edmunds St Mary 81-84; Chapl St Aubyn's Sch Tiverton from 84. *Emmaus, 53 Sylvan Road, Exeter EX4 6EY* Exeter (0392) 51643

BARHAM, Canon Kenneth Lawrence. b 36. Clifton Th Coll. **d** 63 **p** 64. C Worthing St Geo *Chich* 63-65; C Sevenoaks St Nic *Roch* 65-67; C Cheltenham St Mark *Glouc* 67-70; V Malmesbury St Luke *Cant* 70-79; S Area Sec Rwanda Miss 79-84; P-in-c Ashburnham w Penhurst *Chich* from 84. *Rosewood, Canadia Road, Battle, E Sussex TN33 0LR* Battle (04246) 3073

BARKER, Arthur John Willoughby. b 10. Lon Coll of Div 46. **d** 48 **p** 49. V Dent w Cowgill *Bradf* 61-76; rtd 76; Perm to Offic *Bradf* from 76. *West Banks, Dent, Sedbergh, Cumbria LA10 5QT* Dent (05875) 355

BARKER, Arundel Charles. b 24. Tyndale Hall Bris 54. **d** 56 **p** 57. R Passenham *Pet* 65-90; P-in-c Cosgrove 65-66; rtd 90. *7 Bull Farm Mews, Bull Lane, Matlock, Derbyshire DE4 5NB* Matlock (0629) 580321

BARKER, Brian Wallwork. b 26. G&C Coll Cam BA50 MA55. Wells Th Coll 51. **d** 52 **p** 53. V Ashton St Jas *Man* 65-71; R Burnage St Nic 71-85; R Heaton Reddish 85-91; rtd 91. *105 Crossfield Road, Cheadle Hulme, Cheadle, Cheshire* 061-486 0334

BARKER, Charles Gordon. b 19. St Aug Coll Cant 60. **d** 61 **p** 62. Lic to Offic *Heref* 70-78; P-in-c Hopesay w Edgton 78-80; P-in-c Lydbury N 78-80; rtd 83. *25 Lydbury North, Shropshire SY7 8AU* Lydbury North (05888) 257

✠**BARKER, Rt Rev Clifford Conder.** b 26. TD71. Or Coll Ox BA50 MA55 St Chad's Coll Dur DipTh52. **d** 52 **p** 53 **c** 76. C Falsgrave *York* 52-55; C Redcar 55-57; V Sculcoates 57-63; CF (TA) 58-74; P-in-c Sculcoates St Silas *York* 59-61; V Rudby in Cleveland w Middleton 63-70; RD Stokesley 65-70; V York St Olave w St Giles 70-76; RD City of York 71-75; Can and Preb York Minster 73-76; Suff Bp Whitby 76-83; Suff Bp Selby 83-91; rtd 91. *15 Oak Tree Cose, Strensall, York YO3 5TE* York (0904) 490406

BARKER, David Robert. b 45. Worc Coll Ox BA67 MA70. Virginia Th Sem BD72. **d** 72 **p** 73. C Roehampton H Trin *S'wark* 72-75; Chapl Golds Coll Lon 75-79; Min Tr Officer *Cov* 79-85; Selection Sec and Sec for Continuing Minl Educn ACCM 85-90; V Sutton Valence w E Sutton and Chart Sutton *Cant* from 90. *The Vicarage, Chart Road, Sutton Valence, Maidstone, Kent ME17 3AW* Maidstone (0622) 843156

BARKER, Donald Charles. b 05. St Edm Hall Ox BA29 MA67. Ely Th Coll 27. **d** 28 **p** 29. Master Hugh Sexey's Hosp Bruton 67-88; Hon C Bruton w Lamyatt, Wyke and Redlynch *B & W* 67-85; rtd 72; Hon C Bruton and Distr *B & W* from 85. *Denhams, Higher Backway, Bruton, Somerset BA10 0DW* Bruton (0749) 812218

BARKER, Francis Howard. b 41. St Deiniol's Hawarden. **d** 84 **p** 85. NSM Capesthorne w Siddington and Marton *Ches* 84-86; NSM Wilmslow from 86. *The Cedars, Butley Town, Prestbury, Macclesfield, Cheshire SK10 4DZ* Prestbury (0625) 829409

BARKER, Harold Sidney Michael. b 16. St Chad's Coll Dur BA39. **d** 39 **p** 40. V Brookfield St Mary *Lon* 61-86; rtd 86. *Flat 4, 9 Hendon Avenue, London N3 1UL* 081-346 5111

BARKER, Canon Hugh Remington. b 19. Pemb Coll Cam BA41 MA45. Chich Th Coll 41. **d** 43 **p** 44. V Wisbech St Mary *Ely* 62-75; RD Wisbech 72-75; P-in-c Walpole St Andrew 75-77; V 77-84; P-in-c Walpole St Peter 75-77; R 77-84; RD Lynn Marshland 76-84; Hon Can Ely Cathl 81-84; rtd 84; Perm to Offic *Ely* from 84. *39 Dowgate Road, Leverington, Wisbech, Cambs PE13 5DJ* Wisbech (0945) 585385

BARKER, James Gavin. b 33. Kelham Th Coll 54. **d** 58 **p** 59. C Greenford H Cross *Lon* 58-61; C Bournemouth St Clem w St Mary *Win* 61-66; C Pokesdown St Jas 66-70; V Stanmore 70-77; Chapl Besselsleigh Sch Abingdon 77-86; Hon C S Hinksey *Ox* 77-79; Hon C Wootton (Boars Hill) 79-86; V Southbourne St Chris *Win* from 86. *St Christopher's Vicarage, 81 Watcombe Road, Bournemouth BH6 3LX* Bournemouth (0202) 424886

BARKER, John Frederic Waller. b 18. MBE45. Selw Coll Cam BA49 MA53. Linc Th Coll 49. **d** 51 **p** 52. Chapl Univ Coll Hosp Lon 56-83; rtd 83. *Brambles, East Boldre, Brockenhurst, Hants SO42 7WT* East End (059065) 679

BARKER, John Howard. b 36. Southn Univ BA58. Ripon Coll Cuddesdon 80. **d** 82 **p** 83. C W Leigh *Portsm* 82-84; V Cosham 84-88; Bp's Dom Chapl from 88. *46 Blackbrook Park Avenue, Fareham, Hants PO15 5JL* Fareham (0329) 280247 or 221326

BARKER, Very Rev John Kidman Stuart Ridley. b 12. Lich Th Coll 32. **d** 35 **p** 36. R Over Whitacre w Shustoke *Birm* 60-73; Dean Cloyne *C, C & R* 73-84; Prec Cork Cathl 73-84; rtd 84; Perm to Offic *Bradf* from 85. *Cloyne, Skellbank Close, Ripon, N Yorkshire HG4 2PY* Ripon (0765) 2434

BARKER, John Lawrence. b 26. Middx Poly BA74 NE Lon Poly MSc84. Oak Hill NSM Course 86. **d** 88 **p** 89. NSM Prittlewell *Chelmsf* from 88. *109 Baxter Avenue, Southend-on-Sea SS2 6HX* Southend-on-Sea (0702) 343025

BARKER, John Stuart. b 30. Keele Univ BA55. Wells Th Coll 55. **d** 57 **p** 58. C Oswestry St Oswald *Lich* 57-60; C Portishead *B & W* 60-63; V Englishcombe 63-69; R Priston 63-69; V Chew Magna w Dundry 70-85. *9 West Street, Axbridge, Somerset BS26 2AA* Axbridge (0934) 732740

BARKER, Jonathan. b 55. Hull Univ BA79. Westcott Ho Cam 79. **d** 83 **p** 84. C Sketty *S & B* 83-86; Chapl Sport & Leisure 83-86; C Swansea St Mary w H Trin 83-86; Bermuda 86-90; TV Liv Our Lady and St Nic w St Anne *Liv* from 90. *485 Grafton Street, Liverpool L8 9TA* 051-727 5255

BARKER, Julian Roland Palgrave. b 37. Magd Coll Cam BA61 MA65. Westcott Ho Cam 61. **d** 63 **p** 64. C Stafford St Mary *Lich* 63-66; Chapl Clare Hall Cam 66-69; Chapl Clare Coll Cam 66-70; Lic to Offic *Cant* 70-71; Tutor St Aug Coll Cant 70-71; TV Raveningham *Nor* 71-78; TR 78-82; V Foremark *Derby* from 82; V Repton from 82; RD Repton from 91. *St Wystan's Vicarage, Repton, Derby DE6 6FH* Burton-on-Trent (0283) 703317

BARKER, Leonard Ralph. b 11. ALCD39. **d** 39 **p** 40. R Linby w Papplewick *S'well* 63-78; rtd 78. *53 Lancaster Drive, Long Sutton, Spalding, Lincs PE12 9BD* Holbeach (0406) 363422

BARKER, Canon Leonard Roy. b 24. Selw Coll Cam BA49 MA53. Ridley Hall Cam 49. **d** 51 **p** 52. V Upton (or Overchurch) *Ches* 62-80; Hon Can Ches Cathl 78-80; Dir Past Studies Ridley Hall Cam 80-84; Dir of Ords *Ches* 84-90; Can Res Ches Cathl 84-89; rtd 90. *Parkgate, 1 Dee Hills Park, Chester CH3 5AR* Chester (0244) 314662

BARKER, Neil Anthony. b 52. St Andr Univ BSc73. Ridley Hall Cam 74. **d** 77 **p** 78. C Leic H Apostles *Leic* 77-81; C Camberley St Paul *Guildf* 81-86; R Bradfield *Ox* 86-88; P-in-c Stanford Dingley 86; R Bradfield and Stanford Dingley from 88. *The Rectory, Bradfield, Reading RG7 6EU* Bradfield (0734) 744333

BARKER, Nicholas John Willoughby. b 49. Or Coll Ox BA73 BTh75 MA77. Trin Coll Bris 75. **d** 77 **p** 78. C Watford *St Alb* 77-80; TV Didsbury St Jas and Em *Man* 80-86; TR Kidderminster St Geo *Worc* from 86. *The Rectory, 30 Leswell Street, Kidderminster, Worcs DY10 1RP* Kidderminster (0562) 822131

BARKER, Very Rev Roy Thomas. b 33. K Coll Lon BD57 AKC57. St Boniface Warminster. **d** 58 **p** 59. C Headingley *Ripon* 58-62; C Hawksworth Wood 62-66; S Africa from 66; Sub-Dean Cape Town Cathl 73-80; Can 75-80; Dean and Adn of Grahamstown from 80. *The Deanery, PO Box 102, Grahamstown, 6140 South Africa* Grahamstown (461) 23976

BARKER, Stephen Luke Remington. b 20. Cant Sch of Min. **d** 82 **p** 83. NSM Cranbrook *Cant* 82-90; rtd 90. *St Damian's, High Street, Cranbrook, Kent TN17 3LH* Cranbrook (0580) 712048

BARKER, Timothy Reed. b 56. Qu Coll Cam BA79 MA82. Westcott Ho Cam 78. **d** 80 **p** 81. C Nantwich *Ches* 80-83; V Norton 83-88; V Runcorn All SS from 88; Urban Officer 88-90; Dioc Communications Officer from 91. *All Saints' Vicarage, Highlands Road, Runcorn, Cheshire WA7 4PS* Runcorn (0928) 575666

BARKER, Wallace Hamilton. b 08. Cuddesdon Coll 56. **d** 57 **p** 58. V Newchurch *Portsm* 67-70; V Arreton 67-70; rtd 73. *77 Church Road, Combe Down, Bath BA2 5JQ* Combe Down (0225) 834546

BARKER, Walter Frederick. b 25. Lon Univ BD48 ALCD48. St Jo Coll Lon 44. **d** 51 **p** 52. Home Sec CMJ 66-71; Gen Sec 71-86; Min at large CMJ 86-89; rtd 89. *72 Lime Grove, Ruislip, Middx HA4 8RY* 081-866 6941

BARKER, William Edward. b 28. Kelham Th Coll 49. **d** 54 **p** 55. C Warsop *S'well* 54-55; C Bawtry w Austerfield 55-57; V Frizington *Carl* 57-64; V Barrow St Jas 64-70; V Applethwaite from 70; P-in-c Troutbeck from 78. *St Mary's Vicarage, Ambleside Road, Windermere, Cumbria LA23 1BA* Windermere (09662) 3032

BARKING, Area Bishop of. See SAINSBURY, Rt Rev Roger Frederick

BARKS, Jeffrey Stephen. b 45. Cranmer Hall Dur 66. **d** 71 **p** 72. C Wootton *St Alb* 71-74; C Boscombe St Jo *Win* 74-76; C Ringwood 76-80; P-in-c Spaxton w Charlynch *B & W* 80; P-in-c Enmore w Goathurst 80; P-in-c Spaxton w Goathurst, Enmore and Charlynch 80-81; R from 81; RD Bridgwater from 89. *The Rectory, Church Road, Spaxton, Bridgwater, Somerset TA5 1DA* Spaxton (027867) 265

BARLING, Michael Keith. b 38. Oak Hill Th Coll 63. **d** 66 **p** 67. C Portman Square St Paul *Lon* 66-70; C Enfield Ch Ch Trent Park 70-74; V Sidcup St Andr *Roch* 74-78; Dir Fountain Trust 78-81; Lic to Offic Guildf 78-81; Chich 81-88; Chapl Bethany Fellowship and Roffey Place Tr Cen 81-88; Hon C Kennington St Mark *S'wark* from 88. *Roffey Place, Faygate, Horsham, W Sussex RH12 4SA* Faygate (029383) 543

BARLOW, Alan David. b 36. Worc Coll Ox BA59 MA65. Wycliffe Hall Ox 59. **d** 61 **p** 62. C Wealdstone H Trin *Lon* 61-67; V Neasden cum Kingsbury St Cath 67-73; Chapl Cranleigh Sch Surrey 73-81; Chapl Cheltenham Ladies' Coll from 82. *22 Moorend Road, Leckhampton, Cheltenham, Glos GL53 0EU* Cheltenham (0242) 584668

BARLOW, Arthur Stanley. b 06. Bp Wilson Coll 39. **d** 39 **p** 41. V Runcorn St Mich *Ches* 58-77; rtd 77; Perm to Offic *Ches* from 77. *26 Hallastone Road, Helsby, Warrington* Helsby (0928) 723115

BARLOW, Charles William Moore. b 32. ALCM50 Man Univ BA57. Cuddesdon Coll 56. **d** 58 **p** 59. C Atherton *Man* 58-61; C Swinton St Pet 61-64; V Dobcross 64-76; V Dobcross w Scouthead from 76. *The Vicarage, Woods Lane, Dobcross, Oldham OL3 5AN* Saddleworth (0457) 872342

BARLOW, Clive Christopher. b 42. Linc Th Coll 67. **d** 70 **p** 71. C Surbiton St Mark *S'wark* 70-74; C Spring Park *Cant* 74-77; V Ash w Westmarsh from 77; RD E Bridge from 86. *The Vicarage, Sandpits, Queens Road, Ash, Canterbury, Kent CT3 2BG* Ash (0304) 812296

BARLOW, David. b 50. Leeds Univ BA71 MA. Wycliffe Hall Ox 71. **d** 73 **p** 74. C Horninglow *Lich* 73-75; C Wednesfield St Thos 75-77; C Bloxwich 77-78; Chapl RN from 78. *c/o MOD, Lacon House, Theobald's Road, London WC1X 8RY* 071-430 6847

BARLOW, Edward Burnley. b 29. St Aid Birkenhead 56. **d** 58 **p** 59. C Lenton Abbey *S'well* 58-61; C Ipswich All SS *St E* 61-63; R Fishtoft *Linc* 63-76; V Linc St Giles from 76. *The Vicarage, Shelley Drive, Lincoln LN2 4BY* Lincoln (0522) 527655

BARLOW, Norman Edward. b 09. ALCD36 St Jo Coll Dur LTh36 BA37 MA42. **d** 37 **p** 38. R Windlesham *Guildf* 63-76; rtd 76; Perm to Offic *Guildf* from 77. *Holly Bank, Horseshoe Lane, Cranleigh, Surrey GU6 8QB* Cranleigh (0483) 272839

BARLOW, Paul Benson. b 31. Fitzw Coll Cam BA73 MA77. **d** 64 **p** 65. C Bath Abbey w St Jas *B & W* 64-74; Dep Hd Master Leys High Sch Redditch 74-81; Hd Master Jo Kyrle High Sch Ross-on-Wye from 82; Perm to Offic *Heref* 82-85; Lic to Offic from 85. *The Coach House, Hentland, Ross-on-Wye, Herefordshire HR9 6LP*

BARLOW, Robert Mark. b 53. St Jo Coll Nottm. **d** 86 **p** 87. C Colwich w Gt Haywood *Lich* 86-91; R Crick and Yelvertoft w Clay Coton and Lilbourne *Pet* from 91. *The Rectory, Crick, Northants NN6 7TU* Crick (0788) 822223

BARLOW, Thomas Frank. b 24. W Midl Minl Tr Course. **d** 84 **p** 85. NSM Dudley St Jas *Worc* 84-88; NSM Belbroughton w Fairfield and Clent from 88. *30 The Glebe, Belbroughton, Stourbridge, W Midlands DY9 9TH* Belbroughton (0562) 730426

BARLOW, Timothy David. b 46. Univ Coll Ox BA67 MA71 Lon Univ BD71. Oak Hill Th Coll 71. **d** 71 **p** 72. C Marple All SS *Ches* 71-74; C Northwood Em *Lon* 74-78; Chapl Vevey w Chateau d'Oex and Villars *Eur* 78-84; Switzerland 84-89; V Chadkirk *Ches* from 89. *St Chad's Vicarage, Chadkirk Road, Romiley, Stockport, Cheshire SK6 3JY* 061-430 4652

BARLOW, William George. b 40. Liv Univ BSc62 Univ of Wales BD65. St Mich Coll Llan 76. **d** 76 **p** 77. C Roath St Marg *Llan* 76-79; TV Cyncoed *Mon* 79-83; R Radyr *Llan* from 83. *The Rectory, Radyr, Cardiff CF4 8DY* Cardiff (0222) 842417

BARNABAS, Brother. See LINDARS, Canon Prof Frederick Chevallier

BARNACLE, Ronald William. b 20. Wells Th Coll 66. **d** 66 **p** 67. C Camp Hill w Galley Common *Cov* 69-70; R Etton w Dalton Holme *York* 70-76; R Hinderwell w Roxby 76-78; P-in-c Buckland Newton *Sarum* 78-80; P-in-c Wootton Glanville and Holnest 78-80; P-in-c Pulham 78-80; R Radwinter w Hempstead *Chelmsf* 80-83; V Blackfordby *Leic* 83-84; rtd 84; Perm to Offic Worc from 84; Cov from 87. *26 Meadow Road, Wolston, Coventry CV8 3HL* Wolston (0203) 543552

BARNARD, Canon Anthony Nevin. b 36. St Jo Coll Cam BA60 MA64. Wells Th Coll 61. **d** 63 **p** 64. C Cheshunt *St Alb* 63-65; Tutor Wells Th Coll 65-66; Chapl 66-69; Vice-Prin 69-71; Dep Prin Sarum & Wells Th Coll 71-77; Dir S Dios Minl Tr Scheme 74-77; Can Res and Chan Lich Cathl *Lich* from 77; Warden of Readers 77-91; Dir of Tr 86-91. *13 The Close, Lichfield, Staffs WS13 7LD* Lichfield (0543) 255168 or 250300

BARNARD, Catherine Elizabeth. b 54. York Univ BA76 Dur Univ BA79. Cranmer Hall Dur 77. **dss** 80 **d** 87. Mexborough *Sheff* 80-83; Sheff Manor 83-87; Hon Par Dn 87-90. *The Vicarage, Stonemoor Road, Bolsterstone, Sheffield S30 5ZN* Sheffield (0742) 882149

BARNARD, Canon Harold Reginald. b 07. AKC35. **d** 35 **p** 36. V Fishponds St Mary *Bris* 49-75; RD Stapleton 65-76; Hon Can Bris Cathl 67-81; rtd 75. *68 Oldbury Court Road, Bristol BS16 2JG* Bristol (0272) 659105

BARNARD, Canon John Stuart. b 19. Em Coll Cam BA41 MA45. Ridley Hall Cam 41. **d** 43 **p** 44. V Bromley Common St Aug *Roch* 58-73; Hon Can Roch Cathl 70-82; V Seal St Pet 73-82; Perm to Offic *Chich* from 82; rtd 84. *3 Chanctonbury Close, Rustington, Littlehampton, W Sussex BN16 2JB* Rustington (0903) 771351

BARNARD, Jonathan Dixon. b 46. St Cath Coll Cam BA68. Cuddesdon Coll 69. **d** 71 **p** 72. C Silksworth *Dur* 71-74; C Hatf Hyde St Mary *St Alb* 74-78; TV Hitchin 78-86; TR Penrith w Newton Reigny and Plumpton Wall *Carl* 86-91; rtd 91. *4 Hallin Croft, Penrith, Cumbria CA11 8AA* Penrith (0768) 63000

BARNARD, Kevin James. b 52. Keble Coll Ox BA77 MA79. Cranmer Hall Dur 77. **d** 79 **p** 80. C Swinton *Sheff* 79-83; TV Sheff Manor 83-90; V Bolsterstone from 90. *The Vicarage, Stonemoor Road, Bolsterstone, Sheffield S30 5ZN* Sheffield (0742) 882149

BARNARD, Leslie William. b 24. St Cath Coll Ox BA50 MA55 Southn Univ PhD70. Cuddesdon Coll 51. **d** 51 **p** 52. Sen Lect Leeds Univ 69-83; Dioc Dir of Tr *Ripon* 70-76; Chapl Harrogate Gen Hosp 83-89; rtd 89. *3 Carlton Road, Harrogate, N Yorkshire HG2 8DD* Harrogate (0423) 871289

BARNARD, Robert James. b 15. Lich Th Coll 54. **d** 55 **p** 56. R Clenchwarton *Ely* 65-77; P-in-c Hinxton 77-80; rtd 80; Perm to Offic *Roch* from 80. *Flat 23, Bromley*

College, London Road, Bromley BR1 1PE 081-290 1280

BARNARD, Canon William Henry. b 09. Dorchester Miss Coll 37. **d** 39 **p** 40. C Leic St Paul *Leic* 39-43; C Brighton All So *Chich* 43-51; C Barrowhill *Derby* 51-52; C Newbold and Dunston 51-53; R Hinton Martel *Sarum* from 53; RD Wimborne 75-79; Can and Preb Sarum Cathl from 79. *The Rectory, Hinton Martel, Wimborne, Dorset BH21 7HD* Witchampton (0258) 840256

BARNBY, Canon Bertram Louis. b 13. Ch Coll Cam BA35 MA39. Ridley Hall Cam 36. **d** 38 **p** 39. P-in-c Wilmslow *Ches* 69-72; R 72-76; Hon Can Ches Cathl 74-82; R W Kirby St Andr 76-82; rtd 82. *7 Holbeck Road, Scarborough, N Yorkshire YO11 2XF* Scarborough (0723) 378282

BARNES, Alan Duff. b 42. St Steph Ho Ox 75. **d** 77 **p** 78. C Wanstead H Trin Hermon Hill *Chelmsf* 77-80; C Clacton St Jas 80-82; R Cranham 82-89; V Calcot *Ox* from 89. *St Birinus' House, Langley Hill, Reading RG3 5QX* Reading (0734) 422828

BARNES, Brian. b 42. MA. Cant Sch of Min 79. **d** 82 **p** 83. NSM Maidstone All SS and St Phil w Tovil *Cant* 82-89; C from 89; FE Adv Gen Syn Bd of Educn from 86. *16 Greenside, Maidstone, Kent ME15 7SA* Maidstone (0622) 761476

BARNES, Bruce Roy. b 52. FRSA. St Steph Ho Ox 73. **d** 76 **p** 77. C Birm St Pet *Birm* 76-81; C Portsea St Mary *Portsm* 81-87; V Paulsgrove from 87. *St Michael's Vicarage, Hempsted Road, Portsmouth PO6 4AS* Cosham (0705) 375912

BARNES, Canon Bryan Peter. b 24. Leeds Univ BA50. Coll of Resurr Mirfield 50. **d** 52 **p** 53. V Moorfields *Bris* 66-71; P-in-c Winterbourne Down 71-75; V Fishponds St Mary 75-87; Hon Can Bris Cathl from 84; rtd 87; NSM Duloe w Herodsfoot *Truro* from 91. *Duloe Rectory, Liskeard, Cornwall PL14 4PW* Looe (05036) 2846

BARNES, Canon Charles Peter Kentish. b 19. Ch Coll Cam BA40 MA44. Ridley Hall Cam 40. **d** 42 **p** 43. R Stratford w Bishopton *Cov* 69-81; V Priors Hardwick, Priors Marston and Wormleighton 81-84; rtd 84; Perm to Offic Cov and Glouc from 84. *5 Willow Bank, Welford on Avon, Stratford-upon-Avon, Warks CV37 8HB* Stratford-upon-Avon (0789) 750780

BARNES, Colin. b 33. St Jo Coll York CertEd58. St Aid Birkenhead 61. **d** 64 **p** 65. C Eccles St Mary *Man* 64-66; C Barrow St Geo w St Luke *Carl* 66-68; V Goodshaw *Man* 68-80; P-in-c Wythenshawe St Martin 80-83; New Zealand from 83. *St Matthew's Vicarage, 16 Pearce Crescent, Taita, Lower Hutt, New Zealand* Wellington (4) 677655

BARNES, Very Rev Cyril Arthur. b 26. Edin Th Coll 47. **d** 50 **p** 51. C Aber St Jo *Ab* 50-53; R Forres *Mor* 53-55; C Darrington w Wentbridge *Wakef* 55-58; V Ripponden 58-67; V Thorpe 66-67; R Huntly *Mor* 67-83; R Aberchirder 67-83; Hon Can St Andr Cathl Inverness 71-83; Dioc Sec 71-83; R Keith 74-83; Dean Mor 77-83; Perm to Offic *Ab* from 83. *Pillyarmont Cottage, Bridge of Isla, Huntly, Aberdeenshire AB5 4SP* Rothiemay (046681) 370

BARNES, David John. b 37. Lon Univ DipRS65. Chich Th Coll 65. **d** 68 **p** 69. C Crayford *Roch* 68-71; Chapl RAF 71-75; Chapl Sutton Valence Sch Kent 75-87; C Minster in Sheppey *Cant* from 87. *St Peter's House, 2 St Peter's Close, Sheerness, Kent ME12 3DD* Sheerness (0795) 662399

BARNES, David Keith. b 53. Linc Th Coll. **d** 89 **p** 90. C E Crompton *Man* from 89. *15 Oak Street, Shaw, Oldham OL2 8EJ* Shaw (0706) 844934

BARNES, Derek Ian. b 44. Leeds Univ BA66. Westcott Ho Cam 66. **d** 68 **p** 69. C Far Headingley St Chad *Ripon* 68-71; Chapl Qu Eliz Coll *Lon* 72-77; Warden Lee Abbey Internat Students' Club Kensington 77-81; Hon C Willesden Green St Gabr *Lon* 81-83; P-in-c Southall H Trin from 84; P-in-c Southall St Geo from 89. *Holy Trinity Vicarage, 41 Park View Road, Southall, Middx UB1 3HJ* 081-574 3762

BARNES, Preb Donald Edward. b 26. K Coll Lon BD51 AKC51. **d** 52 **p** 53. C Willesden St Matt *Lon* 52-59; V Cricklewood St Pet 59-79; Lect Bps' Coll Cheshunt 63-68; V Belsize Park *Lon* from 79; Preb St Paul's Cathl from 84; AD N Camden (Hampstead) 83-88. *St Peter's Parsonage, Belsize Square, London NW3 4HY* 071-794 4020

BARNES, Edwin George. b 11. St Aid Birkenhead 45. **d** 47 **p** 48. R Oulton St Mich *Nor* 55-79; rtd 80; Perm to Offic *Nor* from 80. *35 St James's Crescent, Belton, Great Yarmouth NR31 9IN* Great Yarmouth (0493) 781964

BARNES, Edwin Ronald. b 35. Pemb Coll Ox BA58 MA62. Cuddesdon Coll 58. **d** 60 **p** 61. C Portsea N End St Mark

Portsm 60-64; C Woodham *Guildf* 64-67; R Farncombe 67-78; V Hessle *York* 78-87; AD W Hull Deanery 85-87; Prin St Steph Ho Ox from 87. *St Stephen's House, Marston Street, Oxford OX4 1JX* Oxford (0865) 247874

BARNES, Enid Mabel. b 38. Homerton Coll Cam DipT58. W Midl Minl Tr Course 87. **d** 90. Par Dn Walsall St Paul *Lich* from 90. *Emmanuel Vicarage, Bentley, Walsall WS2 0HP* Walsall (0922) 24200

BARNES, Esdaile Lenox. b 13. ALCD40. **d** 40 **p** 41. Australia 70-72; C Folkestone H Trin w Ch Ch *Cant* 72-74; R Grimston w Congham *Nor* 74-75; R Roydon All SS 74-75; rtd 75. *41 Melvin Street South, Beverley Hills, NSW, Australia 2209*

BARNES, James Barrie. b 27. Bps' Coll Cheshunt 51. **d** 53 **p** 54. C Leic St Phil *Leic* 53-59; V Blackfordby 59-76; V Smisby *Derby* 59-69; RD Akeley W (Ashby) *Leic* 69-76; V Broom Leys from 76. *St David's Vicarage, 7 Greenhill Road, Coalville, Leicester LE6 3RL* Coalville (0530) 36262

BARNES, John Barwick. b 32. AKC58. **d** 59 **p** 60. C Brentwood St Thos *Chelmsf* 59-65; R Arkesden w Wicken Bonhunt 65-71; V Gt Ilford St Mary from 71. *26 South Park Road, Ilford, Essex IG1 1SS* 081-478 0546

BARNES, John Christopher. b 43. MA ATI DMS. Linc Th Coll 78. **d** 80 **p** 81. C Guiseley *Bradf* 80-83; TV Guiseley w Esholt 83-86; V Rawdon from 86. *The Vicarage, Rawdon, Leeds LS19 6QQ* Rawdon (0532) 503263

BARNES, John Edgar. b 45. Univ of Wales (Lamp) BA66 St Chad's Coll Dur MA67. St Steph Ho Ox 68. **d** 70 **p** 71. C Newc St Jo *Newc* 70-73; VC 73-77; C St As and Tremeirchion *St As* 73-77; V Walsingham and Houghton *Nor* 77-89; V Wymondham from 89. *The Vicarage, Wymondham, Norfolk NR18 0PL* Wymondham (0953) 602269

BARNES, John Kenneth. b 04. Jes Coll Ox BA27 MA35. Ripon Hall Ox 34. **d** 36 **p** 37. R Kinnersley w Norton Canon *Heref* 57-74; rtd 74; Perm to Offic *Heref* from 74. *12 Falstaff Road, Hereford HR2 7QF*

BARNES, John Seymour. b 30. Qu Coll Birm 58. **d** 61 **p** 62. C Bromsgrove St Jo *Worc* 61-64; C Kingsthorpe *Pet* 64-66; C Styvechale *Cov* 66-69; P-in-c Avon Dassett w Farnborough 69-75; P-in-c Cov St Alb 75-84; R Weddington and Caldecote 84-89; P-in-c Wilnecote *Lich* 89-90; V Bentley from 90. *The Vicarage, Bentley, Walsall WS2 0HP* Walsall (0922) 242000

BARNES, Neil. b 42. Kelham Th Coll 61 Bps' Coll Cheshunt 65. **d** 68 **p** 69. C Poulton-le-Fylde *Blackb* 68-72; C Ribbleton 72-75; V Knuzden 75-81; Chapl Prestwich Hosp Man from 81; Chapl Salford Mental Illness Unit from 90. *65 Rectory Lane, Prestwich, Manchester M25 5BN* 061-798 8234 or 733 2236

BARNES, Paul Nicholas. b 58. Qu Coll Birm 89. **d** 91. NSM Horninglow *Lich* from 91. *St John's House, 41 Field Lane, Horninglow, Burton-on-Trent, Staffs* Burton-on-Trent (0283) 66491

BARNES, Peter Frank. b 52. St Jo Coll Nottm LTh81. **d** 81 **p** 82. C Colne St Bart *Blackb* 81-83; C Melton Mowbray w Thorpe Arnold *Leic* 83-86; P-in-c Barlestone 86-89; V Broughton and Duddon *Carl* from 89. *The Vicarage, Broughton-in-Furness, Cumbria LA20 6HS* Broughton-in-Furness (0229) 716305

BARNES, Ms Sheena Elizabeth. b 56. Reading Univ MFA Cant Coll of Art BA78 Ox Univ BA85. Ripon Coll Cuddesdon 83. **dss** 86 **d** 87. Westmr St Jas *Lon* 86-87; Par Dn 87-89; rtd 89; Lic to Offic *Lon* from 90. *14H Sussex Street, London SW1V 4RS* 071-931 8318

BARNES, Stephen. b 46. Hull Univ BA69 Bris Univ DipTh71. Clifton Th Coll 69. **d** 72 **p** 73. C Girlington *Bradf* 72-74; TV Glyncorrwg w Afan Vale and Cymmer Afan *Llan* 74-79; R 79-86; V Aberavon from 86. *The Vicarage, 68 Pentyla, Aberavon, Port Talbot, W Glam SA12 8AD* Port Talbot (0639) 883824

BARNES, Stephen John. b 59. Univ of Wales (Cardiff) BSc80. Chich Th Coll 83. **d** 86 **p** 87. C Neath w Llantwit *Llan* 86-89; C Coity w Nolton from 89. *Y Lletty, Heol-yr-Ysgol, Coity, Bridgend, M Glam CF35 6BL* Bridgend (0656) 652540

BARNES, Stephen William. b 53. Man Univ BSc. St Jo Coll Nottm DipTh82. **d** 83 **p** 84. C Chadwell Heath *Chelmsf* 83-87; C Becontree St Alb 88-89; Deanery Youth Chapl 88-91; C Becontree S 89-91; TV Worth *Chich* from 91. *St Barnabas's Vicarage, 2 Crawley Lane, Crawley, W Sussex RH10 4EB* Crawley (0293) 513398

BARNES, William Thomas. b 39. Dur Univ BA60. Wycliffe Hall Ox 60. **d** 62 **p** 63. C Scotforth *Blackb* 62-66; C Cleveleys 66-67; V Colne Ch Ch 67-74; V Bamber

Bridge St Sav from 74. *St Saviour's Vicarage, Bamber Bridge, Preston, Lancs PR5 6AJ* Preston (0772) 35374

BARNES-CEENEY, Brian. b 35. St Aid Birkenhead 59. **d** 62 **p** 63. C Plaistow St Andr *Chelmsf* 62-64; C Waltham Abbey 64-66; V Falfield *Glouc* 66-71; R Rockhampton 66-71; Chapl HM Det Cen Eastwood Park 68-71; HM Youth Cust Cen Everthorpe 71-76; HM Pris Coldingley 76-79; Bris 79-87; Chapl HM Pris Ford from 87. *HM Prison, Arundel, W Sussex BN18 0BX* Littlehampton (0903) 717261

BARNES-CLAY, Peter John Granger. b 43. MCollP Cam Univ CertEd69. Chich Th Coll 72. **d** 75 **p** 82. C Earlham St Anne *Nor* 75-76; Asst Master Hewett Sch Nor 76-83; Hon C Eaton 81-83; C 83-87; R Winterton w E and W Somerton and Horsey from 87. *The Rectory, Winterton-on-Sea, Great Yarmouth, Norfolk NR29 4AW* Winterton-on-Sea (0493) 393227

BARNETT, Alec James Leon. b 44. Em Coll Cam BA66 MA70. Cuddesdon Coll. **d** 69 **p** 70. C Preston St Jo *Blackb* 69-72; Asst Chapl Uppingham Sch Leics 72-80; Hd of RE 73-80; Dir of Farmington/Ampleforth Project 79-83; C Witney *Ox* 80-84; P-in-c Lt Compton w Chastleton, Cornwell etc 84-88; Prin Ox Chr Tr Scheme 84-88; P-in-c St Michael Penkevil *Truro* from 88; Dioc Tr Officer from 88. *The Rectory, Tresillian, Truro, Cornwall TR2 4AA* Tresillian (087252) 431

BARNETT, David John. b 33. Magd Coll Ox BA56 BTh58 MA61. St Steph Ho Ox 56. **d** 59 **p** 60. C Styvechale *Cov* 59-62; S Africa 62-69; Rhodesia 70-76; V Colindale St Matthias *Lon* 77-90; R Finchley St Mary from 90. *St Mary's Rectory, Rectory Close, London N3 1TS* 081-346 4600

BARNETT, Dudley Graham. b 36. Ch Ch Ox BA62 MA65. St Steph Ho Ox 62. **d** 64 **p** 65. C Abbey Hey *Man* 64-68; V Swinton H Rood 68-90; R Old Trafford St Hilda from 90. *St Hilda's Rectory, 255 Kings Road, Manchester M16 0JD* 061-881 9332

BARNETT, Miss Jessica Dorothy Anne. b 18. St Paul's Coll Limuru. **dss** 69 **d** 87. Halifax St Jo Bapt *Wakef* 72-80; rtd 80; Perm to Offic *Ox* from 80. *Cotswold Cottage, Thames Street, Charlbury, Oxford OX7 3QL* Charlbury (0608) 810234

BARNETT, John Raymond. b 51. Lon Univ LLB74 BD86. Westcott Ho Cam 74. **d** 77 **p** 78. C Northfield *Birm* 77-81; V Hamstead St Bernard from 81. *The Vicarage, 147 Hamstead Road, Birmingham B43 5BB* 021-358 1286

BARNETT, John Richard. b 28. FCIS72. Portsm Dioc Tr Course 86. **d** 88. NSM Droxford *Portsm* from 88; NSM Meonstoke w Corhampton cum Exton from 88. *Pinfarthings, Coombe Lane, West Meon, Petersfield, Hants GU32 1NB* West Meon (0730) 829380

BARNETT, Canon Norman. b 19. Univ of Wales BA41. St Mich Coll Llan 41. **d** 43 **p** 44. R Liss *Portsm* 53-85; RD Petersfield 70-75; Hon Can Portsm Cathl 76-85; rtd 85. *Banbury House, Burton Street, Marnhull, Sturminster Newton, Dorset DT10 1PS* Sturminster Newton (0258) 820260

BARNETT, Miss Patricia Ann. b 38. Whitelands Coll Lon CertEd. St Jo Coll Dur 75. **dss** 78 **d** 87. Gateacre *Liv* 78-82; Litherland St Paul Hatton Hill 82-87; Par Dn 87-88; Par Dn Platt Bridge from 88. *28 Stanley Road, Platt Bridge, Wigan, Lancs WN2 3TF* Wigan (0942) 866716

BARNETT, Peter Geoffrey. b 46. AKC71. St Aug Coll Cant 71. **d** 72 **p** 73. C Wolv *Lich* 72-77; P-in-c Caldmore 77-83; TR Bris St Agnes and St Simon w St Werburgh *Bris* 83-87; P-in-c Bris St Paul w St Barn 83-87; TR Bris St Paul's from 87. *St Paul's Rectory, 131 Ashley Road, Bristol BS6 5NU* Bristol (0272) 550150

BARNETT, Peter John. b 36. N Ord Course 82. **d** 85 **p** 86. C New Bury *Man* 85-87; TV from 87. *507 Plodder Lane, Farnworth, Bolton BL4 0JZ* Farnworth (0204) 791577

BARNETT, Preb Raymond Michael. b 31. Man Univ BA54. Wells Th Coll 54. **d** 56 **p** 57. C Fallowfield *Man* 56-59; Madagascar 59-60; V Blackrod *Man* 60-67; V Woolavington *B & W* 67-76; RD Bridgwater 72-76; V St Decumans from 76; RD Quantock 78-86; Preb Wells Cathl from 89. *St Decuman's Vicarage, 47A Brendon Road, Watchet, Somerset TA23 0HU* Watchet (0984) 31228

BARNETT, Canon Robert Theodore. b 15. Ch Coll Cam BA37 MA41. Chich Th Coll 38. **d** 40 **p** 41. V Highcliffe w Hinton Admiral *Win* 52-78; Hon Can Win Cathl 71-78; rtd 78; Perm to Offic *Ban* from 78. *Llys Caerwynt, Rhosybol, Amlwch, Gwynedd LL68 9PP* Amlwch (0407) 831917

BARNETT, Russell Scott. b 20. Oak Hill Th Coll 56. **d** 58 **p** 59. V Salterhebble All SS *Wakef* 67-77; R Aikton *Carl* 77-85; R Orton St Giles 77-85; rtd 86; Perm to Offic *Carl* from 86. *8 Jackson Road, Houghton, Carlisle CA3 0NW* Carlisle (0228) 31721

BARNEY, Michael Frank. b 29. New Coll Ox BA53 MA58. Chich Th Coll 53. **d** 55 **p** 56. C Hampstead St Jo *Lon* 55-59; C Wilton Place St Paul 59-68; C Kensington St Mary Abbots w St Geo 68-75; V Chiswick St Mich from 75. *St Michael's Vicarage, 59 Sutton Lane South, London W4 3JR* 081-994 3173

BARNFATHER, Thomas Fenwick. b 52. Linc Th Coll 86. **d** 88 **p** 89. C Sedgefield *Dur* 88-91; TV E Darlington from 91. *343 Yarm Road, Darlington, Co Durham DL1 1BD* Darlington (0325) 357748

BARNSLEY, Melvyn. b 46. Dur Univ BA67 DipTh69 CertEd. St Chad's Coll Dur 64. **d** 71 **p** 72. C Cov St Thos *Cov* 71-74; C Cov St Jo 71-75; V New Bilton 75-82; R Stevenage St Andr and St Geo *St Alb* from 82; RD Stevenage from 89. *The Rectory, Cuttys Lane, Stevenage, Herts SG1 1UP* Stevenage (0438) 351631

BARNSTAPLE, Archdeacon of. See LLOYD, Ven Bertram Trevor

BARON, Noel Spencer Peter. b 15. K Coll Cam BA39 MA42. Linc Th Coll 40. **d** 41 **p** 42. V W Malvern *Worc* 52-83; rtd 83; Perm to Offic *Heref* from 85. *Brindley, 21 The Crescent, Colwall, Malvern, Worcs WR13 6QN* Colwall (0684) 40477

BARON, Thomas Michael. b 63. St Steph Ho Ox 85. **d** 88 **p** 89. C Hartlepool St Paul *Dur* from 88; Chapl Asst Hartlepool Gen Hosp from 89. *50 The Oval, Hartlepool, Cleveland TS26 9QH* Hartlepool (0429) 267598

BARON, Mrs Vanessa Lilian. b 57. SRN79 City Univ BSc79 Fitzw Coll Cam BA85. Ridley Hall Cam 83. **dss** 86 **d** 87. Roxbourne St Andr *Lon* 86-87; Par Dn 87-89. *4 Peterborough House, Grove Hill, Harrow, Middx HA1 3HF* 081-422 1691

BARR, Canon David James Osborne. b 23. TCD BA45 MA. CITC 46. **d** 46 **p** 47. C Derriaghy *Conn* 46-48; C Dub Donnybrook *D & G* 48-51; C Dub St Ann 51-57; I Dub St Mark 57-65; I Dub Booterstown from 65; RD Monkstown from 83; Can Ch Ch Cathl Dub from 84. *The Rectory, Cross Avenue, Blackrock, Co Dublin, Irish Republic* Dublin (1) 288-7118

BARR, John Gourlay Crichton. b 23. Edin Univ BL46. Edin Dioc NSM Course 81. **d** 84 **p** 85. NSM Edin St Mark *Edin* from 84; NSM Edin St Andr and St Aid from 90. *3 Hamilton Terrace, Edinburgh EH15 1NB* 031-669 3300

BARR (nee HAYTER), Dr Mary Elizabeth. b 58. Jes Coll Ox BA80 CertEd81 MA84 DPhil85. Ridley Hall Cam 84. **dss** 86 **d** 87. Chapl Cam Univ Pastorate 86-91; Cam H Trin w St Andr Gt *Ely* 86-87; Par Dn 87-91; Perm to Offic from 91. *12 Searle Street, Cambridge CB4 3DB* Cambridge (0223) 62757

BARR, Michael John Alexander. b 60. Qu Coll Ox BA82 MA86 Pemb Coll Cam BA86 MA90. Ridley Hall Cam 84. **d** 87 **p** 88. C Earley St Pet *Ox* 87-89; C Cam Gt St Mary w St Mich *Ely* from 89; Chapl Girton Coll Cam from 90. *12 Searle Street, Cambridge CB4 3DB* Cambridge (0223) 62757

BARR, Nigel Andrew. b 55. Lon Univ BSc. Wycliffe Hall Ox 80. **d** 83 **p** 84. C Kimberworth Park *Sheff* 83-86; C Cantley 86-90; V New Rossington from 90. *St Luke's Vicarage, The Circle, New Rossington, Doncaster, S Yorkshire DN11 0QP* Doncaster (0302) 868288

BARR, Very Rev William Norman Cochrane. b 20. TCD BA44 MA50 BD50. CITC 45. **d** 46 **p** 46. Bp's Dom Chapl *Conn* 56-71; I Derriaghy w Colin 61-90; RD Derriaghy 72-82; Can Conn Cathl 80-82; Dean Conn 82-90; rtd 90. *45 Killeaton Crescent, Dunmurry, Belfast BT17 9HB* Belfast (0232) 621746

BARRACLOUGH, Dennis. b 35. LCP62 FCP74 CertEd58. Lambeth STh68 Ripon Hall Ox 66. **d** 68 **p** 69. C Woodhouse *Wakef* 68-71; V Gildersome 71-83; V Kirkburton from 83. *The Vicarage, 3B Shelley Lane, Kirkburton, Huddersfield HD8 0SJ* Huddersfield (0484) 602188

BARRACLOUGH, Canon Owen Conrad. b 32. Pemb Coll Cam BA55 MA59. Westcott Ho Cam 56. **d** 57 **p** 58. C Chippenham St Andr w Tytherton Lucas *Bris* 57-62; V Harringay St Paul *Lon* 62-70; Bp's Chapl for Community Relns *Cov* 70-77; P-in-c Baginton 72-77; V Swindon Ch Ch *Bris* from 77; Chapl Princess Marg Hosp Swindon 77-89; Hon Can Bris Cathl *Bris* from 87. *Christ Church Vicarage, 26 Cricklade Street, Swindon SN1 3HG* Swindon (0793) 522832

BARRALL, John Henry. b 31. BEd. Bps' Coll Cheshunt. **d** 61 **p** 62. C Digswell *St Alb* 61-65; C Aldershot St Mich *Guildf* 65-70; TV Hemel Hempstead *St Alb* 70-82; Perm to Offic 83-91; R Meppershall w Campton and Stondon

38

from 91. *The Rectory, Church Road, Meppershall, Shefford, Beds SG17 5NA* Hitchin (0462) 813334

BARRAND, George William. b 33. Lon Coll of Div 59. **d** 62 **p** 63. C Bucknall and Bagnall *Lich* 62-65; C Parr *Liv* 65-70; Australia from 70. *PO Box 222, Warburton, Victoria, Australia 3799* Warburton (59) 671166

BARRATT, Ven Anthony John. b 19. Glas Univ MRCVS. Bible Churchmen's Coll. **d** 49 **p** 50. Argentina 70-84; Adn Tucuman 73-84; rtd 84. *Couchill Villa, Couchill Farm Lane, Seaton, Devon EX12 3AL* Seaton (0297) 21118

BARRATT, Elizabeth June. b 32. ACP65. Trin Coll Bris 75. **dss** 78 **d** 87. W Kilburn St Luke w St Simon and St Jude *Lon* 78-87; Par Dn from 87. *Flat 1, St Luke's Church Centre, Fernhead Road, London W9 3EH* 081-969 9338

BARRATT, Peter. b 29. Down Coll Cam BA53 MA57. Ridley Hall Cam 53. **d** 55 **p** 56. C Bebington *Ches* 55-58; C-in-c Cam St Martin CD *Ely* 58-61; V Cam St Martin 61-68; V Rawtenstall St Mary *Man* 68-83; AD Rossendale 80-83; V Bosley and N Rode w Wincle and Wildboarclough *Ches* from 83. *The Vicarage, Wincle, Macclesfield, Cheshire SK11 0QH* Wincle (0260) 227234

BARRETT, Alan. b 48. Southn Univ BA69. Wycliffe Hall Ox 74. **d** 77 **p** 78. C Conisbrough *Sheff* 77-80; C Lower Homerton St Paul *Lon* 80-81; C Homerton St Barn w St Paul 81; C-in-c Hounslow Gd Shep Beavers Lane CD 81-87; R Langdon Hills *Chelmsf* from 87. *The Rectory, 105A Berry Lane, Langdon Hills, Basildon, Essex SS16 6AP* Basildon (0268) 542156

BARRETT, Brian William. b 28. Lon Univ BA60. Ox NSM Course 72. **d** 75 **p** 76. Hd Master St Edw's Sch Reading 73-88; Hon C Goring *Ox* 75-84; Hon C Goring w S Stoke from 84; rtd 88; C Blewbury *Ox* 89-90; C Hagbourne 89-90; C Blewbury, Hagbourne and Upton from 90. *3 Chestnut Cottages, Wallingford Road, Streatley, Reading RG8 9JQ* Goring-on-Thames (0491) 873337

BARRETT, Christopher Paul. b 49. AKC71 St Aug Coll Cant 71. **d** 72 **p** 73. C Tupsley *Heref* 72-75; C Ex St Thos *Ex* 75-79; R Atherington and High Bickington 79-83; V Burrington 79-83; Asst Dir of Educn 79-87; P-in-c Sticklepath 83-85; P-in-c Barnstaple 83-85; TV 85-90; V Whipton from 90. *The Vicarage, 19 The Mede, Exeter EX4 8ED* Exeter (0392) 67552

BARRETT, Clive. b 55. MA CertEd. St Steph Ho Ox. **d** 83 **p** 84. C Wakef Cathl *Wakef* 83-87; Chapl Leeds Univ *Ripon* from 87; Dioc Development Rep from 89. *30 St Anne's Road, Leeds LS6 3NX* Leeds (0532) 755497

BARRETT, David Brian. b 27. Clare Coll Cam BA48 MA52 BD69 Columbia Univ (NY) PhD65. Union Th Sem (NY) STM63 Ridley Hall Cam 52. **d** 54 **p** 55. Min Can Bradf Cathl *Bradf* 54-57; CMS 57-63 and from 65; Kenya 57-85; USA from 85. *PO Box 6767, Richmond 23250, Virginia, USA*

BARRETT, Canon Derek Leonard. b 25. St Fran Coll Brisbane ThL57. **d** 57 **p** 58. V Kidderminster St Jo *Worc* 67-77; V Stourbridge St Thos 77-90; RD Stourbridge 83-89; Hon Can Worc Cathl from 87; rtd 90. *Barton Cottage, Bourton-on-the-Water, Glos GL54 2AR* Cotswold (0451) 21777

BARRETT, Gary John. b 46. Sarum & Wells Th Coll 87. **d** 90 **p** 91. NSM Guernsey St Peter Port *Win* from 90. *Berachah, Les Ozouets Close, St Peter Port, Guernsey, Channel Islands* Guernsey (0481) 720405

BARRETT, Graham Crichton. b 51. IEng76 FIMEMME78. Linc Th Coll 88. **d** 90 **p** 91. C Torpoint *Truro* from 90. *3 Sydney Road, Torpoint, Cornwall PL11 2LY* Plymouth (0752) 814104

BARRETT, Very Rev John Alan Gardiner. b 29. CITC 57. **d** 59 **p** 60. C Bray *D & G* 59-63; I Kingscourt *M & K* 63-69; I Navan 69-84; RD Ardnurcher and Clonmacnoise 78-84; Can Meath 81-84; I Rathdrum w Glenealy, Derralossary and Laragh *D & G* 84-89; Dean Clonmacnoise *M & K* from 89; I Trim w Bective and Galtrim from 89; Dioc Registrar (Meath) from 90. *St Patrick's Deanery, Trim, Co Meath, Irish Republic* Trim (46) 36698

BARRETT, John Edward. b 40. Cam Inst of Educn DipEd72. E Anglian Minl Tr Course 78. **d** 81 **p** 82. NSM Everton w Tetworth *Ely* 81-86; TV Stanground and Farcet 86-91; V Friday Bridge from 91; V Coldham from 91; V Elm from 91. *The Vicarage, Friday Bridge, Wisbech, Cambs PE14 0HJ* Wisbech (0945) 860382

BARRETT, John Joseph James. b 38. Lon Univ BD65. Sarum & Wells Th Coll. **d** 78 **p** 78. C Danbury *Chelmsf* 78-80; Ind Chapl 80-89; C Dovercourt 80-83; TV Dovercourt and Parkeston 83-89; V Rubery *Birm* from

89. *St Chad's Vicarage, 160A New Road, Rednal, Birmingham B45 9JA* 021-453 3255

BARRETT, Kenneth. b 42. Univ of Wales (Lamp) BA64. St Steph Ho Ox 65. **d** 67 **p** 68. C Poulton-le-Fylde *Blackb* 67-69; C S Shore H Trin 69-72; V Brierfield 72-83; V Chorley St Geo from 83. *St George's Vicarage, Letchworth Place, Chorley, Lancs PR7 2HJ* Chorley (02572) 63064

BARRETT, Canon Kenneth Sydney. b 26. Roch Th Coll 60. **d** 62 **p** 63. C Wollaton *S'well* 62-65; C Hucknall Torkard 65-67; Australia from 67. *PO Box 203, Mandurah, W Australia 6210* Mandurah (9) 535-1308

BARRETT, Peter Francis. b 56. TCD BA78 MA81 DipTh81 MPhil84. CITC. **d** 81 **p** 82. C Drumachose *D & R* 81-83; C Dub St Ann *D & G* 83-85; I Conwal Union w Gartan *D & R* 85-90; RD Kilmacrenan E and W 88-90; I Belf St Geo *Conn* from 90. *28 Myrtlefield Park, Belfast BT9 6NF* Belfast (0232) 667134

BARRETT, Philip Leslie Sibborn. b 47. FRHistS88 Ex Coll Ox BA68 MA72 BD90. Cuddesdon Coll 68. **d** 70 **p** 71. C Pershore w Wick *Worc* 70-73; C Bournemouth St Pet w St Swithun, St Steph etc *Win* 74-76; VC Heref Cathl *Heref* 76-86; P-in-c Otterbourne *Win* 86-87; R Compton and Otterbourne from 87. *The Rectory, Kiln Lane, Otterbourne, Winchester, Hants SO21 2EJ* Twyford (0962) 713400

BARRETT, Raymond William. b 23. St Mich Coll Llan 72. **d** 73 **p** 74. C Cheltenham St Luke and St Jo *Glouc* 73-75; P-in-c Holbeach Hurn *Linc* 75-78; V Baston 78-83; rtd 83; Perm to Offic *Glouc* from 83. *2 Millhouse Drive, Wymans Brook, Cheltenham, Glos GL50 4RG* Cheltenham (0242) 575434

BARRETT, Ronald Reginald. b 30. Roch Th Coll 61. **d** 64 **p** 65. C Spring Park *Cant* 64-66; C Thornton Heath St Jude 66-68; V Greengates *Bradf* 68-73; V Shelf 73-79; V Embsay w Eastby 79-87; V Farndon and Coddington *Ches* from 87. *The Vicarage, Farndon, Chester CH3 6QD* Farndon (0829) 270270

BARRETT, Stephen David Norman. b 54. Aber Univ BSc75 Edin Univ BD78. Edin Th Coll 75. **d** 78 **p** 79. C Ardrossan *Glas* 78-80; R Peterhead *Ab* 80-81; R Renfrew *Glas* 81-87; R Bishopbriggs from 87; Chapl HM Pris Glas (Barlinnie) from 87. *9 Meadowburn, Bishopbriggs, Glasgow G64 3HA* 041-772 4514

BARRETT, Mrs Thelma. b 29. S'wark Ord Course 80. **dss** 82 **d** 87. Newington St Mary *S'wark* 82-84; Chapl Asst St Pet Hosp Chertsey 84-90; Chertsey *Guildf* 84-87; C 87-90; rtd 91; Perm to Offic *Guildf* from 91. *9 Danses Close, Guildford, Surrey GU4 7EE* Guildford (0483) 505215

BARRETT, Theodore Louis Joseph. b 10. Lich Th Coll 55. **d** 56 **p** 57. V Crosthwaite Kendal *Carl* 62-75; V Cartmel Fell 73-75; rtd 75; Perm to Offic *Carl* from 77. *11 Vicarage Road, Levens, Kendal, Cumbria LA8 8PY* Sedgwick (05395) 60863

BARRETT, Wilfred. b 19. Dur Univ BA46 MA49. Wycliffe Hall Ox 55. **d** 57 **p** 58. V Wilmington *Roch* 60-72; Perm to Offic *Chelmsf* from 76; rtd 84. *204 Hockley Road, Rayleigh, Essex SS6 8EU* Rayleigh (0268) 770364

BARRIBAL, Richard James Pitt. b 45. Trin Coll Bris DipTh80. **d** 80 **p** 81. C Northn St Giles *Pet* 80-82; V Long Buckby w Watford 82-86; Perm to Offic from 86. *166 Abington Avenue, Northampton NN1 4QD* Northampton (0604) 233612

BARRIE, John Arthur. b 38. Bps' Coll Cheshunt. **d** 63 **p** 64. C Southgate St Mich *Lon* 63-66; CF 66-88; Sen CF from 88. *c/o MOD (Army), Bagshot Park, Bagshot, Surrey GU19 5PL* Bagshot (0276) 71717

✠BARRINGTON-WARD, Rt Rev Simon. b 30. Magd Coll Cam BA53 MA57. Wycliffe Coll Toronto Hon DD Westcott Ho Cam 54. **d** 56 **p** 57 **c** 85. Chapl Magd Coll Ox 56-60; Nigeria 60-63; Fell and Dean of Chpl Magd Coll Cam 63-69; Prin Crowther Hall CMS Tr Coll Selly Oak 69-74; Gen Sec CMS 75-85; Hon Can Derby Cathl *Derby* 75-85; Chapl to HM The Queen 84-85; Bp Cov from 85. *The Bishop's House, 23 Davenport Road, Coventry CV5 6PW* Coventry (0203) 672244

BARRODALE, George Bryan. b 44. Univ of Wales (Ban) DipTh DipMin88. St Mich Coll Llan 67. **d** 69 **p** 70. C Newport Maindee St Jo Ev *Mon* 69-72; TV Merthyr Tydfil and Cyfarthfa *Llan* 72-76; R Cotgrave *S'well* from 76; P-in-c Owthorpe from 76; CF (TA) 76-86. *The Rectory, Thurman Drive, Cotgrave, Nottingham NG12 3HT* Nottingham (0602) 892223

BARRON, Charles Leslie. b 20. AKC49. St Steph Ho Ox 49. **d** 50 **p** 51. V Millfield St Mary *Dur* 55-87; P-in-c Bishopwearmouth Gd Shep 76-79; rtd 87. *64 Stratford Avenue, Grangetown, Sunderland SR2 8RY* 091-565 3179

BARRON, Leslie Gill. b 44. ACII69. Lich Th Coll 67. d 70 p 71. C Bishopwearmouth Ch Ch *Dur* 70-72; C Bishopwearmouth St Mary V w St Pet CD 72-75; C Harton 75-77; V Lumley 77-88; P-in-c Hendon and Sunderland 88-90; R Hendon from 90. *St Ignatius Rectory, Bramwell Road, Hendon, Sunderland SR2 8BY* 091-567 5575

✠**BARRON, Rt Rev Patrick Harold Falkiner.** b 11. Leeds Univ BA35. Coll of Resurr Mirfield 32. d 38 p 39 c 64. C Clerkenwell H Redeemer w St Phil *Lon* 38-40; S Africa from 40; Adn Germiston 57-59; Dean Johannesburg 59-64; Suff Bp Cape Town 64-66; Adn Caledon 65-66; Bp George 66-77; rtd 77. *37 Edingight Flats, Queen Road, Rondebosch, 7700 South Africa* Cape Town (21) 689-1820

BARRON, Richard Davidson. b 51. Lon Univ BSc74. Trin Coll Bris 75. d 78 p 79. C Bradley *Wakef* 78-81; C Heworth *York* 81-82; TV 82-89; Chapl York Distr Hosp 82-86; R Greenhithe St Mary *Roch* from 89. *The Rectory, Mounts Road, Greenhithe, Kent DA9 9ND* Greenhithe (0322) 842031

BARRON, Victor Robert. b 45. Ex Univ CertEd70. Trin Coll Bris 76. d 78 p 79. C Rainham *Chelmsf* 78-81; V Easton H Trin w St Gabr and St Lawr *Bris* 81-82; V Easton H Trin w St Gabr and St Lawr and St Jude 82-89; TR Kinson *Sarum* from 89. *The Rectory, 51 Millham's Road, Bournemouth BH10 7LJ* Bournemouth (0202) 571996

BARROW, Michael David Johnstone. b 36. St Mich Coll Llan DipTh64. d 64 p 65. C Old Charlton *S'wark* 64-70; C Wadhurst *Chich* 70-71; C Tidebrook 70-71; C Minster in Sheppey *Cant* 72-79; Chapl HM Pris Standford Hill 72-77; P-in-c Tenterden St Mich *Cant* 79-83; V 84; TR Carl H Trin and St Barn *Carl* from 84; Chapl Cumberland Infirmary 84-90. *St Barnabas' Rectory, Brookside, Carlisle CA2 7JU* Carlisle (0228) 515274

BARROW, Norman Beynon. b 09. St Jo Coll Dur BA36 DipTh37 MA39. d 37 p 38. V Liv All So Springwood *Liv* 64-74; rtd 74; Perm to Offic *Ches* from 74. *2 Cottage Road, Westminster Park, Chester CH4 7QB* Chester (0244) 678440

BARROW, Sqn Ldr Wilfrid Edward Lewis. b 10. Worc Ord Coll 60. d 62 p 63. V Heath and Reach *St Alb* 66-86; rtd 86; Perm to Offic Ox & St Alb from 86. *10 Bideford Green, Linslade, Leighton Buzzard, Beds LU7 7TH* Leighton Buzzard (0525) 372751

BARRY, Herbert Brian. b 25. QUB 46. Edin Th Coll 46. d 48 p 49. C Northolt Park St Barn *Lon* 69-72; P-in-c S Acton All SS 72-82; V Acton Green St Alb 75-82; V Acton St Alb w All SS 82-88; V Acton Green 88-90; Sub-Warden Guild of St Raphael from 85; rtd 90; Perm to Offic *Ex* from 90. *9 Livery Dole, Magdalen Road, Exeter EX2 5DT* Exeter (0392) 427835

BARRY, Canon John. b 15. TCD BA38 MA41. CITC 38. d 38 p 39. I Hillsborough *D & D* 49-83; Preb St Patr Cathl Dub 73-83; rtd 83. *16 West Park, Lisburn, Co Antrim BT28 2BQ* Lisburn (0846) 670664

BARRY, Jonathan Peter Oulton. b 47. TCD BA70 MA73 Hull Univ BA73 QUB PhD84. Ripon Hall Ox 73. d 74 p 75. C Dundela *D & D* 74-79; I Ballyphilip w Ardquin 79-85; Dioc Info Officer 80-90; I Comber from 85. *The Rectory, High Street, Comber, Newtownards, Co Down BT23 5HJ* Comber (0247) 872283

BARRY, Nicholas Brian Paul. b 61. Leic Univ BA83. St Steph Ho Ox 84. d 87 p 88. C St Jo Wood *Lon* 87-90; Chapl RAF from 90. *c/o MOD, Adastral House, Theobald's Road, London WC1X 8RU* 071-430 7268

BARRYMORE, Arthur Norman. b 38. Lon Univ DipTh67. Kelham Th Coll 61. d 67 p 68. C Guildf St Nic *Guildf* 67-69; P-in-c Burgess Hill St Jo *Chich* 69-74; P-in-c Portslade Gd Shep Mile Oak CD 74-79; Dir Sussex Dioc Assn for the Deaf from 80. *32 York Avenue, Hove, E Sussex BN3 1PH* Brighton (0273) 671899 or 726527

BARSLEY, Anthony Noel. b 14. St Aid Birkenhead 46. d 47 p 48. V Chebsey *Lich* 61-76; rtd 76. *5 Brookside Close, Bedale, N Yorkshire DL8 2DR* Bedale (0677) 22087

BARSLEY, Ms Margaret Ann. b 39. E Midl Min Tr Course 79. dss 83 d 87. NSM Kirton in Holland *Linc* 83-89; NSM Skirbeck Quarter from 89. *44 Sentance Crescent, Boston, Lincs PE20 1XF* Boston (0205) 722307

BARSLEY, Robin Cairns. b 23. Wadh Coll Ox BA48 MA48. Westcott Ho Cam 48. d 49 p 50. R Man St Mary Hulme *Man* 68-75; Bp's Chapl for Soc Work *Birm* 75-77; P-in-c Ramsbottom St Paul *Man* 77-81; V Ramsbottom St Jo and St Paul 81-88; rtd 88; Perm to Offic *Man* from 88. *4 The Drive, Ramsbottom, Bury, Lancs BL0 0LE* Ramsbottom (0706) 822208

BARTER, Christopher Stuart. b 49. Chich Th Coll. d 84 p 85. C Margate St Jo *Cant* 84-88; R Whitwood *Wakef* from 88. *The Rectory, 10A Lumley Street, Castleford, W Yorkshire WF10 5LB* Castleford (0977) 559215

BARTER, Geoffrey Roger. b 41. Bris Univ BSc63. Clifton Th Coll 65. d 67 p 68. C Normanton *Derby* 67-70; C Rainham *Chelmsf* 70-75; V Plumstead St Jo w St Jas and St Paul *S'wark* 75-82; V Frogmore H Trin *St Alb* from 82. *Holy Trinity Vicarage, 39 Frogmore, St Albans, Herts AL2 2JU* Park Street (0727) 872172

BARTER, John Herbert. b 30. AKC56. d 57 p 58. C Horsham *Chich* 57-62; V Desborough *Pet* 62-71; P-in-c Braybrook 67-71; P-in-c Brampton Ash w Dingley 70-72; V Hounslow H Trin *Lon* 72-88; V Hounslow H Trin w St Paul from 88. *The Vicarage, 66 Lampton Road, Hounslow, Middx TW3 4DJ* 081-570 9943

BARTLAM, Alan Thomas. b 51. Bris Univ BEd74. Linc Th Coll 88. d 90 p 91. C Longdon-upon-Tern, Rodington, Uppington etc *Lich* from 90. *44 Pemberton Road, Admaston, Telford, Shropshire TF5 0BL* Telford (0952) 244255

BARTLAM, Graham Frederick. b 37. Lon Univ BA63. Oak Hill Th Coll 59. d 64 p 65. C Hawkwell *Chelmsf* 64-68; C Gt Warley Ch Ch 68-74; R High and Gd Easter w Margaret Roding from 74. *Good Easter Vicarage, Chelmsford CM1 4RU* Good Easter (024531) 429

BARTLE, Alan. b 45. Ridley Hall Cam 82. d 84 p 85. C Ely 84-87; V from 87; V Chettisham from 87; V Prickwillow from 87. *The Vicarage, St Mary's Street, Ely, Cambs CB7 4ER* Ely (0353) 662308

BARTLE, Canon David Colin. b 29. Em Coll Cam BA53 MA57. Ridley Hall Cam 53. d 55 p 56. C Birm St Martin *Birm* 55-57; C Boscombe St Jo *Win* 57-60; V Lowestoft St Jo *Nor* 60-70; P-in-c Thetford St Cuth w H Trin 70-72; TR Thetford 72-75; P-in-c Kilverstone 70-75; P-in-c Croxton 70-75; Bournemouth Sch 75-83; R Brantham w Stutton *St E* 83-90; RD Samford 86-90; P-in-c Roxwell *Chelmsf* from 90; Dioc Dir of Ords from 90; Dioc Lay Min Adv from 90; Hon Can Chelmsf Cathl from 91. *The Vicarage, Vicarage Road, Roxwell, Chelmsford CM1 4NB* Chelmsford (0245) 48644

BARTLE, George Clement. b 98. d 30 p 31. R Woodham Mortimer w Hazeleigh *Chelmsf* 61-67; R Woodham Walter 61-67; rtd 67; Hon C Saffron Walden *Chelmsf* 69-72; Hon C Saffron Walden w Wendens Ambo 72-75. *Manormead Nursing Home, Tilford Road, Hindhead, Surrey GU26 6RA* Hindhead (0428) 604780

BARTLE, Reginald Stephen. b 24. K Coll Lon AKC51 BD52. d 52 p 53. SAMS 55-79; Chile 55-70; Adn Chile & Can St Andr Cathl Santiago 64-70; C Tunbridge Wells St Jas *Roch* 80-83; rtd 83; Perm to Offic *St D* from 84. *23 Woodlands Park, Betws, Ammanford, Dyfed SA18 2HF* Ammanford (0269) 594700

BARTLE-JENKINS, Canon Leonard Christmas. b 13. Univ of Wales (Lamp) BA35. Lich Th Coll 35. d 38 p 39. V Bassaleg *Mon* 55-73; Can St Woolos Cathl 64-82; RD Bassaleg 67-82; R Michaelston-y-Fedw and Rudry 74-82; rtd 82; Lic to Offic *Mon* from 85. *3 St Teilo's Court, Sturminster Road, Roath, Cardiff* Cardiff (0222) 489378

BARTLE-JENKINS, Paul. b 43. Bris & Glouc Tr Course. d 84 p 86. NSM Bris St Agnes and St Simon w St Werburgh *Bris* 84-87; NSM Bris St Paul's from 87. *51 Henleaze Park Drive, Westbury-on-Trym, Bristol BS9 4LN* Bristol (0272) 624689

✠**BARTLEET, Rt Rev David Henry.** b 29. St Pet Hall Ox BA55 MA61. Westcott Ho Cam 55. d 57 p 58 c 82. C Ipswich St Mary le Tower *St E* 57-60; C Doncaster St Geo *Sheff* 60-64; V Edenbridge *Roch* 64-73; V Bromley SS Pet and Paul 73-82; Hon Can Roch Cathl from 79; Suff Bp Tonbridge from 82. *Bishop's Lodge, 48 St Botolph's Road, Sevenoaks, Kent TN13 3AG* Sevenoaks (0732) 456070

BARTLES-SMITH, Ven Douglas Leslie. b 37. St Edm Hall Ox BA61 MA65. Wells Th Coll 61. d 63 p 64. C Westmr St Steph w St Jo *Lon* 63-68; P-in-c Camberwell St Mich w All So w Em *S'wark* 68-72; V 72-75; V Battersea St Luke 75-85; RD Battersea 81-85; Adn S'wark from 85. *1A Dog Kennel Hill, London SE22 8AA* 071-274 6767

BARTLETT, Alan. b 38. Qu Coll *Birm* 79-81; Hon C Kingstanding St Mark from 82. *43 Delhurst Road, Birmingham B44 9UT* 021-360 7878

BARTLETT, Alan Bennett. b 58. G&C Coll Cam BA81 Birm Univ PhD87 St Jo Coll Dur BA90. Cranmer Hall Dur 88. d 91. C Newc H Cross *Newc* from 91. *2A Lancercost Drive, Newcastle upon Tyne NE5 2DE* 091-274 9574

BARTLETT, Alban Denys. b 26. St Jo Coll Ox BA50 MA55. St Mich Coll Llan 50. d 52 p 53. C Neath w Llantwit *Llan* 52-54; C Newport St Mark *Mon* 54-56; CF 57-81; Chapl Chelsea R Hosp from 81. *Royal Hospital Chelsea, London SW3 4SR*   071-730 0161

BARTLETT, Anthony Martin. b 43. Cranmer Hall Dur 74. d 77 p 78. C Heworth St Mary *Dur* 77-80; V Cleadon 80-84; CF (TA) 81-90; Prec Dur Cathl *Dur* 85-87; V Harton from 87. *182 Sunderland Road, South Shields, Tyne & Wear NE34 6AH*   091-456 1855

BARTLETT, Basil Gordon. b 11. Selw Coll Cam BA34 MA38. Wells Th Coll 34. d 36 p 37. Chapl and Prin R Sch for the Blind Leatherhead 50-76; rtd 76; Perm to Offic B & W & Ex from 76. *Meadow Cottage, North Wootton, Shepton Mallet, Somerset BA4 4AQ*   Pilton (074989) 547

BARTLETT, Clifford William Tudor. b 15. ALCD38. d 38 p 39. V Ovingham *Newc* 60-80; rtd 80; Lic to Offic *Newc* from 85; Perm to Offic *Dur* from 81; Chapl Hunties Moor Hosp from 86. *69 Rectory Lane, Winlaton, Blaydon-on-Tyne, Tyne & Wear NE21 6PJ*   091-414 4236

BARTLETT, Canon David Blandford. b 24. Cam Univ BA49 MA50. Sarum Th Coll. d 51 p 52. Tanganyika 54-64; Tanzania 64-90; rtd 91; P-in-c Heptonstall *Wakef* from 91. *The Vicarage, Heptonstall, Hebden Bridge, W Yorkshire HX7 7NT*   Hebden Bridge (0422) 842004

BARTLETT, David John. b 36. Pemb Coll Ox BA61. Linc Th Coll 63. d 65 p 66. C Wollaton *S'well* 65-70; V Woodthorpe 70-83; P-in-c Kirklington w Hockerton from 83; Chapl Rodney Sch Kirklington from 83; V Farnsfield *S'well* from 83; RD S'well from 83. *The Vicarage, Beck Lane, Farnsfield, Newark, Notts NG22 8ER*   Mansfield (0623) 882247

BARTLETT, David William. b 59. Trin Coll Bris 89. d 91. C Frinton *Chelmsf* from 91. *28 St Mary's Road, Frinton-on-Sea, Essex*   Frinton-on-Sea (0255) 671974

BARTLETT, Canon George. b 32. Oak Hill Th Coll 58. d 60 p 61. C Tollington Park St Mark *Lon* 60-63; C Dagenham *Chelmsf* 63-64; V Samlesbury *Blackb* 64-67; V Blackb St Matt 67-71; P-in-c W Thurrock *Chelmsf* 71-78; Ind Chapl 71-88; P-in-c Fobbing 78-88; Hon Can Chelmsf Cathl from 84; P-in-c Panfield from 88; P-in-c Gt w Lt Saling from 88. *The Rectory, 2 Church End, Panfield, Braintree, Essex CM7 5AT*   Braintree (0376) 24615

BARTLETT, Canon Prof John Raymond. b 37. FSA88 BNC Ox BA59 MA62 BLitt62 TCD MA70. Linc Th Coll 61. d 63 p 64. C W Bridgford *S'well* 63-66; Lect Div TCD 66-86; Assoc Prof Bibl Studies 86-90; Prof Past Th from 90; Treas Ch Ch Cathl Dub *D & G* 86-88; Prec from 88; Prin CITC from 89. *Church of Ireland Theological College, Braemor Park, Rathgar, Dublin 14, Irish Republic*   Dublin (1) 975506 or 975274

BARTLETT, Kenneth Vincent John. b 36. Or Coll Ox BA61 BTh63. Ripon Hall Ox. d 63 p 64. C Paddington St Jas *Lon* 63-67; Lic to Offic from 67. *13 Shaa Road, London W3 7LN*   081-743 3989

BARTLETT, Canon Maurice Edward. b 33. G&C Coll Cam BA59 MA63. Wells Th Coll 59. d 60 p 61. C Batley All SS *Wakef* 60-64; Bp's Dom Chapl 64-66; Dir of Ords 64-66; Asst Chapl HM Pris Wakef 64-66; V Allerton *Liv* 66-81; V Lanc St Mary *Blackb* from 81; Sub-Chapl HM Pris Lanc from 81; Hon Can Blackb Cathl from 87. *Priory Vicarage, Lancaster LA1 1YZ*   Lancaster (0524) 63200

BARTLETT, Michael Fredrick. b 52. Ex Univ BA74 Liv Univ BPhil76 Ox Univ BA79 MA. Ripon Coll Cuddesdon 76 Ven English Coll Rome 78. d 79 p 80. C Kirkby *Liv* 79-82; C Wordsley *Lich* 82-83; Chapl Wordsley Hosp 82-88; TV Wordsley *Lich* 83-88; TV Redditch, The Ridge *Worc* from 88. *St Peter's House, Littlewoods, Crabbs Cross, Redditch, Worcs B97 5LB*   Redditch (0527) 545709

BARTLETT, Michael George. b 35. S Dios Minl Tr Scheme 84. d 87 p 88. NSM Wimborne Minster and Holt *Sarum* 87-90; C Charlestown *Truro* from 90. *St Luke's House, 5 Penhaligon Way, St Austell, Cornwall PL25 3AR*   St Austell (0726) 69857

BARTLETT, Stephen Giles Howard. b 39. Bris Univ CertEd63. Lambeth STh86 Lich Th Coll 65. d 67 p 68. C Old Brumby *Linc* 67-70; C Cleobury Mortimer w Hopton Wafers *Heref* 70-72; C Caversham *Ox* 72-77; V Chalgrove w Berrick Salome 77-88; V W Brompton St Mary w St Pet *Lon* from 88. *24 Fawcett Street, London SW10 9EZ*   071-351 4204

BARTON, Canon Alfred Ernest. b 19. Man Univ BA52. Qu Coll Birm 50. d 52 p 53. C Rochdale *Man* 52-54; V Bolton Sav 54-57; Sen Chapl United Sheff Hosps 57-63; P-in-c Hardwick w Tusmore *Ox* 63-67; R 63-67; P-in-c

Cottisford 63-65; R 65-67; V Benson from 67; RD Cuddesdon 73-85; Hon Can Ch Ch from 85; RD Aston and Cuddesdon 85-88. *The Vicarage, Church Road, Benson, Wallingford, Oxon OX10 6SH*   Wallingford (0491) 38254

BARTON, Andrew Edward. b 53. MRSC St Jo Coll Ox MA77 DPhil80. Ridley Hall Cam 87. d 90 p 91. C Ringwood *Win* from 90. *15 Ashburn Garth, Hightown, Ringwood, Hants BH24 3DS*   Ringwood (0425) 474529

BARTON, Canon Arthur (Michael). b 33. CCC Cam BA57 MA61. Wycliffe Hall Ox 57. d 59 p 60. Min Can Bradf Cathl *Bradf* 59-61; C Maltby *Sheff* 61-63; V Silsden *Bradf* 63-70; V Moor Allerton *Ripon* 70-81; TR 81-82; V Wetherby from 82; Chapl HM Young Offender Inst Wetherby 82-89; RD Harrogate *Ripon* from 88; Hon Can Ripon Cathl from 89. *The Vicarage, Parsons Green, Wetherby, W Yorkshire LS22 4RQ*   Wetherby (0937) 582423

BARTON, Ven Charles John Greenwood. b 36. ALCD63. d 63 p 64. C Cant St Mary Bredin *Cant* 63-66; V Whitfield w W Langdon 66-75; V S Kensington St Luke *Lon* 75-83; AD Chelsea 80-83; Chief Broadcasting Officer for C of E 83-90; Lic to Offic *Lon* 84-90; Adn Aston and Can Res Birm Cathl *Birm* from 90. *26 George Road, Birmingham B15 1PJ*   021-454 5525

BARTON, Canon Cyril Albert. b 28. St Pet Hall Ox BA50 MA54. Ridley Hall Cam. d 52 p 53. C Maghull *Liv* 52-55; Min Can Bradf Cathl *Bradf* 55-58; V Oldham St Paul *Man* 58-68; V Norbury *Ches* 68-90; Hon Can Ches Cathl from 85; R Aldford and Bruera from 90. *The Rectory, Middle Lane, Aldford, Chester CH3 6JA*   Chester (0244) 620281

BARTON, Dale. b 49. Selw Coll Cam BA71 MA76. Linc Th Coll 71. d 73 p 74. C Gosforth All SS *Newc* 73-77; Lesotho 77-81; Dep Warden CA Hostel Cam 82-83; C Shepton Mallet w Doulting *B & W* 83-88; TV Preston St Jo *Blackb* from 88. *St Stephen's Vicarage, 60 Broadgate, Preston, Lancs PR1 8DU*   Preston (0772) 555762

BARTON, David Gerald Story. b 38. Selw Coll Cam BA62 MA66. Cuddesdon Coll 63. d 65 p 66. C Cowley St Jas *Ox* 65-68; C Hambleden 68-72; Hon C Hammersmith St Jo *Lon* 72-77; Hon C Paddington St Jas 77-81; Hd Master Soho Par Sch 81-88; Hon C Westmr St Jas from 81; RE Project Officer Lon Dioc Bd for Schs from 88. *60 Hiley Road, London NW10 5PS*   081-960 2958

BARTON, Edward. b 23. d 75 p 76. C Budock *Truro* 75-79; P-in-c St Stithians w Perranarworthal 79-80; V St Stythians w Perranarworthal and Gwennap 80-82; rtd 88. *The Lock House, Avon Lock, Tewkesbury, Glos GL20 5BE*

BARTON, Eric Alfred. b 13. Clifton Th Coll 38. d 40 p 41. V Buttershaw St Paul *Bradf* 61-70; V Nailsea Ch Ch *B & W* 70-82; rtd 82; Perm to Offic *Ex* from 82. *High Roost, Springhead Road, Uplyme, Lyme Regis, Dorset DT7 3UG*   Lyme Regis (02974) 5436

BARTON, Canon Geoffrey. b 27. Or Coll Ox BA48 MA52. Chich Th Coll 49. d 51 p 52. C Arnold *S'well* 51-53; C E Retford 53-54; V Mirfield Eastthorpe St Paul *Wakef* 54-60; V Boroughbridge w Roecliffe *Ripon* 60-73; V Aldborough w Boroughbridge and Roecliffe 73; P-in-c Farnham w Scotton and Staveley and Copgrove 73-74; R 74-77; Chapl Roundway Hosp Devizes from 77; Can and Preb Sarum Cathl *Sarum* from 86. *The Chaplain's Office, Roundway Hospital, Devizes, Wilts SN10 5DS*   Devizes (0380) 724955

BARTON, Canon John. b 25. MBE91. Keble Coll Ox BA48 MA50. Ely Th Coll 48. d 50 p 51. Chapl Stanley Royd & Pinderfields Hosps Wakef 60-72; RD Wakef 68-72; Chapl Jo Radcliffe Hosp & Radcliffe Infirmary 72-90; Chapl Chu Hosp Ox 72-89; Hon Can Ch Ch *Ox* from 77; RD Cowley from 89; rtd 90. *212 Headington Road, Oxford OX3 7PS*   Oxford (0865) 63918

BARTON, Dr John. b 48. Keble Coll Ox BA69 MA73 DPhil74 DLitt88. d 73 p 73. Lect St Cross Coll Ox 74-89; Fell from 74; Reader in Bibl Studies from 89. *11 Withington Court, Abingdon, Oxon*   Abingdon (0235) 525925

BARTON, John Christopher Peter. b 28. Trin Hall Cam BA51 MA56. Ridley Hall Cam 51. d 53 p 54. C Erith St Paul *Roch* 53-56; C Cockfosters Ch Ch CD *Lon* 56-64; V Welling *Roch* 64-75; P-in-c Malmesbury w Westport *Bris* 75-84; P-in-c Charlton w Brokenborough and Hankerton 80-84; V Malmesbury w Westport and Brokenborough from 84. *Abbey Vicarage, Malmesbury, Wilts SN16 9BA*   Malmesbury (0666) 823126

BARTON, John Michael. b 40. TCD BA62 Div Test. d 63 p 64. C Coleraine *Conn* 63-68; C Portadown St Mark *Arm* 68-71; I Carnteel and Crilly 71-83; I Derryloran from 83. *13 Loy Street, Cookstown, Co Tyrone BT80 8PZ* Cookstown (06487) 62261

BARTON, Dr Margaret Anne. b 54. St Anne's Coll Ox MA80 DPhil81 Selw Coll Cam BA89. Ridley Hall Cam 87. **d** 90. Par Dn Burley Ville *Win* from 90. *15 Ashburn Garth, Hightown, Ringwood, Hants BH24 3DS* Ringwood (0425) 474529

BARTON, Samuel David. b 45. DipTh. **d** 84 **p** 85. C Ballywillan *Conn* 84-86; I Aghadowey w Kilrea *D & R* from 86. *Kilrea Rectory, 2 Moneygran Road, Kilrea, Co Londonderry BT51 5SJ* Kilrea (02665) 40257

BARTON, Stephen William. b 50. St Jo Coll Cam BA73 MA76 Leeds Univ MPhil81. Coll of Resurr Mirfield 75. **d** 77 **p** 78. C Horton *Bradf* 77-80; USPG from 80. *St Thomas Church, 54 Johnson Road, Dhaka 1100, Bangladesh*

BARTON, Canon Sydney Gerald. b 1900. St Jo Coll Dur LTh29 BA33. St Aid Birkenhead 26. **d** 30 **p** 31. R W Kirby St Bridget *Ches* 53-70; Hon Can Ches Cathl 61-70; rtd 70; Hon C Capenhurst *Ches* 71-78; Perm to Offic *Cant* from 82. *1 Gillon Mews, Canterbury, Kent CT1 1LZ* Canterbury (0227) 457138

BARTON, Timothy Charles. b 47. Sarum & Wells Th Coll 73. **d** 76 **p** 77. C Upholland *Liv* 76-80; V Dalton from 80. *88 Lyndhurst Avenue, Skelmersdale, Lancs WN8 6UH* Skelmersdale (0695) 33148

BARTON, Trevor James. b 50. St Alb Minl Tr Scheme 79. **d** 87 **p** 88. NSM Hemel Hempstead *St Alb* from 87. *46 Crossfell Road, Hemel Hempstead, Herts HP3 8RQ* Hemel Hempstead (0442) 51537

BARWELL, Brian Bernard Beale. b 30. AKC59. **d** 60 **p** 61. C Heywood St Jas *Man* 60-63; V Smallbridge 63-69; V Farington *Blackb* 69-72; C Blackb St Luke w St Phil 72-75; C Standish 75-76; Lic to Offic from 76. *70 Claytongate, Coppull, Chorley, Lancs PR7 4PS*

BARWOOD, Frederick James. b 05. Selw Coll Cam BA30 MA34. Ely Th Coll 33. **d** 34 **p** 35. V Hordle *Win* 61-74; rtd 74; Perm to Offic *Win* from 75. *94 Manor Road, New Milton, Hants BH25 5EJ* New Milton (0425) 616150

BASDEN, Canon Maurice Edward. b 25. Linc Coll Ox BA49 MA55. Westcott Ho Cam. **d** 51 **p** 52. C Southn St Mark *Win* 51-54; C Christchurch 54-57; Fiji 57-76; Hon Can H Trin Cathl Suva 67-73 and from 76; Can 73-76; Perm to Offic *Lon* 76-80. *Harescombe, Watford Road, Northwood, Middx*

BASHFORD, Richard Frederick. b 36. Lon Univ DipTh68. Clifton Th Coll. **d** 68 **p** 69. C Bedworth *Cov* 68-71; C Lower Homerton St Paul *Lon* 71-75; V Bordesley Green *Birm* 75-81; R Birm Bishop Latimer w All SS from 81. *The Vicarage, 28 Handsworth New Road, Birmingham B18 4PT* 021-554 2221

BASHFORD, Robert Thomas. b 49. Ch Coll Cam BA70 CertEd72 MA74 Lon Univ BD84 MPhil89. Oak Hill Th Coll 86. **d** 88 **p** 89. C Frinton *Chelmsf* 88-91; C Galleywood Common from 91. *St Michael's House, 13 Roughtons, Galleywood, Chelmsford CM2 8PE* Chelmsford (0245) 74695

BASIL, Brother. See FARRANT, Jonathan

BASINGSTOKE, Archdeacon of. See KNIGHT, Ven Alexander Francis

BASINGSTOKE, Suffragan Bishop of. See MANKTELOW, Rt Rev Michael Richard John

BASKERVILLE, Philip Duncan. b 58. St Chad's Coll Dur BSc79 Or Coll Ox PGCE80. Trin Coll Bris BA87. **d** 88 **p** 89. C Roby *Liv* from 88. *42 Buttermere Road, Liverpool L16 2NN* 051-489 5910

BASON, Brian. b 27. Leeds Univ BA49 Lon Univ BD69. Coll of Resurr Mirfield 49. **d** 51 **p** 52. C Haggerston St Aug w St Steph *Lon* 51-55; C Bow w Bromley St Leon 55-56; V Audenshaw St Hilda *Man* 56-89; Perm to Offic Man & Ches from 89; Audenshaw High Sch from 89. *78 Windsor Road, Denton, Manchester M34 2HE* 061-320 8455

BASS, Colin Graham. b 41. Liv Univ BSc62 Fitzw Ho Cam BA64 MA68. Ox NSM Course 84. **d** 87 **p** 88. Dir of Studies Leighton Park Sch Reading from 87; NSM Earley St Pet *Ox* from 87. *9 Bramley Close, Earley, Reading RG6 2PL* Reading (0734) 663732

BASS, George Michael. b 39. Ely Th Coll 62. **d** 65 **p** 66. C Romaldkirk *Ripon* 65-68; C Kenton Ascension *Newc* 68-71; CF from 71. *c/o MOD (Army), Bagshot Park, Bagshot, Surrey GU19 5PL* Bagshot (0276) 71717

BASS, Mrs Rosemary Jane. b 38. Linc Th Coll 76. dss 79 **d** 87. Bedf All SS *St Alb* 79-84; Leavesden All SS 84-87; Par Dn from 87. *49 Ross Crescent, Watford WD2 6DA* Garston (0923) 673129

BASSETT, Abner Gerwyn. b 25. Univ of Wales (Lamp) BA48 LTh50. **d** 50 **p** 51. P-in-c Llanfair-ar-y-Bryn *St D*

58-73; V Llandyssilio w Egremont and Llanglydwen etc 73-91; rtd 91. *1 Ger-y-Llan, The Parade, Carmarthen, Dyfed SA31 1LY* Carmarthen (0267) 235284

BASSETT, John Edmund. b 33. St Aid Birkenhead 63. **d** 66 **p** 67. C Guiseley *Bradf* 66-67; C Stechford *Birm* 67-71; C Ross *Heref* 71-72; P-in-c Brampton Abbotts 73-75; P-in-c Weston under Penyard 73-75; P-in-c Hope Mansell 73-75; TR Halesworth w Linstead and Chediston *St E* 75-78; P-in-c Irby on Humber *Linc* 78; R Laceby 78-83; V Sale St Paul *Ches* 83-88; P-in-c Southport All SS *Liv* from 88; P-in-c Southport All So from 88. *All Saints' Vicarage, 1 Park Avenue, Southport, Merseyside PR9 9LS* Southport (0704) 533336

BASSETT, Canon Ralph Harry. b 09. Keble Coll Ox BA32 MA35. Dorchester Miss Coll 34. **d** 36 **p** 37. Hon Can Portsm Cathl *Portsm* 61-77; V Hambledon 68-77; rtd 77; Perm to Offic *Portsm* from 77. *17 Frensham Road, Southsea, Hants PO4 8AD* Portsmouth (0705) 738571

BASTEN, Richard Henry. b 40. Codrington Coll Barbados 60. **d** 63 **p** 64. Br Honduras 63-67; Barbados 68-72; C Hartlepool H Trin *Dur* 72-73; Chapl Bedstone Coll 73-88; C Clun w Chapel Lawn *Heref* 73-77; P-in-c Clungunford 77-78; R Clungunford w Clunbury and Clunton, Bedstone etc 78-88; R Rowde and Poulshot *Sarum* from 88. *The Rectory, Cock Road, Rowde, Devizes, Wilts SN10 2PN* Devizes (0380) 724413

BASTIDE, Derek. b 44. Dur Univ BA65 Reading Univ DipEd66 Sussex Univ MA77. Chich Th Coll 76. **d** 77 **p** 78. Hon C Lewes All SS, St Anne, St Mich and St Thos *Chich* 77-84; Prin Lect Brighton Poly from 80; P-in-c Hamsey *Chich* from 84. *The Rectory, Offham, Lewes, E Sussex BN7 3PX* Lewes (0273) 474356

BASTIN, Edward James. b 06. Lon Univ BSc28. Ridley Hall Cam 28. **d** 30 **p** 31. V Keresley and Coundon *Cov* 36-71; rtd 71. *9 Margetts Close, Kenilworth, Warks CV8 1EN* Kenilworth (0926) 59855

BASTOCK, Kenneth William. b 22. Launde Abbey 75. **d** 76 **p** 77. C Glen Parva and S Wigston *Leic* 76-80; V Orton-on-the-Hill w Twycross etc from 80. *The Vicarage, 1 Bilstone Road, Twycross, Atherstone, Warks CV9 3PP* Tamworth (0827) 880295

BASTON, Caroline. b 56. Birm Univ BSc78 CertEd79. Ripon Coll Cuddesdon 87. **d** 89. Par Dn Southn Thornhill St Chris *Win* from 89. *22 Lydgate Green, Southampton SO2 6LP* Bursledon (042121) 6351

BATCHELOR, Alan Harold. b 30. Bris Univ BA54 Hull Univ MA63 DipPM68 LSE. Linc Th Coll 54. **d** 56 **p** 57. C Bishops upon Hull St Alb *York* 56-60; C Attercliffe w Carbrook *Sheff* 60-62; India 63-87; Ind Chapl *Ripon* from 87. *23 Harrowby Road, Leeds LS16 5HX* Leeds (0532) 752709

BATCHELOR, John Millar. b 35. CITC 76. **d** 78 **p** 79. C Belf All SS *Conn* 78-80; I Eglish w Killylea *Arm* from 80. *154 Killylea Road, Armagh BT60 4LN* Caledon (0861) 568320

BATCUP, John Aubrey. b 08. Lon Univ BD54. Lich Th Coll 29. **d** 32 **p** 33. V Bounds Green *Lon* 59-77; rtd 77. *16 Green Close, Mayals, Swansea SA3 5DW* Swansea (0792) 402564

BATE, Bernard Percival. b 12. Selw Coll Cam BA37 MA41. Wells Th Coll 37. **d** 38 **p** 39. R Lurgashall *Chich* 68-77; rtd 77; Perm to Offic *Bradf* 79-85. *4 Courtwood Close, Shady Bower, Salisbury SP1 2RX* Salisbury (0722) 328887

BATE, Canon Herbert Roland. b 95. MC18. Leeds Univ BA20. Coll of Resurr Mirfield 13. **d** 22 **p** 23. R Welwyn *St Alb* 31-63; rtd 63; Perm to Offic *Chich* from 63. *4 Lynford Close, Midsomer Norton, Bath BA3 2UA* Midsomer Norton (0761) 41970

BATE, Lawrence Mark. b 40. Univ Coll Ox BA63. Coll of Resurr Mirfield 65. **d** 67 **p** 68. C Benwell St Jas *Newc* 67-69; C Monkseaton St Pet 69-72; TV Withycombe Raleigh *Ex* 72-84; RD Aylesbeare 81-84; R Alphington from 84. *The Rectory, Alphington, Exeter EX2 8XJ* Exeter (0392) 437662

BATE, Michael Keith. b 42. Lich Th Coll 67. **d** 69 **p** 70. C W Bromwich St Jas *Lich* 69-73; C Thornhill *Wakef* 73-76; V Wrenthorpe 76-82; V Upper Gornal *Lich* from 82; Chapl Burton Rd Hosp Dudley from 82. *St Peter's Vicarage, 35 Eve Lane, Upper Gornal, Dudley, W Midlands DY1 3TY* Sedgley (0902) 883467

BATEMAN, Alfred Neville. b 39. MIMI83. Oak Hill Th Coll 87. **d** 89 **p** 90. C Pendlebury St Jo *Man* from 89. *41 Danesway, Swinton, Manchester M27 1JS* 061-736 3613

BATEMAN, James Edward. b 44. Lon Univ BSc65 Bris Univ DipTh74. Trin Coll Bris 71. **d** 74 **p** 75. C Woodlands *Sheff* 74-77; C Rushden w Newton Bromswold *Pet* 77-84;

R Vange *Chelmsf* from 84. *The Rectory, 782 Clay Hill Road, Vange, Basildon, Essex SS16 4NG*   Basildon (0268) 553248

BATEMAN, John Reinhardt. b 05. Magd Coll Cam BA27 MA31. Ripon Hall Ox 31. **d** 33 **p** 34. Lic to Offic *Birm* 56-80; Res Tutor St Pet Tr Coll Birm 56-62; Sen Tutor 62-69; rtd 69. *263 Penn Road, Wolverhampton, W Midlands WV4 5SF*   Wolverhampton (0902) 335504

BATEMAN, Kenneth William. b 34. ACII58. N Ord Course 85. **d** 88 **p** 89. Hon C Pilling *Blackb* from 88; Chapl Lanc Moor Hosp from 88. *Swallowdale, Sandy Lane, Hambleton, Blackpool FY6 9AA*   Hambleton (0253) 700585

BATEMAN, Martyn Henry. b 31. Jes Coll Cam BA54 MA58. Clifton Th Coll 54. **d** 56 **p** 57. C Heatherlands St Jo *Sarum* 56-59; C New Malden and Coombe *S'wark* 59-60; Iran 60-62; V Charsfield *St E* 62-69; R Monewden and Hoo 62-69; V Wickham Market 69-82; Hon Can St E Cathl 80-85; V Felixstowe SS Pet and Paul 82-85; TR Lydford, Brent Tor, Bridestowe and Sourton *Ex* from 85; RD Tavistock from 90. *The Rectory, Lydford, Okehampton, Devon EX20 4BH*   Lydford (082282) 306

BATEMAN, Richard George. b 46. St Jo Coll Dur. **d** 82 **p** 83. C Wolviston *Dur* 82-85; C Greenside 85-87; V Newburn *Newc* from 87. *The Vicarage, Newburn, Newcastle upon Tyne NE15 8LQ*   091-229 0522

BATEMAN, Richard William. b 36. AKC61. **d** 62 **p** 63. C Pennywell St Thos and Grindon St Oswald CD *Dur* 62-66; Trinidad and Tobago 66-70; R Etherley *Dur* 70-77; Ind Chapl *Roch* 77-83; Hon C Chatham St Steph 78-83; Chapl RN 79-83; V Kemsing w Woodlands *Roch* 83-90; P-in-c Petham and Waltham w Lower Hardres etc *Cant* from 90. *The Rectory, Curtis Lane, Stelling Minnis, Canterbury, Kent*   Petham (022770) 318

BATEMAN-CHAMPAIN, John Nicholas. b 30. Cam Univ BA53. S'wark Ord Course 85. **d** 85 **p** 86. C Harpenden St Jo *St Alb* 85-88; V Northaw from 88. *The Vicarage, 58 Hill Rise, Cuffley, Potters Bar, Herts EN6 4RG*   Potters Bar (0707) 874126

BATES, David William. b 25. Cranmer Hall Dur 59. **d** 61 **p** 62. V Linc St Pet-at-Gowts and St Andr *Linc* 68-77; V Metheringham 77-81; V Metheringham w Blankney 81-91; rtd 91; Perm to Offic *Linc* from 91. *The Vicarage, Drury Street, Metheringham, Lincoln LN4 3EZ*   Metheringham (0526) 20204

BATES, Derek Alvin. b 27. St Mich Coll Llan 57. **d** 59 **p** 60. C Bishop's Cleeve *Glouc* 59-63; V Shebbear *Ex* 67-71; R Buckland Filleigh 67-71; R Highampton w Sheepwash 71; R Coates *Ely* 72-80; R Clovelly *Ex* from 80; V Woolfardisworthy and Buck Mills from 80. *The Rectory, Bucks Cross, Bideford, Devon EX39 5DT*   Clovelly (0237) 431571

✠**BATES, Rt Rev Gordon.** b 34. Kelham Th Coll 54. **d** 58 **p** 59 **c** 83. C New Eltham All SS *S'wark* 58-62; Asst Youth Chapl *Glouc* 62-64; Youth Chapl *Liv* 65-69; Chapl Liv Cathl 65-69; V Huyton St Mich 69-73; Can Res and Prec Liv Cathl 73-83; Dir of Ords 73-83; Suff Bp Whitby *York* from 83. *60 West Green, Stokesley, Middlesbrough, Cleveland TS9 5BD*   Stokesley (0642) 710390

BATES, Harry. b 11. Sheff Univ BSc32. Trin Coll Bris 39. **d** 40 **p** 41. Australia 40-45 and from 54; R Barnwell *Pet* 46-54. *34 Pindari Avenue, Camden, NSW, Australia 2570*   Campbeltown (46) 667920

BATES, James. b 46. Linc Th Coll 73. **d** 75 **p** 76. C Ewell *Guildf* 75-77; C Farncombe 77-80; V Pet St Mary *Pet* from 80. *St Mary's Vicarage, 214 Eastfield Road, Peterborough PE1 4BD*   Peterborough (0733) 343418

BATES, Michael. b 33. Dur Univ BSc57 Hull Univ ADME84. Clifton Th Coll 57. **d** 59 **p** 60. C Drypool St Columba w St Andr and St Pet *York* 59-62; C Cheadle *Ches* 62-67; V Newbottle *Dur* 67-75; Asst Master Bilton Grange High Sch Hull from 76; Hon C Kingston upon Hull H Trin *York* from 81. *68 Davenport Avenue, Hessle, N Humberside HU13 0RW*   Hull (0482) 646392

BATES, Canon Paul Spencer. b 40. CCC Cam BA62 MA66. Linc Th Coll 63. **d** 65 **p** 66. C Bris St Andr Hartcliffe *Bris* 65-69; Chapl Win Coll 69-80; Dir of Tr *Win* 80-90; Hon Can Win Cathl 87-90; Can Westmr Abbey from 90. *5 Little Cloister, Westminster Abbey, London SW1P 3PL*   071-222 6939

BATES, Miss Phyllis Edith. b 29. S'wark Ord Course 80. **dss** 83 **d** 87. Registrar S'wark Ord Course from 83; Fulham St Dionis Parson's Green *Lon* 83-87; Hon Par Dn from 87. *26 St Dionis Road, London SW6 4TT*   071-731 6935

BATES, Rosemary Eileen Hamilton. b 45. Ripon Coll Cuddesdon 87. **d** 89. Par Dn Brackley St Pet w St Jas

Pet from 89. *48 Branbury Road, Brackley, Northants NN13 6AT*   Brackley (0280) 704572

BATES, Stuart Geoffrey. b 61. Univ of Wales (Lamp) BA82. St Steph Ho Ox 83. **d** 85 **p** 86. C Bromley St Mark *Roch* 85-88; C Westmr St Matt *Lon* 88-89; C Gt Ilford St Mary *Chelmsf* from 89. *2 Elizabeth Avenue, Ilford, Essex IG1 1TU*   081-478 5723

BATES, Wilfred Abel. b 11. AKC33. Bps' Coll Cheshunt 33. **d** 34 **p** 36. V Dudley St Jo *Worc* 63-73; V Offenham 73-79; P-in-c Bretforton 76-79; V Offenham and Bretforton 79-91; rtd 91. *29 Bramley Avenue, Worcester WR2 6DQ*   Worcester (0905) 426996

BATES, William Frederic. b 49. St Jo Coll Dur BSc72 BA74. Cranmer Hall Dur DipTh75. **d** 75 **p** 76. C Knutsford St Jo and Toft *Ches* 75-78; C Ripley *Derby* 78-80; R Nether and Over Seale from 81; V Lullington from 81. *The Rectory, Neatherseal, Burton-on-Trent, Staffs DE12 8DF*   Burton (0524) 761179

BATES, William Hugh. b 33. Keble Coll Ox BA56 MA59. Westcott Ho Cam 59. **d** 60 **p** 61. C Horsforth *Ripon* 60-63; Tutor St Chad's Coll Dur 63-70; V Bishop Wilton *York* 70-76; RD Pocklington 74-76; V Pickering 76-82; Tutor NE Ord Course from 79; P-in-c Crayke w Brandsby and Yearsley from 82; P-in-c Stillington and Marton w Moxby from 82. *The Rectory, Crayke, York YO6 4TA*   Easingwold (0347) 21352

BATESON, Bernard Lionel. b 07. Clifton Th Coll 58. **d** 59 **p** 60. V Winsham w Cricket St Thomas *B & W* 69-80; rtd 81; Perm to Offic *B & W* from 81. *26 Summershard, South Petherton, Somerset TA13 5DP*   South Petherton (0460) 41489

BATESON, Canon Geoffrey Frederick. b 27. K Coll Lon BD51 AKC51. **d** 52 **p** 53. V Newc St Geo *Newc* 68-77; RD Newc 75-77; Chapl St Geo and Cottage Hosp Morpeth 77-89; R Morpeth *Newc* 77-89; Hon Can Newc Cathl 80-89; rtd 89. *1 Netherby Close, Sleights, Whitby, N Yorkshire YO22 5HD*   Whitby (0947) 810997

BATESON, James Howard. b 36. CEng64 FIMM88 MSOSc88 Qu Mary Coll Lon BSc57. E Midl Min Tr Course 85. **d** 87 **p** 88. NSM W Bridgford *S'well* 87-88; NSM Wilford Hill from 88. *45 Stamford Road, Nottingham NG2 6GD*   Nottingham (0602) 231820

BATEY, George Thomas. b 16. St Chad's Coll Dur BA38 DipTh39 MA42. **d** 39 **p** 40. V Milnrow *Man* 62-79; Perm to Offic *Carl* from 79; rtd 81. *The Cottage, Old Wall, Irthington, Carlisle CA6 4PP*   Crosby-on-Eden (022873) 243

BATEY, Canon Herbert Taylor. b 22. Qu Coll Ox BA46 MA48. Linc Th Coll 48. **d** 48 **p** 49. Chapl Culham Coll Abingdon 64-68; Prin Lect 68-75; P-in-c Culham *Ox* 68-75; Vice-Prin Coll of Ripon and York St Jo from 75; Hon Can Ripon Cathl *Ripon* from 85; rtd 87. *29 College Road, Ripon, N Yorkshire HG4 2HE*   Ripon (0765) 707096

BATEY, William Abbott. b 20. Cranmer Hall Dur 62. **d** 63 **p** 64. R Moresby *Carl* 66-77; P-in-c Arnside 77-85; V 85-90; rtd 90. *33 Greengate, Levens, Kendal, Cumbria LA8 8NF*   Sedgwick (05395) 66791

BATH, David James William. b 43. Oak Hill NSM Course 87. **d** 89 **p** 90. NSM Henley *Ox* 89-90; Gen Manager Humberside Gd News Trust from 90. *Flat 1, 67 Wright Street, Hull HU2 8JD*   Hull (0482) 28135 or 24040

BATH, Edward Nelson. b 16. Bps' Coll Cheshunt 55. **d** 57 **p** 58. V Charing Heath w Egerton *Cant* 67-82; P-in-c Pluckley w Pevington 78-82; rtd 82; Perm to Offic *Cant* from 82. *6 Lindens, Dental Street, Hythe, Kent CT21 5LH*   Hythe (0303) 264896

BATH AND WELLS, Bishop of. *See* THOMPSON, Rt Rev James Lawton

BATH, Archdeacon of. *See* BURGESS, Ven John Edward

BATHURST, William Henry. b 07. **d** 35. V Folkestone St Sav *Cant* 47-60; rtd 72. *34 Broadstairs Road, Broadstairs, Kent*   Thanet (0843) 62970

BATSLEER, Canon Albert. b 21. Selw Coll Cam BA46 MA54. Cuddesdon Coll 46. **d** 48 **p** 49. R Staveley *Derby* 65-72; V Riddings 72-81; RD Alfreton 76-81; V New Mills 81-85; RD Glossop 81-85; Hon Can Derby Cathl 81-85; rtd 85. *21 Dene Close, Skellingthorpe, Lincoln LN6 5SU*   Lincoln (0522) 690901

BATSON, David Frederick. b 38. AKC61. **d** 62 **p** 63. C Southport H Trin *Liv* 62-64; Asst Chapl Hurstpierpoint Coll Hassocks 64; C Cleator Moor w Cleator *Carl* 65-66; Asst Chapl K Geo V Sch Southport 66-67; Lic to Offic *Worc* 68-83. *Address temp unknown*

BATSON, John Gordon Kemp. b 38. Kelham Th Coll 60 Bps' Coll Cheshunt 64. **d** 65 **p** 66. C Lamorbey H Redeemer *Roch* 65-69; Trinidad and Tobago 69-74; V Boro Green *Roch* 74-83; V Perry Street from 83. *All*

Saints' Vicarage, Perry Street, Northfleet, Gravesend, Kent DA11 8RD   Gravesend (0474) 534398

BATSON, Paul Leonard. b 47. Southn Univ BTh79. Sarum & Wells Th Coll 73. **d** 75 **p** 76. C Chesham St Mary *Ox* 75-79; Dioc Youth Adv *Newc* 79-85; V Earley St Pet *Ox* from 85. *St Peter's Vicarage, 129 Whiteknights Road, Reading RG6 2BB*   Reading (0734) 62009

BATSON, William Francis Robert. b 43. Nottm Univ DipTP69 St Jo Coll Dur BA72. **d** 73 **p** 74. C Eastwood *S'well* 73-77; R Long Marton w Dufton and w Milburn *Carl* 77-79; V Flimby 79-85; TR Raveningham *Nor* from 85. *The Rectory, Thurlton, Norwich NR14 6RN* Raveningham (050846) 8835

BATT, Joseph William. b 39. Keele Univ BA62. Ripon Hall Ox 63. **d** 64 **p** 65. C Bushbury *Lich* 64-68; C Walsall 68-71; Nigeria 71-75; Area Sec (Dios Guildf and Chich) CMS 75-84; V Ottershaw *Guildf* from 84. *Christ Church Vicarage, Coach Road, Ottershaw, Chertsey, Surrey KT16 0PA*   Ottershaw (0932) 873160

BATT, Kenneth Victor. b 41. Wycliffe Hall Ox 68. **d** 71 **p** 72. C Yateley *Win* 71-76; R The Candover Valley 76-82; R Durrington *Sarum* 82-89; V Kempshott *Win* from 89. *The Vicarage, 171 Kempshott Lane, Kempshott, Basingstoke, Hants RG22 5LF*   Basingstoke (0256) 56400

BATTELL, Canon Colin Frank. b 44. Keble Coll Ox BA66 MA71. St Steph Ho Ox 66. **d** 68 **p** 69. C Wellingborough St Mary *Pet* 68-71; Lic to Offic *Eur* 70-71; C Wanstead St Mary *Chelmsf* 71-76; Ethiopia from 76; Hon Can All SS Cathl Cairo from 86. *PO Box 109, Addis Ababa, Ethiopia*   Addis Ababa (1) 112623

BATTEN, George William John. b 34. Bris & Glouc Tr Course 76. **d** 80 **p** 81. NSM Dean Forest St Paul *Glouc* from 80. *39 Bells Place, Coleford, Glos GL16 8BX* Dean (0594) 32291

BATTEN, Graham John. b 39. Open Univ BA81. St D Coll Lamp DipTh66. **d** 66 **p** 67. C Llangynwyd w Maesteg *Llan* 66-70; C St Andrew's Major and Michaelston-le-Pit 70-72; Chapl RN from 72. *c/o MOD, Lacon House, Theobald's Road, London WC1X 8RY*   071-430 6847

BATTEN, Thomas Cyril. b 10. St Jo Coll Dur BA37 DipTh38 MA40. **d** 38 **p** 39. V Mellor *Blackb* 59-70; rtd 70; Lic to Offic *Blackb* from 70. *40 Belgrave Avenue, Penwortham, Preston, Lancs PR1 0BH*   Preston (0772) 746473

BATTERSBY, David George Sellers. b 32. AKC57 Lambeth STh80. St Boniface Warminster 57. **d** 58 **p** 59. C Glas St Marg *Glas* 58-60; C Burnley St Pet *Blackb* 60-62; V Warton St Paul 62-71; Chapl K Wm's Coll Is of Man 71-91; C Ashchurch *Glouc* from 91. *The Old Stables, Back Lane, Beckford, Tewkesbury, Glos GL20 7AF* Evesham (0386) 881137

BATTERSBY, Harold. b 16. **d** 79 **p** 80. Hon C Werneth *Ches* 79-84; V 84-88; rtd 89. *3 Cote Green Lane, Marple Bridge, Stockport, Cheshire SK1 5DZ*   061-427 1789

BATTERSBY, Paul Clifford. b 49. Bede Coll Dur CertEd70 St Jo Coll Dur BA74. Cranmer Hall Dur DipTh75. **d** 75 **p** 76. C Sunderland St Chad *Dur* 75-78; Argentina 78-81; P-in-c Holme *Carl* 81-85; Dioc Youth Officer 81-85; Nat Officer for Youth Work Gen Syn Bd of Educn from 85. *c/o Church House, Great Smith Street, London SW1P 3NZ*   071-222 9011

BATTLE, Dean of. *See* CUMMINGS, Very Rev William Alexander Vickery

BATTMAN, John Brian. b 37. ALCD61. **d** 61 **p** 62. C Fulham Ch Ch *Lon* 61-64; Argentina 64-69; Paraguay 69-76; Adn Paraguay 70-76; Ext Sec SAMS 77-80; V Romford Gd Shep Collier Row *Chelmsf* from 80. *Good Shepherd Vicarage, Collier Row Lane, Romford RM5 3BA*   Romford (0708) 45626

BATTY, John Ivan. b 35. Clifton Th Coll 59. **d** 62 **p** 63. C Clayton *Bradf* 62-67; V Toxteth Park St Clem *Liv* 67-73; R Darfield *Sheff* 73-90; Chapl Dusseldorf *Eur* from 90. *Christ Church, Rotterdamerstrasse 135, 4000 Dusseldorf 30, Germany*   Dusseldorf (211) 452759

BATTY, Mark Alan. b 56. BSc. Ripon Coll Cuddesdon. **d** 82 **p** 83. C Bottesford w Ashby *Linc* 82-86; V Scunthorpe All SS from 86. *All Saints' Vicarage, 159 Warwick Road, Scunthorpe, S Humberside DN16 1HH*   Scunthorpe (0724) 869081

BATTY, Stephen Roy. b 58. Chich Th Coll 88. **d** 90 **p** 91. C Wimborne Minster and Holt *Sarum* from 90. *8 Minister View, Wimborne, Dorset BH21 1BA*   Poole (0202) 885268

BATTYE, John Noel. b 42. TCD BA64 MA73. CITC 66. **d** 66 **p** 67. C Drumglass *Arm* 66-69; C Ballynafeigh St Jude *D & D* 70-73; Chapl Pemb Coll Cam 73-78; Bp's C Knocknagoney *D & D* 78-80; I Cregagh from 80. *St*

Finnian's Rectory, 3 Upper Knockbreda Road, Belfast BT6 9QH   Belfast (0232) 793822

BATY, Edward. b 30. ARICS59 Open Univ BA77 UEA PhD88. St Aid Birkenhead 60. **d** 62 **p** 63. C Acomb St Steph *York* 62-64; Succ Chelmsf Cathl *Chelmsf* 64-67; V Becontree St Cedd 67-71; R Hope Bowdler w Eaton-under-Heywood *Heref* 71-79; R Rushbury 71-79; P-in-c Cardington 71-79; R Fincham *Ely* 79-82; OCF from 82; CF (ACF) from 86; R Long Stanton w St Mich *Ely* from 82; P-in-c Lolworth 85-88. *The Rectory, 2 High Street, Longstanton, Cambridge CB4 5BP*   Crafts Hill (0954) 81180

BATY, Ernest John. b 20. Univ of Wales BA42. St Mich Coll Llan 42. **d** 44 **p** 45. V Lydiate *Liv* 62-67; Hon C Sefton 69-85; rtd 85. *7 Delph Park Avenue, Ormskirk, Lancs L39 5DE*   Aughton Green (0695) 423711

BAUERSCHMIDT, John Crawford. b 59. Kenyon Coll Ohio BA81. Gen Th Sem (NY) MDiv84. **d** 84 **p** 85. USA 84-87; Lib Pusey Ho from 87; Lic to Offic *Ox* from 88. *Pusey House, Oxford OX1 3LZ*   Oxford (0865) 278415

✠**BAUGHEN, Rt Rev Michael Alfred.** b 30. Lon Univ BD55. Oak Hill Th Coll 51. **d** 56 **p** 57 **c** 82. C Hyson Green *S'well* 56-59; C Reigate St Mary *S'wark* 59-61; Ord Cand Sec CPAS 61-64; R Rusholme *Man* 64-70; TV St Marylebone All So w SS Pet and Jo *Lon* 70-75; R 75-82; AD Westmr St Marylebone 78-82; Preb St Paul's Cathl 79-82; Bp Ches from 82. *Bishop's House, Abbey Square, Chester CH1 2JD*   Chester (0244) 350864

BAULCH, Preb John Francis. b 28. Bps' Coll Cheshunt 56. **d** 59 **p** 60. C Mill Hill Jo Keble Ch *Lon* 59-64; V Hillingdon All SS 64-70; R Dewsall w Callow *Heref* 71-84; V Upper and Lower Bullinghope w Grafton 71-84; RD Heref City 75-84; Preb Heref Cathl from 80; V Heref St Martin 71-81; TR 81-84; V Holme Lacy w Dinedor 81-84; V Lt Dewchurch, Aconbury w Ballingham and Bolstone 81-84; R Ludlow from 84; P-in-c Caynham from 84; P-in-c Richard's Castle from 84; P-in-c Ludford from 84; P-in-c Ashford Carbonell w Ashford Bowdler from 84. *The Rectory, 4 College Street, Ludlow, Shropshire SY8 1AN*   Ludlow (0584) 872073

BAULCOMB, Geoffrey Gordon. b 46. K Coll Lon AKC68 BD86. **d** 69 **p** 70. C Crofton Park St Hilda w St Cypr *S'wark* 69-74; TV Padgate *Liv* 74-79; R Whitton and Thurleston w Akenham *St E* from 79. *The Rectory, Whitton Church Lane, Ipswich IP1 6LT*   Ipswich (0473) 741389

✠**BAVIN, Rt Rev Timothy John.** b 35. Worc Coll Ox BA59 MA61. Cuddesdon Coll 59. **d** 61 **p** 62 **c** 74. S Africa 61-69 and 73-85; C Uckfield *Chich* 69-71; V Brighton Gd Shep Preston 71-73; Dean and Adn Johannesburg 73-74; Bp Johannesburg 74-85; Bp Portsm from 85; OGS from 87. *Bishopswood, The Avenue, Fareham, Hants PO14 1NT*   Fareham (0329) 280247

BAWTREE, Robert John. b 39. Oak Hill Th Coll 62. **d** 67 **p** 68. C Foord St Jo *Cant* 67-70; C Boscombe St Jo *Win* 70-73; C Kinson *Sarum* 73-75; TV Bramerton w Surlingham *Nor* 76-82; R Arborfield w Barkham *Ox* 82-91; V Hildenborough *Roch* from 91. *The Vicarage, 194 Tonbridge Road, Hildenborough, Tonbridge, Kent TN11 9HR*   Hildenborough (0732) 833596

BAXANDALL, Peter. b 45. Tyndale Hall Bris 67. **d** 70 **p** 72. C Kidsgrove *Lich* 70-71; C St Helens St Mark *Liv* 71-75; C Ardsley *Sheff* 76-77; Rep Leprosy Miss (E Anglia) 77-86; P-in-c March St Wendreda *Ely* 86-87; R from 87. *St Wendreda's Rectory, 21 Wimblington Road, March, Cambs PE15 9QW*   March (0354) 53377

BAXENDALE, John Richard. b 48. Cranmer Hall Dur 89. **d** 91. C Carl St Jo *Carl* from 91. *68 Greystone Road, Carlisle CA1 2DG*   Carlisle (0228) 20893

BAXENDALE, Rodney Douglas. b 45. Ex Univ BA66 Nottm Univ DipTh79. Linc Th Coll 78. **d** 80 **p** 81. C Maidstone All SS and St Phil w Tovil *Cant* 80-83; Chapl RN from 83. *c/o MOD, Lacon House, Theobald's Road, London WC1X 8RY*   071-430 6847

BAXTER, Brian Raymond. b 31. Tyndale Hall Bris. **d** 58 **p** 59. C Heworth H Trin *York* 58-61; C Belper *Derby* 61-65; R Leverton *Linc* 65-67; C Mile Cross *Nor* 74-76; C Farnborough *Guildf* 76-79; Ldr Southgate Chr Project Bury St Edm 79-84; Chapl W Suffolk Hosp 79-81; R Ringsfield w Redisham, Barsham, Shipmeadow etc *St E* 82-88; V Nor Heartsease St Fran *Nor* from 88. *The Vicarage, Rider Haggard Road, Norwich NR7 9UQ* Norwich (0603) 300591

BAXTER, David Norman. b 39. Open Univ BA87. Kelham Th Coll 59. **d** 64 **p** 65. C Tonge Moor *Man* 64-68; Chapl RN 68-84; P-in-c Becontree St Pet *Chelmsf* 84-85; TV Becontree W 85-86; TR from 86. *St Peter's Vicarage, 29 Warrington Road, Dagenham, Essex RM8 3JH* 081-590 2740

BAXTER, Mrs Elizabeth Mary. b 49. Leeds Univ CCouns91 Leeds Poly DipCombStuds91. N Ord Course 81. **dss** 84 **d** 87. Leeds St Marg *Ripon* 84-87; Leeds All Hallows w Wrangthorn 85-87; Par Dn Leeds St Marg and All Hallows from 87; Abbey Grange Sch 85-87; Chapl from 87. *St Margaret's Vicarage, 145 Cardigan Road, Leeds LS6 1JL* Leeds (0532) 751729

BAXTER, Harold Leslie. b 11. Roch Th Coll 62. **d** 64 **p** 65. C Corsham *Bris* 64-67; C Bath Lyncombe *B & W* 67-70; V Shapwick w Ashcott 70-88; P-in-c Burtle 75-88; V Shapwick w Ashcott and Burtle from 88. *The Vicarage, Vicarage Lane, Bridgwater, Somerset TA7 9LR* Ashcott (0458) 210260

BAXTER, Peter James. b 29. St Chad's Coll Dur BA53 DipTh55. **d** 55 **p** 56. R Eynesbury *Ely* 62-89; rtd 89. *15 Bromley College, London Road, Bromley, Kent BR1 1PE*

BAXTER, Canon Richard David. b 33. Kelham Th Coll 53. **d** 57 **p** 58. C Carl St Barn *Carl* 57-59; C Barrow St Matt 59-64; V Drighlington *Wakef* 64-73; V Penistone 73-80; V Carl St Aid and Ch Ch *Carl* 80-86; Can Res and Prec Wakef Cathl *Wakef* from 86. *4 The Cathedral Close, Margaret Street, Wakefield, W Yorkshire WF1 2DQ* Wakefield (0924) 361922

BAXTER, Stanley Robert. b 31. AMIWO69 Leeds Univ MA90. Chich Th Coll 79. **d** 80 **p** 81. C Far Headingley St Chad *Ripon* 80-82; P-in-c Leeds St Marg 82-85; P-in-c Leeds All Hallows w Wrangthorn 85-87; P-in-c Leeds St Marg and All Hallows from 87; Dir Leeds Cen for Urban Th Studies from 89. *St Margaret's Vicarage, 145 Cardigan Road, Leeds LS6 1JL* Leeds (0532) 751729

BAXTER, Stuart. b 43. Liv Univ BA65 Nottm Univ PGCE66. Cuddesdon Coll 66. **d** 70 **p** 71. C Kirkby *Liv* 70-73; C Ainsdale 73-76; Sierra Leone 77-83; CMS 83-84; V Nelson in Lt Marsden *Blackb* from 84. *St Mary's Vicarage, 111 Manchester Road, Nelson, Lancs BB9 7HB* Nelson (0282) 614919

BAYCOCK, Philip Louis. b 33. Wells Th Coll 64. **d** 66 **p** 67. C Kettering SS Pet and Paul *Pet* 66-68; C St Peter-in-Thanet *Cant* 68-72; V Bobbing w Iwade 72-73; Perm to Offic 73-76; V Thanington w Milton 77-84; R Chagford w Gidleigh and Throwleigh *Ex* from 84. *The Rectory, Chagford, Newton Abbot, Devon TQ13 8BW* Chagford (0647) 432265

BAYES, Paul. b 53. Birm Univ BA75 DipTh78. Qu Coll Birm 76. **d** 79 **p** 80. C Tynemouth Cullercoats St Paul *Newc* 79-82; Chapl Qu Eliz Coll *Lon* 82-87; Chapl Chelsea Coll 85-87; TV High Wycombe *Ox* 87-90; TR from 90. *136 Desborough Avenue, High Wycombe, Bucks HP11 2SU* High Wycombe (0494) 29586

BAYFORD, Mrs Daphne Jean. b 32. Lon Univ TCert53. Qu Coll Birm 84. **d** 87. NSM Brinklow *Cov* from 87; NSM Harborough Magna from 87; NSM Monks Kirby w Pailton and Stretton-under-Fosse from 87. *Warwick House, 36 Lutterworth Road, Pailton, Rugby, Warks CV23 0QE* Rugby (0788) 832797

BAYLEY, Albert William David. b 15. Lon Coll of Div 66. **d** 68 **p** 69. C St Giles-in-the-Fields *Lon* 71-78; rtd 78; Perm to Offic *St Alb* from 82. *30 Braithwaite Court, Malzeard Road, Luton LU3 1BE* Luton (0582) 36419

BAYLEY, Dr Anne Christine. b 34. Girton Coll Cam BA55 MB, ChB58. St Steph Ho Ox 90. **d** 91. NSM Wembley Park St Aug *Lon* from 91. *c/o The Vicarage, 13 Forty Avenue, Wembley, Middx HA9 8JL* 081-904 4089

BAYLEY, Miss Barbara Alice. b 31. Cranmer Hall Dur. **d** 87. Par Dn Trowbridge H Trin *Sarum* from 87; Par Dn Trowbridge St Jas from 87. *52 Avenue Road, Trowbridge, Wilts BA14 0AQ* Trowbridge (0225) 764691

BAYLEY, Canon John Benson. b 39. K Coll Cam BA60 MA64. Qu Coll Birm 61. **d** 63 **p** 64. C Clee *Linc* 63-68; V Gainsborough H Trin 68-73; P-in-c Linc St Mich 73-75; P-in-c Linc St Pet in Eastgate w St Marg 73-75; P-in-c Linc St Mary Magd w St Paul 73-75; R Linc Minster Gp from 75; Can and Preb Linc Cathl from 75; Hon PV from 77. *St Peter's Vicarage, Lee Road, Lincoln LN2 4BH* Lincoln (0522) 525741

BAYLEY, Michael John. b 36. CCC Cam BA60 Sheff Univ PhD72. Linc Th Coll 60. **d** 62 **p** 63. C Leeds Gipton Epiphany *Ripon* 62-66; Lic to Offic *Sheff* from 67. *27 Thornsett Road, Sheffield S7 1NB* Sheffield (0742) 585248

BAYLEY, Oliver James Drummond. b 49. Mansf Coll Ox MA PGCE. St Jo Coll Nottm 81. **d** 83 **p** 84. C Bath Weston St Jo w Kelston *B & W* 83-88; P-in-c Bathampton from 88. *Bathampton Vicarage, Bath BA2 6SW* Bath (0225) 463570

BAYLEY, Dr Raymond. b 46. Keble Coll Ox BA68 MA72 Dur Univ DipTh69 Ex Univ PhD86. St Chad's Coll Dur 68. **d** 69 **p** 70. C Mold *St As* 69-74; C Llan w Capel Llanilterne *Llan* 74; PV Llan Cathl 74-77; V Cwmbach 77-80; Dir Past Studies St Mich Coll Llan 80-84; V Ynysddu *Mon* 84-86; V Griffithstown from 86. *St Hilda's Vicarage, 2 Sunnybank Road, Griffithstown, Pontypool, Gwent NP4 5LT* Pontypool (0495) 763641

BAYLISS, David Neil Jean-Marie. b 58. Leic Poly BA80. St Steph Ho Ox 85. **d** 88 **p** 89. C Leic St Chad *Leic* from 88. *292 Coleman Road, Leicester LE5 4LN* Leicester (0533) 767127

BAYLISS, Miss Joan Edith. b 34. RGN55. Qu Coll Birm 80. **dss** 83 **d** 87. Halesowen *Worc* 83-87; Hon Par Dn 87-89; Par Dn Bromsgrove St Jo from 90; Chapl Bromsgrove and Redditch Distr Gen Hosp from 90. *6 Rock Hill, Bromsgrove, Worcs B61 7LJ* Bromsgrove (0527) 32087

BAYLISS, Maurice Selwyn. b 13. Univ of Wales BA36. St Mich Coll Llan 36. **d** 37 **p** 38. V Bush Hill Park St Steph *Lon* 57-80; rtd 80; Perm to Offic Lon from 80; St Alb from 85. *19 Canford Close, Enfield, Middx EN2 8QN* 081-367 7436

BAYLOR, Nigel Peter. b 58. NUI BA80 TCD DipTh84 MPhil88. **d** 84 **p** 86. C Carrickfergus *Conn* 84-87; C Dundela *D & D* 87-89; I Galloon w Drummully *Clogh* from 89; Adult Educn Adv from 91. *The Rectory, Newtownbutler, Co Fermanagh* Newtownbutler (036573) 245

BAYLY, Samuel Niall Maurice. b 36. TCD BA64 MA. CITC Div Test65. **d** 65 **p** 66. C Belf St Matt *Conn* 65-68; Miss to Seamen 68-69; C Belf St Pet *Conn* 69-74; I Belf Ch Ch from 74. *25 Beechlands, Malone Road, Belfast BT9 5HU* Belfast (0232) 668732

BAYNE, David William. b 52. St Andr Univ MA75. Edin Th Coll 88. **d** 90 **p** 91. C Dumfries *Glas* from 90. *39 Barnton Road, Georgetown, Dumfries DG1 4HN* Dumfries (0387) 52158

BAYNES, Matthew Thomas Crispin. b 62. UEA BA83. Westcott Ho Cam BA86. **d** 87 **p** 88. C Southgate Ch Ch *Lon* 87-90; C Gt Berkhamsted *St Alb* from 90. *All Saints' House, Shrubland Road, Berkhamsted, Herts HP4 3HY* Berkhamsted (0442) 866161

BAYNES, Simon Hamilton. b 33. New Coll Ox BA57 DipTh58 MA62. Wycliffe Hall Ox 57. **d** 59 **p** 60. C Rodbourne Cheney *Bris* 59-62; Japan 63-80; C Keynsham *B & W* 80-84; P-in-c Winkfield *Ox* 84-85; V Winkfield and Cranbourne from 85. *The Vicarage, Winkfield Street, Winkfield, Windsor, Berks SL4 4SW* Winkfield Row (0344) 882322

BAYNES, Timothy Francis de Brissac. b 29. Ely Th Coll 59. **d** 61 **p** 62. C Hockerill *St Alb* 61-65; C Mansf Woodhouse *S'well* 65-67; Ind Chapl *Man* from 67; P-in-c Miles Platting St Jo 67-72. *2 The Thorns, Manchester M21 2DX* 061-881 2081

BAYNES, William Hendrie. b 39. Adelaide Univ BA60. S'wark Ord Course 77. **d** 79 **p** 80. C Notting Hill All SS w St Columb *Lon* 79-85; Perm to Offic 86-88; C Paddington St Sav from 88. *39E Westbourne Gardens, London W2 5NR* 071-727 9522

BAYNES CLARKE, Godfrey. b 25. CEng60 FIStructE60. Oak Hill Th Coll 71. **d** 73 **p** 74. C Ches Square St Mich w St Phil *Lon* 73-75; R Beeston Regis *Nor* 76-80; Santiago Community Ch Chile 80-88; R Roughton and Felbrigg, Metton, Sustead etc 88-91; rtd 91. *13 The Croft, Cromer, Norwich NR27 9EH* Cromer (0263) 511356

BAYNHAM, Canon George Thorp. b 19. TCD BA41. **d** 42 **p** 43. I Castlemacadam *D & G* 52-89; I Kilbride (Arklow) 64-73; Can Ch Ch Cathl Dub 71-89; I Castlemacadam w Ballinaclash, Aughrim etc 73-89; rtd 89. *2 St Peter's Place, Drogheda, Co Louth, Irish Republic* Drogheda (41) 36260

BAYNHAM, Matthew Fred. b 57. BA. Wycliffe Hall Ox 80. **d** 83 **p** 84. C Yardley St Edburgha *Birm* 83-87; TV Bath Twerton-on-Avon *B & W* from 87. *The Ascension Vicarage, 35A Claude Avenue, Bath BA2 1AF* Bath (0225) 421971

BAYNHAM, William Benjamin. b 11. Fitzw Ho Cam BA34 MA37. Cuddesdon Coll 34. **d** 35 **p** 36. C Maidstone All SS *Cant* 35-37; CR from 44; rtd 81. *House of the Resurrection, Mirfield, W Yorkshire WF14 0BN* Mirfield (0924) 494318

BAZELY, William Francis. b 53. Sheff Univ BEng75. St Jo Coll Nottm DipTh79 DPS. **d** 81 **p** 82. C Huyton St Geo *Liv* 81-84; TV Netherthorpe *Sheff* from 84. *The Vicarage, 73 Burgoyne Road, Sheffield S6 3QB* Sheffield (0742) 336977

BAZEN, David Peter. b 44. Birm Univ BPhil78 St Chad's Coll Dur BA65 DipTh69. **d** 69 **p** 71. C Acton Green St Pet *Lon* 69-70; Hon C Wylde Green *Birm* 70-78; Hon C Bordesley St Benedict 78-82; Hon C Bordesley SS Alb and Patr from 82. *66 Station Road, Sutton Coldfield, W Midlands B73 5LA* 021-354 5626 or 366 6600

BAZIN, Lewis Charles John Wadsworth. b 09. ALCD43. **d** 43 **p** 44. R Southfleet *Roch* 60-70; V Underriver 70-80; rtd 80; Perm to Offic *Cant* from 81. *9 Bartholomew Lane, Saltwood, Hythe, Kent CT21 4BX* Hythe (0303) 64896

✠**BAZLEY, Rt Rev Colin Frederick.** b 35. St Pet Coll Ox MA57. Tyndale Hall Bris 57. **d** 59 **p** 60 **c** 69. C Bootle St Leon *Liv* 59-62; Chile from 62; Asst Bp Cavtin and Malleco 69-75; Asst Bp Santiago 75-77; Bp Chile from 77; Primate CASA 77-83 and from 89. *Casilla 50675, Correo Central, Santiago, Chile* Santiago (2) 821-2478 or 383009

BAZLINTON, Stephen Cecil. b 46. MRCS Lon Univ BDS LDS. Ridley Hall Cam 78. **d** 85 **p** 86. NSM Stebbing w Lindsell *Chelmsf* from 85. *St Helens, High Street, Stebbing, Dunmow, Essex CM6 3SE* Stebbing (037186) 86495

BEACH, Mark Howard Francis. b 62. Kent Univ BA83. St Steph Ho Ox 85. **d** 87 **p** 88. C Beeston *S'well* 87-90; C Hucknall Torkard from 90. *149 Beardall Street, Hucknall, Notts NG15 7HA* Nottingham (0602) 641088

BEACHAM, Ian William Henry. b 17. Dur Univ LTh41. ALCD41. **d** 41 **p** 42. R Kidlington *Ox* 58-70; R Hampton Poyle 58-70; V Banbury 70-77; TR Banbury 77-82; rtd 82. *11 West Lea Road, Weston, Bath BA1 3RL* Bath (0225) 421682

BEACHAM, Peter Martyn. b 44. Ex Coll Ox BA65 MA70 Lon Univ MPhil67. Sarum Th Coll 70. **d** 73 **p** 74. NSM Ex St Martin, St Steph, St Laur etc *Ex* 73-74; NSM Cen Ex from 74. *Bellever, Barrack Road, Exeter, Devon EX2 6AB* Exeter (0392) 35074

BEACOM, Canon Thomas Ernest. b 12. TCD BA33 MA40 BD40. **d** 36 **p** 36. I Belf St Kath *Conn* 58-82; Can Belf Cathl from 66; rtd 82. *93 Islandmagee Road, Whitehead, Carrickfergus, Co Antrim* Whitehead (09603) 78904

BEACON, Ralph Anthony. b 44. Univ of Wales (Ban) DipTh70. St Mich Coll Llan 70. **d** 71 **p** 72. C Neath w Llantwit *Llan* 71-74; TV Holyhead w Rhoscolyn *Ban* 74-78; R Llanenddwyn w Llanddwywe, Llanbedr w Llandanwg from 78; RD Ardudwy from 89. *The Rectory, Dyffryn Ardudwy, Gwynedd LL44 2EY* Dyffryn (03417) 207

BEADLE, David Alexander. b 37. St And Dioc Tr Course. **d** 88 **p** 89. NSM St Andrews St Andr *St And* from 88. *166 Lamond Drive, St Andrews, Fife KY16 8JP* St Andrews (0334) 72210

BEAK, Richard John. b 34. Open Univ BA75. St Aid Birkenhead 59. **d** 62 **p** 63. C Leic St Pet *Leic* 62-64; C Glen Parva and S Wigston 64-66; Jamaica 66-69; V Thurnby Lodge *Leic* 69-74; Perm to Offic 80-82. *Address temp unknown*

✠**BEAK, Rt Rev Robert Michael Cawthorn.** b 25. OBE90. Lon Bible Coll DipTh51. **d** 53 **p** 54 **c** 84. C Tunbridge Wells St Jo *Roch* 53-55; BCMS 55-56 and 84-89; Kenya 56-69 and 84-89; R Heanton Punchardon *Ex* 70-84; OCF RAF 70-80; RD Barnstaple *Ex* 77-81; R Heanton Punchardon w Marwood 79-84; Preb Ex Cathl 82-84; Asst Bp Mt Kenya E 84-89; rtd 90. *Hillcrest, Newton Road, Tibshelf, Derby DE5 5PA* Alfreton (0773) 872154

BEAKE, Christopher Martyn Grandfield. b 36. K Coll Lon BA AKC60. **d** 61 **p** 62. C Berwick H Trin *Newc* 61-66; V Tynemouth H Trin W Town 66-78; V Hanslope w Castlethorpe *Ox* from 78. *The Vicarage, Park Road, Hanslope, Milton Keynes MK19 7LT* Milton Keynes (0908) 510542

BEAKE, Kenneth George. b 37. Ripon Coll Cuddesdon 75. **d** 77 **p** 78. C Guisborough *York* 77-80; V Kingston upon Hull St Martin 80-84; V Hull St Martin w Transfiguration 84-88; P-in-c Gt Wishford *Sarum* from 88; P-in-c S Newton from 88; Dir of Ords from 88. *The Rectory, Wishford, Salisbury SP2 0PQ* Salisbury (0722) 790363

BEAKE, Stuart Alexander. b 49. Em Coll Cam BA72 MA76. Cuddesdon Coll 72. **d** 74 **p** 75. C Hitchin St Mary *St Alb* 74-76; C Hitchin 77-79; TV Hemel Hempstead 79-85; Bp's Dom Chapl *S'well* 85-87; V Shottery St Andr *Cov* from 87. *The Vicarage, Church Lane, Stratford-upon-Avon, Warks CV37 9HQ* Stratford-upon-Avon (0789) 293381

BEAKEN, Robert William Frederick. b 62. SS Paul & Mary Coll Cheltenham BA83. Lambeth STh90 Ripon Coll Cuddesdon 85 Ven English Coll and Pontifical Gregorian Univ Rome 87. **d** 88 **p** 89. C Forton *Portsm* from 88. *39 Heaton Road, Gosport, Hants PO12 4PL* Gosport (0705) 589429

BEAL, David Michael. b 61. Nottm Univ BTh89. St Jo Coll Nottm 86. **d** 89 **p** 90. C Marton *Blackb* from 89. *74 Worcester Road, Blackpool FY3 9SZ* Blackpool (0253) 792118

BEAL, Malcolm. b 31. Bris Univ BA52. Ridley Hall Cam 57. **d** 59 **p** 60. C Keynsham w Queen Charlton *B & W* 59-62; C Speke All SS *Liv* 62-65; Uganda 65-74; V Salford Priors *Cov* 74-83; R Jersey St Clem *Win* from 83. *St Clement's Rectory, Jersey, Channel Islands JE2 6RB* Jersey (0534) 51992

BEAL, Royston David. b 35. K Coll Lon BD60 AKC60. **d** 61 **p** 62. C Chesterfield All SS *Derby* 61-64; C Chiswick St Nic w St Mary *Lon* 64-70; V Kensal Green St Jo from 70. *St John's Vicarage, Kilburn Lane, London W10 4AA* 081-969 2615

BEALE, Wilfred Henry Ellson. b 11. FCCA FCIS. **d** 69 **p** 71. Hon C Northwood H Trin *Lon* 69-82; Perm to Offic from 82. *23 Woodridge Way, Northwood, Middx HA6 2BE* Northwood (09274) 26301

BEALE, William Edgar. b 11. K Coll Lon 37. Bps' Coll Cheshunt 40. **d** 42 **p** 43. R Kedington *St E* 64-72; C Brighton St Paul *Chich* 72-73; C Bingley All SS *Bradf* 73-77; rtd 77. *Charterhouse, Charterhouse Square, London EC1M 6AN*

BEALES, Christopher Leader Day. b 51. Dur Univ BA72. Cranmer Hall Dur 72. **d** 76 **p** 77. C Upper Armley *Ripon* 76-79; Ind Chapl 76-79; Ind Chapl *Dur* 79-84; Sen Ind Chapl 82-84; Sec Ind Cttee of Gen Syn Bd for Soc Resp from 85. *10 Dallinger Road, London SE12 0TL* 081-851 5735

BEALES, John David. b 55. St Hild & Bede Coll Dur BA77 Univ of W Aus DipEd79 Nottm Univ DipTh82. St Jo Coll Nottm DPS83. **d** 83 **p** 84. Australia 83-89; Dir Educn and Tr Philo Trust 89-90; NSM Nottm St Nic *S'well* from 89. *17 Bramcote Drive, Beeston, Nottingham NG9 1AT* Nottingham (0602) 225031

BEALING, Andrew John. b 42. Sarum Th Coll 67. **d** 69 **p** 70. C Auckland St Andr and St Anne *Dur* 69-73; P-in-c Eastgate 73-76; P-in-c Rookhope 73-76; V Frosterley 76-85; V Rekendyke from 85. *The Vicarage, St Jude's Terrace, South Shields, Tyne & Wear NE33 5PB* 091-455 2338

BEALING, Patricia Ramsey. b 39. dss 63 **d** 87. Rekendyke *Dur* 85-87; Par Dn from 87; Chapl S Shields Gen Hosp from 88. *The Vicarage, St Jude's Terrace, South Shields, Tyne & Wear NE33 5PB* 091-455 2338

BEALL, John. b 19. Clare Coll Cam BA41 MA45. Westcott Ho Cam 41. **d** 42 **p** 43. V Oswaldtwistle Immanuel *Blackb* 61-82; rtd 82; Perm to Offic *Bris* from 82. *12 Golf Crescent, Troon, Ayrshire KA10 6JZ* Troon (0292) 318055

BEAMENT, Owen John. b 41. Bps' Coll Cheshunt 61. **d** 64 **p** 65. C Deptford St Paul *S'wark* 64-68; C Peckham St Jo 69-73; C Vauxhall St Pet 73-74; V Hatcham Park All SS from 74. *22 Erlanger Road, London SE14 5TG* 071-639 3497

BEAMER, Neville David. b 40. Univ of Wales (Lamp) BA62 Jes Coll Ox BA65 MA70. Wycliffe Hall Ox 64. **d** 65 **p** 66. C Hornchurch St Andr *Chelmsf* 65-68; C Warw St Mary *Cov* 68-72; V Holton-le-Clay *Linc* 72-75; P-in-c Stoneleigh w Ashow *Cov* 75-79; P-in-c Baginton 77-79; V Fletchamstead 79-86; Warden Whatcombe Ho Blandford Forum 86-90; V Jersey Millbrook St Matt *Win* from 90; R Jersey St Lawr from 90. *St Matthew's Vicarage, Millbrook, Jersey, Channel Islands JE3 1LN* Jersey (0534) 20934

BEAMISH, Canon Frank Edwin. b 28. TCD BA49 MA. **d** 50 **p** 52. C Templecorran *Conn* 50-53; C Drumglass *Arm* 53-61; I Caledon w Brantry from 61; Preb Arm Cathl from 88. *The Rectory, Caledon, Co Tyrone* Caledon (0861) 568205

BEAMISH, John William. b 25. TCD BA47 MA81. **d** 49 **p** 50. I Brackaville *Arm* 53-84; I Brackaville w Donaghendry and Ballyclog 84-89; rtd 89. *62 Farlough Lane, Newmills, Dungannon, Co Tyrone BT71 4DU* Coalisland (08687) 48288

BEAN, Alan Evison. b 13. Ch Coll Cam BA35 MA39. Ely Th Coll 35. **d** 36 **p** 37. CF 42-45; SSJE from 47; Lic to Offic *Ox* from 55; rtd 83. *SSJE Priory, 228 Iffley Road, Oxford OX4 1SE* Oxford (0865) 242227

BEAN, Douglas Jeyes Lendrum. b 25. Worc Coll Ox BA50 MA53. Ely Th Coll 50. **d** 51 **p** 52. C Croydon Woodside *Cant* 51-54; Min Can Windsor 54-59; V Reading St Laur *Ox* 59-68; Chapl HM Borstal Reading 61-68; RD Reading *Ox* 65-68; Min Can St Paul's Cathl *Lon* 68-72; Hon Min Can from 72; V St Pancras w St

Jas and Ch Ch from 72; PV Westmr Abbey 75-80. *12 Fitzroy Square, London W1P 5HQ* 071-387 6460
BEAN, Canon John Victor. b 25. Down Coll Cam BA47 MA51. Sarum Th Coll 48. **d** 50 **p** 51. V Cowes St Mary *Portsm* 66-91; RD W Wight 68-72; Hon Can Portsm Cathl 70-91; P-in-c Cowes St Faith 77-80; C-in-c Gurnard All SS CD 78-91; Chapl to HM The Queen from 80; rtd 91. *4 Parkmead Court, Park Road, Ryde, Isle of Wight PO33 2HD* Isle of Wight (0983) 812516
BEAN, Kevin Douglas. b 54. Edin Univ BD78. Edin Th Coll 75. **d** 81 **p** 82. USA 81-88 and from 89; C Edin St Marg *Edin* 88-89; C Edin Old St Paul 88-89. *79 Montclair Drive, W Hartford, Connecticut 06107, USA*
BEANEY, John. b 47. Trin Coll Bris DipHE79. **d** 79 **p** 80. C Bromley Ch Ch *Roch* 79-84; V Broadheath *Ches* from 84. *The Vicarage, Lindsell Road, West Timperley, Altrincham, Cheshire WA14 5NX* 061-928 4820
BEARCROFT, Bramwell Arthur. b 52. Homerton Coll Cam BEd82. E Anglian Minl Tr Course 87. **d** 90 **p** 91. Chapl and Hd Relig Studies Kimbolton Sch from 90; NSM Tilbrook *Ely* from 90; NSM Covington from 90; NSM Catworth Magna from 90; NSM Keyston and Bythorn from 90. *White House, High Street, Kimbolton, Huntingdon, Cambs PE18 0HB* Huntingdon (0480) 860469
BEARD, Christopher Robert. b 47. Chich Th Coll 81. **d** 83 **p** 84. C Chich St Paul and St Pet *Chich* 83-86; TV Ifield from 86. *St Leonard's House, 10 Martyr's Avenue, Crawley, W Sussex RH11 7RZ* Crawley (0293) 518419
BEARD, Laurence Philip. b 45. Lon Univ BA68. Trin Coll Bris 88. **d** 90 **p** 91. C Trentham *Lich* from 90. *4 Oakshaw Grove, Trentham, Stoke-on-Trent ST4 8UB* Stoke-on-Trent (0782) 643457
BEARD, Peter Harley. b 39. Coll of Resurr Mirfield 60. **d** 71 **p** 72. S Africa 71-75; Miss to Seamen 75-82; V St Osyth *Chelmsf* 81-86; P-in-c Wellington Ch Ch *Lich* from 86. *Christ Church Vicarage, 1 Church Walk, Wellington, Telford, Shropshire TF1 1RW* Telford (0952) 3185
BEARD, Robert John Hansley. b 61. St Andr Univ BD85. Ripon Coll Cuddesdon 86 Ch Div Sch of the Pacific (USA) 87. **d** 88 **p** 89. C Sheff Manor *Sheff* from 88. *146 Manor Lane, Sheffield S2 1UG* Sheffield (0742) 700437
BEARDALL, Raymond. b 32. St Jo Coll Nottm 70. **d** 72 **p** 73. C Ilkley All SS *Bradf* 72-74; C Seasalter *Cant* 74-79; V Farndon *S'well* 79-84; R Thorpe 79-84; V Blidworth from 84. *2 Kirk's Croft, Wain Street, Mansfield, Notts NG21 0QH* Mansfield (0623) 792306
BEARDMORE, John Keith. b 42. FCP85 Bris Univ BEd74 K Coll Lon MA90. **d** 77 **p** 78. NSM Newport Maindee St Jo Ev *Mon* from 77. *16 Hove Avenue, Newport, Gwent NP9 7QP* Newport (0633) 263272
BEARDSHAW, David. b 37. JP. DPS. Wells Th Coll 65. **d** 67 **p** 68. C Wood End *Cov* 67-69; C Stoke 70-73; V Whitley 73-77; Dioc Educn Officer 77-87; P-in-c Offchurch from 87; Warden Offa Retreat Ho from 87. *The Vicarage, Offchurch, Leamington Spa, Warks CV33 9AL* Leamington Spa (0926) 24401
BEARDSLEY, Christopher. b 51. Sussex Univ BA73. Westcott Ho Cam 76. **d** 78 **p** 79. C Portsea N End St Mark *Portsm* 78-85; V Catherington and Clanfield from 85. *The Vicarage, 330 Catherington Lane, Catherington, Portsmouth PO8 0TD* Horndean (0705) 593139
BEARDSMORE, Alan. b 45. Wycliffe Hall Ox 67. **d** 70 **p** 71. C Prittlewell St Mary *Chelmsf* 70-72; C Epsom St Martin *Guildf* 72-77; P-in-c Burbage and Savernake Ch Ch *Sarum* 78-79; P-in-c E Grafton, Tidcombe and Fosbury 78-79; TV Wexcombe 79-80; Chapl RN 80-83; TV Haverhill w Withersfield, the Wrattings etc *St E* 83-87; V Gt Barton from 87. *The Vicarage, Church Road, Great Barton, Bury St Edmunds, Suffolk IP31 2QR* Great Barton (028487) 274
BEARDSMORE, John. b 19. Kelham Th Coll 46. **d** 51 **p** 51. V Bromley H Trin *Roch* 69-70; V Buttershaw St Paul *Bradf* 70-88; rtd 88; Perm to Offic *Bradf* from 88. *41 Nab Wood Grove, Shipley, W Yorkshire BD18 4HR* Bradford (0274) 596197
BEARE, Canon William. b 33. TCD BA58 DipCSM77. **d** 59 **p** 60. C Waterford St Patr *C & O* 59-62; C Cork H Trin w Shandon St Mary *C, C & R* 62-64; I Rathcormac 64-68; I Marmullane w Monkstown 68-76; Dioc C 76-82; I Stradbally w Ballintubbert, Coraclone etc *C & O* from 82; Preb Ossory Cathl 88-90; Preb Leighlin Cathl 88-90; Chan Leighlin Cathl from 90; Chan Ossory Cathl from 90. *The Rectory, Church Lane, Stradbally, Laois, Irish Republic* Portlaoise (502) 25173
BEARMAN, Leslie Raymond Livingstone. b 09. ALCD35. **d** 35 **p** 36. R Sherington w Chicheley *Ox* 61-74; R N

Crawley and Astwood w Hardmead 74; rtd 74; Perm to Offic *Pet* from 75. *395A Kettering Road, Northampton NN3 1LW* Northampton (0604) 42326
BEARN, Hugh William. b 62. Man Univ BA84. Cranmer Hall Dur 86. **d** 89 **p** 90. C Heaton Ch Ch *Man* from 89. *39 Welbeck Road, Bolton BL1 5LE* Bolton (0204) 42816
BEARPARK, Canon John Michael. b 36. Ex Coll Ox BA59 MA63. Linc Th Coll 59. **d** 61 **p** 62. C Bingley H Trin *Bradf* 61-64; C Baildon 64-67; V Fairweather Green 67-77; Chapl Airedale Gen Hosp from 77; V Steeton *Bradf* from 77; Hon Can Bradf Cathl from 89. *2 Halsteads Way, Steeton, Keighley, W Yorkshire BD20 6SN* Steeton (0535) 652004
BEASLEY, Canon Arthur James. b 12. Hertf Coll Ox BA33 MA38. Ridley Hall Cam 34. **d** 36 **p** 37. V Heaton Ch Ch *Man* 48-81; Hon Can Man Cathl 72-81; rtd 81; Perm to Offic *Man* from 81. *40 Chorley New Road, Lostock, Bolton BL6 4AL* Bolton (0204) 494450
BEASLEY, Bernard Robinson. b 07. OBE66. Leeds Univ BA30 MA45. Coll of Resurr Mirfield 25. **d** 31 **p** 32. V Easebourne *Chich* 62-72; RD Midhurst 64-72; rtd 72. *Agra Cottage, Worton, Devizes, Wilts SN10 5SE* Devizes (0380) 3383
BEASLEY, Michael John. b 41. Dur Univ BA63. Sarum Th Coll 63. **d** 65 **p** 66. C Weston St Jo *B & W* 65-67; C Pinner *Lon* 67-69; C E Grinstead St Swithun *Chich* 69-72; Chapl St Mary's Hosp and Qu Hosp Croydon 72-77; Mayday Hosp Thornton Heath 72-77; TV Swanborough *Sarum* 77-82; V Stourbridge Norton St Mich *Worc* from 82. *St Michael's House, Westwood Avenue, Stourbridge, W Midlands DY8 3EN* Stourbridge (0384) 3647
BEASLEY, Canon Walter Sydney. b 33. Nottm Univ BA57. Linc Th Coll 57. **d** 59 **p** 60. C Harworth *S'well* 59-64; V Forest Town 64-70; R Bulwell St Mary from 70; Hon Can S'well Minster from 85. *The Rectory, Station Road, Bulwell, Nottingham NG6 9AA* Nottingham (0602) 278468
BEASLEY, William Isaac (Hilary). b 23. Leeds Univ BA47. Coll of Resurr Mirfield 47. **d** 49 **p** 50. C Cov St Mark *Cov* 49-53; Lic to Offic *Wakef* from 54; CR from 56. *House of the Resurrection, Mirfield, W Yorkshire WF14 0BN* Mirfield (0924) 494318
BEATER, David MacPherson. b 41. Chich Th Coll 66. **d** 69 **p** 70. C Withington St Crispin *Man* 69-72; C Lightbowne 72-74; V Prestwich St Hilda 74-81; V Northfleet *Roch* 81-85; C Bickley 86-90; TV Stanley *Dur* from 90. *St Thomas's Vicarage, Lowery Lane, Stanley, Co Durham DH9 6EN* Stanley (0207) 230316
BEATTIE, Noel Christopher. b 41. TCD BTh65 Cranfield Inst of Tech MSc86. **d** 68 **p** 69. C Belf H Trin *Conn* 68-70; C Belf St Bart 70-73; C Doncaster St Mary *Sheff* 73-77; TV Northn Em *Pet* 77-88; Ind Chapl 85-88; Ind Chapl *Linc* from 88. *17 Becket Close, Washingborough, Lincoln LN4 1EA* Lincoln (0522) 793145
BEATTY, Robert Harold. b 27. W Ontario Univ BA48 Keble Coll Ox BA55 MA58 McGill Univ Montreal PhD62. **d** 51 **p** 52. Canada 51, 55-57 and 58-67; Perm to Offic *Ox* 52-55; Tutor Bps' Coll Cheshunt 57-58; C W Byfleet *Guildf* 67-71; C Oseney Crescent St Luke w Camden Square St Paul *Lon* 71-72; R Cosgrove *Pet* 72-83; V Hebburn St Oswald *Dur* from 83. *St Oswald's Vicarage, St Oswald's Road, Hebburn, Tyne & Wear NE31 1HR* 091-483 2082
BEAUCHAMP, Anthony Hazlerigg Proctor. b 40. MICE68 Trin Coll Cam BA62 MA66. St Jo Coll Nottm 73. **d** 75 **p** 76. C New Humberstone *Leic* 75-77; C-in-c Polegate *Chich* 77-80; Chapl Bethany Sch Goudhurst 80-86; Chapl Luckley-Oakfield Sch Wokingham 86-88; Chapl Clayesmore Sch Blandford Forum from 89. *Clayesmore School, Iwerne Minster, Blandford Forum, Dorset DT11 8LJ* Fontmell Magna (0747) 811655
BEAUCHAMP, Gerald Charles. b 55. Hull Univ BA78. Coll of Resurr Mirfield 78. **d** 80 **p** 81. C Hatcham St Cath *S'wark* 80-83; S Africa 83-86; C Ealing St Steph Castle Hill *Lon* 86-88; P-in-c Brondesbury St Anne w Kilburn H Trin 88-89; V from 89. *49 Keslake Road, London NW6 6DH* 081-968 3898
BEAUMONT of Whitley, Rev and Rt Hon Lord (Timothy Wentworth). b 28. Ch Ch Ox BA52 MA56. Westcott Ho Cam 55. **d** 55 **p** 56. Lic to Offic *Lon* 63-73; Hon C Balham Hill Ascension *S'wark* 85-86; P-in-c Richmond St Luke 86-87; P-in-c N Sheen St Phil and All SS 86-87; V Kew St Phil and All SS w St Luke 87-91; rtd 91; Perm to Offic *S'wark* from 91. *40 Elms Road, London SW4 9EX* 071-498 8664
BEAUMONT, Albert Edward. b 10. Kelham Th Coll 31. **d** 37 **p** 38. V Knottingley *Wakef* 54-70; rtd 70; Lic to

Offic *Eur* from 80. *3 Furniss Walk, Elmbridge Road, Cranleigh, Surrey GU6 8BE* Cranleigh (0483) 275963

BEAUMONT, Arthur. b 98. Em Coll Cam BA22 MA26. Wycliffe Hall Ox 27. **d** 29 **p** 30. V Marbury *Ches* 60-69; rtd 69. *Nuneham Nursing Home, 41 Victoria Road, Macclesfield, Cheshire SK10 3JA* Macclesfield (0625) 420266

BEAUMONT, Arthur Ralph. b 37. Open Univ BA82 Salford Univ MSc86. Ely Th Coll 61. **d** 64 **p** 87. C Grimsby All SS *Linc* 64-65; Perm to Offic *S'well* 70-72; NSM Addingham, Edenhall, Langwathby and Culgaith *Carl* from 87. *Brookside, Melmerby, Penrith, Cumbria CA10 1HF* Langwathby (076881) 270

BEAUMONT, Canon Brian Maxwell. b 34. Nottm Univ BA56. Wells Th Coll 58. **d** 59 **p** 60. C Clifton *S'well* 59-62; C E Stoke w Syerston 62; C Edgbaston St Geo *Birm* 62-65; V Smethwick St Alb 65-70; Asst Dir RE *Blackb* 70-73; V Blackb H Trin 70-77; Hon Can Blackb Cathl 73-77; Can Res from 77; Dir RE from 73. *St John's House, Clarence Street, Blackburn, Lancs BB1 8AN* Blackburn (0254) 57088

BEAUMONT, Canon John Philip. b 32. Leeds Univ BA55. Coll of Resurr Mirfield 55. **d** 57 **p** 58. C Leeds St Marg *Ripon* 57-60; C Wellingborough All Hallows *Pet* 60-64; Chapl HM Borstal Wellingborough 64-70; V Wellingborough St Andr *Pet* 64-70; V Finedon from 70; Can Pet Cathl from 80; RD Higham 83-87. *The Vicarage, Finedon, Wellingborough, Northants NN9 5NR* Wellingborough (0933) 680285

BEAUMONT, John William. b 19. MBE48. RMC 38. Qu Coll Birm 48. **d** 51 **p** 52. V S w N Hayling *Portsm* 59-74; R Droxford 74-86; R Meonstoke w Corhampton cum Exton 78-86; rtd 86; Perm to Offic *Portsm* from 86. *134 The Dale, Widley, Portsmouth PO7 5DF* Cosham (0705) 377492

BEAUMONT, Stephen Martin. b 51. K Coll Lon BD73 AKC74. St Aug Coll Cant 73. **d** 74 **p** 75. C Benwell St Jas *Newc* 74-77; Asst Chapl Marlborough Coll Wilts 77-81; R Ideford, Luton and Ashcombe *Ex* 81-84; Bp's Dom Chapl 81-84; Chapl Taunton Sch Somerset from 85. *Taunton School, Taunton, Somerset TA2 6AD* Taunton (0823) 284359

BEAUMONT, Terence Mayes. b 41. Lon Univ BA63 Nottm Univ DipTh69. Linc Th Coll 68. **d** 71 **p** 72. C Hitchin St Mary *St Alb* 71-74; C Harpenden St Nic 75-79; V Stevenage St Pet Broadwater 79-87; V St Alb St Mich from 87. *St Michael's Vicarage, St Michael's Street, St Albans, Herts AL3 4SL* St Albans (0727) 835037

BEAVAN, Charles Kenneth. b 15. JP63. Lon Univ BA49. St Deiniol's Hawarden 66. **d** 67 **p** 68. Hd Master Meole Brace Sch 53-76; Hon C Meole Brace *Lich* 67-71; P-in-c Shrewsbury St Alkmund 71-89; Perm to Offic from 89. *School House, 5 Vicarage Road, Shrewsbury SY3 9EZ* Shrewsbury (0743) 4172

BEAVAN, Edward Hugh. b 43. Ex Coll Ox BA70 MA74. Cuddesdon Coll 69. **d** 71 **p** 72. C Ashford St Hilda *Lon* 71-74; C Newington St Mary *S'wark* 74-76; R Sandon *Chelmsf* 76-86; V Thorpe Bay from 86. *The Vicarage, 86 Tyrone Road, Southend-on-Sea, Essex SS1 3HB* Southend-on-Sea (0702) 587597

BEAVER, Christopher Martin. b 31. AKC56. **d** 60 **p** 61. C Leek All SS *Lich* 60-64; C Uttoxeter w Bramshall 64-67; V Normacot 67-77; V Pheasey 77-83; V Dordon *Birm* 83-89; V Langley St Mich from 89. *The Vicarage, 33 Moat Road, Oldbury, Warley, W Midlands B68 8EB* 021-552 1809

BEAVER, Frederick William. b 1900. Worc Ord Coll 60. **d** 61 **p** 62. V Gretton *Pet* 66-73; rtd 73; Lic to Offic *Pet* 73-86; Perm to Offic from 86. *19 St Anne's Close, Oakham, Leics LE15 6AZ* Oakham (0572) 723275

BEAVER, Maurice John. b 15. Qu Coll Birm 77. **d** 77 **p** 78. NSM Hagley *Worc* 77-85; Perm to Offic from 85. *37 Park Road, Hagley, Stourbridge, W Midlands DY9 0NS* Hagley (0562) 883566

BEAVER, William Carpenter. b 45. Colorado Coll BA Wolfs Coll Ox DPhil. Ox NSM Course. **d** 82 **p** 83. NSM Kennington St Jo w St Jas *S'wark* from 82. *7 Shardcroft Avenue, London SE24 0DS* 071-733 8616

BEAZLEY, Prof John Milner. b 32. DRCOG59 MRCOG62 FRCOG73 FACOG89 Man Univ MB, ChB57 MD64. St Deiniol's Hawarden 83. **d** 86 **p** 87. NSM W Kirby St Bridget *Ches* from 86. *Gourley Grange, Gourley's Lane, West Kirby, Wirral, Merseyside L48 8AS* 051-625 5353

BEAZLEY, Miss Margaret Sheila Elizabeth Mary. b 32. Nor City Coll CertEd59. St Alb Minl Tr Scheme 86. **d** 89. NSM Ware St Mary *St Alb* from 89. *38 Fanshawe Crescent, Ware, Herts SG12 0AS* Ware (0920) 462349

BEBB, John. b 08. St Chad's Coll Dur BA34 DipTh35 MA37. **d** 35 **p** 36. V Offenham *Worc* 59-73; rtd 73. *33 Leslie Close, Littleover, Derby DE3 7AW*

BEBB, John Edwin. b 13. St Jo Coll Dur BA35 MA38. Wycliffe Hall Ox 35. **d** 36 **p** 37. Asst Master Blackpool Gr Sch 67-72; V Sandown Ch Ch *Portsm* 73-80; rtd 80; Perm to Offic *Carl* from 86. *2 Wandales Lane, Natland, Kendal, Cumbria LA9 7QY* Sedgwick (05395) 60035

BEBBINGTON, Myles. b 35. Kelham Th Coll 56. **d** 61 **p** 62. C Horbury *Wakef* 61-64; C Ardwick St Benedict *Man* 64-66; V Cudworth *Wakef* 66-73; P-in-c Kensington St Jo the Bapt *Lon* 73-78; P-in-c Walthamstow St Mich *Chelmsf* 78-80; V 80-89; V Sunderland Red Ho *Dur* from 89. *St Cuthbert's Vicarage, Rotherham Road, Sunderland SR5 5QS* 091-549 1261

BECK, Alan. b 28. AKC50. **d** 53 **p** 54. V Puriton *B & W* 69-78; P-in-c Pawlett 74-78; V Puriton and Pawlett 78-79; P-in-c Staplegrove 79-84; R 84-88; rtd 88. *12 Newlands Crescent, Ruishton, Taunton, Somerset TA3 5LA* Taunton (0823) 443030

BECK, Ashley Cranston. b 58. Or Coll Ox BA81 MA84. St Steph Ho Ox 82. **d** 85 **p** 86. C Walham Green St Jo w St Jas *Lon* 85-90; C Camberwell St Giles w St Matt *S'wark* from 90. *St Matthew's House, 77 Coldharbour Lane, London SE5 9NS* 071-274 3778

BECK, Mrs Gillian Margaret. b 50. Sheff Univ CertEd71 Nottm Univ BTh78. Linc Th Coll 74. **dss** 78 **d** 87. Gt Grimsby St Mary and St Jas *Linc* 78-83; St Paul's Cathl *Lon* 84-87; Hon Par Dn St Botolph Aldgate w H Trin Minories 87-88; Par Dn Monkwearmouth St Andr *Dur* from 88. *St Andrew's Vicarage, Park Avenue, Sunderland SR6 9PU* 091-548 6607

BECK, John Edward. b 28. ARCM52 FRCO59 St Jo Coll Ox BA56 MA59. Wells Th Coll 56. **d** 58 **p** 59. C Dursley *Glouc* 58-61; C Glouc St Paul 61-63; S Rhodesia 63-65; Rhodesia 65-70; C Cheltenham Ch Ch *Glouc* 70-77; C Cirencester from 77. *38 Cecily Hill, Cirencester, Glos GL7 2EF* Cirencester (0285) 653778

BECK, Michael Leonard. b 50. K Coll Lon BD77 AKC77. Linc Th Coll 77. **d** 78 **p** 79. C Gt Grimsby St Mary and St Jas *Linc* 78-83; Min Can and Succ St Paul's Cathl *Lon* 83-88; V Monkwearmouth St Andr *Dur* from 88. *St Andrew's Vicarage, Park Avenue, Sunderland SR6 9PU* 091-548 6607

BECK, Peter George Cornford. b 36. Dur Univ BA61. Ridley Hall Cam 61. **d** 63 **p** 64. C Slade Green *Roch* 63-65; C Aylesford 65-68; C-in-c Brampton St Mark CD *Derby* 68-70; V Brampton St Mark 71-75; P-in-c Alvaston 75-89. *Mixon Mines Farm, Onecote, Leek, Staffs*

BECK, Ven Peter John. b 48. Mert Coll Ox BA69 MA75. Sarum Th Coll 69. **d** 72 **p** 73. C Banbury *Ox* 72-75; TV 75-78; Dioc Youth and Community Officer 75-78; P-in-c Linc St Mary-le-Wigford w St Benedict etc *Linc* 78-81; New Zealand from 81; Adn Waitemata from 87. *704 New North Road, Auckland 3, New Zealand* Auckland (9) 864747 or 866046

BECK, Preb Raymond Morris. b 13. Magd Coll Ox BA36 MA40. Cuddesdon Coll 37. **d** 38 **p** 39. V Taunton St Jo *B & W* 56-80; Preb Wells Cathl 78-80; C Hedworth *Dur* 80-82; rtd 82; Hon C Fairwarp *Chich* 82-87; Perm to Offic *Ex* from 87. *Shepherd's House, East Prawle, Kingsbridge, Devon TQ7 2BY* Chivelstone (054851) 247

BECK, Roger William. b 48. Chich Th Coll 79. **d** 81 **p** 82. C St Marychurch *Ex* 81-85; TV Torre 85-88; V Torquay St Jo and Ellacombe from 88. *The Vicarage, 1A Lower Ellacombe Church Road, Torquay TQ1 1JH* Torquay (0803) 293441

BECK, Canon Stephen. b 16. St Pet Hall Ox BA44 MA45. Westcott Ho Cam 45. **d** 47 **p** 48. V Moseley St Agnes *Birm* 59-83; RD Moseley 71-81; Hon Can Birm Cathl 76-83; rtd 83. *Artro View, Llanbedr, Gwynedd LL45 2DQ* Llanbedr (034123) 545

BECKERLEG, Barzillai. b 20. Selw Coll Cam BA43 MA46. Westcott Ho Cam 42. **d** 44 **p** 45. V Kippington *Roch* 64-75; R E Bergholt *St E* 75-79; Chapl St Mary's Sch Wantage 79-85; rtd 85; Perm to Offic *Roch* from 86. *Upper Treasurer's House, Bromley College, Bromley BR1 1PE* 081-290 1544

BECKETT, Michael Shaun. b 55. ACA79. Oak Hill Th Coll BA88. **d** 88 **p** 89. C Cam St Barn *Ely* from 88. *80 St Barnabas Road, Cambridge* Cambridge (0223) 67578

BECKETT, Canon Stanley. b 20. Linc Th Coll. **d** 64 **p** 65. C Barnston *Ches* 64-71; V Daresbury 71-87; Hon Can Ches Cathl 82-87; P-in-c Aston by Sutton 86-87; Hon C 87-90; rtd 87; Hon C Grappenhall *Ches* from 90. *13 Wilson Close, Thelwall, Warrington WA4 2ET* Warrington (0925) 63639

BECKETT, William Vincent. b 12. ALCD50. d 50 p 51. V Nottm St Steph *S'well* 57-83; rtd 84. *44 Brook Avenue, Caister-on-Sea, Great Yarmouth, Norfolk NR30 5RL* Great Yarmouth (0493) 728737

BECKHAM, John Francis. b 25. Bps' Coll Cheshunt 65. d 67 p 68. C Leytonstone St Jo *Chelmsf* 67-70; C Colchester St Mary V 70-73; R Lawford 73-80; V Gt w Lt Chesterford 80-90; rtd 90; Perm to Offic *St E* from 91. *Mayplace Cottage, Queen Street, Southwold, Suffolk IP18 6EQ* Southwold (0502) 724919

BECKLEY, Peter William. b 52. Lon Univ BSc73 CertEd. Trin Coll Bris 76. d 79 p 80. C Plymouth St Jude *Ex* 79-83; C Ecclesall *Sheff* 83-88; V Greystones from 88. *1 Cliffe Farm Drive, Sheffield S11 7JW* Sheffield (0742) 667686

BECKLEY, Simon Richard. b 38. Lon Univ BA61. Oak Hill Th Coll 58. d 63 p 64. C Watford St Luke *St Alb* 63-67; C New Ferry *Ches* 67-70; C Chadderton Ch Ch *Man* 70-73; V Friarmere 73-80; V Tranmere St Cath *Ches* from 80. *St Catherine's Vicarage, 9 The Wiend, Birkenhead, Merseyside L42 6RY* 051-645 4533

BECKWITH, Canon John Douglas. b 33. AKC57. d 58 p 65. C Streatham St Leon *S'wark* 58-59; Lic to Offic *Ripon* 59-60; Nigeria 60-62; C Bedale *Ripon* 62-63; C Mottingham St Andr *S'wark* 64-69; Chapl Gothenburg w Halmstad and Jonkoping *Eur* 69-70; Chapl to Suff Bp Edmonton 70-77; Lic to Offic *Lon* 70-77; Dir of Ords 70-77; V Highgate Rise St Anne Brookfield 77-88; Can Gib Cathl *Eur* from 84; P-in-c Bladon w Woodstock *Ox* from 88. *The Rectory, Woodstock, Oxford OX7 1UQ* Woodstock (0993) 811415

BECKWITH, Roger Thomas. b 29. St Edm Hall Ox BA52 MA56 Ox Univ BD85. Ripon Hall Ox 51 Tyndale Hall Bris 52 Cuddesdon Coll 54. d 54 p 55. C Harold Wood *Chelmsf* 54-57; C Bedminster St Luke w St Silas *Bris* 57-59; Tutor Tyndale Hall Bris 59-63; Lib Latimer Ho Ox 63-73; Warden from 73; Lect Wycliffe Hall Ox from 71; Hon C Wytham *Ox* 88-90; Hon C N Hinksey and Wytham from 90. *Latimer House, 131 Banbury Road, Oxford OX2 7AJ* Oxford (0865) 513879

BEDDER, William Lewis Johnson. b 04. d 44 p 45. V Portland St Jo *Sarum* 58-74; Chapl Portland Hosp Weymouth 58-74; rtd 74. *Fortuneswell, 107 Chafey's Avenue, Weymouth, Dorset DT4 0EN* Weymouth (0305) 4361

BEDDINGTON, Peter Jon. b 36. ACP68 DipEd81. NW Ord Course 71. d 74 p 75. C Bury St Pet *Man* 74-77; Hon C Bury Ch King 77-82; Hon C Elton All SS from 82. *18 Throstle Grove, Bury, Lancs BL8 1EB* 061-764 3292

BEDDOES, Very Rev Ronald Alfred. b 12. St Chad's Coll Dur BA35 MA50. d 36 p 37. Provost Derby 53-80; V Derby All SS 53-80; rtd 80; P-in-c Beeley and Edensor *Derby* from 80. *The Vicarage, Edensor, Bakewell, Derbyshire DE4 1PH* Baslow (024688) 582130

BEDDOW, Arthur Josiah Comyns. b 13. Ch Coll Cam BA35 MA41. Linc Th Coll 38. d 40 p 41. R Bere Ferrers *Ex* 63-78; rtd 78; Perm to Offic Sarum from 78; B & W from 84. *Flat 5, Hillside, South Street, Sherborne, Dorset DT9 3NH* Sherborne (0935) 81534

BEDDOW, Nicholas Mark Johnstone-Wallace. b 47. Birm Univ BA69. Qu Coll Birm 69. d 71 p 72. C Blackheath *Birm* 71-75; Zambia 75-80; V Escomb *Dur* from 80; V Witton Park from 80; Bp's Dom Chapl 80-85. *The Vicarage, Escomb, Bishop Auckland, Co Durham DL14 7ST* Bishop Auckland (0388) 602861

BEDELL, Anthony Charles. b 59. Worc Coll Ox BA81. Linc Th Coll 87. d 90 p 91. C Newbold and Dunston *Derby* from 90. *80 Highfield Lane, Chesterfield S41 8AY* Chesterfield (0246) 234759

BEDFORD, Christopher John Charles. b 46. K Coll Lon BD69 AKC69. St Aug Coll Cant 69. d 70 p 71. C Doncaster Ch Ch *Sheff* 70-73; C St Pancras H Cross w St Jude and St Pet *Lon* 73-76; Selection Sec ACCM 76-81; P-in-c Old St Pancras w Bedf New Town St Matt *Lon* 76-81; P-in-c Bethnal Green St Matt 81-84; R Bethnal Green St Matt w St Jas the Gt from 84. *The Rectory, Hereford Street, London E2 6EX* 071-739 7586

BEDFORD, Colin Michael. b 35. ALCD60. d 61 p 62. C Woking St Mary *Guildf* 61-63; C Guildf St Sav 63-65; C Morden *S'wark* 65-69; V Toxteth Park St Philemon *Liv* 69-75; P-in-c Toxteth Park St Gabr 69-75; P-in-c Toxteth Park St Jas and St Matt 69-75; P-in-c Prince's Park St Paul 70-75; P-in-c Toxteth Park St Cleopas 73-78; TR Toxteth St Philemon w St Gabr 75-89; TR Toxteth St Philemon w St Gabr and St Cleopas from 89. *St Philemon's Vicarage, 40 Devonshire Road, Liverpool L8 3TZ* 051-727 1248

BEDFORD, Norman Stuart. b 28. Oak Hill Th Coll 66. d 68 p 69. C Iver *Ox* 68-71; V Warfield 71-75; V Southwold *St E* 75-83; V Dedham *Chelmsf* from 83. *The Vicarage, High Street, Dedham, Colchester, Essex CO7 6DE* Colchester (0206) 322136

BEDFORD, Richard Derek Warner. b 27. Clare Coll Cam BA52. ALCD54. d 54 p 55. C Wallington H Trin *S'wark* 54-56; C Sanderstead All SS 56-57; C Weybridge *Guildf* 57-59; C Addlestone 59-62; C-in-c New Haw CD 62-66; V Epsom Common Ch Ch 66-81; R Walton-on-the-Hill 81-87; Asst Chapl Burrswood Home of Healing from 87. *2 Lealands Close, Groombridge, Tunbridge Wells, Kent TN3 9ND* Tunbridge Wells (0892) 864550

BEDFORD, Archdeacon of. See BOURKE, Ven Michael Gay

BEDFORD, Suffragan Bishop of. See FARMBROUGH, Rt Rev David John

BEDLOE, Horace Walter. b 11. Keble Coll Ox. Sarum Th Coll 37. d 37 p 38. Jamaica 49-56, 60-69 and 72-75; Can Res Bradf Cathl *Bradf* 70-71; P-in-c Brighton St Jo *Chich* 76-78; rtd 78; Chapl Malaga w Almunecar and Nerja *Eur* 81-83; Perm to Offic Chich and S'wark from 83; Roch from 84. *College of St Barnabas, Blackberry Lane, Lingfield, Surrey RH7 6NJ* Dormans Park (034287) 753

BEDWELL, Stanley Frederick. b 20. MPS42. Ox NSM Course 77. d 80 p 81. NSM Farnham Royal *Ox* 80-81; NSM Farnham Royal w Hedgerley 81-90; Perm to Offic from 90. *18 Ingleglen, Farnham Common, Slough SL2 3QA* Farnham Common (0753) 644522

BEEBY, Lawrence Clifford. b 28. S'wark Ord Course 70. d 73 p 74. C Notting Hill St Jo *Lon* 73-74; C Sunbury 74-76; C-in-c Hounslow Gd Shep Beavers Lane CD 76-80; Chapl Botleys Park Hosp Chertsey 80-89; Hon Chapl from 89; rtd 89. *54 Bingley Road, Sunbury-on-Thames, Middx TW16 7RB* Sunbury-on-Thames (0932) 788922

BEECH, Miss Ailsa. b 44. Newc Univ TDip65. Trin Coll Bris DipHE80. dss 80 d 87. Pudsey St Lawr *Bradf* 80-82; Pudsey St Lawr and St Paul 82-87; Par Dn 87-88; C Attleborough *Cov* 88-89; Par Dn Cumnor *Ox* from 89. *2 Ashcroft Close, Oxford OX2 9SE* Oxford (0865) 863224

BEECH, Albert Edward. b 06. St Aid Birkenhead. d 50 p 51. R Swynnerton *Lich* 63-67; rtd 69. *101 Oxford Gardens, Stafford ST16 3JD* Stafford (0785) 53558

BEECH, Frank Thomas. b 36. Tyndale Hall Bris 64. d 66 p 67. C Penn Fields *Lich* 66-70; C Attenborough w Chilwell *S'well* 70-74; P-in-c 74-75; P-in-c Attenborough 75-76; V 76-84; V Worksop St Anne from 84; Chapl Welbeck Coll from 84. *The Vicarage, 11 Poplar Close, Worksop, Notts S80 3BZ* Worksop (0909) 472069

BEECH, Canon Harold. b 17. Univ of Wales BA39. Chich Th Coll 39. d 41 p 42. Chapl Cell Barnes Hosp and Hill End Hosp St Alb 59-82; Hon Can St Alb 77-83; rtd 82; Perm to Offic *St Alb* from 83. *Milfraen House, 32 Campfield Road, St Albans, Herts AL1 5JA* St Albans (0727) 863608

BEECH, John. b 41. St Jo Coll Nottm. d 83 p 83. C York St Paul *York* 83-84; P-in-c Bubwith w Ellerton and Aughton 84-85; P-in-c Thorganby w Skipwith and N Duffield 84-85; V Bubwith w Skipwith 85-87; V Acomb H Redeemer from 87. *The Vicarage, 108 Boroughbridge Road, York YO2 6AA* York (0904) 798593

BEECH, John Thomas. b 38. St Aid Birkenhead 64. d 67 p 68. C Burton St Paul *Lich* 67-70; Chapl RN 70-85; V Ellingham and Harbridge and Ibsley *Win* from 85. *The Vicarage, Ellingham, Ringwood, Hants BH24 3PJ* Ringwood (0425) 43723

BEECH, Michael John. b 48. ARCM86 ABSM89 Jes Coll Cam BA70 MA82. Westcott Ho Cam 72. d 75 p 76. C Catford St Andr *S'wark* 75-81; C All Hallows by the Tower etc *Lon* 81-87. *St Benedict's Vicarage, 55 Hob Moor Road, Birmingham B10 9AY* 021-772 2726

BEECH, Peter John. b 34. Bps' Coll Cheshunt 58. d 61 p 62. C Fulham All SS *Lon* 61-64; S Africa 64-67; V S Hackney St Mich *Lon* 68-71; P-in-c Haggerston St Paul 68-71; V S Hackney St Mich w Haggerston St Paul 71-75; V Wanstead H Trin Hermon Hill *Chelmsf* 75-89; P-in-c St Mary-at-Latton 89-90; V from 90. *St Mary-at-Latton Vicarage, The Gowers, Harlow, Essex CM20 2JP* Harlow (0279) 424005

BEECHAM, Clarence Ralph. b 35. S'wark Ord Course. d 83 p 84. NSM Leigh-on-Sea St Jas *Chelmsf* from 83. *27 Scarborough Drive, Leigh-on-Sea, Essex SS9 3ED* Southend-on-Sea (0702) 574923

BEEDELL, Trevor Francis. b 31. ALCD65. d 65 p 66. C Walton *St E* 65-68; R Hartshorne *Derby* 68-79; RD Repton 74-79; V Doveridge 79-86; Chapl HM Det Cen

Foston Hall 79-80; Dioc Dir of Chr Stewardship *Derby* from 79. *1 River View, Milford, Derby DE5 0QR*   Derby (0332) 842381

BEEDON, David Kirk. b 59. Birm Univ BA89. Qu Coll Birm 86. **d** 89 **p** 90. C Cannock *Lich* from 89. *44 Manor Avenue, Cannock, Staffs WS11 1AA*   Cannock (0543) 502896

BEEK, Canon Michael Peter. b 27. Em Coll Cam BA50 MA55. Linc Th Coll 50. **d** 52 **p** 53. C Mitcham St Barn *S'wark* 52-55; C Talbot Village *Sarum* 55-58; V Higham and Merston *Roch* 58-66; R Gravesend St Geo 66-74; R Gravesend St Jas 66-74; RD Gravesend 70-74; Hon Can Roch Cathl from 73; RD Tunbridge Wells 74-83; R Speldhurst w Groombridge 74-77; P-in-c Ashurst 77; R Speldhurst w Groombridge and Ashurst 77-83; V Bromley SS Pet and Paul from 83. *The Vicarage, 9 St Paul's Square, Bromley BR2 0XH*   081-460 6275

BEENY, Canon Reginald Charles Morris. b 10. OBE75. Leeds Univ BA32. Coll of Resurr Mirfield 32. **d** 34 **p** 35. Lic to Offic *S'wark* from 41; Dir CECS 64-75; rtd 75. *30 Kennet Court, Wokingham, Berks RG11 9DB*   Wokingham (0734) 772416

BEER, Mrs Janet Margaret. b 43. Golds Coll Lon CertEd64. Oak Hill Th Coll 83. **dss** 86 **d** 87. Colney St Pet *St Alb* 86-87; Hon C from 87. *St Peter's Vicarage, London Colney, St Albans, Herts AL2 1QT*   Bowmansgreen (0727) 22122

BEER, Canon John Stuart. b 44. Pemb Coll Ox BA65 MA70 Fitzw Coll Cam MA78. Westcott Ho Cam 69. **d** 71 **p** 72. C Knaresborough St Jo *Ripon* 71-74; Chapl Fitzw Coll and New Hall Cam 74-80; Lic to Offic *Ely* 74-80; P-in-c Toft w Caldecote and Childerley 80-83; R 83-87; P-in-c Hardwick 80-83; R 83-87; V Grantchester from 87; Dir of Ords, Post-Ord Tr and Student Readers from 88; Hon Can Ely Cathl from 89. *The Vicarage, 44 High Street, Grantchester, Cambridge CB3 9NF*   Cambridge (0223) 840460

BEER, Michael Trevor. b 44. Chich Th Coll 66. **d** 69 **p** 70. C Leagrave *St Alb* 69-73; St Vincent 73-74; C Thorley w Bishop's Stortford H Trin *St Alb* 74-80; V Colney St Pet from 80. *The Vicarage, Riverside, London Colney, St Albans, Herts AL2 1QT*   Bowmansgreen (0727) 22122

BEER, William Barclay. b 43. ACT ThA68 St Steph Ho Ox. **d** 71 **p** 72. C St Marychurch *Ex* 71-76; V Pattishall w Cold Higham *Pet* 76-82; V Northn St Benedict 82-85; V Chislehurst Annunciation *Roch* from 85. *The Vicarage, 2 Foxhome Close, Chislehurst, Kent BR7 5XT*   081-467 3606

BEESLEY, Michael Frederick. b 37. **d** 61 **p** 64. C Eastleigh *Win* 61-69. *42 Highland Road, Parkstone, Poole, Dorset*   Poole (0202) 730497

BEESLEY, Ramon John. b 27. Magd Coll Ox BA51 MA55. Wycliffe Hall Ox 51. **d** 53 **p** 56. C Gerrards Cross *Ox* 53-54; Asst Chapl Embley Park Sch Romsey 54-58; Perm to Offic Guildf 59-63; Win from 63; Hd Master Bellemoor Sch Southn from 74. *Wayfarers, Burley, Ringwood, Hants BH24 4HW*   Burley (04253) 2284

BEESLEY, Symon Richard. b 27. Bris Univ BA53. Tyndale Hall Bris 47. **d** 53 **p** 54. V Leic H Trin *Leic* 64-72; Dep Chapl HM Pris Leic 69-72; Jt Gen Sec CCCS 72-76; Lic to Offic *Lon* 73-76; P-in-c St Leonards St Leon *Chich* 76-77; R 77-82; Kenya 82-84; V Rush *Liv* 84-89; rtd 89. *8 Shales Road, Bitterne, Southampton SO2 5RN*   Southampton (0703) 463671

BEESON, Christopher George. b 48. Man Univ BSc70. Qu Coll Birm 72. **d** 75 **p** 76. C Flixton St Mich *Man* 75-78; C Newton Heath All SS 78-80; R Gorton St Jas 80-90; Dioc Communications Officer *Blackb* from 91. *24 Arnold Close, Ribbleton, Preston PR2 6DX*   Preston (0772) 702675

BEESON, Very Rev Trevor Randall. b 26. K Coll Lon MA76. **d** 51 **p** 52. C Leadgate *Dur* 51-54; C Norton St Mary 54-56; C-in-c Stockton St Chad CD 56-60; V Stockton St Chad 60-65; C St Martin-in-the-Fields *Lon* 65-71; V Ware St Mary *St Alb* 71-76; Can Westmr Abbey 76-87; Treas 78-82; Chapl to Speaker of Ho of Commons 82-87; R Westmr St Marg 82-87; Dean Win from 87; FKC from 87. *The Deanery, The Close, Winchester, Hants SO23 9LS*   Winchester (0962) 853738

BEETHAM, Anthony. b 32. Lon Univ BSc53. Ox NSM Course. **d** 75 **p** 76. NSM Ox St Clem *Ox* from 75; Dir Chr Enquiry Agency from 88. *44 Rose Hill, Oxford OX4 4HS*   Oxford (0865) 770923

BEETON, David Ambrose Moore. b 39. Chich Th Coll 62. **d** 65 **p** 66. C Forest Gate St Edm *Chelmsf* 65-71; V Rush Green 71-81; V Coggeshall w Markshall from 81. *The Vicarage, 4 Church Green, Coggeshall, Colchester CO6 1UD*   Coggeshall (0376) 561234

BEEVER, Miss Alison Rosemary. b 59. Man Univ BA80. Linc Th Coll 88. **d** 90. Par Dn Watford Ch Ch *St Alb* from 90. *77 Northfield Gardens, Watford, Herts WD2 4RF*   Watford (0923) 225411

BEEVERS, Dr Colin Lionel. b 40. CEng70 MIEE70 MBIM73 K Coll Lon BSc62 PhD66 DMS72. Sarum & Wells Th Coll 87. **d** 89 **p** 90. C Ledbury w Eastnor *Heref* from 89; C Lt Marcle from 89. *21 Biddulph Way, Ledbury, Herefordshire HR8 2HP*   Ledbury (0531) 4873

BEEVERS, Reginald. b 22. Dur Univ BA48. Qu Coll Birm 48. **d** 50 **p** 51. Chapl Guy's Hosp Lon 65-70; Chapl Liv Coll 70-81; R Hatch Beauchamp w Beercrocombe, Curry Mallet etc *B & W* 81-88; rtd 88; P-in-c Oare w Culbone *B & W* from 90. *The Rectory, Oare, Lynton, Devon EX35 6NX*   Brendon (05987) 270

BEEVOR, Michael Branthwayt. b 24. Sarum Th Coll 64. **d** 66 **p** 66. C Alton St Lawr *Win* 68-70; C Christchurch 70-73; C Bournemouth St Clem w St Mary 73-75; C S w N Hayling *Portsm* 76-77; rtd 79. *38 Hart Plain Avenue, Cowplain, Portsmouth PO8 8RX*   Portsmouth (0705) 250264

BEGBIE, Jeremy Sutherland. b 57. ARCM LRAM MSSTh Edin Univ BA Aber Univ BD PhD. Ridley Hall Cam. **d** 82 **p** 83. C Egham *Guildf* 82-85; Chapl Ridley Hall Cam 85-87; Dir of Studies from 87. *Ridley Hall, Cambridge CB3 9HG*   Cambridge (0223) 60995

BEGERNIE, Miss Doreen Myrtle. b 27. dss 78 **d** 87. CPAS Staff 76-87; rtd 87; Perm to Offic *Cant* from 87. *11 Leaside Court, Clifton Gardens, Folkestone, Kent CT20 2ED*   Folkestone (0303) 45184

BEGGS, Norman Lindell. b 32. N Lon Poly CQSW77 DipSocWork77. S Dios Minl Tr Scheme 86. **d** 89 **p** 90. NSM Milborne St Andrew w Dewlish *Sarum* from 89. *Wallingford House, Dewlish, Dorchester, Dorset DT2 7LX*   Milborne St Andrew (025887) 320

BEGLEY, Frank William. b 18. Univ of Wales (Lamp) BA48. **d** 49 **p** 50. Guyana 66-70; C Roath St Marg *Llan* 70-74; V Cardiff St Dyfrig and St Samson 74-83; R Llanwenarth Ultra *Mon* 83-87; rtd 87. *24 St Teilo's Court, Church Terrace, Cardiff CF2 5AX*   Cardiff (0222) 489375

BEGLEY, Mrs Helen. b 59. Kingston Poly BA81. N Ord Course 87. **d** 89. Par Dn Leeds H Trin *Ripon* 89-90; Chapl to the Deaf from 89; Par Dn Leeds City from 91. *34 Dale Park Avenue, Leeds LS16 7PU*   Leeds (0532) 613009

BEHENNA, Miss Gillian Eve. b 57. CertEd78. St Alb Minl Tr Scheme 82. **dss** 85 **d** 87. Chapl to the Deaf *Sarum* 85-90; Chapl to the Deaf *Ex* from 90. *16 Mayflower Avenue, Pennsylvania, Exeter, Devon EX4 5DS*   Exeter (0392) 215174

BEHRENS, Andrew James. b 50. AKC73. St Aug Coll Cant 73. **d** 74 **p** 75. C Swanley St Mary *Roch* 74-76; C Crayford 76-79; C Doncaster St Leon and St Jude *Sheff* 79-82; V New Bentley 82-88; R Gt and Lt Houghton w Brafield on the Green *Pet* from 88. *The Rectory, Rectory Close, Great Houghton, Northampton NN4 0AF*   Northampton (0604) 761708

BELBEN, Kenneth Frank. b 30. TD77. Cranmer Hall Dur 51. **d** 55 **p** 56. C Plaistow St Mary *Chelmsf* 55-58; C Chadwell Heath 58-60; C-in-c Marks Gate 60-64; V Gt w Lt Maplestead 64-76; CF (TA) from 65; P-in-c Gestingthorpe *Chelmsf* 75-76; V Gt and Lt Maplestead w Gestingthorpe from 76; ChStJ from 77. *The Vicarage, Church Street, Great Maplestead, Halstead, Essex CO9 2RG*   Hedingham (0787) 60294

BELCHER, David John. b 44. Ch Ch Ox BA65 MA69. Cuddesdon Coll 68. **d** 70 **p** 71. C Gateshead St Mary *Dur* 70-73; C Stockton St Pet 73-76; Lic to Offic *Lich* 76-81; P-in-c W Bromwich Ch Ch 81-85; P-in-c W Bromwich Gd Shep w St Jo 85-89; V from 89; RD W Bromwich from 90. *The Vicarage, 4 Bromford Lane, West Bromwich, W Midlands B70 7HP*   021-525 5530

BELCHER, Derek George. b 50. MRSH73 MBIM82 DipDiet Lon Univ PGCE82 Univ of Wales MEd86. Chich Th Coll 74. **d** 77 **p** 78. C Newton Nottage *Llan* 77-81; V Llan w Capel Llanilterne 81; PV Llan Cathl 81-87; V Margam from 87. *The Vicarage, 59A Bertha Road, Margam, Port Talbot, W Glam SA13 2AP*   Port Talbot (0639) 891067

BELCHER, Frederick William. b 30. Kelham Th Coll 50 Chich Th Coll 53. **d** 54 **p** 55. C Catford St Laur *S'wark* 54-58; C-in-c Plumstead Wm Temple Ch Abbey Wood CD 58-62; V Eltham Park St Luke 62-64; Lic to Offic 65-81; NSM Charminster and Stinsford *Sarum* from 88. *Little Mead, North Street, Charminster, Dorchester, Dorset DT2 9QZ*   Dorchester (0305) 260688

BELCHER, Nicholas Arthur John. b 59. Oak Hill Th Coll BA89. d 89 p 90. C Danbury *Chelmsf* from 89. *40 Millfields, Danbury, Essex* Danbury (024541) 2125

BELFAST, Dean of. *See* SHEARER, Very Rev John

BELHAM, John Edward. b 42. K Coll Lon BSc65 AKC65 PhD70. Oak Hill Th Coll 69. d 72 p 73. C Cheadle Hulme St Andr *Ches* 72-75; C Cheadle 75-83; R Gressenhall w Longham w Wendling etc *Nor* from 83. *The Rectory, Gressenhall, Dereham, Norfolk NR20 4EB* Dereham (0362) 860211

BELHAM, Michael. b 23. Lon Univ BScEng50. d 67 p 68. C Hendon St Mary *Lon* 69-73; V Tottenham H Trin 73-78; V Hillingdon St Jo 78-85; P-in-c Broughton *Ox* 85; R Broughton w N Newington and Shutford 85-90; Chapl Horton Gen Hosp Banbury from 85; rtd 90. *6 Blackwood Place, Bodicote, Banbury, Oxon OX15 4BE* Banbury (0295) 253923

BELING, David Gibson. b 30. Fitzw Ho Cam BA54 MA58. d 56 p 57. C Radipole *Sarum* 56-59; C Broadwater St Mary *Chich* 59-61; R W Knighton w Broadmayne *Sarum* 61-73; V Paignton St Paul Preston *Ex* from 73. *St Paul's Vicarage, Locarno Avenue, Preston, Paignton, Devon TQ3 2DH* Paignton (0803) 522872

BELITHER, John Roland. b 36. Oak Hill Th Coll 83. d 86 p 87. NSM Bushey Heath *St Alb* from 86. *33 Merry Hill Mount, Bushey, Watford WD2 1DJ* 081-950 2906

BELL, Adrian Christopher. b 48. AKC70. St Aug Coll Cant 70. d 72 p 72. C Sheff St Aid w St Luke *Sheff* 71-74; C Willesborough w Hinxhill *Cant* 74-78; P-in-c Wormshill 78; P-in-c Hollingbourne w Hucking 78-82; P-in-c Leeds w Broomfield 79-82; V Hollingbourne and Hucking w Leeds and Broomfield 82-84; V Herne Bay Ch Ch 84-91; R Washingborough w Heighington and Canwick *Linc* from 91. *The Rectory, Church Hill, Washingborough, Lincoln LN4 1EJ* Lincoln (0522) 794071

BELL, Alan. b 29. Linc Th Coll 64. d 65 p 65. C Spilsby w Hundleby *Linc* 65-67; R Ludford Magna w Ludford Parva 67-76; V Burgh on Bain 68-76; V Kelstern, Calcethorpe and E Wykeham 68-76; Clerical Org Sec CECS 76-78. *16 Lagham Road, Godstone, Surrey RH9 8HB* South Godstone (0342) 893717

BELL, Alan John. b 47. Liv Univ BA68. Ridley Hall Cam 69. d 72 p 73. C Speke St Aid *Liv* 72-77; P-in-c Halewood 77-81; R Wavertree St Mary 81-88; Chapl Mabel Fletcher Tech Coll Liv 81-88; Chapl Olive Mt Hosp 81-88; R Fakenham w Alethorpe *Nor* from 88. *The Rectory, Gladstone Road, Fakenham, Norfolk NR21 9BZ* Fakenham (0328) 862268

BELL, Allan McRae. b 49. Moray Ho Teacher Tr Coll Edin CertEd80 E Lon Poly BA90. S'wark Ord Course 86. d 91. NSM Bow H Trin and All Hallows *Lon* from 91. *83 Gore Road, London E9 7HW* 081-986 8546

BELL, Anthony Lawson. b 47. AKC72. St Aug Coll Cant 71. d 72 p 73. C Peterlee *Dur* 72-77; C-in-c Stockton St Jas CD 82-89; P-in-c Byers Green from 89; Ind Chapl Teesside from 89. *St Peter's Rectory, Byers Green, Spennymoor, Co Durham DL16 7NW* Bishop Auckland (0388) 606659

BELL, Antony Fancourt. b 28. Magd Coll Ox BA51 MA58. Wells Th Coll 54. d 56 p 57. C Clapham H Trin *S'wark* 56-59; C Gillingham *Sarum* 59-61; V Stanway *Chelmsf* from 61; RD Dedham and Tey 81-91. *The Rectory, Church Lane, Stanway, Colchester CO3 5LR* Colchester (0206) 210407

BELL, Arthur Francis. b 17. Leeds Univ BA39. Bps' Coll Cheshunt 40. d 41 p 42. R Charlcombe *B & W* 61-85; rtd 85; Perm to Offic *B & W* from 86. *31 New Road, Bradford-on-Avon, Wilts BA15 1AR* Bradford-on-Avon (02216) 7624

BELL, Arthur James. b 33. Ch Coll Cam BA55 MA60. Coll of Resurr Mirfield 57. d 59 p 60. C New Cleethorpes *Linc* 59-63; C Upperby St Jo *Carl* 63-66; Canada 67-72 and 77-83; Perm to Offic *Carl* 73-75; Lic to Offic *Carl* 75-76; Host Retreat of the Visitation Rhandirmwyn from 83. *Nantymwyn, Retreat of the Visitation, Rhandirmwyn, Llandovery, Dyfed SA20 0NR* Rhandirmwyn (05506) 247

BELL, Bryan Bland. b 07. Wadh Coll Ox BA30. Tyndale Hall Bris 38. d 40 p 41. R Nedging w Naughton *St E* 68-72; rtd 72; P-in-c Chawleigh w Cheldon *Ex* 78-81; Perm to Offic from 81. *3 Cod Meadow, Hatherleigh, Okehampton, Devon EX20 3JB* Okehampton (0837) 810593

BELL, Catherine Ann. b 63. Trin Coll Bris BA88. d 89. Par Dn Southsea St Jude *Portsm* from 89. *45 Great South Street, Southsea, Hants PO5 3BY* Portsmouth (0705) 863056

BELL, Charles William. b 43. TCD BA66 MA69. d 67 p 68. C Newtownards *D & D* 67-70; C Larne and Inver *Conn* 70-74; C Ballymena w Ballyclug 74-80; Bp's C Belf Ardoyne 80-88; RD M Belf 86-89; Bp's C Belf Ardoyne w H Redeemer 88-89; I Eglantine from 89; Dioc Info Officer from 89. *All Saints' Rectory, 16 Eglantine Road, Lisburn, Co Antrim BT27 5RQ* Lisburn (0846) 662634

BELL, Colin Ashworth. b 52. FCCA83. Westcott Ho Cam 89. d 91. C Lytham St Cuth *Blackb* from 91. *11 Milner Road, Ansdell, Lytham St Annes, Lancs FY8 4EY* Lytham (0253) 733048

BELL, Cyril John. b 22. Hull Univ BA48. Wycliffe Hall Ox 52. d 53 p 54. C Monkwearmouth St Pet *Dur* 53-56; India 56-60; Hon C Westlands St Andr *Lich* 66-71; Lic to Offic *Ches* 71-82; Perm to Offic from 82. *1 Churchill Crescent, Marple, Stockport, Cheshire SK6 6HL* 061-427 5280

BELL, David James. b 62. QUB BSc84 BTh. d 91. C Ballyholme *D & D* from 91. *61 Windmill Road, Ballyholme, Bangor, Co Down BT20 5QY* Bangor (0247) 469614

BELL, David Mark Bowers. b 63. Hertf Coll Ox MA89. St Steph Ho Ox 88. d 91. C Walham Green St Jo w St Jas *Lon* from 91. *The Vicarage Flat, 40 Racton Road, London SW6 1LP* 071-381 3368

BELL, David Owain. b 49. Dur Univ BA69 Nottm Univ DipTh70 Fitzw Coll Cam BA72 MA80. Westcott Ho Cam 70. d 72 p 73. C Houghton le Spring *Dur* 72-76; C Norton St Mary 76-78; P-in-c Worc St Clem *Worc* 78-84; R 84-85; R Old Swinford Stourbridge from 85; RD Stourbridge from 90. *The Rectory, Oldswinford, Stourbridge, W Midlands DY8 2HA* Stourbridge (0384) 395410

BELL, Derek Arthur. b 35. K Coll Lon BD61 AKC61. St Boniface Warminster. d 62 p 63. C Blackpool H Cross *Blackb* 62-66; Lic to Offic from 67; Asst Master Arnold Sch Blackpool from 67. *4 Mersey Road, Blackpool FY4 1EN*

BELL, Donald John. b 50. Sarum & Wells Th Coll 73. d 76 p 77. C Jarrow St Paul *Dur* 76-77; C Jarrow 77-80; C Darlington St Cuth w St Hilda 80-83; V Wingate Grange 83-89; V Sherburn w Pittington from 89. *The Vicarage, 89 Front Street, Sherburn, Durham DH6 1HD* 091-372 0374

BELL, Edwin Lucius Wyndham. b 19. Worc Coll Ox BA41 MA45. Westcott Ho Cam 41. d 43 p 44. V Maidstone St Paul *Cant* 63-78; P-in-c Nonington w Barfreystone 78-85; P-in-c Womenswold 78-85; rtd 85; Perm to Offic *Cant* from 85. *2 Boarley Court, Sandling Lane, Maidstone, Kent ME14 2NL* Maidstone (0622) 756924

BELL, Edwin Ray. b 23. Clifton Th Coll 60. d 62 p 63. V Rashcliffe *Wakef* 65-76; V Holmebridge 76-89; rtd 89. *10 Hill Walk, Leyland, Preston, Lancs PR5 1NY* Preston (0772) 432774

BELL, Canon Francis William Albert. b 28. TCD BA52 MA57 BD57. d 53 p 54. C Belf St Mich *Conn* 53-55; C Belf All SS 55-61; C Ballynafeigh St Jude *D & D* 61-63; P-in-c Ballyhalbert 63-71; P-in-c Ardkeen 67-71; I Ballyhalbert w Ardkeen from 71; Miss to Seamen from 71; RD Ards *D & D* from 73; Can Belf Cathl from 89. *187 Main Road, Portavogie, Newtownards, Co Down BT22 1DA* Portavogie (02477) 71234

BELL, Godfrey Bryan. b 44. Oak Hill Th Coll 72. d 75 p 76. C Penn Fields *Lich* 75-79; R Dolton *Ex* 79-89; R Iddesleigh w Dowland 79-89; R Monkokehampton 79-89; R Tollard Royal w Farnham, Gussage St Michael etc *Sarum* from 89. *The Rectory, Farnham, Blandford Forum, Dorset DT11 8DE* Tollard Royal (0725) 516221

BELL, Graham Dennis Robert. b 42. ALCM K Coll Lon BSc63 AKC63 Nottm Univ MTh73. Tyndale Hall Bris 65. d 68 p 69. C Stapleford *S'well* 68-71; C Barton Seagrave *Pet* 71-73; C Barton Seagrave w Warkton 73-76; Perm to Offic *Nor* 76-82; V Wickham Market St E 82-86; V Wickham Market w Pettistree and Easton from 86. *The Vicarage, Crown Lane, Wickham Market, Woodbridge, Suffolk IP13 0SA* Wickham Market (0728) 746314

BELL, Canon Jack Gorman. b 23. Lon Univ BSc48. Oak Hill Th Coll 51. d 53 p 54. V Mosley Common *Man* 69-89; Hon Can Man Cathl 87-89; rtd 89; Perm to Offic *Carl* from 89. *36 Sandgate, Kendal, Cumbria LA9 6HT* Kendal (0539) 725807

BELL, James Harold. b 50. St Jo Coll Dur BA72 St Pet Hall Ox BA74 MA78. Wycliffe Hall Ox 72. d 75 p 76. Hon C Ox St Mich w St Martin and All SS *Ox* 75-76; Chapl and Lect BNC Ox 76-82; Lic to Offic 76-82; R

Northolt St Mary *Lon* from 82. *The Rectory, Ealing Road, Northolt, Middx UB5 6AA* 081-841 5691

BELL, James Samuel. b 40. MBE71. St Chad's Coll Dur BA69. Coll of Resurr Mirfield 71. **d** 72 **p** 73. C Lambeth St Phil *S'wark* 72-74; P-in-c St Ninian Invergordon 74-77; C N Lambeth 74; P-in-c Dornoch *Mor* 74-77; P-in-c Brora 74-77; V Pet H Spirit Bretton *Pet* 77-83; P-in-c Marholm 82-83; Chapl Tonbridge Sch Kent from 83. *High Trees, 8 Bourne Lane, Tonbridge, Kent TN9 1LG* Tonbridge (0732) 352802

BELL, Jeffrey William. b 37. Sarum Th Coll 60. **d** 63 **p** 64. C Northn St Matt *Pet* 63-66; C Portishead *B & W* 66-68; C Digswell *St Alb* 68-72; V Pet St Jude *Pet* 72-79; V Buckm *Ox* from 79; RD Buckm 84-88 and 89-90. *The Vicarage, Church Street, Buckingham MK18 1BY* Buckingham (0280) 813178

BELL, Jeremy Aidan. b 46. DipHE. Oak Hill Th Coll 80. **d** 82. C St Paul's Cray St Barn *Roch* 82-83; Perm to Offic *Ex* from 83. *Ford Down Farm, Exeter Road, South Molton, Devon EX36 4MY* South Molton (07695) 3911

BELL, John Alfred Collingwood. b 23. Fitzw Coll Cam BA47 MA52 St Jo Coll Dur DipTh51 DipEd59. **d** 51 **p** 52. CF (TAVR) 56-84; Perm to Offic *Roch* 60-74; C Beverley Minster *York* 74-77; TV Thornaby on Tees 77-78; C Scalby w Ravenscar and Staintondale 78-79; C Luton All SS w St Pet *St Alb* 79-80; C Hykeham *Linc* 81-85; Chapl Sea Cadet Corps RNVR 83-85; R Castle Douglas *Glas* 85-88; rtd 88; Perm to Offic Linc 88-89; Ripon 89-91; B & W from 91. *Flat 6, The Judges Lodging, 19 New Street, Wells, Somerset BA5 2LD* Wells (0749) 672053

BELL, Canon John Christopher. b 33. TCD BA56 MA66. TCD Div Sch Div Test. **d** 56 **p** 57. C Newtownards *D & D* 56-59; C Willowfield 59-62; I Carrowdore 62-70; I Drumbo from 70; RD Hillsborough from 81; Can Down Cathl from 87. *The Rectory, 5 Pinehill Road, Drumbo, Ballylesson, Belfast BT8 8LA* Belfast (0232) 826225

BELL, John Edward. b 34. Cranmer Hall Dur. **d** 67 **p** 68. C Harraby *Carl* 67-70; C Dalton-in-Furness 70-72; V Pennington 72-75; V Carl St Herbert w St Steph 75-84; V Wreay 84-85. *189 Brampton Road, Carlisle, Cumbria CA3 9AX* Carlisle (0228) 22746

BELL, John Holmes. b 50. Sheff City Coll of Educn CertEd71. Oak Hill Th Coll DipHE79 BA80. **d** 80 **p** 81. C Leic St Phil *Leic* 80-83; C Portswood Ch Ch *Win* 83-86; TV S Molton w Nymet St George, High Bray etc *Ex* from 86. *The Rectory, Kings Nympton, Umberleigh, Devon EX37 9ST* Chulmleigh (0769) 80457

BELL, Joseph William. b 30. Pemb Coll Cam BA53 MA57. Wycliffe Hall Ox 53. **d** 55 **p** 56. C Blundellsands St Nic *Liv* 55-58; CF 58-68; V Roby *Liv* 68-70; CF 70-86; P-in-c Fovant, Sutton Mandeville and Teffont Evias etc *Sarum* 86-89. *61 St Ann Place, Salisbury SP1 2SU* Salisbury (0722) 22576

BELL, Kenneth Murray. b 30. Sarum & Wells Th Coll 75. **d** 74 **p** 76. Perm to Offic *Guildf* 74-76; C Hartley Wintney and Elvetham *Win* 76-77; C Hartley Wintney, Elvetham, Winchfield etc 77-80; V Fair Oak from 80. *The Vicarage, Fair Oak Court, Fair Oak, Eastleigh, Hants SO5 7BG* Southampton (0703) 692238

BELL, Kevin David. b 58. Selly Oak Coll CPS87 Aston Tr Scheme 78 Sarum & Wells Th Coll 80. **d** 83 **p** 84. C Weoley Castle *Birm* 83-87; C Acocks Green 87-89; CF from 89. *c/o MOD (Army), Bagshot Park, Bagshot, Surrey GU19 5PL* Bagshot (0276) 71717

BELL, Nicholas Philip Johnson. b 46. St Jo Coll Dur BSc69 Nottm Univ DipTh72. St Jo Coll Nottm 70. **d** 73 **p** 74. C Chadderton Ch Ch *Man* 73-77; C Frogmore H Trin *St Alb* 77-81; V Bricket Wood 81-91; RD Aldenham 87-91; V Luton St Mary from 91. *The Vicarage, 48 Crawley Green Road, Luton LU2 0QX* Luton (0582) 28925

BELL, Paul Joseph. b 35. Dur Univ BA56 DipEd57. Trin Coll Bris 77. **d** 77 **p** 78. CMS 77-82; C Highbury Ch Ch w St Jo and St Sav Lon 82-85; V Middleton w E Winch *Nor* from 85. *The Vicarage, 12 Hall Orchards, Middleton, King's Lynn, Norfolk PE32 1RY* King's Lynn (0553) 840252

BELL, Philip Harold. b 19. Leeds Univ BA45. Coll of Resurr Mirfield 38. **d** 44 **p** 45. R Crawley w Littleton *Win* 61-72; V Holdenhurst 72-78; P-in-c Hilperton w Whaddon *Sarum* 78-84; P-in-c Staverton 78-84; R Hilperton w Whaddon and Staverton etc 85-86; rtd 86. *31 Duxford Close, Larksfield, Bowerhill, Melksham, Wilts SN12 6XN* Melksham (0225) 709732

BELL, Reginald Leslie. b 13. Trin Coll Bris 72. **d** 74 **p** 75. NSM Stoke Bishop *Bris* 74-75 and from 78; NSM

Horfield H Trin 75-77. *September Cottage, 14 Pitch and Pay Lane, Bristol BS9 1NH* Bristol (0272) 681510

BELL, Dr Richard Alexander. b 14. St Pet Hall Ox BA37 MA42. Westcott Ho Cam 37. **d** 39 **p** 39. R Clayton w Keymer *Chich* 58-70; V Amberley w N Stoke 70-75; Israel 76-83; rtd 83; Perm to Offic *Glouc* from 83. *41 Lansdown Road, Gloucester GL1 3JU* Gloucester (0452) 516668

BELL, Robert Clarke. b 30. Roch Th Coll 63. **d** 65 **p** 66. C Leeds All SS *Ripon* 65-67; C Claxby w Normanby-le-Wold *Linc* 67-69; R Newark St Leon *S'well* 69-71; V Gosberton Clough *Linc* 71-74; P-in-c Quadring 73-74; Chapl to the Deaf 74-85; V Harmston from 85; V Coleby from 85. *The Vicarage, Harmston, Lincoln LN5 9SL* Lincoln (0522) 720282

BELL, Robert Mason. b 35. Lon Coll of Div 66. **d** 68 **p** 69. C Burgess Hill St Andr *Chich* 68-78; R Lewes St Jo sub Castro from 78. *St John's Rectory, 1 The Avenue, Lewes, E Sussex BN7 1BA* Lewes (0273) 473080

BELL, Simon Barnaby. b 48. Bris Univ CertEd70. Sarum & Wells Th Coll 87. **d** 89 **p** 90. C Ewyas Harold w Dulas *Heref* 89-90; C Ewyas Harold w Dulas, Kenderchurch etc from 90. *Brightwell, Old Shoppe Lands, Ewyas Harold, Hereford HR2 0HQ* Golden Valley (0981) 240473

BELL, Stuart Rodney. b 46. Ex Univ BA67. Tyndale Hall Bris 69. **d** 71 **p** 72. C Henfynyw w Aberaeron and Llanddewi Aber-arth *St D* 71-74; V 81-88; V Llangeler 74-80; R Abth from 88. *The Rectory, Laura Place, Aberystwyth, Dyfed SA23 2AU* Aberystwyth (0970) 617184

BELL-RICHARDS, Douglas Maurice. b 23. St Steph Ho Ox 59. **d** 61 **p** 62. C Chipping Campden *Glouc* 61-62; C Thornbury 62-67; V Dymock w Donnington 67-75; V Fairford from 75. *The Vicarage, Fairford, Glos GL7 4BB* Cirencester (0285) 712467

BELLAIRS-COX, Miss Diana Geraldine. b 27. LTCL CertEd47. S Dios Minl Tr Scheme 87. **d** 90. NSM Oakdale St Geo *Sarum* from 90. *24 Chalbury Close, Poole, Dorset BH17 8BS* Poole (0202) 600219

BELLAMY, Charles Gordon. b 15. St Chad's Coll Dur BA42. St Deiniol's Hawarden 36. **d** 42 **p** 43. V Overton *Blackb* 67-80; rtd 80; Hon C Monkseaton St Mary *Newc* from 80. *60 Davison Avenue, Whitley Bay, Tyne & Wear NE26 1SH* 091-251 3355

BELLAMY, David Quentin. b 62. Univ of Wales (Cardiff) BMus84. Ripon Coll Cuddesdon 87 Ch Div Sch of the Pacific (USA). **d** 90 **p** 91. C Rhyl w Rhyl St Ann *St As* from 90. *The Close, Paradise Street, Rhyl, Clwyd LL18 3LW* Rhyl (0745) 337130

BELLAMY, Mrs Dorothy Kathleen. b 33. Gilmore Course 74. **dss** 82 **d** 87. Feltham *Lon* 82-84; Twickenham St Mary 84; Hampton St Mary 84-85; Hampton Wick 85-87; Par Dn 87-88; Par Dn Teddington St Mark and Hampton Wick St Jo 88-90; Par Dn Westbury *Sarum* from 90. *11 Laverton Green, Westbury, Wilts BA13 3RP* Westbury (0373) 858866

BELLAMY, John Stephen. b 55. Jes Coll Ox BA77 MA81 DipTh82 DPS84. St Jo Coll Nottm. **d** 84 **p** 85. C Allerton *Liv* 84-87; C Southport Ch Ch 87-89; Bp's Dom Chapl from 89. *48 Babbacombe Road, Liverpool L16 9JW* 051-722 9543

BELLAMY, Mervyn Roger Hunter. b 47. Sussex Univ CertEd. St Mich Coll Llan DipTh81. **d** 81 **p** 82. C Frecheville and Hackenthorpe *Sheff* 81-85; V Shiregreen St Hilda from 85. *St Hilda's House, 2 Firth Park Crescent, Sheffield S5 6HE* Sheffield (0742) 436308

BELLAMY, Peter Charles William. b 38. Birm Univ MA70 PhD79 AKC61. **d** 62 **p** 63. C Allestree *Derby* 62-65; Chapl All SS Hosp Birm 65-73; Chapl St Pet Coll Saltley 73-78; Lic to Offic *Birm* 78-90; Chapl Qu Eliz Hosp Birm from 78; Perm to Offic *Birm* from 90. *District Offices, Vincent Drive, Birmingham B15 2TZ* 021-627 2052

BELLENES, Peter Charles. b 49. Pontifical Univ Salamanca DipPhil68 CQSW72. Linc Th Coll 79. **d** 81 **p** 90. C Penistone *Wakef* 81-82; NSM Liskeard, St Keyne, St Pinnock, Morval etc *Truro* from 89. *Fernlea, Beneathway, Dobwalls, Liskeard, Cornwall PL14 6JN* Liskeard (0579) 20031

BELLINGER, Canon Denys Gordon. b 29. Sheff Univ BA49. Westcott Ho Cam 51. **d** 53 **p** 54. C Ribbleton *Blackb* 53-56; C Lanc St Mary 56-58; V Colne H Trin 58-68; V Scotforth from 68; RD Lanc 82-89; Hon Can Blackb Cathl from 86. *St Paul's Vicarage, 24 Scotforth Road, Lancaster LA1 4ST* Lancaster (0524) 32106

BELOE, Archibald John Martin. b 15. Qu Coll Cam BA37 MA41. Man Egerton Hall 37. **d** 39 **p** 40. R Hilgay *Ely* 61-79; V Fordham St Mary 71-79; rtd

79. *132 Newmarket Road, Norwich NR4 6SB* Norwich (0603) 502610

BELOE, Robert Francis. b 39. Sarum Th Coll. **d** 65 **p** 71. C Nor Heartsease St Fran *Nor* 65-66; C Edmonton St Mary w St Jo *Lon* 68-70; C St Marylebone Ch Ch w St Paul 70-74; P-in-c Wicken *Ely* 74-76; V from 76. *The Vicarage, Wicken, Ely, Cambs CB7 5XT* Ely (0353) 720243

BEMAN, Donald Oliver. b 37. Southn Univ BA58. Coll of Resurr Mirfield 58. **d** 60 **p** 65. C Forton *Portsm* 60-61; Hon C Hound *Win* 64-68; Lic to Offic 69-82. *8 Avon Court, Netley Abbey, Southampton* Southampton (0703) 453239

BENBOW, Mrs Susan Catherine. b 47. Birm Univ BEd70. St Alb Minl Tr Scheme 82. **dss** 85 **d** 87. Gt Wyrley *Lich* 85-87; Par Dn 87-88; Par Dn Whitstable *Cant* from 88. *64 Cromwell Road, Whitstable, Kent CT5 1NN* Whitstable (0227) 262590

BENCE, Canon Graham Edwin. b 16. Lon Univ BA54. Sarum Th Coll 64. **d** 65 **p** 66. R Barlborough *Derby* 68-86; RD Bolsover 70-73; RD Bolsover and Staveley 73-78; Hon Can Derby Cathl 78-86; rtd 86; Perm to Offic *Lich* from 87. *Flat 3, 4 Quarry Place, Shrewsbury SY1 1JN* Shrewsbury (0743) 23533

BENCE, Norman Murray. b 34. Ripon Hall Ox 63. **d** 63 **p** 64. C Eling *Win* 63-66; Australia 66 and 75; Lic to Offic *Win* 67-74 and from 75; Hon C Iford from 81. *72 Corhampton Road, Bournemouth BH6 5PB* Bournemouth (0202) 421992

BENCE, Roy. b 21. Chich Th Coll 55. **d** 57 **p** 58. V Bethnal Green St Jas the Gt w St Jude *Lon* 69-72; V Bush Hill Park St Mark 72-79; V Highgate St Aug 79-86; rtd 87. *5 St James's Close, Bishop Street, London N1 8PH* 071-359 0885

BENDELL, David James. b 38. S'wark Ord Course. **d** 87 **p** 88. NSM Surbiton Hill Ch Ch *S'wark* from 87. *3 Pine Walk, Surbiton, Surrey KT5 8NJ* 081-399 7143

BENDELOW, Thomas Arthur. b 11. Dur Univ BA37. Westcott Ho Cam 37. **d** 38 **p** 39. V High Harrogate Ch Ch *Ripon* 54-70; C Friern Barnet St Jas *Lon* 70-72; V Warter w Huggate *York* 72-85; rtd 85. *Dulverton Hall, St Martin's Square, Scarborough YO11 2DB* Scarborough (0723) 373082

BENDING, Richard Clement. b 47. Southn Univ BSc68. Ridley Hall Cam 87. **d** 89 **p** 90. Par Dn St Neots *Ely* from 89. *20 Avenue Road, St Neots, Huntingdon, Cambs PE19 1LJ* Huntingdon (0480) 219207

BENFIELD, Gordon. b 29. LGSM. Lon Univ BD60 STh79 Birm Univ MA81 Leeds Univ 60. **d** 80 **p** 81. NSM Warw *Cov* 80-85; Prin Westhill Coll of HE Birm 85-90; Perm to Offic *Birm* 85-90; Chmn Ch Educn Movement from 86; R Barford w Wasperton and Sherbourne *Cov* from 90. *The Rectory, Barford, Warwick CV35 8ES* Barford (0926) 624238

BENFIELD, Paul John. b 56. Barrister-at-Law (Lincoln's Inn) 78 Newc Univ LLB77 Southn Univ BTh89. Chich Th Coll 86. **d** 89 **p** 90. C Shiremoor *Newc* from 89. *31 Horsley Avenue, Shiremoor, Newcastle upon Tyne NE27 0UF* 091-251 3067

BENFORD, Brian. b 47. Sheff Univ BA Hull Univ MEd PhD88. N Ord Course 82. **d** 85 **p** 86. NSM Stocksbridge *Sheff* 85-91. *Address temp unknown*

BENGE, Charles David. b 40. Cranmer Hall Dur 63. **d** 68 **p** 69. C Millfield St Mark *Dur* 68-72; C Hensingham *Carl* 72-74; TV Maghull *Liv* 75-82; V Bootle St Leon from 82. *St Leonard's Vicarage, 60 Peel Road, Bootle, Merseyside L20 4RW* 051-922 1434

BENIAMS, Alec Charles. b 28. AKC52. **d** 53 **p** 54. V Willington *Newc* 67-71; CF (TA - R of O) from 67; V Haydon Bridge *Newc* 71-85; R Yardley Hastings, Denton and Grendon etc *Pet* 85-90; rtd 90. *12 Dickson Drive, Highford Park, Hexham, Northd NE46 2RB* Hexham (0434) 600226

BENIANS, Martin Ackland. b 19. St Jo Coll Cam BA41 MA45. Ridley Hall Cam 59. **d** 59 **p** 60. R Rackheath *Nor* 62-89; V Salhouse 62-89; rtd 89. *26 Victoria Street, Sheringham, Norfolk NR26 8JZ* Sheringham (0263) 822563

BENISON, Brian. b 41. K Coll Lon 61. Bps' Coll Cheshunt 63. **d** 66 **p** 67. C Tynemouth Ch Ch *Newc* 66-70; C Gosforth All SS 70-72; TV Cullercoats St Geo 73-81; V Denton from 81. *The Vicarage, Dunblane Crescent, Newcastle upon Tyne NE5 2BE* 091-267 4376

BENJAMIN, Adrian Victor. b 42. Wadh Coll Ox BA66 MA68. Cuddesdon Coll 66. **d** 68 **p** 69. C Gosforth All SS *Newc* 68-71; C Stepney St Dunstan and All SS *Lon* 71-75; V Friern Barnet All SS from 75; Relig Ed ITV Oracle from 83. *14 Oakleigh Park South, London N20 9JU* 081-445 4645 or 445 6831

BENN, Wallace Parke. b 47. UCD BA69 Lon Univ DipTh71. Trin Coll Bris 69. **d** 72 **p** 73. C New Ferry *Ches* 72-76; C Cheadle 76-82; V Audley *Lich* 82-87; V Harold Wood *Chelmsf* from 87; Chapl Harold Wood Hosp Chelmsf from 87. *The Vicarage, 15 Athelstan Road, Harold Wood, Romford RM3 0QB* Ingrebourne (04023) 42080

BENNELL, Canon Richard. b 25. Leeds Univ BA45 DipEd45. Coll of Resurr Mirfield 46. **d** 48 **p** 49. V Knowle St Martin *Bris* 68-73; RD Brislington 73-79; TR Knowle 73-80; Hon Can Bris Cathl 76-91; Chapl St Monica Home Bris 80-91; rtd 91. *1B Cooper Road, Bristol BS9 3QZ* Bristol (0272) 622364

BENNET, Hon George Arthur Grey. b 25. CCC Cam BA46 MA51. Clifton Th Coll 68. **d** 69 **p** 70. C Radipole *Sarum* 69-71; P-in-c Motcombe 71-73; TV Shaston 73-80; R Redenhall w Harleston and Wortwell *Nor* 80-82; P-in-c Needham w Rushall 80-82; R Redenhall, Harleston, Wortwell and Needham 82-90; rtd 90; Perm to Offic *Nor* from 90. *112 Norwich Road, Wymondham, Norfolk NR18 0SZ* Wymondham (0953) 601284

BENNET, Gordon Duncan Affleck. b 31. Lon Univ BSc(Econ)55. Clifton Th Coll 55. **d** 58 **p** 59. C Carl St Jo *Carl* 57-60; C W Kilburn St Luke w St Simon and St Jude *Lon* 60-63; C-in-c Dallam CD *Liv* 63-69; Lic to Offic *Man* 69-75; N W Area Sec CPAS 69-75; R Edgware *Lon* 75-91; V Walton le Soken *Chelmsf* from 91. *The Vicarage, Martello Road, Walton on the Naze, Essex CO14 8TA* Frinton-on-Sea (0255) 75452

BENNETT, Alan Robert. b 31. Roch Th Coll 62. **d** 64 **p** 65. C Asterby w Goulceby *Linc* 64-67; C St Alb St Pet *St Alb* 67-70; R Banham *Nor* 70-72; CF 72-77; P-in-c Colchester St Mary Magd *Chelmsf* 77; TV Colchester St Leon, St Mary Magd and St Steph 77-81; R Colne Engaine 81-88; P-in-c Stoke Ferry w Wretton *Ely* 88-89; V from 89. *The Vicarage, Low Road, Wretton, King's Lynn, Norfolk* Stoke Ferry (0366) 501075

BENNETT, Alan William. b 42. Sarum Th Coll 65. **d** 68 **p** 69. C Fareham H Trin *Portsm* 68-71; C Brighton St Matthias *Chich* 71-73; C Stanmer w Falmer and Moulsecoomb 73-75; C Moulsecoomb 76; V Lower Sandown St Jo *Portsm* 76-80; V Soberton w Newtown 80-87; R Aston Clinton w Buckland and Drayton Beauchamp *Ox* from 87. *The Rectory, Aston Clinton, Aylesbury, Bucks HP22 5JD* Aylesbury (0296) 631626

BENNETT, Anthony. b 31. Qu Coll Birm 72. **d** 74 **p** 74. C Hobs Moat *Birm* 74-76; C Hill 76-79; R Grendon 79-82; R Upwell Ch Ch *Ely* 82-86; R Welney 82-86; P-in-c Coates 86-88; R from 88. *The Rectory, North Green, Coates, Whittlesey, Peterborough PE7 2BQ* Turves (073120) 254

BENNETT, Arnold Ernest. b 29. K Coll Lon BD59 AKC53. **d** 54 **p** 55. C S w N Hayling *Portsm* 54-59; C Stevenage *St Alb* 59-64; R N w S Wootton *Nor* 64-74; V Hykeham *Linc* 74-85; V Heckfield w Mattingley and Rotherwick *Win* from 85. *The Vicarage, Mattingley, Basingstoke, Hants RG27 8LF* Heckfield (0734) 326385

BENNETT, Canon Arthur. b 15. Lon Univ DipTh68. Lambeth STh77 Clifton Th Coll 40. **d** 42 **p** 43. R Sacombe *St Alb* 64-81; R Lt Munden 64-81; Hon Can St Alb 70-81; R Lt Munden w Sacombe 81; rtd 81; Lic to Offic *St Alb* 81-86; Perm to Offic from 86; Vice-Pres CMS from 86. *Munden, 5 Green Lane, Clapham, Bedford MK41 6EP* Bedford (0234) 54462

BENNETT, Arthur Harling. b 22. Ripon Hall Ox 70. **d** 71 **p** 72. C Standish *Blackb* 71-74; TV Darwen St Pet w Hoddlesden 75-79; V Whitechapel 79-89; V Whitechapel w Admarsh-in-Bleasdale 89-90; rtd 90. *1 Eden Gardens, Mersey Street, Longridge, Preston PR3 3WF* Longridge (0772) 784924

BENNETT, Basil Edward. b 02. FRSA. Roch Th Coll 21. **d** 25 **p** 26. Asst ChStJ from 42; V Stoke by Clare w Wixoe *St E* 65-84; rtd 84. *Cornerways, Studley Road, Ripon, N Yorkshire HG4 2QJ* Ripon (0765) 2063

BENNETT, Bernard Michael. b 27. Leeds Univ CertEd52 DipPE54. St Aid Birkenhead 55. **d** 58 **p** 59. V Birkenhead St Bede w All SS *Ches* 62-71; V Latchford St Jas 71-75; Chapl HM Pris Appleton Thorn 75-82; V Appleton Thorn and Antrobus *Ches* 75-86; Chapl HM Rem Cen Risley 81-84; rtd 86. *7 Montpelier Avenue, Blackpool FY2 9AE* Blackpool (0253) 51139

BENNETT, Bryan James. b 39. Tyndale Hall Bris 64. **d** 67 **p** 68. C Consett *Dur* 67-70; CF 70-84; R Leadenham *Linc* from 84; R Welbourn from 84. *The Rectory, Church End, Leadenham, Lincoln LN5 0PX* Loveden (0400) 73253

BENNETT, Clifford Orford. b 32. St Mich Coll Llan 73. **d** 75 **p** 76. C Holywell *St As* 75-79; V Pontblyddyn from

53

79. *The Vicarage, Pontblyddyn, Mold, Clwyd CH7 4HG* Pontybodkin (0352) 771489

BENNETT, David Edward. b 35. Fitzw Ho Cam BA56 MA60 Lon Univ PGCE. Wells Th Coll 58. **d** 60 **p** 61. C Lightcliffe *Wakef* 60-62; NE Area Sec Chr Educn Movement 62-68; Lic to Offic *S'well* 68-71; Gen Insp RE Nottm Co Coun from 68; Hon C Holme Pierrepont w Adbolton 71-85; Hon C Radcliffe-on-Trent and Shelford etc from 85. *The Old Farmhouse, Main Street, Gunthorpe, Nottingham NG14 7EY* Nottingham (0602) 663451

BENNETT, David Lawrence. b 38. Liv Univ BA61. Ripon Hall Ox 61. **d** 63 **p** 64. C Harlington *Lon* 63-66; Zambia from 67. *c/o University of Zambia, PO Box 2379, Lusaka, Zambia*

BENNETT, David Satterly. b 37. Lanc Univ BA79 Linc Coll Ox CertEd80. English Coll Valladolid 57. **d** 62 **p** 63. In RC Ch 62-72; RAChD 72-75; RE 77-84; NSM Alresford *Chelmsf* 83-84; C Chandler's Ford *Win* from 84. *8 Bassett Close, Southampton SO2 3FP* Chandler's Ford (0703) 769404

BENNETT, Dennis Stanley. b 13. Chich Th Coll 37. **d** 39 **p** 40. R Frampton Cotterell *Bris* 65-72; C Wrington w Butcombe *B & W* 73-78; rtd 78. *Ashcombe, West Hay Road, Wrington, Bristol BS18 7NN* Wrington (0934) 862529

BENNETT, Edwin James. b 23. St Barn Coll Adelaide ThL47 STh52. **d** 47 **p** 48. Australia 47-74; V Oldham St Barn *Man* 74-78; V Alderney *Win* 78-84; V Hatherden w Tangley, Weyhill and Penton Mewsey 84-89; rtd 89. *35 Charlton Village, Andover, Hants SP10 4AP* Andover (0264) 56358

BENNETT, Garry Raymond. b 46. K Coll Lon 66. **d** 70 **p** 71. C Mitcham St Mark *S'wark* 70-73; C Mortlake w E Sheen 73-75; TV 76-78; V Herne Hill St Paul 78-88; P-in-c Ruskin Park St Sav and St Matt 82-88; V Herne Hill 89; Sen Dioc Stewardship Adv *Chelmsf* from 89. *Christian Stewardship Department, Council for Mission and Unity, New Street, Chelmsford CM1 1NG* Chelmsford (0245) 266731

BENNETT, Geoffrey Kenneth. b 56. Oak Hill Th Coll. **d** 89 **p** 90. C Ipswich St Matt *St E* from 89. *70 Orford Street, Ipswich IP1 3PE* Ipswich (0473) 210539

BENNETT, George Darley. b 21. ACIS47. **d** 66 **p** 67. Zambia 66-76; R Hulland, Atlow and Bradley *Derby* 76-78; P-in-c Hulland, Atlow, Bradley and Hognaston 76-78; R 78-86; RD Ashbourne 81-86; rtd 87; Perm to Offic *Derby* from 87. *11 Freemantle Road, Mickleover, Derby DE3 5HW* Derby (0332) 510212

BENNETT, George Edward. b 51. Univ of Wales (Abth) BA72. St Steph Ho Ox 73. **d** 76 **p** 77. C Clifton All SS w Tyndalls Park *Bris* 76-78; C Clifton All SS w St Jo 78-82; Chapl Newbury and Sandleford Hosps from 82; TV Newbury *Ox* from 82. *St John's Vicarage, Newbury, Berks RG14 7QA* Newbury (0635) 40387

BENNETT, Graham Eric Thomas. b 53. Sarum & Wells Th Coll 88. **d** 90 **p** 91. C Baswich (or Berkswich) *Lich* from 90. *21 Lansdowne Way, Wildwood, Stafford ST17 4RD* Stafford (0785) 662333

BENNETT, Guy. b 33. St Edm Hall Ox BA56. Wells Th Coll 56. **d** 58 **p** 59. C Norbury St Phil *Cant* 58-61; C Minehead *B & W* 61-63; Chapl Butlin's Clacton-on-Sea 63; C Raynes Park St Sav *S'wark* 63-66; C Motspur Park H Cross CD 66-72; R Oxted from 72. *The Rectory, 29 Chichele Road, Oxted, Surrey RH8 0AE* Oxted (0883) 712955

BENNETT, Handel Henry Cecil. b 33. Cant Sch of Min 79. **d** 82 **p** 83. NSM St Margarets-at-Cliffe w Westcliffe etc *Cant* 82-85; Dir Holy Land Chr Tours from 85; Perm to Offic *St Alb* from 85. *23 The Marsh, Carlton, Bedford MK43 7JU* Bedford (0234) 720745

BENNETT, Harold Archibald Timson. b 11. Keble Coll Ox BA33 MA45. St Steph Ho Ox 34. **d** 35 **p** 36. V Kennington *Ox* 65-79; rtd 79; C Ox St Mary Magd *Ox* 79-87; Perm to Offic from 87. *St John's Home, St Mary's Road, Oxford OX4 1QE* Oxford (0865) 246937

BENNETT, Canon Ian Frederick. b 30. Ch Coll Cam BA54 MA62. Westcott Ho Cam 61. **d** 63 **p** 64. C Hemel Hempstead *St Alb* 63-68; Asst Chapl Man Univ *Man* 69-73; Sen Chapl 73-79; C Chorlton upon Medlock 69-73; P-in-c 73-79; TR Man Whitworth 79; Dioc Tr Officer *Birm* 79-88; Hon Can Birm Cathl 86-88; Can Res Newc Cathl *Newc* 88-90; Dioc Dir of Min and Tr from 90. *21 Otterburn Avenue, Gosforth, Newcastle upon Tyne NE3 4RR* 091-285 1967

BENNETT, James Kenneth Bretherton. b 11. St Jo Coll Ox BA33 DipTh34 MA37. Wycliffe Hall Ox 33. **d** 35 **p** 36. Asst Master Loretto Sch Musselburgh 67-73; Chapl

Caldicott Sch Farnham Royal 73-76; rtd 76. *c/o The Acorns, Church Lane, Oakley, Bedford MK43 7RJ*

BENNETT, John David. b 58. Ox Univ BA79 MA83. Westcott Ho Cam 81. **d** 83 **p** 84. C Taunton St Andr *B & W* 83-86; Chapl Trowbridge Coll *Sarum* 86-90; AP Studley 86-90; V Yeovil H Trin *B & W* from 90. *Holy Trinity Vicarage, 24 Turners Barn Lane, Yeovil, Somerset BA20 2LM* Yeovil (0935) 23774

BENNETT, John Walker. b 09. Hatf Coll Dur BA39 LTh39 MA41. St Aug Coll Cant 35. **d** 39 **p** 40. R Bradfield St Clare *St E* 64-77; R Bradfield St Geo w Rushbrooke 64-77; rtd 77; Perm to Offic *St E* from 77. *5 Orchard Way, Barrow, Bury St Edmunds, Suffolk* Bury St Edmunds (0284) 810617

BENNETT, Dr Joyce Mary. b 23. OBE79. Westf Coll Lon BA44 DipEd45 K Coll Lon DipTh61 Hon DSocSc84. **d** 62 **p** 71. Hong Kong 62-83; NSM St Martin-in-the-Fields *Lon* from 84; Perm to Offic *Ox* from 87. *88 Wrights Lane, Prestwood, Great Missenden, Bucks HP16 0LG* Great Missenden (02406) 2647

BENNETT, Kenneth Leigh. b 18. Jes Coll Ox BA42 MA46. **d** 44 **p** 45. V Sneinton St Matthias *S'well* 55-90; rtd 90. *1 Grafton Avenue, Woodthorpe, Nottingham NG5 4GD* Nottingham (0602) 265469

BENNETT, Michael Edgar. b 32. Keble Coll Ox BA53 MA58 DipEd. Wells Th Coll 59. **d** 61 **p** 62. C Calne and Blackland *Sarum* 61-64; C Tewkesbury w Walton Cardiff *Glouc* 64-69; R Swindon w Uckington and Elmstone Hardwicke from 69; Ed Glouc Dioc Gazette from 73; Chapl Sue Ryder Home Cheltenham from 80. *The Rectory, Swindon, Cheltenham, Glos GL51 9RD* Cheltenham (0242) 522786

BENNETT, Michael John. b 43. AKC66. St Boniface Warminster. **d** 67 **p** 68. C Ches le Street *Dur* 67-71; C Portland All SS w St Pet *Sarum* 71-74; Chapl Portland Hosp Weymouth 74-85; V Portland St Jo *Sarum* 74-85; R Alveley and Quatt *Heref* from 85. *The Vicarage, Alveley, Bridgnorth, Shropshire WV15 6ND* Bridgnorth (0746) 780326

BENNETT, Nigel John. b 47. Lon Univ DipTh69. Oak Hill Th Coll 66. **d** 71 **p** 72. C Tonbridge St Steph *Roch* 71-75; C Heatherlands St Jo *Sarum* 75-79; P-in-c Kingham w Churchill, Daylesford and Sarsden *Ox* 79; R 80-85; Chapl Blue Coat Sch Reading from 85. *13 Wilmington Close, Woodley, Reading RG5 4LR* Reading (0734) 699223

BENNETT, Osmond Shirley. b 36. Or Coll Ox BA67. Ripon Hall Ox 64. **d** 68 **p** 69. C Stocking Farm *Leic* 68-71; C Thurcaston 71-72; V Leic St Marg 72-82; V Leic St Marg and All SS 83-89; R Houghton-on-the-Hill, Keyham and Hungarton from 89. *16 Main Street, Houghton-on-the-Hill, Leicester LE7 9GD* Leicester (0533) 415828

BENNETT, Paul John. b 47. Univ of Wales (Cardiff) DPS89. St Mich Coll Llan 88 Llan Dioc Tr Scheme 79. **d** 85 **p** 86. NSM Ystrad Rhondda w Ynyscynon *Llan* 85-89; C Tylorstown w Ynyshir 89-91; V Ferndale w Maerdy from 91. *The Vicarage, North Terrace, Maerdy, Rhondda CF43 4DD* Ferndale (0443) 755651

BENNETT, Paul Jonathan. b 61. Ex Univ BA85. Ripon Coll Cuddesdon 85. **d** 87 **p** 88. C Henleaze *Bris* 87-91; P-in-c Swindon All SS from 91. *All Saints' Vicarage, Southbrook Street, Swindon SN2 1HF* Swindon (0793) 523572

BENNETT, Peter Harry Edward. b 19. Chich Th Coll 53. **d** 55 **p** 56. V Heathfield St Rich *Chich* 61-71; V Goring-by-Sea 71-84; rtd 84; Perm to Offic *Chich* from 84. *40 Elm Park, Ferring, Worthing, W Sussex BN12 5RW* Worthing (0903) 48219

BENNETT, Peter Hugh. b 22. K Coll Lon 46. **d** 50 **p** 51. V Hillmorton *Cov* 64-76; R Beaudesert w Henley-in-Arden 76-81; P-in-c Ullenhall cum Aspley 76-81; R Beaudesert and Henley-in-Arden w Ullenhall 81-87; rtd 87; Perm to Offic *Cov* from 87. *20 Avon Crescent, Stratford-upon-Avon, Warks CV37 7EY* Stratford-upon-Avon (0789) 296278

BENNETT, Reginald George. b 11. K Coll Lon 32. **d** 35 **p** 36. V Kirtlington *Ox* 61-83; P-in-c Weston on the Green 76-83; rtd 83; Perm to Offic *Ox* from 83. *13 Kennett Road, Headington, Oxford OX3 7BH* Oxford (0865) 750826

BENNETT, Richard Edward Stuart. b 24. St Jo Coll Ox BA49 MA55. Wells Th Coll 50. **d** 51 **p** 52. R Camerton *B & W* 63-80; R Dunkerton 63-80; R Camerton w Dunkerton, Foxcote and Shoscombe 80-88; RD Midsomer Norton 86-88; rtd 88. *Xlendi, 21 Kings Oak Meadow, Clutton, Bristol BS18 4SU*

BENNETT, Robert Francis Henry. b 12. TCD BA40 MA47. NW Ord Course 73. **d** 73 **p** 74. C Feniscliffe *Blackb*

73-78; Lic to Offic from 78. *28 Tower Road, Blackburn BB2 5LE* Blackburn (0254) 21815

BENNETT, Roger Sherwood. b 35. Nottm Univ BA56. Wells Th Coll 58. **d** 59 **p** 60. C Mansf Woodhouse *S'well* 59-60; C Spalding *Linc* 60-63; V Gedney 63-69; Chapl RNR 65-68; Chapl RN 69-90; V Amport, Grateley, Monxton and Quarley *Win* from 90. *The Vicarage, Amport, Andover, Hants SP11 8BE* Weyhill (026477) 2950

BENNETT, Roy Donald. b 40. St Jo Coll Nottm 78. **d** 80 **p** 81. C Fletchamstead *Cov* 80-83; C Bedworth 83-87; P-in-c Studley from 87. *3 Manor Mews, Manor Road, Studley, Warks B80 7NA* Studley (052785) 2830

BENNETT, Stanley Gilbert. b 08. Bonn Univ PhD35. Ridley Hall Cam 36. **d** 37 **p** 38. V Lothersdale *Bradf* 70-76; rtd 76; Perm to Offic *Bradf* from 76. *12 Poplar Close, Burley in Wharfedale, Ilkley, W Yorkshire LS29 7RH* Burley-in-Wharfedale (0943) 862893

BENNETT, William Leslie. TCD Div Sch DipTh90. **d** 90 **p** 91. C Carrickfergus *Conn* from 90. *7 Macroom Gardens, North Road, Carrickfergus, Co Antrim BT38 8NB* Carrickfergus (09603) 62126

BENNETTS, Canon Colin James. b 40. Jes Coll Cam BA63 MA67. Ridley Hall Cam 63. **d** 65 **p** 66. C Tonbridge St Steph *Roch* 65-69; Chapl Ox Pastorate 69-79; C Ox St Aldate w H Trin *Ox* 69-73; Lic to Offic 73-78; Asst Chapl Jes Coll Ox 73-75; Chapl 75-78; P-in-c Ox St Andr *Ox* 79-80; V 80-90; RD Ox 84-89; Can Res Ches Cathl and Dioc Dir of Ords *Ches* from 90. *5 Abbey Street, Chester CH1 2JF* Chester (0244) 315532

BENNETTS, Gordon Vivian. b 15. TD62. Open Univ BA78. **d** 77 **p** 78. NSM Phillack w Gwithian and Gwinear *Truro* 77-79; NSM Redruth 79-80; NSM Redruth w Lanner 80-82; Chapl Tehidy Hosp Camborne 82-87; Lic to Offic *Truro* from 82; Chapl Duchy Hosp Truro from 87. *66 Tregolls Road, Truro, Cornwall TR1 1LD* Truro (0872) 41857

BENNIE, Stanley James Gordon. b 43. Edin Univ MA65. Coll of Resurr Mirfield 66. **d** 68 **p** 69. C Ashington *Newc* 68-70; Prec St Andr Cathl Inverness *Mor* 70-74; Itinerant Priest 74-81; R Portsoy *Ab* 81-84; R Buckie 81-84; R Stornoway *Arg* from 84; Miss to Seamen from 84. *St Peter's House, 10 Springfield Road, Stornoway, Isle of Lewis PA87 2PT* Stornoway (0851) 703609

BENNION, John Richard. b 15. Leeds Univ BA36. Coll of Resurr Mirfield 36. **d** 38 **p** 39. C Ashley Green *Ox* 63-90; rtd 90. *16 Marroway, Weston Turville, Aylesbury, Bucks HP22 5TQ* Aylesbury (0296) 612281

BENNISON, Philip Owen. b 42. Dur Univ BA64. Coll of Resurr Mirfield. **d** 66 **p** 67. C Guisborough *York* 66-67; C S Bank 67-71; C Thornaby on Tees St Paul 71-72; TV Thornaby on Tees 72-74; R Skelton in Cleveland 74-78; R Upleatham 75-78; Chapl Freeman Hosp Newc 78-84; V Ashington *Newc* from 84. *Holy Sepulchre Vicarage, Ashington, Northd NE63 8HZ* Ashington (0670) 813358

BENSON, Christopher Hugh. b 53. Bath Academy of Art BA75 Keble Coll Ox BA78 MA83. Chich Th Coll 78. **d** 80 **p** 81. C Heavitree w Ex St Paul *Ex* 80-83; P-in-c Broadclyst 83-85; TV Pinhoe and Broadclyst 85-90; V Kingsteignton from 90. *8 Vicarage Hill, Kingsteignton, Newton Abbot, Devon TQ12 3BA* Newton Abbot (0626) 54915

BENSON, Donald. b 26. NW Ord Course 75. **d** 78 **p** 79. NSM Edge Hill St Dunstan *Liv* 78-84; NSM Liv St Paul Stoneycroft from 84. *114 Claremont Road, Liverpool L13 3HL* 051-733 8706

BENSON, Douglas Arthur Terrell. b 08. St Jo Coll Dur BA36. Lon Coll of Div 32. **d** 36 **p** 37. V Clapham *St Alb* 48-76; rtd 76; Perm to Offic *Ox* from 76. *2 Beech Court, Tower Street, Taunton, Somerset TA1 4BH* Taunton (0823) 337963

BENSON, Gareth Neil. b 47. HNC71 Jordan Hill Coll Glas FETC80. St And NSM Tr Scheme 77. **d** 81 **p** 82. NSM Glenrothes *St And* from 81; NSM Kinghorn from 88; NSM Kirkcaldy from 88. *129 Waverley Drive, Glenrothes, Fife KY6 2LZ* Glenrothes (0592) 759278

BENSON, George Patrick. b 49. Ch Ch Ox BA70 Lon Univ BD77. All Nations Chr Coll 78 St Jo Coll Nottm 89. **d** 91. C Upton (or Overchurch) *Ches* from 91. *43 Grafton Drive, Upton, Wirral, Merseyside L49 0TX* 051-678 1235

BENSON, Mrs Hilary Christine. b 51. Man Univ BA72 St Hugh's Coll Ox CertEd73. Trin Coll Bris 81. **dss** 84 **d** 87. Starbeck *Ripon* 84-86; Birm St Martin w Bordesley St Andr *Birm* 86-87; Hon Par Dn from 87. *341 George Road, Birmingham B23 7RY* 021-382 4109

BENSON, James Christopher Reginald. b 14. TCD BA35 MA60. **d** 37 **p** 38. I Mullaghdun *Clogh* 57-61; rtd

61. *4 Morston Avenue, Bangor, Co Down* Bangor (0247) 61049

BENSON, John. b 02. **d** 38 **p** 39. V Felixkirk w Boltby *York* 65-70; V Kirby Knowle 66-70; rtd 70. *12 St Giles's Close, York Road, Thirsk, N Yorkshire YO7 3BU* Thirsk (0845) 525456

BENSON, John David. b 36. Lon Univ DipTh61 Hull Univ DipTh82. St Aid Birkenhead 58. **d** 61 **p** 62. C Kingston upon Hull St Martin *York* 61-65; C Marfleet 65-68; V Ingleby Greenhow 68-72; P-in-c Kildale 68-72; Asst Youth Chapl 68-72; Youth Chapl *Sheff* 72-78; V Thorne 78-91; V Totley from 91. *All Saints' Vicarage, 37 Sunnyvale Road, Sheffield S17 4FA* Sheffield (0742) 362322

BENSON, John Patrick. b 51. Univ of Wales (Ban) BSc72. Trin Coll Bris 83. **d** 85 **p** 86. C Stoke Damerel *Ex* 85-88; P-in-c Petrockstowe, Petersmarland, Merton and Huish 88; TV Shebbear, Buckland Filleigh, Sheepwash etc from 89. *The Rectory, Petrockstowe, Okehampton, Devon EX20 3HQ* Okehampton (0837) 810499

BENSON, John Patrick. b 52. Ch Coll Cam BA73 MA76 PhD76. Trin Coll Bris 78. **d** 81 **p** 82. C Walmley *Birm* 81-84; C Chadkirk *Ches* 84-86; Singapore from 87. *St George's Church, Minden Road, Singapore 1024*

BENSON, John Simmonds. b 06. Tyndale Hall Bris 36. **d** 39 **p** 40. V Bucknell *Heref* 69-76; rtd 76; Perm to Offic *Glouc* from 76. *5 Brock Hollands, Lydney, Glos GL15 4PP* Dean (0594) 562860

BENSON, Nicholas Henry. b 53. Trin Coll Bris. **d** 84 **p** 85. C Starbeck *Ripon* 84-86; C Birm St Martin w Bordesley St Andr *Birm* from 86; Chapl to the Markets from 86. *341 George Road, Birmingham B23 7RY* 021-342 4109

BENSON, Peter Leslie. b 60. Leeds Univ BA81. Westcott Ho Cam 81. **d** 85 **p** 86. C Kippax w Allerton Bywater *Ripon* 85-88; C Potternewton 88-91; Asst Chapl St Jas Univ Hosp Leeds from 91. *8 Granton Road, Leeds LS7 3LZ* Leeds (0532) 626225

BENSON, Mrs Rachel Candia. b 43. JP76. TCD MA66 Lon Univ PGCE67 DipRS87. S'wark Ord Course 84. **d** 87. NSM Putney St Marg *S'wark* from 87. *34 St John's Avenue, London SW15 6AN* 081-788 3828

BENSON, Richard Edmund Miller. b 12. TCD BA35 MA50. **d** 36 **p** 37. I Sixmilecross w Termonmaguirke *Arm* 69-76; rtd 76. *14 Dellmount Park, Bangor, Co Down* Bangor (0247) 455175

BENSON, Preb Riou George. b 14. QGM79. Linc Th Coll 38. **d** 39 **p** 40. V Clun w Chapel Lawn *Heref* 61-79; V Bettws-y-Crwyn w Newc 63-79; P-in-c Clungunford 63-79; Preb Heref Cathl from 65; P-in-c Bedstone w Hopton Castle 65-79; P-in-c Llanfair Waterdine w Stowe 73-79; P-in-c Clunbury 75-79; V Clun w Chapel Lawn, Bettws-y-Crwyn and Newc 79; rtd 79. *Maiden Hill Wood, All Stretton, Church Stretton, Shropshire SY6 6LA* Church Stretton (0694) 723610

BENSON, Roy William. b 32. Em Coll Saskatoon LTh76 MDiv76. **d** 76 **p** 77. Canada 76-79 and 80-83; C E Wickham *S'wark* 79-80; V Southea w Murrow and Parson Drove *Ely* 83-85; P-in-c Guyhirn w Ring's End 83-84; V 84-85; Canada from 85. *1102-4th Street, Prince Albert, Saskatchewan, Canada, S6V 0L2*

BENSON, Terence Edward Benjamin. b 17. TCD BA37. **d** 41 **p** 42. I Brinny *C, C & R* 52-56; Perm to Offic *Clogh* from 56; rtd 79. *30 Willoughby Place, Enniskillen, Co Fermanagh BT74 7EX* Enniskillen (0365) 2817

BENSON, William George. b 26. Lon Univ BA51 CertEd52 Ex Univ BA56. Sarum & Wells Th Coll 76. **d** 79 **p** 80. Hon C Heanton Punchardon w Marwood *Ex* 79-88; TR Newport, Bishops Tawton and Tawstock from 88. *The Vicarage, Newport, Barnstaple, Devon EX32 9EH* Barnstaple (0271) 72733

BENSON, Canon William John Robinson. b 02. QUB BA25 DipHE40. **d** 26 **p** 27. I Coleraine *Conn* 62-76; Preb St Patr Cathl Dub 63-76; rtd 76. *16 Ratheane Avenue, Mountsandel Road, Coleraine, Co Londonderry BT52 1JH* Coleraine (0265) 51922

BENSTED, James de Carl Sowerby. b 11. Ex Coll Ox BA34 MA46. Ripon Hall Ox 34. **d** 36 **p** 37. R Ewhurst *Guildf* 56-76; rtd 76; Perm to Offic *Portsm* from 81. *15 Madeline Road, Petersfield, Hants GU31 4AL* Petersfield (0730) 62455

BENT, Canon Michael Charles. b 31. Kelham Th Coll 51. **d** 55 **p** 56. C Wellingborough St Mary *Pet* 55-60; New Zealand 60-85 and from 89; Adn Taranaki 76-85; Dean H Trin Cathl Suva Fiji 85-89; Can St Pet Cathl Hamilton from 90. *The Vicarage, PO Box 38, Te Awamutu, New Zealand* Te Awamutu (7) 871-4627

BENTHAM, John William. b 58. Loughb Univ BSc80 Nottm Univ LTh. St Jo Coll Nottm 82. **d** 85 **p** 86. C Burmantofts St Steph and St Agnes *Ripon* 85-88; C

Horsforth 88-90; P-in-c Nottm St Sav *S'well* from 90. *St Barnabas's Vicarage, Derby Road, Beeston, Nottingham NG9 2SN* Nottingham (0602) 864046

BENTINCK, Richard. b 13. Madras Univ BA35. **d** 43 **p** 44. V Kirkby-in-Cleveland *York* 67-75; V Middlesb St Martin 75-85; rtd 85; P-in-c Clifford *York* 86-89. *21 Beech Avenue, Bishopthorpe, York YO2 1RL* York (0904) 708486

✠**BENTLEY, Rt Rev David Edward.** b 35. Leeds Univ BA56. Westcott Ho Cam 58. **d** 60 **p** 61 **c** 86. C Bris St Ambrose Whitehall *Bris* 60-62; C Guildf H Trin w St Mary *Guildf* 62-66; R Headley All SS 66-73; R Esher 73-86; RD Emly 77-82; Hon Can Guildf Cathl 80-86; Chmn Dioc Coun Soc Resp 80-86; Suff Bp Lynn *Nor* from 86; Chmn Cand Cttee ACCM 87-91; ABM from 91. *The Old Vicarage, Castle Acre, King's Lynn, Norfolk PE32 2AA* Swaffham (0760) 755553

BENTLEY, Edward John. b 35. Bris Univ BA61. Tyndale Hall Bris 58. **d** 63 **p** 64. C Wolv St Luke *Lich* 63-66; BCMS 66-72; C Cheltenham St Mark *Glouc* 72-78; V Wallasey St Nic *Ches* from 78. *St Nicholas' Vicarage, 22 Groveland Road, Wallasey, Merseyside L45 8JY* 051-639 3589

BENTLEY, Frank Richard. b 41. K Coll Lon BD67 AKC67. **d** 68 **p** 69. C Feltham *Lon* 68-72; P-in-c Bethnal Green St Bart 72-77; R Bow w Bromley St Leon 77-88; P-in-c Mile End Old Town H Trin 77-88; P-in-c Bromley All Hallows 77-88; AD Tower Hamlets 83-88; TR E Ham w Upton Park *Chelmsf* from 88. *The Rectory, Navarre Road, London E6 3AQ* 081-470 0011

BENTLEY, Ven Frank William Henry. b 34. AKC57. **d** 58 **p** 59. C Shepton Mallet *B & W* 58-62; R Kingsdon w Podymore-Milton 62-66; P-in-c Yeovilton 62-66; P-in-c Babcary 64-66; V Wiveliscombe 66-76; RD Tone 73-76; V St Jo in Bedwardine *Worc* 76-84; RD Martley and Worc W 80-84; Hon Can Worc Cathl 81-84; P-in-c Worc St Mich 82-84; Adn Worc and Can Res Worc Cathl from 84. *Archdeacon's House, 7 College Yard, Worcester WR1 2LA* Worcester (0905) 25046

BENTLEY, Canon Geoffrey Bryan. b 09. K Coll Cam BA32. MA35. Cuddesdon Coll 32. **d** 33 **p** 34. Can Windsor 57-82; Hon Can from 82; rtd 82. *5 The Cloisters, Windsor Castle, Windsor, Berks SL4 1NJ* Windsor (0753) 863001

BENTLEY, Graham John. b 29. S'wark Ord Course 77. **d** 80 **p** 81. NSM Mert St Mary *S'wark* 80-83; C Balham St Mary 83-84; C Wimbledon 85-86; V Raynes Park St Sav from 86. *St Saviour's Vicarage, Church Walk, London SW20 9DW* 081-542 2787

BENTLEY, Ian Ronald. b 51. BA79. Oak Hill Th Coll 76. **d** 79 **p** 80. C Northwood Em *Lon* 79-85; C St Marylebone All So w SS Pet and Jo 85-88; C Langham Place All So from 88. *12 De Walden Street, London W1M 7PH* 071-935 9811

BENTLEY, James. b 37. TD. Mert Coll Ox BA59 BTh61 MA63 BD75 Sussex Univ DPhil80. St Steph Ho Ox 59. **d** 62 **p** 63. C Elton St Steph *Man* 62-64; C Swinton St Pet 64-66; CF (TA) 65-82; R Stretford All SS *Man* 66-73; V Oldham St Mary w St Pet 73-77; Sen Chapl Eton Coll 79-82. *6 Arborfield Close, Slough, Berks SL1 2JW* Slough (0753) 573522

BENTLEY, Mrs Lesley. b 55. RMN80 Univ of Wales (Lamp) BA76 Nottm Univ MTh82. St Jo Coll Nottm DPS83. **dss** 82 **d** 87. Mickleover St Jo *Derby* 82-84; Thornton *Liv* 84-87; Par Dn 87-89; Dir Diaconal Mins from 89. *39 Brenda Crescent, Thornton, Liverpool L23 4TY* 051-924 8211

BENTLEY, William. Univ Coll Dur BA39 DipTh40 MA42. St Andr Whittlesford 40. **d** 41 **p** 42. R Hartlepool St Hilda *Dur* 59-82; rtd 82. *4 Lindisfarne, High Shincliffe, Durham DH1 2PH* 091-384 9876

BENTON, John Anthony. b 27. Ex Coll Ox BA48 MA52. Sarum Th Coll 49. **d** 50 **p** 51. C N Keyham *Ex* 50-52; C Tavistock and Gulworthy 52-55; C Heavitree 55-56; R Lower Gravenhurst *St Alb* 56-61; V Silsoe 56-61; V Upper Gravenhurst 56-61; S Africa 61-68; R Moretonhampstead *Ex* 68-74; RD Moreton 73-74; R Holsworthy w Cookbury and Hollacombe 74-80; TR Withycombe Raleigh from 80; RD Aylesbeare 84-89. *The Rectory, 74 Withycombe Village Road, Exmouth, Devon EX8 3AE* Exmouth (0395) 264182

BENTON, Canon Michael John. b 34. MSOSc Lon Univ BSc60. Sarum & Wells Th Coll 72. **d** 74 **p** 74. Hon C Weeke *Win* 74-76; Sen Lect K Alfred Coll Win 74-76; C Bursledon 76-78; R Over Wallop w Nether Wallop 78-83; Dir of Educn from 79; R Win St Lawr and St Maurice w St Swithun 83-90; Hon Can Win Cathl from 89. *28 Denham Close, Winchester SO23 7BL* Winchester (0962) 855964

✠**BENZIES, Rt Rev Keith John.** b 38. Glas Univ MA60. Sarum Th Coll 60. **d** 62 **p** 63 **c** 82. C Kingston upon Hull St Nic *York* 62-66; Madagascar from 66; Prin Ambatoharanana Th Coll 66-79; Bp Antsiranana from 82. *Misiona Anglikana, BP 278, 201 Antsiranana, Madagascar* Diego Suarez (8) 22650

BERDINNER, Clifford. b 24. SS Mark & Jo Coll Plymouth BA88. **d** 64 **p** 65. R Heather *Leic* 67-72; NSM Totnes and Berry Pomeroy *Ex* from 86; rtd 89. *Hilltop Cottage, Ashprington, Totnes, Devon TQ9 7UW* Harbertonford (080423) 518

BERESFORD, Charles Edward. b 45. St Jo Coll Nottm. **d** 86 **p** 87. C Bushbury *Lich* 86-90; TV Stoneydelph St Martin *Cov* 90; TV Glascote and Stonydelph from 90. *The New Vicarage, Bamford Street, Tamworth, Staffs B77 2AS* Tamworth (0827) 62612

BERESFORD, Prof Eric Brian. b 57. Liv Univ BSc78 Ox Univ BA82 MA86. Wycliffe Hall Ox. **d** 82 **p** 83. C Upton (or Overchurch) *Ches* 82-85; Canada from 85; Asst Prof Ethics McGill Univ Montreal from 88. *5521 Beaminster Place, Montreal, Quebec, Canada, H3W 2M4*

BERESFORD, Mrs Florence. b 33. Cranmer Hall Dur 75. **dss** 78 **d** 87. Eighton Banks *Dur* 78-86; Lobley Hill 86-87; Par Dn 87-90; Par Dn Ches le Street 90-91; rtd 91. *Gilead, 39 Picktree Lodge, Chester-le-Street, Co Durham DH3 4DH* 091-388 7425

BERESFORD, Peter Marcus de la Poer. b 49. Cranmer Hall Dur 74. **d** 77 **p** 78. C Walney Is *Carl* 77-80; C Netherton 80-83; TV Wednesfield *Lich* 83-88; TV Rugby St Andr *Cov* from 88. *The Vicarage, St Johns Avenue, Hillmorton, Rugby, Warks CV22 5HR* Rugby (0788) 577331

BERESFORD-DAVIES, Thomas. b 14. Univ of Wales (Lamp) BD67. **d** 42 **p** 43. V Twigworth w Down Hatherley *Glouc* 63-85; rtd 85; P-in-c Glouc St Mark *Glouc* 86-87. *Islwyn Tewkesbury Road, Twigworth, Gloucester GL2 9PQ* Gloucester (0452) 730362

BERESFORD-PEIRSE, Mark de la Poer. b 45. Qu Coll Birm 73. **d** 76 **p** 77. C Garforth *Ripon* 76-79; C Beeston 79-83; V Barton and Manfield w Cleasby 83-90; V Pannal w Beckwithshaw from 90. *The Vicarage, 21 Crimple Meadows, Pannal, Harrogate, N Yorkshire HG3 1EL* Harrogate (0423) 870202

BERG, John Russell. b 36. MBE78. Sarum Th Coll 57. **d** 60 **p** 61. C Ipswich St Aug *St E* 60-64; C Whitton and Thurleston w Akenham 64-65; Miss to Seamen from 65; Hong Kong 65-72; Japan from 72. *c/o The Missions to Seamen, Port PO Box 139, Yokohama 231, Japan* Yokohama (45) 662-1871

BERG, Canon Paul Michael. b 31. Lon Univ BA53. Oak Hill Th Coll 54. **d** 56 **p** 57. C Woodford Wells *Chelmsf* 56-60; V Tittensor *Lich* 60-65; V Rainham *Chelmsf* 65-74; R Wennington 65-74; V Clifton Ch Ch w Em *Bris* from 74; Hon Can Bris Cathl from 82; RD Clifton from 87. *Christ Church Vicarage, 16 Mortimer Road, Bristol BS8 4EY* Bristol (0272) 736524

BERGER, Otto. b 19. CEng FIMechE. Oak Hill Th Coll. **d** 83 **p** 84. NSM Dovercourt and Parkeston *Chelmsf* from 83. *35 Gordon Road, Dovercourt, Harwich, Essex CO12 3TL* Harwich (0255) 502806

BERGQUIST, Dr Anders Karim. b 58. Peterho Cam BA79 MA83 PhD90. St Steph Ho Ox BA85 MA90. **d** 86 **p** 87. C Abbots Langley *St Alb* 86-89; C Cam St Mary Less *Ely* 89; Hon C from 89; Tutor Westcott Ho Cam from 89. *Westcott House, Jesus Lane, Cambridge CB5 8BP* Cambridge (0223) 350074

BERKSHIRE, Archdeacon of. See GRIFFITHS, Ven David Nigel

BERNARD, Brother. See APPS, Canon Michael John

BERNARDI, Frederick John. b 33. JP75 KCT89. Chich Th Coll 55. **d** 58 **p** 59. C Blackb St Luke *Blackb* 58-60; C Ribbleton 60-63; V Brinsley w Underwood *S'well* 63-66; Barbados 67-71; V Sparkbrook St Agatha *Birm* 71-77; P-in-c Sparkbrook Ch Ch 73-75; V Haywards Heath St Wilfrid *Chich* 77-80; TR 80-87; Chapl Madrid *Eur* 87-90; NSM Tooting All SS *S'wark* 90-91; V Hanger Hill Ascension and W Twyford St Mary *Lon* from 91. *The Ascension Vicarage, Beaufort Road, London W5 3EB* 081-566 9920

BERNERS-WILSON, Angela Veronica Isabel (Mrs Sillett). b 54. St Andr Univ MTh76 St Jo Coll Dur DipTh78. **dss** 79 **d** 87. Southgate Ch Ch *Lon* 79-82; St Marylebone Ch Ch 82-84; Ind Chapl 82-84; Chapl Thames Poly *S'wark* from 84. *35 Elmdene Road, London SE18 6TZ* 081-855 6858

BERNERS-WILSON, Daniel Downing. b 10. ALCD37. **d** 36 **p** 37. R Frant *Chich* 53-72; rtd 72. *Hamstede, Parkham Hill, Rotherfield, Crowborough, E Sussex TN6 3HR*

BERRETT, Paul Graham. b 49. St Chad's Coll Dur BA70. St Steph Ho Ox 71. **d** 74 **p** 75. C Hockerill *St Alb* 74-77; C Leighton Buzzard 77-81; C Leighton Buzzard w Eggington, Hockliffe etc 81-83; V Bournemouth St Fran *Win* from 83. *St Francis's Clergy House, Charminster Road, Bournemouth BH8 9SH* Bournemouth (0202) 529336

BERRIDGE, Grahame Richard. b 38. S'wark Ord Course 71. **d** 72 **p** 73. NSM Beddington *S'wark* 72-75; NSM Mert St Jas 75-81. *11 Cedar Walk, Kingswood, Tadworth, Surrey KT20 6HW* Burgh Heath (0737) 358882

BERRIMAN, Gavin Anthony. b 60. S'wark Ord Course 87. **d** 90 **p** 91. C Greenwich St Alfege w St Pet and St Paul *S'wark* from 90. *88 Ashburnham Grove, London SE10 8UJ* 081-691 9916

BERROW, Philip Rees. b 36. St D Coll Lamp 58. **d** 62 **p** 63. C Neath w Llantwit *Llan* 62-66; CF 67-87; R Welford w Weston and Clifford Chambers *Glouc* from 87. *The Rectory, Church Lane, Welford on Avon, Stratford-upon-Avon, Warks CV37 8EL* Stratford-upon-Avon (0789) 750808

BERRY, Adrian Charles. b 50. Mert Coll Ox BA71 MA. Cuddesdon Coll 72. **d** 75 **p** 76. C Prestbury *Glouc* 75-79; C Cirencester 79-83; V Cam w Stinchcombe 83-88; Dioc Ecum Officer from 83; P-in-c Twyning from 88. *The Vicarage, Church End, Twyning, Tewkesbury, Glos GL20 6DA* Tewkesbury (0684) 292553

BERRY, Alan Peter. b 36. NW Ord Course 74. **d** 77 **p** 78. NSM Headingley *Ripon* 77-78; NSM Chapel Allerton from 78. *4 Carr Manor Garth, Leeds LS17 5AS* Leeds (0532) 684968

BERRY, Anthony Nigel. b 53. Lon Bible Coll BA80 Sarum & Wells Th Coll 84. **d** 87 **p** 88. NSM Howell Hill *Guildf* 87-90; C 90; C Farnham from 90. *23 Hazell Road, Farnham, Surrey GU9 7BW* Farnham (0252) 714521

BERRY, Brian. b 10. St Mich Coll Llan 42. **d** 44 **p** 45. V Colaton Raleigh *Ex* 66-81; rtd 81; Perm to Offic *Ex* from 81. *63 Polsloe Road, Exeter EX1 2EA* Exeter (0392) 55234

BERRY, David Llewellyn Edward. b 39. St Jo Coll Cam BA61 MA65. Wells Th Coll 64. **d** 66 **p** 67. C Poplar All SS w St Frideswide *Lon* 66-69; C Ellesmere Port *Ches* 69-73; V Brafferton w Pilmoor and Myton on Swale *York* 73-79; P-in-c Thormanby 78-79; R Skelton in Cleveland 79; R Skelton w Upleatham 79-87; V Barrow St Aid *Carl* from 87. *The Vicarage, 31 Middle Hill, Barrow-in-Furness, Cumbria LA13 9HD* Barrow-in-Furness (0229) 830445

BERRY, Geoffrey Wilbur Ronald. b 22. Ridley Hall Cam 54. **d** 56 **p** 57. V Poplar St Matthias *Lon* 59-70; V Westacre *Nor* 70-79; R Gayton Thorpe w E Walton 71-79; P-in-c Maresfield *Chich* 79; R 79-87; P-in-c Nutley 79; V 79-87; rtd 87; Perm to Offic *Bris* from 87. *13 Manor Park, Great Somerford, Chippenham, Wilts SN15 5EQ* Chippenham (0249) 720530

BERRY, Graham Renwick (Brother Superior Silvanus). b 24. Univ of NZ BA54. Coll of Resurr Mirfield 55. **d** 57 **p** 58. C Earl's Court St Cuth w St Matthias *Lon* 57-61; Lic to Offic *Wakef* from 63; CR from 64; Lic to Offic *Ripon* 68-75; Prior CR 75-87; Superior from 87. *House of the Resurrection, Mirfield, W Yorkshire WF14 0BN* Mirfield (0924) 493272

BERRY, John. b 41. Dur Univ BA62. Oak Hill Th Coll 63. **d** 65 **p** 66. C Burnage St Marg *Man* 65-68; C Middleton 68-70; Travelling Sec IVF 70-73; V Derby St Pet *Derby* 73-76; P-in-c Derby Ch Ch and H Trin 73-76; V Derby St Pet and Ch Ch w H Trin 76-81; Bp's Officer for Evang *Carl* 81-86; P-in-c Bampton and Mardale 81-86; TR N Wingfield, Pilsley and Tupton *Derby* 86-89; Evang Sec Evang Alliance from 89. *75 Ashgate Road, Chesterfield S40 4AH* Chesterfield (0246) 201742

BERRY, Michael. b 22. Ex Coll Ox BA49 DipEd53 MA54. Westcott Ho Cam 69. **d** 71 **p** 72. C Didcot *Ox* 71-75; R Farthinghoe w Hinton-in-the-Hedges w Steane *Pet* from 75. *The Rectory, Farthinghoe, Brackley, Northants NN13 5NY* Banbury (0295) 710946

BERRY, Very Rev Peter Austin. b 35. Keble Coll Ox BA59 BTh61 MA63. St Steph Ho Ox 59. **d** 62 **p** 63. C Cov St Mark *Cov* 62-66; Dioc Community Relns Officer 64-70; C Cov Cathl 66-73; Can Res 73-86; Vice-Provost 77-86; Bp's Adv for Community Relns 77-86; Provost Birm from 86. *The Provost's House, 16 Pebble Mill Road, Birmingham B5 7SA* 021-472 0709

BERRY, Miss Susan Patricia. b 49. Bris Univ BA70 CertEd72. Qu Coll Birm 77. **dss** 86 **d** 87. Chapl Barn Fellowship Whatcombe Ho 86-89; Chapl Lee Abbey from 89; Lic to Offic *Ex* from 89. *Lee Abbey, Lynton, Devon EX35 6JJ* Lynton (0598) 52621

BERRY, Timothy Hugh. b 50. Reading Univ BA72. Oak Hill NSM Course 81. **d** 84 **p** 85. NSM Swanley St Paul *Roch* 84-88; Perm to Offic *S'wark* 86-88; C Gorleston St Andr *Nor* from 88. *1 South Garden, Gorleston, Great Yarmouth, Norfolk NR31 6TL* Great Yarmouth (0493) 669401

BERRY, William James. b 25. Bps' Coll Cheshunt 62. **d** 63 **p** 64. V Lidlington *St Alb* 67-72; R Dunton w Wrestlingworth and Eyeworth 72-83; V Earby *Bradf* 83-89; rtd 89. *34 Severn Way, Cressage, Shrewsbury SY5 6DS* Cressage (0952) 510462

BERRYMAN, Canon Carl. b 39. Ex Coll Ox BA61 MA65. Qu Coll Birm DipTh62. **d** 63 **p** 64. C Penwortham St Mary *Blackb* 63-66; C Altham w Clayton le Moors 66-68; V Chorley St Pet 68-86; RD Chorley 73-86; Hon Can Blackb Cathl from 80; V Poulton-le-Fylde from 86; RD Poulton 88-91. *The Vicarage, Vicarage Road, Poulton-le-Fylde, Lancs FY6 7BE* Poulton-le-Fylde (0253) 883086

BERRYMAN, William Arthur David. b 47. Lon Univ BD69 St Pet Coll Ox CertEd71. Sarum & Wells Th Coll 75. **d** 76 **p** 77. Asst Master Preston Sch Yeovil 76-80; Hon C Yeovil St Mich *B & W* 76-80; C Ex St Dav *Ex* 80-83; Chapl Ex Coll 80-83; Chapl RN 83-89; C Highertown and Baldhu *Truro* from 89. *All Saints' House, Highertown, Truro, Cornwall TR1 3LS* Truro (0872) 76688

BERSON, Alan Charles. b 31. Michigan Univ BA52 MA53 Lon Univ PhD62. St Steph Ho Ox 63. **d** 65 **p** 66. C Leeds St Giles-in-the-Fields *Ripon* 65-68; C St Giles-in-the-Fields *Lon* 68; Lic to Offic 69-80; Perm to Offic from 80. *74 Ridgmount Gardens, London WC1E 7AX* 071-636 1990

BERSWEDEN, Nils Herry Stephen. b 57. Newc Univ BSc78. Ripon Coll Cuddesdon 88. **d** 90 **p** 91. C Mirfield *Wakef* from 90. *16 Towngate Grove, Mirfield, W Yorkshire WF14 9JF* Mirfield (0924) 495288

BERTRAM, Canon Richard Henry. b 27. TCD BA50 MA64. CITC 50. **d** 53 **p** 54. C Sligo Cathl *K, E & A* 53-56; C Dub Booterstown *D & G* 56-58; I Stranorlar w Meenglas and Kilteevogue *D & R* 58-65; I Dub St Cath w St Jas *D & G* 65-73; I Dub Irishtown 73-74; I Dub Irishtown w Donnybrook from 74; Can Ch Ch Cathl Dub from 86. *2 Ailesbury Grove, Dublin 4, Irish Republic* Dublin (1) 269-2090

BESS, Canon Cyril Henry George. b 20. AKC50. **d** 50 **p** 51. V E Grinstead St Mary *Chich* 60-75; RD E Grinstead 70-75; Can and Preb Chich Cathl from 75; RD Eastbourne 75-88; V Eastbourne St Mary 75-88; C-in-c Hydneye CD 82-84; rtd 88. *43 Desmond Road, Eastbourne, E Sussex BN22 7LE* Eastbourne (0323) 38545

BESSANT, Brian Keith. b 32. Roch Th Coll 65. **d** 67 **p** 68. C Chatham St Wm *Roch* 67-70; C Cove St Jo *Guildf* 71-74; V Frimley Green from 74. *The Vicarage, 37 Sturt Road, Frimley Green, Camberley, Surrey GU16 6HY* Deepcut (0252) 835179

BESSANT, Idwal Brian. b 39. Cardiff Coll of Art NDD61 ATD62 Univ of Wales DipTh68. St Mich Coll Llan 65. **d** 68 **p** 69. C Llantwit Major and St Donat's *Llan* 68-73; C Llangammarch w Garth, Llanlleonfel etc *S & B* 73-77; C Crickhowell 77-78; CMS Miss 78-83; Cyprus 80-83; V Crickhowell w Cwmdu and Tretower *S & B* 83-91; RD Crickhowell from 86; V Llanwrtyd w Llanddulas in Tir Abad etc from 91. *The Vicarage, Llanwrtyd Wells, Powys LD5 4SA* Llanwrtyd Wells (05913) 231

BESSANT, Simon David. b 56. Sheff Univ BMus77. St Jo Coll Nottm DipTh79. **d** 81 **p** 82. C Litherland St Jo and St Jas *Liv* 81-84; C Holloway Em w Hornsey Road St Barn *Lon* 84-86; C Holloway St Mark w Em from 86. *43 Eden Grove, London N7 8EE* 071-607 3980

BESSENT, Stephen Lyn. b 53. Bris Univ BA75. Wycliffe Hall Ox 75. **d** 77 **p** 78. C Patchway *Bris* 77-80; TV Swindon St Jo and St Andr 80-83; TV Eston w Normanby *York* 83-90; V Cogges *Ox* from 90; P-in-c S Leigh from 90. *Cogges Priory, Church Lane, Witney, Oxon OX8 6LA* Witney (0993) 702155

BEST, Frank Milner. b 21. Linc Coll Ox BA49 MA49. Bps' Coll Cheshunt 49. **d** 50 **p** 51. R Sibson *Leic* 63-75; P-in-c Quendon w Rickling *Chelmsf* 75-78; R Quendon w Rickling and Wicken Bonhunt 78-86; rtd 86; Perm to Offic *Heref* from 87. *Besley House, Bishops Frome, Worcester WR6 5AP* Kyre (0885) 490675

BEST, Harold Arthur Frank. b 15. Cuddesdon Coll 44. **d** 47 **p** 48. TR Dorchester *Ox* 57-74; P-in-c Leigh w Batcombe *Sarum* 74-76; V High Stoy 76-80; rtd 80. *Flat 21, Manormead, Tilford Road, Hindhead, Surrey GU26 6RA*

BEST, Raymond. b 42. Sarum & Wells Th Coll 71. **d** 74 **p** 75. C Whorlton *Newc* 74-78; C Seaton Hirst 78-83; C Benwell St Jas 83-85; TV Benwell Team 85-89; V Walker from 89. *37 Lesbury Road, Newcastle upon Tyne NE6 5LB* 091-265 8467

BESTELINK, William Meindert Croft. b 48. Hull Univ BA70. Cuddesdon Coll 71. **d** 73 **p** 74. C Holt *Nor* 73-74; C E Dereham w Hoe 74-76; C Nor St Andr 76-80; R Colby w Banningham and Tuttington 80-90; R Felmingham 80-90; R Suffield 80-90; P-in-c Roydon St Remigius from 90. *The Rectory, High Road, Roydon, Diss, Norfolk IP22 3RD* Diss (0379) 642180

BESWETHERICK, Andrew Michael. b 55. SS Mark & Jo Coll Plymouth BEd80. S'wark Ord Course 87. **d** 90 **p** 91. Dep Hd Maze Hill Sch Greenwich from 88; NSM Blackheath St Jo S'wark from 90. *28 Eastcombe Avenue, London SE7 7JE* 081-853 0853

BESWICK, Canon Colin Edward. b 28. Leeds Univ BA51 Ex Univ MA75. Sarum Th Coll 58. **d** 60 **p** 61. C Shrewsbury St Mary *Lich* 60-63; Min Can Worc Cathl *Worc* 63-73; R Bredon w Bredon's Norton 73-79; RD Pershore 76-79; Hon Can Worc Cathl 78-84; Dir of Min 79-84; P-in-c Overbury w Alstone, Teddington and Lt Washbourne 81-84; Can Res Nor Cathl *Nor* from 84; P-in-c Nor St Mary in the Marsh 84-87. *52 The Close, Norwich NR1 4DZ* Norwich (0603) 620375

BESWICK, Canon Gary Lancelot. b 38. ALCD63. **d** 63 **p** 64. C Walthamstow St Mary *Chelmsf* 63-67; C Laisterdyke *Bradf* 67-70; V Idle H Trin 70-78; Perm to Offic Ches, Carl, Blackb, Lich, St As, Ban, Bradf, Liv and Derby from 78; Lic to Offic *Man* from 78; Area Sec (NW England) SAMS from 78; Hon Can N Argentina from 87. *1 Abercorn Road, Smithills, Bolton BL1 6LF* Bolton (0204) 43565

BESWICK, Dr Joseph Hubert. b 25. Birm Univ MB, ChB48 Lon Univ DipTh58. **d** 59 **p** 60. Lic to Offic *S'well* from 59. *38 Hallams Lane, Beeston, Nottingham NG9 5FH* Nottingham (0602) 256719

BESWICK, Canon Walter. b 13. St Aid Birkenhead 46. **d** 48 **p** 49. R Dalby w Whenby *York* 64-85; R Terrington 64-85; RD Malton 75-80; Can and Preb York Minster from 79; rtd 85. *Halcyon Reach, Normanby, Sinnington, York YO6 6RH* Kirkbymoorside (0751) 31766

BETSON, Stephen. b 53. Sarum & Wells Th Coll 89. **d** 91. C Sittingbourne St Mich *Cant* from 91. *112 East Street, Sittingbourne, Kent ME10 4RX* Sittingbourne (0795) 471546

BETTELEY, John Richard. b 46. Sarum & Wells Th Coll 81. **d** 83 **p** 84. C Auchterarder *St And* 83-85; C Dunblane 83-85; Chapl RAF 85-89; R Callander *St And* from 89; P-in-c Aberfoyle from 89; P-in-c Doune from 89. *43 Lagrannoch Drive, Callander, Perthshire FK17 8DW* Callander (0877) 30972

BETTIS, Miss Margaret Jean. b 42. Gilmore Ho 72. **dss** 77 **d** 87. Kenya 77-79; Tutor Crowther Hall CMS Tr Coll Selly Oak 79-82; Hodge Hill *Birm* 82-87; Par Dn 87; Par Dn Flitwick *St Alb* from 87. *32 St Albans Close, Flitwick, Bedford MK45 1UA* Flitwick (0525) 718561

BETTRIDGE, Canon Graham Winston. b 39. Kelham Th Coll 60. **d** 65 **p** 66. C Burley in Wharfedale *Bradf* 65-67; C Baildon 67-70; V Harden and Wilsden 70-81; TR Kirkby Lonsdale *Carl* from 81; Hon Can Carl Cathl from 89. *The Rectory, Vicarage Lane, Kirkby Lonsdale, Carnforth, Lancs LA6 2BA* Kirkby Lonsdale (05242) 71320

BETTS, Anthony Clive. b 40. Wells Th Coll 63. **d** 65 **p** 66. C Leeds All Hallows w St Simon *Ripon* 65-67; C Wetherby 67-70; C Adel 70-73; V Leeds All SS 73-79; V Leeds Richmond Hill 79-84; R Knaresborough from 84; Chapl Knaresborough Hosp from 84. *The Rectory, High Bond End, Knaresborough, N Yorkshire HG5 9BT* Harrogate (0423) 865273

BETTS, Canon Anthony Percy. b 26. Lon Univ BD52. ALCD52. **d** 52 **p** 53. C Guildf St Sav *Guildf* 52-56; C Hanworth St Geo *Lon* 56-59; V Derby St Aug *Derby* 59-74; RD Derby 71-74; V Bracebridge *Linc* 74-83; P-in-c Fenny Bentley, Thorpe and Tissington *Derby* 83; P-in-c Kniveton w Hognaston 83; R Fenny Bentley, Kniveton, Thorpe and Tissington from 83; RD Ashbourne 86-91; Hon Can Derby Cathl from 87. *Otterbourne House, Windley, Derby DE5 2LP* Cowers Lane (077389) 677

BETTS, David John. b 38. Lon Univ BSc61. Oak Hill Th Coll 63. **d** 65 **p** 66. C Slough *Ox* 65-70; C Welling *Roch* 70-75; V Swanley St Paul from 75. *The Vicarage, Rowhill Road, Hextable, Swanley, Kent BR8 7RL* Swanley (0322) 62320

BETTS, Edmund John. b 51. St Chad's Coll Dur BA72 Lanc Univ MA81. Qu Coll Birm DipTh75 DPS76.

d 76 **p** 77. C Leagrave *St Alb* 76-79; Asst Chapl R Albert Hosp Lanc 79-81; Chapl Lea Castle Hosp and Kidderminster Gen Hosp 81-86; Prov Officer Educn for Min Ch in Wales 86-88; Exec Sec for Min 88-90; TR Haverhill w Withersfield, the Wrattings etc *St E* from 90; RD Clare from 91. *The Rectory, Great Thurlow, Haverhill, Suffolk CB9 7LF* Thurlow (044083) 372

BETTS, George William John. b 23. Ex Univ BA51. Westcott Ho Cam 51. **d** 53 **p** 54. C Sherborne w Castleton and Lillington *Sarum* 68-69; C Highgate Rise St Anne Brookfield *Lon* 69; rtd 88. *Flat 2, 13A Cranley Gardens, London SW7* 071-373 8351

BETTS, Ivan Ringland. b 38. TCD BA61 MA67. **d** 62 **p** 63. C Ballyholme *D & D* 62-65; C Dundela 65-69; Miss to Seamen 69-73; Sudan 69-71; Trinidad and Tobago 71-73; C Drumglass *Arm* 73-81; I Augher w Newtownsaville and Eskrahoole *Clogh* 81-86; Bp's C Ballymacarrett St Martin *D & D* from 86. *7 Greenwood Park, Belfast BT4 3NJ* Belfast (0232) 658659

BETTS, Paul Robert. b 31. Lon Univ BSc51. Oak Hill Th Coll 53. **d** 56 **p** 57. C Plymouth St Jude *Ex* 56-59; C Cheltenham St Mark *Glouc* 59-63; V Finchley St Paul Long Lane *Lon* 63-76; Warden St Columba Cen Cam 76-79; R Datchworth w Tewin *St Alb* from 79. *The Rectory, Brookbridge Lane, Datchworth, Knebworth, Herts SG3 6SU* Stevenage (0438) 813067

✠**BETTS, Rt Rev Stanley Woodley.** b 12. CBE67. Jes Coll Cam MA37. Ridley Hall Cam 33. **d** 35 **p** 36 **c** 56. C Cheltenham St Paul *Glouc* 35-38; Chapl RAF 38-47; Chapl Clare Coll Cam 47-49; V Cam H Trin *Ely* 49-57; Suff Bp Maidstone *Cant* 56-66; Abp's Rep w HM Forces 57-66; Dean Roch 66-77; rtd 77. *2 Kings Houses, Pevensey, E Sussex* Eastbourne (0323) 762421

BETTS, Steven James. b 64. York Univ BSc86. Ripon Coll Cuddesdon 87. **d** 90 **p** 91. C Bearsted w Thurnham *Cant* from 90. *55 The Landway, Bearsted, Maidstone, Kent ME14 4BG* Maidstone (0622) 38674

BEUKES, Douglas. b 22. Oak Hill Th Coll 45. **d** 51 **p** 52. Chapl Utrecht w Arnhem, Zwolle, Amersfoort etc *Eur* 59-90; rtd 90. *Vogelzang Laan 6, 3571 ZM Utrecht, The Netherlands*

BEVAN, Alan John. b 29. Bris Univ BA54. Oak Hill Th Coll 54. **d** 56 **p** 59. C Darfield *Sheff* 68-71; C Drypool St Columba w St Andr and St Pet *York* 71-79; Chapl HM Pris Wandsworth 79-83; Kirkham 83-86; rtd 86; Perm to Offic *Ex* from 86. *41 Bellever Close, Princetown, Yelverton, Devon PL20 6RT* Princetown (082289) 625

BEVAN, Bryan David. Lon Univ BD60 MA70 CertEd65 DipEd66 MPhil84. Lambeth STh62 St Aug Coll Cant 62. **d** 64 **p** 66. C E Dereham w Hoe *Nor* 64-65; C Hove All SS *Chich* 65-67; Lect St Mich Coll Salisbury 67-70; The Coll Bedf from 70. *4A De Parys Lodge, De Parys Avenue, Bedford MK40 2TZ* Bedford (0234) 43622

BEVAN, Canon Charles Joseph Godfrey. b 22. TCD BA44 MA52. **d** 45 **p** 46. C Dub St Geo *D & G* 45-49; I Rathvilly *C & O* 49-59; I Carbury *M & K* 59-64; I Drogheda St Pet w Ballymakenny, Beaulieu etc *Arm* from 64; Miss to Seamen from 64; Can Arm Cathl *Arm* from 83; Chan from 88; RD Creggan and Louth from 90. *St Peter's Rectory, Drogheda, Co Louth, Irish Republic* Drogheda (41) 38441

BEVAN, David Graham. b 34. Univ of Wales (Lamp) BA54 LTh56. Gen Th Sem (NY) MDiv57. **d** 57 **p** 58. C Llanelly *St D* 57-60; CF 60-76. *148 Bromley Heath Road, Downend, Bristol BS16 6JJ* Bristol (0272) 560946

BEVAN, Dennis Butler. b 24. Bris Univ BA51. St Mich Coll Llan 53. **d** 54 **p** 55. V Cymmer and Porth *Llan* 67-79; V St Brides Major 79-89; rtd 89. *Glenside, 50 Allen Street, Mountain Ash, M Glam CF45 4BB* Mountain Ash (0443) 477585

BEVAN, Donald Keith. b 16. Lon Univ BD40. ALCD40. **d** 40 **p** 41. C Huyton St Mich *Liv* 56-59; rtd 59. *9B Hoscote Park, West Kirby, Wirral, Merseyside L48 0QN*

BEVAN, Gordon Richard. b 26. NW Ord Course. **d** 75 **p** 76. C Spondon *Derby* 75-80; R Upper Langwith w Langwith Bassett etc 80-87; P-in-c Scarcliffe 82-87; R Upper Langwith w Langwith Bassett etc from 87. *Langwith Bassett Rectory, Upper Langwith, Mansfield, Notts NG20 9RE* Mansfield (0623) 742413

BEVAN, Herbert Richard. b 28. Birm Univ DipTh56 MA67. **d** 57 **p** 58. C Sutton Coldfield H Trin *Birm* 57-60; C Chelsea All SS *Lon* 60-62; R Abberley *Worc* from 62; RD Mitton 72-74; P-in-c Pensax 80-84. *The Rectory, Abberley, Worcester WR6 6BN* Great Witley (0299) 248

BEVAN, Hubert Basil Henry. b 24. Univ of Wales (Lamp) BA52 LTh54 MTh77 PhD78. **d** 54 **p** 55. V Gilfach Goch w Llandyfodwg *Llan* 66-73; R Cregina *S & B* 73-78; V

Bettws Disserth w Llansantffraed in Elwell 73-78; V Glascwm and Rhulen 76-78; R Llanferres, Nercwys and Eryrys *St As* 78-80; Tutor St Deiniol's Lib Hawarden 79-89; V Treuddyn and Nercwys and Erryrys *St As* 80-85; R Llanfynydd 85-89; rtd 89. *Creiglys, Bangor Road, Caernarfon, Gwynedd LL55 1LR*

BEVAN, John Vernon. b 16. Univ of Wales BA38. St Mich Coll Llan 38. **d** 39 **p** 40. R Enmore w Goathurst *B & W* 57-71; V Carhampton 71-81; rtd 82; Perm to Offic *B & W* from 84. *12 Spring Gardens, Alcombe, Minehead, Somerset* Minehead (0643) 702897

✠**BEVAN, Rt Rev Kenneth Graham.** b 98. Lon Coll of Div 20. **d** 23 **p** 24 **c** 40. C Tunbridge Wells H Trin *Roch* 23-25; China 25-50; Bp E Szechwan 40-50; V Woolhope *Heref* 51-66; R Putley 53-66; RD Heref S 55-66; Preb Heref Cathl 56-66; rtd 66; Master Abp Holgate's Hosp Hemsworth 66-77; Asst Bp Wakef 68-77. *Grove Cottage, Crockey Hill, York YO1 4SN* York (0904) 51895

BEVAN, Noel Haden. b 34. St Aid Birkenhead 61. **d** 63 **p** 64. C Girlington *Bradf* 63-66; C Worksop St Jo *S'well* 66-68; V Everton w Mattersey 68-70; R Everton and Mattersey w Clayworth 70-77; TV Barton Mills *St E* 77-80; TV Barton Mills, Beck Row w Kenny Hill etc 80-85; TV Mildenhall 85-86; P-in-c Sternfield w Benhall and Snape 86-89; R from 89. *The Rectory, Benhall Green, Benhall, Saxmundham, Suffolk IP17 1RS* Saxmundham (0728) 603825

BEVAN, Paul John. b 49. Bris Sch of Min 84. **d** 87. NSM Bishopsworth *Bris* from 87. *10 Brookdale Road, Headley Park, Bristol BS13 7PZ* Bristol (0272) 646330

BEVAN, Peter John. b 54. K Coll Lon BA76 AKC76 MA86. St Steph Ho Ox BA79. **d** 80 **p** 81. C Brighouse *Wakef* 80-83; C Chapelthorpe 83-86; V Scholes from 86. *The Vicarage, Scholes Lane, Scholes, Cleckheaton, W Yorkshire BD19 6PA* Cleckheaton (0274) 873024

BEVAN, Philip Frank. b 41. Chich Th Coll 65. **d** 67 **p** 68. C Walton St Mary *Liv* 67-71; Bahamas from 71. *c/o N-963, Nassau, Bahamas*

BEVAN, Reginald Morgan. b 10. Keble Coll Ox BA33 MA37. St D Coll Lamp BA31 St Mich Coll Llan 33. **d** 34 **p** 35. V Montacute *B & W* 67-77; rtd 77; Perm to Offic *Mon* from 82. *1 Northfield Close, Caerleon, Newport, Gwent NP6 1EZ* Caerleon (0633) 421333

BEVAN, Canon Richard Justin William. b 22. LTh42 St Chad's Coll Dur BA45 DTh72 PhD80. St Aug Coll Cant 39. **d** 45 **p** 46. Chapl Dur Univ *Dur* 61-74; V Dur St Oswald 64-74; R Dur St Mary le Bow w St Mary the Less 67-74; Bp's Exam Chapl *Carl* from 69; R Grasmere 74-82; Can Res, Lib and Treas Carl Cathl 82-89; Vice-Dean Carl 86-89; Chapl to HM The Queen from 86; rtd 89; Perm to Offic *Carl* from 89. *Beck Cottage, West End, Burgh-by-Sands, Carlisle CA5 6BT* Burgh-by-Sands (0228) 576781

BEVAN, Trevor. b 07. St D Coll Lamp BA28 St Mich Coll Llan 29. **d** 30 **p** 31. R St Nicholas w Bonvilston and St George-s-Ely *Llan* 70-76; rtd 76; Perm to Offic *Llan* from 78. *Hawthorne, The Drope, St George's-super-Ely, Cardiff* Peterston-super-Ely (0446) 760324

BEVER, Michael Charles Stephen. b 44. Selw Coll Cam BA66 MA70. Cuddesdon Coll. **d** 69 **p** 70. C Steeton *Bradf* 69-72; C Northn St Mary *Pet* 72-74; Niger 75-79; P-in-c Elmstead *Chelmsf* 80-83; V 83-85; V Bocking St Pet from 85. *The Vicarage, 6 St Peter's in the Fields, Bocking, Braintree, Essex CM7 6AR* Braintree (0376) 22698

BEVERIDGE, Mrs Freda Joy. b 38. Qu Mary Coll Lon BA59 Lon Inst of Educn PGCE60. Ripon Coll Cuddesdon 83. **dss** 85 **d** 87. Ox St Giles and SS Phil and Jas w St Marg *Ox* 85-87; Par Dn 87-88; Par Dn Woughton from 88. *Epiphany House, 205 Beadlemead, Milton Keynes MK6 4HU* Milton Keynes (0908) 606409

BEVERIDGE, Simon Alexander Ronald. b 61. Nottm Univ BA84. Chich Th Coll 84. **d** 87 **p** 88. C Braunton *Ex* 87-90; TV N Creedy from 90. *The Vicarage, Down St Mary, Crediton, Devon EX17 6EF* Crediton (0363) 84835

BEVERIDGE, Wilbert Esler. b 16. AFBPsS TCD BA38 Div Test40 BLitt52 MLitt60 Lon Univ MA64. **d** 40 **p** 41. Lic to Offic *Lon* 61-81; Prin Lect Middx Poly 69-81; rtd 81; Perm to Offic *Win* from 83. *33 Harewood Avenue, Boscombe, Bournemouth BH7 6NJ* Bournemouth (0202) 420463

BEVERLEY, Canon Arthur Leslie. b 14. Dur Univ BA37. Ely Th Coll 37. **d** 39 **p** 40. V Dorrington *Linc* 59-78; R Ruskington 59-78; Can and Preb Linc Cathl 72-79; RD Lafford 73-78; C Linc St Nic w St Jo Newport 78-79; rtd 79; Perm to Offic *Linc* from 79. *3 Middleton's Field, Lincoln LN2 1QP* Lincoln (0522) 523637

BEVERLEY, David John. b 46. Univ of Wales (Lamp) BA68. Linc Th Coll 71. **d** 73 **p** 74. C Cov E *Cov* 73-76; C Immingham *Linc* 76-84; V Bracebridge Heath 84-86; Ind Chapl from 86. *161 Ashby Road, Scunthorpe, S Humberside DN16 2AQ* Scunthorpe (0724) 844606

BEVINGTON, Colin Reginald. b 36. ALCD63. Lon Coll of Div 63. **d** 63 **p** 64. C Devonport St Budeaux *Ex* 63-65; C Attenborough w Chilwell *S'well* 65-68; R Benhall w Sternfield *St E* 68-74; P-in-c Snape w Friston 73-74; V Selly Hill St Steph *Birm* 74-81; P-in-c Selly Oak St Wulstan 80-81; V Selly Park St Steph and St Wulstan 81-88; Dioc Ecum Officer and Adv on Miss *St E* from 88. *48 Thorney Road, Capel St Mary, Ipswich IP9 2UY* Great Wenham (0473) 311358

BEVINGTON, David John. b 51. Ch Coll Cam BA72 MA76. Trin Coll Bris 73. **d** 76 **p** 77. C Tulse Hill H Trin S'wark 76-79; C Galleywood Common *Chelmsf* 79-82; TV Hanley H Ev *Lich* 82-90; TV Hemel Hempstead *St Alb* from 90. *6 Arkley Road, Woodhall Farm, Hemel Hempstead, Herts HP2 7JT* Hemel Hempstead (0442) 248008

BEVINGTON, Preb George Herbert Woodyear. b 18. Ch Coll Cam BA39 MA43. Ridley Hall Cam 39. **d** 41 **p** 42. R Ex St Leon w H Trin *Ex* 60-83; Preb Ex Cathl 70-83; rtd 83; Perm to Offic *Ex* from 83. *White Briar Cottage, 15 Ascerton Road, Sidmouth, Devon EX10 9BT* Sidmouth (0395) 577814

BEVIS, Anthony Richard. b 34. Chich Th Coll 87. **d** 87 **p** 89. NSM Hamble le Rice *Win* from 87; Chapl Moorgreen Hosp W End Southn from 90. *Lynwood, High Street, Hamble, Southampton SO3 5HA* Southampton (0703) 453102

BEVIS, Derek Harold. **d** 90 **p** 91. NSM Guildf Ch Ch *Guildf* from 90. *94 Woodeland Avenue, Guildford, Surrey GU2 5LD* Guildford (0483) 61968

BEWES, Emmanuel John. b 21. Edin Th Coll 49. **d** 52 **p** 53. V Hesket in the Forest *Carl* 70-76; V Hesket-in-the-Forest and Armathwaite 76-87; rtd 87; Perm to Offic *Carl* from 87. *1 Jennet Croft, Wetheral, Carlisle CA4 8JJ* Wetheral (0228) 61534

BEWES, Preb Richard Thomas. b 34. Em Coll Cam BA58 MA61. Ridley Hall Cam 57. **d** 59 **p** 60. C Beckenham Ch Ch *Roch* 59-65; V Harold Wood *Chelmsf* 65-74; V Northwood Em *Lon* 74-83; R Marylebone All So w SS Pet and Jo 83-88; P-in-c Portman Square St Paul 87-88; R Langham Place All So from 88; Preb St Paul's Cathl from 88. *12 Weymouth Street, London W1N 3FB* 071-580 6029 or 580 4357

BEWES, Canon Thomas Francis Cecil. b 02. Em Coll Cam BA23 MA27. Ridley Hall Cam 23. **d** 25 **p** 26. RD Tonbridge *Roch* 59-70; V Tonbridge SS Pet and Paul 59-70; rtd 70; Perm to Offic *Chich* from 70. *28 Salisbury Road, Moseley, Birmingham B13 8JT* 021-449 7496

BEWLEY, Albert Latham. b 38. Leeds Univ BA61. Ely Th Coll 61. **d** 63 **p** 64. C Wigan St Mich *Liv* 63-65; C Caister *Nor* 65-69; R W Lynn 69-76; V Lakenham St Jo from 76. *Old Lakenham Vicarage, Harwood Road, Norwich NR1 2NG* Norwich (0603) 625678

BEWLEY, Guy Patrick. b 16. Ripon Hall Ox. **d** 58 **p** 59. Area Sec (Dios Glouc, Heref, Cov & Worc) Chr Aid 65-74; Lic to Offic *Carl* 74-81; rtd 81. *Southcot, Turners Lane, Gillingham, Dorset SP8 4BG* Gillingham (0747) 823804

BEXON, Miss Mavis Adelaide. b 31. St Mich Ho Ox. **d** 87. Bestwood St Matt *S'well* 77-86; Chaddesden St Mary *Derby* 86-87; Par Dn from 87. *11 Appledore Drive, Oakwood, Derby DE2 2LN* Derby (0332) 669213

BEYNON, David Griffith. b 09. St D Coll Lamp BA34. **d** 41 **p** 42. V Llanwinio, Eglwys Fair A Churig and Llanfyrnach *St D* 64-78; rtd 78. *33 St Nons Avenue, Carmarthen, Dyfed* Carmarthen (0267) 231239

BEYNON, Ven James Royston. b 07. Dur Univ LTh31. St Aug Coll Cant 27. **d** 31 **p** 32. V Twyford *Win* 48-73; Adn Win 62-73; Hon Can Win Cathl 62-73; rtd 73. *1511 Geary Avenue, London, Ontario N5X 1G6, Canada*

BEYNON, Malcolm. b 36. Univ of Wales (Lamp) BA56 Univ of Wales (Swansea) DipSocSc59 Univ of Wales (Cardiff) PGCE71. St Mich Coll Llan 56. **d** 59 **p** 60. C Aberavon *Llan* 59-62; C Whitchurch 63-68; V Llanwynno 68-73; Chapl Old Hall Sch Wellington Shropshire 74-75; Perm to Offic *Leic* 75-82; Chapl Nevill Holt Sch Market Harborough 75-82; Chapl Denstone Coll Prep Sch from 82. *Denstone College Preparatory School, Smallwood Manor, Uttoxeter, Staffs ST14 8NS* Uttoxeter (0889) 562014

BEYNON, Sidney James. b 09. St D Coll Lamp BA34. **d** 35 **p** 36. V Newport St Andr *Mon* 65-76; rtd 76; Perm to Offic *Mon* from 76. *37 Fairfield Road, Caerleon, Newport, Gwent NP6 1DQ* Newport (0633) 422098

BEYNON, Vincent Wyn. b 54. CertEd76 Univ of Wales DipTh81. St Mich Coll Llan 78. **d** 81 **p** 82. C Llantrisant *Llan* 81-83; C Caerphilly 84-85; R Gellygaer 85-88; TV Gtr Corsham *Bris* from 88. *The Vicarage, Wadswick Lane, Neston, Corsham, Wilts SN13 9TA* Hawthorn (0225) 810572

BIANCHI, Mrs Margaret Ruth. b 56. St Mary's Coll Dur BA77. Cranmer Hall Dur 78. **dss** 80 **d** 91. Ches le Street *Dur* 80-83; W Pelton 83-91; NSM from 91. *9 St Paul's Terrace, West Pelton, Stanley, Co Durham DH9 6RT* 091-370 2146

BIANCHI, Robert Frederick. b 56. St Jo Coll Dur BA77. Cranmer Hall Dur 78. **d** 80 **p** 81. C Ches le Street *Dur* 80-83; C W Pelton 83-86; P-in-c from 86. *The Vicarage, West Pelton, Stanley, Co Durham DH9 6RT* 091-370 2146

BIBBY, Frank. b 37. ACP60 K Coll Lon BD64 AKC64. **d** 65 **p** 66. C Upholland *Liv* 65-67; Lect Birm Coll of Educn 67-72; V Prestwich St Gabr *Man* 72-76; Dir of Ords 72-76; V Hope St Jas 76-86; AD Salford 82-86; R Prestwich St Mary from 86. *The Rectory, Church Lane, Prestwich, Manchester M25 5AN* 061-773 2912

BIBBY, Paul Benington. b 27. Magd Coll Cam BA51 MA56. Westcott Ho Cam 55. **d** 57 **p** 58. C Flixton St Mich *Man* 57-60; C Woolwich St Mary w H Trin *S'wark* 60-62; V Hurst *Man* 62-69; Hd of Cam Ho Camberwell 69-76; R Shepton Mallet *B & W* 76-81; P-in-c Doulting w E and W Cranmore and Downhead 78-81; R Shepton Mallet w Doulting 81-82; Sen Chapl Eton Coll 82-87; R Hambleden Valley *Ox* from 87. *The Rectory, Hambleden, Henley-on-Thames, Oxon RG9 6RP* Henley-on-Thames (0491) 571231

BICK, David Jim. b 33. ALCD59 LTh74. **d** 59 **p** 60. C Glouc St Cath *Glouc* 59-61; C Coleford w Staunton 61-63; R Blaisdon w Flaxley 63-72; V Coaley 72-83; P-in-c Arlingham 80-83; P-in-c Frampton on Severn 80-83; Hon C Saul w Fretherne and Framilode 83-84; Perm to Offic from 84. *St Joseph's, Prinknash Park, Cranham, Glos GL4 8EX* Painswick (0452) 812973

BICKERDYKE, James Clifford. b 17. St Jo Coll Dur BA42 MA45. Oak Hill Th Coll LTh41. **d** 42 **p** 43. C Stockport St Geo *Ches* 42-43; C Cannock *Lich* 43-45; Normanton Sch Buxton 45-48; Chadderton Gr Sch 48-51; CF 51-67; Launceston Coll 67-75; Grove Sch Hindhead 75-81. *Lonningarth, Hawkshead, Ambleside, Cumbria LA22 0PU* Hawkshead (05394) 36245

BICKERSTAFF, John Austin Isaac. b 10. Birm Univ BA34. Qu Coll Birm 31. **d** 36 **p** 37. V Brighton Ch Ch *Chich* 61-80; rtd 80; Perm to Offic *Chich* from 80. *Victoria Nursing Home, 96 The Drive, Hove, E Sussex BN3 6GP* Brighton (0273) 723937

BICKERSTETH, Anthony Cyril. b 33. K Coll Lon 54. Bps' Coll Cheshunt 55. **d** 58 **p** 59. V Stoke Newington Common St Mich *Lon* 68-74; V Nayland w Wiston *St E* 74-82; R Tolleshunt Knights w Tiptree *Chelmsf* 82-87; R Tolleshunt Knights w Tiptree and Gt Braxted 87; rtd 87; Perm to Offic *Chelmsf* from 87. *Lanreath, 125 Woodland Avenue, Hove, E Sussex BN3 6BJ* Brighton (0273) 564663

BICKERSTETH, David Craufurd. b 50. Wycliffe Hall Ox 71. **d** 75 **p** 76. C Beverley Minster *York* 75-79; C Farnborough *Guildf* 79-81; P-in-c Dearham *Carl* 81-85; V 85-86; R Gosforth w Nether Wasdale and Wasdale Head from 86. *The Rectory, Gosforth, Seascale, Cumbria CA20 1AZ* Gosforth (09467) 25251

BICKERSTETH, Edward Piers. b 56. ARICS80. Wycliffe Hall Ox 89. **d** 91. NSM Bebington *Ches* from 91. *c/o The Rectory, Bebington, Cheshire L63 3EX* 051-645 6478

BICKERSTETH, John David. b 26. Ch Ch Ox BA50 MA53. Oak Hill Th Coll 52. **d** 54 **p** 55. Dir Ashburnham Chr Trust 60-88; R Ashburnham w Penhurst *Chich* 62-84; Hon C from 84; rtd 90. *Agmerhurst House, Ashburnham, Battle, E Sussex TN33 9NB* Ninfield (0424) 892253

✠**BICKERSTETH, Rt Rev John Monier.** b 21. KCVO89. Ch Ch Ox BA49 MA53. Wells Th Coll 48. **d** 50 **p** 51 **c** 70. C Moorfields *Bris* 50-54; C-in-c Hurst Green CD *S'wark* 54-62; V Chatham St Steph *Roch* 62-70; Hon Can Roch Cathl 68-70; Suff Bp Warrington *Liv* 70-75; Bp B & W 75-87; ChStJ and Sub-Prelate from 77; Clerk of the Closet to HM The Queen 79-89; rtd 87. *Beckfords, Newtown, Tisbury, Salisbury SP3 6NY* Tisbury (0747) 870479

BICKERTON, David John Theodore. b 09. Lon Univ BA30. Coll of Resurr Mirfield 31. **d** 33 **p** 34. R Sampford Courtenay w Honeychurch *Ex* 61-85; RD Okehampton 66-72; P-in-c Exbourne w Jacobstowe 77-85; rtd 85;

Perm to Offic *Ex* from 86. *3 Domehayes, Okehampton, Devon EX20 1JN* Okehampton (0837) 53412

BICKLEY, John. b 12. Magd Coll Ox BA34 MA38. Sarum Th Coll 35. **d** 36 **p** 37. R Huntingfield w Cookley *St E* 70-77; rtd 77; Perm to Offic *St E* from 77. *Breckland Cottage, Santon Downham, Brandon, Suffolk IP27 0TQ* Thetford (0842) 810497

BIDDELL, Canon Christopher David. b 27. Ch Coll Cam BA48 MA52. Ridley Hall Cam 51. **d** 51 **p** 52. C Hornchurch St Andr *Chelmsf* 51-54; Succ S'wark Cathl *S'wark* 54-56; P-in-c Wroxall *Portsm* 56-61; R Bishops Waltham 62-75; RD Bishops Waltham 69-74; V Stockport St Geo *Ches* 75-86; Hon Can Ches Cathl 81-86; RD Stockport 85-86; Can Res Ches Cathl from 86. *13 Abbey Street, Chester CH1 2JF* Chester (0244) 314408

BIDDELL, John Herman. b 15. Worc Coll Ox BA38 MA45. Wells Th Coll 38. **d** 47 **p** 48. V Milverton *B & W* 65-80; R Fitzhead 77-80; rtd 80; Perm to Offic *B & W* from 81. *Snape Cottage, Wiltown, Curry Rivel, Langport, Somerset TA10 0JF* Langport (0458) 251435

BIDDER, John. b 19. Cuddesdon Coll. **d** 62 **p** 63. R Croft *Leic* 65-71; R Witcham w Mepal *Ely* 71-80; R Coates 80-85; rtd 85; Perm to Offic *Blackb* from 86. *Carinya, 83 Main Street, Nether Kellett, Carnforth, Lancs LA6 1EF* Carnforth (0524) 734993

BIDDINGTON, Dr Terence Eric. b 56. MCollP83 Hull Univ BA77 Trin & All SS Coll Leeds PGCE78 Leeds Univ PhD86 Nottm Univ BTh88. Linc Th Coll 85. **d** 88 **p** 89. C Harpenden St Jo *St Alb* 88-90; Chapl Keele Univ *Lich* from 90. *51 Quarry Bank Road, Keele, Staffs ST5 5AE* Newcastle-under-Lyme (0782) 627385

BIDDLE, Rodney William Dennis. b 44. St Jo Coll Nottm. **d** 85 **p** 86. C Penn *Lich* 85-89; P-in-c Shrewsbury St Geo 89-90; V from 90; P-in-c Montford w Shrawardine and Fitz 89; Chapl HM Pris Shrewsbury from 90. *The Vicarage, St George's Street, Shrewsbury SY3 8QA* Shrewsbury (0743) 235461

BIDDLE, Miss Rosemary. b 44. CertEd67. St Jo Coll Dur 76. **dss** 79 **d** 87. Sheldon *Birm* 79-83; Burntwood *Lich* 83-87; Par Dn 87-89; Par Dn Gt Wyrley from 89. *131 High Street, Cheslyn Hay, Walsall WS6 7HT* Cheslyn Hay (0922) 419032

BIDDLECOMBE, Francis William. b 30. St Mich Coll Llan 57. **d** 59 **p** 60. C Llangynwyd w Maesteg *Llan* 59-62; C Roath St Marg 62-65; V Llanddewi Rhondda w Bryn Eirw 65-71; V Berse and Southsea *St As* 71-79; P-in-c Teme Valley S *Worc* 79-85. *Wyre Farm Bungalow, Cleobury Mortimer, Kidderminster, Worcs DY14 8HJ* Cleobury Mortimer (0299) 270417

BIDDLESTONE, Joseph. b 15. Wycliffe Hall Ox 67. **d** 68 **p** 68. C Woodley *Ox* 68-71; P-in-c Dunsden 71-77; P-in-c Kiddington w Asterleigh 77-85; P-in-c Wootton by Woodstock 77-85; rtd 85; Perm to Offic *Ox* from 85. *6 Dashwood Rise, Duns Tew, Oxford OX5 4JQ* Steeple Aston (0869) 40350

BIDE, Peter William. b 12. St Cath Soc Ox BA39 MA45. Wells Th Coll 38. **d** 49 **p** 50. Chapl LMH Ox 68-80; rtd 80; Prec Ch Ch Ox 80-82; Perm to Offic *Portsm* from 84. *Meadow Corner, The Street, Boxgrove, Chichester, W Sussex PO18 0DY* Chichester (0243) 774134

BIDEN, Neville Douglas. b 31. Lon Univ DipRS80. S'wark Ord Course 76. **d** 79 **p** 80. C Ash *Guildf* 79-82; NSM Surbiton St Andr and St Mark *S'wark* 87-91; Chapl Asst Long Grove Hosp Epsom 90-91; Perm to Offic *Guildf* 90-91; C Coulsdon St Jo *S'wark* from 91. *8 Waddington Avenue, Coulsdon, Surrey CR5 1QE* Reigate (0737) 556043

BIDGOOD, Kevin Patrick. b 46. Chich Th Coll 78. **d** 80 **p** 81. C Leigh Park *Portsm* 80-83; C Southsea H Spirit 83-86; V Portsea All SS 86-91; V Hamble le Rice *Win* from 91. *The Vicarage, Hamble, Southampton SO3 5JF* Southampton (0703) 452148

BIERLEY, George Leslie. b 11. Worc Ord Coll 58. **d** 60 **p** 61. R Gt Coates *Linc* 63-71; R N Thoresby 71-82; R Grainsby 71-82; V Waithe 71-82; rtd 82; Perm to Offic *Linc* from 82. *57 Brackenborough Road, Louth, Lincs LN11 0AD* Louth (0507) 602516

BIGBY, Preb John Harman. b 16. Sarum Th Coll 46. **d** 48 **p** 49. V Ettingshall *Lich* 59-79; R Moreton Say 79-86; P-in-c Tilstock 83-84; Preb Lich Cathl 81-86; RD Hodnet 82-86; P-in-c Tilstock 83-84; rtd 86. *75 Glan y Mor Road, Penrhyn Bay, Gwynedd LL30 3PF* Colwyn Bay (0492) 44722

BIGG, Howard Clive. b 40. Jes Coll Cam BA68 MA72. Ridley Hall Cam 73. **d** 74 **p** 75. C Worksop St Jo *S'well* 74-76; Min Can St Alb 76-77; Perm to Offic *Ches* 78-82; Ely from 82; Vice-Prin Romsey Ho Cam from 86. *Romsey House, 274 Mill Road, Cambridge CB1 3NQ*

BIGGAR, Dennis Alfred. b 21. Ripon Hall Ox 55. **d** 57 **p** 58. V Skegby *S'well* 64-72; V The Brents and Davington w Oare and Luddenham *Cant* 72-80; V Cheriton All So w Newington 80-87; rtd 87. *250A Kingsnorth Road, Ashford, Kent TN23 2LU* Ashford (0233) 22945

BIGGAR, Dr Nigel John. b 55. Worc Coll Ox BA76 MA88 Chicago Univ PhD86 AM81. **d** 90. Lib Latimer Ho Ox from 85; Asst Lect in Chr Ethics Wycliffe Hall Ox from 87; Chapl Or Coll Ox from 90. *The Chaplain's Office, Oriel College, Oxford OX1 4EW* Oxford (0865) 276580

BIGGERSTAFF, Richard. b 65. K Coll Lon BD87 AKC87. Coll of Resurr Mirfield 88. **d** 90 **p** 91. C Brighton Resurr *Chich* from 90. *6 Edinburgh Road, Brighton BN2 3HY* Brighton (0273) 620232

BIGGIN, Ronald. b 20. NW Ord Course 70. **d** 73 **p** 74. C Thelwall *Ches* 73-79; V 79-87; rtd 87; NSM Lt Leigh and Lower Whitley *Ches* from 90. *44 Richmond Avenue, Grappenhall, Warrington, Cheshire WA4 2ND* Warrington (0925) 61531

BIGGS, David James. b 55. St Jo Coll Auckland LTh82. **d** 81 **p** 82. New Zealand 81-86; C Stevenage St Andr and St Geo *St Alb* 86-89; TV Moulsecoomb *Chich* from 89. *Barn Lodge, Norwich Drive, Brighton BN2 4LA* Brighton (0273) 602325

BIGGS, George Ramsay. b 45. Liv Univ BA67 Qu Coll Cam BA73. Westcott Ho Cam 72. **d** 74 **p** 75. C Lee St Aug *S'wark* 74-78; TV Eling, Testwood and Marchwood *Win* 78; TV Totton from 78. *The Vicarage, Netley Marsh, Totton, Southampton SO4 2GX* Southampton (0703) 862124

BIGGS, Canon Ivan Richard. b 22. Edgehill Th Coll Belf 49. **d** 73 **p** 73. Bp's C Killea *C & O* 73-82; I Kiltoghart w Drumshambo, Annaduff and Kilronan *K, E & A* 82-91; Preb Elphin Cathl 84-91; Dioc and Glebes Sec and Info Officer (Elphin and Ardagh) 87-91; rtd 91. *Carrowkeel Lodge, Castlebaldwin, Co Sligo, Irish Republic* Castlebaldwin (79) 66015

BIGGS, Philip John. b 51. Ripon Hall Ox 74 Ripon Coll Cuddesdon 75. **d** 77 **p** 78. C Maidstone All SS w St Phil and H Trin *Cant* 77-80; Dioc Youth Officer *Truro* 80-84; Australia from 84; Hon Chapl Miss to Seamen from 84. *118 Waddell Road, Bicton, W Australia 6157* Perth (9) 330-4938

BIGNELL, Alan Guy. b 39. Lon Univ BA64. Ox NSM Course. **d** 81 **p** 82. NSM Upton cum Chalvey *Ox* 81-90. *2 Wheatlands Road, Slough SL3 7PB* Slough (0753) 23005

BIGNELL, David Charles. b 41. E Midl Min Tr Course 76. **d** 79 **p** 80. C Porchester *S'well* 79-82; V Awsworth w Cossall 82-86; Bp's Ecum Officer from 84; V Edwalton from 86. *The Vicarage, Edwalton, Notts NG12 4AB* Nottingham (0602) 232034

BILES, David George. b 35. Open Univ BA75 AKC58. **d** 59 **p** 60. C Cockerton *Dur* 59-62; C Winlaton 62-67; P-in-c Dipton 67-74; R Wolviston 74-89; P-in-c Thirkleby w Kilburn and Bagby *York* 89-90; V from 90; RD Thirsk 90-91. *The Vicarage, Kilburn, York YO6 4AH* Coxwold (03476) 234

BILES, Canon Timothy Mark Frowde. b 35. Univ of Wales DipTh64. St Mich Coll Llan 60. **d** 64 **p** 66. C Middleton St Cross *Ripon* 64-66; Chapl St Fran Sch Hooke 66-72; P-in-c Toller Porcorum w Hooke *Sarum* 72-79; P-in-c Melplash w Mapperton 74-79; P-in-c Beaminster 77-79; TR Beaminster Area from 79; Can and Preb Sarum Cathl from 83; RD Beaminster 84-89. *The Rectory, Barnes Lane, Beaminster, Dorset DT8 3BU* Beaminster (0308) 862150

BILL, Alan. b 29. K Coll Lon BD66 AKC66. **d** 67 **p** 68. C Gt Burstead *Chelmsf* 67-70; TV Thornaby on Tees *York* 71-76; R E Gilling 76-81; V Ormesby 81-91; rtd 91. *13 Wilmington Close, Tudor Grange, Newcastle upon Tyne NE3 2SF* 091-271 3556

BILL, Denis Aubrey. b 20. Coll of Resurr Mirfield 48. **d** 50 **p** 51. V Holy Is *Newc* 64-89; rtd 89. *The Annexe, Etal Manor, Berwick-upon-Tweed TD15 2PU* Crookham (089082) 378

BILL, Herbert Sydney. b 12. Keble Coll Ox BA34 DipTh35. Wells Th Coll 35. **d** 36 **p** 37. Dioc Missr *Worc* 54-82; R Feckenham w Bradley 60-82; rtd 82; Perm to Offic *Worc* from 82. *31 Tredington Close, Woodrow, Redditch, Worcs B98 7UR*

BILL, Thomas Andrew Graham. b 47. Dur Univ BA76 DipTh78. Cranmer Hall Dur 78. **d** 77 **p** 78. C Penwortham St Mary *Blackb* 77-80; C Torrisholme 80-82; P-in-c Accrington St Pet 82-89; P-in-c Haslingden St Jo Stonefold 82-89; V Skerton St Chad from 89. *St Chad's Vicarage, 1 St Chad's Drive, Lancaster LA1 2SE* Lancaster (0524) 63816

BILLETT, Anthony Charles. b 56. Bris Univ BEd. Wycliffe Hall Ox 82. **d** 85 **p** 86. C Waltham Abbey *Chelmsf* 85-88; C Nor St Pet Mancroft w St Jo Maddermarket *Nor* from 88. *63 Recreation Road, Norwich NR2 3PA* Norwich (0603) 51878

BILLINGHAM, Peter Charles Geoffrey. b 34. Leeds Univ BA56. Westcott Ho Cam 61. **d** 62 **p** 63. C Halesowen *Worc* 62-66; R Addingham *Bradf* 66-70; R Droitwich St Nic w St Pet *Worc* 70-72; TR Droitwich 72-83; P-in-c Salwarpe 76-80; RD Droitwich 78-83; P-in-c Gt Malvern H Trin 83; P-in-c W Malvern 83; V Malvern H Trin and St Jas from 84. *The Vicarage, 2 North Malvern Road, Malvern, Worcs WR14 4LR* Malvern (0684) 54380

BILLINGHURST, Peter John. b 30. St Deiniol's Hawarden 77. **d** 79 **p** 80. C Hawarden *St As* 79-89; P-in-c from 89. *Kemendene, Plot 19, Dinghouse Wood, Burntwood Road, Buckley, Clwyd CH3 7LH* Buckley (0244) 547673

BILLINGHURST, Richard George. b 48. FIA76 St Jo Coll Cam BA70 MA74. Ridley Hall Cam 76. **d** 79 **p** 80. C Caverswall *Lich* 79-81; C Cullompton *Ex* 81-84; R Redgrave cum Botesdale w Rickinghall *St E* from 84. *The Rectory, Botesdale, Diss, Norfolk IP22 1DT* Diss (0379) 898685

BILLINGS, Dr Alan Roy. b 42. Em Coll Cam BA65 MA69 Bris Univ CertEd Leic Univ MEd75. NY Th Sem DMin87 Linc Th Coll 66. **d** 68 **p** 69. C Knighton St Mary Magd *Leic* 68-72; P-in-c Sheff St Silas *Sheff* 72-76; V Beighton 76-77; Perm to Offic Sheff 77-81; Ox 86-91; V Walkley 81-86; Dir Ox Inst for Ch and Soc 86-91; Vice-Prin Ripon Coll Cuddesdon from 88. *Ripon College, Cuddesdon, Oxford OX9 9EX* Wheatley (08677) 4595

BILLINGS, Derek Donald. b 30. Fitzw Ho Cam BA54 MA59. Tyndale Hall Bris 55. **d** 56 **p** 57. C Attenborough w Bramcote and Chilwell *S'well* 56-58; R Ashley w Silverley *Ely* 59-66; V Bottisham 66-80; R Houghton w Wyton from 80. *The Rectory, 3 Rectory Lane, Wyton, Huntingdon, Cambs PE17 2AQ* St Ives (0480) 62499

BILLINGS, Roger Key. b 41. AIB. Oak Hill Th Coll BA80. **d** 80 **p** 81. C Tunbridge Wells St Jas *Roch* 80-84; V Chatham St Paul w All SS from 84. *The Vicarage, 29 Waghorn Street, Chatham, Kent ME4 5LT* Medway (0634) 845419

BILLINGSLEY, Raymond Philip. b 48. FCMA80. Qu Coll Birm 87. **d** 89 **p** 90. C Yardley St Edburgha *Birm* from 89. *424 Church Road, Birmingham B33 8PB* 021-783 4291

BILLINGTON, Charles Alfred. b 30. Leeds Univ BA53. Coll of Resurr Mirfield 53. **d** 55 **p** 56. C Carl H Trin *Carl* 55-59; Lic to Offic *Wakef* 60-64; R Man St Aid *Man* 64-66; V Gt Crosby St Faith *Liv* 66-72; R Harrold and Carlton w Chellington *St Alb* 72-80; R Tintinhull w Chilthorne Domer, Yeovil Marsh etc *B & W* 80-81; Chapl Leybourne Grange Hosp W Malling 81-85; Lic to Offic *Roch* 81-85; V Walsden *Wakef* 85-88; R Llanfair Talhaiarn and Llansannan *St As* from 88. *The Rectory, Llanfairtalhaiarn, Abergele, Clwyd LL22 8ST* Llanfairtalhaiarn (074584) 273

BILLINGTON, John Keith. b 16. **d** 61 **p** 62. C-in-c Seacroft CD *Ripon* 68-73; rtd 73; Perm to Offic *Bradf* from 86. *46 Skipton Road, Ilkley, W Yorkshire LS29 9EP* Burley (04253) 602732

BILLOWES, David. b 20. Chich Th Coll. **d** 76 **p** 77. NSM Cowes St Mary *Portsm* 76-91; Chapl St Mary's Hosp Newport 82-91; rtd 91. *45 Solent View Road, Gurnard, Cowes, Isle of Wight PO31 8JZ* Isle of Wight (0983) 297366

BILLS, Reginald. b 18. TCert47. Lich Th Coll 68 Wm Temple Coll Rugby DipTh68. **d** 70 **p** 71. C Wednesfield St Thos *Lich* 70-73; C Wolv St Pet 73-79; Chapl St Pet Colleg Sch 73-79; C Wolv St Andr 79-81; P-in-c Brockmoor 81-87; rtd 87. *43 Kewstoke Road, Willenhall, W Midlands WV12 5DY* Bloxwich (0922) 405049

BILNEY, Kenneth Henry. b 25. FBCS. St Deiniol's Hawarden 75. **d** 75 **p** 76. Hon C Knighton St Mary Magd *Leic* 75-78; C Leic St Jas 78-80; R Leire w Ashby Parva and Dunton Bassett 80-90; rtd 90. *20 Ferndale Road, Leicester LE2 6GN* Leicester (0533) 810383

BILTON, Paul Michael. b 52. AKC74. St Aug Coll Cant 74. **d** 75 **p** 76. C Skipton Ch Ch *Bradf* 75-79; Ind Chapl *Worc* 79-81; V Greetland and W Vale *Wakef* 81-88; R Mablethorpe w Trusthorpe *Linc* 88-91; V Bradf St Wilfrid Lidget Green *Bradf* from 91. *St Wilfrid's Vicarage, Lidget Green, Bradford, W Yorkshire BD7 2LU* Bradford (0274) 572504

BINDER, Charles Louis Laurence. b 23. St Pet Hall Ox BA46 MA48. Wycliffe Hall Ox 58. **d** 58 **p** 59. V Clapham Common St Barn *S'wark* 67-73; V Fulham St Mary N

End *Lon* 73-79; V Hammersmith St Simon 76-79; V Jersey Millbrook St Matt *Win* 79-89; R Jersey St Lawr 80-89; rtd 90. *22 Salisbury Road, Steeple Langford, Salisbury SP3 4NF*

BINDOFF, Stanley. b 54. Sarum & Wells Th Coll 79. d 82 p 83. C Thirsk *York* 82-86; Chapl HM Young Offender Inst Northallerton 85-89; P-in-c Rounton w Welbury *York* 86-89; Chapl HM Pris Gartree from 89. *HM Prison Gartree, Market Harborough, Leics LE16 7RP* Market Harborough (0858) 410234

BINDON, David Charles. b 33. Lon Univ BSc58. Sarum & Wells Th Coll 77. d 79 p 80. C Yeovil *B & W* 79-83; R Kilmersdon w Babington 83-89; R Radstock w Writhlington 83-89; Chapl St Swithun's Sch Win from 89. *Pond View Cottage, 16 The Soke, Alresford, Hants SO24 9DB* Alresford (0962) 735334

BINDON, Joan Vereker. b 19. K Coll Lon DipTh47. St Chris Coll Blackheath 47. dss 67 d 73. New Zealand from 67; rtd 79. *3/149 Church Street, Onehunga, Auckland 6, New Zealand* Auckland (9) 643920

BING, Alan Charles. b 56. St Edm Hall Ox BA78 DipInstM83. Oak Hill Th Coll DipHE91. d 91. C Fremington *Ex* from 91. *22 Beards Road, Fremington, Barnstaple, Devon EX31 2PG* Barnstaple (0271) 75877

BINGHAM, Mrs Marie Joyce Phyllis. b 27. Glouc Sch of Min 80. dss 84 d 87. Glouc St Mary de Crypt w St Jo and Ch Ch *Glouc* 84-85; Glouc St Mary de Lode and St Nic 85-87; Hon C from 87. *Hazel Cottage, Sandhurst, Gloucester GL2 9NP* Gloucester (0452) 730285

BINGHAM, Norman James Frederick. b 26. Lon Univ BSc51. Tyndale Hall Bris 61. d 63 p 64. C Macclesfield St Mich *Ches* 67-71; P-in-c Macclesfield St Pet 71-73; V Leyton St Mary w St Edw *Chelmsf* 73-91; RD Waltham Forest 81-86; P-in-c Leyton St Luke 82-91; rtd 91. *97 Monks Walk, Buntingford, Herts SG9 9DP*

BINKS, Edmund Vardy. b 36. K Coll Lon BD61 AKC61. d 62 p 63. C Selby Abbey *York* 62-65; Asst Chapl Univ Coll of Ripon & York St Jo 65-83; Prin St Kath Coll Liv 83-87; Prin Ches Coll *Ches* from 87. *Chester College, Cheyney Road, Chester CH1 4BJ* Chester (0244) 375444

BINLEY, Miss Teresa Mary. b 37. Dalton Ho Bris 61. d 87. Par Dn Ashton on Mersey St Mary *Ches* from 87; Bp's Officer for Women in Min from 87. *10 Thirsk Avenue, Sale, Cheshire M33 4GN* 061-969 7858

BINNEY, Mark James Gurney. b 58. K Coll Lon BD80. Qu Coll Birm 84. d 86 p 87. C Hornchurch St Andr *Chelmsf* 86-89; C Hutton 89-91; V Pheasey *Lich* from 91. *St Chad's Vicarage, Hillingford Avenue, Pheasey, Birmingham B43 7HN* 021-360 7556

BINNIAN, Mrs Jennifer Ann. b 34. Qu Coll Birm 81. dss 84 d 87. Chaddesley Corbett and Stone *Worc* 84-85; Bewdley Far Forest 85-87; Chapl Home Care Hospice from 87; Chapl Asst Kidderminster Gen Hosp from 87. *Bodenham Farm, Wolverley, Kidderminster, Worcs DY11 5SY* Kidderminster (0562) 850382

BINNIE, Alexander David. b 22. Ripon Hall Ox 67. d 68 p 69. C Sutton Coldfield H Trin *Birm* 68-72; V Dosthill 72-88; C-in-c Wood End St Mich CD 72-83; rtd 88; Perm to Offic Lich and Birm from 88. *3 Walkers Croft, Lichfield, Staffs WS13 6TR* Lichfield (0543) 254250

BINNIE, Graham Alfred. b 04. AKC37. d 37 p 38. RD Witham *Chelmsf* 61-76; V Hatf Peverel w Ulting 74; rtd 74. *Silvermere, Llandygwydd, Cardigan, Dyfed SA43 2QT* Llechryd (023987) 271

BINNS, Dr John Richard. b 51. Cam Univ MA76 Lon Univ PhD89. Coll of Resurr Mirfield 74. d 76 p 77. C Clapham H Trin *S'wark* 76-78; C Clapham Old Town 78-80; TV Mortlake w E Sheen 80-87; V Upper Tooting H Trin from 87. *Holy Trinity Vicarage, 14 Upper Tooting Park, London SW17 7SW* 081-672 4790

BINNS, Peter Rodney. b 44. St Andr Univ MA66. Ox NSM Course 72. d 75 p 76. NSM Amersham on the Hill *Ox* 75-90; NSM Wingrave w Rowsham, Aston Abbotts and Cublington from 90; NSM Hawridge w Cholesbury and St Leonard from 90. *16 Turnfurlong Row, Turnfurlong Lane, Aylesbury, Bucks HP21 7FF* Aylesbury (0296) 22705

BINNY, John Wallace. b 46. Univ of Wales (Lamp) BA70. St Mich Coll Llan 69. d 71 p 72. C Llantrisant *Llan* 71-77; V Troedrhiwgarth 77-82; R Eglwysbrewis w St Athan, Flemingston, Gileston from 82. *The Rectory, Rectory Drive, St Athan, Barry, S Glam CF6 9PD* St Athan (0446) 750540

BIRBECK, Anthony Leng. b 33. MBE90. Linc Coll Ox BA59 MA63. Linc Th Coll 58. d 60 p 61. C Redcar *York* 60-74; Chapl Teesside Ind Miss 62-74; Can Res and Treas Wells Cathl *B & W* 74-78; Lic to Offic from 78. *4 Mount Pleasant Avenue, Wells, Somerset BA5 2JQ* Wells (0749) 73246

BIRBECK, John Trevor. b 49. AIB77. St Jo Coll Nottm 86. d 88 p 89. C Eccleshill *Bradf* from 88. *3 Hall Road, Eccleshill, Bradford, W Yorkshire BD2 2DP* Bradford (0274) 640286

BIRCH, Arthur James Fleet. b 14. Univ Coll Dur BA36 MA39. d 37 p 38. R Lymm *Ches* 70-79; rtd 79; Perm to Offic *Ches* from 79. *21 Arran Drive, Frodsham, Warrington WA6 6AL* Frodsham (0928) 33709

BIRCH, Arthur Kenneth. b 15. Qu Coll Birm 46. d 48 p 49. Uganda 71-75; V Fence in Pendle *Blackb* 75-76; C Bollington St Jo *Ches* 77-79; R Church Lawton 79-81; rtd 81; Perm to Offic *Sarum* from 81. *58 Manor Gardens, Warminster, Wilts BA12 8PW* Warminster (0985) 215172

BIRCH, Derek. b 31. Univ of Wales (Lamp) BA58. Coll of Resurr Mirfield 58. d 60 p 61. C S Elmsall *Wakef* 60-62; C Penistone w Midhope 62-66; V Silkstone 66-89; Chapl Stainborough 76-89; P-in-c Hoyland Swaine 85-89; V Hoylandswaine and Silkstone w Stainborough from 89. *The Vicarage, 12 High Street, Silkstone, Barnsley, S Yorkshire S75 4JN* Barnsley (0226) 790232

BIRCH, Gordon Clifford. b 20. RD66. Dur Univ BA45 MA66. Oak Hill Th Coll 39. d 43 p 44. Chapl RNR 58-75; V Middlesb St Oswald *York* 68-74; Chapl St Luke's Mental Hosp Middlesb 68-74; R Yarm 74-85; rtd 85. *598 Acklam Road, Acklam, Middlesbrough, Cleveland TS5 8BH* Middlesbrough (0642) 595309

BIRCH, Henry Arthur. b 24. St Jo Coll Dur BA48. Tyndale Hall Bris 48. d 49 p 50. Australia 69-81 and from 84; S Africa 81-84; rtd 90. *Camelot Court, 9/87 Yathong Road, Caringbah, NSW, Australia 2229* Sydney (2) 529-1763

BIRCH, Janet Ann. St Alb Minl Tr Scheme 77. dss 80 d 87. Luton St Mary *St Alb* 80-87; Par Dn Streatley 87-91; rtd 91. *3 Market Cross House, Wentworth Road, Aldeburgh, Suffolk IP15 5BJ* Aldeburgh (0728) 453371

BIRCHALL, Maurice Molyneux. b 11. Dur Univ LTh41 BA45. Edin Th Coll 36. d 39 p 40. Clerical Org Sec CECS 65-73; C Habergham Eaves H Trin *Blackb* 73-77; rtd 77. *33 South Avenue, Morecambe, Lancs LA4 5RJ* Morecambe (0524) 414136

BIRCHALL, Robert Gary. b 59. Sheff Univ BA81. St Jo Coll Nottm 85. d 88 p 89. C Manston *Ripon* 88-91; C Leic Martyrs *Leic* from 91. *63 Ashleigh Road, Leicester LE3 0FB* Leicester (0533) 541341

BIRCHARD, Canon Thaddeus Jude. b 45. Louisiana State Univ BA66 Nottm Univ DipTh68. Kelham Th Coll 66. d 70 p 71. C Devonport St Mark Ford *Ex* 70-73; C Southend St Jo w St Mark, All SS w St Fran etc *Chelmsf* 73-76; TV Poplar *Lon* 76-80; V Paddington St Jo w St Mich from 80; Hon Can Louisiana from 90. *18 Somers Crescent, London W2 2PN* 071-262 1732

BIRCHBY, Martin Cecil. b 17. Worc Ord Coll 66. d 68 p 69. C Bromyard *Heref* 68-70; P-in-c Bredenbury and Wacton w Grendon Bishop 70-75; P-in-c Edwyn Ralph and Collington w Thornbury 71-75; P-in-c Pembridge 75-80; P-in-c Shobdon 79-80; R Pembridge w Moor Court and Shobdon 80-83; P-in-c Staunton-on-Arrow w Byton 81-83; R Pembridge w Moorcourt, Shobdon, Staunton etc 83-85; rtd 85; Perm to Offic *Heref* from 85. *Cornerways, 9 Bearcroft, Weobley, Hereford HR4 8TA* Weobley (0544) 318185

BIRCHMORE, Brian Leonard. b 35. ALCD59. d 59 p 60. C Rusthall *Roch* 59-62; C Rainham 62-64; C Belvedere All SS 64-66; V Meopham 66-74; R Chatham St Mary w St Jo 74-75; Perm to Offic *Chelmsf* 81-83; Ind Chapl Harlow from 83; P-in-c Bush End 83-89; P-in-c Hatf Broad Oak 83-89; P-in-c Greenstead juxta Colchester from 89. *The Rectory, 74 Howe Close, Greenstead, Colchester CO4 3XD* Colchester (0206) 865762

BIRCHNALL, Canon Simeon Robert. b 18. St Jo Coll Dur BA42 MA45 DipTh43. d 43 p 44. C Pitsmoor w Wicker *Sheff* 43-46; C Conisbrough 46-47; C Clifton St Jas 47-50; C Chingford SS Pet and Paul *Chelmsf* 50-53; C-in-c Chingford St Anne 53-55; V 56-64; R Woodford St Mary 64-71; R Woodford St Mary w St Phil and St Jas from 71; Hon Can Chelmsf Cathl from 76; RD Redbridge 77-90; P-in-c Barkingside St Cedd 83-90. *8 Chelmsford Road, South Woodford, London E18 2PL* 081-504 3472

BIRD, Alfred. b 10. Keble Coll Ox BA32 MA39. Melbourne Coll of Div MTh75 Bps' Coll Cheshunt 33. d 34 p 35. C Carl St Aid and Ch Ch *Carl* 34-38; Chapl Asst St Thos Hosp Lon 38-41; Lic to Offic *S'wark* 38-41; C Cockington *Ex* 41-42; Chapl RNVR 42-46; Australia 46-48 and from 51; Chapl Eastbourne Coll E Sussex 48-51. *Unit 19, Pittwater Village, Brinawa Street, Mona Vale, Australia 2103* Sydney (2) 998-0119

BIRD, Dr Anthony Peter. b 31. St Jo Coll Ox BA54 BTh55 MA57 Birm Univ MB, ChB70. Cuddesdon Coll 55. **d** 57 **p** 58. C Stafford St Mary *Lich* 57-60; Chapl Cuddesdon Coll 60-61; Vice-Prin Cuddesdon Coll 61-64; C Selly Oak St Wulstan *Birm* 64-68; Lic to Offic 68-79; Prin Qu Coll Birm 74-79; Perm to Offic *Birm* from 85. *93 Bournbrook Road, Birmingham B29 7BX*

BIRD, Archibald Brian. b 02. AKC28. **d** 28 **p** 31. V Edwardstone w Groton *St E* 46-71; rtd 71; Perm to Offic *St E* from 72. *38 Maidenburgh Street, Colchester CO1 1UB* Colchester (0206) 44757

BIRD, Canon Arthur Leyland. b 02. Linc Th Coll 23. **d** 25 **p** 26. R Walton-on-the-Hill *Guildf* 62-71; Hon Can Guildf Cathl 62-71; rtd 71; Hon C Dorking w Ranmore *Guildf* 72-81; Perm to Offic from 81. *3 Queens Close, Walton-on-the-Hill, Tadworth, Surrey KT20 7SU* Tadworth (0737) 813228

BIRD, Ven Colin Richard Bateman. b 33. Selw Coll Cam BA56 MA61. Cuddesdon Coll 56. **d** 58 **p** 59. S Africa 58-70; C Limpsfield and Titsey *S'wark* 70-75; V Hatcham St Cath 75-88; RD Deptford 80 85; Hon Can S'wark Cathl 82-88; Adn Lambeth from 88; P-in-c Brixton Hill St Sav from 91. *7 Hoadly Road, London SW16 1AE* 081-769 4384 or 780 2308

BIRD, David John. b 46. Univ of Wales (Lamp) BA70 Pittsburgh Univ PhD87. Gen Th Sem (NY) STM74. **d** 70 **p** 71. C Kidderminster St Geo *Worc* 70-72; USA from 72. *Grace Church, 1041 Wisconsin Avenue, Northwest, Georgetown, Washington DC 20007, USA* Washington DC (202) 333-7100

BIRD, David Ronald. b 55. York Univ BA76. St Jo Coll Nottm 83. **d** 86 **p** 87. C Kinson *Sarum* 86-90; R Thrapston *Pet* from 90. *The Rectory, Thrapston, Kettering, Northants NN14 4PD* Thrapston (08012) 2393

BIRD, Donald Wilfred Ray. b 27. Dur Univ BA52. Linc Th Coll 61. **d** 63 **p** 64. C E w W Barkwith *Linc* 63-65; Rhodesia 66-80; R Scotter w E Ferry *Linc* from 80. *The Rectory, Scotter, Gainsborough, Lincs DN21 3RZ* Scunthorpe (0724) 762662

BIRD, Edward Herbert John Richards. b 14. St Deiniol's Hawarden 77. **d** 77 **p** 78. NSM Partington and Carrington *Ches* from 77. *1 Westbrook Cottages, Manchester Road, Carrington, Manchester M31 4BD* 061-775 9142

BIRD, Frederick Hinton. b 38. St Edm Hall Ox BA62 MA66 Univ of Wales MEd81 PhD86. St D Coll Lamp BD65. **d** 65 **p** 66. C Mynyddislwyn *Mon* 65-67; Min Can St Woolos Cathl 67-70; Chapl Anglo-American Coll Farringdon 70-71; Perm to Offic Ox 70-78; Cant 72-78; Mon 76-82; V Rushen *S & M* from 82. *Kirk Rushen Vicarage, Port St Mary, Isle of Man* Port St Mary (0624) 832275

BIRD, Canon Geoffrey Neville. b 22. AKC48. St Boniface Warminster 48. **d** 49 **p** 50. R Edge w Pitchcombe *Glouc* 56-82; P-in-c Brookthorpe w Whaddon and Harescombe 76-82; R The Edge, Pitchcombe, Harescombe and Brookthorpe 82-90; Hon Can Glouc Cathl from 83; RD Bisley 84-90; rtd 90. *Ivy Croft, Winstone, Cirencester, Glos GL7 7JZ* Cirencester (0285) 821644

BIRD, Henry John Joseph. b 37. ARCO58 Qu Coll Cam BA59 MA63. Linc Th Coll 62. **d** 64 **p** 65. C Harbledown *Cant* 64-68; C Skipton H Trin *Bradf* 68-70; V Oakworth 70-81; Chapl Abingdon Sch 81-82; P-in-c Doncaster St Geo *Sheff* 82-85; V from 85. *98 Thorne Road, Doncaster, S Yorkshire DN2 5BJ* Doncaster (0302) 368796 or 323748

BIRD, Dr Hugh Claud Handley. b 24. FRCGP SS Coll Cam MA MB BCh. Ridley Hall Cam. **d** 86 **p** 86. NSM Coxheath w E Farleigh, Hunton and Linton *Roch* from 86. *Heath House, Linton, Maidstone, Kent ME17 4PF* Maidstone (0622) 743438

BIRD, Jeffrey David. b 54. Nottm Univ BCombStuds85. Linc Th Coll 82. **d** 85 **p** 86. C Frome St Jo *B & W* 85-88; Asst Chapl HM Pris Pentonville 88-89; Chapl HM Pris Dartmoor from 89. *HM Prison Dartmoor, Princetown, Yelverton, Devon PL20 6RR* Princetown (082289) 261

BIRD, Jeremy Paul. b 56. Ex Univ BSc77 DipTh78 Hull Univ MA88. Sarum Th Coll 78. **d** 80 **p** 81. C Tavistock and Gulworthy *Ex* 80-83; Chapl Teesside Poly *York* 83-88; R Chipstable w Huish Champflower and Clatworthy *B & W* from 88; Rural Affairs Officer from 88. *The Rectory, Chipstable, Taunton, Somerset TA4 2PZ* Wiveliscombe (0984) 23619

BIRD, Maurice Pidding. b 19. Linc Coll Ox BA40 MA44. Cuddesdon Coll 40. **d** 42 **p** 43. R Winterton w E Somerton *Nor* 59-71; V Heigham St Barn 71-75; V Heigham St Barn w St Bart 75-82; P-in-c Edington and Imber *Sarum* 82-83; P-in-c Erlestoke and Gt Cheverell 82-83; P-in-c Edington and Imber, Erlestoke and E

Coulston 83-88; rtd 88. *61 Beechwood, Woodlesford, Leeds LS26 8PQ* Leeds (0532) 820865

BIRD, Norman David. b 32. CQSW73. Coll of Resurr Mirfield 87. **d** 89 **p** 90. NSM Willesden Green St Andr and St Fran of Assisi *Lon* from 89. *5 Oldfield Road, London NW10 9UD* 081-451 4160

BIRD, Peter Andrew. b 40. Wadh Coll Ox BA62 MA68. Ridley Hall Cam 63. **d** 65 **p** 66. C Keynsham w Queen Charlton *B & W* 65-68; C Strood St Nic *Roch* 68-72; TV Strood 72-79; V S Gillingham 79-89; V Westerham from 89. *The Vicarage, Borde Hill, Vicarage Hill, Westerham, Kent TN16 1TL* Westerham (0959) 63127

BIRD, Rex Alan. b 30. Trin Coll Bris 54. **d** 57 **p** 58. C Wellington Ch Ch *Lich* 57-59; C St Alb St Paul *St Alb* 59-61; V Rainham *Chelmsf* 61-65; R Wennington 61-65; R Lavenham *St E* 65-75; CF (TA) from 65; RD Lavenham *St E* 72-75; Dean Battle *Chich* 75-84; V Battle 75-84; V Castle Hedingham *Chelmsf* 84-91; R Monks Eleigh w Chelsworth and Brent Eleigh etc *St E* from 91. *The Rectory, Monks Eleigh, Ipswich IP7 7AU* Bildeston (0449) 740244

BIRD, Roger Alfred. b 49. AKC72. St Aug Coll Cant 72. **d** 73 **p** 74. C Prestatyn *St As* 73-78; R Llandysilio and Penrhos and Llandrinio etc from 78; Dioc RE Adv from 84; Dioc Dir of Educn from 89. *The Rectory, Rhos Common, Four Crosses, Llanymynech, Powys SY22 6RW* Llanymynech (0691) 830533

BIRDSEYE, Miss Jacqueline Ann. b 55. Sussex Univ BEd78 Southn Univ BTh88. Sarum & Wells Th Coll 85. **d** 88. C Egham Hythe *Guildf* 88-91; C Fleet from 91. *38 Oasthouse Drive, Ancells Farm, Fleet, Aldershot, Hants GU13 8UL*

BIRDWOOD, William Halhed. b 51. St Jo Coll Dur BA73. Sarum & Wells Th Coll 76. **d** 78 **p** 79. C Royston *St Alb* 78-82; C Thorley w Bishop's Stortford H Trin 82-89; Chapl HM Pris Ex from 89; Lic to Offic *Ex* from 89. *HM Prison Exeter, New North Road, Exeter EX4 4EX* Exeter (0392) 78321

BIRKENHEAD, Suffragan Bishop of. See BROWN, Rt Rev Ronald

BIRKET, Cyril. b 28. ACIS70. NW Ord Course 71. **d** 74 **p** 75. C Broughton *Blackb* 74-79; V Wesham 79-86; V Overton from 86. *St Helen's Vicarage, Chapel Lane, Overton, Morecambe, Lancs LA3 3HU* Overton (052471) 234

BIRKETT, Joyce. b 38. W Midl Minl Tr Course 84. **d** 87. Par Dn Hill *Birm* 87-91; Asst Chapl Highcroft Hosp Birm 87-91; Par Dn Rowley Regis *Birm* from 91. *194 Hanover Road, Rowley Regis, Warley, W Midlands B65 9EQ* 021-559 3830

BIRKETT, Neil Warren. b 45. Lanc Univ BEd74 Southn Univ MA84. Kelham Th Coll 65. **d** 77 **p** 77. NSM Win St Matt *Win* from 77. *Corrymeela, 132 Teg Down Meads, Winchester, Hants SO22 5NS* Winchester (0962) 64910

BIRKETT, Peter. b 13. Univ Coll Dur BA35 MA39. **d** 36 **p** 37. R Holford w Dodington *B & W* 70-77; rtd 78; Perm to Offic *B & W* from 82. *14 Long Street, Williton, Taunton, Somerset TA4 4QN* Williton (0984) 32220

BIRLEY, John Lindsay. b 19. Kelham Th Coll 37. **d** 43 **p** 44. Asst Chapl St Jo Sch Leatherhead 54-64; Perm to Offic *Ox* 64-76; rtd 76. *Abtei Himmerod, D5561 Grosslittgen, Germany* Grosslittgen (6575) 4110

BIRMINGHAM, Archdeacon of. See DUNCAN, Ven John Finch

BIRMINGHAM, Bishop of. See SANTER, Rt Rev Mark

BIRMINGHAM, Provost of. See BERRY, Very Rev Peter Austin

BIRT, David Edward. b 26. St Steph Ho Ox 86. **d** 86 **p** 87. NSM Ealing Ch the Sav *Lon* from 86. *10 Manor Court Road, London W7 3EL* 081-579 4871

BIRT, Malcolm Douglas. b 33. Trin Coll Cam BA56 MA60. Ridley Hall Cam 56. **d** 58 **p** 59. C Barrow St Mark *Carl* 58-60; C Tunbridge Wells St Jo *Roch* 60-63; V Constable Lee *Man* 63-72; V Anslow *Lich* from 72; R Rolleston from 72. *The Rectory, Rolleston, Burton-on-Trent, Staffs DE13 9BE*

BIRT, Patrick. b 34. Glouc Th Course 71. **d** 75 **p** 75. NSM Bisley *Glouc* 75-76; NSM Whiteshill 76-81; C Stroud H Trin 81; R Ruardean 81-86; V Newbridge-on-Wye and Llanfihangel Brynpabuan *S & B* 86-88; TV Gillingham *Sarum* from 88. *The Vicarage, Stour Provost, Gillingham, Dorset SP8 5RU* East Stour (074785) 216

BIRT, Richard Arthur. b 43. Ch Ch Ox BA66 MA69. Cuddesdon Coll 67. **d** 69 **p** 70. C Sutton St Mich *York* 69-71; C Wollaton *S'well* 71-75; R Kirkby in Ashfield 75-80; P-in-c Duxford *Ely* 80-87; R 87-88; P-in-c Hinxton 80-87; V 87-88; P-in-c Ickleton 80-87; V 87-88; V Weobley w Sarnesfield and Norton Canon *Heref* from 88; P-in-c Letton w Staunton, Byford, Mansel Gamage etc from 88. *The Vicarage, Church Road, Weobley, Hereford HR4 8SD* Weobley (0544) 318415

BIRT, Ven William Raymond. b 11. Ely Th Coll 55. **d** 56 **p** 57. P-in-c Enbourne w Hampstead Marshall *Ox* 68-70; RD Newbury 70-73; R W Woodhay 71-81; Adn Berks 73-77; Hon Can Ch Ch 79-82; rtd 81; C W Woodhay w Enborne, Hampstead Marshall etc *Ox* 81-91. *1 The Old Bakery, George Street, Kingsclere, Newbury, Berks RG15 8NQ* Newbury (0635) 297426

BIRTWISTLE, Canon James. b 33. FCA66. Ely Th Coll 57. **d** 59 **p** 60. C Southport St Luke *Liv* 59-63; V Cleator Moor w Cleator *Carl* 63-70; R Letchworth *St Alb* 70-73; P-in-c Wareside 73-80; Dep Dir of Educn 77-80; Dir of Educn from 80; Hon Can St Alb from 85; P-in-c Hertingfordbury from 88. *The Rectory, St Mary's Lane, Hertford SG14 2LE* Hertford (0992) 554450

BISCOE, Clive. b 45. **d** 86 **p** 87. C Llansamlet *S & B* 86-90; V Landore 90-91. *6 Hazelwood Row, Cwmavon, Port Talbot, W Glam SA12 9DP*

BISH, Donald. b 26. Ripon Hall Ox. **d** 75 **p** 75. C S Gillingham *Roch* 75-79; R Wateringbury w Teston and W Farleigh from 79. *The Rectory, Church Road, Teston, Maidstone, Kent ME18 5AJ* Maidstone (0622) 812494

BISHOP, Anthony John. b 43. G&C Coll Cam BA66 MA69 Lon Univ MTh69. ALCD67. **d** 69 **p** 70. C Eccleston St Luke *Liv* 69-73; C Gt Baddow *Chelmsf* 73-77; Nigeria 77-84; Lect Lon Bible Coll 84-85; TV Chigwell *Chelmsf* from 85. *The Vicarage, Manor Road, Chigwell, Essex IG7 5PS* 081-500 4608

BISHOP, Anthony Peter. b 46. FRSA87. St Jo Coll Nottm LTh74 MPhil84 ALCD71. **d** 71 **p** 72. C Beckenham St Geo *Roch* 71-75; Chapl RAF 75-91; Asst Chapl-in-Chief RAF from 91. *c/o MOD, Adastral House, Theobald's Road, London WC1X 8RU* 071-430 7268

BISHOP, Arthur Jack. b 07. St Jo Coll Dur BA28 MA31. **d** 30 **p** 31. R Scotter w E Ferry *Linc* 66-72; R Lympsham *B & W* 72-75; rtd 75; Australia from 76. *PO Box 6, Gordon, Victoria, Australia 3345* Gordon (53) 689007

BISHOP, Miss Cecil Marie. b 18. Lon Univ DipTh48. St Chris Coll Blackheath 46 Gilmore Ho 56. **dss** 57 **d** 87. Jamaica 57-74; Gambia 74-76; Lic to Offic *Ex* 76-87; rtd 78; Hon Par Dn Paignton St Jo *Ex* from 87. *Flat 5, Lancaster House, Belle Vue Road, Paignton, Devon TQ4 6HD* Paignton (0803) 523522

BISHOP, Christopher. b 48. K Coll Lon. St Aug Coll Cant 71. **d** 72 **p** 73. C Gt Ilford St Mary *Chelmsf* 72-75; C Upminster 75-78; Adn's Youth Chapl 77-80; Youth Officer 80-86; Chapl Stansted Airport from 86; P-in-c Manuden w Berden from 86; RD Newport and Stansted from 89. *24 Mallows Green Road, Manuden, Bishop's Stortford, Herts CM23 1DG* Bishop's Stortford (0279) 812228

✠**BISHOP, Rt Rev Clifford Leofric Purdy.** b 08. Ch Coll Cam BA31 MA63. Linc Th Coll 31. **d** 32 **p** 33 **c** 62. C Walworth St Jo *S'wark* 32-38; C Middlesb St Jo the Ev *York* 38-41; V Camberwell St Geo *S'wark* 41-49; RD Camberwell 43-49; C-in-c Camberwell All So 44-47; R Blakeney w Lt Langham *Nor* 49-53; RD Walsingham 51-53; R Bishopwearmouth St Mich *Dur* 53-62; RD Wearmouth 53-62; Hon Can Dur Cathl 58-62; Suff Bp Malmesbury *Bris* 62-73; Can Res Bris Cathl 62-73; rtd 73; Perm to Offic *Nor* 73-76 and from 78; P-in-c Cley w Wiveton 76-78. *The Rectory Cottage, Cley, Holt, Norfolk NR25 7BA* Cley (0263) 740250

BISHOP, Canon David Harold. b 28. ARIBA53 FRSA75. Westcott Ho Cam 55. **d** 57 **p** 58. C Cannock *Lich* 57-61; C Gt Barr 61-67; V All Hallows Lon Wall *Lon* 67-80; Can Res Nor Cathl *Nor* from 80. *26 The Close, Norwich NR1 4DZ* Norwich (0603) 624825

BISHOP, David Henry Ryder. b 27. Lon Univ DipTh57. Tyndale Hall Bris. **d** 57 **p** 58. C Sevenoaks St Nic *Roch* 57-59; C Branksome St Clem *Sarum* 59-64; Uganda 64-67; Dep Sec CCCS 68; R Ox St Clem *Ox* 69-91; Zimbabwe from 91. *2 Church Road, Avondale, Harare, Zimbabwe* Harare (4) 39697

BISHOP, Donald. b 22. Lon Univ BSc48. Qu Coll Birm 56. **d** 57 **p** 58. V Bodicote *Ox* 63-87; P-in-c Broughton 71-85; rtd 87; Perm to Offic *Cov* from 87. *66 Hanson Avenue, Shipston-on-Stour, Warks CV36 4HS* Shipston-on-Stour (0608) 63431

BISHOP, Huw Daniel. b 49. Univ of Wales (Lamp) BA71 DipTh73. Bp Burgess Hall Lamp CPS73. **d** 73 **p** 74. C Carmarthen St Pet *St D* 73-77; Prov Youth Chapl Wales 77-79; V Llanybyther and Llanwenog w Llanwnnen 79-80; Youth and Community Officer 80-81; Hd of Relig Studies Carre's Gr Sch Sleaford 81-85; K Sch Pet from 85; Lic to Offic *Linc* from 83; CF (TA) from 85; Perm to Offic *Pet* from 86. *11 Dean Close,*

Leasingham, Sleaford, Lincs NG34 8NW Sleaford (0529) 306723

BISHOP, Ian Gregory. b 62. ARICS87 Portsm Poly BSc84. Oak Hill Th Coll BA91. **d** 91. C Purley Ch Ch *S'wark* from 91. *132 Whytecliffe Road North, Purley, Surrey CR8 2AS* 081-660 5086

BISHOP, Jeremy Simon. b 54. Nottm Univ BSc75 Yonsei Univ S Korea 84. All Nations Chr Coll 82 Wycliffe Hall Ox 89. **d** 91. C Macclesfield Team Par *Ches* from 91. *7 Brocklehurst Way, Macclesfield, Cheshire SK10 2HY* Macclesfield (0625) 617680

BISHOP, John Albert. b 11. Lon Coll of Div 39. **d** 41 **p** 42. R Carlton-in-the-Willows *S'well* 59-74; R Gamston w Eaton and W Drayton 74-78; Canada from 78; rtd 84. *227 William Roe Boulevard, Newmarket, Ontario, Canada, L3Y 1B4* Newmarket (416) 895-1526

BISHOP, John Baylis. b 32. Selw Coll Cam BA54 MA58. Cuddesdon Coll 54. **d** 56 **p** 57. C Middlesb St Oswald *York* 56-59; C Romsey *Win* 59-62; Chapl RN 62-66; P-in-c Linc St Mary-le-Wigford w St Martin *Linc* 66-67; V Linc St Faith 66-68; V Linc St Faith and St Martin w St Pet 69-71; Lic to Offic *Bris* 72-84; C Henbury 84-87; TV Bris St Agnes and St Simon w St Werburgh 87; TV Bris St Paul's from 87. *16 Chesterfield Road, St Andrews, Bristol BS6 5DL* Bristol (0272) 240104

BISHOP, John Charles Simeon. b 46. Chich Th Coll 77. **d** 79 **p** 79. SSF 66-86; P-in-c Edin St Dav *Edin* 82-86; Chapl to the Deaf *Birm* from 86. *183 Bankes Road, Birmingham B10 9PN* 021-772 1380 or 455 0601

BISHOP, John David. b 36. Liv Univ BEng MIMechE. E Midl Min Tr Course. **d** 85 **p** 86. NSM Ockbrook *Derby* from 85. *143 Victoria Avenue, Borrowash, Derby DE7 3HF* Derby (0332) 663828

BISHOP, John Graham. b 30. Bris Univ BA52 Lon Univ BD59 PhD73. Chich Th Coll 54. **d** 56 **p** 57. Tutor and Lib Chich Th Coll 61-70; C Tamerton Foliot *Ex* 70-71; R Dartington 71-90; RD Totnes 75-90; V Rattery 79-90; rtd 90. *188B Orchard Street, Chichester, W Sussex PO19 1DE* Chichester (0243) 784832

BISHOP, John Harold. b 09. Univ Coll Dur BA31 MA45. Cuddesdon Coll 34. **d** 35 **p** 36. R Singleton *Chich* 60-79; V E Dean 60-79; V W Dean 75-79; RD Westbourne 73-78; rtd 80; Perm to Offic *Chich* from 80. *6 Tregarth Road, Chichester, W Sussex PO19 4QU* Chichester (0243) 527612

BISHOP, Malcolm Geoffrey. b 33. Leeds Univ BA59. Coll of Resurr Mirfield 59. **d** 61 **p** 62. C Kingswinford St Mary *Lich* 61-67; V Birches Head 67-72; P-in-c Oakamoor w Cotton 72-78; TV Billingham St Aid *Dur* 78-85; R Burnmoor from 85. *The Rectory, Burnmoor, Houghton le Spring, Tyne & Wear DH4 6EX* 091-385 2695

BISHOP, Mark Wreford. b 20. Ex Coll Ox BA42 MA45. Wycliffe Hall Ox 42. **d** 43 **p** 44. Lic to Offic *Bradf* 67-71; V Helme *Wakef* 71-77; Dioc Ecum Officer 71-77; P-in-c Graveley w Papworth St Agnes w Yelling etc *Ely* 77-78; R 78-85; rtd 85; Perm to Offic *Bradf* from 85. *5 Rowantree Avenue, Baildon, Shipley, W Yorkshire BD17 5LQ* Bradford (0274) 596006

BISHOP, Michael George. b 27. Wycliffe Hall Ox 63. **d** 65 **p** 66. C Cheltenham St Mary *Glouc* 65-68; P-in-c Edale *Derby* 68-71; V Doveridge 71-79; Chapl HM Det Cen Foston Hall 73-79; V Cotmanhay *Derby* 79-81; Chapl Ilkeston Gen Hosp 79-81; USA 81-89; Perm to Offic *Chich* from 89. *Kingsley, 50 Filsham Road, St Leonards-on-Sea, E Sussex TN38 0PA* Hastings (0424) 423539

BISHOP, Philip Michael. b 47. Lon Univ BD69 AKC69. St Aug Coll Cant 70. **d** 71 **p** 72. C Mansf Woodhouse *S'well* 71-76; C Liscard St Mary w St Columba *Ches* 76-78; V Thornton le Moors w Ince and Elton 78-90; V Sutton w Carlton and Normanton upon Trent etc *S'well* from 90. *The Vicarage, Old North Road, Sutton-on-Trent, Newark, Notts NG23 6PL* Newark (0636) 821797

BISHOP, Phillip Leslie. b 44. K Coll Lon BD66 AKC66. **d** 67 **p** 68. C Albrighton *Lich* 67-70; C St-Geo-in-the-East St Mary *Lon* 70-71; C Middlesb Ascension *York* 71-73; P-in-c Withernwick 73-77; Ind Chapl 73-82; V Gt Ayton w Easby and Newton in Cleveland 82-89; RD Stokesley 85-89; R Guisborough from 89. *The Rectory, Guisborough, Cleveland TS14 6BS* Guisborough (0287) 632588

BISHOP, Thomas Harold. b 21. Ridley Hall Cam 60. **d** 61 **p** 62. V Rainford *Liv* 69-87; rtd 87. *14 Keswick Road, Liverpool L18 9UH* 051-724 6647

BISHOP, Thomas Harveyson. b 25. Coll of Resurr Mirfield 54. **d** 56 **p** 57. S Africa 56-79 and from 87; Lic to Offic *Lon* 79-87; Lon Sec USPG 79-87; rtd 91. *19 Alexandra Avenue, Oranjezicht, Cape Town, 8000 South Africa* Cape Town (21) 461-3289

BISHOP, Miss Waveney Joyce. b 38. Westf Coll Lon BSc60. Cranmer Hall Dur DipTh72. **dss** 82 **d** 87. Leyton St Mary w St Edw *Chelmsf* 82-84; Bishopsworth *Bris* 84-87; Hon Par Dn from 87. *2 Bishop's Cove, Bishopsworth, Bristol BS13 8HH* Bristol (0272) 642588

BISHTON, Gerald Arthur. b 32. MRSH76 Ruskin Coll Ox DipEcon56 St Pet Hall Ox BA59 MA63. Qu Coll Birm 60. **d** 61 **p** 62. C Forest Gate St Edm *Chelmsf* 61-64; Asst Chapl Lon Univ *Lon* 64-67; Chapl NE Lon Poly 68-73; Sen Lect 73-80; Chapl St Mary's Hosp Gt Ilford 68-80; Ind Chapl *Chelmsf* from 80; P-in-c Shopland 80-89; P-in-c Sutton 80-89; P-in-c Sutton w Shopland from 89. *The Rectory, Sutton Road, Rochford, Essex SS4 1LQ* Southend-on-Sea (0702) 544587

BISSEX, Mrs Janet Christine Margaret. b 50. Westhill Coll Birm CertEd72. Trin Coll Bris 76. **dss** 86 **d** 87. Toxteth Park St Bede *Liv* 86-87; Par Dn 87-89 and from 90; Hon Par Dn 89-90. *46 Boswell Street, Liverpool L8 0RW* 051-733 9636

BLACK, Canon Alexander Stevenson. b 28. Glas Univ MA53. Edin Th Coll 53. **d** 55 **p** 56. C Dumfries *Glas* 55-58; Chapl Glas Univ 58-61; C Glas St Mary 58-61; P-in-c E Kilbride 61-69; R Edin St Columba *Edin* 69-79; TV Edin St Jo 79-83; R Haddington from 83; R Dunbar from 83; Can St Mary's Cathl from 88. *The Rectory, Church Street, Haddington, East Lothian EH41 3EX* Haddington (062082) 2203

BLACK, Douglas John. b 58. **d** 91. C Wrexham *St As* from 91. *16 Foster Road, Wrexham, Clwyd LL11 2LT* Wrexham (0978) 365841

BLACK, Mrs Elizabeth Anne. b 47. Qu Coll Birm 80 Cranmer Hall Dur 81. **dss** 82 **d** 87. Cleadon *Dur* 82-85; S Westoe 85-87; Par Dn 87-88; Par Dn Ches le Street from 88. *68 Rydal Road, Garden Farm Estate, Chester le Street, Co Durham DH2 3DT* 091-388 0117

BLACK, Henry. b 40. Edin Th Coll 64. **d** 67 **p** 68. C Horden *Dur* 67-69; C Cleadon Park 69-73; C Winlaton 73-78; R S Ockendon *Chelmsf* from 78. *The Rectory, North Road, South Ockendon, Essex RM15 6QJ* South Ockendon (0708) 853349

BLACK, Ian Forbes. b 29. St Aid Birkenhead 55. **d** 58 **p** 59. C Bramhall *Ches* 58-61; C Witton 61-63; P-in-c Prestonpans *Edin* 63-68; R Edin Ch Ch-St Jas 68-71; Asst Chapl HM Pris Liv 71-72; Chapl HM Pris Haverigg 72-73; R Bootle w Corney *Carl* 73-75; P-in-c Whicham w Whitbeck 73-75; R Bootle, Corney, Whicham and Whitbeck 75-86; P-in-c Orton St Giles 86-89; R from 89; P-in-c Aikton 86-89; R from 89. *The Rectory, Aikton, Wigton, Cumbria CA7 0HP* Wigton (06973) 42229

BLACK, Leonard Albert. b 49. Edin Th Coll 69. **d** 72 **p** 73. C Aber St Marg *Ab* 72-75; Chapl St Paul's Cathl Dundee *Bre* 75-77; P-in-c Aber St Ninian *Ab* 77-80; Miss to Seamen from 80; R Inverness St Mich *Mor* from 80; P-in-c Balloch New Town Distr 80-87; R Inverness St Jo 80-87; Relig Progr Producer Moray Firth Radio from 87. *St Michael's Rectory, 28 Abban Street, Inverness IV3 6HH* Inverness (0463) 233797

BLACK, Canon Neville. b 36. DMS85. Oak Hill Th Coll 61. **d** 64 **p** 65. C Everton St Ambrose w St Tim *Liv* 64-69; P-in-c Everton St Geo 69-71; P-in-c Everton St Benedict 70-72; P-in-c Everton St Chad w Ch Ch 70-72; V Everton St Geo 71-81; P-in-c Edge Hill St Nath 81; TR St Luke in the City from 81; Chapl Liv Women's Hosp from 82; Dioc Adv Urban Leadership *Liv* from 84; Hon Can Liv Cathl from 87; N Ord Course from 88. *445 Aigburth Road, Liverpool L19 3PA* 051-427 9803

BLACK, Robert John Edward Francis Butler. b 41. TCD BA65 HDipEd70 DipG&C80 MA85. CITC 66. **d** 66 **p** 67. C Jordanstown *Conn* 66-68; C Dub St Steph and St Ann *D & G* 68-73; C Stillorgan w Blackrock 73-85; Hd Master Dundalk Gr Sch *Arm* from 85. *Dundalk Grammar School, Dundalk, Co Louth, Irish Republic* Dundalk (42) 34459

BLACK, Samuel James. b 38. CITC. **d** 68 **p** 69. C Cloughfern *Conn* 68-72; C Lisburn St Paul 72-78; I Rasharkin w Finvoy 78-82; I Belf Upper Malone (Epiphany) from 82. *The Rectory, 74 Locksley Park, Upper Lisburn Road, Belfast BT10 0AS* Belfast (0232) 601588

BLACK, William. d 88 **p** 89. NSM Malahide w Balgriffin *D & G* 88-89; NSM Dub St Ann w St Mark and St Steph from 89; Asst Hon Chapl Miss to Seamen from 89. *27 Greendale Avenue, Dublin 5, Irish Republic* Dublin (1) 323141

BLACKALL, Mrs Margaret Ivy. b 38. St Kath Coll Lon CertEd58. E Anglian Minl Tr Course 82. **dss** 86 **d** 87. NSM Wickham Market w Pettistree and Easton *St E* 86-88; Par Dn Leiston from 88. *46 Buller Road, Leiston, Suffolk IP16 4HA* Leiston (0728) 831364

BLACKALL, Robin Jeremy McRae. b 35. Ridley Hall Cam 67. **d** 69 **p** 70. C Stowmarket *St E* 69-72; R Stanstead w Shimplingthorne and Alpheton 72-77; R Bradwell on Sea *Chelmsf* 77-79; R St Lawrence 77-79; Warden Bede Ho Staplehurst 79-81; Chapl HM Det Cen Blantyre Ho 81-82; R Edith Weston w N Luffenham and Lyndon w Manton *Pet* from 86. *The Rectory, 8 Church Lane, Edith Weston, Oakham, Leics LE15 8EY* Stamford (0780) 720931

BLACKBURN, David James. b 45. Hull Univ BA67. Trin Coll Bris DipHE87. **d** 87 **p** 88. C Bromsgrove St Jo *Worc* 87-90; V Cradley from 90. *34 Beecher Road, Halesowen, W Midlands B63 2DJ* Cradley Heath (0384) 66928

BLACKBURN, Canon Donald. b 02. OBE. St Jo Coll Dur BA30 MA33. Wycliffe Hall Ox 30. **d** 31 **p** 32. P-in-c Steventon *Ox* 68-71; rtd 71. *Maes y Llan, Llanfechain, Powys SY22 6UU*

BLACKBURN, Frederick John Barrie. b 28. TD73. Lich Th Coll 52. **d** 55 **p** 56. CF (TA) 61-87; V Eighton Banks *Dur* 64-75; R Stella 75-87; TV Bellingham/Otterburn Gp *Newc* 87-89; rtd 89. *47 Coldstream Road, Newcastle upon Tyne NE15 7BY* 091-274 7851

BLACKBURN, John. b 47. Univ of Wales (Cardiff) DipTh69 DPS71 Open Univ BA88. St Mich Coll Llan 66. **d** 71 **p** 72. C Risca *Mon* 71-76; CF (TA) 73-76; CF from 76. *c/o MOD (Army), Bagshot Park, Bagshot, Surrey GU19 5PL* Bagshot (0276) 71717

BLACKBURN, Keith Christopher. b 39. K Coll Lon BD63 AKC63. **d** 64 **p** 65. C Surbiton St Andr *S'wark* 64-66; C Battersea St Mary 67-70; Teacher Sir Walter St Jo Sch Battersea 67-70; Hon C Eltham H Trin 70-76; Hd of Ho Crown Woods Sch Eltham 70-76; Dep Hd Master Altwood C of E Sch 76-82; Lic to Offic *Ox* 76-82; Hd Master St Geo Sch Gravesend from 83; Hon C Fawkham and Hartley *Roch* from 83. *31 Billings Hill Shaw, Hartley, Longfield, Dartford DA3 8EU* Longfield (04747) 5456

BLACKBURN, Peter James Whittaker. b 47. Sydney Univ BA69. Coll of Resurr Mirfield DipTh71. **d** 72 **p** 73. C Felixstowe St Jo *St E* 72-76; C Bournemouth St Pet w St Swithun, St Steph etc *Win* 76-79; R Burythorpe, Acklam and Leavening w Westow *York* 79-85; Chapl Naples Ch Ch *Eur* 85-91; Chapl Algarve from 91. *Casa Raquel, Boliqueime, 8100 Loule, Portugal* Loule (89) 366720

BLACKBURN, Richard Finn. b 52. St Jo Coll Dur BA74. Westcott Ho Cam 81. **d** 83 **p** 84. C Stepney St Dunstan and All SS *Lon* 83-87; P-in-c Isleworth St Jo from 87. *The Vicarage, St John's Road, Isleworth, Middx TW7 6NY* 081-560 4916

BLACKBURN, Archdeacon of. See ROBINSON, Ven William David

BLACKBURN, Bishop of. See CHESTERS, Rt Rev Alan David

BLACKBURN, Provost of. See JACKSON, Very Rev Lawrence

✠**BLACKBURNE, Rt Rev Hugh Charles.** b 12. Clare Coll Cam BA34 MA39. Westcott Ho Cam 36. **d** 37 **p** 38 **c** 77. C Almondbury *Wakef* 37-39; CF (R of O) 39-77; Chapl Clare Coll Cam 39-46; Chapl RMC 46-47; R Milton *Win* 47-53; Chapl to HM The Queen 61-77; R Hilborough w Bodney *Nor* 61-72; RD Swaffham 64-69; Hon Can Nor Cathl 65-80; Bp's Chapl Norfolk Broads 72-77; V Ranworth w Panxworth 72-77; Suff Bp Thetford 77-80; rtd 80; Perm to Offic Nor from 80; St E from 81. *39 Northgate, Beccles, Suffolk NR34 9AU* Beccles (0502) 716374

BLACKER, Herbert John. b 36. Bris Univ BSc59. Cranmer Hall Dur DipTh61. **d** 61 **p** 62. C Wednesbury St Bart *Lich* 61-63; C Chasetown 63-65; C Chigwell *Chelmsf* 65-69; TV Barnham Broom w Kimberley, Bixton etc *Nor* 69-76; R Burgh Parva w Briston from 76; P-in-c Melton Constable w Swanton Novers from 86. *The Vicarage, Briston, Melton Constable, Norfolk NR24 2LG* Melton Constable (0263) 860280

BLACKETT, James Gilbert. b 27. Tyndale Hall Bris 52. **d** 55 **p** 56. C Heworth H Trin *York* 55-57; C Newburn *Newc* 57-58; C Newc St Barn and St Jude 58-61; V Broomfleet *York* 61-67; V Ledsham 67-74; V Burton All SS *Lich* 74-82; V Burton All SS w Ch Ch from 82. *242 Blackpool Street, Burton-on-Trent, Staffs DE14 3AU* Burton-on-Trent (0283) 65134

BLACKFORD, David Walker. b 25. Univ of Wales DipTh69. **d** 70 **p** 71. C Holyhead w Rhoscolyn w Llanfair-yn-Neubwll *Ban* 70-72; Lic to Offic *Blackb* 72-80; Hon C Bassaleg *Mon* 80-85; V Treuddyn and Nercwys and Erryrys *St As* 85-90; rtd 90. *11 White Chapel Walk, Magor, Gwent* Magor (0633) 880507

BLACKIE, Richard Footner (Brother Edmund). b 37. St Cath Coll Cam BA59 MA63 Worc Coll Ox BA59 BSc61. Ely Th Coll 60. **d** 62 **p** 63. C Saffron Walden *Chelmsf* 62-65; SSF from 66. *14/15 Botolph Lane, Cambridge CB2 3RD* Cambridge (0223) 353903

BLACKLAWS, Frederick William. d 90. NSM Dioc Hosp Chapl Team *Ab* from 90. *24 Dalvenie Road, Banchory AB3 3UX* Banchory (03302) 2588

BLACKMAN, Brian David Eric. b 38. Ox NSM Course 82. **d** 85 **p** 86. NSM Reading St Luke *Ox* 85-86; NSM Reading St Luke w St Bart from 86. *138 St Saviour's Road, Reading, Berkshire RG1 6ET* Reading (0734) 572232

BLACKMAN, Clive John. b 51. Hull Univ BSc73 MSc74 Birm Univ DipTh77. Qu Coll Birm 75. **d** 78 **p** 79. C Folkestone St Sav *Cant* 78-81; Chapl Birm Univ *Birm* 81-86; V Thorpe St Matt *Nor* from 86. *St Matthew's Vicarage, Albert Place, Norwich NR1 4JR* Norwich (0603) 20820

BLACKMAN, James Bentley. b 57. SS Hild & Bede Coll Dur BEd80 Nottm Univ BTh88. Linc Th Coll 85. **d** 88 **p** 89. C Nether Hoyland St Pet *Sheff* 88-91; C Harrogate St Wilfrid and St Luke *Ripon* from 91. *7 Lindrick Way, Harrogate HG3 2SU* Harrogate (0423) 508128

BLACKMAN, John Franklyn. b 34. LRAM70 DipRS75. S'wark Ord Course 72. **d** 75 **p** 76. NSM Cov H Trin *Cov* 75-81; Succ Cov Cathl from 81; TV Cov E from 88. *St Margaret's Vicarage, 18 South Avenue, Coventry CV2 4DR* Coventry (0203) 457344

BLACKMAN, Michael Orville. b 46. Univ of W Ontario BMin80 Univ of W Indies LTh70. Codrington Coll Barbados 67. **d** 71 **p** 71. Antigua 71-73; Barbados 73-78 and 80-86 and from 91; Canada 78-80; TV E Ham w Upton Park *Chelmsf* 86-91. *The Rectory, St Peter's Church, Barbados* Barbados (1809) 422-2181

BLACKMAN, Peter Richard. b 28. Sarum Th Coll 52. **d** 55 **p** 56. C Aylestone *Leic* 55-60; V Ratby w Groby 60-84; TR from 84. *The Rectory, 15 Groby Road, Ratby, Leicester LE6 0LJ* Leicester (0533) 393009

BLACKMORE, Cuthbert. b 17. Qu Coll Birm 57. **d** 59 **p** 60. V Seamer w E Ayton *York* 66-83; rtd 84. *The Little Portion, Wrench Green, Hackness, Scarborough, N Yorkshire* Scarborough (0723) 882331

BLACKMORE, Frank Ellis. b 43. Univ of Wales (Lamp) BA66. Wells Th Coll 65. **d** 67 **p** 68. C S'wark St Geo S'wark 67-70; Hon C Camberwell St Giles 70-79; NSM Paddington St Sav *Lon* from 79. *65 Sutherland Avenue, London W9 2HS* 071-289 3020

BLACKMORE, Robert Ivor. b 37. Univ of Wales (Lamp) 59 Open Univ BA78. **d** 62 **p** 63. C Llangynwyd w Maesteg *Llan* 62-65; C Dowlais 65-67; C Neath w Llantwit 67-71; V Pontlottyn 71-73; V Troedrhiwgarth 73-80; V Seven Sisters from 80. *The Vicarage, Seven Sisters, Neath, W Glam SA10 9DT* Seven Sisters (0639) 700286

BLACKMORE, Vernon John. b 50. Southn Univ BSc Man Univ MSc Lon Univ DipTh K Coll Lon MTh. Oak Hill Th Coll DipHE. **d** 82 **p** 83. C Ecclesall *Sheff* 82-87; Bp's Adv on Youth 85-87; Ed Lion Publishing 87-90; Dir Par Resources CPAS from 90. *48 Stephen Street, Rugby CV21 2ES* Rugby (0788) 560404

BLACKSHAW, Alfred. b 14. St Jo Coll Dur BA39 DipTh40 MA42. **d** 40 **p** 41. V Chesham Ch Ch *Ox* 66-72; V Copp *Blackb* 72-79; rtd 79; Perm to Offic *Blackb* from 79. *Apartment 19, Croft House, Derby Road, Poulton-le-Fylde, Blackpool FY6 7AH* Poulton-le-Fylde (0253) 891989

BLACKSHAW, Brian Martin. b 43. Lanc Univ MA74. Ox NSM Course 87. **d** 90. NSM Amersham *Ox* from 90. *De Fontenay, Hyde Heath, Amersham, Bucks HP6 5SG* Chesham (0494) 783564

BLACKSHAW, Trevor Roland. b 36. GIMechE. Lon Coll of Div 67. **d** 69 **p** 70. C New Catton St Luke *Nor* 69-73; C Luton Lewsey St Hugh *St Alb* 73-78; V Llandinam w Trefeglwys w Penstrowed *Ban* 78-85; Youth Chapl 82-93; Dioc Dir of Adult Educn 84-85; Perm to Offic St As from 86; Lich from 87. *Cambrian House, Nantmawr, Oswestry, Shropshire SY10 9HL*

BLACKTOP, Graham Leonard. b 33. St Alb Minl Tr Scheme. **d** 85 **p** 86. NSM Rickmansworth *St Alb* from 85. *52 Shepherd's Way, Rickmansworth, Herts WD3 2NL* Rickmansworth (0923) 772022

BLACKWALL, David D'Arcy Russell. b 35. Southn Univ BSc60 Imp Coll Lon DIC62. Wycliffe Hall Ox 63. **d** 65 **p** 66. C Southn Thornhill St Chris *Win* 65-68; V Long Sutton 69-72; Chapl Ld Wandsworth Coll Long Sutton 69-74; Hon C Odiham w S Warnborough *Win* 72-75; Chapl St Lawr Coll Ramsgate from 75. *Kerrison Cottage, Felderland Lane, Worth, Deal, Kent CT14 0BN* Sandwich (0304) 617708

BLACKWELL, Geoffrey Albert. b 27. Lon Coll of Div 62. **d** 65 **p** 66. Chapl RN 69-73; Warden St Mich Home of Healing Cleadon 73-75; V S Hetton *Dur* 75-82; rtd 82; CSWG from 89. *The Monastery, Crawley Down, Crawley, W Sussex RH10 4LH* Copthorne (0342) 712074

BLACKWELL, Geoffrey David. b 34. Jes Coll Ox BA57 MA61. Chich Th Coll 57. **d** 59 **p** 60. C Romford St Edw *Chelmsf* 59-62; S Africa 62-68; Chapl Westcott Ho Cam 68-73; V Forest Gate St Edm *Chelmsf* 73-81; Pilsdon Community from 83; Perm to Offic *Sarum* from 83. *Pilsdon Community, Pilsdon, Bridport, Dorset DT6 5NZ* Broadwindsor (0308) 68308

BLACKWELL, Nicholas Alfred John. b 54. St Jo Coll Nottm BTh85. **d** 85 **p** 86. C Birkenhead Priory *Ches* 85-88; C Stratford w Bishopton *Cov* 88-91; TV Cov E from 91. *St Anne's Vicarage, 129A London Road, Coventry CV1 2JQ* Coventry (0203) 223381

BLACKWELL-SMYTH, Dr Charles Peter Bernard. b 42. TCD BA64 MA71 MB73. Gen Th Sem (NY) MDiv65. **d** 65 **p** 66. C Ban Abbey *D & D* 65-67; C Dub Ch Ch Leeson Park *D & G* 67-69; P-in-c Carbury *M & K* 73-75; Hon C St Stephen in Brannel *Truro* from 87. *Parcgwyn, Rectory Road, St Stephen, St Austell, Cornwall PL26 7RL* St Austell (0726) 822465

BLACOE, Brian Thomas. b 36. Oak Hill Th Coll 63. **d** 66 **p** 67. C Dundonald *D & D* 66-69; C Drumcree *Arm* 69-74; I Ardtrea w Desertcreat 74-78; I Annalong *D & D* from 78. *173 Kilkeel Road, Annalong, Newry, Co Down BT34 4TN* Annalong (03967) 68246

BLADE, Brian Alan. b 24. ACCS55 ASCA66. Roch Th Coll 67. **d** 69 **p** 70. C Barnehurst *Roch* 69-71; C Crayford 71-76; V Buttershaw St Aid *Bradf* 76-80; R Etton w Helpston *Pet* 80-86; V Hardingstone and Horton and Piddington 86-90; rtd 90. *25 Dan Drive, The Chestnuts, Faversham, Kent ME13 7SW* Faversham (0795) 531842

BLADES, Canon Joseph Henry. b 13. St Chad's Coll Dur BA34 DipTh35 MA37. **d** 36 **p** 37. Hon Can Derby Cathl *Derby* 67-82; V Darley Abbey 68-82; rtd 82; Perm to Offic *Derby* from 82. *105 Cavendish Court, Willow Row, Derby DE1 1UB* Derby (0332) 383185

BLADON, Ernest Albert. b 19. Ex Univ DipEd58. Glouc Sch of Min 75. **d** 78 **p** 78. Hon C Cinderford St Jo *Glouc* 78-89; rtd 89; Perm to Offic *Glouc* from 89. *Valista, Grange Road, Littledean, Cinderford, Glos GL14 3NJ* Dean (0594) 822702

BLAGDON-GAMLEN, Peter Eugene. b 20. KLJ. AKC48. St Boniface Warminster 48. **d** 49 **p** 50. CF (R of O) 59-75; R & V Eastchurch *Cant* 68-71; R & V Eastchurch w Leysdown and Harty 71-87; CF (TA) 78-85; rtd 87; Perm to Offic *Ex* from 87. *Blagdon House, 73 New Street, Great Torrington, Devon EX38 8BT* Torrington (0805) 24472

BLAGG, Colin. b 31. Leeds Univ BA57. Coll of Resurr Mirfield 57. **d** 59 **p** 60. C Edin Old St Paul *Edin* 59-63; R Gourock *Glas* 63-68; Chapl to the Deaf RADD Lon 68-74; Hon C Stoke Newington St Olave *Lon* 73-74; Chapl to the Deaf *Chich* 74-80; V Shoreham Beach from 80. *The Vicarage, West Beach, Shoreham-by-Sea BN43 5LF* Shoreham-by-Sea (0273) 453768

BLAIN, Michael Winston. b 44. Cant Univ (NZ) BA65 MA66. Coll of Resurr Mirfield 66. **d** 67 **p** 68. C Goldthorpe *Sheff* 67-70; New Zealand 70-87; Zimbabwe from 87. *PO Box 119, Guruve, Zimbabwe*

BLAIR, John Wallace. b 48. Lon Univ BSc70. Qu Coll Birm 79. **d** 81 **p** 82. C Chorlton-cum-Hardy St Werburgh *Man* 81-83; CF from 83. *c/o MOD (Army), Bagshot Park, Bagshot, Surrey GU19 5PL* Bagshot (0276) 71717

BLAIR, Patrick Allen. b 31. Trin Coll Cam BA54 MA. Ridley Hall Cam 54. **d** 56 **p** 57. C Harwell *Ox* 56-59; Chapl Oundle Sch *Pet* 59-64; Jerusalem 64-66; Sudan 67-71; Provost Khartoum 67-71; R Ches le Street *Dur* 71-77; Chapl Barking Hosp 77-87; TR Barking St Marg w St Patr *Chelmsf* 77-87; Tunisia from 87. *5 rue Ahmed Beyrem, 1006 Tunis Bab Sovika, Tunisia* Tunis (1) 243648

BLAIR, Philip Hugh. b 39. St Edm Hall Ox BA62 MA67. Ridley Hall Cam 62. **d** 64 **p** 65. C Camborne *Truro* 64-68; C Kenwyn 68-70; Sudan 70-73 and from 78; P-in-c St Enoder *Truro* 73-76; Tutor Ex Univ *Ex* 76-77. *PO Box 322, Khartoum, Sudan*

BLAIR-BROWN, Dennis. b 17. LTh. Em Coll Saskatoon 52. **d** 56 **p** 56. Canada 56-63; C Lymington *Win* 63-70; V Wellow from 70. *The Vicarage, Church Lane, East Wellow, Romsey, Hants SO5 6DR* West Wellow (0794) 22295

BLAIR-FISH, Canon John Christopher. b 20. Linc Coll Ox BA46 MA47. Cuddesdon Coll 48. **d** 49 **p** 50. V Surbiton St Mark *S'wark* 55-72; R Chipstead 73-89; Hon

Can S'wark Cathl 79-88; rtd 89. *39 Beehive Lane, Ferring, Worthing, W Sussex BN12 5NR* Worthing (0903) 41480

BLAKE, Colin David. b 52. CertEd BEd BD. Trin Coll Bris 81. **d** 84 **p** 85. C Hucclecote *Glouc* 84-88; C Patchway *Bris* from 88. *106 Cooks Close, Bradley Stoke, Bristol BS12 0BB* Almondsbury (0454) 617569

BLAKE, Derek Gordon. b 10. St Jo Coll Dur 32. **d** 36 **p** 37. V Holme Cultram St Cuth *Carl* 69-88; P-in-c Allonby 77-81; rtd 89; Perm to Offic *Carl* from 89. *The Mount, Moor Road, Great Broughton, Cockermouth, Cumbria CA13 0YT* Cockermouth (0900) 827483

BLAKE, Ian Martyn. b 57. BA79. Oak Hill Th Coll 76. **d** 80 **p** 81. C Widford *Chelmsf* 80-84; C Barton Seagrave w Warkton *Pet* 84-90; V Sneinton St Chris w St Phil *S'well* from 90. *St Christopher's Vicarage, 180 Sneinton Boulevard, Nottingham NG2 4GL* Nottingham (0602) 505303

BLAKE, Jonathan Clive. b 56. St Jo Coll Dur BA78. St Jo Coll Nottm 79. **d** 81 **p** 82. C Allerton *Bradf* 81-84, C Wyke 84-85; C Roch 85-88; V Barnehurst from 88; Member World Conf Relig & Peace from 89. *The Vicarage, 93 Pelham Road, Barnehurst, Bexleyheath, Kent DA7 4LY* Crayford (0322) 523344

BLAKE, Preb Patrick John. b 30. Univ of Wales BA51 St Edm Hall Ox BA54 MA58. St Mich Coll Llan 54. **d** 55 **p** 56. C Buckley *St As* 55-59; C Oystermouth *S & B* 59-63; V Cleeve *B & W* 63-71; R Bruton w Lamyatt, Wyke and Redlynch 71-83; Dioc Ecum Officer 79-84; Preb Wells Cathl from 79; TR Yeovil 83-88; R Yeovil w Kingston Pitney 88; P-in-c Backwell 88-89; R from 89. *The Rectory, 72 Church Lane, Backwell, Bristol BS19 3JJ* Flax Bourton (027583) 2391

BLAKE, Peta Ruth. b 44. Episc Div Sch Cam Mass STh89 MA90 Trin Coll Bris 82. **dss** 83 **d** 87. New Swindon St Barn Gorse Hill *Bris* 83-87; Par Dn 87-88; Perm to Offic from 88. *The Vicarage, Purton, Swindon SN5 9DS* Swindon (0793) 770210

BLAKE, Canon Peter Douglas Stuart. b 27. BNC Ox BA52 MA57. Westcott Ho Cam 52. **d** 54 **p** 55. V Leek St Edw *Lich* 70-76; P-in-c Hartfield *Chich* 76-78; R Hartfield w Coleman's Hatch 78-87; rtd 87; P-in-c Breamore *Win* 89-90. *Oakleigh, Stedham, Midhurst, W Sussex GU29 0NZ* Midhurst (073081) 2277

BLAKE, Philip Charles. b 29. FAIW88 MACC88 Lon Univ DipTh57 Mitchell Coll (USA) BA80 Macquarie Univ (NSW) MA86. Melbourne Coll of Div DipRE76 DPS80 Oak Hill Th Coll 54. **d** 57 **p** 58. C Slough *Ox* 57-60; C Uphill *B & W* 60-62; V Branston *Lich* 62-69; Australia from 69. *11 Montgomery Road, Carlingford, NSW, Australia 2118* Sydney (2) 261-9539

BLAKE, Richard Arthur (Brother Francis). b 12. Lon Univ BSc33. Bps' Coll Cheshunt 33. **d** 35 **p** 36. CR from 46; S Africa 49-80; Zimbabwe from 80; rtd 82. *House of the Resurrection, Mirfield, W Yorkshire WF14 0BN* Mirfield (0924) 494318

BLAKE, Canon Roy Harold David. b 25. Chich Th Coll 54. **d** 57 **p** 58. C Westbury-on-Trym H Trin *Bris* 57-61; C Bishopston 61-65; V Bris St Agnes w St Simon 65-72; TR Bris St Agnes and St Simon w St Werburgh 72-74; RD Bris City 73-74; V Purton from 74; RD Cricklade 76-82; Hon Can Bris Cathl from 77. *The Vicarage, 4 Church Street, Purton, Swindon SN5 9DS* Swindon (0793) 770210

BLAKE, William Cornford. b 18. Ripon Hall Ox. **d** 67 **p** 68. C Putney St Mary *S'wark* 67-73; C Diss *Nor* 73-76; C Roydon St Remigius 73-76; P-in-c 76-79; R 79-85; rtd 85; Perm to Offic *Derby* from 85. *4 Farnway, Darley Abbey, Derby DE3 2BN* Derby (0332) 550431

BLAKELEY, Julian Graham. b 60. Oak Hill Th Coll BA88. **d** 88 **p** 89. C Bedworth *Cov* 88-91; C Harlow St Mary V *Chelmsf* from 91. *134 East Park, Harlow, Essex CM17 0SR* Harlow (0279) 427357

BLAKELEY, Robert Daniel. b 29. Saskatchewan Univ BA63 St Pet Coll Ox BA67 MA70. Em Coll Saskatchewan LTh56. **d** 56 **p** 57. Canada 56-59; USA 59-68 and 71-75; C High Wycombe *Ox* 68-70; C St Marylebone St Mary *Lon* 75-82; P-in-c Tasburgh *Nor* 82-85; P-in-c Tharston 82-85; P-in-c Forncett St Mary w St Pet 82-85; P-in-c Flordon 82-85; Chapl Hill Ho Sch Knightsbridge from 85. *Hill House Prep School, Hans Place, London SW1* 071-584 1331

BLAKEMAN, Mrs Janet Mary. b 36. Man Univ BA57 CertEd58. Carl Dioc Tr Course 87. **d** 90. NSM Brampton Deanery from 90. *Langstrath, Greenfield Lane, Brampton, Cumbria CA8 1AU* Brampton (06977) 2008

BLAKEMAN, Walter John. b 37. Qu Coll Birm 74. **d** 76 **p** 77. C Gnosall *Lich* 76-83; C Cheadle 83-86; Res Min

Hednesford 86-90; Min Roundshaw LEP *S'wark* from 90. *32 Waterer Rise, Wallington, Surrey SM6 9DN* 081-773 2842

BLAKESLEY, John. b 50. Keble Coll Ox BA72 MA76. St Steph Ho Ox 72. **d** 74 **p** 75. C Egremont *Carl* 74-77; C Doncaster Ch Ch *Sheff* 77-79; V Auckland St Helen *Dur* from 79; Lect Th Dur Univ from 91. *The Vicarage, 8 Manor Road, Bishop Auckland, Co Durham DL14 9EN* Bishop Auckland (0388) 604152

BLAKEWAY-PHILLIPS, Richard John. b 19. St Chad's Coll Dur BA43. **d** 43 **p** 44. V Arrington *Ely* 69-77; R Orwell 69-77; R Wimpole 69-77; P-in-c Gt w Lt Abington 77-86; P-in-c Hildersham 77-86; rtd 86; Perm to Offic *Heref* from 86. *Church Cottage, Clun, Craven Arms, Shropshire SY7 8JW* Clun (05884) 494

BLAKEY, Cedric Lambert. b 54. Fitzw Coll Cam BA76 MA80. St Jo Coll Nottm 77. **d** 79 **p** 80. C Cotmanhay *Derby* 79-83; C-in-c Blagreaves St Andr CD 83-89; P-in-c Sinfin Moor 84-89; V Heanor from 89. *The Vicarage, 1A Mundy Street, Heanor, Derbyshire DE7 7EB* Langley Mill (0773) 719800

BLAKEY, William George. b 51. Southn Univ BSc72 PGCE73. Oak Hill Th Coll BA82. **d** 82 **p** 83. C Cheltenham St Mark *Glouc* 82-85; P-in-c Parkham, Alwington, Buckland Brewer etc *Ex* 85-86; R from 86; RD Hartland from 89. *The Rectory, Parkham, Bideford, Devon EX39 5PL* Horns Cross (0237) 451204

BLAKISTON, Patrick. b 14. Magd Coll Cam BA36 MA42. Linc Th Coll 36. **d** 39 **p** 40. V Whittingham *Newc* 68-79; rtd 80. *Jasmine Cottage, 97 Monkton Deverill, Warminster, Wilts BA12 7EU* Maiden Bradley (09853) 282

BLAMIRE-BROWN, Charles Richard. b 21. St Cath Soc Ox BA49 MA53. Cuddesdon Coll 49. **d** 51 **p** 52. R Tewin *St Alb* 67-75; RD Hatf 71-75; V Chipperfield St Paul 75-86; rtd 86; Perm to Offic *Cov* from 87. *7 Willoughby Avenue, Kenilworth, Warks CV8 1DG* Kenilworth (0926) 50808

BLAMIRES, Canon Norman. b 11. Linc Coll Ox BA34 MA37. Ely Th Coll 34. **d** 35 **p** 36. CR from 66; Barbados 66-69; rtd 81. *House of the Resurrection, Mirfield, W Yorkshire WF14 0BN* Mirfield (0924) 494318

✠**BLANCH of Bishopthorpe, Most Rev and Rt Hon Lord (Stuart Yarworth).** b 18. PC75. St Cath Soc Ox BA48 MA52 Liv Univ Hon LLD75 Hull Univ Hon DD77. Wycliffe Hall Ox 46. **d** 49 **p** 50 **c** 66. C Highfield *Ox* 49-52; V Eynsham 52-57; Vice-Prin Wycliffe Hall Ox 57-60; Warden Roch Th Coll 60-66; Can Res Roch Cathl *Roch* 60-66; Bp Liv 66-75; ChStJ from 74; Abp York 75-83; rtd 83. *Bryn Celyn, The Level, Shenington, Banbury, Oxon OX15 6NA*

BLANCH, Paul Frederick. b 56. Chich Th Coll. **d** 86 **p** 87. C Chaddesden St Phil *Derby* 86-88; C Auckland St Andr and St Anne *Dur* 88-91; P-in-c Hunwick from 91. *The Vicarage, Hunwick, Crook, Co Durham DL15 0JU* Bishop Auckland (0388) 604456

BLANCHARD, Christopher John. b 46. Univ of Wales (Lamp) BA70. St Mich Coll Llan 86. **d** 79 **p** 80. NSM Chepstow *Mon* 79-81; NSM Itton and St Arvans w Penterry and Kilgwrrwg etc 81-86; C Ebbw Vale 87-88; R 88-89; V Llangenny and Llanbedr Ystradyw w Patricio *S & B* from 89. *The Rectory, Llangenni, Crickhowell, Powys NP8 1HD* Crickhowell (0873) 810348

BLANCHARD, Ernest Desmond. b 26. St Jo Coll Dur BA55 DipTh56. **d** 56 **p** 57. C Bedlington *Newc* 56-60; R Salford St Bart *Man* 60-66; V Ashton Ch Ch 66-83; RD Ashton-under-Lyne 74-83; Hon Can Man Cathl 78-83; V Kettlewell w Conistone and Hubberholme *Bradf* 83-84; P-in-c Arncliffe w Halton Gill 83-84; V Kettlewell w Conistone, Hubberholme etc from 84. *The Vicarage, Kettlewell, Skipton, N Yorkshire BD23 5QU* Kettlewell (075676) 237

BLANCHARD, Frank Hugh. b 30. St Jo Coll Dur BA54 DipTh55 MA62. **d** 55 **p** 56. C Bottesford *Linc* 55-58; CMS 58-65; C Kirby Grindalythe *York* 65-67; V 67-71; C N Grimston w Wharram Percy and Wharram-le-Street 65-67; V 67-71; P-in-c Thorpe Bassett 67-71; P-in-c Settrington 67-68; V Scarborough St Jas 71-79; P-in-c Scarborough H Trin 78-79; V Scarborough St Jas and H Trin 79-86; R Stockton-on-the-Forest w Holtby and Warthill from 87. *The Rectory, Sandy Lane, Stockton on the Forest, York* York (0904) 400337

BLANCHARD, Ms Jean Ann. b 43. St Alb Minl Tr Scheme 79. **dss** 85 **d** 87. Mill End and Heronsgate w W Hyde *St Alb* 85-87; Hon Par Dn from 87. *10 Longlees, Maple Cross, Rickmansworth, Herts WD3 2UQ* Rickmansworth (0923) 778801

BLANCHARD, Canon Lawrence Gordon. b 36. Edin Univ MA60. Linc Th Coll 63. **d** 65 **p** 66. C Woodhouse *Wakef* 65-67; C Cannock *Lich* 67-70; Swaziland 70-76; TV Raveningham *Nor* 76-80; V Ancaster *Linc* 80-87; Dir LNSM Linc 80-87; Hon Can Linc Cathl from 85; Dir of Tr CA from 88. *Church Army, Independents Road, London SE3 9LG* 081-318 1226

BLANCHETT, John Eric. b 08. Qu Coll Cam BA31 MA38. Ridley Hall Cam 31. **d** 32 **p** 33. RD Chalke *Sarum* 69-74; R Fovant w Compton Chamberlayne etc 72-74; rtd 74; Perm to Offic *Cant* from 74. *2 Hayden Avenue, Purley, Surrey CR2 4AE*

BLAND, Albert Edward. b 14. St Mich Coll Llan. **d** 62 **p** 63. V Feniscowles *Blackb* 67-84; rtd 85; Perm to Offic *Blackb* from 85. *30 Woodlands Avenue, Blackburn BB2 5NN* Blackburn (0254) 202667

BLAND, Jean Elspeth. b 42. K Coll Lon BA63. Glouc Sch of Min 87. **d** 90. Par Dn Cen Telford *Lich* from 90. *9 Chiltern Gardens, Dawley, Telford, Shropshire TF4 2QG* Telford (0952) 504999

BLAND, Thomas. b 12. Clifton Th Coll 39. **d** 42 **p** 43. R Stratford w Bishopton *Cov* 63-69; rtd 77. *1 Costard Avenue, Shipston-on-Stour, Warks CV36 4HW*

BLANDFORD, Robert Holmes. b 07. ALCD38. **d** 38 **p** 39. V Budbrooke *Cov* 64-73; rtd 73. *4 St Davids Road, Tavistock, Devon PL19 9AN* Tavistock (0822) 615120

BLANEY, Laurence. b 41. Lon Univ DipTh69 Open Univ BA85 Essex Univ MA88. Oak Hill Th Coll 66. **d** 69 **p** 70. C Leyton St Mary w St Edw *Chelmsf* 69-73; P-in-c Wimbish w Thunderley 73-77; P-in-c Steeple 77-82; P-in-c Mayland 77-82; R Pitsea from 82. *The Rectory, Rectory Road, Basildon, Essex SS13 2AA* Basildon (0268) 553240

BLANKENSHIP, Charles Everett. b 42. Santa Clara Univ BA64. Cuddesdon Coll 71. **d** 74 **p** 75. C Catford (Southend) and Downham *S'wark* 74-78; P-in-c Battersea St Phil w St Bart 78-83; V 83-85; TV Wimbledon from 85. *St Matthew's House, 61 Melbury Gardens, London SW20 0DL* 081-946 0092

BLANKLEY, Roger Henry. b 32. ARICS60. Clifton Th Coll 62. **d** 66 **p** 67. C Peckham St Mary Magd *S'wark* 66-69; SAMS 70-74; Brazil 74-80; R Gillingham w Geldeston, Stockton, Ellingham etc *Nor* from 80. *The Rectory, The Street, Geldeston, Beccles, Suffolk NR34 0LN* Beccles (0502) 712255

BLANT, Edgar. b 18. St Chad's Coll Dur BA47 DipTh48. **d** 48 **p** 49. Antigua 55-85; St Kitts-Nevis 60-85; Adn St Kitts 78-85; rtd 86; Perm to Offic *Lich* from 86. *326 Sandon Road, Stoke-on-Trent ST3 7EB* Blythe Bridge (0782) 398300

BLATCHLY, Owen Ronald Maxwell. b 30. Bps' Coll Cheshunt 62. **d** 64 **p** 65. C Boxmoor St Jo *St Alb* 64-67; C Boreham Wood All SS 67-69; C Frimley *Guildf* 69-77; V Manaccan w St Anthony-in-Meneage *Truro* 77-82; R Binfield *Ox* from 82. *The Rectory, Terrace Road North, Bracknell, Berks RG12 5JG* Bracknell (0344) 54406

BLATHWAYT, Canon Linley Dennys. b 16. Qu Coll Cam BA38 MA44. Wells Th Coll 38. **d** 40 **p** 41. R Gussage St Michael and Gussage All Saints *Sarum* 69-71; R Corscombe 71-75; P-in-c Frome St Quintin w Evershot and Melbury Bubb 71-75; R Evershot, Frome St Quinton, Melbury Bubb etc 75-79; RD Beaminster 75-81; Can and Preb Sarum Cathl 79-81; TR Melbury 79-81; rtd 81. *50 Wentworth Park, Allendale, Hexham, Northd NE47 9DR* Hexham (0434) 683448

BLATHWAYT, Canon Wynter. b 18. St Pet Hall Ox BA40 MA44. Ripon Hall Ox 40. **d** 41 **p** 42. V Horning *Nor* 66-85; P-in-c Beeston St Laurence w Ashmanhaugh 78-85; Hon Can Nor Cathl 81-85; rtd 85; Perm to Offic *Nor* from 85. *155 Sir William Close, Aylsham, Norwich NR11 6AY* Aylsham (0263) 734502

BLAY, Ian. b 65. Man Univ BA88. Westcott Ho Cam 89. **d** 91. C Withington St Paul *Man* from 91. *5 Westbourne Grove, Withington, Manchester M20 8JA* 061-445 5498

BLEAKLEY, Melvyn Thomas. b 43. K Coll Lon BD66 AKC66. **d** 67 **p** 68. C Cross Heath *Lich* 67-70; TV High Wycombe *Ox* 70-77; Perm to Offic from 77. *294 Hughenden Road, High Wycombe, Bucks* High Wycombe (0494) 29315

BLEASE, Anthony. b 28. Southn Univ CQSW75. Wells Th Coll 67. **d** 68 **p** 69. C Bognor St Jo *Chich* 68-71; Perm to Offic 71-75; NSM Felpham w Middleton 75-80; Coun for Soc Resp *Win* 80-90; Perm to Offic 80-90; rtd 90; NSM Lymington *Win* from 90. *Bridge Cottage, Bridge Road, Lymington, Hants SO41 9BZ* Lymington (0590) 672526

BLEASE, John Thomas. b 19. Edin Th Coll 41. **d** 43 **p** 44. Chapl RN 47-74; rtd 74. *180 Manor Road North, Thames Ditton, Surrey KT7 0BQ* 081-398 5117

BLENCOE, Charles Dennis. b 17. Lon Univ BA38. Bps' Coll Cheshunt 38. **d** 41 **p** 42. C Sutton in Ashfield St Mary *S'well* 41-43; Chapl RAF 43-61; Canada from 61. *526 Bay View Place, Duncan, British Columbia, Canada, V9L 1M3*

BLENKIN, Hugh Linton. b 16. Trin Coll Cam BA39 MA43. Lambeth STh56 Westcott Ho Cam 39. **d** 40 **p** 41. Lect Sarum & Wells Th Coll 66-78; rtd 81. *31 Abbey Mews, Amesbury, Salisbury SP4 7EX* Amesbury (0980) 624813

BLENNERHASSETT, Canon Richard Noel Rowland. b 09. TCD BA33 MA52. **d** 33 **p** 34. I Timoleague *C, C & R* 69-73; rtd 72. *The Moorings, Fenit, Tralee, Co Kerry, Irish Republic* Tralee (66) 36198

BLENNERHASSETT, Canon Thomas Francis. b 15. TCD BA37 BD43 HDipEd56 MA68. **d** 39 **p** 40. I Howth *D & G* 58-90; Can Ch Ch Cathl Dub from 76; rtd 90; C Dalkey St Patr *D & G* from 90. *25 Bayside Square West, Sutton, Dublin 13, Irish Republic* Dublin (1) 323720

BLEWETT, Roy. b 32. BSc MPhil. Edin Th Coll. **d** 82 **p** 83. C Newc St Fran *Newc* 82-85; P-in-c Cornhill w Carham from 85; P-in-c Branxton from 85. *The Vicarage, Cornhill-on-Tweed, Northd TD12 4EQ* Coldstream (0890) 2105

BLIGH, Peter Alan. b 27. NE Ord Course 78. **d** 81 **p** 82. NSM Thornaby on Tees *York* 81; NSM Stockton *Dur* from 87. *52 Cambridge Road, Thornaby, Stockton-on-Tees, Cleveland TS17 6LR* Stockton-on-Tees (0642) 612700

BLIGH, Philip Hamilton. b 36. MInstP75 Lon Univ BSc57 PhD61 MEd79 St Cath Coll Ox BA63. S'wark Ord Course 86. **d** 88 **p** 89. C Abington *Pet* 88-90; V Bozeat w Easton Maudit from 90. *St Mary's Vicarage, 41 London Road, Bozeat, Wellingborough, Northants NN9 7LZ* Wellingborough (0933) 663216

BLINSTON, John. b 29. St Aug Coll Cant 56. **d** 56 **p** 57. V Harrogate St Luke *Ripon* 69-75; Lic to Offic from 77; C Padiham *Blackb* 90-91; rtd 91. *14 Ash Road, Harrogate, N Yorkshire HH2 8EG* Harrogate (0423) 870414

BLISS, Alfred Charles. b 22. Bps' Coll Cheshunt 45. **d** 46 **p** 47. V Battersea St Steph *S'wark* 57-67; rtd 67. *c/o Stafford, Sticklepath Hill, Barnstaple, Devon EX31 2BT*

BLISS, Allan Ernest Newport. b 29. K Coll Lon. **d** 54 **p** 57. C Sundon w Streatley *St Alb* 68-74; P-in-c Caldecote All SS 74-78; V 78-91; V Old Warden 81-91; rtd 91. *6 Jubilee Gardens, Biggleswade, Beds SG18 0JW* Biggleswade (0767) 313797

BLISS, David Charles. b 52. Aston Univ BSc75 Cranfield Inst of Tech MSc82. St Jo Coll Nottm 87. **d** 89 **p** 90. C Burntwood *Lich* from 89. *9 Derwent Grove, Burntwood, Walsall WS7 9JN* Burntwood (0543) 674324

BLISS, John Derek Clegg. b 40. Sarum Th Coll. **d** 68 **p** 69. C Wymondham *Nor* 68-73; V Easton 73-80; R Colton 73-80; USA from 80. *Box 1168, Madera, California 93637, USA*

BLISS, Canon Leslie John. b 12. K Coll Lon 48. **d** 49 **p** 50. V Sutton le Marsh *Linc* 70-79; Can and Preb Linc Cathl 74-79; rtd 80. *15 Mattock Crescent, Morecambe, Lancs LA4 6QT* Morecambe (0524) 419688

BLISS, Neil Humberstone. b 29. TCD BA54 MA59. Coll of Resurr Mirfield 55. **d** 57 **p** 58. C N Keyham *Ex* 57-60; Swaziland 61-65 and 68-80; S Africa 65-67; P-in-c Osmington w Poxwell *Sarum* 80-81; TV Preston w Sutton Poyntz and Osmington w Poxwell 81-84; V Ernesettle *Ex* 84-88; R S Tawton and Belstone from 88. *The Vicarage, South Tawton, Okehampton, Devon EX20 2LQ* Okehampton (0837) 840337

BLISS, Rupert Geoffrey. b 05. MIMechE27 K Coll Cam BA31 MA45. Ridley Hall Cam 32. **d** 50 **p** 50. P-in-c Melbury Abbas *Sarum* 66-73; rtd 73; Perm to Offic Sarum 73-81; S'wark 81-82; Lon 82-86; Glouc from 86. *13 Manormead, Tilford Road, Hindhead, Surrey GU26 6RA* Hindhead (0428) 607274

BLISSARD-BARNES, Christopher John. b 36. ARCO55 Linc Coll Ox BA61 MA64. Ridley Hall Cam 61. **d** 63 **p** 64. C Woking St Paul *Guildf* 63-67; C Orpington Ch Ch *Roch* 67-71; P-in-c Heref St Jas *Heref* 71-78; Chapl Heref Gen Hosp 71-78; R Hampreston *Sarum* 78-88; TR 88-89; RD Wimborne 80-85; P-in-c Hambledon *Guildf* from 89. *The Rectory, Hambledon, Godalming, Surrey GU8 4DR* Wormley (0428) 682753

BLOCK, Robert Allen. b 62. Univ of Wales (Lamp) BA84. Coll of Resurr Mirfield 86. **d** 88 **p** 89. C Hampton *Worc* from 88. *183 Pershore Road, Hampton, Evesham, Worcs WR11 6NB* Evesham (0386) 40380

BLOFELD, Thomas Guest. b 35. St D Coll Lamp BA59 Cranmer Hall Dur 59. **d** 62 **p** 63. C Ely 68-70; C Pemberton St Jo *Liv* 70-72; V Walton St Jo 72-74; V Barkisland w W Scammonden *Wakef* 74-80; V

Smallbridge *Man* 80-82; C Irlam 83-86; rtd 87. *River View, Morington Road, St Dogmaels, Cardigan, Dyfed*

BLOOD, David John. b 36. G&C Coll Cam BA60 MA64. Westcott Ho Cam 64. **d** 62 **p** 63. C Rushmere *St E* 62-66; C Harringay St Paul *Lon* 66-71; Lic to Offic 71-81. *33 Rosebery Gardens, London N8 8SH* 081-340 3312

BLOOD, Michael William. b 44. AKC67. **d** 69 **p** 70. C Moseley St Agnes *Birm* 69-75; V Cotteridge from 75. *27 Middleton Hall Road, Birmingham B30 1AB* 021-458 2815

BLOOD, Stephen John. b 28. Keble Coll Ox BA53 MA58. Coll of Resurr Mirfield 53. **d** 55 **p** 56. C Greenford H Cross *Lon* 55-58; C Forest Gate St Edm *Chelmsf* 58-61; C-in-c Ashford St Hilda CD *Lon* 61-73; V Ashford St Hilda from 73. *St Hilda's Vicarage, 8 Station Crescent, Ashford, Middx TW15 3HH* Ashford (0784) 54237

BLOOMFIELD, Gillian. b 38. Leeds Univ BA59. W Midl Minl Tr Course 84. **d** 87. Par Dn Highters Heath *Birm* 87-89; TM Chelmsley Wood from 89. *19 Silhill Hall Road, Solihull, W Midlands B91 1JX* 021-705 0145

BLOOMFIELD, Harry. b 29. Chich Th Coll 57. **d** 60 **p** 61. C Brighton St Mich *Chich* 60-64; C Wantage *Ox* 64-84; V Kennington from 84. *The Vicarage, Kennington, Oxford OX1 5PG* Oxford (0865) 735135

BLOOMFIELD, John Michael. b 35. Univ of Wales (Lamp) BA57. Sarum Th Coll 59. **d** 61 **p** 62. C Fordington *Sarum* 61-64; C Branksome St Aldhelm 64-66; Youth Chapl *Win* 66-69; R Win All SS w Chilcomb and Chesil 71-79; P-in-c Corsley *Sarum* 79-81; C Swanage and Studland 83-86; Chapl HM Pris Dorchester 87-89; C Dorchester *Sarum* 87-89; Chapl HM Pris The Verne from 89. *The Chaplain's Office, HM Prison, The Verne, Portland, Dorset DT5 1EG* Portland (0305) 820124

BLOOMFIELD, John Stephen. b 56. Southn Univ. Chich Th Coll 83. **d** 86 **p** 87. C Chich St Paul and St Pet *Chich* 86-89; TV Littlehampton and Wick from 89. *76 Arundel Road, Littlehampton, W Sussex BN17 7DF* Littlehampton (0903) 724311

BLOOMFIELD, Canon Peter Grayson. b 19. ACIS50 K Coll Lon BD60 AKC61. **d** 60 **p** 61. S Rhodesia 61-65; Rhodesia 65-78; Can Matabeleland 75-78; P-in-c Chideock *Sarum* 78-83; P-in-c Symondsbury 78-83; P-in-c Winterbourne Came w Whitcombe etc 83; Perm to Offic from 84; rtd 85. *Pilgrim's Rest, 62A Jestys Avenue, Weymouth, Dorset DT3 5NN* Upwey (0305) 813330

BLORE, John Francis. b 49. Jes Coll Ox BA72 MA76. Wycliffe Hall Ox 73. **d** 75 **p** 76. C Waltham Abbey *Chelmsf* 75-78; C E Ham St Geo 78-81; R Colchester St Mich Myland from 81; Chapl Oxley Parker Sch Colchester from 81. *Myland Rectory, Rectory Close, Colchester, Essex CO4 5DN* Colchester (0206) 853076

BLORE, Robert William. b 12. AKC39. **d** 39 **p** 40. V Thorpe Bay *Chelmsf* 56-79; rtd 79. *10 Victoria Close, Wivenhoe, Colchester CO7 9PL* Wivenhoe (0206) 824550

BLOUNT, Robin George. b 38. Lon Univ DipTh68. Lon Coll of Div 61 Wycliffe Hall Ox 67. **d** 68 **p** 69. C Bletchley *Ox* 68-71; C Washington *Dur* 71-74; TV Chelmsley Wood *Birm* 74-76; Ind Chapl *Worc* 76-89; AP Dudley St Jo 76-89; AP Dudley St Thos and St Luke 88-89; Ind Chapl (Eurotunnel Development) *Cant* from 89. *Rivendell, School Lane, Newington, Folkestone, Kent CT18 8AY* Folkestone (0303) 279222

BLOWERS, Canon Ralph Barrie. b 28. Fitzw Ho Cam BA50 MA61. Ridley Hall Cam 51. **d** 53 **p** 54. C Higher Openshaw *Man* 53-56; R Man Albert Memorial Ch 56-68; RD Cheetham 63-69; R Man Albert Memorial Ch w Newton Heath 68-69; V Normanton *Derby* from 69; RD Derby 74-79; RD Derby S 79-87; Hon Can Derby Cathl from 85. *The Vicarage, Browning Street, Normanton, Derby DE3 8DN* Derby (0332) 767483

BLOWS, Canon Derek Reeve. b 26. MSAnPsych75 Linc Coll Ox BA50 MA52. Cuddesdon Coll 50. **d** 52 **p** 53. C Cov St Mark *Cov* 52-56; Lic to Offic *Sarum* 57-58; Chapl Warlingham Park Hosp Croydon 58-65; V Purley St Mark Woodcote *S'wark* 65-70; Dir Past Care and Counselling 70-80; Dir Westmr Past Foundn from 80; Lic to Offic from 80; Ed SPCK from 80. *14 Woodcote Valley Road, Purley, Surrey CR8 3AL* 081-660 5788 or 071-937 6956

BLOXAM-ROSE, Simon Franklyn. b 61. Southn Univ BTh MA Hon FLCM88. Chich Th Coll 85. **d** 88 **p** 89. C Bassaleg *Mon* 88-89; Chapl Aldenham Sch Herts from 90; Perm to Offic *Ex* from 90. *The Chaplain's Lodge, Aldenham School, Elstree, Borehamwood, Herts WD6 3AJ* Radlett (0923) 853360

BLOXHAM, Oliver. b 27. Ely Th Coll 60. **d** 62 **p** 63. C Newc H Cross *Newc* 62-65; C Ponteland 65-69; V Dudley 69-79; P-in-c Balkwell 79-81; V from 81. *St Peter's*

Vicarage, The Quadrant, North Shields, Tyne & Wear NE29 7JA 091-257 0952

BLOY, Philip Penrose. b 19. Ox Univ MA49 Lanc Univ MA71. Wells Th Coll 49. **d** 51 **p** 53. N Rhodesia 60-64; Zambia 64-70; C-in-c Bris St Geo *Bris* 72-73; Chapl Gatwick Airport *Chich* 73-88; Can and Preb Chich Cathl from 86; rtd 89. *Greenholm, Marston Road, Sherborne, Dorset DT9 4BJ* Sherborne (0935) 812985

BLUNDELL, Canon Derek George. b 32. Tyndale Hall Bris 58. **d** 61 **p** 62. C Fazakerley Em *Liv* 61-64; C-in-c Bath Odd Down *B & W* 64-69; V 69-74; V Tulse Hill H Trin *S'wark* 74-81; Org and Admin African Pastor Fund from 81; Perm to Offic *Cov* from 81; Hon Can Mityana from 90. *12 Ibex Close, Coventry CV3 2FB* Coventry (0203) 448068

BLUNDEN, Miss Jacqueline Ann. b 63. Leic Univ BA86 SS Coll Cam BA(Theol)90. Ridley Hall Cam 88. **d** 91. Par Dn Bedf St Paul *St Alb* from 91. *54 The Grove, Bedford MK40 3JN* Bedford (0234) 218563

BLUNSUM, Charles Michael. b 28. ACIB51 MBIM86. **d** 74 **p** 75. C Stoke Bishop *Bris* 74-79; Chapl Brunel Manor Chr Cen Torquay from 79. *Brunel Manor, Watcombe Park, Torquay TQ1 4SF* Torquay (0803) 329333

BLUNT, Paul David. b 44. Lon Univ BSc65 Leeds Univ DipTh70. Coll of Resurr Mirfield 67. **d** 70 **p** 71. C Norbury St Steph *Cant* 70-73; Canada from 73. *1093 Chateau Crescent, Gloucester, Ontario, Canada, K1C 2C9*

BLYDE, Ian Hay. b 52. Liv Univ BSc74 Edin Univ BD80. Edin Th Coll 77. **d** 80 **p** 81. C Ainsdale *Liv* 80-83; Chapl Birkenhead Sch Merseyside 83-90; Perm to Offic *Ches* 83-90; V Over St Chad from 90. *The Vicarage, 1 Over Hall Drive, Over, Winsford, Cheshire CW7 1EY* Winsford (0606) 593222

BLYTH, Bryan Edward Perceval. b 22. Linc Coll Ox BA49 MA52. Wells Th Coll 48. **d** 50 **p** 51. Teacher Westwood Co Jun Sch 68-72; Dep Hd 72-87; Hon C Thundersley *Chelmsf* 80-84; rtd 87. *5 Deansleigh Close, Preston, Weymouth, Dorset DT3 6QQ* Preston (0305) 834594

BLYTH, Canon Drummond Gwyn. b 26. K Coll Lon 53. **d** 54 **p** 55. R Carlton Colville *Nor* 62-70; V Stalham w Brunstead 70-77; P-in-c E Ruston 76-77; RD Waxham 77-89; V Stalham and E Ruston w Brunstead 77-91; Hon Can Nor Cathl 87-91; rtd 91; Perm to Offic *Nor* from 91. *15 Cliff Road, Overstrand, Cromer, Norfolk NR27 0PP* Overstrand (026378) 724

BLYTH, John Reddie. b 25. Wadh Coll Ox BA48 MA50. Ridley Hall Cam 48. **d** 50 **p** 51. Area Sec (E Midl) CPAS 63-70; V Parkstone St Luke *Sarum* 70-90; Chapl Uplands Sch Parkstone 70-73; rtd 90. *5 Powell Road, Newick, E Sussex BN8 4LS* Newick (082572) 2011

BLYTH, John Stuart. b 36. Lon Univ BD64 DipTh. Lich Th Coll 63. **d** 65 **p** 66. C Knowle St Barn *Bris* 65-68; C Whitchurch *B & W* 68-70; P-in-c Sutton St Nicholas w Sutton St Michael *Heref* 70-73; Dioc RE Adv 70-73; Chapl RAF 73-77; C-in-c Launton *Ox* 77-79; TV Bicester w Bucknell, Caversfield and Launton 79-84; P-in-c Hanborough 84-86; R Hanborough and Freeland 86-89. *12 Green Ridges, Oxford OX3 9PL*

BLYTH, Kenneth Henry. b 35. Lon Univ DipTh60. Oak Hill Th Coll 58. **d** 61 **p** 62. C St Alb St Paul *St Alb* 61-65; P-in-c Aspenden and Layston w Buntingford 65-66; R 66-72; R Washfield, Stoodleigh, Withleigh etc *Ex* 72-82; P-in-c Cruwys Morchard 72-74; RD Tiverton 76-82; V Eastbourne H Trin *Chich* from 82. *Holy Trinity Vicarage, Trinity Trees, Eastbourne, E Sussex BN21 3BE* Eastbourne (0323) 29046

BLYTH, Dr Michael Graham. b 53. Jes Coll Ox BA75 MA78 Dur Univ PhD79. Qu Coll Birm 82. **d** 84 **p** 85. C Nantwich *Ches* 84-86; C Coppenhall 86-88; TV Southend *Chelmsf* from 88. *The Vicarage, 39 St John's Road, Westcliff-on-Sea, Essex SS0 7JY* Southend-on-Sea (0702) 433327

BOADEN, John Edward. b 15. Down Coll Cam BA41 MA45. Ridley Hall Cam 41. **d** 43 **p** 44. R Blackley St Andr *Man* 67-77; P-in-c Parkfield in Middleton 77-81; rtd 81; Hon C Constable Lee *Man* 81-83; Perm to Offic from 83. *11 Horncliffe Close, Rawtenstall, Rossendale, Lancs BB4 6EE* Rossendale (0706) 223696

BOAG, David. b 46. Edin Th Coll 69. **d** 72 **p** 73. C Edin Old St Paul *Edin* 72-75; P-in-c Edin St Andr and St Aid 75-88; Lic to Offic from 88. *26 Noble Place, Edinburgh EH6 8AX* 031-554 7876

BOAK, Donald Kenneth. b 30. MAOT53. S'wark Ord Course DipRS85. **d** 85 **p** 86. C Tulse Hill H Trin and St Matthias *S'wark* 85-88; C Surbiton St Matt 88-91; Intercon Ch Soc and Miss to Seamen from 91; Peru from 91. *Church of the Good Shepherd, Apartado 5152, Lima 18, Peru*   Lima (14) 45-7908

BOAKE, Canon Henry Vaux. b 16. TCD BA38 MA52. CITC 38. **d** 39 **p** 40. I Crosspatrick Gp *C & O* 46-79; Chan Ferns Cathl 71-79; rtd 79. *Little Orton, Rutland, Palatine, Carlow, Irish Republic*   Carlow (503) 43065

BOAKES, Norman. b 50. Univ of Wales (Swansea) BA71 Univ of Wales (Lamp) LTh73. Bp Burgess Hall Lamp 71. **d** 73 **p** 74. C Swansea St Mary w H Trin *S & B* 73-78; Chapl Univ of Wales (Swansea) 76-78; Chapl K Alfred Coll *Win* 78-82; V Colbury 82-91; Chapl Ashurst Hosp from 82; V Southn Maybush St Pet *Win* from 91. *Maybush Vicarage, Sedbergh Road, Southampton SO1 9HJ*   Southampton (0703) 771996

BOAR, Alan Bennett. b 23. Sarum Th Coll 56. **d** 58 **p** 59. R Beeston St Laurence w Ashmanhaugh and Hoveton *Nor* 67-78; P-in-c Tunstead w Sco' Ruston 67-78; P-in-c Marsham 78-89; P-in-c Burgh 78-89; rtd 89; Perm to Offic *Nor* from 89. *20 Emelson Close, Dereham, Norfolk NR19 2ES*   Dereham (0362) 698944

BOARDMAN, Dr Frederick Henry. b 25. Liv Univ BSc46 St Cath Soc Ox BA49 MA54 Birm Univ MEd71 PhD77. Wycliffe Hall Ox 47. **d** 50 **p** 51. V Stechford *Birm* 57-63; Lic to Offic *Liv* from 71; Hon C Sutton 76-89; Hon C Burtonwood from 89; rtd 90. *Woodside, Burtonwood Road, Great Sankey, Warrington WA5 3AN*   Warrington (0925) 35079

BOARDMAN, John Frederick. b 37. Bolton Coll of Art NDD57 Leeds Univ ATD58 AKC64. **d** 65 **p** 66. C Harrogate St Wilfrid *Ripon* 65-68; C Fleetwood *Blackb* 68-71; C Cen Torquay *Ex* 71-77; Chapl S Devon Tech Coll Torbay 71-77; P-in-c Ellacombe *Ex* 76-77; V Milber from 77. *St Luke's Vicarage, Milber, Newton Abbot, Devon TQ12 4LQ*   Newton Abbot (0626) 65837

BOARDMAN, Jonathan. b 63. Magd Coll Cam BA89 Magd Coll Ox MA90. Westcott Ho Cam 87. **d** 90 **p** 91. C W Derby St Mary *Liv* from 90. *2 The Village, West Derby, Liverpool L12 5HW*   051-256 6600

BOARDMAN, Ms Philippa Jane. b 63. Jes Coll Cam BA85 MA89. Ridley Hall Cam 87. **d** 90. C Walthamstow St Mary w St Steph *Chelmsf* from 90. *10 Church End, London E17 9RJ*   081-520 2225

BOARDMAN, William. b 21. AKC52. **d** 53 **p** 54. V Barton *Portsm* 67-86; RD W Wight 78-82; rtd 86; Perm to Offic *Portsm* from 86. *41 Culver Way, Sandown, Isle of Wight PO36 8QJ*   Isle of Wight (0983) 404552

BOASE, David John. b 49. St Jo Coll Dur BA71 Trin Coll Ox PGCE73. Cuddesdon Coll 71. **d** 73 **p** 74. C Penrith *Carl* 73-76; Tutor Greystoke Coll Carl 76-78; Prec Gib Cathl *Eur* 78-80; Miss to Seamen 78-80; Chapl Gothenburg w Halmstad and Jonkoping *Eur* 80-82; TV Thornaby on Tees *York* 82-88; V Kirkby-in-Cleveland from 88; Resp for Clergy In-Service Tr Cleveland W from 88. *3 Holmemead, The Holme, Great Broughton, Middlesbrough TS9 7HF*   Middlesbrough (0642) 710005

BOCKING, Dean of. *See* HAIG, Very Rev Alistair Matthew; ARRAND, Very Rev Geoffrey William

BODDINGTON, Alan Charles Peter. b 37. Lon Univ DipH66. Oak Hill Th Coll 63. **d** 66 **p** 67. C Bushbury *Cov* 66-69; Bp's Officer for Min 69-75; Bp's Chapl for Miss 69-75; P-in-c Wroxall 72-75; P-in-c Honiley 72-75; V Westwood 75-85; Asst Chapl Warw Univ 78-85; R Farnborough *Guildf* from 85; RD Aldershot from 88. *The Rectory, 66 Church Avenue, Farnborough, Hants GU14 7AP*   Farnborough (0252) 544754

BODDINGTON, Clive Frederick Malcolm. b 35. Qu Coll Cam BA59 MA63. Ridley Hall Cam 59. **d** 61 **p** 62. C Tonbridge SS Pet and Paul *Roch* 61-64; C St Leonards St Leon *Chich* 64-66; Kenya from 67. *PO Box 8802, Nairobi, Kenya*

BODDINGTON, John Slater. b 17. Wells Th Coll 63. **d** 64 **p** 65. C Roxbourne St Andr *Lon* 68-71; V W Acton St Martin 71-85; rtd 85; Perm to Offic Ban and St As from 85. *Lane End, Aber Place, Llandudno, Gwynedd LL30 3AR*   Llandudno (0492) 47080

BODDY, Alan Richard. b 47. Ripon Coll Cuddesdon. **d** 84 **p** 85. C Eastcote St Lawr *Lon* 84-87; C Kensington St Mary Abbots w St Geo 87-90; Chapl HM Pris Brixton 90-91; Chapl HM Pris Send and Downview from 91; Lic to Offic *Guildf* from 91. *c/o The Chaplain's Office, HM Prison Send, Guildford, Surrey*

BODDY, Canon William Kenneth. b 16. TD63. St Jo Coll Dur BA39 DipTh40. Westcott Ho Cam 40. **d** 40 **p** 41. V Wylam *Newc* 65-82; RD Corbridge 71-82; Hon Can Newc Cathl 74-82; rtd 82. *21 Dukes Road, Hexham, Northd NE46 3AW*   Hexham (0434) 602807

BODMIN, Archdeacon of. *See* WHITEMAN, Ven Rodney David Carter

BODY, Andrew. b 46. Pemb Coll Cam BA68 MA71. Ridley Hall Cam 68. **d** 70 **p** 71. C New Bury *Man* 70-73; TV Droylsden St Mary 73-78; V Low Harrogate St Mary *Ripon* from 78; Trustee FLAME from 90. *St Mary's Vicarage, 22 Harlow Oval, Harrogate, N Yorkshire HG2 0DS*   Harrogate (0423) 502614

BODY, Richard Sidney. b 25. CEng FIEE55 FIHospE72 BSc46 CertRS88. S'wark Ord Course 86. **d** 88 **p** 89. Hon C Chelsfield *Roch* from 88. *Beechwood, 96 Goddington Lane, Orpington, Kent BR6 9DY*   Orpington (0689) 829990

BODYCOMB, Peter Lionel. b 28. Roch Th Coll 65. **d** 67 **p** 68. C Gravesend St Jas *Roch* 67-70; C Hawley H Trin *Guildf* 70-75; V Egham Hythe 75-77. *Address temp unknown*

BODYCOMBE, Stephen John. b 58. Lanchester Poly BA. St Mich Coll Llan DipTh83. **d** 83 **p** 84. C Cardiff St Jo *Llan* 83-86; V Dinas and Penygraig w Williamstown from 86. *The Vicarage, 1 Llanfair Road, Penygraig, Tonypandy, M Glam CF40 1TA*   Tonypandy (0443) 422677

BOFF, Charles Roy. b 31. Pemb Coll Ox BA57 MA60. Clifton Th Coll 55. **d** 57 **p** 58. C Plumstead All SS *S'wark* 57-61; V Gipsy Hill Ch Ch 61-68; V Felbridge 68-79; V Steyning *Chich* 79-84; R Ashurst 79-84; R Storrington 81-84; R Romaldkirk w Laithkirk *Ripon* from 84; RD Richmond from 90. *The Rectory, Romaldkirk, Barnard Castle, Co Durham DL12 9EE*   Teesdale (0833) 50202

BOFFEY, Ian. b 40. Glas Univ MA63. **d** 75 **p** 78. Hon C Dalry *Glas* from 75. *2 Kinloch Avenue, Stewarton, Kilmarnock, Ayrshire KA3 3HF*   Stewarton (0560) 82586

BOGGIS, Canon Augustine Thomas Isaac. b 08. Ex Coll Ox BA30 MA45. Sarum Th Coll 34. **d** 34 **p** 35. Chapl Sedbergh Sch Cumbria 38-74; Hon Can Bradf Cathl *Bradf* 68-86; rtd 75; Lic to Offic *Bradf* from 86. *Beamsmoor, Sedbergh, Cumbria LA10 5JN*   Sedbergh (05396) 21286

BOGGUST, Mrs Patricia Anne. Portsm Dioc Tr Course. **d** 90. NSM Hook w Warsash *Portsm* from 90. *21 Beverley Close, Park Gate, Southampton SO3 6QU*   Locks Heath (0489) 573586

BOGLE, James Main Lindam Linton. b 33. Peterho Cam BA56 MA60. Wells Th Coll 59. **d** 61 **p** 62. Chapl York Univ *York* 65-72; V Brayton 72-76; V Forest Hill St Aug *S'wark* 76-83; C Hatcham St Cath 83-85; C Herne Hill St Paul 86-87; rtd 87. *8 Waller Road, London SE14 5LA*   071-732 9420

BOHUN, Roger Alexander. b 32. Lon Univ BSc58. Cuddesdon Coll 65. **d** 68 **p** 69. C Rugby St Andr *Cov* 68-74; SSF from 74; Lic to Offic Sarum 74-76; Newc 76-78; Tanzania 78-86; Zimbabwe 86-88. *The Friary, Hilfield, Dorchester, Dorset DT2 7BE*   Cerne Abbas (0300) 341345

BOIT, Mervyn Hays. b 38. Univ of Wales (Lamp) BA59. St Mich Coll Llan 59. **d** 61 **p** 62. C Roath St German *Llan* 61-63; C Skewen 63-69; V Pontycymmer and Blaengarw from 69. *The Vicarage, Pontycymmer, Bridgend, M Glam*   Bridgend (0656) 870280

BOLAND, Geoffrey. b 56. DipHE89. Oak Hill Th Coll 87. **d** 89 **p** 90. C Ormskirk *Liv* from 89. *18 Lea Crescent, Ormskirk, Lancs L39 1PQ*   Ormskirk (0695) 77577

BOLE, Malcolm Dennis. b 30. Oak Hill Th Coll 65. **d** 67 **p** 68. C Bridlington Priory *York* 67-70; Rwanda 71-73; P-in-c Combe Hay *B & W* 74-81; V Bath Odd Down 74-81; P-in-c Taunton St Jas 81-84; V 84-90; R Bicknoller w Crowcombe and Sampford Brett from 90. *The Rectory, 11 Trendle Lane, Bicknoller, Taunton, Somerset TA4 4EG*   Stogumber (0984) 56262

BOLLARD, Canon Richard George. b 39. Fitzw Ho Cam BA61 MA65 K Coll Lon BD63 AKC63. **d** 64 **p** 65. C Southn Maybush St Pet *Win* 64-68; Chapl Aston Univ *Birm* 68-74; TR Chelmsley Wood 74-82; V Coleshill from 82; V Maxstoke from 82; RD Coleshill from 82; Hon Can Birm Cathl from 85. *The Vicarage, High Street, Coleshill, Birmingham B46 3BP*   Coleshill (0675) 462188

BOLLEN, Bryan Hayward. b 26. **d** 77 **p** 78. NSM Chippenham St Pet *Bris* from 77. *27 The Tinings, Chippenham, Wilts SN15 3LY*   Chippenham (0249) 652515

BOLLOM, Canon David. b 23. Lambeth MA88 Wycliffe Hall Ox 72. **d** 74 **p** 75. C Norbiton *S'wark* 74-77; Dioc Sec 77-88; Hon Can S'wark Cathl 78-88; AP Upper Mole Valley Gp 88-90; rtd 91. *Karanga, North Street, South Petherton, Somerset TA13 5DA*   South Petherton (0460) 42427

BOLSIN, Canon Cyril Edward. b 10. AKC41. **d** 41 **p** 42. R Colchester St Mich Myland *Chelmsf* 62-80; Hon Can

Chelmsf Cathl 76-80; rtd 80. *10 Bedford Road, Colchester CO4 5LS* Colchester (0206) 63718

BOLSTER, David Richard. b 50. BA. St Jo Coll Nottm. **d** 84 **p** 85. C Luton Lewsey St Hugh *St Alb* 84-87; V Woodside w E Hyde from 87. *The Vicarage, Church Road, Slip End, Luton* Luton (0582) 424363

BOLT, David Dingley. b 18. St Jo Coll Cam LLB58 LLM85. Westcott Ho Cam 66. **d** 68 **p** 69. Malawi 68-70; C Chesterton Gd Shep· *Ely* 70-71; P-in-c Gt Wilbraham 71-74; V 74-86; P-in-c Lt Wilbraham 71-74; R 74-86; RD Quy 75-81; rtd 86; Perm to Offic *Ely* from 86. *24 Warwick Road, Cambridge CB4 3HN* Cambridge (0223) 66361

BOLT, George Henry. b 34. MInstP75 CPhys Sir John Cass Coll Lon BSc60 Bath Univ MSc75. Sarum & Wells Th Coll 85. **d** 88 **p** 89. Chapl Chippenham Tech Coll from 89; NSM Kington *Bris* from 90; NSM Draycot Cerne from 90. *Mill Cottage, Cherhill, Calne, Wilts SN11 8XS* Calne (0249) 816157

BOLT, Philip John Mitchell. b 15. Bps' Coll Cheshunt 49. **d** 52 **p** 53. R Nunney *B & W* 65-74; P-in-c Wanstrow w Cloford 72-74; R Nunney w Wanstrow and Cloford 74-80; V Rotherham Ferham Park *Sheff* 80-84; rtd 84; Perm to Offic *B & W* from 85; C Stoke Lacy, Moreton Jeffries w Much Cowarne etc *Heref* 87-90. *37 Main Road, Westonzoyland, Bridgewater, Somerest TA7 0EB* Weston Zoyland (0278) 691686

BOLTON, Christopher Leonard. b 60. Llan St Mich DipTh83. **d** 83 **p** 84. C Lamp *St D* 83-86; P-in-c Llanarth and Capel Cynon w Talgarreg etc 86-87; V from 87. *The Vicarage, Llanarth, Dyfed SA47 0NJ* Llanarth (0545) 580745

BOLTON, John. b 43. SS Paul & Mary Coll Cheltenham DipEd64. Trin Coll Bris 83. **d** 85 **p** 86. C Minehead *B & W* 85-89; R Winford w Felton Common Hill from 89. *The Rectory, 4 Parsonage Lane, Winford, Bristol BS18 8DG* Lulsgate (0275) 474636

BOLTON, Peter Richard Shawcross. b 58. Warw Univ BA79. Sarum & Wells Th Coll 80. **d** 83 **p** 84. C Beckenham St Jas *Roch* 83-86; C Bedf Leigh *Man* 86-88; V Royton St Paul from 88. *11 Holderness Drive, Royton, Oldham OL2 5DW* 061-624 2388

BOLTON, Richard David Edward. b 52. MA. St Steph Ho Ox 79. **d** 81 **p** 82. C Rawmarsh w Parkgate *Sheff* 81-84; Chapl Wellingborough Sch from 85; Lic to Offic *Pet* from 85. *The School, Wellingborough, Northants NN8 2BX* Wellingborough (0933) 222428

BOLTON, Sidney Robert. b 15. Dur Univ LTh45. Edin Th Coll 42. **d** 44 **p** 45. V Bloxham and Milcombe *Ox* 59-81; V Bloxham w Milcombe and S Newington 81-84; rtd 84; Perm to Offic *Ox* from 84. *Finches, 1 Brookside, Hook Norton, Banbury, Oxon OX15 5NS* Hook Norton (0608) 737153

BOLTON, William. b 05. Tyndale Hall Bris 31. **d** 33 **p** 34. V Douglas St Ninian *S & M* 65-74; rtd 74; Perm to Offic *S & M* 74-91. *Carolyn Residential Home, 2 Beefold Lane, Atherton, Manchester*

BOLTON, Archdeacon of. See BRISON, Ven William Stanly

BOLTON, Suffragan Bishop of. See BONSER, Rt Rev David

BOMFORD, Rodney William George. b 43. BNC Ox BA64 DipTh66 MA68. Coll of Resurr Mirfield 67 Union Th Sem (NY) STM69. **d** 69 **p** 70. C Deptford St Paul *S'wark* 69-77; V Camberwell St Giles w St Matt from 77; RD Camberwell from 87. *St Giles's Vicarage, Benhill Road, London SE5 8RB* 071-703 4504

BOMYER, Julian Richard Nicholas Jeffrey. b 55. AKC78. Sarum & Wells Th Coll 78. **d** 79 **p** 80. C Rugby St Andr *Cov* 79-84; TV 85-88; P-in-c Clifton upon Dunsmore w Brownsover 84-85; Prec Ch Ch *Ox* from 88. *Christ Church Cathedral, Oxford OX1 1DP* Oxford (0865) 276214

BOND, Alan Richard. b 49. MBIM75 AFIMA75 MIIM79 Lon Univ BSc71 Imp Coll Lon ARCS71 Portsm Poly DMS74. S Dios Minl Tr Scheme 80. **d** 83 **p** 84. NSM Westbourne *Chich* 83-86. *14 Fraser Gardens, Southbourne, Emsworth, Hants PO10 8PY* Emsworth (0243) 378478

BOND, Arthur Edward (Brother Stephen). b 44. St Steph Ho Ox 68. **d** 69 **p** 69. S Africa 69-70; OGS 70-73; C Hendon St Alphage *Lon* 70-73; OSB from 75; Asst Sec ACS from 75; Hon C Sparkbrook St Agatha w Balsall Heath St Barn *Birm* from 86. *264A Washwood Heath Road, Birmingham B8 2XS* 021-354 9885 or 328 0749

✠**BOND, Rt Rev Charles (Derek).** b 27. AKC51. **d** 52 **p** 53 c 76. C Friern Barnet St Jas *Lon* 52-56; Lic to Offic *Birm* 56-58; Midl Sch Sec SCM 56-58; V Harringay St Paul *Lon* 58-62; V Harrow Weald All SS 62-72; P-in-c

Pebmarsh *Chelmsf* 72-73; Adn Colchester 72-76; Suff Bp Bradwell 76-84; Area Bp Bradwell from 84. *Bishop's House, 21 Elmhurst Avenue, Benfleet, Essex SS7 5RY* South Benfleet (0268) 755175

BOND, Charles Robert. b 25. Trin Coll Bris DipHE80. **d** 80 **p** 81. C Wythenshawe Wm Temple Ch *Man* 80-82; TV Cwmbran *Mon* 82-88; Chapl Corfu *Eur* 88-91; rtd 91; Chapl Playa de Las Americas *Eur* from 91. *Edificio I-3A, Jardines Canarios, Los Cristianos, Tenerife, Canary Islands* Tenerife (22) 793143

BOND, Clifford Frank. b 24. St Aid Birkenhead 60. **d** 62 **p** 63. C Kirkham *Blackb* 62-64; C Wallingford St Mary w All Hallows and St Leon *Ox* 64-69; PM Reading St Barn CD 69-73; R Reading St Barn from 73. *St Barnabas's Rectory, 14 Elm Road, Reading RG6 2TS* Reading (0734) 871718

BOND, David. b 36. Oak Hill Th Coll 72. **d** 74 **p** 75. C Leyton St Mary w St Edw *Chelmsf* 74-78; C Slough *Ox* 78-80; V Selby St Jas *York* from 80; P-in-c Wistow 80-82; V from 82; RD Selby from 89. *St James's Vicarage, St James's Terrace, Selby, N Yorkshire YO8 0HL* Selby (0757) 702861

BOND, David Matthew. b 38. Leic Univ BA59 Nottm Univ MA85. Sarum Th Coll 59. **d** 61 **p** 62. C Leic St Anne *Leic* 61-64; Hon C Nor St Pet Mancroft *Nor* 64-67; E England Sec SCM from 64; Sen Lect Pet Regional Coll from 67; Hon C Stamford All SS w St Pet *Linc* 74-81; Hon C Stamford All SS w St Jo from 81; Perm to Offic *Pet* from 85. *2 The Courtyard, Cotterstock, Peterborough PE8 5HB* Cotterstock (08326) 255

BOND, David Warner. b 32. BSc. Cant Sch of Min. **d** 82 **p** 83. NSM Otham w Langley *Cant* from 82. *229 Willington Street, Maidstone, Kent ME15 8EW* Maidstone (0622) 761257

BOND, Douglas Gregory. b 39. Edin Th Coll 74. **d** 76 **p** 77. NSM Edin St Paul and St Geo *Edin* 76-83; P-in-c Abthorpe w Slapton *Pet* 83-84; P-in-c Silverstone and Abthorpe w Slapton 84; R 84-89; V Pet St Jude from 89. *St Jude's Vicarage, 49 Atherstone Avenue, Peterborough PE3 6TZ* Peterborough (0733) 264169

BOND, Elton Howard. b 31. McGill Univ Montreal BA54 Harvard Univ MA55 Lon Univ BA57 BD60 Birm Univ DipTh61 PhD64 Bris Univ MEd75 Newc Univ MLitt79 MPhil79 Aston Univ MSc82. Qu Coll Birm 60. **d** 62 **p** 63. Lic to Offic Sarum 69-74; Newc 74-78; Chapl Blue Coat Comp Sch Walsall 78-91; rtd 91. *Vesey, 42A Jesson Road, Walsall WS1 3AX* Walsall (0922) 21152

BOND, Gordon. b 44. Chich Th Coll 68. **d** 71 **p** 72. C Wisbech St Aug *Ely* 71-74; C Wembley Park St Aug *Lon* 74-77; C York Town *Guildf* 77-80; C Haywards Heath St Wilfrid *Chich* 80; TV 80-82; V Lower Beeding 82-86; V E Grinstead St Mary from 86. *The Vicarage, Windmill Lane, East Grinstead, W Sussex RH19 2DS* East Grinstead (0342) 323439

BOND, Canon John Albert. b 35. St Cath Soc Ox BA61 MA65 MPhil77 LRAM55 GGSM56. Wycliffe Hall Ox 58 Seabury-Western Th Sem BD62. **d** 62 **p** 63. C Chelmsf Cathl *Chelmsf* 62-63; Succ 63-64; Prec 64-66; Lect St Osyth Coll Clacton-on-Sea 66-69; Lic to Offic Chelmsf 66-69; Cant from 69; Lect Ch Ch Coll Cant 69-73; Hon Min Can Cant Cathl *Cant* 70-85; Hon Can from 85; Sen Lect Ch Ch Coll Cant 73-85; Prin Lect and Hd Relig Studies Ch Ch Coll from 85. *St Lawrence Priory, 136 Old Dover Road, Canterbury, Kent CT1 3NX* Canterbury (0227) 765575

BOND, John Frederick Augustus. b 45. Open Univ BA75. CITC 64. **d** 67 **p** 69. C Lisburn St Paul *Conn* 67-70; C Finaghy 70-77; I Ballynure and Ballyeaston from 77. *The Rectory, 11 Church Road, Ballynure, Ballyclare, Co Antrim BT39 9UF* Ballyclare (09603) 22350

BOND, Miss Kim Mary. b 58. SRN79. Trin Coll Bris BA87. **d** 87. Par Dn Cullompton *Ex* 87-91; Asst Chapl N Staffs R Infirmary Stoke-on-Trent from 91. *c/o Bishop's House, The Close, Lichfield WS13 7LG* Lichfield (0543) 262251

BOND, Mark Francis Wilson. b 53. Sarum & Wells Th Coll 89. **d** 91. C Taunton Lyngford *B & W* from 91. *1 Kirke Grove, Taunton, Somerset TA2 8SB* Taunton (0823) 321801

BOND, Norman. b 23. Wycliffe Hall Ox. **d** 70 **p** 71. C Warrington St Ann *Liv* 70-73; P-in-c 73-77; P-in-c Warrington St Pet 73-77; V Wigan St Cath 77-88; rtd 88. *Bridge House, Old Hutton, Kendal, Cumbria LA8 0NH* Kendal (0539) 722293

BOND, Paul Maxwell. b 36. TD70. ACIB58. Oak Hill Th Coll 76. **d** 79 **p** 80. Hon C Wisley w Pyrford *Guildf* from 79. *Fosters, Pyrford Heath, Pyrford, Woking, Surrey GU22 8SS* Byfleet (0932) 347537

BOND, Richard Jack. b 16. Lich Th Coll 38. **d** 41 **p** 42. V Balkwell *Newc* 68-78; R Allendale 78-79; R Allendale w Whitfield 79-83; rtd 83. *82 Brantwood Avenue, Whitley Bay, Tyne & Wear NE25 8NL* 091-252 9798

BOND, Ven Thomas James. b 18. TCD BA41 MA68. CITC 41. **d** 42 **p** 43. I Bailieborough *K, E & A* 55-60; I Templemichael w Clongish, Clooncumber etc 60-91; Preb Elphin Cathl 67-91; Adn Elphin and Ardagh 78-91; rtd 91. *Halstow, Drumelis, Cavan, Co Cavan, Irish Republic* Cavan (49) 61812

BOND-THOMAS, David Harradence. b 23. Ch Coll Cam BA44 MA51. **d** 59 **p** 60. C Earley St Pet *Ox* 62-71; P-in-c Middleton Stoney 71-77; P-in-c Bucknell 71-76; P-in-c Weston on the Green 72-76; P-in-c Chesterton w Wendlebury 76-77; V Chesterton w Middleton Stoney and Wendlebury 77-89; rtd 89. *35 Greet Road, Winchcombe, Cheltenham, Glos GL54 5JT* Cheltenham (0242) 603150

✠**BONE, Rt Rev John Frank Ewan.** b 30. St Pet Coll Ox BA54 MA59 Whitelands Coll Lon PGCE71. Ely Th Coll 54. **d** 56 **p** 57 **c** 89. C Pimlico St Gabr *Lon* 56-60; C Henley *Ox* 60-63; V Datchet 63-76; RD Burnham 74-77; R Upton cum Chalvey 76-78; Adn Buckm 77-89; Area Bp Reading from 89. *Greenbanks, Old Bath Road, Sonning, Reading RG4 0SY* Reading (0734) 692187

BONE, Michael Thomas. b 33. ACMA62 Open Univ BA82. Brechin NSM Ord Course 79. **d** 83 **p** 84. Chapl Dundee Inst of Tech from 83; Hon C Broughty Ferry *Bre* 83-84; Hon C Arbroath 84-87; Hon C Dundee St Mary Magd from 87. *5 Roxburgh Terrace, Dundee DD2 1NZ* Dundee (0382) 66897

BONE, Noel Francis. b 18. TD64. Clifton Th Coll. **d** 59 **p** 60. Lic to Offic *Lon* 69-71; V Boxmoor St Jo *St Alb* 71-72; V Aston w Benington 72-83; C St Giles-in-the-Fields *Lon* 83; rtd 83; Perm to Offic St Alb from 84; Nor from 87. *Crofters, The Croft, Cromer, Norfolk NR27 9EH* Cromer (0263) 513873

BONE, Canon Trevor Hubert. b 25. Ch Ch Ox BA49 MA50. Qu Coll Birm. **d** 51 **p** 52. V Barnsley St Edw *Wakef* 69-85; Hon Can Wakef Cathl 82-85; rtd 85; Perm to Offic *Wakef* from 85. *28 Downs Crescent, Barnsley, S Yorkshire S75 2JE* Barnsley (0226) 240216

BONHAM, Frederick Thomas. b 37. St Deiniol's Hawarden 70. **d** 72 **p** 73. C Northwood Hills St Edm *Lon* 72-75; C Clewer St Andr *Ox* 75-90; V Reading H Trin from 90. *Holy Trinity Presbytery, 32 Baker Street, Reading RG1 7XY* Reading (0734) 572650

BONHAM-CARTER, Gerard Edmund David. b 31. Lon Univ BSc53 DCAe55. S'wark Ord Course. **d** 87 **p** 88. NSM Wandsworth St Paul *S'wark* from 87; Perm to Offic *St E* from 87. *85 Victoria Drive, London SW19 6HW* 081-788 1230

BONIFACE, Lionel Ernest George. b 36. Lon Coll of Div ALCD63 BD64. **d** 64 **p** 65. C Attenborough w Chilwell *S'well* 64-69; C Farndon 69-71; C Thorpe 69-71; P-in-c Mansf St Aug 71-77; V Oughtibridge *Sheff* from 77; Ind Chapl 79-81. *The Vicarage, Church Street, Oughtibridge, Sheffield S30 3FU* Oughtibridge (074286) 2317

BONIWELL, Timothy Richard. b 51. AKC73. St Aug Coll Cant 74. **d** 75 **p** 76. C Walthamstow St Mich *Chelmsf* 75-78; C Wigmore Abbey *Heref* 78-83; C Studley *Sarum* 83-86; Chapl Trowbridge Coll 83-86; V Bath St Barn w Englishcombe *B & W* from 86. *The Vicarage, Mount View, Bath BA2 1JX* Bath (0225) 21838

BONNER, David Robert. b 28. ASCA66 FCIS72 FCIB74 DipRS78. S'wark Ord Course 74. **d** 77 **p** 78. NSM Hampton All SS *Lon* 77-84; P-in-c Twickenham All SS 84-91; rtd 91. *17 St James's Road, Hampton Hill, Hampton, Middx TW12 1DH* 081-979 1565

BONNER, Frederick Charles. b 10. Worc Ord Coll 63. **d** 65 **p** 66. R W Ilsley w Farnborough *Ox* 69-75; P-in-c E Ilsley 70-74; rtd 75. *4 Ham View, Upton-upon-Severn, Worcester WR8 0QE* Upton-upon-Severn (06846) 2087

BONNER, James Maxwell Campbell. Sydney Univ BSc48 DipEd49 Lon Univ BD59. Oak Hill Th Coll. **d** 60 **p** 61. C Walthamstow St Mary *Chelmsf* 60-63; C Morden *S'wark* 63-65; Australia from 65. *13 Waratah Street, Croydon Park, NSW, Australia 2133* Sydney (2) 744-9832

BONNET, Tom. b 51. Univ of Wales (Ban) DipTh89 Univ of Wales (Cardiff) BTh90. St Mich Coll Llan 90. **d** 90 **p** 91. C Criccieth w Treflys *Ban* from 90. *Clydfan, Garddyr-Esgob, Criccieth, Gwynedd LL52 0DU* Criccieth (0766) 522568

BONNEY, Mark Philip John. b 57. St Cath Coll Cam BA78 MA82. St Steph Ho Ox BA84 MA89. **d** 85 **p** 86. C Stockton St Pet *Dur* 85-88; Chapl St Alb Abbey *St Alb* 88-90; Prec St Alb Abbey from 90. *Flat 1, The Deanery,*

Sumpter Yard, St Albans, Herts AL1 1BY St Albans (0727) 55321

BONNEY, Stuart Campbell. b 51. Edin Univ BD83. Edin Th Coll 81. **d** 83 **p** 84. C Edin St Luke *Edin* 83-86; C Edin St Martin 83-86; P-in-c Auchterarder *St And* 86-90; P-in-c Muthill 86-90; Dep Chapl HM Pris Leeds 90-91; Chapl HM Pris Moorland from 91. *HM Prison Moorland, Bowtree Road, Hatfield Woodhouse, Doncaster, S Yorkshire DN7 6EE* Doncaster (0302) 846600

BONNEYWELL, Christine Mary. b 57. Univ of Wales (Lamp) BA78 LTh80. Sarum & Wells Th Coll 80. **d** 81. C Swansea St Pet *S & B* 81-84; C Llangyfelach 84-86; Chapl Univ of Wales (Lamp) *St D* 86-90; Educn Officer Wells Cathl *B & W* from 90. *14 Vicar's Close, Wells, Somerset BA5 2UJ* Wells (0749) 74483

BONSALL, Charles Henry Brash. b 42. Ex Univ BA66. Ridley Hall Cam 66. **d** 68 **p** 69. C Cheltenham St Mary *Glouc* 68-72; Sudan 72-78 and 79-83; Perm to Offic *Nor* 78-79; Development Sec Intercon Ch Soc from 83; Perm to Offic *Birm* from 91. *3 Pakenham Road, Birmingham B15 2NE* 021-440 6143

✠**BONSER, Rt Rev David.** b 34. Man Univ MA75 AKC61. **d** 62 **p** 63 **c** 91. C Heckmondwike *Wakef* 62-65; C Sheff St Geo *Sheff* 65-68; R Chorlton-cum-Hardy St Clem *Man* 68-82; Bp's Ecum Adv 73-81; Hon Can Man Cathl 81-82; AD Hulme 81-82; Adn Rochdale 82-91; TR Rochdale 82-91; Suff Bp Bolton from 91. *4 Sandfield Drive, Lostock, Bolton BL6 4DU* Bolton (0204) 43400

BONSEY, Hugh Richmond Lowry. b 49. Sarum & Wells Th Coll 74. **d** 76 **p** 77. C Bedminster *Bris* 76-80; TV Sutton *Liv* 80-88; P-in-c Yatton Keynell *Bris* 88-89; P-in-c Biddestone w Slaughterford 88-89; P-in-c Castle Combe 88-89; P-in-c W Kington 88-89; P-in-c Nettleton w Littleton Drew 88-89; C Westbury-on-Trym H Trin 89-90; V Peasedown St John w Wellow *B & W* from 90. *The Vicarage, 18 Church Road, Peasedown St John, Bath BA2 8AA* Radstock (0761) 32293

BONSEY, Thory Richmond. b 18. St Chad's Coll Dur 37. Cuddesdon Coll 46. **d** 47 **p** 48. R Ecton *Pet* 67-73; V Ketton 73-77; Australia from 77; rtd 83. *33 Laughton Street, Chisholm, ACT, Australia 2905*

BOOCOCK, John Walter. b 31. Wells Th Coll 63. **d** 65 **p** 66. C Guisborough *York* 65-67; C Bottesford *Linc* 67-73; TV Bottesford w Ashby 73-74; V Riddlesden *Bradf* 74-83; V Darlington H Trin *Dur* 83-91; P-in-c Denton and Ingleton from 91; Dioc Par Development Officer from 91. *The Vicarage, Ingleton, Darlington, Co Durham DL2 3HS* Darlington (0325) 730382

BOOKER, Gerald Dennis. b 30. St Pet Coll Ox BA52 MA56. Ridley Hall Cam 53 Oak Hill Th Coll 80. **d** 81 **p** 82. Hon C Hertf All SS *St Alb* 81-83; R Bramfield w Stapleford and Waterford from 83. *St Mary's Rectory, Stapleford, Hertford SG14 3NB* Hertford (0992) 581169

BOOKER, James Howard. b 57. CD (US Air)83. Edin Th Coll 88. **d** 90 **p** 91. C Longside *Ab* from 90; C Old Deer from 90; C Peterhead from 90; C Strichen from 90. *3 Pitfour Place, Mintlaw, Peterhead AB42 8FJ* Mintlaw (0771) 22876

BOOKER, Mrs Margaret Katharine. b 20. MCSP42. Westcott Ho Cam 82. **dss** 83 **d** 87. Stansted Mountfitchet *Chelmsf* 83-87; Par Dn 87-90; Hon Par Dn from 90; rtd 90. *Moorlands Cottage, Burton End, Stansted, Essex CM24 8VE* Bishop's Stortford (0279) 812684

BOOKER, Michael Charles. b 36. LLCM57 ARCO58. Lon Coll of Div LTh63. **d** 63 **p** 64. C Royston *St Alb* 63-66; C Mildenhall *St E* 66-68; Min Can St E Cathl 68-83; Prec St E Cathl 70-83; Chapl Framlingham Coll Suffolk from 84. *29 The Mowbrays, Framlingham, Woodbridge, Suffolk IP13 9DL* Framlingham (0728) 723122

BOOKER, Michael Paul Montague. b 57. Jes Coll Ox BA79 Bris Univ CertEd80. Trin Coll Bris 84. **d** 87 **p** 88. C Cant St Mary Bredin *Cant* from 87. *38 Nunnery Road, Canterbury, Kent CT1 3LS* Canterbury (0227) 455723

BOOKLESS, John Guy. b 19. Clare Coll Cam BA40 MA46 Serampore Univ MTh72. Ridley Hall Cam 47. **d** 49 **p** 50. India 53-72; C St Alb St Mich *St Alb* 73-76; C Harlow New Town w Lt Parndon *Chelmsf* 76-78; TV 78-79; P-in-c Widmerpool *S'well* 79-85; V Willoughby-on-the-Wolds w Wysall 79-85; V Willoughby-on-the-Wolds w Wysall and Widmerpool 85; rtd 85; Perm to Offic S'well and Leic from 85. *84 Kirkstone Drive, Loughborough, Leics LE11 3RW* Loughborough (0509) 263650

BOOKLESS, Mrs Rosemary. b 26. Westf Coll Lon BA47 DipEd49 Serampore Univ BD72. St Mich Ho Ox 56. **dss** 80 **d** 91. Willoughby-on-the-Wolds w Wysall and Widmerpool *S'well* 80-85; rtd 85; Perm to Offic *Leic* 85-89; Loughb Em 89-91; NSM from 91. *84 Kirkstone*

Drive, Loughborough, Leics LE11 3RW Loughborough (0509) 263650

BOOLE, Robert Hugh Philip. b 12. Linc Th Coll 46. **d** 47 **p** 48. V Metheringham *Linc* 66-77; rtd 77. *37 Liddell Drive, Llandudno, Gwynedd LL30 1UH* Llandudno (0492) 75304

BOON, Nigel Francis. b 39. St Jo Coll Nottm. **d** 83 **p** 84. C St Helens St Helen *Liv* 83-86; V Kirkdale St Lawr from 86. *St Lawrence's Vicarage, 21 Westminster Close, Liverpool L4 1XB* 051-922 5794

BOON, William John. b 54. Glouc Sch of Min 84. **d** 88 **p** 89. Hon C Matson *Glouc* 88-91; NSM Gt Witcombe from 91. *57 Ermine Park, Brockworth, Gloucester GL3 4DD* Gloucester (0452) 610774

BOOTES, Michael Charles Edward. b 35. ACP70. Sarum Th Coll 58. **d** 61 **p** 62. C Winchmore Hill St Paul *Lon* 61-64; Chapl and Hd Master Rosenberg Coll Switzerland 64-65; Chapl Aiglon Coll Switzerland 65-67; C St Marylebone All SS *Lon* 67-68; OGS from 68; Chapl Kingsley St Mich Sch W Sussex 69-75; V Brandon *Dur* 75-78; Chapl Shoreham Gr Sch 78-79; C Clayton w Keymer *Chich* 80-84; TV Ovingdean w Rottingdean and Woodingdean 84-85; TR Ovingdean 85-88; V Lundwood *Wakef* from 88. *The Vicarage, Littleworth Lane, Lundwood, Barnsley, S Yorkshire S71 5RG* Barnsley (0226) 203194

BOOTH, Alexander John. b 23. Ripon Hall Ox. **d** 66 **p** 67. C Walkden Moor *Man* 66-69; R Oldham St Andr 69-75; V Cadishead 75-86; Perm to Offic from 86; V Hollinfare *Liv* from 86. *St Helen's Vicarage, 54 Glazebrook Lane, Hollinfare, Warrington WA3 6LL* 061-775 2160

BOOTH, Charles Robert. b 48. Leeds Univ CertEd75. N Ord Course 79. **d** 82 **p** 83. C Eccleshill *Bradf* 82-84; C Jersey St Brelade *Win* 84-88; Australia 88-90; V Blurton *Lich* from 90. *The Vicarage, School Lane, Stoke-on-Trent ST3 3DU* Stoke-on-Trent (0782) 312163

BOOTH, David. b 44. Coll of Resurr Mirfield 72. **d** 74 **p** 75. C Osmondthorpe St Phil *Ripon* 74-77; C St Bart Armley w St Mary New Wortley 77-79; V Leeds St Wilfrid from 79. *St Wilfrid's Vicarage, Chatsworth Road, Leeds LS8 3RS*

BOOTH, Canon David Herbert. b 07. MBE44. Pemb Coll Cam BA31 MA36. Ely Th Coll 31. **d** 32 **p** 33. Chapl to HM The Queen 57-77; Adn Lewes *Chich* 59-72; rtd 72; Can and Preb Chich Cathl *Chich* 72-77; Hd Master Shoreham Gr Sch 72-77. *Courtyard Cottage, School Road, Charing, Ashford, Kent TN27 0HX* Charing (023371) 3349

BOOTH, Derek. b 36. LTCL ALCM AKC61. **d** 62 **p** 63. C Woodchurch *Ches* 62-65; C Penrith St Andr *Carl* 65-67; C Tranmere St Paul *Ches* 67-70; V Wilmslow 70-72; V Micklehurst from 73. *All Saints' Vicarage, Mossley, Ashton-under-Lyne, Lancs* Mossley (0457) 832393

BOOTH, Eric James. b 43. Open Univ BA84. N Ord Course 86. **d** 89 **p** 90. NSM Nelson St Phil *Blackb* from 89. *5 Round Hill Place, Park Road, Cliviger, Burnley BB10 4UA* Burnley (0282) 50708

BOOTH, George Kenneth. b 12. Pemb Coll Ox BA37 MA40. Wells Th Coll 37. **d** 39 **p** 50. Lic to Offic *Ex* 59-78; Chapl St Luke's Coll Ex 59-78; rtd 78. *Furcroft, Rock, Wadebridge, Cornwall PL27 6LD* Bodmin (0208) 2476

BOOTH, Graham Richard. b 55. Birm Univ BSocSc75. St Jo Coll Nottm 89. **d** 91. C Woodthorpe *S'well* from 91. *22 Barden Road, Nottingham NG3 5QD* Nottingham (0602) 264731

BOOTH, Ian George. b 64. Chich Th Coll 85 Linc Th Coll 87. **d** 88 **p** 89. C Pet St Mary *Pet* 88-90; C Hawley H Trin *Guildf* from 90. *295 Fernhill Road, Farnborough, Hants GU14 9EW* Camberley (0276) 34241

BOOTH, James Roger. b 46. Keble Coll Ox BA71 MA74 BTh77. Wycliffe Hall Ox 75. **d** 78 **p** 79. C Bridlington Priory *York* 78-83; V Nafferton w Wansford from 83. *The Vicarage, Nafferton, Driffield, N Humberside YO25 0JS* Driffield (0377) 44372

BOOTH, Jon Alfred. b 42. Nottm Univ BA64 Lon Univ MPhil72. Coll of Resurr Mirfield 78. **d** 80 **p** 81. C Elland *Wakef* 80-84; C Royston from 84. *The Vicarage, Church Street, Royston, Barnsley, S Yorkshire S71 4QZ* Barnsley (0226) 722410

BOOTH, Joseph Arthur Paul. b 31. Lon Univ DipTh59. St Aid Birkenhead. **d** 60 **p** 61. C Blackley St Andr *Man* 60-63; C Wickford *Chelmsf* 63-65; V New Thundersley 65-72; R Gorton St Jas *Man* 72-80; R Bradwell on Sea *Chelmsf* 80-87; R Warmsworth *Sheff* from 87. *The Rectory, 187 Warmsworth Road, Doncaster, S Yorkshire DN4 0TW* Doncaster (0302) 853324

BOOTH, Leonard William. b 46. K Coll Lon BD70 AKC70. **d** 71 **p** 72. C Cockerton *Dur* 72-75; C Hove St Barn

Chich 75-77; TV Brighton Resurr 77-78; C E Grinstead St Mary 78-81; USA from 81. *254 St Joseph Avenue, Long Beach, California 90803, USA* Long Beach (213) 433-6531

BOOTH, Michael Kevin. b 47. Louvain Univ Belgium BA. St Jo Coll Nottm 88 Oscott Coll (RC) 65. **d** 71 **p** 72. In RC Ch 71-87; C N Reddish *Man* 88-89; R Heaton Norris Ch w All SS from 89. *6 Glenfield Road, Stockport, Cheshire SK4 2QP* 061-432 6838

BOOTH, Paul Harris. b 49. St Jo Coll Nottm LTh79. **d** 79 **p** 80. C Thorpe Edge *Bradf* 79-82; P-in-c Frizinghall 82-83; TV Shipley St Paul and Frizinghall from 83. *St Margaret's Vicarage, 213 Bradford Road, Frizinghall, Shipley, W Yorkshire BD18 3AA* Bradford (0274) 581470

BOOTH, Percy Elliott. b 26. Lich Th Coll 55. **d** 58 **p** 59. C Walsall St Gabr Fullbrook *Lich* 58-61; C Whitchurch 61-64; V St Martin's 64-67; V Silverdale and Knutton Heath 67-83; Ind Chapl *Ches* from 83. *The Vicarage, Crewe Green, Crewe CW1 1UN* Crewe (0270) 580118

BOOTH, Raymond Lister. b 15. FIL43 Leeds Univ BA37 MA43. Lich Th Coll 37. **d** 39 **p** 40. P-in-c Whitwood St Phil *Wakef* 69-74; P-in-c Whitwood 74-80; rtd 81; Perm to Offic *Bradf* from 81. *460 Silver Grove, Skipton Road, Utley, Keighley, W Yorkshire BD20 6DT* Keighley (0535) 664665

BOOTH, Wallace. b 14. **d** 62 **p** 63. V Woodnesborough *Cant* 66-79; P-in-c Staple 77-79; rtd 79; Perm to Offic *Chich* from 87. *3 St Augustine's Close, Bexhill-on-Sea, E Sussex* Bexhill-on-Sea (0424) 214524

BOOTH, William James. b 39. TCD BA60 MA75. **d** 62 **p** 63. C Belf St Luke *Conn* 62-64; Chapl Cranleigh Sch Surrey 65-74; Chapl Westmr Sch from 74; Lic to Offic *Lon* from 74; P-in-O to HM The Queen from 76; PV Westmr Abbey from 87; Sub Dean Chpls Royal and Dep Clerk of the Closet from 91; Sub Almoner and Dom Chapl to HM The Queen from 91. *Marlborough Gate, St James's Palace, London SW1* 071-930 3007

✠BOOTH-CLIBBORN, Rt Rev Stanley Eric Francis. b 24. Or Coll Ox BA51 MA56. Westcott Ho Cam 50. **d** 52 **p** 53 **c** 79. C Heeley *Sheff* 52-54; C Attercliffe w Carbrook 54-56; Kenya 56-67; P-in-c Linc St Mary-le-Wigford w St Martin *Linc* 67-70; P-in-c Linc St Mark 67-70; V Cam Gt St Mary w St Mich *Ely* 70-79; Hon Can Ely Cathl 76-79; Bp Man from 79. *Bishopscourt, Bury New Road, Manchester M7 0LE* 061-792 2096 or 792 1779

BOOTHMAN, Canon Samuel. b 09. TCD BA34 Div Test35 MA37. **d** 35 **p** 35. R Farley Chamberlayne w Braishfield *Win* 46-81; RD Romsey 71-79; Hon Can Win Cathl 73-81; R Michelmersh, Timsbury, Farley Chamberlayne etc 81; rtd 81; Perm to Offic *Win* from 81. *Boldbrook Lodge, Pound Lane, Ampfield, Romsey, Hants SO51 9BP* Braishfield (0794) 68143

BOOTHROYD, John Hubert. b 14. St Edm Hall Ox BA36 MA43. Wycliffe Hall Ox 36. **d** 38 **p** 39. Perm to Offic *Chich* from 69; Chapl Brighton Coll E Sussex 69-79; rtd 79. *19 Manormead, Tilford Road, Hindhead, Surrey GU26 6RA* Hindhead (0428) 4873

BOOTS, Claude Donald Roy. b 26. Roch Th Coll 67. **d** 69 **p** 70. C Midsomer Norton *B & W* 69-73; V Westf 73-80; P-in-c Hambridge w Earnshill and Isle Brewers 80; R Ilton w Hambridge, Earnshill, Isle Brewers etc from 80. *The Vicarage, Rod Lane, Ilton, Ilminster, Somerset TA19 9ET* Ilminster (0460) 52860

BOOTY, John Robert. b 04. AKC31. **d** 31 **p** 32. V Colney St Pet *St Alb* 49-79; rtd 79. *18 Larch Avenue, Bricket Wood, St Albans, Herts* St Albans (0727) 661602

BOREHAM, Harold Leslie. b 37. S'wark Ord Course. **d** 72 **p** 73. C Whitton and Thurleston w Akenham *St E* 72-77; R Saxmundham 77-85; V Felixstowe SS Pet and Paul from 85. *The Vicarage, 14 Picketts Road, Felixstowe, Suffolk IP11 7JT* Felixstowe (0394) 284135

BORRETT, Ven Charles Walter. b 16. Em Coll Cam BA39 MA43. Ridley Hall Cam 39. **d** 41 **p** 43. V Tettenhall Regis *Lich* 49-70; RD Trysull 58-70; Preb Lich Cathl 64-71; Hon Can Lich Cathl 71-82; Adn Stoke 70-82; P-in-c Sandon 76-82; Chapl to HM The Queen 80-86; rtd 82; Perm to Offic *St E* from 82. *34 Queensway, Mildenhall, Bury St Edmunds, Suffolk IP28 7JL* Mildenhall (0638) 712718

BORRILL, John. b 19. Lon Univ BD41 AKC41. Westcott Ho Cam 41. **d** 42 **p** 43. V St Pancras w St Jas and Ch Ch *Lon* 59-71; V Hendon St Mary 71-82; Chapl Puerto de la Cruz Tenerife *Eur* 82-84; rtd 84; Hon C Tenerife *Eur* 84-87. *Loganberry Cottage, Strand Hill, Winchelsea, E Sussex TN36 4JT* Rye (0797) 226489

BORROWDALE, Geoffrey Nigel. b 61. Southn Univ BSc83. Chich Th Coll 87. **d** 90. C Tilehurst St Mich *Ox*

90-91. *34 Prince Andrew Way, Ascot, Berks SL5 8NL* Winkfield Row (0344) 883882

BORSBEY, Alan. b 38. Linc Th Coll 71. **d** 73 **p** 73. C Bardsley *Man* 73-75; C Elton All SS 75-78; V Bury St Paul from 78. *St Paul's Vicarage, Parsonage Street, Bury, Lancs BL9 6BG* 061-761 6991

BORTHWICK, Alexander Heywood. b 36. MBPsS90 Open Univ BA80 Surrey Univ MSc89. Lich Th Coll 57. **d** 60 **p** 61. C Glas Ch Ch *Glas* 60-62; C Landore *S & B* 62-64; C Swansea St Thos and Kilvey 64-65; Br Guiana 65-66; Guyana 66-70; C Oystermouth *S & B* 70-71; Lic to Offic *Man* 71-76; Area Sec (Dios Man and Liv) USPG 71-76; (Dios Blackb and S & M) 73-76; Sch and Children's Work Sec USPG 76-83; Chapl Tooting Bec Hosp Lon from 83. *4 Worple Avenue, London SW19 4JQ* 081-672 9933

BOSHER, Philip Ross. b 61. Sarum & Wells Th Coll 84. **d** 87 **p** 88. C Warminster St Denys *Sarum* 87-90; P-in-c Farley w Pitton and W Dean w E Grimstead 90-91; TV Alderbury Team from 91. *The Rectory, West Dean, Salisbury SP5 1JL* Lockerley (0794) 40271

BOSSOM, Peter Emery. b 28. St D Dioc Tr Course. **d** 82 **p** 83. NSM Llandyssilio w Egremont and Llanglydwen etc *St D* 82-86; Lic to Offic from 86. *Glyn-y-Fran, Crymych, Dyfed* Crymych (0239) 831347

BOSTOCK, Canon Geoffrey Kentigern. b 30. Sarum Th Coll 66. **d** 68 **p** 69. SSF 50-60; C Shrewsbury St Chad *Lich* 68-72; C Hanley w Hope 72-74; P-in-c Wednesbury St Jo 74-79; V Dudley Holly Hall St Aug *Worc* 79-80; V Sheff Parson Cross St Cecilia *Sheff* from 80. *St Cecilia's Priory, 98 Chaucer Close, Sheffield S5 9QE* Sheffield (0742) 321084

BOSTOCK, Peter Anthony. b 64. Nottm Univ BA85 Fitzw Coll Cam BA89. Westcott Ho Cam 87. **d** 90 **p** 91. C Brighton St Matthias *Chich* from 90. *116 Brentwood Road, Brighton BN1 7ES* Brighton (0273) 553239

BOSTOCK, Canon Peter Geoffrey. b 11. Qu Coll Ox BA33 MA37. Wycliffe Hall Ox 33. **d** 35 **p** 37. Asst Sec Miss and Ecum Coun of Ch Assembly 67-70; Dep Sec Bd Miss and Unity Gen Syn 71-73; Clergy Appts Adv 74-76; rtd 77; Perm to Offic *Ox* from 77. *6 Moreton Road, Oxford OX2 7AX* Oxford (0865) 515460

BOSTON, Jonathan Bertram. b 40. Ely Th Coll 61. **d** 64 **p** 65. C Eaton *Nor* 64-70; Sen Chapl ACF Norfolk from 70; V Horsham St Faith w Newton St Faith 70-90; V Horsford 71-90; V Horsford and Horsham St Faith from 90. *The Vicarage, Horsford, Norwich NR10 3DB* Norwich (0603) 898266

BOSWELL, Colin John Luke. b 47. Sarum & Wells Th Coll 72. **d** 74 **p** 75. C Upper Tooting H Trin *S'wark* 74-78; C Sydenham St Phil 78-79; C St Helier 80-83; P-in-c Caterham from 83; P-in-c Chaldon from 85; RD Caterham from 85. *The Rectory, 5 Whyteleafe Road, Caterham, Surrey CR3 5EG* Caterham (0883) 42062

BOTHAM, Norman. b 29. MRTS84 Nottm Univ MPhil80 Lon Univ CertEd55 DBRS66. S'wark Ord Course 63. **d** 66 **p** 67. Lect Coll SS Mark & Jo Chelsea 66-69; C Englefield Green *Guildf* 66-69; Sen Lect Shoreditch Coll Egham 69-74; C Bagshot 69-73; C-in-c Bath H Trin *B & W* 74; Asst Dir RE 74; Sen Lect Doncaster Inst of HE 74-82; Public Preacher *S'well* 75; Perm to Offic *Sheff* 75; Hon AP Bawtry w Austerfield and Misson 75-85; OCF RAF from 85. *Rufford, Mattersey Road, Ranskill, Retford, Notts DN22 8NF* Retford (0777) 818234

BOTT, Dr Theodore Reginald. b 27. CEng58 FIChemE68 Birm Univ BSc52 PhD68 DSc84. W Midl Minl Tr Course 85. **d** 86 **p** 87. NSM Harborne St Faith and St Laur *Birm* from 86. *17 Springavon Croft, Harborne, Birmingham B17 9BJ* 021-427 4209

BOTTERILL, David Darrell. b 45. Open Univ BA. Sarum & Wells Th Coll. **d** 83 **p** 84. C Blandford Forum and Langton Long etc *Sarum* 83-86; TV Shaston from 86; Chapl HM Young Offender Inst Guys Marsh from 89. *St James's Vicarage, 34 Tanyard Lane, Shaftesbury, Dorset SP7 8HW* Shaftesbury (0747) 2193

BOTTING, Canon Michael Hugh. b 25. K Coll Lon BSc51 AKC K Coll Lon PGCE52. Ridley Hall Cam 54. **d** 56 **p** 57. V Fulham St Matt *Lon* 61-72; V Leeds St Geo *Ripon* 72-84; RD Headingley 81-84; Hon Can Ripon Cathl 82-84; R Aldford and Bruera *Ches* 84-90; rtd 90; Jt Dir Lay Tr *Ches* from 90. *25 Woodfield Grove, Hoole, Chester CH2 3NY* Chester (0244) 321133

BOTTING, Paul Lloyd. b 43. St Mich Coll Llan 69. **d** 71 **p** 72. C Hucknall Torkard *S'well* 71-74; C Torquay H Trin *Ex* 74-76; P-in-c Sutton in Ashfield St Mich *S'well* 77; V 77-88; Chapl King's Mill Hosp Sutton-in-Ashfield from 85. *9 Orchard Close, Radcliffe-on-Trent, Nottingham* Nottingham (0602) 332591

BOTTLEY, David Thomas. b 39. Clifton Th Coll 64. **d** 67 **p** 68. C Burley *Ripon* 67-75; V Owlerton *Sheff* from 75; Chapl St Geo Hosp Sheff from 82. *The Vicarage, Forbes Road, Sheffield S6 2NW* Sheffield (0742) 343560

BOTTOMLEY, George Edward. b 06. St Jo Coll Dur LTh34. Bible Churchmen's Coll 30. **d** 35 **p** 36. V Cheltenham St Mark *Glouc* 61-76; rtd 76; Hon C Camborne *Truro* from 77. *Salem, Reskadinnick Road, Camborne, Cornwall TR14 7LR* Camborne (0209) 713028

BOTTOMLEY, Gordon. b 31. Oak Hill Th Coll 51. **d** 55 **p** 56. C Kinson *Sarum* 55-58; Lic to Offic *Man* 58-63; N Area Sec BCMS 58-63; V Hemswell w Harpswell *Linc* 63-72; V Glentworth 63-72; Chapl RAF 63-71; R Bucknall and Bagnall *Lich* 72-80; TR 80-82; P-in-c Worthing H Trin *Chich* 82-88; V Camelsdale from 88. *The Vicarage, School Road, Camelsdale, Haslemere, Surrey GU27 3RN* Haslemere (0428) 2983

BOTTOMLEY, Philip. b 45. Cranmer Hall Dur BA67 DipTh69. **d** 70 **p** 71. C Harlow New Town w Lt Parndon *Chelmsf* 70-74; C W Kilburn St Luke w St Simon and St Jude *Lon* 74-78; Midl Sec CMJ 78-84; Hon C Selly Park St Steph and St Wulstan *Birm* 81-84; USA from 84. *78 Main Street, Fair Oaks, Pennsylvania 15003, USA*

BOTWRIGHT, Adrian Paul. b 55. St Jo Coll Ox MA PGCE. Westcott Ho Cam 80. **d** 82 **p** 83. C Chapel Allerton *Ripon* 82-85; Chapl Chapl Allerton Hosp 82-85; C Bourne *Guildf* 85-88; V Weston from 88. *All Saints' Vicarage, 1 Chestnut Avenue, Esher, Surrey KT10 8JL* 081-398 1849

BOUCHER, Brian Albert. b 39. Univ of Wales (Lamp) BA61. Chich Th Coll 61. **d** 63 **p** 64. C Hoxton H Trin w St Mary *Lon* 63-67; Chapl RN 67-68; Lic to Offic *Lon* 68-86; Asst Chapl Harrow Sch Middx 68-73; Chapl 73-86; P-in-c Clerkenwell H Redeemer w St Phil *Lon* from 86; P-in-c Myddleton Square St Mark from 86. *Holy Redeemer Clergy House, Exmouth Market, London EC1R 4QE* 071-837 1861

BOUGHEY, Richard Keith. b 26. Man Univ MEd71. Qu Coll Birm 77. **d** 80 **p** 82. NSM Upper Tean *Lich* 80-81; NSM Stoke-upon-Trent 80-81; NSM Uttoxeter w Bramshall 82-88; rtd 88; Perm to Offic *Lich* from 88. *Kontokali, The Old Lane, Checkley, Stoke-on-Trent* Tean (0538) 722013

BOUGHTON, Michael John. b 37. Kelham Th Coll 57. **d** 62 **p** 63. C Grantham St Wulfram *Linc* 62-66; C Kingsthorpe *Pet* 66-68; C Linc St Nic w St Jo Newport *Linc* 68-72; V Scunthorpe All SS 72-79; V Crowle 79-89; R Epworth 80-89; TR Bottesford w Ashby from 89. *St Paul's Rectory, Ashby, Scunthorpe, S Humberside DN16 3DL* Scunthorpe (0724) 856863

BOULCOTT, Thomas William. b 16. Bps' Coll Cheshunt 47. **d** 49 **p** 50. V N Evington *Leic* 61-73; Chapl Leic Gen Hosp 62-73; V Loppington w Newtown *Lich* 73-85; RD Wem and Whitchurch 83-85; rtd 85; Perm to Offic *Lich* from 85. *Silver Birch, Tilley Road, Wem, Shrewsbury SY4 5HA* Wem (0939) 33602

BOULD, Preb Arthur Roger. b 32. Selw Coll Cam BA54 MA58 Wadh Coll Ox BA55 DipTh56 DipEd57 MA58. St Steph Ho Ox 54. **d** 57 **p** 58. C Wednesfield St Thos *Lich* 57-64; V Wellington Ch Ch 64-71; R Cheadle 71-88; P-in-c Freehay 84-88; R Cheadle w Freehay 88-91; Chapl Cheadle Hosp 71-91; Sub-Chapl HM Pris Moorcourt 72-82; RD Cheadle 72-91; Preb Lich Cathl from 83; Asst to Bp Wolv from 91. *10 Paradise Lane, Pelsall, Walsall, W Midlands WS3 4NH* Pelsall (0922) 694299

BOULD, Stephen Frederick. b 49. K Coll Lon BD78 AKC78. Sarum & Wells Th Coll 78. **d** 79 **p** 80. C Cantril Farm *Liv* 79-82; AV Hindley St Pet 82-85; C Wigan All SS 85; Hon C Leic H Spirit *Leic* 85-88; Chapl Leic Univ 85-88; V Leic St Pet 88; P-in-c Leic St Sav 88; V Leic Ch Sav from 88. *St Saviour's Vicarage, Wood Hill, Leicester LE5 3JB* Leicester (0533) 513396

BOULLIER, Kenneth John. b 51. Trin Coll Bris. **d** 84 **p** 85. C Heref St Pet w St Owen and St Jas *Heref* 84-88; V Nutley *Chich* from 88; R Maresfield from 88. *The Vicarage, Nutley, Uckfield, E Sussex TN22 3HH* Nutley (082571) 2692

BOULSOVER, Philip John. b 16. ACT ThL55 Kelham Th Coll 34. **d** 40 **p** 41. C Middlesb St Cuth *York* 40-41; C Northallerton 41-43; C Bexhill St Pet *Chich* 43-51; Australia from 51. *21 Chillagoe Street, Fisher, Canberra, Australia 2611* Canberra (62) 887589

BOULT, Audrey. Qu Coll Birm. dss 85 **d** 87. Sheldon *Birm* 85-87; Hon Par Dn from 87. *17 Fulford Grove, Sheldon, Birmingham B26 3XX* 021-743 9993

BOULT, Geoffrey Michael. b 56. Southn Univ BTh88 Bris Univ DPhil90. Sarum & Wells Th Coll 77. **d** 80 **p** 81. C Newark w Hawton, Cotham and Shelton *S'well* 80-83; TV Melksham *Sarum* 83-90; P-in-c Charminster and Stinsford from 90. *The Vicarage, Mill Lane, Charminster, Dorchester, Dorset DT2 8DX* Dorchester (0305) 262477

BOULTBEE, John Michael Godolphin. b 22. Oak Hill Th Coll 66. **d** 68 **p** 69. C Hawkwell *Chelmsf* 68-71; C St Keverne *Truro* 71-73; V Constantine 74-79; P-in-c St Merryn 79-81; V 81-87; rtd 87. *8 Williams Close, Dawlish, Devon EX7 9SP* Dawlish (0626) 865761

BOULTER, Michael Geoffrey. b 32. Lon Univ BD56. Tyndale Hall Bris 53. **d** 57 **p** 58. C Tranmere St Cath *Ches* 57-60; R Cheetham Hill *Man* 60-65; R Tollard Royal w Farnham *Sarum* 65-66; Chapl Alderney Hosp Poole from 66; V Branksome St Clem *Sarum* from 66. *The Vicarage, Parkstone Heights, Branksome, Poole, Dorset BH14 0QE* Parkstone (0202) 748058

BOULTER, Robert George. b 49. Man Univ BA90. St Aug Coll Cant 72. **d** 75 **p** 76. C Langley All SS and Martyrs *Man* 75-80; V Lower Kersal 80-84; Oman 84-86; Community Chapl Slough *Ox* 86-87; R Whalley Range St Marg *Man* from 87. *St Margaret's Rectory, Rufford Road, Whalley Range, Manchester M16 8AE* 061-226 1289

BOULTON, Christopher David. b 50. Keble Coll Ox BA71 MA80. Cuddesdon Coll 71. **d** 74 **p** 75. C Harlow St Mary V *Chelmsf* 74-77; C Shrub End 77-80; P-in-c Gt Bentley 80-83; V 83-89; V Cherry Hinton St Andr *Ely* from 89; P-in-c Teversham from 90. *Cherry Hinton Vicarage, Fulbourn Old Drift, Cambridge CB1 4LR* Cambridge (0223) 247740

BOULTON, Canon Peter Henry. b 25. St Chad's Coll Dur BA49. Ely Th Coll 49. **d** 50 **p** 51. C Coppenhall *Ches* 50-54; C Mansf St Mark *S'well* 54-55; V Clipstone 55-60; V Carlton 60-67; Chapl Victoria Hosp Worksop 67-87; V Worksop Priory *S'well* 67-87; Hon Can S'well Minster from 75; Dir of Educn from 87; Chapl to HM The Queen from 91. *Dunham House, Westgate, Southwell, Notts NG25 0JL* Southwell (0636) 814504

BOULTON, Preb Thomas Oswald. b 10. Keble Coll Ox BA35 MA39. Wycliffe Hall Ox 35. **d** 36 **p** 37. RD Oswestry *Lich* 60-76; V Oswestry St Oswald 60-76; Preb Lich Cathl 67-76; rtd 76. *21 Rayleigh Road, Harrogate, N Yorkshire HG2 8QR* Harrogate (0423) 871753

BOULTON, Wallace Dawson. b 31. Lon Coll of Div 65. **d** 67 **p** 68. C Bramcote *S'well* 67-71; Dioc Public Relns Officer 69-71; Hon C St Bride Fleet Street w Bridewell etc *Lon* 71-86; Publicity Sec CMS 71-79; Media Sec 79-86; Lic to Offic *Chich* from 84; Guild Chapl from 86; Ed C of E Newspaper 86-88. *44 Winterbourne Close, Hastings, E Sussex TN34 1XQ* Hastings (0424) 713743

BOULTON-LEA, Peter John. b 46. St Jo Coll Dur BA68. Westcott Ho Cam 69. **d** 71 **p** 72. C Farlington *Portsm* 72-75; C Darlington St Jo *Dur* 75-77; R E and W Horndon w Lt Warley *Chelmsf* 77-82; V Hersham *Guildf* from 82. *The Vicarage, 5 Burwood Road, Hersham, Walton-on-Thames, Surrey KT12 4AA* Walton-on-Thames (0932) 227445

BOUNDS, John Henry. b 11. Clifton Th Coll 36. **d** 40 **p** 41. V Leigh *Roch* 57-80; rtd 80; Perm to Offic *Chich* 80-81 and from 84; Hon C Uckfield 81-84. *39 Manor End, Uckfield, E Sussex TN22 1DN* Uckfield (0825) 5604

BOUNDY, David. b 34. Kelham Th Coll 55. **d** 59 **p** 60. C Stirchley *Birm* 59-64; Chapl E Birm Hosp 64-74; V Bordesley St Oswald 64-70; V S Yardley St Mich 70-74; R Bideford *Ex* 74-82; RD Hartland 80-82; R Northfield *Birm* 82-88; P-in-c Penzance St Mary w St Paul *Truro* 88-90; V from 90. *St Mary's Vicarage, Chapel Street, Penzance, Cornwall TR18 4AP* Penzance (0736) 63079

BOUNDY, Gerald Neville. b 36. BA. Linc Th Coll. **d** 65 **p** 66. C Bris St Mary Redcliffe w Temple etc *Bris* 65-70; P-in-c Southmead 70-72; V 72-81; V Cotham St Sav w St Mary from 81. *182 St Michael's Hill, Cotham, Bristol BS2 8DE* Bristol (0272) 743198 or 733395

BOURDEAUX, Canon Michael Alan. b 34. St Edm Hall Ox BA57 MA61 BD68. Wycliffe Hall Ox 57. **d** 60 **p** 61. C Enfield St Andr *Lon* 60-64; C Old Charlton *S'wark* 65-66; Lic to Offic *Roch* 66-70; Gen Dir Keston Coll Kent from 70; Hon Can Roch Cathl from 90. *Keston Research, 33A Canal Street, Oxford OX2 6BQ* Oxford (0865) 311022

BOURKE, Very Rev Francis Robert. b 16. TCD BA40 BD46 PhD61. CITC 41. **d** 42 **p** 42. Dean Kilfenora *L & K* 72-86; Dean Killaloe 72-86; I Killaloe 72-76; Can Killaloe Cathl 72-86; I Killaloe w Abington, Kiltinanlea etc 76-86; rtd 86. *Tinnaview, Inchanore, Ballina, Killaloe, Co Clare, Irish Republic* Killaloe (61) 76461

BOURKE, Ven Michael Gay. b 41. CCC Cam BA63 MA67. Cuddesdon Coll 65. **d** 67 **p** 68. C Gt Grimsby St Jas *Linc* 67-71; C Digswell *St Alb* 71-73; C-in-c Panshanger CD 73-78; Course Dir St Alb Minl Tr Scheme 75-87; V Southill 78-86; Adn Bedf from 86. *84 Bury Road, Shillington, Hitchin, Herts SG5 3NZ* Hitchin (0462) 711958

BOURKE, Ronald Samuel James. b 50. MA HDipEd. **d** 79 **p** 80. C Portadown St Mark *Arm* 79-83; I Carnteel and Crilly 83-90; I Mountmellick w Coolbanagher, Rosenallis etc *M & K* from 90. *The Rectory, Mountmellick, Co Laois, Irish Republic* Mountmellick (502) 24143

BOURKE, Stanley Gordon. b 48. CITC 78. **d** 78 **p** 79. C Dundonald *D & D* 78-80; C Lurgan Ch Ch 81-82; I Dungiven w Bovevagh *D & R* 82-89; I Lurgan St Jo *D & D* from 89. *St John's Rectory, Sloan Street, Lurgan, Craigavon, Co Armagh BT66 8NT* Lurgan (0762) 322770

BOURNE, Canon Charles Wittwer Wilfrid. b 02. AKC30. **d** 30 **p** 31. V Grove *Ox* 36-71; V Denchworth 40-71; Hon Can Ch Ch 64-71; rtd 71. *4 Thoroughgood Road, Clacton-on-Sea, Essex CO15 6AN* Clacton-on-Sea (0225) 421827

BOURNE, David James. b 54. Reading Univ BA76. Trin Coll Bris 77. **d** 79 **p** 80. C W Bromwich Gd Shep w St Jo *Lich* 79-84; V Riseley w Bletsoe *St Alb* from 84. *The Vicarage, Church Lane, Riseley, Bedford* Bedford (0234) 708234

BOURNE, Dennis John. b 32. Loughb Coll of Educn DLC55. Ridley Hall Cam 58. **d** 60 **p** 61. C Gorleston St Andr *Nor* 60-64; Min Gorleston St Mary CD 64-79; V Costessey 79-86; R Hingham w Woodrising w Scoulton from 86; RD Hingham and Mitford from 90. *The Rectory, Hingham, Norwich NR9 4HP* Attleborough (0953) 850211

BOURNE, Henry. b 34. Spurgeon's Coll 55. **d** 64 **p** 65. C Handsworth St Mary *Birm* 64-67; Chapl RAF 67-85; Asst Chapl-in-Chief RAF 85-87; P-in-c Bourn *Ely* 87-88; V 88-89; P-in-c Kingston 87-88; V 88-89; V Caxton 88-89; R Bourn and Kingston w Caxton and Longstowe from 89. *The Rectory, Short Street, Bourn, Cambridge CB3 7SG* Caxton (0954) 719728

BOURNE, Michael. b 30. AKC58. **d** 59 **p** 60. C Southmead *Bris* 59-62; C-in-c W Leigh CD *Portsm* 62-67; V Wroxall 67-73; TR Poplar *Lon* 73-89; Sec and Dir Tr Gen Syn Hosp Chapl Coun from 89. *c/o Church House, Great Smith Street, London SW1P 3NZ* 071-222 9011

BOURNE, Philip John. b 61. Sussex Univ BEd83 Aber Univ MLitt86. Cranmer Hall Dur 85. **d** 87 **p** 88. C Gildersome *Wakef* 87-89; Chapl Ex Univ *Ex* from 89; Lic to Offic from 89. *29 Barnardo Road, Exeter EX2 4ND* Exeter (0392) 420162

BOURNER, Paul. b 48. CA Tr Coll. **d** 90 **p** 91. CA from 79; C Ipswich St Mary at Stoke w St Pet & St Mary Quay *St E* from 90. *6 Stone Lodge Lane, Ipswich, Suffolk IP2 9PA* Ipswich (0473) 601617

BOURNON, Dennis Harry. b 20. St Cuth Soc Dur LTh48 BA49. Oak Hill Th Coll 46. **d** 49 **p** 50. R Eastrop *Win* 65-80; R Nursling and Rownhams 80-85; rtd 85. *47 Stoneleigh Avenue, Hordle, Lymington, Hants SO41 0GS* New Milton (0425) 614016

BOURNON, Canon John Raymond. b 18. St Cath Soc Ox BA48 MA52. Oak Hill Th Coll 48. **d** 50 **p** 51. V Ware Ch Ch *St Alb* 60-85; RD Hertf 71-77; Hon Can St Alb 80-85; rtd 85; Perm to Offic Linc from 86; Pet from 87. *Hawkesbury, 14 Cambridge Road, Stamford, Lincs PE9 1BN* Stamford (0780) 54394

BOUTLE, David Francis. b 44. Leeds Univ BSc67 Lon Univ DipTh72. Cuddesdon Coll 69. **d** 72 **p** 73. C Boston *Linc* 72-77; C Waltham 77-80; P-in-c Morton 80-81; V from 81; Chapl Jo Coupland Hosp Gainsborough from 80. *The Vicarage, Morton Front, Gainsborough, Lincs DN21 3AD* Gainsborough (0427) 612654

BOVEY, Denis Philip. b 29. Ely Th Coll 50. **d** 53 **p** 54. C Southwick St Columba *Dur* 53-57; Perm to Offic *Ox* 57-59; Lic to Offic *Chich* 62-64; C W Hartlepool St Aid *Dur* 64-66; R Aber St Jas *Ab* 66-74; R Old Deer 74-89; R Longside 74-89; R Strichen 74-89; Can St Andr Cathl 75-88; Syn Clerk 78-83; Dean Ab 83-88; R Dufftown from 89; R Inverurie from 89; R Auchindoir from 89; R Alford from 89; P-in-c Kemnay from 89. *The Rectory, St Mary's Place, Inverurie, Aberdeenshire AB51 9QN* Inverurie (0467) 20470

BOVILL, Francis William. b 34. Lon Univ DipTh58. St Aid Birkenhead 55. **d** 58 **p** 59. C Bispham *Blackb* 58-61; C Crosthwaite Keswick *Carl* 61-64; V Radcliffe St Andr *Man* 64-68; P-in-c Woodside St Steph *Glouc* 68; V 69-73; V Scotby *Carl* from 73. *The Vicarage, Lambley Bank, Scotby, Carlisle CA4 8BX* Scotby (022872) 205

BOWDEN, Frank James. b 12. Lon Univ BA35. **d** 38 **p** 40. Lic to Offic *Nor* from 38. *52 Heigham Road, Norwich NR2 3AU* Norwich (0603) 624481

BOWDEN, John Stephen. b 35. CCC Ox BA59 MA62 Edin Univ Hon DD81. Linc Th Coll 59. **d** 61 **p** 62. C Nottm St Mary *S'well* 61-64; Lect Nottm Univ 64-66; Ed and Managing Dir SCM Press from 66; Hon C Highgate All SS *Lon* from 66; Hon C Brentford St Faith 80-87; Hon C Brentford from 87. *20 Southwood Avenue, London N6 5RZ* 081-340 7548

BOWDEN, John-Henry David. b 47. Magd Coll Cam BA69 MA73 Man Poly DMS77. S Dios Minl Tr Scheme 81. **d** 84 **p** 85. NSM Redlynch and Morgan's Vale *Sarum* 84-88; NSM Cuckfield *Chich* from 88. *Greenwood, Bolney Road, Ansty, Haywards Heath, W Sussex RH17 5AW* Haywards Heath (0444) 450213

BOWDEN, Canon Robert Andrew. b 38. Worc Coll Ox BA62 DipTh63 MA67 BDQ68. Cuddesdon Coll 63. **d** 65 **p** 66. C Wolv St Geo *Lich* 65-69; C Duston *Pet* 69-72; R Byfield 72-79; Chapl R Agric Coll Cirencester from 79; R Coates, Rodmarton and Sapperton etc *Glouc* from 79; Bp's Adv on Rural Soc from 81; Hon Can Glouc Cathl from 90. *Coates Rectory, Cirencester, Glos GL7 6NR* Cirencester (0285) 770235

BOWDER, Reginald (William) Maxwell. b 46. TCD BA68 MA81 Kent Univ DipSocWork71. S'wark Ord Course 78. **d** 80 **p** 81. C Bush Hill Park St Steph *Lon* 81-84; I Fiddown w Clonegam, Guilcagh and Kilmeaden *C & O* 84-87; I Lismore w Cappoquin, Kilwatermoy, Dungarvan etc 87-89; Dean Lismore 87-89; Chapl Kent Univ and KIAD *Cant* from 90. *The Chaplaincy, University of Kent, Canterbury, Kent CT2 7NX* Canterbury (0227) 764000

BOWDLER, Ernest Roy. b 10. Lich Th Coll 32. **d** 34 **p** 36. V Wolv Ch Ch *Lich* 57-71; Chapl CGA 71-73; C Langley Marish 73-76; rtd 75; Hon C Worc St Martin w St Pet *Worc* 76-85; Hon C Walsall Pleck and Bescot *Lich* 85-88; Perm to Offic from 87. *1 Vicarage Road West, Woodsetton, Dudley, W Midlands DY1 4NN* Wolverhampton (0902) 674797

BOWEN, Colin Wynford. b 48. St D Coll Lamp DipTh71. **d** 71 **p** 72. C Hubberston w Herbrandston and Hasguard etc *St D* 71-75; R Cosheston w Nash and Upton 75-77; V Carew and Cosheston w Nash and Upton 77-85; V Pemb St Mary and St Mich from 85. *The Vicarage, 18 Grove Hill, Pembroke, Dyfed SA71 5PT* Pembroke (0646) 682710

BOWEN, Daniel Austin. b 11. St D Coll Lamp BA33 St Steph Ho Ox 33. **d** 35 **p** 36. V Monkton *St D* 67-78; rtd 78; Perm to Offic *Chich* from 78. *38 Harwood Avenue, Goring-by-Sea, Worthing, W Sussex BN12 6EJ* Worthing (0903) 49233

BOWEN, David Gregory. b 47. Lanchester Poly BSc69. Cuddesdon Coll 70. **d** 74 **p** 75. C Rugby St Andr *Cov* 74-77; C Charlton St Luke w H Trin *S'wark* 78-80; TV Stantonbury *Ox* 80-82. *Address temp unknown*

BOWEN, David John. b 46. Glouc Th Course 83. **d** 86 **p** 88. NSM Ross w Brampton Abbotts, Bridstow and Peterstow *Heref* 86-88; C Kingstone w Clehonger, Eaton Bishop etc from 88. *The Vicarage, Church Road, Clehonger, Hereford HR2 9SE* Hereford (0432) 277786

BOWEN, Mrs Delyth. St D Coll Lamp BA. St Mich Coll Llan. **d** 91. C Llandybie *St D* from 91. *Nantyffin, 38 Ffordd y Betws, Ammanford, Dyfed SA18 2HE* Ammanford (0269) 595492

BOWEN, Glyn. b 18. Univ of Wales BA40. St Steph Ho Ox 40. **d** 42 **p** 43. V Port Talbot St Theodore *Llan* 71-84; rtd 84; Perm to Offic *Llan* from 84. *49 Beechwood Road, Margam, Port Talbot, W Glam SA13 2AD* Port Talbot (0639) 885866

BOWEN, Gwyn Humphrey. b 21. Univ of Wales (Lamp) BA54. **d** 56 **p** 57. C Penarth w Lavernock *Llan* 56-63; C Pontycymmer and Blaengarw 63-65; V Cwmaman from 65. *The Vicarage, 27 Byron Street, Cwmaman, Aberdare, M Glam CF44 6HP* Aberdare (0685) 872902

BOWEN, Howard Charles Campbell. b 13. Univ of Wales BA36. **d** 36 **p** 37. V N Newton w St Mich Ch *B & W* 63-74; P-in-c Langford Budville w Runnington 74-79; rtd 80; Hon C Ash Priors *B & W* 81-85; Perm to Offic from 86. *22 Drakes Park, Wellington, Somerset TA21 8TB* Wellington (0823) 472226

BOWEN, Miss Jennifer Ethel. b 46. Liv Univ BSc68 CertEd69. N Ord Course 80. **dss** 83 **d** 87. Blundellsands St Nic *Liv* 83-86; W Derby St Mary 86-87; Par Dn from 87. *4 The Armoury, West Derby, Liverpool L12 5EL* 051-256 6600

BOWEN, John. b 39. Univ of Wales DipTh63 Aus Nat Univ BA88. St Mich Coll Llan 60. **d** 68 **p** 69. C Aberavon *Llan* 68-73; Australia from 73. *c/o Radford College, College Street, Bruce, ACT, Australia 2607* Bruce (6) 251-4488

BOWEN, John Roger. b 34. St Jo Coll Ox BA59 MA62. Tyndale Hall Bris 59. **d** 61 **p** 62. C Cam St Paul *Ely* 61-65; Tanzania 65-76; Kenya 76-80; Lic to Offic *S'well* from 80; Dir Past Studies St Jo Coll Nottm 80-85; Tutor from 85. *St John's College, Bramcote, Nottingham NG9 3DS* Nottingham (0602) 224086

BOWEN, Very Rev Lawrence. b 14. Univ of Wales BA36. St Mich Coll Llan 37. **d** 38 **p** 39. R Tenby w Gumfreston *St D* 63-72; Can St D Cathl 72; Dean and Prec St D 72-84; V St D Cathl 72-84; rtd 84. *Sladeway, Fishguard, Dyfed SA65 9NY* Fishguard (0348) 874563

BOWEN, Lionel James. b 16. S'wark Ord Course 63. **d** 64 **p** 65. C Sanderstead All SS *S'wark* 67-74; V Pill *B & W* 74-79; Perm to Offic *Chich* from 79; rtd 81. *43 Sussex Court, Eaton Road, Hove, E Sussex BN3 3AS* Brighton (0273) 775945

BOWEN, Philip Jackson. b 10. St D Coll Lamp BA33 St Steph Ho Ox 33. **d** 35 **p** 36. V Llandeilo Fawr w Llandyfeisant *St D* 70-72; rtd 72. *3 Ger-y-Llan, The Parade, Carmarthen, Dyfed* Carmarthen (0267) 233731

BOWEN, Roger William. b 47. Magd Coll Cam BA69 MA73. St Jo Coll Nottm 69. **d** 72 **p** 73. C Rusholme *Man* 72-75; Rwanda Miss 75-84; Burundi 77-84; Tutor and Lect All Nations Chr Coll Ware from 85; Lic to Offic *St Alb* from 86. *All Nations Christian College, Easneye, Ware, Herts SG12 8LX* Ware (0920) 61243

BOWEN, Stephen Guy. b 47. Qu Coll Cam BA68 MA72 Bris Univ MA72. Clifton Th Coll 69. **d** 71 **p** 72. C Chelsea St Jo *Lon* 71-73; C Chelsea St Jo w St Andr 73; C Guildf St Sav *Guildf* 73-76; C Guildf St Sav w Stoke-next-Guildf 76-77; C Wallington H Trin *S'wark* 77-79; V Felbridge from 79. *The Vicarage, The Glebe, Felbridge, East Grinstead, W Sussex RH19 2QT* East Grinstead (0342) 321524

BOWEN, Thomas Raymond. b 20. Univ of Wales (Lamp) BA42. **d** 48 **p** 49. Chapl RAF 53-75; Chapl Gresham's Sch Holt 75-83; rtd 83; Perm to Offic *St D* from 83. *35 Gail Rise, Llangwm, Haverfordwest* Johnston (0437) 891179

BOWEN, Vincent Paul. b 26. Qu Coll Cam BA50 MA55. Ely Th Coll 51. **d** 53 **p** 54. R Cranham *Chelmsf* 61-71; R Wanstead St Mary 71-91; rtd 91. *44 Nunnery Fields, Canterbury CT1 3JT* Canterbury (0227) 472036

BOWER, Brian Mark. b 60. QUB BA DipTh. **d** 85 **p** 86. C Orangefield w Moneyreagh *D & D* 85-87; I Inver w Mountcharles, Killaghtee and Killybegs *D & R* from 87; Miss to Seamen from 87. *The Rectory, Inver, Donegal, Irish Republic* Donegal (73) 36013

BOWER, James Hugh Marsh. b 17. St Chad's Coll Dur BA39 DipTh40 MA43. **d** 40 **p** 41. V Wolv St Andr *Lich* 58-74; R Cavendish *St E* 74-83; P-in-c Stansfield 78-83; RD Clare 82-83; rtd 83; Perm to Offic *St E* from 83. *142 Melford Road, Sudbury, Suffolk CO10 6JZ* Sudbury (0787) 72683

BOWERING, John Anthony. b 34. SS Coll Cam BA57 MA. Wycliffe Hall Ox 57. **d** 59 **p** 60. C Hornchurch St Andr *Chelmsf* 59-62; Succ Chelmsf Cathl 62; Prec Chelmsf Cathl 63; V Brampton Bierlow *Sheff* 64-70; V Norton Woodseats St Paul 70-80; V Tickhill w Stainton from 80; RD W Doncaster from 87. *2 Sunderland Street, Tickhill, Doncaster, S Yorkshire DN11 9QJ* Doncaster (0302) 742224

BOWERING, Ven Michael Ernest. b 35. Kelham Th Coll 55. **d** 59 **p** 60. C Middlesb St Oswald *York* 59-62; C Huntington 62-64; V Brayton 64-72; RD Selby 71-72; V Saltburn-by-the-Sea 72-81; Can Res York Minster 81-87; Sec for Miss and Evang 81-87; Adn Lindisfarne *Newc* from 87. *12 Rectory Park, Morpeth, Northd NE61 2SZ* Morpeth (0670) 513207

BOWERS, David. b 55. Man Univ BA79. Wycliffe Hall Ox 82. **d** 84 **p** 85. C Lawton Moor *Man* 84-87; C Walmsley from 87. *38 Queen's Avenue, Bromley Cross, Bolton BL7 9BL* Bolton (0204) 53080

BOWERS, Francis Malcolm. b 44. Chan Sch Truro 79. **d** 82 **p** 83. NSM Penzance St Mary w St Paul *Truro* 82-83; C 86-88; NSM Madron 83-86; TV Redruth w Lanner and Treleigh 88-91; V St Blazey from 91. *The Vicarage, St Blazey, Par, Cornwall PL24 2NG* Par (072681) 2113

BOWERS, Canon John Edward. b 23. TD68. AKC50. **d** 51 **p** 52. V Ashby-de-la-Zouch St Helen w Coleorton *Leic* 63-88; CF (R of O) 67-78; RD Akeley W (Ashby) *Leic* 76-88; Hon Can Leic Cathl from 78; rtd 88; Perm to Offic Derby & Leic from 88; Chapl to High Sheriff of Derbyshire 89-90. *50 The Woodlands, Packhorse Road, Melbourne, Derbyshire DE7 1DQ* Melbourne (0332) 864067

BOWERS, Canon John Edward William. b 32. St Aid Birkenhead 60. **d** 63 **p** 64. C Bromborough *Ches* 63-68; Ind Chapl 68-74; P-in-c Crewe St Pet 69-71; V Crewe St Mich 71-74; TR Ellesmere Port 74-79; V Hattersley from 79; Hon Can Ches Cathl from 80; RD Mottram from 88. *St Barnabas' Vicarage, Hattersley Road East, Hyde, Cheshire SK14 3EQ* 061-368 2795

BOWERS, Julian Michael. b 48. Edin Th Coll 69. **d** 72 **p** 73. C Chippenham St Andr w Tytherton Lucas *Bris* 72-74; C Henbury 74-77; Sri Lanka 77-82; P-in-c Evercreech w Chesterblade and Milton Clevedon *B & W* 82-83; V 83-89; V Enfield St Jas *Lon* from 89. *St James's Vicarage, 144 Hertford Road, Enfield, Middx EN3 5AY* 081-804 1966

BOWERS, Michael Charles. b 52. Sarum & Wells Th Coll 89. **d** 91. C St Peter-in-Thanet *Cant* from 91. *64 High Street, St Peter's, Broadstairs, Kent CT10 2TD* Thanet (0843) 65229

BOWERS, Peter. b 47. Linc Th Coll 72. **d** 76 **p** 77. C Mackworth St Fran *Derby* 76-78; C Maidstone St Martin *Cant* 78-83; V Elmton *Derby* 83-89; V Swimbridge and W Buckland *Ex* from 89. *The Vicarage, Swimbridge, Barnstaple, Devon EX32 0PH* Swimbridge (0271) 830257

BOWERS, Peter William Albert. b 36. K Coll Lon BD61 AKC61. **d** 62 **p** 63. C Chorley St Pet *Blackb* 62-64; C New Sleaford *Linc* 64-67; C Folkestone H Trin w Ch Ch *Cant* 67-72; V Deal St Geo 72-80; Dir Galilee Community 80-85; R River from 86. *The Vicarage, 23 Lewisham Road, Dover, Kent CT17 0QG* Dover (0304) 822037

BOWERS, Raymond Franklin. b 16. Lon Univ BD40. ALCD40. **d** 40 **p** 41. V Bath St Steph *B & W* 66-76; P-in-c Gosforth *Carl* 76-78; P-in-c Wasdale Head and Nether Wasdale 76-78; R Gosforth w Nether Wasdale and Wasdale Head 78-80; rtd 81; Perm to Offic *Carl* from 81. *Brow House, Blackbeck, Egremont, Cumbria CA22 2NY* Beckermet (0946) 841345

BOWERS, Stanley Percival. b 20. Lon Univ BD45. Wells Th Coll. **d** 66 **p** 66. C Lawrence Weston *Bris* 66-69; V Two Mile Hill St Mich from 69. *St Michael's Vicarage, Bristol BS15 1BE* Bristol (0272) 671371

BOWES, Ernest Ward. b 04. Trin Coll Cam BA27 MA30. Ridley Hall Cam 27. **d** 29 **p** 30. V Weston-super-Mare Em *B & W* 52-70; rtd 70; Perm to Offic *Chich* from 70. *40 Exmoor Drive, Worthing, W Sussex BN13 2PH* Worthing (0903) 60741

BOWES, John Anthony Hugh. b 39. Ch Ch Ox BA62 DipTh63 MA65. Westcott Ho Cam 63. **d** 65 **p** 66. C Langley All SS and Martyrs *Man* 65-68; Asst Chapl Bris Univ *Bris* 68-73; TV Cramlington *Newc* 73-76; P-in-c Oldland *Bris* 76-80; TR 80-84; V Westbury-on-Trym St Alb from 84. *St Alban's Vicarage, 21 Canowie Road, Bristol BS6 7HR* Bristol (0272) 735844

BOWETT, Richard Julnes. b 45. E Anglian Minl Tr Course 86. **d** 89 **p** 90. C Hunstanton St Mary w Ringstead Parva, Holme etc *Nor* from 89. *The Little House, 2 Hamilton Road, Hunstanton, Norfolk PE36 6JA* Hunstanton (04853) 2276

BOWHILL, Allan Harold Leslie. b 43. Trin Coll Bris DipHE80. **d** 82 **p** 83. C Wolv St Luke *Lich* 82-84; C-in-c Reading St Mary Castle Street Prop Chpl *Ox* 84-90; R Keinton Mandeville w Lydford on Fosse *B & W* from 90. *The Rectory, Church Street, Keinton Mandeville, Somerton, Somerset TA11 6EP* Charlton Mackrell (045822) 3216

BOWIE, Michael Nicholas Roderick. b 59. Sydney Univ BA78 CCC Ox DPhil90. St Steph Ho Ox MA90. **d** 91. C Swanley St Mary *Roch* from 91. *25 Irving Way, Swanley, Kent BR8 7EP* Swanley (0322) 667601

BOWKER, Archibald Edward. b 18. Univ of Manitoba BA52. St Jo Coll Winnipeg LTh51. **d** 51 **p** 52. V Blackhill *Dur* 61-79; rtd 80. *19 Greenside, Greatham, Hartlepool, Cleveland TS25 2HS* Hartlepool (0429) 871973

BOWKER, Canon Prof John Westerdale. b 35. Worc Coll Ox BA58. Ripon Hall Ox. **d** 61 **p** 62. C Endcliffe *Sheff* 61-62; Fell Lect and Dir of Studies CCC Cam 62-74; Lect Div Cam Univ 70-74; Prof of Relig Studies Lanc Univ 74-86; Hon Can Cant Cathl *Cant* from 85; Dean of Chpl Trin Coll Cam from 86. *Trinity College, Cambridge* Cambridge (0223) 338400

BOWKETT, Canon Cyril Edward Vivian. b 11. St Jo Coll Dur LTh38 BA39 MA68. Clifton Th Coll 35. **d** 39 **p** 40. R S'wark St Geo *S'wark* 64-82; Hon Can S'wark Cathl 66-82; P-in-c S'wark St Jude 75-82; rtd 82; Perm to Offic *B & W* from 82. *The Lookout, Warren Road, Brean, Burnham-on-Sea, Somerset TA8 2RP* Brean Down (027875) 517

✣**BOWLBY, Rt Rev Ronald Oliver.** b 26. Trin Coll Ox BA50 MA54. Westcott Ho Cam 50. **d** 52 **p** 53 **c** 73. C Pallion *Dur* 52-56; C Billingham St Cuth 56-57; C-in-c Billingham St Aid CD 57-60; V Billingham St Aid 60-66; V Croydon *Cant* 66-73; Hon Can Cant Cathl 70-73; Bp Newc 73-80; Bp S'wark 80-91; rtd 91; Asst Bp Lich from 91. *4 Uppington Avenue, Shrewsbury SY3 7JL* Shrewsbury (0743) 244192

BOWLER, Christopher William. b 61. Nottm Univ BA83 Ch Ch Ox PGCE84 Down Coll Cam BA89. Ridley Hall Cam 87. **d** 90 **p** 91. C Downend *Bris* from 90. *5 Queensholm Close, Bristol BS16 6LD* Bristol (0272) 562081

BOWLER, David Henderson. b 54. Kent Univ BA75. St Jo Coll Nottm 75. **d** 78 **p** 79. C Bramcote *S'well* 78-82; TV Kirby Muxloe *Leic* 82-88; V Quorndon from 88. *6 Loughborough Road, Quorn, Loughborough, Leics LE12 8DX* Quorn (0509) 412593

BOWLER, Denis Charles Stanley. b 16. **d** 66 **p** 67. C Coleford w Staunton *Glouc* 69-72; V Coney Hill 72-77; V Lydbrook 77-82; rtd 82; Perm to Offic *Glouc* from 82. *22 Harpfield Road, Bishops Cleeve, Cheltenham, Glos GL52 4EB* Bishops Cleeve (024267) 4307

BOWLER, Frederick Wallace. b 11. MBE46. AKC34. **d** 34 **p** 35. V Alcombe *B & W* 66-71; rtd 72. *43 Upcot Crescent, Taunton, Somerset TA1 5PJ* Taunton (0823) 272352

BOWLER, Preb Kenneth Neville. b 37. K Coll Lon 57. **d** 61 **p** 62. C Buxton *Derby* 61-67; R Sandiacre 67-75; V E Bedfont *Lon* 75-87; AD Hounslow 82-87; Preb St Paul's Cathl from 85; V Fulham All SS from 87. *All Saints' Vicarage, 70 Fulham High Street, London SW6 3LG* 071-736 6301

BOWLER, Roy Harold. b 27. Wadh Coll Ox BA48 MA57. Wells Th Coll 52. **d** 53 **p** 54. C Clerkenwell H Redeemer w St Phil *Lon* 53-55; C Tottenham All Hallows 55-57; Lic to Offic *Cant* 57-61; S Rhodesia 61-65; Rhodesia 65-80; Zimbabwe from 80. *Address temp unknown*

✣**BOWLES, Rt Rev Cyril William Johnston.** b 16. Em Coll Cam Jes Coll Cam BA38 MA41. Ridley Hall Cam 37. **d** 39 **p** 40 **c** 69. C Barking St Marg *Chelmsf* 39-41; Chapl Ridley Hall Cam 42-44; Vice-Prin 44-51; Prin 51-63; Hon Can Ely Cathl *Ely* 59-63; Adn Swindon *Bris* 63-69; Hon Can Bris Cathl 63-69; Bp Derby 69-87; rtd 87. *Rose Lodge, Tewkesbury Road, Stow on the Wold, Cheltenham, Glos GL54 1EN* Cotswold (0451) 31965

BOWLES, David Anthony. b 44. Kelham Th Coll 63. **d** 68 **p** 69. C Bilborough w Strelley *S'well* 68-72; C Beeston 72-75; Ascension Is 75-77; V Wellingborough St Mark *Pet* 77-83; P-in-c Wilby 78-83; R Burton Latimer 83-90; V Sheff St Oswald *Sheff* 90-91. *64 Church Street, Matlock, Derbyshire DE4 3BY*

BOWLES, John. b 32. N Ord Course. **d** 89 **p** 90. NSM Stockport St Mary *Ches* from 89. *13 Trajan Drive, Offerton, Stockport, Cheshire SK2 5QX* 061-483 9566

BOWLES, Preb Michael Hubert Venn. b 36. Selw Coll Cam BA59 MA63. Ridley Hall Cam 59. **d** 61 **p** 62. C Woodside Park St Barn *Lon* 61-64; C Swanage *Sarum* 64-67; Lect St Mich Coll Llan 67-72; Chapl St Mich Coll Llan 67-70; Lect Th Univ of Wales (Cardiff) 67-72; Lib St Mich Coll Llan 70-72; Lic to Offic *Llan* 71-72; R Gt Stanmore *Lon* from 72; Preb St Paul's Cathl from 85. *The Rectory, Rectory Lane, Stanmore, Middx HA7 4AQ* 081-954 0276

BOWLES, Peter John. b 39. Lon Univ BA60. Linc Th Coll 71. **d** 73 **p** 74. C Clay Cross *Derby* 73-76; C Boulton 76-79; R Brailsford w Shirley 79-85; P-in-c Osmaston w Edlaston 81-85; R Brailsford w Shirley and Osmaston w Edlaston 85-89; TR Old Brampton and Loundsley Green from 89. *The Rectory, 25 Oldridge Close, Chesterfield, Derbyshire S40 4UF* Chesterfield (0246) 236663

BOWLES, Ronald Leonard. b 24. K Coll Lon BD52 AKC52. **d** 53 **p** 54. V Woolston *Win* 66-75; V Moordown 75-89; rtd 89. *25 Cherry Tree Avenue, Cowplain, Portsmouth* Portsmouth (0705) 267376

BOWLEY, John Richard Lyon. b 46. MRTPI76 Dur Univ BA68 QUB MSc72. CITC. **d** 79 **p** 80. C Knock *D & D* 79-81; Bp's C Knocknagoney 81-90; I Ballywalter w Inishargie from 90. *The Vicarage, 2 Whitechurch Road, Ballywalter, Newtownards, Co Down BT22 2LB* Ballywalter (02477) 58416

BOWLZER, Ronald. b 41. CEng69 MIMechE69. **d** 84 **p** 84. NSM Rosyth *St And* 84-85; NSM Lochgelly 84-85; NSM Inverkeithing 84-85; NSM Dunfermline 85-89; C Whitehaven *Carl* from 89. *13 Rowan Tree Close, Whitehaven, Cumbria CA28 6LB* Whitehaven (0946) 691462

BOWMAN, Miss Alison Valentine. b 57. St Andr Univ MA79. St Steph Ho Ox 86. **d** 89. Par Dn Peacehaven *Chich* from 89. *24 Woodlands Close, Peacehaven, E Sussex BN10 7SF* Brighton (0273) 581356

BOWMAN, Clifford William. b 57. St Jo Coll Dur BA78. Ridley Hall Cam. **d** 82 **p** 83. C Sawley *Derby* 82-85; C Hucknall Torkard *S'well* 85-89; R Warsop from 89. *The Rectory, Church Road, Warsop, Mansfield, Notts NG20 0SL* Mansfield (0623) 843290

BOWMAN, George Henry Lindsay. b 15. Linc Th Coll 45. **d** 47 **p** 48. V Steeton *Bradf* 66-76; C Cleethorpes *Linc* 76-77; C Cleethorpes 77-80; rtd 80. *14 Broadway, Lincoln LN2 1SH* Lincoln (0522) 526579

BOWMAN-EADIE, Russell Ian. b 45. ACP68 K Coll Lon BD71 AKC71. St Aug Coll Cant 71. **d** 72 **p** 73. C Hammersmith St Pet *Lon* 72-74; V Leic St Nic *Leic* 74-81; Chapl Leic Univ 74-81; Adult Educn Adv *Dur* 81-84; Dir of Tr *B & W* from 84; Preb Wells Cathl from 90. *2 The Liberty, Wells, Somerset BA5 2SU* Wells (0749) 74702

BOWN, Francis Adrian Charles Simon. b 48. Jes Coll Cam BA72 MA74 Jes Coll Ox BA75 MA78 Hull Univ MA88. Linc Th Coll 76. **d** 77 **p** 78. C Howden *York* 77-79; C Howden Team Min 80; P-in-c Hull Sculcoates St Steph 80-85; V from 85. *St Stephen's Presbytery, 29 Westbourne Avenue, Hull HU5 3HN* Hull (0482) 46075

BOWN, Canon John Frederick Olney. b 13. TD. MA. **d** 37 **p** 38. QHC 67-70; R Fordingbridge w Ibsley *Win* 70-79; RD Christchurch 74-78; rtd 79; P-in-c Longstock w Leckford *Win* 79-87. *Dawlish House, 7 Trafalgar Way, Stockbridge, Hants SO20 6ET* Andover (0264) 810672

BOWNESS, William Gary. b 48. Warw Univ BSc69. Ripon Coll Cuddesdon 80. **d** 82 **p** 83. C Lanc St Mary *Blackb* 82-86; V Lostock Hall from 86. *76A Brownedge Road, Lostock Hall, Preston, Lancs PR5 5AD* Preston (0772) 35366

BOWSER, Alan. b 35. Univ of Wales (Lamp) BA60 DipTh63. **d** 63 **p** 64. C Gateshead St Chad Bensham *Dur* 63-67; C Owton Manor CD 67-72; V Horden from 72. *The Vicarage, Horden, Peterlee, Co Durham SR8 4JF* 091-586 4423

BOWSHER, Andrew Peter. b 59. Reading Univ BA81 Nottm Univ DipTh84. St Jo Coll Nottm DPS86. **d** 86 **p** 87. C Grenoside *Sheff* 86-89; C Darfield 89-91; P-in-c Halifax All So *Wakef* from 91. *All Souls' Vicarage, 13 Booth Town Road, Halifax, W Yorkshire HX3 6EU* Halifax (0422) 321731

BOWSKILL, Robert Preston. b 48. S Dios Minl Tr Scheme 88. **d** 91. NSM Eastrop *Win* from 91. *Old Sarum, 1 Camfield Close, Basingstoke, Hants RG21 3AQ* Basingstoke (0256) 27301

BOWTELL, Paul William. b 47. Lon Univ BSc68. St Jo Coll Nottm. **d** 82 **p** 83. C Gorleston St Andr *Nor* 82-85; TV Forest Gate St Sav w W Ham St Matt *Chelmsf* 85-91; R Spitalfields Ch Ch w All SS *Lon* from 91. *The Rectory, 2 Fournier Street, London E1 6QE* 071-247 7202

BOWYER, Frank. b 28. Man Univ BA49 BD56. Oak Hill Th Coll 53. **d** 55 **p** 56. C Halliwell St Paul *Man* 55-57; C Crosthwaite Keswick *Carl* 57-59; V Thornham w Gravel Hole *Man* 59-63; R Burnage St Marg 63-81; R Gosforth w Nether Wasdale and Wasdale Head *Carl* 81-85; R Holcombe *Man* from 85. *The Rectory, 12 Carrwood Hey, Ramsbottom, Bury, Lancs BL0 9QT* Ramsbottom (0706) 822312

BOWYER, Geoffrey Charles. b 54. ACA79 ATII82 Lanc Univ BA76. St Jo Coll Nottm 85. **d** 87 **p** 88. C Walton St E 87-89; C Macclesfield Team Par *Ches* 89-91; V Cinderford St Steph w Littledean *Glouc* from 91. *The Vicarage, St Annal's Road, Cinderford, Glos GL14 2AS* Dean (0594) 822286

BOWYER, Dr Richard Astley. b 55. Jes Coll Ox MA Ex Univ PhD. Chich Th Coll 82. **d** 84 **p** 85. C Ex St Jas *Ex* 84-87; TV Ex St Thos and Em from 87. *St Andrew's Vicarage, 78 Queens Road, Exeter EX2 9EW* Exeter (0392) 433656

BOWYER, Robert Joscelyn. b 13. St Jo Coll Dur LTh36 BA37. St Aid Birkenhead 33. **d** 37 **p** 38. R Brook w Mottistone *Portsm* 53-78; rtd 78; Perm to Offic *Portsm* from 78. *Southbrook, Brook, Newport, Isle of Wight PO30 4EJ* Isle of Wight (0983) 740482

BOX, David Norman. b 28. K Coll Lon BD48 AKC48. **d** 51 **p** 52. C Grays Thurrock *Chelmsf* 51-53; Hon C Aldershot St Mich *Guildf* 53-55; Asst Master St Benedict's Sch Aldershot 53-55; C Weston 55-58; C Camberley St Paul 58-61; V Blackheath and Chilworth 61-69; V Allerton *Bradf* 69-75; R Exford w Exmoor *B & W* 75-80; V Castle Cary w Ansford 80-90; P-in-c Childe Okeford, Manston, Hammoon and Hanford *Sarum* from 90. *The Rectory, Child Okeford, Blandford Forum, Dorset DT11 8DX* Child Okeford (0258) 860547

BOX, Reginald Gilbert (Brother Reginald). b 20. Lon Univ BD41 AKC41 Em Coll Cam BA52 MA57. Westcott Ho Cam 41. **d** 43 **p** 44. SSF from 51; New Zealand, Australia and Melanesia 69-84; Perm to Offic Sarum from 84; Ely from 85; rtd 90; Chapl Chich Th Coll from 90. *St Francis House, 15 Botolph Lane, Cambridge CB2 3RD* Cambridge (0223) 353903

BOXALL, David John. b 41. Dur Univ BA63 DipTh65. Sarum Th Coll 65. **d** 66 **p** 67. C Ipswich St Aug *St E* 66-69; C Bourne *Linc* 69-71; C Woodside Park St Barn *Lon* 71-72; C Thundersley *Chelmsf* 72-76; P-in-c Farcet *Ely* 76-77; TV Stanground and Farcet 77-85; V Guyhirn w Ring's End 85-90; V Southea w Murrow and Parson Drove 85-90; P-in-c Fletton from 90. *The Rectory, 152 Fletton Avenue, Peterborough PE2 8DF* Peterborough (0733) 62783

BOXALL, Keith Michael. b 37. Trin Coll Bris. **d** 82 **p** 83. C Staines St Pet *Lon* 82-83; C Staines St Mary and St Pet 83-85; C Lydiard Millicent w Lydiard Tregoz *Bris* 85-86; TV The Lydiards from 86. *The Vicarage, Shaw, Swindon SN5 9PH* Swindon (0793) 770568

BOXALL, Martin Alleyne. b 37. Wells Th Coll 65. **d** 67 **p** 68. C Crowthorne *Ox* 67-70; C Tilehurst St Mich 70-76; V Tilehurst St Cath 76-78; V Padstow *Truro* from 78; Miss to Seamen from 78. *The Vicarage, Station Road, Padstow, Cornwall PL28 8DA* Padstow (0841) 532224

BOXALL, Simon Roger. b 55. St Jo Coll Cam BA76. Ridley Hall Cam 77. **d** 79 **p** 80. C Eaton *Nor* 79-82; SAMS from 82. *c/o SAMS, Allen Gardiner House, Pembury Road, Tunbridge Wells, Kent TN2 3QU* Tunbridge Wells (0892) 38647

BOXLEY, Christopher. b 45. K Coll Lon BD68 AKC68 Southn Univ CertEd73 Reading Univ MA84. **d** 69 **p** 70. C Bitterne Park *Win* 69-73; Perm to Offic *Chich* 73-78; Hd of Relig Studies Midhurst Gr Sch from 73; Dir Midhurst and Petworth Relig Studies Cen from 78; P-in-c Heyshott from 78. *The Rectory, Heyshott, Midhurst, W Sussex GU29 0DH* Midhurst (073081) 4405

BOXLEY, John Edwin. b 15. Ch Coll Cam BA38 MA41. Ridley Hall Cam 37. **d** 39 **p** 40. Chapl Dulwich Coll 61-76; R W w E Mersea *Chelmsf* 76-80; rtd 80; Perm to Offic *B & W* from 81. *16 Market Street, Wells, Somerset BA5 2DS* Wells (0749) 75073

BOYCE, Canon Brian David Michael. b 32. Fitzw Ho Cam BA55 MA62. Wells Th Coll 55. **d** 57 **p** 58. C Tavistock and Gulworthy *Ex* 57-60; C Paignton St Jo 60-62; S Africa from 62. *8 Eton Road, Parktown, 2193 South Africa* Johannesburg (11) 482-1606

BOYCE, Christopher Allan. b 44. RIBA Brighton Poly DipArch68. S Dios Minl Tr Scheme. **d** 87 **p** 88. NSM Eastbourne All SS *Chich* from 87. *53 Summerdown Road, Eastbourne, E Sussex BN20 8DR* Eastbourne (0323) 647780

BOYCE, John Frederick. b 33. ALCD57. **d** 57 **p** 58. C Earlsfield St Andr *S'wark* 57-60; C Westerham *Roch* 60-63; C Farnborough 63-66; V Sutton at Hone 66-73; P-in-c Chiddingstone 73-74; R Chiddingstone w Chiddingstone Causeway 74-84; V Brenchley from 84. *The Vicarage, Brenchley, Tonbridge, Kent TN12 7NN* Brenchley (089272) 2140

BOYCE, Kenneth. b 21. St Aid Birkenhead 59. **d** 60 **p** 61. R N Reddish *Man* 66-86; rtd 86. *150 Overdale Road, Romiley, Stockport, Cheshire SK6 6NF* 061-494 0934

BOYCE, Kenneth Albert. b 51. St Edm Hall Ox BA72 MA76 Selw Coll Cam BA75 MA79. Westcott Ho Cam 73. **d** 75 **p** 76. C Evington *Leic* 75-78; P-in-c Gt Bowden w Welham 78-81; Dioc Stewardship Adv 78-81; Chapl Leic Poly 81-86; TV Leic H Spirit 82-86; Chapl to the Deaf *Worc* from 86; P-in-c Astwood Bank from 86. *The Vicarage, Church Road, Astwood Bank, Redditch, Worcs B96 6EH* Astwood Bank (0527) 892489

BOYCE, Robert Albert Wright. b 19. BA. St Alb Minl Tr Scheme. **d** 82 **p** 83. NSM Hatf *St Alb* 82-89; Perm to Offic from 89; rtd 90. *92 Park Meadow, Hatfield, Herts AL9 5HE* Hatfield (0707) 267531

BOYD, Alan McLean. b 50. St Jo Coll Nottm BTh79. **d** 79 **p** 80. C Bishops Waltham *Portsm* 79-83; Chapl Reading Univ *Ox* 83-88; Chapl E Birm Hosp from 88. *38 Rodborough Road, Dorridge, Solihull, W Midlands B93 8EF* Knowle (0564) 730115

BOYD, Alexander Jamieson. b 46. MIBiol FSAScot St Chad's Coll Dur BSc68 Nottm Univ PGCE69. Coll of Resurr Mirfield 69. **d** 79 **p** 80. NSM Musselburgh *Edin* 79-83; CF from 83. *c/o MOD (Army), Bagshot Park, Bagshot, Surrey GU19 5PL* Bagshot (0276) 71717

BOYD, Allan Gray. b 41. St Jo Coll Nottm 84. **d** 87 **p** 88. NSM Glas St Gabr *Glas* from 87; Miss to Seamen from

87. *47 Holms Crescent, Erskine, Renfrewshire PA8 6DJ* 041-812 2754

BOYD, Allan Newby. b 31. MInstM73 Ball Coll Ox MA. St Alb Minl Tr Scheme 81. **d** 84 **p** 85. NSM Watford St Luke *St Alb* 84-88; C Ardsley *Sheff* 88-91; V Barrow St Jo *Carl* from 91. *St John's Vicarage, James Watt Terrace, Barrow-in-Furness, Cumbria LA14 2TS*   Barrow-in-Furness (0229) 821101

BOYD, David Anthony. b 42. Sarum & Wells Th Coll 72. **d** 75 **p** 76. C Ches H Trin *Ches* 75-79; R from 85; V Congleton St Jas 79-85. *Holy Trinity Rectory, Norris Road, Chester CH1 5DZ*   Chester (0244) 372721

BOYD, Michael Victor. b 33. St Chad's Coll Dur BA57 DipAdEd69 MEd77 PhD81. Coll of Resurr Mirfield 57. **d** 59 **p** 60. C Warsop *S'well* 59-61; Chapl St Geo Coll Quilmes Argent 62-63; Wolsingham Sch 63-67; Lect St Hild Coll Dur 67-75; Lect SS Hild & Bede Dur 75-79; Lect Dur Univ 79-84. *4 Aykley Green, Whitesmocks, Durham DH1 4LN*   091-384 9473

BOYD, Robert Henry. b 36. **d** 66 **p** 67. C Drumcree *Arm* 66-69; I Annaghmore 69-83; Bp's C Lissan 83-90; I from 90. *The Rectory, 150 Moneymore Road, Cookstown, Co Tyrone BT80 8PY*   Cookstown (06487) 66112

BOYD, Samuel Robert Thomas. b 62. **d** 90 **p** 91. NSM Derryloran *Arm* from 90. *10 Shankey Road, Stewartstown, Dungannon, Co Tyrone BT71 5PN* Stewartstown (086873) 8159

BOYD, William Green. b 07. K Coll Lon BA29 AKC29. Oak Hill Th Coll 74. **d** 75 **p** 76. Hon C Chingford SS Pet and Paul *Chelmsf* 75-81; Hon C Buckhurst Hill 81-86; rtd 86. *2 Leyland Gardens, Woodford Green, Essex IG8 7QT*   081-505 5752

BOYD, Canon William John Peter. b 28. Lon Univ BA48 BD53 PhD77 Birm Univ MA60. **d** 57 **p** 58. C Aston SS Pet and Paul *Birm* 57-60; V W Smethwick 60-63; V St Breward *Truro* 63-68; Adult Educn Chapl 64-85; Dioc Ecum Officer 65-83; R St Ewe 68-73; Preb St Endellion 73-85; V St Kew 73-77; R Falmouth K Chas 77-85; RD Carnmarth S 84-85; Dir of Tr from 85; Prin SW Minl Tr Course from 85; Can Res and Chan Truro Cathl *Truro* from 85. *25 Bosvean Gardens, Truro, Cornwall TR1 3NQ*   Truro (0872) 76491 or 76782

BOYD, William Thomas. b 15. TCD BA38 MA43. **d** 39 **p** 40. R W Parley *Sarum* 70-76; rtd 76. *Turlough, 4 Heath Farm Close, Ferndown, Wimborne, Dorset BH22 8JP* Ferndown (0202) 892055

BOYD-WILLIAMS, Anthony Robert. b 46. Univ of Wales (Cardiff) DPS88. St Mich Coll Llan 86. **d** 88 **p** 89. C Tonyrefail w Gilfach Goch *Llan* 88-91; V Treharris w Bedlinog from 91. *The Vicarage, 13 The Oaks, Quakers Yard, Treharris, M Glam*   Tonyrefail (0443) 410280

BOYDEN, Peter Frederick. b 41. Lon Univ BSc62 AKC62 Em Coll Cam BA64 MA68 MLitt69. Ridley Hall Cam 63. **d** 66 **p** 67. C Chesterton St Andr *Ely* 66-68; C Wimbledon *S'wark* 68-72; Chapl K Sch Cant 72-89; Chapl Radley Coll Abingdon from 89. *Radley College, Abingdon, Oxon*   Abingdon (0235) 530750

BOYES, David Arthur Stiles. b 30. Lon Coll of Div 62. **d** 63 **p** 64. C Islington St Mary *Lon* 63-71; V Canonbury St Steph 71-75; V St Paul's Cray St Barn *Roch* 75-85; P-in-c Earl Soham w Cretingham and Ashfield cum Thorpe *St E* from 85; Dioc Development Officer from 86. *The Rectory, Church Lane, Earl Soham, Woodbridge, Suffolk IP13 7SD*   Earl Soham (072882) 778

BOYES, Michael Charles. b 27. Lon Univ BA53 BD58. Wells Th Coll 53. **d** 55 **p** 56. C Heavitree *Ex* 55-61; C Exwick 61-68; V Broadclyst 68-83; RD Aylesbeare 77-81; TV Sampford Peverell, Uplowman, Holcombe Rogus etc 83-85; TR Sampford Peverell, Uplowman, Holcombe Rogus etc from 85. *The Rectory, Sampford Peverell, Tiverton, Devon EX16 7BP*   Tiverton (0884) 820206

BOYLAND, David Henry. b 58. TCD BA79 BAI79. **d** 91. C Seapatrick *D & D* from 91. *16 Bannview Heights, Banbridge, Co Down BT32 4LY*   Banbridge (08206) 28303

BOYLAND, Henry Hubert. b 23. DipMan. CITC. **d** 84 **p** 85. NSM Dunboyne w Kilcock, Maynooth, Moyglare etc *M & K*   84-87; Bp's C Carrickmacross w Magheracloone *Clogh* 87-90; I from 90. *The Rectory, Drumconrath Road, Carrickmacross, Co Monaghan, Irish Republic*   Carrickmacross (42) 61931

BOYLE, Andrew McKenzie. b 45. Down Coll Cam BA67 MA71 CEng72 MICE72. W Midl Minl Tr Course 82. **d** 85 **p** 86. NSM Woodthorpe *S'well* 85-87; Perm to Offic *Roch* 88-90; Hon C Sevenoaks St Luke CD 90-91. *31 Lambarde Drive, Sevenoaks, Kent TN13 3HX* Sevenoaks (0732) 456546

BOYLE, Christopher John. b 51. AKC75. St Aug Coll Cant 75. **d** 76 **p** 77. C Wylde Green *Birm* 76-80; Bp's Dom Chapl 80-83; R Castle Bromwich SS Mary and Marg from 83. *The Rectory, Rectory Lane, Birmingham B36 9DH*   021-747 2281

BOYLE, Canon Richard Henry. b 08. TCD BA30 LLB37 MA47. **d** 45 **p** 46. I Banagher *M & K* 60-82; Can Meath from 69; rtd 82. *Shannon Cottage, West End, Banagher, Birr, Co Offaly, Irish Republic*   Birr (509) 51134

BOYLE, Terence Robert. b 26. **d** 77 **p** 78. NSM Wexham *Ox* 77-84. *1 Wexham Springs Cottages, Framewood Road, Wexham, Slough SL2 4QR*   Fulmer (0753) 662134

BOYLES, Peter John. b 59. Univ of Wales (Lamp) BA84. Sarum & Wells Th Coll 86. **d** 88 **p** 89. C Ches St Mary *Ches* 88-91; C Neston from 91. *139 West Vale, Little Neston, South Wirral L64 0TJ*   051-336 6449

BOYLING, Canon Denis Hudson. b 16. Keble Coll Ox BA38 DipTh39 MA42. Cuddesdon Coll 39. **d** 40 **p** 41. V Almondbury *Wakef* 68-75; Can Res Wakef Cathl 75-82; rtd 82; Perm to Offic *Heref* from 82. *Brendon, Berrington Road, Tenbury Wells, Worcs WR15 8EN*   Tenbury Wells (0584) 810360

BOYLING, Mark Christopher. b 52. Keble Coll Ox BA74 BA76 MA78. Cuddesdon Coll 74. **d** 77 **p** 78. C Kirkby *Liv* 77-79; P-in-c 79-80; TV 80-85; Bp's Dom Chapl 85-89; V Formby St Pet from 89. *St Peter's Vicarage, Cricket Path, Formby, Liverpool L37 7DP* Formby (07048) 73369

BOYNS, Martin Laurence Harley. b 26. St Jo Coll Cam BA49 MA51. Ridley Hall Cam 50. **d** 52 **p** 53. C Woodmansterne *S'wark* 52-55; C Folkestone H Trin w Ch Ch *Cant* 55-58; V Duffield *Derby* 58-71; V Rawdon *Bradf* 71-76; Chapl Woodlands Hosp Rawdon 71-76; R Melton *St E* 76-85; R Gerrans w St Antony in Roseland *Truro* from 85; Miss to Seamen from 85. *The Rectory, Gerrans, Portscatho, Truro, Cornwall TR2 5EB* Portscatho (087258) 277

BOYNS, Timothy Martin Harley. b 58. Warw Univ BA80 Nottm Univ BCombStuds84. Linc Th Coll 81. **d** 84 **p** 85. C Oxhey St Matt *St Alb* 84-87; TV Solihull *Birm* from 87. *St Francis's House, 52 Redlands Close, Solihull, W Midlands B91 2LZ*   021-705 3234

BOYS SMITH, Canon John Sandwith. b 01. St Jo Coll Cam BA22 MA26 Hon LLD70. Westcott Ho Cam 22. **d** 26 **p** 27. Lic to Offic *Ely* from 44; Master St Jo Coll Cam 59-69; rtd 69. *Trinity House, Castle Street, Saffron Walden, Essex CB10 1BP*   Saffron Walden (0799) 23692

BOYSE, Felix Vivian Allan. b 17. LVO78. CCC Cam BA39 MA42. Cuddesdon Coll 39. **d** 40 **p** 41. HM Chapl Hampton Court Palace 65-82; Preacher Lincoln's Inn from 82; rtd 83. *Rose Cottage, Rookwood Road, West Wittering, Chichester, W Sussex PO20 8LT*   Birdham (0243) 514320

BOZON, David Hamish. b 28. Fitzw Ho Cam BA52 MA56. Linc Th Coll 53. **d** 55 **p** 56. C Baswich (or Berkswich) *Lich* 55-58; S Rhodesia 58-64; C Westbury-on-Trym H Trin *Bris* 64-65; Chapl to the Deaf 66-68; Info Officer RADD 68-84; Lic to Offic *Chelmsf* 74-84; R Sundridge w Ide Hill *Roch* from 84. *The Rectory, Chevening Road, Sundridge, Sevenoaks, Kent TN14 6AB*   Westerham (0959) 63749

BRABY, Peter. b 11. Ch Ch Ox BA32 MA37. Wells Th Coll 37. **d** 38 **p** 39. V Badsey *Worc* 58-76; V Wickhamford 58-76; RD Evesham 71-76; V Temple Guiting w Cutsdean *Glouc* 73-76; V The Guitings, Cutsdean and Farmcote 76; rtd 76; Perm to Offic *Guildf* from 85. *119 Clare Park, Crondall, Farnham, Surrey GU10 5DT* Aldershot (0252) 850004

BRACE, Stuart. b 49. Bp Burgess Hall Lamp DipTh74. **d** 74 **p** 75. C Llanelly Ch Ch *St D* 74-76; C Tenby w Gumfreston 76-77; V Ystradmeurig and Strata Florida 77-79; CF 79-86; Chapl HM Youth Cust Cen Everthorpe 86-88; Chapl HM Pris Stafford from 88. *HM Prison Stafford, 54 Gaol Road, Stafford ST16 3AW*   Stafford (0785) 54421

BRACEGIRDLE, Christopher Andrew. b 56. Dur Univ BEd79 St Edm Ho Cam BA84 MA89. Ridley Hall Cam 82. **d** 85 **p** 86. C Livesey *Blackb* 85-88; TV E Farnworth and Kearsley *Man* from 88. *The Vicarage, 93 Bradford Street, Farnworth, Bolton BL4 9JY*   Bolton (0204) 73842

BRACEGIRDLE, Mrs Cynthia Wendy Mary. b 52. LMH Ox BA73 MA77 Liv Univ DipAE82. N Ord Course. **d** 87. Chapl Asst Man R Infirmary 85-88; Dir Dioc Local Ord Min Scheme Man from 89. *The Rectory, Parsonage Close, Salford M5 3GT*   061-872 0800

BRACEGIRDLE, Robert Kevin Stewart. b 47. Univ Coll Ox BA69 MA73. St Steph Ho Ox 70. **d** 73 **p** 74. C Dorchester *Sarum* 73-75; C Woodchurch *Ches* 75-78; V Bidston 78-82; P-in-c Salford St Ignatius *Man* 82-86; R

Salford St Ignatius and Stowell Memorial from 86. *The Rectory, Parsonage Close, Salford M5 3GT*   061-872 0800

BRACEWELL, David John. b 44. Leeds Univ BA66 Man Univ MA82. Tyndale Hall Bris 67. **d** 69 **p** 70. C Tonbridge St Steph *Roch* 69-72; C Shipley St Pet *Bradf* 72-75; V Halliwell St Paul *Man* 75-84; R Guildf St Sav *Guildf* from 84. *St Saviour's Rectory, Wharf Road, Guildford GU1 4RP* Guildford (0483) 61867

BRACEWELL, Howard Waring. b 35. FRGS73. Tyndale Hall Bris. **d** 63 **p** 63. Canada 63-72; Travel Missr World Radio Miss Fellowship 72-77; P-in-c Ashill *Nor* 72-74; Hon C Bris St Phil and St Jacob w Em *Bris* 77-84; Perm to Offic *St Alb* 84-86; R Odell 86-88; V Pavenham 86-88; rtd 88. *13 Ashbee Street, Asterley Bridge, Bolton, Manchester* Bolton (0204) 591576

BRACEY, David Harold. b 36. AKC63. **d** 64 **p** 65. C Westleigh St Pet *Man* 64-67; C Dunstable *St Alb* 67-70; V Benchill *Man* 70-76; V Elton St Steph 76-87; V Howe Bridge from 87. *The Vicarage, Leigh Road, Atherton, Manchester M29 0PH* Atherton (0942) 883359

BRACHER, Paul Martin. b 59. Solicitor 84 Ex Univ LLB80. Trin Coll Bris BA90. **d** 90 **p** 91. C Sparkhill St Jo *Birm* 90; C Sparkhill w Greet and Sparkbrook from 90. *132 Oakwood Road, Sparkhill, Birmingham B11 4HD* 021-777 6093

BRACK, Christopher Francis. b 07. Em Coll Cam BA30 MA34. Westcott Ho Cam. **d** 66 **p** 67. C Cheltenham St Luke and St Jo *Glouc* 66-72; Perm to Offic *Chich* from 74; Chapl Cottesmore Sch Crawley 75-86. *Ground Floor Flat, 43 Walsingham Road, Hove, E Sussex BN3 4FE* Brighton (0273) 726255

BRACK, Edward James. b 37. Sarum Th Coll 67. **d** 69 **p** 70. C Gravesend St Aid *Roch* 69-73; C Woodside Park St Barn *Lon* 73-77; C Wood Green St Mich 77-80; V Whitton SS Phil and Jas 80-83; TV Bethnal Green St Jo w St Bart 83-86; TV St Jo on Bethnal Green from 87. *St Bartholomew's Vicarage, Buckhurst Street, London E1 5QT* 071-247 8013

BRACKENBURY, Ven Michael Palmer. b 30. Linc Th Coll 64. **d** 66 **p** 67. C S Ormsby w Ketsby, Calceby and Driby *Linc* 66-69; V Scothern w Sudbrooke 69-77; RD Lawres 73-78; Bp's Personal Asst 77-88; Dioc Dir of Ords 77-87; Can and Preb Linc Cathl from 79; Dioc Lay Min Adv 86-87; Adn Linc from 88. *2 Ashfield Road, Sleaford, Lincs NG34 7DZ* Sleaford (0529) 307149

BRACKLEY, Ian James. b 47. Keble Coll Ox BA69 MA73. Cuddesdon Coll 69. **d** 71 **p** 72. C Bris Lockleaze St Mary Magd w St Fran *Bris* 71-74; Asst Chapl Bryanston Sch Blandford 74-77; Chapl 77-80; V E Preston w Kingston *Chich* 80-88; RD Arundel and Bognor 82-87; TR Haywards Heath St Wilfrid from 88; RD Cuckfield from 89. *The Rectory, St Wilfrid's Way, Haywards Heath, W Sussex RH16 3QH* Haywards Heath (0444) 413300

BRADBERRY, John. b 20. Clifton Th Coll 46. **d** 47 **p** 48. V Siddal *Wakef* 61-72; R Bentham St Jo *Bradf* 72-85; rtd 85; Perm to Offic Wakef from 85; Bradf from 86. *18 Moor Bottom Road, Halifax, W Yorkshire HX2 9SR* Halifax (0422) 244944

BRADBERRY, John Stephen. b 47. Hull Univ BSc70 Leeds Univ CertEd71 MEd86. NW Ord Course 76. **d** 79 **p** 80. NSM Warley *Wakef* from 79. *129 Paddock Lane, Halifax, W Yorkshire HX2 0NT* Halifax (0422) 58282

BRADBROOK, Peter David. b 33. Kelham Th Coll 54. **d** 60 **p** 61. C Ches St Oswald St Thos *Ches* 60-63; C Fulham St Etheldreda *Lon* 64-65; V Congleton St Jas *Ches* 65-79; V Wheelock from 79. *The Vicarage, Crewe Road, Wheelock, Sandbach, Cheshire CW11 0RE* Crewe (0270) 762377

BRADBROOKE, Canon Edward. b 06. Qu Coll Ox BA32 MA32. Bps' Coll Cheshunt 36. **d** 37 **p** 38. CF (R of O) 39-74; Can and Preb Chich Cathl *Chich* 65-74; R Graffham w Woolavington 66-74; rtd 74; Perm to Offic *B & W* from 81. *68 Moorlands Park, Martock, Somerset TA12 6DW* Martock (0935) 823415

BRADBURY, Alan Harry. b 32. K Coll Lon BD56 AKC56. **d** 57 **p** 58. C Leytonstone St Jo *Chelmsf* 57-60; Prec Chelmsf Cathl 60-63; V Gt Ilford St Jo 63-68; C-in-c Plumstead Wm Temple Ch Abbey Wood CD *S'wark* 68-70; Chapl St Pet Coll Saltley 70-73; Lic to Offic *Win* 74-84. *Address temp unknown*

BRADBURY, George Graham. b 35. AKC58. **d** 59 **p** 60. C Portsea St Mary *Portsm* 59-62; C Melksham *Sarum* 62-64; R Winfrith Newburgh w Chaldon Herring 64-88; CF 68-71. *16 Bread Street, Warminster, Wilts BA12 8DF* Warminster (0985) 213179

BRADBURY, Canon Herbert Cedric. b 30. Linc Th Coll 64. **d** 66 **p** 67. C Blackpool St Steph *Blackb* 66-71; TV Hempnall *Nor* 71-74; R Fritton w Morningthorpe w

Shelton and Hardwick 74-77; TR Hempnall 74-81; RD Depwade 77-81; V Wroxham w Hoveton 81; P-in-c Belaugh 81; R Wroxham w Hoveton and Belaugh from 81; RD Tunstead from 83; Hon Can Nor Cathl from 90. *The Vicarage, Church Lane, Wroxham, Norwich NR12 8SH* Wroxham (06053) 2678

BRADBURY, Julian Nicholas Anstey. b 49. BNC Ox BA71 MA75 Birm Univ MA84. Cuddesdon Coll 71. **d** 73 **p** 74. C S'wark H Trin *S'wark* 73-76; USA 76-79; V Tottenham H Trin *Lon* 79-85; Dir Past Th Sarum & Wells Th Coll 85-90; P-in-c Yatton Keynell *Bris* from 90; P-in-c Biddestone w Slaughterford from 90; P-in-c Castle Combe from 90; P-in-c W Kington from 90; P-in-c Nettleton w Littleton Drew from 90. *The Rectory, Yatton Keynell, Chippenham, Wilts SN14 7BA* Castle Combe (0249) 782663

BRADBURY, Kenneth James Frank. b 23. Qu Coll Birm 72. **d** 75 **p** 76. NSM Cen Telford *Lich* 75-77; C 77-80; V Chirbury *Heref* 80-88; V Marton 80-88; V Trelystan 80-88; rtd 88. *The Glebe, Rodington, Shrewsbury SY4 4QX* Telford (0952) 770312

BRADBURY, Norman Lunn. b 15. K Coll Lon BA36 AKC36. N Ord Course 76. **d** 77 **p** 78. NSM Paddock *Wakef* 77-81; NSM Rashcliffe and Lockwood 81-84; Perm to Offic from 84. *23 Springwood Hall Gardens, Huddersfield HD1 4HA* Huddersfield (0484) 427548

BRADBURY, Robert Douglas. b 50. Ripon Coll Cuddesdon 75. **d** 76 **p** 77. C Harlescott *Lich* 76-81; V Ruyton 81-88; P-in-c Gt w Lt Ness 84-88; V Ruyton XI Towns w Gt and Lt Ness from 88. *The Vicarage, The Village, Ruyton Eleven Towns, Shrewsbury SY4 1LQ* Baschurch (0939) 260254

BRADBURY, Roy Albert. b 30. Chich Th Coll 72. **d** 74 **p** 75. C Earlsdon *Cov* 74-76; C Cov Caludon 76-78; P-in-c Calow *Derby* 78-82; V Pensnett *Lich* 82-90; V Pattingham w Patshull from 90. *The Vicarage, Pattingham, Wolverhampton WV6 7BG* Pattingham (0902) 700257

BRADDOCK, Arthur Derek. b 25. Bolton Inst of Educn BA90. Lich Th Coll 56. **d** 59 **p** 60. V Kearsley Moor *Man* 65-79; C Ellesmere Port *Ches* 79-85; rtd 85; Perm to Offic *Man* from 85. *1 Corrie Drive, Kearsley, Bolton BL4 8RG* 061-794 8953

BRADFORD, John. b 34. FRSA FRGS Lon Univ BA60 Birm Univ MEd81 Ox Univ ACertEd70. Oak Hill Th Coll 55. **d** 60 **p** 61. C Walcot *B & W* 60-64; Perm to Offic Ox 66-70; Birm 70-71; Lic from 71; Perm Cov from 77; Nat Chapl-Missr CECS from 77; Gen Perm to Offic Ch in Wales from 89. *27 Marsh Lane, Solihull, W Midlands B91 2PG* 021-704 9895 or 071-837 4299

BRADFORD, Peter. b 38. Sarum Th Coll 69. **d** 70 **p** 71. C Holdenhurst *Win* 70-73; C Stanmore 73-77; P-in-c Eling, Testwood and Marchwood 77-78; R Marchwood 78-86; C Christchurch 86-90; C Andover w Foxcott from 90. *17 Sunnyside Close, Charlton, Andover SP10 4AL* Andover (0264) 62065

BRADFORD, Archdeacon of. See SHREEVE, Ven David Herbert

BRADFORD, Bishop of. See WILLIAMSON, Rt Rev Robert Kerr

BRADFORD, Provost of. See RICHARDSON, Very Rev John Stephen

BRADLEY, Anthony David. b 56. Wye Coll Lon BSc76. St Jo Coll Nottm DPS88. **d** 88 **p** 89. C Southchurch Ch Ch *Chelmsf* 88-91; C Cov H Trin *Cov* from 91. *466 Tile Hill Lane, Coventry CV4 9DY* Coventry (0203) 471047

BRADLEY, Brian Hugh Granville. b 32. Lon Coll of Div 58. **d** 62 **p** 63. C E Twickenham St Steph *Lon* 62-65; C Herne Bay Ch Ch *Cant* 65-69; Miss to Seamen Teesside 69-71; Ceylon 71-72; Sri Lanka 72-74; Chapl Amsterdam w Haarlem and Den Helder *Eur* 75-79; Chapl Lyon w Grenoble and Aix-les-Bains 79-85; TV Bucknall and Bagnall *Lich* from 87. *St Chad's Parsonage, Bagnall, Stoke-on-Trent ST9 9JR* Stoke-on-Trent (0782) 503696

BRADLEY, Canon Cecil Robert Jones. b 23. TCD BA47 MA50. CITC 48. **d** 48 **p** 49. C Clooney *D & R* 48-50; C Derry Cathl 50-67; Dean's V St Patr Cathl Dub from 67; Preb Maynooth St Patr Cathl Dub from 81. *The Vicarage, St Patrick's Close, Dublin 8, Irish Republic* Dublin (1) 754817

BRADLEY, Clifford James. b 36. Lon Univ BA60. St Aid Birkenhead 60. **d** 62 **p** 63. C Stoneycroft All SS *Liv* 62-65; C Chipping Sodbury and Old Sodbury *Glouc* 65-68; Br Honduras 68-70; C Leckhampton SS Phil and Jas *Glouc* 70-71; V Badgeworth w Shurdington 71-79; Dioc Missr *S & M* 79-84; V Santan 79-84; V Braddan 79-84; Bp's Dom Chapl 81-84; V Stroud and Uplands w Slad *Glouc* 84-89; C Shepshed *Leic* from 90. *28 Forest*

Street, Shepshed, Loughborough LE12 9DA Shepshed (0509) 503316

BRADLEY, Canon Colin John. b 46. Edin Univ MA69 Hertf Coll Ox 71. Sarum & Wells Th Coll 72. **d** 75 **p** 76. C Easthampstead *Ox* 75-79; V Shawbury *Lich* 79-90; R Moreton Corbet 80-90; P-in-c Stanton on Hine Heath 81-90; Can Res Portsm Cathl *Portsm* from 90; Dir of Ords from 90. *61 St Thomas Street, Portsmouth PO1 2EZ* Portsmouth (0705) 824621

BRADLEY, Connla John Osman. b 08. Bible Churchmen's Coll. **d** 47 **p** 47. V Havering-atte-Bower *Chelmsf* 68-76; rtd 76; Perm to Offic *Chich* from 76. *57 Davis Court, Marlborough Road, St Albans, Herts AL1 3XU* St Albans (0727) 46795

BRADLEY, Canon Donald John Walter. b 19. Em Coll Cam BA40 MA44. Westcott Ho Cam 40. **d** 42 **p** 43. Lic to Offic *Birm* 63-70; Hon Can Birm Cathl 70-84; V Edgbaston St Geo 71-84; RD Edgbaston 77-84; rtd 84. *32 St Mark's Road, Salisbury SP1 3AZ* Salisbury (0722) 334653

BRADLEY (nee DRAPER), Mrs Elizabeth Ann. b 38. Nottm Univ BTh75 Birm Univ DipTh77. Linc Th Coll 71. **dss** 84 **d** 87. Ind Chapl *Linc* 84-91; Bracebridge 84-87; Hon C 87-90; Chapl to GFS in Lon Ind Chapl *Lon* from 91. *26 Dewpond Road, Flitwick, Bedford MK45 1RT* Flitwick (0525) 712369

BRADLEY, Gary Scott. b 53. Lon Univ LLB75. Ripon Coll Cuddesdon 75. **d** 78 **p** 79. C St Jo Wood *Lon* 78-83; V Paddington St Sav from 83. *24 Formosa Street, London W9 2QA* 071-286 4962

BRADLEY, George Herbert. b 99. Liv Univ BCom25. Bps' Coll Cheshunt 27. **d** 28 **p** 29. V Gt Sutton *Ches* 37-73; rtd 73; Perm to Offic *Ches* from 74. *The Rectory, Church Lane, Gawsworth, Macclesfield, Cheshire SK11 9RJ* North Rode (02603) 201

BRADLEY, John Owen. b 30. Jes Coll Ox BA55 MA56. St Mich Coll Llan 52. **d** 56 **p** 57. C Cardiff St Mary *Llan* 56-59; Lect St Mich Coll Llan 59-61; C Caerau w Ely *Llan* 60; C Newton Nottage 61-64; V Aberavon H Trin 65-69; Lic to Offic *Cov* 70-76; C W Kirby St Bridget *Ches* 76-79; TV Knowle *Bris* 79-80; TR 80-91; RD Brislington 83-89; Chapl St Monica Home Bris from 91. *St Augustine, Cote Lane, Bristol BS9 3UL* Bristol (0272) 623310 or 629281

BRADLEY, Kenneth Sutton. b 08. ALCD39. **d** 38 **p** 39. R Dogmersfield w Winchfield *Win* 53-72; rtd 73. *12 Mildway Court, Odiham, Basingstoke, Hants RG25 1AX* Basingstoke (0256) 704897

BRADLEY, Michael Frederick John. b 44. Qu Coll Birm 76. **d** 77 **p** 78. C Sheff St Cuth *Sheff* 77-78; C Alford w Rigsby *Linc* 78-83; V Bracebridge 83-90; V Flitwick *St Alb* from 90. *The Vicarage, 26 Dew Pond Road, Flitwick, Bedford MK45 1RT* Flitwick (0525) 712369

BRADLEY, Peter David Douglas. b 49. Nottm Univ BTh79. Linc Th Coll 75. **d** 79 **p** 80. C Upholland *Liv* 79-83; V Dovecot from 83; Dir Continuing Minl Educn from 89. *Holy Spirit Vicarage, Dovecot Avenue, Liverpool L14 7QJ* 051-220 6611

BRADLEY, Peter Edward. b 64. Trin Hall Cam BA86 Trin Coll Cam MA90. Ripon Coll Cuddesdon 86. **d** 88 **p** 89. C Northn St Mich w St Edm *Pet* 88-91; Chapl G&C Coll Cam from 91. *Gonville and Caius College, Cambridge CB2 1TA* Cambridge (0223) 332400

BRADLEY, Ronald Percival. b 25. ACP51 FRSA52 TCert49. Ex 4 Truro NSM Scheme 80. **d** 83 **p** 84. C Honiton, Gittisham, Combe Raleigh, Monkton etc *Ex* 83-86; P-in-c Halberton 86-87; rtd 90. *Flat 5 Adams House, Adams Way, Alton, Hants GU34 2UY* Alton (0420) 80257

BRADNUM, Mrs Ella Margaret. b 41. CertEd64 St Hugh's Coll Ox MA65. **dss** 69 **d** 87. Illingworth *Wakef* 69-72; Batley All SS 72-73; Lay Tr Officer 77-82; Min Tr Officer from 82; Warden of Readers from 88. *The Vicarage, 1 Sunnybank Road, Mixenden, Halifax, W Yorkshire HX2 8RX* Halifax (0422) 244761 or 240669

BRADNUM, Richard James. b 39. Pemb Coll Ox BA62 MA67. Ridley Hall Cam 62. **d** 64 **p** 65. C Birm St Martin *Birm* 64-68; C Sutton St Jas *York* 68-69; Perm to Offic *Wakef* 71-72; C Batley All SS 72-74; V Gawthorpe and Chickenley Heath 74-86; V Mixenden from 86. *The Vicarage, 1 Sunny Bank Road, Mixenden, Halifax, W Yorkshire HX2 8RX* Halifax (0422) 244761

BRADSHAW, Charles Anthony. b 44. Birm Univ MA76. Qu Coll Birm DipTh74. **d** 75 **p** 76. C Whickham *Dur* 75-78; C Bilton *Cov* 78-81; TV Cov Caludon 81-89; V Birstall and Wanlip *Leic* from 89. *The Rectory, 251 Birstall Road, Birstall, Leicester LE4 4DJ* Leicester (0533) 674517

BRADSHAW, Denis Matthew. b 52. Chich Th Coll 77. **d** 80 **p** 81. C Ruislip St Martin *Lon* 80-84; C Northolt Park St Barn 84-86; V Northolt W End St Jos from 86. *St Joseph's Vicarage, 430 Yeading Lane, Northolt, Middx UB5 6JS* 081-845 6161

BRADSHAW, George Henry. b 28. Wycliffe Hall Ox. **d** 62 **p** 63. Chapl RAF 65-84; R Wittering w Thornhaugh and Wansford *Pet* 65-84; Ascension Is 84-85; V The Suttons w Tydd *Linc* 85-87; rtd 87; Perm to Offic *Linc* from 87. *8 Brown's Hospital, Broad Street, Stamford, Lincs PE8 1PD* Stamford (0780) 56614

BRADSHAW, Gordon George. b 31. St Pet Coll Ox BA56 MA59. Wycliffe Hall Ox 56. **d** 58 **p** 59. V W Derby St Jas *Liv* 68-75; TR Keynsham *B & W* 75-83; rtd 83. *36 Oakleigh Gardens, Oldland Common, Bristol* Bristol (0272) 322629

BRADSHAW, Graham. b 58. Edin Univ BD86. Edin Th Coll 83. **d** 86 **p** 87. C Thornton-le-Fylde *Blackb* 86-89; C Kirkby Lonsdale *Carl* 89-91; V Langford *St Alb* from 91. *The Vicarage, 65 Church Street, Langford, Biggleswade, Beds SG18 9QT* Hitchin (0462) 700248

BRADSHAW, Miss Jennie McNeille. b 47. UEA BA69. Cranmer Hall Dur 85. **d** 90. Par Dn Herne *Cant* from 90. *9 Darrell Close, Herne Bay, Kent CT6 7QQ* Herne Bay (0227) 362429

BRADSHAW, Jolyon Anthony. b 51. St Jo Coll Dur BA73. Trin Coll Bris 73. **d** 76 **p** 77. C Normanton *Wakef* 76-82; TV Wreningham *Nor* 82-89; R Bermondsey St Mary w St Olave, St Jo etc *S'wark* 89-90; P-in-c from 90. *The Rectory, 193 Bermondsey Street, London SE1 3UW* 071-407 5273

BRADSHAW, Kenneth Allan. b 23. Roch Th Coll 60. **d** 62 **p** 63. C Preston *Chich* 67-71; C Haywards Heath St Wilfrid 71-82; C Sidley 82-88; rtd 88; Hon C Roath St Sav *Llan* from 88. *The Cottage, 115A Splott Road, Cardiff CF2 2BY* Cardiff (0222) 465998

BRADSHAW, Malcolm McNeille. b 45. Lon Univ DipTh69. Kelham Th Coll 65. **d** 70 **p** 71. C New Addington *Cant* 70-76; Chapl Milan w Cadenabbia, Varese and Lugano *Eur* 77-82; V Boxley w Detling *Cant* from 82. *St John's House, 7 Samphire Close, Weavering, Maidstone, Kent ME14 5UD* Maidstone (0622) 39294

BRADSHAW, Canon Prof Paul Frederick. b 45. Clare Coll Cam BA66 MA70 K Coll Lon PhD71. Westcott Ho Cam 67. **d** 69 **p** 70. C W Wickham St Jo *Cant* 69-71; C St Martin and St Paul 71-73; Tutor Chich Th Coll 73-78; V Flamstead *St Alb* 78-82; Dir of Minl Tr Scheme 78-82; Vice-Prin Ripon Coll Cuddesdon 83-85; USA from 85; Prof Th Notre Dame Univ from 85; Hon Can N Indiana from 90. *Department of Theology, University of Notre Dame, Notre Dame, Indiana 46556, USA* Notre Dame (219) 239-7811

BRADSHAW, Philip Hugh. b 39. Qu Coll Ox BA64 MA67 Lon Univ DipRS91. S'wark Ord Course 88. **d** 91. NSM Bletchingley *S'wark* from 91; Ldr Community of Celebration from 91. *Community of Celebration, Berry House, 58 High Street, Bletchingley, Redhill RH1 4PA* Godstone (0883) 743737

BRADSHAW, Roy John. b 49. Sarum & Wells Th Coll 85. **d** 87 **p** 88. FSJ from 84; C Gainsborough All SS *Linc* 87-90; V New Waltham from 90. *The Vicarage, 41 Dunbar Avenue, New Waltham, Grimsby DN36 4PY* Grimsby (0472) 827765

BRADSHAW, Dr Timothy. b 50. PhD Keble Coll Ox BA72 MA78. St Jo Coll Nottm BA75. **d** 76 **p** 77. C Clapton Park All So *Lon* 76-79; Lect Trin Coll Bris 80-91; Hon C Sea Mills *Bris* 83-91; Tutor Regent's Park Coll Ox from 91. *54 St Giles, Oxford BS9 1HD* Oxford (0865) 515951

BRADSHAW, Mrs Veronica. b 52. St Jo Coll Dur BA75. Cranmer Hall Dur. **dss** 82 **d** 87. Borehamwood *St Alb* 82-84; Watford Ch Ch 84-85; Stevenage St Mary Shephall 85-87; Par Dn Stevenage St Mary Sheppall w Aston 87-88. *31 Harefield, Shephall, Stevenage, Herts SG2 9NG* Stevenage (0438) 365714

BRADWELL, Area Bishop of. See BOND, Rt Rev Charles (Derek)

BRADY, Canon Ernest William. b 17. Dur Univ LTh42. Edin Th Coll 39. **d** 42 **p** 43. Can St Mary's Cathl *Edin* 67-83; Syn Clerk 69-76; P-in-c S Queensferry 74-82; Dean Edin 76-82 and 85-86; rtd 82; Dioc Supernumerary *Edin* 82-90; Hon Can St Mary's Cathl from 83. *44 Glendevon Place, Edinburgh EH12 5UJ* 031-337 9528

BRADY, Mrs Madalaine Margaret. BD. **d** 89. NSM Angl Chapl Cen Ban from 89. *4 Salem Place, Llanllechid, Bangor, Gwynedd LL57 3ES* Bangor (0248) 600567

BRAIN, George. b 19. St Chad's Coll Dur BA41 DipTh43 MA44. **d** 43 **p** 44. V Leic St Leon *Leic* 54-81; Perm to

Offic from 81; rtd 84. *1 Steyning Crescent, Glenfield, Leicester LE3 8PL* Leicester (0533) 878451

BRAIN, Michael Charles. b 39. ACP65. Lich Th Coll 68. **d** 70 **p** 71. C Stone St Mich *Lich* 70-73; C Harlescott 73-76; C Longton St Jas 76-77; P-in-c Dudley St Edm *Worc* 77-79; V from 79. *St Edmund's Vicarage, 9 Ednam Road, Dudley, W Midlands DY1 1JX* Dudley (0384) 252532

BRAIN, Vernon Roy. b 15. St D Coll Lamp BA38 Ripon Hall Ox 41. **d** 42 **p** 43. V Seaham w Seaham Harbour *Dur* 61-80; rtd 80. *61 Vicarage Close, Silksworth, Sunderland SR3 1JF* 091-521 0847

BRAITHWAITE, Albert Alfred. b 24. Clifton Th Coll. **d** 59 **p** 60. Chapl RN 62-81; QHC from 77; C Southsea St Jude *Portsm* 82-90; Lic to Offic from 90; rtd 90. *3 Lorne Road, Southsea, Hants PO5 1RR* Portsmouth (0705) 738753

BRAITHWAITE, Michael Royce. b 34. Linc Th Coll 71. **d** 73 **p** 74. C Barrow St Geo w St Luke *Carl* 73-77; V Kells 77-88; RD Calder 84-88; V Lorton and Loweswater w Buttermere from 88. *The Vicarage, Loweswater, Cockermouth, Cumbria CA13 0RU* Lorton (090085) 237

BRAITHWAITE, Roy. b 34. Dur Univ BA56. Ridley Hall Cam 58. **d** 60 **p** 61. C Blackb St Gabr *Blackb* 60-63; C Burnley St Pet 63-66; V Accrington St Andr 66-74; V Blackb St Jas from 74; RD Blackb 86-91. *St James's Vicarage, Cromer Place, Blackburn BB1 8EL* Blackburn (0254) 56465

BRAITHWAITE, Wilfrid. b 14. St Chad's Coll Dur BA41 MA44. **d** 42 **p** 43. V Lanercost w Kirkcambeck *Carl* 62-79; P-in-c Walton 78-79; rtd 79; Perm to Offic *Carl* from 82. *Brougham Lodge, Eamont Bridge, Penrith, Cumbria CA10 2BZ* Penrith (0768) 62939

BRALESFORD, Nicholas Robert. b 53. St Jo Coll Nottm LTh79 BTh79. **d** 79 **p** 80. C Leic St Chris *Leic* 79-82; C Heeley *Sheff* 82-85; TV Kings Norton *Birm* 85-90; V Chapel-en-le-Frith *Derby* from 90. *The Vicarage, 71 Manchester Road, Chapel-en-le-Frith, Stockport, Cheshire SK12 6TH* Chapel-en-le-Frith (0298) 812134

BRALEY, Robert James. b 57. Ch Ch Ox BA82 Down Coll Cam BA83 MA87. Ridley Hall Cam 81. **d** 84 **p** 85. C Thames Ditton *Guildf* 84-87; C Gravesend St Geo *Roch* from 87. *71 Peacock Street, Gravesend, Kent DA12 1EG* Gravesend (0474) 320886

BRAMELD, Peter John. b 40. AKC62. **d** 63 **p** 64. C Hucknall Torkard *S'well* 63-66; C Ordsall 66-70; C Carlton 70-74; C Colwick 70-74; P-in-c Overton w Fyfield and E Kennett *Sarum* 74-75; TV Upper Kennett 75-80; R Hickling w Kinoulton and Broughton Sulney *S'well* from 80; RD Bingham S 86-91. *The Rectory, Main Street, Kinoulton, Notts NG12 3EA* Kinoulton (0949) 81657

BRAMHALL, Eric. b 39. St Cath Coll Cam BA61 MA65. Tyndale Hall Bris 61. **d** 63 **p** 64. C Eccleston St Luke *Liv* 63-66; C Bolton Em *Man* 66-69; Perm to Offic *Ches* 70-74; Chapl Ormskirk Hosp *Liv* from 75; V Aughton Ch Ch *Liv* from 75. *Christ Church Vicarage, 22 Long Lane, Aughton, Ormskirk, Lancs L39 5AT* Aughton Green (0695) 422175

BRAMLEY, Canon Charles Edward. b 14. Keble Coll Ox BA37 MA50. Lich Th Coll 36. **d** 38 **p** 38. R Standish *Blackb* 56-80; Hon Can Blackb Cathl 66-80; rtd 80; Lic to Offic *Blackb* from 83. *2 Primrose Cottages, Dawbers Lane, Euxton, Chorley, Lancs PR7 6EL* Chorley (02572) 65011

BRAMMER, Charles Harold. b 08. Ripon Hall Ox 54. **d** 54 **p** 55. V St Cleer *Truro* 65-75; rtd 75; Perm to Offic *Liv* 75-85; Man 85-90. *20 The Windrush, Shawclough, Healey Gardens, Rochdale, Lancs OL12 6DY* Rochdale (0706) 342818

BRAMPTON, Ms Fiona Elizabeth Gordon. b 56. St Jo Coll Dur BA78. Cranmer Hall Dur BA83. dss 84 **d** 87. Bris St Andr Hartcliffe *Bris* 84-87; Par Dn 87-90; C Orton Waterville *Ely* from 90. *5 Riseholme, Orton Goldhay, Peterborough PE2 0SP* Peterborough (0733) 238691

BRANCHE, Brian Maurice. b 37. Chich Th Coll 73. **d** 75 **p** 76. C Brighton Resurr *Chich* 75-78; C Upper Norwood St Jo *Cant* 78-81; P-in-c Croydon St Martin 81-84; V Croydon St Martin *S'wark* 85-88; V St Helier from 88. *St Peter's Vicarage, Bishopsford Road, Morden, Surrey SM4 6BH* 081-648 6050

BRAND, Frank Ronald Walter. b 25. Lon Coll of Div ALCD56 LTh74. **d** 56 **p** 57. V N Greenford All Hallows *Lon* 67-91; rtd 91. *23 Hawthorn Grove, Combe Down, Bath BA2 5QA* Bath (0225) 834572

BRAND, Peter John. b 32. Lon Univ BSc54. Edin Dioc NSM Course 75. **d** 83 **p** 84. NSM Edin St Jo *Edin* from

83. *24 Drum Brae Park, Edinburgh EH12 8TF* 031-339 4406

BRAND, Richard Harold Guthrie. b 65. Dur Univ BA87. Ripon Coll Cuddesdon 87. **d** 89 **p** 90. C N Lynn w St Marg and St Nic *Nor* from 89. *33 All Saints' Street, King's Lynn, Norfolk PE30 5AD* King's Lynn (0553) 691727

BRAND, Stuart William. b 30. Leeds Univ BSc53. Coll of Resurr Mirfield. **d** 55 **p** 56. C Stepney St Dunstan and All SS *Lon* 55-59; C Acton Green St Pet 59-60; C-in-c Godshill CD *Portsm* 60-64; Malawi 64-67; V Widley w Wymering *Portsm* 67-72; Chapl Fieldhead Hosp Wakef 72-80; Pinderfields & Stanley Royd Hosps Wakef 72-80; Chapl Brook Gen Hosp *Lon* from 80; Chapl Greenwich Distr Hosp *Lon* from 80. *4A Queen's Road, London SE15 2PT* 071-635 9550

BRANDES, Simon Frank. b 62. Univ of Wales (Ban) BA83. Edin Th Coll 83. **d** 85 **p** 86. C Barton w Peel Green *Man* 85-88; Asst Dioc Youth Officer from 88; C Longsight St Jo w St Cypr 88-90; R from 90. *The Rectory, St John's Road, Longsight, Manchester M13 0WU* 061-224 2744

BRANDIE, Canon Beaumont Lauder. b 40. K Coll Lon AKC64 BD66. **d** 65 **p** 66. C Whitton St Aug *Lon* 65-71; C Portsea St Mary *Portsm* 71-77; TR Brighton Resurr *Chich* from 77; Can and Preb Chich Cathl from 87. *St Martin's Rectory, Upper Wellington Road, Brighton BN2 3AN* Brighton (0273) 604687

BRANDON, Dennis Ralph. b 24. Leeds Univ BA50. Linc Th Coll 53. **d** 55 **p** 56. C Pickering *York* 68-71; P-in-c Newton-on-Rawcliffe 71-74; Hon C Newton Kyme 74-80; P-in-c 80-83; rtd 83. *21 The Coppice, Bishopthorpe, York YO2 1QP* York (0904) 707486

BRANDON, Canon Ernest Arthur. b 19. TCD BA42 MA45. CITC 43. **d** 43 **p** 44. C Kilkenny St Canice Cathl *C & O* 43-46; C Belf St Donard *D & D* 46-47; C Belf St Clem 47-49; C Dub Booterstown w Carysfort *D & G* 49-51; I Celbridge w Straffan 51-63; I Taghmon w Horetown and Bannow *C & O* from 63; Preb Ferns Cathl from 81; Chan from 85; Prec from 91. *Horetown Rectory, Foulksmills, Wexford, Irish Republic* Wexford (53) 63688

BRANDON, Michael Charles. b 56. Em Coll Cam BA78 MA82. Coll of Resurr Mirfield 78. **d** 80 **p** 81. C Pinner *Lon* 80-85; C Heston 85-88; V Shepshed *Leic* from 88. *The Vicarage, 36 Church Street, Shepshed, Loughborough, Leics LE12 9RH* Shepshed (0509) 502255

BRANDON, Owen Rupert. b 08. Bris Univ MA51 Dur Univ MLitt62. ALCD34. **d** 34 **p** 35. R Fordwich *Cant* 66-73; rtd 73. *Condover House, 10-12 Burlington Place, Eastbourne, E Sussex BN21 4AZ*

BRANDON, Miss Vera Eileen. b 12. Univ of Wales (Abth) CertEd35 BSc40 Lon Univ DipEd42 BD53. St Mich Ho Ox 51. **dss** 60 **d** 87. Tutor CA Wilson Carlile Coll of Evang 64-74; Community of the Word of God from 75; Lower Homerton St Paul *Lon* 75-80; Clapton Park All So 75-80; Tottenham St Ann 80-83; rtd 83; Tunbridge Wells St Pet *Roch* 83-87; Hon Par Dn from 87. *Esther Porritt House, Trinity Close, Tunbridge Wells TN2 3PP*

BRANDWOOD, Herbert. b 05. Wadh Coll Ox BA27 BA29 Lon Univ DipEd50. St Aid Birkenhead 38. **d** 39 **p** 40. R Croxton Kerrial and Knipton w Harston etc *Leic* 63-73; rtd 73; Lic to Offic *Nor* 73-75; P-in-c Bodham 75-79; P-in-c E w W Beckham 75-78; Perm to Offic from 83. *37 Nelson Road, Sheringham, Norfolk NR26 8BX* Sheringham (0263) 823514

BRANFORD, David Charles. b 62. Qu Coll Ox BA85 MA88. Ripon Coll Cuddesdon 85. **d** 88 **p** 89. C Poulton-le-Fylde *Blackb* 88-91; C St Barn w St Mary New Wortley *Ripon* from 91. *c/o Armley Vicarage, Wesley Road, Leeds LS12 1SR* Leeds (0532) 638620

BRANNAGAN, Alan McKenzie. b 34. Chich Th Coll 66. **d** 68 **p** 69. C N Hull St Mich *York* 68-70; C Dunstable *St Alb* 70-75; R E w W Rudham *Nor* 75-81; V Houghton 75-81; TV Wolv *Lich* 81-87; R W Felton from 87. *St Michael's Rectory, West Felton, Oswestry, Shropshire SY11 4LE* Queens Head (069188) 228

BRANSON, Canon Charles Stanley. b 07. St Aug Coll Cant 34. **d** 37 **p** 38. V Brampton SS Pet and Paul *Derby* 69-76; TR Old Brampton and Loundsley Green 76-78; Hon Can Derby Cathl 74-78; rtd 78; Perm to Offic *Derby* from 78. *5 Westbourne Grove, Chesterfield, Derbyshire S40 3QD* Chesterfield (0246) 569321

BRANSON, Robert David. b 46. Linc Th Coll 74. **d** 77 **p** 78. C Kempston Transfiguration *St Alb* 77-80; C Goldington 80-82; V Marsh Farm 82-91; V Aylsham *Nor* from 91. *The Vicarage, 64 Holman Road, Aylsham, Norwich NR11 6BZ* Aylsham (0263) 733871

BRANT, Anthony Richard. b 44. S Dios Minl Tr Scheme. d 82 p 83. NSM Felpham w Middleton *Chich* 82-84; C Clymping 84-85; NSM 85-87; NSM Clymping and Yapton w Ford from 87. *23 Somerstown, Chichester PO19 4AG* Chichester (0243) 780550

BRANT, Anthony William. b 31. TD67. Linc Th Coll 73. d 75 p 76. C Cove St Jo *Guildf* 75-79; P-in-c Puttenham and Wanborough 79-83; V Lightwater from 83. *The Vicarage, Broadway Road, Lightwater, Surrey GU18 5SJ* Bagshot (0276) 72270

BRANT, Leslie Harold. b 11. d 71 p 72. C Lower Sandown St Jo *Portsm* 71-74; P-in-c Newchurch 75-80; rtd 80; Perm to Offic *Portsm* from 82. *Seaspray, 22 The Esplanade, Ryde, Isle of Wight PO33 2DZ* Isle of Wight (0983) 64054

BRANWELL, Edward Bruce. b 20. St Cath Coll Cam BA42 MA46. Linc Th Coll 42. d 44 p 45. Chapl Aldenham Sch Herts 64-70; Asst Master Burlington Sch Lon 70-77; Perm to Offic St Alb from 81; Ches from 84; rtd 85. *16 King's Crescent West, Chester CH3 5HQ* Chester (0244) 313641

BRASIER, Ralph Henry (Jim). b 30. Cant Sch of Min 82. d 85 p 86. C S Ashford Ch Ch *Cant* 85-89; V Pembury *Roch* from 89. *The Vicarage, 4 Hastings Road, Pembury, Tunbridge Wells, Kent TN2 4PD* Pembury (089282) 4761

BRASNETT, Canon Leslie Stanley. b 97. Ch Ch Ox BA21 MA24. Cuddesdon Coll 21. d 21 p 22. V Runcorn All SS *Ches* 47-55; rtd 62. *Cranford Nursing Home, 15 Cranford Avenue, Exmouth, Devon EX8 2HT* Exmouth (0395) 263383

BRASSELL, Canon Kenneth William. b 23. Kelham Th Coll 46. d 50 p 51. V Beckenham St Jas *Roch* 63-88; P-in-c Beckenham St Aug 66-77; P-in-c Beckenham St Mich 77-78; P-in-c Beckenham St Mich w St Aug 77-78; Hon Can Roch Cathl 82-88; rtd 88. *20 College Green, Gloucester GL1 2LR* Gloucester (0452) 309080

BRATLEY, David Frederick. b 42. Linc Th Coll 80. d 82 p 83. C Holbeach *Linc* 82-85; R Fleet w Gedney from 85. *The Rectory, Fleet, Spalding, Lincs PE12 8NQ* Holbeach (0406) 23795

BRAUND, George Basil. b 26. SS Coll Cam BA50 MA54. Ely Th Coll 51. d 53 p 54. OGS from 52; Superior OGS 69-75; C Chesterton St Luke *Ely* 53-60; Chapl SS Coll Cam 60-68; Lic to Offic Ely 60-68; Lon 68-69; Travel Missr USPG 68-73; Overseas Sec 73-79; Lic to Offic *Ox* 69-88; Assoc Sec Miss & Ecum Affairs ACC 79-85; Co Sec Angl Reformed Internat Commn 80-86; TV Wallingford w Crowmarsh Gifford etc *Ox* from 88. *34 Thames Mead, Crowmarsh Gifford, Wallingford, Oxon OX10 8EY* Wallingford (0491) 37626

BRAY, Anthony Markham. b 16. Magd Coll Cam BA37 MA43. Cuddesdon Coll 38. d 39 p 40. V Posbury Chap Ex 53-75; P-in-c Otterton *Ex* 76-80; rtd 81. *Quince, King Street, Colyton, Devon EX13 6LA* Colyton (0297) 53149

BRAY, Christopher Laurence. b 53. Leeds Univ BSc74 Qu Univ Kingston Ontario MSc76. St Jo Coll Nottm DipTh79 DPS81. d 81 p 82. C Aughton Ch Ch *Liv* 81-84; Hon C Scarborough St Mary w Ch Ch and H Apostles *York* 84-88; Chapl Scarborough Coll 84-88; V St Helens St Matt Thatto Heath *Liv* from 88. *The Vicarage, St Matthew's Grove, St Helens, Merseyside WA10 3SE* St Helens (0744) 24644

BRAY, Gerald Lewis. b 48. McGill Univ Montreal BA69. Ridley Hall Cam 76. d 78 p 79. C Canning Town St Cedd *Chelmsf* 78-80; Tutor Oak Hill NSM Course from 80; Lic to Offic *Lon* from 81. *Oak Hill College, London N14 4PS* 081-449 3064

BRAY, Jeremy Grainger. b 40. Man Univ BA62. Wells Th Coll 62. d 64 p 65. C Bris St Andr w St Bart *Bris* 64-67; C Bris H Cross Inns Court 67-71; C-in-c Stockwood CD 71-73; V Bris Ch the Servant Stockwood 73-83; RD Brislington 79-83; P-in-c Chippenham St Pet 83-88; V from 88. *St Peter's Vicarage, Lords Mead, Chippenham, Wilts SN14 0LL* Chippenham (0249) 654835

BRAY, Joyce. b 32. CA Tr Coll. dss 80 d 87. Bloxwich *Lich* 80-84; Derringham Bank *York* 84-87; Par Dn from 87. *413 Willerby Road, Hull HU5 5JD* Hull (0482) 502193

BRAY, Kenneth John. b 31. St Mich Coll Llan 65. d 67 p 72. C Killay *S & B* 67-68; C S Harrow St Paul *Lon* 71-73; C Hillingdon St Jo 73-76; C Chipping Sodbury and Old Sodbury *Glouc* 76-79; C Worle *B & W* 79-80; Lic to Offic *Ches* 80-83; TV Wrexham *St As* 83-85; V Llay from 85. *The Vicarage, Llay, Wrexham, Clwyd LL12 0TN* Gresford (0978) 832262

BRAY, Richard. b 29. Linc Th Coll 55. d 57 p 58. C Lt Ilford St Barn *Chelmsf* 57-62; R Tye Green w Netteswell from 62. *The Rectory, Tawneys Road, Tye Green, Harlow, Essex CM18 6QR* Harlow (0279) 425138

BRAY, Thomas Chadwick. b 08. Qu Coll Birm 46. d 48 p 49. V Bolam *Newc* 69-74; rtd 74. *26 Post Office Lane, Moreton, Newport, Shropshire TF10 9DR* Great Chatwell (095270) 225

BRAYBROOKE, Marcus Christopher Rossi. b 38. Magd Coll Cam BA62 MA65 Lon Univ MPhil68. Wells Th Coll 63. d 64 p 65. C Frindsbury w Upnor *Roch* 67-72; TV Strood St Fran 72-73; P-in-c Swainswick w Langridge *B & W* 73-76; R 76-79; Dir of Tr 79-84; Hon C Bath Ch Ch Prop Chpl from 84; Exec Dir Coun of Chrs and Jews 84-87; rtd 88; Perm to Offic *Bris* from 88; Preb Wells Cathl *B & W* from 90. *2 The Bassetts, Box, Wilts SN14 9ER* Box (0225) 742827

BRAYBROOKE, Oliver Henry. b 08. Pemb Coll Cam BA30 MA58. Wells Th Coll 58. d 58 p 59. R Bredfield w Boulge *St E* 61-73; R Debach 61-73; rtd 73; Perm to Offic *St E* from 73. *9 Chapel Street, Woodbridge, Suffolk IP12 4NF* Woodbridge (03943) 7006

BRAZELL, Denis Illtyd Anthony. b 42. Trin Coll Cam BA64 MA68. Wycliffe Hall Ox 78. d 80 p 81. C Cheltenham Ch Ch *Glouc* 80-84; V Reading St Agnes w St Paul *Ox* from 84. *The Vicarage, 290 Northumberland Avenue, Reading RG2 8DE* Reading (0734) 874448

BRAZELL, Mrs Elizabeth Jane. b 44. LRAM64 ARCM65 GGSM65 AGSM65. Wycliffe Hall Ox 85. dss 86 d 87. Reading St Agnes w St Paul *Ox* 86-87; Hon Par Dn 87-90; Par Dn from 90. *The Vicarage, 290 Northumberland Avenue, Reading RG2 8DE* Reading (0734) 874448

BRAZIER, Eric James Arthur. b 37. Qu Coll Birm 84. d 86 p 87. C Lighthorne *Cov* 86-89; P-in-c from 89; P-in-c Chesterton from 89; P-in-c Newbold Pacey w Moreton Morrell from 89. *The Rectory, Lighthorne, Warwick CV35 0AR* Leamington Spa (0926) 651247

BRAZIER, Raymond Venner. b 40. Wells Th Coll 68. d 71 p 72. C Horfield St Greg *Bris* 71-75; P-in-c Bris St Nath w St Kath 75-79; V 79-84; P-in-c Kingsdown 80-84; V Bris St Matt and St Nath from 84; RD Horfield 85-91. *The Vicarage, 11 Gletworth Road, Bristol BS6 7EG* Bristol (0272) 424186

BRAZINGTON, David Albert. b 36. Open Univ BA86. Glouc Th Course 75. d 78 p 79. Hon C Wotton St Mary *Glouc* 78-82; P-in-c Huntley 82-83; P-in-c Longhope 82-83; R Huntley and Longhope 83-89; R Glouc St Mary de Crypt w St Jo and Ch Ch from 89. *The Rectory, 17 Brunswick Road, Gloucester GL1 1HG* Gloucester (0452) 22843

BREADEN, Very Rev Robert William. b 37. Edin Th Coll 58. d 61 p 62. C Broughty Ferry *Bre* 61-65; R Carnoustie 65-72; R Broughty Ferry from 72; Can St Paul's Cathl Dundee from 77; Dean Bre from 84. *46 Seafield Road, Broughty Ferry, Dundee DD5 3AN* Dundee (0382) 77477

BREAR, Alvin Douglas. d 87 p 88. NSM Leic H Spirit *Leic* 87-88; NSM Leic St Pet 88; NSM Leic Ch Sav from 88. *84 Parkland Drive, Oadby, Leicester LE2 4DG* Leicester (0533) 714137

BREARLEY, Janet Mary. b 48. Cranmer Hall Dur 88. d 90. C Prudhoe *Newc* from 90. *11 Westwood View, Ryton, Tyne & Wear NE40 4HR* 091-413 7648

BREAY, John. b 19. Selw Coll Cam BA41 MA45 St Chad's Coll Dur DipTh42. d 42 p 43. V Shepreth *Ely* 59-77; V Barrington 77; V Gt w Lt Chesterford *Chelmsf* 77-79; rtd 79; Perm to Offic *Ely* from 79. *66 Montague Road, Cambridge CB4 1BX* Cambridge (0223) 358448

BREBNER, Martin James. b 47. ARCS68 Imp Coll Lon BSc68. St Alb Minl Tr Scheme 87. d 90 p 91. Hon C Letchworth St Paul w Willian *St Alb* from 90. *42 Farthing Drive, Letchworth, Herts SG6 2TR* Letchworth (0462) 679129

BRECHIN, Bishop of. See HALLIDAY, Rt Rev Robert Taylor

BRECHIN, Dean of. See BREADEN, Very Rev Robert William

BRECKLES, Robert Wynford. b 48. St Edm Hall Ox BA72 MA74 CertEd. St Jo Coll Dur DipTh79. d 79 p 80. C Bulwell St Mary *S'well* 79-84; P-in-c Lady Bay 84; V from 84. *The Vicarage, 121 Holme Road, Nottingham NG2 5AG* Nottingham (0602) 813565

BRECKNELL, David Jackson. b 32. Keble Coll Ox BA53 MA57. St Steph Ho Ox 56. d 58 p 59. C Streatham St Pet *S'wark* 58-62; C Sneinton St Steph w St Alb *S'well* 62-64; C Solihull *Birm* 64-68; V Streatham St Paul *S'wark* 68-75; R Rumboldswyke *Chich* 75-81; P-in-c Portfield 79-81; R Whyke w Rumboldswhyke and

Portfield from 81. *St George's Rectory, 199 Whyke Road, Chichester PO19 2HQ*   Chichester (0243) 782535

BRECKWOLDT, Peter Hans. b 57. Man Poly BA79. Oak Hill Th Coll BA88. **d** 88 **p** 89. C Knutsford St Jo and Toft *Ches* from 88. *86 Grove Park, Knutsford, Cheshire WA16 8QB*   Knutsford (0565) 632894

BRECON, Archdeacon of. See REES, Ven John Wynford Joshua

BRECON, Dean of. See JONES, Very Rev David Huw

BREE, Reginald Hooper. b 13. **d** 61 **p** 62. V Broadwaters *Worc* 66-78; rtd 78. *14 Highfield Way, Aldridge, Walsall, W Midlands WS9 8XF*

BREED, Kenneth Wilfred. b 11. Leeds Univ BA33. Coll of Resurr Mirfield 33. **d** 35 **p** 36. V Shirley *Birm* 51-77; rtd 77; Hon C St Andr Holborn *Lon* 77-79; Perm to Offic *B & W* from 86. *4 Yard Court, East Street, Warminster, Wilts BA12 9NY*   Warminster (0985) 213230

BREEDS, Christopher Roger. b 51. LGSM83 ACertCM87 Lon Univ CertEd73. Chich Th Coll 84. **d** 87 **p** 88. C E Grinstead St Swithun *Chich* 87-90; TV Aldrington from 90. *18 Amesbury Crescent, Hove, E Sussex BN3 5RD*   Brighton (0273) 28973

BREEN, Michael James. b 58. Oak Hill Th Coll BA79 MA85 LTh Cranmer Hall Dur 81. **d** 83 **p** 84. C Cam St Martin *Ely* 83-87; V Clapham Park All SS *S'wark* from 87. *All Saints' Vicarage, 250 Lyham Road, London SW2 5NP*   081-674 4994

BREENE, Timothy Patrick Brownell. b 59. Kent Univ BA81 CCC Cam BA89. Ridley Hall Cam 87. **d** 90. C Hadleigh w Layham and Shelley *St E* from 90. *85 Cliff Road, Felixstowe, Suffolk IP11 9SQ*   Felixstowe (0394) 283718

BREESE, Kenneth Edmund. b 11. Qu Coll Birm 46. **d** 49. C Radford *Cov* 49-51. *129 Carlingford Drive, Westcliff-on-Sea, Essex*

BREFFITT, Geoffrey Michael. b 46. CChem MRIC72 Trent Poly CertEd77 DipPSE82. Qu Coll Birm 87. **d** 89 **p** 90. C Prenton *Ches* from 89. *91 Woodchurch Lane, Birkenhead, Merseyside L42 9PL*   051-608 9793

BRENDON-COOK, John Lyndon. b 37. FRICS. SW Minl Tr Course. **d** 81 **p** 82. NSM Bodmin *Truro* 81-82; NSM St Breoke and Egloshayle 82-90; NSM Helland from 90; NSM Cardynham from 90. *Treworder Byre, Egloshayle, Wadebridge, Cornwall PL27 6HX*   Wadebridge (0208) 812488

BRENNAN, Dr John Lester. b 20. MRCP51 FRCPath77 Barrister-at-Law (Middle Temple) 71 Lon Univ MB, BS44 DipTh47 MD52 LLM86. St Aug Coll Cant 54. **d** 55 **p** 56. India 55-65; Hon C Woodside Park St Barn *Lon* 65-69; Lic to Offic *Lich* 69-88; P-in-c Chrishall *Chelmsf* 88-89; Hon C 89-91; Hon C Heydon, Gt and Lt Chishill, Chrishall etc from 91. *5 Engleric, Chrishhall, Royston, Herts SG8 8QZ*   Royston (0763) 838752

BRENNAN, Samuel James. b 16. St Aid Birkenhead. **d** 57 **p** 58. I Aghalee *D & D* 69-84; RD Shankill 77-84; rtd 84. *71 Bangor Road, Newtownards, Co Down BT23 3BZ*   Newtownards (0247) 819139

BRENNEN, Canon Dr Colin. b 15. Lon Univ BA47 BD56 Dur Univ PhD88. Linc Th Coll 46. **d** 48 **p** 49. V Whitworth w Spennymoor *Dur* 58-78; RD Auckland 74-82; Hon Can Dur Cathl from 78; V Hamsterley 78-82; rtd 82. *13 Springwell Road, Durham DH1 4LR*   091-386 9386

BRENTNALL, David John. b 53. UEA BA75 MPhil82. Ridley Hall Cam 84. **d** 86 **p** 87. C Eaton *Nor* 86-90; V Stevenage St Pet Broadwater *St Alb* from 90. *St Peter's House, 1 The Willows, Stevenage, Herts SG2 8AN*   Stevenage (0438) 352447

BRENTON, Basil. b 28. Sarum Th Coll. **d** 55 **p** 56. C Kensington St Mary Abbots w St Geo *Lon* 55-59; CF 59-62; Chapl Sliema *Eur* 62-65; C-in-c Hayes St Edm CD *Lon* 65-68; V Cowfold *Chich* from 68. *The Vicarage, Cowfold, Horsham, W Sussex RH13 8AH*   Cowfold (0403) 864296

BRETEL, Keith Michael. b 51. St Mich Coll Llan 79. **d** 81 **p** 82. C Thundersley *Chelmsf* 81-84; CF from 84. *c/o MOD (Army), Bagshot Park, Bagshot, Surrey GU19 5PL*   Bagshot (0276) 71717

BRETHERTON, Donald John. b 18. Lon Univ BD57. Handsworth Coll Birm 38 Headingley Coll Leeds 38 St Aug Coll Cant 59. **d** 60 **p** 61. In Meth Ch 42-59; V Thornton Heath St Jude *Cant* 62-70; V Herne 70-82; RD Reculver 74-80; rtd 82; Perm to Offic *Cant* from 84. *30 Bramley Avenue, Canterbury, Kent CT1 3XW*   Canterbury (0227) 765418

BRETHERTON, Canon William Alan. b 22. St Cath Coll Cam BA43 MA47. Lon Coll of Div BD49 ALCD49. **d** 49 **p** 50. V Ince Ch Ch *Liv* 65-72; V Kirkdale St Mary

72-73; V Kirkdale St Mary and St Athanasius 73-87; RD Liv 81-87; Hon Can Liv Cathl 81-87; rtd 87. *3 Bradville Road, Liverpool L9 9BH*   051-525 0866

BRETHERTON-HAWKSHEAD-TALBOT,   Richard Dolben. b 11. Trin Coll Cam BA32 MA56. Ely Th Coll 32. **d** 34 **p** 35. R Eccleston *Blackb* 58-78; rtd 78; Lic to Offic *Blackb* from 79. *The Delph, 71 Marsh Lane, Longton, Preston PR4 5ZL*   Preston (0772) 612893

BRETT, Dennis Roy Anthony. b 46. Sarum & Wells Th Coll 86. **d** 88 **p** 89. C Bradford-on-Avon *Sarum* from 88. *126 Trowbridge Road, Bradford-on-Avon, Wilts BA15 1EW*   Bradford-on-Avon (02216) 2516

BRETT, Donald Angus Adair. b 17. Chich Th Coll 52. **d** 55 **p** 56. C Findon *Chich* 66-81; rtd 81; Perm to Offic *Chich* from 81. *Irene Residential Club, 1 Parkfield Road, Worthing, W Sussex BN13 1EN*   Worthing (0903) 30418

BRETT, Canon Paul Gadsby. b 41. St Edm Hall Ox BA62 MA66. Wycliffe Hall Ox 64. **d** 65 **p** 66. C Bury St Pet *Man* 65-68; Asst Ind Chapl 68-72; Ind Chapl *Worc* 72-76; Sec Ind Cttee of Gen Syn Bd for Soc Resp 76-84; Dir Soc Resp *Chelmsf* from 85; Can Res Chelmsf Cathl from 85. *11 Millers' Croft, Great Baddow, Chelmsford CM2 8JL*   Chelmsford (0245) 73167

BRETT, Canon Peter Graham Cecil. b 35. Em Coll Cam BA59 MA63. Cuddesdon Coll 59. **d** 61 **p** 62. C Tewkesbury w Walton Cardiff *Glouc* 61-64; C Bournemouth St Pet *Win* 64-66; Chapl Dur Univ *Dur* 66-72; R Houghton le Spring 72-83; RD Houghton 80-83; Can Res Cant Cathl *Cant* from 83. *22 The Precincts, Canterbury, Kent CT1 2EP*   Canterbury (0227) 459757

BRETTELL, Robert Michael. b 20. St Cath Soc Ox BA49 MA54. Lon Coll of Div 46 Wycliffe Hall Ox 47. **d** 49 **p** 50. V Clifton Ch Ch w Em *Bris* 62-73; V Eastbourne H Trin *Chich* 73-82; V Bexhill St Steph 82-86; rtd 86; Perm to Offic *Chich* from 86. *229 Little Ridge Avenue, St Leonards-on-Sea, E Sussex TN37 7HN*   Hastings (0424) 752035

BREUKELMAN, Stephen Peter. b 55. Keble Coll Ox BA77 DPhil79. Trin Coll Bris 83. **d** 86 **p** 87. C Gt Horton *Bradf* 86-90; V Sunnyside w Bourne End *St Alb* from 90. *St Michael's Vicarage, Berkhamsted, Herts HP4 2PP*   Berkhamsted (0442) 865100

BREW, William Kevin Maddock. b 49. BA MSc. **d** 78 **p** 79. C Raheny w Coolock *D & G* 78-80; Bp's C Dub Finglas 80-83; I Mountmellick w Coolbanagher, Rosenallis etc *M & K* 83-89; I Aghoghill w Portglenone *Conn* from 89. *42 Church Street, Ahoghill, Ballymena, Co Antrim BT42 2PA*   Ahoghill (0266) 871240

BREW, William Philip. b 43. FCollP84 Derby Coll of Educn CertEd64 Liv Univ DSpEd72. N Ord Course 84. **d** 87 **p** 88. In Independent Meth Min 70-83; Hd Master Birtenshaw Sch 78-90; NSM Holcombe *Man* 87-90; TV Horwich from 91. *St Elizabeth's Vicarage, Cedar Avenue, Horwich, Bolton BL6 6HT*   Horwich (0204) 669120

BREWER, Barry James. b 44. Oak Hill Th Coll 72. **d** 75 **p** 76. C Hove Bp Hannington Memorial Ch *Chich* 75-78; C Church Stretton *Heref* 78-81; TV Bishopsnympton, Rose Ash, Mariansleigh etc *Ex* 81-87; R Swynnerton and Tittensor *Lich* from 87. *St Luke's Vicarage, Stone Road, Tittensor, Stoke-on-Trent ST12 9HE*   Barlaston (078139) 2312

BREWER, Canon John Herbert. b 13. DDEd. St Steph Ho Ox 37. **d** 39 **p** 40. V Isleworth St Fran *Lon* 66-78; rtd 78; Lic to Offic *Nor* 78-86; Perm to Offic from 86. *36 Cleaves Drive, Walsingham, Norfolk NR22 6EQ*   Walsingham (0328) 820579

BREWIN, Dr David Frederick. b 39. Leic Poly BSc PhD. Lich Th Coll. **d** 66 **p** 67. C Shrewsbury H Cross *Lich* 66-69; C Birstall *Leic* 69-73; V Eyres Monsell 73-79; V E Goscote 79-82; V E Goscote w Ratcliffe and Rearsby 82-90; R Thurcaston from 90. *The Rectory, 74 Anstey Lane, Thurcaston, Leicester LE7 7JA*   Leicester (0533) 362525

BREWIN, Donald Stewart. b 41. Ch Coll Cam BA62 MA66. Ridley Hall Cam 68. **d** 71 **p** 72. C Ecclesall *Sheff* 71-75; V Anston 75-81; V Walton H Trin *Ox* 81-89; TR from 89; RD Aylesbury from 90. *Holy Trinity Vicarage, 147 Wendover Road, Aylesbury, Bucks HP21 9NL*   Aylesbury (0296) 82068 or 29142

BREWIN, Canon Eric Walter. b 15. Hertf Coll Ox BA38 MA42. Ripon Hall Ox 38. **d** 40 **p** 41. RD Forest S *Glouc* 57-81; Hon Can Glouc Cathl 65-81; R Leckhampton St Pet 70-81; rtd 81; Perm to Offic *Glouc* from 82. *The Pleck, Llangrove, Ross-on-Wye, Herefordshire HR9 6EU*   Llangarron (098984) 487

BREWIN, Karan Rosemary. b 42. CA Tr Coll Glas NSM Course. **dss** 84 **d** 85. Clarkston *Glas* 84-86; Hon C 86-89;

Hon Par Dn from 91; OHP from 89. c/o 8 Golf Road, Clarkston, Glasgow G76 7LZ
BREWIN, Wilfred Michael. b 45. Nottm Univ BA69. Cuddesdon Coll 69. **d** 70 **p** 71. C Walker Newc 70-73; C Alnwick St Paul 73-74; C Alnwick w Edlingham and Bolton Chpl 74-77; Fell Sheff Univ 77-79; C Greenhill Sheff 79; P-in-c Eggleston Dur 79-81; V Norton St Mich 81-87; V Headington Ox from 87. The Vicarage, 33 St Andrew's Road, Oxford OX3 9DL   Oxford (0865) 61094
BREWSTER, David Pearson. b 30. Clare Coll Cam BA54 MA58 Lon Univ BA65 Or Coll Ox MA66 DPhil76. Ridley Hall Cam. **d** 58 **p** 59. C Southn St Mary w H Trin Win 58-61; C N Audley Street St Mark Lon 61-62 and 63-65; Tunisia 62-63; Home Sec JEM 65-66; C Ox St Mary V w St Cross and St Pet Ox 66-68; Lect Lady Spencer-Churchill Coll Ox 68-71; New Zealand 71-78; V Brockenhurst Win from 78. The Vicarage, Meerut Road, Brockenhurst, Hants SO42 7TD   Lymington (0590) 22150
BREWSTER, Lester Arnold. b 27. Fitzw Ho Cam BA51 MA55. Wycliffe Hall Ox 51. **d** 53 **p** 54. C Swanley St Paul Roch 53-55; C High Wycombe All SS Ox 55-57; Clerical Deputation Sec Dr Barnardo's Homes 57-60; Hon C Carshalton S'wark from 60; Org Sec Ox Miss to Calcutta 60-67. 155 Demesne Road, Wallington, Surrey SM6 8EW   081-647 4174
BREWSTER, Noel Theodore. b 16. CCC Cam BA38 MA42. Qu Coll Birm 38. **d** 39 **p** 40. R Chilcomb w Win All SS and Chesil Win 69-70; V Grantchester Ely 71-86; rtd 86; Perm to Offic Ely 86-90; Chapl St Cross Win 86-90. 5 Carthagena, Sutton Scotney, Hants SO21 3LJ   Winchester (0962) 760667
BREWSTER, William Taylor. b 26. Bps' Coll Cheshunt 58. **d** 59 **p** 60. R Woolfardisworthy w Kennerleigh Ex 61-71; R Washford Pyne w Puddington 61-71; P-in-c Cruwys Morchard 68-71; RD Cadbury 68-71; P-in-c Poughill w Stockleigh English 71; Asst Chapl HM Pris Man 71; Chapl HM Pris Maidstone 72-77; Blundeston 77-84; Featherstone 84-89; rtd 89; Perm to Offic Lich from 89. 4 Pinfold Road, Lichfield, Staffs WS13 7BX   Lichfield (0543) 254983
BRIAN, Stephen Frederick. b 54. Brighton Coll of Educn CertEd76 Sussex Univ BEd77 Birm Univ DipTh84. Qu Coll Birm 82. **d** 85 **p** 86. C Scotforth Blackb 85-88; V Freckleton from 88. Holy Trinity Vicarage, 3 Sunnyside Close, Freckleton, Preston PR4 1YJ   Freckleton (0772) 632209
BRICE, Christopher John. b 48. St Edm Ho Cam MA80. Wycliffe Hall Ox 82. **d** 82 **p** 83. C N Hinksey Ox 82-86; Chapl Nuff Coll Ox 84-86; V S Hackney St Mich w Haggerston St Paul Lon from 86. 97 Lavender Grove, London E8 3LR   071-249 4440
BRICE, Neil Alan. b 59. Man Univ BA81 Hughes Hall Cam CertEd87. Westcott Ho Cam 82. **d** 84 **p** 85. C Longton Lich 84-86; Hd of Relig Studies Coleridge Community Coll Cam 87-89; NSM Cherry Hinton St Andr Ely 88-89; C Fulbourn from 89; C Gt Wilbraham from 89; C Lt Wilbraham from 89. The Vicarage, Great Wilbraham, Cambridge CB1 5JS   Cambridge (0223) 880332
BRICE, Paul Earl Philip. b 54. Bath Univ BSc77. Wycliffe Hall Ox 83. **d** 86 **p** 87. C Gt Baddow Chelmsf 86-89; Chapl Imp Coll Lon from 89; St Mary's Hosp Med Sch from 89; RCA from 90. 1 Porchester Gardens, London W2 3LA   071-229 5089
BRIDCUT, William John. b 38. CITC 67. **d** 70 **p** 71. C Lisburn Ch Ch Cathl Conn 71-74; Dub Irish Ch Miss D & G from 74. Irish Church Missions, 28 Bachelors Walk, Dublin 1, Irish Republic   Dublin (1) 730829 or 212165
BRIDGE, Very Rev Antony Cyprian. b 14. FSA. Linc Th Coll 53. **d** 55 **p** 56. Dean Guildf 68-86; rtd 86. 34 London Road, Deal, Kent CT14 9TE   Deal (0304) 366792
BRIDGE, Miss Helen Cecily. b 25. SRN47 SCM49 Open Univ BA80. Lambeth STh78 Dalton Ho Bris 70 Trin Coll Bris 70. **dss** 74 **d** 87. Tonbridge St Steph Roch 74-75; Countess of Ches Hosp 75-84; Plemstall w Guilden Sutton Ches 85-87; Hon Par Dn 87-88; Hon Par Dn Stockport St Mary from 88. 25 Rectory Fields, Stockport, Cheshire SK1 4BX   061-477 2154
BRIDGE, Martin. b 45. Lon Univ BA66 Linacre Coll Ox BA71 MA73. St Steph Ho Ox 69. **d** 72 **p** 73. C St Peter-in-Thanet Cant 72-77; New Zealand from 77. 5 Landscape Road, Papatoetoe, PO Box 23-073, New Zealand   Auckland (9) 278-0656
BRIDGE-COLLYNS, Douglas Herbert. b 26. Nottm Univ BSc48 MPhil71. St Steph Ho Ox 51. **d** 53 **p** 54. C Leic St Pet Leic 53-57; S Rhodesia 58-65; C Nottm St Pet and St Jas S'well 65-68; Lic to Offic Derby 68-85; Perm

to Offic S'well 76-84; Chapl Abbots Bromley Sch 84-87; V Whatton w Aslockton, Hawksworth, Scarrington etc S'well from 87. The Vicarage, Main Street, Aslockton, Nottingham NG13 9AL   Whatton (0949) 51040
BRIDGEN, John William. b 40. K Coll Cam BA62 MA66. Ripon Hall Ox 66. **d** 70 **p** 72. C Headstone St Geo Lon 70-71; C Hanwell St Mary 71-75; C Tolladine Worc 75; TV Worc St Barn w Ch Ch 76; R Barrow St E 76-83; V Denham St Mary 76-83; Perm to Offic Ely 84-88 and from 91; rtd 88; Perm to Offic Glas 89-91. 57 St Philip's Road, Cambridge CB1 3DA   Cambridge (0223) 248096
BRIDGEN, Mark Stephen. b 63. K Coll Lon BD85. Cranmer Hall Dur 86. **d** 88 **p** 89. C Kidderminster St Jo Worc 88-90; C Kidderminster St Jo and H Innocents from 90. 59 Stretton Road, Kidderminster, Worcs DY11 6NQ   Kidderminster (0562) 754194
BRIDGER, Francis William. b 51. Pemb Coll Ox BA73 MA78 Bris Univ DipTh75 PhD80. Trin Coll Bris 74. **d** 78 **p** 79. C Islington St Jude Mildmay Park Lon 78-82; Lic to Offic S'well 82-90; C Mildmay Grove St Jude and St Paul Lon 82; Lect St Jo Coll Nottm 82-90; Dir of Courses 88-89; Dir of Studies 89-90; V Woodthorpe S'well from 90. St Mark's Vicarage, 37A Melbury Road, Nottingham NG5 4PG   Nottingham (0602) 267859
BRIDGER, Canon Gordon Frederick. b 32. Selw Coll Cam BA53 MA. Ridley Hall Cam 54. **d** 56 **p** 57. C Islington St Mary Lon 56-60; C Cam St Sepulchre Ely 60-62; V Fulham St Mary N End Lon 62-69; C Edin St Thos Edin 69-76; R Heigham H Trin Nor 76-87; RD Nor S 79-86; Hon Can Nor Cathl 84-87; Prin Oak Hill Th Coll from 87. 10 Farm Lane, London N14 4PP   081-441 7091
BRIDGER, Malcolm John. b 36. AKC62. **d** 63 **p** 64. C Sheff St Cuth Sheff 63-66; C Wythenshawe Wm Temple Ch CD Man 66-67; C-in-c Lower Kersal CD 67-72; V Lower Kersal 72-74; C Ifield Chich 75-78; TV 78-84; P-in-c Brentford St Paul w St Lawr and St Geo Lon 84-87; P-in-c Gunnersbury St Jas 85-87; TR Brentford from 87. The Rectory, 3 The Butts, Brentford, Middx TW8 8BJ   081-568 6502
BRIDGER, Nigel Egerton. b 23. Dartmouth RN Coll 40. Wells Th Coll 59. **d** 61 **p** 62. C Neston Ches 61-64; S Africa from 64. PO Box 119, Queenstown, 5320 South Africa   Queenstown (451) 4377
BRIDGER, Renee Winifred. b 45. Lon Univ BD76. Trin Coll Bris. **dss** 80 **d** 87. Islington St Jude Mildmay Park Lon 80-82; Mildmay Grove St Jude and St Paul 82; St Jo Coll Nottm from 87; Hon Par Dn Chilwell S'well 87-88; Assoc Min Woodthorpe from 90. St Mark's Vicarage, 37A Melbury Road, Nottingham NG5 4PG   Nottingham (0602) 267859
✠**BRIDGES, Rt Rev Dewi Morris.** b 33. Univ of Wales (Lamp) BA54 CCC Cam BA56 MA60. Westcott Ho Cam 57. **d** 57 **p** 58 **c** 88. C Rhymney Mon 57-60; C Chepstow 60-63; V Tredegar St Jas 63-65; Lic to Offic Worc 65-69; V Kempsey 69-79; RD Upton 74-79; R Tenby and Gumfreston St D 79-85; RD Narberth 80-82; Adn St D 82-88; R Tenby 85-88; Bp S & B from 88. Ely Tower, Brecon, Powys LD3 9DE   Brecon (0874) 622008
BRIDGES, Mrs Gillian Mary. b 43. E Anglian Minl Tr Course 85. **d** 88. Hon C Hellesdon Nor from 88. 2 Vera Road, Norwich, Norfolk NR6 5HU   Norwich (0603) 789634
BRIDGES, Harry. b 05. Lon Coll of Div 27. **d** 31 **p** 32. R Saxlingham Nethergate w Saxlingham Thorpe Nor 71-76; rtd 76; Perm to Offic Nor from 77. 11 Merchant Way, Felbrigg Green, Hellesdon, Norwich NR6 5HF   Norwich (0603) 787245
BRIDGES, Ven Peter Sydney Godfrey. b 25. ARIBA51 Birm Univ DipL&A67. Linc Th Coll 56. **d** 58 **p** 59. Perm to Offic Birm 65-72; Lect Aston Univ 68-72; Dir Dioc Research and Development Unit 72-77; Adn Southend Chelmsf 72-77; P-in-c Southend St Jo w St Mark, All SS w St Fran etc 72-77; Adn Cov 77-83; Can Th Cov Cathl 77-90; Adn Warw 83-90; rtd 90; Dioc Adv for Chr Spirituality from 90. Saint Clare, 1 Bellcourt, The Maltings, Leamington Spa, Warks CV32 5FH   Leamington Spa (0926) 335491
BRIDGEWATER, Guy Stevenson. b 60. Ch Ch Ox BA83. Trin Coll Bris BA87. **d** 87 **p** 88. C Radipole and Melcombe Regis Sarum 87-90; Chapl Lee Abbey from 90. Lee Abbey, Lynton, Devon EX35 6JJ   Lynton (0598) 52621
BRIDGLAND, Cyril John Edwin. b 21. Tyndale Hall Bris 42. **d** 45 **p** 46. V Redhill H Trin S'wark 58-87; rtd 87. 3 Barned Court, Barming, Maidstone, Kent ME16 9EL   Maidstone (0622) 728451
BRIDGMAN, Canon Gerald Bernard. b 22. St Cath Coll Cam BA50 MA55. Wycliffe Hall Ox 50. **d** 51 **p** 52. V

Kingston upon Hull H Trin *York* 67-87; AD Cen and N Hull 81-86; Can and Preb York Minster 83-87; rtd 87; Perm to Offic *Chich* from 87. *69 William Allen Lane, Lindfield, W Sussex RH16 2ST* Haywards Heath (0444) 456181

BRIDGWATER, Edward Roden Gresham. b 98. Union Th Sem (NY) MDiv28 K Coll (NS) BA22 MA23. **d** 24 **p** 25. V Chilworth *Win* 62-72; rtd 72. *Flat 30, Capel Court, The Burgage, Prestbury, Cheltenham GL52 3EL* Cheltenham (0242) 571812

BRIDLE, Geoffrey Peter. b 52. CITC 87. **d** 87 **p** 88. C Lurgan (Shankill) *D & D* 87-91; I Carnteel and Crilly *Arm* from 91. *St James' Rectory, 22 Carnteel Road, Aughnacloy, Co Tyrone BT69 6DU* Aughnacloy (066252) 682

BRIDLE, Reginald. b 05. Lon Univ BA30 BD50. Ripon Hall Ox 34. **d** 34 **p** 35. Chile 55-66; Nigeria 67-73; rtd 71; Perm to Offic *Win* from 73. *65 Barlows Lane, Andover, Hants SP10 2HB* Andover (0264) 352666

BRIDSON, Raymond Stephen. b 58. Southn Univ BTh82. Chich Th Coll. **d** 82 **p** 83. C St Luke in the City *Liv* 82-86; TV Ditton St Mich from 86. *All Saints' Vicarage, Hough Green Road, Widnes, Cheshire WA8 9SZ* 051-420 4963

BRIDSTRUP, Juergen Walter. b 44. St Alb Minl Tr Scheme 84. **d** 87 **p** 88. C Leagrave *St Alb* 87-90; V Goff's Oak St Jas from 90. *St James's Vicarage, St James' Road, Goffs Oak, Herts EN7 6TP* Cuffley (0707) 872328

BRIERLEY, David James. b 53. Bris Univ BA75. Oak Hill Th Coll 75. **d** 77 **p** 78. C Balderstone *Man* 77-80; P-in-c Eccles St Andr 80-81; Bp's Ecum Adv 81-88; TV Eccles 81-85; V Harwood from 85; Sec Bd Miss and Unity from 88. *The Vicarage, Stitch-mi-Lane, Bolton BL2 4HU* Bolton (0204) 25196

BRIERLEY, Eric. b 21. St Aid Birkenhead 47. **d** 50 **p** 51. V Horwich St Cath *Man* 66-74; V Irlam 74-81; V Farndon and Coddington *Ches* 81-86; rtd 86; Perm to Offic *Blackb* from 86. *6 Derbyshire Avenue, Garstang, Preston PR3 1DX* Garstang (0995) 602047

BRIERLEY, John Michael. b 32. Lon Univ BD71. Lich Th Coll 57. **d** 60 **p** 61. C Lower Mitton *Worc* 60-62; C-in-c Dines Green St Mich CD 62-68; V Worc St Mich 69-71; R Eastham w Rochford 71-79; P-in-c Knighton-on-Teme 76-79; P-in-c Reddal Hill St Luke 79-81; V from 81. *St Luke's Vicarage, Upper High Street, Cradley Heath, Warley, W Midlands B64 5HX* Cradley Heath (0384) 69940

BRIERLEY, William Peter. b 13. Dur Univ BSc38. Cranmer Hall Dur 65. **d** 66 **p** 67. C Otterburn w Elsdon and Horsley w Byrness *Newc* 69-75; V Greenhead 75-78; P-in-c Lambley w Knaresdale 77-78; rtd 78; Perm to Offic *Carl* 79-87. *7 Hitcombe Bottom Cottage, Horningsham, Warminster, Wilts* Warminster (0985) 844720

BRIERLY, Henry Barnard Lancelot. b 30. Or Coll Ox BA55 MA63. Clifton Th Coll 55. **d** 58 **p** 59. C Normanton *Derby* 58-61; C St Helens St Helen *Liv* 61-63; V Tebay *Carl* 63-69; R Ashwellthorpe w Wreningham *Nor* 69-74; P-in-c Fundenhall 70-74; P-in-c Tacolneston 70-74; TR Wreningham 74-86; R Tetsworth, Adwell w S Weston, Lewknor etc *Ox* from 86. *The Rectory, 46 High Street, Tetsworth, Oxford OX9 7AS* Tetsworth (084428) 267

BRIGGS, Ven Archie. b 17. Dur Univ BA39 DipTh40 MA42. **d** 41 **p** 42. Malaya 59-63; Malaysia 63-74; Dean Kota Kinabalu 70-74; Taiwan 75-85; rtd 85. *46 Kell Crescent, Sherburn Hill, Durham DH6 1PP* 091-372 2013

BRIGGS, Christopher Ronald. b 58. K Coll Lon BD79 AKC79 PGCE80. Sarum & Wells Th Coll 87. **d** 89 **p** 90. C Horsell *Guildf* from 89. *6 Waldens Park Road, Horsell, Woking, Surrey GU21 4RN* Woking (0483) 715440

BRIGGS, Derek. b 26. Lon Univ DipTh55. St Aid Birkenhead 52. **d** 55 **p** 56. V Farsley *Bradf* 67-90; rtd 90. *6 College Court, Bradley, Keighley, W Yorkshire BD20 9EA* Keighley (0535) 630585

✠**BRIGGS, Rt Rev George Cardell.** b 10. CMG80. SS Coll Cam BA33 MA37. Cuddesdon Coll 33. **d** 34 **p** 35 **c** 73. C Stockport St Alb Hall Street *Ches* 34-37; Tanzania 37-73; OGS from 39; Adn Newala 55-64; Can Zanzibar 64-65; Can Dar-es-Salaam 65-69; Can Masasi 69-73; Bp Seychelles 73-79; Asst Bp Derby 79-80; C Matlock and Tansley 79-80; rtd 80. *Beauchamp Community, Newland, Malvern, Worcester WR13 5AX* Malvern (0684) 572941

BRIGGS, Herbert. b 15. Linc Th Coll 43. **d** 45 **p** 46. R Gt Ponton *Linc* 68-84; R Stoke 68-84; P-in-c Lt Ponton 73-84; P-in-c Skillington 76-84; rtd 84. *The Lodge, Little Ponton, Grantham, Lincs NG33 5BS* Great Ponton (047683) 382

BRIGGS, John. b 39. Edin Univ MA61. Ridley Hall Cam 61. **d** 63 **p** 64. C Jesmond Clayton Memorial *Newc* 63-66; Schs Sec Scripture Union 66-79; Tutor St Jo Coll Dur 67-74; Lic to Offic Dur 67-74; Edin 74-79; V Chadkirk *Ches* 79-88; RD Chadkirk 85-88; TR Macclesfield Team Par from 88. *The Rectory, 85 Beech Lane, Macclesfield, Cheshire SK10 2DY* Macclesfield (0625) 426110

BRIGGS, Canon John Arthur. b 12. St Jo Coll Dur BA34 MA38 Lon Univ BD43. Wycliffe Hall Ox 34. **d** 35 **p** 36. V Formby H Trin *Liv* 62-78; Hon Can Liv Cathl 69-78; rtd 78; Perm to Offic *Liv* from 78. *3 Clifden Court, Formby, Liverpool L37 3QE* Formby (07048) 77739

BRIGGS, Michael Weston. b 40. Edin Th Coll 61. **d** 64 **p** 65. C Sneinton St Steph w St Alb *S'well* 64-67; C Beeston 67-70; P-in-c Kirkby Woodhouse 70-74; V Harworth 74-81; R Harby w Thorney and N and S Clifton from 81. *The Rectory, Front Street, South Clifton, Newark, Notts NG23 7AA* Spalford (052277) 258

BRIGGS, Ralph Irvin. b 27. Lon Univ BD66. Westcott Ho Cam 66. **d** 68 **p** 69. C Chadwell Heath *Chelmsf* 68-73; C Canning Town St Matthias 73-75; P-in-c from 75. *The Gate House, 230B Grange Road, London E13 0HG* 071-476 9318

BRIGGS, Roger Edward. b 36. ALCD61. **d** 61 **p** 61. Canada 61-71 and from 72; C Upper Armley *Ripon* 71-72. *317 Chapel Street, Ottawa, Ontario, Canada, K1N 7Z2*

BRIGHAM, John Keith. b 48. FSAScot Man Univ CertEd70. St Steph Ho Ox 71. **d** 74 **p** 75. C Ches H Trin *Ches* 74-77; C Ealing Ch the Sav *Lon* 77-85; P-in-c Fulwell St Mich and St Geo 85-88; P-in-c Upper Teddington SS Pet and Paul 85-88; V Southport St Luke *Liv* from 88; Dioc Chapl to the Deaf from 88. *The Clergy House, 71 Hawkshead Street, Southport, Merseyside PR9 9BT* Southport (0704) 538703

BRIGHOUSE, George Alexander. b 46. N Ord Course 87. **d** 90 **p** 91. NSM Ingrow cum Hainworth *Bradf* from 90. *7 Cliffe Terrace, Spring Bank, Keighley, W Yorkshire BD21 5DP* Keighley (0535) 681342

BRIGHT, George Frank. b 50. Peterho Cam BA71 MA75 Leeds Univ DipTh73 LSE MSc83. Coll of Resurr Mirfield 71. **d** 74 **p** 75. C Notting Hill *Lon* 74-77; Perm to Offic 77-84; P-in-c Kentish Town St Benet and All SS 84-89; P-in-c Kensington St Jo the Bapt from 89. *The Vicarage, 176 Holland Road, London W14 8AH* 071-602 4655

BRIGHT, Patrick John Michael. b 36. Keble Coll Ox BA59 MA64. Chich Th Coll 59. **d** 61 **p** 62. C Bracknell *Ox* 61-68; V Hitchin H Sav *St Alb* 68-76; V Royston 76-90; RD Buntingford from 88; R Ashwell from 90. *The Rectory, Ashwell, Baldock, Herts SG7 6QG* Ashwell (046274) 2277

BRIGHT, Reginald. b 26. Tyndale Hall Bris 57. **d** 60 **p** 61. C Toxteth Park St Philemon w St Silas *Liv* 60-63; P-in-c Everton St Polycarp 63-65; R Orton St Giles *Carl* 65-72; V Holme 72-79; P-in-c W Newton 79-81; V Bromfield w Waverton 79-81; R Bowness from 81. *The Rectory, Bowness-on-Solway, Carlisle CA5 5AF* Kirkbride (06973) 51328

BRIGHTMAN, Peter Arthur. b 30. Lon Coll of Div ALCD61 LTh74. **d** 64 **p** 65. C Westgate St Jas *Cant* 64-67; C Lydd 67-70; C Lt Coates *Linc* 70; C Heaton Ch Ch *Man* 71-72; V Bolton SS Simon and Jude 72-77; R Bath St Sav *B & W* 77-85; R Farmborough, Marksbury and Stanton Prior 85-90; C Coney Hill *Glouc* from 90. *3 Oxmoor, Abbeydale, Gloucester GL4 9XW* Gloucester (0452) 500569

BRIGHTON, Herbert Ernest. b 96. Bris Univ BA22. St Aid Birkenhead 23. **d** 24 **p** 25. R Burnsall *Bradf* 47-57; rtd 57. *44 Cusden Drive, Artist's Way, Andover, Hants SP10 3TF* Andover (0264) 59248

BRIGHTON, Terrence William. b 43. SW Minl Tr Course 85. **d** 88 **p** 89. C Dawlish *Ex* from 88. *15 Cousens Close, Dawlish, Devon EX7 9TE* Dawlish (0626) 862944

BRIGNALL, Simon Francis Lyon. b 54. St Jo Coll Dur BA78. Wycliffe Hall Ox 80. **d** 83 **p** 84. C Colne St Bart *Blackb* 83-86; SAMS from 86. *c/o SAMS, Allen Gardiner House, Pembury Road, Tunbridge Wells, Kent TN2 3QU* Tunbridge Wells (0892) 38647

BRIMICOMBE, Mark. b 44. Nottm Univ BA66 CertEd. SW Minl Tr Course 83. **d** 85 **p** 86. NSM Plympton St Mary *Ex* from 85. *4 David Close, Stoggy Lane, Plympton, Plymouth PL7 3BQ* Plymouth (0752) 338454

BRINDLE, John Harold. b 21. St Jo Coll Dur LTh42 BA43 MA46. St Aid Birkenhead 39. **d** 44 **p** 44. V Grimsargh *Blackb* 51-88; rtd 88. *8 Sussex Drive, Garstang, Preston PR3 1ET* Garstang (0995) 606588

BRINDLE, Peter John. b 47. MIStructE72. N Ord Course 78. **d** 81 **p** 82. NSM Bingley All SS *Bradf* 81-84; NSM Bingley H Trin 84-86; V Keighley All SS 86-91; V Kirkstall *Ripon* from 91. *The Vicarage, Vicarage View, Leeds LS5 3HF* Leeds (0532) 781007

BRINDLEY, Canon Brian Dominick Frederick Titus. b 31. Ex Coll Ox BA54 MA59. **d** 62 **p** 63. C Clewer St Andr *Ox* 62-67; V Reading H Trin 67-89; Hon Can Ch Ch 85-89; Asst Dioc Sec *Chich* from 89; Dioc Past Sec from 89. *Flat 1, 17 Devonshire Place, Brighton BN2 1QA* Brighton (0273) 608895 or 279023

BRINDLEY, David Charles. b 53. K Coll Lon BD75 AKC75 MTh76 MPhil81. St Aug Coll Cant 75. **d** 76 **p** 77. C Epping St Jo *Chelmsf* 76-79; Lect Coll of SS Mary and Paul Cheltenham 79-82; Lic to Offic *Glouc* 79-82; Dioc Dir of Tr *Leic* 82-86; V Quorndon 82-86; Prin Glouc Sch for Min *Glouc* from 87; Dir of Minl Tr from 87; Dioc Officer for NSM from 88. *4 The Vineys, Sandhurst, Gloucester GL2 9NX* Gloucester (0452) 731132

BRINDLEY, Stuart Geoffrey Noel. b 30. St Jo Coll Dur BA53 DipTh55. **d** 55 **p** 56. C Newc St Anne *Newc* 55-58; C Tynemouth Cullercoats St Paul 58-60; C Killingworth 60-63; V Newsham 63-69; W Germany 69-76; Asst Master Wyvern Sch Weston-super-Mare 76-80; V Stocksbridge *Sheff* 80-88; RD Tankersley 85-88; V Rotherham from 88. *2 Heather Close, Rotherham, S Yorkshire S60 2TQ* Rotherham (0709) 364341

BRINKWORTH, Christopher Michael Gibbs. b 41. Lanc Univ BA70. Kelham Th Coll 62. **d** 67 **p** 68. C Lanc St Mary *Blackb* 67-70; C Milton *Portsm* 70-74; V Ault Hucknall *Derby* 74-84; V Derby St Anne and St Jo from 84. *The Vicarage, 25 Highfield Road, Derby DE3 1GX* Derby (0332) 32681

BRINSMEAD, Keith. b 06. DSO44. **d** 78 **p** 78. NSM Ebbesbourne Wake w Fifield Bavant and Alvediston *Sarum* 78-81; NSM Chalke Valley W 81-84; Perm to Offic from 84. *38 Harnham Road, Salisbury SP2 8JJ* Salisbury (0722) 332519

BRINSON, David Wayne Evans. b 32. Univ of Wales (Lamp) BA53 LTh55. **d** 55 **p** 56. P-in-c Swansea St John-juxta-Swansea *S & B* 63-82; V Llanrhidian w Llanmadoc and Cheriton 82-90; rtd 90. *Rosenberg, 157 Terrace Road, Mount Pleasant, Swansea SA1 6HU* Swansea (0792) 474069

BRION, Martin Philip. b 33. Ex Univ BA55. Ridley Hall Cam 57. **d** 59 **p** 60. C Balderstone *Man* 59-62; C Morden *S'wark* 62-66; V Low Elswick *Newc* 66-73; P-in-c Giggleswick *Bradf* 73-77; V 77-80; V Camerton H Trin W Seaton *Carl* 80-86; V Dearham from 86. *The Vicarage, Church Street, Dearham, Maryport, Cumbria CA15 7HX* Maryport (0900) 812320

BRISCOE, Canon Frances Amelia. b 35. Univ of Wales CertEd55 Leeds Univ DipRE62 Man Univ BA71 MA74. Gilmore Course 74. **dss** 77 **d** 87. Gt Crosby St Luke *Liv* 77-81; Dioc Lay Min Adv 81-89; Chapl Liv Cathl 81-89; Dir Diaconal Mins 87-89; Lect St Deiniol's Minl Tr Scheme from 88; Hon Can Liv Cathl *Liv* from 88; AD Sefton from 89; Dir of Reader Studies from 89. *20 Ascot Park, Crosby, Liverpool L23 2XH* 051-931 3573

BRISCOE, Gordon Michael. b 24. Ely Th Coll 51. **d** 53 **p** 54. C Isleworth St Fran *Lon* 53-54; Hon C 66-67; C Ealing Ch the Sav 54-57; Chapl Prince Rupert Sch Wilhelmshaven, W Germany 57-62; C Twickenham St Mary *Lon* 62-65; Chapl Fortescue Ho Sch Twickenham 62-65; Hon C Highgate Rise St Anne Brookfield *Lon* 67-77; Hon C Paddington St Steph w St Luke 77-80; Chapl St Marylebone Annunciation Bryanston Street 80-83; Chapl Bedf Modern Sch 83-84; Hon Chapl from 84; R Dunton w Wrestlingworth and Eyeworth *St Alb* from 84. *The Rectory, 7 Braggs Lane, Wrestlingworth, Sandy, Beds SG19 2ER* Wrestlingworth (076723) 596

BRISCOE, Henry Ellis. b 15. QUB BA44 TCD MA49. CITC 46. **d** 46 **p** 47. V Sneyd *Lich* 62-77; V Llanyblodwel 77-82; rtd 82; P-in-c Clyro w Bettws *S & B* 82-85; Perm to Offic St As and Lich from 85. *Gwynfa, Llansilin, Oswestry, Shropshire SY10 7QB* Llansilin (069170) 265

BRISON, Ven William Stanly. b 29. Alfred Univ NY BSc51 Connecticut Univ MDiv57 STM71. Berkeley Div Sch. **d** 57 **p** 57. USA 57-72; V Davyhulme Ch Ch *Man* 72-81; R Newton Heath All SS 81-85; AD N Man 81-85; Hon Can Man Cathl 82-85; Adn Bolton from 85; TV E Farnworth and Kearsley 85-89; C Bolton St Thos from 89. *All Souls' Vicarage, 2 Myrrh Street, Bolton BL1 8XE* Bolton (0204) 27269

BRISTOL, Archdeacon of. *See* BANFIELD, Ven David John

BRISTOL, Bishop of. *See* ROGERSON, Rt Rev Barry

BRISTOL, Dean of. *See* CARR, Very Rev Arthur Wesley

BRISTOW, Arthur George Raymond. b 09. Lich Th Coll 32. **d** 35 **p** 36. V Willenhall St Steph *Lich* 57-75; rtd 75; C Emscote *Cov* from 75; Perm to Offic *Lich* from 85. *41 Badgers Way, Heath Hayes, Cannock, Staffs WS12 5XQ* Heath Hayes (0543) 275530

BRISTOW, Keith Raymond Martin. b 56. Ex Univ BA78. Chich Th Coll 87. **d** 89 **p** 90. C Kirkby *Liv* from 89. *45 Alvanley Road, Kirkby, Merseyside L32 0SZ* 051-547 2769

BRISTOW, Peter. b 49. Pontificium Institutum Internationale Angelicum Rome JCL77 St Jos Coll Upholland 67. **d** 72 **p** 73. In RC Church 72-87; C Poplar *Lon* from 89; Lay Tr Officer 89-90. *St Nicholas Church Flat, Aberfeldy Street, London E14 0QD* 071-515 8405

BRISTOW, Roger. b 60. Aston Tr Scheme 81 Ridley Hall Cam 83. **d** 86 **p** 87. C Leyton St Mary w St Edw *Chelmsf* 86-90; TV Kings Norton *Birm* from 90. *53 Wychall Park Grove, King's Norton, Birmingham B38 8AG* 021-458 1836

BRITT, Eric Stanley. b 47. St Jo Coll Nottm LTh74 BTh75. **d** 74 **p** 75. C Chorleywood Ch Ch *St Alb* 74-78; C Frimley *Guildf* 78-80; P-in-c Alresford *Chelmsf* 80-88; R Takeley w Lt Canfield from 88. *The Rectory, Parsonage Road, Takeley, Bishop's Stortford, Herts CM22 6QX* Bishop's Stortford (0279) 870837

BRITTAIN, John. b 23. St Aug Coll Cant 59. **d** 60 **p** 61. V Highley *Heref* 62-88; rtd 88. *1 Mead Close, Leckhampton, Cheltenham, Glos GL53 7DX* Cheltenham (0242) 525987

BRITTON, Basil. b 29. Bris Univ BA50. S'wark Ord Course 66. **d** 69 **p** 70. C Roehampton H Trin *S'wark* 69-73; Hon C Hedsor and Bourne End *Ox* from 77. *5 Coach Ride, Marlow, Bucks* Marlow (0628) 484339

BRITTON, Cyril Edward. b 06. Kelham Th Coll 26. **d** 31 **p** 32. C Bethnal Green St Jo *Lon* 31-34; Australia 34-39; C Stoke-upon-Trent *Lich* 39-42; P-in-c Tunstall St Chad CD 42-47; S Africa from 47. *15 St Michael's Village, Weltevreden Park, 1715 South Africa* Johannesburg (11) 475-2431

BRITTON, John Anthony. b 39. Dur Univ BA60. Wycliffe Hall Ox 61. **d** 63 **p** 64. C Sheff St Swithun *Sheff* 63-64; C Sheff St Aid w St Luke 64-66; C Doncaster St Geo 66-68; C Grantham St Wulfram *Linc* 68-72; V Surfleet 72-76; V Bolsover *Derby* 76-86; V Harworth *S'well* from 86. *The Vicarage, Tickhill Road, Harworth, Doncaster, S Yorkshire DN11 8PD* Doncaster (0302) 744157

BRITTON, John Timothy Hugh. b 50. Dundee Univ BSc73. Trin Coll Bris 73. **d** 76 **p** 77. C Cromer *Nor* 76-79; P-in-c Freethorpe w Wickhampton 79-82; P-in-c Beighton and Moulton 79-82; P-in-c Halvergate w Tunstall 79-82; CMS 82-89; Uganda 83-89; R Allesley *Cov* from 89. *The Rectory, Allesley, Coventry CV5 9EQ* Coventry (0203) 402006

BRITTON, Neil Bryan. b 35. Em Coll Cam BA59 MA63. Clifton Th Coll 61. **d** 63 **p** 64. C Eastbourne All SS *Chich* 63-67; C Ashtead *Guildf* 67-70; Chapl Scargill Ho N Yorkshire 70-74; Asst Chapl Villars *Eur* 74-81. *Address temp unknown*

BRITTON, Canon Paul Anthony. b 29. SS Coll Cam BA52 MA57. Linc Th Coll 52. **d** 54 **p** 55. C Upper Norwood St Jo *Cant* 54-57; C Wantage *Ox* 57-61; V Stanmore *Win* 61-70; V Bitterne Park 70-80; Can Res Win Cathl from 80; Lib 81-85; Treas from 85. *11 The Close, Winchester, Hants SO23 9LS* Winchester (0962) 868580

BRITTON, Robert. b 37. Oak Hill Th Coll 78. **d** 79 **p** 80. C St Helens St Helen *Liv* 79-83; V Lowton St Mary from 83; AD Winwick from 89. *The Vicarage, 1 Barford Drive, St Mary's Park, Lowton, Warrington WA3 1DD* Leigh (0942) 607705

BRITTON, Robert. b 40. Univ of Wales DipTh64. St Mich Coll Llan 61. **d** 64 **p** 65. C Aberdare *Llan* 64-67; C Coity w Nolton 67-71; V Abercynon 71-75; V Tycoch *S & B* from 75. *The Vicarage, 26 Hendrefoilan Road, Swansea SA2 9LS* Swansea (0792) 204476

BRITTON, Ronald George Adrian. Oklahoma City SW Coll BA76 NY State Univ BSc78 Clayton Univ St Louis PhD82 Nova Coll Edmonton EdD83 Hon LittD84 Univ de la Romande Basle JD86. St D Coll Lamp 63 Bapt Coll Louisiana MA79 Lambeth STh82 St Deiniol's Hawarden 85. **d** 85 **p** 85. Chapl Alassio *Eur* 85-86; Chapl San Remo 86-90; Hon C Southbourne St Kath *Win* from 90. *The Parsonage, 121 Broadway, Bournemouth BH6 4EJ* Bournemouth (0202) 426171

BRIXWORTH, Suffragan Bishop of. *See* BARBER, Rt Rev Paul Everard

BROACKES, Ronald Reginald. b 17. Wells Th Coll. **d** 72 **p** 73. NSM Bath St Steph *B & W* 72-78; NSM Bath Ch Ch Prop Chpl 78-83; rtd 84; Perm to Offic *B & W* from

84. *5 Cambridge Place, Widcombe Hill, Bath, Avon BA2 6AB* Bath (0225) 317713

BROAD, David. b 59. Man Univ BA. Edin Th Coll. **d** 87 **p** 88. C Fulham All SS *Lon* 87-90; TV Clare w Poslingford, Cavendish etc *St E* from 90. *The Rectory, 23 Greys Close, Cavendish, Sudbury, Suffolk CO10 8BT* Glemsford (0787) 280330

BROAD, Donald. b 19. **d** 82 **p** 83. Hon C Purley St Swithun *S'wark* from 82. *15 Wheat Knoll, Kenley, Surrey CR8 5JT* 081-668 3128

BROAD, Hugh Duncan. b 37. Lich Th Coll 64. **d** 67 **p** 68. C Heref H Trin *Heref* 67-72; Asst Master Bp's Sch Heref 72-73; C Fareham SS Pet and Paul *Portsm* 74-76; V Heref All SS *Heref* 76-90; R Matson *Glouc* from 90. *The Rectory, Matson Lane, Gloucester GL4 9DX* Gloucester (0452) 22698

BROAD, Hugh Robert. b 49. St Mich Coll Llan 67. **d** 72 **p** 73. C Tenby w Gumfreston *St D* 72-75; C Caerau w Ely *Llan* 75-79; V Llanharan w Peterston-s-Montem 79-89; RD Bridgend 88-89; Ex-Paroch Officer 90; V Whatborough Gp of Par *Leic* from 90. *The Vicarage, Oakham Road, Tilton on the Hill, Leicester LE7 9LB* Tilton (053754) 244

BROAD, Paul Martin. b 56. St Jo Coll Dur BA79. Coll of Resurr Mirfield 79. **d** 81 **p** 82. C Kells *Carl* 81-83; C Pet St Jo *Pet* 83-87; R Corby Epiphany w St Jo from 87; Chapl Corby Community Hosp from 89. *The Rectory, 18 Argyll Street, Corby, Northants NN17 1RU* Corby (0536) 203314

BROAD, William Ernest Lionel. b 40. Ridley Hall Cam 64. **d** 66 **p** 67. C Ecclesfield *Sheff* 66-69; Chapl HM Pris Wormwood Scrubs 69; Albany 70-74; HM Rem Cen Risley 74-76; V Ditton St Mich *Liv* 76-81; TR 82-83; P-in-c Mayland *Chelmsf* 83-91; P-in-c Steeple 83-91; V Blackhall *Dur* from 91. *The Vicarage, Blackhall, Hartlepool, Cleveland TS27 4LE* 091-586 4202

BROADBENT, Edward Ronald. b 23. Man Univ BSc44. Westcott Ho Cam 53. **d** 55 **p** 56. SPCK Staff 63-87; Hon C Wilton w Netherhampton and Fugglestone *Sarum* 78-80; P-in-c S Newton 80-83; Hon C Chalke Valley W from 84; rtd 88. *2 Marlborough Road, Salisbury SP1 3TH* Salisbury (0722) 326809

BROADBENT, Hugh Patrick Colin. b 53. Selw Coll Cam BA75 MA. Wycliffe Hall Ox DipTh78. **d** 78 **p** 79. C Chatham St Steph *Roch* 78-82; C Shortlands 82-84; C Edenbridge 84-87; C Crockham Hill H Trin 84-87; V Bromley H Trin from 87. *Holy Trinity Vicarage, Church Lane, Bromley BR2 8LB* 081-462 1280

BROADBENT, Michael Tom. b 45. Down Coll Cam BA66 MA70. Cuddesdon Coll 67. **d** 68 **p** 69. C Leeds St Aid *Ripon* 68-71; S Africa 71-77; V Luddenden *Wakef* 77-78; P-in-c Luddenden Foot 77-78; V Luddenden w Luddenden Foot 78-79; Swaziland 79-86; Adn W Swaziland 83-86; R Middleham w Coverdale and E Witton *Ripon* from 87; RD Wensley from 88. *The Rectory, The Springs, Middleham, Leyburn, N Yorkshire DL8 4RB* Wensleydale (0969) 22276

BROADBENT, Neil Seton. b 53. Qu Coll Birm DipTh80. **d** 81 **p** 82. C Knaresborough *Ripon* 81-83; C Knaresborough 83-84; C Leeds Gipton Epiphany 84-87; Lic to Offic from 87; Chapl Minstead Community *Derby* 89. *The Vicarage, Main Road, Horsley Woodhouse, Derby DE7 6BB* Derby (0332) 780598

BROADBENT, Paul John. b 41. Oak Hill Th Coll DipTh83. **d** 85 **p** 86. C Duston *Pet* 85-88; TV Ross w Brampton Abbotts, Bridstow and Peterstow *Heref* from 88. *The Rectory, Brampton Abbotts, Ross-on-Wye, Herefordshire HR9 7JD* Ross-on-Wye (0989) 64876

BROADBENT, Peter Alan. b 52. Jes Coll Cam BA74 MA78. St Jo Coll Nottm DipTh75. **d** 77 **p** 78. C Dur St Nic *Dur* 77-80; C Holloway Em w Hornsey Road St Barn *Lon* 80-83; Chapl Poly of N Lon 83-89; Hon C Islington St Mary 83-89; V Harrow H Trin St Mich from 89. *The Vicarage, 39 Rusland Park Road, Harrow, Middx HA1 1UN* 081-427 2616 or 863 6131

BROADBENT, Ralph Andrew. b 55. K Coll Lon BD76 AKC76. Chich Th Coll 77. **d** 78 **p** 79. C Prestwich St Mary *Man* 78-82; R Man Miles Platting 82-84; CF 84-87; TV Wordsley *Lich* from 88. *1 Denleigh Road, Kingswinford, W Midlands DY6 8QB* Kingswinford (0384) 278692

BROADBENT, Thomas William. b 45. Chu Coll Cam BA66 MA70 PhD70. Ridley Hall Cam 75. **d** 78 **p** 79. C Allington and Maidstone St Pet *Cant* 78-82; Chapl Mid Kent Coll of H&FE 80-82; C Kings Heath *Birm* 82-84; Chapl Salford Univ *Man* from 84; Hon C Pendleton St Thos 84-89; TV Pendleton St Thos w Charlestown from 89; Chair Man Coun of Chrs & Jews from 89.

16 Beaminster Walk, Longsight, Manchester M13 9DD 061-273 3671

BROADBERRY, Canon Richard St Lawrence. b 31. TCD BA53 BD59 MLitt66. **d** 54 **p** 55. C Dub St Thos *D & G* 54-56; C Dub Grangegorman 56-62; Min Can St Patr Cathl Dub 58-62; Hon CV Ch Ch Cathl Dub *D & G* 62-64; C Dub Clontarf 62-64; C Thornton Heath St Jude *Cant* 64-66; V Norwood All SS 66-82; RD Croydon N 81-84; Hon Can Cant Cathl 82-84; V Upper Norwood All SS w St Marg 82-84; Hon Can S'wark Cathl *S'wark* from 85; RD Croydon N 85; V Mert St Mary from 85. *The Vicarage, Church Path, London SW19 3HJ* 081-542 1760

BROADHEAD, Dr Alan John. b 38. Lon Univ MD62. Cuddesdon Coll 65. **d** 66 **p** 67. C Willenhall H Trin *Lich* 66-68; USA from 71. *PO Box 255, Jamestown, N Dakota 58402, USA*

BROADHEAD, Malcolm Keith. b 33. Nottm Univ BA63. Kelham Th Coll 54. **d** 62 **p** 63. Chapl and Tutor Kelham Th Coll 63-70; SSM St Paul's Priory Lanc 70-73; C Huddersfield St Jo *Wakef* 73-75; P-in-c March St Pet *Ely* 75-76; R 76-84; R March St Mary 78-84; V Stainton-in-Cleveland *York* from 84; Chapl Cleveland Police from 89. *The Vicarage, 21 Thornton Road, Stainton, Middlesbrough, Cleveland TS8 9BS* Middlesbrough (0642) 590423

BROADHURST, John Charles. b 42. AKC65. Lambeth STh82. **d** 66 **p** 67. C Southgate St Mich *Lon* 66-70; C Wembley Park St Aug 70-73; P-in-c 73-75; V 75-85; AD Brent 82-85; TR Wood Green St Mich w Bounds Green St Gabr etc from 85; AD E Haringey from 85. *St Michael's Rectory, 39 Bounds Green Road, London N22 4HE* 081-888 1968 or 881 0202

BROADHURST, John James. b 08. Birm Univ BA31. **d** 32 **p** 33. R S Hill w Callington *Truro* 59-73; rtd 73. *18 Monmouth Gardens, Beaminster, Dorset DT8 3BT* Beaminster (0308) 862509

BROADHURST, Jonathan Robin. b 58. Univ Coll Ox BA81 MA86. Wycliffe Hall Ox 85. **d** 88 **p** 89. C Hull Newland St Jo *York* 88-91; P-in-c Burton Fleming w Fordon, Grindale etc from 91. *The Vicarage, Back Street, Burton Fleming, Driffield, N Humberside YO25 0RD* Bridlington (0262) 87668

BROADHURST, Kenneth. b 33. Lon Coll of Div 56. **d** 59 **p** 60. R Clitheroe St Jas *Blackb* 67-82; V Leyland St Andr 82-88; rtd 89. *Paris House, 12 Ramsgreave Road, Ramsgreave, Blackburn BB1 9BH* Blackburn (0254) 240924

BROCK, Michael John. b 52. Birm Univ BSc74 Nottm Univ BA77. St Jo Coll Nottm 75. **d** 78 **p** 79. C Stapleford *S'well* 78-82; C Bestwood St Matt 82-86; TV Bestwood 86-90; R Epperstone from 90; R Gonalston from 90; V Oxton from 90. *The Rectory, Main Street, Epperstone, Notts NG14 6AG* Nottingham (0602) 664220

BROCK, Preb Patrick Laurence. b 18. MBE45. Trin Coll Ox BA46 MA48. Ripon Hall Ox 55. **d** 57 **p** 58. V Belsize Park *Lon* 62-72; R Finchley St Mary 72-89; Preb St Paul's Cathl 80-89; AD Cen Barnet 80-85; rtd 89. *10 Albert Street, London NW1 7NZ* 071-383 0198

BROCKBANK, Arthur Ross. b 51. Wigan Coll of Tech BTEC ND85. N Ord Course 87. **d** 90 **p** 91. C Haughton St Mary *Man* from 90. *6 Ripley Way, Denton, Manchester M34 1WY* 061-336 3785

BROCKBANK, Donald Philip. b 56. Univ of Wales (Ban) BD78. Sarum & Wells Th Coll 79. **d** 81 **p** 82. C Prenton *Ches* 81-85; TV Birkenhead Priory 85-91; V Altrincham St Jo from 91; Urban Officer from 91. *St John's Vicarage, 52 Ashley Road, Altrincham, Cheshire WA14 2LY* 061-928 3236

BROCKBANK, John Keith. b 44. Dur Univ BA65. Wells Th Coll 66. **d** 68 **p** 69. C Preston St Matt *Blackb* 68-71; C Lanc St Mary 71-73; V Habergham All SS 73-83; P-in-c Gannow 81-83; V W Burnley 83-86; Dioc Stewardship Adv from 86; P-in-c Shireshead from 86. *Shireshead Vicarage, Forton, Preston PR3 0AE* Forton (0524) 791355

BROCKBANK, Leslie David. b 35. St Aid Birkenhead 60. **d** 63 **p** 64. C Corby SS Pet and Andr *Pet* 63-66; C Darley w S Darley *Derby* 66-72; New Zealand from 72. *The Vicarage, Maungaturoto, Northland, New Zealand* Whangarei (89) 38193

BROCKHOUSE, Grant Lindley. b 47. Adelaide Univ BA71 Ex Univ MA81. St Barn Coll Adelaide 70 ACT ThL72. **d** 73 **p** 74. Australia 73-78; C St Jas *Ex* 78-80; Asst Chapl Ex Univ 80-83; Dep PV Ex Cathl from 81; V Marldon from 83. *The Vicarage, Marldon, Paignton, Devon TQ3 1NH* Paignton (0803) 557294

BROCKIE, William James Thomson. b 36. Pemb Coll Ox BA58 MA62. Linc Th Coll 58. **d** 60 **p** 61. C Lin St Jo

Bapt CD *Linc* 60-63; V Gt Staughton *Ely* 63-68; Chapl HM Youth Cust Cen Gaynes Hall 63-68; TV Edin St Jo *Edin* 68-76; Chapl Edin Univ 71-76; R Edin St Martin from 76; P-in-c Edin St Luke 79-90. *15 Ardmillan Terrace, Edinburgh EH11 2JW* 031-337 5493 or 337 9714

BROCKLEBANK, John. b 32. **d** 86 **p** 87. NSM Warrington St Barn *Liv* from 86. *55 St Mary's Road, Penketh, Warrington WA5 2DT* Penketh (092572) 2398

BROCKLEHURST, John Richard. b 51. Univ Coll Ox BA72 Lon Univ CertD74. Oak Hill Th Coll BA81. **d** 81 **p** 82. C Harwood *Man* 81-85; V Hopwood from 85. *St John's Vicarage, Manchester Road, Heywood, Lancs OL10 2EQ* Heywood (0706) 369324

BROCKLEHURST, Simon. b 63. Cranmer Hall Dur 86. **d** 89 **p** 90. C Clifton *S'well* from 89. *6 Myrtus Close, Barton, Nottingham NG11 8SN* Nottingham (0602) 844606

BRODDLE, Christopher Stephen Thomas. b 57. **d** 87 **p** 88. C Lisburn St Paul *Conn* 87-90; CF from 90. *c/o MOD (Army), Bagshot Park, Bagshot, Surrey GU19 5PL* Bagshot (0276) 71717

BRODY, Paul. b 40. N Ord Course 85. **d** 88 **p** 89. C Leigh St Mary *Man* 88-90; C Peel from 90. *88 Treen Road, Tyldesley, Manchester M29 7HA* Atherton (0942) 875001

BROGGIO, Bernice Muriel Croager. b 35. Bedf Coll Lon BA57 K Coll Lon BD66 IDC66 Glas Univ DSocStuds71 DASS72. K Coll Lon 63. **dss** 84 **d** 87. Bris St Paul w St Barn *Bris* 84-87; Hon Par Dn Bris St Paul's 87-88; Par Dn Charlton St Luke w H Trin *S'wark* from 88. *73 Elliscombe Road, London SE7 7PF* 081-858 0296

BROMAGE, Kenneth Charles. b 51. E Anglian Minl Tr Course. **d** 90 **p** 91. NSM Woolpit w Drinkstone *St E* from 90. *17 Briar Hill, Woolpit, Bury St Edmunds, Suffolk IP30 9SD* Beyton (0359) 40138

BROMFIELD, Michael. b 32. Lich Th Coll 59. **d** 62 **p** 63. C Sedgley All SS *Lich* 62-64; C Tunstall Ch Ch 64-67; P-in-c Grindon 67-70; R 70-80; P-in-c Butterton 67-70; V 70-80; R Hope Bowdler w Eaton-under-Heywood *Heref* from 80; R Rushbury from 80; V Cardington from 80. *The Rectory, Hope Bowdler, Church Stretton, Shropshire SY6 7DD* Church Stretton (0694) 722918

BROMFIELD, Richard Allan. b 47. Chich Th Coll 86. **d** 88 **p** 89. C Durrington *Chich* from 88. *8 Greenland Walk, Worthing, W Sussex BN13 2NS* Worthing (0903) 63304

BROMHAM, Ivor John. b 18. Univ of Wales (Swansea) BA40. Clifton Th Coll 40. **d** 42 **p** 43. V Swansea St Matt w Greenhill *S & B* 49-86; rtd 86. *Cowleaze, Plaisters Lane, Sutton Poyntz, Weymouth, Dorset DT3 6LQ* Weymouth (0305) 835368

BROMIDGE, Robert Harold. b 28. K Coll Lon BD52 AKC52. **d** 53 **p** 54. Min Arbourthorne CD *Sheff* 61-70; Lic to Offic from 71; rtd 86. *4 Barnfield Close, Sheffield S10 5TF* Sheffield (0742) 307889

BROMILEY, Paul Nigel. b 49. Univ of Wales (Cardiff) BSc71. Oak Hill Th Coll 88. **d** 90 **p** 91. C Gee Cross *Ches* from 90. *36 Baron Road, Hyde, Cheshire SK14 5RW* 061-368 3037

BROMLEY, William James. b 44. Edin Univ BD74. Edin Th Coll 70. **d** 74 **p** 75. C Glas St Mary *Glas* 74-77; Bangladesh 77-80; R Glas H Cross *Glas* 80-89; R Stottesdon w Farlow, Cleeton and Silvington *Heref* from 89. *The Rectory, Stottesdon, Kidderminster, Worcs DY14 8UE* Stottesdon (074632) 297

BROMLEY, Archdeacon of. See FRANCIS, Ven Edward Reginald

BROMWICH, Edmund Eustace. b 15. Bris Univ BA35 St Cath Soc Ox BA39 MA43 TCD MA50. Ripon Hall Ox 37. **d** 40 **p** 41. R Wanstrow w Cloford *B & W* 49-57; Lic to Offic *Ches* from 68; rtd 80. *5B London Road, Alderley Edge, Cheshire SK9 7JT* Alderley Edge (0625) 585366

BROMWICH, John. b 09. AKC39. **d** 39 **p** 40. V Banwell *B & W* 49-76; rtd 76. *Westholme, Westfield Lane, Draycott, Cheddar, Somerset BS27 3TP* Cheddar (0934) 743141

BRONNERT, David Llewellyn Edward. b 36. Ch Coll Cam BA57 MA61 PhD61 Lon Univ BD62. Tyndale Hall Bris 60. **d** 63 **p** 64. C Cheadle Hulme St Andr *Ches* 63-67; C Islington St Mary *Lon* 67-69; Chapl Poly of N Lon 69-75; V Southall Green St Jo from 75; AD Ealing W 84-90. *St John's Vicarage, Church Avenue, Southall, Middx UB2 4DH* 081-574 2055

BRONNERT, John. b 33. FCA57 Lon Univ DipTh68 Man Univ MA(Theol)84. Tyndale Hall Bris 65. **d** 68 **p** 69. C Hoole *Ches* 68-71; P-in-c Parr *Liv* 71-73; TV 73-85; V Runcorn St Jo Weston *Ches* from 85. *The Vicarage,*

Weston, Runcorn, Cheshire WA7 4LY Runcorn (0928) 573798

BROOK, John Llewellyn. b 11. St Aid Birkenhead 47. **d** 49 **p** 50. V Allonby w W Newton *Carl* 63-76; rtd 76; Perm to Offic Carl 78-90; Linc from 91. *9 Egerton Road, Lincoln LN2 4PJ* Lincoln (0522) 523419

BROOK, Kathleen Marjorie. b 23. IDC. Lightfoot Ho Dur 57. **dss** 66 **d** 87. Linthorpe *York* 66-75; Ormesby 75-83; rtd 83. *6 Station Square, Saltburn-by-the-Sea, Cleveland TS12 1AG* Guisborough (0287) 24006

BROOK, Peter Watts Pitt. b 06. Em Coll Cam BA31 MA36. Ridley Hall Cam 31. **d** 33 **p** 35. Asst Chapl Canford Sch 33-35; C Fisherton Anger *Sarum* 35-36; Chapl Clifton Coll Bris 36-72; CF (EC) 44-46; Perm to Offic *Bris* from 72. *Orford House, 65 Clifton Park Road, Bristol BS8 3HN* Bristol (0272) 639948

BROOK, Stephen Edward. b 44. Univ of Wales (Abth) BSc65. Wycliffe Hall Ox 71. **d** 74 **p** 75. C Heworth *York* 74-77; C Linthorpe 77-80; TV Deane *Man* 80-85; BCMS from 87; Portugal from 87. *Bairro do Padre Nabeto, Lote 82-U, Aires, 2950 Palmela, Portugal* Lisbon (1) 235-3192

BROOK, Timothy Cyril Pitt. b 06. St Cath Coll Cam BA28 MA32. Ridley Hall Cam 28. **d** 31 **p** 32. R Over w Nether Compton and Trent *Sarum* 66-73; rtd 73. *15 Raleigh Court, Long Street, Sherborne, Dorset DT9 3EQ* Sherborne (0935) 812484

BROOK, William Neville. b 31. S'wark Ord Course 66. **d** 69 **p** 70. C Maidstone St Martin *Cant* 69-75; V Hartlip w Stockbury 75-80; R Willesborough w Hinxhill 80-86; R Willesborough 87-89; V Gt Staughton *Ely* from 89; R Hail Weston from 90. *St Andrew's Vicarage, The Causeway, Great Staughton, Huntingdon, Cambs PE19 4BA* Huntingdon (0480) 861554

BROOKE, Miss Bridget Cecilia. b 31. DBO51. Coll of Resurr Mirfield 88. **d** 89. Hon Par Dn Ranmoor *Sheff* from 89. *166 Tom Lane, Sheffield S10 3PG* Sheffield (0742) 302147

BROOKE, Michael Zachery. b 21. G&C Coll Cam BA43 MA46. Cuddesdon Coll 46. **d** 48 **p** 49. R Old Trafford St Cuth *Man* 57-63; rtd 86. *21 Barnfield, Urmston, Manchester M31 1EW*

BROOKE, Robert. b 44. Birm Univ DPS77. Qu Coll Birm 70. **d** 73 **p** 74. C Man Resurr *Man* 73-76; C Bournville *Birm* 76-77; Chapl Qu Eliz Coll *Lon* 77-82; C Bramley *Ripon* 82-85; TV 85-86; V Hunslet Moor St Pet and St Cuth from 86; Community Chapl for Mental Handicap from 86. *St Peter's Vicarage, 139 Dewsbury Road, Leeds LS11 5NW* Leeds (0532) 772464

BROOKE, Rosemary Jane. b 53. Cam Univ BEd75 Open Univ BA83. N Ord Course 86. **d** 89. NSM Poynton *Ches* from 89. *45 Brookfield Avenue, Poynton, Stockport, Cheshire SK12 1JE* Poynton (0625) 872822

BROOKE, Timothy Cyril. b 38. Jes Coll Cam BA60 MA70 Middx Poly CQSW76. Ripon Coll Cuddesdon 84. **d** 86 **p** 87. C Hillmorton *Cov* 86-90; V Earlsdon from 90. *St Barbara's Vicarage, 24 Rochester Road, Coventry CV5 6AG* Coventry (0203) 674057

BROOKE, Vernon. b 41. St Aid Birkenhead 62. **d** 65 **p** 66. C Crofton Park St Hilda w St Cypr *S'wark* 65-68; C Eccleshill *Bradf* 68-70; Ind Chapl *Linc* 70-84; Ind Chapl *Derby* from 84. *10 Oldridge Close, Chesterfield, Derbyshire S40 4UF* Chesterfield (0246) 270197

BROOKE, Canon William Edward. b 13. Birm Univ BA34 MA35. Westcott Ho Cam 35. **d** 37 **p** 38. R Castle Bromwich SS Mary and Marg *Birm* 60-78; Hon Can Birm Cathl 61-78; rtd 78; Perm to Offic *Heref* from 78. *Ivy Cottage, Tarrington, Hereford HR1 4HZ* Tarrington (043279) 357

BROOKER, David George. b 34. Ely Th Coll 56. **d** 58 **p** 59. C Ealing St Pet Mt Park *Lon* 58-60; C Holborn St Alb w Saffron Hill St Pet 60-66; C W Wycombe *Ox* 67-68; C Winchmore Hill St Paul *Lon* 68; V Somers Town St Mary 68-79; V Bush Hill Park St Mark from 79. *St Mark's Vicarage, Bush Hill Park, Enfield, Middx EN1 1BE* 081-363 2767

BROOKER, Mrs Wendy Ann. b 41. St Alb Minl Tr Scheme 82. **dss** 85 **d** 87. Pinner *Lon* 85-87; Greenhill St Jo 87; Par Dn 87-88; Ind Chapl from 89. *16 Rosecroft Walk, Pinner, Middx HA5 1LL* 081-866 0795

BROOKES, Albert. b 06. K Coll Lon 51. **d** 53 **p** 54. V Barnton *Ches* 68-76; rtd 76; Perm to Offic *Ches* from 76. *The Gables, West Road, Bowdon, Altrincham, Cheshire WA14 2LD* 061-928 1238

BROOKES, Arthur George. b 21. ACIB52. Worc Ord Coll 64. **d** 66 **p** 67. C Fladbury w Throckmorton, Wyre Piddle and Moor *Worc* 67-70; C Abberton w Bishampton 67-70; R 70-73; V Cradley 73-78; P-in-c Castle Morton 78-79; P-in-c Holly Bush w Birtsmorton 78-79; P-in-c

Castlemorton, Hollybush and Birtsmorton 79-80; P-in-c Norton w Whittington 80-81; TV Worc St Martin w St Pet, St Mark etc 81-86; rtd 86; Perm to Offic *Worc* from 86. *9 Bredon Lodge, Main Road, Bredon, Tewkesbury, Glos GL20 7LT* Bredon (0684) 72338

BROOKES, David Charles. b 45. St Mich Coll Llan 84. **d** 86 **p** 87. C Llanishen and Lisvane *Llan* 86-88; TV Brighouse *Wakef* from 89. *St Chad's Vicarage, 161 Halifax Road, Brighouse, W Yorkshire HD6 2EQ* Brighouse (0484) 713649

BROOKES, Derrick Meridyth. b 17. Trin Hall Cam BA38 MA42. Westcott Ho Cam 39. **d** 40 **p** 41. C Macclesfield St Mich *Ches* 40-44; Chapl RAFVR 44-46; C Wilmslow *Ches* 47-49; V Chipping Sodbury and Old Sodbury *Glouc* 49-53; Youth Chapl 51-53; Chapl RAF 53-71. *Woodpeckers, Pilcorn Street, Wedmore, Somerset BS28 4AW* Wedmore (0934) 712352

BROOKES, Keith Roy. b 37. St Aid Birkenhead 64. **d** 80 **p** 81. Hon C Stockport St Thos *Ches* 80-86; Hon C Stockport St Thos w St Pet 86-91; C from 91. *Dryden House, 1 Cliff Grove, Stockport, Cheshire SK4 4HR* 061-432 3580

BROOKES, Robin Keenan. b 47. Trin Coll Bris 72. **d** 75 **p** 76. C Livesey *Blackb* 75-78; C Burnley St Pet 78-80; P-in-c Bawdeswell w Foxley *Nor* 80-83; I Donagh w Tyholland and Errigal Truagh *Clogh* 83-91; RD Monaghan 86-91; Dioc Info Officer 90-91; I Dub Drumcondra w N Strand *D & G* from 91. *74 Grace Park Road, Drumcondra, Dublin 9, Irish Republic* Dublin (1) 372505

BROOKES, Steven David. b 60. Lanc Univ BA81. Ripon Coll Cuddesdon 82. **d** 85 **p** 86. C Stanley *Liv* 85-88; C W Derby St Mary 88-90; Chapl RN from 90. *c/o MOD, Lacon House, Theobald's Road, London WC1X 8RY* 071-430 6847

BROOKFIELD, Patricia Anne. b 50. St Mary's Coll Dur BA72. Cranmer Hall Dur DipTh73 MA74. **dss** 84 **d** 87. Kingston upon Hull St Nic *York* 84-86; Acomb St Steph 86-87; Par Dn from 87. *12 Askham Lane, Acomb, York YO2 3HA* York (0904) 791511

BROOKHOUSE, Leslie. b 28. Ridley Hall Cam 69 St Aid Birkenhead 68. **d** 70 **p** 71. C Tonge *Man* 70-72; C Didsbury Ch Ch 72-74; V Newall Green 74-80; V High Crompton 80-86; R Ashwater, Halwill, Beaworthy, Clawton etc *Ex* from 86. *The Rectory, Ashwater, Beaworthy, Devon EX21 5EZ* Ashwater (040921) 205

BROOKS, Andrew Richard. b 44. Leeds Univ BA Birm Poly PGCE DipInstAM. Qu Coll Birm 83. **d** 86 **p** 87. C Olton *Birm* 86-87; C Sheldon 87-89; V Erdington St Chad from 89. *St Chad's Vicarage, 10 Shepherd's Green Road, Birmingham B24 8EX* 021-373 3915 or 373 8984

BROOKS, Christine Ellen. b 43. Sheff Univ BA65 Lon Univ BD81. Lambeth STh81 E Anglian Minl Tr Course 86. **d** 88. NSM Palgrave w Wortham and Burgate *St E* 88-89; Par Dn Thorndon w Rishangles, Stoke Ash, Thwaite etc from 89. *Netherfields, Crossing Road, Palgrave, Diss, Norfolk IP22 1AW* Diss (0379) 643042

BROOKS, Edward Charles. b 18. Leeds Univ PhD71. Coll of Resurr Mirfield 42. **d** 44 **p** 45. P-in-c Herringfleet *Nor* 69-83; R Somerleyton w Ashby 69-83; rtd 83; Perm to Offic *St E* from 83. *Wheelwrights, Thorpe Morieux, Bury St Edmunds, Suffolk IP30 0NR* Bury St Edmunds (0284) 828353

BROOKS, Canon Francis Leslie. b 35. Kelham Th Coll 55. **d** 59 **p** 60. C Woodlands *Sheff* 59-61; Ind Missr S Yorkshire Coalfields 61-66; V Moorends 66-72; Chapl HM Borstal Hatf 67-72; HM Pris Acklington 72-75; HM Borstal Wellingborough 75-79; HM Pris Wakef 79-83; Area Sec (Dios Wakef and Bradf) USPG 83-88; V Carleton *Wakef* from 88; V E Hardwick from 88; Hon Can Mara (Tanzania) from 88. *The Vicarage, 10 East Close, Pontefract, W Yorkshire WF8 3NS* Pontefract (0977) 702478

BROOKS, George Edward Thomas. b 02. St Aug Coll Cant. **d** 37 **p** 39. R Leven *St And* 55-69; rtd 69; Perm to Offic *Cant* from 69. *1 Juniper Close, Stuppington Lane, Canterbury, Kent CT1 3LL* Canterbury (0227) 765918

BROOKS, Henry Craven. b 12. CITC 62. **d** 64 **p** 65. I Dunlavin w Ballymore Eustace and Hollywood *D & G* 67-85; rtd 85; Lic to Offic *D & G* from 87. *9 Orwell Court, Braemor Road, Churchtown, Dublin 14, Irish Republic* Dublin (1) 985659

BROOKS, Ian George. b 47. Selw Coll Cam BA68 MA72. Chich Th Coll 68. **d** 70 **p** 71. C Stoke Newington St Mary *Lon* 70-74; C Hoxton St Anne w St Sav and St Andr 74-75; C Hoxton St Anne w St Columba 75-80; P-in-c Croxteth St Paul CD *Liv* 80-81; V Croxteth from 81. *St Paul's Vicarage, Delabole Road, Liverpool L11 6LG* 051-548 9009

BROOKS, John Cowell. b 09. St Jo Coll Cam BA31 MA35. Coll of Resurr Mirfield 46. **d** 47 **p** 48. N Rhodesia 61-64; Zambia 64-71; Lic to Offic *Cant* 71-74; Chapl Dover Coll Kent 71-74; R Northbourne, Tilmanstone w Betteshanger and Ham *Cant* 74-86; rtd 86; Perm to Offic *Cant* from 86. *3 Mill Road, Deal, Kent CT14 9AB* Deal (0304) 367961

BROOKS, Jonathan Thorburn. b 53. G&C Coll Cam BA75 DipHE Solicitor 76. Trin Coll Bris 84. **d** 86 **p** 87. C Dagenham *Chelmsf* 86-88. *12 Hyde Avenue, Thornbury, Bristol BS12 1JA* Thornbury (0454) 411853

BROOKS, Canon Joseph. b 27. Univ Coll Dur BA53. St Aid Birkenhead 52. **d** 54 **p** 55. C Birch St Agnes *Man* 54-57; C Davyhulme St Mary 57-59; R Oldham St Andr 59-65; V Ipswich St Fran *St E* 65-75; R Freston w Woolverstone 75-76; P-in-c Holbrook 75-76; R Holbrook w Freston and Woolverstone 76-82; R Horringer cum Ickworth 82-88; Chapl Asst Ipswich Hosp 88-90; Chapl from 90; Hon Can St E Cathl *St E* from 90. *339 Colchester Road, Ipswich IP4 4SE* Ipswich (0473) 713095

BROOKS, Leslie Frederick. b 08. Wells Th Coll 68. **d** 69 **p** 70. C Northn H Sepulchre w St Andr *Pet* 69-73; C Desborough 73-77; rtd 77; Perm to Offic *Ches* from 77. *93 Weston Grove, Chester CH2 1QP* Chester (0244) 27691

BROOKS, Malcolm David. b 45. Univ of Wales (Lamp) DipTh71. **d** 71 **p** 72. C Pontlottyn w Fochriw *Llan* 71-72; C Caerphilly 72-78; V Ferndale w Maerdy 78-81; C Port Talbot St Theodore 82-84; V Ystrad Mynach 84-85; V Ystrad Mynach w Llanbradach from 85. *The Vicarage, Ystrad Mynach, Hengoed, M Glam CF8 7EG* Hengoed (0443) 813246

BROOKS, Neville Charles Wood. b 16. Bps' Coll Cheshunt 50. **d** 53 **p** 54. R Gilmorton w Peatling Parva *Leic* 66-86; R Gilmorton w Peatling Parva and Kimcote etc 86; rtd 86. *1 Cherry Tree Walk, Southam, Leamington Spa, Warks CV33 0EF*

BROOKS, Patrick John. b 27. Man Univ BA49 DipEd. Oak Hill Th Coll 78. **d** 77 **p** 79. Burundi 77-80; Perm to Offic *Ex* 80-83; P-in-c Phillack w Gwithian and Gwinear Truro 83-88; R from 88. *The Rectory, 15 Lethlean Lane, Phillack, Hayle, Cornwall TR27 5AW* Hayle (0736) 753541

BROOKS, Paul John. b 59. Loughb Univ BSc81 DTS89 DPS90. St Jo Coll Nottm 87. **d** 90 **p** 91. C Long Eaton St Jo *Derby* from 90. *66 Curzon Street, Long Eaton, Nottingham NG10 4FT* Nottingham (0602) 460557

BROOKS, Peter Joseph. b 54. **d** 83 **p** 84. C Portslade St Nic and St Andr *Chich* 83-86; C Kingstanding St Luke *Birm* 86-91; V Nork *Guildf* from 91. *The Vicarage, Warren Road, Banstead, Surrey SM7 1LG* Burgh Heath (0737) 353849

BROOKS, Peter Newman. b 31. Trin Coll Cam BA54 Peterho Cam MA58 PhD60. Cuddesdon Coll 67. **d** 67 **p** 68. C Hackington *Cant* 67-70; Lect Kent Univ 67-70; Dean Down Coll Cam 70-82; Lect Div Cam Univ from 70; Lic to Offic *Ely* from 70; Tutor Rob Coll Cam from 82. *Robinson College, Cambridge CB3 9AN* Cambridge (0223) 311431

BROOKS, Philip David. b 52. MA Cam Univ MTh. St Jo Coll Nottm 80. **d** 83 **p** 84. C Ipsley *Worc* 83-87; V Fulford w Hilderstone *Lich* from 87. *20 Tudor Hollow, Fulford, Stoke-on-Trent ST11 9NP* Blythe Bridge (0782) 7073

BROOKS, Raymond Samuel. b 11. ARIBA39. Clifton Th Coll 63. **d** 65 **p** 66. V Hastings Em and St Mary in the Castle *Chich* 71-82; rtd 82. *Brighnorton, Eight Acre Lane, Three Oaks, Hastings, E Sussex TN25 4NL* Hastings (0424) 754432

BROOKS, Stephen. b 54. Trin Coll Carmarthen CertEd75 Univ of Wales BEd76. St Steph Ho Ox BA78 MA83. **d** 79 **p** 80. C Oystermouth *S & B* 79-81; Min Can Brecon Cathl 81-84; C Brecon w Battle 81-84; Youth Chapl 82-84; Dir of Ords from 83; V Landore 84-90; V Sketty from 90. *The Vicarage, De La Beche Road, Sketty, Swansea SA2 9AR* Swansea (0792) 202767

BROOKS, Mrs Susan Vera. b 51. N Ord Course 87. **d** 90. Par Dn Carleton *Wakef* from 90; Par Dn E Hardwick from 90. *108 Churchbalk Lane, Pontefract, W Yorkshire WF8 2QW* Pontefract (0977) 797379

BROOKS, Mrs Vivien June. b 47. Univ of Wales (Ban) BA68 Southn Univ MA70. Ridley Hall Cam 87. **d** 89. C Exning St Martin w Landwade *St E* from 89. *3 Norfolk Avenue, Newmarket, Suffolk CB8 0DE* Newmarket (0638) 661120

BROOKS, Mrs Vivienne Christine. See ARMSTRONG-MacDONNELL, Mrs Vivienne Christine

BROOKSBANK, Alan Watson. b 43. Univ of Wales (Lamp) BA64 Edin Univ MEd76. Edin Th Coll 64. **d** 66 **p** 67. C Cleator Moor w Cleator *Carl* 66-70; V Dalston

70-80; P-in-c Greystoke, Matterdale and Mungrisdale 80-81; R 81-83; R Watermillock 81-83; R Hagley *Worc* from 83; Bp's Officer for NSM from 88. *The Rectory, 6 Middlefield Lane, Hagley, Stourbridge, W Midlands DY9 0PX* Kidderminster (0562) 882442

BROOKSTEIN, Canon Royston. b 29. Qu Coll Birm 60. **d** 62 **p** 63. C Rubery *Birm* 62-66; V Cotteridge 66-75; V Hall Green St Pet from 75; Hon Can Birm Cathl from 84. *St Peter's Vicarage, 33 Paradise Lane, Birmingham B28 0DY* 021-777 1935

BROOM, Bernard William. b 21. Roch Th Coll 64. **d** 66 **p** 67. R Alderford w Attlebridge and Swannington *Nor* 69-75; RD Sparham 73-75; R Drayton 75-80; P-in-c Felthorpe w Haveringland 77-80; R Drayton w Felthorpe 80-81; TV Eckington w Handley and Ridgeway *Derby* 84-88; rtd 88; Perm to Offic *Nor* from 88. *119A High Street, Blakeney, Holt, Norfolk NR25 7NU* Cley (0263) 740001

BROOM, Donald Rees. b 14. St Cath Soc Ox BA38 MA42. St D Coll Lamp BA36 BD45 Wycliffe Hall Ox 36. **d** 38 **p** 39. V Middleton Tyas and Barton *Ripon* 62-75; V Barton and Manfield w Cleasby 75-82; rtd 82. *47 Linden Avenue, Darlington, Co Durham DL3 8PS* Darlington (0325) 284216

BROOME, David Curtis. b 36. Leeds Univ BA63. Coll of Resurr Mirfield. **d** 65 **p** 66. C Winshill *Derby* 65-69; C Leigh-on-Sea St Marg *Chelmsf* 69-74; V Leeds St Marg *Ripon* 74-81; V Stoke H Cross w Dunston *Nor* from 81. *The Vicarage, Stoke Holy Cross, Norwich NR14 8AB* Framingham Earl (05086) 2305

BROOME, Gordon Alty. b 13. Ripon Hall Ox 65. **d** 65 **p** 66. C Portchester *Portsm* 65-72; R Brighstone 72-79; R Brighstone and Brooke w Mottistone 79-80; rtd 80; Perm to Offic *Portsm* from 81. *St Saviour's Vicarage, Queens Road, Shanklin, Isle of Wight PO37 6AN* Isle of Wight (0983) 862786

BROOME, William Harold. b 09. Man Egerton Hall 32. **d** 34 **p** 35. R Nairn *Mor* 64-73; Can St Andr Cathl Inverness 66-73; R Selkirk *Edin* 73-75; rtd 75; Lic to Offic *Newc* 75-77; Hon C Morpeth 77-80; Hon C St Andrews St Andr *St And* from 80. *122 North Street, St Andrews, Fife KY16 9AF* St Andrews (0334) 73204

BROOMFIELD, David John. b 37. Reading Univ BA59. Oak Hill Th Coll 64. **d** 66 **p** 67. C Gresley *Derby* 66-71; C Rainham *Chelmsf* 71-77; R High Ongar w Norton Mandeville 77-88; RD Ongar 83-88; P-in-c Stanford Rivers 84-86; P-in-c Loughton St Mary and St Mich from 88. *St Mary's Vicarage, High Road, Loughton, Essex IG10 1BB* 081-508 3643

BROOMFIELD, Canon Frederick Harry. b 08. Lon Univ BA29 BD39. Sarum Th Coll 39. **d** 40 **p** 41. V Southbourne St Chris *Win* 51-75; Hon Can Win Cathl 74-75; rtd 75. *31 Cowper Road, Bournemouth BH9 2UJ* Bournemouth (0202) 521380

BROOMFIELD, Iain Jonathan. b 57. Univ Coll Ox MA. Wycliffe Hall Ox 80. **d** 83 **p** 84. C Beckenham Ch Ch *Roch* 83-87; Perm to Offic *Ox* from 87. *91 Walton Street, Oxford OX2 6EB* Oxford (0865) 59006

BROPHY, Raymond Paul. b 58. G&C Coll Cam BA80 MA84. Chich Th Coll 82. **d** 84 **p** 85. C Swansea St Pet *S & B* 84-86; C Landore 86-88; Succ Heref Cathl *Heref* 88-90; P-in-c Cranham *Chelmsf* from 90. *All Saints' House, 51 Courtenay Gardens, Upminster, Essex RM14 1DM* Upminster (04022) 28200

BROSTER, Godfrey David. b 52. Ealing Tech Coll BA75. Ripon Coll Cuddesdon 78. **d** 81 **p** 82. C Crayford *Roch* 81-82; C Brighton Resurr *Chich* 82-86; C-in-c Hydneye CD 86-91; R Plumpton from 91. *The Rectory, Station Road, Plumpton, Lewes, E Sussex BN7 3BU* Plumpton (0273) 890570

BROTHERSTON, Miss Isabel Mary. b 42. Cranmer Hall Dur 81. **dss** 83 **d** 87. Coleshill *Birm* 83-87; Par Dn Duddeston w Nechells from 87. *St Clement's House, 14 Stanley Road, Birmingham B7 5QS* 021-328 3781

BROTHERTON, Canon John Michael. b 35. St Jo Coll Cam BA59 MA63. Cuddesdon Coll 59. **d** 61 **p** 62. C Chiswick St Nic w St Mary *Lon* 61-65; Trinidad and Tobago 65-75; V Cowley St Jo *Ox* 76-81; Chapl St Hilda's Coll Ox 76-81; RD Cowley *Ox* 78-81; V Portsea St Mary *Portsm* from 81; Hon Can Kobe Japan from 86. *St Mary's Vicarage, Fratton Road, Portsmouth PO1 5PA* Portsmouth (0705) 822687

BROTHERTON, Leslie Charles. b 22. OStJ FSCA MInstAM. St Steph Ho Ox 68. **d** 68 **p** 69. C Fenny Stratford *Ox* 68-70; C Solihull *Birm* 71-76; V Moseley St Anne from 76. *15 Park Hill, Birmingham B13 8DU* 021-449 1071

BROTHERTON, Michael. b 56. Univ of Wales (Abth) BD80. Wycliffe Hall Ox 80. **d** 81 **p** 82. Hon Chapl Miss to Seamen 81-84; C Pemb Dock *St D* 81-84; Chapl RN from 84. *c/o MOD, Lacon House, Theobald's Road, London WC1X 8RY* 071-430 6847

BROTHERWOOD, Nicholas Peter. b 50. Oak Hill Th Coll BA83. **d** 83 **p** 84. C Nottm St Nic *S'well* 83-86; Canada from 86. *3498 Harvard, Montreal, Quebec, Canada, H4A 2W3* Montreal (514) 489-4158

BROTHWELL, Canon Paul David. b 37. Lich Th Coll 62. **d** 65 **p** 66. C Honley *Wakef* 65-68; Min Can Wakef Cathl 68-71; V Whittington St Giles *Lich* 71-83; P-in-c Weeford 78-83; V Whittington w Weeford from 83. *The Vicarage, Whittington, Lichfield, Staffs WS14 9LH* Whittington (0543) 432233

BROTHWOOD, Ian Sidney. b 56. K Coll Lon BD84. Linc Th Coll 87. **d** 89 **p** 90. C Selsdon St Jo w St Fran *S'wark* from 89. *4 Turnstone Close, South Croydon, Surrey CR2 8SP* 081-651 4930

BROTHWOOD, Dr John. b 31. Peterho Cam MA55 MB, ChB55. S'wark Ord Course 89. **d** 91. NSM Dulwich St Barn *S'wark* from 91. *81 Calton Avenue, London SE21 7DF* 081-693 8273

BROUGH, Gerald William. b 32. Trin Coll Cam BA55 MA59. Ridley Hall Cam 55. **d** 57 **p** 58. C Westgate St Jas *Cant* 57-60; C New Addington 60-62; V Mancetter *Cov* 62-73; P-in-c Bourton w Frankton and Stretton on Dunsmore etc 73-74; R from 74. *The Rectory, Frankton, Rugby, Warks CV23 9PB* Marton (0926) 632805

BROUGHTON, Canon Harry. b 09. Dur Univ LTh32. Lich Th Coll 29. **d** 32 **p** 33. V Coxwold *York* 56-69; Can and Preb York Minster from 66; rtd 70; RD Helmsley *York* 74-75. *Charters Garth, Hutton-le-Hole, York YO6 6UD* Lastingham (07515) 288

BROUGHTON, James Roger. b 48. Leeds Univ BA71 Nottm Univ CertEd72. Wycliffe Hall Ox 87. **d** 89 **p** 90. C Stoneycroft All SS *Liv* from 89. *38 Saville Road, Stoneycroft, Liverpool L13 4DP* 051-228 9445

BROUGHTON, Stuart Roger. b 36. Univ of Wales DipTh65. St Mich Coll Llan 61. **d** 64 **p** 65. C Bromley Ch Ch *Roch* 64-67; SAMS 67-79; V Stoke sub Hamdon *B & W* 79-83; V Blackb Ch Ch w St Matt *Blackb* 83-86; Portugal from 86. *Avenue dos Aviadores, 17 r/c, Esq, 7580 Alcacer do Sal, Portugal* Setubal (65) 62190

BROUN, Canon Claud Michael. b 30. BNC Ox BA55. Edin Th Coll 56. **d** 58 **p** 59. Chapl St Mary's Cathl *Edin* 58-62; P-in-c Cambuslang *Glas* 62-70; R 70-75; R Hamilton 75-88; Can St Mary's Cathl from 84; R Gatehouse of Fleet from 88; R Kircudbright from 88. *Greyfriars Rectory, 54 High Street, Kirkcudbright DG6 4JX* Kirkcudbright (0557) 30580

BROWN, Alan. b 37. Tyndale Hall Bris 59. **d** 63 **p** 64. C Braintree *Chelmsf* 63-66; C Tooting Graveney St Nic *S'wark* 66-68; C Chesham St Mary *Ox* 68-70; V Hornsey Rise St Mary *Lon* 70-75; V Sidcup Ch Ch *Roch* 75-88; V Newport St Jo *Portsm* from 88; RD W Wight from 91. *St John's Vicarage, 3 Cypress Road, Newport, Isle of Wight PO30 1EY* Isle of Wight (0983) 522148

BROWN, Alan Michael Ernest. b 52. St Chad's Coll Dur BA74. St Jo Coll Nottm 81. **d** 83 **p** 84. C Bridlington Priory *York* 83-86; V Morton St Luke *Bradf* from 86. *The Vicarage, Morton, Keighley, W Yorkshire BD20 5RS* Bradford (0274) 563829

BROWN, Albert Harry Alfred Victor. b 12. **d** 81 **p** 83. Hon C Kennington Park St Agnes *S'wark* from 81. *61 Brittany Point, Lollard Street, London SE11 6PX* 071-274 5982

BROWN, Alec Charles. b 33. AKC58. **d** 59 **p** 60. C S Mimms St Mary and Potters Bar *Lon* 59-63; C S Ashford Ch Ch *Cant* 63-66; New Zealand from 66. *24 Examiner Street, Nelson, New Zealand* Nelson (54) 83644

BROWN, Alexander Peter-Aidan. b 48. Sarum & Wells Th Coll. **d** 82 **p** 83. C Ifield *Chich* 82-86; TV 86-91; V St Leonards SS Pet and Paul from 91. *The Vicarage, 10 Bloomfield Road, St Leonards-on-Sea, E Sussex TN37 6HH* Hastings (0424) 445606

BROWN, Alexander Thomas. b 21. **d** 79 **p** 80. NSM Irvine St Andr LEP *Glas* 79-83; NSM Ardrossan 79-83; rtd 83. *44 Ravenscroft, Irvine, Ayrshire KA12 9DE* Irvine (0294) 74354

BROWN, Allan James. b 47. K Coll Lon BD69 AKC69 MTh70. St Aug Coll Cant 69. **d** 73 **p** 74. Jerusalem 73-75; C Clifton *S'well* 75-77; CF from 77. *c/o MOD (Army), Bagshot Park, Bagshot, Surrey GU19 5PL* Bagshot (0276) 71717

BROWN, Andrew. b 55. St Pet Hall Ox BA80 MA82. Ridley Hall Cam 79. **d** 80 **p** 81. C Burnley St Pet *Blackb* 80-82; C Elton All SS *Man* 82-85; P-in-c Ashton St Pet from 86. *The Vicarage, Chester Square, Ashton-under-Lyne, Lancs OL7 0LB* 061-330 4285

BROWN, Anthony. d 91. NSM Woodford St Mary w St Phil and St Jas *Chelmsf* from 91. *c/o 8 Chelmsford Road, South Woodford, London E18 2PL* 081-504 3472

BROWN, Anthony Frank Palmer. b 31. Fitzw Ho Cam BA56 Fitzw Coll Cam MA84. Cuddesdon Coll 56. **d** 58 **p** 59. C Aldershot St Mich *Guildf* 58-61; C Chiswick St Nic w St Mary *Lon* 61-66; Asst Chapl Lon Univ 65-70; Lic to Offic 70-72; C-in-c Hammersmith SS Mich and Geo White City Estate CD 72-74; P-in-c Upper Sunbury St Sav 74-80; V from 80. *St Saviour's Vicarage, 205 Vicarage Road, Sunbury-on-Thames TW16 7TP* Sunbury-on-Thames (0932) 782800

BROWN, Anthony Paul. b 55. ARICS87 Reading Univ BSc75. Qu Coll Birm 77. **d** 80 **p** 81. C Pelsall *Lich* 80-83; C Leighton Buzzard w Eggington, Hockliffe etc *St Alb* 83-87; TV Langley Marish *Ox* from 87. *St Mary's Vicarage, 180 Langley Road, Slough SL3 7EE* Slough (0753) 46659

BROWN, Anthony Storey. b 34. Open Univ BA73. NW Ord Course 75. **d** 78 **p** 79. NSM Leyburn w Bellerby *Ripon* 78-82; NSM Middleham and Coverham w Horsehouse 82-86; NSM Middleham w Coverdale and E Witton from 86. *Milton House, Castle Hill, Middleham, Leyburn, N Yorkshire DL8 4QR* Wensleydale (0969) 22730

BROWN, Antony William Keith. b 26. Trin Coll Bris 86. **d** 87 **p** 88. NSM Lawrence Weston *Bris* 87-89; Chapl Casablanca *Eur* from 89. *60 rue des Landes, Ain Diab, Casablanca, Morocco* Morocco (212) 365104

BROWN, Arthur Basil Etheredge. b 17. Reading Univ BA39. Wycliffe Hall Ox 46. **d** 47 **p** 48. R Camborne *Truro* 66-82; rtd 82. *14 Tregenna Fields, Camborne, Cornwall TR14 7QS* Camborne (0209) 716196

BROWN, Canon Arthur Henry. b 18. St Pet Hall Ox BA39 MA43. Wycliffe Hall Ox 39. **d** 41 **p** 42. V Worksop St Anne *S'well* 56-83; P-in-c Scofton w Osberton 66-83; RD Worksop 72-83; Hon Can S'well Minster 77-83; rtd 83; Perm to Offic S'well from 83; Ex from 87. *Gentians, Plymouth Road, Chudleigh Knighton, Newton Abbot, Devon TQ13 0HE* Chudleigh (0626) 853786

BROWN, Arthur William Neville. b 08. Kelham Th Coll 30. **d** 36 **p** 38. Hon CF from 44; V Ellington *Ely* 66-74; R Grafham 66-74; rtd 74. *85 Pirehill Lane, Stone, Staffs ST15 0AS* Stone (0785) 812538

BROWN, Arthur William Stawell. b 26. St Jo Coll Ox BA50 MA51. Cuddesdon Coll 63. **d** 65 **p** 66. C Petersfield w Sheet *Portsm* 67-75; V Portsea St Alb 75-79; R Smithfield St Bart Gt *Lon* 79-91; R St Sepulchre w Ch Ch Greyfriars etc 81-91; rtd 91; Chapl Madeira *Eur* from 91. *Rua do Quebra Costas 20, 9000 Funchal, Madeira, Portugal* Madeira (91) 20674

BROWN, Barry Ronald. b 48. Ridley Coll Melbourne ThL72. **d** 73 **p** 74. Australia 73-77 and from 82; C Richmond St Mary *S'wark* 78-79; C Richmond St Mary w St Matthias and St Jo 79; C Edin Old St Paul *Edin* 79-80; Chapl Belgrade w Zagreb *Eur* 81-82. *290 Burnley Street, Burnley, Victoria, Australia 3121* Burnley (3) 428-3284

BROWN, Canon Bernard Herbert Vincent. b 26. Mert Coll Ox BA50 MA52. Westcott Ho Cam 50. **d** 52 **p** 53. C Rugby St Andr *Cov* 52-56; C Stoke Bishop *Bris* 56-59; Youth Chapl 56-62; Ind Chapl *Roch* 62-73; Bp's Dom Chapl 66-73; R Crawley *Chich* 73-79; TR 79-83; Ind Chapl *Bris* from 83; Bp's Soc and Ind Adv from 84; Hon Can Bris Cathl from 85; RD Bris City 85-91. *St John's Vicarage, 55 Apsley Road, Bristol BS8 2SW* Bristol (0272) 736794

BROWN, Bernard Maurice Newall. b 26. Oak Hill Th Coll 47. **d** 51 **p** 52. V Stapenhill w Cauldwell *Derby* 68-72; C Weston-super-Mare Ch Ch *B & W* 72-74; R Spaxton w Charlynch 74-80; rtd 80. *12 Ewart Road, Weston-super-Mare, Avon BS22 8NU* Weston-super-Mare (0934) 412170

BROWN, Bill. b 44. Linc Th Coll 87. **d** 89 **p** 90. C Moulsham St Luke *Chelmsf* from 89. *235 Linnet Drive, Chelmsford, Essex CM2 8AZ* Chelmsford (0245) 494167

BROWN, Brian Ernest. b 36. ALA64. Oak Hill NSM Course 82. **d** 85 **p** 86. NSM Wallington H Trin *S'wark* from 85. *27 Morton Gardens, Wallington, Surrey SM6 8EU* 081-647 5882

BROWN, Charles Hubert. b 21. S'wark Ord Course 82. **d** 84 **p** 85. NSM Shortlands *Roch* 84-86; P-in-c Seal St Lawr 86-90; P-in-c Underriver 86-90; rtd 90. *Barton Croft, 11 St Mary's Close, Sevenoaks, Kent TN15 8NH* Sevenoaks (0732) 882893

BROWN, Christopher. b 38. AKC62. **d** 63 **p** 64. C Crofton Park St Hilda w St Cypr *S'wark* 63-64; C S Beddington St Mich 64-67; C Herne Hill St Paul 67-68; Lic to Offic

S'well 68-72; Lich 72-76; Worc 77-79; Ox 79-86; Chelmsf from 86; Dir NSPCC from 89. *7 Baronia Croft, Highwoods, Colchester CO4 4EE* Colchester (0206) 844705

BROWN, Christopher. b 43. Linc Th Coll 79. **d** 81 **p** 82. C Stafford St Jo *Lich* 81-85; C Stafford St Jo and Tixall w Ingestre 85; V Alton w Bradley-le-Moors and Oakamoor w Cotton from 85. *The New Vicarage, Limekiln Lane, Alton, Stoke-on-Trent ST10 4AR* Oakamoor (0538) 702469

BROWN, Christopher Charles. b 58. Solicitor 82 Univ of Wales (Cardiff) LLB79. Westcott Ho Cam 87. **d** 90 **p** 91. C Taunton St Mary *B & W* from 90. *25 Laburnum Street, Taunton, Somerset TA1 1LB* Taunton (0823) 257439

BROWN, Christopher Edgar Newall. b 31. Oak Hill Th Coll 51. **d** 55 **p** 56. C Surbiton Hill Ch Ch *S'wark* 55-57; C Gipsy Hill Ch Ch 57-61; V Plumstead All SS 61-70; V Sissinghurst *Cant* 70-73; P-in-c Frittenden 72-73; V Sissinghurst w Frittenden 73-76; Perm to Offic *S & M* 84-91; Bp's Dom Chapl from 91. *21 College Green, Castletown, Isle of Man* Castletown (0624) 822364

BROWN, Christopher Francis. b 44. Sarum Th Coll 68. **d** 71 **p** 72. C High Wycombe *Ox* 71-74; C Sherborne w Castleton and Lillington *Sarum* 74-77; P-in-c Wylye, Fisherton Delamere and the Langfords 77-79; R Yarnbury 79-82; R Portland All SS w St Pet 82-88; RD Weymouth 85-88; R Trowbridge St Jas from 88. *The Rectory, Union Street, Trowbridge, Wilts BA14 8RU* Trowbridge (0225) 755121

BROWN, Clive Lindsey. b 33. Southn Univ BA55. Oak Hill Th Coll 57. **d** 59 **p** 60. C Becontree St Mary *Chelmsf* 59-62; Australia from 62. *30 William Street, Roseville, NSW, Australia 2069* Sydney (2) 407-2377

BROWN, Prof Colin. b 32. Liv Univ BA53 Lon Univ BD58 Nottm Univ MA61 Bris Univ PhD70. Tyndale Hall Bris 55. **d** 58 **p** 59. C Chilwell *S'well* 58-61; Lect Tyndale Hall Bris 61-78; Vice Prin 67-70; Dean of Studies 70-71; USA from 78; Prof Systematic Th Fuller Th Sem California from 78; Assoc Dean Adv Th Studies from 88. *1024 Beverly Way, Altadena, California 91001, USA* Pasadena (818) 584-5239

BROWN, Cyril James. b 04. OBE56. Keble Coll Ox BA26 MA39. St Steph Ho Ox 26. **d** 27 **p** 28. R Warbleton *Chich* 70-77; R Warbleton and Bodle Street Green 77; rtd 77; Perm to Offic *Chich* from 78. *16 Merlynn, Devonshire Place, Eastbourne, E Sussex BN21 4AQ* Eastbourne (0323) 23849

BROWN, David. b 44. DipTh80 TCD BTh90. **d** 86 **p** 87. C Cregagh *D & D* 86-91; Bp's C Knocknagoney from 91. *54 Rochester Avenue, Belfast BT6 9JW* Belfast (0232) 791296

BROWN, David Charles Girdlestone. b 42. Solicitor 67. S'wark Ord Course 87. **d** 90. NSM Milford *Guildf* from 90. *Tallboys, Courts Hill Road, Haslemere, Surrey GU27 2NG* Haslemere (0428) 651889

BROWN, David Frederick. b 38. Illinois Univ BA60. Seabury-Western Th Sem MDiv67. **d** 67 **p** 67. USA 67-78; Hon C Battersea Ch Ch and St Steph *S'wark* 78-83; Chapl R Marsden Hosp Lon and Surrey from 83. *Royal Marsden Hospital, Fulham Road, London SW3 6JJ* 071-352 8171 or 351 6082

BROWN, David Victor Arthur. b 44. Em Coll Cam BA66 MA70 CertEd. Linc Th Coll 72. **d** 74 **p** 75. C Bourne *Linc* 74-77; Chapl St Steph Coll Broadstairs 77-79; TV Grantham *Linc* 79-81; Chapl Asst N Gen Hosp Sheff 81-84; C Sheff St Cuth *Sheff* 81-84; Chapl Ridge Lea Hosp Lanc from 84; Chapl Lanc Moor Hosp from 84; Chapl Lanc R Infirmary from 87. *Lancaster Moor Hospital, Quernmore Road, Lancaster LA1 3JR* Lancaster (0524) 65241

BROWN, Prof David William. b 48. Edin Univ MA70 Or Coll Ox BA72 Clare Coll Cam PhD76. Westcott Ho Cam 75. **d** 76 **p** 77. Chapl, Fell and Tutor Or Coll Ox 76-90; Van Mildert Prof Div Dur Univ from 90. *14 The College, Durham DH1 3EQ* 091-386 4657

BROWN, Canon Dr Denis Arthur Whitlock. b 10. LCP63 Hatf Coll Dur LTh35 BA36 MA47 BCL55 Lon Univ BD50. St Boniface Warminster 32. **d** 36 **p** 37. CF (TA - R of O) 39-75; V North St Jas *Pet* 57-70; R Gayton w Tiffield 70-89; Can Pet Cathl 79-89; rtd 89; Perm to Offic *Pet* from 89. *3 Meeting Lane, Towcester, Northants NN12 7JX* Towcester (0327) 359317

BROWN, Dennis Cockburn. b 27. Hatf Coll Dur BSc48 K Coll Dur PhD54. W Midl Minl Tr Course 79. **d** 82 **p** 83. C Bilton *Cov* 82-84; V Wolford w Burmington from 84; R Cherington w Stourton from 84; R Barcheston from 84. *The Vicarage, Great Wolford, Shipston-on-Stour, Warks CV36 5NQ* Barton-on-the-Heath (060874) 361

BROWN, Canon Derek Frederick. b 27. St Fran Coll Brisbane ThL52. **d** 52 **p** 54. Australia 52-58; C Merstham and Gatton *S'wark* 59-61; R Deptford St Paul 61-69; Chapl RNR from 62; R Havant *Portsm* from 69. *St Faith's Rectory, Emsworth Road, Havant, Hants PO9 2FR* Havant (0705) 483485

BROWN, Donald Evans. b 10. Ch Coll Cam BA34 MA38. Lon Coll of Div 34. **d** 37 **p** 38. V Hemingford Grey *Ely* 55-77; rtd 77. *21 Manor Drive, Fenstanton, Huntingdon, Cambs PE18 9QZ* Huntingdon (0480) 67073

BROWN, Canon Donald Fryer. b 31. St Jo Coll Dur BA56 DipTh61. Cranmer Hall Dur 60. **d** 61 **p** 62. Min Can Bradf Cathl *Bradf* 61-64; C Bingley All SS 64-66; V Low Moor H Trin from 66; Hon Can Bradf Cathl from 85; RD Bowling and Horton from 87. *Holy Trinity Vicarage, Park House Road, Low Moor, Bradford, W Yorkshire BD12 0HR* Bradford (0274) 678859

BROWN, Mrs Doreen Marion. b 39. Cam Univ CertEd67 DCouns85. N Ord Course 85. **d** 88. Par Dn Axminster, Chardstock, Combe Pyne and Rousdon *Ex* from 88. *14 Cridlake, Axminster, Devon EX13 5BT* Axminster (0297) 34641

BROWN, Douglas Adrian Spencer. Univ of W Aus BA50. St Mich Th Coll Crafers ThL50. **d** 53 **p** 54. SSM from 54; Australia 53-60 and 67-90; Lic to Offic *S'wark* 60-67; Tutor and Chapl Kelham Th Coll 60-67; Chapl Bucharest w Sofia *Eur* from 90. *Church of the Resurrection, Str Xenopol 2, Bucharest, Romania* Bucharest (0) 110211

BROWN, Eric. b 28. NW Ord Course 73. **d** 76 **p** 77. NSM S Kirkby *Wakef* 76-83; NSM Knottingley from 83; NSM Kellington w Whitley from 89; Sub-Chapl HM Pris Lindholme from 90. *Wynberg, Barnsley Road, South Kirby, Pontefract, W Yorkshire WF9 3BG* Pontefract (0977) 43683

BROWN, Ernest Frederick Leonard. b 15. Edin Th Coll 46. **d** 49 **p** 50. R S Ockendon *Chelmsf* 59-77; R Pentlow, Foxearth, Liston and Borley 77-83; rtd 83. *20 Pasture Road, Barton-on-Humber, S Humberside DN18 5HN* Barton-on-Humber (0652) 32844

BROWN, Canon Ernest George. b 23. Em Coll Cam BA51 MA56. Oak Hill Th Coll 52. **d** 53 **p** 54. V Thurnby w Stoughton *Leic* 67-90; RD Gartree II (Wigston) 78-90; Hon Can Leic Cathl from 82; rtd 90. *16 Holbeck Drive, Broughton Astley, Leics LE9 6UR* Sutton Elms (0455) 285458

BROWN, Ernest Harry. b 32. St Mich Coll Llan. **d** 59 **p** 60. C Swansea St Pet *S & B* 59-62; CF (TA) from 62; C Gowerton w Waunarlwydd *S & B* 62-68; Chapl to the Deaf from 68. *Montreaux, 30 Lon Cedwyn, Sketty, Swansea SA2 0TH* Swansea (0792) 207628

BROWN, Frank Edward. b 02. Roch Th Coll 62. **d** 63 **p** 64. V Pendlebury St Aug *Man* 68-86; rtd 86. *20 Ranelagh Road, Pendlebury, Manchester M27 1HQ* 061-743 1053

BROWN, Frank Seymour. b 10. S'wark Ord Course 62 St Aug Coll Cant 65. **d** 65 **p** 66. C Bexleyheath Ch Ch *Roch* 65-70; R Cratfield w Heveningham and Ubbeston *St E* 70-76; rtd 76; Perm to Offic *St E* 76-86; P-in-c Ixworth and Ixworth Thorpe 78; P-in-c Euston w Barnham and Fakenham 80; Perm to Offic *St Alb* from 86. *3 Windsor Gardens, Kimbolton Road, Bedford MK40 3BU* Bedford (0234) 210999

BROWN, Geoffrey Gilbert. b 38. Dur Univ BA62 Fitzw Coll Cam BA69 MA73. Westcott Ho Cam 67. **d** 70 **p** 71. C Gosforth All SS *Newc* 70-73; Chapl Dauntsey's Sch Devizes 73-76; New Zealand 76-78 and from 86; V Barrow St Aid *Carl* 79-86. *7 Gloucester Street, Christchurch 1, New Zealand* Christchurch (3) 660535

BROWN, Canon Geoffrey Harold. b 30. Trin Hall Cam BA54 MA58. Cuddesdon Coll 54. **d** 56 **p** 57. C Plaistow St Andr *Chelmsf* 56-60; C Birm St Pet *Birm* 60-63; R Birm St Geo 63-73; TR Gt Grimsby St Mary and St Jas *Linc* 73-85; Can and Preb Linc Cathl 79-85; V St Martin-in-the-Fields *Lon* from 85. *St Martin's Place, London WC2N 4JH* 071-930 1862

BROWN, Geoffrey Peter. b 44. Lon Univ BD69 AKC69 MTh70. St Aug Coll Cant 69. **d** 70 **p** 71. C Woodford St Mary w St Phil and St Jas *Chelmsf* 71-74; Chapl Westf Coll and Bedf Coll *Lon* 74-80; V Bush Hill Park St Steph 80-86; Admin Sec Gen Syn Bd for Miss and Unity 86-91. *29 Orchard Crescent, Enfield, Middx EN1 3NS* 081-367 5247

BROWN, Ven Gerald Arthur Charles. b 35. CCC Cam BA56 MA60 CCC Ox BA58 DipTh59. St Steph Ho Ox 58. **d** 60 **p** 61. C Wolv St Pet *Lich* 60-66; V Trent Vale 66-74; V Wolv St Andr 74-82; Chapl Milan w Cadenabbia and Varese *Eur* 82-90; Adn Scandinavia from 90; Chapl Oslo w Bergen, Trondheim, Stavanger etc from 90. *c/o The British Embassy, BFPO 50, Oslo, Norway* Oslo (2) 552400 or 559786

BROWN, Graham Stanley. b 51. Sarum & Wells Th Coll 82. **d** 84 **p** 85. C Crediton and Shobrooke *Ex* 84-87; Chapl RAF from 87. *c/o MOD, Adastral House, Theobald's Road, London WC1X 8RU* 071-430 7268

BROWN, Harold. b 53. SEN74 SRN77 RMN82 RCN CCT84. Edin Th Coll 86. **d** 88 **p** 89. C Upperby St Jo *Carl* 88-90; C Carl H Trin and St Barn 90-91; C Workington St Mich from 91. *8 Dean Street, Workington, Cumbria CA14 2XA* Workington (0900) 61169

BROWN, Mrs Harriet Nina. b 37. Open Univ BA77 Lon Univ CertEd. Gilmore Course 80. **dss** 83 **d** 87. Greenstead juxta Colchester *Chelmsf* 83-87; Par Dn 87-90; Asst Chapl R Hosp Sch Holbrook from 90. *Three Hollies, Royal Hospital School, Holbrook, Ipswich IP9 2RU* Holbrook (0473) 327310

BROWN, Henry. b 27. Lon Univ BSc51 BSc52. NW Ord Course 72. **d** 75 **p** 76. NSM Padiham *Blackb* 75-80; V Warton St Paul 80-90; rtd 90. *18 Windsor Gardens, Garstang, Preston, Lancs PR3 1EG* Garstang (0995) 606592

BROWN, Canon Dr Howard Miles. b 11. Lon Univ BSc35 BD42 PhD47. Man Egerton Hall 39. **d** 40 **p** 40. V St Veep *Truro* 62-89; V St Winnow 62-89; Hon Can Truro Cathl from 64; RD Bodmin 71-76; Preb St Endellion 73-89; P-in-c Lostwithiel 87-89; P-in-c Boconnoc w Bradoc 87-89; rtd 90. *30 Chirgwin Road, Truro, Cornwall TR1 1TT* Truro (0872) 70350

BROWN, Ian. b 48. Nor Ord Course 89. **d** 91. C Burnage St Marg *Man* from 91. *29 Bournelea Avenue, Burnage, Manchester M19 1AE* 061-431 7272

BROWN, Ian Barry. b 53. Ruskin Coll Ox 75 St Cuth Soc Dur BA80 PGCE81. Westmr Past Foundn CCouns90 Sarum & Wells Th Coll 84. **d** 86 **p** 87. C Winchmore Hill St Paul *Lon* 86-89; Hon Chapl Chase Farm Hosp Enfield 86-88; Hon Chapl Harley Street Area Hosps 88-90; Hon Chapl RAM 89; C St Marylebone w H Trin from 89. *38 Nottingham Place, London W1M 3FD* 071-487 3551

BROWN, Ian David. b 53. UEA BA76. Wycliffe Hall Ox BA80. **d** 81 **p** 82. C Southsea St Jude *Portsm* 81-84; Chapl Coll of SS Mary and Paul Cheltenham 84-89; V Lt Heath *St Alb* from 89. *The Vicarage, Thornton Road, Potters Bar, Herts EN6 1JJ* Potters Bar (0707) 54414

BROWN, Ivan James. b 24. Cant Sch of Min 84. **d** 86 **p** 87. NSM St Nicholas at Wade w Sarre and Chislet w Hoath *Cant* from 86. *Hurst Cottage, Millbank, Hoath, Canterbury, Kent CT3 4LP* Chislet (022786) 210

BROWN, Jack Robin. b 44. Linc Th Coll 67. **d** 69 **p** 70. C Canning Town St Cedd *Chelmsf* 69-72; C Dunstable *St Alb* 72-78; V Luton St Andr 78-85; V Kempston Transfiguration from 85. *Transfiguration Vicarage, Cleveland Street, Kempston, Bedford MK42 8DW* Bedford (0234) 854788

BROWN, Canon James Philip. b 30. Ex Coll Ox BA54 MA55. Westcott Ho Cam 54. **d** 56 **p** 57. C Hemel Hempstead *St Alb* 56-63; V Hellesdon *Nor* 63-71; P-in-c Kirkley w Lowestoft St Jo 71-79; TV Lowestoft St Marg 76-78; TV Lowestoft and Kirkley 79-81; P-in-c Northleach w Hampnett and Farmington *Glouc* from 81; RD Northleach from 83; P-in-c Cold Aston w Notgrove and Turkdean from 86; Hon Can Glouc Cathl from 91. *The Vicarage, Northleach, Cheltenham, Glos GL54 3HL* Cotswold (0451) 60293

BROWN, Canon James Russell. b 19. Qu Coll Ox BA52 MA56 Nashotah Ho Wisconsin DD70 Winnipeg Univ LLD77 LTh DD. **d** 43 **p** 44. C Bris St Jude w St Matthias *Bris* 43-45; C Portishead *B & W* 47-49; USA 52-55; C Brighton Gd Shep Preston *Chich* 55-47; C Abbots Langley *St Alb* 55-56; Canada from 56; Prof Nashotah Ho Wisconsin 61-70; Warden and Vice-Chan St Jo Coll Winnipeg 70-80; Can St Jo Cathl Winnipeg 70-80; Hon Can from 80; Lect Manitoba Univ from 80. *96 Kingsway Avenue, Winnipeg, Manitoba, Canada, R3M 0G9*

BROWN, Mrs Joan Leslie. b 31. SS Hild & Bede Coll Dur CertEd55. Oak Hill Th Coll BA85. **dss** 85 **d** 87. Fulwood *Sheff* 85-87; Par Dn 87-88; TM Netherthorpe from 88. *32 Roebuck Road, Sheffield S6 3GP* Sheffield (0742) 682046

BROWN, John. b 21. **d** 50 **p** 51. I Clabby *Clogh* 62-75; V Dunham w Darlton and Ragnall *S'well* 75-87; R Fledborough 76-87; rtd 87. *The Groton, Norbury, Bishops Castle, Shropshire SY9 5DX* Linley (058861) 272

BROWN, John. b 24. St Paul's Cheltenham 67. Oak Hill Th Coll 50. **d** 53 **p** 54. Teacher Middlecroft Sch Staveley 69-75; Hd of RE Silverdale Sch Sheff 75-87; rtd 87.

17 Avondale Road, Inkersall, Chesterfield, Derbyshire S43 3EQ Chesterfield (0246) 473394

BROWN, John. b 64. Kent Univ BA86. Westcott Ho Cam 87. **d** 90 **p** 91. C Lt Ilford St Mich *Chelmsf* from 90. *The Froud Centre, Toronto Avenue, London E12 7JF* 081-553 4627

BROWN, John Bruce. b 42. Nottm Univ BA64 MA68. Cuddesdon Coll 64. **d** 66 **p** 67. C Warw St Nic *Cov* 66-71; C Hatf *St Alb* 71-78; V Watford St Mich from 78. *St Michael's Vicarage, 5 Mildred Avenue, Watford WD1 7DY* Watford (0923) 32460

BROWN, Canon John Derek. b 41. Linc Th Coll 71. **d** 73 **p** 74. C Rotherham *Sheff* 73-76; P-in-c W Pinchbeck *Linc* 76-78; V Surfleet 76-78; V Surfleet 78-82; R Boultham from 83; RD Christianity from 85; Hon Can Linc Cathl from 88. *The Rectory, 2A St Helen's Avenue, Boultham, Lincoln LN6 7RA* Lincoln (0522) 682026

BROWN, John Dixon. b 28. Pemb Coll Cam BA52. Oak Hill Th Coll 52. **d** 54 **p** 55. V W Hampnett *Chich* 63-91; rtd 91. *3 Manor Way, Elmer Sands, Bognor Regis, W Sussex PO22 6LA* Bognor Regis (0243) 583449

BROWN, John Duncan. b 43. St Pet Coll Ox BA64 BA66 MA68 Lon Univ BSc. Wycliffe Hall Ox 65. **d** 67 **p** 68. C Kingston upon Hull H Trin *York* 67-69; C St Leonards St Leon *Chich* 69-72; Hon C Norbiton *S'wark* 72-75; C Kirkcaldy *St And* 75-78; Prec and Chapl Chelmsf Cathl *Chelmsf* 78-86; P-in-c Kelvedon Hatch from 86; P-in-c Navestock from 86. *The Rectory, Church Road, Kelvedon Common, Brentwood, Essex CM14 5TJ* Coxtie Green (0277) 372466

✠**BROWN, Rt Rev John Edward.** b 30. Lon Univ BD68. Kelham Th Coll 50. **d** 55 **p** 56 **c** 87. Jerusalem 55-57; C Reading St Mary V *Ox* 57-60; Sudan 60-64; V Stewkley *Ox* 64-69; V Maidenhead St Luke 69-73; V Bracknell 73-77; RD Sonning 74-77; Adn Berks 78-87; Warden Ascot Priory 80-87; Bp Cyprus and the Gulf from 87. *2 Afxentiou Street, PO Box 2075, Nicosia 118, Cyprus* Nicosia (2) 451338

BROWN, Preb John Roger. b 37. AKC60. **d** 61 **p** 62. C New Eltham All SS *S'wark* 61-64; C Bexhill St Pet *Chich* 64-68; V Eastbourne St Eliz 68-75; V E Grinstead St Swithun from 75; Chapl Qu Victoria's Hosp E Grinstead from 75; RD E Grinstead *Chich* from 82; Can and Preb Chich Cathl from 89. *St Swithun's Vicarage, East Grinstead, Sussex RH19 3AZ* East Grinstead (0342) 323307

BROWN, Canon John Simpson. b 10. TCD BA46 MA49 BD54 Cam Univ MA50. TCD Div Sch. **d** 47 **p** 48. Warden Div Hostel Dub 61-80; Prof Past Th TCD 64-80; Prec St Patr Cathl Dub 75-80; rtd 80. *25 Pasadena Gardens, Belfast BT5 6HU* Belfast (0232) 654953

BROWN, John William Etheridge. b 13. St Pet Hall Ox BA35 MA39. Wycliffe Hall Ox 35. **d** 37 **p** 38. V Leusden *Ex* 61-79; V Widecombe in the Moor 61-79; P-in-c Holne 70-74; P-in-c Princetown 74-79; RD Moreton 74-80; Asst Chapl HM Pris Dartmoor 75-82; V Widecombe, Leusden and Princetown etc *Ex* 79-82; rtd 82. *8 Emmetts Park, Ashburton, Newton Abbot, Devon TQ13 7DB* Ashburton (0364) 53072

BROWN, Jonathan. b 60. Univ Coll Dur BA83 MA85 Ex Univ CertEd86. Ripon Coll Cuddesdon 86 Ch Div Sch of the Pacific (USA) 88. **d** 89 **p** 90. C Esher *Guildf* from 89. *Hazel Cottage, Hillbrow Road, Esher, Surrey KT10 9UD* Esher (0372) 66865

BROWN, Julian Keith. b 57. Magd Coll Ox BA79. St Jo Coll Nottm 82. **d** 85 **p** 86. C Kidlington w Hampton Poyle *Ox* 85-88; C Luton All SS w St Pet *St Alb* 88-91. *Address temp unknown*

BROWN, Kenneth Arthur Charles. b 27. ACP65. Local NSM Course 85. **d** 84 **p** 85. NSM Ingoldsby *Linc* from 84. *11 Ingoldsby Road, Lenton, Grantham, Lincs NG33 4HB* Ingoldsby (047685) 763

BROWN, Canon Kenneth Edward. b 22. Qu Coll Cam BA43 MA47. Ridley Hall Cam 46. **d** 47 **p** 48. V Southbroom *Sarum* 69-83; RD Devizes 77-83; Can and Preb Sarum Cathl from 77; TV Tisbury 83-87; rtd 87. *24 Broadleas Road, Devizes, Wilts SN10 5DG* Devizes (0380) 78254

BROWN, Kenneth Roger. b 48. Dur Univ BA69 St Chad's Coll Dur DipLit72. Liturg Inst Trier DipLit73. **d** 73 **p** 74. C Patchway *Bris* 73-77; C Fishponds St Jo 77-79; C Fishponds All SS 77-79; Chapl RAF from 79. *c/o MOD, Adastral House, Theobald's Road, London WC1X 8RU* 071-430 7268

✠**BROWN, Rt Rev Laurence Ambrose.** b 07. Qu Coll Cam BA31 MA46. Cuddesdon Coll 31. **d** 32 **p** 33 **c** 60. C Kennington St Jo *S'wark* 32-35; C Luton Ch Ch *St Alb* 35-40; V Hatf Hyde St Mary 40-46; Can Res and Prec S'wark Cathl *S'wark* 50-56; Asst Sec S Lon Ch Fund

and S'wark DBF 46-52; Sec 52-60; Adn Lewisham 55-60; Vice Provost S'wark 56-60; Suff Bp Warrington *Liv* 60-69; Bp Birm 69-77; rtd 77; Perm to Offic *Sarum* 77-78 and from 84; P-in-c Odstock w Nunton and Bodenham 78-84. *7 St Nicholas Road, Salisbury* Salisbury (0722) 333138

BROWN, Lawrence Richard. b 08. S'wark Ord Course 63. **d** 66 **p** 67. Hon C Lee Gd Shep w St Pet *S'wark* 66-78; rtd 78; Perm to Offic *S'wark* 78-90. *30 Scotsdale Road, London SE12 8BP* 081-852 1527

BROWN, Leslie Maurice. b 04. FRSE47 Bris Univ BSc24 MSc25 St Andr Univ PhD38. Edin Th Coll 74. **d** 74 **p** 74. Hon C Edin St Jo *Edin* 74-88; rtd 88. *26 Falcon Court, Edinburgh EH10 4AE* 031-447 5387

✠**BROWN, Rt Rev Leslie Wilfrid.** b 12. CBE65. Lon Univ BD36 MTh44 DD57 Cam Univ Hon MA53. ALCD35. **d** 35 **p** 36 **c** 53. C Milton *Portsm* 35-38; India 38-43 and 44-50; Chapl Down Coll Cam 43-44; C Cam H Trin *Ely* 43-44; Chapl Jes Coll Cam 50-51; Bp Uganda 53-60; Abp Uganda, Rwanda and Burundi 60-65; Bp Namirembe 60-65; Bp St E 66-78; ChStJ from 68; rtd 78. *47 New Square, Cambridge CB1 1EZ* Cambridge (0223) 352465

BROWN, Miss Louise Margaret. b 53. Trin Coll Bris DipHE82. dss 83 **d** 87. Woodley *Ox* 84-87; Par Dn from 87. *St John's Church House, 35 Comet Way, Reading RG5 4PQ* Reading (0734) 692981

BROWN, Malcolm Arthur. b 54. Or Coll Ox BA76 MA82. Westcott Ho Cam 77. **d** 79 **p** 80. C Riverhead w Dunton Green *Roch* 79-83; TV Southn (City Cen) *Win* 83-91; Lic to Offic *Man* from 91; Assoc Dir Wm Temple Foundn from 91. *c/o William Temple Foundation, Manchester Business School, Manchester M15 6PB* 061-275 6534

BROWN, Mark Edward. b 61. Southn Univ BSc83 Cam Univ PGCE84. Trin Coll Bris DipHE87 BA88. **d** 88 **p** 89. C Egham *Guildf* from 88. *33 Grange Road, Egham, Surrey TW20 9QP* Egham (0784) 434137

BROWN, Martin Douglas. b 53. Oak Hill Th Coll 78. **d** 81 **p** 82. C New Malden and Coombe *S'wark* 81-85; C Cheadle *Ches* 85-87; V Preston All SS *Blackb* 87-91; R Darfield *Sheff* from 91. *The Rectory, Darfield, Barnsley, S Yorkshire S73 9JX* Barnsley (0226) 752236

BROWN, Martin Easdale. b 27. Ely Th Coll 53. **d** 55 **p** 66. C Surbiton St Andr *S'wark* 55-59; C Blandford Forum *Sarum* 59-62; V France Lynch *Glouc* 62-75; P-in-c Aysgarth *Ripon* 75-77; V 77-80; P-in-c Bolton w Redmire 78-80; V Aysgarth and Bolton cum Redmire from 80. *The Vicarage, Carperby, Leyburn, N Yorkshire DL8 4DQ* Aysgarth (09693) 235

BROWN, Michael Coningsby. b 23. St Jo Coll Ox BA47 MA49. Linc Th Coll 47. **d** 49 **p** 50. C Mill Hill St Mich *Lon* 49-53; C Wilton Place St Paul 53-56; V Bures *St E* 56-62; P-in-c Mt Bures *Chelmsf* 58-62; V Godalming *Guildf* from 62; RD Godalming 74-79. *The Vicarage, Godalming, Surrey GU7 1ES* Godalming (0483) 421057

BROWN, Ven Michael Rene Warneford. b 15. St Pet Coll Ox BA37 MA41. St Steph Ho Ox 38. **d** 41 **p** 42. Adn Nottm *S'well* 60-77; Perm to Offic *Cant* from 77; rtd 80; Hon OCF R Marines Sch of Music Deal from 85. *Faygate, 72 Liverpool Road, Deal, Kent CT14 7LR* Deal (0304) 361326

BROWN, Nicholas Francis Palgrave. b 23. Fitzw Ho Cam BA51 MA54. **d** 53 **p** 54. Gen Sec Ind Chr Fellowship 66-76; V St Kath Cree *Lon* 66-71; Chapl and Dir of Studies Holland Ho Cropthorne 76-80; P-in-c Cropthorne w Charlton *Worc* 76-88; Adult Educn Officer 80-85; rtd 88. *Bredon View, Rear of 40 Bridge Street, Pershore, Worcs WR10 1AT* Pershore (0386) 556816

BROWN, Canon Norman Charles Harry. b 27. Univ of Wales BSc46. St Mich Coll Llan 48. **d** 50 **p** 51. C Canton St Jo *Llan* 50-57; C Llanishen and Lisvane 58-63; V Miskin from 63; RD Aberdare from 82; Can Llan Cathl from 86. *The Vicarage, Miskin, Mountain Ash, M Glam CF45 3NE* Mountain Ash (0443) 473247

BROWN, Norman John. b 34. Thames Poly MA90. Ripon Hall Ox 72. **d** 74 **p** 75. C High Wycombe *Ox* 74-78; V Tilehurst St Cath 78-82; V Boyne Hill from 82. *All Saints' Vicarage, Westmorland Road, Maidenhead, Berks SL6 4HB* Maidenhead (0628) 26921

BROWN, Paul David Christopher. b 50. Lon Univ LLB71. E Midl Min Tr Course 81. **d** 84 **p** 85. NSM Wollaton *S'well* from 84. *32 Benington Drive, Wollaton, Nottingham NG8 2TF* Nottingham (0602) 284493

BROWN, Peter. b 38. Leeds Univ BSc62 PhD65. Nashotah Ho 85. **d** 87 **p** 88. USA 87-89; C Sprowston *Nor* 89-90; C Sprowston w Beeston from 90. *6 Wroxham Road, Sprowston, Norwich NR7 8TZ* Norwich (0603) 484438

BROWN, Peter. b 47. RMN69. Kelham Th Coll 69. d 74
p 75. C Hendon Dur 74-80; C Byker St Ant Newc 80-90;
C Brandon Dur from 90. The Clergy House, Sawmill
Lane, Brandon, Durham DH7 8NS 091-378 0845

BROWN, Peter. b 53. St Chad's Coll Dur BA75. Sarum
& Wells Th Coll 75. d 77 p 78. C Tunstall Ch Ch Lich
77-79; C Tunstall 79-80; C Willenhall H Trin 80-83; V
Weston Rhyn 83-88; Australia 88-90; R Hubbertson
St D from 90. Hubbertson Rectory, 35 Westaway Drive,
Hubbertson, Milford Haven SA73 3EQ   Milford Haven
(0646) 692251

BROWN, Canon Peter Kimpton. b 34. ALCD58. d 60 p 61.
C Folkestone H Trin w Ch Ch Cant 60-63; C Swanage
Sarum 63-67; Australia from 67. 43 Hamersely Drive,
Bunbury, W Australia 6230

BROWN, Peter Russell. b 43. Oak Hill Th Coll. d 71 p 72.
C Gt Faringdon w Lt Coxwell Ox 71-73; C Reading
Greyfriars 73-74; V Forty Hill Jes Ch Lon 74-81; V
Laleham from 81. The Vicarage, Laleham, Staines,
Middx TW18 1SB   Staines (0784) 457330

BROWN, Philip Anthony. b 54. Oak Hill Th Coll BA91.
d 91. C Rock Ferry Ches from 91. 35 Browning Avenue,
Rock Ferry, Wirral L42 2DE   051-645 7468

BROWN, Philip Roy. b 41. St Steph Ho Ox 78. d 80 p 81.
C Highters Heath Birm 80-83; P-in-c Washwood Heath
83-87; V Tysoe w Oxhill and Whatcote Cov from 87.
The Vicarage, Peacock Lane, Tysoe, Warwick CV35 0SE
Tysoe (029588) 201

BROWN, Phillip Murray. b 59. Keele Univ BSc80. Trin
Coll Bris DipTh86 ADPS87. d 87 p 88. C Greasbrough
Sheff 87-91; Ind Chapl from 87; V Thorne from 91.
The Vicarage, 2 Brooke Street, Thorne, Doncaster, S
Yorkshire DN8 4AZ   Thorne (0405) 814055

BROWN, Raymond Isaac Harry. b 14. Kelham Th Coll
36. d 42 p 43. V Tintinhull B & W 66-74; RD Martock
70-75; Lesotho from 76; rtd 79. Community of the Holy
Name, PO Box 43, Leribe 300, Lesotho

BROWN, Raymond John. b 49. Ox Univ BEd71. Wycliffe
Hall Ox 72. d 75 p 76. C Barking St Marg w St Patr
Chelmsf 75-78; C Walton H Trin Ox 78-82; V Enfield St
Mich Lon 82-91; Chapl St Mich Hosp Enfield 82-91; R
Springfield All SS Chelmsf from 91. The Rectory,
9 Mulberry Way, Chelmsford CM1 5SN   Chelmsford
(0245) 356720

BROWN, Reginald. b 16. St Jo Coll Dur BA38 DipTh40
MA41. d 39 p 40. V Bishopwearmouth Ch Ch Dur 63-77;
R Shincliffe 77-87; Chapl Dur High Sch 79-85; rtd 87.
Sherburn Hospital, Sherburn House, Durham DH1 2SE
091-372 0421

BROWN, Richard. b 47. Open Univ BA90. St Steph Ho
Ox 71. d 74 p 75. C Toxteth Park St Marg Liv 74-77; C
Reading St Giles Ox 77-80; V Earley St Nic 80-84; V
Kenton Lon from 84. St Mary's Vicarage, 3 St Leonard's
Avenue, Harrow, Middx HA3 8EJ   081-907 2914

BROWN, Richard George. b 38. Dur Univ BSc63. Wells
Th Coll 63. d 65 p 66. C Norton St Mary Dur 65-69; C
N Gosforth Newc 69-71; Chapl Wells Cathl Sch 71-81;
P-in-c Dulverton and Brushford B & W 81-83; R 83-86;
Chapl Millfield Jun Sch Somerset 86-89; Chapl Brighton
Coll E Sussex from 89. 8 Walpole Road, Brighton
BN2 2EA

BROWN, Richard Lessey. b 27. Keble Coll Ox
BA51 MA55. Qu Coll Birm 51. d 53 p 54. C York St
Lawr w St Nic York 53-55; C Fulford 55-57; V
Fridaythorpe w Fimber and Thixendale 57-61; V York
St Luke 61-75; V Barlby from 75. The Vicarage, York
Road, Barlby, Selby, N Yorkshire YO8 7JP   Selby
(0757) 702384

BROWN, Ven Robert Saville. b 14. Selw Coll Cam
BA39 MA43. Linc Th Coll 39. d 40 p 41. Hon Can
St Alb 63-74; V Bedf St Paul 69-74; Adn Bedf 74-79;
P-in-c Old Warden 74-79; rtd 79; Perm to Offic Ox
79-87. The Rowans, 29 The Rise, Amersham, Bucks
HP7 9AG   Amersham (0494) 728376

BROWN, Robin. b 38. Leeds Univ BA60 MPhil69. Qu
Coll Birm 89. d 91. C Far Headingley St Chad Ripon
from 91. 64 Beckett's Park Crescent, Leeds LS6 3PF
Leeds (0532) 743636

BROWN, Roger Lee. b 42. Univ of Wales (Lamp)
BA63 Univ Coll Lon MA73. Wycliffe Hall Ox 66. d 68
p 69. C Dinas w Penygraig Llan 68-70; C Bargoed and
Deri w Brithdir 70-72; TV Glyncorrwg w Afan Vale and
Cymmer Afan 72-74; R 74-79; V Tongwynlais from 79.
The Vicarage, 1 Merthyr Road, Tongwynlais, Cardiff
CF4 7LE   Cardiff (0222) 810437

✠BROWN, Rt Rev Ronald. b 26. St Jo Coll Dur
BA50 DipTh52. d 52 p 53 c 74. C Chorley St Laur Blackb
52-56; V Whittle-le-Woods 56-61; V Halliwell St Thos

Man 61-69; R Ashton St Mich 69-74; RD Ashton-under-
Lyne 69-74; Suff Bp Birkenhead Ches from 74. Trafford
House, Victoria Crescent, Chester CH4 7AX   Chester
(0244) 675895

BROWN, Ronald Glyn. b 34. Lich Th Coll 70. d 73 p 74.
C Weymouth St Paul Sarum 73-78; C Swanage 78-79;
P-in-c Bromham 79-80; P-in-c Chittoe 79-80; R
Bromham, Chittoe and Sandy Lane from 80. The
Rectory, Bromham, Chippenham, Wilts SN15 2HA
Bromham (0380) 850322

BROWN, Ms Shelagh Margaret. b 30. Gilmore Course 78.
dss 80 d 87. Reigate St Mark S'wark 80-81; St Marylebone
Ch Ch Lon 81-82; Caterham Valley S'wark 82-86; Dir
Abp Coggan's Tr Services Cen 86-89; rtd 89; Par Dn
Reigate St Mary S'wark from 89. 1 The Clears, Reigate,
Surrey RH2 9JL   Reigate (0737) 245223

BROWN, Simon Nicolas Danton. b 37. Clare Coll Cam
BA61 MA65. S'wark Ord Course 61 Linc Th Coll 63.
d 64 p 65. C Lambeth St Mary the Less S'wark 64-66;
Chapl and Warden LMH Settlement 66-72; P-in-c Southn
St Mary w H Trin Win 72-73; TV Southn (City Cen)
73-79; R Gt Brickhill w Bow Brickhill and Lt Brickhill
Ox 79-84; TR Burnham w Dropmore, Hitcham and
Taplow from 84; RD Burnham from 87. The Rectory,
The Precincts, Burnham, Slough SL1 7HU   Burnham
(0628) 604173

BROWN, Stanley George. b 19. Bps' Coll Cheshunt 66.
d 67 p 68. C Shrub End Chelmsf 67-71; R Dengie w
Asheldham 71-89; V Tillingham 71-89; RD Maldon and
Dengie 82-89; rtd 89. 134 Lynn Road, Ely, Cambs
CB6 1DE   Ely (0353) 662888

BROWN, Stephen Charles. b 60. Leeds Univ BA83
Reading Univ PGCE89 Leeds Univ BA89. Coll of
Resurr Mirfield 87. d 90 p 91. C Whitkirk Ripon from
90. 6 Hollyshaw Crescent, Whitkirk, Leeds LS15 7AN
Leeds (0532) 606355

BROWN, Stephen James. b 44. Bradf Univ BSc69. Westcott
Ho Cam 71. d 72 p 73. C Seaton Hirst Newc 72-75; C
Marton-in-Cleveland York 75-77; Dioc Youth Adv Dur
77-82; V Thorner Ripon from 82; Dioc Officer for Local
Min from 90. The Vicarage, Thorner, Leeds LS14 3EG
Leeds (0532) 892437

BROWN, Victor Charles. b 31. S'wark Ord Course 67.
d 71 p 72. C Pinhoe Ex 71-73; C Egg Buckland 73-74; C
Oakdale St Geo Sarum 74-77; R Old Trafford St Hilda
Man 77-83; R Chigwell Row Chelmsf from 83. The
Rectory, Romford Road, Chigwell, Essex IG7 4QD
081-500 2805

BROWN, Wallace. b 44. Oak Hill Th Coll 77. d 79 p 80. C
Oadby Leic 79-85; V Quinton Road W St Boniface Birm
from 85. St Boniface Vicarage, Quinton Road West,
Birmingham B32 2QD   021-427 1939

BROWN, Walter Bertram John. b 09. K Coll Lon 43. d 43
p 44. Ex and Devon Miss to Adult Deaf & Dumb 53-73;
Chapl to the Deaf Chich 73-75; rtd 75; Perm to Offic
Chich from 80. High Trees, 31 Knowle Road, Fairlight,
Hastings, E Sussex TN35 4AT   Hastings (0424) 813347

BROWN, William Martyn. b 14. Pemb Coll Cam
BA36 MA47. Nor Ord Course 76. d 76 p 77. NSM
Thornage w Brinton w Hunworth and Stody Nor 76-77;
NSM Field Dalling w Saxlingham 77-84; RD Holt 84-88;
NSM Gunthorpe w Bale w Field Dalling, Saxlingham
etc 84-88; Perm to Offic from 88. Lodge Cottage,
Field Dalling, Holt, Norfolk NR25 7AS   Binham (0328)
830403

BROWNBRIDGE, Bernard Alan. b 19. NW Ord Course
74. d 77 p 78. NSM Huntington York 77-80; V Sand
Hutton 80-86; rtd 87; Hon C Birdsall w Langton York
from 87. 127 Langton Road, Norton, Malton, N
Yorkshire YO17 9AE   Malton (0653) 697626

BROWNBRIDGE, Peter John. b 31. BD. d 81 p 82. NSM
Wingham w Elmstone and Preston w Stourmouth Cant
81-87; V from 87. St Mary's House, 5 St Mary's Meadow,
Wingham, Canterbury, Kent CT3 1DF   Canterbury
(0227) 721530

BROWNE, Anthony Douglas. b 40. BD69 Aston Univ
MSc74. Oak Hill NSM Course 88. d 91. NSM Woodford
St Mary w St Phil and St Jas Chelmsf from 91. 1 Bradfield
Way, Buckhurst Hill, Essex IG9 5AG

BROWNE, Arnold Samuel. b 52. St Jo Coll Ox BA73 MA77
SS Coll Cam PhD87 Surrey Univ MSc89. Westcott Ho
Cam 76. d 78 p 79. C Esher Guildf 78-81; C Worplesdon
81-86; Chapl R Holloway and Bedf New Coll from 86.
10 Willow Walk, Egham, Surrey TW20 0DQ   Egham
(0784) 432025 or 443070

BROWNE, Arthur Donal. b 11. MC44. St Edm Hall Ox
BA34 DipTh35 MA54. Wycliffe Hall Ox 34. d 35 p 36.
V S Kensington St Jude Lon 62-78; rtd 78; P-in-c
Lydgate w Ousden and Cowlinge St E 80-81; P-in-c

Glenurquhart *Mor* 84-89. *Ham Farm, Dunnet, Thurso, Caithness KW14 8XP* Thurso (0847) 85232

BROWNE, Aubrey Robert Caulfeild. b 31. Moore Th Coll Sydney 54. **d** 55 **p** 56. Australia 55-71; Producer of Relig Radio Progr USPG 72-84; Hon C S Kensington St Steph *Lon* 78-88; Hd of Area Sec Dept USPG 84-87; P-in-c Nunhead St Antony *S'wark* 88-90; V Nunhead St Antony w St Silas from 90. *St Anthony's Vicarage, 2A Carden Road, London SE15 3UD* 071-639 4261

BROWNE, Very Rev Cecil Charles Wyndham. b 16. TCD BA38 BD44. **d** 40 **p** 41. I Sligo w Knocknarea *K, E & A* 47-83; RD N Elphin 53-83; Dean Elphin and Ardagh 67-83; rtd 83. *9 St Mantan's Road, Wicklow, Irish Republic* Wicklow (404) 67917

BROWNE, Miss Christine Mary. b 53. Nottm Univ BEd75. E Midl Min Tr Course 87. **d** 90. Par Dn Bulwell St Mary *S'well* from 90. *47 Henrietta Street, Bulwell, Nottingham NG6 9JB*

BROWNE, Cyril Theodore Martin. b 12. Tyndale Hall Bris 30. **d** 35 **p** 36. V Greenwich H Trin and St Paul *S'wark* 62-74; R Tilston and Shocklach *Ches* 74-78; rtd 78; C-in-c Reading St Mary Castle Street Prop Chpl *Ox* 78-84; Perm to Offic *Roch* from 85. *14 St Philip's Court, Sandhurst Road, Tunbridge Wells, Kent TN2 3SW* Tunbridge Wells (0892) 546356

BROWNE, Herman Beseah. b 65. K Coll Lon BD90 AKC90. Cuttington Univ Coll BA86. **d** 87. Liberia 87-90; C N Lambeth *S'wark* from 90; Lect Simon of Cyrene Th Inst from 90. *Flat 2, 3/5 Lambeth Road, London SE1 7DG* 071-735 4568

BROWNE, Ian Cameron. b 51. St Cath Coll Ox BA74 MA78 Fitzw Coll Cam BA76 MA80. Ridley Hall Cam 74. **d** 77 **p** 78. C Cheltenham Ch Ch *Glouc* 77-80; Hon C Shrewsbury St Chad *Lich* 80-83; Asst Chapl Shrewsbury Sch 80-83; Hd of RE Bedf Sch from 83. *32 The Grove, Bedford MK40 3JW* Bedford (0234) 56004

BROWNE, John Burnell. b 15. MC45. Qu Coll Cam BA36 MA40. Westcott Ho Cam 46. **d** 47 **p** 48. V Billingham St Cuth *Dur* 71-80; rtd 80; Perm to Offic *Wakef* from 80. *40 Slack Top, Heptonstall, Hebden Bridge, W Yorkshire HX7 7HA* Hebden Bridge (0422) 843099

BROWNE, Leonard Joseph. b 58. St Cath Coll Cam BA81 MA84. Trin Coll Bris 87. **d** 89 **p** 90. C Reading Greyfriars *Ox* from 89. *26 Prospect Street, Reading RG1 7YG* Reading (0734) 599930

BROWNE, Norman Desmond. b 21. TCD BA42 BD46 MA61. CITC 43. **d** 44 **p** 45. R Hedgerley *Ox* 61-80; rtd 80. *8 Brett House Close, West Hill, London SW15 3JD* 081-788 1365

BROWNE, Peter Clifford. b 59. SRN82 Bris Univ BA80. Ripon Coll Cuddesdon 88. **d** 90 **p** 91. C Southgate Ch Ch *Lon* from 90. *6 The Green, London N14 7EG* 081-882 0293

BROWNING, Canon Denys James. b 07. Keble Coll Ox BA29 MA59. Coll of Resurr Mirfield 38. **d** 40 **p** 41. C Oxley *Lich* 40-42; CF (EC) 42-47; C Leeds St Aid *Ripon* 48-50; CF (TA) 49-50; Australia 50-55; Area Sec (Dios Ox and Cov) USPG 55-59; Papua New Guinea 59-81; Hon Prov Can Papua from 81; New Zealand from 81. *RD9, Hamilton, New Zealand*

BROWNING, Canon George Henry. b 06. OBE46. Dur Univ LTh32. St Aug Coll Cant 28. **d** 32 **p** 33. V Edgbaston St Geo *Birm* 56-71; Hon Can Birm Cathl 69-71; rtd 71; Lic to Offic *Worc* from 71. *43 Camp Hill Road, Worcester WR5 2HE* Worcester (0905) 355947

BROWNING, Canon John William. b 36. Keele Univ BA61. Ripon Hall Ox 61. **d** 63 **p** 64. C Baswich (or Berkswich) *Lich* 63-66; Chapl Monyhull Hosp Birm 67-71; Chapl Wharncliffe Hosp Sheff 71-78; Chapl Middlewood Hosp Sheff from 71; Hon Can Sheff Cathl *Sheff* from 84; Chapl Sheff Mental Health Unit from 85. *131 Low Road, Stannington, Sheffield S6 5FZ* Sheffield (0742) 343740 or 852222

BROWNING, Julian. b 51. St Jo Coll Cam BA72 MA76. Ripon Coll Cuddesdon 77. **d** 80 **p** 81. C Notting Hill *Lon* 80-81; C W Brompton St Mary w St Pet 81-84; Perm to Offic 84-91. *82 Ashworth Mansions, Grantully Road, London W9 1LN* 071-286 6034

BROWNING, Canon Richard Geoffrey Claude. b 25. Selw Coll Cam BA50 MA55. Lon Coll of Div BD53 ALCD53. **d** 53 **p** 54. C Walthamstow St Mary *Chelmsf* 53-56; V E Ham St Paul 56-65; V Old Hill H Trin *Worc* 65-91; Hon Can Worc Cathl from 77. *The Vicarage, 35 Beeches Road, Rowley Regis, Warley, W Midlands B65 0AT* 021-559 7407

BROWNING, Robert Frank. b 11. K Coll Lon 56. **d** 57 **p** 58. V Lightwater *Guildf* 63-76; rtd 76; Perm to Offic

Guildf from 76. *Braeholme, Rectory Lane, Windlesham, Surrey GU20 6BW* Bagshot (0276) 74813

BROWNING, Thomas Clive. b 35. Lon Univ DipTh65 BD67. Wycliffe Hall Ox 63. **d** 67 **p** 68. C Ipswich St Jo *St E* 67-69; Chapl Scargill Ho N Yorkshire 69-70; C Downend *Bris* 70-73; C Hagley *Worc* 73-76; Asst Master Bay Ho Sch Gosport from 77; Perm to Offic *Portsm* from 82. *81 Oval Gardens, Gosport, Hants* Gosport (0705) 584738

BROWNING, Canon Wilfrid Robert Francis. b 18. Ch Ch Ox BA40 MA44 BD49. Cuddesdon Coll 40. **d** 41 **p** 42. Lect Cuddesdon Coll 65-70; Can Res Ch Ch *Ox* 65-87; Dir of Post-Ord Tr 65-85; Dir of Ords 65-85; Lect Wycliffe Hall Ox 67-69; Dir Ox NSM Course 72-89; rtd 87; Hon Can Ch Ch *Ox* from 87. *42 Alexandra Road, Oxford OX2 0DB* Oxford (0865) 723464

BROWNLESS, Brian Paish. b 25. TD72. Keble Coll Ox BA50 MA50. Wells Th Coll 50. **d** 52 **p** 53. Area Sec (Dio Lich) USPG 66-77; Lic to Offic *Lich* 66-77; CF (TA - R of O) 66-72; R Yoxall *Lich* 77-82; V S Ramsey *S & M* 82-87; rtd 87; Perm to Offic *Heref* from 87. *10 Caple Avenue, Kings Caple, Hereford HR1 4TX* Carey (0432) 840246

BROWNLESS, Philip Paul Stanley. b 19. Selw Coll Cam BA41 MA45. Ridley Hall Cam 46. **d** 47 **p** 48. Chapl & Hd Master Lambrook Sch Bracknell 54-71; V Heckfield cum Mattingley *Win* 71-74; V Heckfield w Mattingley and Rotherwick 74-84; RD Odiham 83-84; rtd 85; Perm to Offic *Chich* from 85. *The Hornpipe, Oakmeadow, Birdham, Chichester, W Sussex PO20 7BH* Birdham (0243) 512177

BROWNLIE, Caroline Heddon. b 47. CQSW75. St Jo Coll Nottm DPS80 Qu Coll Birm 81. **d** 87. Asst Chapl Fairfield Hosp Hitchin from 87. *8 Swan Street, Ashwell, Herts SG7 5NX* Hitchin (0462) 742611

BROWNRIDGE, Allan John Michael. b 32. Local NSM Course 80. **d** 82 **p** 83. C St Keverne *Truro* 82-86; P-in-c Werrington, St Giles in the Heath and Virginstow from 86. *The Vicarage, Werrington, Launceston, Cornwall PL15 8TP* Launceston (0566) 773932

BROWNRIGG, Canon Ronald Allen. b 19. Em Coll Cam BA47 MA50. Westcott Ho Cam 47. **d** 49 **p** 50. R Bletchingley *S'wark* 60-74; V Petersham 74-85; Hon Can S'wark Cathl 78-85; Consultant Inter-Ch Travel from 83; rtd 85. *6 Stoneleigh Lodge, Branston Road, Kew, Richmond, Surrey TW9 3LD* 081-940 3506

BROWNSELL, John Kenneth. b 48. Hertf Coll Ox BA69 BA72 MA89. Cuddesdon Coll 70. **d** 73 **p** 74. C Notting Hill All SS w St Columb *Lon* 73-74; C Notting Hill 74-76; TV 76-82; V Notting Hill All SS w St Columb from 82; AD Kensington from 84. *All Saints' Vicarage, Powis Gardens, London W11 1JG* 071-727 5919

BRUCE, David Ian. b 47. Univ of Wales (Cardiff) DipTh73. St Mich Coll Llan 70. **d** 73 **p** 74. C Bordesley St Benedict *Birm* 73-74; C Llanishen and Lisvane *Llan* 74-81; V Canley *Cov* 81-90; V Longford from 90. *St Thomas's Vicarage, Hurst Road, Coventry CV6 6EL* Coventry (0203) 364078

BRUCE, Francis Bernard. b 30. Trin Coll Ox BA52 MA56. Westcott Ho Cam 52. **d** 54 **p** 55. C Bury St Mary *Man* 54-59; C Sherborne w Castleton and Lillington *Sarum* 59-61; R Croston *Blackb* 61-86; V Bibury w Winson and Barnsley *Glouc* from 86. *The Vicarage, Bibury, Cirencester, Glos GL7 5NT* Bibury (028574) 387

BRUCE, James Hamilton. b 57. Newc Univ MSc79 Dur Univ BSc78. Trin Coll Bris DipTh84. **d** 84 **p** 85. C Walmley *Birm* 84-86; Perm to Offic *Carl* from 87; W Cumbria Sch Worker N Schs Chr Union from 87. *An Beannaich, Eaglesfield, Cockermouth, Cumbria CA13 0SP* Cockermouth (0900) 823074

BRUCE, John. b 26. **d** 50 **p** 51. V Carl St Herbert w St Steph *Carl* 66-74; P-in-c Kendal St Geo 74-76; V 76-83; V Coundon *Dur* 83-86; rtd 86; Perm to Offic *Carl* from 86. *9 Penton Close, Carlisle CA3 0PX*

BRUCE, Dr Leslie Barton. b 23. Liv Univ MB, ChB48. **d** 71 **p** 72. NSM Wavertree H Trin *Liv* from 71. *3 Childwall Park Avenue, Liverpool L16 0JE* 051-722 7664

BRUCE, Lewis Stewart. b 07. Sarum Th Coll 34. **d** 37 **p** 38. V Brockworth *Glouc* 54-75; rtd 76; P-in-c Bourton on the Hill *Glouc* 76-78; Hon C Hardwicke, Quedgeley and Elmore w Longney 78-87. *Sarum House, 1 Ryelands, Gloucester GL4 0QA* Gloucester (0452) 414292

BRUMPTON, Canon John Charles Kenyon. b 16. Selw Coll Cam BA38 MA42. Linc Th Coll 38. **d** 40 **p** 41. Chapl Asst Barnsley Gen Hosp 65-88; RD Barnsley *Wakef* 65-88; R Barnsley St Mary 66-88; Hon Can Wakef Cathl from 67; rtd 88; Perm to Offic *Linc* from 88.

Greenside, 199 Legsby Avenue, Grimsby, S Humberside DN32 0AD Grimsby (0472) 753258

BRUMWELL, Francis John Thomas. b 33. Lich Th Coll 57. d 61 p 62. C Birm St Geo *Birm* 61-63; C Gorton St Mark *Man* 63-64; V Calderbrook 65-73; V Bradley St Martin *Lich* 73-89; P-in-c Bilston St Mary 75-78; R Gorton St Phil *Man* from 89. *St Philip's Rectory, Lavington Grove, Gorton, Manchester M18 7ET* 061-231 2201

BRUNDLE, Michael Roy. b 52. Qu Coll Birm. d 84 p 85. C Swindon New Town *Bris* 84-88; TV Halifax *Wakef* from 88. *Holy Trinity Vicarage, 9 Love Lane, Halifax, W Yorkshire HX1 2BQ* Halifax (0422) 52446

BRUNDRITT, Cyril. b 17. AKC34. d 34 p 35. V Grateley cum Quarley *Win* 59-66; rtd 66; Perm to Offic *Win* from 67. *The Old Malt House, Middle Wallop, Stockbridge, Hants SO20 6ET* Andover (0264) 781353

BRUNING, Arthur Frederick. b 17. ALCD54. d 54 p 55. V Deptford St Luke *S'wark* 66-72; V Sprowle w Gt and Lt Palgrave *Nor* 72-81; rtd 81; Perm to Offic *Nor* from 81. *3 Adams Road, Norwich NR7 8QT* Norwich (0603) 400457

BRUNNER, William Thomas. b 47. K Coll Lon BD AKC. St Steph Ho Ox 83. d 85 p 86. C Clifton All SS w St Jo *Bris* 85-88; C Willesden Green St Andr and St Fran of Assisi *Lon* 88-90; rtd 90. *3 Cochrane Street, London NW8 7PA* 071-483 1827

BRUNNING, David George. b 32. Univ of Wales (Lamp) BA53. St Mich Coll Llan 53. d 55 p 56. C Llantwit Major and St Donat's *Llan* 55-59; C Usk and Monkswood w Glascoed Chpl and Gwehelog *Mon* 59-62; V Abercarn 62-71; V Llanfrechfa Upper 71-89; RD Pontypool from 89; R Panteg from 90. *Panteg Rectory, The Highway, New Inn, Pontypool, Gwent NP4 0PH* Pontypool (0495) 763724

BRUNNING, Neil. b 29. NW Ord Course 73. d 76 p 77. C Cheadle Hulme All SS *Ches* 76-79; V 79-88; V Glentworth *Linc* from 88; P-in-c Hemswell w Harpswell from 88. *The Vicarage, 1 Stoney Lane, Glentworth, Gainsborough, Lincs DN21 5DF* Gainsborough (0427) 73203

BRUNNING, Sidney John George. b 13. Ely Th Coll 46. d 49 p 50. R Sunningwell *Ox* 55-81; rtd 81; Perm to Offic *Nor* from 81. *Woodlands, Church Close, West Runton, Cromer, Norfolk NR27 9QY* West Runton (026375) 495

BRUNO, Allan David. b 34. AKC59. d 60 p 61. C Darlington H Trin *Dur* 60-64; S Africa 64-65 and 76-80; Rhodesia 65-70; Overseas Chapl Scottish Episc Ch 70-75; C Edin Old St Paul *Edin* 75-76; Namibia 80-86; Dean Windhoek 81-86; R Falkirk *Edin* from 86. *The Rectory, Kerse Lane, Falkirk FK1 1RX* Falkirk (0324) 23709

BRUNSDEN, Canon Maurice Calthorpe. b 21. St Paul's Grahamstown 48. d 49 p 50. S Africa 49-77; V Earley St Bart *Ox* 78-85; rtd 85; Perm to Offic *Ox* from 87. *12 Manchester Road, Reading, Berks RG1 3QW* Reading (0734) 666064

BRUNSDON, Canon Thomas Kenneth. b 08. Univ of Wales BA33. St Mich Coll Llan 33. d 34 p 35. V Newton St Pet *S & B* 61-76; rtd 76. *121 Homegower House, St Helen's Road, Swansea SA1 4DW* Swansea (0792) 463473

BRUNSWICK, Robert John. b 38. TD86. St Aid Birkenhead 60. d 63 p 64. C Neston *Ches* 63-66; CF (TA - R of O) from 65; C Warrington St Paul *Liv* 66-68; V Liv St Paul Stoneycroft 68-78; V Southport St Luke 78-87; R Croston *Blackb* from 87; Chapl Bp Rawstorne Sch Croston Preston from 88. *St Michael's Rectory, Croston, Preston PR5 7RR* Croston (0772) 600877

BRUNYEE, Miss Hilary. b 46. Linc Th Coll 76. dss 81 d 87. Longsight St Jo w St Cypr *Man* 81-87; Par Dn Peel from 87. *7 Trent Drive, Little Hulton, Worsley, Manchester M28 5TF* 061-790 7761

BRUSH, Sally. b 47. Lon Univ BD. Trin Coll Bris 73. dss 76 d 80. Flint *St As* 76-80; C 80-83; C Cefn 83-87; Chapl St As Cathl 83-87; C St As and Tremeirchion 83-87; Dn-in-c Cerrig-y-Drudion w Llanfihangel GM etc from 87. *The Rectory, Cerrigydrudion, Corwen, Clwyd LL21 0RU* Cerrigydrudion (049082) 313

BRUSSELS, Dean of. *See* HOLLAND, Rt Rev Edward

BRUTTON, Robert Springett. b 14. Trin Coll Cam BA34 MA55. Cuddesdon Coll 54. d 55 p 56. V Sonning *Ox* 65-74; rtd 79. *7 North Street, Langton Matravers, Swanage, Dorset BH19 3HL* Swanage (0929) 425681

BRYAN, Cecil William. b 43. TCD BA66 MA73. CITC 66. d 68 p 69. C Dub Zion Ch *D & G* 68-72; Chapl RAF 72-75; Dioc Info Officer *D & G* 75-90; I Castleknock w Mulhuddart, Clonsilla etc 75-89; Chapl K Hosp Sch Palmerstown Dub from 89. *King's Hospital School,*

Palmerstown, Dublin 20, Irish Republic Dublin (1) 626-5933

BRYAN, Charles Rigney. b 10. TCD BA47 MA50 Leeds Univ MA60. Bps' Coll Cheshunt 36. d 37 p 38. V Sheff St Nath *Sheff* 65-77; rtd 78. *Ormond Nursing Home, Elm Lane, Lane Top, Sheffield S5 7TW* Sheffield (0742) 456026

BRYAN, Dr David John. b 56. Liv Univ BSc77 Hull Univ BTh85 Qu Coll Ox DPhil89. Ox Min Course 89. d 90 p 91. C Abingdon *Ox* from 90. *33 Mattock Way, Abingdon, Oxon OX14 2PQ* Abingdon (0235) 555083

BRYAN, Leslie Harold. b 48. Div Hostel Dub 70. d 73 p 74. C Cork St Fin Barre's Cathl *C, C & R* 73-75; I Templebreedy w Tracton and Nohoval 75-79; CF from 79. *c/o MOD (Army), Bagshot Park, Bagshot, Surrey GU19 5PL* Bagshot (0276) 71717

BRYAN, Michael John Christopher. b 35. MSBiblLit MCBiblAA Wadh Coll Ox BA58 BTh59 MA63 Ex Univ PhD83. Ripon Hall Ox 59. d 60 p 61. C Reigate St Mark *S'wark* 60-64; Tutor Sarum & Wells Th Coll 64-69; Vice-Prin 69-71; USA 71-74; Sen Officer Educn and Community Dept *Lon* 74-79; Chapl Ex Univ *Ex* from 79. *6 Park Place, St Leonard's, Exeter EX4 4QJ* Exeter (0392) 215675

BRYAN, Nigel Arthur. b 39. Univ of Wales (Lamp) BA61. d 63 p 64. C Llanstadwell *St D* 63-69; Chapl RAF from 69. *c/o MOD, Adastral House, Theobald's Road, London WC1X 8RU* 071-430 7268

BRYAN, Patrick Joseph. b 41. St Jo Coll Cam BA63 MA67. St Steph Ho Ox 73. d 75 p 76. C Rushall *Lich* 75-78; C Brierley Hill 78-80; P-in-c Walsall St Mary and All SS Palfrey 80-87. *49 Hawthorn Road, Shelfield, Walsall* Walsall (0922) 963234

BRYAN, Canon Percival John Milward. b 19. St Pet Coll Ox BA40 MA46 BTh47. Wycliffe Hall Ox 46. d 48 p 49. R Kings Cliffe *Pet* 56-85; Can Pet Cathl 73-86; rtd 86; Perm to Offic Pet from 86; Linc from 91. *3 Saxon Road, Barnack, Stamford, Lincs PE9 3EQ* Stamford (0780) 740906

BRYAN, Philip Richard. b 40. Dur Univ BA61. Wycliffe Hall Ox 72. d 74 p 75. C Macclesfield St Mich *Ches* 74-77; V St Bees *Carl* from 77; Chapl St Bees Sch Cumbria from 77; RD Calder *Carl* from 88. *The Priory, St Bees, Cumbria CA27 0DR* Egremont (0946) 822279

BRYAN, Sherry Lee. b 49. W Midl Minl Tr Course 88. d 91. C St Columb Minor and St Colan *Truro* from 91. *46 Willow Close, Quintrell Downs, Newquay* Newquay (0637) 851936

BRYAN, Thomas John. b 06. St D Coll Lamp BA48. d 49 p 50. V Tremeirchion *St As* 68-76; rtd 76. *Bryn Haf, Cae Glas Estate, Trefnant, Denbigh, Clwyd* Trefnant (074574) 279

BRYAN, Timothy James Bryan. b 23. d 54 p 55. C Weybridge *Guildf* 54-57; Lebanon from 65. *PO Box 4008, Beirut, Lebanon*

BRYAN, William Terence. b 38. Chich Th Coll 73. d 75 p 76. C Shrewsbury St Giles *Lich* 75-79; V Churchstoke w Hyssington and Sarn *Heref* from 79. *The Vicarage, Church Stoke, Montgomery, Powys SY15 6AF* Church Stoke (05885) 228

BRYANS, Joseph. b 15. TCD BA39 MA43. CITC 40. d 42 p 43. I Tamlaghtard w Aghanloo *D & R* 60-90; rtd 90. *4 Duncrun Road, Limavady, Co Londonderry BT49 0JD* Bellarena (05047) 50239

BRYANT, Andrew Watts. b 57. MA. Qu Coll Birm. d 83 p 84. C Pelsall *Lich* 83-87; Perm to Offic from 87. *Kaleidoscope Theatre, 19 Mellish Road, Walsall WS4 2DQ* Walsall (0922) 642751

BRYANT, Canon Christopher. b 32. AKC60. d 61 p 62. C Fareham H Trin *Portsm* 61-65; C Yatton Keynell *Bris* 65-71; V Chirton, Marden and Patney *Sarum* 71-76; V Chirton, Marden, Patney, Charlton and Wilsford 76-78; P-in-c Devizes St Jo w St Mary 78-79; R from 79; RD Devizes from 83; Can and Preb Sarum Cathl from 87. *The Rectory, Long Street, Devizes, Wilts SN10 1NS* Devizes (0380) 723705

BRYANT, Christopher John. b 62. Mansf Coll Ox BA83 MA87. Ripon Coll Cuddesdon 83. d 86 p 87. C High Wycombe *Ox* 86-89; Youth Chapl Pet 89-91. *1st Floor Flat, The Blockmakers Arms, 133 Shepherdess Walk, London N1*

BRYANT, David Charles. b 48. St Andr Univ BSc71. St Mich Coll Llan 71. d 74 p 75. C Llanilid w Pencoed *Llan* 74-78; C Caerphilly 78-79; V Crynant 79-84; V Llanegryn and Llanfihangel-y-Pennant w Talyllyn *Ban* from 84. *The Vicarage, Llanegryn, Tywyn, Gwynedd LL36 9SS* Tywyn (0654) 710320

BRYANT, David Henderson. b 37. K Coll Lon BD60 AKC60. d 61 p 62. C Trowbridge H Trin *Sarum*

61-63; C Ewell *Guildf* 63-67; V Leiston *St E* 67-73; Chapl RN 73; P-in-c Northam w Westward Ho and Appledore *Ex* 74-75; P-in-c Clavering w Langley *Chelmsf* 76-77; Teacher Mountview High Sch Harrow 77-85; P-in-c Boosbeck w Moorsholm *York* 85-89; V 89-90; V Sowerby from 90; P-in-c Sessay from 90. *The Vicarage, The Close, Sowerby, Thirsk, N Yorkshire YO7 1JA* Thirsk (0845) 523546

BRYANT, Donald Thomas. b 29. FSS59 SE Essex Coll BSc56 Birkb Coll Lon BSc58. S'wark Ord Course 85. d 88 p 89. NSM Redhill St Matt *S'wark* from 88. *21 Windermere Way, Reigate, Surrey RH2 0LW* Redhill (0737) 762382

BRYANT, Canon Douglas William. b 17. St Boniface Warminster. d 41 p 42. V Burpham *Guildf* 57-70; V Egham Hythe 70-75; Hon Can Guildf Cathl 70-83; R Fetcham 75-83; rtd 83; Perm to Offic *Guildf* from 83. *4 Clandon Road, Guildford GU1 2DR* Guildford (0483) 572682

BRYANT, Edgar James. b 28. Univ of Wales (Swansea) BA49. St Mich Coll Llan 49. d 51 p 52. C Brynmawr *S & B* 51-55; C Llandrindod w Cefnllys 55-59; V Bettws Disserth w Llansantffraed in Elwell 59-73; V Disserth 59-68; Perm to Offic *Heref* 70-73 and 82-86; C Aymestrey and Leinthall Earles w Wigmore etc 73-82 and Priest (w Past Care) from 86. *The Vicarage, Wigmore, Leominster, Herefordshire HR6 9UW* Wigmore (056886) 272

BRYANT, Edward Francis Paterson. b 43. Man Univ BA64 Golds Coll Lon CertEd65 Lille Univ LesL67 Lon Univ DipRS78 City Univ MBA82. S'wark Ord Course 75. d 78 p 79. NSM Hadlow *Roch* 78-84; C Dartford St Alb 84-87; R Hollington St Leon *Chich* from 87. *The Rectory, Tile Barn Road, St Leonards-on-Sea, E Sussex TN38 9PA* Hastings (0424) 852257

BRYANT, Graham Trevor. b 41. Keble Coll Ox BA63 DipTh64 MA67. Chich Th Coll 64. d 66 p 67. C Leeds St Wilfrid *Ripon* 66-69; C Haywards Heath St Wilfrid *Chich* 69-74; V Crawley Down All SS 74-79; V Bexhill St Aug 79-85; V Charlton Kings St Mary *Glouc* from 85. *63 Church Street, Charlton Kings, Cheltenham, Glos GL53 8AT* Cheltenham (0242) 580067

BRYANT, Mark Watts. b 49. St Jo Coll Dur BA72. Cuddesdon Coll 72. d 75 p 76. C Addlestone *Guildf* 75-79; C Studley *Sarum* 79-83; V 83-88; Chapl Trowbridge Coll 79-83; Voc Development Adv *Cov* from 88. *35 Wood Lane, Shilton, Coventry CV7 9LA* Coventry (0203) 617512

BRYANT, Max Gordon. b 09. Univ of NZ BA30 MA31 Lon Univ BD34. d 32 p 33. V Northaw *St Alb* 51-78; rtd 78; Perm to Offic *St D* from 78. *Llanina, Aberporth, Cardigan, Dyfed SA43 2EY* Aberporth (0239) 810124

BRYANT, Michael Hedley. b 39. St Chad's Coll Dur BA62 DipTh64. d 64 p 65. C Brighton St Paul *Chich* 64-67; Dean's V Lich Cathl 67-70; VC York Minster *York* 70-73; C Cheam *S'wark* 73-76; V Copmanthorpe *York* 76-79; C-in-c Stockton St Mark CD *Dur* 82-83; V Stockton St Mark 83-86; V Bordesley SS Alb and Patr *Birm* from 86. *St Alban's Vicarage, Stanhope Street, Birmingham B12 0XB* 021-440 4605

BRYANT, Patricia Ann. b 46. d 91. NSM Llanbadoc *Mon* from 91. *Island House, Usk, Gwent NP5 1SY* Usk (02913) 2082

BRYANT, Richard Kirk. b 47. Ch Coll Cam BA68 MA72 Nottm Univ DipTh70. Cuddesdon Coll 70. d 72 p 73. C Newc St Gabr *Newc* 72-75; C Morpeth 75-78; C Benwell St Jas 78-82; V Earsdon and Backworth from 82. *Earsdon Vicarage, 5 Front Street, Whitley Bay, Tyne & Wear NE25 9JU* 091-252 9393

BRYANT, Royston George. b 09. St Aid Birkenhead 54. d 56 p 57. V Fishponds All SS *Bris* 69-76; rtd 76; Perm to Offic *Bris* from 76. *2 Beaufort, Harford Drive, Bristol BS16 1NP* Bristol (0272) 564874

BRYANT, Sidney John. b 29. Linc Coll Ox BA52 MA56. St Steph Ho Ox 52. d 54 p 55. C Southgate St Andr *Lon* 54-58; C Tottenham Ch Ch W Green 58-60; V New Southgate St Paul 60-71; R Gt Leighs *Chelmsf* from 71. *The Rectory, Boreham Road, Great Leighs, Chelmsford CM3 1PP* Chelmsford (0245) 361218

BRYANT, William George. b 22. Selw Coll Cam MA48. St Alb Minl Tr Scheme 78. d 81 p 82. NSM Welwyn w Ayot St Peter *St Alb* 81-82; NSM Balsall Heath St Paul *Birm* 82-85; P-in-c Teme Valley S *Worc* 85-89; rtd 89. *28 De Havilland Way, Christchurch, Dorset BH23 3JE* Christchurch (0202) 499231

BRYARS, Peter John. b 54. BA MEd PhD. St Jo Coll Nottm. d 84 p 85. C Kingston upon Hull St Martin *York* 84; C Hull St Martin w Transfiguration 84-87; TV Drypool 87-90; TV Glendale Gp *Newc* from 90. *Church House, 2 Queens Road, Wooler, Northd NE71 6DR* Wooler (0668) 81468

BRYCE, Michael Adrian Gilpin. b 47. TCD BA. CITC 74. d 77 p 78. C Dub Ch Ch Cathl Gp *D & G* 77-79; Chapl Univ Coll Dub 79-82; I Ardamine w Kiltennel, Glascarrig etc *C & O* 82-84; CF from 84. *c/o MOD (Army), Bagshot Park, Bagshot, Surrey GU19 5PL* Bagshot (0276) 71717

BRYER, Anthony Colin. b 51. Lon Univ BSc72 Bris Univ DipTh75. Trin Coll Bris 72. d 75 p 76. C Preston St Cuth *Blackb* 75-78; C Becontree St Mary *Chelmsf* 78-81; TV Loughton St Mary and St Mich 81-88; C Clifton St Paul *Bris* from 88. *9 Leigh Road, Clifton, Bristol BS8 2DA* Bristol (0272) 737427

BRYER, Paul Donald. b 58. Sussex Univ BEd80. St Jo Coll Nottm DipTh90. d 90 p 91. C Tonbridge St Steph *Roch* from 90. *35 Waterloo Road, Tonbridge, Kent TN9 2SW*

BUBBERS, David Bramwell. b 23. Lambeth MA84 Oak Hill Th Coll 51. d 54 p 55. V Northwood Em *Lon* 65-74; Perm to Offic *St Alb* from 74; Lic to Offic *Lon* from 74; Gen Sec CPAS 74-88; rtd 88. *2 Earlsmead Court, 15 Granville Road, Eastbourne, E Sussex BN20 7HE* Eastbourne (0323) 37077

BUBBINGS, Charles Gardam. b 26. Qu Coll Birm 68. d 69 p 70. C Scarborough St Mary w Ch Ch, St Paul and St Thos *York* 69-72; C Fulford 72-74; V Middlesb St Oswald 74-81; V Ringley *Man* 81-88; rtd 88; Perm to Offic *Man* from 88. *4 Hilton Grove, Worsley, Manchester M28 5SX* 061-702 9402

BUCHAN, Ven Eric Ancrum. b 07. St Chad's Coll Dur BA32. d 33 p 34. Adn Cov 65-77; rtd 77; Perm to Offic *Glouc* from 78. *6B Millers Green, Gloucester GL1 2BN* Gloucester (0452) 415944

BUCHANAN, Barrington Cromwell. b 51. Univ of W Indies BA(Theol)81 DipEd82 Birm Univ MEd91. W Indies United Th Coll DMinlStuds81. d 81 p 84. Jamaica 81-91; Perm to Offic *Birm* from 91. *College of the Ascension, Weoley Park Road, Birmingham B29 6RD* 021-472 1667

✠**BUCHANAN, Rt Rev Colin Ogilvie.** b 34. Linc Coll Ox MA. Tyndale Hall Bris 59. d 61 p 62 c 85. C Cheadle *Ches* 61-64; Tutor St Jo Coll Nottm 64-85; Lib 64-69; Registrar 69-74; Dir of Studies 74-75; Vice-Prin 75-78; Prin 79-85; Hon Can S'well Minster *S'well* 81-85; Suff Bp Aston *Birm* 85-89; Asst Bp Roch from 89; V Gillingham St Mark from 91; Asst Bp S'wark from 90. *St Mark's Vicarage, 173 Canterbury Street, Gillingham, Kent ME7 5UA* Medway (0634) 51818

BUCHANAN, Canon Eric. b 32. Leeds Univ BA54. Coll of Resurr Mirfield 54. d 56 p 57. C Cov St Mark *Cov* 56-59; Asst Chapl Lon Univ *Lon* 59-64; C Bloomsbury St Geo w St Jo 59-64; V Duston *Pet* 64-79; RD Wootton 75-79; Can Pet Cathl from 77; V Wellingborough All Hallows 79-90; V Higham Ferrers w Chelveston from 90. *The Vicarage, Higham Ferrers, Wellingborough, Northants NN9 8DL* Rushden (0933) 312433

BUCHANAN, Canon Frank. b 03. St Edm Hall Ox BA25 MA29. Cuddesdon Coll 25. d 26 p 27. Hon Can Birm Cathl *Birm* 57-71; V Sutton Coldfield St Columba 65-71; rtd 71. *Greenwood, Oakdene Road, Godalming, Surrey GU7 1QF* Godalming (0483) 417406

BUCHANAN, George Rowland. b 15. St Aug Coll Cant. d 59 p 60. R Gt Wishford *Sarum* 67-73; R Lt Langford 67-73; RD Wylye and Wilton 69-73; Org Sec (Dios Ex and B & W) CECS 73-77; Perm to Offic *Sarum* from 77; rtd 80. *Cobblers, Greenhill, Sherborne, Dorset DT9 4EP* Sherborne (0935) 812263

BUCK, Eric Joseph. b 14. Lon Univ BA35 DipEd54. Ridley Hall Cam 60. d 61 p 62. V Wicklewood and Crownthorpe *Nor* 62-79; P-in-c Deopham w Hackford 75-79; rtd 79; Perm to Offic *Nor* from 80. *62 Chapel Lane, Wymondham, Norfolk NR18 0DL* Wymondham (0953) 602153

BUCK, Nicholas John. b 57. BScEng. Ridley Hall Cam 81. d 84 p 85. C Oakwood St Thos *Lon* 84-87; C Attercliffe *Sheff* 87-90; C Darnall H Trin 87-90; C Kimberworth from 90. *331 Kimberworth Road, Kimberworth, Rotherham, S Yorkshire S61 1HD* Rotherham (0709) 554441

BUCK, Canon Richard Peter Holdron. b 37. AKC64. d 65 p 66. C Mill Hill Jo Keble Ch *Lon* 65-68; C St Marylebone All SS 68-74; Can Res and Treas Truro Cathl *Truro* 74-76; V Primrose Hill St Mary w Avenue Road St Paul *Lon* 76-84; Bp's Ecum Adv *S'wark* 84-91; P-in-c Dulwich Common St Pet 84-86; Hon Can S'wark Cathl from 90; C Rotherhithe St Kath w St Barn from 91. *30 Rotherhithe New Road, London SE16 2AP* 071-237 9244

BUCK, William Ashley. b 61. Man Univ BA82 Ox Univ BA86. Ripon Coll Cuddesdon 84. **d** 87 **p** 88. C Addington *S'wark* from 87. *56 Viney Bank, Courtwood Lane, Croydon CR0 9JT* 081-657 2478

BUCKETT, Canon James Frederick. b 27. ACP. Roch Th Coll 60. **d** 62 **p** 63. C Rowner *Portsm* 62-64; Lic to Offic 64-66; Chapl Highbury Tech Coll Portsm 64-66; V St Helens *Portsm* 66-72; CF (TA) from 72; V Newport St Thos *Portsm* from 72; Hon Can Portsm Cathl from 81. *The Vicarage, Mount Pleasant Road, Newport, Isle of Wight PO30 1ES* Isle of Wight (0983) 522733

BUCKINGHAM, Ven Hugh Fletcher. b 32. Hertf Coll Ox BA57 MA60. Westcott Ho Cam 55. **d** 57 **p** 58. C St Thos *Man* 57-60; C Sheff St Silas *Sheff* 60-65; V Hindolveston *Nor* 65-70; V Guestwick 65-70; R Fakenham w Alethorpe 70-88; Chmn Dioc Bd Soc Resp 81-88; RD Burnham and Walsingham 81-87; Hon Can Nor Cathl 85-88; Adn E Riding *York* from 88. *Brimley Lodge, 27 Molescroft Road, Beverley, N Humberside HU17 7DX* Hull (0482) 881659

BUCKINGHAM, Patrick Anthony. b 34. St Steph Ho Ox. **d** 62 **p** 86. C Elland *Wakef* 62-66; Novice CSWG 66-69; Hon C Nor St Mary Magd w St Jas *Nor* 69-73; Hon C Wandsworth St Faith *S'wark* 73-77; Shrine of Our Lady Walsingham 77-78; CSWG from 78. *The Monastery, 23 Cambridge Road, Hove, E Sussex BN3 1DE*

BUCKINGHAM, Richard Arthur John. b 49. Univ of Wales (Cardiff) BA71 PGCE72. Chich Th Coll 73. **d** 76 **p** 77. C Llantwit Major *Llan* 76-80; C Leigh-on-Sea St Marg *Chelmsf* 80-84; C Westmr St Matt *Lon* 84-87; R Stock Harvard *Chelmsf* from 87. *The Rectory, 61 High Street, Stock, Ingatestone, Essex CM4 9BN* Stock (0277) 840453

BUCKINGHAM, Archdeacon of. See MORRISON, Ven John Anthony

BUCKINGHAM, Area Bishop of. See BURROWS, Rt Rev Simon Hedley

BUCKLAND, Geoffrey Douglas. b 36. Lon Univ DipTh61. Clifton Th Coll 59. **d** 62 **p** 63. C Spitalfields Ch Ch w All SS *Lon* 62-68; C Romford Gd Shep Collier Row *Chelmsf* 68-71; V Kirkdale St Lawr *Liv* 71-85; V Grassendale from 85. *St Mary's Vicarage, 22 Eaton Road, Liverpool L19 0PW* 051-427 1474

BUCKLE, Graham Martin. b 62. Southn Univ BTh89. Sarum & Wells Th Coll 85. **d** 89 **p** 90. C Paddington St Jas *Lon* from 89. *16 Crastock Court, 7/9 Queens Gardens, London W2 3BA* 071-724 2881

BUCKLER, George Anthony (Tony). b 35. Open Univ BA74. Lich Th Coll 58. **d** 61 **p** 62. C Old Swinford *Worc* 61-65; C Droitwich St Nic w St Pet 65-67; C Droitwich St Andr w St Mary 65-67; Chapl Claybury Hosp Woodford Bridge 67-78; St Geo and Co Hosps Linc 78-87; Lawn Hosp Linc 78-81; Wexham Park Hosp Slough 87-90; Chapl Nottm Mental Illness & Psychiatric Unit and Mapperley and Community Hosp Nottm from 90. *The Chaplaincy, Mapperley Hospital, Porchester Road, Nottingham NG3 6AA* Nottingham (0602) 691300

BUCKLER, Guy Ernest Warr. b 46. ACA69 FCA79. Linc Th Coll 71. **d** 74 **p** 75. C Dunstable *St Alb* 74-77; C Houghton Regis 77-86; TV Willington Team *Newc* 86-88; TR from 88. *The Vicarage, 2 Burlington Court, Wallsend, Tyne & Wear NE28 9YH* 091-263 7922

BUCKLER, Canon Peter. b 17. OBE79. Lon Univ BSc38. Linc Th Coll. **d** 66 **p** 67. R Grendon *Birm* 68-71; P-in-c Burton Dassett *Cov* 71-74; Hon Can Cov Cathl 76-83; P-in-c Baxterley w Hurley and Wood End and Merevale etc *Birm* 80-83; rtd 83; Perm to Offic Cov and Birm from 83. *9 St Michael's Close, Atherstone, Warks CV9 1LU* Atherstone (0827) 712627

BUCKLER, Philip John Warr. b 49. St Pet Coll Ox BA70 MA74. Cuddesdon Coll 70. **d** 72 **p** 73. C Bushey Heath *St Alb* 72-75; Chapl Trin Coll Cam 75-81; Min Can and Sacr St Paul's Cathl *Lon* 81-87; V Hampstead St Jo from 87. *The Vicarage, 14 Church Row, London NW3 6UU* 071-435 0553

BUCKLEY, Alan. b 40. Tyndale Hall Bris. **d** 67 **p** 68. C Owlerton *Sheff* 67-70; C Mansf St Pet *S'well* 70-73; C Charlesworth *Derby* 73-75; P-in-c Whitfield 76-84; V Moldgreen *Wakef* 84-90; V Hadfield *Derby* from 90. *St Andrew's Vicarage, 122 Hadfield Road, Hadfield, Hyde, Cheshire SK14 8DR* Glossop (0457) 852431

BUCKLEY, Alexander Christopher. b 67. **d** 91. C Llandudno *Ban* from 91. *The Parsonage, Morfa Road, West Shore, Llandudno, Gwynedd*

BUCKLEY, Alfred John. b 07. St Pet Coll Jamaica 37. **d** 37 **p** 38. V Mottingham St Edw *S'wark* 58-73; rtd 73. *Maresk Vasparth Road, Crantock, Newquay, Cornwall TR8 5RQ*

BUCKLEY, Basil Foster. b 11. Dorchester Miss Coll. **d** 38 **p** 39. R Salford St Ignatius *Man* 42-81; rtd 82; Hon C Salford St Paul w Ch Ch *Man* from 82. *22 Alresford Road, Salford M6 7RF* 061-743 1420

BUCKLEY, Christopher Ivor. b 48. Chich Th Coll. **d** 86 **p** 87. C Felpham w Middleton *Chich* 86-89; C Jersey St Brelade *Win* from 89; Chapl HM Pris Jersey from 90. *The Parsonage, High Street, St Aubin, Jersey, Channel Islands* Jersey (0534) 44009

BUCKLEY, David Rex. b 47. Ripon Coll Cuddesdon 75. **d** 77 **p** 78. C Witton *Ches* 77-81; V Backford 81-85; Youth Chapl from 81; V Barnton from 85. *The Vicarage, Barnton, Northwich, Cheshire CW8 4JH* Northwich (0606) 74358

BUCKLEY, Canon Derek Haslam. b 17. Bps' Coll Cheshunt 52. **d** 54 **p** 55. V Scropton *Derby* 67-73; R Boylestone 67-73; HM Det Cen Foston Hall 67-73; RD Longford *Derby* 71-81; P-in-c Ch Broughton w Boylestone & Sutton on the Hill 73-76; V 76-83; P-in-c Dalbury, Long Lane and Trusley 77-83; Hon Can Derby Cathl 79-83; rtd 83; Perm to Offic *Derby* from 83. *St Oswald's House, Belle Vue Road, Ashbourne, Derbyshire DE6 1AT* Ashbourne (0335) 45155

BUCKLEY, Ernest Fairbank. b 25. Jes Coll Cam BA49 MA50. Jes Coll Ox BLitt53. Westcott Ho Cam 55. **d** 55 **p** 56. V Baguley *Man* 64-79; V Clun w Chapel Lawn, Bettws-y-Crwyn and Newc *Heref* 79-87; RD Clun Forest 82-87; rtd 88. *Hawthorn Bank, Clunton, Craven Arms, Shropshire SY7 0HP* Little Brampton (05887) 281

BUCKLEY, Michael. b 49. St Jo Coll Dur Cranmer Hall Dur 77. **d** 79 **p** 80. C Birkdale St Jo *Liv* 79-82; TV Maghull 82-88; V Earlestown from 88. *The Vicarage, 63 Market Street, Newton-le-Willows, Merseyside WA12 9BS* Newton-le-Willows (0925) 224771

BUCKLEY, Canon Michael Richard. b 20. Lon Univ BD42 AKC42. Cuddesdon Coll 42. **d** 43 **p** 44. R Weybridge *Guildf* 67-85; Hon Can Guildf Cathl 76-85; rtd 85; Perm to Offic *Chelmsf* from 85; Ely from 86. *Bourn Cottage, High Street, Great Chesterford, Saffron Walden, Essex CB10 1PL* Saffron Walden (0799) 30398

BUCKLEY, Richard Francis. b 44. Ripon Hall Ox 69. **d** 72 **p** 73. C Portsea' St Cuth *Portsm* 72-75; C Portsea All SS w St Jo Rudmore 75-79; Chapl RN from 79. *c/o MOD, Lacon House, Theobald's Road, London WC1X 8RY* 071-430 6847

BUCKLEY, Dr Richard John. b 43. Hull Univ BSc64 PhD87 Strathclyde Univ MSc69. Sarum Th Coll 64. **d** 66 **p** 67. C Huddersfield St Jo *Wakef* 66-68; C Sutton St Jas *York* 69-71; TV Sutton St Jas and Wawne 71-75; V Handsworth Woodhouse *Sheff* 75-85; R Adwick-le-Street from 85. *The Rectory, Adwick-le-Street, Doncaster, S Yorkshire DN6 7AD* Doncaster (0302) 723224

BUCKLEY, Robert William. b 50. MInstP75 CPhys75 MCollP83 MInstE90 Grey Coll Dur BSc70 PhD73. N Ord Course 85. **d** 87 **p** 88. Hd Teacher Twyford High Sch Ealing from 86; NSM N Greenford All Hallows *Lon* from 87. *68 Robin Hood Way, Greenford, Middx UB6 7QN* 081-902 7448

BUCKLEY, Stephen Richard. b 45. Cranmer Hall Dur 82. **d** 84 **p** 85. C Iffley *Ox* 84-88; TV Halesowen *Worc* from 88. *St Margaret's Vicarage, 55 Quarry Lane, Halesowen, W Midlands B63 4PD* 021-550 8744

BUCKLEY, Timothy Denys. b 57. BA. St Jo Coll Nottm DipTh. **d** 83 **p** 84. C S Westoe *Dur* 83-85; C Paddington Em Harrow Road *Lon* 85-88; C Binley *Cov* from 88; Min Binley Woods LEP from 88. *20 Daneswood Road, Coventry CV3 2BJ* Coventry (0203) 543003

BUCKLEY, Wyndham Awdry. b 13. St Boniface Warminster 34. **d** 37 **p** 38. V Langham *Pet* 67-79; Chapl HM Pris Ashwell 67-79; rtd 79; Perm to Offic *Pet* from 85. *8 Uppingham Road, Oakham, Leics* Oakham (0572) 56844

BUCKMAN, Rossly David. b 36. TCD BA64 MA67 St Pet Coll Ox BA65. Moore Th Coll Sydney ACT ThL59. **d** 59 **p** 60. Australia 59-61 and 76-80 and from 89; C Dub Harold's Cross *D & G* 61-64; C Ox St Mich *Ox* 64-65; Lect Th Bris Univ 65-69; Lic to Offic *Bris* 65-69; CF 69-76; P-in-c Mid Marsh Gp *Linc* 81-82; R 82-89. *St Martin's Rectory, 9 Centre Street, Blakehurst, Sydney, NSW, Australia 2221* Sydney (2) 546-6523

BUCKMASTER, Charles. b 20. St Jo Coll Dur BA50. Wells Th Coll 50. **d** 51 **p** 52. Prin St Pet Coll Birm 68-78; Cyprus 78-82; P-in-c Viney Hill *Glouc* 82-89; rtd 89. *Rose Cottage, Church Walk, Viney Hill, Lydney, Glos GL15 4NY* Dean (0594) 510435

BUCKMASTER, Cuthbert Harold Septimus. b 03. Cuddesdon Coll 25. **d** 26 **p** 27. R Chagford *Ex* 59-71; rtd 71. *47 Carlyle Street, Byron Bay, NSW, Australia 2481*

BUCKNALL, Allan. b 35. ALCD62. Lon Coll of Div 62. **d** 62 **p** 63. C Harlow New Town w Lt Parndon *Chelmsf* 62-69; Chapl W Somerset Miss to Deaf 69-71; Perm to Offic *Bris* 71-77; P-in-c Wisborough Green *Chich* 77-79; R Tillington 78-86; R Duncton 82-86; R Up Waltham 82-86; C Henfield w Shermanbury and Woodmancote 86-89; Asst Chapl Princess Marg Hosp Swindon from 89. *7 Vicarage Lane, Highworth, Swindon, Wilts SN5 7AD*

BUCKNALL, Miss Ann Gordon. b 32. K Coll Lon BSc53 Hughes Hall Cam DipEd54. Qu Coll Birm 80. **dss** 81 **d** 87. Birm St Aid Small Heath *Birm* 81-85; Balsall Heath St Paul 85-87; Par Dn from 87. *51 Alpha Close, Birmingham B12 9HF* 021-440 7867

BUCKNALL, William John. b 44. Lon Univ DipTh67. Kelham Th Coll 63. **d** 68 **p** 69. C Carl H Trin *Carl* 68-71; C Baswich (or Berkswich) *Lich* 71-73; P-in-c Ilam w Blore Ray and Okeover 73-76; V Wednesbury St Paul Wood Green 76-84; RD Wednesbury 78-84; TR Wordsley 84-90. *198 The Broadway, Dudley DY1 3DR* Dudley (0384) 214047

BUCKNER, Richard Pentland. b 37. Keble Coll Ox BA61 MA64. Wells Th Coll 60. **d** 62 **p** 63. C Crediton *Ex* 62-65; C Ex St Matt 65-66; Chapl Grenville Coll Bideford 66-74; Lic to Offic *Ex* 66-74; S'well 74-82; Chapl Worksop Coll Notts 74-82; Chapl Merchant Taylors' Sch Northwood and St Helen's Sch Northwood 82-91; Lic to Offic *Lon* & *St Alb* from 82; Chapl Gresham's Sch Holt from 91. *c/o Gresham's School, Holt, Norfolk* Holt (0263) 713271

BUCKS, Michael William. b 40. K Coll Lon BD63 AKC63. **d** 64 **p** 65. C Workington St Mich *Carl* 64-69; Chapl RN from 69. *c/o MOD, Lacon House, Theobald's Road, London WC1X 8RY* 071-430 6847

BUDD, John Christopher. b 51. DLIS QUB BA73 TCD DipTh82. **d** 82 **p** 83. C Ballymena *Conn* 82-85; C Jordanstown w Monkstown 85-88; I Craigs w Dunaghy and Killagan from 88; RD Ballymena from 89. *Craigs Rectory, 95 Hillmount Road, Cullybackey, Ballymena, Co Antrim BT42 1NZ* Cullybackey (0266) 880248

BUDD, John Victor. b 31. CCC Ox BA55 MA58. Bps' Coll Cheshunt 57. **d** 59 **p** 60. C Friern Barnet St Jas *Lon* 59-64; C Harrow Weald All SS 64-70; Lic to Offic *St Alb* 70-73; V Lt Amwell from 73; RD Hertf 83-88. *The Vicarage, 17 Barclay Close, Hertford Heath, Hertford SG13 7RW* Hertford (0992) 589140

BUDD, Philip John. b 40. Bris Univ PhD78. Cranmer Hall Dur BA63 DipTh65 MLitt71. **d** 66 **p** 67. C Attenborough w Chilwell *S'well* 66-69; Lect Clifton Th Coll 69-71; Lect Trin Coll Bris 72-80; Tutor Ripon Coll Cuddesdon 80-88; Tutor Westmr Coll Ox from 80; Lect from 88. *Westminster College, Oxford OX2 9AT* Oxford (0865) 242788

BUDDEN, Clive John. b 39. Chich Th Coll. **d** 84 **p** 86. C Gaywood, Bawsey and Mintlyn *Nor* 84-87; TV Brixham w Churston Ferrers and Kingswear *Ex* 87-90; R Exton and Winsford and Cutcombe w Luxborough *B & W* from 90. *The Rectory, Winsford, Minehead, Somerset TA24 7JE* Winsford (064385) 301

BUDGE, Leonard Percival. b 11. Dur Univ LTh40. St Aug Coll Cant 37. **d** 40 **p** 41. V Frithelstock *Ex* 64-76; V Monkleigh 64-76; V Littleham 70-76; rtd 76; Perm to Offic *Ex* from 76. *2 Chestnut Close, Braunton, Devon EX33 2EH* Braunton (0271) 814313

BUDGELL, Peter Charles. b 50. Lon Univ BD. **d** 83 **p** 84. C Goodmayes All SS *Chelmsf* 83-86; C Chipping Barnet w Arkley *St Alb* 86-88; V Luton St Anne from 88. *The Vicarage, 7 Blaydon Road, Luton LU2 0RP* Luton (0582) 20052

BUDGELL, Rosemary Anne. b 51. Lon Bible Coll BD73 CertEd76. **dss** 83 **d** 87. Goodmayes All SS *Chelmsf* 83-86; Chipping Barnet w Arkley *St Alb* 86-87; Hon Par Dn 87-88; Hon Par Dn Luton St Anne from 88. *7 Blaydon Road, Luton, Beds LU2 0RP* Luton (0582) 20052

BUDGETT, Preb Anthony Thomas. b 26. TD60. Or Coll Ox BA50 MA57. Wells Th Coll 57. **d** 59 **p** 60. V Somerton *B & W* 68-80; RD Ilchester 72-81; P-in-c Compton Dundon 76-80; R Somerton w Compton Dundon 80-81; R Somerton w Compton Dundon, the Charltons etc 81-84; Preb Wells Cathl 83-90; P-in-c Bruton w Lamyatt, Wyke and Redlynch 84-85; P-in-c Batcombe w Upton Noble 84-85; P-in-c S w N Brewham 84-85; TR Bruton and Distr 85-90; rtd 90; Perm to Offic *Ex* from 90. *Cornerways, White Ball, Wellington, Somerset TA21 0LS*

BUDGETT, Robert Brackenbury. b 08. Ch Coll Cam BA30 MA34 DIC31. Ridley Hall Cam 34. **d** 36 **p** 37. R Overstrand *Nor* 61-73; rtd 73; P-in-c Salle *Nor* 74-78; Perm to Offic from 79. *Bellamy Cottage, Mill Yard,*

Burnham Market, King's Lynn, Norfolk PE31 8HH Fakenham (0328) 738342

BUFFEE, Canon Leslie John. b 30. AKC53 Open Univ BA88. **d** 54 **p** 55. C Lewisham St Swithun *S'wark* 54-57; Australia 57-62; C Cheam *S'wark* 63-65; P-in-c Becontree St Pet *Chelmsf* 65-67; V 67-72; Min Parkeston CD 72-83; TV Dovercourt and Parkeston 83-89; Miss to Seamen 83-89; C Southend St Sav Westcliff *Chelmsf* from 89. *46 Grosvenor Road, Westcliff-on-Sea, Essex SS0 8EN* Southend-on-Sea (0702) 343905

BUFFETT, Frederick. b 11. Keble Coll Ox BA34 MA39. St Steph Ho Ox 34. **d** 35 **p** 36. V Ipplepen w Torbryan *Ex* 64-82; rtd 82; Perm to Offic *Ex* from 82. *20 Woodland Road, Denbury, Newton Abbot, Devon TQ12 6DY* Ipplepen (0803) 813149

BUFFREY, Canon Samuel John Thomas. b 28. Keble Coll Ox BA52 MA57. Cuddesdon Coll 52. **d** 54 **p** 55. C Lower Tuffley St Geo CD *Glouc* 54-56; C Branksome St Aldhelm *Sarum* 56-61; R Gussage St Michael and Gussage All Saints 61-69; V Amesbury 69-80; RD Avon 77-80; P-in-c Broadstone 80-82; V from 82; Can and Preb Sarum Cathl from 87. *St John's Vicarage, Macauley Road, Broadstone, Dorset BH18 8AR* Broadstone (0202) 694109

BUGBY, Timothy. b 53. AKC75. Chich Th Coll 76. **d** 77 **p** 78. C Hockerill *St Alb* 77-81; C Pimlico St Mary Graham Terrace *Lon* 81-87; V Highgate St Aug from 87. *St Augustine's Vicarage, Langdon Park Road, London N6 5BH* 081-340 3567

BUGDEN, Ernest William. b 16. Lich Th Coll 56. **d** 58 **p** 59. C Esher *Guildf* 58-68; Hon C 68-81; rtd 81. *32 French's Road, Cambridge CB4 3LA* Cambridge (0223) 311306

BUGG, Peter Richard. b 33. Univ of BC BA62. Wells Th Coll 63. **d** 64 **p** 64. C Whitley Ch Ch *Ox* 64-67; C Ludlow *Heref* 67-69; Zambia 69-72; P-in-c Brill w Boarstall *Ox* 72-78; P-in-c Chilton w Dorton 77-78; V Brill, Boarstall, Chilton and Dorton from 78. *The Vicarage, Brill, Aylesbury, Bucks HP18 9ST* Brill (0844) 238325

BUIK, Allan David. b 39. St Andr Univ BSc61. Coll of Resurr Mirfield 66. **d** 68 **p** 69. Perm to Offic *Win* 68-69; C Eastleigh 69-72; C Brighton St Bart *Chich* 72-74; C Lavender Hill Ascension *S'wark* 74-78; V Kingstanding St Mark *Birm* 78-86; Guyana 86-91. *c/o St Oswald's Vicarage, 228 Jardine Crescent, Coventry CV4 9PL* Coventry (0203) 465072

BUIKE, Desmond Mainwaring. b 32. Ex Coll Ox BA55 MA69 Leeds Univ CertEd72. Qu Coll Birm DipTh57. **d** 57 **p** 58. C Man St Aid *Man* 57-60; C Ox SS Phil and Jas *Ox* 60-63; V Queensbury *Bradf* 63-71; Perm to Offic 71-85; V Glaisdale *York* from 85. *The Vicarage, Glaisdale, Whitby, N Yorkshire YO21 2PL* Whitby (0947) 87214

BULFIELD, Miss Kathleen Linda. b 29. S'wark Ord Course 87. **d** 90. NSM Sanderstead All SS *S'wark* from 90. *29 Farm Fields, Sanderstead, Surrey CR2 0HQ* 081-657 8555

BULL, Albert Henry. b 12. Lon Univ BD39. ALCD39. **d** 39 **p** 40. Asst Master Coombe Girls' Sch 60-73; Perm to Offic *Guildf* from 75; rtd 77. *40 The Warren, Worcester Park, Surrey* 081-337 2265

BULL, Christopher Bertram. b 45. Lon Bible Coll BA87. Wycliffe Hall Ox 88. **d** 90 **p** 91. C Leominster *Heref* from 90. *10 The Meadows, Leominster, Herefordshire HR6 8RF* Leominster (0568) 2124

BULL, Christopher David. b 59. St Jo Coll Nottm 89. **d** 91. C Bowbrook S *Worc* from 91. *The Parsonage, Church Lane, Tibberton, Droitwich WR9 7NW* Spetchley (090565) 316

BULL, Canon Frank Spencer. b 19. Lon Univ BD43. ALCD43. **d** 43 **p** 44. V Kenilworth St Nic *Cov* 66-85; RD Kenilworth 73-83; Hon Can Cov Cathl 74-85; rtd 85; Perm to Offic *Cant* from 85. *74 Riverside Close, Bridge, Canterbury, Kent CT4 5TN* Canterbury (0227) 830440

BULL, Malcolm Harold. b 44. BDS. St Alb Minl Tr Scheme. **d** 83 **p** 84. NSM Bedf St Paul *St Alb* from 83. *27 Cardington Road, Bedford MK42 0BN* Bedford (0234) 68163

BULL, Malcom George. b 35. Portsm Dioc Tr Course. **d** 87. NSM Farlington *Portsm* 87-90. *20 Charleston Close, Hayling Island, Hants PO11 0JY* Hayling Island (0705) 462025

BULL, Martin Wells. b 37. Worc Coll Ox BA61 MA68. Ripon Hall Ox 61. **d** 63 **p** 64. C Blackley St Andr *Man* 63-67; C Horton *Bradf* 67-68; V Ingrow cum Hainworth 68-78; RD S Craven 74-77; V Bingley All SS 78-80; TR from 80. *The Vicarage, Hallbank Drive, Bingley, W Yorkshire BD16 4BZ* Bradford (0274) 563113

BULL, Michael John. b 35. Roch Th Coll 65. **d** 67 **p** 68. C N Wingfield *Derby* 67-69; C Skegness *Linc* 69-72; R Ingoldmells w Addlethorpe 72-79; Area Sec (Dio S'wark) USPG 79-85; Area Org RNLI (Lon) 86-88; C Croydon St Jo *S'wark* from 89. *37 Alton Road, Croydon CR0 4LZ* 081-760 9626

BULL, Dr Norman John. b 16. Trin Coll Ox BTh38 BA39 MA48 Reading Univ PhD67. Linc Th Coll 38. **d** 39 **p** 40. C Colchester St Botolph w H Trin and St Giles *Chelmsf* 39-41; C Loughton St Mary 41-43; P-in-c Petersfield w Sheet *Portsm* 44-45; C Croydon *Cant* 45-46; Dioc Youth Chapl 46-48; Chapl St Luke's Coll Ex 49-60; Lect 49-75. *21 Wonford Road, Exeter EX4 2LH* Exeter (0392) 55806

BULL, Robert David. b 51. Man Univ DSPT86. Ripon Coll Cuddesdon 74. **d** 77 **p** 78. C Worsley *Man* 77-80; C Peel 80-81; TV 81-86; P-in-c Wisbech St Aug *Ely* 86-88; V from 88. *St Augustine's Vicarage, Lynn Road, Wisbech, Cambs PE13 3DL* Wisbech (0945) 583724

BULL, Robert Humphrey. b 06. FIMarE73 CEng73. Ox Ord Course 72. **d** 74 **p** 74. Hon C Reading St Jo *Ox* 74-88; Perm to Offic trom 88. *1 Tamarisk Avenue, Reading RG2 8JB* Reading (0734) 871441

BULL, William George. b 28. Sarum Th Coll 65. **d** 66 **p** 67. C Salisbury St Mich *Sarum* 66-69; V Swallowcliffe w Ansty 69-75; Dioc Youth Officer 69-71; P-in-c Laverstock 75-81; V from 81. *The Vicarage, 14 Church Road, Laverstock, Salisbury SP1 1QX* Salisbury (0722) 334036

BULLEN, Richard David Guy. b 43. Brasted Place Coll 71. Ripon Hall Ox 73. **d** 75 **p** 76. C Pocklington w Yapham-cum-Meltonby, Owsthorpe etc *York* 75-78; TV Thornaby on Tees 78-84; V New Marske 84-90; P-in-c Wilton 84-90; Ind Chapl from 90. *26 Chestnut Close, Saltburn-by-the-Sea, Cleveland TS12 1PE* Guisborough (0287) 623287

BULLEY, Roger Charles. b 12. Lon Univ BCom34 BA37. Wells Th Coll 38. **d** 40 **p** 41. Chapl Community St Jo Bapt Clewer 71-79; rtd 78; Chapl Convent of Sisters of Charity Knowle 79-88. *Lindsay House, Lindsey Street, Epping, Essex CM16 6RB* Epping (0378) 78518

BULLEY, William Joseph. b 28. Chich Th Coll 65. **d** 67 **p** 68. C Littleham w Exmouth *Ex* 67-72; V Harberton w Harbertonford 72-77; R Chagford 77-79; R Chagford w Gidleigh and Throwleigh 79-84; V Widecombe, Leusden and Princetown etc 84-85; TR Widecombe-in-the-Moor, Leusdon, Princetown etc 85-88; P-in-c Inverness St Jo *Mor* from 88; Chapl Raigmore Hosp Inverness from 88. *Dalcharn Cottage, Cawdor, Nairn IV12 5XU* Croy (06678) 215

BULLIVANT, Canon Ronald. b 13. Nashdom Abbey. **d** 43 **p** 43. V Brighton Annunciation *Chich* 53-89; Can and Preb Chich Cathl 78-89; rtd 89. *9 Farm Close, Castle Park, Whitby, N Yorkshire YO21 3LS* Whitby (0947) 601495

BULLIVANT, Ronald. b 32. CertEd DCouns. St Mich Coll Llan. **d** 59 **p** 60. C Roath St German *Llan* 59-61; P-in-c Bradf H Trin *Bradf* 61-66; V Horbury *Wakef* 66-69; Lic to Offic Ripon 70-78; Perm Nor 78-81; Lic from 81. *22 Cleaves Drive, Walsingham, Norfolk NR22 6EQ* Fakenham (0328) 820526

BULLOCK, Andrew Timothy. b 56. Southn Univ BTh91. Sarum & Wells Th Coll 89. **d** 91. C Erdington St Barn *Birm* from 91. *62 Dunvegan Road, Erdington, Birmingham B24 9HH* 021-382 6169

BULLOCK, John Philip. b 26. Birm Univ BSc47. Qu Coll Birm 79. **d** 81 **p** 82. NSM Helston *Truro* 81-85; NSM Helston and Wendron from 85. *St Clair, Breage, Helston, Cornwall TR13 9PD* Helston (0326) 564177

BULLOCK, Canon John Raymond. b 16. Ch Ch Ox BA37 MA46. Westcott Ho Cam 46. **d** 48 **p** 49. RD Hartlepool *Dur* 62-78; V Hartlepool St Paul 62-86; P-in-c Hartlepool Ch Ch 65-73; Hon Can Dur Cathl 71-86; rtd 86. *4 The Green, Greatham, Hartlepool, Cleveland TS25 2HG* Hartlepool (0429) 870600

BULLOCK, Kenneth Poyser. b 27. Down Coll Cam BA50 MA55. Ridley Hall Cam 50. **d** 52 **p** 53. V Ainsworth *Man* 63-91; rtd 91. *26 Plas Penrhyn, Penrhyn Bay, Llandudno, Gwynedd LL30 3EU* Llandudno (0492) 543343

BULLOCK, Michael. b 49. Hatf Coll Dur BA71 Leeds Univ DipTh74. Coll of Resurr Mirfield 72. **d** 75 **p** 76. C Pet St Jo *Pet* 75-79; Zambia 79-86; V Longthorpe *Pet* 86-91; Chapl Naples w Sorrento, Capri and Bari *Eur* from 91. *Christ Church, via S Pasquala a Chiaia 15B, 80121 Naples, Italy* Naples (81) 411842

BULLOCK, Miss Rosemary Joy. b 59. Portsm Poly BA81. Sarum & Wells Th Coll 89. **d** 91. Par Dn Warblington

and Emsworth *Portsm* from 91. *104 Westbourne Avenue, Emsworth, Hants PO10 7QJ* Emsworth (0243) 377640

BULLOCK-FLINT, Peter. b 22. Kelham Th Coll 39. **d** 45 **p** 46. C-in-c Tilehurst St Mary CD *Ox* 56-72; V Hughenden 72-83; V Ivinghoe w Pitstone and Slapton 83-91; RD Mursley 86-91; rtd 91. *1 Wellow Cottage, Salisbury Road, Pimperne, Blandford Forum, Dorset DT11 8UW*

BULLOUGH, Canon Walter Herbert. b 15. AKC39. **d** 39 **p** 40. R Halsall *Liv* 59-91; RD Ormskirk 69-78; Hon Can Liv Cathl from 71; rtd 91. *49 Moss Lane, Southport, Merseyside PR9 7QS*

BULMAN, Madeline Judith. b 61. K Coll Lon BD AKC. dss 86 **d** 87. Shepperton *Lon* 86-87; Par Dn 87-88; Par Dn Brentford from 88. *34 Brook Road South, Brentford, Middx TW8 0NN* 081-568 6518

BULMAN, Michael Thomas Andrew. b 34. Jes Coll Cam BA59 MA62. Ridley Hall Cam 58. **d** 60 **p** 61. C Blackpool St Mark *Blackb* 60-63; C Branksome St Clem *Sarum* 63-67; V York St Barn *York* 67-84; Israel from 84. *5 Isaiah Street, PO Box 191, 91001 Jerusalem, Israel* Jerusalem (2) 224584

BUNCE, Michael John. b 49. FRSA FSA St Andr Univ MTh79. Westcott Ho Cam DipTh. **d** 80 **p** 81. C Grantham *Linc* 80-83; TV 83-85; R Tarfside *Bre* from 85; R Bre from 85; R Auchmithie from 91. *St Andrew's Rectory, 39 Church Street, Brechin, Angus DD9 6HB* Brechin (03562) 2708

BUNCE, Raymond Frederick. b 28. Lon Univ DipSocSc53. Ely Th Coll 54. **d** 57 **p** 58. V Ealing All SS *Lon* 67-89; rtd 89; Chapl Ascot Priory 89-90; Perm to Offic *Portsm* from 91. *Dwarf Croft, Steephill Road, Ventnor, Isle of Wight PO38 1UF* Isle of Wight (0983) 855145

BUNCH, Andrew William Havard. b 53. Selw Coll Cam BA74 MA78 PhD79. Ox NSM Course 84. **d** 87 **p** 88. NSM Wantage *Ox* 87-91; C New Windsor from 91. *The Vicarage, Hermitage Lane, Windsor, Berks SL4 4AZ* Windsor (0753) 858720

BUNDAY, Canon Paul. b 30. Wadh Coll Ox BA54 MA58. ALCD56. **d** 56 **p** 57. C Woking St Jo *Guildf* 56-60; Chapl Reed's Sch Cobham 60-66; R Landford w Plaitford *Sarum* 66-77; RD Alderbury 73-77; TR Radipole and Melcombe Regis 77-86; RD Weymouth 82-85; Can and Preb Sarum Cathl from 83; TV Whitton 86-91; TR from 91. *The Vicarage, Chilton Foliat, Hungerford, Berks RG27 0TF* Hungerford (0488) 682470

BUNDOCK, Anthony Francis. b 49. Qu Coll Birm 81. **d** 83 **p** 84. C Stansted Mountfitchet *Chelmsf* 83-86; TV Borehamwood *St Alb* from 86. *Holy Cross Vicarage, 1 Warren Grove, Borehamwood, Herts WD6 2QU* 081-953 2183

BUNDOCK, John Nicholas Edward. b 45. Wells Th Coll 66. **d** 70 **p** 71. C Chingford SS Pet and Paul *Chelmsf* 70-74; P-in-c Gt Grimsby St Matt Fairfield CD *Linc* 74-81; V Hindhead *Guildf* from 81; RD Farnham from 91. *The Vicarage, Wood Road, Hindhead, Surrey GU26 6PX* Hindhead (0428) 605305

BUNDOCK, Ronald Michael. b 44. Leeds Univ BSc65. Ox NSM Course 87. **d** 90. NSM Buckm *Ox* from 90. *1 Holton Road, Buckingham MK18 1PQ* Buckingham (0280) 813887

BUNKER, Harry. b 28. Oak Hill Th Coll. **d** 59 **p** 60. C Longfleet *Sarum* 59-63; R Blisworth *Pet* from 63. *The Rectory, Blisworth, Northampton* Blisworth (0604) 858412

BUNKER, John Herbert George. b 31. AKC56. **d** 57 **p** 58. C Newc St Jo *Newc* 57-60; C Cullercoats St Geo 61-65; V Byker St Mich 65-74; V Ashington 74-84; V Halifax St Aug *Wakef* from 84. *St Augustine's Vicarage, Hanson Lane, Halifax, W Yorkshire HX1 5PG* Halifax (0422) 65552

BUNKER, Preb Michael. b 37. Oak Hill Th Coll 59. **d** 63 **p** 64. C Alperton *Lon* 63-66; C St Helens St Helen *Liv* 66-70; V Muswell Hill St Matt *Lon* 70-79; V Muswell Hill St Jas 78-79; V Muswell Hill St Jas w St Matt from 79; AD W Haringey 85-90; Preb St Paul's Cathl from 90. *St James's Vicarage, 2 St James's Lane, London N10 3DB* 081-883 6277

BUNKER, Neil John. b 59. K Coll Lon BD77 AKC77. Ripon Coll Cuddesdon 82. **d** 83 **p** 84. C Bromley St Andr *Roch* 83-87; Chapl Farnborough Psychiatric Unit 85-87; Chapl Farnborough Hosp and Orpington Hosp from 87; Distr Chapl Bromley HA from 89. *6 Ruskin Road, Belvedere, Kent DA17 5BH* Erith (03224) 42621

BUNNELL, Adrian. b 49. Univ of Wales (Abth) BSc72. St Mich Coll Llan 74. **d** 75 **p** 76. C Wrexham *St As* 75-78; C Rhyl w Rhyl St Ann 78-79; CF from 79. *c/o MOD (Army), Bagshot Park, Bagshot, Surrey GU19 5PL* Bagshot (0276) 71717

BUNT, Brian William. b 34. Bris Univ BA63 Lon Univ BD67. Tyndale Hall Bris. **d** 68 **p** 69. C Chich St Pancras and St Jo *Chich* 68-72; C Camborne *Truro* 72-75; P-in-c Kenwyn St Jo from 75. *St John's Vicarage, 52 Daniell Road, Truro, Cornwall TR1 2DA* Truro (0872) 79873

BUNTING, Ian David. b 33. Ex Coll Ox BA58 MA61. Tyndale Hall Bris 57 Princeton Th Sem ThM60. **d** 60 **p** 61. C Bootle St Leon *Liv* 60-63; V Waterloo St Jo 64-71; Dir Past Studies St Jo Coll Dur 71-78; R Ches le Street *Dur* 78-87; RD Ches le Street 79-84; Kingham Hill Fellow 87-89; Dioc Dir of Ords *S'well* from 90; C Lenton from 90. *13 Rolleston Drive, Lenton, Nottingham NG7 1JS* Nottingham (0602) 472777

BUNTING, Jeremy John. b 34. St Cath Coll Cam BA56 MA60 Worc Coll Ox BA58 MA60. St Steph Ho Ox 57. **d** 59 **p** 60. C Bickley *Roch* 59-62; C Luton St Mary Less *Ely* 62-66; USA 66-68; R Stock Harvard *Chelmsf* 68-87; RD Wickford 73-79; V Hampstead Garden Suburb *Lon* from 87. *St Jude's Vicarage, 1 Central Square, London NW11 7AH* 081-455 7206

BUNYAN, Richard Charles. b 43. Oak Hill Th Coll 63 Ridley Hall Cam 69. **d** 71 **p** 72. C Luton Ch Ch *Roch* 71-74; C Bexleyheath Ch Ch 74-76; C Bexley St Jo 76-79; TV Northn Em *Pet* 79-81; V Erith St Jo *Roch* 81-86; V S Woodham Ferrers *Chelmsf* 86-89; Chapl Scargill Ho from 89. *Scargill House, Kettlewell, Skipton, N Yorkshire BD23 5HU* Kettlewell (075676) 234

BURBERY, Ian Edward. b 37. Univ of Wales (Lamp) BA59. Coll of Resurr Mirfield 59. **d** 61 **p** 62. C Penarth w Lavernock *Llan* 61-68; V Porth 68-77; V Cainscross w Selsley *Glouc* 77-89; P-in-c Cheltenham Em from 89. *Emmanuel Vicarage, 115 Old Bath Road, Cheltenham, Glos GL53 7DE* Cheltenham (0242) 525059

BURBIDGE, Canon Edward Humphrey. b 07. Qu Coll Cam BA30 MA34. St Aug Coll Cant 30. **d** 31 **p** 32. C Castleford All SS *Wakef* 31-34; Australia from 34. *48 Ullapool Road, Mount Pleasant, W Australia 6153* Perth (9) 364-1019

BURBRIDGE, Very Rev John Paul. b 32. FSA89 K Coll Cam BA54 MA58 New Coll Ox BA54 MA58. Wells Th Coll 58. **d** 59 **p** 60. C Eastbourne St Mary *Chich* 59-62; VC York Minster *York* 62-66; Can Res and Prec 66-76; Adn Richmond *Ripon* 76-83; Can Res Ripon Cathl 76-83; Dean Nor from 83. *The Deanery, Cathedral Close, Norwich NR1 4EG* Norwich (0603) 666835 or 760140

BURBRIDGE, Richard James. b 47. Univ of Wales (Ban) BSc68. Oak Hill Th Coll 68. **d** 72 **p** 73. C Rodbourne Cheney *Bris* 72-75; C Downend 75-78; P-in-c Bris H Cross Inns Court 78-83; P-in-c Fishponds All SS 83-86; V from 86; RD Stapleton from 89. *All Saints' Vicarage, Grove Road, Fishponds, Bristol BS16 2BW* Bristol (0272) 654143

BURCH, Cyril John. b 18. AKC49. **d** 49 **p** 50. V Stoke Mandeville *Ox* 63-86; rtd 86. *4 Gange Mews, Middle Row, Faversham, Kent* Faversham (0795) 538166

BURCH, John Anthony. b 37. Open Univ BA75. Wycliffe Hall Ox 67. **d** 69 **p** 70. C Guildf Ch Ch *Guildf* 69-72; C Cove St Jo 72-75; TV Fincham *Ely* 75-79; V Huntington St Barn 79-81; Perm to Offic 82-90. *Address temp unknown*

BURCH, John Christopher. b 50. Trin Coll Cam BA71 MA76. St Jo Coll Nottm 73. **d** 76 **p** 77. C Sheff St Jo *Sheff* 76-79; C Holbeck *Ripon* 79-82; V Burmantofts St Steph and St Agnes from 82. *St Agnes Vicarage, 21 Shakespeare Close, Leeds LS9 7UQ* Leeds (0532) 482648

BURCH, Peter John. b 36. ACA60 FCA71. Ripon Hall Ox 62. **d** 64 **p** 65. C Brixton St Matt *S'wark* 64-67; Sierra Leone 67-72; P-in-c Chich St Pet *Chich* 72-76; V Broadwater Down 76-85; V Steyning from 85; R Ashurst from 85. *St Andrew's Vicarage, Steyning, W Sussex BN44 3YL* Steyning (0903) 813256

BURCH, Sidney Alfred Richard. b 09. Bps' Coll Cheshunt 63. **d** 65 **p** 66. C Southend St Sav Westcliff *Chelmsf* 68-82; rtd 82; Perm to Offic *Chelmsf* from 82. *42 Cleveland Drive, Westcliff-on-Sea, Essex SS0 0SU* Southend-on-Sea (0702) 345742

BURCH, Stephen Roy. b 59. St Jo Coll Nottm LTh82. **d** 85 **p** 86. C Ipswich St Aug *St E* 85-89; P-in-c Kinwarton w Gt Alne and Haselor *Cov* from 89; Youth Chapl from 89. *The Rectory, Great Alne, Alcester, Warks B49 6HY* Great Alne (0789) 488344

BURCH, Victor Ernest Charles. b 18. Nor Ord Course 73. **d** 76 **p** 77. NSM Heigham St Barn w St Bart *Nor* 76-80; NSM Lakenham St Jo from 80. *35 Oaklands, Framingham Earl, Norwich NR14 7QS* Framingham Earl (05086) 2790

BURCHILL, Dr Jane. b 31. Dalhousie Univ Canada BSc54 Aber Univ PhD81. Moray Ho Edin CertEd56 St Jo Coll

Nottm 85. **d** 88. NSM Inverurie *Ab* from 88; NSM Auchindoir from 88; NSM Alford from 88; NSM Kemnay from 88. *5 Hopetoun Avenue, Bucksburn, Aberdeen AB2 9QU* Aberdeen (0224) 712931

BURDEN, Miss Anne Margaret. b 47. Ex Univ BSc69 LSE DSA70 DipSocWork72 CQSW72. Linc Th Coll 89. **d** 91. Par Dn Mill Hill Jo Keble Ch *Lon* from 91. *27 Sefton Avenue, London NW7 3QB* 081-959 2724

BURDEN, Arthur Theodore. b 11. St Pet Hall Ox BA35 MA42. Wycliffe Hall Ox 35. **d** 37 **p** 38. V Dorking St Paul *Guildf* 63-73; V Defford w Besford *Worc* 73-78; V Eckington 73-78; rtd 78; Perm to Offic Glouc and Worc from 78; P-in-c Ripple, Earls Croome w Hill Croome and Strensham *Worc* 87. *Wellspring, 7 Golden Valley, Castlemorton, Malvern, Worcs WR13 6AA* Birtsmorton (068481) 341

BURDEN, Derek. b 29. St Edm Hall Ox BA52 MA56. Wells Th Coll 56. **d** 58 **p** 59. V N Bradley *Sarum* 69-79; V Steeple Ashton w Semington 79-84; V Keevil 79-84; V Steeple Ashton w Semington and Keevil 84-89; rtd 89. *9 Farleigh Avenue, Trowbridge, Wilts BA14 9DS* Trowbridge (0225) 754759

BURDEN, Derek Ronald. b 37. Sarum Th Coll 59. **d** 62 **p** 63. C Cuddington *Guildf* 62-64; C Leamington Priors All SS *Cov* 64-66; C Stamford All SS w St Pet *Linc* 66-74; C-in-c Stamford Ch Ch CD 71-74; P-in-c Ashbury w Compton Beauchamp *Ox* 74-77; V 77-81; V Ashbury, Compton Beauchamp and Longcot w Fernham 81-84; V Wokingham St Sebastian from 84. *St Sebastian's Vicarage, Nine Mile Ride, Wokingham, Berks RG11 3AT* Crowthorne (0344) 761050

BURDEN, Michael Henry. b 36. Selw Coll Cam BA59 MA63 Hull Univ MEd81. Ridley Hall Cam 60. **d** 62 **p** 63. C Ashton on Mersey St Mary *Ches* 62-65; Chapl St Pet Sch York 65-70; Asst Master Beverley Gr Sch 70-74; R Walkington *York* 74-77; Chapl Asst Berwick R Infirmary from 82; P-in-c Berwick H Trin *Newc* 82-87; V 87-89; P-in-c Berwick St Mary 82-87; V Berwick H Trin and St Mary from 89. *Holy Trinity Vicarage, 77 Ravensdowne, Berwick-upon-Tweed TD15 1DX* Berwick-upon-Tweed (0289) 306136

BURDETT, John Fergusson. b 25. Pemb Coll Cam BA47 MA79. **d** 79 **p** 80. C Edin St Jo *Edin* 79-87; Cyprus from 87. *4 Hillpark Avenue, Edinburgh EH4 7AT* 031-312 8178

BURDETT, Stephen Martin. b 49. AKC72. St Aug Coll Cant 73. **d** 74 **p** 75. C Walworth St Pet *S'wark* 74-75; C Walworth 75-77; C Benhilton 77-80; P-in-c Earlsfield St Jo 80-83; V 83-89; V N Dulwich St Faith from 89. *St Faith's Vicarage, Red Post Hill, London SE24 9JQ* 071-274 1338

BURDITT, Jeffrey Edward. b 46. Ex Univ BA67 CertEd68 Lon Univ MPhil79. Westcott Ho Cam 86. **d** 88 **p** 89. C Saffron Walden w Wendens Ambo and Littlebury *Chelmsf* from 88. *17 Saxon Way, Saffron Walden, Essex CB11 4EQ* Saffron Walden (0799) 24808

BURDON, Anthony James. b 46. Ex Univ LLB67 Lon Univ BD73. Oak Hill Th Coll 71. **d** 73 **p** 74. C Ox St Ebbe w St Pet *Ox* 73-76; C Church Stretton *Heref* 76-78; Cand Sec CPAS 78-81; Hon C Bromley Ch Ch *Roch* 78-81; V Filkins w Broadwell, Broughton, Kelmscot etc *Ox* 81-84; R Broughton Poggs w Filkins, Broadwell etc 84-85; V Reading St Jo from 85. *St John's Vicarage, 50 London Road, Reading RG1 5AS* Reading (0734) 872366

BURDON, Christopher John. b 48. Jes Coll Cam BA70 MA74 Leeds Univ DipTh73. Coll of Resurr Mirfield 71. **d** 74 **p** 75. C Chelmsf All SS *Chelmsf* 74-78; TV High Wycombe *Ox* 78-84; P-in-c Olney w Emberton 84-90; R from 90. *9 Orchard Rise, Olney, Bucks MK46 5HB* Bedford (0234) 713308

BURDON, Edward Arthur. b 11. Linc Th Coll 44. **d** 46 **p** 47. V Gosfield *Chelmsf* 54-72; V Coggeshall w Markshall 72-80; rtd 80; Perm to Offic *St E* from 81. *The Nutshell, 20 Naverne Meadows, Woodbridge, Suffolk IP12 1HU* Woodbridge (03943) 4787

BURDON, Pamela Muriel. b 46. Ex Univ BA68 Reading Univ DipEd69. Wycliffe Hall Ox 88. **d** 90. Par Dn Reading St Jo *Ox* from 90. *St John's Vicarage, 50 London Road, Reading, Berks RG1 5AS* Reading (0734) 872366

BURDON, William. b 23. Leeds Univ BA51. Coll of Resurr Mirfield 51. **d** 53 **p** 54. V Skirwith *Carl* 64-73; V Skirwith w Ousby and Melmerby 73-84; R Maidwell w Draughton, Scaldwell, Lamport etc *Pet* 84-88; rtd 88. *The Rectory, Church Park, Tenby, Dyfed SA70 7EE* Tenby (0834) 2068

BURFORD, Alfred Graham. b 10. Leic Univ DipEd51. St D Coll Lamp BA50. **d** 58 **p** 59. V Leic St Paul *Leic* 65-74; V Long Clawson and Hose 74-80; rtd 80; Perm to Offic *Leic* from 80. *West End Cottage, Long Clawson, Melton Mowbray, Leics LE14 4PQ* Melton Mowbray (0664) 822183

BURGER, David Joseph Cave. b 31. Selw Coll Cam BA58 MA62 Leic Univ 68. Coll of Resurr Mirfield 58. **d** 60 **p** 61. C Chiswick St Paul Grove Park *Lon* 60-63; C Charlton St Luke w H Trin *S'wark* 63-65; Chapl Moor Park Coll Farnham 66; Teacher Ysgol y Gader Dolgellau Gwynedd 68-85; Resettlement Officer Ches Aid to the Homeless from 88. *Roodee House, 22 Grosvenor Street, Chester CH1 2DD*

BURGESS, Alan James. b 51. Ridley Hall Cam 87. **d** 89 **p** 90. C Glenfield *Leic* from 89. *47 Clovelly Road, Glenfield, Leicester LE3 8AE* Leicester (0533) 875488

BURGESS, Alfred George. b 18. Univ of Wales BA39. St Mich Coll Llan 39. **d** 41 **p** 42. V Alveston *Cov* 58-81; R Ilmington w Stretton on Fosse and Ditchford 81-84; rtd 84; Perm to Offic *Cov* from 84. *139 Evesham Road, Stratford-upon-Avon, Warks CV37 9BP* Stratford-upon-Avon (0789) 293321

BURGESS, Colin. b 38. St Aid Birkenhead 63. **d** 65 **p** 66. C Blackb St Steph *Blackb* 65-68; Trinidad and Tobago 68-71; Miss to Seamen 71-73 and 76-84; Tanzania 73-76; Prov Sec and Sen Chapl Wales 79-84; Asst Chapl HM Pris Pentonville 85; Chapl HM Youth Cust Cen E Sutton Park 85-88; HM Pris Maidstone 85-88; Chapl HM Pris Holloway from 88. *The Chaplain's Office, HM Prison, Parkhurst Road, London N7 0NU* 071-607 6747

BURGESS, David James. b 58. **d** 89 **p** 90. C S Mimms Ch Ch *Lon* from 89. *8 Wentworth Road, Barnet, Herts* 081-441 0645

BURGESS, David John. b 39. Trin Hall Cam BA62 MA66 Univ Coll Ox MA66. Cuddesdon Coll 62. **d** 65 **p** 66. C Maidstone All SS w St Phil *Cant* 65; Asst Chapl Univ Coll Ox 66-70; Chapl 70-78; Can and Treas Windsor 78-87; Chapl to HM The Queen from 87; V St Lawr Jewry *Lon* from 87. *St Lawrence Jewry Vicarage, Next Guildhall, London EC2V 5AA* 071-600 9478

BURGESS, Edwin Michael. b 47. Ch Coll Cam BA69 MA73. Coll of Resurr Mirfield 70. **d** 72 **p** 73. C Beamish *Dur* 72-77; C Par *Truro* 77-80; Jt Dir SW Min T1 Course *Ex* 80-86; P-in-c Duloe w Herodsfoot *Truro* 80-83; R 83-86; Sub-Warden St Deiniol's Lib Hawarden from 86. *St Deiniol's Library, Hawarden, Deeside, Clwyd CH5 3DF* Hawarden (0244) 532350

BURGESS, Frederick William. b 12. FRCO39 St Jo Coll Cam BA33 MA37. Ridley Hall Cam 34. **d** 36 **p** 39. Lic to Offic *St Alb* 59-77; R Gt Oakley *Chelmsf* 77-82; rtd 82; Perm to Offic *Chelmsf* from 82. *Rose Cottage, Beaumont Road, Great Oakley, Harwich, Essex CO12 5BG* Ramsey (0255) 880840

BURGESS, Canon Henry James. b 08. Lon Univ BA31 MA49 PhD54. Wycliffe Hall Ox 35. **d** 36 **p** 37. Can Res Sheff Cathl *Sheff* 70-75; Dioc Dir of Educn 70-75; rtd 75; Perm to Offic *Truro* 75-85; Roch from 85. *Flat 21, Bromley College, London Road, Bromley BR1 1PE* 081-290 1362

BURGESS, Canon Henry Percival. b 21. Leeds Univ BA48. Coll of Resurr Mirfield 48. **d** 50 **p** 51. V Wylde Green *Birm* 62-89; Hon Can Birm Cathl 75-90; RD Sutton Coldfield 76-88; rtd 90. *84 Fairholme Road, Hodge Hill, Birmingham B36 8HP* 021-373 1224

BURGESS, James Graham. b 30. Lon Univ BA51 St Cath Coll Ox DipTh55. Ripon Hall Ox 53. **d** 55 **p** 56. C Northn St Jas *Pet* 55-58; C Mortlake w E Sheen *S'wark* 58-61; R Morley *Nor* 61-63; Perm to Offic *Derby* from 71; Hd Relig Studies Coalville Gr Sch 63-71; St Elphin's Sch Darley Dale 71-88; Hd Hist from 88. *Appletrees, 7 Church Road, Darley Dale, Matlock, Derbyshire DE4 2GG* Matlock (0629) 734038

BURGESS, Ven John Edward. b 30. Lon Univ BD57. ALCD56. **d** 57 **p** 58. C Bermondsey St Mary w St Olave and St Jo *S'wark* 57-60; C Southn St Mary w H Trin *Win* 60-62; V Dunston w Coppenhall *Lich* 62-67; Chapl Stafford Coll of Tech 63-67; V Keynsham w Queen Charlton *B & W* 67-75; R Burnett 67-75; RD Keynsham 72-75; Adn Bath and Preb Wells Cathl from 75. *Birnfels, 56 Grange Road, Saltford, Bristol BS18 3AG* Saltford (0225) 873609

BURGESS, John Michael. b 36. ALCD61. **d** 61 **p** 62. C Eccleston St Luke *Liv* 61-64; S Rhodesia 64-65; Rhodesia 65-74; V Nottm St Andr *S'well* 74-79; Bp's Adv on Community Relns 77-79; V Earlestown *Liv* 79-87; RD Warrington 82-87; TR Halewood from 87. *22 Kenton Road, Liverpool, Merseyside L26 9TS* 051-486 3180

BURGESS, John Mulholland. b 32. Cranmer Hall Dur 58. **d** 61 **p** 62. C Frimley *Guildf* 61-67; C Cheltenham St Luke and St Jo *Glouc* 67-69; P-in-c Withington w Compton Abdale 69-74; R Woolstone w Gotherington

and Oxenton 74-75; Chapl Rotterdam w Schiedam etc *Eur* 75-78; Sliema 78-80; C Nottm All SS *S'well* 80; C Rolleston w Morton 80-83; C Rolleston w Fiskerton, Morton and Upton 83-84; V Mansf St Aug from 84; Asst RD Mansfield from 88. *St Augustine's Vicarage, 46 Abbott Road, Mansfield, Notts NG19 6DD* Mansfield (0623) 21247

BURGESS, Michael Anglin. b 34. St Deiniol's Hawarden 81. **d** 83 **p** 84. C Habergham Eaves St Matt *Blackb* 83-85; C Burnley (Habergham Eaves) St Matt w H Trin 85-86; V Preston St Matt from 86. *St Matthew's Vicarage, 20 Fishwick View, Preston, Lancs PR1 4YA* Preston (0772) 794312

BURGESS, Michael James. b 42. Coll of Resurr Mirfield 74. **d** 76 **p** 77. C Leigh-on-Sea St Marg *Chelmsf* 76-79; C St Peter-in-Thanet *Cant* 79-82; Canada from 82. *46 Spencer Avenue, Toronto, Ontario, Canada, M6K 2J6* Toronto (416) 531-4037

BURGESS, Michael Walter. Bps' Coll Cheshunt 66. **d** 68 **p** 70. C Hammersmith St Matt *Lon* 68-70; C Boreham Wood All SS *St Alb* 70-73; V Flamstead 74-77; V St Marylebone Annunciation Bryanston Street *Lon* from 77. *4 Wyndham Place, London W1H 1AP* 071-262 4329

BURGESS, Neil. b 53. Univ of Wales (Lamp) BA75 Nottm Univ MTh87. St Mich Coll Llan 75. **d** 77 **p** 78. C Cheadle *Lich* 77-79; C Longton 79-82; TV Hanley H Ev 82-86; C Uttoxeter w Bramshall 86-87; Lect Linc Th Coll from 87. *Lincoln Theological College, The Bishop's Hostel, Drury Lane, Lincoln LN1 3BP* Lincoln (0522) 538885

BURGESS, Sister Patricia Jean. b 16. Edin Univ BSc38. dss 69 **d** 86. NSM Roslin (Rosslyn Chpl) *Edin* 69-73; Community of the Transfiguration Midlothian from 72. *House of the Transfiguration, 70E Clerk Street, Loanhead, Midlothian EH20 9RG*

BURGESS, Paul Christopher James. b 41. Qu Coll Cam BA63 MA67. Lon Coll of Div 66. **d** 68 **p** 69. C Islington St Mary *Lon* 68-72; C Church Stretton *Heref* 73-74; Pakistan 74-83; Warden Carberry Tower (Ch of Scotland) 84-86; TV Livingston LEP *Edin* from 88. *124 Mowbray Rise, Livingston, West Lothian EH54 6JP* Livingston (0506) 417158

BURGESS, Robin. b 49. St D Coll Lamp BA. St Steph Ho Ox 81. **d** 83 **p** 84. C Willesden Green St Andr and St Fran of Assisi *Lon* 83-86; C Ealing St Pet Mt Park 86-90; C Hanger Hill Ascension and W Twyford St Mary from 90; Chapl Cen Middx Hosp from 90. *48 Brentmead Gardens, London NW10 7ED* 081-961 9089

BURGESS, Roy. b 32. S Dios Minl Tr Scheme 80. **d** 83 **p** 84. NSM Bentworth and Shalden and Lasham *Win* 83-89; R Ingoldsby *Linc* from 89. *The Rectory, Back Lane, Ingoldsby, Grantham, Lincs NG33 4EW* Ingoldsby (047685) 746

BURGHALL, Kenneth Miles. b 34. Selw Coll Cam BA57 MA61. Qu Coll Birm 57. **d** 59 **p** 60. C Macclesfield St Mich *Ches* 59-63; CF 63-66; P-in-c Birkenhead Priory *Ches* 67-71; V Macclesfield St Paul 71-87; V Nether Peover from 87. *The Vicarage, Lower Peover, Knutsford, Cheshire WA16 9PZ* Lower Peover (0565) 812304

BURGIN, Henry Kenneth. b 36. S'wark Ord Course 70. **d** 71 **p** 72. C Caterham Valley *S'wark* 71-73; C Benhilton 73-77; V Cheam Common St Phil 77-82; P-in-c Blackheath All SS 82-89; V from 89. *All Saints' Vicarage, 10 Duke Humphrey Road, London SE3 0TY* 081-852 4280

BURGON, George Irvine. b 41. Edin Th Coll. **d** 65 **p** 66. C Dundee St Mary Magd *Bre* 65-68; C Wellingborough All Hallows *Pet* 68-71; P-in-c Norton 71-73; TV Daventry w Norton 73-75; V Northn St Mary from 75. *St Mary's Vicarage, Towcester Road, Northampton NN4 9EZ* Northampton (0604) 761104

BURGOYNE, Edward Geoffrey. b 27. Univ of Wales (Abth) BA49. St Mich Coll Llan 49. **d** 51 **p** 52. C Aberavon *Llan* 51-55; C Ynyshir 55-63; V Bockleton w Leysters *Heref* 63-70; Lic to Offic from 70. *Lawnswood, Tupsley, Hereford HR1 1UT* Hereford (0432) 268860

BURGOYNE, Percy John. b 19. OBE74. Univ of Wales (Cardiff) BSc41. St Mich Coll Llan. **d** 43 **p** 44. Chapl RN 52-78; QHC 72-75; P-in-c Kelsale w Carlton *St E* 78-85; R Kelsale-cum-Carlton, Middleton-cum-Fordley etc 85-90; rtd 90; Perm to Offic *St E* from 90. *St Dyfrig, Woods Lane, Melton, Woodbridge, Suffolk IP12 1JF*

BURGOYNE-JOHNSON, Philip Simon (Brother Thaddeus). b 51. S'wark Ord Course 81. **d** 84 **p** 85. SSF from 71; Lic to Offic *Heref* from 84. *Holy Trinity House, Orsett Terrace, London W2 6AH* 071-723 9135

BURKE, Charles Michael. b 28. Keble Coll Ox BA51 MA54 Ox Univ DipEd52. Glouc Th Course. **d** 84 **p** 85. C Colwall w Upper Colwall and Coddington *Heref* 84-88; V Canon Pyon w Kings Pyon and Birley from

88. *The Vicarage, Brookside, Canon Pyon, Hereford HR4 8NY*   Canon Pyon (043271) 802

BURKE, Eric John. b 44. Llan Dioc Tr Scheme 81. **d** 85 **p** 86. NSM Cardiff St Jo *Llan* from 85. *81 Ty Mawr Road, Rumney, Cardiff CF3 8BS*   Cardiff (0222) 798147

BURKE, Jonathan. b 53. Lon Univ BEd. Westcott Ho Cam 79. **d** 82 **p** 83. C Weymouth H Trin *Sarum* 82-85; R Bere Regis and Affpuddle w Turnerspuddle from 85. *The Vicarage, Bere Regis, Wareham, Dorset BH20 7HQ*   Bere Regis (0929) 471262

BURKE, Michael Robert. b 61. Leeds Univ BA83. Trin Coll Bris BA89. **d** 89 **p** 90. C Anston *Sheff* from 89. *20 St James Avenue, Anston, Sheffield S31 7DR*   Dinnington (0909) 550579

BURKETT, Christopher Paul. b 52. Warw Univ BA75 Birm Univ DipTh77. Qu Coll Birm 75. **d** 78 **p** 79. C Streetly *Lich* 78-81; C Harlescott 81-83; TV Leek and Meerbrook 83-89; Area Sec (Dio Ches) USPG from 89. *282 London Road, Northwich, Cheshire CW9 8AJ*   Northwich (0606) 47159

BURKILL, Mark Edward. b 56. MA PhD. Trin Coll Bris. **d** 84 **p** 85. C Cheadle *Ches* 84-88; C Harold Wood *Chelmsf* 88-91; V Leyton Ch Ch from 91. *The Vicarage, 52 Elm Road, London E11 4DN*   081-539 4980

BURKITT, Paul Adrian. b 49. RMN75 SRN77 Coll of Ripon & York St Jo CCouns89. St Steph Ho Ox 84. **d** 86 **p** 87. C Whitby *York* 86-90; V Egton w Grosmont from 90. *St Hilda's Vicarage, Egton, Whitby, N Yorkshire YO21 1UT*   Whitby (0947) 85315

BURKITT, Richard Francis. b 49. Leeds Univ BA71 CertEd72. Sarum Th Coll 82. **d** 90 **p** 90. R Fraserburgh w New Pitsligo *Ab* from 90. *6 Crimond Court, Fraserburgh, Aberdeenshire AB43 5QW*   Fraserburgh (0346) 28158

BURLAND, Clive Beresford. b 37. Sarum & Wells Th Coll 81. **d** 85 **p** 86. C Warblington and Emsworth *Portsm* 85-87; C Cowes St Mary from 87. *22 The Avenue, Cowes, Isle of Wight PO31 8JL*   Isle of Wight (0983) 292050

BURLEIGH, David John. b 42. FCII69. St Deiniol's Hawarden 84. **d** 87 **p** 88. NSM Lache cum Saltney *Ches* 87-88; NSM Eastham from 89. *5 Rowcliffe Avenue, Chester CH4 7PN*   Chester (0244) 679139

BURLEIGH, Walter Coleridge. b 41. W Midl Minl Tr Course 89. **d** 89 **p** 90. NSM N Evington *Leic* from 90. *90 Farrier Lane, Leicester LE4 0WA*   Leicester (0533) 359663

BURLES, Robert John. b 54. Bris Univ BSc75. St Jo Coll Nottm LTh86. **d** 88 **p** 89. C Mansf St Pet *S'well* 88-91; C The Lydiards *Bris* from 91. *1 Brandon Close, Swindon SN5 6AA*   Swindon (0793) 870244

BURLEY, John Anderson. b 11. Selw Coll Cam BA33 MA37. Ely Th Coll 33. **d** 34 **p** 35. V Clacton St Jas *Chelmsf* 59-70; Hon Can Utrecht Old Cathl Ch *Eur* from 69; R Gt and Lt Braxted *Chelmsf* 70-83; rtd 83. *Braxted, Church Road, Lyminge, Kent CT18 8JL*   Lyminge (0303) 862610

BURLEY, John Roland James. b 46. St Jo Coll Cam BA67 MA70. Ball Coll Ox DipGeochem68. Trin Episc Sch for Min Ambridge Penn MDiv88. **d** 81 **p** 82. SAMS 81-90; Chile 81-90; TV Southgate *Chich* from 90. *Holy Trinity Vicarage, Titmus Drive, Crawley, W Sussex RH10 5EU*   Crawley (0293) 25809

BURLEY, Michael. b 58. Ridley Hall Cam 86. **d** 89 **p** 90. C Scarborough St Mary w Ch Ch and H Apostles *York* from 89. *13 Woodall Avenue, Scarborough, N Yorkshire YO12 7TH*   Scarborough (0723) 361188

BURLTON, Aelred Harry. b 49. Sarum & Wells Th Coll 75. **d** 78 **p** 79. C Feltham *Lon* 78-82; Chapl Heathrow Airport from 83. *1 Dingle Road, Ashford, Middx TW15 1HF*   Ashford (0784) 57078

BURLTON, Robert Michael. b 18. Ely Th Coll 40 Chich Th Coll 41. **d** 42 **p** 43. R Lound *Nor* 65-76; P-in-c Fritton St Edm 65-83; R Blundeston w Flixton and Lound 76-83; rtd 83. *Heatherley, 3 Furze Park, Trelights, Port Isaac, Cornwall PL29 3TG*

BURLTON, William Frank. b 12. K Coll Lon. **d** 43 **p** 44. R Cromhall *Glouc* 51-78; HM Pris Leyhill 54-89; R Cromhall w Tortworth *Glouc* 78-82; rtd 82; Perm to Offic Glouc from 82; Truro from 89. *24 Godolphin Terrace, Marazion, Penzance, Cornwall TR17 0EX*   Penzance (0736) 710699

BURMAN, Philip Harvey. b 47. Kelham Th Coll 66. **d** 70 **p** 71. C Huyton St Mich *Liv* 70-75; C Farnworth 75-77; TV Kirkby 77-83; V Hindley All SS from 83. *The Vicarage, 192 Atherton Road, Hindley, Wigan, Lancs WN2 3XA*   Wigan (0942) 551757

BURMAN, Thomas George. b 41. S'wark Ord Course 86. **d** 89 **p** 90. NSM Forest Hill Ch Ch *S'wark* from 89.

131 Como Road, Forest Hill, London SE23 2JN   081-699 8929

BURMAN, William Guest. b 26. St Cath Coll Cam MA55 Worc Coll Ox MA63. St Steph Ho Ox 81. **d** 83 **p** 84. C Weymouth H Trin *Sarum* 83-86; R Exton and Winsford and Cutcombe w Luxborough *B & W* 86-89; TV Langport Area Chs from 89. *The Vicarage, New Street, Long Sutton, Langport, Somerset TA10 9JW*   Langport (0458) 241260

BURN, Canon Alan Edward. b 24. St Chad's Coll Dur BA49 DipTh51. **d** 51 **p** 52. V Binley *Cov* 67-73; R Allesley 73-89; RD Cov E 71-73; RD Cov N 79-87; Hon Can Cov Cathl from 87; rtd 89. *3 Church Farm, South Kilvington, Thirsk, N Yorkshire YO7 2NL*   Thirsk (0845) 524184

BURN, James Douglas. b 60. St Jo Coll Nottm BTh90. **d** 90 **p** 91. C Hucclecote *Glouc* from 90. *18 Millfields, Hucclecote, Gloucester GL3 3NH*   Gloucester (0452) 371003

BURN, Leonard Louis. b 44. K Coll Lon BD67 AKC67. **d** 68 **p** 69. C Kingswinford St Mary *Lich* 68-70; C S Ascot *Ox* 70-72; C Caversham 72-76; Chapl Selly Oak Hosp Birm 76-81; Bris City Hosp 81-82; P-in-c Bris St Mich *Bris* 81-83; R Peopleton and White Ladies Aston etc *Worc* 83-88; V Bengeworth from 88. *The Vicarage, 1 Broadway Road, Bengeworth, Evesham, Worcs WR11 6BB*   Evesham (0386) 446164

BURN, Richard James Southerden. b 34. Pemb Coll Cam BA56. Wells Th Coll 56. **d** 58 **p** 59. C Cheshunt *St Alb* 58-62; C Leighton Buzzard 65-66; C Glastonbury St Jo *B & W* 66-68; P-in-c Prestonpans *Edin* 68-71; P-in-c Stokesay *Heref* 71-75; P-in-c Dorrington 75-81; P-in-c Stapleton 75-81; P-in-c Leebotwood w Longnor 75-81; P-in-c Smethcott w Woolstaston 81; TR Melbury *Sarum* 81-87; P-in-c Quendon w Rickling and Wicken Bonhunt *Chelmsf* from 87. *The Vicarage, Cambridge Road, Quendon, Saffron Walden, Essex CB11 3XJ*   Rickling (079988) 238

BURN, Dr Robert Pemberton. b 34. Peterho Cam BA56 MA60 Lon Univ PhD68. CMS Tr Coll Chislehurst 60. **d** 63 **p** 81. India 63-71; Perm to Offic *Ely* 71-81; P-in-c Foxton 81-88; Perm to Offic *Ex* from 89. *Flat 4, 9 Lansdowne Terrace, Exeter EX2 4JJ*   Exeter (0392) 430028

BURN-MURDOCH, Aidan Michael. b 35. Trin Coll Cam BA60 MA63. Ridley Hall Cam. **d** 61 **p** 62. C Bishopwearmouth St Gabr *Dur* 61-63; Tutor Ridley Hall Cam 63-67; CMS Miss 67-70; R Hawick *Edin* 70-77; Bp's Co-ord of Evang *S & B* 77-89; R Reynoldston w Penrice and Llangennith 77-83; V Port Eynon w Rhosili and Llanddewi and Knelston 83-89; R Uddingston *Glas* from 89; R Cambuslang from 89. *5 Brownside Road, Cambuslang, Glasgow G72 8NL*   041-641 1173

BURNE, Christopher John Sambrooke. b 16. DSO45. Linc Th Coll 58. **d** 59 **p** 60. V N Leigh *Ox* 63-81; rtd 81; Perm to Offic *Win* from 81. *Beam Ends, Middle Road, Tiptoe, Lymington, Hants SO41 6FX*   Lymington (0590) 682898

BURNE, Canon Wilfrid Durnford Elvis. b 07. OBE65. Keble Coll Ox BA29 MA57. Bps' Coll Cheshunt 30. **d** 31 **p** 32. V Manea *Ely* 67-72; rtd 72. *1 Waterloo Road, Salisbury SP1 2JR*   Salisbury (0722) 24396

BURNESS, John Alfred. b 91. Qu Coll Cam BA14. Ridley Hall Cam 13. **d** 14 **p** 15. R Helmingham *St E* 29-60; C-in-c Framsden 53-60; rtd 60; Perm to Offic *St E* from 82. *The Five Gables, Witnesham, Ipswich*   Witnesham (047385) 243

BURNET, Norman Andrew Gray. b 32. Aber Univ BEd77. Edin Th Coll 53. **d** 55 **p** 56. C Ayr *Glas* 55-58; S Africa 58-69; R Leven *St And* 69-72; Perm to Offic Aber, Bre and Ely 73-81; P-in-c Brinkley, Burrough Green and Carlton *Ely* 82-83; P-in-c Westley Waterless 82-83; Australia 83-84; R Fraserburgh w New Pitsligo *Ab* 85-89; P-in-c Bicker *Linc* 89; V Bicker and Wigtoft from 89. *St Swithin's Vicarage, 14 Old Main Road, Bicker, Boston, Lincs PE20 3EF*   Spalding (0775) 820574

BURNETT, Canon John Capenhurst. b 19. AKC49. **d** 49 **p** 50. R Wroughton *Bris* 56-76; RD Cricklade 70-76; Hon Can Bris Cathl 74-85; V Bris St Andr w St Bart 76-85; rtd 85; Perm to Offic *Bris* from 85. *7 Queen Victoria Road, Bristol BS6 7PD*   Bristol (0272) 738856

BURNETT, Canon Philip Stephen. b 14. Lon Univ BA34 Ball Coll Ox BA45 MA46. Westcott Ho Cam 46. **d** 47 **p** 48. Can Res Sheff Cathl *Sheff* 61-70; Adult Educn Officer Gen Syn Bd of Educn 70-80; rtd 81; C St Botolph without Bishopgate *Lon* 81-84; Lic to Offic 84-88; Perm to Offic *S'wark* from 84. *91 Chelverton Road, London SW15 1RW*   081-789 9934

BURNETT, Susan Mary. b 50. Lon Univ BEd73 St Jo Coll Dur DipTh76. **dss** 78 **d** 87. Welling *S'wark* 78-83; E

Greenwich Ch Ch w St Andr and St Mich 83-87; Par Dn 87-91; Par Dn Sydenham All SS from 91; Par Dn Lower Sydenham St Mich from 91. *St Michael's Vicarage, Champion Crescent, London SE26 4HH*   081-778 7196

BURNHAM, Andrew. b 48. ARCO New Coll Ox BA69 BA71 Westmr Coll Ox CertEd72. St Steph Ho Ox 81. **d** 83 **p** 84. Hon C Clifton *S'well* 83-85; C Beeston 85-87; V Carrington from 87. *Carrington Vicarage, 6 Watcombe Circus, Nottingham NG5 2DT*   Nottingham (0602) 621291

BURNHAM, Cecil Champneys. b 14. AKC39. **d** 39 **p** 40. V Westham *Chich* 66-74; R Harting 74-79; rtd 79; Perm to Offic *Chich* from 87. *25 Sovereign Court, Campbell Road, Bognor Regis, W Sussex PO21 1AH*   Bognor Regis (0243) 822119

BURNHAM, Frank Leslie. b 23. Edin Th Coll 52. **d** 55 **p** 56. TR Marfleet *York* 62-74; V Acomb St Steph 74-85; C Fulford 85-88; rtd 88. *Dulverton Hall, St Martin's Square, Scarborough YO11 2DB*   Scarborough (0723) 373082

BURNINGHAM, Frederick George. b 34. ALCD60. **d** 60 **p** 61. C New Beckenham St Paul *Roch* 60-63; Canada 63-67 and from 89; C Wisley w Pyrford *Guildf* 68-69; P-in-c Sydenham H Trin *S'wark* 69-71; C Broadwater St Mary *Chich* 72-77; R Sotterley, Willingham, Shadingfield, Ellough etc *St E* 77-82; R Ipswich St Clem w H Trin 82-89. *The Good Shepherd Mission, Spence Bay, NWT, Canada, X0E 1B0*   Spence Bay (403) 561-6151

BURNINGHAM, George Walter. b 13. Leeds Univ BA34 MA35. Coll of Resurr Mirfield 34. **d** 36 **p** 37. R Morley *Derby* 67-72; V Derby St Anne and St Jo 72-83; rtd 84; Perm to Offic *Pet* from 84. *5 Uppingham Road, Caldecot, Market Harborough, Leics LE16 8RX*   Rockingham (0536) 771669

BURNISTON, Aubrey John. b 53. St Jo Coll Dur BA. Cranmer Hall Dur. **d** 83 **p** 84. C Owton Manor *Dur* 83-86; TV Rugby St Andr *Cov* from 86. *Peterhouse, 71 Hillmorton Road, Rugby, Warks CV22 5AG*   Rugby (0788) 4381

BURNLEY, William Francis Edward. b 06. Lon Univ BD40. Sarum Th Coll 32. **d** 35 **p** 36. Hon CF from 45; V Westwood *Sarum* 68-74; rtd 74. *Sunnyhill, 2A Perry's Lane, Seend, Melksham, Wilts SN12 6QA*   Devizes (0380) 828510

BURNLEY, Suffragan Bishop of. See MILNER, Rt Rev Ronald James

BURNS, Clifford John Sexstone. b 10. **d** 71 **p** 72. Hon C Canton St Cath *Llan* 71-77; Perm to Offic *Roch* from 77. *2 Bromley College, London Road, Bromley BR1 1PE*   081-464 5075

BURNS, Dane. b 51. DipTh. **d** 85 **p** 86. C Enniskillen *Clogh* 85-87; I Augher w Newtownsaville and Eskrahoole from 87; Dioc Info Officer from 91. *16 Knockmany Road, Augher, Co Tyrone BT77 0DE*   Clogher (06625) 48008

BURNS, Douglas. **d** 85 **p** 86. NSM Dub Crumlin *D & G* 85-91; NSM Dub Crumlin w Chapelizod from 91. *100 Cherryfield Road, Dublin 12, Irish Republic*   Dublin (1) 502010

BURNS, Canon Edward Joseph. b 38. Liv Univ BSc58 St Cath Soc Ox BA61 MA64. Wycliffe Hall Ox 58. **d** 61 **p** 62. C Leyland St Andr *Blackb* 61-64; C Burnley St Pet 64-67; V Chorley St Jas 67-75; V Fulwood Ch Ch from 75; RD Preston 79-86; Chapl Sharoe Green Hosp Preston from 81; Hon Can Blackb Cathl *Blackb* from 86; Bp's Adv on Hosp Chapls from 89. *The Vicarage, 6 Watling Street Road, Fulwood, Preston, Lancs PR2 4DY*   Preston (0772) 719210

BURNS, James Denis. b 43. Lich Th Coll 69. **d** 72 **p** 73. C Gt Wyrley *Lich* 72-75; C Atherton *Man* 75-76; Asst Chapl Sheff Ind Miss *Sheff* 76-79; C-in-c Masborough St Paul w St Jo 76-78; C-in-c Northfield St Mich 76-78; V Rotherham Ferham Park 78-79; V Lanc Ch Ch *Blackb* 79-81; V Lanc Ch Ch w St Jo and St Anne 81-86; V Chorley St Pet from 86. *St Peter's Vicarage, Harpers Lane, Chorley, Lancs PR6 0DW*   Chorley (02572) 63423

BURNS, Michael John. b 53. AKC76. Chich Th Coll 76. **d** 77 **p** 78. C Broseley w Benthall *Heref* 77-81; C Stevenage All SS Pin Green *St Alb* 81-84; V Tattenham Corner and Burgh Heath *Guildf* from 84. *St Mark's Vicarage, Tattenham Corner, Epsom, Surrey KT18 5RD*   Burgh Heath (0737) 353011

BURNS, Robert Joseph. b 34. Wycliffe Hall Ox 67. **d** 71 **p** 72. C Portswood Ch Ch *Win* 71-73; C Woking St Jo *Guildf* 73-77; C Glas St Mary *Glas* 77; Bp's Dom Chapl 77-78; R Glas Gd Shep w Ascension from 78. *The Rectory, 31 Westfield Drive, Glasgow G52 2SG*   041-882 1842

BURNS, Stuart Maitland. b 46. Leeds Univ BA67. Coll of Resurr Mirfield 67. **d** 69 **p** 70. C Wyther Ven Bede *Ripon* 69-73; Asst Chapl Leeds Univ 73-77; Asst Chapl Leeds Poly 73-77; P-in-c Thornthwaite w Thruscross and Darley 77-84; V Leeds Gipton Epiphany 84-89; OSB from 89; Priory of Our Lady Burford from 89; Lic to Offic *Ox* from 89. *The Priory of Our Lady, Burford, Oxford OX8 4SQ*   Burford (099382) 3605

BURR, Mrs Ann Pamela. b 39. S Dios Minl Tr Scheme 83. **dss** 86 **d** 87. Fareham H Trin *Portsm* 86-87; Hon C from 87. *3 Bruce Close, Fareham, Hants PO16 7QJ*   Fareham (0329) 281375

BURR, Brian Gilbert. b 23. AKC49. St Boniface Warminster 50. **d** 50 **p** 51. V Churston Ferrers w Goodrington *Ex* 63-76; RD Ipplepen 69-77; V Brixham 76-77; V Brixham w Churston Ferrers 77; R Cen Torquay 77-81; TR Torre 81-87; rtd 87; Perm to Offic *Ex* from 89. *The Chaplain's House, The Quadrangle, Newland, Malvern, Worcs WR13 5AX*

BURR, Raymond Leslie. b 43. NE Ord Course 82 Edin Th Coll 84. **d** 85 **p** 86. C Hartlepool St Paul *Dur* 85-87; C Sherburn w Pittington 87-89; R Lyons from 89. *The Rectory, High Street, Easington Lane, Houghton le Spring DH5 0JN*   091-526 5505

BURRELL, Arthur Lewis. b 12. Qu Coll Ox BA34 MA39. Westcott Ho Cam 35. **d** 36 **p** 37. R Sulhamstead Abbots and Bannister w Ufton Nervet *Ox* 66-80; rtd 80; Perm to Offic *Ox* from 86. *15 Church End, Haddenham, Bucks HP18 AE*   Haddenham (0844) 290357

BURRELL, David Philip. b 56. Southn Univ BTh90. Sarum & Wells Th Coll 85. **d** 88 **p** 89. C Ixworth and Bardwell *St E* 88-91; P-in-c Haughley w Wetherden from 91. *The Vicarage, Haughley, Stowmarket, Suffolk IP14 3NS*   Stowmarket (0449) 673467

BURRELL, Godfrey John. b 49. Reading Univ BSc70 Qu Coll Ox CertEd71. Wycliffe Hall Ox 84. **d** 86 **p** 87. C Didcot All SS *Ox* 86-89; S Africa from 90. *St Alban's College, Private Bag 1, Alkantrant, Pretoria, 0005 South Africa*

BURRELL, Canon Maurice Claude. b 30. Bris Univ BA54 MA63 Lanc Univ PhD78. Tyndale Hall Bris. **d** 55 **p** 56. C Wandsworth St Steph *S'wark* 55-57; C Whitehall Park St Andr Hornsey Lane *Lon* 57-59; R Kirby Cane *Nor* 59-63; R Ellingham 61-63; Chapl K Sch Gutersloh, W Germany 63-67; R Widford *Chelmsf* 67-71; Chapl and Lect St Mary's Coll Cheltenham 71-75; Dir of Educn *Nor* 75-86; Hon Can Nor Cathl from 87; Dioc Dir of Tr from 87. *8 Old Grove Court, Norwich NR3 3NL*   Norwich (0603) 402122

BURRIDGE, Richard Alan. b 55. Univ Coll Ox BA77 MA81 Nottm Univ CertEd78 DipTh83 PhD89. St Jo Coll Nottm 82. **d** 85 **p** 86. C Bromley SS Pet and Paul *Roch* 85-87; Chapl Ex Univ *Ex* from 87. *3 Glenthorne Road, Exeter, Devon EX4 4QU*   Exeter (0392) 435384

✠**BURROUGH, Rt Rev John Paul.** b 16. MBE46. St Edm Hall Ox BA37 DipTh38 MA45. Ely Th Coll 45. **d** 46 **p** 47 **c** 68. C Aldershot St Mich *Guildf* 46-51; Korea 51-59; Chapl to Overseas Peoples *Birm* 59-67; Hon Can Birm Cathl 65-67; Can Res Birm Cathl 67-68; Bp Mashonaland 68-81; R Empingham *Pet* 81-85; Asst Bp Pet 81-85; RD Rutland 82-85; rtd 85; Perm to Offic *Ox* from 85. *6 Mill Green Close, Bampton, Oxford OX8 2HF*   Bampton Castle (0993) 850952

BURROUGHS, Edward Graham. b 36. K Coll Lon BD AKC. **d** 60 **p** 61. C Walton St Mary *Liv* 60-63; S Rhodesia 63-65; Rhodesia 65-80; Zimbabwe from 80. *Box 8045, Belmont, Bulawayo, Zimbabwe*   Bulawayo (9) 78711

BURROW, Alison Sarah. b 59. Homerton Coll Cam BEd82. Westcott Ho Cam 84. **d** 87. Par Dn Hebden Bridge *Wakef* 87-88; Par Dn Prestwood and Gt Hampden *Ox* 88-90; Par Dn Olney w Emberton from 90. *4 Oxleys, Olney, Bucks MK46 5PH*   Bedford (0234) 712878

BURROW, Ronald. b 31. Univ Coll Dur BA55. St Steph Ho Ox 83. **d** 85 **p** 86. C Dawlish *Ex* 85-87; TV Ottery St Mary, Alfington, W Hill, Tipton etc 87-91; P-in-c Pyworthy, Pancrasweek and Bridgerule from 91. *The Rectory, Pyworthy, Holsworthy, Devon EX22 6SU*   Holsworthy (0409) 254062

BURROWES, Thomas Cecil. b 13. TCD BA36 MA43. TCD Div Sch Div Test36. **d** 37 **p** 38. I Killinchy *D & D* 50-78; RD Killinchy 71-78; rtd 78. *1 Kilmood Church Road, Killinchy, Newtownards, Co Down BT23 6SA*   Killinchy (0238) 541942

BURROWS, Canon Brian Albert. b 34. Lon Univ DipTh59. St Aid Birkenhead. **d** 59 **p** 60. C Sutton St Geo *Ches* 59-62; Canada 62-69 and from 74; V Stratton St Margaret *Bris* 70-74; Hon Can Frobisher Bay 78-80. *705 Main Street East, Hamilton, Ontario, Canada, L8M 1K8*

BURROWS, Clifford Robert. b 37. MIMechE68 Univ of Wales BSc62 Lon Univ PhD69. Chich Th Coll 75. **d** 76 **p** 77. NSM Brighton St Pet *Chich* 76-78; NSM Brighton St Pet w Chpl Royal 78-80; NSM Brighton St Pet w Chpl Royal and St Jo 80-82; Perm to Offic *Glas* 82-85 and 86-89; NSM Clarkston 85-86. *Address temp unknown*

BURROWS, David. b 62. Leeds Univ BA85. Linc Th Coll 86. **d** 88 **p** 89. C Kippax w Allerton Bywater *Ripon* 88-91; C Manston from 91. *21 Pendas Grove, Manston, Leeds LS15 8HE* Leeds (0532) 649666

BURROWS, David MacPherson. b 43. N Ord Course. **d** 82 **p** 83. NSM Newburgh *Liv* from 82. *34 Woodrow Drive, Newburgh, Wigan, Lancs WN8 7LB* Parbold (0257) 462948

BURROWS, Canon George Henry Jerram. b 10. TCD BA31 MA37. TCD Div Sch 31. **d** 33 **p** 38. P-in-c Dub St Luke *D & G* 71-78; rtd 78; CV Ch Ch Cathl Dub *D & G* 81-90. *22 Longwood Avenue, Dublin 8, Irish Republic* Dublin (1) 543629

BURROWS, Graham Charles. b 47. Leeds Univ CertEd69 Open Univ BA81. N Ord Course 87. **d** 90 **p** 91. C Chorlton-cum-Hardy St Clem *Man* from 90. *94 Hardy Lane, Chorlton-cum-Hardy, Manchester M21 2DN* 061-881 9458

BURROWS, Miss Jean. b 54. CertEd75. Trin Coll Bris 89. **d** 91. C Allesley *Cov* from 91. *c/o The Rectory, Allesley, Coventry CV5 9EQ* Coventry (0203) 402006

BURROWS, John Edward. b 36. Leeds Univ BA60 PGCE63. Coll of Resurr Mirfield. **d** 63 **p** 65. C Much Hadham *St Alb* 63-65; Hon C Haggerston St Mary w St Chad *Lon* 65-73; P-in-c Finsbury St Clem w St Barn and St Matt 73-76; Chapl Woodbridge Sch Suffolk 76-83; Lic to Offic *St E* 76-83; V Ipswich St Bart from 83. *St Bartholomew's Vicarage, Newton Road, Ipswich IP3 8HQ* Ipswich (0473) 727441

BURROWS, Joseph Atkinson. b 32. St Aid Birkenhead 57. **d** 61 **p** 62. C Hoole Ches 61-67; Jamaica 67-68; C Ayr *Glas* 68-74; R Prestwick 74-78; Australia from 78. *60 Memorial Avenue, St Ives, NSW, Australia 2075* St Ives (2) 488-9393

BURROWS, Leonard Ernest. b 14. Roch Th Coll. **d** 62 **p** 63. V Thurmaston *Leic* 70-79; V Leic St Eliz Nether Hall 79-81; rtd 81; Lic to Offic *Ely* from 81. *44 Humberley Close, Eynesbury, St Neots, Huntingdon, Cambs PE19 2SE* Huntingdon (0480) 213524

BURROWS, Michael Andrew James. b 61. TCD BA82 MA85 MLitt86 DipTh87. **d** 87 **p** 88. C Douglas Union w Frankfield *C, C & R* 87-91; Dean of Residence TCD from 91; Lic to Offic *D & G* from 91; Min Can St Patr Cathl Dub from 91. *27 Trinity College, Dublin 2, Irish Republic* Dublin (1) 772941 or 985811

BURROWS, Paul Anthony. b 55. Nottm Univ BA77. Gen Th Sem (NY) STM88 St Steph Ho Ox 77. **d** 79 **p** 80. C Camberwell St Giles *S'wark* 79-81; C St Helier 81-83; C Fareham SS Pet and Paul *Portsm* 83-85; USA from 85. *13207 L'Enfant Drive, Fort Washington, Maryland 20744, USA* Fort Washington (301) 203-9521

BURROWS, Peter. b 55. BTh. Sarum & Wells Th Coll 80. **d** 83 **p** 84. C Baildon *Bradf* 83-87; R Broughton Astley *Leic* from 87. *The Rectory, Frolesworth Road, Broughton Astley, Leicester LE9 6PF* Sutton Elms (0455) 282261

BURROWS, Reginald Wilfred. b 36. Qu Coll Cam BA57 MA62. Clifton Th Coll 61. **d** 63 **p** 64. C Muswell Hill St Jas *Lon* 63-65; C Bootle St Leon *Liv* 65-69; R Man Albert Memorial Ch w Newton Heath *Man* 69-72; V Newc St Barn and St Jude *Newc* from 72. *The Vicarage, 1 Springbank Road, Newcastle upon Tyne NE2 1PD* 091-232 7837

BURROWS, Samuel Reginald. b 30. AKC57. **d** 58 **p** 59. C Shildon *Dur* 58-62; C Heworth St Mary 62-67; C-in-c Leam Lane CD 67-72; C-in-c Bishopwearmouth St Mary V w St Pet CD 72-77; R Bewcastle and Stapleton *Carl* 77-82; R Harrington 82-90; P-in-c Millom 90; V from 90. *The Vicarage, St George's Drive, Millom, Cumbria LA18 4JA* Millom (0229) 773805

✠**BURROWS, Rt Rev Simon Hedley.** b 28. K Coll Cam BA52 MA56. Westcott Ho Cam 52. **d** 54 **p** 55 **c** 74. C St Jo Wood *Lon* 54-57; Chapl Jes Coll Cam 57-60; V Wyken *Cov* 60-67; V Fareham H Trin *Portsm* 67-71; TR 71-74; Suff Bp Buckm *Ox* 74-87; Area Bp Buckm from 87. *Sheridan, Grimms Hill, Great Missenden, Bucks HP16 9BD* Great Missenden (02406) 2173

BURSELL, Chan Rupert David Hingston. b 42. QC. Ex Univ LLB63 St Edm Hall Ox BA67 MA72 DPhil72. St Steph Ho Ox 67. **d** 68 **p** 69. NSM St Marylebone w H Trin *Lon* 68-69; NSM Almondsbury *Bris* 69-71; NSM Bedminster St Fran 71-75; Lic to Offic *B & W* from 72; NSM Bedminster *Bris* 75-82; NSM Bris Ch Ch w St

Ewen and All SS 83-88; NSM City of Bris 83-88; Lic to Offic from 88. *Brookside, 74 Church Road, Winscombe, Avon BS25 1BP* Winscombe (093484) 3542

BURSLEM, Christopher David Jeremy Grant. b 35. AKC85. **d** 59 **p** 60. C Bocking St Mary *Chelmsf* 59-63; C Glouc All SS *Glouc* 64-67; R Amberley 67-87; P-in-c Withington and Compton Abdale w Haselton from 87. *The Rectory, Withington, Cheltenham, Glos GL54 4BG* Withington (024289) 242

BURSON-THOMAS, Michael Edwin. b 52. Sarum & Wells Th Coll 84. **d** 86 **p** 87. C Bitterne Park *Win* 86-89; V Lockerley and E Dean w E and W Tytherley from 89. *The Vicarage, The Street, Lockerley, Romsey, Hants SO51 0JF* Lockerley (0794) 40635

BURSTON, Robert Benjamin Stuart. b 45. St Chad's Coll Dur BA68 DipTh70. **d** 70 **p** 71. C Whorlton *Newc* 70-77; V Alwinton w Holystone and Alnham 77-83; TR Glendale Gp from 83. *The Rectory, 5 Fenton Drive, Wooler, Northd NE71 6DT* Wooler (0668) 81551

BURT, Leslie Reginald. b 22. ACIS49. St Aug Coll Cant 65. **d** 66 **p** 67. C Petersfield w Sheet *Portsm* 66-70; Perm to Offic from 82. *44B Victoria Road South, Southsea, Hants PO5 2BT* Portsmouth (0705) 730989

BURT, Noel Bryce. b 21. Clare Coll Cam BA49 MA53. Cuddesdon Coll 49. **d** 51 **p** 52. R Invergowrie *Bre* 67-76; R Glencarse 71-76; V Denton and Ingleton *Dur* 76-88; rtd 88. *8 North Terrace, Gainford, Darlington, Co Durham DL2 3EE* Darlington (0325) 730075

BURT, Paul Andrew. b 52. Leeds Univ BA74. Ridley Hall Cam 82. **d** 84 **p** 85. C Edin St Thos *Edin* 84-88; CMS 88-90; Bahrain 88-90; R Melrose *Edin* from 91. *20 High Cross Avenue, Melrose, Roxburghshire TD6 9SU* Melrose (089682) 2626

BURT, Robert. b 08. Lich Th Coll 31. **d** 34 **p** 35. V Darlington St Matt *Dur* 61-77; rtd 77. *Dulverton Hall, St Martin's Square, Scarborough YO11 2DB* Scarborough (0723) 373082

BURT, Roger Malcolm. b 45. St Jo Coll Auckland LTh74 SSC. **d** 73 **p** 74. New Zealand 73-80; P-in-c Colton *Nor* 80; P-in-c Easton 80; V Easton w Colton and Marlingford 80-88; CF from 88. *c/o MOD (Army), Bagshot Park, Bagshot, Surrey GU19 5PL* Bagshot (0276) 71717

BURT, William Henry John. b 14. BA. **d** 38 **p** 39. Chapl St Mary's Gen Hosp Portsm 51-76; P-in-c Elmsted w Hastingleigh *Cant* 77-78; P-in-c Crundale w Godmersham 77-78; rtd 79; P-in-c Upper Hardres w Stelling *Cant* 79-85. *18 Oaten Hill Place, Canterbury, Kent CT1 3HJ* Canterbury (0227) 69351

BURTON, Andrew John. b 63. St Kath Coll Liv BA84 CertDiv84. Cranmer Hall Dur 86. **d** 88 **p** 89. C Harlescott *Lich* from 88. *14 Maple Drive, Shrewsbury SY1 3SE* Shrewsbury (0743) 350907

BURTON, Antony William James. b 29. Ch Coll Cam BA52 MA56. Cuddesdon Coll 52. **d** 54 **p** 55. C Linc St Nic w St Jo Newport *Linc* 54-57; C Croydon *Cant* 57-62; V Winterton *Linc* 62-82; V Roxby w Risby 70-82; RD Manlake 76-82; V Nettleham from 82. *The Vicarage, 2 Vicarage Lane, Nettleham, Lincoln LN2 2RH* Lincoln (0522) 754752

BURTON, Cecil John. b 17. Tyndale Hall Bris 39. **d** 43 **p** 44. V Muswell Hill St Matt *Lon* 63-70; Perm to Offic S'wark 70-81; Ches 71-78; rtd 82. *6 Lawman Court, 262 Kew Road, Richmond, Surrey TW9 3EF* 081-940 1578

BURTON, Christopher Paul. b 38. FCA75. Clifton Th Coll 67. **d** 69 **p** 70. C Wandsworth All SS *S'wark* 69-72; C York St Paul *York* 72-75; V Castle Vale *Birm* 75-82; R Gt Parndon *Chelmsf* from 82. *Great Parndon Rectory, Perry Road, Harlow, Essex CM18 7NP* Harlow (0279) 432626

BURTON, David Alan. b 53. St Jo Coll Dur BA. Westcott Ho Cam 81. **d** 84 **p** 85. C Bedf St Andr *St Alb* 84-87; C Leighton Buzzard w Eggington, Hockliffe etc 87-91; V Kingsbury Episcopi w E Lambrook *B & W* from 91. *The Vicarage, Folly Road, Kingsbury Episcopi, Martock, Somerset TA12 6BH* Martock (0935) 824605

BURTON, Desmond Jack. b 49. Sarum & Wells Th Coll 70. **d** 73 **p** 74. C Lakenham St Jo *Nor* 73-77; C Gt Yarmouth 77-80; R Tidworth *Sarum* 80-83; Chapl HM Pris Pentonville 83-84; Standford Hill 84-88; Chapl HM Pris Swaleside from 88. *6 Range Road, Eastchurch, Sheerness, Kent ME12 4DY* Eastchurch (0795) 880656

BURTON, Ven Douglas Harry. b 13. OBE62. Univ Coll Dur LTh37 BA38. St Aug Coll Cant. **d** 39 **p** 40. Argentina from 40; Adn River Plate 71-84; rtd 84. *11 De Setiembre 2130 2 Fl, 1428 Buenos Aires, Argentina*

BURTON, Edward Arthur. b 15. Tyndale Hall Bris 39. **d** 42 **p** 43. V Beckford w Ashton under Hill *Glouc* 63-78; rtd 78; Perm to Offic *Chich* from 83. *B5 Hatfield Court,*

Salisbury Road, Hove, E Sussex BN3 3AA   Brighton (0273) 727560

BURTON, Edward Arthur. b 40. AKC63. **d** 64 **p** 65. C Upper Teddington SS Pet and Paul *Lon* 64-69; C-in-c Hammersmith SS Mich and Geo White City Estate CD 69-71; C Addlestone *Guildf* 71-74; V Harlesden All So *Lon* 75-89; V Notting Dale St Clem w St Mark and St Jas from 89. *St Clement's House, Sirdar Road, London W11 4EQ*   071-727 5450

BURTON, Frank George. b 19. AKC42. **d** 42 **p** 43. V Edmonton All SS *Lon* 66-77; rtd 77. *15 Lincoln Crescent, Enfield, Middx EN1 1JN*   081-366 3620

BURTON, Frank Victor. b 10. Linc Th Coll 76. **d** 76 **p** 77. Hon C Folkingham w Laughton *Linc* 76-77; Hon C S Lafford 77-79; Hon C Helpringham 79; Hon C New Sleaford 79-80; Perm to Offic from 80. *27 Gardenfield, Skellingthorpe, Lincoln LN6 5SP*   Lincoln (0522) 688697

BURTON, Geoffrey Robert William. b 20. Ridley Hall Cam. **d** 63 **p** 64. R Scarning w Wendling *Nor* 67-71; V Bacton w Edingthorpe 71-80; P-in-c Witton w Ridlington 75-80; V Bacton w Edingthorpe w Witton and Ridlington 80-87; rtd 87; Perm to Offic *Nor* from 87; Hon C Duns *Edin* from 87. *Harelawside Farm, Grantshouse, Duns, Berwickshire TD11 3RP*   Grantshouse (03615) 209

BURTON, Graham John. b 45. Bris Univ BA69. Tyndale Hall Bris 69. **d** 71 **p** 72. C Leic St Chris *Leic* 71-75; C Southall Green St Jo *Lon* 75-79; CMS from 80; Pakistan from 80. *House No 44, 27th Street, Islamabad F-6/2, Pakistan*   Islamabad (51) 826770

BURTON, Harold Alban. b 10. Worc Ord Coll. **d** 53 **p** 54. C Worthing St Paul *Chich* 69-74; rtd 74; Hon C Leek and Meerbrook *Lich* 83-90. *Ramsay Hall, Byron Road, Worthing, W Sussex BN11 3HW*   Worthing (0903) 200838

BURTON, Hugh Anthony. b 56. Edin Univ BD79. Cranmer Hall Dur 81. **d** 83 **p** 84. C Coalville and Bardon Hill *Leic* 83-87; P-in-c Packington w Normanton-le-Heath from 87. *The Vicarage, Mill Street, Packington, Ashby-de-la-Zouch, Leics LE6 5WL*   Ashby-de-la-Zouch (0530) 412215

BURTON, John Harold Stanley. b 13. Univ Coll Ox BA35 MA38. Westcott Ho Cam 36. **d** 36 **p** 38. Gen Sec Ch Lads' Brigade 54-64 and 73-76; rtd 78. *45 Westbourne Terrace, London W2 3UR*   071-262 8470

BURTON, John Richard. b 22. Em Coll Cam BA47 MA51. Wycliffe Hall Ox 49. **d** 50 **p** 51. V Ellacombe *Ex* 59-74; TV Cen Torquay 74-76; Warden Maillard Ho of Healing 76-87; Hon C Torre 76-82; rtd 82; Perm to Offic *Ex* from 87. *Manor House, Coffinswell, Newton Abbot, Devon TQ12 4SW*   Kingskerswell (0803) 873758

BURTON, Leonard Barcham. b 13. St Deiniol's Hawarden 60. **d** 60 **p** 61. V Lower Darwen St Jas *Blackb* 69-75; V Stalmine 75-81; rtd 82; Lic to Offic *Blackb* from 82. *34 Roylen Avenue, Poulton-le-Fylde, Blackpool FY6 7PH*   Poulton-le-Fylde (0253) 883118

BURTON, Leslie Samuel Bertram. b 23. **d** 91. NSM St Cleer *Truro* from 91. *41 Park View, Liskeard, Cornwall PL14 3EF*   Liskeard (0579) 44891

BURTON, Michael John. b 55. Leeds Univ BSc76 Leeds Poly BSc80. St Jo Coll Nottm LTh88. **d** 88 **p** 89. C Charles w St Matthias Plymouth *Ex* from 88. *18 Dale Gardens, Plymouth PL4 6PX*   Plymouth (0752) 669087

BURTON, Nicholas John. b 52. St Steph Ho Ox 77. **d** 80 **p** 81. C Leic St Matt and St Geo *Leic* 80-82; C Leic Resurr 82-83; TV 83-88; C Narborough and Huncote 88-90; R from 90. *All Saints' Rectory, 15 Church View, Narborough, Leicester LE9 5GY*   Leicester (0533) 867658

BURTON, Norman George. b 30. N Ord Course. **d** 83 **p** 84. C Rothwell w Lofthouse *Ripon* 83-86; C Rothwell 86-87; V Lofthouse from 87. *8 Church Farm Close, Lofthouse, Wakefield, W Yorkshire WF3 3SA*   Wakefield (0924) 823286

BURTON, Philip. b 04. Or Coll Ox BA26 MA31. Sarum Th Coll 31. **d** 31 **p** 32. V Aberford *York* 59-77; V Saxton 59-77; V Aberford w Saxton 77; rtd 77; Hon C Ryther *York* 80-81. *De Brome Cottage, Aberford, Leeds LS25 3DP*   Leeds (0532) 813267

BURTON, Richard Peter. b 56. Nottm Univ BA80. Cranmer Hall Dur 80. **d** 82 **p** 83. C Linthorpe *York* 82-85; R Bishop Burton w Walkington from 85. *The Rectory, Walkington, Beverley, N Humberside HU17 8SP*   Hull (0482) 868379

BURTON EVANS, David. *See* EVANS, David Burton

BURTT, Andrew Keith. b 50. Massey Univ (NZ) BA72 MA74. DipEd76. St Jo Coll (NZ) LTh82. **d** 81 **p** 82. New Zealand 81-83; CF from 84. *c/o MOD (Army),*

Bagshot Park, Bagshot, Surrey GU19 5PL   Bagshot (0276) 71717

BURTWELL, Stanley Peter. b 32. Leeds Univ BA55. Coll of Resurr Mirfield 55. **d** 57 **p** 58. C Leeds St Hilda *Ripon* 57-61; S Africa 61-72; P-in-c Gt Hanwood *Heref* 72-78; R 78-83; RD Pontesbury 80-83; V Upper Norwood St Jo *Cant* 83-84; V Upper Norwood St Jo *S'wark* 85-90; RD Croydon N 85-90; TR Bourne Valley *Sarum* from 90. *The Rectory, Newton Tony Road, Allington, Salisbury SP4 0BZ*   Idmiston (0980) 610663

BURWELL, Peter William Gale. b 45. Edin Th Coll 72. **d** 75 **p** 76. C Edin St Jo *Edin* 75-79; R Lasswade 79-86; R Dalkeith 80-86; Dioc Stewardship Adv *Bradf* from 86. *93 Hoyle Court Road, Baildon, Shipley, W Yorkshire BD17 6EL*   Bradford (0274) 594790

BURY, Herbert John Malcolm. b 28. Linc Coll Ox BA52 MA56. Roch Th Coll 68. **d** 69 **p** 70. C Bexleyheath Ch Ch *Roch* 69-72; V Ryarsh w Birling 72-83; P-in-c Addington w Trottiscliffe 76-83; R Knockholt w Halstead from 83. *The Rectory, Church Road, Halstead, Sevenoaks, Kent TN14 7HQ*   Knockholt (0959) 2133

BURY, Nicholas Ayles Stillingfleet. b 43. Qu Coll Cam BA65 MA69 Ch Ch Ox MA71. Cuddesdon Coll. **d** 68 **p** 69. C Liv Our Lady and St Nic *Liv* 68-71; Chapl Ch Ch *Ox* 71-75; V Stevenage St Mary Shephall *St Alb* 75-84; V St Peter-in-Thanet *Cant* from 84. *The Vicarage, 14 Vicarage Street, St Peters, Broadstairs, Kent CT10 2SG*   Thanet (0843) 62728 or 69169

BUSBY, Canon Geoffrey. b 10. Lich Th Coll 30. **d** 33 **p** 34. R Wirksworth w Carsington *Derby* 51-83; V Idridgehay 55-83; V Middleton 55-83; Hon Can Derby Cathl 57-83; R Kirk Ireton 57-83; rtd 83; Perm to Offic *Derby* from 83. *8 Yokecliffe Crescent, Wirksworth, Derby DE4 4ER*   Wirksworth (062982) 2567

BUSBY, Ian Frederick Newman. b 32. Roch Th Coll 61. **d** 64 **p** 65. C Bedale *Ripon* 64-67; C Stevenage St Geo *St Alb* 67-71; V Stevenage St Mary Shephall 71-75; V Kildwick *Bradf* from 75. *The Vicarage, Kildwick, Keighley, W Yorkshire BD20 9BB*   Cross Hills (0535) 633307

BUSBY, Jack Wright. b 12. Leeds Univ BA35. Coll of Resurr Mirfield 35. **d** 37 **p** 38. R Barkestone cum Plungar and Redmile *Leic* 70-77; rtd 77. *43 Chestnut Avenue, Waltham, Grimsby, S Humberside DN37 0DF*   Grimsby (0472) 823208

BUSH, Alfred Edward Leonard. b 09. ALCD39. **d** 39 **p** 40. V Oakwood St Thos *Lon* 58-75; rtd 75; Perm to Offic Chich 75-78; St E 78-86; Ox from 86. *11 Pitford Road, Woodley, Reading RG5 4QF*   Reading (0734) 698115

BUSH, David. b 25. FRIBA47 Liv Univ BArch47. S'wark Ord Course 73. **d** 77 **p** 77. C Douglas St Geo and St Barn *S & M* 77-80; Chapl Ballamona Hosp and Cronk Grianagh 80-86; V Marown 80-87; R The Rissingtons *Glouc* from 87. *The Rectory, Great Rissington, Cheltenham, Glos GL54 2LL*   Cotswold (0451) 20560

BUSH, George Raymond. b 57. St Jo Coll Cam BA81 MA84. Ripon Coll Cuddesdon BA85 MA88. **d** 85 **p** 86. C Leeds St Aid *Ripon* 85-89; Chapl St Jo Coll Cam from 89. *St John's College, Cambridge*   Cambridge (0223) 338600

BUSH, Roger Charles. b 56. K Coll Lon BA78 Leeds Univ BA85. Coll of Resurr Mirfield 83. **d** 86 **p** 87. C Newbold and Dunston *Derby* 86-90; TV Leic Resurr *Leic* from 90. *St Albans House, Weymouth Street, Leicester LE4 6FN*   Leicester (0533) 661002

BUSHAU, Reginald Francis. b 49. St Steph Ho Ox BA73. **d** 74 **p** 75. C Deptford St Paul *S'wark* 74-77; C Willesden St Andr *Lon* 77; C Gladstone Park St Fran 77-82; P-in-c Brondesbury St Anne w Kilburn H Trin 83-88; V Paddington St Mary Magd from 88. *St Mary Magdalene Clergy Ho, Rowington Close, London W2 5TF*   071-289 1818

BUSHELL, Roy. b 32. **d** 79 **p** 80. NSM Croft w Southworth *Liv* 79-87; C Netherton 87-89; R Newton in Makerfield Em from 89. *The Rectory, Wargrave Road, Newton-le-Willows, Merseyside WA12 8RR*   Newton-le-Willows (0925) 24920

BUSK, David Westly. b 60. Magd Coll Cam BA. Cranmer Hall Dur. **d** 89 **p** 90. C Old Swinford Stourbridge *Worc* from 89. *8 Bedcote Place, Stourbridge, W Midlands*   Stourbridge (0384) 390367

BUSK, Horace. b 34. Clifton Th Coll 56. **d** 60 **p** 61. C Burton All SS *Lich* 60-63; Paraguay 63-66; C Silverhill St Matt *Chich* 66-67; Lic to Offic *Sarum* 67-69; C W Kilburn St Luke w St Simon and St Jude *Lon* 69-74; TV Ashwellthorpe w Wreningham *Nor* 74-81; TV Wreningham 81; P-in-c Meysey Hampton w Marston Meysey and Castle Eaton *Glouc* from 81. *The Rectory,*

Meysey Hampton, Cirencester, Glos GL7 5JX Poulton (028585) 249

BUSS, Gerald Vere Austen. b 36. CCC Cam PhD87. St Steph Ho Ox 59. **d** 63 **p** 64. C Petersham *S'wark* 63-66; C Brompton H Trin *Lon* 66-69; Asst Chapl Hurstpierpoint Coll Hassocks 70-73; Chapl 74-90; Ho Master from 90. *Hurstpierpoint College, Hassocks, W Sussex BN6 9JS* Hurstpierpoint (0273) 833636

BUSS, Philip Hodnett. b 37. Ch Coll Cam BA59 MA63. Tyndale Hall Bris 61. **d** 63 **p** 64. Tutor Lon Coll of Div 62-66; Chapl 66-69; Hon C Northwood Em *Lon* 63-70; V Handsworth Woodhouse *Sheff* 70-74; V Fulham Ch *Lon* 74-82; V Woking St Pet *Guildf* 82-88. *80 Woodville Road, Ham, Richmond, Surrey TW10 7QN*

BUSSELL, Greader Edmund. b 02. AKC34. **d** 34 **p** 35. R Buckerell *Ex* 61-68; R Feniton 61-68; rtd 68; Hon C Ottery St Mary *Ex* 69-84; Area Sec (S and W) Melanesian Miss 70-76; Lic to Offic *Lich* from 84. *Flat 111, The Cedars, Abbey Foregate, Shrewsbury SY2 6BY* Shrewsbury (0743) 271430

BUSSELL, Ronald William. b 34. CA Tr Coll 57 St Deiniol's Hawarden 81. **d** 83 **p** 84. C Claughton cum Grange *Ches* 83-85; P-in-c Preston St Oswald *Blackb* 85-87; V Fleetwood St Nic from 87. *St Nicholas's Vicarage, Highbury Avenue, Fleetwood, Lancs FY7 7DJ* Fleetwood (03917) 4402

BUSSEY, Norman. b 22. Clifton Th Coll 63. **d** 65 **p** 66. V Bradley *Wakef* 69-88; rtd 88. *43 Crispin Road, Winchcombe, Cheltenham, Glos GL54 5JX* Cheltenham (0242) 602754

BUSTARD, Guy Nicholas. b 51. K Coll Lon BD77 AKC77. St Steph Ho Ox 77. **d** 78 **p** 79. C Hythe *Cant* 78-81; Chapl RN 81-85; V Haddenham *Ely* 85-89; V Wilburton 85-89; Chapl Qu Eliz Hosp Welwyn Garden City from 89. *The Chaplain's Office, Queen Elizabeth II Hospital, Welwyn Garden City, Herts AL6 9DQ* Welwyn Garden (0707) 328111

BUSTIN, Canon Peter Ernest. b 32. Qu Coll Cam BA56 MA60. Tyndale Hall Bris 56. **d** 57 **p** 58. C Welling *Roch* 57-60; C Farnborough *Guildf* 60-62; V Hornsey Rise St Mary *Lon* 62-70; R Barnwell *Pet* 70-78; RD Oundle 76-84; P-in-c Luddington w Hemington and Thurning 77-78; R Barnwell w Thurning and Luddington 78-84; V Southwold *St E* from 84; RD Halesworth from 90; Hon Can St E Cathl from 91. *The Vicarage, Gardner Road, Southwold, Suffolk IP18 6HJ* Southwold (0502) 722397

BUSTIN, Peter Laurence. b 54. St Steph Ho Ox. **d** 83 **p** 84. C Northolt St Mary *Lon* 83-86; C Pimlico St Pet w Westmr Ch Ch 86-88; C Heston 88-91; P-in-c Twickenham All SS from 91. *All Saints' Vicarage, 18 Belmont Road, Twickenham TW2 5DA*

BUSTON, Dudley Graham. b 06. Trin Coll Cam BA28 MA32 Ox Univ DipTh33. Wycliffe Hall Ox 32. **d** 34 **p** 35. P-in-c Enbourne w Hampstead Marshall *Ox* 70-74; rtd 74; Perm to Offic Ox from 74; Lon 74-80; Hon C Chelsea Ch Ch *Lon* 80-87; Hon C Chelsea St Luke and Ch Ch from 87. *c/o 3 Mill End Cottages, Little Missenden, Amersham, Bucks HP7 0RG* Great Missenden (02406) 4686

BUTCHER, Andrew John. b 43. Trin Coll Cam BA66 MA69. Cuddesdon Coll 66. **d** 68 **p** 69. C Sheff Broomhall St Mark *Sheff* 68-70; P-in-c Louth H Trin *Linc* 70-72; Chapl RAF 72-87; Lic to Offic *Ox* 85-87; TR Cove St Jo *Guildf* from 87. *The Rectory, 55 Cove Road, Farnborough, Hants GU14 0EX* Farnborough (0252) 544544

BUTCHER, Canon Douglas Claude. b 08. Ch Coll Cam BA29 MA44. Oak Hill Th Coll 50. **d** 51 **p** 52. Egypt 60-72; C Swanage *Sarum* 72-78; rtd 78. *7 Brookside, Shreen Way, Gillingham, Dorset SP8 4HR* Gillingham (0747) 823865

BUTCHER, Francis Walter Lowndes. b 17. Bps' Coll Cheshunt 49. **d** 52 **p** 53. V Malden St Jas *S'wark* 63-80; rtd 82; Perm to Offic S'wark from 82. *12 Glenavon Close, Claygate, Esher, Surrey KT10 0HP* Esher (0372) 64597

BUTCHER, Dr Hubert Maxwell. b 24. Ch Coll Cam BA48 MA53. Trin Coll Toronto BD68 San Francisco Th Sem DMin78 Wycliffe Hall Ox 49. **d** 51 **p** 52. P-in-c Bradf St Jo *Bradf* 58-62; Canada from 63; rtd 88. *Box 129, Sorrento, British Columbia, Canada, V0E 2W0* Sorrento (604) 675 2783

BUTCHER, Norman. b 13. Wycliffe Hall Ox 40. **d** 42 **p** 43. R Barwick in Elmet *Ripon* 59-79; rtd 79; P-in-c Middleton w Cropton *York* 81-83. *4 Pippin Road, Mount Park, Malton, N Yorkshire* Malton (0653) 695707

BUTCHER, Philip Warren. b 46. Trin Coll Cam BA68 MA70. Cuddesdon Coll 68. **d** 70 **p** 71. C Bris St

Mary Redcliffe w Temple etc *Bris* 70-73; Hon C W Wickham St Fran *Cant* 73-78; Chapl Abingdon Sch 78-85; Chapl K Edw VI Sch Nor from 85. *70 Bishopgate, Norwich NR1 4AA* Norwich (0603) 664042

BUTCHER, Richard Peter. b 50. St Chad's Coll Dur BA71. Chich Th Coll 73. **d** 74 **p** 75. C Yeovil St Mich *B & W* 74-77; Chapl Wellingborough Sch 77-83; R Gt w Lt Billing *Pet* 83-88; Chapl Bp Stopford Sch Kettering 88-90. *4 Field Street Avenue, Kettering, Northants NN16 8EP* Kettering (0536) 522733

BUTCHERS, Mark Andrew. b 59. Trin Coll Cam BA81 Southn Univ BTh87 K Coll Lon MTh90. Chich Th Coll 84. **d** 87 **p** 88. C Chelsea St Luke *Lon* 87; C Chelsea St Luke and Ch Ch 87-90; C Mitcham SS Pet and Paul *S'wark* from 90. *32 Lewis Road, Mitcham, Surrey CR4 3DE* 081-646 2268

BUTLAND, Cameron James. b 58. BA. Ripon Coll Cuddesdon 81. **d** 84 **p** 85. C Tettenhall Regis *Lich* 84-88; V Bodicote *Ox* from 88. *The Vicarage, Bodicote, Banbury, Oxon OX15 4BN* Banbury (0295) 270174

BUTLAND, Godfrey John. b 51. Grey Coll Dur BA72. Wycliffe Hall Ox 73. **d** 75 **p** 76. C Much Woolton *Liv* 75-78; Bp's Dom Chapl 78-81; V Everton St Geo from 81; AD Liv N from 89. *St George's Vicarage, Northumberland Terrace, Liverpool L5 3QG* 051-263 1945

BUTLAND, William Edwin. b 09. Lon Coll of Div 49. **d** 51 **p** 52. V Colney Heath St Mark *St Alb* 59-80; rtd 80; Perm to Offic *St Alb* from 80. *9 Studley Road, Wootton, Bedford MK43 9DL* Bedford (0234) 767620

BUTLER, Alan. b 51. Carl Dioc Tr Inst 86. **d** 89 **p** 90. NSM Flookburgh *Carl* from 89. *25 Main Street, Flookburgh, Grange-over-Sands, Cumbria LA11 7LA* Flookburgh (05395) 58227

BUTLER, Alan. b 57. Leic Univ BA78. Coll of Resurr Mirfield 80. **d** 83 **p** 84. C Skerton St Luke *Blackb* 83-87; C Birch w Fallowfield *Man* 87-90; V Claremont H Angels from 90. *The Vicarage, Moorfield Road, Salford M6 7EY* 061-736 3064

BUTLER, Ven Alan John. b 30. Kelham Th Coll 51. **d** 56 **p** 57. S Africa 56-65 and from 79; Bechuanaland 65-66; Botswana 66-70; V Fletchamstead *Cov* 71-79; Adn Griqualand W 79-86; Adn Kuruman 79-86; Dir Moffat Miss, Kuruman from 81. *PO Box 34, Kuruman, 8460 South Africa* Kuruman (1471) 21352

BUTLER, Ms Angela Elizabeth. b 31. Studley Coll DipHort53. Gilmore Ho 60 DipTh64 Lambeth STh64. **dss** 81 **d** 87. Cookham *Ox* 81-86; Wheatley w Forest Hill and Stanton St John 86-87; Dom Par Dn 87-89; rtd 91. *10 River Gardens, Purley, Reading RG8 8BX* Reading (0734) 422055

BUTLER, Angela Madeline. b 47. Oak Hill NSM Course 87. **d** 90. Hon Par Dn Chipperfield St Paul *St Alb* from 90. *Springhill, Flaunden Lane, Bovingdon, Herts HP3 0PA* Hemel Hempstead (0442) 832135

BUTLER, Christopher John. b 25. Leeds Univ BA50. Chich Th Coll 50. **d** 52 **p** 53. C Kensington St Mary Abbots w St Geo *Lon* 52-57; Australia 57-59; V Blackmoor *Portsm* 60-70; V Wellingborough St Andr *Pet* 70-79; P-in-c Garsington *Ox* 79-83; P-in-c Garsington and Horspath 80-83; R from 83. *The Rectory, 17 Southend, Garsington, Oxford OX9 9DH* Garsington (086736) 381

BUTLER, Colin Sydney. b 59. Bradf Univ BSc81. Wycliffe Hall Ox 81. **d** 84 **p** 85. C Farsley *Bradf* 84-87; C Bradf St Aug Undercliffe 87-89; P-in-c Darlaston All SS *Lich* from 89; Ind Missr from 89. *All Saints' Vicarage, Walsall Road, Darlston, Wednesbury, W Midlands WS10 9SQ* 021-568 6618

BUTLER, Ven Cuthbert Hilary. b 13. St Jo Coll Cam BA35 MA39. Westcott Ho Cam. **d** 40 **p** 41. Canada 58-84; Adn Colombia 77-78; rtd 78; Perm to Offic *Ex* from 85. *Four Chimneys, Bratton Clovelly, Okehampton, Devon EX20 4JS* Bratton Clovelly (083787) 409

BUTLER, David Edwin. b 56. ACA83 Jes Coll Ox BA79 BA86. St Steph Ho Ox MA87. **d** 87 **p** 88. C Hulme Ascension *Man* 87-90; V Patricroft from 90. *Christ Church Vicarage, Cromwell Road, Eccles, Manchester M30 0GT* 061-789 1234

BUTLER, Derek John. b 53. BSc. Cranmer Hall Dur. **d** 82 **p** 83. C Bramcote *S'well* 82-86; Perm to Offic Roch and Portsm from 86; Lon and SE Co-ord CPAS from 86. *130 Farnaby Road, Bromley BR1 4BH* 081-464 2759

BUTLER, Donald Arthur. b 31. **d** 79 **p** 80. Hon C Apsley End *St Alb* 79-80; Hon C Chambersbury (Hemel Hempstead) from 80. *143 Belswains Lane, Hemel Hempstead, Herts HP3 9UZ*

BUTLER, Edward Daniel. b 42. Rhodes Univ Grahamstown BA65 MA70. Qu Coll Birm. **d** 68 **p** 69. C

Edgbaston St Bart *Birm* 68-72; Perm to Offic *Birm* 72-73, Chich from 74. *43 Princes Terrace, Brighton BN2 5JS*

BUTLER, Frederick Walter. b 28. Chich Th Coll 67. **d** 69 **p** 70. C Seaford w Sutton *Chich* 69-73; V Peacehaven 73-75; P-in-c Copthorne 75-81; V 81-83; TR Moulsecoomb 83-86; R Etchingham from 86; V Hurst Green from 86. *The Rectory, High Street, Etchingham, E Sussex BN19 7AH* Etchingham (058081) 235

BUTLER, George James. b 53. AKC74. St Aug Coll Cant 75. **d** 76 **p** 77. C Ellesmere Port *Ches* 76-79; C Eastham 79-81; Chapl RAF 81-83; C W Kirby St Bridget *Ches* 83-84; V Newton 84-86; CF 86-91; V Folkestone St Sav *Cant* from 91. *St Saviour's Vicarage, 134 Canterbury Road, Folkestone, Kent CT19 5PH* Folkestone (0303) 54686

BUTLER, George William. **d** 90 **p** 91. C Drung w Castleterra, Larah and Lavey etc *K, E & A* from 90. *Drung Vicarage, Drung, Co Cavan, Irish Republic* Cavan (49) 38204

BUTLER, Henry. b 25. Ridley Hall Cam 73. **d** 75 **p** 76. C Cam St Paul *Ely* 75-77; P-in-c Stilton w Denton and Caldecote 77-83; P-in-c Folksworth w Morborne 77-83; V Histon 83-90; P-in-c Impington 84-90; rtd 90. *85 High Street, Cherry Hinton, Cambridge CB1 4LU*

BUTLER, Ian Malcolm. b 39. Bris Univ BA67. Clifton Th Coll 67. **d** 69 **p** 70. C Clapham Common St Barn *S'wark* 69-73; C Reigate St Mary 73-78; V Sissinghurst w Frittenden *Cant* from 78. *The Rectory, Frittenden, Cranbrook, Kent TN17 2DD* Cranbrook (0580) 80275

BUTLER, Ivor John. b 36. Dur Univ BA58. Ely Th Coll 58. **d** 60 **p** 61. C W Bromwich All SS *Lich* 60-64; V Upper Gornal 64-72; V Tividale 72-79; V Dartmouth *Ex* from 79; Chapl RN from 79; RD Totnes *Ex* from 90. *The Vicarage, North Ford Road, Dartmouth, Devon TQ6 9EP* Dartmouth (0803) 832415

BUTLER, John. b 38. Univ of Wales DipTh67 DPS68 Gwent Coll Newport CertEd77. St Mich Coll Llan. **d** 68 **p** 69. C Ebbw Vale *Mon* 68-70; TV 70-75; Perm to Offic 76-77 and 79-88; P-in-c Crumlin 77-78; R Gt and Lt Casterton w Pickworth and Tickencote *Pet* from 88. *The Rectory, Great Casterton, Stamford, Lincs PE9 4AP* Stamford (0780) 64036

BUTLER, John Kenneth. b 27. Keele Univ DipAdEd75. St Aid Birkenhead 56. **d** 58 **p** 59. Perm to Offic *Ches* 69-70 and from 75; C Witton 70-72; Hon C Knutsford St Cross 73-75; rtd 88. *4 School Close, Knutsford, Cheshire WA16 0BJ* Knutsford (0565) 634949

BUTLER, John Philip. b 47. Leeds Univ BA70. Coll of Resurr Mirfield 70. **d** 72 **p** 73. C Elton All SS *Man* 72-75; C Bolton St Pet 75-78; Chapl Bolton Colls of FE 75-78; Hon C Clifton St Paul *Bris* 78-81; Asst Chapl Bris Univ 78-81; V Llansawel w Briton Ferry *Llan* 81-84; Warden Bp Mascall Cen *Heref* 84-88; Vice-Prin Glouc Sch for Min 85-88; Warden Angl Chapl Cen Ban from 88. *Anglican Chaplaincy Centre, Prince's Road, Bangor, Gwynedd LL57 2BD* Bangor (0248) 370566

BUTLER, Linda Jane. b 56. SRN77. St Jo Coll Nottm 85. **d** 88. Par Dn Burbage w Aston Flamville *Leic* 88-90; Chapl Leic R Infirmary from 91. *45 Boyslade Road, Burbage, Hinckley, Leics L10 2RF* Hinkley (0455) 611180

BUTLER, Malcolm. b 40. Linc Th Coll 76. **d** 78 **p** 79. C Whickham *Dur* 78-82; V Leam Lane 82-87; R Penshaw 87-90; rtd 90. *2 Lapwing Court, Barcus Close Lane, Burnopfield, Newcastle upon Tyne NE16 4DZ* Burnopfield (0207) 71559

BUTLER, Michael. b 41. Univ of Wales (Ban) DipTh62. Llan St Mich 62 St Deiniol's Hawarden 63. **d** 64 **p** 65. C Welshpool *St As* 64; C Welshpool w Castle Caereinion 65-73; TV Abth *St D* 73-80; Chapl Univ of Wales (Abth) 73-80; V St Issell's and Amroth from 80. *St Issell's Vicarage, Saundersfoot, Dyfed SA69 9BD* Saundersfoot (0834) 812375

BUTLER, Canon Michael John. b 32. Keble Coll Ox BA58 MSW. Coll of Resurr Mirfield. **d** 59 **p** 60. C Poplar All SS w St Frideswide *Lon* 59-68; Hon C St Steph Walbrook and St Swithun etc 68-73; C Godalming *Guildf* 73-76; P-in-c Brighton St Anne *Chich* 77-79; Dioc Communications Officer & Dir Soc Resp 77-83; Asst Dir Dioc Bd of Soc Resp from 83; Can and Preb Chich Cathl from 85. *30 Bigwood Avenue, Hove, E Sussex BN3 6FD* Brighton (0273) 725811

BUTLER, Michael Weeden. b 38. Clare Coll Cam BA60 MA65. Westcott Ho Cam 63. **d** 65 **p** 66. C Bermondsey St Mary w St Olave, St Jo etc *S'wark* 65-68; Ind Chapl 68-72; Sierra Leone 73-77; Ind Chapl *Cant* 77-86; R Gt Chart 77-86; RD E Charing 81-86; V Glouc St Jas and All SS *Glouc* from 86. *The Vicarage, 1 The*

Conifers, Upton Street, Gloucester GL1 4LP Gloucester (0452) 422349

BUTLER, Ms Pamela. b 53. Nottm Univ BTh86. Linc Th Coll 83. **dss** 86 **d** 87. Rotherhithe H Trin *S'wark* 86-87; Par Dn 87-88; Par Dn Old Trafford St Jo *Man* 88-89; Par Dn Claremont H Angels from 90. *The Vicarage, Moorfield Road, Salford M6 7EY* 061-736 3064

BUTLER, Paul Roger. b 55. Nottm Univ BA77. Wycliffe Hall Ox BA82. **d** 83 **p** 84. C Wandsworth All SS *S'wark* 83-87; Scripture Union from 87; Inner Lon Evang from 87. *102 Lincoln Road, London E7 8QW* 081-472 3237

BUTLER, Perry Andrew. b 49. York Univ BA70 Jes Coll Ox DPhil78 Nottm Univ DipTh79. Linc Th Coll 78. **d** 80 **p** 81. C Chiswick St Nic w St Mary *Lon* 80-83; C S Kensington St Steph 83-87; V Bedf Park from 87. *St Michael's Vicarage, Priory Gardens, London W4 1TT* 081-994 1380

BUTLER, Philip Owen. b 24. St D Coll Lamp 49. **d** 53 **p** 54. C Amlwch *Ban* 53-55; C Llanbeblig w Caernarfon 55-57; R Llanymawddwy 57-63; V Pentir from 63. *The Vicarage, Pentir, Bangor, Gwynedd LL57 4YB* Bangor (0248) 362016

BUTLER, Richard Charles Burr. b 34. St Pet Hall Ox BA59 MA62. Linc Th Coll 58. **d** 60 **p** 61. C St Jo Wood *Lon* 60-63; V Kingstanding St Luke *Birm* 63-75; R Lee St Marg *S'wark* from 75. *St Margaret's Rectory, Brandram Road, London SE13 5EA* 081-852 0633

BUTLER, Robert Clifford. b 25. AKC54. **d** 55 **p** 56. C Gt Berkhamsted *St Alb* 55-59; C Dunstable 59-63; V Stanbridge w Tilsworth 63-73; R Maulden 73-80; R Oldbury *Sarum* 80-83; R Oldbury from 83. *The Rectory, Heddington, Calne, Wilts SN11 0PR* Bromham (0380) 850411

BUTLER, Robert Edwin. b 37. Ely Th Coll 60. **d** 62 **p** 63. C Lewisham St Jo Southend *S'wark* 62-65; C Eastbourne St Eliz *Chich* 65-69; V Langney from 69. *St Richard's Rectory, 7 Priory Road, Eastbourne, E Sussex BN23 7AX* Eastbourne (0323) 761158

BUTLER, Robert George. b 13. FCCA ACIS35. Oak Hill Th Coll 74. **d** 76 **p** 77. Lic to Offic *Chelmsf* from 76. *Grianan, Debden, Saffron Walden, Essex CB11 3LE* Saffron Walden (0799) 40665

BUTLER, Sidney. b 07. Dur Univ LTh35. St Aid Birkenhead 33. **d** 35 **p** 36. R Bilsthorpe *S'well* 69-73; R Eakring 71-73; rtd 73; Perm to Offic *S'well* 73-88. *17 Chestnut Avenue, Nottingham NG3 6FU* Nottingham (0602) 625228

✠**BUTLER, Rt Rev Thomas Frederick.** b 40. Leeds Univ BSc61 MSc62 PhD72. Coll of Resurr Mirfield 62. **d** 64 **p** 65 **c** 85. C Wisbech St Aug *Ely* 64-66; C Folkestone St Sav *Cant* 66-67; Zambia 68-73; Chapl Kent Univ *Cant* 73-80; Six Preacher Cant Cathl 79-84; Adn Northolt *Lon* 80-85; Area Bp Willesden 85-91; Bp Leic from 91. *Bishop's Lodge, 10 Springfield Road, Leicester LE2 3BD* Leicester (0533) 708985

BUTLER, Canon William Hamilton Arthur. b 14. **d** 40 **p** 47. V Kensington St Mary Abbots w St Geo *Lon* 69-72; Gen Sec Rwanda Miss 72-77; V Laleham *Lon* 77-80; rtd 80; Perm to Offic *Chich* from 85. *28 Francome House, Brighton Road, Worthing, W Sussex BN15 8RP* Worthing (0903) 764453

BUTLER-SMITH, Basil George. b 30. Bps' Coll Cheshunt 66. **d** 67 **p** 68. C Bray and Braywood *Ox* 67-71; R Norton St E 71-74; P-in-c Tostock 71-74; R Rotherfield Peppard *Ox* from 76; P-in-c Rotherfield Greys 79-80; R from 80. *The Rectory, Rotherfield Peppard, Henley-on-Thames, Oxon RG9 5JN* Rotherfield Greys (04917) 603

BUTLIN, Claude Charles Jack. b 07. ALCD36. **d** 36 **p** 37. R Gt Horkesley *Chelmsf* 64-74; rtd 74; Perm to Offic *Sheff* from 80. *12 Rustlings Court, Graham Road, Sheffield S10 3HQ* Sheffield (0742) 307033

BUTLIN, David Francis Grenville. b 55. Bris Univ BA77 Ox Univ CertEd78. Sarum & Wells Th Coll 85. **d** 87 **p** 88. C Bedf St Andr *St Alb* 87-90; C Milton Portsm from 90. *51 Goldsmith Avenue, Southsea, Hants PO4 8DU* Portsmouth (0705) 751132

BUTLIN, Timothy Greer. b 53. St Jo Coll Dur BA75 Ox Univ CertEd76. Wycliffe Hall Ox 85. **d** 87 **p** 88. C Eynsham and Cassington *Ox* 87-91; V Loudwater from 91. *The Vicarage, Loudwater, High Wycombe, Bucks HP10 9QL* Bourne End (06285) 26087

BUTT, Adrian. b 37. **d** 71 **p** 72. S Africa 71-76; C Ilkeston St Mary *Derby* 76-79; P-in-c Sturton w Littleborough *S'well* 79-84; P-in-c Bole w Saundby 79-84; R N and S Wheatley w W Burton 79-84; R N Wheatley, W Burton, Bole, Saundby, Sturton etc 84-85; R Kirkby in Ashfield from 85. *The Rectory, 12 Church Street, Kirkby-in-Ashfield, Nottingham NG17 8LE* Mansfield (0623) 753790

BUTT, Christopher Martin. b 52. St Pet Coll Ox BA74 Fitzw Coll Cam BA77. Ridley Hall Cam 75. **d** 79 **p** 80. C Cam St Barn *Ely* 79-82; Hong Kong 82-89; P-in-c Windermere *Carl* from 89. *The Rectory, Longlands, Windermere, Cumbria LA23 3AJ* Windermere (09662) 3063

BUTT, Edward. b 46. Huddersfield Poly DipSocWork80 CQSW80. Trin Coll Bris DipHE88. **d** 88 **p** 89. C Erith St Paul *Roch* from 88. *113 Belmont Road, Erith, Kent DA8 1LF* Dartford (0322) 334762

BUTT, Martin James. b 52. Sheff Univ LLB75. Trin Coll Bris 75. **d** 78 **p** 79. C Aldridge *Lich* 78-84; C Walsall 84-87; TV from 87. *21 Buchanan Road, Walsall WS4 2EW* Walsall (0922) 34859

BUTT, Rowland Donald. b 31. Oak Hill Th Coll 70. **d** 72 **p** 73. C Hailsham *Chich* 72-74; C Worthing St Paul 74-77; V Lynesack *Dur* 77-83; R Ebchester from 83. *The New Rectory, Shaw Lane, Ebchester, Consett, Co Durham DH8 0PY* Ebchester (0207) 560301

BUTT, William Arthur. b 44. Kelham Th Coll 70 Linc Th Coll 71. **d** 71 **p** 72. C Mackworth St Fran *Derby* 71-75; C Aston cum Aughton *Sheff* 76-79; V Dalton 79-88; TR Staveley and Barrow Hill *Derby* from 88. *The Rectory, Staveley, Chesterfield, Derbyshire S43 3XZ* Chesterfield (0246) 472270

BUTTANSHAW, Graham Charles. b 59. TCD BA(Econ)80 BA85. St Jo Coll Nottm 88. **d** 91. C Toxteth St Cypr w Ch Ch *Liv* from 91. *37 Nuttall Street, Edge Hill, Liverpool*

BUTTERFIELD, David John. b 52. Lon Univ BMus73. St Jo Coll Nottm DipTh75. **d** 77 **p** 78. C Southport Ch Ch *Liv* 77-81; Min Aldridge St Thos CD *Lich* from 81. *14 St Thomas' Close, Aldridge, Walsall WS9 8SC* Walsall (0922) 53942

BUTTERFIELD, John Kenneth. b 52. Nottm Univ BCombStuds. Linc Th Coll 79. **d** 82 **p** 83. C Cantley *Sheff* 82-84; C Doncaster St Leon and St Jude 84-86; TV Ilfracombe, Lee, Woolacombe, Bittadon etc *Ex* 86-88; V Thurcroft *Sheff* from 88. *The Vicarage, 122 Green Arbour Road, Thurcroft, Rotherham, S Yorkshire S66 9ED* Rotherham (0709) 542261

BUTTERWORTH, Antony James. b 51. Hull Univ BSc73 Bris Univ DipTh76. Trin Coll Bris 73. **d** 76 **p** 77. C Halliwell St Pet *Man* 76-81; V Werneth 81-90; V Tonge Fold from 90. *St Chad's Vicarage, Tonge Fold Road, Bolton BL2 6AW* Bolton (0204) 25809

BUTTERWORTH, Derek. b 27. Wells Th Coll 63. **d** 65 **p** 65. C Bottesford *Linc* 65-73; TV Bottesford w Ashby 73-83; Chapl St Hilda's Sch Whitby 83-85; V Derringham Bank *York* 85-90; rtd 90. *52 Whitethorn Close, Huntington, York*

BUTTERWORTH, Elsie. b 27. Linc Th Coll 81. **dss** 83 **d** 87. OHP 83-85; Derringham Bank *York* 85-87; Par Dn 87-88; Par Dn Filey from 88. *15 St Oswald's Court, Queen Street, Filey, N Yorkshire YO14 9EY* Scarborough (0723) 515781

BUTTERWORTH, Dr George Michael. b 41. Man Univ BSc63 Lon Univ BD67 PhD89 Nottm Univ MPhil71. Tyndale Hall Bris. **d** 67 **p** 68. C S Normanton *Derby* 67-71; India 72-79; Lect Oak Hill Th Coll from 80; Perm to Offic *St Alb* from 80. *6 Farm Lane, Oak Hill College, Southgate, London N14 4PP* 081-441 5889

BUTTERWORTH, Ian Eric. b 44. Aber Univ MA67 MTh79. Edin Th Coll 67. **d** 69 **p** 70. C Langley All SS and Martyrs *Man* 69-71; Prec St Andr Cathl *Ab* 71-75; V Bolton St Matt w St Barn *Man* 75-85; C-in-c Lostock CD from 85. *32 Kilworth Drive, Lostock, Bolton BL6 4RL* Bolton (0204) 43559

BUTTERWORTH, James Frederick. b 49. St Chad's Coll Dur BA70. Cuddesdon Coll 70. **d** 72 **p** 73. C Kidderminster St Mary *Worc* 72-76; P-in-c Dudley St Barn 76-79; V 79-82; Prec Worc Cathl 82-88; Min Can Worc Cathl 82-88; TR Bridgnorth, Tasley, Astley Abbotts, Oldbury etc *Heref* from 88. *The Rectory, 16 East Castle Street, Bridgnorth, Shropshire WV16 4AL* Bridgnorth (0746) 763256

BUTTERWORTH, James Kent. b 49. Southn Univ BTh79. Chich Th Coll 75. **d** 79 **p** 80. C Heckmondwike *Wakef* 79-83; V Wrenthorpe from 83. *121 Wrenthorpe Road, Wrenthorpe, Wakefield, W Yorkshire WF2 0JS* Wakefield (0924) 373758

BUTTERWORTH, John Walton. b 49. St Jo Coll Dur BSc70 DipTh73. **d** 74 **p** 75. C Todmorden *Wakef* 74-77; Chapl Wakef Cathl 77-78; C Wakef Cathl 77-78; V Outwood from 78. *Outwood Vicarage, 424 Leeds Road, Wakefield, W Yorkshire WF1 2JB* Wakefield (0924) 823150

BUTTERWORTH, Ms Julia Kay. b 42. Edin Univ MA64 Bris Univ CertEd66 Nottm Univ DipTh75. Linc Th Coll 73. **dss** 77 **d** 87. Cov E *Cov* 77-79; Cant Cathl *Cant* 79-84; Dioc Adv in Women's Min from 82; Faversham 84-87; Par Dn from 87. *78 Cyprus Road, Faversham, Kent ME13 8HB* Faversham (0795) 538334

BUTTERWORTH, Keith. b 45. St Paul's Cheltenham CertEd66. Linc Th Coll 69. **d** 72 **p** 73. C Hollinwood *Man* 72-75; C Failsworth H Family CD 75-76; R Man Clayton St Cross w St Paul 76-87; V Lawton Moor from 87. *140 Wythenshawe Road, Northern Moor, Manchester M23 0PD* 061-998 2461

BUTTERWORTH, Roy. b 31. Selw Coll Cam BA55 MA59. Wells Th Coll 55. **d** 57 **p** 58. C Bathwick w Woolley *B & W* 57-61; Prec St Paul's Cathl Dundee *Bre* 61-63; V Dearnley *Man* 63-81; V Tyldesley w Shakerley 81-83; V Healey from 83. *Healey Vicarage, Gandy Lane, Rochdale, Lancs OL12 6EF* Rochdale (0706) 57386

BUTTERY, Graeme. b 62. York Univ BA84. St Steph Ho Ox 85. **d** 88 **p** 89. C Peterlee *Dur* 88-91; C Sunderland from 91. *19 Thornhill Terrace, Sunderland, Tyne & Wear SR2 7JL* 091-567 5570

BUTTIMORE, Canon John Charles. b 27. St Mich Coll Llan 55. **d** 57 **p** 58. C Treherbert *Llan* 57-60; C Aberdare St Fagan 60-64; V Williamstown 64-71; Chapl Ely Hosp Cardiff from 71; V Caerau w Ely *Llan* from 71; RD Cardiff 83-89; Can Llan Cathl from 87. *The Vicarage, Cowbridge Road West, Ely, Cardiff CF5 5BQ* Cardiff (0222) 563254

BUTTLE, Leslie Albert. b 32. Open Univ BA89. Edin Th Coll 61. **d** 64 **p** 65. C Sowerby Bridge w Norland *Wakef* 64-66; C Plymstock *Ex* 66-69; C Ilfracombe H Trin 69-71; V Woolfardisworthy and Buck Mills 71-76; C Sticklepath 76-77; Asst Chapl HM Pris Leeds 77-80; Lic to Offic *Ripon* 77-80; Chapl HM Youth Cust Cen Hindley 80-84; Perm to Offic *Ex* from 86. *Bakes Meade, 21 Burvill Street, Lynton, Devon EX35 6HA* Lynton (0598) 52319

BUTTLE, Leslie Ronald Frank. b 07. Lon Univ BA28. **d** 34 **p** 35. R Lowick w Sudborough and Slipton *Pet* 67-73; rtd 73. *5 Castle Street, Launceston, Cornwall PL15 8BA* Launceston (0566) 2052

BUTTON, David Frederick. b 27. St Chad's Coll Dur BA53 DipTh54. **d** 54 **p** 55. C Jarrow Docks *Dur* 54-58; C Seacroft *Ripon* 58-60; V Holland Fen *Linc* 60-64; V Surfleet 64-71; R Belton SS Pet and Paul 71-78; V Barkston w Syston 72-78; V Honington 73-78; R Gunhouse w Burringham 78-82; P-in-c Gt w Lt Hockham w Wretham w Illington *Nor* 82-84; P-in-c Shropham w Larling and Snetterton 82-84; V Hockham w Shropham Gp of Par from 84. *The Vicarage, 1 Peddars Way, East Wretham, Thetford, Norfolk IP24 1SE* Great Hockham (095382) 708

BUXTON, Canon Derek Major. b 31. Lon Univ BD63. Ripon Hall Ox 58. **d** 60 **p** 61. C Leic St Nic *Leic* 60-64; Chapl Leic Univ 60-64; Chapl Leic Coll of Art and Tech 61-65; Min Can Leic Cathl 64-69; Prec Leic Cathl 67-69; R Ibstock 69-76; R Ibstock w Heather 76-87; Chapl ATC from 78; OCF and Cen and E Regional Chapl from 87; RD Akeley S (Coalville) *Leic* 84-87; P-in-c Woodhouse Eaves from 87; Chapl Roecliffe Manor Cheshire Home from 87; Chapl Coun OStJ from 87; Hon Can Leic Cathl *Leic* from 89. *The Vicarage, 32 Church Hill, Woodhouse Eaves, Loughborough, Leics LE12 8RI* Woodhouse Eaves (0509) 890226

BUXTON, Canon Digby Hugh. b 16. Trin Coll Cam BA38 MA41. Wycliffe Hall Ox 39. **d** 41 **p** 42. Canada 50-77; C Gt Burstead *Chelmsf* 77-78; C Sandhurst *Ox* 78-81; rtd 81; Hon C Barkway, Reed and Buckland w Barley *St Alb* 81-87. *Rosemary Holt, Edward Road, St Cross, Winchester, Hants SO23 9RB* Winchester (0962) 860877

BUXTON, Preb Edmund Digby. b 08. Trin Coll Cam BA29 MA33. Ridley Hall Cam 29. **d** 33 **p** 34. V Milborne Port w Goathill *B & W* 54-74; rtd 74; Perm to Offic *Win* 74-75 and from 78; Tristan da Cunha 75-78. *10 Pound Hill, Alresford, Hants SO24 9BW* Alresford (0962) 732353

BUXTON, Edmund Francis. b 42. Trin Coll Cam BA65 MA68 DPS74. Linc Th Coll 65. **d** 67 **p** 68. C Wanstead St Mary *Chelmsf* 67-70; C Cam Gt St Mary w St Mich *Ely* 70-73; C Barking St Marg w St Patr *Chelmsf* 74-75; India 75-79; Chapl Bath Univ *B & W* 79-89; TR Willenhall H Trin *Lich* from 89. *The Rectory, Short Heath, Willenhall, W Midlands WV12 5PT* Bloxwich (0922) 476416

BUXTON, Edward Brian. b 41. AKC65 BEd79. **d** 66 **p** 67. C Laindon w Basildon *Chelmsf* 66-73; P-in-c Grays All SS 73-76; Perm to Offic from 76. *2 Fieldway, Basildon, Essex SS13 3DB*

BUXTON, Graham. b 45. BA MSc. St Jo Coll Nottm 83. **d** 83 **p** 84. C Ealing Dean St Jo *Lon* 83-84; C W Ealing St Jo w St Jas 84-86; C S Harrow St Paul 86-89; P-in-c 89-91; Australia from 91. *c/o D Hoyle Esq, Midland Bank plc, 235 Northolt Road, Harrow, Middx HA2 8HP* 081-422 9404

BUXTON, Richard Fowler. b 40. Lon Univ BSc62 Linacre Coll Ox BA67 MA71 Ex Univ PhD73. St Steph Ho Ox 65. **d** 68 **p** 69. C Whitley Ch Ch *Ox* 68-70; C Pinhoe *Ex* 70-71; Asst Chapl Ex Univ 71-73; Tutor Sarum & Wells Th Coll 73-77; Vice-Prin 77; Perm to Offic *Ches* from 77; Lect Liturgy Man Univ from 80; Perm to Offic *Man* from 81. *221 Dane Road, Sale, Cheshire M33 2LZ* 061-973 4727

BUXTON, Trevor George. b 57. Ex Univ BEd78. Chich Th Coll 81. **d** 83 **p** 84. C Hove All SS *Chich* 83-87; C Burgess Hill St Jo from 87. *St Edward's House, 7 Dunstall Avenue, Burgess Hill, W Sussex RH15 8PJ* Burgess Hill (0444) 241300

BUXTON, William Arnold Greaves. b 33. FBIM78. Sarum & Wells Th Coll 80. **d** 82 **p** 83. C Durrington *Chich* 82-85; R Kingston Buci 85-89; TR Rye from 89. *St Mary's Rectory, Gungarden, Rye, E Sussex TN31 7HH* Rye (0797) 222430

BYE, Dennis Robert. b 20. **d** 86 **p** 87. NSM Bishop's Cleeve *Glouc* 86-90; rtd 90. *The Old Coach House, Lye Lane, Cleeve Hill, Cheltenham, Glos GL52 3QD* Bishops Cleeve (024267) 3587

BYE, Peter John. b 39. Lon Univ BD65. Clifton Th Coll 62. **d** 67 **p** 68. C Hyson Green *S'well* 67-70; C Dur St Nic *Dur* 70-73; V Lowestoft Ch Ch *Nor* 73-80; V Carl St Jo *Carl* from 80; Chapl Carl Gen Hosp from 80. *St John's Vicarage, London Road, Carlisle CA1 2QQ* Carlisle (0228) 21601

BYERS, Christopher Martin. b 33. Jes Coll Ox BA59 MA62. Wycliffe Hall Ox 59. **d** 60 **p** 61. C Bermondsey St Mary w St Olave, St Jo etc *S'wark* 60-66; R Mottingham St Andr 66-86; TR Thamesmead from 86. *Thamesmead Rectory, 22 Manor Close, London SE28 8EY* 081-311 7278

BYFORD, Canon David Charles. b 30. Bps' Coll Cheshunt 58. **d** 61 **p** 62. C Short Heath *Birm* 61-63; C Londonderry 63-65; Chapl Selly Oak Hosp Birm 65-70; V Rowley Regis *Birm* 70-78; V Polesworth from 78; RD Polesworth from 84; Hon Can Birm Cathl from 87. *Polesworth Vicarage, Tamworth, Staffs B78 1DU* Tamworth (0827) 892340

BYLES, Ernest William. b 09. Lon Univ BA31 BD39. Bps' Coll Cheshunt 34. **d** 36 **p** 37. V Chingford St Edm *Chelmsf* 56-71; V Coleford *B & W* 72-74; rtd 74; Perm to Offic Ex 74-77; B & W 78-90. *Ashover House, 133 Long Ashton Road, Bristol BS18 9JQ* Bristol (0272) 392110

BYLES, Canon Raymond Vincent. b 30. Univ of Wales (Lamp) BA52. St Mich Coll Llan 52. **d** 54 **p** 55. C Llanfairisgaer *Ban* 54-57; C Llandudno 57-59; V Carno 59-64; V Trefeglwys 63; V Newmarket and Gwaenysgor *St As* 64-72; V Llysfaen 72-80; R Bodelwyddan and St George 80-85; V Bodelwyddan from 85; Hon Can St As Cathl from 89. *The Vicarage, Bodelwyddan, Rhyl, Clwyd LL18 5UR* St Asaph (0745) 583034

BYLLAM-BARNES, Paul William Marshall. b 38. Birm Univ BCom Lon Univ MSc. Sarum & Wells Th Coll. **d** 84 **p** 85. C Gt Bookham *Guildf* 84-87; R Cusop w Clifford, Hardwicke, Bredwardine etc *Heref* from 87. *The Vicarage, Cusop, Hay-on-Wye, Hereford HR3 5RF* Hay-on-Wye (0497) 820634

BYNON, William. b 43. St Aid Birkenhead 63. **d** 66 **p** 67. C Huyton St Mich *Liv* 66-69; C Maghull 69-72; TV 72-75; V Highfield 75-82; V Southport All SS 82-88; P-in-c Southport All So 86-88; V Newton in Makerfield St Pet from 88. *St Peter's Vicarage, Church Street, Newton-le-Willows, Merseyside WA12 9SR* Newton-le-Willows (0925) 224815

BYRNE, David Patrick. b 48. St Jo Coll Nottm 74. **d** 77 **p** 78. C Bordesley Green *Birm* 77-79; C Weoley Castle 79-82; TV Kings Norton from 82. *195 Monyhull Road, Kings Norton, Birmingham B30 3QN* 021-458 3483

BYRNE, David Rodney. b 47. St Jo Coll Cam BA70 MA73. Cranmer Hall Dur 71. **d** 73 **p** 74. C Maidstone St Luke *Cant* 73-77; C Patcham *Chich* 77-83; TV Stantonbury *Ox* 83-87; TV Stantonbury and Willen from 87. *Bradwell Church House, Atterbrook, Bradwell, Milton Keynes MK13 9EY* Milton Keynes (0908) 320850

BYRNE, John Victor. b 47. FCA. St Jo Coll Nottm LTh73. **d** 73 **p** 74. C Gillingham St Mark *Roch* 73-76; C Crosland Park *Chelmsf* 76-80; V Balderstone *Man* 80-87; V Southsea St Jude *Portsm* from 87. *St Jude's Vicarage,*

7 Hereford Road, Southsea, Hants PO5 2DH Portsmouth (0705) 821071

BYRNE, Very Rev Matthew. b 27. Man Univ MA69 TCD HDipEd81. Tyndale Hall Bris 47. **d** 51 **p** 52. C Rawtenstall St Mary *Man* 51-54; OCF 54-57; R Moss Side St Jas *Man* 57-62; R Whalley Range St Marg 62-80; P-in-c Chapelizod *D & G* 80-83; Chapl K Hosp Sch Palmerstown Dub 83-89; Dean Kildare *M & K* from 89; I Kildare w Kilmeague and Curragh from 89; Producer Relig Dept RTE from 83; Chapl Defence Forces from 89. *Dean's House, Curragh Camp, Co Kildare, Irish Republic* Curragh (45) 41654

BYRNE, Miriam Alexandra Frances. b 46. Westcott Ho Cam. **d** 87. Par Dn Beoley *Worc* 87-90; C Ayr *Glas* from 90. *2A Ailsa Place, Ayr KA7 1JG* Ayr (0292) 284243

BYRNE, Rodney Edmund. b 18. **d** 84 **p** 84. Hon C Leckhampton SS Phil and Jas w Cheltenham St Jas *Glouc* 84-88; rtd 88; Perm to Offic *Glouc* from 88. *39 Collum End Rise, Cheltenham, Glos GL53 0PA* Cheltenham (0242) 526428

BYRNE, Ronald Brendan Anthony. b 31. **d** 64. Chapl Cov Cathl *Cov* from 87; Chapl Lanchester Poly from 87. *The Chaplaincy, Priory Hall, Coventry Polytechnic, Coventry CV1 5FB* Coventry (0203) 24166

BYROM, Canon John Kenneth. b 20. Selw Coll Cam BA41 MA45. Westcott Ho Cam 41. **d** 43 **p** 44. Warden Brasted Place Coll Westerham 64-74; V Swaffham Prior *Ely* 74-88; Dir of Ords 75-87; Dir of Post-Ord Tr 75-87; Hon Can Ely Cathl 78-88; RD Fordham 78-83; rtd 88. *62 Cambridge Road, Great Shelford, Cambridge CB2 5JS* Cambridge (0223) 844015

BYROM, Malcolm Senior. b 37. Edin Th Coll 65. **d** 67 **p** 68. C Allerton *Bradf* 67-69; C Padstow *Truro* 69-72; V Hessenford 72-77; P-in-c St Martin by Looe 72-77; V Kenwyn 77-91; R Kenwyn w St Allen from 91; Sub-Warden Community of the Epiphany Truro from 85; RD Powder *Truro* 88-90. *The Vicarage, Kenwyn Close, Truro, Cornwall TR1 3DX* Truro (0872) 72664

BYRON, Frederick. b 14. Dur Univ BA38. St Jo Coll Dur 38. **d** 39 **p** 40. V Out Rawcliffe *Blackb* 68-78; C Standish 78-79; rtd 79. *18 Scott Avenue, Hindley, Wigan, Lancs WN2 4DG* Wigan (0942) 53807

BYRON, Frederick Thomas Christopher. b 16. Mert Coll Ox BA39 MA43. St Steph Ho Ox 39. **d** 40 **p** 41. V Ruislip St Martin *Lon* 62-70; V Kensington St Jas Norlands 70-83; rtd 83. *63 Belvedere Court, 372/4 Upper Richmond Road, London SW15 6HZ* 081-785-7567

BYRON, Terence Sherwood. b 26. Keble Coll Ox BA50 MA54. Linc Th Coll 50. **d** 52 **p** 53. C Melton Mowbray w Burton Lazars, Freeby etc *Leic* 52-55; C Whitwick St Jo the B 55-60; India 60-76; C-in-c Beaumont Leys (Ex-paroch Distr) *Leic* 76-85; V Beaumont Leys 85-86; RD Christianity (Leic) N from 86; P-in-c Leic St Phil 86-88; V from 88. *St Philip's House, 2A Stoughton Drive North, Leicester LE5 5UB* Leicester (0533) 736204

BYRON-DAVIES, Peter. b 49. K Coll Lon BD75 AKC75 Nottm Univ MTh85. St Aug Coll Cant 75. **d** 76 **p** 77. C Wootton Bassett *Sarum* 76-79; Chapl Charterhouse Godalming 79-80; R Bassingham *Linc* 80-85; V Aubourn w Haddington 80-85; V Carlton-le-Moorland w Stapleford 80-85; R Thurlby w Norton Disney 80-85; Canada 85-88; R Chalke Valley E *Sarum* from 88. *The Rectory, Bishopstone, Salisbury SP5 4AN* Coombe Bissett (072277) 330

BYSOUTH, Paul Graham. b 55. Oak Hill Th Coll. **d** 84 **p** 85. C Gorleston St Andr *Nor* 84-87; C Ripley *Derby* 87-91; TV N Wingfield, Clay Cross and Pilsley from 91. *Pilsley Vicarage, Chesterfield, Derbyshire S45 8EF* Ripley (0773) 590529

BYWATER, Hector William Robinson. b 10. ALCD32. **d** 33 **p** 34. V Derby St Alkmund *Derby* 40-84; rtd 84; Perm to Offic *Derby* from 84. *15 Bath Road, Mickleover, Derby DE3 5BW* Derby (0332) 513281

BYWORTH, Christopher Henry Briault. b 39. Or Coll Ox BA61 MA65 Bris Univ BA63. Lon Coll of Div 64. **d** 65 **p** 66. C Low Leyton *Chelmsf* 65-68; C Rusholme *Man* 68-70; Lic to Offic *Lon* 71-75; TR Thetford *Nor* 75-79; Warden Cranmer Hall Dur 79-83; TR Fazakerley Em *Liv* 83-90; P-in-c St Helens St Helen from 90; AD St Helens from 90. *The Vicarage, 51A Rainford Road, St Helens WA10 6BZ* St Helens (0744) 22067

C

CABLE, Patrick John. b 50. AKC72. **d** 74 **p** 75. C Herne Cant 74-78; CF from 78. c/o MOD (Army), Bagshot Park, Bagshot, Surrey GU19 5PL Bagshot (0276) 71717

CADDELL, Richard Allen. b 54. Auburn Univ Alabama BIE77. Trin Coll Bris BA88. **d** 88 **p** 89. C Uphill B & W from 88. 6 Ellesmere Road, Weston-super-Mare, Avon BS23 4UT Weston-super-Mare (0934) 415802

CADDEN, Brian Stuart. b 58. BSc BTh TCD. **d** 89 **p** 90. C Lecale Gp D & D from 89. 48 High Street, Ardglass, Downpatrick, Co Down BT30 7TU Ardglass (0396) 841311

CADDEN, Terence John. b 60. MChS82 TCD BTh89. CITC 86. **d** 89 **p** 90. C Coleraine Conn from 89. 42 Kenvarra Park, Coleraine, Co Londonderry BT52 1RT Coleraine (0265) 57828

CADDICK, Jeremy Lloyd. b 60. St Jo Coll Cam BA82 MA86. Ripon Coll Cuddesdon BA86. **d** 87 **p** 88. C Kennington St Jo w St Jas S'wark 87-90; Chapl Lon Univ Lon from 90; Chapl R Free Medical Sch from 90; Chapl R Veterinary Coll Sch of Pharmacy from 90. 3 Carleton Villas, Leighton Grove, London NW5 2TU 071-482 2133

CADDICK, Lloyd Reginald. b 31. Bris Univ BA56 St Cath Coll Ox BA58 MA62 Nottm Univ MPhil73 K Coll Lon PhD78 Open Univ Hon MA79. St Steph Ho Ox 56. **d** 59 **p** 59. C N Lynn w St Marg and St Nic Nor 59-62; Chapl Oakham Sch Leics 62-66; P-in-c Bulwick, Harringworth w Blatherwycke and Laxton Pet 66-67; R Bulwick, Blatherwycke w Harringworth and Laxton 67-77; V Oundle from 77. The Vicarage, Oundle, Peterborough PE8 4EA Oundle (0832) 73595

CADDY, Dennis Gordon James. b 27. Bps' Coll Cheshunt 62. **d** 64 **p** 65. C Greenhill St Jo Lon 64-67; C Harlington 67-69; C-in-c Harlington Ch Ch CD 69-72; V N Harrow St Alb 72-83; R Corsley Sarum from 83. The Rectory, Corsley, Warminster, Wilts BA12 7QD Chapmanslade (037388) 224

CADDY, Michael George Bruce Courtenay. b 45. K Coll Lon. **d** 71 **p** 72. C Walton St Mary Liv 71-76; C Solihull Birm 76-79; TV 79-81; V Shard End 81-87; TV Shirley 87; TR from 87. The Vicarage, 2 Bishopton Close, Shirley, Solihull, W Midlands B90 4AH 021-744 3123

CADMAN, Kenneth Claude. b 14. St Jo Coll Dur BA40. **d** 40 **p** 41. R Guernsey St Pierre du Bois Win 69-81; R Guernsey St Philippe de Torteval 80-81; Vice Dean Guernsey 70-81; rtd 81; Perm to Offic Win from 82. Marske, Rue de St Apolline, St Saviour's, Guernsey, Channel Islands Guernsey (0481) 63720

CADMAN, Reginald Hugh. b 09. Man Univ LLB30 LLM52. Wycliffe Hall Ox 32. **d** 34 **p** 35. V Paul Truro 66-82; RD Penwith 76-82; rtd 82. Pendle, Drift, Penzance, Cornwall Penzance (0736) 68551

CADMAN, Robert Hugh. b 49. Nottm Univ DipTh76. St Jo Coll Nottm 77. **d** 78 **p** 79. C Ecclesall Sheff 78-82; C Worting Win 82-84; C-in-c Winklebury CD 84-87; R Widford Chelmsf from 87. The Rectory, 3 Canuden Road, Widford, Chelmsford CM1 2SU Chelmsford (0245) 355989

CADMORE, Albert Thomas. b 47. Open Univ BA81 NE Lon Poly Nor City Coll DMS84 SS Mark & Jo Coll Plymouth Lon Inst of Educn CertEd68. E Anglian Minl Tr Course 85. **d** 88 **p** 89. NSM Gorleston St Andr Nor from 88. 10 Upper Cliff Road, Gorleston, Great Yarmouth, Norfolk NR31 6AL Great Yarmouth (0493) 668762

CADOGAN, Paul Anthony Cleveland. b 47. AKC74. **d** 75 **p** 76. C Fishponds St Jo Bris 75-79; C Swindon New Town 79-81; P-in-c Swindon All SS 81-82; V 82-90; R Lower Windrush Ox from 90. The Rectory, Stanton Harcourt, Oxford OX8 1RP Oxford (0865) 880249

CAESAR, Canon Anthony Douglass. b 24. LVO87. FRCO47 Magd Coll Cam BA47 MusB47 MA49. St Steph Ho Ox 59. **d** 61 **p** 62. Chapl RSCM Addington 65-70; ACCM 66-70; P-in-O to HM The Queen 68-70; C Bournemouth St Pet Win 70-73; Prec and Sacr Win Cathl 74-79; Hon Can Win Cathl 75-76 and from 79; Can Res 76-79; Dom Chapl to HM The Queen 79-91; Extra Chapl from 91; Dep Clerk of the Closet and Sub-Almoner 79-91; Sub-Dean of the Chpls Royal 79-91; rtd 91; Chapl St Cross Hosp Win from 91. Chaplain's Lodge, St Cross Hospital, Winchester SO23 9SD Winchester (0962) 853525

CAFFYN, Douglas John Morris. b 36. ACIS77 Peterho Cam MA60 Nairobi Univ MSc69 Westmr Coll Ox DipEd61. S Dios Minl Tr Scheme 87. **d** 90 **p** 91. NSM Hampden Park Chich from 90. 255 King's Drive, Eastbourne, E Sussex BN21 2UR Eastbourne (0323) 500977

CAHILL, Nigel. b 59. Llan St Mich DipTh80 DPS82. **d** 82 **p** 83. C Whitchurch Llan 82-86; V Tonypandy w Clydach Vale from 86. The Vicarage, St Andrew's Church Grounds, Tonypandy, M Glam CF40 2LD Tonypandy (0443) 437759

CAIGER, Canon Douglas George Colley. b 23. Kelham Th Coll 39. **d** 46 **p** 48. R Lowestoft St Marg Nor 69-78; Hon Can Nor Cathl 73-78; TR Shaston Sarum 78-86; rtd 86; Perm to Offic Portsm and Chich from 86. 11 Record Road, Emsworth, Hants PO10 7NS Emsworth (0243) 376058

CAIN, Andrew David. b 63. Aber Univ BSc86. Ripon Coll Cuddesdon BA89. **d** 90 **p** 91. C Walworth St Jo S'wark from 90. 16 Larcom Street, London SE17 1NQ 071-703 4375

CAIN, Frank Robert. b 56. Oak Hill Th Coll BA88. **d** 88 **p** 89. C Aughton Ch Ch Liv from 88. 25 Peet Avenue, Ormskirk, Lancs L39 4SH Ormskirk (0695) 77958

CAIN, Michael John. b 62. Chich Th Coll 88. **d** 91. C Cainscross w Selsley Glouc from 91. 13 Frome Gardens, Cainscross, Stroud, Glos GL5 4LE Stroud (0453) 751040

CAIN, Richard Douglas. b 20. Edin Univ MA51 Cam Univ MA73. Edin Th Coll 51. **d** 53 **p** 54. Chapl Warw Univ Cov 67-73; Chapl Chu Coll Cam 73-81; rtd 85. San Sebastian 8, Frigiliana, Malaga, Spain

CAINE (nee BALDWIN), Mrs Joyce Gertrude. b 21. Nottm Univ BA42 Cam Univ CertEd43 Lon Univ BD58. **d** 87. NSM Redland Bris from 87. 164 Bishop Road, Bishopston, Bristol BS7 8NB Bristol (0272) 427113

CAINK, Richard David Somerville. b 37. Lich Th Coll 68. **d** 71 **p** 72. C Prittlewell St Mary Chelmsf 71-74; C Gt Yarmouth Nor 74-76; P-in-c Blickling w Ingworth 76-80; P-in-c Saxthorpe and Corpusty 76-80; P-in-c Oulton SS Pet and Paul 76-80; R Cheddington w Mentmore and Marsworth Ox 80-87; P-in-c Wooburn 87-90; V from 90. Wooburn Vicarage, Windsor Hill, Wooburn Green, High Wycombe, Bucks HP10 0EH Bourne End (06285) 20030

✠**CAIRD, Most Rev Donald Arthur Richard.** b 25. TCD BA49 MA55 BD55 Hon DD88. CITC 49. **d** 50 **p** 51 **c** 70. C Dundela D & D 50-54; Asst Master and Chapl Portora R Sch 54-57; Lect St D Coll Lamp 57-58; I Rathmichael D & G 60-69; Lect TCD 62-63; Lect CITC 65-69; Dean Ossory C & O 69-70; Preb Leighlin Cathl 69-70; I Kilkenny 69-70; Bp Limerick, Ardfert and Aghadoe L & K 70-76; Bp M & K 76-85; Abp Dub D & G from 85; Preb Cualaun St Patr Cathl Dub from 85. The See House, 17 Temple Road, Milltown, Dublin 6, Irish Republic Dublin (1) 977849

CAIRNS, Henry Alfred. b 20. Melbourne Univ BA49 Ridley Coll Melbourne. ACT ThL43. **d** 42 **p** 43. Australia 42-81; Can Gippsland 59-60; Perm to Offic Cant & St Alb from 81; Hon C Radlett St Alb 83-85. 47 Westminster Court, St Stephen's Hill, St Albans, Herts AL1 2DX St Albans (0727) 50949

CAIRNS, Robert Hill. b 21. Aber Univ MA50. St Deiniol's Hawarden. **d** 83 **p** 83. Lic to Offic Ab 83-86; Portsoy 86-88. Flat 3, South College House, Elgin, Morayshire IV30 1EP Elgin (0343) 541190

CALAMINUS, Peter Andrew Franz. b 14. Lon Univ BA44. Cuddesdon Coll 69. **d** 71 **p** 71. C Westbury Sarum 71-73; P-in-c Pitcombe w Shepton Montague and Bratton St Maur B & W 73-76; V 76-78; rtd 79. 6 Banksia Avenue, Sun Valley, Gladstone, Queensland, Australia 4680

CALCOTT-JAMES, Colin Wilfrid. b 25. Bris Univ BSc48. S'wark Ord Course 77. **d** 80 **p** 81. NSM Barnes H Trin S'wark 80-85; C Hykeham Linc 85-88; R Barrowby from 88. 16 Thorold Road, Barrowby, Grantham, Lincs NG32 1TD Grantham (0476) 76307

CALDER, Ian Fraser. b 47. York Univ BA68 CertEd69. Glouc Sch of Min 84. **d** 87 **p** 88. NSM Lydney w Aylburton Glouc from 87. 3 Cambourne Place, Lydney, Glos GL15 5PT Dean (0594) 843687

CALDER, Roger Paul. b 53. Hatf Coll Dur BA75. Chich Th Coll 76. **d** 79 **p** 80. C Addlestone Guildf 79-82; C Grangetown Dur 82-84; TV Brighton Resurr Chich 84-87; CF from 87. c/o MOD (Army), Bagshot Park, Bagshot, Surrey GU19 5PL Bagshot (0276) 71717

CALDERBANK, Geoffrey Randall. b 59. Man Poly BA81 Man Univ MA89. Ripon Coll Cuddesdon. **d** 86 **p** 87. C Flixton St Mich Man 86-89; P-in-c Dixon Green 89-91; Ecum Chapl Wales Poly (Pontypridd) Llan from

91. *Neuadd Maes yr Eglwys, Upper Church Village, Pontypridd, M Glam* Pontypridd (0443) 208784

CALDICOTT, Anthony. b 31. ARCO52 FRCO62 ADCM66 St Jo Coll Dur BA53. Ripon Hall Ox 55. **d** 57 **p** 58. C Finham *Cov* 57-61; C Bedf St Andr *St Alb* 61-64; Chapl Lindisfarne Coll 64-67; C W Bromwich All SS *Lich* 67-69; Lic to Offic *Cov* 69-75; Hon C Twickenham St Mary *Lon* 75-89. *56 Durham Road, Feltham, Middx TW14 0AD* 081-890 1575

CALDICOTT, John Michael Parlane. b 46. Selw Coll Cam BA69. St Steph Ho Ox 69. **d** 71 **p** 72. C Mayfield *Chich* 71-74; Hon C Deptford St Paul *S'wark* 74-76; P-in-c Sydenham St Phil 76-83; P-in-c Forest Hill Ch Ch from 83; P-in-c Forest Hill St Paul from 84; RD W Lewisham 87. *The Vicarage, 20 Gaynesford Road, London SE23* 081-699 6538

CALDWELL, Alan. b 29. Oak Hill Th Coll 65. **d** 67 **p** 68. C Aldershot H Trin *Guildf* 67-69; C New Malden and Coombe *S'wark* 69-73; C Edgware St Andr CD *Lon* 73-78; P-in-c Pettaugh and Winston *St E* 78; R Helmingham w Framsden and Pettaugh w Winston 78-87; R Cowden w Hammerwood *Chich* from 87. *The Rectory, Cowden, Edenbridge, Kent TN8 7JE* Cowden (0342) 850221

CALDWELL, Alan Alfred. b 48. Loughb Univ BSc70 PhD83. Linc Th Coll DipTh71. **d** 73 **p** 74. C Bulwell St Mary *S'well* 73-80; Chapl Nottm Univ 80-87; R Baxterley w Hurley and Wood End and Merevale etc *Birm* 87-91. *Address temp unknown*

CALDWELL, David Denzil. b 24. TD70. Bps' Coll Cheshunt 53. **d** 55 **p** 56. I Kilwaughter w Cairncastle *Conn* 61-90; CF (TAVR) 67-90; RD Carrickfergus *Conn* 70-90; CF (R of O) 70-80; Asst ChStJ from 80; rtd 90. *Clogher Croft, 193 Straid Road, Bushmills, Co Antrim BT57 8XW* Bushmills (02657) 32336

CALDWELL, Ian Charles Reynolds. b 43. St Mich Coll Llan 68. **d** 70 **p** 71. C Oakham w Hambleton and Egleton *Pet* 70-74; C Swindon New Town *Bris* 74-78; P-in-c Honicknowle *Ex* 78-80; V 80-88; V Norton St Mich *Dur* from 88. *The Vicarage, 13 Imperial Avenue, Norton, Stockton-on-Tees, Cleveland TS20 2EW* Stockton-on-Tees (0642) 553984

CALDWELL, Canon John Donaldson. b 19. TCD BA41. **d** 42 **p** 43. I Kilmegan w Maghera *D & D* 55-89; RD Kilmegan 62-89; Can Dromore Cathl 85-89; rtd 89; Lic to Offic *D & D* from 90. *66 Castlewellan Road, Newcastle, Co Down BT33 0JP* Newcastle (03967) 24874

CALDWELL, Robert McKinley. b 20. Pittsburgh Univ BSc42. Nashotah Ho MDiv64. **d** 64 **p** 64. USA 64-85; P-in-c Kenmare w Sneem, Waterville etc *L & K* from 87. *St Patrick's Rectory, Kenmare, Killarney, Co Kerry, Irish Republic* Killarney (64) 41121

CALDWELL, Roger Fripp. b 31. Cranmer Hall Dur. **d** 64 **p** 65. C Sugley Newc 67-74; R Helmdon w Stuchbury and Radstone *Pet* 74-91; R Greatworth 74-91; rtd 91. *Quiet Waters, Station Road, Lower Heyford, Oxford OX5 3PD*

CALE, Clifford Roy Fenton. b 38. St Mich Coll Llan 65. **d** 67 **p** 68. C Griffithstown *Mon* 67-72; V Cwm 72-73; V Abersychan 73-79; V Abersychen and Garndiffaith 79-82; R Goetre w Llanover and Llanfair Kilgeddin 82-85; R Goytrey w Llanover from 85; RD Raglan-Usk from 90. *The Rectory, Nantyderry, Abergavenny, Gwent NP7 9DW* Nantyderry (0873) 880378

CALEY, Charles Joseph. b 16. AKC47. Bp Wilson Coll 35. **d** 39 **p** 40. V E Farleigh and Coxheath *Roch* 62-82; rtd 82; Perm to Offic *Roch* from 82; Cant from 83. *1 Bakery Cottages, Oakvale, Chatham Road, Sandling, Maidstone, Kent ME14 3BE* Maidstone (0622) 673397

CALLAGHAN, Harry. b 34. AKC59 Open Univ BA83. **d** 60 **p** 61. C Sheff Parson Cross St Cecilia *Sheff* 60-63; Br Guiana 63-66; Guyana 66-70; Barbados 70-74; Lic to Offic *Man* 74-84; Miss to Seamen 74-76; Area Sec (Dios Blackb, Man and S & M) USPG 76-84; P-in-c Wythenshawe St Martin *Man* 84-85; V 85-91; V Bolton St Jo from 91. *St John's Vicarage, 7 Alford Close, Bolton BL2 6NR* Bolton (0204) 31191

CALLAGHAN, Robert Paul. b 59. K Coll Lon BD81. Linc Th Coll 81. **d** 83 **p** 85. C Winchmore Hill St Paul *Lon* 83-85; C Paddington St Jo w St Mich 85-91; V Dartford St Edm *Roch* from 91. *The Vicarage, St Edmund's Road, Temple Hill, Dartford, Kent DA1 5ND* Dartford (0322) 225335

CALLAN, Canon Terence Frederick. b 26. CITC 55. **d** 57 **p** 58. C Monaghan *Clogh* 57-58; I Clogh 58-64; C Derriaghy *Conn* 64-66; P-in-c Ballymacash 67-70; I Belf St Aid 70-79; I Agherton from 79; Can Conn Cathl from 86; Treas Conn Cathl from 90. *59 Strand Road,*

Portstewart, Co Londonderry BT55 7LU Portstewart (026583) 2538

CALLARD, David Kingsley. b 37. St Pet Coll Ox BA61 MA65. Westcott Ho Cam 61. **d** 63 **p** 64. C Leamington Priors H Trin *Cov* 63-66; C Wyken 66-68; C Hatf *St Alb* 68-73; R Bilton *Cov* 73-83; TR Swanage and Studland *Sarum* from 83. *The Rectory, 12 Church Hill, Swanage, Dorset BH19 1HU* Swanage (0929) 422916

CALLENDER, Thomas Henry. b 13. SS Coll Cam BA35 MA39. Sarum Th Coll 35. **d** 37 **p** 38. V Carbrooke *Nor* 66-76; R Ovington 66-76; V Carbrooke w Ovington, Woodrising and Scoulton 76-78; rtd 78; Perm to Offic *Nor* from 78. *4 Bickley Close, Mill Lane, Attleborough, Norfolk NR17 2NT* Attleborough (0953) 454727

CALLER, Laurence Edward Harrison. b 19. Lon Univ BMus77 MA82. Lich Th Coll 39. **d** 42 **p** 43. V Harlescott *Lich* 63-67; rtd 84. *103 Fronks Road, Dovercourt, Harwich, Essex* Harwich (0255) 504501

CALLON, Andrew McMillan. b 56. Chich Th Coll 77. **d** 80 **p** 81. C Wigan All SS *Liv* 80-85; V Abram 85-90; V Bickershaw 89-90; Chapl RN from 90. *c/o Royal Naval Base, Portland, Dorset* Portland (0305) 820311

CALTHROP-OWEN, William Gordon. b 35. Chich Th Coll 62. **d** 63 **p** 64. C Egremont St Jo *Ches* 63-68; C Bawtry w Austerfield *S'well* 68-69; P-in-c Radford All So w Ch Ch 69-73; P-in-c Radford St Mich 69-73; R Bilsthorpe 73-90; R Eakring 73-90; P-in-c Winkburn 77-90; P-in-c Maplebeck 77-90; V Woodborough from 90; Chapl HM Young Offender Inst Lowdham Grange from 90. *The Vicarage, Lingwood Lane, Woodborough, Nottingham NG14 6DX* Nottingham (0602) 652250

CALVER, Nicholas James. b 58. Nottm Univ BTh83 Dur Univ MA(Theol)90. Cranmer Hall Dur 86. **d** 88 **p** 89. C Forest Hill Ch Ch *S'wark* from 88. *12 Ewelme Road, London SE23 3BH* 081-699 1588

CALVER, Sydney Bertram. b 10. Keble Coll Ox BA33. Chich Th Coll 33. **d** 35 **p** 36. R Stonesfield *Ox* 56-75; rtd 75; Perm to Offic Ox 75-77; B & W from 77. *8 Parkfield Drive, Taunton, Somerset TA1 5BT* Taunton (0823) 72535

CALVERT, Geoffrey Richard. b 58. Edin Univ BSc79 PhD84 Leeds Univ BA86. Coll of Resurr Mirfield 84. **d** 87 **p** 88. C Curdworth w Castle Vale *Birm* 87-90; C Barnsley St Mary *Wakef* from 90. *St Paul's House, 33 Queen's Drive, Barnsley, S Yorkshire S75 2QG* Barnsley (0226) 284775

CALVERT, Mrs Jean. b 34. Lightfoot Ho Dur IDC. **dss** 78 **d** 87. S Bank *York* 84-90; Chapl Asst Rampton Hosp Retford from 84; Dn-in-c Dunham w Darlton and Ragnall *S'well* 88-89; Dn-in-c E Drayton w Stokeham 88-89; Dn-in-c Fledborough 88-89; Dn-in-c Dunham-on-Trent w Darlton, Ragnall etc from 89. *The Vicarage, Dunham-on-Trent, Newark, Notts NG22 0UL* Dunham-on-Trent (077785) 707

CALVERT, John Raymond. b 42. Lon Coll of Div 64. **d** 67 **p** 68. C Kennington St Mark *S'wark* 67-70; C Southborough St Pet *Roch* 70-72; C Barton Seagrave *Pet* 72-75; Asst Master Shaftesbury High Sch 78-79; Dioc Children's Officer *Glouc* 79-87; P-in-c S Cerney w Cerney Wick and Down Ampney 87-89; V from 89. *The Vicarage, South Cerney, Cirencester, Glos GL7 5TP* Cirencester (0285) 860221

CALVERT, Peter Noel. b 41. Ch Coll Cam BA63 MA67. Cuddesdon Coll 64. **d** 66 **p** 67. C Brighouse *Wakef* 66-71; V Heptonstall 71-82; V Todmorden from 82; P-in-c Cross Stone from 83; RD Calder Valley from 84. *The Vicarage, Todmorden, Lancs OL14 7BS* Todmorden (0706) 813180

CALVIN-THOMAS, David Nigel. b 43. Univ of Wales (Cardiff) BSc64 Lon Univ BD77 Leeds Univ DipC&G88. St Mich Coll Llan 77. **d** 78 **p** 79. C Pontypridd St Cath *Llan* 78-80; Malawi 81-84; V Rastrick St Matt *Wakef* 84-88; V Birchencliffe from 88; Chapl Huddersfield R Infirmary from 88. *The Vicarage, 1 Marling Road, Birchincliffe, Huddersfield HD2 2EE* Elland (0422) 372679

CALWAY, Geoffrey. b 45. Bris Sch of Min. **d** 87 **p** 88. NSM Cotham St Sav w St Mary *Bris* from 87. *59 Hamilton Road, Bristol BS3 1NZ* Bristol (0272) 664402

CAM, Julian Howard. b 48. York Univ BA69 Birm Univ DipTh74. Qu Coll Birm 73. **d** 75 **p** 76. C St Ives *Truro* 75-80; C Lelant 78-80; V Flookburgh *Carl* 80-82; V St Stephen by Saltash *Truro* 82-83; V Low Marple *Ches* from 83. *St Martin's Vicarage, 15 Brabyns Brow, Marple Bridge, Stockport, Cheshire SK6 5DT* 061-427 2736

CAMENISCH, Richard Frank. b 12. Univ Coll Dur BA34. Wells Th Coll 34. **d** 35 **p** 36. V Bicker *Linc* 68-77; rtd 77; Perm to Offic *S'well* from 77; *Sheff* from 86. *The*

113

Whipping Post, Norwell Lane, Newark, Notts NG23 6JE
Newark (0636) 821423

CAMERON, Andrew Bruce. b 41. New Coll Edin CPS72. Sheff Urban Th Unit 82 Edin Th Coll 61. **d** 64 **p** 65. C Helensburgh *Glas* 64-67; C Edin H Cross *Edin* 67-71; Prov Youth Chapl 69-75; Dioc Youth Chapl 69-75; Chapl St Mary's Cathl 71-75; R Dalmahoy 75-82; Chapl Heriot-Watt Univ 75-82; TV Livingston LEP 82-88; R Perth St Jo *St And* from 88; Convener Prov Miss Board from 88. *23 Comeley Bank, Perth PH2 7HU* Perth (0738) 25394

CAMERON, David Alan. b 59. Glas Univ MA81 DipEd82 PGCE82. Ripon Coll Cuddesdon 88. **d** 91. C Farncombe *Guildf* from 91. *73 Binscombe Crescent, Farncombe, Godalming, Surrey GU7 3RA* Godalming (0483) 428972

CAMERON, David Alexander. b 42. MRTPI Reading Univ BA63 Leeds Art Coll DipTP69. St And Dioc Tr Course 80. **d** 90. NSM Blairgowrie *St And* from 90. *Firgrove, Golf Course Road, Blairgowrie, Perthshire PH10 6LF* Blairgowrie (0250) 3272

CAMERON, Donald Eric Nelson. b 29. St Jo Coll Dur 68. **d** 70 **p** 71. C Kingston upon Hull H Trin *York* 70-73; V Eston 73-82; R Balerno *Edin* 82-88. *6 Redford Terrace, Edinburgh EH13 0BT* 031-441 3022

CAMERON, Canon Douglas MacLean. b 35. Univ of S Tennessee 61. Edin Th Coll 59. **d** 62 **p** 63. C Falkirk *Edin* 62-65; Papua New Guinea 66-74; Adn New Guinea Mainland 72-74; P-in-c Edin St Fillan *Edin* 74-78; R 78-87; R Edin St Hilda 77-87; R Dalkeith from 87; R Lasswade from 87; Syn Clerk from 90; Can St Mary's Cathl from 90. *The Rectory, 7 Ancrum Bank, Dalkeith, Midlothian EH22 3AY* 031-663 7000

CAMERON, Gregory Kenneth. b 59. Linc Coll Ox BA80 MA84 Down Coll Cam BA82 MA85 Univ of Wales (Cardiff) DPS83 Univ of Wales MPhil90. St Mich Coll Llan 82. **d** 83 **p** 84. C Newport St Paul *Mon* 83-86; Tutor St Mich Coll Llan 86-89; C Llanmartin *Mon* 86-87; TV 87-88; Chapl Wycliffe Coll Stonehouse Glos from 88. *Cornerways, 44 Bath Road, Stonehouse, Glos GL10 2AD* Stonehouse (0453) 822607

CAMERON, Mrs Margaret Mary. b 48. Qu Mary Coll Lon BA69 Liv Univ DAA70. SW Minl Tr Course 87. **d** 90. NSM Budleigh Salterton *Ex* from 90. *Belair, 9 Cyprus Road, Exmouth, Devon EX8 2DZ* Exmouth (0395) 263180

CAMERON, Peter Samuel Griswold. b 30. TD76. New Coll Ox BA53 MA56. Wells Th Coll 53. **d** 55 **p** 56. C Westbury-on-Trym St Alb *Bris* 55-58; C Henbury 58-60; CF (TA) 59-70 and 72-78 and 80-87; Perm to Offic *Ely* 60-63; Chapl K Coll Cam 60-63; C-in-c Davyhulme CD *Man* 63-69; V Davyhulme Ch Ch 69-72; V Worsley 72-79; V Waterbeach *Ely* 79-83; R Landbeach 79-83; RD Quy 81-83; V Chesterton Gd Shep from 83. *The Good Shepherd Vicarage, 51 Highworth Avenue, Cambridge CB4 2BQ* Cambridge (0223) 312933 or 351844

CAMERON, William Hugh Macpherson. b 59. Edin Univ LLB82 BD86. Edin Th Coll 83. **d** 86 **p** 87. C Cheadle Hulme All SS *Ches* 86-89; Asst Chapl and Hd Relig Studies Wellington Coll from 89. *c/o Wellington College, Crowthorne, Berks RG11 7PT* Crowthorne (0344) 780375

CAMERON, William James. b 35. St Aid Birkenhead 60. **d** 64 **p** 65. C Halewood *Liv* 64-66; C-in-c Halewood St Mary CD 66-68; Asst Chapl Leeds Univ *Ripon* 68-71; Ind Chapl *Liv* 71-77; Tr Officer Gen Syn Bd of Educn 77-84; V Hickling and Waxham w Sea Palling *Nor* from 89. *The Vicarage, Stubb Road, Hickling, Norwich NR12 0BQ* Hickling (069261) 227

CAMIER, Canon James. b 12. TCD BA33 MA67 Div Test. **d** 35 **p** 36. I Borrisokane w Ardcroney, Aglishclohane etc *L & K* 61-86; RD Ely O'Carroll 82-86; Can Killaloe Cathl from 65; Prec Killaloe Cathl 72-86; rtd 86. *Ferndale, Shillelagh, Co Wicklow, Irish Republic* Shillelagh (55) 29227

CAMM, Howard Arthur. b 56. Newc Univ BEd79 Lon Univ BD82 DipTh82. St Jo Coll Dur MA91. **d** 91. C S Westoe *Dur* from 91. *5 Tynedale Road, South Shields, Tyne & Wear NE34 6EX* 091-456 0932

CAMM, Joseph Arnold. b 12. Worc Ord Coll 68 Ridley Hall Cam 69. **d** 69 **p** 70. C Gt and Lt Driffield *York* 69-72; V Stillingfleet w Naburn 72-78; rtd 78. *61 St James's Road, Bridlington, N Humberside YO15 3PQ* Bridlington (0262) 675052

CAMP, Brian Arthur Leslie. b 50. St Jo Coll Nottm. **d** 83 **p** 84. C Blackheath *Birm* 83-86; TV Halesowen *Worc* from 86. *19 Lapal Lane North, Halesowen, W Midlands B62 0BE* 021-550 5458

CAMP, Frederick Walter. b 19. Sarum Th Coll 47. **d** 49 **p** 50. V Brigham *Carl* 58-80; V Whittingham *Newc* 80-84; V Whittingham and Edlingham w Bolton Chapel 84-85; rtd 85; Perm to Offic *Carl* from 85. *10 Meadow Close, Maryport, Cumbria CA15 7AS* Maryport (0900) 817936

CAMP, John Edward. b 44. Barrister 69 Jes Coll Ox MA68 Brunel Univ MTech69. Ripon Coll Cuddesdon DipTh88. **d** 88 **p** 89. NSM High Wycombe *Ox* 88-89; Chapl St Andr Hosp Northn from 89. *4 Elwes Way, Great Billing, Northampton NN3 4EA* Northampton (0604) 785130 or 29696

CAMP, Michael Maurice. b 52. BTh CertEd. Sarum & Wells Th Coll 78. **d** 81 **p** 82. C Loughton St Jo *Chelmsf* 81-84; C Chingford SS Pet and Paul 84-87; V Northfleet *Roch* from 87. *The Vicarage, The Hill, Northfleet, Gravesend, Kent DA11 9EU* Gravesend (0474) 566400

CAMPBELL, Allan. b 14. Selw Coll Cam BA36 MA40. Westcott Ho Cam 36. **d** 38 **p** 39. R Amersham *Ox* 63-86; Chapl Amersham Gen Hosp 63-86; rtd 86; Perm to Offic *Carl* from 86. *Bridge House, Cockermouth, Cumbria CA13 0HF* Cockermouth (0900) 826748

CAMPBELL, Andrew Victor. b 20. St Chad's Coll Dur 39. Linc Th Coll 46. **d** 49 **p** 50. S Africa 52-72; Adn N Transvaal 67-72; V Hunstanton St Edm *Nor* 72-74; Chapl Coll of the Ascension Selly Oak 74-75; TV Devonport St Aubyn *Ex* 75-76; P-in-c Whitleigh 76-80; V 80-83; RD Plymouth 79-82; P-in-c Harberton w Harbertonford 83-85; rtd 85; Perm to Offic *Ex* from 85. *5 Lovell Close, Exmouth, Devon EX8 1HJ* Exmouth (0395) 270525

CAMPBELL, Frederick David Gordon. b 15. Ex Coll Ox BA39. Wells Th Coll 39. **d** 40 **p** 41. V Isleworth St Mary *Lon* 51-54; SSJE from 57; Superior Gen SSJE 76-91; Lic to Offic *Lon* from 69; rtd 85. *St Edward's House, 22 Great College Street, London SW1P 3QA* 071-222 9234

CAMPBELL, George St Clair. b 32. Lon Univ BSc53. Clifton Th Coll 58. **d** 60 **p** 61. C Tunbridge Wells St Pet *Roch* 60-64; C Clitheroe St Jas *Blackb* 64-70; V Tibshelf *Derby* 70-86; V W Bromwich H Trin *Lich* from 86; Chapl Heath Lane Hosp from 87. *The Vicarage, 1 Burlington Road, West Bromwich, W Midlands B70 6LF* 021-525 3595

CAMPBELL, Canon Ian David. b 33. AKC57. **d** 58 **p** 59. C Liv Our Lady and St Nic w St Anne *Liv* 58-62; V Edge Hill St Dunstan 62-70; R Loughb Em *Leic* 70-80; V Leamington Priors All SS *Cov* 80-91; Hon Can Cov Cathl 87-91; RD Warw and Leamington 87-91; TR Brixham w Churston Ferrers and Kingswear *Ex* from 91. *The Rectory, Durleigh Road, Brixham, Devon TQ5 9JJ* Brixham (08045) 4924

CAMPBELL, James Duncan. b 55. Qu Eliz Coll Lon BSc77. St Jo Coll Dur 85. **d** 87 **p** 88. C Hendon St Paul Mill Hill *Lon* from 87. *46 Shakespeare Road, London NW7 4BE* 081-959 8461

CAMPBELL, James Larry. b 46. Indiana Univ BSc69 E Kentucky Univ MA73 Hull Univ MA91. Linc Th Coll 86. **d** 88 **p** 89. C N Hull St Mich *York* from 88. *1 St Michael's Church, Orchard Park Road, Hull HU6 9BX* Hull (0482) 804458

CAMPBELL, James Malcolm. b 55. ARICS81 R Agric Coll Cirencester DipREM77. Wycliffe Hall Ox 89. **d** 91. C Scole, Brockdish, Billingford, Thorpe Abbots etc *Nor* from 91. *18 St Leonard's Close, Scole, Diss, Norfolk IP21 4DW* Diss (0379) 740250

CAMPBELL, James Norman Thompson. b 49. DipTh. **d** 86 **p** 87. C Arm St Mark w Aghavilly *Arm* 86-89; I Belf H Trin and Ardoyne *Conn* from 89. *The Rectory, 313 Ballysillan Road, Belfast BT14 6RD* Belfast (0232) 713958

CAMPBELL, John Frederick Stuart. b 25. Open Univ BA80. ACT ThL50 Oak Hill Th Coll 51. **d** 52 **p** 53. Australia 65-74; V Bath Weston St Jo *B & W* 74-80; R Bath Weston St Jo w Kelston 81-90; rtd 90; Chapl Shepton Mallet Hosps from 91. *22 Drake Road, Wells, Somerset BA5 3JX* Wells (0749) 675016

CAMPBELL, Canon John Norman. b 16. Ch Coll Cam BA38 MA42. Ridley Hall Cam 38. **d** 40 **p** 41. Uganda 49-70; R Stapleton *Bris* 70-85; rtd 85; Perm to Offic *Bris* from 85. *71 Gloucester Road, Malmesbury, Wilts SN16 0AJ* Malmesbury (0666) 822730

CAMPBELL, Kenneth Scott. b 47. BA82. Oak Hill Th Coll. **d** 82 **p** 83. C Aughton St Mich *Liv* 82-85; V Brough w Stainmore *Carl* 85-90; R Brough w Stainmore, Musgrave and Warcop from 90. *The Vicarage, Church Brough, Kirkby Stephen, Cumbria CA17 4EJ* Brough (09304) 238

CAMPBELL, Lawrence Henry. b 41. TCD BA63 MA66. **d** 63 **p** 65. C Larne and Inver *Conn* 63-66; C Finaghy

66-67; Chapl RN 67-83; R Brancaster w Burnham Deepdale and Titchwell *Nor* from 83. *The Rectory, Brancaster, King's Lynn, Norfolk PE31 8AU* Brancaster (0485) 210268

CAMPBELL, Nelson James. b 10. AKC33. **d** 33 **p** 34. V Whitton SS Phil and Jas *Lon* 68-79; rtd 79; Perm to Offic St E from 79; Lon from 84; Portsm & Win from 90. *Karen House, Hilbrow, Liss, Hants GU33 7PB* Liss (0730) 893640

CAMPBELL, Patrick Alistair. b 36. Qu Coll Birm 64. **d** 67 **p** 68. C Paston *Pet* 67-71; C Stockton Heath *Ches* 71-73; V Egremont St Jo 73-78; V Bredbury St Mark 78-85; R Astbury and Smallwood from 85. *The Rectory, Astbury, Congleton, Cheshire CW12 4RQ* Congleton (0260) 2625

CAMPBELL, Robin William. b 41. TCD BA63 MA67. Ridley Hall Cam 63. **d** 65 **p** 66. C Netherton *Liv* 65-68; C Liv Our Lady and St Nic w St Anne 68-70; V Hooton *Ches* from 70. *Hooton Vicarage, Chester Road, Wirral, Merseyside L66 1QH* 051-339 2020

CAMPBELL, Roger Stewart. b 40. Birm Univ BSc61 PhD65 St Jo Coll Dur BA71. Cranmer Hall Dur 68. **d** 71 **p** 72. C Jesmond Clayton Memorial *Newc* 71-77; Singapore 78-85; C Nottm St Nic *S'well* 86-90; V Holloway St Mark w Em *Lon* from 90. *St Mark's Vicarage, 1 Moray Road, London N4 3LD* 071-272 5376

CAMPBELL, Stephen James. b 60. **d** 91. C Lisburn Ch Ch *Conn* from 91. *74 Woodland Park, Lisburn BT28 1LD* Belfast (0232) 602124

CAMPBELL-SMITH, Robert Campbell. b 38. CCC Cam BA61 MA66 Ibadan Univ Nigeria 62. Linc Th Coll 61. **d** 63 **p** 64. C Norbury St Steph *Cant* 63-66; C W Wickham St Mary 66-71; V Croydon St Aug 71-81; V Goudhurst 81-87; RD W Charing 82-89; P-in-c Kilndown 83-87; V Goudhurst w Kilndown from 87. *The Vicarage, Goudhurst, Cranbrook, Kent TN17 1AN* Goudhurst (0580) 211332

CAMPBELL-WILSON, Allan. b 43. Dur Univ BEd74. NE Ord Course 79. **d** 82 **p** 83. NSM Boosbeck w Moorsholm *York* 82-85; R Easington w Skeffling, Kilnsea and Holmpton 85-87; P-in-c Middlesb St Jo the Ev from 89. *St John's Vicarage, 45 Lothian Road, Middlesbrough, Cleveland TS4 2HS* Middlesbrough (0642) 242926

CAMPEN, William Geoffrey. b 50. Liv Univ CertEd71 Southn Univ BTh81. Sarum & Wells Th Coll 76. **d** 79 **p** 80. C Peckham St Jo w St Andr *S'wark* 79-83; P-in-c Mottingham St Edw from 83. *St Edward's Vicarage, St Keverne Road, London SE9 4AQ* 081-857 6278

CAMPION, Keith Donald. b 52. S Dios Minl Tr Scheme. **d** 84 **p** 87. NSM Scilly Is *Truro* from 84. *20 Launceston Close, St Mary's, Isles of Scilly TR21 0LN* Scillonia (0720) 22606

CAMPION, Peter Robert. **d** 90 **p** 91. C Belf H Trin and Ardoyne *Conn* from 90. *27 Wheatfield Gardens, Belfast BT14 7HU* Belfast (0232) 715478

CAMPLING, Very Rev Christopher Russell. b 25. St Edm Hall Ox BA50 MA54. Cuddesdon Coll 50. **d** 51 **p** 52. C Basingstoke *Win* 51-55; Min Can Ely Cathl *Ely* 55-60; Chapl K Sch Ely 55-60; Chapl Lancing Coll Sussex 60-68; P-in-c Birlingham w Nafford *Worc* 68-75; V Pershore w Wick 68-75; RD Pershore 70-76; Hon Can Worc Cathl 74-84; V Pershore w Pinvin, Wick and Birlingham 75-76; Dioc Dir of Educn 76-84; Adn Dudley 76-84; P-in-c Dodderhill 76-84; Dean Ripon from 84; Chmn CCC from 88. *The Minster House, Ripon, N Yorkshire HG4 1PE* Ripon (0765) 3615

CAMPLING, Michael. b 27. Trin Coll Cam BA50 MA61. Wells Th Coll 51. **d** 53 **p** 54. C Calne *Sarum* 53-57; C Roehampton H Trin *S'wark* 57-61; V Crowthorne *Ox* 61-75; P-in-c Foleshill St Laur *Cov* 75-81; V 81-83; R Old Alresford and Bighton *Win* from 83. *The Rectory, Old Alresford, Alresford, Hants SO24 9DY* Alresford (0962) 732780

CANDLER, David Cecil. b 24. Cape Town Univ BSc47 Keble Coll Ox BA50 MA55. St Paul's Grahamstown 56. **d** 56 **p** 57. S Rhodesia 57-65; Rhodesia 65-80; Zimbabwe 80-85; R Barningham w Matlaske w Baconsthorpe etc *Nor* from 85. *The Rectory, Matlaske, Norwich NR11 7AQ* Matlaske (026377) 420

CANE, Anthony William Nicholas Strephon. b 61. Cape Town Univ BA81. Westcott Ho Cam 87. **d** 90 **p** 91. C Kings Heath *Birm* from 90. *14 All Saints' Road, Birmingham B14 7LL* 021-444 2491

CANE, Peter Geoffrey. b 14. MC44. Ridley Hall Cam 62. **d** 63 **p** 64. V Comberton *Ely* 65-74; V Ilyde Common *Win* 74-82; rtd 82. *1 Maners Way, Cambridge CB1 4SL* Cambridge (0223) 240155

CANEY, Robert Swinbank. b 37. St Jo Coll Cam 57. Lich Th Coll 58. **d** 61 **p** 62. C Kingswinford H Trin *Lich*

61-64; C Castle Church 64-67; V Bradwell *Derby* 67-73; V Fairfield 73-84; RD Buxton 78-84; P-in-c Peak Forest and Wormhill 79-83; R Wirksworth w Alderwasley, Carsington etc from 84. *The Rectory, Wirksworth, Derby DE4 4FB* Wirksworth (0629) 824707

CANHAM, John Graham. b 33. Univ of Wales (Lamp) BA55. Chich Th Coll 55. **d** 57 **p** 58. C Hawarden *St As* 57-64; Asst Chapl Ellesmere Coll Shropshire 64-66; Chapl Ches Cathl Choir Sch 66-73; Chapl Choral Ches Cathl *Ches* 66-73; Asst Chapl Rossall Sch Fleetwood 73-76 and from 83; Chapl 76-83. *Dragon and Crescent House, Rossall School, Fleetwood, Lancs FY7 8JW* Fleetwood (03917) 2739

CANHAM, John Rowland Brindley. b 17. St Steph Ho Ox 56. **d** 58 **p** 59. V Raunds *Pet* 67-82; rtd 82; Perm to Offic *Worc* 84-85. *8B Cliff Road, Bridgnorth, Shropshire* Bridgnorth (0746) 761154

CANHAM, Philip Edward. b 15. St Aid Birkenhead 46. **d** 46 **p** 47. V Dalston *Carl* 65-70; V Irthington 70-76; P-in-c Addingham 76-79; P-in-c Edenhall w Langwathby and Culgaith 76-79; P-in-c Greenhead *Newc* 79-80; P-in-c Lambley w Knaresdale 79-80; rtd 80. *6 Eden Park Crescent, Carlisle CA1 2UF* Carlisle (0228) 47236

CANHAM, Robert Edwin Francis. b 24. FRCO59 ARCM. **d** 74 **p** 75. NSM Newlyn St Pet *Truro* 74-75; C Phillack w Gwithian 75-79; C Phillack w Gwithian and Gwinear 78-79; P-in-c 79-83; V Greenham *Ox* from 83. *The Vicarage, New Road, Greenham, Newbury, Berks RG14 7RZ* Newbury (0635) 41075

CANHAM, William Alexander. b 26. Clare Coll Cam BA47 MA56. Roch Th Coll 65. **d** 67 **p** 68. C Orpington St Andr *Roch* 67-70; C Guernsey St Steph *Win* 70-75; Chapl Eliz Coll Guernsey 72-75; R Tadley St Pet 75-83; V Bournemouth St Luke 83-91; R Guernsey St Marguerite de la Foret from 91. *The Rectory, Le Bourg, Foret, Guernsey, Channel Islands* Guernsey (0481) 38392

CANN, Christopher James. b 64. **d** 91. C Newport St Julian *Mon* from 91. *142 Ennerdale Court, Old Barn, St Julian's, Newport, Gwent NP9 7BQ* Newport (0633) 211791

CANN, Stanley George. b 16. St Boniface Warminster 40 Linc Th Coll. **d** 43 **p** 44. V Sidley *Chich* 66-84; P-in-c 84; RD Battle and Bexhill 77-84 and 85-86; rtd 84; Perm to Offic *Chich* from 86. *45 First Avenue, Bexhill-on-Sea, E Sussex TN40 2PL* Bexhill-on-Sea (0424) 211867

✠**CANNAN, Rt Rev Edward Alexander Capparis.** b 20. K Coll Lon BD49 AKC49. **d** 50 **p** 51 **c** 79. C Blandford Forum *Sarum* 50-53; Chapl RAF 53-69; Asst Chapl-in-Chief RAF 69-74; Vice-Prin RAF Chapl Sch 66-69; Prin 73-74; QHC 71-74; Chapl St Marg Sch Bushey 74-79; Bp St Helena 79-85; rtd 86. *Church Cottage, Allensmore, Hereford HR2 9AQ* Hereford (0432) 277357

CANNER, Canon Peter George. b 24. St Chad's Coll Dur BA49 DipTh51 MA55. **d** 51 **p** 52. V Tynemouth Ch Ch *Newc* 63-77; V Ponteland 77-89; Hon Can Newc Cathl 80-89; rtd 89. *The Rigg, 4 Back Croft, Rothbury, Morpeth, Northd NE65 7YB* Rothbury (0669) 21319

CANNING, Arthur Brian. b 12. St Jo Coll Dur BA(Theol)37 MA40. **d** 37 **p** 38. V New Romney w Hope and St Mary's Bay etc *Cant* 66-71; V Boughton Monchelsea 71-79; rtd 79; Perm to Offic *Heref* from 81. *Harp Cottage, Old Radnor, Presteigne, Powys LD8 2RH* New Radnor (054421) 312

CANNING, Arthur James. b 45. St Jo Coll Dur BA66 Linacre Coll Ox BA70 MA74. Lambeth STh90 Ripon Hall Ox 67. **d** 71 **p** 72. C Coleshill *Birm* 71-74; C Frome St Jo B & W 75-76; V Frizington and Arlecdon *Carl* 76-80; P-in-c Foleshill St Paul *Cov* 80-81; V from 81. *St Paul's Vicarage, 13 St Paul's Road, Foleshill, Coventry CV6 5DE* Coventry (0203) 688283

CANNING, Graham Gordon Blakeman. b 33. S'wark Ord Course 73. **d** 76 **p** 77. NSM Mill Hill Jo Keble Ch *Lon* 76-78; TV Dorchester *Ox* 78-85; V Shipton-under-Wychwood w Milton-under-Wychwood from 85. *The Vicarage, Shipton-under-Wychwood, Oxford OX7 6BP* Shipton-under-Wychwood (0993) 830257

CANNING, John Graham. b 21. Edin Th Coll 47. **d** 49 **p** 50. V Hammersmith St Jo *Lon* 62-90; rtd 90. *11 Circus Field Road, Glastonbury, Somerset BA6 9PE* Glastonbury (0458) 33708

CANNING, Peter Christopher. b 52. Birm Poly DipSocWork78 CQSW. St Jo Coll Nottm 87. **d** 89 **p** 90. C Cov St Mary *Cov* from 89. *193 Allesley Road, Coventry CV5 8FL* Coventry (0203) 691392

CANNING, Canon Richard Dandridge. b 16. St Chad's Coll Dur BA41 DipTh42 MA44. **d** 42 **p** 43. Hon Can Antigua from 64; St Kitts-Nevis 68-75; Grenada 76-81;

rtd 81. *Chantimelle, Blowing Point, Anguilla* Anguilla (1809497) 6884

CANNING, Robert Kingswood. b 03. St Boniface Warminster 61. d 52 p 53. V Marden *Cant* 65-72; rtd 72. *c/o J R Canning Esq, 5 Rechner Place, Flynn, ACT, Australia 2615*

CANNON, Alan George. b 35. FRSA MBIM Lon Univ BA57 MA63 PhD71 AKC. Sarum & Wells Th Coll 76. d 80 p 81. Hon C Whipton *Ex* 80-89; Perm to Offic from 89. *The Stable, Sowden's Mews, Brampford Speke, Exeter EX5 5HL* Exeter (0392) 841045

CANNON, Mark Harrison. b 60. Keble Coll Ox BA82. Cranmer Hall Dur 83. d 85 p 86. C Skipton Ch Ch *Bradf* 85-88; Dioc Youth Officer from 88; C Baildon from 88. *7 Park Mount Avenue, Baildon, Shipley, W Yorkshire BD17 6DS* Bradford (0274) 581482

CANSDALE, George Graham. b 38. Mert Coll Ox BA60 MA64 DipEd61. Clifton Th Coll 62. d 64 p 65. C Heatherlands St Jo *Sarum* 64-67; Kenya 68-76; P-in-c Clapham *St Alb* 76-80; V 80-89; Bedf Sch from 89. *62 High Street, Oakley, Bedford* Oakley (02302) 5011

CANT, David Edward. b 49. Sheff Univ LLB70. Oak Hill Th Coll DipTh89. d 89 p 90. C Newburn *Newc* from 89. *153 Hallow Drive, Throckley, Newcastle upon Tyne NE15 9PS* 091-264 4075

CANTERBURY, Archbishop of. See CAREY, Most Rev and Rt Hon George Leonard

CANTERBURY, Archdeacon of. See TILL, Ven Michael Stanley

CANTERBURY, Dean of. See SIMPSON, Very Rev John Arthur

CANTI, Mrs Christine. b 24. St Alb Minl Tr Scheme 82. dss 85 d 87. Radlett *St Alb* 85-86; Hon C Pitminster w Corfe *B & W* from 87. *Brook Farm House, Corfe, Taunton, Somerset TA3 7BU* Blagdon Hill (082342) 623

CANTRELL, David Grindon. b 59. Bris Univ BSc80 Nottm Univ PhD83 Pemb Coll Cam BA88. Ridley Hall Cam 86. d 89 p 90. C Low Harrogate St Mary *Ripon* 89-90; C Horsforth from 90. *7 Featherbank Walk, Horsforth, Leeds LS18 4QN* Leeds (0532) 589567

CAPEL-EDWARDS, Dr Maureen. b 36. Southn Univ BSc60 Reading Univ PhD69. St Alb Minl Tr Scheme 84. d 87. NSM Ware St Mary *St Alb* from 87; Chapl Ware Coll from 87; NSM Hertf All SS from 90. *5 Pearman Drive, Dane End, Ware, Herts* Dane End (0920) 438365

CAPENER, Herbert Francis. b 30. Jes Coll Ox BA53 MA58. Cuddesdon Coll 53. d 55 p 56. V Shirley St Geo *Cant* 63-70; V Folkestone St Pet 70-89; rtd 90. *1 Baldric Road, Folkestone, Kent CT20 2NR* Folkestone (0303) 54579

CAPERON, John Philip. b 44. Bris Univ BA66 Open Univ MPhil80 Ox Univ MSc83. Ox NSM Course 80. d 83 p 84. NSM Hook Norton w Gt Rollright, Swerford etc *Ox* 83-86; NSM Knaresborough *Ripon* from 86; Dep Hd St Aid Sch Harrogate from 86. *Sarum, Birkhills, Burton Leonard, Harrogate, N Yorkshire HG3 3SF* Ripon (0765) 87083

CAPES, Arthur Geoffrey. b 33. Bps' Coll Cheshunt 58. d 61 p 62. C Seacroft *Ripon* 61-66; Guyana 66-80; V Claremont H Angels *Man* 80-85; V Blyton w Pilham *Linc* 85-90; V E Stockwith 86-90; V Laughton w Wildsworth 86-90; R Broad Town, Clyffe Pypard and Tockenham *Sarum* from 90. *The Rectory, Clyffe Pypard, Swindon SN4 7PY* Swindon (0793) 731623

CAPES, Dennis Robert. b 34. Handsworth Coll Birm 55 Linc Th Coll 64. d 64 p 65. In Meth Ch (Malaysia) 59-63; C Lt Coates *Linc* 64-66; Malaysia 66-69; V Gosberton Clough *Linc* 69-71; V Kirton in Holland 71-80; Area Sec (Dios Cov, Heref and Worc) USPG 80-87; Chapl Copenhagen w Aarhus *Eur* from 87. *Stigaardsvej 6, 2900 Hellerup, Denmark* Denmark (45) 3162-7736

CAPIE, Fergus Bernard. b 47. Auckland Univ BA68 MA71. Wycliffe Hall Ox BA77. d 77 p 78. C Ox St Mich w St Martin and All SS *Ox* 77-80; Chapl Summer Fields Sch Ox 80-91; Hon C Wolvercote w Summertown *Ox* 87-91; Perm to Offic *St E* 91; C E Ham w Upton Park *Chelmsf* from 91. *1 Norman Road, London E6 4HN* 081-471 8751

CAPLE, Stephen Malcolm. b 55. Chich Th Coll 86. d 88 p 89. C Newington St Mary *S'wark* from 88. *89 Ambergate Street, London SE17 3RZ* 071-820 0786

CAPON, Canon Anthony Charles. b 26. Trin Coll Cam BA51 MA55. Wycliffe Coll Toronto BD65 DD82 Oak Hill Th Coll 51. d 53 p 54. C Portman Square St Paul *Lon* 53-56; Canada from 56; Hon Can Montreal from

78; Prin Montreal Dioc Th Coll 78-91. *5 Loradean Crescent, Kingston, Ontario, Canada, K7K 6X9*

CAPON, Canon Martin Gedge. b 09. Magd Coll Cam BA31 MA36. Wycliffe Hall Ox 34. d 35 p 36. V Breage w Germoe *Truro* 70-74; rtd 74; Perm to Offic *Ex* from 74. *Flat 2, 26 Alexandra Terrace, Exmouth, Devon EX8 1BB* Exmouth (0395) 265128

✠CAPPER, Rt Rev Edmund Michael Hubert. b 08. OBE61. Dur Univ LTh32. St Aug Coll Cant 28. d 32 p 33 c 67. C Strood St Mary *Roch* 32-36; Tanganyika 36-62; Adn Lindi 48-54; Adn Dar-es-Salaam 54-57; Provost 57-62; Chapl Palma *Eur* 62-67; Bp St Helena 67-73; Aux Bp Eur from 73; Chapl Malaga 73-76; Asst Bp S'wark from 81; rtd 86. *Morden College, London SE3 0PW* 081-858 9169

CAPPER, Mrs Elizabeth Margaret. b 31. St Chris Coll Blackheath 52. dss 79 d 87. The Dorothy Kerin Trust Burrswood from 79; Whitstable *Cant* 80-87; Hon Par Dn from 87. *26 Swalecliffe Road, Whitstable, Kent CT5 2PR* Whitstable (0227) 272800

CAPPER, Ian Parode. b 05. Sarum Th Coll. d 47 p 48. R High Halden *Cant* 71-75; rtd 75; Perm to Offic *Cant* from 75. *26 Swalecliffe Road, Whitstable, Kent CT5 2PR* Whitstable (0227) 272800

CAPPER, Canon James Frank. b 18. Qu Coll Ox BA40 MA44. Westcott Ho Cam 48. d 48 p 49. V Erdington St Barn *Birm* 64-75; V Coleshill 75-82; V Maxstoke 75-82; RD Coleshill 77-82; Perm to Offic *Ex* from 82; rtd 83. *Martlets, Harpford, Sidmouth, Devon EX10 0NQ* Colaton Raleigh (0395) 68198

CAPPER, John Raymond. b 29. Liv Univ BA53. Coll of Resurr Mirfield 53. d 55 p 56. C Birm St Aid Small Heath *Birm* 55-58; C Widley w Wymering *Portsm* 60-63; C Portsea St Sav 63-68; V Gosport H Trin from 68. *Holy Trinity Vicarage, Trinity Green, Gosport, Hants PO12 1HL* Gosport (0705) 580173

CAPPER, Richard. b 49. Leeds Univ BSc70 Fitzw Coll Cam BA72 MA79. Westcott Ho Cam 70. d 73 p 74. C Wavertree H Trin *Liv* 73-76; P-in-c Ince St Mary 76-79; V 79-83; V Gt Crosby St Faith from 83; AD Bootle from 89. *St Faith's Vicarage, Crosby Road North, Liverpool L22 4RE* 051-928 3342

CAPPER, Robert Melville. b 52. Chu Coll Cam BA74 MA. Wycliffe Hall Ox 74. d 77 p 78. C Newport Maindee St Jo Ev *Mon* 77-81; Chapl Univ of Wales (Abth) *St D* 81-87; TV Malpas *Mon* from 87; V Malpas *Mon* from 87. *The Vicarage, Malpas, Newport, Gwent NP9 6GQ* Newport (0633) 852047

CAPPER, William Alan. QUB BTh. d 88 p 89. C Dundonald *D & D* 88-91; C Lisburn Ch Ch *Conn* from 91. *Flat 8, Dalboyne House, 5 Belsize Road, Lisburn, Co Antrim BT27 4AL* Lisburn (0846) 671439

CAPRON, David Cooper. b 45. Open Univ BA80. Sarum & Wells Th Coll 71. d 75 p 76. C Cov St Mary *Cov* 75-79; V Shottery St Andr 79-86; TV Stratford w Bishopton 79-86; V Newton Aycliffe *Dur* 86-89; TR 89-90; P-in-c Alcester and Arrow w Oversley and Weethley *Cov* from 90. *3 Greville Road, Alcester, Warks B49 5QN* Alcester (0789) 764261

CAPRON, Ronald Beresford. b 35. Clifton Th Coll. d 62 p 63. R Gaddesby w S Croxton *Leic* 67-71; R Beeby 67-71; Chapl RAF 71-83; rtd 83. *c/o MOD, Adastral House, Theobald's Road, London WC1X 8RU* 071-430 7268

CAPSTICK, John Nowell. b 30. AKC54. d 55 p 56. C Skipton Ch Ch *Bradf* 55-57; C Buxton *Derby* 57-61; V Codnor and Loscoe 61-63; C-in-c Rawthorpe CD *Wakef* 63-64; V Rawthorpe 64-70; V Netherthong 70-89; TV Upper Holme Valley from 89. *The Vicarage, Netherthong, Holmfirth, Huddersfield HD7 2UQ* Holmfirth (0484) 682430

CAPSTICK, William Richard Dacre. b 32. Pemb Coll Ox. Chich Th Coll 61. d 64 p 65. C Hunslet St Mary and Stourton St Andr *Ripon* 64-67; C Knaresborough H Trin 67-71; V Stratfield Mortimer *Ox* 71-76; P-in-c St Marylebone Ch Ch w St Paul *Lon* 76-78; TV St Marylebone Ch Ch 78-79; TR Newbury *Ox* 79-89; TV Brighton St Pet and St Nic w Chpl Royal *Chich* from 89. *13 Ditchling Road, Brighton BN1 4SB* Brighton (0273) 609144

CARBERRY, Leon Carter. b 54. Pennsylvania Univ BSc76. St Steph Ho Ox 81. d 84 p 85. C Peterlee *Dur* 84-87; C Newton Aycliffe 87-89; VC York Minster *York* from 89. *2A Sycamore Terrace, York YO3 7DN* York (0904) 646727

CARBERRY, Robin Linton. b 28. Chich Th Coll 51. d 53 p 54. R York St Clem w St Mary Bishophill Senior *York* 65-89; rtd 89. *55 Middlethorpe Grove, Dringhouses, York* York (0904) 709289

CARBUTT, George Maurice. b 06. d 44 p 45. OSP 25-69; rtd 69; Perm to Offic *Wakef* from 71. *865 Bradford Road, Batley, W Yorkshire WF17 8NN*

CARD, Terence Leslie. b 37. K Coll Lon BD68 AKC68 Heythrop Coll Lon MTh84. d 69 p 70. C Thundersley *Chelmsf* 69-72; Lic to Offic *Bradf* 72-75; V Chingford St Anne *Chelmsf* 75-81; RD Waltham Forest 78-81; R Springfield All SS 81-83; C Becontree St Jo 85-87; rtd 87. *39 Kings Chase, Brentwood, Essex CM14 4LD*

CARD, Thomas Ian. b 36. RD76. Master Mariner 61. Portsm Dioc Tr Course 88. d 89. NSM Binstead *Portsm* from 89; NSM Swanmore St Mich w Havenstreet from 89. *Dolphins, 49 Mayfield Road, Ryde, Isle of Wight PO33 3PR* Isle of Wight (0983) 64749

CARDALE, Charles Anthony. b 21. St D Coll Lamp BA47 Lich Th Coll 55. d 56 p 57. V Staverton w Landscove *Ex* 69-87; R Broadhempston, Woodland, Staverton etc 88-89; Perm to Offic from 89; rtd 90. *Keyberry, 13 Woodland Close, Staverton, Totnes, Devon TQ9 6PQ* Staverton (080426) 277

CARDALE, Edward Charles. b 50. CCC Ox BA72. Cuddesdon Coll 72 Union Th Sem (NY) STM74. d 74 p 75. C E Dulwich St Jo *S'wark* 74-77; USA 77-80; V Ponders End St Matt *Lon* 80-84; V Lytchett Minster *Sarum* from 84. *The Vicarage, Lytchett Minster, Poole, Dorset BH16 6JQ* Wimborne (0202) 622253

CARDELL-OLIVER, John Anthony. b 43. Em Coll Cam BA67 MA72 Univ of W Aus BEd75 MEd85. Westcott Ho Cam 86. d 86 p 88. Australia 86-88; Perm to Offic *Ely* from 88; C Stansted Mountfitchet *Chelmsf* from 89. *43 Gilbey Crescent, Stansted, Essex CM24 8DT* Bishop's Stortford (0279) 814463

CARDEN, Edwin William. b 54. Cranmer Hall Dur 85. d 87 p 88. C Thundersley *Chelmsf* 87-91; CUF from 91. *14 Grangeway, Thundersley, Benfleet, Essex SS7 3RP* Rayleigh (0268) 773462

CARDEN, John Brumfitt. b 24. Lon Coll of Div 48. d 52 p 53. Asia Sec CMS 70-76; Hon C Croydon St Sav *Cant* 75-76; C-in-c Bath St Steph *B & W* 76-82; V 82-84; CMS 84-89; Jerusalem 84-87; Exec Asst WCC Geneva 87-89; rtd 89; Miss Partner CMS from 89. *81 The Village, Haxby, York YO3 8JE* York (0904) 750035

CARDIGAN, Archdeacon of. *See* JONES, Ven Benjamin Jenkin Hywel

CARDINAL, Ian Ralph. b 57. Qu Coll Birm 81. d 84 p 85. C Whitkirk *Ripon* 84-87; C Knaresborough 87-89; P-in-c Wilsford *Linc* 89; P-in-c Ancaster 89; R Ancaster Wilsford Gp from 89. *The Rectory, 117 Ermine Street, Ancaster, Grantham, Lincs NG32 3QL* Loveden (0400) 30398

CARDWELL, Edward Anthony Colin. b 42. Trin Coll Cam BA63 MA68. St Jo Coll Nottm 73. d 75 p 76. C Stapenhill w Cauldwell *Derby* 75-78; C Bramcote *S'well* 78-81; V S'well H Trin from 81. *Holy Trinity Vicarage, Westhorpe, Southwell, Notts NG25 0NB* Southwell (0636) 813243

CARDWELL, Joseph Robin. b 47. Qu Coll Cam BA68 MA77. Trin Coll Bris 73. d 76 p 77. C Bromley Ch Ch *Roch* 76-79; C Shirley *Win* 79-82; V Somborne w Ashley 82-90; V Derry Hill *Sarum* from 90; Community Affairs Chapl from 90. *The Vicarage, Derry Hill, Calne, Wilts SN11 9NN* Calne (0249) 812172

CARE, Canon Charles Richard. b 21. Univ of Wales (Lamp) BA42. St Mich Coll Llan 42. d 44 p 45. R St Brides Minor *Llan* 57-88; RD Bridgend 75-88; Can Llan Cathl from 83; Prec Llan Cathl 87-88; rtd 88. *31 Laburnum Drive, Danygraig, Porthcawl, M Glam* Porthcawl (065671) 5446

CAREFULL, Alan Vincent. b 24. Magd Coll Ox BA50 MA60. St Steph Ho Ox DipTh51. d 52 p 53. V Newc St Jo *Newc* 65-73; Admin of Shrine of Our Lady of Walsingham 73-81; P-in-c E w N and W Barsham *Nor* 73-80; Lic to Offic 80-86; Asst Chapl HM Pris *Nor* 83-89; E Anglian Minl Tr Course from 84; P-in-c N Lynn w St Marg and St Nic *Nor* 86-88; rtd 89. *30 Park Lane, Fakenham, Norfolk NR21 7BE* East Rudham (048522) 680

CAREW, Bryan Andrew. b 38. AIB63 ACIB87. St D Coll Lamp DipTh69. d 67 p 68. C Pemb Dock *St D* 67-70; CF 70-74; P-in-c Gt and Lt Henny w Middleton *Chelmsf* 74-76; P-in-c Wickham St Paul w Twinstead 75-76; R Gt and Lt Henny w Middleton, Wickham St Paul etc from 76. *The Rectory, Great Henny, Sudbury, Suffolk CO10 7NW* Twinstead (0787) 269336

CAREY, Alan Lawrence. b 29. AKC53. d 54 p 55. C Radford *Cov* 54-57; C Burnham *Ox* 57-65; C-in-c Cippenham CD 65-77. *12 Ormsby Street, Reading RG1 7YR* Reading (0734) 584217

CAREY, Charles John. b 29. K Coll Lon BD53 AKC53. St Aug Coll Cant 71. d 72 p 73. C Spring Park *Cant* 72-74; C Ifield *Chich* 74-78; C Burgess Hill St Jo 78-80; Chapl Rush Green and Oldchurch Hosps Romford from 80. *The Chaplain's Office, Oldchurch Hospital, Romford RM7 0BE* Romford (0708) 46090

CAREY, Christopher Lawrence John. b 38. St Andr Univ BSc61 Lon Univ BD64. Clifton Th Coll 61. d 64 p 65. C Battersea Park St Sav *S'wark* 64-67; Kenya 68-79; Overseas Regional Sec for E Africa CMS from 79; Perm to Offic *Roch* from 81. *5 Downs Avenue, Chislehurst, Kent BR7 6HG* 081-467 4417

✠**CAREY, Most Rev and Rt Hon George Leonard.** b 35. PC91. Lon Univ BD62 MTh65 PhD71. ALCD61. d 62 p 63 c 87. C Islington St Mary *Lon* 62-66; Lect Oak Hill Th Coll 66-70; Lect St Jo Coll Nottm 70-75; V Dur St Nic *Dur* 75-82; Chapl HM Rem Cen Low Newton 77-81; Prin Trin Coll Bris 82-87; Hon Can Bris Cathl *Bris* 84-87; Bp B & W 87-91; Abp Cant from 91. *Lambeth Palace, London SE1 7JU or, The Old Palace, Canterbury CT1 2EE* 071-928 8282 or 928 7207

CAREY, Graham Charles. b 33. Kelham Th Coll 53. d 57 p 58. C Millfield St Mary *Dur* 57-66; V Northfield St Mich *Sheff* 66-76; P-in-c Jarrow St Mark *Dur* 76-77; TV Jarrow 77-84; P-in-c Southwick St Pet *Chich* from 84; Miss to Seamen from 84. *St Peter's Vicarage, Gardner Road, Southwick, Brighton BN4 1PN* Brighton (0273) 592474

CAREY, Very Rev James Maurice George. b 26. TCD BA49 MA52 BD52. CITC 51. d 52 p 53. C Larne and Inver *Conn* 52-55; USA 55-56; C Dub St Ann *D & G* 57-58; Hon CV Ch Ch Cathl Dub 58; Dean of Residences QUB 58-64; I Dub St Bart *D & G* 64-71; I Cork St Fin Barre's Cathl *C, C & R* 71-87; I Cork St Fin Barre's Union from 87; I Cork St Nic w H Trin 71-75; Dean Cork from 71; Radio Officer (Cork) from 90. *The Deanery, 9 Dean Street, Cork, Irish Republic* Cork (21) 964742

CAREY, Canon Ronald Clive Adrian. b 21. K Coll Cam BA46 MA48. Chich Th Coll 47. d 48 p 49. V Claygate *Guildf* 68-78; RD Emly 72-77; Hon Can Guildf Cathl 78-86; R Guildf H Trin w St Mary 78-86; RD Guildf 84-86; rtd 86; Perm to Offic *Roch* from 86. *4 Chart View, Kemsing, Sevenoaks, Kent TN15 6PP* Sevenoaks (0732) 62629

CARHART, John Richards. b 29. Bris Univ BA50 Salford Univ MSc77. St Deiniol's Hawarden 63. d 65 p 66. C Ches St Oswald w Lt St Jo *Ches* 65-72; Lect Ches Coll of HE 65-72; Prin Lect from 72; Dean Academic Studies from 88; C Ches 72; Lic to Offic 73-85; Hon C Ches St Mary from 85. *29 Abbot's Grange, Chester CH2 1AJ* Chester (0244) 380923

CARLESS, Canon Frank. b 22. Lon Univ BD56. St Aid Birkenhead 53. d 56 p 57. V Warley *Wakef* 64 87; RD Halifax 82-86; Hon Can Wakef Cathl 86-87; rtd 87. *130 Savile Park Road, Halifax, W Yorkshire HX1 2EX* Halifax (0422) 348379

CARLILE, Edward Wilson. b 15. ACA39 FCA59 K Coll Lon AKC43 BD46. d 43 p 44. V Leic St Pet *Leic* 60-73; R Swithland 73-76; P-in-c Belgrave St Mich 76-81; rtd 81; Perm to Offic *Leic* from 81. *120A Mount View Road, Sheffield S8 8PL* Sheffield (0742) 581098

CARLILL, Adam Jonathan. b 66. Keble Coll Ox BA88. Linc Th Coll 88. d 90 p 91. C Romford St Edw *Chelmsf* from 90. *54 Parkside Avenue, Romford RM1 4ND* Romford (0708) 727960

CARLILL, Richard Edward. b 38. Westcott Ho Cam 77. d 79 p 80. C Prittlewell *Chelmsf* 79-83; TV Saffron Walden w Wendens Ambo and Littlebury 83-89; V Langtoft w Foxholes, Butterwick, Cottam etc *York* from 89. *The Vicarage, Langtoft, Driffield, N Humberside YO25 0TN* Driffield (0377) 87226

CARLIN, William Patrick Bruce. b 53. St Steph Ho Ox 75. d 78 p 79. C Penistone *Wakef* 78-81; C Barnsley St Mary 81-83; V Stockton St Chad *Dur* from 83. *The Vicarage, Ragpath Lane, Stockton-on-Tees, Cleveland TS19 9JN* Stockton-on-Tees (0642) 674737

CARLING, Mrs Bronwen Noel. b 43. SRN65 SCM73. Linc Th Coll 89. d 91. C Blakeney w Cley, Wiveton, Glandford etc *Nor* from 91. *Rivendell, The Fairstead, Cley-next-the-Sea, Holt, Norfolk NR25 7RJ* Cley (0263) 740539

CARLISLE, Christopher John. b 39. Sheff Univ BEng62. NW Ord Course 72. d 75 p 76. C Bury St Paul *Man* 75-80; C Walkden Moor 80-82; V Lytham St Jo *Blackb* from 82. *The Vicarage, East Beach, Lytham, Lytham St Annes, Lancs FY8 5EX* Lytham (0253) 734396

CARLISLE, Archdeacon of. *See* STANNARD, Ven Colin Percy

CARLISLE, Bishop of. *See* HARLAND, Rt Rev Ian

CARLISLE, Dean of. *See* STAPLETON, Very Rev Henry Edward Champneys

CARLOS, Francis John. b 29. Jes Coll Cam BA54 MA57. Wells Th Coll 52. **d** 55 **p** 56. C Canning Town St Matthias *Chelmsf* 55-57; C-in-c Thundersley CD *St E* 57-64; V New Thundersley *Chelmsf* 64-65; R Wentnor and Ratlinghope w Myndtown and Norbury *Heref* 65-89; P-in-c More w Lydham 82-89; P-in-c Snead 85-89; R Wentnor w Ratlinghope, Myndtown, Norbury etc from 89. *The Rectory, Wentnor, Bishops Castle, Shropshire SY9 5EE* Linley (058861) 244

CARLTON, Roger John. b 51. **d** 80 **p** 81. NSM Downend *Bris* 80-83; NSM Heavitree w Ex St Paul *Ex* 83-87; Chapl St Marg Sch Ex 83-87; Chapl Ex Sch 83-87; TV Bickleigh (Plymouth) *Ex* from 87. *The Vicarage, 2 Blackeven Close, Roborough, Plymouth PL6 7AX* Plymouth (0752) 702119

CARMARTHEN, Archdeacon of. *See* GOULSTONE, Ven Thomas Richard Kerry

CARMICHAEL, Peter Iain. b 28. Chich Th Coll 75. **d** 75 **p** 76. C Rye w Rye Harbour and Playden *Chich* 75-79; C Rye, Rye Harbour and Playden and Iden 79-80; R Earnley and E Wittering from 80. *The Rectory, East Wittering, Chichester, W Sussex PO20 8PS* Brackleshaw Bay (0243) 672260

CARMODY, Canon Dermot Patrick Roy. b 41. CITC 77. **d** 77 **p** 78. C Dub Zion Ch *D & G* 77-79; I Dunganstown w Redcross 79-84; I Dub Ch Ch Cathl Gp from 84; Can Ch Ch Cathl Dub from 84. *All Saints' Vicarage, 30 Phibsborough Road, Dublin 7, Irish Republic* Dublin (1) 728814

CARMYLLIE, Robert Jonathan. b 63. Cov Poly BSc85. St Jo Coll Dur 85. **d** 88 **p** 89. C Horwich *Man* from 88. *27 Brownlow Road, Horwich, Bolton BL6 7DW* Bolton (0204) 696923

CARNE, Canon Brian George. b 29. FSA Liv Univ BCom50. Qu Coll Birm 53. **d** 55 **p** 56. C Swindon St Aug *Bris* 55-58; C Bris St Andr w St Bart 58-60; R Lydiard Millicent w Lydiard Tregoz 60-68; V Bris St Andr Hartcliffe 68-74; V Almondsbury from 74; RD Westbury and Severnside 80-86; Hon Can Bris Cathl from 82; P-in-c Littleton on Severn w Elberton from 83; P-in-c Olveston from 83. *The Vicarage, Almondsbury, Bristol BS12 4DS* Almondsbury (0454) 613223

CARNE, Norman David John. b 27. Roch Th Coll 59. **d** 62 **p** 63. C Roch St Justus *Roch* 62-66; C Strood St Mary 66-68; R Westcote Barton and Steeple Barton *Ox* 68-74; P-in-c Enstone and Heythrop 74-82; V from 82. *The Vicarage, Little Tew Road, Church Enstone, Oxford OX7 4NL* Chipping Norton (0608) 677319

CARNE-ROSS, Stewart Pattison. b 24. Wycliffe Hall Ox 58. **d** 59 **p** 60. V Champion Hill St Sav *S'wark* 64-70; P-in-c Stanton Lacy *Heref* 70-72; V 72-77; V Bromfield 70-77; R Culmington w Onibury 70-77; V Hambledon *Portsm* 77-79; Chapl HM Pris Kingston 79-90; C Portsea St Mary *Portsm* 86-90; rtd 90. *7 Hanover Court, Highbury Street, Portsmouth PO1 2BN* Portsmouth (0705) 752698

CARNELL, Canon Geoffrey Gordon. b 18. St Jo Coll Cam BA40 MA44. Cuddesdon Coll 40. **d** 42 **p** 43. R Isham *Pet* 53-71; V Gt w Lt Harrowden 53-71; Dir of Ords 62-85; Can Pet Cathl 65-85; R Boughton 71-85; Chapl to HM The Queen from 81; rtd 85; Perm to Offic *Pet* from 86. *52 Walsingham Avenue, Kettering, Northants NN15 5ER* Kettering (0536) 511415

CARNELLEY, Ven Desmond. b 29. Open Univ BA77 Leeds Univ CertEd Ex Univ CertRE. Ripon Hall Ox 59. **d** 60 **p** 61. C Aston cum Aughton *Sheff* 60-63; C-in-c Ecclesfield St Paul CD 63-67; V Balby w Hexthorpe 67-73; P-in-c Mosborough 73-74; V 74-85; RD Attercliffe 79-84; Adn Doncaster from 85; Dioc Dir of Educn from 91. *1 Balmoral Road, Doncaster, S Yorkshire DN2 5BZ* Doncaster (0302) 25787

CARNELLEY, Ms Elizabeth Amy. b 64. St Aid Coll Dur BA85 Selw Coll Cam MPhil87. Ripon Coll Cuddesdon 88. **d** 90. Par Dn Sheff Sharrow *Sheff* from 90. *18 Raven Road, Sheffield S7 1SB* Sheffield (0742) 580926

CARNES, Gerald Lambton. b 12. Episc Th Sem Haiti 58. **d** 61 **p** 61. P-in-c Hampton Wick *Lon* 68-75; V 75-84; rtd 85; Perm to Offic *Lon* from 85. *46 Kingston Road, Teddington, Middx TW11 9HX* 081-943 3687

CARNEY, Mrs Mary Patricia. b 42. Univ of Wales (Ban) BSc62 DipEd63. Wycliffe Hall Ox. **d** 90. Par Dn Carterton *Ox* from 90. *8 Alderley Close, Carterton, Oxon OX8 3QP* Carterton (0993) 845116

CARNLEY, Ronald Birch. b 18. Pemb Coll Ox BA47 MA47. Cuddesdon Coll 47. **d** 49 **p** 50. V Matfield *Roch* 59-78; Perm to Offic Roch & Chich from 79; rtd 83. *5 Cleeve Avenue, Hawkenbury, Tonbridge, Kent TN2 4TY* Tunbridge Wells (0892) 30045

CARPENTER, Bruce Leonard Henry. b 32. Lon Univ BA54 St Chad's Coll Dur DipTh59. **d** 59 **p** 60. C Portsea N End St Mark *Portsm* 59-63; C Fareham H Trin 63-67; TR 74-84; V Locks Heath 67-74; RD Alverstoke 71-77; Hon Can Portsm Cathl 81-84; V Richmond St Mary w St Matthias and St Jo *S'wark* from 84. *The Vicarage, Ormond Road, Richmond, Surrey TW10 6TH* 081-940 0362

CARPENTER, David James. b 52. St Steph Ho Ox 74. **d** 76 **p** 77. C Newport St Julian *Mon* 76-77; C Pontypool 77-79; C Ebbw Vale 79-81; TV 81-85; V Pontnewynydd 85-88; V Bedwellty from 88. *The Rectory, Bedwellty, Blackwood, Gwent NP2 0BE* Bargoed (0443) 831078

CARPENTER, Derek George Edwin. b 40. K Coll Lon BD62 AKC62. **d** 63 **p** 64. C Friern Barnet All SS *Lon* 63-66; C Chingford SS Pet and Paul *Chelmsf* 66-70; V Dartford St Alb *Roch* 70-79; R Crayford 79-90; RD Erith 82-90; R Beckenham St Geo from 90. *The Rectory, 14 The Knoll, Beckenham, Kent BR3 2JW* 081-650 0983

CARPENTER, Donald Arthur. b 35. Roch Th Coll 65. **d** 67 **p** 68. C Thornton Heath St Jude *Cant* 67-73; V Earby *Bradf* 73-78; V Skipton Ch Ch 78-88; V Baildon from 88. *The Vicarage, Baildon, Shipley, W Yorkshire BD17 6BY* Bradford (0274) 594941

CARPENTER, Very Rev Edward Frederick. b 10. K Coll Lon BA32 MA34 BD35 AKC35 PhD43. Lambeth DD79. **d** 35 **p** 36. Can Westmr Abbey 51-74; Treas 59-74; Adn Westmr 63-74; Dean Westmr 74-85; rtd 85. *6 Selwyn Avenue, Richmond, Surrey* 081-940 3896

CARPENTER, Ven Frederick Charles. b 20. SS Coll Cam BA47 MA49 St Cath Soc Ox DipTh48. Wycliffe Hall Ox 47. **d** 49 **p** 50. Can Res Portsm Cathl *Portsm* 68-77; Dir RE 68-75; Adn Is of Wight 77-86; P-in-c Binstead 77-86; rtd 86; Perm to Offic Portsm & Sarum from 86. *Gilston, Mount Pleasant, Stoford, Salisbury SP2 0PP* Salisbury (0722) 790335

CARPENTER, Gilbert Lant. b 10. Down Coll Cam BA34 MA38. Ely Th Coll 34. **d** 35 **p** 36. V Willesden St Andr *Lon* 57-76; rtd 76. *2 Rushbury Court, Station Road, Hampton, Middx TW12 2DD* 081-941 1449

✠**CARPENTER, Rt Rev Harry James.** b 01. Lon Univ BA21 Qu Coll Ox BA25 MA28 Hon DD55. Cuddesdon Coll 26. **d** 27 **p** 28 **c** 55. C Leatherhead *Guildf* 27; Tutor Keble Coll Ox 27-39; Warden 39-55; Lic to Offic *Ox* 27-55; Can Th Leic Cathl *Leic* 41-55; Bp Ox 55-70; rtd 70. *St John's Home, St Mary's Road, Oxford OX4 1QE* Oxford (0865) 249953

CARPENTER, Justin David William. b 43. Dur Univ BA65. Westcott Ho Cam 65. **d** 67 **p** 68. C Newlyn St Pet *Truro* 67-69; C Gt Marlow *Ox* 69-73; C Forrabury w Minster and Trevalga *Truro* 73-74; C Davidstow w Otterham 73-74; C Boscastle w Davidstow 73-74; TV 74-75; P-in-c Mawgan in Pyder 75-77; P-in-c Mawgan w St Martin-in-Meneage 75-77; R St Mawgan w St Ervan and St Eval 77-78; Chapl St Wilfrid's Sch Ex 78-90. *Address temp unknown*

CARPENTER, Leonard Richard. b 32. E Midl Min Tr Course. **d** 85 **p** 86. NSM Leic H Apostles *Leic* 85-90; P-in-c Barlestone from 90. *The New Vicarage, 22 Bosworth Road, Barlestone, Nuneaton, Warks CV13 0EL* Market Bosworth (0455) 290249

CARPENTER, William Brodie. b 35. St Alb Minl Tr Scheme 76. **d** 79 **p** 80. NSM Hemel Hempstead *St Alb* 79-85; C Hatf 85-88; C Caversham and Mapledurham *Ox* 88-89; R Caversham St Andr from 89. *St Andrew's Vicarage, Harrogate Road, Reading RG4 7PW* Reading (0734) 472788

CARR, Alan Cobban. b 49. Nottm Univ BTh88. Linc Th Coll 85. **d** 88 **p** 89. C Rustington *Chich* from 88. *23 Henry Avenue, Rustington, Littlehampton, W Sussex BN16 2PA* Rustington (0903) 787612

CARR, Very Rev Arthur Wesley. b 41. Jes Coll Ox BA64 MA67 Jes Coll Cam BA66 MA70 Sheff Univ PhD75. Ridley Hall Cam 65. **d** 67 **p** 68. C Luton w E Hyde *St Alb* 67-71; Tutor Ridley Hall Cam 70-71; Chapl 71-72; Hon C Ranmoor *Sheff* 72-74; Chapl Chelmsf Cathl *Chelmsf* 74-78; Dep Dir Cathl Cen for Research and Tr 74-82; Dioc Dir of Tr 76-84; Can Res Chelmsf Cathl 78-87; Dean Bris from 87. *The Deanery, 20 Charlotte Street, Bristol BS1 5PZ* Bristol (0272) 264879 or 262443

CARR, Bernard John Bedford. b 23. Oak Hill Th Coll 59. **d** 61 **p** 62. R Greenhithe St Mary *Roch* 65-74; R Georgeham *Ex* 74-88; rtd 88; Perm to Offic *Ex* from 89. *Fivestones, 145 Yelland Road, Yelland, Barnstaple, Devon EX31 3EE* Barnstaple (0271) 860431

CARR, Douglas Nicholson. b 20. Jes Coll Cam BA47 MA50. Cranmer Hall Dur. **d** 65 **p** 66. Home Dir OMF 69-85; Lic to Offic *S'wark* 77-86; rtd 85. *Willow*

Cottage, 435 Paiswick Road, Gloucester GL4 9BY Gloucester (0452) 455

CARR, Geoffrey. b 09. Ch Coll Cam BA33. Ridley Hall Cam 34. **d** 35 **p** 36. R Arborfield *Ox* 63-76; rtd 76; Chapl St Luke's Hosp Guildf 77-78; Hon Chapl from 78. *Flat 8, Harvey Lodge, Harvey Road, Guildford GU1 3NJ* Guildford (0483) 502923

CARR, Preb James Arthur. b 28. St Aid Birkenhead 62. **d** 64 **p** 65. C Cannock *Lich* 64-68; V Edensor 68-72; V Caverswall 72-85; P-in-c Dilhorne 83-85; P-in-c St Martin's 85-86; V from 86; RD Oswestry from 87; Preb Lich Cathl from 89. *The Vicarage, St Martins, Oswestry, Shropshire SY11 3AP* Oswestry (0691) 772295

CARR, John Mabey. b 05. Univ Coll Dur BA27 MA30. Westcott Ho Cam 27. **d** 28 **p** 29. V Shiplake *Ox* 67-74; rtd 74. *8 Monkswood Avenue, Morecambe, Lancs LA4 6TW* Morecambe (0524) 420455

CARR, John Robert. b 40. ACII62. Oak Hill Th Coll 63. **d** 66 **p** 67. C Tonbridge St Steph *Roch* 66-70; C Cheadle Hulme St Andr *Ches* 70-79; R Widford *Chelmsf* 79-87; TV Becontree W from 87. *The Vicarage, Burnside Road, Dagenham, Essex RM8 2JN* 081-590 6190

CARR, Miss Joy Vera. b 32. DipEd52. Dalton Ho Bris 56. **dss** 80 **d** 87. Scarborough St Jas and H Trin *York* 80-82; Kingston upon Hull St Matt w St Barn 82-87; Par Dn 87-89; Par Dn Elloughton and Brough w Brantingham from 89. *78 Hunter Road, Elloughton, Brough, N Humberside HU15 1LN* Hull (0482) 667054

CARRE, Canon John Trenchard. b 23. Lich Th Coll 42 Linc Th Coll 45. **d** 46 **p** 47. V Steeple Morden *Ely* 60-74; V Guilden Morden 60-74; RD Shingay 67-74; V Wendy w Shingay 69-74; R Croydon w Clopton 69-74; R Hatley 69-74; V Litlington w Abington Pigotts 69-74; V Tadlow w E Hatley 69-74; V Chesterton St Andr 74-88; Hon Can Ely Cathl 79-88; rtd 88. *North Barn, 17 Cromwell Road, Ely, Cambs CB6 1AS* Ely (0353) 662471

CARRICK, Canon Ian Ross. b 13. Clare Coll Cam BA35 MA39. Chich Th Coll 35. **d** 37 **p** 38. C Sculcoates St Paul *York* 37-39; C Staveley *Derby* 39-43; Min St Barn CD Northolt 43-54; V Northolt Park St Barn *Lon* 54-58; S Africa from 58. *65 First Crescent, Fish Hoek, 7975 South Africa* Cape Town (21) 825586

CARRINGTON, Mrs Elizabeth Ashby (Liz). b 46. **d** 90. NSM Nottm St Ann w Em *S'well* from 90. *98 Repton Road, West Bridgford, Nottingham NG2 7EL* Nottingham (0602) 231206

CARRINGTON, Philip John. b 48. MIEE MBIM Leeds Poly CEng. Chich Th Coll 83. **d** 85 **p** 86. C W Acklam *York* 85-88; V Middlesb St Agnes from 88. *St Agnes Vicarage, 1 Broughton Avenue, Middlesbrough TS4 3PX* Middlesbrough (0642) 316144

CARRIVICK, Derek Roy. b 45. Birm Univ BSc66. Ripon Hall Ox 71. **d** 74 **p** 75. C Enfield St Jas *Lon* 74-78; C-in-c Woodgate Valley CD *Birm* 78-83; TR Chelmsley Wood from 83; Dioc Ecum Officer from 86. *The Rectory, Pike Drive, Chelmsley Wood, Birmingham B37 7US* 021-770 5155 or 770 1511

CARROLL, Ven Charles William Desmond. b 19. TCD BA43 MA46. St Chad's Coll Dur. **d** 48 **p** 49. Dir RE *Blackb* 59-73; Can Res Blackb Cathl 64-75; Adn Blackb 73-86; V Balderstone 73-86; rtd 86; Lic to Offic *Blackb* from 86. *11 Assheton Road, Blackburn BB2 6SF* Blackburn (0254) 51915

CARROLL, Frederick Albert. b 16. Worc Coll Ox BA51 MA55. Ripon Hall Ox 46. **d** 51 **p** 52. V Castle Vale *Birm* 68-74; V Coughton *Cov* 74-87; R Spernall, Morton Bagot and Oldberrow 74-87; RD Alcester 84-87; rtd 87. *10 Greenway Close, Shurdington, Cheltenham, Glos GL51 5TL* Cheltenham (0242) 862606

CARROLL, James Thomas. b 41. Pittsburgh Univ MA85. St Deiniol's Hawarden 89 Oblate Fathers Sem Dub 59. **d** 63 **p** 64. C Dub St Patr Cathl Gp *D & G* from 89; Min Can St Patr Cathl Dub from 90. *St Kevin's Rectory, 258 South Circular Road, Dublin 8, Irish Republic* Dublin (1) 542726

CARROLL, John Hugh. b 31. Bris Univ BA57. Tyndale Hall Bris 54. **d** 58 **p** 59. C Slough *Ox* 58-61; V S Lambeth St Steph *S'wark* 61-72; V Norwood 72-81; P-in-c Purley Ch St 81-85; V from 85. *The Vicarage, 38 Woodcote Valley Road, Purley, Surrey CR8 3AJ* 081-660 1790

CARROLL, Miss Joy Anne. b 59. SS Mark & Jo Coll Plymouth BEd82. Cranmer Hall Dur 85. **d** 88. Par Dn Hatcham St Jas *S'wark* from 88. *3 St Michael's Church Centre, Desmond Street, London SE14 6JF* 081-691 2167

CARRUTHERS, Alan. b 15. **d** 60 **p** 61. V Wigan St Jas *Liv* 65-70; P-in-c Wigan St Thos 65-70; V Wigan St Jas w St Thos 70-87; rtd 87. *Low Meadow, Cat Tree Road,*

Grange-over-Sands, Cumbria LA11 7ED Grange-over-Sands (05395) 33037

CARRUTHERS, Arthur Christopher. b 35. St Jo Coll Nottm LTh60. **d** 60 **p** 61. C Addiscombe St Mary *Cant* 60-62; Prec Bradf Cathl *Bradf* 62-64; CF from 64. *c/o MOD (Army), Bagshot Park, Bagshot, Surrey GU19 5PL* Bagshot (0276) 71717

CARRY, Canon Edward Austin. b 18. TCD BA41 MA47. **d** 42 **p** 43. I Killiney H Trin *D & G* 56-86; Preb St Patr Cathl Dub 83-86; rtd 86. *2 Roxboro Close, Ballinclea Road, Killiney, Co Dublin, Irish Republic* Dublin (1) 858847

CARSON, Ernest. b 17. S'wark Ord Course 68. **d** 71 **p** 72. C Baldock w Bygrave and Clothall *St Alb* 71-75; R Hertingfordbury 75-86; rtd 86; Perm to Offic *Worc* from 86. *16 Woodward Close, Pershore, Worcs WR10 1LP* Pershore (0386) 553511

CARSON, Gerald James Alexander. b 24. TCD BA49 MA52. **d** 49 **p** 50. RD Kilmacrenan W *D & R* 60-85; Can Raphoe Cathl 67-81; I Urney w Sion Mills 68-85; Can Derry Cathl 81-85; I Clonallon w Warrenpoint *D & D* 85-90; rtd 90. *84 Avonbrook Gardens, Mountsandel, Coleraine, Co Derry BT52 1SS* Coleraine (0265) 56047

CARSON, Harold. b 05. AKC30. **d** 30 **p** 31. V Kilburn St Mary *Lon* 61-71; rtd 71. *10 St Nicholas Road, Weston-super-Mare, Avon BS23 4XE* Weston-super-Mare (0934) 415705

CARSON, Herbert Moore. b 22. TCD BA43 BD45. **d** 45 **p** 46. V Cam St Paul *Ely* 58-65; rtd 87. *19 Hillcrest Road, Leicester LE2 6HG* Leicester (0533) 882720

CARSON, James Irvine. b 59. TCD BA DipTh84. **d** 84 **p** 85. C Willowfield *D & D* 84-87; C Lecale Gp 87-89; I Devenish w Boho *Clogh* from 89; Dioc Youth Adv from 91. *The Rectory, Monea, Enniskillen, Co Fermanagh* Springfield (036589) 228

CARSON-FEATHAM, Lawrence William. b 53. SSM 77 AKC DipTh74. **d** 78 **p** 79. C Walton St Mary *Liv* 78-82; Chapl Bolton Colls of FE 82-87; C Bolton St Pet *Man* 82-87; TV Oldham from 87. *Holy Trinity Vicarage, 46 Godson Street, Oldham OL1 2DB* 061-627 1640

CARTER, Anthony James. b 24. Sarum Th Coll 54. **d** 56 **p** 57. V Walton-on-Thames *Guildf* 68-78; P-in-c Lytchett Minster *Sarum* 78-81; V 81-83; V Teddington St Mark *Lon* 83-88; V Teddington St Mark and Hampton Wick St Jo 88-89; rtd 89. *3 Westport Cottages, West Street, Wareham, Dorset BH20 4LF* Wareham (0929) 554255

CARTER, Barry Graham. b 54. K Coll Lon BD76 AKC76. St Steph Ho Ox 76. **d** 77 **p** 78. C Evesham *Worc* 77-81; C Amblecote 81-84; TV Ovingdean w Rottingdean and Woodingdean *Chich* 84-85; TR Woodingdean from 85. *The Vicarage, Downsway, Woodingdean, Brighton BN2 6BD* Brighton (0273) 681582

CARTER, Celia. b 38. JP74. Glouc Sch of Min 86. **d** 89. NSM Avening w Cherington *Glouc* from 89; Asst Chapl Stoud Gen Hosp from 89. *Avening Park, Avening, Tetbury, Glos GL8 8NE* Nailsworth (045383) 2716

CARTER, Canon Charles Trevelyan Aubrey. b 14. TCD BA36 MA46. TCD Div Sch Div Test37. **d** 37 **p** 38. I Dub Sandford *D & G* 67-85; Can Ch Ch Cathl Dub 71-85; I Dub Sandford w Milltown 82-85; rtd 85. *7 South Hill, Dartry, Dublin 6, Irish Republic* Dublin (1) 971171

CARTER (nee SMITH), Mrs Christine Lydia. b 43. SRN SCM RNT. Trin Coll Bris. **d** 91. NSM Penkridge Team *Lich* from 91. *24 Poplar Way, Stafford ST17 9LJ* Stafford (0785) 224672

CARTER, Christopher Franklin. b 37. Wadh Coll Ox BA59 MA63. Wycliffe Hall Ox 60. **d** 64 **p** 65. C Clifton St Jas *Sheff* 64-67; C Handsworth 67-70; C Clun w Chapel Lawn *Heref* 70-74; Lic to Offic 74-76; P-in-c Ironbridge 76-78; C Coalbrookdale, Iron-Bridge and Lt Wenlock 78-80; V Llansilin w Llangadwaladr and Llangedwyn *St As* from 80; RD Llanfyllin from 88. *The Vicarage, Llansilin, Oswestry, Shropshire SY10 7PX* Llansilin (069170) 209

CARTER, Clifford Stanley. b 24. Oak Hill Th Coll 72. **d** 74 **p** 75. C Becontree St Mary *Chelmsf* 74-77; V Harold Hill St Paul from 77. *St Paul's Vicarage, Redcar Road, Romford RM3 9PT* Ingrebourne (04023) 41225

CARTER, David John. b 37. Chich Th Coll 64. **d** 67 **p** 68. C Plaistow St Andr *Chelmsf* 67-70; C Wickford 70-73; Chapl Asst Runwell Hosp Essex 71-73; Chapl Basingstoke Distr Hosp 73-80; R E Woodhay and Woolton Hill *Win* from 80. *The Rectory, The Mount, Woolton Hill, Newbury, Berks RG15 9QZ* Highclere (0635) 253323

CARTER, Canon Donald George. b 32. Keble Coll Ox BA54 MA57. Ely Th Coll 54. **d** 56 **p** 57. C St Leonards Ch Ch *Chich* 56-66; R 77-80; V Mayfield 66-77; RD

Dallington 71-77; RD Hastings from 78; P-in-c Hastings St Mary Magd 78-80; R St Leonards Ch Ch and St Mary from 81; Can and Preb Chich Cathl from 81; P-in-c St Leonards SS Pet and Paul 82-85. *Flat 3, 20 Carisbrooke Road, St Leonards-on-Sea, E Sussex TN38 0JN*

CARTER, Dudley Herbert. b 25. Peterho Cam BA49 MA51. Ridley Hall Cam 49. **d** 51 **p** 52. Chapl Colston's Sch Bris 65-67; Lic to Offic *B & W* 67-85; Perm to Offic from 85; rtd 90. *24 Caernarvon Way, Burnham-on-Sea, Somerset TA8 2DQ* Burnham-on-Sea (0278) 789572

CARTER, Duncan Robert Bruton. b 58. Univ of Wales (Cardiff) BA79 Cam Univ BA83 MA89. Ridley Hall Cam 81. **d** 84 **p** 85. C Harold Wood *Chelmsf* 84-88; C S Kensington St Luke *Lon* 88-90; V Rotherfield Greys H Trin *Ox* from 90. *Holy Trinity Vicarage, Church Street, Henley-on-Thames, Oxon RG9 1SE* Henley-on-Thames (0491) 574822

CARTER, Eric. b 17. **d** 58 **p** 59. V Adlington *Blackb* 69-75; V Garstang St Thos 75-84; rtd 84. *1 Arncliffe Road, Harrogate, N Yorkshire HG2 8NQ* Harrogate (0423) 884867

CARTER, Frank Howard James. b 23. Chich Th Coll 58. **d** 59 **p** 60. V Haggerston All SS *Lon* 65-75; V Alexandra Park St Andr 75-88; rtd 88. *53 Naylor Road, London N20 0HE* 081-445 0982

CARTER, Grayson Leigh. b 53. Univ of S California BSc76 Ch Ch Ox DPhil90. Fuller Th Sem California MA84 Wycliffe Hall Ox 89. **d** 90 **p** 91. C Bungay H Trin w St Mary *St E* from 90. *27 Old Grammar School Lane, Bungay, Suffolk NR35 1PU* Bungay (0986) 892478

CARTER, Hector Thomas. b 26. St Paul's Grahamstown LTh51. **d** 52 **p** 54. C Ludford *Heref* 67-70; S Africa 71-83; V Barrow St Jas *Carl* 83; Perm to Offic *Heref* from 84; rtd 87. *21 Brooklands Park, Craven Arms, Shropshire*

CARTER, Ian Sutherland. b 51. Trin Coll Ox BA73 MA77 DPhil77 Leeds Univ BA80. Coll of Resurr Mirfield 78. **d** 81 **p** 82. C Shildon *Dur* 81-84; C Darlington H Trin 84-87; Chapl Liv Univ *Liv* from 87. *The Beeches, 71 Woodlands Road, Aigburth, Liverpool L17 0AL* 051-727 6291

CARTER, John Henry. b 24. Oak Hill Th Coll 66. **d** 68 **p** 69. C Halliwell St Paul *Man* 68-71; V Bolton St Phil 71-76; Chapl to the Deaf (Dios Man and Blackb) 76-82; V Childs Ercall *Lich* 82-87; R Stoke upon Tern 82-87; rtd 87. *3 Chestnut Drive, Hemingbrough, Selby, N Yorkshire YO8 7UE* Selby (0757) 638197

CARTER, John Howard Gregory. b 55. York Univ BA76. St Jo Coll Nottm LTh87. **d** 87 **p** 88. C Nailsea H Trin *B & W* 87-91; TV Camberley St Paul *Guildf* from 91. *61 Goldney Road, Camberley, Surrey GU15 1DW* Camberley (0276) 20897

✠**CARTER, Rt Rev John Stanley.** b 21. Lon Univ BA47. Oak Hill Th Coll 46 Wycliffe Hall Ox 48. **d** 49 **p** 50 **c** 68. C Walthamstow St Mary *Chelmsf* 49-52; C Streatham Immanuel w St Anselm *S'wark* 52-53; S Africa from 53; Suff Bp Johannesburg 68-77. *The Rectory, 43 Pypies Plein, Devil's Peak, Cape Town, 8001 South Africa* Cape Town (21) 461-5350

CARTER, Leslie Alfred Arthur. b 27. K Coll Lon 50 St Boniface Warminster 53. **d** 54 **p** 55. C Northolt Park St Barn *Lon* 54-56; S Africa 57-62; C Wimbledon *S'wark* 63-68; Chapl Quainton Hall Sch Harrow 68-77; TV Brighton Resurr *Chich* 77-81; TV Southend St Jo w St Mark, All SS w St Fran etc *Chelmsf* 81-82; TV Southend 82-88; V Gt Waltham w Ford End from 88. *The Vicarage, Great Waltham, Chelmsford CM3 1AR* Chelmsford (0245) 360334

CARTER, Michael John. b 32. St Alb Minl Tr Scheme 81. **d** 84 **p** 85. NSM Radlett *St Alb* 84-88; Chapl SW Herts HA from 88; Chapl Watford Gen Hosp from 88. *42 Oakridge Avenue, Radlett, Herts WD7 8ER* Radlett (0923) 856009

CARTER, Nicholas Adrian. b 47. Ripon Hall Ox 71. **d** 74 **p** 75. C Sowerby *Wakef* 74-79; V Hanging Heaton 79-83; CF 83-86; V Elton All SS *Man* 86-90; C Milton Win from 90. *25 Ashley Common Road, Ashley, New Milton, Hants BH25 5AU* New Milton (0425) 612644

CARTER, Noel William. b 53. Birm Univ BSc75 Bris Univ CertEd76 Nottm Univ BSc83. Linc Th Coll. **d** 83 **p** 84. C Penrith w Newton Reigny and Plumpton Wall *Carl* 83-86; C Barrow St Matt 86-87; V Netherton from 87. *The Vicarage, Church Terrace, Maryport, Cumbria CA15 7PS* Maryport (0900) 812200

CARTER, Canon Norman. b 23. Leeds Univ BSc48. Coll of Resurr Mirfield 48. **d** 50 **p** 51. V Orford St Marg *Liv* 56-71; V Knotty Ash H Spirit 71-74; V Dovecot 74-83; RD W Derby 78-83; Hon Can Liv Cathl from 82; V

Formby St Pet 83-88; rtd 88. *34 Granby Close, Southport, Merseyside PR9 9QG* Southport (0704) 232821

CARTER, Canon Paul Brian. b 22. AKC49. **d** 50 **p** 51. R Ainderby Steeple and Scruton *Ripon* 60-79; P-in-c Danby Wiske w Yafforth and Hutton Bonville 76-79; R Ainderby Steeple w Yafforth and Scruton 79-87; Hon Can Ripon Cathl 86-87; rtd 87. *Cliffe Cottage, West Tanfield, Ripon, N Yorkshire HG4 5JR* Bedale (0677) 70203

CARTER, Paul Joseph. b 67. St Chad's Coll Dur BA(Theol)88. St Steph Ho Ox 89. **d** 91. C Ipswich All Hallows *St E* from 91. *13 Swatchbury Close, Ipswich, Suffolk IP3 0SF* Ipswich (0473) 717424

CARTER, Paul Mark. b 56. BA78 MA90. Ridley Hall Cam 79. **d** 81 **p** 82. C Kidsgrove *Lich* 81-84; CF from 84. *c/o MOD (Army), Bagshot Park, Bagshot, Surrey GU19 5PL* Bagshot (0276) 71717

CARTER, Paul Rowley. b 45. Lon Bible Coll BD69 Southn Univ PGCE70. Trin Coll Bris. **d** 91. C Penkridge Team *Lich* from 91. *24 Poplar Way, Stafford ST17 9LJ* Stafford (0785) 224672

CARTER, Raymond Timothy. b 27. Qu Coll Birm 57. **d** 59 **p** 60. C Wembley St Jo *Lon* 59-62; C Hatch End St Anselm 62-67; V Harrow Weald St Mich 67-79; V Teddington St Mary w St Alb from 79. *11 Twickenham Road, Teddington, Middx TW11 8AG* 081-977 2767

CARTER, Richard Neville. b 35. K Coll Lon 59. Chich Th Coll 63. **d** 65 **p** 66. C St Alb St Sav *St Alb* 65-69; S Africa 70-71; Perm to Offic *St Alb* 72-87; V Kempston from 87. *The Vicarage, Church Road, Kempston, Bedford MK43 8RH* Bedford (0234) 852241

CARTER, Robert Desmond. b 35. Cranmer Hall Dur 62. **d** 65 **p** 66. C Otley *Bradf* 65-69; C Keighley 69-73; V Cowling from 73. *The Vicarage, Gill Lane, Cowling, Keighley, W Yorkshire BD22 0DD* Cross Hills (0535) 632050

CARTER, Robert Edward. b 44. Univ of Wales (Ban) BSc65. St Jo Coll Nottm 79. **d** 81 **p** 82. C Caverswall *Lich* 81-86; V Biddulph from 86. *The Vicarage, Congleton Road, Biddulph, Stoke-on-Trent ST8 7RG* Stoke-on-Trent (0782) 513247

CARTER, Robin. b 46. Chich Th Coll 71. **d** 74 **p** 75. C Wortley de Leeds *Ripon* 74-76; C Hutton *Chelmsf* 76-78; C Wickford 78-81; TV Wickford and Runwell 81-83; Chapl HM Pris Leeds 83-85; Reading 85-89; Chapl HM Young Offender Inst Huntercombe 85-89; Finnamore Wood Camp 86-89; Lic to Offic *Ox* 85-89; Gov HM Pris Channings Wood from 89; Perm to Offic *Ex* from 90. *HM Prison Channings Wood, Denbury, Newton Abbot, Devon TQ12 6DW* Ipplepen (0803) 812361

CARTER, Ronald George. b 31. Leeds Univ BA58. Coll of Resurr Mirfield 58. **d** 60 **p** 61. C Wigan St Anne *Liv* 60-63; Prec Wakef Cathl *Wakef* 63-66; V Woodhall *Bradf* 66-77; Chapl Qu Marg Sch Escrick Park 77-83; Min Can, Prec and Sacr Pet Cathl *Pet* 83-88; R Upper St Leonards St Jo *Chich* from 88. *53 Brittany Road, St Leonards-on-Sea, E Sussex TN38 0RD* Hastings (0424) 423367

CARTER, Ronald William. b 01. ATCL25 ALCD31. **d** 31 **p** 32. V Staines St Pet *Lon* 41-78; rtd 78; Perm to Offic *Win* from 78. *24 Vespasian Way, Eastleigh, Hants SO5 2DF* Chandler's Ford (0703) 269520

CARTER, Russell James Wigney. b 29. Chich Th Coll 80. **d** 82 **p** 83. C Aldwick *Chich* 82-86; R Buxted and Hadlow Down 86-90; rtd 90. *6 Lucerne Court, Aldwick, Bognor Regis, W Sussex PO21 4XL* Bognor Regis (0243) 862858

CARTER, Samuel. b 49. St Jo Coll Dur BA71 DipTh72. Cranmer Hall Dur 73. **d** 74 **p** 75. C Kingswinford St Mary *Lich* 74-77; C Shrewsbury H Cross 77-84; V Normacot from 84. *The Vicarage, Upper Belgrave Road, Stoke-on-Trent ST3 4QJ* Stoke-on-Trent (0782) 319695

CARTER, Stanley Reginald. b 24. St Jo Coll Dur BA49 DipTh50. **d** 50 **p** 51. V Sneinton St Chris w St Phil *S'well* 69-89; rtd 89; Perm to Offic *S'well* from 89. *31 Pateley Road, Nottingham NG3 5QF* Nottingham (0602) 264054

CARTER, Stephen. b 56. Univ of Wales (Lamp) BA77 Southn Univ BTh81. Sarum & Wells Th Coll 78. **d** 81 **p** 82. C Halstead St Andr w H Trin and Greenstead Green *Chelmsf* 81-84; C Loughton St Jo 84-89; V N Shoebury from 89. *The Vicarage, 2 Weare Gifford, Shoeburyness, Southend-on-Sea SS3 8AB* Southend-on-Sea (0702) 584053

CARTER, Stephen Howard. b 47. City Univ BSc72. St Jo Coll Nottm LTh85. **d** 85 **p** 86. C Hellesdon *Nor* 85-88; Chapl Asst Birm Children's Hosp 88-91; Chapl Asst Birm Maternity Hosp 88-91; Lic to Offic *Birm* 88-91; TV Tettenhall Wood *Lich* from 91; Chapl Compton

Hall Hospice Wolv from 91. *The Vicarage, 12 Windmill Lane, Wolverhampton WV3 8HJ* Wolverhampton (0902) 761170

CARTER, Terence John. b 31. K Coll Lon BD57 AKC57 Lon Univ BA68 PGCE69. **d** 58 **p** 59. R Ockham w Hatchford *Guildf* 63-69; Lic to Offic S'wark 69-78; Portsm 78-82; Perm from 82; rtd 91. *15 Balliol Road, Portsmouth PO2 7PP* Portsmouth (0705) 699167

CARTLEDGE, Mark John. b 62. BA85 MPhil89. Lon Bible Coll 82 Oak Hill Th Coll 86. **d** 88 **p** 89. C Formby H Trin *Liv* from 88. *24 Roe Lane, Southport, Merseyside PR9 9DX* Southport (0704) 538560

CARTMAN, James. b 10. OBE55. Man Univ BA37 MA50 Lon Univ BD44 MTh48. Westcott Ho Cam 51. **d** 51 **p** 51. Prin Lect Relig Studies Heref Coll of Educn 69-78; Lic to Offic *Heref* 69-78; rtd 78; Perm to Offic Win from 78; Guildf from 79. *9 Handcroft Close, Crondall, Farnham, Surrey GU10 5RY* Aldershot (0252) 850234

CARTMELL, Richard Peter. b 43. Cranmer Hall Dur 77. **d** 79 **p** 80. C Whittle-le-Woods *Blackb* 79-85; V Lower Darwen St Jas from 85; RD Darwen from 91. *The Vicarage, Stopes Brow, Lower Darwen, Darwen, Lancs BB3 0QP* Blackburn (0254) 53898

CARTMILL, Ralph Arthur. b 40. St Jo Coll Dur BA62 Em Coll Cam MA64. Ridley Hall Cam 63. **d** 65 **p** 66. C Dukinfield St Jo *Ches* 65-68; C Wilmslow 68-69; Warden Walton Youth Cen Liv 69-70; Asst Master Aylesbury Gr Sch 70-74; Perm to Offic *Ox* 72-74; V Terriers 74-85; P-in-c Chinnor w Emmington and Sydenham 85-86; R Chinnor w Emmington and Sydenham etc from 86. *The Rectory, Chinnor, Oxford OX9 4DH* Kingston Blount (0844) 51309

CARTWRIGHT, Cyril Hicks. b 13. Selw Coll Cam BA35 MA44. Linc Th Coll 36. **d** 38 **p** 39. C Forest Row *Chich* 62-70; V Whitehawk 70-75; C Hove All SS 76-80; rtd 80; Perm to Offic *Chich* from 80. *c/o Bunker and Co, 7 The Drive, Hove, E Sussex BN3 3JS* Brighton (0273) 737814

✠**CARTWRIGHT, Rt Rev Edward David.** b 20. Selw Coll Cam BA41 MA45. Westcott Ho Cam 41. **d** 43 **p** 44 **c** 84. C Boston *Linc* 43-48; V Bris St Leon Redfield *Bris* 48-52; V Olveston 52-60; V Bishopston 60-73; Hon Can Bris Cathl 70-73; AdV Win 73-84; Hon Can Win Cathl 73-88; V Sparsholt w Lainston 73-84; Suff Bp Southn 84-88; rtd 88. *Bargate House, 25 Newport, Warminster, Wilts BA12 8RH* Warminster (0985) 216298

CARTWRIGHT, Frank. b 15. Chich Th Coll 47. **d** 49 **p** 50. V Wigan St Anne *Liv* 62-73; V Walton *Ches* 73-80; rtd 80; Perm to Offic Ches from 80; Liv from 83. *38 Gaskell Street, Stockton Heath, Warrington WA4 2UN* Warrington (0925) 67469

CARTWRIGHT, Preb Hugh Bent. b 07. St Steph Ho Ox 30. **d** 32 **p** 33. V Alexandra Park St Andr *Lon* 46-73; rtd 73; Perm to Offic *Heref* from 73. *21 Queens Court, Ledbury, Herefordshire HR8 2AL* Ledbury (0531) 3123

CARTWRIGHT, John Walter Deryk. b 25. Lon Univ BSc. Ox NSM Course. **d** 82 **p** 83. NSM Welford w Wickham and Gt Shefford *Ox* 82-85; TV Newbury from 85. *St Mary's Vicarage, 14 Strawberry Hill, Newbury, Berks RG13 1XJ* Newbury (0635) 40889

CARTWRIGHT, Michael John. b 42. Birm Univ DipL&A70. Qu Coll Birm 67. **d** 70 **p** 71. C Astwood Bank w Crabbs Cross *Worc* 70-75; P-in-c Worc St Mich 75-77; V Stockton St Paul *Dur* 77-87; V Market Rasen *Linc* from 87; RD W Wold from 89. *The Vicarage, 13 Lady Frances Drive, Market Rasen, Lincs LN8 3JJ* Market Rasen (0673) 843424

✠**CARTWRIGHT, Rt Rev Richard Fox.** b 13. Pemb Coll Cam BA35 MA39 Univ of the South (USA) Hon DD69. Cuddesdon Coll 35. **d** 36 **p** 37 **c** 72. C Kennington Cross St Anselm *S'wark* 36-40; C Kingswood 40-45; V Surbiton St Andr 45-52; V Bris St Mary Redcliffe w Temple etc *Bris* 52-72; Hon Can Bris Cathl 60-72; Suff Bp Plymouth *Ex* 72-81; rtd 82; Asst Bp Truro from 82; Asst Bp Ex from 88. *5 Old Vicarage Close, Ide, Exeter, Devon EX2 9RT* Exeter (0392) 211270

CARTWRIGHT, Roy Arthur. b 29. CCC Cam BA52 MA56. Wycliffe Hall Ox. **d** 54 **p** 55. V Prittlewell St Steph *Chelmsf* 69-72; rtd 72; Hon C S Shoebury *Chelmsf* from 77. *72 Raphael Drive, Shoeburyness, Southend-on-Sea SS3 9UX* Southend-on-Sea (0702) 293245

CARTWRIGHT, Samuel. b 27. Cuddesdon Coll 71. **d** 72 **p** 72. C Rochdale *Man* 72-76; V Roundthorn 76-83; V Ashton Ch Ch from 83. *The Vicarage, Vicarage Road, Ashton-under-Lyne, Lancs OL7 9QY* 061-330 1601

CARTWRIGHT, Sidney Victor. b 22. Launde Abbey 73. **d** 74 **p** 75. C Braunstone *Leic* 74-78; P-in-c Arnesby w Shearsby 78-86; R Arnesby w Shearsby and Bruntingthorpe 86-87; rtd 87; Perm to Offic Leic & Pet

from 87. *32 Northleigh Grove, Market Harborough, Leics LE16 9QX* Market Harborough (0858) 463915

CARTY, Very Rev Hilton Manasseh. b 21. OBE85. Dur Univ BA45 LTh45. Codrington Coll Barbados. **d** 45 **p** 45. C Cowley St Jas *Ox* 65-73; V Earley St Bart 73-77; Dean Antigua 77-86; rtd 86. *Carnival Gardens, PO Box 1447, St Johns, Antigua* Antigua (1809) 461-1440

CARUANA, Mrs Rosemary Anne. b 38. St Alb Minl Tr Scheme 81. dss 84 **d** 87. Hertf St Andr *St Alb* 84-87; Par Dn Hertingfordbury from 87. *36 Holly Croft, Sele Farm Estate, Hertford SG14 2DR* Hertford (0992) 587625

CARVER, Arthur Tregarthen. b 15. Tyndale Hall Bris 37. **d** 41 **p** 42. R Uphill *B & W* 69-80; rtd 80; Perm to Offic *Ches* from 80. *Copinsay, 20 Hayton Street, Knutsford, Cheshire WA16 0DR* Knutsford (0565) 651622

CARVOSSO, John Charles. b 45. ACA71 FCA79. Oak Hill Th Coll 75. **d** 78 **p** 79. C Chelsea St Jo w St Andr *Lon* 78-81; Chapl RAF 81-84; P-in-c Tawstock *Ex* 84-85; TV Newport, Bishops Tawton and Tawstock from 85. *The Rectory, Tawstock, Barnstaple, Devon EX31 3HZ* Barnstaple (0271) 74963

CASE, Catherine Margaret. b 44. Ripon Coll Cuddesdon 86. **d** 88. C Blurton *Lich* from 88. *St Alban's House, 51 Ripon Road, Stoke-on-Trent ST3 3BS* Stoke-on-Trent (0782) 315029

CASE, Philip Thomas Charles. b 17. Lon Univ BSc(Econ)51. Sarum Th Coll 51. **d** 53 **p** 54. V Witley *Guildf* 84-89; RD Godalming 79-84; rtd 84; Perm to Offic *Ex* from 85. *The Old Malthouse, Vine Street, Winkleigh, Devon EX19 8HN* Winkleigh (0837) 83283

CASEBOW, Ronald Philip. b 31. Roch Th Coll 59. **d** 61 **p** 62. C Southgate Ch Ch *Lon* 61-64; C Oseney Crescent St Luke w Camden Square St Paul 64-70; V Colchester St Steph *Chelmsf* 70-74; V Burnham 74-89. *The Priory, Priory Road, Palgrave, Diss, Norfolk IP22 1AJ* Diss (0379) 651804

CASEY, Ernest George. b 14. St Chad's Coll Dur BA36 DipTh. **d** 37 **p** 38. V Dur St Giles *Dur* 59-79; rtd 79. *7 Hampshire Road, Belmont, Durham DH1 2DJ* 091-384 9228

CASHEL, Dean of. See WOODWORTH, Very Rev Gerald Mark David

CASHEL, WATERFORD AND LISMORE, Archdeacon of. See WOODWORTH, Very Rev Gerald Mark David

CASHEL AND OSSORY, Bishop of. See WILLOUGHBY, Rt Rev Noel Vincent

CASHMORE, Cyril. b 01. St Aug Coll Cant 20. **d** 25 **p** 32. V Bilsby w Farlesthorpe *Linc* 68-71; R Hannah cum Hagnaby w Markby 68-71; rtd 71. *Connaught Court, St Oswald's Road, Fulford, York YO1 4QA*

CASIOT, David John. b 39. St Pet Coll Ox BA63 MA67. Clifton Th Coll 63. **d** 65 **p** 66. C Drypool St Columba w St Andr and St Pet *York* 65-67; C Barking St Marg *Chelmsf* 67-71; R Whalley Range St Edm *Man* 71-84; V Wandsworth St Mich *S'wark* from 84. *St Michael's Vicarage, 73 Wimbledon Park Road, London SW18 5TT* 081-874 7682

CASON, Preb Ronald Arthur. b 28. Kelham Th Coll 48. **d** 53 **p** 54. C Fenton *Lich* 53-56; V Brereton 56-63; V Hugglescote w Donington *Leic* 63-67; R Blakenall Heath *Lich* 67-74; R Stoke upon Trent 74-80; Preb Lich Cathl from 75; RD Stoke 78-88; TR Stoke-upon-Trent 80-91; Lect Tettenhall Par from 91. *60 Cherrington Gardens, Bramstead Avenue, Compton, Wolverhampton*

CASSAM, Victor Reginald. b 33. Chich Th Coll 59. **d** 62 **p** 63. C Portsea St Jo Rudmore *Portsm* 62-64; C W Leigh CD 64-66; V Torquay St Martin Barton *Ex* 66-69; C Stanmer w Falmer and Moulsecoomb *Chich* 69-73; P-in-c Catsfield 73-76; R Catsfield and Crowhurst 76-81; R Selsey from 81. *The Rectory, St Peter's Crescent, Selsey, Chichester, W Sussex PO20 0NA* Selsey (0243) 602363

CASSELTON, John Charles. b 43. DipTh67. Oak Hill Th Coll 64. **d** 68 **p** 69. C Upton *Ex* 68-73; C Braintree *Chelmsf* 73-80; V Ipswich St Jo *St E* from 80; RD Ipswich from 86. *St John's Vicarage, Cauldwell Hall Road, Ipswich IP4 4QE* Ipswich (0473) 728034

CASSIDY, Ven George Henry. b 42. QUB BSc65 Lon Univ MPhil67. Oak Hill Th Coll 70. **d** 72 **p** 73. C Clifton Ch Ch w Em *Bris* 72-75; V Sea Mills 75-82; V Portman Square St Paul *Lon* 82-87; Adn Lon and Can Res St Paul's Cathl from 87; P-in-c St Ethelburga Bishopsgate 89-91. *2 Amen Court, Warwick Lane, London EC4M 7BU* 071-248 3312

CASSIDY, Very Rev Herbert. b 35. TCD BA57 MA65. CITC 58. **d** 58 **p** 59. C Belf H Trin *Conn* 58-60; C Londonderry Ch Ch *D & R* 60-62; I Aghavilly w Derrynoose *Arm* 62-65; Hon VC Arm Cathl 63-85; C Portadown St Columba 65-67; I 67-85; Dean Kilmore

K, E & A 85-89; I Kilmore w Ballintemple 85-86; I Kilmore w Ballintemple, Kildallon etc 86-89; Dir of Ords 89; Dean Arm and Keeper of Public Lib *Arm* from 89; I Arm St Patr from 89; Hon Sec Gen Syn from 90. *The Library, Abbey Street, Armagh BT61 7DY* Armagh (0861) 523142

CASSIDY, Patrick Nigel. b 40. TCD BA63 MA66. Sarum Th Coll 64. **d** 66 **p** 67. C Heaton St Barn *Bradf* 66-68; Asst Chapl Brussels *Eur* 68-70; Chapl SW France 70-72; V Oseney Crescent St Luke w Camden Square St Paul *Lon* 72-83; Chapl Strasbourg w Stuttgart and Heidelberg *Eur* 83-84; Perm to Offic *Chich* 86-90; Chapl Marseille w Aix-en-Provence *Eur* from 90; Hon Chapl Miss to Seamen from 90. *399 rue Paradis, 13008 Marseille, France* France (33) 91 22 01 78

CASSIDY, Ronald. b 43. Lon Univ BD66 Man Univ MPhil85. Tyndale Hall Bris 63. **d** 68 **p** 69. C Kirkdale St Lawr *Liv* 68-70; C Bolton Em *Man* 70-74; V Roughtown 74-89; R Denton St Lawr from 89. *St Lawrence's Rectory, 131 Town Lane, Denton. Manchester M34 2DJ* 061-320 4895

CASSON, David Christopher. b 41. Qu Coll Cam BA64 MA68. Ridley Hall Cam 65. **d** 67 **p** 68. C Birm St Martin *Birm* 67-72; C Luton St Mary *St Alb* 72-77; P-in-c 77; V Luton St Fran 77-84; V Richmond H Trin and Ch Ch *S'wark* from 84. *Holy Trinity Vicarage, Sheen Park, Richmond, Surrey TW9 1UP* 081-940 3995

CASSON, Donald Trench. b 12. Qu Coll Cam BA34 MA38. Wycliffe Hall Ox 34. **d** 36 **p** 37. V Framfield *Chich* 69-77; rtd 77; C Broughton Poggs w Filkins, Broadwell etc *Ox* from 88. *The Hermitage, Broad Street, Bampton, Oxon OX8 2LS* Bampton Castle (0993) 850372

CASSON, Frank Alfred. b 06. Qu Coll Cam BA28 MA32. Ridley Hall Cam 28. **d** 30 **p** 31. V Eastbourne All SS *Chich* 55-69; rtd 69; Perm to Offic *Chich* from 69. *12 Parkgates, Chiswick Place, Eastbourne, E Sussex BN21 4BE* Eastbourne (0323) 33693

CASSON, James Stuart. b 32. Liv Univ BA54 Nottm Univ MPhil70. Ridley Hall Cam. **d** 61 **p** 62. C Eccleston Ch Ch *Liv* 61-64; C Littleover *Derby* 64-67; V Dearham *Carl* 67-76; V Holme Eden from 76. *St Paul's Vicarage, Warwick Bridge, Carlisle CA4 8RF* Wetheral (0228) 60332

CASSWELL, David Oriel. b 52. Loughb Coll of Educn CertEd74 Leeds Univ CQSW79. Oak Hill Th Coll DipHE87. **d** 87 **p** 88. C Acomb St Steph *York* 87-91; Dep Chapl HM Pris Leeds from 91. *HM Prison, Armley, Leeds LS12 2TJ* Leeds (0532) 636411

CASSWELL, Canon Peter Joyce. b 22. Trin Coll Cam BA48 MA50. Ridley Hall Cam 48. **d** 50 **p** 51. Chapl Forest Gate Hosp Lon 64-78; R Buckhurst Hill *Chelmsf* 64-78; Hon Can Chelmsf Cathl 75-78; R Lutterworth w Cotesbach *Leic* 78-90; RD Guthlaxton II (Lutterworth) 89-90; rtd 90. *74 Coventry Road, Broughton Astley, Leics LE9 6QA* Sutton Elms (0455) 282630

CASTERTON, Michael John. b 39. Univ of Wales (Lamp) BA62. St Mich Coll Llan 63. **d** 65 **p** 66. C Sidcup St Jo *Roch* 65-67; C Brighouse *Wakef* 67-73; Chapl Choral Ches Cathl *Ches* 73-75; V Roberttown *Wakef* 75-87; V Birkenshaw w Hunsworth from 87. *6 Vicarage Gardens, Bradford Road, Birkenshaw, Bradford, W Yorkshire BD11 2EF* Bradford (0274) 683776

CASTLE, Dr Brian Colin. b 49. Lon Univ BA72 Ox Univ BA77 MA80 Birm Univ PhD89. Cuddesdon Coll 74. **d** 77 **p** 78. C Sutton St Nic *S'wark* 77; C Limpsfield and Titsey 77-81; V N Petherton w Northmoor Green *B & W* from 85. *The Dower House, North Petherton, Bridgwater, Somerset TA6 6SE* North Petherton (0278) 662429

CASTLE, Brian Stanley. b 47. Oak Hill Th Coll 70. **d** 73 **p** 74. C Barnsbury St Andr w St Thos and St Matthias *Lon* 73-76; C Lower Homerton St Paul 76-79; P-in-c Bethnal Green St Jas Less from 79. *St James the Less Vicarage, St James's Avenue, London E2 9JD* 081-980 1612

CASTLE, Charles. b 01. AKC35. Bps' Coll Cheshunt 35. **d** 35 **p** 36. V Thurnham w Detling *Cant* 66-71; rtd 71. *16 Pannal Ash Crescent, Harrogate, N Yorkshire HG2 0HT* Harrogate (0423) 567731

CASTLE, Michael David. b 38. Wells Th Coll 69. **d** 71 **p** 72. C Acocks Green *Birm* 71-75; C Weoley Castle 76-78; V from 78. *St Gabriel's Vicarage, 83 Marston Road, Birmingham B29 5LS* 021-475 1194

CASTLE, Roger James. b 39. St Jo Coll Cam BA62 MA66. Clifton Th Coll 63. **d** 65 **p** 66. C Rushden w Newton Bromswold *Pet* 65-68; C Stapenhill w Cauldwell *Derby* 68-72; V Hayfield 72-89; R Coxheath w E Farleigh, Hunton and Linton *Roch* from 89. *The Vicarage, 19 Westerhill Road, Coxheath, Maidstone, Kent ME17 4DQ* Maidstone (0622) 747570

CASTLE, Vincent Clifton. b 15. ALCD37 St Jo Coll Dur LTh38 BA39. **d** 39 **p** 40. Miss to Seamen 63-71; V Creeksea w Althorne *Chelmsf* 71-79; RD Dengie 74-82; V Creeksea w Althorne, Latchingdon and N Fambridge 80-82; rtd 82; Perm to Offic *Chelmsf* from 82. *49 Winstree Road, Burnham-on-Crouch, Essex CM0 8ET* Maldon (0621) 782807

CASTLE, Wilfrid Thomas Froggatt. b 11. Qu Coll Cam BA33 MA37. Wycliffe Hall Ox 33. **d** 35 **p** 36. V Bocking St Pet *Chelmsf* 65-72; R Paisley St Barn *Glas* 72-77; P-in-c 77-79; rtd 77. *5 Freemen's Court, Water Lane, Clifton, York YO3 6PR* York (0904) 640185

CASTLEDINE, Canon John. b 17. AKC40. **d** 40 **p** 41. V Northallerton w Kirby Sigston *York* 63-85; RD Northallerton 63-85; Can and Preb York Minster 76-85; rtd 85; Perm to Offic *S'well* from 85. *35 Landseer Road, Southwell, Notts NG25 0LX* Southwell (0636) 812063

CASTLETON, David Miles. b 39. Oak Hill Th Coll 69. **d** 72 **p** 73. C Canonbury St Steph *Lon* 72-76; C Stoke-next Guildf St Jo *Guildf* 76; C Guildf St Sav w Stoke-next-Guildf 76-89. *26 Keswick Road, Great Bookham, Surrey KT23 4BH*

CASWELL, Roger John. b 47. St Chad's Coll Dur BA70. St Steph Ho Ox 75. **d** 77 **p** 78. C Brighton Resurr *Chich* 77-83; TV Crawley 83-90; TR Littlehampton and Wick from 90. *34 Fitzalan Road, Littlehampton, W Sussex BN17 5ET* Littlehampton (0903) 724410

CATCHPOLE, Geoffrey Alan. b 53. AKC. Westcott Ho Cam 76. **d** 77 **p** 78. C Camberwell St Luke *S'wark* 77-80; C Dulwich St Barn 80-82; TV Canvey Is *Chelmsf* 82-87; Ind Chapl from 83; P-in-c Bradwell on Sea from 87. *The Rectory, East End Road, Bradwell-on-Sea, Southminster, Essex CM0 7PX* Maldon (0621) 76203

CATCHPOLE, Guy St George. b 30. **d** 82 **p** 83. Kenya 82-89; C Woodford Wells *Chelmsf* from 89. *7 Marion Grove, Woodford Green, Essex IG8 9TA* 081-505 1431

CATCHPOLE, Canon Keith William. b 30. AKC56. **d** 57 **p** 58. C Woodchurch *Ches* 57-61; C W Kirby St Bridget 61-64; C-in-c Upton Priory CD 64-72; R Lavant *Chich* 72-82; RD Chich from 80; Can and Preb Chich Cathl from 82; V Chich St Paul and St Pet from 82. *The Vicarage, Tower Close, Chichester, W Sussex PO19 1QN* Chichester (0243) 531624

CATCHPOLE, Roy. b 46. St Jo Coll Nottm LTh74. **d** 74 **p** 75. C Rainham *Chelmsf* 74-76; C Hyson Green *S'well* 76-79; V Broxtowe 79-86; V Calverton from 86. *The Vicarage, Calverton, Nottingham NG14 6GF* Nottingham (0602) 652552

CATCHPOOL, Terence David Housden. b 34. MIBiol Hatf Coll Dur BSc56. Trin Coll Bris 85. **d** 86 **p** 87. NSM Bath Odd Down w Combe Hay *B & W* from 86. *119 Rush Hill, Bath BA2 2QT* Bath (0225) 424828

CATER, Henry Derek. b 17. Chich Th Coll 49. **d** 51 **p** 52. rtd 69; Lic to Offic *Eur* 69-84. *5 Furniss Court, Cranleigh, Surrey GU6 8TN* Cranleigh (0483) 275541

CATER, Lois May. b 37. S Dios Minl Tr Scheme 81. **dss** 84 **d** 87. Calne and Blackland *Sarum* 84-87; Hon Par Dn 87-89; Hon Par Dn Devizes St Jo w St Mary from 89. *Pear Cottage, 28 Pans Lane, Devizes, Wilts SN10 5AF* Devizes (0380) 723034

CATERER, James Albert Leslie Blower. b 44. New Coll Ox BA67 MA81. Sarum & Wells Th Coll 79. **d** 81 **p** 82. C Cheltenham St Luke and St Jo *Glouc* 81-85; V Standish w Haresfield and Moreton Valence etc from 85. *The Vicarage, Church Lane, Moreton Valence, Gloucester GL2 7NB* Gloucester (0452) 720258

CATES, Canon Geoffrey Charles. b 18. Leeds Univ BA42. Coll of Resurr Mirfield 42. **d** 44 **p** 45. Br Guiana 61-66; Guyana 66-71; Dean Georgetown 61-71; R Salford Sacred Trin *Man* 71-82; RD Salford 71-82; Hon Can Man Cathl 80-82; Soc Resp Adv *St E* 82-88; Hon Can St E Cathl from 85; rtd 88. *55 Berners Street, Ipswich IP1 3LN* Ipswich (0473) 216629

CATHCART, Adrian James. b 51. N Ord Course. **d** 87 **p** 88. C Blackley St Andr *Man* 87-90. *54 Tweedlehill Road, Higher Blackley, Manchester M9 3LG* 061-740 6774

CATHIE, Sean Bewley. b 43. Dur Univ BA67. Cuddesdon Coll 67. **d** 69 **p** 70. C Kensal Rise St Martin *Lon* 69-73; C Paddington H Trin w St Paul 73-75; P-in-c Bridstow w Peterstow *Heref* 76-79; Hon C Westmr St Jas *Lon* from 85. *23 Brookfield Mansions, Highgate West Hill, London N6 6AS* 081-340 6603

CATLEY, John Howard. b 37. AKC60. **d** 61 **p** 62. C Sowerby Bridge w Norland *Wakef* 61-64; C Almondbury 64-67; V Earlsheaton 67-75; V Brownhill 75-86; V Morley St Pet w Churwell from 86. *St Peter's Vicarage, Rooms Lane, Morley, Leeds LS27 9PA* Morley (0532) 532052

CATLIN, John Howard. b 39. St Chad's Coll Dur BA62. **d** 64 **p** 65. C Portsea N End St Mark *Portsm* 64-67; C Fareham SS Pet and Paul 67-70; Bahamas 70-71; Turks and Caicos Is 71-72; C Forton *Portsm* 72-73; V Paulsgrove 73-80; V Portsea St Alb 80-83; TV Bournemouth St Pet w St Swithun, St Steph etc *Win* 83-87; TV Kirkby *Liv* from 87; AD Walton from 89. *St Chad's Vicarage, Old Hall Lane, Kirkby, Liverpool L32 5TH* 051-546 5109

CATLING, Charles Skene. Bris Univ BA38. Lich Th Coll 38. **d** 40 **p** 41. Asst Chapl Keele Univ *Lich* 64-65; Hd Master Bethany Sch Kent 65-87; Perm to Offic Cant 71-87; Truro from 72; rtd 81; Perm to Offic *Ex* from 87. *Ground Floor Flat, 31 Cranford Avenue, Exmouth, Devon EX8 2QA* Exmouth (0395) 267896

CATLING, Michael David. b 56. Golds Coll Lon CertEd77 DipEd84 Whitelands Coll Lon DipC&S88. Cranmer Hall Dur 88. **d** 90 **p** 91. C Cullercoats St Geo *Newc* from 90. *42 Shorestone Avenue, Cullercoats, North Shields NE30 3NE* 091-253 4847

CATLING, Canon Robert Mason. b 19. St Jo Coll Ox BA41 MA44. St Steph Ho Ox 41. **d** 43 **p** 44. V Beckenham St Barn *Roch* 64-72; V Devoran *Truro* 72-87; Hon Can Truro Cathl from 77; rtd 87; Perm to Offic Ex and Truro from 87. *Ground Floor Flat, 31 Cranford Avenue, Exmouth, Devon EX8 2QA* Exmouth (0395) 267896

CATO, Percy William Frederick. b 06. OBE51. AKC35. **d** 35 **p** 36. R Cottesmore *Pet* 64-75; rtd 75. *20 Torkington Gardens, Stamford, Lincs PE9 2EW* Stamford (0780) 62460

CATON, David Arthur. b 25. Trin Coll Ox BA50 MA50. St Steph Ho Ox 49. **d** 51 **p** 52. C Seaton Hirst *Newc* 51-55; S Africa 55-61; V Stapleford *Ely* 61-69; V Hurst *Man* 69-75; V Hanwell St Thos *Lon* 75-84; AD Ealing W 82-84; V Staincross *Wakef* from 84. *Priest's Lodge, 48 Greenside, Barnsley, S Yorkshire S75 6AY* Barnsley (0226) 382261

CATON, Philip Cooper. b 47. Oak Hill Th Coll 79. **d** 81 **p** 82. C Much Woolton *Liv* 81-85; TV Parr from 85. *St Paul's Vicarage, 75 Chain Lane, St Helens, Merseyside WA11 9QF* St Helens (0744) 34335

CATT, Albert Henry. b 08. St Steph Ho Ox 34. **d** 37 **p** 38. V Hornsey St Geo *Lon* 49-74; rtd 74; Perm to Offic Ely from 75. *48 Green Park, Chatteris, Cambs PE16 6DL* Chatteris (03543) 3102

CATT, Douglas Gordon. b 23. MCSP49 SRP67. Roch Th Coll 61. **d** 63 **p** 64. R Croughton *Pet* 66-75; R Hinton in the Hedges w Steane 66-75; V Evenley 72-75; Chapl St Andr Hosp Northn 75-89; Lic to Offic *Pet* from 75; rtd 88. *195 Billing Road, Northampton NN1 5RS* Northampton (0604) 27110

CATTANACH, Alexander Hamilton Avery. b 16. Univ of Wales BA37. St Mich Coll Llan 38. **d** 39 **p** 40. V Lt Thornton *Blackb* 61-81; rtd 81; Lic to Offic *Blackb* from 81. *4 Dawson Road, St Annes, Lytham St Annes, Lancs FY8 3AJ* St Annes (0253) 727099

CATTELL, Ven Jack. b 15. Univ Coll Dur BA37 DipTh38 MA40 Lon Univ BD53. Sarum & Wells Th Coll 38. **d** 39 **p** 40. C Royston *Wakef* 39-41; Perm to Offic *Sarum* 41-42; CF (EC) 42-46; Lic to Offic *Ripon* 46-49; Chapl R Wanstead Sch 49-53; Bermuda 53-82; Adn Bermuda 61-82; Perm to Offic *Mon* from 82. *39A Risca Road, Newport, Gwent* Newport (0633) 54529

CATTELL, John Eugene Brownlow. b 11. TD62. Selw Coll Cam BA34 MA44. Wells Th Coll 35. **d** 36 **p** 37. V Piddletrenthide w Alton Pancras and Plush *Sarum* 65-74; R Piddlehinton 73-74; P-in-c Kington Magna and Buckhorn Weston 74-77; rtd 77. *Tredinnock, Bishops Hill Road, New Polzeath, Wadebridge, Cornwall PL27 6UF* Trebetherick (020886) 2388

CATTERALL, David Arnold. b 53. ARCS Lon Univ BSc74. Cranmer Hall Dur DipTh78. **d** 78 **p** 79. C Swinton St Pet *Man* 78-81; C Wythenshawe St Martin 81-83; R Heaton Norris Ch w All SS 83-88; I Fanlobbus Union C, C & R from 88. *The Rectory, Sackville Street, Dunmanway, Co Cork, Irish Republic* Dunmanway (23) 45151

CATTERALL, Mrs Janet Margaret. b 53. Univ of Wales (Ban) BA74. Cranmer Hall Dur DipTh77. dss 81 **d** 87 **p** 90. Wythenshawe St Martin *Man* 81-83; Heaton Norris Ch w All SS 83-87; Par Dn 87-88; C Bandon Union C, C & R 88-89; Dioc Youth Adv (Cork) from 89. *The Rectory, Sackville Street, Dunmanway, Co Cork, Irish Republic* Dunmanway (23) 45151

CATTLE, Richard John. b 40. W Midl Minl Tr Course 88. **d** 90 **p** 91. NSM Brixworth Deanery *Pet* from 90. *Cedar Hay Farm, School Lane, Yelvertoft, Northants NN6 7LH* Crick (0788) 822087

CATTLEY, Richard Melville. b 49. Trin Coll Bris DipTh73. **d** 73 **p** 74. C Kendal St Thos *Carl* 73-77; Nat Sec Pathfinders, CPAS 77-82; Exec Sec 82-85; V Dalton-in-Furness *Carl* 85-90; V Dulwich St Barn *S'wark* from 90; Chapl Alleyn's Foundn Dulwich from 90. *St Barnabas's Vicarage, Calton Avenue, London SE21 7DG* 081-693 2936

CATTON, Canon Cedric Trevor. b 36. JP. DipRJ. Wells Th Coll 70. **d** 72 **p** 73. C Solihull *Birm* 72-74; R Whepstead w Brockley *St E* 74-75; R Hawstead and Nowton w Stanningfield etc 74-79; Dioc Stewardship Adv 77-83; R Cockfield 79-83; V Exning St Martin w Landwade from 83; Chapl Newmarket Gen Hosp from 85; Hon Can St E Cathl *St E* from 90. *The Vicarage, New River Green, Exning, Newmarket, Suffolk CB8 7HS* Exning (063877) 413

CAUDWELL, Charles Leopold. b 17. Sarum & Wells Th Coll 75. **d** 77 **p** 78. NSM Offwell, Widworthy, Cotleigh, Farway etc *Ex* 77-80; TV 80-83; rtd 86; Perm to Offic B & W from 86. *Old Inn, Langford Budville, Wellington, Somerset TA21 0RT* Milverton (0823) 400287

CAUDWELL, Cyril. b 12. **d** 75 **p** 76. Hon C Bexhill St Barn *Chich* 75-78; Hon C Sidley 78-82; P-in-c Bexhill St Andr CD 82-90; rtd 90; Perm to Offic *Chich* from 90. *52 The Fieldings, Southwater, Horsham, W Sussex RH13 7LZ* Horsham (0403) 733417

CAULDWELL, Wallace Harrison. b 01. Chich Th Coll 42. **d** 42 **p** 43. V Grendon w Castle Ashby *Pet* 53-75; rtd 75; Lic to Offic *Pet* 76-85; Perm to Offic from 85. *11 The Square, Yardley Hastings, Northampton NN7 1EU* Yardley Hastings (060129) 883

CAVAGAN, Dr Raymond. b 35. Hull Univ MA86 PhD87. Oak Hill Th Coll DipTh62. **d** 63 **p** 64. C Upper Holloway St Pet *Lon* 63-66; C Hurworth *Dur* 66-68; V New Shildon 68-76; P-in-c Toxteth Park St Andr Aigburth Road *Liv* 76-77; V Toxteth Park St Mich 76-77; V Toxteth Park St Mich w St Andr 78-88; V Stamfordham w Matfen *Newc* from 88; Hon CF from 90. *The Vicarage, Stamfordham, Newcastle upon Tyne NE18 0QQ* Stamfordham (06616) 456

CAVAGHAN, Dennis Edgar. b 45. St Jo Coll Nottm BTh74. **d** 74 **p** 75. C Hartford *Ches* 74-77; C Plymouth St Andr w St Paul and St Geo *Ex* 77-80; V Cofton w Starcross 80-88; P-in-c W *Exe* from 88. *St Paul's Vicarage, Bakers Hill, Tiverton, Devon EX16 5NE* Tiverton (0884) 255705

CAVAN, Lawrence Noel. b 38. Trin Coll Bris 72. **d** 75 **p** 76. C Lurgan Ch Ch *D & D* 75-78; C Chorleywood Ch Ch *St Alb* 78-82; I Durrus *C, C & R* 82-85; I Portarlington w Cloneyhurke and Lea *M & K* 85-90; TV Eston w Normanby *York* from 90. *The Vicarage, 73A High Street, Eston, Middlesbrough, Cleveland TS6 9EH* Eston Grange (0642) 456755

CAVANAGH, Charles Terrence. b 49. Oklahoma Univ BLitt70 Trin Hall Cam BA74 MA77. Ripon Coll Cuddesdon 75. **d** 77 **p** 80. Hon C Camberwell St Geo *S'wark* 77-78; Perm to Offic 78-80 and 84-85; Hon C Clapham Old Town 80-84; Hon C Streatham St Pet from 85. *34 Tasman Road, London SW9 9LU* 071-737 2269

CAVANAGH, Capt Kenneth Joseph. b 41. **d** 77 **p** 77. CA from 64; Paraguay 77-83; P-in-c Gt w Lt Snoring *Nor* 83-85; R Gt w Lt Snoring w Kettlestone and Pensthorpe 85-88; P-in-c Glencarse *Bre* from 88; CA Co-ord (Scotland and Ireland) & Regional Voc Adv from 90. *The Rectory, Glencarse, Perth PH2 7LY* Glencarse (073886) 386

CAVANAGH, Peter Bernard. b 49. Sarum & Wells Th Coll 71. **d** 73 **p** 74. C Gt Crosby St Faith *Liv* 73-76; C Stanley 76-79; V Anfield St Columba from 79. *St Columba's Vicarage, Pinehurst Avenue, Liverpool L4 2TZ* 051-263 3031

CAVE, Canon Alan John. b 17. IPFA52 Lon Univ DipTh65. Cuddesdon Coll 64. **d** 65 **p** 66. C Ribbleton *Blackb* 68-72; V Burnley St Cath 72-78; P-in-c Burnley St Alb w St Paul 77-78; R Ribchester w Stidd 78-85; Hon Can Blackb Cathl 81-85; rtd 85; Perm to Offic Guildf from 86. *Mellstock, 23 Portmore Park Road, Weybridge, Surrey KT13 8ET* Weybridge (0932) 851635

CAVE, Anthony Sidney. b 32. E Midl Min Tr Course. **d** 84 **p** 85. C Immingham *Linc* 84-88; V Keelby 88-89; V Riby 88-89; V Keelby w Riby and Aylesby from 89. *The Vicarage, Keelby, Grimsby, S Humberside DN37 8EH* Roxton (0469) 60251

CAVE, Brian Malcolm. b 37. St Cath Soc Ox BA60 MA64. Oak Hill Th Coll. **d** 63 **p** 64. C Streatham Park St Alb *S'wark* 63-66; C Ruskin Park St Sav and St Matt 66-68; C Tunbridge Wells St Jas *Roch* 68-71; V Bootle St Leon *Liv* 71-75; Min St Mary w St John Bootle 73-75; Area Sec Leprosy Miss 75-81; V Hurst Green *Bradf* 81-82;

P-in-c Mitton 81-82; V Hurst Green and Mitton from 82. *The Vicarage, Hurst Green, Blackburn BB6 9QR* Stonyhurst (025486) 686

CAVE, Cyril Hayward. b 20. Nottm Univ MA60 BD63. AKC49. **d** 50 **p** 51. Lect Th Ex Univ 65-80; Sen Lect 80-85; rtd 85. *Berry House, Cheriton Fitzpaine, Crediton, Devon EX17 4HZ* Cheriton Fitzpaine (03636) 548

CAVE, Douglas Lionel. b 26. Lon Bible Coll 50 Lon Coll of Div 64. **d** 66 **p** 67. C Barking St Marg *Chelmsf* 69-73; V Blackb St Barn *Blackb* 73-81; Ind Chapl *Lon* 81-91; rtd 91. *8 Wood Rise, Pinner, Middx HA5 2JD* Uxbridge (0895) 677426

CAVE, Ven Guy Newell. b 19. TCD BA41 MA58. CITC 41. **d** 42 **p** 43. P-in-c Kildrumferton w Ballymachugh *K, E & A* 45-73; Preb St Patr Cathl Dub 65-72; Adn Kilmore *K, E & A* 72-87; P-in-c Ballymachugh w Kildrumferton and Ballyjamesduff 73-87; rtd 87. *5 Yew Point, Hodson's Bay, Athlone, Co Westmeath, Irish Republic* Athlone (902) 92718

CAVE, John Edwin Dawson. b 43. Cranmer Hall Dur 71. **d** 74 **p** 75. C Gt Ayton w Easby and Newton in Cleveland *York* 74-77; C Redcar w Kirkleatham 77-78; C Redcar 78-80; P-in-c Aislaby and Ruswarp 80-81; V 81-87; V Dormanstown from 87. *All Saints' Vicarage, South Avenue, Redcar, Cleveland TS10 5LL* Redcar (0642) 478334

CAVE, Robert Philip. b 23. Roch Th Coll 64. **d** 67 **p** 68. C York Town *Guildf* 67-71; C Yaxley *Ely* 71-75; R Cottenham 75-88; rtd 88; Perm to Offic *Pet* from 89. *14 St Mary's Way, Roade, Northampton NN7 2PQ* Roade (0604) 864420

CAVE BERGQUIST, Julie Anastasia. b 59. St Jo Coll Dur BA80 Franciscan Univ Rome STL87. St Steph Ho Ox 85. **d** 87. Par Dn Kennington *Cant* 87-89; Chapl Trin Coll Cam from 89. *Trinity College, Cambridge CB2 1TQ* Cambridge (0223) 338435

CAVE-BROWNE-CAVE, Bernard James William. b 54. Trin Hall Cam BA76 MA80 Bradf Univ MA90. Westcott Ho Cam 77. **d** 79 **p** 80. C Chesterton Gd Shep *Ely* 79-83; Chapl Lanc Univ *Blackb* from 83. *The Chaplaincy Centre, The University, Bailrigg, Lancaster LA1 4YW* Lancaster (0524) 65201 or 382337

✠**CAVELL, Rt Rev John Kingsmill.** b 16. Qu Coll Cam BA39 MA44. Wycliffe Hall Ox 39. **d** 40 **p** 41 **c** 72. C Folkestone H Trin *Cant* 40; C Addington 40-44; Lic to Offic *Ox* 45-52; Area Sec (Dio Ox) CMS 44-52; Dioc Sec 44-49; Tr Officer 49-52; V Cheltenham Ch Ch *Glouc* 52-62; V Plymouth St Andr *Ex* 62-72; RD Plymouth 67-72; Preb Ex Cathl 67-72; V E Stonehouse 68-72; Suff Bp Southn *Win* 72-84; Hon Can Win Cathl 72-84; rtd 84; Perm to Offic *Win* from 84; Asst Bp Sarum from 88; Can and Preb Sarum Cathl from 88. *5 Constable Way, West Harnham, Salisbury SP2 8LN* Salisbury (0722) 334782

CAVELL-NORTHAM (formerly NORTHAM), Canon Cavell Herbert James. b 32. St Steph Ho Ox 53. **d** 56 **p** 57. C W Wycombe *Ox* 56-61; CF (TA) 60-63; V Lane End *Ox* 61-68; V Stony Stratford from 68; P-in-c Calverton 69-72; R from 72; Hon Can Ch Ch from 91. *The Vicarage, London Road, Stony Stratford, Milton Keynes MK11 1JA* Milton Keynes (0908) 562148

CAWLEY, David Lewis. b 44. FSA81. AKC71 St Aug Coll Cant 71. **d** 72 **p** 73. C Sprowston *Nor* 72-75; Chapl HM Pris *Nor* 74-75; C Wymondham *Nor* 75-77; C Buckland in Dover w Buckland Valley *Cant* 77-83; V Eastville St Anne w St Mark and St Thos *Bris* from 83. *St Anne's Vicarage, 75 Greenbank Road, Bristol BS5 6HD* Bristol (0272) 520202

CAWLEY, Stephen. b 42. RMCM GRSM63. St Deiniol's Hawarden 81. **d** 84 **p** 85. C Tranmere St Paul w St Luke *Ches* 84-88; TV Hawarden *St As* from 88. *St Mary's Parsonage, Church Road, Broughton, Clwyd CH4 0NW* Hawarden (0244) 520148

CAWRSE, Christopher William. b 60. Univ of Wales (Cardiff) DipTh. Westcott Ho Cam. **d** 84 **p** 85. C Stoke Newington St Mary *Lon* 84-86; Chapl St Mark's Hosp Lon 86-90; C Islington St Jas w St Phil *Lon* 86-87; C Islington St Jas w St Pet 87-90; Chapl Charing Cross Hosp Lon from 90. *15A Golding House, Charing Cross Hospital, Fulham Palace Road, London W6 8RF* 081-846 1039

CAWTE, Canon David John. b 30. St Mich Coll Llan. **d** 65 **p** 66. C Chorley St Laur *Blackb* 65-67; C Boyne Hill *Ox* 67-74; C-in-c Cox Green CD 75-78; V Cox Green from 78; Hon Can Ch Ch from 88. *9 Warwick Close, Maidenhead, Berks SL6 3AL* Maidenhead (0628) 22139 or 32567

CAWTHORNE, Henry Howarth. b 03. Lon Univ BSc24 AKC24. Lich Th Coll 63. **d** 64 **p** 65. R Hinstock *Lich*

67-75; rtd 75. *25 Preston Trust Homes, Preston, Telford, Shropshire TF6 6DQ* Telford (0952) 603663

CAWTHORNE, Jack. b 22. ATD50 Lon Univ DipTh71. Cuddesdon Coll 69. **d** 71 **p** 72. NSM Newchurch *Man* 71-86; NSM Garforth *Ripon* from 87. *21 Lazch Lane, Garforth, Leeds LS25 2JP* Leeds (0532) 869527

CAYTON, John. b 32. Bps' Coll Cheshunt 54. **d** 57 **p** 58. C Hindley All SS *Liv* 57-59; C Littleham w Exmouth *Ex* 59-63; V Burnley St Cath *Blackb* 63-72; V Marton 72-87; V Fleetwood from 87; Miss to Seamen from 87. *St Peter's Vicarage, 39 Mount Road, Fleetwood, Lancs FY7 6EX* Fleetwood (03917) 71642

CECIL, Kevin Vincent. b 54. BA PGCE. St Mich Coll Llan DipTh82. **d** 82 **p** 83. C Llanilid w Pencoed *Llan* 82-85; C Coity w Nolton 85-88; Area Sec (Dios St D, Llan, Mon and S & B) CMS from 88. *Gronw House, Llanharri, Pontyclun, M Glam CF7 9LH* Llantrisant (0443) 225035

CHADD, Jeremy Denis. b 55. Jes Coll Cam BA77 MA81. Coll of Resurr Mirfield 78. **d** 81 **p** 82. C Seaton Hirst *Newc* 81-84; C N Gosforth 84-88; V Sunderland St Chad *Dur* from 88. *St Chad's Vicarage, Charter Drive, Sunderland SR3 3PG* 091-528 2397

CHADD, Canon Leslie Frank. b 19. Leeds Univ BSc41. Coll of Resurr Mirfield 41. **d** 43 **p** 44. C Portsea All SS w St Jo Rudmore *Portsm* 43-46; Chapl RNVR 46-48; C Greenford H Cross *Lon* 48-54; C Littlehampton St Mary *Chich* 54-58; V Hanworth All SS *Lon* 58-65; V Fareham SS Pet and Paul *Portsm* from 65; Relig Adv STV 72-81; Hon Can Portsm Cathl from 81. *The Vicarage, 30 Osborn Road, Fareham, Hants PO16 7DS* Fareham (0329) 280256

CHADWICK, Charles John Peter. b 59. Birm Univ BA81 Slough Coll DMS84 Southn Univ BTh90. Sarum & Wells Th Coll 85. **d** 88 **p** 89. C Chalfont St Peter *Ox* 88-91; C Gt Marlow from 91. *71 Seymour Park, Marlow, Bucks* Marlow (0628) 481056

CHADWICK, David Guy Evelyn St Just. b 36. Bps' Coll Cheshunt 61. **d** 68 **p** 69. C Edmonton All SS *Lon* 68-71; C Edmonton St Mary w St Jo 71-72; C Greenhill St Jo 72-74; Bp's Dom Chapl *Truro* 74-79; Chapl Community of the Epiphany Truro 77-78; P-in-c Crantock *Truro* 79-83; R Clydebank *Glas* 83-87; R Renfrew from 87. *The Rectory, 2 Oxford Road, Renfrew PA4 0SJ* 041-886 7858

CHADWICK, Francis Arnold Edwin. b 30. AKC54. **d** 55 **p** 56. C Chapel Allerton *Ripon* 55-58; C Hayes *Roch* 58-61; V Arreton *Portsm* 61-67; V Newchurch 61-67; V Kingshurst *Birm* 67-73; V York Town *Guildf* 73-83; P-in-c Long Sutton w Long Load *B & W* 83-87; R Stockbridge and Longstock and Leckford *Win* from 87. *The Rectory, 11 Trafalgar Way, Stockbridge, Hants SO20 6ET* Andover (0264) 810810

CHADWICK, Canon George Bancroft. b 12. Linc Th Coll 40. **d** 42 **p** 43. V Cullercoats St Geo *Newc* 55-70; RD Tynemouth 67-70; V Corbridge w Halton 70-81; Hon Can Newc Cathl 74-82; P-in-c Newton Hall 79-81; V Corbridge w Halton and Newton Hall 82; rtd 82. *14 Alexandra Terrace, Hexham, Northd NE46 3JH* Hexham (0434) 602092

✠**CHADWICK, Rt Rev Graham Charles.** b 23. Keble Coll Ox BA49 MA53. St Mich Coll Llan 49. **d** 50 **p** 51 **c** 76. C Oystermouth *S & B* 50-53; Basutoland 53-63; Chapl Univ of Wales (Swansea) *S & B* 63-68; Sen Bursar Qu Coll Birm 68-69; Lic to Offic *S'wark* 69-70; Lesotho 70-76; S Africa 76-82; Bp Kimberley and Kuruman 76-82; Dioc Adv on Spirituality *St As* 83-90; Chapl St As Cathl 83-90; rtd 90; Asst Bp Liv from 90. *423 Eaton Road, West Derby, Liverpool L12 2AJ* 051-228 2891

CHADWICK, Ms Helen Jane. b 63. UEA BA84 Nottm Univ MTh91. St Jo Coll Nottm LTh88 DPS91. **d** 91. Par Dn Easton H Trin w St Gabr and St Lawr and St Jude *Bris* from 91. *7 Villiers Road, Bristol BS5 0JH* Bristol (0272) 518516

CHADWICK, Henry. b 20. KBE89. FBA60 MRIA Magd Coll Cam BA MusBac41 MA45 DD57 Yale Univ Hon DD75. Ridley Hall Cam 42. **d** 43 **p** 44. C S Croydon Em *Cant* 43-45; Asst Chapl Wellington Coll Berks 45-46; Chapl Qu Coll Cam 46-50; Dean 50-55; Can Ch Ch *Ox* 59-69; Regius Prof Div Ox 59-69; Vice-Pres Br Academy 68-69; Dean Ch Ch *Ox* 69-79; Regius Prof Div Cam Univ 79-82; Hon Can Ely 79-83; Lic to Offic from 83; Master Peterho Cam from 87. *Peterhouse, Cambridge CB2 1RD* Cambridge (0223) 338200

CHADWICK, Canon Martin James. b 27. Trin Hall Cam BA51 MA54. Cuddesdon Coll 52. **d** 54 **p** 55. C Earl's Court St Cuth w St Matthias *Lon* 54-58; Chapl Trin Hall Cam 58-63; Chapl Ch Ch Ox 63-67; V Market

Lavington and Easterton *Sarum* 67-79; V Charlbury w Shorthampton *Ox* from 79; RD Chipping Norton from 79; Hon Can Ch Ch from 91. *The Vicarage, Charlbury, Oxford OX73PX* Charlbury (0608) 810286

CHADWICK, Martin John. b 55. Univ of Wales (Ban) BMus77. Coll of Resurr Mirfield 78. **d** 81 **p** 82. C Stoke-upon-Trent *Lich* 81-85; TV from 85. *All Saints' Vicarage, 540 Leek Road, Stoke-on-Trent ST13HH* Stoke-on-Trent (0782) 29806

CHADWICK, Peter MacKenzie. b 21. Lich Th Coll 63. **d** 65 **p** 66. Jt Hd Master Forres Sch Swanage 56-81; Chapl 66-85; NSM Kingston, Langton Matravers and Worth Matravers *Sarum* from 85; rtd 89. *Cull's, Langton Matravers, Swanage, Dorset BH193HJ* Swanage (0929) 422258

CHADWICK, Roger Vernon. b 39. Dur Univ BA60. Cranmer Hall Dur DipTh62. **d** 62 **p** 63. C Swinton St Pet *Man* 62-65; C Heworth St Mary *Dur* 65-68; Hon C 68-74; V Hartlepool St Aid 74-84; R Egglescliffe from 84. *The Rectory, 10 Butts Lane, Egglescliffe, Stockton-on-Tees, Co Durham TS169BT* Eaglescliffe (0642) 780185

CHADWICK, Prof William Owen. b 16. KBE82. FBA62 St Jo Coll Cam BA39 MA42 BD51 DD55 Ox Univ Hon DD73. Cuddesdon Coll 39. **d** 40 **p** 41. C Huddersfield St Jo *Wakef* 40-42; Chapl Wellington Coll Berks 42-46; Lic to Offic *Ely* from 47; Fell Trin Hall Cam 47-56; Dean 49-56; Master Selw Coll Cam 56-83; Dixie Prof Ecclesiastical Hist 58-68; Regius Prof Modern Hist 68-83; Pres Br Academy 81-85; Chan UEA from 85. *67 Grantchester Street, Cambridge CB79HZ* Cambridge (0223) 314000

CHADWIN, James William. b 01. Glas Univ MA23 Lon Univ BA39. Edin Dioc NSM Course 75. **d** 76 **p** 77. NSM Edin H Cross *Edin* 76-83; rtd 83. *35 Carlogie Road, Carnoustie, Angus DD76ER* Carnoustie (0241) 55781

CHAFFEY, Jane Frances. b 59. Somerville Coll Ox BA80 MA84 St Jo Coll Dur BA86. Cranmer Hall Dur 84. **d** 88. Par Dn Roby *Liv* 88-90. *9 Eider Avenue, Lyneham, Chippenham, Wilts SN154QG*

CHAFFEY, Jonathan Paul Michael. b 62. St Chad's Coll Dur BA83. Cranmer Hall Dur 84. **d** 87 **p** 88. C Gateacre *Liv* 87-90; Chapl RAF from 90. *c/o MOD, Adastral House, Theobald's Road, London WC1X 8RU* 071-430 7268

CHAFFEY, Michael Prosser. b 30. Lon Univ BA51. St Steph Ho Ox 53. **d** 55 **p** 56. C Victoria Docks Ascension *Chelmsf* 55-59; C Leytonstone H Trin Harrow Green 59-62; V Walthamstow St Mich 62-69; R Cov St Jo *Cov* 69-85; P-in-c Cov St Thos 69-75; Hon C Bideford *Ex* 85; P-in-c Charlestown *Man* 85-88; V Sutton St Mich *York* from 88. *St Michael's Vicarage, 751 Marfleet Lane, Hull HU94TJ* Hull (0482) 74509

CHALCRAFT, Christopher Warine Terrell. b 37. Oak Hill Th Coll. **d** 67 **p** 68. C Egham *Guildf* 67-70; P-in-c Slough *Ox* 70-73; TV Bramerton w Surlingham *Nor* 73-87; P-in-c Cockley Cley w Gooderstone from 87; P-in-c Gt and Lt Cressingham w Threxton from 87; P-in-c Didlington from 87; P-in-c Hilborough w Bodney from 87; P-in-c Oxborough w Foulden and Caldecote from 87. *The Rectory, Gooderstone, King's Lynn, Norfolk PE339BS* Gooderstone (036621) 425

CHALK, Francis Harold. b 25. Lich Th Coll 61. **d** 62 **p** 63. R Gt Gonerby *Linc* 69-89; rtd 89. *Chalkleigh, 3 Church Street, St Just, Penzance, Cornwall TR197HA* Penzance (0736) 787925

CHALK, Norman Albert. b 25. S'wark Ord Course 69. **d** 71 **p** 72. C Northwood Hills St Edm *Lon* 71-76; R Cowley 76-90; rtd 91. *23 Rushmoor Avenue, Hazelmere, High Wycombe, Bucks HP157NT* High Wycombe (0494) 813438

CHALKLEY, Henry Roy. b 23. St Aid Birkenhead 58. **d** 59 **p** 60. Miss to Seamen 63-88; rtd 88. *2 Spriteshall Lane, Felixstowe, Suffolk IP119QY* Felixstowe (0394) 277600

CHALLEN, Canon Peter Bernard. b 31. Clare Coll Cam BA56 MA60. Westcott Ho Cam 56. **d** 58 **p** 59. C Goole *Sheff* 58-61; V Dalton 61-67; Sen Ind Chapl *S'wark* from 67; R S'wark Ch Ch from 67; Hon Can S'wark Cathl from 74. *Christ Church Rectory, 49 Colombo Street, London SE18DP* 071-928 4707

CHALLEN, Victor Stanley. b 14. Bede Coll Dur BSc39. **d** 41 **p** 43. V Bedf St Martin *St Alb* 52-83; rtd 83; Perm to Offic St Alb and Nor from 83. *57 Hunstanton Road, Dersingham, King's Lynn, Norfolk PE316ND* Dersingham (0485) 540964

CHALLENDER, Canon Clifford. b 32. CITC 67. **d** 67 **p** 68. C Belf St Luke *Conn* 67-70; C Kilkenny w Aghour and Odagh *C & O* 70-71; Bp's V and Lib Kilkenny Cathl

70-71; Dioc Registrar (Ossory, Ferns and Leighlin) 70-71; I Fenagh w Myshall and Kiltennel 71-76; I Fenagh w Myshall, Aghade and Ardoyne 76-79; I Crosspatrick Gp from 79; Preb Ferns Cathl 85-88; Dioc Glebes Sec (Ferns) from 86; Treas Ferns Cathl 88-91; Chan from 91; RD Gorey from 89. *The Rectory, Tinahely, Arklow, Co Wicklow, Irish Republic* Arklow (402) 38178

CHALLENGER, Cyril George. b 02. Peterho Cam BA24 Jes Coll Cam MA28. Ripon Hall Ox 26. **d** 27 **p** 28. V Almeley *Heref* 67-70; RD Weobley 67-70; rtd 70. *52 Walliscote Road, Weston-super-Mare, Avon BS23 1XF* Weston-super-Mare (0934) 26341

CHALLENGER, Peter Nelson. b 33. St Jo Coll Cam BA57 MA61. Ripon Hall Ox 57. **d** 59 **p** 60. C Bushbury *Lich* 59-62; V Horsley Woodhouse *Derby* 62-67; V Derby St Barn 67-75; Brazil 75-80; TV New Windsor *Ox* 80-89; V Wootton (Boars Hill) from 89. *Wootton Vicarage, Boars Hill, Oxford OX15JL* Oxford (0865) 735661

CHALLENGER, Miss Susanne Christine. b 41. Bp Grosseteste Coll TCert64 Leeds Poly DipSocSc68 Teesside Poly DMS86. NE Ord Course 88. **d** 91. NSM Middlesb St Cuth *York* from 91. *Hundlebrook, 11 Garbutts Lane, Hutton, Rudby, Yarm, Cleveland TS150UN* Stokesley (0642) 700391

CHALLICE, John Richard. b 34. ACP65. Sarum & Wells Th Coll 73. **d** 75 **p** 76. C Warminster St Denys *Sarum* 75-78; R Longfield *Roch* from 78. *The Rectory, 67 Main Road, Longfield, Kent DA3 7PQ* Longfield (0474) 702201

CHALLIS, Ian. b 46. St Jo Coll Nottm 82. **d** 84 **p** 85. C Heatherlands St Jo *Sarum* 84-86; C Lytchett Minster 86-88. *9 Haven Road, Corfe Mullen, Wimborne, Dorset BH21 3SY* Wimborne (0202) 691300

CHALLIS, Preb James Dobb. b 16. St Jo Coll Cam BA38 MA42. Ridley Hall Cam 39. **d** 40 **p** 41. V Penn Fields *Lich* 67-81; Preb Lich Cathl 80-81; rtd 81. *21 Seymour Avenue, Louth, Lincs LN11 9EW* Louth (0507) 602637

CHALLIS, Terence Peter. b 40. St Aid Birkenhead 65. **d** 68 **p** 69. C Billericay St Mary *Chelmsf* 68-71; Kenya 72-75; P-in-c Sparkbrook Ch Ch *Birm* 76-80; V Enfield St Jas *Lon* 80-89; V Astley Bridge *Man* from 89. *St Paul's Vicarage, Sweetloves Lane, Bolton BL1 7ET* Bolton (0204) 54119

CHALLIS, William George. b 52. Keble Coll Ox BA73 K Coll Lon MTh75. Oak Hill Th Coll 73. **d** 75 **p** 76. C Islington St Mary *Lon* 75-79; Lect Trin Coll Bris 79-81; C Stoke Bishop *Bris* 79-81; Lect Oak Hill Th Coll 82; Burundi 82-85; P-in-c Bishopston *Bris* 86-89; TR from 89. *Bishopston Vicarage, 25 Morley Square, Bristol BS79DW* Bristol (0272) 424359

CHALMERS, Brian. b 42. Or Coll Ox BA64 MA68 DPhil70 BA71. Wycliffe Hall Ox 71. **d** 72 **p** 73. C Luton St Mary *St Alb* 72-76; Chapl Cranfield Inst of Tech 76-81; Chapl Kent Univ *Cant* 81-89; Six Preacher Cant Cathl from 85; V Charing w Charing Heath and Lt Chart from 89. *The Vicarage, Pett Lane, Charing, Ashford, Kent TN270QL* Charing (023371) 2598

CHALMERS, Robert Alan. b 66. QUB LLB88 TCD BTh91. **d** 91. C Lurgan etc w Ballymachugh, Kildrumferton etc *K, E & A* from 91. *Kildrumferton Rectory, Corsserlough, Killaneck, Co Cavan, Irish Republic* Cavan (49) 36211

CHALONER, Stephen Mason. b 34. Dur Univ BA57. Ridley Hall Cam 57. **d** 59 **p** 60. C Aspley *S'well* 59-62; Chapl RNR from 61; P-in-c Eakring *S'well* 62-65; R 65-69; R Bilsthorpe 62-69; Chapl Saxondale Hosp Radcliffe-on-Trent 69-73; P-in-c Holme Pierrepont w Adbolton *S'well* 69-73; V Shelford 69-73; V Radcliffe-on-Trent 69-73; C Rowner *Portsm* 73-74; Hon C 74-81; Miss to Seamen 81-86; P-in-c Binstead *Portsm* from 86; P-in-c Swanmore St Mich w Havenstreet from 86; RD E Wight from 88. *The Rectory, Pitts Lane, Ryde, Isle of Wight PO33 3SU* Isle of Wight (0983) 62890

CHAMBERLAIN, David (Bernard). b 28. Fitzw Ho Cam BA51. Linc Th Coll 52. **d** 54 **p** 55. C Brighouse *Wakef* 54-57; C Sheff Parson Cross St Cecilia *Sheff* 57-61; CR 63-85; S Africa 68-70; Bp's Adv on Community Relns *Wakef* 71-85; Bp's Adv Community Relns & Inter-Faith Dialogue *Bris* from 86; V Easton All Hallows from 86. *The Vicarage, All Hallows' Road, Easton, Bristol BS50HH* Bristol (0272) 552477

CHAMBERLAIN, David Murray. b 22. Cuddesdon Coll 55. **d** 57 **p** 58. Japan 60-71 and 76-81; V Edgbaston St Germain *Birm* 71-76; Miss to Seamen N Australia 81-88; rtd 88. *42 Tresawls Road, Truro, Cornwall TR1 3LE* Truro (0872) 72270

CHAMBERLAIN, Eric Edward. b 34. Lon Univ DipTh64. Tyndale Hall Bris 62. **d** 65 **p** 66. C Chell *Lich* 65-73; P-in-c Preston St Mary *Blackb* 73-76; V 76-89; P-in-c Preston St Luke 81-83; R S Normanton *Derby* from 89. *The Rectory, Church Street, South Normanton, Derby DE55 2BT* Ripley (0773) 811273

CHAMBERLAIN, Frederick George. b 19. Univ of Wales (Lamp) BA50. Chich Th Coll 50. **d** 52 **p** 53. R Tilshead, Orcheston and Chitterne *Sarum* 71-80; P-in-c Handley w Gussage St Andrew and Pentridge 80-82; R 82-84; rtd 84. *Mill Cottage, Codford St Mary, Warminster, Wilts BA12 0ND* Warminster (0985) 50519

CHAMBERLAIN, Canon Neville. b 39. Nottm Univ BA61 MA73 CQSW73. Ripon Hall Ox 61. **d** 63 **p** 64. C Balsall Heath St Paul *Birm* 63-64; C Hall Green Ascension 64-66; C-in-c Gospel Lane CD 66-69; V Gospel Lane St Mich 69-72; Lic to Offic *Lic* 73-74; Soc Resp Sec 74-82; Can and Preb Linc Cathl from 79; R Edin St Jo *Edin* from 82. *1 Ainslie Place, Edinburgh EH3 6AR* 031-225 5004

CHAMBERLAIN, Nicholas Alan. b 63. St Chad's Coll Dur BA85 PhD91 New Coll Edin BD91. **d** 91. C Cockerton *Dur* from 91. *The Vicarage, Newton Lane, Cockerton, Darlington, Co Durham DL3 9EX* Darlington (0325) 463705

CHAMBERLAIN, Roger Edward. b 53. BEd76 BA87. Trin Coll Bris 84. **d** 87 **p** 88. C Plymouth Em w Efford *Ex* 87-90; C Selly Park St Steph and St Wulstan *Birm* from 90. *98 Bournbrook Road, Selly Oak, Birmingham B29 7BU* 021-472 5378

CHAMBERLAIN, Canon Roy. b 10. Selw Coll Cam BA31 MA35. Wycliffe Hall Ox 32. **d** 33 **p** 34. V Brockenhurst *Win* 69-78; RD Lyndhurst 74-77; rtd 78; Perm to Offic Win from 78; Ely from 88. *81 Woodland Road, Sawston, Cambridge CB2 4DT* Cambridge (0223) 834786

CHAMBERLAIN, Russell Charles. b 51. **d** 78 **p** 79. C Harold Hill St Geo *Chelmsf* 78-80; C Uckfield *Chich* 80-83; R Balcombe 83-90; V Okehampton w Inwardleigh *Ex* from 90. *The Vicarage, 1 Church Path, Okehampton, Devon EX20 1LW* Okehampton (0837) 52731

CHAMBERLIN, John Malcolm. b 38. Carl Dioc Tr Course 84. **d** 87 **p** 88. NSM Cockermouth w Embleton and Wythop *Carl* from 87. *45 Dale View, Cockermouth, Cumbria CA13 9EW* Cockermouth (0900) 822849

CHAMBERS, Anthony Frederick John. b 40. Sarum Th Coll 69. **d** 71 **p** 72. C Hall Green St Pet *Birm* 71-74; C Holdenhurst *Win* 74-77; P-in-c Ropley w W Tisted 77-79; P-in-c Bishop's Sutton 79; R Bishop's Sutton and Ropley and W Tisted 79-83; V Pokesdown St Jas from 83. *St James's Vicarage, 12 Harewood Avenue, Bournemouth BH7 6NQ* Bournemouth (0202) 425918

CHAMBERS, Preb George William. b 24. TCD BA46 MA57. CITC 47. **d** 47 **p** 48. C Conwall *D & R* 47-50; Chapl Portora R Sch Enniskillen 50-51; I Tullyaughnish w Milford *D & R* 51-61; I Adare *L & K* 61-81; Dioc Registrar 62-81; Adn Limerick 69-81; Dean Limerick 81-86; I Killeshin w Cloydagh and Killabban *C & O* from 86; Preb Ossory Cathl from 90; Preb Leighlin Cathl from 90. *The Rectory, Ballickmoyler, Carlow, Irish Republic* Athy (507) 25321

CHAMBERS, Canon Peter Lewis. b 43. Imp Coll Lon BScEng64. St Steph Ho Ox 64. **d** 66 **p** 67. C Llan w Capel Llanilterne *Llan* 66-70; Chapl Ch in Wales Youth Coun 70-73; Youth Chapl *Bris* 73-78; V Bedminster St Mich 78-84; RD Bedminster 81-84; Adv Ho of Bps Marriage Educn Panel Gen Syn 84-88; Dir Dioc Coun for Soc Resp *Guildf* from 88; Hon Can Guildf Cathl from 89. *72 West Hill, Epsom, Surrey KT19 8LF* Guildford (0483) 571826

CHAMBERS, Roland Arthur Blake. b 07. AKC32. **d** 32 **p** 33. V Bedf St Leon *St Alb* 54-73; rtd 73; Perm to Offic *St Alb* from 74. *33 Eversleigh Road, London N3* 081-349 2138

CHAMIER, Peter Lewis Deschamps. b 13. Ch Ch Ox BA35 BCL38 MA40. Ely Th Coll 39. **d** 39 **p** 40. V Carlton on Trent *S'well* 71-80; V Sutton on Trent 71-80; P-in-c Marnham 77-80; P-in-c Normanton on Trent 77-80; rtd 80; Perm to Offic *Ely* from 80. *9 Sherlock Road, Cambridge CB3 0HR* Cambridge (0223) 354563

CHAMPION, Canon John Oswald Cecil. b 27. St Chad's Coll Dur BA49 DipTh51. **d** 51 **p** 52. C Worc St Martin *Worc* 51-53; Chapl RN 53-57; C Cant St Martin w St Paul *Cant* 57-60; C-in-c Stourbridge St Mich Norton CD *Worc* 60-64; V Astwood Bank w Crabbs Cross 64-68; V Redditch St Steph 68-75; R Fladbury, Wyre Piddle and Moor from 75; RD Pershore 79-85; Hon Can Worc Cathl from 81. *The Rectory, Fladbury, Pershore, Worcs WR10 2QW* Evesham (0386) 860356

CHAMPNEYS, Michael Harold. b 46. LRAM67 GRSM67 ARCO67. Linc Th Coll 69. **d** 72 **p** 83. C Poplar *Lon* 72-73; C Bow w Bromley St Leon 73-75; P-in-c Bethnal Green St Barn 75-76; C Tewkesbury w Walton Cardiff *Glouc* 76-78; V Bedf Park *Lon* 78-83; V Shepshed *Leic* 84-87; Community Educn Tutor Bolsover from 88; Perm to Offic *Derby* from 90. *36 Sterland Street, Brampton, Chesterfield, Derbyshire S40 1BP* Chesterfield (0246) 220610

CHANCE, David Newton. b 44. Univ of Wales (Lamp) BA68. St Steph Ho Ox 68. **d** 70 **p** 71. C Selsdon St Jo w St Fran *Cant* 70-73; C Plymstock *Ex* 73-77; P-in-c Northam 77-79; TR Northam w Westward Ho and Appledore from 79. *The Vicarage, Fore Street, Northam, Bideford, Devon EX39 1AW* Bideford (0237) 474379

CHAND, Wazir. b 29. Punjab Univ BA56 BT59. Ox NSM Course. **d** 90. NSM Cowley St Jo *Ox* from 90. *7 Frederick Road, Cowley, Oxford OX4 3HL* Oxford (0865) 714160

CHANDA, Daniel Khazan. b 28. Punjab Univ BA57 MA62 Saharanputh Coll. **d** 70 **p** 70. Hon C Handsworth St Jas *Birm* 70-83; Hon C Perry Barr 83-89; C Small Heath St Greg from 89. *22 Tennyson Road, Birmingham B10 0HB* 021-772 7673

CHANDLER, Preb Arthur Stanley. b 06. St Edm Hall Ox BA29 MA38. Westcott Ho Cam 29. **d** 30 **p** 31. V Ilfracombe H Trin *Ex* 52-72; V W Downe 58-72; V Lee 58-72; RD Barnstaple 67-77; Preb Ex Cathl from 67; TR Ilfracombe, Lee and W Down 72-78; V Woolacombe 76-78; TR Ilfracombe, Lee, W Down, Woolacombe and Bittadon 78-83; rtd 83. *The Hollies, Lee, Ilfracombe, Devon EX34 8LR* Ilfracombe (0271) 62622

CHANDLER, John Edmond Owen. b 18. St Cath Soc Ox BA48 MA48. Cuddesdon Coll 68. **d** 68 **p** 69. Hon C Quarndon *Derby* 68-72; Lic to Offic *S'well* 73-78; P-in-c Oxton 79-85; R Epperstone 79-85; R Gonalston 79-85; rtd 85; Perm to Offic *S'well* from 85. *18 Thoresby Dale, Hucknall, Nottingham NG15 7UG* Nottingham (0602) 635945

CHANDLER, Michael John. b 45. Lon Univ DipTh75 K Coll Lon PhD87. Lambeth STh80 Linc Th Coll 70. **d** 72 **p** 73. C Cant St Dunstan w H Cross *Cant* 72-75; C Margate St Jo 75-78; V Newington w Bobbing and Iwade 78-83; P-in-c Hartlip w Stockbury 80-83; V Newington w Hartlip and Stockbury 83-88; RD Sittingbourne 84-88; R Hackington from 88. *St Stephen's Rectory, St Stephen's Green, Canterbury, Kent CT2 7JU* Canterbury (0227) 765391

CHANING-PEARCE, David. b 32. Roch Th Coll 63. **d** 65 **p** 66. C Plaistow St Mary *Roch* 65-69; C Rustington *Chich* 69-73; R Slinfold 73-83; P-in-c Itchingfield 82-83; R Itchingfield w Slinfold 83-85; V Midhurst from 85; R Woolbeding from 85. *The Vicarage, June Lane, Midhurst, W Sussex GU29 9EW* Midhurst (073081) 3339

CHANNER, Christopher Kendall. b 42. K Coll Lon BD64 AKC64. **d** 65 **p** 66. C Norbury St Steph *Cant* 65-68; C S Elmsall *Wakef* 68-70; V Dartford St Edm *Roch* 70-75; Chapl Joyce Green Hosp Dartford 73-75; V Bromley St Andr *Roch* 75-81; V Langton Green from 81. *The Vicarage, Speldhurst Road, Langton Green, Tunbridge Wells TN3 0JB* Langton (0892) 862072

CHANT, Edwin John. b 14. Lon Univ BA62. Clifton Th Coll 46. **d** 47 **p** 48. V Gentleshaw *Lich* 56-80; V Farewell 56-80; rtd 80; Perm to Offic *Lich* from 80. *31 Huntsmans Gate, Burntwood, Staffs WS7 9LL*

CHANT, Harry. b 40. Oak Hill Th Coll DipHE78. **d** 78 **p** 79. C Heatherlands St Jo *Sarum* 78-81; P-in-c Bramshaw 81-83; P-in-c Landford w Plaitford 81-83; R Bramshaw and Landford w Plaitford 83-87; V Fareham St Jo *Portsm* from 87. *St John's Vicarage, 3A St Michael's Grove, Fareham, Hants PO14 1DN* Fareham (0329) 280762

CHANT, Kenneth William. b 37. St Deiniol's Hawarden 67. **d** 70 **p** 71. C Ynyshir *Llan* 70-74; C Bargoed and Deri w Brithdir 74; P-in-c Aberpergwm and Blaengwrach 74-77; V 77-81; V Cwmavon from 81. *The Vicarage, Coed Parc, Cwmavon, Port Talbot, W Glam SA12 9BL* Port Talbot (0639) 896254

CHANT, Maurice Ronald. b 26. Chich Th Coll 51. **d** 54 **p** 55. Chapl Miss to Seamen Tilbury 67-71; Gt Yarmouth 71-77; Australia 77-84 and 85-91; Singapore 84-85; rtd 91; Australia from 91. *47 Regent Street, Wynnum West, Queensland, Australia 4178* Brisbane (7) 893-1251

CHANTER, Canon Anthony Roy. b 37. ACP60 Open Univ BA72 Lon Univ MA75. Sarum Th Coll 64. **d** 66 **p** 67. C W Tarring *Chich* 66-69; Chapl St Andr Sch Worthing 69-70; Hd Master Bp K Sch Linc 70-73; Hon PV Linc Cathl *Linc* 70-73; Hd Master Grey Court Comp Sch Richmond 73-76; Hon C Kingston All SS *S'wark* 73-76; Hd Master Bp Reindorp Sch Guildf 77-84; Hon Can

Guildf Cathl *Guildf* from 84; Dir of Educn from 84. *Grasshoppers, Woodland Avenue, Cranleigh, Surrey GU6 7HU*   Cranleigh (0483) 273833 or 571826

CHANTREY, David Frank. b 48. K Coll Cam BA70 PhD73 MA74. Westcott Ho Cam 83. **d** 86 **p** 87. C Wordsley *Lich* 86-89; C Beckbury 89-90; P-in-c from 90. *The Rectory, Beckbury, Shifnal, Shropshire TF11 9DG* Ryton (095287) 474

CHANTRY, Helen Fiona. b 59. Bradf Univ BSc82 Leeds Univ CertEd83. Trin Coll Bris BA89. **d** 89. NSM Hyde St Geo *Ches* from 89. *121 Dowson Road, Hyde, Cheshire SK14 5HJ*   061-367 9353

CHANTRY, Peter Thomas. b 62. Bradf Univ BSc83. Trin Coll Bris BA89. **d** 89 **p** 90. C Hyde St Geo *Ches* from 89. *121 Dowson Road, Hyde, Cheshire SK14 5HJ* 061-367 9353

CHANTRY, Richard Michael. b 31. Hertf Coll Ox BA55 MA57. Ridley Hall Cam 55. **d** 57 **p** 57. C Boulton *Derby* 57-59; C Ox St Aldate w H Trin *Ox* 59-68; P-in-c 74-75; Chapl Hertf Coll Ox from 61. *11 Talbot Road, Oxford OX2 8LL*   Oxford (0865) 58286 or 279411

CHANTRY, Mrs Sandra Mary. b 41. Cam Inst of Educn CertEd63. E Midl Min Tr Course 83. **dss** 86 **d** 87. Loughb Gd Shep *Leic* 86-87; Par Dn 87-89; Par Dn Belton and Osgathorpe 89-90; Par Dn Hathern, Long Whatton and Diseworth w Belton etc from 90. *The Rectory, Presents Lane, Belton, Loughborough, Leics LE12 9UN* Coalville (0530) 222266

CHAPLIN, Colin. b 33. **d** 76 **p** 77. NSM Penicuik *Edin* 76-91; NSM Bathgate from 91. *26 Broomhill Road, Penicuik, Midlothian EH26 9EE*   Penicuik (0968) 72050

CHAPLIN, Douglas Archibald. b 59. Em Coll Cam BA81. St Jo Coll Nottm DipTh84. **d** 86 **p** 87. C Glouc St Geo w Whaddon *Glouc* 86-89; C Lydney w Aylburton from 89. *21 Orchard Road, Lydney, Glos GL15 5QL*   Dean (0594) 44180

CHAPLIN, Frederick David. b 20. CCC Ox BA49 MA54. Cuddesdon Coll 49. **d** 51 **p** 52. Trinidad and Tobago 61-72; Asst to Gen Sec ACC 72-78; Sec C of E Partnership for World Miss 79-85; Perm to Offic *Ox* from 83; rtd 86. *19 Granville Court, Cheney Lane, Oxford OX3 0HS*   Oxford (0865) 240489

CHAPLIN, Paul. b 57. Hull Univ BA80 CertEd81 K Coll Lon MA89. St Steph Ho Ox 85. **d** 87 **p** 88. C Ex St Jas *Ex* 87-90; C Wokingham St Paul *Ox* from 90. *St Nicholas House, 13 Brook Close, Wokingham, Berks RG11 1ND* Wokingham (0734) 780034

CHAPMAN, Canon Albert Aidan. b 09. TD. Em Coll Cam BA35 MA39. Lon Coll of Div. **d** 37 **p** 38. Hon Can Roch Cathl *Roch* 64-76; V Westerham 64-76; rtd 76; Perm to Offic *St E* from 76. *41 Honeymeade Close, Stanton, Bury St Edmunds, Suffolk IP31 2EF*   Stanton (0359) 50518

CHAPMAN, Barry Frank. b 48. Trin Coll Bris. **d** 82 **p** 83. NSM Bradford-on-Avon Ch Ch *Sarum* from 82; Assoc Chapl Bath Univ from 83. *16 Church Acre, Bradford-on-Avon, Wilts BA15 1RL*   Bradford-on-Avon (02216) 6861

CHAPMAN, Celia. b 32. Whitelands Coll Lon TCert53 Open Univ BA82. W Midl Minl Tr Course 84. **d** 87. NSM Bilston *Lich* from 87. *St Leonard's Vicarage, Dover Street, Bilston, W Midlands WV14 6AW*   Bilston (0902) 491560

CHAPMAN, Christopher Robin. b 37. Nottm Univ DipAdEd71 Cam Univ DipRK74. Ripon Hall Ox 72. **d** 73 **p** 74. C Kidbrooke St Jas *S'wark* 73-77; V Corton *Nor* 77-80; V Hopton 77-80; RD Lothingland 80-86; V Hopton w Corton from 80. *The Vicarage, 51 The Street, Corton, Lowestoft, Suffolk NR32 5HT*   Lowestoft (0502) 730977

CHAPMAN, Colin. b 38. St Andr Univ MA60 Lon Univ BD62. Ridley Hall Cam. **d** 64 **p** 65. C Edin St Jas *Edin* 64-67; Egypt 68-74; Perm to Offic *Birm* 74-77; Lebanon 77-83; Lect Trin Coll Bris 83-90; Prin Crowther Hall CMS Tr Coll Selly Oak from 90. *Crowther Hall, Weoley Park Road, Birmingham B29 6QT*   021-471 4380

CHAPMAN, David. b 06. Bps' Coll Cheshunt 67. **d** 68 **p** 69. V Merrington *Dur* 71-79; rtd 79; Perm to Offic *Portsm* from 81. *c/o J B Chapman Esq, Barnacle Building, Amacre Drive, Plymouth PL9 9RT*

CHAPMAN, David John. b 28. Jes Coll Ox BA52 MA56. Wells Th Coll 52. **d** 54 **p** 55. C Sedgley All SS *Lich* 54-57; C Cannock 57-60; V Tipton St Matt 60-69; R Sawley *Derby* 69-79; P-in-c Holkham w Egmere and Waterden *Nor* 79-83; P-in-c Warham w Wighton 79-83; R Wells next the Sea 79-83; R Holkham w Egmere w Warham, Wells and Wighton 83; V Feltham *Lon* from 83. *The Vicarage, Cardinal Road, Feltham, Middx TW13 5AL*   081-890 6681 or 890 2011

CHAPMAN, Canon Derek. b 22. Westcott Ho Cam 52. **d** 53 **p** 54. V E Malling *Roch* 58-79; R Hever w Mark Beech 79-89; P-in-c Four Elms 80-89; Hon Can Roch Cathl 84-89; rtd 89; Perm to Offic Roch and Chich from 89. *1 Moat Lane, Sedlescombe, E Sussex TN33 0RZ* Hastings (0424) 754455

CHAPMAN, Mrs Dorothy. b 38. Nottm Univ CTPS. E Midl Min Tr Course. **d** 89. Par Dn Bingham *S'well* from 89; Sub-Chapl HM Pris Whatton from 89. *86 Kenrick Road, Nottingham NG3 6FB*   Nottingham (0602) 503088

CHAPMAN, Drummond John. b 36. Cant Sch of Min. **d** 83 **p** 86. C Kington w Huntington, Old Radnor, Kinnerton etc *Heref* 83-84; C Llanidloes w Llangurig *Ban* 86-90; V Llanwnnog and Caersws w Carno from 90. *The Vicarage, Llanwnnog, Caersws, Powys SY17 5JG* Caersws (0686) 688318

CHAPMAN, Edwin Thomas. b 32. Man Univ BA60. St Mich Coll Llan 62. **d** 63 **p** 64. C Cleveleys *Blackb* 63-65; C Ox St Mary V w St Cross and St Pet *Ox* 65-67; Chapl LMH Ox 67-68; Asst Dir of Educn *York* 68-75; R E Gilling 68-76; P-in-c Hockley *Chelmsf* 76-77; V 77-82; P-in-c Gosberton Clough and Quadring *Linc* 82-83; Chapl St Cath Sch Bramley 83-86; R Bulmer w Dalby, Terrington and Welburn *York* from 86; RD Bulmer and Malton from 91. *The Rectory, Terrington, York YO6 4PU* Coneysthorpe (065384) 226

CHAPMAN, Canon Eric Ronald. b 19. Man Univ BA41 BD59. Bps' Coll Cheshunt 41. **d** 43 **p** 44. RD Whitehaven *Carl* 66-70; R Egremont 66-81; Hon Can Carl Cathl 79-85; TR Egremont and Haile 81-85; rtd 85; Perm to Offic *Carl* from 86. *Bernaville, Highfield Road, Grange-over-Sands, Cumbria LA11 7JA*   Grange-over-Sands (05395) 34351

CHAPMAN, Miss Ethel Winifred. b 96. K Coll Lon LLA20. Lambeth STh28. **dss** 27 **d** 87. rtd 66; Hon Par Dn Newport w Widdington *Chelmsf* from 87. *St Mark's College, Audley End, Saffron Walden, Essex CB11 4JB* Saffron Walden (0799) 22006

CHAPMAN, Gorran. b 55. Dur Univ BA. Westcott Ho Cam 78. **d** 80 **p** 81. C Par *Truro* 80-82; C Kenwyn 82-84; P-in-c Penwerris 84-89; V from 89. *Penwerris Vicarage, 12 Stratton Terrace, Falmouth, Cornwall TR11 2SY* Falmouth (0326) 314263

CHAPMAN, Canon Guy Godfrey. b 33. Southn Univ BSc57. Clifton Th Coll 60. **d** 62 **p** 63. C Chadderton Ch Ch *Man* 62-67; V Edgeside 67-70; P-in-c Shipton Bellinger *Win* 70-72; V 72-83; RD Andover 75-85; Hon Can Win Cathl from 79; R Over Wallop w Nether Wallop from 83. *The Rectory, Over Wallop, Stockbridge, Hants SO20 8HT*   Andover (0264) 781345

CHAPMAN, Henry Davison. b 31. Bris Univ BA55. Tyndale Hall Bris 52. **d** 56 **p** 57. C St Helens St Mark *Liv* 56-60; R Clitheroe St Jas *Blackb* 60-67; V Tipton St Martin *Lich* 67-68; Area Sec (SW) CPAS 68-72; V Eccleston St Luke *Liv* 72-78; P-in-c Ringshall w Battisford, Barking w Darmsden etc *St E* 78-80; R 80; RD Bosmere from 87. *The Rectory, Barking, Ipswich IP6 8HJ*   Needham Market (0449) 720394

CHAPMAN, Mrs Janet Elizabeth. b 58. St Jo Coll Dur BSc80. Cranmer Hall Dur 84. **d** 87. Par Dn Darlington St Cuth *Dur* from 87. *15 Southend Avenue, Darlington, Co Durham DL3 7HL*   Darlington (0325) 486562

CHAPMAN, John. b 24. St Cuth Soc Dur BA51 St Chad's Coll Dur DipTh53. **d** 53 **p** 54. C Billingham St Cuth *Dur* 53-55; C Harton 55-57; V Hedgefield 57-63; V Annfield Plain 63-78; V Bolton All So w St Jas *Man* 78-85; V Baddesley Ensor w Grendon *Birm* from 85. *The Vicarage, Baddesley Ensor, Atherstone, Warks CV9 2BY* Atherstone (0827) 712149

CHAPMAN, Mary Elizabeth. NE Ord Course. **dss** 84 **d** 87. Newc St Gabr *Newc* 84-87; Hon C from 87. *9 Sefton Avenue, Newcastle upon Tyne NE6 5QR*   091-265 9931

CHAPMAN, Ven Michael Robin. b 39. Leeds Univ BA61. Coll of Resurr Mirfield 61. **d** 63 **p** 64. C Southwick St Columba *Dur* 63-68; Chapl RN 68-84; V Hale *Guildf* 84-91; RD Farnham 88-91; Adn Northn *Pet* from 91. *11 The Drive, Northampton NN1 4RZ*   Northampton (0604) 714015

CHAPMAN, Patricia Ann. b 42. **dss** 84 **d** 87. Rainworth *S'well* 84-87; Par Dn from 87. *8 Hartington Court, Oak Tree Lane Estate, Mansfield, Notts NG18 3QJ* Mansfield (0623) 645030

CHAPMAN, Canon Percy Frank. b 06. Bris Univ BSc27 MA31. **d** 36 **p** 37. V Aldbourne and Baydon *Sarum* 65-72; R Whitton 65-72; V Coombe Bissett w Homington 72-81; P-in-c Bishopstone w Stratford Tony 80-81; R Chalke Valley E 81-88; Can and Preb Sarum Cathl from

83; rtd 88. *College of St Barnabas, Blackberry Lane, Lingfield, Surrey RH7 6NJ* Dormans Park (034287) 762

CHAPMAN, Peter Harold White. b 40. AKC64. **d** 65 **p** 66. C Havant *Portsm* 65-69; C Stanmer w Falmer and Moulsecoomb *Chich* 69-73; Chapl RN 73-86; Chapl Chigwell Sch Essex 86-90; P-in-c Stapleford Tawney w Theydon Mt *Chelmsf* from 87. *The Rectory, Theydon Mount, Epping, Essex CM16 7PW* Epping (0378) 78723

CHAPMAN, Peter John. b 33. Dur Univ BA56. Cranmer Hall Dur DipTh59. **d** 59 **p** 60. C Boulton *Derby* 59-62; Uganda 63-70; P-in-c Southn St Matt *Win* 71-73; TV Southn (City Cen) 73-78; V Bilston St Leon *Lich* 78-79; P-in-c Bilston St Mary 78-79; TR Bilston from 80; RD Wolv from 89. *St Leonard's Vicarage, Dover Street, Bilston, W Midlands WV14 6AW* Bilston (0902) 491560

CHAPMAN, Raymond. b 24. FRSA90 Jes Coll Ox BA45 MA59 Lon Univ MA47 BD75 PhD78. S'wark Ord Course 72. **d** 74 **p** 75. NSM St-Mary-le-Strand w St Clem Danes *Lon* 74-82; NSM St Barnes St Mary *S'wark* from 82; Perm to Offic *Lon* from 82. *6 Kitson Road, London SW13 9HJ* 081-748 9901

CHAPMAN, Raymond. b 41. Linc Th Coll 68. **d** 71 **p** 72. C Dronfield *Derby* 71-74; C Delaval *Newc* 75-76; TV Whorlton 76-79; V Newc St Hilda 79-83; V Blyth St Cuth 83-89. *42 Drewbridge Road, Newsham Farm Estate, Blyth, Northd NE24*

CHAPMAN, Canon Rex Anthony. b 38. Univ Coll Lon BA62 St Edm Hall Ox BA64 MA68 Birm Univ DPS67. Wells Th Coll 64. **d** 65 **p** 66. C Stourbridge St Thos *Worc* 65-68; Chapl Aber Univ *Ab* 68-78; Can St Andr Cathl 76-78; Bp's Adv for Educn *Carl* 78-85; Can Res Carl Cathl from 78; Dir of Educn from 85. *1 The Abbey, Carlisle CA3 8TZ* Carlisle (0228) 21614 or 38086

CHAPMAN, Rodney Andrew. b 53. AKC75. St Aug Coll Cant 75. **d** 76 **p** 77. C Hartlepool St Aid *Dur* 76-81; Lic to Offic 81-83; AP Owton Manor from 83; P-in-c Kelloe from 87. *The Vicarage, Glengarth, Front Street, Kelloe, Co Durham DH6 4PG* 091-377 1053

CHAPMAN, Roger John. b 34. AKC58. **d** 59 **p** 60. C Guildf Ch Ch *Guildf* 59-61; Kenya 61-67; R S Milford *York* 68-77; RD Selby 72-77; V Beverley St Mary 77-88; RD Beverley 85-88; V Desborough *Pet* from 88; R Brampton Ash w Dingley and Braybrooke from 88. *St Giles' Vicarage, Desborough, Kettering, Northants NN14 2NP* Kettering (0536) 760324

CHAPMAN, Mrs Sally Anne. b 55. Lanchester Poly BSc76 Univ of Wales (Swansea) PGCE77. W Midl Minl Tr Course 87. **d** 90. Par Dn Stoneydelph St Martin CD *Lich* 90; Par Dn Glascote and Stonydelph from 90. *78 Linty, Tamworth, Staffs B77 4LN* Tamworth (0827) 896363

CHAPMAN, Mrs Sarah Jean. b 55. **d** 89. NSM Rogate w Terwick and Trotton w Chithurst *Chich* from 89. *Church House, Rogate, Petersfield, Hants GU31 5EA* Rogate (0730) 80784

CHAPMAN, Sydney William. b 12. Didsbury Meth Coll 32 Sarum Th Coll 55. **d** 56 **p** 57. In Meth Ch 32-55; V Walberton w Binsted *Chich* 60-81; rtd 81; Perm to Offic *Win* from 82. *16 Walberton Park, Walberton, Arundel, W Sussex BN18 0PJ* Bognor Regis (0243) 551777

CHAPMAN, Thomas Graham. b 33. Trin Coll Bris 73. **d** 75 **p** 76. C Branksome St Clem *Sarum* 75-81; V Quarry Bank *Lich* from 81. *The Vicarage, Maughan Street, Brierley Hill, W Midlands DY5 2DN* Cradley Heath (0384) 65480

CHAPMAN, William Henry Stanley (Peter). b 08. OBE58. St Chad's Coll Dur BA31. **d** 32 **p** 33. V W Dean *Chich* 63-73; rtd 73; Perm to Offic *Chich* from 73. *Moons, Green Lane, Crowborough, E Sussex TN6 2DE* Crowborough (0892) 61568

CHAPMAN, William Howard Dale. b 11. Edin Th Coll 33. **d** 38 **p** 39. R Brookthorpe w Whaddon and Harescombe *Glouc* 71-76; rtd 76; Perm to Offic *Glouc* from 85. *35A Winchester Road, Chandlers Ford, Eastleigh, Hants SO5 2GF* Chandler's Ford (0703) 268907

CHAPPELL, Allan. b 27. Selw Coll Cam BA51 MA56. Coll of Resurr Mirfield 51. **d** 53 **p** 54. C Knowle *Bris* 53-57; Zanzibar 57-63; C Long Eaton St Laur *Derby* 64-67; C-in-c Broxtowe CD *S'well* 67-73; P-in-c Flintham 73-82; R Car Colston w Screveton 73-82; V Mansf St Lawr from 82. *St Lawrence's Vicarage, 3 Shaw Street, Mansfield, Notts NG18 2NP* Mansfield (0623) 23698

CHAPPELL, Edward Michael. b 32. Glouc Sch of Min 84. **d** 87 **p** 88. NSM Wotton-under-Edge w Ozleworth and N Nibley *Glouc* from 87. *20 Old Town, Wotton-under-Edge, Glos GL12 7DH* Dursley (0453) 844250

CHAPPELL, Eric Richardson. b 08. Keble Coll Ox BA30 MA34. Cuddesdon Coll 30. **d** 31 **p** 32. V Goodnestone H Cross w Chillenden and Knowlton *Cant*

64-78; P-in-c Adisham 75-78; rtd 78; Perm to Offic *Cant* from 78. *33 Sandgate Hill, Folkestone, Kent CT20 3AX* Folkestone (0303) 48141

CHAPPELL, Frank Arnold. b 37. Dur Univ BA58. Bps' Coll Cheshunt. **d** 60 **p** 61. C Headingley *Ripon* 60-65; V Beeston Hill St Luke 65-73; R Garforth from 73. *The Rectory, Garforth, Leeds LS25 1NR* Leeds (0532) 863737

CHAPPELL, Preb George Thomas. b 04. St Jo Coll Dur LTh28 BA29 MA32. Lon Coll of Div 24. **d** 28 **p** 29. V Paddington St Jas *Lon* 43-71; Preb St Paul's Cathl 63-71; rtd 71; C S Kensington H Trin w All SS *Lon* 71-74; P-in-c 74-75; Perm to Offic from 75. *Flat 3, 19 Burton Road, Poole, Dorset BH13 6DT* Poole (0202) 764665

CHAPPELL, Henry Pegg. b 09. DSC42. St Cath Coll Cam BA31 MA35. Wells Th Coll 33. **d** 34 **p** 35. P-in-c How Caple w Sollers Hope *Heref* 71-76; rtd 76; Perm to Offic *Heref* from 76. *Walcote House, West Street, Pembridge, Leominster, Herefordshire* Pembridge (05447) 559

CHAPPELL, Michael Paul. b 35. Selw Coll Cam BA57 MA61 ACertCM65. Cuddesdon Coll 60. **d** 62 **p** 63. C Pershore w Pinvin, Wick and Birlingham *Worc* 62-65; Malaysia 65-67; VC and Chapl Heref Cathl *Heref* 67-71; Min Can Dur Cathl *Dur* 71-76; Prec 72-76; Chapl H Trin Sch Stockton 76-87; C-in-c Stockton Green Vale H Trin CD *Dur* 82-87; V Scarborough St Luke *York* from 87; Chapl Scarborough Gen Hosp from 87. *The Vicarage, 37 Woodland Ravine, Scarborough, N Yorkshire YO12 6TA* Scarborough (0723) 372831

CHARD, Canon Francis Eric. b 24. Dur Univ BA53 MLitt81. St Jo Coll Dur DipTh55. **d** 55 **p** 56. C Cleveleys *Blackb* 55-57; C Preston St Jo 57-60; V Ewood 60-72; V Downham 72-88; RD Whalley 83-89; Hon Can Blackb Cathl from 86; Co Ecum Officer from 88. *21 Moorland Crescent, Clitheroe, Lancs BB7 4PY* Clitheroe (0200) 27480

CHARD, Reginald Jeffrey. b 40. Univ of Wales (Lamp) BA62 Birm Poly CQSW75. Coll of Resurr Mirfield 62. **d** 64 **p** 65. C Ystrad Mynach *Llan* 64-67; C Aberdare St Fagan 67-71; V Hirwaun 71-74; Hon C Stechford *Birm* 74-78; TV Banbury *Ox* 78-86; Ind Chapl from 86; P-in-c Claydon w Mollington from 86. *18 Bignold's Close, Claydon, Banbury, Oxon OX17 1ER* Farnborough (029589) 315

CHARE, Frederic Keith. b 16. Hatf Coll Dur LTh38 BA39. Edin Th Coll 35. **d** 39 **p** 40. V Barming Heath *Cant* 69-73; V Upchurch 74-75; V Upchurch w Lower Halstow 75-82; rtd 82; Perm to Offic *Cant* from 82. *71 Douglas Road, Maidstone, Kent ME16 8ER* Maidstone (0622) 761370

CHARING CROSS, Archdeacon of. *See* KLYBERG, Rt Rev Charles John

CHARKHAM, Rupert Anthony. b 59. Ex Univ BA81. Wycliffe Hall Ox 83. **d** 89 **p** 89. C Ox St Aldate w St Matt *Ox* from 89. *100A Divinity Road, Oxford OX4 1LN* Oxford (0865) 250786

CHARLES, Canon Hubert Edward Richard. b 09. Trin Coll Cam BA31 MA35. Westcott Ho Cam 33. **d** 35 **p** 36. R Dunstable *St Alb* 66-73; P-in-c Lidlington 73-77; rtd 77; Perm to Offic *St Alb* from 77; Vice Pres Chr Peace Conf from 83; Chr Socialist Movement from 85. *46 St Albans Road, Codicote, Hitchin, Herts SG4 8UT* Stevenage (0438) 820024

CHARLES, Jack William. b 16. Bps' Coll Cheshunt 50. **d** 53 **p** 54. C Kensington St Jas Norlands *Lon* 59-76; rtd 76; Hon C Chiswick St Nic w St Mary *Lon* from 76. *37 Brackley Road, London W4 2HW* 081-995 9580

CHARLES, John Hugo Audley. b 04. Worc Coll Ox BA25 MA46. Cuddesdon Coll 27. **d** 29 **p** 30. V Lyme Regis *Sarum* 62-74; rtd 74. *Badgeworth Court, Axbridge, Somerset BS18 7QD* Axbridge (0934) 732843

CHARLES, Canon Jonathan. b 42. Ripon Coll Cuddesdon 78. **d** 79 **p** 80. C Leagrave *St Alb* 79-82; Chapl Denstone Coll Uttoxeter 82-86; Chapl Malvern Girls' Coll Worcs from 86; K Sch Worc from 89; Min Can Worc Cathl *Worc* from 89. *12A College Green, Worcester WR1 2LH*

CHARLES, Martin. b 40. **d** 90 **p** 91. C Market Harborough *Leic* 90-91; P-in-c Higham-on-the-Hill w Fenny Drayton and Witherley from 91. *The Rectory, Old Forge Road, Fenny Drayton, Nuneaton, Warks CV13 6BD* Atherstone (0827) 714638

CHARLES, Meedperdas Edward. b 28. Fitzw Ho Cam BA60 MA64. Bangalore Th Coll BD54. **d** 54 **p** 55. V Gravelly Hill *Birm* 66-78; V Endcliffe *Sheff* 79-90; rtd 91. *60 Ringinglow Road, Ecclesall, Sheffield* Sheffield (0742) 664980

CHARLES, Robert Sidney James. b 40. Lon Univ CertEd77 Open Univ BA79. St Mich Coll Llan DipTh65. **d** 65 **p** 66. C Merthyr Tydfil *Llan* 65-68; C Shotton *St As*

68-70; R Stock and Lydlinch *Sarum* 70-74; R Hubberston *St D* 74-76; Perm to Offic *Chelmsf* 81-83; V Crossens *Liv* from 83. *The Vicarage, Rufford Road, Southport, Merseyside PR9 8JH*   Southport (0704) 27662

CHARLES, Robin. b 50. N Staffs Poly HND72. Sarum & Wells Th Coll. **d** 86 **p** 87. C Chesterton *Lich* 86-89; C Rugeley 89-90; TV from 90. *The Vicarage, 14 Peakes Road, Etching Hill, Rugeley, Staffs WS15 2LY*   Rugeley (0889) 582809

CHARLES, Theodore Arthur Barker. b 24. K Coll Cam BA45 MA48. Lon Univ DipRS71. S'wark Ord Course 68. **d** 71 **p** 72. C Cuckfield *Chich* 71-77; V Rudgwick 77-89; rtd 89: Perm to Offic *Ox* from 89. *1 Herringcote, Dorchester-on-Thames, Wallingford, Oxon OX10 7RD*   Oxford (0865) 341321

CHARLESWORTH, Eric Charlesworth. b 29. Kelham Th Coll 49. **d** 54 **p** 56. C Woodbridge St Mary *St E* 54-57; Asst Chapl Oslo St Edm *Eur* 57-59; Canada 60-66; R Huntingfield w Cookley *St E* 66-70; R Slimbridge *Glouc* from 70. *The Rectory, Slimbridge, Gloucester GL2 7BJ*   Cambridge (0453) 890233

CHARLESWORTH, Gerald Edward. b 16. K Coll Lon 37. **d** 41 **p** 42. C Newfoundpool *Leic* 41-44; CF (EC) 44-46; Stepney St Dunstan and All SS *Lon* 47; Malaya 48-49; R Croft *Ripon* 49-58; V Liverton *York* 58-62; S Africa from 66. *43 Tennant Street, Barrydale, 6750 South Africa*

CHARLEY, Julian Whittard. b 30. New Coll Ox BA55 MA58. Ridley Hall Cam 55. **d** 57 **p** 58. C St Marylebone All So w SS Pet and Jo *Lon* 57-64; Lect Lon Coll of Div 64-70; Vice-Prin St Jo Coll Nottm 70-74; Warden Shrewsbury Ho 74-87; TR Everton St Pet *Liv* 74-87; P-in-c Gt Malvern St Mary *Worc* from 87. *Priory Vicarage, Clarence Road, Malvern, Worcs WR14 3EN*   Malvern (0684) 563707

CHARLTON, Canon Arthur David. b 23. Open Univ BA73 BPhil83. Chich Th Coll. **d** 66 **p** 67. C Rotherfield *Chich* 66-70; C Uckfield 70-72; C Isfield 70-72; C Lt Horsted 70-72; R Cocking w Bepton 72-79; P-in-c W Lavington 78-79; R Cocking, Bepton and W Lavington 79-90; Can and Preb Chich Cathl 88-90; rtd 90. *33 High Cross Field, Crowborough, E Sussex TN6 2SN*   Crowborough (0892) 661351

CHARLTON, Colin. b 32. Em Coll Cam BA56 MA60. Oak Hill Th Coll 56. **d** 58 **p** 59. C Gateshead St Geo *Dur* 58-59; C Houghton le Spring 59-62; V Newbottle 62-66; Area Sec (Dios Chelmsf and St Alb) CMS 66-72; P-in-c Becontree St Eliz *Chelmsf* 72-78; P-in-c Bentley Common from 78. *The Vicarage, 6 Applegate, Pilgrims Hatch, Brentwood, Essex CM14 5PL*   Coxtie Green (0277) 372200

CHARLTON, William. b 48. Coll of Ripon & York St Jo CertEd. Chich Th Coll 76. **d** 79 **p** 80. C Sheff Parson Cross St Cecilia *Sheff* 79-80; C Cantley 80; C Doncaster Ch Ch 80-82; V Thurcroft 82-87; V Kingston upon Hull St Alb *York* from 87. *St Alban's Vicarage, 62 Hall Road, Hull HU6 8SA*   Hull (0482) 446639

CHARMAN, Arthur Ernest. b 09. Bible Churchmen's Coll. **d** 37 **p** 38. V Litherland St Jo and St Jas *Liv* 57-73; rtd 73. *29 Hawksworth Close, Grovelands, Wantage, Oxon OX12 0NU*   Wantage (02357) 3785

CHARMAN, Jane Ellen Elizabeth. b 60. St Jo Coll Dur BA81 Selw Coll Cam BA84 MA88. Westcott Ho Cam 82. **d** 87. Glouc St Geo w Whaddon *Glouc* 85-87; C 87-90; Chapl and Fell Clare Coll Cam from 90. *69 Alpha Road, Cambridge CB4 3DQ*   Cambridge (0223) 66266 or 333229

CHARNLEY, John Trevor. b 12. Ex Coll Ox BA36 MA39. Wells Th Coll 36. **d** 37 **p** 38. V Ashburton w Buckland-in-the-Moor *Ex* 63-84; V Bickington 63-84; rtd 84. *24 Devon House, Bovey Tracey, Newton Abbot, Devon TQ13 9HB*   Bovey Tracey (0626) 833824

CHARNOCK, Deryck Ian. b 47. Oak Hill Th Coll 78. **d** 80 **p** 81. C Rowner *Portsm* 80-84; TV Southgate *Chich* 84-90; V Penge St Paul *Roch* from 90. *St Paul's Vicarage, Hamlet Road, Upper Norwood, London SE19 2AW*   081-653 0978

CHARNOCK, Ernest Burrell. b 14. ACIS42 AACCA50 Lon Univ DipTh60. **d** 61 **p** 62. V Buglawton *Ches* 64-70; R Tattenhall 70-77; P-in-c Handley 72-77; R Tattenhall and Handley 77-80; rtd 80; Perm to Offic Ches from 85; Glouc from 87. *26 Pegasus Court, St Stephen's Road, Cheltenham, Glos GL51 5AB*   Cheltenham (0242) 578651

CHARRETT, Geoffrey Barton. b 36. ALCM Nottm Univ BSc57. Ridley Hall Cam 65. **d** 67 **p** 68. C Clifton *York* 67-68; Lic to Offic *Blackb* 69-80; C Walthamstow St Mary w St Steph *Chelmsf* 81-82; TV 82-87; Chapl Gordon's Sch Woking from 87. *Gordon's School, West*

End, Woking, Surrey GU24 9PT   Chobham (0276) 857585

CHARRINGTON, Nicholas John. b 36. MA. Cuddesdon Coll 60. **d** 62 **p** 63. C Shrewsbury St Chad *Lich* 62-65; C Gt Grimsby St Mary and St Jas *Linc* 65-72; P-in-c Wellington Ch Ch *Lich* 72-78; R Edgmond 78-89; R Edgmond w Kynnersley and Preston Wealdmoors 89-91; C Plymstock *Ex* from 91; Chapl St Luke's Hospice Plymouth from 91. *5 Campbell Road, Plymstock, Plymouth, Devon PL9 8UF*   Plymouth (0752) 481061

CHARTERS, Alan Charles. b 35. Trin Hall Cam BA60 MA63. Linc Th Coll 60. **d** 62 **p** 63. C Gt Grimsby St Mary and St Jas *Linc* 62-65; Chapl Eliz Coll Guernsey 65-70; Dep Hd Master Park Sch Swindon 70-74; Chapl St Jo Sch Leatherhead 74-77; Dep Hd Master 77-83; Master K Sch Glouc from 83. *King's School House, Gloucester GL1 2LR*   Gloucester (0452) 21251

CHARTERS, John Nicholson. b 27. Trin Hall Cam BA51 MA55. Westcott Ho Cam 51. **d** 53 **p** 54. C Selby Abbey *York* 53-55; C Hornsea and Goxhill 55-57; C Milton *Portsm* 57-60; Chapl RN 60-64; R Thorndon w Rishangles *St E* 64-68; Hon C Beeford w Lissett *York* 68-77; Hon C Beeford w Frodingham and Foston 77-89; R from 90. *The Rectory, 2 Alton Road, Beeford, Driffield, N Humberside YO25 8BZ*   Beeford (026288) 485

CHARTRES, Richard John Carew. b 47. Trin Coll Cam BA68 MA73 BD83. Cuddesdon Coll 69 Linc Th Coll 72. **d** 73 **p** 74. C Bedf St Andr *St Alb* 73-75; Bp's Dom Chapl 75-80; Abp's Chapl *Cant* 80-84; P-in-c Westmr St Steph w St Jo *Lon* 84-85; V from 86; Dir of Ords from 85; Prof Div Gresham Coll from 86; Six Preacher Cant Cathl *Cant* from 91. *The Vicarage, 21 Vincent Square, London SW1P 2NA*   071-834 0950

CHASE, Canon Frank Selby Mason. b 15. Univ Coll Dur BSc37 DipTh39. St Aug Coll Cant 39. **d** 39 **p** 40. V S Westoe *Dur* 60-78; Hon Can Dur Cathl from 71; RD Jarrow 75-77; V Lanchester 78-82; rtd 82. *21 Broadoak Drive, Lanchester, Durham DH7 0PN*   Lanchester (0207) 520393

CHASE, Lt-Col Frederick Jack. b 14. Westcott Ho Cam 61. **d** 62 **p** 63. Rhodesia 69-70; V St Columb Minor *Truro* 71-73; V St Columb Minor and St Colan 73-76; P-in-c Arreton *Portsm* 76-82; rtd 82; Perm to Offic *Cant* from 82. *60 Stade Street, Hythe, Kent CT21 6BD*   Hythe (0303) 265663

CHASE, Geoffrey Hugh. b 25. Tyndale Hall Bris 48. **d** 51 **p** 52. Chapl Deva Hosp Cheshire 62-70; W Cheshire Hosp Ches 71-84; Countess of Ches Hosp 84-90; rtd 90. *78 Liverpool Road, Chester CH2 1AU*   Chester (0244) 382910

CHATER, Very Rev John Leathley. b 29. Qu Coll Cam BA54 MA58. Ridley Hall Cam 54. **d** 56 **p** 57. C Bath Abbey w St Jas *B & W* 56-60; V Bermondsey St Anne S'wark 60-64; Ind Chapl 60-64; V Heslington *York* 64-69; Chapl York Univ 64-69; V Lawrence Weston *Bris* 69-73; Perm to Offic 74-80; P-in-c Wraxall *B & W* 80-82; R 82-84; V Battle *Chich* 84-90; Dean Battle 84-90; RD Battle and Bexhill 86-90; R St Marylebone w H Trin *Lon* from 90. *21 Beaumont Street, London W1N 1FF*   071-935 8965

CHATFIELD, Adrian Francis. b 49. Leeds Univ BA71 MA72 MPhil89. Coll of Resurr Mirfield 71. **d** 72 **p** 73. Trinidad and Tobago 72-83; TV Barnstaple, Goodleigh and Landkey *Ex* 83-84; TV Barnstaple 85; TR 85-88; Lect St Jo Coll Nottm from 88. *5 Peatfield Road, Stapleford, Nottingham NG9 8GN*   Nottingham (0602) 391287

CHATFIELD, Preb Frederick Roy. b 06. **d** 32 **p** 33. V Cockington *Ex* 47-72; Preb Ex Cathl 71-82; rtd 72. *Warberry Cottage, Lower Warberry Road, Torquay TQ1 1QP*   Torquay (0803) 296033

CHATFIELD, Canon Norman. b 37. Fitzw Ho Cam BA59 MA68. Ripon Hall Ox 60. **d** 62 **p** 63. C Burgess Hill St Jo *Chich* 62-65; C Uckfield 65-69; V Lower Sandown St Jo *Portsm* 69-76; V Locks Heath 76-83; Bp's Chapl for Post Ord Tr 78-85; R Alverstoke from 83; Chapl HM Pris Haslar 83-90; Chapl Gosport War Memorial Hosp from 83; Hon Can Portsm Cathl *Portsm* from 85. *The Rectory, Little Anglesey Road, Alverstoke, Gosport, Hants PO12 2JA*   Gosport (0705) 81979

CHATFIELD, Roderick Money. b 18. Bps' Coll Cheshunt 40. **d** 44 **p** 45. R Ashreigney *Ex* 63-72; V Burrington 63-72; R Ilchester w Northover, Limington, Yeovilton etc *B & W* 72-76; C Yarlington 76-79; C Camelot Par 78-79; R Stonton Wyville w Glooston, Slawston and Cranoe *Leic* 79-83; rtd 83; Perm to Offic *Ex* from 83. *19 Atherton Way, Tiverton, Devon EX16 4EW*   Tiverton (0884) 253642

CHATFIELD, Thomas William. b 19. Lon Univ. Chich Th Coll 44. **d** 46 **p** 47. P-in-c Hastings St Mary Magd *Chich* 68-71; R 71-78; P-in-c Bishopstone 78-84; rtd 84; Perm to Offic *Chich* from 84. *5 Leeds Close, Victoria Avenue, Ore Village, Hastings, E Sussex TN35 5BX* Hastings (0424) 437413

CHATFIELD-JUDE, Canon Henry. b 09. OBE76. AKC32. **d** 32 **p** 33. Chapl Lisbon *Eur* 66-76; rtd 76; Perm to Offic *Win* from 76. *8 Lansdowne Court, Winchester, Hants SO23 9TJ* Winchester (0962) 863249

CHATHAM, Richard Henry. b 28. Launde Abbey 71. **d** 71 **p** 72. C Aylestone *Leic* 71-76; R Hoby cum Rotherby 76-77; P-in-c Brooksby 76-77; R Hoby cum Rotherby w Brooksby, Ragdale & Thru'ton 77-85; R Overstrand *Nor* from 85. *The Rectory, Harbord Road, Overstrand, Cromer, Norfolk NR27 0PN* Overstrand (026378) 350

CHATTERJI DE MASSEY, Robert Arthur Sovan Lal. b 15. Chich Th Coll 54. **d** 56 **p** 57. R Abberton w Langenhoe *Chelmsf* 60-90; rtd 90. *Clare House, 82 Main Street, Witchford, Ely, Cambs CB6 2HQ*

CHATWIN, Barbara. b 07. MCSP33. Selly Oak Coll 62. **dss** 65 **d** 87. Birm St Dav *Birm* 63-67; Londonderry 67-69; Pershore w Pinvin, Wick and Birlingham *Worc* 69-87; Hon C from 87. *Myrtle Cottage, Broad Street, Pershore, Worcs WR10 1BB* Pershore (0386) 552080

CHATWIN, Ronald Ernest. b 34. St Aid Birkenhead 58. **d** 60 **p** 61. C Selsdon St Jo *Cant* 60-64; C Crawley *Chich* 64-68; V Coldwaltham 68-74; TV Ovingdean w Rottingdean and Woodingdean 74-83; V Saltdean from 83. *St Nicholas' Vicarage, Saltdean, Brighton BN2 8HE* Brighton (0273) 32345

CHAVE, Brian Philip. b 51. Open Univ BA. Trin Coll Bris. **d** 84 **p** 85. C Cullompton *Ex* 84-87; TV Bishopsnympton, Rose Ash, Mariansleigh etc from 87. *The Vicarage, Molland, South Molton, Devon EX36 3NG* Bishops Nympton (07697) 551

CHAVE-COX, Guy. b 56. St Andr Univ BSc79. Wycliffe Hall Ox 83. **d** 86 **p** 87. C Wigmore Abbey *Heref* 86-88; C Bideford *Ex* 88-91; TV Barnstaple from 91. *St Paul's Vicarage, Old Sticklepath Hill, Barnstaple, Devon EX31 2BG* Barnstaple (0271) 44400

CHEADLE, Preb Robert. b 24. MBE71 TD66. Leeds Univ BA49. Coll of Resurr Mirfield 49. **d** 51 **p** 52. V Bloxwich *Lich* 60-72; V Penkridge w Stretton 72-89; Preb Lich Cathl 79-89; P-in-c Dunston w Coppenhall 79-82; V 82-89; P-in-c Acton Trussell w Bednall 80-82; V 82-89; rtd 89. *26 Audley Place, Newcastle, Staffs ST5 3RS* Newcastle-under-Lyme (0782) 618685

CHEAL, Kenneth Herbert. b 12. Sarum Th Coll 46. **d** 48 **p** 49. R Rodborough *Glouc* 61-77; rtd 78; Perm to Offic Glouc from 78; Bris from 79. *6 The Ferns, Tetbury, Glos GL8 8JE* Tetbury (0666) 503100

CHEALL, Henry Frederick Knowles. b 34. Ex Coll Ox BA56 MA60. Ripon Hall Ox 58. **d** 60 **p** 61. C Sutton *Liv* 60-63; C Blundellsands St Mich 63-66; Nigeria 66-68; R Crumpsall St Matt *Man* 68-76; R Crumpsall 76-84; V Chipping and Whitewell *Blackb* from 84. *The Vicarage, Chipping, Preston PR3 2QH* Chipping (0995) 61252

CHEATLE, Adele Patricia. b 46. York Univ BA73. Trin Coll Bris 76. **d** 87. Par Dn Harborne Heath *Birm* 87. *27 Carrisbrooke Road, Birmingham B17 8NN* 021-420 2742

CHEEK, Richard Alexander. b 35. Lon Univ LDS60. Ox NSM Course 72. **d** 75 **p** 76. NSM Maidenhead St Luke *Ox* from 75. *Windrush, Sheephouse Road, Maidenhead, Berks SL6 8EX* Maidenhead (0628) 28484

CHEESEMAN, Colin Henry. b 47. Reading Univ BA. Sarum & Wells Th Coll 82. **d** 84 **p** 85. C Cranleigh *Guildf* 84-87; C Godalming 87-89; V Cuddington from 89. *The Vicarage, St Mary's Road, Worcester Park, Surrey KT4 7JL* 081-337 4026

CHEESEMAN, John Anthony. b 50. Or Coll Ox BA73 MA75. Trin Coll Bris DipTh76. **d** 76 **p** 77. C Sevenoaks St Nic *Roch* 76-79; C Egham *Guildf* 79-82; V Leyton St Mary Ch Ch *Chelmsf* 82-90; V Westgate St Jas *Cant* from 90. *St James's Vicarage, Orchard Gardens, Westgate-on-Sea, Kent CT9 5JT*

CHEESEMAN, Kenneth Raymond. b 29. Roch Th Coll 63. **d** 66 **p** 67. C Crayford *Roch* 66-69; C Beckenham St Jas 69-75; V Belvedere St Aug 75-83; V Thorley *Portsm* from 83; R Yarmouth from 83. *The Rectory, Yarmouth, Isle of Wight PO41 0NU* Isle of Wight (0983) 760247

CHEESMAN, Ashley Frederick Bruce. b 53. Oak Hill Th Coll. **d** 83 **p** 84. C Tranmere St Cath *Ches* 83-88; R Gaulby *Leic* from 88. *The Rectory, Gaulby, Leicester LE7 9BB* Billesdon (053755) 228

CHEESMAN, Peter. b 43. ACA65 FCA76 MBIM. Ridley Hall Cam 66. **d** 69 **p** 70. C Herne Bay Ch Ch *Cant* 69-74; TV Lowestoft St Marg *Nor* 75-78; TV Lowestoft and

Kirkley 79-81; Ind Chapl *Glouc* 81-84; P-in-c Saul w Fretherne and Framilode 84-85; V Frampton on Severn, Arlingham, Saul etc from 85. *The Vicarage, Frampton on Severn, Gloucester GL2 7ED* Gloucester (0452) 740966

CHEETHAM, Eric. b 34. Trin Hall Cam BA57 MA61. Coll of Resurr Mirfield 57. **d** 59 **p** 60. C S Kirkby *Wakef* 59-62; C-in-c Mixenden CD 62-65; Bahamas 65-69; V Grimethorpe *Wakef* 69-81; V Featherstone 81-90; V Leeds Belle Is St Jo and St Barn *Ripon* from 90. *The Vicarage, Low Grange View, Leeds LS10 3DT* Leeds (0532) 717821

CHEETHAM, Gilbert Stanley. b 14. Bps' Coll Cheshunt 49. **d** 52 **p** 53. V Basford St Leodegarius *S'well* 64-77; V Clipstone 77-82; rtd 82; Perm to Offic *S'well* from 82. *6 St Peter's Court, 398 Woodborough Road, Nottingham* Nottingham (0602) 608794

CHEETHAM, Richard Ian. b 55. CCC Ox BA77 CertEd78 MA82. Ripon Coll Cuddesdon 85. **d** 87 **p** 88. C Newc H Cross *Newc* 87-90; V Luton St Aug Limbury *St Alb* from 90. *The Vicarage, 215 Icknield Way, Luton LU3 2JR* Luton (0582) 572415

CHEEVERS, George Alexander. b 42. CITC 70. **d** 73 **p** 74. C Carrickfergus *Conn* 73-81; C Kilroot 78-81; I Kilmakee 82-91; I Magheragall from 91. *Magheragall Rectory, 70 Ballinderry Road, Lisburn, Co Antrim BT28 2QS* Maze (0846) 621273

CHELMSFORD, Bishop of. See WAINE, Rt Rev John

CHELMSFORD, Provost of. See MOSES, Very Rev Dr John Henry

CHELTENHAM, Archdeacon of. See LEWIS, Ven John Arthur

CHELTON, James Howard. b 35. Oak Hill Th Coll. **d** 67 **p** 68. C Pitsea *Chelmsf* 67-71; P-in-c Nevendon 71-74; P-in-c Harwich 74-80; Ind Chapl 74-80; Miss to Seamen from 80; Tanzania 80-81; Nigeria from 81. *c/o St Michael Paternoster Royal, College Hill, London EC4R 2RL* 071-248 5202 or 248 7442

CHENNELL, Capt Arthur John. b 28. St Deiniol's Hawarden 77. **d** 77 **p** 78. CA from 58; C Prenton *Ches* 77-79; V Liscard St Thos 79-82; V Lt Thornton *Blackb* from 82. *St John's Vicarage, 35 Station Road, Thornton Cleveleys, Blackpool FY5 5HY* Cleveleys (0253) 825107

CHERRILL, John Oliver. b 33. Bath Univ MArch75 DipArch61. Sarum & Wells Th Coll 76. **d** 79 **p** 80. NSM Blackmoor *Portsm* 79-83; NSM Headley All SS *Guildf* 83-85; C 86-90. *7 Oaktree Road, Whitehill, Bordon, Hants GU35 9DF* Bordon (0420) 473193

CHERRIMAN, Colin Wilfred (Brother Colin Wilfred). b 37. Leeds Univ BA63. Coll of Resurr Mirfield 63. **d** 65 **p** 66. C Bournemouth St Fran *Win* 65-69; SSF from 69; Lic to Offic Chelmsf 73-75; Cant 75-77; Edin 77-79; Sarum 79-82, Newc 82-88; Perm to Offic *Lon* from 88; Adv HIV/AIDS Unit from 91. *HIV/AIDS Unit, St Paul's, Lorrimore Square, London SE17 3QU* 071-793 0338

CHERRY, David. b 30. Roch Th Coll 59. **d** 61 **p** 62. R Bamford *Derby* 67-75; Chapl Malaga w Almunecar and Nerja *Eur* 83-91; rtd 91. *La Huerta del Molino, La Molinetta, Frigiliana, Malaga, Spain* Malaga (52) 533084

CHERRY, Malcolm Stephen. b 28. Open Univ BA81. Sarum Th Coll 51. **d** 54 **p** 55. C Mill Hill Jo Keble Ch *Lon* 54-57; C Hendon All SS Childs Hill 57-59; V Colchester St Anne *Chelmsf* 59-68; V Horndon on the Hill 68-79; Ind Chapl 69-79; Voc Officer Southend Adnry 74-79; R Lochgilphead *Arg* 79-82; V Mill End and Heronsgate w W Hyde *St Alb* 82-90; TV Chipping Barnet w Arkley from 90. *3 Raebarn Gardens, Arkley, Barnet, Herts EN5 3DB* 081-440 2046

CHERRY, Stephen Arthur. b 58. St Chad's Coll Dur BSc79 Fitzw Coll Cam BA85. Westcott Ho Cam 84. **d** 86 **p** 87. C Baguley *Man* 86-89; Chapl K Coll Cam from 89. *King's College, Cambridge* Cambridge (0223) 350411

CHESHAM, William Gerald. b 23. MIMechE55 Birm Univ DPS66. Wells Th Coll 61. **d** 63 **p** 64. V Smethwick *Birm* 68-72; Lic to Offic *Heref* 72-78; TV Glendale Gp *Newc* 78-84; rtd 84; Asst Chapl Algarve *Eur* from 84. *Casita de Paz, Pedreiras, 8375 Sao Bartolomeu de Messines, Algarve, Portugal* Portimao (82) 50659

CHESSUN, Christopher Thomas James. b 56. Univ Coll Ox BA78 MA82 Trin Hall Cam BA82. Westcott Ho Cam. **d** 83 **p** 84. C Sandhurst *Ox* 83-87; C Portsea St Mary *Portsm* 87-89; Min Can and Chapl St Paul's Cathl *Lon* from 89; Voc Adv from 90. *7B Amen Court, London EC4M 7BU* 071-248 6151

CHESTER, Mark. b 55. Lanc Univ BA79. Wycliffe Hall Ox 86. **d** 88 **p** 89. C Plymouth St Andr w St Paul and St

Geo *Ex* from 88. *117 Lipson Road, Plymouth, Devon PL4 7NQ* Plymouth (0752) 661334

CHESTER, Philip Anthony Edwin. b 55. Birm Univ LLB76. St Jo Coll Dur 77. **d** 80 **p** 81. C Shrewsbury St Chad *Lich* 80-85; C St Martin-in-the-Fields *Lon* 85-88; Chapl K Coll Lon from 88; PV Westmr Abbey from 90. *King's College, Strand, London WC2R 2LS* 071-873 2373

CHESTER, Archdeacon of. See GEAR, Ven Michael Frederick

CHESTER, Bishop of. See BAUGHEN, Rt Rev Michael Alfred

CHESTER, Dean of. See SMALLEY, Very Rev Stephen Stewart

CHESTERFIELD, Archdeacon of. See PHIZACKERLEY, Ven Gerald Robert

CHESTERMAN, Canon Dr George Anthony. b 38. Man Univ BSc62 DipAdEd Nottm Univ PhD89. Coll of Resurr Mirfield 62. **d** 64 **p** 65. C Newbold and Dunston *Derby* 64-68; C Derby St Thos 68-70; Adult Educn Officer 70-79; R Mugginton and Kedleston 70-89; Vice-Prin E Midl Min Tr Course from 79; Can Res Derby Cathl *Derby* from 89; Dioc Clergy In-Service Tr Adv from 89. *13 Newbridge Road, Ambergate, Derby DE5 2GR* Ambergate (0773) 852236

CHESTERMAN, Lawrence James. b 16. K Coll Lon 48 St Boniface Warminster. **d** 49 **p** 50. V Idmiston *Sarum* 69-73; TR Bourne Valley 73-81; rtd 81; Perm to Offic *Sarum* from 81. *2 Beacon Close, Amesbury, Salisbury SP4 7EG* Amesbury (0980) 622205

✠**CHESTERS, Rt Rev Alan David.** b 37. St Chad's Coll Dur BA59 St Cath Soc Ox BA61 MA65. St Steph Ho Ox 59. **d** 62 **p** 63 **c** 89. C Wandsworth St Anne *S'wark* 62-66; Hon C 66-68; Chapl Tiffin Sch Kingston-upon-Thames 66-72; Hon C Ham St Rich *S'wark* 68-72; Dioc Dir of Educn *Dur* 72-85; R Brancepeth 72-85; Hon Can Dur Cathl 75-85; Adn Halifax *Wakef* 85-89; Bp Blackb from 89. *Bishop's House, Ribchester Road, Blackburn BB1 9EF* Blackburn (0254) 248234

CHESTERS, Peter Durrant. b 17. ACII52. K Coll Lon 54. **d** 56 **p** 57. R Ludgershall and Faberstown *Sarum* 66-82; rtd 82; Perm to Offic *Heref* from 82. *8 Ash Grove Close, Bodenham, Herefordshire HR1 3LT* Bodenham (056884) 591

CHESTERTON, Robert Eric. b 31. St Aid Birkenhead 63. **d** 65 **p** 66. C Kirby Muxloe *Leic* 65-67; Canada 67-68 and 75-78; C St Annes *Blackb* 68-69; V Southminster *Chelmsf* 69-75; V Wythenshawe Wm Temple Ch *Man* 78-82; TV Marfleet *York* 82-85; V Marshchapel *Linc* 85-88; R N Coates 85-88; V Grainthorpe w Conisholme 85-88; V Langtoft Gp from 88. *The Vicarage, East End, Langtoft, Peterborough PE6 9LP* Market Deeping (0778) 346812

CHETWOOD, Noah. b 14. St Jo Coll Dur BA38 DipTh39 MA41 Nottm Univ MEd58. **d** 39 **p** 40. C Ludlow *Heref* 39-45; Lic to Offic *Derby* 45-54; Ox from 54. *Evergreens, 10 Longfield Drive, Amersham, Bucks HP6 5HD* Amersham (0494) 725259

CHETWYND, Edward Ivor. b 45. Leeds Univ DipTh68. Coll of Resurr Mirfield 68. **d** 70 **p** 71. C Westgate Common *Wakef* 70-74; C Penistone w Midhope 74-75; V Smawthorpe St Mich from 75. *St Michael's Vicarage, St Michael's Close, Castleford, W Yorkshire WF10 4ER* Castleford (0977) 557079

CHEVALIER, Harry Ensor Estienne. b 23. Mert Coll Ox BA49 MA56. Ely Th Coll 49. **d** 51 **p** 52. V Bradninch *Ex* 66-71; Perm to Offic from 71; Hon C Christchurch *Win* 74-75; rtd 75; Perm to Offic *Win* from 75. *c/o M Chevalier Esq, 13 Broughton Close, Bournemouth BH10 6JB* Bournemouth (0202) 524318

CHEVERTON, David. b 22. ARIBA. Lon Coll of Div 65. **d** 67 **p** 68. C Wealdstone H Trin *Lon* 67-71; V Budleigh Salterton *Ex* 71-82; Warden Spennithorne Hall Ripon 82-85; N of England Chr Healing Trust 82-87; rtd 87. *Cruachan Cottage, Preston under Scar, Leyburn, N Yorkshire DL8 4AS* Wensleydale (0969) 23951

CHEYNE, Robert Douglas. b 17. Wycliffe Hall Ox 65. **d** 67 **p** 68. C Oakwood St Thos *Lon* 67-70; C Brackley St Pet w St Jas *Pet* 70-72; R Cottesbrooke w Gt Creaton 72-74; P-in-c Thornby w Cold Ashby 72-74; R Cottesbrooke w Gt Creaton and Thornby 74-82; rtd 83. *89 Chaucer Drive, Lincoln* Lincoln (0522) 43239

CHICHESTER, Archdeacon of. See HOBBS, Ven Keith Waldram

CHICHESTER, Bishop of. See KEMP, Rt Rev Eric John David

CHICHESTER, Dean of. See TREADGOLD, Very Rev John David

CHICKEN, Peter Lindsay. b 46. St Andr Univ BSc71. Chich Th Coll 77. **d** 79 **p** 80. C High Wycombe *Ox* 79-83;

V The Stanleys *Glouc* from 83. *The Vicarage, Leonard Stanley, Stonehouse, Glos GL10 3NP* Stonehouse (045382) 3161

CHIDLAW, Richard Paul. b 49. St Cath Coll Cam BA71 MA. Ripon Hall Ox 72. **d** 74 **p** 81. C Ribbesford w Bewdley and Dowles *Worc* 74-76; NSM Coaley *Glouc* 81-83; NSM Frampton on Severn 81-83; NSM Arlingham 81-83; NSM Saul w Fretherne and Framilode 83-84; NSM Cam w Stinchcombe 85-90; Perm to Offic from 90. *Peak View, 86 Kingshill Road, Dursley, Glos GL11 4EF* Dursley (0453) 547838

CHIDWICK, Alan Robert. b 49. MIL MA. Oak Hill NSM Course. **d** 84 **p** 85. NSM Pimlico St Pet w Westmr Ch Ch *Lon* from 84. *24 Chester Square, London SW1W 9HS* 071-730 4354

CHIDZEY, Canon Leonard Whitehead. b 08. Ridley Hall Cam 47. **d** 48 **p** 49. V Gt and Lt Driffield *York* 68-78; rtd 78. *Inchmarlo House, Banchory, Kincardineshire AB3 4AL* Banchory (03302) 4981

CHIGNELL, Preb Wilfred Rowland. b 08. Sarum Th Coll 31. **d** 33 **p** 34. R Whitbourne *Heref* 64-73; Preb Heref Cathl from 64; rtd 73. *Dene Hollow, Whitbourne, Worcester* Knightwick (0886) 21293

CHILD, Canon Rupert Henry. b 29. St Jo Coll Dur 50 K Coll Lon DipTh56 St Boniface Warminster 57. **d** 58 **p** 59. C Tavistock and Gulworthy *Ex* 58-61; C Dunstable *St Alb* 61-65; V Luton St Chris Round Green 65-74; V Sawbridgeworth from 74; Hon Can St Alb from 86. *The Vicarage, 144 Sheering Mill Lane, Sawbridgeworth, Herts CM21 9ND* Bishop's Stortford (0279) 723305

CHILD, Theodore Hilary. b 09. MA. **d** 33 **p** 34. V Southwold *St E* 59-74; rtd 74; P-in-c Starston *Nor* 75-87; Perm to Offic St E & Nor from 87. *37 Loam Pit Lane, Halesworth, Suffolk IP19 8EZ* Halesworth (09867) 4426

CHILDS, Ernest Edmund. b 23. Lich Th Coll 63. **d** 65 **p** 66. Clerical Org Sec CECS (Dios Pet, Leic and Ely) 69-72; V Staverton w Helidon and Catesby *Pet* 72-76; rtd 77; Perm to Offic *Nor* from 77. *19 Wells Road, Walsingham, Norfolk NR22 6DL* Walsingham (0328) 820828

CHILDS, Miss Julie Mary. b 39. Lon Univ BA60 Southn Univ CertEd61. St Alb Minl Tr Scheme 81. **dss** 84 **d** 87. Harpenden St Nic *St Alb* 84-87; C from 87. *86 Tuffnells Way, Harpenden, Herts AL5 3HG* Harpenden (0582) 762485

CHILDS, Leonard Neil. b 43. Leeds Univ BA65. Wells Th Coll 66. **d** 68 **p** 69. C Matlock and Tansley *Derby* 68-72; C Chesterfield All SS 72-74; P-in-c Stonebroom 74-81; P-in-c Morton 78-81; R Morton and Stonebroom 81-84; TV Buxton w Burbage and King Sterndale from 84. *17 Lismore Road, Buxton, Derbyshire SK17 9AN* Buxton (0298) 22151

CHILDS, Stanley Herbert. b 1900. Ch Coll Cam BA23 MA26. Ridley Hall Cam 23. **d** 24 **p** 25. V Combertons *Worc* 63-70; rtd 70; Perm to Offic *Glouc* from 70. *The White House, Gretton Road, Winchcombe, Cheltenham, Glos GL54 5EG* Cheltenham (0242) 602424

CHILDS, Theodore John. b 12. St Edm Hall Ox BA34 MA47 BLitt47. Ripon Hall Ox 37. **d** 40 **p** 41. R Chelvey w Brockley *B & W* 61-70; R Ballaugh *S & M* 70-77; rtd 77; Perm to Offic *S & M* from 77. *9 Ballagorry Drive, Glen Mona, Ramsey, Isle of Man* Ramsey (0624) 861993

CHILLINGWORTH, David Robert. b 51. TCD BA73 Or Coll Ox BA75 MA81. Ripon Coll Cuddesdon 75. **d** 76 **p** 77. C Belf H Trin *Conn* 76-79; Ch of Ireland Youth Officer 79-83; C Ban Abbey *D & D* 83-86; I Seagoe from 86. *8 Upper Church Lane, Portadown, Craigavon, Co Armagh BT63 5JE* Portadown (0762) 332538

CHILTON, Kenneth Chapman. b 20. St Cuth Soc Dur BA49 DipTh51. **d** 51 **p** 52. V Thorpe St Matt *Nor* 57-85; rtd 85; Perm to Offic *Nor* from 85. *3 Hillcrest Road, Norwich NR7 0JZ* Norwich (0603) 36948

CHING, Derek. b 37. MA. Qu Coll Birm. **d** 83 **p** 84. C Finham *Cov* 83-87; V Butlers Marston and the Pillertons w Ettington from 87. *The Vicarage, Ettington, Stratford-upon-Avon, Warks CV37 7SH* Stratford-upon-Avon (0789) 740225

CHIPLIN, Christopher Gerald. b 53. Lon Univ BSc75. St Steph Ho Ox BA77 MA81. **d** 78 **p** 79. C Chesterfield All SS *Derby* 78-80; C Thorpe *Nor* 80-84; V Highbridge *B & W* from 84. *The Vicarage, 81A Church Street, Highbridge, Somerset TA9 3HS* Burnham-on-Sea (0278) 783671

CHIPLIN, Gareth Huw. b 50. Worc Coll Ox BA71 MA. Edin Th Coll 71. **d** 73 **p** 74. C Friern Barnet St Jas *Lon* 73-75; C Eastcote St Lawr 76-79; C Notting Hill St Mich and Ch Ch 79-84; V Hammersmith St Matt from 84. *St Matthew's Vicarage, 1 Fielding Road, London W14 0LL* 071-603 9769

CHIPLIN, Howard Alan. b 43. Sarum & Wells Th Coll 84. **d** 86 **p** 87. C Caerleon *Mon* 86-89; V Ferndale w Maerdy *Llan* 89-91; V Ysbyty Cynfyn w Llantrisant and Eglwys Newydd *St D* from 91. *The Vicarage, Ysbyty Cynfyn, Ponterwyd, Aberystwyth, Dyfed SY23 3JR* Ponterwyd (097085) 663

CHIPLIN, Malcolm Leonard. b 42. **d** 88 **p** 89. C Newton Nottage *Llan* 88-91; V Pwllgwaun w Llanddewi Rhondda from 91. *The Vicarage, Lanelay Crescent, Maesycoed, Pontypridd, M Glam CF37 1JB* Pontypridd (0443) 402417

CHIPPENDALE, Peter David. b 34. Dur Univ BA55. Linc Th Coll 57. **d** 59 **p** 60. C Claines St Jo *Worc* 59-63; V Defford w Besford 63-73; P-in-c Eckington 66-69; V 69-73; V Kidderminster St Geo 73-76; V The Lickey *Birm* from 76. *The Vicarage, 30 Lickey Square, Rednal, Birmingham B45 8HB* 021-445 1425

CHIPPENDALE, Robert William. b 42. DipTh68 BA79 DipT84. **d** 67 **p** 68. Australia 67-72 and from 79; V Shaw *Man* 72-78. *PO Box 290, Southport, Queensland, Australia 4215* Southport (75) 324922

CHIPPINGTON, George Ernest. b 16. Ch Coll Cam BA38 MA42. **d** 61 **p** 62. V Orton-on-the-Hill w Twycross etc *Leic* 65-70; R Milton Damerel and Newton St Petrock etc *Ex* 70-83; rtd 84; Perm to Offic *Ex* from 84. *West Meddon, Hartland, Bideford, Devon EX39 6HD* Morwenstow (028883) 200

CHISHOLM, David Whitridge. b 23. Keble Coll Ox BA48 MA48. Linc Th Coll 48. **d** 50 **p** 51. V N Harrow St Alb *Lon* 66-72; V Paddington St Jas 72-78; RD Westmr Paddington 74-79; C Paddington St Jas 78-79; V Hurley *Ox* 79-90; rtd 90. *32 Herons Place, Marlow, Bucks SL7 3HP* Marlow (0628) 483243

CHISHOLM, Ian Keith. b 36. AKC62. **d** 63 **p** 64. C Lich St Chad *Lich* 63-66; C Sedgley All SS 66-69; V Rough Hills 69-77; V Harrow Weald All SS *Lon* 77-88; V W Moors *Sarum* from 88. *The Vicarage, 57 Glenwood Road, West Moors, Wimborne, Dorset BH22 0EN* Ferndown (0202) 893197

CHISHOLM, Ian Stuart. b 37. ALCD63. **d** 63 **p** 64. C Worksop St Jo *S'well* 63-66; Succ Sheff Cathl *Sheff* 66-68; Bp's Chapl for Soc Resp 68-72; C Ox St Andr *Ox* 72-76; Tutor Wycliffe Hall Ox 72-76; V Conisbrough *Sheff* from 76; RD W Doncaster 82-87. *The Vicarage, 8 Castle Avenue, Conisbrough, Doncaster, S Yorkshire DN12 3BT* Rotherham (0709) 864695

CHISHOLM, Canon Reginald Joseph. b 13. TCD BA40 MA51. CITC 42. **d** 42 **p** 43. I Newtownards *D & D* 51-82; Treas Down Cathl 80-82; rtd 82. *20 Glendun Park, Bangor, Co Down BT20 4UX* Bangor (0247) 450100

CHISHOLM, Samuel James. b 20. **d** 86 **p** 87. NSM Eastriggs *Glas* from 86. *29 Kennels Road, Annan, Dumfriesshire DG12 5EU* Annan (04612) 205415

CHISWELL, Russell James. b 52. Univ of Wales (Lamp) BA73. Wycliffe Hall Ox 74. **d** 76 **p** 77. C Gabalfa *Llan* 76-80; V Hirwaun from 80; Asst Chapl HM Pris Cardiff 86-88. *The Vicarage, High Street, Hirwaun, Aberdare, M Glam CF44 9SL* Aberdare (0685) 811316

CHITHAM, Ernest (John). b 57. LSE BSc79 PGCE80 Dur Univ MA84. **d** 91. C Swanborough *Sarum* from 91. *4 Rushall Road, Pewsey, Wilts SN9 6JY* Stonehenge (0980) 630564

CHITTENDEN, John Bertram d'Encer. b 24. ASCA. Lon Coll of Div 56. **d** 58 **p** 59. R Acrise *Cant* 64-82; R Hawkinge 64-82; R Hawkinge w Acrise and Swingfield 82-90; rtd 91. *19 Hasborough Road, Folkestone, Kent CT19 6BQ* Folkestone (0303) 41773

CHITTENDEN, Reginald Henry. b 18. Bps' Coll Cheshunt 46. **d** 49 **p** 50. R Meavy w Sheepstor *Ex* 69-83; rtd 83; Perm to Offic *Ex* 83-86; Hon C Diptford, N Huish, Harberton and Harbertonford from 86. *23 Bridgetown, Totnes, Devon TQ9 5BA* Totnes (0803) 862754

CHITTY, Philip Crofts. b 27. Roch Th Coll 61. **d** 63 **p** 64. V Long Ichington *Cov* 68-77; R Ufton 69-77; P-in-c Cov St Marg 77-84; rtd 84. *17 Rotherham Road, Coventry CV6 4FF* Coventry (0203) 685398

✠**CHIU, Rt Rev Joshua Ban It.** b 18. Barrister-at-Law (Inner Temple) 41 K Coll Lon AKC41 LLB41. Westcott Ho Cam 43. **d** 45 **p** 46 **c** 66. C Bournville *Birm* 45-47; Malaya 47-50; Singapore 50-59 and 66-82; Hon Can St Andr Cathl Singapore 56-59; Australia 59-62; Service Laymen Abroad WCC Geneva 62-65; Fell St Aug Coll Cant 65-66; Bp Singapore and Malaya 66-70; Bp Singapore 70-82; Member Cen Cttee WCC 68-75; Member ACC 75-79; rtd 82; Perm to Offic *Sarum* from

82. *12 Dewlands Road, Verwood, Wimborne, Dorset BH21 6PL* Verwood (0202) 822307

CHIVERS, Ernest Alfred John. b 34. Bris & Glouc Tr Course. **d** 83 **p** 84. NSM Bedminster *Bris* 83-87; NSM Whitchurch from 87. *40 Calcott Road, Bristol BS4 2HD* Bristol (0272) 777867

CHIVERS, Ronald. b 27. Dur Univ BA52. Oak Hill Th Coll 52. **d** 53 **p** 54. N Sec CCCS 61-71; Lic to Offic Ripon 61-65; Blackb 66-71; V Woodside *Ripon* 71-91; rtd 91. *18 Spen Road, West Park, Leeds LS16 5BT* Leeds (0532) 747709

CHIVERS, Royston George. b 34. Glouc Th Course. **d** 83 **p** 84. NSM Gorsley w Cliffords Mesne *Glouc* 83-85; NSM Newent and Gorsley w Cliffords Mesne from 85. *Mayfield, Gorsley, Ross-on-Wye, Herefordshire HR9 7SJ* Gorsley (098982) 492

CHIVERS, Thomas Harry. b 19. Clifton Th Coll 60. **d** 60 **p** 61. C-in-c Thwaites Brow CD *Bradf* 65-70; V Oxenhope 70-87; rtd 87; Perm to Offic *Bradf* from 87. *1 Camargue Fold, Kings Road, Bradford, W Yorkshire BD2 1HB* Bradford (0274) 308085

CHIVERS, William Herbert. b 20. Univ of Wales (Cardiff) BA42. Coll of Resurr Mirfield 42. **d** 44 **p** 45. R Bushey *St Alb* 60-81; Australia 81-83; R Llandogo and Tintern *Mon* 83-86; rtd 86; Asst Chapl Athens w Kyfissia, Patras, Thessaloniki & Voula *Eur* from 86. *40 Kokinaki/Markou, Botsari 83, 145 61 Kyfissia, Athens, Greece* Athens (1) 807-5335

CHIVERTON, Dennis Lionel Dunbar. b 26. St D Coll Lamp BA51. **d** 53 **p** 54. R Llanfabon *Llan* 67-91; rtd 91. *3 Park Terrace, Treharris, M Glam CF46 6BT*

CHOULES, Edward Frank. b 16. St Steph Ho Ox 75. **d** 78 **p** 79. NSM Boyne Hill *Ox* 78-84; Lic to Offic from 84. *c/o Chantry House, 6 Benyon Mews, Bath Road, Reading, Berks RG1 6HX*

CHOW, Ting Suie Roy. b 46. Brasted Th Coll 68 Sarum & Wells Th Coll 70. **d** 72 **p** 73. C Weaste *Man* 72-74; C Swinton St Pet 74-78; R Blackley St Paul 78-85; Sec SPCK (Dio Man) from 80; R Burnage St Nic *Man* from 85. *St Nicholas's Rectory, Fog Lane, Burnage, Manchester M19 1PL* 061-432 3384

CHOWN, Ernest John Richard. b 17. St Steph Ho Ox 48. **d** 51 **p** 52. C Ox St Paul *Ox* 51-53; C Brighton St Paul *Chich* 53-65; V Swanley St Mary *Roch* 65-72; V Worthing St Andr *Chich* from 72. *St Andrew's Vicarage, 21 Victoria Road, Worthing, W Sussex BN11 1XB* Worthing (0903) 33442

CHOWN, William Richard Bartlett. b 27. AKC54. **d** 55 **p** 56. R Romford St Andr *Chelmsf* 61-78; R Newton Longville w Stoke Hammond, Whaddon etc *Ox* 78-83; P-in-c Kidmore End 83-90; rtd 90. *26 Lovell Close, Henley-on-Thames, Oxon RG9 1PX* Henley-on-Thames (0491) 575735

CHRISMAN, John Aubrey. b 33. US Naval Academy BS58. Westcott Ho Cam 86. **d** 88 **p** 89. NSM Orwell *Ely* 88-89; NSM Wimpole 88-89; NSM Arrington 88-89; NSM Croydon w Clopton 88-89; Asst Chapl Oslo St Edm *Eur* 89-91; USA from 91. *St George's Episcopal Church, 14 Rhode Island Avenue, Newport, Rhode Island 02840, USA*

CHRISTENSEN, Canon Norman Peter. b 37. Univ of Wales (Lamp) BA63. Ridley Hall Cam 63. **d** 65 **p** 66. C Barnston *Ches* 65-70; V Over St Jo 70-77; R Bromborough from 77; RD Wirral S from 86; Hon Can Ches Cathl from 90. *The Rectory, Mark Rake, Bromborough, Wirral, Merseyside L62 2DH* 051-334 1466

CHRISTIAN, Anthony Clive Hammond. b 46. Kent Univ BA74. K Coll Lon 74 St Aug Coll Cant 74. **d** 76 **p** 77. C Faversham *Cant* 76-79; C St Laurence in Thanet 79-81; P-in-c 81-84; R Gt Mongeham w Ripple and Sutton by Dover 84-88; V Pevensey *Chich* from 88. *The Vicarage, Church Lane, Pevensey, E Sussex BN24 5LD* Eastbourne (0323) 762247

CHRISTIAN, Brother. *See* PEARSON, Christian David John

CHRISTIAN, Gerald. b 29. MBIM SSC FCP. Qu Coll Birm 74. **d** 77 **p** 77. NSM Stirchley *Birm* 77-82; S Africa from 82. *The Rectory, Swartberg, Griqualand East, Private Bag 61, 4710 South Africa*

CHRISTIAN, Paul. b 49. Cant Sch of Min 84. **d** 87 **p** 88. C Folkestone St Sav *Cant* 87-91; R Temple Ewell w Lydden from 91. *The Rectory, Green Lane, Temple Ewell, Dover, Kent CT16 3AS* Dover (0304) 822865

CHRISTIAN, Richard. b 37. Nottm Univ DipEd74 Ox Univ MA81. AKC62. **d** 63 **p** 65. C Camberwell St Mich w All So w Em *S'wark* 63-66; C Woolwich St Mary w H Trin 66-70; Chapl and Lect Bp Lonsdale Coll Derby 70-74; Keble Coll Ox 74-76; P-in-c Hurley *Ox* 76-79;

Chapl Lancing Coll Sussex 79-81; Chapl Harrow Sch Middx 82-89; Lic to Offic *Lon* 82-91; Chapl Chich HA 89-91; Chapl R W Sussex Hosp Chich 89-91; P-in-c Cowley *Lon* from 91. *The Rectory, Church Road, Cowley, Uxbridge, Middx UB8 3NB* Uxbridge (0895) 32728

CHRISTIAN, Canon Ronald George. b 20. AKC48. **d** 49 **p** 50. V Bramford *St E* 62-91; Dioc Ecum Officer 66-88; Hon Can St E Cathl from 75; Bruges Link Dioc Co-ord from 88; rtd 91; Perm to Offic *St E* from 91. *54 Pine View Road, Ipswich, Suffolk IP1 4HR* Ipswich (0473) 463031

CHRISTIAN-EDWARDS, Canon Michael Thomas. b 36. Down Coll Cam BA60 MA64. Clifton Th Coll 60. **d** 62 **p** 63. C Ex St Leon w H Trin *Ex* 62-67; V Trowbridge St Thos *Sarum* 67-75; R Wingfield w Rowley 67-75; P-in-c Fisherton Anger 75-81; R from 81; Ind Chapl from 85; RD Salisbury 85-90; Can and Preb Sarum Cathl from 87. *St Paul's Rectory, Salisbury SP2 7QW* Salisbury (0722) 334005

CHRISTIE, David James. b 58. York Univ BA80 MA83 PGCE81 Leeds Univ MPhil88. Cranmer Hall Dur 89. **d** 91. C Drypool *York* from 91. *2 Pavilion Close, Chamberlain Road, Hull HU8 8EA* Hull (0482) 712597

CHRISTIE, Canon Graham. b 08. Leeds Univ BA31. Coll of Resurr Mirfield 31. **d** 33 **p** 34. Tutor Hull Univ 55-80; V Millington w Gt Givendale *York* 60-81; V Pocklington w Yapham-cum-Meltonby, Owsthorpe etc 60-81; RD Pocklington 60-75; Can and Preb York Minster 62-91; rtd 81; Perm to Offic *York* from 91. *Pax Intranti, 66 Wold Road, Pocklington, York YO4 2QG* Pocklington (0759) 304200

CHRISTIE, Leonard Douglas. b 16. AKC39. Bps' Coll Cheshunt 39. **d** 39 **p** 40. Lic to Offic *Guildf* 70-76; V Easington w Skeffling and Kilnsea *York* 76-85; P-in-c Holmpton 83-85; rtd 85; Perm to Offic *Ox* from 85; C Combe 88-89; C Stonesfield w Combe 89-90. *33 Isis Close, Long Hanborough, Oxford OX7 3JN* Freeland (0993) 881855

CHRISTIE, Canon Thomas Richard. b 31. CCC Cam BA53 MA57. Linc Th Coll 55. **d** 57 **p** 58. C Portsea N End St Mark *Portsm* 57-60; C Cherry Hinton St Andr *Ely* 60-62; C-in-c Cherry Hinton St Jas CD 62-66; V Wisbech St Aug 66-73; V Whitstable All SS *Cant* 73-75; V Whitstable All SS w St Pet 75-80; Can Res and Treas Pet Cathl *Pet* from 80; RD Pet from 87. *Prebendal House, Minster Precincts, Peterborough PE1 1XX* Peterborough (0733) 69441

CHUBB, John Nicholas. b 33. St Cath Soc Ox BA55 MA58. Qu Coll Birm 57. **d** 59 **p** 60. C Kirby Moorside w Gillamoor *York* 59-62; C Scarborough St Mary 62-64; V Potterspury w Furtho and Yardley Gobion *Pet* 64-69; V Brixworth 69-74; P-in-c Holcot 73-74; V Brixworth w Holcot 74-81; V Hampton Hill *Lon* 81-88; Perm to Offic Linc and Nor from 88; Chapl Pet Distr Hosps and Edith Cavell Hosp from 88. *40 Bathurst, Orton Goldhay, Peterborough PE2 0QH* Peterborough (0733) 234089 or 67451

CHUBB, Richard Henry. b 45. Univ of Wales (Cardiff) BMus67. Linc Th Coll 67. **d** 70 **p** 71. C Chippenham St Andr w Tytherton Lucas *Bris* 71-72; C-in-c Stockwood CD 72-73; C Bris Ch the Servant Stockwood 73-76; Perm to Offic 76-79; Min Can and Succ Bris Cathl from 79; Chapl to the Deaf from 83. *45 Claremont Road, Bristol BS7 8DN* Bristol (0272) 423905

CHUDLEY, Cyril Raymond. b 29. Lon Univ BA53 DipEd. Wells Th Coll 70. **d** 72 **p** 73. C Newark St Mary *S'well* 72-75; C Egg Buckland *Ex* 75-77; P-in-c Plymouth St Aug 77-80; V 80-83; V Milton Abbot, Dunterton, Lamerton etc 83-91; TV Wickford and Runwell *Chelmsf* from 91. *St Andrew's Vicarage, 8 Friern Walk, Wickford, Essex SS12 0HZ* Wickford (0268) 734077

CHURCH, Geoffrey Arthur. b 09. Clare Coll Cam BA31 MA35. Wells Th Coll 31. **d** 32 **p** 33. C Watford Ch Ch *St Alb* 70-76; rtd 76; Hon C Lt Berkhamsted and Bayford, Essendon etc *St Alb* 76-81; Perm to Offic *Cant* from 81. *5 Bell Meadow, Sutton Road, Maidstone, Kent ME15 9NB* Maidstone (0622) 682245

CHURCH, Howard Joseph. b 05. Em Coll Cam BA28 MA33. Ridley Hall Cam 29. **d** 30 **p** 31. Kenya 69-72; rtd 72. *52 Mill Road, Salisbury SP1 7RZ* Salisbury (0722) 329637

CHURCHILL, Canon Aubrey Gilbert Roy. b 12. Southn Univ 36. Sarum Th Coll 37. **d** 39 **p** 40. R Wilmcote w Billesley *Cov* 55-76; Hon Can Cov Cathl 72-76; rtd 76; Perm to Offic *Cov* from 76. *9 Farley Avenue, Harbury, Leamington Spa, Warks CV33 9LX* Harbury (0926) 613309

CHURCHMAN, David Ernest Donald. b 21. Clifton Th Coll 45. **d** 48 **p** 49. V Southsea St Jude *Portsm* 59-74; V Enfield Ch Ch Trent Park *Lon* 74-86; RD Enfield 75-82; rtd 86. *Heronsbrook, 158 Havant Road, Hayling Island, Hants PO11 0LJ* Hayling Island (0705) 463216

CHURCHUS, Eric Richard Ivor. b 28. Lon Univ BSc MSc56. **d** 78 **p** 79. Hon C Withington w Westhide *Heref* 78-82; C Heref St Martin 82-85; P-in-c Woolhope from 85. *The Vicarage, Woolhope, Hereford HR1 4QR* Hereford (0432) 77287

CHYNCHEN, John Howard. b 38. FRICS72. Sarum & Wells Th Coll 88. **d** 89 **p** 90. Bp's Dom Chapl *Sarum* 89-90; Hong Kong from 90. *Flat B-2, On Lee, 2 Mount Davies Road, Hong Kong* Hong Kong (852) 523-4157

CIANCHI, Dalbert Peter. b 28. Lon Univ BSc57. Westcott Ho Cam 69. **d** 70 **p** 71. C Harpenden St Nic *St Alb* 70-74; TV Woughton *Ox* 74-80; P-in-c Wavendon w Walton 74-80; P-in-c Lavendon w Cold Brayfield 80-84; R Lavendon w Cold Brayfield, Clifton Reynes etc from 84. *The New Rectory, 7A Northampton Road, Lavendon, Olney, Bucks MK46 4AY* Bedford (0234) 712647

CIECHANOWICZ, Edward Leigh Bundock. b 52. Keble Coll Ox BA73. St Steph Ho Ox 74. **d** 76 **p** 77. C Malvern Link w Cowleigh *Worc* 76-80; C-in-c Portslade Gd Shep Mile Oak CD *Chich* 80-88; V Wisborough Green from 88. *The Vicarage, Wisborough Green, Billingshurst, W Sussex RH14 0DZ* Wisborough Green (0403) 700339

CIRCUS, Robert William. b 19. Lon Univ BSc(Econ)90. Wycliffe Hall Ox 52. **d** 54 **p** 55. V Werrington *Pet* 60-70; R The Quinton *Birm* 70-76; P-in-c Wolverley *Worc* 76-82; V Wolverley and Cookley 82-84; rtd 84; Perm to Offic *Worc* from 84. *5 Berrow Hill Road, Franche, Kidderminster, Worcs DY11 5LH* Kidderminster (0562) 753067

CLABON, Harold William George. b 31. **d** 85 **p** 86. NSM Newport St Julian *Mon* from 85. *38 St Julian's Avenue, Newport, Gwent NP9 7JU* Newport (0633) 215419

CLACEY, Derek Phillip. b 48. LTh. St Jo Coll Nottm 76. **d** 79 **p** 80. C Gt Parndon *Chelmsf* 79-82; C Walton H Trin *Ox* 82-88; R Bramshaw and Landford w Plaitford *Sarum* from 88. *The Vicarage, Bramshaw, Lyndhurst, Hants SO4 7JF* Romsey (0794) 390256

CLACK, Joseph John. b 14. Dur Univ LTh38. Clifton Th Coll 34. **d** 37 **p** 38. V Kelbrook *Bradf* 61-76; P-in-c Weston w Denton 76-79; V 79-81; rtd 81. *9 Victoria Avenue, Ilkley, W Yorkshire LS29 9BL* Ilkley (0943) 607176

CLANCEY, Ms Blanche Elizabeth Fisher. b 28. SRN50 Lon Univ CertEd71. Gilmore Ho 64. **dss** 78 **d** 87. Bromley Common St Aug *Roch* 78-83; Hanley H Ev *Lich* 83-87; Dn-in-c 87-89; rtd 89; NSM Gamston and Bridgford *S'well* from 91. *5 Sloane Court, Nottingham NG2 7SY* Nottingham (0602) 216997

CLANCY, Michael. b 24. Kensington Univ (USA) BA82. Glas NSM Course 76. **d** 79 **p** 80. Hon C Glas St Silas Glas from 79. *33 Highfield Drive, Clarkston, Glasgow G76 7SW* 041-638 4469

CLAPHAM, John. b 47. Open Univ BA76. Sarum & Wells Th Coll 77. **d** 80 **p** 81. Dep PV Ex Cathl *Ex* from 80; C Lympstone 85-87; P-in-c from 87. *The Rectory, Lympstone, Exmouth, Devon EX8 5HP* Exmouth (0395) 273343

CLAPHAM, Kenneth. b 47. Trin Coll Bris 76. **d** 78 **p** 79. C Pemberton St Mark Newtown *Liv* 78-81; C Darfield *Sheff* 81-83; P-in-c Over Kellet *Blackb* 83-88; V from 88. *The Vicarage, Over Kellet, Carnforth, Lancs LA6 1DJ* Carnforth (0524) 734189

CLAPP, Andrew Gerald Drummond. b 58. Coll of Resurr Mirfield 87. **d** 90 **p** 91. C Tilbury Docks *Chelmsf* from 90. *4 Pepys Close, Tilbury, Essex RM18 8JT* Tilbury (0375) 843195

CLAPP, Nicholas Michel Edward. b 48. Univ of Wales (Cardiff) DipTh74. St Mich Coll Llan 71. **d** 74 **p** 75. C Walsall St Gabr Fullbrook *Lich* 74-77; C Burnley St Cath *Blackb* 77-80; R Blackley H Trin *Man* 80-87; V Carl St Aid and Ch Ch *Carl* from 87. *St Aidan's Vicarage, 6 Lismore Place, Carlisle CA1 1LX* Carlisle (0228) 22942

CLAPSON, Clive Henry. b 55. Leeds Univ BA76. Trin Coll Toronto MDiv79. **d** 79 **p** 80. Canada 79-83; USA 83-88; C Hawley H Trin *Guildf* 88-90; Miss to Seamen from 90; R Invergordon *Mor* from 90; I Invergordon St Ninian from 90; Vice Prin Ord and Lay Tr Course from 90. *St Ninian's Rectory, 132 High Street, Invergordon, Ross-shire IV18 0AE* Invergordon (0349) 852392

CLARE, Arthur Hargreaves. b 14. St Aid Birkenhead 46. **d** 48 **p** 49. V Sutton St Geo *Ches* 64-77; V Aston by Sutton 77-83; rtd 83; Perm to Offic *Ches* from 83.

27 Wayford Close, Frodsham, Warrington WA6 7QB Frodsham (0928) 31435

CLARE, Lionel Philip. b 19. St Aid Birkenhead 46. **d** 49 **p** 50. V Sunnyside w Bourne End *St Alb* 66-74; V Kirkbymoorside w Gillamoor, Farndale & Bransdale *York* 74-84; rtd 84; Perm to Offic *Bradf* from 84. *Flat 1, Regent Court, 20 Regent Road, Ilkley, W Yorkshire LS29 9EA* Ilkley (0943) 609330

CLAREY, Harry. b 09. Worc Ord Coll 65. **d** 66 **p** 67. P-in-c Nettleton *Linc* 70-78; rtd 78. *11 South Dale, Caistor, Lincoln LN7 6LS* Caistor (0472) 851494

CLARIDGE, Antony Arthur John. b 37. LRAM Hull Univ MA. Bris & Glouc Tr Course. **d** 84 **p** 85. NSM Keynsham *B & W* from 84; Bp's Officer for NSM's from 90. *62 Cranwells Park, Weston, Bath BA1 2YE* Bath (0225) 27462

CLARINGBULL, Canon Denis Leslie. b 33. MIPM85 K Coll Lon BD57 AKC57. **d** 58 **p** 59. C Croydon St Aug *Cant* 58-62; Ind Chapl to Bp Croydon 62-71; Ind Chapl *Cov* 71-75; Chapl Cov Cathl 71-75; Succ 72-75; V Norbury St Phil *Cant* 75-80; Sen Ind Chapl *Birm* from 80; P-in-c Birm St Paul 85-88; V from 88; Hon Can Birm Cathl from 87. *197 Russell Road, Birmingham B13 8RR* 021-449 1435

CLARINGBULL (nee DAVID), Mrs Faith Caroline. b 55. St Aid Coll Dur BA77. Ripon Coll Cuddesdon 87. **d** 89. Par Dn Is of Dogs Ch Ch and St Jo w St Luke *Lon* from 89. *Flat 2, St Mildred's House, Roserton Street, London E14 3PG* 071-515 7975

CLARK, Albert Percival. b 17. Hatf Coll Dur LTh39 BA39. St Boniface Warminster 36. **d** 40 **p** 41. R The Quinton *Birm* 61-70; V Werrington *Pet* 70-77; S Africa 77-80; R Chipping Warden w Edgcote and Aston le Walls *Pet* 80-83; rtd 83; Perm to Offic S'wark from 83; Guildf from 86. *3 Falconhurst, The Crescent, Surbiton, Surrey KT6 4BP* 081-399 2032

CLARK, Alexander Rees. b 19. Univ of Wales (Lamp) BA48 Hull Univ CertEd50. St D Coll Lamp 50. **d** 51 **p** 52. V Eglwyswenwydd *St D* 84-90; V Pontyates 61-74; V Ysbyty Cynfyn w Llantrisant 74-90; rtd 90. *Llety'r Dryw, 1 Lon Tyllwyd, Llanfarian, Aberystwyth, Dyfed SY23 4UH* Aberystwyth (0970) 612736

CLARK, Alfred Reeves. b 06. MC44. Lon Coll of Div 53. **d** 55 **p** 57. Pakistan 56-63; Chapl HM Pris Liv 64; Parkhurst 65-69; Lic to Offic Sarum 70-71; Ox from 71. *St John's Hospital, Heytesbury, Warminster, Wilts* Warminster (0985) 40441

CLARK, Andrew Mark. b 62. W Midl Coll of Educn BEd85. Coll of Resurr Mirfield 87. **d** 90 **p** 91. C Cov St Fran N Radford *Cov* from 90. *361 Grangemouth Road, Coventry CV6 3FH* Coventry (0203) 594771

CLARK, Antony. b 61. York Univ BA83. Wycliffe Hall Ox 84. **d** 88 **p** 89. C Ashton on Mersey St Mary *Ches* from 88. *12 Willoughby Close, Sale, Cheshire M33 1PJ* 061-962 5204

CLARK, Arthur. b 30. MIBiol FRSC Sheff Univ BSc MCB. St D Dioc Tr Course. **d** 88 **p** 89. NSM Haverfordwest St Mary and St Thos w Haroldston *St D* from 88. *84 Portfield, Haverfordwest, Dyfed SA61 1BT* Haverfordwest (0437) 762694

CLARK, Arthur Towers. b 08. OBE45. AKC36. **d** 36 **p** 37. V Robertttown *Wakef* 56-58; Perm to Offic from 73; rtd 86. *32 Broomcroft Road, Ossett, W Yorkshire WF5 8LH* Wakefield (0924) 261139

CLARK, Bernard Charles. b 34. Open Univ BA81. S'wark Ord Course 65. **d** 68 **p** 69. C Pemberton St Jo *Liv* 68-71; C Winwick 71-73; P-in-c Warrington St Barn 74-76; V 76-78; V Hindley All SS 78-83; Perm to Offic from 86. *34 Lander Close, Old Hall, Great Sankey, Warrington WA5 5PJ* Warrington (0925) 53770

CLARK, Charles Gordon Froggatt. b 07. Em Coll Cam BA29 MA33. Wycliffe Hall Ox 29. **d** 31 **p** 32. V Crowborough *Chich* 48-67; Chapl Crowborough Hosp 59-67; rtd 67; Chapl Kent and Sussex Hosp Tunbridge Wells 68-80; Hon C Tunbridge Wells H Trin w Ch Ch *Roch* 68-80; Hon C Penshurst and Fordcombe 80-84; Asst Chapl Dorothy Kerin Trust 80-87; Perm to Offic Roch from 84; Pet from 89. *4 Village Farm Close, Castor, Peterborough PE5 7BX* Peterborough (0733) 380527

CLARK, Canon David George Neville. b 25. Linc Coll Ox BA49 MA59. Wells Th Coll 49. **d** 51 **p** 52. V Sutton New Town St Barn S'wark 59-72; R Charlwood 72-90; P-in-c Sidlow Bridge 76-77; R 77-90; P-in-c Buckland 85-87; P-in-c Leigh 87-90; Hon Can S'wark Cathl from 88; rtd 90. *12 Marlborough Road, Coventry CV2 4EP* Coventry (0203) 442400

CLARK, David Gordon. b 29. Clare Coll Cam BA52 MA57. Ridley Hall Cam 52. **d** 54 **p** 55. C Walthamstow St Jo *Chelmsf* 54-57; V 60-69; C Gt Ilford St Andr

57-60; R Stansted *Roch* 69-82; R Stansted w Fairseat and Vigo from 82. *The Rectory, Fairseat, Sevenoaks, Kent TN15 7LT* Fairseat (0732) 822494

CLARK, David Humphrey. b 39. G&C Coll Cam BA60. Wells Th Coll 62. **d** 64 **p** 65. C Leigh St Mary *Man* 64-68; Min Can and Prec Man Cathl 68-70; Ind Chapl *Nor* 70-85; P-in-c Nor St Clem and St Geo 70-76; P-in-c Nor St Sav w St Paul 70-76; V Norwich-over-the-Water Colegate St Geo 76-79; Hon AP Nor St Pet Mancroft 79-85; R Oadby *Leic* from 85. *St Peter's Rectory, 1 Leicester Road, Oadby, Leicester LE2 5BD* Leicester (0533) 712135 or 720080

CLARK, David John. b 40. CEng MIStructE Surrey Univ MPhil75. Ridley Hall Cam 81. **d** 83 **p** 84. C Combe Down w Monkton Combe and S Stoke *B & W* 83-89; Voc Adv Bath Adnry from 89; R Freshford, Limpley Stoke and Hinton Charterhouse from 89. *The Rectory, Crowe Lane, Freshford, Bath BA3 6EB* Bath (0225) 723135

CLARK, Dennis Henry Graham. b 26. St Steph Ho Ox 52. **d** 55 **p** 56. C Southall St Geo *Lon* 55-58; C Barbourne *Worc* 58-61; Chapl RAF 61-78; Asst Chapl-in-Chief RAF 78-82; Chapl St Clem Danes (RAF Ch) 79-82; V Godmanchester *Ely* from 82. *The Vicarage, 59 Post Street, Godmanchester, Huntingdon, Cambs PE18 8AQ* Huntingdon (0480) 453354

CLARK, Douglas Austin. b 15. Dur Univ LTh41 Lon Univ BA51. Oak Hill Th Coll 38. **d** 41 **p** 42. V Rugby St Matt *Cov* 66-81; rtd 82; Australia 82-90; Hon C Tiverton St Andr *Ex* from 90. *Sundale, St Paul's Square, Tiverton, Devon EX15 5JD* Tiverton (0884) 242944

CLARK, Edward Robert. b 39. Ex Coll Ox BA61 MA65 Bris Univ DSA68 CASS69. St Steph Ho Ox 61. **d** 63 **p** 64. C Solihull *Birm* 63-67; Perm to Offic Bris 67-69; Leic 69-71; Ox 71-80; St Alb 80-84; Cant from 84. *41 The Street, Kingston, Canterbury, Kent CT4 6JQ* Canterbury (0227) 830074

CLARK, Eric Douglas Colbatch. b 08. OBE66 MBE62. St Jo Coll Ox BA29. Wycliffe Hall Ox 39. **d** 40 **p** 41. Dir Overseas Studies Commendation Cen Lon 70-71; Warden Student Res Cen Wimbledon 72-77; rtd 77; Perm to Offic S'wark from 82. *11 Rosemary Cottages, The Drive, London SW20 8TQ* 081-879 0344

CLARK, Frederick Albert George. b 15. MBE68. ACP66. **d** 67 **p** 68. Hon C Stroud *Glouc* 67-84; Hon C Stroud and Uplands w Slad 84-85; Perm to Offic from 85. *2 Terrace Cottages, Thrupp, Stroud, Glos GL5 2BN* Brimscombe (0453) 882060

CLARK, Henry. b 23. AKC52. **d** 53 **p** 54. V Middlesb St Chad *York* 63-91; rtd 91. *Broadview, Ferry Road, Fingringhoe, Colchester CO5 7BY* Colchester (0206) 729248

CLARK, Hugh Lockhart. b 44. Oak Hill Th Coll 69. **d** 72 **p** 73. C Islington St Jude Mildmay Park *Lon* 72-75; C N Walsham w Antingham *Nor* 75-78; TV S Molton, Nymet St George, High Bray etc *Ex* 78-81; CF 81-83; V Gisburn *Bradf* 83-89; R Clitheroe St Jas *Blackb* from 89. *St James's Rectory, Woone Lane, Clitheroe, Lancs BB7 1BJ* Clitheroe (0200) 23608

CLARK, Ian. b 31. Lich Th Coll 63. **d** 65 **p** 66. C Droylsden St Mary *Man* 65-68; C Bedf Leigh 68-70; V Broughton Moor *Carl* 70-80; R Kirton S'well from 80; V Walesby from 80; P-in-c Egmanton 80-81; V from 81. *St Edmund's Vicarage, Walesby, Newark, Notts NG22 9PA* Mansfield (0623) 860522

CLARK, Dr Ian Duncan Lindsay. b 35. K Coll Cam BA59 MA63 PhD64 Ox Univ DipTh63. Ripon Hall Ox 62. **d** 64 **p** 65. C Willington *Newc* 64-66; India 66-76; Chapl St Cath Coll Cam 76; Tutor 78-85; Dean of Chpl 80-85. *4 Yewtree Lane, Yetholm, Kelso, Roxburghshire TD5 8RZ* Yetholm (057382) 323

CLARK, Mrs Jean Robinson. b 32. K Coll Lon AKC BD79. St Chris Coll Blackheath 53. **dss** 85 **d** 87. Cov E *Cov* 85-87; C 87-88; NSM Upper Mole Valley Gp S'wark 89-90; Hon Par Dn Charlwood 89-90; Lic to Offic *Cov* from 90. *12 Marlborough Road, Coventry CV2 4EP* Coventry (0203) 442400

CLARK, John David Stanley. b 36. Dur Univ BA64. Ridley Hall Cam 64. **d** 66 **p** 67. C Benchill *Man* 66-69; C Beverley Minster *York* 69-74; Perm to Offic S'well 74-76; Lic 76-77; Lic to Offic *Chelmsf* 77-80; Perm York 80-83; Miss to Seamen 77-80; V Egton w Grosmont *York* 83-89; R Thornton Dale and Ellerburne w Wilton from 89. *Thornton Dale Rectory, Pickering, N Yorkshire YO18 7QH* Pickering (0751) 74244

CLARK, John Edward Goodband. b 49. Chich Th Coll 70. **d** 73 **p** 74. C Thorpe *Nor* 73-76; C Earlham St Anne 76-78; Chapl RN 78-82; P-in-c Tittleshall w Godwick, Wellingham and Weasenham *Nor* 82-85; P-in-c

Helhoughton w Raynham 82-85; R S, E w W Raynham, Helhoughton, etc 85-90; R Taverham w Ringland from 90. *The Rectory, Taverham, Norwich NR8 6TE* Norwich (0603) 868217

CLARK, John Michael. b 35. DSMSC63 DipYW65 Leic Poly DCEd80. E Midl Min Tr Course 87. **d** 90. Chapl to the Deaf *Linc* from 86. *3 Hawthorn Road, Cherry Willingham, Lincoln LN3 4JU* Lincoln (0522) 751759

CLARK, Dr John Patrick Hedley. b 37. St Cath Coll Cam BA61 MA65 Worc Coll Ox BA63 MA72 BD74. Lambeth DD89 St Steph Ho Ox 61. **d** 64 **p** 65. C Highters Heath *Birm* 64-67; C Eglingham *Newc* 67-72; P-in-c Newc St Anne 72-77; V Longframlington w Brinkburn from 77. *The Vicarage, Rothbury Road, Longframlington, Morpeth, Northd NE65 8AQ* Longframlington (066570) 272

CLARK, John Ronald Lyons. b 47. TCD BA69 MA72. Div Hostel Dub 67. **d** 70 **p** 71. C Dundela *D & D* 70-72; CF 72-75; C Belf St Aid *Conn* 75-76; I Stranorlar w Meenglas and Kilteevogue *D & R* 76-81; Chapl Wythenshawe Hosp Man from 81. *8 Heath Road, Timperley, Altrincham, Cheshire WA15 6BH* 061-962 1081 or 998 7070

CLARK, Jonathan Dunnett. b 61. Ex Univ BA83 DipHE86 Bris Univ MLitt90. Trin Coll Bris 84. **d** 88 **p** 89. C Stanwix *Carl* from 88. *77 Brackenridge, Carlisle CA3 9TB* Carlisle (0228) 402625

CLARK, Jonathan Jackson. b 57. Linc Coll Ox 79 Down Coll Cam 83. Ridley Hall Cam 81. **d** 84 **p** 85. C W Derby St Luke *Liv* 84-87; C St Clacton *Chelmsf* from 87. *257 St John's Road, Clacton-on-Sea, Essex CO16 8DE* Clacton-on-Sea (0225) 434329

CLARK, Miss Kathleen Christine. b 33. St Mich Ho Ox DipHE58 Trin Coll Bris 89. **d** 90. NSM Eastbourne H Trin *Chich* from 90. *4 Hydney Street, Eastbourne, E Sussex BN22 7NX* Eastbourne (0323) 640294

CLARK, Ven Kenneth James. b 22. DSC44. St Cath Soc Ox BA48 MA52. Cuddesdon Coll 52. **d** 52 **p** 53. C Brinkworth *Bris* 52-53; C Cricklade w Latton 53-56; C-in-c Filwood Park CD 56-59; V Bris H Cross Inns Court 59-61; V Westbury-on-Trym H Trin 61-72; V Bris St Mary Redcliffe w Temple etc 72-82; P-in-c Bedminster St Mich 73-78; RD Bedminster 73-79; Hon Can Bris Cathl from 74; Adn Swindon from 82. *70 Bath Road, Swindon, Wilts SN1 4AY* Swindon (0793) 695059

CLARK, Lance Edgar Dennis. b 52. Linc Th Coll 74. **d** 77 **p** 78. C Arnold *S'well* 77-82; V Brinsley w Underwood 82-87; Chapl RAF from 87. *c/o MOD, Adastral House, Theobald's Roads, London WC1X 8RU* 071-430 7268

CLARK, Canon Malcolm Aiken. b 05. Lich Th Coll 32. **d** 34 **p** 35. R Edin Gd Shep *Edin* 56-77; I Edin St Vin from 77; rtd 77; Can St Mary's Cathl *Edin* 82-85; Dean Edin 82-85; Hon Can St Mary's Cathl from 85. *12 St Vincent Street, Edinburgh EH3 6SH* 031-557 3662

CLARK, Martin Hudson. b 46. K Coll Lon BD68 AKC68. **d** 71 **p** 72. C S'wark H Trin S'wark 71-74; C Parkstone St Pet w Branksea and St Osmund *Sarum* 74-77; V E Wickham *S'wark* 77-86; V Wandsworth St Anne from 86; RD Wandsworth from 90. *St Anne's Vicarage, 182 St Ann's Hill, London SW18 2RS* 081-874 2809

CLARK, Michael Arthur. b 46. S Dios Minl Tr Scheme. **d** 83 **p** 84. NSM Monkton Farleigh, S Wraxall and Winsley *Sarum* from 83. *62 Tyning Road, Winsley, Bradford-on-Avon, Wilts BA15 2JW* Bradford-on-Avon (02216) 6652

CLARK, Michael David. b 45. Ox Univ MA68. Trin Coll Bris DipTh72. **d** 72 **p** 73. C Cheadle *Ches* 72-76; Brazil 77-86; Bolivia 86-88; C Wilton *B & W* 89-90; TV from 90. *1 Comeytrowe Lane, Taunton, Somerset TA1 5PA* Taunton (0823) 337458

CLARK, Michael Wilford. b 23. OBE91 JP75. Loughb Univ TCert49. **d** 87 **p** 88. In Meth Ch 57-87; Chapl Asst Nightingale MacMillan Hospice Derby 87-89; Hon C Marston on Dove w Scropton *Derby* 87-89; P-in-c Longford, Long Lane, Dalbury and Radbourne from 89. *Ashleigh House, Grassy Lane, Burnaston, Etwall, Derby DE6 6LN* Derby (0332) 516968

CLARK, Patricia Mary. b 36. Liv Univ BSc. **d** 88. Par Dn Leasowe *Ches* from 88; Bp's Officer for Women in Min from 89. *4 Leasoweside, Leasowe, Wirral, Merseyside L46 3RW* 051-638 8568

CLARK, Peter. b 39. Ch Coll Cam BA61 MA65. Chich Th Coll 61. **d** 63 **p** 64. C Huddersfield SS Pet and Paul *Wakef* 63-67; C Notting Hill St Jo *Lon* 67-74; Grenada 75-79; C Hove All SS *Chich* 79; P-in-c Hove St Patr 79-82; V Hove St Patr w Ch Ch and St Andr 82-83; V Battersea Ch Ch and St Steph *S'wark* from 83; RD Battersea from 90. *Christ Church Vicarage, Candahar Road, London SW11 2PU* 071-228 1225

CLARK, Peter. b 45. Sarum & Wells Th Coll 87. **d** 89 **p** 90. C Portsea St Cuth *Portsm* from 89. *20 Highgrove Road, Portsmouth PO3 6PR* Portsmouth (0705) 661890

CLARK, Peter Norman. b 53. Qu Coll Cam BA79. Westcott Ho Cam 78. **d** 80 **p** 81. C Bris St Mary Redcliffe w Temple etc *Bris* 80-83; C Potternewton *Ripon* 83-86; R Longsight St Luke *Man* from 86. *St Luke's Rectory, Stockport Road, Longsight, Manchester M13 9AB* 061-273 6662

CLARK, Reginald Isaac. b 16. AKC47. **d** 47 **p** 48. Chapl Shenley Hosp Radlett Herts 65-84; rtd 84. *1 Monks Walk, Spalding, Lincs PE11 3LG*

CLARK, Richard Martin. b 60. Ch Coll Cam MA81. Trin Coll Bris BA86. **d** 86 **p** 87. C Orpington Ch Ch *Roch* 86-89; C Marple All SS *Ches* from 89. *125 Church Lane, Marple, Stockport, Cheshire SK6 7LD* 061-427 1467

CLARK, Robert Henry. b 32. Oak Hill Th Coll 61. **d** 64 **p** 65. C Haydock St Mark *Liv* 64-67; C Tranmere St Cath *Ches* 67-75; V Platt Bridge *Liv* 75-84; V Litherland St Paul Hatton Hill from 84. *St Paul's Vicarage, Watling Avenue, Liverpool L21 9NU* 051-928 2705

CLARK, Canon Robert James Vodden. b 07. Edin Th Coll 40. **d** 41 **p** 42. R Lasswade *Edin* 69-79; Hon Can St Mary's Cathl from 76; rtd 79. *15 North Street, St Andrews, Fife KY16 9PW* St Andrews (0334) 76237

CLARK, Canon Robin. b 27. Lon Univ BA49 BD69 MPhil77 St Jo Coll Dur DipTh54. **d** 54 **p** 55. C Newton Heath All SS *Man* 54-58; Asst Master Woodhouse Gr Sch Sheff 58-61; R Brant Broughton w Stragglethorpe *Linc* 61-90; P-in-c Welbourn 65-66; RD Loveden from 72; Can and Preb Linc Cathl from 85; R Brant Broughton and Beckingham from 90. *The Rectory, Brant Broughton, Lincoln LN5 0SL* Loveden (0400) 72449

CLARK, Preb Roland Mark Allison. b 21. St Cath Coll Cam BA48 MA53. Wells Th Coll 48. **d** 50 **p** 51. V Wilton *B & W* 56-79; Preb Wells Cathl from 63; R Backwell 79-88; RD Portishead 82-86; rtd 88. *16 Court Close, Portishead, Bristol BS20 9UX* Bristol (0272) 842089

CLARK, Roy. b 21. MBE64. Roch Th Coll 65. **d** 67 **p** 68. C New Sleaford *Linc* 67-70; R Stickney 70-72; rtd 87. *35 Princess Anne Road, Boston, Lincs PE21 9AR*

CLARK, Stephen Kenneth. b 52. Bris Univ BEd74. Wycliffe Hall Ox 80. **d** 83 **p** 84. C Pitsea *Chelmsf* 83-86; Chapl Scargill Ho N Yorkshire 86-89; R Elmley Castle w Bricklehampton and Combertons *Worc* from 89. *The Rectory, 22 Parkwood, Elmley Castle, Pershore, Worcs WR10 3HT* Elmley Castle (038674) 394

CLARK, Trevor Bartholomew. b 44. Qu Coll Birm 68. **d** 71 **p** 72. C Maltby *Sheff* 71-75; V New Rossington 75-80; V Campsall from 80. *The Vicarage, High Street, Campsall, Doncaster DN6 9AD* Doncaster (0302) 700286

CLARK, Vivian George. b 08. TD56. Chich Th Coll 31. **d** 34 **p** 36. V Boningale *Lich* 59-74; V Shifnal 59-74; rtd 74; Hon C Acton Burnell w Pitchford *Heref* 74-84; Perm to Offic *Ex* from 84. *87 Fore Street, Plympton, Plymouth PL7 3NB* Plymouth (0752) 344901

CLARKE, Alan John. b 55. St Jo Coll Dur BA77 MA85. Westcott Ho Cam 78. **d** 80 **p** 81. C Heworth St Mary *Dur* 80-83; C Darlington St Jo 83-87; Asst Chapl Bryanston Sch Blandford from 87. *Bryanston School, Blandford Forum, Dorset DT11 0PX* Blandford (0258) 52411

CLARKE, Alan Keith. b 38. SW Minl Tr Course. **d** 87 **p** 88. NSM Wolborough w Newton Abbot *Ex* from 87. *Headmaster's House, 3 College Road, Newton Abbot, Devon TQ12 1EF* Newton Abbot (0626) 63515

CLARKE, Alfred Charles Reginald. b 19. ACII. Qu Coll Birm 71. **d** 74 **p** 74. Hon C Yardley St Cypr Hay Mill *Birm* 74-80; Hon C Packwood w Hockley Heath 80-89; rtd 89; Lic to Offic *Birm* from 89. *15 Newton Road, Knowle, Solihull, W Midlands B93 9HL* Knowle (0564) 773861

CLARKE, Andrew John. b 58. New Coll Edin BD82 Graduate Soc Dur PGCE89. Linc Th Coll 84. **d** 86 **p** 87. C High Harrogate Ch Ch *Ripon* 86-88; RE Teacher Royds Hall High Sch Huddersfield from 88; NSM Thornbury *Bradf* from 91. *43 Victoria Road, Keighley, W Yorkshire BD21 1HQ* Keighley (0535) 669948

CLARKE, Arthur. b 01. Wycliffe Coll Toronto. **d** 33 **p** 34. V Bleasby w Halloughton *S'well* 59-69; C Witheridge *Ex* 69-73; rtd 72. *The Long House, Upper Westwood, Bradford-on-Avon, Wilts* Bradford-on-Avon (02216) 6460

CLARKE, Arthur. b 34. Lon Univ BD66 Nottm Univ MPhil77 DipEd. Sarum & Wells Th Coll 75. **d** 76 **p** 77. C Wollaton *S'well* 76-79; P-in-c Normanton on Soar 79-91; R Sutton Bonington 79-91; R Sutton Bonington w Normanton-on-Soar from 91. *St Anne's Rectory, Sutton Bonington, Loughborough, Leics LE12 5PF* Kegworth (05097) 2236

CLARKE, Miss Audrey May. b 35. Gilmore Ho 65. **dss** 75 **d** 87. Crofton Park St Hilda w St Cypr *S'wark* 75-79; Chapl Asst Middx Hosp Lon 80-84; Mottingham St Andr *S'wark* 84-87; Par Dn 87-89; C Westborough *Guildf* from 89. *1 Grantley Road, Guildford, Surrey GU2 6BW* Guildford (0483) 68866

CLARKE, Benjamin Blanchard. b 08. Birm Univ BSc31 MSc34 St Cath Soc Ox BA33 MA37. Ripon Hall Ox 31. **d** 33 **p** 34. V Padstow *Truro* 53-73; rtd 73. *4 Athelstan Park, Bodmin, Cornwall PL31 1DS* Bodmin (0208) 73989

CLARKE, Bernard Ronald. b 53. Ridley Hall Cam 74. **d** 77 **p** 78. C Leigh Park *Portsm* 77-78; C Petersfield w Sheet 78-81; Chapl RN from 81. *c/o MOD, Lacon House, Theobald's Road, London WC1X 8RY* 071-430 6847

CLARKE, Charles David. b 37. LCP77 Univ of Wales BA76 DPS90 Cam Univ DipEd77. St Mich Coll Llan 88. **d** 90 **p** 91. C Whitchurch *Llan* from 90. *47 Penydre, Rhiwbina, Cardiff CF4 6EJ* Cardiff (0222) 627531

CLARKE, Miss Christine Vera. b 45. Lon Univ CertEd66. Qu Coll Birm 79. **dss** 81 **d** 87. Bris St Mary Redcliffe w Temple etc *Bris* 81-86; Ind Chapl from 86. *St Leonard's Vicarage, Parkfield Avenue, Bristol BS5 8DP* Bristol (0272) 556286

CLARKE, Christopher George. b 43. Sarum Th Coll 67. **d** 68 **p** 69. C Sprowston *Nor* 68-72; V Hemsby 72-77; V Sutton Courtenay w Appleford *Ox* 77-84; TR Bracknell from 84; RD Bracknell from 90. *The Rectory, 26 Park Road, Bracknell, Berks RG12 2LU* Bracknell (0344) 423869

CLARKE, Colin David Emrys. b 42. Leeds Univ DipAdEd82 MEd84. Wells Th Coll 67. **d** 68 **p** 69. C Plumstead St Nic *S'wark* 68-71; C N Lynn w St Marg and St Nic *Nor* 71-75; Miss to Seamen 71-75; Asst Chapl HM Pris Wakef 75-77; V Birkenshaw w Hunsworth *Wakef* 77-87; V Illingworth from 87. *St Mary's Vicarage, 157 Keighley Road, Illingworth, Halifax HX2 9LL* Halifax (0422) 244322

CLARKE, Daniel. b 17. TCD BA39 MA44 BD66. **d** 41 **p** 42. C Dub St Bart *D & G* 41-44; Dioc Curate Killaloe *L & K* 44-46; Chapl Roscrea Hosp Inst 46-48; C-in-c Corbally 46-48; I Borrisokane 48-59; RD Upper Ormond 55-57; RD Lower Ormond 58-59; Asst Master Robert Bloomfield Sch Shefford 59-62; Hd Relig Studies Rcigate Gr Sch 62-82; Chapl 75-84; Chapl Reigate St Mary's Sch from 85. *4 Orchard Way, Reigate, Surrey RH2 8DT* Reigate (0737) 246169

CLARKE, Canon David George Alexander. b 23. TCD BA47 MA51 BD55 PhD57. **d** 48 **p** 49. I Kilrossanty *C & O* 61-73; Preb Newc St Patr Cathl Dub 65-89; Prec Waterford and Lismore *C & O* 67-73; Dean Cashel 73-83; I Cashel St Jo 73-83; I Ballymascanlan w Creggan, Forkhill etc *Arm* 83-89; rtd 89; Lic to Offic Arm & D & D from 90. *2 Ashley Court, Warrenpoint, Newry, Co Down BT34 3RN* Warrenpoint (06937) 72416

CLARKE, Dr David James. b 55. Univ of Wales (Abth) BSc(Econ)77 Keele Univ MA78 DLib PhD83. Trin Coll Bris DipTh84. **d** 84 **p** 85. C Cardigan and Mount and Verwick *St D* 84-87; P-in-c Llansantffraed and Llanbadarn Trefeglwys etc 87-88; V 88-91; Chapl Coll of St Mark and St Jo Plymouth *Ex* from 91. *Staff House 5, College of St Mark & St John, Derriford Road, Plymouth PL6 8BH* Plymouth (0752) 770809 or 777188

CLARKE, Denis John. b 23. Local NSM Course. **d** 87 **p** 88. NSM Brothertoft Gp *Linc* from 87. *49 Punchbowl Lane, Boston, Lincs PE21 8HU* Boston (0205) 363512

CLARKE, Douglas Charles. b 33. Bps' Coll Cheshunt 65. **d** 66 **p** 67. C Chingford SS Pet and Paul *Chelmsf* 66-72; V Romford Ascension Collier Row 72-79; V Bembridge *Portsm* 79-83; V Bournemouth St Mary *Win* 83-87; R High Wych and Gilston w Eastwick *St Alb* from 87. *The Rectory, High Wych, Sawbridgeworth, Herts CM21 0HX* Bishop's Stortford (0279) 723346

CLARKE, Edward. b 02. Dur Univ LTh28 St Jo Coll Dur BA30 MA32. St Aid Birkenhead 25. **d** 29 **p** 30. V Kirkburton *Wakef* 64-70; rtd 70; Perm to Offic *Wakef* from 70. *Timinets, Northgate, Honley, Huddersfield*

CLARKE, Edwin Joseph Alfred. b 18. Ripon Hall Ox 64. **d** 66 **p** 67. C Yardley St Edburgha *Birm* 66-70; R Nether Whitacre 70-88; rtd 89. *114 Main Street, Clifton Campville, Tamworth, Staffs B79 0AP* Clifton Campville (082786) 587

CLARKE, Eric Samuel. b 26. Nottm Univ BSc51 St Cath Coll Ox BA69 MA69. Wycliffe Hall Ox 51. **d** 54 **p** 55. C Gedling *S'well* 54-57; C Nottm St Pet and St Jas 57-69;

Perm to Offic *Derby* from 63. *16 Menin Road, Allestree, Derby DE3 2NL*

CLARKE, Frank. b 21. St Jo Coll Nottm. **d** 85 **p** 87. NSM Farnsfield *S'well* from 85. *Belvedere, Tippings Lane, Farnsfield, Newark, Notts NG22 8EP* Mansfield (0623) 882528

CLARKE, Canon Harold George. b 29. St D Coll Lamp 58. **d** 61 **p** 62. C Ebbw Vale Ch Ch *Mon* 61-64; C Roath St German *Llan* 64-73; Chapl Glam Poly 73-74; V Glyntaff 73-84; V Roath St Martin from 84; RD Cardiff from 89; Can Llan Cathl from 91. *St Martin's Vicarage, Strathnairn Street, Roath, Cardiff CF2 3JL* Cardiff (0222) 482295

CLARKE, Ven Herbert Lewis. b 20. Jes Coll Ox BA43 MA46. Union Th Sem (NY) STM50 Linc Th Coll 44. **d** 45 **p** 46. R Caerphilly *Llan* 67-77; Can Llan Cathl 75-77; Adn Llan 77-88; R St Fagans w Michaelston-s-Ely 77-90; rtd 90. *First Floor Flat, St Andrew, High Street, Llandaff, Cardiff* Cardiff (0222) 578581

CLARKE, Canon Hilary James. b 41. JP. Univ of Wales (Lamp) BA64 Ox Univ DipEd65. St Steph Ho Ox 64. **d** 66 **p** 67. C Kibworth Beauchamp *Leic* 66-68; Chapl to the Deaf 68-71; Prin Officer Ch Miss for Deaf Walsall 71-73; Prin Officer and Sec Leic & Co Miss for the Deaf 73-89; TV Leic H Spirit *Leic* 82-89; Hon Can Leic Cathl from 87; Sec Gen Syn Coun for the Deaf from 89. *c/o Church House, Great Smith Street, London SW1P 3NZ* 071-222 9011

CLARKE, Jason Scott. b 65. Leeds Univ BA87. Coll of Resurr Mirfield 89. **d** 91. C Hendon St Mary *Lon* from 91. *Christchurch House, 76 Brent Street, London NW4 2EF* 081-202 8123

CLARKE, John Cecil. b 32. St Jo Coll Dur BA70 DipTh71. Cranmer Hall Dur. **d** 75 **p** 76. Dioc Ecum Officer and Adv in Miss 75-87; Hon C Ches St Mary *Ches* 75-78; R Barrow 78-87; V Thornton Hough from 87; Dioc Projects Officer from 87. *All Saints' Vicarage, Thornton Hough, Wirral, Merseyside* 051-336 3429

CLARKE, John David Maurice. b 60. **d** 89. C Dub Whitechurch *D & G* from 89; Asst Chapl St Vin Hosp Donnybrook from 89. *8 Heather Park, Marlay Wood, Rathfarnham, Dublin 16, Irish Republic* Dublin (1) 931526

CLARKE, John Martin. b 52. Hertf Coll Ox BA89 MA89 Edin Univ BD76. Edin Th Coll 73. **d** 76 **p** 77. C Kenton Ascension *Newc* 76-79; Prec St Ninian's Cathl Perth *St And* 79-82; Info Officer to Scottish Episc Gen Syn 82-87; Greece 87-88; V Battersea St Mary *S'wark* 89-91; V Battersea St Mary from 91. *St Mary's Vicarage, 32 Vicarage Crescent, London SW11 3LD* 071-228 9648

CLARKE, John Patrick Hatherley. b 46. Pemb Coll Ox MA Man Univ MBA. St Jo Coll Nottm 81. **d** 83 **p** 84. C Leic H Trin w St Jo *Leic* 83-87; C Selly Park St Steph and St Wulstan *Birm* from 87. *927 Pershore Road, Selly Park, Birmingham B29 7PS* 021-472 2514

CLARKE, John Percival. b 44. TCD BA67. **d** 69 **p** 70. C Belf St Simon *Conn* 69-72; C Monkstown *D & G* 72-76; Asst Chapl TCD 76-78; I Durrus *C, C & R* 79-82; I Carrigrohane Union 82-89; Tanzania from 89. *Msalato Bible College, PO Box 264, Dodoma, Tanzania*

CLARKE, John Philip. b 31. Trin Hall Cam BA54 MA62. Linc Th Coll. **d** 57 **p** 58. C Walworth Lady Marg w St Mary *S'wark* 57-59; C Warlingham w Chelsham and Farleigh 59-62; C Mottingham St Andr 62-67; C Eltham Park St Luke 67-72; Chapl Leeds Gen Infirmary 72-91; C Far Headingley St Chad *Ripon* from 91; Bp's Adv on Chr Healing from 91. *75 Weetwood Lane, Leeds L16 5NU* Leeds (0532) 759526 or 432799

CLARKE, Miss Joyce Nancy. b 32. CertEd58. N Ord Course 82. **dss** 85 **d** 87. Prestbury *Ches* 85-87; Par Dn from 87. *2 Peterborough Close, Macclesfield, Cheshire SK10 3DT* Macclesfield (0625) 611809

CLARKE, Mrs Joyce Willoughby Price. b 36. Gilmore Course 78. **dss** 81 **d** 87. Heston *Lon* 81-87; Par Dn 87-89; Deanery Youth Chapl *Sarum* from 90. *Ankadown, 22 Sherford Close, Wareham, Dorset BH20 4JL* Wareham (0929) 554115

CLARKE, Kenneth Herbert. b 49. TCD BA71. **d** 72 **p** 73. C Magheralin *D & D* 72-75; C Dundonald 75-78; Chile 78-82; I Crinken *D & G* 82-86; I Coleraine Conn from 86. *St Patrick's Rectory, Mountsandel Road, Coleraine, Irish Republic BT52 1JE* Coleraine (265) 43429

CLARKE, Canon Leslie Reginald Minchin. b 10. TCD BA40 MA46. **d** 40 **p** 41. Dioc C and Sec *C, C & R*

71-80; Can Cloyne Cathl 76-80; rtd 80. *Adamstown, Fivemilebridge, Ballinhassig, Co Cork, Irish Republic* Cork (21) 888165

CLARKE, Canon Malcolm Methuen. b 08. K Coll Cam BA36 MA40. Cuddesdon Coll 37. **d** 38 **p** 39. V Wellingborough All Hallows *Pet* 49-78; rtd 78; Hon C Northn St Matt *Pet* from 78. *11A Kingsley Road, Northampton NN2 7BN* Northampton (0604) 713695

CLARKE, Canon Margaret Geraldine. b 33. Dalton Ho Bris 62. **dss** 68 **d** 87. Wells St Thos w Horrington *B & W* 68-74; Easthampstead *Ox* 74-87; Par Dn from 87; Hon Can Ch Ch from 90. *St Michael's House, Crowthorne Road, Bracknell, Berks RG12 4DR* Bracknell (0344) 429397

CLARKE, Martin Geoffrey. b 45. Dur Univ BA66. Wells Th Coll 67. **d** 69 **p** 70. C Atherstone *Cov* 69-72; C Keresley and Coundon 72-75; R Scorborough w Leconfield *York* 75-79; P-in-c Lockington w Lund 78-79; R Lockington and Lund and Scorborough w Leconfield 79-81; R Romsley *Worc* from 81; Chapl Halesowen Coll from 81. *The Rectory, St Kenelm's Road, Romsley, Halesowen, W Midlands B62 0PH* Romsley (0562) 710216

CLARKE, Martin Howard. b 47. AKC70. St Aug Coll Cant 70. **d** 71 **p** 72. C Saffron Walden w Wendens Ambo *Chelmsf* 71-74; C Ely 74-78; V Messing w Inworth *Chelmsf* 78-90; V Layer-de-la-Haye from 90. *45 Malting Green Road, Layer-de-la-Haye, Colchester, Essex CO2 0JJ* Layer-de-la-Haye (020634) 243

CLARKE, Mary Margaret. b 65. K Coll Lon BD86 AKC86. Linc Th Coll 87. **d** 89. Par Dn Northn St Jas *Pet* from 89. *54 Bowden Road, Northampton NN5 5LT* Northampton (0604) 759841

CLARKE, Maurice Fulford Lovell. b 12. Clare Coll Cam BA34 MA38. Wells Th Coll 35. **d** 36 **p** 37. R Ashley *Lich* 65-77; rtd 77; Perm to Offic *Heref* from 77. *8 St Mary's Mews, Ludlow, Shropshire SY8 1DZ* Ludlow (0584) 874111

CLARKE, Maurice Harold. b 30. K Alfred's Coll Win CertEd56 Sussex Univ MA79 LCP69. Cuddesdon Coll 65. **d** 67 **p** 68. Hd Master Co Sec Sch Cowplain (Lower Sch) 67-72; Hon C Waterlooville *Portsm* 67-70; Hon C Fareham SS Pet and Paul 70-72; Hon C Higham and Merston *Roch* 72-83; Dep Hd Master Thamesview High Sch 72-80; Hd Master Eltham Green Comp Sch 80-83; V Hamble le Rice *Win* 83-90; rtd 91. *10 Worcester Road, Chichester, W Sussex* Chichester (0243) 775646

CLARKE, Michael. b 39. Ely Th Coll 60. **d** 62 **p** 63. C S Stoneham *Win* 62-64; C Greenford H Cross *Lon* 64-69; Hon C Milton *Portsm* 69-74; Chapl St Jas Hosp Portsm 69-91; Chapl Hurstpierpoint Coll Hassocks from 91. *Hurstpierpoint College, Hassocks, E Sussex BN6 9JS* Hurstpierpoint (0273) 83363

CLARKE, Michael Charles. b 12. TD59. Ch Ch Ox BA36 MA38. Cuddesdon Coll 36. **d** 37 **p** 38. V Eastbury and E Garston *Ox* 64-83; V Lambourne Woodlands 64-83; rtd 83; Perm to Offic *Ox* 84-89. *Steep Meadows, 17 Chilton Way, Hungerford, Berks RG17 0JR* Hungerford (0488) 682131

CLARKE, Norman. b 12. Keble Coll Ox BA52 MA58. St Steph Ho Ox 52. **d** 54 **p** 55. C Ellesmere Port *Ches* 54-57; C Kettering St Mary *Pet* 57-60; Ghana 60-62; C Friern Barnet All SS *Lon* 62-63; Lic to Offic *Leic* 63-74; C Knighton St Mary Magd 74-81; Dioc Communications Officer 81-88; P-in-c Sproughton w Burstall *St E* 81-88; P-in-c Dunsford and Doddiscombsleigh *Ex* from 88; P-in-c Cheriton Bishop from 88. *The Vicarage, Dunsford, Exeter EX6 7AA* Christow (0647) 52490

CLARKE, Oswald Reeman. b 12. Liv Univ BA35 St Cath Soc Ox BA37 MA40. Ripon Hall Ox 34. **d** 36 **p** 37. V Upper Chelsea St Simon *Lon* 58-85; rtd 85; Perm to Offic *Lon* 85-90; P-in-c St Mary Abchurch from 90. *Flat 8, 55-56 Oakley Street, London SW3 5HB* 071-351 6333

CLARKE, Canon Peter. b 25. Lon Univ BSc49 St Chad's Coll Dur DipTh51. **d** 52 **p** 52. V Bardney *Linc* 68-75; V Apley w Stainfield 68-75; V Linc St Nic w St Jo Newport 75-88; RD Christianity 78-85; Can and Preb Linc Cathl from 79; rtd 88. *46 Swallow Avenue, Skellingthorpe, Lincoln LN6 5XW* Lincoln (0522) 684261

CLARKE, Peter Gerald. b 38. Cuddesdon Coll 74. **d** 76 **p** 77. Hon C Marston Magna w Rimpton *B & W* 76-79; Hon C Queen Camel, Marston Magna, W Camel, Rimpton etc 79-87; Hon C Chilton Cantelo, Ashington, Mudford, Rimpton etc 87-88; R Tintinhull w Chilthorne Domer, Yeovil Marsh etc from 88. *The Rectory, Tintinhull, Yeovil, Somerset BA22 8PY* Martock (0935) 822655

CLARKE, Philip John. b 44. Bris Univ BA65 Univ of Wales (Abth) DipEd66. N Ord Course 84. **d** 87 **p** 88.

NSM Crewe Ch Ch and St Pet *Ches* 87-88; NSM Coppenhall 88-90; Lic to Offic from 90. *30 Warmingham Road, Crewe, Cheshire CW1 4PU* Crewe (0270) 585381

CLARKE, Canon Reginald Gilbert. b 06. Qu Coll Cam BA29 MA34. Wycliffe Hall Ox 30. **d** 31 **p** 32. Perm to Offic *Wakef* from 68; V Leck *Blackb* 68-71; rtd 71; Perm to Offic *Carl* from 77. *11 Fairgarth Drive, Kirkby Lonsdale, Carnforth, Lancs LA6 2DT* Kirkby Lonsdale (05242) 71950

CLARKE, Richard Leon. b 37. Sarum Th Coll 62. **d** 65 **p** 66. C Fordington *Sarum* 65-68; C Haywards Heath St Rich *Chich* 68-72; C Goring-by-Sea 72-76; P-in-c Portslade St Andr 76-77; P-in-c Southwick St Pet 76-77; V Portslade St Pet and St Andr 77-79; R Clayton w Keymer from 79; RD Hurst from 90. *The Rectory, Keymer, Hassocks, W Sussex BN6 8RB* Hassocks (07918) 3570

CLARKE, Canon Dr Richard Lionel. b 49. TCD BA71 MA79 PhD90 K Coll Lon BD75 AKC75. **d** 75 **p** 76. C Holywood *D & D* 75-77; C Dub St Bart w Ch Ch Leeson Park *D & G* 77-79; Dean of Residence TCD 79-84; I Bandon Union *C, C & R* from 84; Bp's Exam Chapl from 84; Dir of Ords from 85; Cen Dir of Ords from 82; Can Cork and Ross Cathls from 91. *The Rectory, Bandon, Co Cork, Irish Republic* Bandon (23) 41259

CLARKE, Richard Maximilian Arnold. b 59. Hull Univ BA. St Steph Ho Ox. **d** 86 **p** 87. C Hartlepool St Oswald *Dur* 86-89; C Sedgefield from 91. *9 Belsay Court, Sedgefield, Co Durham* Sedgefield (0740) 20829

CLARKE, Dr Robert George. b 36. Natal Univ PhD83. Cranmer Hall Dur BA65 DipTh67. **d** 67 **p** 68. C Basingstoke *Win* 67-70; S Africa from 71. *26 Somerset Street, Grahamstown, 6140 South Africa* Grahamstown (461) 27803 or 311100

CLARKE, Robert Graham. b 28. Sarum & Wells Th Coll 77. **d** 81 **p** 82. NSM Worting *Win* 81-82; NSM Woolston from 83; NSM Portswood St Denys from 89. *Flat 10, River Green, Hamble, Southampton SO3 5JA* Southampton (0703) 454230

CLARKE, Robert James. b 22. ACP58. CITC 67. **d** 69 **p** 70. C Belf St Mary *Conn* 69-70; C and Min Can Limerick Cathl *L & K* 70-72; Asst Chapl Wilson's Hosp Sch Multyfarnham 72-85; Chapl 85-87; Lic to Offic *M & K* from 87. *c/o W Coleborn Esq, Kilgullen Street, Dunlavin, Co Wicklow, Irish Republic* Naas (45) 51231

CLARKE, Robert Michael. b 45. Lon Univ BD71. Oak Hill Th Coll 66 Sarum & Wells Th Coll 77. **d** 78 **p** 79. Hon C Glastonbury St Jo w Godney *B & W* 78-81; Chapl Felsted Sch Essex 81-85; Asst Chapl from 85. *Deacon's House, Felsted School, Felsted, Dunmow, Essex CM6 3JQ* Great Dunmow (0371) 820465

CLARKE, Robert Sydney. b 35. AKC64. **d** 65 **p** 66. C Hendon St Mary *Lon* 65-69; C Langley Marish *Ox* 69-70; Chapl New Cross Hosp Wolv 70-74; Herrison Hosp Dorchester 74-80; Westmr Hosp Lon 80-85; Chapl R Hants Co Hosp Win from 85; Sen Chapl Win HA from 88; Chapl to HM The Queen from 87. *Royal Hants County Hospital, Romsey Road, Winchester, Hants SO22 5DG* Winchester (0962) 63535

CLARKE, Robert William. b 56. TCD DipTh83. **d** 83 **p** 84. C Cloughfern *Conn* 83-85; C Drumragh w Mountfield *D & R* 85-87; I Edenderry w Clanabogan from 87. *Edenderry Rectory, 91 Crevenagh Road, Omagh, Co Tyrone BT79 0EZ* Omagh (0662) 245525

CLARKE, Roger David. b 58. Man Univ BA Ox Univ MA. Ripon Coll Cuddesdon 80. **d** 83 **p** 84. C Frodsham *Ches* 83-86; C Wilmslow 86-88; V High Lane from 88. *The Vicarage, 85 Buxton Road, High Lane, Stockport, Cheshire SK6 8DX* Disley (0663) 762627

CLARKE, Roland. b 22. St Aid Birkenhead 49. **d** 52 **p** 53. V Pendlebury Ch Ch *Man* 59-78; rtd 78. *79 Hilton Lane, Prestwich, Manchester M25 8SD* 061-773 5198

CLARKE, Ronald George. b 31. Oak Hill Th Coll. **d** 64 **p** 65. C Carlton-in-the-Willows *S'well* 64-68; V Bestwood St Matt 68-76; V Barnsbury St Andr w St Thos and St Matthias *Lon* 76-77; V Barnsbury St Andr 77-78; V Barnsbury St Andr w H Trin 79-80; P-in-c Battle Bridge All SS w Pentonville St Jas 79-81; V Barnsbury St Andr and H Trin w All SS 81-86; TR Bath Twerton-on-Avon *B & W* from 86. *The Rectory, Watery Lane, Bath BA2 1RL* Bath (0225) 21438

CLARKE, Roy Langridge. b 21. St Chad's Coll Dur BA48 DipTh50 DipEd51. **d** 51 **p** 52. Chapl Caldicott Sch Ox 68-69; Hon C Boyne Hill *Ox* 69-81; Perm to Offic from 81; rtd 86. *26 Furrow Way, Maidenhead, Berks SL6 3NY* Littlewick Green (062882) 4082

CLARKE, Royston James. b 33. ALCD58. **d** 58 **p** 59. C Guildf St Sav *Guildf* 58-61; C Otley *Bradf* 61-65; R

Stockton *Cov* 65-72; P-in-c Leamington Priors St Mary 72-75; V 75-91; R Gunton St Pet *Nor* from 91. *The Rectory, 36 Gunton Church Lane, Lowestoft, Suffolk NR32 4LF* Lowestoft (0502) 572600

CLARKE, Thomas Percival. b 15. Univ of Wales BA39. Lich Th Coll 39. **d** 41 **p** 42. V Blackheath All SS *S'wark* 59-73; Chapl Charing Cross Hosp Lon 73-81; rtd 80. *1 Trenos Gardens, Llanharan, Pontyclun, M Glam CF79SZ* Llantrisant (0443) 227662

CLARKE, Vernon Douglas. b 18. Jes Coll Cam BA48 MA50. Bps' Coll Cheshunt 47. **d** 49 **p** 50. V Millom H Trin *Carl* 63-71; V Cockermouth All SS w Ch Ch 71-74; P-in-c Kirkland 75-83; P-in-c Gt Salkeld 79-80; C Gt Salkeld w Lazonby 80-83; rtd 83; Perm to Offic *Carl* from 84. *Birchfield, Great Salkeld, Penrith, Cumbria CA11 9LW* Lazonby (076883) 380

CLARKE, Mrs Yvonne Veronica. b 58. CA Tr Coll. **dss** 86 **d** 87. Nunhead St Silas *S'wark* 86-87; Par Dn 87-90; Par Dn Nunhead St Antony w St Silas 90-91; Par Dn Mottingham St Andr from 91. *St Alban's Parsonage, 132 William Barefoot Drive, London SE9 3BP* 081-857 7702

CLARKSON, Ven Alan Geoffrey. b 34. Ch Coll Cam BA57 MA61. Wycliffe Hall Ox 57. **d** 59 **p** 60. C Penn Lich 59-60; C Oswestry St Oswald 60-63; C Wrington *B & W* 63-65; V Chewton Mendip w Emborough 65-74; Dioc Ecum Officer 65-75; V Glastonbury St Jo w Godney 74-84; P-in-c W Pennard 80-84; P-in-c Meare 81-84; P-in-c Glastonbury St Benedict 82-84; V Glastonbury w Meare, W Pennard and Godney 84; Hon Can Win Cathl *Win* from 84; Adn Win from 84; V Burley Ville from 84. *The Vicarage, Church Corner, Burley, Ringwood, Hants BH24 4AP* Burley (04253) 2303

CLARKSON, David James. b 42. St Andr Univ BSc66. N Ord Course 85. **d** 88 **p** 89. NSM Slaithwaite w E Scammonden *Wakef* 88-89; C Morley St Pet w Churwell 89-91; P-in-c Cumberworth w Denby Dale from 91. *The Rectory, 43 Hollybank Avenue, Upper Cumberworth, Huddersfield HD8 8NY* Huddersfield (0484) 606225

CLARKSON, Eric George. b 22. St Jo Coll Dur BA48 DipTh50. **d** 50 **p** 51. C Birkdale St Jo *Liv* 50-52; C Grassendale 52-54; PC W Derby St Luke 54-66; V Blackb St Mich *Blackb* 66-75; V Blackb St Mich w St Jo 75; V Chapeltown *Sheff* 75-86; C Ranmoor 86-87; C Crosspool from 87. *110 Darwin Lane, Sheffield S10 5RH* Sheffield (0742) 660840

CLARKSON, Geoffrey. b 35. AKC61. **d** 62 **p** 63. C Shildon *Dur* 62-65; Asst Chapl HM Pris Liv 65-66; Chapl HM Borstal Feltham 66-71; Hon C Hampton St Mary *Lon* from 71; Chapl HM Rem Cen Ashford 88-90; Chapl HM Pris Coldingley from 90. *HM Prison Coldingley, Bisley, Woking, Surrey GU24 9EX* Brookwood (04867) 76721

CLARKSON, John Thomas. b 30. AKC54. St Boniface Warminster 55. **d** 54 **p** 55. C Luton St Sav *St Alb* 54-59; Australia 59-73 and from 77; V Dallington *Pet* 73-77. *PO Box 125, Blayney, NSW, Australia 2799* Blayney (63) 682065

CLARKSON, Michael Livingston. b 48. California Univ BA70 Loyola Univ JD73. Wycliffe Hall Ox 87. **d** 89 **p** 90. C Kensington St Barn *Lon* from 89. *St Barnabas's Vicarage, 23 Addison Road, London W14 8LH* 071-371 1451

CLARKSON, Richard. b 33. Man Univ BSc54 Ball Coll Ox DPhil57. Oak Hill Th Coll 89. **d** 91. NSM Sunnyside w Bourne End *St Alb* from 91. *Kingsmead, Gravel Path, Berkhamsted, Herts HP4 2PH* Berkhamsted (0442) 873014

CLARKSON, Richard Michael. b 38. Dur Univ BA60. Cranmer Hall Dur DipTh62. **d** 62 **p** 63. C St Annes *Blackb* 62-66; Hon C from 70; C Lanc St Mary 66-68. *35 Westby Street, Lytham, Lytham St Annes, Lancs FY8 5JF* Lytham (0253) 733719

CLARKSON, Robert Christopher. b 32. Dur Univ BA53 DipEd54. S Dios Minl Tr Scheme 85. **d** 87 **p** 88. NSM Wonston and Stoke Charity w Hunton *Win* from 87. *27 Wrights Way, South Wonston, Winchester, Hants SO21 3HE* Winchester (0962) 881692

CLARRIDGE, Donald Michael. b 41. DipOT86. Oak Hill Th Coll 63. **d** 66 **p** 67. C Newc St Barn and St Jude *Newc* 66-70; C Pennycross *Ex* 70-76; R Clayhanger 76-83; R Petton 76-83; R Huntsham 76-83; V Bampton 76-83. *Winkley Broad Road, Hambrook, Chichester, W Sussex PO18 8RF* Chichester (0243) 572796

CLASBY, Michael Francis Theodore. b 37. Lon Univ BA59. Chich Th Coll 59. **d** 61 **p** 62. C Leigh-on-Sea St Marg *Chelmsf* 61-64; C Forest Gate St Edm 64-69; V Walthamstow St Mich 69-70; Chapl Community of Sisters of the Love of God 87-89; Perm to Offic *St Alb*

87-89; NSM Hemel Hempstead from 90. *47 Wrensfield, Hemel Hempstead, Herts HP1 1RP* Hemel Hempstead (0442) 254400

CLASPER, John. b 42. AKC67. **d** 68 **p** 69. C Leeds All Hallows w St Simon *Ripon* 68-71; C Hawksworth Wood 72-74; Ind Chapl *Dur* from 74; TV Jarrow St Paul 75-77; TV Jarrow 77-91; Dioc Urban Development Officer 90-91; TR E Darlington from 91. *East Darlington House, 30 Smithfield Road, Darlington, Co Durham DL1 4DD* Darlington (0325) 369523

CLASSON, Michael Campbell. b 32. TCD BA52 HDipEd54 MA55. CITC 87. **d** 89 **p** 91. NSM Conwal Union w Gartan *D & R* 89-90; NSM Ardara w Glencolumbkille, Inniskeel etc from 90. *Summy, Portnoo, Co Donegal, Irish Republic* Portnoo (75) 45242

CLATWORTHY, Jonathan Richard. b 48. Univ of Wales BA70. Sarum & Wells Th Coll 71. **d** 76 **p** 77. C Man Resurr *Man* 76-78; C Bolton St Pet 78-81; V Ashton St Pet 81-85; Chapl Sheff Univ *Sheff* from 85. *119 Ashdell Road, Sheffield S10 3DB* Sheffield (0742) 669243 or 78555

CLATWORTHY, Thomas Donald Vaughan. b 08. Univ of Wales BA30. St Mich Coll Llan 31. **d** 33 **p** 34. V Weston-super-Mare All SS *B & W* 71-77; rtd 77; Perm to Offic *Ex* from 77. *3 Copplestone Road, Budleigh Salterton, Devon EX9 6DS* Budleigh Salterton (03954) 5381

CLAUSEN, John Frederick. b 37. Sarum Th Coll 65. **d** 68 **p** 69. C Kentish Town St Jo *Lon* 68-71; C Rainham *Roch* 71-77; R Stone 77-89; Lic to Dartford RD from 89. *14 Watling Street, Dartford DA1 1RF* Dartford (0322) 279570

CLAWSON, Derek George. b 35. AMCST62. Qu Coll Birm 63. **d** 66 **p** 67. C Ditton St Mich *Liv* 66-70; C Speke All SS 70-72; V Hindley Green 72-85; V Wigan St Mich from 85. *St Michael's Vicarage, Duke Street, Wigan, Lancs WN1 2DN* Wigan (0942) 42381

✠**CLAXTON, Rt Rev Charles Robert.** b 03. Qu Coll Cam BA26 MA33. Lambeth DD60 Ridley Hall Cam 26. **d** 27 **p** 28 **c** 46. C Stratford St Jo *Chelmsf* 27-29; C Redhill St Jo *S'wark* 29-33; V Bris H Trin *Bris* 33-38; Bp's Chapl 38-46; Hon Can Bris Cathl 42-46; Home Sec Miss Coun of Ch Assemblies 43-46; Lic to Offic *Roch* 43-46; C St Martin-in-the-Fields *Lon* 44-46; R W Derby St Mary 46-48; Suff Bp Warrington *Liv* 48-60; R Halsall 48-58; Bp Blackb 60-71; rtd 71; Asst Bp Ex 71-89. *St Martins, 18 Prestbury Park, Prestbury, Macclesfield, Cheshire SK10 4AF* Macclesfield (0625) 829864

CLAXTON, Leslie Edward Mitchell. b 10. MC46. ARCM61 Peterho Cam BA33 MA48. Cuddesdon Coll 34. **d** 35 **p** 36. R St Olave Hart Street w All Hallows Staining etc *Lon* 68-85; rtd 85. *Flat 5, 83 St George's Drive, London SW1V 4DB* 071-834 9407

CLAXTON, Louis Allen. b 15. Worc Ord Coll 62. **d** 63 **p** 64. P-in-c Pencoys w Carnmenellis *Truro* 68-71; Chapl Rotterdam Miss to Seamen *Eur* 71-74; Chapl Cadenabbia 74-77; Chapl Costa Blanca 77-78; C-in-c Bexhill St Andr CD *Chich* 78-82; rtd 82; Perm to Offic *Chich* from 83. *c/o Mrs Baker, 2 Bellbanks Bungalows, Bellbanks Road, Hailsham, E Sussex*

CLAY, Colin Peter. b 32. Ch Coll Cam BA55 MA59. Em Coll Saskatoon Hon DD91 Wells Th Coll 55. **d** 57 **p** 58. C Malden St Jas *S'wark* 57-59; Canada from 59; Asst Prof Relig Studies Laurentian Univ 69-72. *College of St Emmanuel and St Chad, 1337 College Drive, Saskatoon, Saskatchewan, Canada, S7N 0W6* Saskatoon (306) 966-8500

CLAY, Elizabeth Jane. b 50. **dss** 86 **d** 87. Birstall *Wakef* 86-87; Hon Par Dn Lupset 87-90; Par Dn from 90. *St George's Vicarage, Broadway, Lupset, Wakefield, W Yorkshire WF2 8AA* Wakefield (0924) 373088

CLAY, Geoffrey. b 51. CertEd. Ridley Hall Cam. **d** 86 **p** 87. C Birstall *Wakef* 86-90; V Lupset from 90. *The Vicarage, Broadway, Lupset, Wakefield, W Yorkshire WF2 8AA* Wakefield (0924) 373088

CLAY, Peter Herbert. b 31. Lich Th Coll 62. **d** 64 **p** 65. C Ross *Heref* 64-67; C Leamington Priors All SS *Cov* 67-70; P-in-c Temple Grafton w Binton 70-73; V 73-75; P-in-c Exhall w Wixford 70-73; V 73-75; TV Cen Telford *Lich* 75-86; USPG 86-90; V Loughb Gd Shep *Leic* from 90. *Good Shepherd Vicarage, 2 Bramcote Road, Loughborough, Leics LE11 2SA* Loughborough (0509) 211005

CLAYDEN, David Edward. b 42. Oak Hill Th Coll 74. **d** 76 **p** 77. C Worksop St Jo *S'well* 76-79; V Clarborough w Hayton 79-84; C Bloxwich *Lich* 87-90; TV from 90. *6 Cresswell Crescent, Mossley, Bloxwich, Walsall WS3 2UW* Bloxwich (0922) 476647

CLAYDON, Graham Leonard. b 43. K Coll Lon BA65. Clifton Th Coll 66. d 68 p 69. C Walthamstow St Mary w St Steph *Chelmsf* 68-73; Hon C St Marylebone All So w SS Pet and Jo *Lon* 73-81; V Islington St Mary from 81. *St Mary's Vicarage, Upper Street, London N1 2TX* 071-226 3400

CLAYDON, John Richard. b 38. St Jo Coll Cam BA61 MA65. Trin Coll Bris DipTh72. d 73 p 74. C Finchley Ch Ch *Lon* 73-76; Asst Chapl K Edw Sch Witley 76-77; C Macclesfield St Mich *Ches* 77-81; V Marple All SS 81-91; CMJ from 91; Israel from 91. *Immanuel House, PO Box 2773, Tel Aviv 61027, Israel* Tel Aviv (3) 821459

CLAYPOLE WHITE, Douglas Eric. b 29. FCA ATII. St Alb Minl Tr Scheme 77. d 80 p 81. NSM Sharnbrook and Knotting w Souldrop *St Alb* 80-82; NSM Felmersham 82-87; P-in-c from 87. *Homelands, Turvey, Bedford MK43 8DB* Turvey (023064) 661

CLAYTON, Anthony Edwin Hay. b 36. Sarum Th Coll 61. d 63 p 64. C Tooting All SS *S'wark* 63-68; Perm to Offic Leic 69-74; S'well 73-80; Hon C Lockington w Hemington *Leic* 74-80; P-in-c Eastwell 80-83; P-in-c Eaton 80-83; P-in-c Croxton Kerrial, Knipton, Harston, Branston etc 83-84; R from 84; Chapl Belvoir Castle from 85; RD Framland (Melton) from 90. *High Framland Rectory, Harston, Grantham, Lincs NG32 1PP* Grantham (0476) 870329

CLAYTON, Geoffrey Buckroyd. b 26. Newc Univ BA67. Roch Th Coll 62. d 64 p 65. C Newc St Geo *Newc* 64-67; C Byker St Ant 67-68; C Cheddleton *Lich* 69-72; V Arbory *S & M* from 72; RD Castletown from 82; V Santan from 88. *Arbory Vicarage, Ballabeg, Castletown, Isle of Man* Castletown (0624) 823595

CLAYTON, Canon Giles. b 21. Keble Coll Ox BA42 MA47. St Steph Ho Ox 42. d 44 p 45. R Durrington *Sarum* 52-70; RD Avon 67-70; R Salisbury St Martin 70-86; RD Salisbury 72-77; Can and Preb Sarum Cathl from 73; rtd 86; Master St Nic Hosp Salisbury from 86. *The Master's House, St Nicholas' Hospital, Salisbury SP1 2SW* Salisbury (0722) 336874

CLAYTON, Canon John. b 11. Leeds Univ BA33 MA43. Wells Th Coll 34. d 35 p 36. V Otley *Bradf* 65-76; rtd 76; Perm to Offic Bradf and Ripon from 76. *10 Sandy Walk, Bramhope, Leeds LS16 9DW* Leeds (0532) 611388

CLAYTON, Michael John. b 32. Ox NSM Course. d 79 p 80. NSM Wokingham St Paul *Ox* 79-81; C 82-84; C Christchurch *Win* from 84. *22 Kestrel Drive, Christchurch, Dorset BH23 4DE* Highcliffe (0425) 276267

CLAYTON, Norman James. b 24. AKC52. d 53 p 54. S Africa 60-78; Dioc Communications Officer *Derby* 78-88; P-in-c Risley 78-87; R 87-89; rtd 89; Perm to Offic *Derby* from 89. *6 Allendale Avenue, Beeston, Nottingham* Nottingham (0602) 250060

CLAYTON, Sydney Cecil Leigh. b 38. Pemb Coll Ox BA62 MA65 Lon Univ BD65. Linc Th Coll. d 65 p 66. C Birch St Jas *Man* 65-68; Lect Bolton Par Ch 68-77; V Denshaw from 77. *The Vicarage, Huddersfield Road, Denshaw, Oldham OL3 5SB* Saddleworth (0457) 874575

CLAYTON, Wilfred. b 10. Worc Ord Coll 57. d 59 p 60. R Whitwell *Derby* 68-73; P-in-c Calow 74-77; rtd 77; Perm to Offic *Derby* from 77. *The Haven, Hodthorpe, Worksop, Notts S80 4UZ* Worksop (0909) 720006

CLAYTON, William Alan. b 32. Liv Univ BSc54 Lon Univ BD60. d 63 p 64. C Wallasey St Hilary *Ches* 63-67; R Burton Agnes w Harpham *York* 67-69; V Batley St Thos *Wakef* 69-72; Lic to Offic *Ripon* 73-85; Hon C Grinton 75-85; R Barningham w Hutton Magna and Wycliffe from 85. *The Rectory, Barningham, Richmond, N Yorkshire DL11 7DW* Teesdale (0833) 21217

CLAYTON-JONES, Roger Francis. b 39. AKC64. d 66 p 67. C Oxton *Ches* 66-69; Asst Chapl R Hosp Sch Ipswich 69-71; Jamaica 71-73; CF from 73. *c/o MOD (Army), Bagshot Park, Bagshot, Surrey GU19 5PL* Bagshot (0276) 71717

CLEAR, Peter Basil. b 13. New Coll Ox BA35 MA40. Chich Th Coll 35. d 36 p 37. R Pen Selwood *B & W* 52-68; rtd 69. *21 Portland Court, Lyme Regis, Dorset* Lyme Regis (02974) 2273

CLEASBY, Very Rev Thomas Wood Ingram. b 20. Magd Coll Ox BA47 MA47. Cuddesdon Coll 47. d 49 p 50. V Chesterfield All SS *Derby* 63-70; Hon Can Derby Cathl 63-78; Adn Chesterfield 63-78; R Morton 70-78; Dean Ches 78-86; rtd 86; Perm to Offic Carl from 86; Bradf from 87. *Low Barth, Dent, Sedbergh, Cumbria* Dent (05875) 476

CLEAVER, Gerald. b 20. Lon Univ BSc52. St Jo Coll Nottm 85. d 86 p 87. NSM W Bridgford *S'well* from 86. *62 South Road, Nottingham NG2 7AH* Nottingham (0602) 810196

CLEAVER, Gordon Philip. b 29. SW Minl Tr Course. d 78 p 79. NSM St Ruan w St Grade *Truro* 78-86; Perm to Offic from 86. *Bryn-Mor, Cadgwith, Ruan Minor, Helston, Cornwall TR12 7JZ* The Lizard (0326) 290328

CLEAVER, John Martin. b 42. K Coll Lon BD64 AKC64. d 65 p 66. C Bexley St Mary *Roch* 65-69; C Ealing St Steph Castle Hill *Lon* 69-71; P-in-c Bostall Heath *Roch* 71-76; V Green Street Green 76-85; RE Adv Lon Dioc Bd of Schs from 85. *8 Poynings Close, Orpington, Kent* Orpington (0689) 29726

CLEAVER, Stuart Douglas. b 46. ACIS. Oak Hill Th Coll. d 83 p 84. C Portsdown *Portsm* 83-86; C Blendworth w Chalton w Idsworth & Rowlands Castle 86-88; P-in-c Whippingham w E Cowes from 88. *The Rectory, 73 Cambridge Road, East Cowes, Isle of Wight PO32 6AH* Isle of Wight (0983) 292130

CLEEVE, Admire William. b 43. ACIS78 MBIM81 CPPS83. Sierra Leone Th Hall 78. d 82 p 83. Sierra Leone 82-86; NSM Douglas St Geo and St Barn *S & M* 87-91; TV Langley Marish *Ox* from 91. *Christ the Worker Vicarage, Parlaunt Road, Slough SL3 8BB* Slough (0753) 45167

CLEEVE, Martin. b 43. ACP67 Open Univ BA80. Bp Otter Coll TCert65 Oak Hill Th Coll 69. d 72 p 73. C Margate H Trin *Cant* 72-76; V Southminster *Chelmsf* 76-86; Teacher Castle View Sch Canvey Is 86-91; Hd RE Bromfords Sch Wickford from 91. *44 Ditton Court Road, Westcliffe-on-Sea, Essex SS0 7HF*

CLEEVES, David John. b 56. Univ of Wales (Lamp) BA Fitzw Coll Cam MA85. Westcott Ho Cam. d 82 p 83. C Cuddington *Guildf* 82-85; C Dorking w Ranmore 85-87; V Ewell St Fran from 87. *St Francis's Vicarage, 61 Ruxley Lane, Ewell, Surrey KT19 0JG* 081-393 5616

CLEGG, David Kneeshaw. b 46. N Ord Course 77. d 80 p 81. C Briercliffe *Blackb* 80-83; Chapl Lancs (Preston) Poly 83-89; rtd 89. *Field House, Albert Street, Durham DH1 4RL* 091-386 5806

CLEGG, Herbert. b 24. Fitzw Ho Cam BA59 MA63 Bris Univ MA65. Sarum Th Coll 52. d 54 p 55. P-in-c Aldsworth *Glouc* 70-75; P-in-c Sherborne w Windrush 70-75; V Marcham w Garford *Ox* 75-83; R Chipping Warden w Edgcote and Aston le Walls *Pet* 83-89; rtd 89; C Ox St Giles and SS Phil and Jas w St Marg *Ox* from 90. *19 Cunliffe Close, Oxford OX2 7BJ*

CLEGG, Jeffrey Thomas. b 50. Padgate Coll of Educn BEd79 DAES85. Nor Ord Course 87. d 90 p 91. C Gateacre *Liv* from 90. *24 Lee Vale Road, Gateacre, Liverpool L25 3RW* 051-487 9391

CLEGG, John Anthony Holroyd. b 44. Kelham Th Coll 65. d 70 p 71. C St Annes *Blackb* 70-74; C Lanc St Mary 74-76; V Lower Darwen St Jas 76-80; TV Shaston *Sarum* 80-86; Chapl HM Youth Cust Cen Guys Marsh 80-86; R Poulton-le-Sands w Morecambe St Laur *Blackb* from 86; RD Lanc from 89. *The Rectory, Church Walk, Morecambe, Lancs LA4 5PR* Morecambe (0524) 410941

CLEGG, John Lovell. b 48. Qu Coll Ox BA70 MA74. Trin Coll Bris DipTh75. d 75 p 76. C Barrow St Mark *Carl* 75-79; R S Levenshulme *Man* from 79. *St Andrew's Rectory, 27 Errwood Road, Levenshulme, Manchester M19 2PN* 061-224 5877

CLEGG, Peter Douglas. b 49. Sarum & Wells Th Coll 83. d 85 p 86. C Hangleton *Chich* 85-88; C-in-c Portslade Gd Shep Mile Oak CD from 88. *35 Stanley Avenue, Portslade, Brighton BN4 2WN* Brighton (0273) 419518

CLEGG, Roger Alan. b 46. St Jo Coll Dur BA68 Nottm Univ DipTh76. St Jo Coll Nottm 75. d 78 p 79. C Harwood *Man* 78-81; TV Sutton St Jas and Wawne *York* 81-87; V Kirk Fenton w Kirkby Wharfe and Ulleskelfe from 87; OCF from 87. *The Vicarage, Church Street, Church Fenton, Tadcaster, N Yorkshire LS24 9RD* Tadcaster (0937) 557387

CLELAND, Richard. b 26. MPS47. St Aid Birkenhead 58. d 60 p 61. C Lisburn Ch Ch *Conn* 60-63; C Ballynafeigh St Jude *D & D* 63-66; C Portman Square St Paul *Lon* 66-67; V Ilkley All SS *Bradf* 67-83; Master Wyggeston's Hosp Leic from 83. *The Master's House, Wyggeston's Hospital, Leicester LE3 0UX* Leicester (0533) 548682 or 541803

CLEMAS, Nigel Antony. b 53. Wycliffe Hall Ox. d 83 p 84. C Bootle St Mary w St Paul *Liv* 83-87; V Kirkdale St Mary and St Athanasius 87-91; TV Netherthorpe *Sheff* from 91. *The Vicarage, 115 Upperthorpe Road, Sheffield S6 3EA* Sheffield (0742) 767130

CLEMENCE, Paul Robert Fraser. b 50. MRTPI82 Man Univ DipTP74 St Edm Hall Ox MA90. Wycliffe Hall Ox 88. **d** 90 **p** 91. C Lanc St Mary *Blackb* from 90; Chapl HM Pris Lanc from 90. *25 Bishopdale Road, Lancaster LA1 5NF*   Lancaster (0524) 844672

CLEMENT, Miss Barbara Winifred. b 20. Gilmore Ho 49. **dss** 56 **d** 87. Hd Dss *Guildf* 66-74; Dioc Adv Lay Min 74-82; Frimley 74-82; Frimley Hosp 74-87; rtd 82; Perm to Offic *Guildf* from 82. *9 Merlin Court, The Cloisters, Frimley, Camberley, Surrey GU16 5JN* Camberley (0276) 22527

CLEMENT, David Elwyn. b 17. St D Coll Lamp BA39 St Mich Coll Llan 46. **d** 46 **p** 48. R New Radnor w Llanfihangel Nantmelan etc *S & B* 60-78; rtd 78. *Marston House, Pembridge, Leominster, Herefordshire* Pembridge (05447) 448

CLEMENTS, Alan Austin. b 39. ACIB66. Linc Th Coll 74. **d** 76 **p** 77. C Woodley *Ox* 76-79; C Wokingham All SS 79-83; V Felton *Newc* from 83. *The Vicarage, 1 Benlaw Grove, Felton, Morpeth, Northd NE65 9NG* Felton (067087) 263

CLEMENTS, Andrew. b 48. K Coll Lon BD72 AKC72. St Aug Coll Cant 72. **d** 73 **p** 74. C Langley All SS and Martyrs *Man* 73-76; C Westhoughton 76-81; R Thornton Dale and Ellerburne w Wilton *York* 81-89; Prec Leic Cathl *Leic* from 89. *154 Barclay Street, Leicester LE3 0JB* Leicester (0533) 557327

CLEMENTS, Anthony John. b 37. AKC60. St Boniface Warminster 60. **d** 61 **p** 62. C Highters Heath *Birm* 61-63; C Guildf St Nic *Guildf* 63-66; P-in-c N Lynn w St Marg and St Nic *Nor* 66-70; Lic to Offic 71-78; P-in-c Tilney All Saints w Tilney St Lawrence *Ely* 79-80; P-in-c W Lynn *Nor* from 90. *26 Chapel Road, Terrington St Clement, King's Lynn, Norfolk PE34 4ND*   King's Lynn (0553) 829627

CLEMENTS, Edwin George. b 41. Chich Th Coll 77. **d** 79 **p** 80. C Didcot St Pet *Ox* 79-83; C Brixham w Churston Ferrers *Ex* 83; TV 84-86; TV Brixham w Churston Ferrers and Kingswear 86-88; P-in-c Hagbourne *Ox* 88; V 88-90; P-in-c Blewbury 89-90; P-in-c Upton 89-90; R Blewbury, Hagbourne and Upton from 90. *The Rectory, Blewbury, Didcot, Oxon OX11 9QH*   Blewbury (0235) 850267

CLEMENTS, John Derek Howard. b 65. Man Univ BA88. St Steph Ho Ox 88. **d** 90 **p** 91. C Ex St Jas *Ex* from 90. *St Anne's House, 103 Old Tiverton Road, Exeter, Devon EX4 6LD*   Exeter (0392) 51976

CLEMENTS, Philip Christian. b 38. K Coll Lon BD64 AKC64. **d** 65 **p** 66. C S Norwood St Mark *Cant* 65-68; Chapl R Russell Sch Croydon 68-75; Asst Chapl Denstone Coll Uttoxeter 75-76; Chapl 76-81; Chapl Lancing Coll Sussex 82-90; R Ninfield *Chich* from 90; V Hooe from 90. *The Rectory, Church Lane, Ninfield, Battle, E Sussex TN33 9JW*   Ninfield (0424) 892308

CLEMENTS, Philip John Charles. b 42. Nottm Univ CertEd64. Ridley Hall Cam. **d** 85 **p** 86. C Aylestone St Andr w St Jas *Leic* 85-87; P-in-c Swinford w Catthorpe, Shawell and Stanford from 87. *The Vicarage, Kilworth Road, Swinford, Lutterworth, Leics LE17 6BQ*   Rugby (0788) 860221

CLEMENTS, Roy Adrian. b 44. Dur Univ BA68 DipTh69 MA. St Chad's Coll Dur 65. **d** 69 **p** 70. C Royston *Wakef* 69-73; V Clifton 73-77; V Rastrick St Matt 77-84; V Horbury Junction from 84; Dioc Communications Officer from 84. *The Vicarage, Millfield Road, Horbury, Wakefield, W Yorkshire WF4 5DU*   Wakefield (0924) 275274

CLEMETSON, Thomas Henry. b 22. **d** 62 **p** 63. V Hurdsfield *Ches* 65-76; V Stockport St Sav 76-88; rtd 88. *23 Old Field Crescent, Lache Lane, Chester* Chester (0244) 676492

CLEMETT, Peter Thomas. b 33. Univ of Wales (Lamp) BA60. Sarum Th Coll 59. **d** 61 **p** 62. CF 66-88; Chapl R Memorial Chpl Sandhurst 84-88; rtd 88. *c/o MOD (Army), Bagshot Park, Bagshot, Surrey GU19 5PL* Bagshot (0276) 71717

CLENCH, Brian Henry Ross. b 31. Ripon Coll Cuddesdon. **d** 82 **p** 83. C Fulham All SS *Lon* 82-85; Ind Chapl *Truro* from 85; P-in-c St Mewan from 85. *The Rectory, St Mewan, St Austell, Cornwall PL26 7DP*   St Austell (0726) 72679

CLENDON, David Arthur. b 33. Em Coll Cam BA56 MA61. Wells Th Coll 56. **d** 58 **p** 59. C Hockerill *St Alb* 58-62; C Digswell 62-63; C Luton Ch 63-65; P-in-c 71-76; V Caddington 65-71; P-in-c Pirton 75-85; V from 85; P-in-c Offley w Lilley 85-88. *The Vicarage, Crabtree Lane, Pirton, Hitchin, Herts SG5 3QE*   Hitchin (0462) 712230

CLEVELAND, Michael Robin. b 52. Warw Univ BA73. St Jo Coll Nottm 86 Serampore Th Coll BD88. **d** 88 **p** 89. C Bushbury *Lich* from 88. *27 Morrison Avenue, Wolverhampton WV10 9TZ*   Wolverhampton (0902) 864548

CLEVELAND, Archdeacon of. See HAWTHORN, Ven Christopher John

CLEVERLEY, Michael Frank. b 36. Man Univ BScTech57. Wells Th Coll 61. **d** 63 **p** 64. C Halifax St Aug *Wakef* 63; C Huddersfield St Jo 63-66; C Brighouse 66-69; V Gomersal 69-83; P-in-c Clayton W w High Hoyland 83-89; P-in-c Scissett St Aug 83-89; R High Hoyland, Scissett and Clayton W from 89. *The Rectory, Church Lane, Clayton West, Huddersfield HD8 9LY* Huddersfield (0484) 862321

CLEVERLY, Charles St George. b 51. Ox Univ MA. Trin Coll Bris. **d** 82 **p** 83. C Cranham Park *Chelmsf* 82-89; V from 89. *201 Front Lane, Upminster, Essex RM14 1LD* Upminster (0708) 225262

CLEWS, Nicholas. b 57. CIPFA85 SS Coll Cam BA80 MA84 Leeds Univ BA87. Coll of Resurr Mirfield 85. **d** 88 **p** 89. C S Elmsall *Wakef* from 88. *40A Beech Street, South Elmsall, Pontefract, W Yorkshire WF9 2LS* South Elmsall (0977) 643241

CLIFF, Frank Graham. b 38. Lon Univ DipTh66. Clifton Th Coll. **d** 66 **p** 67. C Park Estate St Chris CD *Leic* 66-69; C Whitton and Thurleston w Akenham St *E* 69-71; USA from 71. *3010 Pioneer Avenue, Pittsburgh, Pennsylvania 15226, USA*   Pittsburgh (412) 561-4520

CLIFF, Maisie. **d** 87. Asst CF 87-90. *Address temp unknown*

CLIFF, Philip Basil. b 15. Lon Univ BSc61 Birm Univ PhD. Independent Coll Bradf. **d** 77 **p** 77. Hon C Northfield *Birm* from 77. *4 Fox Hill Close, Birmingham B29 4AH*   021-472 1556

CLIFFORD, Douglas Newson. b 16. **d** 83 **p** 84. NSM Strontian *Arg* from 83; NSM Fort William 83-91; NSM Kinlochmoidart from 83; Bp's Dom Chapl from 83. *Bellsgrove Lodge, Strontian, Acharacle, Argyll PH36 4JB* Strontian (0967) 2152

CLIFT, Canon John Wilfred. b 04. MBE65. St Paul's Coll Burgh 29. **d** 30 **p** 31. Miss to Seamen 49-72; rtd 72. *34 Priory Close, Beeston Regis, Sheringham, Norfolk* Sheringham (0263) 823465

CLIFT, Norman Charles. b 21. Kelham Th Coll 40. **d** 45 **p** 46. V Leytonstone St Marg w St Columba *Chelmsf* 61-75; V Gt and Lt Bardfield 75-91; rtd 91. *Squirrels, High Street, Great Chesterford, Saffron Walden, Essex CB10 1TL*   Saffron Walden (0799) 31319

CLIFTON, Robert Walter. b 39. Solicitor. Westcott Ho Cam 82. **d** 84 **p** 85. C Bury St Edmunds St Geo *St E* 84-87; P-in-c Culford, W Stow and Wordwell 87-88; R Culford, W Stow and Wordwell w Flempton etc from 88. *The Rectory, West Stow, Bury St Edmunds, Suffolk IP28 6ET*   Culford (028484) 556

CLIFTON, Roger Gerald. b 45. ACA70 FCA. Sarum & Wells Th Coll 70. **d** 73 **p** 74. C Winterbourne *Bris* 73-76; P-in-c Brislington St Cuth 76-83; P-in-c Colerne w N Wraxall from 83; RD Chippenham from 89. *The Rectory, Colerne, Chippenham, Wilts SN14 8DF*   Box (0225) 742742

CLINCH, Christopher James. b 60. Nottm Univ BEd82 BTh89. Linc Th Coll 86. **d** 89 **p** 90. C Newc St Geo *Newc* from 89. *Tower House, St George's Close, Newcastle upon Tyne NE2 2TF*   091-281 3871

CLINCH, Kenneth Wilfred. b 22. Bps' Coll Cheshunt 62. **d** 64 **p** 65. C Lancing St Mich *Chich* 67-73; R Upper St Leonards St Jo 73-88; rtd 88. *Brae Cottage, 193 Hastings Road, Battle, E Sussex TN33 0TP*   Battle (04246) 4130

CLITHEROW, Andrew. b 50. St Chad's Coll Dur BA72 Ex Univ MPhil87. Sarum & Wells Th Coll 79. **d** 79 **p** 80. Hon C Bedf Ch Ch *St Alb* 79-84; Asst Chapl Bedf Sch 79-84; Chapl Caldicott Sch Farnham Royal 84-85; C Penkridge w Stretton *Lich* 85-88; Min Acton Trussell w Bednall 85-88; Chapl Rossall Sch Fleetwood from 89. *4 The Cop, Thornton Cleveleys, Blackpool FY5 1JQ* Cleveleys (0253) 856826

CLODE, Arthur Raymond Thomas. b 35. Roch Th Coll 67. **d** 69 **p** 70. C Blackheath *Birm* 69-72; V Londonderry 73-75; R Bride *S & M* 75-79; UAE 80-83; Min Stewartly LEP 86-90; C Wootton *St Alb* 86-90; C St Alb St Paul from 90. *46 Brampton Road, St Albans, Herts AL1 4PT* St Albans (0727) 41245

CLOETE, Richard James. b 47. AKC71. St Aug Coll Cant 72. **d** 72 **p** 73. C Redhill St Matt *S'wark* 72-76; V Streatham St Paul 76-84; P-in-c W Coker *B & W* 84-88; P-in-c Hardington Mandeville w E Chinnock and Pendomer 84-88; R W Coker w Hardington Mandeville, E Chinnock etc 88; R Wincanton from 88; R Pen

Selwood from 88; Sec and Treas Dioc Hosp Chapl Fellowship from 91. *The Rectory, Bayford Hill, Wincanton, Somerset BA9 9LQ* Wincanton (0963) 33367

CLOGHER, Archdeacon of. *See* PRINGLE, Ven Cecil Thomas

CLOGHER, Bishop of. *See* HANNON, Rt Rev Brian Desmond Anthony

CLOGHER, Dean of. *See* McCARTHY, Very Rev John Francis

CLONMACNOISE, Dean of. *See* BARRETT, Very Rev John Alan Gardiner

CLOSE, Brian Eric. b 49. St Chad's Coll Dur BA74 MA76. Ridley Hall Cam 74. **d** 76 **p** 77. C Far Headingley St Chad *Ripon* 76-79; C Harrogate St Wilfrid 79-80; C Harrogate St Wilfrid and St Luke 80-82; P-in-c Alconbury w Alconbury Weston *Ely* 82-83; V 83-86; P-in-c Buckworth 82-83; R 83-86; P-in-c Upton and Copmanford 82-83; Chapl Reed's Sch Cobham from 86. *Clover, Sandy Lane, Cobham, Surrey KT11 2EL* Cobham (0932) 64057

CLOSS-PARRY, Ven Selwyn. b 25. Univ of Wales (Lamp) BA50. St Mich Coll Llan 50. **d** 52 **p** 53. R Llangystenyn *St As* 66-71; V Holywell 71-77; Can St As Cathl 76-82; Prec 82-84; Preb 82-90; V Colwyn 77-84; Adn St As 84-90; R Trefnant 84-90; rtd 91. *3 Llys Brompton, Brompton Avenue, Rhos-on-Sea, Clwyd LL28 4ZB* Colwyn Bay (0492) 45801

CLOTHIER, Gerald Harry. b 34. Oak Hill Th Coll 75. **d** 78 **p** 79. Hon C Highwood *Chelmsf* 78-79; Hon C Writtle w Highwood 79-83; P-in-c Westhall w Brampton and Stoven *St E* 83-86; TV Beccles St Mich from 86. *Hillcrest, 17 Upper Grange Road, Beccles, Suffolk NR34 9NU* Beccles (0502) 712317

CLOTHIER, Canon Harry Legg. b 05. G&C Coll Cam BA27 MA36. Ely Th Coll 28. **d** 29 **p** 30. V Sharnbrook *St Alb* 54-69; R Knotting w Souldrop 54-69; rtd 69; Perm to Offic *St D* from 69. *Glenview, Aberporth, Cardigan, Dyfed SA43 2ER* Aberporth (0239) 810618

CLOUGH, Harry. b 11. AKC39. **d** 39 **p** 40. V Upper Hopton *Wakef* 68-76; rtd 76; Perm to Offic *Wakef* from 76. *2 Kirkgate Lane, South Hiendley, Barnsley, S Yorkshire S72 9DS* Barnsley (0226) 711470

CLOVER, Brendan David. b 58. LTCL MA. Ripon Coll Cuddesdon. **d** 82 **p** 83. C Friern Barnet St Jas *Lon* 82-85; C W Hampstead St Jas 85-87; Chapl Em Coll Cam from 87. *Emmanuel College, Cambridge CB2 3AP* Cambridge (0223) 334264

CLOWES, John. b 45. AKC67. **d** 68 **p** 69. C Corby St Columba *Pet* 68-71; R Itchenstoke w Ovington and Abbotstone *Win* 71-74; V Acton w Gt and Lt Waldingfield *St E* 74-80; Asst Dioc Chr Stewardship Adv 75-80; TV Southend St Jo w St Mark, All SS w St Fran etc *Chelmsf* 80-82; TV Southend 82-85; Ind Chapl 80-85; R Ashwick w Oakhill and Binegar *B & W* from 85. *The Rectory, Fosse Road, Oakhill, Bath BA3 5HU* Oakhill (0749) 840226

CLOYNE, Dean of. *See* HILLIARD, Very Rev George Percival St John

CLUCAS, Robert David. b 55. Cranmer Hall Dur. **d** 82 **p** 83. C Gateacre *Liv* 82-86; P-in-c Bishop's Itchington *Cov* from 86. *The Vicarage, Bishop's Itchington, Leamington Spa CV33 0QT* Harbury (0926) 613466

CLUER, Donald Gordon. b 21. S'wark Ord Course 61. **d** 64 **p** 65. C Bexhill St Pet *Chich* 68-73; V Shoreham Beach 73-77; V Heathfield St Rich 77-86; C Eastbourne St Mary 86-90; rtd 90; Perm to Offic *Ox* from 90. *10 Windsor Street, Oxford OX3 7AP* Oxford (0865) 67270

CLUES, David Charles. b 66. K Coll Lon BD87. St Steph Ho Ox 88. **d** 90 **p** 91. C Notting Hill All SS w St Columb *Lon* from 90. *12 Powis Gardens, London W11 1JG* 071-221 2857

CLUETT, Michael Charles. b 53. Kingston Poly BSc78. St Steph Ho Ox 84. **d** 86 **p** 87. C Pontesbury I and II *Heref* 86-90; TV Wenlock from 90. *14 Stretton Road, Much Wenlock, Shropshire TF13 6AS* Much Wenlock (0952) 728211

CLULEE, Miss Elsie Ethel. b 18. St Andr Ho Portsm 46. **dss** 56 **d** 87. Stirchley *Birm* 66-87; Hon Par Dn from 87. *42 Woodbrooke Road, Birmingham B30 1UD* 021-472 2662

CLUTTERBUCK, Herbert Ivan. b 16. Ch Coll Cam BA38 MA42. Chich Th Coll 38. **d** 39 **p** 40. Org Sec Ch Union 66-74; Chapl Qu Marg Sch Escrick Park 74-76; Roedean Sch Brighton 76-81; rtd 82; Master St Jo Hosp Lich from 82. *The Master's Lodge, St John's Hospital, Lichfield, Staffs WS13 6PB* Lichfield (0543) 264169

CLUTTERBUCK, John Michael. b 28. Qu Coll Ox BA53. St Steph Ho Ox BTh55. **d** 56 **p** 57. C Tewkesbury w Walton Cardiff *Glouc* 56-59; C Clerkenwell H Redeemer w St Phil *Lon* 59-64; R Filton *Bris* 65-72; P-in-c Frampton Cotterell from 72. *The Rectory, Frampton Cotterell, Bristol BS17 2BP* Winterbourne (0454) 772112

CLYDE, John. b 39. CITC BTh70. **d** 71 **p** 72. C Belf St Aid *Conn* 71-74; I Belf St Barn 74-80; I Belf H Trin 80-89; Bp's C Acton w Drumbanagher *Arm* from 89. *Drumbanagher Vicarage, 128 Tandragee Road, Newry, Co Down BT35 6LW* Jerrettspass (069382) 298

CLYNES, William. b 33. Sarum & Wells Th Coll 78. **d** 79 **p** 80. C Winterbourne *Bris* 79-83; TV Swindon St Jo and St Andr 83-91; rtd 91. *185A Claverham Road, Claverham, Bristol BS19 4LE*

COATES, Alan Thomas. b 55. St Jo Coll Nottm 87. **d** 89 **p** 90. C Heeley *Sheff* 89-90; C Bramley and Ravenfield from 90. *28 Ferndale Drive, Bramley, Rotherham, S Yorkshire S66 0YD* Rotherham (0709) 544001

COATES, Christopher Ian. b 59. Qu Coll Birm 81. **d** 84 **p** 85. C Cottingham *York* 84-87; TV Howden Team Min from 87. *The Vicarage, 3 Thimblehall Lane, Newport, Brough, N Humberside HU15 2PX* Howden (0430) 440546

COATES, Canon Francis Gustav. b 10. OBE63. G&C Coll Cam BA32 MA36. Ridley Hall Cam 32. **d** 52 **p** 54. R Heydon w Irmingland *Nor* 68-82; rtd 82; Perm to Offic *Nor* from 82. *13 Stuart Court, Recorder Road, Norwich NR1 1NP* Norwich (0603) 664910

COATES, John David Spencer. b 41. Dur Univ BA64 DipTh66. Cranmer Hall Dur 64. **d** 66 **p** 67. C Chipping Campden *Glouc* 66-69; CF from 69. *c/o MOD (Army), Bagshot Park, Bagshot, Surrey GU19 5PL* Bagshot (0276) 71717

COATES, Canon Kenneth Will. b 17. St Jo Coll Dur LTh45 BA46. Tyndale Hall Bris 39. **d** 42 **p** 43. V St Helens St Helen *Liv* 60-88; Hon Can Liv Cathl 71-88; rtd 88. *122 Broadway, Eccleston, St Helens WA10 5DH* St Helens (0744) 29629

COATES, Maxwell Gordon. b 49. Trin Coll Bris 75. **d** 77 **p** 78. C Blackheath Park St Mich *S'wark* 77-79; Perm to Offic *Win* from 79. *2 Tolstoy Road, Parkstone, Poole, Dorset*

COATES, Nigel John. b 51. Reading Univ BSc MA. Trin Coll Bris. **d** 83 **p** 84. C Epsom St Martin *Guildf* 83-86; C Portswood Ch Ch *Win* 86-88; Chapl Southn Univ from 89. *5 Chetwynd Road, Southampton SO2 3JA* Southampton (0703) 760075

COATES, Peter Frederick. b 50. K Coll Lon BD79 AKC79. St Steph Ho Ox 79. **d** 80 **p** 81. C Woodford St Barn *Chelmsf* 80-83; C E and W Keal *Linc* 83-86; R The Wainfleets and Croft from 86. *The Rectory, Wainfleet St Mary, Skegness, Lincs PE24 4JJ* Skegness (0754) 880401

COATES, Raymond Frederick William. b 14. AKC39. Bps' Coll Cheshunt 39. **d** 39 **p** 40. R Kings Somborne w Lt Somborne, Up Somborne etc *Win* 69-76; V Kings Somborne w Ashley 76-81; rtd 81; Perm to Offic *St E* 82-85. *Jameson, 26 St Matthew's Road, Winchester, Hants SO22 9BU* Winchester (0962) 861467

COATES, Robert Charles. b 44. Open Univ BA76. Cant Sch of Min 83. **d** 86 **p** 87. C Deal St Leon and St Rich and Sholden *Cant* 86-89; V Loose from 89. *The Vicarage, 17 Linton Road, Loose, Maidstone, Kent ME15 0AG* Maidstone (0622) 743513

COATES, Robert James. b 16. Lon Coll of Div 57. **d** 59 **p** 60. Chapl St Geo Hosp Stafford 67-81; rtd 81; Perm to Offic *Lich* 81-89; Ex from 89. *34 Home Farm Road, Fremington, Barnstaple, Devon EX31 3DH* Barnstaple (0271) 73946

COATES, Stuart Murray. b 49. Lon Univ BA70. Wycliffe Hall Ox 71. **d** 75 **p** 76. C Rainford *Liv* 75-78; C Orrell 78-79; V 79-86; Chapl Strathcarron Hospice Falkirk from 86; Hon C Stirling *Edin* 86-90; NSM Doune *St And* from 90. *Westwood Smithy, Chalmerston Road, Stirling FK9 4AG* Gargunnock (078686) 531

COATHAM, Canon Sydney. b 16. Leeds Univ BA40. Coll of Resurr Mirfield 40. **d** 42 **p** 43. V Lundley *Wakef* 63-81; rtd 82; Perm to Offic *Wakef* and *Leic* from 82. *9 Rossall Drive, Ashby-de-la-Zouch, Leics LE6 5QN* Ashby-de-la-Zouch (0530) 416107

COATSWORTH, Nigel George. b 39. Trin Hall Cam BA61 MA. Cuddesdon Coll 61. **d** 63 **p** 64. C Hellesdon *Nor* 63-66; Ewell Monastery 66-80; TV Folkestone H Trin and St Geo w Ch Ch *Cant* 83-85; C Milton next Sittingbourne 85-86; P-in-c Selattyn *Lich* from 86; P-in-c Weston Rhyn from 88. *The Rectory, Selattyn, Oswestry, Shropshire SY10 7DH* Oswestry (0691) 659755

COBB, Douglas Arthur. b 25. Kelham Th Coll 49. **d** 54 **p** 55. C Notting Hill St Mich and Ch Ch *Lon* 54-57; C Ruislip St Mary 57-63; V Kentish Town St Silas 63-87; P-in-c Kentish Town St Martin w St Andr 81-85; Chapl Convent of St Mary at the Cross Edgware from 87. *St John's House, 27 Highview Avenue, Edgware, Middx HA8 9TX* 081-958 8980

COBB, George Reginald. b 50. Oak Hill Th Coll BA81. **d** 81 **p** 82. C Ware Ch Ch *St Alb* 81-84; C Uphill *B & W* 84-89; R Alresford *Chelmsf* from 89. *The Rectory, St Andrew's Close, Alresford, Colchester CO7 8BL* Colchester (0206) 822088

COBB, Jeremy William Levi. b 62. Southn Univ BA84. Coll of Resurr Mirfield 84. **d** 86 **p** 87. C Greenhill *Sheff* 86-91; TV Redruth w Lanner and Treleigh *Truro* from 91. *Pencoys Vicarage, Four Lanes, Redruth, Cornwall TR16 6LR* Redruth (0209) 215035

COBB, John Philip Andrew. b 43. Man Univ BSc65 New Coll Ox BA67 MA71. Wycliffe Hall Ox 66. **d** 68 **p** 69. Par Dn Reading St Jo *Ox* 68-71; Par Dn Romford Gd Shep Collier Row *Chelmsf* 71-73; Chile from 74. *Iglesia Anglicana, Casilla 50675, Santiago, Chile* Santiago (2) 227-5713

COBB, Miss Marjorie Alice. b 24. St Chris Coll Blackheath IDC52. **dss** 61 **d** 87. CSA 56-85; rtd 85; Perm to Offic *Cant* from 87; Chapl Jes Hosp Cant from 90. *8 Jesus Hospital, Sturry Road, Canterbury, Kent CT1 1BS* Canterbury (0227) 768357

COBB, Mark Robert. b 64. Lanc Univ BSc86. Ripon Coll Cuddesdon 88. **d** 91. C Hampstead St Jo *Lon* from 91. *1 Holly Bush Vale, London NW3 6TX* 071-794 6838

COBB, Michael Hewett. b 28. K Coll Lon 53. **d** 54 **p** 56. Quest Community 70-83; Perm to Offic *Birm* 71-83; V Gravelly Hill 83-90; rtd 90. *27 Mount Pleasant Avenue, Exmouth, Devon*

COBB, Peter George. b 37. Ch Ch Ox BA59 MA63. St Steph Ho Ox 64. **d** 65 **p** 66. C Solihull *Birm* 65-69; Lib Pusey Ho 69-71; Sen Tutor St Steph Ho Ox 71-76; Cust Lib Pusey Ho 76-78; V Clandown *B & W* 78-83; V Midsomer Norton 78-83; V Midsomer Norton w Clandown 83-84; RD Midsomer Norton 83-84; V Clifton All SS w St Jo *Bris* from 84. *All Saints' Vicarage, 68 Pembroke Road, Bristol BS8 3ED* Bristol (0272) 741355

COBB, Peter Graham. b 27. St Jo Coll Cam BA48 MA52. Ridley Hall Cam 66. **d** 68 **p** 69. C Porthkerry *Llan* 68-71; P-in-c Penmark 71-72; V Penmark w Porthkerry 72-81; V Magor w Redwick and Undy *Mon* from 82. *The Vicarage, Magor, Newport, Gwent NP6 3BZ* Magor (0633) 880266

COBERN, Canon Charles John Julian. b 14. Keble Coll Ox BA36 MA62. Cuddesdon Coll 36. **d** 37 **p** 38. V Woburn Sands *St Alb* 68-79; rtd 79; Perm to Offic *Chich* from 89. *Maison Francaise de Retraite, De Courcel Road, Brighton BN2 5TF*

COCHLIN, Maurice Reginald. b 19. ACP60 FFChM Sussex Univ CertEd70. Cen Sch of Religion MA Lambeth STh74 Chich Th Coll 70. **d** 70 **p** 71. C Rowlands Castle *Portsm* 70-72; Chapl Paulsgrove Sch Cosham 71; C Warblington and Emsworth *Portsm* 72-75; C S w N Bersted *Chich* 76-78; Hd Littlemead Upper Sch Chich 78-79; C Saltdean *Chich* 79-83; V Kirdford 83-88; rtd 88. *56 Farnhurst Road, Barnham, Bognor Regis, W Sussex PO22 0JW* Yapton (0243) 553584

COCHRANE, Alan George. b 28. S'wark Ord Course. **d** 82 **p** 83. NSM Clapham Old Town *S'wark* 82-85; C Spalding St Jo w Deeping St Nicholas *Linc* 85-87; R Southery *Ely* from 87; V Fordham St Mary 87-91; R Hilgay 87-91; R Hilgay from 91. *The Rectory, Hilgay, Downham Market, Norfolk PE38 0JL* Downham Market (0366) 384418

COCHRANE, Canon Kenneth Wilbur. b 27. TCD BA58 MA61 Trin Coll Newburgh PhD88. **d** 58 **p** 59. C Belf St Aid *Conn* 58-61; C Belf St Nic 61-62; C Lisburn Ch Ch 62-63; P-in-c Lisburn St Paul 63-65; I from 65; Can Belf Cathl from 84; Preb Clonmethan St Patr Cathl Dub from 90. *3 Ballinderry Road, Lisburn, Co Antrim BT28 1UD* Lisburn (0846) 663520

COCHRANE, Norman John Michael Antony Ferguson. b 24. QUB BA46. Linc Th Coll 49. **d** 51 **p** 52. C Horsham *Chich* 56-76; V Aldwick 76-90; rtd 90. *41 Grindstone Crescent, Knaphill, Woking, Surrey GU21 2RZ* Brookwood (04867) 87981

COCHRANE, Canon Roy Alan. b 25. AKC53. **d** 54 **p** 55. V Glanford Bridge *Linc* 69-89; Chapl Glanford Hosp 69-89; RD Yarborough 76-81; Can and Preb Linc Cathl 77-90; Chapl and Warden St Anne's Bedehouses 89-90; rtd 90. *St Anne's Lodge, 29 Sewell Road, Lincoln LN2 5RY* Lincoln (0522) 28354

COCKBILL, Douglas John. b 53. Chicago Univ BA75. Gen Th Sem (NY) MDiv78. **d** 78 **p** 79. Virgin Is 79-80; Bahamas 80-83; USA 84-90; P-in-c Roxbourne St Andr *Lon* from 90. *St Andrew's Vicarage, Malvern Avenue, Harrow, Middx HA2 9ER* 081-422 3633

COCKBURN, Sidney. b 14. Leeds Univ BA36. Coll of Resurr Mirfield 36. **d** 38 **p** 40. V Long Eaton St Jo *Derby* 51-85; rtd 85; Perm to Offic *Derby* from 85. *10 Poplar Road, Breaston, Derby DE7 3BH* Draycott (03317) 2363

COCKCROFT, Basil Stanley. CEng MICE Leeds Univ BSc49. Wells Th Coll 64. **d** 66 **p** 67. C Featherstone *Wakef* 66-69; C Norton St Mary *Dur* 69-71; P-in-c Eldon 71-75; NSM Elland *Wakef* from 75. *9 Dene Close, South Parade, Elland, W Yorkshire HX5 0NS* Elland (0422) 374465

COCKE, James Edmund. b 26. Wadh Coll Ox BA50 MA55. Wells Th Coll 50. **d** 52 **p** 53. C Christchurch *Win* 52-57; V Highfield *Ox* from 57; Chapl Wingfield-Morris Hosp Ox 57-90; Chapl Nuff Orthopaedic Cen Ox from 90. *All Saints' Vicarage, 85 Old Road, Oxford OX3 7LB* Oxford (0865) 62536

COCKERELL, David John. b 47. Univ of Wales (Cardiff) BA71 Univ of Wales (Swansea) MA74 Qu Coll Cam BA75. Westcott Ho Cam 73. **d** 76 **p** 77. C Chapel Allerton *Ripon* 76-79; C Farnley 79-81; TV Hitchin *St Alb* 81-89; TV Dorchester *Ox* from 89. *The Vicarage, Cherwell Road, Berinsfield, Wallingford, Oxon OX10 7PB* Oxford (0865) 340460

COCKERTON, Canon John Clifford Penn. b 27. Liv Univ BA48 St Cath Soc Ox BA54 MA58. Wycliffe Hall Ox 51. **d** 54 **p** 55. C St Helens St Helen *Liv* 54-58; Tutor Cranmer Hall Dur 58-60; Chapl 60-63; Warden 68-70; Vice-Prin St Jo Coll Dur 63-70; Prin 70-78; R Wheldrake *York* 78-84; R Wheldrake w Thorganby from 84; Can and Preb York Minster from 87. *The Rectory, Church Lane, Wheldrake, York YO4 6AW* Wheldrake (090489) 230

COCKERTON, Thomas Charles. b 24. **d** 88. NSM Bermondsey St Mary w St Olave, St Jo etc *S'wark* from 88. *30 Carrick Court, Kennington Park Road, London SE11 4EE* 071-735 6966

COCKETT, Elwin Wesley. b 59. Aston Tr Scheme 86 Oak Hill Th Coll DipHE90 BA91. **d** 91. C Chadwell Heath *Chelmsf* from 91. *3 St Chad's Road, Chadwell Heath, Romford RM6 6JB* 081-597 2811

COCKIN, Canon Charles Munby. b 12. MBE46. Em Coll Cam BA34 MA38. Westcott Ho Cam 46. **d** 48 **p** 48. V Oundle *Pet* 63-77; rtd 77; Hon C Much Hadham *St Alb* 77-84; Perm to Offic *Ox* from 84. *32 Lapwing Lane, Cholsey, Oxon OX10 9QS* Cholsey (0491) 651585

✠**COCKIN, Rt Rev George Eyles Irwin.** b 08. Leeds Univ BA31. Linc Th Coll 52. **d** 53 **p** 54 **c** 59. C Kimberworth *Sheff* 53-55; Nigeria 55-69; Bp Owerri 59-69; Asst Bp York from 69; V Bainton 69-78; RD Harthill 73-78; rtd 79. *42 Carr Lane, Willerby, Hull HU10 6JW* Hull (0482) 653086

COCKING, Kermode Neil. b 48. TD. St Pet Coll Birm CertEd69. Sarum & Wells Th Coll 71. **d** 74 **p** 75. C Shirley *Birm* 74-76; CF (TA) 75-89; C Ealing Ch the Sav *Lon* 76-78; Hon C Streatham Ch Ch *S'wark* 78-81; Hon C Deptford St Paul 81-84; Lic to Offic *Lon* from 84; Hd Master Melcombe Primary Sch Lon from 90. *51 Melrose Avenue, London SW19 8BU* 081-947 7042

COCKING, Martyn Royston. b 53. Trin Coll Bris 83. **d** 85 **p** 86. C Weston-super-Mare Cen Par *B & W* 85-88; C Kingswood *Bris* 88-89; TV from 89. *60 Lavers Close, Cock Road, Bristol BS15 2ZG* Bristol (0272) 352658

COCKMAN, David Willie. b 32. Ex & Truro NSM Scheme. **d** 82 **p** 83. Warden Mercer Ho from 82; NSM Exwick Ex 82-86; Lic to Offic from 86. *Mercer House, Exwick Road, Exeter EX4 2AT* Exeter (0392) 219609

✠**COCKS, Rt Rev Francis William.** b 13. CB59. St Cath Coll Cam BA35 MA43. Westcott Ho Cam 35. **d** 37 **p** 37 **c** 70. C Portswood Ch Ch *Win* 37-39; Chapl RAFVR 39-45; Chapl RAF 45-50; Asst Chapl-in-Chief RAF 50-59; Chapl-in-Chief RAF 59-65; QHC 59-65; Can and Preb Linc Cathl *Linc* 59-65; R Wolv St Pet *Lich* 65-70; RD Wolv 65-70; P-in-c Wolv All SS 66-70; P-in-c Wolv St Geo 67-70; Preb Lich Cathl 68-70; Hon Can Lich Cathl from 70; Suff Bp Shrewsbury 70-80; rtd 80; Perm to Offic *St E* from 80. *4 Beatrice Avenue, Felixstowe, Suffolk IP11 9HB* Felixstowe (0394) 283574

COCKS, Howard Alan Stewart. b 46. St Barn Coll Adelaide 78 ACT ThD. **d** 82 **p** 81. Australia 80-82; C Prestbury *Glouc* 82-87; P-in-c Stratton w Baunton from 87; P-in-c N Cerney w Bagendon from 91. *The Rectory, 94 Gloucester Road, Stratton, Cirencester, Glos GL7 2LJ* Cirencester (0285) 653359

COCKS, Canon John Cramer. b 14. Lon Univ BD50. ALCD50. **d** 50 **p** 51. V Rothwell w Orton *Pet* 62-83; rtd 83; Perm to Offic *Pet* from 85. *23 Southgate Drive, Kettering, Northants NN15 7AQ*   Kettering (0536) 514039

COCKSEDGE, Hugh Francis. b 26. Magd Coll Cam BA50 MA52. **d** 88 **p** 89. NSM Alton All SS *Win* 88-89; Lic to Offic from 89. *Allerton, Hall Lane, Farringdon, Alton, Hants GU34 3EA*   Tisted (042058) 684

COCKSWORTH, Dr Christopher John. b 59. Man Univ BA80 PGCE81 PhD89. St Jo Coll Nottm 84. **d** 88 **p** 89. C Epsom Common Ch Ch *Guildf* from 88. *278 The Greenway, The Wells, Epsom, Surrey KT18 7JF*   Epsom (0372) 722698

CODLING, Timothy Michael (Tim). b 62. Trin Coll Ox BA84 MA91. St Steph Ho Ox 89. **d** 91. C N Shoebury *Chelmsf* from 91. *7 Sandpipers Close, Shoeburyness, Southend-on-Sea SS3 9YJ*   Southend-on-Sea (0702) 298069

CODRINGTON, Canon George Herbert. b 13. ALCD34 St Jo Coll Dur BA36 LTh36 MA39. **d** 36 **p** 37. V Melton Mowbray w Thorpe Arnold *Leic* 65-80; rtd 81; C Welsh Newton w Llanrothal *Heref* 81-85; C St Weonards w Orcop, Garway, Tretire etc 85-87. *Glebe Cottage, Staunton-on-Arrow, Leominster, Hereford HR6 9HR*   Pembridge (05447) 378

COE, Andrew Derek John. b 58. Nottm Univ BTh86. St Jo Coll Nottm 83. **d** 86 **p** 87. C Pype Hayes *Birm* 86-88; C Erdington St Barn 88-91; C Birm St Martin w Bordesley St Andr from 91. *175 St Andrew's Road, Bordesley Gardens, Birmingham B9 4NB*   021-771 0237

COE, David. b 45. **d** 69 **p** 70. C Belf St Matt *Conn* 69-72; C Belf St Donard *D & D* 72-75; I Tullylish 75-81; I Lurgan St Jo 81-89; I Ballymacarrett St Patr from 89. *St Patrick's Vicarage, 155 Upper Newtownards Road, Belfast BT4 3HX*   Belfast (0232) 657180

COE, John Norris. b 31. Oak Hill Th Coll 57. **d** 59 **p** 60. C Stoughton *Guildf* 59-61; C Guernsey St Michel du Valle *Win* 61-63; C Norbiton *S'wark* 63-67; V Bath Widcombe *B & W* 67-84; R Publow w Pensford, Compton Dando and Chelwood from 84. *The Rectory, Compton Dando, Bristol BS18 4LA*   Compton Dando (0761) 490221

COEKIN, Richard John. b 61. Solicitor 86 Jes Coll Cam BA83 MA87. Wycliffe Hall Ox 89. **d** 91. NSM Cheadle *Ches* from 91. *1 Warren Avenue, Cheadle, Cheshire*   061-428 3001

COFFIN, Stephen. b 52. Pemb Coll Ox BA74 MA79. Trin Coll Bris 74. **d** 77 **p** 78. C Illogan *Truro* 77-80; C Liskeard w St Keyne and St Pinnock 80-82; C Liskeard w St Keyne, St Pinnock and Morval 82; CMS 82-86; Burundi 82-86; V St Germans *Truro* from 86. *The Vicarage, Quay Road, St Germans, Saltash, Cornwall PL12 5LY*   St Germans (0503) 30275

✠**COGGAN of Canterbury and Sissinghurst, Most Rev and Rt Hon Lord (Frederick Donald).** b 09. PC61. St Jo Coll Cam BA31 MA35 Leeds Univ Hon DD58. Wycliffe Coll Toronto BD41 DD44 Lambeth DD57 Wycliffe Hall Ox 34. **d** 34 **p** 35 **c** 56. C Islington St Mary *Lon* 34-37; Canada 37-44; Prin Lon Coll of Div 44-56; Bp Bradf 56-61; Bp York 61-74; Abp Cant 74-80; rtd 80; Asst Bp Cant 80-88. *28 Lions Hall, St Swithun Street, Winchester SO23 9HW*   Winchester (0962) 864289

COGGINS, Edwin Stanley Claude. b 14. Bris Univ BSc36 DipEd37. Leic Dioc Th Course 63. **d** 64 **p** 65. Hon C Knighton St Mary Magd *Leic* 64-72; V Barlestone 72-77; P-in-c e w W Beckham *Nor* 78-84; rtd 84; Perm to Offic *Nor* from 84. *21 Caxton Park, Beeston Regis, Sheringham, Norfolk NR26 8ST*   Sheringham (0263) 824119

COGGINS, Richard James. b 29. Ex Coll Ox BA50 MA54 DipTh53 BD75. St Steph Ho Ox 52. **d** 54 **p** 55. C Withycombe Raleigh *Ex* 54-57; Tutor St Steph Ho Ox 57-60; Chapl 60-62; Asst Chapl Ex Coll Ox 57-62; Chapl Magd Coll Ox 60-62; Lic to Offic *Lon* from 64; Sub-Warden K Coll Lon 62-67; Lect 62-81; Sen Lect from 81. *8 Gateley Road, London SW9 9SZ*   071-274 6942

COGHLAN, Patrick John. b 47. Cam Univ BA69 Nottm Univ MA73. St Jo Coll Nottm LTh72. **d** 73 **p** 74. C Crookes St Thos *Sheff* 73-78; Brazil from 78. *Rua Marcos de Andrade, No. 20, Guaiba, RS, Brazil 92500*   Guaiba (80) 2141

COGMAN, Canon Frederick Walter. b 13. Lon Univ BD38 AKC38. **d** 38 **p** 39. R Guernsey St Martin *Win* 48-76; Dean *Win* 67-78; Dean Guernsey 67-78; R Guernsey St Peter Port 76-78; rtd 78; Perm to Offic *Win* from 78. *Oriana Lodge, rue des Fontenelles, Forest, Guernsey, Channel Islands*   Guernsey (0481) 64940

COHEN, Clive Ronald Franklin. b 46. ACIB71. Sarum & Wells Th Coll 79. **d** 81 **p** 82. C Esher *Guildf* 81-85; R

Winterslow *Sarum* from 85; RD Alderbury from 89. *The Rectory, Winterslow, Salisbury SP5 1RE*   Winterslow (0980) 862231

COHEN, David Mervyn Stuart. b 42. Sydney Univ BA63 MA79. **d** 67 **p** 68. Mauritius 68-70; New Zealand 70-72; Regional Sec (Africa) Bible Soc 72-75; Australia 75-86; Gen Dir Scripture Union (England and Wales) from 86. *c/o Scripture Union, 130 City Road, London EC1V 2NJ*   071-782 0013 or 081-851 7029

COHEN, Ian Geoffrey Holland. b 51. Nottm Univ BA74. Ripon Coll Cuddesdon 77. **d** 79 **p** 80. C Sprowston *Nor* 79-83; TV Wallingford w Crowmarsh Gifford etc *Ox* 83-88; V Chalgrove w Berrick Salome from 88. *The Vicarage, 58 Brinkinfield Road, Chalgrove, Oxford OX9 7QX*   Stadhampton (0865) 890392

COHEN, John Arthur. b 47. SS Hild & Bede Coll Dur BA68 CertEd69. E Anglian Minl Tr Course 84. **d** 87 **p** 88. Lic to Offic *St E* from 87. *The Rectory, Rayden, Ipswich IP7 5LT*   Great Wenham (0473) 310612

COHEN, Malcolm Arthur. b 38. Canberra Coll of Min DipTh79. **d** 78 **p** 79. Australia 79 84; Chapl Asst Thurrock Hosp 84-86; Hon Chapl ATC from 86; R Stifford *Chelmsf* from 84. *The Rectory, High Road, North Stifford, Grays, Essex RM16 1UE*   Grays Thurrock (0375) 72733

COKE, William Robert Francis. b 46. St Edm Hall Ox BA48 MA79 Lon Univ BD78. Trin Coll Bris 75. **d** 79 **p** 80. C Blackb Sav *Blackb* 79-83; V Fence in Pendle 83-84; P-in-c Newchurch-in-Pendle 83-84; V Fence and Newchurch-in-Pendle 84-89; Chapl Aiglon Coll Switzerland from 89. *Aiglon College, Villars, Switzerland*

COKER, Dr Alexander Bryan. b 48. MCollP84 K Coll Lon BD75 AKC76 MTh76 ThD81 MA84 MEd87. St Aug Coll Cant 75. **d** 86 **p** 87. Overstone Coll Northn 82-87; NSM Belsize Park *Lon* 86-90; Thames Educn Inst 87-90; C Croydon Woodside *S'wark* from 90. *24 Swinburn Crescent, Addiscombe, Croydon CR0 7BY*   081-654 0913

COKER, Barry Charles Ellis. b 46. K Coll Lon BD69 AKC69. **d** 70 **p** 71. C Newton Aycliffe *Dur* 70-74; Trinidad and Tobago 74-78; R Matson *Glouc* 78-90; V Stroud and Uplands w Slad from 90. *The Vicarage, Church Street, Stroud, Glos GL5 1JL*   Stroud (0453) 764555

COLBOURN, John Martin Claris. b 30. Selw Coll Cam BA52 MA56. Ridley Hall Cam 52. **d** 54 **p** 55. C Cheadle *Ches* 54-58; V Trowbridge St Thos *Sarum* 59-65; V Fareham St Jo *Portsm* 65-87; V Crich *Derby* from 87; RD Alfreton from 88. *The Vicarage, Coasthill, Crich, Matlock, Derbyshire DE4 5DS*   Ambergate (0773) 852449

COLBY, David Allan. b 33. Ox NSM Course 78. **d** 81 **p** 82. NSM Gt Faringdon w Lt Coxwell *Ox* 81-83; TV Ewyas Harold w Dulas, Kenderchurch etc *Heref* 83-84; TV Ewyas Harold w Dulas, Kenderchurch etc 84-91; V Westbury-on-Severn w Flaxley and Blaisdon *Glouc* from 91. *The Vicarage, Westbury-on-Severn, Glos GL14 1LW*   Westbury-on-Severn (045276) 592

COLBY, Robert James. b 31. Roch Th Coll 62. **d** 64 **p** 65. C Luton Ch St Alb 64-68; C Chirbury *Heref* 68-70; P-in-c 70-78; V 78-79; P-in-c Trelystan 70-78; V 78-79; P-in-c Marton 70-78; V 78-79; P-in-c Whitbourne 79-82; P-in-c Tedstone Delamere and Edvin Loach etc 80-82; P-in-c Upper Sapey w Wolferlow 80-82; R Edvin Loach w Tedstone Delamere etc from 82. *The Rectory, Whitbourne, Worcester WR6 5RP*   Knightwick (0886) 21285

COLCHESTER, Halsey Sparrowe. b 18. OBE60 CMG68. Magd Coll Ox BA39 MA45. Cuddesdon Coll 72. **d** 73 **p** 74. C Minchinhampton *Glouc* 73-76; V Bollington St Jo *Ches* 76-81; P-in-c Gt w Lt Tew *Ox* 81-87 and from 90; rtd 87. *The Vicarage, Great Tew, Oxford OX7 4AG*   Great Tew (060883) 293

COLCHESTER, Archdeacon of. See STROUD, Ven Ernest Charles Frederick

COLCHESTER, Area Bishop of. See VICKERS, Rt Rev Michael Edwin

COLCLOUGH, Michael John. b 44. Leeds Univ BA69. Cuddesdon Coll 69. **d** 71 **p** 72. C Burslem St Werburgh *Lich* 71-75; C Ruislip St Mary *Lon* 75-79; P-in-c Hayes St Anselm 79-85; V 85-86; AD Hillingdon from 85; P-in-c Uxbridge St Marg 86-88; P-in-c Uxbridge St Andr w St Jo 86-88; TR Uxbridge from 88. *The Rectory, Nursery Waye, Uxbridge, Middx UB8 2BJ*   Uxbridge (0895) 39055

COLDERWOOD, Alfred Victor. b 26. Bps' Coll Cheshunt 58. **d** 60 **p** 61. V Edmonton St Aldhelm *Lon* 66-91; rtd 91. *11 Mill Road, Birchington, Kent CT7 9TT*   Thanet (0843) 41544

COLDHAM, Miss Geraldine Elizabeth. b 35. FLA66 Trevelyan Coll Dur BA80. Cranmer Hall Dur 82. **dss** 83 **d** 87. S Normanton *Derby* 83-87; Par Dn 87; Par Dn Barking St Marg w St Patr *Chelmsf* 87-90; C Stifford from 90. *22 Prince Philip Avenue, Stifford, Grays, Essex RM16 2BT* Grays Thurrock (0375) 379830

COLDWELLS, Canon Alan Alfred. b 30. Univ Coll Ox BA55 MA57. Wells Th Coll 53. **d** 55 **p** 56. C Rugby St Andr *Cov* 55-62; V Sprowston *Nor* 62-73; R Beeston St Andr 62-73; RD Nor N 70-72; R Rugby St Andr *Cov* 73-82; TR 83-87; RD Rugby 73-78; Hon Can Cov Cathl from 83; Can Windsor from 87. *6 The Cloisters, Windsor Castle, Windsor, Berks SL4 1NJ* Windsor (0753) 866313

COLE, Alan John. b 35. Bps' Coll Cheshunt. **d** 66 **p** 67. C Boreham Wood All SS *St Alb* 66-69; C St Alb St Mich 69-72; V Redbourn 72-80; R Thorley w Bishop's Stortford H Trin 80-87; Chapl St Edw King & Martyr Cam *Ely* from 87; Chapl Arthur Rank Hospice Cam from 87. *The Rectory, Robin's Lane, Lolworth, Cambridge CB3 8HH* Crafts Hill (0954) 782930

COLE, Alan Michael. b 40. Melbourne Univ DipEd74 BA74. ACT DipTh67. **d** 66 **p** 67. Australia 66-75 and from 90; Chapl Bp Otter Coll Chich 76-77; Chapl Ardingly Coll Haywards Heath 77-82; Chapl Bonn w Cologne *Eur* 82-86; Chapl Helsinki w Moscow 86-90. *9 Allee Street, Brighton, Victoria, Australia 3186* Melbourne (3) 592-3886

COLE, Brian Robert Arthur. b 35. Nottm Univ BA57. Ridley Hall Cam 59. **d** 61 **p** 62. C Tye Green w Netteswell *Chelmsf* 61-64; C Keighley *Bradf* 64-67; Chapl Halifax Gen Hosp 67-73; V Copley *Wakef* 67-73; R Gt w Lt Dunham *Nor* 73-82; R Gt w Lt Fransham 74-82; P-in-c Sporle w Gt and Lt Palgrave 81-82; R Gt and Lt Dunham w Gt and Lt Fransham and Sporle from 83. *The Rectory, Great Dunham, King's Lynn, Norfolk PE32 2LQ* Fakenham (0328) 701466

COLE, Charles Vincent. b 26. Kelham Th Coll 47. **d** 51 **p** 52. V Blackhall *Dur* 56-91; rtd 91. *66 Scott Green Crescent, Gildersome, Leeds LS27 7DF* Leeds (0532) 530021

COLE, David. b 40. Qu Coll Birm 66. **d** 66 **p** 67. C Kensington St Helen w H Trin *Lon* 66-69; C Altham w Clayton le Moors *Blackb* 69-72; P-in-c Preston St Luke 72-75; V Inskip 75-80; C-in-c Chelmsley Wood St Aug CD *Birm* 80-87; C Cannock *Lich* from 87. *18 Queen Street, Cannock, Staffs WS11 1AE* Cannock (05435) 77392

COLE, David Henry. b 30. ALCD56 San Francisco Th Sem DMin87. **d** 56 **p** 57. C Ashtead *Guildf* 56-59; C Farnham 59-60; Canada from 60. *10922 79A Avenue, Delta, British Columbia, Canada, V4C 1T4* New Westminster (604) 596-4987

COLE, Donald Robertson. b 24. Edin Th Coll 57. **d** 59 **p** 60. C Edin Ch Ch *Edin* 59-62; R Lasswade 62-69; R Edin St Cuth from 69. *6 Westgarth Avenue, Edinburgh EH13 0BD* 031-441 3557

COLE, Guy Spenser. b 63. Univ of Wales (Ban) BA84 Jes Coll Cam BA88. Westcott Ho Cam 85. **d** 88 **p** 89. C Eastville St Anne w St Mark and St Thos *Bris* from 88. *14 Rosemary Lane, Bristol BS5 6YF* Bristol (0272) 512682

COLE, Henry Frederick Charles. b 23. ALCD52. **d** 52 **p** 53. Ind Chapl *Sheff* 67-72; V Wadsley 72-88; RD Hallam 83-87; rtd 88. *Julians, 217 Tullibardine Road, Sheffield S11 7GQ* Sheffield (0742) 684719

COLE, John Charles. b 22. CQSW. E Midl Min Tr Course 79. **d** 82 **p** 83. NSM Skirbeck H Trin *Linc* from 82. *27 Blackthorn Lane, Boston, Lincs PE21 9BG* Boston (0205) 366255

COLE, John Gordon. b 43. Magd Coll Cam BA65 MA69. Cuddesdon Coll 66. **d** 68 **p** 69. C Leeds St Pet *Ripon* 68-71; C Moor Allerton 71-75; P-in-c Pendleton *Blackb* 75-86; Dioc Communications Officer 75-86; Dioc Missr *Linc* from 86. *Pelham House, Little Lane, Wrawby, Brigg, S Humberside DN20 8RW* Brigg (0652) 57484

COLE, John Spensley. b 39. FCA65 Clare Coll Cam BA62 MA66 Nottm Univ DipTh79. Linc Th Coll 78. **d** 80 **p** 81. C Cowes St Mary *Portsm* 80-83; C Portchester 83-87; V Modbury *Ex* from 87; R Aveton Gifford from 87. *The Vicarage, Modbury, Ivybridge, Devon PL21 0QN* Modbury (0548) 830260

COLE, John Wilfrid. b 06. Keble Coll Ox BA30 DipTh31 MA34 DipPsych48 BSc51. Wycliffe Hall Ox 30. **d** 32 **p** 33. R Lyford w Charney *Ox* 47-71; rtd 71. *36 Plantation Road, Oxford OX2 6HE* Oxford (0865) 57927

COLE, Lawrence Howard. b 09. ALCD39 Dur Univ BA47. **d** 39 **p** 40. V Cogges *Ox* 60-77; rtd 77; Perm to Offic *Worc* from 77. *Perrins House, Moorlands Road, Malvern, Worcs WR14 2TZ* Malvern (0684) 563732

COLE, Melvin George Merriman. b 05. Fourah Bay Coll Freetown. **d** 48 **p** 53. Sierra Leone 69-76; rtd 74; Perm to Offic *S'wark* from 76. *101 Pendle Road, London SW16* 081-769 2704

COLE, Dr Michael George. b 35. CD75. Wesley Th Sem Washington DMin88 Kelham Th Coll 56 Lich Th Coll 57. **d** 60 **p** 61. C Doncaster Ch Ch *Sheff* 60-63; Chapl RAF 63-68; Canada 68-82; USA from 82. *110 Montclair Road, Gettysburg, Pennsylvania 17325, USA* Pennsylvania (717) 334-4205

COLE, Michael John. Ab Dioc Tr Course. **d** 80 **p** 81. Miss to Seamen from 81. *Seafarers' Centre, Immingham Dock, Grimsby, S Humberside DN40 2NN* Grimsby (0472) 74195

COLE, Canon Michael John. b 34. St Pet Hall Ox BA56 MA60. Ridley Hall Cam 56. **d** 58 **p** 59. C Finchley Ch Ch *Lon* 58; C Leeds St Geo *Ripon* 58-61; Travelling Sec IVF 61-64; V Crookes St Thos *Sheff* 64-71; R Rusholme *Man* 71-75; V Woodford Wells *Chelmsf* from 75; Chapl Leytonstone Ho Hosp from 85; Hon Can Chelmsf Cathl *Chelmsf* from 89. *All Saints' Vicarage, 4 Inmans Row, Woodford Green, Essex IG8 0NH* 081-504 0266

COLE, Norman George. b 05. **d** 28 **p** 29. V Stainland *Wakef* 60-63; rtd 70. *2 Corondale Road, Beacon Park, Plymouth PL2 2RF* Plymouth (0752) 559348

COLE, Canon Peter George Lamont. b 27. Pemb Coll Cam BA49 MA52. Cuddesdon Coll 50. **d** 52 **p** 53. C Aldershot St Mich *Guildf* 52-55; S Rhodesia 55-65; V Bromley St Andr *Roch* 65-72; V Folkestone St Mary and St Eanswythe *Cant* 72-87; Hon Can Cant Cathl 80-87; V E and W Worldham, Hartley Mauditt w Kingsley etc *Win* from 87; RD Alton from 89. *The Vicarage, East Worldham, Alton, Hants GU34 3AS* Alton (0420) 82392

COLE, Richard Leslie. b 08. Ball Coll Ox BA31 MA35. St Steph Ho Ox DipTh32. **d** 32 **p** 33. Br Guiana 61-66; Guyana 66-84; rtd 84; Perm to Offic *Llan* from 84. *18 Plantagenet Street, Riverside, Cardiff* Cardiff (0222) 229605

COLE, Ven Ronald Berkeley. b 13. Bps' Coll Cheshunt 40. **d** 42 **p** 43. Adn Leic 63-80; Can Res Leic Cathl 78-80; rtd 80; RD Repps *Nor* 83-86; Perm to Offic from 86. *Harland Rise, 70 Cromer Road, Sheringham, Norfolk NR26 8RT* Sheringham (0263) 824955

COLE, Timothy Alexander Robertson. b 60. Aber Univ MA83 Edin Univ BD86. Edin Th Coll 83. **d** 86 **p** 87. C Dunfermline *St And* 86-89; Vice-Provost St Andr Cathl Inverness *Mor* 89-90; R Inverness St Andr 89-90; R Edin St Mich and All SS *Edin* from 90. *15 Leven Terrace, Edinburgh EH3 9LW* 031-229 6104

COLE, Walter John Henden. b 04. Bps' Coll Cheshunt 25. **d** 27 **p** 28. V W Hampstead St Jas *Lon* 55-76; rtd 76. *87 College Road, Isleworth, Middx* 081-568 2708

COLE, William Pritchard. b 09. OBE51. St D Coll Lamp BA32. **d** 33 **p** 35. Chapl Upper Chine Sch Shanklin 65-76; rtd 76. *27 Burton Road, Bridport, Dorset DT6 4JD* Bridport (0308) 56289

COLE-KING, Dr Susan Mary. b 34. Lon Univ MB, BS62 DTPH71. Gen Th Sem (NY) 84. **d** 87. USA 87-88; Par Dn Dorchester *Ox* from 89. *1 Clock Cottage, Burcot, Abingdon, Oxon OX14 3DW* Clifton Hampden (086730) 7911

COLEBROOK, Christopher John. b 36. Qu Mary Coll Lon BA60 BD69. St D Coll Lamp DipTh62. **d** 62 **p** 63. C Llandilo Talybont *S & B* 62-66; C Llansamlet 66-71; V Nantmel w St Harmon's and Llanwrthwl 71-76; V Glantawe 76-85; V Gowerton from 85. *The Vicarage, Church Street, Gowerton, Swansea SA4 3EA* Swansea (0792) 872266

COLEBROOK, Peter Acland. b 29. Coates Hall Edin 52. **d** 55 **p** 56. C Bideford *Ex* 62-66; rtd 89. *Vale Cottage, Ham Lane, Marnhull, Sturminster Newton, Dorset DT10 1JN* Marnhull (0258) 820246

COLEBY, Andrew Mark. b 59. FRHistS88 Linc Coll Ox MA85 DPhil85 Dur Univ BA90. Cranmer Hall Dur 88. **d** 91. C Heeley *Sheff* from 91. *145 St Ann's Road North, Sheffield S2 3DJ* Sheffield (0742) 588841

COLEMAN, Mrs Ann Valerie. b 51. K Coll Lon BD72. St Aug Coll Cant. **dss** 80 **d** 87. Hampstead Garden Suburb *Lon* 80-84; Golders Green 85-87; Selection Sec and Voc Adv ACCM 87-91; ABM from 91. *c/o Church House, Great Smith Street, London SW1P 3NZ* 071-222 9011

COLEMAN, Beverley Warren. b 20. Leeds Univ BA41. Coll of Resurr Mirfield 41. **d** 43 **p** 44. CF (TA) 52-87; V Albrighton *Lich* 64-71; R Jersey St Sav *Win* 71-84; rtd 87. *44 Walnut Crescent, Fruit Lands, Malvern Wells, Worcs WR14 4AX* Malvern (0684) 563535

COLEMAN, Brian James. b 36. K Coll Cam BA58 MA61. Ripon Hall Ox 58. **d** 60 **p** 61. C Allestree *Derby* 60-65; V Allestree St Nic 65-69; Chapl and Lect St Mich Coll Sarum 69-77; P-in-c Matlock Bank 77-86; R Frimley *Guildf* from 86. *The Rectory, Frimley, Camberley, Surrey GU16 5AG* Camberley (0276) 23309

COLEMAN, Charles Romaine Boldero. b 10. Clifton Th Coll 46. **d** 39 **p** 40. R Sampford Brett *B & W* 61-77; rtd 78; Perm to Offic *Nor* from 81. *1 The Firs, Redgate Hill, Hunstanton, Norfolk* Hunstanton (04853) 2946

COLEMAN, David. b 49. K Coll Lon BD72 AKC72. St Aug Coll Cant 72. **d** 73 **p** 74. C Is of Dogs Ch Ch and St Jo w St Luke *Lon* 73-77; C Greenford H Cross 77-80; V Cricklewood St Pet 80-85; V Golders Green 85-90; V Eastcote St Lawr from 90. *St Lawrence Vicarage, 2 Bridle Road, Pinner, Middx HA5 2SJ* 081-866 1263

COLEMAN, Edward William. b 20. Lon Coll of Div 62. **d** 64 **p** 65. C Barking St Marg *Chelmsf* 67-70; C Dagenham 70-78; P-in-c High Laver w Magdalen Laver and Lt Laver 78-86; R High Laver w Magdalen Laver and Lt Laver etc 86-90; P-in-c Matching 84-86; V 86-90; rtd 90; Perm to Offic *Chelmsf* from 90. *Brandon, 28 Manor Road, Great Holland, Essex CO13 0JT* Frinton-on-Sea (0255) 679115

COLEMAN, Dr Frank. b 58. Hull Univ BA Ox Univ BA83 MA87 PhD88. St Steph Ho Ox 80. **d** 83 **p** 84. C Brandon *Dur* 83-85; C Newton Aycliffe 85-88; V Denford w Ringstead *Pet* from 88. *The Vicarage, Ringstead, Kettering, Northants NN14 4DF* Wellingborough (0933) 624627

COLEMAN, Frederick Philip. b 11. Lon Univ BSc(Econ)33. St Steph Ho Ox 38. **d** 40 **p** 41. R St Andr-by-the-Wardrobe w St Ann, Blackfriars *Lon* 71-84; Warden Community of St Jo Bapt Clewer 68-79; P-in-c St Nic Cole Abbey 78-82; AD The City 79-82; rtd 84; Hon C St Botolph Aldgate w H Trin Minories *Lon* from 85. *Charterhouse, Charterhouse Square, London EC1M 6AN* 071-608 1077

COLEMAN, John Edward Noel. b 15. St Chad's Coll Dur BA37 DipTh39 MA49. **d** 39 **p** 40. V Silverdale *Blackb* 55-82; rtd 82; Perm to Offic Blackb from 82; Carl from 83. *16 Hillside, Holme, Carnforth, Lancs* Carnforth (0524) 781294

COLEMAN, John Harold. b 38. Cant Sch of Min 83. **d** 86 **p** 87. NSM Dover St Martin *Cant* from 86. *1 Suffolk Gardens, Elms Vale, Dover, Kent CT17 9NH* Dover (0304) 213803

COLEMAN, John Wycliffe. **d** 77 **p** 78. CMS 84-91; Egypt 84-91. *25 Southborough Road, London E9 7EF* 081-985 7525

COLEMAN, Miss Mary Eileen. b 30. dss 84 **d** 87. Harlesden All So *Lon* 84-87; Par Dn 87-89; Par Dn Brondesbury St Anne w Kilburn H Trin 89-90; rtd 90. *37 Willoughby Road, Langley, Slough, Berks SL3 8JH* Slough (0753) 581940

✠COLEMAN, Rt Rev Peter Everard. b 28. Barrister 65 AKC53 Lon Univ LLB53 Bris Univ MLitt76. Westcott Ho Cam 53. **d** 55 **p** 56 **c** 84. C Bedminster St Fran *Bris* 55-58; C St Helen Bishopsgate w St Martin Outwich *Lon* 58-60; Asst Sec SCM 58-60; Chapl and Lect K Coll Lon 60-66; V Clifton St Paul *Bris* 66-71; Chapl Bris Univ 66-71; Can Res Bris Cathl 71-81; Dir Ord Tr 71-81; Dir Bris & Glouc Tr Course 77-81; Adn Worc and Can Res Worc Cathl *Worc* 81-84; Suff Bp Crediton *Ex* from 84. *10 The Close, Exeter EX1 1EZ* Exeter (0392) 73509

COLEMAN, Peter Nicholas. b 42. St Mich Coll Llan 83. **d** 85 **p** 86. C Skewen *Llan* 85-88; V Ystradyfodwg from 88. *The Vicarage, St David's Close, Pentre, M Glam CF41 7AX* Tonypandy (0443) 434201

COLEMAN, Robert William Alfred. b 16. Ch Coll Cam BA39 MA42. Bible Churchmen's Coll 39. **d** 40 **p** 41. Chapl Seaford Coll Sussex 60-81; rtd 81; Perm to Offic *Chich* from 83. *Villa Florence, 24 West Drive, Bognor Regis, W Sussex PO22 7TS* Middleton-on-Sea (0243) 583410

COLEMAN, Sybil Jean. b 30. St Deiniol's Hawarden 83. **d** 85. NSM Manselton *S & B* 85-90; C Swansea St Mark and St Jo from 90. *Beckley, 25 Beverley Gardens, Fforestfach, Swansea SA5 5DR* Swansea (0792) 584280

COLEMAN, Terence Norman. b 37. St Mich Coll Llan 83. **d** 85 **p** 86. C Machen *Mon* 85-87; C Penmaen and Crumlin 87-89; V from 89. *The Vicarage, Central Avenue, Oakdale, Blackwood, Gwent NP2 0JS* Blackwood (0495) 223043

COLEMAN, Timothy. b 57. CEng80 MIChemE86 Southn Univ BSc79. Ridley Hall Cam 87. **d** 89 **p** 90. C Bisley and W End *Guildf* from 89. *12 Bolding House Lane, West End, Woking, Surrey GU24 9JJ* Chobham (0276) 858435

COLERIDGE, Francis Arthur Wilson. b 10. Clifton Th Coll 58. **d** 59 **p** 60. R Berrington and Betton Strange *Heref* 61-68; Perm to Offic *Chich* from 68; rtd 75. *Flat 10, Cleaver Court, Station Road, Kettering, Northants NN15 7HH* Kettering (0536) 520001

COLES, Francis Herbert. b 35. Selw Coll Cam BA59 MA63. Coll of Resurr Mirfield 59. **d** 61 **p** 62. C Wolvercote *Ox* 61-65; C Farnham Royal 65-69; V Lynton and Brendon *Ex* 69-73; V Countisbury 70-73; TR Lynton, Brendon, Countisbury, Lynmouth etc 73-76; P-in-c Iffley *Ox* 76-88; V Ivybridge w Harford *Ex* from 88. *The Vicarage, Ivybridge, Devon PL21 0AD* Plymouth (0752) 690193

COLES, Geoffrey Herbert. b 38. Nottm Univ CertEd59 TCert60 Loughb Coll of Educn DLC60. N Ord Course 77. **d** 80 **p** 81. NSM Shelf *Bradf* 80-85; C Manningham 85-86; TV from 86. *1 Selborne Grove, Manningham, Bradford, W Yorkshire BD9 4NL* Bradford (0274) 541110

COLES, John Spencer Halstaff. b 50. Hertf Coll Ox BA72 MA76. Wycliffe Hall Ox 72. **d** 75 **p** 76. C Reading Greyfriars *Ox* 75-79; C Clifton Ch Ch w Em *Bris* 79-82; V Woodside Park St Barn *Lon* from 82. *St Barnabas' Vicarage, 68 Westbury Road, London N12 7PD* 081-445 3598

COLES, Robert Charles. b 41. Bps' Coll Cheshunt 66. **d** 68 **p** 69. C Northn St Alb *Pet* 68-72; C Durrington *Chich* 72-74; C Portslade St Nic 74-78; C Horsham 78-82; C-in-c Parklands St Wilfrid CD 82-87; V Eastbourne St Phil from 87. *1 St Philip's Avenue, Eastbourne, E Sussex BN22 8LU* Eastbourne (0323) 32381

COLES, Robert Reginald. b 47. Surrey Univ BSc69. Cant Sch of Min 82. **d** 85 **p** 86. NSM Sittingbourne St Mich *Cant* 85-87; C St Laurence in Thanet from 87. *St Mary's House, 1 Sandwich Road, Cliffs End, Ramsgate, Kent CT12 5HX* Thanet (0843) 597123

COLES, Stephen Richard. b 49. Univ Coll Ox BA70 MA74 Leeds Univ BA80. Coll of Resurr Mirfield 78. **d** 81 **p** 82. C Stoke Newington St Mary *Lon* 81-84; Chapl K Coll Cam 84-89; V Finsbury Park St Thos *Lon* from 89. *25 Romilly Road, London N4 2QY* 071-359 5741

COLES, William Dennis. b 17. St Cath Soc Ox BA40 QUB PhD71. Edin Th Coll 38. **d** 40 **p** 41. Magee Univ Coll Londonderry 64-81; rtd 81; Hon C Leverburgh *Arg* from 81. *Carragh Ban, An-t-Ob, Na Hearadh, Isle of Harris PA83 3UD* Leverburgh (085982) 223

COLESHILL, Archdeacon of. *See* COOPER, Ven John Leslie

COLEY, Frederick Albert. b 13. Lich Th Coll 65. **d** 66 **p** 67. C Tardebigge *Worc* 68-72; P-in-c Stoke Bliss w Kyre Wyard 72-73; P-in-c Hanley William w Hanley Child 72-73; P-in-c Stoke Bliss w Kyre Wyard, Hanley William etc 73-78; rtd 78; Perm to Offic *Worc* from 78. *Greenfields, Kyre Wood, Tenbury Wells, Worcs WR15 8SQ* Tenbury Wells (0584) 810961

COLEY, Peter Leonard. b 45. CEng MIMechE Bath Univ BSc67 City Univ MSc84. Oak Hill Th Coll 85. **d** 87 **p** 88. C Mile Cross *Nor* from 87. *Glebe House, 140 Mile Cross Road, Norwich NR3 2LD* Norwich (0603) 45493

✠COLIN, Rt Rev Gerald Fitzmaurice. b 13. TCD BA34 MA46. CITC 36. **d** 36 **p** 37 **c** 66. C Ballywillan *Conn* 36-38; C Dub St Geo *D & G* 38-47; Chan V St Patr Cathl Dub 38-47; Chapl RAFVR 39-47; V Frodingham *Linc* 47-66; Can and Preb Linc Cathl from 60; RD Manlake 60-66; Suff Bp Grimsby 66-78; rtd 79; Asst Bp Linc from 79. *Orchard Close, 52A St Mary's Lane, Louth, Lincs LN11 0DT* Louth (0507) 602600

COLIN WILFRED, Brother. *See* CHERRIMAN, Colin Wilfred

COLLARD, Fred. b 25. Lon Bible Coll 51 Wycliffe Hall Ox 61. **d** 61 **p** 63. OMF 61-81; Malaya 61-63; Malaysia 63-75; Perm to Offic *Ox* 71-81; TV Cheltenham St Mary, St Matt, St Paul and H Trin *Glouc* from 81. *85 Brunswick Street, Cheltenham, Glos GL50 4HA* Cheltenham (0242) 524572

COLLARD, Canon Harold. b 27. Wycliffe Hall Ox 51. **d** 53 **p** 54. C Rainham *Chelmsf* 53-56; C Kingston upon Hull H Trin *York* 56-59; V Upper Armley *Ripon* 59-68; R Chesterfield H Trin *Derby* 68-77; P-in-c Matlock Bath 77-83; V from 83; Hon Can Derby Cathl from 87; RD Wirksworth from 88. *Holy Trinity Vicarage, Derby Road, Matlock, Derbyshire DE4 3PU* Matlock (0629) 2947

COLLARD, John Cedric. b 30. Pemb Coll Cam BA53 MA76. St Alb Minl Tr Scheme 77. **d** 80 **p** 81. NSM Roxton w Gt Barford *St Alb* 80-84; C Liskeard w St Keyne, St Pinnock and Morval *Truro* 84-87; TV Liskeard, St Keyne, St Pinnock, Morval etc from 87.

The New Vicarage, 1 Maddever Crescent, Liskeard, Cornwall PL14 3PT Liskeard (0579) 42136

COLLARD, Norton Harvey. b 22. Open Univ BA80. Roch Th Coll 63. **d** 65 **p** 66. C Dartford H Trin *Roch* 67-70; V Grantham St Anne *Linc* 70-87; rtd 87. *1 Kenwick Drive, Grantham, Lincs NG31 9DP* Grantham (0476) 77345

COLLAS, Canon Victor John. b 23. Pemb Coll Ox BA44 MA48. Wycliffe Hall Ox 49. **d** 51 **p** 52. R Guernsey St Andr *Win* 58-81; Perm to Offic from 81; rtd 88. *Paradis, Vale, Guernsey, Channel Islands* Guernsey (0481) 44450

COLLEDGE, Christopher Richard. b 58. Chich Th Coll. **d** 82 **p** 83. C Deal St Leon *Cant* 82-83; C Deal St Leon and St Rich and Sholden 83-85; Bermuda 85-88; TV Wickford and Runwell *Chelmsf* 88-90; Chapl Runwell Hosp Essex 88-90; Chapl RAD from 90. *St Saviour's Centre, 1 Armstrong Road, London W3 7JL* 081-743 2209

COLLETT, Albert Ernest Jack. b 15. S'wark Ord Course 62. **d** 65 **p** 66. C Lewisham St Jo Southend *S'wark* 65-73; C-in-c Reigate St Phil CD 73-82; rtd 83; Perm to Offic *S'wark* from 83. *42 Wimborne Avenue, Redhill RH1 5AG* Redhill (0737) 763218

COLLETT, Maurice John. b 28. S'wark Ord Course 76. **d** 79 **p** 80. NSM Feltham *Lon* from 79. *58 Shakespeare Avenue, Feltham, Middx TW14 9HX* 081-751 4144

COLLETT-WHITE, Thomas Charles. b 36. Trin Coll Cam BA61 MA86. Ridley Hall Cam 60. **d** 62 **p** 63. C Gillingham St Mark *Roch* 62-66; V 79-90; C Normanton *Wakef* 66-69; V Highbury New Park St Aug *Lon* 69-76; Canada 76-79; Chapl Medway Hosp Gillingham 79-85; P-in-c Clerkenwell St Jas and St Jo w St Pet *Lon* from 90. *4 Owens Row, London EC1V 4NP* 071-833 8947

COLLIE, Dr Bertie Harold Guy. b 28. Glas Univ MB, ChB56. **d** 76 **p** 77. NSM Ayr *Glas* 76-84; NSM Maybole from 76; NSM Girvan from 76; NSM Pinmore from 76. *Hillside, Cargill Road, Maybole, Ayrshire KA19 8AF* Maybole (0655) 83564

COLLIE, Canon John Norman. b 25. Em Coll Cam BA51 MA56. Ridley Hall Cam 52. **d** 54 **p** 55. V Ecclesall *Sheff* 68-90; Hon Can Sheff Cathl 83-90; RD Ecclesall 85-89; rtd 90. *46 Sunnyvale Road, Totley, Sheffield S17 4FB* Sheffield (0742) 352249

COLLIER, Anthony Charles. b 45. Peterho Cam BA68 MA72 Or Coll Ox DipTh70 Whitelands Coll Lon CertEd76. Cuddesdon Coll 68. **d** 71 **p** 72. C N Holmwood *Guildf* 71-75; Perm to Offic *S'wark* 75-79; Chapl Colfe's Sch Lon from 80; Hon C Shirley St Jo *Cant* 80-84; Hon C Shirley St Jo *S'wark* from 85. *56 Bennetts Way, Shirley, Croydon CR0 8AB* 081-777 5719

COLLIER, Clive. b 53. Trin Coll Bris 80. **d** 82 **p** 83. C Hazlemere *Ox* 82-90; V from 90. *The New Vicarage, 260 Amersham Road, High Wycombe, Bucks HP15 7PZ* High Wycombe (0494) 439404

COLLIER, Michael Francis. b 29. Wycliffe Hall Ox 71. **d** 73 **p** 74. C Hamstead St Paul *Birm* 73-75; P-in-c Castleton *Derby* 75-80; P-in-c Hope 78-80; V Hope and Castleton from 80; RD Bakewell and Eyam from 90. *The Vicarage, Hope, Sheffield S30 2RN* Hope Valley (0433) 20534

COLLIER, Richard John Millard. b 45. E Anglian Minl Tr Course 78. **d** 81 **p** 82. NSM Nor St Pet Mancroft *Nor* 81-82; NSM Nor St Pet Mancroft w St Jo Maddermarket from 82. *11 The Close, Norwich NR1 4DH* Norwich (0603) 624204

COLLIER, Robert Howard. b 25. St Cath Soc Ox BA46 MA50. **d** 54 **p** 55. V Shabbington *Ox* 59-84; V Worminghall 59-84; P-in-c Ickford 64-84; RD Waddesdon 66-73; Sec Dioc Adv Cttee for the Care of Chs 85-89; Lic to Offic from 85; rtd 89; Lic to Offic *Arg* from 89. *Morar House, Connel by Oban, Argyll PA37 1PA* Connel (063174) 644

COLLIN, Anthony Garth. b 27. Roch Th Coll 64. **d** 66 **p** 67. C Hove 69-72; R Rumboldswyke *Chich* 72-75; Chapl R W Sussex & Graylingwell Hosps Chich 75-88; rtd 88. *6 Muirfield Avenue, Doncaster, S Yorkshire DN4 6UP* Doncaster (0302) 538512

COLLIN, Terry. b 39. St Aid Birkenhead 65. **d** 67 **p** 68. C Bolton St Jas w St Chrys *Bradf* 67-71; C Keighley 71-74; V Greengates from 74. *The Vicarage, 138 New Line, Greengates, Bradford, W Yorkshire BD10 0BX* Bradford (0274) 613111

COLLING, Canon James Oliver. b 30. Man Univ BA50. Cuddesdon Coll 52. **d** 54 **p** 55. C Wigan All SS *Liv* 54-59; V Padgate Ch Ch 59-71; R Padgate 71-73; RD Warrington 70-82; AD from 89; R Warrington St Elphin from 73; Hon Can Liv Cathl from 76; Chapl to The Queen from 90. *The Rectory, Warrington WA1 2TL* Warrington (0925) 35020

COLLING, Terence John. b 47. Linc Th Coll 84. **d** 86 **p** 87. C Wood End *Cov* 86-90; V Willenhall from 90. *The Vicarage, Robin Hood Road, Coventry CV3 3AY* Coventry (0203) 303266

COLLINGS, Neil. b 46. K Coll Lon BD69 AKC69. **d** 70 **p** 71. C Littleham w Exmouth *Ex* 70-72; TV 72-74; Chapl Westmr Abbey 74-79; Preb Heref Cathl Heref 79-86; Dir of Ords and Post Ord Tr 79-86; R Heref St Nic 79-86; Bp's Dom Chapl 82-86; R Harpenden St Nic *St Alb* from 86. *The Rectory, 9 Rothamsted Avenue, Harpenden, Herts AL5 2DD* Harpenden (0582) 712202

COLLINGS, Robert Frank. b 26. Lon Univ BD53. ALCD52. **d** 52 **p** 53. C Bayswater *Lon* 52-55; Australia from 55; rtd 87. *Lot 6, Maguire Place, Dardanup, W Australia 6236* Dardanup (97) 281264

COLLINGWOOD, Christopher Paul. b 54. MA BMus. Ripon Coll Cuddesdon. **d** 83 **p** 84. C Tupsley *Heref* 83-86; Prec St Alb Abbey *St Alb* 86-90; V Bedf St Paul from 90. *St Paul's Vicarage, 12 The Embankment, Bedford MK40 3PD* Bedford (0234) 352314

COLLINGWOOD, Deryck Laurence. b 50. St Jo Coll Cam BA72. Edin Th Coll BD85. **d** 85 **p** 85. Chapl Napier Coll Edin from 85; C Edin Ch Ch *Edin* 85-88; Edin Th Inst Coll from 89. *66 Marchmont Crescent, Edinburgh EH9 1HD* 031-662 0228

COLLINGWOOD, John Jeremy Raynham. b 37. Barrister 64 CCC Cam BA60 MA68 Lon Univ BD78. Trin Coll Bris 75. **d** 78 **p** 79. C Henleaze *Bris* 78-80; P-in-c Clifton H Trin, St Andr and St Pet 80-81; V from 81; RD Clifton 84-87; Bp's Officer for Miss and Evang from 87. *Holy Trinity Vicarage, 6 Goldney Avenue, Bristol BS8 4RA* Bristol (0272) 734751

COLLINS, Adelbert Andrew. b 15. Lich Th Coll. **d** 61 **p** 62. C Sedgley All SS *Lich* 61-77; P-in-c Enville 77-81 and 86-88; R 81-86; C Kinver and Enville 88-90; rtd 90. *West Cottage, Enville, Stourbridge, W Midlands DY7 5JA* Kinver (0384) 873733

COLLINS, Barry Douglas. b 47. Kelham Th Coll 66. **d** 70 **p** 71. C Peel Green *Man* 70-73; C Salford St Phil w St Steph 73-75; R Blackley H Trin 75-79; Perm to Offic Ripon from 80; Pet from 83; Cov from 85. *c/o 10 Onley Park, Willoughby, Rugby, Warks CV23 8AN* Rugby (0788) 817579

COLLINS, Bruce Churton. b 47. BSc. Oak Hill Th Coll. **d** 83 **p** 84. C Notting Hill St Jo *Lon* 83-87; C Notting Hill St Jo and St Pet 87-90; V Roxeth Ch Ch and Harrow St Pet from 90; P-in-c S Harrow St Paul from 91. *Christ Church Vicarage, Harrow, Middx HA2 0JN* 081-422 3241

COLLINS, Christopher. b 46. K Coll Lon BSc67 AKC67 Pemb Coll Ox BA70. St Steph Ho Ox 68. **d** 71 **p** 72. C Pennywell St Thos and Grindon St Oswald CD *Dur* 71-74; C Pallion 74-76; C Millfield St Mary 74-76; C Bishopwearmouth Gd Shep 74-76; C Harton Colliery 76-78; TV Winlaton 78-85; V Grangetown from 85. *St Aidan's Vicarage, Grangetown, Sunderland SR2 9RS* 091-514 3485

COLLINS, Christopher David. b 43. Sheff Univ BA(Econ)64. Tyndale Hall Bris 65. **d** 68 **p** 69. C Rusholme *Man* 68-71; C Bushbury *Lich* 71-74; V Fairfield *Liv* 74-81; V Tunbridge Wells St Jo *Roch* from 81. *St John's Vicarage, 1 Amherst Road, Tunbridge Wells, Kent TN4 9LG* Tunbridge Wells (0892) 21183

COLLINS, Donard. b 55. TCD BA. Oak Hill Th Coll. **d** 83 **p** 84. C Lurgan (Shankill) *D & D* 83-87; I Ardmore w Craigavon from 87. *Ardmore Rectory, Lurgan, Craigavon, Co Armagh BT66 6QR* Derryadd (0762) 340357

COLLINS, Canon Frederick Spencer. b 36. FACCA Birm Univ DipTh67. Ripon Hall Ox. **d** 67 **p** 68. C Evington *Leic* 67-71; C Hall Green Ascension *Birm* 71-73; V Burney Lane 73-79; Dioc Stewardship Adv 79-84; V Yardley St Edburgha from 84; RD Yardley from 86; Hon Can Birm Cathl from 89. *The Vicarage, Yardley, Birmingham B33 8PH* 021-783 2085

COLLINS, George Martyn. b 36. Bris Univ BA58. Coll of Resurr Mirfield. **d** 62 **p** 63. C Widley w Wymering *Portsm* 62-64; C Kingstanding St Mark CD *Birm* 64-69; V Weoley Castle 69-78; R Curdworth 78-83; TR Curdworth w Castle Vale 83-88; V Westbury-on-Trym H Trin *Bris* from 88. *Holy Trinity Vicarage, 44 Eastfield Road, Westbury-on-Trym, Bristol BS9 4AG* Bristol (0272) 621536

COLLINS, Canon Ian Geoffrey. b 37. Hull Univ BA60 CertEd. Sarum Th Coll 60. **d** 62 **p** 63. C Gainsborough All SS *Linc* 62-65; Min Can Windsor 65-81; Succ Windsor 67-81; R Kirkby in Ashfield *S'well* 81-85; Can Res S'well Minster from 85. *5 Vicar's Court, Southwell, Notts NG25 0HP* Southwell (0636) 815056

146

COLLINS, James Frederick. b 10. St Jo Coll Cam BA34 MA38. Westcott Ho Cam 34. **d** 35 **p** 36. Dir of Ords *Sarum* 68-73; Hon C Devizes St Jo w St Mary 68-75; rtd 75; Perm to Offic *St Alb* from 81. *3 Parkinson Close, Marford Road, Wheathampstead, St Albans, Herts AL4 5DP* Wheathampstead (058283) 3944

COLLINS, Miss Janet May. b 55. Qu Mary Coll Lon BA78 St Jo Coll Dur BA84. Cranmer Hall Dur 82. **dss** 85 **d** 87. Willington Team *Newc* 85-87; C 87-88; Par Dn Stevenage St Hugh Chells *St Alb* 88-90; Par Dn Goldington from 90. *9 Heather Gardens, Goldington, Bedford MK41 0TB* Bedford (0234) 347393

COLLINS, John Brenton. b 06. Trin Coll Cam BA28 MA32. Ridley Hall Cam 30. **d** 33 **p** 34. R Hever w Mark Beech *Roch* 69-73; rtd 73; Perm to Offic *Heref* from 74. *26 Marlow Road, Leominster, Hereford HR6 8SN* Leominster (0568) 3413

COLLINS, John Gilbert. b 32. S'wark Ord Course 67. **d** 71 **p** 72. C Coulsdon St Jo S'wark 71-75; Chapl St Fran Hosp Haywards Heath 75-84; Hurstwood Park Hosp Haywards Heath 75-84; R Stedham w Iping, Elsted and Treyford-cum-Didling *Chich* from 84. *The Rectory, Stedham, Midhurst, W Sussex GU29 0NQ* Midhurst (073081) 3342

COLLINS, Preb John Theodore Cameron Bucke. b 25. Clare Coll Cam BA49 MA52. Ridley Hall Cam 49. **d** 51 **p** 52. V Gillingham St Mark *Roch* 57-71; Chapl Medway Hosp Gillingham 70-71; V Canford Magna *Sarum* 71-80; RD Wimborne 79-80; V Brompton H Trin w Onslow Square St Paul *Lon* 80-85; C 85-89; AD Chelsea 84-88; Preb St Paul's Cathl 85-89; rtd 89; Perm to Offic *Lon* & *Win* from 89. *7 Solent Court, Cornwallis Road, Milford on Sea, Lymington, Hants SO41 0NH* Lymington (0590) 645961

COLLINS, Maurice Arthur Reily. b 19. Clare Coll Cam BA41 MA45. Westcott Ho Cam 45. **d** 47 **p** 48. R Ockley *Guildf* 53-82; R Ockley w Okewood and Forest Green 82-85; rtd 85; Perm to Offic *Portsm* from 86. *Old Wheatsheaf, Privett, Alton, Hants GU34 3NX* Privett (073088) 287

COLLINS, Norman Hilary. b 33. Mert Coll Ox BA55 MA58. Wells Th Coll 58. **d** 60 **p** 61. C Ystrad Mynach *Llan* 60-62; C Gellygaer 62-67; V Maerdy 67-77; R Penarth w Lavernock from 77; RD Penarth and Barry from 87. *The Rectory, 13 Hickman Road, Penarth, S Glam CF6 2AJ* Penarth (0222) 709463

COLLINS, Paul David Arthur. b 50. K Coll Lon BD72 AKC72. **d** 73 **p** 74. C Rotherhithe St Mary w All SS S'wark 73-76; C Stocking Farm *Leic* 76-78; V 78-83; R Husbands Bosworth w Mowsley and Knaptoft etc 83-87; Soc Resp Officer *Blackb* from 87. *St Mary's House, Cathedral Close, Blackburn BB1 5AA* Blackburn (0254) 57759

COLLINS, Paul Myring. b 53. St Jo Coll Dur BA75. St Steph Ho Ox BA78. **d** 79 **p** 80. C Meir *Lich* 79-82; C Fenton 82-83; TV Leek and Meerbrook 83-87; Tutor in Th and Liturgy Chich Th Coll from 87. *Chichester Theology College, Chichester, W Sussex PO19 3ES* Chichester (0243) 783369

COLLINS, Canon Peter Churton. b 13. Lon Univ BD35. Ely Th Coll 35. **d** 36 **p** 37. R Crayford *Roch* 60-78; V Dartford St Alb 42-60; Hon Can Roch Cathl 63-79; RD Erith 65-79; rtd 79; Chapl Huggens Coll Northfleet 79-87. *College of St Barnabas, Blackberry Lane, Lingfield, Surrey RH7 6NJ* Dormans Park (034287) 260

COLLINS, Peter John. b 33. Open Univ BA. Oak Hill Th Coll 64. **d** 66 **p** 67. C Low Leyton *Chelmsf* 66-69; C Portsdown *Portsm* 69-72; V Gatten St Paul 72-79; C-in-c Ingrave St Steph CD *Chelmsf* 79-85; V Roydon from 85. *St Peter's Vicarage, Church Mead, Roydon, Harlow, Essex CM19 5EY* Roydon (027979) 2103

COLLINS, Philip Howard Norton. b 50. AKC73. St Aug Coll Cant 73. **d** 74 **p** 75. C Stamford Hill St Thos *Lon* 74-78; C Upwood w Gt and Lt Raveley *Ely* 78-81; C Ramsey 78-81; R Leverington from 81; P-in-c Wisbech St Mary from 89; RD Wisbech from 90. *The Rectory, Gorefield Road, Leverington, Wisbech, Cambs PE13 5AS* Wisbech (0945) 581486

COLLINS, Rodney Harry. b 20. Open Univ BA74. S'wark Ord Course 75. **d** 78 **p** 79. NSM Swanley St Mary *Roch* from 78. *16 Stanhope Road, Sidcup, Kent DA15 7AA* 081-302 0867

COLLINS, Roger Richardson. b 48. Birm Univ BPhil88. W Midl Minl Tr Course 78. **d** 81 **p** 82. NSM Cotteridge *Birm* from 81. *6 Chesterfield Court, Middleton Hall Road, Birmingham B30 1AF* 021-459 4009

COLLINS, Mrs Stella Vivian. b 32. Sarum Th Coll 74. **dss** 77 **d** 87. Harnham *Sarum* 77-87; Hon Par Dn from 87; Dioc Lay Min Adv from 82; Hon Par Dn Wilton w

Netherhampton and Fugglestone from 88; RD Wylye and Wilton from 89. *Shawmeare, Coombe Road, Salisbury SP2 8BT* Salisbury (0722) 336420

COLLINS, William Arthur Donovan. b 21. AKC49. **d** 50 **p** 51. S Africa 66-80; Adn Cape Town 75-80; V Birchington w Acol and Minnis Bay *Cant* 80-85; Warden Coll of St Barn Lingfield 85-88; rtd 88. *16 Chatsworth Avenue, Haslemere, Surrey GU27 1BA* Haslemere (0428) 2045

COLLINS, William Carpenter. b 35. BA55 MA57 MDiv65. Ch Div Sch of the Pacific (USA) 63. **d** 66 **p** 67. USA 66-71; Hon C Newlyn St Pet *Truro* from 82. *Cape House, Cape Cornwall, St Just, Penzance, Cornwall TR19 7NN* Penzance (0736) 787112

COLLINS, William Francis Martin. b 43. St Cath Coll Cam BA66 MA70. Cuddesdon Coll 68. **d** 70 **p** 71. C Man Victoria Park *Man* 70-73; P-in-c Ancoats 73-78; Chapl Abraham Moss Cen 78-91; Hon C Cheetham Hill 81-84; Chs' FE Officer for Gtr Man 84-91; V Norbury *Ches* from 91. *Norbury Vicarage, 75 Chester Road, Hazel Grove, Stockport, Cheshire SK7 5PE* 061-483 8640

COLLINS, Winfield St Clair. b 41. Univ of W Indies BA83 Man Univ BA88. Codrington Coll Barbados LTh77. **d** 76 **p** 76. Asst Chapl HM Pris Wakef 76; Barbados 76-84; Asst Chapl HM Pris Wandsworth 85; Chapl HM Young Offender Inst Thorn Cross 85-91; Chapl HM Pris Pentonville from 91. *HM Prison Pentonville, Caledonian Road, London N7 8TT* 071-607 5353

COLLINSON, Ernest John. b 12. ALCD36. **d** 36 **p** 37. V Tiverton St Geo *Ex* 66-73; Perm to Offic from 74; rtd 77. *Cleve Cottage, Flower Lane, Woodbury, Exeter EX5 1LX* Woodbury (0395) 32548

COLLINSON, Canon Joan Irene. b 31. ALA55 Westf Coll Lon BA52. **dss** 63 **d** 87. Westmr St Steph w St Jo *Lon* 65-68; R Foundn of St Kath 68-73; Qu Mary Coll 68-73; Notting Hill St Jo 73-74; Kent Univ *Cant* 74-82; Dean of Women's Min S'wark 82-89; Hon Can S'wark Cathl from 88; TM Newc Epiphany *Newc* from 89; Adv for Accredited Lay Min from 89. *St Hugh's Vicarage, Wansbeck Road, Gosforth, Newcastle upon Tyne NE3 2LR* 091-285 8792

COLLIS, Michael Alan. b 35. K Coll Lon BD60 AKC60. **d** 61 **p** 62. C Worc St Martin *Worc* 61-63; C Dudley St Thos 63-66; C St Peter-in-Thanet *Cant* 66-70; V Croydon H Trin 70-77; P-in-c Norbury St Steph 77-81; V 81-82; V Sutton Valence w E Sutton and Chart Sutton 82-89; R New Fishbourne *Chich* from 89. *12 Fishbourne Road, Chichester, W Sussex PO19 3HX* Chichester (0243) 783364

COLLIS, Stephen Thomas. b 47. Cranmer Hall Dur 80. **d** 82 **p** 83. C Crewe All SS and St Paul *Ches* 82-84; C Wilmslow 84-86; Chapl RAF from 86. *c/o MOD, Adastral House, Theobald's Road, London WC1X 8RU* 071-430 7268

COLLIS SMITH, Charles Philip. b 39. St Cath Coll Cam BA61. Lich Th Coll 61. **d** 63 **p** 64. C Wednesfield St Thos *Lich* 63-66; C Hednesford 66-71; V High Offley 71-80; R Myddle from 80; V Broughton from 80. *The Rectory, Myddle, Shrewsbury SY4 3RX* Bomere Heath (0939) 290811

COLLISHAW, Arthur Beecroft. b 13. Qu Coll Cam BA35 MA48. Chich Th Coll 38. **d** 40 **p** 41. Ghana 69-78; rtd 78; Perm to Offic *Lon* from 85. *15 Up The Quadrant, Morden College, St German's Place, London SE3 0PW* 081-293 5486

COLLISON, Christopher John. b 48. Oak Hill Th Coll 68. **d** 72 **p** 73. C Cromer *Nor* 72-75; C Costessey 76-78; V from 87; C Heckmondwike *Wakef* 78-79; P-in-c Shepley 79-83; Dioc Communications Officer 79-83; Chapl Flushing Miss to Seamen *Eur* 83-85; Asst Min Sec Miss to Seamen 85-87; C St Mich Paternoster Royal *Lon* 85-87. *The Vicarage, Folgate Lane, Costessey, Norwich NR8 5DP* Norwich (0603) 742818

COLLISON, Ms Elizabeth. b 38. Man Univ CertEd58. N Ord Course 85. **d** 88. C Huyton St Mich *Liv* from 88. *54 Jacqueline Drive, Huyton, Liverpool L36 1TU* 051-489 1074

COLLYER, David John. b 38. JP. Keble Coll Ox BA61 Ox Univ MA86. Westcott Ho Cam 61. **d** 63 **p** 64. C Perry Beeches *Birm* 63-65; Bp's Chapl for Special Youth Work 65-70; P-in-c Deritend 66-70; Bp's Youth Chapl and Dioc Youth Officer 70-73; R Northfield 73-78; Hon Chapl Birm Cathl 78-81; Hon C Birm St Geo 81-86; V Handsworth St Andr from 86. *St Andrew's Vicarage, Laurel Road, Birmingham B21 9PB* 021-551 2097

COLLYER, John Gordon Llewellyn. b 15. Lon Univ BA. Sarum Th Coll 69. **d** 70 **p** 71. C Portchester *Portsm* 70-74; C Portsea All SS w St Jo Rudmore 74-75; TV

Boscastle w Davidstow *Truro* 75-77; rtd 80; P-in-c Copdock w Washbrook and Belstead *St E* 80-83; Perm to Offic Glouc from 83; Truro from 86. *Stonecote, 12 The Street, Ovington, Thetford, Norfolk IP25 6RT* Watton (0953) 881569

COLMAN, Cyril Vickers. b 14. ALCD40. **d** 40 **p** 41. R Orlestone w Ruckinge *Cant* 58-70; V Lower Halstow 70-72; V Guernsey St Matt *Win* 72-84; rtd 84; Perm to Offic *Win* from 84. *Les Mouettes Cottage, rue de la Lande, Castel, Guernsey, Channel Islands* Guernsey (0481) 55060

COLMAN, Geoffrey Hugh. b 29. Univ Coll Ox BA53 MA68. Wells Th Coll 67. **d** 68 **p** 69. C Wanstead St Mary *Chelmsf* 68-72; V Barking St Erkenwald 72-77; Youth Chapl 78-81; C Maidstone All SS and St Phil w Tovil *Cant* 85-88; P-in-c Teynham from 88. *76 Station Road, Teynham, Sittingbourne, Kent ME9 9SN* Teynham (0795) 522510

COLMER, Malcolm John. b 45. Sussex Univ MSc67 Nottm Univ BA73. St Jo Coll Nottm 71. **d** 73 **p** 74. C Egham *Guildf* 73-76; C Chadwell *Chelmsf* 76-79; V S Malling *Chich* 79-85; V Hornsey Rise St Mary w St Steph *Lon* 85-87; TR Hornsey Rise Whitehall Park Team from 87; AD Islington from 90. *St Mary's Vicarage, 3 Highcroft Road, London N19 3AQ* 071-272 1783

COLQUHOUN, Canon Frank. b 09. Univ Coll Dur LTh32 BA33 MA37. Bible Churchmen's Coll 29. **d** 33 **p** 34. Can Res S'wark Cathl *S'wark* 61-73; Chan 66-73; Prin S'wark Ord Course 66-71; Can Res Nor Cathl *Nor* 73-78; rtd 78; Perm to Offic *Chich* from 80. *21 Buckholt Avenue, Bexhill-on-Sea, E Sussex TN40 2RS* Bexhill-on-Sea (0424) 221138

COLSON, Major Alexander Francis Lionel. b 21. MBE45. St Jo Coll Cam BA43 MA61. Tyndale Hall Bris 60. **d** 62 **p** 63. R Elmswell *St E* 65-73; V W Kilburn St Luke w St Simon and St Jude *Lon* 73-82; R Thrandeston, Stuston and Brome w Oakley *St E* 82-86; rtd 86; Perm to Offic *Nor* from 86. *10 Soanes Court, Lyng, Norwich NR9 5RE* Norwich (0603) 872812

COLSON, Ian Richard. b 65. Wolv Poly BSc86 Nottm Univ BTh89. Linc Th Coll 86. **d** 89 **p** 90. C Nunthorpe *York* from 89. *15 Ripon Road, Nunthorpe, Middlesbrough, Cleveland TS7 0HX* Middlesbrough (0642) 310834

COLSTON, John Edward. b 43. Lich Th Coll 65. **d** 68 **p** 69. C Bromsgrove All SS *Worc* 68-71; C Tettenhall Wood *Lich* 71-74; V Alrewas 74-88; V Wychnor 74-88; R Ainderby Steeple w Yafforth and Kirby Wiske etc *Ripon* from 88; Warden of Readers from 90. *The Rectory, Ainderby Steeple, Northallerton, N Yorkshire DL7 9PY* Northallerton (0609) 773346

COLTHURST, Ven Reginald William Richard. b 22. TCD BA44. CITC 45. **d** 45 **p** 46. C Portadown St Mark *Arm* 45-48; C Belf All SS *Conn* 48-55; I Ardtrea w Desertcreat *Arm* 55-66; I Richhill from 66; RD Kilmore from 79; Adn Arm from 85. *15 Annareagh Road, Richhill, Armagh* Richhill (0762) 871232

COLTON, Leonard Henry. b 35. Bris & Glouc Tr Course 81. **d** 84 **p** 85. NSM Swindon Ch Ch *Bris* 84-90; NSM Lyddington w Wanborough 90-91; NSM Bishopstone w Hinton Parva 90-91; NSM Lyddington and Wanborough and Bishopstone etc from 91. *5 Callows Cross, Brinkworth, Chippenham, Wilts SN15 5DY* Brinkworth (066641) 336

COLTON, William Paul. b 60. NUI BCL81 TCD DipTh84 MPhil87. **d** 84 **p** 85. C Lisburn St Paul *Conn* 84-87; Bp's Dom Chapl 85-90; VC Belf Cathl 87-90; I Castleknock and Mulhuddart w Clonsilla *D & G* from 90; Min Can Belf Cathl 89-90; Hon Sec of Coun for the Ch Overseas from 90; CV Ch Ch Cathl Dub *D & G* from 90. *12 Hawthorn Lawn, Castleknock, Dublin 15, Irish Republic* Dublin (1) 213083

COLVEN, Canon Christopher George. b 45. Leeds Univ BA66. Coll of Resurr Mirfield 66. **d** 68 **p** 69. C Tottenham St Paul *Lon* 68-74; C Notting Hill St Mich and Ch Ch 74-76; V W Hampstead St Jas 76-81; P-in-c Hampstead All SS 78-81; Admin of Shrine of Our Lady Walsingham 81-86; P-in-c E w N and W Barsham *Nor* 81-84; Hon Can Nor Cathl 86-87; V S Kensington St Steph *Lon* from 87. *9 Eldon Road, London W8 5PU* 071-937 5083

COLVER, Canon John Lawrence. b 14. Keble Coll Ox BA36 MA40. Cuddesdon Coll 36. **d** 37 **p** 38. V Bembridge *Portsm* 65-79; rtd 79; Perm to Offic *Portsm* from 81. *Lynton, 10 Yelfs Road, Ryde, Isle of Wight PO33 2LY* Isle of Wight (0983) 66498

COLWILL, Raymond William. b 06. Ripon Hall Ox. **d** 71 **p** 71. Hon C Wilton *B & W* from 71. *Hamara, Comeytrowe Lane, Taunton, Somerset TA1 5JB* Taunton (0823) 331833

COMBE, Edward Charles. b 40. N Ord Course. **d** 89 **p** 90. NSM Broadheath *Ches* from 89. *4 Holly Close, Altrincham, Cheshire WA15 6NE* 061-980 6410

COMBE, Very Rev John Charles. b 33. TCD BA53 MA56 BD57 MLitt65 PhD70. **d** 56 **p** 57. C Cork St Luke w St Ann *C, C & R* 56-58; C Ballynafeigh St Jude *D & G* 58-61; I Crinken *D & G* 61-66; Hon CV Ch Ch Cathl Dub 63-66; C Belf St Bart *Conn* 66-70; I Belf St Barn 70-74; I Portadown St Mark *Arm* 74-84; I Arm St Mark w Aghavilly 84-90; Can Arm Cathl 85-90; Dean Kilmore *K, E & A* from 90; I Kilmore w Ballintemple, Kildallon etc from 90. *The Deanery, Danesfort, Cavan, Irish Republic* Cavan (49) 31918

COMBER, Ven Anthony James. b 27. Leeds Univ BSc49 MSc52. St Chad's Coll Dur 53. **d** 56 **p** 57. C Manston *Ripon* 56-60; V Oulton 60-69; V Hunslet St Mary 69-77; RD Armley 72-75 and 79-81; R Farnley 77-82; Hon Can Ripon Cathl from 80; Adn Leeds from 82. *712 Foundry Lane, Leeds LS14 6BL* Leeds (0532) 602069

COMBER, Keith Charles. b 15. Wycliffe Hall Ox 71. **d** 73 **p** 74. C Walmley *Birm* 73-76; V Barston 76-79; rtd 80; Perm to Offic Ely & Nor 80-86; Lic Chich 86-88; Perm from 88. *6 Saunders Close, Hastings, E Sussex TN34 3UG* Hastings (0424) 720334

COMBER, Michael. b 35. **d** 71 **p** 72. CA 59-72; C Carl H Trin and St Barn *Carl* 72-73; C Upperby St Jo 73-76; V Dearham 76-81; V Harraby 81-84; R Orton and Tebay w Ravenstonedale etc 84-90; I Clonfert Gp of Par *L & K* from 90. *The Rectory, Banagher, Co Offaly, Irish Republic* Birr (509) 51269

COMBES, Roger Matthew. b 47. K Coll Lon LLB69. Ridley Hall Cam 72. **d** 74 **p** 75. C Onslow Square St Paul *Lon* 74-77; C Brompton H Trin 76-77; C Cam H Sepulchre w All SS *Ely* 77-86; R Silverhill St Matt *Chich* from 86. *The Rectory, St Matthew's Road, St Leonards-on-Sea, E Sussex TN38 0TN* Hastings (0424) 423790

COMER, Michael John. b 30. St Mich Coll Llan 79. **d** 81 **p** 82. C Bistre *St As* 81-84; R Llanfyllin and Bwlchycibau 84-91; V Hattersley *Ches* from 91. *58 Callington Drive, Hyde, Cheshire SK14 3EL* 061-366 7036

COMERFORD, Peter Morris. b 35. AKC61. **d** 62 **p** 63. C Catford St Laur *S'wark* 62-65; C Bournemouth St Clem w St Mary *Win* 65-66; C Berry Pomeroy *Ex* 66-68; Asst Chapl HM Pris Wormwood Scrubs 68-69; Chapl HM Pris Grendon 69-74; HM Youth Cust Cen Feltham 74-78; HM Pris Brixton 78-85; Pentonville 85-89; R Marytavy *Ex* from 89; R Peter Tavy from 89. *The Rectory, Mary Tavy, Tavistock, Devon PL19 9PP* Mary Tavy (0822) 810516

COMLEY, Thomas Hedges. b 36. Leeds Univ BA62 Birm Univ DipSocWork78. Coll of Resurr Mirfield 62. **d** 64 **p** 65. C Leadgate *Dur* 64-67; C Shirley *Birm* 67-71; V Smethwick St Alb 71-76; Perm to Offic 76-82; V N Wembley St Cuth *Lon* from 82. *St Cuthbert's Vicarage, 214 Carlton Avenue West, Wembley, Middx HA0 3QY* 081-904 7657

COMMANDER, Reginald Arthur. b 20. RGN Aston Univ DHSA BA. Qu Coll Birm 75. **d** 78 **p** 79. NSM Wolv *Lich* from 78. *15 Coulter Grove, Perton, Wolverhampton WV6 7UA* Wolverhampton (0902) 744276

COMPTON, Barry Charles Chittenden. b 33. Linc Th Coll 60. **d** 62 **p** 63. C Beddington *S'wark* 62-65; C Limpsfield and Titsey 66-68; Hon C from 71; R Ridley *Roch* 69-70; R Ash 69-70. *Highlands, Limpsfield Chart, Oxted, Surrey* Oxted (0883) 714896

COMPTON, Frank Edward. b 12. St Jo Coll Dur BSc34 St Cath Soc Ox BA36 MA40. Ripon Hall Ox 34. **d** 36 **p** 37. V Caynham *Heref* 60-77; rtd 77; Perm to Offic *Heref* from 79. *The School House, Leysters, Leominster, Herefordshire HR6 0HS* Leominster (0568) 611608

COMYNS, Clifford John. b 28. TCD BA50 HDipEd53 MA53 BD67. **d** 51 **p** 52. C Chapelizod *D & G* 51-55; CF 55-75; Asst Master Eastbourne Coll from 75; Asst Chapl from 85. *Eastbourne College, Eastbourne, E Sussex BN21 4JY* Eastbourne (0323) 37411

CONANT, Fane Charles. b 44. Oak Hill Th Coll 83. **d** 85 **p** 86. C Hoole *Ches* 85-89; V Kelsall from 89. *St Philip's Vicarage, Chester Road, Kelsall, Tarporley, Cheshire CW6 0SA* Kelsall (0829) 51472

CONAWAY, Barry Raymond. b 41. CertEd69 Nottm Univ BEd70. Sarum & Wells Th Coll 86. **d** 88 **p** 89. C Ross w Brampton Abbotts, Bridstow and Peterstow *Heref* from 88. *Little House, Sussex Avenue, Ross-on-Wye, Herefordshire HR9 5AJ* Ross-on-Wye (0989) 64635

CONDELL, Canon Joseph Alfred Ambrose. b 48. CITC 70. **d** 73 **p** 74. C Donaghcloney *D & D* 73-76; I Achonry w Tubbercurry and Killoran *T, K & A* 76-79; I Roscrea w Kyle, Bourney and Corbally *L & K* from 79; Can Killaloe Cathl 83-89; RD Killaloe and Roscrea from 89;

Prec Limerick and Killaloe Cathls from 89. *St Conan's Rectory, Roscrea, Co Tipperary, Irish Republic* Roscrea (505) 21725

CONDER, Paul Collingwood Nelson. b 33. St Jo Coll Cam BA56 MA60. Ridley Hall Cam 56. **d** 58 **p** 59. C Grassendale *Liv* 58-61; Tutor St Jo Coll Dur 61-67; R Sutton *Liv* 67-74; TR 74-75; V Thames Ditton *Guildf* 75-86; RD Emly 82-86; V Blundellsands St Mich *Liv* from 86. *St Michael's Vicarage, 41 Dowhills Road, Liverpool L23 8SJ* 051-924 3424

CONDRY, Edward Francis. b 53. UEA BA74 Ex Coll Ox DipSocAnth75 BLitt77 DPhil80 Nottm Univ DipTh81. Linc Th Coll 80. **d** 82 **p** 83. C Weston Favell *Pet* 82-85; V Bloxham w Milcombe and S Newington *Ox* from 85. *The Vicarage, Church Street, Bloxham, Banbury, Oxon OX15 4ET* Banbury (0295) 720252

CONEY, Miss Mary Margaret. b 37. K Coll Lon BD58 CertEd59 DipAdEd78 Ex Univ MA87. **d** 87. NSM Penzance St Mary w St Paul *Truro* 87-90; Public Preacher from 90. *Stony Rocks, 3 Polgoon Close, Tredarvah, Penzance, Cornwall TR18 4JZ* Penzance (0736) 65671

CONEY, Preb Peter Norman Harvey. b 28. Keble Coll Ox BA51 MA55. Cuddesdon Coll 51. **d** 53 **p** 54. C Northallerton w Kirby Sigston *York* 53-56; C Wakef Cathl *Wakef* 56-59; V Milverton *B & W* 59-65; Chapl K Coll Taunton 65-70; V Martock *B & W* 70-72; V Martock w Ash from 72; RD Martock 80-89; Dioc Press Officer 83-88; Preb Wells Cathl from 85. *The Vicarage, Water Street, Martock, Somerset TA12 6JN* Martock (0935) 822579

CONEYS, Stephen John. b 61. Sheff Univ LLB82. St Jo Coll Nottm 87. **d** 90 **p** 91. C Plymouth Em w Efford *Ex* from 90. *27 Efford Crescent, Efford, Plymouth PL3 6NH* Plymouth (0752) 786250

CONGDON, John Jameson. b 30. St Edm Hall Ox BA53 MA57. Wycliffe Hall Ox 53. **d** 55 **p** 56. C Aspley *S'well* 55-58; C-in-c Woodthorpe CD 59-63; V Woodthorpe 63-69; V Spring Grove St Mary *Lon* 70-84; V Woodley *Ox* 84-89; Chapl W Middx Hosp Isleworth from 89. *95 Harewood Road, Isleworth, Middlesex TW7 5HN* 081-568 6504 or 867 5447

CONLEY, James Alan. b 29. Dur Univ BSc51. St Jo Coll Nottm. **d** 87 **p** 88. NSM Cropwell Bishop w Colston Bassett, Granby etc *S'well* from 87. *8 Willow Lane, Langar, Nottingham NG13 9HL* Harby (0949) 60820

CONN, Alistair Aberdein. b 37. Down Coll Cam BA60 MA64. Linc Th Coll 60. **d** 62 **p** 63. C W Hartlepool St Paul *Dur* 62-65; Uganda 65-66; Chapl Shrewsbury Sch 66-73; R Coupar Angus *St And* 73-78; V Ravenshead *S'well* from 78; RD Newstead from 90. *The Vicarage, 55 Sheepwalk Lane, Ravenshead, Nottingham NG15 9FD* Mansfield (0623) 792716

CONN, Robert Edwin. b 14. TCD BA38 MA44. **d** 39 **p** 40. I Killyleagh *D & D* 65-88; rtd 88. *9 Drumkeen Court, Belfast BT8 4FY* Belfast (0232) 644305

CONNELL, Miss Heather Josephine. b 38. SRN60 SCM61 Open Univ BA86. S'wark Ord Course 77. **dss** 79 **d** 87. Heston *Lon* 79-84; Gillingham St Barn *Roch* 84-87; Par Dn 87-90; Chapl Medway HA from 91. *Church House, 63 Stopford Road, Gillingham, Kent ME7 4NQ* Medway (0634) 576343

CONNER, Charles Borthwick. b 20. Keble Coll Ox BA43 MA49. St Steph Ho Ox 48. **d** 50 **p** 51. C Saltburn-by-the-Sea *York* 50-52; Chapl Ely Th Coll 52-53; CF 53-70; Perm to Offic *Sarum* from 80. *Angel Cottage, West Knighton, Dorchester, Dorset DT2 8PE* Warmwell (0305) 852465

CONNER, David John. b 47. Ex Coll Ox BA69 MA77. St Steph Ho Ox 69. **d** 71 **p** 72. Hon C Summertown *Ox* 71-76; Asst Chapl St Edw Sch Ox 71-73; Chapl 73-80; TV Wolvercote w Summertown *Ox* 76-80; Chapl Win Coll 80-87; V Cam Gt St Mary w St Mich *Ely* from 87; RD Cam from 89. *Great St Mary's Vicarage, 39 Madingley Road, Cambridge CB3 0EL* Cambridge (0223) 355285

CONNOCK, Gilbert Ronald. b 14. St Cath Soc Ox BA49 MA53. St Steph Ho Ox. **d** 49 **p** 50. R Hayes St Mary *Lon* 68-77; R The Sampfords *Chelmsf* 77-84; rtd 84; Perm to Offic *Bris* from 85. *16 Hengrove Road, Bristol BS4 2PS* Bristol (0272) 721630

CONNOLL, Miss Helen Dorothy. b 45. Oak Hill Th Coll BA86. **dss** 86 **d** 87. Leytonstone St Jo *Chelmsf* 86-87; Par Dn 87-90; Asst Chapl Grimsby Distr Gen Hosp from 90. *4 Worlaby Road, Grimsby, S Humberside DN33 3JY* Grimsby (0472) 74729

CONNOLLY, Daniel. b 51. BEng. St Jo Coll Nottm DPS84. **d** 84 **p** 85. C Bedgrove *Ox* 84-87; C-in-c Crookhorn Ch Cen CD *Portsm* 87-88; V Crookhorn from 88. *The*

Vicarage, 87 Perseus Place, Portsmouth PO7 8AW Portsmouth (0705) 267647

CONNOLLY, Sydney Herbert. b 40. Leeds Univ BA66. Coll of Resurr Mirfield 66. **d** 68 **p** 69. C W Derby St Mary *Liv* 68-71; C Prescot 71-74; V Burtonwood 74-80; V Walker *Newc* 80-89; TR Whorlton from 89. *The Vicarage, 8 Frenton Close, Newcastle upon Tyne NE5 1EH* 091-267 4069

CONNOR, Dennis George Austin. b 16. K Coll Lon BD40 AKC40. **d** 40 **p** 41. C Shoreditch St Leon *Lon* 40-42; C Mill Hill Jo Keble Ch 42-47; C Enfield St Andr 47-52; V Harefield from 52; Chapl Harefield Hosp Middx from 52; RD Hillingdon *Lon* 70-75. *The Vicarage, Church Hill, Harefield, Middx UB9 6DF* Harefield (089582) 3221

CONNOR, Ellis Jones. b 16. Univ of Wales BA38. St Mich Coll Llan 38. **d** 39 **p** 41. R Desford *Leic* 55-73; R N Hill *Truro* 73-75; R Llanddewi Skirrid w Llanvetherine etc *Mon* 75-78; C Spalding St Jo *Linc* 79-82; rtd 82; Perm to Offic *Leic* from 82. *35 Sycamore Street, Blaby, Leicester LE8 3FL* Leicester (0533) 777725

CONNOR, Geoffrey. b 46. K Coll Lon BD73 AKC73. St Aug Coll Cant. **d** 74 **p** 75. C Cockerton *Dur* 74-79; Dioc Recruitment Officer 79-87; Chapl St Chad's Coll Dur 84-87; Vice-Provost St Mary's Cathl *Edin* 87-90; R Edin St Mary 87-90; Dioc Dir of Ords (Dios Edin and Arg) 87-90; V Whitechapel w Admarsh-in-Bleasdale *Blackb* from 90; Dir of Ords from 90. *The Vicarage, Whitechapel, Preston, Lancs PR3 2EP* Brock (0995) 40282

CONNOR, Patrick Francis Latham. b 25. Ex Coll Ox BA47 MA52. Gen Th Sem (NY) STB53. **d** 53 **p** 53. R Sparkford w Weston Bampfylde *B & W* 64-85; P-in-c Sutton Montis 70-85; R Mawnan *Truro* 85-89; rtd 89; Perm to Offic *Truro* from 89. *Trelatham, Boyton, Launceston, Cornwall PL15 9RJ* Launceston (0566) 776078

CONNOR, Stephen John. b 58. MA. Ridley Hall Cam. **d** 84 **p** 85. C Beamish *Dur* 84-86; C Wordsley *Lich* 86-90; TV Langport Area Chs *B & W* from 90. *The Vicarage, 2 Mill Road, High Ham, Langport, Somerset TA10 9DJ* Langport (0458) 251293

CONNOR, Archdeacon of. See ROLSTON, Ven John Ormsby

CONNOR, Bishop of. See POYNTZ, Rt Rev Samuel Greenfield

CONNOR, Dean of. See FAIR, Very Rev James Alexander

CONRAD, Paul Derick. b 54. Worc Coll Ox BA76 MA82. St Steph Ho Ox 78. **d** 80 **p** 81. C Wanstead St Mary *Chelmsf* 80-83; C Somers Town St Mary *Lon* 83-85; P-in-c Kentish Town St Martin w St Andr 85-91; V from 91. *The Vicarage, 26 Vicars Road, London NW5 4NN* 071-485 3807

CONSTABLE, Douglas Brian. b 40. Lon Univ BA62. Linc Th Coll 63. **d** 65 **p** 66. C Stockwood CD *Bris* 65-70; Hon C Clifton St Paul 70-72; Asst Chapl Bris Univ 70-72; Chapl Lee Abbey 72-77; V Derby St Thos *Derby* 77-85; TV Southn (City Cen) *Win* from 85. *12 The Avenue, Southampton SO1 2SQ* Southampton (0703) 222574

CONSTANT, Arden. b 09. K Coll Cam BA32 MA36. Cuddesdon Coll. **d** 34 **p** 35. V Kirkby Malham *Bradf* 66-73; rtd 72. *38 Bushwood Road, Kew, Richmond, Surrey TW9 3BQ* 081-940 3156

CONSTANTINE, Miss Elaine Muriel. b 50. Univ of Wales (Swansea) BSc72 CertEd73 DipEd75 Lon Univ MEd78. St Alb Minl Tr Scheme. **dss** 86 **d** 87. Bedf St Martin *St Alb* 86-87; Par Dn 87-88; Par Dn Leighton Buzzard w Eggington, Hockliffe etc from 88. *138 Brooklands Drive, Leighton Buzzard, Beds LU7 8PQ* Leighton Buzzard (0525) 373167

CONSTANTINE, Leonard. b 30. AKC57. **d** 58 **p** 59. C W Hartlepool St Aid *Dur* 58-61; C Sheff St Geo and St Steph *Sheff* 61-62; Nyasaland 62-64; Malawi 64-69; V W Pelton *Dur* 69-73; V Shotton 73-78; V Stillington 78-80; V Grindon and Stillington 80-82; V Corbridge w Halton and Newton Hall *Newc* from 82. *St Andrew's Vicarage, Corbridge, Northd NE45 5DW* Hexham (0434) 632128

CONVERY, Arthur Malcolm. b 42. Sheff Univ BSc63 DipEd64. N Ord Course 79. **d** 82 **p** 83. NSM Parr *Liv* 82-87; V Marown *S & M* from 87. *The Vicarage, Marown, Crosby, Isle of Man* Marown (0624) 851378

CONWAY, Alfred Sydney. b 22. Kelham Th Coll 40. **d** 45 **p** 46. V Croxley Green All SS *St Alb* 63-81; V Walton St Jo *Liv* 81-89; rtd 89; Perm to Offic *Ex* from 89. *14 Mount Close, Honiton, Devon EX14 8QZ* Honiton (0404) 46052

CONWAY, Glyn Haydn. b 38. St Mich Coll Llan DipTh65. **d** 65 **p** 66. C Wrexham *St As* 65-71; TV 71-77; V Holywell

77-83; V Upton Ascension *Ches* from 83. *The Vicarage, Demage Lane, Chester CH2 1EL*   Chester (0244) 383518

CONWAY, Irvine Claude. b 31. ACP62 FLCM62 LGSM64 Em Coll Cam BA56 MA60 Man Univ PGCE57 Lon Univ DipEd65 Keele Univ DASE70 Sheff Univ MA73 PhD84 Nottm Univ ME85 MTh88. Qu Coll Birm 72. **d** 75 **p** 76. NSM Lich Ch Ch *Lich* 75-78; NSM Burton St Modwen 79-86; NSM The Ridwares and Kings Bromley from 86. *1 Preedy's Close, Abbots Bromley, Rugeley, Staffs WS15 3EE*   Burton-on-Trent (0283) 840513

CONWAY, Canon Owen Arnott. b 35. Dur Univ BA58. St Steph Ho Ox 58. **d** 60 **p** 61. C Manston *Ripon* 60-64; V Osmondthorpe St Phil 64-70; Warden Dioc Ho Barrowby 70-73; V St Bart Armley w St Mary New Wortley 73-81; V Headingley 81-91; RD Headingley 87-91; Hon Can Ripon Cathl 87-91; Can Res Ches Cathl *Ches* from 91. *9 Abbey Street, Chester CH1 2JF*   Chester (0244) 316144

CONWAY, Reginald Henry. b 02. St Aid Birkenhead 29. **d** 33 **p** 34. R Conington *Ely* 64-69; rtd 69. *50 Knights Croft, New Ash Green, Dartford DA3 8HT*   Dartford (0322) 873783

CONWAY, Stephen David. b 57. Keble Coll Ox BA80 MA84 CertEd81 Selw Coll Cam BA85. Westcott Ho Cam 83. **d** 86 **p** 87. C Heworth St Mary *Dur* 86-89; C Bishopwearmouth St Mich w St Hilda 89-90; Hon C Dur St Marg from 90; Dir of Ords from 90. *36 Archery Rise, Durham DH1 4LA*   091-386 0968

CONWAY, Thomas Robertson. b 36. DipTh. **d** 86 **p** 87. C Ban Abbey *D & D* 86-89; I Dungiven w Bovevagh *D & R* from 89. *14 Main Street, Dungiven, Londonderry BT47 4LB*   Dungiven (05047) 41226

CONWAY-LEE, Stanley. b 17. Linc Th Coll 68. **d** 70 **p** 71. C Dedham *Chelmsf* 70-72; C Lt Ilford St Mich 72-74; V Tollesbury 74-75; V Tollesbury w Salcot Virley 75-79; V Bocking St Pet 79-85; rtd 85; Perm to Offic *Chelmsf* from 85. *51 Bedells Avenue, Black Notley, Braintree, Essex CM7 8LZ*   Braintree (0376) 550117

COOGAN, Ven Robert Arthur William. b 29. Univ of Tasmania BA51 St Jo Coll Dur DipTh53. **d** 53 **p** 54. C Plaistow St Andr *Chelmsf* 53-56; Australia 56-62; V N Woolwich *Chelmsf* 62-73; P-in-c W Silvertown St Barn 62-73; V Hampstead St Steph *Lon* 73-77; P-in-c N St Pancras All Hallows 74-77; RD S Camden (Holborn & St Pancras) 75-81; P-in-c Old St Pancras w Bedf New Town St Matt 76-80; V Hampstead St Steph w All Hallows 77-85; P-in-c Kentish Town St Martin w St Andr 78-81; AD N Camden (Hampstead) 78-83; Preb St Paul's Cathl 82-85; Adn Hampstead from 85. *27 Thurlow Road, London NW3 5PP*   071-435 5890

COOK, Alan. b 27. St Deiniol's Hawarden 79. **d** 80 **p** 81. Hon C Gatley *Ches* 80-83; Chapl Man R Eye Hosp 83-86; Chapl Asst Man R Infirmary 80-83 and 86-88; V Congleton St Jas *Ches* from 89. *St James's Vicarage, 116 Holmes Chapel Road, Congleton, Cheshire CW12 4NX*   Congleton (0260) 273722

COOK, Brian Edwin. b 36. Sarum & Wells Th Coll 78. **d** 80 **p** 81. C E Wickham *S'wark* 80-83; C Petersfield w Sheet *Portsm* 83-86; R Liss from 86; RD Petersfield from 91. *The Rectory, Station Road, Liss, Hants GU33 7AQ*   Liss (0730) 3175

COOK, Brian Robert. b 43. Chich Th Coll 83. **d** 85 **p** 86. C Whyke w Rumboldswhyke and Portfield *Chich* 85-87; C Worth 87-90; TV from 90. *3 Mayflower Close, Maidenblower, Crawley, W Sussex RH10 4WH*   Crawley (0293) 884309

COOK, Charles Peter. b 32. St Jo Coll Dur BA54 DipTh58. **d** 58 **p** 59. C Kingston upon Hull H Trin *York* 58-64; V High Elswick St Paul *Newc* 64-74; V Cheadle Hulme St Andr *Ches* from 74. *St Andrew's Priory, Cheadle Road, Cheadle Hulme, Cheshire SK8 5EU*   061-485 1112 or 485 2648

COOK, Christopher. b 44. Qu Coll Birm 68. **d** 69 **p** 70. C Gt Ilford St Mary *Chelmsf* 69-72; C Corringham 72-77; R E Donyland 77-84; R Pentlow, Foxearth, Liston and Borley 84-88; Chapl RAD Essex Area 88-89; rtd 89; Perm to Offic *Chelmsf* from 89. *Oak Mill, Field View Lane, Little Totham, Maldon, Essex CM9 8ND*

COOK, David. b 46. Hertf Coll Ox BA MA72. Wycliffe Hall Ox 69. **d** 73 **p** 74. C Hartlepool All SS Stranton *Dur* 74-75; Lect Qu Coll Birm 75-81; Chapl Cranbrook Sch Kent from 81. *33 Oatfield Drive, Cranbrook, Kent TN17 3LA*   Cranbrook (0580) 713310

COOK, David Arthur. b 50. St Jo Coll Dur BA74. St Steph Ho Ox 86. **d** 88 **p** 89. C S Bank *York* from 88. *13 Poplar Grove, South Bank, Middlesbrough, Cleveland TS6 6SY*   Middlesbrough (0642) 467928

COOK, David Charles Murray. b 41. MA. Wycliffe Hall Ox 65. **d** 67 **p** 68. C Chatham St Phil and St Jas *Roch*

67-71; S Africa 71-89; TR Newbury *Ox* from 89. *The Rectory, 64 North Croft Lane, Newbury, Berks RG13 1BN*   Newbury (0635) 40326

COOK, Canon David Reginald Edmund. b 25. Wells Th Coll 65. **d** 67 **p** 68. C Gt Ilford St Clem *Chelmsf* 67-71; P-in-c Langdon Hills 71-75; R 75-79; RD Basildon 76-79; P-in-c W Bergholt 79-80; R 80-90; Hon Can Chelmsf Cathl 86-90; rtd 90. *177 Straight Road, Lexden, Colchester CO3 5DG*   Colchester (0206) 573231

COOK, David Smith. b 47. Hull Univ BTh88. Lich Th Coll 68. **d** 71 **p** 72. C Tudhoe Grange *Dur* 71-75; C Bishopwearmouth St Mary V w St Pet CD 75-77; V Copley *Wakef* 77-80; V Birstall 80-83; V Holme-on-Spalding Moor *York* from 83. *The Vicarage, Holme-on-Spalding Moor, York YO4 4AG*   Market Weighton (0430) 860248

COOK, Canon Derek Edward. b 23. AKC51. **d** 52 **p** 53. V Luton St Paul *St Alb* 64-78; P-in-c Stanbridge w Tilsworth 78-80; V Totternhoe, Stanbridge and Tilsworth 80-88; Hon Can St Alb 85-88; rtd 88. *8 Ridgeway, Eynesbury, St Neots, Huntingdon, Cambs PE19 2QY*   Huntingdon (0480) 75141

COOK, Canon Edward Rouse. b 28. Linc Coll Ox BA51 MA55. Linc Th Coll 51. **d** 53 **p** 54. C Louth H Trin *Linc* 53-56; C Crosby 56-57; Lect of Boston 58-60; R Lt Coates 60-67; V Saxilby 67-90; R Broxholme 69-90; P-in-c Burton by Linc from 78; Can and Preb Linc Cathl from 79; Chmn Dioc Readers from 86; RD Corringham from 87; R Saxilby w Ingleby and Broxholme from 90. *The Vicarage, Saxilby, Lincoln LN1 2PT*   Lincoln (0522) 702427

COOK, Mrs Elspeth Jean. b 34. Edin Univ BSc56 PhD66. S Dios Minl Tr Scheme 85. **d** 88. C Yateley *Win* from 88. *120 Manor Park Drive, Yateley, Camberley, Surrey GU17 7JB*   Yateley (0252) 874323

COOK, George Basil Frederick. b 21. K Coll Lon BA42 St Cath Soc Ox BA48 MA52. Ripon Hall Ox 46. **d** 49 **p** 50. V Mitcham St Barn *S'wark* 55-91; rtd 91; Perm to Offic *S'wark* from 91. *6 Cranmer Road, Mitcham, Surrey CR4 4LD*   081-648 1980

COOK, Ian Bell. b 38. NW Ord Course 70. **d** 73 **p** 74. C Oldham St Paul *Man* 73-75; Ind Chapl 76-79; P-in-c Newton Heath St Wilfrid and St Anne 76-79; V Middleton Junction from 79. *The Vicarage, Greenhill Road, Middleton Junction, Manchester M24 2BD*   061-643 5064

COOK, Ian Brian. b 38. MBIM73 Aston Univ MSc72 Birm Univ MA76. Kelham Th Coll 58. **d** 63 **p** 64. C Langley Marish *Ox* 63-66; C Stokenchurch and Cadmore End 66-68; V Lane End 68-72; P-in-c Ibstone w Fingest 68-72; Tutor W Bromwich Coll of Comm & Tech 72-74; Sen Tutor 74-80; Perm to Offic *Lich* 75-77; NSM W Bromwich St Pet 77-80; P-in-c Wednesbury St Jo 80; P-in-c Wednesbury St Jas and St Jo 80; R from 80; Dir St Jas Tr Inst from 81; RD Wednesbury from 88. *The Rectory, 1 Hollies Drive, Wednesbury, W Midlands WS10 9EQ*   021-505 1188 or 505 1568

COOK, James Christopher Donald. b 49. Ch Ch Ox BA70 MA74. St Steph Ho Ox 79. **d** 80 **p** 81. C Witney *Ox* 80-83; CF from 83. *c/o MOD (Army), Bagshot Park, Bagshot, Surrey GU19 5PL*   Bagshot (0276) 71717

COOK, Mrs Joan Lindsay. b 46. SRN70. St Jo Coll Dur 86. **d** 88. Par Dn Hartlepool St Hilda *Dur* from 88. *8 Gladstone Street, Hartlepool, Cleveland TS24 0PE*   Hartlepool (0429) 265371

COOK, John. b 32. Linc Th Coll 87. **d** 89 **p** 90. C Bourne *Linc* from 89. *5 Hawthorne Road, Bourne, Lincs PE10 9SN*   Bourne (0778) 393239

COOK, John Edward. b 35. AKC61. **d** 62 **p** 63. C York Town *Guildf* 62-67; Singapore 67-77; P-in-c Beoley *Worc* 78-83; V 83-89; V Bromsgrove All SS from 89. *All Saints' Vicarage, 20 Burcot Lane, Bromsgrove, Worcs B60 1AE*   Bromsgrove (0527) 579849

COOK, John Henry. b 11. Mert Coll Ox BA34 BSc35 MA39 MSc81. Clifton Th Coll 36. **d** 38 **p** 39. R Witney *Ox* 68-78; rtd 79; Hon C Witney *Ox* from 79. *9 Church View Road, Witney, Oxon OX8 7HT*   Witney (0993) 704609

COOK, John Michael. b 48. Coll of Resurr Mirfield 72. **d** 74 **p** 75. C Weymouth H Trin *Sarum* 74-76; C Felixstowe St Jo *St E* 76-79; P-in-c Gt and Lt Whelnetham 79-84; P-in-c Cockfield 84-85; P-in-c Bradfield St George w Bradfield St Clare etc 84-85; R Cockfield w Bradfield St Clare, Felsham etc 85-87; V Workington St Jo *Carl* from 87. *St John's Vicarage, 59 Thorncroft Gardens, Workington, Cumbria CA14 4DP*   Workington (0900) 602383

COOK, John Richard Millward. b 61. St Jo Coll Dur BA. Wycliffe Hall Ox 83. **d** 85 **p** 86. C Brampton St Thos

Derby 85-89; C Farnborough *Guildf* from 89. *7 Syon Place, Farnborough, Hants GU14 7EH* Farnborough (0252) 513225

COOK, Kenneth George Thomas. b 36. ACA59 AHA69 FCA70 Man Univ DSA65. Coll of Resurr Mirfield 86. **d** 88 **p** 89. C Stocking Farm *Leic* 88-91; Chapl Leics Hospice from 91. *c/o Leicestershire Hospice, Groby Road, Leicester LE3 9QE* Leicester (0533) 313771

COOK, Canon Kenneth Hugh. b 30. ALAM. AKC55. **d** 56 **p** 57. C Netherfield *S'well* 56-59; C Newark w Coddington 59-61; V Basford St Aid 61-67; V Gargrave *Bradf* 67-77; Dir of Ords 77-89; Can Res Bradf Cathl from 77. *3 Cathedral Close, Bradford BD1 4EG* Bradford (0274) 727720

COOK, Kenneth Robert. b 42. Huddersfield Poly BA86. Chich Th Coll 66. **d** 68 **p** 69. C Upton *Ox* 68-72; C Duston *Pet* 72-76; V Halifax St Hilda *Wakef* 76-79; Chapl Huddersfield Poly 79-90; V Linc St Mary-le-Wigford w St Benedict etc *Linc* from 90. *220 Boultham Park Road, Lincoln LN6 7SU* Lincoln (0522) 540549

COOK, Marcus John Wyeth. b 41. Chich Th Coll 67. **d** 70 **p** 71. C Friern Barnet St Jas *Lon* 70-73; Hon C St-Geo-in-the-East w St Paul from 73. *St George-in-the-East Church, Cannon Street Road, London E1 0BH*

COOK, Nicholas Leonard. b 59. Nottm Univ BCombStuds. Linc Th Coll 81. **d** 84 **p** 85. C Leic St Pet *Leic* 84-85; C Knighton St Mich 85-86; Chapl Asst Towers Hosp Humberstone 86-90; Chapl from 90; Chapl Leics Mental Health Service Unit from 89; CF (TA) from 88. *Towers Hospital, Gipsy Lane, Humberstone, Leicester LE5 0TD* Leicester (0533) 460460

COOK, Peter John Arthur. b 42. Reading Univ BA64 Brandeis Univ (USA) MA65 QUB PhD81. Tyndale Hall Bris 68. **d** 71 **p** 72. C Everton St Chrys *Liv* 71-74; Chapl Stranmillis Coll of Educn Belf 74-87; Hon C Belf All SS *Conn* 81-87; USA from 87. *4419 Lake Lawrence, Baton Rouge, Louisiana 70816, USA*

COOK, Richard John Noel. b 49. Univ Coll Ox BA70 MA74 PGCE72. Wycliffe Hall Ox MA77. **d** 78 **p** 79. C Fulwood *Sheff* 78-80; C Bolton St Paul w Em *Man* 81-86; TV from 86. *Emmanuel Vicarage, Edward Street, Bolton BL3 5LQ* Bolton (0204) 393282 or 20837

COOK, Robert Bond. b 28. Dur Univ BSc54. Ripon Hall Ox 54. **d** 56 **p** 57. C Benwell St Jas *Newc* 56-60; C Sugley 60-64; V Denton 64-75; V Haltwhistle 75-88; P-in-c Greenhead 84-88; V Haltwhistle and Greenhead from 88; RD Hexham from 88. *The Vicarage, Haltwhistle, Northd NE49 0AB* Haltwhistle (0434) 320215

COOK, Ronald Thomas. b 50. St Steph Ho Ox BA79 MA83. **d** 80 **p** 81. C Willesden St Andr *Lon* 80-83; USA 83-87; C Northolt Park St Barn *Lon* 87-90; Chapl HM Pris Blundeston from 90. *The Chaplain's Office, HM Prison Blundeston, Lowestoft, Suffolk NR32 5BG* Lowestoft (0502) 730591

COOK, Stephen William. b 57. BA DipHE. Lambeth STh87 Trin Coll Bris. **d** 85 **p** 86. C Heref St Pet w St Owen and St Jas *Heref* 85-89; TV Keynsham *B & W* from 89. *St Francis's Vicarage, Warwick Road, Keynsham, Bristol BS18 2PW* Bristol (0272) 863968

COOK, Trevor Vivian. b 43. Sarum Th Coll 67. **d** 69 **p** 70. C Lambeth St Phil *S'wark* 69-73; C St Buryan, St Levan and Sennen *Truro* 73-75; V The Ilketshalls *St E* 75-79; P-in-c Rumburgh w S Elmham 75-79; R Rumburgh w S Elmham w the Ilketshalls 79-84; TR Langport Area Chs *B & W* from 84. *The Rectory, Huish Episcopi, Langport, Somerset TA10 9QR* Langport (0458) 250480

COOK, Canon William George. b 14. St Jo Coll Dur LTh36 BA37. St Aid Birkenhead 33. **d** 37 **p** 38. V Allestree *Derby* 68-79; Hon Can Derby Cathl 78-79; rtd 79; Perm to Offic St E from 79; Pet from 85; P-in-c Starston *Nor* 85. *1 Orchard Grove, Diss, Norfolk 1P22 3LX* Diss (0379) 642058

COOKE, Alan. b 50. Nottm Univ BTh74 Lanc Univ PGCE75. Kelham Th Coll 69. **d** 75 **p** 76. C Tyldesley w Shakerley *Man* 75-78; C Salford Ordsall St Clem 78; C Langley All SS and Martyrs 80-82; TV Langley and Parkfield 82-83; P-in-c Chadderton St Mark 83-85; V from 85. *St Mark's Vicarage, Milne Street, Chadderton, Oldham OL9 0HR* 061-624 2005

COOKE, Canon Alfred Gordon. b 05. AKC28. Ripon Hall Ox 29. **d** 29 **p** 30. R St Columb Major *Truro* 49-72; Hon Can Truro Cathl from 57; R St Columb Major w St Wenn 72-84; rtd 84. *Lawhitton, 13 Marlborough Crescent, Falmouth, Cornwall TR11 2RJ* Falmouth (0326) 312706

COOKE, Alfred Hunt. b 08. Lon Univ MRCS35 LRCP35. **d** 68 **p** 69. Hon C Hendon St Mary *Lon* from 68. *3 Hendon Lodge, Sunningfields Road, London NW4* 081-203 4603

COOKE, Angela Elizabeth. b 42. SRN65 SCM67 MTD72. St Jo Coll Nottm 85. **d** 87. Par Dn Walton H Trin *Ox* from 87. *107 Orwell Drive, Aylesbury, Bucks HP21 9HE* Aylesbury (0296) 26678

COOKE, Arthur Lewis. b 16. Keble Coll Ox BA38 MA43 Univ of Wales BD48. St Mich Coll Llan 39. **d** 39 **p** 41. R Hope *St As* 59-82; rtd 82. *144 Gresford Road, Llay, Wrexham, Clwyd LL12 0NW* Gresford (0978) 853644

COOKE, Mrs Beatrice Lilian. b 21. Gilmore Ho 67 Linc Th Coll. **dss** 77 **d** 87. Northaw St Alb 77-87; Hon Par Dn from 87. *154 Brookside Crescent, Cuffley, Potters Bar, Herts EN6 4QL* Cuffley (0707) 872169

COOKE, Christopher Stephen. b 54. Lon Univ BA76 MA77 Ox Univ BA81 MA88. Ripon Coll Cuddesdon 79. **d** 82 **p** 83. C Cen Telford *Lich* 82-86; R Uffington, Upton Magna and Withington from 86. *The Rectory, Upton Magna, Shrewsbury SY4 4TZ* Upton Magna (074377) 283

COOKE, David John. b 31. Linc Th Coll 60. **d** 62 **p** 63. C Brighton Gd Shep Preston *Chich* 62-65; C Clayton w Keymer 65-70; R Stone w Hartwell w Bishopstone *Ox* 70-77; R Stone w Dinton and Hartwell from 77. *The Rectory, Stone, Aylesbury, Bucks HP17 8RZ* Aylesbury (0296) 748215

COOKE, Edward Alan. b 18. St D Coll Lamp BA41. **d** 46 **p** 47. R Ightfield w Calverhall *Lich* 73-83; P-in-c Ash 78-83; rtd 83. *Guadalest, Hollins Lane, Tilstock, Whitchurch, Shropshire* Whixall (094872) 421

COOKE, Frederic Ronald. b 35. Selw Coll Cam BA58 MA61. Ridley Hall Cam 59. **d** 61 **p** 62. C Flixton St Mich *Man* 61-64; C-in-c Flixton St Jo CD 64-67; V Flixton St Jo 68-74; R Ashton St Mich 74-77; Jerusalem 77-80; V Walmsley *Man* 80-85; AD Walmsley 81-85; Malaysia 85-90; Prin Ho of Epiphany Th Coll Borneo 85-90; P-in-c Accrington *Blackb* 90-91; TR from 91. *St Paul's Vicarage, Barnfield Street, Accrington, Lancs BB5 2AQ* Accrington (0254) 399322

COOKE, Geoffrey. b 38. Sarum Th Coll 61. **d** 64 **p** 65. C Eastover *B & W* 64-67; Chapl RAF 67-71; C Bridgwater St Jo *B & W* 71-76; R N Newton w St Michaelchurch and Thurloxton 76-78; R N Newton w St Michaelchurch, Thurloxton etc 78-83; TV Yeovil 83-88; V Yeovil H Trin 88-89; R Staple Fitzpaine, Orchard Portman, Thurlbear etc from 89. *The Rectory, Thurlbear, Taunton, Somerset TA3 5BW* Taunton (0823) 443581

COOKE, Ms Gillian Freda. b 39. Lon Univ DipTh70 BD73 Leeds Univ MA87. Linc Th Coll 74. **dss** 78 **d** 87. Middx Poly *Lon* 78-80; Cricklewood St Pet CD 78-80; Leeds Poly *Ripon* 80-87; N Humberside Ind Chapl *York* 87-90; Sub-Chapl HM Pris Hull from 90. *7 Northfield, Swanland, North Ferriby, N Humberside HU14 3RG* Hull (0482) 633462

COOKE, Gordon Ewart. b 28. Lon Univ BSc57 MSc64. Cuddesdon Coll 58 Lich Th Coll 59. **d** 60 **p** 61. C Kidderminster St Mary *Worc* 60-62; C Hagley 62-66; R Brinklow *Cov* 66-75; R Areley Kings *Worc* from 75; RD Stourport from 88. *The Rectory, Areley Kings, Stourport-on-Severn, Worcs DY13 0TH* Stourport (02993) 2868

COOKE, Harry Burford. b 18. **d** 64 **p** 65. C Slad *Glouc* 64-68; Chapl Marling Sch Stroud 68-78; Hon C Bisley, Oakridge, Miserden and Edgeworth *Glouc* 83-88; Perm to Offic from 88. *Norman Cottage, Miserden, Stroud, Glos GL6 7JA* Miserden (028582) 672

COOKE, Hereward Roger Gresham. b 39. ACA64 K Coll Lon BD69 AKC70. **d** 70 **p** 71. C Rugby St Andr *Cov* 70-76; P-in-c St Kath Cree *Lon* 76-82; P-in-c St Botolph without Aldersgate 82-89; AD The City 82-85; P-in-c St Edm the King and St Mary Woolnoth etc 82-89; TV Nor St Pet Parmentergate w St Jo *Nor* from 89; Ind Miss from 89. *St John's Vicarage, 31 Bracondale, Norwich NR1 2AT* Norwich (0603) 624827

COOKE, Ian Kirk Hamel. b 36. Birm Univ BA39. Chich Th Coll 39. **d** 41 **p** 42. V Addlestone *Guildf* 63-75; R Tittleshall w Godwick and Wellingham *Nor* 75-76; R Tittleshall w Godwick, Wellingham and Wesenham 76-82; rtd 82; Perm to Offic *Nor* from 82. *Crugmeer, Croft Yard, Wells-next-the-Sea, Norfolk NR23 1JS* Fakenham (0328) 710358

COOKE, James Percy. b 13. St D Coll Lamp BA51. **d** 52 **p** 54. R Derwen and Llanelidan *St As* 57-83; rtd 83. *28 Maes Cantaba, Ruthin, Clwyd* Ruthin (08242) 4905

COOKE, John. b 21. Lon Univ BD60 Man Univ MA65. Maynooth JCL47 Liv RC Sem Upholland. **d** 44 **p** 45. Hon C Eccleston St Thos *Liv* 68-71; V 76-81; C Rainhill 71-76; R Caston w Griston, Mert and Thompson *Nor* 81-83; P-in-c Stow Bedon w Breckles 82-83; R Caston w Griston, Merton, Thompson etc 83-90; rtd 90.

51 Sharman Avenue, Watton, Thetford, Norfolk IP25 6EG Watton (0953) 882730

COOKE, John Frederick. b 51. Southn Univ. Sarum & Wells Th Coll 72. **d** 75 **p** 76. C Sheff Parson Cross St Cecilia *Sheff* 75-78; C Goldthorpe w Hickleton 78-82; V Balby from 82; Chapl Doncaster HA from 82. *St John's Vicarage, 6 Greenfield Lane, Doncaster, S Yorkshire DN4 0PT* Doncaster (0302) 853278

COOKE, John Stephen. b 35. K Coll Lon BD58 AKC58. **d** 59 **p** 60. C W Bromwich St Fran *Lich* 59-62; C Chalfont St Peter *Ox* 62-66; V Cross Heath *Lich* 66-72; R Haughton 72-86; P-in-c Ellenhall w Ranton 72-80; V Eccleshall from 86; Chapl HM Pris Drake Hall from 86. *The Vicarage, Church Street, Eccleshall, Stafford ST21 6BY* Eccleshall (0785) 850351

COOKE, Kenneth John. b 29. Linc Coll Ox BA53 MA57. Ely Th Coll 53. **d** 55 **p** 56. C Nuneaton St Mary *Cov* 55-58; C Cov St Thos 58-61; V Willenhall 61-66; V Meriden 66-76; V Cov St Geo 76-84; V Leamington Spa and Old Milverton from 84. *Holy Trinity Vicarage, Clive House, Kenilworth Road, Leamington Spa CV32 5TL* Leamington Spa (0926) 424016

COOKE, Dr Michael David. b 46. New Coll Ox BA68 MA71 DPhil71. Ox NSM Course 75. **d** 78 **p** 79. NSM Newport Pagnell *Ox* 78-85; NSM Newport Pagnell w Lathbury and Moulsoe 85-88; NSM Beckenham Ch Ch *Roch* from 90. *70 Kingswood Avenue, Bromley BR2 0NP* 081-460 8748

COOKE, Michael John. Ab Dioc Tr Course. **d** 80 **p** 81. Perm to Offic *Ab* 80-81; Miss to Seamen Tilbury 81-91; Hon C Immingham *Linc* 81-91; Ind Chapl Teesside *Dur* from 91. *41 Arncliffe Gardens, Hartlepool, Cleveland TS26 9JG* Hartlepool (0429) 277591

COOKE, Miss Priscilla Garland Hamel. b 24. Gilmore Ho 69. **dss** 80 **d** 87. Bromsgrove St Jo *Worc* 80-82; Lee Abbey 82-85; Torquay St Matthias, St Mark and H Trin *Ex* 86-87; Hon Par Dn from 87. *Roydon Flat, Asheldon Road, Torquay, Devon TQ1 2QN* Torquay (0803) 297366

COOKE, Raymond. b 34. Liv Univ BSc56. Wells Th Coll 58. **d** 60 **p** 61. C Newton Heath All SS *Man* 60-64; C-in-c Failsworth H Family CD 64-75; R Failsworth H Family 75-83; P-in-c Man Gd Shep 83-88; V Westleigh St Pet from 88. *St Peter's Vicarage, 6 Malham Close, Leigh, Lancs WN7 4SD* Leigh (0942) 673626

COOKE, Richard James. b 60. Pemb Coll Ox BA82 MA88. Trin Coll Bris 85. **d** 88 **p** 89. C Rugby St Matt *Cov* from 88. *14 York Street, Rugby, Warks CV21 2BL* Rugby (0788) 68359

COOKE, Samuel. b 17. Tyndale Hall Bris. **d** 49 **p** 50. V Scarborough H Trin *York* 62-77; rtd 82. *303 2888 273rd Street, Lions Grove Estate, Aldergrove, British Columbia, Canada, V0X 1A0*

COOKMAN, Alan George. b 26. Keble Coll Ox BA50 MA56. St Steph Ho Ox 50. **d** 52 **p** 53. C Plymouth St Pet *Ex* 52-60; C Richmond St Jo *S'wark* 60-61; R Lower Broughton Ascension *Man* 61-65; V Lavender Hill Ascension *S'wark* 65-72; R Lympstone *Ex* 72-81; V Laira 81-88; Chapl Convent of Sisters of Charity Knowle from 88. *The Chaplaincy, St Agnes Avenue, Knowle, Bristol BS4 2HH* Bristol (0272) 777738

COOKSON, Miss Diane Veronica. b 51. Nor Ord Course 81. **dss** 84 **d** 87. Gt Sutton *Ches* 84-86; Neston 86-87; Par Dn from 87. *Alphega House, 26 Stratford Road, Little Neston, South Wirral L64 0SH* 051-336 3059

COOKSON, Graham Leslie. b 37. Sarum Th Coll 64. **d** 67 **p** 68. C Upton Ascension *Ches* 67-69; C Timperley 69-75; V Godley cum Newton Green 75-83; R Tarporley from 83. *The Rectory, Tarporley, Cheshire CW6 0AG* Tarporley (0829) 732491

COOLING, Derrick William. b 35. AKC58 Lon Univ BD69 DipEd71 Univ of Wales (Cardiff) MEd81. **d** 59 **p** 60. C Haydock St Jas *Liv* 59-61; C Hove St Barn *Chich* 61-63; V Llangattock-J-Usk w Llanfair Kilgedain etc *Mon* 63-68; R Blaina 68-70; Perm to Offic *Sarum* 70-74; Chapl Windsor Girls' Sch Hamm 74-75; Asst Master Croesyceiliog Sch Cwmbran 75-81; Perm to Offic *Mon* 79-81; Chapl Epsom Coll Surrey 81-84; V Bettws *Mon* from 84. *St David's Rectory, Bettws Hill, Bettws, Newport, Gwent NP9 6AD* Newport (0633) 855193

COOLING (nee YOUNG), Mrs Margaret Dorothy. b 37. K Coll Lon BA59 AKC Univ Coll Lon BD69 PGCE70 Univ of Wales MEd82. St Deiniol's Hawarden. **d** 90. NSM Bettws *Mon* from 90. *St David's Rectory, Bettws Hill, Bettws, Newport, Gwent NP9 6AD* Newport (0633) 855193

COOMBE, James Anthony. b 31. Em Coll Cam BA53 MA57 Lon Univ BD60. Tyndale Hall Bris 57. **d** 60 **p** 61. C Chadderton Ch Ch *Man* 60-63; C Worthing

St Geo *Chich* 63-65; V Wandsworth St Mich *S'wark* 65-74; P-in-c Warboys *Ely* 74-76; R 76-87; RD St Ives 83-87; P-in-c Broughton 84-87; P-in-c Wistow 84-87; V Alconbury w Alconbury Weston from 87; R Buckworth from 87. *The Vicarage, Alconbury, Huntingdon, Cambs PE17 5DX* Huntingdon (0480) 890284

COOMBE, John Morrell (Brother Martin). b 25. Chich Th Coll 56. **d** 57 **p** 58. SSF from 49; Lic to Offic *Sarum* 57-59; C Hillfield and Hermitage 59-66; Asst Chapl Ellesmere Coll Shropshire 66-69; Chapl Ranby Ho Sch Retford 69-71; V Cam St Benedict *Ely* 71-85; Jerusalem 85-86; Prov Sec SSF from 86; Lic to Offic *Linc* from 86. *St Francis House, Normanby Road, Scunthorpe, S Humberside DN15 6AR* Scunthorpe (0724) 853899

COOMBE, Kenneth Harry Southcott. b 24. Clifton Th Coll 61. **d** 63 **p** 64. C Cullompton *Ex* 63-66; C-in-c Elburton CD 66-73; V Elburton from 73. *St Matthew's Vicarage, Shesford Road, Plymouth PL9 8DQ* Plymouth (0752) 402771

COOMBE, Michael Thomas. b 31. Lon Univ BA64. Ox NSM Course 73. **d** 75 **p** 76. Chapl St Piran's Sch Maidenhead 75-81; Hon C Furze Platt *Ox* 76-81; C 86-88; Asst Chapl Oslo St Edm *Eur* 81-84; Chapl Belgrade w Zagreb 84-86; Chapl Marseille 86-89. *Address temp unknown*

COOMBER, Ian Gladstone. b 47. Ch Ch Coll Cant CertEd68 Southn Univ BTh79. Sarum & Wells Th Coll 73. **d** 76 **p** 77. C Weeke *Win* 76-79; TV Saffron Walden w Wendens Ambo and Littlebury *Chelmsf* 79-82; V Weston *Win* 82-90; R Bedhampton *Portsm* from 90. *The Rectory, Bidbury Lane, Bedhampton, Havant, Hants PO9 3JG* Havant (0705) 483013

COOMBES, Derek Fennessey. b 42. Edin Th Coll 61. **d** 65 **p** 66. Prec St Andr Cathl Inverness *Mor* 65-68; Bp's Chapl 65-68; Perm to Offic *Nor* 76-79; V Happisburgh w Walcot 79-83; C Tewkesbury Abbey 84-85; Ind Chapl *S'wark* 85-89; R Asterby Gp *Linc* from 89. *The Rectory, Butt Lane, Goulceby, Louth, Lincs LN11 9UP* Stenigot (050784) 345

COOMBES, Edward David. b 39. Dur Univ BA61. Qu Coll Birm DipTh63. **d** 63 **p** 64. C Claines St Jo *Worc* 63-65; C Halesowen 65-69; V Beoley 69-77; V Edgbaston St Bart *Birm* from 77; Chapl Birm Univ from 77. *Edgbaston Vicarage, 1B Arthur Road, Birmingham B15 2UW* 021-454 0070

COOMBES, Frederick Brian John. b 34. FRTPI63 Nottm Univ BA56 Univ Coll Lon DipTP63 Plymouth Poly MPhil73. SW Minl Tr Course 85. **d** 88 **p** 89. NSM Bodmin w Lanhydrock and Lanivet *Truro* from 88. *5 Valley View, Bodmin, Cornwall PL31 1BE* Bodmin (0208) 3036

COOMBS, John Allen. b 46. Portsm Poly BSc70. Oak Hill Th Coll DipHE88 Sarum & Wells Th Coll 89. **d** 89 **p** 90. C Leverington *Ely* from 89; C Wisbech St Mary from 89. *The Vicarage, Church Road, Wisbech St Mary, Wisbech, Cambs PE13 4RN* Wisbech St Mary (094581) 814

COOMBS, John Kendall. b 47. Culham Coll Ox BEd73. Sarum & Wells Th Coll 75. **d** 77 **p** 78. C Fareham H Trin *Portsm* 77-80; C Petersfield w Sheet 80-83; TV Beaminster Area *Sarum* 83-87; TR Preston w Sutton Poyntz and Osmington w Poxwell from 87. *The Rectory, Sutton Road, Preston, Weymouth, Dorset DT3 6BX* Preston (0305) 833142

COOMBS, Ven Peter Bertram. b 28. Bris Univ BA58 MA61. Clifton Th Coll 55. **d** 60 **p** 61. C Beckenham Ch Ch *Roch* 60-63; R Nottm St Nic *S'well* 63-68; V New Malden and Coombe *S'wark* 68-75; RD Kingston 71-75; Adn Wandsworth 75-88; Adn Reigate from 88. *89 Nutfield Road, Redhill RH1 3HD* Redhill (0737) 642375

COOMBS, Richard John. b 29. MBE87. K Coll Lon BD53 AKC53. **d** 54 **p** 55. C Methley *Ripon* 54-57; C Bourne *Guildf* 57-60; USA 60-61; V Burghill *Heref* 61-70; Chapl St Mary's Hosp Burghill 61-70; CF (TA) 62-70; CF 70-87; CF (R of O) from 87. *c/o MOD (Army), Bagshot Park, Bagshot, Surrey GU19 5PL* Bagshot (0276) 71717

COOMBS, Richard Murray. b 63. St Chad's Coll Dur BSc85 Rob Coll Cam BA89. Ridley Hall Cam 87. **d** 90. C Enfield Ch Ch Trent Park *Lon* from 90. *c/o Christ Church Vicarage, Chalk Lane, Barnet, Herts EN4 9NQ* 081-441 1230

COOMBS, Stephen John. b 54. Open Univ BA86. Trin Coll Bris 85. **d** 87 **p** 88. C Norton Canes *Lich* 87-90; Chapl Trowbridge Coll *Sarum* from 90; C Studley from 90. *18 Balmoral Road, Trowbridge, Wilts BA14 0JS* Trowbridge (0225) 752166

COOMBS, Canon Walter James Martin. b 33. Keble Coll Ox BA57 MA61. Cuddesdon Coll 59. **d** 61 **p** 62. C Kennington St Jo *S'wark* 61-64; Chapl Em Coll Cam 64-68; Bp's Dom Chapl *S'wark* 68-70; V E Dulwich St Jo 70-77; V Pershore w Pinvin, Wick and Birlingham *Worc* from 77; Hon Can Worc Cathl from 84; RD Pershore 85-91. *The Vicarage, Church Street, Pershore, Worcs WR10 1DT* Pershore (0386) 552071

COON, Clayton Hollis. b 37. California Univ BA60. Episc Th Sch Cam Mass BD66. **d** 66 **p** 67. USA 66-71; C Hove St Jo *Chich* 71-74; C Brighton St Paul 74-79; V Linthwaite *Wakef* from 79. *The Vicarage, Church Lane, Linthwaite, Huddersfield HD7 5TA* Huddersfield (0484) 842591

COONEY, Michael Patrick. b 55. City of Lon Poly BA77. Ripon Coll Cuddesdon 77. **d** 80 **p** 81. C Cov E *Cov* 80-83; C Old Brumby *Linc* 83-85; V Linc St Jo 85-90; V Frodingham from 90. *The Vicarage, Vicarage Gardens, Scunthorpe, S Humberside DN15 7AZ* Scunthorpe (0724) 842726

COONEY, William Barry. b 47. K Coll Lon 69. **d** 70 **p** 71. C W Bromwich All SS *Lich* 70-73; C Wolv St Pet 73-75; C Rugeley 75-78; V Sneyd Green 78-87; R Sandiacre *Derby* from 87. *St Giles's Rectory, Church Drive, Sandiacre, Nottingham NG10 5EE* Sandiacre (0602) 397163

COOPER, Andrew John. b 62. W Sussex Inst of HE BA87. St Steph Ho Ox 88. **d** 91. C Rawmarsh w Parkgate *Sheff* from 91. *3 Thorogate, Rawmarsh, Rotherham, S Yorkshire S62 7HU* Rotherham (0709) 719222

COOPER, Andrew John Gearing. b 48. Sir John Cass Coll Lon BSc70. Ripon Coll Cuddesdon 73. **d** 76 **p** 77. C Potternewton *Ripon* 76-79; Antigua 79-81; Anguilla 81-87; V W Bromwich St Andr w Ch Ch *Lich* from 88. *St Andrew's Vicarage, Oakwood Street, W Bromwich B70 9SN* 021-553 1871

COOPER, Mrs Annette Joy. b 53. Open Univ BA80 Lon Univ CQSW84 DipSocWork84. S'wark Ord Course DipRS88. **d** 88. NSM Pembury *Roch* 88; Chapl Tunbridge Wells Hosps, Kent and Sussex Hosp Tunbridge Wells and Leybourne Grange Hosp W Malling 88-91; Bassetlaw Distr Gen from 91. *51 Blyth Road, Worksop, Notts S81 0JJ* Worksop (0909) 500990

COOPER, Barrie Keith. b 56. Oak Hill Th Coll. **d** 85 **p** 86. C Partington and Carrington *Ches* 85-89; V Stockport St Mark from 89. *St Mark's Vicarage, 66 Berlin Road, Stockport, Cheshire SK3 9QD* 061-480 5896

COOPER, Barry Jack. Sarum Th Coll 59. **d** 61 **p** 62. C Norbury St Oswald *Cant* 61-64; C Crook *Dur* 64-68; R Cheriton *Cant* 68-84; V Cant All SS from 84. *All Saints' Vicarage, Military Road, Canterbury, Kent CT1 1PA* Canterbury (0227) 63505

COOPER, Canon Bede Robert. b 42. Ex Univ BA69. Coll of Resurr Mirfield 69. **d** 71 **p** 72. C Weymouth H Trin *Sarum* 71-74; P-in-c Broad Town 74-79; V Wootton Bassett 74-86; R Wilton w Netherhampton and Fugglestone from 86; Can and Preb Sarum Cathl from 88. *The Rectory, 27A West Street, Wilton, Salisbury SP2 0DL* Salisbury (0722) 743159

COOPER, Brian Hamilton. b 35. Keble Coll Ox BA58 MA67. Ripon Hall Ox 58. **d** 60 **p** 61. C Woolwich St Mary w H Trin *S'wark* 60-64; Canada 64-66; Vice-Prin Westcott Ho Cam 66-71; R Downham Market w Bexwell *Ely* 71-82; RD Fincham 80-82; V Chesterfield All SS *Derby* 82-91; V Herringthorpe *Sheff* from 91. *493 Herringthorpe Valley Road, Rotherham, S Yorkshire S60 4LB* Rotherham (0709) 363526

COOPER, Carl Norman. b 60. Univ of Wales (Lamp) BA82. Wycliffe Hall Ox 82. **d** 85 **p** 86. C Llanelly *St D* 85-87; P-in-c Llanarchaeron w Ciliau Aeron and Dihewyd etc 87-88; R from 88. *The Rectory, Ciliau Aeron, Lampeter, Dyfed SA48 7SG* Aeron (0570) 470901

COOPER, Cecil Clive. b 26. TD75. AKC52. **d** 53 **p** 54. C Chipping Campden *Glouc* 53-55; C Cheltenham St Mary 55-60; V Stroud 60-65; CF (TA) 65-79; V Woodmansterne *S'wark* from 65; RD Sutton 80-90. *The Rectory, Woodmansterne, Banstead, Surrey SM7 3NL* Burgh Heath (0737) 352849

COOPER, Canon Cecil William Marcus. b 32. TCD BA58 MA66. CITC 57. **d** 59 **p** 60. C Cork St Fin Barre and St Nic *C, C & R* 59-62; Bp's V, Lib and Registrar Kilkenny Cathl *C & O* 62-64; C Knockbreda *D & D* 65-67; Asst Ed Ch of Ireland Gazette 66-82; I Magheradroll 67-82; Dioc Registrar 81-90; Ed Ch of Ireland Gazette from 82; I Drumbeg from 82; Can Down Cathl from 86; Prec Down Cathl from 90. *Drumbeg, Dunmurry, Belfast BT17 9LE* Belfast (0232) 613265

COOPER, Clive Anthony Charles. b 38. Lon Univ BEd74. ALCD62. **d** 62 **p** 63. C Morden *S'wark* 62-65; Argentina 65-71; Hon C Cranleigh *Guildf* 78-79; Hon C Ewhurst 80-82; Hon Chapl Duke of Kent Sch from 83. *1 Ellery Close, Cranleigh, Surrey GU6 8DF* Cranleigh (0483) 276393

COOPER, Colin. b 55. Open Univ BA. St Jo Coll Nottm 83. **d** 86 **p** 87. C Cheadle Hulme St Andr *Ches* 86-89; C Tunbridge Wells St Jo *Roch* from 89. *112 Stephens Road, Tunbridge Wells, Kent TN4 9QA* Tunbridge Wells (0892) 21767

COOPER, Colin Charles. b 40. Oak Hill Th Coll 62. **d** 66 **p** 67. C Islington St Andr w St Thos and St Matthias *Lon* 66-69; Bermuda 69-76; V Gorleston St Andr *Nor* from 77. *The Vicarage, Duke Road, Gorleston, Great Yarmouth, Norfolk NR31 6LL* Great Yarmouth (0493) 663477

COOPER, David. b 44. AKC69. **d** 69 **p** 70. C Wortley de Leeds *Ripon* 69-73; CF 73-83; Lic to Offic *Ox* from 84. *Eton College, Windsor, Berks* Windsor (0753) 869991

COOPER, David Jonathan. b 44. Sarum & Wells Th Coll 70. **d** 74 **p** 75. C Charlton-in-Dover *Cant* 74-79; TV Wednesfield *Lich* 79 83; SSF 83-85; V Grimsby St Aug *Linc* 85-89; TV Trowbridge H Trin *Sarum* from 89. *The Team Vicarage, 1 Chepston Place, Trowbridge, Wilts BA14 9TA* Trowbridge (0225) 768671

COOPER, Dennis Bradley. b 29. New Coll Ox BA52 MA57. Cuddesdon Coll 52. **d** 54 **p** 55. C Bedf St Mary *St Alb* 54-56; C Hackney Wick St Mary of Eton w St Aug *Lon* 56-59; V York St Chad *York* 59-67; V Middlesb St Martin 67-74; V Norton from 74; RD Buckrose 85-90. *The Vicarage, 80 Langton Road, Norton, Malton, N Yorkshire YO17 9AE* Malton (0653) 692741

COOPER, Derek Edward. b 30. Bps' Coll Cheshunt 61. **d** 62 **p** 63. C Bishop's Stortford St Mich *St Alb* 62-66; V Westcliff St Cedd *Chelmsf* 66-89; R Camerton w Dunkerton, Foxcote and Shoscombe *B & W* from 89. *The Rectory, Camerton, Bath BA3 1PU* Timsbury (0761) 70249

COOPER, Donald Martin. b 12. K Coll Lon BD35 AKC35 MTh40 PhD44. **d** 35 **p** 36. Chapl Tooting Bec Hosp Lon 51-77; rtd 77; Perm to Offic *Guildf* from 82. *82 Nork Way, Banstead, Surrey SM7 1HW* Burgh Heath (0737) 353163

COOPER, Eric John. b 22. Cam Univ MA47. Chich Th Coll 52. **d** 53 **p** 54. V Bedminster Down *Bris* 66-72; rtd 87. *6 Deveron Grove, Keynsham, Bristol BS18 1UJ* Bristol (0272) 867339

COOPER, Frederick. b 30. Cranmer Hall Dur 68. **d** 70 **p** 71. C Preston All SS *Blackb* 70-72; C Preston St Jo 72-76; TV 76-78; V Higher Walton 78-91; P-in-c Preston All SS from 91. *All Saints' Vicarage, 94 Watling Street Road, Fulwood, Preston PR2 4BP* Preston (0772) 700672

COOPER, George Frank. b 19. St Aid Birkenhead 41. **d** 45 **p** 46. V Countesthorpe w Foston *Leic* 61-74; R Thurlaston 74-76; R Thurlaston and Peckleton w Kirkby Mallory 76-82; R Croft and Stoney Stanton 82-84; rtd 84; Perm to Offic Leic and Linc from 84. *Breezy Mere, 30 Signal Road, Grantham, Lincs NG31 9BL* Grantham (0476) 60689

COOPER, Graham Denbigh. b 48. Nottm Univ BTh75. St Jo Coll Nottm LTh75. **d** 75 **p** 76. C Collyhurst *Man* 75-78; C Stambermill *Worc* 78-80; V The Lye and Stambermill 80-90; P-in-c Frome H Trin *B & W* 90; V from 91. *Holy Trinity Vicarage, Orchard Street, Frome, Somerset BA11 3BX* Frome (0373) 62586

COOPER, Herbert William. b 29. Chich Th Coll 77. **d** 79 **p** 80. C Leigh Park *Portsm* 79-82; C-in-c Hayling St Pet CD 82-85; V Whitwell from 85; R St Lawrence from 85; P-in-c Niton from 89. *The Vicarage, Whitwell, Ventnor, Isle of Wight PO38 2PP* Isle of Wight (0983) 730745

COOPER, Ian Clive. b 48. FCA Ex Univ BA76. Linc Th Coll 76. **d** 78 **p** 79. C Sunbury *Lon* 78-81; P-in-c Astwood Bank *Worc* 81-85; P-in-c Feckenham w Bradley 82-85; TV Hemel Hempstead *St Alb* from 85. *St Mary's Vicarage, 51 Walnut Grove, Hemel Hempstead HP2 4AP* Hemel Hempstead (0442) 256708

COOPER, Jack. b 44. St Jo Coll Nottm 76. **d** 78 **p** 79. C Roundhay St Edm *Ripon* 78-80; C Ripley *Derby* 81-82; V Willington 82-88; V Findern 82-88; P-in-c Parwich w Alsop en le Dale from 88. *The Vicarage, Parwich, Ashbourne, Derbyshire DE6 1QD* Parwich (033525) 226

COOPER, James Peter. b 61. Westf Coll Lon BSc82. Sarum & Wells Th Coll 82. **d** 85 **p** 86. C Durrington *Chich* 85-88; C Clayton w Keymer from 88. *11 The Spinney, Hassocks, W Sussex BN6 8EJ* Hassocks (07918) 2599

COOPER, Jeremy John. b 45. Kelham Th Coll 65 Linc Th Coll 71. **d** 71 **p** 72. C Derby St Luke *Derby* 71-76; TV

Malvern Link w Cowleigh *Worc* 76-79; P-in-c Claypole *Linc* 79-80; P-in-c Westborough w Dry Doddington and Stubton 79-80; C Eye w Braiseworth and Yaxley *St E* 80-82; P-in-c Hundon w Barnardiston 82-85; R from 85. *The Vicarage, 5 Armstrong Close, Hundon, Sudbury, Suffolk CO10 8HD* Hundon (044086) 617

COOPER, John. b 34. BEd. N Ord Course. **d** 83 **p** 84. C Tong *Bradf* 83-87; V Bingley H Trin from 87. *Holy Trinity Vicarage, Oak Avenue, Bingley, W Yorkshire BD16 1ES* Bradford (0274) 563909

COOPER, John. b 47. Sarum & Wells Th Coll 71. **d** 74 **p** 75. C Spring Grove St Mary *Lon* 74-77; C Shepherd's Bush St Steph w St Thos 77-82; V Paddington St Pet 82-89; V Darwen St Cuth w Tockholes St Steph *Blackb* from 89. *St Cuthbert's Vicarage, Earnsdale Road, Darwen, Lancs BB3 1JA* Darwen (0254) 775039

COOPER, John Edward. b 40. K Coll Lon BD63 AKC63. **d** 64 **p** 65. C Prittlewell St Mary *Chelmsf* 64-67; C Up Hatherley *Glouc* 67-69; C-in-c Dorridge CD *Birm* 69-71; P-in-c Alkmonton w Yeaveley *Derby* 71-76; V Longford 71-76; TV Canvey Is *Chelmsf* 76-82; R Spixworth w Crostwick *Nor* 82-91; R Frettenham w Stanninghall 82-91; V Gt w Lt Harrowden and Orlingbury *Pet* from 91. *The Vicarage, 18 Kings Lane, Little Harrowden, Wellingborough, Northants NN9 5BL* Wellingborough (0933) 678225

COOPER, Ven John Leslie. b 33. Lon Univ BD65 MPhil78. Chich Th Coll 59. **d** 62 **p** 63. C Kings Heath *Birm* 62-65; Asst Chapl HM Pris Wandsworth 65-66; Chapl HM Borstal Portland 66-68; HM Pris Bris 68-72; P-in-c Balsall Heath St Paul *Birm* 73-81; V 81-82; Adn Aston and Can Res Birm Cathl 82-90; Adn Coleshill from 90. *93 Coleshill Road, Birmingham B37 7HT* 021-779 4959

COOPER, John Richard. b 34. Lon Univ DipTh60. Bps' Coll Cheshunt 60. **d** 62 **p** 63. C Old St Pancras w Bedf New Town St Matt *Lon* 71-74; rtd 75. *54 Longlands Road, Welwyn Garden City, Herts AL7 3PZ*

COOPER, Jonathan Mark Eric. b 62. Man Univ BSc83 Edin Univ BD88. Edin Th Coll 85. **d** 88 **p** 89. C Stainton-in-Cleveland *York* 88-91; C W Bromwich All SS *Lich* from 91. *50 Wilford Road, West Bromich, W Midlands B71 1QN* 021-588 3440

COOPER, Joseph Trevor. b 32. Linc Th Coll 65. **d** 67 **p** 68. C Fletchamstead *Cov* 67-69; Ind Chapl 69-90. *16 Trevor Close, Tile Hill, Coventry CV4 9HP* Coventry (0203) 462341 or 27597

COOPER, Kenneth Cantlay. b 17. Qu Coll Cam BA39 MA43. Ridley Hall Cam 39. **d** 41 **p** 42. R Fisherton Anger *Sarum* 65-74; P-in-c Fovant w Compton Chamberlayne etc 74-79; R Fovant, Sutton Mandeville and Teffont Evias etc 79-82; rtd 82; Perm to Offic *B & W* from 83. *8 Helena Road, East Coker, Yeovil, Somerset BA20 2HQ* West Coker (093586) 2291

COOPER, Kenneth Roland. b 23. Ox NSM Course. **d** 85 **p** 86. NSM Reading St Matt *Ox* from 85. *221 Southcote Lane, Reading RG3 3AY* Reading (0734) 573921

COOPER, Leslie Martin. b 17. Jes Coll Cam BA39 MA43. Lon Coll of Div 39. **d** 40 **p** 41. Chapl Wrekin Coll Shropshire 71-79; Perm to Offic *Glouc* from 79; rtd 82. *87 Corinium Gate, Cirencester, Glos GL7 2PX* Cirencester (0285) 654094

COOPER, Malcolm Tydeman. b 37. Pemb Coll Ox BA61 MA64. Linc Th Coll 63. **d** 63 **p** 64. C Spennithorne *Ripon* 63-66; C Caversham *Ox* 66-71; Hon C Blackbird Leys CD 71-75; Lic to Offic Sarum 75-78; B & W 78-82; NSM Sutton *Ely* from 82; NSM Witcham w Mepal from 82. *91 The Row, Sutton, Ely, Cambs CB6 2PB* Ely (0353) 777310

COOPER, Sister Margery. b 26. Cam Inst of Educn CertRK52. CA Tr Coll 49. **dss** 79 **d** 87. Evang Family Miss (Dios Dur, Newc and York) 79-86; rtd 86; Perm to Offic *York* from 86. *7 Grange Street, Fulford Road, York YO1 4BH* York (0904) 633990

COOPER, Maxwell Edgar. b 11. CD63. Jes Coll Cam BA37 MA41. Wycliffe Hall Ox 37. **d** 39 **p** 40. C Meole Brace *Lich* 39-41; CF (EC) 41-46; CF 46-54; Canada from 55. *624-1701 Cedar Hill Cross Road, Victoria, British Columbia, Canada, V8P 2P9* Victoria (604) 477-1798

COOPER, Canon Michael Leonard. b 30. St Jo Coll Cam BA53 MA58. Cuddesdon Coll 53. **d** 55 **p** 56. C Croydon *Cant* 55-61; V Spring Park 61-71; V Boxley 71-82; RD Sutton 74-80; Hon Can Cant Cathl from 76; P-in-c Detling 77-82; V Cranbrook from 82. *The Vicarage, Waterloo Road, Cranbrook, Kent TN17 3JQ* Cranbrook (0580) 712150

COOPER, Michael Sydney. b 41. Univ of Wales (Lamp) BA63. Westcott Ho Cam 63. **d** 65 **p** 66. C Farlington *Portsm* 65-69; Pakistan 70-71; Mauritius 71-73; C-in-c

Hayling St Pet CD *Portsm* 74-81; V Carisbrooke St Mary from 81; V Carisbrooke St Nic from 81; P-in-c Gatcombe 85-86. *The Vicarage, Carisbrooke, Newport, Isle of Wight PO30 1PA* Isle of Wight (0983) 522095

COOPER, Nigel Scott. b 53. CBiol MIBiol Ox Univ MA Cam Univ MA PGCE. Ripon Coll Cuddesdon. **d** 83 **p** 84. C Moulsham St Jo *Chelmsf* 83-88; R Rivenhall from 88. *The Rectory, 40 Church Road, Rivenhall, Witham, Essex CM8 3PQ* Witham (0376) 511161

COOPER, Noel. b 49. Oak Hill Th Coll. **d** 88 **p** 89. C Plymouth St Jude *Ex* from 88. *120 Salisbury Road, Plymouth PL4 8TB* Plymouth (0752) 261178

COOPER, Norman Mortimer. b 32. FRGS79. St Mich Coll Llan 63. **d** 65 **p** 66. C Llangynwyd w Maesteg *Llan* 65-70; P-in-c Matthewstown w Ynysboeth 70-72; V Oakwood 72-79; V Cadoxton-juxta-Neath from 79. *St Catwg's Vicarage, Cadoxton, Neath, W Glam SA10 8AS* Neath (0639) 644625

COOPER, Peter David. b 48. Sarum & Wells Th Coll 70. **d** 73 **p** 74. C Yateley *Win* 73-78; C Christchurch 78-81; P-in-c Southn St Mark 81-83; V from 83. *St Mark's Vicarage, 54 Archers Road, Southampton SO1 2LU* Southampton (0703) 636425

COOPER, Richard Thomas. b 46. Leeds Univ BA69. Coll of Resurr Mirfield 69. **d** 71 **p** 72. C Rothwell *Ripon* 71-75; C Adel 75-78; C Knaresborough 78-81; P-in-c Croft 81-90; P-in-c Eryholme 81-90; P-in-c Middleton Tyas and Melsonby 81-90; RD Richmond 86-90; V Aldborough w Boroughbridge and Roecliffe from 90. *The Vicarage, Church Lane, Boroughbridge, York YO5 9BA* Boroughbridge (0423) 322433

COOPER, Robert James. b 52. Bris Univ BA75. Ridley Hall Cam 76. **d** 78 **p** 79. C Street w Walton *B & W* 78-82; C Batheaston w St Cath 82-86; Asst Chapl to Arts and Recreation from 86; P-in-c Sadberge *Dur* from 86. *The Rectory, Middleton Road, Sadberge, Darlington, Co Durham DL2 1RP* Dinsdale (0325) 333771

COOPER, Roger Charles. b 48. GRSM ARMCM69 PGCE70. Coll of Resurr Mirfield 79. **d** 81 **p** 82. C Monkseaton St Mary *Newc* 81-83; C Morpeth 83-87; Min Can and Prec Man Cathl *Man* 87-90; V Blackrod from 90. *St Katharine's Vicarage, Blackhorse Street, Blackrod, Bolton BL6 5EN* Horwich (0204) 68150

COOPER, Stephen. b 54. Chich Th Coll 74. **d** 77 **p** 78. C Horbury *Wakef* 77-78; C Horbury w Horbury Bridge 78-81; C Barnsley St Mary 81-84; TV Elland from 84. *All Saints' Vicarage, Charles Street, Elland, W Yorkshire HX5 0JF* Elland (0422) 373184

COOPER, Sydney Bernard Nikon. b 27. K Coll Lon BD49 AKC49. **d** 51 **p** 52. V Stoke Newington St Olave *Lon* 66-76; R Chigwell Row *Chelmsf* 76-83; P-in-c Easton on the Hill, Collyweston w Duddington etc *Pet* 83; R 84-88; rtd 88. *Chase View, Church Road, Walpole St Peter, Wisbech, Cambs PE14 7NU* Wisbech (0945) 780473

COOPER, Thomas. b 20. Man Univ BA42. Edin Th Coll 42. **d** 44 **p** 45. V Bolton le Sands *Blackb* 63-85; rtd 85; Perm to Offic *Blackb* from 85. *Hillcrest, 21 Hazelmount Drive, Warton, Carnforth, Lancs LA5 9HR* Carnforth (0524) 732507

COOPER, Wallace Peter. b 24. Kelham Th Coll 47. **d** 51 **p** 52. C New Brompton St Luke *Roch* 54-56; Perm to Offic *Ox* 62-81; Hon C Earley St Pet 81-83; Hon C Earley St Nic from 83; rtd 90. *10 Morton Court, Christchurch Road, Reading RG2 7BB* Reading (0734) 860528

COOPER, Very Rev William Hugh Alan. b 09. Ch Coll Cam BA31 MA35. Lon Coll of Div 31. **d** 32 **p** 33. Provost Bradf 62-77; rtd 77; P-in-c Chrishall *Chelmsf* 81-88. *4 Eastgate Gardens, Guildford, Surrey GU1 4AZ* Guildford (0483) 67128

COOPER-SMITH, Alfred Riddington. b 13. TD63. St Deiniol's Hawarden 74. **d** 74 **p** 75. Hon C Smeeton Westerby w Saddington *Leic* 74-80; Perm to Offic Leic & Pet from 80. *63 Stockerston Crescent, Uppingham, Oakham, Leics LE15 9UA* Uppingham (0572) 822412

COOTE, Bernard Albert Ernest. b 28. Lon Univ BD53. Chich Th Coll 54. **d** 55 **p** 56. Chapl HM Borstal E Sutton Park 63-74; V Sutton Valence w E Sutton *Cant* 63-76; P-in-c Chart next Sutton Valence 71-76; Chapl and Dir R Sch for the Blind Leatherhead 76-91; rtd 91. *6 Coxham Lane, Steyning, W Sussex BN44 3JG* Steyning (0903) 813762

✠COOTE, Rt Rev Roderic Norman. b 15. TCD BA37 MA41 DD54. TCD Div Sch. **d** 38 **p** 39 **c** 51. C Dub St Bart *D & G* 38-41; Gambia 41-57; Bp Gambia and Rio Pongas 51-57; Suff Bp Fulham *Lon* 57-66; Suff Bp Colchester *Chelmsf* 66-84; Area Bp Colchester

84-87; Adn Colchester 69-72; rtd 87. *58 Broom Park, Teddington, Middx TW11 9RS* 081-943 3648

COPE, James Brian Andrew. b 58. Chich Th Coll 80. **d** 83 **p** 84. C Poulton-le-Fylde *Blackb* 83-86; C Fleetwood 86-87; V Fleetwood St Dav from 87. *St David's Vicarage, 211 Broadway, Fleetwood, Lancs FY7 8AZ* Fleetwood (0253) 779725

COPE, Miss Olive Rosemary. b 29. Birm Univ DPS73. Gilmore Ho 63. **dss** 69 **d** 87. Kentish Town St Martin w St Andr *Lon* 69-72; Enfield St Andr 73-87; Par Dn 87-89; Hon Par Dn from 89; rtd 89. *7 Calder Close, Enfield, Middx EN1 3TS* 081-363 8221

COPE, Peter John. b 42. Mert Coll Ox BA64 MA68 Lon Univ MSc74. Cuddesdon Coll 64. **d** 66 **p** 67. C Chapel Allerton *Ripon* 66-69; Ind Chapl *Lon* 69-76; Min Can Worc Cathl *Worc* 76-85; Ind Chapl 76-85; P-in-c Worc St Mark 76-81; Min W Bromwich St Mary Magd CD *Lich* from 85; Ind Chapl from 85. *7 Hopkins Drive, West Bromwich, W Midlands B71 3RR* 021-588 3744

COPE, Stephen Victor. b 60. St Jo Coll Ox BA81 DipTh84 MA87. Chich Th Coll 86. **d** 89 **p** 90. C Newmarket St Mary w Exning St Agnes *St E* from 89. *5 St Mary's Square, Newmarket, Suffolk CB8 0HZ* Newmarket (0638) 664959

COPELAND, Christopher Paul. b 38. AKC64. **d** 65 **p** 66. C Luton St Andr *St Alb* 65-67; C Droitwich St Nic w St Pet *Worc* 67-71; C Kings Norton *Birm* 71-72; TV 73-78; V Tyseley 78-88; P-in-c Grimley w Holt *Worc* from 88; Dioc Stewardship Missr from 88. *8 Holt Vicarage, Holt Heath, Worcester WR6 6NJ* Worcester (0905) 620646

COPELAND, Derek Norman. b 38. Worc Coll Ox BA62 MA68. Westcott Ho Cam 63. **d** 64 **p** 65. C Portsea St Mary *Portsm* 64-71; P-in-c Avonmouth St Andr *Bris* 71-77; P-in-c Chippenham St Paul w Langley Burrell 78-79; Ind Chapl from 78; TR Chippenham St Paul w Hardenhuish etc 79-89; V Kington 79-89. *51B Lowden, Chippenham, Wilts SN15 2BG* Chippenham (0249) 443879

COPELAND, Norman. b 1900. OBE54. Univ Coll Dur BA25 MA30. **d** 25 **p** 26. R Gotham *S'well* 54-71; rtd 71. *16 Normans, Normans Road, Winchester, Hants SO23 9AW* Winchester (0962) 62186

COPESTAKE, Leslie. b 13. ALCD39. **d** 39 **p** 40. V Beckermet St Jo *Carl* 61-71; V Egton w Newland 71-78; rtd 78; Perm to Offic *Carl* from 78. *Valley Howe, Cartmel, Grange-over-Sands, Cumbria LA11 7SB* Cartmel (05395) 36357

COPINGER, Stephen Hubert Augustine (Brother Hubert). b 18. Lon Univ BA48. Ely Th Coll 60. **d** 62 **p** 63. SSF from 61; P-in-c Hilfield and Hermitage *Sarum* 68-76; Lic to Offic Conn from 76; M & K 78-80; Chapl R Victoria Hosp Belf 83-86; rtd 86. *St Francis House, 75 Deerpark Road, Belfast BT14 7PW* Belfast (0232) 351480

COPLAND, Carole Jean. b 37. Man Univ BA60. Wm Temple Coll Rugby DipRK67. **d** 87. NSM Northallerton w Kirby Sigston *York* 87-90; Dioc Adv in Children's Work 81-90; Par Dn Dunnington from 90; Faith in the City Link Officer from 90. *30 Curlew Glebe, Dunnington, York YO1 5PQ* York (0904) 488755

COPLAND, Canon Charles McAlester. b 10. CCC Cam BA33 MA36. Cuddesdon Coll 33. **d** 34 **p** 35. R Oban St Jo *Arg* 59-79; Provost St Jo Cathl Oban 59-79; Hon Can from 79; Dean Arg 77-79; rtd 79. *Fir Cottage, South Crieff Road, Comrie, Crieff, Perthshire PH6 2HF* Comrie (0764) 70185

COPLEY, Dr Colin. b 30. FRSA. Kelham Th Coll 51. **d** 55 **p** 56. C Linc St Swithin *Linc* 55-58; C Bottesford 58-60; Chapl HM Borstal Hollesley 60-66; HM Pris Liv 66-70; Styal 70-73; Drake Hall 73-75; N Regional Chapl HM Pris and Borstals 70-73; Midl Region 73-75; Asst Chapl Gen of Pris (Midl) 75-90; Chapl HM Open Pris Sudbury and Foston Hall from 90. *The Chaplain's Office, HM Prison, Sudbury, Derby DE6 5HW* Sudbury (028378) 511

COPLEY, David Judd. b 15. Linc Coll Ox BA48 MA53. Wycliffe Hall Ox 48. **d** 50 **p** 51. V Tardebigge *Worc* 67-81; rtd 81; Perm to Offic *Worc* from 82. *220 Bromsgrove Road, Hunnington, Halesowen, W Midlands B62 0JS* Romsley (0562) 710247

COPLEY, Edmund Miles. b 27. Lon Univ BScEng50 Birm Univ DipTh57. Qu Coll Birm 55. **d** 57 **p** 58. C Allestree *Derby* 57-61; R Banff *Ab* 61-65; R Portsoy 61-65; R Uggeshall w Sotherton, Wangford and Henham *St E* from 65. *Bullions, Uggeshall, Beccles, Suffolk NR34 8BB* Wangford (050278) 235

COPNER, Thomas Herbert Woodward. b 08. Bp Wilson Coll 36. **d** 38 **p** 39. V Lonan *S & M* 59-75; rtd 75; Perm

to Offic *S & M* from 75. *Ellan Vannim Home, Kingswood Grove, Douglas, Isle of Man* Douglas (0624) 823005

COPPEN, Colin William. b 53. BCombStuds85. Linc Th Coll. **d** 85 **p** 86. C Tokyngton St Mich *Lon* 85-88; C Somers Town St Mary 88-90; P-in-c Edmonton St Alphege from 90. *St Alphege's Vicarage, Rossdale Drive, London N9 7LG* 081-804 2255

COPPEN, Martin Alan. b 48. Ex Univ BA69 Nottm Univ DipTh84. St Jo Coll Nottm 83. **d** 85 **p** 86. C Bitterne *Win* 85-88; V St Mary Bourne and Woodcott from 88. *The Vicarage, St Mary Bourne, Andover, Hants SP11 6AY* St Mary Bourne (0264) 738308

COPPEN, Peter Euan. b 39. Ripon Coll Cuddesdon 79. **d** 81 **p** 82. C New Sleaford *Linc* 81-86; V Scawby and Redbourne 86-89; V Scawby, Redbourne and Hibaldstow from 89. *The Vicarage, Scawby, Brigg, S Humberside DN20 9LX* Brigg (0652) 52451

COPPEN, Robert George. b 39. Cape Town Univ BA66. St Jo Coll Dur 79. **d** 81 **p** 82. C Douglas St Geo and St Barn *S & M* 81-84; TV Kidlington w Hampton Poyle *Ox* from 84; Chapl HM Young Offender Inst Campsfield Ho from 84. *St John's Vicarage, The Broadway, Kidlington, Oxon OX5 1EF* Kidlington (08675) 5611

COPPIN, Canon Ronald Leonard. b 30. Birm Univ BA52. Ridley Hall Cam 54. **d** 56 **p** 57. C Harrow Weald All SS *Lon* 56-59; Bp's Dom Chapl *Man* 59-63; Chapl St Aid Birkenhead 63-65; Vice-Prin 65-68; Selection Sec ACCM 68-71; Selection Sec and Sec Cttee for Th Educn 71-74; Lib Dur Cathl from 74; Can Res from 74; Dir of Clergy Tr *Dur* from 74; Warden NE Ord Course 76-84; Dir Post-Ord Tr from 86. *3 The College, Durham DH1 3EQ* 091-384 2415

COPPING, John Frank Walter Victor. b 34. K Coll Lon BD58 AKC58. **d** 59 **p** 60. C Hampstead St Jo *Lon* 59-62; C Bray and Braywood *Ox* 62-65; V Langley Mill *Derby* 65-71; V Cookham Dean *Ox* from 71; RD Maidenhead from 87. *The Vicarage, Cookham Dean, Maidenhead, Berks SL6 9PN* Marlow (06284) 3342

COPPING, Raymond. b 36. Wycliffe Hall Ox 72. **d** 74 **p** 75. C High Wycombe *Ox* 74-77; TV 77-87; TV Digswell and Panshanger *St Alb* from 87. *69 Hardings, Welwyn Garden City, Herts AL7 2HA* Welwyn Garden (0707) 333272

COPSEY, Canon Harry Charles Frederick. b 05. Linc Th Coll 31. **d** 34 **p** 35. V E Grinstead St Swithun *Chich* 54-75; Chapl Qu Victoria's Hosp E Grinstead 55-75; Chapl Sackville Coll E Grinstead 56-75; Can and Preb Chich Cathl *Chich* from 70; rtd 75. *Town House, South Pallant, Chichester, W Sussex PO19 1SY* Chichester (0243) 784509

COPSEY, Nigel John. b 52. K Coll Lon BD75 AKC75 Surrey Univ MSc. St Aug Coll Cant 72. **d** 76 **p** 77. C Barkingside St Fran *Chelmsf* 76-78; C Canning Town St Cedd 78-80; P-in-c Victoria Docks Ascension 80-87; Chapl Cane Hill Hosp Coulsdon from 87; Chapl Netherne Hosp Coulsdon from 87; E Surrey Mental Health Unit from 90. *Netherne Hospital, PO Box 150, Coulsdon, Surrey CR5 1YE* Downland (07375) 56700

COPUS, Brian George. b 36. AKC59. **d** 60 **p** 61. C Croydon St Mich *Cant* 60-63; C Swindon New Town *Bris* 63-69; V Colebrooke *Ex* 69-73; P-in-c Hittisleigh 69-73; R Perivale *Lon* 73-82; V Ruislip St Mary from 82. *St Mary's Vicarage, 9 The Fairway, South Ruislip, Middx HA4 0SP* 081-845 3485

COPUS, James Lambert. b 19. Edin Th Coll 47. **d** 50 **p** 51. V S Lambeth All SS and St Barn *S'wark* 58-77; TV Eling, Testwood and Marchwood *Win* 77-78; TV Totton 78-79; rtd 80. *94 Moorfield, Harlow, Essex CM18 7QG*

COPUS, John Cecil. b 38. BA DipEd. Cant Sch of Min. **d** 83 **p** 84. Hon C Folkestone H Trin and St Geo w Ch Ch *Cant* 83-85; Hon C Midsomer Norton w Clandown *B & W* from 85. *108 North Road, Midsomer Norton, Bath BA3 2QW* Midsomer Norton (0761) 418812

COPUS, Jonathan Hugh Lambert. b 44. AKC59 BNC Ox BA66 MA71. S'wark Ord Course 68. **d** 71 **p** 72. C Horsell *Guildf* 71-73; Producer Relig Progr BBC Radio Solent 73-87; Lic to Offic *Win* from 74. *55 Lower Ashley Road, New Milton, Hants BH25 5QF* New Milton (0425) 619400

CORBETT-MILWARD, Canon Richard George Corbet. b 12. K Coll Cam BA36 MA40. Cuddesdon Coll 37. **d** 38 **p** 39. V Portsea St Alb *Portsm* 48-74; RD Portsm 65-70; V Ryde H Trin 74-79; RD E Wight 75-78; rtd 80; Perm to Offic *Portsm* from 82. *2 Pembroke Close, Portsmouth PO1 2NX* Portsmouth (0705) 825072

CORBETT, Albert Ernest. b 20. FCA62. Qu Coll Birm 71. **d** 74 **p** 74. Hon C Sheldon *Birm* 74-77; Hon C Coleshill 77-85; Hon C Sandbach *Ches* from 85.

9 Capesthorne Close, Sandbach, Cheshire CW11 0ED
Crewe (0270) 765427

CORBETT, Canon Charles Eric. b 17. Jes Coll Ox BA39 MA43. Wycliffe Hall Ox 39. **d** 40 **p** 41. V Farnworth *Liv* 61-71; Adn Liv 71-79; Can Res Liv Cathl 71-79; Can Res and Treas Liv Cathl 79-83; rtd 83; Perm to Offic *Ches* from 85. *80 Latham Avenue, Helsby, Cheshire WA6 0EB* Helsby (0928) 724184

CORBETT, George. b 18. Bible Churchmen's Coll 47. **d** 50 **p** 51. V Hatherleigh *Ex* 63-78; P-in-c Ringmore and Kingston 78-84; R Bigbury, Ringmore and Kingston 84-86; rtd 86; Perm to Offic *Heref* from 87. *2 Quantock Close, Hereford HR4 0TD* Hereford (0432) 269211

CORBETT, Henry. b 53. CCC Cam BA75. Wycliffe Hall Ox DipTh78. **d** 78 **p** 79. C Everton St Pet *Liv* 78-84; TV 84-87; TR from 87. *Shrewsbury House, Langrove Street, Liverpool L5 3LT* 051-207 1948

CORBETT, Canon Ian Deighton. b 42. St Cath Coll Cam BA64 MA68 Salford Univ MSc83. Westcott Ho Cam 67. **d** 69 **p** 70. C New Bury *Man* 69-72; C Bolton St Pet 72-75; Chapl Bolton Colls of FE 72-75; Dioc FE Officer 74-83; R Man Victoria Park *Man* 75-80; Chapl Salford Univ 80-83; Hon Can Man Cathl 83-87; P-in-c Salford Sacred Trin 83-87; Dir of In-Service Tr 83-87; Lesotho from 87. *Lelapa la Jesu Seminary, NUL, Roma 180, Lesotho*

CORBETT, John David. b 32. Or Coll Ox BA55 MA59. St Steph Ho Ox 55. **d** 57 **p** 58. C Plymouth St Pet *Ex* 57-64; V Marldon 64-74; TV Bournemouth St Pet w St Swithun, St Steph etc *Win* 74-83; V Beckenham St Barn *Roch* 83-88; V King's Sutton and Newbottle and Charlton Pet from 88. *The Vicarage, Church Avenue, Kings Sutton, Banbury, Oxon OX17 3RJ* Banbury (0295) 811364

CORBETT, Miss Phyllis. b 34. Cranmer Hall Dur 76. dss 80 **d** 87. Walsall Wood *Lich* 80-87; Par Dn Baswich (or Berkswich) from 87. *18 Hartland Avenue, Baswich, Stafford ST17 0EJ* Stafford (0785) 664598

CORBETT, Stephen Paul. b 57. BA80. St Jo Coll Nottm 83. **d** 85 **p** 86. C Tollington Park St Mark w St Anne *Lon* 85-86; C Holloway St Mark w Em 86-91; V Chitts Hill St Cuth from 91. *St Cuthbert's Vicarage, 85 Wolves Lane, London N22 5JD* 081-888 6178

CORBIN, Frederick Athelston. b 42. S Dios Minl Tr Scheme 80. **d** 83 **p** 85. NSM Basingstoke *Win* 83-84; C Hulme Ascension *Man* 84-86; Lic to Hulme Deanery 86-87; C E Crompton 87-89; V Oldham St Barn from 89. *St Barnabas's Vicarage, 1 Arundel Street, Oldham OL4 1NL* 061-624 7708

CORBIN, Robert Charles Henry. b 17. AKC49. **d** 49 **p** 50. C Boscombe St Andr *Win* 69-72; C Bournemouth St Pet 72-74; P-in-c Newton Valence 74-79; P-in-c Selborne 74-79; P-in-c Old Alresford 79; Public Preacher *Chelmsf* from 80; Chapl Community of the Sacred Passion Chelmsf 81-83; Chapl St Giles's Hosp E Hanningfield 81-83; rtd 83. *1 Rectory Close, Stock, Ingatestone, Essex CM4 9BP* Stock (0277) 840830

CORBY, Mrs Jennifer Marjorie. b 40. SRN62. Cant Sch of Min 87. **d** 90. NSM Kemsing w Woodlands *Roch* from 90; Chapl Stone Ho Hosp Kent from 90. *7 Copperfields Walk, Kemsing, Sevenoaks, Kent TN15 6QF* Sevenoaks (0732) 62006

CORBYN, John. b 58. Man Univ BA79 Ven English Coll and Pontifical Gregorian Univ Rome 83. Wycliffe Hall Ox BA83 MA87. **d** 84 **p** 85. C Deane *Man* 84-87; C Lanc St Mary *Blackb* 87-90; Chapl HM Pris Lanc 89-90; V Blackb St Gabr *Blackb* from 90. *St Gabriel's Vicarage, 284 Pleckgate Road, Blackburn BB1 8QU* Blackburn (0254) 248430

CORBYN, John Robert. b 54. Qu Coll Birm. **d** 82 **p** 83. C Northolt W End St Jos *Lon* 82-86; Urban Miss Priest *York* 86-88; C Sutton St Mich 86-88; V Dalton *Sheff* from 88. *The Vicarage, Dalton, Rotherham, S Yorkshire S65 3QL* Rotherham (0709) 850377

CORDELL, Derek Harold. b 34. Chich Th Coll 57. **d** 60 **p** 61. C Whitstable All SS *Cant* 60-63; C Moulsecoomb *Chich* 63-69; Chapl Bucharest *Eur* 69-71; V Brighton St Wilfrid *Chich* 71-74; Chapl HM Borstal Roch 74-80; Asst Chapl HM Pris Man 80-81; Chapl HM Pris The Verne 81-89; Channings Wood *Man* 89-90; Chapl Milan w Genoa and Varese *Eur* 90-91; Chapl Mojacar from 91. *Apartment 157, 04630 Garrucha, Almeria, Spain* Almeria (51) 475278

CORDINGLEY, Canon Brian Lambert. b 30. St Aid Birkenhead 55. **d** 57 **p** 58. Ind Chapl *Sheff* 57-63; C Clifton St Jas 57-61; C Rotherham 61-63; Ind Chapl *Man* from 63; R Old Trafford St Cuth 63-81; V Hamer from 81; Hon Can Man Cathl from 87. *All Saints'*

Vicarage, Foxholes Road, Rochdale, Lancs OL12 0EF
Rochdale (0706) 355591

CORDINGLEY, Francis Andre Annandale. b 26. **d** 67 **p** 68. C Wooler *Newc* 67-70; V Broadhembury *Ex* 70-73; V Rillington *York* 73-76; V Scampston 74-76; V Wintringham 74-76; P-in-c Thorpe Bassett 76; V Rillington w Scampston, Wintringham etc 77-83; C Askham Bryan w Askham Richard 83; V Healaugh w Wighill and Bilbrough 83; V Healaugh w Wighill, Bilbrough and Askham Richard 83-85; rtd 85. *Pantile Cottage, 6 Fowberry, Wooler, Northd NE71 6ER*

CORDINGLEY, Fred. b 11. St Jo Coll Dur BA40 MA43. **d** 40 **p** 41. R Birdbrook w Sturmer *Chelmsf* 63-71; rtd 71. *8 Ashwood Close, Helmsley, York YO6 5HW* Helmsley (0439) 70595

CORDY, Gordon Donald. b 30. **d** 63 **p** 64. C Kirkley *Nor* 63-65; C Stroud *Glouc* 66-68; V Badgeworth w Shurdington 68-71; V Coleford w Staunton 71-73; C Digswell *St Alb* 73-75; TV Lilleshall w Abington Pigotts *Ely* 75-78; R March St Jo 78-83; Perm to Offic *Nor* 84-87; P-in-c Smallburgh w Dilham w Honing and Crostwight from 87. *The Rectory, Honing, North Walsham, Norfolk NR28 9AB* Smallburgh (0692) 536466

CORE, Edward. b 54. BTh. Sarum & Wells Th Coll. **d** 82 **p** 83. C Newbold and Dunston *Derby* 82-86; Chapl RAF from 86. *c/o MOD, Adastral House, Theobald's Road, London WC1X 8RU* 071-430 7268

CORFE, David Robert. b 35. Pemb Coll Cam BA58 MA62. Lambeth DipTh70 Cuddesdon Coll 58. **d** 60 **p** 61. C Wigan All SS *Liv* 60-63; India 63-68 and 70-75; C Northwood Em *Lon* 75; V Westwell *Cant* 75-80; R Eastwell w Boughton Aluph 75-80; V Hildenborough *Roch* 80-91; Lic Preacher Stretford St Bride *Man* from 91. *3 Blair Street, Old Trafford, Manchester M16 9AZ*

CORFIELD, John Bernard. b 24. Jes Coll Cam BA49 MA51. Ridley Hall Cam 64. **d** 66 **p** 67. P-in-c Bledlow Ridge *Ox* 69-75; P-in-c Bradenham 71-75; R Sherington w Chicheley, N Crawley, Astwood etc 75-82; V Terrington St Clement *Ely* 82-90; rtd 90; Perm to Offic *Ox* from 90. *13 Sturt Road, Charlbury, Oxon OX7 3SX* Charlbury (0608) 811464

CORK, CLOYNE AND ROSS, Archdeacon of. See MAYES, Ven Michael Hugh Gunton

CORK, CLOYNE AND ROSS, Bishop of. See WARKE, Rt Rev Robert Alexander

CORK, Dean of. See CAREY, Very Rev James Maurice George

CORKE, Colin John. b 59. St Pet Coll Ox BA81. Cranmer Hall Dur 83. **d** 85 **p** 86. C Chapel Allerton *Ripon* 85-88; C Burmantofts St Steph and St Agnes 88-91; P-in-c Tatsfield *S'wark* from 91. *The Rectory, Ricketts Hill Road, Tatsfield, Westerham, Kent TN16 2NA* Tatsfield (0959) 77289

CORKE, John Harry. b 29. AKC55. **d** 56 **p** 57. C Stockingford *Cov* 56-58; C Nuneaton St Nic 58-60; V Hartshill 60-80; R Hampton Lucy w Charlecote and Loxley from 80. *The Vicarage, Charlecote, Warwick CV35 9EW* Stratford-upon-Avon (0789) 840244

CORKER, John Anthony. b 37. AKC63. **d** 64 **p** 65. C Lindley *Wakef* 64-68; V Brotherton 68-72; Perm to Offic 72-82; Hon C Askham Bryan *York* 82-91; TV York All SS Pavement w St Crux and St Martin etc from 91. *All Saints Rectory, 52 St Andrewgate, York YO1 2BZ* York (0904) 631116

CORKER, Canon Ronald. b 30. Ely Th Coll 51. **d** 54 **p** 55. C Whitworth w Spennymoor *Dur* 54-58; Min Dunstan St Nic ED 58-65; Chapl Dunston Hill Hosp Gateshead 58-68; V Dunston St Nic *Dur* 65-68; R Willington 68-75; P-in-c Sunnybrow 73-75; R Willington and Sunnybrow 75-80; V Billingham St Cuth 80-85; RD Stockton 83-85; TR Jarrow from 85; Hon Can Dur Cathl from 90. *St Peter's House, York Avenue, Jarrow, Tyne & Wear NE32 5LP* 091-489 1925 or 489 0946

CORKETT, Canon Cecil Harry. b 10. Dur Univ LTh41. Sarum Th Coll 32. **d** 35 **p** 36. V Whitechapel *Wakef* 43-80; rtd 80; Perm to Offic *Wakef* from 80. *1 Fernlea Close, Crofton, Wakefield, W Yorkshire* Wakefield (0924) 864427

CORLESS, Keith Ronald. b 37. Edin Th Coll 58. **d** 61 **p** 62. C Pittville *Glouc* 61-64; C Leckhampton SS Phil and Jas 66-69; R Ashchurch from 69. *The Rectory, Ashchurch, Tewkesbury, Glos GL20 8JZ* Tewkesbury (0684) 293729

CORLETT, Dr Ewan Christian Brew. b 23. OBE85. FRSA FIMarE Qu Coll Ox MA47 K Coll Dur PhD50. Local NSM Course. **d** 91. NSM Maughold *S & M* from 91. *Cottimans, Port-e-Vullen, Ramsey, Isle of Man* Ramsey (0624) 814009

CORNE, Ronald Andrew. b 51. Sarum & Wells Th Coll 87. d 89 p 90. Par Dn Bitterne Park *Win* from 89. *24 Lacon Close, Southampton SO2 4JA* Southampton (0703) 584640

CORNECK, Canon Warrington Graham. b 35. FCA ACA60. Clifton Th Coll. d 65 p 66. C Islington St Jude Mildmay Park *Lon* 65-67; C Southgate *Chich* 67-73; P-in-c Deptford St Nic w Ch Ch *S'wark* 73-76; P-in-c Deptford St Luke 73-76; V Deptford St Nic and St Luke from 76; RD Deptford from 85; Hon Can S'wark Cathl from 91. *St Nicholas' Vicarage, 41 Creek Road, London SE8 3BU* 081-692 2749

CORNELIUS, Donald Eric. b 31. K Coll Lon BD AKC. d 84 p 85. Hon C Crowle *Linc* from 84. *4 Mulberry Drive, Crowle, Scunthorpe, S Humberside DN17 4JF* Scunthorpe (0724) 710279

CORNELL, Frederick William. b 12. St Pet Hall Ox BA34 MA38. Wells Th Coll 38. d 40 p 41. V Barrington *B & W* 61-77; R Puckington w Bradon and Stocklynch 61-77; rtd 77. *Pinneys Cottage, Chardstock, Axminster, Devon* South Chard (0460) 20883

CORNELL, Jean Cranston. b 36. Man Univ CertEd59 BA64 York Univ BPhil71. Ripon Coll Cuddesdon 87. d 89. C Matson *Glouc* from 89. *58 Haycroft Drive, Gloucester GL4 9XX* Gloucester (0452) 502150

CORNELL, John Lister. b 12. St Pet Hall Ox BA34 MA39. Wycliffe Hall Ox 35. d 35 p 36. R Mickleham *Guildf* 53-78; rtd 78. *Staddles, Windmill Hill, Ashill, Ilminster, Somerset TA19 9NT* Hatch Beauchamp (0823) 480012

CORNELL, Michael Neil. b 45. Ripon Coll Cuddesdon 79. d 81 p 82. C Gt Bookham *Guildf* 81-84; C York Town from 84. *St Martin's Vicarage, Hampshire Road, Camberley, Surrey GU15 4DW* Camberley (0276) 23958

CORNES, Andrew Charles Julian. b 49. CCC Ox BA70 MA73 St Jo Coll Dur DipTh73. Wycliffe Hall Ox 70 Cranmer Hall Dur 72. d 73 p 74. C York St Mich-le-Belfrey *York* 73-76; C St Marylebone All So w SS Pet and Jo *Lon* 76-85; USA 85-88; V Crowborough *Chich* from 89. *The Vicarage, Chapel Green, Crowborough, E Sussex TN6 1ED* Crowborough (0892) 667384

CORNISH, Anthony. b 30. Roch Th Coll 64. d 67 p 68. C Goodmayes All SS *Chelmsf* 67-71; C Buckhurst Hill 71-73; V Westcliff St Andr 73-83; R Rawreth w Rettendon from 83. *The Rectory, Church Road, Rawreth, Wickford, Essex SS11 8SH* Wickford (0268) 766766

CORNISH, Dennis Henry Ronald. b 31. FCIB72 FCIS81. S'wark Ord Course 83. d 86 p 87. NSM Uxbridge *Lon* 86-89; R Lurgashall, Lodsworth and Selham *Chich* from 89. *The Vicarage, Lodsworth, Petworth, W Sussex GU28 9DE* Lodsworth (07985) 274

CORNISH, Canon Edward Maurice John. b 14. TD51. Qu Coll Birm 48. d 48 p 49. V Chorley St Geo *Blackb* 56-70; Bp's Dom Chapl 70-78; R Ribchester w Stidd 70-78; Hon Can Blackb Cathl 74-81; C Fairhaven 78-87; rtd 79; Perm to Offic *Blackb* from 87. *16 Ripon Road, Ansdell, Lytham St Annes, Lancs FY8 4DS* Lytham (0253) 739845

CORNISH, Francis John. b 14. Hertf Coll Ox BA36 MA42. Wycliffe Hall Ox 37. d 38 p 39. R Poynings *Chich* 57-79; R Edburton 57-79; rtd 79. *Four Winds, Clapham, Worthing, W Sussex BN13 3UU* Patching (090674) 359

CORNISH, Graham Peter. b 42. Dur Univ BA67. NE Ord Course 82. d 84 p 85. NSM Harrogate St Wilfrid and St Luke *Ripon* from 84. *33 Mayfield Grove, Harrogate, N Yorkshire HG1 5HD* Harrogate (0423) 562747

CORNISH, Ian. Reading Univ BSc61 DipEd62 ADipR79. Ox Min Course 86. d 89 p 90. NSM Aston Clinton w Buckland and Drayton Beauchamp *Ox* from 89. *79 Weston Road, Aston Clinton, Aylesbury, Bucks HP22 5EP* Aylesbury (0296) 630345

CORNISH, John Douglas. b 42. Lich Th Coll 67. d 70 p 71. C Lt Stanmore St Lawr *Lon* 70-73; C Harefield from 73. *23 High Street, Harefield, Middx UB9 6BX* Harefield (089582) 2510

CORNISH, Peter Andrew. b 55. Ch Ch Ox BA77 MA80 Ex Univ CertEd78. St Jo Coll Nottm 84. d 87 p 88. C Sanderstead All SS *S'wark* from 87. *285 Limpsfield Road, South Croydon, Surrey CR2 9DG* 081-657 0613

CORNISH, Philip Gordon Pym. b 01. K Coll Lon AKC25 BD28. d 26 p 27. R Lt Waltham *Chelmsf* 59-67; rtd 67. *75A Penn Hill Avenue, Poole, Dorset* Parkstone (0202) 747085

CORNWALL, Canon John Whitmore. b 1900. Cuddesdon Coll 29. d 31 p 32. UMCA (Masasi) 33-54; R Minchinhampton *Glouc* 59-72; rtd 72; Perm to Offic *Glouc* from 77. *6 Southgate Crescent, Rodborough, Stroud, Glos GL5 3TS* Stroud (0453) 764816

CORNWALL-JONES, Canon Guy Rupert. b 30. Jes Coll Cam BA54 MA59. Westcott Ho Cam 55. d 57 p 58. C Longton St Jas *Lich* 57-60; C Wood End *Cov* 60-64; R Caldecote 64-84; R Weddington 64-84; RD Nuneaton 79-84; Hon Can Cov Cathl from 80; R Bilton from 84. *The Rectory, Church Walk, Rugby, Warks CV22 7RN* Rugby (0788) 812613

CORNWALL, Archdeacon of. See RAVENSCROFT, Ven Raymond Lockwood

CORNWALL, Christopher Richard. b 43. Dur Univ BA67. Cuddesdon Coll 67. d 69 p 70. C Cannock *Lich* 69-75; P-in-c Hadley 75-80; V 80-81; Bp's Dom Chapl 81-86; Subchanter Lich Cathl 81-86; V Ellesmere 86-89; V Welsh Frankton 86-89; V Ellesmere and Welsh Frankton from 89. *The Vicarage, Church Hill, Ellesmere, Shropshire SY12 0HB* Ellesmere (0691) 622571

CORNWELL, Gertrude Florence. b 21. CertEd48 Nottm Univ DipEd72. Gilmore Ho 56 Lambeth STh60. dss 62 d 87. Sen Lect Bp Grosseteste Coll Linc 64-81; rtd 81. *14/2A Minster Yard, Lincoln LN2 1PW* Lincoln (0522) 27249

CORNWELL, Canon Reginald George. b 09. St Edm Hall Ox BA31 DipTh32 MA35. Cuddesdon Coll 32. d 33 p 34. Can Res Newc Cathl *Newc* 68-76; Bp's Ind and Community Adv 68-76; rtd 76; Hon Can Newc Cathl *Newc* 76-79. *Eothen House, 45 Elmfield Road, Gosforth, Newcastle upon Tyne NE3 4BB*

CORRADINE, John. b 29. St Aid Birkenhead. d 58 p 59. C Tarporley *Ches* 58-61; C Wilmslow 61-64; V Moulton from 64. *The Vicarage, Moulton, Northwich, Cheshire CW9 8NR* Winsford (0606) 3355

CORRAN, Dr Henry Stanley. b 15. Trin Coll Cam BA36 PhD41. CITC 76. d 77 p 78. NSM Bray Ch Ch *D & G* 77-85; rtd 85. *71 Alderley Road, Hoylake, Wirral, Merseyside L47 2AU* 051-632 2750

CORREY, William Henry. b 14. Liv Univ BA37. ALCD49. d 49 p 50. V Bishopwearmouth St Gabr *Dur* 68-73; R Gt Parndon *Chelmsf* 73-80; RD Harlow 80-83; V Hatf Broad Oak 80-83; rtd 83; Perm to Offic *Chich* from 83. *Ramsay Hall, Byron Road, Worthing, W Sussex BN11 3HW* Worthing (0903) 771847

CORRIE, John. b 48. Imp Coll Lon BScEng69 MSc70 DIC70 PhD73 Lon Univ DipTh77 Nottm Univ MTh86. Trin Coll Bris 74. d 77 p 78. C Kendal St Thos *Carl* 77-80; C Attenborough *S'well* 80-86; Chapl Intercon Chr Soc 86-91; Peru 86-91; Tutor and Lect All Nations Chr Coll Ware from 91. *10 Peters Wood Hill, Ware, Herts SG12 9NR* Ware (0920) 462676

CORRIE, Paul Allen. b 43. St Jo Coll Nottm 77. d 79 p 80. C Beverley Minster *York* 79-82; V Derby St Werburgh *Derby* 82-84; V Derby St Alkmund and St Werburgh from 84. *The Vicarage, 200 Duffield Road, Derby DE3 1BL* Derby (0332) 48339

CORRIGAN, Ven Thomas George. b 28. CITC 56. d 58 p 59. C Cavan and Drung *K, E & A* 58-60; I Drung 60-67; I Belf St Mich *Conn* 67-70; I Kingscourt w Drumconrath, Syddan and Moybologue *M & K* from 70; Adn Meath from 81; Dioc Reg (Meath) 87-90. *St Ernan's Rectory, Kingscourt, Co Cavan, Irish Republic* Dundalk (42) 67255

CORSER, Peter Robert Mosse. b 18. Bps' Coll Cheshunt 47. d 49 p 50. R Wainfleet All SS w St Thos *Linc* 66-74; V Wainfleet St Mary 74; V Holland Fen 74-80; R Claypole 80-81; R Westborough w Dry Doddington and Stubton 80-81; R Claypole 81-83; rtd 83; Perm to Offic *Linc* from 84. *39 Abbey Road, Swineshead, Boston, Lincs PE20 3EN* Boston (0205) 820793

CORSTORPHINE, Miss Margaret. b 34. SRN57 SCM59. Cranmer Hall Dur 70. dss 84 d 87. Colchester St Jo *Chelmsf* 84-87; Par Dn from 87. *18 Craven Drive, Colchester CO4 4BE* Colchester (0206) 845588

CORTEEN, Robert. b 18. ACII. Coll of Resurr Mirfield 77. d 79 p 80. NSM Chorlton-cum-Hardy St Clem *Man* 79-88; Perm to Offic from 88. *23 Meadow Bank, Manchester M21 2EF* 061-881 1118

CORY, Valerie Ann. b 44. CertEd65 Nottm Univ BEd85. E Midl Min Tr Course 85. d 88. Area Sec (Dios Linc and Pet) CMS from 87; NSM Grantham *Linc* from 88. *23 North Parade, Grantham, Lincs NG31 8AT* Grantham (0476) 61244

COSBY, Ingrid St Clair. b 34. ALCM LLCM DipEd Lon Univ DipTh. dss 71 d 86. Cumbernauld *Glas* 71-73; Asst CF 73-83; NSM Kirkwall *Ab* 83-91; Stromness 83-91; rtd 91. *Quarrybrae, Hillside Road, Stromness, Orkney KW16 3HR* Stromness (0856) 850832

COSENS, William Edward Hyde. b 38. Lich Th Coll 61. d 64 p 65. C W Drayton *Lon* 64-68; C Roehampton H Trin *S'wark* 68-70; ILEA Youth Ldr 69-70; Miss to Seamen from 70; Chapl Rotterdam Miss to Seamen *Eur*

70-72; Tilbury 72-76; Australia 76-81; New Zealand 81-89; Chapl Immingham Seafarers' Cen from 89; Hon C Immingham *Linc* from 89. *342 Pelham Road, Immingham, Grimsby, S Humberside DN40 1PU* Immingham (0469) 572818 or 574195

COSH, Roderick John. b 56. Lon Univ BSc78. St Steph Ho Ox 78. **d** 81 **p** 82. C Swindon New Town *Bris* 81-86; Chapl Asst R Marsden Hosp Lon and Surrey 86-91; V Whitton St Aug *Lon* from 91. *St Augustine's Vicarage, Hospital Bridge Road, Whitton, Middx TW2 6DE* 081-894 3764

COSLETT, Anthony Allan. b 49. Cuddesdon Coll. **d** 84 **p** 85. C Notting Hill St Clem and St Mark *Lon* 84-85; C Brentford 85-87; C-in-c Hounslow Gd Shep Beavers Lane CD 87-90; V Hounslow W Gd Shep from 90. *Good Shepherd House, 360 Beavers Lane, Hounslow, Middx TW4 6HJ*

COSSAR, David Vyvyan. b 34. Lon Univ BA63. Chich Th Coll 63. **d** 65 **p** 66. C Upper Clapton St Matt Lon 65-68; C Withycombe Raleigh *Ex* 68-72; V Honicknowle 72-78; V Brixham w Churston Ferrers 78-86; P-in-c Kingswear 85-86; TR Brixham w Churston Ferrers and Kingswear 86-90; V Lamorbey H Trin *Roch* from 90. *Holy Trinity Vicarage, 1 Hurst Road, Sidcup, Kent DA15 9AE* 081-300 8231

COSSAR, Miss Heather (Jillian) Mackenzie. b 27. dss 83 **d** 91. Miss Partner CMS 83-90; Kenya 83-90; Slindon, Eartham and Madehurst *Chich* 90-91; NSM from 91. *31 Madehurst, Arundel, W Sussex BN18 0NJ* Slindon (024365) 291

COSSAR, John Robert Mackenzie. b 26. Oak Hill Th Coll 53. **d** 56 **p** 57. C Rainham *Chelmsf* 56-59; C Hastings Em and St Mary in the Castle *Chich* 59-61; P-in-c Madehurst 61-62; V 62-81; Dioc Youth Chapl 61-78; P-in-c Slindon w Eartham 81; R Slindon, Eartham and Madehurst from 81. *The Rectory, Slindon, Arundel, W Sussex BN18 0RE* Slindon (024365) 275

COSSINS, John Charles. b 43. Hull Univ BSc65. Oak Hill Th Coll 65. **d** 67 **p** 68. C Kenilworth St Jo *Cov* 67-70; C Huyton St Geo *Liv* 70-73; TV Maghull 73-79; Chapl Oakwood Hosp Maidstone 79-85; Maidstone Hosp 85-88; Park Lane, Moss Side and Ashworth Hosps, Liv from 88. *50 Parkbourn Square, Maghull, Liverpool L31 1JD* 051-531 9481

COSSINS, Roger Stanton. b 40. K Coll Lon BD67 AKC67. **d** 68 **p** 69. C Bramley *Ripon* 68-71; C W End *Win* 71-76; V Bramley 76-91; P-in-c Bournemouth H Epiphany from 91. *The Vicarage, 81 Castle Lane West, Bournemouth BH9 3LH* Bournemouth (0202) 512481

COSSLETT, Ronald James. b 38. St D Coll Lamp DipTh70. **d** 70 **p** 71. C Newport St Teilo *Mon* 70-74; C Epsom St Barn *Guildf* 74-78; C Shrewsbury St Mary w All SS and St Mich *Lich* 78-80; V Smallthorne from 80. *St Saviour's Vicarage, Smallthorne, Stoke-on-Trent ST6 1NX* Stoke-on-Trent (0782) 835941

COSTELOE, Frederick John. b 14. TCD BA41 MA45. **d** 40 **p** 41. V Kewstoke *B & W* 60-75; V Brent Knoll 75-80; rtd 81; Perm to Offic *B & W* from 81. *3 Regency Close, Burnham-on-Sea, Somerset TA8 2PB* Burnham-on-Sea (0278) 789310

COSTERTON, Alan Stewart. b 40. Bris Univ BA67. Clifton Th Coll 67. **d** 69 **p** 70. C Peckham St Mary Magd *S'wark* 69-73; C Forest Gate St Sav w W Ham St Matt *Chelmsf* 73-76; TV 76-79; V Thornton cum Bagworth *Leic* 79-85; V Thornton, Bagworth and Stanton from 85. *The Vicarage, Main Street, Thornton, Leicester LE6 1AF* Bagworth (0530) 230268

COTGROVE, Alan Edward. b 26. AKC51. **d** 52 **p** 53. C Earl's Court St Cuth w St Matthias *Lon* 52-55; Perm to Offic *Ox* 56-58; Lic to Offic 58-62 and 65-76; SSJE from 58; India 62-65; Lic to Offic *Lon* from 76. *St Edward's House, 22 Great College Street, London SW1P 3QA* 071-222 9234

COTGROVE, Canon Edwin John. b 23. Kelham Th Coll 42. **d** 47 **p** 48. V Hampton All SS *Lon* 64-82; RD Hampton 72-82; R Bartlow *Ely* 82-91; V Linton 82-91; P-in-c Shudy Camps 85-91; P-in-c Castle Camps 85-91; RD Linton from 88; Hon Can Ely Cathl from 89; rtd 91. *96 The High Street, Great Abington, Cambridge CB1 6AE* Cambridge (0223) 893735

COTGROVE, Norman James. b 24. CCC Cam BA53 MA57. Kelham Th Coll 46. **d** 50 **p** 51. R Ashingdon w S Fambridge *Chelmsf* 60-80; P-in-c Gt w Lt Tey 80-81; P-in-c Wakes Colne w Chappel 80-81; R Gt Tey and Wakes Colne w Chappel 81-90; rtd 90. *42 Manchester Drive, Leigh-on-Sea, Essex SS9 3HR* Southend-on-Sea (0702) 711046

COTMAN, John Sell Granville. b 44. St Jo Coll Dur BA69 Bris Univ DSA72. Wells Th Coll 70. **d** 73 **p** 74. C

Leigh St Mary *Man* 73-76; P-in-c Coldhurst 76-78; TV Oldham 78-82; TV E Ham w Upton Park *Chelmsf* 82-85; C Hove All SS *Chich* from 88. *Church House Flat, Wilbury Road, Hove, E Sussex BN3 3PB* Brighton (0273) 736643

COTTEE, Christopher Paul. b 54. Newc Univ BSc75. Wycliffe Hall Ox 77. **d** 80 **p** 81. C Much Woolton *Liv* 80-84; C Prescot 84-88; NSM Parr 89-91; V Watford St Pet *St Alb* from 91. *St Peter's Vicarage, 61 Westfield Avenue, Watford WD2 4HT* Watford (0923) 226717

COTTEE, Mary Jane. b 43. CertEd64 Open Univ BA81. Oak Hill Th Coll 87. **d** 90. Hon Par Dn Gt Baddow *Chelmsf* from 90. *19 Avenue Road, Great Baddow, Chelmsford, Essex CM2 9TY* Chelmsford (0245) 266225

COTTER, Graham Michael. b 50. Univ of Wales (Ban) BA72. Ridley Hall Cam 75. **d** 78 **p** 79. C Headley All SS *Guildf* 78-81; C Plymouth St Andr w St Paul and St Geo *Ex* 81-84; V Buckland Monachorum from 84. *The Vicarage, Buckland Monachorum, Yelverton, Devon PL20 7LQ* Yelverton (0822) 852227

COTTER, James England. b 42. G&C Coll Cam BA64 MA67. Linc Th Coll 65. **d** 67 **p** 68. C Stretford St Matt *Man* 67-70; Lect Linc Th Coll 70-73; Lic to Offic *Lon* 73-74; Chapl G&C Coll Cam 74-77; C Leavesden All SS *St Alb* 77-83; Asst Prin St Alb Minl Tr Scheme 77-83; Course Dir 83-86; Perm to Offic *Ex* 86-88; Sheff 88-89; Lic to Offic *Sheff* from 89. *47 Firth Park Avenue, Sheffield S5 6HF* Sheffield (0742) 431182

COTTER, Canon John Beresford Dolmage. b 20. TCD BA47 BD55. **d** 47 **p** 48. Bahrain 69-75; V Towednack *Truro* 76-89; V Zennor 76-89; Past Tr Chapl 82-89; rtd 89. *Thimble Cottage, 64 Mount Road, Bath BA2 1LH* Bath (0225) 337414

COTTERELL, Michael Clifford. b 54. Oak Hill Th Coll 81. **d** 84 **p** 85. C Lutterworth w Cotesbach *Leic* 84-87; C Belper *Derby* 87-91; V Locking *B & W* from 91. *The Vicarage, The Green, Locking, Weston-super-Mare, Avon BS24 8DA* Banwell (0934) 823556

COTTINGHAM, Peter John Garnet. b 24. Wadh Coll Ox BA48 MA50. Ridley Hall Cam 48. **d** 50 **p** 51. V S Mimms Ch Ch *Lon* 68-81; V Derby St Pet and Ch Ch w H Trin *Derby* 81-89; rtd 89. *5 Broadway, Rhos-on-Sea, Colwyn Bay, Clwyd LL28 4AR* Colwyn Bay (0492) 548840

COTTINGHAM, Ronald Frederick. b 27. Bps' Coll Cheshunt 55. **d** 58 **p** 59. C Biscot *St Alb* 58-60; C Bushey Heath 60-64; C-in-c Enfield St Giles CD *Lon* 64-68; C S Mymms K Chas *St Alb* 68-69; R Hardwick *Pet* 70-86; V Mears Ashby 70-86; St Helena and Ascension Is from 86. *St Mary's Vicarage, Ascension Island, South Atlantic*

COTTON, Canon John Alan. b 24. Qu Coll Ox BA48 MA52. Chich Th Coll 50. **d** 51 **p** 52. V Fairwarp *Chich* 69-82; Dir of Educn 72-78; Can and Preb Chich Cathl 72-89; Bp's Adv on Min 79-89; Dir of Ords 79-89; rtd 89. *1 Newhaven, Thursby, Carlisle CA5 6PH* Carlisle (0228) 711506

COTTON, John Horace Brazel. b 28. MIMechE St Jo Coll Cam BA50 MA76. St Alb Minl Tr Scheme 78. **d** 81 **p** 82. NSM Lt Berkhamsted and Bayford, Essendon etc *St Alb* 81-87; P-in-c from 87. *49 Sherrardspark Road, Welwyn Garden City, Herts AL8 7LD* Welwyn Garden (0707) 321815

COTTON, John Kenneth. b 25. Westcott Ho Cam 57. **d** 58 **p** 59. C S Ormsby w Skendleby, Calceby and Driby *Linc* 58-61; R Wrentham w Benacre, Covehithe and Henstead *St E* 61-68; R Sotterley w Willingham 63-68; R Shadingfield 63-68; Canada 68-71; TV Sandringham w W Newton *Nor* 71-76; P-in-c Assington *St E* 80-86; P-in-c Lt Cornard 80-86; P-in-c Newton 80-86; P-in-c Eyke w Bromeswell, Rendlesham, Tunstall etc from 87; P-in-c Alderton w Ramsholt and Bawdsey from 89. *The Rectory, Eyke, Woodbridge, Suffolk IP12 2QW* Eyke (0394) 460289

COTTON, John Wallis. b 31. Wells Th Coll 57. **d** 59 **p** 60. C Stepney St Dunstan and All SS *Lon* 59-64; C Hanworth All SS 64-67; V Hammersmith St Sav 67-74; R Lancing w Coombes *Chich* 75-86; RD Worthing 83-85; R Bexhill St Pet 86-90; TR from 90. *The Rectory, Old Town, Bexhill-on-Sea, E Sussex TN40 2HE* Bexhill-on-Sea (0424) 211115

COTTON, John William. b 53. DipHE86. Oak Hill Th Coll 84. **d** 86 **p** 87. C New Clee *Linc* 86-89; P-in-c Middle Rasen Drax 89; P-in-c W Rasen 89; P-in-c Newton and Toft 89; R Middle Rasen Gp from 89. *The Vicarage, North Street, Middle Rasen, Market Rasen, Lincs LN8 3TS* Market Rasen (0673) 842249

COTTON, Mrs Margaret Elizabeth. b 30. JP79. Newnham Coll Cam BA53 MA66. St Alb Minl Tr Scheme 78. dss 82 **d** 87. Lt Berkhamsted and Bayford, Essendon etc

St Alb 82-87; Hon Par Dn from 87. *49 Sherrardspark Road, Welwyn Garden City, Herts AL8 7LD* Welwyn Garden (0707) 321815

COTTON, Norman Joseph. b 39. Kelham Th Coll 59. **d** 64 **p** 65. C Auckland St Helen *Dur* 64-67; C Withington St Chris *Man* 67-68; C Hucknall Torkard *S'well* 69-71; TV 71-73; TV Fenny Stratford *Ox* 73-75; TV Fenny Stratford and Water Eaton 75-82; P-in-c Broughton and Milton Keynes 82; P-in-c Wavendon w Walton 82; R Walton 82-90; TR Walton Milton Keynes from 90. *The Rectory, Walton Road, Wavendon, Milton Keynes MK17 8LW* Milton Keynes (0908) 582839

COTTON, Miss Patricia Constance. b 32. Gilmore Ho 54. **dss** 60 **d** 87. Forest Gate St Edm *Chelmsf* 60-64; Reading St Giles *Ox* 64-65; Basildon St Martin w H Cross and Laindon *Chelmsf* 65-79; Gt Burstead 79-87; Par Dn Maldon All SS w St Pet from 87. *2 Acacia Drive, Maldon, Essex CM9 6AP* Maldon (0621) 50924

COTTON, Patrick Arthur William. b 46. Essex Univ BA67 Cam Univ MA73. Linc Th Coll 68. **d** 71 **p** 72. C Earlham St Anne *Nor* 71-73; Chapl Down Coll Cam 73-78; V Eaton Socon *St Alb* 78-84; TR Newc Epiphany *Newc* 84-90; V Tunstall w Melling and Leck *Blackb* from 90. *The New Vicarage, Church Lane, Tunstall, Carnforth, Lancs* Tunstall (046834) 376

COTTON, Peter John. b 45. BNC Ox BA66 Bris Univ CQSW76. Cuddesdon Coll 67. **d** 69 **p** 70. C Salford St Phil w St Steph *Man* 69-73; Asst Educn Officer *St Alb* 73-75; C Bris St Geo *Bris* 75-76; C-in-c Portsea St Geo CD *Portsm* 76-80; Soc Resp Adv 78-88; Can Res Portsm Cathl 84-88; V St Laurence in Thanet *Cant* from 88. *St Laurence Vicarage, 2 Newington Road, Ramsgate, Kent CT11 0QT* Thanet (0843) 592478

COTTON, Richard William. b 35. Hertf Coll Ox BA58 MA62. Clifton Th Coll 58. **d** 60 **p** 61. C Harold Wood *Chelmsf* 60-64; C Higher Openshaw *Man* 64-67; Lic to Offic *Man* 67-71; *St Alb* 73-76; Ch Youth Fellowships Assn & Pathfinders 67-71; Nat Sec Pathfinders, CPAS 71-76; V Chislehurst Ch Ch *Roch* from 76. *Christ Church Vicarage, 62 Lubbock Road, Chislehurst, Kent BR7 5JX* 081-467 3185

COTTON, Robert Lloyd. b 58. Mert Coll Ox MA79 Louvain Univ Belgium DipTh81. Westcott Ho Cam 81. **d** 83 **p** 84. C Plaistow St Mary *Roch* 83-86; C Bisley and W End *Guildf* 87-89; P-in-c E Molesey St Paul from 89; Dir of Reader Tr from 90. *St Paul's Vicarage, 101 Palace Road, East Molesey, Surrey KT8 9DU* 081-979 1580

COTTON, Roy William. b 29. Jes Coll Ox BA53 MA61. Chich Th Coll 66. **d** 66 **p** 67. C Eastney *Portsm* 66-71; R Harting *Chich* 71-74; P-in-c Eastbourne St Andr 74-76; V 76-84; R Brede w Udimore from 84. *The Rectory, Brede, Rye, E Sussex TN31 6DX* Brede (0424) 882457

COTTRELL, Bertram Lionel. b 23. Lich Th Coll 51. **d** 54 **p** 56. V Isleworth St Jo *Lon* 63-83; rtd 83; Perm to Offic *Lon* from 83. *13 Sutton Square, Heston, Middx TW5 0JB* 081-572 5034

COTTRELL, Francis St John. b 02. St Chad's Coll Dur BA27 DipTh28 MA30. **d** 28 **p** 29. V Lakenham St Mark *Nor* 38-69; V Nor St Jo Sepulchre 54-57; rtd 69; Perm to Offic *Nor* from 70. *24 Neville Street, Norwich NR2 2PR* Norwich (0603) 660623

COTTRELL, Stephen Geoffrey. b 58. Cen Lon Poly BA79. St Steph Ho Ox 81. **d** 84 **p** 85. C Forest Hill Ch Ch *S'wark* 84-88; C-in-c Parklands St Wilfrid CD *Chich* from 88; Asst Dir of Past Studies Chich Th Coll from 88. *7 Durnford Close, Parklands, Chichester, W Sussex PO19 3AG* Chichester (0243) 783853

COTTRILL, Derek John. b 43. MA. Qu Coll Birm. **d** 82 **p** 83. C Southn Maybush St Pet *Win* 82-85; V Barton Stacey and Bullington etc from 85. *The Rectory, Longparish, Andover, Hants SP11 6PG* Longparish (026472) 215

COUCH, Andrew Nigel. b 48. K Coll Lon BD70 AKC70 Ox Univ CertEd72. St Aug Coll Cant 70. **d** 71 **p** 72. C St Ives *Truro* 71-74; C St Martin-in-the-Fields *Lon* 74-78; USPG from 78; Uruguay 78-85; Argentina from 85. *25 De Mayo 282, 1002 Buenos Aires, Argentina*

COUCHMAN, Anthony Denis. b 37. Sarum Th Coll 66. **d** 69 **p** 70. C Barkingside St Fran *Chelmsf* 69-71; C Chingford SS Pet and Paul 71-76; P-in-c Walthamstow St Barn and St Jas Gt 76-80; V from 80. *St Barnabas' Vicarage, St Barnabas Road, London E17 8JZ* 081-520 5323

COUGHTREY, Miss Sheila Frances. b 48. RSCN73 SRN73 S Bank Poly BSc79. Qu Coll Birm 79. **dss** 84 **d** 87. Sydenham St Bart *S'wark* 81-85; Roehampton H Trin 85-87; Par Dn 87-91; Par Dn Brixton Hill St Sav from

91; Min K Acre LEP from 91. *6 Blenheim Gardens, London SW2 5ET* 081-674 6914

COULING, Albert James. b 10. Linc Th Coll 43. **d** 44 **p** 45. R Bleadon *B & W* 59-78; rtd 78; Perm to Offic *B & W* from 79. *36 Brockley Crescent, Bleadon, Weston-super-Mare, Avon BS24 9LL* Bleadon (0934) 812056

COULING, David Charles. b 36. Open Univ BA89. Qu Coll Birm 61. **d** 63 **p** 64. C Harborne St Faith and St Laur *Birm* 63-66; C E Grinstead St Mary *Chich* 66-70; V Copthorne 70-75; V Eastbourne St Mich 75-82; V Brighton St Matthias 82-83; C-in-c Harton St Lawr CD *Dur* 84-90; V Horsley Hill S Shields from 91. *St Lawrence House, 84 Centenary Avenue, South Shields NE34 6SF* 091-456 1747

COULSON, Louis Morton. b 36. K Coll Lon BA59. Wells Th Coll 59. **d** 61 **p** 62. C E Greenwich Ch Ch w St Andr and St Mich *S'wark* 61-64; C Streatham St Paul 64-67; PV Truro Cathl *Truro* 67-70; R Gidleigh *Ex* 70-72; P-in-c Throwleigh 70-72; R Gidleigh w Throwleigh 72-78; P-in-c Hartland and Welcombe 78-80; V from 80. *The Vicarage, Hartland, Bideford, Devon EX39 6BP* Hartland (0237) 441240

COULSON, Robert Gustavus. b 99. Wycliffe Hall Ox 45. **d** 45 **p** 45. R Stansted *Roch* 50-61; rtd 68. *The Old Vicarage, Moulsford, Wallingford, Oxon* Cholsey (0491) 651368

COULSON, Stephen Hugh. b 60. St Edm Hall Ox BA82 MA88 Lon Univ CertEd83. Wycliffe Hall Ox 85. **d** 88 **p** 89. C Summerfield *Birm* from 88. *Flat 1, Crowther Hall, Weoley Park Road, Selly Oak, Birmingham* 021-472 4744

COULSON, Canon Thomas Stanley. b 32. TCD BA54 MA68. TCD Div Sch 55. **d** 55 **p** 56. C Maghera *D & R* 55-62; I Aghalurcher and Tattykeeran *Clogh* 62-63; I Woodschapel w Gracefield *Arm* from 63; Preb Arm Cathl from 88; RD Tullyhogue from 90. *140 Ballyronan Road, Magherafelt, Co Derry BT45 6HU* Ballyronan (064887) 87230

COULSON, Tony Erik Frank. b 32. St Edm Hall Ox BA55 DipTh56 MA59. Wycliffe Hall Ox 55. **d** 57 **p** 58. C Walthamstow St Mary *Chelmsf* 57-60; C Reading St Jo *Ox* 60-63; V Iver 63-86; R White Waltham w Shottesbrooke from 86. *The Vicarage, White Waltham, Maidenhead, Berks SL6 3JD* Littlewick Green (062882) 2000

COULTER, Edmond James. b 60. QUB BSc82 TCD DipTh87. **d** 87 **p** 88. C Ballymena w Ballyclug *Conn* 87-90; C Knockbreda *D & D* from 90. *28 Church Road, Newtownbreda, Belfast BT8 4AQ* Belfast (0232) 641339

COULTER, John James. b 09. TCD BA32. **d** 32 **p** 33. V Cauldon *Lich* 57-78; V Waterfall 57-78; rtd 78. *8 Hawkestone Avenue, Newport, Shropshire TF10 7SE* Newport (0952) 810230

COULTER, Richard Samuel Scott. b 09. Dur Univ LTh39. Clifton Th Coll 35. **d** 38 **p** 39. Hon CF from 46; V Upton Snodsbury w Broughton Hackett etc *Worc* 61-77; rtd 77. *29 Greenheart Way, Southmoor, Abingdon, Oxon OX13 5DF* Longworth (0865) 820912

COULTHURST, Jeffrey Evans. b 38. Man Univ BA. Local NSM Course 85. **d** 84 **p** 85. NSM Ancaster *Linc* 84-89; NSM Ancaster Wilsford Gp from 89. *5 North Drive, Ancaster, Grantham, Lincs NG32 3RB* Loveden (0400) 30280

COULTON, David Stephen. b 41. Sarum Th Coll 64. **d** 67 **p** 68. C Guildf H Trin w St Mary *Guildf* 67-70; Asst Chapl Radley Coll Abingdon 70-83; Chapl from 83. *Radley College, Abingdon, Oxon OX14 2HR* Abingdon (0235) 34651

COULTON, Very Rev Nicholas Guy. b 40. Lon Univ BD72. Cuddesdon Coll 65. **d** 67 **p** 68. C Pershore w Wick *Worc* 67-70; Bp's Dom Chapl *St Alb* 71-75; P-in-c Bedf St Paul 75-79; V 79-90; Hon Can St Alb 89-90; Provost Newc from 90. *The Cathedral Vicarage, 26 Mitchell Avenue, Jesmond, Newcastle upon Tyne NE2 3LA* 091-281 6554 or 232 1939

COULTON, Philip Ernest. b 31. St Cath Coll Cam BA54 MA58 TCD BD68 Open Univ BA84. Ely Th Coll 55. **d** 57 **p** 58. C Newark w Coddington *S'well* 57-61; Min Can and Sacr Cant Cathl *Cant* 61-63; Min Can Ripon Cathl *Ripon* 63-68; Hd of RE Ashton-under-Lyne Gr Sch 69-84; Perm to Offic *Ches* 70-71; Lic to Offic 71-84; V Ulceby Gp *Linc* 85-89; P-in-c Ingatestone w Buttsbury *Chelmsf* from 89; P-in-c Fryerning w Margaretting from 89. *51 Willow Green, Ingatestone, Essex CM4 0DH* Ingatestone (0277) 353768

COULTON-TORDOFF, Neville Stephen. b 43. Open Univ BA York Univ MSc. N Ord Course 79. **d** 82 **p** 83. NSM Low Harrogate St Mary *Ripon* 82-86; C Horsforth 86-88; V Langcliffe w Stainforth and Horton *Bradf* from 88.

The Vicarage, Stainforth, Settle, N Yorkshire BD24 9PG Settle (0729) 823010

COUND, David Bryan. b 32. Univ of Wales (Lamp) BA52. St Mich Coll Llan. **d** 55 **p** 56. C Aberdare St Fagan *Llan* 55-60; C Roath St Sav 60-61; C Llan w Capel Llanilterne 61-63; V Porth 63-68; P-in-c Englefield *Ox* 68-73; R 73-76; Asst Dioc Youth Officer 68-75; Lic to Offic from 76. *Benny's Cottage, Southend Road, Bradfield, Reading* Bradfield (0734) 744368

COUNSELL, Edwin Charles Robert. b 63. Univ of Wales (Cardiff) BA84. St Steph Ho Ox 85. **d** 88 **p** 89. C Cardiff St Mary and St Steph w St Dyfrig etc *Llan* from 88; Sub-Chapl HM Pris Cardiff from 90. *43 Pentre Street, Grangetown, Cardiff CF1 7QX* Cardiff (0222) 230054

COUNSELL, Michael John Radford. b 35. Pemb Coll Cam BA59 MA63. Ripon Hall Ox 59. **d** 61 **p** 62. C Handsworth St Mary *Birm* 61-63; Singapore 64-68; Vietnam and Cambodia 68-71; Seychelles 72-76; Dean Mahe 73-76; V Harborne St Pet *Birm* 76-89; Relig Consultant to Inter-Ch Travel Ltd 89-90; V Forest Hill St Aug *S'wark* from 90. *St Augustine's Vicarage, 8 Hengrave Road, London SE23 3NW* 081-699 1535

COUPAR, Thomas. b 50. BA. **d** 80 **p** 81. NSM Dunbar *Edin* 80-86; NSM Haddington 80-86; Hd Master Pencaitland Primary Sch E Lothian 80-81; K Meadow Sch E Lothian 81-87; Dioc Supernumerary *Edin* from 87; Primary Educn Adv Fife from 88. *St John's House, 4 Duddingston Crescent, Edinburgh EH15 3AS* 031-669 3390

COUPER, Donald George. b 21. St Jo Coll Dur BA44 LTh44. Tyndale Hall Bris 39. **d** 45 **p** 46. V Hunmanby w Muston *York* 69-74; V Ledsham w Fairburn 74-86; rtd 86. *49 Marton Road, Bridlington, N Humberside YO16 5PR* Bridlington (0262) 676437

COUPER, Jeanette Emily. b 40. S'wark Ord Course 85. **d** 88. Par Dn Mitcham SS Pet and Paul *S'wark* from 88. *55 Brookfield Avenue, Mitcham, Surrey CR4 4BQ* 081-640 7370

COUPER, Jonathan George. b 51. St Jo Coll Dur BA73. Wycliffe Hall Ox 73. **d** 75 **p** 76. C Clifton *York* 75-78; C Darfield *Sheff* 78-81; V Bridlington Quay Ch Ch *York* from 81. *Christ Church Vicarage, 2 Quay Road, Bridlington, N Humberside YO15 2AP* Bridlington (0262) 673538

COUPLAND, Simon Charles. b 59. St Jo Coll Cam BA82 PGCE83 MA85 PhD87. Ridley Hall Cam 88. **d** 91. C Bath St Luke *B & W* from 91. *59 Longfellow Avenue, Bath BA2 4SH* Bath (0225) 480189

COURAGE, Roy Kenneth. b 25. ACCS63 ACIS70. St D Coll Lamp 67. **d** 69 **p** 70. C Blaenavon w Capel Newydd *Mon* 69-71; R Blaina 71-78; V Blackwood 78-89; rtd 89. *Ysgubor Wen, Tylsaf Farm, Llechryd, Rhymney, Gwent NP2 5QU* Rhymney (0685) 841260

COURT, David. b 58. **d** 91. C Barton Seagrave w Warkton *Pet* from 91. *Rectory Cottage, St Botolph's Road, Kettering, Northants NN15 6SR* Kettering (0536) 517760

COURT, Kenneth Reginald. b 36. AKC60. **d** 61 **p** 62. C Garforth *Ripon* 61-63; C Harrogate St Wilfrid 63-65; V Thornbury *Bradf* 65-73; Prec Leic Cathl *Leic* 73-76; V Douglas St Matt *S & M* 76-84; V Syston *Leic* from 84; RD Goscote from 90. *The Vicarage, Upper Church Street, Syston, Leicester LE7 8HR* Leicester (0533) 608276

COURT, Martin Jeremy. b 61. GRNCM84 Nottm Univ BTh89. Linc Th Coll 86. **d** 89 **p** 90. C Thurmaston *Leic* from 89. *118 Dovedale Road, Thurmaston, Leicester LE4 8ND* Leicester (0533) 695440

COURT, Nicholas James Keble. b 56. Chich Th Coll 86. **d** 88 **p** 89. C Golders Green *Lon* 88-91; C Westbury-on-Trym H Trin *Bris* from 91. *16 Southfield Road, Bristol BS9 3BH* Bristol (0272) 621336

COURTAULD, Augustine Christopher Caradoc. b 34. Trin Coll Cam BA58. Westcott Ho Cam 58. **d** 60 **p** 61. C Oldham St Mary *Man* 60-63; Chapl Trin Coll Cam 63-68; Chapl The Lon Hosp (Whitechapel) 68-78; V Wilton Place St Paul *Lon* from 78. *St Paul's Vicarage, 32 Wilton Place, London SW1X 8SH* 071-235 1810 or 235 3460

COURTIE, Dr John Malcolm. b 42. BNC Ox BA65 DPhil72 St Jo Coll Dur BA76 DipTh77. Cranmer Hall Dur 74. **d** 77 **p** 78. C Mossley Hill St Matt and St Jas *Liv* 77-80; V Litherland St Paul Hatton Hill 80-84; Wellingborough Sch 84-89; Hon C Wollaston and Strixton *Pet* 84-89; V Woodford Halse w Eydon from 89. *The Vicarage, Woodford Halse, Daventry, Northants NN11 6RE* Byfield (0327) 61477

COURTNEY, Brian Joseph. b 44. CITC 70. **d** 73 **p** 74. C Willowfield *D & D* 73-78; I Aghavea *Clogh* 78-83; I Carrickfergus *Conn* from 83. *The Rectory, 12 Harwood* Gardens, Carrickfergus, Co Antrim BT38 7LZ Carrickfergus (09603) 63244

COURTNEY, Michael Monlas. b 19. Coll of Resurr Mirfield 58. **d** 60 **p** 61. V N Keyham *Ex* 68-73; TV Sidmouth, Woolbrook and Salcombe Regis 73-79; TV Sidmouth, Woolbrook, Salcombe Regis etc 79-84; rtd 84; Perm to Offic *Ex* from 86. *Furzehill Farm House, Sidbury, Sidmouth EX10 0RE* Sidbury (03957) 440

COUSINS, Christopher William. b 44. Oak Hill Th Coll DipHE87. **d** 87 **p** 88. C Wallasey St Hilary *Ches* 87-90; R Rollesby w Burgh w Billockby w Ashby w Oby etc *Nor* from 90. *The Rectory, Rollesby, Great Yarmouth, Norfolk NR29 5HJ* Great Yarmouth (0493) 740323

COUSINS, Graham John. b 55. Oak Hill Th Coll BA91. **d** 91. C Birkenhead St Jas w St Bede *Ches* from 91. *3 Buckingham Avenue, Claughton, Birkenhead L43 8TD* 051-652 9180

COUSINS, Herbert Ralph. b 13. Bps' Coll Cheshunt 52. **d** 54 **p** 55. R Clophill *St Alb* 71-78; rtd 78. *Evensong, Sand Road, Weston-super-Mare, Avon BS22 9UF* Weston-super-Mare (0934) 413260

COUSINS, Chan Philip John. b 35. K Coll Cam BA58 MA62. Cuddesdon Coll 59. **d** 61 **p** 62. C Marton *Blackb* 61-63; PV Truro Cathl *Truro* 63-67; Ethiopia 67-75; V Henleaze *Bris* 75-84; RD Clifton 79-84; Provost All SS Cathl Cairo 84-89; Chan Malta Cathl *Eur* from 89; Chapl Valletta w Sliema from 89. *Chancellor's Lodge, Valletta, Malta* Malta (356) 225714

COUSSENS, Mervyn Haigh Wingfield. b 47. St Jo Coll Nottm BTh74. **d** 74 **p** 75. C Clifton Ch Ch w Em *Bris* 74-77; C Morden *S'wark* 77-83; V Patchway *Bris* 83-91; R Lutterworth w Cotesbach *Leic* from 91. *The Rectory, Coventry Road, Lutterworth, Leics LE17 4SH* Lutterworth (0455) 552669

COUSSMAKER, Canon Colin Richard Chad. b 34. Worc Coll Ox BA57 BSc58 MA63 MSc85. Chich Th Coll 59. **d** 60 **p** 61. C Newtown St Luke *Win* 60-64; C Whitley Ch Ch *Ox* 64-67; Chapl Istanbul *Eur* 67-72; Chapl Sliema 72-77; Chapl Antwerp St Boniface from 77; Can Brussels Cathl from 81. *Gretrystraat 39, 2018 Antwerp, Belgium* Antwerp (3) 239-3339

COUTTS, Ian. b 56. Warw Univ BA77 Jes Coll Ox MSc80 CQSW80. St Jo Coll Nottm DipTh89. **d** 89 **p** 90. C Hamstead St Bernard *Birm* from 89. *33 Hamstead Road, Birmingham B43 5BA* 021-357 4741

COUTTS, James Allan. b 58. Fitzw Coll Cam MA. St Jo Coll Nottm MTh84. **d** 84 **p** 85. C Dishley and Thorpe Acre *Leic* 84-88; TV Kirby Muxloe from 88. *106 Hinckley Road, Leicester Forest East, Leicester LE3 3JS* Leicester (0533) 386344

COUTTS, James Walter Cargill. b 35. Univ of Wales (Lamp) BA57 CCC Cam BA59. St Mich Coll Llan 59. **d** 60 **p** 61. C Cardiff St Mary *Llan* 60-63; C Greenford H Cross *Lon* 63-67; C Swansea St Gabr *S & B* 67-71; V Llanwrtyd w Llanddulas in Tir Abad etc 71-78; V Brecon St Dav 78-80; V Brecon St David w Llanspyddid and Llanilltyd 80-84; V Mon from 84. *The Vicarage, The Parade, Monmouth, Gwent NP5 3PA* Monmouth (0600) 3141

COUTTS, Robin Iain Philip. b 52. Sarum & Wells Th Coll. **d** 83 **p** 84. C Alverstoke *Portsm* 83-86; Min Leigh Park St Clare CD 86-89; V Warren Park St Clare 89-91; V Purbrook from 91. *The Vicarage, Purbrook, Portsmouth PO7 5RS* Waterlooville (0705) 262307

COVE, Kenneth John. b 34. Lich Th Coll 58. **d** 60 **p** 61. C Crosland Moor *Wakef* 60-63; C Halifax St Jo Bapt 63-65; V Wakef St Jo 65-73; V Appleby *Carl* 73-78; RD Appleby 74-78; V Ambleside w Brathay 78-87; V Thames Ditton *Guildf* from 87. *The Vicarage, Summer Road, Thames Ditton, Surrey KT7 0QQ* 081-398 3446

COVE, Tom Griffiths William. b 10. **d** 64 **p** 65. OSB from 59; Lic to Offic *Ox* 65-84; Australia from 84. *St Mark's Priory, PO Box 111, Camperdown, Victoria 3260, Australia* Camperdown (55) 932848

COVENTRY, Preb Frank. b 13. K Coll Lon BA35 Em Coll Cam PhD42. Linc Th Coll 45. **d** 46 **p** 47. R St Marylebone w H Trin *Lon* 58-78; Preb St Paul's Cathl 73-78; rtd 78; Perm to Offic *Lon* from 80. *2B Upper Park Road, London NW3 2UP* 071-722 7298

COVENTRY, Archdeacon of. See RUSSELL, Ven Harold Ian Lyle

COVENTRY, Bishop of. See BARRINGTON-WARD, Rt Rev Simon

COVENTRY, Provost of. See PETTY, Very Rev John Fitzmaurice

COVINGTON, Canon Michael William Rock. b 38. Open Univ BA78. Sarum Th Coll 60. **d** 63 **p** 64. C Daventry *Pet* 63-66; C Woolwich St Mary w H Trin *S'wark* 66-68; C Northn All SS w St Kath *Pet* 68-71; V Longthorpe

71-86; Hon Min Can Pet Cathl 75-86; Can Pet Cathl from 86; V Warmington, Tansor, Cotterstock and Fotheringhay from 86; Warden Dioc Assn of Readers from 87; RD Oundle from 89. *The Vicarage, Warmington, Peterborough PE8 6TE* Oundle (0832) 280263

COWARD, Colin Charles Malcolm. b 45. Westcott Ho Cam 75. **d** 78 **p** 79. C Camberwell St Geo *S'wark* 78-82; P-in-c Wandsworth St Faith 82-90; V from 90. *2 Alma Road, London SW18 1AB* 081-874 8567

COWARD, Frederic Edward. b 06. Man Univ BA31. Ripon Hall Ox 30. **d** 31 **p** 32. R Tockenham *Sarum* 66-73; V Clyffe Pypard 66-73; V Clyffe Pypard and Tockenham 73-80; rtd 80; Perm to Offic *Ox* from 83. *Flat 17, Purcells Court, George Lane, Marlborough, Wilts SN8 4BS* Marlborough (0672) 516205

COWARD, Raymond. b 41. NW Ord Course 79. **d** 82 **p** 83. C Turton *Man* 82-84; C Heaton Ch Ch 84-86; V Rochdale St Geo w St Alb from 86. *13 Brooklands Court, Bury Road, Rochdale, Lancs OL11 4EJ* Rochdale (0706) 39743

COWBURN, John Charles. b 48. Sarum & Wells Th Coll 88. **d** 90 **p** 91. C Andover w Foxcott *Win* from 90. *2 Madrid Road, Andover, Hants SP10 1JR* Andover (0264) 359625

COWDREY, Herbert Edward John. b 26. Trin Coll Ox BA49 MA51. St Steph Ho Ox 50. **d** 52 **p** 53. Tutor St Steph Ho Ox 52-56; Chapl 54-56; Asst Chapl Ex Coll Ox 52-56; Lic to Offic *Ox* from 52; Fell St Edm Hall Ox from 56; Chapl 56-78. *St Edmund Hall, Oxford OX1 4AR* Oxford (0865) 279015

COWDRY, Gilbert. b 26. Wells Th Coll 70. **d** 72 **p** 73. C Bath Twerton-on-Avon *B & W* 72-76; V Long Sutton w Long Load 76-82; TV S Molton, Nymet St George, High Bray etc 82-86; TV S Molton w Nymet St George, High Bray etc from 86; RD S Molton from 87. *Springfield, East Street, North Molton, Devon EX36 3HX* North Molton (05984) 325

COWELL, Arthur John. b 10. Wycliffe Hall Ox 40. **d** 41 **p** 42. V Prittlewell St Pet *Chelmsf* 60-80; Chapl Southend Gen Hosp 68-80; rtd 80; Perm to Offic *Chelmsf* from 80. *Nazareth House, London Road, Southend-on-Sea* Southend-on-Sea (0702) 345627

COWELL, Peter James. b 58. Peterho Cam BA80 MA84. Coll of Resurr Mirfield 80. **d** 82 **p** 83. C Folkestone St Sav *Cant* 82-86; Chapl Asst St Thos Hosp Lon 86-90; Chapl R Lon Hosps (Mile End and Whitechapel) from 90. *The Chaplain's Office, The Royal London Hospital, London E1 1BB* 071-377 7000 or 377 7385

COWEN, Brian. b 45. Nottm Univ BTh77. Linc Th Coll 73. **d** 77 **p** 78. C Hexham *Newc* 77-80; C Eastnor *Heref* 80-81; C Ledbury 80-81; C Ledbury w Eastnor 81; TV Glendale Gp *Newc* 81-90; V Lesbury w Alnmouth from 90. *The Vicarage, Lesbury, Alnwick, Northd NE66 3AU* Alnwick (0665) 830281

COWEN, Peter Stewart. b 42. AKC65. **d** 67 **p** 68. C Wandsworth St Paul *S'wark* 67-71; Refugee Projects Officer Middle E Coun Ch 71-75; Hon C Harringay St Paul *Lon* 75; V 78-80; Cyprus 75-78. *Address temp unknown*

COWEN, Richard James. b 48. St Jo Coll Nottm. **d** 83 **p** 84. C Kenilworth St Jo *Cov* 83-87; TV Becontree W *Chelmsf* from 87. *St Cedd's Vicarage, 185 Lodge Avenue, Dagenham, Essex RM8 2HQ* 081-592 5900

COWGILL, Michael. b 48. Linc Th Coll 84. **d** 86 **p** 87. C Bolton St Jas w St Chrys *Bradf* 86-89; V Buttershaw St Paul from 89. *The Vicarage, Wibsey Park Avenue, Bradford, W Yorkshire BD6 3QA* Bradford (0274) 676735

COWIE, Derek Edward. b 33. S'wark Ord Course 70. **d** 73 **p** 74. C Maldon All SS w St Pet *Chelmsf* 73-76; R Bowers Gifford w N Benfleet 76-79; V Chelmsf Ascension 79-84; V Shrub End from 84. *All Saints' Vicarage, 270 Shrub End Road, Colchester CO3 4RL* Colchester (0206) 574178

COWIE, Leonard Wallace. b 19. Pemb Coll Ox BA41 DipTh43 MA46 Lon Univ PhD54. Ripon Hall Ox 42. **d** 43 **p** 44. C High Wycombe All SS *Ox* 43-45; Tutor Coll SS Mark and Jo Chelsea 45-68; Chapl 45-47; Tutor Whitelands Coll Putney 68-82; Lic to Offic *S'wark* from 68. *38 Stratton Road, London SW19 3JG* 081-542 5036

COWLAN, William Thomas. b 12. OBE. Leeds Univ BD. **d** 79 **p** 79. NSM Kenton w Mamhead and Powderham *Ex* 79-82; Perm to Offic from 82. *4 Court Hull, Kenton, Exeter EX6 8NA* Starcross (0626) 890210

COWLEY, Charles Frederick. b 27. Trin Coll Cam BA53 MA56. Wells Th Coll 53. **d** 55 **p** 56. V Aldringham *St E* 61-86; rtd 86; Perm to Offic *St E* from 86.

The Vicarage, Aldringham, Leiston, Suffolk IP16 4QF Leiston (0728) 830632

COWLEY, Canon Colin Patrick. b 02. Hertf Coll Ox BA25 MA28. Wells Th Coll. **d** 26 **p** 27. R Wonston *Win* 55-71; rtd 71. *Brendon House, Park Road, Winchester SO23 7BE* Winchester (0962) 66621

COWLEY, Geoffrey Willis. b 17. FICE50 FRTPI54. St Alb Minl Tr Scheme 77. **d** 80 **p** 81. NSM Stevington *St Alb* 80-87; rtd 87; Lic to Offic *St Alb* from 87. *The Cottage, 30 High Street, Carlton, Bedford MK43 7LA* Bedford (0234) 720451

COWLEY, Herbert Kenneth. b 20. Glouc Sch of Min 75. **d** 79 **p** 80. Hon C Lydney w Aylburton *Glouc* 79-89; rtd 89. *17 Kimberley Drive, Lydney, Glos GL15 5AD* Dean (0594) 842880

COWLEY, Leslie. b 22. St Jo Coll Nottm 70. **d** 71 **p** 72. C Worksop St Jo *S'well* 71-73; P-in-c Awsworth 74-77; V Basford St Leodegarius 77-88; rtd 88; Perm to Offic *Linc* from 88. *12 Ridgeway, Nettleham, Lincoln* Lincoln (0522) 752447

COWLEY, Samuel Henry. b 44. St Jo Coll Nottm 85. **d** 87 **p** 88. C Hadleigh w Layham and Shelley *St E* from 90. *74 Anne Beaumont Way, Hadleigh, Ipswich IP7 6SB* Hadleigh (0473) 823235

COWLING, Canon Douglas Anderson. b 19. Leeds Univ BA40. Coll of Resurr Mirfield 40. **d** 42 **p** 43. V Spalding St Paul *Linc* 61-84; Can and Preb Linc Cathl from 77; rtd 84. *24 Campbell's Close, Spalding, Lincs PE11 2UH* Spalding (0775) 767044

COWLING, John Francis. b 32. K Coll Cam BA56. Linc Th Coll 56. **d** 58 **p** 59. C Leigh St Mary *Man* 58-61; Sec SCM in Schs Liv and Ches 61-65; V Bolton St Matt 65-71; V Bolton St Matt w St Barn 71-75; V Southport H Trin *Liv* 75-91; R St Olave Hart Street w All Hallows Staining etc *Lon* from 91. *St Olave's Rectory, 8 Hart Street, London EC3R 7NB* 071-488 4318

COWLING, Simon Charles. b 59. G&C Coll Cam BA80 MA88 K Coll Lon PGCE82. Linc Th Coll BTh91. **d** 91. C Potternewton *Ripon* from 91. *8 Granton Road, Leeds LS7 3LZ* Leeds (0532) 626225

COWLING, Wilfred Edmund. b 14. Dur Univ BA38 MA42. St Aid Birkenhead 38. **d** 40 **p** 41. V Kirkburn *York* 57-83; V Garton on the Wolds 57-83; RD Harthill 63-73 and 78-80; rtd 83. *14 Ashleigh Drive, Beeford, Driffield, N Humberside YO25 8AU* Beeford (026288) 277

COWMEADOW, Derek Lowe. b 28. Wells Th Coll 68. **d** 70 **p** 71. C Ledbury *Heref* 70-72; C Llanrhos *St As* 72-74; V Bringhurst w Gt Easton *Leic* 74-77; P-in-c Coln St Aldwyn w Hatherop and Quenington *Glouc* 77-82; V Coln St Aldwyn, Hatherop, Quenington etc from 82. *The Vicarage, Coln St Aldwyns, Cirencester, Glos GL7 5AG* Coln St Aldwyns (028575) 207

COWPER, Christopher Herbert. b 44. AKC67 Open Univ BA76. **d** 68 **p** 69. C Pitsmoor *Sheff* 68-71; C Ulverston St Mary w H Trin *Carl* 71-74; R Kirklinton w Hethersgill and Scaleby 74-83; V Bridekirk from 83; Chapl Dovenby Hall Hosp Cockermouth from 83. *The Vicarage, Bridekirk, Cockermouth, Cumbria CA13 0PE* Cockermouth (0900) 822257

COWPERTHWAITE, John. b 20. St Jo Coll Dur. **d** 53 **p** 54. V Ryhill *Wakef* 65-74; V Royston 74-80; V Felkirk w Brierley 80-87; rtd 87. *99 Fishponds Drive, Crigglestone, Wakefield, W Yorkshire WF4 3PD* Wakefield (0924) 257604

COX, Alan John. b 34. Lon Coll of Div ALCD65 LTh. **d** 65 **p** 66. C Kirkheaton *Wakef* 65-67; C Keynsham w Queen Charlton *B & W* 67-71; R Chipstable w Huish Champflower and Clatworthy 71-76; TV Strood *Roch* 76-80; V Strood St Fran 80-83; R Keston from 83. *The Rectory, 24 Commonside, Keston, Kent BR2 6BP* Farnborough (0689) 853186

COX, Alexander James. b 12. Pemb Coll Ox BA34 MA43. Westcott Ho Cam 34. **d** 36 **p** 37. CR from 63; Barbados 64-75; rtd 82. *House of the Resurrection, Mirfield, W Yorkshire WF14 0BN* Mirfield (0924) 494318

COX, Bryan Leslie. b 41. Qu Coll Birm 77. **d** 79 **p** 80. C Stantonbury *Ox* 79-82; TV Fenny Stratford and Water Eaton 82-89; P-in-c Elford *Lich* from 89; Dioc Past Counsellor from 89. *The Vicarage, Church Road, Elford, Tamworth, Staffs B79 9DA* Harlaston (082785) 212

COX, Canon Christopher George Stuart. b 17. St Jo Coll Dur BA38 DipTh39 MA41. **d** 40 **p** 41. V Knighton St Jo *Leic* 69 77; R Appleby 77-81; R Appleby Magna and Swepstone w Snarestone 81-83; rtd 83; Perm to Offic *Leic* from 83. *Fairhaven, South Street, Ashby-de-la-Zouch, Leics LE6 5BR* Ashby-de-la-Zouch (0530) 414198

COX

COX, David. b 20. SS Coll Cam BA46 MA48 BD57. Qu Coll Birm 47. **d** 48 **p** 49. V Chatham All SS *Roch* 55-75; V Southborough St Thos 75-87; rtd 87. *9 Hollicondane Road, Ramsgate, Kent CT11 7JP* Thanet (0843) 585775

COX, David John. b 51. S Bank Poly HNC76. Qu Coll Birm 76. **d** 79 **p** 80. C Brampton Bierlow *Sheff* 79-82; Miss Partner CMS 82-88; Malaysia 83-88; V Friarmere *Man* from 88. *The Vicarage, 1 Cobler's Hill, Delph, Oldham OL3 5HT* Saddleworth (0457) 874209

COX, Canon Eric William. b 30. Dur Univ BA54. Wells Th Coll 54. **d** 56 **p** 57. C Sutton in Ashfield St Mary *S'well* 56-59; Asst Chapl Brussels *Eur* 59-62; V Winnington *Ches* 62-71; V Middlewich 71-76; Chapl Leighton Hosp Crewe from 73; P-in-c Biley *Ches* 73-76; V Middlewich w Byley from 76; RD Middlewich from 80; Hon Can Ches Cathl from 84. *St Michael's Vicarage, 37 Queen Street, Middlewich, Cheshire CW10 9AR* Middlewich (060684) 3124

COX, Frank Allen. b 09. Dur Univ LTh51. Lon Coll of Div 29. **d** 32 **p** 33. P-in-c Ashbourne St Jo *Derby* 70-74; rtd 74. *c/o Flint, Bishop & Barnett, 825A Osmaston Road, Allenton, Derby DE2 9BQ* Derby (0332) 365497

COX, Geoffrey Sidney Randel. b 33. Mert Coll Ox BA56 MA60. Tyndale Hall Bris. **d** 58 **p** 59. C St Paul's Cray St Barn CD *Roch* 58-61; C Bromley Ch Ch 61-64; V Gorsley w Cliffords Mesne *Glouc* 64-79; V Hucclecote 79-89; V Wollaston and Strixton *Pet* from 89. *The Vicarage, Wollaston, Wellingborough, Northants NN9 7RW* Wellingborough (0933) 664256

COX, George William. b 25. St Steph Ho Ox 83. **d** 86 **p** 87. NSM Abingdon *Ox* from 86. *103 Bath Street, Abingdon, Oxon OX14 1EG* Abingdon (0235) 521375

COX, James Edward Thomas. b 20. Sheff Univ BA47. Cuddesdon Coll 47. **d** 49 **p** 50. Chapl Abbey Sch Malvern 64-79; V Lt Malvern *Worc* 65-85; P-in-c 85-90; rtd 85. *Hazel Hollow, 18 Kings Road, Malvern Wells, Worcs WR14 4HL* Malvern (0684) 564392

COX, Canon James Gordon. b 12. Poitiers Univ Diplome d'Etudes Francaises31 Hertf Coll Ox BA34 MA38. Cuddesdon Coll 37. **d** 38 **p** 39. R Thorpe Malsor *Pet* 63-76; Dir of Educn 53-76; Can Pet Cathl 75-80; V Warmington 76-80; rtd 80; Lic to Offic *Pet* 80-85; Perm to Offic Ely from 80; Pet from 85. *9 De Vere Road, Thrapston, Kettering, Northants NN14 4JN* Thrapston (08012) 3553

COX, John Anthony. b 45. Hull Univ BA67 Birm Univ DipTh72. Qu Coll Birm 71. **d** 73 **p** 74. C Buckm *Ox* 73-76; C Whitley Ch Ch 76-81; V Reading St Agnes w St Paul 81-83; V Chaddesley Corbett and Stone *Worc* from 83. *The Vicarage, Butts Lane, Stone, Kidderminster, Worcs DY10 4BH* Kidderminster (0562) 69438

COX, John Edgar. b 26. CEng MIEE56 Lon Univ BSc50 MSc69. Bps' Coll Cheshunt 67. **d** 68 **p** 69. NSM Harlow St Mary Magd *Chelmsf* 68-76; C S Petherwin w Trewen *Truro* 77-79; P-in-c 79-82; P-in-c Lawhitton 81-82; P-in-c Lezant 81-82; R Lezant w Lawhitton and S Petherwin w Trewen 82-83; V Breage w Germoe from 83. *The Vicarage, Breage, Helston, Cornwall TR13 9PN* Helston (0326) 573449

COX, John Hamilton. b 23. Univ of Wales (Cardiff) BA48. St Mich Coll Llan 49. **d** 51 **p** 52. V Tylorstown *Llan* 61-85; V Llansawel w Briton Ferry 85-89; rtd 89. *59 Cwrt Sart, Briton Ferry, Neath, W Glam SA11 2SR* Briton Ferry (0639) 820515

COX, Canon John Stuart. b 40. Fitzw Ho Cam BA62 MA66 Linacre Coll Ox BA67 Birm Univ DPS68. Wycliffe Hall Ox 64. **d** 68 **p** 69. C Prescot *Liv* 68-71; C Birm St Geo *Birm* 71-73; R 73-78; Selection Sec ACCM 78-83; Hon C Orpington All SS *Roch* 78-83; Dioc Dir of Ords *S'wark* 83-91; Can Res and Treas S'wark Cathl 83-91; V Roehampton H Trin from 91. *The Vicarage, 7 Ponsonby Road, London SW15 4LA* 081-788 9460

COX, Leonard James William. b 27. Sarum & Wells Th Coll 79. **d** 81 **p** 82. C Hythe *Cant* 81-84; V Thanington from 84. *The Vicarage, 70 Thanington Road, Canterbury, Kent CT1 3XE* Canterbury (0227) 464516

COX, Martin Lloyd. b 57. **d** 88 **p** 89. C Risca *Mon* 88-91; TV Pontypool from 91. *St Luke's Vicarage, Pontnewynydd, Pontypool, Gwent NP4 8LW*

COX, Paul Graham. b 40. Keele Univ BA62 DipEd62 Ibadan Univ Nigeria 63. Westcott Ho Cam 77. **d** 78 **p** 79. NSM Kemsing w Woodlands *Roch* 78-80; Hd Master and Chapl St Mich Sch Otford 81-90; C Petham and Waltham w Lower Hardres etc *Cant* from 90; Bp's Officer for NSM from 91. *The Vicarage, Pilgrims Lane, Hastingleigh, Ashford, Kent TN25 5HP* Elmsted (023375) 414

COX, Peter Allard. b 55. Univ of Wales (Lamp) BA76. Wycliffe Hall Ox 77. **d** 79 **p** 80. C Penarth All SS *Llan*

79-82; V Aberpergwm and Blaengwrach 82-86; V Bargoed and Deri w Brithdir from 86. *The Vicarage, Moorland Road, Bargoed, M Glam CF8 8UH* Bargoed (0443) 831069

COX, Mrs Sheila Stuart. b 41. Robert Gordon's Inst of Tech TDDSc62 Aber Coll of Educn CertEd63. Edin Dioc NSM Course 85. **d** 88. NSM Livingston LEP *Edin* from 88; Asst Chapl St Jo and Bangour Hosps W Lothian from 89. *The Shieling, 6 Pentland Park, Livingston, West Lothian EH54 5NR* Livingston (0506) 34874

COX, Dr Simon John. b 53. MIBiol79 CBiol79 Qu Mary Coll Lon BSc74 Liv Univ PhD81 Selw Coll Cam BA81 MA85 Lanc Univ MA87. Ridley Hall Cam 79. **d** 82 **p** 83. C Livesey *Blackb* 82-85; C Cheadle Hulme St Andr *Ches* 85-89; V Disley from 89. *37 Martlett Avenue, Disley, Stockport, Cheshire SK12 2JH* Disley (0663) 762068

COX, Stephen. b 38. Open Univ BA80. Bps' Coll Cheshunt 65. **d** 68 **p** 69. C Gaywood, Bawsey and Mintlyn *Nor* 68-72; Youth Chapl 72-82; C N Lynn w St Marg and St Nic 73-82; Chapl Guildf Coll of Tech 82-87; Chapl Surrey Univ *Guildf* from 82. *6 Cathedral Close, Guildford, Surrey GU2 5TL* Guildford (0483) 576380

COX, Stephen John Wormleighton. b 54. New Coll Ox MA79 Fitzw Coll Cam BA79. Ridley Hall Cam 77. **d** 80 **p** 81. C Clapton Park All So *Lon* 80-85; TV Hackney Marsh 85-87; V Holloway St Mary w St Jas 87-88; P-in-c Barnsbury St Dav w St Clem 87-88; V Holloway St Mary Magd from 88. *St Mary Magdalene Vicarage, 28 Witherington Road, London N5 1PP* 071-607 3919

COX, Vernon James Frederick. b 37. Birm Univ DPS83. Sarum Th Coll 66. **d** 69 **p** 70. C Salisbury St Fran *Sarum* 69-72; P-in-c Winterbourne Earls w Winterbourne Dauntsey etc 72-73; TV Bourne Valley 73-80; Chapl Jos Sheldon Hosp Birm from 80; Chapl Rubery Hill Hosp Birm from 80. *39 Ashmead Drive, Rednal, Birmingham B45 8AB* 021-445 4468 or 453 3771

COX, Wallace Francis. b 13. Bris Univ BA34. Sarum Th Coll 33. **d** 36 **p** 37. V Burrington *B & W* 71-78; rtd 78; Perm to Offic *B & W* from 79. *9 Carlton Court, Wells, Somerset BA5 1FF* Wells (0749) 670406

COX, Canon William Arthur Moncrieff. b 13. TCD BA35 MA50. **d** 37 **p** 38. I Bunclody *C & O* 68-83; Treas Ferns Cathl 81-83; rtd 83. *c/o Kilgolan House, Kilcormac, Birr, Co Offaly, Irish Republic*

COX, William John Francis. b 24. SW Minl Tr Course. **d** 77 **p** 78. NSM Liskeard w St Keyne and St Pinnock *Truro* 77-82; NSM Liskeard w St Keyne, St Pinnock and Morval 82-86; NSM N Hill w Altarnon, Bolventor and Lewannick 86-87; TV Bolventor from 87. *The Rectory, North Hill, Launceston, Cornwall PL15 7PQ* Coads Green (0566) 82806

COYLE, Matthew Ernest. b 11. Lon Coll of Div 31. **d** 34 **p** 35. R Weare Giffard w Landcross *Ex* 62-69; rtd 69. *Flat 20, The Octagon, Middle Street, Taunton, Somerset TA1 1RT* Taunton (0823) 322142

COYNE, John Edward. b 55. Oak Hill Th Coll BA79. **d** 79 **p** 80. C Cheadle Hulme St Andr *Ches* 79-81; C Macclesfield St Mich 81-83; V Stalybridge H Trin and Ch Ch 83-88; Chapl RAF from 88. *c/o MOD, Adastral House, Theobald's Road, London WC1X 8RU* 071-430 7268

COYNE, Terence Roland Harry. b 39. Chich Th Coll 64. **d** 66 **p** 67. C Meir *Lich* 66-69; C Horninglow 69-72; V Walsall St Gabr Fullbrook from 72. *St Gabriel's Vicarage, Walstead Road, Walsall WS5 4LZ* Walsall (0922) 22583

COZENS, Mrs Audrey Lilian. b 35. St Hugh's Coll Ox BA56 MA84. Gilmore Course 79. **dss** 82 **d** 87. Shenfield *Chelmsf* 82-87; Par Dn 87-89; Par Dn Westcliff St Andr from 89. *40 Beedell Avenue, Westcliff-on-Sea, Essex SS0 9JU* Southend-on-Sea (0702) 433902

COZENS, Daniel Harry. b 44. Oak Hill Th Coll DipTh70. **d** 71 **p** 72. C St Paul's Cray St Barn *Roch* 71-74; C Deptford St Nic w Ch Ch *S'wark* 74-76; C Deptford St Nic and St Luke 76-78; Dioc Missr *Ely* from 78. *The Rectory, 73 High Street, Coton, Cambridge CB3 7PL* Madingley (0954) 210239

✠**CRABB, Most Rev Frederick Hugh Wright.** b 15. Lon Univ BD. Wycliffe Coll Toronto 80 ALCD39. **d** 39 **p** 40 **c** 75. C W Teignmouth *Ex* 39-41; C Plymouth St Andr 41-42; CMS 42-51; Sudan 42-51; Prin Bp Gwynne Coll 42-51; Vice-Prin Lon Coll of Div 51-57; Chaplain from 57; Prin Em Coll Saskatoon 57-67; Bp Athabasca 75-83; Abp Rupertsland 77-83. *3483 Chippendale Drive, Calgary, Alberta, Canada, T2L 0W7*

CRABB, Paul Anthony. b 58. St Chad's Coll Dur BSc79 Leeds Univ PGCE80. Qu Coll Birm 90. **d** 91. C Gomersal *Wakef* from 91. *12 Woodlands Crescent, Gomersal,*

Cleckheaton, W Yorkshire BD19 4SP Cleckheaton (0274) 870396

CRABTREE, Stephen. b 56. Nottm Univ BTh80. Linc Th Coll 76. **d** 80 **p** 81. C Chorley St Pet *Blackb* 80-83; C Blackpool St Steph 83-84; C Penwortham St Mary 84-88; R Mareham-le-Fen and Revesby *Linc* from 88. *The Rectory, Mareham-le-Fen, Boston, Lincs PE22 7QU* Mareham-le-Fen (065886) 502

CRABTREE, Victor. b 18. Kelham Th Coll 36. **d** 43 **p** 44. R Shirland *Derby* 66-84; P-in-c Brackenfield w Wessington 77-79; rtd 84. *31 Pinelands, Briergate, Haxby, York YO3 8YT* York (0904) 761941

CRACE, John Allan. b 21. DSC43. Master Mariner 62. Wells Th Coll 62. **d** 64 **p** 65. V Milton Lilbourne w Easton Royal *Sarum* 67-86; R Wootton Rivers 71-86; RD Pewsey 79-84; rtd 86; Perm to Offic Win & Portsm from 86. *Venables, Steep Marsh, Petersfield, Hants GU32 2BP* Petersfield (0730) 63553

CRADDOCK, Brian Arthur. b 40. Chich Th Coll 67. **d** 70 **p** 71. C Stoke-upon-Trent *Lich* 70-74; Bermuda 75-89; P-in-c Bury and Houghton *Chich* from 89; Chapl St Mich Sch Burton Park from 89. *The Vicarage, Church Lane, Bury, Pulborough, W Sussex RH20 1PB* Bury (0798) 831677

CRADDUCK, Martin Charles. b 50. Hull Univ BSc71. St Jo Coll Nottm DipTh77. **d** 79 **p** 80. C W Kilburn St Luke w St Simon and St Jude *Lon* 79-83; C Oxhey All SS *St Alb* 83-86; Asst Chapl HM Pris Man 86-87; Dep Chapl HM Young Offender Inst Glen Parva 87-89; Chapl HM Pris Stocken from 89. *35 Worcester Road, Grantham, Lincs NG31 8SF* Grantham (0476) 71351

CRAFT, William Newham. b 46. MIPM70 Lon Univ BSc68. Oak Hill Th Coll 87. **d** 89 **p** 90. C Werrington *Pet* from 90. *66 Barbers Hill, Werrington, Peterborough PE4 5ED* Peterborough (0733) 323146

✠**CRAGG, Rt Rev Albert Kenneth.** b 13. Jes Coll Ox BA34 MA38 DPhil50 Huron Coll Hon DD63. Tyndale Hall Bris 34. **d** 36 **p** 37 **c** 70. C Tranmere St Cath *Ches* 36-39; Lebanon 39-47; R Longworth *Ox* 47-51; USA 51-56; Can Res Jerusalem 56-59; St Aug Coll Cant 59-60; Sub-Warden 60-61; Warden 61-67; Hon Can Cant Cathl *Cant* 61-80; Hon Can Jerusalem 65-73; Asst Bp 70-73; Bye-Fellow G&C Coll Cam 69-70; Asst Bp Chich 73-78; Asst Bp Wakef 78-81; V Helme 78-81; rtd 81; Asst Bp Ox from 82. *49 Shipton Road, Ascott-under-Wychwood, Oxford OX7 6AG* Shipton-under-Wychwood (0993) 830911

CRAGG, Canon Leonard Albert. b 28. TCD BA53 MA56. Cuddesdon Coll 54. **d** 55 **p** 56. C Morecambe St Barn *Blackb* 55-57; C Skerton St Luke 57-60; V Brierfield 60-63; Chapl Whittingham Hosp Preston 63-69; V Padiham *Blackb* 69-80; V Lytham St Cuth from 80; Hon Can Blackb Cathl from 84; RD Fylde 85-88. *The Vicarage, Church Road, Lytham St Annes, Lancs FY8 5PX* Lytham (0253) 736168

CRAGGS, Colin Frederick. b 41. Open Univ BA80. Sarum & Wells Th Coll 85. **d** 88 **p** 89. NSM Wilton *B & W* 88-90; NSM Taunton St Andr from 90. *18 Manor Road, Taunton, Somerset TA1 5BD* Taunton (0823) 271989

CRAGGS, Michael Alfred. b 43. Open Univ BA79. St Mich Coll Llan 66. **d** 69 **p** 70. C Clee *Linc* 69-72; C Old Brumby 72-76; TV Kingsthorpe w Northn St Dav *Pet* 76-83; P-in-c Gt w Lt Addington 83-89; RD Higham 88-89; TR Corby SS Pet and Andr w Gt and Lt Oakley from 89; RD Corby from 90. *The Rectory, 40 Beanfield Avenue, Corby NN18 0EH* Corby (0536) 67620

CRAGO, Geoffrey Norman. b 44. Linc Th Coll 67. **d** 70 **p** 71. C Matson *Glouc* 70-75; V Dean Forest H Trin 75-80; Relig Progr Producer Radio Severn Sound 80-85; P-in-c Huntley 80-82; Perm to Offic 82-90; Dioc Communications Officer 84; Gen Syn Broadcasting Dept 85-88; Hon C Highnam, Lassington, Rudford, Tibberton etc from 90. *Milestones, 2 Two Mile Lane, Highnam, Gloucester GL2 8DW* Minsterworth (045275) 575

CRAIG, Canon Alan Stuart. b 38. Leeds Univ BA59. Cranmer Hall Dur DipTh61. **d** 61 **p** 62. C Newc w Butterton *Lich* 61-65; C Scarborough St Mary w Ch Ch, St Paul and St Thos *York* 65-67; V Werrington *Lich* 67-72; Asst Chapl HM Pris Man 72-73; Chapl HM Borstal Hindley 73-78; HM Pris Acklington 78-84; RD Morpeth *Newc* from 84; V Longhirst 84-90; R Morpeth from 90; Hon Can Newc Cathl from 90. *The Rectory, Cottingwood Lane, Morpeth, Northd NE61 1ED* Morpeth (0670) 513517

CRAIG, Eric. b 39. Birm Univ BA62 DipTh63. Qu Coll Birm 62. **d** 64 **p** 65. C Todmorden *Wakef* 64-68; C Hurstpierpoint *Chich* 68-70; C Cobham *Guildf* 70-73; V Dawley St Jerome *Lon* 73-76; V Stainland *Wakef* 76-87; R Yarnton w Begbroke and Shipton on Cherwell *Ox*

from 87. *The Rectory, 26 Church Lane, Yarnton, Oxford OX5 1PY* Kidlington (08675) 5749

CRAIG, Gillean Weston. b 49. York Univ BA72 Qu Coll Cam BA76 MA80. Westcott Ho Cam 76. **d** 77 **p** 78. C St Marylebone Ch Ch *Lon* 77-82; C Ealing St Barn 82-88; P-in-c St-Geo-in-the-East w St Paul 88-89; R from 89. *St George's Rectory Flat, Cannon Street Road, London E1 0BH* 071-481 1345

CRAIG, John Newcome. b 39. Selw Coll Cam BA63 MA67. Linc Th Coll 63. **d** 65 **p** 66. C Cannock *Lich* 65-71; V Gt Wyrley 71-79; TR Wednesfield from 79. *9 Vicarage Road, Wednesfield, Wolverhampton WV11 1SB* Wolverhampton (0902) 731462

CRAIG, Miss Julie Elizabeth. *See* LEAVES, Julie Elizabeth

CRAIG, Patrick Thomas. b 36. BA. St D Coll Lamp 59 Bps' Coll Cheshunt 59. **d** 61 **p** 62. C Belf St Mary *Conn* 61-65; C Belf St Pet 65-69; CF 69-88; R Hartfield w Coleman's Hatch *Chich* from 88. *The Rectory, Hartfield, E Sussex TN7 4AG* Hartfield (089277) 259

CRAIG, Richard Harvey. b 31. Em Coll Cam BA58. Linc Th Coll. **d** 60 **p** 61. C Bottesford *Linc* 60-65; Bp's Ind Chapl 65-69; Dioc Adv on Laity Tr *Bris* 69-74; V Whitchurch 74-86; TV N Lambeth *S'wark* from 86; Bp's Ecum Adv from 88; Ecum Officer from 90. *Lambeth Mission, 1-5 Lambeth Road, London SE1 7DQ or, 10 Wincott Street, London SE11 4NT* 071-735 2926 or 582 2120

CRAIG, Robert Henry. b 13. St Jo Coll Dur BA47 DipTh49. **d** 49 **p** 50. R Mersham *Cant* 68-78; rtd 78. *Jasmine House, 54A St Leonard's Road, Hythe, Kent CT21 6HW* Hythe (0303) 269222

CRAIG, Robert Joseph. b 43. TCD BA65 Div Test66 Birm Univ CertEd70. **d** 66 **p** 67. C Carrickfergus *Conn* 66-69; Chapl Ld Wandsworth Coll Long Sutton 75-85; Chapl K Sch Macclesfield from 85; Hd of Lower Sch from 85. *King's School, Macclesfield, Cheshire SK10 1DA* Macclesfield (0625) 618586

CRAIG-WILD, Dorothy Elsie. b 54. Birm Univ BA77. Qu Coll Birm 79. dss 81 **d** 87. Middleton St Mary *Ripon* 81-87; Par Dn Chapeltown *Sheff* from 88. *The Vicarage, 23 Housley Park, Chapeltown, Sheffield S30 4UE* Sheffield (0742) 467295

CRAIG-WILD, Peter John. b 55. Leeds Univ BA77. Qu Coll Birm 77. **d** 80 **p** 81. C Rothwell w Lofthouse *Ripon* 80-83; C Beeston 83-87; V Chapeltown *Sheff* from 87. *The Vicarage, 23 Housley Park, Chapeltown, Sheffield S30 4UE* Sheffield (0742) 467295

CRAMERI, Mrs Mary Barbara. b 44. K Coll Lon BD65 CertEd66. S Dios Minl Tr Scheme 86. **d** 88. Par Dn Whitton SS Phil and Jas *Lon* 88-91; Tutor Sarum & Wells Th Coll from 91. *Sarum and Wells Theological College, 19 The Close, Salisbury, Wilts SP1 2EE* Salisbury (0722) 332235

CRAMPTON, John Leslie. b 41. CITC 64. **d** 67 **p** 68. C Lurgan Ch Ch *D & D* 67-71; C Dundela 71-73; Rhodesia 73-80; Zimbabwe 80-82; I Killanne w Killegney, Rossdroit and Templeshanbo *C & O* 82-88; Preb Ferns Cathl 85-88; Chapl Wilson's Hosp Sch Multyfarnham *M & K* 88-91; C Mullingar, Portnashangan, Moyliscar, Kilbixy etc 89-91; I Athy w Kilberry, Fontstown and Kilkea *D & G* from 91. *The Rectory, Church Road, Athy, Co Kildare, Irish Republic* Athy (507) 31446

CRAN, Preb Alexander Strachan. b 09. St Jo Coll Dur BA31 MA43. St Aid Birkenhead 31. **d** 32 **p** 33. V Congresbury *B & W* 48-73; Preb Wells Cathl from 61; P-in-c Puxton w Hewish St Ann and Wick St Lawrence 71-73; rtd 73. *Rowan Wick, Wolvershill Road, Banwell, Weston-super-Mare, Avon BS24 6DR* Banwell (0934) 823209

CRANCH, Peter Kenneth. b 47. St Chad's Coll Dur BA70 DipTh71 PGCE72. **d** 73 **p** 74. C Tavistock and Gulworthy *Ex* 73-78; TV Cen Torquay 78-80; C Heavitree w Ex St Paul 80-84; TV Withycombe Raleigh from 84. *All Saints' Vicarage, Church Road, Exmouth, Devon EX8 1RZ* Exmouth (0395) 263572

CRANE, Bryant Frederick Francis. b 13. Qu Coll Cam BA35 MA39. Ridley Hall Cam 35. **d** 37 **p** 38. R Astbury and Smallwood *Ches* 64-78; rtd 78; Perm to Offic Ches and Lich from 78. *6 Ridgefields, Biddulph Moor, Stoke-on-Trent ST8 7JE* Stoke-on-Trent (0782) 513752

CRANE, John Walter. b 32. Chich Th Coll. **d** 58 **p** 59. Min Can and Chapl Windsor 67-79; Chapl St Geo Sch Ascot 67-79; Warden Dioc Retreat Ho (Holland Ho) Cropthorne *Worc* 79-83; P-in-c Harvington, Norton and Lenchwick 84-87; rtd 87. *16 Allesborough Drive, Pershore, Worcs* Pershore (0386) 556444

CRANE, Robert Bartlett. b 14. Clare Coll Cam BA36 MA40. Qu Coll Birm 37. **d** 39 **p** 40. Area Sec (Dio S'wark) USPG 70-79; rtd 79; Hon C Bellingham St

Dunstan *S'wark* from 79. *8 Bromley College, London Road, Bromley, Kent BR1 1PE* 081-460 4578

CRANE, Ronald Edward. b 48. Wilson Carlile Coll 73 St Steph Ho Ox 83. **d** 85 **p** 86. C Bicester w Bucknell, Caversfield and Launton *Ox* 85-88; P-in-c Washwood Heath *Birm* from 88. *St Mark's Vicarage, 266 Washwood Heath Road, Birmingham B8 2XS* 021-327 1461

CRANE, Vincent James. b 10. St Aid Birkenhead 62. **d** 64 **p** 65. C Penn *Lich* 64-70; R Himley 70-78; V Swindon 70-78; rtd 78. *14 Holcroft Road, Wall Heath, Kingswinford, W Midlands DY6 0HP* Kingswinford (0384) 292208

CRANFIELD, Dr Nicholas William Stewart. b 56. Mert Coll Ox BA77 MA81 DPhil89 Leeds Univ BA81. Coll of Resurr Mirfield 79 Union Th Sem (NY) STM84. **d** 86 **p** 87. C Ascot Heath *Ox* 86-89; Prin Berks Chr Tr Scheme from 89; Hon C Reading St Mary w St Laur from 89. *St Mary's House, Chain Street, Reading, Berks RG1 2HX* Reading (0734) 504197 or 571057

CRANIDGE, Mrs Wendy Ann. b 31. Sheff Univ CertEd52. Cant Sch of Min 81. **dss** 84 **d** 87. Roch 84-87; Hon Par Dn 87-88; Soc Resp Adv (Dios Cant and Roch) 86-88; Hon C Washingborough w Heighington and Canwick *Linc* from 88. *The Vines, Hall Drive, Canwick, Lincoln LN4 2RG* Lincoln (0522) 544209

CRANKSHAW, Ronald. b 41. Coll of Resurr Mirfield 74. **d** 76 **p** 77. C Orford St Andr *Liv* 76; C N Meols 76-79; V Abram 79-85; V Wigan St Anne from 85. *St Anne's Vicarage, 154 Beech Hill Avenue, Wigan, Lancs WN6 7TA* Wigan (0942) 41930

CRANSTON, Robert William. b 23. Bris Univ BSc47. Oak Hill Th Coll 76. **d** 79 **p** 80. Hon C Heanton Punchardon w Marwood *Ex* from 79. *Broom Cottage, Middle Marwood, Barnstaple, Devon EX31 4EG* Barnstaple (0271) 72426

CRANWELL, Brian Robert. b 32. Sheff Poly MSc. Cranmer Hall Dur. **d** 84 **p** 85. C Ecclesfield *Sheff* 84-86; V Handsworth Woodhouse from 86. *St James's Vicarage, Tithe Barn Lane, Woodhouse, Sheffield S13 7LL* Sheffield (0742) 694146

CRASKE, Leslie Gordon. b 29. AKC54. Lambeth STh80. **d** 55 **p** 56. C Malden St Jo *S'wark* 55-58; C Streatham St Leon 58-60; S Rhodesia 60-65; Rhodesia 65-66; V Upper Norwood St Jo *Cant* 67-83; R Guernsey St Sav *Win* from 83. *St Saviour's Rectory, Guernsey, Channel Islands* Guernsey (0481) 63045

CRASTON, Canon Richard Colin. b 22. Bris Univ BA49 Lon Univ BD51. Tyndale Hall Bris 46. **d** 51 **p** 52. C Dur St Nic *Dur* 51-54; V Bolton St Paul *Man* 54-76; P-in-c Bolton Em 64-66; V 66-76; Hon Can Man Cathl from 68; RD Bolton from 72; V Bolton St Paul w Em 77-86; TR from 86; Chapl to HM The Queen from 85. *St Paul's Vicarage, 174 Chorley New Road, Bolton BL1 4PF* Bolton (0204) 42303

CRATE, Canon George Frederick Jackson. b 28. Lon Univ BD56. ALCD55. **d** 56 **p** 57. C Penge St Jo *Roch* 56-58; C Tonbridge St Steph 58-60; R Knossington and Cold Overton *Leic* 60-64; V Owston and Withcote 60-64; V Mountsorrel Ch Ch 64-83; RD Akeley E (Loughb) from 75; Hon Can Leic Cathl from 80; V Mountsorrel Ch Ch and St Pet from 83. *Christ Church Vicarage, 2 Rothley Road, Mountsorrel, Loughborough, Leics LE12 7JU* Leicester (0533) 302235

CRAVEN, Alan. b 32. N Ord Course. **d** 87. NSM Hessle *York* from 87. *28 Weelsby Way, Bootherferry Road, Hessle, N Humberside HU13 0JW* Hull (0482) 643214

CRAVEN, Allan. b 35. LTCL77 Univ of Wales (Lamp) BA57 Lon Univ BD72. Chich Th Coll 57. **d** 59 **p** 60. C Blaenau Ffestiniog *Ban* 59-61; C Milford Haven *St D* 61-65; V Llwynhendy 65-68; R Nolton w Roch from 68; RD Roose from 85. *The Rectory, Nolton, Haverfordwest, Dyfed SA62 3NW* Haverfordwest (0437) 710213

CRAVEN, Colin Peter. b 48. Dartmouth RN Coll. St Steph Ho Ox 83. **d** 85 **p** 86. C Holbeach *Linc* 85-88; Chapl Fleet Hosp from 86; TV Grantham *Linc* from 88; OCF from 88. *St Anne's Vicarage, Harrowby Road, New Somerby, Grantham, Lincs NG31 9ED* Grantham (0476) 62822

CRAVEN, Gordon Forster. b 26. Qu Coll Cam BA50 MA55. Wells Th Coll 51. **d** 53 **p** 54. V King Sterndale *Derby* 57-72; V Fairfield 57-72; Perm to Offic *B & W* from 81; rtd 91. *Kingfisher Cottage, 41 Southover, Wells, Somerset BA5 1UH* Wells (0749) 72282

CRAVEN, Archdeacon of. See SMITH, Ven Brian Arthur

CRAWFORD, Albert Edward. b 13. TCD BA37 MA43. **d** 37 **p** 38. I Camlough *Arm* 65-78; rtd 78. *Shalom, 54 Edenvale Avenue, Banbridge, Co Down* Banbridge (08206) 22924

CRAWFORD, Canon Arthur Edward. b 14. TCD BA39 MA51. TCD Div Sch Div Test39. **d** 40 **p** 41. I Clara *M & K* 66-85; Can Meath 84-85; rtd 85. *Klosters, Crookedwood, Mullingar, Co Westmeath, Irish Republic* Mullingar (44) 72272

CRAWFORD, Duncan Alexander. b 59. Newc Univ BA81 MA83 K Coll Lon CertEd83. St Jo Coll Nottm 86. **d** 89 **p** 90. C Hatcham St Jas *S'wark* from 89. *26 Millmark Grove, London SE14 6QR* 081-692 4645

CRAWFORD, Miss Ivy Elizabeth. b 50. Trin Coll Bris DipTh85. **dss** 85 **d** 87. Collier Row St Jas *Chelmsf* 85; Collier Row St Jas and Havering-atte-Bower 86-87; Par Dn 87-89; Par Dn Harlow New Town w Lt Parndon from 89. *64 Hare Street Springs, Harlow, Essex CM19 4AW* Harlow (0279) 453601

CRAWFORD, John. b 22. TCD BA50. **d** 51 **p** 53. C Lt Marlow *Ox* 67-83; rtd 83. *33 Wenlock Edge, Charvil, Reading* Reading (0734) 341848

CRAWFORD, Canon John William Rowland. b 53. AKC75 Open Univ BA81. CITC 75. **d** 76 **p** 77. C Dundela *D & D* 76-79; C Taney Ch Ch *D & G* 79-84; I Dub St Patr Cathl Gp from 84; Preb Tipperkevin St Patr Cathl Dub from 84. *248 South Circular Road, Dolphin's Barn, Dublin 8, Irish Republic* Dublin (1) 542274

CRAWFORD, Peter. b 22. Trin Coll Cam BA49 MA54. Wycliffe Hall Ox 49. **d** 51 **p** 52. V Masham *Ripon* 60-75; RD Ripon 70-75; V Masham and Healey 75-79; R E Bergholt *St E* 79-87; RD Samford 82-86; rtd 87; Perm to Offic *St E* from 87. *3 Burl's Yard, Crown Street, Needham Market, Ipswich IP6 8AJ* Needham Market (0449) 722343

CRAWFORD, Philip Hugh Southern. b 16. Lon Univ BA40. Chich Th Coll 41. **d** 42 **p** 43. V Healaugh w Wighill and Bilbrough *York* 60-78; P-in-c Slingsby 78-86; P-in-c Hovingham 78-86; V 86; RD Bulmer and Malton 80-85; rtd 86; C Hovingham *York* 86-88. *44 Bootham Crescent, York YO3 7AH* York (0904) 30386

CRAWFORD, Robin. b 33. Pemb Coll Cam BA57 MA61. **d** 67 **p** 80. Ghana 67-69; Dep Sec Chrs Abroad 69-73; Nigeria 77-78; Perm to Offic *Win* 78-80; Dep Sec Buttle Trust 78-86; Sec 86-90; Dir from 90; Hon C *Win* H Trin *Win* 80-82; Hon C Notting Hill All SS w St Columb *Lon* 82-87; Hon C Westmr St Matt from 87. *Audley House, 13 Palace Street, London SW1E 5HS* 071-828 7311

CRAWLEY, David. b 47. St Steph Ho Ox 75. **d** 78 **p** 79. C Solihull *Birm* 78-81; TV Newbury *Ox* 81-84; Lic to Offic from 84; Distr Chapl from 88. *Stoke Mandeville Hospital, Mandeville Road, Aylesbury, Bucks HP20 8AL* Aylesbury (0296) 84111

CRAWLEY, John Lloyd Rochfort. b 22. Selw Coll Cam BA47 MA52. Cuddesdon Coll 47. **d** 49 **p** 50. Chapl Newc Univ *Newc* 69-74; C-in-c Newc St Thos Prop Chpl 69-74; P-in-c Cockermouth All SS w Ch Ch *Carl* 74-77; TR Cockermouth w Embleton and Wythop 77-86; Perm to Offic *Arg* from 86; rtd 87. *Cove, Tarbert, Argyll PA29 6SX* Tarbert (0880) 820842

CRAWLEY, Leonard Frank. b 38. ARCA. NW Ord Course 74. **d** 77 **p** 78. NSM Bradf St Wilfrid Lidget Green *Bradf* from 77. *185 Highgate, Bradford, W Yorkshire BD9 5PU* Bradford (0274) 487249

CRAWLEY, Nicholas Simon. b 58. ACIB82 AMSIA85 Southn Univ BSc79. Wycliffe Hall Ox 85. **d** 88 **p** 89. C E Twickenham St Steph *Lon* from 88. *29 St Margaret's Road, Twickenham TW1 2LN* 081-892 6809

CRAWLEY, Simon Ewen. b 31. Em Coll Cam BA57 MA60. Ridley Hall Cam 56. **d** 58 **p** 59. C Denton Holme *Carl* 58-61; P-in-c Cinderford St Steph w Littledean *Glouc* 61-67; V Margate H Trin *Cant* 67-74; V Folkestone H Trin w Ch Ch 74-81; R Patterdale *Carl* 81-87; RD Penrith 83-86; R Culworth w Sulgrave and Thorpe Mandeville *Pet* from 87; RD Brackley from 89; R Chipping Warden w Edgcote and Aston le Walls from 89. *The Rectory, Culworth, Banbury, Oxon OX17 2AT* Sulgrave (029576) 383

CRAWLEY-BOEVEY, Robert Arthur. b 12. Hertf Coll Ox BA34 MA38. Cuddesdon Coll 35. **d** 37 **p** 38. V Seer Green *Ox* 59-78; rtd 78. *3 St Michael's Close, Urchfont, Devizes, Wilts SN10 4QJ* Devizes (0380) 840635

CRAWSHAW, Charles Barritt. b 14. Leeds Univ BA36. Coll of Resurr Mirfield 36. **d** 38 **p** 39. V Smethwick H Trin *Birm* 54-60; Lect Ashton Coll of FE 60-63; Hd of Humanities Brunel Coll of Tech 63-80; rtd 79; Lic to Offic *B & W* from 80. *Crow Wood, 30 Hillcrest Road, Portishead, Bristol BS20 8HP* Bristol (0272) 842659

CRAWSHAW, Henry Michael Aitken. b 15. Em Coll Cam BA37 MA43. Westcott Ho Cam 39. **d** 40 **p** 41. R Barnham Broom w Kimberley, Bixton etc *Nor* 64-70; R Brandon Parva 64-70; P-in-c Wramplingham w Barford

64-70; P-in-c Coston w Runhall 64-70; P-in-c Hardingham 64-70; P-in-c Garveston w Thuxton 64-70; R Brancaster 70-80; R Burnham Deepdale 71-80; R Brancaster w Burnham Deepdale and Titchwell 80-83; rtd 83; Perm to Offic *Nor* from 83. *85 Waveney Close, Wells-next-the-Sea, Norfolk NR23 1HT* Fakenham (0328) 710080

CRAY, Graham Alan. b 47. Leeds Univ BA68. St Jo Coll Nottm 69. **d** 71 **p** 72. C Gillingham St Mark *Roch* 71-75; N Area Co-ord CPAS Youth Dept 75-78; C York St Mich-le-Belfrey *York* 78-82; V from 82. *Half, The Avenue, York YO3 6AS* York (0904) 628539 or 624190

CREAN, Patrick John Eugene. b 38. TCD BA81 MA84. Edin Th Coll 82. **d** 84 **p** 85. C Perth St Jo *St And* 84-86; P-in-c Liv St Phil w St Dav *Liv* 86-87; V 87-90; R Cupar *St And* from 90; R Ladybank from 90. *The Rectory, Castlebank Road, Cupar, Fife KY15 4BN* Cupar (0334) 52372

CREASER, Canon David Edward. b 35. St Cath Coll Cam BA58 MA62. Clifton Th Coll 59. **d** 61 **p** 62. C Cheadle *Ches* 61-67; V Weston *Bradf* 67-69; P-in-c Denton 67-69; V Weston w Denton 69-74 and from 82; Dir Educn from 73; V Frizinghall *Bradf* 71-82; Hon Can Bradf Cathl from 80. *The Vicarage, Askwith, Otley, W Yorkshire LS21 2HX* Otley (0943) 461139

CREASEY, Graham. b 51. Trent Poly BA. Cranmer Hall Dur 80. **d** 83 **p** 84. C Birstall and Wanlip *Leic* 83-87; C-in-c Wheatley Park St Paul CD *Sheff* from 87. *278 Thorne Road, Doncaster, S Yorkshire DN2 5AJ* Doncaster (0302) 326041 or 322459

CREBER, Arthur Frederick. b 45. Lon Univ DipTh67. N Ord Course 84. **d** 87 **p** 88. C Rickerscote *Lich* 87-91; V Gt Wyrley from 91. *St Mark's Vicarage, 1 Cleves Crescent, Cheslyn Hay, Walsall WS6 7LR* Cheslyn Hay (0922) 414309

CRECY, Hugh Charles. b 05. Worc Ord Coll 56. **d** 57 **p** 58. R Bentworth cum Shalden *Win* 62-77; rtd 77; Perm to Offic *Ex* 77-87. *2 Weirfield Road, Exeter EX2 4DN* Exeter (0392) 436777

CREDITON, Suffragan Bishop of. *See* COLEMAN, Rt Rev Peter Everard

CREE, John Richard. b 44. Open Univ BA74. Coll of Resurr Mirfield. **d** 83 **p** 84. C Blackb St Jas *Blackb* 83-86; V Feniscowles from 86. *732 Preston Old Road, Feniscowles, Blackburn BB2 5EN* Blackburn (0254) 21236

CREER, Mrs Irene. b 45. Gilmore Course 80 NE Ord Course 82. **dss** 83 **d** 87. Elloughton and Brough w Brantingham *York* 83-86; Westborough *Guildf* 86-87; C 87-88; C Shottermill from 88. *1 Manor Lea, Haslemere, Surrey GU27 1PD* Haslemere (0428) 52594

CREERY-HILL, Anthony Thomas. b 23. BNC Ox BA49 MA54. Ridley Hall Cam 49. **d** 51 **p** 52. Chapl Dean Close Sch Cheltenham 59-74; Dep Hd Master Larchfield Sch Helensburgh 75-77; Kenya 77-83; Chapl Chantilly *Eur* 83-86; rtd 87; Perm to Offic *Heref* from 87. *Under Down, Ledbury, Herefordshire HR8 2JE* Ledbury (0531) 5608

CREES, Geoffrey William. b 35. ONC Open Univ BA85. Cranmer Hall Dur 65. **d** 67 **p** 68. C Hoddesdon *St Alb* 67-70; C Harwell *Ox* 70-73; C Chilton All SS 70-73; V Greenham 73-82; AD E Hull Deanery 82-88; TR Marfleet *York* 82-88; TR Rodbourne Cheney *Bris* from 88. *St Mary's Rectory, 298 Cheney Manor Road, Swindon SN2 2PF* Swindon (0793) 522379

CREIGHTON, Frederick David. b 50. ACII74 TCD BTh88. **d** 88 **p** 89. C Lisburn Ch Ch *Conn* 88-91; I Drumclamph w Lower and Upper Langfield *D & R* from 91. *The Rectory, 70 Greenville Road, Castlederg, Co Tyrone BT81 7NU* Castlederg (06626) 71433

CREIGHTON, Mrs Judith. b 36. Reading Univ BSc57. Trin Coll Bris 80 Edin Th Coll 81. **dss** 83 **d** 87. Greenock *Glas* 83-85; Lawrence Weston *Bris* 85-87; Par Dn Kingswood 87-90; Chapl Stoke Park and Purdown Hosps Stapleton from 90. *Home Farm Cottage, West Littleton, Marshfield, Chippenham, Wilts SN14 8JE* Bath (0225) 891021

CRELLIN, Howard Joseph. b 30. Magd Coll Cam BA52 MA56 Magd Coll Ox BA54 DipTh55 MA56. Wycliffe Hall Ox 53. **d** 55 **p** 56. R Theydon Garnon *Chelmsf* 58-70; Select Preacher Ox Univ 68; Perm to Offic *Ox* 70-82; Hon C High Wycombe 72-77; Master K Chas I Sch Kidderminster 74-80; rtd 77; Perm to Offic *Chelmsf* from 82; Master Caldicott Sch Farnham 80-82; Fryerns Sch Basildon 82-88; St Anselm's Sch Basildon 88-91; P-in-c Whatfield w Semer, Nedging and Naughton *St E* from 91. *The Rectory, Whatfield, Ipswich IP7 6QU* Ipswich (0473) 822100

CRESSALL, Paul Richard. b 51. UEA BA74. Ripon Coll Cuddesdon 86. **d** 88 **p** 89. C Stevenage H Trin *St Alb*

from 88. *413 Scarborough Avenue, Stevenage, Herts SG1 2QA* Stevenage (0438) 361179

CRESSEY, Roger Wilson. b 35. Chich Th Coll 72. **d** 74 **p** 75. C Pontefract St Giles *Wakef* 74-77; Hon C Dewsbury All SS 77-80; Chapl Pinderfields, Carr Gate and Fieldhead Hosps Wakef from 80. *Pinderfields Hospital, Aberford Road, Wakefield WF1 4DG* Wakefield (0924) 375217

CRESSWELL, Howard Rex. b 31. Ely Th Coll 56. **d** 59 **p** 60. C Dovercourt *Chelmsf* 59-61; C Victoria Docks Ascension 61-64; V 64-71; R E w W Harling *Nor* 71-72; TV Quidenham w Eccles and Snetterton 72-75; V Arminghall 75-82; R Caistor w Markshall 75-82; V Trowse 75-82; V Heigham St Barn w St Bart from 82. *The Vicarage, Russell Street, Norwich NR2 4QT* Norwich (0603) 27859

CRESSWELL, Canon Jack Joseph. b 11. Qu Coll Cam BA39 MA43. Wycliffe Hall Ox 39. **d** 40 **p** 41. R Busbridge *Guildf* 70-78; Perm to Offic *Glouc* from 75; rtd 78; C Broughton Poggs w Filkins, Broadwell etc *Ox* from 88. *12 Eastleach, Cirencester, Glos GL7 3NQ* Southrop (036785) 261

CRESSWELL, Jeremy Peter. b 49. St Jo Coll Ox BA72 MA78. Ridley Hall Cam 73. **d** 75 **p** 76. C Wisley w Pyrford *Guildf* 75-78; C Weybridge 78-82; P-in-c E Clandon 82-83; P-in-c W Clandon 82-83; R E and W Clandon 83-90; V Oxshott from 90. *The Vicarage, Steel's Lane, Oxshott, Leatherhead, Surrey KT22 0QH* Oxshott (037284) 2071

CRESSWELL, Preb Kenneth Benjamin. b 17. St D Coll Lamp BA50. **d** 51 **p** 52. V Horninglow *Lich* 67-81; Preb Lich Cathl 80-83; TV Stoke-upon-Trent 81-83; rtd 83; Perm to Offic *Lich* from 83. *1 Chartwell Close, Woodsetton, Dudley, W Midlands DY1 4LY* Sedgley (0902) 663354

CRIBB, Robert John. b 22. Spurgeon's Coll 45. **d** 85 **p** 86. NSM Curry Rivel w Fivehead and Swell *B & W* 85-89; rtd 89. *4 Heale Lane, Curry Rivel, Langport, Somerset TA10 0PG* Langport (0458) 252333

CRICHTON, James Kenneth. b 35. Glouc Sch of Min 78. **d** 80 **p** 80. NSM Minchinhampton *Glouc* 80-83; NSM Nailsworth 83-86; Dep Chapl HM Pris Pentonville 86-87; Chapl HM Pris The Mount from 87. *15 Lysander Close, The Mount, Bovingdon, Hemel Hempstead, Herts HP3 0NZ* Hemel Hempstead (0442) 832636

CRICK, Peter. b 39. Lon Univ BD68 NY Univ DMin84. Wells Th Coll 66. **d** 67 **p** 68. C Horsham *Chich* 67-71; Asst Dioc Youth Officer *Ox* 71-75; R Denham 75-88; Bp's Adv for Continuing Minl Educn *Dur* from 88; P-in-c Coniscliffe from 88. *76 Merrybent Village, Darlington, Co Durham DL2 2LE* Darlington (0325) 374510

CRICK, Philip Benjamin Denton. b 33. Bris Univ BA63. Clifton Th Coll 60. **d** 64 **p** 65. C Clerkenwell St Jas and St Jo w St Pet *Lon* 64-67; CF 67-72; C Southall Green St Jo *Lon* 72-75; P-in-c Southall H Trin 75-83; P-in-c Kidbrooke St Jas *S'wark* 83-85; TV from 85. *91 Telemann Square, London SE3 9YU* 081-319 3874

CRINGLE, William Edward James. b 15. Lon Univ BD40. **d** 41 **p** 41. V Lezayre St Olave Ramsey *S & M* 61-80; rtd 80; Perm to Offic *S & M* from 80. *3 Queens Drive West, Ramsey, Isle of Man* Ramsey (0624) 814608

CRIPPS, Harold Ernest. b 04. AKC47. **d** 47 **p** 48. V Burtonwood *Liv* 59-74; rtd 74; Perm to Offic *Chich* from 77. *Flat A, 41 Broadmark Lane, Rustington, Littlehampton, W Sussex BN16 2HH* Rustington (0903) 782603

CRIPPS, Keith Richard John. b 21. Trin Coll Cam BA43 MA47 Newc Univ PhD80. Ridley Hall Cam 43. **d** 45 **p** 47. Lic to Offic Newc 65-84; Ely 84-86; Lect Newc Poly 74-79; Chapl Jes Coll Cam 84; rtd 86. *9 Pentlands Court, Pentlands Close, Cambridge CB4 1JN* Cambridge (0223) 354216

CRIPPS, Martyn Cyril Rowland. b 46. Birm Univ LLB68. Wycliffe Hall Ox 80. **d** 82 **p** 83. C Canford Magna *Sarum* 82-86; V Preston St Cuth *Blackb* from 87. *St Cuthbert's Vicarage, 20 Black Bull Lane, Fulwood, Preston PR2 3PX* Preston (0772) 717346

CRIPPS, Michael Frank Douglas. b 28. Ch Ch Ox BA50 MA53. Ridley Hall Cam 58. **d** 59 **p** 60. C Cam Gt St Mary w St Mich *Ely* 59-62; Ceylon 62-66; C-in-c Swindon Covingham CD *Bris* 66-72; V Swindon St Paul 72-73; P-in-c Aldbourne and Baydon *Sarum* 73; TV Whitton 73-81; C Marlborough from 81. *9 Silverless Street, Marlborough, Wilts SN8 1JQ* Marlborough (0672) 512748

CRISALL, Christopher James Philip. b 34. St Deiniol's Hawarden 87. **d** 89 **p** 90. NSM Low Marple *Ches* 89-90; C Woodchurch from 90. *23 Mavis Drive, Upton, Wirral, Merseyside L49 0UN* 051-677 7578

CRISP, Ronald Leslie. b 11. Worc Ord Coll 52. **d** 56 **p** 57. V Dudley Wood *Worc* 63-87; rtd 88. *34 Whitegate Drive, Kidderminster, Worcs DY11 6LQ*

CRITCHLEY, Colin. b 41. Dur Univ BA63 Liv Univ MA69. NW Ord Course 75. **d** 78 **p** 79. NSM Halewood *Liv* from 78. *53 Elwyn Drive, Halewood, Liverpool L26 0UX* 051-487 5710

CRITCHLEY, Ronald John. b 15. Kelham Th Coll 31. **d** 38 **p** 39. V Fylingdales *York* 63-80, V Hawsker 63-80; rtd 80. *4A North Promenade, Whitby, N Yorkshire YO21 3JX* Whitby (0947) 600238

CRITCHLOW, Trevor Francis. b 61. Lanc Univ BA83. Westcott Ho Cam 88. **d** 90 **p** 91. C Croydon St Jo *S'wark* from 90. *8 The Ridgeway, Waddon, Croydon CR0 4AB* 081-686 3947 or 688 8104

CRITTALL, Richard Simon. b 47. Sussex Univ BA69 Linacre Coll Ox BA71. St Steph Ho Ox 69. **d** 72 **p** 73. C Oswestry H Trin *Lich* 72-75; C E Grinstead St Mary *Chich* 75-78; TV Brighton Resurr 78-83; R E Blatchington from 83. *The Rectory, 25 Blatchington Hill, Seaford, E Sussex BN25 2AJ* Seaford (0323) 892964

CRITTLE, Wilfrid. b 04. Birm Univ BCom24. **d** 30 **p** 31. V Worthing Ch Ch *Chich* 49-74; rtd 74; Perm to Offic *Chich* from 74. *23 Seabright, West Parade, Worthing, W Sussex BN11 3QR* Worthing (0903) 33120

CROAD, Arthur Robert. b 35. Down Coll Cam BA58 MA61. Clifton Th Coll 58. **d** 61 **p** 62. C Sneinton St Chris w St Phil *S'well* 61-64; C Kinson *Sarum* 64-72; R Sherfield English *Win* 72-74; R Awbridge w Sherfield English from 74. *The Rectory, Sherfield English, Romsey, Hants SO5 6FP* West Wellow (0794) 22352

CROAD, David Richard. b 31. Reading Univ BSc55. Clifton Th Coll. **d** 57 **p** 58. C Iver *Ox* 57-60; C Rushden *Pet* 60-63; V Loudwater *Ox* 63-72; SW Area Sec CPAS 72-78; V Bovingdon *St Alb* 78-91; Min Hampstead St Jo Downshire Hill Prop Chpl *Lon* from 91. *The Parsonage, 64 Pilgrim's Lane, London NW3 1SM* 071-435 8404

CROCKER, Keith Gwillam. b 49. Lanchester Poly BSc70 DipTh78. Oak Hill Th Coll 74. **d** 77 **p** 78. C Whitnash *Cov* 77-80; C Gt Horton *Bradf* 80-83; C Grays SS Pet and Paul, S Stifford and W Thurrock *Chelmsf* 83-84; TV Grays Thurrock 84-88; TR Wreningham *Nor* from 88. *The Rectory, Bracon Ash, Norwich NR14 8HJ* Mulbarton (0508) 78207

CROCKER, Richard Campbell. b 54. BSc Nottm Univ MA. Wycliffe Hall Ox. **d** 82 **p** 83. C Summerfield *Birm* 82-84; Chapl K Edw Sch Birm from 84. *318 Bristol Road, Birmingham B5 7SN* 021-471 4631

CROCKETT, Peter James Sinclair. b 44. Sarum & Wells Th Coll 74. **d** 77 **p** 78. C Heavitree *Ex* 77; C Heavitree w Ex St Paul 78-80; TV Ex St Thos and Em 80-87; V Wear St Luke from 87. *The Vicarage, 375 Topsham Road, Exeter EX2 6HB* Topsham (039287) 3263

CROCKETT, Phillip Anthony. b 45. K Coll Lon BA67 BD70 AKC70. Llan St Mich DPS71. **d** 71 **p** 72. C Aberdare *Llan* 71-74; C Whitchurch 74-78; V Llanfihangel-y-Creuddyn, Llanafan w Llanwnnws *St D* 78-86; Sec Prov Selection Panel 83-87; V Ysbyty Ystwyth 84-86; R Dowlais *Llan* 86-91; Exec Sec for Min from 91. *39 Cathedral Road, Cardiff CF1 9XF* Cardiff (0222) 231638

CROFT, Bernard Theodore. b 10. Kelham Th Coll 30. **d** 35 **p** 36. V Reighton w Speeton *York* 68-75; rtd 75; Perm to Offic *York* from 75. *4 Freeman's Court, Water Lane, York YO3 6PR* York (0904) 656611

CROFT, James Stuart. b 57. K Coll Lon BD80. Ripon Coll Cuddesdon 83. **d** 85 **p** 86. C Friern Barnet St Jas *Lon* 85-88; R Lea *Linc* from 88; V Knaith from 88; V Upton from 88; R Gate Burton from 88. *The Rectory, 18 Gainsborough Road, Lea, Gainsborough, Lincs DN21 5HZ* Gainsborough (0427) 613188

CROFT, John Armentieres. b 15. MC44. Sarum Th Coll 56. **d** 57 **p** 58. V Gwinear *Truro* 60-70; rtd 70; Perm to Offic Truro, Sarum and B & W from 70. *Vine House, Common Road, Wincanton, Somerset BA9 9RB* Wincanton (0963) 32253

CROFT, Michael Peter. b 60. GradIPM. Trin Coll Bris BA88. **d** 88 **p** 89. C Drypool *York* 88-91; P-in-c Sandal St Cath *Wakef* from 91; Chapl Manygates Maternity Hosp Wakef from 91. *The Vicarage, 157 Agbrigg Road, Wakefield, W Yorkshire WF1 4AU* Wakefield (0924) 252249741210

CROFT, Canon Peter Gardom. b 25. St Jo Coll Cam BA48 MA50. Wells Th Coll 50. **d** 52 **p** 53. C Rugby St Andr *Cov* 52-58; V Stockingford 58-65; R Washington *Dur* 65-78; Dioc Info Officer *Sheff* 78-83; Can Res and Sub-Dean Guildf Cathl *Guildf* from 83. *4 Cathedral Close, Guildford GU2 5TL* Guildford (0483) 575140

CROFT, Ronald. b 30. St Aid Birkenhead 61. **d** 63 **p** 64. C Lawton Moor *Man* 63-65; C Withington St Crispin 65-66; R 74-86; C Prestwich St Marg 66-67; V Oldham St Ambrose 67-71; P-in-c Oldham St Jas 67-68; V 68-71; V Prestwich St Hilda 71-74; R Heaton Norris St Thos from 86. *St Thomas's Rectory, 6 Heaton Moor Road, Stockport, Cheshire SK4 4NS* 061-432 1912

CROFT, Simon Edward Owen. b 51. St Steph Ho Ox 75. **d** 78 **p** 79. C Heavitree w Ex St Paul *Ex* 78-83; V Seaton from 83. *The Vicarage, Colyford Road, Seaton, Devon EX12 2DF* Seaton (0297) 20391

CROFT, Stephen John Lindsey. b 57. MA PhD. Cranmer Hall Dur 80. **d** 83 **p** 84. C Enfield St Andr *Lon* 83-87; V Ovenden *Wakef* from 87. *St George's Vicarage, Bracewell Drive, Wheatley, Halifax, W Yorkshire HX3 5BT* Halifax (0422) 54153

CROFT, William Alan. b 15. Lich Th Coll 55. **d** 57 **p** 58. V Cornworthy *Ex* 59-73; TR Cheriton Fitzpaine, Woolfardisworthy etc 74-76; TR N Creedy 76-80; rtd 80. *33 Holyoak Road, Oxford OX3 8AF*

CROFT, William Hammond. b 08. Jes Coll Ox BA30 MA35. Wells Th Coll 31. **d** 31 **p** 32. R Alphington *Ex* 54-73; rtd 73. *Dolphins Rest Home, 5 Moor Lane, Budleigh Salterton, Devon*

CROFT, William Stuart. b 53. Trin Hall Cam BA76 MA79 MTh88. Ripon Coll Cuddesdon BA80. **d** 80 **p** 81. C Friern Barnet St Jas *Lon* 80-83; Tutor Chich Th Coll from 83; Vice-Prin from 88. *The Theological College, Tollhouse Close, Chichester, W Sussex PO19 1SG* Chichester (0243) 783369

CROFTON, Edwin Alan. b 46. Univ Coll Ox BA68 MA72. Cranmer Hall Dur DipTh72. **d** 73 **p** 74. C Hull Newland St Jo *York* 73-77; C Worksop St Jo *S'well* 77-81; Chapl Kilton Hosp Worksop 80-81; V Scarborough St Mary w Ch Ch and H Apostles *York* from 81; Miss to Seamen from 81; Chapl St Mary's Hosp Scarborough from 82; RD Scarborough *York* 91. *The Vicarage, The Crescent, Scarborough, N Yorkshire YO11 2PP* Scarborough (0723) 371354

CROFTS, Charles Arthur. b 14. Ball Coll Ox BA38 MA48. Lich Th Coll 38. **d** 39 **p** 40. V Hexton *St Alb* 69-77; Hon Can St Alb 69-71; C Merstham and Gatton *S'wark* 77-80; Dir RE and Chapl St Bede's Sch Redhill 77-80; rtd 80. *5 Manaton Close, Haywards Heath, W Sussex RH16 3HS* Haywards Heath (0444) 457190

CROFTS, Ian Hamilton. b 55. BSc. St Jo Coll Nottm 79. **d** 82 **p** 83. C Leamington Priors St Paul *Cov* 82-86; C Oadby *Leic* 86; TV 86-91; V Maidstone St Faith *Cant* from 91. *St Faith's Vicarage, Moncktons Lane, Maidstone, Kent ME14 2PY* Maidstone (0622) 751079

CROMBIE, William Ian. b 52. Ex Coll Ox BA76 MA79. Ripon Coll Cuddesdon 76. **d** 78 **p** 79. C Broadstone *Sarum* 78; C Warminster St Denys 78-81; C Fleetwood *Blackb* 81-85; Tanzania from 85. *PO Box 2184, Dar-es-Salaam, Tanzania*

CROMPTON, Roger Martyn Francis. b 47. Sheff Univ BA69 PGCE73. St Jo Coll Dur Cranmer Hall Dur BA84. **d** 85 **p** 86. C Woodford Wells *Chelmsf* 85-89; V Golcar *Wakef* from 89. *The Vicarage, Church Street, Golcar, Huddersfield HD7 4PX* Huddersfield (0484) 654647

CROOK, Colin. b 44. JP. Brighton Poly ALA67 DMS81 Lon Univ BSc(Econ)74. S'wark Ord Course 87. **d** 90 **p** 91. NSM Dartford Ch Ch *Roch* from 90. *Walliscote, 4 Swaisland Road, Dartford, Kent DA1 3DA* Dartford (0322) 272957

CROOK, David Creighton. b 37. Trin Coll Cam BA61 MA68. Cuddesdon Coll 61. **d** 63 **p** 64. C Workington St Mich *Carl* 63-66; C Penrith St Andr 66-70; V Barrow St Jas 70-78; V Maryport 78-81; TV Greystoke, Matterdale and Mungrisdale 81-87; TV Watermillock 84-87; V Hesket-in-the-Forest and Armathwaite from 87. *The Vicarage, High Hesket, Carlisle CA4 0HU* Southwaite (06974) 73320

CROOK, Canon Dennis Eric. b 40. AKC65. **d** 66 **p** 67. C Penwortham St Mary *Blackb* 66-69; C Kirkham 69-71; V Accrington St Jo 72-89; RD Accrington 82-90; P-in-c Huncoat 86-89; Hon Can Blackb Cathl from 89; V Accrington St Jo w Huncoat from 89. *St John's Vicarage, 11 Queen's Road, Accrington, Lancs BB5 6AR* Accrington (0254) 234587

CROOK, Frederick Herbert. b 17. Oak Hill Th Coll. **d** 52 **p** 53. C Bournemouth St Jo *Win* 52-55; V Margate H Trin *Cant* 55-66; Gen Sec Commonwealth and Continental Ch Soc 66-71; Canada 71-89; Perm to Offic *Ches* from 89. *4 Heathfield Road, Bebington, Wirral, Merseyside L63 3BS* 051-645 2664

CROOK, George Brian. b 56. Univ of Ottawa BAdmin78. Wycliffe Hall Ox. **d** 86 **p** 87. C Chaddesden St Mary

Derby 86-89; Chapl Asst Gt Ormond Street Hosp for Sick Children *Lon* 89-91; Perm to Offic Roch and Edmonton Episc Area 89-91; Asst Chapl Vevey w Chateau d'Oex and Villars *Eur* from 91. *Av E Bieler 21, 1800 Vevey, Switzerland*   Lausanne (21) 922-9913

CROOK, Graham Leslie. b 49. Chich Th Coll 74. **d** 76 **p** 77. C Withington St Crispin *Man* 76-79; C Prestwich St Marg 79-82; V Nelson St Bede *Blackb* from 82. *St Bede's Vicarage, Railway Street, Nelson, Lancs BB9 0LT* Nelson (0282) 614197

CROOK, Canon John Michael. b 40. Univ of Wales (Lamp) BA62. Coll of Resurr Mirfield 62. **d** 64 **p** 65. C Horninglow *Lich* 64-66; C Bloxwich 66-70; R Inverness St Mich *Mor* 70-78; R Inverness St Jo 74-78; Dioc Youth Chapl *St And* 78-86; R Aberfoyle 78-87; R Doune 78-87; R Callander 78-87; Can St Ninian's Cathl Perth from 85; R Bridge of Allan from 87. *21 Fountain Road, Bridge of Allan, Stirling FK9 4AT*   Bridge of Allan (0786) 832368

CROOK, Malcolm Geoffrey. b 53. St Steph Ho Ox 88. **d** 90 **p** 91. C Pet St Jude *Pet* from 90. *57 Brookfurlong, Peterborough PE3 7LQ*   Peterborough (0733) 260231

CROOK, Rowland William. b 39. Lon Univ DipTh63. Tyndale Hall Bris 61. **d** 64 **p** 65. C Penn Fields *Lich* 64-68; C Lower Broughton St Clem w St Matthias *Man* 68-70; C Bucknall and Bagnall *Lich* 70-76; V New Shildon *Dur* 76-86; V Northwich St Luke and H Trin *Ches* from 86. *St Luke's Vicarage, Dyar Terrace, Northwich, Cheshire CW8 4DL*   Northwich (0606) 74632

CROOKES, Canon Richard John. b 17. Pemb Coll Cam BA38 MA42. Linc Th Coll 39. **d** 41 **p** 42. R Cleethorpes *Linc* 60-75; Can and Preb Linc Cathl from 72; R Binbrook 75-83; rtd 83. *176 Grimsby Road, Humberston, Grimsby, S Humberside DN36 4AG*   Grimsby (0472) 813678

CROOKS, Christopher John (Kip). b 53. St Bede's Coll Dur CertEd75. Trin Coll Bris BA90. **d** 90 **p** 91. C The Quinton *Birm* from 90. *84 Highfield Lane, Quinton, Birmingham B32 1QX*   021-422 3596

CROOKS, David William Talbot. b 52. TCD BA75 MA78 BD83. **d** 77 **p** 78. C Glendermott *D & R* 77-81; C Edin Old St Paul *Edin* 81-84; I Taughboyne, Craigadooish, Newtowncunningham etc *D & R* from 84; Bp's Dom Chapl from 88. *Taughboyne Rectory, Churchtown, Carrigans, Lifford, Co Donegal, Irish Republic* Letterkenny (74) 40135

CROOKS, Eric. b 34. Oak Hill Th Coll 68. **d** 70 **p** 71. C Chadderton Ch Ch *Man* 70-73; C Bolton St Paul 73-75; C Lurgan Ch Ch *D & D* 75-77; I Aghaderg w Donaghmore 77-80; I Dundonald from 80. *26A Ballyregan Road, Dundonald, Belfast BT16 0HY* Belfast (0232) 483153

CROOKS, Frederick Walter. b 18. TCD BA41 MA45. TCD Div Sch Div Test41. **d** 41 **p** 42. V Epsom St Martin *Guildf* 69-74; V Shalfleet *Portsm* 74-80; V Thorley 75-80; Perm to Offic from 80; rtd 83. *Millstream Cottage, Station Road, Yarmouth, Isle of Wight PO41 0QT*   Isle of Wight (0983) 760240

CROOKS, Henry Cecil. b 15. Edin Th Coll 71. **d** 72 **p** 72. P-in-c Kinross *St And* 72-75; R 75-81; P-in-c Dollar 76-81; rtd 81; Perm to Offic Bris 81-86; Chich from 87. *Terry's Cross, Bungalow 8, Brighton Road, Henfield, W Sussex BN5 9SX*   Henfield (0273) 493802

CROOKS, Very Rev John Robert Megaw. b 14. TCD BA38 MA48. CITC 38. **d** 38 **p** 39. VC Arm Cathl *Arm* 56-73; Can 71-73; Dioc Sec 63-79; Hon Sec Gen Syn 70-89; Adn Arm 73-79; Dean Arm and Keeper of Public Lib 79-89; rtd 89. *44 Abbey Street, Armagh BT61 7DZ* Armagh (0861) 522540

CROOKS, Kenneth Robert. b 36. CEng FBIM FIEE. S'wark Ord Course 80. **d** 83 **p** 84. NSM Wisley w Pyrford *Guildf* from 83. *Combley Wood, Hurst Way, Woking, Surrey GU22 8PH*   Byfleet (0932) 336600

CROOKS, Very Rev Peter James. b 50. St Jo Coll Cam BA72. Cranmer Hall Dur 74. **d** 76 **p** 77. C Onslow Square St Paul *Lon* 76-78; C Brompton H Trin w Onslow Square St Paul 78-79; C Wembley St Jo 79-82; CMS from 83; Lebanon 83-85; Syria 85-89; Dean Jerusalem from 89. *St George's Cathedral, PO Box 19018, Jerusalem, 91190 Israel*   Jerusalem (2) 283261

CROOKSHANK, Stephen Graham. b 08. Lon Univ BA37. Westcott Ho Cam 39. **d** 40 **p** 41. V Seal St Pet *Roch* 66-73; Lic to Offic Cant, Roch and S'wark 73-76; rtd 73; Perm to Offic Roch from 76. *23 Vinson Close, Orpington, Kent BR6 0EQ*   Orpington (0689) 38729

CROSBY, Bernard Edward. b 47. Oak Hill Th Coll 86. **d** 88 **p** 89. C Springfield H Trin *Chelmsf* 88-91; C Penn

Fields *Lich* from 91. *149 Mount Road, Pennfields, Wolverhampton*   Wolverhampton (0902) 343778

CROSFIELD, George Philip Chorley. b 24. OBE90. Selw Coll Cam BA50 MA55. Edin Th Coll 46. **d** 51 **p** 52. Can St Mary's Cathl *Edin* from 68; Vice-Provost 68-70; Provost 70-90; R Edin St Mary 70-90; rtd 90. *21 Biggar Road, Silverburn, Penicuik, Midlothian EH26 9LQ* Penicuik (0968) 76607

CROSS, Alan. b 43. Chich Th Coll 68. **d** 70 **p** 71. C Bordesley St Oswald *Birm* 70; C S Yardley St Mich 70-73; C Colchester St Jas, All SS, St Nic and St Runwald *Chelmsf* 73-77; V Leigh-on-Sea St Jas 77-89; V Woodford St Barn from 89. *127 Snakes Lane East, Woodford Green, Essex IG8 7HX*   081-504 4687

CROSS, Christopher Francis. b 02. New Coll Ox BA24 MA27. Cuddesdon Coll 26. **d** 27 **p** 28. R Aston Tirrold w Aston Upthorpe *Ox* 48-61; rtd 61. *Trebrown Gate, Blunts, Saltash, Cornwall PL12 5AX*   Landrake (0752) 851242

CROSS, Miss Elizabeth Mary. b 46. Leeds Univ BA69 CertEd70. Sarum Th Coll 80. **dss** 83 **d** 87. Wootton Bassett *Sarum* 83-86; Westbury 86-87; Par Dn 87-89; C Glastonbury w Meare, W Pennard and Godney *B & W* from 89; Asst Dir of Ords from 89. *St Nicholas Cottage, Newtown Lane, West Pennard, Glastonbury, Somerset BA6 8NL* Glastonbury (0458) 32317

CROSS, Greville Shelly. b 49. Birm Univ DPS80. Sarum & Wells Th Coll 73. **d** 76 **p** 77. C Kidderminster St Mary *Worc* 76-80; P-in-c Worc St Mark 80-81; TV Worc St Martin w St Pet, St Mark etc 81-85; R Inkberrow w Cookhill and Kington w Dormston from 85. *The Vicarage, High Street, Inkberrow, Worcester WR7 4DU* Inkberrow (0386) 792222

CROSS, James Stuart. b 36. Magd Coll Ox BA65 MA72. Ripon Hall Ox 62. **d** 65 **p** 66. C Leckhampton SS Phil and Jas *Glouc* 65-67; CF from 67; QHC from 89. *c/o MOD (Army), Bagshot Park, Bagshot, Surrey GU19 5PL* Bagshot (0276) 71717

CROSS, Jeremy Burkitt. b 45. St Pet Coll Ox BA68 MA71. Wycliffe Hall Ox 67. **d** 69 **p** 70. C Mildenhall *St E* 69-72; C Lindfield *Chich* 72-77; V Framfield 77-89; R St Leonards St Leon from 89. *81A Filsham Road, St Leonards-on-Sea, E Sussex TN38 0PE*   Hastings (0424) 422199

CROSS, John Henry Laidlaw. b 30. Peterho Cam BA53 MA57. Ridley Hall Cam 53. **d** 55 **p** 56. C Ealing Dean St Jo *Lon* 55-58; C Gt Baddow *Chelmsf* 58-60; V Maidenhead St Andr and St Mary Magd *Ox* 60-68; News Ed C of E Newspaper 68-71; Dir Chr Weekly Newpapers Ltd 71-79; Assoc Ed 71-72; Ed 72-75; Hon C St Pet Cornhill *Lon* 68-87; P-in-c from 87; Hon C Chelsea All SS from 76. *4 Coombe Hill Glade, Kingston-upon-Thames, Surrey KT2 7EF*   081-942 7563

CROSS, Leslie Howard. b 10. ACP65 Lanc Coll TCert47 Lon Univ CTOSc58. Cranmer Hall Dur 63. **d** 64 **p** 65. C Tynemouth St Jo *Newc* 64-70; C-in-c Old Benwell 70-72; V Matfen 72-80; P-in-c Stamfordham 76-80; rtd 80. *14 Birkdene, Painshawfield Road, Stocksfield, Northd NE43 7EN*   Stocksfield (0661) 843245

CROSS, Michael Anthony. b 45. Leeds Univ BA67 BA69. Coll of Resurr Mirfield 68. **d** 70 **p** 71. S Africa 70-73; C Adel *Ripon* 74-76; Chapl Birm Univ *Birm* 76-81; V Chapel Allerton *Ripon* from 81. *The Vicarage, Wood Lane, Chapel Allerton, Leeds LS7 3QF*   Leeds (0532) 683072

CROSS, Michael Harry. b 28. Liv Univ BVSc50. Cuddesdon Coll 74. **d** 76 **p** 77. C Ledbury *Heref* 76-79; P-in-c Bosbury 79-82; P-in-c Coddington 79-82; P-in-c Wellington Heath 79-82; V Bosbury w Wellington Heath etc 82-83; V Bishop's Castle w Mainstone 83-84; P-in-c Snead 83-84; V Morland, Thrimby and Gt Strickland *Carl* from 84. *The Vicarage, Morland, Penrith, Cumbria CA10 3AX*   Morland (09314) 655

CROSSE, Canon Michael Selby. b 09. Linc Th Coll 29. **d** 33 **p** 34. V Hazelwood *Derby* 68-74; rtd 74. *Astell, Overton Park Road, Cheltenham, Glos GL50 3BT* Cheltenham (0242) 517823

CROSSEY, Nigel Nicholas. b 59. Cam Univ BA TCD DipTh84. **d** 84 **p** 85. C Drumglass w Moygashel *Arm* 84-87; I Magheraculmoney *Clogh* from 87. *The Rectory, Kesh, Co Fermanagh*   Kesh (03656) 31217

CROSSLAND, Felix Parnell. b 20. CEng MIMechE57 Univ of Wales (Swansea) BSc49. St Deiniol's Hawarden 73. **d** 75 **p** 76. Hon C Skewen *Llan* 75-78; Hon C Neath w Llantwit 78-85; rtd 85; Perm to Offic *Llan* from 85. *21 Cimla Road, Neath, W Glam SA11 3PR*   Neath (0639) 643560

CROSSLAND, Joyce. d 87. Hon Par Dn Bedf St Paul *St Alb* from 87. *4 Conduit Road, Bedford* Bedford (0234) 52299

CROSSLEY, Dennis Thomas. b 23. AKC52 St Boniface Warminster. **d** 53 **p** 54. C Crofton Park St Hilda *S'wark* 53-56; C Beddington 56-59; C Talbot Village *Sarum* 59-62; R Finchampstead *Ox* from 62. *The Rectory, Finchampstead, Wokingham, Berks RG11 3SE* Eversley (0734) 732102

CROSSLEY, George Alan. b 34. Dur Univ BA56. Cranmer Hall Dur DipTh60. **d** 60 **p** 61. C Blackb St Steph *Blackb* 60-63; C Ashton-on-Ribble St Andr 63-65; V Oswaldtwistle St Paul 65-72; R Dufton *Carl* 72-73; P-in-c Milburn w Newbiggin 72-73; R Long Marton w Dufton and w Milburn 73-76; P-in-c Beckermet St Jo 76-78; P-in-c Beckermet St Bridget w Ponsonby 78; V Beckermet St Jo and St Bridget w Ponsonby 78-84; Chapl Furness Gen Hosp 84-89; TV Newbarns w Hawcoat *Carl* 84-89; Chapl Princess R Hosp Telford from 89. *28 Appledore Gardens, Wellington, Telford, Shropshire TF1 1RR* Telford (0952) 53802

CROSSLEY, Hugh Vaughan. b 20. AKC42. Bps' Coll Cheshunt. **d** 47 **p** 48. S Africa 60-73; Adn Mafeking 66-70; R Orsett *Chelmsf* 73-85; P-in-c Bulphan 77-85; rtd 85; Perm to Offic *Nor* from 86. *15 Knyvett Green, Ashwellthorpe, Norwich NR16 1HA* Fundenhall (050841) 489

CROSSLEY, James Salter Baron. b 39. Linc Th Coll 70. **d** 72 **p** 73. C Chesterfield All SS *Derby* 72-75; Chapl Doncaster R Infirmary, St Cath Hosp and Tickhill Road Hosp Doncaster from 75; Hon C Doncaster Intake *Sheff* from 78. *143 Thorne Road, Doncaster, S Yorkshire* Doncaster (0302) 326306 or 366666

CROSSLEY, Canon Dr Robert Scott. b 36. Lon Univ BSc61 BD68 PhD75. ALCD64. **d** 64 **p** 65. C Beckenham St Jo *Roch* 64-68; C Morden *S'wark* 68-72; Chapl Ridley Hall Cam 72-75; V Camberley St Paul *Guildf* 75-83; TR from 83; RD Surrey Heath 81-84; Hon Can Guildf Cathl from 89. *St Paul's Rectory, Crawley Ridge, Camberley, Surrey GU15 2AD* Camberley (0276) 22773

CROSSLEY, William Jeremy Hugh. b 55. St Jo Coll Dur BA76. Cranmer Hall Dur 81. **d** 84 **p** 85. C Gillingham St Mark *Roch* 84-87; C Ches Square St Mich w St Phil *Lon* from 87. *107B Pimlico Road, London SW1W 8PH* 071-730 4371

CROSTHWAITE, George Roger. b 38. Dur Univ BSc62. Ridley Hall Cam 62. **d** 65 **p** 66. C Bradf Cathl Par *Bradf* 65-67; C Ox St Aldate w H Trin *Ox* 67-70; Youth Adv CMS 70-73; P-in-c Derby St Werburgh *Derby* 73-78; V 78-82; V Anston *Sheff* 82-83; C St Giles-in-the-Fields *Lon* 83-86; V Barnes St Mich *S'wark* 86-88. *18 Croft Road, Godalming, Surrey GU7 1BY*

CROUCH, Raymond. b 21. Cuddesdon Coll 66. **d** 68 **p** 69. C Bracknell *Ox* 68-71; P-in-c Littlemore 71-78; C Boxgrove *Chich* 78-81; C Tangmere 78-81; P-in-c Oving w Merston 78-81; V Winkfield *Ox* 81-84; P-in-c Cranbourne 81-84; C Thame w Towersey 84-86; rtd 86; Perm to Offic *Ox* from 86. *9 Orchard Close, Chalgrove, Oxford OX9 7RA* Stadhampton (0865) 890653

CROUCHMAN, Eric Richard. b 30. Bps' Coll Cheshunt 64. **d** 66 **p** 67. C Ipswich H Trin *St E* 66-69; C Ipswich All Hallows 69-72; R Crowfield w Stonham Aspal and Mickfield 72-81; R Combs 81-90; RD Stowmarket 84-90; P-in-c Lydgate w Ousden and Cowlinge from 90. *The Rectory, Lidgate, Newmarket, Suffolk CB8 9PW* Ousden (063879) 437

CROW, Arthur. b 26. St Chad's Coll Dur BA51 DipTh52. **d** 52 **p** 53. V Flockton cum Denby Grange *Wakef* 63-91; rtd 91. *2 Thatchers Croft, Copmanthorpe, York YO2 3YD* York (0904) 709861

CROW, Michael John. b 35. AKC63. **d** 64 **p** 65. C Welwyn Garden City *St Alb* 64-67; C Sawbridgeworth 67-69; C Biscot 69-71; V Luton St Aug Limbury 71-79; TR Borehamwood 79-87; V Markyate Street from 87. *The Vicarage, High Street, Markyate, St Albans, Herts AL3 8PD* Luton (0582) 841701

CROWDER, Ven Norman Harry. b 26. St Jo Coll Cam BA48 MA52. Westcott Ho Cam 50. **d** 52 **p** 53. C Radcliffe-on-Trent *S'well* 52-55; Bp's Res Chapl *Portsm* 55-59; Asst Chapl Canford Sch Wimborne 59-64; Chapl 64-72; V Oakfield St Jo *Portsm* 72-75; Can Res Portsm Cathl 75-85; Dir RE 75-85; Adn Portsm from 85. *Victoria Lodge, 36 Osborn Road, Fareham, Hants PO16 7DS* Fareham (0329) 280101

CROWE, Anthony Murray. b 34. St Edm Hall Ox BA58 MA61. Westcott Ho Cam 57. **d** 59 **p** 60. C Stockingford *Cov* 59-62; C New Eltham All SS *S'wark* 62-66; V Clapham St Jo 66-73; R Charlton St Luke w H Trin from 73. *The Rectory, 185 Charlton Church Lane, London SE7 7AA* 081-858 0791

CROWE, Eric Anthony. b 29. St Jo Coll Dur BA53. Cuddesdon Coll 53. **d** 55 **p** 56. V Battyeford *Wakef* 68-74; P-in-c Pitminster w Corfe *B & W* 75-76; V 76-90; rtd 90. *70 Woolbrook Road, Sidmouth, Devon EX10 9XB* Sidmouth (0395) 579085

CROWE, John Yeomans. b 39. Keble Coll Ox BA62 MA66. Linc Th Coll 62. **d** 64 **p** 65. C Tettenhall Regis *Lich* 64-67; C Caversham *Ox* 67-71; V Hampton *Worc* 72-76; P-in-c Leek St Edw *Lich* 76-79; TR Leek 79-83; TR Leek and Meerbrook 83-87; RD Leek 82-87; TR Dorchester *Ox* from 87. *The Rectory, Dorchester-on-Thames, Wallingford, Oxon OX10 7HZ* Oxford (0865) 340007

CROWE, Laurence. b 32. Linc Th Coll 60. **d** 61 **p** 62. C Cov St Jo *Cov* 61-66; V New Bilton 66-75; V Washwood Heath *Birm* 75-82; V Tividale *Lich* from 82. *St Michael's Vicarage, Tividale, Warley, W Midlands B69 2LQ* 021-520 7766

CROWE, Leonard Charles. b 25. S Dios Minl Tr Scheme 80. **d** 82 **p** 83. NSM Buxted and Hadlow Down *Chich* 82-84; NSM Fairlight 84-86; P-in-c 86-89; V from 89. *Church House, Waites Lane, Fairlight, Hastings, E Sussex TN35 4AX* Hastings (0424) 813104

CROWE, Canon Norman Charles. b 23. ADipR62. Launde Abbey. **d** 63 **p** 64. V Leic St Chad *Leic* 68-73; V Market Harborough 73-88; RD Gartree I (Harborough) 76-81; Hon Can Leic Cathl 80-88; rtd 88; Perm to Offic Pet & Leic from 88. *8 Wilton Close, Desborough, Kettering, Northants NN14 2QJ* Kettering (0536) 760820

CROWE, Philip Anthony. b 36. Selw Coll Cam BA60 MA64. Ridley Hall Cam 60. **d** 62 **p** 63. Tutor Oak Hill Th Coll 62-67; C Enfield Ch Ch Trent Park *Lon* 62-65; Ed C of E Newspaper 67-71; Lect Birm St Martin 71-76; R Breadsall *Derby* 77-88; Prin and Tutor Sarum & Wells Th Coll from 88. *19A The Close, Salisbury, Wilts SP1 2EE* Salisbury (0722) 332235

CROWE, Canon Sydney Ralph. b 32. Edin Th Coll 61. **d** 63 **p** 64. C Bingley H Trin *Bradf* 63-66; C Bierley 66-69; V Manningham St Chad from 69; Hon Can Bradf Cathl from 85. *St Chad's Vicarage, 54 Toller Lane, Bradford, W Yorkshire BD8 8QH* Bradford (0274) 43957

CROWHURST, David Brian. b 40. Qu Coll Birm 77. **d** 80 **p** 81. NSM Ribbesford w Bewdley and Dowles *Worc* 80-82; Hon Chapl Birm Cathl *Birm* 81-82; C Kidderminster St Jo *Worc* 82-83; C-in-c Wribbenhall 83-84; P-in-c 84-87; V Oswestry St Oswald *Lich* from 87; P-in-c Rhydycroesau from 90. *St Oswald's Vicarage, Penylan Lane, Oswestry, Shropshire SY11 2AN* Oswestry (0691) 653467 or 652861

CROWIE, Hermon John. b 41. Kelham Th Coll 61. **d** 69 **p** 73. C Sneinton St Cypr *S'well* 69; C Balderton 72-75; V Basford St Aid 75-78; R Everton and Mattersey w Clayworth 78-84; St Helena 84-89; Chapl HM Pris Nor 89-91; Chapl HM Pris Cant from 91. *The Chaplain's Office, HM Prison, Longport, Canterbury* Canterbury (0227) 762244

CROWLEY, Brian Golland. b 01. Keble Coll Ox BA23 MA28. Westcott Ho Cam 26. **d** 27 **p** 28. V Clifton Hampden *Ox* 54-69; rtd 69. *2 Woodlands Paddock, Penn Road, Wolverhampton* Wolverhampton (0902) 330544

✠**CROWTHER, Rt Rev Clarence Edward. b** 29. Leeds Univ BA50 LLB52 LLM53 California Univ PhD75. Cuddesdon Coll 55. **d** 56 **p** 57 **c** 65. C Ox SS Phil and Jas *Ox* 56-59; USA 59-64 and from 67; S Africa 64-67; Bp Kimberley and Kuruman 65-67; Asst Bp California from 73. *210 San Ysidro Road, Santa Barbara, California 93108, USA*

CROWTHER, Donald James. b 23. Oak Hill NSM Course. **d** 82 **p** 83. NSM Seal St Lawr *Roch* 82-85; NSM Sevenoaks St Nic 85-87; P-in-c Sevenoaks Weald from 87. *Midhope, Pilgrims Way, Kemsing, Sevenoaks, Kent TN15 6LS* Sevenoaks (0732) 61035

CROWTHER, Frank. b 28. Qu Coll Birm 68. **d** 69 **p** 70. C Bulwell St Mary *S'well* 74; TV Clifton 72-77; R Kirkby in Ashfield St Thos 77-85; rtd 86; Perm to Offic *S'well* from 86. *14 Ivy Grove, Kirkby-in-Ashfield, Nottingham NG17 8JL* Mansfield (0623) 756325

CROWTHER, Ronald. b 22. Sarum Th Coll. **d** 53 **p** 54. V Tooting All SS *S'wark* 67-73; R Brinkley, Burrough Green and Carlton *Ely* 73-80; P-in-c Westley Waterless 78-80; R Brandon and Santon Downham *St E* 80-87; rtd 87. *5 Kestrel Drive, Brandon, Suffolk IP27 0UA* Thetford (0842) 811258

CROWTHER, Stephen Alfred. b 59. TCD DipTh87. **d** 87 **p** 88. C Willowfield *D & D* 87-89; I Belf St Chris from

89. St Christopher's Rectory, 412 Upper Newtownards Road, Belfast BT4 3EZ Belfast (0232) 471522

CROWTHER-ALWYN, Benedict Mark. b 53. Kent Univ BA74. Qu Coll Birm 74. **d** 77 **p** 78. C Fenny Stratford and Water Eaton *Ox* 77-80; C Moulsecoomb *Chich* 80-81; TV 81-83; R Glas St Serf *Glas* 83-87; R Baillieston 83-87; R Bassingham *Linc* 87-90; V Aubourn w Haddington 87-90; V Carlton-le-Moorland w Stapleford 87-90; R Thurlby w Norton Disney 87-90; V Elmton *Derby* from 90. *The Vicarage, Creswell, Worksop, Notts S80 4HD* Worksop (0909) 721264

CROWTHER-GREEN, Canon John Patrick Victor. b 18. Hatf Coll Dur LTh41 BA42. St Boniface Warminster 39. **d** 42 **p** 44. V Leic St Sav *Leic* 58-73; V Blaby 73-87; RD Guthlaxton I (Blaby) 81-87; Hon Can Leic Cathl 82-87; rtd 87. *40 Craighill Road, Knighton, Leicester LE2 3FB* Leicester (0533) 707615

CROWTHER-GREEN, Michael Leonard. b 36. K Coll Lon 56. **d** 60 **p** 61. C Caterham *S'wark* 60-64; C Lewisham St Jo Southend 64-69; Chr Aid Area Sec (Berks, Oxon and Bucks) 69-78; Lic to Offic *Ox* 78-83; Dioc Stewardship Adv from 83. *8 Egerton Road, Reading RG2 8HQ* Reading (0734) 872502

CROYDON, Archdeacon of. See HAZELL, Ven Frederick Roy

CROYDON, Area Bishop of. See WOOD, Rt Rev Dr Wilfred Denniston

CRUICKSHANK, Jonathan Graham. b 52. K Coll Lon BD74 AKC74 Ox Univ PGCE75. St Aug Coll Cant 75. **d** 76 **p** 77. C Stantonbury *Ox* 76-79; C Burnham 79-82; Chapl RNR 80-83; C Burnham w Dropmore, Hitcham and Taplow *Ox* 82-83; Chapl RN 83-89; TV New Windsor *Ox* from 89. *Holy Trinity Rectory, 73 Alma Road, Windsor, Berks SL4 3HD* Windsor (0753) 853585

CRUISE, Brian John Alexander. Bris Univ BA TCD BTh. **d** 88 **p** 89. C Lurgan (Shankill) *D & D* from 88. *35 Gilford Road, Lurgan, Craigavon, Co Armagh BT66 7DZ* Lurgan (0762) 6040

CRUMP, John. b 27. AKC54. **d** 55 **p** 56. V Highams Park All SS *Chelmsf* 65-78; RD Waltham Forest 75-78; R Lambourne w Abridge and Stapleford Abbotts 78-83; V Walton le Soken 83-90; rtd 90. *14 Kenilworth Road, Holland-on-Sea, Clacton-on-Sea, Essex CO15 5NX* Clacton-on-Sea (0225) 814511

CRUMPTON, Colin. b 38. AKC61. **d** 64 **p** 65. C Billingham St Cuth *Dur* 64-66; C Shirley *Birm* 66-69; V Mossley *Ches* 69-75; Miss to Seamen 75-77; V Burslem St Paul *Lich* 77-82; V Edensor from 82. *The Vicarage, 131 Longton Hall Road, Stoke-on-Trent ST3 2EL* Stoke-on-Trent (0782) 319210

CRUMPTON, Michael Reginald. b 33. Chich Th Coll 66. **d** 69 **p** 70. C Longton St Mary and St Chad *Lich* 69-72; C Rugeley 72-76; C Kingswinford St Mary 76-87; V Moxley 87-91; Chapl Moxley Hosp Lich 88-91. *69 The Lea, Trentham, Stoke-on-Trent ST4 8DY*

CRUSE, Jack. b 35. ARIBA67. Sarum & Wells Th Coll 76. **d** 79 **p** 80. NSM V Teignmouth *Ex* 79-85; NSM Ideford, Luton and Ashcombe 85-87; C 87-89; NSM Bishopsteignton 85-87; C 87-89; C Teignmouth, Ideford w Luton, Ashcombe etc 90; R Broadhempston, Woodland, Staverton etc from 90. *The Rectory, Broadhempston, Totnes, Devon TQ9 6AU* Ipplepen (0803) 813646

CRUSE, John Jeremy. b 58. Univ of Wales (Lamp) BA79 Hughes Hall Cam CertEd87. Sarum & Wells Th Coll 81. **d** 82 **p** 83. C Newton St Pet *S & B* 82-84; P-in-c Newbridge-on-Wye and Llanfihangel Brynpabuan 84-86; Perm to Offic *Heref* 88-89; C Waltham H Cross *Chelmsf* from 89. *Abbey Lodge, 5A Greenyard, Waltham Abbey, Essex EN9 1RS* Lea Valley (0992) 715314

CRUSHA, Edwin Herbert William. b 12. St Cath Coll Ox BA35 MA38 Bris Univ BA36. St Steph Ho Ox 39. **d** 40 **p** 41. R Charlton on Otmoor and Oddington *Ox* 65-78; rtd 78; Perm to Offic *Nor* from 78. *31 Pyghtle Close, Trunch, North Walsham, Norfolk NR28 0QF* Mundesley (0263) 721219

CRUST, John Allen. b 40. Linc Th Coll. **d** 68 **p** 69. C Spalding *Linc* 68-73; C Cullercoats St Geo *Newc* 73-75; V Scotswood 75-82; V Old Leake w Wrangle *Linc* 82-87; R Crowland from 87. *The Abbey Rectory, East Street, Crowland, Peterborough PE6 0EN* Peterborough (0733) 210499

CRUTTENDEN, Leslie Roy. b 39. Cant Sch of Min. **d** 84 **p** 85. NSM Maidstone St Luke *Cant* 84-86; NSM Charlton-in-Dover from 86; NSM River from 88. *6 Citadel Heights, Dover, Kent* Dover (0304) 205281

CRYER, Gordon David. b 34. St D Coll Lamp BA63 DipTh64. **d** 64 **p** 65. C Mortlake w E Sheen *S'wark* 64-67; C Godstone 67-70; R Stoke Damerel *Ex* from

71; Chapl St Dunstan's Abbey Sch *Ex* from 71; P-in-c Devonport St Aubyn *Ex* from 88. *The Rectory, 6 Underhill Road, Plymouth PL3 4BP* Plymouth (0752) 562348

CRYER, Neville Barker. b 24. Hertf Coll Ox BA48 MA52. Ridley Hall Cam. **d** 50 **p** 51. Sec Conf Br Miss Socs 67-70; Gen Sec BFBS 70-86; rtd 86. *14 Carmires Road, Haxby, York YO3 8NN* York (0904) 763371

CRYER, Percival. b 11. AKC39. **d** 39 **p** 40. Chapl Princess Chr Hosp Hildenborough Kent 62-82; Leybourne Grange Hosp W Malling 62-82; rtd 82; Perm to Offic *Chich* from 86. *19 Ascot Close, St John's Road, Eastbourne, E Sussex BN20 7HL* Eastbourne (0323) 35211

CUFFE-FULLER, Anette Elizabeth Dora. b 61. Ex Univ BA83. Ripon Coll Cuddesdon BA87. **d** 88. C Heref St Martin w St Fran (S Wye Team Min) *Heref* 88-90; C Walton-on-Thames *Guildf* from 90. *50 Misty's Field, Walton-on-Thames, Surrey KT12 2BG* Walton-on-Thames (0932) 248945

CUFFE-FULLER, Robert Charles. b 59. Westmr Coll Ox BA84. Ripon Coll Cuddesdon 84. **d** 86 **p** 87. C Heref St Martin w St Fran (S Wye Team Min) *Heref* 86-90; NSM Walton-on-Thames *Guildf* from 90. *50 Misty's Field, Walton-on-Thames, Surrey KT12 2BG* Walton-on-Thames (0932) 248945

CULBERTSON, Eric Malcolm. b 54. Ch Ch Ox BA76 MA80. Edin Th Coll 78. **d** 80 **p** 81. C Edin St Thos *Edin* 80-83; C Ealing St Mary *Lon* 83-87; R Clarkston *Glas* 87-89; Area Sec BCMS from 89; Hon C Halliwell St Luke *Man* from 90. *52 Rydal Road, Bolton, Lancs BL1 5LJ* Bolton (0204) 494921

CULL, Ernest Geoffrey. b 20. Coll of Resurr Mirfield 57. **d** 57 **p** 58. V Barrowhill *Derby* 61-70; V Derby St Paul 71-80; V Mackworth St Fran 80-90; rtd 90. *15 Lodge Lane, Spondon, Derby DE2 7GD* Derby (0332) 674562

CULL, Canon Francis Cyril Duncan. b 15. Natal Univ BA63 York Univ MPhil73 Univ of S Africa DLitt79. Clifton Th Coll 35. **d** 38 **p** 39. C Waltham Abbey *Chelmsf* 38-40; C Streatham St Paul *S'wark* 40-42; C Newington St Mary 42-45; Min St Mary's CD Welling 46-52; V Battersea St Steph 52-57; S Africa from 58; Lect Rhodes Univ 65-73; Witwatersrand Univ 74-78; Prov Can from 88. *Bishopscourt, Bishopscourt Drive, Claremont, South Africa* Cape Town (21) 797-6451

CULL, John. b 31. Oak Hill Th Coll 56. **d** 59 **p** 60. C Radipole *Sarum* 59-66; Chapl Mariners' Ch Glouc 66-70; R Woodchester *Glouc* 70-90; RD Stonehouse 85-89; V Walton *St E* from 90. *194A Grange Road, Felixstowe, Suffolk IP11 8QF* Felixstowe (0394) 284803

CULLEN, Henry d'Aubri. b 17. Leeds Univ BA39. Coll of Resurr Mirfield 39. **d** 41 **p** 42. R Shottisham w Sutton *St E* 66-86; rtd 86. *2 Meadow Rise, Barton under Needwood, Staffs DE13 8DT* Barton under Needwood (0283) 716701

CULLEN, Henry William Robert. b 07. Liv Univ BA31 Fitzw Ho Cam BA34 MA38. Ely Th Coll 34. **d** 34 **p** 35. V Cranwell *Linc* 62-78; V N w S Rauceby 62-78; rtd 78. *9 Victoria Avenue, Sleaford, Lincs NG34 4LN* Sleaford (0529) 304964

CULLEN, Dr John Austin. b 43. FRSA89 Auckland Univ BA67 Otago Univ BD76 Keble Coll Ox DPhil86 St Jo Coll Auckland 66. **d** 69 **p** 70. New Zealand 69-78; Asst Chapl Keble Coll Ox 79-82; Perm to Offic *Lon* 82-84; Chapl and Lect Worc Coll Ox 84-86; C St Botolph Aldgate w H Trin Minories *Lon* 86-87; Hon AP St Marylebone All SS 87-91; Dir Inst of Chr Studies 87-91; Dir of Tr Win from 91. *28 Lark Hill Rise, Badger Farm, Winchester SO22 4LX* Winchester (0962) 849584

CULLIFORD, Michael. b 26. Qu Coll Birm 56. **d** 58 **p** 59. V Heald Green St Cath *Ches* 62-80; Perm to Offic *Man* from 89; rtd 91. *23 Field Vale Drive, Stockport, Cheshire SK5 6XZ* 061-432 1706

CULLING, Elizabeth Ann. b 58. St Mary's Coll Dur BA79 St Jo Coll Dur PhD87 Rob Coll Cam BA88. Ridley Hall Cam 86. **d** 89. C S Cave and Ellerker w Broomfleet *York* 89-90; Par Dn from 90. *11 St Katherine's Road, South Cave, Brough, N Humberside HU15 2JB* Howden (0430) 421014

CULLINGWORTH, Anthony Robert. b 42. BSc. Ox NSM Course. **d** 83 **p** 84. NSM Slough *Ox* from 83. *375 Goodman Park, Slough SL2 5NW* Slough (0753) 36274

CULLIS, Andrew Stanley Weldon. b 48. Hertf Coll Ox BA69 LTh. St Jo Coll Nottm 70. **d** 73 **p** 74. C Reigate St Mary *S'wark* 73-78; C Yateley *Win* 78-82; V Dorking St Paul *Guildf* from 82. *St Paul's Vicarage, South Terrace, Dorking, Surrey RH4 2AB* Dorking (0306) 883023

CULLWICK, Christopher John. b 53. Hull Univ BA75 Reading Univ Ox Univ BA80 MA85. Wycliffe Hall Ox 78. **d** 81 **p** 82. C Nottm St Jude *S'well* 81-84; C York St Mich-le-Belfrey *York* 84-87; TV Huntington from 87. *The Vicarage, 64 Strensall Road, Huntington, York YO3 9SH* York (0904) 764608

CULLY, Miss Elizabeth Faith. b 46. SRN67 SCM69 RGN72. Trin Coll Bris BA88. **d** 88. Par Dn Filton *Bris* from 88. *16 Branksome Drive, Bristol BS12 7EF* Bristol (0272) 791288

CULPIN, Albert. b 16. Open Univ BA75. St Deiniol's Hawarden 76. **d** 77 **p** 78. NSM Bidston *Ches* 77-87; Perm to Offic from 87. *27 Derwent Road, Meols, Wirral, Merseyside L47 8XY* 051-632 3542

CULROSS, James Fred. b 17. Lon Univ BD51. Bps' Coll Cheshunt 47. **d** 50 **p** 51. Chapl R Wanstead Sch 67-71; Chapl Sir Roger Manwood's Sch Sandwich 71-79; R Barrowden and Wakerley w S Luffenham *Pet* 79-82; rtd 82; Perm to Offic *B & W* from 83. *34 Heritage Court, Magdalene Street, Glastonbury, Somerset BA6 9ER* Glastonbury (0458) 34179

CULVERWELL, Keith Francis. b 57. Leeds Univ BA78 Leic Univ MA90. St Steph Ho Ox 79. **d** 81 **p** 82. C Knighton St Mary Magd *Leic* 81-84; C Amblecote *Worc* 84-86; V Leic St Chad *Leic* from 86. *St Chad's Clergy House, 145 Coleman Road, Leicester LE5 4LH* Leicester (0533) 766062

CULVERWELL, Martin Phillip. b 48. Sarum & Wells Th Coll 72. **d** 75 **p** 76. C Ashford St Hilda *Lon* 75-78; C Chelsea St Luke 78-80; Chapl RN 80-83; TV Yeovil *B & W* 83-87; P-in-c Sarratt *St Alb* 87-90. *The Rectory, The Green, Sarrat, Rickmansworth, Herts WD3 6BT* Kings Langley (09277) 64377

CUMBERLAND, Barry John. b 44. Birm Univ BA67 Worc Coll Ox DipEd68 Trin Coll Singapore MDiv88. **d** 88 **p** 89. NSM Westmr St Matt *Lon* 88-90; Perm to Offic from 90; Philippines from 90. *Makati Central PO Box 8, 1299 Makati, Metro Manila, The Philippines* Manila (2) 673-7651

CUMBERLAND, Leslie Hodgson. b 15. Leeds Univ BA37. Coll of Resurr Mirfield 37. **d** 39 **p** 40. V Bradf St Columba *Bradf* 55-64; Lic to Offic 64-85; rtd 80; Perm to Offic *Bradf* from 85. *29 Union Road, Low Moor, Bradford, W Yorkshire BD12 0DW* Bradford (0274) 676138

CUMBERLEGE, Francis Richard. b 41. AKC65. **d** 66 **p** 67. C Leigh Park St Fran CD *Portsm* 66-71; Papua New Guinea 71-81; Adn N Papua 74-81; C Portsea St Mary *Portsm* 81; R Hastings St Clem and All SS *Chich* 81-86; V Broadwater Down 86-91; V Tunbridge Wells St Mark *Roch* from 91. *The Vicarage, 1 St Mark's Road, Tunbridge Wells, Kent TN2 5LT* Tunbridge Wells (0892) 26069

CUMBERLIDGE, Anthony Wynne. b 49. ACIB75. Sarum & Wells Th Coll 79. **d** 82 **p** 83. C Llanrhos *St As* 82-85; R Llanfair Talhaiarn and Llansannan etc 85-87; CF from 87. *c/o MOD (Army), Bagshot Park, Bagshot, Surrey GU19 5PL* Bagshot (0276) 71717

CUMBRAE, Provost of. *See* McCUBBIN, Very Rev David

CUMING, Mark Alexander. b 53. AKC75. Westcott Ho Cam 76. **d** 77 **p** 78. C Newc H Cross *Newc* 77-80; Perm to Offic *Birm* from 87. *6 All Saints' Road, King's Heath, Birmingham B14 7LL* 021-443 4783

CUMINGS, Llewellyn Frank Beadnell. b 29. Natal Univ BA50 St Cath Coll Cam CertEd53. Ridley Hall Cam 65. **d** 67 **p** 68. C Leamington Priors St Mary *Cov* 67-70; V Lobley Hill *Dur* 70-74; R Denver *Ely* 74-82; V Ryston w Roxham 74-82; R St Leonards St Leon *Chich* 82-88; V Billinghay *Linc* from 88. *The Vicarage, Billinghay, Lincoln LN4 4HN* Billinghay (0526) 861321

CUMMING, Nigel Patrick. b 42. St Jo Coll Nottm 73. **d** 75 **p** 76. C Castle Hall *Ches* 75-77; C Stalybridge H Trin and Ch Ch 77-78; C Tadley St Pet *Win* 78-82; R Overton w Laverstoke and Freefolk from 82; RD Whitchurch from 89. *54 Lordsfield Gardens, Overton, Basingstoke, Hants RG25 3EW* Basingstoke (0256) 770207

CUMMING, Ms Susan Margaret. b 47. Man Univ BSc68 Makerere Univ Kampala DipEd69. E Midl Min Tr Course 79. **dss** 82 **d** 87. Cinderhill *S'well* 82-85; Dioc Adv in Adult Educn from 85. *11 Clumber Crescent North, The Park, Nottingham NG7 1EY* Nottingham (0602) 417156

CUMMINGS, Elizabeth. b 45. St Jo Coll Dur BA84. NE Ord Course. **d** 87. NSM Dur St Giles *Dur* 87-89; Chapl HM Pris Dur 89-90; Chapl HM Rem Cen Low Newton from 90. *8 Homelands Crescent, Durham DH1 5AR* 091-386 8469

CUMMINGS, George Osmond. b 21. St Chad's Coll Dur BA43 MA48 DipTh45. **d** 45 **p** 46. P-in-c New Cantley

CD *Sheff* 67-72; V Campsall 72-80; V Arksey 80-86; RD Adwick 82-84; rtd 86; Lic to Offic *Sheff* from 87. *7 Lidget Close, Cantley, Doncaster, S Yorkshire DN4 6EE* Doncaster (0302) 536999

CUMMINGS, Richard Vivian Payn. b 21. Lon Univ BSc41. Chich Th Coll 51. **d** 53 **p** 54. V Wellingborough St Barn *Pet* 69-73; RD Wellingborough 70-73; P-in-c Milton Malsor 73-80; R Collingtree w Courteenhall 73-80; R Collingtree w Courteenhall and Milton Malsor 80-90; rtd 90. *55 Watersmeet, Northampton NN1 5SQ* Northampton (0604) 37027

CUMMINGS, Very Rev William Alexander Vickery. b 38. Ch Ch Ox BA62 MA64. Wycliffe Hall Ox 64 **p** 65. C Leytonstone St Jo *Chelmsf* 64-67; C Writtle 67-71; R Stratton St Mary w Stratton St Michael *Nor* 71-73; R Wacton Magna w Parva 71-73; R Stratton St Mary w Stratton St Michael etc 73-91; RD Depwade 81-91; Hon Can Nor Cathl from 90; V Battle *Chich* from 91; Dean Battle from 91. *The Deanery, Mount Street, Battle, E Sussex TN33 0JY* Battle (04246) 2693

CUMMINS, Ashley Wighton. b 56. St Andr Univ BD82. Edin Th Coll 82. **d** 84 **p** 85. C Broughty Ferry *Bre* 84-87; P-in-c Dundee St Ninian from 87. *St Ninian's Church House, Kingsway East, Dundee DD4 7RW* Dundee (0382) 459626

CUMMINS, James Ernest. b 32. Westcott Ho Cam 57. **d** 60 **p** 61. C Baswich (or Berkswich) *Lich* 60-64; V Hales w Heckingham *Nor* 64-70; V Raveningham 70-76; Perm to Offic *Heref* from 76. *Skyborry, Knighton, Powys LD7 1TW* Knighton (0547) 528369

CUMMINS, Canon Nicholas Marshall. b 36. CITC. **d** 67 **p** 68. C Ballymena *Conn* 67-70; C Belf St Nic 70-73; I Buttevant Union *C, C & R* 73-78; I Mallow Union 78-83; I Kilmoe Union from 83; Preb Cork Cathl from 90. *Altar Rectory, Toormore, Goleen, Co Cork, Irish Republic* Skibbereen (28) 28249

CUMMINS, William Frederick. b 17. St Pet Hall Ox BA39 DipTh40 MA44. Wycliffe Hall Ox 39. **d** 41 **p** 42. Chapl R Gr Sch Worc 67-75; P-in-c Peopleton *Worc* 70-75; R 75-78; P-in-c White Ladies Aston w Spetchley and Churchill 76-78; R Peopleton and White Ladies Aston etc 78-83; rtd 83; Perm to Offic Birm from 84; Cov from 86. *27 The Birches, Bulkington, Nuneaton, Warks CV12 9PW* Nuneaton (0203) 317830

CUMPSTY, Prof John Sutherland. b 31. Barrister-at-Law (Middle Temple) K Coll Dur BSc53 PhD56 St Jo Coll Dur DipTh60 Carnegie-Mellon Univ MS58. **d** 60 **p** 61. C Normanton *Wakef* 60-62; Tutor St Jo Coll Dur 62-66; Lect Glas Univ 66-69; S Africa from 70; Prof Relig Studies Cape Town Univ from 70. *Department of Religious Studies, University of Cape Town, Rondebosch, 7700 South Africa* Cape Town (21) 650-3455

CUNDIFF, Mrs Margaret Joan. b 32. Man Univ DMS60. St Mich Ho Ox 51. **dss** 77 **d** 87. Broadcasting Officer *York* from 75; Angl Adv Yorkshire TV 79-90; Selby St Jas *York* 77-87; Par Dn from 87. *37 Oaklands, Camblesforth, Selby, N Yorkshire YO8 8HH* Selby (0757) 618148

CUNDY, Ian Patrick Martyn. b 45. Trin Coll Cam BA67 MA71. Tyndale Hall Bris 67. **d** 69 **p** 70. C New Malden and Coombe *S'wark* 69-73; Lect Oak Hill Th Coll 73-77; TR Mortlake w E Sheen *S'wark* 78-83; Warden Cranmer Hall Dur from 83. *St John's College, Durham, DH1 3RJ or, 7 South Bailey, Durham DH1 3EE* 091-374 3585 or 384 0016

CUNLIFFE, Christopher John. b 55. Ch Ch Ox BA77 MA81 DPhil81 Trin Coll Cam BA82 MA86. Westcott Ho Cam 80. **d** 83 **p** 84. C Chesterfield All SS *Derby* 83-85; Chapl Linc Coll Ox 85-89; Chapl Guildhall Sch of Music & Drama from 89; Chapl City Univ *Lon* from 89; Voc Officer and Selection Sec ABM from 91. *St Paul's Vicarage, Rectory Grove, London SW4 0DX* 071-627 3315

CUNLIFFE, Gerald Thomas. b 35. Linc Th Coll 74. **d** 76 **p** 77. C Sidcup St Jo *Roch* 76-80; C Pembury 80-82; V Lamorbey H Redeemer 82-89; V Riverhead w Dunton Green from 89. *The Vicarage, Riverhead, Sevenoaks, Kent TN13 3BS* Sevenoaks (0732) 455736

CUNLIFFE, Harold. b 28. St Aid Birkenhead 57. **d** 60 **p** 61. C Hindley All SS *Liv* 60-64; V Everton St Chad w Ch Ch 64-69; R Golborne from 70. *The Rectory, Golborne, Warrington WA3 3TH* Ashton-in-Makerfield (0942) 728305

CUNLIFFE, Ms Helen Margaret. b 54. St Hilda's Coll Ox BA77 MA78. Westcott Ho Cam 81. **dss** 83 **d** 87. Chesterfield All SS *Derby* 84-87; St Mary V w St Cross and St Pet *Ox* 86-87; Par Dn 87-89; Chapl Nuff Coll Ox 86-89; TM Clapham Team Min *S'wark* from

89. *St Paul's Vicarage, Rectory Grove, London SW4 0DX*
071-622 2128

CUNNINGHAM, John Colpoys. b 10. Or Coll Ox
BA34 MA37. Cuddesdon Coll 34. **d** 35 **p** 36. R Churchill
w Blakedown *Worc* 68-77; rtd 77. *7A Devonshire
Crescent, Roundhay, Leeds LS8 1AX* Leeds (0532)
666148

CUNNINGHAM, Canon Robert Stewart. b 16. **d** 59 **p** 60. I
Portglenone *Conn* 63-74; I Belf Whiterock 74-83; I
Sallaghy *Clogh* 83-86; I Monaghan w Tydavnet and
Kilmore 86-91; Can Clogh Cathl 88-89; Preb Clogh Cathl
from 89; rtd 91. *Flat 3, 16 Cathedral Close, Armagh
BT61 7EE* Armagh (0861) 527868

CUNNINGTON, Andrew Thomas. b 56. Southn Univ
BTh86. Sarum & Wells Th Coll 82. **d** 85 **p** 86. C Ifield
Chich 85-89; TV Haywards Heath St Wilfrid from 89.
*The Vicarage, Franklands Village, Haywards Heath, W
Sussex RH16 3RL* Haywards Heath (0444) 456894

CUNNINGTON, Edgar Alan. b 37. Oak Hill Th Coll 68.
d 70 **p** 71. C Highbury Ch Ch *Lon* 70-73; P-in-c W Holl
St Dav 73-76; V Martham *Nor* 76-83; V W Somerton
76-83; V Martham w Repps w Bastwick 83-89; RD Flegg
84-87; TV Trunch from 89. *The Rectory, Trunch,
North Walsham, Norfolk NR28 0QE* Mundesley (0263)
720420

CUPITT, Don. b 34. Trin Hall Cam BA55 MA59. Westcott
Ho Cam 57. **d** 59 **p** 60. C Salford St Phil w St Steph
Man 59-62; Vice-Prin Westcott Ho Cam 62-66; Lic to
Offic *Ely* from 63; Dean Em Coll Cam from 66; Asst
Lect Div Cam Univ 68-73; Lect from 73. *Emmanuel
College, Cambridge CB2 3AP* Cambridge (0223)
334200

CURD, Christine Veronica Letsom. b 51. Bris Univ BA.
Oak Hill Th Coll 84 W Midl Minl Tr Course 88. **d** 89.
NSM Widecombe-in-the-Moor, Leusdon, Princetown etc
Ex from 89. *Leusdon Vicarage, Poundsgate, Newton
Abbot, Devon TQ13 7PE* Poundsgate (03643) 559

CURD, Clifford John Letsom. b 45. RNT Qu Eliz Coll
Lon SRN. Oak Hill Th Coll 84. **d** 86 **p** 87. C Stone Ch
Ch *Lich* 86-89; C Stone Ch Ch and Oulton 89; TV
Widecombe-in-the-Moor, Leusdon, Princetown etc *Ex*
from 89. *Leusdon Vicarage, Poundsgate, Newton Abbot,
Devon TQ13 7PE* Poundsgate (03643) 559

CURGENVEN, Peter. b 10. MBE45. CCC Cam
BA33 MA36. Cuddesdon Coll 48. **d** 49 **p** 50. R
Rotherfield *Chich* 70-79; RD E Grinstead 75-77; rtd 79;
Perm to Offic *B & W* from 81. *Tretawn, 2 Church
Hill, Marnhull, Sturminster Newton, Dorset DT10 1PU*
Marnhull (0258) 820802

CURL, Roger William. b 50. BA BD DPhil. Oak Hill Th
Coll. **d** 82 **p** 83. C Cromer *Nor* 82-86; C Sevenoaks St
Nic *Roch* 86-88; V Fulham St Mary N End *Lon* from
88. *St Mary's Vicarage, 2 Edith Road, London W14 9BA*
071-602 1996

CURL, Trevor Charles Harvey. b 50. K Coll Lon
BD74 AKC74 Univ Coll Lon PGCE75 MA85. Oak Hill
Th Coll 89. **d** 91. NSM Kensington St Mary Abbots w
St Geo *Lon* from 91. *11 Kempsford Gardens, London
SW5 9LA* 071-244 9780

CURNEW, Brian Leslie. b 48. Qu Coll Ox BA69 DPhil77
MA77 DipTh78. Ripon Coll Cuddesdon 77. **d** 79 **p** 80.
C Sandhurst *Ox* 79-82; Tutor St Steph Ho Ox 82-87; V
Fishponds St Mary *Bris* from 87. *St Mary's Vicarage,
Vicar's Close, Bristol BS16 3TH* Bristol (0272) 654462

CURNOW, Terence Peter. b 37. Univ of Wales (Lamp)
BA62 DipTh63. **d** 63 **p** 64. C Llanishen and Lisvane *Llan*
63-71; Youth Chapl 67-71; Asst Chapl K Coll Taunton
71-74; Chapl Taunton Sch Somerset 74-84; Ho Master
from 84. *Fairwater, Taunton School, Taunton, Somerset
TA2 6AD* Taunton (0823) 275988

CURRAN, Patrick Martin Stanley. b 56. Southn Univ
BTh. K Coll (NS) BA80 Chich Th Coll 80. **d** 84 **p** 85. C
Heavitree w Ex St Paul *Ex* 84-87; Bp's Chapl to Students
Bradf from 87. *2 Ashgrove, Bradford, W Yorkshire
BD7 1BN* Bradford (0274) 727034

CURRAN, Thomas Heinrich. b 49. Toronto Univ
BA72 Dalhousie Univ Canada MA75 Hatf Coll Dur
PhD91. Atlantic Sch of Th MTS80. **d** 78 **p** 79. Canada
77-81; Chapl Hatf Coll Dur from 88. *Hatfield College,
Durham DH1 3RQ* 091-374 3175

CURRIE, Piers William Edward. b 13. MC44. BNC Ox
BA35 MA62. E Anglian Minl Tr Course 79. **d** 80 **p** 81.
Hon C Holt *Nor* 80-82; P-in-c Baconsthorpe and
Hempstead 84-85; Perm to Offic 85-86; Hon C Blakeney
w Cley, Wiveton, Glandford etc 86-89; Hon C Nor St
Mary in the Marsh from 90. *48 The Close, Norwich
NR1 4EG* Norwich (0603) 764247

CURRIE, Stuart William. b 53. Hertf Coll Ox MA79 Fitzw
Coll Cam BA85 CertEd. Westcott Ho Cam 82. **d** 85

p 86. C Whitley Ch Ch *Ox* 85-89; TV Banbury from
89. *4 Longfellow Road, Banbury, Oxon OX16 9LB*
Banbury (0295) 264961

CURRIE, William George. b 08. Clifton Th Coll 38. **d** 41
p 42. V Lt Bedwyn *Sarum* 65-81; V Gt Bedwyn 65-81;
V Savernake Forest 65-81; rtd 81. *The Old School House,
Savernake, Marlborough, Wilts SN8 3BG* Marlborough
(0672) 870267

CURRY, Anthony Bruce. b 31. ARCO49 St Edm Hall Ox
BA53 MA57. Wells Th Coll 53. **d** 55 **p** 56. C Northfleet
Roch 55-56; Chapl K Sch Cant 56-61; R Penshurst *Roch*
61-75; Dir Music Kelly Coll Tavistock 76-85; Hon C
Calstock *Truro* 76-85; Lic to Offic *Ex* 78-85; R Brasted
Roch from 85. *The Rectory, Brasted, Westerham, Kent
TN16 1NH* Westerham (0959) 63491

CURRY, Bruce. b 39. Dur Univ BA61. Wells Th Coll 61.
d 63 **p** 64. C Shepton Mallet *B & W* 63-67; C Cheam
S'wark 67-71; R W Walton *Ely* 71-78; V St Neots from
78; RD St Neots from 90. *The Vicarage, Church Street,
St Neots, Huntingdon, Cambs PE19 2BU* Huntingdon
(0480) 72297

CURRY, David John. b 24. St Cath Coll Cam BA48 MA58
DipTh. Oak Hill Th Coll 73. **d** 74 **p** 75. C Watford *St Alb*
74-77; V Whitehall Park St Andr Hornsey Lane *Lon*
77-82; P-in-c Heydon w Lt Chishall *Chelmsf* 82; R
Heydon w Gt and Lt Chishill 82-88; rtd 89. *3 St
Mary's Cottages, Rectory Lane, Pulborough, W Sussex
RH20 2AD* Pulborough (07982) 3409

CURRY, Canon George Christopher. b 14. TCD
BA42 MA55 Div Test. **d** 44 **p** 45. I Edenderry w
Clanabogan *D & R* 64-86; Can Derry Cathl 79-86; rtd
86. *8 Rutherglen Park, Bangor, Co Down BT19 1DX*
Bangor (0247) 455970

CURRY, George Robert. b 51. JP90. Bede Coll Dur BA72.
Cranmer Hall Dur DipTh74 Oak Hill Th Coll DPS76.
d 76 **p** 77. C Denton Holme *Carl* 76-81; V Low Elswick
Newc from 81. *St Stephen's Vicarage, Clumber Street,
Newcastle upon Tyne NE4 7ST* 091-273 4680

CURRY, Thomas Christopher. b 47. Sarum & Wells Th
Coll 71. **d** 74 **p** 75. C Bradford-on-Avon *Sarum* 74-78;
Asst Chapl Hurstpierpoint Coll Hassocks 78-82; P-in-c
The Donheads *Sarum* from 82; RD Chalke from 87.
*The Rectory, Donhead St Andrew, Shaftesbury, Dorset
SP7 9DZ* Donhead (074788) 370

CURSON, James Desmond. b 30. Keble Coll Ox
BA54 MA60. St Steph Ho Ox 54. **d** 56 **p** 57. C Teddington
St Alb *Lon* 56-58; C Ruislip St Martin 58-62; V
Tottenham St Paul 62-67; V Hockley *Chelmsf* 67-75;
Chapl HM Borstal Bullwood Hall 68-75; V Treverbyn
Truro 75-79; P-in-c Marazion 79-85; P-in-c St Hilary w
Perranuthnoe 81-83; R from 83. *The Rectory, St Hilary
Churchtown, Penzance, Cornwall TR20 9DQ* Penzance
(0736) 710294

CURTIS, Bert. b 20. **d** 46 **p** 47. Perm to Offic *Carl*
from 74. *Greystones, Embleton, Cockermouth, Cumbria
CA13 9YP* Bassenthwaite Lake (059681) 503

CURTIS, Clement Ernest. b 09. Ch Coll Cam BA32 MA36.
Ely Th Coll 32. **d** 33 **p** 35. V Gateshead St Chad Bensham
Dur 61-74; rtd 74. *Steel House, Alston, Cumbria CA9 3SL*
Alston (0434) 381346

CURTIS, Canon Douglas Henry. b 04. St Cath Coll Cam
BA32 MA36. Westcott Ho Cam 32. **d** 33 **p** 34. V
Towcester w Easton Neston *Pet* 53-81; rtd 81; Perm to
Offic *Pet* from 81. *15 Benham Road, Green Norton,
Towcester, Northants* Towcester (0327) 51401

✠**CURTIS, Most Rev Ernest Edwin.** b 06. CBE76. ARCS27
Lon Univ BSc27. Wells Th Coll 32. **d** 33 **p** 34 **c** 66. C
Waltham Cross *St Alb* 33-36; Mauritius 37-44; C Portsea
St Mary *Portsm* 44-47; V Portsea All SS 47-55; Chapl
Portsm R Hosp 47-55; C-in-c Portsea St Agatha 54-55;
V Locks Heath *Portsm* 55-66; RD Alverstoke 64-66; Bp
Mauritius 66-76; Abp Indian Ocean 72-76; rtd 76; Asst
Bp Portsm from 76. *5 Elizabeth Gardens, Havenstreet,
Ryde, Isle of Wight PO33 4DU* Isle of Wight (0983)
883049

CURTIS, Frederick John. b 36. SS Coll Cam MA64. Ridley
Hall Cam 77. **d** 79 **p** 80. C Chilvers Coton w Astley *Cov*
79-82; V Claverdon w Preston Bagot 82-87; V Allesley
Park and Whoberley from 87. *St Christopher's Vicarage,
Buckingham Rise, Coventry CV5 9HF* Coventry (0203)
672879

CURTIS, Canon Geoffrey John. b 35. Dur Univ BA57.
Ripon Hall Ox 59. **d** 61 **p** 62. C Gosport Ch Ch *Portsm*
61-65; C Bedhampton 65-68; Producer Schs Broadcasting
Dept BBC Lon 68-75; Dioc Communications Adv *Guildf*
from 75; P-in-c Grayswood 75-91; Dir Grayswood Studio
from 84; Hon Can Guildf Cathl from 87. *The Vicarage,
Clammer Hill Road, Grayswood, Haslemere, Surrey
GU27 2DZ* Haslemere (0428) 4208

CURTIS, Gerald Arthur. b 46. Lon Univ BA69. Sarum & Wells Th Coll 85. **d** 87 **p** 88. C Allington and Maidstone St Pet *Cant* 87-90; TV Gt Grimsby St Mary and St Jas *Linc* from 90. *4 Freshney Drive, Grimsby, S Humberside DN31 1TP* Grimsby (0472) 359332

CURTIS, Jacqueline Elaine. b 60. Sarum & Wells Th Coll 87. **d** 90. Par Dn Bridport *Sarum* from 90. *40 Alexandra Road, Bridport, Dorset DT6 5AJ* Bridport (0308) 23812

CURTIS, John Durston. b 43. Lich Th Coll 65. **d** 68 **p** 69. C Coseley Ch Ch *Lich* 68-71; C Sedgley All SS 71-74; CF 74-79; P-in-c Newton Valence *Win* 79-82; P-in-c Selborne 79-82; R Newton Valence, Selborne and E Tisted w Colemore 82-87; R Marchwood from 87. *St John's Vicarage, Vicarage Road, Marchwood, Southampton SO4 4UZ* Southampton (0703) 861496

CURTIS, Peter Bernard. b 35. St Pet Hall Ox BA60 MA64. Westcott Ho Cam 60. **d** 62 **p** 63. C Warsop *S'well* 62-65; Chapl Dur Univ *Dur* 65-69; V Worle *B & W* 69-78; R Crewkerne w Wayford from 78. *The Rectory, Gouldsbrook Terrace, Crewkerne, Somerset TA18 7JA* Crewkerne (0460) 72047

CURTIS, Philip. b 17. Ball Coll Ox BA39 MA42. **d** 40 **p** 41. Chapl Giggleswick Sch N Yorkshire 55-82; rtd 82. *68 Llandudno Road, Penrhyn Bay, Llandudno LL30 3HA* Llandudno (0492) 49498

CURTIS, Thomas John. b 32. Pemb Coll Ox BA55 MA59 Lon Univ BD58. Clifton Th Coll 55. **d** 58 **p** 59. C Wandsworth All SS *S'wark* 58-61; Chile 61-71; R Saxmundham *St E* 71-77; V Cheltenham St Mark *Glouc* 77-84; TR 84-86; V Chipping Norton *Ox* from 86. *The Vicarage, Church Street, Chipping Norton, Oxon OX7 5NT* Chipping Norton (0608) 642688

CURTIS, Very Rev Wilfred Frank. b 23. AKC51. **d** 52 **p** 53. Lic to Offic *Ex* 55-74; Home Sec CMS 65-74; Provost Sheff 74-88; Hon Can N Maseno from 82; rtd 88; Perm to Offic *Ex* from 88; RD Okehampton from 89. *Ashplant's Fingle Cottage, Church Gate, Drewsteignton, Exeter EX6 6QX* Drewsteignton (0647) 21253

CURTIS, Wilfrid Fitz-Harold. b 23. St Aug Coll Cant 47 Linc Th Coll 49. **d** 51 **p** 52. CF (TA) 58-90; V Filey *York* 67-90; Chapl Speedway Riders' Assn from 86; rtd 90. *23 Scholes Park Road, Scarborough, N Yorkshire YO12 6RE* Scarborough (0723) 366410

CURWEN, David. b 38. St Cath Coll Cam BA62. Cuddesdon Coll 62. **d** 64 **p** 65. C Orford St Andr *Liv* 64-67; Ind Chapl *Cant* 67-77 and 83-84; C S'wark Ch Ch *S'wark* 78-83; Ind Chapl 78-83 and 85-88; Dioc Soc Resp Adv *St E* from 88. *41 Cuckfield Avenue, Ipswich IP3 8SA* Ipswich (0473) 727632

CUTCLIFFE, Neil Robert. b 50. NUU BA72 TCD BA72. **d** 75 **p** 76. C Belf St Mary *Conn* 75-78; C Lurgan (Shankill) *D & D* 78-80; I Garrison w Slavin and Belleek *Clogh* 80-86; I Mossley *Conn* from 86. *558 Doagh Road, Mossley, Newtownabbey, Co Antrim BT36 6TA* Glengormley (0232) 832726

CUTHBERT, Frederick Norton. b 07. Worc Ord Coll 67. **d** 68 **p** 69. C Cov St Marg *Cov* 68-73; C Cov Caludon 73-79; rtd 79; Perm to Offic *Cov* from 79. *2 Harefield Road, Coventry CV2 4DF* Coventry (0203) 452248

CUTHBERT, John Hamilton. b 34. Univ of Wales (Lamp) BA59. Coll of Resurr Mirfield 59. **d** 61 **p** 62. C Cov St Pet *Cov* 61-64; Australia 64-69; C Willesden St Andr *Lon* 69-72; C Sheff Parson Cross St Cecilia *Sheff* 72-74; V Lavender Hill Ascension *S'wark* from 74. *The Ascension Clergy House, Pountney Road, London SW11 5TU* 081-228 5340

CUTHBERTSON, Christopher Martin. b 48. K Coll Lon BD74 AKC74 CertEd75 MTh80. St Aug Coll Cant 75. **d** 76 **p** 77. C Whitstable All SS w St Pet *Cant* 76-79; Chapl Princess Marg R Free Sch Windsor 79-84; Perm to Offic *Win* from 84; Chapl Bp Wordsworth Sch Salisbury from 84. *14 Stephen Martin Gardens, Parsonage Park, Fordingbridge, Hants SP6 1RF* Fordingbridge (0425) 655865

CUTHBERTSON, John Dickon. b 19. Lon Univ BSc49. Oak Hill Th Coll 51. **d** 53 **p** 54. V Upper Holloway St Jo *Lon* 69-77; R Stanstead w Shimplingthorne and Alpheton *St E* 77-84; P-in-c Lawshall 80-84; rtd 84; Perm to Offic *Ox* from 84. *86 Evans Road, Eynsham, Oxon OX8 1QS* Oxford (0865) 880904

CUTHBERTSON, Raymond. b 52. AKC75. Coll of Resurr Mirfield 76. **d** 77 **p** 78. C Darlington St Mark w St Paul *Dur* 77-81; C Usworth 81-83; C Darlington St Cuth 83-86; V Shildon w Eldon from 86. *St John's Vicarage, Central Parade, Shildon, Co Durham DL4 1DW* Bishop Auckland (0388) 772122

CUTLER, Francis Bert. b 15. Kelham Th Coll 32. **d** 38 **p** 39. R Crowland *Linc* 64-80; rtd 80. *35 St Andrew's Road, Spalding, Lincs PE11 2SJ* Spalding (0775) 68010

CUTLER, Herbert. b 06. Kelham Th Coll 26. **d** 31 **p** 32. V Dunsden *Ox* 64-70; Lic to Offic from 70; Chapl Jes Hosp Bray 70-89; rtd 72. *21 Glenthorn Road, Bexhill-on-Sea, E Sussex TN39 3QH* Bexhill-on-Sea (0424) 214493

CUTLER, Roger Charles. b 49. MInstPkg76. Coll of Resurr Mirfield 86. **d** 88 **p** 89. C Walney Is *Carl* 88-91; Chapl RN from 91. *c/o MOD, Lacon House, Theobald's Road, London WC1X 8RU* 071-430 7268

CUTT, Canon Samuel Robert. b 25. Selw Coll Cam BA50 MA54. Cuddesdon Coll 51. **d** 53 **p** 54. C W Hartlepool St Aid *Dur* 53-56; Tutor St Boniface Coll Warminster 56-59; Sub Warden St Boniface Coll Warminster 59-65; Tutor Chich Th Coll 65-71; PV Chich Cathl *Chich* 66-71; Min Can St Paul's Cathl *Lon* 71-79; Lect K Coll Lon 73-79; P-in-O to HM The Queen 75-79; Can Res Wells Cathl *B & W* from 79; Chan 79-85; Treas from 85; Dir of Ords 79-86; Warden Community of St Denys Warminster from 87. *8 The Liberty, Wells, Somerset BA5 2SU* Wells (0749) 78763

CUTTELL, Canon Colin. b 08. OBE77. Bp's Univ Lennox BA37 STM68. **d** 37 **p** 38. V All Hallows by the Tower etc *Lon* 63-76; rtd 76. *25 Withyholt Court, Charlton Kings, Cheltenham, Glos GL53 9BQ* Cheltenham (0242) 512025

CUTTELL, Jeffrey Charles. b 59. Birm Univ BSc80 PhD83. Trin Coll Bris DipHE86. **d** 87 **p** 88. C Normanton *Wakef* 87-91; V from 91. *The Vicarage, High Street, Normanton, W Yorkshire WF6 1NR* Wakefield (0924) 893100

CUTTER, John Douglas. b 31. Lon Univ BD61. Chich Th Coll 56. **d** 59 **p** 60. V Rocester *Lich* 65-73; V Shrewsbury St Giles 73-83; R Yoxall 83-91; Dean's V Lich Cathl 83-91; rtd 91. *Little Wykeham, 111 Teg Down Meads, Winchester SO22 5NN* Winchester (0962) 852203

CUTTING, Alastair Murray. b 60. Westhill Coll Birm BEd83. St Jo Coll Nottm LTh86 DPS87. **d** 87 **p** 88. C Woodlands *Sheff* 87-88; C Wadsley from 89. *3 Overton Road, Sheffield S6 1WG* Sheffield (0742) 344697

CUTTS, David. b 52. Van Mildert Coll Dur BSc73 Nottm Univ BA79. St Jo Coll Nottm BA77. **d** 80 **p** 81. C Ipswich St Matt *St E* 80-82; Bp's Dom Chapl 82-85; R Coddenham w Gosbeck and Hemingstone w Henley from 85. *The Rectory, School Road, Coddenham, Ipswich IP6 9PS* Coddenham (044979) 419

CUTTS, Nigel Leonard. b 57. Sheff Univ BA86 BTh. Linc Th Coll 83. **d** 87 **p** 88. C Old Brampton and Loundsley Green *Derby* 87-89; C Chesterfield All SS from 89. *5 Queen Street, Chesterfield, Derbyshire S40 4SF* Chesterfield (0246) 279063

✠**CUTTS, Rt Rev Richard Stanley.** b 19. AKC47. Coll of Resurr Mirfield 47. **d** 51 **p** 52 **c** 75. C Godalming *Guildf* 51-56; S Africa 56-71; Adn Kuruman 69-71; Rhodesia 71-75; Dean Salisbury 71-75; Bp of Argentina and Uruguay 75-89; rtd 90; Asst Bp Linc from 90; Hon C S Lafford from 90. *29 High Street, Osbournby, Sleaford, Lincs NG34 0DN*

CYSTER, Canon Raymond Frederick. b 13. CCC Ox BA35 MA40. Wycliffe Hall Ox 40. **d** 42 **p** 43. R Fenny Compton and Wormleighton *Cov* 64-76; Hon Can Cov Cathl 74-80; P-in-c Hampton Lucy w Charlecote 76-79; R Hampton Lucy w Charlecote and Loxley 79-80; rtd 80; Perm to Offic *Cov* from 80. *47 Cherry Orchard, Stratford-upon-Avon, Warks CV37 9AP* Stratford-upon-Avon (0789) 295012

D

DABBS, Roger Stevens. b 09. Bp Wilson Coll 29. **d** 32 **p** 33. R Jersey Grouville *Win* 53-74; rtd 74; Perm to Offic *Ex* from 74. *9 Highfield, Walden Meadows, Honiton, Devon EX14 8JD* Honiton (0404) 3370

DABORN, Robert Francis. b 52. Keble Coll Ox BA74 MA78 Fitzw Coll Cam BA77. Ridley Hall Cam 75. **d** 78 **p** 79. C Mortlake w E Sheen *S'wark* 78-81; Chapl Collingwood and Grey Coll Dur 82-86; V Lapley w Wheaton Aston *Lich* from 86; P-in-c Blymhill w Weston-under-Lizard from 89. *The Vicarage, Pinfold Lane, Lapley, Stafford ST19 9PD* Wheaton Aston (0785) 840395

DACK, Paul Marven. K Coll Lon BD51 AKC51. St Boniface Warminster. **d** 52 **p** 53. R Quedgeley *Glouc* 61-82; P-in-c Hasfield w Tirley and Ashleworth 82-90;

rtd 90. *19 Arle Gardens, Cheltenham, Glos GL51 8HP* Cheltenham (0242) 261627

DACRE, Roy Aubrey. b 17. AKC41 Lon Univ BD41. Linc Th Coll 41. **d** 41 **p** 42. Lic to Offic *Sheff* 66-82; rtd 82; Perm to Offic *Chich* from 83. *27 The Lawns, Sompting, Lancing, W Sussex BN15 0DT* Lancing (0903) 754840

DADD, Alan Edward. b 50. St Jo Coll Nottm 77. **d** 78 **p** 79. C Bishopsworth *Bris* 78-81; V Springfield *Birm* 81-85; Chapl Poly of Cen Lon 85-86; V Tottenham St Ann from 86. *St Ann's Vicarage, South Grove, London N15 5QG* 081-800 3506

DADD, Canon Peter Wallace. b 38. Sheff Univ BA59. Qu Coll Birm 59. **d** 61 **p** 62. C Grays Thurrock *Chelmsf* 61-65; C Grantham St Wulfram *Linc* 65-70; C Grantham w Manthorpe 70-72; TV 72-73; V Haxey 73-90; RD Is of Axholme 82-90; V Gainsborough All SS from 90; Can and Preb Linc Cathl from 91. *All Saints' Vicarage, 32 Morton Terrace, Gainsborough, Lincs DN21 2RQ* Gainsborough (0427) 612965

DADSON, Stephen Michael. b 57. BA. Cuddesdon Coll. **d** 84 **p** 85. C Wednesfield *Lich* 84-87; Lic to Offic *Ox* from 88; Chapl Asst John Radcliffe Hosp Ox 88-91; Chapl Asst Radcliffe Infirmary Ox 88-91. *Laurel Cottage, Wareham, Dorset BH20 7AB* Wareham (0929) 556786

DADSWELL, David Ian. b 58. New Coll Ox BA80 MA83. Westcott Ho Cam 80. **d** 83 **p** 84. C W Derby St Mary *Liv* 83-87; Chapl Brunel Univ *Lon* from 87. *26 Church Road, Cowley, Uxbridge, Middx UB8 3NA* Uxbridge (0895) 38815 or 74000

DAFFURN, Lionel William. b 19. DFC43. AKC49. **d** 50 **p** 51. R Brampton St Thos *Derby* 57-74; P-in-c Hindon w Chicklade w Pertwood *Sarum* 74-76; R E Knoyle, Hindon w Chicklade and Pertwood 76-84; rtd 84; Perm to Offic *Cov* from 84. *Bankside, Quineys Road, Stratford-upon-Avon, Warks CV37 9BW* Stratford-upon-Avon (0789) 292703

DAGGER, John Henry Kynaston. b 07. Selw Coll Cam BA31 MA35. Cuddesdon Coll. **d** 32 **p** 34. R Sutton w Bignor *Chich* 61-77; R Barlavington 62-77; rtd 77; Perm to Offic *Win* from 78. *Greenways, Copthorne Lane, Fawley, Southampton SO4 1DP* Fawley (0703) 891582

DAGGER, Kenneth. b 46. Bernard Gilpin Soc Dur 72 Cranmer Hall Dur 73. **d** 76 **p** 77. C Blackb St Jas *Blackb* 76-79; C Colne St Bart 79-81; R Hesketh w Becconsall 81-85; Deputation Appeals Org Children's Soc 85-89; C Lowton St Mary *Liv* 89-91; C Rainhill from 91. *26 Calder Drive, Prescot, Merseyside L35 0NW* 051-426 3853

DAGGETT, Micheal Wayne. b 47. Portland State Univ BSc72. Ridley Hall Cam 84. **d** 86 **p** 87. C Tyldesley w Shakerley *Man* 86-90; V Swinton H Rood from 90. *Holy Rood Vicarage, 33 Moorside Road, Swinton, Manchester M27 3EL* 061-794 2464

DAGLEISH, John. b 38. ACIB74 MBAC85 Lon Univ DipRS78. S'wark Ord Course 75. **d** 78 **p** 79. NSM Riddlesdown *S'wark* from 78; NSM All Hallows by the Tower etc *Lon* from 79; Chapl Asst Guy's Hosp Lon 87-89. *42 Brancaster Lane, Purley, Surrey CR8 1HF* 081-660 6060

DAGLISH, John Davis. b 44. RMCS BSc70. Cranmer Hall Dur 76. **d** 77 **p** 78. C Ormesby *York* 77-79; C Kirk Ella 79-82; V Hull St Cuth from 82. *St Cuthbert's Vicarage, 112 Marlborough Avenue, Hull HU5 3JX* Hull (0482) 42848

DAGNALL, Bernard. b 44. CChem MRSC K Coll Lon BSc65 AKC65 Ox Univ BA75 MA78. St Steph Ho Ox 72. **d** 75 **p** 76. C Stanningley St Thos *Ripon* 75-76; C Lightbowne *Man* 76-78; P-in-c Grahame Park St Aug CD *Lon* 78-84; V Earley St Nic *Ox* 84-91; Ind Chapl 85-91; TR N Huddersfield *Wakef* from 91. *The Vicarage, 75 St John's Road, Huddersfield HD1 5EA* Huddersfield (0484) 427071

d'AGUIAR, Carlos. b 20. St Chad's Coll Dur BA43 DipTh44. **d** 44 **p** 45. V Bowes *Ripon* 64-80; V Startforth w Bowes 80-86; rtd 86. *2 St Nicholas Close, Richmond, N Yorkshire DL10 7SP* Richmond (0748) 4572

DAILEY, Arthur John Hugh. b 25. Lon Univ BScEng45. Clifton Th Coll 63. **d** 65 **p** 66. C Wandsworth All SS *S'wark* 65-70; V Frogmore H Trin *St Alb* 70-81; RD Aldenham 75-79; C St Alb St Paul 82-90; rtd 90. *24 Clifton Street, St Albans, Herts AL1 3RY* St Albans (0727) 50639

DAILEY, Douglas Grant. b 56. Nottm Univ BTh88. Linc Th Coll 85. **d** 88 **p** 89. C Leominster *Heref* 88-91; USA from 91. *Church of the Ascension, 726 First Avenue, North-West Hickory, N Carolina 28601, USA*

DAIMOND, John Ellerbeck. b 39. Dur Univ BA61. Ripon Hall Ox 61. **d** 63 **p** 64. C Caverswall *Lich* 63-66;

Chapl RAF 66-85; Asst Chapl-in-Chief RAF from 85; QHC from 89. *c/o MOD, Adastral House, Theobald's Road, London WC1X 8RU* 071-430 7268

✠**DAIN, Rt Rev Arthur John.** b 12. OBE79. Ridley Hall Cam 59. **d** 59 **p** 65. Australia 59-82; Asst Bp Sydney 65-82; rtd 82; Perm to Offic *Chich* from 87. *14 Kipling Court, Winnals Park, Haywards Heath, W Sussex RH16 1EX* Haywards Heath (0444) 453091

DAIN, Frederick Ronald. OBE80. Jes Coll Ox BA31 MA43. St Aug Coll Cant 61. **d** 62 **p** 64. Kenya 62-80; Perm to Offic *St Alb* from 80. *2 Eastbury Court, Lemsford Road, St Albans, Herts* St Albans (0727) 863923

DAINES, John Wilfred. b 13. Lon Univ BD36 AKC36 MTh45 DipEd46 PhD49. **d** 36 **p** 37. Lic to Offic *Derby* 47-79; Tutor Nottm Univ *S'well* 58-78; rtd 78; Hon C Ockbrook *Derby* from 79. *161 The Ridings, Ockbrook, Derby DE7 3SG* Derby (0332) 673668

DAINTREE, Geoffrey Thomas. b 54. Bris Univ BSc77. Trin Coll Bris 78. **d** 81 **p** 82. C Old Hill H Trin *Worc* 81-85; C Tunbridge Wells St Jo *Roch* 85-89; V Framfield *Chich* from 89. *The Vicarage, Framfield, Uckfield, E Sussex TN22 5NH* Framfield (0825) 890365

DAINTY, James Ernest. b 46. BA Lon Univ DipTh68. Cranmer Hall Dur 71. **d** 73 **p** 74. C Normanton *Wakef* 73-76; C Gillingham St Mark *Roch* 76-78; V Barnsley St Geo *Wakef* 78-88; Chapl Barnsley Distr Gen Hosp 78; Chapl Seacroft and Killingbeck Hosps and Meanwood Park Hosp Leeds from 88. *4 Carter Avenue, Leeds LS15 7AL* Leeds (0532) 606491

DAKIN (nee HOLLETT), Mrs Catherine Elaine. b 53. Qu Eliz Coll Lon BSc74 DipTh90. St Jo Coll Nottm 88. **d** 90. Par Dn Horley *S'wark* from 90. *39 Church Road, Horley, Surrey RH6 8AB* Horley (0293) 772217

DAKIN, Canon John Edward Clifford. b 10. AKC40. **d** 40 **p** 41. R Thrapston *Pet* 57-78; Can Pet Cathl 71-78; rtd 78; Lic to Offic *Pet* 78-85; Perm to Offic from 85. *8 Derling Drive, Raunds, Wellingborough, Northants NN9 6LF* Wellingborough (0933) 623069

DAKIN, Peter David. b 57. Wye Coll Lon BSc79. St Jo Coll Nottm DipTh91. **d** 91. NSM Southgate *Chich* from 91. *39 Church Road, Horley, Surrey RH6 8AB* Horley (0293) 772217

DAKIN, Reginald James Blanchard. b 25. S'wark Ord Course 66. **d** 70 **p** 71. C Preston Ascension *Lon* 70-74; C Greenhill St Jo 74-76; P-in-c Littleton 76-80; R from 80; CF (ACF) from 78; Warden for Readers (Kensington Episc Area) from 88. *Littleton Rectory, Squires Bridge Road, Shepperton, Middx TW17 0QE* Chertsey (0932) 562249

DAKIN, Canon Stanley Frederick. b 30. Roch Th Coll 63. **d** 65 **p** 66. C Meole Brace *Lich* 65-68; V 68-72; R Sutton 68-72; Kenya 72-75; P-in-c Nettlebed *Ox* 75-81; P-in-c Bix w Pishill 77-81; P-in-c Highmore 78-81; R Nettlebed w Bix and Highmore 81; V Ealing Dean St Jo *Lon* 81-84; P-in-c Ealing St Jas 81-84; V W Ealing St Jo w St Jas from 84; Hon Can Mombasa from 89. *St John's Vicarage, 23 Culmington Road, London W13 9NJ* 081-566 3462

DALAIS, Duncan John. b 56. St Paul's Grahamstown. **d** 83 **p** 84. S Africa 83-87; C Chingford SS Pet and Paul *Chelmsf* from 87. *2 Sunnyside Drive, London E4 7DZ* 081-529 3929

DALBY, John. b 43. Cuddesdon Coll 72. **d** 74 **p** 75. C Baildon *Bradf* 74-78; P-in-c Austwick 78-85; P-in-c Clapham 84-85; V Clapham-with-Keasden and Austwick from 85. *The Vicarage, Austwick, Lancaster LA2 8BE* Clapham (04685) 313

DALBY, Ven Dr John Mark Meredith. b 38. Ex Coll Ox BA61 MA65 Nottm Univ PhD77. Ripon Hall Ox 61. **d** 63 **p** 64. C Hambleden *Ox* 63-68; C Medmenham 66-68; V Birm St Pet *Birm* 68-75; RD Birm City 73-75; Hon C Tottenham All Hallows *Lon* 75-80; Selection Sec and Sec Cttee for Th Educn ACCM 75-80; V Worsley *Man* 80-84; TR 84-91; AD Eccles 87-91; Adn Rochdale from 91. *21 Belmont Way, Rochdale, Lancs OL12 6HR* Rochdale (0706) 48640

DALE, Miss Barbara. b 48. Cranmer Hall Dur 78. **dss** 81 **d** 87. N Wingfield, Pilsley and Tupton *Derby* 81-87; Par Dn 87-90; Par Dn N Wingfield, Clay Cross and Pilsley from 90. *20 Hambleton Avenue, North Wingfield, Chesterfield, Derbyshire S42 5LT* Chesterfield (0246) 852856

DALE, David William. b 35. Open Univ BA74 MPhil87 Hereford Coll of FE CertEd78. Wells Th Coll 61. **d** 63 **p** 64. C Weybridge *Guildf* 63-66; C Farnham 67-69; P-in-c Downton w Burrington and Aston and Elton *Heref* 69-76; P-in-c Brampton Bryan w Lingen 69-76; V Leintwardine 69-76; P-in-c Wigmore w Leinthall Starkes

72-76; V Heref H Trin 76-81; Chapl Shiplake Coll Henley 81-91; Lic to Offic *Ox* from 85; Chapl Reading Sch from 91. *48 Cardinal Close, Caversham, Reading RG4 8BZ* or, *Reading School, Erleigh Road, Reading RG1 5LW* Reading (0734) 261406 or 461116

DALE, Eric Stephen. b 24. Roch Th Coll 63. **d** 65 **p** 66. V Askham Bryan *York* 69-70; V Askham Richard 69-70; V Askham Bryan w Askham Richard 70-78; Chapl HM Pris Askham Grange 69-78; Wakef 78-79; Gartree 79-82; Leeds 82-89; rtd 89. *28 Armley Grange Avenue, Armley, Leeds LS12 3QN*

DALE, Canon John Anthony. b 42. Qu Coll Birm 72. **d** 75 **p** 76. C Elmley Castle w Bricklehampton and Combertons *Worc* 75-81; P-in-c 81-83; R 83-88; Hon Can Worc Cathl from 87; V Hallow from 88. *The Vicarage, Hallow, Worcester WR2 6PF* Worcester (0905) 640348

DALES, Douglas John. b 52. FRHistS90 Ch Ch Ox BA74 MA78 BD89. Cuddesdon Coll 74. **d** 77 **p** 78. C Shepperton *Lon* 77-81; C Ely 81-83; Chapl Marlborough Coll Wilts from 84; Hd of RE from 84. *Hillside, Bath Road, Marlborough, Wilts SN8 1NN* Marlborough (0672) 514557

DALEY, Victor Leonard. b 38. Chich Th Coll 76. **d** 78 **p** 79. C Durrington *Chich* 78-81; C Somerton w Compton Dundon, the Charltons etc *B & W* 81-87; P-in-c Cheddar 87-88; V from 88. *The Vicarage, Church Street, Cheddar, Somerset BS27 3RF* Cheddar (0934) 742535

DALL, Kathleen Ria Agnes. b 32. St Andr Univ MA54 Edin Univ DipEd57 HDipRE57. **dss** 82 **d** 86. NSM Dundee St Paul *Bre* 82-89; Dn-in-c Muchalls from 89. *St Ternan's Rectory, Muchalls, Stonehaven, Kincardineshire AB3 2PP* Stonehaven (0569) 30625

DALLAWAY, Philip Alan. b 48. Chich Th Coll 80. **d** 81 **p** 82. C Newbury *Ox* 81-83; C Newport Pagnell w Lathbury 83-85; C Newport Pagnell w Lathbury and Moulsoe 85; V Stewkley w Soulbury and Drayton Parslow from 85. *The Vicarage, Stewkley, Leighton Buzzard, Beds LU7 0OH* Leighton Buzzard (0525) 240287

DALLING, Antony Fraser. b 26. Magd Coll Cam MA50. Westcott Ho Cam 64. **d** 65 **p** 66. C Ipswich St Mary le Tower *St E* 65-67; C Hemel Hempstead *St Alb* 67-70; Ind Chapl 70-76; Hon C Bexley St Jo *Roch* from 76; Ind Chapl from 76. *30 Maiden Erlegh Avenue, Bexley, Kent DA5 3PD* Crayford (0322) 529776

DALLING, Roger Charles. b 26. Lon Univ BSc53 DChemEng55. S Dios Minl Tr Scheme 79. **d** 83 **p** 84. NSM Lewes St Jo sub Castro *Chich* 83-84; NSM Uckfield from 84. *The Parsonage, Isfield, Uckfield, E Sussex TN22 5TX* Isfield (082575) 439

DALLISTON, Christopher Charles. b 56. Ox Univ BA Cam Univ MA. St Steph Ho Ox 81. **d** 84 **p** 85. C Halstead St Andr w H Trin and Greenstead Green *Chelmsf* 84-87; Bp's Dom Chapl 87-91; V Forest Gate St Edm from 91. *St Edmund's House, 264 Plashet Grove, London E6* 081-552 1444

DALLY, Keith Richard. b 47. FCCA77. St Jo Coll Nottm 80. **d** 82 **p** 83. C Southend St Sav Westcliff *Chelmsf* 82-85; Ind Chapl from 85; C Southend 85-86; TV from 86. *93 Cambridge Road, Southend-on-Sea SS1 1EP* Southend-on-Sea (0702) 330494

DALRIADA, Archdeacon of. See STONEY, Ven Thomas Vesey

DALTON, Anthony Isaac. b 57. Em Coll Cam BA78 MA82 Leeds Univ BA82. Coll of Resurr Mirfield. **d** 82 **p** 83. C Carl St Aid and Ch Ch *Carl* 82-86; C Caversham and Mapledurham *Ox* 86-88; P-in-c Accrington St Mary *Blackb* from 88; Chapl Victoria Hosp Accrington from 88. *St Mary Magdalen's Vicarage, 5 Queens Road, Accrington, Lancs BB5 6AR* Accrington (0254) 33763

DALTON, Canon Arthur Benjamin. b 07. Univ Coll Lon BA27 Ox Univ BA30 MA35. Ripon Hall Ox 27. **d** 30 **p** 31. V Forest Hill St Aug *S'wark* 49-75; Hon Can S'wark Cathl 71-75; rtd 75. *43 Empress Drive, Chislehurst, Kent BR7 5BQ* 081-467 8727

DALTON, Bertram Jeremy. b 32. AIB64. Sarum & Wells Th Coll 81. **d** 83 **p** 84. C Ringwood *Win* 83-86; R Norton sub Hamdon, W Chinnock, Chiselborough etc *B & W* from 86. *The Rectory, Cat Street, Chiselborough, Stoke-sub-Hamdon, Somerset TA14 6TT* Chiselborough (093588) 202

DALTON, Derek. b 40. N Ord Course. **d** 84 **p** 85. NSM Pool w Arthington *Ripon* 84-87; P-in-c Thornton Watlass w Thornton Steward *Ripon* 87-90; C Bedale 87-90; R Wensley from 90. *The Rectory, Wensley, Leyburn, N Yorkshire DL8 4HS* Wensleydale (0969) 23736

DALTON, Kevin. b 32. TCD BA65. Ch Div Sch of the Pacific (USA) BD67 CITC 66. **d** 66 **p** 67. C Stillorgan

D & G 66-72; I Dub Drumcondra w N Strand 72-79; I Monkstown from 79. *62 Monkstown Road, Monkstown, Blackrock, Co Dublin, Irish Republic* Dublin (1) 280-6596

DALTON, Lawrence Richard. b 18. Qu Coll Birm 57. **d** 58 **p** 59. Chapl Antwerp Seafarers' Cen *Eur* 68-71; V Birstall *Wakef* 71-79; V Darrington w Wentbridge 79-84; rtd 84; Perm to Offic *Wakef* from 84. *31 Barnsley Road, Cawthorne, Barnsley, S Yorkshire S75 4HW* Barnsley (0226) 790696

DALTON, Ronald. b 20. St Deiniol's Hawarden 60. **d** 61 **p** 62. V Rillington *York* 64-73; V Scampston 64-73; rtd 73. *15 Ambrey Close, Hunmanby, Filey, N Yorkshire YO14 0LZ* Scarborough (0723) 890037

DALY, Jeffrey. b 50. Bris Univ BA73 Cam Univ BA82 MA86. Ridley Hall Cam 80. **d** 83 **p** 84. C Tilehurst St Mich *Ox* 83-89; P-in-c Steventon w Milton from 89. *Steventon Rectory, Steventon, Abingdon, Oxon OX13 6TF* Abingdon (0235) 831243

✠DALY, Rt Rev John Charles Sydney. b 03. K Coll Cam BA24 MA28. Cuddesdon Coll 25. **d** 26 **p** 27 **c** 35. C Rekendyke *Dur* 26-29; C-in-c Airedale CD *Wakef* 29-30; V Airedale w Fryston 30-35; Bp Gambia and Rio Pongas 35-51; Bp Accra 51-55; Bp Korea 55-65; Bp Taejon 65-68; Asst Bp Cov from 68; P-in-c Honington w Idlicote and Whatcote 68-70; V Bishop's Tachbrook 70-75; rtd 75. *32 Rainbow Fields, Shipston-on-Stour, Warks CV36 4BU* Shipston-on-Stour (0608) 62140

DAMIAN, Brother. See KIRKPATRICK, Roger James

DAMMERS, Very Rev Alfred Hounsell. b 21. Pemb Coll Cam BA45 MA47. Westcott Ho Cam 46. **d** 48 **p** 49. Can Res Cov Cathl *Cov* 65-73; Dean Bris 73-87; rtd 87. *4 Bradley Avenue, Shirehampton, Bristol BS11 9SL* Avonmouth (0272) 829121

DAMPIER, Robert Cecil Walter. b 19. Pemb Coll Cam BA40 MA47. Ely Th Coll 46. **d** 48 **p** 49. V Tettenhall Wood *Lich* 67-82; V Coven 82-90; rtd 90; Hon C Lapley w Wheaton Aston *Lich* from 90; Hon C Blymhill w Weston-under-Lizard from 90. *Blymhill Rectory, Shifnal, Shropshire TF11 8LL* Weston-under-Lizard (095276) 273

DAMS, John Lockton. b 17. FRCO40. AKC45. **d** 46 **p** 47. R Ex St Petrock w St Mary Major *Ex* 69-74; Dep PV Ex Cathl from 73; TV Cen Ex 74-77; rtd 77. *4 Wonford Road, Exeter, Devon EX2 4EQ* Exeter (0392) 71448

DANA, Canon Edmund Francis Kinnaird. b 15. ALCD40. **d** 40 **p** 41. R Northwood *Portsm* 63-80; Hon Can Portsm Cathl 77-80; V W Cowes H Trin 78-80; rtd 80; Perm to Offic *Portsm* from 82. *15 Littlestairs Road, Shanklin, Isle of Wight PO37 6HR* Isle of Wight (0983) 864153

DANCE, Peter Patrick. b 31. Em Coll Saskatoon. **d** 69 **p** 69. Canada 69-71; C Hednesford *Lich* 71-75; P-in-c Westcote Barton and Steeple Barton *Ox* 76-77; P-in-c Sandford St Martin 76-77; R Westcote Barton w Steeple Barton, Duns Tew etc 77-89; R Castle Douglas *Glas* from 89. *68 St Andrew Street, Castle Douglas, Kirkcudbrightshire DG7 1EN* Castle Douglas (0556) 3818

DAND, Robert William Scrymgour. b 17. Pemb Coll Ox BA MA45. Cuddesdon Coll. **d** 47 **p** 48. V Bracknell *Ox* 68-72; C Upton cum Chalvey 73-82; rtd 82; Perm to Offic *Cov* from 82. *11 Foxes Way, Warwick CV34 6AX* Warwick (0926) 490864

DANDO, Stephen. b 49. Golds Coll Lon TCert70. Coll of Resurr Mirfield 81. **d** 83 **p** 84. C Wandsworth St Anne *S'wark* 83-87; V Stainland *Wakef* from 87. *The Vicarage, 295 Stainland Road, Holywell Green, Halifax, W Yorkshire HX4 9EH* Halifax (0422) 374767

DANE, Henry Arthur. b 12. ARCS34 Lon Univ BSc35 DIC35. Clifton Th Coll 37. **d** 39 **p** 40. V Worthington *Leic* 49-72; Lic to Offic 72-79; P-in-c Mackworth All SS *Derby* 79-86; P-in-c Kirk Langley 79-86; rtd 86; Perm to Offic Derby and Leic from 86. *31 Millfield Close, Ashby-de-la-Zouch, Leics LE6 5JS* Ashby-de-la-Zouch (0530) 416088

DANES, Charles William. b 28. Chich Th Coll 54. **d** 56 **p** 57. C N Greenford All Hallows *Lon* 56-59; C Caversham *Ox* 59-63; V Walsgrave on Sowe *Cov* 63-65; P-in-c Hanworth All SS *Lon* 65-67; V 68-76; P-in-c Wick *Chich* 76-78; V Littlehampton St Jas 76-78; P-in-c Littlehampton St Mary 76-78; V W Worthing St Jo 78-87; Chapl Monte Carlo *Eur* from 87. *St Paul's Church House, Avenue de Grande-Bretagne, Monte Carlo, MC98000 Monaco* Monaco (3393) 307106

DANGERFIELD, Andrew Keith. b 63. Univ of Wales (Ban) BD87. St Steph Ho Ox 87. **d** 89 **p** 90. C St Marychurch *Ex* from 89. *100 Hartop Road, St Marychurch, Torquay, Devon TQ1 4QJ* Torquay (0803) 311629

DANIEL, Alan Noel. b 09. AKC35. Ripon Hall Ox 35. **d** 36 **p** 37. V Dormansland *S'wark* 58-76; rtd 76; Perm to Offic *Chich* from 76. *31 Large Acres, Selsey, Chichester, W Sussex PO20 9BA* Selsey (0243) 4566

DANIEL, Arthur Guy St John. b 12. K Coll Cam BA33 MA37. Cuddesdon Coll 34. **d** 35 **p** 36. V Colnbrook *Ox* 46-78; TV Riverside 78-80; rtd 80; Perm to Offic *Ox* 80-87. *2 Gervis Court, Penwerris Avenue, Osterley, Middx TW7 4QU* 081-572 1848

DANIEL, Herrick Haynes. b 38. Open Univ BA81. Trin Coll Bris 73. **d** 75 **p** 76. C Harlesden St Mark *Lon* 75-78; C Livesey *Blackb* 78-81; V Blackb St Barn from 81. *20 Buncer Lane, Blackburn BB2 6SE*

DANIEL, Isaac Thomas. b 11. Univ of Wales BA34. St D Coll Lamp 35. **d** 36 **p** 37. V Wolv St Chad *Lich* 55-76; rtd 76. *113 Brynian Road, West Shore, Llandudno, Gwynedd* Llandudno (0492) 870487

DANIEL, Mrs Joy. b 44. Gilmore Course 81 Oak Hill Th Coll 82. **dss** 84 **d** 87. Luton St Fran *St Alb* 84-87; Par Dn from 87. *22 Rowelfield, Luton, Beds LU2 9HN* Luton (0582) 35237

DANIEL, Michael George. b 23. Magd Coll Cam BA49 MA52 Lon Univ BSc64 MPhil67. Linc Th Coll 49. **d** 51 **p** 52. C Ches Square St Mich w St Phil *Lon* 61-64; Adv R Foundn of St Kath Stepney 64-66; rtd 66. *84 North Lane, Rustington, Littlehampton, W Sussex BN16 3PW* Rustington (0903) 773837

DANIEL, Philip Sharman. b 62. Man Univ BA83 Rob Coll Cam CertEd84. Wycliffe Hall Ox 84. **d** 86 **p** 87. C Macclesfield Team Par *Ches* 86-89; C Cheadle from 89. *The Curatage, 4 Cuthbert Road, Cheadle, Cheshire SK8 2HY* 061-428 3983

DANIEL, Rajinder Kumar. b 34. St Steph Coll Delhi 55 Westcott Ho Cam 61. **d** 63 **p** 64. C Purley St Barn *S'wark* 63-66; C Battersea St Pet 66-67; C N Harrow St Alb *Lon* 67-72; TV Beaconsfield *Ox* 72-75; V Smethwick St Matt w St Chad *Birm* 75-87; Dioc Adv on Black Min from 87. *133 Church Lane, Handsworth Wood, Birmingham B20 2HJ* 021-551 5445

DANIELS, Alan Henry. b 14. Keble Coll Ox BA35 BSc39 MA39. Wycliffe Hall Ox 63. **d** 64 **p** 65. R Yarmouth *Portsm* 67-82; rtd 82; Perm to Offic *Portsm* from 82. *11 Queens Close, Freshwater, Isle of Wight PO40 9EU* Isle of Wight (0983) 752681

DANIELS, Geoffrey Gregory. b 23. St Pet Coll Ox BA48 MA53. Lambeth STh60 Linc Th Coll 73. **d** 73 **p** 75. NSM Diss *Nor* 73-74; NSM Bexhill St Pet *Chich* 74-83; C Eastbourne St Andr 83-84; V Horam 84-88; rtd 88; Chapl Convent of Dudwell St Mary from 88; NSM Bexhill St Andr CD *Chich* from 90. *The Parsonage, 18 Woodville Road, Bexhill-on-Sea, E Sussex TN39 3EU* Bexhill-on-Sea (0424) 215460

DANIELS, Hubert Frederick. b 05. Hon CF46 TD50. Richmond Th Coll 28 Qu Coll Birm 51. **d** 52 **p** 53. In Meth Ch 28-51; V Alfriston and Lullington *Chich* 66-85; rtd 85. *45 Clementine Avenue, Seaford, E Sussex BN25 2UU* Seaford (0323) 898619

DANIELS, Kenneth Percival Thomas. b 17. AKC50. St Boniface Warminster 50. **d** 51 **p** 52. V Lamorbey H Redeemer *Roch* 58-75; V Kemsing w Woodlands 75-82; rtd 82; Perm to Offic *Roch* from 83. *Shepherd's Hey, 21 Priestley Drive, Tonbridge, Kent TN10 4RS* Tonbridge (0732) 352677

DANIELS, Norman. b 38. Leeds Univ BA60. St Mich Coll Llan 71. **d** 73 **p** 74. C Pontnewynydd *Mon* 73-76; Chapl Qu Sch Rheindahlen 76-82; Chapl Giggleswick Sch N Yorkshire from 82. *Giggleswick School, Giggleswick, Settle, N Yorkshire BD24 0DE* Settle (07292) 2637

DANKS, Alan Adam. b 41. Edin Th Coll 61. **d** 64 **p** 65. C Dumfries *Glas* 64-67; C Earl's Court St Cuth w St Matthias *Lon* 68-71; C St Steph Walbrook and St Swithun etc 71-74; C Brookfield St Mary 75-76; V Hendon St Mary 76-85. *130 Clarence Gate Gardens, Glentworth Street, London NW1 6AN* 071-723 3806

DANSEY, Desmond Henry Roger. b 17. Bible Churchmen's Coll. **d** 43 **p** 44. India 68-78; Chapl to Ethnic Minorities *Birm* 78-84; C Lozells St Paul and St Silas 84-85; rtd 85; Perm to Offic *Birm* from 85. *80 Portland Road, Birmingham B16 9QU* 021-454 7049

DANSKIN, William Campbell. b 35. Edin Th Coll 78. **d** 80 **p** 81. C Largs *Glas* 80-81; C Gourock 80-81; P-in-c 81-84; P-in-c Pinmore 84-87; R Girvan 84-87; R Maybole 84-87; R Challoch w Newton Stewart from 87. *All Saints' Rectory, Challoch, Newton Stewart, Wigtownshire DG8 6RB* Newton Stewart (0671) 2107

DANSON, Mrs Mary Agatha. Strathclyde Univ MPS48. St Jo Coll Nottm 82. **d** 88. NSM Uddingston *Glas* from 88; NSM Cambuslang from 88. *3 Golf Road, Rutherglen, Glasgow G73 4JW* 041-634 4330

DARBY, Anthony Ernest. b 26. Linc Th Coll 74. **d** 76 **p** 77. C Chilvers Coton w Astley *Cov* 76-79; P-in-c Longford 79-81; V 81-84; V Cov St Mary from 84; RD Cov S from 88. *St Mary Magdalen's Vicarage, Craven Street, Coventry CV5 8DT* Coventry (0203) 675838

✠**DARBY, Rt Rev Harold Richard.** b 19. St Jo Coll Dur BA49 Nottm Univ Hon DD88. **d** 50 **p** 51 **c** 75. C Low Leyton *Chelmsf* 50-51; C Harlow St Mary V 51-53; P-in-c Berechurch 53-54; V 54-59; V Stanway and Lexden 53-59; V Waltham Abbey 59-70; V Battle *Chich* 70-75; Suff Bp Sherwood *S'well* 75-89; rtd 89; Asst Bp Linc from 89. *Sherwood, Main Street, Claypole, Lincs NG23 5BJ* Newark (0636) 626748

DARBY, Michael Barwick. b 34. St D Coll Lamp BA61 Tyndale Hall Bris 61. **d** 63 **p** 64. C Islington St Andr w St Thos and St Matthias *Lon* 63-66; C Ealing Dean St Jo 66-68; Area Sec (Dios York and Sheff) CCCS 68-72; V Broomfleet *York* 68-73; Lic to Offic *Sheff* 69-73; V Paddington Em Harrow Road *Lon* 73-78; Iran 78-79; Brazil 80-83; Perm to Offic *Cant* 80-84; V Maidstone St Faith 84-90; UAE from 90. *PO Box 7415, Dubai, United Arab Emirates* Sharjah (6) 357530

DARBY, Nicholas Peter. b 50. Kent Univ BA82. Sarum & Wells Th Coll 71. **d** 74 **p** 75. C Walton-on-Thames *Guildf* 74-78; C Horsell 78-80; Perm to Offic *Cant* 81-84; Chapl Lon Univ *Lon* 84-89; C Shepherd's Bush St Steph w St Thos 89; Chapl Lon Hosp (Whitechapel) 89-90; Chapl R Lon Hosp (Whitechapel) 90-91; V Kew St Philip and All SS from 91. *St Philip's Vicarage, 70 Marksbury Avenue, Richmond, Surrey TW9 4JF* 081-392 1425

DARBY, Philip William. b 44. Bede Coll Dur TCert66. Qu Coll Birm DipTh70. **d** 70 **p** 71. C Kidderminster St Geo *Worc* 70-74; P-in-c Dudley St Jo 74-79; V 79-80; P-in-c Catshill 80-82; V Catshill and Dodford 82-88; V Ipplepen w Torbryan *Ex* from 88. *The Vicarage, Ipplepen, Newton Abbot, Devon TQ12 5RY* Ipplepen (0803) 812215

DARBYSHIRE, Brian. b 48. Kent Univ DipTh81 BA83. Oak Hill Th Coll. **d** 83 **p** 84. C Enfield St Jas *Lon* 83-86; R Slaidburn *Bradf* from 86. *The Rectory, Slaidburn, Clitheroe, Lancs BB7 3ER* Slaidburn (02006) 238

DARCH, John Henry. b 52. Univ of Wales (Lamp) BA73 Lon Univ CertEd74 MA77 DipHE82. Trin Coll Bris 80. **d** 82 **p** 83. C Meole Brace *Lich* 82-85; C Hoole *Ches* 85-88; V Hyde St Geo from 88; P-in-c Godley cum Newton Green from 89. *The Vicarage, 85 Edna Street, Hyde, Cheshire SK14 1DR* 061-367 8787

DARE, Charles Gilbert Francis. b 22. Dur Univ BA48. St Jo Coll Dur 46. **d** 48 **p** 49. V S Harrow St Paul *Lon* 60-74; V Ealing St Pet Mt Park 74-81; V Wisborough Green *Chich* 81-87; rtd 87; Perm to Offic *Chich* from 87. *39 Langdale Avenue, Oving, Chichester, W Sussex PO19 2JQ* Chichester (0243) 782798

DARK, Ronald Henry Richard. b 31. Oak Hill Th Coll. **d** 85 **p** 86. NSM Fyfield *Chelmsf* 85-89; NSM Fyfield and Moreton w Bobbingworth from 90. *74 Warescot Road, Brentwood, Essex CM15 9HE* Brentwood (0277) 214797

DARLEY, Canon Shaun Arthur Neilson. b 36. Dur Univ BA61 DipTh63 Reading Univ MSc75. Cranmer Hall Dur 61. **d** 63 **p** 64. C Hyde *St Alb* 63-67; Chapl Bris Tech Coll 67-69; Lic to Offic *Bris* 67-69; Bp's Cathl Chapl from 69; Chapl Bris Poly from 69; Lect 69-75; Sen Lect from 75; Hon Can Bris Cathl from 89. *24 Downs Park East, Bristol BS6 7QD* Bristol (0272) 629219 or 656261

✠**DARLING, Rt Rev Edward Flewett.** b 33. TCD BA55 MA58. **d** 56 **p** 57 **c** 85. C Belf St Luke *Conn* 56-59; C Orangefield *D & D* 59-62; C-in-c Carnalea 62-72; Chapl Ban Hosp 63-72; I Belf Malone (St Jo) *Conn* 72-85; Bp L & K from 85. *Bishop's House, North Circular Road, Limerick, Irish Republic* Limerick (61) 51532

DARLING, John. b 47. CMBHI. Sarum & Wells Th Coll 76. **d** 79 **p** 80. NSM Trowbridge St Thos *Sarum* 79-82; NSM Trowbridge St Thos and W Ashton from 82. *24 Eastbourne Road, Trowbridge, Wilts BA14 7HN* Trowbridge (0225) 762864

DARLINGTON, Preb David John. b 14. Oak Hill Th Coll 33. **d** 37 **p** 38. V Tollington Park St Mark w St Anne *Lon* 65-81; Preb St Paul's Cathl 79-81; rtd 81; Perm to Offic St Alb from 81; Lon from 84. *29 Grasmere Road, Luton, Beds LU3 2DT* Luton (0582) 591547

DARLISON, Geoffrey Stuart. b 49. MRTPI80 Liv Poly DipTP74 DipCM91. St Jo Coll Nottm 89. **d** 91. C Horncastle w Low Toynton *Linc* from 91. *6 Park Road, Horncastle, Lincs LN9 5EF* Horncastle (0507) 524564

DARRAH, Reginald Geoffrey. b 30. Jes Coll Ox BA54. Coll of Resurr Mirfield 54. **d** 56 **p** 57. TR Winfarthing w Shelfanger *Nor* 68-79; V Earlham St Anne 79-83;

rtd 83. *Kiln Cottage, Hunts Lane, Banham, Norwich* Quidenham (095387) 462

DARRALL, Charles Geoffrey. b 32. Nottm Univ BA55 MA57. Qu Coll Birm 56. **d** 57 **p** 58. C Cockermouth All SS w Ch Ch *Carl* 57-63; Chapl Dioc Youth Cen from 63; V St Johns-in-the-Vale w Wythburn from 63; P-in-c Threlkeld from 85. *The Vicarage, St Johns-in-the-Vale, Naddle, Keswick, Cumbria CA12 4TF* Keswick (07687) 72542

DARRALL, John Norman. b 34. Nottm Univ BA57. Ripon Hall Ox 57. **d** 60 **p** 61. C Nottm St Mary *S'well* 60-65; Chapl Nottm Children's Hosp 64-65; V Bole w Saundby *S'well* 65-66; V Sturton w Littleborough 65-66; Chapl Oakham Sch Leics from 84; Lic to Offic *Pet* from 84. *Choir Close, 3 Church Passage, Oakham, Leics LE15 6DR* Oakham (0572) 723136

DARROCH, Ronald Humphrey. b 45. Trin Coll Cam BA67 MA71 Ch Ch Ox BA67 MA71. Ripon Hall Ox 67. **d** 70 **p** 71. C Kingston upon Hull St Nic *York* 70-73; Hon C 73-74; Hon C Perth St Jo *St And* from 74; Chapl Stancliffe Hall Derby 84-87; Perm to Offic *Worc* from 87; Chapl Old Swinford Hosp Sch Worc from 89. *17 Viewlands Terrace, Perth PH1 1BN* Perth (0738) 28880

DART, John Peter. b 40. St Jo Coll Ox BA63. Cuddesdon Coll 62. **d** 64 **p** 65. C W Hartlepool St Aid *Dur* 64-67; C Alverthorpe *Wakef* 67-70; Lic to Offic from 70. *3 Springhill Avenue, Crofton, Wakefield, W Yorkshire* Wakefield (0924) 863782

DARVILL, Christopher Mark. b 61. Ox Univ BA83. St Steph Ho Ox 84. **d** 86 **p** 87. C Tottenham St Paul *Lon* 86-88; C Oystermouth *S & B* 88-90; Chapl Univ of Wales (Swansea) from 90. *106 Glen Road, West Cross, Swansea, W Glam* Swansea (0792) 403652

DARVILL, Geoffrey. b 43. Aston Univ DipHE81. Oak Hill Th Coll 79. **d** 81 **p** 82. C Barking St Marg w St Patr *Chelmsf* 81-84; C Widford 84-86; P-in-c Ramsden Crays w Ramsden Bellhouse 86-90; Dep Chapl HM Pris Pentonville 90-91; Chapl HM Young Offender Inst Onley from 91. *HM Young Offender Institute Onley, Willoughby, Rugby, Warks CV23 8AP* Rugby (0788) 52202

DARVILL, George Collins. b 36. Kelham Th Coll 56. **d** 61 **p** 62. C Middlesb St Chad *York* 61-64; C Manston *Ripon* 64-66; V Kippax 66-79; V Catterick 79-88; RD Richmond 80-86; P-in-c Adel 88-89; R from 89; RD Headingley from 91. *The Rectory, 25 Church Lane, Adel, Leeds LS16 8DQ* Leeds (0532) 673676

✠**DARWENT, Rt Rev Frederick Charles.** b 27. JP87. ACIB. Wells Th Coll 61. **d** 63 **p** 64 c 78. C Pemberton St Jo *Liv* 63-65; R Strichen *Ab* 65-71; R New Pitsligo 65-71; R Fraserburgh w New Pitsligo 71-78; Can St Andr Cathl 71-78; Dean Ab 73-78; Bp Ab from 78. *Bishop's House, 107 Osborne Place, Aberdeen AB2 4DD* Aberdeen (0224) 646497

DARWIN, Oliver Maurice. b 17. Bps' Coll Cheshunt. **d** 57 **p** 58. Canada 68-72; C Spondon *Derby* 72-74; V Manea *Ely* 74-82; R Wimblington 74-82; rtd 82; Perm to Offic St E & Chelmsf from 82. *284 Norwich Road, Ipswich IP1 4HB* Ipswich (0473) 251337

DATSON, Sheila Mary. CertEd67. S'wark Ord Course 76. **dss** 78 **d** 87. Bexleyheath Ch Ch *Roch* 78-87; Hon Par Dn from 87. *106 Lion Road, Bexleyheath, Kent DA6 8PQ* 081-303 2755

DAUBNEY, Howard. b 49. Woolwich Poly BA70. S'wark Ord Course 86. **d** 89 **p** 90. NSM Roch from 89. *Trehaun, 20 City Way, Rochester, Kent ME1 2AB* Medway (0634) 401691

DAUBNEY, Kenneth Crocker. b 18. Cuddesdon Coll 69. **d** 70 **p** 71. C Swindon New Town *Bris* 70-73; C Highcliffe w Hinton Admiral *Win* 73-75; P-in-c Froyle 75-83; rtd 83; Perm to Offic *Win* from 84. *40 Rookswood, Alton, Hants GU34 2LD* Alton (0420) 87091

DAUBUZ, Michael Claude. b 19. Trin Coll Cam BA40 MA53. Wells Th Coll 40. **d** 42 **p** 43. C Twyford *Win* 64-70; V Colden 70-84; rtd 84. *31 St Osmund Close, Yetminster, Sherborne, Dorset DT9 6LU* Yetminster (0935) 872584

DAUGHTRY, Norman. b 26. St Chad's Coll Regina 51. **d** 53 **p** 54. Canada 53-63 and 65-67; V Smawthorpe St Mich *Wakef* 63-65; C Claxby w Normanby-le-Wold *Linc* 67-69; V Taddington and Chelmorton *Derby* 69-73; P-in-c Dalbury, Long Lane and Trusley 73-77; P-in-c Radbourne 74-77; Chapl Pastures Hosp Derby 77-81; V Clifton *Derby* 81-90; R Norbury w Snelston 81-90; V Hazelwood from 90; V Turnditch from 90. *The Vicarage, Hazelwood, Duffield, Derby DE6 4AL* Derby (0332) 840161

DAULMAN, John Henry. b 33. Lich Th Coll 60. **d** 62 **p** 63. C Monkseaton St Mary *Newc* 62-65; Min Can Newc Cathl 65-67; Chapl Crumpsall & Springfield Hosp 67-73; V Tyldesley w Shakerley *Man* 73-81; V Turton from 81. *St Anne's Vicarage, High Street, Turton, Bolton BL7 0EH* Turton (0204) 852222

DAUNTON-FEAR, Andrew. b 45. Univ of Tasmania BSc64 Qu Coll Cam BA67 MA72 Lon Univ DipLib74 St Andr Univ BPhil76. Ridley Hall Cam 67 ACT ThL68. **d** 68 **p** 70. Australia 68-71; P-in-c Islington H Trin Cloudesley Square *Lon* 71-75; Hon C Islington St Mary 71-75; C Stoke Bishop *Bris* 76-79; R Thrapston *Pet* 79-89; R Barming *Roch* from 89. *The Rectory, Barming, Maidstone, Kent ME16 9HA* Maidstone (0622) 726263

DAUNTON-FEAR, Ven Richard Daunton. b 08. Hon DD46. **d** 32 **p** 32. Australia 60-72; Hon C Jersey Millbrook St Matt *Win* 72-79; rtd 73; Perm to Offic *Chich* from 87. *38 Ladydell Road, Worthing, W Sussex BN11 2LE* Worthing (0903) 32756

DAVAGE, William Ernest Peter. b 50. BA80 PGCE81 MPhil. St Steph Ho Ox 89. **d** 91. C Eyres Monsell *Leic* from 91. *11 Dixon Drive, Leicester LE2 1RA*

DAVENPORT (nee HILL), Ms Elizabeth Jayne Louise. b 55. St Hugh's Coll Ox BA77 MA81. Fuller Th Sem California ThM89 N Ord Course 79. **dss** 82 **d** 87 **p** 91. Halliwell St Pet *Man* 82-83; Paris St Mich *Eur* 83-85; Lic to Offic *St Alb* 85-87; Hon Par Dn Chorleywood St Andr 87-89; USA from 89. *132 N Euclid, Pasadena, California 91101, USA* Pasadena (818) 796-1172

DAVENPORT, Ian Arthan. b 54. Linc Th Coll 85. **d** 87 **p** 88. C Ches H Trin *Ches* from 87. *114 Saughall Road, Chester CH1 5EZ* Chester (0244) 373955

DAVENPORT, Michael Arthur. b 38. Kelham Th Coll 58 Lich Th Coll 60. **d** 62 **p** 63. C Bilborough w Strelley *S'well* 62-66; C Kettering St Mary *Pet* 66-69; V Tottenham St Benet Fink *Lon* from 69. *St Benet's Vicarage, Walpole Road, London N17 6BH* 081-888 4541

DAVENPORT, Miss Sybil Ann. b 36. Nottm Univ DipTh88. E Midl Min Tr Course 85. **d** 89. NSM Thurgarton w Hoveringham and Bleasby etc *S'well* from 89. *Holmedale, North Muskham, Newark, Notts NG23 6HQ* Newark (0636) 701552

DAVEY, Andrew John. b 57. Magd Coll Ox BA78 MA83. Wycliffe Hall Ox 80. **d** 83 **p** 84. C Bermondsey St Jas w Ch Ch *S'wark* 83-87; Chapl Trin Coll Cam from 87. *Trinity College, Cambridge CB2 1TQ* Cambridge (0223) 338465

DAVEY, Andrew Paul. b 61. Southn Univ BA82. Westcott Ho Cam 85. **d** 87 **p** 88. C S'wark H Trin w St Matt *S'wark* 87-91; V Camberwell St Luke from 91. *St Luke's Vicarage, 123 Farnborough Way, London SE15 6HL* 071-703 5587

DAVEY, Canon Clive Herbert George. b 09. St Jo Coll Dur BA31 MA34. Wycliffe Hall Ox 31. **d** 32 **p** 33. V Guildf Ch Ch *Guildf* 63-78; RD Guildf 73-78; Hon Can Guildf Cathl 76-78; rtd 78; Perm to Offic *B & W* from 78. *24 Preywater Road, Wookey, Wells, Somerset BA5 1LE* Wells (0749) 77865

DAVEY, Dr Colin Hugh Lancaster. b 34. Em Coll Cam BA56 MA60 PhD89. Cuddesdon Coll 59. **d** 61 **p** 62. C Moseley St Agnes *Birm* 61-64; Lic to Offic *Eur* 64-65; Sub Warden St Boniface Coll Warminster 66-69; C Bath Weston St Jo *B & W* 69-70; Asst Gen Sec C of E Coun on Foreign Relns 70-74; Hon C St Dunstan in the West *Lon* 71-73; Hon C Kennington St Jo *S'wark* 73-74; V S Harrow St Paul *Lon* 74-80; V Paddington St Jas 80-83; Lic to Offic from 83; Asst Gen Sec BCC 83-90; Ch Life Sec CCBI from 90. *30 Westwick Gardens, London W14 0BU* 071-602 6860 or 620 4444

DAVEY, Canon Deryck Harry Percival. b 23. St Jo Coll Dur BA48 DipTh50. **d** 50 **p** 51. C Madron w Morvah *Truro* 50-53; V Paul 53-59; V Liskeard w St Keyne 59-76; RD W Wivelshire 65-68 and 71-73; Hon Can Truro Cathl from 75; V Liskeard w St Keyne and St Pinnock 76-82; P-in-c Morval 80-82; TR Liskeard, St Keyne, St Pinnock, Morval etc from 82; P-in-c Boconnoc w Bradoc 82-90. *The Rectory, Church Street, Liskeard, Cornwall PL14 3AQ* Liskeard (0579) 42178

DAVEY, Eric Victor. b 28. Wycliffe Hall Ox 53 Ridley Hall Cam. **d** 56 **p** 57. C Stockton St Thos *Dur* 56-59; C Stretford St Matt *Man* 59-61; V Slaithwaite w E Scammonden *Wakef* 61-68; V Pontefract St Giles 68-83; V Wakef St Jo from 83. *St John's Vicarage, 65 Bradford Road, Wakefield, W Yorkshire WF1 2AA* Wakefield (0924) 371029

DAVEY, Canon Frederick Hutley David. b 14. Cranmer Hall Dur 58. **d** 60 **p** 62. E Pakistan 69-71; Bangladesh 71-76; Chapl De Beer Miss to Seamen *Eur* 77-82; rtd 82.

126 Ashtree Road, Frome, Somerset BA11 2SF   Frome (0373) 67545

DAVEY, James Garland. b 21. **d** 75 **p** 76. C Liskeard w St Keyne and St Pinnock *Truro* 75-77; Perm to Offic *B & W* 77-80; TV S Molton w Nymet St George, High Bray etc *Ex* 80-86; rtd 86; Perm to Offic *B & W* from 86. *Keeper's Cottage, Ham Lane, Compton Dundon, Somerton, Somerset TA11 6PQ*   Somerton (0458) 45991

DAVEY, John. b 35. FRSH Lon Univ BSc MPhil PhD90. Chich Th Coll 67. **d** 69 **p** 70. C Eastbourne St Eliz *Chich* 69-72; C Eastbourne St Mary 72-74; V W Wittering 74-77; Min Can Windsor 78-81; R The Rissingtons *Glouc* 81-85; R Alfriston w Lullington, Litlington and W Dean *Chich* from 85. *The Rectory, Sloe Lane, Alfriston, Polegate, E Sussex BN26 5UY*   Eastbourne (0323) 870376

DAVEY, John Michael. b 31. St Chad's Coll Dur BA54 DipTh56. **d** 56 **p** 61. C Southwick H Trin *Dur* 56-57; C Harton 60-64; C Bawtry w Austerfield *S'well* 64-67; V Stillington *Dur* 67-70; Lic to Offic 70-78; Perm to Offic *Sheff* from 78. *254 Albert Road, Sheffield S8 9QU*   Sheffield (0742) 588734

DAVEY, Julian Metherall. b 40. Jes Coll Ox BA62 MA65. Wells Th Coll 62. **d** 64 **p** 65. C Weston-super-Mare St Jo *B & W* 64-66; Perm to Offic *St Alb* 66-68; Chapl St Alb Sch 68-73; Chapl Merchant Taylors' Sch Crosby 73-82; Perm to Offic *Truro* 82-83; P-in-c Meavy w Sheepstor *Ex* 83-85; P-in-c Walkhampton 83-85; R Meavy, Sheepstor and Walkhampton 85; Chapl Warw Sch 86-89; P-in-c The Winterbournes and Compton Valence *Sarum* from 89. *The Rectory, Martinstown, Dorchester, Dorset DT2 9JZ*   Martinstown (0305) 889241

DAVEY, Dr Julian Warwick. b 45. LRCPI DCH DRCOG. Qu Coll Birm 78. **d** 81 **p** 82. NSM Ipsley *Worc* from 81. *2 Meeting Lane, Alcester, Warks B49 5QT*   Alcester (0789) 764640

DAVEY, Kenneth William. b 41. Lanc Coll HNC. Qu Coll Birm 84. **d** 86 **p** 87. C Baswich (or Berkswich) *Lich* 86-90; V Lostock Gralam *Ches* from 90. *The Vicarage, Lostock Gralam, Northwich, Cheshire CW9 7PS*   Northwich (0606) 43806

DAVEY, Preb Norman John. b 23. Bps' Coll Cheshunt 51. **d** 53 **p** 54. C Ex St Martin, St Steph, St Laur etc *Ex* 67-70; R Ex St Mary Arches 70-73; TR Cen Ex 74-77; P-in-c Ide 75-77; Dioc Dir of Educn 77-88; Preb Ex Cathl 77-88; V Holcombe Burnell 77-88; rtd 88. *2 The Poplars, Park Lane, Pinhoe, Exeter EX6 9HH*

DAVEY, Peter Francis. b 40. Trin Coll Cam BA63 MA68. Cuddesdon Coll 63. **d** 65 **p** 66. C Atherton *Man* 65-69; C Leesfield 69-72; V High Crompton 72-79; V Blackrod 79-89; P-in-c Ringley from 89. *Ringley Vicarage, 1A Fold Road, Radcliffe, Manchester M26 9FT*   Farnworth (0204) 73742

DAVEY, Piers Damer. b 57. Dur Univ BSc. Coll of Resurr Mirfield 80. **d** 83 **p** 84. C Heworth St Mary *Dur* 83-86; C Barnard Castle w Whorlton 86-89; V Aycliffe from 89. *The Vicarage, Aycliffe, Newton Aycliffe, Co Durham DL5 6JT*   Aycliffe (0325) 313395

DAVEY, William Edwin. b 15. TCD BA39 MA42. TCD Div Sch. **d** 41 **p** 42. V Gt Harwood St Jo *Blackb* 67-72; R Mamble w Bayton *Worc* 72-80; rtd 80. *2 Garfield Villas, High Street, Tisbury, Salisbury SP3 6LA*   Tisbury (0747) 871063

DAVID, Brother. See JARDINE, David John

DAVID, Canon Colin Mackie. b 20. St Mich Coll Llan 46. **d** 48 **p** 49. R Merthyr Dyfan *Llan* 67-84; Hon Can Llan Cathl from 83; rtd 84. *10 Cwrtvil Road, Penarth, S Glam CF6 2HN*   Penarth (0222) 711341

DAVID, Edmund Watcyn Rees. b 15. St D Coll Lamp BA37. **d** 38 **p** 39. V Shoreham *Roch* 68-80; RD Shoreham 77-80; rtd 80; Perm to Offic *Chich* from 80. *Hampton Place, 71 Hampton Dene Road, Hereford HR1 1UK*   Hereford (0432) 279497

DAVID, Evan David Owen Jenkin. b 10. St D Coll Lamp BA34. **d** 34 **p** 35. R Llandyrnog and Llangwyfan *St As* 67-77; rtd 77. *Flat 29, Cromer Court, 81 Alderley Road, Hoylake, Wirral, Merseyside L47 2AU*   051-632 6474

DAVID, Miss Faith Caroline. See CLARINGBULL, Mrs Faith Caroline

DAVID, Canon Kenith Andrew. b 39. Natal Univ BA64. Coll of Resurr Mirfield 64. **d** 66 **p** 67. C Harpenden St Nic *St Alb* 66-69; S Africa 69-71; Th Educn Sec Chr Aid 72-75; Project Officer India and Bangladesh 75-81; Hon C Kingston All SS *S'wark* 72-76; Hon C Kingston All SS w St Jo 76-81; Botswana 81-83; Hon C Geneva *Eur* from 83; Co-ord Urban Rural Miss WCC from 83; Can Dio Lundi Zimbabwe from 84. *c/o WCC/CWME Urban Rural Mission, PO Box 2100, CH-1211 Geneva 20, Switzerland*   Geneva (22) 791-6134

DAVID, Michael Anthony Louis. b 29. AKC58. **d** 59 **p** 60. V Gravesend St Mary *Roch* 63-78; V Foremark *Derby* 78-81; V Repton 78-81; TV Buxton w Burbage and King Sterndale 81-85; R Warlingham w Chelsham and Farleigh *S'wark* 85-90; rtd 91. *95 Lulworth Avenue, Hamworthy, Poole, Dorset BH15 4DH*   Poole (0202) 684475

DAVID, Philip Evan Nicholl. b 31. Jes Coll Ox BA53 MA57 Univ of Wales BA61 Nottm Univ MPhil86 Leic Univ MEd88. St Mich Coll Llan 56. **d** 57 **p** 58. C Llanblethian w Cowbridge *Llan* 57-60; C Cardiff St Jo 60-64; Chapl Ch Coll Brecon 64-75; P-in-c Aberyscir and Llanfihangel Nantbran *S & B* 70-75; Chapl Loretto Sch Musselburgh 75-82; Lic to Offic *Derby* from 80; Chapl Trent Coll Nottm from 83. *Trent College, Long Eaton, Nottingham NG10 4AD*   Long Eaton (0602) 729941

DAVID COLUMBA, Brother. See HARE, David

DAVID STEPHEN, Brother. See STEVENS, Canon David Johnson

DAVIDSON, Canon Charles Hilary. b 29. St Edm Hall Ox BA52 MA56 Leic Univ MPhil89. Lich Th Coll 52. **d** 54 **p** 55. C Abington *Pet* 54-59; C Pet St Jo 59-60; R Sywell w Overstone 60-66; P-in-c Lamport w Faxton 66-76; R Maidwell w Draughton and Scaldwell 67-76; R Maidwell w Draughton, Scaldwell, Lamport etc 77-80; RD Brixworth 77-79; Can Pet Cathl from 79; V Roade 80-87; V Roade and Ashton w Hartwell from 87. *The Vicarage, Roade, Northampton NN7 2NT*   Northampton (0604) 862284

DAVIDSON, George Morley. b 10. AKC33. **d** 33 **p** 34. V Clavering w Langley *Chelmsf* 68-75; rtd 75; Perm to Offic Ches from 78; Lon from 87. *10 Woodridings Close, Pinner, Middx HA5 4RF*

DAVIDSON, Ian George. b 32. Lon Univ BSc53. Linc Th Coll 55. **d** 58 **p** 59. C Waltham Cross *St Alb* 58-60; C St Alb Abbey 61-63; Hon PV S'wark Cathl *S'wark* 63-67; V Gt Cornard *St E* 67-72; R Lt Cornard 67-70; Lic to Offic 72-79; Student Counsellor Suffolk Coll 72-79; P-in-c Witnesham w Swilland and Ashbocking 79-83; Warden Scargill Ho N Yorkshire 83-88; Chapl Chr Fellowship of Healing (Scotland) from 88. *St Hilda's House, 1A Oxgangs Avenue, Edinburgh EH13 9JA*   031-441 1235

DAVIDSON, John. b 34. Edin Th Coll. **d** 66 **p** 67. C Helensburgh *Glas* 66-69; C Kirkby *Liv* 69-70; TV 70-74. *Flat 19, 153-155 Seymour Place, London W1H 5TQ*   071-723 4262

DAVIDSON, John Lindsay. b 27. LRCP51 St Cath Soc Ox DipTh57. St Steph Ho Ox. **d** 58 **p** 59. C Croydon St Mich *Cant* 58-61; P-in-c H Cross Miss 62-66; V Lewisham St Steph *S'wark* 67-70; V Croydon St Mich *Cant* 70-80; V Croydon St Mich w St Jas 80-81; TR N Creedy *Ex* from 81; RD Cadbury 86-90. *The Rectory, Cheriton Fitzpaine, Crediton, Devon EX17 4JB*   Cheriton Fitzpaine (03636) 352

DAVIDSON, Canon John Noble. b 15. Edin Th Coll 52. **d** 54 **p** 55. V Southport H Trin *Liv* 69-75; V Blackford w Scaleby *Carl* 75-78; V Rockcliffe 75-78; rtd 78; Perm to Offic *Carl* from 78; Hon Can Malta Cathl *Eur* 81-84. *6 Netherend Road, Penrith, Cumbria CA11 8PF*   Penrith (0768) 63274

DAVIDSON, John Stuart. b 27. RMA 48. Linc Th Coll 62. **d** 64 **p** 65. C Hexham *Newc* 64-66; CF 66-78; P-in-c Rockcliffe *Carl* 78-79; P-in-c Blackford w Scaleby 78-79; V Rockcliffe and Blackford 79-83; R Kelso *Edin* from 83. *The Rectory, Forestfield, Kelso, Roxburghshire TD5 7BX*   Kelso (0573) 24163

DAVIDSON, Jonathan Eric. b 18. TCD BA41 MA65. **d** 42 **p** 43. I Kildress w Altedesert *Arm* 51-83; rtd 83. *51 Burn Road, Cookstown, Co Tyrone*   Cookstown (06487) 63733

DAVIDSON, Norman Martin. b 24. BSc. W Midl Minl Tr Course. **d** 85 **p** 86. NSM Allesley *Cov* 85-90; rtd 90; Perm to Offic *Cov* from 90. *77 Four Pounds Avenue, Coventry CV5 8DH*   Coventry (0203) 673682

DAVIDSON, Air Vice-Marshal Sinclair Melville. b 22. CBE68. CEng FRaeS FIEE. Chich Th Coll 79. **d** 81 **p** 81. Hon C High Hurstwood *Chich* 81-82; P-in-c 83-88; Perm to Offic from 88. *Trinity Cottage, Chilles Lane, High Hurstwood, Uckfield, E Sussex TN22 4AA*   Buxted (082581) 2151

DAVIDSON, Trevor John. b 49. CertEd DipHE. Oak Hill Th Coll 80. **d** 85 **p** 86. C Drypool *York* 85-88; V Bessingby from 88; V Carnaby from 88; Chapl Bridlington and Distr Gen Hosp from 88. *The Vicarage, Kent Road, Bessingby, Bridlington, N Humberside YO16 4RU*   Bridlington (0262) 670399

DAVIDSON, William Watkins. b 20. Wadh Coll Ox BA48 MA53. Westcott Ho Cam 49. **d** 50 **p** 51. V Westmr St Steph w St Jo *Lon* 65-83; rtd 85. *Chedworth*

*House, Highfield Road, West Byfleet, Weybridge, Surrey
KT14 6QT* Weybridge (0932) 342711

DAVIE (nee JONES), Mrs Alyson Elizabeth. b 58. Ex Univ
BA86. Wycliffe Hall Ox 86. **d** 88. Par Dn Ipswich St
Fran *St E* from 88. *76 Holcombe Crescent, Ipswich
IP2 9PW* Ipswich (0473) 688339

DAVIE, Peter Edward Sidney. b 36. Lon Univ BSc57
MPhil78 Birm Univ MA73 Kent Univ PhD91. Coll of
Resurr Mirfield 57. **d** 60 **p** 61. C De Beauvoir Town St
Pet *Lon* 60-63; C-in-c Godshill CD *Portsm* 63-67; R
Upton St Leonards *Glouc* 67-73; Sen Lect Ch Ch Coll
Cant from 73. *8 Brockenhurst Close, Canterbury, Kent
CT2 7RX* Canterbury (0227) 451572

DAVIES, Adrian Paul. b 43. K Coll Lon. **d** 69 **p** 70. C
Nottm St Mary *S'well* 69-74; C Gt w Lt Billing *Pet*
74-75; P-in-c Marholm 75-82; R Castor 75; R Castor w
Sutton and Upton 76-82; V Byker St Mich w St Lawr
Newc from 82. *St Michael's Vicarage, Headlam Street,
Newcastle upon Tyne NE6 2DX* 091-265 3720

DAVIES, Alan Arthur. b 35. Sarum & Wells Th Coll 83.
d 85 **p** 86. C Eastleigh *Win* 85-88; C Portsea N End St
Mark *Portsm* 88-90; V Lydiate *Liv* from 90. *The
Vicarage, Lydiate, Liverpool L31 4HL* 051-526 0512

DAVIES, Alastair John. b 56. Nottm Univ BA MTh.
Westcott Ho Cam. **d** 84 **p** 85. C Eltham St Jo *S'wark*
84-87; C Dulwich St Barn 87-89; Chapl RAF from 89.
*c/o MOD, Adastral House, Theobald's Road, London
WC1X 8RU* 071-430 7268

DAVIES, Alcwyn Ivor. b 09. Univ of Wales BA32 DipEd33.
St D Coll Lamp 36. **d** 38 **p** 39. R Fowlmere *Ely* 53-76; V
Thriplow 53-76; rtd 76. *17 Station Road, Lode,
Cambridge CB5 9HB* Cambridge (0223) 811867

DAVIES, Aldwyn Ivan. b 09. St D Coll Lamp BA31. St
Mich Coll Llan. **d** 32 **p** 33. Miss to Seamen 39-43, 46-54,
56-57 and 69-78; V Port Eynon w Rhosili and Llanddewi
and Knelston *S & B* 69-74; V Llangennith 75-77; rtd 77.
*Cherry Trees, North Avenue, Llandrindod Wells, Powys
LD1 6BY* Llandrindod Wells (0597) 822198

DAVIES, Alexander Richard. b 12. St Deiniol's Hawarden
63. **d** 64 **p** 65. V Llanfihangel Crucorney w Oldcastle etc
Mon 69-77; rtd 77; Perm to Offic St As from 77; Ches
83-89; Ban from 90. *9 Glan Gors, Harlech, Gwynedd
LL46 2NJ* Harlech (0766) 780639

DAVIES, Canon Alfred Joseph. b 23. St D Coll Lamp
BA49. **d** 50 **p** 51. V Llangeler *St D* 54-74; RD Emlyn
70-73; Chapl Cardigan Hosp 74-88; V Cardigan and
Mount and Verwick *St D* 74-88; Can St D Cathl from
79; rtd 88. *19 Penbryn Avenue, Carmarthen, Dyfed
SA31 3DH* Carmarthen (0267) 234045

DAVIES, Alun Edwards. b 13. Univ of Wales BA40. St D
Coll Lamp 45. **d** 46 **p** 47. R Lower Crumpsall *Man* 62-84;
rtd 84; Perm to Offic *Man* from 84. *48 Ashtree Road,
Crumpsall, Manchester M8 6AT* 061-720 8345

DAVIES, Very Rev Alun Radcliffe. b 23. Univ of Wales
BA45 Keble Coll Ox BA47 MA51. St Mich Coll Llan
47. **d** 48 **p** 49. C Roath St Marg *Llan* 48-49; Lect St
Mich Coll Llan 49-53; Warden of Ords *Llan* 50-71; Dom
Chapl to Abp of Wales 52-57; Chapl RNVR 53-58; Dom
Chapl Bp Llan 57-59; Chapl RNR 58-60; V Ystrad
Mynach *Llan* 59-75; Chan Llan Cathl 69-71; Adn Llan
71-77; Can Res Llan Cathl 75-77; Dean Llan from 77;
V Llan w Capel Llanilterne from 77. *The Deanery,
Cathedral Green, Llandaff, Cardiff CF5 2YF* Cardiff
(0222) 561545 or 564554

DAVIES, Anthony John. b 41. New Coll Ox BA65 MA71.
St Steph Ho Ox 64. **d** 66 **p** 67. C Longton St Mary and
St Chad *Lich* 66-68; C Trent Vale 68-72; V Cross Heath
from 72. *St Michael's Presbytery, Linden Grove, Cross
Heath, Newcastle, Staffs ST5 9LJ* Newcastle-under-
Lyme (0782) 617241

DAVIES, Anthony William. b 29. St Jo Coll Ox
BA52 MA58 Man Univ MEd73. S Dios Minl Tr Scheme
84. **d** 87 **p** 88. C Burnham *B & W* 87-89; R Westcote
Barton w Steeple Barton, Duns Tew etc *Ox* from 89.
*The Rectory, 29 Enstone Road, Middle Barton, Oxford
OX5 4AA* Steeple Aston (0869) 40510

DAVIES, Canon Arthur Cadwaladr. b 19. Univ of Wales
BA41. Wells Th Coll 41. **d** 43 **p** 44. V Stockton Heath
Ches 64-85; RD Gt Budworth 81-85; rtd 85; Perm to Offic
Ban from 85. *Highfield, Treforris Road, Penmaenmawr,
Gwynedd LL34 6RH* Penmaenmawr (0492) 623739

DAVIES, Arthur Cecil Francis. b 11. Keble Coll Ox
BA34 MA42. Bps' Coll Cheshunt 35. **d** 37 **p** 38. V
Horncastle w Low Toynton *Linc* 59-80; rtd 80; Perm to
Offic Pet from 80; Linc from 81. *30 Church Lane,
Greetham, Oakham, Leics LE15 7NF* Oakham (0572)
812600

DAVIES, Arthur Gerald Miles. b 29. Univ of Wales (Ban)
BA51. St Mich Coll Llan. **d** 53 **p** 54. C Shotton *St As*

53-60; R Nannerch 60-63; V Llansilin and Llangadwaladr
63-68; V Llansilin w Llangadwaladr and Llangedwyn
68-71; V Llanfair Caereinion w Llanllugan 71-75; TV
Wrexham 75-83; V Hanmer, Bronington, Bettisfield,
Tallarn Green from 83. *The Vicarage, Hanmer,
Whitchurch, Shropshire SY13 3DE* Hanmer (094874)
316

DAVIES, Arthur Lloyd. b 31. Univ of Wales BA55.
Cuddesdon Coll 55. **d** 57 **p** 58. C Tonypandy w Clydach
Vale *Llan* 57-59; C Merthyr Dyfan 59-62; C Amersham
Ox 62-65; V Tilehurst St Geo 65-73; R Wokingham St
Paul 73-84; R Nuthurst *Chich* 84-90; I Fiddown w
Clonegam, Guilcagh and Kilmeaden *C & O* from 90.
Piltown Rectory, Piltown, Co Kilkenny, Irish Republic
Waterford (51) 43275

DAVIES, Arthur Philip. b 99. Lon Coll of Div 24. **d** 27
p 28. V Ketley *Lich* 40-69; rtd 69; Perm to Offic *Heref*
from 69. *The Gaff Flat, Foy, Ross-on-Wye, Herefordshire
HR9 6RA* Ross-on-Wye (0989) 63806

DAVIES, Basil Tudor. b 18. Keble Coll Ox BA40 MA48.
Westcott Ho Cam 40. **d** 42 **p** 43. V Wigston Magna *Leic*
57-73; R Upwell St Pet *Ely* 73-77; P-in-c Nordelph 75-77;
Chapl Community of St Mary V Wantage 77-88; Lic to
Offic *Ox* 77-88 and from 89; rtd 88; P-in-c Steventon w
Milton *Ox* 88-89. *38 Chapel Lands, Alnwick, Northd
NE66 1EN* Alnwick (0665) 510343

DAVIES, Benjamin John. b 27. Glouc Sch of Min 80 Trin
Coll Bris 87. **d** 88 **p** 89. NSM Cinderford St Steph w
Littledean *Glouc* from 88. *Mannings Weil, The Ruffit,
Littledean, Cinderford, Glos GL14 3LA* Dean (0594)
22352

DAVIES, Bernard. b 24. St D Coll Lamp BA49. **d** 51 **p** 52.
V Stand Lane St Jo *Man* 63-66; rtd 84. *7 Maritoba Close,
Lakeside, Cardiff CF2 6HD*

DAVIES, Bernard. b 34. Lon Univ BD63. Oak Hill Th
Coll 59. **d** 63 **p** 64. C Rawtenstall St Mary *Man* 63-69;
Sec Rwanda Miss 69-71; R Widford *Chelmsf* 71-78; V
Braintree from 78; RD Braintree from 87. *St Michael's
Vicarage, 10A Marshalls Road, Braintree, Essex
CM7 7LL* Braintree (0376) 22840

DAVIES, Bruce Edmund. b 22. Univ of Wales BA44. St
Mich Coll Llan 44. **d** 46 **p** 47. Chapl Univ of Wales
(Cardiff) *Llan* 56-78; R Peterston-super-Ely w St Brides-
super-Ely 78-87; rtd 87. *7 St Paul's Court, Heol Fair,
Llandaff, Cardiff CF5 2ES* Cardiff (0222) 553144

DAVIES, Cadoc Trevor. b 28. Keble Coll Ox BA52 MA57.
Cuddesdon Coll 57. **d** 57 **p** 58. C Cheltenham St Steph
Glouc 57-60; C Shalford *Guildf* 60-64; V Water Orton
Birm 64-83; R Kislingbury w Rothersthorpe *Pet* from
83. *The Rectory, Kislingbury, Northampton NN7 4AG*
Northampton (0604) 830592

DAVIES, Carl Joseph. b 53. Chich Th Coll 85. **d** 87 **p** 88.
C Lancing w Coombes *Chich* 87-90; C Walthamstow St
Sav *Chelmsf* from 90. *212 Markhouse Road, London
E17 8EP*

DAVIES, Catharine Mary. b 48. Lon Univ CertEd73.
E Midl Min Tr Course 85. **d** 88. C Spalding *Linc*
from 88. *2 Mulberry Way, Spalding, Lincs PE11 4QJ*
Spalding (0775) 766987

DAVIES, Charles William Keith. b 48. MIOT71. Linc Th
Coll. **d** 83 **p** 84. C Hythe *Cant* 83-86; Perm to Offic *Bris*
from 86; Chapl RAF from 86. *c/o MOD, Adastral House,
Theobald's Road, London WC1X 8RU* 071-430 7268

DAVIES, Christopher John. b 55. St Alb Minl Tr Scheme
83. **d** 86 **p** 87. C Tooting All SS *S'wark* 86-90; V Malden
St Jas from 90. *St James's Vicarage, 7 Bodley Road,
New Malden, Surrey KT3 5QD* 081-942 1860

DAVIES, Clifford Morgan. b 19. Univ of Wales BA41. St
Mich Coll Llan 41. **d** 43 **p** 44. Chapl Duke of York's
R Mil Sch Dover 61-77; rtd 84. *37 Applegarth Avenue,
Guildford, Surrey* Guildford (0483) 579415

DAVIES, Clifford O'Connor. b 17. Lon Univ BCom37. St
Aug Coll Cant 42. **d** 44 **p** 45. C Lamorbey H Trin *Roch*
44-46; S Africa from 46. *64 Schuller Street, Forest Hill,
2091 South Africa* Johannesburg (11) 683-3680

DAVIES, Clifford Thomas. b 41. Glouc Th Course. **d** 83
p 84. NSM Dean Forest H Trin *Glouc* 83-87; C Huntley
and Longhope 87; R Ruardean from 87. *The Rectory,
Ruardean, Glos GL17 9US* Dean (0594) 542214

DAVIES, David Anthony. b 57. ARICS84 Thames Poly
BSc81. Coll of Resurr Mirfield 85. **d** 88 **p** 89. C
Stalybridge *Man* 88-91; C (and TV designate) Swinton
and Pendlebury from 91. *4 Banbury Mews, Wardley,
Swinton, Manchester M27 3QZ* 061-794 5934

DAVIES, David Arthur Guy Hampton. b 27. St Jo Coll
Ox BA50 DipTh51 MA55. Ely Th Coll 51. **d** 53 **p** 54. R
Stamford St Mary and St Mich *Linc* 62-90; rtd 90.
8 Holywell Terrace, Shrewsbury SY2 5DF Shrewsbury
(0743) 245086

DAVIES, David Barry Grenville. b 38. St Jo Coll Dur BA60 MA77. Sarum Th Coll 61. **d** 63 **p** 64. C Abth St Mich *St D* 63-66; Min Can St D Cathl 66-72; R Stackpole Elidor w St Petrox 72-83; V Laugharne w Llansadurnen and Llandawke from 83. *The Vicarage, King Street, Laugharne, Dyfed SA33 4QE* Laugharne (0994) 427218

DAVIES, David Christopher. b 52. Lon Univ BSc73 Leeds Univ DipTh75. Coll of Resurr Mirfield 73. **d** 76 **p** 77. C Bethnal Green St Jo w St Simon *Lon* 76-78; C Bethnal Green St Jo w St Bart 78-80; C-in-c Portsea St Geo CD *Portsm* 80-81; Relig Affairs Producer Radio Victory 81-86; V Portsea St Geo 81-87; Chapl Ham Green and Southmead Hosps Bris from 87. *Southmead Hospital, Westbury-on-Trym, Bristol BS10 5NB* Bristol (0272) 505050

DAVIES, Canon David Eldred. b 18. St Edm Hall Ox 39. St Mich Coll Llan 46. **d** 49 **p** 50. R Market Deeping *Linc* 62-86; V Langtoft 65-71; Can and Preb Linc Cathl from 77; RD Aveland and Ness w Stamford 77-80; rtd 86. *3 Lindsey Avenue, Market Deeping, Peterborough PE6 8DZ* Market Deeping (0778) 346815

DAVIES, David Francis Jeffrey. b 01. Keble Coll Ox BA22 MA40. Sarum Th Coll 24. **d** 26 **p** 27. R Upton St Leonards *Glouc* 55-67; rtd 67; Perm to Offic *Glouc* from 74. *Romanway, Church Lane, North Woodchester, Stroud, Glos GL5 5NE* Amberley (0453) 872366

DAVIES, David Geoffrey George. b 24. Univ of Wales (Ban) BA49 Lon Univ BD55 Chorley Coll of Educn PGCE75. St Mich Coll Llan 49. **d** 51 **p** 52. Warden of Ords *St As* 62-70; V Ruabon 63-70; Can St As Cathl 69-70; NSM W Derby (or Tuebrook) St Jo *Liv* 70-81; Chapl to Welsh-speaking Angl in Liv 74-81; TV Bourne Valley *Sarum* 81-87; TR 87-89; Bp's Chapl to Schs from 83; RD Alderbury 86-89; rtd 89; Hon Chapl Liv Cathl *Liv* from 89. *55 Hattons Lane, Liverpool L16 7QR* 051-722 1415

DAVIES, Chan David Hywel. b 13. Univ of Wales BA40. St Mich Coll Llan 41. **d** 42 **p** 43. V Carmarthen St Pet *St D* 67-83; Can St D Cathl 72-82; Chan 82-83; rtd 83. *The Vicarage, Llanfihangel Abercywyn, St Clears, Dyfed SA33 4ND* St Clears (0994) 231019

DAVIES, Canon David Ioan Gwyn. b 19. Univ of Wales BA41 MA54. Lich Th Coll 41. **d** 43 **p** 44. V Blackpool St Paul *Blackb* 59-86; RD Blackpool 73-84; Hon Can Blackb Cathl 77-86; rtd 86. *37 Oakfield Street, Pontardulais, Swansea SA4 1LN* Swansea (0792) 883947

DAVIES, David Islwyn. b 42. St Deiniol's Hawarden 83. **d** 85 **p** 86. C Llanguicke *S & B* 85-87; C Swansea St Pet 87-89; Chapl Schiedam Miss to Seamen *Eur* from 89. *Jan Steenstraat 69, 3117 TC Schiedam, The Netherlands* Schiedam (10) 427-0063

DAVIES, Canon David Jeremy Christopher. b 46. CCC Cam BA68 MA72. Westcott Ho Cam 68. **d** 71 **p** 72. C Stepney St Dunstan and All SS *Lon* 71-74; Chapl Qu Mary Coll 74-78; Chapl Univ of Wales (Cardiff) *Llan* 78-85; Can Res Sarum Cathl *Sarum* from 85. *Hungerford Chantry, 54 The Close, Salisbury SP1 2EL* Salisbury (0722) 330914

DAVIES, David John. b 36. St Cath Soc Ox BA58 MA62. St D Coll Lamp 58. **d** 60 **p** 61. C Rhosddu *St As* 60-68; Chr Aid Area Sec (Glos, Herefordshire and Wilts) from 68; Midl Regional Co-ord from 78; Area Sec (Devon and Cornwall) from 86. *8 Carne Road, Newlyn, Penzance, Cornwall* Penzance (0736) 60401

DAVIES, David Leslie Augustus. b 25. St D Coll Lamp BA50. **d** 51 **p** 52. Chapl May Day, Qu and St Mary's Hosps Croydon 65-71; V Penrhyncoch and Elerch *St D* 71-74; Chapl R Berks and Reading Distr Hosps 74-89; rtd 90; Perm to Offic *Win* from 90. *Basset Down, 31 Three Acre Drive, New Milton, Hants BH25 7LG* New Milton (0425) 610376

DAVIES, David Michael Cole. b 44. St D Coll Lamp DipTh69. **d** 68 **p** 69. C Carmarthen St Pet *St D* 68-72; R Dinas 72-77; V Ty-Croes w Saron 77-80; V Llanedy w Tycroes and Saron 80-90; RD Dyffryn Aman 85-90; V Dafen and Llwynhendy from 90. *The Vicarage, Bryngwyn Road, Dafen, Llanelli, Dyfed SA14 8LW* Llanelli (0554) 774730

DAVIES, David Philip. b 09. St Aid Birkenhead 34. **d** 36 **p** 37. V W End *Guildf* 51-74; rtd 74; Perm to Offic *St Alb* from 74. *25 Hilton Avenue, Dunstable, Beds LU6 3QF* Dunstable (0582) 667655

DAVIES, Prof David Protheroe. b 39. CCC Cam BA62 MA66 CCC Ox MA BD69. Ripon Hall Ox 62. **d** 64 **p** 65. C Swansea St Mary w H Trin *S & B* 64-67; Lect T Univ of Wales (Lamp) 67-75; Sen Lect 75-86; Dean Faculty of Th 75-77 and from 81; Hd of Th and Relig Studies from 84; Prof Th Univ of Wales (Lamp)

from 86; Bp's Chapl for Th Educn *S & B* from 79. *St David's College, Lampeter, Dyfed SA48 7ED* Lampeter (0570) 422351

DAVIES, Canon David Thomas. b 09. Jes Coll Ox BA33 MA36. St D Coll Lamp BA31 St Steph Ho Ox. **d** 33 **p** 34. R Holyhead w Rhoscolyn w Llanfair-yn-Neubwll *Ban* 71-77; rtd 77; Perm to Offic *Ban* from 85. *2 Rock Terrace, Bethesda, Bangor, Gwynedd LL57 3AA* Bethesda (0248) 600440

DAVIES, David Vernon. b 14. AFBPsS68 Univ of Wales (Swansea) BA35 BD38 St Cath Coll Ox MA40 K Coll Lon PhD56. St D Coll Lamp 41. **d** 41 **p** 42. Lic to Offic *Llan* from 68; Prin Lect Llan Coll of Educn 68-77; Sen Lect Univ of Wales (Cardiff) 77-79; rtd 79. *41 Cefn Coed Avenue, Cyncoed, Cardiff CF2 6HF* Cardiff (0222) 757635

DAVIES, David William. b 64. **d** 90 **p** 91. C Newton St Pet *S & B* from 90. *72 Croftfield Crescent, Newton, Swansea SA3 4UL* Swansea (0792) 363157

DAVIES, Dennis William. b 24. Leeds Univ BA46 K Coll Lon AKC54 BD65. **d** 54 **p** 55. C Aylesbury *Ox* 54-58; Lic to Offic from 60; rtd 90. *45 Green End Street, Aston Clinton, Aylesbury, Bucks HP22 5JE* Aylesbury (0296) 630989

DAVIES, Dewi Caradog. b 14. St D Coll Lamp BA35. **d** 38 **p** 39. R Canton St Jo *Llan* 66-79; rtd 79. *10 Insole Gardens, Llandaff, Cardiff* Cardiff (0222) 563743

DAVIES, Canon Dillwyn. b 30. St Mich Coll Llan 52. **d** 54 **p** 55. C Laugharne w Llansadurnen and Llandawke *St D* 54-57; Lic to Offic *Dur* 57-58; Miss to Seamen 57-58; Ceylon 58-62; R Winthorpe *S'well* 62-71; V Langford w Holme 62-71; V Mansf Woodhouse 71-85; R Gedling from 85; RD Gedling 85-90; Hon Can S'well Minster from 90. *The Rectory, Gedling, Nottingham NG4 4BG* Nottingham (0602) 613214

DAVIES, Canon Dilwyn Morgan. b 10. Univ of Wales BA32 DipEd33. St Mich Coll Llan 32. **d** 34 **p** 35. Hon Can Cov Cathl *Cov* 65-80; P-in-c Ilmington w Stretton on Fosse and Ditchford 72-76; R 77-80; rtd 80; Perm to Offic *Cov* from 80. *6 Manor Barns, Ilmington, Shipston-on-Stour, Warks CV36 4LS* Ilmington (060882) 568

DAVIES, Donald Alfred. b 11. Linc Th Coll 62. **d** 63 **p** 64. R Bow w Broad Nymet *Ex* 65-77; P-in-c Colebrooke 75-77; rtd 77; Perm to Offic *Ex* from 79. *5 Homefield Close, Ottery St Mary, Devon EX11 1HS* Ottery St Mary (040481) 2562

DAVIES, Dorrien Paul. b 34. **d** 88 **p** 89. C Llanelly *St D* 88-91; V Llanfihangel Ystrad and Cilcennin w Trefilan etc from 91. *Ystrad Vicarage, Felinfach, Lampeter, Dyfed SA48 8AE* Aeron (0570) 470331

DAVIES, Douglas James. b 47. St Jo Coll Dur BA69 St Pet Coll Ox MLitt72 Nottm Univ PhD80. Cranmer Hall Dur 71. **d** 75 **p** 76. Lect Nottm Univ from 75; Sen Lect from 90; Hon C Wollaton *S'well* 75-83; Hon C Attenborough from 83; Hon C E Leake from 85. *The Warden, Derby Hall, University Park, Nottingham NG7 2QT* Nottingham (0602) 504110

DAVIES, Canon Douglas Tudor. b 20. Univ of Wales (Ban) BA44. Coll of Resurr Mirfield 44. **d** 46 **p** 47. V Treboeth *S & B* 65-90; RD Penderi 78-90; Hon Can Brecon Cathl 82-83; Can Brecon Cathl from 83; rtd 90. *245A Swansea Road, Waunarlwydd, Swansea SA5 4SN* Swansea (0792) 879587

DAVIES, Canon Ebenezer Thomas. b 03. Univ of Wales BA27 MA40. St Mich Coll Llan 35. **d** 36 **p** 37. R Llangybi *Mon* 48-73; Dioc Dir of RE 49-73; Can St Woolos Cathl 53-73; RD Raglan-Usk 63-72; P-in-c Llanfair Kilgeddin and Llanover 77-82; rtd 82; Perm to Offic *Mon* from 82. *11 Ty Brith Gardens, Usk, Gwent* Usk (02913) 2458

DAVIES, Edward Earl. b 40. **d** 90 **p** 91. C Pontypridd St Cath w St Matt *Llan* from 90. *26 East Street, Trallwn, Pontypridd, M Glam CF37 4PL* Pontypridd (0443) 406101

DAVIES, Edward William Llewellyn. b 51. Nottm Univ BTh77. St Jo Coll Nottm 73. **d** 78 **p** 79. C Southsea St Jude *Portsm* 78-81; C Alverstoke 81-84; R Abbas and Templecombe w Horsington *B & W* 84-89; Perm to Offic Ches from 89. *46 Barber Street, Macclesfield, Cheshire SK10 5HT*

DAVIES, Canon Edwin Isaac. b 21. Univ of Wales BA43. St Mich Coll Llan 43. **d** 45 **p** 46. V Llantrisant *Llan* 57-78; V Cardiff St Jo 78-86; Can Res Llan Cathl 78-86; Prec 86; rtd 86; Perm to Offic *Llan* from 87. *52 Prospect Drive, Llandaff, Cardiff CF5 2HN* Cardiff (0222) 554721

DAVIES, Elizabeth Jean. b 39. MRCS LRCP65 Lon Univ MB, BS63. S Dios Minl Tr Scheme 86 Chich Th Coll 86. **d** 89. Par Dn Southwick *Chich* 89-91; Par Dn Littlehampton and Wick from 91. *13 Peregrine Road,*

Littlehampton, W Sussex BN17 6DT Littlehampton (0903) 723908

DAVIES, Eric Brian. b 36. St Jo Coll Nottm. **d** 87 **p** 89. NSM Castle Donington and Lockington cum Hemington *Leic* 87-88; Hon C Hathern, Long Whatton and Diseworth 88-90; Hon C Hathern, Long Whatton and Diseworth w Belton etc from 90. *26 The Green, Castle Donington, Derby DE7 2JX* Derby (0332) 811127

DAVIES, Evan Wallis. b 08. Bps' Coll Cheshunt. **d** 42 **p** 43. V Pirton *St Alb* 48-52; rtd 71. *7 Treetops, Swiss Valley Park, Llanelli, Dyfed*

DAVIES, Francis James Saunders. b 37. Univ of Wales (Ban) BA60 Selw Coll Cam BA62 MA66 Bonn Univ 63. St Mich Coll Llan 62. **d** 63 **p** 64. C Holyhead w Rhoscolyn *Ban* 63-67; Chapl Ban Cathl 67-69; R Llanllyfni 69-75; Can Missr Ban Cathl 75-78; V Gorseinon *S & B* 78-86; RD Llwchwr 83-86; V Cardiff Dewi Sant *Llan* from 86. *Hafod-lon, 51 Heath Park Avenue, Cardiff CF4 3RF* Cardiff (0222) 751418

DAVIES, Frank Ernest. b 13. Dur Univ LTh43. Clifton Th Coll 39. **d** 43 **p** 44. R Bigbury *Ex* 60-84; rtd 84; Perm to Offic *Ches* from 84. *93 Heywood Boulevard, Thingwall, Wirral, Merseyside L61 3XE* 051-648 3561

DAVIES, Gareth Rhys. b 51. DipHE. Oak Hill Th Coll. **d** 83 **p** 84. C Gt Warley Ch *Chelmsf* 83-86; C Oxhey All SS *St Alb* 86-90; C Aldridge *Lich* from 90. *227 Walsall Road, Aldridge, Walsall* Aldridge (0922) 57732

DAVIES, Gary. b 37. AKC62. **d** 63 **p** 64. C Dovercourt *Chelmsf* 63-65; C Lambeth St Phil *S'wark* 65-68; P-in-c 68-70; V W Brompton St Mary *Lon* 70-72; V W Brompton St Mary w St Pet 73-83; RD Chelsea 76-80; Dir Post-Ord Tr 78-81; Perm to Offic from 83. *21 Margravine Gardens, London W6* 081-741 9315

DAVIES, Canon Geoffrey Lovat. b 30. St Aid Birkenhead. **d** 62 **p** 63. C Davenham *Ches* 62-65; C Higher Bebington 65-67; V Witton 67-80; R Lymm from 80; Clergy Widows and Retirement Officer from 87; Hon Can Ches Cathl from 88; RD Gt Budworth from 91. *The Rectory, Rectory Lane, Lymm, Cheshire WA13 0AL* Lymm (092575) 2164

DAVIES, George Vivian. b 21. CCC Cam BA47 MA49. Ely Th Coll. **d** 49 **p** 50. R Warehorne w Kenardington *Cant* 59-74; R Rounton w Welbury *York* 74-86; rtd 86; Perm to Offic *Derby* from 86. *12 Rectory Drive, Wingerworth, Chesterfield, Derbyshire S42 6RT* Chesterfield (0246) 79222

DAVIES, George William. b 51. MITD MBIM Open Univ BA84 MPhil89. Sarum & Wells Th Coll 83. **d** 85 **p** 86. C Mansf St Pet *S'well* 85-89; Chapl Cen Notts HA 86-89; P-in-c Fobbing *Chelmsf* from 89; Ind Chapl from 89. *The Rectory, High Road, Fobbing, Stanford-le-Hope, Essex SS17 9JH* Stanford-le-Hope (0375) 672002

DAVIES, Glanmor Adrian. b 51. St D Coll Lamp DipTh73. **d** 73 **p** 75. C Llanstadwell *St D* 73-78; R Dinas w Llanllawer and Pontfaen w Morfil etc 78-84; V Lamphey w Hodgeston 84-85; V Lamphey w Hodgeston and Carew from 85. *The Vicarage, Lamphey, Pembroke, Dyfed SA71 5NR* Lamphey (0646) 672407

DAVIES, Glyn Richards. b 28. Solicitor 52. **d** 79 **p** 80. NSM Michaelston-y-Fedw and Rudry *Mon* 79-88; NSM St Mellons and Michaelston-y-Fedw from 88. *Ty Golau, 8 Tyr Winch Road, St Mellons, Cardiff CF3 9UX* Cardiff (0222) 792813

DAVIES, Glyndwr George. b 36. Glouc Sch of Min 88. **d** 91. NSM Clodock and Longtown w Craswall, Llanveynoe etc *Heref* from 91. *White House Farm, Llanfihangel Crucorney, Abergavenny, Gwent NP7 8HW* Crucorney (0873) 890251

DAVIES, Graham James. b 35. Univ of Wales BD72 St D Coll Lamp BA56. St Mich Coll Llan 56 Episc Th Sch Cam Mass 58. **d** 59 **p** 60. C Johnston w Steynton *St D* 59-62; C Llangathen w Llanfihangel Cilfargen 62-64; Min Can St D Cathl 64-66; R Burton 66-71; R Hubberston 71-74; Hon C Lenham w Boughton Malherbe *Cant* 74-80; V Cwmddauddwr w St Harmon's and Llanwrthwl *S & B* 80-86; V Kidwelly and Llandefaelog *St D* from 86. *The Vicarage, Kidwelly, Dyfed SA17 4SY* Kidwelly (0554) 890295

DAVIES, Harry Bertram. b 11. Chich Th Coll 70. **d** 70 **p** 71. C Fareham H Trin *Portsm* 70-74; R Lowick w Sudborough and Slipton *Pet* 74-81; P-in-c Islip 78-81; rtd 81; Perm to Offic *Lich* from 81. *22 Beachwood Avenue, Wall Heath, Kingswinford, W Midlands DY6 0HL* Kingswinford (0384) 292000

DAVIES, Hedleigh Llewelyn. b 17. Worc Coll Ox BA40 MA44. Westcott Ho Cam 40. **d** 41 **p** 42. Sacr Nor Cathl *Nor* 66-71; V Nor St Andr 66-72; P-in-c Nor St Mich at Plea and St Pet Hungate 66-72; V Nor St Mary in the Marsh 67-72; R Brooke w Kirstead 72-82; Hon Min Can Nor Cathl from 78; rtd 82; Perm to Offic *Nor* from 91. *April Rise, Rectory Road, East Carleton, Norwich NR14 8HT* Mulbarton (0508) 70420

DAVIES, Henry Joseph. b 38. Univ of Wales (Cardiff) BSc61. St Mich Coll Llan 75. **d** 76 **p** 77. C Griffithstown *Mon* 76-79; TV Cwmbran 79-85; V Newport St Andr from 85. *The Vicarage, 1 Brookfield Close, Liswerry, Newport, Gwent NP9 0LA* Newport (0633) 271904

DAVIES, Canon Henry Lewis. b 20. St Jo Coll Dur BA42 DipTh43 MA45. **d** 43 **p** 44. R Old Swinford *Worc* 65-78; R Old Swinford Stourbridge 78-85; rtd 85; Perm to Offic *Worc* from 87. *15 Bramley Road, Bewdley, Worcs DY12 2BU* Bewdley (0299) 402713

DAVIES, Herbert John. b 30. Glouc Sch of Min 84. **d** 87 **p** 88. NSM Cheltenham St Mark *Glouc* from 87. *45 Farmington Road, Benhall, Cheltenham, Glos GL51 6AG* Cheltenham (0242) 515996

DAVIES, Herbert Lewis Owen. b 08. CBE. Ox Univ BA31 MA36. St Steph Ho Ox 31. **d** 32 **p** 33. R Bourton on the Hill *Glouc* 68-75; rtd 75. *Conway, Croft Drive West, Caldy, Wirral, Merseyside L48 2JQ* 051-625 1866

✠DAVIES, Rt Rev Howell Haydn. b 27. ARIBA55 DipArch54. Tyndale Hall Bris 56. **d** 59 **p** 60 **c** 81. C Heref St Pet w St Owen *Heref* 59-61; Kenya 61-79; Adn N Maseno 71-74; Provost Nairobi 74-79; V Woking St Pet *Guildf* 79-81; Uganda 81-87; Bp Karamoja 81-87; V Wolv St Jude *Lich* from 87. *St Jude's Vicarage, St Jude's Road, Wolverhampton WV6 0EB* Wolverhampton (0902) 753360

DAVIES, Hugh Middlecott. b 19. Worc Ord Coll 58. **d** 59 **p** 60. R Ightfield w Calverhall *Lich* 66-72; Chapl HM Borstal Stoke Heath 70-72; R Catfield *Nor* 72-74; Chapl Nor Hosp 74-75; Asst Chapl HM Pris Nor 74-77; R Bunwell w Carleton Rode 75-77; Master Charterhouse Hull 77-80; rtd 80; Chapl Addenbrooke's Hosp Cam 80-81; Perm to Offic *Nor* from 81. *2 The Beeches, Station Road, Holt, Norfolk NR25 6BS* Sheringham (0263) 713479

DAVIES, Ian Charles. b 51. Sarum & Wells Th Coll 78. **d** 81 **p** 82. C E Bedfont *Lon* 81-84; C Cheam *S'wark* 84-87; V Mert St Jas from 87. *St James's Vicarage, Beaford Grove, London SW20 9LB* 081-540 3122

DAVIES, Ian Elliott. b 64. Univ of Wales (Ban) BD85 Univ of Tibet DLitt90. Ridley Hall Cam 86. **d** 88 **p** 89. C Baglan *Llan* 88-90; C Skewen from 90. *Manod, 21 Drummau Road, Neath Abbey, W Glam SA10 6NT* Swansea (0792) 321324

DAVIES, Ieuan. b 39. Lon Univ BSc60 K Coll Cam 60 New Coll Ox 63. St Steph Ho Ox 63. **d** 65 **p** 66. C Pimlico St Gabr *Lon* 65-68; USA 68-89; The Netherlands from 89. *Jan Steenstraat 69, 3177 TC Schidam, Rotterdam, The Netherlands* Rotterdam (10) 427-0063

DAVIES, Iorwerth Vernon. b 34. Univ of Wales BA55 Fitzw Ho Cam BA57 MA62. St Mich Coll Llan 57. **d** 58 **p** 59. Lect Trin Coll Carmarthen 65-91; rtd 91. *7 Penllwyn Park, Carmarthen, Dyfed* Carmarthen (0267) 235019

DAVIES, Ven Ivor Gordon. b 17. Univ of Wales BA49 Lon Univ BD51. St Steph Ho Ox 39. **d** 41 **p** 42. Can Res S'wark Cathl *S'wark* 57-72; Adn Lewisham 72-85; rtd 85; Perm to Offic *St E* from 85. *10 Garfield Road, Felixstowe, Suffolk IP11 7PU* Felixstowe (0394) 271546

DAVIES, Canon Ivor Llewellyn. b 35. Univ of Wales BA56 St Cath Soc Ox BA58 MA63. Wycliffe Hall Ox 56. **d** 62 **p** 63. C Wrexham *St As* 62-64; India 65-71; V Connah's Quay *St As* 71-79; P-in-c Gorsley w Cliffords Mesne *Glouc* 79-84; P-in-c Hempsted 84-90; Dir of Ords 84-90; Hon Can Glouc Cathl from 89; V Dean Forest St Paul from 90. *The Vicarage, Parkend, Lydney, Glos GL15 4HL* Dean (0594) 562284

DAVIES, Canon Ivor Llewelyn. b 23. Univ of Wales (Swansea) BA49 St Cath Soc Ox DipTh52 Fitzw Coll Cam BA56 MA60. Wycliffe Hall Ox 49. **d** 51 **p** 52. R Llanfeugan w Llanddetty and Glyncollwg *S & B* 59-70; P-in-c Llansantffraed-juxta-Usk 67-70; V Hay 70-72; RD Hay 73-82; V Hay w Llanigon and Capel-y-Ffin 72-87; Hon Can Brecon Cathl 76-79; Can Brecon Cathl 79-89; RD Hay 85-87; V Knighton and Norton 87-89; Treas Brecon Cathl 88-89; rtd 89. *Holly Cottage, 5 The Cwm, Knighton, Powys LD7 1HF* Knighton (0547) 520253

DAVIES, James Alan. b 38. St Jo Coll Nottm. **d** 83 **p** 84. C Fletchamstead *Cov* 83-87; P-in-c Hartshill 87-89; V from 89; Asst RD Nuneaton from 90. *The Vicarage, Hartshill, Nuneaton, Warks CV10 0LY* Chapel End (0203) 392266

DAVIES, James Owen. b 26. St Aid Birkenhead 60. **d** 61 **p** 62. C Drayton in Hales *Lich* 61-65; V Tipton St Jo 65-69; P-in-c Lt Drayton 70-73; V from 73. *The Vicarage,*

Little Drayton, Market Drayton, Shropshire TF9 1DY Market Drayton (0630) 2801

DAVIES, Canon James Trevor Eiddig. b 17. St D Coll Lamp BA39. AKC41. **d** 41 **p** 42. V Llantarnam *Mon* 68-71; R Cwmbran 71-86; Hon Can St Woolos Cathl from 83; rtd 86. *34 Rockfield Road, Monmouth, Gwent* Monmouth (0600) 6649

DAVIES, James William. b 51. Trin Hall Cam BA72 MA76 St Jo Coll Dur BA79. **d** 80 **p** 81. C Croydon Ch Ch Broad Green *Cant* 80-83; CMS 83-86; Chapl Bethany Sch Goudhurst 86-90; P-in-c Parkstone St Luke *Sarum* from 90. *The Vicarage, 2 Birchwood Road, Parkstone, Poole, Dorset BH14 9NP* Parkstone (0202) 741030

DAVIES, Joan Margaret (Sister Joanna). b 06. Lon Univ BA. **dss** 37 **d** 87. CSA from 34; Notting Hill St Clem *Lon* 37-43; Paddington St Steph w St Luke 48-69; Shadwell St Paul w Ratcliffe St Jas 69-73. *St Andrew's House, 2 Tavistock Road, London W11 1BA* 071-229 2662

DAVIES, Canon John Arthur. b 06. St D Coll Lamp BA37 Qu Coll Birm 37. **d** 38 **p** 39. R Taxal and Fernilee *Ches* 61-73; C Chapel-en-le-Frith *Derby* 73-75; rtd 75. *53 Milldale Avenue, Temple Meads, Buxton, Derbyshire SH7 9BG* Buxton (0298) 2050

DAVIES, John Atcherley. b 27. St Jo Coll Dur BA55. Wycliffe Hall Ox 55. **d** 57 **p** 58. C Eastbourne St Jo *Chich* 57-61; Chapl RN 61-82; V Hyde Common *Win* from 82. *The Vicarage, Hyde, Fordingbridge, Hants SP6 2QJ* Fordingbridge (0425) 653216

DAVIES, John Aubrey. b 15. St D Coll Lamp BA37. **d** 41 **p** 42. R Essendon and Woodhill *St Alb* 64-76; R Lt Berkhampsted 74-76; R Lt Berkhamsted and Bayford, Essendon etc 76-80; rtd 80; Perm to Offic *Roch* from 84. *15 Staleys Road, Borough Green, Sevenoaks, Kent TN15 8RL* Borough Green (0732) 882926

DAVIES, John Barden. b 47. Univ of Wales (Ban) DipTh70. St D Coll Lamp 70. **d** 71 **p** 72. C Rhosllan-erchrugog *St As* 71-75; R Llanbedr-y-Cennin *Ban* 75-86; Adult Religious Educn Officer from 86; V Bettws-y-Coed and Capel Curig w Penmachno etc from 86. *The Vicarage, Betws-y-Coed, Gwynedd LL24 0AD* Betws-y-Coed (06902) 313

DAVIES, Preb John Conway de la Tour. b 16. Jes Coll Cam BA38 MA42. Ripon Hall Ox 39. **d** 40 **p** 41. C Chipping Norton *Ox* 40-44; CF 44-52; V Highters Heath *Birm* 52-57; V Vowchurch and Turnastone *Heref* 57-83; V Peterchurch 57-83; P-in-c Bredwardine w Brobury 77-83; RD Abbeydore 78-84; Preb Heref Cathl from 79; R Peterchurch w Vowchurch, Turnastone and Dorstone from 83. *Peterchurch Vicarage, Peterchurch, Hereford HR2 0SJ* Peterchurch (09816) 374

DAVIES, John David Edward. b 53. Southn Univ LLB74 Univ of Wales (Cardiff) DipTh84. St Mich Coll Llan 82. **d** 84 **p** 85. C Chepstow *Mon* 84-86; C Michaelston-y-Fedw and Rudry 86-89; R Bedwas and Rudry from 89. *The Rectory, Bryn Goleu, Bedwas, Newport, Gwent NP1 9AU* Caerphilly (0222) 885220

✠**DAVIES, Rt Rev John Dudley.** b 27. Trin Coll Cam BA51 MA63. Linc Th Coll 52. **d** 53 **p** 54 **c** 87. C Leeds Halton St Wilfrid *Ripon* 53-56; S Africa 57-71; Sec Chapls in HE Gen Syn Bd of Educn 71-74; P-in-c Keele *Lich* 74-76; Chapl Keele Univ 74-76; Lic to Offic *Birm* 76-81; Prin USPG Coll of the Ascension Selly Oak 76-81; Preb Lich Cathl *Lich* 76-87; Hon Can from 87; Can Res, Preb and Sacr St As Cathl *St As* 82-85; Dioc Missr 82-87; V Llanrhaeadr-ym-Mochnant, Llanarmon, Pennant etc 85-87; Suff Bp Shrewsbury from 87. *Athlone House, 68 London Road, Shrewsbury SY2 6PG* Shrewsbury (0743) 235867

DAVIES, John Edwards Gurnos. b 18. Ch Coll Cam BA41 MA45. Westcott Ho Cam 40. **d** 42 **p** 43. CF 46-73; R Monk Sherborne and Pamber *Win* 73-76; P-in-c Sherborne 76; R The Sherbornes w Pamber 76-83; rtd 83. *3 Parsonage Lane, Edington, Westbury, Wilts* Devizes (0380) 830479

DAVIES, John Gwylim. b 27. Ripon Hall Ox 67. **d** 70 **p** 71. C Ox St Mich *Ox* 70-71; C Ox St Mich w St Martin and All SS 71-72; TV New Windsor 73-77; R Hagley *Worc* 77-83; TV Littleham w Exmouth *Ex* from 83; Asst Dioc Stewardship Adv from 83. *The Vicarage, 96 Littleham Road, Exmouth, Devon EX8 2QX* Exmouth (0395) 272061

DAVIES, John Gwyn. b 12. St Cath Coll Cam BA36 MA40. Ely Th Coll 36. **d** 37 **p** 38. V Rowington *Cov* 54-77; rtd 78; Perm to Offic *Cov* from 78. *Lapwater, Pinley, Claverdon, Warwick CV35 8NA* Claverdon (092684) 2597

DAVIES, John Harverd. b 57. Keble Coll Ox BA80 MA84 CCC Cam MPhil82. Westcott Ho Cam 82. **d** 84 **p** 85. C

Liv Our Lady and St Nic w St Anne *Liv* 84-87; C Pet St Jo *Pet* 87-90; Min Can Pet Cathl 88-90; V Anfield St Marg *Liv* from 90. *St Margaret's Vicarage, Rocky Lane, Liverpool L6 4BA* 051-263 3118

DAVIES, Canon John Howard. b 29. St Jo Coll Cam BA50 MA54 Nottm Univ BD62. Westcott Ho Cam 54. **d** 55 **p** 56. Succ Derby Cathl *Derby* 55-58; Chapl Westcott Ho Cam 58-63; Lect Th Southn Univ 63-81; Lic to Offic *Win* 63-81; Sen Lect 74-81; Dir Th and Relig Studies Southn Univ from 81; Can Th Win Cathl *Win* 81-91; Hon C Southn St Alb from 88. *13 Glen Eyre Road, Southampton SO23GA* Southampton (0703) 679359

DAVIES, Canon John Howard. b 35. Ely Th Coll 62. **d** 64 **p** 65. C Bromsgrove All SS *Worc* 64-67; C Astwood Bank w Crabbs Cross 67-70; R Worc St Martin 70-74; P-in-c Worc St Pet 72-74; R Worc St Martin w St Pet 74-79; RD Worc E 77-79; TR Malvern Link w Cowleigh from 79; Hon Can Worc Cathl from 81; RD Malvern from 83. *St Matthias' Rectory, 12 Lambourne Avenue, Malvern, Worcs WR14 1NL* Malvern (0684) 573834

DAVIES, John Hugh Conwy. b 42. CEng MICE72 Bris Univ BSc64 PhD67. Linc Th Coll 84. **d** 86 **p** 87. C Gt Limber w Brocklesby *Linc* 86-89; R Wickenby Gp from 89. *The Rectory, Snelland Road, Wickenby, Lincoln LN3 5AB* Wickenby (06735) 721

DAVIES, John Hywel Morgan. b 45. St D Coll Lamp BA71 LTh73. **d** 73 **p** 74. C Milford Haven *St D* 73-77; V from 89; R Castlemartin w Warren and Angle etc 77-82; R Walton W w Talbenny and Haroldston W 82-89. *St Katharine's Vicarage, 1 Sandhurst Road, Milford Haven, Dyfed SA73 3JU* Milford Haven (0646) 693314

DAVIES, John Ifor. b 20. ACP DipEd. **d** 80 **p** 81. Hon C Allerton *Liv* 80-84; Hon C Ffynnongroew *St As* 84-87; Hon C Whitford 87-88. *Hafan Deg, Ffordd-y-Graig, Lixwm, Holywell, Clwyd CH8 8LY* Halkyn (0352) 781151

DAVIES, John Keith. b 33. St Mich Coll Llan 80. **d** 82 **p** 83. C Llanbadarn Fawr w Capel Bangor *St D* 82-84; V Llandygwydd and Cenarth w Cilrhedyn etc 84-89; V Abergwili w Llanfihangel-uwch-Gwili etc from 89. *The Vicarage, Wellfield Road, Abergwili, Carmarthen, Dyfed SA31 2JQ* Carmarthen (0267) 234189

DAVIES, John Melvyn George. b 37. Wycliffe Hall Ox 68. **d** 71 **p** 72. C Norbury *Ches* 71-75; C Heswall 76-78; V Claughton cum Grange 78-83; R Waverton from 83; RD Malpas from 90. *The Vicarage, Waverton, Chester* Chester (0244) 335581

DAVIES, John Neville Milwyn. b 15. MBE45. Univ of Wales BA37. St Steph Ho Ox 37. **d** 38 **p** 39. CF 42-73; QHC 69-73; V Clapham H Spirit *S'wark* 73-80; rtd 80; Perm to Offic *B & W* from 91. *Brooklands Durcott Lane, Camerton, Bath BA3 1QE* Bath (0225) 71361

DAVIES, John Oswell. b 27. St D Coll Lamp 74. **d** 75 **p** 76. C Henfynyw w Aberaeron and Llanddewi Aber-arth *St D* 75-76; P-in-c Eglwyswrw w Ysbyty Ystwyth 76-77; V 77-83; R Manordeifi and Capel Colman w Llanfihangel etc from 83; RD Cemais and Sub-Aeron from 87. *The Rectory, Manordeifi, Llechryd, Cardigan, Dyfed SA43 2PN* Llechryd (023987) 568

DAVIES, John Rees. b 07. St D Coll Lamp BA38. **d** 41 **p** 42. V Resolven *Llan* 67-77; rtd 77; Perm to Offic *Llan* from 78. *24 Broniestyn Terrace, Trecynon, Aberdare, M Glam CF44 8EG* Aberdare (0685) 875049

DAVIES, Ven John Stewart. b 43. MSOTS Univ of Wales BA72 Qu Coll Cam MLitt74. Westcott Ho Cam 72. **d** 74 **p** 75. C Hawarden *St As* 74-78; Tutor St Deiniol's Lib Hawarden 76-83; V Rhosymedre *St As* 78-87; Dir Dioc Minl Tr Course from 83; Warden of Ords 83-91; Hon Can St As Cathl from 86; V Mold from 87; Adn St As from 91. *The Vicarage, Church Lane, Mold, Clwyd CH7 1BW* Mold (0352) 2960

DAVIES, Canon John Treharne. b 14. St D Coll Lamp BA36. **d** 38 **p** 39. V Potterne *Sarum* 59-73; V Worton 67-73; Can and Preb Sarum Cathl 72-82; P-in-c Ramsbury 73-74; R Whitton 74-76; TR Whitton 76-81; rtd 81; Perm to Offic *Heref* from 82. *16 Lambourne Close, Ledbury, Herefordshire HR8 2HW* Ledbury (0531) 4629

DAVIES, John Vernon. b 16. Or Coll Ox BA40 MA43. Cuddesdon Coll 40. **d** 41 **p** 42. R Radyr *Llan* 69-83; rtd 83. *8 Insole Gardens, Llandaff, Cardiff* Cardiff (0222) 562130

DAVIES, John Vernon. b 20. Clifton Th Coll 66. **d** 68 **p** 69. C Surbiton Hill Ch Ch *S'wark* 68-70; C Heatherlands St Jo *Sarum* 70-71; V Wandsworth St Mich *S'wark* 75-83; rtd 83. *11 Pearson Avenue, Parkstone, Poole, Dorset BH14 0DT* Poole (0202) 731591

DAVIES, Johnston ap Llynfi. b 28. St D Coll Lamp BA51 St Mich Coll Llan 51. **d** 53 **p** 54. Perm to Offic *Ox* 67-72; Perm to Offic *York* 72-86; V Creeksea w Althorne,

Latchingdon and N Fambridge *Chelmsf* 86-88; rtd 88; Asst Chapl Costa Blanca *Eur* from 88. *Pasionaria, 10B Las Adelfas, Calpe, Alicante, Spain*

DAVIES, Joseph Henry. b 17. St D Coll Lamp BA40 St Mich Coll Llan 40. **d** 41 **p** 42. V Barlaston *Lich* 66-78; R Mucklestone 78-82; rtd 82; Perm to Offic *St As* from 82. *5 Dinas Road, Llandudno, Gwynedd* Llandudno (0492) 878526

DAVIES, Joseph Thomas. b 32. **d** 71 **p** 72. C St-Geo-in-the-East w St Paul *Lon* 71-79; R Roos and Garton in Holderness w Tunstall etc *York* 79-89; R Pentlow, Foxearth, Liston and Borley *Chelmsf* from 89. *The Rectory, The Street, Foxearth, Sudbury, Suffolk CO10 7JG* Sudbury (0787) 75697

DAVIES, Kenneth John. b 42. Ripon Coll Cuddesdon 79. **d** 80 **p** 81. C Buckm *Ox* 80-83; V Birstall *Wakef* 83-91; TV Crookes St Thos *Sheff* from 91. *352 Crookesmoor Road, Crookes, Sheffield S10 1BH* Sheffield (0742) 664463

DAVIES, Laurence Gordon. b 28. Down Coll Cam BA52 MA56. Linc Th Coll 52. **d** 54 **p** 55. R Gt w Lt Billing *Pet* 69-83; V Welton w Ashby St Ledgers 83-88; rtd 88; Perm to Offic *Ox* from 89. *Cherry Pie, 56 Couching Street, Watlington, Oxford OX9 5PU* Watlington (049161) 2446

DAVIES, Lawford Idwal. b 32. St D Coll Lamp DipTh63. **d** 63 **p** 64. C Llanelly *St D* 63-70; TV Tenby 70-78; V Penally and St Florence w Redberth 78-85; V Caerwent w Dinham and Llanfair Discoed etc *Mon* 85-86; rtd 86. *Lamera, 35 Glanwern Avenue, Newport, Gwent NP9 9BW* Newport (0633) 281849

DAVIES, Lawrence. b 14. Univ of Wales (Lamp) BA36. Chich Th Coll 36. **d** 38 **p** 39. V Longdon *Worc* 54-78; V Queenhill w Holdfast 54-78; V Longdon, Bushley and Queenhill w Holdfast 78-86; RD Upton 80-86; rtd 86; Perm to Offic *Worc* from 86. *Theocsbury, Bushley, Tewkesbury, Glos GL20 6HX* Tewkesbury (0684) 294220

DAVIES, Lawrence. b 20. BEM45. Tyndale Hall Bris 46. **d** 49 **p** 50. V Preston All SS *Blackb* 61-73; V St Michaels on Wyre 73-85; rtd 85; Perm to Offic Blackb and Carl from 85. *23 Inglemere Gardens, Arnside, Carnforth, Lancs LA5 0BX* Carnforth (0524) 762141

DAVIES, Lawrence Vercoe. b 40. Lich Th Coll 67. **d** 70 **p** 71. C Glan Ely *Llan* 70-77; V Grangetown from 77. *St Paul's Vicarage, Llanmaes Street, Cardiff CF1 7LR* Cardiff (0222) 228707

DAVIES, Leslie Lobbett John. b 07. MC43. Keble Coll Ox BA30 MA38. Wells Th Coll 33. **d** 34 **p** 35. Can St D Cathl *St D* 65-77; V Haverfordwest St Mary 68-77; rtd 77. *Greystones, 59 London Road, Datchet, Slough* Slough (0753) 41883

DAVIES, Canon Lorys Martin. b 36. JP. ALCM52 Univ of Wales (Lamp) BA57. Wells Th Coll 57. **d** 59 **p** 60. C Tenby w Gumfreston *St D* 59-62; Brentwood Sch Essex 62-66; Chapl Solihull Sch Warks 66-68; V Moseley St Mary *Birm* 68-81; Can Res Birm Cathl from 81; Dioc Dir of Ords 82-90. *119 Selly Park Road, Birmingham B29 7HY* 021-472 0146 or 236 4333

DAVIES, Malcolm. b 35. St Mich Coll Llan 82. **d** 84 **p** 85. C Roath St Marg *Llan* 84-88; C Pentre from 88. *The Vicarage, 7 Llewellyn Street, Pentre, M Glam CF41 7BY* Tonypandy (0443) 433651

DAVIES, Malcolm Thomas. b 36. Open Univ BA81. St Mich Coll Llan 71. **d** 73 **p** 74. C Bettws St Dav *St D* 73-76; V Cilycwm and Ystradffin w Rhandir-mwyn etc 76-80; V Llangyfelach *S & B* 80-85; V Lougher from 85. *The Rectory, 109 Glebe Road, Loughor, Swansea SA4 2SR* Gorseinon (0792) 891958

DAVIES, Mark. b 62. BA85. Coll of Resurr Mirfield 86. **d** 89 **p** 90. C Barnsley St Mary *Wakef* from 89. *19 Smithies Street, Barnsley, S Yorkshire S71 1RB* Barnsley (0226) 296815

DAVIES, Martyn John. b 60. Chich Th Coll 82. **d** 85 **p** 86. C Llantrisant *Llan* 85-87; C Whitchurch 87-90; V Porth w Trealaw from 90. *St Paul's Vicarage, Birchgrove Street, Porth, M Glam CF39 9UU* Porth (0443) 682401

DAVIES, Canon Mervyn Morgan. b 25. Univ of Wales BA49. Coll of Resurr Mirfield 49. **d** 51 **p** 52. C Penarth w Lavernock *Llan* 51-58; Lic to Offic *Wakef* 58-60; C Port Talbot St Theodore *Llan* 60-63; V Pontycymmer and Blaengarw 63-69; V Fairwater from 69; RD Llan from 81; Ed Welsh Churchman from 82; Can Llan Cathl 84-89; Prec from 89. *The Vicarage, St Fagan's Road, Fairwater, Cardiff CF5 3DW* Cardiff (0222) 562551

DAVIES, Meurig Ceredig. b 21. Univ of Wales (Abth) BA43. St Mich Coll Llan 43. **d** 45 **p** 46. Perm to Offic *Pet* 64-74; V St Dogmael's w Moylgrove and Monington

St D 74-86; rtd 86. *Geinfe, Gelliwen, Llechryd, Cardigan, Dyfed* Llechryd (023987) 550

DAVIES, Miss Moira Kathleen. b 41. Cant Sch of Min. **d** 88. Par Dn Walmer *Cant* from 88. *9 Roselands, Deal, Kent CT14 7QE* Deal (0304) 368656

DAVIES, Mostyn David. b 37. AKC64. **d** 65 **p** 66. C Corby St Columba *Pet* 65-69; Ind Chapl from 69; P-in-c Pet St Barn from 80. *16 Swanspool, Peterborough PE3 7LS* Peterborough (0733) 262034

DAVIES, Myles Cooper. b 50. Sarum & Wells Th Coll 71. **d** 74 **p** 75. C W Derby St Mary *Liv* 74-77; C Seaforth 77-80; V 80-84; Chapl Rathbone Hosp Liv from 84; V Stanley *Liv* from 84. *St Anne's Vicarage, 8 Derwent Square, Liverpool L13 6QT* 051-228 5252

DAVIES, Neil Anthony Bowen. b 52. Ex Univ BSc74. Westcott Ho Cam 75. **d** 78 **p** 79. C Llanblethian w Cowbridge and Llandough etc *Llan* 78-80; C Aberdare 80-82; V Troedyrhiw w Merthyr Vale 82-88; Min Lower Earley LEP *Ox* from 88. *15 Caraway Road, Lower Earley, Reading RG6 2XR* Reading (0734) 868615

DAVIES, Nigel Eric. b 20. Codrington Coll Barbados 39. **d** 43 **p** 44. V Leeming *Ripon* 57-86; rtd 86. *8 Seth Ward Drive, Bishopdown, Salisbury SP1 3JA* Salisbury (0722) 331509

DAVIES, Nigel Lawrence. b 55. Lanc Univ BEd77. Sarum & Wells Th Coll 84. **d** 87 **p** 88. C Heywood St Luke w All So *Man* 87-91; V Burneside *Carl* from 91. *St Oswald's Vicarage, Burneside, Kendal, Cumbria LA9 6QJ* Kendal (0539) 731398

DAVIES, Noel Paul. b 47. Chich Th Coll 83. **d** 85 **p** 86. C Milford Haven *St D* 85-89; R Jeffreyston w Reynoldston and E Williamston etc from 89. *The Rectory, Jeffreyston, Kilgetty, Dyfed SA68 0SG* Carew (0646) 651269

DAVIES, Norman Edward. b 37. Worc Coll Ox BA62. Cuddesdon Coll 62. **d** 64 **p** 65. C Mottingham St Andr *S'wark* 64-67; Hon C 67-75 and 83-87; Hd Master W Hatch Sch Chigwell 76-82; Hd Master Sedghill Sch Lon 82-87; Hon C Eltham H Trin *S'wark* 77-82; V Plumstead St Mark and St Marg from 87. *St Mark's Vicarage, 11 Old Mill Road, London SE18 1QE* 081-854 2973

DAVIES, Oliver. b 04. St Jo Coll Dur 50. **d** 52 **p** 53. R Knightwick w Doddenham and Broadwas *Worc* 56-72; rtd 72. *Cartref, The Strand, Charlton, Pershore, Worcs WR10 3JZ* Evesham (0386) 860157

DAVIES, Miss Patricia Elizabeth. b 36. Westf Coll Lon BA58 Hughes Hall Cam CertEd59 Leeds Univ MA74. NE Ord Course 83. **dss** 86 **d** 87. Killingworth *Newc* 86-87; Hon C 87-90; Hon C Newc H Cross from 91. *27 Crossway, Jesmond, Newcastle upon Tyne NE2 3QH* 091-281 3520

DAVIES, Paul Lloyd. b 46. Solicitor 71 Bris Univ LLB68 Trin Coll Carmarthen 84. **d** 87 **p** 88. NSM Newport w Cilgwyn and Dinas w Llanllawer *St D* from 87. *Priors Wood, The Paddock, Fishguard, Dyfed SA65 9NU* Fishguard (0348) 873306 or 873223

DAVIES, Paul Martin. b 35. Lon Univ BD75. Sarum & Wells Th Coll 75. **d** 75 **p** 76. C Walthamstow St Mary w St Steph *Chelmsf* 75-79; Kenya 79-86; R Leven w Catwick *York* from 86; RD N Holderness from 90. *The Rectory, West Street, Leven, Hull HU17 5LR* Hornsea (0964) 543793

DAVIES, Paul Scott. b 59. Cranmer Hall Dur 85. **d** 88 **p** 89. C New Addington *S'wark* 88-91; C Croydon H Sav from 91. *96A Lodge Road, Croydon, Surrey CR0 2PF* 081-684 8017

DAVIES, Percy Sharples. b 10. Univ of Wales BA32. St Steph Ho Ox 32. **d** 34 **p** 35. V Plumstead St Mark and St Marg *S'wark* 68-77; rtd 77; Perm to Offic *Cant* from 77. *China Cottage, 149A Middle Street, Deal, Kent* Deal (0304) 372515

DAVIES, Peter Huw. b 57. Crewe & Alsager Coll BEd79. Wycliffe Hall Ox 87. **d** 89 **p** 90. C Moreton *Ches* from 89. *40 Carnsdale Road, Moreton, South Wirral L46 9QR* 051-605 1241

DAVIES, Peter Richard. b 32. St Jo Coll Ox BA55 MA58. Westcott Ho Cam 56. **d** 58 **p** 59. C Cannock *Lich* 58-62; Kenya 63-75; Chapl Bedf Sch 76-85; V Dale and St Brides w Marloes *St D* from 85. *The Vicarage, Dale, Haverfordwest, Dyfed SA62 3RN* Dale (0646) 636255

DAVIES, Peter Timothy William. b 50. Leeds Univ BSc74. Oak Hill Th Coll 75. **d** 78 **p** 79. C Kingston Hill St Paul *S'wark* 78-81; C Hove Bp Hannington Memorial Ch *Chich* 81-88; V Audley *Lich* from 88. *The Vicarage, Wilbraham Walk, Audley, Stoke-on-Trent ST7 8HL* Stoke-on-Trent (0782) 720392

DAVIES, Ven Philip Bertram. b 33. Cuddesdon Coll 61. **d** 63 **p** 64. C Atherton *Man* 63-66; V Winton 66-71; R Salford St Phil w St Steph 71-76; V Radlett *St Alb* 76-87;

RD Aldenham 79-87; Adn St Alb from 87. *6 Sopwell Lane, St Albans, Herts AL1 1RR*   St Albans (0727) 57973

DAVIES, Philip James. b 58. UEA BA79 Keswick Hall Coll PGCE80. Ridley Hall Cam 86. **d** 89 **p** 90. C Rainham *Roch* 89-90; C Gravesend St Geo from 90. *St Mark's Vicarage, 123 London Road, Rosherville, North Fleet, Kent DA11 9NH*   Gravesend (0474) 534430

DAVIES, Raymond Emlyn Peter. b 25. St Mich Coll Llan 51. **d** 53 **p** 54. V Penrhiwceiber w Matthewstown and Ynysboeth *Llan* 68-72; C Whitchurch 72-73; V Childs Ercall *Lich* 73-81; R Stoke upon Tern 73-81; P-in-c Hamstall Ridware w Pipe Ridware 81-82; P-in-c Kings Bromley 81-82; P-in-c Mavesyn Ridware 81-82; R The Ridwares and Kings Bromley 83-90; rtd 90. *78 Thorley Drive, Cheadle, Stoke-on-Trent, Staffs ST10 1SA*   Cheadle (0538) 750522

DAVIES, Reginald Charles. b 33. Tyndale Hall Bris 58. **d** 64 **p** 65. C Heywood St Jas *Man* 64-66; C Drypool St Columba w St Andr and St Pet *York* 66-69; V Denaby Main *Sheff* from 69. *The Vicarage, Denaby Main, Doncaster, S Yorkshire*   Rotherham (0709) 862297

DAVIES, Rendle Leslie. b 29. St Chad's Coll Dur BA52 DipTh54. **d** 54 **p** 55. C Mon 54-58; V Llangwm Uchaf w Llangwm Isaf w Gwernesney etc 58-63; V Usk and Monkswood w Glascoed Chpl and Gwehelog from 63; Chpl HM Young Offender Inst Usk from 63. *The Vicarage, Castle Parade, Usk, Gwent NP5 1AA*   Usk (02913) 2653

DAVIES, Richard Henry. b 44. Mansf Coll Ox BA72 MA78. St Steph Ho Ox 68. **d** 72 **p** 73. C Higham Ferrers w Chelveston *Pet* 72-80; C Cantley *Sheff* 80-82; V Leic St Aid *Leic* 82-85; C Tronge Moor *Man* from 85. *St Augustine's Vicarage, Ainsworth Lane, Bolton BL2 2QW*   Bolton (0204) 23899

DAVIES, Richard James. b 42. **d** 69 **p** 70. Rhodesia 69-72 and 75-80; Zimbabwe from 80; C Southwick *Chich* 72-74; P-in-c Malmesbury w Westport *Bris* 75. *James's Mission, PO Box 23, Nyamandlovu, Zimbabwe*

DAVIES, Richard Paul. b 48. Wycliffe Hall Ox 72. **d** 75 **p** 76. C Everton St Sav w St Cuth *Liv* 75-78; Chapl Asst Basingstoke Distr Hosp 78-80; TV Basingstoke *Win* 80-85; V Southn Thornhill St Chris from 85. *St Christopher's Vicarage, 402 Hinkler Road, Southampton SO2 6DF*   Southampton (0703) 448537

DAVIES, Robert Emlyn. b 56. N Staffs Poly BA79. Coll of Resurr Mirfield 83. **d** 86 **p** 87. C Cardiff St Jo *Llan* 86-90; V Cwmparc from 90. *St George's Vicarage, Cwmparc, Treorchy, M Glam CF42 6NA*   Treorchy (0443) 773303

DAVIES, Robert Mark. b 53. St Jo Coll Nottm BTh79. **d** 79 **p** 80. C Tonbridge SS Pet and Paul *Roch* 79-83; NSM 84-86; Chapl Amsterdam w Haarlem and Den Helder *Eur* 83-84; NSM Littleover *Derby* 84; NSM Kentish Town St Benet and All SS *Lon* 86-87; TV N Lambeth *S'wark* from 87. *22 Wincott Street, London SE11 4NT*   071-582 4915

DAVIES, Roger Charles. b 46. Univ of Wales BD73. St Mich Coll Llan 69. **d** 73 **p** 74. C Llanfabon *Llan* 73-76; CF (TAVR) from 75; C Llanblethian w Cowbridge and Llandough etc *Llan* 76-78; CF 78-84; TV Halesworth w Linstead, Chediston, Holton etc *St E* 84-87; R Claydon and Barham 87-91; R Lavant *Chich* from 91. *The Rectory, Lavant, Chichester, W Sussex PO18 0AH*   Chichester (0243) 527313

DAVIES, Canon Ronald. b 14. Univ of Wales BA36. St Steph Ho Ox 36. **d** 39 **p** 40. V Abergavenny H Trin *Mon* 60-84; Can St Woolos Cathl 76-84; rtd 84; Lic to Offic *Mon* from 84. *The Bungalow, 11 Ysgubarwen, Abergavenny, Gwent NP7 6EE*   Abergavenny (0873) 4401

DAVIES, Ross Owen. b 55. Melbourne Univ BA77 LLB79. ACT ThL81. **d** 81 **p** 82. Australia 81-91; P-in-c Mundford w Lynford *Nor* from 91; P-in-c Ickburgh w Langford from 91; P-in-c Cranwich from 91. *The Rectory, St Leonard's Street, Mundford, Thetford, Norfolk IP26 5HG*   Thetford (0842) 878220

DAVIES, Canon Roswell Morgan. b 22. St D Coll Lamp BA46. **d** 48 **p** 49. V Rhayader *S & B* 63-76; V Rhayader and Nantmel 76-89; Hon Can Brecon Cathl 84-87; Can Res from 87; RD Maelienydd 87-89; rtd 90. *28 Maesyderi, Rhayader, Powys LD6 5DG*   Rhayader (0597) 810995

DAVIES, Preb Roy Basil. b 34. Bris Univ BA55. Westcott Ho Cam 57. **d** 59 **p** 60. C Ipswich St Mary le Tower *St E* 59-63; C Clun w Chapel Lawn *Heref* 63-70; V Bishop's Castle w Mainstone 70-83; RD Clun Forest 72-83; Preb Heref Cathl from 82; P-in-c Billingsley w Sidbury 83-86; P-in-c Chelmarsh 83-86; P-in-c Chetton w Deuxhill and Glazeley 83-86; P-in-c Middleton Scriven 83-86; R

Billingsley w Sidbury, Middleton Scriven etc 86-89; RD Bridgnorth 87-89; TR Wenlock from 89. *The Rectory, Much Wenlock, Shropshire TF13 6BN*   Much Wenlock (0952) 727396

DAVIES, Roy Gabe. b 38. Univ of Wales DipTh64. St Mich Coll Llan 61. **d** 64 **p** 65. C St Issells *St D* 64-65; C Milford Haven 65-67; C Codsall *Lich* 67-70; V Wolv St Steph 70-79; V Newport St Julian *Mon* 79-89; V Lakenheath *St E* from 89. *The Vicarage, Lakenheath, Brandon, Suffolk IP27 9EW*   Thetford (0842) 860683

✠**DAVIES, Rt Rev Roy Thomas.** b 34. St D Coll Lamp BA55 Jes Coll Ox DipTh58 BLitt59. St Steph Ho Ox 57. **d** 59 **p** 60 **c** 85. C Llanelly St Paul *St D* 59-64; V Llanafan y Trawscoed and Llanwnnws 64-67; Chapl Univ of Wales (Abth) 67-73; C Abth 67-69; TV 70-73; Sec Ch in Wales Prov Coun for Miss and Unity 73-79; V Carmarthen St Dav *St D* 79-83; Adn Carmarthen 82-85; V Llanegwad w Llanfynydd 83-85; Bp Llan from 85. *Llys Esgob, The Cathedral Green, Llandaff, Cardiff CF5 2YE*   Cardiff (0222) 562400

DAVIES, Sarah Isabella. b 39. **d** 91. NSM Pontypridd St Cath w St Matt *Llan* from 91. *St Matthew's House, 26 East Street, Trallwn, Pontypridd, M Glam CF37 4PL*   Pontypridd (0443) 406101

DAVIES, Sidney. b 16. St D Coll Lamp BA40. **d** 41 **p** 42. R Llanerch Aeron w Ciliau Aeron and Dihewyd *St D* 69-82; rtd 82. *12 Pontfaen, Porthyrhyd, Carmarthen, Dyfed*   Llanddarog (0267) 275525

DAVIES, Stanley James. b 18. MBE54. St Chad's Coll Dur BA40 DipTh41 MA44. **d** 41 **p** 42. CF 45-68; Asst Chapl Gen Lon 68-70; BAOR 70-73; QHC from 72; R Uley w Owlpen and Nympsfield *Glouc* 73-84; rtd 84; Perm to Offic *Ex* from 86. *Peverell Cottage, Doddiscombsleigh, Exeter EX6 7PR*   Christow (0647) 52616

DAVIES, Stephen Walter. b 26. AKC54. **d** 55 **p** 56. C Plympton St Mary *Ex* 55-58; C Ex St Mark 58-61; Chapl RAF 61-77; R Feltwell *Ely* 78-84; R N Newton w St Michaelchurch, Thurloxton etc *B & W* from 84. *The Rectory, Thurloxton, Taunton, Somerset TA2 8RH*   West Monkton (0823) 412479

DAVIES, Stuart Simeon. b 13. St Chad's Coll Dur BA41 DipTh42 MA44. Knutsford Test Sch 37. **d** 42 **p** 43. R Fifield w Idbury *Ox* 65-74; rtd 74. *Wing 3, Home of St Monica, Cote Lane, Westbury-on-Trym, Bristol BS9 3UN*   Bristol (0272) 629281

DAVIES, Canon Thomas. b 15. Man Univ BA38. Ridley Hall Cam 38. **d** 40 **p** 41. V Westhoughton *Man* 53-80; Hon Can Man Cathl 70-80; RD Deane 74-80; rtd 80; Perm to Offic St As and Ban from 80. *9A College Avenue, Rhos-on-Sea, Colwyn Bay, Clwyd LL28 4NT*   Colwyn Bay (0492) 534-9339

DAVIES, Preb Thomas Derwent. b 16. St D Coll Lamp BA38 St Mich Coll Llan 39. **d** 39 **p** 41. Preb Ex Cathl *Ex* from 69; V Cadbury 74-81; V Thorverton 74-81; rtd 82. *12 Blagdon Rise, Crediton, Devon EX17 1EN*   Crediton (03632) 3856

DAVIES, Thomas Neville James. b 27. St Mich Coll Llan 54. **d** 56 **p** 57. C Wrexham *St As* 56-62; V Bronnington and Bettisfield 62-65; CF 65-83. *7 Surrey Lodge, 19 Surrey Road, Bournemouth BH4 9HN*

DAVIES, Canon Thomas Philip. b 27. Univ of Wales (Ban) BEd73. St Mich Coll Llan 55. **d** 56 **p** 57. C Ruabon *St As* 56-59; C Prestatyn 59-62; V Penley 62-69; V Bettisfield 66-69; V Holt and Isycoed 69-77; Dioc Dir of Educn from 76; Dioc RE Adv from 76; RD Wrexham 76-77; R Hawarden from 77; Can St As Cathl from 79. *The Rectory, 2 Birch Rise, Hawarden, Clwyd CH5 3DD*   Hawarden (0244) 520091

DAVIES, Thomas Stanley. b 10. Nashdom Abbey 33. **d** 37 **p** 38. V Stansted Mountfitchet *Chelmsf* 71-78; rtd 78; Perm to Offic *Chelmsf* from 78. *54 Newbiggen Street, Thaxted, Essex CM6 2QT*   Thaxted (0371) 830110

DAVIES, Tommy. b 16. St D Coll Lamp. **d** 39 **p** 40. V Llanfihangel y Pennant and Talyllin *Ban* 54-63; rtd 63. *Gwynfro, Ciliau Aeron, Lampeter, Dyfed*   Cardigan (0239) 614018

DAVIES, Canon Trevor Gwesyn. b 28. Univ of Wales (Ban) BEd73. St Mich Coll Llan 55. **d** 56 **p** 57. C Holywell *St As* 56-63; V Cwm 63-74; V Colwyn Bay from 74; Can St As Cathl from 79. *The Vicarage, Woodland Road East, Colwyn Bay, Clwyd LL29 7DT*   Colwyn Bay (0492) 532403

DAVIES, Victor George. b 08. St Jo Coll Dur BA33 MA36. **d** 34 **p** 35. Lect Liv Univ 49-57; V Walton *Ches* 59-73; Sec Dioc Adv Cttee 59-73; Dioc Insp of Schs 60-73; rtd 73. *Ground Floor, 15 Wennington Road, Southport, Merseyside PR9 7ER*   Southport (0704) 29117

DAVIES, Vincent Anthony. b 46. Brasted Th Coll 69 St Mich Coll Llan 71. **d** 73 **p** 74. C Owton Manor CD *Dur* 73-76; C Wandsworth St Faith *S'wark* 76-78; P-in-c 78-81; V Walworth St Jo from 81; RD S'wark and Newington from 88. *St John's Vicarage, Larcom Street, London SE17 1NQ* 071-703 4375

DAVIES, Canon Vincent James. b 22. St D Coll Lamp BA48. **d** 50 **p** 51. V Llangorse *S & B* 58-72; V Llangorse w Cathedine 72-91; RD Brecon I 77-91; Hon Can Brecon Cathl from 89; rtd 91. *Blaen Nant, 29 Blackfriars Court, Llanfaes, Brecon, Powys*

DAVIES, Walter Hugh. b 28. St Deiniol's Hawarden 64. **d** 66 **p** 67. C Ban St Mary *Ban* 66-69; P-in-c Rhosybol and Llandyfrydog 70; TV Amlwch, Rhosybol and Llandyfrydog 71-74; R Llanfaethlu w Llanfwrog and Llanrhyddlad etc from 74; RD Llifon and Talybolion from 85. *The Rectory, Llanfaethlu, Holyhead, Gwynedd LL65 4PB* Llanfaethlu (0407) 730251

DAVIES, Ven Walter Merlin. b 10. St D Coll Lamp BA36 Westcott Ho Cam 37. **d** 38 **p** 39. C Bris St Mich *Bris* 38-40; New Zealand 40-44; Dir of Educn *Bris* 45-49; V Baswich (or Berkswich) *Lich* 49-59; New Zealand from 59; Adn Akaroa and Ashburton 59-69; Adn Sumner 69-73; Hon Can H Trin Cathl Auckland 74-76. *St Hilda's Retreat House, 20 Queen Street, Auckland 9, New Zealand* Auckland (9) 480-7225

DAVIES, Canon William David. b 19. Bris Univ BA41. St Mich Coll Llan 48. **d** 43 **p** 44. R Porthkerry *Llan* 68-72; R Barry All SS 72-85; RD Penarth and Barry 75-85; Can Llan Cathl from 82; rtd 85. *3 Brookfield Park Road, Cowbridge, S Glam CF7 7HS* Bridgend (0656) 5259

DAVIES, Canon William John Morgan. b 10. St D Coll Lamp BA32. **d** 36 **p** 37. V Defynnog w Rhydybriw and Llandeilo'r Fan *S & B* 54-84; RD Brecon II 76-80; Can Brecon Cathl 78-84; rtd 84. *Bronwysg, Sennybridge, Brecon, Powys LD3 8PG* Sennybridge (0874) 636226

DAVIES, William Kenneth (Brother Edgar). b 24. St Pet Hall Ox BA47 MA50. Wycliffe Hall Ox 48. **d** 50 **p** 51. C Netherton St Andr *Worc* 50-53; CF 53-57; C-in-c Birchen Coppice St Pet CD *Worc* 57-61; R Stoke Bliss w Kyre Wyard 61-69; SSF from 69; Lic to Offic Ely 72-75 and 80-85; Liv 77-80; Chapl Arthur Rank Ho Brookfields Hosp Cam 81-85; Chapl Hengrave Hall Community 85-86; Perm to Offic *Lich* 86-88; Zimbabwe from 88. *St Barnabas's Friary, 191 Westwood, PO Kambuzuma, Harare, Zimbabwe* Harare (4) 762391

DAVIES, William Martin. b 56. Univ of Wales (Cardiff) BSc78. Wycliffe Hall Ox 78. **d** 81 **p** 82. C Gabalfa *Llan* 81-84; P-in-c Beguildy and Heyope *S & B* 84-85; V 85-87; V Swansea St Thos and Kilvey from 87; Asst Chapl Miss to Seamen from 89. *St Thomas's Vicarage, Lewis Street, Swansea SA1 8BP* Swansea (0792) 652891

DAVIES, William Morris. b 19. LCP56 Univ of Wales (Lamp) BA41 Jes Coll Ox BA43 MA47 Man Univ DipEd61 Liv Univ MEd68. St Mich Coll Llan 43. **d** 44 **p** 45. Lect Div Crewe Coll Educn 65-68; Sen Lect 68-71; Hd of Div Dept 71-75; Tutor Th & Educn Crewe & Alsager Coll of HE 75-79; Tutor Open Univ 78-81; V Norley *Ches* 79-85; Tutor St Deiniol's Lib Hawarden from 83; rtd 85; Sub-Chapl HM Young Offender Inst Thorn Cross 85-89; Lic to Offic *Ches* from 85. *Eastwood, Willington, Tarporley, Cheshire CW6 0NE* Kelsall (0829) 52181

DAVIES, William Morris. b 23. St Mich Coll Llan 66. **d** 68 **p** 68. C Llanguicke *S & B* 68-72; V Bryngwyn and Newchurch and Llanbedr etc 72-77; R Bedwas *Mon* 77-88; rtd 88. *31 Landore Avenue, Killay, Swansea SA2 7BP* Swansea (0792) 206704

DAVIES, William Paul Seymour. b 27. Ex Coll Ox BA51 MA55. St Mich Coll Llan 53. **d** 54 **p** 56. C Chirk *St As* 54-55; C Minera 55-57; V Bwlchgwyn 57-61; V Llandrinio and Criggion 61-66; Tristan da Cunha 66-68; R Pont Robert w Pont Dolanog *St As* 68-71; V Llansilin w Llangadwaladr and Llangedwyn 71-80; V Meifod and Llangynyw 80-88; RD Caereinion 86-88; P-in-c Llangynog from 88. *Iscoed, Pennant Melangell, Llangynog, Oswestry, Shropshire SY10 0HQ* Pennant (069174) 455

DAVILL, Robin William. b 51. CertEd73 SS Paul & Mary Coll Cheltenham BEd74 Leic Univ MA79. Westcott Ho Cam 86. **d** 88 **p** 89. C Broughton *Blackb* 88-91; C Howden Team Min *York* from 91. *6 Sandholme Way, Howden, Goole, N Humberside DN14 7LN* Howden (0430) 431920

DAVIS, Alan. b 34. Birm Univ BSc56. Ox NSM Course. **d** 75 **p** 76. NSM Chesham St Mary *Ox* 75-80; NSM Gt Chesham from 80. *18 Cheyne Walk, Chesham, Bucks HP5 1AY* Chesham (0494) 782124

DAVIS, Alan John. b 33. St Alb Minl Tr Scheme 77. **d** 80 **p** 81. NSM Goldington *St Alb* 80-84; C Benchill *Man* 84-86; R Gt Chart *Cant* from 86. *The Rectory, Great Chart, Ashford, Kent TN23 3AY* Ashford (0233) 620371

DAVIS, Alan Norman. b 38. Open Univ BA75. Lich Th Coll. **d** 65 **p** 66. C Kingstanding St Luke *Birm* 65-68; C-in-c Ecclesfield St Paul CD *Sheff* 68-72; I 72-73; V Sheff St Paul Wordsworth Avenue 73-75; V Shiregreen St Jas and St Chris 75-80; R Maltby 80-81; TR 81-89; Abp's Officer for UPA from 90; Lic to Offic *St Alb* from 90. *11 Potters Road, Barnet, Herts EN5 5HS* 081-447 1250

DAVIS, Allan. b 15. ALCD54. **d** 54 **p** 55. V Colchester St Jo *Chelmsf* 67-80; rtd 80; Perm to Offic *St Alb* from 80. *5 Pipit Close, Flitwick, Beds MK45 1NJ* Flitwick (0525) 713854

DAVIS, Andrew Fisher. b 46. St Chad's Coll Dur BA67. St Steph Ho Ox 68. **d** 70 **p** 71. C Beckenham St Jas *Roch* 70-74; C Kensington St Mary Abbots w St Geo *Lon* 74-80; V Sudbury St Andr 80-90; AD Brent 85-90; V Ealing Ch the Sav from 90. *The Clergy House, The Grove, London W5 5DX* 081-567 1288

DAVIS, Andrew George. b 63. Bath Univ BSc Edin Univ BD. Edin Th Coll. **d** 89 **p** 90. C Alverstoke *Portsm* from 89. *32 Privett Place, Alverstoke, Gosport, Hants PO12 3SQ* Portsmouth (0705) 581999

DAVIS, Anthony David Hugh. b 52. Southn Univ BTh80. Chich Th Coll 75. **d** 78 **p** 79. C Roath St German *Llan* 78-82; C Roath St Sav 82-85; V Pontlottyn w Fochriw from 85. *St Tyfaelog's Vicarage, Southend Terrace, Pontlottyn, Bargoed, M Glam CF8 9RL* Rhymney (0685) 841322

DAVIS, Arthur Vivian. b 24. Clifton Th Coll 60. **d** 62 **p** 63. V Cam St Andr Less *Ely* 68-75; V Kirtling 75-86; V Wood Ditton w Saxon Street 75-86; P-in-c Cheveley 83-86; P-in-c Ashley w Silverley 83-86; rtd 86. *408 Aureole Walk, Studlands Park, Newmarket, Suffolk CB8 7BB* Newmarket (0638) 661709

DAVIS, Canon Bernard Rex. b 33. FRSA87 Sydney Univ BA55 Newc Univ MA67. Gen Th Sem (NY) MDiv60 Coll of Resurr Mirfield. **d** 57 **p** 58. C Guildf St Nic *Guildf* 57-59; USA 59-61; Australia 62-68; Exec Sec Unit 3 WCC Geneva 68-77; Warden Edw King Ho from 77; Can Res and Sub Dean Linc Cathl *Linc* from 77; Treas from 85. *The Subdeanery, 18 Minster Yard, Lincoln LN2 1PX* Lincoln (0522) 521932

DAVIS, Brian. b 40. AKC69 BD69. St Aug Coll Cant 69. **d** 70 **p** 71. C Humberstone *Leic* 70-73; C Kirby Muxloe 73-74; V Countesthorpe w Foston from 74; RD Guthlaxton I (Blaby) from 90. *The Vicarage, 102 Station Road, Countesthorpe, Leicester LE8 3TB* Leicester (0533) 784442 or 778643

DAVIS, Christopher Eliot. b 28. Pemb Coll Cam BA50 MA55. Wells Th Coll 53. **d** 54 **p** 55. C Dudley Holly Hall St Aug *Worc* 54-56; C Bromyard *Heref* 56-57; Min Can Carl Cathl *Carl* 57-59; Prec Worc Cathl *Worc* 59-62; P-in-c Lich St Mary *Lich* 65-66; PV Lich Cathl 65-67; Chapl Magd Coll Ox 71-74; Perm to Offic *Lich* from 77. *28 Newbridge Crescent, Wolverhampton WV6 0LH* Wolverhampton (0902) 759220

DAVIS, Clinton Ernest Newman. b 46. Solicitor 71. Wycliffe Hall Ox 78. **d** 80 **p** 81. C Margate H Trin *Cant* 80-84; C St Laurence in Thanet 84-87; V Sandgate St Paul from 87. *The Vicarage, 10 Meadowbrook, Sandgate, Folkestone, Kent CT20 3NY* Folkestone (0303) 48675

DAVIS, David John. b 35. St Steph Ho Ox 79. **d** 81 **p** 82. C Reading St Mark *Ox* 81-84; C Gt Grimsby St Mary and St Jas *Linc* 84-85; TV 85-89; V Caistor w Clixby from 89. *The Vicarage, 1 Cromwell View, Caistor, Lincoln LN7 6OH* Caistor (0472) 339

DAVIS, Edwin John Charles. b 36. Dur Univ BA60 St Cath Soc Ox BA62 MA66. Ripon Hall Ox 60. **d** 62 **p** 63. C Kington w Huntington *Heref* 62-65; Lect Lich Th Coll 65-66; Chapl Edin Th Coll 66-70; Hon Chapl St Mary's Cathl *Edin* 66-70; P-in-c Hope w Shelve *Heref* 70-78; R 78-81; P-in-c Middleton *W* 78-81; P-in-c Worthen 75-78; R 78-81; V S Hinksey *Ox* from 81; Dep Dir Tr Scheme for NSM from 84. *New Hinksey Vicarage, Vicarage Road, Oxford OX1 4RD* Oxford (0865) 245879

DAVIS, Harold Horace. b 19. Worc Ord Coll 66. **d** 67 **p** 68. C Gt Clacton *Chelmsf* 67-73; V Heybridge w Langford 73-77; P-in-c W w S Hanningfield 77-78; R W Hanningfield 78-87; rtd 87; Perm to Offic *Chelmsf* from 87. *35 Highview Avenue, Clacton-on-Sea, Essex CO15 4DX* Clacton-on-Sea (0225) 251315

DAVIS, Herbert Roger. b 36. Kelham Th Coll 60. **d** 65 **p** 66. C Barkingside St Fran *Chelmsf* 65-69; C Harpenden St Nic *St Alb* 69-73; P-in-c Eaton Bray 73-75; V Eaton

Bray w Edlesborough 75-81; RD Dunstable 77-81; R Gt Berkhamsted from 81. *The Rectory, Berkhamsted, Herts HP4 2DH* Berkhamsted (0442) 864194

DAVIS, Ian Andrew. b 58. MIBiol85 CBiol85 Sheff Univ BSc79 PGCE80. St Jo Coll Nottm LTh89 DPS90. **d** 90 **p** 91. C Hatf *Sheff* from 90. *St Mary's House, 11 High Street, Hatfield, Doncaster, S Yorkshire DN7 6RS* Doncaster (0302) 840283

DAVIS, Ivor Leslie. b 23. TCD BA48 MA53. **d** 48 **p** 49. V Eccleston Park *Liv* 61-70; R Maghull 70-72; TR 72-88; rtd 88. *3 Oxford Gardens, Oxford Road, Southport, Merseyside PR8 2JR* Southport (0704) 69480

DAVIS, Jack. b 35. LRSC63 CChem80 MRSC80 Sheff City Poly HNC59 Sheff Univ MSc88. Oak Hill Th Coll DipHE88. **d** 88 **p** 89. C Owlerton *Sheff* 88-91; V Manea *Ely* from 91; R Wimblington from 91. *The Vicarage, High Street, Manea, March, Cambs PE15 0JD* Manea (035478) 415

DAVIS, James Raymond. b 17. Mert Coll Ox BA40 MA44. Wells Th Coll 40. **d** 41 **p** 42. V Borden *Cant* 66-84; rtd 84; Perm to Offic *Llan* from 85. *3 St Teilo Close, Dinas Powys, S Glam CF6 4TY* Cardiff (0222) 514600

DAVIS, John Basil. b 20. Lon Univ BA69. Bps' Coll Cheshunt 46. **d** 49 **p** 50. V Bacton w Edingthorpe *Nor* 61-66; Perm to Offic *S'well* 71-86; rtd 85; Hon C Bingham *S'well* from 86. *1 Banks Crescent, Bingham, Nottingham NG13 8BP* Bingham (0949) 837721

DAVIS, John Brian. b 33. Linc Th Coll 72. **d** 75 **p** 76. Hon C Bungay H Trin w St Mary *St E* 75-84; P-in-c Barrow 84-85; P-in-c Denham St Mary 84-85; R Barrow w Denham St Mary and Higham Green from 85. *The Rectory, Barrow, Bury St Edmunds, Suffolk IP29 5AA* Bury St Edmunds (0284) 810279

DAVIS, John Harold. b 54. St Jo Coll Dur BSc76 DipTh78 MA86. Cranmer Hall Dur 76. **d** 79 **p** 80. C Marske in Cleveland *York* 79-82; C Pocklington w Yapham-cum-Meltonby, Owsthorpe etc 82-83; TV Pocklington Team 84-86; V Carlton and Drax from 86; Ind Chapl from 88. *The Vicarage, 2 Church Dike Lane, Drax, Selby, Yorkshire YO8 8NZ* Selby (0757) 618313

DAVIS, John Stephen. b 51. N Staffs Poly BSc75. Wycliffe Hall Ox 75. **d** 78 **p** 79. C Meole Brace *Lich* 78-81; C Bloxwich 81-85; V Walsall St Paul from 85. *St Paul's Vicarage, 57 Mellish Road, Walsall WS4 2DG* Walsall (0922) 24963

DAVIS, Kenneth Gordon. b 18. Selw Coll Cam BA40 MA43. Qu Coll Birm 40. **d** 42 **p** 43. V Exbury *Win* 63-77; V Beaulieu and Exbury 77-83; rtd 83; Perm to Offic *Win* from 83; Hon C Highcliffe w Hinton Admiral from 85. *2 Chatsworth Way, New Milton, Hants BH25 5UL* New Milton (0425) 618520

DAVIS, Preb Kenneth William. b 25. Ripon Hall Ox 60. **d** 62 **p** 63. C Lyngford *B & W* 62-65; R Axbridge 65-72; V Wells St Cuth 72-73; V Wells St Cuth w Wookey Hole from 73; RD Shepton Mallet 79-86; Preb Wells Cathl from 83. *The Vicarage, 1 St Cuthbert Street, Wells, Somerset BA5 2AW* Wells (0749) 73136

DAVIS, Martyn Kevin. b 59. Chich Th Coll 84. **d** 87 **p** 88. C Hove All SS *Chich* from 87. *Flat 1, 28 Tisbury Road, Hove, E Sussex BN3 3BA* Brighton (0273) 821439

DAVIS, Nicholas Anthony Wylie. b 56. BA. Chich Th Coll. **d** 84 **p** 85. C N Lambeth *S'wark* 84-88; TV Catford (Southend) and Downham from 88. *233 Bellingham Road, London SE6 1EH* 081-698 4094

DAVIS, Norman. b 38. FCII66. Oak Hill Th Coll 77. **d** 79 **p** 80. C Walton *St E* 79-82; P-in-c Bredfield w Boulge 86-91; P-in-c Grundisburgh w Burgh 82-91; RD Woodbridge from 90; R Boulge w Burgh and Grundisburgh from 91. *The Rectory, Grundisburgh, Woodbridge, Suffolk IP13 6UF* Grundisburgh (047335) 749

DAVIS, Norman John. b 41. Oak Hill Th Coll 63. **d** 66 **p** 67. C Wellington w Eyton *Lich* 66-70; C Higher Openshaw *Man* 70-72; R S Levenshulme 72-79; P-in-c Berrow w Pendock and Eldersfield *Worc* 79-81; R 81-87; R Churchill-in-Halfshire w Blakedown and Broome from 87. *The Rectory, 5 Mill Lane, Blakedown, Kidderminster, Worcs DY10 3ND* Kidderminster (0562) 700293

DAVIS, Paul Montague. b 29. St Jo Coll Dur BA52. Ely Th Coll 52. **d** 54 **p** 55. C Malden St Jas *S'wark* 54-56; C Boreham Wood All SS *St Alb* 56-57; C Colchester St Jas, All SS, St Nic and St Runwald *Chelmsf* 57-61; Hon C 72-81; CF 61-63; C Leigh St Clem *Chelmsf* 63-67; C Hockley 67-70; V Lt Horkesley 81-85; R The Bromleys from 85. *The Rectory, Hull Road, Great Bromley, Colchester CO7 7TS* Colchester (0206) 230344

DAVIS, Peter Thomas. b 61. Flinders Univ Aus BTh87. Adelaide Coll of Div DPS88 St Barn Coll Adelaide 83. **d** 87 **p** 91. Australia 87-91; TV Gt and Lt Coates w

Bradley *Linc* from 91. *The Vicarage, Wingate Road, Grimsby, S Humberside DN37 9EL* Grimsby (0472) 885709

DAVIS, Ronald Frank. b 26. Oak Hill Th Coll 62. **d** 64 **p** 65. V N and S Otterington *York* 67-77; C Rainham *Chelmsf* 77-82; V Hainault 82-88; rtd 88. *Home View, Westview Grove, Keighley, W Yorkshire BD20 6JJ* Keighley (0535) 681294

DAVIS, Ronald Geoffrey. b 47. St Jo Coll Nottm 79. **d** 81 **p** 81. C Maidstone St Luke *Cant* 81-84; P-in-c Lostwithiel *Truro* 84-86; P-in-c Lanhydrock 84-86; Asst Dioc Youth Officer 84-86; P-in-c Boughton Monchelsea *Cant* 86-88; V from 88. *The Vicarage, Church Hill, Boughton Monchelsea, Maidstone, Kent ME17 4BU* Maidstone (0622) 743321

DAVIS, Ronald Huthwaite. b 03. Lon Univ BSc23. **d** 43 **p** 44. Chapl Win Ho Sch Brackley from 43; Lic to Offic *Pet* from 43. *57A Manor Road, Brackley, Northants* Brackley (0280) 702246

DAVIS, Royston Grandfield. b 33. Sarum & Wells Th Coll 86. **d** 88 **p** 89. C Cainscross w Selsley *Glouc* 88-90; TV Hugglescote w Donington, Ellistown and Snibston *Leic* from 90. *St James' Vicarage, Highfield Street, Coalville, Leicester LE6 2BN* Coalville (0530) 32679

DAVIS, Sidney Charles. b 31. DMA61 ACIS61 FCIS73. S Dios Minl Tr Scheme 80. **d** 83 **p** 84. NSM Amesbury *Sarum* from 83; Nat Chapl Ex-Prisoners of War Assn from 90. *4 Stonehenge Road, Amesbury, Salisbury SP4 7BA* Amesbury (0980) 623248

DAVIS, Stephen Charles. b 19. AKC48 St Cath Soc Ox BA50 MA54. Wycliffe Hall Ox 48. **d** 50 **p** 51. R Dur St Marg *Dur* 64-87; rtd 87. *6 Juniper Way, Malvern Wells, Worcs WR14 4XG* Malvern (0684) 561039

DAVIS, Thomas Edward. b 20. **d** 83 **p** 84. NSM Cen Telford *Lich* from 83. *14 Bembridge, Telford, Shropshire TF3 1NA* Telford (0952) 592352

DAVIS, Timothy Charles. b 59. Reading Univ BA81 Homerton Coll Cam PGCE82. Trin Coll Bris DipHE91. **d** 91. C Normanton *Wakef* from 91. *8 Prospect Avenue, Ashgap Lane, Normanton, Wakefield, W Yorkshire WF6 2DS* Wakefield (0924) 892773

DAVIS, William Henry. b 17. Open Univ BA84. Bps' Coll Cheshunt. **d** 67 **p** 68. C Sudbury St Andr *Lon* 67-70; V Wickhambrook *St E* 70-72; V Wickhambrook w Stradishall and Denston from 72; P-in-c Stansfield 76-78. *The Vicarage, Wickhambrook, Newmarket, Suffolk CB8 8XH* Wickhambrook (0440) 820288

DAVIS-JONES, Noel Jenkin. b 10. St D Coll Lamp BA32. **d** 33 **p** 34. R Amcotts w Luddington and Garthorpe *Linc* 65-76; RD Is of Axholme 69-76; P-in-c Althorpe 70-76; rtd 76; P-in-c Llanddewi Ystradenni and Abbey Cwmhir *S & B* 76-84; P-in-c Llanddewi Ystradenny from 84; P-in-c Llanbister and Llanbadarn Fynydd w Llananno 84-87. *Llandewi Vicarage, Llandrindod Wells, Powys LD1 6SE* Penybont (059787) 424

DAVISON, Beryl. b 37. Lightfoot Ho Dur 62. **d** 87. Par Dn Consett *Dur* from 87. *13 Barr House Avenue, Consett, Co Durham DH8 5NE* Consett (0207) 505173

DAVISON, Canon Paul. b 15. Ex Coll Ox BA37 MA41. Ripon Hall Ox 37. **d** 39 **p** 40. V Needham Market w Badley *St E* 64-86; RD Bosmere 70-86; Hon Can St E Cathl 75-86; P-in-c Creeting St Mary 75-86; rtd 86; Perm to Offic *St E* from 87. *58 Stowmarket Road, Needham Market, Ipswich* Needham Market (0449) 722191

DAVISON, Ralph Guild. b 13. Ely Th Coll 33. **d** 36 **p** 37. R Bagborough *B & W* 63-78; rtd 78; Chapl Franciscans Posbury from 78. *St Mary of the Angels, Posbury, Crediton, Devon EX17 3QF* Crediton (03632) 3280

DAVISON, Richard Ireland. b 42. St Chad's Coll Dur BSc63. Linc Th Coll 64. **d** 66 **p** 67. C Cockerton *Dur* 66-70; C Houghton le Spring 70-73; V Heworth St Alb 73-80; Ascension Is 80-82; V Dunston *Dur* 82-85; V Bishopwearmouth Ch Ch from 85. *Christ Church Vicarage, 7 St Bede's Park, Sunderland SR2 7DZ* 091-565 8077

DAVISON, Richard John. b 32. St Andr Univ MA56. Linc Th Coll 56. **d** 58 **p** 59. C S Shields St Hilda *Dur* 58-61; C Dur St Cuth 61-63; R Wyberton *Linc* 63-86; RD Holland W 84-86; TR Swan *Ox* 86-91; V Streatley w Moulsford from 91. *The Vicarage, Streatley, Reading RG8 9HX* Goring-on-Thames (0491) 872191

DAVISON, Canon Roger William. b 20. Kelham Th Coll 46. **d** 51 **p** 52. V Higham Ferrers w Chelveston *Pet* 65-88; rtd 88; Perm to Offic *Roch* from 88. *17 Hermitage Road, Higham, Rochester, Kent ME3 7DB* Shorne (047482) 3824

DAVISON, Thomas Alfred. b 28. St Aug Coll Cant 48 St Chad's Coll Dur 52. **d** 60 **p** 61. C Tetbury w Beverston *Glouc* 60-62; C Malvern Link St Matthias *Worc* 62-65;

R Coates *Glouc* 65-76; R Coates, Rodmarton and Sapperton etc 76-78; P-in-c Bleadon *B & W* 78-81; Chapl HM Pris Leeds 81-84; Channings Wood 84-89; P-in-c Pyworthy, Pancrasweek and Bridgerule *Ex* 89-91; P-in-c Otterton and Colaton Raleigh from 91. *The Vicarage, Otterton, Budleigh Salterton, Devon EX9 7JQ* Colaton Raleigh (0395) 67003

DAVISON, William. b 18. St D Coll Lamp 58. **d** 60 **p** 61. R Mareham le Fen *Linc* 66-76; Lic to Offic 77-78; P-in-c Barkestone cum Plungar and Redmile *Leic* 78; R 78-81; rtd 82. *29 Bedford Road, Cleethorpes, S Humberside DN35 0PZ* Cleethorpes (0472) 814282

DAVOLL, Ivan John (Snowy). b 33. DipYW67. Local NSM Course 87. **d** 88 **p** 90. NSM Bermondsey St Jas w Ch Ch *S'wark* from 88. *2 Thurland Road, London SE16 4AA* 071-237 8741

DAW, Geoffrey Martin. b 57. Oak Hill Th Coll 81. **d** 84 **p** 85. C Hollington St Leon *Chich* 84-87; C Seaford w Sutton 87-90; V Iford w Kingston and Rodmell from 90. *The Vicarage, Well Green Lane, Kingston, Lewes, E Sussex BN7 3NS* Lewes (0273) 472384

DAWE, David Fife Purchas. b 20. Keble Coll Ox BA41 MA45. Wells Th Coll 41. **d** 43 **p** 44. V Criftins *Lich* 61-77; V Dudleston 63-77; P-in-c Alkmonton w Yeaveley *Derby* 77-81; P-in-c Cubley w Marston Montgomery 77-81; V Alkmonton, Cubley, Marston, Montgomery etc 81-85; rtd 85; Perm to Offic Derby and Lich from 85. *8 West Drive, Doveridge, Derby DE6 5NG* Uttoxeter (0889) 563434

DAWES, Alexander Barton. b 09. Bps' Coll Cheshunt 44. **d** 46 **p** 47. V Pill *B & W* 70-74; rtd 74. *Fairlawn, 2 Battery Road, Portishead, Avon BS20 9HP* Portishead (0272) 842378

DAWES, Dori Katherine. b 37. ARCM. Oak Hill NSM Course 85. **d** 88. Par Dn Watford St Luke *St Alb* 88-90; Par Dn Watford from 90. *135 Abbots Road, Abbots Langley, Watford, Herts WD5 0BJ* Kings Langley (0923) 262516

DAWES, Hugh William. b 48. Univ Coll Ox BA71 MA76. Cuddesdon Coll 71. **d** 74 **p** 75. C Purley St Mark Woodcote *S'wark* 74-77; Chapl G&C Coll Cam 77-82; Lic to Offic *Ely* 78-87; Chapl Em Coll Cam 82-87; V Cam St Jas *Ely* from 87. *St James's Vicarage, 110 Wulfstan Way, Cambridge CB1 4QJ* Cambridge (0223) 246419

DAWES, Julian Edward. b 27. RAF Coll Cranwell 49. Bps' Coll Cheshunt 58. **d** 59 **p** 60. V Overbury w Alstone, Teddington and Lt Washbourne *Worc* 65-70; V Cropthorne w Charlton 70-76; Chapl Dioc Conf Cen 70-76; Chapl Exe Vale Hosp Gp 76-84; Bromsgrove and Redditch Distr Gen Hosp 84-86; rtd 91. *41 Thornton Hill, Exeter, Devon EX4 4NR* Exeter (0392) 77928

DAWES, Peter Martin. b 24. Westmr Coll Cam 52. **d** 81 **p** 81. C Dunscroft *Sheff* 81-83; V 83-89; rtd 89. *4 Vancouver Road, London SE23 2AF* 081-699 9413

✠**DAWES, Rt Rev Peter Spencer.** b 28. Hatf Coll Dur BA52. Tyndale Hall Bris 53. **d** 54 **p** 55 **c** 88. C Whitehall Park St Andr Hornsey Lane *Lon* 54-57; C Ox St Ebbe *Ox* 57-60; Tutor Clifton Th Coll 60-65; V Romford Gd Shep Collier Row *Chelmsf* 65-80; Hon Can Chelmsf Cathl 78-80; Adn W Ham 80-88; Dioc Dir of Ords 80-86; Bp Derby from 88. *The Bishop's House, 6 King Street, Duffield, Derby DE6 4EY* Derby (0332) 840132 or 46744

DAWES, Victor. b 18. Wycliffe Hall Ox 63. **d** 64 **p** 65. V Andreas St Jude *S & M* 67-73; V Jurby 67-73; Warden Baycliff Healing Cen 73-83; Perm to Offic from 85; rtd 89. *48 Ballakane Close, Port Erin, Isle of Man* Port Erin (0624) 832921

DAWES, William Henry. b 41. AKC68. **d** 69 **p** 73. S Africa 69-72; C Noel Park St Mark *Lon* 72-76; C N Greenford All Hallows 76; C Hillingdon St Andr 76-78; Perm to Offic Lon 82-87; Pet 87-91; Lich from 91. *Chez Guillaume, 4 Hawthorne Gardens, Talke, Stoke-on-Trent ST7 1TD* Stoke-on-Trent (0782) 773563

DAWKES, Peter. b 31. Roch Th Coll 64. **d** 66 **p** 67. C Newbold and Dunston *Derby* 66-69; C Buxton 69-72; V Somercotes from 72. *The Vicarage, Nottingham Road, Somercotes, Derby DE55 4LY* Leabrooks (0773) 602840

DAWKIN, Peter William. b 60. Nottm Univ BTh88. St Jo Coll Nottm 85. **d** 88 **p** 89. C Birkdale St Jo *Liv* from 88. *23 Carnarvon Road, Southport, Merseyside PR8 4SE* Southport (0704) 68389

DAWKINS, Canon Alan Arthur Windsor. b 26. Lon Univ DipTh54. St Aid Birkenhead 53. **d** 55 **p** 56. C Preston Em *Blackb* 55-57; C S Shore H Trin 57-59; V Slade Green *Roch* 59-61; V St Mary Cray and St Paul's Cray 61-63; V White Colne *Chelmsf* 63-66; R Pebmarsh 63-66; P-in-c Mt Bures 65-66; V Westgate St Jas *Cant* 66-74; V

Herne Bay Ch Ch 74-83; Hon Can Cant Cathl from 79; P-in-c Chilham 83-85; Adv for Miss and Unity from 85. *5 Randolph Close, Canterbury, Kent CT1 3AZ* Canterbury (0227) 452009

DAWKINS, Anthony Norman. b 32. HNC55. NW Ord Course 70. **d** 73 **p** 74. C Man Clayton St Cross w St Paul *Man* 73-74; C Chorlton-cum-Hardy St Werburgh 74-77; C Scarborough St Martin *York* 77-78; P-in-c Kexby w Wilberfoss 78-84; R Dodleston *Ches* 84-88; V Felkirk w Brierley *Wakef* from 88. *The Vicarage, George Street, South Hiendley, Barnsley, S Yorkshire S72 9BX* Barnsley (0226) 715315

DAWKINS, Canon Cuthbert Howard. b 10. Peterho Cam BA32 MA47. St Andr Coll Pampisford 47. **d** 47 **p** 48. Kenya from 56; rtd 75. *Trinity Fellowship, PO Box 376, Kisumu, Kenya* Kisumu (35) 2948

DAWKINS, Michael Howard. b 44. BTh. Tyndale Hall Bris 67. **d** 69 **p** 69. C Drypool St Columba w St Andr and St Pet *York* 69-73; CF 74-80; P-in-c Bulford *Sarum* 80-81; P-in-c Figheldean w Milston 80-81; R Meriden and Packington *Cov* from 85. *The Rectory, The Green, Meriden, Coventry CV7 7LN* Meriden (0676) 22719

DAWSON, Alan. b 28. St Jo Coll Dur BA54 Liv Univ MA67. Clifton Th Coll 54. **d** 56 **p** 57. V Birkdale St Pet *Liv* 69-91; rtd 91. *8 Dunbar Avenue, Kirkcudbright DG6 4HD* Kirkcudbright (0557) 30017

DAWSON, Arthur Roger. b 38. Sarum Th Coll 64. **d** 66 **p** 66. C Addiscombe St Mildred *Cant* 66-67; C Cove St Jo *Guildf* 67-69; C-in-c Newton-in-Makerfield Em CD *Liv* 75-77; R Newton in Makerfield Em 77-83; BCC 83-87; Hon C Dulwich St Barn *S'wark* from 84. *49 Pymers Mead, London SE21 8NH*

DAWSON, Barry. b 38. Lon Univ DipTh65. Oak Hill Th Coll 63. **d** 66 **p** 67. C Fulham St Mary N End *Lon* 66-69; C St Marylebone All So w SS Pet and Jo 69-73; Bp's Chapl *Nor* 73-76; Gen Sec CEMS 76-81; V Rye Park St Cuth *St Alb* 81-89; V Attenborough *S'well* from 89. *The Vicarage, 6 St Mary's Close, Attenborough, Notts NG9 6AT* Nottingham (0602) 259602

DAWSON, Brian. b 33. Leeds Univ BA54 Lon Univ DipTh57 Man Univ MA84. Coll of Resurr Mirfield 56. **d** 58 **p** 59. C Hollinwood *Man* 58-62; C Rawmarsh w Parkgate *Sheff* 62-63; V Royton St Anne *Man* 63-75; V Urswick *Carl* 75-86; V Bardsea 75-86; R Skelton and Hutton-in-the-Forest w Ivegill from 86. *The Rectory, Skelton, Penrith, Cumbria CA11 9SE* Skelton (08534) 295

DAWSON, Christopher John Rowland. b 26. OBE QPM. Lon Univ DipTh86. S'wark Ord Course 82. **d** 86 **p** 87. NSM Sevenoaks St Jo *Roch* from 86. *Craggan House, 58 Oak Hill Road, Sevenoaks, Kent TN13 1NT* Sevenoaks (0732) 458037

DAWSON, Clifford Mildmay Asquith. b 22. Wycliffe Hall Ox. **d** 58 **p** 59. R Bradfield *Sheff* 68-77; V Brodsworth 77; V Brodsworth w Hooton Pagnell, Frickley etc 77-80; V Wentworth 80-87; rtd 87; Perm to Offic *Linc* from 87. *2A Trinity Lane, Louth, Lincs LN11 8DL* Louth (0507) 603167

DAWSON, Canon Cyril. b 34. St Chad's Coll Dur BA58 DipTh59. **d** 59 **p** 60. C Honicknowle *Ex* 59-63; C Paignton St Jo 63-66; V Heptonstall *Wakef* 66-71; V Todmorden 71-82; RD Calder Valley 75-82; Can Res Wakef Cathl from 82; Vice-Provost from 86. *3 Cathedral Close, Margaret Street, Wakefield, W Yorkshire WF1 2DQ* Wakefield (0924) 374349

DAWSON, Edward. b 81 **p** 83. Hon C Newington St Paul *S'wark* 81-85; Hon C Walworth St Jo from 85; Chapl Asst Maudsley Hosp Lon from 87. *3 Ethal Street, London SE17 1NH* 071-701 8923

DAWSON, Francis Andrew Oliver Duff. b 48. Keble Coll Ox BA70 MA74. St Jo Coll Nottm 74. **d** 76 **p** 77. C Billericay St Mary *Chelmsf* 76-77; C Billericay and Lt Burstead 77-80; C Childwall All SS *Liv* 80-84; Chapl St Kath Coll 80-84; V Shevington *Blackb* from 84. *St Anne's Vicarage, Gathurst Lane, Shevington, Wigan, Lancs WN6 8HW* Appley Bridge (02575) 2136

DAWSON, Frederick William. b 44. St Chad's Coll Dur BA66 Nottm Univ MTh74. Linc Th Coll 69. **d** 69 **p** 70. C Caversham *Ox* 69-72; C Ranmoor *Sheff* 72-79; R Kibworth Beauchamp *Leic* 79-82; R Kibworth and Smeeton Westerby and Saddington from 82. *The Rectory, 25 Church Road, Kibworth Beauchamp, Leicester LE8 0NB* Kibworth (0533) 792294

DAWSON, George Alfred. b 98. K Coll Lon 21. **d** 22 **p** 23. V Tolleshunt D'Arcy *Chelmsf* 42-72; rtd 72. *Brandons, 17 Barnhall Road, Tolleshunt Knights, Maldon, Essex* Maldon (0621) 815822

DAWSON, George Cuming. b 17. Ch Ch Ox BA38 TCD BA56. TCD Div Sch. **d** 58 **p** 59. Hon CV Ch Ch Cathl

Dub *D & G* from 68; P-in-c Dub St Werburgh 74-79; C Dub Ch Ch Cathl Gp 79-84; rtd 84. *Kilronan, Cloghran, Co Dublin, Irish Republic*   Dublin (1) 401224

DAWSON, Ian Douglas. b 52. Liv Univ BSc73. N Ord Course 83. **d** 86 **p** 87. NSM Southport SS Simon and Jude *Liv* from 86. *15 Melling Road, Southport, Merseyside PR9 9DY*   Southport (0704) 33172

DAWSON, John Thomas Merrilees. b 22. Newc Univ CertBS64. Wycliffe Hall Ox 81. **d** 82 **p** 83. C Kingston upon Hull H Trin *York* 82-86; P-in-c Settrington w N Grimston and Wharram from 86. *The Rectory, Settrington, Malton, N Yorkshire YO17 8NP*   North Grimston (09446) 275

DAWSON, Nicholas Anthony. b 52. St Jo Coll Nottm 88. **d** 90 **p** 91. C Mortomley *Sheff* from 90. *45 Oaklodge Road, High Green, Sheffield S30 4QA*   Sheffield (0742) 845049

DAWSON, Norman William. b 41. K Coll Lon BD63 AKC63. **d** 65 **p** 66. C Salford St Phil w St Steph *Man* 65-68; C Heaton Ch Ch 68-70; R Longsight St Jo 70-75; R Longsight St Jo w St Cypr 75-82; R Withington St Paul from 82; AD Withington from 91. *The Rectory, 491 Wilmslow Road, Withington, Manchester M20 9AW*   061-445 3781

DAWSON, Paul Christopher Owen. b 61. Leeds Univ BA82. Ripon Coll Cuddesdon 83. **d** 85 **p** 86. C Dovecot *Liv* 85-89; V Westbrook St Phil from 89. *St Philip's Vicarage, 89 Westbrook Crescent, Warrington WA5 5TE*   Warrington (0925) 574932

DAWSON, Ven Peter. b 29. Keble Coll Ox BA52 MA56. Ridley Hall Cam 52. **d** 54 **p** 55. C Morden *S'wark* 54-59; R 68-77; V Barston *Birm* 59-63; R Higher Openshaw *Man* 63-68; RD Merton *S'wark* 75-77; Adn Norfolk *Nor* from 77. *Intwood Rectory, Norwich NR4 6TG*   Norwich (0603) 51946

DAWSON, Peter. b 34. E Midl Min Tr Course 73. **d** 76 **p** 77. NSM Blyton w Pilham *Linc* 76-80; NSM Laughton w Wildsworth 76-80; C E Stockwith 77-80; C Blyth St Mary *Newc* 80-84; P-in-c Lowick and Kyloe w Ancroft 84-89; P-in-c Ford 87-89; P-in-c Sleekburn from 89. *St John's Vicarage, North View, Bedlington, Northd NE22 7ED*   Bedlington (0670) 822309

DAWSON, Thomas Douglas. b 52. Newc Univ BA. St Steph Ho Ox. **d** 80 **p** 82. C N Gosforth *Newc* 80-81; C Leic St Chad *Leic* 82-85; TV Catford (Southend) and Downham *S'wark* 85-88; V Chevington *Newc* from 88. *The Vicarage, 98 The Farnes, South Broomhill, Morpeth, Northd NE65 9SE*   Morpeth (0670) 760273

DAWSON, William James Andrew. MA. CITC 88. **d** 88 **p** 89. NSM Killyman *Arm* 88-91; NSM Newtownhamilton w Ballymoyer and Pomeroy etc from 91. *Tamlaght, Coagh, Cookstown, Co Tyrone BT80 0AB*   Coagh (06487) 37151

DAWSON, William John. b 26. ACP68 TEng74 MIEE74. CITC 77. **d** 80 **p** 81. NSM Lisburn St Paul *Conn* 80-85; Dioc C from 85. *55 Thornleigh Drive, Lisburn, Co Antrim BT28 2DA*   Lisburn (0846) 670252

DAWSON, William Norman. b 27. Leeds Univ BA50. Coll of Resurr Mirfield 50. **d** 52 **p** 53. V Blackpool H Cross *Blackb* 65-91; rtd 91. *88A Grange Road, Southport, Merseyside*

DAWSON-WALKER, Eric Dawson. b 07. St Jo Coll Dur BA29 MA32. Ripon Hall Ox 31. **d** 32 **p** 33. R New Windsor H Trin *Ox* 45-72; rtd 72. *Sherburn House, Durham DH1 2SE*   091-372 0600

DAXTER, Gregory. b 42. Lon Univ DipTh66. Oak Hill Th Coll 64. **d** 68 **p** 69. C Paignton St Paul Preston *Ex* 68-72; C Woodford Wells *Chelmsf* 72-75; Hon C Harold Hill St Paul 75-77; Hon C Wilmington *Roch* 77-87; Chapl Ex Cathl Sch from 87; PV Ex Cathl *Ex* from 87. *6A The Close, Exeter EX1 1EZ*   Exeter (0392) 58892

DAY, Sister Audrey. b 30. CA Tr Coll IDC57. **d** 88. CA from 57; Par Dn Mildenhall *St E* 88-91; Dioc Officer for the Care of the Elderly from 91; Perm to Offic from 91. *Peace Haven, Duke Street, Stanton, Bury St Edmunds, Suffolk IP33 2AB*   Stanton (0359) 50742

DAY, Charles Ian. b 48. Univ of Wales (Ban) BA72. St Mich Coll Llan 73. **d** 75 **p** 76. C Llanrhos *St As* 75-79; V Mochdre 79-83; CF 83; V Minera *St As* from 83; Dioc Soc Resp Officer from 89. *The Vicarage, Church Road, Minera, Wrexham, Clwyd LL11 3DA*   Wrexham (0978) 755679

DAY, Colin Michael. b 40. Lon Univ BSc62 AKC62 Em Coll Cam BA66 MA71. Ridley Hall Cam 65. **d** 67 **p** 68. C Heworth w Peasholme St Cuth *York* 67-70; C Ox St Clem *Ox* 70-76; V Kidsgrove *Lich* 76-86; Exec Officer Angl Evang Assembly & C of E Coun 86-90; Adv on Miss and Evang *Sarum* from 90. *Bowmoor House, Anvil*

Road, Blandford, Dorset DT11 8UQ   Blandford (0258) 480606

DAY, David John. b 44. CEng72 MICE72. Trin Coll Bris DipHE. **d** 90 **p** 91. C Stratton St Margaret w S Marston etc *Bris* from 90. *54 Nythe Road, Swindon, Wilts SN3 4AP*   Swindon (0793) 822653

DAY, David William. b 37. St Andr Univ MA58 BD61 CertEd73. **d** 76 **p** 77. C St Andrews All SS *St And* 76-77; P-in-c Dundee St Ninian *Bre* 77-84; Itinerant Priest *Arg* 84-91; R Duror from 91. *St Adamnan's Rectory, Duror of Appin, Argyll PA38 4BS*   Duror (063174) 218

DAY, Fergus William. b 09. TCD BA40 MA45. **d** 41 **p** 41. Dean Waterford *C & O* 67-79; I Waterford w Killea, Drumcannon and Dunhill 67-79; rtd 79. *13 Brabazon Court, Gilford Road, Sandymount, Dublin 4, Irish Republic*   Dublin (1) 283-0204

DAY, Frank Henry. b 18. Clifton Th Coll 40. **d** 43 **p** 44. R Stanton St Quintin w Grittleton etc *Bris* 68-76; R Stanton St Quintin, Hullavington, Grittleton etc 76-81; rtd 81; Perm to Offic *Bris* from 81. *17 Avon Mead, Chippenham, Wilts SN15 3PP*

DAY, George Chester. b 45. Ex Univ BA66 Lon Univ BD70. Clifton Th Coll 67. **d** 71 **p** 72. C Reading St Jo *Ox* 71-75; C Morden *S'wark* 75-81; Sec for Voc and Min CPAS 81-86; Hon C Bromley Ch Ch *Roch* 83-86; V St Paul's Cray St Barn from 86. *The Vicarage, Rushet Road, St Paul's Cray, Orpington, Kent BR5 2PU*   Orpington (0689) 821353

DAY, Hilary Paul Wilfrid. b 13. Qu Coll Birm 47. **d** 48 **p** 49. V Slade Green *Roch* 62-71; R Milton next Gravesend w Denton 71-87; rtd 87. *1 Killick Road, Hoo St Werburgh, Rochester, Kent ME3 9EP*   Medway (0634) 252960

DAY, Canon James Alfred. b 23. DFC44. AKC49. **d** 50 **p** 51. V Tattershall *Linc* 66-80; R Coningsby 66-80; RD Horncastle 73-80; Can and Preb Linc Cathl from 77; V Heckington 80-89; rtd 89. *22 Ancaster Drive, Sleaford, Lincs NG34 7LY*   Sleaford (0529) 305318

DAY, John. b 44. Oak Hill NSM Course 87. **d** 90 **p** 91. NSM Bexleyheath St Pet *Roch* from 90. *56 Barrington Road, Bexleyheath, Kent DA7 4UW*   081-301 2053

DAY, Canon John Alfred. b 25. TCD BA51. **d** 51 **p** 52. I Maguiresbridge w Derrybrusk *Clogh* 67-91; Can Clogh Cathl from 78; rtd 91. *Killeenifinane Cottage, 40 Ballylucas Road, Tamlaght, Enniskillen, Co Fermanagh BT74 4HD*   Enniskillen (0365) 87835

DAY, John Cuthbert. b 36. Sarum Th Coll 66. **d** 68 **p** 69. C Bedhampton *Portsm* 68-72; V Froxfield 72-73; V Froxfield w Privett 73-77; V Warminster Ch Ch *Sarum* 77-81; R Pewsey 81-90; Chapl Pewsey Hosp Wilts 81-90; P-in-c Sturminster Newton and Hinton St Mary *Sarum* from 90; P-in-c Stock and Lydlinch from 90. *The Vicarage, Sturminster Newton, Dorset DT10 1DB*   Sturminster Newton (0258) 72531

DAY, John Kenneth. b 58. Hull Univ BA85. Cranmer Hall Dur 85. **d** 87 **p** 88. C Thornbury *Bradf* 87-90; V from 90. *The Vicarage, Upper Rushton Road, Thornbury, Bradford, W Yorkshire BD3 7HX*   Bradford (0274) 664702

DAY, John Nathaniel. b 36. Kelham Th Coll 59. **d** 64 **p** 65. C Mansf St Mark *S'well* 64-69; C W Wycombe *Ox* 69-75; TV High Wycombe 75-77; C-in-c Britwell St Geo CD 77-78; TV W Slough 78-87; TV Langley Marish from 87. *21 Lynwood Avenue, Langley, Slough SL3 7BJ*   Slough (0753) 27903

DAY, Michael. b 37. RCA(Lon) MA75 AKC61. **d** 62 **p** 63. C Hulme St Phil *Man* 62-65; Asst Chapl Newc Univ *Newc* 65-70; Chapl Chelsea Coll *Lon* 70-85; Chapl R Coll of Art 70-90; Chapl Cen, Chelsea and St Martin's Schs of Art *Lon* 85-90; P-in-c Bloomsbury St Geo w Woburn Square Ch Ch from 91. *6 Gower Street, London WC1 6DP*   071-580 4010

DAY, Paul Geoffrey. b 51. Dur Univ BEd75. Trin Coll Bris 76. **d** 78 **p** 79. C Roxeth Ch Ch *Lon* 78-82; C Roxeth Ch Ch and Harrow St Pet 82; TV Barking St Marg w St Patr *Chelmsf* 82-87; V Barrow St Mark *Carl* from 87. *St Mark's Vicarage, Rawlinson Street, Barrow-in-Furness LA14 1BX*   Barrow-in-Furness (0229) 820405

DAY, Paul Geoffrey. b 56. St Pet Coll Ox BA77. St Jo Coll Nottm 87. **d** 89 **p** 90. C Mildmay Grove St Jude and St Paul *Lon* from 89. *94 Mildmay Grove, London N1 4PJ*   071-249 6233

DAY, Peter. b 50. BPharm71. Coll of Resurr Mirfield 85. **d** 87 **p** 88. C Eastcote St Lawr *Lon* 87-91; C Wembley Park St Aug from 91. *194 Windermere Avenue, Wembley, Middx HA9 8QT*   081-908 2252

DAY, Canon Philip Henry Maurice. b 45. TCD BA69 MA78. **d** 70 **p** 71. C Crumlin *Conn* 70-73; Asst Chapl K Hosp Sch Dub 73-76; I Mountmellick *M & K* 76-83; Can

Kildare Cathl 82-83; Warden Wilson's Hosp 83-85; I Maryborough w Dysart Enos and Ballyfin *C & O* from 85; Preb Stagonil St Patr Cathl Dub from 87. *Portlaoise, Co Laoise, Irish Republic* Portlaoise (502) 21154

DAY, Robert Clifford. b 08. **d** 70 **p** 71. C Lt Stanmore St Lawr *Lon* 70-75; Perm to Offic *Worc* from 75. *10 Forge Lane, Blakedown, Kidderminster, Worcs DY10 3JF* Kidderminster (0562) 700205

DAY, Roy Frederick. b 24. S'wark Ord Course 63. **d** 67 **p** 68. C Newington St Paul *S'wark* 67-70; C Radlett *St Alb* 70-72; P-in-c Ponsbourne 72-76; R Campton 76-82; V Shefford 76-82; R Shenley 82-89; rtd 89. *11 Hill End Lane, St Albans, Herts AL4 0TX* St Albans (0727) 45782

DAY, Canon Samuel Richard. b 14. Reading Univ BSc36 Ch Ch Ox BA48 MA52 DPhil56. St D Coll Lamp 37. **d** 38 **p** 39. V Gt Marlow *Ox* 66-89; RD Wycombe 68-74; Hon Can Ch Ch from 70; rtd 89. *3 Leighton House, Glade Road, Marlow, Bucks* Marlow (06284) 2660

DAY, Stephen Philip. b 61. St Pet Coll Ox BA82 MA86. Coll of Resurr Mirfield 84. **d** 86 **p** 87. C Streetly *Lich* 86-89; C Tividale from 89. *Holy Cross House, Ashleigh Road, Tividale, Warley, W Midlands B69 1LL* Dudley (0384) 257060

DAY, William Charles. b 47. Portsm Poly BEd86. Ripon Coll Cuddesdon 88. **d** 90 **p** 91. C Bishops Waltham *Portsm* from 90. *15 Denewulf Close, Bishops Waltham, Southampton SO3 1GZ* Bishops Waltham (0489) 894729

DAYBELL, Canon Cecil John Richmond. b 16. Univ Coll Ox BA38 MA47. Westcott Ho Cam 39. **d** 40 **p** 42. V Old Dalby and Nether Broughton *Leic* 61-83; RD Framland II 79-84; rtd 83; Perm to Offic *Leic* from 84. *36 Beckingthorpe Drive, Bottesford, Notts NG13 0DN* Bottesford (0949) 42874

DAYKIN, Timothy Elwin. b 54. Lon Univ BSc75 Dur Univ DipTh77 MA81. Cranmer Hall Dur 75. **d** 78 **p** 79. C Bourne *Guildf* 78-81; Chapl K Alfred Coll *Win* 82-87; C-in-c Valley Park CD 87-91; V Valley Park from 91. *35 Raglan Close, Eastleigh, Hants SO5 3NH* Eastleigh (0703) 255749

DAYNES, Andrew John. b 47. Jes Coll Cam BA69 MA73. Westcott Ho Cam 69. **d** 72 **p** 73. C Radlett *St Alb* 72-76; Chapl St Alb Abbey 76-80; Chapl Bryanston Sch Blandford from 80. *Bryanston School, Blandford Forum, Dorset DT11 0PX* Blandford (0258) 456863

DAZELEY, Mrs Lorna. b 31. CertEd53 New Hall Cam BA82 MA86. E Anglian Minl Tr Course 82. **dss** 84 **d** 87. Chesterton St Andr *Ely* 84-87; C from 87. *Chesterton House, Church Street, Chesterton, Cambridge CB4 1DT* Cambridge (0223) 356243

de BERRY, Andrew Piers. b 44. St Jo Coll Dur BA66. Ripon Hall Ox 70. **d** 74 **p** 75. C Aylesbury *Ox* 74-77; USA 78; TV Clyst St George, Aylesbeare, Clyst Honiton etc *Ex* 78-80; Asst Chapl HM Pris Wormwood Scrubs 80-82; Chapl HM Pris Sudbury 82-84; V Blackwell *Derby* from 84. *St Werburgh's Vicarage, Blackwell, Derby DE55 5HY* Ripley (0773) 863242

de BERRY, Oscar Keith de la Tour. b 07. St Jo Coll Cam BA29 MA33 Ball Coll Ox MA52. Ridley Hall Cam 29. **d** 30 **p** 31. R Ox St Aldate w H Trin *Ox* 52-74; Hon Can Ch Ch 70-74; rtd 74; Hon C Portman Square St Paul *Lon* 74-88; Hon C Langham Place All So from 88. *9 Wilton Place, Hyde Park Corner, London SW1X 8SH* 071-235 5583

de BERRY, Robert Delatour. b 42. Qu Coll Cam BA64 MA68. Ridley Hall Cam 65. **d** 67 **p** 68. Min Can Bradf Cathl *Bradf* 67-70; Uganda 71-75; V Attercliffe *Sheff* 75-83; V W Kilburn St Luke w St Simon and St Jude *Lon* from 83. *The Vicarage, 19 Macroom Road, London W9 3HY* 081-969 0876

de BOWEN, Alfred William. b 24. Leeds Univ DipHort. ThL St Paul's Grahamstown 76. **d** 78 **p** 86. S Africa 78-86; NSM Cilycwm and Ystradffin w Rhandir-mwyn etc *St D* 86-88; Lic to Offic *Linc* from 88; rtd 90. *The Shambles, 14 Cowgate, Heckington, Sleaford, Lincs NG34 9RL* Sleaford (0529) 60772

de BRETT, Rodney John Harry. b 13. Open Univ BA89. Wells Th Coll 63. **d** 64 **p** 65. V Stoke St Gregory *B & W* 66-75; V Stoke St Gregory w Burrowbridge 75-78; V Stoke St Gregory w Burrowbridge and Lyng 78-81; RD Taunton N 80-81; rtd 81; Perm to Offic *Ex* from 81. *106 Whipton Lane, Exeter EX1 3DJ* Exeter (0392) 55940

de BURGH-THOMAS, George Albert. b 30. Univ of Wales (Ban) BA50. St Mich Coll Llan 51. **d** 53 **p** 54. C Hawarden *St As* 53-56 and 60-63; C Roath St Martin *Llan* 56-58; C Llangeinor 58-60; V Bampton and Mardale *Carl* 63-70; V Fritwell *Ox* 70-83; R Souldern 70-83; R

Fritwell w Souldern and Ardley w Fewcott 83-87; R Hawridge w Cholesbury and St Leonard from 87; V Lee from 87. *The Vicarage, The Lee, Great Missenden, Bucks HP16 9LZ* The Lee (024020) 315

de CANDOLE, Charles Patrick. b 07. Chich Th Coll 34. **d** 34 **p** 36. R Witchampton and Hinton Parva, Long Crichel etc *Sarum* 62-82; rtd 82. *1 Redway, Wimborne, Dorset BH21 1AF* Wimborne (0202) 887507

de CASABIANCA, Louis Edward Philip. b 09. Codrington Coll Barbados LTh38. **d** 38 **p** 39. R Woodford w Twywell *Pet* 67-80; rtd 80. *5 Grove House, The Grove, Epsom, Surrey KT17 4DJ* Epsom (0372) 720189

de CHAZAL, John Robert. b 16. Bris Univ. Wycliffe Hall Ox 53. **d** 55 **p** 56. R Caldecote *Cov* 64-71; R Bradf Peverell w Stratton *Sarum* 72-77; P-in-c Sydling St Nic 77; P-in-c Frampton 77; R Bradf Peverell, Stratton, Frampton etc 77-80; rtd 81. *Lavender Cottage, East Street, Sydling St Nicholas, Dorchester, Dorset DT2 9NX* Cerne Abbas (0300) 341693

de CHAZAL, Mrs Nancy Elizabeth. b 28. Bedf Coll Lon BA52. Lambeth STh90 Sarum & Wells Th Coll 81. **dss** 84 **d** 87. NSM Melbury *Sarum* from 84. *Lavender Cottage, East Street, Sydling St Nicholas, Dorchester, Dorset DT2 9NX* Cerne Abbas (0300) 341693

de FORTIS, Paul Maurice Georges Pierre Guichot. b 53. K Coll Lon BD80 AKC80. Ridley Hall Cam 80. **d** 81 **p** 82. C W Hackney St Barn *Lon* 81-84; Chapl Asst Middx Hosp Lon 84-90; Assoc Chapl from 90. *The Middlesex Hospital, Mortimer Street, London W1N 8AA* 071-636 8333

DE GROOSE, Leslie John. b 28. Oak Hill Th Coll 62. **d** 64 **p** 65. C Gunton St Pet *Nor* 64-67; Chapl RN 67-83; P-in-c Gt Oakley *Chelmsf* 83-85; R Gt Oakley w Wix from 85. *The Rectory, Wix Road, Great Oakley, Harwich, Essex CO12 5BJ* Ramsey (0255) 880230

DE GRUYTHER, Albert Alfred. b 14. Magd Coll Ox BA48 MA60. Ridley Hall Cam. **d** 50 **p** 51. R Ulverston St Mary w H Trin *Carl* 67-73; R Gt Salkeld 73-79; rtd 79; Perm to Offic *Carl* from 82. *The Mill House, Lindale, Grange-over-Sands, Cumbria LA11 6LF* Grange-over-Sands (05395) 32968

DE HOOP, Thomas Anthony (Brother Thomas Anthony). b 38. Bp's Univ Lennox BA63 LTh63. **d** 68 **p** 69. Canada 68-79; SSF from 79; P-in-c Cam St Benedict *Ely* 85-88; V from 88. *St Francis House, 15 Botolph Lane, Cambridge CB2 3RD* Cambridge (0223) 353903

de JONGE, Frank Hermann. b 03. Or Coll Ox BA24 MA45 Kiel Univ Hon DTh49. Ely Th Coll 25. **d** 26 **p** 27. R Hitcham *Ox* 62-73; rtd 73. *Oriel House, Thames Road, Goring-on-Thames, Oxon RG8 9AH* Goring-on-Thames (0491) 872134

DE KEYSER, Nicholas David Llewellyn. b 49. Nottm Univ BTh75 MTh86. St Jo Coll Nottm 71. **d** 75 **p** 76. C Portswood Ch Ch *Win* 75-77; C Yateley 77-81; TV Grantham *Linc* 81-86; V Heyside *Man* 86-91; R Charlton-in-Dover *Cant* from 91. *The Rectory, St Alphege Road, Dover, Kent CT16 2PU* Dover (0304) 201143

de la BAT SMIT, Reynaud. b 50. St Edm Hall Ox BA80 MA86. Ripon Coll Cuddesdon. **d** 82 **p** 83. C Headington *Ox* 82-85; Chapl St Hild and St Bede Coll Dur from 85. *College of SS Hild and Bede, University of Durham, Durham DH1 1SZ* 091-374 3069

de la HOYDE, Denys Ralph Hart. b 33. G&C Coll Cam BA57 MA61. Westcott Ho Cam 57. **d** 59 **p** 60. C Moss Side Ch Ch *Man* 59-60; Chapl G&C Coll Cam 60-64; India 64-68; C Eltham H Trin *S'wark* 68-69; Chapl Bromsgrove Sch Worcs 69-71; Lic to Offic *Ripon* 71-78; V Pool w Arthington from 86; Dioc Dir of Ords from 86. *The Vicarage, Old Pool Bank, Pool in Wharfedale, Otley, W Yorkshire LS21 1LH* Leeds (0532) 843706

de la MARE, Benedick James Hobart. b 38. Trin Coll Ox BA63 MA67. Cuddesdon Coll 63. **d** 65 **p** 66. C Gosforth All SS *Newc* 65-68; Chapl Trin Coll Cam 68-73; V Newc St Gabr *Newc* 73-81; V Dur St Oswald *Dur* from 81. *St Oswald's Vicarage, Church Street, Durham DH1 3DG* 091-386 4313

de la MOUETTE, Norman Harry. b 39. Southn Univ BEd73. Sarum & Wells Th Coll 76. **d** 79 **p** 80. NSM Win St Lawr and St Maurice w St Swithun *Win* from 79; Deputation Appeals Org (Win and Portsm) CECS from 83. *146 Greenhill Road, Winchester, Hants SO22 5DR* Winchester (0962) 853191

DE LACEY, Thomas. b 46. HNC68. Carl Dioc Tr Inst 88. **d** 91. NSM Ingol *Blackb* from 91. *5 Fulwood Hall Lane, Fulwood, Preston, Lancs PR2 4DA* Preston (0772) 700923

DE MEL, Basil William. b 18. Keble Coll Ox BA41 MA47 BLitt47. Westcott Ho Cam 41. **d** 43 **p** 44. Chapl Manor Hosp Epsom 53-83; rtd 83; Perm to Offic *Guildf* from

85. *83 Manor Green Road, Epsom, Surrey* Epsom (03727) 22134

de MELLO, Gualter Rose. b 34. Ridley Hall Cam 63. **d** 64 **p** 65. C S Hackney St Jo w Ch Ch *Lon* 64-66; Toc H Chapl (Hackney) 66-72; Dir Friends Anonymous Service from 73; Hon C All Hallows by the Tower etc *Lon* from 73; Dir Community of Reconciliation & Fellowship from 88. *Prideaux House, 10 Church Crescent, London E9 7DL* 081-986 2233

DE MURALT, Robert Willem Gaston. b 25. Utrecht Univ LLM48 DLSc54. Chich Th Coll 90. **d** 90 **p** 91. Asst Chapl The Hague *Eur* from 90. *Zuidwerflaan 5, 2594 CW, The Hague, The Netherlands* The Hague (70) 383-8520

✠de PINA CABRAL, Rt Rev Daniel Pereira dos Santos. b 24. Lisbon Univ LLB47. Lon Coll of Div. **d** 47 **p** 49 **c** 67. Portugal 47-67; Portuguese E Africa 67-75; Mozambique 75-76; Asst Bp Lebombo 67-68; Bp 68-76; Aux Bp Eur from 76; Hon Can Gib Cathl 79-87; Adn Gib from 87; rtd 89. *R Fernao Lopes Castanheda 51, 4100 Oporto, Portugal* Oporto (2) 617-7772

DE PURY, Andrew Robert. b 28. K Coll Lon BD57 AKC57. **d** 58 **p** 59. C Epping St Jo *Chelmsf* 58-60; C Loughton St Jo 60-65; V Harold Hill St Geo 65-72; Missr Swan Par Gp *Ox* 72-76; TR Swan 76-85; R Worminghall w Ickford, Oakley and Shabbington from 85. *The Rectory, 32A The Avenue, Worminghall, Aylesbury, Bucks HP18 9LE* Ickford (08447) 338839

DE SAUSMAREZ, Canon John Havilland Russell. b 26. Lambeth Univ MA81 Wells Th Coll 54. **d** 56 **p** 57. C N Lynn w St Marg and St Nic *Nor* 56-58; C Hythe *Cant* 58-61; V Maidstone St Martin 61-68; V St Peter-in-Thanet 68-81; RD Thanet 74-81; Hon Can Cant Cathl 78-81; Can Res Cant Cathl from 81. *15 The Precincts, Canterbury, Kent CT1 2EP* Canterbury (0227) 463056

DE SILVA, David Ebenezer Sunil. b 48. Sri Lanka Nat Sem DipTh. **d** 72 **p** 73. Sri Lanka 72-84; C Elm Park St Nic Hornchurch *Chelmsf* 84-87; R Mistley w Manningtree and Bradfield 87-90; TR Stanground and Farcet *Ely* from 90. *The Rectory, 9 Mace Road, Stanground, Peterborough PE2 8RQ* Peterborough (0733) 890552

DE SMET, Andrew Charles. b 58. Ex Univ BSc79 Southn Univ BTh88. Sarum & Wells Th Coll 85. **d** 88 **p** 89. C Portsea St Mary *Portsm* from 88. *St Faith's House, Fyning Street, Portsmouth* Portsmouth (0705) 823451

de VERE, Anthony George Augustine. b 31. Ch Ch Ox BA54 MA58. St Steph Ho Ox 54. **d** 56 **p** 57. C Poplar All SS w St Frideswide *Lon* 56-59; S Africa 59-70; V Elsfield *Ox* from 71; P-in-c Beckley 71-73; V from 73; P-in-c Horton-cum-Studley 71-73; V from 73. *The Vicarage, Elsfield, Oxford OX3 9UH* Stanton St John (086735) 260

de VIAL, Raymond Michael. b 39. Oak Hill Th Coll 77. **d** 80 **p** 81. NSM Beckenham St Jo *Roch* 80-84; C Morden *S'wark* 84-88; TV from 88. *140 Stonecot Hill, Sutton, Surrey SM3 9HQ* 081-337 6421

de WAAL, Canon Hugo Ferdinand. b 35. Pemb Coll Cam BA58 MA63. Ridley Hall Cam 59. **d** 60 **p** 61. C Birm St Martin *Birm* 60-64; Chapl Pemb Coll Cam 64-68; P-in-c Dry Drayton *Ely* 64-68; R 68-74; Min Bar Hill LEP 68-74; V Blackpool St Jo *Blackb* 74-78; Prin Ridley Hall Cam from 78; Lic to Offic *Ely* 78-86; Hon Can Ely Cathl from 86. *Principal's Lodge, Ridley Hall, Cambridge CB3 9HG* Cambridge (0223) 353040

de WAAL, Dr Victor Alexander. b 29. Pemb Coll Cam BA49 MA53 Nottm Univ Hon DD83. Ely Th Coll 50. **d** 52 **p** 53. Can Res and Chan Linc Cathl *Linc* 69-76; Dean Cant 76-86; Perm to Offic *Heref* from 88; rtd 90; Chapl Soc of Sacred Cross Tymawr from 90; Lic to Offic *Mon* from 90. *Cwm Cottage, Rowlestone, Hereford HR2 0DP* Golden Valley (0981) 240391

DE WIT, John. b 47. Or Coll Ox BA69 MA73 Clare Coll Cam BA78 MA84. Westcott Ho Cam 75. **d** 78 **p** 79. C The Quinton *Birm* 78-81; TV Solihull 81-85; V Kings Heath from 85; RD Moseley from 91. *All Saints' Vicarage, 2 Vicarage Road, Birmingham B14 7RA* 021-444 1207

DEACON, Donald (Brother Angelo). Chich Th Coll 66. **d** 68 **p** 69. SSF from 63; Lic to Offic *Man* 69-70; USA 70-72; C Kennington St Jo *S'wark* 72-74; C Wilton Place St Paul *Lon* 74-75; Angl-Franciscan Reg Ecum Cen Assisi *Eur* 75; Franciscanum Sem 76-78; Perm to Offic *Sarum* 78-82; Lic to Offic Chelmsf 82-90; Birm from 90. *St Francis House, 113 Gillott Road, Birmingham B16 0ET* 021-454 8302

DEACON, Edwin William Frederick. b 18. Oak Hill Th Coll 46. **d** 48 **p** 49. R Lustleigh *Ex* 55-85; Perm to Offic from 85; rtd 86. *Dunoon, 17A Highweek Village, Newton Abbot, Devon TQ12 1QA* Newton Abbot (0626) 65433

DEACON, Frederick George Raymond. b 15. Tyndale Hall Bris 63. **d** 65 **p** 66. C Leckhampton SS Phil and Jas *Glouc* 69-71; V Longcot *Ox* 71-72; V Longcot w Fernham and Bourton 72-77; Zambia 77-80; P-in-c Cressage w Sheinton *Heref* 80-81; P-in-c Harley w Kenley 80-81; TV Wenlock 81-85; rtd 85; Perm to Offic *Heref* from 85. *29 Robinson Meadow, Ledbury, Herefordshire* Ledbury (0531) 4500

DEACON, John. b 37. Arm Aux Min Course 87. **d** 90 **p** 91. NSM Enniscorthy w Clone, Clonmore, Monart etc *C & O* from 90. *Creagh, Gorey, Co Wexford, Irish Republic* Gorey (55) 20354

DEACON, Canon Peter Olford. b 26. MBIM84 MInstAM84. K Coll Lon 48. **d** 52 **p** 53. C Lewisham St Mary *S'wark* 52-58; C Whippingham w E Cowes *Portsm* 58-61; Chapl City of Lon Freeman's Sch Ashtead Park 61-62; C-in-c Gurnard All SS CD *Portsm* 62-68; Chapl RN 68-85; V-Gen to Bp Eur from 85; Can Gib Cathl from 86. *5A Gregory Place, London W8 4NG* 071-937 2796

DEACON, Timothy Randall. b 55. Ex Univ BA78. Chich Th Coll 79. **d** 80 **p** 81. C Whiteleigh *Ex* 80-83; P-in-c Devonport St Aubyn 83-88; P-in-c Newton Ferrers w Revelstoke from 88. *The Rectory, Court Road, Newton Ferrers, Plymouth, Devon PL8 1DL* Plymouth (0752) 872530

DEADMAN, Richard George Spencer. b 63. Ex Univ BA85. Coll of Resurr Mirfield 86. **d** 88 **p** 89. C Grangetown *York* from 88. *2 Oldgate, Eston, Middlesbrough, Cleveland TS6 9LP* Middlesbrough (0642) 454838

DEAKIN, Preb John Hartley. b 27. K Coll Cam BA50 MA63. Cranmer Hall Dur DipTh65. **d** 65 **p** 66. C Newc St Geo *Lich* 65-70; V Cotes Heath 70-84; RD Eccleshall from 82; R Standon and Cotes Heath from 84; Preb Lich Cathl from 88; Sub-Chapl HM Pris Drake Hall from 89. *The Vicarage, Cotes Heath, Stafford ST21 6RX* Standon Rock (078270) 268

DEAN, Alan. b 38. Hull Univ BA61. Qu Coll Birm DipTh63. **d** 63 **p** 64. C Clitheroe St Mary *Blackb* 65-67; C Burnley St Pet 67-68; CF from 68. *c/o MOD (Army), Bagshot Park, Bagshot, Surrey GU19 5PL* Bagshot (0276) 71717

DEAN, Alan Shacklock. b 24. Lon Univ BSc54. St Jo Coll Dur 79. **d** 81 **p** 82. C Habergham All SS *Blackb* 81-84; P-in-c Holme-in-Cliviger 84-89; rtd 89. *The Old School House, 35 Church Square, Worsthorne, Burnley, Lancs BB10 3NH* Burnley (0282) 26987

DEAN, Andrew Duncan. b 40. Sarum Th Coll 62. **d** 64 **p** 65. C Stockton Heath *Ches* 64-68; C Mottram in Longdendale w Woodhead 68-71; P-in-c Over Tabley 71-73; P-in-c Over Tabley and High Legh 73; V 73-79; R Astbury and Smallwood 79-85; R Woodchurch from 85. *The Rectory, Church Lane, Woodchurch, Upton, Wirral, Merseyside L49 7LS* 051-677 5352

DEAN, Archibald Charles. b 13. Wycliffe Hall Ox 52. **d** 54 **p** 55. R Odcombe *B & W* 61-91; R Brympton 61-91; R Lufton 61-91; P-in-c Montacute 78-86; rtd 91. *3 Chur Lane, West Coker, Yeovil, Somerset BA22 9BH* West Coker (0935) 862224

DEAN, Arthur. b 32. CQSW80. S Dios Minl Tr Scheme 89. **d** 90 **p** 90. NSM Eastney *Portsm* from 90. *9 Kingsley Road, Southsea, Hants PO4 8HJ* Portsmouth (0705) 735773

DEAN, Canon Desmond Keable. b 06. ALCD30 St Jo Coll Dur LTh30 BA31 MA37 BD41. **d** 30 **p** 31. R Tooting Graveney St Nic *S'wark* 51-76; Hon Can S'wark Cathl 63-76; rtd 76; Perm to Offic *Chich* from 76. *68 Milland Road, Harmers Hay, Hailsham, E Sussex BN27 1TY* Hailsham (0323) 843910

DEAN, Francis John Michael. b 15. Univ Coll Ox BA38 MA42. Cuddesdon Coll 38. **d** 39 **p** 40. V Regents Park St Mark *Lon* 64-81; rtd 81. *74 Temple Fortune Lane, London NW11 7TT* 081-455 6309

DEAN, John Milner. b 27. S'wark Ord Course 69. **d** 72 **p** 73. C Lewisham St Mary *S'wark* 72-75; C Mert St Mary 75-77; V S Beddington St Mich from 77. *St Michael's Vicarage, Milton Road, Wallington, Surrey SM6 9RP* 081-647 1201

DEAN, Malcolm. b 34. Tyndale Hall Bris 67. **d** 69 **p** 70. C Daubhill *Man* 69-73; P-in-c Constable Lee 73-74; V 74-79; P-in-c Everton St Sav w St Cuth *Liv* 79-86; P-in-c Anfield SS Simon and Jude 81-86; V Walton Breck Ch Ch 86-89; rtd 89. *6 Sunny Lea Street, Rawtenstall, Rossendale, Lancs BB4 8JE* Rossendale (0706) 215953

DEAN, Canon Maurice. b 12. Birm Univ BA37. Ripon Hall Ox 37. **d** 38 **p** 39. V Bromsgrove St Jo *Worc* 68-77; RD Bromsgrove 73-77; Hon Can Worc Cathl 76-77; rtd 77. *42 Crane Drive, Verwood, Wimborne, Dorset* Verwood (0202) 825932

DEAN, Preb Raymond Charles. b 27. Bris Univ BA51. Wycliffe Hall Ox 51. **d** 53 **p** 54. C Weston-super-Mare St Jo *B & W* 53-59; V Lyngford 59-70; V Burnham from 70; Preb Wells Cathl from 73; RD Burnham 82-91; RD Axbridge from 87. *The Vicarage, Rectory Road, Burnham-on-Sea, Somerset TA8 2BZ* Burnham-on-Sea (0278) 782991

DEAN, Simon Timothy Michael Rex. b 62. Liv Univ BEng83. Ridley Hall Cam 86. **d** 89 **p** 90. C St German's Cathl *S & M* from 89. *3 Peveril Avenue, Peel, Isle of Man* Peel (0624) 843588

DEANE, Gilbert Ernest. b 06. Lon Univ BD38. Lon Coll of Div 34. **d** 38 **p** 39. Teacher Forest Sch Horsham 64-74; rtd 74. *1 Barnfield Close, Lower Park Road, Braunton, Devon EX33 2HL* Braunton (0271) 812949

DEANE, Nicholas Talbot Bryan. b 46. Bris Univ BA69. Clifton Th Coll 70. **d** 72 **p** 73. C Accrington Ch Ch *Blackb* 72-75; OMF 75-89; Korea 75-89; P-in-c Newburgh *Liv* from 90; P-in-c Westhead from 90. *The Vicarage, Back Lane, Newburgh, Wigan, Lancs WN8 7XB* Parbold (0257) 463267

DEANE, Robert William. b 52. DipTh85. CITC 85. **d** 85 **p** 86. C Raheny w Coolock *D & G* 85-88; I Clonsast w Rathangan, Thomastown etc *M & K* from 88; Dioc Youth Officer (Kildare) from 90. *The Rectory, Edenderry, Co Offaly, Irish Republic* Edenderry (405) 31585

DEANE, Stuart William. b 45. Sarum & Wells Th Coll 86. **d** 88 **p** 89. C Bromyard *Heref* from 88. *Somerset, 12 Lower Thorn, Bromyard, Herefordshire HR7 4DZ* Bromyard (0885) 82620

DEANE-HALL, Henry Michael. b 21. Leeds Univ BA46. Coll of Resurr Mirfield 47. **d** 49 **p** 50. R Duloe w Herodsfoot *Truro* 71-79; V Morval 71-79; P-in-c Donhead St Mary *Sarum* 79-80; R The Donheads 80-82; rtd 82; Perm to Offic *Ex* from 82. *The College of St Barnabas, Blackberry Lane, Lingfield, Surrey RH7 6NJ* Dormans Park (034287) 260

DEAR, Graham Frederick. b 44. St Luke's Coll Ex CertEd66. Wycliffe Hall Ox 67. **d** 70 **p** 71. C Chigwell *Chelmsf* 70-73; C Chingford SS Pet and Paul 73-75; V Southchurch Ch Ch 75-82; CF 82-89; P-in-c The Cowtons *Ripon* from 89; RE Adv from 89. *The Vicarage, East Cowton, Northallerton, N Yorkshire DL7 0BN* Darlington (0325) 378230

DEAR, Neil Douglas Gauntlett. b 35. Linc Th Coll 87. **d** 89 **p** 90. C Framlingham w Saxtead *St E* from 89. *10 Brook Lane, Framlingham, Woodbridge, Suffolk IP13 9RN* Framlingham (0728) 724352

DEARDEN, James Varley. b 22. Wycliffe Hall Ox 61. **d** 62 **p** 63. V Newington Transfiguration *York* 66-75; V Huddersfield H Trin *Wakef* 75-87; rtd 87. *26 Sycamore Avenue, Meltham, Huddersfield HD7 3EE* Huddersfield (0484) 852519

DEARDEN, Philip Harold. b 43. AKC65. **d** 66 **p** 67. C Haslingden w Haslingden Grane *Blackb* 66-69; C Burnley St Pet 69-71; V Langho Billington 71-78; TR Darwen St Pet w Hoddlesden 78-91; RD Darwen 86-91; V Altham w Clayton le Moors from 91. *The Vicarage, Church Street, Clayton le Moors, Accrington, Lancs BB5 5HT* Accrington (0254) 384321

DEARING, Trevor. b 33. Lon Univ BD58. Qu Coll Birm MA63. **d** 61 **p** 62. C Harlow New Town w Lt Parndon *Chelmsf* 68-70; V Hainault 70-75; Dir Healing Miss 75-79; Hon C Gt Ilford St Andr 75-79; Perm to Offic *Linc* 80-81; USA 81-83; rtd 83. *2 West Street, Easton on the Hill, Stamford, Lincs PE9 3LS* Stamford (0780) 51680

DEARNLEY, Mark Christopher. b 59. Cranmer Hall Dur 84. **d** 87 **p** 88. C Purley Ch Ch *S'wark* 87-91; C Addiscombe St Mary from 91. *68 Elgin Road, Croydon, Surrey CR0 6XA* 081-654 6925

DEARNLEY, Preb Patrick Walter. b 34. Nottm Univ BA55 LTh75. ALCD64. **d** 64 **p** 65. C New Malden and Coombe *S'wark* 64-68; C Portswood Ch Ch *Win* 68-71; C Leeds St Geo *Ripon* 71-74; Hon C Nottm St Nic *S'well* 74-77; P-in-c Holloway Em w Hornsey Road St Barn *Lon* 77-85; AD Islington 80-85; Abp's Officer for UPA 85-90; Preb St Paul's Cathl *Lon* 86-91; V Waterloo St John *Liv* from 91. *St John's Vicarage, 16 Adelaide Terrace, Liverpool L22 8QD* 051-928 3793

DEAS, Leonard Stephen. b 52. New Coll Ox BA75 CertEd76 MA78. St Mich Coll Llan 81. **d** 82 **p** 83. C Dowlais *Llan* 82-84; Chapl St Mich Coll Llan 84-85; Chapl Univ of Wales (Cardiff) *Llan* 85-86; V Newbridge *Mon* from 86. *The Vicarage, High Street, Newbridge, Newport, Gwent NP1 4FW* Newbridge (0495) 243975

DEAVE, Mrs Gillian Mary. b 31. E Midl Min Tr Course 79. **dss** 82 **d** 87. Nottm St Pet and St Jas *S'well* 82-87;

Par Dn 87-91; rtd 91. *Greensmith Cottage, Stathern, Melton Mowbray, Leics LE14 4HE* Harby (0949) 60340

DEBENHAM, Mrs Joan Winifred. b 26. LRAM57 Lon Univ BA47 Cam Univ DipEd48. SW Minl Tr Course. **dss** 82 **d** 87. Plymouth St Jas Ham *Ex* 82-86; Asst Chapl Coll of SS Mark and Jo Plymouth from 87; Par Dn Teignmouth, Ideford w Luton, Ashcombe etc *Ex* from 89. *Radway Lodge, Radway Street, Bishopsteignton, Teignmouth, Devon TQ14 9SS* Teignmouth (0626) 775540

DEBNEY, Canon Wilfred Murray. b 26. ACA48 FCA60. Wycliffe Hall Ox 58. **d** 60 **p** 61. C Leic H Apostles *Leic* 60-65; V Thorpe Edge *Bradf* 65-69; TV Wendy w Shingay *Ely* 69-75; R Brampton from 75; OCF RAF from 75; RD Huntingdon *Ely* from 81; Hon Can Ely Cathl from 85. *The Rectory, Brampton, Huntingdon, Cambs PE18 8PF* Huntingdon (0480) 453341

DEDMAN, Roger James. b 45. Oak Hill Th Coll 68. **d** 71 **p** 72. C Gresley *Derby* 71-74; C Ipswich St Fran *St E* 74-79; P-in-c Bildeston w Wattisham from 79. *The Rectory, 176 High Street, Bildeston, Ipswich IP7 7EF* Bildeston (0449) 740530

DEE, Clive Hayden. b 61. Ripon Coll Cuddesdon 86. **d** 89 **p** 90. C Bridgnorth, Tasley, Astley Abbotts, Oldbury etc *Heref* from 89. *9 Fir Trees, Bridgnorth, Shropshire WV15 5EA* Bridgnorth (0746) 761069

DEEDES, Canon Arthur Colin Bouverie. b 27. Bede Coll Dur BA51. Wells Th Coll 51. **d** 53 **p** 54. C Milton *Portsm* 53-58; C Worplesdon *Guildf* 58-60; V Weston 60-66; V Fleet 66-73; RD Aldershot 69-73; TR Bournemouth St Pet w St Swithun, St Steph etc *Win* 73-80; RD Bournemouth 74-80; Hon Can Win Cathl from 78; Master Win St Cross w St Faith from 80. *The Master's Lodge, St Cross Hospital, Winchester, Hants SO23 9SD* Winchester (0962) 852888

DEEGAN, Arthur Charles. b 49. CertEd71 Birm Univ BEd86. Qu Coll Birm 86. **d** 88 **p** 89. C Leic St Jas *Leic* 88-91; C Melton Gt Framland from 91. *26 Firwood Road, Melton Mowbray, Leicester LE13 1SA* Melton Mowbray (0664) 61066

DEEMING, Paul Leyland. b 44. CA Tr Coll 65 CMS Tr Coll Selly Oak 70. **d** 80 **p** 80. CMS 71-82; Pakistan 71-82; R E and W Horndon w Lt Warley *Chelmsf* 83-89; V Gt Ilford St Andr from 89. *The Vicarage, St Andrew's Road, Ilford, Essex IG1 3PE* 081-554 3858

DEETH, William Stanley. b 38. St Pet Coll Ox BA59 MA67. St Steph Ho Ox 66. **d** 68 **p** 69. C Eastbourne St Mary *Chich* 68-71; C Benwell St Jas *Newc* 71-75; C-in-c Byker St Martin CD 75-76; P-in-c Byker St Martin 76; V 76-89; P-in-c Bothal from 89. *Bothal Rectory, Longhirst Road, Pegswood, Morpeth, Northd NE61 6XF* Morpeth (0670) 510793

DEFTY, Henry Gordon. b 14. St Chad's Coll Dur BA38 MA41 DipTh41. **d** 39 **p** 40. V Hartlepool St Aid *Dur* 68-73; Can Res Ches Cathl *Ches* 73-74; V Gainford *Dur* 74-80; R Winston 76-80; rtd 80. *39 Crossgate, Durham DH1 4PS* 091-384 4334

DEGG, Ralph William. b 26. Lon Univ BSc57. Wells Th Coll 61. **d** 63 **p** 64. C The Lickey *Birm* 66-71; R Grendon 71-78; V Tanworth St Patr Salter Street 78-86; rtd 89; Perm to Offic *Birm* from 89. *23 Wayfield Road, Shirley, Solihull, W Midlands B90 3HF* 021-744 3564

✠**DEHQANI-TAFTI, Rt Rev Hassan Barnaba.** b 20. Tehran Univ BA43. Virginia Th Sem DD81 Ridley Hall Cam 47. **d** 49 **p** 50 **c** 61. Iran 49-61; Bp Iran 61-90; Pres Bp Episc Ch Jerusalem and Middle E 76-86; Asst Bp Win from 82; rtd 90. *Sohrab House, 1 Camberry Close, Basingstoke RG21 3AG* Basingstoke (0256) 27457

DEIGHTON, Ian Armstrong. b 19. Glas Univ MA40. Edin Th Coll. **d** 43 **p** 44. R Musselburgh *Edin* 57-84; P-in-c Prestonpans 76-84; rtd 84. *6 Duddingston Park South, Edinburgh EH15 3PA* 031-669 5108

DEIMEL, Richard Witold. b 49. Lon Univ BA84. Cranmer Hall Dur 86. **d** 88 **p** 89. C Bilton *Cov* from 88. *51 Falstaff Drive, Bilton, Rugby, Warks CV22 6LJ* Rugby (0788) 810761

DELACOUR, Arthur Winter. b 14. Lon Univ BSc52. Sarum & Wells Th Coll 79. **d** 80 **p** 81. NSM Gtr Corsham *Bris* 80-83; Perm to Offic *Win* 83-86; Chapl St Jo Win Charity 86-89; Perm to Offic *Cov* from 89. *3 Margetts Close, Kenilworth, Warks CV8 1EN* Kenilworth (0926) 55667

DELAMERE, Allen Stephen. **d** 90 **p** 91. C Ban Abbey *D & D* from 90. *33 Donard Court, Bangor, Co Down BT20 3QN* Bangor (0247) 455749

DELANEY, Canon Peter Anthony. b 37. AKC65. St Boniface Warminster. **d** 66 **p** 67. C St Marylebone w H Trin *Lon* 66-70; Chapl Nat Heart and Orthopaedic Hosps Lon 66-70; Chapl Res Univ Ch of Ch the King

Lon 70-73; Can Res and Prec S'wark Cathl *S'wark* 73-77; V All Hallows by the Tower etc *Lon* from 77; Can Cyprus and the Gulf from 88. *All Hallows-by-the-Tower, Byward Street, London EC3R 5BJ* 071-481 2928 or 488 4772

DELANY, Michael Edward. b 34. Lon Univ BSc55 PhD58. S'wark Ord Course 80. **d** 83 **p** 84. NSM Hampton St Mary *Lon* 83-87; R Copythorne and Minstead *Win* from 87. *The Rectory, Minstead, Lyndhurst, Hants SO43 7FY* Southampton (0703) 812221

DELEVINGNE, Gordon Gresswell. b 21. Oak Hill Th Coll 59. **d** 61 **p** 62. V W Ham St Matt *Chelmsf* 65-72; R Langley *Cant* 72-79; rtd 79. *33 Culverden Avenue, Tunbridge Wells, Kent TN4 9RE* Tunbridge Wells (0892) 22451

DELFGOU, John. b 35. Oak Hill Th Coll 81. **d** 84 **p** 85. NSM Loughton St Mary and St Mich *Chelmsf* 84-90; NSM Loughton St Jo from 90. *20 Carroll Hill, Loughton, Essex IG10 1NN* 081-508 6333

DELIGHT, Ven John David. b 25. Liv Univ CSocSc48 Open Univ BA75. Oak Hill Th Coll 49. **d** 52 **p** 53. R Aldridge *Lich* 52-57; Preb Lich Cathl 80-90; RD Walsall 81-82; Adn Stoke 82-90; rtd 90; Hon Co-ord Th Educn Dio Machakos Kenya from 90. *42 Little Tixal Lane, Great Haywood, Stafford ST19 0SE*

DELIGHT, Paul Charles. b 31. Loughb Coll of Educn DipEd54. Oak Hill Th Coll 59. **d** 62 **p** 63. C Macclesfield Ch Ch *Ches* 62-65; Ho Master Mobberley Sch Knutsford 65-68; Perm to Offic Ches 65-68; Chich 68-71; Asst Master Mile Oak Sch Portslade 68-71; Dep Prin Thorntoun Sch Kilmarnock 71-75; Perm to Offic *Glas* 71-75; R Snodland All SS w Ch Ch *Roch* 75-81; V Guernsey H Trin *Win* from 81. *Holy Trinity Vicarage, Brock Road, St Peter Port, Guernsey, Channel Islands* Guernsey (0481) 724382

DELL, Dr Murray John. b 31. Cape Town Univ BA51 BSc54 Edin Univ MB, ChB59. Westcott Ho Cam 63. **d** 65 **p** 65. S Africa 65-70; Dean Windhoek 71-80; V Lyme Regis *Sarum* from 80. *The Vicarage, West Hill Road, Lyme Regis, Dorset DT7 3LW* Lyme Regis (02974) 3134

DELL, Ven Robert Sydney. b 22. Em Coll Cam BA46 MA50. Ridley Hall Cam 46. **d** 48 **p** 49. C Islington St Mary *Lon* 48-50; C Cam H Trin *Ely* 50-53; Lic to Offic *Lich* 53-55; Asst Chapl Wrekin Coll Shropshire 53-55; R Mildenhall *St E* 55-57; Vice-Prin Ridley Hall Cam 57-65; V Chesterton St Andr *Ely* 66-73; Hon Can Derby Cathl *Derby* 73-81; Can Res from 81; Adn Derby from 73. *72 Pastures Hill, Littleover, Derby DE3 7BB* Derby (0332) 512700

DELVE, Albert William John. b 15. Leeds Univ BA38. Coll of Resurr Mirfield 38. **d** 40 **p** 41. R Thurlestone *Ex* 69-83; R Thurlestone w S Milton 83-85; rtd 85; Perm to Offic *Ex* from 85. *Jalmar, Littlemead Lane, Exmouth, Devon EX8 3BU* Exmouth (0395) 278373

DELVE, Eric David. b 42. Trin Coll Bris. **d** 89 **p** 90. NSM Bris St Matt and St Nath *Bris* from 89. *61 Cranbrook Road, Bristol BS6 7BS* Bristol (0272) 429415

DELVES, Anthony James. b 47. Brunel Univ BSocSc70. St Steph Ho Ox 83. **d** 85 **p** 86. C Cantley *Sheff* 85-90; V Goldthorpe w Hickleton from 90. *The Vicarage, Lockwood Road, Goldthorpe, Rotherham, S Yorkshire S63 9JY* Rotherham (0709) 898426

DELVES-BROUGHTON, Simon Brian Hugo. b 33. Ex Coll Ox BA56 MA64. Kelham Th Coll 56. **d** 59 **p** 60. India 59-64; C Skirbeck St Nic *Linc* 64-67; E Pakistan 67-71; Bangladesh 71-74; V Northn Ch Ch *Pet* from 74; Chapl Northn Gen Hosp 77-87. *Christ Church Vicarage, 3 Christ Church Road, Northampton NN1 5LL* Northampton (0604) 33254

DENBY, Paul. b 47. NW Ord Course 73. **d** 76 **p** 77. C Stretford All SS *Man* 76-80; V Stalybridge 80-87; Chapl Tameside Distr Gen Hosp Ashton-under-Lyne from 82; Dir of Ords *Man* from 87. *9 Bettwood Drive, Higher Crumpsall, Manchester M8 6JY* 061-740 5711

DENCH, Christopher David. b 62. RGN83. Aston Tr Scheme 86 Sarum & Wells Th Coll 88. **d** 91. C Crayford *Roch* from 91. *1A Iron Mill Place, Crayford, Dartford DA1 4RT* Crayford (0322) 558789

DENERLEY, John Keith Christopher. b 34. Qu Coll Ox BA58 MA61. St Steph Ho Ox 58. **d** 61 **p** 62. C Airedale w Fryston *Wakef* 61-64; Chapl Sarum Th Coll 64-68; Min Can Cov Cathl *Cov* 68-76; Chapl Lanchester Poly 70-76; Chapl The Dorothy Kerin Trust Burrswood 76-85; V Trellech and Cwmcarvan *Mon* 85-87; V Penallt 85-87; V Penallt and Trellech from 87; Chapl Ty Mawr Convent (Wales) from 85. *The Vicarage, Penallt, Monmouth, Gwent NP5 4SE* Monmouth (0600) 716622

DENFORD, Keith Wilkie. b 35. AKC62. **d** 63 **p** 64. C Gunnersbury St Jas *Lon* 63-66; C Brighton St Pet *Chich* 66-71; Min Can Cant Cathl *Cant* 71-75; R W Tarring *Chich* 75-85; V Burgess Hill St Jo 85-90; R Pulborough from 90. *The Rectory, Church Place, Pulborough, W Sussex RH20 1AF* Pulborough (07982) 5773

DENGATE, Richard Henry. b 39. Cant Sch of Min 82. **d** 85 **p** 86. NSM Wittersham w Stone-in-Oxney and Ebony *Cant* 85; R Sandhurst w Newenden from 90. *The Rectory, Sandhurst, Hawkhurst, Kent TN18 5LE* Sandhurst (0580) 850213

DENHAM, Nicholas Philip. b 50. Salford Univ BSc72 Birm Univ CertEd74. Wycliffe Hall Ox 87. **d** 89 **p** 90. C Bishopwearmouth St Gabr *Dur* 89-90; C Ches le Street from 90. *2 Glencoe Avenue, Chester-le-Street, Co Durham DH2 2JJ* 091-388 0931

DENHAM, Thomas William. b 17. Wycliffe Hall Ox 58. **d** 59 **p** 60. Area Sec CMS 62-82; Perm to Offic *Liv* 62-73; P-in-c Bishopwearmouth St Gabr *Dur* 73-82; rtd 82. *The Laurels, Corwen Road, Pontblyddyn, Mold, Clwyd CH7 4HR* Mold (0352) 770046

DENHOLM, Edward Godfrey Denholm. b 08. AKC34. **d** 35 **p** 36. Chapl St Kath Convent Parmoor 68-73; rtd 73. *Round Lodge, Godstone, Surrey RH9 8DB*

DENHOLM, Canon Robert Jack. b 31. Edin Th Coll 53. **d** 56 **p** 57. R N Berwick *Edin* 69-80; R Gullane 76-80; R Edin St Mark 80-90; rtd 90. *Cluan, Ledaig, Connel, Argyll* Ledaig (063172) 250

DENING, John Cranmer. b 21. Clare Coll Cam BA48 MA52. Qu Coll Birm 50. **d** 52 **p** 53. C Moulsham St Jo *Chelmsf* 69-70; C W Teignmouth *Ex* 70-73; C N Stoneham *Win* 73-80; C Sholing 80-85; rtd 86. *27 The Paddocks, Brandon, Suffolk IP27 0DX*

DENISON, Keith Malcolm. b 45. Down Coll Cam BA67 MA71 PhD70. Westcott Ho Cam 70. **d** 71 **p** 72. C Chepstow *Mon* 71-72; C Bassaleg 72-75; Post-Ord Tr Officer 75-85; V Mathern and Mounton 75-80; V Mathern and Mounton w St Pierre 80-85; RD Chepstow 82-85; V Risca from 85. *The Vicarage, 1 Gelli Crescent, Risca, Newport, Gwent NP1 6QG* Risca (0633) 612307

DENISON, Philip. b 55. York Univ BA77 CertEd. St Jo Coll Nottm 83. **d** 86 **p** 87. C Barnoldswick w Bracewell *Bradf* 86-88; P-in-c Basford St Leodegarius *S'well* 88-91; C Basford w Hyson Green from 91. *Basford Vicarage, 152 Perry Road, Nottingham NG5 1GL* Nottingham (0602) 605602

DENMAN, Frederick George. b 46. Chich Th Coll 67. **d** 70 **p** 71. C Stafford St Mary *Lich* 70-72; C Ascot Heath *Ox* 72-75; P-in-c Culham 75-77; P-in-c Sutton Courtenay w Appleford 75-77; P-in-c Clifton Hampden 77; TV Dorchester 78-81; C Ox St Mich w St Martin and All SS 80; Chapl Henley Memorial Hosp 81-82; P-in-c W Hill *Ex* 82; TV Ottery St Mary, Alfington and W Hill 82-87; V Sparkwell from 87; V Shaugh Prior from 87. *The Vicarage, Sparkwell, Plymouth PL7 5DB* Cornwood (075537) 218

DENMAN, Preb Ronald. b 19. St Chad's Coll Dur LTh44 BA46. St Aug Coll Cant 40. **d** 44 **p** 45. V Cheddar *B & W* 57-86; Preb Wells Cathl from 77; rtd 86. *3 Gardenhurst Close, Burnham-on-Sea, Somerset TA8 2EQ* Burnham-on-Sea (0278) 781386

DENNEN, Lyle. b 42. Harvard Univ LLB67 Trin Coll Cam BA70 MA75. Cuddesdon Coll 72. **d** 72 **p** 73. C S Lambeth St Ann *S'wark* 72-75; C Richmond St Mary 75-78; P-in-c Kennington St Jo 78-79; V Kennington St Jo w St Jas from 79; P-in-c Brixton Rd Ch Ch 81-89. *The Vicarage, 92 Vassall Road, London SW9 6IA* 071-735 9340

DENNESS, Mrs Linda Christine. b 51. Portsm Dioc Tr Course. **d** 89. NSM Milton *Portsm* from 89. *88 Mayles Road, Portsmouth PO4 8NS* Portsmouth (0705) 738353

DENNETT, John Edward. b 36. Tyndale Hall Bris 66. **d** 68 **p** 69. C Chell *Lich* 68-71; C Bispham *Blackb* 71-73; C Cheltenham Ch Ch *Glouc* 73-75; V Coppull *Blackb* 75-79; P-in-c Parkham, Alwington and Buckland Brewer *Ex* 79-80; R 80-84; V Blackpool St Thos *Blackb* from 84. *St Thomas's Vicarage, 80 Devonshire Road, Blackpool FY3 8AE* Blackpool (0253) 32544

✠**DENNIS, Rt Rev John.** b 31. St Cath Coll Cam BA54 MA59. Cuddesdon Coll 54. **d** 56 **p** 57 **c** 79. C Armley St Bart *Ripon* 56-60; C Kettering SS Pet and Paul *Pet* 60-62; V Is of Dogs Ch Ch and St Jo w St Luke *Lon* 62-71; V Mill Hill Jo Keble Ch 71-79; RD W Barnet 73-79; Preb St Paul's Cathl 77-79; Suff Bp Knaresborough *Ripon* 79-86; Dioc Dir of Ords 80-86; Bp St E from 86. *Bishop's House, 4 Park Road, Ipswich IP1 3ST* Ipswich (0473) 252829

DENNIS, Canon John Daniel. b 20. LLCM. St D Coll Lamp BA41 LTh43. **d** 43 **p** 44. R Worthenbury w Tallarn

Green *St As* 62-71; V Chirk 71-86; RD Llangollen 74-86; Hon Can St As Cathl 83-86; rtd 86; Perm to Offic *St As* from 86. *Mount Cottage, Chirk, Wrexham, Clwyd LL14 5HD* Chirk (0691) 773382

DENNIS, John William. b 13. St Pet Hall Ox BA38 MA45. Linc Th Coll 38. **d** 39 **p** 40. V Linc St Swithin *Linc* 60-82; rtd 83; Perm to Offic *Linc* from 83. *17 Eastbrook Road, Swallowbeck, Lincoln LN6 7ER* Lincoln (0522) 680373

DENNIS, Keith Aubrey Lawrence. b 55. City of Lon Poly BA79. Cranmer Hall Dur 88. **d** 90 **p** 91. C Bushbury *Lich* from 90. *11 Wistwood Hayes, Bushbury, Wolverhampton WV10 8UQ* Wolverhampton (0902) 784907

DENNIS, Patrick John. b 44. Linc Th Coll 67. **d** 70 **p** 71. C Eccleshill *Bradf* 70-72; C Ponteland *Newc* 73-75; Chr Aid Org Leic and Linc 75-78; TV Cullercoats St Geo *Newc* 78-82; Dioc Ecum Officer 79-82; R Bradfield *Sheff* from 82; Dioc Ecum Adv from 82; Sec & Ecum Officer S Yorkshire Ecum Coun from 91. *The Rectory, Bradfield, Sheffield S6 6LG* Sheffield (0742) 851225

DENNIS, Canon Peter Gwyn Morgan. b 99. Bris Univ BA26. **d** 31 **p** 32. V Long Benton *Newc* 58-72; RD Newc E 64-72; Hon Can Newc Cathl 66-72; rtd 72. *Sherburn House, Durham DH1 2SE* 091-372 0253

DENNIS, Robert Ernest. b 08. TCD BA34 MA38. **d** 35 **p** 36. V Bootle Ch Ch *Liv* 61-75; rtd 75; Hon C Ormskirk *Liv* 75-84; Perm to Offic from 84; Hon C Blundellsands St Mich from 89. *7 Warrenhurst Court, Warren Road, Blundellsands, Liverpool L23 6TY* 051-931 2855

DENNIS, Trevor John. b 45. St Jo Coll Cam BA68 MA71 PhD74. Westcott Ho Cam 71. **d** 72 **p** 73. C Newport Pagnell *Ox* 72-75; Chapl Eton Coll Windsor 75-82; Tutor Sarum & Wells Th Coll from 82; Vice-Prin and Admissions Tutor from 89. *The Theological College, The Close, Salisbury SP1 2EE* Salisbury (0722) 332235

DENNISON, Philip Ian. b 52. Nottm Univ BTh81. St Jo Coll Nottm 77. **d** 81 **p** 82. C Stalybridge H Trin and Ch Ch *Ches* 81-84; C Heswall 84-91; TV Bushbury *Lich* from 91. *131 Taunton Avenue, Wolverhampton* Wolverhampton (0902) 781944

DENNISTON, Robin Alastair. b 26. Ch Ch Ox MA48. **d** 78 **p** 79. NSM Clifton upon Teme *Worc* 78-81; NSM Clifton-on-Teme, Lower Sapey and the Shelsleys 81-85; NSM S Hinksey *Ox* 85-87; NSM Gt w Lt Tew 87-90; NSM Burntisland *St And* from 90; NSM Aberdour from 90. *16A Inverleith Row, Edinburgh EH3 5LS* 031-556 8949

DENNO, Basil. b 52. Dundee Univ BSc74. Oak Hill Th Coll BA81. **d** 81 **p** 83. C Chaddesden St Mary *Derby* 81-83; Hon C 83-84. *21 Parkside Road, Chaddesden, Derby DE2 6QR* Derby (0332) 672687

DENNY, Laurence Eric. b 29. Oak Hill Th Coll 54. **d** 57 **p** 58. C Wallington H Trin *S'wark* 57-61; V Leyton St Edw *Chelmsf* 61-64; P-in-c 65-69; V Leyton St Mary w St Edw 64-72; V Pennycross *Ex* from 73. *St Pancras Vicarage, 66 Glentor Road, Plymouth PL3 5TR* Plymouth (0752) 774332

DENNY, Michael Thomas. b 47. Kelham Th Coll 68 St Jo Coll Nottm 71. **d** 73 **p** 74. C Gospel Lane St Mich *Birm* 73-77; P-in-c Frankley 77-82; R from 82. *The Rectory, Frankley Green, Birmingham B32 4AS* 021-475 3724

DENNY, Peter Bond. b 17. Lon Univ BA41. Bps' Coll Cheshunt 41. **d** 43 **p** 44. V Newlyn St Newlyn *Truro* 56-83; RD Pydar 74-81; rtd 83. *Tralee, The Crescent, Truro, Cornwall TR1 3ES* Truro (0872) 74492

DENT, Christopher Mattinson. b 46. K Coll Lon BA68 AKC68 MTh69 Jes Coll Cam BA72 MA76 New Coll Ox MA76 DPhil80. Westcott Ho Cam 70. **d** 72 **p** 73. C Chelsea St Luke *Lon* 72-76; Asst Chapl New Coll Ox 76-79; Dean of Div 79-84; V Hollingbourne and Hucking w Leeds and Broomfield *Cant* from 84. *The Vicarage, Hollingbourne, Maidstone, Kent ME17 1UJ* Maidstone (0622) 880243

DENT, Nigel Clive. b 56. K Coll Lon BD77 Keble Coll Ox DPhil85. St Steph Ho Ox 83. **d** 85 **p** 86. C High Wycombe *Ox* 85-89; Asst Chapl HM Pris Wormwood Scrubs 89-90; Chapl HM Young Offender Inst Wellingborough from 90. *c/o HM Prison Wellingborough, Millers Park, Doddington Road, Wellingborough, Northants NN8 2NH* Wellingborough (0933) 224151

DENT, Raymond William. b 47. Birm Coll of Educn CertEd68 Open Univ BA84. Ridley Hall Cam 70. **d** 73 **p** 74. C Hyde St Geo *Ches* 73-76; C Eastham 76-79; TV E Runcorn w Halton 79-80; V Hallwood 80-83; V New Brighton Em from 83. *Emmanuel Vicarage, 32 Magazine Brow, New Brighton, Wallasey, Wirral L45 1HP* 051-639 2885

DENT, Richard William. b 32. Down Coll Cam BA56 MA LLB59. Bris Sch of Min 73. **d** 77 **p** 78. NSM Southmead *Bris* 77-81; NSM Henleaze 81-85; V Highworth w

Sevenhampton and Inglesham etc 85-88; TV Oldland 88-91; V Longwell Green from 91. *85 Bath Road, Longwell Green, Bristol BS15 6DF* Bristol (0272) 322414

DENTON, Kenneth Percival. b 14. Clifton Th Coll 54. **d** 55 **p** 56. V Middlesb St Thos *York* 69-73; C Rufforth w Moor Monkton and Hessay 73-76; P-in-c Escrick 76-80; rtd 80; Perm to Offic *B & W* from 81. *46 Pedlars Grove, Packsaddle Way, Frome, Somerset BA11 2SX* Frome (0373) 63875

DENTON, Peter Brian. b 37. Kelham Th Coll 57. **d** 62 **p** 63. C Ellesmere Port *Ches* 62-66; Chapl HM Borstal Hollesley 66-69; CF 69-90; Warden Bridge Cen from 90; C Hounslow H Trin w St Paul *Lon* from 90. *Holy Trinity Church, High Street, Hounslow, Middx TW3 1HG*

DENTON, Peter Charles. St Jo Coll Dur BA52. Oak Hill Th Coll 49. **d** 52 **p** 53. Lect City of Newc Coll of Educn 67-75; Sen Lect Newc Poly 75-90; rtd 90. *10 Whitesmocks Avenue, Durham DH1 4HP* 091-384 3247

DENYER, Alan Frederick. b 31. Wycliffe Hall Ox 80. **d** 82 **p** 83. C Rodbourne Cheney *Bris* 82-84; P-in-c Garsdon w Lea and Cleverton 84-87; R Garsdon, Lea and Cleverton and Charlton 87-91; R Lydbury N w Hopesay and Edgton *Heref* from 91. *The Vicarage, Lydbury North, Shropshire SY7 8AU* Lydbury North (05888) 609

DENYER, Paul Hugh. b 46. Lon Univ BA68. Ripon Coll Cuddesdon 74. **d** 77 **p** 78. C Horfield H Trin *Bris* 77-82; TV Yate New Town 82-88; V Bris Lockleaze St Mary Magd w St Fran from 88. *The Parsonage, Copley Gardens, Bristol BS7 9YE* Bristol (0272) 512516

DENZIL, Sister. *See* ONSLOW, Denzil Octavia

DERBRIDGE, Roger. b 39. Clifton Th Coll 63. **d** 66 **p** 69. C Surbiton Hill Ch Ch *S'wark* 66-67; C Richmond Ch Ch 67-70; C Toxteth Park St Philemon *Liv* 70-75; TV Toxteth St Philemon w St Gabr 75-84; V Woking St Mary *Guildf* from 84. *St Mary of Bethany Vicarage, West Hill Road, Woking, Surrey GU22 7UJ* Woking (0483) 761269

DERBY, Archdeacon of. *See* DELL, Ven Robert Sydney

DERBY, Bishop of. *See* DAWES, Rt Rev Peter Spencer

DERBY, Provost of. *See* LEWERS, Very Rev Benjamin Hugh

DERBYSHIRE, Alan George. b 16. Lon Univ BA41. Linc Th Coll 41. **d** 43 **p** 44. R Merrow *Guildf* 67-81; rtd 81; Perm to Offic *Heref* from 81. *2A Abbey Cottages, Abbey Precinct, Tewkesbury, Glos GL20 5SR*

DERBYSHIRE, Mrs Anne Margaret. b 31. Lon Univ CertEd75 Open Univ BA87. SW Minl Tr Course. **d** 87. NSM Tiverton St Pet *Ex* 87-90; Perm to Offic from 90. *50 Carew Road, Tiverton, Devon EX16 6BN* Tiverton (0884) 257357

DERBYSHIRE, Arnold Sydney. b 06. **d** 50 **p** 52. R Horsington *B & W* 61-75; rtd 75; Perm to Offic *B & W* from 76. *Flat 2, Sutledge House, Langford, Bristol BS18 7HP* Wrington (0934) 862271

DERBYSHIRE, Douglas James. b 26. **d** 81 **p** 82. Hon C Heald Green St Cath *Ches* 81-86; Hon C Stockport St Geo 86-89; C 89-91; rtd 91. *91 East Avenue, Heald Green, Cheshire SK8 3BR* 061-437 3748

DERBYSHIRE, Philip Damien. b 50. Sarum & Wells Th Coll 80. **d** 82 **p** 83. C Chatham St Wm *Roch* 82-86; Zimbabwe 86-88; TV Burnham w Dropmore, Hitcham and Taplow *Ox* from 88. *Hitcham Vicarage, 1 The Precincts, Burnham, Slough SL1 7HU* Burnham (0628) 602881

DERHAM, Miss Hilary Kathlyn. b 50. MRPharmS Nottm Univ BPharm71. Chich Th Coll 89. **d** 91. Par Dn Stevenage H Trin *St Alb* from 91. *413 Scarborough Avenue, Stevenage, Herts SG1 2QA* Stevenage (0438) 361179

DERISLEY, Canon Albert Donald. b 20. Ely Th Coll 60. **d** 62 **p** 63. V Gt w Lt Plumstead *Nor* 66-72; V N Elmham w Billingford 72-85; RD Brisley and Elmham 77-85; Hon Can Nor Cathl 78-85; rtd 85; Perm to Offic *Nor* from 85. *22 Stuart Road, Aylsham, Norwich NR11 6HN* Aylsham (0263) 734579

DERMOTT, David John. b 34. Hull Univ BA60. Cuddesdon Coll 67. **d** 68 **p** 69. C Howden *York* 68-71; C W Acklam 71-74; TV Thornaby on Tees 74-79; R Hinderwell w Roxby from 79. *The Rectory, Hinderwell, Saltburn, Cleveland TS13 5JH* Whitby (0947) 840249

DERRETT, Canon Leslie John. b 14. St Jo Coll Dur BA41 MA45. **d** 41 **p** 42. V Witham *Chelmsf* 68-76; Hon Can Chelmsf Cathl 76-80; V Thorpe-le-Soken 76-80; rtd 80. *15 Larkfield Road, Great Bentley, Colchester CO7 8PX* Great Bentley (0206) 251315

DERRICK, David John. b 46. S'wark Ord Course. **d** 84 **p** 85. NSM Angell Town St Jo *S'wark* from 84; NSM

St-Mary-le-Strand w St Clem Danes *Lon* from 86. *319 Shakespeare Road, London SE24 0QD* 071-737 3809

DERRIMAN, Graham Scott. b 39. Bps' Coll Cheshunt 63. **d** 66 **p** 67. C Wandsworth St Mich *S'wark* 66-70; C Mert St Mary 70-74; P-in-c Earlsfield St Andr 75-81; V Camberwell St Luke 81-90; V Croydon St Aug from 90. *The Vicarage, 23A St Augustine's Avenue, Croydon, Surrey CR2 6JN* 081-688 2663

DERRY, Eric Leonard Stobart. b 15. Worc Ord Coll 62. **d** 64 **p** 65. V Luddenden *Wakef* 68-73; V Dodworth 73-83; rtd 84; Perm to Offic *Wakef* from 84. *29 Barnsley Road, Cawthorne, Barnsley, S Yorkshire S75 4HW* Barnsley (0226) 790697

DERRY, Hugh Graham. b 10. Or Coll Ox BA35 MA50. Ely Th Coll 46. **d** 48 **p** 49. S Africa 58-72; rtd 72; Perm to Offic *Ex* from 74. *Beech Tree Cottage, Cheriton Fitzpaine, Crediton, Devon EX17 4JJ* Cheriton Fitzpaine (03636) 438

DERRY AND RAPHOE, Bishop of. *See* MEHAFFEY, Rt Rev James

DERRY, Archdeacon of. *See* SIMPSON, Ven Samuel

DERRY, Dean of. *See* ORR, Very Rev David Cecil

DESBRULAIS, Mrs Patricia Mary. b 27. Qu Coll Birm 77. **dss** 79 **d** 87. Gt Bowden w Welham *Leic* 79-83; Market Harborough 83-87; Hon Par Dn 87-89; rtd 89. *14 Dunslade Road, Market Harborough, Leics LE16 8AQ* Market Harborough (0858) 64726

DESERT, Thomas Denis. b 31. Bps' Coll Cheshunt 54. **d** 56 **p** 57. C Goldington *St Alb* 56-60; C-in-c Luton St Hugh Lewsey CD 60-63; C St Alb St Sav 63-65; C Cheshunt 65-68; V Bedf All SS 68-89; R Northill w Moggerhanger from 89. *The Rectory, Bedford Road, Northill, Biggleswade, Beds SG18 9AH* Northill (076727) 262

DESON, Rolston Claudius. b 39. Qu Coll Birm 85. **d** 84 **p** 85. NSM Saltley *Birm* 84-86; C Edgbaston SS Mary and Ambrose 86-90; V W Bromwich St Phil *Lich* from 90. *The Vicarage, 33 Reform Street, West Bromwich, W Midlands B70 7PF* 021-525 1985

DESPARD, Canon Eric Herbert. b 17. TCD BA40 BD48. CITC 41. **d** 41 **p** 42. C Roscommon *K, E & A* 41-43; C Dub St Pet *D & G* 43-51; I Blessington w Kilbride 51-65; RD Rathdrum 63-77; I Lucan w Leixlip from 65; Can Ch Ch Cathl Dub from 73; RD Ballymore 77-85; RD Omorthy from 86. *The Rectory, Lucan, Co Dublin, Irish Republic* Dublin (1) 628-0339

DETTMER, Douglas James. b 64. Univ of Kansas BA86 Yale Univ MDiv90. Berkeley Div Sch 90. **d** 90 **p** 91. C Ilfracombe, Lee, Woolacombe, Bittadon etc *Ex* from 90. *St Peter's House, Highfield Road, Ilfracombe, Devon EX34 9LH* Ilfracombe (0271) 864119

DEUCHAR, Andrew Gilchrist. b 55. Southn Univ BTh86. Sarum & Wells Th Coll 81. **d** 84 **p** 85. C Alnwick St Mich and St Paul *Newc* 84-88; TV Heref St Martin w St Fran (S Wye Team Min) *Heref* 88-90; Adv to Coun for Soc Resp (Cant and Roch) from 90. *57 Queen Elizabeth Square, Maidstone, Kent ME15 9DE* Maidstone (0622) 687722

DEUCHAR, John. b 24. Or Coll Ox BA49 MA50. Westcott Ho Cam 49. **d** 51 **p** 52. R Woolwich St Mary w H Trin *S'wark* 68-72; V Whitley Ch Ch *Ox* 72-84; Chapl and Tutor Whittington Coll Felbridge 84-89; rtd 89; Perm to Offic Sarum & Win from 89. *2 The Leys, 63 Church Street, Fordingbridge, Hants SP6 1BB* Fordingbridge (0425) 655407

DEVAMANIKKAM, Trevor. b 47. Ripon Hall Ox 74. **d** 76 **p** 77. C Manston *Ripon* 76-79; P-in-c Moor Allerton 79-81; P-in-c Harrogate St Wilfrid and St Luke 81-84; V Buttershaw St Aid *Bradf* 84-85; Succ St D Cathl *St D* 85-87; V Llanwnda, Goodwick, w Manorowen and Llanstinan 87-90; Chapl RN from 90. *c/o MOD, Lacon House, Theobald's Road, London WC1X 8RM* 071-430 6847

DEVENNEY, Raymond Robert Wilmont. b 47. TCD BA69 MA73. CITC 70. **d** 70 **p** 71. C Ballymena *Conn* 70-75; C Ballyholme *D & D* 75-81; I Killinchy w Kilmood and Tullynakill from 81. *The Rectory, 11 Whiterock Road, Killinchy, Newtownards, Co Down BT23 6PR* Killinchy (0238) 541249

✠DEVENPORT, Rt Rev Eric Nash. b 26. Open Univ BA74. Kelham Th Coll 46. **d** 51 **p** 52 **c** 80. C Leic St Mark *Leic* 51-54; C Barrow St Matt *Carl* 54-56; Succ Leic Cathl *Leic* 56-59; V Shepshed 59-64; R Oadby 64-73; Hon Can Leic Cathl 73-80; Dioc Missr 73-80; Suff Bp Dunwich *St E* from 80. *The Old Vicarage, Church Road, Stowupland, Stowmarket, Suffolk IP14 4BQ* Stowmarket (0449) 678234

DEVEREUX, Canon John Swinnerton. b 32. Lon Univ BSc53. Wells Th Coll. **d** 58 **p** 59. C Wigan St Mich *Liv*

58-60; C Goring-by-Sea *Chich* 60-69; Ind Chapl from 69; Can and Preb Chich Cathl from 90. *4 The Driveway, Shoreham by Sea, Sussex BN4 5GG* Shoreham-by-Sea (0273) 454093

DEVONSHIRE, Roger George. b 40. AKC62. **d** 63 **p** 64. C Rotherhithe St Mary w All SS *S'wark* 64-67; C Kingston Hill St Paul 67-71; Chapl RN from 71. *c/o MOD, Lacon House, Theobald's Road, London WC1X 8RY* 071-430 6847

DEW, Lindsay Charles. b 52. Cranmer Hall Dur 85. **d** 86 **p** 86. C Knottingley *Wakef* 86-89; V Batley St Thos from 89. *The Vicarage, 16 Stockwell Drive, Batley, W Yorkshire WF17 5PA* Batley (0924) 473901

DEW, Robert David John. b 42. St Pet Coll Ox BA63. St Steph Ho Ox 63. **d** 65 **p** 66. C Abington *Pet* 65-69; Chapl Tiffield Sch Northants 69-71; Ind Chapl *Pet* 71-79; Ind Chapl *Liv* 79-87; Sen Ind Missr 88-91; R Skelsmergh w Selside and Longsleddale *Carl* from 91; Bp's Research Officer from 91. *The Vicarage, Skelsmergh, Kendal, Cumbria LA9 6NU* Kendal (0539) 724498

DEWAR, Francis John Lindsay. b 33. Keble Coll Ox BA56 MA59. Cuddesdon Coll 58. **d** 60 **p** 61. C Hessle *York* 60-63; C Stockton St Chad *Dur* 63-66; V Sunderland St Chad 66-81; Org Journey Inward, Journey Outward Project from 82. *2 Hillcrest Mews, Durham DH1 1RD* 091-384 1509

DEWAR, John. b 32. Chich Th Coll 58. **d** 61 **p** 62. C Leeds St Hilda *Ripon* 61-65; C Cullercoats St Geo *Newc* 65-69; V Newsham 69-76; C Kenton Ascension 76-86; R Wallsend St Pet from 86. *St Peter's Rectory, Wallsend, Tyne & Wear NE28 6PY* 091-262 3852

DEWAR, Canon Michael Willoughby. b 21. Em Coll Cam BA47 MA49 Lon Univ DipTh57 QUB PhD60. St Aid Birkenhead 47. **d** 49 **p** 50. C-in-c Magherally w Annaclone *D & D* 64-73; I Helen's Bay 73-86; Preb Castleknock St Patr Cathl Dub 83-86; rtd 86; Perm to Offic *Glouc* from 86. *4 St Kenelms, Shurdington Road, Cheltenham, Glos GL53 0JH* Cheltenham (0242) 523030

DEWEY, David Malcolm. b 43. Lon Univ BA72 LSE MSc(Econ)87. Westcott Ho Cam 76. **d** 78 **p** 79. Sen Lect Middx Poly from 72; Hon C Enfield St Mich *Lon* 78-79; Hon C Bush Hill Park St Steph 79-84; Hon C Palmers Green St Jo 84-90; Perm to Offic from 90. *11 Amberley Gardens, Enfield, Middx EN1 2NE* 081-360 8614

DEWEY, Peter Lewis. b 38. Wycliffe Hall Ox 69. **d** 71 **p** 72. C Hammersmith St Sav *Lon* 71-73; Chapl to Bp Kensington 73-75; C Isleworth All SS 75-81; TV Dorchester *Ox* from 81. *The Vicarage, Clifton Hampden, Abingdon, Oxon OX14 3EF* Clifton Hampden (086730) 7784

DEWEY, Sanford Dayton. b 44. Syracuse Univ AB67 MA72. Gen Th Sem (NY) MDiv79. **d** 79 **p** 80. USA 79-87; C St Mary le Bow w St Pancras Soper Lane etc *Lon* from 87. *St Mary-le-Bow Church, Cheapside, London EC2V 6AU* 071-248 5139

DEWHURST, George. b 34. TD76. AKC58. **d** 59 **p** 60. C Chorley St Pet *Blackb* 59-61; C-in-c Oswaldtwistle All SS CD 61-65; CF (TA) 63-67; V Shevington *Blackb* 65-83; CF (TAVR) 67-83; CF (TA - R of O) 83-88; V Horsley and Newington Bagpath w Kingscote *Glouc* from 83. *The Vicarage, Horsley, Stroud, Glos GL6 0PR* Nailsworth (045583) 3814

DEWHURST, George Gabriel. b 30. **d** 59 **p** 60. In RC Ch 60-69; C Darlington St Jo *Dur* 70; C Bishopwearmouth St Nic 71-81; C-in-c Stockton St Mark CD 73-81; V Harton 81-86; R Castle Eden w Monkhesleden from 86. *The Rectory, Castle Eden, Hartlepool, Cleveland TS27 4SL* Wellfield (0429) 836846

DEWIS, Harry Kenneth. b 19. NW Ord Course 75. **d** 78 **p** 79. NSM Bedale *Ripon* from 78. *11 Masham Road, Bedale, N Yorkshire DL8 2AF* Bedale (0677) 23588

DEXTER, Frank Robert. b 40. Cuddesdon Coll 66. **d** 68 **p** 69. C Newc H Cross *Newc* 68-71; C Whorlton 71-73; V Pet Ch Carpenter *Pet* 73-80; V High Elswick St Phil *Newc* 80-85; RD Newc W 81-85; P-in-c Newc St Aug 85; V Newc St Geo from 85. *St George's Vicarage, St George's Close, Jesmond, Newcastle upon Tyne NE2 2TF* 091-281 1628

DEY, Charles Gordon Norman. b 46. Lon Coll of Div DipTh70. **d** 71 **p** 72. C Almondbury *Wakef* 71-76; V Mixenden 76-85; TR Tong *Bradf* from 85. *The Rectory, Holmewood Road, Tong, Bradford, W Yorkshire BD4 9EJ* Bradford (0274) 682100

DEY, John Alfred. b 33. AI.CD57 ALCM57. **d** 57 **p** 58. C Man Albert Memorial Ch *Man* 57-60; C Pennington 60-62; V Mosley Common 62-69; V Chadderton Em 69-79; V Flixton St Jo from 79. *St John's Vicarage, Irlam Road, Flixton, Manchester M31 3WA* 061-748 6754

DIAMOND, Canon David John. b 35. Leeds Univ BA60. St Steph Ho Ox 60. **d** 62 **p** 63. C W Derby (or Tuebrook) St Jo *Liv* 62-68; R Deptford St Paul *S'wark* from 69; Hon Can S'wark Cathl from 73; RD Deptford 74-80. *St Paul's Rectory, Deptford High Street, London SE8 3PQ* 081-692 1419

DIAMOND, Gordon Ernest. b 08. ALCD37. **d** 36 **p** 37. R Newick *Chich* 56-73; RD Uckfield 64-73; rtd 73; Hon C Battle *Chich* 74-83. *203 The Welkin, Lindfield, Haywards Heath, W Sussex RH16 2PW* Lindfield (0444) 484201

DIAMOND, Michael Lawrence. b 37. St Jo Coll Dur BA60 MA74 Sussex Univ DPhil84. Lon Coll of Div ALCD62 LTh74. **d** 62 **p** 63. C Wandsworth St Mich *S'wark* 62-64; C Patcham *Chich* 64-69; R Hamsey 70-75; P-in-c Cam St Andr Less *Ely* 75-86; V from 86. *The Vicarage, Parsonage Street, Cambridge CB5 8DN* Cambridge (0223) 353794

DIAPER, James Robert. b 30. Portsm Dioc Tr Course 84. **d** 85. NSM Portsea St Sav *Portsm* 85-89 and from 91; NSM Milton 89-91. *48 Wallington Road, Portsmouth PO2 0HB* Portsmouth (0705) 691372

DIAPER, Trevor Charles. b 51. ALA79. Coll of Resurr Mirfield 88. **d** 90 **p** 91. C N Walsham w Antingham *Nor* from 90. *35 Kimberley Road, North Walsham, Norfolk NR28 2DZ* North Walsham (0692) 404755

DIBB SMITH, John. b 29. Ex & Truro NSM Scheme 78. **d** 81 **p** 82. NSM Carbis Bay *Truro* 81-82; NSM Carbis Bay w Lelant 82-84; Warden Trelowarren Fellowship Helston 84-91; Chapl 89-91; NSM Halsetown *Truro* from 91. *St John in the Fields Vicarage, St Ives, Cornwall TR26 2HG* Penzance (0736) 796035

DIBBENS, Hugh Richard. b 39. Lon Univ BA63 MTh67 St Pet Coll Ox BA65 MA74. Oak Hill Th Coll 60. **d** 67 **p** 68. C Holborn St Geo w H Trin and St Bart *Lon* 67-72; CMS 73-74; Japan 74-77; TR Chigwell *Chelmsf* from 78. *The Rectory, High Road, Chigwell, Essex IG7 6QB* 081-500 3510

DIBBS, Canon Geoffrey. b 24. Man Univ BA51 ThD69. Wycliffe Hall Ox 51. **d** 53 **p** 54. R Burton Agnes w Harpham *York* 59-66; Canada from 66; rtd 88. *116 Hawthorne, London, Ontario, Canada, N6G 2W8*

DIBDEN, Alan Cyril. b 49. Hull Univ LLB70 Fitzw Coll Cam BA72 MA76. Westcott Ho Cam 70. **d** 73 **p** 74. C Camberwell St Luke *S'wark* 73-77; TV Walworth 77-79; TV Langley Marish *Ox* 79-84; C Chalfont St Peter 84-90; TV Burnham w Dropmore, Hitcham and Taplow from 90. *Taplow Rectory, Maidenhead, Berks SL6 0ET* Maidenhead (0628) 661182

DIBDIN, Ronald Frank. b 20. Glouc Sch of Min 84 Trin Coll Bris 84. **d** 84 **p** 84. NSM Newent *Glouc* 84-85; NSM Newent and Gorsley w Cliffords Mesne 85-90; Perm to Offic *Glouc* from 90. *The Retreat, High Street, Newent, Glos GL18 1AS* Newent (0531) 822090

DICK, Alexander Walter Henry. b 20. Lon Univ BSc49 BSc(Econ)56. Sarum & Wells Th Coll 73. **d** 74 **p** 75. C Totnes *Ex* 74-77; Min Estover LEP 77-80; V Estover 80-81; P-in-c Broadwoodwidger 81-83; V 83-86; P-in-c Kelly w Bradstone 81-83; R 83-86; P-in-c Lifton 81-83; R 83-86; rtd 86; Perm to Offic Ex and Lon from 86. *Flat 1, Fairfield, Huxtable Hill, Torquay, Devon TQ2 6RN* Torquay (0803) 605126

DICK, Mrs Caroline Ann. b 61. Nottm Univ BTh88. Linc Th Coll 85. **d** 88. Par Dn Houghton le Spring *Dur* from 88. *The Rectory, Houghton Road, Hetton-le-Hole, Houghton le Spring, Tyne & Wear DH5 9PH* 091-526 3198

DICK, Cecil Bates. b 42. Selw Coll Cam BA68 MA72. E Midl Min Tr Course 73. **d** 76 **p** 78. NSM Cinderhill *S'well* 76-79; Chapl Dame Allan's Schs Newc 79-85; C Gosforth All SS *Newc* 85-87; Chapl HM Pris Dur 88-89; Chapl HM Pris Hull from 89. *The Chaplain's Office, HM Prison Hull, Hedon Road, Hull HU9 5LS* Hull (0482) 20673

DICK, Norman MacDonald. b 32. ACIB. Ox NSM Course 87. **d** 90. NSM Bedgrove *Ox* from 90. *21 Columbine Avenue, Aylesbury, Bucks HP21 7UH* Aylesbury (0296) 85530

DICK, Raymond Owen. b 53. Edin Univ BD77. Edin Th Coll 73. **d** 77 **p** 78. C Glas St Mary *Glas* 77-84; Perm to Offic *St Alb* 84-85; P-in-c Edin St Paul and St Geo *Edin* 85; P-in-c Edin SS Phil and Jas 85-86; P-in-c Edin St Marg 85-87; TV Edin Old St Paul 87-88; R Hetton-le-Hole *Dur* from 88. *The Rectory, Houghton Road, Hetton-le-Hole, Tyne & Wear DH5 9PH* 091-526 3198

DICK, Mrs Valerie Ann. b 33. Girton Coll Cam MA56. Gilmore Ho 57. **dss** 78 **d** 87. Estover LEP *Ex* 78-80; Estover 80-81; Broadwoodwidger 81-86; Kelly w Bradstone 81-86; Lifton 81-86; Par Dn Tufnell Park St Geo and All SS *Lon* 87-90; Par Dn W Holl St Luke

from 90. *25 Freegrove Road, London N7 9RG* 071-607 7799

DICKEN, Dr Eric William Trueman. b 19. Ex Coll Ox BA39 MA46 DD64. Cuddesdon Coll 49. **d** 49 **p** 50. Warden Lenton Hall Nottm Univ 65-80; R Maidwell w Draughton, Scaldwell, Lamport etc *Pet* 80-84; rtd 84. *Monks Barn, Maugersbury, Stow on the Wold, Cheltenham, Glos GL54 1HP* Stow (05783) 30562

DICKENS, Philip Henry Charles. b 28. S'wark Ord Course 76. **d** 79 **p** 80. NSM Headley All SS *Guildf* 79-81; C 81-84; V Wrecclesham from 84. *The Vicarage, 2 Kings Lane, Wrecclesham, Farnham, Surrey GU10 4QB* Farnham (0252) 716431

DICKENS, Timothy Richard John. b 45. Leeds Univ BSc68. Westcott Ho Cam 68. **d** 71 **p** 72. C Meole Brace *Lich* 71-74; C-in-c Stamford Ch Ch CD *Linc* 74-80; V Anlaby St Pet *York* from 80. *The Vicarage, Church Street, Anlaby, Hull HU10 7DG* Hull (0482) 653024

DICKENSON, Charles Gordon. b 29. Bps' Coll Cheshunt 53. **d** 56 **p** 57. C Ellesmere Port *Ches* 56-61; R Egremont St Columba 61-68; V Latchford Ch Ch 68-74; P-in-c Hargrave 74-79; V Birkenhead St Jas w St Bede 79-83; R Tilston and Shocklach from 83. *The Rectory, Inveresk Road, Tilston, Malpas, Cheshire* Tilston (08298) 289

DICKENSON, Geoffrey. b 20. Kelham Th Coll 38. **d** 44 **p** 45. V Frecheville *Derby* 67-70; RD Staveley 68-70; V Scarcliffe 70-75; R Walton on Trent w Croxall 75-83; Perm to Offic *Heref* from 83; rtd 85. *26 Churchill Road, Church Stretton, Shropshire SY6 6EP* Church Stretton (0694) 723015

DICKENSON, Oswald Clare. b 08. Qu Coll Newfoundland 32. **d** 37 **p** 38. V Clapham Ch Ch *S'wark* 63-76; rtd 76; Lic to Offic *Newc* from 78. *17 Hugh Street, Wallsend, Tyne & Wear NE28 6RL* 091-262 7068

DICKER, David. b 31. St Pet Hall Ox BA57 MA58. Linc Th Coll 55. **d** 57 **p** 58. C Wootton Bassett *Sarum* 57-60; C Broad Town 57-60; C Weymouth H Trin 60-63; Antigua 63-64; R Tisbury *Sarum* 64-71; Argentina 71-77; Miss to Seamen 77-81; Chapl Dunkerque w Lille Arras etc Miss to Seamen *Eur* 81-86; TR Shaston *Sarum* from 86; RD Blackmore Vale from 90. *The Rectory, 7 Bimport, Shaftesbury, Dorset SP7 8AT* Shaftesbury (0747) 52547

DICKER, Ms Jane Elizabeth. b 64. Whitelands Coll Lon BA87. Linc Th Coll 87. **d** 89. Par Dn Mert St Jas *S'wark* from 89. *7 Westcroft Gardens, Morden, Surrey SM4 4DJ* 081-540 2217

DICKER, Miss Mary Elizabeth. b 45. Girton Coll Cam BA66 MA70 Sheff Univ MSc78. Cranmer Hall Dur 83. **dss** 85 **d** 87. Mortlake w E Sheen *S'wark* 85-87; Par Dn 87-88; Par Dn Irlam *Man* from 88. *21 Addison Road, Irlam, Manchester M30 6FP* 061-775 3175

DICKIE, James Graham Wallace. b 50. Worc Coll Ox BA72 MA BLitt77. Westcott Ho Cam 78. **d** 81 **p** 82. C Bracknell *Ox* 81-84; Lic to Offic *Ely* 84-89; Chapl Trin Coll Cam 84-89; Chapl Clifton Coll Bris from 89. *Clifton College, Bristol* Bristol (0272) 732580

DICKINSON, Anthony William. b 48. New Coll Ox BA71 MA74 Nottm Univ DipHE82. Linc Th Coll 80. **d** 82 **p** 83. C Leavesden All SS *St Alb* 82-86; TV Upton cum Chalvey *Ox* from 86. *St Peter's Parsonage, 52 Montem Lane, Slough SL1 2QJ* Slough (0753) 520725

DICKINSON, Henry. b 29. St Deiniol's Hawarden 84. **d** 86 **p** 87. NSM Blackb St Mich w St Jo and H Trin *Blackb* 86-89; NSM Burnley St Cath w St Alb and St Paul from 89. *47 Culshaw Street, Burnley, Lancs BB10 4LL* Burnley (0282) 55739

DICKINSON, Very Rev the Hon Hugh Geoffrey. b 29. Trin Coll Ox BA53 DipTh54 MA56. Cuddesdon Coll 54. **d** 56 **p** 57. C Melksham *Sarum* 56-58; Chapl Trin Coll Cam 58-63; Chapl Win Coll 63-69; P-in-c Milverton *Cov* 69-77; V St Alb St Mich *St Alb* 77-86; Dean Sarum from 86. *The Deanery, 7 The Close, Salisbury SP1 2EF* Salisbury (0722) 22457

DICKINSON, John Frederick. b 48. Hull Univ BA CertEd. Qu Coll Birm 84. **d** 86 **p** 87. C Gt Parndon *Chelmsf* 86-89; C Harrogate St Wilfrid and St Luke *Ripon* from 89. *59 Coppice Way, Harrogate, N Yorkshire HG1 2DJ* Harrogate (0423) 522194

✠**DICKINSON, Rt Rev John Hubert.** b 01. Jes Coll Ox BA24 MA28. Cuddesdon Coll 24. **d** 25 **p** 26 **c** 31. C Middlesb St Jo the Ev *York* 25-29; Japan 29-31; Bp Melanesia 31-37; V Felkirk w Brierley *Wakef* 37-42; V Warkworth *Newc* 42-59; Hon Can Newc Cathl 47-71; R Chollerton w Birtley and Thockrington 59-71; rtd 71. *Ravenstone Rest Home, Ladycutter Lane, Corbridge, Northd NE45 5RZ* Hexham (0434) 633500

DICKINSON, Matthew Lewis. b 22. SRN51 MRIPHH54. Launde Abbey 77. **d** 79 **p** 80. C Leic St Anne *Leic* 79-81; C Leic St Eliz Nether Hall 81-87; OStJ from 80; rtd 87; Perm to Offic Leic from 87; Pet from 88. *32 Glebe Way, Oakham, Leicester LE15 6XL* Oakham (0572) 722680

DICKINSON, Robert Edward. b 47. Nottm Univ BTh74. St Jo Coll Nottm 70. **d** 74 **p** 75. C Birm St Martin *Birm* 74-78; P-in-c Liv St Bride w St Sav *Liv* 78-81; TV St Luke in the City 81-86; Chapl Liv Poly from 86. *45 Queen's Drive, Liverpool L18 2DT* 051-722 1625 or 207 3581

DICKINSON, Stephen Paul. b 54. SRN75. N Ord Course 85. **d** 88 **p** 89. Hon C Purston cum S Featherstone *Wakef* from 88. *174 Featherstone Lane, Featherstone, Pontefract, W Yorkshire WF7 6AD* Pontefract (0977) 796483

DICKINSON, Victor Tester. b 48. Univ of Wales (Cardiff) BSc70. St Steph Ho Ox 70. **d** 73 **p** 74. C Neath w Llantwit *Llan* 73-76; Asst Chapl Univ of Wales (Cardiff) 76-79; TV Willington Team *Newc* 79-86; V Kenton Ascension from 86. *The Vicarage, Creighton Avenue, Newcastle upon Tyne NE3 4UN* 091-285 7803

DICKINSON, Wilfrid Edgar. b 21. AKC42 Lon Univ BD42. Linc Th Coll. **d** 44 **p** 45. V Chigwell *Chelmsf* 54-74; TR 74-78; V Hatf Heath 78-86; rtd 86; Perm to Offic *Heref* from 86. *4 Bearcroft, Weobley, Hereford HR4 8TA* Weobley (0544) 318641

DICKSON, Anthony Edward. b 59. Nottm Univ BTh88. Linc Th Coll 85. **d** 88 **p** 89. C Portsea St Alb *Portsm* 88-91; C Cleobury Mortimer w Hopton Wafers *Heref* from 91. *The Glebe House, New Road Gardens, Cleobury Mortimer, Kidderminster, Worcs DY14 8AW* Cleobury Mortimer (0299) 270559

DICKSON, Brian John. b 19. Reading Univ BSc41 Birm Univ DipTh51. Qu Coll Birm 49. **d** 51 **p** 52. Lic to Offic *Bris* 67-74; Chapl Colston's Sch Bris 67-74; V Bishopston *Bris* 74-85; RD Horfield 80-85; rtd 85; Perm to Offic *Worc* from 85. *One Acre Cottage, Abberley, Worcester WR6 6BS* Great Witley (0299) 896442

DICKSON, Dr Richard John. b 48. Ch Coll Cam BA70 BChir73 MB74. Coll of Resurr Mirfield 74. **d** 77 **p** 78. C Paulsgrove *Portsm* 77-80; C Forton 80-84; V Southsea St Pet from 84. *St Peter's Vicarage, Playfair Road, Southsea, Hants PO5 1EQ* Portsmouth (0705) 822786

DICKSON, Samuel Mervyn James. b 41. CITC. **d** 66 **p** 67. C Ballyholme *D & D* 66-70; C Knockbreda 70-75; I Clonallon w Warrenpoint 75-84; RD Kilbroney from 82; I Down H Trin w Hollymount from 84; RD Lecale from 85. *50 St Patrick's Avenue, Downpatrick, Co Down BT30 6DW* Downpatrick (0396) 612286

DILL, Peter Winston. b 44. ACP66 K Coll Lon BD72 AKC72. **d** 73 **p** 74. C Warsop *S'well* 73-75; C Rhyl w Rhyl St Ann *St As* 75-77; C Oxton *Ches* 77-78; V Newton in Mottram 78-82; P-in-c Oxon and Shelton *Lich* 82-84; V 84-87; Chapl Clifton Coll Bris from 87. *7 College Fields, Clifton, Bristol BS8 3HP* Bristol (0272) 738605

DILLISTONE, Canon Frederick William. b 03. BNC Ox BA24 DipTh25 MA28 BD33 DD51. Wycliffe Coll Toronto Hon DD57 Wycliffe Hall Ox 25. **d** 27 **p** 28. Chapl Or Coll Ox 64-70; rtd 70. *11 Eyot Place, Meadows Lane, Oxford OX4 1SA* Oxford (0865) 241324

DILNOT, Canon John William. b 36. Selw Coll Cam BA60 MA64. Cuddesdon Coll 60. **d** 62 **p** 63. C Stafford St Mary *Lich* 62-66; C Stoke upon Trent 66-67; V Leek All SS 67-74; V Leeds w Broomfield *Cant* 74-79; P-in-c Aldington 79-81; P-in-c Bonnington w Bilsington 79-81; P-in-c Fawkenhurst 79-81; R Aldington w Bonnington and Bilsington 81-87; RD N Lympne 82-87; Hon Can Cant Cathl from 85; V Folkestone St Mary and St Eanswythe from 87. *The Vicarage, Priory Gardens, Folkestone, Kent CT20 1SW* Folkestone (0303) 52947

DILWORTH, Anthony. b 41. St Deiniol's Hawarden. **d** 90 **p** 91. NSM Gt Saughall *Ches* from 90. *49 Hermitage Road, Saughall, Chester CH1 6AQ* Chester (0244) 881587

DIMMER, Harry James. b 12. Chich Th Coll 73. **d** 73 **p** 73. NSM Fareham H Trin *Portsm* 73-82; rtd 82; Perm to Offic *Portsm* 82-90. *9 Bradley Road, Fareham, Hants PO15 5BW* Titchfield (0329) 47131

DIMOLINE, Keith Frederick. b 22. Clifton Th Coll 48. **d** 51 **p** 52. V Coalpit Heath *Bris* 65-74; V Hanham 74-83; C Cudworth w Chillington *B & W* 83-84; P-in-c Dowlishwake w Chaffcombe, Knowle St Giles etc 83-84; R Dowlishwake w Chaffcombe, Knowle St Giles etc 84-88; rtd 88. *16 Exeter Road, Weston-super-Mare, Avon BS23 4DB* Weston-super-Mare (0934) 635006

DIMOND, Canon Edward William. b 27. TCD BA50. **d** 51 **p** 52. C Belf St Mary *Conn* 51-54; Chapl Rotterdam

---

Miss to Seamen *Eur* 54-55; C Portadown St Mark *Arm* 55-59; R Higher Broughton *Man* from 59; Hon Can Man Cathl from 84; P-in-c Broughton from 87. *St James's Rectory, Higher Broughton, Salford M7 0UH* 061-792 1208

DINES, Anthony Bernard. b 25. Clifton Th Coll 57. **d** 60 **p** 61. R Glas St Silas *Glas* 67-78; R Gunton St Pet *Nor* 78-90; rtd 90; NSM Flixton w Homersfield and S Elmham *St E* from 90. *The Rectory, Flixton, Bungay, Suffolk NR35 1NL* Bungay (0986) 895530

DINES, Philip Joseph (Griff). b 59. BSc PhD MA. Westcott Ho Cam 83. **d** 86 **p** 87. C Northolt St Mary *Lon* 86-89; C Withington St Paul *Man* 89-91; V Wythenshawe St Martin from 91. *St Martin's Vicarage, 2 Blackcarr Road, Manchester M23 8LX* 061-998 3408

DINGLE, Geoffrey Philip Warren. b 27. Trin Hall Cam BA51 MA55. Westcott Ho Cam 51. **d** 53 **p** 54. R Berkswell *Cov* 66-87; V Bournemouth St Aug *Win* 87-91; rtd 91. *8 Halton Close, Bransgore, Christchurch, Dorset BH23 8HZ*

DINGLE, John Rodger. b 14. Keble Coll Ox BA37 MA41. Westcott Ho Cam 38. **d** 39 **p** 40. C Billingham St Cuth *Dur* 39-42; Lic to Offic *Worc* 42-43; C Hartlepool H Trin *Dur* 43-44; C Shadforth 44-46; C Worc St Martin-in-the-Cornmarket *Worc* 76-80; C Worc City St Paul and Old St Martin etc 80-82; Perm to Offic from 83. *34 Beech Avenue, Worcester WR3 8PY* Worcester (0905) 53053

DINNEN, John Frederick. b 42. TCD BA65 BD72. **d** 66 **p** 67. C Belf All SS *Conn* 66-68; ICM Dub 69-71; C Carnmoney 71-73; Asst Dean of Residences QUB 73-74; Dean 74-84; I Hillsborough *D & D* from 84. *17 Dromore Road, Hillsborough, Co Down BT26 6HS* Hillsborough (0846) 682366

DINNIS, Richard Geoffrey. b 40. AKC63. **d** 64 **p** 65. C Plymouth St Pet *Ex* 64-68; C Tividale *Lich* 68-70; V Goldenhill 70-79; R Letchworth *St Alb* 79-88; V Withyham St Jo *Chich* from 88. *St John's Vicarage, St John's Road, Crowborough, E Sussex TN6 1ST* Crowborough (0892) 654660

DINSMORE, Stephen Ralph. b 56. Wye Coll Lon BSc78. Cranmer Hall Dur 82. **d** 85 **p** 86. C Haughton le Skerne *Dur* 85-88; C Edgware *Lon* from 88. *St Andrew's Parsonage, 1 Beulah Close, Edgware, Middx HA8 8SP* 081-958 9730

DISNEY, Peter James. b 13. Univ of BC BA36. BC Th Coll LTh37. **d** 37 **p** 38. V Halstead H Trin *Chelmsf* 69-78; rtd 78; Perm to Offic *St E* from 78. *16 Lower Byfield, Monks Eleigh, Ipswich IP7 7JJ* Bildeston (0449) 740994

DISS, Canon Ronald George. b 31. Sarum Th Coll 58. **d** 61 **p** 62. C Greenwich St Alfege w St Pet *S'wark* 61-65; Lic to Offic *S'wark* 65-80; Lon 68-77; Chapl Lon Univ *Lon* 68-71; Bp's Dom Chapl *Win* 78-80; V Southn Maybush St Pet 80-91; Hon Can Win Cathl from 85; R Freemantle from 91. *The Rectory, 129 Paynes Road, Southampton SO1 3BW* Southampton (0703) 221804

DITCH, David John. b 45. St Cath Coll Cam BA67 MA70 Leeds Univ PGCE68. W Midl Minl Tr Course 88. **d** 91. C Biddulph *Lich* from 91. *48 Thames Drive, Biddulph, Stoke-on-Trent ST8 7HL* Biddulph (0782) 522428

DITCHBURN, Hazel. b 44. NE Ord Course 82. **dss** 84 **d** 87. Scotswood *Newc* 84-86; Ind Chapl *Dur* from 86. *2 Woburn Way, Westerhope, Newcastle upon Tyne NE5 5JD* 091-283 0553

DITCHFIELD, Timothy Frederick. b 61. CCC Cam BA83. Cranmer Hall Dur 85. **d** 88 **p** 89. C Accrington St Jo *Blackb* 88-89; C Accrington St Jo w Huncoat 89-91; C Whittle-le-Woods from 91. *65 Daisy Meadow, Clayton Brook, Preston PR5 8DL* Preston (0772) 312186

DITTMER, Canon Michael William. b 17. St Edm Hall Ox BA39 MA43. Sarum Th Coll 40. **d** 41 **p** 42. V Yatton Keynell *Bris* 52-88; R Biddestone w Slaughterford 53-88; R Castle Combe 53-88; RD Chippenham 66-76; R W Kington 75-88; Hon Can Bris Cathl 84-88; P-in-c Nettleton w Littleton Drew 85-88; rtd 88. *Greenacres, Summerhedge Lane, Othery, Bridgwater, Somerset TA7 0JD* Burrowbridge (082369) 288

DIVALL, David Robert. b 40. New Coll Ox BA64 Sussex Univ DPhil74. Sarum & Wells Th Coll 75. **d** 77 **p** 78. Hon C Catherington and Clanfield *Portsm* from 77. *17 Pipers Mead, Clanfield, Portsmouth PO8 0ST* Horndean (0705) 594845

DIXON, Aidan Geoffrey Wilson. b 15. Bp Wilson Coll. **d** 44 **p** 45. V Appleby and Murton cum Hilton *Carl* 60-72; R Kinnersley *Lich* 72-76; R Tibberton 72-76; R Preston on the Weald Moors 74-76; rtd 76; Perm to Offic *Lich* from 76. *Hay House, Tibberton, Newport, Shropshire TF10 8NR* Telford (0952) 603224

DIXON, Miss Anne Nicholson. b 28. Lightfoot Ho Dur 54. **dss** 60 **d** 87. Dioc RE Adv *Dur* 62-83; RE Consultant Gateshead 83-89; rtd 89. *12 Wellbank Road, Washington, Tyne & Wear NE37 1NH* 091-416 1130

DIXON, Bruce Richard. b 42. Lon Univ BScEng63. Sarum Th Coll 66. **d** 68 **p** 69. C Walton St Mary *Liv* 68-70; C Harnham *Sarum* 70-73; C Streatham St Leon *S'wark* 73-77; R Thurcaston *Leic* 77-83; R Cranborne w Boveridge, Edmondsham etc *Sarum* from 83. *The Rectory, Grugs Lane, Cranborne, Wimborne, Dorset BH21 5PX* Cranborne (07254) 232

DIXON, Charles William. b 41. NW Ord Course 78. **d** 81 **p** 82. C Almondbury *Wakef* 81-82; C Almondbury w Farnley Tyas 82-84; P-in-c Shepley 84-88; P-in-c Shelley 84-88; V Shelley and Shepley 88-89; V Ripponden from 89; V Barkisland w W Scammonden from 89. *St Bartholomew's Vicarage, Ripponden, Sowerby Bridge, W Yorkshire HX6 4DF* Halifax (0422) 822239

DIXON, Canon David. b 19. Lich Th Coll 57. **d** 58 **p** 59. Warden Rydall Hall 68-84; P-in-c Rydal *Carl* 78-84; rtd 84; Hon Can Carl Cathl *Carl* 84-85. *Rheda, The Green, Millom, Cumbria LA18 5JA* Millom (0229) 774300

DIXON, Edward Ashby. b 15. K Coll Lon AKC40 BD45. **d** 40 **p** 41. V Frampton on Severn *Glouc* 66-75; V Frampton on Severn w Whitminster 75-80; P-in-c Arlingham 66-80; RD Glouc S 67-79; rtd 80; Perm to Offic *Glouc* from 80. *3 Grange Close, Minchinhampton, Stroud, Glos GL6 9DF* Brimscombe (0453) 882560

DIXON, Edward Michael. b 42. St Chad's Coll Dur BA64 DipTh66. **d** 66 **p** 67. C Hartlepool H Trin *Dur* 66-70; C Howden *York* 70-73; Chapl HM Pris *Liv* 73; Onley 74-82; Frankland 82-87; Chapl HM Pris *Dur* from 87. *3 Richmond Road, Newton Hall, Durham DH1 5NT* 091-386 5002 or 386 2621

DIXON, Eric. b 31. MPS. E Midl Min Tr Course 78. **d** 81 **p** 82. NSM Kirk Langley *Derby* from 81; NSM Mackworth All SS from 81. *Silverdale, Lower Road, Mackworth, Derby DE3 4NG* Kirk Langley (033124) 543

DIXON, Mrs Francesca Dorothy. b 52. Cam Univ MA73 Birm Univ DipTh83. **dss** 84 **d** 87. W Bromwich All SS *Lich* 84-87; Par Dn from 87. *139 Church Vale, West Bromwich, W Midlands B71 4DR* 021-588 2854

DIXON, Canon Guy Kenneth. b 08. Hertf Coll Ox BA30 MA34. Cuddesdon Coll 30. **d** 31 **p** 32. R Thrybergh *Sheff* 45-73; Asst RD Rotherham 47-73; Hon Can Sheff Cathl 64-73; rtd 73; Perm to Offic *Chich* from 74. *20 Alderton Court, West Parade, Bexhill-on-Sea, E Sussex TN39 3HF* Bexhill-on-Sea (0424) 218834

DIXON, John Kenneth. b 40. Linc Th Coll 79. **d** 81 **p** 82. C Goldington *St Alb* 81-85; V Cardington from 85; RD Elstow from 89. *The Vicarage, Cardington, Bedford MK44 3SS* Bedford (0234) 838203

DIXON, John Martin. b 42. Kelham Th Coll Lich Th Coll. **d** 72 **p** 73. C Ellesmere Port *Ches* 72-74; C Bredbury St Mark 74-75; P-in-c Greenlands *Blackb* 75-78; Chapl Victoria Hosp Blackpool 75-78; Chapl RAF 78-81; Asst Chapl HM Pris Featherstone 81-85; Dep Chapl HM Pris Wormwood Scrubs 85-87; Chapl HM Pris Rudgate and Thorp Arch 87-89; Chapl HM Pris Leeds from 89. *HM Prison, Armley, Leeds LS12 2TJ* Leeds (0532) 636411

DIXON, Canon John Wickham. b 18. St Jo Coll Dur BA43 MA46. St Aid Birkenhead LTh41. **d** 43 **p** 44. V Blackb St Steph *Blackb* 54-85; Can Res Blackb Cathl 65-73; Hon Can 74-85; rtd 86; Perm to Offic *Blackb* from 86. *11A Sunnyside Avenue, Wilpshire, Blackburn BB1 9LW* Blackburn (0254) 246145

DIXON, Nicholas Scarth. b 30. G&C Coll Cam BA54 MA63. Westcott Ho Cam 54. **d** 56 **p** 57. C Walney Is *Carl* 56-59; CF 59-62; V Whitehaven Ch Ch w H Trin *Carl* 62-70; R Blofield w Hemblington *Nor* 70-77; P-in-c Bowness *Carl* 77-79; R 79-81; V Frizington and Arlecdon 81-87; V Barton, Pooley Bridge and Martindale from 87. *The Vicarage, Pooley Bridge, Penrith, Cumbria CA10 2LT* Pooley Bridge (07684) 86220

DIXON, Dr Peter. b 36. Qu Coll Ox BA58 MA62. Qu Coll Birm DipTh60 BD65 PhD75. **d** 60 **p** 61. C Mountain Ash *Llan* 60-63; C Penrhiwceiber w Matthewstown and Ynysboeth 63-68; P-in-c Penrhiwceiber and Matthewstown w Ynysboeth 68-70; V Bronllys and Llanvillo w Llandefaelog Tregraig *S & B* from 70. Bp's Chapl for Readers from 80; Bp's Chapl for Th Educn from 83; RD Hay from 90. *The Vicarage, Bronllys, Brecon, Powys LD3 0HS* Talgarth (0874) 711200

DIXON, Peter David. b 48. Edin Univ BSc71. **d** 79 **p** 80. NSM Prestonpans *Edin* 79-91; NSM Musselburgh 79-91; NSM Edin St Barn from 91. *c/o 112 St Alban's Road, Edinburgh EH9 2PG* 031-667 1280

DIXON, Philip. b 48. Leeds Univ BSc69. St Jo Coll Nottm 77. **d** 80 **p** 81. C Soundwell *Bris* 80-82; C Stoke Bishop 82-84; TV Hemel Hempstead *St Alb* 84-85; Chapl Westonbirt Sch from 85; Perm to Offic *Bris* from 86. *East Lodge, Westonbirt, Tetbury, Glos GL8 8QG* Westonbirt (066688) 345

DIXON, Philip Roger. b 54. CCC Ox BA77 MA80. Oak Hill Th Coll BA80. **d** 80 **p** 81. C Droylsden St Mary *Man* 80-84; TV Rochdale 84-91; V Audenshaw St Steph from 91. *St Stephen's Vicarage, 176 Stamford Road, Audenshaw, Manchester M34 5WW* 061-370 1863

DIXON, Richard Russell. b 32. Dur Univ BA60. Chich Th Coll 60. **d** 62 **p** 70. C Scarborough St Martin *York* 62-63; C Thirsk w S Kilvington 69-73; P-in-c Swine 73-81; Youth Officer 73-78; V Beverley St Nic from 81. *St Nicholas' Vicarage, 72 Grovehill Road, Beverley, N Humberside HU17 0ER* Hull (0482) 881458

DIXON, Robert. b 50. Univ of Wales (Lamp) BA80. Chich Th Coll 80. **d** 81 **p** 82. C Maidstone St Martin *Cant* 81-84; Chapl HM Youth Cust Cen Dover 84-88; C All Hallows by the Tower etc *Lon* 88-90; P-in-c Southwick H Trin *Dur* from 90. *5 Carlisle Terrace, Sunderland SR5 2DF* 091-548 1349

DIXON, Roger John. b 33. Magd Coll Cam MA. E Anglian Minl Tr Course. **d** 79 **p** 80. NSM Fakenham w Alethorpe *Nor* 79-82; C Brandeston w Kettleburgh *St E* 82-84; P-in-c from 84; Asst Chapl Framlingham Coll Suffolk from 82. *The Rectory, Kettleburgh, Woodbridge, Suffolk IP13 7JP* Framlingham (0728) 723080

DIXON, Royston Clarence. b 15. Leeds Univ BA36. Coll of Resurr Mirfield 36. **d** 38 **p** 39. V Appledore *Ex* 53-72; C-in-c Lundy Is 53-72; V Exwick 72-81; rtd 81. *45 Greenways, Crediton, Devon EX17 3LP* Crediton (03632) 3971

DIXON, Victor. b 08. Bible Churchmen's Coll 37. **d** 38 **p** 40. R Winteringham *Linc* 70-75; rtd 75; Perm to Offic *Linc* from 76. *12 Bradley Road, Grimsby, S Humberside DN33 1QW* Grimsby (0472) 79800

D'MORIAS, Sydney James. b 07. Madras Univ BA29 Serampore Coll BD32. Bp's Coll Calcutta 30. **d** 32 **p** 33. V Finsbury Park St Thos *Lon* 68-78; rtd 78; Hon C Wood Green St Mich w Bounds Green St Gabr etc *Lon* from 83. *Ground Floor Flat, 21 Albert Road, London N22 4AA* 081-888 6427

DOAN, Charles Bryce. b 24. Michigan Univ AS48 AB50 MA52 MDiv65 STM79. **d** 65 **p** 65. USA 65-87; Warden Spennithorne Hall *Ripon* from 87. *Necht, Spennithorne Hall, Leyburn, N Yorkshire DL8 5PR* Wensleydale (0969) 23308

DOBB, Canon Arthur Joseph. b 31. ARIBA54 Man Coll of Art DA52 ACertCM80. Oak Hill Th Coll 56. **d** 58 **p** 59. C Bolton St Paul *Man* 58-60; C Rawtenstall St Mary 60-62; V Bircle 62-72; V Harwood 72-84; Hon Can Man Cathl from 81; V Wingates from 84. *Wingates Vicarage, 91 Chorley Road, Westhoughton, Bolton BL5 3PG* Westhoughton (0942) 812119

DOBB, Christopher. b 46. Dur Univ BA68. Cuddesdon Coll 68. **d** 70 **p** 71. C Portsea St Mary *Portsm* 70-73; Lic to Offic S'wark 73-77; Bris 79-81; Perm to Offic *Bris* 77-79; V Swindon St Aug from 81. *St Augustine's Vicarage, Morris Street, Swindon SN2 2HT* Swindon (0793) 22741

DOBBIE, Gary. b 51. FSA St Andr Univ MA75 BD77 Magd Coll Cam CertEd80. **d** 83 **p** 83. Kimbolton Sch Cambs 83-84; Hon C Kimbolton *Ely* 83-84; Ch Hosp Horsham 84-85; Chapl from 85. *Whites, Christ's Hospital, Horsham, W Sussex RH13 7LP* Horsham (0403) 66305

DOBBIN, Charles Philip. b 51. Jes Coll Cam BA73 MA77 Or Coll Ox BA75 MA88. St Steph Ho Ox 74. **d** 76 **p** 77. C New Addington *Cant* 76-79; C Melton Mowbray w Thorpe Arnold *Leic* 79-83; V Loughb Gd Shep 83-89; V Ashby-de-la-Zouch St Helen w Coleorton from 89. *The Rectory, Prior Park, Ashby-de-la-Zouch, Leics LE6 5BH* Ashby-de-la-Zouch (0530) 412180

DOBBIN, Harold John. b 47. Liv Univ BSc69. St Steph Ho Ox 70. **d** 73 **p** 74. C Newbold and Dunston *Derby* 73-77; C Leckhampton SS Phil and Jas w Cheltenham St Jas *Glouc* 77-80; V Hebburn St Cuth *Dur* 80-86; R Barlborough *Derby* from 86. *The Rectory, Barlborough, Chesterfield, Derbyshire S43 4EP* Chesterfield (0246) 810401

DOBBS, George Christopher. b 43. Linc Th Coll 66. **d** 68 **p** 69. C Hykeham *Linc* 68-71; Asst Master Heneage Sch Grimsby 71-78; Perm to Offic *S'well* 78-80; TV Chelmsley Wood *Birm* 80-84; TV Rochdale *Man* from 84. *St Aidan's Vicarage, 498 Manchester Road, Rochdale, Lancs OL11 3HE* Rochdale (0706) 31812

DOBBS, John Hedley. b 03. Magd Coll Cam BA26 MA32. Ridley Hall Cam 26. **d** 27 **p** 28. V Durnford *Sarum* 59-74;

RD Avon 70-74; rtd 74; Perm to Offic Win 74-84; Guildf from 85. *25 Stanton Close, Cranleigh, Surrey GU6 8UH* Cranleigh (0483) 275991

DOBBS, Michael John. b 48. Linc Th Coll 74. **d** 77 **p** 78. C Warsop *S'well* 77-82; V Worksop St Paul 82-89; P-in-c Mansf St Mark from 89. *St Mark's Vicarage, Nottingham Road, Mansfield, Notts NG18 1BP* Mansfield (0623) 655548

DOBSON, Christopher John. b 62. Univ of Wales (Abth) BA84 Ox Univ BA88. Wycliffe Hall Ox 86. **d** 89 **p** 90. C Biggin Hill *Roch* from 89. *22 Foxearth Close, Biggin Hill, Westerham, Kent TN16 3HQ* Biggin Hill (0959) 75900

DOBSON, Geoffrey Norman. b 46. ACP70 MCCEd71 Leeds Univ CertEd68 BA77 Open Univ BA73. Sarum & Wells Th Coll 72. **d** 74 **p** 75. C S Woodford H Trin CD *Chelmsf* 74-76; Colchester Adnry Youth Chapl 76-78; C Halstead St Andr w H Trin and Greenstead Green 76-78; Asst Dir Youth Educn *Carl* 78-82; P-in-c Kirkandrews-on-Eden w Beaumont and Grinsdale 78-82; V Illingworth *Wakef* 82-86; V Roxton w Gt Barford *St Alb* from 86. *The Vicarage, Great Barford, Bedford MK44 3JJ* Bedford (0234) 870363

DOBSON, John Francis Alban. b 12. **d** 38 **p** 45. V New Groombridge *Chich* 57-58; Canada from 58. *10 Kensington Road, Suite 1509, Bramalea, Ontario, Canada, L6T 3V4*

DOBSON, John Haselden. b 29. Mert Coll Ox BA52 MA55 Lon Univ BD58. Oak Hill Th Coll 54. **d** 56 **p** 57. C Rugby St Matt *Cov* 56-59; C W Hampstead St Luke *Lon* 59-60; Uganda 60-72; C Gorleston St Andr *Nor* 73-77; V Shotesham 77-90; R Saxlingham Nethergate w Saxlingham Thorpe 77-90; R Saxlingham Nethergate and Shotesham from 90. *The Rectory, Saxlingham Nethergate, Norwich NR15 1AJ* Hempnall (050842) 454

DOBSON, John Richard. b 64. Van Mildert Coll Dur BA87. Ripon Coll Cuddesdon 87. **d** 89 **p** 90. C Benfieldside *Dur* from 89. *36 Barley Mill Crescent, Consett, Co Durham DH8 8JX* Consett (0207) 590650

DOBSON, Kenneth Shuard. b 26. Oak Hill Th Coll 53. **d** 56 **p** 57. Chapl Eccles Hall Sch Quidenham 74-78; R Elvedon *St E* 78-84; R Eriswell 78-84; R Icklingham 78-84; RD Mildenhall 80-81; rtd 84; Lic to Offic *Nor* from 84. *57 Hargham Road, Attleborough, Norfolk NR17 2HG*

DOBSON, Philip. b 52. Lanc Univ BA73 CertEd74. Trin Coll Bris DipHE89. **d** 89 **p** 90. C Grenoside *Sheff* from 89. *49 Penistone Road, Grenoside, Sheffield S30 3QH* Sheffield (0742) 400723

DOBSON, Robert Christopher. b 28. Reading Univ BSc49. Clifton Th Coll 65. **d** 67 **p** 68. C Bilston St Leon *Lich* 67-70; C Cromer *Nor* 70-74; V Upton 74-81; R S Walsham 74-81; Chapl Lt Plumstead Hosp 74-81; Chapl R Albert Hosp Lanc from 81; Lanc R Infirmary from 84; Lanc Moor Hosp and Qu Victoria's Hosp Morecambe from 87. *The Chaplains' Room, Royal Albert Hospital, Ashton Road, Lancaster LA1 5AJ* Lancaster (0524) 68771

DOBSON, Robert William. b 19. Univ of Wales BA41. Coll of Resurr Mirfield 41. **d** 43 **p** 44. Chapl St Mary's Coll Ban 63-71; V Holt and Isycoed *St As* 77-83; V Holt 83-84; rtd 84. *Martin's Rise, Ellesmere Road, Tetchill, Ellesmere, Shropshire SY12 9AP*

DOBSON, Stuart Joseph. b 51. Westmr Coll Ox BA85. Chich Th Coll 86. **d** 88 **p** 89. C Costessey *Nor* 88-90; C Chaddesden St Phil *Derby* from 90. *St Philip's House, 2 Somerby Way, Oakwood, Derby DE2 2DY* Derby (0332) 834029

DOBSON, Theodore Edward. b 16. K Coll Cam BA38 MA42. Ridley Hall Cam 38. **d** 40 **p** 41. V Wembley St Jo *Lon* 65-74; P-in-c Stradbroke w Horham and Athelington *St E* 74-78; R 78-81; RD Hoxne 78-81; rtd 81. *31 Bishopdown Road, Salisbury, Wilts SP1 3DS* Salisbury (0722) 332663

✠**DOCKER, Rt Rev Ivor Colin.** b 25. Birm Univ BA46 St Cath Soc Ox BA49 MA52. Wycliffe Hall Ox 46. **d** 49 **p** 50 **c** 75. C Normanton *Wakef* 49-52; C Halifax St Jo Bapt 52-54; Area Sec (Dios Derby Linc and S'well) CMS 54-58; Metrop Sec (S) 58-59; V Midhurst *Chich* 59-64; RD Midhurst 61-64; R Woolbeding 61-64; V Seaford w Sutton 64-71; Can and Preb Chich Cathl from 66; V Eastbourne St Mary 71-75; RD Eastbourne 71-75; Suff Bp Horsham 75-91; rtd 91; Asst Bp Ex from 91. *Braemar, Bradley Road, Bovey Tracey, Newton Abbot, Devon TQ13 9EU* Newton Abbot (0626) 832468

DOCKRELL, George Thomas. b 29. TCD BA51 MA66. **d** 51 **p** 53. C Belf St Luke *Conn* 51-54; C Portadown St Columba *Arm* 54-59; I Newtownhamilton w Ballymoyer

---

59-63; Area Sec (Dios Ox and Win) CMS 63-68; V Jersey St Andr *Win* 68-80; Chapl HM Pris Pentonville 80-81; Coldingley 81-84; Chapl HM Pris Wayland from 84. *Chaplain's Office, HM Prison Wayland, Griston, Thetford, Norfolk IP25 6RL* Watton (0953) 884103 or 882107

DODD, Alan Henry. b 42. Man Univ BA70 MA79. Chich Th Coll 82. **d** 82 **p** 83. C Fareham H Trin *Portsm* 82-84; TV 84-89; V Osmotherley w E Harlsey and Ingleby Arncliffe *York* from 89. *The Vicarage, Osmotherley, Northallerton, N Yorkshire DL6 3BB* Osmotherley (060983) 282

DODD, Cyril. b 20. SS Hild & Bede Coll Dur MA48 DipEd. Coll of Resurr Mirfield 80. **d** 81 **p** 82. Hon C Guiseley *Bradf* 81-83; Hon C Guiseley w Esholt 83-90; rtd 90; Perm to Offic *Bradf* from 90. *Brierley, 37 Croft Park, Menston, Ilkley, W Yorkshire LS29 6LY* Menston (0943) 72132

DODD, Ian Neville. b 16. ACA39 FCA52. LTh. **d** 67 **p** 68. Canada 67-74; C Kingstanding St Mark *Birm* 74-75; P-in-c Smallburgh w Barton Turf w Dinham *Nor* 75-76; P-in-c Smallburgh w Dilham 77-80; P-in-c Smallburgh w Dilham w Honing and Crostwight 80-81; rtd 81; Perm to Offic *Chich* from 81. *Flat 2, High Trees, Carew Road, Eastbourne, E Sussex BN21 2JB* Eastbourne (0323) 644809

DODD, James Henry Birchenough. b 25. CPsychol AFBPsS Ox Univ MA. Westcott Ho Cam 85. **d** 85 **p** 86. NSM Epping Upland *Chelmsf* from 85. *The Chequers, Epping, Essex CM16 6PH* Epping (0378) 72561

DODD, John Dudley. b 15. Liv Univ BA36 Lon Univ BD51 DipEd54. Westcott Ho Cam 54. **d** 54 **p** 55. C Jersey St Helier *Win* 54-78; rtd 78; P-in-c Jersey Gouray St Martin *Win* from 78. *Gouray Vicarage, Gorey St Martin, Jersey, Channel Islands* Jersey (0534) 53255

DODD, John Stanley. b 24. Huron Coll Ontario 46. **d** 50 **p** 51. V Meanwood *Ripon* 65-89; rtd 89. *3 Shawdene, Burton Crescent, Leeds LS6 4DN* Leeds (0532) 789069

DODD, Lawrence Walter. b 04. Wells Th Coll 45. **d** 47 **p** 47. V Stratton *Truro* 55-69; rtd 69. *Sliggon Field, Trebetherick, Wadebridge, Cornwall PL27 6SB* Trebetherick (0208) 862341

DODD, Malcolm Ogilvie. b 46. Dur Univ BSc67 Loughb Univ MSc90. Edin Th Coll 67. **d** 70 **p** 71. C Hove All SS *Chich* 70-73; C Crawley 73-78; P-in-c Rusper 79-83; Chapl Brighton Coll Jun Sch 83; Perm to Offic *Derby* from 84; Chapl Stancliffe Hall Sch from 84. *40 Jackson Road, Matlock, Derbyshire DE4 3JQ* Matlock (0629) 582000

DODD, Michael Christopher. b 33. Ch Coll Cam BA55 MA59. Ridley Hall Cam 59. **d** 59 **p** 60. V Quinton Road W St Boniface *Birm* 62-72; TV Paston *Pet* 72-77; TR Hodge Hill *Birm* 77-89; rtd 90. *39 Regency Gardens, Birmingham B14 4JS* 021-474 6945

DODD, Canon Peter Curwen. b 33. St Jo Coll Cam BA57. Linc Th Coll 58 Wm Temple Coll Rugby 59. **d** 60 **p** 61. C Eastwood *Sheff* 60-63; Ind Chapl 63-67; Ind Chapl *Newc* from 67; RD Newc E 78-83; Hon Can Newc Cathl from 82. *Glenesk, 26 The Oval, Benton, Newcastle upon Tyne NE12 9PP* 091-266 1293

DODD, Peter Lawrence. b 38. MBE. Leeds Univ BA61. Qu Coll Birm DipTh62. **d** 63 **p** 64. CF 70-89; rtd 89; V Selby Abbey *York* from 90. *32A Leeds Road, Selby, N Yorkshire YO8 0HX* Selby (0757) 709218

DODD, Roy. b 30. S'wark Ord Course 67. **d** 70 **p** 71. NSM Farnborough *Guildf* 70-75; NSM Walton-on-Thames 75-76; Perm to Offic 76-81; NSM Woodham 81-90; R Headley w Box Hill from 90. *The Rectory, Headley, Epsom, Surrey KT18 6LE* Leatherhead (0372) 377327

DODD, Walter Herbert. b 96. Qu Coll Birm 33. **d** 35 **p** 36. V Weston upon Trent *Lich* 40-63; rtd 63. *Flat 1, Brunswick House, 112 Graham Road, Great Malvern, Worcs WR14 2HX*

DODD, William Samuel. b 31. Oak Hill Th Coll 64. **d** 66 **p** 67. C Dagenham *Chelmsf* 66-67; C Stratford St Jo and Ch Ch w Forest Gate St Jas 67-70; C Woodford Wells 70-72; V E Ham St Paul 72-77; Perm to Offic 77-82; V Harwich 82-89; Chapl Jes Hosp Bray 89-90; Perm to Offic *Ox* from 90. *37 Brunel Road, Maidenhead, Berks SL6 2RP* Maidenhead (0628) 76876

DODDS, Canon Arthur Whitfield. b 20. FRMetS Qu Coll Ox BA48 MA53. Wells Th Coll 49. **d** 50 **p** 51. V Chedworth w Yanworth and Stowell *Glouc* 64-75; RD Northleach 73-83; V Chedworth, Yanworth and Stowell, Coln Rogers etc 75-85; Hon Can Glouc Cathl from 78; rtd 86. *Church Lane Cottage, Harnhill, Cirencester, Glos GL7 5PT* Cirencester (0285) 851288

DODDS, Brian Martin. b 37. AKC62. **d** 63 **p** 64. C Morpeth *Newc* 63-67; Guyana 67-71; V Willington *Newc* 71-74;

TV Brayton *York* 75-79; V Gravelly Hill *Birm* 79-83; V Winterton *Linc* 83-85; V Winterton Gp 85-90; V Gainsborough St Jo from 90. *St John's Vicarage, 97A Sandsfield Lane, Gainsborough, Lincs DN21 1DA* Gainsborough (0427) 2847

DODDS, Graham Michael. b 58. GTCL80. Trin Coll Bris. **d** 84 **p** 85. C Reigate St Mary *S'wark* 84-91; R Bath Walcot *B & W* from 91. *The Rectory, 6 Rivers Street, Walcot, Bath BA1 2PZ* Bath (0225) 425570

DODDS, Canon Neil Sutherland. b 35. ARCO59 Keble Coll Ox BA59 DipTh61 MA63. Linc Th Coll 60. **d** 62 **p** 63. C Handsworth St Jas *Birm* 62-65; V Highters Heath 65-75; V Olton from 75; RD Solihull 79-89; Hon Can Birm Cathl from 82. *St Margaret's Vicarage, 5 Old Warwick Road, Solihull, W Midlands B92 7JU* 021-706 2318

DODDS, Norman Barry. b 43. Open Univ BA. CITC 73. **d** 76 **p** 77. C Ballynafeigh St Jude *D & D* 76-80; I Belf St Mich *Conn* from 80. *5 Sunningdale Park, Belfast BT14 6RU* Belfast (0232) 715463

DODDS, Peter. b 35. W Midl Minl Tr Course 88 Qu Coll Birm 88. **d** 91. NSM Hartshill *Cov* from 91. *Wem House, 51 Magyar Crescent, Nuneaton, Warks CV11 4SQ* Nuneaton (0203) 384061

DODGSON, Ronald. b 27. Sarum & Wells Th Coll 72. **d** 74 **p** 75. Sub Warden Barn Fellowship Blandford Forum 74-85; Hon C Canford Magna *Sarum* 78-85; C Hartley Wintney, Elvetham, Winchfield etc *Win* from 85. *Winton, 40 Pool Road, Hartley Wintney, Basingstoke, Hants RG27 8RD* Hartley Wintney (025126) 3602

DODHIA, Hitesh Kishorilal. b 57. Cranmer Hall Dur 85. **d** 88 **p** 89. C Leamington Priors All SS *Cov* 88-91; Chapl HM Young Offender Inst Glen Parva from 91. *HM Youth Custody Centre, Glen Parva, Tigers Road, South Wigston, Leicester LE8 2TN* Leicester (0533) 772022

DODSON, Canon Gordon. b 31. Barrister 56 Em Coll Cam BA54 LLB55 MA58. Ridley Hall Cam 57. **d** 59 **p** 60. C Belhus Park *Chelmsf* 59-60; C Barking St Marg 60-63; CMS 63-67; C New Malden and Coombe *S'wark* 67-69; V Snettisham *Nor* 69-81; RD Heacham and Rising 76-81; P-in-c Reepham and Hackford w Whitwell and Kerdiston 81-83; P-in-c Salle 81-83; P-in-c Thurning w Wood Dalling 81-83; R Reepham, Hackford w Whitwell, Kerdiston etc from 83; Hon Can Nor Cathl from 85. *The Rectory, Station Road, Reepham, Norwich NR10 4LJ* Norwich (0603) 870220

DODSON, James Peter. b 32. DipMin88. Lich Th Coll 58. **d** 61 **p** 62. C Chasetown *Lich* 61-63; C Hednesford 63-68; V Halifax St Hilda *Wakef* 68-76; V Upperthong 76-85; TV York All SS Pavement w St Crux and St Martin etc *York* 85-90. *117 The Village, Stockton-on-Forest, York YO3 9UP* York (0904) 400237

DODSWORTH, George Brian Knowles. b 34. Univ of Wales DipTh62 Birm Univ DPS66. St Mich Coll Llan 59. **d** 62 **p** 63. C Kidderminster St Mary *Worc* 62-67; Asst Chapl HM Pris Man 67-68; Chapl HM Pris Eastchurch 68-70; Wakef 70-74; Wormwood Scrubs 74-83; Asst Chapl Gen of Pris (SE) 83-90; Asst Chapl Gen of Pris (HQ) from 90; Lic to Offic *Lon* from 83. *c/o HM Prison Service Chaplaincy, Home Office, Cleland House, Page Street, London SW1P 4LN* 071-217 6398 or 081-693 9976

DOE, Canon Francis Harold. b 22. S'wark Ord Course 68. **d** 71 **p** 72. C Sompting *Chich* 71-74; C Stopham 74-78; C Hardham 74-78; P-in-c Sutton w Bignor 79-81; P-in-c Barlavington 79-81; V Warnham 81-87; R Stopham and Fittleworth from 87; RD Petworth from 88; Can and Preb Chich Cathl from 89. *The Rectory, Fittleworth, Pulborough, W Sussex RH20 1JG* Fittleworth (079882) 455

DOE, Martin Charles. b 54. Lon Univ BSc(Econ)75 PGCE87. St Steph Ho Ox 89. **d** 91. C Portsea St Mary *Portsm* from 91. *1 Glebe Flats, Nutfield Place, Fratton, Portsmouth, Hants PO1 4JF* Portsmouth (0705) 830154

DOE, Canon Michael David. b 47. St Jo Coll Dur BA69. Ripon Hall Ox 69. **d** 72 **p** 73. C St Helier *S'wark* 72-76; Youth Sec BCC 76-81; C-in-c Blackbird Leys CD *Ox* 81-88; RD Cowley 86-89; V Blackbird Leys 88-89; Soc Resp Adv *Portsm* from 89; Can Res Portsm Cathl from 89. *15 Grays Court, Gunwharf Gate, Portsmouth PO1 2PN* Portsmouth (0705) 733575 or 821137

DOE, William Frank. b 11. AKC46. **d** 46 **p** 47. V Maidstone St Martin *Cant* 68-72; V Preston next Faversham 72-73; V Preston next Faversham, Goodnestone and Graveney 73-78; RD Ospringe 76-78; rtd 78; Perm to Offic Guildf from 81; S'wark from 89. *Flat 3, Waterslade, Elm Road, Redhill, Surrey RH1 6AJ* Redhill (0737) 778242

DOHERTY, Deana Rosina Mercy. b 21. dss 82 **d** 87. Sutton St Jas and Wawne *York* 82-87; Par Dn from 87. *Sutton*

Rectory, Hull, N Humberside HU7 4TK Hull (0482) 782154

DOHERTY, Ven Raymond William Patrick. b 39. TCD BA63 MA71. **d** 65 **p** 66. C Clooney *D & R* 65-67; C Conwall 67-70; I Drumholm 70-75; I Tralee w Ballymacelligott, Kilnaughtin etc *L & K* 75-88; RD Tralee 78-79; Adn Ardfert and Aghadoe 80-88; Treas Limerick Cathl 80-88; I Kinsale Union *C, C & R* 88-90; Miss to Seamen 88-90; I Drumcliffe w Kilnasoolagh *L & K* from 90. *St Columba's Rectory, Bindon Street, Ennis, Co Clare, Irish Republic* Ennis (65) 20109

DOHERTY, Terence William. b 30. Shoreditch Coll Lon TCert St Jo Coll Dur BA56. Ripon Hall Ox 56. **d** 58 **p** 59. C Church Stretton *Heref* 58-60; C Halesowen *Worc* 60-62; Lic to Offic 62-64 and 69-78; R Hagley 64-69; Warden Dioc Conf Cen *Ches* 69-78; Lic to Offic *B & W* 70-78; TR Sutton St Jas and Wawne *York* from 78. *Sutton-on-Hull Rectory, Hull, N Humberside HU7 4TK* Hull (0482) 782154

DOHERTY, Thomas Alexander. b 48. Chich Th Coll 73. **d** 76 **p** 77. VC Derry Cathl *D & R* 76-79; C Llan w Capel Llanilterne *Llan* 79-80; PV Llan Cathl 80-84; V Penmark w Porthkerry 84-90; R Merthyr Dyfan from 90. *Merthyr Dyfan Rectory, 10 Buttrills Road, Barry, S Glam CF6 6AB* Barry (0446) 735943

DOIG, Dr Allan George. b 51. Univ of BC BA69 K Coll Cam BA73 MA80 PhD82. Ripon Coll Cuddesdon 86. **d** 88 **p** 89. C Abingdon *Ox* from 88. *3 River Close, Abingdon, Oxon OX14 5LU* Abingdon (0235) 533598

DOLMAN, Derek Alfred George Gerrit. b 40. ALCD64. **d** 64 **p** 65. C St Alb St Paul *St Alb* 65-68; C Bishopwearmouth St Gabr *Dur* 68-72; R Jarrow Grange 72-80; V New Catton St Luke *Nor* from 80. *St Luke's Vicarage, Aylsham Road, Norwich NR3 2HF* Norwich (0603) 425959

DOMINY, Peter John. b 36. Qu Coll Ox BA60 MA64 Aber Univ MLitt83. Oak Hill Th Coll 60. **d** 62 **p** 63. C Bedworth *Cov* 62-66; Nigeria 67-84; R Broadwater St Mary *Chich* from 84. *8 Sompting Avenue, Worthing, W Sussex BN14 8HT* Worthing (0903) 823916

DOMMETT, Canon Richard Radmore. b 19. St Jo Coll Ox BA41 MA45. Wells Th Coll 41. **d** 43 **p** 44. R Caister *Nor* 60-81; Hon Can Nor Cathl 77-85; P-in-c Saxthorpe and Corpusty 81-85; P-in-c Oulton SS Pet and Paul 81-85; P-in-c Blickling w Ingworth 81-85; P-in-c Heydon w Irmingland 82-85; rtd 85; Perm to Offic St E and Nor from 85. *14 Norwich Road, Halesworth, Suffolk IP19 8HN* Halesworth (0986) 873778

DONALD, Andrew William. b 19. St Jo Coll Morpeth 47 ACT ThL50. **d** 49 **p** 50. Chapl Halmstad *Eur* 65-68; Australia from 68; rtd 84. *18A Cobham Way, Westfield Park, Kelmscott, W Australia 6112* Perth (9) 390-8425

DONALD, Brother. See GREEN, Donald Pentney

DONALD, Dennis Curzon. b 38. Oak Hill Th Coll 68. **d** 70 **p** 71. C Carl St Jo *Carl* 70-73; Lic to Offic 73-77; Warden Blaithwaite Ho Chr Conf Cen Wigton from 73; Perm to Offic *Carl* from 77. *Blaithwaite House, Wigton, Cumbria CA7 0AZ* Wigton (06973) 42319

DONALD, Malcolm Collighan. b 15. Chich Th Coll 37. **d** 40 **p** 41. R Stow Bardolph w Wimbotsham and Stow Bridge *Ely* 64-77; P-in-c Crimplesham w Stradsett 68-73; V Thriplow 77-82; R Fowlmere 77-82; rtd 82; Perm to Offic *Ely* from 83. *4 St John's Close, Waterbeach, Cambs CB5 9HL* Cambridge (0223) 862281

DONALD, Robert Francis. b 49. St Jo Coll Nottm BTh75 LTh. **d** 75 **p** 76. C New Barnet St Jas *St Alb* 75-79; C St Alb St Paul 79-86; C St Alb St Mary Marshalswick 86-87; Lic to Offic from 87. *85A Abbots Park, St Albans, Herts AL1 1TN* St Albans (0727) 41647

DONALD, Steven. b 55. CertEd76. Oak Hill Th Coll BA88. **d** 88 **p** 89. C Cheadle All Hallows *Ches* 88-91; C Ardsley *Sheff* from 91. *St Andrew's House, Gerald Walk, Barnsley, S Yorkshire S70 3AT* Barnsley (0226) 203906

DONALD, William. b 30. Lon Univ DipTh61. Tyndale Hall Bris 58. **d** 61 **p** 62. C Stapenhill w Cauldwell *Derby* 61-63; Perm to Offic *Ox* 63-66; Lic to Offic Bris 66-70; Glouc from 82; C Cheltenham St Mark *Glouc* 70-77; C Glouc St Jas 77-82. *82 Forest View Road, Gloucester GL4 0BY* Gloucester (0452) 506993

DONALDSON, Christopher William. b 17. Lon Univ BD49. Kelham Th Coll. **d** 42 **p** 43. R Cant St Martin and St Paul *Cant* 63-76; Six Preacher Cant Cathl 72-78; rtd 82; Perm to Offic *B & W* from 82. *The Cottage, 13 Beadon Lane, Merriott, Crewkerne, Somerset TA16 5QT* Crewkerne (0460) 7259

DONALDSON, Miss Elizabeth Anne. b 55. Univ of Wales (Ban) BSc76 Surrey Univ MSc80 Nottm Univ BA82. St Jo Coll Nottm DPS83. dss 83 **d** 87. Guildf Ch Ch *Guildf* 83-86; Cuddington 86-87; C 87-90; C Keresley and

Coundon *Cov* from 90. *32 Parkfield Road, Keresley, Coventry CV7 8LR* Keresley (020333) 3694

DONALDSON, John Colvin. b 22. TCD BA49 MA57. **d** 50 **p** 51. V Ilsington *Ex* 59-73; RD Moreton 69-73; V Cockington 73-87; RD Ipplepen 78-82; rtd 87; Perm to Offic *Ex* from 87. *42 Bidwel Brook Drive, Paignton, Devon TQ4 7NF* Churston (0803) 843296

DONALDSON, Malcolm Alexander. b 48. Cranmer Hall Dur 84. **d** 86 **p** 87. C Heworth *York* 86-89; Chapl York Distr Hosp 86-89; C Marfleet *York* 89-90; TV from 90. *St Hilda's House, 256 Annendale Road, Greatfield, Hull, N Humberside HU9 4JX* Hull (0482) 799100

DONALDSON, Maurice Coburne. b 19. Univ of Wales BA40 Lon Univ BD47. St Mich Coll Llan 41. **d** 42 **p** 43. V Ruabon *St As* 70-77; V Abergele 77-84; rtd 84; Perm to Offic St As & Ban from 84. *35 Llys Mair, Bryn Eithinog, Bangor, Gwynedd* Bangor (0248) 354589

DONALDSON, Roger Francis. b 50. Jes Coll Ox BA71 MA75. Westcott Ho Cam 72. **d** 74 **p** 75. C Mold *St As* 74-78; V Deneio w Abererch *Ban* from 78. *The Vicarage, Yr Ala, Pwllheli, Gwynedd LL53 5BL* Pwllheli (0758) 612305

DONALDSON, William Richard. b 56. St Cath Coll Cam BA78 MA81. Ridley Hall Cam 79. **d** 82 **p** 83. C Everton St Sav w St Cuth *Liv* 82-85; C Reigate St Mary *S'wark* 85-89; V Easton H Trin w St Gabr and St Lawr and St Jude *Bris* from 89. *The Vicarage, 69 Stapleton Road, Easton, Bristol BS5 0PQ* Bristol (0272) 554255

DONCASTER, Reginald Arthur. b 23. Leeds Univ BA48. Coll of Resurr Mirfield. **d** 50 **p** 51. C Chesterfield All SS *Derby* 50-54; R Pleasley 54-73; V Ardleigh *Chelmsf* from 73. *The Vicarage, The Street, Ardleigh, Colchester, Essex CO7 7LD* Colchester (0206) 230231

DONCASTER, Archdeacon of. See CARNELLEY, Ven Desmond

DONCASTER, Suffragan Bishop of. See PERSSON, Rt Rev William Michael Dermot

DONELLA, Sister. See MATHIE, Patricia Jean

DONKIN, Robert. b 50. Univ of Wales (Cardiff) DipTh74. St Mich Coll Llan 71. **d** 74 **p** 75. C Mountain Ash *Llan* 74-77; C Coity w Nolton 77-79; V Oakwood 79-84; V Aberaman and Abercwmboi from 84. *St Margaret's Vicarage, Aberaman, Aberdare, M Glam CF44 6RT* Aberdare (0685) 872871

DONNELLY, Canon Arthur Ferguson. b 14. St Jo Coll Dur BA36 MA39. **d** 37 **p** 38. V Hartburn and Meldon *Newc* 65-83; V Netherwitton 66-83; RD Morpeth 76-83; Hon Can Newc Cathl 77-83; rtd 83. *20 Birchwood Avenue, Woodlands Park South, Newcastle upon Tyne NE13 6PZ* 091-236 6114

DONNELLY, James Alexander. b 20. TCD BA42. **d** 43 **p** 44. I Saul w Inch *D & D* 64-83; rtd 83. *29 Downpatrick Road, Clough, Downpatrick, Co Down BT30 8NL* Seaforde (039687) 273

DONSON, Miss Helen Cripps. b 32. Somerville Coll Ox DipEd55 MA58. Dalton Ho Bris 58 Gilmore Ho 69. **dss** 79 **d** 87. Staines St Pet *Lon* 80-83; Staines St Mary and St Pet 83-87; Par Dn 87-90; Par Dn Herne Bay Ch Ch *Cant* from 90. *19 Central Avenue, Herne Bay, Kent CT6 8RX* Herne Bay (0227) 360902

DOOLAN, Brian James. b 43. ACP65. St Steph Ho Ox 66. **d** 68 **p** 69. C Milton *Win* 68-71; C Bournemouth St Pet 71-73; C Kilburn St Aug w St Jo *Lon* 73-76; V Bordesley St Oswald *Birm* 76-82; Guyana 82-85; V Tile Hill *Cov* from 85. *St Oswald's Vicarage, 228 Jardine Crescent, Tile Hill, Coventry CV4 9PL* Coventry (0203) 465072

DOOLAN, Leonard Wallace. b 57. St Andr Univ MA79 Ox Univ BA82 MA88. Ripon Coll Cuddesdon 80. **d** 83 **p** 84. C High Wycombe *Ox* 83-85; C Bladon w Woodstock 85-88; C Wootton by Woodstock 85-88; P-in-c 88-90; C Kiddington w Asterleigh 85-88; P-in-c 88-90; P-in-c Glympton 88-90; R Wootton w Glympton and Kiddington from 90. *The Vicarage, Wootton, Abingdon, Oxon OX7 1HA* Woodstock (0993) 812543

DOONAN, Robert John. b 13. TCD BA36. **d** 37 **p** 38. I Magheraculmoney *Clogh* 53-78; rtd 78. *Crevnish Road, Kesh, Co Fermanagh* Kesh (03656) 31677

DORAN, Edward Roy. b 47. St Jo Coll Nottm. **d** 85 **p** 86. C Roby *Liv* 85-88; V Ravenhead from 88. *St John's Vicarage, Crossley Road, Ravenhead, St Helens, Merseyside WA10 3ND* St Helens (0744) 23601

DORAN, Sidney William. b 12. AKC40. **d** 40 **p** 41. V Bray and Braywood *Ox* 61-77; RD Maidenhead 74-77; rtd 77; Hon C Boscastle w Davidstow *Truro* from 85. *St Michael's, Combe Lane, Widemouth Bay, Bude, Cornwall EX23 0AA* Widemouth Bay (028885) 386

DORBER, Adrian John. b 52. St Jo Coll Dur BA74. Westcott Ho Cam 76. **d** 79 **p** 80. C Easthampstead *Ox*

79-85; C Caversham and Mapledurham 85-88; Chapl Portsm Poly *Portsm* from 88. *40 Worthing Road, Southsea, Hants PO5 2RN* Portsmouth (0705) 839029 or 843161

DORCHESTER, Area Bishop of. See RUSSELL, Rt Rev Anthony John

DORE, Eric George. b 47. S Dios Minl Tr Scheme 87. **d** 90 **p** 91. NSM Hove Bp Hannington Memorial Ch *Chich* from 90. *20 Tongdean Road, Hove, E Sussex BN3 6QE* Brighton (0273) 553488

DORE, Robert Edward Frederick. b 28. Birm Univ BCom51. Wycliffe Hall Ox. **d** 58 **p** 59. C Cheltenham Ch Ch *Glouc* 58-62; C Bridgnorth St Mary *Heref* 62-67; R Billingsley w Sidbury 67-82; R Chetton w Deuxhill and Glazeley 67-82; R Middleton Scriven 67-82; RD Bridgnorth 71-78; Preb Heref Cathl 75-82; P-in-c Chelmarsh 80-82; V 82; P-in-c Carhampton *B & W* 82-84; P-in-c Dunster 82-84; R Dunster, Carhampton and Withycombe w Rodhuish from 84. *The Rectory, St George's Street, Dunster, Minehead, Somerset TA24 6RS* Dunster (0643) 821812

DOREY, Trevor Eric. b 30. ACIS53. S Dios Minl Tr Scheme 87. **d** 90 **p** 91. NSM E Woodhay and Woolton Hill *Win* from 90. *Little Oxleas, Woolton Hill, Newbury, Berks RG15 9XQ* Newbury (0635) 253391

DORKING, Archdeacon of. See HERBERT, Ven Christopher William

DORKING, Suffragan Bishop of. See WILCOX, Rt Rev David Peter

DORMAN, John Richard. b 16. Keble Coll Ox BA38 MA55. Ely Th Coll 38. **d** 39 **p** 40. R Threlkeld *Carl* 46-57; Br Guiana 57-66; Guyana from 66; rtd 85. *c/o Paul James Esq, A44 Barima Avenue, Bel Air Park, Georgetown, Guyana*

DORMANDY, Richard Paul. b 59. Univ Coll Lon BA81 St Edm Ho Cam BA88. Ridley Hall Cam 86. **d** 89 **p** 90. C Sydenham H Trin *S'wark* from 89. *56 Sydenham Park Road, London SE26 4DL* 081-699 0271

DORMER, Christopher Robert. b 39. Bris Univ BA61. Lich Th Coll 61. **d** 63 **p** 64. C Sheff Parson Cross St Cecilia *Sheff* 63-67; C Greenford H Cross *Lon* 67-69; Australia 69-74; Sec (Ireland) USPG 74-75; R Catton *York* 75-78; R Stamford Bridge Gp of Par 78-81; RD Pocklington 80-81; Itinerant Priest *Mor* from 81; R Ullapool from 81; Miss to Seamen from 81. *25 Market Street, Ullapool, Ross-shire IV26 2XE* Ullapool (0854) 612143

DORMOR, Duncan Stephen. b 36. St Edm Hall Ox BA60. Cuddesdon Coll 60. **d** 62 **p** 63. C Headington *Ox* 62-66; USA 66-72; R Hertf St Andr *St Alb* 72-88; RD Hertf 77-83; R Burford I *Heref* from 88; TR Tenbury from 88. *The Vicarage, Tenbury Wells, Worcs WR15 8BP* Tenbury Wells (0584) 810702

DORRINGTON, Brian Goodwin. b 32. Leeds Univ CertEd55. St Deiniol's Hawarden 65. **d** 66 **p** 67. C Poynton *Ches* 66-71; Perm to Offic *Truro* 71-78; Hd Master Veryan Sch Truro 71-84; Hon C Veryan *Truro* 78-84; C N Petherwin 84-87; C Boyton w N Tamerton 84-87; TV Bolventor 87-90; R Kilkhampton w Morwenstow from 90. *The Rectory, East Road, Kilkhampton, Bude, Cornwall EX23 9QS* Kilkhampton (028882) 314

DORRINGTON, Richard Bryan. b 48. Linc Th Coll 79. **d** 81 **p** 82. C Streetly *Lich* 81-84; C Badger 84-85; C 85-88; C Ryton 84-85; R 85-88; C Beckbury 84-85; R 85-88; V Geddington w Weekley *Pet* from 88. *The Vicarage, Geddington, Kettering, Northants NN14 1BD* Kettering (0536) 742200

DORSET, Archdeacon of. See WALTON, Ven Geoffrey Elmer

DOSSETOR, Robert Francis. b 14. St Pet Hall Ox BA37 MA62 Lon Univ BA63 MA67. Ripon Hall Ox 37. **d** 37 **p** 38. V Lower Streatham St Andr *S'wark* 61-80; rtd 80; P-in-c Tilshead, Orcheston and Chitterne *Sarum* 80-85. *42 Fowlers Road, Salisbury SP1 2PU* Salisbury (0722) 20725

DOSSOR, John Haley. b 41. Leeds Univ BA62. E Anglian Minl Tr Course 82. **d** 90 **p** 91. NSM Hadleigh w Layham and Shelley *St E* from 90. *Butterfly Hall, Hadleigh, Ipswich, Suffolk IP7 5JZ* Ipswich (0473) 823338

DOTCHIN, Joan Marie. b 47. NE Ord Course 84. **d** 87. C Newc St Gabr *Newc* from 87. *33 Swindon Terrace, Heaton, Newcastle upon Tyne NE6 5RB* 091-265 5738

DOTY, Joseph Bonn. b 27. Woodstock Coll PhL51 STL58 Fordham Univ MA63. **d** 57 **p** 57. In RC Ch 57-70; USA 57-85; Prec St Ninian's Cathl Perth *St And* 85-88; R Church Brampton, Chapel Brampton, Harleston etc *Pet* from 88. *The Rectory, Church Brampton, Northampton NN6 8AU* Northampton (0604) 846213

DOUBLE, Richard Sydney (Brother Samuel). b 47. K Coll Lon BD69 AKC69. St Aug Coll Cant 69. **d** 70 **p** 71. C Walton St Mary *Liv* 70-74; SSF from 75; Lic to Offic *Liv* from 88. *St Francis House, 68 Laurel Road, Liverpool L7 0LW* 051-263 8581

DOUBTFIRE, Samuel. b 33. Edin Th Coll 63. **d** 66 **p** 66. C Knottingley *Wakef* 66-68; V Ripponden 68-76; V Crosthwaite Keswick *Carl* 76-81; V Barrow St Matt 81-87; R N Reddish *Man* from 87. *The Rectory, 551 Gorton Road, Stockport, Cheshire SK5 6NF* 061-223 0692

DOUGALL, David Brian. b 23. CBE. Oak Hill Th Coll. **d** 81 **p** 82. C Sandringham w W Newton *Nor* 81-83; P-in-c Fritton St Edm 83-84; R Somerleyton w Ashby 83-84; R Somerleyton w Ashby, Fritton and Herringfleet from 84. *The Rectory, Somerleyton, Lowestoft, Suffolk NR32 5PT* Lowestoft (0502) 731885

DOUGHTY, Andrew William. b 56. K Coll Lon BD AKC. Westcott Ho Cam. **d** 82 **p** 83. C Alton St Lawr *Win* 82-85; TV Basingstoke 85-91; V Chilworth w N Baddesley from 91. *The Vicarage, 33 Crescent Road, North Baddesley, Southampton S05 9HU* Southampton (0703) 732393

DOUGLAS, Canon Alexander Joseph. b 18. TCD BA45 MA61. CITC 45. **d** 45 **p** 46. I Orangefield w Moneyreagh *D & D* 63-86; rtd 86. *6 Rannoch Road, Holywood, Co Down BT18 0NA* Holywood (02317) 3661

DOUGLAS, Ann Patricia. b 49. Lon Univ CertEd71. Oak Hill NSM Course 85. **d** 88. Par Dn Chorleywood Ch Ch *St Alb* from 88. *98 Long Lane, Rickmansworth, Herts WD3 2YG* Rickmansworth (0923) 720300

DOUGLAS, Anthony Victor. b 51. St Jo Coll Nottm 74. **d** 76 **p** 77. C Gt Crosby St Luke *Liv* 76-79; TV Fazakerley Em 79-84; TR Speke St Aid 84-90; TR Gt and Lt Coates w Bradley *Linc* from 90. *St Michael's Rectory, 34 Great Coates Road, Grimsby, S Humberside DN34 4NE* Grimsby (0472) 44570

DOUGLAS, Canon Archibald Sholto. b 14. TD50. Selw Coll Cam BA37 MA46. Wells Th Coll 38. **d** 47 **p** 48. V Capesthorne w Siddington and Marton *Ches* 69-82; Hon Can Ches Cathl 78-82; rtd 82; Perm to Offic *Ches* from 82. *Monks Heath Hall Farm, Chelford, Macclesfield, Cheshire SK10 4SY* Chelford (0625) 861154

DOUGLAS, Brother. See NEEDHAM, Peter

DOUGLAS, Charles David. b 29. Leeds Univ BSc50. Linc Th Coll 68. **d** 70 **p** 71. C Royton St Anne *Man* 70-73; V Edenfield 73-83; V Spotland 83-88; P-in-c Calderbrook from 88. *St James's Vicarage, Stansfield Hall, Littleborough OL15 9RH* Littleborough (0706) 378414

DOUGLAS, George Gawain. b 35. Qu Coll Birm 59. **d** 61 **p** 62. C Workington St Jo *Carl* 61-64; C Upperby St Jo 64-67; C-in-c Carl St Luke Morton CD 67-68; V Carl St Luke Morton 68-72; V Aspatria w Hayton from 72. *The Vicarage, King Street, Aspatria, Carlisle CA5 3AL* Aspatria (06973) 20398

DOUGLAS, Ian Alexander. b 11. St Aug Coll Cant 71. **d** 71 **p** 72. C Palmers Green St Jo *Lon* 71-81; rtd 81; Perm to Offic *Lon* from 82. *62 Compton Road, London N21 3NS* 081-360 3472

DOUGLAS, Janet Elizabeth. b 60. SS Paul & Mary Coll Cheltenham BEd83. Cranmer Hall Dur 88. **d** 90. Par Dn Yardley St Edburgha *Birm* from 90. *422 Church Road, Yardley, Birmingham B33 8PB* 021-783 7318

DOUGLAS, John Beresford. b 36. Sarum & Wells Th Coll 78. **d** 81 **p** 82. NSM Bath Bathwick *B & W* from 81. *241 Bailbrook Lane, Bath* Bath (0225) 858936

DOUGLAS, John Howard Barclay. b 23. St Jo Coll Dur BA48. Bps' Coll Cheshunt 48. **d** 50 **p** 51. V Thirkleby w Kilburn and Bagby *York* 60-88; rtd 88. *6 St Giles Close, York Road, Thirsk, N Yorkshire YO7 3BU* Thirsk (0845) 524573

DOUGLAS, Martyn Graham. b 59. St Steph Ho Ox 85. **d** 88 **p** 89. C Stanmore *Win* from 88. *St Mark's House, Oliver's Battery Crescent, Winchester, Hants SO22 4EU* Winchester (0962) 861970

DOUGLAS, Robert Vernon. b 24. Pemb Coll Cam BA48 MA53. Wells Th Coll 48. **d** 50 **p** 51. C Worsley *Man* 50-53; C Brindle Heath 53-55; C Pendleton St Thos 53-55; PC Chatham St Phil and St Jas ED *Roch* 55-62; V Chatham St Phil and St Jas 62-65; R N Cray w Ruxley 66-80; V Platt from 80. *The Vicarage, Comp Lane, Sevenoaks, Kent TN15 8NR* Borough Green (0732) 885482

DOUGLAS-JONES, Ian Elliott. b 14. Trin Hall Cam BA35 MA39. Wycliffe Hall Ox 35. **d** 37 **p** 38. V Mayfield *Lich* 68-79; rtd 79; Perm to Offic *Worc* from 79. *32 Hanley Road, Malvern Wells, Worcester WR14 4PH* Malvern (0684) 575822

DOUGLASS, John Edward. b 20. St D Coll Lamp 60. **d** 62 **p** 63. R Llanddewi Skirrid w Llanvetherine etc *Mon* 66-70; V Newport H Trin and St Steph 70-76; V Trellech and Cwmcarvan 76-84; V Newport St Teilo 84-89; rtd 89. *16 Coulson Close, Newport, Gwent NP9 2QF* Newport (0633) 243162

DOUGLASS, Philip. b 48. Open Univ BA88. St Steph Ho Ox 87. **d** 89 **p** 90. C Peterlee *Dur* from 89. *27 St Leonard's Close, Peterlee, Co Durham SR8 2NW* 091-586 1018

DOULL, Iain Sinclair. b 43. Univ of Wales (Cardiff) DPS88. **d** 88 **p** 89. C Malpas *Mon* 88-91; P-in-c Newport All SS from 91. *The Vicarage, Brynglas Road, Newport, Gwent NP9 5QY* Newport (0633) 854657

DOULTON, Dick. b 32. St Cath Coll Cam BA60 MA64. Ridley Hall Cam 61. **d** 63 **p** 64. C Gedling *S'well* 63-65; C Danbury *Chelmsf* 65; Lic to Offic *Ox* from 88. *Thornton Hall, Thornton, Milton Keynes MK17 0HB* Buckingham (0280) 5272

DOVE, Reginald George James Thomas. b 16. Leeds Univ BA38. Coll of Resurr Mirfield 38. **d** 40 **p** 41. C Blyth St Mary *Newc* 40-43; S Africa from 43; rtd 88. *PO Box 2263, Edenvale, 1610 South Africa*

DOVER, Canon Oswald Leslie Simpson. b 18. Edin Th Coll 46. **d** 47 **p** 48. R Melrose *Edin* 59-85; Hon Can St Mary's Cathl from 77; rtd 85. *12 Shielswood Court, Tweedbank, Galashiels, Selkirkshire TD1 3RH* Galashiels (0896) 56946

DOVER, Suffragan Bishop of. See THIRD, Rt Rev Richard Henry McPhail

DOW, Andrew John Morrison. b 46. Univ Coll Ox BA67 MA71. Oak Hill Th Coll 69. **d** 71 **p** 72. C Watford St Luke *St Alb* 71-74; C Chadderton Ch Ch *Man* 75-78; V Leamington Priors St Paul *Cov* 78-88; V Knowle *Birm* from 88. *The Vicarage, 1811 Warwick Road, Knowle, Solihull, W Midlands B93 0DS* Knowle (0564) 773666

DOW, Canon Geoffrey Graham. b 42. Qu Coll Ox BA63 BSc65 MA68 Birm Univ DipTh74 Ox Univ MSc Nottm Univ MPhil82. Clifton Th Coll 66. **d** 67 **p** 68. C Tonbridge SS Pet and Paul *Roch* 67-72; Chapl St Jo Coll Ox 72-75; Lect St Jo Coll Nottm 75-81; V Cov H Trin *Cov* from 81; Can Th Cov Cathl from 88. *The Vicarage, 6 Davenport Road, Coventry CV5 6PY* Coventry (0203) 674996 or 220418

DOW, George Francis. b 11. ALCD32. **d** 34 **p** 35. V Manaccan w St Anthony-in-Meneage *Truro* 66-76; rtd 76; Perm to Offic *Ox* 76-86; *St Alb* from 86. *Stanstead Lodge, Stanstead Abbotts, Ware, Herts SG12 8LD* Roydon (027979) 2146

DOWD, Garfield George. b 60. QUB BSc TCD DipTh83. **d** 86 **p** 87. C Monkstown *D & G* 86-90; I Carlow w Urglin and Staplestown *C & O* from 90. *The School House, Green Road, Carlow, Irish Republic* Carlow (503) 32565

DOWDEN, Gordon Frederick. b 25. Selw Coll Cam BA51 MA55. Chich Th Coll 51. **d** 53 **p** 54. R Hulme St Phil *Man* 58-70; R Hulme Ascension 70-78; RD Hulme 73-78; P-in-c Holybourne cum Neatham *Win* 78-82; RD Alton 79-82; C Man Resurr *Man* 82; AD Ardwick 82-90; C Man Gd Shep 82-91; Chapl Ancoats Hosp Man 85-90; rtd 91. *41 Rozel Square, Manchester M3 4FQ* 061-832 5592

DOWDING, Edward Brinley. b 47. St Mich Coll Llan 70 St D Coll Lamp BA71. **d** 72 **p** 73. C Canton St Cath *Llan* 72-75; C Aberdare 75-78; V Aberavon H Trin 78-85; R Sully from 85. *The Rectory, 26 South Road, Sully, Penarth, S Glam CF6 2TG* Cardiff (0222) 530221

DOWDING, Jeremy Charles. b 51. **d** 91. C Newport St Steph and H Trin *Mon* from 91. *St John the Baptist's Vicarage, Upper Flat, Oakfield Road, Newport, Gwent NP9 4LP* Newport (0633) 221873

DOWDING, Stanley Frederick. b 10. ALCD32 St Jo Coll Dur BA33 LTh33. **d** 34 **p** 35. V Nelson in Lt Marsden *Blackb* 55-75; rtd 75; Lic to Offic *Blackb* from 76. *4 Hillside Avenue, Reedley, Burnley, Lancs BB10 2NF* Nelson (0282) 693030

DOWDLE, Miss Cynthia. b 48. Cranmer Hall Dur 88. **d** 90. C Allerton *Liv* from 90. *120 Abbottshey Avenue, Liverpool L18 7TJ* 051-724 1454

DOWELL, Graham Moffat. b 26. Magd Coll Cam BA48 MA53. Ely Th Coll 51. **d** 53 **p** 54. C Derby Cathl *Derby* 53-56; Chapl Derby Cathl 53-56; Cyprus 56-59; C Sheff St Geo and St Steph *Sheff* 59-63; Chapl Sheff Univ 59-63; Ethiopia 64-67; Zambia 68-70; Chapl Lon Univ *Lon* 70-74; V Hampstead St Jo 74-86; Perm to Offic *Heref* from 87. *Riversdale, 8 Bridge Street, Clun, Craven Arms, Shropshire* Clun (05884) 521

DOWLAND, Martin John. b 48. Lon Univ BD70 Southn Univ PGCE71. Wycliffe Hall Ox 75. **d** 77 **p** 78. C

Jesmond Clayton Memorial *Newc* 77-80; C Chadderton Ch Ch *Man* 80-85; R Haughton St Mary from 85. *Haughton Green Rectory, Meadow Lane, Denton, Manchester M34 1GD* 061-336 4529

DOWLEN, Edward Mark. b 25. DLC47 Cranfield Inst of Tech MSc49. St Jo Coll Dur 79. **d** 79 **p** 80. C Rhyl w Rhyl St Ann *St As* 79-82; C Warton St Paul *Blackb* 83-90; rtd 90; Lic to Offic *Sarum* from 90. *33 Hythe Road, Poole, Dorset BH15 3NN* Poole (0202) 737699

DOWLING, Donald Edward. b 43. St Jo Coll Dur DipTh74 St Andr Univ MA66. **d** 74 **p** 75. C Thame w Towersey *Ox* 74-77; C Norton *St Alb* 77-80; V Wilbury from 81. *Church House, 103 Bedford Road, Letchworth, Herts SG6 4DU* Letchworth (0462) 679236

DOWLING, Paul Martin. b 55. ACA G&C Coll Cam MA79. Cranmer Hall Dur 88. **d** 90 **p** 91. C Redhill St Jo *S'wark* from 90. *15 Earlsbrook Road, Redhill, Surrey RH1 6DR* Redhill (0737) 778834

DOWMAN, John Frederick. b 26. AKC52. **d** 53 **p** 54. C Frodingham *Linc* 53-55; C Clee 55-57; C Horncastle w Low Toynton 57-59; P-in-c S Kyme 59-64; V Legbourne w Lt Cawthorpe 64-81; R Muckton w Burwell and Walmsgate 64-81; P-in-c Withcall 79-81; P-in-c Tathwell w Haugham 79-81; V Legbourne from 81; R Raithby from 81. *The Vicarage, Legbourne, Louth, Lincs LN11 8LN* Louth (0507) 602535

DOWMAN, Peter Robert. b 52. City Univ BSc. Wycliffe Hall Ox 82. **d** 84 **p** 85. C Cheltenham Ch Ch *Glouc* 84-87; C Danbury *Chelmsf* 87-90; R Woodham Ferrers and Bicknacre from 90. *Church House, Main Road, Bicknacre, Chelmsford CM3 4HA* Danbury (024541) 4895

DOWN, Martin John. b 40. Jes Coll Cam BA62 MA68. Westcott Ho Cam 63. **d** 65 **p** 66. C Bury St Mary *Man* 65-68; C Leigh St Mary 68-70; R Fiskerton *Linc* 70-75; V Irnham w Corby 75-79; RD Beltisloe 76-84; P-in-c Creeton w Swinstead 78-79; P-in-c Swayfield 78-79; V Corby Glen 79-84; Good News Trust 84-88; Perm to Offic Linc 84-88; Pet 86-88; P-in-c Ashill w Saham Toney *Nor* from 88. *The Rectory, Ashill, Thetford, Norfolk IP25 7BT* Holme Hale (0760) 440247

DOWN, Peter Michael. b 54. K Coll Lon BD78 AKC. Coll of Resurr Mirfield 78. **d** 79 **p** 80. C Swindon Ch Ch *Bris* 79-82; C Southmead 82-84; TV Cannock *Lich* from 84. *St John's Vicarage, 226 Hednesford Road, Heath Hayes, Cannock, Staffs WS12 5DZ* Heath Hayes (0543) 278478

DOWN, Philip Roy. b 53. Melbourne Coll of Div MTh. **d** 89 **p** 89. C Gt Grimsby St Mary and St Jas *Linc* 89-91; TV from 91. *62A Brighowgate, Grimsby DN32 0QW* Grimsby (0472) 250877

DOWN, Canon Wilfred Samuel. b 26. Keble Coll Ox BA50 MA54. Linc Th Coll 50. **d** 51 **p** 52. R Monkton Farleigh w S Wraxall *Sarum* 69-76; TR Marlborough 76-91; Can and Preb Sarum Cathl 83-91; RD Marlborough 86-90; rtd 91. *14 Eyres Drive, Alderbury, Salisbury* Marlborough (0672) 512357

✠**DOWN, Rt Rev William John Denbigh.** b 34. St Jo Coll Cam BA57 MA61. Ridley Hall Cam 57. **d** 59 **p** 60 **c** 90. C Fisherton Anger *Sarum* 59-63; Miss to Seamen 63-90; Australia 71-74; Dep Gen Sec Miss to Seamen 75; Gen Sec 76-90; C St Mich Paternoster Royal *Lon* 76-90; Perm to Offic *St Alb* 78-90; Hon Can Gib Cathl *Eur* from 85; Hon Can Kobe Japan from 87; Bp Bermuda from 90. *Bishop's Lodge, PO Box HM 769, Hamilton HM CX, Bermuda* Bermuda (1809) 292-2967

DOWN AND DROMORE, Bishop of. See McMULLAN, Rt Rev Gordon

DOWN, Archdeacon of. See MOORE, Ven James Edward

DOWN, Dean of. See LECKEY, Very Rev Hamilton

DOWNER, Cuthbert John. b 18. S'wark Ord Course 60. **d** 74 **p** 75. Hon C Kirdford *Chich* 74-76; C Halesworth w Linstead and Chediston *St E* 76-79; P-in-c Knodishall w Buxlow 79-80; P-in-c Friston 79-80; R Bacton w Wyverstone 80-83; P-in-c Cotton and Wickham Skeith 80-83; R Bacton w Wyverstone and Cotton 83-84; rtd 84; Perm to Offic St E 84-87; B & W from 88. *Andros, 9 Little Orchard, Cheddar, Somerset BS27 3LS* Cheddar (0934) 744295

DOWNEY, John Stewart. b 38. QUB CertEd60 Open Univ BA76. Oak Hill Th Coll 63. **d** 66 **p** 67. C Londonderry St Aug *D & R* 66-71; I Dungiven w Bovevagh 71-82; Bp's Dom Chapl 75-82; V Bishopwearmouth St Gabr *Dur* 82-91; V New Malden and Coombe *S'wark* from 91. *The Vicarage, 93 Coombe Road, New Malden, Surrey KT3 4RE* 081-942 0915

DOWNHAM, Canon Peter Norwell. b 31. Man Univ BA52. Ridley Hall Cam 54. **d** 56 **p** 57. C Cheadle *Ches* 56-62; V Rawtenstall St Mary *Man* 62-68; Chapl Rossendale Gen Hosp from 62; V Denton Holme *Carl* 68-79; V

Reading Greyfriars *Ox* from 79; Can Ch Ch from 90. *Greyfriars Vicarage, 64 Friar Street, Reading RG1 1EH* Reading (0734) 573822

DOWNING, Edward Nalder. b 10. Worc Coll Ox BA33 MA36. Westcott Ho Cam 34. **d** 35 **p** 36. V Shaw *Man* 68-72; P-in-c Heaton Norris Ch Ch 72-75; rtd 75; Hon C Davyhulme Ch Ch *Man* 75-77; P-in-c Roslin (Rosslyn Chpl) *Edin* from 77. *St Matthew's House, 51 Moat View, Roslin, Midlothian EH25 9NZ* 031-440 1678

DOWNING, Francis Gerald. b 35. Qu Coll Ox BA56 MA60. Linc Th Coll. **d** 58 **p** 59. C Filwood Park CD *Bris* 58-60; Tutor Linc Th Coll 60-64; V Unsworth *Man* 64-80; Tutor N Ord Course 80-82; Vice-Prin 82-90; Lic to Offic *Man* 80-90; V Bolton SS Simon and Jude from 90. *The Vicarage, 15 Lowick Avenue, Bolton BL3 2DS* Bolton (0204) 23919

DOWNS, Miss Geinor. b 47. UEA BA72 Southn Univ BTh89. Chich Th Coll 85. **d** 87. Par Dn Wellingborough All SS *Pet* 87-89; Development Officer Chich Th Coll from 89. *The Theological College, Chichester, W Sussex PO19 3ES* Chichester (0243) 783369

DOWNS, Ivan Frederick. b 26. Chich Th Coll 65. **d** 66 **p** 67. C Corbridge w Halton *Newc* 66-70; C Tynemouth Ch Ch 70-74; V Walker 74-79; V Dudley 79-89; V Weetslade from 90. *The Vicarage, Dudley, Cramlington, Northd NE23 7HR* 091-250 0251

DOWNS, Thomas Greaves. b 19. BA. Qu Coll Birm 74. **d** 76 **p** 79. Hon C Tenbury *Heref* 76-78; C Crosthwaite Keswick *Carl* 79-81; Lic to Offic 81-83; Hon C Kirkland 83-84; Hon C Addingham, Edenhall, Langwathby and Culgaith from 85. *Woodlands, Edenhall, Penrith, Cumbria CA11 8SR* Penrith (0768) 63131

DOWSE, Edgar. b 10. Dur Univ LTh35 Lon Univ BD37 Fitzw Coll Cam BA72 MA74 Lon Univ MPhil90. Clifton Th Coll 32. **d** 35 **p** 36. St Dunstan-in-the-Wall Lon 70-71; V Acton Green St Alb *Lon* 72-75; rtd 75. *87 College Road, Isleworth, Middx TW7 5DP* 081-568 2548

DOWSE, Ivor Roy. b 35. St Deiniol's Hawarden 66. **d** 68 **p** 70. C Harrow St Pet *Lon* 68-69; C Sudbury St Andr 69-71; C Weeke *Win* 71-73; Min Can Ban Cathl *Ban* 73-78; V Hollym w Welwick and Holmpton *York* 78-81; R Bearwood *Ox* 81-82; P-in-c Rothesay *Arg* 83-86; C Boxmoor St Jo *St Alb* from 86. *23 Beechfield Road, Hemel Hempstead, Herts HP1 1PP* Hemel Hempstead (0442) 253102

DOWSETT, Alan Charles. b 27. Selw Coll Cam BA51 MA55 Bris Poly CQSW76. Cuddesdon Coll 51. **d** 53 **p** 54. C Stoke Bishop *Bris* 65-68; Lic to Offic from 69; rtd 89. *23 Upper Cranbrook Road, Bristol BS6 7UW* Bristol (0272) 243227

DOWSETT, Marian Ivy Rose. b 40. **d** 88. NSM Rumney *Mon* from 88. *114 Ridgeway Road, Rumney, Cardiff CF3 9AB* Cardiff (0222) 792635

DOWSON, Roger Christopher. b 32. Clifton Th Coll 60. **d** 63 **p** 64. C Virginia Water *Guildf* 63-66; C Darfield *Sheff* 66-68; V Thorpe Edge *Bradf* 68-80; V Wyke from 80. *The Vicarage, Vicarage Close, Wyke, Bradford, W Yorkshire BD12 8QW* Bradford (0274) 678216

DOXSEY, Roy Desmond. St D Coll Lamp 64. **d** 67 **p** 68. C Pemb St Mary and St Mich *St D* 67-70; C Milford Haven 70-73; C Loughton *Ox* 73-75; Chapl Llandovery Coll 75-81; Zambia 81-86; Chapl Epsom Coll Surrey from 86. *The Chaplain's Office, Epsom College, Epsom, Surrey KT17 4JQ* Epsom (03727) 21973 or 41863

DOYLE, Canon Alan Holland. b 22. JP. Lon Univ BD55 Birm Univ MA86. Wycliffe Hall Ox 52. **d** 52 **p** 53. R Salwarpe *Worc* 64-74; RD Droitwich 69-78; P-in-c Himbleton w Huddington 74-78; Hon Can Worc Cathl 74-87; P-in-c Ombersley w Doverdale 78-83; R 83-87; rtd 87. *3 Graham Court, Graham Road, Malvern, Worcs WR14 2HX* Malvern (0684) 892133

DOYLE, Canon Alfred Thomas Laurence. b 10. St Jo Coll Dur BA32 DipTh33 MA35. **d** 33 **p** 34. V Edgbaston SS Mary and Ambrose *Birm* 50-75; Hon Can Birm Cathl 69-75; rtd 75. *Norr Rock, The Cleave, Kingsand, Plymouth PL10 1NF* Plymouth (0752) 822944

DOYLE, Andrew Michael. b 63. K Coll Lon BD85 AKC85. Ripon Coll Cuddesdon 86. **d** 88 **p** 89. C Lytchett Minster *Sarum* from 88. *15 Guest Road, Poole, Dorset BH16 5LQ* Poole (0202) 623637

DOYLE, Graham Thomas. b 48. Worc Coll Ox BA85 MA90. St Barn Coll Adelaide ThL73 ThSchol77. **d** 73 **p** 74. Australia 73-83; Perm to Offic *Ox* 83-85; C Cobbold Road St Sav w St Mary *Lon* 86; P-in-c Bradf St Oswald Chapel Green *Bradf* 86-91; Chapl Belgrade w Zagreb *Eur* from 91. *The Chaplain's Flat, Generale*

Zdanova 46, 11000 Belgrade, Yugoslavia Belgrade (11) 660186

DOYLE, Robin Alfred. b 43. Dur Univ BA65. Westcott Ho Cam 66. **d** 68 **p** 69. C Edgbaston St Geo *Birm* 68-70; C Erdington St Barn 70-73; P-in-c Oldbury 73-81; V Maker w Rame *Truro* from 81. *The Vicarage, Fore Street, Torpoint, Cornwall PL10 1NB* Plymouth (0752) 822302

DOYLE, William. b 31. RMN61. Sarum Th Coll 87. **d** 87 **p** 88. NSM Heene *Chich* 87-91; Chapl Qu Alexandra's Hosp Worthing 89-91; Chapl Gifford Ho Chich 89-91; C W Tarring *Chich* from 91. *6 Lansdowne Court, Lansdowne Road, Worthing, W Sussex BN11 5HD* Worthing (0903) 40149

DRACKLEY, John Oldham. b 36. Em Coll Cam BA57 MA61. Wells Th Coll 57. **d** 59 **p** 60. C Eckington *Derby* 59-62; C Lee Gd Shep w St Pet *S'wark* 62-63; C Derby St Thos *Derby* 63-67; C Matlock and Tansley 67-77; P-in-c Radbourne 77-82; P-in-c Dalbury, Long Lane and Trusley 77-82; P-in-c Longford 77-82; Sec Dioc Cttee for Care of Chs from 82. *The Vicarage, Turnditch, Derby DE5 2LH* Cowers Lane (077389) 357

DRAFFAN, Prof Ian William. b 42. FBCS77 CEng88 Aston Univ BSc65 MSc66. N Ord Course 83. **d** 86 **p** 87. NSM Millhouses H Trin *Sheff* from 86. *8 Silverdale Crescent, Sheffield S11 9JH* Sheffield (0742) 720911

DRAIN, Walter. b 39. ACP66 Open Univ BA76. NW Ord Course 76. **d** 79 **p** 80. NSM Cheadle *Ches* 79-81; C 81-84; V Chatburn *Blackb* from 84. *The Vicarage, Chatburn, Clitheroe, Lancs BB7 4AA* Clitheroe (0200) 41317

DRAKE, Graham. b 46. Linc Th Coll 81. **d** 83 **p** 85. C Alford w Rigsby *Linc* 83-84; Perm to Offic *Wakef* 84-85; Hon C Purston cum S Featherstone 85-89; NSM Castleford All SS from 89. *8A Broomhill, Castleford, W Yorkshire WF10 4QP* Castleford (0977) 518407

DRAKE, Graham Rae. b 45. Fitzw Coll Cam BA68 MA72. Qu Coll Birm 70. **d** 73 **p** 74. C New Windsor *Ox* 73-77; TV 77-78; P-in-c Bath Ascension *B & W* 78-81; TV Bath Twerton-on-Avon 81-86; P-in-c Buxton w Oxnead *Nor* 86-90; P-in-c Lammas w Lt Hautbois 86-90; RD Ingworth from 88; R Buxton w Oxnead, Lammas and Brampton from 90. *The Vicarage, Buxton, Norwich NR10 5HD* Buxton (0603) 279394

DRAKE, John Paul. b 19. Qu Coll Ox BA41 MA44. Cuddesdon Coll 46. **d** 47 **p** 48. V Stewkley *Ox* 69-75; V Stewkley w Soulbury and Drayton Parslow 75-85; RD Mursley 77-83; rtd 85; Perm to Offic *St Alb* from 85. *3 The Cloisters, Welwyn Garden City, Herts AL8 6DU* Welwyn Garden (0707) 325379

DRAKE, Leslie Sargent. b 47. Boston Univ BA69 MTh72 Hull Univ BPhil74. Coll of Resurr Mirfield 78. **d** 78 **p** 79. C Oldham *Man* 78-81; TV Rochdale 81-83; V Palmers Green St Jo *Lon* 83-89; St Mary's Sch Cheshunt from 89. *29 Arundel Gardens, London N21* 081-886 9104

DRAKE-BROCKMAN, Archibald David. b 12. Magd Coll Cam BA34 MA37. Ely Th Coll 35. **d** 36 **p** 37. C Ox St Mary V *Ox* 36; Lic to Offic 36-39; Chapl Bradfield Coll Berks 38-41; Asst Master 41-48; V Framfield *Chich* 48-49; Chapl Bedf Sch 49-65; Lic to Offic *St E* 70-79; Perm to Offic from 79. *Rosemary Cottage, Grundisburgh, Woodbridge, Suffolk IP13 6RA* Grundisburgh (047335) 449

DRAKELEY, Stephen Richard Francis. b 51. Aston Univ BSc73. Chich Th Coll 76. **d** 76 **p** 77. C Yardley Wood *Birm* 76-79; V Rednal 79-89; TV Bodmin w Lanhydrock and Lanivet *Truro* from 89. *The Vicarage, Rectory Road, Lanivet, Bodmin, Cornwall PL30 5HG* Bodmin (0208) 831743

DRAPER, Ven Alfred James. b 23. Natal Univ BA50. St Aug Coll Cant DipTh59 St Paul's Grahamstown LTh54. **d** 54 **p** 54. S Africa 54-63 and 75-87; V Tile Cross *Birm* 63-72; V Olton 72-75; Adn Durban 79-87; R S Ferriby *Linc* from 87; V Horkstow from 87; R Saxby All Saints from 87. *The Rectory, Main Street, Saxby-All-Saints, Brigg, S Humberside DN20 0QF* Saxby-All-Saints (065261) 747

DRAPER, Charles. b 59. Dur Univ BSc80 Cam Univ BA86. Ridley Hall Cam 84. **d** 87 **p** 88. C Wareham *Sarum* 87-90; C Maltby *Sheff* from 90. *86 Braithwell Road, Maltby, Rotherham, S Yorkshire S66 8JT* Rotherham (0709) 817152

DRAPER, Derek Vincent. b 38. Linc Th Coll 65. **d** 68 **p** 69. C Orpington All SS *Roch* 68-72; C Bramley *Guildf* 72-74; P-in-c Kempston *St Alb* 74-76; Min Kempston Transfiguration CD 77-79; V Kempston Transfiguration 79-84; RD Bedf 79-84; V Bromham w Oakley 84-88; P-in-c Stagsden 84-88; V Bromham w Oakley and Stagsden from 88; Chapl Bromham Hosp from 84.

The Vicarage, 47 Stagsden Road, Bromham, Bedford MK43 8PY Oakley (02302) 3268

DRAPER, Miss Elizabeth Ann. *See* BRADLEY, Mrs Elizabeth Ann

DRAPER, Dr Ivan Thomas. b 32. FRCP FRCPGlas Aber Univ MB, ChB56. St Jo Coll Nottm 87. **d** 90 **p** 91. NSM Glas St Bride *Glas* from 90. *13/1 Whistlefield Court, 2 Canniesburn Road, Bearsden, Glasgow G61 1PX* 041-943 0954

DRAPER, Jack William. b 18. Oak Hill Th Coll 51. **d** 53 **p** 54. R Bramerton w Surlingham *Nor* 62-70; RD Loddon 71-75; P-in-c Hoxne w Denham St Jo *St E* 75-79; P-in-c Hoxne w Denham St Jo and Syleham 79-80; V 80-84; rtd 84; Lic to Offic *St E* 84-85; Hon C Yoxford from 85. *52 Pier Avenue, Southwold, Suffolk IP18 6BO* Southwold (0502) 722810

DRAPER, Jean Margaret. b 31. **d** 80. NSM Llanfrechfa Upper *Mon* 80-83; BRF from 82; NSM Llantillio Pertholey w Bettws Chpl etc *Mon* from 83. *Govilon House, Govilon, Abergavenny, Gwent* Abergavenny (0873) 830380

DRAPER, John William. b 54. Aston Tr Scheme 86 Qu Coll Birm 88. **d** 90 **p** 91. C Stepney St Dunstan and All SS *Lon* from 90. *St Faith's House, Shandy Street, London E1 4ST* 071-790 9961

DRAPER, Jonathan Lee. b 52. Gordon Coll Mass BA76 St Jo Coll Dur BA78 PhD84. Ripon Coll Cuddesdon 83. **d** 83 **p** 84. C Baguley *Man* 83-85; Dir of Academic Studies Ripon Coll Cuddesdon from 85. *3 Church Close, Cuddesdon, Oxford OX9 9HD* Wheatley (08677) 4310

DRAPER, Martin Paul. b 50. Birm Univ BTh79 Southn Univ BTh79. Chich Th Coll 72. **d** 75 **p** 76. C Primrose Hill St Mary w Avenue Road St Paul *Lon* 75-78; C Westmr St Matt 79-84; Chapl Paris St Geo *Eur* from 84. *7 rue Auguste-Vacquerie, 75116 Paris, France* Paris (331) 47 20 22 51

DRAPER, Paul Richard. b 64. Glas Univ MA87 TCD BTh90. **d** 90 **p** 91. C Drumragh w Mountfield *D & R* from 90. *3 Anderson Gardens, Omagh, Co Tyrone BT78 1HY* Omagh (0662) 247200

DRAPER, Raymond James. b 48. Ex Coll Ox BA70 MA75 Em Coll Cam BA73 MA78. Ridley Hall Cam 71. **d** 74 **p** 75. C Sheff Manor *Sheff* 74-78; Ind Chapl 78-82; R Wickersley from 82. *The Rectory, Church Lane, Wickersley, Rotherham, S Yorkshire S66 0ES* Rotherham (0709) 543111

DRAPER, Sylvia Edith. b 39. ARCM60. Nor Ord Course 86. **d** 89. C Aughton St Mich *Liv* from 89. *6 Brookfield Lane, Aughton, Ormskirk, Lancs L39 6SP* Aughton Green (0695) 422138

DRAY, Robert William. b 30. Wells Th Coll 62. **d** 64 **p** 65. C Bushey Heath *St Alb* 64-68; C-in-c Marsh Farm CD 68-71; V Hatf Hyde St Mary 71-86; Chapl Hastings HA from 86; Chapl R E Sussex Hosp Hastings from 86. *Royal East Sussex Hospital, Cambridge Road, Hastings, E Sussex TN34 1LY* Hastings (0424) 434513

DRAYCOTT, Christopher John Philip. b 55. Cuddesdon Coll 77. **d** 79 **p** 80. C Horninglow *Lich* 79-82; C Tividale 82-85; V Willenhall St Anne from 85. *St Anne's Vicarage, Ann Street, Willenhall, W Midlands WV13 1EN* Willenhall (0902) 66516

DRAYCOTT, John. b 53. Sheff Univ BA84 DCEd82. Br Nazarene Coll DipTh77 Linc Th Coll 85. **d** 85 **p** 86. In Wesleyan Reform Ch 77-82; C Wombwell *Sheff* 85-87; V V Bessacarr from 87. *39 Sturton Close, West Bessacarr, Doncaster, S Yorkshire DN4 7JG* Doncaster (0302) 538487

DRAYCOTT, Philip John. b 27. Sarum & Wells Th Coll. **d** 83 **p** 84. C Bishop's Cleeve *Glouc* 83-86; V Chedworth, Yanworth and Stowell, Coln Rogers etc from 86. *The Vicarage, Chedworth, Cheltenham, Glos GL54 4AE* Fossebridge (028572) 392

DRAYTON, James Edward. b 30. St Deiniol's Hawarden 81. **d** 84 **p** 86. Hon C Heald Green St Cath *Ches* 84-88; C Bollington St Jo from 88. *5 Sandy Close, Bollington, Macclesfield, Cheshire SK10 5DT* Bollington (0625) 572856

DREDGE, David John. b 32. Cranmer Hall Dur 69. **d** 71 **p** 72. C Goole *Sheff* 71-74; P-in-c Eastoft 74-77; V Whitgift w Adlingfleet 74-77; V Whitgift w Adlingfleet and Eastoft 77-78; V Walkley 78-81; TV Bicester w Bucknell, Caversfield and Launton *Ox* 81-86; V N Brickhill and Putnoe *St Alb* 86-90; P-in-c Sarratt from 90. *The Rectory, The Green, Sarratt, Rickmansworth, Herts WD3 6BP* Rickmansworth (0923) 264377

DREDGE, David Julian. b 36. ALA74 Sheff Univ BA59. Cranmer Hall Dur 61 Ban Ord Course 85. **d** 87 **p** 88. NSM Penmaenmawr *Ban* from 87. *Westfield, Treforris*

Road, Dwygyfylchi, Penmaenmawr, Gwynedd LL34 6RH Penmaenmawr (0492) 623439

DREW, Emlyn Floyd. b 06. Lich Th Coll. **d** 57 **p** 57. V Branscombe Ex 68-71; rtd 71; Perm to Offic Ex from 84. 3 James Close, Elburton, Plymouth PL9 8PX Plymouth (0752) 401411

DREW, Gerald Arthur. b 36. Bps' Coll Cheshunt 59. **d** 61 **p** 62. C Lyonsdown H Trin St Alb 61-67; C Tring 67-71; R Bramfield w Stapleford and Waterford 71-78; V Langleybury St Paul 78-90; P-in-c Hormead, Wyddial, Anstey, Brent Pelham etc from 90. The Vicarage, Great Hormead, Buntingford, Herts SG9 0NT Great Hormead (076389) 258

DREW, John Whatley. b 24. CCC Cam BA54 MA58. Kelham Th Coll 46. **d** 51 **p** 52. C Cam St Andr Gt Ely 51-54; C Northolt Park St Barn Lon 54-57; C Bethnal Green St Jas the Gt w St Jude 57-60; V Thorington w Wenhaston St E 60-76; V Wenhaston w Thorington and Bramfield w Walpole 76; V Leiston 76-82; Chapl St Audry's Hosp Melton 82-89; P-in-c Ufford St E 82-91; P-in-c Bredfield w Boulge 86-91; P-in-c Hasketon 89-91; R Ufford w Bredfield and Hasketon from 91. The Rectory, Ufford, Woodbridge, Suffolk IP13 6DS Eyke (0394) 460455

DREW, Joseph Harold. b 09. St D Coll Lamp BA30. St Mich Coll Llan 30. **d** 32 **p** 33. Chapl and Sec Pris Chapl Coun 64-74; Asst Chapl Gen of Pris 64-74; rtd 74; Perm to Offic S'wark from 82. 58 Cambridge Drive, London SE12 8AJ 081-852 8031

DREW, Michael Edgar Cecil. b 31. Or Coll Ox BA55 MA59. St Steph Ho Ox 55. **d** 57 **p** 58. C Plymouth St Pet Ex 57-63; Missr Pemb Coll Cam Miss Walworth 63-67; Asst Chapl All Hallows Sch Rousdon 67-75; Chapl 80-81; Lic to Offic Ex 76-83; Chapl Ex Sch 81-83; V Hungarton Leic 83-87; V Scraptoft from 83; P-in-c Leic St Eliz Nether Hall from 87. The Vicarage, Scraptoft, Leicester LE7 9ST Leicester (0533) 412318

DREWETT, Canon Mervyn Henry. b 27. Wadh Coll Ox BA50 MA53. Linc Th Coll 52. **d** 54 **p** 55. C Filwood Park CD Bris 54-58; C Bishopston 58-61; V Brislington St Chris 61-67; V Henbury 67-80; RD Westbury and Severnside 79-80; Hon Can Bris Cathl from 80; TR Gtr Corsham from 80; RD Chippenham 82-88. The Rectory, Lacock Road, Corsham, Wilts SN13 9HS Corsham (0249) 713232

DREWETT, Robert John. b 40. Ripon Hall Ox 64. **d** 66 **p** 67. C Fishponds St Jo Bris 66-70; C Oldland 70-74; P-in-c Coalpit Heath 74-76; TV Cannock Lich from 90; Chapl Chase Hosp Cannock from 90. St Chad's Vicarage, Cannock Road, Chadsmoor, Cannock, Staffs WS11 2TH Cannock (05435) 79381

DREYER, Rodney Granville. b 55. **d** 81 **p** 82. NSM Northolt St Mary Lon 86-87; C Portsea St Mary Portsm 87-90; V Sudbury St Andr Lon from 90. St Andrew's Vicarage, 956 Harrow Road, Wembley, Middx HA0 2QA 081-904 4016

DRINKWATER, Frank. b 10. K Coll Lon BSc32 AKC34. **d** 34 **p** 35. C Earley St Pet Ox 69-72; V Coley Wakef 72-77; rtd 77; Perm to Offic Glouc from 78. 11 Lawn Crescent, Shurdington, Cheltenham, Glos GL51 5UR Cheltenham (0242) 862684

DRISCOLL, David. b 42. Lon Univ BSc64 Nottm Univ DipTh69. Linc Th Coll 68. **d** 71 **p** 72. C Walthamstow St Jo Chelmsf 71-76; Chapl NE Lon Poly 71-79; C-in-c Plaistow St Mary 76-79; P-in-c Stratford St Jo and Ch Ch w Forest Gate St Jas 79-89; V Theydon Bois from 89. The Vicarage, 2 Piercing Hill, Theydon Bois, Epping, Essex CM16 7JN Theydon Bois (0992) 814725

DRISCOLL, Edward Llewellyn. b 09. Kelham Th Coll 33. **d** 38 **p** 39. V Fairhaven Blackb 67-74; rtd 75; Lic to Offic Blackb from 75. 32 Ashley Road, Lytham St Annes, Lancs FY8 3AS St Annes (0253) 727026

DRIVER, Anthony. b 28. Chich Th Coll 76. **d** 76 **p** 77. Prec Gib Cathl Eur 76-78; C Harton Dur 78-82; V Tow Law 82-91; rtd 91. 34 Minster Avenue, Long Lane, Beverley, N Humberside HU17 0NL Hull (0482) 864448

DRIVER, Arthur John Roberts. b 44. SS Coll Cam MA70 Nottm Univ DipTh75. Linc Th Coll 74. **d** 76 **p** 77. C S'wark H Trin w St Matt S'wark 76-80; TV N Lambeth 80-85; CMS from 85; Sri Lanka from 86. 368/1 Bauddhaloka Mawatha, Colombo 7, Sri Lanka

DRIVER, Bruce Leslie. b 42. Lon Univ LLB73 Nottm Univ DipTh77. Linc Th Coll 76. **d** 78 **p** 79. C Dunstable St Alb 78-81; TV 81-86; V Rickmansworth from 86; RD Rickmansworth from 91. The Vicarage, Bury Lane, Rickmansworth, Herts WD3 1BS Rickmansworth (0923) 772627

DRIVER, Geoffrey. b 41. Chich Th Coll 86. **d** 88 **p** 89. C Pontefract St Giles Wakef 88-91; V Glasshoughton from

91. The Vicarage, Churchfield Lane, Glasshoughton, Castleford, W Yorkshire WF10 4BW Castleford (0977) 551031

DRIVER, Geoffrey Lester. b 59. Liv Poly BA83. Chich Th Coll 86. **d** 89 **p** 90. C Walton St Mary Liv from 89. The Rectory Flat, Walton Rectory, Liverpool L4 6TJ 051-523 0683

DRIVER, Penelope May. b 52. N Ord Course. **d** 87. Dioc Youth Adv Newc 86-88; C Cullercoats St Geo 87-88; Youth Chapl Ripon from 88; Dioc Adv Women's Min from 91. 7 Loxley Grove, Wetherby, W Yorkshire LS22 4YG Wetherby (0937) 65440

DRIVER, Roger John. b 64. Trin Coll Bris BA88. **d** 90 **p** 91. C Much Woolton Liv from 90. 46 Linkstor Road, Liverpool L25 6DH 051-428 3339

DRIVER, Canon Stuart Clare. b 15. Ch Coll Cam BA37 MA41. Ridley Hall Cam 37. **d** 38 **p** 39. V Werneth Man 45-80; Hon Can Man Cathl 76-80; RD Oldham 76-80; rtd 80; Perm to Offic Ches and Man from 80. 9 Brookside Lane, High Lane, Stockport, Cheshire SK6 8HL Disley (0663) 2263

DROMORE, Archdeacon of. See NEILL, Ven William Barnet

DROMORE, Dean of. See WILSON, Very Rev Mervyn Robert

DROWLEY, Arthur. b 28. Oak Hill Th Coll 54. **d** 56 **p** 57. C Longfleet Sarum 56-59; C Wallington H Trin S'wark 59-62; V Taunton St Jas B & W 62-73; RD Taunton N 72-73; V Rodbourne Cheney Bris 73-87; R Bigbury, Ringmore and Kingston Ex from 87. The Rectory, Ringmore, Kingsbridge, Devon TQ7 4HR Bigbury-on-Sea (0548) 810565

DROWN, Richard. b 19. BNC Ox BA41 MA43. Wycliffe Hall Ox 41. **d** 42 **p** 43. Kenya 65-73; Hd Master Edin Ho Sch New Milton 73-84; rtd 84; Hon C Brockenhurst Win from 85. Milton Lodge, Ossemsley South Drive, New Milton, Hants BH25 5TN New Milton (0425) 614480

DRUCE, Brian Lemuel. b 31. ARICS55. Bps' Coll Cheshunt 58. **d** 60 **p** 61. C Whitton St Aug Lon 60-63; C Minehead B & W 63-66; R Birch St Agnes Man 66-70; V Overbury w Alstone, Teddington and Lt Washbourne Worc 70-81; Ind Chapl 81-91. Park Cottage, Elmley Castle, Pershore, Worcs WR10 3HU Elmley Castle (038674) 577

DRUCE, John Perry. b 34. ALCM86 Em Coll Cam BA57 MA61. Wycliffe Hall Ox 57. **d** 59 **p** 60. C Wednesbury St Bart Lich 59-62; C Bushbury 62-64; V Walsall Wood 64-74; R Farnborough Roch 74-87; R E Bergholt St E from 87. The Rectory, White Horse Road, Colchester CO7 6TR Colchester (0206) 298076

DRUMMOND, Canon Christopher John Vaughan. b 26. Magd Coll Ox BA51 MA51. Ridley Hall Cam 51. **d** 53 **p** 54. C Barking St Marg Chelmsf 53-56; Tutor Ridley Hall Cam 56-59; Lic to Offic Ely 57-62; Chapl Clare Coll Cam 59-62; Nigeria 63-69; V Walthamstow St Jo Chelmsf 69-74; P-in-c Stantonbury Ox 74-75; R 75-84; P-in-c Ducklington 84-88; Dioc Ecum Officer 84-88; Can Ibadan from 87; Home Sec Gen Syn Bd for Miss and Unity 88-91; Can for Chr Unity from 91. 28 Westfield, The Marld, Ashtead, Surrey KT21 1RH Ashtead (0372) 277031

DRUMMOND, John Malcolm. b 44. Nottm Univ CertEd65. Edin Th Coll 68. **d** 71 **p** 72. C Kirkholt Man 71-74; C Westleigh St Pet 74-76; Hd of RE Leigh High Sch from 76; Lic to Offic 76-84; Hon C Leigh St Jo from 84. 14 Bull's Head Cottages, Turton, Bolton BL7 0HS Bolton (0204) 852232

DRUMMOND, Josceline Maurice Vaughan. b 29. Lon Univ DipTh58 BD70. Wycliffe Hall Ox. **d** 58 **p** 59. C Tunbridge Wells St Jo Roch 58-60; C Walthamstow St Mary Chelmsf 60-62; V Oulton Lich 62-68; V Leyton St Cath Chelmsf 71-85; Gen Dir CMJ from 85. 30C Clarence Road, St Albans, Herts AL1 4JJ St Albans (0727) 33114

DRURY, Esmond Peter. b 24. Sheff Univ BSc43 Newc Univ DipEd64. Coll of Resurr Mirfield 47. **d** 49 **p** 50. Min Hackenthorpe Ch Ch CD Derby 57-60. 74 Beach Road, North Shields, Tyne & Wear NE30 2QW 091-257 4350

DRURY, John Henry. b 36. Trin Hall Cam BA61. Westcott Ho Cam 61. **d** 63 **p** 64. C St Jo Wood Lon 63-66; Chapl Down Coll Cam 66-69; Chapl Ex Coll Ox 69-73; Can Res Nor Cathl Nor 73-79; Vice-Dean 78-79; Lect Sussex Univ 79-81; Dean and Chapl K Coll Cam 81-91; Dean Ch Ch Ox from 91. Christ Church College, Oxford Oxford (0865) 276150

DRURY, Michael Dru. b 31. Trin Coll Ox BA55 MA59 DipTh57. Wycliffe Hall Ox 56. **d** 58 **p** 59. C Fulham St

Mary N End *Lon* 58-62; C Blackheath St Jo *S'wark* 62-64; Asst Chapl Canford Sch Wimborne 64-72; Chapl 72-80; Chapl Fernhill Manor Sch New Milton 80-81; P-in-c Stowe *Ox* from 82; Asst Master Stowe Sch Bucks from 82. *Stowe Vicarage, Dadford, Buckingham MK18 5JX* Buckingham (0280) 812285

DRURY, Thomas Frank. b 06. Westcott Ho Cam. **d** 45 **p** 46. P-in-c Nor St Laur w St Greg *Nor* 66-75; V Nor St Giles 64-76; rtd 76; Perm to Offic *Nor* 77-78; Chapl St Nic Hosp Gt Yarmouth from 76; Hon C Gt Yarmouth from 90. *Flat 24, The Lawns, 55 Caister Road, Great Yarmouth NR30 4DQ* Great Yarmouth (0493) 842199

DRURY, William. b 30. Qu Coll Cam BA53 MA56. Trin Coll Toronto STB61. **d** 61 **p** 61. Canada 61-66; C Ashford *Cant* 66-70; V Milton next Sittingbourne from 70. *The Vicarage, Vicarage Road, Milton Regis, Sittingbourne, Kent ME10 2BL* Sittingbourne (0795) 72016

DRY, John Malcolm. b 24. Ely Th Coll 53. **d** 55 **p** 56. C Bourne *Guildf* 67-71; V Andover St Mich *Win* 71-74; P-in-c Knights Enham 74-76; R 76-79; P-in-c Hatherden cum Tangley 79-81; P-in-c Weyhill cum Penton Newsey 79-81; P-in-c Hatherden w Tangley, Weyhill and Penton Mewsey 81-83; C Headbourne Worthy 83-89; C King's Worthy 83-89; rtd 89. *12 Bunton Road, Herestock, Winchester, Hants SO22 6HX* Winchester (0962) 885168

DRYDEN, Canon Leonard. b 29. MIEE59 MIMechE59 Lon Univ BD64 Bath Univ MSc73. Ridley Hall Cam. **d** 61 **p** 62. C-in-c Bedminster *Bris* 65-74; Bp's Soc and Ind Adv 65-74; Chapl Bris Cathl 66-70; Hon Can Bris Cathl 70-74; Dir CORAT 74-76; Sec from 76; Team Ldr and Convener Lon Ind Chapl *Lon* 77-85; V Frindsbury w Upnor *Roch* 85-91; rtd 91; P-in-c Sevenoaks Weald *Roch* from 91. *The Vicarage, Weald, Sevenoaks, Kent TN14 6LT* Sevenoaks (0732) 61035

DRYE, Douglas John. b 37. Man Univ BSc61. Clifton Th Coll. **d** 63 **p** 64. C Whalley Range St Edm *Man* 63-66; C Drypool St Columba w St Andr and St Pet *York* 66-68; V Worsbrough Common *Sheff* 68-86; R Armthorpe from 86. *The Rectory, Church Street, Armthorpe, Doncaster, S Yorkshire DN3 3AD* Doncaster (0302) 831231

du HEAUME, Cecil Cabot. b 04. Keble Coll Ox BA29 MA40. Wycliffe Hall Ox 27. **d** 31 **p** 32. Sec Leprosy Miss (Ireland) 56-74; P-in-c Glympton *Ox* 74-80; rtd 80; Perm to Offic *Mon* from 80. *Hillgrove, Rockfield, Monmouth, Gwent NP5 4EZ* Monmouth (0600) 713806

du PRE, Wilfrid de Vaumorel. b 04. St Paul's Coll Mauritius LTh30. **d** 28 **p** 30. Hon C Northwood Hills St Edm *Lon* 61-72; rtd 72; Perm to Offic *Chelmsf* from 72. *Abbeyfield House, 90 Herman Hill, London E18 1QB* 081-518 8722

DUBLIN, Archbishop of and Bishop of Glendalough. *See* CAIRD, Most Rev Donald Arthur Richard

DUBLIN, Archdeacon of. *See* LINNEY, Ven Gordon Charles Scott

DUBLIN (Christ Church), Dean of. *See* PATERSON, Very Rev John Thomas Farquhar

DUBLIN (St Patrick's), Dean of. *Vacant*

DUCE, Alan Richard. b 41. St Pet Coll Ox BA65 MA68. Cuddesdon Coll 65. **d** 67 **p** 68. C Harrow St Mary *Lon* 67-71; Chapl St Geo Hosp Gp *Lon* 71-75; Chapl HM Pris Pentonville 75-76; The Verne 76-81; Chapl HM Pris Linc from 81. *The Chaplain's Office, HM Prison, Greetwell Road, Lincoln LN2 4BD* Lincoln (0522) 533633

DUCKER, Vere Townshend. b 04. Wadh Coll Ox BA26 MA30. Wycliffe Hall Ox 27. **d** 28 **p** 29. R Hanborough *Ox* 61-66; Perm to Offic *Guildf* from 66; rtd 69; Perm to Offic *Chich* from 69. *Paddock Corner, Farnham Lane, Haslemere, Surrey GU27 1HB* Haslemere (0428) 2827

DUCKETT, Brian John. b 45. ALCD70. **d** 70 **p** 71. C S Lambeth St Steph *S'wark* 70-73; C Norwood 73-75; C Bushbury *Lich* 75-77; TV 77-79; V Dover St Martin *Cant* from 79. *St Martin's Vicarage, 339 Folkestone Road, Dover, Kent CT17 9JG* Dover (0304) 205391

DUCKETT, Edward. b 36. Keble Coll Ox BA59 MA61. Cuddesdon Coll 59. **d** 61 **p** 62. C Portsea St Cuth *Portsm* 61-65; C Rotherham *Sheff* 65-68; Lic to Offic *Portsm* 68-69; Hon Chapl Portsm Cathl 69-75; Perm to Offic *Ely* 75-82; R Rampton 82-89; R Willingham 82-89; RD N Stowe 86-89; P-in-c Ramsey 89-90; P-in-c Upwood w Gt and Lt Raveley 89-90; TR The Ramseys and Upwood from 90; RD St Ives from 89. *The Rectory, Hollow Lane, Ramsey, Huntingdon, Cambs PE17 1DE* Ramsey (0487) 813271

DUCKETT, John Dollings. b 41. Nottm Univ BA62 BTh81. Linc Th Coll 79. **d** 81 **p** 82. C Boston *Linc* 81-84; V Baston 84-86; V Langtoft Gp 86-88; V Sutterton and Wigtoft 88-89; R Sutterton w Fosdyke and Algarkirk from 89. *The Vicarage, Sutterton, Boston, Lincs PE20 2JH* Boston (0205) 460285

DUCKWORTH, Capt Brian George. b 47. CA79. Edin Th Coll 85. **d** 87 **p** 88. C Sutton in Ashfield St Mary *S'well* from 87; C Sutton in Ashfield St Mich from 89. *St Michael's Vicarage, Deepdale Gardens, Sutton-in-Ashfield, Notts NG17 2AQ* Mansfield (0623) 555031

DUCKWORTH, Derek. b 29. Fitzw Ho Cam BA52 MA58 Lon Univ PGCE66 Lanc Univ PhD72. Oak Hill Th Coll 52. **d** 54 **p** 55. C Preston All SS *Blackb* 54-57; C Sutton *Liv* 57-58; Hon C Wakef St Jo *Wakef* 58-60; Public Preacher *Blackb* 60-64; C Whalley 64-73; Hon C Newbury *Ox* 73-80; Perm to Offic *Ox* 80-81; Cant 81-84 and 85-86; P-in-c Dymchurch w Burmarsh and Newchurch *Cant* 84-85; Chapl Leybourne Grange Hosp W Malling 85-86; P-in-c Rampton w Laneham, Treswell, Cottam and Stokeham *S'well* 86-89; R from 89. *The Vicarage, Rampton, Retford, Notts DN22 0HR* Rampton (077784) 8143

DUDDING, Edward Leslie (Father Superior Gregory). b 30. Auckland Univ MSc52 St Jo Coll Auckland LTh56. **d** 57 **p** 57. New Zealand 57-60; Lic to Offic *Chich* from 62; CSWG from 62; Father Superior from 73. *The Monastery, Crawley Down, Crawley, W Sussex RH10 4LH* Copthorne (0342) 712074

DUDLEY, Harold George. b 14. St Mich Coll Llan 68. **d** 70 **p** 70. C Fleur-de-Lis *Mon* 70-73; V Goldcliffe and Whiston and Nash 73-83; rtd 83; Lic to Offic *Mon* from 83. *4 St Stephen's Close, Caerwent, Newport, Gwent NP6 4JJ* Caldicot (0291) 421951

DUDLEY, Mrs Janet Carr. b 36. E Midl Min Tr Course 86. **d** 89. Hon C Countesthorpe w Foston *Leic* from 89. *31 Westfield Avenue, Countesthorpe, Leicester LE8 3PL* Leicester (0533) 772109

DUDLEY, John Rea. b 31. Pemb Coll Cam BA54 MA58. St Steph Ho Ox. **d** 57 **p** 58. C Kennington St Jo *S'wark* 57-61; C Merstham and Gatton 61-68; V N Gosforth *Newc* 68-79; RD Newc Cen 77-82; V Newc St Jo from 79. *St John's Vicarage, 5 Summerhill Grove, Newcastle upon Tyne NE4 6EE* 091-232 7194

DUDLEY, Martin Raymond. b 53. K Coll Lon BD77 AKC77 MTh78 DPS79. St Mich Coll Llan 78. **d** 79 **p** 80. C Whitchurch *Llan* 79-83; V Weston *St Alb* 83-88; P-in-c Ardeley 87-88; V Owlsmoor *Ox* from 88. *107 Owlsmoor Road, Owlsmoor, Camberley, Surrey GU15 4SS* Crowthorne (0344) 771286

DUDLEY, Mrs Wendy Elizabeth. b 46. City of Sheff Coll CertEd68. Cranmer Hall Dur 79. **dss** 81 **d** 87. Cumnor *Ox* 81-87; Par Dn 87-89; Par Dn Hodge Hill *Birm* from 89. *95 Hodge Hill Road, Hodge Hill, Birmingham B34 6DX* 021-783 0140

✠**DUDLEY-SMITH, Rt Rev Timothy.** b 26. Pemb Coll Cam BA47 MA51. Lambeth MLitt91 Ridley Hall Cam 48. **d** 50 **p** 51 **c** 81. C Erith St Paul *Roch* 50-53; Lic to Offic *S'wark* 53-62; Hd of Cam Univ Miss Bermondsey 53-55; Chapl 55-60; Ed Sec Evang Alliance and Ed Crusade 55-59; Asst Sec CPAS 59-65; Gen Sec 65-73; Adn Nor 73-81; Suff Bp Thetford from 81. *The Rectory Meadow, Bramerton, Norwich NR14 7DW* Surlingham (05088) 251

DUDLEY, Archdeacon of. *See* GATHERCOLE, Ven John Robert

DUDLEY, Suffragan Bishop of. *See* DUMPER, Rt Rev Anthony Charles

DUERDEN, Martin James. b 55. Liv Poly BA77. Oak Hill Th Coll 86. **d** 88 **p** 89. C Tunbridge Wells St Jas *Roch* from 88. *3 Andrews Close, Tunbridge Wells, Kent TN2 3PA* Tunbridge Wells (0892) 31297

DUFF, Adam Alexander Howard. b 16. Linc Coll Ox BA38 DipTh43 MA46. Wycliffe Hall Ox 42. **d** 43 **p** 44. V Paddington H Trin w St Paul *Lon* 62-79; C Kilburn St Aug w St Jo 79-81; rtd 81. *Cedar Cottage, Water Eaton Road, Summertown, Oxford OX2 7QQ* Oxford (0865) 58621

DUFF, Canon Harold Patterson. b 23. Edin Th Coll 48. **d** 51 **p** 52. C Motherwell *Glas* 51-54; P-in-c Bathgate *Edin* 54-56; R Glas St Jas *Glas* 56-62; P-in-c Dundee St Martin *Bre* 62-75; R Dundee St Salvador from 69; Can St Paul's Cathl Dundee from 76. *35 Sherbrook Street, Dundee DD3 8LU* Dundee (0382) 825053

DUFFETT, Canon Paul Stanton. b 33. Keble Coll Ox BA55 MA59. Ripon Hall Ox DipTh58. **d** 59 **p** 60. C Portsea St Cuth *Portsm* 59-63; S Africa 63-80; P-in-c Greatham w Empshott *Portsm* 80-85; R 85-88; Hon Can Zululand from 87; R Papworth Everard *Ely* from 88; Chapl Papworth Hosps from 88. *The Rectory, Papworth Everard, Cambridge CB3 8QJ* Huntingdon (0480) 830061

DUFFIELD, Dr Ian Keith. b 47. K Coll Lon BD71 AKC71 MTh73. NY Th Sem DMin84. **d** 73 **p** 74. C Broxbourne *St Alb* 73-77; C Harpenden St Nic 77-81; TV Sheff Manor *Sheff* 81-87; V Walkley from 87. *St Mary's Vicarage, 150 Walkley Road, Sheffield S6 2XQ* Sheffield (0742) 345029

DUFFIELD, John Ernest. b 55. BA86. Oak Hill Th Coll 83. **d** 86 **p** 87. C Walton Breck Ch Ch *Liv* 86-89; TV Fazakerley Em from 89. *St George's Vicarage, 72 Stopgate Lane, Liverpool L9 6AR* 051-523 1536

DUFFY, James Walter. b 17. Leeds Univ BA48. Coll of Resurr Mirfield 48. **d** 50 **p** 51. R Curdworth *Birm* 64-70; R Ballachulish *Arg* 70-74; R Glencoe 70-74; R Auchterarder *St And* 74-83; rtd 83; Hon C Edin Old St Paul *Edin* 83-91; Hon C Edin St Fillan from 91. *75 Buckstone Crescent, Edinburgh EH10 6TR* 031-445 4442

DUFFY, Thomas Patrick. b 26. Clifton Th Coll 55. **d** 57 **p** 58. S Africa 57-69 and 73-78; Ascension 69-73; Chapl Gothenburg *Eur* 78-80; V Acton w Gt and Lt Waldingfield *St E* 80-82; V Aycliffe *Dur* 83-88; P-in-c Satley 88-90; rtd 90. *4 Founder's Court, Greatham, Hartlepool, Cleveland TS25 2HS*

DUFTON, Francis Trevor. b 29. Trin Coll Cam BA51 MA55. Ridley Hall Cam 51. **d** 53 **p** 54. R Elmdon and Wendon Lofts *Chelmsf* 67-80; R Strethall 67-80; P-in-c Bottisham *Ely* 80-85; rtd 85; Perm to Offic *Ely* from 85. *9 Shelford Park Avenue, Great Shelford, Cambridge CB2 5LU* Cambridge (0223) 841438

DUGDALE, Canon Dennis. b 19. OBE78. Worc Ord Coll 65. **d** 68 **p** 69. C Shalford *Guildf* 68-70; V Sandon and Wallington w Rushden *St Alb* 71-74; Chapl Ghent w Ypres *Eur* 74-84; Hon Can Brussels Cathl 82-84; rtd 84; Perm to Offic *Chich* from 85. *12 High Trees, Carew Road, Eastbourne, E Sussex BN21 2JB* Eastbourne (0323) 26661

✠**DUGGAN, Rt Rev John Coote.** b 18. TCD BA40 BD47. CITC 41. **d** 41 **p** 42 **c** 70. C Cork St Luke *C, C & R* 41-43; C Taney Ch Ch *D & G* 43-48; R Portarlington *M & K* 48-55; I Glenageary *D & G* 55-69; I Aughaval *T, K & A* 69-70; Adn Tuam 69-70; Bp T, K & A 70-85; rtd 85. *15 Beechwood Lawn, Rochestown Avenue, Dunlaoghaire, Co Dublin, Irish Republic* Dublin (1) 285-7581

DUGUID, Reginald Erskine. b 29. S'wark Ord Course. **d** 88 **p** 89. NSM Notting Hill All SS w St Columb *Lon* from 88. *c/o The Rev J Brownsell, All Saints' Vicarage, Powis Gardens, London W11 1JG* 071-727 5919

DUKE, Alan Arthur. b 38. Tyndale Hall Bris 59. **d** 64 **p** 65. C Whalley Range St Marg *Man* 64-67; C Folkestone H Trin w Ch Ch *Cant* 67-71; V Queenborough 71-76; V Bearsted w Thurnham 76-86; P-in-c Thurnham w Detling 77-82; P-in-c Torquay St Luke *Ex* from 86. *St Luke's Vicarage, St Luke's Road North, Torquay TQ2 5NX* Torquay (0803) 297974

DUKE, Brian Peter. b 33. Pemb Coll Cam BA55 MA59. Ely Th Coll 55. **d** 57 **p** 58. C Blyth St Mary *Newc* 57-61; C Newc St Andr 61-63; Perm to Offic *Guildf* from 64. *24 Regent Close, Fleet, Aldershot, Hants GU13 9NS* Fleet (0252) 614548

DULFER, John Guidi. b 37. Lich Th Coll 62. **d** 64 **p** 65. C Fenny Stratford and Water Eaton *Ox* 64-67; C Cheshunt *St Alb* 67-68; C Kennington Cross St Anselm *S'wark* 68-74; C N Lambeth 74-76; P-in-c Kensington St Phil Earl's Court *Lon* 76-79; V 79-84; Chapl Odstock and Distr Hosp Salisbury 84; USA from 84. *162 Harrison Avenue, Jersey City, New Jersey 07304, USA*

DULLEY, Arthur John Franklyn. b 32. Mert Coll Ox BA54 MA57. St Jo Coll Nottm 69. **d** 71 **p** 72. Lect St Jo Coll Nottm from 71; Hon C Attenborough w Chilwell *S'well* 71-73; C Penn Fields *Lich* 73-74; Chapl Aldenham Sch Herts 74-79; Chapl HM Pris Ashwell 79-87; V Langham *Pet* from 79. *The Vicarage, Langham, Oakham, Leics LE15 7JE* Oakham (0572) 2969

DUMAT, Mrs Jennifer. b 42. ARCM62. Qu Coll Birm 80 E Midl Min Tr Course 82. **dss** 83 **d** 87. Chapl Asst Pilgrim Hosp Boston from 83. *11 Sea Lane, Butterwick, Boston, Lincs PE22 0HG* Boston (0205) 760883

✠**DUMPER, Rt Rev Anthony Charles.** b 23. Ch Coll Cam BA45 MA48. Westcott Ho Cam. **d** 47 **p** 48 **c** 77. C E Greenwich Ch Ch w St Andr and St Mich *S'wark* 47-49; Malaya 49-63; Malaysia 63-64; Dean Singapore 64-70; V Stockton St Pet *Dur* 70-77; P-in-c Stockton H Trin 76-77; RD Stockton 70-77; Suff Bp Dudley *Worc* from 77. *366 Halesowen Road, Cradley Heath, W Midlands B64 7JF* 021-550 3407

DUNBAR, George Alban Charles. b 08. AKC40. **d** 40 **p** 41. V Whetstone St Jo *Lon* 56-81; rtd 81; Perm to Offic *Linc* from 82. *63 Harrowby Road, Grantham, Lincs NG31 9ED* Grantham (0476) 62935

DUNBAR, Peter Lamb. b 46. Bede Coll Dur DipEd68. Lambeth STh77 N Ord Course 78. **d** 81 **p** 82. NSM Knaresborough *Ripon* 81-82; C 82-84; R Farnham w Scotton, Staveley, Copgrove etc from 84. *The Rectory, Staveley, Knaresborough, N Yorkshire HG5 9LO* Boroughbridge (0423) 340275

DUNCAN, Alexander Stewart. b 17. **d** 83 **p** 84. NSM Aberchirder *Mor* from 83; NSM Keith from 83. *2 Market Street, Aberchirder, Huntly, Aberdeen AB5 5TN* Aberchirder (04665) 662

DUNCAN, Canon Anthony Douglas. b 30. Chich Th Coll 60. **d** 62 **p** 63. C Tewkesbury w Walton Cardiff *Glouc* 62-65; V Dean Forest St Paul 65-69; R Highnam w Lassington and Rudford 69-73; V Newc St Jo *Newc* 73-79; V Warkworth and Acklington 79-87; Hon Can Newc Cathl from 84, V Whitley from 87. *The Vicarage, Whitley, Hexham, Northd NE46 2LA* Hexham (0434) 673379

DUNCAN, Canon Bruce. b 38. FRSA Leeds Univ BA60. Cuddesdon Coll 65. **d** 67 **p** 68. C Armley St Bart *Ripon* 67-69; Lic to Offic *Ely* 69-70; Chapl Vienna w Budapest and Prague *Eur* 71-75; V Crediton *Ex* 75-82; R Crediton and Shobrooke 82-86; RD Cadbury 76-81 and 84-86; Can Res Man Cathl *Man* from 86. *1 Barnhill Road, Prestwich, Manchester M25 8WH* 061-773 3171 or 833 2220

DUNCAN, Charles Patrick Maxwell. b 37. Ch Ch Ox MA62. St Jo Coll Dur 78. **d** 81 **p** 82. C York St Mich-le-Belfrey *York* 81-84; Perm to Offic 84-86; Chapl Asst Ch Hosp Horsham from 86. *Christ's Hospital, Horsham, W Sussex RH13 7LS* Horsham (0403) 58195

DUNCAN, Christopher Robin. b 41. AKC71. **d** 72 **p** 73. C Allington *Cant* 72-77; P-in-c Wittersham 77 82; R Wittersham w Stone-in-Oxney and Ebony 82-85; P-in-c Chilham 85-86; V from 86; P-in-c Challock w Molash from 87. *The Vicarage, 3 Hambrook Close, Chilham, Canterbury, Kent CT4 8EJ* Canterbury (0227) 730235

DUNCAN, Colin Richard. b 34. SS Coll Cam BA58 MA60. Ripon Coll Cuddesdon 83. **d** 85 **p** 86. C Stafford *Lich* 85-89; C Wednesfield 89-90; TV from 90. *St Alban's House, Griffiths Drive, Wednesfield, Wolverhampton WV11 2LJ* Wolverhampton (0902) 732317

DUNCAN, George Ballie. b 12. Edin Univ MA32. Clifton Th Coll 35. **d** 37 **p** 38. I Cockfosters Ch Ch CD *Lon* 51-58; rtd 77; Perm to Offic *Chich* from 80. *41 Merchiston Crescent, Edinburgh* 031-229 2071

DUNCAN, Gregor Duthie. b 50. Glas Univ MA72 Clare Coll Cam PhD77 Or Coll Ox BA83. Ripon Coll Cuddesdon 81. **d** 83 **p** 84. C Oakham, Hambleton, Egleton, Braunston and Brooke *Pet* 83-86; Edin Th Coll 87-89; R Largs *Glas* from 89. *St Columba's Rectory, Aubery Crescent, Largs, Ayrshire KA30 8PR* Largs (0475) 673143

DUNCAN, Harold Norton. b 03. Bible Churchmen's Coll 28. **d** 29 **p** 37. R Easton w Letheringham *St E* 66-72; C-in-c Dub St Thos *D & G* 72-75; Lic to Offic *Cant* 75-79; rtd 82; Perm to Offic *Chich* from 82. *Flat 4, 45 Blackwater Road, Eastbourne, E Sussex BN20 7DH* Eastbourne (0323) 641866

DUNCAN, James Montgomerie. b 29. Edin Th Coll 53. **d** 56 **p** 57. C Edin St Pet *Edin* 56-59; C Edin Old St Paul 59-60; S Africa 60-65; Prov Youth Org Scotland 65-69; Chapl HM Pris Saughton 69-86; R Edin St Salvador *Edin* 69-86; R Aberlour *Mor* from 86; R Fochabers from 86. *Gordon Chapel House, Castle Street, Fochabers, Morayshire IV32 7DW* Fochabers (0343) 820337

DUNCAN, John. b 22. Open Univ BA. Roch Th Coll 64. **d** 66 **p** 67. C Boultham *Linc* 68-71; V W Pinchbeck 72-76; Canada 76-81; R Ridgewell w Ashen, Birdbrook and Sturmer *Chelmsf* 81-88; rtd 88. *20 Westcott Way, Northampton NN3 3BE* Northampton (0604) 30797

DUNCAN, Ven John Finch. b 33. Univ Coll Ox BA57 MA63. Cuddesdon Coll 57. **d** 59 **p** 60. C S Bank *York* 59-61; SSF 61-62; C Birm St Pet *Birm* 62-65; Chapl Birm Univ 65-76; V Kings Heath 76-85; Hon Can Birm Cathl 83-85; Adn Birm from 85. *122 Westfield Road, Birmingham B15 3JQ* 021-454 3402

DUNCAN, Peter Harold Furlong. b 25. AKC52 Lon Univ BA68 Golds Coll Lon BA71 MPhil79. **d** 53 **p** 54. C Sheff St Geo and St Steph *Sheff* 53-56; C Wealdstone H Trin *Lon* 56-57; V Battersea St Pet *S'wark* 57-64; Nigeria 64-66; Hon C All Hallows by the Tower etc *Lon* 67-73; Ind Chapl Lon Docks 67-73; Sen Lect Sociology City of Lon Poly 73-87; Hon C Gt Ilford St Andr *Chelmsf* 73-80; P-in-c Gt Canfield 80-87; P-in-c N Woolwich w Silvertown from 87. *St John's Vicarage, Manwood Street, London E16 2JY* 071-476 2388

DUNCAN, Virginia Elinor. b 39. DNEd. W Midl Minl Tr Course 86 Qu Coll Birm 86. **d** 89. Par Dn Wednesfield *Lich* from 89. *St Alban's House, Griffiths Drive, Wednesfield, Wolverhampton WV11 2LJ* Wolverhampton (0902) 732317

DUNCAN, William Albert. b 30. TCD BA53 MA61 BD66. CITC 54. **d** 54 **p** 55. C Ban Abbey *D & D* 54-57; C Larne and Inver *Conn* 57-61; Hd of Trin Coll Miss Belf 61-66; I Rasharkin w Finvoy 66-78; I Ramoan w Ballycastle and Culfeightrin from 78. *12 Novally Road, Ballycastle, Co Antrim* Ballycastle (02657) 62461

DUNCAN-JONES, Andrew Roby. b 14. St Edm Hall Ox BA38 MA41. Linc Th Coll 39. **d** 40 **p** 41. R Lochgilphead *Arg* 70-79; rtd 79. *Barrachourin, Kilmartin, Lochgilphead, Argyll PA31 8QP* Kilmartin (05465) 204

DUNCANSON, Derek James. b 47. AKC69 Open Univ BA80. St Aug Coll Cant 69. **d** 70 **p** 71. C Norbury St Oswald *Cant* 70-72; CF (TAVR) from 71; C Woodham *Guildf* 72-76; CF 76-79; V Burneside *Carl* 79-84; R Coppull St Jo *Blackb* 84-86; Chapl Bloxham Sch Oxon from 86. *Courtington House, Courtington Lane, Bloxham, Banbury, Oxon OX15 4PQ* Banbury (0295) 720626

DUNDAS, Edward Paul. b 67. NUU BSc88. TCD Div Sch BTh91. **d** 91. C Portadown St Mark *Arm* from 91. *4 Killycomaine Drive, Portadown, Co Armagh BT63 5JJ* Portadown (0762) 335813

DUNDAS, Edward Thompson. b 36. TCD BA63. **d** 64 **p** 65. C Conwall *D & R* 64-67; I Kilbarron 67-78; I Donagheady 78-84; I Kilmore St Aid w St Sav *Arm* from 84. *38 Vicarage Road, Portadown, Craigavon, Co Armagh* Portadown (0762) 332664

DUNDEE, Provost of. *See* SANDERSON, Very Rev Peter Oliver

DUNFORD, Ernest Charles. b 09. St Cath Soc Ox BA33 MA37. Cuddesdon Coll 34. **d** 35 **p** 36. V Gt Missenden *Ox* 39-76; rtd 76; Perm to Offic *Ox* from 77. *26 Bacombe Lane, Wendover, Aylesbury, Bucks HP22 6EQ* Aylesbury (0296) 622022

DUNFORD, Evelyn Cecil Braley. b 11. Jes Coll Cam BA34 MA39. Wells Th Coll 36. **d** 37 **p** 38. R Marhamchurch *Truro* 62-76; rtd 76; Perm to Offic *Truro* from 76. *College of St Barnabas, Blackberry Lane, Lingfield, Surrey RH7 6NJ* Lingfield (0342) 87522

DUNFORD, Malcolm. b 34. FCA74. E Midl Min Tr Course 73. **d** 76 **p** 77. NSM Frodingham *Linc* from 76. *57 Rowland Road, Scunthorpe, S Humberside DN16 1SP* Scunthorpe (0724) 840879

DUNFORD, Reginald John. b 15. Worc Ord Coll. **d** 60 **p** 61. V Lenton *S'well* 68-80; rtd 80; Perm to Offic *S'well* from 80. *Mosley, 33 Cow Lane, Bramcote, Nottingham* Nottingham (0602) 256841

DUNGAN, Canon Victor Samuel. b 17. TCD BA39 BD42. CITC 41. **d** 42 **p** 43. I Killiney H Trin *D & G* 71-84; rtd 84. *Brambles, Monart Church Lane, Enniscorthy, Co Wexford, Irish Republic* Enniscorthy (54) 35239

DUNHILL, Robin Arnold. b 15. BNC Ox BA38 MA46. Cuddesdon Coll. **d** 46 **p** 47. V Hampstead Garden Suburb *Lon* 63-73; RD W Barnet 70-73; Perm to Offic *Pet* from 74; rtd 80; Perm to Offic *Linc* from 91. *Market Cross, Bridge Street, Kings Cliffe, Peterborough PE8 6XH* Kings Cliffe (0780) 470342

DUNK, Michael Robin. b 43. Oak Hill Th Coll BA82. **d** 82 **p** 83. C Northn All SS w St Kath *Pet* 82-86; Ind Chapl *Birm* from 86. *68 Oakfield Road, Birmingham B29 7EG* 021-427 5141 or 472 0034

DUNK, Peter Norman. b 43. Sarum Th Coll 67. **d** 69 **p** 70. C Sheff St Mary w St Simon w St Matthias *Sheff* 69-71; C Margate St Jo *Cant* 71-74; Dioc Youth Officer *Birm* 74-78; R Hulme Ascension *Man* 78-83; V E Farleigh and Coxheath *Roch* 83; P-in-c Linton w Hunton 83; R Coxheath w E Farleigh, Hunton and Linton 83-88; Australia from 88. *105 Shenton Road, Swanbourne, W Australia 6010* Perth (9) 384-2958

DUNKERLEY, James Hobson. b 39. Seabury-Western Th Sem BD69 STh70. **d** 64 **p** 65. C Stirchley *Birm* 64-66; C Perry Barr 66-70; USA from 70. *621 Belmont Avenue, Chicago, Illinois 60657, USA*

DUNKLEY, Christopher. b 52. Edin Univ MA74 Ox Univ BA77 MA81. St Steph Ho Ox 75. **d** 78 **p** 79. C Newbold and Dunston *Derby* 78-82; C Chesterfield All SS 82; Chapl Leic Univ *Leic* 82-85; P-in-c Leic St Aid 85; TV Leic Ascension from 85. *St Aidan's Vicarage, St Oswald's Road, Leicester LE3 6RJ* Leicester (0533) 872342

DUNKLEY, Reginald Alfred Lorenz. b 13. Clifton Th Coll 56. **d** 58 **p** 59. R Longfield *Roch* 64-78; rtd 78. *33 Sheriff Drive, Chatham, Kent ME5 9PU* Medway (0634) 862143

DUNLOP, Canon Arthur John. b 27. AKC52. **d** 53 **p** 54. C Loughton St Jo *Chelmsf* 53-57; C-in-c Chelmsf All SS CD 57-65; R Laindon w Basildon 65-72; RD Basildon 65-72; V Maldon All SS w St Pet from 72; RD Maldon 73-82; Hon Can Chelmsf Cathl from 80; RD Maldon and Dengie from 89. *All Saints' Vicarage, Church Walk, Maldon, Essex CM9 7PY* Maldon (0621) 54179

DUNLOP, Canon Ian Geoffrey David. b 25. FSA New Coll Ox BA48 MA56. Linc Th Coll 54. **d** 56 **p** 57. C Hatf St Alb 56-60; Chapl Westmr Sch 60-62; C Bures St E 62-72; Dir Post-Ord Tr from 72; Chan and Can Res Sarum Cathl *Sarum* from 72; Dir of Ords from 73; Lect Sarum & Wells Th Coll from 76. *24 The Close, Salisbury SP1 2EH* Salisbury (0722) 336809

DUNLOP, Peter John. b 44. TCD BA68 MA72 Dur Univ DipTh70 CertEd71. Cranmer Hall Dur. **d** 71 **p** 72. C Barking St Marg w St Patr *Chelmsf* 71-75; C Gt Malvern Ch Ch *Worc* 75-78; Chapl K Sch Tynemouth 78-89; V Monkseaton St Pet *Newc* from 90. *St Peter's Vicarage, 6 Elmwood Bay, Whitley Bay, Tyne & Wear NE25 8EX* 091-252 1991

DUNN, Alastair Matthew Crusoe. b 40. Lon Univ LLB64 AKC64. Wycliffe Hall Ox 78. **d** 80 **p** 81. C Yardley St Edburgha *Birm* 80-83; R Bishop's Sutton and Ropley and W Tisted *Win* 83-90; V Milford from 90. *The Vicarage, Lymington Road, Milford on Sea, Lymington, Hants SO41 0QN* Lymington (0590) 643289

DUNN, Brian. b 40. St Aid Birkenhead 66. **d** 69 **p** 70. C Over Darwen H Trin *Blackb* 69-71; C Burnley St Pet 71-74; V Darwen St Barn 74-84; V S Shore H Trin from 84; Chapl Arnold Sch Blackpool from 84. *Holy Trinity Vicarage, 1 Windermere Road, Blackpool FY4 2BX* Blackpool (0253) 42362

DUNN, Christopher George Hunter. b 28. Pemb Coll Cam BA49 MA53. Oak Hill Th Coll 51. **d** 53 **p** 54. C Tunbridge Wells H Trin *Roch* 53-54; C Broadwater St Mary *Chich* 54-58; R Garsdon w Lea and Cleverton *Bris* 58-74; V Tiverton St Geo *Ex* from 74; Chapl Marie Curie Foundn (Tidcombe Hall) from 74; RD Tiverton *Ex* from 84. *St George's Vicarage, St Andrew Street, Tiverton, Devon EX16 6PH* Tiverton (0884) 252184

DUNN, David. b 42. Univ of Wales DipTh65. St Mich Coll Llan 62. **d** 66 **p** 67. C Brighton St Wilfrid *Chich* 66-69; C Tunbridge Wells St Barn *Roch* 69-74; TV Brighton Resurr *Chich* 74-77; V Southsea H Spirit *Portsm* 77-88; P-in-c Bournemouth St Mary *Win* from 88. *St Mary's Vicarage, 49 Thistlebarrow Road, Bournemouth BH7 7AL* Bournemouth (0202) 398376

DUNN, David James. b 47. CertEd79 BA82 DipHE90. Trin Coll Bris 88. **d** 90 **p** 91. C Magor w Redwick and Undy *Mon* from 90. *3 The Meadows, Magor, Newport, Gwent NP6 3LA* Magor (0633) 881714

DUNN, David Michael. b 47. AKC70. St Aug Coll Cant 70. **d** 71 **p** 72. C Padgate *Liv* 71-74; C Halliwell St Marg *Man* 74-76; V Lever Bridge 76-84; V Bradshaw from 84. *The New Vicarage, Bolton Road, Bolton BL2 3EU* Bolton (0204) 54240

DUNN, David Whitelaw Thomas. b 34. Trin Coll Carmarthen CertEd54. St Mich Coll Llan 87 St Deiniol's Hawarden 83. **d** 83 **p** 85. NSM Brecon St Mary and Battle w Llanddew *S & B* 83-87; Min Can Brecon Cathl 87-88; V Llanfihangel Crucorney w Old Castle etc *Mon* from 88. *The Vicarage, Llanfihangel Crucorney, Abergavenny, Gwent NP7 8DH* Crucorney (0873) 890349

DUNN, Derek William Robert. b 48. AMusTCL74 LTCL75 Stranmillis Coll CertEd70 Open Univ BA81 QUB DASE86. **d** 85 **p** 87. NSM Carnalea *D & D* 85-91; Lic to Offic from 91. *13 Wandsworth Park, Carnalea, Bangor, Co Down BT19 1BD* Bangor (0247) 456898

DUNN, John Frederick. b 44. Trin Coll Bris 71. **d** 74 **p** 75. C Carl St Jo *Carl* 74-77; C Tooting Graveney St Nic *S'wark* 77-82; V Attleborough *Cov* 85; Perm to Offic *Cant* from 86. *73 St Luke's Avenue, Ramsgate, Kent* Thanet (0843) 581632

DUNN, John Samuel. b 39. CEng MIM HNC. Llan Dioc Tr Scheme. **d** 88 **p** 89. NSM Aberavon *Llan* from 88. *46 Vivian Terrace, Port Talbot, W Glam SA12 6ET* Port Talbot (0639) 886786

DUNN, Kevin Samuel. b 31. QUB BA52 Cam Univ MA54 Toronto Univ MDiv74. **d** 73 **p** 74. USA 73-90; I Rathkeale w Askeaton and Kilcornan *L & K* from 90. *The Rectory, Askeaton, Co Limerick, Irish Republic* Limerick (61) 398269

DUNN, Michael Henry James. b 34. Em Coll Cam BA56 MA62. Cuddesdon Coll 57 and 62. **d** 62 **p** 63. C Chatham St Steph *Roch* 62-66; C Bromley SS Pet and Paul 66-70; V Roch St Justus 70-83; P-in-c Malvern Wells and Wyche *Worc* 83-85; P-in-c Lt Malvern,

Malvern Wells and Wyche from 85. *1 The Moorlands, Malvern Wells, Malvern, Worcs WR14 4PS* Malvern (0684) 575123

DUNN, Nicholas John Eaton. b 12. Keble Coll Ox BA36 MA46. **d** 68 **p** 69. Hon C Leebotwood w Longnor *Heref* 68-80; Hon C Dorrington 74-80; Hon C Stapleton 74-80; Lic to Offic from 80. *82 Stretton Farm Road, Church Stretton, Shropshire SY6 6DX* Church Stretton (0694) 723964

DUNN, Paul James Hugh. b 55. Ripon Coll Cuddesdon. **d** 83 **p** 84. C Wandsworth St Paul *S'wark* 83-87; C Richmond St Mary w St Matthias and St Jo from 88. *19 Old Deer Park Gardens, Richmond, Surrey TW9 2TM* 081-940 8359

DUNN, Reginald Hallan. b 31. Oak Hill NSM Course. **d** 82 **p** 83. NSM Enfield St Andr *Lon* from 82. *3 Conway Gardens, Enfield, Middx* 081-366 3982

DUNN, Struan Huthwaite. b 43. Ch Coll Hobart 66 Moore Th Coll Sydney ThL68 Clifton Th Coll 68. **d** 70 **p** 71. C Orpington Ch Ch *Roch* 70-74; C Cheltenham St Mary *Glouc* 74-76; C Cheltenham St Mary, St Matt, St Paul and H Trin 76; C Welling *Roch* 76-79; Chapl Barcelona w Casteldefels *Eur* 79-83; R Addington w Trottiscliffe *Roch* 83-89; P-in-c Ryarsh w Birling 83-89; P-in-c S Gillingham 89-90; TR from 90; RD Gillingham from 91. *The Rectory, 4 Drewery Drive, Wigmore, Gillingham, Kent ME8 0NX* Medway (0634) 31071

DUNNAN, Donald Stuart. b 59. Harvard Univ AB80 AM81 Ch Ch Ox BA85 MA90. Gen Th Sem (NY). **d** 86 **p** 87. USA 86-87; Lib Pusey Ho 87-89; Lic to Offic *Ox* from 87; Perm to Offic *Cant* from 87; Chapl Linc Coll Ox from 90. *Lincoln College, Oxford OX1 3DR* Oxford (0865) 279789

DUNNE, Kevin Headley. b 43. Cranmer Hall Dur 85. **d** 87 **p** 88. C Ches le Street *Dur* 87-90; V S Hetton w Haswell from 90. *The Vicarage, South Hetton, Durham DH6 2SW* 091-526 1157

DUNNE, Nigel Kenneth. BA BTh. **d** 90 **p** 91. C Dub St Bart w Ch Ch Leeson Park *D & G* from 90. *St Mary's Lodge, Clyde Lane, Bullsbridge, Dublin 4, Irish Republic* Dublin (1) 602904

DUNNETT, John Frederick. b 58. CQSW82 SS Coll Cam MA84 Worc Coll Ox MSc83. Trin Coll Bris BA87. **d** 88 **p** 89. C Kirkheaton *Wakef* from 88. *423 Wakefield Road, Huddersfield HD5 8DB* Huddersfield (0484) 429885

DUNNETT, Robert Curtis. b 31. SS Coll Cam BA54 MA58. Oak Hill Th Coll 56. **d** 58 **p** 59. C Markfield *Leic* 58-60; C Bucknall and Bagnall *Lich* 60-73; Perm to Offic *Birm* from 72; Chapl and Tutor Birm Bible Inst from 72; Vice-Prin from 84. *7 Pakenham Road, Edgbaston, Birmingham B15 2NN* 021-440 3105

DUNNILL, Dr John David Stewart. b 50. UEA BA72 Birm Univ DipTh82 PhD88. Ripon Coll Cuddesdon 86. **d** 88 **p** 89. C Tupsley *Heref* from 88. *6 Gaisford Close, Tupsley, Hereford HR1 1YG* Hereford (0432) 357284

DUNNING, David John. b 52. Liv Univ BA Ox Univ CertEd. Ripon Coll Cuddesdon 79. **d** 82 **p** 84. C N Gosforth *Newc* 82-83; C Willington Team 83-85; C Bellingham/Otterburn Gp 85-86; Chapl Magd Coll Sch Ox from 86. *Magdalen College School, Oxford OX4 1DZ* Oxford (0865) 243026

DUNNING, George Henry John. b 27. Sarum Th Coll 57. **d** 59 **p** 60. C Seaton Hirst *Newc* 59-61; C Hedworth *Dur* 61-64; V Auckland St Pet 64-75; V Clay Cross *Derby* 75-83; V S Norwood St Alb *Cant* 83-85; V S Norwood St Alb *S'wark* from 85. *The Vicarage, 6 Dagmar Road, London SE25 6HZ* 081-653 6092

DUNNING, John Stanley. b 19. Lon Univ BSc41. E Midl Min Tr Course 78. **d** 81 **p** 82. NSM Nottm St Pet and St Jas *S'well* 81-85; rtd 85. *12 Brookhill Drive, Wollaton, Nottingham NG8 2PS* Nottingham (0602) 283357

DUNNINGS, Reuben Edward. b 36. Clifton Th Coll 62. **d** 66 **p** 67. C Longfleet *Sarum* 66-70; C Melksham 70-73; TV 73-78; R Broughton Gifford w Gt Chalfield 78-84; V Holt St Kath 78-84; R Broughton Gifford, Gt Chalfield and Holt 85-86; V Salisbury St Fran from 86. *The Vicarage, 52 Park Lane, Salisbury SP1 3NP* Salisbury (0722) 333762

DUNSETH, George William. b 52. Multnomah Sch of the Bible Oregon BRE79. Oak Hill Th Coll BA85. **d** 85 **p** 86. C Cheadle All Hallows *Ches* 85-88; C New Boro and Leigh *Sarum* 88-91; V Thurnby w Stoughton *Leic* from 91. *The Vicarage, Thurnby, Leicester LE7 9PN* Leicester (0533) 412263

DUNSTAN, Canon Alan Leonard. b 28. Wadh Coll Ox BA49 MA52. Ripon Hall Ox 50. **d** 52 **p** 53. C Barford *Cov* 52-55; C Brompton H Trin *Lon* 55-57; V Gravesend St Mary *Roch* 57-63; Chapl Wycliffe Hall Ox 63-66; Vice-Prin 66-70; Hon C Ox St Mary V w St Cross and

St Pet *Ox* 70-78; Chapl Keble Coll Ox 70-71; Vice-Prin Ripon Hall Ox 71-74; Acting Prin 74-75; Vice-Prin Ripon Coll Cuddesdon 75-78; Can Res Glouc Cathl *Glouc* from 78. *7 College Green, Gloucester GL1 2LX* Gloucester (0452) 23987

DUNSTAN, Prof Gordon Reginald. b 17. CBE89. Hon MRCP87 Leeds Univ BA38 MA39 Ex Univ Hon DD73. Coll of Resurr Mirfield 39. **d** 41 **p** 42. Hon Can Leic Cathl *Leic* 66-82; Prof Moral and Soc Th K Coll Lon 67-82; Chapl to HM The Queen 76-87; rtd 82; Perm to Offic *Ex* from 82. *9 Maryfield Avenue, Exeter EX4 6JN* Exeter (0392) 214691

DUNSTAN, Gregory John Orchard. b 50. Cam Univ MA75 TCD BTh90. **d** 90 **p** 91. C Ballymena w Ballyclug *Conn* from 90. *38 Ballee Road East, Ballymena, Co Antrim BT42 3DH* Ballymena (0266) 47038

DUNSTAN, Kenneth Ian. b 40. ACP Golds Coll Lon BEd71. Oak Hill NSM Course 86. **d** 88 **p** 89. NSM Creeksea w Althorne, Latchingdon and N Fambridge *Chelmsf* from 88. *35 Ely Close, Southminster, Essex CM0 7AQ* Maldon (0621) 772199

DUNSTAN, Sydney James. b 33. St Deiniol's Hawarden 71. **d** 72 **p** 73. C Llangynwyd w Maesteg *Llan* 72-75; TV Ystradyfodwg 75-79; V Llanbradach 79-84; V Skewen from 84; Miss to Seamen from 84. *The Vicarage, Hill Road, Skewen, Neath, W Glam SA10 7NP* Skewen (0792) 814116

DUNSTAN-MEADOWS, Victor Richard. b 63. Chich Th Coll BTh90. **d** 90 **p** 91. C Clacton St Jas *Chelmsf* from 90. *8 Trafalgar Road, Clacton-on-Sea, Essex CO15 1LR* Clacton-on-Sea (0225) 434763

DUNTHORNE, Paul. b 63. K Coll Lon LLB85 Paris Sorbonne 85 St Jo Coll Dur BA90. Cranmer Hall Dur 88. **d** 91. C Heacham and Sedgeford *Nor* from 91. *27 School Road, Heacham, King's Lynn, Norfolk PE31 7EQ* Heacham (0485) 70268

DUNWICH, Suffragan Bishop of. *See* DEVENPORT, Rt Rev Eric Nash

DUNWOODY, Canon Thomas Herbert Williamson. b 35. TCD BA58 MA64. TCD Div Sch Div Test59. **d** 59 **p** 60. C Newc *D & D* 59-61; C Ballymacarrett St Martin 61-63; C Lurgan Ch Ch 63-66; I Ardglass w Dunsford 66-74; V Urmston *Man* 74-85; Miss to Seamen from 85; I Wexford w Ardcolm and Killurin *C & O* from 85; Can Ferns Cathl from 88. *The Rectory, Park, Wexford, Irish Republic* Wexford (53) 43013

DUPLOCK, Canon Peter Montgomery. b 16. OBE76. Qu Coll Cam BA38 MA42. Ridley Hall Cam 38. **d** 40 **p** 41. Chapl Brussels w Charleroi, Liege and Waterloo *Eur* 71-81; Chan Brussels Cathl 81; Adn NW Eur 81; rtd 81; Hon Can Brussels Cathl *Eur* 81-84; V Breamore Win 81-86; Perm to Offic from 86. *14 Broomfield Drive, Alderholt, Fordingbridge, Hants SP6 3HY* Fordingbridge (0425) 656000

DUPREE, Hugh Douglas. b 50. Univ of the South (USA) BA72 Ch Ch Ox MA86 Ball Coll Ox DPhil88. Virginia Th Sem MDiv75. **d** 75 **p** 76. USA 75-80; Hon C Ox St Mich w St Martin and All SS *Ox* 80-87; Asst Chapl Ball Coll Ox 84-87; Chapl from 87; Chapl HM Pris Ox from 88. *Balliol College, Oxford OX1 3BJ* Oxford (0865) 277716

DURAND, Sir Henry Mortimer Dickon Marion St George, Bt. b 34. Sarum Th Coll 66. **d** 69 **p** 70. C Fulham All SS *Lon* 69-72; C Heston 72-75; C Upper Sunbury St Sav 75-79; I Kilbixy w Almoritia *M & K* 79-82; I Youghal Union *C, C & R* from 82. *The Rectory, Upper Strand, Youghal, Co Cork, Irish Republic* Youghal (24) 92350

DURAND, Noel Douglas. b 33. Jes Coll Cam BA57 MA61 BD76. Westcott Ho Cam 72. **d** 74 **p** 75. C Eaton *Nor* 74-78; V Cumnor *Ox* from 78. *The Vicarage, 1 Abingdon Road, Cumnor, Oxford OX2 9QN* Oxford (0865) 862198

DURANT, Robert-Ashton. b 23. OSB Univ of Wales (Lamp) BA47. Bp Burgess Hall Lamp. **d** 48 **p** 49. C Brynmawr *S & B* 48-49; C Fleur-de-Lis *Mon* 49-51; C Bassaleg 51-56; CF (TA) 53-55; V Trellech and Cwmcarvan *Mon* 56-69; Priest Tymawr Convent 56-69; V Slapton *Ex* 69-81; V Strete 69-81; R E Allington, Slapton and Strete from 81. *The Rectory, Strete, Dartmouth, Devon TQ6 0RS* Stoke Fleming (0803) 770378

DURANT, Ven Stanton Vincent. b 42. S'wark Ord Course 69. **d** 72 **p** 73. C Ickenham *Lon* 72-76; C Paddington Em Harrow Road 76-78; V 78-87; AD Westmr Paddington 84-87; TR Hackney Marsh 87-91; Adn Liv from 91. *All Saints' Vicarage, West Oak Hill Park, Liverpool L13 4BW* 051-228 3581

DURANT, William John Nicholls. b 55. K Coll Lon BA76 DipTh DPS. St Jo Coll Nottm 77. **d** 80 **p** 81. C

Norwood *S'wark* 80-83; C Morden 83-88; TV from 88. *49 Camborne Road, Morden, Surrey SM4 4JL* 081-542 2966

DURBIN, Roger. b 41. Bris Sch of Min 83. **d** 85 **p** 86. NSM Bedminster *Bris* from 85. *13 Charbury Walk, Bristol BS11 9UU* Bristol (0272) 827858

DURELL, Miss Jane Vavasor. b 32. Bedf Coll Lon BSc55. Gilmore Ho 61 Lambeth STh64. **dss** 86 **d** 87. Banbury *Ox* 86-87; Par Dn from 87. *79 Warwick Road, Banbury, Oxon OX16 7AL* Banbury (0295) 255022

DURHAM, John Francis Langton. b 03. TD50. Ely Th Coll 27. **d** 28 **p** 29. V Sudbury St Andr *Lon* 60-68; rtd 68. *31 Alexandra Road, London SW19 7JZ* 081-946 3476

DURHAM, Archdeacon of. *See* PERRY, Ven Michael Charles

DURHAM, Bishop of. *See* JENKINS, Rt Rev David Edward

DURHAM, Dean of. *See* ARNOLD, Very Rev John Robert

DURKIN, Anthony Michael. b 45. Sarum & Wells Th Coll 87. **d** 89 **p** 90. C Faversham *Cant* from 89. *12 Stonebridge Way, Faversham, Kent ME13 7RZ* Faversham (0795) 537874

DURN, Edward Nelson. b 06. St Fran Coll Brisbane 62. **d** 63 **p** 63. Australia 63-67; Perm to Offic Ox 67-69; Blackb 69-70; C Preston St Jo *Blackb* 70-72; C Cov H Trin *Cov* 73-75; C Cainscross w Selsley *Glouc* 75-78; Perm to Offic from 79. *Lyttleholme, Selsley West, Stroud, Glos GL5 5LG* Stonehouse (045382) 4105

DURNDELL, Miss Irene Frances. b 43. Nottm Univ DipRE78. Trin Coll Bris DipHE86. **dss** 86 **d** 87. Erith Ch Ch *Roch* 86-87; Par Dn from 87. *St John's Church House, 100 Park Crescent, Erith, Kent DA8 3DZ* Dartford (0322) 332555

DURNELL, John. b 32. St Aid Birkenhead 64. **d** 66 **p** 67. C Newport w Longford *Lich* 66-69; P-in-c Church Aston 69-72; R 72-77; V Weston Rhyn 77-82; P-in-c Petton w Cockshutt and Weston Lullingfield etc 82-83; R Petton w Cockshutt, Welshampton and Lyneal etc from 83. *The Rectory, Cockshutt, Ellesmere, Shropshire SY12 0JQ* Cockshutt (093922) 211

DURNFORD, Miss Catherine Margaret. b 36. St Mary's Coll Dur BA57 DipEd58. Gilmore Course 78 NW Ord Course 77. **d** 87. Area Sec (Dios York and Ripon) USPG 82-89; Par Dn Whitby *York* from 89. *9 Grove Street, Whitby, N Yorkshire YO21 1PP* Whitby (0947) 601413

DURNFORD, John Edward. b 30. CCC Cam BA53 MA61. Linc Th Coll 53. **d** 55 **p** 56. C Selby Abbey *York* 55-58; C Newland St Jo 58-62; S Rhodesia 62-65; Rhodesia 65-76; V Hebden Bridge *Wakef* 76-84; RD Calder Valley 82-84; P-in-c Blanchland w Hunstanworth *Newc* 84-90; P-in-c Edmundbyers w Muggleswick *Dur* 84-90; RD Corbridge *Newc* from 88; R Blanchland w Hunstanworth and Edmundbyers etc from 90. *The Vicarage, Blanchland, Consett, Co Durham DH8 9ST* Hexham (0434) 675207

DURNFORD, Comdr Peter Jeffrey. b 20. Bps' Coll Cheshunt 63. **d** 65 **p** 66. R St Just in Roseland *Truro* 70-82; P-in-c Ruan Lanihorne w Philleigh 70-82; P-in-c St Mewan 82-85; Chapl Mount Edgcumbe Hospice 82-88; rtd 85. *8 Tredennam Road, St Mawes, Truro, Cornwall TR2 5AN* St Mawes (0326) 270793

DURRAN, Ms Margaret (Maggie). b 47. Lady Spencer Chu Coll of Educn CertEd70. S'wark Ord Course 88. **d** 91. Par Dn Brixton St Matt *S'wark* from 91. *4 Edithna Street, London SW9 9JP* 071-733 1209

DURRANS, Canon Anthony. b 37. Leeds Univ BA59. Linc Th Coll 60. **d** 62 **p** 63. C Stanningley St Thos *Ripon* 62-64; C Chorlton upon Medlock *Man* 64-69; SCM Field Sec Man 64-66; NW Sec 66-68; Asst Gen Sec 68-69; R Old Trafford St Jo *Man* 69-80; V Langley All SS and Martyrs 80-82; TR Langley and Parkfield 82-85; R Man Miles Platting 85-87; P-in-c Man Apostles 85-87; R Man Apostles w Miles Platting from 87; Hon Can Man Cathl from 86; AD Ardwick from 91. *The Rectory, Ridgway Street, Manchester M10 7FY* 061-205 1742

DURRANT, Reginald Patrick Bickersteth. b 37. AKC64. **d** 65 **p** 66. C Summertown *Ox* 65-68; C Ascot Heath 68-71; C Heene *Chich* 71-76; R Burwash from 76. *The Rectory, Burwash, Etchingham, E Sussex TN19 7BH* Burwash (0435) 882301

DURSTON, Preb David Michael Karl. b 36. Em Coll Cam BA60 MA64. Clifton Th Coll 61. **d** 63 **p** 64. C Wednesfield Heath *Lich* 63-66; Project Officer Grubb Inst 67-78; Ind Chapl *Lich* 78-84; P-in-c W Bromwich St Paul Golds Hill 78-82; V 82-84; Adult Educn Officer from 84; Preb Lich Cathl from 89. *The Vicarage,*

Sheriffhales, Shifnal, Shropshire TF11 8RA Telford (0952) 460606

DUTFIELD, Canon Alan. b 20. Linc Th Coll 54. **d** 55 **p** 56. V New Rossington *Sheff* 60-71; R Old Brumby *Linc* 71-77; TR 77-86; Can and Preb Linc Cathl 81-86; RD Manlake 82-86; rtd 86; Perm to Offic *Linc* from 89. *30 Barnes Green, Scotter, Gainsborough, Lincs DN21 3RW* Scunthorpe (0724) 764220

DUTHIE, Elliot Malcolm. b 31. Clifton Th Coll 63. **d** 66 **p** 67. C Eccleston St Luke *Liv* 66-69; Malaysia 70-75; P-in-c Bootle St Leon *Liv* 76-78; V 78-81; V Charlton Kings H Apostles *Glouc* from 81. *The Vicarage, Langton Grove Road, Charlton Kings, Cheltenham, Glos GL52 6JA* Cheltenham (0242) 512254

DUTSON, Bruce Martin. b 45. Man Univ BA67 Nottm Univ DipTh69. Chich Th Coll 67. **d** 70 **p** 71. C Plymouth St Pet *Ex* 70-73; C Bordesley SS Alb and Patr *Birm* 73-82; V Saltley 82-89; R Reading St Giles *Ox* from 89. *St Giles's Rectory, Church Street, Reading RG1 2SB* Reading (0734) 572831

DUTTON, Arthur Mander. b 10. St Aid Birkenhead 37. **d** 39 **p** 40. V Ipstones *Lich* 62-63; rtd 63; Lic to Offic *Lich* from 64. *54 Armitage Road, Rugeley, Staffs WS15 1BZ* Rugeley (0889) 574672

DUTTON, Leonard Arthur. b 35. Bps' Coll Cheshunt 63. **d** 66 **p** 67. C Knighton St Jo *Leic* 66-70; C Chilvers Coton w Astley *Cov* 70-73; R Hathern *Leic* 73-79; V Ashby-de-la-Zouch H Trin from 79. *Holy Trinity Vicarage, 1 Trinity Close, Ashby-de-la-Zouch, Leics LE6 5GQ* Ashby-de-la-Zouch (0530) 412339

DUVAL, Canon David. b 14. St Chad Ox BA36 MA41. Wells Th Coll 36. **d** 38 **p** 39. Hon Can St E Cathl *St E* 62-83; R Withersfield 73-79; P-in-c 79-82; rtd 79; TV Haverhill w Withersfield, the Wrattings etc *St E* 82-83; Perm to Offic from 83. *25 Whiting Street, Bury St Edmunds, Suffolk IP33 1NP* Bury St Edmunds (0284) 61232

DUVAL, Canon Philip Ernest. b 18. MBE45. Mert Coll Ox BA45 MA45. Westcott Ho Cam 47. **d** 47 **p** 48. R Merstham and Gatton *S'wark* 66-86; Hon Can S'wark Cathl 78-86; rtd 86. *2 The Holt, Frogs Hill, Newenden, Hawkhurst, Kent TN18 5PX* Northiam (0797) 252578

DUVALL, Michael James. b 31. **d** 79 **p** 80. Hon C Kings Langley *St Alb* 79-89; Hon C Selworthy and Timberscombe and Wootton Courtenay *B & W* from 89; Hon C Luccombe from 89. *The Parsonage, Luccombe, Minehead, Somerset TA24 8TE* Minehead (0643) 862834

DUXBURY, James Campbell. b 33. Tyndale Hall Bris 58. **d** 61 **p** 62. C Southport SS Simon and Jude *Liv* 61-65; V Tittensor *Lich* 65-70; V W Bromwich Gd Shep w St Jo 70-75; P-in-c Wellington w Eyton 75-80; V 80-85; V Padiham *Blackb* from 85. *The Vicarage, 1 Arbory Drive, Padiham, Burnley, Lancs BB12 8JS* Padiham (0282) 72442

DUXBURY, Miss Margaret Joan. b 30. JP81. DipEd52. St Jo Coll Nottm 83. **dss** 84 **d** 87. Thornthwaite w Thruscross and Darley *Ripon* 84-86; Middleton St Cross 86-87; C 87-90; Par Dn Dacre w Hartwith and Darley w Thornthwaite from 90. *Scot Beck House, Darley, Harrogate HG3 2QN* Harrogate (0423) 780451

DYALL, Henry. b 19. ARICS51 Lon Univ BSc51 LLB58. S'wark Ord Course 81. **d** 82 **p** 83. Hon C St Mary Cray and St Paul's Cray *Roch* 82-84; Perm to Offic 84-86; Hon C Sidcup Ch Ch from 86. *8 Saxville Road, Orpington, Kent BR5 3AW* Orpington (0689) 872598

DYAS, Stuart Edwin. b 46. Lon Univ BSc67. Ridley Hall Cam 78. **d** 80 **p** 81. C Bath Weston St Jo *B & W* 80; C Bath Weston St Jo w Kelston 81-83; C Tunbridge Wells St Jas *Roch* 83-90; V Nottm St Jude *S'well* from 90. *St Jude's Vicarage, Woodborough Road, Mapperley, Nottingham NG3 5HE* Nottingham (0602) 604102

DYER, Anne Catherine. b 57. St Anne's Coll Ox MA80 Lon Univ MTh89. Wycliffe Hall Ox 84. **d** 87. NSM Beckenham St Jo *Roch* 87-88; NSM Beckenham St Geo 88-89; Hon Par Dn Luton Ch Ch from 89. *6 Thrush Close, Chatham, Kent ME5 7TG* Medway (0634) 685828

DYER, Ms Catherine Jane. b 46. Westf Coll Lon BA68. Ox NSM Course 85. **d** 88. Hon C Wokingham All SS *Ox* 88-90; C from 90. *6 Barkhart Gardens, Wokingham, Berks RG11 1ET* Wokingham (0734) 787720

DYER, Mrs Christine Anne. b 53. Nottm Univ BEd75. E Midl Min Tr Course 84. **dss** 84 **d** 87. Mickleover St Jo *Derby* 85-87; Par Dn 87-90; Voc Adv 86-90; Par Educn Adv from 90. *4 Chain Lane, Mickleover, Derby DE3 5AJ* Derby (0332) 514390

DYER, Mrs Gillian Marie. b 50. Sheff Univ BA71 Leic Univ CertEd72. S Dios Minl Tr Scheme 81. **dss** 84 **d** 87.

Witney *Ox* 84-85; Carl St Cuth w St Mary *Carl* 86-87; Par Dn 87-89; Dioc Communications Officer 86-89; Par Dn Kirkbride w Newton Arlosh from 89. *The Rectory, Kirkbride, Carlisle CA5 5HY*   Kirkbride (06973) 51256

DYER, Canon James Henry. b 14. ALCD39. **d** 39 **p** 40. C S Hackney St Jo w Ch Ch *Lon* 39-43; C New Malden and Coombe *S'wark* 43-50; New Zealand from 50; Hon Can Nelson Cathl from 85. *41 Oxford Street, Richmond, Nelson, New Zealand*   Nelson (54) 47440

DYER, Janet. b 35. dss 85 **d** 86. Balerno *Edin* 85-86; NSM from 86. *499 Lanark Road West, Balerno, Midlothian EH14 7AL*   031-449 3767

DYER, John Alan. b 31. **d** 56 **p** 57. C Weston-super-Mare Ch Ch *B & W* 56-60; V Battersea St Geo w St Andr *S'wark* 60-69; Australia from 69. *The Rectory, 9 Janice Place, Narreweena, NSW, Australia 2099*   Sydney (2) 981-3758

DYER, Stephen Roger. b 57. Brunel Univ BSc. Wycliffe Hall Ox 83. **d** 86 **p** 87. C Beckenham St Jo *Roch* 86-89; C Luton Ch Ch from 89. *6 Thrush Close, Chatham, Kent ME5 7TG*   Medway (0634) 685828

DYER, Sydney Charles George. b 03. ALCD33 St Jo Coll Dur LTh33 BA34 MA38. **d** 34 **p** 35. V Redhill St Jo *S'wark* 55-69; rtd 69; Hon C Tenerife *Eur* 72-75. *85 Old Fort Road, Shoreham-by-Sea, W Sussex BN43 5HA*   Shoreham-by-Sea (0273) 454422

DYER, Terence Neville. b 50. Sheff Univ BEng71 Leic Univ PGCE72. Carl Dioc Tr Course 86. **d** 89 **p** 90. NSM Kirkbride w Newton Arlosh *Carl* from 89. *The Rectory, Kirkbride, Carlisle CA5 5HY*   Kirkbride (06973) 51256

DYKE, George Edward. b 22. TCD BA65 BCom65 MA80. CITC. **d** 79 **p** 80. NSM Dub St Geo *D & G* 79-82; NSM Tallaght 83-89; NSM Killiney (Ballybrack) 89-90; Bp's C Dub St Geo and St Thos from 90. *45 Thornhill Road, Mount Merrion, Co Dublin, Irish Republic*   Dublin (1) 288-9376

DYKE, Kenneth Aubrey. b 30. Sarum Th Coll 61. **d** 63 **p** 64. C Bournville *Birm* 63-66; Chapl RAF 66-82; R Bottesford and Muston *Leic* from 82. *The Rectory, 4 Rutland Lane, Bottesford, Nottingham NG13 0BX*   Bottesford (0949) 42335

DYKES, John Edward. b 33. DipHE84. Trin Coll Bris 82. **d** 84 **p** 85. C Rushden w Newton Bromswold *Pet* 84-87; R Heanton Punchardon w Marwood *Ex* from 87. *The Rectory, Heanton, Barnstaple, Devon EX31 4DG*   Braunton (0271) 812249

DYKES, Lawrence Gregson Fell. b 06. Wycliffe Hall Ox. **d** 34 **p** 35. R Hartfield *Chich* 51-76; rtd 76; Perm to Offic *Carl* from 77. *Garden Cottage, Holker Hall, Cark in Cartmel, Grange-over-Sands, Cumbria*   Flookburgh (044853) 581

DYKES, Michael David Allan. b 42. Chich Th Coll 68. **d** 71 **p** 72. C Pocklington w Yapham-cum-Meltonby, Owsthorpe etc *York* 72-75; C Howden 75-77; V Eskdaleside w Ugglebarnby and Sneaton 77-85; R Stokesley from 85; P-in-c Hilton in Cleveland from 85; P-in-c Seamer in Cleveland from 85. *The Rectory, Leven Close, Stokesley, Middlesbrough, N Yorkshire TS9 5AP*   Stokesley (0642) 710405

DYKES, Philip John. b 61. Loughb Univ BSc83 DIS83. Trin Coll Bris DTS90 ADPS91. **d** 91. C Morden *S'wark* from 91. *23 Cedars Road, Morden, Surrey SM4 5AB*   081-542 4877

DYMOCK, Michael James Paul. b 45. AKC69. St Aug Coll Cant 70. **d** 70 **p** 71. C Benhilton *S'wark* 70-73; V Clapham St Jo 73-77; P-in-c Clapham Ch Ch 76-77; V Clapham Ch Ch and St Jo 77-80; V Hackbridge and N Beddington 80-84; V Plumstead St Nic from 84; Sub-Dean of Woolwich from 87. *St Nicholas's Vicarage, 64 Purrett Road, London SE18 1JP*   081-854 0461

DYSON, Prof Anthony Oakley. b 35. Em Coll Cam BA59 MA63 Ex Coll Ox BD64 DPhil68. Ripon Hall Ox 59. **d** 61 **p** 62. C Putney St Mary *S'wark* 61-63; Chapl Ripon Hall Ox 63-68; Prin 69-74; Can Windsor 74-77; Lect Kent Univ 77-80; Perm to Offic *Man* from 80; Prof of Soc and Past Th Man Univ from 80. *33 Danesmoor Road, West Didsbury, Manchester M20 9JT*   061-434 5410

DYSON, Frank. b 28. Open Univ BA. Oak Hill Th Coll 60. **d** 62 **p** 63. C Parr *Liv* 62-65; V Newchapel *Lich* 65-77; R Bunwell w Carleton Rode *Nor* 77-79; P-in-c Tibenham 78-80; R Bunwell w Carleton Rode and Tibenham 80-81; R Pakefield from 81. *The Rectory, Pakefield, Lowestoft, Suffolk NR33 0JZ*   Lowestoft (0502) 574040

DYSON, Peter Whiteley. b 51. Man Univ BA73 LLB75. Qu Coll Birm DipTh80. **d** 81 **p** 82. C Swindon Ch Ch *Bris* 81-84; P-in-c Brislington St Luke 84-91; V Bourne *Guildf* from 91. *Bourne Vicarage, 2 Middle Avenue, Farnham, Surrey GU9 8JL*   Farnham (0252) 715505

DYSON, Philip. b 45. AKC67. **d** 68 **p** 69. C Kennington St Jo *S'wark* 68-71; C Petersham 71-74; C Ham St Rich 71-74; V Ponders End St Matt *Lon* 74-80; P-in-c Old St Pancras w Bedf New Town St Matt 80-87; V from 87; V Somers Town St Mary from 80; P-in-c Oseney Crescent St Luke w Camden Square St Paul 84-87; P-in-c Oseney Crescent St Luke 87-89; AD S Camden (Holborn & St Pancras) from 86; V Camden Square St Paul from 87; P-in-c Kentish Town St Silas 88-89. *St Mary's Church House, Eversholt Street, London NW1 1BN*   071-387 7301

DYSON, Ven Thomas. b 17. OBE91. Man Univ BA38 Lon Univ BD44 St Edm Hall Ox DipEd47 BA50 MA53. Ely Th Coll 38. **d** 40 **p** 41. C Kennington Cross St Anselm *S'wark* 40-43; Chapl RNVR 43-47; V Ox St Pet in the E w St Jo *Ox* 47-54; Chapl St Edm Hall Ox 47-54; Chapl and Asst Master (Hamm) BAOR 54-55; V Colne Ch Ch *Blackb* 55-57; Bermuda from 57; Miss to Seamen from 57; Can and Adn Bermuda from 81. *The Rectory, 15 Longford Road, Warwick, PO Box 248WK, Bermuda WK06*   Bermuda (1809) 236-5744

DYTOR, Clive Idris. b 56. MC82. Trin Coll Cam MA80 Ox Univ BA88. Wycliffe Hall Ox 86. **d** 89 **p** 90. C Rushall *Lich* from 89. *61 Daw End Lane, Walsall WS4 1JP*   Walsall (0922) 35116

E

EADE, John Christopher. b 45. Ch Coll Cam BA68 MA72. Linc Th Coll 68. **d** 70 **p** 71. C Portsea N End St Mark *Portsm* 70-73; C Henleaze *Bris* 73-77; V Slad *Glouc* 77-82; V N Bradley, Southwick and Heywood *Sarum* 82-91; R Fovant, Sutton Mandeville and Teffont Evias etc from 91. *The Rectory, Brookwood House, Fovant, Salisbury SP3 5JA*   Salisbury (0722) 70826

EADE, Stephen David. b 29. Wells Th Coll 67. **d** 69 **p** 70. C Soundwell *Bris* 69-72; C Chippenham St Paul w Langley Burrell 72-75; P-in-c Pilning 76-80; C Bath Twerton-on-Avon *B & W* 80-81; TV Bath Twerton-on-Avon 81-91; rtd 91; Perm to Offic *B & W* from 91. *41A Stafford Street, Weston-super-Mare, Avon BS23 3BP*   Weston-super-Mare (0934) 612252

EADES, Jonathan Peter. b 51. Dundee Univ MA74 Edin Univ BD77. Coates Hall Edin 74. **d** 77 **p** 78. Chapl St Paul's Cathl Dundee *Bre* 77-88; Chapl Dundee Univ 79-88; TV Leek and Meerbrook *Lich* from 88. *All Saints' Vicarage, Compton, Leek, Staffs ST13 5PT*   Leek (0538) 382588

EADY, David Robert. b 43. Salford Univ BSc Birm Univ DSocStuds. Glouc Th Course 82. **d** 85 **p** 86. NSM Highnam, Lassington, Rudford, Tibberton etc *Glouc* from 85. *113 Sussex Gardens, Hucclecote, Gloucester GL3 3SP*   Gloucester (0452) 619931

EADY, Timothy William. b 57. Open Univ BA. Cranmer Hall Dur 82. **d** 85 **p** 86. C Boulton *Derby* 85-88; C Portchester *Portsm* from 88; Relig Progr Adv Ocean Sound Radio from 88. *190 Dore Avenue, Portchester, Fareham, Hants PO16 8EP*   Fareham (0329) 288716

EAGLE, John Frederick Laurence. b 16. St Chad's Coll Dur BA39 DipTh40 MA42. **d** 41 **p** 41. R Stanwick *Pet* 58-72; P-in-c Hargrave 59-72; R Stanwick w Hargrave 72-87; rtd 87; Perm to Offic *Pet* from 87. *Mandell House, Minster Precincts, Peterborough PE1 1XX*   Peterborough (0733) 61807

EAGLE, Canon Julian Charles. b 32. Qu Coll Cam BA56 MA60. Westcott Ho Cam. **d** 58 **p** 59. C Billingham St Aid *Dur* 58-61; C Eastleigh *Win* 61-65; Ind Chapl from 65; Hon Can Win Cathl from 83. *24 Butterfield Road, Southampton SO1 7EE*   Southampton (0703) 791097

EAGLES, Anthony Arthur. b 39. S'wark Ord Course 81. **d** 84 **p** 85. NSM Hillingdon All SS *Lon* 84-87; C Uxbridge 87-90; C Gt Marlow *Ox* from 91. *165 Marlow Bottom Road, Marlow, Bucks*

EAGLES, Peter Andrew. b 59. K Coll Lon BA82 AKC82 Ox Univ BA88. St Steph Ho Ox 86. **d** 89 **p** 90. C Ruislip St Martin *Lon* from 89. *34 Midcroft, Ruislip, Middx HA4 8HB*   Ruislip (0895) 632605

EALES, Howard Bernard. b 46. Sarum & Wells Th Coll 73. **d** 76 **p** 77. C Timperley *Ches* 76-78; C Stockport St Thos 78-82; V Wythenshawe Wm Temple Ch *Man* from 82. *William Temple Vicarage, Robinswood Road, Woodhouse Park, Manchester M22 6BU* 061-437 3194

EALES WHITE, Donald James. b 16. MC. St Jo Coll Ox BA44 MA44. St Deiniol's Hawarden 60. **d** 61 **p** 62. Lic to Offic *Arg* 69-71; V Mendham *St E* 71-72; P-in-c Metfield w Withersdale 71-72; Perm to Offic 73-74; P-in-c Eorrapaidh *Arg* 74-77 and 79-81; R Dalbeattie *Glas* 77-79; rtd 81; P-in-c Dornoch *Mor* 81-82; P-in-c Brora 81-82. *Dell Cottage, South Dell, Isle of Lewis PA86 0SP* Port-of-Ness (085181) 726

EAMAN, Michael Leslie. b 47. Ridley Hall Cam 87. **d** 89 **p** 90. C Wharton *Ches* from 89. *School House, 2 School Road, Wharton, Winsford, Cheshire CW7 3EF* Winsford (0606) 554584

✠**EAMES, Most Rev Robert Henry Alexander.** b 37. QUB LLB60 PhD63 LLD89. CITC. **d** 63 **p** 64 **c** 75. C Ban St Comgall *D & D* 63-66; I Gilnahirk 66-74; I Dundela 74-75; Bp D & R 75-80; Bp D & D 80-86; Abp Arm from 86. *The See House, Cathedral Close, Armagh BT61 7EE* Armagh (0861) 522851

EARDLEY, John. b 38. Ch Coll Cam BA61. Ridley Hall Cam 60. **d** 62 **p** 63. C Barnston *Ches* 62-65; C Wilmslow 65-67; V Hollingworth 67-75; V Leasowe 75-91; RD Wallasey 86-91; V Church Hulme from 91. *The Vicarage, Holmes Chapel, Crewe CW4 7BD* Holmes Chapel (0477) 33124

EARDLEY, Canon John Barry. b 35. MEd87. AKC62. **d** 63 **p** 64. C Mert St Jas *S'wark* 63-66; C St Helier 66-69; C Bilton *Cov* 69-70; C Canley CD 70-74; P-in-c Church Lawford w Newnham Regis 74-80; P-in-c Leamington Hastings and Birdingbury 74-88; Dioc Educn Officer from 82; Hon Can Cov Cathl from 87. *The Rectory, Bubbenhall, Coventry CV8 3BD* Coventry (0203) 302345

EARDLEY, Paul Wycliffe. b 19. ALCD42. **d** 42 **p** 43. R Ripe w Chalvington *Chich* 62-71; V Kemp Town St Mark and St Matt 71-84; rtd 84; Perm to Offic *Chich* from 84. *Saxons, 2 Falmer Road, Rottingdean, Brighton BN2 7DA* Brighton (0273) 32255

EAREY, Mark Robert. b 65. Lough Univ BSc87. Cranmer Hall Dur BA91. **d** 91. C Glen Parva and S Wigston *Leic* from 91. *163 Little Glen Road, Glen Parva, Leicester LE2 9TX* Leicester (0533) 774275

EARIS, Stanley Derek. b 50. Univ Coll Dur BA71 BCL80. Ripon Hall Ox BA73 MA80. **d** 74 **p** 75. C Sutton St Jas and Wawne *York* 74-77; C Acomb St Steph 77-81; V Skelmanthorpe *Wakef* 81-87; R Market Deeping *Linc* from 87. *The Rectory, Church Street, Market Deeping, Peterborough PE6 8DA* Market Deeping (0778) 342237

EARL, David Arthur. b 34. Hartley Victoria Coll 63 Coll of Resurr Mirfield. **d** 83 **p** 83. In Meth Ch 67-83; P-in-c Paddock *Wakef* 83-84; C Huddersfield St Pet and All SS from 84. *All Saints Vicarage, 17 Cross Church Street, Huddersfield HD1 4SN* Huddersfield (0484) 530814

EARL, Very Rev David Kaye Lee. b 28. TCD BA54. **d** 55 **p** 56. C Chapelizod *D & G* 55-58; I Rathkeale *L & K* 58-65; I Killarney 65-79; RD Tralee 71-77; Prec Limerick Cathl 77-79; Dean Ferns *C & O* from 79; I Ferns w Kilbride, Toombe, Kilcormack etc from 79. *The Deanery, Ferns, Co Wexford, Irish Republic* Ferns (54) 66124

EARL, Victor Charles. b 22. Bede Coll Dur BA49. ALCD51. **d** 51 **p** 52. Lic to Offic *Man* 67-82; R Gorton St Phil 82-88; rtd 88; Perm to Offic *Derby* from 88. *4 Burdekin Close, Chapel-en-le-Frith, Stockport, Cheshire SK12 6QA* Chapel-en-le-Frith (0298) 815312

EARLE, Charles Walter. b 08. Keble Coll Ox BA31 MA35. Linc Th Coll 31. **d** 32 **p** 33. R Newent *Glouc* 69-76; rtd 76. *39 Kingsfield Road, Dane End, Ware, Herts SG12 0LZ* Ware (0920) 438514

EARLE, Ven Edward Ernest Maples. b 1900. Dur Univ LTh24 St Jo Coll Dur BA27 MA30. Lon Coll of Div. **d** 24 **p** 25. Hon Can Roch Cathl *Roch* 49-77; Adn Tonbridge 53-77; V Shipbourne 59-86; rtd 86. *Butcher's Cottage, Stumble Hill, Shipbourne, Tonbridge, Kent* Plaxtol (0732) 810648

EARLE, John Nicholas Francis. b 26. Trin Coll Cam BA47 MA54. Westcott Ho Cam 50. **d** 52 **p** 53. Lic to Offic *S'wark* 61-71; Hd Master Bromsgrove Sch Worcs 71-85; rtd 85. *1 Red Post Hill, London SE21 7BX* 081-693 5829

EARLE, Kenneth Noel Morris. b 07. St D Coll Lamp BA30 St Mich Coll Llan 30. **d** 31 **p** 32. Missr to the Deaf (Northants and Rutland) 53-72; rtd 73; Perm to Offic *Pet* from 76. *1 St Christopher's Walk, Abington Park Crescent, Northampton NN3 3AE* Northampton (0604) 31411

EARNEY, Graham Howard. b 45. AKC67. **d** 68 **p** 69. C Auckland St Helen *Dur* 68-72; C Corsenside *Newc* 72-76; P-in-c 76-79; TV Willington Team 79-83; TR

83-87; Dioc Soc Resp Officer *B & W* from 87. *176 Somerton Road, Street, Somerset BA16 0SB* Street (0458) 46621

EARNSHAW, Alan Mark. b 36. CQSW81. Lon Coll of Div LTh60. **d** 60 **p** 61. C Fazakerley Em *Liv* 60-65; V Ovenden *Wakef* 65-79; NSM Halifax St Jude 79-90; V Coley from 90. *41 Ing Head Terrace, Shelf, Halifax, W Yorkshire HX3 7LB* Halifax (0422) 202292

EARNSHAW, Robert Richard. b 42. N Ord Course 78. **d** 81 **p** 82. NSM Liv All So Springwood *Liv* 81-85; R Hinton Ampner w Bramdean and Kilmeston *Win* 85-87; Chapl HM Young Offender Inst Huntercombe and Finnamore Wood Camp from 87. *HM Young Offender Institute, Huntercombe, Oxon* Nettlebed (0491) 641711

EARP, John William. b 19. Jes Coll Cam BA42 MA45. Ridley Hall Cam 42. **d** 43 **p** 44. V Hartley Wintney and Elvetham *Win* 62-77; RD Odiham 76-83; V Hartley Wintney, Elvetham, Winchfield etc 77-88; rtd 88; Perm to Offic *Nor* from 89. *3 The Driftway, Sheringham, Norfolk NR26 8LD* Sheringham (0263) 825487

EARWAKER, John Clifford. b 36. Keble Coll Ox BA59 MA63 Man Univ MEd71. Linc Th Coll 59. **d** 61 **p** 62. C Ecclesall *Sheff* 61-64; Succ St Mary's Cathl *Edin* 64-65; Lic to Offic Man 65-69; Sheff from 69; Chapl and Lect Sheff Poly from 81. *24 Newbould Lane, Sheffield S10 2PL* Sheffield (0742) 665745 or 720911

EASON, Canon Cyril Edward. b 21. Leeds Univ BA43 MA67. Coll of Resurr Mirfield 43. **d** 45 **p** 46. Area Sec (Dio B & W) USPG 65-86; (Dios Ex and Truro) 75-86; Perm to Offic *Truro* 75-86; Hon Can Mufulira from 85; rtd 86; P-in-c Tilshead, Orcheston and Chitterne *Sarum* from 86. *The Vicarage, High Street, Tilshead, Salisbury SP3 4RZ* Shrewton (0980) 620517

EAST, Mark Richard. b 57. Trin Coll Bris BA89. **d** 89 **p** 90. C Dalton-in-Furness *Carl* from 89. *4 Fair View, Dalton-in-Furness, Cumbria LA15 8RZ* Dalton-in-Furness (0229) 64402

EAST, Reginald Walter. b 16. St Jo Coll Dur BA49 DipTh50. **d** 50 **p** 51. V W Mersea *Chelmsf* 57-71; R E Mersea 57-71; C Winterborne Whitechurch w Clenston *Sarum* 71-75; Warden Barn Fellowship Whatcombe Ho 75-80; Lic to Offic 80-85; rtd 85. *Shepherds Cottage, Winterborne Whitechurch, Blandford Forum DT11 0NZ* Milton Abbas (0258) 880190

EAST, Richard Kenneth. b 47. Oak Hill Th Coll 86. **d** 88 **p** 89. C Necton w Holme Hale *Nor* from 88. *21 Chantry Lane, Necton, Swaffham, Norfolk PE37 8ES* Swaffham (0760) 22694

EAST, Stuart Michael. b 50. Chich Th Coll 86. **d** 88 **p** 89. C Middlesb St Martin *York* from 88. *127 Oxford Road, Middlesbrough, Cleveland TS5 5EA* Middlesbrough (0642) 825163

EAST, Dr William Gordon. b 48. Keble Coll Ox BA69 MA77 DipTh77 Yale Univ MPhil71 PhD74. St Steph Ho Ox 77. **d** 78 **p** 79. C Newington St Mary *S'wark* 78-81; C Kennington St Jo w St Jas 81-83; P-in-c Pallion *Dur* 83-86; V from 86. *St Luke's Vicarage, Pallion, Sunderland SR4 6SF* 091-565 6554

EAST RIDING, Archdeacon of. See BUCKINGHAM, Ven Hugh Fletcher

EASTELL, John Kevin. b 42. Liv Univ DSocStuds77 DipAdEd80 MEd86 Open Univ BA83. Lambeth STh82 Kelham Th Coll 61 Wells Th Coll 64. **d** 66 **p** 67. C Horbury *Wakef* 66-69; C Armley St Bart *Ripon* 69-72; V Toxteth St Marg *Liv* 72-76; V Formby St Pet 76-82; V Royston St Paul *Man* 82-88; Dir Professional Min *Lon* from 88. *23A Culmington Road, London W13 9NJ* 081-579 8083

EASTEN, Edmund John Attlee. b 07. CCC Cam BA29 MA33. Bps' Coll Cheshunt 29. **d** 30 **p** 31. R Thurning w Wood Dalling *Nor* 61-79; rtd 79; Perm to Offic *Nor* from 79. *Churchill Cottage, Reepham, Norwich NR10 4JL*

EASTER, Sister Ann Rosemarie. SRN68 DipRS78. Qu Coll Birm. dss 80 **d** 87. Chapl Asst Newham Gen Hosp 80-89; Stratford St Jo and Ch w Forest Gate St Jas *Chelmsf* 80-87; Par Dn 87-89; Hon Par Dn Forest Gate Em w Upton Cross from 89. *St Alban's House, 147 Katherine Road, London E6 1ES* 081-470 2498

EASTER, Brian James Bert. b 33. Lon Univ DipTh55 Birm Univ DPS75 PhD83. Tyndale Hall Bris 53 St Aug Coll Cant 56. **d** 57 **p** 58. C Tipton St Martin *Lich* 57-59; Midl Area Sec BCMS 59-64; V Barston *Birm* 64-72; Chapl Mentally Handicapped S Birm HA from 72; Chapl Monyhull Hosp Birm from 72; Lect Birm Univ from 86. *995 Yardley Wood Road, Birmingham B14 4BS* 021-474 2622 or 444 2271

EASTER, Stephen Talbot. b 22. St Cath Coll Cam BA47 MA53. Ely Th Coll. **d** 50 **p** 51. V St Margarets-at-Cliffe w Westcliffe etc *Cant* 61-85; rtd 85; Perm to Offic *Cant* from 85. *9/11 Blenheim Road, Deal, Kent* Deal (0304) 368021

EASTGATE, Canon John. b 30. Kelham Th Coll 47. **d** 54 **p** 55. C Ealing St Pet Mt Park *Lon* 54-58; C-in-c Leic St Gabr CD *Leic* 58-64; V Leic St Gabr 64-69; Asst RD Christianity 64-69; V Glen Parva and S Wigston 69-74; V Woodley *Ox* 74-83; V Hughenden from 83; RD Wycombe 87-90; Hon Can Ch Ch from 90. *The Vicarage, Valley Road, Hughenden Valley, High Wycombe, Bucks HP14 4PF* Naphill (024024) 3439

EASTOE, Robin Howard Spenser. b 53. Lon Univ BD75 AKC75. Coll of Resurr Mirfield 77. **d** 78 **p** 79. C Gt Ilford St Mary *Chelmsf* 78-81; C Walthamstow St Sav 81-84; V Barkingside St Fran from 84. *St Francis's Vicarage, Fencepiece Road, Ilford, Essex IG6 2LA* 081-500 2970

EASTON, Christopher Richard Alexander. b 60. TCD BA DipTh. **d** 84 **p** 85. C Belf St Donard *D & D* 84-89; I Inishmacsaint *Clogh* from 89. *The Rectory, Derrygonnelly, Co Fermanagh BT93 6HW* Derrygonnelly (036564) 683

EASTON, Dr Donald Fyfe. b 48. St Edm Hall Ox BA69 Nottm Univ CertEd70 Univ Coll Lon MA76 PhD90. Westcott Ho Cam 89. **d** 90. NSM Fulham St Andr Fulham Fields *Lon* from 90. *19 Perham Road, London W14 9SR* 071-385 1002

EASTON, John. b 34. St Cath Soc Ox BA59 MA63. Chich Th Coll 59. **d** 61 **p** 62. C Rugeley *Lich* 61-64; TR 72-87; C Shrewsbury All SS 64-66; Ind Chapl *Sheff* 66-72; V Bolsover *Derby* from 87. *The Vicarage, Bolsover, Chesterfield, Derbyshire S44 6BG* Chesterfield (0246) 824888

EASTON, Richard Huntingford. b 26. Or Coll Ox BA51 MA51. Westcott Ho Cam 53. **d** 54 **p** 55. C Bris St Ambrose Whitehall *Bris* 54-57; New Zealand from 57. *Muriwai Road, RD1 Waimauku, Auckland, New Zealand* Auckland (9) 411-8320

EASTWOOD, Arthur Christopher John. b 17. St Edm Hall Ox BA45 MA45. Westcott Ho Cam 45. **d** 47 **p** 48. V Cowplain *Portsm* 62-86; rtd 86; Perm to Offic *Bris* from 87. *40 Templar Road, Yate, Bristol BS17 5TG* Chipping Sodbury (0454) 322405

EASTWOOD, Colin Foster. b 34. Leeds Univ BA56 MA66. Linc Th Coll 65. **d** 67 **p** 68. C Cottingham *York* 67-70; C Darlington St Cuth *Dur* 70-75; V Eighton Banks 75-81; V Sutton St Jas *Ches* from 81. *St James's Vicarage, Sutton, Macclesfield, Cheshire SK11 0DS* Sutton (02605) 2228

EASTWOOD, Canon Dennis Townend. b 05. Man Univ BA29. Wells Th Coll 29. **d** 30 **p** 31. V Hart w Elwick Hall *Dur* 63-73; rtd 73. *Bishop Stitchill Cottage, Greatham, Hartlepool, Cleveland TS25 2HR* Hartlepool (0429) 870888

EASTWOOD, Harry. b 26. Man Univ BSc48. Ridley Hall Cam 81. **d** 82 **p** 83. NSM Barton Seagrave w Warkton *Pet* from 82. *22 Poplars Farm Road, Kettering, Northants* Kettering (0536) 513271

EASTWOOD, Irvine Thomas. b 17. Sheff Univ BSc38. CITC 88. **d** 90 **p** 91. NSM Wexford w Ardcolm and Killurin *C & O* from 90. *Dubross, Trinity Street, Wexford, Irish Republic* Wexford (53) 23604

EASTWOOD, Miss Janet. b 54. Wycliffe Hall Ox 83. **dss** 86 **d** 87. Ainsdale *Liv* 86-87; Par Dn 87-90; TM Kirkby Lonsdale *Carl* from 90; Dioc Youth Officer from 90. *The Vicarage, Vicarage Lane, Kirkby Lonsdale, Carnforth, Lancs LA6 2BA* Kirkby Lonsdale (05242) 72078

EATOCK, John. b 45. Lanc Univ MA83. Lich Th Coll 67. **d** 70 **p** 71. C Crumpsall St Mary *Man* 70-73; C Atherton 73-74; C Ribbleton *Blackb* 74-77; V Ingol 77-83; V Laneside from 83; RD Accrington from 90. *St Peter's Vicarage, Laneside, Haslingden, Rossendale, Lancs BB4 4BG* Rossendale (0706) 213838

EATON, David Andrew. b 58. ACA83 Man Univ BSc79. Trin Coll Bris BA89. **d** 89 **p** 90. C Barking St Marg w St Patr *Chelmsf* from 89. *12 Thorpe Road, Barking, Essex IG11 9XJ* 081-591 1238

EATON, David John. b 45. Nottm Univ LTh BTh74. St Jo Coll Nottm 70. **d** 74 **p** 75. C Headley All SS *Guildf* 74-77; Ind Chapl *Worc* 77-82; TV Halesowen 80-82; V Rowledge *Guildf* 82-89; V Leatherhead from 89. *The Vicarage, 2 St Mary's Road, Leatherhead, Surrey KT22 8EZ* Leatherhead (0372) 372313

✠**EATON, Rt Rev Derek Lionel.** b 41. QSM85. DMSchM68 Neuchatel Univ Switz Certificate Francais 69 Internat Inst Chr Communication Nairobi 74 Univ of Tunis CertFAI70 Univ of Missouri MA78. Trin Coll Bris DipTh66 WEC Miss Tr Coll DipTh66. **d** 71 **p** 71 **c** 90. C Brislington St Luke *Bris* 71-72; Chapl Br Emb Tunisia 72-78; Provost All SS Cathl Cairo and Chapl Br Emb 78-83; Hon Can from 85; New Zealand from 84; Bp Nelson from 90. *Bishopdale, PO Box 100, Nelson, New Zealand* Christchurch (3) 548-8991 or 548-3124

EATON, Julie Elizabeth. b 57. SEN81. Trin Coll Bris DipHE89. **d** 89. Par Dn Gt Ilford St Andr *Chelmsf* from 89. *12 Thorpe Road, Barking, Essex IG11 9XJ* 081-591 1238

EATON, Mrs Margaret Anne. b 44. **dss** 84 **d** 86. NSM Ellon *Ab* from 84; NSM Cruden from 84. *55 Eilean Rise, Ellon, Aberdeenshire AB4 9NF* Ellon (0358) 21806

EATON, Oscar Benjamin. b 37. Puerto Rico Th Coll STB66. **d** 66 **p** 67. Ecuador 66-69; C Wandsworth St Anne *S'wark* 69-71; C Aldrington *Chich* 71-73; TV Littleham w Exmouth *Ex* 74-79; R Alphington 79-84; Chapl Barcelona w Casteldefels *Eur* 84-88; Chapl Maisons-Laffitte from 88. *15 Avenue Carnot, 78600 Maisons-Laffitte, France* Paris (331) 39 62 34 97

EATON, Canon Peter David. b 58. K Coll Lon BA82 AKC82 Qu Coll Cam BA85 MA89. Westcott Ho Cam 83. **d** 86 **p** 87. C Maidstone All SS and St Phil w Tovil *Cant* 86-89; Fells' Chapl Magd Coll Ox 89-91; Lic to Offic *Ox* from 89; USA from 91; Can Th Dio Utah from 91. *261 South 9000 East, Salt Lake City, Utah 84102, USA* Salt Lake City (801) 322-5869

EATON, Miss Phyllis Mary. b 42. SRD Qu Eliz Coll Lon BSc63 Univ of S Africa BA79. W Midl Minl Tr Course 87. **d** 90. NSM Washwood Heath *Birm* from 90. *Flat 14, Mark House, 14 Wake Green Road, Birmingham B13 9HA* 021-449 2431

EAVES, Alan Charles. b 37. Lon Univ DipTh64. Tyndale Hall Bris 62. **d** 65 **p** 66. C Southport SS Simon and Jude *Liv* 65-66; C Eccleston Ch Ch 66-70; V Earlestown 70-79; V Orpington Ch Ch *Roch* from 79. *Christ Church Vicarage, 165 Charterhouse Road, Orpington, Kent BR6 9EP* Orpington (0689) 870923

EAVES, Brian Maxwell. b 40. Tyndale Hall Bris 66. **d** 69 **p** 70. C Wolv St Jude *Lich* 69-72; C Fazeley 72-75; TV Ipsley *Worc* 75-79; Chapl Amsterdam *Eur* 79-86; Chapl Bordeaux w Riberac, Chares, Duras etc 86-91; Monaco from 91. *Address temp unknown*

EBBITT, Francis Simon. b 20. TCD BA42 MA49 BD56. TCD Div Sch 40. **d** 43 **p** 44. V Rainhill *Liv* 65-74; V Stanford in the Vale w Goosey and Hatford *Ox* 74-80; RD Vale of White Horse 75-80; V Furze Platt 80-87; Chapl St Mark's and Clarefield Hosps Ox 80-87; rtd 87; Asst Chapl Malaga *Eur* 87-90. *Cleeves Lea, Station Road, Lower Heyford, Oxon OX5 3PD* Stonehaven (0569) 40302

EBBITT, Robert David. b 22. TCD BA44 MA56. TCD Div Sch 44. **d** 45 **p** 46. Ireland 45-47; CF 47-65; Dep Asst Chapl Gen 65-72; Asst Chapl Gen 72-78. *13 The Meadow, Groomsport, Co Down BT19 2JH* Bangor (0247) 464443

ECCLES, Ernest Pattison. b 23. Kelham Th Coll 46. **d** 50 **p** 51. R Braithwell w Bramley *Sheff* 56-88; P-in-c Hooton Roberts w Ravenfield 62-75; rtd 88. *Stonegates, Back Lane, Maltby, Rotherham, S Yorkshire S66 7RA* Rotherham (0709) 867910

ECCLES, James Henry. b 30. DLC64 Lon Univ CertPsych70 DipEd. Wycliffe Hall Ox 86. **d** 87 **p** 88. NSM Llandudno *Ban* 87-91. *Lowlands, 7 St Seiriol's Road, Llandudno, Gwynedd LL30 2YY* Llandudno (0492) 78524

ECCLESTONE, Alan. b 04. St Cath Coll Cam BA25 MA29. Wells Th Coll 30. **d** 31 **p** 32. V Darnall H Trin *Sheff* 42-69; rtd 69. *Raceside Cottage, Wellington, Seascale, Cumbria* Gosforth (09467) 25528

ECKERSLEY, Mrs Nancy Elizabeth. b 50. York Univ BA72 Leeds Univ CertEd73. NE Ord Course 86. **d** 89. NSM Clifton *York* from 89. *30 Howard Drive, Rawcliffe, York YO3 6XB* York (0904) 658905

ECKERSLEY, Canon Richard Hugh. b 25. Trin Coll Cam BA48 MA50. Chich Th Coll 49. **d** 51 **p** 52. C Portsea St Jo Rudmore *Portsm* 51-57; C Portsea N End St Mark 57-62; V Paulsgrove 62-73; V Brighton St Nic *Chich* 73-84; Can Res Portsm Cathl *Portsm* from 84. *44 St Thomas's Street, Portsmouth PO1 2EZ* Portsmouth (0705) 816766

EDDERSHAW, Lionel Francis Trevor. b 34. Down Coll Cam BA58 MA62. Linc Th Coll 58. **d** 60 **p** 61. C Wallsend St Luke *Newc* 60-63; C Balkwell CD 63-68; R Falstone 68-75; R St Jo Lee 75-84; R Rothbury from 84. *The Rectory, Rothbury, Morpeth, Northd NE65 7TL* Rothbury (0669) 20482

EDDISON, Frederick Donald Buchanan. b 19. Trin Coll Cam BA41 MA46. Ridley Hall Cam 47. **d** 48 **p** 49. V

Tunbridge Wells St Jo *Roch* 65-80; rtd 80; Perm to Offic *Roch* from 81. *43 East Cliff Road, Tunbridge Wells, Kent TN4 9AG* Tunbridge Wells (0892) 20991

EDDISON, Robert John Buchanan. b 16. Trin Coll Cam BA38 MA42. Ridley Hall Cam 38. **d** 39 **p** 40. Travelling Sec Scripture Union 42-80; rtd 81; Perm to Offic *Chich* from 81. *Durham Lodge, Crowborough, E Sussex TN6 1EW* Crowborough (0892) 2606

EDDLESTON, William. b 08. St Jo Coll Dur BA31 MA34. Wycliffe Hall Ox 31. **d** 32 **p** 33. R Shilling Okeford *Sarum* 65-72; P-in-c Okeford Fitzpaine 67-72; rtd 73; Perm to Offic *Ex* from 73. *25 Springfields, Colyford, Colyton, Devon EX13 6RE* Colyton (0297) 52047

EDE, Albert Alfred. b 11. Dur Univ LTh44 BA45. Clifton Th Coll 36. **d** 39 **p** 40. R Fulletby w Greetham and Ashby Puerorum *Linc* 46-87; V High Toynton 52-87; V Mareham on the Hill 57-87; R Hameringham w Scrafield and Winceby 63-87; rtd 87; Perm to Offic *Linc* from 90. *The Chantry, Greetham, Horncastle, Lincs LN9 6NT* Winceby (065888) 211

EDE, Ven Dennis. b 31. Nottm Univ BA55 Birm Univ MSocSc73. Ripon Hall Ox 55. **d** 57 **p** 58. C Sheldon *Birm* 57-60; C Castle Bromwich SS Mary and Marg 60-64; Chapl E Birm Hosp 60-76; C-in-c Hodge Hill CD *Birm* 64-70; V Hodge Hill 70-72; V Bromwich 72-76; Chapl Sandwell Distr Gen Hosp 76-90; V W Bromwich All SS *Lich* 76-90; P-in-c W Bromwich Ch Ch 76-79; RD W Bromwich 76-90; Preb Lich Cathl 83-90; Adn Stoke from 90; Hon Can Lich Cathl from 90. *39 The Brackens, Clayton, Newcastle-under-Lyme ST5 4JL* Newcastle-under-Lyme (0782) 663066

EDE, Preb Oswald George. b 16. Lich Th Coll 37. **d** 39 **p** 40. V Marchington w Marchington Woodlands *Lich* 46-82; rtd 82; Perm to Offic *Lich* from 82. *19 St Mary's Crescent, Uttoxeter, Staffs ST14 7BH* Uttoxeter (0889) 566106

EDEN, Henry. b 36. G&C Coll Cam BA59 MA64. Ox NSM Course. **d** 87 **p** 88. NSM Abingdon w Shippon *Ox* 87-88; Chapl Brentwood Sch Essex from 89. *Mitre House, 6 Shenfield Road, Brentwood, Essex CM15 8AA* Brentwood (0277) 224442

EDEN, Leslie Thomas Ernest. b 19. ACII55. S'wark Ord Course. **d** 69 **p** 70. NSM Kidbrooke St Jas *S'wark* from 69. *47 Begbie Road, London SE3 8DA* 081-856 3088

EDEN, Michael William. b 57. Nottm Univ BTh86. Linc Th Coll 83. **d** 86 **p** 87. C Daventry *Pet* 86-89; TV Northn Em from 89. *4 Booth Lane North, Northampton NN3 1JG* Northampton (0604) 648974

EDGAR, Brother. *See* DAVIES, William Kenneth

EDGAR, David. b 59. Newc Univ BA81. Linc Th Coll BTh86. **d** 86 **p** 87. C Wednesbury St Paul Wood Green *Lich* 86-91; V Winterton Gp *Linc* from 91. *The Vicarage, High Street, Winterton, Scunthorpe, S Humberside DN15 9PU* Scunthorpe (0724) 732262

EDGAR, Canon Granville George. b 25. St Pet Hall Ox BA46 MA50. St Mich Coll Llan 46. **d** 48 **p** 49. V Llantilio Crossenny and Llanfihangel Ystern etc *Mon* 69-73; Dioc Dir RE 73-86; R Llangybi 73-91; Can St Woolos Cathl from 73; rtd 91. *28 Manor Court, Baron Street, Usk, Gwent*

EDGAR, Timothy Roy. b 56. K Coll Lon BD78 AKC78. Coll of Resurr Mirfield 79. **d** 80 **p** 81. C Hampstead Garden Suburb *Lon* 80-82; C Cantley *Sheff* 82-86; V Sheff St Cath Richmond Road 86-90; Dir Past Studies Coll of the Resurr Mirfield from 90. *Hall Cottage, 440 Huddersfield Road, Mirfield, W Yorkshire WF14 0EE* Mirfield (0924) 492199

EDGE, Canon John Francis. b 32. Ex Coll Ox BA54 MA58. St Steph Ho Ox 54. **d** 58 **p** 59. C Oswestry H Trin *Lich* 58-62; V 64-79; Tutor Lich Th Coll 62-64; Malaysia 79-88; Warden Ho of the Epiphany Kuching 79-88; Hon Can Kuching from 88; TV Wolv *Lich* from 88. *All Saints' Vicarage, Vicarage Road, Wolverhampton WV2 1DT* Wolverhampton (0902) 450753

EDGE, Michael MacLeod. b 45. St Andr Univ BSc68 Qu Coll Cam BA70 MA74. Westcott Ho Cam 68. **d** 72 **p** 73. C Allerton *Liv* 72-76; R Bretherton *Blackb* 76-82; P-in-c Kilpeck *Heref* 82-84; P-in-c St Devereux w Wormbridge 82-84; TR Ewyas Harold w Dulas, Kenderchurch etc from 82; RD Abbeydore 84-90. *The Rectory, Ewyas Harold, Hereford HR2 0EY* Golden Valley (0981) 240484

EDGE, Philip John. b 54. Ripon Coll Cuddesdon 77. **d** 80 **p** 81. C N Harrow St Alb *Lon* 80-83; C St Giles Cripplegate w St Bart Moor Lane etc 83-86; P-in-c Belmont 86-88; V from 88. *St Anselm's Vicarage, Ventnor Avenue, Stanmore, Middx HA7 2HU* 081-907 3186

EDGE, Ms Renate Erika. b 50. Bonn Chamber of Commerce TransDip75 DIL77. Cranmer Hall Dur 86.

d 88. Par Dn Leic H Spirit *Leic* 88-89; Asst Chapl Leic and Co Miss for the Deaf 88-89; Par Dn Leic H Apostles *Leic* from 89. *47 Duncan Road, Leicester LE2 8EG* Leicester (0533) 834462

EDGE, Timothy Peter. b 55. CEng85 MIEE85 FRAS80 Brighton Poly BSc80. Westcott Ho Cam 85. **d** 88 **p** 89. C Norton *Ches* from 88. *10 Moorland Drive, Abbot's Lodge, Murdishaw, Runcorn, Cheshire WA7 6HL* Runcorn (0928) 716942

EDGELL, Hugh Anthony Richard. b 31. ARHistS84. AKC57. **d** 58 **p** 59. C N Lynn w St Marg and St Nic *Nor* 58-64; R S Walsham 64-74; V Upton w Fishley 64-74; R Hingham 74-81; R Hingham w Woodrising w Scoulton 81-85; OStJ 79-88; SBStJ from 88; V Horning *Nor* 85-89; P-in-c Beeston St Laurence w Ashmanhaugh 85-89; R Horning w Beeston St Laurence and Ashmanhaugh from 89; Prior St Benet's Abbey Horning from 87. *The Vicarage, Horning, Norwich NR12 8PZ* Horning (0692) 630216

EDGELL, William John Raymond. b 15. St Aid Birkenhead 63. **d** 65 **p** 66. V Bury St Paul *Man* 68-77; rtd 80. *Dunromin, 18 Greenbrock Close, Bury, Lancs BL9 6NS* 061-797 1513

EDGINGTON, Harold James Figg. b 05. LCP49. Cuddesdon Coll 60. **d** 60 **p** 61. R Boyton w Sherrington *Sarum* 67-76; rtd 76; Hon C Bladon w Woodstock *Ox* 76-80; Hon C Cottisford 81-83; Perm to Offic from 83. *Balney Grounds, Hanslope Road, Castle Thorpe, Milton Keynes MK19 7HD* Milton Keynes (0908) 510385

EDINBOROUGH, David. b 36. BA MEd. E Midl Min Tr Course. **d** 82 **p** 83. NSM Bramcote *S'well* from 82; Dioc Officer for NSMs from 89. *105A Derby Road, Beeston, Nottingham NG9 3GZ* Nottingham (0602) 251066

EDINBURGH, Bishop of. *See* HOLLOWAY, Rt Rev Richard Frederick

EDINBURGH, Dean of. *See* HARDY, Very Rev Brian Albert

EDINBURGH, Provost of. *See* FORBES, Very Rev Graham John Thompson

EDIS, John Oram. b 26. ACIS50 ACP52 FCP89 CDipAF78 Open Univ BA81. Ox NSM Course 85. **d** 88 **p** 89. Hon Warden and Chapl E Ivor Hughes Educn Foundn from 88; NSM St Chesham *Ox* from 88. *21 Greenway, Chesham, Bucks HP5 2BW* Chesham (0494) 785815

EDMEADS, Andrew. b 53. Linc Th Coll 84. **d** 86 **p** 87. C Sholing *Win* 86-89; R Knights Enham from 89. *The Rectory, 1 Ryon Close, Knights Enham, Andover, Hants SP10 4DG* Andover (0264) 57032

EDMONDS, Bernard Bruce. b 10. Ch Coll Cam BA32 MA36. St Steph Ho Ox 36. **d** 37 **p** 38. V Caxton *Ely* 61-72; rtd 73; Perm to Offic *St Alb* from 74. *Pilgrims Rest, Poslingford Corner, Clare, Sudbury, Suffolk CO10 8QT* Clare (0787) 277442

EDMONDS, Clive. b 42. ACII. S'wark Ord Course 78. **d** 81 **p** 82. C Horsell *Guildf* 81-85; R Bisley and W End from 85; RD Surrey Heath from 90. *The Rectory, Clews Lane, Bisley, Woking, Surrey GU24 9DY* Brookwood (04867) 3377

EDMONDS, Canon John Herbert. b 16. BNC Ox BA38 MA41. Cuddesdon Coll 39. **d** 40 **p** 41. C Northolt St Mary *Lon* 40-44; Chapl Woodbridge Sch Suffolk 44-47; Perm to Offic *Cant* 47-49, 56-74 and from 80; Chapl K Sch Cant 47-56; Min Can Cant Cathl *Cant* 49-56; Hd Master K Jun Sch Cant 56-78; Hon Can Cant Cathl *Cant* 74-80. *15 Burgate, Canterbury, Kent CT1 2HG* Canterbury (0227) 455840

EDMONDS, Canon Joseph William. b 12. Bps' Coll Cheshunt 46. **d** 49 **p** 50. R Dickleburgh w Thelveton and Frenze *Nor* 69-80; RD Redenhall 73-88; R Dickleburgh w Thelveton w Frenze and Shimpling 80-81; rtd 81; Hon Can Nor Cathl *Nor* from 84. *Rookery Nook, Plot 4, Sunnyside, Diss, Norfolk IP22 3DS* Diss (0379) 643369

EDMONDS, Richard Henry. b 11. Em Coll Cam BA34 MA39. Chich Th Coll 35. **d** 36 **p** 37. V Torquay St Jo *Ex* 67-74; R Cen Torquay 74-77; rtd 77; Lic to Offic *Ex* from 77. *Larksborough, Rectory Road, Newton Abbot, Devon TQ12 6AH* Newton Abbot (0626) 62857

EDMONDS, Sidney. b 20. Oak Hill Th Coll. **d** 58 **p** 59. Chapl HM Pris *Liv* 61-63; Dur 63-69; Parkhurst 69-74; Reading 74-85; V Aldworth and Ashampstead *Ox* 74-85; rtd 85. *22 Sandlea Park, West Kirby, Wirral, Merseyside L48 0QF* 051-625 6147

EDMONDS-SEAL, Dr John. b 34. FFARCS63 Lon Univ MB, BS58. Ox NSM Course WInTh90. **d** 90. NSM Ox St Aldate w St Matt *Ox* from 90. *Otway, Wood Perry Road, Oxford OX3 9UY* Stanton St John (086735) 582

EDMONDSON, Christopher Paul. b 50. Dur Univ BA71 MA81 St Jo Coll Dur DipTh72. **d** 73 **p** 74. C

Kirkheaton *Wakef* 73-79; V Ovenden 79-86; Bp's Adv on Evang 81-86; P-in-c Bampton w Mardale *Carl* from 86; Dioc Officer for Evang from 86. *The Vicarage, Bampton Grange, Penrith, Cumbria CA10 2QR* Bampton (09313) 239

EDMONDSON, Christopher Talbot. b 32. Wycliffe Hall Ox 64. **d** 66 **p** 67. C Buckhurst Hill *Chelmsf* 66-70; V Leytonstone St Jo 70-84; rtd 84; Perm to Offic *B & W* from 86. *Danesboro, Castle Street, Keinton Mandeville, Somerton, Somerset TA11 6DX* Charlton Mackrell (045822) 3239

EDMONDSON, John James William. b 55. St Jo Coll Dur BA83 MA91. Cranmer Hall Dur 80. **d** 83 **p** 84. C Gee Cross *Ches* 83-86; C Camberley St Paul *Guildf* 86-88; TV 88-90; V Foxton w Gumley and Laughton and Lubenham *Leic* from 90. *The Vicarage, Vicarage Drive, Foxton, Market Harborough, Leics LE16 7RJ* East Langton (085884) 245

EDMONDSON, Canon Norman Ross. b 16. St Jo Coll Dur BA39. **d** 39 **p** 40. R Crook *Dur* 55-72; RD Stanhope 61-72; Hon Can Dur Cathl from 66; R Sedgefield 72-84; RD Sedgefield 78-84; rtd 84. *2 Spring Lane, Sedgefield, Stockton-on-Tees, Cleveland TS21 2DG* Sedgefield (0740) 20629

EDMONTON, Area Bishop of. See MASTERS, Rt Rev Brian John

EDMUND, Brother. See BLACKIE, Richard Footner

EDMUNDS, Andrew Charles. b 57. Lon Univ BEd80 CQSW83. Oak Hill NSM Course. **d** 89 **p** 90. NSM Hawkwell *Chelmsf* from 89. *30 Hawkwell Park Drive, Hawkwell, Hockley, Essex SS5 4HB* Southend-on-Sea (0702) 203476

EDMUNDS, Eric John. b 39. Univ of Wales TCert60. W Midl Minl Tr Course 87. **d** 90 **p** 91. NSM Brewood *Lich* from 90; Chapl R Wolv Sch from 91. *15 Fern Leys, Wolverhampton WV3 9EJ* Wolverhampton (0902) 763572

EDMUNDS, Gerald. b 12. ACIB. Glouc Th Course 72. **d** 72 **p** 73. NSM Tewkesbury w Walton Cardiff *Glouc* 72-82; Perm to Offic from 82. *29 Manor Park, Tewkesbury, Glos GL20 8BQ* Tewkesbury (0684) 294150

EDMUNDSON, Thomas. b 09. Oak Hill Th Coll 58. **d** 59 **p** 60. V Halliwell St Paul *Man* 61-75; rtd 75; Lic to Offic *Blackb* from 76. *10 The Hayels, Blackburn BB1 9HZ* Blackburn (0254) 246408

EDNEY, William Henry. b 13. Birm Univ BA34. Qu Coll Birm 77. **d** 78 **p** 79. Hon C Cov St Geo *Cov* 78-85; Perm to Offic from 85. *20 Loudon Avenue, Coventry CV6 1JH* Coventry (0203) 592168

EDSON, Michael. b 42. Birm Univ BSc64 Leeds Univ BA71. Coll of Resurr Mirfield 69. **d** 72 **p** 73. C Barnstaple St Pet w H Trin *Ex* 72-77; TV Barnstaple and Goodleigh 77-79; TV Barnstaple, Goodleigh and Landkey 79-82; V Roxbourne St Andr *Lon* 82-89; AD Harrow 85-89; P-in-c S Harrow St Paul 86-89; Warden Lee Abbey from 89. *Garden Lodge, Lee Abbey, Lynton, Devon EX35 6JJ* Lynton (0598) 52621

EDWARD, Brother. See LEES-SMITH, Christopher John

EDWARDS, Canon Alan Henry. b 07. Qu Coll Ox BA30 MA33. Westcott Ho Cam 33. **d** 34 **p** 35. V Marbury *Ches* 69-74; rtd 74; Perm to Offic *Lich* from 75. *1 Mercian Court, Market Drayton, Shropshire TF9 1PB* Market Drayton (0630) 3778

EDWARDS, Preb Albert. b 20. Univ of Wales (Lamp) BA48. St Mich Coll Llan 48. **d** 50 **p** 51. V Tamworth *Lich* 65-86; RD Tamworth 69-81; Preb Lich Cathl 73-86; rtd 86; Perm to Offic *Lich* from 86. *Broom Cottage, Mount Street, Welshpool, Powys SY21 7LW* Welshpool (0938) 4008

EDWARDS, Aled. b 55. Univ of Wales (Lamp) BA77. Trin Coll Bris 77. **d** 79 **p** 80. C Glanogwen *Ban* 79-82; V Llandinorwig w Penisa'r-waen 82-85; R Meyllteyrn w Botwnnog and Llandygwnnin etc from 85. *The Rectory, Botwnnog, Pwllheli, Gwynedd LL53 8PY* Botwnnog (075883) 450

EDWARDS, Andrew Colin. b 55. ACA81 Pemb Coll Cam BA77 MA80. St Mich Coll Llan BD89. **d** 89 **p** 90. C Newport St Paul *Mon* 89-91; C Newport St Woolos from 91; Min Can St Woolos Cathl from 91. *10 Clifton Road, Newport, Gwent NP9 4EW* Newport (0633) 264805

EDWARDS, Andrew David. b 42. Tyndale Hall Bris 67. **d** 70 **p** 71. C Blackpool Ch Ch *Blackb* 70-73; C W Teignmouth *Ex* 73-76; P-in-c Ilfracombe SS Phil and Jas 76-85; C-in-c Lundy Is 79-89; V Ilfracombe SS Phil and Jas w W Down 85-89; TV Canford Magna *Sarum* from 89. *The Vicarage, 11 Plantagenet Crescent, Bournemouth BH11 9PL* Bournemouth (0202) 573872

EDWARDS, Andrew James. b 54. York Univ BA76. Wycliffe Hall Ox 77. **d** 80 **p** 81. C Beckenham St Jo *Roch* 80-83; C Luton Ch Ch 83-87; V Skelmersdale Ch at Cen *Liv* from 87. *10 Ferndale, Skelmersdale, Lancs WN8 6QZ* Skelmersdale (0695) 28356

EDWARDS, Anthony Stuart. b 40. Queensland Univ BA60 DipEd61 Caen Univ LesL63 Linacre Coll Ox BA65 MA70 Lon Univ AcDipEd75 MA77 MTh88. St Steph Ho Ox 63. **d** 66 **p** 68. C Pimlico St Gabr *Lon* 66-67; C Balham Hill Ascension *S'wark* 68-69; C Bedf St Andr *St Alb* 69-73; C Bedf St Paul 73-75; Chapl Bancroft's Sch Woodford Green 75-81; Lic to Offic *Chelmsf* 75-82; Hon C Loughton St Mary and High Beech 82-86; Chapl Roedean Sch Brighton 86-87; Chapl St Olave and St Sav Sch Orpington 87-91; Chapl RAF 90-91; Chapl Dulwich Coll from 91. *Foxwood, 6 Church Row, Chislehurst, Kent BR7 5PG* 081-468 7743

EDWARDS, Canon Arthur John. b 42. Qu Mary Coll Lon BA64 MPhil66. St Mich Coll Llan 66. **d** 68 **p** 69. C Newport St Woolos *Mon* 68-71; V Llantarnam 71-74; Chapl The Bp of Llan High Sch 74-78; V Griffithstown *Mon* 78-86; Dioc Dir RE from 86; R Cwmbran from 86; Hon Can St Woolos Cathl 88-91; Can St Woolos Cathl from 91. *The Rectory, Clomendy Road, Cwmbran, Gwent NP44 3LS* Cwmbran (0633) 34880

EDWARDS, Miss Carol Rosemary. b 46. Lon Univ DipTh76. Trin Coll Bris 74. **dss** 81 **d** 87. Hengrove Bris 81-82; Filton 82-85; Brislington St Chris 85-87; Dn-in-c from 87. *24 Hampstead Road, Brislington, Bristol BS4 3HJ* Bristol (0272) 773670

EDWARDS, Charles Grayson. b 37. Macalester Coll (USA) BSc59. Ripon Hall Ox 64. **d** 66 **p** 67. C Bletchley *Ox* 66-68; C Ware St Mary *St Alb* 68-73; TV Basingstoke *Win* 73-80; P-in-c Sandford w Upton Hellions *Ex* 80-82; R from 82. *The Rectory, Sandford, Crediton, Devon EX17 4LZ* Crediton (03632) 2530

EDWARDS, Cyril Arthur. b 28. Ripon Hall Ox 54. **d** 56 **p** 57. C Rotherham *Sheff* 56-61; Lic to Offic *Bris* from 61. *1A Colston Parade, Bristol BS1 6RA* Bristol (0272) 262770

EDWARDS, Cyril Herbert Charles. b 03. AKC31. **d** 31 **p** 32. R Hawridge w Cholesbury *Ox* 61-72; rtd 72. *7 Warwick Road, Reading RG2 7AX* Reading (0734) 873259

EDWARDS, David Arthur. b 26. Wadh Coll Ox BA50 MA51. Wycliffe Hall Ox 50. **d** 52 **p** 53. C Didsbury St Jas and Em *Man* 52-55; Liv Sec SCM 55-58; Chapl Liv Univ *Liv* 55-58; R Burnage St Nic *Man* 58-65; V Yardley St Edburgha *Birm* 65-73; Org Sec (Dios Blackb, Carl and Man) CECS 73-78; R Man Resurr *Man* 78-81; V Lorton and Loweswater w Buttermere *Carl* 81-87; Malaysia from 87. *House of the Epiphany, PO Box 347, 93704 Kuching, Sarawak, Malaysia*

EDWARDS, David Forsyth. b 15. Selw Coll Cam BA37 MA41. Ridley Hall Cam 37. **d** 41 **p** 41. Rhodesia 65-80; Zimbabwe from 80; rtd 80. *5 Vanguard Close, Emerald Hill, Harare, Zimbabwe* Harare (4) 304973

EDWARDS, David Henry Oswald. b 16. St D Coll Lamp BA38. **d** 41 **p** 42. C Fishguard w Llanychar *St D* 71-81; rtd 81. *Walmer House, West Street, Fishguard, Dyfed* Fishguard (0348) 873329

EDWARDS, David Idwal. b 06. St D Coll Lamp BA29. **d** 29 **p** 30. R St Lawrence and Ford *St D* 57-76; rtd 76. *Garreg Wen, Llanfrynach, Dyfed SA35 0BA* Llanfrynach (087486) 460

EDWARDS, Very Rev David Lawrence. b 29. Magd Coll Ox BA52 MA56. Lambeth DD90 Westcott Ho Cam 53. **d** 54 **p** 55. Fell All So Coll Ox 52-59; Tutor Westcott Ho Cam 54-55; SCM Sec 55-58; C Hampstead St Jo *Lon* 55-58; C St Martin-in-the-Fields 58-66; Ed SCM Press 59-66; Gen Sec SCM 65-66; Dean K Coll Cam 66-70; Six Preacher Cant Cathl *Cant* 69-76; Can Westmr Abbey 70-78; R Westmr St Marg 70-78; Chmn Chr Aid 71-78; Chapl to Speaker of Ho of Commons 72-78; Sub-Dean Westmr 74-78; Dean Nor 78-83; Provost S'wark from 83. *51 Bankside, London SE1 9JE* 071-928 6414 or 407 3708

EDWARDS, Ms Diana Clare. b 56. SRN77 RSCN81 Nottm Univ BTh86. Linc Th Coll 83. **dss** 86 **d** 87. S Wimbledon H Trin and St Pet *S'wark* 86-87; Par Dn 87-90; Par Dn Lingfield and Crowhurst from 90; Chapl St Pier's Hosp Sch Lingfield from 90. *8 Youngman, St Pier's Lane, Lingfield, Surrey RH7 6PN* Lingfield (0342) 833086

EDWARDS, Douglas. b 33. **d** 62 **p** 63. C Weaste *Man* 62-66; C Kersal Moor 66-71; V Gedney *Linc* 71-80. *c/o Gedney Vicarage, Spalding, Lincs PE12 0BU*

EDWARDS, Dudley James Milne. b 15. AKC38. **d** 38 **p** 39. V Mackworth St Fran *Derby* 68-75; R Ashwick w Oakhill and Binegar *B & W* 75-80; rtd 80; Perm to Offic *B & W*

from 81. *Trefechan, The Street, Draycott, Cheddar, Somerset BS27 3TH* Cheddar (0934) 743573

EDWARDS, Canon Emrys Llewelyn. b 14. St D Coll Lamp BA37. **d** 39 **p** 41. V Llanelly Ch Ch *St D* 60-72; R Llanbadarn Fawr 72-79; Can St D Cathl 72-79; rtd 79. *Llys-y-Coed, New Quay, Dyfed SA45 9SB* New Quay (0545) 560143

EDWARDS, Canon Geoffrey Lewis. b 14. Lon Univ BD39 AKC39. **d** 39 **p** 40. V Mill End *St Alb* 47-72; V W Hyde St Thos 47-72; RD Watford 68-70; RD Rickmansworth 70-72; V Hockerill 72-84; RD Bishop's Stortford 74-84; Hon Can St Alb 76-84; rtd 84; Perm to Offic *Heref* from 84. *Appleyard, Ashfield Crescent, Ross-on-Wye, Herefordshire HR9 5PH* Ross-on-Wye (0989) 67782

EDWARDS, Geraint Wyn. b 47. St D Coll Lamp DipTh70. **d** 71 **p** 72. C Llandudno *Ban* 71-73; C Ban St Mary 73-74; V Penisarwaen and Llanddeiniolen 74-77; V Llandinorwig w Penisarwaun and Llanddeiniolen 77-78; R Llanfechell w Bodewryd w Rhosbeirio etc from 78. *The Rectory, Llanfechell, Amlwch, Gwynedd LL68 0RE* Cemaes Bay (0407) 710356

EDWARDS, Gerald Claude Francis. b 04. Keble Coll Ox BA27 MA31. Cuddesdon Coll 27. **d** 28 **p** 29. R Blunham *St Alb* 54-70; rtd 70. *Worlington Flat, Kington Langley, Chippenham, Wilts SN15 5NN* Kington Langley (024975) 515

EDWARDS, Canon Gerald Lalande. b 30. Bris Univ MEd72. Glouc Th Course 75. **d** 76 **p** 76. NSM Pittville *Glouc* 76-79; NSM Cheltenham St Mich from 79; Hon Can Glouc Cathl from 91. *26 Monica Drive, Cheltenham, Glos GL50 4NQ* Cheltenham (0242) 516863

EDWARDS, Gordon Henry. b 33. FRICS60 FCILA67 FCIArb72 Reading Univ PhD87. Ripon Coll Cuddesdon 89. **d** 90 **p** 91. Hon C Sherston Magna, Easton Grey, Luckington etc *Bris* from 90. *The Old Vicarage, Sherston, Malmesbury, Wilts SN16 0LR* Malmesbury (0666) 840405

EDWARDS, Canon Graham Arthur. b 32. St D Coll Lamp 56. **d** 61 **p** 62. C Bettws St Dav *St D* 61-65; V Castlemartin and Warren 65-69; R Castlemartin w Warren and Angle etc 69-77; V St Clears w Llangynin and Llanddowror 77-83; CF (TAVR) from 78; V St Clears w Llangynin and Llanddowror etc *St D* from 83; Hon Can St D Cathl from 90. *The Vicarage, High Street, St Clears, Carmarthen, Dyfed SA33 4EE* St Clears (0994) 230266

EDWARDS, Graham Charles. b 40. Qu Coll Birm 80. **d** 82 **p** 83. C Baswich (or Berkswich) *Lich* 82-86; C Tamworth 86-88; R Hertf St Andr *St Alb* from 88. *St Andrew's Rectory, 43 North Road, Hertford SG14 1LZ* Hertford (0992) 582726

EDWARDS, Harold James. b 50. Lon Univ CertEd72. Ridley Hall Cam 84 Qu Coll Birm 78. **d** 81 **p** 82. NSM The Quinton *Birm* 81-84; C Highters Heath 84-85; V Llanwddyn and Llanfihangel and Llwydiarth *St As* 85-88; V Ford *Heref* from 88; V Alberbury w Cardeston from 88. *The Vicarage, Ford, Shrewsbury SY5 9LZ* Shrewsbury (0743) 850254

EDWARDS, Harry Steadman. b 37. St Aid Birkenhead 64. **d** 66 **p** 67. Hon C Handsworth St Jas *Birm* 66-83; Hon C Curdworth w Castle Vale 83-85; P-in-c Small Heath St Greg 85-88; V High Crompton *Man* from 88. *St Mary's Vicarage, 18 Rushcroft Road, High Crompton, Shaw, Oldham OL2 7GG*

EDWARDS, Helen. b 57. SRN79 RMN81. Wycliffe Hall Ox 88. **d** 90. Par Dn Clapham St Jas *S'wark* from 90. *Church House, 10 West Road, London SW4 7DN*

EDWARDS, Henry Victor. b 48. AKC71 Open Univ BA85. St Aug Coll Cant 72. **d** 73 **p** 74. C W Leigh CD *Portsm* 73-77; V Cosham 77-84; V Reydon *St E* from 84; Chapl Blythburgh Hosp from 86; P-in-c Walberswick w Blythburgh *St E* from 86. *The Vicarage, Wangford Road, Reydon, Southwold, Suffolk IP18 6PZ* Southwold (0502) 722192

EDWARDS, Herbert Joseph. b 29. Nottm Univ BA51. Wells Th Coll 54. **d** 56 **p** 57. C Leic St Pet *Leic* 56-61; C-in-c Broom Leys CD 61-65; V Broom Leys 65-68; Lect Lich Th Coll 68-71; Rhodesia 71-79; Botswana 74-75; V Bloxwich *Lich* 80-84; R Asfordby *Leic* from 84. *The Rectory, Church Lane, Asfordby, Melton Mowbray, Leics LE14 3RU* Melton Mowbray (0664) 812327

EDWARDS, James Frederick. b 36. ALCD62. **d** 62 **p** 63. C Kenwyn *Truro* 62-68; V Tuckingmill 68-76; V St Columb Minor and St Colan from 76; RD Pydar from 84. *The Vicarage, Parkenbutts, St Columb Minor, Newquay, Cornwall TR7 3HE* Newquay (0637) 3496

EDWARDS, John Gregory. b 29. Univ of Wales BA49 MA53. St Steph Ho Ox 64. **d** 66 **p** 67. C Ealing Ch the Sav *Lon* 66-70; C Greenford H Cross 70-75;

P-in-c Poundstock *Truro* 75-82; R Week St Mary w Poundstock and Whitstone from 82. *The Rectory, The Glebe, Week St Mary, Holsworthy, Devon EX22 6UY* Week St Mary (028884) 265

EDWARDS, Canon Jonathan Gilbert. b 19. Keble Coll Ox BA41 MA50. Linc Th Coll 41. **d** 43 **p** 44. R Gt Bookham *Guildf* 67-80; RD Leatherhead 77-80; Hon Can Guildf Cathl 78-85; V Bramley 80-81; V Grafham 80-81; RD Cranleigh 81-85; V Bramley and Grafham 81-85; rtd 85. *Cyprus Cottage, Bath Road, Sturminster Newton, Dorset DT10 1DU* Sturminster Newton (0258) 72933

EDWARDS, Kenneth Barnsley. b 19. **d** 72 **p** 73. C Henley *Ox* 74-77; P-in-c Hatch Beauchamp w Beercrocombe *B & W* 77-80; P-in-c W Hatch 77-80; P-in-c Curry Mallet 79-80; C Ex St Thos and Em *Ex* 81; Perm to Offic *B & W* from 82; R Tollard Royal w Farnham, Gussage St Michael etc *Sarum* 87-89; rtd 89. *6 Stephens Cottages, Buckland St Mary, Chard, Somerset TA20 3SL* Buckland St Mary (046034) 673

EDWARDS, Leigh Cameron. b 17. St Cath Soc Ox BA38 MA42. St Steph Ho Ox 38. **d** 40 **p** 41. C Roath St Marg *Llan* 40-43; P-in-c Llangeview *Mon* 43-46; P-in-c Gwernesney 43-46; C Bournemouth St Mary *Win* 46-49; V Southn St Jas 49-54; C Win St Jo cum Winnall 54-58; R Carshalton *S'wark* from 58. *The Rectory, 2 Talbot Road, Carshalton, Surrey SM5 3BS* 081-647 2366

EDWARDS, Leslie. b 27. Univ of Wales (Ban) DipTh54. St D Coll Lamp 54. **d** 55 **p** 56. C Rhyl w Rhyl St Ann *St As* 55-59; V Llawrybettws and Bettws Gwerfyl Goch 59-62; V Caerfallwch 62-66; R Halkyn and Caerfallwch from 66; P-in-c Rhesycae from 74. *The New Rectory, Halkyn, Holywell, Clwyd CH8 8BU* Halkyn (0352) 780670

EDWARDS, Malcolm Ralph. b 27. Man Univ 49. Cranmer Hall Dur 57. **d** 59 **p** 60. C Withington St Paul *Man* 59-62; C Chadderton Em 62-64; R Longsight St Jo 64-70; V Halliwell St Thos 70-81; V Milnrow from 81. *The Vicarage, 40 Eafield Avenue, Milnrow, Rochdale, Lancs OL16 3UN* Rochdale (0706) 42988

EDWARDS, Michael Norman William. b 34. St Paul's Grahamstown 62. **d** 63 **p** 65. S Africa 63-81; Tristan da Cunha 81-83; R Aston-on-Trent and Weston-on-Trent *Derby* 84-87; V Derby St Thos from 87. *St Thomas's Vicarage, 159 Pear Tree Road, Derby DE3 8NQ* Derby (0332) 43470

EDWARDS, Nicholas John. b 53. UEA BA75 Fitzw Coll Cam BA77 MA80. Westcott Ho Cam 75. **d** 78 **p** 79. C Kirkby *Liv* 78-81; V Cantril Farm 81-87; V Hale from 87. *The Vicarage, Hale, Liverpool L24 4AX* 051-425 3195

EDWARDS, Mrs Patricia Anne. b 52. E Midl Min Tr Course 79. **dss** 79 **d** 87. Hon Par Dn Clifton *S'well* from 87. *148 Wilford Road, Ruddington, Nottingham NG11 6FB* Nottingham (0602) 843402

EDWARDS, Peter Aubrey. b 30. Qu Coll Birm. **d** 58 **p** 59. V Didcot St Pet *Ox* 65-73; P-in-c Letcombe Regis w Letcombe Bassett 73-77; P-in-c Childrey 75-77; P-in-c Sparsholt w Kingston Lisle 75-77; RD Wantage 77-84; R Ridgeway 77-86; P-in-c Grazeley and Beech Hill 86-88; P-in-c Spencer's Wood 86-88; V Beech Hill, Grazeley and Spencers Wood 88-91; rtd 91. *Shalom, Newbury Street, Lambourn, Newbury, Berks RE16 7PD* Lambourn (0488) 72205

EDWARDS, Peter Clive. b 50. Lon Univ BA72. St Steph Ho Ox 83. **d** 85 **p** 86. C Lee St Aug *S'wark* 85-90; V Salfords from 90. *The Vicarage, Honeycrock Lane, Salfords, Redhill RH1 5DF* Redhill (0737) 762232

EDWARDS, Very Rev Peter Graham. b 50. St Steph Ho Ox 72. **d** 75 **p** 76. C Upper Teddington SS Pet and Paul *Lon* 75-81; Zambia 81-89; Dean Lusaka Cath 85-89; Can Lusaka from 89; Perm to Offic *Lon* from 85; V Swanley St Mary *Roch* from 89. *St Mary's Vicarage, London Road, Swanley, Kent BR8 7AQ* Swanley (0322) 662201

EDWARDS, Peter John. b 59. Dur Univ BA. Ripon Coll Cuddesdon 81. **d** 83 **p** 84. C Banstead *Guildf* 83-86; C Upminster *Chelmsf* 86-88; R Kedington *St E* from 88. *The Rectory, Kedington, Haverhill, Suffolk CB9 7NN* Haverhill (0440) 712052

EDWARDS, Canon Peter John Smaliman. b 48. Univ of Wales (Ban) BD72 MTh75. Linc Th Coll 72. **d** 73 **p** 74. C Llanelly *St D* 73-76; Prec St Andr Cathl Inverness *Mor* 76-77; R Walton W w Talbenny and Haroldston W *St D* 77-81; P-in-c Invergordon St Ninian *Mor* 81-86; I 86-89; Prin Moray Dioc Ord Course 81-88; Can St Andr Cathl Inverness 81-89; OCF RAF 82-88; Syn Clerk *Mor* 85-89; V Caldicot *Mon* from 89; Hon Can St Andr Cathl Inverness *Mor* from 90. *The Vicarage, 39 Church Road,*

Caldicot, Newport, Gwent NP6 4HT   Caldicot (0291) 420221

EDWARDS, Canon Philip John. b 28. Lon Univ MRCS51 LRCP51. Chich Th Coll 58. **d** 60 **p** 61. C Mayfield *Chich* 67-71; V Haywards Heath St Rich 71-91; Can and Preb Chich Cathl 84-91; rtd 91. *21 Haywards Road, Haywards Heath, W Sussex RH16 4HX*   Haywards Heath (0444) 457880

EDWARDS, Philip Osbert Clifford. b 11. St Jo Coll Ox BA33 MA47. Wycliffe Hall Ox 35. **d** 35 **p** 36. Chapl Algarve *Eur* 74-77; rtd 77; Perm to Offic *Heref* from 86. *Tan House Cottage, Dilwyn, Hereford HR4 8JW* Weobley (0544) 318209

EDWARDS, Phillip Gregory. b 52. MSOSc90 Lon Univ BSc73 Imp Coll Lon ARCS73. Qu Coll Birm DipTh80. **d** 81 **p** 82. C Lillington *Cov* 81-85; P-in-c Cov St Alb 85-86; TV Cov E from 86. *St Alban's Vicarage, Mercer Avenue, Coventry CV2 4PQ*   Coventry (0203) 452493

EDWARDS, Raymond Lewis. Keble Coll Ox BA46 MA47. St Deiniol's Hawarden 69. **d** 70 **p** 71. Prin Educn Cen Penmaenmawr 56-81; Hon C Penmaenmawr *Ban* 70-81; P-in-c Llandwrog St Thos w Llandwrog 81-82; V 82-90; Dioc Dir of Educn from 84; rtd 90. *Dulyn View, 23 Rhiwlas Road, Talysarn, Penygroes, Gwynedd LL54 6HU* Penygroes (0286) 880844

EDWARDS, Rhys Meurig. b 16. St D Coll Lamp BA37. **d** 39 **p** 41. V Kenley *S'wark* 55-74; V Kingston Vale St Jo 74-84; rtd 84; Perm to Offic *Chich* from 84. *5 Paddock Close, Fernhurst, Haslemere, Surrey GU27 3JZ* Haslemere (0428) 56695

EDWARDS, Richard Sinclair. b 46. **d** 71 **p** 72. C Bushey *St Alb* 71-75; C Hitchin H Sav 75-76; TV Hitchin 77-81. *Address temp unknown*

EDWARDS, Roger Brian. b 41. Sarum & Wells Th Coll 87. **d** 89 **p** 90. C Wellington and Distr *B & W* from 89. *25 Drakes Park, Wellington, Somerset TA21 8TB* Wellington (0823) 660058

EDWARDS, Ronald. b 14. DSO44. BA. St D Coll Lamp 37. **d** 38 **p** 39. Chapl Lic Victuallers' Sch Slough 65-76; Lic to Offic *St D* 76-80; rtd 79; Perm to Offic *Chich* from 83. *33 Saltdean Drive, Saltdean, Brighton BN2 8SB* Brighton (0273) 305196

EDWARDS, Canon Ronald William. b 20. Kelham Th Coll 37. **d** 43 **p** 44. C Perry Street *Roch* 43-46; S Africa 46-57; V Godmanchester *Ely* 57-62; Australia from 62; Adn of the Coast 71-74; Dean Bathurst 74-77; Can Perth from 79. *2/31 Park Street, Como, W Australia 6152*   Perth (9) 450-6272

EDWARDS, Rowland Thomas. b 62. **d** 88 **p** 89. C Llanguicke *S & B* 88-90; C Morriston from 90. *St David's House, 2 Monmouth Place, Parc Gwernfadog, Swansea SA6 6RF*   Swansea (0792) 793197

EDWARDS, Dr Ruth Blanche. b 39. Girton Coll Cam BA61 MA65 PhD68 Aber Coll of Educn CertEd75. Ab Dioc Tr Course 77. **d** 87. Lect Aber Univ *Ab* 77-90; Sen Lect from 90; NSM Aber St Jas 87-88; NSM Aber St Jo from 88. *39 Woodstock Road, Aberdeen AB2 4EX* Aberdeen (0224) 314734

EDWARDS, Stephen. b 44. S'wark Ord Course. **d** 82 **p** 83. C Benhilton *S'wark* 82-86; P-in-c Clapham Ch Ch and St Jo 86-87; TV Clapham Team Min from 87. *Christ Church Vicarage, 39 Union Grove, London SW8 2QJ* 071-622 3552

EDWARDS, Stephen Zachary. b 04. Down Coll Cam BA30 MA33. **d** 31 **p** 32. R Siddington w Preston *Glouc* 65-69; rtd 70. *38 Richmond Road, Pelynt, Looe, Cornwall PL13 2NH*   Lanreath (0503) 20788

EDWARDS, Stuart. b 46. Lon Univ DipTh70 Lanc Univ BA73. Kelham Th Coll 66. **d** 71 **p** 72. C Skerton St Luke *Blackb* 71-76; C Ribbleton 76-80; TV 80-82; V Blackb St Mich w St Jo and H Trin from 82. *St Michael's Vicarage, Whalley New Road, Blackburn BB1 6LB* Blackburn (0254) 57121

EDWARDS, Mrs Susan. b 54. R Holloway Coll Lon BSc75 SS Hild & Bede Coll Dur PGCE76. Qu Coll Birm 78. **dss** 81 **d** 87. Lillington *Cov* 81-85; Cov E 85-87; C 87-91; Par Dn from 91. *St Alban's Vicarage, Mercer Avenue, Coventry CV2 4PQ*   Coventry (0203) 452493

EDWARDS, Very Rev Thomas Erwyd Pryse. b 33. Univ of Wales (Lamp) BA56. St Mich Coll Llan 56. **d** 58 **p** 59. C Llanbeblig w Caernarfon *Ban* 58-63; Chapl Asst St Geo Hosp Gp Lon 63-66; Lic to Offic *S'wark* 63-72; Chapl K Coll Hosp Lon 66-72; R Penmon and Llangoed w Llanfihangel Dinsylwy *Ban* 72-75; V Llandysilio and Llandegfan 75-81; V Glanadda 81-85; Chapl St D Hosp Ban 81-84; Gwynedd Hosp Ban 84-86; V Caer Rhun w Llangelynin w Llanbedr-y-Cennin *Ban* 86-88; Hon Can Ban Cathl from 88; Dean Ban from 88; R Ban from 88.

The Deanery, Bangor, Gwynedd LL57 1LH   Bangor (0248) 370693 or 352304

EDWARDS, Thomas Harold David. b 16. Jes Coll Ox BA38 MA46. Westmr Coll Cam 38 St Aug Coll Cant 58. **d** 58 **p** 59. V Bledlow *Ox* 64-73; RD Aylesbury 72-77; R Bledlow w Saunderton and Horsenden 73-89; rtd 89; Perm to Offic *Heref* from 89. *Baymount, Clee Hill Road, Tenbury Wells, Worcs WR15 8HL*   Tenbury Wells (0584) 811926

EDWARDS, Thomas Victor. b 22. Univ of Wales (Lamp) BA52 LTh54 Birm Univ MA57. **d** 54 **p** 55. V Oxley *Lich* 65-71; R Kingsley 71-90; rtd 90. *14 Pastoral Close, Madeley, Crewe CW3 9PU*   Stoke-on-Trent (0782) 751502

EDWARDS, Walter Harry. b 12. Launde Abbey 59. **d** 60 **p** 61. R Dunkeld *St And* 70-72; rtd 80. *Dail an t-Sagairt, Calvine, Pitlochry, Perthshire PH18 5UR*

EDWARDS, William Emrys. b 13. Univ of Wales BA35. St Mich Coll Llan 35. **d** 36 **p** 37. Asst Master Caernarvon Gr Sch 52-72; V Llandwrog St Thos w Llandwrog *Ban* 72-78; rtd 78; Lic to Offic *Ban* from 78. *Menai, Campbell Road, Caernarfon, Gwynedd*   Caernarfon (0286) 3115

EDWARDSON, David Roger Hately. b 54. Edin Th Coll. **d** 91. C Edin St Jo *Edin* from 91. *135 Craiglea Drive, Edinburgh EH10 5PP*

EDWARDSON, Joseph Philip. b 28. Dur Univ BA52 Leeds Univ PGCE53. Wells Th Coll 61. **d** 63 **p** 64. C Macclesfield St Mich *Ches* 63-66; V Egremont St Jo 66-72; V Eastham 72-81; V Poulton from 81. *St Luke's Vicarage, Mill Lane, Wallasey, Merseyside L44 3BP* 051-638 4663

EDYE, Ian Murray. b 21. K Coll Lon BD AKC. S'wark Ord Course 66. **d** 69 **p** 70. NSM E Grinstead St Swithun *Chich* from 69. *Thrush Field, Coombe Hill Road, East Grinstead, W Sussex RH19 4LY*   East Grinstead (0342) 323157

EFEMEY, Raymond Frederick. b 28. Ball Coll Ox BA51 MA64. Cuddesdon Coll 51. **d** 53 **p** 54. C Croydon St Mich *Cant* 53-57; C Hendford *B & W* 57-60; V Upper Arley *Worc* 60-66; Ind Chapl 60-66; P-in-c Dudley St Jas 66-69; V Dudley St Thos 66-69; V Dudley St Thos and St Luke 69-75; Hon C Stretford All SS *Man* 76-82; SSF from 81; P-in-c Weaste *Man* 82-87; V from 87. *The Vicarage, Derby Road, Salford M6 5BA*   061-736 5819

EGERTON, George. b 28. S'wark Ord Course 70. **d** 73 **p** 74. NSM Shere *Guildf* from 73. *6 Heathrow, Gomshall, Guildford, Surrey GU5 9QD*   Shere (048641) 2549

EGERTON, Ronald. b 14. St D Coll Lamp BA37 St Mich Coll Llan 37. **d** 38 **p** 39. R Rhydycroesau *Lich* 63-77; V Selattyn 63-77; R Chewton Mendip w Ston Easton, Litton etc *B & W* 77-80; rtd 80; Perm to Offic *Lich* from 80. *10 Rosehill Close, Whittington, Oswestry, Shropshire SY11 4DY*   Oswestry (0691) 662453

EGGERT, Max Alexander. b 43. AKC67 Birkb Coll Lon BSc74 Cen Lon Poly MA87 CPsychol90. **d** 67 **p** 68. C Whitton St Aug *Lon* 67-69; Hon C Hackney 72-74; Hon C Llantwit Major *Llan* 74-76; NSM Haywards Heath St Rich *Chich* from 78. *94 High Street, Lindfield, W Sussex RH16 2HP* Lindfield (0444) 483057

EGGINGTON, William Charles. b 10. Lon Univ BSc31. Coll of Resurr Mirfield 32. **d** 34 **p** 35. V Barnet Vale St Mark *St Alb* 60-80; rtd 80; Perm to Offic *St Alb* from 80. *The Rectory, Pirton Road, Holwell, Hitchin, Herts SG5 3SS*   Hitchin (0462) 712307

EGLIN, Ian. b 55. St Jo Coll Dur BA76. Coll of Resurr Mirfield 77. **d** 79 **p** 80. C Cov St Mary *Cov* 79-83; TV Kingsthorpe w Northn St Dav *Pet* 83-87; Chapl RN from 87. *c/o MOD, Lacon House, Theobald's Road, London WC1X 8RY*   071-430 6847

EGLIN, Reginald Martin. b 97. Bps' Coll Cheshunt 29. **d** 31 **p** 32. V Offton, Nettlestead and Willisham *St E* 61-74; rtd 74. *70 Springfield Road, Somersham, Ipswich IP8 4PQ*   Ipswich (0473) 831238

EICHELMAN, Canon George Charles. b 14. Roch Univ NY BA37. **d** 40 **p** 40. USA 40-78; rtd 79; Hon C Costa Blanca *Eur* 83-86; Hon Can Gib Cathl 85-86. *6C Marisol Park, Calpe, Alicante, Spain*

EKE, Canon Robert Foord Stansfield. b 17. K Coll Lon BD39 AKC39. Ely Th Coll 40. **d** 40 **p** 41. St Kitts-Nevis 62-72; V Alton St Lawr *Win* 72-89; Bp's Ecum Officer 80-82; Hon Can Win Cathl from 82; RD Alton 82-89; rtd 89; Perm to Offic *Chich* from 89. *77 Hangleton Way, Hove, E Sussex BN3 8AF*   Brighton (0273) 421443

EKIN, Tom Croker. b 29. Linc Th Coll 59. **d** 60 **p** 61. C Leamington Priors All SS *Cov* 60-63; R Ilmington w Stretton-on-Fosse 63-72; S Africa 72-77; R Moreton-in-Marsh w Batsford *Glouc* 77-83; R Moreton-in-Marsh w

Batsford, Todenham etc from 83. *The Rectory, Moreton-in-Marsh, Glos GL56 0BG*   Moreton-in-Marsh (0608) 50389

ELBOURNE, Keith Marshall. b 46. Nottm Univ BTh74 Lon Univ BD76. Westmr Past Foundn DAPC89 St Jo Coll Nottm 70. **d** 74 **p** 75. C Romford Gd Shep Collier Row *Chelmsf* 74-78; C Victoria Docks St Luke 78-81; P-in-c from 81. *St Luke's Vicarage, 105 Tarling Road, London E16 1HN*   071-476 2076

ELBOURNE, Raymond Nigel Wilson. b 43. Dur Univ BA66. Linc Th Coll 67. **d** 69 **p** 70. C Liscard St Mary *Ches* 69-72; V Hattersley 72-77; R Odd Rode from 77. *Odd Rode Rectory, Scholar Green, Cheshire ST7 3QN*   Alsager (0270) 882195

ELBOURNE, Timothy. b 60. Selw Coll Cam BA81 PGCE82 MA85. Westcott Ho Cam 84. **d** 86 **p** 87. C Tottenham H Trin *Lon* 86-88; Chapl York Univ *York* from 88. *Bede House, Field Lane, Heslington, York YO1 5HX*   York (0904) 413925

ELCOAT, Canon George Alastair. b 22. Qu Coll Birm. **d** 51 **p** 52. C Corbridge w Halton *Newc* 51-55; V Spittal 55-62; V Chatton w Chillingham 62-70; V Sugley 70-81; RD Newc W 77-81; Hon Can Newc Cathl from 79; P-in-c Tweedmouth 81-87; V from 87; Miss to Seamen from 81; Chapl to HM The Queen from 82; RD Norham *Newc* from 82. *The Vicarage, Main Street, Tweedmouth, Berwick-upon-Tweed TD15 2AW*   Berwick-upon-Tweed (0289) 306409

ELDER, David. b 28. **d** 79 **p** 80. NSM Dundee St Salvador *Bre* from 79. *21 Law Road, Dundee DD3 6PZ*   Dundee (0382) 827844

ELDER, Nicholas John. b 51. Hatf Poly BA73. Cuddesdon Coll 73. **d** 76 **p** 77. C Mill End *St Alb* 76-77; C Mill End and Heronsgate w W Hyde 77-79; TV Borehamwood 79-85; V Bedf St Mich 85-90; V Bedf All SS from 90. *All Saints' Vicarage, 1 Cutliffe Place, Bedford MK40 4DF*   Bedford (0234) 266945

ELDRID, John Gisborne Charteris. b 25. AKC52. **d** 53 **p** 54. C St Steph Walbrook and St Swithun etc *Lon* 72-81; V Portsea All SS *Portsm* 64-71; P-in-c Portsea St Jo Rudmore 69-71; V Portsea All SS w St Jo Rudmore 71-72; Gen Consultant Cen Lon Samaritans 72-74; Dir The Samaritans 74-87; Gen Consultant-Dir from 87; Lic to Offic *Lon* from 82; rtd 90. *46 Marshall Street, London W1V 1LR*   071-439 1406

ELDRIDGE, Francis Henry Bixby. b 16. AKC47. **d** 48 **p** 49. V Kettering St Mary *Pet* 68-78; R Walgrave w Hannington and Wold 78-82; rtd 82; Lic to Offic *Pet* 82-85; Perm to Offic from 85. *73 St Catherine's Road, Kettering, Northants NN15 5EN*   Kettering (0536) 510004

ELDRIDGE, Canon Richard Henry. b 21. Lon Univ BSc48 MSc50 BD61. Ridley Hall Cam 56. **d** 58 **p** 59. V Lt Heath *St Alb* 67-76; P-in-c Belper *Derby* 76-88; RD Duffield 81-87; Hon Can Derby Cathl from 83; rtd 88; Perm to Offic *Pet* from 89. *16 Polwell Lane, Kettering, Northants NN15 6UA*   Kettering (0536) 83138

ELDRIDGE, Stephen William. b 50. Chich Th Coll 87. **d** 89 **p** 90. C Stroud and Uplands w Slad *Glouc* from 89. *St Hugh's Lodge, 11 Hillier Close, Stroud, Glos GL5 1XF*   Stroud (0453) 751935

ELEY, John Edward. b 49. Sarum & Wells Th Coll 74. **d** 77 **p** 78. C Sherborne w Castleton and Lillington *Sarum* 77-80; Min Can Carl Cathl *Carl* 80-84; V Bromsgrove All SS *Worc* 84-88; Perm to Offic *St E* from 90. *Topos, Lackford, Bury St Edmunds IP28 6HR*   Bury St Edmunds (0284) 84511

ELFORD, Keith Anthony. b 59. Em Coll Cam BA80 MA84. Wycliffe Hall Ox 87. **d** 90 **p** 91. C Chertsey *Guildf* from 90. *Maple Tree Cottage, 73 Eastworth Road, Chertsey, Surrey KT16 8DJ*   Chertsey (0932) 560527

ELFORD, Robert John. b 39. Man Univ MA71 Ex Univ PhD74. Brasted Th Coll 64 Ridley Hall Cam 66. **d** 68 **p** 69. C Denton St Lawr *Man* 68-71; P-in-c Gwinear *Truro* 71-74; R Phillack w Gwithian and Gwinear 74-78; Lect Man Univ 78-87; Hon C Withington St Paul *Man* 79-83; Warden St Anselm Hall 82-87; Lic to Offic *Man* 84-87; Liv from 88; Hd and Pro-Rector Liv Inst of HE from 88. *St Katharine's College, Stand Park Road, PO Box 6, Liverpool L16 9JD*   051-722 2361

ELFRED, Michael William. b 48. BA76 MPhil. Linc Th Coll 77. **d** 79 **p** 80. C Boultham *Linc* 79-82; C Croydon H Sav *Cant* 82-84; C Upper Norwood All SS w St Marg 84; C Upper Norwood All SS *S'wark* 85-88; V Sanderstead St Mary from 88. *The Vicarage, Purley Oaks Road, South Croydon, Surrey CR2 0NY*   081-657 1725

ELGAR, Frederick Stanton. b 20. AKC56. **d** 56 **p** 57. C-in-c Pound Hill CD *Chich* 60-80; rtd 85. *31 Byrefield*

Road, Guildford, Surrey GU2 6UB   Guildford (0483) 37587

ELIOT, Ven Peter Charles. b 10. MBE TD. Magd Coll Cam BA31 MA35. Westcott Ho Cam 53. **d** 54 **p** 55. Adn Worc 61-75; Can Res Worc Cathl 65-75; Perm to Offic *Heref* from 72; rtd 75. *Old House, Kingsland, Leominster, Herefordshire HR6 9QS*   Kingsland (056881) 285

ELIOT, Whately Ian. b 12. **d** 39 **p** 40. R Ex St Paul *Ex* 64-77; rtd 77; Perm to Offic *Ex* from 77. *21 Rydon Lane, Countess Wear, Exeter EX2 7AN*   Topsham (0392) 873034

ELIZABETH, Sister. *See* WEBB, Marjorie Valentine

ELKINGTON, David John. b 51. Nottm Univ BTh76 Leic Univ MEd81. St Jo Coll Nottm 73. **d** 76 **p** 77. C Leic Martyrs *Leic* 76-78; C Kirby Muxloe 78-80; Asst Chapl Leic Univ 80-82; Hon C Leic H Spirit 82; Chapl UEA *Nor* 82-88; TV Newc Epiphany *Newc* 88-91; TR from 91. *12 Shannon Court, Kingston Park, Newcastle upon Tyne NE3 2XF*   091-286 4050

ELKINGTON, Stephen Lumsden. b 27. FCA51. E Midl Min Tr Course 82. **d** 85 **p** 86. NSM Ashford w Sheldon *Derby* 85-88; Chapl Costa del Sol W *Eur* from 88. *Apartado 106, San Pedro de Alcantara, Malaga, Spain*   Malaga (52) 786091

ELKINS, Alan Bernard. b 47. Sarum & Wells Th Coll 70. **d** 73 **p** 74. C Wareham *Sarum* 73-77; P-in-c Codford, Upton Lovell and Stockton 77-79; P-in-c Boyton w Sherrington 77-79; C Ashton Gifford 79; R Bishopstrow and Boreham from 79. *The Rectory, 8 Rock Lane, Warminster, Wilts BA12 9JZ*   Warminster (0985) 213000

ELKINS, Canon Patrick Charles. b 34. St Chad's Coll Dur BA57 DipTh60 DipEd. **d** 60 **p** 61. C Moordown Win 60-63; C Basingstoke 64-67; V Bransgore from 67; Hon Can Win Cathl from 89. *The Vicarage, Ringwood Road, Bransgore, Christchurch, Dorset BH23 8JH*   Bransgore (0425) 72327

ELLA, David John. b 51. Trin Coll Bris DipTh83. **d** 85 **p** 86. C Canford Magna *Sarum* 85-89; TV Southend *Chelmsf* from 89; Youth Development Officer from 89. *All Saints' Vicarage, 1 Sutton Road, Southend-on-Sea SS2 5PA*   Southend-on-Sea (0702) 613440

ELLAM, Stuart William. b 53. Westcott Ho Cam. **d** 85 **p** 86. C Ditton St Mich *Liv* 85-88; C Greenford H Cross *Lon* 88-91. *St Edward's House, Medway Drive, Greenford, Middx UB6 8LN*   081-997 4953

ELLEANOR, David John. b 48. Leic Univ LLB70 St Jo Coll Dur BA88. Cranmer Hall Dur 85. **d** 88 **p** 89. C Consett *Dur* 88-90. *c/o 2 Farm Cottages, Ellingham, Chathill, Northd*

ELLEL, Thomas Fielding. b 20. Cranmer Hall Dur. **d** 63 **p** 64. V Huncoat *Blackb* 67-74; V Worsthorne 74-88; rtd 88. *9 Harefield Rise, Burnley, Lancs BB12 0EZ*   Burnley (0282) 24440

ELLEM, Peter Keith. b 58. CQSW. St Jo Coll Nottm BTh90. **d** 90 **p** 91. C Islington St Mary *Lon* from 90. *St Peter's House, Oakley Crescent, London EC1V 1LQ*   071-251 3565

ELLERY, Arthur James Gabriel. b 28. St Jo Coll Dur BSc49. Linc Th Coll 51. **d** 53 **p** 54. C Milton next Sittingbourne *Cant* 53-56; C St Laurence in Thanet 56-58; C Darlington St Cuth *Dur* 58-62; V Tanfield 62-70; Chapl St Olave's Sch York 70-78; V Gt Ayton w Easby and Newton in Cleveland *York* 78-81; Chapl Bancroft's Sch Woodford Green 81-86; V Chipperfield St Paul *St Alb* from 86. *The Vicarage, Chipperfield, Kings Langley, Herts WD4 9BJ*   Kings Langley (0923) 263054

ELLERY, Ian Martyn William. b 56. K Coll Lon BD AKC. Chich Th Coll. **d** 82 **p** 83. C Hornsey St Mary w St Geo *Lon* 82-85; VC York Minster *York* 85-89; Subchanter York Minster 86-89; R Patrington w Hollym, Welwick and Winestead from 89. *The Rectory, Patrington, Hull HU12 0PB*   Withernsea (0964) 630327

ELLERY, Robert Martin. b 53. Jes Coll Ox BA76. St Mich Coll Llan 74. **d** 77 **p** 80. C Earlsfield St Jo *S'wark* 77-80; C Clapham Ch Ch and St Jo 81-85; Perm to Offic 85-89. *Christ Church Vicarage, Union Grove, London SW8 2QJ*   071-622 3552

ELLINGTON, David John. b 39. Or Coll Ox BA63 MA. Cuddesdon Coll 63. **d** 65 **p** 66. C Timperley *Ches* 68-72; P-in-c Altrincham St Jo 72-74; V 74-79; P-in-c Ashley 82-86; rtd 86; Perm to Offic *Ches* from 87. *6 Hough Green, Ashley, Altrincham, Cheshire WR15 0QS*   061-928 2173

ELLIOT, Hugh Riversdale. b 25. Bps' Coll Cheshunt. **d** 62 **p** 65. C Swaffham *Nor* 62-64; C Kessingland 64-67; C Mutford w Rushmere 65-67; P-in-c 67-68; P-in-c Gisleham 67-68; P-in-c Welborne 68-72; P-in-c Yaxham

68-80; P-in-c N Tuddenham 72-80; R E w W Harling 80-90; R Bridgham and Roudham 81-90; R E w W Harling and Bridgham w Roudham from 90. *The Rectory, East Harling, Norwich NR16 2NF*   East Harling (0953) 717235

ELLIOT, William. b 33. Glouc Sch of Min 84. **d** 87 **p** 88. C Kington w Huntington, Old Radnor, Kinnerton etc *Heref* 87-90; C Heref H Trin from 90. *79 Bridle Road, Kings Acre, Hereford HR4 0PW*   Hereford (0432) 341033

ELLIOT, William Brunton. b 41. **d** 84 **p** 85. NSM Lasswade *Edin* from 84; NSM Dalkeith from 84. *157 Newbattle Abbey Crescent, Dalkeith, Midlothian EH22 3LR* 031-663 1369

ELLIOT-NEWMAN, Christopher Guy. b 43. Bede Coll Dur TCert67 Hull Univ BTh83 MEd87. Westcott Ho Cam 67. **d** 70 **p** 71. C Ditton St Mich *Liv* 70-73; C Hazlemere *Ox* 73-77; R Stockton-on-the-Forest w Holtby and Warthill *York* 77-87; Dir of Educn *Cant* from 87. *4 Mill Hamlet, Wickhambreaux, Canterbury, Kent CT3 1RF*   Canterbury (0227) 720997

ELLIOTT, Brian. b 49. Dur Univ BA73. Coll of Resurr Mirfield 73. **d** 75 **p** 76. C Nunthorpe *York* 75-77; CF from 77. *c/o MOD (Army), Bagshot Park, Bagshot, Surrey GU19 5PL*   Bagshot (0276) 71717

ELLIOTT, Charles. b 15. Lon Univ BA55. St Steph Ho Ox 51. **d** 53 **p** 54. V Lower Gornal *Lich* 61-80; rtd 80; Lic to Offic Lich from 80; Worc 81-83; Perm to Offic *Worc* from 83. *1 The Village, Kingswinford, W Midlands DY6 8AY*   Kingswinford (0384) 279360

ELLIOTT, Preb Charles Middleton. b 39. Linc Coll Ox BA60 DPhil63. Linc Th Coll 62. **d** 64 **p** 65. C Wilford *S'well* 64-65; Zambia 65-69; WCC and Pontifical Commn Justice & Peace 69-73; Hon Min Can Nor Cathl *Nor* 74-78; Asst Gen Sec BCC 82-84; Preb Lich Cathl *Lich* 87-89; Dean Trin Hall Cam from 90. *11 Perowng Street, Cambridge CB1 1XU*   Cambridge (0223) 69233

ELLIOTT, Christopher John. b 44. Sarum Th Coll 66. **d** 69 **p** 70. C Walthamstow St Pet *Chelmsf* 69-71; C Witham 71-74; P-in-c Gt and Lt Bentley 74-80; R Colchester Ch Ch w St Mary V 80-85; R Sible Hedingham from 85. *The Rectory, Prayors Hill, Sible Hedingham, Halstead, Essex CO9 3LE*   Hedingham (0787) 61118

ELLIOTT, Canon Colin. b 23. St Pet Coll Ox BA48 DipTh49 MA52. Wycliffe Hall Ox 48. **d** 49 **p** 50. R Windermere St Martin *Carl* 59-88; RD Windermere 79-84; Hon Can Carl Cathl from 81; rtd 88. *Fairbank View, Brow Lane, Staveley, Kendal, Cumbria LA8 9PJ*   Staveley (0539) 821758

ELLIOTT, Colin David. b 32. AKC55. **d** 56 **p** 57. C W Wickham St Jo *Cant* 56-59; C Dover St Mary 59-64; V Linton 64-66; V Gillingham H Trin *Roch* 66-81; V Belvedere All SS 81-88; V Bromley St Jo from 88. *St John's Vicarage, 9 Orchard Road, Bromley, Kent BR1 2PR*   081-460 1844

ELLIOTT, Very Rev David. b 31. Bps' Coll Cheshunt 60. **d** 63 **p** 64. C Chingford St Anne *Chelmsf* 63-64; C Woodford St Mary 64-66; Trucial States 67-69; Prec St Alb Abbey *St Alb* 69-72; Zambia 72-75; Dean Ndola 72-75; Can Ndola Cathl from 75; TR Borehamwood *St Alb* 75-79; Dean Jerusalem 79-86; OStJ 80-82; CStJ from 82; R Covent Garden St Paul *Lon* from 86. *St Paul's Rectory, 14 Burleigh Street, London WC2E 7PX* 071-379 7488 or 836 5221

ELLIOTT, Derek John. b 26. Pemb Coll Cam BA50 MA55. Oak Hill Th Coll 48. **d** 51 **p** 53. C Ealing Dean St Jo *Lon* 51-53; C New Milverton *Cov* 53-55; C Boscombe St Jo *Win* 55-57; V Biddulph *Lich* 57-63; R Rushden w Newton Bromswold *Pet* 63-68; RD Higham 66-68; Chapl Bedf Modern Sch 68-83; V Potten End w Nettleden *St Alb* from 83. *The Vicarage, Church Road, Potten End, Berkhamsted, Herts HP4 2QY*   Berkhamsted (0442) 865217

ELLIOTT, George Evan. b 17. Sarum Th Coll. **d** 58 **p** 59. V Kimblesworth *Dur* 64-71; V Sutton St James *Linc* 71-77; V Sutton St Edmund 73-77; P-in-c Bishop Norton 77-80; R Wadingham w Snitterby 77-80; R Bishop Norton, Wadingham and Snitterby 80-82; rtd 82; Perm to Offic *Nor* from 82. *10 Dugard Avenue, Norwich NR1 4NQ*   Norwich (0603) 35806

ELLIOTT, Gordon. b 25. St Aid Birkenhead 63. **d** 65 **p** 66. C Bollington St Jo *Ches* 68-70; V Dukingfield St Mark 70-73; TV Tenbury *Heref* 74-78; V Bromfield 78-82; R Culmington w Onibury 78-82; V Stanton Lacy 78-82; P-in-c Withybrook w Copston Magna *Cov* 82-83; P-in-c Wolvey, Burton Hastings and Stretton Baskerville 82-83; V Wolvey w Burton Hastings, Copston Magna etc 83-90; rtd 90. *39 Beech Close, Ludlow, Shropshire SY8 2PD* Ludlow (0584) 875084

ELLIOTT, Harry. b 04. Dur Univ LTh30. St Aug Coll Cant 26. **d** 30 **p** 32. V Rathmell *Bradf* 70-73; rtd 73; Perm to Offic *Bradf* from 76. *22 Grassington Road, Skipton, N Yorkshire BD23 1LL*

ELLIOTT, Ian David. b 40. Qu Coll Cam BA61 MA65. Tyndale Hall Bris 64. **d** 66 **p** 67. C Halewood *Liv* 66-71; C Gt Crosby St Luke 71-74; C-in-c Dallam CD 74-80; V Dallam 80-83; TV Fazakerley Em from 83. *St Paul's House, Formosa Drive, Liverpool L10 7LB*   051-521 3344

ELLIOTT, John George. b 15. Qu Coll Ox BA37 MA46. Westcott Ho Cam 46. **d** 47 **p** 48. Chapl Loughb Gr Sch 61-80; rtd 80; Perm to Offic *Leic* from 80. *14 Victoria Street, Loughborough, Leics LE11 2EN*   Loughborough (0509) 263365

ELLIOTT, John Philip. b 37. MIChemE61 MBIM Salford Univ CEng. Glouc Th Course 79. **d** 80 **p** 80. NSM Brimscombe *Glouc* 80-86; C Caverswall *Lich* 86-91; R Tredington and Darlingscott w Newbold on Stour *Cov* from 91. *The Rectory, Tredington, Shipston-on-Stour, Warks CV36 4NG*   Shipston-on-Stour (0608) 61264

ELLIOTT, Joseph William. b 37. Chich Th Coll. **d** 66 **p** 67. C Whickham *Dur* 66-72; V Lamesley 72-78; TR Usworth from 78. *4 Highbury Close, Springwell, Gateshead, Tyne & Wear NE9 7PU*   091-416 3533

ELLIOTT, Leslie Aidan. b 13. Qu Coll Cam BA35 MA39. TCD Div Sch 35. **d** 37 **p** 38. Can Ch Cathl Dub *D & G* 66-82; I Kilmoe Union *C, C & R* 78-82; rtd 82. *Fresh Springs, Colla, Schull, Co Cork, Irish Republic* Skibbereen (28) 28216

ELLIOTT, Michael James. b 58. LTh. St Jo Coll Nottm 80. **d** 83 **p** 84. C Pontypridd St Cath *Llan* 83-86; C Leamington Priors St Paul *Cov* 86-89; Chapl RAF from 89. *c/o MOD, Adastral House, Theobald's Road, London WC1X 8RU*   071-430 7268

ELLIOTT, Canon Peter. b 41. Hertf Coll Ox BA63 MA68. Linc Th Coll 63. **d** 65 **p** 66. C Gosforth All SS *Newc* 65-68; C Balkwell 68-72; V High Elswick St Phil 72-80; V N Gosforth 80-87; V Embleton w Rennington and Rock from 87; RD Alnwick from 89; Hon Can Newc Cathl from 90. *The Vicarage, Embleton, Alnwick, Northd NE66 3UW*   Embleton (066576) 660

ELLIOTT, Peter Wolstenholme. b 31. CChem MRSC. NE Ord Course 78. **d** 81 **p** 82. NSM Yarm *York* from 81. *48 Butterfield Drive, Eaglescliffe, Stockton-on-Tees TS16 0EZ*   Eaglescliffe (0642) 782788

ELLIOTT, Stanley Griffin. b 19. Lon Univ BA50. Ridley Hall Cam 50. **d** 52 **p** 53. R Ashton upon Mersey St Martin *Ches* 59-80; V Tile Hill *Cov* 80-85; rtd 85; Perm to Offic *Win* from 85. *Flat 3 Chartwell, 8 The Avenue, Branksome Park, Poole, Dorset BH13 6AG*   Poole (0202) 766080

ELLIOTT, William. b 20. Lon Univ BA56. Ripon Hall Ox 60. **d** 61 **p** 62. C Kidderminster St Mary *Worc* 61-70; V Bewdley Far Forest 70-78; V Rock w Heightington w Far Forest 78-82; V Mamble w Bayton, Rock w Heightington etc 82-85; rtd 85; Perm to Offic Heref and Worc from 85. *8 Lea View, Cleobury Mortimer, Kidderminster DY14 8EE*   Cleobury Mortimer (0299) 270993

ELLIOTT, William Charles. b 10. **d** 67 **p** 68. C Harlington *Lon* 69-72; C-in-c Harlington Ch Ch CD 72-76; rtd 76; Perm to Offic *Ches* from 82. *3 Rowcliffe Avenue, Chester* Chester (0244) 677073

ELLIOTT, William Henry Venn. b 34. K Coll Cam BA55 MA59. Wells Th Coll 59. **d** 61 **p** 62. C Almondbury *Wakef* 61-66; V Bramshaw *Sarum* 66-81; P-in-c Landford w Plaitford 77-81; V Mere w W Knoyle and Maiden Bradley from 81. *The Vicarage, Angel Lane, Mere, Warminster, Wilts BA12 6DH*   Mere (0747) 860292

ELLIOTT, William James. b 38. Jes Coll Cam BA62 MA66 Birm Univ MA69 PhD74. Qu Coll Birm 62. **d** 64 **p** 65. C Hendon St Paul Mill Hill *Lon* 64-67; C St Pancras w St Jas and Ch Ch 67-69; P-in-c Preston St Paul *Blackb* 69-74; R Elstree *St Alb* from 74. *The Rectory, St Nicholas' Close, Elstree, Borehamwood, Herts WD6 3EW* 081-953 1411

ELLIOTT, William Norman. b 20. Kelham Th Coll 37. **d** 43 **p** 44. V S Crosland *Wakef* 64-85; rtd 85; Chapl Community of St Pet Horbury from 85. *St Peter's Convent, Dovecote Lane, Horbury, Wakefield, W Yorkshire WF4 6BB*   Wakefield (0924) 272181 or 270197

ELLIS, Anthony Colin. b 56. Keble Coll Ox BA77 Man Univ PhD80. Linc Th Coll 80. **d** 81 **p** 82. C Mill Hill Jo Keble Ch *Lon* 81-83; Staff Tutor in Relig Studies Man Univ from 83; C Stretford St Pet *Man* 83-87; NSM Shore 87-89; Lic to Offic from 89. *2 Crowther Terrace, Blackshaw, Hebden Bridge, W Yorkshire HX7 6DE* Hebden Bridge (0422) 844242

ELLIS, Canon Bryan Stuart. b 31. Qu Coll Cam BA54 MA58. Ridley Hall Cam 55. **d** 57 **p** 58. C Ramsgate St Luke *Cant* 57-59; C Herne Bay Ch Ch 59-62; V Burmantofts St Steph and St Agnes *Ripon* 62-81; RD Wakef from 81; V Wakef St Andr and St Mary from 81; Hon Can Wakef Cathl from 89. *2 Kilnsey Road, Wakefield WF1 4RW* Wakefield (0924) 372105

ELLIS, Charles Harold. b 50. N Ord Course 78. **d** 81 **p** 82. C Davyhulme St Mary *Man* 81-85; V Tonge w Alkrington 85-91; P-in-c Radcliffe St Thos and St Jo from 91; P-in-c Radcliffe St Mary from 91. *St Thomas's Vicarage, Heber Street, Radcliffe, Manchester M26 9TG* 061-723 2123

ELLIS, Christopher Charles. b 55. Societas Oecumenica 90 Edin Univ BD78 Hull Univ MA80. Edin Th Coll 76 Irish Sch of Ecum 78. **d** 79 **p** 80. C Selby Abbey *York* 79-82; C Fulford 82-85; Dioc Ecum Officer from 81; Dioc Ecum Adv from 90; Lect Ecum Th Hull Univ from 84; P-in-c Kexby w Wilberfoss *York* 85-90; Ecum Officer S Cleveland & N Yorkshire Ecum Coun from 88. *21 Sandstock Road, Pocklington, York YO4 2HN* Pocklington (0759) 305881

ELLIS, David Craven. b 34. Man Univ BA56 MA57. St Aid Birkenhead 59. **d** 61 **p** 62. C Gt Crosby St Luke *Liv* 61-65; Hong Kong 65-69; P-in-c Sawrey *Carl* 69-74; Dioc Youth Officer 69-74; V Halifax St Aug *Wakef* 74-84; R Greystoke, Matterdale and Mungrisdale *Carl* 84-87; TR Greystoke, Matterdale, Mungrisdale & W'millock from 88; R Watermillock 84-87; RD Penrith from 87. *The Rectory, Greystoke, Penrith, Cumbria CA11 0TJ* Greystoke (08533) 293

ELLIS, Hugh William. b 54. Sussex Univ BSc76. Ridley Hall Cam 88. **d** 90 **p** 91. C Reading St Jo *Ox* from 90. *1 Church House, Orts Road, Reading RG1 3JN* Reading (0734) 669545

ELLIS, Ian Morton. b 52. QUB BD75 MTh82 TCD PhD89. CITC. **d** 77 **p** 78. C Portadown St Columba *Arm* 77-79; C Arm St Mark 79-85; Chapl Arm R Sch 79-85; Hon VC Arm Cathl from 82; I Mullavilly from 85; Dom Chapl to Abp Arm from 86; Tutor for Aux Min (Arm) from 90. *89 Mullavilly Road, Tandragee, Co Armagh BT62 2LX* Tandragee (0762) 840221

ELLIS, Ian William. b 57. QUB BSc78 CertEd79 TCD BTh89. CITC 86. **d** 89 **p** 90. C Arm St Mark w Aghavilly *Arm* from 89. *6 Ashley Avenue, Armagh, Co Armagh BT60 1HD* Armagh (0861) 522389

ELLIS, John. b 27. Glouc Th Course 82. **d** 85 **p** 86. NSM Dowdeswell and Andoversford w the Shiptons etc *Glouc* from 85. *18 Hunter's Way, Andoversford, Cheltenham, Glos GL54 4JW* Cheltenham (0242) 820746

ELLIS, John Anthony. b 47. Univ of Wales (Lamp) DipTh70 Open Univ BA80. Coll of Resurr Mirfield 70. **d** 72 **p** 73. C Sketty *S & B* 72-75; C Duston *Pet* 75-80; R Lichborough w Maidford and Farthingstone 80-85; V Stratfield Mortimer *Ox* from 85; P-in-c Mortimer W End w Padworth from 85. *St John's House, Loves Wood, Mortimer, Reading RG7 2JX* Mortimer (0734) 332404

ELLIS, John Beaumont. b 45. Univ of Wales (Lamp) BA67 LTh69. Bp Burgess Hall Lamp. **d** 69 **p** 70. C Abergavenny St Mary w Llanwenarth Citra *Mon* 69-72; C Swansea St Gabr *S & B* 72-75; V Llanbister and Llanbadarn Fynydd w Llananno 75-77; V Newport St Andr *Mon* 77-80; V Risca 80-84; V Cheadle Heath *Ches* from 84. *The Vicarage, 8 Tillard Avenue, Cheadle Heath, Stockport, Cheshire SK3 0UB* 061-477 3541

ELLIS, John Franklyn. b 34. Leeds Univ BA58. Linc Th Coll 58. **d** 60 **p** 61. C Ladybarn *Man* 60-63; C Stockport St Geo *Ches* 63-66; V High Lane 66-81; V Chelford w Lower Withington from 81. *The Vicarage, Chelford, Macclesfield, Cheshire SK11 9AH* Chelford (0625) 861231

ELLIS, John Frederick Alexander. b 23. Sarum Th Coll 50. **d** 52 **p** 53. V Harnham *Sarum* 65-80; RD Salisbury 77-80; Can and Preb Sarum Cathl 77-80; P-in-c Belstone *Ex* 80-81; P-in-c S Tawton 80-81; R S Tawton and Belstone 81-87; RD Okehampton 82-87; TR Yelverton, Meavy, Sheepstor and Walkhampton 87-89; rtd 89. *55 Church Street, Tisbury, Salisbury SP3 6NH* Tisbury (0747) 871447

ELLIS, John George. b 31. Worc Coll Ox BA54 MA56. Wells Th Coll. **d** 58 **p** 59. C Poplar All SS w St Frideswide *Lon* 58-65; V Diddlebury w Bouldon *Heref* 65-67; R Diddlebury w Bouldon and Munslow 67-72; V N Hammersmith St Kath *Lon* from 72. *St Katherine's Vicarage, London W12 0SD* 081-743 3951

ELLIS, John Roland. b 32. Wells Th Coll 67. **d** 69 **p** 70. C Kettering SS Pet and Paul *Pet* 69-71; C Kingsthorpe 71-73; TV 73-74; TV Ebbw Vale *Mon* 74-76; V Llanddewi Rhydderch w Llanvapley etc 76-83; Miss to Seamen from 79; V New Tredegar *Mon* 83-86; V Llanelly *S & B*

from 86; RD Crickhowell from 91. *Llanelly Rectory, Gilwern, Abergavenny, Gwent NP7 0EL* Gilwern (0873) 830280

ELLIS, John Wadsworth. b 42. TCD BA64. **d** 66 **p** 67. C Lisburn Ch Ch Cathl *Conn* 66-69; C Norbiton *S'wark* 69-72; C New Clee *Linc* 72-85; V from 85. *120 Queen Mary Avenue, Cleethorpes, S Humberside DN35 7SZ* Cleethorpes (0472) 696521

ELLIS, Joseph Walter. b 08. St D Coll Lamp BA32. **d** 32 **p** 33. V Gt w Lt Chesterford *Chelmsf* 64-77; rtd 77. *5 Southfield, Back Lane, Ickleton, Saffron Walden, Essex* Saffron Walden (0799) 30334

ELLIS, Malcolm Railton. b 35. LTCL71 Univ of Wales (Lamp) BA56. Sarum Th Coll 56. **d** 58 **p** 59. C Llangynwyd w Maesteg *Llan* 58-61; C Llantrisant 61-67; V Troedrhiwgarth 67-70; PV Truro Cathl *Truro* 70-73; V Egloshayle 73-81; V Margam *Llan* 81-87; V Cardiff St Jo from 87; Offic Chapl Priory for Wales OStJ from 87. *The Vicarage, 39A Cathedral Road, Cardiff CF1 9HB* Cardiff (0222) 230692

ELLIS, Preb Mark Durant. b 39. Ex Univ BA62. Cuddesdon Coll 62. **d** 64 **p** 65. C Lyngford *B & W* 64-67; V Weston-super-Mare St Andr Bournville 67-76; TV Yeovil 76-88; V Yeovil St Mich from 88; Preb Wells Cathl from 90. *St Michael's Vicarage, Yeovil, Somerset BA21 4LH* Yeovil (0935) 75752

ELLIS, Peter Andrew. b 46. St D Coll Lamp 65. **d** 69 **p** 70. C Milford Haven *St D* 69-71; R Walwyn's Castle w Robeston W 71-74; Miss to Seamen from 74; Hong Kong 74-75; Singapore 75-82; The Tees and Hartlepool from 82. *15 Bowland Close, Nunthorpe, Cleveland TS7 0RE* Middlesbrough (0642) 312802

ELLIS, Robert Albert. b 48. K Coll Lon BD70 AKC70. St Aug Coll Cant 70. **d** 72 **p** 73. C Liv Our Lady and St Nic w St Anne *Liv* 72-76; P-in-c Meerbrook *Lich* 76-80; Producer Relig Progr BBC Radio Stoke 76-80; V Highgate All SS *Lon* 80-81; Dioc Communications Officer *Lich* from 81; P-in-c Longdon 81-87. *The Pump House, Jack's Lane, Marchington, Uttoxeter, Staffs ST14 8LW* Burton-on-Trent (0283) 820732

ELLIS, Robert Charles Ross-Lewin. b 06. TCD BA28. CITC 29. **d** 29 **p** 30. I Dunmurry *Conn* 32-79; Prec Conn Cathl 73-79; rtd 79. *26 Glenshesk Park, Dunmurry, Belfast BT17 9BA* Belfast (0232) 621266

ELLIS, Ven Robin Gareth. b 35. Pemb Coll Ox BA57 BCL58 MA62. Chich Th Coll 58. **d** 60 **p** 61. C Swinton St Pet *Man* 60-63; Asst Chapl Worksop Coll Notts 63-66; V Swaffham Prior *Ely* 66-74; Asst Dir Educn 66-74; V Wisbech St Aug 74-82; V Yelverton *Ex* 82-86; Adn Plymouth from 82. *33 Leat Walk, Roborough, Plymouth PL6 7AT* Plymouth (0752) 793397

ELLIS, Roger Henry. b 40. Natal Univ BA61 Selw Coll Cam BA64 MA68 Linacre Coll Ox BLitt69. **d** 66 **p** 67. C Ox St Mich *Ox* 66-68; S Africa 68-76; P-in-c Wortham *St E* 77; V Wheatley Hills *Sheff* 77-84; Chapl St Edm Sch Cant from 84. *St Edmund's School, Canterbury, Kent CT2 8HU* Canterbury (0227) 454575

ELLIS, Miss Sheila. b 39. Lon Univ CertRK. St Mich Ho Ox 67 Dalton Ho Bris 68. **dss** 80 **d** 87. Kirkdale St Mary and St Athanasius *Liv* 80-86; Earlestown 86-87; Par Dn 87-91; C W Derby St Luke from 91. *66 Baycliff Road, West Derby, Liverpool L12 6QX* 051-228 5455

ELLIS, Timothy William. b 53. AKC75. St Aug Coll Cant 75. **d** 76 **p** 77. C Old Trafford St Jo *Man* 76-80; V Pendleton St Thos 80-87; Chapl Salford Coll of Tech 80-87; V Sheff Norwood St Leon *Sheff* from 87. *St Leonard's Vicarage, Everingham Road, Sheffield S5 7LE* Sheffield (0742) 436689

ELLIS, Canon Vorley Michael Spencer. b 15. St Edm Hall Ox BA38 MA41. St Steph Ho Ox 37. **d** 39 **p** 40. V Keswick St Jo *Carl* 50-83; Hon Can Carl Cathl 78-83; P-in-c Threlkeld 80-83; rtd 83; Perm to Offic *Leic* from 83. *12 Brookfield Way, Kibworth, Leicester LE8 0SA* Kibworth (0533) 793138

ELLIS JONES, Betty Mary. CertEd41. Bps' Coll Cheshunt. **dss** 62 **d** 87. Perm to Offic *St E* from 62. *St Martin's Cottage, 8 Old Kirton Road, Trimley, Ipswich IP10 0QH* Felixstowe (0394) 275233

✠**ELLISON, Rt Rev and Rt Hon Gerald Alexander.** b 10. KCVO81 PC73. New Coll Ox BA32 DipTh34 MA36. Lambeth DD55 Westcott Ho Cam 34. **d** 35 **p** 36 **c** 50. C Sherborne w Castleton and Lillington *Sarum* 35-37; Sec Dioc Youth Movement 37-42; Bp's Dom Chapl *Win* 37-42; Chapl RNVR 39-43; Abp's Dom Chapl *York* 43-46; V Portsea N End St Mark *Portsm* 46-50; Hon Can Portsm Cathl 50; P-in-c St Botolph without Bishopgate *Lon* 50-53; Suff Bp Willesden 50-55; Bp Ches 55-73; Bp Lon 73-81; Dean of the Chpls Royal

73-81; rtd 81. *Billey's House, 16 Long Street, Cerne Abbas, Dorset DT2 7JF* Cerne Abbas (03003) 247

✠**ELLISON, Rt Rev John Alexander.** b 40. ALCD67. d 67 p 68. c 88. C Woking St Paul *Guildf* 67-74; Argentina 80-83; R Aldridge *Lich* 83-88; Bp Paraguay from 88. *Iglesia Anglicana, Casilla de Correo 1124, Asuncion, Paraguay*

ELLISTON, John Ernest Nicholas. b 37. ALCD61. d 61 p 62. C Gipsy Hill Ch Ch *S'wark* 61-64; C Whitton and Thurleston w Akenham *St E* 64-68; P-in-c New Clee *Linc* 68-71; V Grimsby St Steph 71-75; V New Clee 75-76; P-in-c Mildenhall *St E* 77-79; P-in-c Barton Mills, Beck Row w Kenny Hill etc 80; R 80-84; RD Mildenhall 81-84; V Ipswich St Aug from 84. *St Augustine's Vicarage, 2 Bucklesham Road, Ipswich IP3 8TJ* Ipswich (0473) 728654

ELLMORE, Geoffrey Richard. b 36. CEng68 MIMechE68 Leic Coll of Art & Tech BScEng57. S'wark Ord Course 86. d 87 p 88. NSM Coxheath w E Farleigh, Hunton and Linton *Roch* from 87. *31 Parkway, Coxheath, Maidstone, Kent ME17 4HH* Maidstone (0622) 744737

ELLMORE, Peter Robert. b 44. Sarum & Wells Th Coll 84. d 86 p 87. C Bridgemary *Portsm* 86-89; C Portsea N End St Mark 89-91; Asst Chapl St Mary's Gen Hosp Portsm from 91. *90A Compton Road, Portsmouth PO2 0SR* Portsmouth (0705) 660657

ELLSLEY, Howard. b 23. Roch Th Coll 65. d 67 p 68. C Glas St Marg *Glas* 67-71; R Dalbeattie 71-77; TV Melton Mowbray w Thorpe Arnold *Leic* 77-78; R Balcombe *Chich* 78-83; R Airdrie *Glas* 83-88; R Gartcosh 83-88; rtd 88. *Auchencraig, Lower Barcaple, Ringford, Castle Douglas, Kirkcudbrightshire DG7 2AP* Ringford (055722) 228

ELLSON, Montague Edward. b 33. Birm Univ BA56 Cam Univ ACertEd67. E Anglian Minl Tr Course 84. d 87 p 88. Hon C Freethorpe w Wickhampton, Halvergate etc *Nor* 87-90; C Gaywood, Bawsey and Mintlyn from 90; Miss to Seamen from 90. *5 Gayton Road, Gaywood, King's Lynn, Norwich PE30 3EA* King's Lynn (0553) 768667

ELLSWORTH, Dr Lida Elizabeth. b 48. Columbia Univ (NY) BA70 Girton Coll Cam PhD76. E Midl Min Tr Course. d 88. NSM Bakewell *Derby* from 88. *Apple Croft, Granby Gardens, Bakewell, Derbyshire DE4 1ET* Bakewell (0629) 814255

ELLWOOD, Keith Brian. b 36. AIGCM58 FRSA65 ACP66 FCollP83 Curwen Coll Lon BA58 CertEd59 MMus65 DipRIPH&H65. Bps' Coll Cheshunt 64. d 64 p 65. Chapl R Wanstead Sch 64-66; C Wanstead St Mary *Chelmsf* 64-66; CF 66-70; Hong Kong 70-71; P-in-c Bicknoller *B & W* 71-73; Chapl Roedean Sch Brighton 73-76; Perm to Offic *B & W* 74-79; W Germany 76-79; Chapl Trin Coll Glenalmond 79-81; Hd Master St Chris Sch Burnham-on-Sea 82-86; Hon C Burnham *B & W* 82-86; R Staple Fitzpaine, Orchard Portman, Thurlbear etc 86-89; P-in-c Hugill *Carl* from 89; Educn Adv from 89. *The Rectory, Ings, Kendal, Cumbria LA8 9PU* Kendal (0539) 821383

ELLMORE, Graeme Martin. b 47. Sarum & Wells Th Coll 71. d 74 p 75. C Norbury St Oswald *Cant* 74-77; P-in-c St Allen *Truro* 77-79; P-in-c St Erme 77-79; V Newlyn St Pet 79-85; CF (TA) 80-86; R Redruth w Lanner *Truro* 85-86; Chapl RN from 86. *c/o MOD, Lacon House, Theobald's Road, London WC1X 8RY* 071-430 6847

ELPHICK, Robin Howard. b 37. ALCD63. d 64 p 65. C Clapham Common St Barn *S'wark* 64-67; C Woking St Pet *Guildf* 67-71; R Rollesby w Burgh w Billockby *Nor* 71-80; P-in-c Ashby w Oby, Thurne and Clippesby 79-80; R Rollesby w Burgh w Billockby w Ashby w Oby etc 80-84; R Frinton *Chelmsf* from 84. *The Rectory, 22 Queen's Road, Frinton-on-Sea, Essex CO13 9BL* Frinton-on-Sea (0255) 674664

ELPHICK, Miss Vivien Margaret. b 53. Solicitor 77 Kent Univ BA74. Trin Coll Bris BA90. d 90. C Oulton Broad *Nor* from 90. *95 Westwood Avenue, Oulton, Lowestoft, Suffolk NR33 9RS* Lowestoft (0502) 508905

ELPHIN AND ARDAGH, Archdeacon of. See JACKSON, Ven Robert Stewart

ELPHIN AND ARDAGH, Dean of. *Vacant*

ELSDON, Bernard Robert. b 29. Roch Th Coll 65. d 67 p 68. C Wallasey St Hilary *Ches* 67-71; C Liv Our Lady and St Nic w St Anne *Liv* 71-72; V Anfield St Marg 73-89; Dioc Exec Dir for Chr Resp 80-83; rtd 89. *31 Douglas Road, Hazel Grove, Stockport, Cheshire SK7 4JE* 061-456 6824

ELSEY, Cyril. b 08. Ridley Hall Cam 65. d 66 p 67. R Petton w Cockshutt *Lich* 69-75; rtd 75; Perm to Offic *Ex* from 82. *9 Raleigh Court, Raleigh Road, Budleigh*

Salterton, *Devon EX9 6HR* Budleigh Salterton (03954) 5504

ELSON, Christopher John. b 52. K Coll Lon BD75 AKC75. St Aug Coll Cant. d 76 p 77. C New Haw *Guildf* 76-79; C Guildf H Trin w St Mary 79-82; C Hale 85-87; V Ripley from 87; Sub-Chapl HM Pris Send from 88. *The Vicarage, High Street, Ripley, Woking, Surrey GU23 6AE*

ELSON, John Frederick. Roch Th Coll 62. d 64 p 65. C Tenterden St Mildred w Smallhythe *Cant* 64-68; P-in-c Chart next Sutton Valence 68-71; V Fletching *Chich* from 71. *The Vicarage, Fletching, Uckfield, E Sussex TN22 3SR* Newick (082572) 2498

ELSTOB, Stephen William. b 57. Sarum & Wells Th Coll. d 86 p 87. C Sunderland Springwell w Thorney Close *Dur* 86-88; C Upholland *Liv* 88-89; TV from 89. *158 Birleywood, Skelmersdale, Lancs WN8 9BX* Skelmersdale (0695) 28091

ELSTON, Philip Herbert. b 35. RD80. Leeds Univ MA76 AKC63. d 64 p 65. C Thurnby Lodge *Leic* 64-66; Hon C 66-67; Chapl RNR from 67; Malawi 68-75; Hon C Far Headingley St Chad *Ripon* 75-79; V Knowl Hill w Littlewick *Ox* 79-84; Chapl RN Sch Haslemere 85-89; C Felpham w Middleton *Chich* 89-90. *Corona, Barn Road, East Wittering, Chichester, W Sussex PO20 8NL* Middleton-on-Sea (0243) 671049

ELTON, Clarence Edward. b 09. ALCD36. d 36 p 37. R Hambledon *Guildf* 57-74; rtd 74; Perm to Offic Guildf from 74; Chich from 83. *76 Church Road, Milford, Godalming, Surrey GU8 5JD* Godalming (0483) 417959

ELTON, Derek Hurley. b 31. Lon Univ BSc52. Wycliffe Hall Ox 53. d 55 p 56. C Ashton-on-Ribble St Andr *Blackb* 55-58; India 58-71; R Wickmere w Lt Barningham and Itteringham *Nor* 71-79; R Lt w Gt Ellingham 79-83; P-in-c Rockland All SS and St Andr w St Pet 81-83; R Lt w Gt Ellingham w Rockland 83-88; Chapl Wayland Hosp Norfolk 86-88; CMS from 88; Algeria from 88. *64 Avenue Souidani, Boudjemma, Algiers, Algeria*

ELTRINGHAM, Mrs Fiona Ann. b 48. CertEd69. NE Ord Course 86. d 89. Par Dn Willington Team *Newc* from 89. *10 Churchill Street, Wallsend, Tyne & Wear NE28 7SZ* 091-263 6140

ELVERSON, Ronald Peter Charles. b 50. St Edm Hall Ox BA73 MA86. St Jo Coll Nottm 84. d 86 p 87. C Whitnash *Cov* 86-90; V Dunchurch from 90. *The Vicarage, 11 Critchley Drive, Dunchurch, Rugby, Warks CV22 6PJ* Rugby (0788) 810274

ELVIN, Keith Vernon. b 24. Bris Univ BSc52. d 65 p 65. C St Clement *Truro* 65-66 and 67-75 and 76-79; Chapl Truro Cathl Sch 66-67; C St John w Millbrook *Truro* 75-76; Hon C Truro St Paul and St Clem 79-80; Vice-Prin Chan Sch & SW Minl Tr Sch (Truro) 80-82; Lic to Offic 80-84; Perm to Offic from 84. *26 Westfield House, Cote Lane, Bristol BS9 3UN* Bristol (0272) 628328

ELVY, Canon Peter David. b 38. Lon Univ BA62 Fitzw Ho Cam BA64 MA68. Ridley Hall Cam. d 65 p 66. C Herne *Cant* 65-66; C New Addington 66-68; C Addiscombe St Mildred 69-71; Youth Chapl *Chelmsf* 71-80; V Gt Burstead from 75; Dioc Can Chelmsf Cathl from 80. *The Vicarage, 111 Church Street, Great Burstead, Billericay, Essex CM11 2TR* Billericay (0277) 625947

ELWIN, Ernest John. b 31. Selw Coll Cam BA54 MA58. Ridley Hall Cam 54. d 56 p 57. C Wandsworth All SS *S'wark* 56-59; C Harlow New Town w Lt Parndon *Chelmsf* 59-61; Tidworth Down Sch Dorset 61-63; V Soundwell *Bris* 63-66; Perm to Offic *Sarum* from 66; Master Seldown Sch Dorset 66-68; Wareham Modern Sch 68-69; S Dorset Tech Coll Weymouth 70-85; Weymouth Coll 85-88. *4 Portesham Hill, Portesham, Weymouth, Dorset DT3 4EU* Weymouth (0305) 871358

ELY, Archdeacon of. See WALSER, Ven David

ELY, Bishop of. See SYKES, Rt Rev Stephen Whitefield

ELY, Dean of. See HIGGINS, Very Rev Michael John

EMBERTON, John Nicholas. b 45. FCA69. Oak Hill NSM Course 85. d 88 p 89. NSM Purley Ch Ch *S'wark* from 88. *49 Oakwood Avenue, Purley, Surrey CR8 1AR* 081-668 2684

EMBLETON, Harold. b 21. Ch Coll Cam BA47 MA52. Qu Coll Birm 47. d 49 p 50. Chapl RN 53-76; QHC 74-76; V Bognor *Chich* 76-84; RD Arundel and Bognor 77-82; V Skirwith, Ousby and Melmerby w Kirkland *Carl* 84-87; rtd 87; Perm to Offic *Carl* from 87. *3 Brisco Road, Carlisle CA2 4PG* Carlisle (0228) 47240

EMBLIN, Richard John. b 48. BEd71 MA81. S Dios Minl Tr Scheme 83. d 86 p 87. C S w N Hayling *Portsm* 86-89; P-in-c Wootton from 89. *The Rectory, 32 Church Road, Wootton, Ryde, Isle of Wight PO33 4PX* Isle of Wight (0983) 882213

EMBRY, Miss Eileen Margaret. b 38. Westf Coll Lon BA60 Lon Univ BD71. **dss** 81 **d** 87. Lect Trin Coll Bris 81-83; Bishopsworth *Bris* 83-87; Par Dn 87-89. *2 Bishop's Cove, Bishopsworth, Bristol BS13 8HH* Bristol (0272) 642588

EMERSON, Arthur Edward Richard. b 24. Lich Th Coll 69. **d** 72 **p** 73. C Barton upon Humber *Linc* 72-74; V Chapel St Leonards 75-88; P-in-c Hogsthorpe 77-88; V Chapel St Leonards w Hogsthorpe from 88. *The Vicarage, Chapel St Leonards, Skegness, Lincs PE24 5HQ* Skegness (0754) 72666

EMERSON, David. b 43. BNC Ox BA66 MA70 DPhil70. **d** 86 **p** 87. NSM Edin St Hilda *Edin* from 86; NSM Edin St Fillan from 86. *25 Little Road, Liberton, Edinburgh EH16 6SH* 031-664 3035

EMERSON, Donald Godfrey. b 11. CBE73. Trin Coll Cam BSc32. **d** 88 **p** 88. Hon C Boxwell, Leighterton, Didmarton, Oldbury etc *Glouc* from 88. *Meads House, Leighterton, Tetbury, Glos GL8 8UW* Leighterton (0666) 890259

EMERTON, Canon John Adney. b 28. FBA79 CCC Ox BA50 MA54 CCC Cam BD60 DD73 Edin Univ Hon DD77. Wycliffe Hall Ox 50. **d** 52 **p** 53. C Birm Cathl *Birm* 52-53; Asst Lect Th Birm Univ 52-53; Lect Hebrew Dur Univ 53-55; Lect Div Cam Univ 55-62; Reader in Semitic Philology Ox Univ 62-68; Lic to Offic *Ely* from 68; Regius Prof Hebrew Cam Univ from 68; Fell St Jo Coll Cam from 70; Hon Can Jerusalem from 84. *34 Gough Way, Cambridge CB3 9LN* Cambridge (0223) 63219

EMERY, Frank. b 07. **d** 67 **p** 68. C Holyhead w Rhoscolyn *Ban* 67-71; C Holyhead w Rhoscolyn w Llanfair-yn-Neubwll 71-80; rtd 80. *Bodhyfryd, 16 Seabourne Road, Holyhead, Gwynedd LL65 1AL* Holyhead (0407) 762491

EMES, Leonard Bingham. b 10. Wycliffe Hall Ox 69. **d** 70 **p** 70. C Thame *Ox* 70-73; P-in-c Tetsworth 73-77; P-in-c Adwell w S Weston 73-77; rtd 77; Perm to Offic St E 77-83; Cant from 83. *47 Summerlands Lodge, Wellbrook Road, Farnborough, Kent BR6 8ME* Farnborough (0689) 51076

EMM, Robert Kenneth. b 46. K Coll Lon BD68 AKC68. **d** 69 **p** 70. C Hammersmith SS Mich and Geo White City Estate CD *Lon* 69-72; C Keynsham *B & W* 72-75; C Yeovil 75-80; TV Gt Grimsby St Mary and St Jas *Linc* 80-85; R N Thoresby from 85; R Grainsby from 85; V Waithe from 85. *The Rectory, Church Lane, North Thoresby, Grimsby, S Humberside DN36 5QG* Grimsby (0472) 840029

EMMEL, Canon Malcolm David. b 32. Qu Coll Birm DipTh58. **d** 58 **p** 59. C Hessle *York* 58-62; Canada 62-66; V Catterick *Ripon* 66-73; V Pateley Bridge and Greenhow Hill 73-77; P-in-c Middlesmoor w Ramsgill 76-77; V Upper Nidderdale 77-88; RD Ripon 79-86; Hon Can Ripon Cathl from 84; R Bedale from 88. *The Rectory, Bedale, N Yorkshire DL8 1AB* Bedale (0677) 22103

EMMERSON, Peter Barrett. b 29. Fitzw Ho Cam BA54 MA58. Tyndale Hall Bris 50. **d** 54 **p** 57. Canada 54-58; V Fazakerley St Nath *Liv* 59-64; Perm to Offic 64-70; Distr Sec BFBS 64-72; Midl Regional Sec 72-74; Hon C Boldmere *Birm* 71-74; C-in-c Crown E CD *Worc* 74-77; P-in-c Crown E and Rushwick 77-81; R Stoke Prior, Wychbold and Upton Warren from 81. *The Rectory, Fish House Lane, Stoke Prior, Bromsgrove, Worcs B60 4JT* Bromsgrove (0527) 32501

✠**EMMERSON, Rt Rev Ralph.** b 13. AKC38 Lon Univ BD38. Westcott Ho Cam 38. **d** 38 **p** 39 **c** 72. C Leeds St Geo *Ripon* 38-41; C-in-c Seacroft CD 41-48; C Methley 48-49; P-in-c 49-52; R 52-56; P-in-c Mickletown 49-52; R 52-56; V Headingley 56-66; Hon Can Ripon Cathl 64-66; Can Res Ripon Cathl 66-72; Suff Bp Knaresborough 72-79; rtd 79; Asst Bp Ripon from 86. *Flat 1, 15 High St Agnes Gate, Ripon, N Yorkshire HG4 1QR* Ripon (0765) 701626

EMMET, Herbert Gerald. b 18. Trin Coll Cam BA40. Linc Th Coll 40. **d** 42 **p** 43. V Harpenden St Jo *St Alb* 64-73; V Kings Langley 73-80; rtd 80; Perm to Offic *St Alb* from 80. *39 Linwood Grove, Leighton Buzzard, Beds LU7 8RP* Leighton Buzzard (0525) 377360

EMMETT, Kerry Charles. b 46. St Jo Coll Dur BA68. St Jo Coll Nottm 71. **d** 73 **p** 74. C Attenborough w Chilwell *S'well* 73-75; C Chilwell 75-76; C Wembley St Jo *Lon* 76-79; V Hanworth St Rich 79-89; R Ravenstone and Swannington *Leic* from 89. *The Rectory, 9 Orchard Close, The Limes, Ravenstone, Leicester LE6 2JW* Coalville (0530) 39802

EMMETT, Thomas. b 40. Chich Th Coll 67. **d** 70 **p** 71. C Shiremoor *Newc* 70-73; C Haltwhistle 73-75; V Newc Ch Ch 75-80; P-in-c Newc St Anne 77-80; V Newc Ch Ch w St Ann 81-87; V Bywell St Pet from 87. *St Peter's Vicarage, Meadowfield Road, Bywell, Stocksfield, Northd NE43 7PY* Stocksfield (0661) 842272

EMMOTT, David Eugene. b 41. St Chad's Coll Dur BA63 DipTh66. **d** 66 **p** 67. C Bingley H Trin *Bradf* 66-69; C Anfield St Marg *Liv* 69-70; C Kirkby 70-75; Chapl Newc Poly *Newc* 75-78; Hon C Toxteth Park St Marg *Liv* 78-80; TV Upholland 80-88; V Southfields St Barn *S'wark* from 88. *St Barnabas's Vicarage, 430 Merton Road, London SW18 5AE* 081-874 7768

EMMOTT, Douglas Brenton. b 45. K Coll Lon BD78 AKC78. Linc Th Coll 79. **d** 80 **p** 81. C Kingston upon Hull St Alb *York* 80-83; V Scarborough St Sav w All SS 83-91; V York St Chad from 91. *St Chad's Vicarage, Campleshon Road, York YO2 1EY* York (0904) 654707

EMPEY, Canon Clement Adrian. b 42. TCD BA64 MA68 PhD71. CITC. **d** 74 **p** 75. Hon Chapl Miss to Seamen from 75; C Dub St Ann *D & G* 75-76; I Kells-Inistioge Gp *C & O* 76-84; Preb Tassagard St Patr Cathl Dub from 82; I Clane w Donadea and Coolcarrigan *M & K* 84-88; I Dub St Ann w St Mark and St Steph *D & G* from 88; Treas St Patr Cathl Dub from 89. *St Ann's Vicarage, 88 Mount Anville Wood, Dublin 14, Irish Republic* Dublin (1) 288-0663

✠**EMPEY, Most Rev Walton Newcome Francis.** b 34. TCD BA57. K Coll (NS) BD69. **d** 58 **p** 59 **c** 81. C Glenageary *D & G* 58-60; Canada 60-66; I Stradbally *C & O* 66-71; I Limerick St Mich *L & K* 71-81; Dean Limerick 71-81; Preb Taney St Patr Cathl Dub 73-81; Bp *L & K* 81-85; Bp M & K from 85. *Bishop's House, Moyglare, Maynooth, Co Kildare, Irish Republic* Dublin (1) 628-9354

EMRYS-JONES, John. b 09. St Andr Coll Pampisford 46. **d** 46 **p** 47. V Thames Ditton *Guildf* 66-75; rtd 75. *Collin House, 108 Ridgway, London SW19 4RD* 081-947 8513

EMSLEY, John Stobart. b 13. Qu Coll Birm 39. **d** 41 **p** 41. V Ycadon St Andr *Bradf* 71-79; rtd 79. *11 Bishop Garth, Pateley Bridge, Harrogate, N Yorkshire HG3 5LL* Harrogate (0423) 711835

EMSON, Stanley George. b 26. Glouc Sch of Min. **d** 89 **p** 90. NSM Cirencester *Glouc* from 89. *17 Cecily Hill, Cirencester, Glos GL7 2EF* Cirencester (0285) 640051

EMTAGE, Miss Susan Raymond. b 34. St Mich Ho Ox 63. **dss** 79 **d** 87. SW Area Sec CPAS Women's Action 75-82; Leic St Chris *Leic* 82-86; Bramerton w Surlingham *Nor* 86-87; C 87-88; C Rockland St Mary w Hellington, Bramerton etc 88-89; Par Dn W Bromwich St Jas *Lich* from 89; Par Dn W Bromwich St Paul Golds Hill from 89. *St Paul's Vicarage, 93 Bagnall Street, West Bromwich, W Midlands B70 0TS* 021-520 3468

ENDALL, Peter John. b 38. Linc Th Coll 83. **d** 85 **p** 86. C Burley in Wharfedale *Bradf* 85-88; V Thwaites Brow from 88. *The Vicarage, Spring Avenue, Thwaites Brow, Keighley, W Yorkshire BD21 4TA* Keighley (0535) 602830

ENDEAN, Michael George Devereux. b 33. Ox NSM Course. **d** 84 **p** 85. NSM Wantage Downs *Ox* from 84. *2 Mount Pleasant, East Hendred, Wantage, Oxon OX12 8LA* Abingdon (0235) 833497

ENDICOTT, Oliver Brian. b 31. Sarum Th Coll. **d** 57 **p** 58. C Lt Ilford St Barn *Chelmsf* 57-60; C Barking St Marg 60-66; V Gt w Lt Saling 66-70; USA from 70. *2818 Century, Bakersfield, California 93306-1516, USA*

ENEVER, Mrs Rosemary Alice Delande. b 45. Oak Hill Th Coll 86. **d** 88. NSM Gt Ilford St Jo *Chelmsf* from 88. *211 Aldborough Road South, Ilford, Essex IG3 8HY* 081-590 2851

ENEVER, Vivian John. b 61. Collingwood Coll Dur BA82 Cam Univ PGCE85. Westcott Ho Cam 88. **d** 91. C Gt Crosby St Faith *Liv* from 91. *31 Allenby Avenue, Crosby, Liverpool L23 0SU* 051-920 4644

ENGEL, Jeffrey Davis. b 38. Man Univ BA59 Liv Univ PGCE60 Keele Univ ADC69 Aston Univ MSc82 FCP83. St Deiniol's Hawarden 86. **d** 89 **p** 90. NSM Formby St Pet *Liv* from 89. *Rose Lodge, 14 Blundell Avenue, Birkdale, Southport PR8 4TA* Southport (0704) 67989

ENGELSEN, Christopher James. b 57. Nottm Univ BTh86. Linc Th Coll 83. **d** 86 **p** 87. C Sprowston *Nor* 86-89; C High Harrogate Ch Ch *Ripon* from 89. *7 Kingsway Drive, Harrogate, N Yorkshire HG1 5NJ* Harrogate (0423) 526846

ENGH, Timm Gray. b 38. Univ of the South (USA) 79 Arizona Univ BSc66 Michigan State Univ MSc69. **d** 81 **p** 82. USA 81-86; R Melrose *Edin* 86-90; R Edin St Mark from 90; R Edin St Andr and St Aid from 90. *27 Argyle Crescent, Portobello, Edinburgh EH15 2QE* 031-669 3452

ENGLAND, Robert Gordon. b 39. TCD BA62 QUB MTh76. TCD Div Sch Div Test65. d 66 p 67. C Raheny w Coolock *D & G* 66-69; C Lisburn Ch Ch *Conn* 72-73; Lic to Offic *D & D* from 74; Hd of RE Regent Ho Sch Newtowards from 74. *65 Cabin Hill Park, Belfast BT5 7AN* Newtownards (0247) 813234

ENGLISH, Peter Gordon. b 31. Edin Univ MA55. Ripon Hall Ox 59. d 61 p 62. C Bingley All SS *Bradf* 61-64; V Cottingley 64-66; Uganda from 66. *PO Box 7062, Kampala, Uganda*

ENGLISH, Peter Redford. b 26. Ridley Hall Cam 70. d 72 p 73. C Tyldesley w Shakerley *Man* 72-74; C Worsley 74-76; R Levenshulme St Mark 76-81; R Heytesbury and Sutton Veny *Sarum* 81-91; rtd 91. *The Old Rectory, Bromsberrow, Ledbury, Herefordshire HT8 1RU* Ledbury (0531) 650362

ENNION, Peter. b 56. Aston Tr Scheme 85 Coll of Resurr Mirfield 87. d 89 p 90. C Middlewich w Byley *Ches* 89-91; C Aylestone St Andr w St Jas *Leic* from 91. *58 Belvoir Drive, Leicester LE2 8PA* Leicester (0533) 833653

ENNIS, Alfred Reginald. b 07. TCD BA29 MA34 BD35. d 34 p 35. R Stanton-by-Bridge and Swarkestone *Derby* 60-80; rtd 80. *Manormead Residential Home, Tilford Road, Hindhead, Surrey GU26 6RA* Hindhead (0428) 604780

ENNIS, Martin Michael. b 58. MCollP84 Man Univ BSc80. Sarum & Wells Th Coll 87. d 89 p 90. C Newquay *Truro* from 89. *2 St Michael's Road, Newquay, Cornwall TR7 1QZ* Newquay (0637) 877302

ENOCH, David John. b 34. Univ of Wales (Ban) BA55 Univ of Wales (Abth) MA69. United Th Coll Abth 55 Glouc Sch of Min 89. d 91. NSM Much Birch w Lt Birch, Much Dewchurch etc *Heref* from 91. *Fayre Oaks, King's Thorn, Hereford HR2 8AZ* Golden Valley (0981) 540661

ENOCH, William Frederick Palmer. b 30. E Midl Min Tr Course 76. d 79 p 80. NSM Ilkeston St Mary *Derby* 79-85; P-in-c Ilkeston H Trin from 85. *Holy Trinity Vicarage, 1 Cotmanhay Road, Ilkeston, Derbyshire DE7 8HR* Ilkeston (0602) 320833

ENRIGHT, James Leslie. b 06. d 66 p 66. I Dromod *L & K* 67-76; Can Limerick Cathl 72-76; Prec Limerick Cathl 72-76; rtd 76. *8 Seafield, Newtown Hill, Tramore, Waterford, Irish Republic* Tramore (51) 81855

ENSOR, David Alec. b 25. Cape Town Univ BA67. Cuddesdon Coll 48. d 50 p 51. V Quadring *Linc* 68-73; V Gt Grimsby St Andr and St Luke 73-74; V Grimsby St Aug 73-84; R Claypole 84-86; V Whaplode Drove 86-91; V Gedney Hill 86-91; rtd 91. Perm to Offic *Linc* from 91. *73 Monks Dyke Road, Louth, Lincs LN11 8QN* Louth (0507) 604341

ENSOR, Keith Victor. b 08. Dur Univ LTh32. Lon Coll of Div 27. d 31 p 32. C Holloway St Jas *Lon* 31-34; Org Sec (N Province) BCMS 34-38; Algeria 38-39; Chapl RAFVR 39-47; V Wolvey, Burton Hastings and Stretton Baskerville *Cov* 47-50; Chapl RAF 50-63; R Horton and Lt Sodbury *Glouc* from 64. *The Rectory, Horton, Chipping Sodbury, Bristol BS17 6QP* Chipping Sodbury (0454) 313256

ENSOR, Paul George. b 56. Ripon Coll Cuddesdon. d 82 p 83. C Newington St Mary *S'wark* 82-87; TV Croydon St Jo from 87. *The Church House, Barrow Road, Croydon CR0 4EZ* 081-688 7006

ENSOR, Stephen Herbert Paulett. b 07. ALCD31 St Jo Coll Dur LTh31 BA32. d 32 p 33. R Bedworth *Cov* 70-81; rtd 81; Perm to Offic *B & W* from 82. *Hillside Cottage, South Street, Castle Cary, Somerset BA7 7ES* Castle Cary (0963) 51003

ENSOR, Terrence Bryon. b 45. K Coll Lon BD78 AKC78. Westcott Ho Cam 78. d 79 p 80. C S'wark St Sav w All Hallows *S'wark* 79-82; Seychelles 82-85; V Northn St Benedict *Pet* 85-90; Uruguay from 90. *c/o Holy Trinity Cathedral, Montevideo, Uruguay*

ENTWISLE, Canon George Barry. b 43. St Jo Coll Ox BA66 MA73. Linc Th Coll 73. d 75 p 76. C Rawmarsh w Parkgate *Sheff* 75-78; New Zealand from 78; Can St Paul's Cathl Dunedin from 87. *15 Trafford Street, Gore, New Zealand* Gore (20) 87366

ENTWISLE, Alan. b 41. ACP69 Nottm Univ CertEd67 Open Univ BA80 Man Univ MEd85. NW Ord Course 72. d 75 p 76. C Bury H Trin *Man* 75-78; Hd Master Hazlehurst Sch Bury from 78; Lic to Offic *Man* from 78. *1 Alderwood Grove, Edenfield, Bury, Lancs BL0 0HQ* Ramsbottom (0706) 824221

ENTWISLE, Christopher John. b 47. N Ord Course 79. d 82 p 83. NSM Colne H Trin *Blackb* 82-84; C Poulton-le-Fylde 84-87; V Blackpool St Paul from 87. *St Paul's Vicarage, Edgerton Road, Blackpool FY1 2NP* Blackpool (0253) 25308

ENTWISTLE, Frank Roland. b 37. Dur Univ BA59 DipTh60. Cranmer Hall Dur 59. d 61 p 62. C Harborne Heath *Birm* 61-65; S Area Sec BCMS 65-66; Educn Sec 66-73; Hon C Wallington H Trin *S'wark* 68-73; UCCF from 73; Hon C Ware Ch Ch *St Alb* 73-76; Hon C Leic H Trin w St Jo *Leic* from 76. *157 Shanklin Drive, Leicester LE2 3QG* Leicester (0533) 700759

ENTWISTLE, Harry. b 40. St Chad's Coll Dur BSc61 DipTh63. d 63 p 64. C Fleetwood *Blackb* 63-69; P-in-c Aston Abbots w Cublington *Ox* 69-74; P-in-c Hardwick St Mary 69-74; Chapl HM Pris Aylesbury 69-74; Lewes 74-77; HM Rem Cen Risley 77-81; HM Pris Wandsworth 81-88; Australia from 88. *PO Box 50, Fremantle, W Australia 6160* Willeton (9) 335-4911

ENTWISTLE, Howard Rodney. b 36. Ball Coll Ox BA61. Linc Th Coll 61. d 63 p 64. C Langley St Aid *CD Man* 63-64; C Langley All SS and Martyrs 64-66; V Wythenshawe St Martin 66-73; R Stretford St Matt from 73. *St Matthew's Rectory, 39 Sandy Lane, Stretford, Manchester M32 9DB* 061-865 2535

EPERSON, Canon Donald Birkby. b 04. Ch Ch Ox BA27 MA30. Ripon Hall Ox 30. d 30 p 31. Perm to Offic *Cant* from 64; rtd 71. *12 Puckle Lane, Canterbury, Kent CT1 3JX* Canterbury (0227) 766477

EPPINGSTONE, Preb Rudolph Oscar Herbert. b 19. Kelham Th Coll 47. d 51 p 52. R Clovelly *Ex* 59-78; RD Hartland 67-74; V Woolfardisworthy and Buck Mills 77-78; V Beer 78-86; Preb Ex Cathl from 82; C Combe Martin and Berrynarbor 86; rtd 87; Hon C Combe Martin and Berrynarbor *Ex* from 87. *Parson's Pightle, Berrynarbor, Ilfracombe, Devon EX34 9TB* Combe Martin (027188) 2802

EPPS, Gerald Ralph. b 31. Open Univ BA79. Oak Hill Th Coll 52 K Coll Lon 54. d 57 p 58. C Slade Green *Roch* 57-60; V Freethorpe w Wickhampton *Nor* 60-70; P-in-c Halvergate w Tunstall 62-67; V 67-70; R Pulham St Mary Magd 70-80; P-in-c Alburgh 76-77; P-in-c Denton 76-77; P-in-c Pulham St Mary V 76-80; R Pulham from 80. *The Rectory, Pulham Market, Diss, Norfolk IP21 4TE* Pulham Market (0379) 676256

EPPS, Stanley Moorcroft. b 1900. St Jo Coll Cam BA22 MA26 K Coll Lon BD52. d 23 p 24. V Wimborne Minster *Sarum* 57-66; rtd 66; Lic to Offic *B & W* 67-86. *c/o The Rectory, Manningford Bruce, Pewsey, Wilts SN9 6JW* Stonehenge (0980) 630308

EQUEALL, David Edward Royston. b 41. Open Univ BA. St Mich Coll Llan 68. d 71 p 72. C Mountain Ash *Llan* 71-74; C Gabalfa 74-77; Chapl Asst Univ Hosp of Wales Cardiff 74-77; Chapl 77-79; Chapl N Gen Hosp Sheff from 79. *Norwood Cottage, 2 Longley Lane, Sheffield S5 7JD* Sheffield (0742) 438713 or 434343

ERDAL, Miss Ayshe Anne. b 61. Nottm Univ BA84. Ripon Coll Cuddesdon 88. d 90. C Daventry *Pet* 90-91; C Corby SS Pet and Andr w Gt and Lt Oakley from 91. *7 Thetford Close, Corby, Northants NN18 9PH* Kettering (0536) 460240

ERREY, Albert George. b 18. Lon Univ BA44 MA48 BD50. Cuddesdon Coll. d 65 p 66. Hon C Leamington Priors H Trin *Cov* 65-72; C 72-74; P-in-c Wolverton w Norton Lindsey and Langley 74-78; R 78-84; rtd 84; Perm to Offic *Chich* from 84. *33 Mill Mead, Ringmer, Lewes, E Sussex BN8 5JG* Ringmer (0273) 813007

ERRIDGE, David John. b 45. Lon Univ DipTh68. Tyndale Hall Bris 66. d 69 p 70. C Bootle St Matt *Liv* 69-72; C Horwich H Trin *Man* 72-77; R Blackley St Andr from 77; AD N Man from 85. *The Vicarage, Churchdale Road, Higher Blackley, Manchester M9 3ND* 061-740 2961

ERRINGTON, John Robert. b 59. St Jo Coll Cam BA80 MA84. Coll of Resurr Mirfield 82. d 84 p 85. C Walker *Newc* 84-86; C Ponteland 86-88; TV Whorlton from 88. *St Wilfred's House, Trevelyan Drive, Newcastle upon Tyne NE5 4DA* 091-286 0343

ERSKINE, Canon Samuel Thomas. b 19. TCD BA42 MA46. d 43 p 44. RD Canewdon and Southend *Chelmsf* 68-84; V Prittlewell St Mary 68-77; V Prittlewell 77-84; rtd 84; Perm to Offic *St E* from 85. *11 Kembold Close, Moreton Rise, Bury St Edmunds, Suffolk IP32 7EF* Bury St Edmunds (0284) 706337

ESCOLME, Miss Doreen. b 29. St Jo Coll Nottm 82. dss 83 d 87. Hunslet Moor St Pet and St Cuth *Ripon* 83-87; C 87-88; Par Dn Wyther Ven Bede from 88. *6 Heather Gardens, Leeds LS13 4LF* Leeds (0532) 579055

ESCRITT, Mrs Margaret Ruth. b 37. Selly Oak Coll 60. d 87. Chapl Asst York Distr Hosp 81-83; Dioc Adv for Diaconal Mins *York* from 85. *The Rectory, 3 Westfield Close, Haxby, York YO3 8JG* York (0904) 766658

ESCRITT, Michael William. b 35. Birm Univ DipTh67. Qu Coll Birm 64. d 67 p 68. C Huntington *York* 67-69; Abp's Dom Chapl 69-72; V Bishopthorpe 72-83; V Acaster Malbis 73-83; V Selby Abbey 83-90; TR Haxby w Wigginton from 90. *The Rectory, 3 Westfield Close, Haxby, York YO3 8JG* York (0904) 760455

ESDAILE, Adrian George Kennedy. b 35. Mert Coll Ox BA57 MA61. Wells Th Coll 59. d 61 p 62. C St Helier *S'wark* 61-64; C Wimbledon 64-68; V Hackbridge and N Beddington 68-80; RD Sutton 76-80; TR Chipping Barnet w Arkley *St Alb* from 80; RD Barnet from 89. *The Rectory, 38 Manor Road, Barnet, Herts EN5 2JJ* 081-449 3894

ESLING, Edwin. b 07. Dur Univ LTh36. Qu Coll Birm 33. d 36 p 37. Australia 60-70; V Alvingham w N and S Cockerington *Linc* 70-73; R Yarburgh 71-73; rtd 73. *Ty Newydd, Llanfynydd, Carmarthen, Dyfed SA32 7TQ* Llandeilo (0558) 668691

ESSER, Lindsay Percy David. b 53. BA. Oak Hill Th Coll. d 84 p 85. C Barnsbury St Andr and H Trin w All SS *Lon* 84-87; Chapl Paris St Mich *Eur* 87-90; C Spring Grove St Mary *Lon* from 90. *16 Spencer Road, Isleworth, Middx TW7 6BH* 081-560 7141

ESSERY, Canon Eric Albert. b 28. TD ED78. Univ of Wales (Lamp) BA53 Reading Univ CertEd76. St Mich Coll Llan 53. d 55 p 56. C Skewen *Llan* 55-57; C Oakwood 57-59; C Sunbury *Lon* 59-63; Ind Chapl *Chich* 63-64; P-in-c Crawley 63-64; V Hammersmith St Paul *Lon* 64-74; CF (TAVR) from 65; V Shinfield *Ox* 74-84; V Whitley Ch Ch from 84; RD Reading from 85; Hon Can Ch Ch from 88. *Christ Church Vicarage, 4 Vicarage Road, Reading RG2 7AJ* Reading (0734) 871250

ESTDALE, Canon Francis Albert. b 26. ALCD53. d 53 p 54. C Penn *Lich* 53-56; C Watford Ch Ch *St Alb* 56-61; V Stopsley from 61; Hon Can St Alb Abbey from 90. *The Vicarage, 702 Hitchin Road, Luton LU2 7UJ* Luton (0582) 29194

ETCHELLS, Peter. b 26. Kelham Th Coll 48. d 52 p 53. C Chesterton St Geo *Ely* 52-55; C Leic St Marg *Leic* 55-58; R Willoughby Waterleys, Peatling Magna etc from 58. *The Vicarage, Gilmorton Road, Ashby Magna, Lutterworth, Leics LE17 5NF* Leire (0455) 209406

ETCHES, Haigh David. b 45. St Jo Coll Dur BA71 DipTh72. d 73 p 74. C Whitnash *Cov* 73-77; C Wallingford *Ox* 77-79; C Wallingford w Crowmarsh Gifford etc 79-83; P-in-c Bearwood 83-86; R from 86. *The Rectory, 6 St Catherine's Close, Wokingham, Berks RG11 5BZ* Wokingham (0734) 794364

ETHERIDGE, Mrs Marjorie. b 18. Univ of Wales (Ban) BA38 Open Univ BA84. St Alb Minl Tr Scheme 80. dss 83 d 87. Hitchin *St Alb* 83-87; Hon Par Dn from 87. *10 Balmoral Road, Hitchin, Herts SG5 1XG* Hitchin (0462) 50496

ETHERIDGE, Richard Thomas. b 32. Lon Univ BD62. ALCD61. d 62 p 63. C Wilmington *Roch* 62-65; C Rainham 65-69; V Langley St Jo *Birm* from 69; P-in-c Oldbury from 83. *The Vicarage, St John's Road, Oldbury, Warley, W Midlands B68 9RF* 021-552 5005

ETHERIDGE, Terry. b 44. Wells Th Coll 68. d 70 p 71. C Barrow St Jo *Carl* 70-73; C Wilmslow *Ches* 73-76; V Knutsford St Cross 76-85; R Malpas and Threapwood from 85. *The Rectory, Malpas, Cheshire SY14 8PP* Malpas (0948) 860209

ETHERINGTON, Ernest Hugh. b 12. CCC Cam BA34 MA39. Linc Th Coll 34. d 35 p 36. Asst Master Horbury Sec Sch 61-77; Perm to Offic *Wakef* from 72; rtd 77. *61 Fairfield Avenue, Ossett, W Yorkshire WF5 0LZ* Wakefield (0924) 277074

ETHERINGTON, Robert Barry. b 37. Man Univ BA62. Linc Th Coll 62. d 64 p 65. C Linc St Jo *Linc* 64-67; C Frodingham 67-69; V Reepham 69-78; Ind Chapl 70-78; Ind Chapl *St Alb* 78-88; V Luton St Chris Round Green from 88. *St Christopher's Vicarage, 33 Felix Avenue, Luton LU2 7LE* Luton (0582) 24754

ETTERLEY, Peter Andrew Gordon. b 39. Kelham Th Coll 63 Wells Th Coll 66. d 68 p 69. C Gillingham St Aug *Roch* 68-71; Papua New Guinea 71-80; V Cleeve w Chelvey and Brockley *B & W* 80-84; V Seaton Hirst *Newc* 84-86; TR from 86. *The Vicarage, Newbiggin Road, Ashington, Northd NE63 0TQ* Ashington (0670) 813218

ETTLINGER, Max Brian. b 28. Sarum & Wells Th Coll 70. d 72 p 73. C Mill Hill Jo Keble Ch *Lon* 72-74; Min Cricklewood St Pet CD 74-78; R Monken Hadley 78-88; Bp's Dom Chapl *St E* 88-91; Dioc Communications Officer 88-91; P-in-c Stratford St Mary from 91; P-in-c Raydon from 91; P-in-c Holton St Mary w Gt Wenham from 91. *The Rectory, Stratford St Mary, Colchester CO7 6LZ* Colchester (0206) 322128

ETTRICK, Peter Alured. b 14. TD56 and Bars OBE67. Ch Coll Cam BA36 MA41. Qu Coll Birm 36. d 37 p 38. V Bisley *Glouc* 70-79; rtd 79; Perm to Offic *Glouc* from 80. *Meiktila, The Ridge, Bussage, Stroud, Glos GL6 8BB* Brimscombe (0453) 883272

EUSTICE, Peter Lafevre. b 32. AKC56. d 57 p 58. C Finsbury Park St Thos *Lon* 57-60; C Redruth *Truro* 60-63; V Treslothan 63-71; V Falmouth All SS 71-76; R St Stephen in Brannel from 76. *70 Rectory Road, St Stephen, St Austell, Cornwall PL26 7RL* St Austell (0726) 822236

EVA, Nigel James. b 29. Pemb Coll Cam BA53 MA57. Ely Th Coll 53. d 55 p 56. Asst Missr Pemb Coll Miss Walworth 55-57; C Greenwich St Alfege w St Pet *S'wark* 57-60; C Mottingham St Andr 60-62; V Eltham H Trin 62-80; R Portishead *B & W* 80-90; R Mawnan *Truro* from 90. *The Rectory, Mawnan, Falmouth, Cornwall TR11 5HY* Falmouth (0326) 250280

EVA, Canon Owen Vyvyan. b 17. MBE83. Selw Coll Cam BA39 MA43. Ridley Hall Cam 46. d 47 p 48. R Halewood *Liv* 62-83; TR 83-86; RD Farnworth 71-81; Hon Can Liv Cathl from 74; rtd 86; Perm to Offic Ches & Liv from 87. *10 Saddlers Rise, Norton, Runcorn, Cheshire WA7 6PG* Runcorn (0928) 717119

EVANS, Alan David Carter. b 35. Clifton Th Coll 62. d 65 p 66. C Gt Baddow *Chelmsf* 65-68; C Walthamstow St Mary 68-72; V Forest Gate St Mark 72-77; V Chadwell Heath 77-86; V Squirrels Heath from 86. *The Vicarage, 36 Ardleigh Green Road, Hornchurch, Essex RM11 2LQ* Hornchurch (04024) 46571

EVANS, Alun Wyn. b 47. Down Coll Cam BA70 MA73. Cuddesdon Coll 70. d 72 p 73. C Bargoed w Brithdir *Llan* 72-74; C Bargoed and Deri w Brithdir 74-75; C Coity w Nolton 75-77; V Cwmavon 77-81; Warden of Ords 80-81; V Llangynwyd w Maesteg 81-86; Prov Officer for Soc Resp from 86. *9 Cosmeston Drive, Penarth, S Glam CF6 2FA* Penarth (0222) 705856

EVANS, Andrew. b 57. Southn Univ BEd80. S Dios Minl Tr Scheme 88. d 91. NSM Cricklade w Latton *Bris* from 91. *35 Pittsfield, Cricklade, Wilts SN6 6AW* Swindon (0793) 751688

EVANS, Anthony Nigel. b 53. Nottm Univ BA74 Fitzw Coll Cam BA76. Westcott Ho Cam 74. d 77 p 78. C Sneinton St Cypr *S'well* 77-80; C Worksop Priory 80-83; V Nottm St Geo w St Jo 83-88; R Ordsall from 88. *The Rectory, All Hallows Street, Retford, Notts DN22 7TP* Retford (0777) 702515

EVANS, Benjamin John. b 13. JP. St Mich Coll Llan 75. d 76 p 77. NSM Barry All SS *Llan* from 76. *167 Pontypridd Road, Barry, S Glam CF6 8LW* Barry (0446) 734742

EVANS, Brian. b 34. Univ of Wales (Cardiff) DipTh58 Open Univ BA86. St Deiniol's Hawarden 70. d 71 p 72. C Porthkerry *Llan* 71-72; C Barry All SS 72-75; V Abercynon 75-82; V Pendoylan and Welsh St Donats 82-87; R Maentwrog w Trawsfynydd *Ban* from 87. *The Rectory, Trawsfynydd, Blaenau Ffestiniog, Gwynedd LL41 4RY* Trawsfynydd (076687) 482

✠**EVANS, Rt Rev Bruce Read.** b 29. ACIS DipTh Witwatersrand Univ 47. Oak Hill Th Coll 54. d 57 p 58 c 75. C Redhill H Trin *S'wark* 57-59; C Portman Square St Paul *Lon* 59-62; S Africa from 62; Bp Port Elizabeth from 75. *Bishop's House, 75 River Road, Walmer, 6070 South Africa* Port Elizabeth (41) 514296

EVANS, Caroline Mary. b 46. CertEd69 DipTh86. St Jo Coll Nottm 84. d 86. C Llanbeblig w Caernarfon and Betws Garmon etc *Ban* 86-88; Dn-in-c Bodedern, Llechcynfarwy, Llechylched etc from 88. *The Vicarage, Bodedern, Holyhead, Gwynedd LL65 3SU* Valley (0407) 740340

EVANS, Charles Wyndham. b 28. Univ of Wales (Ban) BA49 St Cath Soc Ox BA51 MA55. St Steph Ho Ox 49. d 52 p 53. C Denbigh *St As* 52-56; Lic to Offic *St D* 56-79; Chapl Llandovery Coll 56-67; Chapl and Sen Lect Trin Coll Carmarthen 67-79; V Llanrhaiadr yn Cinmerch and Prion *St As* from 79; Dioc RE Adv from 82; Tutor St Deiniol's Lib Hawarden from 84; Chapl Ruthin Sch from 84; RD Denbigh *St As* from 84. *The Vicarage, Llanrhaeadr, Denbigh, Clwyd LL16 4NN* Llanynys (074578) 250

EVANS, Prof Christopher Francis. b 09. CCC Cam BA32 MA38 Ox Univ MA48 Southn Univ Hon DLitt77. Linc Th Coll 33. d 34 p 35. Prof NT Studies K Coll Lon 62-77; rtd 77. *4 Church Close, Cuddesdon, Oxford OX9 9EX* Wheatley (08677) 4406

EVANS, Christopher Idris. b 51. Chich Th Coll 74. d 77 p 78. C Gellygaer *Llan* 77-80; C St Andrew's Major and Michaelston-le-Pit 80-81; V Llangeinor 81-87; V Watlington w Pyrton and Shirburn *Ox* from 87. *The*

Vicarage, Hill Road, Watlington, Oxford OX9 5AD Watlington (049161) 2494

EVANS, Christopher Jonathan. b 43. AKC67 AKC88. **d** 68 **p** 69. C Wednesfield St Thos *Lich* 68-71; C Dorridge *Birm* 71-74; V Marston Green 74-81; V Acocks Green 81-86; RD Yardley 84-86; V Hill 86-88; Area Officer COPEC Housing Trust 88-91; V Harborne St Pet from 91. *The Vicarage, Old Church Road, Birmingham B17 0BB* 021-427 1949

EVANS, Canon Colin Rex. b 24. Reading Univ BA49. Linc Th Coll. **d** 57 **p** 58. R Bassingham *Linc* 66-74; V Aubourn w Haddington 66-74; V Carlton-le-Moorland w Stapleford 66-74; R Skinnand 66-74; R Thurlby w Norton Disney 66-74; RD Graffoe 69-74; RD Elloe E 74-89; Can and Preb Linc Cathl 74-89; V Holbeach 74-89; rtd 90. *24 Sweetbriar Lane, Holcombe, Dawlish, Devon EX7 0JZ* Dawlish (0626) 862860

EVANS, Miss Daphne Gillian. b 41. Bible Tr Inst Glas 67 Trin Coll Bris IDC75. **dss** 83 **d** 87. Wenlock *Heref* 83-87; TM 87-88; rtd 88. *12 Greenmeadow Grove, Endon, Stoke-on-Trent ST9 9EU* Stoke-on-Trent (0782) 504686

EVANS, David. b 37. Keble Coll Ox BA60 MA65 Lon Univ BD64. Wells Th Coll 62. **d** 64 **p** 65. Min Can Brecon Cathl *S & B* 64-68; C Brecon w Battle 64-68; C Swansea St Mary and H Trin 68-71; Chapl Univ of Wales (Swansea) 68-71; Bp's Chapl for Samaritan and Soc Work *Birm* 71-75; Jt Gen Sec Samaritans 75-84; Gen Sec 84-89; Lic to Offic *Ox* 75-89; R Heyford w Stowe Nine Churches *Pet* from 89. *The Rectory, Nether Heyford, Northampton NN7 3LQ* Weedon (0327) 40487

EVANS, David. b 37. Open Univ BA73. St Mich Coll Llan 65. **d** 67 **p** 68. C Swansea St Pet *S & B* 67-70; C St Austell *Truro* 70-75; R Purley *Ox* 75-90; RD Bradfield 85-90; R Bryanston Square St Mary w St Marylebone St Mark *Lon* from 90; P-in-c St Marylebone Ch Ch 90-91. *73 Gloucester Place, London W1H 3PF* 071-935 2200

EVANS, David Alexander Noble. b 13. Pemb Coll Ox BA36 MA41. Wells Th Coll 38. **d** 40 **p** 41. V Sunningdale *Ox* 67-80; rtd 80; Perm to Offic *Ex* from 80. *High Bank, Manaton, Newton Abbot, Devon TQ13 9UA* Manaton (064722) 336

EVANS, David Aylmer. b 28. Lon Univ CertEd62 Reading Univ DipC&G73. St D Coll Lamp BA49 LTh51. **d** 51 **p** 52. C Brecon St David w Llanspyddid and Llanilltyd *S & B* 51-53; C Colwyn Bay *St As* 53-54; C Macclesfield St Mich *Ches* 54-56; V Lostock Gralam 56-59; Perm to Offic Chelmsf 58-65; Ox 65-73; Chapl Endsleigh Sch 59-65; Wokingham Gr Sch 65-72; Counsellor S Molton Sch & Commun Coll Devon 73-87; V Middlezoy and Othery and Moorlinch *B & W* from 87. *The Vicarage, Othery, Bridgwater, Somerset TA7 0QG* Burrowbridge (082369) 700

EVANS, David Burton. b 35. Open Univ BA87. K Coll Lon 58 Edin Th Coll 60. **d** 62 **p** 63. C Leeds St Hilda *Ripon* 62-63; C Cross Green St Sav and St Hilda 63-67; Min Can Dur Cathl *Dur* 67-71; Chapl Prebendal Sch Chich 71-74; PV Chich Cathl *Chich* 71-74; V Lynch w Iping Marsh 74-79; Chapl K Edw VII Hosp Midhurst 77-86; V Easebourne *Chich* 79-86; R St Mich Cornhill w St Pet le Poer etc *Lon* from 86. *St Michael's Vestry, Cornhill, London EC3V 9DS* 071-626 8841

EVANS, Canon David Conrad. b 16. St D Coll Lamp BA40. **d** 42 **p** 43. V Llanfihangel Abercywyn *St D* 63-83; Hon Can St D Cathl from 79; rtd 83. *17 Penbryn Avenue, Carmarthen, Dyfed SA31 3DH* Carmarthen (0267) 234333

EVANS, Ven David Eifion. b 11. Univ of Wales BA32 MA51. St Mich Coll Llan 33. **d** 34 **p** 35. Adn Cardigan *St D* 67-79; V Newc Emlyn 69-79; rtd 79. *31 Bryncastell, Bow Street, Aberystwyth, Dyfed SY24 5DE* Aberystwyth (0970) 828747

EVANS, David Elwyn. b 43. St Mich Coll Llan 71. **d** 73 **p** 74. C Llandybie *St D* 73-75; C Llanelly 75-78; V Trelech-a'r-Bettws w Abernant and Llanwinio from 78. *Tre-Lech Vicarage, Pen-y-Bont, Carmarthen, Dyfed* Madox (09948) 335

EVANS, David Frederick Francis. b 35. Univ of Wales BSc59. Wells Th Coll 59. **d** 61 **p** 62. C Eltham St Jo *S'wark* 61-64; C Banbury *Ox* 64-69; V Brize Norton and Carterton 69-73; V Tilehurst St Geo 73-84; V Lydney w Aylburton *Glouc* from 84; RD Forest S from 90. *The Vicarage, Lydney, Glos GL15 5EG* Dean (0594) 42321

EVANS, Canon David Geraint. b 24. Univ of Wales BA47. St D Coll Lamp 49. **d** 49 **p** 50. C St Ishmael's w Llansaint and Ferryside *St D* 49-54; C Llandeilo Fawr and Llandefeisant 54-58; V Strata Florida 58-68; R Ystradgynlais *S & B* from 68; Hon Can Brecon Cathl

from 86. *The Rectory, Ystradgynlais, Swansea* Glantawe (0639) 843200

EVANS, David John. b 49. Univ of Wales (Ban) BSc72 Bath Univ CertEd73 Leeds Univ DipTh77. Coll of Resurr Mirfield 75. **d** 78 **p** 79. C Wandsworth St Anne *S'wark* 78-81; C Angell Town St Jo 81-82; TV Catford (Southend) and Downham 82-90; P-in-c Somersham w Pidley and Oldhurst *Ely* from 90; P-in-c Broughton from 90. *The Rectory, 8 King Street, Somersham, Huntingdon, Cambs PE17 3EL* Ramsey (0487) 840676

EVANS, Canon David Leslie Bowen. b 28. Univ of Wales (Lamp) BA52 LTh54. **d** 54 **p** 55. C Cardigan *St D* 54-57; C Llangathen w Llanfihangel Cilfargen 57-58; C Bettws St Dav 58-60; V Bettws Evan 60-64; V Burry Port and Pwll 64-76; V Cardiff Dewi Sant *Llan* 76-86; Asst Chapl HM Pris Cardiff 76-86; V Llanllwch w Llangain and Llangynog *St D* from 86; Can St D Cathl from 89. *The Vicarage, Llanllwch, Carmarthen, Dyfed SA31 3RN* Carmarthen (0267) 236805

EVANS, David Morgan. b 98. Dur Univ 27. Lich Th Coll 26. **d** 29 **p** 30. R Moulsoe *Ox* 38-85; P-in-c Broughton and Milton Keynes 60-64; rtd 85. *The Rectory, Moulsoe, Newport Pagnell, Bucks MK16 0HL* Newport Pagnell (0908) 615249

EVANS, David Richard. b 47. St Steph Ho Ox 68. **d** 72 **p** 73. C Cardiff St Jo *Llan* 72-76; PV Llan Cathl 76-80; V Cleeve Prior and The Littletons *Worc* from 80. *The Vicarage, South Littleton, Evesham, Worcs WR11 5TJ* Evesham (0386) 830397

✠**EVANS, Rt Rev David Richard John.** b 38. G&C Coll Cam BA63 MA66. Clifton Th Coll 63. **d** 65 **p** 66 **c** 78. C Enfield Ch Ch Trent Park *Lon* 65-68; Argentina 69-77; Peru 77-88; Bp Peru 78-88; Bp Bolivia 82-88; Asst Bp Bradf from 88. *30 Grosvenor Road, Shipley, W Yorkshire BD18 4RN* Bradford (0274) 582033

EVANS, David Ronald. b 59. Man Univ BSc81 Southn Univ BTh87. Chich Th Coll 84. **d** 87 **p** 88. C Goldthorpe w Hickleton *Sheff* 87-90; C Somers Town St Mary *Lon* from 90. *The Vicarage, Camden Square, London NW1 9XG* 071-485 3147

EVANS, David Russell. Liv Univ BA57. Ripon Hall Ox 59. **d** 61 **p** 62. C Netherton CD *Liv* 61-65; Asst Chapl Can Slade Sch Bolton from 65; Lic to Offic *Man* from 66; Perm to Offic *Liv* from 76. *2 Rushford Grove, Bolton* Bolton (0204) 592981

EVANS, David Thomas Pugh. b 95. St Aid Birkenhead 41. **d** 44 **p** 45. C-in-c Birkenhead St Winifred's Welsh Ch *Ches* from 44; Chapl Birkenhead Gen Hosp 46-82; V Birkenhead H Trin 54-74; rtd 82; Perm to Offic *Ches* from 82. *33 Harcourt Street, Birkenhead, Mersyside L42 5LU* 051-652 4617

EVANS, David Vincent. b 22. Keble Coll Ox BA43 MA47. Wells Th Coll 45. **d** 47 **p** 48. Chapl RN 51-81; rtd 81; Perm to Offic *Portsm* from 81. *22 The Ridgeway, Fareham, Hants PO16 8RE* Fareham (0329) 233791

EVANS, Derek. b 45. St D Coll Lamp DipTh68. **d** 68 **p** 69. C Pemb Dock *St D* 68-74; V Ambleston, St Dogwells, Walton E and Llysyfran 74-78; V Wiston w Ambleston, St Dogwells and Walton E 78-81; V Wiston w Ambleston, St Dogwells, Walton E and St-81-85; R Haverfordwest St Mary and St Thos w Haroldston from 85. *The Rectory, Scarrowscant Lane, Haverfordwest, Dyfed SA61 1EP* Haverfordwest (0437) 763170

EVANS, Preb Derek Courtenay. b 29. Down Coll Cam BA52 MA56. St Aid Birkenhead 55. **d** 57 **p** 58. C Taunton St Mary *B & W* 57-61; V Trull 61-77; RD Taunton S 72-77; P-in-c Walton 77; R Street 77; Preb Wells Cathl from 77; R Street w Walton from 78; RD Glastonbury 79-82; R Greinton from 81. *The Rectory, Vestry Road, Street, Somerset BA16 0HX* Street (0458) 42671

EVANS, Desmond. b 26. Univ of Wales (Lamp) BA48 St Cath Soc Ox BA50 MA54. St Steph Ho Ox 48. **d** 51 **p** 52. C Clydach *S & B* 51-54; V 82-87; Chapl Cranleigh Sch Surrey 54-59; Lic to Offic *Ban* 59-78; V Llanwrtyd w Llanddulas in Tir Abad etc *S & B* 78-82; RD Builth Elwell 79-82; V Abercrave and Callwen from 87. *The Vicarage, Abercrave, Swansea SA9 1TJ* Abercrave (0639) 730640

EVANS, Donald Henry. b 13. St D Coll Lamp BA35. **d** 36 **p** 37. V Seighford, Derrington and Cresswell *Lich* 64-78; rtd 78; Perm to Offic *Ches* from 80. *3 Highfields Avenue, Audlem, Crewe* Audlem (0270) 811165

EVANS, Edward John. b 47. Univ of Wales (Cardiff) DipTh71. St Mich Coll Llan 67. **d** 71 **p** 72. C Llantwit Fadre *Llan* 71-77; R Eglwysilan 77-88; V Laleston w Tythegston and Merthyr Mawr from 88. *The Vicarage, Laleston, Bridgend, M Glam CF32 0LB* Bridgend (0656) 654254

✠**EVANS, Rt Rev Edward Lewis.** b 04. Lon Univ BD34 MTh39. Bps' Coll Cheshunt 35. **d** 37 **p** 38 **c** 57. C Prittlewell *Chelmsf* 37-40; Jamaica 40-60; Suff Bp Kingston 57-60; Bp Barbados 60-71; rtd 71. *Bungalow 1, Terry's Cross, Brighton Road, Henfield, W Sussex BN5 9SX* Henfield (0273) 493334

EVANS, Elwyn David. b 36. Keble Coll Ox BA58 MA62. St Mich Coll Llan 60. **d** 61 **p** 62. C Abth H Trin *St D* 61-63; C Llanelly St Paul 63-66; C Roath St German *Llan* 66-69; V Crynant 69-78; R Llanilid w Pencoed from 79. *The Rectory, 60 Coychurch Road, Pencoed, Bridgend, M Glam CF35 5NA* Pencoed (0656) 860337

EVANS, Elwyn Thomas. b 12. Univ of Wales BA36. St D Coll Lamp 37. **d** 38 **p** 39. V Tyseley *Birm* 64-78; rtd 78. *8 Gipsy Lane, Balsall Common, Coventry CV7 7FW*

EVANS, Emrys. b 17. St D Coll Lamp BA41. **d** 42 **p** 43. V Twickenham All SS *Lon* 60-81; rtd 81; Perm to Offic *Chich* from 81. *5 Rowan Drive, Billingshurst, W Sussex RH14 9NE* Billingshurst (0403) 784312

EVANS, Ernest Lloyd Parry. b 14. St D Coll Lamp BA37 Keble Coll Ox BA39 MA45. St Mich Coll Llan 39. **d** 40 **p** 41. V Frensham *Guildf* 69-80; rtd 80; Perm to Offic *Guildf* from 82. *2 Kimbers Lane, Farnham, Surrey GU9 9PT* Farnham (0252) 714954

EVANS, Ernest Maurice. b 28. MIMechE66. St As Minl Tr Course 84. **d** 86 **p** 87. NSM Hope *St As* 86-89; P-in-c Corwen and Llangar 89-90; R Corwen and Llangar w Gwyddelwern and Llawr-y-B from 90. *The Rectory, Maesafallen, Corwen, Clwyd LL21 9AB* Corwen (0490) 3114

EVANS, Evan. b 04. **d** 39 **p** 40. V Churcham w Bulley *Glouc* 61-69; rtd 69; Perm to Offic *Glouc* 69-70 and from 74; C Glouc St Jas 70-74. *4 Oxstalls Way, Gloucester GL2 9JG* Gloucester (0452) 24620

EVANS, Canon Evan Austin. b 02. Keble Coll Ox BA24 MA31. St D Coll Lamp 24. **d** 25 **p** 26. Can Llan Cathl *Llan* 61-72; V Llancarfan 64-72; rtd 72. *30 Bronawelon, Barry, S Glam CF6 8PS* Barry (0446) 734837

EVANS, Evan Walter. b 16. **d** 39 **p** 40. C Cellan w Llanfair Clydogau *St D* 39; C Narberth 39-40; C Cardigan 40-42; CF (EC) 42-47; C Llandyssul *St D* 47; R Didmarton w Oldbury-on-the-Hill and Sopworth *Glouc* 47-52; Chapl Chelsea R Hosp 72-81; Perm to Offic *St D* from 81. *Cilgwyn Row, Llandyssul, Dyfed* Llandyssul (0559) 362275

EVANS, Frank Owen. b 23. Univ of Wales BA44. St D Coll Lamp 44. **d** 46 **p** 63. C Llanelly *St D* 63-81; Hd Master Coleshill Secondary Sch Dyfed 74-82; Hon C Kidwelly and Llandefaelog *St D* 81-82; V Martletwy w Lawrenny and Minwear and Yerbeston 82-87; rtd 87. *35 Stradey Park Avenue, Llanelli, Dyfed SA15 3EG* Llanelli (0554) 777149

EVANS, Frederick Albert. b 29. **d** 83 **p** 84. NSM Maisemore *Glouc* from 83; NSM Glouc St Geo w Whaddon from 86. *10 Hillborough Road, Gloucester GL4 0JQ* Gloucester (0452) 26034

EVANS, Frederick James Stephens. b 21. Qu Coll Cam BA42 MA46. St D Coll Lamp LTh44. **d** 44 **p** 45. R Chalfont St Peter *Ox* 65-78; V Rustington *Chich* 78-86; rtd 86; Perm to Offic *Chich* from 86. *45 Falmer Avenue, Goring-by-Sea, Worthing, W Sussex BN12 4SY* Worthing (0903) 503905

EVANS, Canon Frederick John Margam. b 31. Magd Coll Ox BA53 MA57. St Mich Coll Llan 53. **d** 54 **p** 55. C New Tredegar *Mon* 54-58; C Chepstow 58-60; Asst Chapl United Sheff Hosps 60-62; Chapl Brookwood Hosp Woking 62-70; V Crookham *Guildf* from 70; RD Aldershot 78-83; Hon Can Guildf Cathl from 89. *14 Gally Hill Road, Church Crookham, Fleet, Hants GU13 0LH* Fleet (0252) 617130

EVANS, Gareth Milton. b 39. Bris Univ LLB60 St Cath Coll Ox BA62 MA66. Ripon Hall Ox 60. **d** 63 **p** 64. C Hengrove *Bris* 63-65; Min Can Bris Cathl 65-68; C Bishopston 68-71; C Notting Hill *Lon* 71-83; V Bayswater from 83. *St Matthew's Vicarage, 27 St Petersburgh Place, London W2 4LA* 071-229 2192

EVANS, Ven Geoffrey Bainbridge. b 34. St Mich Coll Llan 56. **d** 58 **p** 59. C Llan All SS CD *Llan* 58-60; C Llan N 60-67; Guyana 67-73; Chapl Izmir w Bornova *Eur* from 73; Adn Aegean from 78. *Pk 1005, Arzu Apartment, 1402 Sokak 6, No 7, Izmir, Turkey* Izmir (51) 212774

EVANS, Geoffrey David. b 44. K Coll Lon BD69 AKC69. St Aug Coll Cant 69. **d** 70 **p** 71. C Lawrence Weston *Bris* 71-73; Chapl Grenville Coll Bideford 74-79; Chapl Eastbourne Coll E Sussex 79-82; Chapl Taunton and Somerset Hosp from 83; Chapl Musgrove Park Hosp from 83. *49 Cheddon Road, Taunton, Somerset* Taunton (0823) 275871 or 333444

EVANS, Gerald Arthur. b 35. Univ of Wales (Swansea) BA57 Lon Univ DipRS77. S'wark Ord Course 74. **d** 77 **p** 78. NSM Balcombe *Chich* 77-81; NSM Cuckfield 81-87; R Tillington from 87; R Duncton from 87; R Up Waltham from 87. *The Rectory, Tillington, Petworth, W Sussex GU28 9AH* Petworth (0798) 42117

EVANS, Mrs Gillian. b 39. Imp Coll Lon BSc61 Univ of Wales (Cardiff) DPS88. **d** 88. NSM Penallt and Trellech *Mon* 88-89; NSM St Thos-over-Monnow w Wonastow and Michel Troy from 89. *Upper Grove, Newcastle, Monmouth, Gwent NP5 4NT* Monmouth (0600) 84241

EVANS, Canon Glyn. b 10. Univ of Wales BA33. St Steph Ho Ox 33. **d** 34 **p** 35. V St Issells *St D* 55-80; RD Narberth 65-80; Treas St D Cathl 77-80; rtd 80. *3 Flemish Close, St Florence, Tenby, Dyfed SA70 8LT* Manorbier (0834) 871434

EVANS, Glyn. b 59. Nene Coll Northampton BA80 Leic Univ BA80 Ch Ch Coll Cant CertEd82 Kent Univ PGCE82 Birm Univ DipTh87. Qu Coll Birm 85. **d** 88 **p** 89. C Denton *Newc* from 88. *17 Langley Road, Newcastle upon Tyne NE5 2AP* 091-264 5229

EVANS, Glyn Peter. b 54. Leeds Univ BA75. Ripon Coll Cuddesdon 76. **d** 77 **p** 78. C Binley *Cov* 77-80; C Clifton upon Dunsmore w Brownsover 80-84; P-in-c Lacock w Bowden Hill *Bris* 84-89; P-in-c Lt Compton w Chastleton, Cornwell etc *Ox* from 89; Agric Chapl from 89. *The Rectory, Little Compton, Moreton-in-Marsh, Glos GL56 0SE* Barton-on-the-Heath (060874) 313

EVANS, Guy Maxwell Lyon. b 23. Univ of Wales (Cardiff) BA50 BA51. Llan Dioc Tr Scheme 81. **d** 82 **p** 83. NSM Cardiff Dewi Sant *Llan* 82-84; P-in-c Llanfihangel-ar-arth *St D* 84-85; V from 85. *The Vicarage, Llanfihangel-ar-arth, Pencader, Dyfed SA39 9HU* Pencader (0559) 384858

EVANS, Gwilym Owen. b 06. St D Coll Lamp BA29 BD55. **d** 29 **p** 30. Lic to Offic *St As* from 67; rtd 72. *7 Kinard Drive, Rhyl, Clwyd LL18 3EF* Rhyl (0745) 351135

EVANS, Miss Gwyneth Mary. b 43. Gilmore Ho Linc Th Coll 69. **dss** 74 **d** 87. Stamford Hill St Thos *Lon* 72-79; Chapl Asst R Free Hosp Lon 79-89; Chapl Salisbury Hosps and Odstock and Distr Hosp Salisbury from 89. *Odstock Hospital, Salisbury SP2 8BJ* Salisbury (0722) 336262 or 412546

EVANS, Harold Vincent. b 99. St D Coll Lamp BA25. **d** 25 **p** 26. V Llantilio Crossenny and Llanfihangel Ystern etc *Mon* 50-58; rtd 58. *8 Isca Close, Ross-on-Wye, Hereford* Ross-on-Wye (0989) 65951

EVANS, Canon Henry Thomas Platt. b 28. Selw Coll Cam BA51 MA55. Linc Th Coll 51. **d** 53 **p** 54. C Lt Ilford St Barn *Chelmsf* 53-56; C-in-c Stocking Farm CD *Leic* 56-58; V Stocking Farm 58-67; R Stretford St Matt *Man* 67-73; V Knighton St Mary Magd *Leic* 73-83; Hon Can Leic Cathl from 76; RD Christianity (Leic) S 81-83; Warden Launde Abbey from 83; P-in-c Loddington *Leic* from 83. *Launde Abbey, East Norton, Leicester LE7 9XB* Belton (057286) 254

EVANS, Ven Hugh Arfon. b 13. St D Coll Lamp BA35 St Mich Coll Llan 35. **d** 36 **p** 37. V Llanfairisgaer *Ban* 52-73; RD Arfon 58-73; Can Treas 66-73; Adn Ban 73-83; rtd 83. *79 Chambers Lane, Mynydd Isa, Mold, Clwyd CH7 6UZ* Mold (0352) 59269

EVANS, Hywel Victor. b 14. Univ of Wales BA36. St Steph Ho Ox 36. **d** 38 **p** 39. V Bunny w Bradmore *S'well* 66-74; V Walesby 74-79; R Kirton 74-79; P-in-c Egmanton 77-79; rtd 79. *2 The Retreat, King's Fee, Monmouth, Gwent NP5 3DU* Monmouth (0600) 2268

EVANS, Ifor Wynne. b 06. Univ Coll Ox BA28 MA31. St Mich Coll Llan 32. **d** 33 **p** 34. V Ampfield *Win* 57-74; rtd 74; Perm to Offic *Win* from 75. *Ridgemount, Haccups Lane, Michelmarsh, Romsey, Hants SO5 0NP* Braishfield (0794) 68383

EVANS, Mrs Jennifer. b 41. Sarum Th Coll. **d** 88. C Bramshott *Portsm* from 88. *49 Haslemere Road, Liphook, Petersfield, Hants GU30 7BB* Liphook (0428) 724595

EVANS, John. b 10. St D Coll Lamp BA34. **d** 34 **p** 35. RD Cyfeiliog and Mawddwy *Ban* 68-72; R Penegoes and Darowen w Llanbrynmair 72-78; rtd 78. *Llys Cadfan, Tywyn, Gwynedd LL36 9HG*

EVANS, Ven John Barrie. b 23. Univ of Wales (Lamp) BA47 St Edm Hall Ox BA49 MA54. St Mich Coll Llan 50. **d** 51 **p** 52. C Trevethin *Mon* 51-57; V Caerwent w Dinham and Llanfair Discoed 57-64; V Chepstow 64-79; Can St Woolos Cathl 71-77; Adn Mon 74-86; R Llanmartin w Wilcrick and Langstone 79-83; R Llanmartin 83-86; Adn Newport from 86. *Draycot, 16 Stow Park Crescent, Newport, Gwent NP9 4HD* Newport (0633) 264919

EVANS, Dr John Daryll. b 39. FCP85 Univ of Wales (Abth) BSc61 Univ of Wales (Cardiff) DipEd62 MA68 PhD72 Cam Univ DipRS83. **d** 73 **p** 74. Sen Lect Cardiff Institute of HE from 66; Hon C Panteg *Mon* 73-83; P-in-c Mamhilad and Pontymoile from 83. *6 Sluvad Road, Panteg, Pontypool, Gwent NP4 0SX* Pontypool (0495) 752042

EVANS, John David Vincent. b 41. CQSW78. Lich Th Coll 66. **d** 68 **p** 70. C Kingsthorpe *Pet* 68-69; C Corby Epiphany w St D Jo 69-72; Bp's Adv in Children's Work 72-74; Perm to Offic 88-90; R Green's Norton w Bradden 90-91; R Greens Norton w Bradden and Lichborough from 91. *The Rectory, Greens Norton, Towcester, Northants NN12 8BL* Towcester (0327) 50279

EVANS, John Eric. b 14. St D Coll Lamp BA38. **d** 38 **p** 39. V Churchstoke w Hyssington *Heref* 64-77; V Churchstoke w Hyssington and Sarn 77-79; rtd 79. *52 Oaklands Road, Chirk Bank, Wrexham, Clwyd*

EVANS, John Griffiths. b 37. Glouc Th Course 76. **d** 77 **p** 77. Hd Master Corse Sch Glos from 70; C Hartpury w Corse and Staunton *Glouc* 77-79; P-in-c from 79. *Gadfield Elm House, Staunton, Gloucester GL19 3PA* Staunton Court (045284) 302

EVANS, Canon John Hopkin. b 17. St D Coll Lamp BA41. **d** 42 **p** 44. R Llanfechain *St As* 60-82; Hon Can St As Cathl 76-82; rtd 82. *The Rectory, Llanfechain, Powys SY22 6UT* Llansantffraid (069181) 446

EVANS, John Laurie. b 34. Pretoria Univ BSc54 Imp Coll Lon BSc55 Rhodes Univ Grahamstown BA59. Ripon Coll Cuddesdon 84. **d** 86 **p** 87. C Bruton and Distr *B & W* 86-89; P-in-c Ambrosden w Mert and Piddington *Ox* 89-91; C Pet St Mary *Pet* from 91. *19 Danes Close, Eastfield, Peterborough PE1 5LJ* Peterborough (0733) 315200

EVANS, Canon John Mascal. b 15. BNC Ox BA37 MA43. Wells Th Coll 37. **d** 38 **p** 39. Adn Surrey *Guildf* 68-80; rtd 80. C Ridgeway *Sarum* 80-84. *60 Swan Meadow, Pewsey, Wilts SN9 5HP* Marlborough (0672) 63290

EVANS, John Morgan. b 14. MBE87. St D Coll Lamp BA37. **d** 37 **p** 38. V Llangenny *S & B* 55-79; CF (EC) 46-48; CF (TA) 61-87; OCF from 55; rtd 79; Lic to Offic *S & B* from 79. *Milfraen, 1 St John's Road, Brecon, Powys LD3 9DS* Brecon (0874) 4054

EVANS, John Rhys. b 45. Hull Univ BSc66. Sarum & Wells Th Coll 77. **d** 79 **p** 80. C Alton St Lawr *Win* 79-82; C Tadley St Pet 82-85; V Colden from 85. *The Vicarage, Colden Common, Winchester, Hants SO21 1TL* Twyford (0962) 712505

EVANS, John Ronald. b 16. Univ of Wales BA40. St Mich Coll Llan 41. **d** 42 **p** 44. V Glyndyfrdwy *St As* 54-81; RD Edeyrnion 64-81; Dioc Sec SPCK 66-81; rtd 81. *21 Bryn Hyfryd, Johnstown, Wrexham, Clwyd LL14 1PR* Rhosllanerchrugog (0978) 842300

EVANS, John Thomas. b 43. Univ of Wales DipTh66 DPS67. St Mich Coll Llan 66. **d** 67 **p** 68. C Connah's Quay *St As* 67-71; C Llanrhos 71-74; Chapl Rainhill Hosp Liv 74-78; TV Wrexham *St As* 78-83; V Holywell from 83. *The Vicarage, Fron Park Road, Holywell, Clwyd CH8 7UT* Holywell (0352) 710010

EVANS, Canon John Wyn. b 46. FSA88 Univ of Wales (Cardiff) BA68 BD71. St Mich Coll Llan 68. **d** 71 **p** 72. C St D Cathl *St D* 71-72; Min Can St D Cathl 72-75; Perm to Offic *Ox* 75-76; Dioc Archivist *St D* 76-82; R Llanfallteg w Clunderwen and Castell Dwyran etc 77-82; Warden of Ords 78-83; Dioc Dir of Educn from 82; Chapl Trin Coll Carmarthen from 82; Dean of Chpl from 90; Hon Can St D Cathl *St D* 88-90; Can from 90. *Trinity College, Carmarthen, Dyfed SA31 7EP* Carmarthen (0267) 237971

EVANS, Joseph Henry Godfrey. b 31. Univ of Wales (Lamp) BA51. Qu Coll Birm 53. **d** 55 **p** 56. C Hackney St Jo *Lon* 55-58; C Stonehouse *Glouc* 58-60; V Selsley 60-65; V Cheltenham St Pet 65-73; R Willersey w Saintbury 73-77; Chapl Tiffin Sch Kingston-upon-Thames from 77. *300 Raeburn Avenue, Surbiton, Surrey KT5 9EF* 081-390 0936

EVANS, Keith. b 57. Trin Coll Carmarthen CertEd81 BEd82. St D Coll Lamp BA84 Sarum & Wells Th Coll 84. **d** 85 **p** 86. C Swansea St Thos and Kilvey *S & B* 85-87; C Gorseinon 87-89; V Oxwich w Penmaen and Nicholaston from 89. *The Rectory, Penmaen, Swansea SA3 2HN* Penmaen (0792) 371241

EVANS, Kenneth. b 50. Bp Burgess Hall Lamp DipTh74. **d** 74 **p** 75. C Llanaber w Caerdeon Ban 74-79; C Upper Clapton St Matt *Lon* 79-82; P-in-c Tottenham St Phil from 82. *St Philip's Vicarage, 226 Philip Lane, London N15 4HH* 081-808 4235

✠**EVANS, Rt Rev Kenneth Dawson.** b 15. Clare Coll Cam BA37 MA41. Ripon Hall Ox 37. **d** 38 **p** 39 **c** 68. C Northn

St Mary *Pet* 38-41; C Northn All SS w St Kath 41-45; R Ockley *Guildf* 45-49; V Ranmore 49-57; V Dorking 49-57; Hon Can Guildf Cathl 55-63 and 79-85; V Dorking w Ranmore 57-63; RD Dorking 57-63; Can Res Guildf Cathl 63-68; Adn Dorking 63-68; Suff Bp Dorking 68-85; rtd 85. *3 New Inn Lane, Guildford, Surrey GU4 7HN* Guildford (0483) 67978

EVANS, Kenneth Percy. b 16. OBE. Keble Coll Ox BA37 MA42. Wells Th Coll 38. **d** 39 **p** 40. QHC 68-72; V Bradninch *Ex* 72-83; RD Cullompton 77-81; rtd 83; Chapl Menton w San Remo *Eur* 83-87; Perm to Offic *St As* from 87. *Heulfron, Pant-y-Ffridd, Berriew, Welshpool, Powys SY21 8BH* Berriew (0686) 650426

EVANS, Kenneth Roy. b 47. Lon Univ BSc. Ridley Hall Cam 79. **d** 81 **p** 81. C Stratford w Bishopton *Cov* 81-82; C Trunch *Nor* 82-85; Chapl Nottm Mental Illness & Psychiatric Unit from 85; Chapl Mapperley and Community Hosp Nottm 85-89; Lic to Offic *S'well* from 85. *Brandon House, 9 Burlington Road, Sherwood, Nottingham NG5 2GR* Nottingham (0602) 603414

EVANS, Kenwyn Harries Price. b 29. Univ of Wales (Lamp) BA52. St Mich Coll Llan 56. **d** 57 **p** 58. C Swansea St Nic *S & B* 57-58; P-in-c Rhayader 58-61; Miss to Seamen 61-62; C Llangynwyd w Maesteg *Llan* 62-65; V Nantymoel w Wyndham 65-71; V Pwllgwaun 71-75; V Pwllgwaun w Llanddewi Rhondda 75-88; R Llandough w Leckwith from 88; Chapl Llandough Hosp from 88. *The Rectory, Llandough, Penarth, S Glam CF6 1XX* Penarth (0222) 703349

EVANS, Lewys Thomas Gareth. b 29. St Mich Coll Llan. **d** 58 **p** 59. C Clydach *S & B* 58-65; R Vaynor and Capel Taffechan 65-80; V Defynnog w Rhydybriw, Llandeilo'r Fan etc 80-83; V Devynock w Rhydybriw and Llandilo'r-fan 83-87; V Ystalyfera from 87. *The Vicarage, Ystalyfera, Swansea SA9 2EP* Glantawe (0639) 842257

EVANS, Ms Linda Mary. b 49. Univ of Wales (Cardiff) BA71 K Coll Lon BD74 AKC74. Yale Div Sch STM76. **dss** 76 **d** 80. Llanishen and Lisvane *Llan* 76-78; Wrexham *St As* 78-80; C 80-82; Chapl Maudsley Hosp Lon 82-84; Bethlem R Hosp Beckenham 82-84; Chapl Lon Univ *Lon* 84-87. *2 Rhes Eldon, Allt Glanrafon, Bangor, Gwynedd LL57 2RA* Bangor (0248) 370561

EVANS, Miss Madeleine Thelma Bodenham. b 30. K Coll Lon BD76 AKC76. Gilmore Course 80. **dss** 85 **d** 87. Chapl Pipers Corner Sch from 85. *Pipers Corner School, Great Kingshill, High Wycombe, Bucks HP15 6LP* High Wycombe (0494) 718255

EVANS, Michael. b 49. St Jo Coll Nottm 88. **d** 90 **p** 91. C Beeston *S'well* from 90. *46 Bramcote Road, Beeston, Nottingham NG9 1DW* Nottingham (0602) 258825

EVANS, Nathaniel. b 06. Univ of Wales BA35. **d** 38 **p** 40. V Durrington *Chich* 49-75; rtd 75; Perm to Offic *Chich* from 77. *Ramsey Hall, Byron Road, Worthing, W Sussex BN11 3HW* Worthing (0903) 36880

EVANS, Neil Glynne. b 55. Lon Univ DipTh78 Leeds Univ BA81. Trin Coll Bris 81. **d** 82 **p** 83. C Llandybie *St D* 82-86; P-in-c Gwaun-cae-Gurwen 90; V from 90. *The Vicarage, 118 Heol Cae Gurwen, Gwauncaergurwen, Ammanford, Dyfed SA18 1PD* Amman Valley (0269) 822430

EVANS, Neil Robert. b 54. Coll of Resurr Mirfield. **d** 84 **p** 85. C Bethnal Green St Jo w St Bart *Lon* 84-86; C St Jo on Bethnal Green 87-88; P-in-c Stoke Newington Common St Mich from 88. *St Michael's Vicarage, 55 Fountayne Road, London N16 7ED* 081-806 4225

EVANS, Nicholas Anthony Paul. b 60. Sheff Univ BA Liv Inst of Educn CertEd. Qu Coll Birm 81. **d** 84 **p** 87. C Ludlow *Heref* 84-85; C Sunbury *Lon* from 86. *82 Peregrine Road, Sunbury-on-Thames, Middx TW16 6JP* Sunbury-on-Thames (0932) 780404

EVANS, Ven Patrick Alexander Sidney. b 43. Linc Th Coll 70. **d** 73 **p** 74. C Lyonsdown H Trin *St Alb* 73-76; C Royston 76-78; V Gt Gaddesden 78-82; V Tenterden St Mildred w Smallhythe *Cant* 82-89; Adn Maidstone from 89; Hon Can Cant Cathl from 89; Dir of Ords from 89. *The Archdeacon's House, Charing, Ashford, Kent TN27 0LU* Ashford (0233) 712294

EVANS, Percy. b 12. **d** 35 **p** 36. R Manordeifi and Llangoedmor w Llechryd *St D* 43-84; rtd 84. *Ucheldir, Lledryd, Cardigan, Dyfed* Llechryd (023987) 239

EVANS, Peter. b 35. St Aid Birkenhead 57. **d** 60 **p** 61. C Higher Bebington *Ches* 60-63; C W Kirby St Bridget 63-66; P-in-c Lower Tranmere 66-68; V Flimby *Carl* 68-74; V Kirkby Ireleth 74-79; P-in-c Kirkbride w Newton Arlosh 79-80; R 80-85; V Beckermet St Jo and St Bridget w Ponsonby from 85. *St John's Vicarage, Beckermet, Cumbria CA21 2YX* Beckermet (0946) 841327

EVANS, Peter. b 40. S'wark Ord Course 75. **d** 75 **p** 76. C Welling *S'wark* 75-78; C Sutton New Town St Barn 78-81; C Kingston All SS w St Jo 81-87; V Croydon Woodside from 87. *St Luke's Vicarage, Portland Road, London SE25 4RB* 081-654 1225

EVANS, Peter Anthony. b 36. Lon Univ BScEng Ox Univ DipTh59. St Steph Ho Ox 58. **d** 60 **p** 61. C Surbiton St Mark *S'wark* 60-63; Asst Chapl Lon Univ *Lon* 63-64; C S Kensington St Luke 64-68; C Surbiton St Andr and St Mark *S'wark* 68-69; C Loughton St Jo *Chelmsf* 69-74; P-in-c Becontree St Geo 74-82; NSM Romford St Alb from 89. *6 Woodhall Crescent, Hornchurch, Essex RM11 3NN* Hornchurch (04024) 74995

EVANS, Peter Gerald. b 41. Man Univ BA72. AKC64. **d** 65 **p** 66. C Kidbrooke St Jas *S'wark* 65-69; C Fallowfield *Man* 69-72; C Brockley Hill St Sav *S'wark* 72-74; P-in-c Colchester St Botolph w H Trin and St Giles *Chelmsf* 74-79; V from 79. *St Botolph's Vicarage, 50 Priory Street, Colchester CO1 2QB* Colchester (0206) 868043

EVANS, Peter Kenneth Dunlop. b 38. Ch Coll Cam BA60. St D Coll Lamp 72. **d** 74 **p** 75. C Roath St Marg *Llan* 74-77; V Buttington and Pool Quay *St As* 77-87; V Llanfair Caereinion w Llanllugan from 87. *The Vicarage, Llanfair Caereinion, Welshpool, Powys SY21 0RR* Llanfair Caereinion (0938) 810146

EVANS, Philip Ronald. b 55. Qu Coll Cam BA77 MA81 Dur Univ CCouns90. Cranmer Hall Dur 88. **d** 90. C Devonport St Budeaux *Ex* from 90. *5 Buckingham Place, St Budeaux, Plymouth PL5 2EN* Plymouth (0752) 368653

EVANS, Reginald Arthur. b 07. Bris Univ BA38. Sarum Th Coll 38 Wells Th Coll 39. **d** 40 **p** 41. V Batheaston w St Cath *B & W* 49-77; Preb Wells Cathl 73-77; rtd 77; Perm to Offic *Bris* from 81. *Heberden House, Bath Road, Cricklade, Wilts SN6 6AS* Swindon (0793) 750109

EVANS, Richard Alan. b 15. Univ of Wales BA37. **d** 38 **p** 39. V Swansea St Thos and Kilvey *S & B* 65-80; rtd 80. *135 Penfilia Road, Brynhyfryd, Swansea SA5 9HX* Swansea (0792) 641513

EVANS, Richard Edward Hughes. b 14. Univ of Wales BA44. St Mich Coll Llan. **d** 45 **p** 46. V Llanybyther and Llanwenog w Llanwnnen *St D* 64-72; V Llanychaiarn 72-79; rtd 79. *23 Gwarfelin, Llanilar, Aberystwyth, Dyfed SY23 4PE* Llanilar (09747) 357

EVANS, Richard Edward Victor. b 21. Linc Th Coll 66. **d** 68 **p** 69. C Aston cum Aughton *Sheff* 68-71; C Prestwich St Mary *Man* 71-74; R Moston St Jo 74-83; R Failsworth H Family 83-91; rtd 91. *508 Edge Lane, Droylesden, Manchester M35 6JW* 061-370 1947

EVANS, Richard Gregory. b 50. Univ of Wales (Cardiff) DipTh72. St Mich Coll Llan 69. **d** 73 **p** 74. C Oystermouth *S & B* 73-76; C Clydach 76-79; CF 78-81; V Llanddew and Talachddu *S & B* 79-83; Youth Chapl 79-83; Hon Min Can Brecon Cathl 79-83; New Zealand from 83. *97 Liverpool Street, Wanganui, New Zealand* Wanganui (64) 345-0587

EVANS, Richard Lee. b 47. Univ of Wales (Cardiff) BA71 LTh. St D Coll Lamp 71. **d** 73 **p** 74. C Llantwit Major *Llan* 73-74; C Roath St Sav 74-77; C Penarth w Lavernock 77-78; C-in-c Rhydyfelin CD 78-82; P-in-c Clydach Vale 78; V Rhydyfelin 82-84; Vice-Prin Chich Th Coll 84-88; V Southsea H Spirit *Portsm* from 89. *The Vicarage, 26 Victoria Grove, Southsea, Hants PO5 1NF* Portsmouth (0705) 736063

EVANS, Richard Neville. b 15. Qu Coll Cam BA36 MA44. Ripon Hall Ox 36. **d** 38 **p** 39. V Cam St Andr Gt *Ely* 60-72; V Waterbeach 72-74; Perm to Offic 75-86; rtd 84; Perm to Offic *Truro* from 86. *2 Hounster Drive, Millbrook, Torpoint, Cornwall PL10 1BZ* Plymouth (0752) 822811

EVANS, Richard Trevor. b 33. Jes Coll Ox MA58 DipEd58. **d** 76 **p** 76. NSM Leven *St And* from 76. *33 Huntingtower Park, Whinnyknowe, Glenrothes, Fife KY6 3QF* Glenrothes (0592) 741670

EVANS, Canon Robert Arthur. b 24. Univ of Wales (Cardiff) BA48. St Mich Coll Llan 48. **d** 50 **p** 51. Chapl Supt Mersey Miss to Seamen 62-74 and 79-89; Chapl RNR from 67; V Rainhill *Liv* 74-79; Perm to Offic *Ches* 79-91; Hon Can Liv Cathl *Liv* 88-89; rtd 89. *35 Hookland Road, Porthcawl, M Glam CF36 5SF* Porthcawl (065671) 3388

EVANS, Robert Charles. b 55. K Coll Lon BA77 AKC77 MA78 MTh89 Qu Coll Cam BA80 MA83 CertEd85. Westcott Ho Cam 79. **d** 81 **p** 87. C St Breoke *Truro* 81-83; C St Columb Minor and St Colan 83-84; Chapl Robinson Coll from 87. *Robinson College, Cambridge CB3 9AN* Cambridge (0223) 311431

EVANS, Robert George Roger. b 49. Cam Univ MA. Trin Coll Bris 74. **d** 77 **p** 78. C Bispham *Blackb* 77-80; C Chadwell *Chelmsf* 80-84; V Ardsley *Sheff* from 84. *The Vicarage, Doncaster Road, Barnsley, S Yorkshire S71 5EF* Barnsley (0226) 203784

EVANS, Ronald. b 47. Univ of Wales (Cardiff) DipTh87. St Mich Coll Llan 85. **d** 87 **p** 88. C Flint *St As* 87-91; TV Wrexham from 91. *The Vicarage, 37 Acton Gate, Wrexham, Clwyd LL11 2PW* Wrexham (0978) 290143

EVANS, Simon. b 55. Newc Univ BA77. St Steph Ho Ox 78. **d** 80 **p** 81. C Pet St Jude *Pet* 80-84; C Wantage *Ox* 84-87; V W Leigh *Portsm* from 87. *St Alban's Vicarage, Martin Road, Havant, Hants PO9 5TE* Havant (0705) 451751

EVANS, Simon Andrew. b 59. Sarum & Wells Th Coll 81. **d** 84 **p** 85. C Norbury St Steph and Thornton Heath *Cant* 84; C Norbury St Steph and Thornton Heath *S'wark* 85-88; C Putney St Mary from 88. *54 Clarendon Drive, London SW15 1AH* 081-785 2257

EVANS, Stanley Munro. b 30. AKC53. **d** 54 **p** 55. C Norbury St Oswald *Cant* 54-57; C St Laurence in Thanet 57-63; V Bredgar 63-71; V Bredgar w Bicknor and Huckinge 71-72; V Westgate-on-Sea St Sav from 72. *St Saviour's Vicarage, Thanet Road, Westgate-on-Sea, Kent CT8 8PB* Thanet (0843) 31869

EVANS, Stephen John. b 60. Dartmouth RN Coll 81 Ox Univ BA85 MA90. St Steph Ho Ox 83. **d** 86 **p** 87. Prec St Andr Cathl Inverness *Mor* 86-89; R Montrose *Bre* from 89; P-in-c Inverbervie from 89; Miss to Seamen from 89. *The Rectory, 17 Panmure Place, Montrose, Angus DD10 8ER* Montrose (0674) 72212

EVANS, Ms Susan Mary. b 55. St Jo Coll Dur BA76 CertEd77 Nottm Univ BCombStuds84. Linc Th Coll 81. **dss** 84 **d** 87. Weaste *Man* 84-87; Par Dn 87-88; Par Dn Longsight St Luke from 88. *16 Beaminster Walk, Longsight, Manchester M13 9DD* 061-273 3671

EVANS, Terence. b 35. St Mich Coll Llan 67. **d** 69 **p** 70. C Lougher *S & B* 69-73; C Gowerton w Waunarlwydd 73-77; V Llanbister and Llanbadarn Fynydd w Llananno 77-82; V Penclawdd from 82. *The Vicarage, Crofty, Penclawdd, Swansea SA4 3RP* Penclawdd (0792) 850285

EVANS, Terence Robert. b 45. N Ord Course 82. **d** 85 **p** 86. C Warrington St Elphin *Liv* 85-88; V Cantril Farm from 88. *St Jude's Vicarage, 168 Round Hey, Liverpool L28 1RQ* 051-220 4524

EVANS, Very Rev Thomas Eric. b 28. Univ of Wales (Lamp) BA50 St Cath Coll Ox BA53 MA57. St Steph Ho Ox. **d** 54 **p** 55. C Margate St Jo *Cant* 54-58; C Bournemouth St Pet *Win* 58-62; Hon Min Can Glouc Cathl *Glouc* 62-69; Dioc Can Res 69-88; Youth Chapl 62-69; Can Missr 69-75; Adn Cheltenham 75-88; Dean St Paul's *Lon* from 88; P-in-c St Martin Ludgate from 89. *The Deanery, 9 Amen Court, London EC4M 7BU* 071-236 2827

EVANS, Thomas Howell. b 13. St Cath Soc Ox BA37 MA40. Ripon Hall Ox 36. **d** 37 **p** 38. V Anstey *St Alb* 58-74; V Brent Pelham w Meesden 58-74; P-in-c Albury 74-79; C Braughing w Albury, Furneux Pelham etc 79; rtd 79; Perm to Offic *St Alb & Chelmsf* from 79. *Home Farm Lodge, High Street, Clavering, Saffron Walden, Essex CB11 4QR* Saffron Walden (0799) 550600

EVANS, Canon Thomas Norman. b 30. K Coll Lon BA51 BD53 AKC56. **d** 56 **p** 57. C Handsworth *Sheff* 56-59; C Mexborough 59-61; V Denaby Main 61-65; V Wythenshawe Wm Temple Ch *Man* 65-78; RD Withington 72-78; R Prestwich St Mary 78-85; AD Radcliffe and Prestwich 78-85; Hon Can Man Cathl 79-85; R Skelton w Upleatham *York* from 87. *The Rectory, North Terrace, Skelton-in-Cleveland, Cleveland TS12 2ES* Guisborough (0287) 50329

EVANS, Thomas Rowland. b 09. Univ of Wales BA41. Coll of Resurr Mirfield 41. **d** 43 **p** 44. V Port Talbot St Agnes *Llan* 60-78; rtd 78. *St Anthony, 128 Victoria Avenue, Porthcawl, M Glam CF36 3HA* Porthcawl (065671) 6410

EVANS, Timothy Simon. b 57. York Univ BA79 Sussex Univ MA81 Fitzw Coll Cam BA85 MA88. Ridley Hall Cam 83. **d** 87 **p** 88. C Whitton St Aug *Lon* 87-90; C Ealing St Steph Castle Hill from 90. *The Vicarage, St Stephen's Road, London W13 8HD* 081-997 4918

EVANS, Canon Trefor Rhys. b 06. Univ of Wales BA32. St Mich Coll Llan 33. **d** 33 **p** 34. V Lamp *St D* 56-74; rtd 74. *60 Penbryn, Lampeter, Dyfed* Lampeter (0570) 422060

EVANS, Canon Trevor Owen. b 37. Univ of Wales BSc59. Coll of Resurr Mirfield 59. **d** 61 **p** 62. C Llanaber w Caerdeon *Ban* 61-64; C Llandudno 64-70; TV 70-75; V

Llanidloes w Llangurig 75-89; RD Arwystli 75-89; Can and Preb Ban Cathl from 82; Dioc Adv on Spirituality from 84; R Trefdraeth 89-90; Dir of Min from 89; R Llanfairpwll w Penmynydd from 90. *The Rectory, Llanfairpwll, Gwynedd LL61 5YH* Llanfairpwll (0248) 714244

EVANS, Walter James. b 29. Huron Coll Ontario LTh58. **d** 58 **p** 59. R Chilthorne Domer, Yeovil Marsh and Thorne Coffin *B & W* 65-70; V Chalford *Glouc* 70-91; rtd 91. *67 Mandara Grove, Gloucester GL4 9XT* Gloucester (0452) 385157

EVANS, Walter Tenniel. b 26. Ox NSM Course. **d** 84 **p** 85. NSM Beaconsfield *Ox* from 84. *Candlemas, Jordans, Beaconsfield, Bucks HP9 2ST* Chalfont St Giles (02407) 3165

EVANS, Canon William Brewster. b 15. TCD BA37 MA43. CITC 37. **d** 38 **p** 39. I Castlerock Union *D & R* 60-82; Can Derry Cathl 72-82; rtd 82. *4 Bells Hill, Limavady, Co Londonderry BT49 0DG* Limavady (05047) 64349

EVANS, William Hill. b 01. Clifton Th Coll 35. **d** 37 **p** 38. R Buscot *Ox* 48-73; R Eaton Hastings 49-73; rtd 73. *56 Brynderwen, Adpar, Newcastle Emlyn, Dyfed SA38 9PS* Velindre (0559) 370952

EVANS, William James Lynn. b 30. St D Coll Lamp 73. **d** 75 **p** 76. P-in-c Penbryn and Blaenporth *St D* 75-77; V Penbryn and Betws Ifan w Bryngwyn 77-79; V Penrhyncoch and Elerch 79-83; V Cynwil Elfed and Newchurch 83-87; V Llandybie from 87. *The Vicarage, 77 Kings Road, Llandybie, Ammanford, Dyfed SA18 2TL* Llandybie (0269) 850337

EVANS, William Thomas. b 10. Univ of Wales BA37. St D Coll Lamp 37. **d** 40 **p** 41. V St Clears w Llangynin and Llanddowror *St D* 69-76; rtd 76. *27 Danlan Road, Burry Port, Dyfed* Burry Port (05546) 3580

EVANS-PUGHE, Thomas Goronwy. b 29. TCD. Wycliffe Hall Ox 59. **d** 61 **p** 62. C Grassendale *Liv* 61-63; P-in-c Mossley Hill St Matt and St Jas 63-64; C 64-65; Prec Chelmsf Cathl *Chelmsf* 65-69; R Birchanger from 69. *202 Birchanger Lane, Birchanger, Bishop's Stortford, Herts CM23 5QH* Bishop's Stortford (0279) 812310

EVASON, Andrew Brian. b 32. Univ of Wales (Lamp) BA57. St Mich Coll Llan 57. **d** 59 **p** 60. C Llangyfelach and Morriston *S & B* 59-66; R Llangammarch w Garth, Llanlleonfel etc 66-73; R Bishopston from 73. *The Rectory, Portway, Bishopston, Swansea SA3 3JR* Bishopston (044128) 2140

EVASON, Stuart Anthony. b 44. Salford Univ BSc. Chich Th Coll 79. **d** 81 **p** 82. C Heref St Martin *Heref* 81-85; TV Cleethorpes *Linc* 85-87; TV Howden Team Min *York* from 87. *The Vicarage, Portington Road, Eastrington, Goole, N Humberside DN14 7QE* Howden (0430) 410282

EVE, Cedric Robert Sutcliff. b 18. Lon Coll of Div 63. **d** 65 **p** 66. C Ipsley *Worc* 69-73; TV 73-78; P-in-c Norton and Lenchwick 78; P-in-c Harvington 78; P-in-c Harvington, Norton and Lenchwick 78-84; rtd 84; Perm to Offic *Chich* from 85. *Flat 2, Woodfold, Fernhurst, Haslemere, Surrey GU27 3ET* Haslemere (0428) 54085

EVE, David Charles Leonard. b 45. AKC74 St Aug Coll Cant 74. **d** 75 **p** 76. C Hall Green Ascension *Birm* 75-79; TV Kings Norton 79-84; V Rowley Regis from 84. *192 Hanover Road, Rowley Regis, Warley, W Midlands B65 9EQ* 021-559 1251

EVE, Hilary Anne. b 57. Lon Univ BEd80. Ripon Coll Cuddesdon 89. **d** 91. Par Dn Coulsdon St Andr *S'wark* from 91. *23 Rickman Hill, Coulsdon, Surrey CR5 3DS* Downland (0737) 557732

EVELEIGH, Raymond. b 36. Univ of Wales (Cardiff) BSc58. NW Ord Course 73. **d** 76 **p** 77. NSM S Cave and Ellerker w Broomfleet *York* 76-79; P-in-c Kingston upon Hull St Mary 79-82; Chapl Hull Coll of FE from 79; V Anlaby Common St Mark *York* from 82. *St Mark's Vicarage, 1055 Anlaby Road, Hull HU4 7PP* Hull (0482) 51977

EVENS, Philip Alistair. b 36. Leic Univ BA61. Trin Coll Bris 84. **d** 86 **p** 87. C Aston SS Pet and Paul *Birm* 86-89; V Tyseley from 89. *St Edmund's Vicarage, 277 Reddings Lane, Tyseley, Birmingham B11 3DD* 021-777 2433

EVENS, Robert John Scott. b 47. ACIB74 DipTh. Trin Coll Bris 74. **d** 77 **p** 78. C Southsea St Simon *Portsm* 77-79; C Portchester 79-83; V Locks Heath from 83. *The Vicarage, 7 Church Road, Locks Heath, Southampton SO3 6LW* Locks Heath (0489) 2497

EVEREST, Harold William. b 26. Lon Univ BD54. Tyndale Hall Bris 51. **d** 54 **p** 55. C Crookes St Thos *Sheff* 54-57; C Leyland St Andr *Blackb* 57-59; V Darwen St Barn 59-67; V Sheff St Jo *Sheff* 67-78; V Tinsley from 78; Ind Chapl from 78. *St Lawrence's Vicarage, 24 Highgate, Sheffield S9 1WL* Sheffield (0742) 441740

EVEREST, Canon John Cleland. b 45. Sarum Th Coll 66. **d** 68 **p** 69. C Moulsecoomb *Chich* 68-71; C Easthampstead *Ox* 71-74; C Southwick *Chich* 74-77; Dioc Soc Services Adv *Worc* 77-84; Ind Chapl from 84; R Worc City St Paul and Old St Martin etc from 84; RD Worc E from 89; Hon Can Worc Cathl from 90. *7 St Catherine's Hill, Worcester WR5 2EA* Worcester (0905) 358944 or 325952

EVERETT, Alan Neil. b 57. St Cath Coll Ox BA79 SS Coll Cam BA84. Westcott Ho Cam 82. **d** 85 **p** 86. C Hindley All SS *Liv* 85-88; Chapl Qu Mary Coll *Lon* from 88. *24 Sidney Square, London E1 2EY* 071-791 1973

EVERETT, Anthony William. b 60. S Bank Poly BA82. Oak Hill Th Coll BA89. **d** 89 **p** 90. C Hailsham *Chich* from 89. *19 St Wilfrid's Green, Hailsham, E Sussex BN27 1DR* Hailsham (0323) 442132

EVERETT, Bryan John. b 25. ALCD54. **d** 54 **p** 55. V Lullington *Derby* 69-80; R Nether and Over Seale 69-80; P-in-c Longstone 80-90; rtd 90. *2 Lime Grove, Ashbourne, Derbyshire DE6 1HP* Ashbourne (0335) 300303

EVERETT, Colin Gerald Grant. b 44. Open Univ BA77 Keswick Hall Coll CertEd. Ripon Coll Cuddesdon 79. **d** 81 **p** 82. C Aston cum Aughton *Sheff* 81-84; R Fornham All SS and St Martin w Timworth *St E* from 84. *The Rectory, Fornham All Saints, Bury St Edmunds, Suffolk IP28 6JR* Bury St Edmunds (0284) 760027

EVERETT, David Gordon. b 45. Pemb Coll Ox BA67 MA. Lon Coll of Div 68. **d** 70 **p** 71. C Hatcham St Jas *S'wark* 70-73; C Reading St Jo *Ox* 73-77; TV Fenny Stratford and Water Eaton 77-83; Hon C Bletchley 83-87; C Loughton 84-85; NSM Stantonbury and Willen from 87. *33 Crosslands, Stantonbury, Milton Keynes MK14 6AY* Milton Keynes (0908) 320116

EVERETT, Canon John Wilfred. b 37. Qu Coll Cam BA61 MA65. Cuddesdon Coll 64. **d** 66 **p** 67. C St Helier *S'wark* 66-69; C Yeovil St Jo w Preston Plucknett *B & W* 69-73; R Wincanton 73-82; R Pen Selwood 80-82; V Ashford *Cant* from 82; Hon Can Cant Cathl from 90. *The College, Church Yard, Ashford, Kent TN23 1QG* Ashford (0233) 620672

EVERETT, Robert Henry. b 60. Em Coll Cam BA82 BA85 MA86. St Steph Ho Ox 83. **d** 86 **p** 87. C Ex St Thos and Em *Ex* 86-88; C Plymstock 88-91; R St Dominic, Landulph and St Mellion w Pillaton *Truro* from 91. *The Rectory, St Mellion, Saltash, Cornwall PL12 6RN* Liskeard (0579) 50329

EVERETT, Robin Nigel. b 34. Dur Univ BA55 DipTh59. Cranmer Hall Dur 57. **d** 59 **p** 60. C New Humberstone *Leic* 59-62; C Humberstone 62-66; V Quorndon 66-74; V Castle Donington 74-82; P-in-c Lockington w Hemington 81-82; V Castle Donington and Lockington cum Hemington 82-86; Antigua 86-87; R Ibstock w Heather *Leic* from 87. *The Rectory, Ibstock, Leicester LE6 1JQ* Ibstock (0530) 60246

EVERETT, Simon Francis. b 58. Oak Hill Th Coll BA89. **d** 89 **p** 90. C Wroughton *Bris* from 89. *21 Anthony Road, Wroughton, Swindon, Wilts SN4 9HN* Swindon (0793) 813929

EVERETT-ALLEN, Clive. b 47. AKC70. St Aug Coll Cant 69. **d** 70 **p** 71. C Minera *St As* 70-72; C Hatcham St Cath *S'wark* 72-75; C Beaconsfield *Ox* 75; TV 75-83; R Southwick *Chich* from 83. *The Rectory, 22 Church Lane, Southwick, Brighton BN42 4GB* Brighton (0273) 592389

EVERITT, Mark. b 34. Linc Coll Ox BA58 MA62. Wells Th Coll. **d** 60 **p** 61. C Hangleton *Chich* 60-63; Chapl Mert Coll Ox from 63. *Merton College, Oxford OX1 4JD* Oxford (0865) 276365

EVERITT, William Frank James. b 38. FCA63 Dur Univ BA68 DipTh69. Cranmer Hall Dur 65. **d** 69 **p** 70. C Leic St Phil *Leic* 69-73; P-in-c Prestwold w Hoton 73-77; R Settrington w N Grimston and Wharram *York* 77-84; RD Buckrose 80-84; V Cheltenham St Pet *Glouc* from 84. *St Peter's Vicarage, 375 Swindon Road, Cheltenham, Glos GL51 9LB* Cheltenham (0242) 524369

EVERSON, Canon Owen Neville. b 32. St Jo Coll Cam BA56 MA61. Wycliffe Hall Ox 56. **d** 58 **p** 59. C Edgbaston St Aug *Birm* 58-63; Tutor Wycliffe Hall Ox 63-66; Chapl 66-67; V Lee Gd Shep w St Pet *S'wark* 67-85; Hon Can S'wark Cathl from 83; V W Wickham St Fran from 85. *St Francis's Vicarage, 2 The Grove, West Wickham, Kent BR4 9JS* 081-777 6010

EVERSON, Simon Charles. b 58. Leeds Univ BA80. Ripon Coll Cuddesdon 80. **d** 83 **p** 84. C Rotherhithe St Mary w All SS *S'wark* 83-87; P-in-c Kennington Park St Agnes from 87. *The Vicarage, 37 St Agnes Place, London SE11 4BB* 071-735 3860

EVERY, Canon Edward. b 09. Mert Coll Ox BA30 MA46. Linc Th Coll 36. **d** 36 **p** 37. Can Jerusalem 52-79; rtd 79; Perm to Offic *Lon* from 82. *College of St Barnabas, Blackberry Lane, Lingfield, Surrey RH7 6NJ* Dormans Park (034287) 260

EVES, Barry. b 51. Sunderland Poly DipHums86. Cranmer Hall Dur 86. **d** 88 **p** 89. C Tadcaster w Newton Kyme *York* 88-91; C York St Paul from 91. *123 Hamilton Drive, York YO2 4NX* York (0904) 785135

EWBANK, Very Rev Robert Arthur Benson. b 22. Ox Univ MA48. Cuddesdon Coll 46. **d** 48 **p** 49. C Boston *Linc* 48-52; Chapl Uppingham Sch Pet 52-56; S Rhodesia 57-65; Rhodesia 65-80; Zimbabwe from 80; Dean Bulawayo 82-90. *45A Leander Avenue, Bulawayo, Zimbabwe*

EWBANK, Robin Alan. b 42. Ex Coll Ox BA64 MA88 Lon Univ BD68. Clifton Th Coll 66. **d** 69 **p** 70. C Woodford Wells *Chelmsf* 69-72; Warden Cam Univ Miss Bermondsey 72-76; TV Sutton St Jas and Wawne *York* 76-82; R Bramshott *Portsm* from 82; Chmn IDWAL (Dios Chich, Guildf and Portsm) from 90. *The Rectory, 6 Portsmouth Road, Bramshott, Liphook, Hants GU30 7AA* Liphook (0428) 723119

EWBANK, Ven Walter Frederick. b 18. Ball Coll Ox BA45 MA45 BD52. Bps' Coll Cheshunt. **d** 46 **p** 47. Hon Can Carl Cathl *Carl* 66-78 and 83-84; V Carl St Cuth 66-71; Adn Westmorland and Furness 71-77; V Winster 71-78; Adn Carl 78-84; Can Res Carl Cathl 78-82; rtd 84; Perm to Offic *Carl* from 84. *7 Castle Court, Castle Street, Carlisle CA3 8TP* Carlisle (0228) 810293

EWEN, Keith John McGregor. b 43. Sarum & Wells Th Coll 77. **d** 79 **p** 80. C Kington w Huntington *Heref* 79-82; C Kington w Huntington, Old Radnor, Kinnerton etc 82-83; P-in-c Culmington w Onibury 83-89; P-in-c Bromfield 83-89; P-in-c Stanton Lacy 83-89; R Culmington w Onibury, Bromfield etc from 90. *The Vicarage, Bromfield, Ludlow, Shropshire SY8 2JP* Ludlow (0584) 77234

EWER, Edward Sydney John (Brother Jonathan). b 36. Univ of New England BA69. ACT ThL63. **d** 62 **p** 63. Australia 62-83; SSM from 68; Perm to Offic *Blackb* 83-84; Lic to Offic *Dur* from 84; Prior SSM Priory Dur from 85. *St Antony's Priory, Claypath, Durham DH1 1QT* 091-384 3747

EWINGTON, John. b 43. ARICS65. Chich Th Coll 74. **d** 78 **p** 79. C Walthamstow St Jo *Chelmsf* 78-81; Papua New Guinea 81-87; V Southend St Sav Westcliff *Chelmsf* from 87. *St Saviour's Vicarage, 33 King's Road, Southend-on-Sea SS0 8LL* Southend-on-Sea (0702) 342920

EXALL, John Aubrey. b 20. Univ Coll Lon BSc41. Cuddesdon Coll 46. **d** 48 **p** 49. V Southn St Barn *Win* 57-85; rtd 86; Perm to Offic *Win* from 86. *Delve Cottage, 36 Church Lane, Romsey, Hants SO51 8EP* Romsey (0794) 522928

EXCELL, Robin Stanley. b 41. AKC64. **d** 65 **p** 66. C Ipswich St Mary Stoke *St E* 65-68; C Melton Mowbray w Thorpe Arnold *Leic* 68-71; R Gt and Lt Blakenham w Baylham *St E* 71-76; R Gt and Lt Blakenham w Baylham and Nettlestead 76-86; RD Bosmere 84-86. *28 Luther Road, Ipswich* Ipswich (0473) 690267

EXELL, Ernest William Carter. b 28. Qu Coll Cam BA52 MA53. Tyndale Hall Bris 49. **d** 52 **p** 53. C Sydenham H Trin *S'wark* 52-54; C E Ham St Paul *Chelmsf* 54-57; Uganda 57-65; Tanzania 66-70; R Abbess and Beauchamp Roding *Chelmsf* 70-71; P-in-c White Roding w Morrell Roding 70-71; R Abbess Roding, Beauchamp Roding and White Roding from 71; RD Roding 75-79. *The Rectory, Abbess Roding, Ongar, Essex CM5 0JN* White Roding (027976) 313

EXELL, Michael Andrew John. b 45. Sarum & Wells Th Coll 87. **d** 89 **p** 90. C Ryde H Trin *Portsm* from 89; C Swanmore St Mich w Havenstreet from 89. *The Croft, 5 Wood Street, Ryde, Isle of Wight PO33 2DH* Isle of Wight (0983) 63783

EXETER, Archdeacon of. *See* RICHARDS, Ven John

EXETER, Bishop of. *See* THOMPSON, Rt Rev Geoffrey Hewlett

EXETER, Dean of. *See* EYRE, Very Rev Richard Montague Stephens

EXLEY, Malcolm. b 33. Cranmer Hall Dur. **d** 67 **p** 68. C Sutton St Jas *York* 67-73; V Mappleton w Goxhill 73-77; V Market Weighton 77-90; P-in-c Goodmanham 77-78; R 78-90; V Bridlington Em from 90. *Emmanuel Vicarage, 72 Cardigan Road, Bridlington, York YO15 3JT* Bridlington (0262) 604948

EYDEN, Christopher David. b 59. DipRSAMDA81. St Steph Ho Ox 88. **d** 91. C Tottenham St Paul *Lon* from

91. *The Vicarage, 1 St Paul's House, Park Lane, London N17 0JW* 081-808 1810

EYDEN, Canon Eric Westley. b 09. Lon Univ BA31 AKC33 BD34. **d** 33 **p** 34. Can Res and Prec Heref Cathl *Heref* 64-75; rtd 75. *Little Croft, 5 The Grange, Chilton Polden, Bridgwater, Somerset TA7 9DW* Chilton Polden (0278) 722622

EYLES, Anthony John. b 34. Bris Univ BSc57. Sarum Th Coll 61. **d** 63 **p** 64. C Wellington w W Buckland *B & W* 63-67; C Wilton 67-74; Ind Chapl *Dur* 74-85; Ind Chapl *Worc* 85-90; P-in-c Bickenhill w Elmdon *Birm* 90; P-in-c Bickenhill St Pet from 90; Chapl Birm Airport from 90. *The Vicarage, Barndale House, Church Lane, Solihull, W Midlands B92 0DT* Coleshill (0675) 52215

EYLES, David William. b 45. Sarum & Wells Th Coll 75. **d** 77 **p** 78. C Knaresborough *Ripon* 77-80; C Chapel Allerton 80-82; P-in-c W Tanfield and Well w Snape and N Stainley 82-83; R from 83. *The Rectory, West Tanfield, Ripon, N Yorkshire HG4 5JJ* Bedale (0677) 70321

EYRE, John Trevor. b 42. BA88. Oak Hill Th Coll 86. **d** 89 **p** 90. C Watton w Carbrooke and Ovington *Nor* from 89. *44 Jubilee Road, Watton, Thetford, Norfolk IP24 3PW* Watton (0953) 883583

EYRE, Very Rev Richard Montague Stephens. b 29. Or Coll Ox BA53 MA56. St Steph Ho Ox 53. **d** 56 **p** 57. C Portsea N End St Mark *Portsm* 56-59; Tutor Chich Th Coll 59-61; Chapl 61-62; Chapl Eastbourne Coll E Sussex 62-65; V Arundel w Tortington and S Stoke *Chich* 65-73; V Brighton Gd Shep Preston 73-75; Dir of Ords 75-79; Adn Chich 75-81; Can Res and Treas Chich Cathl 78-81; Dean Ex from 81. *The Deanery, Exeter EX1 1HT* Exeter (0392) 52891 or 72697

EYRE, Richard Stuart. b 48. Nottm Univ MTh86 Bris Univ BEd81. Linc Th Coll 74. **d** 77 **p** 78. C Henbury *Bris* 77-81; C Bedminster 81-82; TV 82-84; Chapl Bp Grosseteste Coll Linc from 84; Sen Tutor from 89. *West End Lodge, 9 Hewson Road, Lincoln LN1 1RZ* Lincoln (0522) 533648

EYRE-WALKER, John Benson. b 15. St Pet Hall Ox BA40 DipTh41 MA44. Wycliffe Hall Ox. **d** 42 **p** 43. V Burton *Ches* 57-80; rtd 80; Perm to Offic *Carl* from 81. *Sunrise Cottage, Kilmidyke Road, Grange-over-Sands, Cumbria LA11 7AQ* Grange-over-Sands (05395) 32647

EYRES, Canon Leslie. b 10. AKC41. **d** 41 **p** 42. R Aughton St Mich *Liv* 65-78; rtd 78; Hon C N Meols *Liv* from 78. *25 Montrose Drive, Southport, Merseyside PR9 7JA* Southport (0704) 27776

F

FACER, Miss Rosemary Jane. b 44. LTCL72 Hull Univ BA65 Reading Univ CertEd66. Trin Coll Bris DipHE80. **dss** 80 **d** 87. St Paul's Cray St Barn *Roch* 80-87; Par Dn 87-88; C Cheltenham St Mark *Glouc* from 88. *33 Campden Road, Cheltenham, Glos GL51 6AA* Cheltenham (0242) 239477

FACEY, Canon Edward Lincoln. b 13. St Aug Coll Cant 33. **d** 38 **p** 39. V Crosland Moor *Wakef* 66-77; Hon Can Wakef Cathl 71-82; Master Abp Holgate's Hosp Hemsworth 77-82; rtd 78; Perm to Offic *Wakef* from 82. *12 Station Road, Hemsworth, Pontefract, W Yorkshire WF9 4JW* Hemsworth (0977) 612992

FAGAN, John Raymond. b 32. Lon Univ BD69. Ripon Hall Ox 71. **d** 72 **p** 73. C Stalybridge *Man* 72-74; C Madeley *Heref* 74-79; V Amington *Birm* 79-91; P-in-c Stonnall *Lich* from 91; Chapl HM Young Offender Inst Swinfen Hall from 91. *2 St Peter's Close, Stonnall, Walsall WS9 9EN* Brownhills (0543) 373088

FAGAN, Thomas. b 27. NW Ord Course 78. **d** 81 **p** 82. NSM Rainhill *Liv* 81-90; NSM Prescot from 90. *4 Wensleydale Avenue, Prescot, Merseyside L35 4NR* 051-426 4788

FAGERSON, Joseph Leonard Ladd. b 35. Harvard Univ BA57 Lon Univ DipTh62. Ridley Hall Cam 61. **d** 63 **p** 64. C Tonbridge SS Pet and Paul *Roch* 63-67; Afghanistan 67-74; P-in-c Marbury *Ches* 74-75; P-in-c Kinloch Rannoch *St And* from 75; Chapl Rannoch Sch Perthshire from 75. *Rannoch School, Rannoch Station, Perthshire PH17 2QQ* Kinloch Rannoch (08822) 332

FAGG, Alan Gordon. b 06. K Coll Lon 54. **d** 55 **p** 56. V Forest Row *Chich* 63-70; Perm to Offic from 70; rtd 78. *11 Davis Court, Marlborough Road, St Albans AL1 3XU* St Albans (0727) 47146

FAHIE, Mrs Stephanie Bridget. b 48. St Jo Coll Nottm 85. **d** 87. Par Dn Leic St Chris *Leic* 87-90; Chapl Scargill Ho from 90. *Swale Cottage, Kettlewell, Skipton, N Yorkshire BD23 5RW* Kettlewell (075676) 332

FAINT, Paul Edward. b 38. Qu Coll Birm 85. **d** 87 **p** 88. C Cradley *Worc* 87-90; V Hanley Castle, Hanley Swan and Welland from 90. *The Vicarage, 5 Westmere, Hanley Swan, Worcester WR8 0DL* Hanley Swan (0684) 310321

FAIR, Very Rev James Alexander. TCD BA48 MA59. CITC 49. **d** 49 **p** 50. C Monaghan w Tyholland *Clogh* 49-52; C Portadown St Mark *Arm* 52-56; I Woodschapel 56-60; C-in-c Rathcoole *Conn* 62-68; Dioc Chief Insp of Educn 63-81; Miss to Seamen from 68; I Larne and Inver *Conn* from 68; Preb Conn Cathl 82-84; Treas 84-86; Chan 86-90; Dean Conn from 90; Bp's C Glynn w Raloo from 90. *The Rectory, Lower Carncastle Road, Larne, Co Antrim BT40 1PQ* Larne (0574) 272788

FAIRALL, Michael John. b 45. SW Minl Tr Course 88. **d** 90. NSM Southway *Ex* from 90. *132 Lakeview Close, Tamerton Foliot, Plymouth PL5 4LX* Plymouth (0752) 707694

FAIRBAIRN, John Alan. b 46. Trin Coll Cam BA67 MA72. Wycliffe Hall Ox 84. **d** 86 **p** 87. C Boscombe St Jo *Win* 86-89; C Edgware *Lon* from 89. *St Peter's Parsonage, Stonegrove, Edgware, Middx HA8 8AB* 081-958 5791

FAIRBAIRN, Stella Rosamund. **d** 87. NSM Banbury *Ox* from 87; Perm to Offic *Pet* from 88. *Hillside, Overthorpe, Banbury, Oxon OX17 2AF* Banbury (0295) 710648

FAIRBANK, Brian Douglas Seeley. b 53. AKC75. St Steph Ho Ox 77. **d** 78 **p** 79. C Newton Aycliffe *Dur* 78-81; C Stocking Farm *Leic* 81-84; C Ratby w Groby 84; TV 84-91; Chapl RN from 91. *c/o MOD, Lacon House, Theobald's Road, London WC1X 8RY* 071-430 6847

FAIRBROTHER, Robin Harry. b 44. Univ of Wales DipTh68. Ho of Resurr Mirfield 64 Wells Th Coll 68. **d** 69 **p** 70. C Wrexham *St As* 69-74; C Welshpool w Castle Caereinion 74-77; V Bettws Cedewain and Tregynon 77-80; V Bettws Cedewain and Tregynon and Llanwyddelan from 80. *The Vicarage, Bettws Cedewen, Newtown, Powys SY16 3DS* Tregynon (0686) 650345

FAIRBROTHER, Ronald Peter. b 20. St Steph Ho Ox 59. **d** 61 **p** 62. R Newton Ferrers w Revelstoke *Ex* 69-83; V Abbotskerswell 83-89; rtd 90. *3 Chestnut Court, Alphington, Exeter, Devon*

FAIRBURN, Peter. b 16. Linc Th Coll 42. **d** 42 **p** 43. V Arkendale *Ripon* 54-82; R Goldsborough 54-82; rtd 82. *13 Woodpark Drive, Knaresborough, N Yorkshire HG5 9DN* Harrogate (0423) 864851

FAIRCLOUGH, Canon Francis Stanley. b 08. St Jo Coll Dur BA30 DipTh31 MA34. **d** 31 **p** 32. Hon Can Derby Cathl *Derby* 63-70; V Bretby w Newton Solney 67-70; rtd 70; Perm to Offic *Derby* from 70. *30 Penn Lane, Melbourne, Derby DE71EQ* Melbourne (0332) 862805

FAIRCLOUGH, John Frederick. b 40. DMS78 MBIM St Jo Coll Dur BA63 MA68. Coll of Resurr Mirfield 81. **d** 83 **p** 84. C Horninglow *Lich* 83-87; V Skerton St Luke *Blackb* from 87. *St Luke's Vicarage, Slyne Road, Lancaster LA1 2HU* Lancaster (0524) 63249

FAIRHEAD, Jeremy Shay. b 60. St Andr Univ MA83 Southn Univ BTh86. Chich Th Coll 83. **d** 86 **p** 87. C Notting Hill All SS w St Columb *Lon* 86-89; C-in-c Grahame Park St Aug CD from 89. *St Augustine's House, Great Field, London NW9 5SY* 081-205 1979

FAIRHURST, Canon Alan Marshall. b 30. Clare Coll Cam BA52 MA56 Lon Univ BD56. Tyndale Hall Bris 53 Hask's Th Academy Istanbul 54 Wycliffe Hall Ox 55. **d** 56 **p** 57. Tutor St Jo Coll Dur 56-60; C Stockport St Geo *Ches* 60-62; Ceylon 62-66; R Ashley w Silverley *Ely* 67-71; R Stockport St Mary *Ches* from 71; Chapl Stepping Hill Hosp Stockport from 76; Hon Can Ches Cathl *Ches* from 81; RD Stockport from 86. *St Mary's Rectory, Gorsey Mount Street, Stockport, Cheshire SK1 4DU* 061-429 6564

FAIRHURST, John Graham. b 39. Linc Th Coll 86. **d** 88 **p** 89. C Whiston *Sheff* from 88. *37 Flat Lane, Whiston, Rotherham, S Yorkshire S60 4EF* Rotherham (0709) 372438

FAIRWEATHER, David James. b 35. Keele Univ BEd79. Wycliffe Hall Ox 70. **d** 72 **p** 73. C Trentham *Lich* 72-76; C Cheddleton 76; C Hanley H Ev 77-79; C Rugeley 79-86; V Brown Edge from 86. *St Anne's Vicarage, Church Road, Brown Edge, Stoke-on-Trent ST6 8TD* Stoke-on-Trent (0782) 502134

FAIRWEATHER, John. b 39. K Coll Lon AKC66 BD72. **d** 67 **p** 68. C Plymouth St Jas Ham *Ex* 67-69; C Townstal w St Sav and St Petrox w St Barn 69-73; R Corringham w Springthorpe *Linc* 73-78; P-in-c Blyborough 76-78; P-in-c Heapham 76-78; P-in-c Willoughton 76-78; V

Pinchbeck 78-82; V Exwick *Ex* from 82. *Exwick Vicarage, Exwick Road, Exeter EX4 2AT* Exeter (0392) 55500

FALCONER, Ian Geoffrey. b 40. BNC Ox BA62. Cuddesdon Coll 62. **d** 64 **p** 65. C Chiswick St Nic w St Mary *Lon* 64-68; C-in-c Hounslow Gd Shep Beavers Lane CD 68-76; P-in-c Hammersmith St Matt 76-84; P-in-c Byker St Silas *Newc* from 84. *St Silas's Vicarage, 196 Heaton Park Road, Newcastle upon Tyne NE6 5AP* 091-265 5353

FALCONER, John Geikie. b 13. Selw Coll Cam BA33 MA37. Lon Coll of Div 33. **d** 36 **p** 37. Deputation Sec Leprosy Miss 62-70; Perm to Offic Kensington Deanery 71-82; Dio Lon from 82; rtd 78. *10 Hounslow Avenue, Hounslow TW3 2DX* 081-898 1122

FALKNER, Jonathan Michael Shepherd. b 47. Open Univ BA74 St Jo Coll Dur DipTh78. **d** 79 **p** 80. C Penrith *Carl* 79; C Penrith w Newton Reigny 79-81; C Penrith w Newton Reigny and Plumpton Wall 81-82; C Dalton-in-Furness 82-84; V Clifton 84-90; P-in-c Dean 85-89; R 89-90; P-in-c Rumburgh w S Elmham w the Ilketshalls *St E* from 90. *Church House, Ilketshall St Margaret, Bungay, Suffolk NR35 1QZ* Ilketshall (098681) 345

FALL, Harry. b 17. Leeds Univ BA40 BD51 Dur Univ BA42 MA48. **d** 42 **p** 43. R Scrayingham *York* 57-71; R York H Trin w St Jo Micklegate and St Martin 71-84; rtd 84. *20 Weaponness Valley Road, Scarborough, N Yorkshire YO11 2JF* Scarborough (0723) 361822

FALL, John David McPherson. b 29. St Paul's Grahamstown LTh64. **d** 64 **p** 65. S Rhodesia 64-65; Rhodesia 65-80; Zimbabwe 80-82; P-in-c Dorrington *Heref* from 82; P-in-c Leebotwood w Longnor from 82; P-in-c Stapleton from 82; P-in-c Smethcott w Woolstaston from 82. *The Vicarage, Dorrington, Shrewsbury SY5 7JL* Dorrington (074373) 578

FALLONE, Christopher. b 55. Aston Tr Scheme 85 Oak Hill Th Coll 87. **d** 90 **p** 91. C Rochdale *Man* from 90. *1 Castlemere Street, Rochdale, Lancs OL11 3SW* Rochdale (0706) 45826

FALLOWES, Richard Prince. b 01. Pemb Coll Cam BA23 MA27. Dorchester Miss Coll. **d** 24 **p** 25. V Whatton w Aslockton *S'well* 50-59; S Africa from 59; rtd 69. *PO Box 572, Vryheid, 3100 South Africa*

FALLOWS, Stuart Adrian. b 50. Moray Ho Edin 75. **d** 78 **p** 79. Hon C Forres *Mor* 78-81; Hon C Elgin w Lossiemouth 81-86; C Brighton St Geo w St Anne and St Mark *Chich* 86-89; V Wivelsfield from 89. *New Vicarage, Church Lane, Wivelsfield, Haywards Heath, W Sussex RH17 7RD* Wivelsfield Green (044484) 783

FANE, Clifford Charles. b 39. Kelham Th Coll 62. **d** 67 **p** 68. C Heston *Lon* 67-73; C Bedminster St Mich *Bris* 73-76; P-in-c 76-77; C Gaywood, Bawsey and Mintlyn *Nor* 77-81; V Bolton St Jo *Man* 81-90; rtd 90. *10 Booth Road, Little Lever, Bolton* Farnworth (0204) 709420

FANTHORPE, Robert Lionel. b 35. FBIM81 FCP90 CertEd63 Open Univ BA80. Llan Dioc Tr Scheme. **d** 87 **p** 88. NSM Roath St German *Llan* from 87. *Riverdell, 48 Claude Road, Roath, Cardiff CF2 3QA* Cardiff (0222) 498368

FARADAY, John. b 49. Leeds Univ BSc71 MICE78. Oak Hill Th Coll 81. **d** 83 **p** 84. C Sutton *Liv* 83-86; C Rainhill 86-89; Chapl Whiston Hosp 86-89; V Over Darwen St Jas *Blackb* from 89. *St James's Vicarage, Winterton Road, Darwen, Lancs BB3 0ER* Darwen (0254) 702364

FARAH, Mones Anton. b 64. Trin Coll Bris BA88. **d** 88 **p** 89. C Abth *St D* 88-91; Chapl St D Coll Lamp from 91. *Gelli Aur, Bryn Road, Lampeter, Dyfed SA48 7EE* Lampeter (0570) 422984

FARAH, Ven Rafiq Amin. b 21. Beirut Univ BA45. Near E Sch of Th 45. **d** 46 **p** 48. Jerusalem 46-74; Adn and Can Res 74-86; Min to Arab Angl and Evangelicals in Lon from 86; Hon C Herne Hill *S'wark* from 86. *St Saviour's Vicarage, 1 Finsen Road, London SE5 9AK* 071-274 3663

FARBRIDGE, Nicholas Brisco. b 33. FCA. Sarum & Wells Th Coll 75. **d** 77 **p** 78. C Gt Bookham *Guildf* 77-80; C Ewell 80-83; V Addlestone 83-89; R Shere from 89. *The Rectory, Shere, Guildford, Surrey GU5 9HN* Shere (048641) 2394

FARDON, Jean Audrey May. b 24. Westf Coll Lon BA45 DipEd46. Gilmore Ho DipTh69. **dss** 79 **d** 87. St Alb St Pet *St Alb* 79-87; Hon Par Dn from 87. *61 The Park, St Albans, Herts AL1 4RX* St Albans (0727) 61685

FARDON, Raymond George Warren. b 30. St Pet Hall Ox BA52 MA56. Ridley Hall Cam 54. **d** 59 **p** 60. C High Wycombe All SS *Ox* 59-63; Chapl Bedf Secondary Modern Sch 63-68; Hd Master K Sch Grantham 72-82; Travelling Ev from 82; Hon C Longfleet *Sarum* from

82. *26 Kingland Road, Poole, Dorset BH15 1TP*   Poole (0202) 675609

FAREY, David Mark. b 56. St Jo Coll Dur BA85. Cranmer Hall Dur 82. **d** 86 **p** 87. C Brackley St Pet w St Jas *Pet* 86-89; TV Kingsthorpe w Northn St Dav from 89. *St David's Vicarage, 88 Eastern Avenue, Northampton NN2 7QB*   Northampton (0604) 714536

FARGUS, Gavin James Frederick. b 30. AKC54. **d** 55 **p** 57. R Nether Lochaber *Arg* 65-81; R Kinlochleven 65-81; rtd 81; Lic to Offic *Arg* from 82. *Benvheir Cottage, Ballachulish, Argyll PA39 4JX*   Ballachulish (08552) 420

FARGUS, Maxwell Stuart. b 34. Linc Coll Ox BA57 MA61 Leeds Univ DipAdEd79. Cuddesdon Coll 57. **d** 59 **p** 60. C Newc St Fran *Newc* 59-62; C Rothbury 62-64; Dioc Youth Officer *Ripon* 64-76; R Kirkby Wiske 64-76; Perm to Offic Sheff, Wakef and York 77-88; Community Educn Officer Barnsley MBC 76-88; V Rudston w Boynton and Kilham *York* from 88. *The Vicarage, Rudston, Driffield, N Humberside YO25 0XA*   Kilham (026282) 474

FARISH, Alan John. b 58. Lanc Univ BA. St Jo Coll Nottm LTh86 DPS86. **d** 86 **p** 87. C Bishopwearmouth St Gabr *Dur* 86-89; C Fatfield from 89. *17 Whittonstall, Washington, Tyne & Wear NE38 8PH*   091-4155 424

FARLEY, David Stuart. b 53. Univ Coll Dur BA75 Nottm Univ DipTh82. St Jo Coll Nottm. **d** 84 **p** 85. C Bath Weston All SS w N Stoke *B & W* 84-87; Chapl Scargill Ho N Yorkshire 87-90; Min Hedge End N CD *Win* from 90. *16 Elliot Rise, Hedge End, Southampton SO3 4RU*   Botley (0489) 786717

FARLEY, Edward Albert. b 36. Lon Univ BSc59 ARCS59 Em Coll Cam BA61. Ridley Hall Cam 60. **d** 62 **p** 63. C Bitterne *Win* 62-65; C Swindon Ch Ch *Bris* 65-68; V Dunston w Coppenhall *Lich* 68-71; V Blurton 71-82; V Cheddleton from 82; Chapl St Edward's Hosp Cheddleton from 82; RD Leek *Lich* from 87. *The Vicarage, Hollow Lane, Cheddleton, Leek, Staffs ST13 7HP*   Churnet Side (0538) 360226

FARLEY, Ian David. b 56. Linc Coll Ox BA78 MA87 Dur Univ PhD88. Cranmer Hall Dur 84. **d** 87 **p** 88. C Dishley and Thorpe Acre *Leic* from 87. *3 Deane Street, Loughborough, Leics LE11 0NQ*   Loughborough (0509) 231612

FARLEY, James Trevor. b 37. IEng MIEE FRSA. E Midl Min Tr Course 80. **d** 82 **p** 83. NSM Grantham *Linc* from 82. *Highfield Cottage, Station Road, Bottesford, Nottingham NG13 0EN*   Bottesford (0949) 43646

FARLEY, Lionel George Herbert. b 10. Chich Th Coll 32. **d** 35 **p** 36. V Marazion *Truro* 51-78; rtd 78. *Karenza, 22 Chestnut Way, Gillingham, Dorset SP8 4RT*   Gillingham (0747) 823530

FARLEY, Ronald Alexander. b 30. Oak Hill NSM Course. **d** 79 **p** 80. NSM Stoke Newington St Faith, St Matthias and All SS *Lon* from 79. *20 Chaucer Court, Howard Road, London N16 8TS*   071-249 4349

FARLIE, Canon Hugh. b 29. Lon Univ BSc53. Linc Th Coll 53. **d** 55 **p** 56. C Bilston St Leon *Lich* 55-58; C Stoke Newington St Olave *Lon* 58-63; Asst Chapl Bris Univ *Bris* 63-65; Chapl Bris Coll of Science and Tech 63-65; Chapl Bath Univ *B & W* 65-73; P-in-c Knowle St Barn *Bris* 73-85; V from 85; Hon Can Bris Cathl from 89. *St Barnabas' Vicarage, Daventry Road, Bristol BS4 1DQ*   Bristol (0272) 664139

FARMAN, Robert Joseph. b 54. Ridley Hall Cam 86. **d** 88 **p** 89. C Sutton St Nic *S'wark* 88-90; C Cheam Common St Phil from 90. *75 Brinkley Road, Worcester Park, Surrey*   081-337 0224

FARMAN, Mrs Roberta. b 48. Aber Univ MA70 Cam Univ CertEd72. Qu Coll Birm 78. **dss** 82 **d** 87. Ovenden *Wakef* 80-82; Scargill Ho 83-84; Coulsdon St Jo *S'wark* 85-86; Hon Par Dn Cam St Mark *Ely* 86-88; Hon Par Dn Sutton St Nic *S'wark* from 88. *75 Brinkley Road, Worcester Park, Surrey KT4 8JE*   081-337 0224

FARMBOROUGH, James Laird McLelland. b 22. MBE90. Magd Coll Cam BA49 MA54. Tyndale Hall Bris. **d** 52 **p** 53. Org Sec SAMS 65-70; V Marple All SS *Ches* 70-80; Chile from 80; Miss to Seamen from 80; rtd 88. *6 Norte 940, Department 32, Casilla 561, Vina del Mar, Chile*   Vina del Mar (32) 973049

✠**FARMBROUGH, Rt Rev David John.** b 29. Linc Coll Ox BA51 MA53. Westcott Ho Cam 51. **d** 53 **p** 54 **c** 81. C Hatf *St Alb* 53-57; P-in-c 57-63; V Bishop's Stortford St Mich 63-74; RD Bishop's Stortford 73-74; Adn St Alb 74-81; Suff Bp Bedf from 81. *168 Kimbolton Road, Bedford MK41 8DN*   Bedford (0234) 357551

FARMER, George Wilson. b 37. Lich Th Coll 61. **d** 65 **p** 66. C Kingston All SS w Southwark 65-69; C Heston *Lon* 69-74; C Southmead *Bris* 74-75; C Bedminster 75-80; TV Langley Marish *Ox* 80-86; R Wexham from 86.

The Rectory, 7 Grangewood, Wexham, Slough SL3 6LP   Slough (0753) 23852

FARMER, Kenneth William. b 29. CPM. FBIM. Ripon Coll Cuddesdon 75 Launde Abbey 76. **d** 77 **p** 78. C Evington *Leic* 77-80; V Wymeswold and Prestwold w Hoton 80-85; P-in-c Barney w Thursford *Nor* 85-87; P-in-c Fulmodeston w Croxton 85-87; P-in-c Hindringham and Binham 85-87; R Barney, Fulmodeston w Croxton, Hindringham etc from 87; RD Holt from 88. *The Vicarage, Hindringham, Fakenham, Norfolk NR21 0PR*   Thursford (0328) 878338

FARMER, Simon. b 60. Birm Univ BSc82. St Jo Coll Nottm. **d** 89 **p** 90. C Ulverston St Mary w H Trin *Carl* from 89. *41 Devonshire Road, Ulverston, Cumbria LA12 9AL*   Ulverston (0229) 581389

FARMER, Canon William John Cotton. b 19. St Jo Coll Dur LTh42 BA43. St Aid Birkenhead. **d** 43 **p** 44. V Packwood w Hockley Heath *Birm* 64-81; Hon Can Birm Cathl 80-81; rtd 84. *Flat 12, Bowling Green Court, Moreton-in-Marsh, Glos GL56 0BX*   Moreton-in-Marsh (0608) 51082

FARMILOE, Trevor James. b 42. Sarum & Wells Th Coll. **d** 82 **p** 82. C S Petherton w the Seavingtons *B & W* 82-85; R Norton St Philip w Hemington, Hardington from 85; Rural Affairs Officer from 87; RD Frome from 89. *The Rectory, Vicarage Lane, Norton St Philip, Bath BA3 6LY*   Faulkland (037387) 447

FARNHAM, Douglas John. b 30. Ex Univ MEd. S Dios Minl Tr Scheme 80. **d** 83 **p** 84. NSM Barnham and Eastergate *Chich* 83-85; NSM Aldingbourne, Barnham and Eastergate from 85. *Treetops, 10 Downview Road, Barnham, Bognor Regis, W Sussex PO22 0EE*   Yapton (0243) 553033

FARNWORTH, Michael Godfrey Frankland. b 18. Selw Coll Cam BA40 MA46. Westcott Ho Cam 40. **d** 42 **p** 43. CF 50-72; P-in-c Hindringham and Binham *Nor* 72-77; R 77-84; rtd 84; Perm to Offic *Nor* from 85. *15 Skeldrake Close, Fakenham, Norfolk NR21 8ND*   Fakenham (0328) 55211

FARNWORTH, Russell. b 60. Lon Bible Coll BA82 Nottm Univ MTh85. St Jo Coll Nottm DPS84. **d** 84 **p** 85. C Blackpool St Jo *Blackb* 84-87; TV Darwen St Pet w Hoddlesden from 87. *St Paul's Vicarage, Johnson New Road, Hoddlesden, Darwen, Lancs BB3 3NN*   Darwen (0254) 72598

FARQUHAR, Patricia Ann. b 42. dss 78 **d** 87. S Hackney St Jo w Ch Ch *Lon* 80-87; Par Dn from 87. *19 Valentine Road, London E9 7AD*   081-986 6273

FARQUHARSON, Hunter Buchanan. b 58. ALAM LLAM. Edin Th Coll 85. **d** 88 **p** 89. C Dunfermline *St And* 88-91; R Glenrothes from 91. *St Luke's Rectory, 60 Ninian Quadrant, Glenrothes KY7 4HP*   Glenrothes (0592) 759764

FARQUHARSON-ROBERTS, Donald Arthur. b 21. Bps' Coll Cheshunt 64. **d** 65 **p** 66. R Pimperne *Sarum* 68-89; P-in-c Stourpaine, Durweston and Bryanston 77-89; rtd 90. *30 East House Avenue, Fareham, Hants PO14 2RE*   Fareham (0329) 667333

FARR, Arthur Ronald. b 24. JP77. Llan Dioc Tr Scheme 77. **d** 80 **p** 81. NSM Penarth All SS *Llan* 80-90; rtd 90. *3 Cymric Close, Ely, Cardiff CF5 4GR*   Cardiff (0222) 561765

FARR, Mark Julian Richard. b 60. **d** 87 **p** 88. C Clapham Team Min *S'wark* 87-91; TV Wimbledon from 91. *55 Alwyne Road, London SW19 7AE*   081-946 4175

FARR, Richard William. b 55. MA. Ridley Hall Cam. **d** 83 **p** 84. C Enfield Ch Ch Trent Park *Lon* 83-87; C Eastbourne H Trin *Chich* 87-90; P-in-c Henham and Elsenham w Ugley *Chelmsf* from 90. *The Vicarage, Carters Lane, Henham, Bishop's Stortford, Herts CM22 6AQ*   Bishop's Stortford (0279) 850281

FARRAN, Canon George Orman. b 35. Worc Coll Ox BA58 MA62. Wycliffe Hall Ox 58. **d** 60 **p** 61. C Tyldesley w Shakerley *Man* 60-62; Tutor Wycliffe Hall Ox 62-64; V Netherton *Liv* 64-73; R Sefton 69-73; R Credenhill w Brinsop, Mansel Lacey, Yazor etc *Heref* 73-83; RD Heref Rural 81-83; R Ditcheat w E Pennard and Pylle *B & W* from 83; Can and Chan Wells Cathl from 85; Dir of Ords 86-89. *The Rectory, Ditcheat, Shepton Mallet, Somerset BA4 6RE*   Ditcheat (074986) 429

FARRANCE, William Kenneth. b 22. Univ of Wales (Ban) 46. Bps' Coll Cheshunt 49. **d** 52 **p** 53. V Heddon-on-the-Wall *Newc* 63-78; Chapl Tynemouth Hosps 79-82; AP Tynemouth Ch Ch 79-82; rtd 82; Perm to Offic *Newc* from 82. *5 Prestwick Terrace, Prestwick, Ponteland, Newcastle upon Tyne NE20 9BZ*   Ponteland (0661) 25163

FARRANT, David Stuart. b 38. Ripon Coll Cuddesdon 82. **d** 84 **p** 85. C Woodford St Mary w St Phil and St Jas

Chelmsf 84-87; P-in-c Clymping *Chich* 87; V Clymping and Yapton w Ford from 87. *The Vicarage, Church Lane, Yapton, Arundel, W Sussex BN18 0EE* Yapton (0243) 552962

FARRANT, John Frederick Ames. b 30. Aber Univ MA51 BD58 MTh80. Edin Th Coll 51. **d** 53 **p** 54. C Dundee St Mary Magd *Bre* 53-58; R Clydebank *Glas* 58-65; R Motherwell 65-70; Papua New Guinea 70-73 and 81-84; R Glas St Bride *Glas* 73-81; Can St Mary's Cathl 77-81; Provost Rabaul 81-84; R Penicuik *Edin* from 84; R W Linton from 84. *The Rectory, 23 Broomhill Road, Penicuik, Midlothian EH26 9EE* Penicuik (0968) 72862

FARRANT, Jonathan (Brother Basil). b 44. **d** 73 **p** 74. Tanzania 73-78; SSF from 74; Lic to Offic *Heref* 78-80. *3 The Mount, Worcester Park, Surrey* 081-393 4003

FARRANT, Martyn John. b 38. AKC61. **d** 62 **p** 63. C Hampton St Mary *Lon* 62-65; C Shere *Guildf* 65-67; V Stonaleigh 67-75; V Addlestone 75-83; V Ranmore from 83; RD Dorking from 89. *St Martin's Vicarage, Westcott Road, Dorking, Surrey RH4 3DP* Dorking (0306) 882875

FARRAR, James Albert. b 27. TCD BA55 MA57. CITC 56. **d** 56 **p** 57. C Dub Drumcondra w N Strand *D & G* 56-59; C Dub Rathmines 59-61; I Ballinaclash 61-72; I Dunganstown w Redcross 72-79; Warden Ch Min of Healing from 79; Hon CV Ch Ch Cathl Dub from 79. *38 Springfield Road, Templeogue, Dublin 6, Irish Republic* Dublin (1) 906765

FARRELL, Peter Godfrey Paul. b 39. Sarum & Wells Th Coll 72. **d** 74 **p** 75. C St Just in Roseland *Truro* 74-77; C Kenwyn 77-80; V Knighton St Jo *Leic* 80-86; V Clarendon Park St Jo w Knighton St Mich 86-89; V Woodham *Guildf* from 89. *The Vicarage, 25 Woodham Waye, Woodham, Woking, Surrey GU21 5SW* Woking (0483) 762857

FARRELL, Robert Edward. b 54. Univ of Wales (Abth) BA74 Jes Coll Ox BA77 MA81. Qu Coll Birm 85. **d** 86 **p** 87. C Llanrhos *St As* 86-88; C Prestwich St Marg *Man* 89-91; V Moulsham St Luke *Chelmsf* from 91. *St Luke's House, 26 Lewis Drive, Moulsham Lodge, Chelmsford, Essex CM2 9EF* Chelmsford (0245) 354479

FARRELL, Ronald Anthony. b 57. Edin Univ BD84 Birm Univ MA86. Qu Coll Birm 84. **d** 86 **p** 87. C Shard End *Birm* 86-87; C Shirley 87-89; Bp's Officer for Schs and Young People from 89. *77 Bannersgate Road, Sutton Coldfield, W Midlands B73 6TY* 021-355 8497

FARRELL, Thomas Stanley. b 32. Lon Univ BD71. Ridley Hall Cam 69. **d** 71 **p** 72. C Much Woolton *Liv* 71-73; C Gt Sankey 73-74; Asst Chapl Dulwich Coll 74-76; Chapl 76-81; P-in-c Wonersh *Guildf* 81-86; V 86-90; RD Cranleigh 87-90; R St Marg Lothbury and St Steph Coleman Street etc *Lon* from 90; V St Botolph without Aldersgate from 90. *The Rectory, 1 St Olave's Court, London EC2V 8EX* 071-600 2379

FARRER, Miss Carol Elizabeth. b 47. Open Univ BA88. Cranmer Hall Dur 81. dss 83 **d** 87. Newbarns w Hawcoat *Carl* 83-86; Egremont and Haile 86-87; Par Dn from 87; Dioc Lay Min Adv 87-88; Assoc Dir of Ords from 88. *St John's House, 9 St John's Terrace, Bigrigg, Egremont, Cumbria CA22 2TU* Cleator Moor (0946) 811155

FARRER, Canon Michael Robert Wedlake. b 22. St Pet Hall Ox BA52 MA57. Tyndale Hall Bris 47. **d** 52 **p** 53. C Ox St Ebbe *Ox* 52-56; Tutor Clifton Th Coll 56-65; R Barton Seagrave *Pet* 65-73; R Barton Seagrave w Warkton 73-78; V Cam St Paul *Ely* from 78; RD Cam 84-89; Hon Can Ely Cathl from 88. *St Paul's Vicarage, Cambridge CB1 2EZ* Cambridge (0223) 354186

FARRER, Simon James Anthony. b 52. St Cath Coll Cam MA77 BD78. AKC78 Coll of Resurr Mirfield 78. **d** 79 **p** 80. C St Jo Wood *Lon* 79-84; C N Harrow St Alb 84-87; P-in-c Hammersmith St Luke from 87. *St Luke's Vicarage, 450 Uxbridge Road, London W12 0NS* 081-749 7523

FARRINGTON, Miss Christine Marion. b 42. Birkb Coll Lon BA65 Nottm Univ DASS66 Middx Poly MA75. St Alb Minl Tr Scheme 79. dss 82 **d** 87. Redbourn *St Alb* 82-87; Dir Past Studies Linc Th Coll 86-87; HM Pris Linc 86-87; Dir Sarum Chr Cen from 87; Dn Sarum Cathl *Sarum* from 87. *57A The Close, Salisbury SP1 2EL* Salisbury (0722) 323631

FARROW, Edward. b 38. Sarum Th Coll 69. **d** 71 **p** 72. C Parkstone St Pet w Branksea *Sarum* 71-74; R Tidworth 74-79; P-in-c W and E Lulworth 79-80; P-in-c Winfrith Newburgh w Chaldon Herring 79-80; R The Lulworths, Winfrith Newburgh and Chaldon 80-83; V Ensbury Park from 83. *The Vicarage, 42 Coombe Avenue, Bournemouth BH10 5AE* Bournemouth (0202) 514286

FARROW, Elizabeth Maura. Edin Th Coll. **d** 91. NSM Knightswood H Cross Miss *Glas* from 91. *5 Campsie Road, Strathblane G63 9AB* Drymen (0360) 70936

FARROW, Ian Edmund Dennett. b 38. S'wark Ord Course 70. **d** 72 **p** 73. C Tunbridge Wells St Jo *Roch* 72-78; Chapl N Cambs Gen Hosp Gp from 78; P-in-c Walsoken *Ely* 78-80; R from 80. *The Rectory, Walsoken, Wisbech, Cambs PE13 3RA* Wisbech (0945) 583740

FARROW, Peter Maurice. b 44. St Chad's Coll Dur BSc65 DipTh68. **d** 68 **p** 69. C Gt Yarmouth *Nor* 68-71; C N Lynn w St Marg and St Nic 71-75; P-in-c Sculthorpe w Dunton and Doughton 75-77; Perm to Offic 78-89; TV Lowestoft and Kirkley from 89; Ind Miss from 89. *27 Kirkley Park Road, Lowestoft, Suffolk NR33 0LQ* Lowestoft (0502) 567888

FARROW, Ronald. b 46. S'wark Ord Course. **d** 87 **p** 88. NSM Barnes St Mich *S'wark* 87-91; C Streatham St Pet from 91. *21 Ivymount Road, London SE27 0NB* 081-670 4737

FARTHING, Michael Thomas. b 28. St Cuth Soc Dur 48. Lambeth STh81 St Steph Ho Ox. **d** 58 **p** 59. C St Marylebone St Mark w St Luke *Lon* 58-63; C Newport Pagnell *Ox* 63-69; R Standlake 69-76; R Yelford 69-76; R Lower Windrush 76-82; V Wheatley w Forest Hill and Stanton St John from 82. *The Vicarage, 18 London Road, Wheatley, Oxford OX9 1YA* Wheatley (08677) 2224

FARTHING, Ronald Edward. b 27. Oak Hill Th Coll. **d** 58 **p** 59. C Tollington Park St Anne *Lon* 58-61; C Tollington Park St Mark 58-61; V Clodock and Longtown w Craswell and Llanveyno *Heref* 61-67; R Langley *Cant* 67-72; V Bapchild w Tonge and Rodmersham 72-80; TV Widecombe, Leusden and Princetown etc *Ex* 80-84; P-in-c Riddlesworth w Gasthorpe and Knettishall *Nor* 84-87; P-in-c Garboldisham w Blo' Norton 84-87; P-in-c Brettenham w Rushford 84-87; R Garboldisham w Blo' Norton, Riddlesworth etc from 88. *The Rectory, Back Street, Garboldisham, Diss, Norfolk IP22 2SD* Garboldisham (095381) 8101

FASHOLE-LUKE, Edward William. b 34. Dur Univ BA63. Cranmer Hall Dur 61. **d** 62 **p** 63. C Dur St Cuth *Dur* 62-64; Sierra Leone from 64. *Fourah Bay College, Freetown, Sierra Leone*

FATHERS, Canon Derek Esmond. b 27. Magd Coll Ox BA50 MA52. St Aid Birkenhead 50. **d** 56 **p** 57. Tutor St Aid Birkenhead 56-59; C W Kirby St Bridget *Ches* 59-63; V Thornton Hough 63-86; RD Wirral S 78-86; Hon Can Ches Cathl from 82; C Woodchurch 86-89; Chapl Arrowe Park Hosp Birkenhead from 86. *6 Ashton Drive, West Kirby, Wirral, Merseyside L48 0RQ* 051-625 1181

FAULDS, John Parker. b 33. Edin Th Coll 55. **d** 57 **p** 58. C Edin St Dav *Edin* 57-58; C Edin St Jo 58-60; Chapl Dundee Hosps 60-63; Chapl Qu Coll Dundee 60-63; Dioc Supernumerary *Bre* 60-63; Lic to Offic *Birm* 65-66 and from 87; P-in-c Aston Brook 66-69; V Handsworth St Pet 69-87. *6 Little Heath Close, Audlem, Crewe CW3 0HX*

FAULKES, Edmund Marquis. b 62. **d** 91. C Broughty Ferry *Bre* from 91. *45 Abbey Road, West Ferry, Dundee DD5 1NU* Dundee (0382) 736984

FAULKNER, Brian Thomas. b 48. S Dios Minl Tr Scheme. **d** 84 **p** 85. C W Leigh *Portsm* 84-88; R Foulsham w Hindolveston and Guestwick *Nor* from 88. *The Rectory, Foulsham, Dereham, Norfolk NR20 5RZ* Foulsham (036284) 275

FAULKNER, David Ernest. b 43. Univ of Wales (Lamp) DipTh65. St Mich Coll Llan 65. **d** 66 **p** 67. C Abth St Mich *St D* 66-68; C Tenby and Gumfreston 68-69; C Burry Port and Pwll 69-73; R Jeffreyston w Reynalton and E Williamston 73-79; R Jeffreyston w Reynoldston and E Williamston etc 79-89; V Whitland and Kiffig 89-90; V Whitland w Kiffig and Henllan Amgoed and Llangan from 90. *The Vicarage, North Road, Whitland, Dyfed SA34 0BH* Whitland (0994) 240494

FAULKNER, Henry Odin. b 35. G&C Coll Cam BA56 MA60. St Jo Coll Nottm DipTh73. **d** 74 **p** 75. C Heigham H Trin *Nor* 74-76; C Heeley *Sheff* 76-80; TV Netherthorpe 80-84; Perm to Offic *St Alb* from 84. *69 Holywell Hill, St Albans, Herts AL1 1HF* St Albans (0727) 54177

FAULKNER, Peter Charles. b 37. Chich Th Coll 72. **d** 74 **p** 75. C St Bart Armley w St Mary New Wortley *Ripon* 74-76; C Tilehurst St Mich *Ox* 76-80; V Calcot 80-82; V Hagbourne 82-88; TV W Slough from 88. *St George's House, Long Furlong Drive, Slough SL2 2LX* Slough (0753) 25935

FAULKNER, Peter Graham. b 47. Lon Univ CertEd69. Oak Hill Th Coll BA87. **d** 82 **p** 83. C Crofton *Portsm*

87-89; R Mid Marsh Gp *Linc* from 89. *The Vicarage, Grange Lane, Manby, Louth, Lincs LN11 8HF* South Cockerington (050782) 429

FAULKNER, Robert Henry. b 20. St Edm Hall Ox BA48 MA53. Wycliffe Hall Ox 48. **d** 50 **p** 51. V Thame w Towersey *Ox* 60-85; R Aston Sandford 73-85; rtd 85; Perm to Offic *Ox* from 85. *5 Mavor Close, Old Woodstock, Oxford OX7 1YL* Woodstock (0993) 812059

FAULKNER, Canon Roger Kearton. b 36. AKC62. **d** 63 **p** 64. C Oxton *Ches* 63-67; C Ellesmere Port 67-69; V Runcorn H Trin 69-73; TV E Runcorn w Halton 73-76; V Altrincham St Geo 76-90; Chapl Altrincham Gen Hosp from 80; Hon Can Ches Cathl *Ches* from 88; V Higher Bebington from 90. *The Vicarage, Higher Bebington, Wirral, Merseyside L63 8LX* 051-608 4429

FAULKS, David William. b 45. E Midl Min Tr Course 82. **d** 86 **p** 87. C Market Harborough *Leic* 86-88; C Wootton Bassett *Sarum* 88-90; R Clipston w Naseby and Haselbech w Kelmarsh *Pet* from 90. *The Rectory, 18 Church Lane, Clipston, Market Harborough, Leics LE16 9RW* Clipston (085886) 342

FAULL, Canon Cecil Albert. b 30. TCD BA52. **d** 54 **p** 55. C Dub Zion Ch *D & G* 54-57; C Dub St Geo 57-59; Hon CV Ch Ch Cathl Dub 58-63; C Dun Laoghaire 59-63; I Portarlington w Cloneyhurke and Lea *M & K* 63-71; I Dub St Geo and St Thos *D & G* 71-80; I Clondalkin w Rathcoole 81-91; Can Ch Ch Cathl Dub 90-91; I Dunleckney w Nurney, Lorum and Kiltennel *C & O* from 91. *St Mary's Rectory, Dunleckney, Muine Bheag, Co Carlow, Irish Republic* Carlow (503) 21570

FAULL, Vivienne Frances. b 55. St Hilda's Coll Ox BA77 MA82 Clare Coll Cam MA90. St Jo Coll Nottm BA81 DPS82. **dss** 82 **d** 87. Mossley Hill St Matt and St Jas *Liv* 82-85; Chapl Clare Coll Cam 85-90; Chapl Glouc Cathl *Glouc* from 90. *10 College Green, Gloucester GL1 2LX* Gloucester (0452) 300655

FAULL, William Baines. b 29. FRCVS Lon Univ BSc51. NW Ord Course 77. **d** 79 **p** 80. NSM Willaston *Ches* 79-80; NSM Neston 80-82; P-in-c Harthill and Burwardsley 82-86; Perm to Offic 87-91; Sen Fell Liv Univ from 89; V Ashton Hayes *Ches* from 91. *St John's Vicarage, Church Road, Ashton, Chester CH3 8AB* Kelsall (0829) 51265

FAUNCH, Canon Paul. b 13. FPhS46 FTSC65. Hong Kong DD72 St Jo Coll Dur 51. **d** 53 **p** 54. R E Donyland *Chelmsf* 65-75; OSJM from 72; rtd 78; Perm to Offic Lon, Chich and S'wark from 78; Hon Can St Ephraim Solna Sweden from 87. *78 St Andrew's Road, Portslade, Brighton BN4 1DE* Brighton (0273) 414204

FAVELL, Brian Jeffrey. b 23. Cuddesdon Coll 64. **d** 66 **p** 67. Lic to Offic *Birm* 70-76; V Cwmtillery *Mon* 76-86; P-in-c Six Bells 77-86; RD Blaenau Gwent 83-86; V Cwmcarn 86-88; rtd 88. *3 Church Street, Fladbury, Pershore, Worcs WR10 2QB* Pershore (0386) 860585

FAVELL, Canon John Walter Allen. b 25. **d** 72 **p** 73. C Northn St Pet w Upton *Pet* from 72; Chapl to the Deaf from 72; Can Pet Cathl from 85. *66 Main Road, Duston, Northampton NN5 6JN* Northampton (0604) 754694

FAWCETT, Canon Frederick William. TCD BA49 MA52. CITC 50. **d** 50 **p** 51. C Belf St Aid *Conn* 50-52; C-in-c Draperstown *D & R* 52-59; I 59-60; I Cumber Upper w Learmount 60-87; I Camus-juxta-Mourne from 87. *Newtown Street, Strabane, Co Tyrone BT82 8DW* Strabane (0504) 882314

FAWCETT, James Ralph Llewelyn Rees. b 12. AKC38. **d** 38 **p** 39. R Tittleshall w Godwick and Wellingham *Nor* 65-74; P-in-c Weasenham 67-74; P-in-c Rougham 70-74; R Stiffkey w Morston and Langham Episcopi 74-76; R Stiffkey and Cockthorpe w Morston, Langham etc 76-90; rtd 90; Perm to Offic *Nor* from 90. *47A High Street, Mundesley, Norfolk NR11 8JL* Mundesley (0263) 721752

FAWCETT, Kenneth. b 17. **d** 40 **p** 41. V Fewston *Bradf* 64-83; rtd 83. *37 Thumb Creek Road, Taylors Arm, Macksville, NSW, Australia 2447*

FAWCETT, Mrs Pamela Margaret. b 29. Univ Coll Lon BA52 DipEd75. E Anglian Minl Tr Course 83. **dss** 86 **d** 87. Stiffkey w Morston, Langham Episcopi etc *Nor* 86-87; Hon C Stiffkey and Cockthorpe w Morston, Langham etc 87-90; Hon Asst Min Repps Deanery from 91. *Seekings, 47A High Street, Mundesley, Norwich NR11 8JL* Mundesley (0263) 721752

FAWCETT, Timothy John. b 44. K Coll Lon BD66 AKC67 PhD71. **d** 67 **p** 68. C Blackpool St Steph *Blackb* 67-70; Hon C St Marylebone All SS *Lon* 68-70; C Southgate St Mich 70-72; Sacr Dur Cathl *Dur* 72-75; V Wheatley Hill 75-79; V Torrisholme *Blackb* 79-84; V Thaxted *Chelmsf* 84-89; Perm to Offic *Nor* from 89. *Dowitchers, 14 The*

Cornfield, Langham, Holt, Norfolk NR25 7DQ Fakenham (0328) 830415

FAYERS, Henry Douglas Freeman. b 03. Lich Th Coll 55. **d** 56 **p** 57. R Westerfield *St E* 62-71; R Westerfield w Tuddenham St Martin 71-73; rtd 73; Perm to Offic *St E* 78-86; from 91. *25 Morley Avenue, Woodbridge, Suffolk IP12 4AZ* Woodbridge (03943) 2262

FAYERS, Robert Stanley. b 48. DipFD. St Steph Ho Ox 82. **d** 84 **p** 85. C Deptford St Paul *S'wark* 84-88; V Beckenham St Mich w St Aug *Roch* from 88. *St Michael's Vicarage, 120 Birkbeck Road, Beckenham, Kent BR3 4SS* 081-778 6569

FAYLE, David Charles Wilfred. b 51. Sarum & Wells Th Coll. **d** 83 **p** 84. C Parkstone St Pet w Branksea and St Osmund *Sarum* 83-87; TV Dorchester from 87. *The Vicarage, 17A Edward Road, Dorchester, Dorset DT1 2HL* Dorchester (0305) 268434

FEARN, Anthony John. b 34. Lich Th Coll 58. **d** 61 **p** 62. C Redditch St Steph *Worc* 61-64; C Bladon w Woodstock *Ox* 64-66; V Ruscombe and Twyford 67-85; P-in-c Westmill w Gt Munden *St Alb* 85-87; Asst Dioc Stewardship Adv 85-87; Chr Giving Adv *Heref* from 87. *Crozen Cottage, Felton, Hereford HR1 3PW* Hereford (0432) 820161

FEARN, Preb Hugh. b 18. Selw Coll Cam BA48 MA52 Sheff Univ MA52 Lon Univ PhD57 FRHistS60. **d** 58 **p** 59. V Northwood H Trin *Lon* 65-81; Preb St Paul's Cathl 77-88; R St Clem Eastcheap w St Martin Orgar 81-88; rtd 88. *The Northwood Nursing Home, 24 Eastbury Avenue, Northwood, Middx HA6 3LN* Northwood (09274) 26452

FEARN, Robert Benjamin. b 27. Bps' Coll Cheshunt 62. **d** 64 **p** 65. C Newark St Mary *S'well* 64-68; V Basford St Aid 68-74; V Beckingham w Walkeringham 74-83; V N and S Muskham from 83; R Averham w Kelham from 83. *The Vicarage, Marsh Lane, North Muskham, Newark, Notts NG23 6HG* Newark (0636) 702655

FEARON, Mrs Doris Ethel Elizabeth. b 26. Gilmore Ho 66. **dss** 72 **d** 87. Lingfield *S'wark* 68-75; Farnborough *Roch* 75-77; Bitterne *Win* 78-86; rtd 86; Bexhill St Pet *Chich* 86-87; Hon Par Dn 87-89; Perm to Offic from 89. *Delrosa, 32 Dalehurst Road, Bexhill-on-Sea, E Sussex TN39 4BN* Bexhill-on-Sea (0424) 221013

FEAST, Robert Butler. b 08. Trin Hall Cam BA30 MA36. Cuddesdon Coll 30. **d** 31 **p** 32. R Northlew w Ashbury *Ex* 69-73; rtd 73. *Rose Cottage, Boddington Lane, Northleigh, Witney, Oxon OX8 6PU* Freeland (0993) 881396

FEATHERSTONE, Andrew. b 53. St Chad's Coll Dur BA74. Sarum & Wells Th Coll 78. **d** 80 **p** 81. C Newc H Cross *Newc* 80-83; C Seaton Hirst 83-86; TV 86-87; R Crook *Dur* from 87; V Stanley from 87. *The Rectory, 14 Hartside Close, Crook, Co Durham DL15 9NH* Bishop Auckland (0388) 764024

FEATHERSTONE, Gray. b 42. Stellenbosch Univ BA62 LLB64. Cuddesdon Coll. **d** 67 **p** 68. S Africa 67-70; Swaziland 70-72; Portuguese E Africa 73-75; Mozambique 75-76; Miss to Seamen 76-80; V Upper Clapton St Matt *Lon* 80-83; V Stamford Hill St Thos 80-89; Chr Aid Area Sec (NW Lon) from 89. *c/o Inter-Church House, 35-41 Lower Marsh, London SE1 7RL* 071-620 4444

FEATHERSTONE, John. b 23. Kelham Th Coll 40. **d** 46 **p** 47. V Longford *Derby* 66-70; V Alkmonton w Yeaveley 66-70; V Chaddesden St Phil 70-72; V Denby 72-77; R Whitwell 77-84; RD Bolsover and Staveley 78-81; P-in-c Barlow 84-88; rtd 88; Perm to Offic *Derby* from 88. *16 Fern Close, Eckington, Sheffield S31 9HE* Eckington (0246) 432440

FEATHERSTONE, Robert Leslie. b 54. LLCM74 Lon Univ CertEd75. Chich Th Coll 84. **d** 86 **p** 87. C Crayford *Roch* 86-89; V Belvedere St Aug from 89. *The Vicarage, St Augustine's Road, Belvedere, Kent DA17 5HH* 081-311 6307

✠**FEAVER, Rt Rev Douglas Russell.** b 14. Keble Coll Ox BA35 MA39. Wells Th Coll 37. **d** 38 **p** 39 **c** 72. C St Alb Abbey *St Alb* 38-42; Chapl RAFVR 42-46; Can Res and Sub-Dean St Alb 46-58; V Nottm St Mary *S'well* 58-72; RD Nottm 58-72; Hon Can S'well Minster 58-72; Bp Pet 72-84; rtd 84; Perm to Offic *Ely* from 85. *6 Mill Lane, Bruton, Somerset BA10 0AT* Bruton (0749) 813485

FEDDEN, Canon Patrick Vincent. b 17. Ex Coll Ox BA40 MA43. Westcott Ho Cam 40. **d** 41 **p** 42. V Totteridge *St Alb* 59-72; RD Barnet 69-72; V Lower Mitton *Worc* 72-83; RD Stourport 75-80; Hon Can Worc Cathl 79-83; rtd 83; Perm to Offic *Glouc* from 83. *Church House, High Street, Newnham, Glos GL14 1AA* Dean (0594) 516259

FEHRENBACH, Donald Joseph. b 17. Selw Coll Cam BA49 MA53. Qu Coll Birm 49. **d** 51 **p** 52. V Sandford-on-Thames *Ox* 65-84; rtd 84; Perm to Offic *Ox* from 84. *2 Walbury, Bracknell, Berks RG12 3JB* Bracknell (0344) 422759

FEIST, Nicholas James. b 45. Solicitor 70. St Jo Coll Nottm LTh76. **d** 76 **p** 77. C Didsbury St Jas *Man* 76-80; TV Didsbury St Jas and Em 80; V Friarmere 80-88; R Middleton from 88. *St Leonard's Rectory, Mellalieu Street, Middleton, Manchester M24 3DN* 061-643 2693

FEIT, Michael John. b 24. FICE68 FIStructE68. S'wark Ord Course. **d** 69 **p** 71. C Feltham *Lon* 69-76; C Ashford St Matt 76-78; C Hykeham *Linc* 78-81; V Cranwell 81-85; R Leasingham 81-85; R Bishop Norton, Wadingham and Snitterby 85-90; rtd 90. *9167 210th Street, Langley, British Columbia, Canada, V1M 2B4*

FELCE, Brian George. b 30. Jes Coll Ox BA54 MA57. Oak Hill Th Coll. **d** 58 **p** 59. R Bedingfield w Southolt *St E* 64-73; V Preston All SS *Blackb* 73-86; rtd 86. *11 St Barnabas Road, Sutton, Surrey SM1 4NL* 081-642 7885

FELIX, David Rhys. b 55. Solicitor 81 Univ of Wales (Cardiff) LLB76. Ripon Coll Cuddesdon 83. **d** 86 **p** 87. C Bromborough *Ches* 86-89; V Grange St Andr from 89. *37 Lime Grove, Runcorn, Cheshire WA7 5JZ* Runcorn (0928) 574411

FELIX, Donald Cameron. b 24. St Aid Birkenhead 64. **d** 65 **p** 66. C Walsall *Lich* 65-68; V Pype Hayes *Birm* 68-73; V Burslem St Paul *Lich* 73-76; V Bloxwich 76-79; P-in-c Seighford, Derrington and Cresswell 79-81; V 81-86; V Hanbury w Newborough from 86. *The New Vicarage, Hanbury, Burton-on-Trent, Staffs DE13 8TF* Burton-on-Trent (0283) 813357

FELL, Alan William. b 46. Ball Coll Ox BA69 Leeds Univ DipTh70. Coll of Resurr Mirfield 68. **d** 71 **p** 72. C Woodchurch *Ches* 71-74; C Man Clayton St Cross w St Paul *Man* 74-75; C Prestwich St Marg 75-77; V Hyde St Thos *Ches* 77-80; R Tattenhall and Handley 80-86; V Sedbergh, Cautley and Garsdale *Bradf* from 86; Hon C Firbank, Howgill and Killington from 86. *The Vicarage, Sedbergh, Cumbria LA10 5SQ* Sedbergh (05396) 20283

FELL, Stephen. b 18. St Jo Coll Dur LTh41 BA42. Oak Hill Th Coll 38. **d** 42 **p** 43. R Castleford All SS *Wakef* 58-83; rtd 83. *255 Lower Mickletown, Methley, Leeds LS26 9AN* Castleford (0977) 515530

FELL, Willis Marshall. b 29. NW Ord Course 73. **d** 75 **p** 76. C Bolsover *Derby* 75-78; C Clay Cross 78-80; V Brampton St Mark from 80. *The Vicarage, 15 St Mark's Road, Chesterfield, Derbyshire S40 1DH* Chesterfield (0246) 34015

FELLINGHAM, John. b 25. Lon Coll of Div 52. **d** 55 **p** 56. R Coltishall w Gt Hautbois *Nor* 59-70; RD Ingworth 65-70; Chapl HM Pris Nor 69-73; P-in-c Nor St Helen *Nor* 70-73; Perm to Offic from 73; rtd 90; Asst Chapl HM Pris Wayland from 90. *Fielding Cottage, Anchor Corner, Attleborough, Norfolk NR17 1JX* Attleborough (0953) 455185

FELLOWES BROWN, Eldred Joscelyn. b 03. Ch Ch Ox BA25 MA32. Cuddesdon Coll 26. **d** 27 **p** 28. V Worstead w Westwick and Sloley *Nor* 64-69; C Wood Green St Mich *Lon* 69-70; C Tilehurst St Mich *Ox* 70-71; rtd 71; C Burnham Thorpe w Burnham Overy *Nor* 75-77; Hon C Southgate St Andr *Lon* 77-80; Perm to Offic *Nor* from 83. *6 Travers Court, West Runton, Cromer, Norfolk* West Runton (026375) 8251

FELLOWS, Grant. b 56. K Coll Lon BD77 AKC77. Coll of Resurr Mirfield 79. **d** 80 **p** 81. C Addington *Cant* 80-84; C S Gillingham *Roch* 84-86; V Heath and Reach *St Alb* from 86. *The Vicarage, 2 Reach Lane, Heath and Reach, Leighton Buzzard LU7 0AL* Heath and Reach (052523) 633

FELLOWS, John Lambert. b 35. LTCL67 SS Mark & Jo Coll Chelsea CertEd58. Portsm Dioc Tr Course 86. **d** 88. NSM Portsea St Cuth *Portsm* from 88. *7 Court Lane, Portsmouth PO6 2LG* Cosham (0705) 377270

FELLOWS, John Michael. b 46. Or Coll Ox MA77. Coll of Resurr Mirfield 74. **d** 77 **p** 78. C Kings Heath *Birm* 77-80; TV E Ham w Upton Park *Chelmsf* 80-85; P-in-c Wormingford 85-90; P-in-c Mt Bures 85-90; P-in-c Lt Horkesley 85-90; V Wormingford, Mt Bures and Lt Horkesley 90; R Compton w Shackleford and Peper Harow *Guildf* from 90. *The Rectory, Compton, Guildford, Surrey GU3 1ED* Guildford (0483) 810328

FELLOWS, Peter William. b 48. CertEd70 DipEd79. Chich Th Coll 86. **d** 88 **p** 89. C Westmr St Steph w St Jo *Lon* from 88. *Flat C, Napier Hall, Hide Place, London SW1P 4NJ* 071-821 6195

FELLOWS, Roy. b 30. Keble Coll Ox BA53 MA57. St Steph Ho Ox 53. **d** 56 **p** 57. C Tonge Moor *Man* 56-61; C Hulme St Phil 61-63; R Withington St Crispin 63-74;

V Southport St Luke *Liv* 74-78; V Bedf Leigh *Man* 78-81; Warden Co of Miss Priests 81-87; Admin of Shrine of Our Lady Walsingham from 87; Lic to Offic *Nor* from 87. *The College, Walsingham, Norfolk NR22 6EF* Fakenham (0328) 820266

FELSTEAD, Canon Kenneth Walter Harry. b 14. Sheff Univ BSc35 MSc36. Lich Th Coll 35. **d** 37 **p** 38. V Southn St Mich w H Rood, St Lawr etc *Win* 46-70; RD Southn 58-70; Hon Can Win Cathl 62-79; Master St Cross Hosp Win 70-79; V Win St Cross w St Faith *Win* 70-79; RD Win 72-77; rtd 79; Perm to Offic *Sarum* 79-80 and from 82; RD Heytesbury 80-82; Perm to Offic B & W from 85; Ox from 91. *40 Waltham Court, Mill Road, Goring, Reading RG8 9DJ* Goring-on-Thames (0491) 875438

FELTHAM, Keith. b 40. Lon Univ DipTh66. **d** 75 **p** 76. C Plympton St Mary *Ex* 75-79; TV Northam w Westward Ho and Appledore 79-82; TR Lynton, Brendon, Countisbury, Lynmouth etc 82-85; P-in-c Bickleigh (Plymouth) 85-86; TR from 86. *The Rectory, 47 The Heathers, Woolwell, Roborough, Plymouth PL6 7QS* Plymouth (0752) 790293

FELTON, Philip Leonard. b 31. Univ of Wales BD78. St D Coll Lamp BA53. **d** 55 **p** 56. C St Ishmael's w Llansaint and Ferryside *St D* 55-64; V 81-89; V Gwaun-cae-Gurwen 64-81; V Meidrim and Llanboidy and Merthyr from 89. *Arlais, Station Road, St Clears, Carmarthen SA33 4BY* St Clears (0994) 231247

FENN, Norman Alexander. b 20. Kelham Th Coll 37. **d** 43 **p** 44. V Ellesmere *Lich* 61-85; V Welsh Frankton 62-85; RD Ellesmere 70-85; rtd 85; Perm to Offic *Lich* from 85. *1 Larkhill Road, Oswestry, Shropshire SY11 4AW*

FENN, Dr Roy William Dearnley. b 33. FRHistS70 FCP86 FSA88 Jes Coll Ox BA54 MA59 BD68. St Mich Coll Llan 54. **d** 56 **p** 57. C Swansea St Mary and H Trin *S & B* 57-59; C Cardiff St Jo *Llan* 59-60; C Coity w Nolton 60-63; V Glascombe w Rhulen and Gregrina *S & B* 63-68; V Glascwm and Rhulen 68-74; P-in-c Letton w Staunton, Byford, Mansel Gamage etc *Heref* 75-79; Perm to Offic *S & B* 80-85; Heref from 85. *9 Victoria Road, Kington, Herefordshire HR5 3BX* Kington (0544) 230018

FENNELL, Canon Alfred Charles Dennis. b 15. Bp's Coll Calcutta 35. **d** 38 **p** 39. V Yardley St Cypr Hay Mill *Birm* 65-80; Hon Can Birm Cathl 78-80; rtd 80; Perm to Offic *Birm* from 80. *27 Madresfield Road, Malvern, Worcs WR14 2AS* Malvern (0684) 560613

FENNELL, Anthony Frederick Rivers. b 90. NSM Braemar *Ab* from 90; NSM Ballater from 90; NSM Aboyne from 90. *19 Craigendarroch Circle, Ballater AB3 5ZA* Ballater (03397) 55040

FENNEMORE, Nicholas Paul. b 53. Wycliffe Hall Ox 76. **d** 79 **p** 80. C N Mymms *St Alb* 79-82; C Chipping Barnet w Arkley 82-83; TV 83-84; TV Preston w Sutton Poyntz and Osmington w Poxwell *Sarum* 84-86; Chapl St Helier's Hosp Carshalton 86-90; Chapl Jo Radcliffe Hosp Ox from 90. *c/o John Radcliffe Hospital, Oxford OX3 9DU* Oxford (0865) 741166 or 66886

FENNING, John Edward. b 32. CITC 86. **d** 88 **p** 89. NSM Douglas Union w Frankfield *C, C & R* 88-89; Chapl Ashton Sch Cork from 88; NSM Moviddy Union *C, C & R* from 89. *The Rectory, Aherla, Co Cork, Irish Republic* Cork (21) 331511

FENSOME, Anthony David. b 49. DipYL74 Open Univ BA89. Sarum & Wells Th Coll 82. **d** 84 **p** 85. C Gtr Corsham *Bris* 84-88; P-in-c Lyddington w Wanborough 88-91; P-in-c Bishopstone w Hinton Parva 88-91; R Lyddington and Wanborough and Bishopstone etc from 91. *The Vicarage, 19 Church Road, Wanborough, Swindon, Wilts SN4 0BZ* Swindon (0793) 790242

FENTON, Albert George. b 14. Linc Th Coll 42. **d** 43 **p** 44. C Weymouth St Paul *Sarum* 43-46; S Africa 46-61 and 62-84; R Coates *Ely* 61-62; Perm to Offic *Win* from 85. *9 Highfield Lodge, Highfield Lane, Southampton SO2 1WF* Southampton (0703) 559409

FENTON, Barry. b 59. Leeds Univ BA85. Coll of Resurr Mirfield 85. **d** 87 **p** 88. C Leigh Park *Portsm* 87-90; Chapl and Prec Portsm Cathl from 90. *3 Pembroke Road, Portsmouth PO1 2NR* Portsmouth (0705) 827359

FENTON, Christopher Miles Tempest. b 28. MInstPC75 Qu Coll Cam BA50 LLB51 MA55. Ridley Hall Cam 52. **d** 54 **p** 55. C Welling *Roch* 54-57; Lic to Offic *Bradf* 57-63; Chapl Malsis Prep Sch Keighley 57-63; C Hove Bp Hannington Memorial Ch *Chich* 63-65; V Ramsgate Ch Ch *Cant* 65-71; Hd Dept of Gp Studies Westmr Past Foundn 71-82; C Mottingham St Andr *S'wark* 71-73; Perm to Offic *Ely* 73-85; Co-ord of Tr St Alb Past Foundn 82-85; Perm to Offic *Heref* from 85; Dir St Anne's Cen of Psychotherapy & Counselling from

85. *Under Down, Ledbury, Herefordshire HR8 2JE* Ledbury (0531) 2669

FENTON, Heather. b 48. Trin Coll Bris CertEd78. **d** 87. C Corwen and Llangar *St As* 87-89; C Corwen and Llangar w Gwyddelwern and Llawr-y-B from 89; Dioc Rural Min Co-ord from 87. *Coleg y Groes, Corwen, Clwyd LL21 0AU* Corwen (0490) 2169

FENTON, Ian Christopher Stuart. b 40. AKC62. **d** 63 **p** 64. C Banstead *Guildf* 63-67; V N Holmwood 67-84; RD Dorking 80-84; V Witley from 84. *The Vicarage, Petworth Road, Witley, Godalming, Surrey GU8 5LT* Wormley (0428) 682886

FENTON, Canon John Charles. b 21. Qu Coll Ox BA43 MA47 BD53. Linc Th Coll 43. **d** 44 **p** 45. Prin St Chad's Coll Dur 65-78; Can Res Ch Ch *Ox* 78-91; rtd 91. *Christ Church, Oxford OX1 1DP* Oxford (0865) 276200

FENTON, Michael John. b 42. Linc Th Coll 67. **d** 69 **p** 70. C Guiseley *Bradf* 69-72; C Heswall *Ches* 72-75; TV Birkenhead Priory 75-81; V Alvanley from 81; Chapl Crossley Hosp Cheshire from 82. *The Vicarage, 47 Ardern Lea, Alvanley, Warrington WA6 9EQ* Helsby (0928) 722012

FENTON, Wallace. b 32. TCD. **d** 64 **p** 65. C Glenavy *Conn* 64-67; I Tullaniskin w Clonoe *Arm* 67-87; Bp's C Sallaghy Clogh from 87; Warden of Readers from 91. *Sallaghy Rectory, Lisnaskea, Enniskillen, Co Fermanagh BT92 5FG* Lisnaskea (03657) 21372

FENWICK, Edward Hartwig. b 05. Fitzw Coll Cam BA33 MA43. Westcott Ho Cam 32. **d** 33 **p** 34. R Baddesley Clinton *Birm* 60-76; R Lapworth 60-76; rtd 76; C Solihull *Birm* 76-90. *1 St Alphege Close, Church Hill Road, Solihull, W Midlands B91 3RQ* 021-704 4736

FENWICK, Very Rev Jeffrey Robert. b 30. Pemb Coll Cam BA53 MA57. Linc Th Coll 53. **d** 55 **p** 56. C Upholland *Liv* 55-58; S Rhodesia 58-64; Rhodesia 65-78; Area Sec (Dio Ox) USPG 64-65; Adn Charter 73-75; Dean Bulawayo 75-78; adn Bulawayo 75-78; Can Res Worc Cathl *Worc* 78-89; R Guernsey St Peter Port *Win* from 89; Dean Guernsey from 89; Hon Can Win Cathl from 89; Pres Guernsey Miss to Seamen from 89. *The Deanery, St Peter Port, Guernsey, Channel Islands* Guernsey (0481) 20036

FENWICK, John Robert Kipling. b 51. Societas Liturgica Van Mildert Coll Dur BSc72 Nottm Univ BA74 MTh78 K Coll Lon PhD85. Lambeth STh84 St Jo Coll Nottm 72. **d** 77 **p** 78. C Dalton-in-Furness *Carl* 77-80; Lect Trin Coll Bris 80-88; Chapl 80-87; Lic to Offic *Bris* from 81; Abp's Asst Ecum Affairs *Cant* from 88; NSM Purley Ch Ch *S'wark* from 88; Asst ChStJ from 89. *55 Pampisford Road, Purley, Surrey CR8 2NJ* 081-660 8988

FENWICK, Malcolm Frank. b 38. Cranmer Hall Dur 62. **d** 65 **p** 66. C Tynemouth Cullercoats St Paul *Newc* 65-68; C Bywell St Pet 68-73; V Alnmouth 73-75; CF (TAVR) 75-83; V Lesbury w Alnmouth *Newc* 75-80; V Delaval from 80; RD Bedlington 83-88. *The Vicarage, Seaton Sluice, Whitley Bay, Tyne & Wear NE26 4QW* 091-237 1982

FENWICK, Canon Richard David. b 43. FLCM68 FTCL76 Univ of Wales (Lamp) BA66 MA86 TCD MusB79. Ridley Hall Cam 66. **d** 68 **p** 69. C Skewen *Llan* 68-72; C Penarth w Lavernock 72-74; PV, Succ and Sacr Roch Cathl *Roch* 74-78; Min Can St Paul's Cathl *Lon* 78-79; Min Can and Succ 79-83; Warden Coll Min Cans 81-83; PV Westmr Abbey 83-90; V Ruislip St Martin *Lon* 83-90; Can Res and Prec Guildf Cathl *Guildf* from 90. *3 Cathedral Close, Guildford, Surrey GU2 5TL* Guildford (0483) 69682

FEREDAY, Harold James Rodney. b 46. Sheff Univ CEIR76. St Jo Coll Nottm 87. **d** 89 **p** 90. C Rastrick St Matt *Wakef* from 89. *2 Newbury Road, Brighouse, W Yorkshire* Brighouse (0484) 721066

FERGUSON, Aean Michael O'Shaun. **d** 90 **p** 91. NSM Kilmallock w Kilflynn, Kilfinane, Knockaney etc *L & K* 90-91; NSM Killaloe w Stradbally from 91. *Moohane, Lough Gur, Bruff, Co Limerick, Irish Republic* Limerick (61) 85195

FERGUSON, Dr Alastair Stuart. b 45. MRCS69 LRCP69 Ball Coll Ox BA78 MA82 Lon Univ MB, BS69. St Steph Ho Ox. **d** 82 **p** 83. NSM Dengie w Asheldham *Chelmsf* 82-86; NSM Mayland 86-89; NSM Steeple 86-89; Perm to Offic 89-91; Zimbabwe from 91. *St Andrew's Rectory, PO Box 21, Mvurwi, Zimbabwe* Mvurwi (77) 2401

FERGUSON, Ian John. b 51. Aber Univ BD77. Trin Coll Bris 77. **d** 78 **p** 79. C Foord St Jo *Cant* 78-82; C Bieldside *Ab* 82-86; Dioc Youth Chapl 82-86; P-in-c Westhill from 86. *31 Leslie Crescent, Westhill, Skeene, Aberdeenshire AB3 6UY* Aberdeen (0224) 740007

FERGUSON, James Paterson. b 07. Glas Univ MA29 Qu Coll Ox BA33. Wycliffe Hall Ox 33. **d** 33 **p** 34. Swaziland 70-71; rtd 72; Perm to Offic *S & M* from 72. *Creigneish, Albany Road, Douglas, Isle of Man* Douglas (0624) 673130

FERGUSON, John Aitken. b 40. ARCST64 CEng MICE Glas Univ BSc64 Strathclyde Univ PhD74. Linc Th Coll 79. **d** 81 **p** 82. C Morpeth *Newc* 81-85; V Whittingham and Edlingham w Bolton Chapel from 85. *The Vicarage, Whittingham, Alnwick, Northd NE66 4UP* Whittingham (066574) 224

FERGUSON, John Duncan. b 31. Clare Coll Cam BA54 MA58. Kelham Th Coll 54. **d** 59 **p** 60. C Old Charlton *S'wark* 59-63; Ghana 63-75; Lic to Offic Pet 75-76; Ox 75-77; Truro 86-91; V Hessenford *Truro* 77-84; Dioc Development Rep 80-86; RD Trigg Major from 91. *Hampton Manor, Stoke Climsland, Callington, Cornwall PL17 8LZ* Stoke Climsland (0579) 370494

FERGUSON, John Richard Preston. b 34. CITC 63. **d** 65 **p** 66. C Dundela *D & D* 65-70; I Annahilt 70-76; I Belf St Brendan from 76. *St Brendan's Rectory, 36 Circular Road, Belfast BT4 2GA* Belfast (0232) 763458

FERGUSON, Mrs Kathleen. b 46. ALA76 LMH Ox BA68 MA72. **d** 88. NSM Llanidloes w Llangurig *Ban* from 88. *Oerle, Trefeglwys, Caersws, Powys SY17 5QX* Trefeglwys (05516) 626

FERGUSON, Paul John. b 55. FRCO75 New Coll Ox BA76 MA80 K Coll Cam BA84 MA88. Westcott Ho Cam 82. **d** 85 **p** 86. C Ches St Mary *Ches* 85-88; Sacr and Chapl Westmr Abbey from 88; Perm to Offic *Lon* from 89. *4B Little Cloister, London SW1P 3PL* 071-222 4023 or 222 5152

FERGUSON, Peter Carr. b 22. Cranmer Hall Dur 62. **d** 63 **p** 64. V Newington w Dairycoates *York* 69-74; V York St Thos w St Maurice 74-79; V Lythe 79-83; V Coniscliffe *Dur* 83-87; rtd 87. *Gib Stubbin, Wass, York YO6 4BE*

FERGUSON, Richard Archie. b 39. Dur Univ BA62. Linc Th Coll 62. **d** 64 **p** 65. C Stretford St Matt *Man* 64-68; Bp's Dom Chapl *Dur* 68-69; C Newc St Geo *Newc* 69-71; V Glodwick *Man* 71-77; V Tynemouth Ch Ch *Newc* 77-82; P-in-c Tynemouth St Aug 82-87; V Tynemouth Ch Ch w H Trin 82-87; TR N Shields 87-90; TR Upton cum Chalvey *Ox* from 90. *The Rectory, 18 Albert Street, Slough SL1 2BU* Slough (0753) 29988

FERGUSON, Robert Garnett Allen. b 48. Leeds Univ LLB70 Clare Coll Cam. Cuddesdon Coll 71. **d** 73 **p** 74. C Wakef Cathl *Wakef* 73-76; V Lupset 76-83; Chapl Cheltenham Coll 83-87; Sen Chapl Win Coll from 87. *Winchester College, Winchester, Hants* Winchester (0962) 864242

FERGUSON, Robin Sinclair. b 31. Worc Coll Ox BA53 MA57 Lon Univ CertEd63. ALCD55 Wycliffe Coll Toronto 55. **d** 57 **p** 58. C Brompton H Trin *Lon* 57-60; C Brixton St Matt *S'wark* 60-63; Hon C Framlingham w Saxtead *St E* 63-65; Hon C Haverhill 65-67; Chapl St Mary's Sch Richmond 67-75; C Richmond St Mary *S'wark* 68-76; P-in-c Shilling Okeford *Sarum* 76-87; Chapl Croft Ho Sch Shillingstone 76-87; R Milton Abbas, Hilton w Cheselbourne etc *Sarum* from 87. *The Rectory, Ansty, Dorchester, Dorset DT2 7PX* Milton Abbas (0258) 880372

FERGUSON, Ronald Leslie. b 36. Open Univ BA86 BA89 Newc Poly CertFT90. Chich Th Coll 65. **d** 68 **p** 69. C Toxteth Park St Marg *Liv* 68-72; C Oakham w Hambleton and Egleton *Pet* 72-74; Asst Chapl The Dorothy Kerin Trust Burrswood 74-76; V Castleside *Dur* from 76. *The Vicarage, Castleside, Consett, Co Durham DH8 9AP* Consett (0207) 508242

FERGUSON, Wallace Raymond. b 47. Qu Coll Birm BTh CITC 76. **d** 78 **p** 79. C Lurgan Ch Ch *D & D* 78-80; I Newtownards w Movilla Abbey 80-84; I Mullabrack w Markethill and Kilcluney *Arm* from 84. *Mullurg Road, Mullabrack BT60 1UR* Markethill (0861) 551092

FERGUSSON, Miss Catherine Margaret. b 28. MIPM Birm Univ CSocStuds50. Linc Th Coll 77. **dss** 79 **d** 87. Watford St Pet *St Alb* 79-82; Prestwood *Ox* 82-86; Gt Horwood 86-87; Par Dn 87-89; Dir Cottesloe Chr Tr Progr 86-89; rtd 89. *Checkmate, Middle Ground, Fovant, Salisbury SP3 5LP* Fovant (0722) 720314

FERLEY, Canon John Harold. b 07. Lon Coll of Div 25 ALCD29. **d** 30 **p** 31. V Hunstanton St Edm *Nor* 52-72; RD Heacham 66-70; RD Heacham and Rising 70-72; Hon Can Nor Cathl 70-85; rtd 72; P-in-c Nor St Geo Tombland *Nor* 72-85; Perm to Offic from 86. *10 Kingsley Road, Norwich NR1 3RB* Norwich (0603) 610268

FERMER, Michael Thorpe. b 30. Lon Univ BSc52 ARCS52 St Cath Soc Ox BA54. Wycliffe Hall Ox 52. **d** 54 **p** 55. C Upper Holloway All SS *Lon* 54-57; C Plymouth St Andr *Ex* 57-59; V Tamerton Foliot 59-63; Asst Chapl

United Sheff Hosps 63-64; Chapl 64-66; Lic to Offic *Sheff* 66-73; V Holmesfield *Derby* 73-79; TR Old Brampton and Loundsley Green 79-83; V Brightside St Thos and St Marg *Sheff* 83; V Brightside w Wincobank 83-89; V Loscoe *Derby* from 89. *The Vicarage, High Street, Loscoe, Derby DE7 7LE* Langley Mill (0773) 765631

FERN, John. b 36. Nottm Univ BA57 DipRE64 MA88. Coll of Resurr Mirfield 57. d 59 p 60. C Carlton *S'well* 59-61; C Hucknall Torkard 61-68; V Rainworth from 68. *The Vicarage, 27 St Peter's Drive, Rainworth, Mansfield, Notts NG21 0BE* Mansfield (0623) 792293

FERNANDO, Kenneth Michael James. b 32. Ceylon Univ BA55. Cuddesdon Coll 55. d 57 p 58. C Leagrave *St Alb* 57-59; Ceylon 59-72; Sri Lanka from 72. *Ecumenical Institute for Study & Dialogue, 490/5 Havelock Road, Colombo 6, Sri Lanka* Colombo (1) 586998

FERNANDO, Percy Sriyananda. b 49. Dundee Coll DCEU81. St And Dioc Tr Course 85. d 88 p 89. NSM Blairgowrie *St And* from 88; NSM Coupar Angus from 89; NSM Alyth from 89. *Gowrie Cottage, Perth Road, Blairgowrie, Perthshire PH10 6QB* Blairgowrie (0250) 3024

FERNANDO, Mrs Susan Joy. b 50. Nottm Univ CertEd77 BEd78. Linc Th Coll 83. dss 85 d 87. Kingsbury H Innocents *Lon* 85-87; Par Dn 87-88; Par Dn Harmondsworth from 88. *St Mary's Vicarage, Harmondsworth, West Drayton, Middx UB7 0AQ* 081-897 2385

FERNS, Stephen Antony Dunbar. b 61. St Chad's Coll Dur BA84 Ox Univ BA87. Ripon Coll Cuddesdon 85. d 88 p 89. C Billingham St Cuth *Dur* 88-90; Chapl Dur Univ 91; Chapl Van Mildert and Trevelyan Coll Dur from 91. *Trevelyan College, Elvet Hill Road, Durham DH1 3LN* 091-374 3761 or 374 3781

FERNS, Archdeacon of. See WILKINSON, Ven Kenneth Samuel

FERNS, Dean of. See EARL, Very Rev David Kaye Lee

FERNSBY, Jack. b 08. St Chad's Coll Dur BA39 DipTh40 MA42. d 40 p 41. C Billingham St Cuth *Dur* 40-42; C Kennington St Jo *S'wark* 42-46; C St Marylebone All SS *Lon* 46-47; C Upper Norwood St Jo *S'wark* 47-48; V Weoley Castle *Birm* 48-51; V Nether Stowey *B & W* 51-55; Perm to Offic *Lich* from 72. *15 Fairfield Close, Gobowen, Oswestry, Shropshire SY11 3JP* Oswestry (0691) 650473

FERNYHOUGH, Ven Bernard. b 32. St D Coll Lamp BA53. d 55 p 56. Trinidad and Tobago 55-61; R Stoke Bruerne w Grafton Regis and Alderton *Pet* 61-67; RD Preston 65-67; V E Haddon 67-69; V Ravensthorpe 67-69; R Holdenby 67-69; RD Haddon 68-71; V Ravensthorpe w E Haddon and Holdenby 69-77; RD Brixworth 71-77; Can Pet Cathl 74-77 and from 89; Can Res Pet Cathl 77-89; Adn Oakham from 77. *18 Minster Precincts, Peterborough* Peterborough (0733) 62762

FERNYHOUGH, Timothy John Edward. b 60. Leeds Univ BA81. Linc Th Coll 81. d 83 p 84. C Daventry *Pet* 83-86; Chapl Tonbridge Sch Kent from 86. *1 Chiltern Way, Tonbridge, Kent* Tonbridge (0732) 357973

FERRIDAY, Donald Martin. b 30. Univ of Wales (Lamp) BA55. Qu Coll Birm 55. d 57 p 58. C Stockport St Sav *Ches* 57-59; C Heswall 59-64; V Cheadle Hulme All SS 64-72; V Ches 72-76; TR Ches Team 76-77; R W Kirby St Bridget from 77. *The Rectory, West Kirby, Wirral, Merseyside L48 7HL* 051-625 5229

FERRIER, Malcolm. b 38. St Mich Coll Llan 67. d 69 p 70. C Solihull *Birm* 69-73; C E Grinstead St Swithun *Chich* 73-75; V Saltley *Birm* 75-82; V Waterlooville *Portsm* from 82. *The Vicarage, Stakes Hill Road, Waterlooville, Portsmouth PO7 7LB* Waterlooville (0705) 262145

FERRY, David Henry John. b 53. TCD BTh88. d 88 p 89. C Enniskillen *Clogh* 88-90; I Leckpatrick w Dunnalong *D & R* from 90. *1 Lowertown Road, Ballymagorry, Strabane, Co Tyrone BT82 0LE* Strabane (0504) 883545

FESSEY, Annis Irene. b 40. SS Paul & Mary Coll Cheltenham CertEd60. Ripon Coll Cuddesdon 88. d 90. Par Dn Bris St Andr Hartcliffe *Bris* from 90. *404 Bishport Avenue, Bristol BS13 0HX* Bristol (0272) 784052

FESSEY, Brian Alan. b 39. Bris Univ CertEd61 Leeds Univ DipEd71. Ripon Coll Cuddesdon 88. d 90 p 91. Hon C Bishopsworth *Bris* 90; C Withywood CD from 91. *404 Bishport Avenue, Bristol BS13 0HX* Bristol (0272) 784052

FETHNEY, John Garside. b 27. Linc Coll Ox BA53. Linc Th Coll 51. d 53 p 54. C W Hackney St Barn *Lon* 53-55; P-in-c 56; Pakistan 57-68; Area Sec (Dio York) USPG 68-70; (Dio Lon) from 70; Deputation Sec 73-83; Hon C St Botolph without Bishopgate *Lon* 73-86; Educn Sec USPG from 83; Area Sec (Dio Guildf) USPG from 86.

21 *Plover Close, East Wittering, Chichester, W Sussex PO20 8PW* Bracklesham Bay (0243) 670145

FEWKES, Jeffrey Preston. b 47. Wycliffe Hall Ox 72. d 75 p 76. C Ches le Street *Dur* 75-78; C Kennington St Mark *S'wark* 78-81; V Bulwell St Jo *S'well* from 81. *St John's Vicarage, Snape Wood Road, Bulwell, Nottingham NG6 7GH* Nottingham (0602) 278025

FIDDAMAN, Ernest Robert. b 13. d 78 p 78. Hon C Preston *Chich* 78-83; Chapl Wokingham Hosp from 83; Hon C Wokingham All SS *Ox* from 83. *2 Beckett Close, Wokingham, Berks RG11 1YZ* Wokingham (0734) 791451

FIDGIN, Canon Douglas Michael. b 15. Linc Th Coll 46. d 49 p 50. V Hounslow St Steph *Lon* 62-70; R Owermoigne w Warmwell *Sarum* 70-76; R Portland All SS w St Pet 76-81; rtd 81; C Urchfont w Stert *Sarum* 82-85. *50 Rodwell Road, Weymouth, Dorset DT4 8QU* Weymouth (0305) 770943

FIDLER, John Harvey. b 49. Hatf Poly BSc72. St Alb Minl Tr Scheme 84. d 87 p 88. NSM Royston *St Alb* from 87. *8 Stamford Avenue, Royston, Herts SG8 7DD* Royston (0763) 241886

FIELD, David Hibberd. b 36. K Coll Cam BA58. Oak Hill Th Coll 58. d 60 p 61. C Aldershot H Trin *Guildf* 60-63; C Margate H Trin *Cant* 63-66; Sec Th Students Fellowship 66-68; Tutor Oak Hill Th Coll from 68; Vice Prin from 79; Dean Minl Tr Course from 88. *Oak Hill College, Chase Side, London N14 4PS* 081-449 0467

FIELD, Donald Charles. b 21. Lon Univ BSc50. Glouc Th Course 65. d 66 p 67. C Tewkesbury w Walton Cardiff *Glouc* 69-72; V Standish w Hardwicke and Haresfield 72-74; V Standish w Haresfield and Moreton Valence 74-80; V Deerhurst, Apperley w Forthampton and Chaceley 80-86; rtd 86. *27 Highfield Road, Ammanford, Dyfed SA18 1JL* Amman Valley (0269) 822716

FIELD, Geoffrey Alder. b 13. Ely Th Coll. d 47 p 48. V Whittlesey St Andr *Ely* 54-75; V Foxton 75-80; rtd 81. *14 Poplar Close, Great Shelford, Cambridge CB21 5LX* Cambridge (0223) 842089

FIELD, Leonard Frederick. b 34. Man Univ BSc56 Lon Univ CertEd57. E Midl Min Tr Course 85. d 88 p 89. Hon C Holton-le-Clay *Linc* from 88. *35 Bedford Road, Humberston, Grimsby, S Humberside DN35 0PZ* Grimsby (0472) 812489

FIELD, Martin Richard. b 55. Keswick Hall Coll CertEd76 Leic Univ MA87. St Jo Coll Nottm BTh82 LTh. d 82 p 83. C Gaywood, Bawsey and Mintlyn *Nor* 82-85; Perm to Offic *Leic* 85-87; Hon C S'well Minster *S'well* 87-88; Hon C Stand *Man* 88-89; Dioc Press and Communications Officer 88-91. *2 Hamilton Road, Prestwich, Manchester M25 8GG* 061-773 5963

FIELD, Miss Olwen Joyce. b 53. St Jo Coll Nottm 86. d 88. Par Dn Kensal Rise St Mark and St Martin *Lon* 88-91; Par Dn Northwood H Trin from 91; Chapl Mt Vernon Hosp Uxbridge from 91. *81 Mertleside Close, Northwood, Middx* Northwood (09274) 23221

FIELD, Richard Colin. b 33. St Cath Soc Ox BA54 MA63. Clifton Th Coll 63. d 65 p 66. C Highbury Ch Ch *Lon* 65-70; V Tottenham St Ann 70-85; V Leytonstone St Jo *Chelmsf* from 85. *St John's Vicarage, 44 Hartley Road, London E11 3BL* 081-989 5447

FIELD, Miss Susan Elizabeth. b 59. York Univ BA80 Birm Univ CertEd81. Qu Coll Birm 84. d 87. C Coleshill *Birm* 87-90; Chapl Loughb Univ *Leic* from 91. *13 Spinney Hill Drive, Loughborough, Leics LE11 3LB* Loughborough (0509) 268203

FIELD, William Jenkin. b 25. St Deiniol's Hawarden. d 66 p 67. C Cardiff St Jo *Llan* 66-72; V Llancarfan w Llantrithyd from 72. *The Vicarage, Llancarfan, Barry, S Glam* St Athan (0446) 750241

FIELDEN, Robert. b 32. Linc Th Coll 65. d 67 p 68. C Bassingham *Linc* 67-72; R Anderby w Cumberworth 72-88; P-in-c Huttoft 72-88; P-in-c Mumby 77-88; R Fiskerton w Reepham 88-90; rtd 90; Perm to Offic *Linc* from 91. *Woodlands, 32 Sibthorpe Drive, Sudbrooke, Lincoln LN2 2RQ* Lincoln (0522) 595199

FIELDER, Canon Arthur John. b 14. Lon Univ DipTh48. Bps' Coll Cheshunt 46. d 47 p 50. Hon Can Leic Cathl *Leic* 67-77; Dir of Educn 67-77; Master Wyggeston's Hosp Leic 68-78; rtd 78; Perm to Offic *St Alb* from 78. *3 Morley House, College of St Barnabas, Lingfield, Surrey RH7 6NJ* Dormans Park (034287) 407

FIELDGATE, John William Sheridan. b 44. St Jo Coll Dur BA68. Ox NSM Course 75. d 79 p 80. NSM Haddenham w Cuddington, Kingsey etc *Ox* 79-90; C Northleach w Hampnett and Farmington *Glouc* from 90; C Cold Aston w Notgrove and Turkdean from 90. *High View, Farmington Road, Northleach, Cheltenham, Glos GL54 3JA* Cotswold (0451) 60096

FIELDING, John Joseph. b 29. TCD BA53 MA65. **d** 54 **p** 55. C Belf St Luke *Conn* 54-57; C Belf St Mary Magd 57-60; W Germany 61-69; Chapl St Edw Sch Ox 69-73; V Highgate St Mich *Lon* from 73. *The Vicarage, 10 The Grove, London N6 6LB* 081-340 7279

FIELDING, Canon Ronald Jeffrey. b 17. Lon Univ BSc38. Qu Coll Birm 40. **d** 42 **p** 43. C Selly Oak St Mary *Birm* 42-46; S Africa from 46; Hon Can Grahamstown Cathl from 86. *40 Kennington Road, Nahoon, East London, 5241 South Africa* East London (431) 353735

FIELDING, William. b 35. St Jo Coll Dur BA60. Ridley Hall Cam. **d** 62 **p** 63. C Ashton-on-Ribble St Mich *Blackb* 62-64; C Broughton 64-67; V Knuzden 67-75; V Darwen St Cuth 75-85; RD Darwen 77-87; P-in-c Tockholes 79-83; V Darwen St Cuth w Tockholes St Steph 85-87; V St Annes from 87; RD Kirkham from 91. *St Thomas's Vicarage, St Annes, Lytham St Annes, Lancs FY8 1LE* St Annes (0253) 722725

FIELDING-FOX, John Alfred. b 21. Univ of Wales BA42. **d** 48 **p** 49. C Canton St Jo *Llan* 48-50; C Cardiff St Andr and St Teilo 50-59; C-in-c Barry Is CD 59-66; V Hammerwich *Lich* from 66. *The Vicarage, Hammerwich, Walsall WS7 0JT* Burntwood (0543) 686088

FIELDSEND, John Henry. b 31. Nottm Univ BSc54 Lon Univ BD61. ALCD59. **d** 61 **p** 62. C Pennington *Man* 61-64; C Didsbury Ch Ch 64-66; P-in-c Bayston Hill *Lich* 66-67; V 67-88; UK Dir CMJ from 89; Min at large CMJ from 91. *19 The Ridgeway, St Albans, Herts AL4 9AL* St Albans (0727) 869537

FIELDSON, Robert Steven. b 56. Qu Coll Cam BA78 MA79 MSc. St Jo Coll Nottm. **d** 87 **p** 88. C Walmley *Birm* 87-90; Oman from 90. *c/o Oman Protestant Church, PO Box 4982, Ruwi, Sultanate of Oman*

FIFE, Miss Janet Heather. b 53. Sussex Univ BA77. Wycliffe Hall Ox 84. **d** 87. Chapl Bradf Cathl *Bradf* 87-89; Par Dn York St Mich-le-Belfrey *York* from 89. *27 Nunthorpe Grove, York YO2 1DT* York (0904) 652067

FIFIELD, William Herbert. b 04. Univ of Wales BA26. Ripon Hall Ox 27. **d** 28 **p** 29. V Attleborough *Cov* 39-78; rtd 78; Perm to Offic *Cov* from 78. *102 Lutterworth Road, Nuneaton, Warks CV11 6PH* Nuneaton (0203) 342308

FILBY, John Michael. b 34. Oak Hill Th Coll 56. **d** 60 **p** 61. C Penge St Jo *Roch* 60-64; C Foord St Jo *Cant* 64-66; Dioc Ev (Dios *Roch, Guildf* and *Chelmsf*) 66-75; Perm to Offic *Roch* 66-68; *Guildf* 68-71; *Chelmsf* 71-75; V Broxted w Chickney and Tilty and Lt Easton *Chelmsf* 75-85; P-in-c Gt Easton 83-85; R Broxted w Chickney and Tilty etc from 85. *The Rectory, Park Road, Little Easton, Dunmow, Essex CM6 2JJ* Great Dunmow (0371) 2509

FILBY, Ven William Charles Leonard. b 33. Lon Univ BA58. Oak Hill Th Coll 53. **d** 59 **p** 60. C Eastbourne All SS *Chich* 59-62; C Woking St Jo *Guildf* 62-65; V Richmond H Trin *S'wark* 65-71; V Hove Bp Hannington Memorial Ch *Chich* 71-79; R Broadwater St Mary 79-83; RD Worthing 80-83; Can and Preb Chich Cathl 81-83; Adn Horsham from 83. *The Archdeaconry, Itchingfield, Horsham, W Sussex RH13 7NX* Slinfold (0403) 790315

FILE, Ronald Sidney Omer. b 20. Bps' Coll Cheshunt 58. **d** 60 **p** 61. C Clee *Linc* 68-72; R Trusthorpe 72-76; P-in-c Apley w Stainfield 76-78; P-in-c Gautby w Waddingworth 76-78; R Bardney 76-80; Hong Kong 80-85; V Friskney *Linc* 85-90; V Thorpe St Peter 85-90; rtd 91; Perm to Offic *Linc* from 91. *4 Marshall Close, Fishtoft, Boston, Lincs PE21 0RX* Boston (0205) 369199

FILE, Canon Roy Stephen. b 23. Leeds Univ BA50. Coll of Resurr Mirfield 50. **d** 53 **p** 54. S Africa 66-80; V Ilkley St Marg *Bradf* 80-88; rtd 88; Perm to Offic *Bradf* from 88; Hon Can Cape Town from 90. *4 Bowling View, Skipton, N Yorkshire BD23 1SR* Skipton (0756) 795599

FILER, Victor John. b 43. Sarum Th Coll 66. **d** 69 **p** 70. C Mortlake w E Sheen *S'wark* 69-74; SSF 75-82; P-in-c Plaistow SS Phil and Jas w St Andr *Chelmsf* 80-83; Chapl Plaistow Hosp 81-83; TV Plaistow 83; TV Beaconsfield *Ox* 84-90; TR Maltby *Sheff* from 90. *The Rectory, 69 Blyth Road, Maltby, Rotherham, S Yorkshire S66 7LF* Rotherham (0709) 812684

FILES, Ian James. b 54. Loughb Univ BSc76. Chich Th Coll 85. **d** 87 **p** 88. C Prestwich St Mary *Man* 87-89; C Man Clayton St Cross w St Paul from 89. *191 North Road, Clayton, Manchester M11 4NF* 061-220 8597

FILLERY, William Robert. b 42. Univ of Wales BA65. St D Coll Lamp CPS68 BD69. **d** 68 **p** 69. C Llangyfelach and Morriston *S & B* 68-71; C Morriston 71-72; Lic to Offic *Ox* 73-76; Chapl Windsor Girls' Sch Hamm 76-81; Chapl Reed's Sch Cobham 81-86; V Oxshott *Guildf*

86-89; P-in-c Seale from 89; P-in-c Puttenham and Wanborough from 89. *The Rectory, Seale, Farnham, Surrey GU10 1JA* Runfold (02518) 2302

FINCH, Alfred John. b 10. TCD BA33 MA36. CITC 33. **d** 33 **p** 34. I Knocknamuckley *D & D* 55-75; rtd 75. *4 Shimnavale, Newcastle, Co Down* Newcastle (03967) 22202

FINCH, Christopher. b 41. Lon Univ BA63 AKC63 BD69. Sarum Th Coll 63. **d** 65 **p** 66. C High Wycombe *Ox* 65-69; Prec Leic Cathl *Leic* 69-73; R Lt Bowden St Nic 73-81; V Evington from 81. *The Vicarage, Stoughton Lane, Evington, Leicester LE2 2FH* Leicester (0533) 712032

FINCH, David Walter. b 40. FIMLS69 Cam Univ MA74. Ridley Hall Cam. **d** 91. C Ixworth and Bardwell *St E* from 91. *19 Crown Crescent, Ixworth, Bury St Edmunds, Suffolk IP31 2EJ* Pakenham (0359) 31452

FINCH, Canon Edward Albert. b 23. Lon Univ BSc50. Sarum Th Coll 50. **d** 52 **p** 53. V Walthamstow St Pet *Chelmsf* 59-70; Can Res Chelmsf Cathl 70-85; Dir Interface Assn 85-90; rtd 90; Perm to Offic *St E* from 91. *St Clare, The Street, Pakenham, Bury St Edmunds, Suffolk IP31 2LG* Pakenham (0359) 323885

FINCH, Frank. b 33. Qu Coll Birm 72. **d** 74 **p** 75. C Bilston St Leon *Lich* 74-78; R Sudbury and Somersal Herbert *Derby* 78-87; Chapl HM Pris Sudbury 78-87; HM Det Cen Foston Hall 80-87; V Lilleshall and Sheriffhales *Lich* 87-90; R The Ridwares and Kings Bromley from 90. *The Rectory, Alrewas Road, Kings Bromley, Burton-on-Trent, Staffs DE13 7HP* Yoxall (0543) 472932

FINCH, Frederick. b 22. Lon Coll of Div 59. **d** 60 **p** 61. Area Sec (W Midl) CPAS 68-71; V Blackpool Ch Ch *Blackb* 71-77; Canada from 78; rtd 90. *725 Provencher Boulevard, Brossard, Quebec, Canada, J4W 1Y5*

FINCH, Jeffrey Walter. b 45. Man Univ BA(Econ)66 Liv Univ DASE80. Linc Th Coll 82. **d** 84 **p** 85. C Briercliffe *Blackb* 84-87; P-in-c Brindle from 87; Asst Dir of Educn from 87. *The Rectory, Sandy Lane, Brindle, Chorley, Lancs PR6 8JN* Hoghton (025485) 4130

FINCH, John. b 20. Bps' Coll Cheshunt 59. **d** 61 **p** 62. V Habergham Eaves St Matt *Blackb* 68-75; V Garstang St Helen Churchtown 75-86; rtd 86; Perm to Offic *Blackb* from 86. *55 Worcester Avenue, Garstang, Preston PR3 1FJ* Garstang (0995) 602386

FINCH, Paul William. b 50. Oak Hill Th Coll DipTh73 Lon Bible Coll. **d** 75 **p** 76. C Hoole *Ches* 75-78; C Charlesworth *Derby* 78-87; C Charlesworth and Dinting Vale 87-88; TV Radipole and Melcombe Regis *Sarum* from 88. *74 Field Barn Drive, Weymouth, Dorset DT4 0EF* Weymouth (0305) 778995

FINCH, Richard Michael. b 22. Selw Coll Cam BA47 MA49. Cuddesdon Coll 47. **d** 49 **p** 50. V Westf *Chich* 62-79; P-in-c Laughton w Ripe and Chalvington 79-84; R 84-87; rtd 87; Perm to Offic *Nor* from 87. *28 Heathlands Drive, Croxton Road, Croxton, Thetford, Norfolk IP24 1UT* Thetford (0842) 766595

FINCH, Ronald. b 15. Qu Coll Birm 79. **d** 80 **p** 80. Hon C Welford w Weston and Clifford Chambers *Glouc* 80-85; Perm to Offic *Ches* from 85. *Cornerstone, 1 Penrhyd Road, Irby, Wirral L61 2XJ* 051-648 1559

FINCH, Stanley James. b 31. Mert Coll Ox BA55 MA58. Wells Th Coll 55. **d** 57 **p** 58. C Lanc St Mary *Blackb* 57-61; C Leeds St Pet *Ripon* 61-65; V Habergham All SS *Blackb* 65-73; V S Shore H Trin 73-84; V Broughton from 84; RD Preston from 86. *The Vicarage, 410 Garstang Road, Broughton, Preston PR3 5JB* Broughton (0772) 862330

FINCH, Thomas. b 20. Lon Univ BD57. Edin Th Coll 48. **d** 51 **p** 51. V Wellingborough St Mary *Pet* 67-88; rtd 88. *18 Royal Avenue, Leyland, Preston PR5 1BQ* Leyland (0772) 433780

FINCHAM, Nicholas Charles. b 56. St Jo Coll Dur BA78 MA80. Westcott Ho Cam 80 Bossey Ecum Inst Geneva 81. **d** 82 **p** 83. C Seaham w Seaham Harbour *Dur* 82-85; C Lydney w Aylburton *Glouc* 85-87; C Isleworth All SS *Lon* from 87. *3 Lawrence Parade, Lower Square, Isleworth, Middx* 081-569 8609 or 568 4645

FINDLAY, Brian James. b 42. Wellington Univ (NZ) BA62 MA63 BMus66 Magd Coll Ox MA75. Qu Coll Birm DipTh71. **d** 72 **p** 73. C Deptford St Paul *S'wark* 72-75; Chapl and Dean of Div Magd Coll Ox 75-84; V Tonge Moor *Man* from 84. *St Augustine's Vicarage, Ainsworth Lane, Bolton BL2 2QW* Bolton (0204) 23899

FINDLAYSON, Roy. b 44. Sarum & Wells Th Coll 80. **d** 82 **p** 83. C Benwell St Jas *Newc* 82-83; Hon C 83-85; C Morpeth 85-88; C N Gosforth 88; TV Ch the King in the Dio of Newc from 88. *27 Polwarth Drive, Newcastle upon Tyne NE3 5NH* 091-236 4995

FINDON, John Charles. b 50. Keble Coll Ox BA71 MA75 DPhil79. Ripon Coll Cuddesdon DipTh76. **d** 77 **p** 78. C Middleton *Man* 77-80; Lect Bolton St Pet 80-83; V Astley 83-91; V Baguley from 91. *St John's Vicarage, 186 Brooklands Road, Sale, Cheshire M33 3PB* 061-973 5947

FINK, Kevin Burroughs. b 55. BA77. Episc Th Sch Cam Mass MDiv82. **d** 82 **p** 83. C Pet St Mary *Pet* 82-84; C Addington *Cant* 84; C Addington *S'wark* 85-87; V Riddlesdown 87-90; USA from 91. *c/o Ms K Bryan, PO Box 457, Barstow, California 92311, USA*

FINKENSTAEDT, Harry Seymour. b 23. Yale Univ BA49 Mass Univ MA68. Episc Th Sch Cam Mass BD50. **d** 53 **p** 54. USA 53-71; C Hazlemere *Ox* 71-73; C Huntingdon St Mary w St Benedict *Ely* 73-75; R Castle Camps 75-84; R Shudy Camps 75-84; P-in-c W Wickham 79-84; P-in-c Horseheath 79-81; P-in-c Gt w Lt Stukeley 84-88; rtd 88. *4 The Fairway, Bar Hill, Cambridge CB3 8SR* Crafts Hill (0954) 782224

FINLAY, Hueston Edward. b 64. TCD BA84 BAI85 BTh89. CITC 86. **d** 89. C Kilkenny w Aghour and Kilmanagh *C & O* from 89; Bp Ossory Dom Chapl from 89; Lib and Registrar Kilkenny Cathl from 89; Bp's V Ossory Cathl from 90. *St Canice's Library, Kilkenny, Irish Republic* Kilkenny (56) 61910

FINLAY, Michael Stanley. b 45. N Ord Course 78. **d** 81 **p** 82. C Padgate *Liv* 81-85; V Newton-le-Willows 85-90; V Orford St Marg from 90. *St Margaret's Vicarage, St Margaret's Avenue, Orford, Warrington WA2 8DT* Warrington (0925) 31937

FINLAYSON, Duncan. b 24. **d** 76 **p** 76. NSM Bridge of Allan *St And* from 76; NSM Alloa 77-91. *29 Cawdor Road, Bridge of Allan, Stirling FK9 4JJ* Bridge of Allan (0786) 833074

FINLAYSON, Capt Grantley Adrian. b 55. Wilson Carlile Coll 74 Chich Th Coll 87. **d** 89 **p** 90. C Watford St Mich *St Alb* from 89. *57 Whippendell Road, Watford WD1 7LY* Watford (0923) 248739

FINLINSON, Paul. b 58. St Chad's Coll Dur BA79 St Martin's Coll Lanc PGCE81. Carl Dioc Tr Course 86. **d** 89 **p** 90. NSM Kirkby Lonsdale *Carl* from 89. *21 Lower Abbotsgate, Kirkby Lonsdale, Carnforth, Lancs LA6 2JU* Kirkby Lonsdale (05242) 72491

FINN, Gordon Frederick. b 33. Dur Univ BA60. Ely Th Coll 60. **d** 62 **p** 63. C Kingswinford St Mary *Lich* 62-65; C Northn St Mary *Pet* 65-67; Chapl Barnsley Hall Hosp Bromsgrove 67-71; Chapl Lea Hosp Bromsgrove 67-71; C Swanage *Sarum* 71-73; P-in-c Ford End *Chelmsf* 73-79; V S Shields St Oswin *Dur* from 79. *The Vicarage, St Oswin's Street, South Shields, Tyne & Wear NE33 4SE* 091-455 3072

FINN, Ian Michael. b 58. AKC. Chich Th Coll 81. **d** 82 **p** 83. C Habergham All SS *Blackb* 82-83; C W Burnley 83-85; C Torrisholme 85-87; V Lanc Ch w St Jo and St Anne 87-91; P-in-c Tillingham *Chelmsf* from 91; P-in-c Dengie w Asheldham from 91. *Tillingham Vicarage, Southminster, Essex CM0 7TW* Tillingham (062187) 249

FINN, Miss Sheila. b 30. LMH Ox BA68 MA69. Gilmore Ho 68. **dss** 78 **d** 87. Tettenhall Wood *Lich* 78-86; Dioc Ecum Officer from 86; The Ridwares and Kings Bromley 86-87; Par Dn from 87. *The Rectory, 56 Uttoxeter Road, Hill Ridware, Rugeley, Staffs WS15 3QU* Armitage (0543) 492023

FINNEMORE, Ernest Harold. b 28. Keble Coll Ox BA49 MA53. St Steph Ho Ox 51. **d** 53 **p** 54. V Hanford *Lich* 64-90; rtd 90. *24 Belgrave Road, Newcastle-under-Lyme, Staffs ST5 1LR* Newcastle-under-Lyme (0782) 638179

FINNEMORE, James Christopher. b 59. Pemb Coll Cam BA81 MA85. Coll of Resurr Mirfield. **d** 85 **p** 86. C Manston *Ripon* 85-88; C Hessle *York* from 88. *The Clergy House, 167 First Lane, Hessle, N Humberside HU13 9EY* Hull (0482) 642169

FINNEY, Canon Charles William. b 27. **d** 59 **p** 60. C Dunleckney *C & O* 59-62; I Abbeyleix 62-72; I Clonsast w Rathangan, Thomastown etc *M & K* 72-86; RD Kildare, Edenderry, Naas and Newbridge 75-76; Treas Kildare Cathl 76-79; Adn Kildare 79-86; I Clara w Liss, Ardnurcher and Moate from 86; Can Meath from 87. *The Rectory, Clara, Co Offaly, Irish Republic* Clara (506) 31406

FINNEY, David. b 41. St Mich Coll Llan 68. **d** 70 **p** 71. C Wythenshawe Wm Temple Ch *Man* 70-73; C Bedf Leigh 73-75; V Royton St Anne 75-81; V Dearnley from 81. *The Vicarage, Arm Road, Littleborough, Lancs OL15 8NJ* Littleborough (0706) 78466

FINNEY, Canon Fred. b 17. Bris Univ BA38 DipEd39. Wycliffe Hall Ox 61. **d** 62 **p** 63. V Ashton-in-Makerfield

St Thos *Liv* 66-86; Hon Can Liv Cathl 83-86; rtd 86; Perm to Offic Blackb & Liv from 86. *1 Howard Drive, Tarleton, Preston PR4 6DA* Hesketh Bank (0772) 812598

FINNEY, Canon John Thomas. b 27. Sheff Univ BA51 DipEd52. Ripon Hall Ox 60. **d** 62 **p** 63. C Leigh St Mary *Man* 62-65; V from 83; V Peel 65-69; Chapl Hockerill Coll Bishop's Stortford 69-74; V Astley *Man* 74-83; AD Leigh from 85; Hon Can Man Cathl from 87. *The Vicarage, Vicarage Square, Leigh, Lancs WN7 1YD* Leigh (0942) 673546

FINNEY, Canon John Thornley. b 32. Hertf Coll Ox BA55 DipTh57. Wycliffe Hall Ox. **d** 58 **p** 59. C Highfield *Ox* 58-61; C Weston Turville 61-65; R Tollerton *S'well* 65-71; V Aspley 71-80; Bp's Adv on Evang 80-89; Hon Can S'well Minster from 84; Officer for Decade of Evang Ch Ho Westmr from 90. *c/o Church House, Great Smith Street, London SW1P 3NZ* 071-222 9011

FINNEY, Melva Kathleen. b 24. LTh71. Gilmore Ho 55. **dss** 56 **d** 78. E Dulwich St Jo *S'wark* 56-59; New Zealand from 61; rtd 84. *22 Gunn's Crescent, Christchurch 2, New Zealand* Christchurch (3) 332-7100

FINNIE, Robert. **d** 84 **p** 84. NSM Aber St Andr *Ab* from 84; NSM Aber St Ninian from 84. *10 Cairngorm Crescent, Aberdeen AB1 5BL* Aberdeen (0224) 874669

FINNIMORE, Keith Anthony. b 36. **d** 60 **p** 61. C Wanstead H Trin Hermon Hill *Chelmsf* 60-63; C Kingswood *S'wark* 63-65; V Bolney *Chich* 65-67; V Elmstead *Chelmsf* 67-73; R Pentlow, Foxearth, Liston and Borley 73-77. *New House, Quaker Lane, Beyton, Bury St Edmunds, Suffolk IP30 9AN* Beyton (0359) 71097

FIRMIN, Mrs Dorrie Eleanor Frances. b 19. **d** 88. NSM Ellon *Ab* from 88; NSM Cruden from 88. *North Burnside of Schivas, Ythanbank, Ellon, Aberdeenshire AB4 0TY* Schivas (03587) 301

FIRMIN, Paul Gregory. b 57. ACIB80. Trin Coll Bris BA87. **d** 87 **p** 88. C Swindon Ch Ch *Bris* 87-91; V Shrewsbury H Trin w St Julian *Lich* from 91. *Holy Trinity Vicarage, Greyfriars Road, Shrewsbury SY3 7EP* Shrewsbury (0743) 232158

FIRMSTONE, Ian Harry. b 44. Qu Coll Birm. **d** 82 **p** 83. C Warminster St Denys *Sarum* 82-84; C N Stoneham *Win* 84-88; R Freemantle 88-90; V Littleport *Ely* from 90. *St George's Vicarage, 30 Church Lane, Littleport, Ely, Cambs CB6 1PS* Ely (0353) 860207

FIRTH, Barry. b 37. ACA60 FCA71. NW Ord Course 74. **d** 77 **p** 78. NSM Brighouse *Wakef* 77-81; P-in-c Batley St Thos 81-85; V 85-88; V Rastrick St Matt from 88. *St Matthew's Vicarage, 1 Vicarage Gardens, Ogden Lane, Brighouse, W Yorkshire HD6 3HD* Brighouse (0484) 713386

FIRTH, Christopher John Kingsley. b 37. Llan St Mich DipTh66. **d** 66 **p** 67. C Sutton in Ashfield St Mary *S'well* 66-70; V Langold 70-74; C Falmouth K Chas *Truro* 74-77; P-in-c Mabe 77-81; V from 81; RD Carnmarth S from 90. *The Vicarage, Church Road, Mabe, Penryn, Cornwall TR10 9HN* Falmouth (0326) 73201

FIRTH, Cyril Bruce. b 05. Fitzw Ho Cam BA28 MA32. Cheshunt Coll Cam 25. **d** 65 **p** 66. Asia Sec Conf of Miss Socs of GB & Ireland 65-74; Hon C Wellow *Win* 65-88; rtd 88. *Steplake Cottage, Sherfield English, Romsey, Hants SO51 6EP* West Wellow (0794) 22563

FIRTH, George Cuthbert. b 19. Keble Coll Ox BA41 MA45. Lich Th Coll 41. **d** 43 **p** 44. Chapl to the Deaf *Lich* 66-71; P-in-c Patshull 71-73; Lic to Offic *Ex* 74-84; Chapl to the Deaf 74-84; rtd 84. *18 Sydney Road, Exeter EX2 9AH* Exeter (0392) 75568

FIRTH, Graham Alfred. b 38. Man Univ BA60. Ripon Hall Ox. **d** 62 **p** 63. C Norton Woodseats St Paul *Sheff* 62-65; C-in-c Kimberworth Park CD 65-69; V Kimberworth Park 69-71; P-in-c Egmanton *S'well* 71-77; P-in-c Laxton 71-77; V Sibthorpe from 77; R Elston w Elston Chapelry from 77; R E Stoke w Syerston from 77. *The Rectory, Top Street, Elston, Newark, Notts NG23 5PC* East Stoke (0636) 525383

✠**FIRTH, Rt Rev Peter James.** b 29. Em Coll Cam BA52 MA63. St Steph Ho Ox 53. **d** 55 **p** 56 **c** 83. C Barbourne *Worc* 55-58; C Malvern Link St Matthias 58-62; R Abbey Hey *Man* 62-66; Asst Network Relig Broadcasting BBC Man 66-67; Sen Producer/Org Relig Progr TV & Radio BBC Bris 67-83; Hon Can Bris Cathl *Bris* 74-83; Suff Bp Malmesbury from 83; Angl Adv HTV West from 84. *7 Ivywell Road, Bristol BS9 1NX* Bristol (0272) 685931

FIRTH, Ronald Mahlon. b 22. Linc Th Coll 60. **d** 61 **p** 62. V York St Thos w St Maurice *York* 66-73; V Marton-in-Cleveland 73-87; rtd 87. *24 Whenby Grove, Huntington, York YO3 9DS* York (0904) 634531

FISH, Winthrop. b 40. Dalhousie Univ Canada BA63 BEd Birm Univ BPhil76 MEd78. K Coll (NS) 62. **d** 64 **p** 65. Canada 64-74; Perm to Offic *Birm* 74-77; Asst Chapl Solihull Sch W Midl 77-79; Chapl Wroxall Abbey Sch 79-82; C Newquay *Truro* 82-84; V Highertown and Baldhu 84-89; P-in-c Newlyn St Newlyn from 89; Dioc Children's Adv from 89. *The Vicarage, Newlyn East, Newquay, Cornwall TR8 5LJ* Mitchell (0872) 510383

FISHER, Adrian Charles Proctor. b 24. TCD BA48 MA62. TCD Div Sch Div Test47. **d** 49 **p** 50. C Carlow *C & O* 49-52; C Tintern 49-52; C Killesk 49-52; CF 52-57 and 62-69; I Fethard w Killesk, Tintern and Templetown *C & O* 57-62; P-in-c N Stoke w Mongewell and Ipsden *Ox* 70-83; V from 83; Chapl Oratory Prep Sch 73-80. *The Vicarage, North Stoke, Oxford OX10 6BG* Wallingford (0491) 35077

FISHER, Eric William. b 30. Birm Univ BA53. Coll of Resurr Mirfield 70. **d** 72 **p** 73. C Styvechale *Cov* 72-75; C Chesterfield All SS *Derby* 75-78; Chapl Buxton Hosps 78-84; TV Buxton w Burbage and King Sterndale *Derby* 78-84; R Shirland 84-89; V Sheff St Matt *Sheff* from 89. *St Matthew's Vicarage, 5 Broomgrove Crescent, Sheffield S10 2LQ* Sheffield (0742) 662299

FISHER, Ernest George Reginald. b 15. St Aid Birkenhead 66. **d** 68 **p** 69. C Brampton St Thos *Derby* 68-71; P-in-c Langley Mill 71-79; rtd 79; Perm to Offic *Newc* 79-86; *Derby* from 86. *54 Linnet House, Old Whittington, Chesterfield, Derbyshire S41 9LQ* Chesterfield (0246) 453775

FISHER, Ernest William. b 32. St Jo Coll Dur BA56 DipTh58. Cranmer Hall Dur 58. **d** 58 **p** 59. Hong Kong 58-70 and 71-84; C Whiston *Sheff* 70-71; V Malew *S & M* from 84. *Malew Vicarage, St Mark's Road, Ballasalla, Isle of Man* Castletown (0624) 822469

FISHER, George Arnold. b 54. Lon Univ BD75. N Ord Course 81. **d** 84 **p** 85. C Conisbrough *Sheff* from 84. *4 Grasmere Road, Conisbrough, Doncaster, S Yorkshire DN12 3HT* Rotherham (0709) 864911

FISHER, Gordon. b 44. NW Ord Course 74. **d** 77 **p** 78. NSM Airedale w Fryston *Wakef* 77-81; C Barkisland w W Scammonden 81-84; C Ripponden 81-84; V Sutton St Mich *York* 84-87; V Marton-in-Cleveland from 87. *The Vicarage, Stokesley Road, Marton-in-Cleveland, Middlesbrough TS7 8JU* Middlesbrough (0642) 316201

FISHER, Henry John. b 25. Lich Th Coll 64. **d** 66 **p** 67. C Kings Norton *Birm* 66-70; C Weston-super-Mare St Jo *B & W* 70-75; C Weston-super-Mare H Trin 72-75; P-in-c Leigh upon Mendip 75-78; P-in-c Stoke St Michael 75-78; P-in-c Leigh upon Mendip w Stoke St Michael 78-80; C Wilton 80-88; C Street w Walton 88-90; rtd 90. *18 Hawker's Lane, Wells, Somerset BA5 3JL* Street (0458) 42044

FISHER, Humphrey John. b 33. **d** 91. NSM Bryngwyn and Newchurch and Llanbedr etc *S & B* from 91. *Rose Cottage, Newchurch, Kington, Hereford HR5 3QF* Kington (0544) 22632

FISHER, Ian St John. b 59. Down Coll Cam BA80 MA84 Leic Univ PhD84. St Steph Ho Ox BA88. **d** 88 **p** 89. C Colwall w Upper Colwall and Coddington *Heref* from 88. *5 Stone Close, Colwall, Worcs WR13 6QZ* Malvern (0684) 540782

FISHER, James Atherton. b 09. SS Coll Cam BA32 MA45. Cuddesdon Coll 32. **d** 33 **p** 34. Can and Treas Windsor 58-78; rtd 78. *32 High Lawn, Devizes, Wilts SN10 2BA* Devizes (0380) 4254

FISHER, James Victor. b 35. Sarum & Wells Th Coll 75. **d** 77 **p** 78. C Corsham *Bris* 77-79; C Gtr Corsham 79-80; C Bris Ch the Servant Stockwood 80-84; C Swindon Ch Ch 84-87; Lic to Offic 88-89; C Warmley 89-90; rtd 90. *Spring House, Spring Street, Bristol BS3 4PX*

FISHER, John Bertie. b 15. TCD BA36 BD44. CITC 39. **d** 39 **p** 40. I Kilternan *D & G* 51-83; rtd 83. *21 Rathdown Park, Greystones, Co Wicklow* Dublin (1) 287-4904

FISHER, Canon John Douglas Close. b 09. SS Coll Cam BA31 MA47 BD66. Lich Th Coll 36. **d** 38 **p** 39. Can and Preb Chich Cathl *Chich* 66-84; V Cuckfield 67-77; rtd 77; P-in-c Hove St Jo *Chich* 77-81. *Flat 2, 10 Brunswick Square, Hove, E Sussex BN3 1EG* Brighton (0273) 738080

FISHER, Canon John Howard Warren. b 05. Univ Coll Dur LTh30. St Aug Coll Cant. **d** 30 **p** 31. Hon Can Glouc Cathl *Glouc* from 53; V Rangeworthy 67-75; rtd 75. *Greenacres, Church Lane, Rockhampton, Berkeley, Glos GL13 9DX* Falfield (0454) 260470

FISHER, John Victor. b 33. Brasted Th Coll 64 Coll of Resurr Mirfield 66. **d** 68 **p** 69. C Stepney St Dunstan and All SS *Lon* 68-71; C E Ham w Upton Park *Chelmsf* 71-73; P-in-c Becontree St Pet 73-82; V Barkingside St

Geo from 82. *St George's Vicarage, Woodford Avenue, Ilford, Essex IG2 6XQ* 081-550 4149

FISHER, Kenneth Francis McConnell. b 36. K Coll Lon 57. **d** 61 **p** 62. C Sheff St Geo and St Steph *Sheff* 61-63; Chapl Sheff Univ 64-69; Chapl Lon Univ *Lon* 69-75; P-in-c Dean *Carl* 75-80; Soc Resp Officer 75-80; TR Melksham *Sarum* 80-90; P-in-c Stapleford *Ely* from 90; Dioc Ecum Officer from 90. *Stapleford Vicarage, Cambridge CB2 5BG* Cambridge (0223) 842150

FISHER, Canon Michael Harry. b 39. Ex Univ BA61. St Steph Ho Ox 61. **d** 63 **p** 64. C Wolv St Pet *Lich* 63-67; C Newquay *Truro* 67-70; V Newlyn St Pet 70-75; P-in-c Launceston St Steph w St Thos 75-82; V Carbis Bay w Lelant from 82; Hon Can Truro Cathl from 85; RD Penwith from 88. *The Vicarage, Porthrepta Road, Carbis Bay, St Ives, Cornwall TR26 2LD* Penzance (0736) 796206

FISHER, Michael John. b 43. Leic Univ BA64 Keele Univ MA67. Qu Coll Birm 75. **d** 78 **p** 79. NSM Stafford St Mary and St Chad *Lich* 78-79; NSM Stafford from 79. *35 Newland Avenue, Stafford ST16 1NL* Stafford (0785) 45069

FISHER, Paul Vincent. b 43. ARCM73 Worc Coll Ox BA66 MA70. Qu Coll Birm DipTh68. **d** 70 **p** 71. C Redditch St Steph *Worc* 70-73; C Chorlton upon Medlock *Man* 73-79; Chapl Man Univ 73-79; Exec Sec Community Affairs Division BCC 79-81; Asst Dir of Tr and Dir of Lay Tr *Carl* 81-86; P-in-c Raughton Head w Gatesgill 81-85; Lay Tr Officer *S'wark* 86-90; Dir of Tr from 90. *474 Merton Road, London SW18 5AE* 081-870 4623

FISHER, Peter Francis Templar. b 36. CCC Cam BA60 MA. Wells Th Coll 62. **d** 63 **p** 64. C Gt Ilford St Mary *Chelmsf* 63-67; C Colchester St Mary V 67-70; C-in-c Basildon St Andr CD 70-72; P-in-c Edstaston *Lich* 83-87; P-in-c Whixall 83-87; P-in-c Tilstock 84-87; V Oxon and Shelton from 87. *The Vicarage, Shelton Gardens, Bicton, Shrewsbury SY3 8DJ* Shrewsbury (0743) 52774

FISHER, Peter Timothy. b 44. Dur Univ BA68 MA75. Cuddesdon Coll 68. **d** 70 **p** 71. C Bedf St Andr *St Alb* 70-74; Chapl Surrey Univ *Guildf* 74-78; Sub-Warden Linc Th Coll 78-83; R Houghton le Spring *Dur* from 83; RD Houghton from 87. *The Rectory, Dairy Lane, Houghton le Spring, Tyne & Wear DH4 5PR* 091-584 2198

✠**FISHER, Rt Rev Reginald Lindsay (Brother Michael).** b 18. Lambeth MA78 Westcott Ho Cam 51. **d** 53 **p** 54 **c** 79. SSF from 42; Lic to Offic *Ely* 53-62; Newc 62-67; Sarum 67-79; Suff Bp St Germans *Truro* 79-85; Bp HM Pris 85; Min Gen SSF 85-91; rtd 85; Asst Bp Ely from 85. *15 Botolph Lane, Cambridge CB2 3RD* Cambridge (0223) 321576

FISHER, Richard John. b 60. K Coll Lon BA82 AKC82 Selw Coll Cam BA87. Ridley Hall Cam 85. **d** 88 **p** 89. C Woodley *Ox* from 88. *8 Caldbeck Drive, Woodley, Reading RG5 4LA* Reading (0734) 696605

FISHER, Roy Percy. b 22. Lon Univ TCert49. Linc Th Coll 51. **d** 53 **p** 54. V Westgate-on-Sea St Sav *Cant* 66-71; R Staplegrove *B & W* 71-79; TR Eckington w Handley and Ridgeway *Derby* 79-87; rtd 87. *258 New Road, Porthcawl, M Glam CF36 5BA* Porthcawl (065671) 8682

FISHER, Stephen Newson. b 46. CEng82 MIEE82 Univ of Wales (Swansea) BSc67. Linc Th Coll 84. **d** 86 **p** 87. C Nunthorpe *York* 86-89; P-in-c Middlesb St Oswald 89-90; V from 90. *St Oswald's Vicarage, Lambton Road, Middlesbrough, Cleveland TS4 2RG* Middlesbrough (0642) 816156

FISHER, Thomas Andrew. b 35. Sarum & Wells Th Coll 84. **d** 86 **p** 87. C Win Ch Ch *Win* 86-89; Chapl Salisbury Coll of Tech *Sarum* from 89; Chapl Salisbury Coll of FE from 89. *7 Empire Road, Salisbury SP2 9DE* Salisbury (0722) 335155

FISHER, Thomas Ruggles. b 20. Cranmer Hall Dur 58. **d** 60 **p** 61. R Husbands Bosworth *Leic* 63-74; R Husbands Bosworth w Mowsley and Knaptoft 74-79; R Husbands Bosworth w Mowsley and Knaptoft etc 79-82; Perm to Offic Leic from 82; Pet from 83; rtd 85. *12 The Dell, Oakham, Leics LE15 6JG* Oakham (0572) 757630

FISHWICK, Alan. b 48. Chich Th Coll 87. **d** 89 **p** 90. C Laneside *Blackb* from 89. *25 Pine Street, Haslingden, Rossendale, Lancs BB4 5ND* Rossendale (0706) 214245

FISHWICK, Ian Norman. b 54. Lanc Univ BEd. St Jo Coll Nottm DipTh. **d** 82 **p** 83. C High Wycombe *Ox* 82-87; V Walshaw Ch Ch *Man* from 87; Area Voc Adv from 88. *37 Gisburn Drive, Walshaw, Bury, Lancs BL8 3DH* 061-763 1193

FISK, Paul. b 35. St Jo Coll Cam BA60 MA64. Wells Th Coll 60. **d** 62 **p** 63. C Ipswich H Trin *St E* 62-65; C

Wrentham w Benacre, Covehithe and Henstead 65-67; R Copdock w Washbrook and Belstead 67-73; R Brantham 73-75; RD Samford 73-75; TV Old Brumby *Linc* 85-88; W Germany 88-90; Germany from 90. *Erzburgerstrasse 9, D-6540, Hanau 1, Germany*

FISK, Canon William Ernest Gyde. b 09. TD51. Linc Th Coll. **d** 47 **p** 48. Chapl HM Pris Sudbury 59-77; R Sudbury and Somersal Herbert *Derby* 59-77; Hon Can Derby Cathl 68-77; rtd 77; Perm to Offic *Derby* from 77. *Woodlea, 17 Chestnut Grove, Etwall, Derby DE6 6NG* Etwall (028373) 3272

FISKE, Eben Horsford. b 10. Harvard Univ AB35 Trin Coll Cam BA37 MA42. Cuddesdon Coll 38. **d** 40 **p** 41. P-in-c Kinsley *Wakef* 58-85; rtd 85; Perm to Offic *Wakef* from 85. *Park Croft, Pontefract Road, Ackworth, Pontefract, W Yorkshire WF7 7EU* Pontefract (0977) 709114

FISKE, Paul Francis Brading. b 45. St Jo Coll Dur BA68 PhD72. Wycliffe Hall Ox DipTh72. **d** 73 **p** 74. C Sutton *Liv* 73-76; TV Cheltenham St Mary, St Matt, St Paul and H Trin *Glouc* 76-80; C-in-c Hartplain CD *Portsm* 80-84; Hd of Miss UK CMJ 84-86; Hon C Edgware *Lon* 84-86; R Broughton Gifford, Gt Chalfield and Holt *Sarum* from 86. *The Rectory, Holt, Trowbridge, Wilts BA14 6PZ* Trowbridge (0225) 782289

FISON, Geoffrey Robert Martius. b 34. Dur Univ BA59. Ely Th Coll 59. **d** 61 **p** 62. C Heavitree *Ex* 61-64; Australia 64-69; BSB 64-69; C Southn Maybush St Pet *Win* 70-73; TV Strood *Roch* 73-79; TV Swindon Dorcan *Bris* 79-83; P-in-c Brislington St Cuth from 83. *St Cuthbert's Vicarage, 35 Wick Crescent, Bristol BS4 4HG* Bristol (0272) 776351

FITCH, Canon John Ambrose. b 22. CCC Cam BA44 MA48. Wells Th Coll 45. **d** 47 **p** 48. V Reydon *St E* 51-70; R Brandon and Santon Downham 70-80; Hon Can St E Cathl 75-87; RD Mildenhall 78-80; R Monks Eleigh w Chelsworth and Brent Eleigh etc 80-87; rtd 87; Perm to Offic *St E* and *Chelmsf* from 87. *The Oak House, High Street, Great Yeldham, Halstead, Essex CO9 4EX* Great Yeldham (0787) 237058

FITZ, Lionel Alfred. b 24. **d** 87 **p** 88. NSM Cheltenham St Mary, St Matt, St Paul and H Trin *Glouc* from 87. *9 Foxgrove Drive, Cheltenham, Glos GL52 6TQ* Cheltenham (0242) 43405

FITZGERALD, Gerald O'Connell. b 07. K Coll Cam BA29 MA33. Ely Th Coll 29. **d** 30 **p** 31. V Highgate St Aug *Lon* 52-70; rtd 72; Perm to Offic *Chich* from 73. *Flat 3, 41 Ventnor Villas, Hove, E Sussex BN3 3DA* Brighton (0273) 772249

FITZGERALD, John Edward. b 44. Oak Hill Th Coll 74. **d** 76 **p** 77. C Rainham *Chelmsf* 76-79; C Cam St Andr Less *Ely* 79-86; V Holmesfield *Derby* 86-88; Chapl HM Pris Wakef 88-90; Chapl HM Pris Nottm from 90. *The Chaplaincy Office, HM Prison Nottingham, Perry Road, Sherwood, Nottingham NG5 3AG* Nottingham (0602) 625022

FITZGERALD, Thomas Martin William. b 30. Trin Coll Bris 72. **d** 72 **p** 73. C Stapleton *Bris* 72-75; C Gt Yarmouth *Nor* 75-77; Perm to Offic 77-79; P-in-c Forncett St Mary w St Pet 79-81; P-in-c Flordon w Hapton 79-81; P-in-c Tasburgh 79-81; P-in-c Tharston 79-81; Kenya from 81. *Address temp unknown*

FITZGIBBON, Kevin Peter. b 49. St Jo Coll Nottm BTh81. **d** 81 **p** 82. C Corby St Columba *Pet* 81-85; V Newborough from 85. *The Vicarage, Newborough, Peterborough PE6 7QZ* Peterborough (0733) 810682

FITZHARRIS, Barry. b 47. Lon Univ BA69 W Ontario Univ MA70 K Coll Lon BD72 AKC72. St Aug Coll Cant 72. **d** 73 **p** 74. C Whitstable All SS *Cant* 73-75; C Whitstable All SS w St Pet 75-76; Hon C Clapham Old Town S'wark 77-79; Asst Chapl Abp Tenison Gr Sch Kennington 78-84; Hd of Relig Studies from 87; Hon C Streatham Ch Ch *S'wark* 80-84; R Radwinter w Hempstead *Chelmsf* 84-87. *The Chaplain's Office, Archbishop Tenison's School, London* 071-735 4070

FITZHARRIS, Robert Aidan. b 46. Sheff Univ BDS71. Linc Th Coll 87. **d** 89 **p** 90. C Dinnington *Sheff* from 89. *32 Shakespeare Drive, Dinnington, Sheffield S31 7RP* Dinnington (0909) 563682

FITZSIMONS, Mrs Kathryn Anne. b 57. Bedf Coll of Educn CertEd78. NE Ord Course 87. **d** 90. NSM Bilton *Ripon* from 90. *17 Strawberry Dale Avenue, Harrogate, N Yorkshire HG1 5EA* Harrogate (0423) 563074

FITZWILLIAMS, Canon Mark Morshead. b 36. Trin Coll Cam BA59 MA64. Westcott Ho Cam 59. **d** 61 **p** 62. C St Jo Wood *Lon* 61-64; C Hempnall *Nor* 64-70; R Lathbury *Ox* 70-78; R Newport Pagnell 70-78; RD Newport 73-78; TR Beaconsfield from 78; RD Amersham 82-86; Hon Can Ch Ch from 88. *The Rectory, Wycombe End, Beaconsfield, Bucks HP9 1NB* Beaconsfield (0494) 673949

FLACK, Canon John Robert. b 42. Leeds Univ BA64. Coll of Resurr Mirfield 64. **d** 66 **p** 67. C Armley St Bart *Ripon* 66-69; C Northn St Mary *Pet* 69-72; V Chapelthorpe *Wakef* 72-81; V Ripponden 81-85; V Barkisland w W Scammonden 81-85; V Brighouse 85-88; TR from 88; RD Brighouse and Elland from 86; Hon Can Wakef Cathl from 89. *The Vicarage, 11 Slead Avenue, Brighouse, W Yorkshire HD6 2JB* Brighouse (0484) 714032

FLAGG, David Michael. b 50. CCC Cam BA71 MA75 Nottm Univ BA76. St Jo Coll Nottm 74. **d** 77 **p** 78. C Hollington St Leon *Chich* 77-80; C Woodley *Ox* 80-86; Chapl The Dorothy Kerin Trust Burrswood from 86. *The Chaplain's House, Burrswood, Groombridge, Tunbridge Wells, Kent TN3 9PY* Tunbridge Wells (0892) 864459

✠FLAGG, Rt Rev John William Hawkins. b 29. **d** 59 **p** 61 **c** 69. Paraguay 59-63; Argentina 64-73; Adn N Argentina 65-69; Bp Paraguay and N Argentina 69-73; Asst Bp Chile 73-77; Bp Peru 73-77; Asst Bp Liv 78-86; V Toxteth St Cypr w Ch Ch 78-85; P-in-c Litherland Ch Ch 85-86; Gen Sec SAMS from 86; Asst Bp Roch from 87. *Allen Gardiner House, Pembury Road, Tunbridge Wells TN2 3QU* Tunbridge Wells (0892) 38647/8

FLAHERTY, Alan Thomas. b 45. N Ord Course 85. **d** 88 **p** 89. NSM Howe Bridge *Man* 88-90; C from 90. *18 Car Bank Square, Atherton, Manchester M29 9WH* Atherton (0942) 878300

FLATHER, Peter George. b 29. Sarum Th Coll. **d** 59 **p** 60. R E w W Bradenham *Nor* 65-72; P-in-c Speke All SS *Liv* 72-73; P-in-c Sharrington *Nor* 73-87; R Gunthorpe w Bale 73-87; P-in-c Gt w Lt Snoring 77-83; R Gunthorpe w Bale w Field Dalling, Saxlingham etc 87-89; rtd 89. *29 Jannys Close, Aylsham, Norwich NR11 6DL* Aylsham (0263) 733548

FLATMAN, Martin Edward. b 46. Hull Univ BA68. Cuddesdon Coll 69. **d** 71 **p** 72. C Reading St Giles *Ox* 71-75; TV Newbury 75-82; V Cowley St Jo from 82. *The Vicarage, 271 Cowley Road, Oxford OX4 2AJ* Oxford (0865) 242396

FLATT, Donald Clifford. b 15. Worc Ord Coll 63. **d** 65 **p** 66. V Wigginton *St Alb* 67-75; Chapl HM Pris Bedf 75-80; V Biddenham *St Alb* 75-82; rtd 83; P-in-c Oare w Culbone *B & W* 83-86; Perm to Offic from 86. *8 Brushford, Dulverton, Somerset TA22 9AP* Dulverton (0398) 23088

FLATT, Roy Francis Ferguson. b 47. Edin Th Coll 78. **d** 80 **p** 81. C St Andrews St Andr *St And* 80-82; C Elie and Earlsferry 80-82; C Pittenweem 80-82; Dioc Supernumerary 82-83; R Kilmartin *Arg* from 83; Dioc Sec 83-87; Dioc Youth Chapl from 83; R Lochgilphead from 83; R Inveraray 83-90. *Bishopton, Bishopton Road, Lochgilphead, Argyll PA31 8PY* Lochgilphead (0546) 2315

FLATTERS, Clive Andrew. b 56. Sarum & Wells Th Coll 83. **d** 86 **p** 88. C Weston Favell *Pet* 86-87; C Old Brumby *Linc* 88-91; C Syston *Leic* from 91. *The Vicarage, Barkby, Leicester LE7 8QD* Leicester (0533) 695539

FLAVELL, Paul William Deran. b 44. Univ of Wales (Ban) DipTh66. St Mich Coll Llan 67. **d** 68 **p** 69. Australia 68-71; C Blaenavon w Capel Newydd *Mon* 71-74; V Ynysddu 74-84; R Llanaber w Caerdeon *Ban* from 84. *The Rectory, Mynach Road, Barmouth, Gwynedd LL42 1RL* Barmouth (0341) 280516

FLEET, Daniel James Russell. b 60. Wye Coll Lon BSc84. St Jo Coll Nottm LTh88 DPS89. **d** 89 **p** 90. C Boldmere *Birm* from 89. *46 Redacre Road, Sutton Coldfield, W Midlands B73 5EA* 021-354 8432

FLEETWOOD, John Arnold. b 10. K Coll Lon BD39 AKC39. **d** 39 **p** 40. V Canvey Is *Chelmsf* 57-73; R Kelvedon Hatch 73-78; V Navestock 73-78; rtd 78. *15 Orchard Piece, Blackmore, Ingatestone, Essex CM4 0RX* Blackmore (0277) 822683

FLEMING, Ven David. b 37. Kelham Th Coll 58. **d** 63 **p** 64. C Walton St Marg Belmont Road *Liv* 63-67; Chapl HM Borstal Gaynes Hall 68-76; V Gt Staughton *Ely* 68-76; RD St Neots 72-76; V Whittlesey 76-85; RD March 77-82; Hon Can Ely Cathl from 82; P-in-c Ponds Bridge 83-85; Adn Wisbech from 84; V Wisbech St Mary 85-89. *20 Barton Road, Ely, Cambs CB7 4DE* Ely (0353) 663632

FLEMING, George. b 39. IDC. CITC. **d** 78 **p** 79. C Donaghcloney w Waringstown *D & D* 78-80; C Newtownards 80; I Movilla 80; C Heref St Pet w St Owen and St Jas *Heref* 80-85; V Holmer w Huntington from 85. *The Vicarage, Holmer, Hereford HR4 9RG* Hereford (0432) 273200

FLEMING, Very Rev John Robert William. b 07. TCD BA30 MA33 Lon Univ BD63. CITC 40. d 40 p 41. Dean Ross *C, C & R* 78-82; rtd 82. *Ballyvoskillakeen House, Fermoy, Co Cork, Irish Republic* Fermoy (25) 31745

FLEMING, Mrs Penelope Rawling. b 43. Glas Univ MA63. Westcott Ho Cam 87. d 89. C Bourne *Guildf* from 89. *64 Weydon Hill Road, Farnham, Surrey GU9 8NY* Farnham (0252) 715250

FLEMING, Ronald Thorpe. b 29. Codrington Coll Barbados. d 56 p 57. Barbados 56-61; C Delaval *Newc* 61-64; V Cambois 64-69; V Ancroft w Scremerston 69-81; V Longhirst 81-84; Chapl N Tyneside Hosps and Preston R Hosp from 84; Lic to Offic *Newc* from 84. *18 Holly Avenue, Whitley Bay, Tyne & Wear NE26 1ED* 091-252 7414

FLEMING, Canon William Edward Charlton. b 29. TCD BA51 MA65. CITC 52. d 52 p 53. C Dub Santry *D & G* 52-56; C Arm St Mark *Arm* 56-61; I Tartaraghan 61-80; Prov Registrar from 79; I Tartaraghan w Diamond from 80; Can Arm Cathl from 86; Treas from 88. *The Rectory, 5 Tarthlogue Road, Portadown, Co Armagh BT62 1RB* Annaghmore (0762) 851289

FLENLEY, Benjamin Robert Glanville. b 50. Sarum & Wells Th Coll 86. d 88 p 89. C Eastleigh *Win* from 88. *St Francis House, Nightingale Avenue, Eastleigh, Hants SO5 3JB* Eastleigh (0703) 619949

FLETCHER, Albert Reginald. b 20. Leeds Univ BA50. d 51 p 52. V Whyteleafe *S'wark* 63-85; rtd 85. *2 Dharma Court, East Hill Road, Oxted, Surrey RH8 9HZ* Oxted (0883) 715061

FLETCHER, Anthony Peter Reeves. b 46. Bede Coll Dur CertEd Nottm Univ BTh78. Kelham Th Coll 63 Ridley Hall Cam DPT. d 74 p 75. C Luton St Mary *St Alb* 74-78; Chapl RAF from 78. *c/o MOD, Adastral House, Theobald's Road, London WC1X 8RU* 071-430 7268

FLETCHER, Arthur William George. b 24. Leeds Univ BA50. Coll of Resurr Mirfield 50. d 52 p 53. Chapl RAF 61-72; R Challoch w Newton Stewart *Glas* 73-75; R Kilmacolm 75-82; R Bridge of Weir 75-82; R Largs 82-89; rtd 89; Perm to Offic *Glas* from 89. *Westhaven, Main Road, Inverkip, Greenock, Renfrewshire PA16 0EA* Wemyss Bay (0475) 521611

FLETCHER, Dr Christopher Ian. b 43. BSc PhD. Glouc Sch of Min. d 89 p 90. C Tenbury *Heref* from 89. *23 Castle Close, Burford, Tenbury Wells, Worcs WR15 8AY* Tenbury Wells (0584) 811975

FLETCHER, Colin John. b 46. Chich Th Coll. d 83 p 84. C Lt Ilford St Mich *Chelmsf* 83-86; C Hockerill *St Alb* 86-89; V New Cantley *Sheff* from 89. *St Hugh's House, Levet Road, Cantley, Doncaster, S Yorkshire DN4 6JQ* Doncaster (0302) 535739

FLETCHER, Colin William. b 50. Trin Coll Ox BA72 MA76. Wycliffe Hall Ox 72. d 75 p 76. C Shipley St Pet *Bradf* 75-79; Tutor Wycliffe Hall Ox 79-84; Hon C Ox St Andr *Ox* 79-84; V Margate H Trin *Cant* from 84; RD Thanet from 88. *The Vicarage, 5 Offley Close, Northdown Park Road, Margate, Kent CT9 3UT* Thanet (0843) 224037 or 294137

FLETCHER, David Clare Molyneux. b 32. Worc Coll Ox BA55 MA59 DipTh56. Wycliffe Hall Ox 56. d 58 p 59. C Islington St Mary *Lon* 58-62; Hon C 62-83; Field Worker Scripture Union 62-86; Lic to Offic *St Alb* 83-86; R Ox St Ebbe w H Trin and St Pet *Ox* from 86. *St Ebbe's Rectory, 2 Roger Bacon Lane, Oxford OX1 1QE* Oxford (0865) 248154

FLETCHER, David Mark. b 56. Chich Th Coll 84. d 87 p 88. C Taunton St Andr *B & W* 87-91; P-in-c Chard, Furnham w Chaffcombe, Knowle St Giles etc from 91. *Furnham Rectory, Furnham Road, Chard, Somerset TA20 1AE* Chard (0460) 63167

FLETCHER, Douglas. b 40. Coll of Resurr Mirfield 67. d 68 p 69. C Notting Hill St Jo *Lon* 68-73; C Cam St Mary Less *Ely* 73-74; C Fulham St Jo Walham Green *Lon* 74-76; C Walham Green St Jo w St Jas 76-84; P-in-c Kensal Town St Thos w St Andr and St Phil from 84. *St Thomas's Vicarage, 231 Kensal Road, London W10 5DB* 081-960 3703

FLETCHER, Francis Cecil. b 12. Clifton Th Coll 33. d 36 p 38. V Weston upon Trent *Lich* 66-75; rtd 77. *243 Congleton Road, Biddulph, Stoke-on-Trent ST8 7RQ*

FLETCHER, George Henry Yorke. b 11. Wycliffe Hall Ox 58. d 59 p 60. V Hall Green St Pet *Birm* 67-75; V Clive w Grinshill *Lich* 75-80; rtd 80; Perm to Offic *Lich* from 80. *4 Croft Close, Bomere Heath, Shrewsbury SY4 3PZ* Bomere Heath (0939) 290337

FLETCHER, Gordon Wolfe. b 31. Edin Th Coll. d 62 p 63. C Eston *York* 62-65; C Harton Colliery *Dur* 65-68; V Pelton 68-81; V Ryhope from 81. *St Paul's Vicarage, Ryhope, Sunderland SR2 0HH* 091-521 0238

FLETCHER, James Anthony. b 36. St Edm Hall Ox BA60 DipTh61 MA66. St Steph Ho Ox 60. d 62 p 63. C Streatham St Pet *S'wark* 62-65; C Hobs Moat CD *Birm* 65-68; C Cowley St Jo Ox 68-77; V Hanworth All SS *Lon* from 77; P-in-c Hanworth St Geo from 89. *All Saints' Vicarage, Uxbridge Road, Feltham, Middx TW13 5EE* 081-894 9330

FLETCHER, Jeremy James. b 60. Dur Univ BA81. St Jo Coll Nottm DipTh86. d 88 p 89. C Stranton *Dur* 88-91; C Nottm St Nic *S'well* from 91. *4 Balmoral Avenue, West Bridgford, Nottingham NG2 7QU* Nottingham (0602) 815665

FLETCHER, John Alan Alfred. b 33. Oak Hill Th Coll 58. d 61 p 62. C Erith St Paul *Roch* 61-64; C Rushden *Pet* 64-67; R Hollington St Leon *Chich* 67-86; V Chadwell Heath *Chelmsf* from 86; Chapl Chadwell Heath Hosp from 86. *The Vicarage, 10 St Chad's Road, Chadwell Heath, Romford RM6 6JB* 081-590 2054

FLETCHER, Jonathan James Molyneux. b 42. Hertf Coll Ox BA66 MA66. Wycliffe Hall Ox 66. d 68 p 69. C Enfield Ch Ch Trent Park *Lon* 68-72; C Cam St Sepulchre *Ely* 72-76; C St Helen Bishopsgate w St Martin Outwich *Lon* 76-81; Min Wimbledon Em Ridgway Prop Chpl *S'wark* from 82. *Emmanuel Parsonage, 8 Sheep Walk Mews, Ridgway, London SW19 4QL* 081-946 4728

FLETCHER, Keith. b 47. Man Univ DipTh72. Chich Th Coll 79. d 80 p 81. C Haydon Bridge St Paul *Dur* 80-82; V Eighton Banks 82-85; V Haydon Bridge *Newc* from 85. *The New Vicarage, Station Yard, Haydon Bridge, Hexham, Northd NE47 6LL* Haydon Bridge (0434) 684307

FLETCHER, Linden Elisabeth. b 50. Lon Univ BEd73 MA80. St Jo Coll Nottm 87. d 89. C Fakenham w Alethorpe *Nor* from 89. *54 North Park, Fakenham, Norfolk NR21 9RQ* Fakenham (0328) 855707

FLETCHER, Paul Gordon MacGregor. b 61. St Andr Univ MTh84. Edin Th Coll 84. d 86 p 87. C Cumbernauld *Glas* 86-89; C-in-c Glas H Cross from 89. *The Rectory, 64 Cowdenhill Road, Glasgow G13 2HE* 041-954 6078

FLETCHER, Ralph Henry Maurice. b 43. St Steph Ho Ox 71. d 74 p 75. C Chislehurst Annunciation *Roch* 74-77; Chapl Quainton Hall Sch Harrow 77-87; Hon C Hillingdon All SS *Lon* from 87. *19 Denecroft Cres, Uxbridge, Middx UB10 9HU* Uxbridge (0895) 32708

FLETCHER, Robert Alexander. b 52. Ridley Hall Cam. d 84 p 85. C Chalfont St Peter *Ox* 84-88; C Bushey *St Alb* from 88. *Trinity House, Bushey Mill Lane, Bushey, Watford WD2 2AS* Watford (0923) 220565

FLETCHER, Canon Robin Geoffrey. b 32. Nottm Univ BA57. Ridley Hall Cam 57. d 59 p 60. C S Mimms Ch Ch *Lon* 59-64; V Wollaton Park *S'well* 64-71; V Clifton *York* from 71; Chapl Clifton Hosp N Yorkshire 71-88; RD City of York from 86; Can and Preb York Minster from 89. *The Vicarage, Clifton, York YO3 6BH* York (0904) 655071

FLETCHER, Sheila Elizabeth. b 35. Nottm Univ BA57 CertEd58. NE Ord Course 84. d 87. NSM Dringhouses *York* 87-90; Par Dn from 90. *The Vicarage, Clifton, York YO3 6BH* York (0904) 655071

FLETCHER, Stanley Philip. b 27. St Jo Coll Dur BA52 MA73. d 54 p 55. C Knighton St Jo *Leic* 54-58; V Fleckney w Saddington 58-61; Nigeria 61-66; V Bishopton w Gt Stainton *Dur* 66-76; V Cornforth 76-82; R Hartlepool St Hilda from 82; RD Hartlepool 86-91. *The Rectory, Church Close, Hartlepool, Cleveland TS24 0PW* Hartlepool (0429) 267030

FLETCHER, Stephen. b 57. Man Univ BA79 MA84. St Jo Coll Nottm 82. d 84 p 85. C Didsbury St Jas and Em *Man* 84-88; R Kersal Moor from 88. *2 Hilton Drive, Prestwich, Manchester M25 8NN* 061-773 9408

FLETCHER, Stephen William. b 62. Wolv Poly BA84 Birm Univ DipTh87. Qu Coll Birm 85. d 88 p 89. C Rainham *Roch* 88-91; C Shottery St Andr *Cov* from 91; Min Bishopton St Pet from 91. *63 Baker Avenue, Bishopton, Stratford-upon-Avon, Warks CV37 9PN* Stratford-upon-Avon (0789) 415868

FLETCHER, Timothy. b 27. Reading Univ BSc48. Linc Th Coll 50. d 52 p 53. C Oatlands *Guildf* 52-57; Korea 57-61; V Kirkby Ravensworth w Dalton *Ripon* 61-67; R Binfield *Ox* 67-81; R Barcombe *Chich* from 81. *The Rectory, The Grange, Barcombe, Lewes, E Sussex BN5 5AT* Barcombe (0273) 400260

FLETCHER, Valentine. b 14. Or Coll Ox BA38 MA64. Cuddesdon Coll 38. d 39 p 39. V Littlemore *Ox* 64-71; R Stratton Audley w Godington 71-74; rtd 74. *8 Percy Gardens, Blandford Forum, Dorset DT11 7PN* Blandford (0258) 452290

FLETCHER-CAMPBELL, Walter John Fletcher. b 12. Magd Coll Ox BA33 BSc38 MA44. Wells Th Coll 37. **d** 38 **p** 39. V Stanton Harcourt w Northmoor *Ox* 70-75; P-in-c Bampton Aston w Shifford 75-76; P-in-c Bampton Proper w Bampton Lew 75-76; rtd 77; RD Abingdon *Ox* 80-87; C Radley 89-90; C Radley and Sunningwell from 90. *153 Upper Road, Kennington, Oxford OX1 5LR* Oxford (0865) 730467

FLEURY, Dr Phyllis Mary. LRCP Lon Univ MRCS49 Dur Univ MB, BS50. CITC 87. **d** 89 **p** 91. Hon Par Dn Ardara w Glencolumbkille, Inniskeel etc *D & R* from 89. *Inisfree House, Portnoo, Co Donegal, Irish Republic* Ardara (75) 45231

FLEWKER, David William. b 53. Birm Univ BA75. Wycliffe Hall Ox 76. **d** 78 **p** 79. C Netherton *Liv* 78-82; C Prescot 82-84; V Seaforth 84-88; TV Whitstable *Cant* from 88; Miss to Seamen from 88. *St Alphege's Vicarage, 28 West Cliff, Whitstable, Kent CT5 1DN* Whitstable (0227) 277904

FLIGHT, Michael John. b 41. Sarum Th Coll 68. **d** 71 **p** 72. C Wimborne Minster *Sarum* 71-75; R Tarrant Gunville, Tarrant Hinton etc 75-78; P-in-c Tarrant Rushton, Tarrant Rawston etc 77-78; R Tarrant Valley 78-80; V Westbury from 80; RD Heytesbury 83-87. *The Vicarage, Bitham Lane, Westbury, Wilts BA13 3BU* Westbury (0373) 822209

FLINN, Canon John Robert Patrick. b 30. **d** 65 **p** 66. I Baltinglass w Ballynure etc *C & O* 67-76; I Castlepollard and Oldcastle w Loughcrew etc *M & K* 76-84; rtd 84; Treas Leighlin Cathl *C & O* from 90; Treas Ossory Cathl from 90. *The Old School House, Kells, Kilkenny, Irish Republic* Kilkenny (56) 28297

FLINT, John Hedley. b 32. Edin Th Coll 55. **d** 57 **p** 58. C Glas Ch Ch *Glas* 57-60; C Motherwell 60-62; P-in-c Glas St Gabr 62-65; C-in-c Harlow Green *CD Dur* 65-73; V Gannow *Blackb* 74-76; Chapl RADD S Lon 76-79; P-in-c Idridgehay *Derby* 79-84; P-in-c Kirk Ireton 79-84; Chapl to the Deaf 84-87; C Derby St Luke from 87. *75 Otter Street, Derby DE1 3FD* Derby (0332) 45251

FLINT, Nicholas Angus. b 60. Chich Th Coll 84. **d** 87 **p** 88. C Aldwick *Chich* 87-91; Bp's Asst Chapl for the Homeless *Lon* from 91. *1 St James's Close, Bishop Street, London N1 8PH* 071-359 6688

FLITCROFT, John. b 14. Man Univ BA36 MA37. Bps' Coll Cheshunt 37. **d** 38 **p** 39. V Lytham St Cuth *Blackb* 66-79; rtd 79. *34 Blenheim Gardens, Grove, Wantage, Oxon OX12 0NP* Wantage (02357) 69989

FLOATE, Herbert Frederick Giraud. b 25. Keble Coll Ox BA50 MA54. Qu Coll Birm 50. **d** 61 **p** 62. Australia 66-72; R Stroxton *Linc* 72-74; R Harlaxton w Wyville and Hungerton 72-74; Lect Shenston New Coll *Worcs* 74-78; P-in-c Redditch St Geo *Worc* 78-79; Lic to Offic 80-84; R Upton Snodsbury and Broughton Hackett etc 84-89; Chapl Mojacar *Eur* 89-91; rtd 91. *12 Fairways Avenue, Coleford, Glos GL16 8RJ* Dean (0594) 37178

FLORANCE, James Andrew Vernon. b 44. MCIOB. Linc Th Coll 84. **d** 86 **p** 87. C Lt Ilford St Mich *Chelmsf* 86-90; TV Becontree S from 90. *St John's Vicarage, 522 Goresbrook Road, Dagenham, Essex RM9 4XB* 081-517 5712

FLORY, John Richard. b 35. Clare Coll Cam BA59 MA63. Westcott Ho Cam 69. **d** 71 **p** 72. C Shirehampton *Bris* 71-74; V Patchway 74-82; R Lydiard Millicent w Lydiard Tregoz 82-86; TR The Lydiards from 86. *The Rectory, Lydiard Millicent, Swindon SN5 9LR* Swindon (0793) 770217

FLOWER, Roger Edward. b 45. AKC68. **d** 69 **p** 70. C Gt Stanmore *Lon* 69-72; C Wells St Cuth w Coxley and Wookey Hole *B & W* 72-77; V Tatworth 77-82; P-in-c Taunton St Andr 82-84; V from 84; RD Taunton from 90. *118 Kingston Road, Taunton, Somerset TA2 7SR* Taunton (0823) 332544

FLOWERDAY, Andrew Leslie. b 53. Imp Coll Lon BSc75. St Jo Coll Nottm DipTh. **d** 90 **p** 91. C Farnborough *Guildf* from 90. *St Peter's House, 22 Rectory Road, Farnborough, Hants GU14 7BY* Farnborough (0252) 517886

FLOWERDAY, Edward Arthur. b 04. Richmond Th Coll 28. **d** 43 **p** 43. V Acomb St Steph *York* 58-74; rtd 74; Perm to Offic *Carl* from 77. *14 Barton View, Penrith, Cumbria CA11 8AU* Penrith (0768) 64192

FLOWERDAY, Leslie Frank. b 26. DGA ADipR. **d** 87 **p** 88. NSM Gtr Corsham *Bris* from 87. *14 Station Road, Corsham, Wilts SN13 9EX* Corsham (0249) 712236

FLOWERDEW, George Douglas Hugh. b 10. MBE44. Wycliffe Hall Ox 66. **d** 67 **p** 68. C Chandler's Ford *Win* 67-70; R Baughurst w Ramsdale 70-80; rtd 80; Perm to Offic *Ox* from 83. *3 Lovelace Road, Oxford OX2 8LP*

FLOWERDEW, Martin James. b 56. Herts Coll CertEd78 Pemb Coll Cam BEd79 UEA CertCS82. Sarum & Wells Th Coll 89. **d** 91. C Leagrave *St Alb* from 91. *St Luke's House, 39 Butely Road, Leagrave, Luton, Beds LU4 9EW* Luton (0582) 572054

FLOWERS, John Henry. b 33. Qu Coll Birm 63. **d** 65 **p** 66. C Aberdare St Fagan *Llan* 65-68; C Llantrisant 68-72; V Nantymoel w Wyndham 72-76; Chapl HM Pris Wormwood Scrubs 76-78; Birm 78-80; Chapl HM Pris Albany from 80. *HM Prison, Albany, Newport, Isle of Wight PO30 5RS* Isle of Wight (0983) 524055

FLUCK, Paul John Martin. b 46. Hertf Coll Ox BA69 MA78. Cranmer Hall Dur DipTh72. **d** 73 **p** 74. C Burmantofts St Steph and St Agnes *Ripon* 73-76; C Kingswood *Bris* 76-79; TV Ipsley *Worc* 79-83; V Dudley St Barn 83-85; USA from 85. *Address temp unknown*

FLUCK, Canon Peter Ernest. b 29. Linc Th Coll. **d** 61 **p** 62. C Maidstone All SS w St Phil *Cant* 61-64; R Uffington *Linc* 64-70; V Tallington 64-70; P-in-c Barholm w Stowe 65-66; V 66-70; V Linc St Nic w St Jo Newport 70-75; P-in-c Haugh 75-84; P-in-c Harrington w Brinkhill 75-84; P-in-c Oxcombe 75-84; P-in-c Ruckland w Farforth and Maidenwell 75-84; P-in-c Somersby w Bag Enderby 75-84; P-in-c Tetford and Salmonby 75-84; R S Ormsby w Ketsby, Calceby and Driby 75-84; V Boston from 84; Miss to Seamen from 84; Can and Preb Linc Cathl *Linc* from 87. *The Vicarage, Boston, Lincs PE21 6NP* Boston (0205) 362864

FLUDE, Maurice Haddon. b 41. St Aid Birkenhead. **d** 69 **p** 70. C Mottingham St Andr *S'wark* 69-74; Perm to Offic 76-81. *Address temp unknown*

FLUX, Brian George. b 39. Oak Hill Th Coll 68. **d** 71 **p** 72. C Chadderton Ch Ch *Man* 71-74; C Preston All SS *Blackb* 75-76; P-in-c Preston St Luke 76-81; CF (TA) from 78; R Higher Openshaw *Man* 81-88; Chapl HM Pris Haverigg from 88. *HM Prison Haverigg, Millom, Cumbria LA18 4NA* Millom (0229) 775224

FLYNN, Alexander Victor George. b 45. DTh. **d** 90 **p** 91. C Kilsaran w Drumcar, Dunleer and Dunany *Arm* from 90. *Dromena House, Dromiskin Road, Castlebellingham, Co Louth, Irish Republic* Castlebellingham (42) 72699

FLYNN, Peter Murray. b 35. Oak Hill Th Coll 76. **d** 79 **p** 80. Hon C Finchley St Mary *Lon* 79-83; Hon C Mill Hill Jo Keble Ch 84-86; C Mill End and Heronsgate w W Hyde *St Alb* from 86. *St Thomas's House, 46 Chalfont Road, Rickmansworth, Herts WD3 2TB* Rickmansworth (0923) 771022

FOGDEN, Mrs Elizabeth Sally. b 40. MCSP61 DipRS77. Qu Coll Birm 76. dss 78 **d** 87. Chevington w Hargrave and Whepstead w Brockley *St E* 78-84; Honington w Sapiston and Troston 84-87; Par Dn from 87; Par Dn Euston w Barnham, Elvedon and Fakenham Magna from 90; Chapl Center Parc Elvedon from 90; Dioc Adv Women's Min from 90. *The Rectory, Honington, Bury St Edmunds, Suffolk IP31 1RG* Honington (03596) 265

FOIZEY, Michael John. b 24. Trin Coll Cam BA45 MA65. Westcott Ho Cam 45. **d** 47 **p** 48. R Lon Docks St Pet w Wapping St Jo *Lon* 60-82; V Ealing Ch the Sav 82-89; Preb St Paul's Cathl 83-89; rtd 89. *157 Birmingham Road, Kidderminster, Worcs DY10 2SL* Kidderminster (0562) 823277

✠**FOLEY, Rt Rev Ronald Graham Gregory.** b 23. St Jo Coll Dur BA49 DipTh50. **d** 50 **p** 51 **c** 82. C S Shore H Trin *Blackb* 50-54; V Blackb St Luke 54-60; Dir RE *Dur* 60-71; R Brancepeth 60-71; Hon Can Dur Cathl 65-71; Hon Can Ripon Cathl *Ripon* 71-82; V Leeds St Pet 71-82; Chapl to HM The Queen 77-82; Suff Bp Reading *Ox* 82-87; Area Bp Reading 87-89; rtd 89. *3 Poplar Avenue, Kirkbymoorside, York YO6 6ES* Kirkbymoorside (0751) 32439

FOLKARD, Oliver Goring. b 41. Nottm Univ BA63. Lich Th Coll 64. **d** 66 **p** 67. C Carlton S'well 66-67; C Worksop Priory 67-68; C Brewood *Lich* 68-71; C Laughton w Laughton *Linc* 72-75; P-in-c Gedney Hill 76-77; V 77-84; V Whaplode Drove 76-84; V Sutton St Mary from 84; RD Elloe E from 89. *The Vicarage, Long Sutton, Spalding, Lincs PE12 9JJ* Holbeach (0406) 362033

FOLKS, Andrew John. b 42. St Jo Coll Dur BA65 DipTh69. **d** 69 **p** 70. C Stranton *Dur* 69-72; Chapl Sandbach Sch Cheshire 73-80; Lic to Offic *Carl* 80-85; Chapl Casterton Sch Cumbria 80-85; Hd Master Fernhill Manor Sch New Milton from 85; Perm to Offic *Win* from 89. *Fernhill Manor School, New Milton, Hants BH25 5JL* New Milton (0425) 611090

FOLKS, Peter William John. b 30. FRCO56 ARCM. Launde Abbey 72. **d** 72 **p** 73. C Leic St Aid *Leic* 72-76; V Newfoundpool 76-84; V Whetstone from 84. *The Vicarage, Church Lane, Whetstone, Leicester LE8 3LQ* Leicester (0533) 848713

FOLLAND, Mark Wilkins. b 59. Univ of Wales (Cardiff) DipTh86 Southn Univ BTh88. Sarum & Wells Th Coll 86. **d** 88. C Kirkby *Liv* from 88. *92 Gaywood Green, Kirkby, Liverpool L32 6QZ* 051-548 8875

FOLLAND, Ronald George. b 14. AKC48. St Boniface Warminster 48. **d** 49 **p** 50. V E Teignmouth *Ex* 66-79; rtd 79; Public Preacher (*Ex*) 80-89; Perm to Offic *Sarum* from 89. *1 Hollows Close, Salisbury SP2 8JU* Salisbury (0722) 338562

FOLLETT, Jeremy Mark. b 60. Jes Coll Cam BA82. St Jo Coll Nottm DTS90. **d** 91. C Newark-upon-Trent *S'well* from 91. *28 Harewood Avenue, Newark, Notts NG24 4AN* Newark (0636) 700396

FOLLETT, Neil Robert Thomas. b 50. RMCS BSc75 Open Univ BA85. E Anglian Minl Tr Course 86. **d** 89 **p** 90. C Godmanchester *Ely* from 89. *Chestnut House, 7 London Road, Godmanchester, Huntingdon, Cambs PE18 8HZ* Huntingdon (0480) 458036

FOLLIS, Raymond George Carlile. b 23. DFC45. Lich Th Coll 63. **d** 65 **p** 66. R New Fishbourne *Chich* 69-88; P-in-c Appledram 84-88; rtd 88. *47 Old Place, Aldwick, Bognor Regis, W Sussex PO21 3AX* Pagham (0243) 264663

FOOD, Frank Herbert. b 02. Wycliffe Hall Ox 37. **d** 38 **p** 39. R Markfield *Leic* 61-71; rtd 71; Chapl Torbay Hosp Torquay 71-77; Perm to Offic *Ex* from 77. *354A Torquay Road, Paignton, Devon TQ3 2BT* Paignton (0803) 552544

FOOKES, Roger Mortimer. b 24. VRD63 and Bars 73. Ch Ch Ox BA49 MA53. Wells Th Coll 48. **d** 50 **p** 51. Chapl RNR 58-74; V Midsomer Norton *B & W* 62-78; RD Midsomer Norton 72-78; P-in-c Stratton on the Fosse 74-78; P-in-c Clandown 75-78; V Wotton-under-Edge w Ozleworth and N Nibley *Glouc* 78-89; RD Dursley 85-89; rtd 89; Perm to Offic *Ex* from 90. *Feniton Cottage, Feniton, Honiton, Devon EX14 0BE* Honiton (0404) 850300

FOORD, Claude Victor. b 07. Worc Ord Coll. **d** 56 **p** 57. V Cleeve Prior *Worc* 64-72; rtd 72. *9 Lincoln Green, Worcester WR5 1QU* Worcester (0905) 359322

FOOT, Daniel Henry Paris. b 46. Peterho Cam BA67 MA74 Didsbury Coll of Educn CertEd68 Selw Coll Cam 76. Ridley Hall Cam 77. **d** 79 **p** 80. C Werrington *Pet* 79-82; P-in-c Cranford w Grafton Underwood 82; R Cranford w Grafton Underwood and Twywell from 83. *The Rectory, Cranford, Kettering, Northants NN14 4AH* Cranford (053678) 231

FOOT, Leslie Frank. b 07. Dur Univ 30. St Boniface Warminster 27. **d** 32 **p** 33. R Eastergate *Chich* 63-75; rtd 75; Perm to Offic *Chich* from 75. *120 Little Breach, Chichester, W Sussex PO19 4TZ* Chichester (0243) 789640

FOOT, Leslie Robert James. b 33. Bris Univ BSc54. Wells Th Coll 67. **d** 69 **p** 70. Hon C Yeovil *B & W* 69-76; Lic to Offic from 76. *45 The Roman Way, Glastonbury, Somerset BA6 8AB* Glastonbury (0458) 32247

FOOTE, Desmond. b 46. S Dios Minl Tr Scheme. **d** 82 **p** 83. NSM Furze Platt *Ox* from 82. *24 Furze Platt Road, Maidenhead, Berks SL6 7NN* Maidenhead (0628) 25412

FOOTE, Dr John Bruce. b 18. FRCPath G&C Coll Cam BA39 MA43 MD51. St Jo Coll Nottm 78. **d** 79 **p** 80. NSM Crookes St Thos *Sheff* 79-88; Perm to Offic *Derby* from 79; rtd 88. *67 St Thomas Road, Sheffield S10 1UW* Sheffield (0742) 665021

FOOTTIT, Ven Anthony Charles. b 35. K Coll Cam BA57 MA70. Cuddesdon Coll 59. **d** 61 **p** 62. C Wymondham *Nor* 61-64; C Blakeney w Lt Langham 64-67; P-in-c Hindringham w Binham and Cockthorpe 67-71; P-in-c Yarlington *B & W* 71-76; R N Cadbury 71-75; P-in-c S Cadbury w Sutton Montis 75-76; TR Camelot Par 76-81; RD Cary 79-81; Dioc Missr *Linc* 81-87; Hon Can Linc Cathl 86-87; Dioc Rural Officer *Nor* 87; Adn Lynn from 87. *Ivy House, Whitwell Street, Reepham, Norwich NR10 4RA* Norwich (0603) 870340

FOOTTIT, John Guy. b 11. Jes Coll Cam BA34. Wycliffe Hall Ox 34. **d** 35 **p** 36. R Whatfield w Semer *St E* 51-77; P-in-c Nedging w Naughton 74-77; rtd 77. *Dane House, Kettlestone, Fakenham, Norfolk* Fakenham (0328) 878455

FORAN, Andrew John. b 55. Aston Tr Scheme 84 Linc Th Coll 86. **d** 88 **p** 89. C Epping St Jo *Chelmsf* from 88. *St John's House, St John's Road, Epping, Essex CM16 5DN* Epping (0378) 75570

FORBES, Very Rev Graham John Thompson. b 51. Aber Univ MA73 Edin Univ BD76. Edin Th Coll 73. **d** 76 **p** 77. C Edin Old St Paul *Edin* 76-82; Can St Ninian's Cathl Perth *St And* 82-90; R Stanley 82-88; Provost St Ninian's Cathl Perth 82-90; R Perth St Ninian 82-90; Provost St Mary's Cathl *Edin* from 90; R Edin St Mary

from 90. *8 Landsdowne Crescent, Edinburgh EH12 5EQ* 031-225 2978 or 225 6293

FORBES, Iain William. b 56. Ex Univ BA81. Chich Th Coll 83. **d** 85 **p** 86. C Upper Norwood St Jo *S'wark* 85-88; C Lewisham St Mary 88-90; Chapl St Martin's Coll of Educn *Blackb* from 90. *St Martin's College, Bowerham Road, Lancaster LA1 3JD* Lancaster (0524) 63446

FORBES, James Paterson. b 32. **d** 88 **p** 90. NSM Dundee St Jo *Bre* from 88. *6 Gillies Place, Broughty Ferry, Dundee DD5 3LE* Dundee (0382) 79655

FORBES, John Francis. b 29. CITC 85. **d** 88 **p** 90. C Ferns w Kilbride, Toombe, Kilcormack etc *C & O* 88-90; NSM Gorey w Kilnahue from 90. *Ballinabarna House, Enniscorthy, Co Wexford, Irish Republic* Enniscorthy (54) 33353

FORBES, Very Rev John Franey. b 33. AKC57. **d** 58 **p** 59. C Darlington H Trin *Dur* 58-62; S Africa from 62; Dean Pietermaritzburg from 76. *Deanery, PO Box 1639, Pietermaritzburg, 3200 South Africa* Pietermaritzburg (331) 425848

FORBES, Patrick. b 38. Lon Univ DipSoc74 Open Univ BA82. Linc Th Coll 64. **d** 66 **p** 67. C Yeovil *B & W* 66-69; C Plumstead Wm Temple Ch Abbey Wood CD *S'wark* 69-70; Thamesmead Ecum Gp 70-73; TV Thamesmead 73-78; Dioc Communications Officer *St Alb* 78-90; P-in-c Offley w Lilley 78-82; Info Officer Communications Dept Ch Ho Lon from 91. *14 East Street, Lilley, Luton LU2 8LP* Offley (046276) 483 or 071-222 9011

FORBES, Raymond John. b 34. ALCD58. **d** 58 **p** 59. C Wandsworth St Steph *S'wark* 58-61; C Kewstoke *B & W* 61-63; V Fordcombe *Roch* 63-73; R Ashurst 64-73; P-in-c Morden w Almer and Charborough *Sarum* 73-76; P-in-c Bloxworth 73-76; V Red Post 76-84; P-in-c Hamworthy from 84. *St Michael's Rectory, Blandford Road, Hamworthy, Poole, Dorset BH15 4HP* Poole (0202) 674878

FORBES, Stuart. b 33. Lon Univ BD59. Oak Hill Th Coll 56. **d** 61 **p** 62. C Halliwell St Pet *Man* 61-64; P-in-c Wicker w Neepsend *Sheff* 64-69; V Stainforth 69-77; V Salterhebble All SS *Wakef* 77-89; V Toxteth Park St Mich w St Andr *Liv* from 89. *St Michael's Vicarage, St Michael's Church Road, Liverpool L17 7BD* 051-727 2601

FORBES ADAM, Stephen Timothy Beilby. b 23. Ball Coll Ox. Chich Th Coll 59. **d** 61 **p** 62. R Barton in Fabis *S'well* 64-70; V Thrumpton 65-70; P-in-c S Stoke *B & W* 74-81; C Combe Down w Monkton Combe and S Stoke 81-83; Perm to Offic *B & W* 83-86; Ox 86-87; NSM Epwell w Sibford, Swalcliffe and Tadmarton *Ox* from 87; rtd 88. *Baker's Lane, Tadmarton, Banbury, Oxon OX15 5SS* Banbury (0295) 788305

FORCE-JONES, Graham Roland John. b 41. Sarum Th Coll 63. **d** 68 **p** 69. C Calne and Blackland *Sarum* 68-73; TV Oldbury 73-78; R 78-80; TR Upper Kennett from 80; RD Marlborough from 90. *The Rectory, West Overton, Marlborough, Wilts SN8 4ER* Lockeridge (067286) 260

FORD, Adam. b 40. Lanc Univ MA72 K Coll Lon BD63 AKC63. **d** 65 **p** 65. C Cirencester *Glouc* 65-70; V Hebden Bridge *Wakef* 70-76; Chapl St Paul's Girls Sch Hammersmith from 77; P-in-O to HM The Queen from 84. *55 Bolingbroke Road, London W14* 071-602 5902

FORD, Arthur Edward. b 05. Ch Ch Ox BA26 MA31. Cuddesdon Coll 28. **d** 30 **p** 31. R Kilmeston w Beauworth *Win* 66-72; rtd 72; Perm to Offic *Win* from 73. *Mayford, Beeches Hill, Bishops Waltham, Southampton SO3 1FE* Bishops Waltham (04893) 3476

FORD, Benjamin Pierson. b 22. Princeton Univ AB48. Gen Th Sem (NY) MDiv51. **d** 51 **p** 52. USA 51-85 and from 87; C Gt Grimsby St Mary and St Jas *Linc* 85-87. *1544 Union Road, Waldoboro, Maine 04572, USA*

FORD, Christopher Simon. b 51. AKC74 Leeds Univ MPhil86 PhD91. **d** 75 **p** 76. C Wythenshawe Wm Temple Ch *Man* 75-77; C New Bury 77-80; R Old Trafford St Jo from 80. *St John's Rectory, Lindum Avenue, Old Trafford, Manchester M16 9NQ* 061-872 0500

FORD, Colin David. b 28. MIMechE59. Oak Hill Th Coll 60. **d** 62 **p** 63. C Dover St Martin *Cant* 62-67; V Goodnestone St Bart and Graveney 67-71; V Croydon Ch Ch Broad Green 71-84; V Croydon Ch Ch *S'wark* from 85. *Christ Church Vicarage, 34 Longley Road, Croydon CR0 3LH* 081-684 2880

FORD, Canon David George. b 37. Lon Coll of Div ALCD61 LTh74. **d** 61 **p** 62. C Walthamstow St Barn and St Jas *St Alb* 61-64; C Wisbech SS Pet and Paul *Ely* 64-66; C-in-c Cherry Hinton St Jas CD 66-73; V Cam St Jas 73-80; Can Res Ripon Cathl *Ripon* from

80. *St Peter's House, Minster Close, Ripon, N Yorkshire HG4 4QJ* Ripon (0765) 604108

FORD, David John. b 38. Lon Coll of Div BD68. **d** 69 **p** 70. C Blackheath St Jo *S'wark* 69-71; C Westlands St Andr *Lich* 71-75; V Sheff St Steph w St Phil and St Ann *Sheff* 75-77; R Netherthorpe 77-80; TR 80-84; R Thrybergh 82-84; R Thrybergh w Hooton Roberts from 84; Ind Chapl 86-87. *The Rectory, Thrybergh, Rotherham, S Yorkshire S65 4NS* Rotherham (0709) 850336

FORD, Derek Ernest. b 32. St Mich Coll Llan 56. **d** 58 **p** 59. C Roath St Martin *Llan* 58-61; C Newton Nottage 61-67; V Abercanaid 67-70; Perm to Offic *Win* 70-80; SSF from 72; Lic to Offic Sarum 73-80; Newc 75-80; USA from 80. *Little Portion Friary, PO Box 399, Mount Sinai, New York 11766, USA* Mount Sinai (516) 473-0553

FORD, Preb Douglas William Cleverley. b 14. Lon Univ BD36 MTh41. ALCD36. **d** 37 **p** 38. V S Kensington H Trin w All SS *Lon* 55-74; RD Westmr St Marg 67-74; Preb St Paul's Cathl 68-80; Prov Can of York from 69; Chapl to HM The Queen 73-84; Abp's Sen Chapl *Cant* 75-80; rtd 80; Six Preacher Cant Cathl *Cant* from 82; Perm to Offic *S'wark* from 83. *Rostrevor, Lingfield, Surrey RH7 6BZ* Lingfield (0342) 832461

FORD, Eric Charles. b 31. Ely Th Coll 56. **d** 59 **p** 60. C Kettering St Mary *Pet* 59-65; R Bowers Gifford *Chelmsf* 65-69; V Walthamstow St Barn and St Jas Gt 69-76; V Chingford St Edm from 76. *St Edmund's Vicarage, Larkswood Road, London E4 9DS* 081-529 5226

FORD, Eric Copeland. b 20. Linc Th Coll 68. **d** 70 **p** 71. C Lupset *Wakef* 70-73; V Cornholme 73-78; V Sharlston 78; V Wragby w Sharlston 78-85; P-in-c Hightown 85-87; V 87-88; V Hartshead and Hightown 88-90; rtd 90; P-in-c Halifax St Jo Cragg Vale *Wakef* 90-91; Chapl Las Palmas w Lanzarote *Eur* from 91. *Calle Montevideo 2, 35007 Las Palmas, Canary Islands* Las Palmas (28) 267202

FORD, Canon Henry Malcolm. b 33. Em Coll Cam BA54 MA58. Ely Th Coll 58. **d** 59 **p** 69. C Ipswich St Matt *St E* 59-61; Hon C Bury St Edmunds St Jo 66-76; Hon C Hawstead and Nowton w Stanningfield etc 76-89; Hon Can St E Cathl from 86; Hon C Cockfield w Bradfield St Clare, Felsham etc from 89. *Cross Green, Cockfield, Bury St Edmunds, Suffolk IP30 0LG* Cockfield Green (0284) 828479

FORD, Hubert. b 14. Kelham Th Coll 30. **d** 38 **p** 39. V Hurst Green *S'wark* 64-79; rtd 79; Perm to Offic *Chich* from 79. *88 Barrington Road, Worthing, W Sussex BN12 4RS* Worthing (0903) 44428

FORD, John. b 15. Linc Th Coll 38. **d** 40 **p** 41. R Aikton *Carl* 67-72; P-in-c Lambeth St Jo w All SS *S'wark* 72-76; rtd 76. *The Old House, Gornal Ground, Thwaites, Millom, Cumbria* Broughton-in-Furness (0229) 716733

FORD, John. b 31. Sarum Th Coll 58. **d** 61 **p** 62. C Saffron Walden *Chelmsf* 61-64; C Chingford SS Pet and Paul 64-67; VC S'well Minster *S'well* 67-72; R N and S Wheatley w W Burton 72-78; P-in-c Sturton w Littleborough 72-78; P-in-c Bole w Saundby 72-78; V Edwinstowe w Carburton from 78. *The Vicarage, 5 West Lane, Edwinstowe, Mansfield, Notts NG21 9QT* Mansfield (0623) 822430

FORD, Canon John Albert. b 13. TCD BA35 MA38. CITC 36. **d** 36 **p** 37. I Drumcree *Arm* 61-83; Can Arm Cathl 75-83; rtd 83. *84 Bleary Road, Portadown, Co Armagh BT63 5NF* Portadown (0762) 345484

FORD, John Frank. b 52. Chich Th Coll 76. **d** 79 **p** 80. C Forest Hill Ch Ch *S'wark* 79-82; V Lee St Aug 82-91; V Lower Beeding *Chich* from 91; Dom Chapl to Suff Bp Horsham from 91. *The Vicarage, Plummers Plain, Lower Beeding, Horsham, W Sussex RH13 6NU* Lower Beeding (0403) 891367

FORD, Leslie Charles. b 08. S'wark Ord Course 65. **d** 68 **p** 69. C Norwood *S'wark* 68-76; rtd 76. *Capel Court, The Burgage, Prestbury, Cheltenham, Glos GL52 3EL* Cheltenham (0242) 579410

FORD, Canon Lionel Peter. b 32. St Mich Coll Llan 57. **d** 60 **p** 61. C Ribbesford w Bewdley and Dowles *Worc* 60-63; C St Mary in the Marsh *Cant* 63-67; P-in-c 76-78; V Elmsted w Hastingleigh 67-71; V New Romney w Hope 71-78; RD S Lympne 75-81; V New Romney w Hope and St Mary's Bay etc 78-82; Hon Can Cant Cathl from 82; V New Romney w Old Romney and Midley from 82. *The Vicarage, New Romney, Kent TN28 8DR* New Romney (0679) 62308

FORD, Lionel Widdicombe. b 18. Leeds Univ BA40. Coll of Resurr Mirfield 37. **d** 42 **p** 43. V Stonehouse *Glouc* 68-82; rtd 82; Perm to Offic *Cant* from 82. *9 Priors Lees,*

5/6 *The Leas, Folkestone, Kent CT20 2DR* Folkestone (0303) 52601

FORD, Peter. b 46. ACP75 Bede Coll Dur TCert72. Linc Th Coll 76. **d** 78 **p** 79. OGS from 72; C Hartlepool H Trin *Dur* 78-81; Dioc Youth Officer *Wakef* 81-84; C Mirfield Eastthorpe St Paul 82-84; C Upper Hopton 82-84; V Dodworth 84-88; Chapl and Hd Relig Studies Rishworth Sch from 88. *2 Goat House Barn, Shaw Lane, Rishworth, Sowerby Bridge, W Yorkshire HX6 4QL* Halifax (0422) 823622 or 822217

FORD, Peter Collins. b 23. Roch Th Coll 60. **d** 62 **p** 63. V Milton next Gravesend Ch Ch *Roch* 69-72; V Gosfield *Chelmsf* 72-84; RD Colne 79-81; RD Halstead and Coggeshall 81-84; rtd 88. *Little Winster, 12 Upper Fourth Avenue, Frinton-on-Sea CO13 9JS* Frinton-on-Sea (0255) 77151

FORD, Ven Peter Hugh. b 43. St Cath Coll Cam BA65 MA69. Cuddesdon Coll 65. **d** 67 **p** 68. C Is of Dogs Ch Ch and St Jo w St Luke *Lon* 67-70; Canada from 70. *The Rectory, Box 110, Niagara-on-the-Lake, Ontario, Canada, L0S 1J0*

FORD, Richard Graham. b 39. AKC65. **d** 66 **p** 67. C Morpeth *Newc* 66-71; C Fordingbridge w Ibsley *Win* 71-73; TV Whorlton *Newc* 73-80; V Choppington from 80. *The Vicarage, Choppington, Northd NE62 5SX* Bedlington (0670) 822216

FORD, Roger James. b 33. Sarum & Wells Th Coll 81. **d** 83 **p** 84. C Sidcup St Jo *Roch* 83-86; V Darenth from 86. *Darenth Vicarage, Lane End, Dartford, Kent DA2 7JR* Dartford (0322) 227153

FORD, Roger Lindsay. b 47. **d** 91. NSM Fairwater *Llan* from 91. *46 St Michael's Road, Llandaff, Cardiff CF5 2AP* Cardiff (0222) 565716

FORD, Mrs Shirley Elsworth. b 40. Open Univ BA88. Sarum & Wells Th Coll 89. **d** 91. C Farnham *Guildf* from 91. *6 High Park Road, Farnham, Surrey GU9 7JL* Farnham (0252) 726057

FORD, William John. b 50. Linc Th Coll 89. **d** 91. C Marton-in-Cleveland *York* from 91. *37 Lambourne Drive, Marton-in-Cleveland, Middlesbrough, Cleveland TS7 8QF*

FORDE, Stephen Bernard. b 61. Edin Univ BSc TCD DipTh. **d** 86 **p** 87. C Belf St Mary *Conn* 86-89; Chapl QUB from 89; Min Can Belf Cathl from 89; Bp's Dom Chapl *Conn* from 90. *20 Elmwood Avenue, Belfast BT9 6AY* Belfast (0232) 667754

FORDER, Ven Charles Robert. b 07. Ch Coll Cam BA28 MA32. Ridley Hall Cam 28. **d** 30 **p** 31. Adn York 57-72; Can and Preb York Minster 57-76; rtd 72. *Dulverton Hall, St Martin's Square, Scarborough YO11 2DB* Scarborough (0723) 373082

FORDER, Harry Walter. b 15. AKC39. **d** 39 **p** 40. R W Horsley *Guildf* 53-87; rtd 87. *Grove Cottage, 10 Levylsdene, Guildford, Surrey GU1 2RS*

FORDHAM, Canon James Charles Horace Adcock. b 11. MBE47 TD61. St Aid Birkenhead 39. **d** 41 **p** 42. V Preston Em *Blackb* 47-81; Hon Can Blackb Cathl 72-82; rtd 82; Perm to Offic *Blackb* from 82. *56 Hawkhurst Avenue, Fulwood, Preston, Lancs PR2 4XT* Preston (0772) 774836

FORDHAM, Mrs June Erica. b 28. DCR52. Oak Hill Th Coll 83. **dss** 86 **d** 87. Digswell and Panshanger *St Alb* 86-87; Par Dn 87-90; TM from 91. *22 Crossway, Welwyn Garden City, Herts AL8 7EE* Welwyn Garden (0707) 326997

FORDHAM, Philip Arthur Sidney. b 51. Avery Hill Coll DipEd. St Steph Ho Ox. **d** 81 **p** 82. C Wanstead St Mary *Chelmsf* 81-82; C Romford St Edw 82-83; C Shrub End 83-86; TV Brighton St Pet and St Nic w Chpl Royal *Chich* 86-88; V Eastbourne Ch Ch from 88. *18 Addingham Road, Eastbourne, E Sussex BN22 7DX* Eastbourne (0323) 21952

FOREMAN, Joseph Arthur. **d** 86 **p** 87. NSM Win St Bart *Win* from 86. *Willow Tree House, Domum Road, Winchester, Hants SO23 9NN* Winchester (0962) 52138

FOREMAN, Patrick Brian. b 41. CertEd. St Jo Coll Nottm 77. **d** 79 **p** 80. C Gainsborough All SS *Linc* 79-83; V Thornton St Jas *Bradf* 83-91; R Hevingham w Hainford and Stratton Strawless *Nor* from 91. *The Rectory, Westgate Green, Hevingham, Norfolk NR10 5NH* Hevingham (060548) 643

FOREMAN, Roy Geoffrey Victor. b 31. Oak Hill Th Coll 62. **d** 64 **p** 65. C Chitts Hill St Cuth *Lon* 64-67; C Rodbourne Cheney *Bris* 67-70; C Walthamstow St Mary w St Steph *Chelmsf* from 71. *9 Church End, London E17 9RJ* 081-521 1361

FORGAN, Eleanor. b 44. St Andr Univ MA. St And Dioc Tr Course. **d** 89. NSM Alloa *St And* from 89. *8 Crophill,*

Sauchie, Alloa, Clackmannanshire FK10 3EZ   Alloa (0259) 212836

FORMAN, Alastair Gordon. b 48. St Jo Coll Nottm 78. **d** 80 **p** 81. C Pennycross *Ex* 80-83; C Woking St Jo *Guildf* 83-88; V Luton Lewsey St Hugh *St Alb* from 88. *St Hugh's Vicarage, 367 Leagrave High Street, Luton LU4 0ND*   Luton (0582) 664433

FORMAN, Diana Blanche Grant. b 19. DCR. Edin Dioc NSM Course 79. **dss** 83 **d** 86. Edin St Jo *Edin* 83-86; NSM from 86. *7 Myreside Court, Edinburgh EH10 5LX* 031-447 4463

FORRER, Michael Dennett Cuthbert. b 34. St Pet Hall Ox BA59 MA63. Wycliffe Hall Ox 59. **d** 60 **p** 61. C Westwood *Cov* 60-63; Ind Chapl 63-69; C Cov Cathl 63-71; Sen Ind Chapl 69-71; Hon C All Hallows by the Tower etc *Lon* from 76. *117 London Road, Marlborough, Wilts*   Marlborough (0672) 55275

FORREST, Edward William. b 09. Man Univ BA34. Bps' Coll Cheshunt. **d** 62 **p** 63. V Ramsbottom St Paul *Man* 65-76; rtd 77; Perm to Offic *Man* 77-86; *Cov* from 86. *3 Bonds Court, Hill Street, Coventry CV1 4AN* Coventry (0203) 57805

FORREST, John Sagar. b 15. Ridley Hall Cam 65. **d** 66 **p** 67. R Man St Pet Oldham Road w St Jas *Man* 69-75; R Man St Paul New Cross 72-75; Chapl Wythenshawe and Christie Hosps Man 75-80; rtd 80; Perm to Offic *Man* from 80. *11 Allanson Road, Northenden, Manchester M22 4HN*   061-998 2754

FORREST, Canon Kenneth Malcolm. b 38. Linc Coll Ox BA61 MA65. Wells Th Coll 60. **d** 62 **p** 63. C Walton St Mary *Liv* 62-65; Asst Chapl Liv Univ 65-67; Chapl Blue Coat Sch Liv 67-75; R Wavertree H Trin 67-75; R Wigan All SS from 75; Hon Can Liv Cathl from 87; AD Wigan E from 89. *The Hall, Wigan, Lancs WN1 1HN* Wigan (0942) 44459

FORREST, Very Rev Leslie David Arthur. b 46. TCD BA68 MA86. CITC 70. **d** 70 **p** 71. C Conwall *D & R* 70-73; I Tullyaughnish 73-80; I Athenry w Monivea *T, K & A* 80-82; I Galway w Kilcummin from 80; RD Tuam from 82; Dir of Ords from 84; Can Tuam Cathl from 86; Provost Tuam from 91. *The Rectory, Taylor's Hill, Galway, Irish Republic*   Galway (91) 21914

FORREST, Michael Barry Eric. b 38. Lon Univ BA87 MA89. NZ Bd of Th Studies LTh62 Chich Th Coll 64. **d** 66 **p** 67. C Beckenham St Jas *Roch* 66-70; Papua New Guinea 70-76; C Altarnon and Bolventor *Truro* 76-78; TV N Hill w Altarnon, Bolventor and Lewannick 78-79; R St Martin w E and W Looe 79-84; V Kensington St Phil Earl's Court *Lon* from 84. *St Philip's Vicarage, 46 Pembroke Road, London W8 6NU* 071-602 5025 or 373 4847

FORREST, Canon Robin Whyte. b 33. Edin Th Coll 58. **d** 61 **p** 62. C Glas St Mary *Glas* 61-66; R Renfrew 66-70; R Motherwell 70-79; R Wishaw 75-79; R Nairn *Mor* from 79; R Forres from 79; Can St Andr Cathl Inverness from 86; Syn Clerk from 91. *St John's Rectory, Victoria Road, Forres, Morayshire IV36 0BN*   Forres (0309) 72856

FORRESTER, Herbert Howarth. b 19. Liv Univ LLB46. Wycliffe Hall Ox 65. **d** 67 **p** 68. C Blundellsands St Nic *Liv* 67-70; V Liv St Phil 70-76; V Liv St Phil w St Dav 76-85; rtd 85; Perm to Offic *Liv* from 85. *5 Kenilworth Road, Liverpool L16 7PS*   051-722 1365

FORRESTER, Ian Michael. b 56. Chich Th Coll. **d** 82 **p** 83. C Leigh-on-Sea St Marg *Chelmsf* 82-84; Min Can, Succ and Dean's V Windsor 84-86; Prec and Chapl Chelmsf Cathl *Chelmsf* 86-91; Chapl Lancing Coll Sussex from 91. *c/o Lancing College, Lancing, W Sussex BN15 0RW*   Brighton (0273) 452213

FORRESTER, James Oliphant. b 50. SS Coll Cam BA72 MA76. Wycliffe Hall Ox 73. **d** 76 **p** 77. C Hull Newland St Jo *York* 76-80; C Fulwood *Sheff* 80-87; V Lodge Moor St Luke 87-90; V Ecclesfield from 90. *230 The Wheel, Ecclesfield, Sheffield S30 3ZB*   Sheffield (0742) 570002

FORRESTER, Kenneth Norman. b 22. Ely Th Coll 46. **d** 49 **p** 50. C Brighton St Bart *Chich* 68-71; Chapl Montreux *Eur* 71-79; Chapl Malaga w Almunecar and Nerja 79-81; Chapl Pau w Biarritz 81-86; rtd 87. *Residence Callebaste Cristal, 42 rue de Masure, 64100 Bayonne, France*   France (33) 59 42 07 03

FORRESTER, Matthew Agnew. b 31. Univ of Wales (Cardiff) BA64 Lon Univ DipTh72. Trin Coll Bris 70. **d** 72 **p** 73. C Tonbridge SS Pet and Paul *Roch* 72-77; Chapl Elstree Sch Woolhampton 77-78; Chapl Duke of York's R Mil Sch Dover from 78. *Duke of York's Royal Military School, Dover, Kent CT15 5EQ*   Dover (0304) 203012

FORRYAN, John Edward. b 31. Wells Th Coll 58. **d** 60 **p** 61. C Leckhampton SS Phil and Jas *Glouc* 60-63; C Cirencester 63-68; V Glouc St Paul 68-78; R Rodborough 78-91; P-in-c Deerhurst, Apperley w Forthampton and Chaceley from 91. *The Vicarage, 1 The Green, Apperley, Gloucester*   Gloucester (0452) 780880

FORRYAN, Thomas Quested. b 64. Pemb Coll Cam BA85 DipTh86. Wycliffe Hall Ox 87. **d** 90 **p** 91. C Cheadle Hulme St Andr *Ches* from 90. *33 Kingsley Drive, Cheadle Hulme, Cheadle, Cheshire SK8 5LZ* 061-486 9306

FORSE, Reginald Austin. b 43. Oak Hill Th Coll 77. **d** 79 **p** 80. C Crofton *Portsm* 79-84; NSM Gosport Ch Ch from 91. *40 Osprey Gardens, Lee-on-the-Solent, Hants PO13 8LJ*   Portsmouth (0705) 553395

FORSHAW, David Oliver. b 27. Trin Coll Cam BA50 MA52. Qu Coll Birm. **d** 53 **p** 54. C Glen Parva and S Wigston *Leic* 53-55; Singapore 55-59; V Heptonstall *Wakef* 59-66; V Whitehaven St Nic *Carl* 66-76; P-in-c Whitehaven Ch Ch w H Trin 73-76; V Benchill *Man* 76-89; C Elton All SS from 89. *171 Brandlesholme Road, Bury, Lancs BL8 1AZ* 061-764 5231

FORSHAW, Canon Eric Paul. b 42. Lon Univ BSc63 Fitzw Coll Cam BA69 Birm Univ MA78. Ridley Hall Cam 67. **d** 70 **p** 71. C Yardley St Edburgha *Birm* 70-72; Ind Chapl 72-78; Hon C Edgbaston St Geo 72-78; Bp's Adv on Ind Soc *S'well* 78-90; Assoc Min Nottm St Pet and St Jas from 82; Hon Can S'well Minster from 85; Bp's Research Officer from 90. *11 Clumber Crescent North, The Park, Nottingham NG7 1EY*   Nottingham (0602) 417156

FORSTER, Bennet Fermor. b 21. BNC Ox BA48 MA53. Cuddesdon Coll. **d** 51 **p** 52. Chapl Bedf Sch 65-72; C Bedf St Pet *St Alb* 72-73; Lic to Offic 73-78; P-in-c Froxfield w Privett *Portsm* 78-81; V 81-88; P-in-c Hawkley w Priors Dean 78-81; V 81-88; rtd 88. *Flat 2, Holywell House, Holywell Road, Malvern Wells, Worcs WR14 4LF*   Malvern (0684) 572170

FORSTER, Brian John. b 39. Chich Th Coll 64. **d** 68 **p** 69. C Orford St Andr *Liv* 68-71; C Knotty Ash H Spirit 71-74; TV Kirkby 74-79; V Liv St Paul Stoneycroft from 79. *St Paul's Vicarage, Carlton Lane, Liverpool L13 6QS* 051-228 1041

FORSTER, Charles Clifford. b 34. AKC59. **d** 60 **p** 61. C Marske in Cleveland *York* 60-63; C Auckland St Andr and St Anne *Dur* 63-65; V Brafferton w Pilmoor and Myton on Swale *York* 65-72; V Derringham Bank 72-81; V Brompton w Snainton 81-83; V Brompton-by-Sawdon w Snainton, Ebberston etc from 83. *The Vicarage, Pudding Lane, Snainton, Scarborough, N Yorkshire YO13 9AS*   Scarborough (0723) 859805

FORSTER, Eric Lindsay. b 11. Worc Coll Ox BA33 MA38. Wycliffe Hall Ox 34. **d** 39 **p** 40. R Spaldwick w Barham and Woolley *Ely* 57-75; P-in-c Easton 58-75; rtd 75. *50 Way Lane, Waterbeach, Cambridge CB5 9NQ* Cambridge (0223) 860785

FORSTER, Gregory Stuart. b 47. Worc Coll Ox BA69 MA73 DipSocAnth70. Wycliffe Hall Ox 69. **d** 72 **p** 73. C Bath Walcot *B & W* 72-74; C Bolton Em *Man* 74-76; C Bolton St Paul w Em 77-79; R Northenden from 79. *The Rectory, Ford Lane, Northenden, Manchester M22 4NQ*   061-998 2615

FORSTER, Ian Robson. b 33. AKC59. **d** 60 **p** 61. C Leigh St Mary *Man* 60-62; C Chorlton-cum-Hardy St Werburgh 62-64; Grenada 64-66; St Lucia 66-69; P-in-c Alberbury w Cardeston *Heref* 69-76; V Ford 69-76; P-in-c Wolv St Chad *Lich* 76-78; TV Wolv 78-86; V Battersea St Phil w St Bart *S'wark* from 86. *St Philip's Vicarage, Queenstown Road, London SW8 3RT*   071-622 1929

FORSTER, Kenneth. b 27. St Jo Coll Cam BA50 MA52 Salford Univ MSc77 PhD80. NE Ord Course 83. **d** 86 **p** 87. NSM Hessle *York* from 86; Chapl Humberside Poly from 87. *Birchwood, 12 Tower View, Anlaby, Hull HU10 7EG*   Hull (0482) 657931

FORSTER, Peter Robert. b 50. Mert Coll Ox MA73 Edin Univ BD77 PhD. Edin Th Coll 77. **d** 80 **p** 81. C Mossley Hill St Matt and St Jas *Liv* 80-82; Sen Tutor St Jo Coll Dur from 83. *11 South Bailey, Durham DH1 3EE* 091-386 6793

FORSTER, Ven Victor Henry. b 17. TCD BA45 MA49. **d** 45 **p** 46. I Aghalurcher w Tattykeeran, Cooneen etc *Clogh* 67-89; RD Clogh 73-89; Preb Clogh Cathl 80-83; Adn Clogh 83-89; rtd 89; Lic to Offic *D & D* from 90. *4 Ard-Na-Ree, Groomsport, Bangor, Co Down BT19 2JL* Bangor (0247) 464548

FORSYTH, Jeanette Mary Shaw. b 48. **d** 89. NSM Old Deer *Ab* from 89; NSM Longside from 89; NSM Strichen from 89. *Moss-side of Strichen, Bogensourie, Strichen, Fraserburgh AB4 4TN* Strichen (07715) 230

FORSYTH, William. b 10. Lich Th Coll 55. **d** 56 **p** 57. V Netherton *Carl* 65-70; V Levens 70-77; rtd 77; Perm to Offic *Carl* from 77. *2 Vicarage Road, Levens, Kendal, Cumbria LA8 8PY* Sedgwick (05395) 60926

FORSYTHE, John Leslie. b 27. CITC. **d** 65 **p** 66. C Cloughfern *Conn* 65-67; C Carnmoney 67-71; I Mossley 71-80; I Antrim All SS from 80. *10 Vicarage Gardens, Station Road, Antrim BT41 4JP* Antrim (08494) 62188

FORTNUM, Brian Charles Henry. b 48. Hertf Coll Ox MA Imp Coll Lon MSc. Wycliffe Hall Ox 82. **d** 84 **p** 85. C Tonbridge St Steph *Roch* 84-87; V Shorne from 87. *The Vicarage, Butchers Hill, Shorne, Gravesend, Kent DA12 3EB* Shorne (047482) 2239

FORTUNE, John Montague. b 13. St Aid Birkenhead 43. **d** 44 **p** 45. R Berrow w Pendock *Worc* 68-78; rtd 79; Perm to Offic *Worc* from 80. *66 Badsey Lane, Evesham, Worcs* Evesham (0386) 47508

FORTUNE-WOOD, Janet. b 61. Selw Coll Cam BA82 MA88 CertEd83. Trin Coll Bris 86. **d** 88. Par Dn Rotherhithe H Trin *S'wark* from 88. *7 Howland Way, London SE16 1HN* 071-252 2995

FORWARD, Eric Toby. b 50. Nottm Univ BEd72. Cuddesdon Coll 74. **d** 77 **p** 78. C Forest Hill Ch Ch *S'wark* 77-80; Chapl Golds Coll Lon 80-84; Chapl Westwood Ho Sch 84-86; V Brighton St Aug and St Sav *Chich* 86-90; Perm to Offic *York* from 90. *28 Danesway, Beverley HU17 7JQ* Hull (0482) 865587

FORWARD, Canon Ronald George. b 25. Selw Coll Cam BA50 MA54. Ridley Hall Cam 50. **d** 52 **p** 53. V Kendal St Thos *Carl* 66-90; V Crook 78-90; Hon Can Carl Cathl from 79; rtd 90. *51 Mayo Park, Cockermouth, Cumbria CA13 0BJ* Cockermouth (0900) 824359

FOSBUARY, David Frank. b 32. Leeds Univ BA63. Coll of Resurr Mirfield 63. **d** 65 **p** 66. C Fleetwood *Blackb* 65-68; Lesotho 69-76; C Dovercourt *Chelmsf* 76-78; TV 78-79; TV Basildon St Martin w H Cross and Laindon etc 79-82; R Colsterworth *Linc* 82-84; R Colsterworth Gp 84-90; RD Beltisloe 89-90; R Lawshall w Shimplingthorne and Alpheton *St E* from 90. *The Rectory, Harrow Green, Lawshall, Bury St Edmunds, Suffolk IP29 4PB* Bury St Edmunds (0284) 830184

FOSDIKE, Lewis Bertram. b 23. Keble Coll Ox BA52 MA56. Wells Th Coll 52. **d** 54 **p** 55. V Summertown *Ox* 64-76; TR Wolvercote w Summertown 76-89; rtd 89; Chapl St Hugh's Coll Ox from 89. *18 Osberton Road, Oxford OX2 7NU* Oxford (0865) 515817

FOSKETT, Eric William. b 29. Qu Coll Birm 75. **d** 78 **p** 79. NSM Billesley Common *Birm* 78-82; V Allens Cross from 82. *St Bartholomew's Vicarage, 148 Frankley Beeches Road, Birmingham B31 5LW* 021-475 8329

FOSKETT, Canon John Herbert. b 39. St Cath Coll Cam BA62. Chich Th Coll 62. **d** 64 **p** 65. C Malden St Jo *S'wark* 64-70; P-in-c Kingston St Jo 70-76; Chapl Bethlem R Hosp Beckenham from 76; Chapl Maudsley Hosp Lon from 76; Hon Can S'wark Cathl *S'wark* from 88. *Bethlem Royal Hospital, Monk's Orchard Road, Beckenham, Kent BR3 3BX* 081-777 6611 or 776 0849

FOSS, David Blair. b 44. Bris Univ BA65 Dur Univ MA66 Fitzw Coll Cam BA68 MA72 K Coll Lon PhD86. St Chad's Coll Dur 68. **d** 69 **p** 70. C Barnard Castle *Dur* 69-72; Sierra Leone 72-74; Chapl St Jo Coll York 74-75; Chapl Ch Ch Coll Cant 75-80; Chapl Elmslie Girls' Sch Blackpool 80-83; Tutor Coll of Resurr Mirfield 83-88; V Battyeford *Wakef* from 88. *The Vicarage, Stocksbank Road, Mirfield, W Yorkshire WF14 9QT* Mirfield (0924) 493277

FOSS, William Cecil Winn. b 40. Man Univ BA68 MA87 Lon Univ DipTh66 CertEd72 BD76. Ely Th Coll 64. **d** 68 **p** 69. C S'wark St Geo *S'wark* 68-73; Perm to Offic *Ches* 73-79; V Crewe Ch Ch 79-83; V Crewe Ch Ch and St Pet from 83. *Christ Church Vicarage, 3 Heathfield Avenue, Crewe CW1 3BA* Crewe (0270) 213148

FOSSETT, Michael Charles Sinclair. b 30. CEng MIMechE59 Dur Univ BSc54. NE Ord Course 82. **d** 90 **p** 91. Hon C Nether w Upper Poppleton *York* from 90. *20 Fairway Drive, Upper Poppleton, York YO2 6HE* York (0904) 794712

FOSTER, Preb Albert Edward John. b 29. Lich Th Coll 52. **d** 55 **p** 56. C Is of Dogs Ch Ch and St Jo w St Luke *Lon* 55-58; C Notting Hill St Mich and Ch Ch 58-60; C Bethnal Green St Matt 60-62; P-in-c Bethnal Green St Jas the Gt w St Jude 62-69; V Paddington St Mary from 69; Preb St Paul's Cathl from 86; AD Westmr Paddington from 87. *6 Park Place Villas, London W2 1SP* 071-723 1968

FOSTER, Antony John. b 39. Down Coll Cam BA61 MA65. Ridley Hall Cam 65. **d** 66 **p** 67. C Sandal St Helen *Wakef* 66-69; Uganda 69-74; V Mt Pellon *Wakef* from 74. *Christ Church Vicarage, Church Lane, Mount Pellon, Halifax, W Yorkshire HX2 0EF* Halifax (0422) 365027

FOSTER, Christopher Richard James. b 53. Univ Coll Dur BA75 Man Univ MA77 Trin Hall Cam BA79 MA83 Wadh Coll Ox MA83. Westcott Ho Cam 78. **d** 80 **p** 81. C Tettenhall Regis *Lich* 80-82; Chapl Wadh Coll Ox 82-86; C Ox St Mary V w St Cross and St Pet *Ox* 82-86; V Southgate Ch Ch *Lon* from 86; Continuing Minl Educn Officer from 88. *Christ Chuch Vicarage, 1 The Green, London N14 7EG* 081-886 0384

FOSTER, David Brereton. b 55. Selw Coll Cam BA77 MA81 Ox Univ BA80. Wycliffe Hall Ox 78. **d** 81 **p** 82. C Luton St Mary *St Alb* 81-84; C Douglas St Geo and St Barn *S & M* 84-87; V S Ramsey from 87; Dir Dioc Tr Inst from 88. *St Paul's Vicarage, Walpole Drive, Ramsey, Isle of Man* Ramsey (0624) 812275

FOSTER, Donald Wolfe. b 24. St Cath Coll Cam BA48 MA50 TCD BD56. **d** 50 **p** 51. Asst Chapl Loughb Gr Sch 67-80; Chapl 80-87; Perm to Offic *Leic* from 81; rtd 87. *90 Brook Street, Wymeswold, Loughborough, Leics LE12 6TU* Loughborough (0509) 880029

FOSTER, Edward James Graham. b 12. St Jo Coll Cam BA34 MusBac35 MA38. Wells Th Coll 35. **d** 37 **p** 38. V Ashford w Sheldon *Derby* 67-78; rtd 78; Perm to Offic *Derby* from 78. *Montrose, Ashford Road, Bakewell, Derbyshire DE4 1GL* Bakewell (0629) 813718

FOSTER, Edward Philip John. b 49. Trin Hall Cam BA70 MA74. Ridley Hall Cam 77. **d** 79 **p** 80. C Finchley Ch Ch *Lon* 79-82; C Marple All SS *Ches* 82-86; P-in-c Cam St Matt *Ely* from 86. *St Matthew's Vicarage, 24 Geldart Street, Cambridge CB1 2LX* Cambridge (0223) 63545

FOSTER, Francis Desmond. b 11. ALCD33. **d** 34 **p** 35. V Throwley *Cant* 48-75; V Throwley w Stalisfield and Otterden 75-77; rtd 77; Perm to Offic *Chich* from 78. *43 Milton Road, Eastbourne, E Sussex BN21 1SH* Eastbourne (0323) 639430

FOSTER, Gareth Glynne. b 44. Open Univ BA. Chich Th Coll 66. **d** 69 **p** 70. C Fairwater *Llan* 69-71; C Merthyr Tydfil 71-72; C Merthyr Tydfil and Cyfarthfa 72-76; TV 76-87; Dioc Soc Resp Officer from 87; P-in-c Abercanaid from 87. *19 The Walk, Merthyr Tydfil, M Glam CF47 8RU* Merthyr Tydfil (0685) 722375

FOSTER, James. b 29. Man Univ BA52 MA55 Lon Univ CertEd53 Leeds Univ MEd74. NE Ord Course 82. **d** 85 **p** 86. NSM Aldborough w Boroughbridge and Roecliffe *Ripon* 85-91; P-in-c Kirby-on-the-Moor, Cundall w Norton-le-Clay etc from 91. *Ford House, Farnham, Knaresborough, N Yorkshire HG5 9JD* Boroughbridge (0423) 340200

FOSTER, John Anthony. b 18. Ridley Hall Cam 62. **d** 64 **p** 65. V Nassington w Yarwell *Pet* 67-73; R Taxal and Fernilee *Ches* 73-83; rtd 83; Perm to Offic *Lich* from 87. *31 Lindrosa Road, Sutton Coldfield, W Midlands B74 3JZ* 021-353 3340

FOSTER, John Francis. b 13. Chich Th Coll 47. **d** 49 **p** 50. V S Ramsey *S & M* 64-79; rtd 79; P-in-c Leck *Blackb* 79-83; Perm to Offic Blackb from 84; Carl from 85; Bradf from 87. *49 Fairgarth Drive, Kirkby Lonsdale, Carnforth, Lancs LA6 2DT* Kirkby Lonsdale (05242) 71753

FOSTER, Very Rev John William. b 21. BEM. St Aid Birkenhead 51. **d** 54 **p** 55. Hong Kong 57-73; Dean Hong Kong 64-73; Hon Can Hong Kong from 73; V Lythe *York* 73-78; Angl Adv Channel TV 78-88; Hon Can Win Cathl *Win* 78-88; R Guernsey St Peter Port 78-88; Dean Guernsey 78-88; rtd 88; Perm to Offic *York* from 90. *14 Lightfoots Avenue, Scarborough, N Yorkshire YO12 5NS* Scarborough (0723) 379012

FOSTER, Jonathan Guy Vere. b 56. Golds Coll Lon BA78. Wycliffe Hall Ox 83. **d** 86 **p** 87. C Hampreston *Sarum* 86-90; Chapl Chantilly *Eur* from 90. *15F Avenue Marie-Amelie, 60500 Chantilly, France* France (33) 44 58 53 22

FOSTER, Joseph James Frederick. b 22. SS Paul & Mary Coll Cheltenham CertEd42 Birm Univ DipEd59. **d** 88 **p** 88. NSM Elstead *Guildf* from 88. *Wodenscroft, Thursley Road, Elstead, Godaiming, Surrey GU8 6DH* Elstead (0252) 703198

FOSTER, Leslie. b 49. Linc Th Coll 89. **d** 91. C Coseley Ch Ch *Lich* from 91. *12 Ribbesford Crescent, Coseley, Bilston, W Midlands WV14 8XU* Bilston (0902) 493600

FOSTER, Michael John. b 52. St Steph Ho Ox 76. **d** 79 **p** 80. C Wood Green St Mich *Lon* 79-82; C Wood Green St Mich w Bounds Green St Gabr etc 82; TV Clifton *S'well* 82-85; P-in-c Aylesbury *Ox* 85-87; Dep Warden

Durning Hall Chr Community Cen 87-89; V Lydbrook *Glouc* from 89. *The Vicarage, Church Hill, Lydbrook, Glos GL17 9SW* Dean (0594) 60225

FOSTER, Neville Colin. b 34. Aston Univ BSc67. W Midl Minl Tr Course 78. **d** 81 **p** 82. C Castle Bromwich St Clem *Birm* 81-84; V Tile Cross from 84. *The Vicarage, Haywood Road, Birmingham B33 0LH* 021-779 2739

FOSTER, Phillip Deighton. b 38. Lon Univ BD70. St Aid Birkenhead 62. **d** 66 **p** 67. C Castleton Moor *Man* 66-70; V Facit 70-76; R Salford St Phil w St Steph from 76. *St Philip's Rectory, 6 Encombe Place, Salford M3 6FJ* 061-834 2041

FOSTER, Robin. b 46. ACP70 Bede Coll Dur CertEd67 Nottm Univ BTh75 Lanc Univ MA87 Open Univ BA88. Linc Th Coll 71. **d** 75 **p** 76. C Briercliffe *Blackb* 75-77; Asst Dir RE 77-79; P-in-c Tockholes 77-79; Lic to Offic *Blackb* 80-83; *Dur* from 88; Hon C Walmsley *Man* 83-88. *42 Breamish Drive, Washington, Tyne & Wear NE38 9HS* 091-415 4251

FOSTER, Ronald George. b 25. Bris Univ BSc51 AKC51. **d** 52 **p** 53. Chapl Bearwood Coll Wokingham 60-83; R Wantage Downs *Ox* 83-91; rtd 91. *Ascension Cottage, Horn Lane, East Hendred, Wantage, Oxon OX12 8LD* Abingdon (0235) 820790

FOSTER, Simon John Darby. b 57. Qu Mary Coll Lon BSc78. Wycliffe Hall Ox 85. **d** 88 **p** 89. C Bedgrove *Ox* from 88. *16 Patrick Way, Aylesbury, Bucks HP21 7XH* Aylesbury (0296) 434529

FOSTER, Stephen. b 47. Leeds Univ CertEd69. NE Ord Course 83. **d** 86 **p** 87. NSM Kingston upon Hull St Nic *York* 86-89; NSM Aldbrough, Mappleton w Goxhill and Withernwick from 89. *1 Westbourne Road, Hornsea, N Humberside HU18 1PQ* Hornsea (0964) 533679

FOSTER, Stephen Arthur. b 54. Coll of Resurr Mirfield 75. **d** 78 **p** 79. C Ches H Trin *Ches* 78-82; C Tranmere St Paul w St Luke 82-83; V Grange St Andr 83-88; V Cheadle Hulme All SS from 88. *15 Dennison Road, Cheadle Hulme, Cheshire SK8 6LW* 061-485 3455

FOSTER, Steven. b 52. Wadh Coll Ox BA75 MA80. Ridley Hall Cam 76. **d** 79 **p** 80. C Ipsley *Worc* 79-83; TV Woughton *Ox* from 83. *The Vicarage, 47 Garraways, Coffee Hall, Milton Keynes MK6 5DD* Milton Keynes (0908) 670427

FOSTER, Steven Francis. b 55. FRSA90 Lon Univ BD76 AKC76 Open Univ BA91. Coll of Resurr Mirfield 77. **d** 78 **p** 79. C Romford St Edw *Chelmsf* 78-80; C Leigh St Clem 80-83; Ed Mayhew McCrimmon Publishers 84-86; Lic to Offic 84; Hon C Southend 85-86; P-in-c Sandon 86-90; R from 90. *The Rectory, Sandon, Chelmsford CM2 7SQ* Chelmsford (0245) 72262

FOSTER, Stuart Jack. b 47. DipHE79 BA80. Lambeth STh86 Oak Hill Th Coll 77. **d** 80 **p** 81. C Worting *Win* 80-84; C-in-c Kempshott CD 84-88; R Hook from 88. *The Rectory, London Road, Hook, Basingstoke, Hants RG27 9EG* Hook (0256) 762268

FOSTER, Thomas Andrew Hayden. b 43. DipEcum. CITC 70. **d** 73 **p** 74. C Dub Clontarf *D & G* 73-78; I Drumcliffe w Clare Abbey and Kildysart *L & K* 78-80; P-in-c Polstead *St E* 78; I Kilscoran w Killinick and Mulrankin *C & O* 80-85; I Fanlobbus Union *C, C & R* 85-86; R Lasswade *Edin* 86-87; R Dalkeith 86-87; C Woodford St Mary w St Phil and St Jas *Chelmsf* 87-88; I New Ross w Old Ross, Whitechurch, Fethard etc *C & O* 89-91; Dioc Info Officer (Ferns) 90-91. *Address temp unknown*

FOSTER, Thomas Arthur. b 23. Univ of Wales (Lamp) BA47. Cuddesdon Coll 47. **d** 49 **p** 50. C Risca *Mon* 49-52; C Win H Trin *Win* 52-55; C Rhymney *Mon* 55-56; V Cwmtillery 56-59; R Llanfoist and Llanellen from 59. *The Rectory, Llanellen Road, Llanfoist, Abergavenny, Gwent NP7 9NF* Abergavenny (0873) 78168

FOSTER, William Basil. b 23. Worc Ord Coll 65. **d** 67 **p** 68. C Folkingham w Laughton *Linc* 67-71; P-in-c Gedney Hill 71-75; V Whaplode Drove 71-75; R Heydour w Culverthorpe, Welby and Londonthorpe 75-77; P-in-c Ropsley 75-79; R from 79; R Sapperton w Braceby from 79; R Old Somerby from 82. *The Rectory, Ropsley, Grantham, Lincs NG33 4BE* Ingoldsby (047685) 255

FOTHERGILL, Anthony Page. b 36. Dur Univ BA60. Cranmer Hall Dur DipTh62. **d** 62 **p** 63. V Wellington St Luke *Lich* 69-77; TV Hanley H Ev 77-78; V Rocester 78-87; P-in-c Croxden 85-87; RD Uttoxeter 87; rtd 87. *Bowerleigh, 24 Purley Rise, Purley-on-Thames, Reading RG8 8AE* Reading (0734) 842984

FOTHERGILL, Guy Sherbrooke. Lon Coll of Div. **d** 47 **p** 48. V Drax *Sheff* 65-72; V Eldersfield *Worc* 72-77; rtd 77; Perm to Offic *Glouc* from 77. *96 Coiesbourne Road, Cheltenham, Glos GL51 6DN* Cheltenham (0242) 527884

FOTHERGILL, Leslie Gurth. b 09. Tyndale Hall Bris 46. **d** 49 **p** 50. V Poughill *Truro* 65-74; rtd 74; Perm to Offic *Ex* from 74. *Magnolia Cottage, Kingscott, Torrington, Devon EX38 7JJ* Torrington (0805) 23554

FOULDS, John Stuart. b 64. Lanc Univ BA87 Southn Univ BTh91. Chich Th Coll 88. **d** 91. C Eastcote St Lawr *Lon* from 91. *33 Sunningdale Avenue, Eastcote, Ruislip, Middx HA4 9SS* 081-868 9994

FOULGER, Bernard Darwin. b 28. Cant Sch of Min 86. **d** 89 **p** 90. NSM Sittingbourne H Trin w Bobbing *Cant* from 89. *30 Frederick Street, Sittingbourne, Kent ME10 1AU* Sittingbourne (0795) 422724

FOULIS BROWN, Graham Douglas. b 50. JP. St Steph Ho Ox 80. **d** 82 **p** 83. C Hungerford and Denford *Ox* 82-84; C Bicester w Bucknell, Caversfield and Launton 84-85; TV 85-90; V Kidmore End from 90. *The Vicarage, Kidmore End, Reading RG4 9AY* Kidmore End (0734) 723987

FOULKES, Chan Meurig. b 21. St D Coll Lamp BA46. St Mich Coll Llan 46. **d** 47 **p** 48. RD Ardudwy *Ban* 64-76; R Llanaber w Caerdeon 66-76; Can Ban Cathl 71-89; Treas 74-83; Chan 83-89; R Llandegfan and Beaumaris w Llanfaes w Penmon etc 76-89; rtd 90. *Llanaber, 11 Gogarth Avenue, Penmaenmawr, Gwynedd LL34 6PY* Penmaenmawr (0492) 623011

FOULKES, Simon. b 58. Ox Poly BA81. Oak Hill Th Coll BA89. **d** 89 **p** 90. C St Austell *Truro* from 89. *10 Glen View, Truro Road, St Austell, Cornwall PL25 5JG* St Austell (0726) 63028

FOUNTAIN, David Roy (Brother Malcolm). b 48. Qu Coll Birm 85. **d** 87 **p** 88. SSF from 72; NSM Handsworth St Mich *Birm* from 87. *St Michael's Vicarage, Soho Avenue, Birmingham B18 5LB* 021-554 3521

FOUNTAINE, Michael James. b 59. Lon Univ BA81. St Steph Ho Ox. **d** 83 **p** 84. C Northn St Matt *Pet* 83-86; C Swindon New Town *Bris* 86-88; TV from 88. *St Saviour's House, Ashford Road, Swindon SN1 3NR* Swindon (0793) 695688

FOUTS, Arthur Guy. b 44. Washington Univ BA72. Ridley Hall Cam 78. **d** 81 **p** 82. C Alperton *Lon* 81-84; R Pinxton *Derby* 84-87; USA from 88. *3820 Aspen Hill Road, Wheaton, Maryland 20906, USA* Wheaton (301) 871-7660

FOWELL, Graham Charles. b 48. Southn Univ BTh85. Chich Th Coll. **d** 82 **p** 83. C Clayton *Lich* 82-86; C Uttoxeter w Bramshall 86-90; V Oxley from 90. *The Vicarage, Lymer Road, Oxley, Wolverhampton WV10 6AA* Wolverhampton (0902) 783342

FOWKE, Lt-Comdr Thomas Randall. b 07. Master Mariner 33. Chich Th Coll 52. **d** 54 **p** 55. V Brighton St Aug *Chich* 63-76; rtd 76; Perm to Offic *Heref* from 76. *6 Lower Road, Pontesbury, Shrewsbury SY5 0YH* Shrewsbury (0743) 790450

FOWKE, Canon Walter Henry. b 06. Keble Coll Ox BA28 MA32. Cuddesdon Coll 30. **d** 30 **p** 31. V Chaddesley Corbett *Worc* 66-76; RD Kidderminster 72-76; Hon Can Worc Cathl 75-76; rtd 76. *3 Queens Terrace, Church Street, Wiveliscombe, Taunton, Somerset TA4 2LP* Wiveliscombe (0984) 23661

FOWKES, Eric. b 12. Lich Th Coll 54. **d** 55 **p** 56. C Sowerby Bridge w Norland *Wakef* 55-58; V Pontefract All SS from 58. *All Saints' Vicarage, Pontefract, W Yorkshire WF8 1QT* Pontefract (0977) 702286

FOWLE, Ian. b 36. Sarum & Wells Th Coll 74. **d** 76 **p** 77. C S Wimbledon H Trin and St Pet *S'wark* 76-79; C Charlton St Luke w H Trin 79-83; V Brockley Hill St Sav from 83; Lewisham Adnry Ecum Officer from 90. *St Saviour's Vicarage, 5 Lowther Hill, London SE23 1PZ* 081-690 2499

FOWLER, Colin. b 40. Linc Th Coll 80. **d** 82 **p** 83. C Barbourne *Worc* 82-85; TV Worc St Martin w St Pet, St Mark etc 85-86; TV Worc SE from 86. *160 Bath Road, Worcester WR5 3EP* Worcester (0905) 357244

FOWLER, David Mallory. b 51. Lancs Coll of Agric OND72. Trin Coll Bris 75. **d** 78 **p** 79. C Rainhill *Liv* 78-81; C Houghton *Carl* 81-84; P-in-c Grayrigg 84-89; P-in-c Old Hutton w New Hutton 84-89; V Kirkoswald, Renwick and Ainstable from 89. *The Vicarage, Kirkoswald, Penrith, Cumbria CA10 1DQ* Lazonby (076883) 8176

FOWLER, John Douglass. b 22. Worc Ord Coll 61. **d** 63 **p** 64. P-in-c Huish Champflower w Clatworthy *B & W* 67-71; P-in-c Chipstable w Raddington 67-71; R Chelvey w Brockley 71-73; Asst Chapl Scilly Is *Truro* 73; V 74-78; P-in-c Ashbrittle w Bathealton, Stawley and Kittisford *B & W* 78-81; TV Wellington and Distr 81-86; Perm to Offic *Ex* from 86; rtd 87. *Rosedene, 1 Venn Lane, Stoke Fleming, Dartmouth, Devon TQ6 0QH* Stoke Fleming (0803) 770362

FOWLER, John Ronald. b 30. Ely Th Coll 55. d 58 p 59. C Surbiton St Andr *S'wark* 58-61; Guyana 61-70 and 83-89; V Sydenham All SS *S'wark* 70-81; V Wood End *Cov* 81-83; Can St Geo Cathl 86-89; Adn Demerara 86-89; V Bedf St Mich *St Alb* from 90. *St Michael's Vicarage, Faldo Road, Bedford MK42 0EH* Bedford (0234) 266920

FOWLER, Canon John Sims. b 25. Trin Coll Cam BA46 MA50 Lon Univ BD52. Clifton Th Coll 48. d 52 p 53. Nigeria 61-72; Hon Can Ibadan from 71; Hon Can Lagos from 72; R Crieff *St And* 73-78; R Muthill 74-78; R Comrie 77-78; Warden Leasow Ho Selly Oak 78-84; V Fulham St Dionis Parson's Green *Lon* 84-90; rtd 90; Perm to Offic *Worc* from 90. *5 Mason Close, Malvern Link, Worcs WR14 2NF* Malvern (0684) 574463

FOWLER, Miss Morag Margaret. b 45. CertEd67 DipRE67 DipLib76 St Andr Univ MA66. St Jo Coll Nottm 84. dss 85 d 87. Skipton H Trin *Bradf* 85-87; Par Dn 87-89; Par Dn Market Bosworth, Cadeby w Sutton Cheney etc *Leic* from 90. *4 Springfield Avenue, Market Bosworth, Nuneaton, Warks CV13 0NS* Market Bosworth (0455) 292157

FOWLES, Christopher John. b 31. Lich Th Coll 54. d 58 p 59. C Englefield Green *Guildf* 58-63; C Worplesdon 63-69; V Chessington 69-77; V Horsell from 77. *Horsell Vicarage, Woking, Surrey GU21 4QQ* Woking (0483) 772134

FOWLES, Peter. b 30. St Deiniol's Hawarden 71. d 72 p 73. C Connah's Quay *St As* 72-76; V Towyn 76-83; V Esclusham 83-89; rtd 89. *Filiz Casan, Towyn Road, Abergele, Clwyd LL17 7PY* Abergele (0745) 826891

FOX, Albert. b 06. MBE. d 73 p 74. C Bris St Ambrose Whitehall *Bris* 73-75; Hon C E Bris 75-79; rtd 79. *20 New Brunswick Avenue, Bristol BS5* Bristol (0272) 672632

FOX, Alfred Henry Purcell. b 95. AKC21. d 22 p 23. V Halifax St Jo Cragg Vale *Wakef* 59-65; rtd 65; P-in-c Cothelstone *B & W* 65-72. Maywind, West Bay, Bridport, Dorset DT6 4HP* Bridport (0308) 24970

FOX, Canon Bernard John Gurney. b 07. Hertf Coll Ox BA28 MA35. Cuddesdon Coll 31. d 32 p 33. V Warkworth and Acklington *Newc* 68-73; rtd 74; Perm to Offic *Newc* from 74; Hon Can Kuala Lumpur from 87. *Woodside Farm, Chevington, Morpeth, Northd NE61 5AZ* 091-565 7713

FOX, Cecil George. b 15. TCD BA47 MA64. d 48 p 49. Chapl HM Pris Lewes 66-70; V Charsfield *St E* 70-77; R Monewden and Hoo 70-77; V Charsfield w Debach and Monewden w Hoo 77-82; rtd 82; Perm to Offic *St E* from 82. *1 Ivy Cottages, Wangford, Southwold, Suffolk IP18 6UX* Southwold (0502) 724263

FOX, Canon Charles Alfred. b 08. St Aid Birkenhead 31. d 33 p 34. Hon Can Chelmsf Cathl *Chelmsf* 63-78; V Stratford St Jo and Ch Ch w Forest Gate St Jas 66-78; rtd 78; Perm to Offic *Lich* from 78. *5 Limewood Close, Blythe Bridge, Stafford ST11 9NZ* Blythe Bridge (0782) 395164

FOX, Charles Edward. b 36. Lich Th Coll 62. d 66 p 67. C S Bank *York* 66-69; C Stokesley 69-72; P-in-c Ugthorpe 72-82; V Egton w Grosmont 72-82; P-in-c Newbold Verdon *Leic* 82-83; R Newbold de Verdun and Kirkby Mallory from 84. *The Rectory, Main Street, Newbold Verdon, Leicester LE9 9NN* Hinckley (0455) 822528

FOX, Colin George. b 46. TD. Southn Univ DipTh75. Sarum & Wells Th Coll 73. d 75 p 76. C N Hammersmith St Kath *Lon* 75-79; CF (TA) 76-90; C Heston *Lon* 79-81; TV Marlborough *Sarum* 81-90; P-in-c Pewsey 90-91; TR Pewsey Team Min from 91. *The Rectory, Church Street, Pewsey, Wilts SN9 5DL* Marlborough (0672) 63203

FOX, Harvey Harold. b 27. Lich Th Coll 58. d 60 p 61. V Sparkbrook Em *Birm* 65-71; V Dordon 71-77; V Four Oaks 77-82; V Packwood w Hockley Heath 82-90; rtd 90. *3 St James' Close, Kissing Tree Lane, Alveston, Stratford-upon-Avon, Warks CV37 7RH* Stratford-upon-Avon (0789) 268263

FOX, Herbert Frederick. b 26. Leeds Univ BA50. Coll of Resurr Mirfield 50. d 52 p 53. V Turton *Man* 61-72; V Farnworth and Kearsley 72-78; RD Farnworth 77-84; TR E Farnworth and Kearsley 78-84; Hon Can Man Cathl 81-84; V Ashford Hill w Headley *Win* 84-91; rtd 91. *9 Highfield Road, Blackrod, Bolton BL6 5BP* Bolton (0204) 698368

FOX, Ian James. b 44. Selw Coll Cam BA66 MA70. Linc Th Coll 66. d 68 p 69. C Salford St Phil w St Steph *Man* 68-71; C Kirkleatham *York* 71-73; TV Redcar w Kirkleatham 73-77; V Bury St Pet *Man* 77-85; V Northallerton w Kirby Sigston *York* from 85; RD Northallerton 85-91; Chapl Friarage and Distr Hosp Northallerton from 88. *The Vicarage, Northallerton, N Yorkshire DL7 8DJ* Northallerton (0609) 780825

FOX, Miss Jacqueline Frederica. b 43. Ripon Coll of Educn CertEd66 Leeds Univ BEd74 MEd84 RCM 85. S Dios Minl Tr Scheme 83. dss 85 d 87. RCM *Lon* 85-86; Dioc FE Officer from 87. *3 Roman Close, Avenue Gardens, London W3 8HE* 081-993 5042

FOX, Jonathan Alexander. b 56. St Jo Coll Nottm LTh BTh81. d 81 p 82. C Chasetown *Lich* 81-85; TV Fazakerley Em *Liv* 85-89; Perm to Offic *Derby* from 89. *Charity Cottage, Turners Lane, The Delves, Swanwick, Derby DE55 1AS* Leabrooks (0773) 540712

FOX, Canon Joseph Denis. b 06. St Edm Hall Ox BA28 MA33. Cuddesdon Coll 28. d 29 p 30. R Neatishead w Irstead *Nor* 62-76; Hon Can Nor Cathl 75-77; rtd 76. *Seaward, Verriotts Lane, Bridport, Dorset DT6 6DX* Chideock (0297) 397

FOX, Joseph William. b 08. Sarum Th Coll 52. d 52 p 53. C Widecombe in the Moor *Ex* 52-56; Chapl HM Pris Dartmoor 56-57; C Leusden *Ex* 57-60; Perm to Offic from 74. *Craigmoor, Haytor, Newton Abbot, Devon TQ13 9XU* Haytor (0364) 498

FOX, Leonard. b 41. AKC66. d 67 p 68. C Salford Stowell Memorial *Man* 67-68; C Hulme St Phil 68-72; C Portsea All SS w St Jo Rudmore *Portsm* 72-75; V Oakfield St Jo from 75. *St John's Vicarage, Victoria Crescent, Ryde, Isle of Wight PO33 1DQ* Isle of Wight (0983) 62863

FOX, Maurice Henry George. b 24. Lon Univ BD58. St Aid Birkenhead 47. d 49 p 50. V Sutton *Bradf* 62-79; V Grange-over-Sands *Carl* 79-88; rtd 89. *7 Manor Close, Topcliffe, Thirsk, N Yorkshire YO7 3RH* Thirsk (0845) 578322

FOX, Canon Michael John. b 42. Hull Univ BSc63. Coll of Resurr Mirfield 64. d 66 p 67. C Becontree St Eliz *Chelmsf* 66-70; C Wanstead H Trin Hermon Hill 70-72; V Victoria Docks Ascension 72-76; V Chelmsf All SS 76-88; P-in-c Chelmsf Ascension 85-88; RD Chelmsf 86-88; R Colchester St Jas, All SS, St Nic and St Runwald from 88; Hon Can Chelmsf Cathl from 91. *The Rectory, East Hill, Colchester CO1 2QW* Colchester (0206) 866802

FOX, Michael John Holland. b 41. Lon Univ BD68. Oak Hill Th Coll 64. d 69 p 70. C Reigate St Mary *S'wark* 69-73; Hon C from 76; C Guildf St Sav *Guildf* 73-76; C Guildf St Sav w Stoke-next-Guildf 76; Asst Chapl Reigate Gr Sch 76-81; Chapl from 81. *71 Blackborough Road, Reigate, Surrey RH2 7BU* Reigate (0737) 249017

FOX, Michael John Howard. b 32. Coll of Resurr Mirfield 56. d 58 p 59. C Pennywell St Thos and Grindon St Oswald CD *Dur* 58-60; C Birtley 60-62; Asst Master Fairchilds Sec Boys' Sch Croydon 62-66; Saudi Arabia from 66. *Address temp unknown*

FOX, Canon Michael Storrs. b 05. Em Coll Cam BA28 MA32. Bps' Coll Cheshunt 31. d 33 p 34. Can York Minster *York* 63-87; Preb York Minster (Dunnington) 63-90; R Barton le Street 64-77; V Salton 64-77; rtd 77. *Hawthorn Cottage, Coneysthorpe, York YO6 7DD* Coneysthorpe (065384) 358

FOX, Nigel Stephen. b 35. Sarum Th Coll 59. d 62 p 63. C Rainbow Hill St Barn *Worc* 62-65; C Kidderminster St Geo 65-67; C-in-c Warndon CD 67-69; V Warndon 69-74; R S Hill w Callington *Truro* 74-85; RD E Wivelshire 78-81; R St Martin w E and W Looe from 85. *St Martin's Rectory, Barbican Road, Looe, Cornwall PL13 1NX* Looe (05036) 3070

FOX, Norman Stanley. b 39. Univ of Wales DipTh64. St Mich Coll Llan 61. d 64 p 65. C Brierley Hill *Lich* 64-67; C Tettenhall Regis 67-70; V Cradley *Worc* 70-73; Asst Chapl HM Pris Wakef 73-74; Chapl HM Pris The Verne 74-76; R Clayton W w High Hoyland *Wakef* 76-81; R Cumberworth 81-84; C Tettenhall Wood *Lich* 85-89; TV 89-91; V Pensnett from 91. *The Vicarage, Vicarage Lane, Pensnett, Brierley Hill, W Midlands DY5 4JH* Brierley Hill (0384) 262666

FOX, Peter John. b 52. AKC74. St Aug Coll Cant 74. d 75 p 76. C Wymondham *Nor* 75-79; Papua New Guinea 79-85; P-in-c Tattersett *Nor* 85-88; P-in-c Houghton 85-88; P-in-c Syderstone w Barmer and Bagthorpe 85-88; P-in-c Tatterford 85-88; P-in-c E w W Rudham 85-88; R Coxford Gp 88-89; TR Lynton, Brendon, Countisbury, Lynmouth etc *Ex* from 89. *The Rectory, Lynton, Devon EX35 6BP* Lynton (0598) 53251

FOX, Raymond. b 46. QUB BSc69. CITC 71. d 71 p 72. C Holywood *D & D* 71-75; C Min Can Down Cathl 75-78; I Killinchy w Kilmood and Tullynakill 78-81; I Belf St Mary *Conn* 81-88; I Killaney w Carryduff *D & D* from 88. *700 Saintfield Road, Carryduff, Belfast BT8 8BU* Carryduff (0232) 812342

FOX, Robert. b 54. Man Univ BEd76. Nor Ord Course 89. d 91. NSM Stalybridge *Man* from 91. *36 Norman Road, Stalybridge, Cheshire SK15 1LY* 061-338 8481

FOX, Sidney. b 47. Nottm Univ BTh79. Linc Th Coll 75. **d** 79 **p** 80. C Middlesb St Oswald *York* 79-81; P-in-c 81-86; V 86-87; V Newby from 87. *The Vicarage, 77 Green Lane, Newby, Scarborough, N Yorkshire YO12 6HT* Scarborough (0723) 363205

FOX, Timothy William Bertram. b 37. CCC Cam BA61. Qu Coll Birm 66. **d** 68 **p** 69. C Cannock *Lich* 68-72; C Bilston St Leon 72-75; V Essington 75-81; R Buildwas and Leighton w Eaton Constantine etc from 81; RD Wrockwardine from 88. *The Vicarage, Eaton Constantine, Shrewsbury SY5 6RF* Cressage (0952) 510333

FOX-ROBINSON, Wilfred Henry. b 11. Lich Th Coll 32. **d** 35 **p** 36. V Bournemouth St Pet *Win* 57-67; Perm to Offic *Linc* 71-76; rtd 76; Hon C St Giles Cripplegate w St Bart Moor Lane etc *Lon* from 77. *Boothby Hall, Spilsby, Lincs PE23 5TE* Skegness (0754) 810347

FOX-WILSON, Francis James. b 46. Nottm Univ BTh73. Linc Th Coll 69. **d** 73 **p** 74. C Eastbourne St Eliz *Chich* 73-76; C Seaford w Sutton 76-78; P-in-c Hellingly 78-79; P-in-c Upper Dicker 78-79; V Hellingly and Upper Dicker 79-85; V Goring-by-Sea from 85. *The Vicarage, 12 Compton Avenue, Goring-by-Sea, Worthing, W Sussex BN12 4UJ* Worthing (0903) 42525

FOXCROFT, James. b 05. St Andr Coll Pampisford 47. **d** 49 **p** 49. V Louth H Trin *Linc* 65-70; R Cattistock w Chilfrome *Sarum* 70-73; rtd 73; Perm to Offic *S'well* from 74. *Bradleys Cottage, 47 The Holme, Southwell, Notts NG25 0NF* Southwell (0636) 813910

FOY, Malcolm Stuart. b 48. ACP80 FCollP FRSA Univ of Wales (Lamp) BA71 Magd Coll Cam CertEd72 K Coll Lon MA89. Ox NSM Course 84. **d** 87 **p** 88. NSM Tilehurst St Mich *Ox* 87-90; C Ireland Wood *Ripon* from 90; Adv RE Leeds Adnry from 90. *The Clergy House, 9 Bedford View, Leeds LS16 6DL* Leeds (0532) 672599

FRAMPTON, Miss Marcia Ellen. b 36. SRN65 SCM66. Ripon Coll Cuddesdon 86. **d** 88. Par Dn Paston *Pet* 88-89; Par Dn Burford w Fulbrook and Taynton *Ox* from 90. *Cromwell Cottage, 43 High Street, Burford, Oxford OX8 4QE* Burford (099382) 2185

FRAMPTON-MORGAN, Anthony Paul George. b 57. Sarum & Wells Th Coll 89. **d** 91. C Plymstock *Ex* from 91. *93 Holmwood Avenue, Plymstock, Plymouth, Devon PL9 9EZ* Plymouth (0752) 47788

FRANCE, Evan Norman Lougher. b 52. Jes Coll Cam BA74 MA78. Wycliffe Hall Ox 76. **d** 79 **p** 80. C Hall Green Ascension *Birm* 79-82; CMS 82-84; C Bexhill St Pet *Chich* 84-87; V Westf from 87. *The Vicarage, Westfield, Hastings, E Sussex TN35 4SD* Hastings (0424) 751029

FRANCE, Geoffrey. b 37. S Dios Minl Tr Scheme 87. **d** 90 **p** 91. NSM Uckfield *Chich* from 90. *63 Lashbrooks Road, Uckfield, E Sussex TN22 2AY* Uckfield (0825) 767860

FRANCE, Canon Geoffrey Charles. b 23. Ripon Hall Ox 57. **d** 59 **p** 60. V Sneinton St Cypr *S'well* 68-90; Hon Can S'well Minster from 87; rtd 90; Perm to Offic *Nor* from 90. *11 Elsden Close, Holt, Norfolk NR25 6JW* Holt (0263) 711210

FRANCE, Dr Malcolm Norris. b 28. Ch Ch Ox BA53 MA57 Essex Univ PhD75. Westcott Ho Cam 53. **d** 55 **p** 56. C Ipswich St Mary le Tower *St E* 55-58; V Esholt *Bradf* 58-64; Chapl Essex Univ *Chelmsf* 64-73; Perm to Offic *Chich* 77-87; P-in-c Starston *Nor* from 87. *The Old Rectory, Starston, Harleston, Norfolk IP20 9NG* Harleston (0379) 854326

FRANCE, Richard Thomas. b 38. Ball Coll Ox BA60 MA63 Lon Univ BD62 Bris Univ PhD67. Tyndale Hall Bris 60. **d** 66 **p** 67. C Cam St Matt *Ely* 66-69; Nigeria 69-73 and 76-77; Lib Tyndale Ho Cam 73-76; Warden 78-81; Vice-Prin Lon Bible Coll 81-88; Lic to Offic *St Alb* from 83; Prin Wycliffe Hall Ox from 89. *Wycliffe Hall, Oxford OX2 6PW* Oxford (0865) 274205

FRANCIS, Brother. See BLAKE, Richard Arthur

FRANCIS, Claude Vernon Eastwood. b 15. Univ of Wales BA38. Ripon Hall Ox 38. **d** 40 **p** 41. R E Pennard w Pylle *B & W* 55-75; R Ditcheat w E Pennard and Pylle 75-81; rtd 81; Perm to Offic *B & W* from 81. *Millbank, Mill Lane, Alhampton, Shepton Mallet, Somerset BA4 6PX* Ditcheat (074986) 225

FRANCIS, David Carpenter. b 45. Southn Univ BSc66 Loughb Univ MSc71 Sussex Univ MA83. Westcott Ho Cam 85. **d** 87 **p** 88. C Ealing St Mary *Lon* 87-90; Chapl Ealing Coll of HE 87-90; Chapl Clayponds Hosp Ealing 88-90; P-in-c Wembley St Jo *Lon* from 90. *The Vicarage, 3 Crawford Avenue, Wembley, Middx HA0 2HX* 081-902 0273

FRANCIS, David Everton Baxter. b 45. St Deiniol's Hawarden 76. **d** 77 **p** 78. C Llangyfelach *S & B* 77-78; C

Llansamlet 78-80; V Llanrhaeadr-ym-Mochnant, Llanarmon, Pennant etc *St As* 80-85; V Penrhyncoch and Elerch *St D* from 85. *The Vicarage, Penrhyncoch, Aberystwyth, Dyfed* Aberystwyth (0970) 828746

FRANCIS, David Lloyd. b 01. St Jo Coll Auckland. St Jo Coll Morpeth 34. **d** 35 **p** 37. Chapl Westmr Hosp Lon 61-66; rtd 68; Perm to Offic *Chich* from 77. *54 Wordsworth Street, Hove, E Sussex BN3 5BH* Brighton (0273) 733017

FRANCIS, Donald. b 31. Bris Univ BA52. St Mich Coll Llan 52. **d** 54 **p** 55. C Newport St Julian *Mon* 54-59; C Pokesdown St Jas *Win* 59-61; R Wolvesnewton w Kilgwrrwg and Devauden *Mon* 61-74; V Llantilio Pertholey w Bettws Chpl 74-83; V Llantillio Pertholey w Bettws Chpl etc from 83; RD Abergavenny from 87. *St Teilo's Vicarage, Llantillio Pertholey, Abergavenny, Gwent NP7 6NY* Abergavenny (0873) 4323

FRANCIS, Ven Edward Reginald. b 29. Roch Th Coll 59. **d** 61 **p** 62. Chapl TS Arethusa 61-64; C Frindsbury *Roch* 61-64; C-in-c Chatham St Wm CD 64-71; V Chatham St Wm 71-73; RD Roch 73-78; V Roch 73-78; Hon Can Roch Cathl from 79; Ind Chapl 79-89; Dir Continuing Minl Educn from 89; Adn Bromley from 79. *6 Horton Way, Farningham, Dartford DA4 0DQ* Farningham (0322) 864522

FRANCIS, Canon Ernest Walter. b 08. MBE45. Clifton Th Coll 29. **d** 36 **p** 37. S Area Sec BCMS 67-74; rtd 74; Perm to Offic *Cov* from 76; Hon Can Burma from 82. *7 Margetts Close, Kenilworth, Warks CV8 1EN* Kenilworth (0926) 52560

FRANCIS, Garfield. b 12. St D Coll Lamp. **d** 42 **p** 43. R Grafton Flyford w N Piddle and Flyford Flavell *Worc* 62-77; rtd 77. *15 The Bungalows, Pontwillim Estate, Brecon, Powys* Brecon (0874) 611160

FRANCIS, Miss Gillian Cartwright. b 40. CertEd61. Dalton Ho Bris Trin Coll Bris DipTh71. **dss** 85 **d** 87. Blackheath *Birm* 86-87; Par Dn from 87. *25 Garland Crescent, Halesowen, W Midlands B62 9NJ* 021-421 4821

FRANCIS, Graham John. b 45. Univ of Wales (Cardiff) DipTh70. St Mich Coll Llan 66. **d** 70 **p** 71. C Llanblethian w Cowbridge and Llandough etc *Llan* 70-76; V Penrhiwceiber w Matthewstown and Ynysboeth from 76. *The Vicarage, Penrhiwceiber, Mountain Ash, M Glam CF45 3YF* Mountain Ash (0443) 473716

FRANCIS, Hilton Barrington. b 23. Selw Coll Cam BA46 MA48. Ridley Hall Cam 61. **d** 62 **p** 63. P-in-c Gt w Lt Plumstead *Nor* 81-87; rtd 88. *190 Church End, Cherry Hinton, Cambridge CB1 3LB* Cambridge (0223) 212081

FRANCIS, James More MacLeod. b 44. Edin Univ MA65 BD68 PhD74. Yale Div Sch STM69. **d** 87 **p** 87. NSM Sunderland St Chad *Dur* from 87. *73 Hillcrest, Sunderland SR3 3NN* 091-528 1326

FRANCIS, Jeffrey Merrick. b 46. Bris Univ BSc69. Qu Coll Birm 72. **d** 76 **p** 77. C Bris Ch the Servant Stockwood *Bris* 76-79; C Bishopston 79-82; V Bris St Andr Hartcliffe from 82. *St Andrew's Vicarage, Peterson Square, Bristol BS13 0EE* Bristol (0272) 643554

FRANCIS, Jeremy Montgomery. b 31. BNC Ox BA53 MA. Glouc Sch of Min 84. **d** 87 **p** 88. NSM Chedworth, Yanworth and Stowell, Coln Rogers etc *Glouc* 87-90; NSM Coates, Rodmarton and Sapperton etc from 90. *Old Barnfield, Duntisbourne Leer, Cirencester, Glos GL7 7AS* Miserden (028582) 370

FRANCIS, John Sims. b 25. Fitzw Ho Cam BA54 MA58. St D Coll Lamp BA47 LTh49. **d** 49 **p** 50. C Swansea St Barn *S & B* 49-52; C Chesterton St Andr *Ely* 52-54; C Swansea St Mary and H Trin *S & B* 54-58; V Newbridge-on-Wye and Llanfihangel Brynpabuan 58-65; R Willingham *Ely* 65-82; RD N Stowe 78-82; R Rampton 82; P-in-c Buckden from 82. *The Vicarage, Buckden, St Neots, Huntingdon, Cambs PE18 9TL* Huntingdon (0480) 810371

FRANCIS, Jon. b 49. Birm Univ BEd75. Ripon Hall Ox DipTh74. **d** 74 **p** 75. C Bromsgrove St Jo *Worc* 74-75; C Evesham 75-77; Hon C Pimlico St Pet w Westmr Ch Ch *Lon* 78-80; Hon C S Wimbledon All SS *S'wark* from 84. *2A Oxford Avenue, London SW20* 081-542 4474

FRANCIS, Julian Montgomery. b 60. Selw Coll Cam MA83. S'wark Ord Course 88. **d** 91. C S Wimbledon H Trin and St Pet *S'wark* from 91. *50 Evelyn Road, London SW19 8NT* 081-542 6226

FRANCIS, Kenneth. b 30. Em Coll Cam BA56 MA60. Coll of Resurr Mirfield. **d** 58 **p** 59. C De Beauvoir Town St Pet *Lon* 58-61; N Rhodesia 62-64; Zambia 64-70; V Harlow St Mary Magd *Chelmsf* 70-76; V Felixstowe St Jo *St E* from 76. *St John's Vicarage, Princes Road, Felixstowe, Suffolk IP11 7PL* Felixstowe (0394) 284226

FRANCIS, Kenneth Charles. b 22. Oak Hill Th Coll 46. **d** 50 **p** 51. V Summerstown *S'wark* 61-77; R Cratfield w Heveningham and Ubbeston etc *St E* 77-87; rtd 87. *Trenute Barns, Trebullett, Launceston, Cornwall PL15 9QB* Coads Green (0566) 82257

FRANCIS, Canon Kenneth Edgar. b 15. St D Coll Lamp BA38. **d** 39 **p** 40. R Aberdovey *Ban* 55-80; V Beddgelert 80-84; Hon Can Ban Cathl 81-84; rtd 84; Perm to Offic *Ban* from 84. *6 Edmund House, Y Maes, Criccieth, Gwynedd LL52 0AN* Criccieth (0766) 522678

FRANCIS (or ROOSE FRANCIS), Leslie. b 18. Magd Coll Ox BA48 MA52. Westcott Ho Cam 48. **d** 49 **p** 50. V Hilmarton and Highway *Sarum* 68-78; rtd 83. *2 Merton Cottages, Tregatta, Tintagel, Cornwall PL34 0DY* Camelford (0840) 770446

FRANCIS, Leslie John. b 47. FBPsS88 Pemb Coll Ox BA70 BD90 MA74 Qu Coll Cam PhD76 Nottm Univ MTh76 Lon Univ MSc77. Westcott Ho Cam 70. **d** 73 **p** 74. Hon C Haverhill *St E* 73-75; C 75-77; NSM Gt Bradley 78-82; NSM Gt w Lt Wratting 79-82; NSM N Cerney w Bagendon *Glouc* 82-85; Research Officer Culham Coll Inst 82-88; Perm to Offic from 85; Fell Trin Coll Carmarthen from 89. *Trinity College, Carmarthen, Dyfed SA31 3EP* Carmarthen (0267) 237971/2/3

FRANCIS, Martin Rufus. b 37. Pemb Coll Ox BA60 MA64. Linc Th Coll 60. **d** 63 **p** 64. C W Hartlepool St Paul *Dur* 63-67; C Yeovil St Jo w Preston Plucknett *B & W* 67-69; Chapl Tonbridge Sch Kent 69-83; Chapl and Dep Hd St Jo Sch Leatherhead from 83. *Paddock House, Linden Pit Path, Leatherhead, Surrey KT22 7JD* Leatherhead (0372) 372839

FRANCIS, Noel Charles. b 14. St Andr Univ. St D Coll Lamp BA36. **d** 38 **p** 39. V Manningham St Paul and St Jude *Bradf* 69-81; I Aughaval w Burrishoole, Knappagh and Louisburgh *T, K & A* 81-85; rtd 85; Perm to Offic *York* from 87. *5 Foxcroft, Haxby, York YO3 3GY* York (0904) 769160

FRANCIS, Paul Edward. b 52. Southn Univ BTh84. Sarum & Wells Th Coll 78. **d** 81 **p** 82. C Biggin Hill *Roch* 81-85; R Fawkham and Hartley 85-90; V Aylesford from 90. *The Vicarage, Vicarage Close, Aylesford, Maidstone, Kent ME20 7BB* Maidstone (0622) 717143

FRANCIS, Peter Brereton. b 53. St Andr Univ MTh77. Qu Coll Birm 77. **d** 78 **p** 79. C Hagley *Worc* 78-81; Chapl Qu Mary Coll *Lon* 81-87; R Ayr *Glas* from 87; Miss to Seamen from 87. *12 Barns Terrace, Ayr KA7 2DB* Ayr (0292) 262482

FRANCIS, Peter Philip. b 48. St Jo Coll Dur BA73. Wycliffe Hall Ox 73. **d** 75 **p** 76. C Foord St Jo *Cant* 75-78; C Morden *S'wark* 78-83; P-in-c Barford St Martin, Dinton, Baverstock etc *Sarum* 83-88; P-in-c Fovant, Sutton Mandeville and Teffont Evias etc 83-86; R Newick *Chich* from 88. *The Rectory, Church Road, Newick, Lewes, E Sussex BN8 4JX* Newick (082572) 2692

FRANCIS, Philip Thomas. b 58. St D Coll Lamp BA81. Chich Th Coll 81. **d** 82 **p** 83. C Llanelly St Paul *St D* 82-84; C Barnsley St Mary *Wakef* 84-87; V Burton Dassett *Cov* from 87; V Gaydon w Chadshunt from 87. *Burton Dassett Vicarage, Northend, Leamington Spa, Warks CV33 0TH* Fenny Compton (029577) 400

FRANCIS, Canon Roger. b 07. Man Univ BSc29. Ely Th Coll 29. **d** 30 **p** 31. R Areley Kings *Worc* 47-74; Hon Can Worc Cathl 69-75; rtd 74. *St Briavel's, 19 Pickersliegh Road, Malvern, Worcs WR14 2RP* Malvern (0684) 575606

FRANK, Derek John. b 49. Imp Coll Lon BSc70 Warw Univ MSc71. Cranmer Hall Dur 83. **d** 85 **p** 86. C Clay Cross *Derby* 85-87; C Crookes St Thos *Sheff* 87-90; TV from 90. *36 Forres Avenue, Sheffield S10 1WG* Sheffield (0742) 670569

FRANK, Richard Egon. b 15. Lon Univ BSc37. Qu Coll Birm 46. **d** 48 **p** 49. R Kingsnorth *Cant* 65-71; R Shadoxhurst 66-71; V Shirley St Geo 71-78; rtd 80; Perm to Offic *B & W* from 81. *27 Bincombe Drive, Crewkerne, Somerset TA18 7BE* Crewkerne (0460) 73702

FRANK, Richard Patrick Harry. b 40. St Chad's Coll Dur BA66 DipTh68. **d** 68 **p** 69. C Darlington H Trin *Dur* 68-72; C Monkwearmouth St Andr 72-74; C-in-c Harlow Green CD 74-79; R Skelton and Hutton-in-the-Forest w Ivegill *Carl* 79-86; V Carl St Luke Morton from 86; RD Carl 88-89; P-in-c Thursby 89-90; P-in-c Kirkbride w Newton Arlosh from 89. *St Luke's Vicarage, Brownrigg Drive, Carlisle CA2 6PA* Carlisle (0228) 515693

FRANKHAM, Very Rev Harold Edward. b 11. Lon Coll of Div 39. **d** 41 **p** 42. V Luton w E Hyde *St Alb* 61-70; R S'wark St Sav w All Hallows *S'wark* 70-82; Provost S'wark 70-82; rtd 83; Perm to Offic *B & W* from 83.

Garden Flat, Lambridge House, London Road West, Bath BA1 7HY Bath (0225) 333214

FRANKLAND, John Ashlin. b 12. Hatf Coll Dur LTh36 BA37 MA47 Liv Univ DipEd52. Edin Th Coll 35. **d** 37 **p** 38. Sierra Leone 53-59; Perm to Offic *Ches* from 76; rtd 77; Perm to Offic *Man* from 77. *27 Warwick Road, Hale, Altrincham, Cheshire WA15 9NP* 061-928 5178

FRANKLIN, Archibald William. b 01. Lon Univ BD32 AKC32. **d** 32 **p** 33. V Pool *Ripon* 66-74; V Pool w Arthington 74-77; rtd 77. *56 New Adel Lane, Leeds LS16 6AN* Leeds (0532) 610796

FRANKLIN, Arthur Harrington. b 03. MBE45 TD51. Linc Coll Ox BA26 MA29. Bps' Coll Cheshunt 34. **d** 34 **p** 35. R Gt Leighs *Chelmsf* 45-70; RD Roding 62-70; rtd 71. *Hea Corner, Mill Lane, Felsted, Dunmow, Essex CM6 3HQ* Great Dunmow (0371) 820519

FRANKLIN, Eric Edward Joseph. b 29. St Pet Hall Ox BA53 MA58. Qu Coll Birm DipTh55. **d** 55 **p** 56. C Knighton St Mary Magd *Leic* 55-60; Chapl Brasted Place Coll Westerham 60-66; Tutor St Chad's Coll Dur 66-72; Tutor Chich Th Coll 72-74; C Margate St Jo *Cant* 74-83; Vice-Prin St Steph Ho Ox 83-90; Dir of Studies St Steph Ho Ox from 91. *St Stephen's House, 16 Marston Street, Oxford OX4 1JX* Oxford (0865) 247874

FRANKLIN, Joan Mary. b 20. St Andr Ho Portsm 47. **dss** 61 **d** 87. Scunthorpe St Jo *Linc* 66-70; Gt Grimsby St Mary and St Jas 70-86; rtd 86. *56 Vicarage Gardens, Grimsby, S Humberside DN34 4PZ* Grimsby (0472) 242341

FRANKLIN, Kenneth Douglas. b 20. Worc Ord Coll 61. **d** 62 **p** 63. Singapore 69-72 and 78-80; V Southsea St Pet *Portsm* 72-77; C Portsea St Mary 81; Chapl Qu Alexandra Hosp Portsm 81-83; rtd 83; Perm to Offic *Chich* from 84. *56A Langdale Gardens, Hove, E Sussex BN3 4HH* Brighton (0273) 731187

FRANKLIN, Richard Charles Henry. b 48. Ch Ch Coll Cant CertEd70. Sarum & Wells Th Coll 75. **d** 78 **p** 79. C Pershore w Pinvin, Wick and Birlingham *Worc* 78-80; Educn Chapl 80-85; V Wollescote from 85. *The Vicarage, Oakfield Road, Wollescote, Stourbridge, W Midlands DY9 9DG* Stourbridge (0384) 422695

FRANKLIN, Richard Heighway. b 54. Southn Univ BA75 MPhil83. Sarum & Wells Th Coll 75. **d** 78 **p** 79. C Thame w Towersey *Ox* 78-81; Asst Chapl Southn Univ *Win* 81-83; Dir of Studies Chich Th Coll 83-89; P-in-c Stalbridge *Sarum* from 90. *The Rectory, Stalbridge, Sturminster Newton, Dorset DT10 2LR* Stalbridge (0963) 62859

FRANKLIN, Simon George. b 54. Bris Univ BA75. Ridley Hall Cam 77. **d** 79 **p** 80. C Woodmansterne *S'wark* 79-83; C St Peter-in-Thanet *Cant* 83-86; R Woodchurch from 86. *The Rectory, Woodchurch, Ashford, Kent TN26 3QJ* Woodchurch (023386) 257

FRANKLIN, Stephen Alaric. b 58. Lon Univ BD87. Sarum & Wells Th Coll 87. **d** 89 **p** 90. C Chenies and Lt Chalfont, Latimer and Flaunden *Ox* from 89. *St George's Parsonage, White Lion Road, Amersham, Bucks* Little Chalfont (0494) 763244

✠**FRANKLIN, Rt Rev William Alfred.** b 16. OBE64. Kelham Th Coll 33. **d** 40 **p** 41 **c** 72. C Bethnal Green St Jo *Lon* 40-42; C Palmers Green St Jo 43-45; Argentina 45-58; Chile 58-65; Colombia 65-78; Adn 66-71; Bp 72-78; Asst Bp Pet 78-86; rtd 86; Asst Bp Cant from 86. *Flat C, 26 The Beach, Walmer, Deal, Kent CT14 7HJ* Deal (0304) 361807

FRANKLIN, William Henry. b 50. Macquarie Univ (NSW) BA78 Birkb Coll Lon MA82. Moore Th Coll Sydney 76 Melbourne Coll of Div 83 Chich Th Coll 85. **d** 86 **p** 87. C S Leamington St Jo *Cov* 86-89; Chapl RN from 89. *c/o MOD, Lacon House, Theobald's Road, London WC1X 8RY* 071-430 6847

FRANKS, Dennis Leslie. b 24. BEM55. Bps' Coll Cheshunt 65. **d** 67 **p** 68. C Anlaby Common St Mark *York* 67-70; V Middlesb Ascension 71-75; P-in-c Whorlton 76-77; V Whorlton w Carlton and Faceby 77-82; V Saltburn-by-the-Sea 82-87; rtd 87. *26 The Chine, Saltburn-by-the-Sea, Cleveland TS12 1QL* Guisborough (0287) 624012

FRANKS, John Edward. b 29. **d** 61 **p** 62. C Plymouth St Matthias *Ex* 61-66; V Upton Grey w Weston Patrick and Tunworth *Win* 66-77; V Upton Grey, Weston Patrick, Tunworth etc 77-79; P-in-c Wolverton cum Ewhurst and Hannington 79-80; R Baughurst, Ramsdell, Wolverton w Ewhurst etc from 81. *The Rectory, Wolverton, Basingstoke, Hants RG26 5RU* Kingsclere (0635) 298008

FRANZ, Very Rev Kevin Gerhard. b 53. Edin Univ MA74 BD79. Edin Th Coll 76. **d** 79 **p** 80. C Edin St Martin *Edin* 79-83; R Selkirk 83-90; Provost St Ninian's Cathl Perth *St And* from 90; R Perth St Ninian from 90.

St Ninian's House, 40 Hay Street, Perth PH1 5HS   Perth (0738) 26874

FRASER, Alister Douglas. b 26. Qu Coll Cam BA49 MA55. Tyndale Hall Bris 50. **d** 68 **p** 69. C Weymouth St Jo *Sarum* 68-72; R Kingswood *Glouc* 72-80; V Woodside St Steph 80-84; RD Forest S 84-88; V Cinderford St Steph w Littledean 84-90; rtd 90. *4 Stevens Cross Close, Sidmouth, Devon EX10 9QJ*   Sidmouth (0395) 579568

FRASER, Andrew Thomas. b 52. Newc Univ Aus BA81. St Jo Coll (NSW) ThL79. **d** 81 **p** 82. Australia 81-87; C Prestbury *Glouc* 87-91; C Wotton St Mary from 91. *30 Simon Road, Longlevens, Gloucester GL2 0TP*   Gloucester (0452) 23803

FRASER, David Ian. b 32. Em Coll Cam BA54 MA58. Oak Hill Th Coll 56. **d** 58 **p** 59. C Bedf St Jo *St Alb* 58-61; C Cheadle Hulme St Andr *Ches* 61-64; R Fringford w Hethe and Newton Purcell *Ox* 64-67; V Preston St Luke *Blackb* 67-71; V Surbiton Hill Ch Ch *S'wark* from 71. *Parish Office, 8 Christ Church Road, Surbiton, Surrey KT5 8JJ*   081-399 3444

FRASER, Ernest William Emerson. b 04. AKC27. Westcott Ho Cam 28. **d** 28 **p** 29. V Downe *Roch* 51-57; Perm to Offic *Chich* from 57; rtd 69. *The Goodalls, Ellerslie Lane, Bexhill-on-Sea, E Sussex TN39 4LJ*   Bexhill-on-Sea (0424) 211141

FRASER, Geoffrey Michael. b 29. Sarum Th Coll. **d** 59 **p** 60. C Thames Ditton *Guildf* 59-63; C Shere 63-65; C Dunsford and Doddiscombsleigh *Ex* 65-70; V Uffculme from 70. *The Vicarage, Uffculme, Cullompton, Devon EX15 3AX*   Craddock (0884) 841001

FRASER, Air Marshal Sir Henry Paterson. b 07. KBE61 CB53 AFC37. CEng FRAeS Pemb Coll Cam BA29 MA73. **d** 77 **p** 78. APM Ramsey Deanery *S & M* from 77. *803 King's Court, Ramsey, Isle of Man*   Ramsey (0624) 813069

FRASER, James Stuart. b 26. Em Coll Cam BA50 MA53. Westcott Ho Cam 52. **d** 54 **p** 55. C Ipswich St Thos *St E* 54-57; V Rushmere 57-70; V Putney St Mary *S'wark* from 70. *The Vicarage, 45 St John's Avenue, London SW15 6AL*   081-788 4575

FRASER, Jane Alicia. b 44. Man Univ BA. Glouc Sch of Min. **d** 89. NSM Upton-upon-Severn *Worc* from 89. *Dunstall Cottage, Dunstall Common, Earl's Croome, Worcester WR8 9DF*   Severn Stoke (090567) 391

FRASER, Canon John Keys. b 15. TCD BA38. CITC 39. **d** 39 **p** 40. V Scarborough St Mary w Ch H and A Apostles *York* 65-81; Can and Preb York Minster from 76; rtd 81; Perm to Offic *York* from 90. *10 North Leas Avenue, Scarborough, N Yorkshire YO12 6LN*   Scarborough (0723) 377982

FRASER, Canon John Sheean. b 23. TCD BA47 MA52. **d** 47 **p** 50. C Dub St Geo *D & G* 47-48; C Dub St Steph 50-52; I Leney and Kilbixy *M & K* 52-59; I Killucan Union 59-65; I Limerick St Mary *L & K* 65-67; Can Res and Preb Limerick Cathl 67-76; Sub-Dean 74-76; Lic to Offic from 82. *5 Ashbrook, Ennis Road, Limerick, Irish Republic*   Limerick (61) 53502

FRASER, Ross Dominic. b 24. St Jo Coll Morpeth. **d** 47 **p** 48. V Ryhope *Dur* 61-74; P-in-c Elton 74-75; P-in-c Medomsley 75-76; V 76-84; rtd 84. *19 Laburnum Gardens, Low Fell, Gateshead, Tyne & Wear NE9 5JN*

FRASER-SMITH, Keith Montague. b 48. St Jo Coll Dur BA70. Trin Coll Bris DipTh72. **d** 73 **p** 74. C Bishopsworth *Bris* 73-76; Egypt from 77. *Address temp unknown*

FRAYLING, Canon Nicholas Arthur. b 44. Ex Univ BA69. Cuddesdon Coll 69. **d** 71 **p** 72. C Peckham St Jo *S'wark* 71-74; V Tooting All SS 74-83; Can Res and Prec Liv Cathl *Liv* 83-87; R Liv Our Lady and St Nic w St Anne 87-90; TR from 90; Hon Can Liv Cathl from 89. *25 Princes Park Mansions, Sefton Park Road, Liverpool L8 3SA*   051-727 4692 or 236 5287

FRAYNE, Canon David. b 34. St Edm Hall Ox BA58 MA62 Birm Univ DipTh60. Qu Coll Birm 58. **d** 60 **p** 61. C E Wickham *S'wark* 60-63; C Lewisham St Jo Southend 63-67; V N Sheen St Phil and All SS 67-73; R Caterham 73-83; RD Caterham 80-83; Hon Can S'wark Cathl 82; V Bris St Mary Redcliffe w Temple etc *Bris* from 83; RD Bedminster from 86; Hon Can Bris Cathl from 91. *The Vicarage, 10 Redcliffe Parade West, Bristol BS1 6SP*   Bristol (0272) 291962 or 291487

FRAYNE, Derek Arthur Vivian. b 30. Univ of Wales (Swansea) BA52. Wells Th Coll 52. **d** 54 **p** 55. C Aberdare *Llan* 54-58; PV Llan Cathl 58-64; V Llanharan w Peterston-s-Montem 64-79; Chapl St Dav Hosp from 79; R Canton St Jo from 79. *The Rectory, 3A Romilly Road, Cardiff CF1 1FH*   Cardiff (0222) 229683

FRAZER, Ven Albert Henry Victor. b 14. TCD BA38 MA62. CITC 38. **d** 38 **p** 39. I Rathdrum w

Glenealy, Derralossary and Laragh *D & G* 66-84; Adn Glendalough 70-84; rtd 83; Chapl Kingston Coll Co Cork from 84. *The Chaplaincy, Kingston College, Michelstown, Co Cork, Irish Republic*   Fermoy (25) 24429

FRAZER, David. b 60. QUB BSSc TCD DipTh84. TCD Div Sch. **d** 84 **p** 85. C Taney w St Nahi *D & G* 84-87; C Dub Ch Ch Cathl Gp 87-88; I Clane w Donadea and Coolcarrigan *M & K* from 88. *St Michael's Vicarage, Sallins, Naas, Co Kildare, Irish Republic*   Kildare (45) 68276

FRAZER, Ian Martin. b 44. **d** 91. Lic to Offic *D & D* from 91. *Lisroyan, 154 Malone Road, Belfast BT9 5LT*   Belfast (0232) 667100

FRAZER, Canon James Stewart. b 27. TCD. **d** 57 **p** 58. C Belf Whiterock *Conn* 57-59; C Belf St Matt 59-61; I Lack *Clogh* 61-64; I Mullaglass *Arm* 64-65; I Milltown 65-70; Australia 70-74; I Dromore *Clogh* 74-82; RD Kesh 78-82; Bp Dom Chapl 82; I Derryvullen S w Garvary 82-90; Can Clogh Cathl 83-85; Preb from 85; RD Enniskillen 89-90; I Clogh w Errigal Portclare from 90. *Cathedral Rectory, Clogher, Co Tyrone BT76 0AD*   Clogher (06625) 48235

FRAZER, Milburn Ronald. b 18. Worc Ord Coll 63. **d** 65 **p** 66. C Bexhill St Pet *Chich* 67-71; R Tillington 71-78; Chapl Upper Chine Sch Shanklin 78-84; rtd 85; Chapl Shoreham Coll 86-90. *290 Old Shoreham Road, Southwick, Brighton BN42 4LQ*   Brighton (0273) 597224

FREAR, Philip Scott. b 45. Univ of Wales (Lamp) BA66. **d** 80 **p** 81. Hon C Purton *Bris* 80-81; C Rodbourne Cheney 81-85; V Hengrove from 85. *Christ Church Vicarage, 7 Petherton Road, Bristol BS14 9BP*   Whitchurch (0272) 832346

FREARSON, Andrew Richard. b 57. BA. Wycliffe Hall Ox. **d** 83 **p** 84. C Acocks Green *Birm* 83-86; C Moseley St Mary 86-89; P-in-c Holme-in-Cliviger *Blackb* from 89. *St John's Vicarage, Burnley Road, Cliviger, Burnley, Lancs BB10 4SU*   Burnley (0282) 22467

FREATHY, Nigel Howard. b 46. Lon Univ BA68 CertEd. Sarum & Wells Th Coll 79. **d** 81 **p** 82. C Crediton *Ex* 81-82; C Crediton and Shobrooke 82-84; TV Ex St Thos and Em 84-86; V Beer and Branscombe from 86. *The Vicarage, Mare Lane, Beer, Seaton, Devon EX12 3NB*   Seaton (0297) 20996

FREDERICK, John Bassett Moore. b 30. Princeton Univ BA51 Birm Univ PhD73. Gen Th Sem (NY) MDiv54. **d** 54 **p** 55. USA 54-56 and 61-71; C All Hallows Barking *Lon* 56-58; C Ox SS Phil and Jas *Ox* 58-60; R Bletchingley *S'wark* from 74; Reigate Adnry Ecum Officer from 90. *The Rectory, Bletchingley, Redhill RH1 4LR*   Godstone (0883) 743252

FREDERICK, Warren Charles. b 47. Qu Coll Birm 86. **d** 88 **p** 89. C W Leigh *Portsm* 88-91; V N Holmwood *Guildf* from 91. *The Vicarage, North Holmwood, Dorking, Surrey RH5 4JB*   Dorking (0306) 882135

FREDRIKSEN, Martin. b 47. St Chad's Coll Dur BA69 DipTh70. **d** 70 **p** 71. C Bideford *Ex* 70-73; C Guildf St Nic *Guildf* 73-76; R Cossington *B & W* 76-82; V Woolavington 76-82; Asst Chapl K Coll Taunton 82-84; C Hatf *St Alb* from 84. *St John's House, Bishops Rise, Hatfield, Herts AL10 9BZ*   Hatfield (0707) 262689

FREE, Canon James Michael. b 25. K Coll Lon BD50 AKC50. **d** 51 **p** 52. V Pilning *Bris* 67-75; P-in-c Lydiard Millicent w Lydiard Tregoz 75-82; Hon Can Bris Cathl 76-82; Can Res, Prec and Sacr Bris Cathl 82-83; Can Treas 83-90; Bp's Adv for Miss 82-87; Bp's Officer for Miss and Evang 87-89; rtd 90. *23 Manor Drive, Merriott, Somerset TA16 5PB*   Crewkerne (0460) 76053

FREEBAIRN-SMITH, Mrs Jane. b 36. K Coll Lon DipTh59 DipPC86. St Chris Coll Blackheath 59. **d** 88. NSM Uddingston *Glas* 88-91; NSM Cambuslang 88-91; Dioc Missr from 88; NSM Baillieston from 91. *14 Prospect Avenue, Cambuslang, Glasgow G72 8BW*   041-641 5055

FREEBORN, John Charles Kingon. b 30. G&C Coll Cam BA52 MA56. Ridley Hall Cam 53. **d** 55 **p** 56. C Doncaster St Geo *Sheff* 55-57; Tutor Wycliffe Hall Ox 57-61; R Flixton St Mich *Man* 61-72; C Leic H Apostles *Leic* 72-73; C E Crompton *Man* 73-74; Hon C Ashton St Mich 74-76; Perm to Offic 77-80; Hd Master H Trin Sch Halifax 80-88; Lic to Offic *Wakef* from 80; Hon C Sowerby from 83. *27 Crossley Hill, Halifax, W Yorkshire HX3 0PL*   Halifax (0422) 342489

FREEMAN, Canon Alan John Samuel. b 27. SS Coll Cam BA48 MA52. Sarum Th Coll 50. **d** 52 **p** 53. C Tottenham Ch Ch W Green *Lon* 52-55; C Harpenden St Nic *St Alb* 55-60; R Aspley Guise 60-75; RD Fleete 67-70; RD Ampthill 70-75; Hon Can St Alb from 74; V Boxmoor St Jo from 75; Chapl Hemel Hempstead Gen Hosp (W

Herts Wing) from 75; RD Berkhamsted *St Alb* from 85. *The Vicarage, 10 Charles Street, Hemel Hempstead, Herts HP1 1JH* Hemel Hempstead (0442) 255382

FREEMAN, Anthony John Curtis. b 46. Ex Coll Ox BA68 MA72. Cuddesdon Coll 70. **d** 72 **p** 73. C Worc St Martin *Worc* 72-74; C Worc St Martin w St Pet 74-75; Bp's Dom Chapl *Chich* 75-78; C-in-c Parklands St Wilfrid CD 78-82; V Durrington 82-89; P-in-c Staplefield Common from 89; Adv Continuing Minl Educn from 89; Asst Dir of Ords from 89. *The Vicarage, Staplefield, Haywards Heath, W Sussex RH17 6EN* Handcross (0444) 400241

FREEMAN, Canon Douglas Charles. b 29. Lon Univ BD54 AKC54. **d** 55 **p** 56. C Is of Dogs Ch Ch and St Jo w St Luke *Lon* 55-59; V Guyhirn w Ring's End *Ely* 59-63; P-in-c Coldham 60-63; R Duloe w Herodsfoot *Truro* 63-70; V Morval 66-70; V St Ives 70-82; P-in-c Lelant 78-80; Hon Can Truro Cathl 80-82; V Forton *Portsm* 82-89; RD Alverstoke 86-89; V Widley w Wymering from 89. *The Vicarage, Medina Road, Cosham, Portsmouth PO6 3NH* Cosham (0705) 376307

FREEMAN, Douglas James. b 20. Ox NSM Course 80. **d** 83 **p** 84. NSM Ellesborough *Ox* 83-91; NSM Wendover Deanery from 87; NSM Ellesborough, The Kimbles and Stoke Mandeville from 91. *Chadley, Butlers Cross, Aylesbury, Bucks HP17 0TS* Wendover (0296) 623240

FREEMAN, James Henry. b 14. **d** 79 **p** 80. Hon C Wandsworth St Steph *S'wark* from 79. *43 Oakhill Road, London SW15 2QJ* 081-874 1501

FREEMAN, Karl Fredrick. b 57. St Luke's Coll Ex BEd80. **d** 90 **p** 91. C Plymouth St Andr w St Paul and St Geo *Ex* from 90. *18 Glenhurst Road, Plymouth PL3 5LT* Plymouth (0752) 267025

FREEMAN, Malcolm Robin. b 48. **d** 88 **p** 89. NSM Kirkcaldy *St And* from 88; NSM Kinghorn from 91. *Cherrybank Cottage, Main Street, Auchertool, Fife KY2 5XW* Glenrothes (0592) 781439

FREEMAN (nee ADAMS), Mrs Margaret Anne. b 27. AKC48. Gilmore Ho. **dss** 82 **d** 87. Gt Yarmouth *Nor* 80-87; rtd 87; Hon Par Dn Malborough w S Huish, W Alvington and Churchstow *Ex* from 87. *26 Weymouth Park, Hope Park, Kingsbridge, Devon TQ7 3HD* Kingsbridge (0548) 561274

FREEMAN, Michael Charles. b 36. Magd Coll Cam BA61 MA68 Lon Univ BD69. Clifton Th Coll 67. **d** 69 **p** 70. C Bedworth *Cov* 69-72; C Morden *S'wark* 72-77; P-in-c Westcombe Park St Geo 77-85; V Kingston Vale St Jo from 85. *The Vicarage, Robin Hood Lane, London SW15 3PY* 081-546 4079

FREEMAN, Michael Curtis. b 51. Lanc Univ BA72. Cuddesdon Coll 72. **d** 75 **p** 76. C Walton St Mary *Liv* 75-78; C Hednesford *Lich* 78-81; TV Solihull *Birm* 81-86; V Yardley Wood 86-90; V Farnworth *Liv* from 90. *The Vicarage, Farnworth, Widnes, Cheshire WA8 9HY* 051-424 2735

FREEMAN, Michael Raymond. b 58. Chu Coll Cam BA80 MA84 Ox Univ BA87. St Steph Ho Ox 85. **d** 88 **p** 89. C Clifton All SS w St Jo *Bris* from 88. *70 Pembroke Road, Bristol BS8 3ED* Bristol (0272) 741355

FREEMAN, Mrs Pamela Mary. b 45. W Midl Minl Tr Course 83. **dss** 86 **d** 87. Cannock *Lich* 86-87; Par Dn 87-88; Par Dn Oxon and Shelton from 88; Min for Deaf (Salop Adnry) from 88. *4 High Oaks, Bicton Heath, Shrewsbury SY3 5AX* Shrewsbury (0743) 69656

FREEMAN, Philip Martin. b 54. Westcott Ho Cam 76. **d** 79 **p** 80. C Stanley *Liv* 79-82; C Bromborough *Ches* 82-84; Chapl Halton Gen Hosp 84-91; V Runcorn H Trin *Ches* 84-91; R Ashton upon Mersey St Martin from 91. *St Martin's Rectory, 367 Glebelands Road, Sale, Cheshire M33 5GG* 061-973 4204

FREEMAN, Philip Michael. b 25. Jes Coll Cam BA50 MA54. Qu Coll Birm 50. **d** 52 **p** 53. P-in-c Bottesford w Ashby *Linc* 66-73; TR 73-75; P-in-c Warw St Nic *Cov* 75-76; TV Warw 77-87; P-in-c Claverdon w Preston Bagot 87-90; rtd 90. *10 Arundel Close, Warwick CV34 5HZ* Warwick (0926) 411431

FREEMAN, Richard Alan. b 52. Ripon Coll Cuddesdon. **d** 83 **p** 84. C Crayford *Roch* 83-86; V Slade Green from 86. *The Vicarage, Slade Green, Erith, Kent DA8 2HX* Dartford (0322) 333970

FREEMAN, Robert John. b 52. St Jo Coll Dur BSc74 Fitzw Coll Cam BA76 MA. Ridley Hall Cam 74. **d** 77 **p** 78. C Blackpool St Jo *Blackb* 77-81; TV Chigwell *Chelmsf* 81-85; V Leic Martyrs *Leic* from 85. *The Vicarage, 17 Westcotes Drive, Leicester LE3 0QT* Leicester (0533) 546162

FREEMAN, Ronald Mercer. b 24. Trin Coll Cam BA45 MA50. Wycliffe Hall Ox 47. **d** 49 **p** 50. R Kersal

Moor *Man* 67-78; V Walmersley 78-90; rtd 90. *3 High Avenue, Bolton BL2 5AZ* Bolton (0204) 385341

FREEMAN, Shirley Beckett. b 14. Ch Coll Cam BA36 MA40. Ridley Hall Cam 36. **d** 38 **p** 39. R Compton Valence *Sarum* 65-75; R Long Bredy w Lt Bredy and Kingston Russell 65-75; rtd 74. *Eckling Grange, Norwich Road, Dereham, Norfolk NR20 3BB* Dereham (0362) 691189

FREEMAN, Terence. b 40. Wells Th Coll 67. **d** 70 **p** 71. C Hanham *Bris* 70-75; C Cockington *Ex* 75-77; R Sampford Spiney w Horrabridge 77-89; V Wembury from 89. *The Vicarage, Wembury, Plymouth PL9 0JJ* Plymouth (0752) 862319

FREEMAN, William John. b 04. Lon Coll of Div 31. **d** 34 **p** 35. R W Parley *Sarum* 54-69; rtd 69. *133 Heathfield Road, West Moors, Wimborne, Dorset BH22 0DE* Ferndown (0202) 875029

FREER, Andrew Selwyn Bruce. b 26. Wells Th Coll 55. **d** 57 **p** 58. C Yardley St Edburgha *Birm* 57-62; R Byfield *Pet* 62-71; V Brackley St Pet w St Jas 71-81; R Bincombe w Broadwey, Upwey and Buckland Ripers *Sarum* from 81. *The Rectory, 526 Littlemoor Road, Weymouth, Dorset DT3 5PA* Upwey (0305) 812542

FREER, Bernard. b 22. St Aid Birkenhead 60. **d** 62 **p** 63. C Boulton *Derby* 62-65; V Stanley 65-73; P-in-c Scropton 73; P-in-c Marston on Dove 73; V Marston on Dove w Scropton from 74; RD Longford 81-86. *The Vicarage, Back Lane, Hilton, Derby DE6 5GJ* Etwall (028373) 3433

FREESTONE, Herbert Keith. b 14. Ripon Hall Ox. **d** 65 **p** 66. P-in-c Erith St Jo *Roch* 68-73; R Horsmonden 73-79; rtd 79; Perm to Offic *Chich* from 79. *51 Ashdown Road, Worthing, W Sussex BN11 1DE* Worthing (0903) 34956

FREETH, Barry James. b 35. Birm Univ BA60. Tyndale Hall Bris 60. **d** 62 **p** 64. C Selly Hill St Steph *Birm* 62-63; C Birm St Jo Ladywood 63-71; Chapl RAF 71-75; P-in-c Crudwell w Ashley *Bris* 75-81; P-in-c Lanreath *Truro* 81-84; R 84-87; P-in-c Pelynt 81-84; V 84-87; R Harvington, Norton and Lenchwick *Worc* from 87. *The Rectory, Station Road, Harvington, Evesham, Worcs WR11 5NJ* Evesham (0386) 871068

FREETH, Ven John Stanton. b 40. Selw Coll Cam BA62 MA66. Ridley Hall Cam 64. **d** 66 **p** 67. C Gillingham St Mark *Roch* 66-72; TV Heslington *York* 72-80; Chapl York Univ 72-80; S Africa from 80; Adn Athlone from 88. *The Rectory, 16 Waterloo Road, Wynberg, 7800 South Africa* Cape Town (21) 762-4395

FREETH, Richard Hudson de Wear. b 13. Worc Ord Coll. **d** 64 **p** 65. V Mayland *Chelmsf* 67-76; V Steeple 67-76; rtd 76. *Ml Sol Roof 36, Apt 63, Villa de Madrid, Torrevieja, Alicante, Spain*

FRENCH, Basil Charles Elwell. b 19. Edin Th Coll LTh44. **d** 45 **p** 46. S Rhodesia 59-65; Rhodesia 65-80; Zimbabwe 80-85; rtd 85; Hon C Wrington w Butcombe *B & W* from 85. *Christ Church Parsonage, Redhill, Bristol BS18 7SL* Wrington (0934) 862398

FRENCH, Clive Anthony. b 43. AKC70. St Aug Coll Cant 70. **d** 71 **p** 72. C Monkseaton St Mary *Newc* 71-73; Dioc Youth Adv 73-76; Chapl RN from 76; Dir of Ords RN from 84. *c/o MOD, Lacon House, Theobald's Road, London WC1X 8RY* 071-430 6847

FRENCH, Canon Dendle Charles. b 29. Lon Univ BD56. ALCD55. **d** 56 **p** 57. C Gt Yarmouth *Nor* 56-63; Jamaica 63-66; V Sedgeford w Southmere *Nor* 66-71; P-in-c Gt Ringstead 66-67; R 67-71; TV Thetford 71-74; Chapl Hockerill Coll Bishop's Stortford 74-78; P-in-c St Paul's Walden *St Alb* 78-85; V from 85; RD Hitchin 84-89; Hon Can St Alb from 91. *The Vicarage, Whitwell, Hitchin, Herts SG4 8HX* Whitwell (0438) 871658

FRENCH, George Leslie. b 47. AIFST NE Lon Poly BSc70. S'wark Ord Course 86. **d** 89 **p** 90. NSM Reading St Barn *Ox* from 89. *Hawthorne House, 2 Cutbush Close, Lower Earley, Reading RG6 4XA* Reading (0734) 861886

FRENCH, Jonathan David Seabrook. b 60. Westcott Ho Cam 84. **d** 87 **p** 88. C Loughton St Jo *Chelmsf* 87-90; Chapl St Bede's Ch for the Deaf Clapham from 90. *412 Clapham Road, London SW4* 071-622 4969

FRENCH, Ms Judith Karen. b 60. St D Coll Lamp BA89. St Steph Ho Ox 89. **d** 91. Par Dn Botley *Portsm* from 91. *1 Rectory Court, Botley, Southampton, Hants SO3 2SJ* Botley (0489) 787715

FRENCH, Owen John Jason. b 01. K Coll Lon 34. **d** 38 **p** 39. V High Easter w Margaret Roding *Chelmsf* 61-69; V Gd Easter 61-69; rtd 69; Perm to Offic *Nor* from 69. *c/o F W Standley and Son, 22 Middleton Street, Wymondham, Norfolk NR18 0AE*

FRENCH, Peter Robert. b 65. Man Univ BTh87. Qu Coll Birm 88. **d** 90 **p** 91. C Unsworth *Man* from 90. *113 Hollins Lane, Bury, Lancs BL9 8AB*   061-796 9697

FRENCH, Philip Colin. b 50. Sarum & Wells Th Coll 81. **d** 83   **p** 84.   C Llansamlet *S & B* 83-86; P-in-c Waunarllwydd 86-87; V from 87. *St Barnabas' Vicarage, Waunarllwyd, Swansea SA5 4SY*   Gowerton (0792) 872251

FRENCH, Richard John. b 34. Open Univ BA82. Tyndale Hall Bris 62. **d** 64 **p** 65. C Rustington *Chich* 64-68; C Walton H Trin *Ox* 68-72; V Grove from 72. *The Vicarage, Grove, Wantage, Oxon OX12 7LQ*   Wantage (02357) 66484

FRENCH, Stephen Robert James. b 52. St Jo Coll Nottm. **d** 87 **p** 88. C Chell *Lich* 87-91; TV from 91. *The Vicarage, 110 Springbank Road, Stoke-on-Trent ST6 6HZ*   Stoke-on-Trent (0782) 810329

FREND, Prof William Hugh Clifford. b 16. TD59. FSA52 FRHistS54 FRSE79 FBA83 Keble Coll Ox BA37 DPhil40 MA51 DD66 Cam Univ BD64 Edin Univ Hon DD74. **d** 82 **p** 83. Prof Ecclesiastical Hist Glas Univ 69-84; NSM Whittlesford *St And* 82-84; P-in-c Barnwell w Thurning and Luddington *Pet* 84-90; rtd 90. *The Clerk's Cottage, Little Wilbraham, Cambridge CB1 5CB*   Cambridge (0223) 811731

FRERE, Christopher Michael Hanbury. b 21. Roch Th Coll 65. **d** 67 **p** 68. C Spilsby w Hundleby *Linc* 67-71; V N Kelsey 71-76; V Cadney 71-76; P-in-c Aisthorpe w W Thorpe and Scampton 75-79; P-in-c Brattleby 75-79; R Fillingham 76-78; V Ingham w Cammeringham 76-78; RD Lawres 78-84; V Ingham w Cammeringham w Fillingham 79-86; R Aisthorpe w Scampton w Thorpe le Fallows etc 79-86; rtd 86. *164 Newark Road, North Hykeham, Lincoln LN6 8LZ*   Lincoln (0522) 689145

FRESTON, John Samuel Kern. b 28. Lich Th Coll 70. **d** 72 **p** 73. C Walsall *Lich* 72-75; TV Trunch w Swafield *Nor* 75-77; TV Trunch 77-82; R W Winch from 82; Chapl St Jas Hosp 82-85; Qu Eliz Hosp King's Lynn 85-90. *The Rectory, West Winch, King's Lynn, Norfolk PE33 0NR*   King's Lynn (0553) 840835

FRETWELL, Brian George. b 34. TD. CEng MIMechE. Chich Th Coll 79. **d** 81 **p** 82. C Bude Haven *Truro* 81-82; C Saltash 82-85; C Walthamstow St Sav *Chelmsf* 85-87; V Doncaster Intake *Sheff* from 87. *The Vicarage, Kingston Road, Intake, Doncaster, S Yorkshire DN2 6LS*   Doncaster (0302) 323167

FREWIN, William Charles. b 46. Trin Coll Bris 84. **d** 86 **p** 87. C Southchurch H Trin *Chelmsf* 86-89; C Shrub End 89-91; R W Bergholt from 91. *The Rectory, 1 Church Close, West Bergholt, Colchester CO6 3JZ*   Colchester (0206) 240273

FREY, Christopher Ronald. b 44. AKC69 Uppsala Univ BD73 MTh77. St Aug Coll Cant 69. **d** 70 **p** 71. C Addington *Ox* 70-72; Lic to Offic *Eur* 73-78; Chapl Stockholm w Uppsala 78-85; Can Brussels Cathl 81-85; Lic to Offic *Carl* 85-89; Chapl Casterton Sch Cumbria 85-89; Epsom Coll Surrey 89-91; Chapl Worksop Coll Notts from 91. *2 North Copse, Worksop College, Worksop, Notts S80 3AP*

FRIARS, Ian Malcolm George. b 50. Sarum & Wells Th Coll 83. **d** 85 **p** 86. C Norton *St Alb* 85-88; C Ramsey *Ely* 88-90; TV The Ramseys and Upwood from 90. *The Vicarage, Thatcher's Close, Upwood, Huntingdon, Cambs PE17 1PN*   Ramsey (0487) 814473

FRIARS, Robert John. b 32. Trin Coll Cam BA55 MA59. Wells Th Coll 55. **d** 57 **p** 58. C Hackney St Jo *Lon* 57-62; Youth Tr Officer 62-65; C St Andr Holborn 62-70; Sen Youth Chapl 65-70; TV Hackney 70-79; V Sompting *Chich* from 79. *The Vicarage, West Street, Sompting, Lancing, W Sussex BN15 0AX*   Worthing (0903) 34511

FRICKER, Alfred Spartan. b 93. ALCD27. **d** 28 **p** 29. R Meppershall *St Alb* 60-71; R Upper Stondon 60-71; rtd 71. *Sycamore, 28 Greenway, Campton, Shefford, Beds*   Hitchin (0462) 814714

FRICKER, Canon David Duncan. b 27. Lon Univ BA53. Ridley Hall Cam 53. **d** 55 **p** 56. C Ecclesfield *Sheff* 55-58; C Luton St Mary *St Alb* 58-61; V Luton St Paul 61-64; R Bedf St Pet 64-75; RD Bedf 69-79; Hon Can St Alb 74-88; P-in-c Bedf St Paul 75-79; R Bedf St Pet w St Cuth 75-88; R Brightling, Dallington, Mountfield & Netherfield *Chich* from 88; RD Dallington from 88. *The Rectory, Brightling, Robertsbridge, E Sussex TN32 5HE*   Brightling (042482) 281

FRIEND, Frederick James. b 41. BA. Oak Hill NSM Course. **d** 82 **p** 83. NSM Hughenden *Ox* from 82. *The Chimes, Cryers Hill Road, High Wycombe, Bucks HP15 6JS*   Naphill (024024) 3168

FRIESS, Herbert Friedrich. b 09. Leipzig Univ BD. **d** 41 **p** 42. Dean Killala *T, K & A* 67-73; I Achill w Dugort,

Castlebar and Turlough 73-79; rtd 79. *Mulrany, Westport, Co Mayo, Irish Republic*   Westport (98) 36126

FRIGGENS, Canon Maurice Anthony. b 40. Sheff Univ BA65. Westcott Ho Cam 65. **d** 67 **p** 68. C Stocksbridge *Sheff* 67-70; C St Buryan, St Levan and Sennen *Truro* 70-72; R 72-84; RD Penwith 82-84; R St Columb Major w St Wenn 84-91; Hon Can Truro Cathl from 87; Dioc Dir of Ords from 87; V St Cleer from 91. *The Vicarage, St Cleer, Liskeard, Cornwall PL14 5DJ*   Liskeard (0579) 43240

FRITH, Christopher John Cokayne. b 44. Ex Coll Ox BA65 MA69. Ridley Hall Cam 66. **d** 68 **p** 69. C Crookes St Thos *Sheff* 68-71; C Rusholme *Man* 71-74; R Haughton St Mary 74-85; R Brampton St Thos *Derby* from 85. *The Rectory, 481 Chatsworth Road, Chesterfield, Derbyshire S40 3AD*   Chesterfield (0246) 232717

FRITH, David William. b 65. K Coll Lon BD87 PGCE88. Westcott Ho Cam 88 Lambeth STh90. **d** 90 **p** 91. C St Jo Wood *Lon* from 90. *Flat 3, St John's Hall, St John's Wood High Street, London NW8 7NF*   071-722 9188

FRITH, Ivy Florence. b 24. CertEd56. St Chris Coll Blackheath 48. **dss** 79 **d** 87. St Alb Abbey *St Alb* 79-82; Truro St Paul and St Clem *Truro* 82-84; C Truro St Mary from 85; Asst Dioc Dir of Ords from 85; Dioc Lay Min Adv from 85; MU Chapl from 91. *42 Tregolls Road, Truro, Cornwall TR1 1LA*   Truro (0872) 79463

FRITH, Richard Michael Cokayne. b 49. Fitzw Coll Cam BA72 MA76. St Jo Coll Nottm 72. **d** 74 **p** 75. C Mortlake w E Sheen *S'wark* 74-78; TV Thamesmead 78-83; TR Keynsham *B & W* from 83. *The Rectory, 1 The Park, Keynsham, Bristol BS18 2BL*   Bristol (0272) 863354

FRITH, Roger Eatherley. b 12. St Jo Coll Dur BA37 MA40. **d** 38 **p** 39. V Jesmond Clayton Memorial *Newc* 60-72; V Carl St Jo *Carl* 72-80; rtd 80; Perm to Offic *Carl* from 85. *9 Powdrake Crescent, Longtown, Carlisle CA6 5XD*   Longtown (0228) 791515

FRIZELLE, Canon Thomas Herbert. b 07. TCD BA36 MA40. **d** 38 **p** 39. I Dundonald *D & D* 51-80; Treas Down Cathl 74-80; rtd 80. *24 Killeaton Park, Derriaghy, Dunmurry, Belfast BT17 9HE*   Belfast (0232) 621233

FROGGATT, Alan. b 16. Nor Ord Course 73. **d** 76 **p** 77. NSM Gorleston St Andr *Nor* from 76; Perm to Offic *Ely* from 86. *15 Clarke's Road, Gorleston, Great Yarmouth, Norfolk NR31 7AG*   Great Yarmouth (0493) 661663

FROGGATT, Jeffrey. b 27. Ch Coll Cam BA48 MA52. Ridley Hall Cam 49. **d** 51 **p** 52. C Scunthorpe St Jo *Linc* 51-53; C Doncaster St Jas *Sheff* 53-56; V New Edlington 56-62; V Malin Bridge 62-73; Ind Chapl 73-79; V Wortley 73-79; R Todwick 79-85; V Dore from 85. *The Vicarage, 51 Vicarage Lane, Dore, Sheffield S17 3GY*   Sheffield (0742) 363335

FROOM, Ian Leonard John. b 42. Sarum Th Coll 69. **d** 71 **p** 72. C Gillingham and Fifehead Magdalen *Sarum* 71-75; C Parkstone St Pet w Branksea and St Osmund 75-78; V Sedgley St Mary *Lich* 78-85; TV Weston-super-Mare Cen Par *B & W* from 85. *46 Manor Road, Weston-super-Mare, Avon BS23 2SU*   Weston-super-Mare (0934) 623230

FROST, Bruce Alan. b 31. St Barn Coll Adelaide 74. **d** 76 **p** 77. Australia 76-87 and from 88; P-in-c Goldenhill *Lich* 87-88. *129 Morphett Road, Morphetville, S Australia 5043*   Adelaide (8) 295-4759

FROST, Daveth Harold. b 56. Univ Coll Dur BSc77. Ripon Coll Cuddesdon 77. **d** 80 **p** 81. C Cockerton *Dur* 80-83; C Newton Aycliffe 83-87; V Dunston from 87. *Wyndcrest Lodge, 14 Park Avenue, Dunston, Gateshead, Tyne & Wear NE11 9QE*   091-460 9591

FROST, David. b 48. **d** 86 **p** 87. Hon C Upper Norwood All SS *S'wark* 86-89; C Battersea St Luke from 90. *30 Canford Road, London SW11 6NZ*   071-228 7431

FROST, David Richard. b 54. Ridley Hall Cam 84. **d** 86 **p** 87. C Burgess Hill St Andr *Chich* 86-90; TV Rye from 90. *The Vicarage, 21 Fairmeadow, Rye, E Sussex TN31 7NL*   Rye (0797) 222456

FROST, Derek Charles. b 47. Lich Th Coll 69. **d** 71 **p** 72. C Woodley *Ox* 71-76; V Bampton w Clanfield 76-81; V Minster Lovell and Brize Norton 81-88; TV Upper Kennett *Sarum* from 88. *The Vicarage, Broad Hinton, Swindon, Wilts SN4 9PA*   Swindon (0793) 731310

FROST, Ven George. b 35. Dur Univ BA56 MA61. Linc Th Coll 57. **d** 60 **p** 61. C Barking St Marg *Chelmsf* 60-64; C-in-c Marks Gate CD 64-70; V Tipton St Matt *Lich* 70-77; V Penn 77-87; RD Trysull 84-87; Preb Lich Cathl 85-87; Hon Can from 87; Adn Salop from 87; V Tong from 87. *Tong Vicarage, Shifnal, Shropshire TF11 8PW*   Albrighton (0902) 372622

FROST, James Michael. b 29. Liv Univ BA51 DipEd52 DUP54. NE Ord Course 81. **d** 84 **p** 85. NSM Huntington

York 84-89; TV Heworth from 89. *St Wulstan's Vicarage, 8 Abbotsway, York YO3 9LD*   York (0904) 425188

FROST, Julian. b 36. Solicitor 57 Bris Univ BA61 MA65 Lon Univ CertEd70. Clifton Th Coll 64. **d** 65 **p** 66. C Welling *Roch* 65-69; Hon C 70-73; Dep Dir Schs Coun RE Project Lanc Univ 73-78; V New Beckenham St Paul from 78. *St Paul's Vicarage, Brackley Road, Beckenham, Kent BR3 1RB*   081-650 3400

FROST, Philip Frederick Wainwright. b 20. Keble Coll Ox BA42 MA46. Qu Coll Birm 46. **d** 48 **p** 49. V Ainstable w Armathwaite *Carl* 69-74; V Flimby 74-79; V Allithwaite 79-85; rtd 85; Perm to Offic *Blackb* from 85. *12 Taylor Grove, Bare, Morecambe, Lancs LA4 6HT* Morecambe (0524) 412181

FROST, Ronald Andrew. b 48. Cam Univ DipRS77 Univ of S Carolina BTh81. Ridley Hall Cam 86. **d** 87 **p** 88. C Gt Wilbraham *Ely* 87-89; P-in-c Stow Longa 89-91; V from 91; P-in-c Kimbolton 89-91; V from 91. *The Vicarage, Kimbolton, Huntingdon, Cambs PE18 0HB* Huntingdon (0480) 860279

FROST, Stanley. b 37. MIBiol FAEB Univ of Wales MSc Liv Univ Ord Course 79. **d** 82 **p** 83. NSM Lower Kersal *Man* 82-87; NSM Patricroft 87-89; NSM Convenor (Dio Man) from 87; Perm to Offic from 89. *5 Moorside Road, Kersal, Salford M7 0PJ*   061-792 3107

FROST, Thomas Laurence. b 20. Clifton Th Coll 60. **d** 62 **p** 63. V Knaresborough H Trin *Ripon* 69-78; R Stoke Climsland *Truro* 78-79; Chapl Sliema *Eur* 79-81; R Kirriemuir *St And* 81-85; rtd 85. *Ramley House Nursing Home, Ramley Road, Pennington, Lymington, Hants S04 8LH*   Lymington (0590) 677645

FROST, William Henry. b 10. Dur Univ LTh37. Clifton Th Coll 33. **d** 36 **p** 37. V Sea Mills *Bris* 59-75; rtd 75; Perm to Offic *B & W* from 79. *Flat 3, 43 Walliscote Road, Weston-super-Mare, Avon BS23 1EE* Weston-super-Mare (0934) 23666

FROST, Preb William Selwyn. b 29. Wells Th Coll 61. **d** 62 **p** 63. C Cheddleton *Lich* 62-67; V Longdon-upon-Tern 67-81; R Rodington 67-81; RD Wrockwardine 77-84; Preb Lich Cathl from 81; R Longdon-upon-Tern, Rodington, Uppington etc 81-84; R Whittington St Jo 84-86; C Trysull 86-89; TV Wombourne w Trysull and Bobbington from 89. *The Vicarage, Trysull, Wolverhampton WV5 7HR*   Wombourne (0902) 892647

FROSTICK, Alan Norman. b 25. Ripon Hall Ox 74. **d** 75 **p** 76. C Crewkerne w Wayford *B & W* 75-78; P-in-c Brompton Regis w Upton and Skilgate 78-80; V Buttershaw St Aid *Bradf* 80-83; V Aylesham *Cant* 83-85; P-in-c Adisham 84-85; R Aylesham w Adisham 85-90; rtd 90. *18 Hawthorn Close, St Marys Bay, Romney Marsh, Kent TN29 0SZ*   Dymchurch (0303) 875158

FROSTICK, Canon John George. b 23. Wells Th Coll 52. **d** 54 **p** 55. V Frisby-on-the-Wreake w Kirby Bellars *Leic* 58-71; V Shepshed 71-83; Hon Can Leic Cathl 80-83; R Kirton w Falkenham *St E* 83-90; rtd 90. *68 Melton Road, Barrow-upon-Soar, Loughborough, Leics LE12 8NX* Quorn (0509) 620110

FROSTICK, Paul Andrew. b 52. CertEd. Ripon Hall Ox 74 Ripon Coll Cuddesdon 75. **d** 77 **p** 78. C Shepton Mallet *B & W* 77-80; TV Barton Mills, Beck Row w Kenny Hill etc *St E* 80-85; TV Mildenhall 85-86; TV Raveningham *Nor* 86-89; V Bottisham *Ely* 89-90; P-in-c Lode and Longmeadow 89-90; V Bottisham and Lode w Long Meadow from 90. *The Vicarage, 86 High Street, Bottisham, Cambridge CB5 9BA*   Cambridge (0223) 812367

FROUD, James George. b 23. MBE89. **d** 54 **p** 55. Hong Kong 54-58; C All Hallows by the Tower etc *Lon* 58-61; Chapl Durning Hall Chr Community Cen Forest Gate 61-82; P-in-c Forest Gate St Jas *Chelmsf* 61-66; Chapl Forest Gate Hosp Lon 61-69; Chapl Aston Charities Trust from 82; NSM Barking St Marg w St Patr *Chelmsf* from 91. *37 The Drive, Loughton, Essex IG10 1HB* 081-508 6479

FROWLEY, Peter Austin. b 32. W Midl Minl Tr Course. **d** 84 **p** 85. NSM Tardebigge *Worc* 84-88; Hong Kong from 88. *First Floor, 19 County Apartments, 19 Stanley Village Road, Stanley, Hong Kong*   Hong Kong (852) 813-1047

FRY, Barry James. b 49. ACIB. Ripon Coll Cuddesdon 81. **d** 83 **p** 84. C Highcliffe w Hinton Admiral *Win* 83-87; V Southn St Barn from 87. *St Barnabas's Vicarage, 12 Rose Road, Southampton SO2 1AE*   Southampton (0703) 223107

FRY, Christopher David. b 49. St D Coll Lamp DipTh74. **d** 74 **p** 75. C Ynyshir *Llan* 74-75; C Barry All SS 76-79; V Llansawel w Briton Ferry 79-81; C Llanishen and Lisvane 81-85; V Llan N from 85. *All Saints' Vicarage,*

59 Station Road, Llandaff North, Cardiff CF4 2FB Cardiff (0222) 564096

FRY, Canon James Reinhold. b 30. St Cuth Soc Dur BSc53 MA70. Oak Hill Th Coll 55. **d** 57 **p** 58. C Bromley St Jo *Roch* 57-60; V Deptford St Luke *S'wark* 60-66; V Chalk *Roch* from 66; RD Gravesend 81-91; Hon Can Roch Cathl from 87. *The Vicarage, 2A Vicarage Lane, Gravesend, Kent DA12 4TF*   Gravesend (0474) 567906

FRY, Miss Joan Aileen. b 29. Bedf Coll Lon BA50. Qu Coll Birm 79. dss 82 **d** 87. Hendon St Mary *Lon* 82-87; Colindale St Matthias 82-87; Asst Chapl Colindale Hosp 82-87; Hon Par Dn Swanage and Studland *Sarum* from 87. *Flat 1, Richmond House, 27 Rabling Road, Swanage, Dorset BH19 1ED*   Swanage (0929) 423351

FRY, Miss Lorna Sylvia Crawshay. b 21. Dalton Ho Bris 50. dss 60 **d** 87. Chapl Lee Abbey 70-81; rtd 81; Plymouth St Andr w St Paul and St Geo *Ex* 81-87; Hon Par Dn Devonport St Budeaux from 87. *24 Dunstone Road, Plymouth PL5 2HJ*   Plymouth (0752) 360836

FRY, Michael John. b 59. Nottm Univ BA80 Sheff Univ CQSW83 Cam Univ BA85. Westcott Ho Cam 83. **d** 86 **p** 87. C Upholland *Liv* 86-89; C Dovecot 89-91; TV St Luke in the City from 91. *2 Minster Court, Crown Street, Liverpool L7*   051-709 9665

FRY, Roger Joseph Hamilton. b 29. Em Coll Cam BA52 MA56. Clifton Th Coll 52. **d** 54 **p** 55. C Walcot *B & W* 54-57; C Gresley *Derby* 57-61; P-in-c Bowling St Bart and St Luke *Bradf* 61-65; V Bowling St Jo 61-87; V Ingleton w Chapel le Dale from 87. *The Vicarage, Ingleton, Carnforth, Lancs LA6 3HF*   Ingleton (05242) 41440

FRY, Roger Owen. b 30. Sarum Th Coll 58. **d** 60 **p** 61. C Yeovil St Mich *B & W* 60-63; P-in-c Weston-in-Gordano 64-70; R Clapton-in-Gordano 64-70; R Portishead 64-80; V Weston Zoyland w Chedzoy from 80. *The Vicarage, Weston Zoyland, Bridgwater, Somerset TA7 0EP* Weston Zoyland (0278) 691251

FRY, Stephen. b 57. St Steph Ho Ox 83. **d** 86 **p** 87. C Wood Green St Mich w Bounds Green St Gabr etc *Lon* 86-89; C Kentish Town St Jo from 89. *The Church House, Ospringe Road, London NW5 2JB*   071-267 4720

FRYAR, John Davies. b 53. St Steph Ho Ox 77. **d** 80 **p** 81. C Bidston *Ches* 80-81; C Thame w Towersey *Ox* 81-84; C Dorchester 84-85; TV 85-88; TR Catford (Southend) and Downham *S'wark* from 88. *St John's Rectory, 353 Bromley Road, London SE6 2RP*   081-698 3898

FRYER, Anthony Charles. b 18. RMA. Wycliffe Hall Ox. **d** 60 **p** 60. C Furze Platt *Ox* 60-62; V Shinfield 62-73; Perm to Offic *Pet* 85-86; P-in-c Charwelton w Fawsley and Preston Capes from 86. *Byfield House, Byfield, Daventry, Northants NN11 6XN*   Byfield (0327) 60244

FRYER, Charles Eric John. b 14. Lon Univ BA54 PhD84. Linc Th Coll 62. **d** 63 **p** 64. C Finham *Cov* 63-66; Perm to Offic *S'well* 66-75; Lic to Offic 75-79; R Killin *St And* from 79; R Lochearnhead 79-89. *The Shieling, Crianlarich, Perthshire FK20 8RU*   Crianlarich (08383) 237

FRYER, George. b 33. St Jo Coll Cam BA57 MA61. Ox NSM Course 73. **d** 76 **p** 77. NSM Wallingford *Ox* 76-79; C Wokingham St Paul 79-83; V Linc St Swithin *Linc* 83-88; P-in-c Walsden *Wakef* from 88. *6 Stoneley Drive, Todmorden, Lancs OL14 7UR*   Todmorden (0706) 817776

FRYER, Kenneth Wesley. b 34. AKC59. **d** 60 **p** 61. C Heckmondwike *Wakef* 60-62; C Osmondthorpe St Phil *Ripon* 62-65; C Ancoats *Man* 65-66; V Tinsley *Sheff* 73-77; P-in-c Scarcliffe *Derby* 77-80; V Newhall from 80. *The Vicarage, Church Street, Newhall, Burton-on-Trent, Staffs DE11 0HY*   Burton (0524) 213860

FRYER, Michael Andrew. b 56. St Jo Coll Nottm 88. **d** 90 **p** 91. C Hull St Martin w Transfiguration *York* from 90. *87 Parkfield Drive, Anlaby Road, Hull HU3 6TF*   Hull (0482) 566706

FRYER, Preb Peter Hugh. b 25. Linc Th Coll 58. **d** 60 **p** 61. R St Buryan *Truro* 64-72; R St Levan 66-72; R St Sennen 70-72; R Elgin w Lossiemouth *Mor* 72-76; Chapl RAF 72-76; P-in-c Lewannick *Truro* 76-78; P-in-c Altarnon and Bolventor 76-78; P-in-c N Hill 76-78; TR N Hill w Altarnon, Bolventor and Lewannick 78-84; P-in-c Laneast w St Clether and Tresmere 80-84; Preb St Endellion 84-90; R St Endellion w Port Isaac and St Kew 84-90; rtd 90. *Blythswood, Fore Street, Marazion, Cornwall TR17 0AS*   Penzance (0736) 711857

FUDGER, John. b 53. Coll of Resurr Mirfield 76. **d** 77 **p** 78. C Sutton in Ashfield St Mary *S'well* 77-80; C Duston *Pet* 80-82; V Radford All So w Ch Ch and St Mich *S'well* 82-91; Min Bermondsey St Hugh CD *S'wark* from 91. *Charterhouse Mission, 40 Tabard Street, London SE1 4JU*   071-407 1123

FUDGER, Michael Lloyd. b 55. K Coll Lon BD77 AKC77. Coll of Resurr Mirfield 77. **d** 78 **p** 79. C Weston Favell *Pet* 78-82; C Pet H Spirit Bretton 82-84; V Irchester 84-90; TV Darnall-cum-Attercliffe *Sheff* from 90. *66 Mather Road, Sheffield S9 4GQ* Sheffield (0742) 440167

FUGGLE, Francis Alfred. b 13. Selw Coll Cam BA34 MA38. Wells Th Coll 35. **d** 36 **p** 37. C Kingsbury St Andr *Lon* 36-38; S Africa from 38. *360A Florida Road, Durban, 4001 South Africa* Durban (31) 238923

FULFORD, Herbert Anthony. b 31. FRICS70. SW Minl Tr Course. **d** 85 **p** 86. NSM Topsham *Ex* from 85. *Coach House, Grove Hill, Topsham, Exeter EX3 0EG* Topsham (039287) 4296

FULHAM, Suffragan Bishop of. See KLYBERG, Rt Rev Charles John

FULLAGAR, Michael Nelson. b 35. SS Coll Cam BA57 MA61. Chich Th Coll 57. **d** 59 **p** 60. C Camberwell St Giles *S'wark* 59-61; C Northolt Park St Barn *Lon* 61-64; C Hythe *Cant* 64-66; Zambia 66-78; R Freemantle *Win* 78-87; P-in-c Westbury w Turweston, Shalstone and Biddlesden *Ox* from 87. *The Vicarage, Westbury, Brackley, Northants NN13 5JT* Brackley (0280) 704964

FULLALOVE, Miss Brenda Hurst. b 33. Open Univ BA75 Man Univ MPhil86. St Mich Ho Ox 58. dss 80 **d** 87. Bolton St Paul w Em *Man* 80-87; Par Dn from 87. *63 Hargreaves House, Crook Street, Bolton, Lancs BL3 6EF* Bolton (0204) 28209

FULLER, Alison Jane. b 61. St Andr Univ MTheol84. Edin Th Coll 85. **d** 87. C Selkirk *Edin* 87-89; C Melrose 87-89; C Galashiels 87-89; C Edin H Cross from 89. *1 Almondbank Cottages, Edinburgh EH4 6PJ* 031-336 1031

FULLER, Alistair James. b 66. Univ of Wales (Lamp) BA87. Ripon Coll Cuddesdon 88. **d** 90 **p** 91. C Thornton-le-Fylde *Blackb* from 90. *6 Waring Drive, Thornton Cleveleys, Blackpool FY5 2SP* Blackpool (0253) 855103

FULLER, Christopher John. b 53. Chich Th Coll 85. **d** 87 **p** 88. C Swinton St Pet *Man* 87; C Swinton and Pendlebury 87-90; C Chiswick St Nic w St Mary *Lon* from 90. *St Denys Cottage, Church Street, London W4 2PD* 081-995 2019

FULLER, Colin Spencer. b 34. Qu Coll Birm 60. **d** 63 **p** 64. C Walsall *Lich* 63-68; C-in-c Pheasey CD 68-75; V Pheasey 75-76; TV Cockermouth All SS w Ch Ch *Carl* 76-77; TV Cockermouth w Embleton and Wythop 77-87; V Clipstone *S'well* from 87. *The Vicarage, Church Road, Clipstone, Mansfield, Notts NG21 9DG* Mansfield (0623) 23916

FULLER, Canon Frank William. b 22. Chich Th Coll 53. **d** 54 **p** 55. R Cockfield *St E* 61-72; RD Lavenham 64-72; Hon Can St E Cathl 67-87; V Bungay H Trin w St Mary 73-87; RD Beccles and S Elmham 76-83; rtd 87. *23 Middle Street, Puriton, Bridgwater, Somerset TA7 8AU* Bridgwater (0278) 684131

FULLER, Frederick Walter Tom. b 17. St Cath Coll Cam BA48 MA53 Bris Univ MLitt72 Ex Univ PhD74. Union Th Sem (NY) STM54 Cuddesdon Coll 49. **d** 51 **p** 52. Lect and Chapl St Luke's Coll Ex 59-78; Hon C Swindon New Town *Bris* from 79; rtd 82. *29 Oxford Road, Swindon, Wilts SN3 4HP* Swindon (0793) 824980

FULLER, Graham Drowley. b 33. AKC58. **d** 59 **p** 60. C E Grinstead St Swithun *Chich* 59-62; C Coulsdon St Andr *S'wark* 62-64; Chapl RN 64-68; V Battersea St Luke *S'wark* 68-75; V Stoneham *Win* 75-90; Bp's Ecum Officer 84-90; R Eversley from 90. *The Rectory, Eversley, Basingstoke, Hants RG27 0LX* Eversley (0734) 733237

FULLER, Canon Howel Pascal. b 20. St D Coll Lamp BA47. **d** 49 **p** 50. R Ashton w Hartwell *Pet* 60-70; V Camrose *St D* 70-73; Chapl Withybush Gen Hosp Haverfordwest 73-87; R Prendergast w Rudbaxton *St D* 73-87; RD Daugleddau 78-87; Can St D Cathl 80-87; rtd 87. *9 Albert Street, Haverfordwest, Dyfed SA61 1TA* Haverfordwest (0437) 765520

FULLER, Canon John James. b 38. SS Coll Cam BA63. Chich Th Coll 63 Union Th Sem (NY) STM64. **d** 65 **p** 66. C Westmr St Steph w St Jo *Lon* 65-71; Tutor Cuddesdon Coll 71-75; Tutor Ripon Coll Cuddesdon 75-77; Dir S Dios Minl Tr Scheme from 77; Can and Preb Sarum Cathl *Sarum* from 83. *The Theological College, 19 The Close, Salisbury SP1 2EE* Salisbury (0722) 332235

FULLER, Canon Reginald Horace. b 15. Cam Univ BA37 MA41. Qu Coll Birm 39. **d** 40 **p** 41. USA 55-80; Lic to Offic *Derby* from 64; rtd 80. *5001 East Seminary Avenue, Richmond, Virginia 23227, USA* Richmond (804) 226-6010

FULLER, Robert James. b 10. Lon Univ BD53. **d** 55 **p** 56. R Exford w Exmoor *B & W* 61-75; rtd 75. *Verna,*

Trefonen, Oswestry, Shropshire SY10 9DJ Oswestry (0691) 653505

FULLER, Robert Peter. b 49. Bernard Gilpin Soc Dur 71 Trin Coll Bris 72. **d** 75 **p** 76. C Tonbridge SS Pet and Paul *Roch* 75-79; C Welling 79-83; V Nottm St Sav *S'well* 83-89; V Ripley *Derby* from 89. *The Vicarage, 26 Mount Pleasant, Ripley, Derby DE5 3DX* Ripley (0773) 749641

FULLER, Terence James. b 30. Bris Univ BA55. Clifton Th Coll 55. **d** 56 **p** 57. C Uphill *B & W* 56-60; V Islington St Jude Mildmay Park *Lon* 60-67; V Southgate *Chich* 67-80; R Stoke Climsland *Truro* from 80; RD Trigg Major 85-91. *The Rectory, Stoke Climsland, Callington, Cornwall PL17 8NZ* Stoke Climsland (0579) 70501

FULLERTON, Hamish John Neville. b 45. Ball Coll Ox BA68 MA73. S'wark Ord Course 76. **d** 79 **p** 80. NSM Clapham Old Town *S'wark* 79-82; Abp Tennison's Sch Kennington 79-88; Perm to Offic 82-89; Hon C Brixton Rd Ch Ch from 89. *Flat 4, 21 Offerton Road, London SW4 0DJ* 071-622 7890

FULLJAMES, Janet Kathleen Doris. b 43. Open Univ BA79. Qu Coll Birm 85. **d** 87. Par Dn Harborne St Pet *Birm* from 87. *21 Vicarage Road, Birmingham B17 0SN* 021-426 1318

FULLJAMES, Michael William. b 36. AKC60. **d** 61 **p** 62. C Armley St Bart *Ripon* 61-64; C E Wells *B & W* 64-67; R Stanningley St Thos *Ripon* 67-73; Chapl St Aug Hosp *Cant* 73-88; St Martin's Hosp 82-88; RD W Bridge *Cant* 87-88; Sen Chapl Rotterdam Miss to Seamen *Eur* from 88; Chapl Rotterdam St Mary from 88. *Heemraadssingel 44, 3021 DB, Rotterdam, The Netherlands* Rotterdam (10) 476-9765

FULLJAMES, Peter Godfrey. b 38. BNC Ox BA60 MA64. Qu Coll Birm DipTh62. **d** 62 **p** 63. C Mexborough *Sheff* 62-65; India 65-69; Lic to Offic *Lich* 70-79; Moorside High Sch Werrington 71-79; Kenya 80-85; Research Fell Qu Coll Birm 85-87; Perm to Offic *Birm* 85-90; Tutor W Midl Minl Tr Course from 87; Lic to Offic *Birm* from 90. *21 Vicarage Road, Harborne, Birmingham B17 0SN* 021-426 1318

FULLWOOD, William. b 11. St Aid Birkenhead 45. **d** 48 **p** 49. V Laxton w Blacktoft *York* 68-74; V Rudston w Boynton 74-77; rtd 77. *11 Ambrey Close, Hunmanby, Filey, N Yorkshire YO14 0LZ* Scarborough (0723) 891027

FULTON, John William. b 49. Ex Coll Ox BA71 BPhil72 MA75 MPhil79. Wycliffe Hall Ox 72. **d** 76 **p** 77. C Bexleyheath Ch Ch *Roch* 76-79; C Ealing Dean St Jo *Lon* 79-83; V Aldborough Hatch *Chelmsf* 83-87; Chapl Chantilly *Eur* 87-90; R Hepworth, Hinderclay, Wattisfield and Thelnetham *St E* from 90. *The Rectory, Church Lane, Hepworth, Diss, Norfolk IP22 2PU* Stanton (0359) 50285

FUNNELL, Norman Richard James. b 40. Univ of Wales (Lamp) BA64. Ripon Hall Ox 64. **d** 66 **p** 67. C Hackney *Lon* 66-70; Hon C 71-85; TV from 85. *St James's Vicarage, 59A Kenninghall Road, London E5 8BS* 081-985 1804

FURBER, Peter. b 43. Ex Univ BA. Sarum & Wells Th Coll 83. **d** 85 **p** 86. C Stanmore *Win* 85-88; TV Basingstoke from 88. *The Vicarage, Tewkesbury Close, Popley Basingstoke RG24 9DU* Basingstoke (0256) 24734

FURLONGER, Maurice Frank. b 25. AKC50. **d** 51 **p** 52. V St Minver *Truro* 67-70; V St Gluvias 70-74; TV Seacroft *Ripon* 74-77; V Hunslet St Mary 77-81; USA 81-88; C Dalton le Dale *Dur* 88-90; rtd 90; Hon C Diptford, N Huish, Harberton and Harbertonford *Ex* from 91. *Harberton Vicarage, Totnes, Devon TQ9 7SA* Totnes (0803) 867117

FURNELL, Very Rev Raymond. b 35. Linc Th Coll 63. **d** 65 **p** 66. C Cannock *Lich* 65-69; V Clayton 69-75; RD Stoke N 75-81; R Shelton 75-77; TR Hanley H Ev 77-81; Provost St E from 81. *The Provost's House, Bury St Edmunds, Suffolk IP33 1RS* Bury St Edmunds (0284) 754852

FURNESS, Colin. b 43. Lich Th Coll 65. **d** 68 **p** 69. C New Bentley *Sheff* 68; C Sheff Parson Cross St Cecilia 68-74; V Edlington 74-78; C Heavitree w Ex St Paul *Ex* 78-81; TV 81-89; R Sampford Spiney w Horrabridge from 89. *The Rectory, Station Road, Horrabridge, Yelverton, Devon PL20 7RF* Yelverton (0822) 855198

FURNESS, Dominic John. b 53. Bris Univ BA76. Ridley Hall Cam 82. **d** 84 **p** 85. C Downend *Bris* 84-88; V Stoke Hill *Guildf* from 88. *St Peter's House, 37 Hazel Avenue, Guildford, Surrey GU1 1NP* Guildford (0483) 572078

FURNESS, Edward Joseph. b 42. S'wark Ord Course 74. **d** 77 **p** 78. NSM S Lambeth St Steph *S'wark* 77-81; Min Mayflower Family Cen Canning Town *Chelmsf* from

82. *64 Burke Street, London E16 1ET* 071-476 9890 or 476 1171

FURNESS, Edward Peter Alexander. b 29. St Edm Hall Ox BA52 MA56. St Aid Birkenhead 52. **d** 54 **p** 55. C Ashton-on-Ribble St Andr *Blackb* 54-57; C Storrington *Chich* 57-59; C Sullington 57-59; V Worsthorne *Blackb* 59-64 and from 88; V Longridge 64-88. *The Vicarage, Gorple Road, Worsthorne, Burnley, Lancs BB10 3NN* Burnley (0282) 28478

FURNESS, John Alfred. b 31. Chich Th Coll 60. **d** 62 **p** 63. C Leeds St Aid *Ripon* 62-66; C Rickmansworth *St Alb* 66-73; R Wymington 73-75; P-in-c Podington w Farndish 74-75; R Wymington w Podington 75-79; V Waltham Cross 79-89; RD Cheshunt 84-89; R Swyncombe w Britwell Salome *Ox* from 89. *The Rectory, Swyncombe, Henley-on-Thames, Oxon RG9 6EA* Nettlebed (0491) 641249

FURNIVALL, Charles Guy. b 06. Trin Coll Cam BA28 MA37. Westcott Ho Cam 37. **d** 38 **p** 39. Chapl Shrewsbury Sch 41-66; Lic to Offic *Chich* 69-79; rtd 71; Perm to Offic *Chich* from 79. *The Barn, Angel Street, Petworth, W Sussex GU28 0BG* Petworth (0798) 42454

FURST, John William. b 41. Ripon Coll Cuddesdon. **d** 84 **p** 85. C Bris Ch the Servant Stockwood *Bris* 84-88; V Hanham from 88. *The Vicarage, Church Road, Bristol BS15 3AF* Bristol (0272) 673580

FUSSELL, Preb Laurence Walkling. b 14. Keble Coll Ox BA35 MA39. Wells Th Coll 36. **d** 37 **p** 38. R Wraxall *B & W* 59-79; Preb Wells Cathl from 69; rtd 79; Perm to Offic *B & W* from 79. *2 South Meadows, Wrington, Bristol BS18 7PF* Wrington (0934) 862924

FUTCHER, Christopher David. b 58. Edin Univ BD80. Westcott Ho Cam 80. **d** 82 **p** 83. C Borehamwood *St Alb* 82-85; C Stevenage All SS Pin Green 85-88; V from 88. *All Saints' Vicarage, 100 Derby Way, Stevenage, Herts SG1 5TJ* Stevenage (0438) 318706

FUTERS, Michael Roger. b 58. Trin & All SS Coll Leeds BEd80. St Jo Coll Nottm 82. **d** 85 **p** 86. C Narborough and Huncote *Leic* 85-87; C Spondon *Derby* 87-90; P-in-c Derby St Jas from 90. *St James's Vicarage, 224 Osmaston Road, Derby DE3 8JX* Derby (0332) 43911

FUTTER, Canon Ivan Herbert. b 31. Roch Th Coll 62. **d** 64 **p** 65. C Buckhurst Hill *Chelmsf* 64-66; Canada from 66. *2560 Maynard Street, Victoria, British Columbia, Canada, V8N 1K2* Victoria (604) 477-0705

FYFE, Arthur Douglas Cummine. b 98. St Aug Coll Cant. **d** 60 **p** 61. P-in-c Ixworth Thorpe *St E* 65-68; R Bardwell 65-68; rtd 68; Perm to Offic *Chich* from 69; *S'wark* from 82. *College of St Barnabas, Blackberry Lane, Lingfield, Surrey RH7 6NJ* Dormans Park (034287) 513

FYFFE, Robert Clark. b 56. Edin Univ BD78 Bris Poly DAVM87. Edin Th Coll 74. **d** 79 **p** 80. C Edin St Jo *Edin* 79-83; Youth Chapl *B & W* 83-87; Prov Youth Officer Scottish Episc Ch from 87; Co-ord Internat Angl Youth Network from 88. *47 Darnell Road, Edinburgh EH5 3PH* 031-552 3780

FYFFE, Timothy Bruce. b 25. New Coll Ox MA54. Westcott Ho Cam 54. **d** 56 **p** 57. TV Lowestoft St Marg *Nor* 69-80; Chapl HM Pris Blundeston 70-78; TV Tettenhall Regis *Lich* 80-85; Chapl Compton Hall Hospice Wolv 85-87; NSM Wolv St Andr *Lich* 88-90; rtd 90. *21 Sandy Lane, Tettenhall, Wolverhampton WV6 9EB* Wolverhampton (0902) 752066

FYLES, Gordon. b 39. Trin Coll Bris 76. **d** 77 **p** 78. C Islington St Mary *Lon* 77-81; Ext Sec BCMS from 81; Hon C Kingston Hill St Paul *S'wark* 82-88; V Wimbledon Em Ridgway Prop Chpl from 88. *25 Richmond Road, London SW20 0PG* 081-946 9940

G

GABB-JONES, Adrian William Douglas. b 43. ARICS. Ripon Coll Cuddesdon 79. **d** 81 **p** 82. C Northolt Park St Barn *Lon* 81-84; C Ruislip St Martin 84-89; V Minster Lovell and Brize Norton *Ox* from 89. *The Vicarage, Burford Road, Minster Lovell, Oxford OX8 5RA* Witney (0993) 776492

GABE, Eric Sigurd. b 15. Lon Univ BA52. St Aid Birkenhead 54. **d** 55 **p** 55. V Cricklewood St Mich *Lon* 60-72; V Brondesbury St Anne w Kilburn H Trin 72-80; rtd 80; Perm to Offic *St Alb* from 80; *Lon* from 81. *21 Cromer Road, New Barnet, Herts EN5 5HT* 081-449 6779

GABRIEL, Brother. *See* SANFORD, William Henry Steward

GABRIEL, Michael Hunt. b 29. BA. **d** 57 **p** 58. C Waterford Ch Ch *C & O* 57-60; C New Windsor H Trin *Ox* 60-62; C Albany Street Ch Ch *Lon* 62-63; R W and E Shefford *Ox* 63-67; C Hillingdon St Jo *Lon* 67-86; C Kingston Buci *Chich* from 86. *15 The Drive, Shoreham-by-Sea, W Sussex BN4 5GA* Shoreham-by-Sea (0273) 463171

GADD, Alan John. b 44. FRMetS67 Imp Coll Lon BSc65 PhD69. S'wark Ord Course 68. **d** 71 **p** 72. Asst Chapl Lon Univ *Lon* 71-72; Perm to Offic *S'wark* from 73. *100 Prince of Wales Drive, London SW11 4BD* 071-622 3809

GADD, Brian Hayward. b 33. Hatf Coll Dur BA54 DipEd55. Glouc Th Course 82. **d** 85 **p** 85. NSM Cleobury Mortimer w Hopton Wafers *Heref* from 85. *34 Lower Street, Cleobury Mortimer, Kidderminster DY14 8AB* Cleobury Mortimer (0299) 270758

GADD, Bryan Stephen Andrew. b 56. Dur Univ BA Ox Univ CertEd. Chich Th Coll. **d** 81 **p** 82. C Newlyn St Pet *Truro* 81-86; R St Mawgan w St Ervan and St Eval 86-90; Chapl Summer Fields Sch Ox from 90. *Summer Fields School, Oxford OX2 7EN* Oxford (0865) 54433

GADD, Frederick Arthur. b 15. St Jo Coll Dur BA40 MA43. **d** 40 **p** 41. V Gillingham St Mark *Roch* 52-57; Canada from 57; rtd 80. *Box 692, Hampton, New Brunswick, Canada, E0G 1Z0*

GAGE, Robert Edward. b 47. Whitman Coll Washington BA69. Cuddesdon Coll BA75 MA81. **d** 76 **p** 77. C Cheshunt *St Alb* 76-79; C Harpenden St Nic 79-81; V S Mymms 81-82; P-in-c Ridge 81-82; V S Mymms and Ridge from 82. *The Vicarage, Blanche Lane, Potters Bar, Herts EN6 3PE* Potters Bar (0707) 43142

GAINER, Jeffrey. b 51. Jes Coll Ox BA73 MA77. Wycliffe Hall Ox 74. **d** 77 **p** 78. C Baglan *Llan* 77-81; V Cwmbach 81-85; V Tonyrefail w Gilfach Goch and Llandyfodwg 85-87; Dir NT Studies from 87; Dir Past Studies St Mich Coll Llan from 87. *St Michael's College, Llandaff, Cardiff CF5 2YJ* Cardiff (0222) 551639

GAINES, George Yorke. b 15. St Aid Birkenhead 59. **d** 61 **p** 62. V Kilham *York* 64-77; V Lowthorpe w Ruston Parva 64-77; P-in-c Kirk Fenton 77-84; rtd 84. *Colwell, Welbury, Northallerton, N Yorkshire* East Harlsey (060982) 659

GAINEY, Alfred Tom. b 08. **d** 62 **p** 63. V Saul w Fretherne and Framilode *Glouc* 68-84; P-in-c Arlingham 83-84; P-in-c Frampton on Severn 83-84; rtd 84; Perm to Offic *Glouc* from 84. *5 Danell Gardens Bridge Road, Frampton on Severn, Gloucester GL2 7HZ* Gloucester (0452) 740017

GAINS, Peter Eric. b 21. LRAM51 St Cath Soc Ox BA48 MA52. Wycliffe Hall Ox 48. **d** 50 **p** 51. V Church Minshull w Leighton and Minshull Vernon *Ches* 59-86; rtd 86; Perm to Offic *Ox* from 87. *Ellesborough Manor, Butlers Cross, Aylesbury, Bucks HP17 0XF*

GAIR, Andrew Kennon. b 62. Westcott Ho Cam 88. **d** 91. C Clare w Poslingford, Cavendish etc *St E* from 91. *20 March Place, Clare, Sudbury, Suffolk CO10 8RH* Sudbury (0787) 277552

GAISFORD, Ven John Scott. b 34. St Chad's Coll Dur BA59 DipTh60 MA76. **d** 60 **p** 61. C Audenshaw St Hilda *Man* 60-62; C Bramhall *Ches* 62-65; V Crewe St Andr 65-86; Adn Nantwich 74-85; Hon Can Ches Cathl 80-86; Adn Macclesfield from 86. *2 Lovat Drive, Knutsford, Cheshire WA16 8NS* Knutsford (0565) 634456

GAIT, David James. b 48. BNC Ox BA71 BSc72 MA77 Ox Univ MSc83. Ridley Hall Cam 71. **d** 74 **p** 75. C Litherland St Paul Hatton Hill *Liv* 74-77; C Farnworth 77-80; V Widnes St Jo from 80. *St John's House, Greenway Road, Widnes, Cheshire WA8 6HA* 051-424 3134

GAKURU, Griphus. BSc BD. **p** 91. Selw Coll Cam from 91; Hon C Cam H Trin w St Andr Gt *Ely* from 91. *Selwyn College, Cambridge*

GALBRAITH, Alexander Peter James. b 65. Qu Coll Ox BA86 MA90. Wycliffe Hall Ox 87. **d** 90 **p** 91. C Southport Em *Liv* from 90. *49 Ferryside Lane, Crossens, Southport, Merseyside PR9 9FJ* Southport (0704) 29451

GALBRAITH, John Angus Frame. b 44. Sarum Th Coll 68. **d** 71 **p** 72. C Richmond St Mary *S'wark* 71-74; Chapl W Lon Colls 74-79; V S'wark H Trin w St Matt from 79. *Holy Trinity Rectory, Merrick Square, London SE1 4JB* 071-407 1707

GALBRAITH, John Watson Joseph Denham. b 19. Glas Univ MA41. Bps' Coll Cheshunt 47. **d** 48 **p** 49. Dep Asst Chapl Gen 67-72; R Hodnet w Weston under Redcastle *Lich* 72-77; V Deeping St James *Linc* 77-81; Chapl Porto (or Oporto) *Eur* 81-85; rtd 85; Perm to Offic *B & W* from 86. *64 High Street, Rode, Bath BA3 6PB* Frome (0373) 830077

GALBRAITH, Peter John. b 59. QUB BA TCD DipTh.
d 85 p 86. C Knockbreda *D & D* 85-88; C Ballynafeigh
St Jude 88-91; I Broomhedge *Conn* from 91. *Broomhedge
Rectory, 30 Lurganure Road, Broughmore, Lisburn, Co
Antrim BT28 2TR*   Maze (0846) 621229

GALE, Christopher. b 44. ALCD67. d 68 p 69. C Balderton
S'well 68-72; C Bilborough St Jo 72-75; P-in-c Colwick
75-78; V Radford St Pet 78-84; V Sherwood from 84;
AD Nottm N from 90. *St Martin's Vicarage, Trevose
Gardens, Sherwood, Nottingham NG5 3FU*   Notting-
ham (0602) 607547

GALE, Colin Edward. b 49. Lon Univ PGCE74. St Jo
Coll Nottm LTh BTh73. d 79 p 80. C Hoole *Ches* 79-82;
C Woodley *Ox* 82-87; V Clapham St Jas *S'wark* from
87. *St James's Vicarage, 1 Rodenhurst Road, London
SW4 8AE*   081-674 3973

GALE, Denys Jearrad Pickmore. b 08. St Chad's Coll Dur
BA29. d 39 p 42. C Felpham w Middleton *Chich* 39-40;
C Bognor St Jo 40-44; Hd Master Northcliffe Ho Sch
Bognor 44-62; Perm to Offic *Glouc* from 81. *8 Eden
Drive, Bexhill-on-Sea, E Sussex TN39 3RL*   Cooden
(04243) 5169

GALE, Douglas Norman. b 32. Birkb Coll Lon BA72.
Franciscan Ho of Studies E Bergholt 53. d 61 p 61. Asst
Master Judd Sch Tonbridge 72-74; K Sch Ches 74-80; C
Ches Team *Ches* 79-83; TV 83-87; rtd 87. *6 Allen Court,
Hauxton Road, Trumpington, Cambridge CB2 2LU*
Cambridge (0223) 841197

GALE, Edwin Donald. b 12. AKC40. d 40 p 41. V Hebburn
St Oswald *Dur* 69-72; rtd 72. *6 The Peacheries, Bognor
Road, Chichester, W Sussex PO19 2NP*   Chichester
(0243) 776129

GALE, Keith George. b 44. Sarum Th Coll 69. d 70 p 71.
C Sheff St Cuth *Sheff* 70-77; P-in-c Brightside All SS
76-77; C Birm St Martin *Birm* 77-78; C Birm St Martin
78-81; USPG from 81; Malawi from 81. *St Peter's
Rectory, PO Box 294, Lilongwe, Malawi*

GALE, Peter Simon. b 56. BD. St Mich Coll Llan. d 83
p 84. C Caerphilly *Llan* 83-89; Chapl RN from 89. *c/o
MOD, Lacon House, Theobald's Road, London WC1X
8RY*   071-430 6847

GALES, Alan. b 29. Sarum Th Coll 56. d 59 p 60. C
Greenside *Dur* 59-60; C Peterlee 60-63; Ind Chapl 60-70;
V Marley Hill from 63; Asst Chapl HM Pris Dur
74-81. *The Vicarage, Marley Hill, Newcastle upon Tyne
NE16 5DJ*   091-488 7887

GALES, Bernard Henry. b 27. Lon Univ BSc(Econ)51.
Wells Th Coll 62. d 64 p 65. C Sholing *Win* 64-67; C
Fordingbridge w Ibsley 67-71; C S Molton w Nymet St
George *Ex* 71-73; C Thelbridge 73-77; P-in-c 77-78;
P-in-c Creacombe 77-78; P-in-c W w E Worlington
77-78; P-in-c Meshaw 77-78; P-in-c Witheridge 77-78; C
Witheridge, Thelbridge, Creacombe, Meshaw etc 79-80;
R Bow w Broad Nymet from 80; V Colebrooke from
80; R Zeal Monachorum from 80; RD Cadbury from
90. *The Rectory, Bow, Crediton, Devon EX17 6HS*
Bow (0363) 82566

GALILEE, George David Surtees. b 37. Or Coll Ox
BA60 MA64. Westcott Ho Cam 61. d 62 p 63. C
Knighton St Mary Magd *Leic* 62-67; V Stocking Farm
67-69; Tutor Westcott Ho Cam and Homerton Coll
69-71; V Sutton *Ely* 71-80; P-in-c Addiscombe St Mildred
Cant 80-81; V 81-84; V Addiscombe St Mildred *S'wark*
from 85. *St Mildred's Vicarage, Sefton Road, Croydon
CR0 7HR*   081-654 3569

GALLAGHER, Hubert. b 31. Linc Th Coll 78. d 80 p 81.
C Lupset *Wakef* 80-82; C Badsworth 82-86; V Kinsley
86-88; V Kinsley w Wragby from 88. *The Vicarage,
Kinsley, Pontefract, W Yorkshire WF9 5BX*   Hemsworth
(0977) 610497

GALLAGHER, Ian. BTh. d 90 p 91. C Annagh w
Drumgoon, Ashfield etc *K, E & A* from 90. *The Rectory,
Cootehill, Co Cavan, Irish Republic*   Cavan (49) 52004

GALLAGHER, Michael Collins. b 48. Dur Univ BA.
Sarum Th Coll. d 82 p 83. C Bridport *Sarum* 82-86; V
Downton from 86. *The Vicarage, Barford Lane,
Downton, Salisbury SP5 3QA*   Downton (0725) 20326

GALLAGHER, Neville Roy. b 45. Lon Univ CertEd66
AKC70 Lon Univ BD76. d 71 p 72. C Folkestone St
Mary and St Eanswythe *Cant* 71-74; Hon C Sutton
Valence w E Sutton and Chart Sutton 74-76; TV Cen
Telford *Lich* 76-78; P-in-c Gt Mongeham *Cant* 78-80;
P-in-c Ripple 78-80; R Gt Mongeham w Ripple and
Sutton by Dover 80-83; V Kennington 83-88; Chapl
Bedgebury Sch Kent from 88. *3 Beech Drive, Bedgebury
Park, Goudhurst, Kent TN17 2SJ*   Goudhurst (0580)
211989

GALLAGHER, Robert. b 43. St Chad's Coll Dur BSc65
DipTh67. d 67 p 68. C Crosland Moor *Wakef* 67-69; C

Huddersfield SS Pet and Paul 69-71; Chapl Huddersfield
Poly 72-79; Min Coulby Newham Ecum Project *York*
79-90; V Toxteth St Marg *Liv* from 90. *St Margaret's
Vicarage, 3 Princes Road, Toxteth, Liverpool L8 1TG*
051-709 1526

GALLAGHER, Stephen. b 58. Southn Univ BTh89. Chich
Th Coll 86. d 89 p 90. C S Shields All SS *Dur* from 89.
4 Mitford Road, South Shields, Tyne & Wear NE34 0EQ
091-454 6983

GALLETLY, Thomas. b 23. St Chad's Coll Dur
BA50 DipTh52. d 52 p 53. Chapl Aycliffe Approved Sch
Co Dur 56-57; Chapl Chailey Heritage Hosp and Sch
Lewes from 57; Lic to Offic *Chich* from 59; rtd 88.
Beech House, North Chailey, Lewes, E Sussex BN8 4DT
Newick (082572) 2168

GALLEY, Giles Christopher. b 32. Qu Coll Cam
BA56 MA60. Linc Th Coll 56. d 58 p 59. C Gt Yarmouth
Nor 58-62; C N Lynn w St Marg and St Nic 62-66; C
Leeds St Pet *Ripon* 66-69; V N Hull St Mich *York* 70-79;
V Strensall from 79; RD Easingwold from 82. *The
Vicarage, 10 York Road, Strensall, York YO3 5UB*
York (0904) 490683

GALLICHAN, Henry Ernest. b 45. Sarum Th Coll 70.
d 72 p 73. C Kenton Ascension *Newc* 72-76; Tanzania
76-80; Lic to Offic *Truro* from 80. *Karibu, Trevelmond,
Liskeard, Cornwall*   Liskeard (0579) 20530

✠**GALLIFORD, Rt Rev David George.** b 25. Clare Coll
Cam BA49 MA51. Westcott Ho Cam. d 51 p 52 c 75. C
Newland St Jo *York* 51-54; C Eton w Boveney *Ox* 54-56;
Min Can Windsor 54-56; V Middlesb St Oswald *York*
56-61; R Bolton Percy 61-71; Dioc Adult Tr Officer
61-71; Can and Preb York Minster 69-70; Can Res and
Treas 70-75; Suff Bp Hulme *Man* 75-84; Suff Bp Bolton
84-91; rtd 91. *Bishopgarth, Maltongate, Thornton Dale,
Pickering, N Yorkshire YO18 7SA*   Pickering (0751)
74605

GALLON, Edward George. b 16. St Steph Ho Ox 64. d 66
p 67. C Hockley *Chelmsf* 69-74; R Takeley w Lt Canfield
74-83; rtd 83; Perm to Offic *S'wark* from 84. *42 Home
Park, Oxted, Surrey RH8 0JU*   Oxted (0883) 714091

GALLOWAY, Charles Bertram. b 41. Lon Univ
BA62 Birm Univ DipTh64. Qu Coll Birm 64. d 64 p 65.
C Darlington H Trin *Dur* 64-68; Ind Chapl Teesside
68-77; Sen Ind Chapl *Liv* 77-87; Team Ldr and Convener
Lon Ind Chapl *Lon* from 87. *16 Kingswood Avenue,
London NW6 6LG*   081-969 1175

GALLOWAY, Michael Edward. b 41. Chich Th Coll 72.
d 74 p 75. C Aldwick *Chich* 74-77; C Bournemouth St
Clem w St Mary *Win* 78-82; V S Benfleet *Chelmsf* from
83. *St Mary's Vicarage, 105 Vicarage Hill, Benfleet, Essex
SS7 1PD*   South Benfleet (0268) 792294

GALLOWAY, Peter John. b 54. JP89. FRSA88 Golds
Coll Lon BA76 K Coll Lon PhD87. St Steph Ho Ox 80.
d 83 p 84. C St Jo Wood *Lon* 83-86; C St Giles-in-the-
Fields 86-90; OStJ from 86; P-in-c Hampstead Em
W End *Lon* from 90. *Emmanuel Vicarage, Lyncroft
Gardens, London NW6 1JU*   071-435 1911

GALLUP, Peter Whitfield. b 06. Sarum Th Coll 51. d 53
p 54. R Buriton *Portsm* 61-74; rtd 74; Perm to Offic *Win*
from 74. *16 St Swithun's Street, Winchester, Hants
SO23 9JD*   Winchester (0962) 854090

GALT, Ian Ross. b 34. Leeds Univ BSc56. d 76 p 77. NSM
Newport St Julian *Mon* from 76; NSM Newport St Teilo
from 87. *47 Brynglas Avenue, Newport, Gwent NP9 5LR*
Newport (0633) 857134

GAMBLE, David Lawrence. b 34. AKC61. d 62 p 63.
C-in-c Shrub End All SS CD *Chelmsf* 62-65; C Colchester
St Jas, All SS, St Nic and St Runwald 65-69; V Chelmsf
St Andr 69-73; P-in-c Hatf Heath 69-73; C 74-77; TV
Hemel Hempstead *St Alb* 77-82; P-in-c Renhold 82-90;
Chapl HM Pris Bedf 82-90; P-in-c Petersham *S'wark*
from 90; Chapl HM Pris Latchmere Ho from 90.
*99 Barnfield Avenue, Kingston-upon-Thames, Surrey
KT2 5RG*   081-549 8296

GAMBLE, Donald William. b 67. NUU BSc88. TCD Div
Sch BTh91. d 91. C Belf St Mich *Conn* from 91.
17 Westway Park, Belfast BT13 3NW   Belfast (0232)
391619

GAMBLE, Norman Edward Charles. b 50. TCD
BA72 HDipEd73 PhD78. CITC 76. d 79 p 80. C Ban St
Comgall *D & D* 79-83; I Dunleckney w Nurney, Lorum
and Kiltennel *C & O* 83-90; Warden of Readers 84-90;
RD Aghade 85-90; P-in-c Leighlin w Grange Sylvae,
Shankill etc 89-90; Preb Leighlin Cathl 89-90; Preb
Ossory Cathl 89-90; I Malahide w Balgriffin *D & G* from
90. *The Rectory, Church Road, Malahide, Co Dublin,
Irish Republic*   Dublin (1) 462762

GAMBLE, Peter John. b 20. St Cath Soc Ox BA51 MA55 DipEd59. Ripon Hall Ox 48. **d** 52 **p** 53. Prin Anglo-American Coll Faringdon 67-71; Chapl and Tutor Harrow Sch Middx 72-82; rtd 82. *2 Lawn Road, Guildford, Surrey GU2 5DE* Guildford (0483) 576902

GAMBLE, Robin Philip. b 53. Oak Hill Th Coll 74. **d** 77 **p** 78. C Kildwick *Bradf* 77-78; C Laisterdyke 78-80; C York St Paul *York* 80-82; V Bradf St Aug Undercliffe *Bradf* from 82. *St Augustine's Vicarage, Undercliffe Lane, Bradford, W Yorkshire BD3 0DW* Bradford (0274) 637607

GAMBLE, Thomas Richard. b 42. K Coll Lon BD64 AKC. **d** 65 **p** 66. C Gt Ilford St Jo *Chelmsf* 65-68; Hon C 68-73; Asst Master Pettits Sec Sch Romford 68-73; Hall Mead Sch Upminster 73-75; Tabor High Sch Braintree 75-77; Chapl Warminster Sch Wilts 77-80. *Address temp unknown*

GAMBLES, Una Beryl. b 33. Man Univ BEd78. St Chris Coll Blackheath 59. **d** 87. NSM Upton Priory *Ches* from 87; Chapl Parkside Hosp *Ches* from 87. *23 Grangelands, Upton, Macclesfield, Cheshire SK10 4AB* Macclesfield (0625) 21691

GAMESTER, Sidney Peter. b 27. SS Coll Cam BA51 MA55. Oak Hill Th Coll 56. **d** 58 **p** 59. C Surbiton Hill Ch Ch *S'wark* 58-61; C Worthing H Trin *Chich* 61-69; R Silverhill St Matt 69-86; R Bexhill St Mark from 86. *11 Coverdale Avenue, Bexhill-on-Sea, E Sussex TN39 4TY* Cooden (04243) 3733

GAMMON, William Paul Lachlan. b 60. SS Hild & Bede Coll Dur BA82. St Steph Ho Ox 89. **d** 91. C Chalfont St Peter *Ox* from 91. *67 Fieldway, Chalfont St Peter, Gerrards Cross, Bucks SL9 9SQ* Gerrards Cross (0753) 888724

GANDON, Andrew James Robson. b 54. St Jo Coll Dur BA76. Ridley Hall Cam 76. **d** 78 **p** 79. C Aston SS Pet and Paul *Birm* 78-82; CMS from 82; Zaire 82-89; Kenya from 89. *PO Box 40360, Nairobi, Kenya*

GANDON, James Philip. b 31. ALCD56. **d** 56 **p** 57. C Westcliff St Mich *Chelmsf* 56-58; Canada from 58. *13 Kerr Road, Unit 10, Toronto, Ontario, Canada, M4L 1K2* Toronto (416) 466-9062

GANDON, Percy James. b 22. ALCD53. **d** 53 **p** 54. V Hoddesdon *St Alb* 63-83; RD Cheshunt 81-83; Perm to Offic *Nor* 83-85 and from 86; P-in-c Lyng w Sparham 85-86; rtd 87. *The Old Bakery, Hindolveston, Dereham, Norfolk NR20 5DF* Melton Constable (0263) 861325

GANDY, Nicholas John. b 53. CBiol79 MIBiol Westf Coll Lon BSc75 Reading Univ MSc76 Ex Coll Ox CertEd78. St Steph Ho Ox 86. **d** 88 **p** 89. C Crowthorne *Ox* 88-89; C Tilehurst St Mary from 89. *10 Forest Hill, Reading RG3 6XL* Reading (0734) 413588

GANE, Canon Christopher Paul. b 33. Qu Coll Cam BA57 MA61. Ridley Hall Cam 57. **d** 59 **p** 60. C Rainham *Chelmsf* 59-62; C Farnborough *Guildf* 62-64; V Erith St Paul *Roch* 64-71; V Ipswich St Marg *St E* 71-88; Hon Can St E Cathl from 82; R Hopton, Market Weston, Barningham etc from 88. *The Rectory, Nethergate Street, Hopton, Diss, Norfolk IP22 2QZ* Garboldisham (095381) 8239

GANJAVI, John Farhad. b 57. ACGI79 Imp Coll Lon BSc79. Ridley Hall Cam 79. **d** 82 **p** 83. C Yardley St Edburgha *Birm* 82-85; C Knowle 85-89; P-in-c Beaudesert and Henley-in-Arden w Ullenhall *Cov* from 89. *The Rectory, Beaudesert Lane, Henley-in-Arden, Solihull, W Midlands B95 5JY* Henley-in-Arden (0564) 792570

GANN, Canon Anthony Michael. b 37. TCD BA60 MA64 BD64. **d** 62 **p** 63. VC Derry Cathl *D & R* 62-66; Lesotho 66-74; Dioc Officer for Miss and Unity *Carl* 75-80; P-in-c Bampton and Mardale 75-80; TV Cen Telford *Lich* 80-89; TR Wolvercote w Summertown *Ox* from 89. *The Rectory, Lonsdale Road, Oxford OX2 7ES* Oxford (0865) 56079

GANN, John West. b 29. Ex Coll Ox BA55 MA59. Wells Th Coll 55. **d** 57 **p** 58. C Wendover *Ox* 57-59; C Walton St Mary *Liv* 59-62; R Didcot *Ox* 62-70; R Newbury St Nic 70-78; TR Newbury 73-78; V Twickenham St Mary *Lon* 78-87; Dir of Ords 81-87; TR Bridport *Sarum* from 87; RD Lyme Bay from 89. *The Rectory, 84 South Street, Bridport, Dorset DT6 3NW* Bridport (0308) 22138

GANT, Brian Leonard. b 45. K Coll Lon 72. **d** 73 **p** 74. C Hillmorton *Cov* 73-75; C Cov St Geo 76; P-in-c Maldon St Mary *Chelmsf* 76-79; R Muthill *St And* 79-81; R Crieff 79-81; R Comrie 79-81; V Walsall St Paul *Lich* 81-84; Min Can Worc Cathl *Worc* 84-89; Chapl K Sch Worc 84-89; V Tunbridge Wells K Chas *Roch* from 89. *The Vicarage, 5D Frant Road, Tunbridge Wells, Kent TN2 5SB* Tunbridge Wells (0892) 25455

GANT, Peter Robert. b 38. BNC Ox BA60 MA64 G&C Coll Cam BA62 MA67. Ridley Hall Cam 61. **d** 63 **p** 64. C Portsea St Mary *Portsm* 63-67; V Blackheath *Birm* 67-73; Perm to Offic Birm 73-75; Guildf from 75. *8 Sandon Close, Esher, Surrey KT10 8JE* 081-398 5107

GANZ, Timothy Jon. b 36. ARCM63 Univ Coll Ox BA58 MA62. St Steph Ho Ox 58. **d** 61 **p** 62. C Shrewsbury H Cross *Lich* 61-65; Asst Chapl Hurstpierpoint Coll Hassocks 65-69; Chapl 69-73; Chapl Univ of Wales (Swansea) *S & B* 74-75; P-in-c Hanley All SS *Lich* 75-80; TV Stoke-upon-Trent 80-81; V Tutbury from 81. *The Vicarage, Tutbury, Burton-on-Trent, Staffs DE13 9JF* Burton-on-Trent (0283) 813127

GARBUTT, Arthur. b 09. St Paul's Coll Burgh 32. **d** 33 **p** 34. R Catton *York* 62-74; R Stamford Bridge Gp of Par 62-74; rtd 74. *35 Fossway, Stamford Bridge, York YO4 1DS* Stamford Bridge (0759) 71436

GARBUTT, Gerald. b 41. St Aid Birkenhead 65. **d** 67 **p** 68. C Stretford All SS *Man* 67-70; Lic to Offic 70-72; R Salford St Bart 72-74; V Lower Kersal 74-79; V Bethnal Green St Jo w St Bart *Lon* 79-90; P-in-c Stepney St Pet w St Benet 85-87; Chapl Furness Gen Hosp from 90; Chapl S Cumbria HA from 90. *25 Scales Close, Dalton-in-Furness, Cumbria LA15 8PE* Dalton-in-Furness (0229) 64157

GARDEN, Robert Andrew. b 26. MInstP58 FIMA72 Edin Univ BSc49. Cant Sch of Min 87. **d** 90. NSM Sandwich *Cant* from 90. *Naini, 164 St George's Road, Sandwich, Kent CT13 9LD* Sandwich (0304) 612116

GARDINER, Canon Arthur John. b 22. Ch Ch Ox BA46 MA50. Ely Th Coll 49. **d** 50 **p** 51. S Rhodesia 64-65; Rhodesia 65-80; R Rushton and Glendon w Thorpe Malsor *Pet* 81-86; P-in-c Loddington w Cransley 82-86; Chapl Soc of St Marg E Grinstead from 86; rtd 88. *The Cottage, St Margaret's Convent, East Grinstead RH19 3LD* East Grinstead (0342) 322406

GARDINER, Brian John. b 31. Chich Th Coll. **d** 60 **p** 61. C Leighton Buzzard *St Alb* 60-63; C Haywards Heath St Wilfrid *Chich* 63-64; C Brighton St Jo 64-66; V Scaynes Hill 66-71; C Caversham *Ox* 73-77. *Address temp unknown*

GARDINER, James Carlisle. b 18. St Jo Coll Dur LTh48. Tyndale Hall Bris. **d** 49 **p** 50. R Ditton *Roch* 56-83; rtd 83; Perm to Offic *Roch* from 83. *5 Larch Crescent, Tonbridge, Kent TN10 3NN* Tonbridge (0732) 362323

GARDINER, John. b 15. Clifton Th Coll 67. **d** 68 **p** 69. C Halliwell St Pet *Man* 68-71; V Monton 71-80; V Hoghton *Blackb* 80-84; rtd 84; Perm to Offic *Blackb* from 84. *20 Shortlands Drive, Longlands Lane, Heysham, Morecambe, Lancs LA3 2NT* Heysham (0524) 55894

GARDINER, John Kingsmill. b 18. OBE51. Bps' Coll Cheshunt 53. **d** 55 **p** 56. R Hardenhuish *Bris* 62-68; Lic to Offic 69-89; Perm to Offic from 89; rtd 83. *Combe Head, Giddeahall, Chippenham, Wilts SN14 7ES* Castle Combe (0249) 782497

GARDINER, Canon Kenneth Ashton. b 27. S'wark Ord Course 60. **d** 63 **p** 64. C Sydenham H Trin *S'wark* 63-67; C Macclesfield St Mich *Ches* 67-70; V Chatham St Phil and St Jas *Roch* from 70; RD Roch from 88; Hon Can Roch Cathl from 88. *The Vicarage, 289 Walderslade Road, Chatham, Kent ME5 0NU* Medway (0634) 862498

GARDINER, Thomas Alfred. b 30. St Cuth Soc Dur BA52 MA56. Ridley Hall Cam 54. **d** 56 **p** 57. C Stockport St Geo *Ches* 56-60; Asst Chapl Brentwood Sch Essex 60-62; Chapl 62-88; R Greensted-juxta-Ongar w Stanford Rivers *Chelmsf* from 88. *The Rectory, Greensted, Ongar, Essex CM5 9LA* Ongar (0277) 364694

GARDINER, William Gerald Henry. b 46. Lon Univ BD72. Oak Hill Th Coll 68. **d** 72 **p** 73. C Beckenham St Jo *Roch* 72-75; C Cheadle *Ches* 75-81; P-in-c Swynnerton *Lich* 81-83; P-in-c Tittensor 81-83; R Swynnerton and Tittensor 83-86; V Westlands St Andr from 86. *St Andrew's Vicarage, 50 Kingsway West, Westlands, Newcastle, Staffs ST5 3PU* Newcastle-under-Lyme (0782) 619594

GARDNER, Alfred. b 04. **d** 55 **p** 55. R Marton w Birdingbury *Cov* 64-72; rtd 72; Perm to Offic *Cov* from 72. *1 Margotts Close, Kenilworth, Warks CV8 1EM* Kenilworth (0926) 58635

GARDNER, Canon Anthony Brian. b 32. Lon Coll of Div 62. **d** 64 **p** 65. C Stoke *Cov* 64-68; R Whitnash from 68; RD Leamington 78-79; RD Warw and Leamington 79-87; Hon Can Cov Cathl from 83. *St Margaret's Rectory, 2 Church Close, Whitnash, Leamington Spa CV31 2HJ* Leamington Spa (0926) 25070

GARDNER, Charles Graham. b 18. AKC49. **d** 50 **p** 51. C Clapham H Trin *S'wark* 50-54; S Africa from 54.

49 Dahlia Avenue, Virginia, 9430 South Africa Virginia (1722) 28187

GARDNER, Canon Christopher John. b 23. Jes Coll Cam BA47 MA53. Ely Th Coll 48. **d** 50 **p** 51. R Orton Waterville *Ely* 63-89; RD Yaxley 79-82; Hon Can Ely Cathl from 81; P-in-c Alwalton 83-89; P-in-c Chesterton w Haddon 83-89; rtd 89. *73 Five Arches, Orton Wistow, Peterborough PE2 0FQ* Peterborough (0733) 371349

GARDNER, Ven Clifton Gordon. b 15. Toronto Univ BA36 Lon Univ BD39 AKC39. **d** 39 **p** 40. C Maidenhead St Luke *Ox* 39-41 and 46-47; Chapl RNVR 41-46; V Furze Platt *Ox* 47-52; Canada 52-76; Can St Paul's Cathl Lon Ontario 64-74; Adn Middx Ontario 74-76; Perm to Offic *Chelmsf* from 77. *1 Shepherd's Way, Saffron Walden, Essex CB10 2AH* Saffron Walden (0799) 27890

GARDNER, David. b 57. Oak Hill Th Coll BA87. **d** 87 **p** 88. C Ogley Hay *Lich* 87-91; TV Mildenhall *St E* from 91. *The Vicarage, 2 Oak Drive, Beck Row, Bury St Edmunds, Suffolk IP28 8AL* Mildenhall (0638) 717331

GARDNER, David Edward. b 21. Oak Hill Th Coll 44. **d** 49 **p** 50. Chapl Dockland Settlement No 1 Canning Town *Chelmsf* 55-60; Nat Chapl and Evang to Boy's Covenanter Union from 60; rtd 90. *15 Churchmead Close, Barnet, Herts EN4 8UY* 081-449 4213

GARDNER, David Lewis. b 20. Oak Hill Th Coll 49. **d** 52 **p** 53. C Walthamstow St Mary w St Steph *Chelmsf* 78; P-in-c Ramsden Crays w Ramsden Bellhouse 78-85; rtd 85. *5 Roseberry Green, North Stainley, Ripon, N Yorkshire HG4 3HZ* Ripon (0765) 85371

GARDNER, Geoffrey Maurice. b 28. K Coll Lon BA51. Cranmer Hall Dur DipTh59. **d** 59 **p** 60. C Bowling St Jo *Bradf* 59-62; Nigeria 62-72; Hon C Bath St Luke *B & W* 72-81; Perm to Offic 81-90; NSM Bath Widcombe from 90. *17 St Winifred's Drive, Combe Down, Bath BA2 7HR* Combe Down (0225) 832953

GARDNER, Ian Douglas. b 34. St Pet Hall Ox BA58 MA62. Oak Hill Th Coll 58. **d** 60 **p** 61. C Biddulph *Lich* 60-63; C Weston St Jo *B & W* 64; Nigeria 65-76; P-in-c Hurstbourne Tarrant and Faccombe *Win* 77-79; V Hurstbourne Tarrant, Faccombe, Vernham Dean etc 79-85; R Nursling and Rownhams from 85. *The Vicarage, 27 Horns Drove, Rownhams, Southampton SO1 8AH* Southampton (0703) 738293

GARDNER, Canon John Phillip Backhouse. b 21. St Aid Birkenhead 49. **d** 52 **p** 53. R Wisley w Pyrford *Guildf* 70-87; RD Woking 82-87; Hon Can Guildf Cathl 86-87; rtd 87; Perm to Offic *Pet* from 87. *82 Water Lane, Wootton, Northampton NN4 0HG* Northampton (0604) 760254

GARDNER, Leslie John Thomas. b 15. Wells Th Coll 68. **d** 69 **p** 70. C Tiverton St Pet *Ex* 69-70; C Thornton *Leic* 70-72; P-in-c Wilne and Draycott w Breaston *Derby* 72-74; C Fordingbridge w Ibsley *Win* 74-75; C Welwyn w Ayot St Peter *St Alb* 75-78; C Compton Gifford *Ex* 78-82; rtd 82; Perm to Offic *Ex* from 82. *Braelea, Newland Park, Seaton, Devon EX12 2SF* Seaton (0297) 21520

GARDNER, Mark Douglas. b 58. TCD BA80 MA83 DipTh83. **d** 83 **p** 84. C Ballymacarrett St Patr *D & D* 83-87; C Belf St Steph w St Luke *Conn* 87-89; C Hendon and Sunderland *Dur* 89-90; TV Sunderland from 90. *8 Drury Lane, Sunderland SR1 2AW* 091-510 8239

GARDNER, Mary Christine. b 42. SRN65 Liv Univ HVCert71. St Jo Coll Nottm 80. dss 82 **d** 87. Ches St Paul *Ches* 82-84; Macclesfield St Mich 84-85; Macclesfield Team Par 85-87; Par Dn 87; Chapl Asst Nottm City Hosp from 87. *The Chaplain's Office, City Hospital, Hucknall Road, Nottingham NG5 1PB* Nottingham (0602) 608111 or 691169

GARDNER, Dr Paul Douglas. b 50. K Coll Lon BA72 AKC72 SS Coll Cam PhD89. Reformed Th Sem Mississippi MDiv79 Ridley Hall Cam 79. **d** 80 **p** 81. C Cam St Martin *Ely* 80-83; Lect Oak Hill Th Coll 83-90; V Hartford *Ches* from 90. *St John's Vicarage, Hartford, Northwich, Cheshire CW8 1QA* Northwich (0606) 77557

GARDNER, Richard Beverley Twynam. b 11. Chich Th Coll 33. **d** 36 **p** 37. V Botleys and Lyne *Guildf* 54-71; V Long Cross 56-71; V Ewshott 71-76; rtd 76; Perm to Offic *Guildf* from 81. *Kappa Crucis, Hillside Road, Weybourne, Farnham, Surrey GU9 9DW* Aldershot (0252) 25957

GARDNER, Ronald Frederick. b 25. Dur Univ BA51 DipTh52 Birm Univ MA79. **d** 52 **p** 53. V Forsbrook *Lich* 69-83; V Mow Cop 83-89; rtd 89. *Rode Mill House, Church Lane, Scholar Green, Stoke-on-Trent ST7 3QR* Alsager (0270) 872185

GARDOM, Francis Douglas. b 34. Trin Coll Ox BA55 MA59. Wells Th Coll 58. **d** 60 **p** 61. C Greenwich St Alfege w St Pet *S'wark* 60-68; C Lewisham St Steph and St Mark 68-76; Hon C from 76. *79 Maze Hill, London SE10 8XQ* 081-858 7052 or 852 1474

GARDOM, James Theodore Douglas. b 61. St Anne's Coll Ox BA83. Ripon Coll Cuddesdon 88. **d** 90 **p** 91. C Witney *Ox* from 90. *111 Thorney Leys, Witney, Oxon OX8 7AY* Witney (0993) 772191

GARLAND, Christopher John. b 47. Ex Univ BA69 PhD72. Qu Coll Birm 78. **d** 80 **p** 81. C Beckenham St Jas *Roch* 80-82; C Roch 82-85; Papua New Guinea from 85. *Newton Theological College, PO Box 162, Popondetta, Papua New Guinea*

GARLAND, Harry Earle. b 01. St Boniface Warminster. **d** 49 **p** 50. V Parham w Hacheston *St E* 50-69; rtd 69. *Rose Cottage, Hacheston, Woodbridge, Suffolk* Framlingham (0728) 723561

GARLAND, Michael. b 50. St D Coll Lamp DipTh72 Sarum & Wells Th Coll 72. **d** 73 **p** 74. C Swansea St Thos and Kilvey *S & B* 73-76; C Boldmere *Birm* 76-79; V Kingshurst 79-88; P-in-c Curdworth w Castle Vale 88-90; R Curdworth from 90. *The Rectory, Glebe Fields, Curdworth, Sutton Coldfield, W Midlands B76 9ES* Curdworth (0675) 470384

GARLAND, Peter Stephen John. b 52. ALA79 Univ Coll Lon BA73 Univ of W Ontario MA74 Dur Univ PGCE75. Ripon Coll Cuddesdon 88. **d** 90 **p** 91. C Crookham *Guildf* from 90. *29 The Verne, Church Crookham, Aldershot, Hants GU13 0LU* Fleet (0252) 620943

GARLICK, David. b 37. Nottm Univ BA62 Ox Univ DipPSA63. St Steph Ho Ox 62. **d** 64 **p** 65. C Kennington St Jo *S'wark* 64-66; Hon C Newington St Paul 66-68; P-in-c Vauxhall St Pet 68-79; V Lewisham St Mary from 79. *Lewisham Vicarage, 48 Lewisham Park, London SE13 6QZ* 081-690 2682

GARLICK, Dennis. b 26. ACIS. Qu Coll Birm. **d** 84 **p** 85. NSM Dronfield *Derby* 84-88; C 88-89; C-in-c Holmesfield 89-90; TV Dronfield w Holmesfield from 90. *St Swithin's Vicarage, Holmesfield, Sheffield S18 5WT* Sheffield (0742) 890243

GARLICK, Mrs Kathleen Beatrice. b 49. Leeds Univ BA71 Birm Univ CertEd72. Glouc Sch of Min 87. **d** 90. Hon C Much Birch w Lt Birch, Much Dewchurch etc *Heref* from 90. *Birch Lodge, Much Birch, Hereford HR2 8HT* Golden Valley (0981) 540666

GARLICK, Canon Peter. b 34. AKC57. **d** 58 **p** 59. C Swindon All SS *Bris* 58-63; St Kitts-Nevis 63-66; V Heyside *Man* 66-73; R Stretford All SS 73-79; RD Wootton *Pet* 79-88; V Duston 79-91; TR Duston Team from 91; Can Pet Cathl from 85. *The Vicarage, Duston, Northampton NN5 6JB* Northampton (0604) 752591

GARMAN, Canon Bernard Wilfred. b 16. Edin Th Coll 47. **d** 49 **p** 50. V Bywell St Andr *Newc* 66-73; V Riding Mill 66-77; Chapl Dioc Retreat Ho 69-77; Asst Dioc Tr Officer from 77; rtd 77; Hon Can Newc Cathl *Newc* from 77. *Thropton Hill, Physic Lane, Thropton, Morpeth, Northd NE65 7HU* Rothbury (0669) 20840

GARNER, Canon Carl. b 42. Rhodes Univ Grahamstown BA62 Keble Coll Ox BA65 MA70. St Paul's Grahamstown 66. **d** 67 **p** 68. S Africa 67-84; Dioc Missr *St Alb* from 84; Can Res St Alb from 84. *Holywell Close, 43 Holywell Hill, St Albans, Herts AL1 1HE* St Albans (0727) 54832

GARNER, David Henry. b 40. Trin Coll Bris 70. **d** 73 **p** 74. C Tunstead *Man* 73-75; C Fazeley *Lich* 76-78; V Sparkhill St Jo *Birm* 78-85; V Blackheath from 85. *St Paul's Vicarage, 83 Vicarage Road, Halesowen, W Midlands B62 8HX* 021-559 1000

GARNER, Geoffrey Walter. b 40. Ripon Hall Ox 69. **d** 71 **p** 72. C Stoke *Cov* 71-76; V Tile Hill 76-80; TV Hackney *Lon* 80-89; R Bow w Bromley St Leon from 89. *16 Tomlins Grove, London E3 4NX* 081-981 6710

GARNER, Martin Wyatt. b 39. Lon Coll of Div 60 Tyndale Hall Bris 63 Sarum Th Coll 66. **d** 66 **p** 67. C Coleraine *Conn* 66-70; C Cam St Martin *Ely* 70-72; V Edge Hill St Nath *Liv* 72-80; P-in-c Burton in Kendal *Carl* 80-87; R Burghclere w Newtown and Ecchinswell w Sydmonton *Win* from 87. *The Rectory, Well Street, Burghclere, Newbury, Berks RG15 9HS* Burghclere (063527) 470

GARNER, Canon Maurice Heath. b 08. Em Coll Cam BA30 MA34. Ridley Hall Cam 30. **d** 32 **p** 33. R Weymouth St Mary *Sarum* 47-70; R Ashurst *Chich* 71-78; V Steyning 71-78; rtd 78. *3 Southfield Avenue, Weymouth, Dorset DT4 7QN* Weymouth (0305) 784065

GARNER, Peter. b 35. Lon Univ BSc56. Wycliffe Hall Ox 56. **d** 58 **p** 59. C Walthamstow St Jo *Chelmsf* 58-61; V Hainault 61-70; R Theydon Garnon 70-73; P-in-c Kirby le Soken 73-74; V 74-82; P-in-c Fountains *Ripon* 82-88; P-in-c Kirkby Malzeard w Grewelthorpe and Mickley etc 82-88; Par Development Adv from 88; P-in-c

Birstwith from 91. *Churchfields, Darley, Harrogate, N Yorkshire HG3 2QF* Harrogate (0423) 780771

GARNER, Rodney George. b 48. MIPM75 Birm Univ DipTh77 Lon Univ BA87. Qu Coll Birm 75. **d** 78 **p** 79. C Tranmere St Paul w St Luke *Ches* 78-81; V Eccleston St Thos *Liv* 81-90; V Sculcoates St Paul w Ch Ch and St Silas *York* 90; P-in-c from 90; Lay Tr Officer (E Riding Adnry) from 90. *St Paul's Vicarage, Bridlington Avenue, Sculcoates, Hull HU2 0DU* Hull (0482) 224370

GARNER, Thomas Richard. b 43. K Coll Lon. **d** 69 **p** 70. C Tynemouth Ch Ch *Newc* 69-73; C Fenham St Jas and St Basil 73-76; V Hamstead St Bernard *Birm* 76-80; New Zealand from 80. *120 Cambridge Street, Levin, New Zealand* Levin (69) 85955

GARNETT, David Christopher. b 45. Nottm Univ BA67 Fitzw Coll Cam BA69 MA73. Westcott Ho Cam 67. **d** 69 **p** 70. C Cottingham *York* 69-72; Chapl Selw Coll Cam 72-77; P-in-c Putterdale *Carl* 77-80; Dir of Ords 78-80; V Heald Green St Cath *Ches* 80-87; R Christleton from 87. *The Rectory, Birch Heath Lane, Christleton, Chester CH3 7AP* Chester (0244) 335663

GARNETT, James Arthur. b 42. N Ord Course 77. **d** 80 **p** 81. C Kirkby *Liv* 80-91; P-in-c Liv St Phil w St Dav from 91. *The Vicarage, 55 Sheil Road, Liverpool L6 3AD* 051-263 6202

GARNETT, Joseph William. b 20. AKC48. Edin Th Coll 48. **d** 49 **p** 50. V Carl St Aid and Ch Ch *Carl* 69-73; R Nairn *Mor* 73-78; R Greenock *Glas* 78-80; R Castle Douglas 80-83; rtd 85. *Knockelly Cottage, Penpont, Thornhill, Dumfriesshire DG3 4NF* Marrburn (08486) 274

GARNETT, Peter. b 17. Bps' Coll Cheshunt 49. **d** 51 **p** 52. Rhodesia 69-71; C Wyken *Cov* 71-73; C Malden St Jo *S'wark* 73-77; C Headington Quarry *Ox* 77-82; rtd 82. *Dulverton Hall, St Martin's Square, Scarborough YO11 2DQ* Scarborough (0723) 373082

GARNETT, Preb Ralph Henry. b 28. Cuddesdon Coll 58. **d** 60 **p** 61. C Broseley w Benthall *Heref* 60-64; V Leintwardine 64-69; P-in-c Downton w Burrington and Aston and Elton 66-69; RD Ludlow 72-75; R Burford II w Greete and Hope Bagot 69-87; R Burford III w Lt Heref 69-87; P-in-c Burford I 72-74; R 74-87; V Tenbury 69-74; TR 74-87; Preb Heref Cathl from 82; P-in-c Fownhope from 87; P-in-c Brockhampton w Fawley from 87. *The Vicarage, Fownhope, Hereford HR1 4PS* Fownhope (0432) 860365

GARNETT, Roger James. b 58. Dur Univ BA79. Wycliffe Hall Ox 89. **d** 91. C Forest Gate St Sav w W Ham St Matt *Chelmsf* from 91. *52 Bolton Road, London E15 4JY* 081-519 0208

GARNSEY, George Christopher. Qu Coll Ox BA63. **d** 60 **p** 60. Lic to Offic *Wakef* 78-79; C Lupset 80; Australia from 80. *St John's College, 363 Morpeth Road, Morpeth, NSW, Australia 2321* Morpeth (49) 336223

GARRARD, Christine Ann. b 51. LCST75 Open Univ BA86. E Anglian Minl Tr Course 87. **d** 90. C Kesgrave St E 90-91; Par Dn from 91. *2 Wainwright Way, Kesgrave, Ipswich* Ipswich (0473) 623840

GARRARD, Nicholas James Havelock. b 62. Leeds Univ BA83. Westcott Ho Cam 86. **d** 88 **p** 89. C Scotforth *Blackb* 88-91; C Eaton *Nor* from 91. *12 Fulton Close, Eaton, Norwich NR4 6HX* Norwich (0603) 57922

GARRARD, Canon Richard. b 37. K Coll Lon BD60 AKC60. **d** 61 **p** 62. C Woolwich St Mary w H Trin *S'wark* 61-66; C Cam Gt St Mary w St Mich *Ely* 66-68; Chapl Keswick Hall Coll Nor 68-74; Prin CA Wilson Carlile Coll of Evang 74-79; Can Res and Chan S'wark Cathl *S'wark* 79-87; Dir of Tr 79-87; Can Res St E Cathl *St E* from 87; Dioc Adv for Continuing Minl Educn from 87. *2 Abbey Precincts, Bury St Edmunds, Suffolk IP33 1RS* Bury St Edmunds (0284) 753396

GARRARD, Robert Ernest. b 12. St Aid Birkenhead 37. **d** 39 **p** 40. Asst Sec BFBS 65-80; Lic to Offic *Sarum* 65-80; rtd 80. *Firswood, 64 Middlehill Road, Colehill, Wimborne, Dorset BH21 2HH* Wimborne (0202) 882590

GARRATT, Bernard John. b 43. Lon Univ BA65 Linacre Coll Ox BA67 MA71. St Steph Ho Ox 65. **d** 68 **p** 69. C Notting Hill St Jo *Lon* 68-71; C Fareham SS Pet and Paul *Portsm* 71-73; Chapl City of Lon Poly *Lon* 73-79; R Trowbridge H Trin *Sarum* 79-81; TR 81-87; V Wootton Bassett from 87; RD Calne 88-90. *The Vicarage, Glebe Road, Wootton Bassett, Swindon SN4 7DU* Swindon (0793) 854302 or 853272

GARRATT, John William. b 11. **d** 78 **p** 78. Hon C Hounslow H Trin *Lon* 78-88; Hon C Hounslow H Trin w St Paul from 88. *Flat 25, Smoothfield, 130 Hibernia Road, Hounslow TW3 3RJ* 081-570 6009

GARRATT, Peter James. b 37. ALCD64. **d** 64 **p** 65. C Bingham *S'well* 64-67; C Mansf St Pet 67-69; R Purlwell *Wakef* 69-73; R Kirk Sandall and Edenthorpe *Sheff* 73-82; R Whippingham w E Cowes *Portsm* 82-87; V Soberton w Newtown from 87. *The Vicarage, Soberton, Southampton S03 1PF* Droxford (0489) 877400

GARRATT, Roger Charles. b 50. St Jo Coll Dur BA72 DipTh73. Cranmer Hall Dur 73. **d** 74 **p** 75. C Leamington Priors St Paul *Cov* 74-77; Chapl Emscote Lawn Sch Warw from 77. *8 Wasdale Close, Leamington Spa, Warks CV32 6NF* Leamington Spa (0926) 335495

GARRETT, Christopher Hugh Ahlan. b 35. Sarum & Wells Th Coll 72. **d** 75 **p** 76. C Addiscombe St Mildred *Cant* 75-81; V Thornton Heath St Jude w St Aid *S'wark* from 81. *St Jude's Vicarage, 11 Dunheved Road North, Thornton Heath CR7 6AH* 081-684 1630

GARRETT, Edgar Ashton. b 20. S'wark Ord Course 62. **d** 65 **p** 66. C Horsell *Guildf* 65-70; V Send 70-79; Perm to Offic *Chich* from 79; rtd 85. *14 Crosbie Close, Chichester, W Sussex PO19 2RZ* Chichester (0243) 789770

GARRETT, Canon Frederick Henry. b 18. TCD BA43. **d** 43 **p** 44. I Mallow *C, C & R* 55-74; I Kilshannig 57-74; I Castlemagner 71-74; RD Midleton 65-75; I Glengarriff w Berehaven 74-87; Preb Ross Cathl 76-87; Preb Cork Cathl 76-87; rtd 87. *Meadow Cottage, Wood View, Mallow, Co Cork, Irish Republic* Mallow (22) 21748

GARRETT, Geoffrey David. b 57. Oak Hill Th Coll 83. **d** 86 **p** 87. C Trentham *Lich* 86-90; V Rhodes *Man* from 90. *The Vicarage, Rhodes, Middleton, Manchester M24 4PU* 061-643 3224

GARRETT, Ian Lee. b 60. MCSP DipPh81. Sarum & Wells Th Coll 86. **d** 89 **p** 90. C Maidstone St Martin *Cant* from 89. *Church House, Wallis Avenue, Maidstone, Kent ME15 9JJ* Maidstone (0622) 764170

GARRETT, John Watkins. b 09. St Chad's Coll Dur BA35 LTh36. **d** 36 **p** 37. Chapl Carlton Hayes Psychiatric Hosp Narborough 54-90; R Narborough *Leic* 59-75; rtd 75; Lic to Offic *Leic* 75-81; Perm to Offic from 81. *5 Keats Close, Enderby, Leicester LE9 5QP* Leicester (0533) 864666

GARRETT, Kevin George. b 48. Oak Hill Th Coll BA86. **d** 86 **p** 87. C Hoddesdon *St Alb* 86-89; C Loughton St Mary and St Mich *Chelmsf* 89-90; TV from 90. *St Michael's House, Roding Road, Loughton, Essex IG10 3EJ* 081-508 1489

GARRETT, Canon William Edward Richard. b 29. CITC 67. **d** 67 **p** 68. C Drumlease *K, E & A* 67-71; I Kildallon w Newtowngore and Corrawallen 72-75; I Bailieborough w Knockbride, Shercock and Mullagh 75-87; Preb Kilmore Cathl 87-88; I Boyle and Elphin w Aghanagh, Kilbryan etc from 88; Preb Elphin Cathl from 91. *The Rectory, Boyle, Co Roscommon, Irish Republic* Boyle (79) 62398

GARRITY, Canon Robert Peter. b 15. St Jo Coll (NZ). **d** 42 **p** 43. Gen Sec Melanesian Miss 57-75; rtd 75; Perm to Offic *S'wark* from 76. *48 Hook Lane, Welling, Kent DA16 2DP* 081-303 2146

GARRUD, Christopher Charles. b 54. Cranmer Hall Dur DipTh84. **d** 85 **p** 86. C Watford *St Alb* 85-89; C Ireland Wood *Ripon* from 89. *6 Holt Park Gardens, Leeds LS16 7RB* Leeds (0532) 675417

GARRY, Brother. See McCARTNEY, Dr Garfield William Crawford

GARSIDE, Canon Howard. b 24. Leeds Univ BA49. Coll of Resurr Mirfield 49. **d** 51 **p** 52. V Manston *Ripon* 64-78; RD Whitkirk 70-78; Hon Can Ripon Cathl 78-89; V Harrogate St Wilfrid 78-80; P-in-c Harrogate St Luke 78-80; V Harrogate St Wilfrid and St Luke 80-89; RD Harrogate 83-88; rtd 89. *73 Kirkby Road, Ripon, N Yorkshire HG4 2HH* Ripon (0765) 690625

GARSIDE, Melvin. b 42. N Ord Course 85. **d** 88 **p** 89. C Lindley *Wakef* 88-91; C Shelf *Bradf* from 91. *91A Mandale Road, Bradford, W Yorkshire BD6 3JS* Bradford (0274) 675015

GARTLAND, Christopher Michael. b 49. Man Univ BA78. Coll of Resurr Mirfield 82. **d** 84 **p** 85. C Almondbury w Farnley Tyas *Wakef* 84-87; P-in-c Upperthong 87-89; TV Upper Holme Valley 89-91; Chapl Stanley Royd Hosp Wakef from 91. *Fall Hall, Waterside, Marsden, Huddersfield HD7 6BU* Huddersfield (0484) 845851

GARTON, Derek John. b 33. ALCD59. **d** 59 **p** 60. C Bromley Common St Aug *Roch* 59-62; C Gravesend St Aid 62-66; Hon C Gravesend St Geo 66-73; Perm to Offic *Ex* 77-83; Australia from 83. *The Manse, 31 Bekta Street, Mallacoota, Victoria, Australia 3889* Moe (51) 580394

GARTON, Canon John Henry. b 41. Worc Coll Ox BA66 MA DipTh67. Cuddesdon Coll 67. **d** 69 **p** 70. CF

69-73; Lect Linc Th Coll 73-78; TR Cov E *Cov* 78-86; V Cuddesdon *Ox* from 86; Prin Ripon Coll Cuddesdon from 86; Hon Can Worc Cathl *Worc* from 87. *The Old Vicarage, Cuddesdon, Oxford OX9 9HP* Wheatley (08677) 4427 or 4368

GARWELL, John Arthur. b 25. K Coll Lon 48. **d** 52 **p** 53. Chapl RN 60-76; C Guildf St Nic *Guildf* 76-77; Sec Sir Oswald Stoll Foundn Fulham 78-86; rtd 90. *75 Portsmouth Road, Guildford, Surrey GU2 5BS* Guildford (0483) 64255

GARWOOD, Albert Wells. b 14. **d** 59 **p** 60. C Dartford H Trin *Roch* 59-60; Canada from 60. *Apartment 515, 1186 Queen Street, Halifax, Nova Scotia, Canada, B3H 4K9*

GARWOOD, David John Shirley (Brother Damian). b 31. Leeds Univ BA59. Coll of Resurr Mirfield. **d** 61 **p** 62. C Meir *Lich* 61-66; Lic to Offic *Wakef* 67-71 and from 74; CR from 68; S Africa 71-74. *House of the Resurrection, Mirfield, W Yorkshire WF14 0BN* Mirfield (0924) 494318

GARY, Brother. *See* ASKEY, Gary Simon

GASCOIGNE, Peter Francis. b 36. Linc Th Coll 85. **d** 87 **p** 88. C Wath-upon-Dearne w Adwick-upon-Dearne *Sheff* 87-90; R Thurnscoe St Helen from 90. *The Rectory, 4 High Street, Thurnscoe, Rotherham, S Yorkshire S63 0SU* Rotherham (0709) 893186

GASCOIGNE, Philip. b 27. Oak Hill Th Coll. **d** 62 **p** 63. C Blackpool Ch Ch *Blackb* 62-65; V Bootle St Leon *Liv* 65-71; Staff Evang CPAS 71-74; V St Helens St Mark *Liv* 74-77; V Blackpool Ch Ch *Blackb* 77-81; V Blackpool Ch Ch w All SS from 81. *The Vicarage, 23A North Park Drive, Blackpool FY3 8LR* Blackpool (0253) 31235

GASH, Christopher Alan Ronald. b 39. St Andr Univ 57 Nottm Univ CPTS. E Midl Min Tr Course 83. **d** 86 **p** 87. C Thurmaston *Leic* 86-89; P-in-c Stoke Golding w Dadlington from 89. *The Vicarage, High Street, Stoke Golding, Nuneaton, Warks CV13 6HE* Hinckley (0455) 212317

GASH, Canon Wilfred John. b 31. Lon Univ DipTh62. St Aid Birkenhead 60. **d** 62 **p** 63. C St Mary Cray and St Paul's Cray *Roch* 62-65; C Bexley St Jo 65-67; R Levenshulme St Pet *Man* 67-72; V Clifton from 72; AD Eccles 81-87; Hon Can Man Cathl from 86; P-in-c Pendlebury Ch Ch 86-87; P-in-c Pendlebury St Aug 86-87; Dioc Adv on Evang from 89. *The Vicarage, Manchester Road, Manchester M27 2PP* 061-794 1939

GASKELL, David. b 48. Lon Univ BD76. Trin Coll Bris 72. **d** 76 **p** 77. C Eccleston Ch Ch *Liv* 76-80; C Rainhill 80-83; V Over Darwen St Jas *Blackb* 83-88; V Livesey from 88. *St Andrew's Vicarage, 112 Full View, Blackburn BB2 4QB* Blackburn (0254) 59422

GASKELL, Ian Michael. b 51. Nottm Univ BTh81. Linc Th Coll 77. **d** 81 **p** 82. C Wakef St Jo *Wakef* 81-83; Ind Chapl *Sheff* 83-86; V Cleckheaton St Luke and Whitechapel *Wakef* from 86. *The Vicarage, 62 Whitcliffe Road, Cleckheaton, W Yorkshire BD19 3BY* Cleckheaton (0274) 873964

GASKELL, Preb John Bernard. b 28. Jes Coll Ox BA52 MA58. Chich Th Coll 59. **d** 60 **p** 61. C Beckenham St Jas *Roch* 60-64; C St Marylebone All SS *Lon* 64-68; C-in-c Grosvenor Chpl 68-79; Warden Liddon Ho Lon 68-79; V Holborn St Alb w Saffron Hill St Pet *Lon* from 79; AD S Camden (Holborn & St Pancras) 81-86; Preb St Paul's Cathl from 85. *St Alban's Clergy House, Brooke Street, London EC1N 7RD* 071-405 1831

GASKELL, Mary. b 50. Nottm Univ BTh81 Bradf and Ilkley Coll CertEd89. Linc Th Coll 77. **dss** 81 **d** 89. NSM Cleckheaton St Luke and Whitechapel *Wakef* from 89. *The Vicarage, 62 Whitcliffe Road, Cleckheaton, W Yorkshire BD19 3BY* Cleckheaton (0274) 873964

GASKILL, Ernest Raymond. b 17. St Chad's Coll Dur BA39 DipTh41 MA42. **d** 41 **p** 42. V Doncaster Ch Ch *Sheff* 66-82; rtd 82; Perm to Offic *Sheff* from 82. *37 Glamis Road, Doncaster, S Yorkshire DN2 6DP* Doncaster (0302) 320845

GATENBY, Denis William. b 31. Ex Coll Ox BA54 DipTh55 MA58 Man Univ DSPT82. Wycliffe Hall Ox 54. **d** 56 **p** 57. C Deane *Man* 56-60; C Bradf Cathl *Bradf* 60-63; V Bootle St Matt *Liv* 63-72; V Horwich H Trin *Man* 72-84; TR Horwich from 84; AD Deane from 87. *The Rectory, Chorley Old Road, Horwich, Bolton BL6 6BQ* Horwich (0204) 68263

GATENBY, Paul Richard. b 32. Dur Univ BA55. Qu Coll Birm DipTh64. **d** 64 **p** 65. C Wellingborough St Barn *Pet* 64-68; V Braunston w Brooke 68-71; C Langley Marish *Ox* 71-72; TV Basildon St Martin w H Cross and Laindon *Chelmsf* 73-76; R Isham w Pytchley *Pet*

from 77. *The Rectory, Isham, Kettering, Northants* Burton Latimer (0536) 722371

GATENBY, Simon John Taylor. b 62. Nottm Univ BA83. St Jo Coll Nottm 84. **d** 87 **p** 88. C Haughton St Mary *Man* 87-90; C Newburn *Newc* from 90. *St Mary's Parsonage, Throckley, Newcastle upon Tyne NE15 9AB* 091-267 4553

GATER, William George Herbert. b 05. AKC35. Chich Th Coll 35. **d** 35 **p** 36. V Chinley w Buxworth *Derby* 55-60; SSJE from 60; rtd 75; Lic to Offic *Lon* from 76. *St Edward's House, 22 Great College Street, London SW1P 3QA* 071-222 9234

GATES, John Michael. b 35. Dur Univ BA56 DipTh60. Cranmer Hall Dur 58. **d** 60 **p** 61. C Felixstowe St Jo *St E* 60-67; R Boyton w Capel St Andrew and Hollesley from 67; P-in-c Shottisham w Sutton from 87. *The Rectory, Hollesley, Woodbridge, Suffolk IP12 3RE* Shottisham (0394) 411252

GATES, John Richard. b 47. Oak Hill Th Coll DipTh73. **d** 73 **p** 74. C Iver *Ox* 73-76; C Broadwater St Mary *Chich* 76-79; Dioc Youth Officer *Nor* 79-82; V Cosby *Leic* 82-86. *39 Whetstone Court, Wale Road, Whetstone, Leicester LE8 3NJ* Leicester (0533) 861298

GATES, Peter Harvey. b 34. St Steph Ho Ox. **d** 61 **p** 62. P-in-c Godshill *Portsm* 67-71; V Kensington St Phil Earl's Court *Lon* 71-75; V S Farnborough *Guildf* 75-83; rtd 83. *13 Elm View, Ash, Aldershot, Hants GU12 6AN* Aldershot (0252) 310194

GATES, Richard James. b 46. BA85. Oak Hill Th Coll 82. **d** 85 **p** 86. C Heald Green St Cath *Ches* 85-89; V Norton from 89. *The Vicarage, Windmill Hill, Runcorn, Cheshire WA7 6QE* Runcorn (0928) 715225

GATES, Simon Philip. b 60. St Andr Univ MA82 BA86. Cranmer Hall Dur 84. **d** 87 **p** 88. C Southall Green St Jo *Lon* from 87. *9 Derley Road, Southall, Middx UB2 5EJ* 081-574 5016

GATFORD, Canon Ian. b 40. AKC65. **d** 67 **p** 68. C Clifton w Glapton *S'well* 67-71; R 71-75; V Sherwood 75-84; Can Res Derby Cathl *Derby* from 84. *22 Kedleston Road, Derby DE3 1GU* Derby (0332) 41201

GATHERCOLE, Ven John Robert. b 37. Fitzw Ho Cam BA59 MA63. Ridley Hall Cam 59. **d** 62 **p** 63. C Dur St Nic *Dur* 62-66; C Croxdale 66-69; Bp's Soc and Ind Adv 66-69; Ind Chapl *Worc* 69-87; RD Bromsgrove 77-85; Sen Chapl Worcs Ind Miss from 85; Hon Can Worc Cathl from 80; Adn Dudley from 87. *15 Worcester Road, Droitwich, Worcs WR9 8AA* Worcester (0905) 773301

GATLIFFE, David Spenser. b 45. Keble Coll Ox BA67 Fitzw Coll Cam BA69. Westcott Ho Cam 67. **d** 69 **p** 70. C Oxted *S'wark* 69-72; C Roehampton H Trin 72-75; C S Beddington St Mich 76-77; TV Clapham Old Town 78-87; P-in-c Clapham Ch and St Jo 81-87; TV Clapham Team Min 87-89; V S Wimbledon H Trin and St Pet from 89. *The Vicarage, 234 The Broadway, London SW19 1SB* 081-542 7098 or 542 1388

GATRILL, Adrian Colin. b 60. Southn Univ BTh82. Linc Th Coll 83. **d** 85 **p** 86. C W Bromwich St Andr *Lich* 85-88; C W Bromwich St Andr w Ch Ch 88-89; Chapl RAF from 89; Perm to Offic *St D* from 90. *c/o MOD, Adastral House, Theobald's Road, London WC1X 8RU* 071-430 7268

GAUGE, Barrie Victor. b 41. St D Coll Lamp BA62 Selw Coll Cam BA64 MA74 Liv Univ CQSW81. **d** 65 **p** 66. C Newtown w Llanllwchaiarn w Aberhafesp *St As* 65-68; C Prestatyn 68-73; R Bodfari 73-76; Dioc RE Adv 73-76; Perm to Offic *Ches* 77-84; V Birkenhead St Jas w St Bede 84-90; Dir of Resources from 90. *103 Five Ashes Road, Westminster Park, Chester CH4 7QA* Chester (0244) 680804

GAUNT, Arthur Raymond. b 15. St Aid Birkenhead 47. **d** 49 **p** 50. V Kexby w Wilberfoss *York* 66-71; V Scarborough St Columba 71-78; rtd 78; Perm to Offic *Bradf* from 80. *20 Grandage Drive, Harrogate, N Yorkshire HG3 2ST* Harrogate (0423) 504998

GAUNT, Eric Emmerson. b 33. Sarum Th Coll 65. **d** 67 **p** 68. C Hatch End St Anselm *Lon* 67-74; V Neasden cum Kingsbury St Cath 74-80; V Neasden St Cath w St Paul from 80. *The Vicarage, Tanfield Avenue, London NW2 7RX* 081-452 7322

GAUNT, Roger Cecil. b 30. K Coll Cam BA52. Westcott Ho Cam 53. **d** 55 **p** 56. C Barnard Castle *Dur* 55-58; C Newc St Jo *Newc* 58-61; V Coulsdon St Andr *S'wark* 61-66; V St Helier 66-68; R Limpsfield and Titsey 68-77; Dir of Educn *St Alb* 77-79; Can Res St Alb 77-79; Perm to Offic *S'wark* 79-88; Lic 88-91; Perm Truro 77-84; Guildf from 84; Hon C Charlwood *S'wark* from 91. *Apple Hill, Old Road, Buckland, Betchworth, Surrey RH3 7DU* Betchworth (073784) 3393

GEE

GAUNTLETT, Gilbert Bernard. b 36. d 61 p 62. C
Maidenhead St Andr and St Mary Magd *Ox* 61-64; C
Ox St Ebbe w St Pet 64-68; R Nottm St Nic *S'well*
68-72; Asst Master Leys High Sch Redditch 73-79; Asst
Master Stourport High Sch 79-85. *Address temp unknown*
GAUSDEN, Peter James. b 32. Qu Coll Birm 57. d 60
p 61. C Battersea St Pet *S'wark* 60-63; C St Peter-in-
Thanet *Cant* 63-68; V Sturry 68-74; R Sturry w Fordwich
and Westbere w Hersden from 74. *The Rectory, 2 The
Hamels, Church Lane, Sturry, Canterbury, Kent
CT2 0BL* Canterbury (0227) 710320
GAVIN, David Guy. b 63. Birm Univ BA85 Dur Univ
BA90. Cranmer Hall Dur 88. d 91. C Parr *Liv* from 91.
5 Epsom Street, St Helens, Lancs WA9 2DT St Helens
(0744) 31434
GAWITH, Canon Alan Ruthven. b 24. Man Univ
SACert47. Lich Th Coll 54. d 56 p 57. V Kendal St Geo
Carl 67-74; Soc Resp Officer *Man* 74-89; Hon Can Man
Cathl 82-89; Bp's Adv on AIDS from 88; rtd 90.
7 Redwaters, Leigh, Lancs WN7 1JD Leigh (0942)
676641
GAWNE-CAIN, John. b 38. CEng MICE G&C Coll Cam
BA61 MA66. Cuddesdon Coll 74. d 76 p 77. C Cowley
St Jas *Ox* 76-80; P-in-c Ox St Giles 80-85; V Ox St Giles
and SS Phil and Jas w St Marg from 85. *The Vicarage,
Church Walk, Oxford OX2 6LY* Oxford (0865) 510460
GAWTHROP, Miss Sheila Mary. b 37. Birm Univ CertEd.
Dalton Ho Bris 68. dss 79 d 87. Halliwell St Paul *Man*
79-82; New Bury 82-87; Par Dn 87-89; Par Dn Tonge w
Alkrington from 89. *18 Highfield Drive, Alkrington,
Manchester M24 1DJ* 061-653 0543
GAY, Colin James. b 37. Univ of Wales (Lamp) BA63.
Chich Th Coll 63. d 65 p 66. C W Hackney St Barn *Lon*
65-69; C Hitchin *St Alb* 69-74; P-in-c Apsley End 74-80;
TV Chambersbury (Hemel Hempstead) 80-85; V Barnet
Vale St Mark from 85. *St Mark's Vicarage, 56 Potters
Road, New Barnet, Herts EN5 5HN* 081-449 4265
GAY, David Charles. b 46. CCC Cam BA68 MA72 PhD71.
Coll of Resurr Mirfield DipTh74. d 75 p 76. C Sheff
Broomhall St Mark *Sheff* 75-78; Bp's Chapl for
Graduates 78-80; Lib Pusey Ho 78-80; Lic to Offic *Sheff*
80-82; C Warmsworth 82-84; V Worsbrough St Thos
and St Jas from 84. *The Vicarage, 13 Bank End Road,
Worsbrough, Barnsley, S Yorkshire S70 4AF* Barnsley
(0226) 203426
GAY, Dr John Dennis. b 43. St Pet Coll Ox BA64 DipTh65
MA68 DPhil69 MSc78. Ripon Hall Ox 64. d 67 p 68. C
Paddington St Jas *Lon* 67-71; P-in-c 71-72; Lic to Offic
Ox from 72; Chapl Culham Coll Abingdon 72-79; Lect
Ox Univ 78-80; Dir Culham Coll Inst from 80; Perm to
Offic *Chich* 87-89. *Culham College Institute, 60 East St
Helen Street, Abingdon, Oxon OX14 5EB* Abingdon
(0235) 520458 or 532992
GAY, Perran Russell. b 59. St Cath Coll Cam BA81 MA85
Ex Univ CertEd82. Ripon Coll Cuddesdon BA86. d 87
p 88. C Bodmin w Lanhydrock and Lanivet *Truro* 87-90;
Bp's Dom Chapl from 90; Dioc Officer for Unity from
90. *The Flat, Lis Escop, Truro, Cornwall TR3 6QQ*
Truro (0872) 862657
GAYLER, Roger Kenneth. b 44. Lich Th Coll 68. d 70
p 71. C Chingford St Anne *Chelmsf* 70-75; P-in-c Marks
Gate 75-81; V from 81. *The Vicarage, 187 Rose Lane,
Romford RM6 5NR* 081-599 0415
GAZE, Canon Arthur Philip Atkinson. b 14. St Jo Coll
Ox BA36 MA47 Otago Univ MLitt88. Linc Th Coll 39.
d 41 p 42. C Romford St Edw *Chelmsf* 41-48; Master
and Chapl Cumnor Sch 48-50; R Puttenham and
Wanborough *Guildf* 50-57; Dioc Insp of Schs 55-62; V
Horsell 57-62; New Zealand from 62; Hon Can St Paul's
Cathl 75-80. *18 Drivers Road, Maori Hill, Dunedin, New
Zealand* Dunedin (24) 467-5951
GAZE, George Henry. b 23. St Jo Coll Dur BA50 DipTh51
MA56. d 51 p 52. R Slaidburn *Bradf* 56-85; rtd 85;
Perm to Offic *Bradf* 86-90. *6 The Croft, Woods Lane,
Stapenhill, Burton-on-Trent, Staffs DE15 9ED* Burton-
on-Trent (0283) 36513
GAZZARD, Canon Richard George Edward. b 40. Lich
Th Coll. d 67 p 68. C Lewisham St Mary *S'wark* 67-71;
C Milton next Gravesend Ch Ch *Roch* 71-74; R
Gravesend H Family w Ifield 74-81; V S Ashford Ch Ch
Cant from 81; RD E Charing from 86; Hon Can Cant
Cathl from 90. *Christ Church Vicarage, 112 Beaver
Road, Ashford, Kent TN23 1SR* Ashford (0233) 620600
GEACH, Michael Bernard. b 26. Qu Coll Cam
BA51 MA56. Westcott Ho Cam 51. d 53 p 54. C Kenwyn
Truro 53-56; C Bodmin 56-59; C Helland 56-59; R St
Dominic 59-65; Chapl Cotehele Ho Chapl Cornwall
60-65; V Linkinhorne 65-84; R Veryan w Ruan

Lanihorne from 84. *The Vicarage, Veryan, Truro, Cornwall
TR2 5QA* Truro (0872) 501618
GEAKE, Peter Henry. b 17. Trin Hall Cam BA39 MA46.
Cuddesdon Coll 45. d 47 p 48. PC Tattenham Corner
and Burgh Heath Guildf 62-69; V 69-72; R Fulbeck *Linc*
72-82; P-in-c Carlton Scroop w Normanton 72-82; rtd
82. *Fulbeck Cottage, 27 Worgret Road, Wareham, Dorset
BH20 4PH* Wareham (0929) 552175
GEAR, John Arthur. b 37. St Aid Birkenhead 62. d 64
p 66. C Attleborough *Cov* 64-66; C Attercliffe *Sheff*
66-68; C Sheerness H Trin w St Paul *Cant* 68-73; Asst
Youth Adv *S'wark* 73-78; Youth Chapl *Lich* 78-88; V
Stafford St Jo and Tixall w Ingestre from 88. *St
John's Vicarage, Westhead Avenue, Stafford ST16 3RP*
Stafford (0785) 53493
GEAR, Ven Michael Frederick. b 34. Dur Univ
BA59 DipTh61. Cranmer Hall Dur 59. d 61 p 62. C
Bexleyheath Ch Ch *Roch* 61-64; C Ox St Aldate w H
Trin *Ox* 64-67; V Clubmoor *Liv* 67-71; Rhodesia 71-76;
Tutor Wycliffe Hall Ox 76-80; V Macclesheld St Mich
Ches 80-85; RD Macclesfield 84-88; TR Macclesfield
Team Par 85-88; Hon Can Ches Cathl 86-88; Adn
Ches from 88. *25 Bartholomew Way, Chester CH4 7RJ*
Chester (0244) 675417
GEARY, Sidney Thomas William. b 11. St Deiniol's
Hawarden. d 80 p 81. NSM Syston *Leic* 80-82; NSM
Hoby cum Rotherby w Brooksby, Ragdale & Thru'ton
from 82. *Cedarwood, Sixhills Road, Ragdale, Melton
Mowbray, Leics* Rotherby (066475) 289
GEBAUER, George Gerhart. b 25. Sarum & Wells Th
Coll 71. d 73 p 74. C Portsdown *Portsm* 73-78; V
Purbrook 78-91; rtd 91. *52 St John's Road, Locksheath,
Southampton, Hants* Locks Heath (0489) 575172
GEBBIE, Canon John Hewitt. b 05. QUB BA27. Lon Coll
of Div 27. d 31 p 32. I Ardstraw *D & R* 39-72; RD
Newtownstewart 54-72; Can Derry Cathl 65-72; rtd
72. *5 Princetown Road, Bangor, Co Down BT20 3TA*
Bangor (0247) 3489
GEDDES, Gordon David. b 38. St Chad's Coll Dur
BA59 DipTh60. d 61 p 62. C Bishopwearmouth St Mary
V w St Pet CD *Dur* 61-65; P-in-c Jarrow 65-68; Teacher
Crewe Boys' Gr Sch 68-71; Hd of Relig Studies 71-78;
Hd of RE Ruskin Sch Crewe 78-90; Lic to Offic *Ches*
68-90; P-in-c Church Minshull from 90. *The Vicarage,
Minshull Vernon, Crewe CW1 4RD* Church Minshull
(027071) 213
GEDDES, Peter Henry. b 51. DipHE86. Trin Coll Bris 84.
d 86 p 87. C Blackpool St Mark *Blackb* 86-88; C Barnston
Ches from 88. *8 Antons Road, Pensby, Wirral, Merseyside
L61 9PT* 051-648 1512
GEDDES, Roderick Charles. b 47. Man Univ DipEd78
MPhil85. N Ord Course 88. d 91. C Alverthorpe *Wakef*
from 91. *52 Lindale Mount, Wrenthorpe, Wakefield, W
Yorkshire WF2 0BH* Wakefield (0924) 376037
GEDGE, Lloyd Victor. b 23. Cuddesdon Coll 54. d 57
p 58. Canada 66-82 and from 86; P-in-c N Creake *Nor*
82-83; P-in-c S Creake 82-83; R N and S Creake w
Waterden 84-86; rtd 88. *PO Box 187, Holden, Alberta,
Canada, T0B 2C0*
GEDGE, Peter Maurice Sydney. b 10. K Coll Cam
BA32 MA39. Coll of Resurr Mirfield 73. d 73 p 74. C
Scarborough St Mary w Ch Ch and H Apostles York
73-81; Lic to Offic from 81. *Pasture Howe, Hutton
Buscel, Scarborough, N Yorkshire YO13 9LL*
Scarborough (0723) 863151
GEDGE, Simon John Francis. b 44. Keble Coll Ox
BA67 MA73. Cuddesdon Coll 67. d 69 p 70. C Perry
Barr *Birm* 69-73; C Handsworth St Andr 73-75; V Birm
St Pet 75-81; Perm to Offic *Lon* 81-85; Hon C Croydon
St Jo *S'wark* from 85. *121 Albany Road, London
SE8 4EB* 081-692 7328
GEDYE, Timothy Robin William. b 56. Wycliffe Hall Ox.
d 89 p 90. NSM Ox St Aldate w St Matt *Ox* from 89.
42 Thorne Close, Kidlington, Oxford OX5 1SJ
Kidlington (08675) 78808
GEE, Mrs Dorothy Mary. St Jo Coll Nottm 88. d 89.
Asst Chapl Univ Hosp Nottm from 89. *16 The Leys,
Normanton-on-the-Wolds, Keyworth, Notts NG12 5NV*
Plumtree (06077) 4927
GEE, Canon Edward. b 28. St Deiniol's Hawarden 59.
d 61 p 62. C Hanging Heaton *Wakef* 61-65; V Brownhill
65-75; V Alverthorpe 75-84; R Castleford All SS from
84; Hon Can Wakef Cathl from 87. *The Rectory,
15 Barnes Road, Castleford, W Yorkshire WF10 5AA*
Castleford (0977) 552401
GEE, Michael Terence. b 29. Dur Univ BSc54. Tyndale
Hall Bris 60. d 62 p 63. C Blackpool St Thos *Blackb*
62-64; C Selston *S'well* 64-68; V Brimscombe *Glouc*
68-80; V Tidenham w Beachley and Lancaut 80-91;

261

P-in-c Sherborne, Windrush, the Barringtons etc from 91. *The Vicarage, Windrush, Oxford OX8 4TS* Windrush (04514) 276

GEE, Norman. b 11. Lon Univ BA33 St Cath Soc Ox BA35 MA42. Wycliffe Hall Ox 33. **d** 35 **p** 36. V Bath St Bart *B & W* 58-73; V Curry Rivel 73-78; rtd 78; Perm to Offic *B & W* from 79. *Sunrising, Holford, Bridgwater, Somerset TA5 1RY* Holford (027874) 393

GEEN, James William. b 50. Chich Th Coll 76. **d** 79 **p** 80. C Brandon *Dur* 79-84; C Sunderland Red Ho 84-86; P-in-c N Hylton St Marg Castletown 86-89; V 89-91; Dep Chapl HM Pris Dur from 91; Perm to Offic *Dur* from 91. *The Chaplain's Office, HM Prison Durham, Old Elvet, Durham DH1 3HU* 091-386 2621

GEERING, Anthony Ernest. b 43. Lon Univ DipTh66 Columbia Pacific Univ BSc. Kelham Th Coll 62. **d** 68 **p** 69. C Cov St Mary *Cov* 68-71; New Zealand 71-75; P-in-c Brinklow *Cov* 75-77; R 77-81; V Monks Kirby w Pailton and Stretton-under-Fosse 77-81; R Harborough Magna 77-81; V Pilton w Ashford *Ex* 81-86; P-in-c Shirwell w Loxhore 83-86; R Crediton and Shobrooke from 86. *The Vicarage, Crediton, Devon EX17 2AF* Crediton (03632) 2669

GEESON, Brian Alfred. b 30. Qu Coll Ox BA51. Qu Coll Birm 54. **d** 55 **p** 56. C Newbold and Dunston *Derby* 55-59; V Calow 59-64; R Broughton *Bradf* 64-71; TV Seacroft *Ripon* 71-77; Hon C Hanging Heaton *Wakef* 77-87; Hon C Purlwell from 87. *30 Ullswater Avenue, Dewsbury, W Yorkshire WF12 7PL* Dewsbury (0924) 465621

GEILINGER, John Edward. b 27. Lon Univ BSc53 BD58 BA76 MPhil79. Tyndale Hall Bris. **d** 59 **p** 60. C Plymouth St Jude *Ex* 59-61; Nigeria 63-77; Perm to Offic *Portsm* from 79. *Emmaus House, Colwell Road, Freshwater, Isle of Wight* Isle of Wight (0983) 753030

GELDARD, Mark Dundas. b 50. Liv Univ BA71 Bris Univ MA75. Trin Coll Bris 73. **d** 75 **p** 76. C Aughton Ch Ch *Liv* 75-78; Tutor Trin Coll Bris 78-84; V Fairfield *Liv* 84-88; Dir of Ords *Lich* from 88. *10 The Brambles, Boley Park, Lichfield, Staffs* Lichfield (0543) 415318

GELDARD, Peter John Esdale. b 45. AKC69. St Aug Coll Cant 70. **d** 71 **p** 72. C Sheerness H Trin w St Paul *Cant* 71-78; Gen Sec Ch Union 78-87; Lic to Offic *Lon* 79-87; *Cant* 80-87; V The Brents and Davington w Oare and Luddenham from 87. *The Vicarage, Brent Hill, Davington, Faversham, Kent ME13 7EF* Faversham (0795) 533272

GELL, Reginald Arthur Patrick. b 10. ALCD32. **d** 33 **p** 34. V Paignton Ch Ch *Ex* 63-90; rtd 90; Perm to Offic *Ex* from 90. *Town Orchard, Church Close, Abbotskerswell, Newton Abbot, Devon TQ12 5NY* Newton Abbot (0626) 61911

GELLI, Frank Julian. b 43. Birkb Coll Lon BA78 K Coll Lon MTh82. Ripon Coll Cuddesdon 84. **d** 86 **p** 87. C Chiswick St Nic w St Mary *Lon* 86-89; Chapl Ankara *Eur* 89-91; C Kensington St Mary Abbots w St Geo *Lon* from 91. *1 Vicarage Cottage, Vicarage Gate, London W8 4HN*

GELLING, Canon John Drury. b 22. Pemb Coll Ox BA44 DipTh45 MA48. Wycliffe Hall Ox 44. **d** 54 **p** 55. Hd Master Eccles High Sch 50-64; C Irlam *Man* 54-59; V Rushen *S & M* 64-77; RD Castletown 71-77; R Ballaugh from 77; P-in-c Michael 77-78; V from 78; Can St German's Cathl from 80. *The Rectory, Ballaugh, Isle of Man* Sulby (062489) 7873

GELSTON, Dr Anthony. b 35. Keble Coll Ox BA57 MA60 DD85. Ridley Hall Cam 59. **d** 60 **p** 61. C Chipping Norton *Ox* 60-62; Lic to Offic *Dur* from 62; Lect Th Dur Univ 62-76; Sen Lect 76-88; Reader from 89; Dean of Faculty of Div 77-79. *Lesbury, Hetton Road, Houghton le Spring, Tyne & Wear DH5 8JW* 091-584 2256

GEMMELL, Ian William Young. b 52. ALAM. St Jo Coll Nottm LTh77. **d** 77 **p** 78. C Old Hill H Trin *Worc* 77-81; C Selly Hill St Steph *Birm* 81; C Selly Park St Steph and St Wulstan 81-83; V Leic St Chris *Leic* from 83. *The Vicarage, 84A Marriott Road, Leicester LE2 6NU* Leicester (0533) 832679

✠**GENDERS, Rt Rev Roger Alban Marson (Brother Anselm).** b 19. BNC Ox BA47 MA47. Coll of Resurr Mirfield 48. **d** 52 **p** 52 **c** 77. Lic to Offic *Wakef* 52-55; CR from 52; Barbados 55-65; Rhodesia 66-75; Adn E Distr 70-75; Bp Bermuda 77-82; Asst Bp Wakef from 83; rtd 84. *House of the Resurrection, Mirfield, W Yorkshire WF14 0BN* Mirfield (0924) 494318

GENOWER, Arthur Herbert. b 98. Leeds Univ BA30. Ripon Hall Ox 33. **d** 33 **p** 34. R Wootton *Portsm* 40-68; rtd 68. *28 Manormead Nursing Home, Tilford Road, Hindhead, Surrey GU26 6RP* Hindhead (0428) 606823

GENT, Canon Comdr Anthony Leonard. b 20. CEng MIMechE. Sarum Th Coll 66. **d** 67 **p** 68. C Forrabury w Minster and Trevalga *Truro* 67-70; C Davidstow w Otterham 67-70; C Boscastle w Davidstow 67-70; V St Minver from 70; RD Trigg Minor 73-84; P-in-c St Kew 77-78; Hon Can Truro Cathl from 84. *The Vicarage, St Minver, Wadebridge, Cornwall PL27 6QH* Trebetherick (0208) 863356

GENT, Mrs Miriam. b 29. Leeds Univ BA51. SW Minl Tr Course 84. **d** 87. NSM Pinhoe and Broadclyst *Ex* from 87. *The Cottage, Mosshayne, Exeter EX1 3TR* Exeter (0392) 67288

GEOFFREY, Brother. *See* PEARSON, Harold

GEORGE, Alec. b 29. Lich Th Coll 56. **d** 59 **p** 60. C Holbrooks *Cov* 59-65; R Lower Broughton Ascension *Man* 65-71; V Hollinwood from 71. *St Margaret's Vicarage, Chapel Road, Oldham OL8 4QQ* 061-681 4541

GEORGE, Alexander Robert. b 46. K Coll Lon BD69 AKC69. St Aug Coll Cant. **d** 70 **p** 71. C Newmarket St Mary w Exning St Agnes *St E* 70-74; C Swindon Ch Ch *Bris* 74-76; C Henbury 76-79; Lic to Offic 79-80; TV Oldland 80-88; C Ipswich St Aug *St E* 89; C Hadleigh w Layham and Shelley 89-90; P-in-c Assington 90-91; R Assington w Newton Green and Lt Cornard from 91. *The Vicarage, Assington, Colchester CO6 5LQ* Boxford (0787) 210249

GEORGE, Brother. *See* GUIVER, Paul Alfred

GEORGE, Cedric James Noel. b 17. Worc Coll Ox BA39 MA43. Ripon Hall Ox 39. **d** 40 **p** 41. V Seaton *Ex* 57-82; rtd 82; Lic to Offic *Ex* from 82. *77 Slade Close, Ottery St Mary, Devon EX11 1SY* Ottery St Mary (0404) 814953

GEORGE, Charles Roy. b 32. St Edm Hall Ox BA55 MA59. Cuddesdon Coll 55. **d** 57 **p** 58. C Chorley St Laur *Blackb* 57-60; C Norton *Derby* 60-64; V Eltham St Barn S'wark 64-74; V Milton *Portsm* 74-90; R Rowner from 90. *The Rectory, 174 Rowner Lane, Gosport, Hants PO13 9SU* Gosport (0705) 81834

GEORGE, Ven David Michael. b 45. Selw Coll Cam BA66 MA70. Chich Th Coll 70. **d** 73 **p** 74. C Chiswick St Nic w St Mary *Lon* 73-76; C Kensington St Mary Abbots w St Geo 76-78; C Northolt Park St Barn 78-81; Argentina from 81; Adn River Plate from 84. *San Lorenzo 2274, 1640 Martinez, Buenos Aires, Argentina* Buenos Aires (1) 798-0078

GEORGE, Mrs Elizabeth Ann. b 33. Westf Coll Lon BA56. S Dios Minl Tr Scheme. **d** 87. NSM Basingstoke *Win* from 87. *c/o The Rectory, Church Street, Basingstoke RG21 1QT*

GEORGE, Frederick. b 39. St Luke's Coll Ex CertEd61. Chich Th Coll 82. **d** 72 **p** 83. Australia 72-75; Brunei 75-80; Gambia 80-82 and 83-88; C Hellingly and Upper Dicker *Chich* 83; P-in-c Ringsfield w Redisham, Barsham, Shipmeadow etc *St E* from 89. *The Rectory, School Road, Ringsfield, Beccles, Suffolk NR34 8NZ* Beccles (0502) 717862

GEORGE, Preb John Thomas. b 17. St D Coll Lamp BA42 Selw Coll Cam BA44 MA47. Westcott Ho Cam 44. **d** 45 **p** 46. R Backwell *B & W* 62-72; RD Portishead 68-72; V Wellington w W Buckland and Nynehead 72-76; R Wellington and Distr 76-82; Preb Wells Cathl 78-86; rtd 82; Hon C Diptford, N Huish, Harberton and Harbertonford *Ex* from 85. *The Parsonage, Avonwick, South Brent, Devon TQ10 9NB* South Brent (0364) 72756

GEORGE, Martin Walter. b 31. TD85. Bris Univ BEd73. Sarum & Wells Th Coll. **d** 82 **p** 82. C Bruton w Lamyatt, Wyke and Redlynch *B & W* 82-85; V Middlezoy and Othery and Moorlinch 85-87; Perm to Offic from 87. *17 Lewis Crescent, Frome, Somerset BA11 2LF* Frome (0373) 62094

GEORGE, Nicholas Paul. b 58. St Steph Ho Ox 86. **d** 89 **p** 90. C Leeds St Aid *Ripon* from 89. *84 Copgrove Road, Leeds LS8 2ST* Leeds (0532) 480050

GEORGE, William Havard. b 15. St D Coll Lamp BA37 St Mich Coll Llan 38. **d** 41 **p** 42. V Bassenthwaite *Carl* 57-74; P-in-c Isel w Setmurthy 72-74; V Bassenthwaite, Isel and Setmurthy 74-83; rtd 83. *Gwyntmor, West Green, Allonby, Maryport, Cumbria CA15 6PG* Allonby (090084) 475

GEORGE, William Llewelyn John. b 16. St Chad's Coll Dur BA37 DipTh38 MA40. **d** 39 **p** 40. R Cherington w Sutton under Brailes *Cov* 66-73; Chapl HM Pris Wormwood Scrubs 73-74; Perm to Offic 74-79; rtd 79; Perm to Offic *Chich* from 79; *Lon* from 82; *Guildf* from 84; Eur 85-90; Ox from 88. *3 Wythegate, Riverside Road, Staines, Middx TW18 2LE* Staines (0784) 458955

GEORGE-JONES, Canon Gwilym Ifor. b 26. K Coll (NS) 56. d 57 p 57. Canada 57-61; V Kirton in Lindsey *Linc* 61-71; R Grayingham 61-71; R Manton 61-71; V Alford w Rigsby from 71; R Maltby from 71; R Well from 71; V Bilsby w Farlesthorpe from 71; R Hannah cum Hagnaby w Markby from 71; R Saleby w Beesby from 71; RD Calcewaithe and Candleshoe 77-85 and 87-89; Can and Preb Linc Cathl from 81. *The Vicarage, Alford, Lincs LN13 9EW* Alford (0507) 462448

GERARD, John William. b 23. BNC Ox BA47 MA52. d 51 p 51. Canada 51-61; Perm to Offic *Chelmsf* from 74; rtd 81. *Oak Tree Cottage, 31 Wycke Lane, Tollesbury, Maldon, Essex CM9 8ST* Maldon (0621) 869318

GERRANS, Nigel Henry. b 31. Cam Univ MA54. St Steph Ho Ox 79. d 81 p 81. C Bicester w Bucknell, Caversfield and Launton *Ox* 81-84; Chapl Qu Alexandra Hosp Portsm from 84. *11 Lower Bere Wood, Waterlooville, Portsmouth PO7 7NQ* Waterlooville (0705) 251326

GERRARD, Brian James. b 38. Wycliffe Hall Ox 72. d 74 p 75. C Ditton St Mich *Liv* 74-78; V Lydiate 78-89; P-in-c N Meols from 89; P-in-c Banks from 89. *76 Beresford Drive, Southport, Merseyside PR9 7LQ* Southport (0704) 25436

GERRARD, Ven David Keith Robin. b 39. St Edm Hall Ox BA61. Linc Th Coll 61. d 63 p 64. C Stoke Newington St Olave *Lon* 63-66; C Primrose Hill St Mary w Avenue Road St Paul 66-69; V Newington St Paul *S'wark* 69-79; V Surbiton St Andr and St Mark 79-89; RD Kingston 84-88; Hon Can S'wark Cathl from 85; Adn Wandsworth from 89. *68 North Side, London SW18 2QX* 081-874 5766

GERRARD, George Ernest. b 16. TEM. FCIS60. Ridley Hall Cam 66. d 68 p 69. OStJ from 61; C Ramsey *Ely* 70-75; rtd 81; Perm to Offic *Nor* from 86. *1 Goodrick Place, Beech Close, Swaffham, Norfolk PE37 7RP* Swaffham (0760) 23311

GERRISH, David Victor. b 38. St Jo Coll Dur BSc61 MA65. Oak Hill Th Coll 61. d 64 p 65. C Fareham St Jo *Portsm* 64-66; Asst Chapl K Sch Roch 67-71; Asst Chapl Bryanston Sch Blandford 71-73; Chapl 73-77; Chapl Mon Sch 77-86; Warminster Sch Wilts 86-89; R Portland All SS w St Pet *Sarum* from 89. *The Rectory, Easton, Portland, Dorset DT5 1HG* Portland (0305) 820177

GERRY, Brian John Rowland. b 38. Oak Hill Th Coll 69. d 71 p 72. C Hawkwell *Chelmsf* 71-74; C Battersea Park St Sav *S'wark* 74-77; C Battersea St Geo w St Andr 74-77; V Axmouth w Musbury *Ex* 77-86; R Upton from 86. *Upton Rectory, Furzehill Road, Torquay TQ1 3JG* Torquay (0803) 211572

GETHYN-JONES, Canon John Eric. b 09. MBE45 TD50. FSA61 Bris Univ MA66. Qu Coll Birm 32. d 34 p 35. V Berkeley *Glouc* 67-76; Hon Can Glouc Cathl from 68; rtd 76. *Canonbury House, Canonbury Street, Berkeley, Gloucester GL13 9BG* Dursley (0453) 810296

GHEST, Richard William Iliffe. b 31. Em Coll Cam BA53 MA57 Lon Univ BA66. Wells Th Coll 53. d 55 p 56. C Weston-super-Mare St Jo *B & W* 55-57; India 58-63; C Holborn St Geo w H Trin and St Bart *Lon* 63-67; Ceylon 67-68; C Combe Down *B & W* 68-73; C Combe Down w Monkton Combe 73-74; R Tickenham from 74. *The Rectory, 27 Clevedon Road, Tickenham, Clevedon, Avon BS21 6RA* Nailsea (0272) 853278

GHINN, Edward. b 45. Oak Hill Th Coll 71. d 74 p 75. C Purley Ch Ch *S'wark* 74-77; Chile 77-82; V Sevenoaks Weald *Roch* 82-86; Chapl HM Pris Hull 86-89; Pentonville 89-91; Chapl HM Pris Maidstone from 91. *The Chaplain's Office, HM Prison, County Road, Maidstone, Kent ME14 1UZ* Maidstone (0622) 755611

GHOSH, Dipen. b 43. St Jo Coll Nottm 71. d 74 p 75. C Bushbury *Lich* 74-77; Hon C 86-89; C Wednesfield Heath from 89. *18 Collingwood Road, Wolverhampton WV10 8DS* Wolverhampton (0902) 788971

GIBB, Malcolm John. b 45. MIBiol81 CBiol84 Lon Univ BSc67. Ox NSM Course 84. d 87 p 88. NSM Dorchester *Ox* from 88. *1 Cratlands Close, Stadhampton, Oxford OX9 7TU* Stadhampton (0865) 890971

GIBBARD, Roger. b 48. Southn Univ BA73. Cuddesdon Coll 73. d 75 p 76. C Portsea St Mary *Portsm* 75-79; P-in-c New Addington *Cant* 79-81; C Ditton St Mich *Liv* 81-82; TV 82-88; Asst Chapl HM Pris Liv 88-89; Chapl HM Young Offender Inst Hindley from 89. *HM Young Offender Institute, Hindley, Wigan, Lancs WN2 5TH* Wigan (0942) 866255

GIBBARD, Sydney Mark. b 10. Selw Coll Cam BA32 MA37. Cuddesdon Coll 33. d 33 p 34. SSJE from 43; USA 70-71 and 75-76 and 80-81; Asst Chapl Ex Coll Ox 71-75; India 77-78; Australia 78-79; New Zealand 79-80; rtd 80. *St John's Home, St Mary's Road, Oxford OX4 1QE* Oxford (0865) 247725

GIBBINS, John Grenville. b 53. Aston Tr Scheme 89 Linc Th Coll 89. d 91. C Market Harborough *Leic* from 91. *5 Ashfield Road, Market Harborough, Leics* Market Harborough (0858) 431977

GIBBON, Edward Herbert Morgan. b 15. St D Coll Lamp BA37 St Mich Coll Llan 38. d 40 p 41. V Sunninghill *Ox* 66-79; rtd 79; Perm to Offic *Guildf* from 82. *Starlings, Sandpit Hall Road, Chobham, Woking, Surrey GU24 8HA* Chobham (0276) 856863

GIBBON, Gordon Percy. b 17. Oak Hill Th Coll 63. d 64 p 65. V Walthamstow St Gabr *Chelmsf* 68-82; rtd 82; Perm to Offic *Chich* from 82. *20 Black Path, Polegate, E Sussex BN26 5AP* Polegate (03212) 6751

GIBBONS, David Anthony. b 57. Univ Coll Dur BA79 Ox Univ BA83 MA88. St Steph Ho Ox 81. d 84 p 85. C Blackpool St Steph *Blackb* 84-87; C Lon Docks St Pet w Wapping St Jo *Lon* 87-90; P-in-c New Brompton St Luke *Roch* from 90. *St Luke's Vicarage, Sidney Road, Gillingham ME7 1PA* Medway (0634) 853060

GIBBONS, David Robin Christian. b 36. Chich Th Coll 82. d 84 p 85. C Seaford w Sutton *Chich* 84-87; R Harting from 87. *The Rectory, South Harting, Petersfield, Hants GU31 5QB* Harting (0730) 825234

GIBBONS, Eric. b 47. Sarum & Wells Th Coll 69. d 72 p 73. C New Haw *Guildf* 72-76; C Hawley H Trin 76-79; P-in-c Blackheath and Chilworth 79-90; V from 90. *The Vicarage, Blackheath, Guildford, Surrey GU4 8QT* Guildford (0483) 893129

GIBBONS, John. b 31. K Coll Lon 52. Oak Hill Th Coll 55. d 57 p 58. C Islington St Steph w St Bart and St Matt *Lon* 57-60; C Rolleston *Lich* 60-63; C Anslow 60-63; V Bobbington 63-83; V N Axholme Gp *Linc* from 83; RD Is of Axholme from 91. *The Vicarage, 20 Chapel Lane, Keadby, Scunthorpe, S Humberside DN17 3EZ* Scunthorpe (0724) 783612

GIBBONS, Ven Kenneth Harry. b 31. Man Univ BSc52. Cuddesdon Coll 54. d 56 p 57. C Fleetwood *Blackb* 56-60; NE Sch Sec SCM 60-62; Hon C Leeds St Pet *Ripon* 60-62; C St Martin-in-the-Fields *Lon* 62-65; V New Addington *Cant* 65-70; V Portsea St Mary *Portsm* 70-81; RD Portsm 73-79; Hon Can Portsm Cathl 76-81; Dir of Post-Ord Tr *Blackb* 81-83; Acting Chapl HM Forces Weeton 81-85; Dir of Ords 82-90; Adn Lanc from 81; P-in-c Weeton 81-85; V St Michaels on Wyre from 85. *The Vicarage, Hall Lane, St Michael's-on-Wyre, Preston PR3 0TQ* St Michaels (09958) 242

GIBBONS, Paul James. b 37. JP. Chich Th Coll 63. d 65 p 66. C Croydon St Mich *Cant* 65-72; V Maidstone St Mich from 72. *The Vicarage, 109 Tonbridge Road, Maidstone, Kent ME16 8JS* Maidstone (0622) 752710

GIBBONS, Thomas Patrick. b 59. St Jo Coll Dur BA82. St Steph Ho Ox 88. d 90 p 91. C Whorlton *Newc* from 90. *6 Audland Walk, Chapel House, Newcastle upon Tyne NE5 1BD* 091-264 1371

GIBBONS, Canon William Simpson. b 32. TCD BA60 MA64. d 61 p 62. C Londonderry Ch Ch *D & R* 61-65; I Drumholm and Rossnowlagh 65-70; C Dub St Ann w St Steph *D & G* 70-72; I Kill from 72; Can Ch Ch Cathl Dub from 91. *The Rectory, Kill o' the Grange, Blackrock, Co Dublin, Irish Republic* Dublin (1) 280-1721

GIBBS, Colin Hugh. b 35. St Mich Coll Llan 82. d 84 p 85. C Bistre *St As* 84-87; V Penycae from 87. *The Vicarage, Church Street, Penycae, Wrexham, Clwyd LL14 2RL* Rhosllanerchrugog (0978) 840878

GIBBS, Colin Wilfred. b 39. Man Univ BA62. St Jo Coll Nottm 71. d 73 p 74. C Crowborough *Chich* 73-76; C Rodbourne Cheney *Bris* 76-77; C Bickenhill w Elmdon *Birm* 77-80; CF from 80. *c/o MOD (Army), Bagshot Park, Bagshot, Surrey GU19 5PL* Bagshot (0276) 71717

GIBBS, Canon Derek Norman. b 38. Kelham Th Coll. d 62 p 63. C Newc Ch Ch w St Ann *Newc* 62-65; C Shiremoor 65-67; V New Bentley *Sheff* 67-68; V Sheff Parson Cross St Cecilia 68-80; RD Ecclesfield 75-80; V Cantley from 80; RD Doncaster from 82; Hon Can Sheff Cathl from 88; P-in-c Doncaster Ch Ch from 89. *The Vicarage, 200 Cantley Lane, Doncaster, S Yorkshire DN4 6PA* Doncaster (0302) 535133

GIBBS, Prof Edmund. b 38. Lon Univ BD62. Fuller Th Sem California DMin81 Oak Hill Th Coll 58. d 63 p 64. C Wandsworth All SS *S'wark* 63-66; Chile 66-70; Sec SAMS 70-73; Educn Sec 73-77; Ch Progr Manager Bible Soc 77-84; USA from 84; Assoc Prof Evang and Ch Renewal Fuller Th Sem from 84. *Fuller Theological Seminary, Pasadena, California 91182, USA* Pasadena (818) 584-5590

GIBBS, Ian Edmund. b 47. Lon Univ BEd69. St Steph Ho Ox 72. d 75 p 76. C Stony Stratford *Ox* 75-79; V Forest Town *S'well* 79-83; R Diddlebury w Munslow,

Holdgate and Tugford *Heref* from 83; R Abdon from 83. *The Rectory, Munslow, Craven Arms, Shropshire SY7 9ET*

GIBBS, James Millard. b 28. Michigan Univ BSE51 Nottm Univ PhD68. Seabury-Western Th Sem BD57. **d** 57 **p** 57. USA 57-60; Lic to Offic S'well 61-62 and 65-66; Lich 66-71; C Brandon *Dur* 62-64; Vice-Prin Lich Th Coll 66-71; India 72-77; Tutor Qu Coll Birm 78-84; V Stechford *Birm* from 84. *The Vicarage, Albert Road, Birmingham B33 8UA* 021-783 2463

✠**GIBBS, Rt Rev John.** b 17. Bris Univ BA42 Lon Univ BD48. Linc Th Coll 55. **d** 55 **p** 56 **c** 73. C Brislington St Luke *Bris* 55-57; Chapl St Matthias's Coll Bris 57-64; Vice-Prin 61-64; Prin Keswick Hall C of E Coll of Educn 64-73; Lic to Offic *Nor* 64-73; Hon Can Nor Cathl 68-73; Suff Bp Bradwell *Chelmsf* 73-76; Bp Cov 76-85; rtd 85; Asst Bp Bris from 85; Asst Bp Glouc from 85. *Farthingloe, Southfield, Minchinhampton, Stroud, Glos GL6 9DY* Brimscombe (0453) 886211

GIBBS, Dr Jonathan Robert. b 61. Jes Coll Ox MA89 Jes Coll Cam PhD90. Ridley Hall Cam 84. **d** 89 **p** 90. C Stalybridge H Trin and Ch Ch *Ches* from 89. *43 Kay Street, Stalybridge, Cheshire SK15 2EH* 061-338 7848

GIBBS, Martin Franck. b 12. St Steph Ho Ox 32. **d** 35 **p** 36. V Roath St German *Llan* 67-77; rtd 77; Perm to Offic *B & W* from 77. *6 George and Crown Cottages, Hinton St George, Crewkerne, Somerset TA17 8SD* Crewkerne (0460) 72158

GIBBS, Peter Winston. b 50. Ex Univ BA72 Leic Univ DipSocWork75 CQSW75. St Jo Coll Nottm DipTh. **d** 90 **p** 91. C Hampreston *Sarum* from 90. *57 Glenmoor Road, Ferndown, Dorset BH22 8QE* Ferndown (0202) 876552

GIBBS, Canon Philip Roscoe. b 33. Codrington Coll Barbados 57. **d** 60 **p** 61. Br Honduras 60-73; Belize 73-74; Hon Can Br Honduras 71-73; Hon Can Belize from 73; V Stoke Newington Common St Mich *Lon* 74-87; New Zealand from 87. *The Vicarage, 22 Bassett Road, Johnsonville, PO Box 13-253, New Zealand* Wellington (4) 788384

GIBBS, Canon Robert John. b 43. Dur Univ BA64. Westcott Ho Cam 66. **d** 68 **p** 69. C Costessey *Nor* 68-71; C Halesowen *Worc* 71-75; TV 75-76; P-in-c Dudley St Jas 77-79; V 79-82; Dioc Ecum Officer 82-89; R Ribbesford w Bewdley and Dowles from 82; RD Kidderminster 83-89; Hon Can Worc Cathl from 87. *The Rectory, Bewdley, Worcs DY12 2DP* Bewdley (0299) 402275

GIBBS, Canon Roderick Harold. b 25. Leeds Univ BA49. Coll of Resurr Mirfield 49. **d** 51 **p** 52. C Whitton SS Phil and Jas *Lon* 51-56; V Hammersmith St Steph 57-65; R Stepney St Dunstan and All SS 65-72; Dep Hd Master Laindon Sch 72-76; Hon C Langdon Hills *Chelmsf* 74-78; Hd Master Wm Forster Sch Tottenham 77-83; Hon C Bounds Green *Lon* 78-83; P-in-c Purley St Mark Woodcote *S'wark* 83-86; V from 86; Hon Can S'wark Cathl from 89. *St Mark's Vicarage, 22 Peaks Hill, Purley, Surrey CR8 3JE* 081-660 7204

GIBBS, Canon William Gilbert. b 31. Bps' Coll Cheshunt 55. **d** 58 **p** 59. C Wellington w W Buckland *B & W* 58-61; C Kensington St Mary Abbots w St Geo *Lon* 61-68; V Guilsborough *Pet* 68; V Guilsborough w Hollowell 68-74; V Guilsborough w Hollowell and Cold Ashby from 74; P-in-c Cottesbrooke w Gt Creaton and Thornby from 83; Can Pet Cathl from 88; P-in-c Maidwell w Draughton, Lamport w Faxton from 88. *The Vicarage, Guilsborough, Northampton NN6 8PU* Northampton (0604) 740297

GIBBY, Thomas Rees. b 12. St D Coll Lamp BA33 BD42. St Mich Coll Llan 33. **d** 35 **p** 36. V Ivybridge *Ex* 62-75; R Harford 63-75; rtd 75. *Penlon, Cwmann, Lampeter, Dyfed SA48 8DU* Lampeter (0570) 422100

GIBLING, Derek Vivian. b 31. Wadh Coll Ox BA56 MA63. Wycliffe Hall Ox 70. **d** 72 **p** 73. C Fisherton Anger *Sarum* 72-74; C Yatton Keynell *Bris* 74-77; C Castle Combe 74-77; C Biddestone w Slaughterford 74-77; P-in-c Youlgreave *Derby* 77-82; P-in-c Stanton-in-Peak 77-82; V Youlgreave, Middleton, Stanton-in-Peak etc 82-88; P-in-c Hartington and Biggin 88-90; V Hartington, Biggin and Earl Sterndale from 90. *The Vicarage, Hartington, Buxton, Derbyshire SK17 0AW* Hartington (029884) 280

GIBRALTAR IN EUROPE, Bishop of. *See* SATTERTHWAITE, Rt Rev John Richard

GIBRALTAR IN EUROPE, Suffragan Bishop of. *See* HOLLAND, Rt Rev Edward

GIBRALTAR, Archdeacon of. *See* de PINA CABRAL, Rt Rev Daniel Pereira dos Santos

GIBRALTAR, Dean of. *See* HORLOCK, Very Rev Brian William

GIBSON, Alan. b 35. Birm Univ BSc56 Man Univ MSc72. NW Ord Course 71. **d** 74 **p** 75. C Sale St Anne *Ches* 74-77; V Runcorn St Mich 77-82; Educn Adv *Carl* 82-88; P-in-c Hugill 82-88; V Grange-over-Sands from 88. *The Vicarage, Hampsfell Road, Grange-over-Sands, Cumbria LA11 6BE* Grange-over-Sands (05395) 32757

GIBSON, Canon Alan Gordon. b 18. AKC48. **d** 48 **p** 49. V S Beddington St Mich *S'wark* 64-76; RD Sutton 70-76; Hon Can S'wark Cathl from 74; P-in-c Perry Hill St Geo 76-82; RD W Lewisham 79-82; Vice-Chmn Dioc Past Cttee 82-87; RD Clapham and Brixton 83-85; rtd 87. *33 Briarwood Road, London SW4 9PJ* 071-627 1100

GIBSON, Alan Henry. b 11. MBE44. K Coll Lon BD37 AKC37 Ely Th Coll 37. **d** 37 **p** 38. V Sandgate St Paul *Cant* 64-76; rtd 76; Lic to Offic *Cant* from 76; Chapl St Mary's Hosp Etchinghill 80-87. *207 Shorncliffe Road, Folkestone, Kent CT20 3PH* Folkestone (0303) 57813

GIBSON, Alexander Douglas. b 21. Wycliffe Hall Ox 60. **d** 62 **p** 63. V Gresley *Derby* 65-77; V Hartington 77-78; V Biggin 77-78; V Hartington and Biggin 78-88; rtd 88; Perm to Offic *Derby* from 88. *Westmead, Aldern Way, Baslow Road, Bakewell, Derbyshire DE4 1AJ* Bakewell (0629) 812723

GIBSON, Anthony Richard. b 43. Ridley Hall Cam 83. **d** 85 **p** 86. C Rushmere *St E* 85-88; P-in-c N Tawton and Bondleigh *Ex* 88; P-in-c Sampford Courtenay w Honeychurch 88; R N Tawton, Bondleigh, Sampford Courtenay etc from 88. *The Rectory, North Tawton, Devon EX20 2EX* North Tawton (0837) 82645

GIBSON, Catherine (Kate) Snyder. b 39. **d** 86. Colombia 86-87; C Aber St Marg *Ab* 87-88; USA 88-89; Dioc Hosp Chapl *Ab* from 89. *287 North Deeside Road, Cults, Aberdeen AB1 9PA* Aberdeen (0224) 868512

GIBSON, Charles Gatchell. b 18. TCD MA. **d** 43 **p** 44. USA 65-83; rtd 83. *The Breakers, Sandycove, Kinsale, Co Cork, Irish Republic* Cork (21) 772364

GIBSON, Colin Taylor. b 54. Trin Coll Cam BA77. Oak Hill Th Coll DipHE88. **d** 88 **p** 89. C Thrybergh w Hooton Roberts *Sheff* from 88. *4 Park Terrace, Doncaster Road, Thrybergh, Rotherham, S Yorkshire S65 4AQ* Rotherham (0709) 850003

GIBSON, Dr David Francis. b 36. Magd Coll Cam BA57 BChir60 MB61. SW Minl Tr Course 84. **d** 90. NSM Newport, Bishops Tawton and Tawstock *Ex* from 90. *Martins Hill, Bishops Tawton, Barnstaple, Devon EX32 0EE* Barnstaple (0271) 42098

GIBSON, David Innes. b 31. NDD53. Oak Hill Th Coll 56. **d** 59 **p** 60. C S Croydon Em *Cant* 59-62; C Washfield *Ex* 62-63; Asst Master and Chapl Blundells Sch Tiverton 63-64; Chapl Sutton Valence Sch Maidstone 64-68; Chapl Dean Close Sch Cheltenham 68-75; Asst Chapl and Ho Master 75-85; Asst Master Brightlands Sch Newnham-on-Severn 85-90; C Cheltenham St Mary, St Matt, St Paul and H Trin *Glouc* from 91. *2 Withyholt Park, Charlton Kings, Cheltenham, Glos GL53 9BP* Cheltenham (0242) 511612

GIBSON, Douglas Harold. b 20. Portsm Dioc Tr Course. **d** 87. NSM Portsea St Luke *Portsm* from 87. *83 Middle Street, Southsea, Hants PO5 4BW* Portsmouth (0705) 829769

GIBSON, Canon George Granville. b 36. Cuddesdon Coll 69. **d** 71 **p** 72. C Tynemouth Cullercoats St Paul *Newc* 71-73; TV Cramlington 73-77; V Newton Aycliffe *Dur* 77-85; R Bishopwearmouth St Mich w St Hilda 85-90; RD Wearmouth from 85; Hon Can Dur Cathl from 88; TR Sunderland from 90. *The Rectory, 21 Thornhill Terrace, Sunderland SR2 7JL* 091-567 3040

GIBSON, Henry Edward. b 15. Keble Coll Ox BA41 DipTh42 MA46. St Steph Ho Ox 41. **d** 43 **p** 44. V Waterlooville *Portsm* 63-81; rtd 81; Perm to Offic Portsm and Chich from 81. *8 Worcester Road, Chichester, W Sussex PO19 4DJ* Chichester (0243) 779194

GIBSON, Ian. b 48. Open Univ BA85. S Dios Minl Tr Scheme 82. **d** 85 **p** 86. NSM Uckfield *Chich* 85-88; V Fairwarp from 88; V High Hurstwood from 88. *The Vicarage, Fairwarp, Uckfield, E Sussex TN22 3BL* Nutley (082571) 2277

GIBSON, Ian David. b 58. NE Lon Poly BSc80. Westcott Ho Cam 84. **d** 87 **p** 88. C Castle Camps *Ely* 87-90; C Bartlow 87-90; C Linton 87-90; C Shudy Camps 87-90; NSM Gt w Lt Gidding and Steeple Gidding from 91; NSM Hamerton from 91; NSM Winwick from 91; NSM Upton and Copmanford from 91. *The Community of Christ the Sower, Manor Farm, Little Gidding, Huntingdon PE17 5RJ* Winwick (08323) 383

GIBSON, John George. b 20. Chich Th Coll 47. **d** 50 **p** 51. V Gunnersbury St Jas *Lon* 58-70; V Upper Teddington SS Pet and Paul 70-84; rtd 84; Perm to Offic *Chich* from

85. *College of St Barnabas, Blackberry Lane, Lingfield, Surrey RH7 6NJ* Dormans Park (034287) 703

GIBSON, John Murray Hope. b 35. Dur Univ BA58 DipTh60. Cranmer Hall Dur 58. **d** 60 **p** 61. C Ches le Street *Dur* 60-63; C Stockton 63-68; V Denton and Ingleton 68-75; V Swalwell from 75; Chapl Dunston Hill Hosp Dur from 80. *The Vicarage, Whickham Bank, Swalwell, Newcastle upon Tyne NE16 3JL* 091-488 7538

GIBSON, John Noel Keith. b 22. MBE89. Ch Coll Cam MA48 Lon Univ BD59. Coll of Resurr Mirfield 45. **d** 47 **p** 48. Antigua 51-56; Virgin Is from 56; rtd 87; Can All SS Cathl Virgin Is from 89. *PO Box 65, Valley, Virgin Gorda, British Virgin Islands* Virgin Islands (1809) 495-5216

GIBSON, Kenneth George Goudie. b 54. Glas Univ MA83 Edin Univ BD87. Edin Th Coll 83. **d** 88 **p** 89. C Glas St Marg *Glas* 88-90; R E Kilbride from 90. *St Mark's Rectory, Telford Road, East Kilbride, Glasgow G75 0HN* East Kilbride (03552) 25552

GIBSON, Laura Mary. b 50. N Ord Course 85. **d** 88. Par Dn Kidderminster *Worc* 88-90; Par Dn Kidderminster St Jo and H Innocents from 90. *The Vicarage, 35 Sutton Park Road, Kidderminster, Worcs DY11 6LD* Kidderminster (0562) 748213

GIBSON, Mark. b 48. **d** 84. OSB from 67; Abbot of Alton 82-90; Perm to Offic *Win* 84-90; Hon C Paddington St Sav *Lon* from 90; Acting Bp's Dom Chapl 90-91. *24 Formosa Street, London W9 2QA or, Alton Abbey, Alton, Hants GU34 4AP* 071-286 4962 or Alton (0420) 62145

GIBSON, Nigel Stephen David. b 53. St Barn Coll Adelaide DipMin87. **d** 87 **p** 87. Australia 87-89; C Boston *Linc* from 90; Lect from 90. *2 Tower Street, Boston, Lincs PE21 8RX* Boston (0205) 355417

GIBSON, Philip Nigel Scott. b 53. St Jo Coll Dur BA78. Cranmer Hall Dur DipTh79. **d** 79 **p** 80. C Yardley St Edburgha *Birm* 79-82; C Stratford w Bishopton *Cov* 82-84; Chapl SW Hosp Lon from 84. *30 Queensville Road, London SW12 0JJ* 081-671 7667

GIBSON, Raymond. b 23. Ely Th Coll 60. **d** 62 **p** 63. Chapl Leic R Infirmary 67-68; Nottm City Hosp 68-84; V Barlings *Linc* 84-88; rtd 88. *Chapel Cottage, Main Road, Aby, Alford, Lincs LN13 0DT* Alford (0507) 480647

GIBSON, Raymond Frank. b 34. Toronto Bible Coll BTh61 Tyndale Hall Bris 62. **d** 64 **p** 65. C Gt Horton *Bradf* 64-67; C Otley 67-72; V Fairlight *Chich* 72-83; V Hallwood *Ches* 83-85; R Freethorpe w Wickhampton, Halvergate etc *Nor* from 85. *The Vicarage, Freethorpe, Norwich NR13 3AH* Great Yarmouth (0493) 700322

GIBSON, Canon Robert Swinton. b 26. Wadh Coll Ox BA50 MA55. Wells Th Coll 50. **d** 53 **p** 54. C Greenwich St Alfege w St Pet *S'wark* 53-61; Ind Missr 55-62; Hon Chapl to Bp S'wark 56-67; Sen Chapl S Lon Ind Miss 62-67; Nigeria 67-69; R Guisborough *York* 69-83; RD Guisborough 73-83; TR Halifax *Wakef* from 83; Hon Can Wakef Cathl from 85; RD Halifax from 86. *The Vicarage, Skircoat Green Road, Halifax, W Yorkshire HX3 0BQ* Halifax (0422) 65477

GIBSON, Ven Terence Allen. b 37. Jes Coll Cam BA61 MA65. Cuddesdon Coll 61. **d** 63 **p** 64. C Kirkby *Liv* 63-66; TV 72-75; TR 75-84; Warden Cen 63 66-75; Youth Chapl 66-72; RD Walton 79-84; Adn Suffolk *St E* 84-87; Adn Ipswich from 87. *99 Valley Road, Ipswich, Suffolk IP1 4NF* Ipswich (0473) 250333

GIBSON, Thomas Thomson. b 23. Sarum Th Coll 62. **d** 63 **p** 64. C E w W Harnham *Sarum* 63-66; V Rowde 66-74; R Poulshot 67-74; V Badminton w Acton Turville *Glouc* 74-84; P-in-c Hawkesbury 81-84; V Badminton w Lt Badminton, Acton Turville etc from 84. *The Vicarage, Badminton, Avon GL9 1ET* Badminton (045421) 427

GIBSON, William John. b 29. Dur Univ BA58 DipTh59. St Chad's Coll Dur 55. **d** 59 **p** 60. C Elland *Wakef* 59-62; C Huddersfield St Jo 62-66; V Sowerby 66-87; V Honley from 87. *The Vicarage, St Mary's Road, Honley, Huddersfield HD7 2AZ* Huddersfield (0484) 661178

GICK, Alan Gladney. b 11. TCD BA38 MA58. **d** 40 **p** 41. I Lislimnaghan *D & R* 60-80; rtd 80. *107 Old Manor Road, Rustington, W Sussex BN16 3QD* Rustington (0903) 774140

GIDDENS, Leslie Vernon. b 29. Bps' Coll Cheshunt 54. **d** 56 **p** 57. C Harrow St Pet *Lon* 56-58; C Tottenham St Benet Fink 58-63; C-in-c Hayes St Nic CD from 63. *St Nicholas' Vicarage, Raynton Drive, Hayes, Middx UB4 8BG* 081-573 4122

GIDDEY, Canon William Denys. b 17. Leeds Univ BA39. Coll of Resurr Mirfield 39. **d** 41 **p** 42. R Binbrook *Linc* 48-61; R Swinhope w Thorganby 48-61; Chapl Eastbourne Hosp Gp 61-83; Can and Preb Chich Cathl *Chich* 78-90; rtd 82; Perm to Offic *Chich* from 90.

70 Sidley Road, Eastbourne, E Sussex BN22 7JP Eastbourne (0323) 22918

GIDDINGS, John Norton Cornock. b 22. **d** 86 **p** 87. NSM Cromhall w Tortworth and Tytherington *Glouc* 86-90; Hon C Stockland w Dalwood *Ex* from 90. *The Vicarage, Stockland, Honiton, Devon EX14 9EF* Stockland (040488) 401

✠GIGGALL, Rt Rev George Kenneth. b 14. OBE61. Man Univ BA37 St Chad's Coll Dur DipTh38. **d** 39 **p** 40 **c** 73. C Cheetwood St Alb *Man* 39-41; C Reddish 41-45; Chapl RN 45-69; QHC 67-69; Dean Gib *Eur* 69-73; Bp St Helena 73-79; Aux Bp Eur 79-81; Chapl San Remo w Bordighera 80-81; rtd 81; Asst Bp Blackb from 81. *Fosbrooke House, 8 Clifton Drive, Lytham St Annes, Lancs FY8 5RQ* Lytham (0253) 735683

GILBERT, Anthony John David. b 54. LRSC83. Ripon Coll Cuddesdon 83. **d** 86 **p** 87. C Exning St Martin w Landwade *St E* 86-89; Chapl RAF from 89. *c/o MOD, Adastral House, Theobald's Road, London WC1X 8RU* 071-430 7268

GILBERT, Arthur (John). b 57. LTCL76 GBSM79 Reading Univ PGCE80. Coll of Resurr Mirfield 88. **d** 91. C Uppingham w Ayston and Wardley w Belton *Pet* from 91. *41 Ash Close, Uppingham, Oakham, Leics LE15 9PJ* Uppingham (0572) 822528

GILBERT, Barry. b 46. Leeds Univ BA67. Coll of Resurr Mirfield 67. **d** 69 **p** 70. C Malvern Link w Cowleigh *Worc* 69-73; P-in-c Bromsgrove All SS 73-81; V 81-83; P-in-c Lower Mitton 83-88; V from 88. *The Vicarage, Stourport-on-Severn, Worcs DY13 9DD* Stourport (0299) 822041

GILBERT, Caroline Margaret. b 62. Nottm Univ BTh90. St Jo Coll Nottm 87. **d** 90. Hon C Aston SS Pet and Paul *Birm* from 90. *81 Electric Avenue, Birmingham B6 7ED* 021-327 0113

GILBERT, Christine Lesley. b 44. DipHE. Trin Coll Bris 79. dss 85 **d** 86. Par Dn Bilston *Lich* from 87. *107 Wellington Road, Bilston, W Midlands WV14 6BQ* Bilston (0902) 353428

GILBERT, Christopher Anthony. b 60. Aston Univ BSc82. St Jo Coll Nottm 86. **d** 89 **p** 90. C Aston SS Pet and Paul *Birm* from 89. *81 Electric Avenue, Birmingham B6 7ED* 021-327 0113

GILBERT, Frederick Herbert. b 14. Worc Ord Coll 64. **d** 66 **p** 67. C Paignton Ch Ch *Ex* 69-73; TV Offwell, Widworthy, Cotleigh, Farway etc 73-79; rtd 80. *3 Orchard Close, Chudleigh, Newton Abbot, Devon TQ13 0LR* Chudleigh (0626) 852730

GILBERT, Frederick Joseph. b 29. Lich Th Coll 58. **d** 59 **p** 60. C Westhoughton *Man* 59-62; V Goodshaw 62-68; R Crumpsall St Matt 68-75; RD Cheetham 70-74; RD N Man 74-75; V Rochdale St Aid 75-78; TV Rochdale 78-80; V Westhoughton 80-85; TR Deane 85-87; R W Bowbrook *Worc* 87-89; R Bowbrook N from 89. *The Rectory, Droitwich Road, Hanbury, Bromsgrove, Worcs B60 4DB* Hanbury (0527) 821370

GILBERT, John Edwin. b 28. FCA62. Bps' Coll Cheshunt 54. **d** 57 **p** 58. C Luton Ch Ch *St Alb* 57-60; C Gt Berkhamsted 60-64; India 65-71; Perm to Offic *St Alb* 71-77; Lic to Offic 77-86; Hon C Sunnyside w Bourne End 86-89; TV Padgate *Liv* from 89. *The Vicarage, Admiral's Road, Birchwood, Warrington* Padgate (0925) 811906

GILBERT, John Michael. b 06. St Boniface Warminster. **d** 31 **p** 32. V Porthleven *Truro* 63-74; Lic to Offic 74-78; rtd 75. *5 Rigelou, Meade Street, George, 6530 South Africa* George (441) 741748

GILBERT, Joseph. b 12. Chich Th Coll 33. **d** 36 **p** 37. V Lever Bridge *Man* 65-76; rtd 77; Perm to Offic *Man* from 77. *159 Bolton Road, Turton, Bolton, Lancs BL7 0AF* Bolton (0204) 852736

GILBERT, Philip Mark. b 62. Liv Univ BA84. Coll of Resurr Mirfield 84. **d** 87 **p** 88. C Frodsham *Ches* 87-89; C Stockton Heath from 89. *St Mary Magdalene House, 8 St Monica's Close, Appleton, Warrington WA4 3AW* Warrington (0925) 602815

GILBERT, Raymond. b 34. AKC61. **d** 62 **p** 63. C Newbold and Dunston *Derby* 62-66; PV and Succ S'wark Cathl *S'wark* 66-68; P-in-c Stuntney *Ely* 68-74; Prec and Sacr Ely Cathl 68-74; Min Can Cant Cathl *Cant* 74-79; Hon Min Can from 79; P-in-c Patrixbourne w Bridge and Bekesbourne 79-81; V from 81. *The Vicarage, 23 High Street, Bridge, Canterbury, Kent CT4 5JZ* Canterbury (0227) 830250

GILBERT, Roger Charles. b 46. Ex Coll Ox BA69 MA74 Nottm Univ MEd81. St Steph Ho Ox 69. **d** 71 **p** 72. NSM Bridgwater St Mary w Chilton Trinity *B & W* 71-74; NSM Rugeley *Lich* 74-81; NSM Cannock 81-83; NSM Wednesbury St Jas and St Jo from 83. *41 Stafford*

Road, Cannock, Staffs WS11 2AF Cannock (0543) 570531

GILBERT, Roger Geoffrey. b 37. K Coll Lon BD69 AKC69. **d** 70 **p** 71. C Walton-on-Thames *Guildf* 70-74; R St Mabyn *Truro* 74-81; P-in-c Helland 74-81; P-in-c Madron 81-86; R Falmouth K Chas from 86. *The Rectory, Albany Road, Falmouth, Cornwall TR11 3RP* Falmouth (0326) 314176

GILBERT, Roy Alan. b 48. Birm Univ BEd70 Lon Univ DipTh79. Ripon Coll Cuddesdon 74. **d** 76 **p** 77. C Moseley St Mary *Birm* 76-82; Australia from 82. *Guildford Grammar School, 11 Terrace Road, Guildford, S Australia 6055* Guildford (9) 378-1222

GILBERT, Sidney Horace. b 34. Dur Univ BA58 MA69 Univ of Wales BD62 CertEd83. St Mich Coll Llan 58. **d** 61 **p** 62. C Colwyn Bay *St As* 61-63; C Llanrhos 63-69; R Penley and Bettisfield 69-78; V Brymbo and Bwlchgwyn 78-82; Univ of Wales (Swansea) *S & B* 82-83; R Beeston Regis *Nor* from 84; Holiday Chapl 84-91; Sen Chapl from 91. *All Saints' Rectory, Cromer Road, Beeston Regis, Cromer, Norfolk NR27 9NG* Sheringham (0263) 822163

GILCHRIST, David John. b 51. Mert Coll Ox BA75 MA79. St Jo Coll Nottm DPS79. **d** 79 **p** 80. C Gt Ilford St Andr *Chelmsf* 79-81; C Buckhurst Hill 81-84; Chapl Dover Coll Kent from 84. *24 Folkestone Road, Dover, Kent* Dover (0304) 205906

GILCHRIST, Gavin Frank. b 53. AKC74. Coll of Resurr Mirfield 76. **d** 77 **p** 78. C Newbold and Dunston *Derby* 77-80; C Addlestone *Guildf* 80-84; V Blackpool St Mary *Blackb* from 84. *St Mary's Vicarage, 59 Stony Hill Avenue, Blackpool FY4 1PR* Blackpool (0253) 42713

GILCHRIST, Lawrence Edward. b 29. Liv Univ BSc52. NW Ord Course 74. **d** 76 **p** 77. NSM Buxton w Burbage and King Sterndale *Derby* 76-83; V Chinley w Buxworth from 83. *The Vicarage, Buxworth, Stockport, Cheshire SK12 7NH* Whaley Bridge (0663) 732243

GILCHRIST, Spencer. b 66. QUB BA88. BTh. **d** 91. C Ballynafeigh St Jude *D & D* from 91. *15 St John's Park, Belfast BT7 3JF* Belfast (0232) 641447

GILDING, James Peter. b 33. Leeds Univ BA64. Ely Th Coll 61. **d** 63 **p** 64. C Chorley St Geo *Blackb* 63-66; C Pemberton St Fran Kitt Green *Liv* 66-69; P-in-c Terrington St John *Ely* 69-73; P-in-c Walpole St Andrew 69-73; V Elm 74-81; TR Stanground and Farcet 81-89; V Haslingfield from 89; R Harlton from 89. *The Vicarage, Broad Lane, Haslingfield, Cambridge CB3 7JF* Cambridge (0223) 870285

GILDING, Richard Herbert. b 11. St Jo Coll Dur LTh46 BA47. ALCD35. **d** 35 **p** 36. V Studley *Sarum* 56-75; rtd 75. *2 Church Corner, Potterne, Devizes, Wilts SN10 5QY* Devizes (0380) 725644

GILES, Barry James. b 35. Kelham Th Coll 54. **d** 59 **p** 60. C Leytonstone St Marg w St Columba *Chelmsf* 59-62; Prec Gib Cathl *Eur* 62-66; V Darwen St Geo *Blackb* 66-69; V Forest Gate St Edm *Chelmsf* 69-73; R Jersey St Pet *Win* from 73; Vice-Dean Jersey from 84. *St Peter's Rectory, Jersey, Channel Islands* Jersey (0534) 81805

GILES, Brother. See HILL, Michael John

GILES, Brother. See SPRENT, Michael Francis

GILES, Edward Alban. b 34. Bps' Coll Cheshunt. **d** 58 **p** 59. C Colne St Bart *Blackb* 58-61; C Warrington St Paul *Liv* 61-63; S Africa 63-70; Chapl HM Pris Camp Hill 70-75; Stafford 75-83; Chapl HM Young Offender Inst Hollesley Bay Colony from 83. *HM Young Offender Institute, Hollesley, Woodbridge, Suffolk IP12 3JS* Shottisham (0394) 411741

GILES, Eric Francis. b 34. Sarum Th Coll 61. **d** 63 **p** 64. C Plympton St Mary *Ex* 63-71; R Dumbleton w Wormington *Glouc* 71-77; P-in-c Toddington w Stanley Pontlarge 71-77; R Dumbleton w Wormington and Toddington 77-79; V Churchdown St Jo from 79. *St John's Vicarage, Churchdown, Gloucester GL3 2DA* Churchdown (0452) 713421

GILES, Frank Edwin. b 22. St Aid Birkenhead 50. **d** 53 **p** 54. V Sacriston *Dur* 56-70; V Hook *S'wark* 70-81; V Langley St Mich *Birm* 81-88; rtd 88. *5 Victoria Terrace, Bourton-on-the-Water, Cheltenham, Glos* Cotswold (0451) 20486

GILES, Graeme John. b 56. Linc Th Coll 82. **d** 85 **p** 86. C Prestbury *Glouc* 85-88; C Paulsgrove *Portsm* from 88. *47 Lime Grove, Portsmouth PO6 4DG* Cosham (0705) 219800

GILES, Canon John Robert. b 36. Em Coll Cam BA60 MA65. Ripon Hall Ox 60. **d** 61 **p** 62. C Lowestoft St Marg *Nor* 61-65; Chapl UEA 65-72; R Kirkbrooke St Jas *S'wark* 72-79; Sub-Dean of Greenwich 74-79; V Sheff Broomhall St Mark *Sheff* 79-87; Ind Chapl from 79; Can Res Sheff Cathl from 87. *62 Kingfield Road, Sheffield S11 9AU* Sheffield (0742) 557782

GILES, Maurice Alfred Douglas. b 15. Bps' Coll Cheshunt 66. **d** 66 **p** 67. C Southgate St Andr *Lon* 69-71; V New Southgate St Paul 71-75; C Friern Barnet St Jas 75-80; rtd 80; Perm to Offic *Lon* from 80. *66 Granville Road, London N12 0HT* 081-346 0214

GILES, Peter Michael Osmaston. b 40. Solicitor 65. S Dios Minl Tr Scheme 85. **d** 88 **p** 89. Hon C Wootton Bassett *Sarum* from 88. *The Old Vicarage, Honeyhill, Wootton Bassett, Swindon SN4 7AZ* Swindon (0793) 852643

GILES, Richard Stephen. b 40. MRTPI71 Newc Univ BA63 MLitt88. Cuddesdon Coll 64. **d** 65 **p** 66. C Higham Ferrers w Chelveston *Pet* 65-68; Perm to Offic *Ox* 69; C Oakengates *Lich* 70; C Stevenage St Geo *St Alb* 71-75; P-in-c Howdon Panns *Newc* 75-76; TV Willington Team 76-79; Bp's Adv for Planning *Pet* 79-87; V Pet St Jude 79-87; Par Development Officer *Wakef* from 87; P-in-c Huddersfield St Thos from 87. *St Thomas's Vicarage, 78 Bankfield Road, Huddersfield HD1 3HR* Huddersfield (0484) 420660

GILES, Robert Medwin. b 37. Man Univ BA58 PGCE59. Ripon Hall Ox 64. **d** 66 **p** 67. C Peel *Man* 66-68; C Alverstoke *Portsm* 68-71; P-in-c Edale *Derby* 71-79; Youth Officer *York* 79-86; P-in-c Shipley *Chich* 86-87; V from 87. *The Vicarage, Shipley, Horsham, W Sussex RH13 8PH* Horsham (0403) 741238

GILES, Timothy David. b 46. FCA69. Oak Hill Th Coll DipTh90. **d** 90 **p** 91. C Ipswich St Marg *St E* from 90. *44 Corder Road, Ipswich, Suffolk IP4 2XD* Ipswich (0473) 231137

GILFORD, George. b 49. St Kath Coll Liv CertEd72 LTCL86. N Ord Course 88. **d** 91. NSM Gt Crosby St Faith *Liv* from 91. *5 Adelaide Road, Seaforth, Liverpool L21 1AR* 051-920 4537

GILKES, Donald Martin. b 47. St Jo Coll Nottm 78. **d** 80 **p** 81. C Conisbrough *Sheff* 80-84; P-in-c Balne 84-86; P-in-c Hensall 84-86; TV Gt Snaith 86-88; V Whittle-le-Woods *Blackb* from 88. *The Vicarage, Preston Road, Whittle-le-Woods, Chorley, Lancs PR6 7PS* Chorley (02572) 63306

GILKS, Peter Martin. b 51. SRN77 Nottm Univ BMus72. Ripon Coll Cuddesdon 82. **d** 84 **p** 85. C Bitterne Park *Win* 84-87; TV Basingstoke from 87. *45 Beaconsfield Road, Basingstoke, Hants RG21 3DG* Basingstoke (0256) 464616

GILL, Alan Gordon. b 42. Sarum & Wells Th Coll 73. **d** 75 **p** 76. C Wimborne Minster *Sarum* 75-78; R Winterbourne Stickland and Turnworth etc 78-86; V Verwood from 86. *The Vicarage, Dewlands Way, Verwood, Wimborne, Dorset BH21 6JN* Verwood (0202) 822298

GILL, Brian Alvan. b 35. Codrington Coll Barbados 59. **d** 62 **p** 63. St Vincent 62-74; C Clun w Chapel Lawn *Heref* 74-77; P-in-c Bucknell 77-78; V Bucknell w Buckton, Llanfair Waterdine and Stowe 78-86; R Presteigne w Discoed, Kinsham and Lingen from 86. *The Rectory, Presteigne, Powys LD8 2BP* Presteigne (0544) 267777

GILL, Christopher John Sutherland. b 28. Selw Coll Cam BA52 MA70. Ely Th Coll 52. **d** 54 **p** 55. C Portslade St Nic *Chich* 54-58; C Goring-by-Sea 58-60; Chapl St Edm Sch Cant 60-76; Chapl Bennett Memorial Sch Tunbridge Wells from 76; Hon C Tunbridge Wells K Chas *Roch* from 77. *Flat 1, Hurstleigh, Hurstwood Lane, Tunbridge Wells, Kent TN4 8YA* Tunbridge Wells (0892) 28409

GILL, David Brian Michael. b 55. Southn Univ BTh88. Sarum & Wells Th Coll 83. **d** 86 **p** 87. C Honiton, Gittisham, Combe Raleigh, Monkton etc *Ex* 86-89; C E Teignmouth 89; C W Teignmouth 89; C Teignmouth, Ideford w Luton, Ashcombe etc from 90. *51 Higher Coombe Drive, Teignmouth, Devon TQ14 9LR* Teignmouth (0626) 776607

GILL, Dr David Christopher. b 38. FRCPsych DPM St Andr Univ MB, ChB63. S Dios Minl Tr Scheme 76 E Midl Min Tr Course 79. **d** 81 **p** 85. NSM Carrington *S'well* from 81. *1 Malvern Court, 29 Mapperley Road, Nottingham NG3 5AG* Nottingham (0602) 622351

GILL, Donald Maule Harvell. b 08. Keble Coll Ox BA33 MA39. Wells Th Coll 34. **d** 35 **p** 36. V Micheldever *Win* 45-70; R Minstead 71-80; rtd 80; Perm to Offic *Win* from 80. *4 Hereward Close, Romsey, Hants SO51 8RA* Romsey (0794) 514591

GILL, Frank Emmanuel. b 34. Oak Hill Th Coll 73. **d** 75 **p** 76. C Shepherd's Bush St Steph w St Thos *Lon* 76-77; P-in-c Kensal Town St Thos w St Andr and St Phil 79-82; W Indies from 82. *Address temp unknown*

GILL, Mrs Gabrielle Mary. d 90. NSM Timperley *Ches* from 90. *The Croft, 3 Harrop Road, Hale, Altrincham WA15 9BU* 061-928 1800

GILL, Gary George. b 44. Culham Coll Ox CertEd70. Cant Sch of Min 85. d 87 p 88. C Addlestone *Guildf* 87-90; C Buckland in Dover w Buckland Valley *Cant* from 90. *24 Dryden Road, Dover, Kent CT16 2BX* Dover (0304) 822004

GILL, Geoffrey Fitzell. b 17. Selw Coll Cam BA39 MA43. Linc Th Coll 39. d 41 p 42. V Enderby *Leic* 51-82; rtd 82. *The Poplars, Port Eynon, Gower, Swansea* Gower (0792) 390206

GILL, James Joseph. b 45. Pontifical Univ Maynooth BD78. d 77 p 78. In RC Ch 77-82; C Howden Team Min *York* 82-83; TV 83-86; P-in-c Wragby w Sharlston *Wakef* 86-88; V Sharlston from 88. *St Luke's Vicarage, 45 West Lane, Sharlston Common, Wakefield, W Yorkshire WF4 1EW* Wakefield (0924) 862414

✠GILL, Rt Rev Kenneth Edward. b 32. Hartley Victoria Coll. d 58 p 60 c 72. In Ch of S India 58-80; Bp Karnataka Cen 72-80; Asst Bp Newc from 80. *83 Kenton Road, Newcastle upon Tyne NE3 4NL* 091-285 1502 or 285 2220

GILL, Mrs Mary. b 20. Nottm Univ BA42. St Jo Coll Nottm CertCS43. d 88. NSM Alston Team *Newc* 88-90; rtd 90. *Old School, Garrigill, Alston, Cumbria CA9 3DP* Alston (0434) 381594

GILL, Michael John. b 59. AKC81 BA81. Llan St Mich BD85. d 85 p 86. Min Can St Woolos Cathl *Mon* 85-90; Chapl St Woolos Hosp Newport 87-90; Succ Heref Cathl *Heref* from 90; C Heref St Jo from 90. *1 College Cloisters, Cathedral Close, Hereford HR1 2NG* Hereford (0432) 272817

GILL, Richard Ward. b 26. Lon Univ BD53. Oak Hill Th Coll 53. d 54 p 55. C Cam St Andr Less *Ely* 54-56; CMS 56-64; C Dagenham *Chelmsf* 64-65; V St Alb St Paul *St Alb* from 65. *St Paul's Vicarage, 9 Brampton Road, St Albans, Herts AL1 4PN* St Albans (0727) 54619

GILL, Canon Robert Henry. b 01. AKC29. d 29 p 30. R Hertf St Andr *St Alb* 52-70; RD Hertf 64-70; Hon Can St Alb 66-70; rtd 70. *Nazareth House, 118 Harleston Road, Northampton NN5 6AD* Northampton (0604) 751832

GILL, Prof Robin Morton. b 44. K Coll Lon BD66 AKC66 Lon Univ PhD69 Birm Univ MSocSc72. d 68 p 69. C Rugby St Andr *Cov* 68-71; Papua New Guinea 71-72; Lect Th Edin Univ 72-86; Sen Lect 86-88; Assoc Dean Faculty of Div 85-88; P-in-c Edin SS Phil and Jas *Edin* 73-75; P-in-c Ford *Newc* 75-87; Perm to Offic from 87; P-in-c Coldstream *Edin* from 87; Wm Leech Prof Applied Th Newc Univ from 88. *The Old Vicarage, Branxton, Cornhill-on-Tweed, Northd TD12 5SW* Crookham (089082) 248

GILL, Stanley. b 11. Clifton Th Coll 37. d 39 p 40. V Cornhill w Carham *Newc* 67-74; V Branxton 71-74; rtd 76. *37 Castle Terrace, Berwick-upon-Tweed TD15 1NZ* Berwick-upon-Tweed (0289) 330982

GILL, Stanley. b 34. Sarum Th Coll 66. d 68 p 69. C Ipswich St Mary at Stoke w St Pet & St Mary Quay *St E* 68-73 and 78-80; TV 80-82; V Bury St Edmunds St Geo 73-78; P-in-c Childe Okeford, Manston, Hammoon and Hanford *Sarum* 82-89; R The Lulworths, Winfrith Newburgh and Chaldon from 89. *The Rectory, West Road, West Lulworth, Wareham, Dorset BH20 5RY* West Lulworth (092941) 550

GILL, Thomas. b 21. St Aid Birkenhead 62. d 63 p 64. V Burstwick w Thorngumbald *York* 67-78; RD S Holderness 74-78; R Brandesburton 78-86; RD N Holderness 80-86; rtd 87. *Bellfield, Arnold Lane, Arnold, Hull HU11 5HP* Hornsea (0964) 562282

GILL, William. b 08. St Aid Birkenhead 59. d 60 p 61. V Austwick *Bradf* 68-78; rtd 78; Perm to Offic Bradf 79-85; Linc from 85. *14 Woodland Avenue, Skellingthorpe, Lincoln LN6 5TE* Lincoln (0522) 682529

GILLAN, Ian Thomson. b 15. Aber Univ MA37 BD40 Edin Univ PhD43. d 52 p 53. In RC Ch 52-72; C Aber St Andr *Ab* 73-74; P-in-c Fochabers *Mor* 74-75; P-in-c Aberlour 74-75; Provost St Andr Cathl Inverness 75; P-in-c Aber St Clem *Ab* 76-78; rtd 79; Perm to Offic *Ab* from 79. *5 Park Crescent, Oldmeldrum, Aberdeen AB5 0DH* Oldmeldrum (06512) 2308

GILLARD, Geoffrey Vernon. b 48. Man Univ BA70 Nottm Univ MPhil80. Trin Coll Nigeria 72 St Jo Coll Nottm 74. d 78 p 79. C Aughton Ch Ch *Liv* 78-81; Hong Kong 81-87; Dir of Studies Minl Tr Scheme *St Alb* from 87. *17 Eastmoor Park, Harpenden, Herts AL5 1BN* Harpenden (0582) 762005

GILLESPIE, George Henry. b 20. SS Coll Cam BA46 MA55. Cuddesdon Coll 46. d 48 p 49. V Allenton

and Shelton Lock *Derby* 56-71; Chapl Derby High Sch for Girls 58-71; V Bath Ascension *B & W* 71-78; P-in-c Norton St Philip w Hemington, Hardington etc 78-81; R 81-85; rtd 85; Perm to Offic *B & W* from 86. *18 South Lea Road, Bath BA1 3RW* Bath (0225) 339023

GILLESPIE, Michael David. b 41. E Midl Min Tr Course 86. d 89 p 90. NSM Countesthorpe w Foston *Leic* from 89. *3 Penfold Drive, Countesthorpe, Leicester LE8 3TP* Leicester (0533) 775167

GILLETT, Brian Alan Michael. b 42. ARICS73. Chich Th Coll. d 82 p 83. C Tupsley *Heref* 82-86; R Kingstone w Clehonger and Eaton Bishop 86-89; P-in-c Thruxton 89; P-in-c Allensmore 89; R Kingstone w Clehonger, Eaton Bishop etc from 89. *The Rectory, Kingstone, Hereford HR2 9EY* Golden Valley (0981) 250350

GILLETT, Canon David Keith. b 45. Leeds Univ BA65 MPhil68. Oak Hill Th Coll 66. d 68 p 69. C Watford St Luke *St Alb* 68-71; Sec Pathfinders and CYFA N Area 71-74; Lect St Jo Coll Nottm 74-79; Ch of Ireland Renewal Cen 80-82; V Luton Lewsey St Hugh *St Alb* 82-88; Prin Trin Coll Bris from 88; Hon Can Bris Cathl *Bris* from 91. *16 Ormerod Road, Stoke Bishop, Bristol BS9 1BB* Bristol (0272) 682646 or 682803

GILLETT, Victor Henry John. b 31. Open Univ BA83 BTh87. Clifton Th Coll 59. d 62 p 63. C Walton Breck *Liv* 62-65; C Wednesfield Heath *Lich* 65-68; V Tipton St Paul 68-76; V Moulton *Pet* from 76. *The Vicarage, Cross Street, Moulton, Northampton NN3 1RZ* Northampton (0604) 491060

GILLETT, Vincent. b 30. FCollP81 Lon Univ BSc55 UEA MSc72 DipSMan76. Chich Th Coll 59. d 61 p 62. C Blackpool St Mich *Blackb* 61-63; Ghana 63-72; Lic to Offic *Liv* 72-79; *Ex* 79-84; Hd Master St Wilfrid's Sch Ex 79-84; R Atherington and High Bickington *Ex* from 84; V Burrington from 84. *The Rectory, High Bickington, Umberleigh, Devon EX37 9BB* High Bickington (0769) 60283

GILLETT, William Charles. b 05. Sarum Th Coll 28. d 31 p 32. R E w W Anstey *Ex* 51-78; rtd 78; Perm to Offic Ex 78-81; B & W from 81. *Sarum, East Anstey, Tiverton, Devon EX16 9JQ* Anstey Mills (03984) 284

GILLHAM, Martin John. b 45. Qu Coll Birm 72. d 75 p 76. C Whitley Ch Ch *Ox* 75-78; TV Crowmarsh Gifford w Newnham Murren 78-79; TV Wallingford w Crowmarsh Gifford etc 79-83; V Kintbury w Avington from 83; Dioc Adv for Lay Min from 89; Chapl SSF Ox from 83. *Kintbury Vicarage, Newbury, Berks RG15 0TS* Kintbury (0488) 58243

GILLHESPEY, Canon Clive. b 28. Lon Univ DipTh66 BD73. Cranmer Hall Dur 63. d 65 p 66. C Barrow St Geo w St Luke *Carl* 65-69; V Flookburgh 69-74; R Barrow St Geo w St Luke 74-81; TR from 81; Hon Can Carl Cathl from 84. *The Rectory, 98 Roose Road, Barrow-in-Furness, Cumbria LA13 9RL* Barrow-in-Furness (0229) 821641

GILLIAT, Canon Patrick Neville. b 10. G&C Coll Cam BA32 MA36. Tyndale Hall Bris 32. d 34 p 35. Can Res Sheff Cathl *Sheff* 69-76; Succ Sheff Cathl 69-76; rtd 76; Perm to Offic *B & W* from 76. *20 Henrietta Gardens, Bath BA2 6NA* Bath (0225) 461828

GILLIBRAND, John Nigel. b 60. d 88 p 89. C Dolgelly w Llanfachreth and Brithdir etc *Ban* 88-90; C Llanbeblig w Caernarfon and Betws Garmon etc from 90. *The Vicarage, Maesincla, Caernarfon, Gwynedd LL55 1DD* Caernarfon (0286) 5604

GILLIES, Canon Eric Robert. b 19. Worc Ord Coll 61. d 63 p 64. R Aldrington *Chich* 67-82; RD Hove 77-82; Can and Preb Chich Cathl 81-89; P-in-c Clapham w Patching 82-83; V Findon 82-83; V Findon w Clapham and Patching 83-89; rtd 89; P-in-c Burpham *Chich* from 89. *The Vicarage, Burpham, Arundel, W Sussex BN18 9RJ* Arundel (0903) 882948

GILLIES, Robert Arthur. b 51. Edin Univ BD77 St Andr Univ PhD91. Edin Th Coll 73. d 77 p 78. C Falkirk *Edin* 77-80; C Edin Ch Ch 80-84; Chapl Napier Coll 80-84; Chapl Dundee Univ *Bre* 84-90; R St Andrews St Andr *St And* from 91. *St Andrew's Rectory, Queen's Terrace, St Andrews, Fife KY16 9QF* St Andrews (0334) 73344

GILLIGAN, Harry. b 07. Dur Univ 56. d 58 p 59. V Everton St Polycarp *Liv* 66-68; Chapl to the Deaf (Southport) 71-79; rtd 74; Perm to Offic *Portsm* from 88; Win from 82. *4 Lampeter Avenue, Cosham, Portsmouth PO6 2AL* Cosham (0705) 77481

GILLING, John Reginald. b 25. Cam Univ BA49 MA51 MLitt55. Cuddesdon Coll 53. d 55 p 56. Chapl Ch Ch Ox 62-71; V Pimlico St Mary Graham Terrace *Lon* 71-90; AD Westmr St Marg 79-85; rtd 90. *49 Westgate, Chichester, W Sussex PO19 3EZ* Chichester (0243) 775169

GILLINGHAM, John Bruce. b 48. Ch Ch Ox BA69 MA74. St Jo Coll Nottm BA73. **d** 73 **p** 74. C Plymouth St Andr w St Paul and St Geo *Ex* 73-77; C Ox St Aldate w H Trin *Ox* 78; Chapl Jes Coll Ox 78-88; Chapl Ox Pastorate 79-88; Dioc Missr *Birm* from 88. *124 Mill Lane, Solihull, W Midlands B93 8NZ* Knowle (0564) 730125

GILLINGHAM, Michael John. b 46. Univ of Wales (Swansea) DSCE80 Hull Univ MA90. Chich Th Coll 68. **d** 71 **p** 72. C Llanharan w Peterston-s-Montem *Llan* 71-73; C Skewen 73-76; Neath Deanery Youth Chapl 74-76; Perm to Offic 79-80; TV Kirkby *Liv* 76-77; Youth Chapl *Ches* 77-79; Perm to Offic *St Alb* 80-83; Sen Youth Worker 80-83; TV Sheff Manor *Sheff* 83-88; Chapl Sheff Sea Cadets from 87; R Frecheville from 88. *Frecheville Rectory, Brackenfield Grove, Sheffield S12 4XS* Sheffield (0742) 399555

GILLINGHAM, Canon Peter Llewellyn. b 14. MVO55. Or Coll Ox BA35 DipTh36 MA39. Wycliffe Hall Ox 35. **d** 37 **p** 38. V Horsham *Chich* 60-77; RD Horsham 74-77; Chapl Sherborne Sch Dorset 78-79; rtd 79; Perm to Offic *St E* from 82. *Maplestead Cottage, Leiston Road, Aldeburgh, Suffolk IP15 5QD* Aldeburgh (0728) 852739

GILLINGS, Richard John. b 45. St Chad's Coll Dur BA67. Linc Th Coll 68. **d** 70 **p** 71. C Altrincham St Geo *Ches* 70-75; P-in-c Stockport St Thos 75-77; R 77-83; P-in-c Stockport St Pet 78-83; TR Birkenhead Priory from 83; RD Birkenhead from 85. *The Priory Rectory, 124 Cathcart Street, Birkenhead, Merseyside L41 3NE* 051-647 6604

GILLION, Canon Frederick Arthur. b 08. ALCD30 St Jo Coll Dur LTh30 BA31 MA34. **d** 31 **p** 32. R Beeston Regis *Nor* 69-75; rtd 75; Perm to Offic *Nor* from 75. *66 The Street, Ingworth, Norwich NR11 6AE* Aylsham (0263) 732583

GILLION, Robert Alan. b 51. LRAM. Sarum & Wells Th Coll 81. **d** 83 **p** 84. C E Dereham *Nor* 83-86; C Richmond St Mary w St Matthias and St Jo *S'wark* 86-90; Hong Kong from 90. *37A Seahorse Lane, Discovery Bay, Lantau Island, Hong Kong* Hong Kong (852) 987-7106

GILLMAN, Noel Francis. b 26. St D Dioc Tr Course St D Coll Lamp St Mich Coll Llan. **d** 79 **p** 80. NSM Llanelly *St D* 79-83; C 83-85; TV Tenby from 85. *The Vicarage, Penally, Tenby, Dyfed SA70 7PN* Tenby (0834) 2416

GILLMOR, Samuel Frederick. b 29. St Aid Birkenhead. **d** 62 **p** 63. C Carlow Union *C & O* 62-64; I Fenagh Union 64-68; I Maryborough w Dysart Enos 68-79; Preb Ossory Cathl 78-79; Preb Leighlin Cathl 78-79; I Clane w Donadea *M & K* 79-84; I Mullingar, Portnashangan, Moyliscar, Kilbixy etc from 84. *All Saints' Rectory, Mullingar, Co Westmeath, Irish Republic* Mullingar (44) 48376

GILLUM, Thomas Alan. b 55. Ex Univ BSc76. Cranmer Hall Dur 87. **d** 89 **p** 90. C Brompton H Trin w Onslow Square St Paul *Lon* from 89. *Holy Trinity Church, Brompton Road, London SW7 1JA* 071-581 8255

GILMAN, Charles Philip. b 12. Tyndale Hall Bris 39. **d** 41 **p** 42. R Marks Tey *Chelmsf* 64-74; V Leigh *S'wark* 74-81; rtd 81; Perm to Offic *Win* from 81. *36 Canon Street, Winchester, Hants SO23 9JJ* Winchester (0962) 867980

GILMORE, Henry. b 51. Man Univ BA72 TCD BD82. CITC 75. **d** 75 **p** 76. C Arm St Mark w Aghavilly *Arm* 75-78; C Dub St Patr Cathl Gp *D & G* 78-81; I Stranorlar w Meenglas and Kilteevogue *D & R* 81-84; I Achill w Dugort, Castlebar and Turlough *T, K & A* 84-91; I Moville w Greencastle, Donagh, Cloncha etc *D & R* from 91. *The Rectory, Castlebar, Moville, Co Donegal, Irish Republic* Castlebar (94) 23423

GILMORE, Canon Norman. b 16. Leeds Univ BA38. Coll of Resurr Mirfield 38. **d** 40 **p** 41. R Friern Barnet St Jas *Lon* 63-78; RD Cen Barnet 72-78; V Mortimer W End w Padworth *Ox* 78-83; rtd 83; Perm to Offic *Chich* from 83. *12 Ashton Gardens, Rustington, W Sussex BN16 2SH* Rustington (0903) 774683

GILMOUR, Ian Hedley. b 57. Ex Univ LLB Lon Univ BD. Wycliffe Hall Ox 80. **d** 83 **p** 84. C Harold Wood *Chelmsf* 83-86; C Thame w Towersey *Ox* from 86. *8 Victoria Road, Thame, Oxon OX9 3HY* Thame (084421) 3491

GILMOUR, John Logan. b 14. Cuddesdon Coll 46. **d** 48 **p** 49. C Reading St Mary V *Ox* 48-51; Min St Barn CD Reading 51-55; Thailand 55-58; V Ellel *Blackb* 58-60; S Africa from 60. *2 Russell Lodge, Main Road, Constantia, 7800 South Africa* Cape Town (21) 794-1523

GILPIN, Jeremy David. b 59. Pemb Coll Ox BA80 CertEd82. Trin Coll Bris BA88. **d** 88 **p** 89. C Southsea St Jude *Portsm* from 88. *92 Marmion Road, Southsea, Hants PO5 2BB* Portsmouth (0705) 824278

GILPIN, Richard John. b 45. Lon Univ BSc66 Bris Univ DipTh69. Wells Th Coll 67. **d** 70 **p** 71. C Davyhulme Ch Ch *Man* 70-74; Pastor Gustav Adolf Berlin EKD 74-77; R Heaton Norris Ch w All SS 77-83; R Chorlton-cum-Hardy St Clem from 83. *The Rectory, 6 Edge Lane, Chorlton-cum-Hardy, Manchester M21 1JF* 061-881 3063

GILPIN, Preb Richard Thomas. b 39. Lich Th Coll 60. **d** 63 **p** 64. C Whipton *Ex* 63-66; C Tavistock and Gulworthy 66-69; V from 73; V Swimbridge 69-73; Preb Ex Cathl from 82; RD Tavistock 87-90; Dioc Dir of Ords 90-91; Adv for Voc and Dioc Dir of Ords from 91. *Taddyforde Lodge, New North Road, Exeter EX4 4AT* Exeter (0392) 54517

GIMSON, Francis Herbert. b 54. Reading Univ BSc79 LTh. St Jo Coll Nottm 83. **d** 86 **p** 87. C Menston w Woodhead *Bradf* 86-89; C Barnoldswick w Bracewell 89-91; V Langleybury St Paul *St Alb* from 91. *The Vicarage, Langleybury Lane, Kings Langley, Herts WD4 8QR* Kings Langley (09277) 63169

GINEVER, Preb John Haynes. b 20. St Jo Coll Dur. Westcott Ho Cam. **d** 43 **p** 44. V Mill Hill Jo Keble Ch *Lon* 63-70; RD W Barnet 67-70; RD Wolv *Lich* 70-89; P-in-c Wolv St Geo 70-78; P-in-c Wolv All SS 70-78; R Wolv 73-78; Preb Lich Cathl 75-89; P-in-c Wolv St Mark 76-78; P-in-c Wolv St Chad 76-78; TR Wolv 78-89; rtd 89. *Flat 4, 26 Branksome Wood Road, Bournemouth BH4 9JZ* Bournemouth (0202) 763373

GINEVER, Paul Michael John. b 49. AKC71. **d** 72 **p** 73. C Davyhulme Ch Ch *Man* 72-75; Australia 76-77; C Tettenhall Wood *Lich* 77-80; C Halesowen *Worc* 80; TV 80-86; P-in-c Gt Malvern Ch Ch from 86. *The Vicarage, 8 Christchurch Road, Malvern, Worcs WR14 3BE* Malvern (0684) 54106

GINGELL, John Lawrence. b 27. Lon Univ BD55. Lon Coll of Div 54. **d** 55 **p** 56. C Normanton *Derby* 55-58; C Ilkeston St Mary 58-60; Toc H Staff Padre (SE Region) 61-66; N Region 66-70; Asst Chapl S Lon Ind Miss 61-64; Lic to Offic *S'wark* 61-66; *Liv* 67-70; V Somercotes *Derby* 70-72; Bp's Ind Adv 75-80. *Address temp unknown*

GINN, Daniel Vivian. b 33. Univ of Wales (Cardiff) BSc55 DipEd56. Llan Dioc Tr Scheme 79. **d** 82 **p** 83. NSM Llantwit Major w St Donat's *Llan* 82-83; NSM Llantwit Major from 83. *Chenet, 24 Voss Park Drive, Llantwit Major, S Glam CF6 9YE* Llantwit Major (0446) 792774

GINN, Richard John. b 51. ACIB Lon Univ BD77 Dur Univ DipTh78. Lambeth STh85 Cranmer Hall Dur 77. **d** 79 **p** 80. C Hornsey Ch Ch *Lon* 79-82; C Highgate St Mich 82-85; V Westleton w Dunwich *St E* from 85; V Darsham from 85. *The Vicarage, Westleton, Saxmundham, Suffolk IP17 3AQ* Westleton (072873) 271

GINNEVER, Canon John Buckley. b 20. Man Univ BA42. Ridley Hall Cam 46. **d** 48 **p** 49. R Levenshulme St Mark *Man* 57-76; V Chadderton St Matt 76-84; Hon Can Man Cathl 82-85; rtd 85; Perm to Offic *St As* from 85. *22 Glan Ffyddion, Waterfall Road, Dyserth, Rhyl, Clwyd LL18 6EG* Dyserth (0745) 570654

GINNO, Albert Charles. b 31. Lon Coll of Div 66. **d** 68 **p** 69. C Kemp Town St Mark and St Matt *Chich* 68-72; P-in-c E Hoathly 72-83; V Westham from 83. *The Vicarage, Westham, Pevensey, E Sussex BN24 5DE* Eastbourne (0323) 762294

GIRARD, William Nicholas Charles. b 35. Coll of Resurr Mirfield 65. **d** 67 **p** 68. C Yate *Glouc* 67-70; C Westbury-on-Trym St Alb *Bris* 70-73; Chapl K Sch Ely 73-76; V Fenstanton *Ely* 76-85; V Hilton 76-85; R Balsham from 85; P-in-c Horseheath from 85; P-in-c W Wickham from 85. *The Rectory, Balsham, Cambridge CB1 6DX* Cambridge (0223) 894010

GIRLING, Andrew Martin. b 40. Em Coll Cam BA63 MA67. Wycliffe Hall Ox 63. **d** 65 **p** 66. C Luton w E Hyde *St Alb* 65-69; Chapl Hull Univ *York* 69-75; V Dringhouses from 75. *The Vicarage, Dringhouses, York YO2 2QG* York (0904) 706120

GIRLING, David Frederick Charles. b 33. Edin Th Coll 58. **d** 61 **p** 62. C Caister *Nor* 61-65; C Leigh St Clem *Chelmsf* 65-66; CF 66-83; V Prittlewell St Luke *Chelmsf* from 83. *The Vicarage, St Luke's Road, Southend-on-Sea SS2 4AB* Southend-on-Sea (0702) 467620

GIRLING, Francis Richard (Brother Vincent). b 28. Worc Coll Ox BA52 MA56 Lon Univ BD65. Coll of Resurr Mirfield 55. **d** 57 **p** 59. CR from 57. *House of the Resurrection, Mirfield, W Yorkshire WF14 0BN* Mirfield (0924) 494318

GIRLING, Gordon Francis Hulbert. b 15. TD61. Univ Coll Ox BA37 MA41. Wells Th Coll 39. **d** 46 **p** 47. V Kingsbury H Innocents *Lon* 59-79; rtd 79; Perm to Offic

Chich from 80. *212 Coast Road, Pevensey Bay, Pevensey, E Sussex BN24 6NR*   Eastbourne (0323) 766359

GIRLING, Stephen Paul. b 61. Southn Univ BSc83. Trin Coll Bris BA(Theol)91. d 91. C Ogley Hay *Lich* from 91. *50 Lichfield Road, Brownhills, Walsall WS8 6HT* Brownhills (0543) 378542

GIRLING, Timothy Havelock. b 43. St Aid Birkenhead 63. d 67 p 68. C Wickford *Chelmsf* 67-70; C Luton w E Hyde *St Alb* 70-74; Chapl Luton and Dunstable Hosp 74-80; C Luton All SS w St Pet *St Alb* 74-80; R Northill w Moggerhanger 80-89; Chapl Glenfield and Glenfrith Hosps Leic from 89. *36 Winton Avenue, Leicester LE3 1DH*   Leicester (0533) 824022

GIRLING, William Havelock. b 18. Ex Coll Ox BA MA46. Ridley Hall Cam. d 49 p 50. Asst Chapl Bradfield Coll Berks 54-70; P-in-c Stanford Dingley *Ox* 71-86; rtd 86. *Oakthorpe, Charlton Drive, Charlton Kings, Cheltenham, Glos GL53 8ES*   Cheltenham (0242) 577364

GITTINGS, Graham. b 46. Qu Coll Birm 75. d 78 p 79. C Caverswall *Lich* 78-81; C Wolv St Matt 81-82; C Walthamstow St Mary w St Steph *Chelmsf* 82-83; C Dagenham 83-89; V Earl Shilton w Elmesthorpe *Leic* from 89. *The Vicarage, Maughan Street, Earl Shilton, Leicester LE9 7BA*   Earl Shilton (0455) 843961

GITTINS, Thomas Raymond. b 06. St Aid Birkenhead. d 50 p 51. C Wrexham *St As* 50-71; TV 72-73; rtd 73. *29 Elm Grove, Acton Park, Wrexham, Clwyd*   Wrexham (0978) 351972

GIVAN, Canon Desmond George. b 11. Worc Coll Ox BA34 MA38. Wycliffe Hall Ox 34. d 36 p 37. Kenya 64-75; Hon Can Nakuru from 64; Provost Mombasa 71-75; C Huddersfield St Jo *Wakef* 75-76; rtd 76; Perm to Offic *Wakef* from 76. *1 Dingley Road, Edgerton, Huddersfield HD3 3AY*   Huddersfield (0484) 540989

GIVEN, Harold Richard. b 54. d 78 p 79. C Belf St Clem *D & D* 78-83; I Tamlaght O'Crilly, Upper w Lower *D & R* from 83. *Hervey Hill Rectory, Hervey Hill Road, Kilrea, Co Londonderry BT51 5TT*   Kilrea (02665) 40296

GLADWIN, Very Rev John Warren. b 42. Chu Coll Cam BA65 MA68. Cranmer Hall Dur DipTh66. d 67 p 68. C Kirkheaton *Wakef* 67-71; Tutor St Jo Coll Dur 71-77; Dir Shaftesbury Project 77-82; Lic to Offic *S'well* 77-82; Sec Gen Syn Bd for Soc Resp 82-88; Preb St Paul's Cathl *Lon* 84-88; Provost Sheff from 88. *Provost's Lodge, 22 Hallam Gate Road, Sheffield S10 5BS* Sheffield (0742) 662373

GLADWIN, Thomas William. b 35. St Alb Minl Tr Scheme 78. d 81 p 82. NSM Hertf St Andr *St Alb* 81-82; NSM Digswell and Panshanger 82-86; C from 86. *99 Warren Way, Welwyn, Herts AL6 0DL*   Welwyn (043871) 4700

GLAISTER, James Richard. b 30. Oak Hill Th Coll 81. d 83 p 84. NSM Shrub End *Chelmsf* 83-85; NSM Lawshall w Shimplingthorne and Alpheton *St E* 85-87; NSM Lavenham 87-88; C Felixstowe St Jo from 88. *1 Arwela Road, Felixstowe, Suffolk IP11 8DQ*   Felixstowe (0394) 271578

GLAISYER, Ven Hugh. b 30. Or Coll Ox BA51 MA55. St Steph Ho Ox 51. d 56 p 56. C Tonge Moor *Man* 56-62; C Sidcup Ch Ch *Roch* 62-64; V Milton next Gravesend Ch Ch 64-81; RD Gravesend 74-81; V Hove All SS *Chich* 81-91; Can and Preb Chich Cathl 82-91; RD Hove 82-91; P-in-c Hove St Jo 87-91; Adn Lewes and Hastings from 91. *27 The Avenue, Lewes, E Sussex BN7 1QT* Lewes (0273) 479530

GLANVILLE-SMITH, Canon Michael Raymond. b 38. AKC61. d 62 p 63. C St Marylebone St Mark w St Luke *Lon* 62-64; C Penzance St Mary *Truro* 64-68; R Worc St Andr and All SS w St Helen *Worc* 68-74; Dioc Youth Chapl 68-74; V Catshill 74-80; P-in-c Worc St Martin w St Pet 80-81; TR Worc St Martin w St Pet, St Mark etc 81-86; TR Worc SE 86-90; Hon Can Worc Cathl 83-90; Can Res Ripon Cathl *Ripon* from 90. *St Wilfred's House, Minster Close, Ripon, N Yorkshire HG4 1QR*   Ripon (0765) 700211

GLARE, Michael Francis. b 28. Southn Univ BA54. St Steph Ho Ox 56. d 57 p 58. C Withycombe Raleigh *Ex* 57-62; C-in-c Goodrington CD 62-65; C Tamerton Foliot 65-70; R Weare Giffard w Landcross 70-76; RD Hartland 74-76; P-in-c Babbacombe 76-80; V 80-87; V Ilsington from 87. *The Vicarage, Ilsington, Newton Abbot, Devon TQ13 9RW*   Haytor (0364) 661245

GLASBY, Alan Langland. b 46. Nottm Univ LTh77. Linc Th Coll DipMin89 St Jo Coll Nottm 74. d 77 p 78. C Erith St Paul *Roch* 77-80; C Moor Allerton *Ripon* 80-81; TV 81-87; V Middleton St Mary from 87. *Middleton Vicarage, 198 Town Street, Leeds LS10 3TJ*   Leeds (0532) 705689

GLASGOW AND GALLOWAY, Bishop of. *See* TAYLOR, Rt Rev John Mitchell

GLASGOW AND GALLOWAY, Dean of. *See* REID, Very Rev Douglas William John

GLASGOW, Provost of. *See* GRANT, Very Rev Malcolm Etheridge

GLASS, Ven Edward Brown. b 13. St Jo Coll Dur BA35 MA38. d 37 p 38. Adn Man *S & M* 64-78; R Andreas 64-78; rtd 78; Perm to Offic *S & M* from 78. *c/o Mrs J C Clucas, Carhonnag, Regaby, Ramsey, Isle of Man*   Ramsey (0624) 812932

GLASS, Kenneth William. b 23. d 57 p 58. V Ipswich St Nic *St E* 63-73; P-in-c Ipswich St Helen 73; R Sproughton w Burstall 74-76; Perm to Offic from 76; rtd 83. *19 Chalkeith Road, Needham Market, Ipswich IP6 8HA* Needham Market (0449) 720393

GLASSPOOL, John Martin. b 59. RGN87 Kent Univ BA83. Westcott Ho Cam 88. d 90 p 91. C Forest Gate Em w Upton Cross *Chelmsf* from 90. *64 Henderson Road, London E7 8EF*   081-471 1721

GLASSWELL, Mark Errol. b 38. St Chad's Coll Dur BA60 PhD65. Ridley Hall Cam 63 Westcott Ho Cam 66. d 66 p 67. Sierra Leone 66-74; Lic to Offic *Dur* 74-75; Nigeria 75-85; Hd Relig Dept Nigeria Univ 80-84; P-in-c The Sampfords *Chelmsf* 85-88; R from 88. *The Rectory, Finchingfield Lane, Little Sampford, Saffron Waldon CB10 2QT*   Great Sampford (079986) 437

GLAZEBROOK, Ronald Victor. b 19. FRHistS Keble Coll Ox BA41 MA48 DipEd53. St Steph Ho Ox 41. d 43 p 44. Perm to Offic *Cant* 70-77; C Beckenham St Barn *Roch* 72-75; Warden St Marg Ho Bethnal Green 76-83; rtd 83. *Flat 1B, 11 Dane Road, St Leonards-on-Sea, E Sussex TN38 0RN*

GLAZEBROOK, William Leng. b 29. Edin Th Coll 76. d 76 p 77. C Dollar *St And* 76-82; Dioc Supernumerary 83; Chapl Trin Coll Glenalmond 84; P-in-c Glencarse *Bre* 84-87; Dioc Sec 84-87; Chapl HM Pris Perth 85-87; V Broughton Poggs w Filkins, Broadwell etc *Ox* from 87. *The Vicarage, Filkins, Lechlade, Glos GL7 3JQ* Faringdon (0367) 860460

GLEADALL, John Frederick. b 39. Ripon Hall Ox 66 Sarum Th Coll 69. d 70 p 71. C S Ashford Ch Ch *Cant* 70-76; P-in-c Hothfield 76-83; P-in-c Eastwell w Boughton Aluph 81-83; P-in-c Westwell 81-83; V Westwell, Hothfield, Eastwell and Boughton Aluph from 84. *The Vicarage, Westwell, Ashford, Kent TN25 4LQ* Charing (023371) 2576

GLEDHILL, Alan. b 43. Lon Univ BSc(Econ). N Ord Course 81. d 84 p 85. C Knaresborough *Ripon* 84-87; P-in-c Easby 87-88; P-in-c Bolton on Swale 87-88; V Easby w Brompton on Swale and Bolton on Swale from 88. *The Vicarage, St Paul's Drive, Brompton on Swale, Richmond, N Yorkshire DL10 7HQ*   Richmond (0748) 811840

GLEDHILL, Canon James William. b 27. Dur Univ BA52. Westcott Ho Cam 52. d 56 p 57. C Mexborough *Sheff* 56-59; CF 59-61; C Bywell St Pet *Newc* 61-65; V Warden w Newbrough from 65; RD Hexham 78-88; Hon Can Newc Cathl from 88. *The Vicarage, Warden, Hexham, Northd NE46 4SL*   Hexham (0434) 603910

GLEDHILL, Jonathan Michael. b 49. Keele Univ BA72 Bris Univ MA75. Trin Coll Bris 72. d 75 p 76. C Marple All SS *Ches* 75-78; C Folkestone H Trin w Ch Ch *Cant* 78-83; V Cant St Mary Bredin from 83; Tutor Cant Sch of Min from 83; RD Cant from 88. *St Mary Bredin Vicarage, 57 Nunnery Fields, Canterbury, Kent CT1 3JN*   Canterbury (0227) 462479

GLEDHILL, Peter. b 29. Ball Coll Ox BA53 MA54. Cuddesdon Coll 54. d 56 p 57. C Balham St Mary *S'wark* 56-58; C Loughton St Jo *Chelmsf* 58-63; Jamaica 63-66; Barbados 66-67; Asst Master Cheadle Gr Sch 68-70; Lic to Offic *Lich* 70-71; P-in-c Kingstone w Gratwich 71-83; P-in-c Llanyblodwel and Trefonen 83-84; R 84-89; C Menai and Malltraeth *Ban* from 90. *Yr Hen Felin, Pwll Fanogl, Llanfairpwll, Gwynedd LL61 6PD* Llanfairpwll (0248) 714434

GLEED, Roy Edward. b 19. Linc Coll Ox BA48 MA53. Chich Th Coll. d 50 p 51. R Dowdeswell and Andoversford w the Shiptons etc *Glouc* 63-74; P-in-c 69-74; R Avening 74-76; R Avening w Cherington 76-84; rtd 84; Perm to Offic Glouc & Bris from 84. *9 Court Field, Tetbury, Glos GL8 8LF*   Tetbury (0666) 52159

GLEESON, Robert Godfrey. b 49. Man Univ CQSW74. Qu Coll Birm 83. d 85 p 86. C Hall Green St Pet *Birm* 85-88; Asst Chapl Mental Health & Elderly Care Services Birm HA 88-90; Chapl from 90; Chapl Moseley Hall Hosp Birm from 90. *180 Pineapple Road, Birmingham B30 2TY*   021-444 2793

GLEN, Robert Sawers. b 25. Qu Coll Cam BA49 MA56. Sarum & Wells Th Coll 79. **d** 81 **p** 82. Chapl Sherborne Sch Dorset 81-86; C Yetminster w Ryme Intrinseca and High Stoy *Sarum* from 86. *Devan Haye, North Road, Sherborne, Dorset DT9 3BJ* Sherborne (0935) 812018

GLENDALOUGH, Archdeacon of. *See* PRICE, Ven Cecil Johnston

GLENDENNING, Dr Francis John. b 21. FRSA89 Liv Univ BA42 Sheff Univ MA49 Keele Univ PhD75. Linc Th Coll 42. **d** 44 **p** 45. Assoc Dir Chr Aid 64-68; rtd 86. *32 Dartmouth Avenue, Newcastle, Staffs ST5 3NY* Newcastle-under-Lyme (0782) 616368

GLENDINING, Canon Alan. b 24. LVO79. Westcott Ho Cam 58. **d** 60 **p** 61. V Raveninghame *Nor* 63-70; P-in-c Hales w Heckingham 63-70; R Thurlton w Thorpe next Haddiscoe 63-70; V Norton Subcourse 63-70; P-in-c Aldeby w Wheatacre w Burgh St Peter 66-70; P-in-c Haddiscoe w Toft Monks 68-70; Dom Chapl to HM The Queen 70-79; Chapl from 79; R Sandringham w W Newton *Nor* 70-79; RD Heacham and Rising 72-76; Hon Can Nor Cathl 77-89; TR Lowestoft and Kirkley *Nor* 79-85; Sen Chapl to Holidaymakers 85-89; V Ranworth w Panxworth and Woodbastwick 85-89; RD Blofield 87-89; rtd 90. *7 Bellfosters, Kings Staithe Lane, King's Lynn PE30 1LZ* King's Lynn (0553) 760113

GLENFIELD, Samuel Ferran. b 54. QUB BA76 TCD MLitt90 BTh91. **d** 91. C Douglas Union w Frankfield C, C & R from 91. *64 Willow Bank, Church Road, Blackrock, Cork, Irish Republic* Cork (21) 358226

GLENN, Michael David. b 37. Lich Th Coll 67. **d** 70 **p** 71. C Denton Ch Ch *Man* 70-74; Chapl Oldham Hosps 74-77; P-in-c Moss Side Ch Ch *Man* 77-78; Hon C Drayton Bassett *Lich* 78-82; Hon C Hints 78-82; Perm to Offic *Man* 82-90; TV Corby SS Pet and Andr w Gt and Lt Oakley *Pet* from 90. *The Vicarage, 1 Lovap Way, Great Oakley, Corby, Northants NN18 8JL* Corby (0536) 746266

GLENNY, William Richard Harcourt Raeburn. b 21. QUB 51. Bps' Coll Cheshunt 54. **d** 56 **p** 57. Chapl St Gabr Convent Sch Newbury 68-74; Chapl Downe Ho Sch Cold Ash Berks 73-74; V Chelmsf St Andr *Chelmsf* 74-90; rtd 90; Perm to Offic *Portsm* from 90. *28 Butser Walk, Petersfield, Hants GU31 4NU* Petersfield (0730) 65952

GLEW, George William. b 24. Oak Hill Th Coll 64. **d** 66 **p** 67. C Willesborough w Hinxhill *Cant* 69-73; R Burlingham St Edmund, St Andr, St Pet etc *Nor* 73-77; V Burlingham St Edmund w Lingwood 77-83; C Horsham *Chich* 83-85; P-in-c Worthing Ch Ch 85-89; rtd 89; Hon CF from 89. *17 Mead Way, Canterbury, Kent CT2 8BB* Canterbury (0227) 472639

GLOUCESTER, Archdeacon of. *See* WAGSTAFF, Ven Christopher John Harold

GLOUCESTER, Bishop of. *See* YATES, Rt Rev John

GLOUCESTER, Dean of. *See* JENNINGS, Very Rev Kenneth Neal

GLOVER, Brian Reginald. b 38. St D Coll Lamp BA60 Sarum Th Coll 60. **d** 62 **p** 63. C Redditch St Steph *Worc* 62-68; V Redditch St Geo 68-74; V Ellistown *Leic* 74-77; V Leic St Aid 77-82; V Fleckney 82-84; V Fleckney and Kilby from 84; RD Gartree II (Wigston) from 89. *The Vicarage, 12 Saddington Road, Fleckney, Leicester LE8 0AW* Leicester (0533) 402215

GLOVER, David. b 50. Coll of Resurr Mirfield 77. **d** 80 **p** 81. C Hope St Jas *Man* 80-83; C Bedf Leigh 83-85; V Cudworth *Wakef* from 85. *The Vicarage, Cudworth, Barnsley, S Yorkshire S72 8DE* Barnsley (0226) 710297

GLOVER, David Charles. b 66. St Jo Coll Dur BA87 St Jo Coll Cam MPhil91. Ridley Hall Cam 87. **d** 90 **p** 91. C Wath-upon-Dearne w Adwick-upon-Dearne *Sheff* from 90. *7 Coronation Road, Wath-upon-Dearne, Rotherham, S Yorkshire S63 7AP* Rotherham (0709) 878118

GLOVER, George Edward. b 58. Strathclyde Univ BSc80 Edin Univ BD83. Edin Th Coll 80. **d** 83 **p** 86. C Dunblane *St And* 83-84; C Southgate Ch Ch *Lon* 84-85; C Golders Green 85-88; Chapl Sunderland Mental Health Unit 88-90; C Sherburn w Pittington *Dur* from 90. *2 Priors Grange, Pittington, Durham DH6 1DA* 091-372 1086

GLOVER, Henry Arthur. b 32. Lon Univ BSc58. Wycliffe Hall Ox 59. **d** 61 **p** 62. C Fareham St Jo *Portsm* 61-63; C Liv Our Lady and St Nic *Liv* 63-64. *15 Thorncliffe Road, Wallasey, Merseyside L44 3AA* 051-638 6018

GLOVER, John. b 48. Kelham Th Coll 67. **d** 71 **p** 72. C Foley Park *Worc* 71-75; TV Sutton *Liv* 75-79; P-in-c Churchill w Blakedown *Worc* 79-84; R 84-87; R Belbroughton w Fairfield and Clent from 87. *The Rectory, Belbroughton, Stourbridge, W Midlands DY9 9TE* Belbroughton (0562) 730531

GLOVER, Michael John Myers. b 28. Lon Univ BSc48. Cuddesdon Coll 54. **d** 56 **p** 57. C Leic St Pet *Leic* 56-60; S Africa 60-73 and from 86; Bp's Chapl E Area Northn 73-74; TR Northn Em *Pet* 74-86. *PO Box 5048, Nongoma, 3950 South Africa* Nongoma (358) 310044

GLOVER, Richard John. b 47. Nottm Univ BTh77. Linc Th Coll 73. **d** 77 **p** 78. C Barrow St Geo w St Luke *Carl* 77-79; C Netherton 79-80; P-in-c Addingham 80-83; P-in-c Edenhall w Langwathby and Culgaith 80-83; V Addingham, Edenhall, Langwathby and Culgaith 83-84; V Bishops Hull *B & W* 84-89; V Shilbottle *Newc* from 89. *The Vicarage, Shilbottle, Alnwick, Northd NE66 2XR* Shilbottle (066575) 800

GLYN-JONES, Alun. b 38. CCC Cam BA59 MA63. Bps' Coll Cheshunt 60. **d** 61 **p** 62. C Portsea St Mary *Portsm* 61-65; Chapl Hampton Sch Middx 65-76; Hd Master Abp Tenison Gr Sch Croydon 76-88; V Twickenham St Mary *Lon* from 88. *St Mary's Vicarage, Riverside, Twickenham TW1 3DT* 081-892 2318

GOALBY, George Christian. b 55. Leeds Univ BA77. St Jo Coll Nottm DPS81. **d** 81 **p** 82. C Wakef St Andr and St Mary *Wakef* 81-84; Asst Chapl HM Pris Wakef 84-85; Chapl HM Youth Cust Cen Deerbolt 85-87; HM Pris Frankland 87-89; V Swinderby *Linc* from 89. *All Saints' Vicarage, Station Road, Swinderby, Lincoln LN6 6LY* Swinderby (052286) 430

GOATCHER, Sara Jacoba Helena. b 46. Oak Hill NSM Course 86. **d** 89. NSM S Croydon Em *S'wark* from 89. *5 Normanton Road, Croydon, Surrey CR2 7AE* 081-688 6130

GOATER, Charles Frederick. b 16. **d** 82 **p** 82. NSM Fishponds St Mary *Bris* 82-89; Perm to Offic from 89. *72 Queensholme Crescent, Bristol BS16 6LH* Bristol (0272) 561147

GOATER, William Arthur. b 12. Chich Th Coll 33. **d** 36 **p** 37. V N Nibley *Glouc* 53-77; V Stinchcombe 55-77; rtd 77; Perm to Offic *Glouc* from 77. *Church Cottage, Stinchcombe, Dursley, Glos GL11 6BQ* Dursley (0453) 542116

GOBBETT, Michael George Timothy. b 64. St Chad's Coll Dur BSc86. St Steph Ho Ox BA89. **d** 90 **p** 91. C Hartlepool St Aid *Dur* from 90. *St Aidan's Clergy House, St Aidan's Street, Hartlepool TS25 1SN* Hartlepool (0429) 273539

GOBLE, Clifford David. b 41. Oak Hill Th Coll 69. **d** 72 **p** 73. C Erith St Paul *Roch* 72-76; C Tunbridge Wells St Jas 76-79; R Southfleet from 79. *The Rectory, Southfleet, Dartford, Kent DA13 9NQ* Southfleet (047483) 3532

GODBER, Francis Giles. b 48. Open Univ BA79. Ridley Hall Cam 72. **d** 75 **p** 76. C Blackheath *Birm* 75-78; C Wolv St Matt *Lich* 78-80; TV Washfield, Stoodleigh, Withleigh etc *Ex* 80-85; R Shenley and Loughton *Ox* 85-88; R Watling Valley from 88. *The Rectory, Pitcher Lane, Loughton, Milton Keynes MK5 8AU* Milton Keynes (0908) 666253

GODDARD, Charles Douglas James. b 47. CITC 67. **d** 70 **p** 71. C Orangefield *D & D* 70-73; C Stormont 73-75; Miss to Seamen 75-77; Sen Chapl and Sec N Ireland from 77. *7 Abercorn Drive, Carnreagh Road, Hillsborough, Co Down BT26 6LB* Hillsborough (0846) 683592

GODDARD, Christopher. b 45. Sarum & Wells Th Coll 79. **d** 81 **p** 82. C Whitehaven *Carl* 81-83; C Barrow St Geo w St Luke 83-85; P-in-c Hayton St Mary 85-90; V Brigham from 90; V Mosser from 90. *The Vicarage, 1 High Brigham, Cockermouth, Cumbria CA13 0TE* Cockermouth (0900) 825383

GODDARD, Christopher Robert Wynn. b 08. Trin Coll Cam BA30. Cuddesdon Coll 32. **d** 33 **p** 34. V Kersey w Lindsey *St E* 68-73; rtd 73. *188 Thunder Lane, Thorpe St Andrew, Norwich NR7 0AB* Norwich (0603) 38046

GODDARD, David. b 43. FTCL63. Sarum & Wells Th Coll. **d** 83 **p** 84. C Romsey *Win* 83-86; C Southsea H Spirit *Portsm* 86-89; V Lancing St Mich *Chich* from 89. *St Michael's Vicarage, 117 Penhill Road, Lancing, Sussex BN15 8HD* Lancing (0903) 753653

GODDARD, Canon Frederick Paul Preston. b 24. Jes Coll Cam BA49 MA51. Westcott Ho Cam 49. **d** 51 **p** 52. Chapl Yeatman and Coldharbour Hosp Dorset 69-87; V Sherborne w Castleton and Lillington *Sarum* 69-87; RD Sherborne 73-77; Can and Preb Sarum Cathl from 75; rtd 87. *56 West Street, Polruan, Fowey, Cornwall* Polruan (0726) 870339

GODDARD, Harold Frederick. b 42. Keble Coll Ox BA63 DipTh65 MA69. Cuddesdon Coll 64. **d** 66 **p** 67. C Birm St Pet *Birm* 66-70; C Alverstoke *Portsm* 70-72; Chapl Portsm Cathl 73-76; P-in-c Portsea St Geo CD 72-76; P-in-c Stoke Prior *Worc* 76-78; P-in-c Wychbold and Upton Warren 77-78; R Stoke Prior, Wychbold and Upton Warren 78-80; Chapl R Marsden Hosp Lon and

Surrey 80-83; R Martley and Wichenford *Worc* 83-88; P-in-c Knightwick w Doddenham, Broadwas and Cotheridge 85-88; R Martley and Wichenford, Knightwick etc 89-90; Bp's Adv on Min of Healing from 87; Chapl St Rich Hospice Worc from 87; RD Martley and Worc W *Worc* 88-90. *The Red House, Dunley, Stourport-on-Severn, Worcs DY13 0TZ* Stourport (02993) 2080

GODDARD, Canon John William. b 47. St Chad's Coll Dur BA69 DipTh70. **d** 70 **p** 71. C S Bank *York* 70-74; C Cayton w Eastfield 74-75; V Middlesb Ascension 75-82; RD Middlesbrough 81-87; V Middlesb All SS 82-88; Can and Preb York Minster 87-88; Vice-Prin Edin Th Coll from 88. *The Theological College, Rosebery Crescent, Edinburgh EH12 5JT* 031-337 3838 or 337 0478

GODDARD, Ms Marion. b 54. Sarum & Wells Th Coll 87. **d** 89. Par Dn Lewisham St Swithun *S'wark* from 89. *14 Duncrievie Road, London SE13 6TE* 081-318 7531

GODDARD, Matthew Francis. b 45. Lon Univ DipTh69. Kelham Th Coll 65. **d** 69 **p** 70. C Mansf St Mark *S'well* 69-72; C Northolt Park St Barn *Lon* 72-78; P-in-c Acton Green St Pet 78-87; R Norwood St Mary from 87. *The Rectory, Norwood Green, Southall, Middx UB2 4LE* 081-574 1362

GODDARD, Canon Sydney Thomas. b 16. St Aid Birkenhead 46. **d** 49 **p** 50. Warden World Friendship Ho 59-83; V Liv St Sav *Liv* 59-71; Hon Can Liv Cathl 69-83; rtd 84; Perm to Offic *Ban* from 84. *Ynys Thomas Bronaber, Trawsfynydd, Blaenau Ffestiniog, Gwynedd LL41 4UR* Trawsfynydd (076687) 413

GODDARD, Canon William. b 09. Kelham Th Coll 29. **d** 34 **p** 35. R Guildf St Nic *Guildf* 59-74; R Catworth Magna *Ely* 74-77; R Covington 75-77; R Tilbrook 75-77; rtd 77; Perm to Offic *Glouc* from 79. *Flat 13, Capel Court, The Burgage, Prestbury, Cheltenham, Glos GL52 3EL* Cheltenham (0242) 528849

GODDARD, William Edwin George. b 14. Clifton Th Coll 66. **d** 68 **p** 69. C Rodbourne Cheney *Bris* 68-71; R Beaford and Roborough *Ex* 71-78; TV Newton Tracey 76-78; R Beaford, Roborough and St Giles in the Wood 78-79; rtd 79; Perm to Offic *Bris* from 84. *10 Park Farm, The Street, Moredon, Swindon SN2 3ER* Swindon (0793) 525341

GODDEN, Ven Max Leon. b 23. Worc Coll Ox BA50 MA54. Chich Th Coll 50. **d** 52 **p** 53. V Glynde, W Firle and Beddingham *Chich* 62-82; Adn Lewes 72-76; Adn Lewes and Hastings 76-88; rtd 88. *14 Oak Close, Chichester, W Sussex PO19 3AJ* Chichester (0243) 531344

GODDEN, Peter David. b 47. ARCO70 Leeds Univ BA69. Linc Th Coll 85. **d** 87 **p** 88. C Bearsted w Thurnham *Cant* 87-90; C Hykeham *Linc* 90-91; TV from 91. *23 Baildon Crescent, North Hykeham, Lincoln LN6 8HS* Lincoln (0522) 690885

GODDEN, Timothy Richard James. b 62. Univ Coll Lon BA84. St Jo Coll Nottm DPS89. **d** 89 **p** 90. C Tulse Hill H Trin and St Matthias *S'wark* from 89. *132 Trinity Rise, London SW2 2QT* 081-674 3551

GODECK, John William George. b 30. Chich Th Coll 57. **d** 60 **p** 61. C Wadhurst *Chich* 60-62; C Tidebrook 60-62; C Eastbourne 62-63; R Bondleigh *Ex* 63-78; R Zeal Monachorum 63-78; P-in-c Broadwoodkelly 65-67; R 68-78; R Dunchideock and Shillingford St George w Ide from 78; RD Kenn 83-89. *The Rectory, Shillingford St George, Exeter EX2 9UT* Exeter (0392) 832589

GODFREY, Brian Ernest Searles. b 37. Lon Univ BSc60 MSc63 PhD72. S'wark Ord Course 78. **d** 81 **p** 82. NSM Hayes *Roch* 81-86; C 86-88; R Kingsdown from 88. *The Rectory, London Road, West Kingsdown, Sevenoaks, Kent TN15 6JL* West Kingsdown (0474) 852265

GODFREY, Brother. See PAWSON, Geoffrey Philip Henry

GODFREY, David Samuel George. b 35. CITC 64. **d** 66 **p** 67. C Londonderry Ch Ch *D & R* 66-68; I Tomregan w Drumlane *K, E & A* 68-71; I Cloonclare 71-79; I Templebreedy *C, C & R* 79-85; I Bray *D & G* from 85. *The Rectory, Church Road, Bray, Co Wicklow, Irish Republic* Dublin (1) 286-2968

GODFREY, Edward Colin. b 30. Wells Th Coll 63. **d** 65 **p** 66. C Lyndhurst and Emery Down *Win* 65-69; C Paignton Ch Ch *Ex* 69-73; V Stockland w Dalwood 73-77; Chapl HM Pris Man 77-78; Cant 78-85; Chapl HM Young Offender Inst Glen Parva 85-90; Chapl HM Pris Highpoint from 90. *HM Prison Highpoint, Stradishall, Newmarket, Suffolk CB8 9YG* Haverhill (0440) 820611

✠**GODFREY, Rt Rev Harold William.** b 48. AKC71. **d** 72 **p** 73 **c** 87. C Warsop *S'well* 72-75; TV Hucknall Torkard

75-86; Dioc Ecum Officer 81-82; Adn Montevideo 86-88; Asst Bp of Argentina and Uruguay 87-88; Uruguay from 88. *Casa Episcopal, Francisco Araucho 1287, Montevideo 11300, Uruguay* Montevideo (2) 783885

GODFREY, John Frederick. b 31. Solicitor Lon Univ LLB53 AKC54. Cuddesdon Coll 59. **d** 61 **p** 62. C Battersea St Luke *S'wark* 61-65; Min Reigate St Phil CD 65-72; Public Preacher *St Alb* from 73. *Thicketts, Theobald Street, Radlett, Herts WD7 7LS* Radlett (0923) 855558

GODFREY, Joy. b 33. SW Minl Tr Course. **dss** 85 **d** 87. Devonport St Aubyn *Ex* 85-87; Hon Par Dn from 87. *85 Browning Road, Plymouth PL2 3AW* Plymouth (0752) 564253

GODFREY, Preb Michael. b 49. K Coll Lon BD70 AKC72. **d** 72 **p** 73. C Birtley *Dur* 72-75; Ind Chapl 76-79; Ind Chapl *Lich* from 79; TV Bilston St Mary 79; TV Bilston 80-86; TV Wolv from 86; Preb Lich Cathl from 87. *283 Henwood Road, Wolverhampton WV6 8PU* Wolverhampton (0902) 752278

GODFREY, Michael James. b 50. Sheff Univ BEd77. St Jo Coll Nottm DipTh79 CPS79. **d** 82 **p** 83. C Walton H Trin *Ox* 82-86; C Chadderton Ch Ch *Man* 86-91; V Woodlands *Sheff* from 91. *The Vicarage, 9 Great North Road, Woodlands, Doncaster, S Yorkshire DN6 7RB* Doncaster (0302) 723268

GODFREY, Nigel Philip. b 51. MRTPI76 Bris Poly DipTP73 Ox Univ BA78 MA84. Ripon Coll Cuddesdon 77. **d** 79 **p** 80. C Kennington St Jo w St Jas *S'wark* 79-89; Community of Ch the Servant from 84; V Brixton Rd Ch Ch *S'wark* from 89. *Community House, Christ Church, Mowll Street, London SW9 6BE* 071-587 0375

GODFREY, Canon Robert Bernard. b 16. Wells Th Coll 55. **d** 56 **p** 57. R Ipswich St Mary at Stoke w St Mary Quay *St E* 69-76; Hon Can St E Cathl 73-81; RD Samford 75-81; R Sproughton w Burstall 76-81; rtd 81; Perm to Offic *St E* from 81. *Long Acre, London Road, Ipswich, Suffolk IP2 0SS* Ipswich (0473) 689398

GODFREY, Robert John. b 27. ACP St Jo Coll York CertEd48. Sarum Th Coll 52. **d** 54 **p** 55. C Roundhay St Edm *Ripon* 54-57; C Gt Marlow *Ox* 57-59; V Long Crendon 59-61; Chapl RAF 61-63; Chapl Crookham Court Sch Newbury 63-79; P-in-c Yattendon w Frilsham *Ox* 79-80; TV Hermitage and Hampstead Norreys, Cold Ash etc 80-88; Cyprus from 88. *The Chaplain's House, PO Box 1494, Limassol, Cyprus* Limassol (51) 362713

GODFREY, Rumley Myles. b 48. S'wark Ord Course. **d** 83 **p** 84. NSM Dorchester *Ox* from 83. *The Old Malthouse, Warborough, Oxon OX9 8DY* Warborough (086732) 8453

GODFREY, Canon Rupert Christopher Race. b 12. Qu Coll Ox BA34 DipТh35 MA38. Ridley Hall Cam 35. **d** 36 **p** 37. Hon Can St E Cathl *St E* 57-77; V Bury St Edmunds St Mary 59-77; rtd 77; Perm to Offic *St E* from 77. *Archway House, Pytches Road, Woodbridge, Suffolk IP12 1EY* Woodbridge (03943) 2816

GODFREY, Simon Henry Martin. b 55. K Coll Lon BD AKC80. St Steph Ho Ox 80. **d** 81 **p** 82. C Kettering SS Pet and Paul *Pet* 81-84; R Crick and Yelvertoft w Clay Coton and Lilbourne 84-89; V Northn All SS w St Kath from 89. *All Saints' Vicarage, Albion Place, Northampton NN1 1UD* Northampton (0604) 21854 or 32194

GODFREY, Stanley William. b 24. CEng MIEE67. Qu Coll Birm 71. **d** 74 **p** 74. C Sutton Coldfield St Chad Birm 74-78; Hon C Handsworth St Andr 78-86; Hon C Worc City St Paul and Old St Martin etc *Worc* 86-89; Hon C Droitwich Spa from 89. *2 Squires Close, Kempsey, Worcester WR5 3JE* Worcester (0905) 820624

GODFREY, William Thomas. b 12. ACP67. K Coll Lon 68. **d** 69 **p** 70. C Southbourne St Kath *Win* 69-72; V S Petherwin w Trewen *Truro* 72-76; Chapl Upper Chine Sch Shanklin 76-78; rtd 78; Perm to Offic *Portsm* 78; *Win* from 85. *Watersplash Cottage, Blissford, Fordingbridge, Hants SP6 2JQ* Fordingbridge (0425) 657044

GODFREY-THOMAS, Cecil Stephens Godfrey. b 09. St Cath Coll Cam BA45 MA48. St D Coll Lamp BA31. **d** 32 **p** 33. R Woodham Mortimer w Hazeleigh *Chelmsf* 67-79; R Woodham Walter 67-79; rtd 79. *14 St Austins Lane, Harwich, Essex CO12 3EX* Harwich (0255) 554309

GODSALL, Andrew Paul. b 59. Birm Univ BA81. Ripon Coll Cuddesdon 86. **d** 88 **p** 89. C Gt Stanmore *Lon* 88-91; C Ealing All SS from 91. *All Saints' Vicarage, Elm Grove Road W5 3JH* 081-567 8166

GODSALL, Ralph Charles. b 48. Qu Coll Cam BA71 MA75. Cuddesdon Coll 73. **d** 75 **p** 76. C Sprowston *Nor* 75-78; Chapl Trin Coll Cam 78-84; V Hebden Bridge *Wakef* from 84. *St James's Vicarage, Church*

Lane, Hebden Bridge, W Yorkshire HX7 6DL Halifax (0422) 842138

GODSELL, Arthur Norman. b 22. St D Coll Lamp BA47. **d** 49 **p** 50. C Tenby and Gumfreston *St D* 49-62; V Heybridge w Langford *Chelmsf* 62-73; RD Maldon 70-73; R Rochford from 73; RD Rochford 84-89. *The Rectory, Hall Road, Rochford, Essex SS4 1NT* Southend-on-Sea (0702) 544304

GODSELL, David Brian. b 40. Lon Univ BA62. Coll of Resurr Mirfield 65. **d** 67 **p** 68. C Middlesb All SS *York* 67-73; C Stainton-in-Cleveland 73-75; V Byker St Ant *Newc* 75-90; P-in-c Brandon *Dur* from 90. *The Clergy House, Sawmill Lane, Brandon, Durham DH7 8NS* 091-378 0845

GODSELL, Kenneth James Rowland. b 22. Birm Univ DipTh50. Qu Coll Birm. **d** 76 **p** 77. Tutor Westhill Coll of HE Birm from 74; Hon C Selly Hill St Steph *Birm* 76-81; Hon C Selly Park St Steph and St Wulstan from 81. *7 Farquhar Road East, Birmingham B15 3RD* 021-454 3737 or 472 7245

GODSON, Alan. b 31. Ch Coll Cam BA61 MA65. Clifton Th Coll 61. **d** 63 **p** 64. C Preston All SS *Blackb* 63-66; Lic to Offic *Man* 66-69; Asst Chapl Emb Ch Paris 69; Dioc Ev *Liv* from 69; P-in-c Edge Hill St Mary 72-78; V from 78. *The Vicarage, Towerlands Street, Liverpool L7 8TT* 051-709 6710

GODSON, Mark Rowland. b 61. K Coll Lon BD83 AKC83 CertEd84. Linc Th Coll 84. **d** 86 **p** 87. C Hurst Green *S'wark* 86-88; C Fawley *Win* 88-90; TV Wimborne Minster and Holt *Sarum* from 90. *The Vicarage, Holt, Wimborne, Dorset BH21 7DJ* Poole (0202) 882437

GODWIN, David Harold. b 45. Lon Univ DipTh71. Kelham Th Coll 67. **d** 71 **p** 72. C Camberwell St Phil and St Mark *S'wark* 71-75; Asst Chapl The Lon Hosp (Whitechapel) 75-79; Chapl R E Sussex Hosp Hastings 79-86; Chapl Glos R and Over Hosps Glouc from 86. *Gloucestershire Royal Hospital, Great Western Road, Gloucester GL1 3NN* Gloucester (0452) 28555

GODWIN, Canon Michael Francis Harold. b 35. Nottm Univ BSc57. Ely Th Coll 59. **d** 61 **p** 62. C Farnborough *Guildf* 61-65; V Epsom St Barn 66-85; V Bramley and Grafham from 85; Hon Can Guildf Cathl from 89. *The Vicarage, Birtley Rise, Bramley, Guildford, Surrey GU5 0HZ* Guildford (0483) 892109

GODWIN, Canon Noel. b 29. Qu Coll Ox BA52 MA57. St Steph Ho Ox 52. **d** 54 **p** 55. C Streatham St Pet *S'wark* 54-57; Ghana 58-63; V Holbeck *Ripon* 63-65; Lic to Offic *Nor* 65-76; RD Depwade 76-77; R Attleborough 77-80; R Attleborough w Besthorpe 80-82; Hon Can Nor Cathl 81-82; V Croydon St Mich w St Jas *Cant* 82-84; V Croydon St Mich w St Jas *S'wark* from 85; RD Croydon Cen from 86; Hon Can S'wark Cathl from 89. *St Michael's Vicarage, 39 Oakfield Road, Croydon CR0 2UX* 081-680 8413

GODWIN, Peter. b 19. MBE77. Malvern Coll. Ridley Hall Cam 76. **d** 77 **p** 78. C Headley All SS *Guildf* 77-78; Argentina from 78; rtd 88. *Avenida Belgrano 568, 8 Piso A, Buenos Aires, Argentina* Buenos Aires (1) 302287

GOFTON, Canon William Alder. b 31. Dur Univ BA54. Coll of Resurr Mirfield 59. **d** 61 **p** 62. C Benwell St Aid *Newc* 61-64; C N Gosforth 64-69; V Seaton Hirst 69-77; V Newc H Cross 77-89; RD Newc W 85-88; Hon Can Newc Cathl from 88; R Bolam w Whalton and Hartburn w Meldon from 89; P-in-c Netherwitton from 89. *The Rectory, Whalton, Morpeth, Northd NE61 3UX* Whalton (067075) 360

GOLBOURNE, Winston George. b 30. Univ of W Indies BA53. Virginia Th Sem STM69 Sarum & Wells Th Coll 71. **d** 73 **p** 74. C Bitterne Park *Win* 73-76; Jamaica 76-79; C Handsworth St Andr *Birm* 79-83; V Perry Hill St Geo *S'wark* from 83. *St George's Vicarage, 2 Woolstone Road, London SE23 2SG* 081-699 2778

GOLD, Guy Alastair Whitmore. b 16. TD50. Trin Coll Cam BA38 MA48. Qu Coll Birm 55. **d** 55 **p** 56. R Hasketon *St E* 69-76; rtd 76; Perm to Offic *St E* 76-89. *Bridge House, Great Bealings, Woodbridge, Suffolk IP13 6NW* Grundisburgh (047335) 518

GOLDEN, Stephen Gerard. b 61. Lon Univ BA84. St Steph Ho Ox 84. **d** 86 **p** 87. C Reading St Luke w St Bart *Ox* 86-90; CF from 90. *c/o MOD (Army), Bagshot Park, Bagshot, Surrey GU19 5PL* Bagshot (0276) 71717

GOLDENBERG, Ralph Maurice. b 45. City Univ FBCO67 FBOA67. Trin Coll Bris DipHE90. **d** 90 **p** 91. C Kinson *Sarum* from 90. *4 Home Road, Kinson, Bournemouth, Dorset BH11 9BN* Bournemouth (0202) 578355

GOLDIE, Canon David. b 46. Glas Univ MA68 Fitzw Coll Cam BA70 MA74. Westcott Ho Cam 68. **d** 70 **p** 71. C Swindon Ch Ch *Bris* 70-73; C Troon *Glas* 73-75; R

Ardrossan 75-82; Miss Priest Irvine 75-82; PM Milton Keynes *Ox* 82-86; V Milton Keynes from 86; RD Milton Keynes 86-90; Can Ch Ch from 90. *7 Alverton, Great Linford, Milton Keynes MK14 5EF* Milton Keynes (0908) 605150

GOLDIE, Donald Norwood. b 14. St Chad's Coll Dur BA36 DipTh37 MA39. **d** 37 **p** 38. R Bishopwearmouth St Mich *Dur* 62-70; P-in-c Bishopwearmouth St Mich w St Hilda 66-70; Hon Can Dur Cathl 65-70; V Bedlington *Newc* 70-80; rtd 80; Chapl Algarve *Eur* 80-83. *Sunrise, Longframlington, Morpeth, Northd NE65 8DT* Longframlington (0665) 570648

GOLDIE, James Stuart. b 46. Edin Univ BTh73 BEd73 ALCD69. **d** 69 **p** 70. C Blackpool St Paul *Blackb* 69-70; C Gt Sankey *Liv* 70-73; Asst Chapl Greystone Heath Sch 70-73; Chapl Kilmarnock Academy 73-75; V Flixton St Jo *Man* 75-78; Chapl Friars Sch Man 75-78; V Skelmersdale St Paul *Liv* 78-80; Chapl Trin Sch Liv 78-80; Chapl Westbrook Hay Sch, Hemel Hempstead 87-89; V Pennington w Lindal and Marton *Carl* 89-90; Chapl Bp Wand Sch *Lon* from 90. *41 Lyndhurst Avenue, Sudbury on Thames, Middx TW16 6AA* Sunbury-on-Thames (0932) 786890

GOLDING, George Charles. b 11. Univ Coll Dur LTh38 BA39. St Aug Coll Cant 35. **d** 39 **p** 39. C Croydon St Pet S End *Cant* 39-42; Ox Miss Calcutta 42-69; Barisal from 69; Superior Brotherhood of the Epiphany (Ox Miss) from 69; E Pakistan 69-71; Bangladesh from 71. *Oxford Mission, Bogra Road, PO Box 21, Barisal 8200, Bangladesh*

GOLDING, Piers Edwin Hugh. b 26. RD76. St Aug Coll Cant 48 Edin Th Coll 50. **d** 53 **p** 54. C Guildf Ch Ch *Guildf* 53-55; C Enfield St Andr *Lon* 55-58; Chapl RN 58-62; Chapl RNR from 62; V S Bermondsey St Aug *S'wark* from 62. *St Augustine's Vicarage, Lynton Road, London SE1 5DP* 071-237 1446

GOLDING, Simon Jefferies. b 46. Brasted Place Coll 70. Linc Th Coll 72. **d** 74 **p** 75. C Wilton *York* 74-77; Chapl RN from 77. *c/o MOD, Lacon House, Theobald's Road, London WC1X 8RY* 071-430 6847

GOLDING, Canon Terence Brannigan. b 25. Univ of Ottawa MA. Qu Coll Birm 79. **d** 77 **p** 77. Lesotho 77-79; C Walsall *Lich* 79-83; I Currin w Drum and Newbliss *Clogh* 83-86 and from 88; V Eighton Banks *Dur* 86-88. *Scotshouse Rectory, Clones, Co Monaghan, Irish Republic* Clones (47) 56103

GOLDINGAY, Dr John Edgar. b 42. Keble Coll Ox BA64 Nottm Univ PhD83. Clifton Th Coll 64. **d** 66 **p** 67. C Finchley Ch Ch *Lon* 66-69; Lect St Jo Coll Nottm 70-75; Dir Academic Studies St Jo Coll Nottm 76-79; Registrar 79-85; Vice-Prin 85-88; Prin from 88. *St John's College, Bramcote, Nottingham NG9 3DS* Nottingham (0602) 251114 or 224046

GOLDSMITH, Brian Derek. b 36. Leeds Univ BA64. Coll of Resurr Mirfield 64. **d** 66 **p** 67. C Littlehampton St Mary *Chich* 66-69; C Guildf St Nic *Guildf* 69-73; V Aldershot St Aug 73-81; C-in-c Leigh Park St Clare CD *Portsm* 82-85; C Rowner from 85. *74 Tichborne Way, Gosport, Hants PO13 0BN* Fareham (0329) 238020

GOLDSMITH, John Oliver. b 46. K Coll Lon BD69 AKC69. St Aug Coll Cant 69. **d** 70 **p** 71. C Dronfield *Derby* 70-73; C Ellesmere Port *Ches* 73-74; TV Ellesmere Port 74-81; P-in-c Pleasley *Derby* 81-87; P-in-c Pleasley Hill *S'well* 83-87; V Matlock Bank *Derby* from 87. *All Saints' Vicarage, Smedley Street, Matlock, Derbyshire DE4 3JG* Matlock (0629) 582235

GOLDSMITH, Malcolm Clive. b 39. Birm Univ BSocSc60. Ripon Hall Ox 60. **d** 62 **p** 63. C Balsall Heath St Paul *Birm* 62-64; Chapl Aston Univ 64-72; Bp's Adv on Ind Soc *S'well* 72-78; C Sherwood 78-79; R Nottm St Pet and St Jas 79-85; P-in-c Nottm All SS 85; Gen Sec IVS 85-88; Lic to Offic 85-88; Bp's Personal Exec Asst *Bradf* from 88. *25 Syke Road, Heaton, Bradford, W Yorkshire BD9 4AB* Bradford (0274) 544197

GOLDSMITH, Mrs Pauline Anne. b 40. Linc Th Coll 84. dss 84 **d** 87. Waddington *Linc* 86-87; C 87-88; Par Dn Gt and Lt Coates w Bradley from 88. *16 Longfield Road, Grimsby, S Humberside DN34 5SB* Grimsby (0472) 51809

GOLDSMITH, Stephen. b 32. Edin Th Coll. **d** 76 **p** 77. NSM Penicuik *Edin* 76-81; NSM Linc St Nic w St Jo Newport *Linc* from 81. *Cantelupe Chantry North, Minster Yard, Lincoln LN2 1PX* Lincoln (0522) 24171

GOLDSPINK, David. b 35. MBAC88 Open Univ BA81. Lon Coll of Div 62. **d** 65 **p** 66. C St Austell *Truro* 68-70; R Bramerton w Surlingham *Nor* 70-73; Min Gunton St Pet 73-75; R Mutford w Rushmere w Gisleham w N Cove w Barnby 75-81; Asst Chapl HM Pris Man 81-82; Chapl HM Youth Cust Cen Hollesley Bay Colony 82-84;

HM Pris Blundeston 84-88; Perm to Offic *St E* from 87; rtd 88; Perm to Offic *Nor* from 88. *Barsham House, Barsham, Beccles, Suffolk NR34 8HD*

GOLDSPINK, Canon Robert William. b 23. Fitzw Coll Cam BA52 MA56. Trin Coll Bris 47. **d** 52 **p** 53. V Tunbridge Wells St Jas *Roch* 64-83; Hon Can Roch Cathl 83-87; V Seal St Pet 83-87; rtd 87; Perm to Offic *Nor* from 87. *Bethany, 50 Uplands Close, Carlton Colville, Suffolk NR33 8AD* Lowestoft (0502) 515662

GOLDSTRAW, William Henry. b 15. Lich Th Coll 60. **d** 61 **p** 62. V Alton *Lich* 68-82; V Bradley-in-the-Moors 68-82; V Alton w Bradley-le-Moors 82-84; rtd 84; Perm to Offic *Lich* from 84. *36 The Avenue, Cheddleton, Leek, Staffs ST13 7RI* Churnet Side (0538) 360204

GOLDTHORPE, Peter Martin. b 36. K Coll Lon 58. **d** 62 **p** 63. C Lt Ilford St Barn *Chelmsf* 62-66; C Wickford 66-68; P-in-c Luton St Anne *St Alb* 68-78; P-in-c Linby w Papplewick *S'well* 78-82; Perm to Offic S'well from 82; Birm from 85; Linc from 86; Midl Sec CMJ from 84. *39 Somerfield Close, Shelfield, Walsall WS4 1PP* Walsall (0922) 683742

GOLDTHORPE, Ms Shirley. b 42. Linc Th Coll 70. **dss** 76 **d** 87. Thornhill Lees *Wakef* 76-78; Birkenshaw w Hunsworth 78-80; Batley St Thos 80-85; Batley All SS 80-85; Purlwell 80-87; Par Dn 87-88; Dn-in-c from 88. *15 Thornville Mount, Huddersfield Road, Dewsbury, W Yorkshire WF13 3RS* Dewsbury (0924) 464635

GOLIGHTLY, William Michael. b 43. Chich Th Coll 67. **d** 70 **p** 74. C Sleekburn *Newc* 70-71; C Wallsend St Luke 71; C Shiremoor 74-77; C Delaval 77-81; TV Bellingham/Otterburn Gp 81-89; TV N Shields from 89. *The Vicarage, 51 Drummond Terrace, North Shields, Tyne & Wear NE30 2AW* 091-258 3083

GOLLEDGE, Leonard. b 09. St Jo Coll Dur BA36 LTh36. Lon Coll of Div 33. **d** 36 **p** 37. V Merriott *B & W* 63-76; rtd 76; Perm to Offic *B & W* from 79. *7 Priory Close, Castle Cary, Somerset BA7 7DH* Castle Cary (0963) 50854

GOLLOP, Michael John. b 58. Keble Coll Ox BA81 MA85. Llan St Mich BD85. **d** 85 **p** 86. C Newport St Mark *Mon* 85-87; C Bassaleg 87-91; V St Hilary Greenway from 91. *St Hilary's Vicarage, 2 Rhyl Road, Rumney, Cardiff CF3 8PA* Cardiff (0222) 793460

GOLTON, Alan Victor. b 29. St Jo Coll Ox BA51 MA54 DPhil54. Local NSM Course 84. **d** 85 **p** 86. P-in-c Barston *Birm* from 87. *12 Granville Road, Dorridge, Solihull, W Midlands B93 8BY* Knowle (0564) 773058

GOMERSALL, Ian Douglass. b 56. Birm Univ BSc77 Fitzw Coll Cam BA80 MA85. Westcott Ho Cam 78. **d** 81 **p** 82. C Darlington St Mark w St Paul *Dur* 81-84; C Barnard Castle w Whorlton 84-86; Chapl HM Young Offender Inst Deerbolt 85-90; P-in-c Cockfield *Dur* 86-88; R 88-90; Dep Chapl HM Pris Wakef 90-91; Chapl HM Pris Full Sutton from 91. *The Chaplain's Office, HM Prison Full Sutton, York YO4 1PS* Stamford Bridge (0759) 72447

GOMPERTZ, Canon Peter Alan Martin. b 40. ALCD63. **d** 64 **p** 65. C Eccleston St Luke *Liv* 64-69; Scripture Union 69-73; C Yeovil *B & W* 73-75; V Northn St Giles *Pet* from 75; Can Pet Cathl from 88. *St Giles's Vicarage, Spring Gardens, Northampton NN1 1LX* Northampton (0604) 34060

GONIN, Christopher Willett. b 33. AKC59. K Coll Lon. **d** 60 **p** 61. C Camberwell St Geo *S'wark* 60-64; C Stevenage H Trin *St Alb* 64-70; C Bletchley *Ox* 70-73; R Newington St Mary *S'wark* 73-76; Perm to Offic *Bris* 76-77; Hon C Horfield H Trin 77-89; Hon C City of Bris from 89. *14 Remenham Drive, Bristol BS9 4HY* Bristol (0272) 628410

GOOD, Alan Raymond. b 39. Bris Sch of Min 83. **d** 85 **p** 86. NSM Horfield St Greg *Bris* from 85. *177 Filton Road, Horfield, Bristol BS7 0XX* Bristol (0272) 519792

GOOD, Andrew Ronald. b 60. Bris Univ BA82. Linc Th Coll 83. **d** 85 **p** 86. C Epping St Jo *Chelmsf* 85-88; C Cheshunt *St Alb* from 88. *St Clement's House, 44 Hillview Gardens, Cheshunt, Herts* Waltham Cross (0992) 25098

GOOD, Anthony Ernest. b 28. ARIBA51 Heriot-Watt Univ MSc73. Wells Th Coll 54. **d** 56 **p** 57. C Maidstone All SS *Cant* 56-60; C Reading St Mary V *Ox* 60-62; R Sandhurst 62-70; Perm to Offic *Ex* 71-82; TR Wallingford w Crowmarsh Gifford etc *Ox* from 82; RD Wallingford 85-91. *The Rectory, 22 Castle Street, Wallingford, Oxon OX10 8DW* Wallingford (0491) 37280

GOOD, David Howard. b 42. Glouc Sch of Min 84. **d** 87 **p** 88. NSM Bromyard *Heref* from 87. *3 Broxash Close, Bromyard, Herefordshire HR7 4TU* Bromyard (0885) 482276

GOOD, Florence Rose. b 10. SRN44. **dss** 78 **d** 87. Upper Holloway St Pet w St Jo *Lon* 84-87; Hon Par Dn 87-89;

rtd 89. *221 Salisbury Walk, Magdala Avenue, London N19 5DY* 071-272 8652

GOOD, Geoffrey. b 27. St Aid Birkenhead. **d** 61 **p** 62. C Roby *Liv* 61-65; V Staincliffe *Wakef* 65-79; V Thornes St Jas w Ch Ch from 79. *The Vicarage, Thornes, Wakefield, W Yorkshire WF2 8DW* Wakefield (0924) 374009

GOOD, Very Rev George Fitzgerald. b 19. TCD BA41. CITC 42. **d** 42 **p** 43. Dean Derry *D & R* 67-84; rtd 84. *Cliff Cottage, Portnoo, Lifford, Co Donegal, Irish Republic*

GOOD, John Hobart. b 43. Bps' Coll Cheshunt 66 Coll of Resurr Mirfield 68. **d** 69 **p** 70. C Ex St Jas *Ex* 69-73; C Cockington 73-75; C Wolborough w Newton Abbot 75-78; P-in-c Exminster 78-80; P-in-c Kenn 78-80; R Exminster and Kenn from 80; RD Kenn from 89. *The Rectory, Exminster, Exeter EX6 8AD* Exeter (0392) 832283

GOOD, Kenneth Raymond. b 52. TCD BA74 Nottm Univ BA76 NUI HDipEd81 MEd84. St Jo Coll Nottm 75. **d** 77 **p** 78. C Willowfield *D & D* 77-79; Chapl Ashton Sch Cork 79-84; I Dungannstown w Redcross and Conary *D & G* 84-90; I Lurgan (Shankill) *D & D* from 90. *Shankill Rectory, 62 Banbridge Road, Lurgan, Craigavon, Co Armagh BT66 7HG* Lurgan (0762) 323341

GOOD, Canon Kenneth Roy. b 41. K Coll Lon BD66 AKC66. **d** 67 **p** 68. C Stockton St Pet *Dur* 67-70; Chapl Antwerp Miss to Seamen *Eur* 70-74; Japan 74-79; Asst Gen Sec Miss to Seamen 79-85; Asst Chapl St Mich Paternoster Royal *Lon* 79-85; V Nunthorpe *York* from 85; RD Stokesley from 90. *The Vicarage, Nunthorpe, Middlesbrough, Cleveland TS7 0PD* Middlesbrough (0642) 346570

GOOD, Robert Stanley. b 24. TCD BA45 BD47 Kent Univ MA82. **d** 47 **p** 48. Sen Lect Ch Ch Coll Cant 64-78; Fiji 83-87; rtd 87. *44 Ivanhoe Road, Herne Bay, Kent CT6 6EG* Herne Bay (0227) 363561

GOOD, Stuart Eric Clifford. b 37. Wycliffe Hall Ox 63. **d** 64 **p** 65. C Walton H Trin *Ox* 64-67; Australia from 67. *5 Vigna Place, Ferndale, W Australia 6155* Perth (9) 271-9633

GOOD, Canon William Thomas Raymond. b 13. TCD BA39 MA45. **d** 39 **p** 40. Prec Cloyne Cathl *C, C & R* 69-82; I Carrigrohane Union 73-82; Preb Cork Cathl 79-82; rtd 82. *Grange House, Castlemartyr, Co Cork, Irish Republic* Cork (21) 667349

GOODACRE, David Leighton. b 36. Birm Univ DPS69. AKC59. **d** 60 **p** 61. C Stockton St Chad *Dur* 60-63; C Birtley 63-68; Chapl Sunderland Gen Hosp 69-74; P-in-c Ryhope *Dur* 75-81; V Ovingham *Newc* from 81. *St Mary's Vicarage, Ovingham, Northd NE42 6BS* Prudhoe (0661) 32273

GOODACRE, Norman William. b 07. ARIBA32 Liv Univ BArch31 MA33. Westcott Ho Cam 32. **d** 33 **p** 34. V Coniston Cold *Bradf* 45-58; Lic to Offic *Ripon* 58-75; rtd 75; Perm to Offic *Liv* from 76. *81 Holmefield Road, Liverpool L19 3PF* 051-724 4176

GOODALL, George. b 24. LCP. **d** 86 **p** 87. NSM Bretby w Newton Solney *Derby* from 86. *6 Brizlincote Lane, Burton-on-Trent, Staffs DE15 0PR* Burton-on-Trent (0283) 62467

GOODALL, John Llewellyn. b 17. Leeds Univ BA41. Lambeth DipTh59 Sarum & Wells Th Coll 78. **d** 78 **p** 79. Hon C Kentisbeare w Blackborough *Ex* 78-84; rtd 84. *Mayfield, Kentisbeare, Cullompton, Devon EX15 2AA* Kentisbeare (08846) 439

GOODALL, John William. b 45. Hull Univ BA69. Ripon Hall Ox 69. **d** 71 **p** 72. C Loughb Em *Leic* 71-74; C Dorchester *Ox* 74-75; TV Dorchester 75-80; Tutor Sarum & Wells Th Coll 80-88; Asst Dir S Dios Minl Tr Scheme 80-88; P-in-c Gt Wishford *Sarum* 80-83; P-in-c Colehill from 88; Dioc Dir of Readers from 88. *The Vicarage, Smugglers Lane, Colehill, Wimborne, Dorset BH21 2RY* Wimborne (0202) 883721

GOODALL, Jonathan Michael. b 61. R Holloway Coll Lon BMus83. Wycliffe Hall Ox 86. **d** 89 **p** 90. C Bicester w Bucknell, Caversfield and Launton *Ox* from 89. *34 Kennedy Road, Bicester, Oxon OX6 8BQ* Bicester (0869) 253691

GOODALL, Malcolm. b 39. Carl Dioc Tr Course 80. **d** 85 **p** 86. NSM Crosscanonby *Carl* 85-88; NSM Allonby 85-88; C Auckland St Andr and St Anne *Dur* 88-90; V Grindon and Stillington from 90. *The Vicarage, Thorpe Thewles, Stockton-on-Tees, Cleveland TS21 3JU* Sedgefield (0740) 30549

GOODBURN, David Henry. b 41. S'wark Ord Course 73. **d** 76 **p** 77. NSM Enfield SS Pet and Paul *Lon* 76-82; Perm to Offic from 83; NSM Potters Bar *St Alb* 85-88;

Chapl RN from 88. *c/o MOD, Lacon House, Theobald's Road, London WC1X 8RY* 071-430 6847

GOODCHILD, Andrew Philip. b 55. Oak Hill Th Coll BA85. **d** 85 **p** 86. C Barnston *Ches* 85-88; C Hollington St Leon *Chich* 88-89; P-in-c Millbrook *Ches* from 89. *St James's Vicarage, 28 Buckton Vale Road, Stalybridge, Cheshire SK15 3LW* Mossley (0457) 833295

GOODCHILD, Canon John McKillip. b 42. Clare Coll Cam BA64 MA68 Or Coll Ox CertEd69. Wycliffe Hall Ox 67. **d** 69 **p** 70. C Clubmoor *Liv* 69-72; Nigeria 72-83; Hon Can Aba from 74; V Ainsdale *Liv* 83-89; TR Maghull from 89. *The Rectory, 20 Damfield Lane, Maghull, Liverpool L31 6DD* 051-526 5017

✠**GOODCHILD, Rt Rev Ronald Cedric Osbourne.** b 10. Trin Coll Cam BA32 MA35. Bps' Coll Cheshunt 34. **d** 34 **p** 35 **c** 64. C Ealing St Mary *Lon* 34-37; Chapl Oakham Sch Leics 37-42; Chapl RAFVR 42-46; Warden St Mich Ho Hamburg 46-49; Sch Sec SCM 49-53; P-in-c St Helen Bishopsgate w St Martin Outwich *Lon* 51-53; V Horsham *Chich* 53-59; RD Horsham 54-59; Adn Northn *Pet* 59-64; R Ecton 59-64; Can Pet Cathl 62-64; Suff Bp Kensington *Lon* 64-79; Area Bp Kensington 79-80; rtd 80; Asst Bp Ex from 83. *Mead Farm, Welcombe, Hartland, Devon EX39 6HH* Morwenstow (028883) 241

GOODCHILD, Roy John. b 30. Wycliffe Hall Ox 60. **d** 61 **p** 62. C Hayes *Roch* 61-64; C S w N Bersted *Chich* 64-68; R Birdham w W Itchenor 68-73; V Saltdean 74-83; V Hollington St Jo 83-90; V Ticehurst and Flimwell from 90. *The Vicarage, Ticehurst, Wadhurst, E Sussex TN5 7AB* Ticehurst (0580) 200316

GOODDEN, John Maurice Phelips. b 34. Sarum & Wells Th Coll 70. **d** 72 **p** 75. C Weymouth St Mary *Sarum* 72-74; C Harlow New Town w Lt Parndon *Chelmsf* 74-78; Ind Chapl 78-82; Chapl Princess Alexandra Hosp Harlow 78-82; V Moulsham St Jo *Chelmsf* 86-90; R Chipstead *S'wark* from 90; Adv Rural Min from 90. *Tandy Cottage, How Lane, Chipstead, Surrey CR5 3LP* Downland (0737) 552157

GOODE, Allan Kenneth. b 37. S'wark Ord Course. **d** 72 **p** 73. C Belmont *Lon* 72-74; V Liv St Bride w St Sav *Liv* 74-78; V Eccleston Park 78-89; C Billinge from 89. *57 Royden Road, Billinge, Wigan, Lancs WN5 7LP* Billinge (0744) 894557

GOODE, Anthony Thomas Ryall. b 42. Ex Coll Ox BA64 MA71. Cuddesdon Coll 65. **d** 67 **p** 68. C Wolvercote *Ox* 67-71; Chapl RAF 71-91; Asst Chapl-in-Chief RAF from 91; P-in-c Edith Weston w Normanton *Pet* 72-74. *c/o MOD, Adastral House, Theobald's Road, London WC1X 8RU* 071-430 7268

GOODE, John Laurence. b 48. Chich Th Coll. **d** 83 **p** 84. C Crewe St Andr *Ches* 83-86; USPG from 86; Brazil from 87. *c/o USPG, Partnership House, 157 Waterloo Road, London SE1 8XA* 071-928 8681

GOODE, Michael Arthur John. b 40. K Coll Lon BD AKC63. **d** 64 **p** 65. C Sunderland Springwell w Thorney Close *Dur* 64-68; C Solihull *Birm* 68-70; R Fladbury, Wyre Piddle and Moor *Worc* 70-75; P-in-c Foley Park 75-81; V 81-83; RD Kidderminster 81-83; TR Crawley *Chich* from 83. *The Rectory, High Street, Crawley, W Sussex RH10 1BQ* Crawley (0293) 22692

GOODE, Canon Peter William Herbert. b 23. Oak Hill Th Coll 60. **d** 62 **p** 63. C Woodford Wells *Chelmsf* 62-65; V Harold Hill St Paul 65-76; V Gt Warley Ch Ch from 76; RD Brentwood from 89; Hon Can Chelmsf Cathl from 90. *Christ Church Vicarage, 79 Mount Crescent, Brentwood CM14 5DD* Brentwood (0277) 220428

GOODE, William Aubrey. b 08. Bps' Coll Cheshunt 63. **d** 65 **p** 66. V Kirk Fenton *York* 67-76; rtd 76. *Flat 16, Guardian Court, Water Lane, Clifton, York YO3 6PR* York (0904) 655199

GOODER, Martin Lee. b 37. Sheff Univ BSc58. Oak Hill Th Coll 58. **d** 60 **p** 61. C Barrow St Mark *Carl* 60-63; C Halliwell St Pet *Man* 63-66; R Chorlton on Medlock St Sav 66-71; R Brunswick from 71. *The Rectory, Brunswick Street, Manchester M13 9TP* 061-273 2470

GOODERHAM, Daniel Charles. b 24. St Fran Coll Brisbane 49 ACT ThL51. **d** 52 **p** 53. V Ipswich St Bart *St E* 64-71; R Drinkstone 71-78; R Rattlesden 71-78; RD Lavenham 75-78; V Beckenham St Mich w St Aug *Roch* 78-87; P-in-c Whiteparish *Sarum* 87-89; rtd 89. *Limairn, Small Street, Chirton, Devizes, Wilts SN10 3QR* Chirton (038084) 8284

GOODERICK, Peter Handley. b 26. Down Coll Cam BA50 MA52. Linc Th Coll 51. **d** 53 **p** 54. CF (TAVR) 59-74; V Mert St Jas *S'wark* 68-80; P-in-c Baginton *Cov* 80-81; P-in-c Stoneleigh w Ashow 80-81; R Stoneleigh w Ashow and Baginton 81-88; RD Kenilworth 83-90; R Berkswell 88-91; rtd 91; Chapl Malaga w Almunecar

and Nerja *Eur* from 91. *Pasea de Reding 21-2C, 29016 Malaga, Spain* Malaga (52) 225012

GOODERSON, William Dennis. b 09. St Pet Hall Ox BA35 MA39. Wycliffe Hall Ox 35. **d** 36 **p** 37. V Cumnor *Ox* 66-77; rtd 77. *6 Gouldland Gardens, Headington, Oxford OX3 9DQ* Oxford (0865) 62387

GOODFELLOW, Dr Ian. b 37. St Cath Coll Cam BA61 MA65 Lon Univ PGCE76 Dur Univ PhD83. Wells Th Coll 61. **d** 63 **p** 64. C Dunstable *St Alb* 63-67; Chapl Haileybury Coll Herts 67-71; Lect, Chapl and Tutor Bede Coll Dur 71-74; Lect SS Hild & Bede Dur 75-78; Sen Counsellor Open Univ (SW Region) from 79; Perm to Offic *Ex* from 80. *Crosslea, 206 Whitchurch Road, Tavistock, Devon PL19 9DQ* Tavistock (0822) 612069

GOODFIELD, Dudley Francis. b 40. AKC65. **d** 66 **p** 67. C Bath Twerton-on-Avon *B & W* 66-69; C Lache cum Saltney *Ches* 69-71; C Portishead *B & W* 71-76; V Weston-super-Mare St Andr Bournville 76-82; V Ruishton w Thornfalcon from 82. *The Vicarage, Church Lane, Ruishton, Taunton, Somerset TA3 5JW* Henlade (0823) 442269

GOODHAND, Richard. b 51. Sarum & Wells Th Coll 88. **d** 90 **p** 91. C Wollaton *S'well* from 90. *4 Woodbank Drive, Wollaton, Nottingham NG8 2QU* Nottingham (0602) 282779

GOODHEW, Roy William. b 41. Reading Univ BA. S Dios Minl Tr Scheme. **d** 89 **p** 90. C Southn Maybush St Pet Win from 89. *St Peter's House, Lockerley Crescent, Southampton SO1 4BP* Southampton (0703) 775014

GOODIER, Sidney Arthur Richmond. b 17. Kelham Th Coll 34. **d** 41 **p** 42. V S Leigh *Ox* 62-69; rtd 69. *Society of St Francis, The Friary, Hilfield, Dorchester, Dorset* Cerne Abbas (03003) 345

GOODING, Ian Eric. b 42. MIProdE68 CEng69 Leeds Univ BSc63 BCom65. St Jo Coll Nottm 70 Lon Coll of Div LTh72 DPS73. **d** 73 **p** 74. C Wandsworth All SS *S'wark* 73-77; Bp's Ind Adv *Derby* from 77; P-in-c Stanton-by-Dale w Dale Abbey 77-87; R from 87. *The Rectory, Stanton-by-Dale, Ilkeston, Derbyshire DE7 4QA* Ilkeston (0602) 324584

GOODING, John Henry. b 47. St Jo Coll Nottm. **d** 84 **p** 85. C Charles w St Matthias Plymouth *Ex* 84-88; C Leeds St Geo *Ripon* from 88. *45 Clarendon Road, Leeds LS2 9NZ* Leeds (0532) 423833

GOODLAD, Martin Randall. b 39. Sheff City Coll of Educn TDip60. Linc Th Coll 63. **d** 66 **p** 67. C Bramley *Ripon* 66-69; TV Daventry *Pet* 69-71; Asst Dioc Youth Officer 69-71; Asst Dir of Educn *Wakef* 71-74; Youth Work Officer Gen Syn Bd of Educn 74-83; P-in-c Cheam Common St Phil *S'wark* 83-85; V from 85; RD Sutton from 90. *61 Kingsmead Avenue, Worcester Park, Surrey KT4 8UZ* 081-337 1327

GOODLEY, Christopher Ronald. b 47. K Coll Lon BD72 AKC72. **d** 73 **p** 74. C Shenfield *Chelmsf* 73-77; C Hanley H Ev *Lich* 77-78; TV 78-83; Chapl Whittington Hosp Lon 83-86; Chapl St Crispin's Hosp Northn from 88. *24 Eaton Road, Duston, Northampton NN5 6XR* Northampton (0604) 758347

GOODMAN, Preb Denys Charles. b 24. Selw Coll Cam BA49 MA56. Linc Th Coll 49. **d** 51 **p** 52. V Hollington *Man* 57-70; R Bath Bathwick St Mary *B & W* 70-78; P-in-c Bath Bathwick St Jo 76-78; R Bath Bathwick 78-91; RD Bath 81-90; Preb Wells Cathl from 82; rtd 91. *Hollinwood, Johnson Close, Wells, Somerset BH5 3NN* Wells (0749) 675011

GOODMAN, Canon Derek George. b 34. Keble Coll Ox BA57 MA60. Ridley Hall Cam 59. **d** 61 **p** 62. C Attenborough *S'well* 61-65; R Eastwood 65-84; Dioc Insp of Schs 65-89; V Woodthorpe 84-89; Dir of Educn *Leic* from 89; Hon Can Leic Cathl from 90. *1 Brown Avenue, Quorn, Loughborough, Leics LE12 8RH* Quorn (0509) 415692

GOODMAN, Ernest Edwin. b 14. BNC Ox BA49 MA53. Chich Th Coll 53. **d** 54 **p** 55. Perm to Offic *Pet* from 66; R Clayton w Keymer *Chich* 71-79; rtd 79. *52 Roche Way, Wellingborough, Northants NN8 3YD* Wellingborough (0933) 677801

GOODMAN, Frank. b 10. ALCM30 Liv Univ BSc32 DipEd34. Ox NSM Course 73. **d** 75 **p** 76. NSM Beaconsfield *Ox* 75-82; rtd 82; Perm to Offic *Ches* 82-86; Cant 86-89; *Liv* from 89. *38 Somerford House, Nicholas Road, Blundellsands, Liverpool L23 6TS* 051-924 9451

GOODMAN, John. b 20. Selw Coll Cam BA42 MA46. Linc Th Coll 47. **d** 49 **p** 50. V Salisbury St Mark *Sarum* 68-83; R Wool and E Stoke 83-88; rtd 88. *141 Avon Road, Devizes, Wilts SN10 1PY* Devizes (0380) 721267

GOODMAN, John Dennis Julian. b 35. FCA68. Sarum & Wells Th Coll 74. **d** 76 **p** 77. C Cotmanhay *Derby* 76-79; TV Old Brampton and Loundsley Green 79-86; R

Finningley w Auckley *S'well* from 86. *The Rectory, Rectory Lane, Finnigley, Doncaster, S Yorkshire DN9 3DA* Doncaster (0302) 770240

GOODMAN, Mark Alexander Scott. b 61. Lanc Univ BA84 Nottm Univ BTh90. Linc Th Coll 87. **d** 90 **p** 91. C Denton St Lawr *Man* from 90. *17 Town Lane, Denton, Manchester M34 1AF* 061-336 5565

GOODMAN, Peter William. b 60. St Cath Coll Cam BA82. St Jo Coll Nottm 85. **d** 89 **p** 90. C Stapenhill w Cauldwell *Derby* from 89. *27 Brizlincote Street, Burton-on-Trent, Staffs DE15 9DJ* Burton-on-Trent (0283) 34097

GOODMAN, Canon Sidney William. b 10. Kelham Th Coll 27. **d** 33 **p** 34. V Habrough Gp *Linc* 55-71; Can and Preb Linc Cathl 69-79; P-in-c Wold Newton w Hawerby 71-78; rtd 78 *28 Grosvenor Road, Louth, Lincs LN11 0BB* Louth (0507) 603798

GOODMAN, Victor Terence. b 46. CEng MICS Liv Univ BSc. E Midl Min Tr Course. **d** 85 **p** 86. NSM Barwell w Potters Marston and Stapleton *Leic* 85-89; NSM Croft and Stoney Stanton from 89. *1 Washington Close, Barwell, Leicester LE9 8ET* Earl Shilton (0455) 845701

GOODRICH, Very Rev Derek Hugh. b 27. Cam Univ MA. St Steph Ho Ox 50. **d** 52 **p** 53. C Willesden St Andr *Lon* 52-57; Guyana from 57; Adn Bertice 80-84; Dean Georgetown from 84. *The Deanery, 79 Carmichael Street, Georgetown, Guyana* Georgetown (2) 65067

GOODRICH, Canon Peter. b 36. Dur Univ BA58. Cuddesdon Coll 60. **d** 62 **p** 63. C Walton St Jo *Liv* 62-66; C Prescot 66-68; V Anfield St Marg 68-72; V Gt Crosby St Faith 72-83; P-in-c Seaforth 76-80; RD Bootle 78-83; TR Upholland from 83; Hon Can Liv Cathl from 89. *The Rectory, 1A College Road, Up Holland, Skelmersdale, Lancs WN8 0PY* Up Holland (0695) 622936

✠**GOODRICH, Rt Rev Philip Harold Ernest.** b 29. St Jo Coll Cam BA52 MA56. Cuddesdon Coll 52. **d** 54 **p** 55 **c** 73. C Rugby St Andr *Cov* 54-57; Chapl St Jo Coll Cam 57-61; R S Ormsby w Ketsby, Calceby and Driby *Linc* 61-68; R Harrington w Brinkhill 61-68; R Oxcombe 61-68; R Ruckland w Farforth and Maidenwell 61-68; R Somersby w Bag Enderby 61-68; R Tetford and Salmonby 61-68; V Bromley SS Pet and Paul *Roch* 68-73; Suff Bp Tonbridge 73-82; Dioc Dir of Ords 74-82; Bp Worc from 82. *The Bishop's House, Hartlebury Castle, Kidderminster, Worcs DY11 7XX* Hartlebury (0299) 250214

GOODRIDGE, Canon Peter David. b 32. Yale Univ STM84. AKC57. **d** 58 **p** 59. C Eastcote St Lawr *Lon* 58-64; V Tottenham St Phil 64-71; V W Drayton 71-85; P-in-c St Michael Penkevil *Truro* 85-88; P-in-c Lamorran and Merther 85-88; Dir of Educn from 85; Hon Can Truro Cathl from 87. *The Rectory, Ladock, Truro, Cornwall TR2 4PL* St Austell (0726) 882554 or 74352

GOODRIDGE, Canon Sehon Sylvester. b 37. K Coll Lon BD66. Huron Coll Ontario DD77 Codrington Coll Barbados 59. **d** 63 **p** 64. St Lucia 64-66; Jamaica 66-71; Warden & Dep Prin United Th Coll W Indies 69-71; Barbados 71-89; Prin Codrington Coll 71-82; Warden, Counsellor & Sen Lect Univ of W Indies 83-89; Hon Can Barbados from 76; Prin Simon of Cyrene Th Inst from 89. *7 Geraldine Road, London SW18 2NR* 081-874 1353 or 874 8905

GOODRUM, Mrs Alice. b 30. Lightfoot Ho Dur 58. **dss** 80 **d** 87. Fenham St Jas and St Basil *Newc* 80-87; C 87-91; rtd 91. *32 Auburn Gardens, Newcastle upon Tyne NE4 9XP* 091-274 0022

GOODSELL, Patrick. b 32. BA88. Linc Th Coll 62. **d** 64 **p** 65. C Thornton Heath St Jude *Cant* 64-65; C Croydon St Jo *S'wark* 65-70; V Tenterden St Mich *Cant* 70-78; P-in-c Sellindge w Monks Horton and Stowting 78-84; P-in-c Lympne w W Hythe 82-84; V Sellindge w Monks Horton and Stowting etc from 84. *The Vicarage, Harringe Lane, Sellindge, Ashford, Kent TN25 6HP* Sellindge (0303) 813168

GOODSON, Paul Frederick. b 34. Qu Coll Birm DipTh61. **d** 62 **p** 63. C Mile End Old Town H Trin *Lon* 62-65; C Liv Our Lady and St Nic w St Anne *Liv* 65-68; V Skerton St Luke *Blackb* 68-74; V Poulton-le-Fylde 74-85. *30 Tudor Avenue, Stalybridge, Cheshire SK15 3EL* 061-303 2707

GOODWIN, Barry Frederick John. b 48. Birm Univ BSc69 PhD77. St Jo Coll Nottm LTh88. **d** 88 **p** 89. C Ware Ch Ch *St Alb* 88-91; P-in-c Stanstead Abbots from 91. *The Vicarage, 25 Hoddesdon Road, Stanstead Abbotts, Ware, Herts SG12 8EG* Ware (0920) 870115

GOODWIN, Deryck William. b 27. Birm Univ BSc48 MSc49 PhD51. NW Ord Course 74. **d** 77 **p** 78. Sen Lect York Univ 77-86; Hon C Elvington w Sutton on Derwent and E Cottingwith *York* 77-86; V Burton Pidsea and Humbleton w Elsternwick 86-90; R Newton w Newton,

Levisham and Lockton from 90. *The Vicarage, Middleton, Pickering, N Yorkshire YO18 8NX* Pickering (0751) 74858

GOODWIN, Canon John Fletcher Beckles. b 20. Jes Coll Cam BA43 MA46. Ridley Hall Cam 42. **d** 45 **p** 46. V Mert *Ox* 62-70; V Heanor *Derby* 70-74; V Hazelwood 74-85; V Turnditch 74-85; Adv for In-Service Tr and Chapl to Bp 74-88; Hon Can Derby Cathl 81-85; rtd 85; Perm to Offic *Derby* from 85. *63 Ladywood Avenue, Belper, Derby DE5 1HT* Belper (0773) 820844

GOODWIN, Ronald Victor. S'wark Ord Course. **d** 86 **p** 87. NSM Wickford and Runwell *Chelmsf* from 86. *164 Southend Road, Wickford, Essex SS11 8EH* Wickford (0268) 734447

GOODWIN, Stephen. b 58. Sheff Univ BA80. Cranmer Hall Dur 82. **d** 85 **p** 86. C Lytham St Cuth *Blackb* 85-87; C W Burnley 88-90; TV Headley All SS *Guildf* from 90. *St Mark's Vicarage, 58 Forest Road, Bordon, Hants GU35 0BP* Bordon (0420) 477550

GOODWIN, Mrs Susan Elizabeth. b 51. Leeds Poly BSc74 Leeds Univ MSc76. St Jo Coll Dur 82. **dss** 84 **d** 87. Norton Woodseats St Chad *Sheff* 84-87; Par Dn 87; Chapl Scargill Ho N Yorkshire 87-89; NSM W Burnley *Blackb* 89-90; NSM Headley All SS *Guildf* from 90; Past Asst Acorn Chr Healing Trust from 91. *St Mark's Vicarage, 58 Forest Road, Bordon, Hants GU35 0BP* Bordon (0420) 477550

GOODWINS, Christopher William Hedley. b 36. St Jo Coll Cam BA58 MA62. Linc Th Coll 62. **d** 64 **p** 65. C Lowestoft Ch Ch *Nor* 64-69; V Tamerton Foliot *Ex* from 69; P-in-c Southway 78-82. *St Mary's Vicarage, Tamerton Foliot, Plymouth, Devon PL5 4NH* Plymouth (0752) 771033

GOOK, Bernard William James. b 19. Oak Hill Th Coll 40. **d** 43 **p** 44. V Walthamstow St Luke *Chelmsf* 50-55; Australia from 55; rtd 84. *43 Glenview Road, Mount Kuringai, NSW, Australia 2080* Sydney (2) 457-9923

GOOLD, Peter John. b 44. Lon Univ BD74. St Steph Ho Ox 67. **d** 70 **p** 71. C Chiswick St Nic w St Mary *Lon* 70-73; Chapl Asst R Masonic Hosp Lon 73-74; Chapl Asst Basingstoke Distr Hosp 74-77; Chapl from 80; Chapl R Marsden Hosp Lon and Surrey 77-80. *Basingstoke District Hospital, Aldermaston Road, Basingstoke, Hants RG24 9NA* Basingstoke (0256) 473202

GORDON, Alan Rex. b 19. Bps' Coll Cheshunt 51. **d** 53 **p** 54. V Perry Street *Roch* 60-83; C Headington Quarry *Ox* 83-90; rtd 90. *33 North Way, Oxford OX3 9ES* Oxford (0865) 68509

GORDON, Alexander Ronald. b 49. Nottm Univ BPharm71 Leeds Univ DipTh76. Coll of Resurr Mirfield 74. **d** 77 **p** 78. C Headingley *Ripon* 77-80; C Fareham SS Pet and Paul *Portsm* 80-83; V Cudworth *Wakef* 83-85; Hon C Tain *Mor* 85-88; P-in-c Lairg Miss from 87; P-in-c Brora from 88; P-in-c Dornoch from 88; Dioc Dir of Ords from 89. *The Grange, Lochside, Lairg, Sutherland IV27 4EG* Lairg (0549) 2295

✠**GORDON, Rt Rev Archibald Ronald McDonald.** b 27. Ball Coll Ox BA50 MA52. Cuddesdon Coll 50. **d** 52 **p** 53 **c** 75. C Stepney St Dunstan and All SS *Lon* 52-55; Chapl Cuddesdon Coll 55-59; Lic to Offic *Ox* 57-59; V Birm St Pet *Birm* 59-67; Lect Qu Coll Birm 60-62; Can Res Birm Cathl *Birm* 67-71; V Ox St Mary V w St Cross and St Pet *Ox* 71-75; Bp Portsm 75-84; Bp at Lambeth (Hd of Staff) *Cant* from 84; Asst Bp S'wark from 84; Bp HM Forces 85-90. *Lambeth Palace, London SE1 7JU* 071-928 8282

GORDON, Bruce Harold Clark. b 40. Hull Univ DipMin87. St Jo Coll Dur 65. **d** 68 **p** 69. C Edin St Jas *Edin* 68-71; C Blackheath St Jo *S'wark* 71-74; R Duns *Edin* 74-90; R Langton *Glas* from 90; R Douglas from 90. *The Rectory, 1 Cleghorn Road, Lanark ML11 7QT* Lanark (0555) 3065

GORDON, Donald Ian. b 30. Nottm Univ BA52 PhD64. Westcott Ho Cam 71. **d** 71 **p** 72. NSM Newport *Chelmsf* 71-75; NSM Creeksea w Althorne, Latchingdon and N Fambridge from 76. *Holden House, Steeple Road, Latchingdon, Chelmsford CM3 6JX* Maldon (0621) 740296

GORDON, Edward John. b 32. Univ of Wales BA52. St Mich Coll Llan 52. **d** 55 **p** 56. C Baglan *Llan* 55-61; C Newc 61-65; C Laleston w Tythegston 61-65; V Ynyshir 65-69; C Bramhall *Ches* 69-72; V Cheadle Hulme All SS 72-79; V Tranmere St Paul w St Luke 79-88; V Sandbach Heath from 88; Chapl Arclid Hosp from 90. *The Heath Vicarage, School Lane, Sandbach, Cheshire CW11 0LS* Crewe (0270) 768826

✠**GORDON, Rt Rev George Eric.** b 05. St Cath Coll Cam BA27 MA31. Wycliffe Hall Ox 27. **d** 29 **p** 30 **c** 66. C

Leic H Trin *Leic* 29-31; Vice-Prin Bp Wilson Th Coll 31-35; Prin 35-42; Bp's Dom Chapl *S & M* 35-42; R Kersal Moor *Man* 42-45; R Middleton 45-51; RD Middleton 45-51; Provost Chelmsf 51-66; Dean St German's Cathl *S & M* 66-74; Bp S & M 66-74; rtd 74; Perm to Offic *Ox* from 74. *Cobden, 45 Queen Street, Eynsham, Oxford OX8 1HH* Oxford (0865) 881378

GORDON, John Michael. b 30. CITC. d 83 p 84. NSM Dub St Geo *D & G* 83-85; NSM Dub Irishtown w Donnybrook from 85. *Ferndale House, Rathmichael, Shankill, Co Dublin, Irish Republic* Dublin (1) 282-2421

GORDON, Jonathan Andrew. b 61. Keele Univ BA83 Southn Univ BTh88. Sarum & Wells Th Coll. d 87 p 88. C Wallingford w Crowmarsh Gifford etc *Ox* from 87. *23 Charter Way, Wallingford, Oxon OX10 0PA* Wallingford (0491) 36353

GORDON, Canon Kenneth Davidson. b 35. Edin Univ MA57. Tyndale Hall Bris 58. d 60 p 61. C St Helens St Helen *Liv* 60-66; V Daubhill *Man* 66-71; R Bieldside *Ab* from 71; Can St Andr Cathl from 81. *St Devenick's Rectory, Bieldside, Aberdeen AB1 9AP* Aberdeen (0224) 861552

GORDON, Robert Andrew. b 42. d 84 p 85. C Bargoed and Deri w Brithdir *Llan* 84-87; V Aberpergwm and Blaengwrach from 87. *The Vicarage, 11 Roberts Close, Glyn Neath, Neath, W Glam SA11 5HR* Neath (0639) 721964

GORDON, Robert Douglas. b 57. Hull Univ BSc. Trin Coll Bris BA87. d 87 p 88. C Bridgwater St Fran *B & W* 87-90; C Street w Walton from 90. *Walton Rectory, Street, Somerset BA16 9QQ* Street (0458) 42044

GORDON, Robert John. b 56. Edin Univ MA81. Wycliffe Hall Ox 87. d 89 p 90. C Wilnecote *Lich* from 89. *5 Avill, Hockley, Tamworth, Staffs B77 5QE* Tamworth (0827) 251816

GORDON, Thomas William. b 57. QUB BEd80 Univ of Ulster MA86 TCD BTh89. CITC 85. d 89 p 90. C Ballymacash *Conn* 89-91; Min Can Belf Cathl from 90; Chapl & Tutor CITC from 91. *Chaplain's Residence, CITC, Braemor Park, Rathgar, Dublin 14, Irish Republic* Dublin (1) 975506 or 975590

GORDON CLARK, Charles Philip. b 36. Worc Coll Ox BA59 MA61. Cuddesdon Coll 61. d 62 p 63. C Haslemere *Guildf* 62-65; Chapl Tonbridge Sch Kent 65-68; R Keston *Roch* 68-74; V Tunbridge Wells K Chas 74-86; Perm to Offic *S & B* from 86. *4 Danyrallt, Llaneglwys, Builth Wells, Powys LD2 3BJ* Builth Wells (0982) 560656

GORDON CLARK, John Vincent Michael. b 29. FCA DipRS. S'wark Ord Course 73. d 76 p 77. NSM Guildf H Trin w St Mary *Guildf* 76-81; NSM Albury w St Martha from 81. *Hillfield, 8 Little Warren Close, Guildford GU4 8PW* Guildford (0483) 69027

GORDON-CUMMING, Henry Ian. b 28. Called to the Bar (Gray's Inn) 56. Oak Hill Th Coll 54. d 57 p 58. C Southsea St Jude *Portsm* 57-60; Uganda 61-68; V Virginia Water *Guildf* 68-78; R Busbridge 78-87; V Lynch w Iping Marsh and Milland *Chich* from 87. *The Rectory, Milland, Liphook, Hants GU30 7LU* Milland (042876) 285

GORDON-KERR, Canon Francis Alexander. b 39. Dur Univ BA64 MA67 Hull Univ PhD81 DipEd. Wycliffe Hall Ox 65. d 67 p 68. C Heworth St Mary *Dur* 67-70; Chapl Newc Poly *Newc* 70-75; Chapl Hull Univ *York* 75-82; Clergy Tr Officer E Riding from 82; V Welton w Melton from 82; AD W Hull Deanery 87-89; RD Hull from 89; Can and Preb York Minster from 89. *St Helen's Vicarage, Welton, Brough, N Humberside HU15 1ND* Hull (0482) 666677

GORE, Canon John Charles. b 29. Leeds Univ BA52. Coll of Resurr Mirfield 52. d 54 p 55. C Middlesb St Jo the Ev *York* 54-59; N Rhodesia 59-64; Zambia 64-75; Can Lusaka 70-75; R Elland *Wakef* 75-84; TR 84-86; RD Brighouse and Elland 77-86; V Wembley Park St Aug *Lon* from 86; P-in-c Tokyngton St Mich 89-90; AD Brent from 90. *The Vicarage, 13 Forty Avenue, Wembley, Middx HA9 8JL* 081-904 4089

GORE, Canon John Harrington. b 24. Em Coll Cam BA49 MA52. Westcott Ho Cam 49. d 51 p 52. R Deal St Leon *Cant* 67-75; RD Sandwich 70-78; P-in-c Sholden 74-75; R Deal St Leon w Sholden 75-80; R Southchurch H Trin *Chelmsf* 80-90; RD Southend-on-Sea 84-89; Hon Can Chelmsf Cathl 86-90; rtd 90; Perm to Offic *St E* from 90. *8 De Burgh Place, Clare, Suffolk CO10 8QL* Clare (0787) 278558

GORHAM, Andrew Arthur. b 51. Bris Univ BA73 Birm Univ DipTh78 MA87. Qu Coll Birm 77. d 79 p 80. C Plaistow St Mary *Roch* 79-82; Chapl Lanchester Poly *Cov* 82-87; TV Warw from 87. *The Vicarage, The Butts, Warwick CV34 4SS* Warwick (0926) 491132

GORICK, David Charles. b 32. Reading Univ BA55 Nottm Univ DipEd72. E Midl Min Tr Course 81. d 84 p 85. NSM W Bridgford *S'well* 84-89; P-in-c Gotham from 89. *The New Rectory, 39 Leake Road, Gotham, Notts NG11 0JL* Nottingham (0602) 830608

GORICK, Janet Margaret. d 87. Hon Par Dn W Bridgford *S'well* from 87. *The New Rectory, Leake Road, Gotham, Nottingham NG11 0JL* Nottingham (0602) 830608

GORICK, Martin Charles William. b 62. Selw Coll Cam BA84 MA88. Ripon Coll Cuddesdon 85. d 87 p 88. C Birtley *Dur* 87-90; Bp's Dom Chapl *Ox* from 91. *55 Marsh Lane, Oxford OX3 0NQ* Oxford (0865) 67946

GORIN, Walter. b 10. Lon Univ BA32 AKC32. Lich Th Coll 39. d 41 p 43. R Gt and Lt Saxham w Westley *St E* 69-79; rtd 79; Perm to Offic *St E* from 79. *16 Samuel Street Walk, Bury St Edmunds, Suffolk IP33 2PQ* Bury St Edmunds (0284) 702110

GORNALL, William Brian. b 36. OStJ SRN58. Ely Th Coll 61. d 64 p 65. C Blackpool St Mich *Blackb* 64-67; C Cheshunt *St Alb* 67-69; P-in-c Blackb St Pet w All SS *Blackb* 69-75; Hon Chapl and Lect Blackb Coll of Tech 69-75; V Blackb St Pet w All SS 75-79; V Blackpool St Mich 79-84; V Torrisholme from 84. *Ascension Vicarage, 63 Michaelson Avenue, Morecambe, Lancs LA4 6SF* Morecambe (0524) 413144

GORRIE, Richard Bingham. b 27. Univ Coll Ox BA49 MA53. Ridley Hall Cam 49. d 51 p 52. C Ox St Clem *Ox* 51-54; C Morden *S'wark* 54-56; Scripture Union Rep (Scotland) from 56; Chapl Fettes Coll Edin 60-74; Dir Inter-Sch Chr Fellowship (Scotland) 74-80. *9 Canal Street, Glasgow G4 0AB* 041-637 5946

GORRINGE, Timothy Jervis. b 46. St Edm Hall Ox BA69 MPhil75. Sarum Th Coll 69. d 72 p 73. C Chapel Allerton *Ripon* 72-75; C Ox St Mary V w St Cross and St Pet *Ox* 76-78; India 79-86; Chapl St Jo Coll Ox from 86. *St John's College, Oxford OX1 3JP* Oxford (0865) 277351

GORTON, Anthony David Trevor. b 39. Lon Univ BSc65. Oak Hill Th Coll 78. d 81 p 82. Hon C Colney Heath St Mark *St Alb* from 81. *Waterdell, Lane End, Hatfield, Herts AL10 9DU* Hatfield (0707) 263605

GORTON, Ian Charles Johnson. b 62. Bp Otter Coll BA84 Sarum & Wells Th Coll 86. d 89 p 90. C Wythenshawe Wm Temple Ch *Man* from 89. *51 Hilary Road, Woodhouse Park, Manchester M22 6PQ* 061-437 3194

GOSDEN, Timothy John. b 50. Open Univ BA86. Chich Th Coll 74. d 77 p 78. C Cant All SS *Cant* 77-81; Asst Chapl Loughb Univ *Leic* 81-85; Lic to Offic *Cant* 85-87; Chapl Ch Ch Coll Cant 85-87; Sen Chapl Hull Univ *York* from 87. *302 Cottingham Road, Hull HU6 8QA* Hull (0482) 43769

GOSHAI, Miss Veja Helena. b 32. SRN57 SCM59 MTD62. Trin Coll Bris 75. d 87. Asst Chapl St Bart Hosp Lon from 87; rtd 91. *7 Freemens Houses, Ferndale Road, London SW9*

GOSLING, Dr David Lagourie. b 39. MInstP69 CPhys84 Man Univ MSc63 Fitzw Coll Cam MA69 Lanc Univ PhD74. Ridley Hall Cam 63. d 73 p 74. Hon C Lanc St Mary *Blackb* 73-74; Hon C Kingston upon Hull St Matt w St Barn *York* 74-77; Hon C Cottingham 78-83; Lic to Offic *Eur* 83-84 and from 88; Chapl Geneva 84-88; C Cam Gt St Mary w St Mich *Ely* from 89; P-in-c Dry Drayton from 90. *39 Maids Causeway, Cambridge CB5 8DE* Cambridge (0223) 322111

GOSLING, James Albert. b 41. Oak Hill Th Coll. d 84 p 85. Lic to Offic *Chelmsf* from 84. *1 Gardner Road, London E13 8LN* 071-476 4564

GOSLING, John William Fraser. b 34. St Jo Coll Dur BA58 DipTh60 MA71 Ex Univ PhD78. Cranmer Hall Dur 58. d 60 p 61. C Plympton St Mary *Ex* 60-68; V Newport 68-78; Org Sec (Dios St Alb and Ox) CECS 78-82; C Stratford sub Castle *Sarum* 83-86; Adv on Cont Minl Educn 83-86; Perm to Offic 86-91; C Swindon Ch Ch *Bris* from 91. *42 Henrietta Court, Marlborough Road, Swindon SN3 1QJ* Swindon (0793) 619782

GOSNELL, Nicholas. b 58. SRN81 Southn Univ BTh91. Chich Th Coll 85. d 88 p 89. C Prestbury *Glouc* from 88; CF from 89. *Oak Cottage, Blacksmith's Lane, Prestbury, Cheltenham, Glos GL52 5JA* Cheltenham (0242) 235349

GOSS, Arthur John Knill. b 10. St Jo Coll Dur BA34 MA37 DipTh37. d 35 p 36. V Worthing Ch Ch *Chich* 66-71; R Buxted St Marg 71-76; rtd 76. *9 By Sunte, Lindfield, W Sussex RH16 2DG* Haywards Heath (0444) 414471

GOSS, David James. b 52. Nottm Univ BCombStuds. Linc Th Coll. d 83 p 84. C Wood Green St Mich w Bounds Green St Gabr etc *Lon* 83-86; TV Gleadless Valley *Sheff* 86-89; TR from 89. *Holy Cross Vicarage,*

Spotswood Mount, Sheffield S14 1LG   Sheffield (0742) 398852

GOSS, Michael John. b 37. Chich Th Coll 62. **d** 65 **p** 66. C Angell Town St Jo *S'wark* 65-68; C Catford St Laur 68-71; P-in-c Lewisham St Swithun 71-81; V Redhill St Jo 81-88; V Dudley St Thos and St Luke *Worc* from 88. *The Vicarage, King Street, Dudley, W Midlands DY2 8QB*   Dudley (0384) 252015

GOSS, Very Rev Thomas Ashworth. b 12. St Andr Univ MA36. Ridley Hall Cam 35. **d** 37 **p** 38. QHC from 66; R Jersey St Sav *Win* 67-71; Dean Jersey 71-85; Hon Can Win Cathl 71-85; R Jersey St Helier 71-85; rtd 85. *Les Pignons, Mont de la Rosiere, Jersey, Channel Islands*   Jersey (0534) 61433

GOSSWINN, Nicholas Simon. b 50. Birm Poly FGA80. St D Coll Lamp DipTh73. **d** 73 **p** 77. C Abergavenny St Mary *Mon* 73-74; C-in-c Bassaleg 74-80; TV Barrow St Geo w St Luke *Carl* 81-87; C Usworth *Dur* 89-90, TV from 90. *Usworth Vicarage, 14 Prestwick Close, Washington, Tyne and Wear NE37 2LP*   091-415 0843

GOSWELL, Geoffrey. b 34. SS Paul & Mary Coll Cheltenham CertEd68. Glouc Th Course 70. **d** 71 **p** 72. C Cheltenham Em *Glouc* 71-73; C Lydney w Aylburton 73-76; P-in-c Falfield w Rockhampton 76-79; Chapl HM Det Cen Eastwood Park 76-79; Area Sec CMS (Dios Linc and Pet) 79-86; Dio Ely 79-81; CMS Dep Reg Sec (UK) from 86; P-in-c Orton Waterville *Ely* from 90. *The Vicarage, 34 Overton Way, Orton Waterville, Peterborough PE2 0HF*   Peterborough (0733) 238877

GOTELEE, Peter Douglas. b 28. K Coll Lon 50. **d** 54 **p** 55. C Croydon St Pet S End *Cant* 54-57; C Camberley St Paul *Guildf* 57-65; P-in-c Badshot Lea CD 65-75; P-in-c Bisley 75-76; V W End 75-76; R Bisley and W End 76-85; V Yarcombe w Membury and Upottery *Ex* from 85; P-in-c Cotleigh from 85. *The Vicarage, Yarcombe, Honiton, Devon EX14 9BD*   Upottery (040486) 561

GOTT, Joseph Desmond. b 26. Ch Ch Ox BA47 MA51 St Chad's Coll Dur DipTh52. **d** 52 **p** 53. V Down Ampney *Glouc* 66-72; PC Poulton 66-69; V 69-72; V Cheltenham St Steph 72-89; rtd 89. *3 Avonmore, 24 Granville Road, Eastbourne, E Sussex BH20 7HA*   Eastbourne (0323) 36222

GOUGE, Canon Frank. b 16. St Pet Hall Ox BA38 MA45. Wycliffe Hall Ox 38. **d** 40 **p** 41. V Hall Green Ascension *Birm* 67-84; RD Solihull 68-79; Hon Can Birm Cathl 73-84; rtd 84; Perm to Offic *Cov* from 84. *39 Campden Road, Shipston-on-Stour, Warks CV36 4DH*   Shipston-on-Stour (0608) 61789

GOUGH, Andrew Stephen. b 60. Sarum & Wells Th Coll 83. **d** 86 **p** 87. C St Leonards Ch Ch and St Mary *Chich* 86-88; C Broseley w Benthall *Heref* 88-90; V Ketley and Oakengates *Lich* from 90. *Holy Trinity Vicarage, Holyhead Road, Oakengates, Telford, Shropshire TF2 6BN*   Telford (0952) 612926

GOUGH, Anthony Jobson. b 39. FCA62. Ridley Hall Cam 75. **d** 77 **p** 78. C Rushden w Newton Bromswold *Pet* 77-81; V Lyddington w Stoke Dry and Seaton 81-89. *77 Redwood Avenue, Melton Mowbray, Leics*   Melton Mowbray (0664) 67197

GOUGH, Dr Anthony Walter. b 31. Lon Univ DipTh68 Leic Univ MA76. Chicago Th Sem DMin81 Oak Hill Th Coll 57. **d** 60 **p** 61. C Southsea St Simon *Portsm* 60-64; R Peldon *Chelmsf* 64-71; V Rothley *Leic* 71-80; USA 80-81; Chapl St Jo Hosp Aylesbury 81-82; Perm to Offic *Leic* from 82. *410 Hinckley Road, Leicester LE3 0WA*   Leicester (0533) 854284

GOUGH, Colin Richard. b 47. St Chad's Coll Dur BA69. Cuddesdon Coll 73. **d** 75 **p** 76. C Lich St Chad *Lich* 75-78; C Codsall 78-84; V Wednesbury St Paul Wood Green from 84. *The Vicarage, Wood Green Road, Wednesbury, W Midlands WS10 9QT*   021-556 0687

GOUGH, David Norman. b 42. Oak Hill Th Coll 70. **d** 70 **p** 71. C Penn Fields *Lich* 70-73; C Stapenhill w Cauldwell *Derby* 73-77; V Heath 77-86; P-in-c Derby St Chad from 86. *81 Palmerston Street, Derby DE3 6PF*   Derby (0332) 760846

GOUGH, Derek William. b 31. Pemb Coll Cam BA55 MA59. St Steph Ho Ox 55. **d** 57 **p** 58. C E Finchley All SS *Lon* 57-60; C Roxbourne St Andr 60-66; V Edmonton St Mary w St Jo from 66. *St John's Vicarage, Dysons Road, London N18 2DS*   081-807 2767

GOUGH, Ernest Hubert. b 31. TCD BA53 MA57. **d** 54 **p** 55. C Glenavy *Conn* 54-57; C Lisburn Ch Ch 57-61; P-in-c Belf St Ninian 61-62; I 62-71; I Belf St Bart 71-85; I Templepatrick w Donegore from 85. *The Vicarage, 926 Antrim Road, Templepatrick, Ballyclare, Co Antrim BT39 0AT*   Templepatrick (08494) 32300

GOUGH, Frank Peter. b 32. Lon Coll of Div 66. **d** 68 **p** 69. C Weymouth St Mary *Sarum* 68-70; C

Attenborough w Chilwell *S'well* 70-73; R Barrow *Ches* 73-77; P-in-c Summerstown *S'wark* 77-88; RD Tooting 80-88; Dioc Past Sec from 88. *c/o Southwark Diocesan Office, 94 Lambeth Road, London SE1 7PS*   071-928 6637

✠**GOUGH, Rt Rev Hugh Rowlands.** b 05. CMG55 OBE45 TD50. Trin Coll Cam BA27 MA31. Lambeth DD59 ACT Hon ThD59 Lon Coll of Div 28. **d** 28 **p** 29 **c** 48. C Islington St Mary *Lon* 28-31; V 46-48; R Walcot *B & W* 31-34; V Carlisle St Jas 34-39; V Bayswater *Lon* 39-46; CF (TA) 39-45; RD Islington *Lon* 46-48; Preb St Paul's Cathl 48; Adn W Ham *Chelmsf* 48-58; Suff Bp Barking 48-58; Abp Sydney 58-66; Primate of Australia 59-66; R Freshford w Limpley Stoke *B & W* 67-72; rtd 72. *Forge House, Over Wallop, Stockbridge, Hants SO20 8JF*   Andover (0264) 781315

GOUGH, Jonathan Robin Blanning. b 62. Univ of Wales (Lamp) BA83. St Steph Ho Ox 83. **d** 85 **p** 86. C Braunton *Ex* 85-86; C Matson *Glouc* 86-89; CF from 89, *c/o MOD (Army), Bagshot Park, Bagshot, Surrey GU19 5PL*   Bagshot (0276) 71717

GOUGH, Martyn John. b 66. Univ of Wales (Cardiff) 84. St Steph Ho Ox 88. **d** 90 **p** 91. C Port Talbot St Theodore *Llan* from 90. *89 Talbot Road, Port Talbot, W Glam SA13 1LB*   Port Talbot (0639) 897017

GOUGH, Robert. b 50. S'wark Ord Course. **d** 82 **p** 83. C Heston *Lon* 82-83; C Feltham 83-86; TV Hemel Hempstead *St Alb* 86-90. *15 Woodbines Avenue, Kingston upon Thames, Surrey KT1 2AZ*   081-546 2644

GOUGH, Stephen William Cyprian. b 50. Alberta Univ BSc71. Cuddesdon Coll BA80. **d** 79 **p** 80. C Walton St Mary *Liv* 79-83; V New Springs 83-87; V Childwall St Dav from 87. *St David's Vicarage, Rocky Lane, Liverpool L16 1JA*   051-722 4549

GOULD, Alan Charles. b 26. Lon Univ DipTh53. **d** 62 **p** 63. V Audlem and Burleydam *Ches* 67-80; P-in-c Coreley w Doddington *Heref* 80-83; V Knowbury 80-83; P-in-c Berrington and Betton Strange 83-91; P-in-c Cound 83-91; rtd 91. *32 Mytton Oak Road, Shrewsbury SY3 8UD*   Shrewsbury (0743) 244820

GOULD, David Robert. b 59. Cov Poly BA81. Cranmer Hall Dur 87. **d** 90 **p** 91. C Rugby St Andr *Cov* from 90. *12 Park Walk, Rugby, Warks CV21 2QP*   Rugby (0788) 542310

GOULD, Preb Douglas Walter. b 35. St Jo Coll Cam BA59 MA63. Ridley Hall Cam 59. **d** 61 **p** 62. C Clifton York 61-64; C Bridgnorth w Tasley *Heref* 64-67; C Astley Abbotts w Linley 64-67; R Acton Burnell w Pitchford 67-73; P-in-c Cound 68-73; Asst Dioc Youth Officer 68-73; P-in-c Frodesley 69-73; RD Bromyard from 73; Chapl Bromyard Hosp from 73; P-in-c Ocle Pychard *Heref* 76-88; P-in-c Ullingswick 76-88; P-in-c Stoke Lacy, Moreton Jeffries w Much Cowarne etc 76-83; Preb Heref Cathl from 83. *The Vicarage, 28 Church Lane, Bromyard, Herefordshire HR7 4DZ*   Bromyard (0885) 482438

GOULD, Gerald. b 37. S Dios Minl Tr Scheme 84. **d** 86 **p** 87. C Hedge End Win 86-89; V St Goran w St Mich Caerhays *Truro* from 89. *The Vicarage, Gorran, St Austell, Cornwall PL26 6HN*   Mevagissey (0726) 842229

GOULD, Canon Jack. b 15. **d** 45 **p** 47. V Kingswear *Ex* 71-85; rtd 85; Perm to Offic *Ex* from 85. *140 Northfields Lane, Brixham, Devon TQ5 8RH*   Brixham (08045) 55397

GOULD, John Barry. b 38. MICE68. S'wark Ord Course 77. **d** 77 **p** 78. C Streatham St Leon *S'wark* 77-80; V Upper Tooting H Trin 80-87; P-in-c Brockham Green 87-90; P-in-c Betchworth from 87; P-in-c Buckland from 87. *The Vicarage, Old Reigate Road, Betchworth, Surrey RH3 7DE*   Betchworth (073784) 2102

GOULD, Peter Richard. b 34. Univ of Wales BA57. Qu Coll Birm DipTh62. **d** 62 **p** 63. C Rothwell *Ripon* 62-68; V Allerton Bywater 68-73; Lic to Offic *S'well* 73-76; Chapl Lic Victuallers' Sch Ascot from 76. *17 Sussex Place, Slough, Berks SL1 1NH*   Ascot (0344) 882770

GOULD, Robert Douglas. b 21. MBE46. Wells Th Coll 58. **d** 60 **p** 61. OGS from 62; V Upper Clapton St Matt *Lon* 68-79; V Stamford Hill St Thos 70-79; Chapl Community St Jo Bapt Clewer 79-86; rtd 86; Perm to Offic *Ox* 86-89; *Lon* & *S'wark* from 89. *5 Down, The Quadrangle, Morden College, London SE3 0PW*   081-293 4970

GOULD, Robert Ozburn. b 38. Williams Coll Mass BA59 St Andr Univ PhD63. **d** 78 **p** 83. NSM Edin St Columba *Edin* 78-80; TV from 83; Hon Dioc Supernumerary 80-83. *33 Charterhall Road, Edinburgh EH9 3HS*   031-667 7230

GOULD, Ms Susan Judith. b 61. BSc83. St Jo Coll Nottm DTS90. **d** 91. Par Dn Stokesley *York* from

91. *25 Riversdene, Stokesley, Middlesbrough, Cleveland TS9 5DD* Stokesley (0642) 710911

GOULDEN, Joseph Notley. b 19. TCD BA41 Div Test42 TCD MA50. **d** 42 **p** 43. I Ramoan *Conn* 54-78; RD Carey 61-78; rtd 78. *15 Clare Road, Ballycastle, Co Antrim BT54 6DB* Ballycastle (02657) 62778

GOULDING, Charles John. b 18. Sarum Th Coll 56. **d** 58 **p** 59. V Ardleigh *Chelmsf* 63-72; V Shrub End 72-84; RD Colchester 81-84; rtd 84; Hon C Fovant, Sutton Mandeville and Teffont Evias etc *Sarum* 84-86; Hon C Mayfield *Chich* 86-89. *Flat 3, 3 Moat Croft Road, Eastbourne, E Sussex BN21 1ND* Eastbourne (0323) 20208

GOULDING, Edward William. b 23. St Aid Birkenhead 54. **d** 56 **p** 57. Chapl HM Pris Birm 69-72; V Gt Harwood St Bart *Blackb* 73-76; Lic to Offic 76-78; V Wray w Tatham Fells 78-87; rtd 88. *2 The Sycamores, Greenhead, Carlisle CA6 7HB* Gilsland (06977) 47688

GOULDING, John Gilbert. b 29. Univ Coll Dur BA54 MA59. **d** 88 **p** 89. NSM Kemsing w Woodlands *Roch* from 88; Hon Nat Moderator for Reader Tr ACCM 90-91; ABM from 91. *50 Copperfields, Kemsing, Sevenoaks, Kent TN15 6QG* Sevenoaks (0732) 62558

GOULDING, Leonard William. b 08. OBE73. **d** 34 **p** 35. V Canwick *Linc* 63-75; rtd 75. *11 Clarke Avenue, Heighington, Lincoln LN4 1TE* Lincoln (0522) 792970

GOULDSTONE, Preb Timothy Maxwell. b 46. Ex Univ BSc68 MSc76. Trin Coll Bris 76. **d** 78 **p** 79. C Ware Ch Ch *St Alb* 78-81; P-in-c Ansley *Cov* 81-82; V 82-85; V St Keverne *Truro* from 85; Preb St Endellion from 90. *The Vicarage, St Keverne, Helston, Cornwall TR12 6NG* St Keverne (0326) 280227

GOULSTONE, Ven Thomas Richard Kerry. b 36. Univ of Wales (Lamp) BA57. St Mich Coll Llan 57. **d** 59 **p** 60. C Llanbadarn Fawr *St D* 59-61; C Carmarthen St Pet 61-64; V from 84; V Whitchurch w Solva and St Elvis 64-67; V Gorslas 67-76; V Burry Port and Pwll 76-84; Chapl W Wales Gen Hosp Carmarthen from 84; Can St D Cathl *St D* from 86; RD Carmarthen from 88; Adn Carmarthen from 91. *The Vicarage, Carmarthen, Dyfed SA31 1LJ* Carmarthen (0267) 237117

GOUNDRY, Ralph Walter. b 31. St Chad's Coll Dur BA56 DipTh58. **d** 58 **p** 59. C Harton Colliery *Dur* 58-62; Prec Newc Cathl *Newc* 62-65; V Seghill 65-72; V Long Benton from 72. *The Vicarage, 3 Station Road, Benton, Newcastle upon Tyne NE12 8AN* 091-266 2015

GOURLEY, William Robert Joseph. b 48. K Coll Lon BD74. CITC 68. **d** 75 **p** 76. C Newtownards *D & D* 75-78; I Currin w Drum and Newbliss *Clogh* 78-81; I Dub St Geo w St Thos, Finglas and Free Ch *D & G* 81-88; RD St Mary 86-88; I Dub Zion Ch from 88. *The Rectory, 18 Bushy Park Road, Rathgar, Dublin 6, Irish Republic* Dublin (1) 972865

GOVER, Michael Sydney Richard. b 41. Chich Th Coll 67. **d** 71 **p** 72. C Ryde All SS *Portsm* 71-75; C Waterlooville 75-83; Perm to Offic from 83. *333 Twyford Avenue, Portsmouth PO2 8PE* Portsmouth (0705) 671161

GOW, Peter Draffin. b 52. Bede Coll Dur BEd76. St Jo Coll Nottm 83. **d** 85. C Kingston Hill St Paul *S'wark* 85-86; rtd 86. *33 Canbury Avenue, Kingston upon Thames, Surrey KT2 6JP* 081-549 7942

GOW, Canon William Connell. b 09. Dur Univ LTh36. Edin Th Coll 34. **d** 36 **p** 37. R Dingwall *Mor* 40-77; R Strathpeffer 40-77; Dean Mor 60-77; rtd 77; Hon Can St Andr Cathl Inverness *Mor* from 77. *14 Mackenzie Place, Maryburgh, Ross-shire IV7 8DY* Dingwall (0349) 61832

GOW, William Masterton. b 06. **d** 32 **p** 33. V Stamfordham *Newc* 52-76; rtd 76. *32 Castleway, Dinnington, Newcastle upon Tyne NE13 7LS* Ponteland (0661) 25562

GOWARD, Giles Conrad. b 65. St Chad's Coll Dur BSc86. Coll of Resurr Mirfield 88. **d** 91. C Tipton St Jo *Lich* from 91. *4 Field Road, Tipton, W Midlands* 021-557 6165

GOWDEY, Canon Alan Lawrence. b 25. Trin Coll Toronto BA50 Ridley Hall Cam. **d** 52 **p** 53. Ind Chapl *Roch* 62-75; Hon C Gravesend St Geo 66-75; Chapl Heathrow Airport *Lon* 75-82; Hon Can Gib Cathl *Eur* 82-84; Chapl Costa Blanca 82-85; Can Gib Cathl 84-86; Ind Chapl *Roch* 85-86; C Bromley SS Pet and Paul 87-88; rtd 88. *16 Grosvenor Court, Varndean Road, Brighton, E Sussex BN1 6RR*

GOWDEY, Michael Cragg. b 32. Or Coll Ox BA56 MA58 Keele Univ CertEd73. Qu Coll Birm DipTh57. **d** 58 **p** 59. C Ashbourne w Mapleton and Clifton *Derby* 58-63; V Chellaston 63-69; Asst Chapl Ellesmere Coll Shropshire 69-74; Chapl Trent Coll Nottm 74-81; Educn

Chapl *Worc* from 81. *26 Croftwood Road, Wollescote, Stourbridge, W Midlands DY9 7EX* Lye (0384) 896796

GOWEN, John Frank. b 30. **d** 87 **p** 89. NSM Lecale Gp *D & D* 87-91; NSM Cregagh 87-91; Lic to Offic from 91. *36 Downshire Road, Belfast BT6 9JL* Belfast (0232) 701640

GOWER, Christopher Raymond. b 45. FRSA Nottm Univ BA73. St Jo Coll Nottm 70. **d** 73 **p** 74. C Hounslow H Trin *Lon* 73-76; Hon C N Greenford All Hallows 76-77; P-in-c Willesden Green St Gabr 77-82; P-in-c Brondesbury St Anne w Kilburn H Trin 81-82; Perm to Offic 82-84; P-in-c Yiewsley from 84. *The Vicarage, 93 High Street, Yiewsley, Middx UB7 7QH* Uxbridge (0895) 442093

GOWER, Denys Victor. b 33. Cant Sch of Min 85. **d** 87 **p** 88. NSM Gillingham H Trin *Roch* 87-91; NSM Gillingham St Aug 89-91; C Perry Street from 91. *6 Dene Holm Road, Northfleet, Gravesend, Kent DA11 8LE* Gravesend (0474) 332652

GOWER, Nigel Plested. b 37. SS Coll Cam BA62 MA65 Lon Univ PGCE68. Ridley Hall Cam 61. **d** 63 **p** 64. C Walthamstow St Jo *Chelmsf* 63-66; CMS 67-78; Nigeria 67-78; P-in-c Loscoe *Derby* 78-79; V 79-88; RD Heanor 84-88; R Bamford from 88; Dioc World Development Officer from 90. *The Rectory, Bamford, Sheffield S30 2AY* Hope Valley (0433) 51375

GOWER, Patricia Ann. b 44. Wilson Carlile Coll IDC79 Sarum & Wells Th Coll 88. **d** 88. Chapl Bris Univ *Bris* 88-91; Hon Par Dn Clifton St Paul 88-91; Par Dn Spondon *Derby* from 91. *Prospect House, 27 Park Road, Derby DE2 7LH* Derby (0332) 662990

GOWER, Canon Peter Charles Gwynne. b 24. St D Coll Lamp 61. **d** 63 **p** 64. CF(TAVR) 67-72; TV Cwmbran *Mon* 69-75; V Raglan and Llandenny w Llansoy 75-90; V Raglan w Llandenny and Bryngwyn 85-90; Can St Woolos Cathl 84-90; RD Raglan-Usk 84-90; rtd 90; Lic to Offic *Mon* from 90. *19 Manor Court, Baron Street, Usk, Gwent NP5 1DQ* Usk (02913) 3061

GOWER-JONES, Alfred. b 08. Man Univ BA30. Coll of Resurr Mirfield 32. **d** 34 **p** 35. R Gorton Our Lady and St Thos *Man* 44-74; rtd 74. *Messrs Davies, Wallis & Foyster, Harvester House, 37 Peter Street, Manchester M2 5GB* 061-228 3702

GOWER, Archdeacon of. *See* THOMAS, Ven Ilar Roy Luther

GOWING, Ven Frederick William. b 18. OBE85. TCD BA40. CITC 41. **d** 41 **p** 42. I Mullavilly *Arm* 56-84; Adn Arm 79-84; rtd 84. *40 Old Rectory Park, Portadown, Craigavon, Co Armagh BT62 3QH* Portadown (0762) 330933

GOWING, John Ellis. b 18. Magd Coll Ox BA40 MA45. Westcott Ho Cam 40. **d** 41 **p** 42. C-in-c N Aldrington St Rich CD *Chich* 51-53; Hon C Somers Town St Mary *Lon* 53-73; Lic to Offic 73-79; Perm to Offic *Ox* from 79; rtd 83. *7 Thurne Close, Newport Pagnell, Bucks MK16 9DY* Newport Pagnell (0908) 611500

GOYMOUR, Michael Edwyn. b 29. Selw Coll Cam BA51 McGill Univ Montreal BD53. Montreal Dioc Th Coll 51 Wells Th Coll 53. **d** 53 **p** 54. C Bury St Edmunds St Jo *St E* 53-56; C Ipswich St Bart 56-60; R Gamlingay *Ely* 60-68. *56 Church Drive, Orton Waterville, Peterborough* Peterborough (0733) 231535

GRACE, Juliet Christine. b 38. Cam Inst of Educn 60. Sarum & Wells Th Coll 84. **d** 87. NSM Petersfield *Portsm* from 87. *33 Woodbury Avenue, Petersfield, Hants GU32 2ED* Petersfield (0730) 62335

GRACE, Kenneth. b 24. Leeds Univ BA49. Wycliffe Hall Ox 62. **d** 63 **p** 64. R Thwing *York* 66-70; V Wold Newton 66-70; Chapl St Andr Sch Worthing 70-76; R Berwick w Selmeston and Alciston *Chich* 76-81; P-in-c Kingston Buci 81-85; R Westbourne 85-90; rtd 90. *17 Beech Road, Findon, Worthing, W Sussex BN14 0UR* Findon (0903) 877021

GRACE, Richard Maurice. b 29. St Chad's Coll Dur BA53. Chich Th Coll 53. **d** 55 **p** 56. C Toxteth Park St Agnes *Liv* 55-58; C Wolv St Pet *Lich* 58-62; V W Bromwich St Fran 62-78; P-in-c Salt 78-84; P-in-c Sandon w Burston 82-84; V Salt and Sandon w Burston from 84. *The Vicarage, Salt, Stafford ST18 0BW* Sandon (08897) 341

GRACE, Wilfrid Windsor. b 15. ACA39 FCA60. Westcott Ho Cam 52. **d** 53 **p** 54. V Minety w Oaksey *Bris* 57-71; V Oldland 71-76; P-in-c Abbots Leigh w Leigh Woods 76; V 76-80; Chapl Ham Green Hosp 79-87; rtd 80; Perm to Offic *B & W* from 81; Hon Chapl Chesire Home Axbridge from 81. *Cornerways, Bristol Road, Sidcot, Winscombe, Avon BS25 1PN* Winscombe (093484) 3362

GRACIE, Anthony Johnstone. b 25. Ch Coll Cam BA48 MA51. Linc Th Coll 57. d 59 p 60. R Lyndon w Manton and Martinsthorpe *Pet* 62-76; R N Luffenham 66-76; V Odiham w S Warnborough *Win* 76; V Odiham w S Warnborough and Long Sutton 76-85; Perm to Offic *Bris* 85-88; rtd 88. *53 Ashford Road, Swindon, Wilts SN1 3NS* Swindon (0793) 695235

GRACIE, Bryan John. b 45. Open Univ BA81. AKC67. d 68 p 69. C Whipton *Ex* 68-72; Chapl St Jo Sch Tiffield Northants 72-73; Chapl HM Borstal Stoke Heath 74-78; Asst Chapl HM Pris Liv 74; Chapl HM Youth Cust Cen Feltham 78-85; Chapl HM Pris Birm from 85. *HM Prison, Winson Green Road, Birmingham B18 4AS* 021-554 3838

GRAEBE, Canon Denys Redford. b 26. Qu Coll Cam BA48 MA51. Westcott Ho Cam 50. d 51 p 52. C Hitchin St Mary *St Alb* 51 57; R Gt Parndon *Chelmsf* 57-72; V Norton *St Alb* 72-83; R Kimpton w Ayot St Lawrence from 83; RD Wheathampstead from 87; Hon Can St Alb Abbey from 90. *The Vicarage, 11 High Street, Kimpton, Hitchin, Herts SG4 8RA* Kimpton (0438) 833419

GRAESSER, Adrian Stewart. b 42. Tyndale Hall Bris 63. d 67 p 68. C Nottm St Jude *S'well* 67-69; C Slaithwaite w E Scammonden *Wakef* 69-72; CF 72-75; V Earlsheaton *Wakef* 75-81; R Norton Fitzwarren *B & W* 81-86; R Bickenhill w Elmdon *Birm* 86-90; R Elmdon St Nic from 90. *Elmdon Rectory, Tanhouse Farm Road, Solihull, W Midlands B92 9EY* 021-743 6336

GRAFTON, Roger Patrick. b 63. Lon Univ BA85. Trin Coll Bris DipHE90. d 91. C Kennington St Mark *S'wark* from 91. *1 Prima Road, London SW9 0NA* 071-582 5297

GRAHAM, Alan. b 50. TCD LTh. d 74 p 75. Hon CV Ch Ch Cathl Dub *D & G* 74-77; C Howth 74-77; Bp's V and Lib Kilkenny Cathl *C & O* 77-81; Bp Ossory Dom Chapl 80-81; Min Can and Succ Roch Cathl *Roch* 81-86; R Horsmonden 86-90; Chapl HM Pris Blantyre Ho 88-90. *Address temp unknown*

GRAHAM, Alan Robert. b 44. St Edm Hall Ox BA67 MA71. St Steph Ho Ox 67. d 70 p 71. C Clifton All SS *Bris* 70-74; C Tadley St Pet *Win* 74-77; P-in-c Upper Clatford w Goodworth Clatford 77-79; R Abbotts Ann and Upper and Goodworth Clatford 79-84; V Lyndhurst and Emery Down from 84. *The Vicarage, 5 Forest Gardens, Lyndhurst, Hants SO43 7AF* Lyndhurst (0703) 282154

GRAHAM, Alfred. b 34. Bris Univ BA57. Tyndale Hall Bris. d 58 p 59. C Chaddesden St Mary *Derby* 58-61; C Bickenhill w Elmdon *Birm* 61-64; V Kirkdale St Lawr *Liv* 64-70; V Stapleford *S'well* 70-83; V Burton Joyce w Bulcote from 83. *The Vicarage, 9 Chestnut Grove, Burton Joyce, Notts NG14 5DP* Burton Joyce (060231) 2109

✠GRAHAM, Rt Rev Andrew Alexander Kenny. b 29. St Jo Coll Ox BA52 DipTh53 MA57. Ely Th Coll 53. d 55 p 56 c 77. C Hove All SS *Chich* 55-58; Chapl Lect Th and Tutor Worc Coll Ox 58-70; Can and Preb Linc Cathl *Linc* 70-77; Warden Linc Th Coll 70-77; Suff Bp Bedf *St Alb* 77-81; Bp Newc from 81; Chmn Selectors ACCM 84-87; Chmn of Doctrine Commn from 87. *Bishop's House, 29 Moor Road South, Newcastle upon Tyne NE3 1PA* 091-285 2220

GRAHAM, Canon Anthony Nigel. b 40. Univ of Wales (Abth) BA62 CertEd70. Ripon Hall Ox 62. d 64 p 65. C Heref H Trin *Heref* 64-67; C Birm St Martin *Birm* 67-69; C Selly Oak St Mary 71-75; V Edgbaston SS Mary and Ambrose 75-83; CMS Miss Partner Nigeria 84-88; Hon Can Jos from 88; V Highworth w Sevenhampton and Inglesham etc *Bris* from 88. *23 The Willows, Highworth, Swindon SN6 7PG* Swindon (0793) 763862

GRAHAM, Anthony Stanley David. b 36. SS Coll Cam BA56 MA60. Cuddesdon Coll 58. d 60 p 61. C Welwyn Garden City *St Alb* 60-64; Asst Chapl Ipswich Sch 64-65; C Margate St Jo *Cant* 65-68; Chr Aid Area Sec Chich from 68. *48 Springfield Road, Crawley, W Sussex RH11 8AH* Crawley (0293) 26279

GRAHAM, Canon Douglas Wrixon. b 13. TCD BA39. Div Test40. d 41 p 43. I Roscommon w Donamon, Rathcline, Kilkeevin etc *K, E & A* 66-88; Preb Elphin Cathl 79-88; rtd 88. *The Rectory, Circular Road, Roscommon, Irish Republic* Roscommon (903) 25028

GRAHAM, Canon Frederick Lawrence. b 35. TCD BA65 DChCD88. CITC 66. d 66 p 67. C Belf St Matt *Conn* 66-69; TV Chelmsley Wood *Birm* 69-73; Ch of Ireland Youth Officer 73-78; Bp's C Stoneyford *Conn* 78-88; Bp's C Fahan Lower and Upper *D & R* from 88; RD Innishowen from 88; Can Raphoe Cathl from 90. *Fahan Lower Rectory, Church Street, Buncrana, Co Donegal, Irish Republic* Buncrana (77) 61154

GRAHAM, Frederick Louis Roth. b 20. Selw Coll Cam BA47 MA49. Ridley Hall Cam 48. d 50 p 51. R Wombwell *Sheff* 61-71; V Thorne 71-77; P-in-c Chiltons-Polden w Edington *B & W* 77-82; P-in-c Catcott 77-82; V W Poldens 82-86; RD Glastonbury 82-86; rtd 86; Perm to Offic *Win* from 86. *73 Newlands Avenue, Southampton SO1 5EQ* Southampton (0703) 789353

GRAHAM, Geoffrey Noel. b 02. Lon Univ DipTh41. St Andr Coll Pampisford 41. d 41 p 42. V Austwick *Bradf* 63-68; rtd 68; Perm to Offic *Glouc* from 69. *84 Roman Way, Bourton-on-the-Water, Cheltenham, Glos GL54 2HD* Cotswold (0451) 21355

GRAHAM, George David. b 42. Jes Coll Cam BA64 MA68. St Jo Coll Nottm LTh Lon Coll of Div 66. d 71 p 72. C Corby St Columba *Pet* 71-74; C Deptford St S *S'wark* 74-77; P-in-c Deptford St Pet 77-82; C-in-c Wheatley Park St Paul CD *Sheff* 82-87; TV Dunstable *St Alb* from 87. *Priory Vicarage, 20 Friars Walk, Dunstable, Beds LU6 3JA* Dunstable (0582) 600972 or 696725

GRAHAM, George Edgar. b 55. QUB BA91. Sarum & Wells Th Coll 74. d 78 p 79. C Lisburn Ch Ch *Conn* 78-81; C Mossley 81-83; I Broomhedge 83-91; I Derriaghy w Colin from 91. *Derriaghy Vicarage, 18 Derriaghy Road, Magheralave, Lisburn, Co Antrim BT28 3SH* Belfast (0232) 610859

GRAHAM, George Gordon. b 17. St Chad's Coll Dur BA48 DipTh50 MSc71. d 50 p 51. V Hunwick *Dur* 69-88; Chapl Homelands Hosp Dur from 80; rtd 88. *3 The Willows, Bishop Auckland, Co Durham DL14 7HH* Bishop Auckland (0388) 602758

GRAHAM, Gordon Cecil. b 31. JP. Ch Coll Cam BA53 MA57. Ripon Hall Ox 53. d 55 p 56. C Didsbury St Jas and Em *Man* 55-58; C Rochdale 58-60; R Heaton Mersey 60-67; Chapl Hulme Gr Sch Oldham 67-74; Lic to Offic *Ches* from 72. *21 The Crescent, Davenport, Stockport, Cheshire SK3 8SL* 061-483 6011

GRAHAM, Ian Maxwell. b 50. CertEd76. Chich Th Coll 86. d 88 p 89. C Middlesb St Thos *York* 88-90; C Stainton-in-Cleveland from 90. *1 Southdene Drive, Hemlington, Middlesbrough TS8 9HH* Middlesbrough (0642) 590496

GRAHAM, James Hamilton. b 54. Solicitor 78 Cam Univ MA76 Ox Univ MA83. Ripon Coll Cuddesdon. d 84 p 85. C Harlescott *Lich* 84-88; C Moreton Say from 88. *The Rectory, Moreton Saye, Market Drayton, Shropshire TF9 3RS* Tern Hill (063083) 241

GRAHAM, John. b 24. d 84 p 84. Hon C Glas St Kentigern *Glas* from 84; Chapl Glas H Infirmary from 84. *121 Garthland Drive, Glasgow G31 2SQ* 041-554 5718

GRAHAM, John Francis Ottiwell Skelton. b 15. G&C Coll Cam BA37 MA48. Wells Th Coll 37. d 39 p 40. V Winterbourne Earls w Winterbourne Dauntsey etc *Sarum* 58-72; R Bincombe w Broadwey 72-80; R Bincombe w Broadwey, Upwey and Buckland Ripers 80-81; rtd 81; Perm to Offic *Win* from 81. *15A Belmore Lane, Lymington, Hants SO41 9NL* Lymington (0590) 673256

GRAHAM, John Galbraith. b 21. K Coll Cam BA43 MA46. Ely Th Coll 46. d 48 p 49. Chapl Reading Univ *Ox* 62-72; C Pimlico St Pet w Westmr Ch Ch *Lon* 72-74; R Houghton w Wyton *Ely* 74-78; rtd 86; Lic to Offic St E and Ely from 86. *4 King Street, Somersham, Huntingdon, Cambs PE17 3EJ* Ramsey (0487) 841137

GRAHAM, Very Rev Malcolm Frederick. b 15. TCD BA37 MA69. d 40 p 41. I Kilbroney *D & D* 60-79; RD Newry and Mourne 61-79; RD Kilbroney 61-79; Preb St Patr Cathl Dub 69-72; Dean Killala *T, K & A* 79-89; I Killala w Dunfeeny, Crossmolina etc 79-89; rtd 89. *Kilbroney, Rathnamaugh, Crossmolina, Co Mayo, Irish Republic* Ballina (96) 31717

GRAHAM, Mrs Marion McKenzie. b 39. St As Minl Tr Course. d 89. NSM Bagillt *St As* from 89. *Sharondale, Bryntirion Road, Bagillt, Clwyd CH6 6BZ* Flint (03526) 4139

GRAHAM, Canon Matthew. b 30. Univ Coll Dur BSc54. K Coll (NS) BD71 Ridley Hall Cam 54. d 56 p 57. C Littleover *Derby* 56-59; C Fazakerley Em *Liv* 59-61; V Huyton St Geo 61-65; Canada 65-71; V Sutton Coldfield St Columba *Birm* 71-85; V Warley Woods from 85; RD Warley from 87; Hon Can Birm Cathl from 90. *St Hilda's Vicarage, Abbey Road, Smethwick, Warley, W Midlands B67 5NQ* 021-429 1384

GRAHAM, Michael. b 30. Westcott Ho Cam 61. d 61 p 62. C Withington St Paul *Man* 61-64; V Lawton Moor 64-87; R Mobberley *Ches* from 87. *The Rectory, Mobberley, Knutsford, Cheshire WA16 7RA* Mobberley (0565) 873218

GRAHAM, Michael Alistair. b 47. CITC 67. d 70 p 71. C Dub Clontarf *D & G* 71-75; C Ox St Mich w St Martin and All SS *Ox* 76-78; P-in-c Dub Sandymount *D & G*

80-86; I Stillorgan w Blackrock from 86. *The Rectory, Stillorgan, Blackrock, Co Dublin, Irish Republic* Dublin (1) 288-1091

GRAHAM, Peter. b 32. CEng MIMechE. d 86 p 87. NSM Minchinhampton *Glouc* from 86. *2 Dr Browns Close, Minchinhampton, Stroud, Glos GL6 9DW* Brimscombe (0453) 886747

GRAHAM, Peter Bartlemy. b 23. K Coll Cam BA47 MA52. Ely Th Coll 50. d 52 p 53. R Harpenden St Nic *St Alb* 64-73; V Aylesbury *Ox* 73-82; Hon Can Ch Ch 79-82; R Elford *Lich* 82-88; Dioc Adv Past Care and Counselling 82-88; rtd 88. *Carriers Cottage, Buckland Newton, Dorchester, Dorset DT2 7DW* Buckland Newton (03005) 287

GRAHAM, Canon Robert John. b 15. Lon Univ BD54 Hull Univ DipAdEd. Bp Wilson Coll 39. d 42 p 43. V Howden *York* 58-78; V Barmby on the Marsh 62-78; V Wressell 62-78; RD Howden 70-78; C Worksop Priory *S'well* 78-80; rtd 80. *Cranley, Flat 11, Wellington Square, Cheltenham, Glos*

GRAHAM, Ronald Fleming. b 33. Edin Th Coll 67. d 69 p 69. Chapl St Andr Cathl *Ab* 69-73; R Glas Gd Shep *Glas* 73-75; CF (TA) 74-76; R Glas Gd Shep w Ascension *Glas* 75-76; Chapl RAF 76-80; R Peterhead *Ab* 76-80; Bp's Dom Chapl *Arg* 80-84; Itinerant Priest 80-84; R Lanark *Glas* 84-89; R Douglas 84-89; rtd 89; Hon C Glas St Ninian *Glas* from 91. *77 Merryvale Avenue, Merrylee Park, Giffnock, Glasgow G46 6DE* 041-637 4761

GRAHAM, Ronald Gaven. d 90 p 91. NSM Adare w Kilpeacon and Croom *L & K* from 90; Dioc Info Officer (Limerick) from 91. *The Pyramids, Old Schoolhouse Road, Castletroy, Limerick, Irish Republic* Limerick (61) 330190

GRAHAM, Roy Richard Arthur. b 39. Lon Univ BD63 Open Univ BA78. ALCD62. d 63 p 64. C Southsea St Jude *Portsm* 63-66; C Morden *S'wark* 66-70; V Tittensor *Lich* 70-79; R Dinsdale w Sockburn *Dur* from 79; R Hurworth from 79. *The Rectory, 3 Croft Road, Hurworth, Darlington, Co Durham DL2 2HD* Darlington (0325) 720362

GRAHAM-BROWN, John George Francis. b 34. CA60. Wycliffe Hall Ox 60. d 63 p 64. C Darlington St Cuth *Dur* 63-67; C Rufforth w Moor Monkton and Hessay *York* 67-73; Sec York Dioc Redundant Chs Uses Cttee 69-89; Asst Sec DBF 73-84; Dioc Past Cttee 73-89; Hon C York St Barn 73-85; P-in-c from 85. *St Barnabas's Vicarage, Jubilee Terrace, Leeman Road, York YO2 4YZ* York (0904) 654214

GRAHAM-ORLEBAR, Ian Henry Gaunt. b 26. New Coll Ox BA49 MA56. Cuddesdon Coll 60. d 62 p 63. C Hemel Hempstead *St Alb* 62-70; R Barton-le-Cley w Higham Gobion 70-80; R Barton-le-Cley w Higham Gobion and Hexton from 80. *The Rectory, Barton-le-Clay, Bedford MK45 4LA* Luton (0582) 881226

GRAIN, Anthony Ernest. b 07. CCC Cam BA31 MA35. Ely Th Coll 31. d 32 p 33. P-in-c Edin St Barn *Edin* 55-58; S Rhodesia 63-65; Rhodesia 65-80; Zimbabwe 80-86; rtd 73; Perm to Offic *Chich* from 86. *College of St Barnabas, Blackberry Lane, Lingfield, Surrey RH7 6NJ* Dormans Park (034287) 260

GRAIN, Canon Keith Charles. b 27. St Boniface Warminster 47 AKC51. d 52 p 53. C Liversedge *Wakef* 52-55; C Barnsley St Mary 55-60; V Hanging Heaton 60-70; V Heckmondwike 70-82; Hon Can Wakef Cathl 74-82; RD Birstall 79-82; V Gargrave *Bradf* from 82. *The Vicarage, Gargrave, Skipton, N Yorkshire BD23 3NQ* Gargrave (0756) 749392

GRAINGE, Alan Herbert. b 16. Dur Univ BA49 MA53. Sarum Th Coll 49. d 51 p 52. V Immingham *Linc* 61-70; Perm to Offic *Ox* 70-74; Lic to Offic 74-81; SSJE from 76; Lic to Offic *Leic* 80-86; rtd 86; Lic to Offic *Lon* from 86. *St Edward's House, 22 Great College Street, London SW1P 3QA* 071-222 9234

GRAINGER, Canon Bruce. b 37. Nottm Univ BA62 Hull Univ MA83. Cuddesdon Coll 62. d 64 p 65. C Bingley All SS *Bradf* 64-67; Chapl K Sch Cant 67-72; Hon Min Can Cant Cathl *Cant* 69-72; V Baildon *Bradf* 72-88; Hon Can Bradf Cathl from 84; V Oxenhope from 88; Dir of Ords from 88. *The Vicarage, Oxenhope, Keighley, W Yorkshire BD22 9SA* Keighley (0535) 42529

GRAINGER, Horace. b 34. Carl Dioc Tr Course 82. d 85 p 86. NSM Barrow St Matt *Carl* 85-89; C Carl St Herbert w St Steph from 89. *93 Beaumont Road, Carlisle CA2 4RJ* Carlisle (0228) 515778

GRAINGER, Michael Noel Howard. Trin Coll Carmarthen. d 91. NSM Haverfordwest St Martin w Lambston *St D* from 91. *Derlwyn Forge, Haycastle Cross, Haverfordwest, Dyfed SA62 5PW* Treffgarne (043787) 660

GRAINGER, Dr Roger Beckett. b 34. FRAI FRSA Birm Univ MA70 Leeds Univ PhD79 Lon Univ BA80 DD90 Huddersfield Poly MPhil88. Lambeth STh83 Lich Th Coll 64. d 66 p 69. C Walsall *Lich* 69-73; Chapl Stanley Royd Hosp Wakef 73-90; rtd 91. *7 Park Grove, Horbury, Wakefield, W Yorkshire WF4 6EE* Wakefield (0924) 272742

GRANGE, Tom Wilkinson. b 01. St Cath Coll Cam BA25 MA29. Ridley Hall Cam 25. d 27 p 28. V Melling w Tatham *Blackb* 56-66; rtd 66. *14 Haverbreaks Place, Lancaster LA1 5BH* Lancaster (0524) 65405

GRANGER, Arthur Charles. b 99. St Paul's Coll Burgh 22. d 25 p 26. R Jersey H Trin *Win* 56-76; rtd 76. *Springfield House, Trinity, Jersey, Channel Islands JE3 5JN* Jersey (0534) 63347

GRANGER, Canon Ronald Harry. b 22. Selw Coll Cam BA49 MA53. Cuddesdon Coll 49. d 51 p 52. V Ryde All SS *Portsm* 63-70; RD E Wight 65-70; Hon Can Portsm Cathl 67-90; V Petersfield w Sheet 70-90; V Petersfield 90; RD Petersfield 75-80; P-in-c Buriton 79-84; R 84-90; rtd 90. *45 Siskin Close, Bishops Waltham, Hants SO3 1RP* Bishops Waltham (0489) 894378

GRANT, Alistair Sims. b 25. SS Coll Cam BA49 MA53. Sarum Th Coll 49. d 51 p 52. V Haddenham *Ely* 58-65; rtd 90. *56 The Causeway, Burwell, Cambridge CB5 0DU* Newmarket (0638) 741670

GRANT, Andrew Richard. b 40. Univ of Wales BA62. Chich Th Coll 63. d 65 p 66. C Kennington St Jo *S'wark* 65-69; Hon C 70-72; C Stockwell Green St Andr 69-70; V Nunhead St Antony 72-79; TR N Lambeth from 79. *St Anselm's Rectory, Kennington Cross, London SE11 5DU* 071-735 3415

GRANT, Antony Richard Charles. b 34. Ch Ch Ox BA59 MA64. Coll of Resurr Mirfield 72. d 74 p 75. C St Jo Wood *Lon* 74-77; Novice CR 77-79; CR from 79; Lic to Offic *Wakef* from 80. *House of the Resurrection, Mirfield, W Yorkshire WF14 0BN* Mirfield (0924) 494318

GRANT, Arthur Glyndwr Webber. b 28. St Luke's Coll Ex CertEd49. Wells Th Coll 52. d 54 p 55. C Cannock *Lich* 54-57; S Rhodesia 57-63; C Paignton St Jo *Ex* 63-68; C Brighton Gd Shep Preston *Chich* 68-76; C Moulsecoomb 76-80; Chapl HM Pris Northeye 80-83; P-in-c Wartling *Chich* 80-83; C Seaford w Sutton 83-87; Sub-Chapl HM Pris Lewes from 86. *Glebelands Cottage, Gilberts Drive, East Dean, Eastbourne, E Sussex BN20 0DJ* East Dean (0323) 422049

GRANT, David Francis. b 32. Chich Th Coll. d 60 p 61. C Acton Green St Pet *Lon* 60-63; C Ruislip St Martin 63-68; V Oving w Merston *Chich* 68-75; Bp's Dom Chapl 68-75; R Graffham w Woolavington 75-86; R Hastings St Clem and All SS 86-91; R Petworth from 91. *The Rectory, Petworth, W Sussex GU28 0DB* Petworth (0798) 42505

GRANT, Canon Douglas Wyndham Maling. b 22. Trin Coll Cam BA48 MA52. Edin Th Coll 53. d 55 p 56. R Lenzie *Glas* 65-70; R Alyth *St And* 70-78; R Blairgowrie 70-78; R Inverurie *Ab* 78-88; R Auchindoir 78-88; R Alford 78-88; P-in-c Kemnay 78-88; Can St Andr Cathl from 87; rtd 89; Perm to Offic *Mor* from 89. *Shewglie, 8 Ardross Place, Inverness IV3 5EL* Inverness (0463) 242870

GRANT, Canon Edward Francis. b 14. TCD BA37. TCD Div Sch Div Test. d 40 p 41. Prec Ferns Cathl *C & O* 69-85; I Wexford w Ardcolm 70-85; Preb Stagonil St Patr Cathl Dub 76-85; rtd 85. *9 Kingston College, Mitchelstown, Co Cork, Irish Republic* Fermoy (25) 84214

GRANT, Evert Ronald. b 09. K Coll Lon BA32 BD34 AKC34. d 36 p 37. V Cheswardine *Lich* 56-71; rtd 71; Perm to Offic *Win* from 71. *17 Naish Road, Barton-on-Sea, New Milton, Hants BH25 7PT* New Milton (0425) 610314

GRANT, Canon Geoffrey. b 27. Lich Th Coll 55. d 58 p 59. C Swindon New Town *Bris* 58-62; V Eastville St Thos 62-67; V Sherston Magna w Easton Grey 67-75; P-in-c Luckington w Alderton 71-75; P-in-c Woolcott Park 75-78; V Cotham St Mary 76-78; V Cotham St Sav w St Mary 78-81; TR Yate New Town 81-88; Hon Can Bris Cathl from 82; Dir St Jo Home Bris from 89. *5 Hawthorn Coombe, Worle, Weston-super-Mare, Avon BS22 9EE* Weston-super-Mare (0934) 513295

GRANT, Geoffrey Leslie. b 33. Trin Coll Cam BA57 MA61. Ridley Hall Cam 57. d 59 p 60. C Chelsea St Luke *Lon* 59-64; Chapl Orwell Park Sch Nacton from 64; R Nacton w Levington *St E* 64-78; P-in-c Bucklesham w Brightwell and Foxhall 75-76; R Nacton and Levington w Bucklesham and Foxhall from 78; RD Colneys from 86.

The Rectory, Nacton, Ipswich IP10 0HY Ipswich (0473) 659232

GRANT, James Neil. b 57. Toorak Coll of Educn DipEd77. Trin Coll Melbourne 80. **d** 85 **p** 86. Australia 85-87 and from 89; C Feltham *Lon* 87-89. *Geelong CEGS, Corio, Victoria, Australia 3214* Geelong (52) 739200

GRANT, John Peter. b 19. TD50. Wycliffe Hall Ox. **d** 62 **p** 63. Chapl Warneford Hosp Ox 67-71; Rhodesia 71-80; V Gayton *Nor* 80-82; rtd 82; S Africa from 82. *15 De Villiers Road, Kommetjie, 7975 South Africa* Cape Town (21) 833206

GRANT, Kenneth Gordon. b 21. ARCM54 BA. K Coll Lon. **d** 55 **p** 56. C Wotton-under-Edge *Glouc* 55-58; R Charfield from 58. *The Rectory, 36 Wotton Road, Charfield, Wotton-under-Edge, Glos GL12 8TG* Falfield (0454) 260489

GRANT, Very Rev Malcolm Etheridge. b 44. Edin Univ BSc66 BD69. Edin Th Coll 66. **d** 69 **p** 70. C St Mary's Cathl *Glas* 69-72; C Grantham w Manthorpe *Linc* 72-78; TV Grantham 78; P-in-c Invergordon *Mor* 78-81; Provost St Mary's Cathl *Glas* from 81; Can from 81; R Glas St Mary from 81. *45 Rowallan Gardens, Glasgow G11 7LH* 041-339 4956

GRANT, Murray William. b 36. Chich Th Coll 64. **d** 66 **p** 67. C Stanley *Liv* 66-70; C Munster Square St Mary Magd *Lon* 70-74; C Westmr St Sav and St Jas Less 74-82; P-in-c Albany Street Ch Ch 82; P-in-c Hammersmith H Innocents from 83. *Holy Innocents Vicarage, 35 Paddenswick Road, London W6 0VA* 081-748 5195

GRANT, Rodney Arthur. b 26. AKC52. **d** 53 **p** 54. C Edin St Jas *Edin* 53-56; R 72-80; C Musselburgh 56-59; P-in-c Prestonpans 59-60; P-in-c Edin St Aid Miss Niddrie Mains 60-72; R Edin Ch Ch 72-80; R Edin Ch Ch-St Jas 80-86; R Edin SS Phil and Jas from 86; Chapl St Columba's Hospice Edin from 86. *5 Wardie Road, Edinburgh EH5 3QE* 031-552 4300

GRANT, William Frederick. b 23. Fitzw Ho Cam BA48 MA50. Wycliffe Hall Ox 51. **d** 53 **p** 54. V Islington All SS *Lon* 57-60; Perm to Offic *Guildf* from 66; rtd 88. *50 Hillside Gardens, Brockham, Betchworth, Surrey RH3 7EW* Betchworth (073784) 2551

GRANT, Very Rev William James. b 29. **d** 58 **p** 59. Asst Missr S Ch Miss Ballymacarrett *D & D* 58-60; C Belf St Geo *Conn* 60-63; Canada 63-66; Miss to Seamen 66-70; I Fethard w Tintern and Killesk *C & O* 70-77; I Cong, Ballinrobe and Aasleagh *T, K & A* 77-81; Adn Tuam from 80; I Tuam w Cong and Aasleagh from 81; Dean Tuam from 81. *Deanery Place, Cong, Claremorris, Co Mayo, Irish Republic* Cong (92) 46017

GRANTHAM, Michael Paul. b 47. Linc Th Coll. **d** 84 **p** 85. C Gainsborough All SS *Linc* 84-87; R S Kelsey Gp from 87. *The Rectory, South Kelsey, Lincoln LN76 6PH* North Kelsey (06527) 251

GRANTHAM, Suffragan Bishop of. See IND, Rt Rev William

GRATY, Canon John Thomas. b 33. Univ Coll Ox BA58 MA60. Coll of Resurr Mirfield 58. **d** 60 **p** 61. C Cov St Mark *Cov* 60-63; C Hitchin St Mary *St Alb* 63-67; R Cov St Alb *Cov* 67-75; P-in-c Radway w Ratley 75-77; P-in-c Warmington w Shotteswell 75-77; RD Dassett Magna 76-79; R Warmington w Shotteswell and Radway w Ratley 77-84; Hon Can Cov Cathl from 80; P-in-c Nuneaton St Mary 84-89; V from 89. *St Mary's Abbey Vicarage, Nuneaton, Warks CV11 5JB* Nuneaton (0203) 382936

GRAVELL, John Hilary. b 45. Univ of Wales (Abth) BA65 DipEd66. Burgess Hall Lamp 66. **d** 68 **p** 69. C Abth *St D* 68-72; V Blaenpennal and Llangeitho 72-81; V Betws Leuci 73-81; V Llan-non from 81. *The Vicarage, 23 Morlais Road, Llan-non, Llanelli, Dyfed SA14 6BD* Cross Hands (0269) 841358

GRAVELLE, John Elmer. b 25. St Jo Coll Dur BA50 DipTh51. **d** 51 **p** 52. V Hatf Hyde St Mary *St Alb* 64-71; P-in-c Gt Munden 71-74; Dep Dir Clinical Th Assn 71-80; P-in-c Fryerning w Margaretting *Chelmsf* 80-87; Dep Dir Cathl Cen for Research and Tr 82-84; Bp's Adv in Care and Counselling 87-90; rtd 90. *8 Gordon Road, Chelmsford CM2 9LL* Chelmsford (0245) 491795

GRAVES, Canon Eric Arthur. b 13. Leeds Univ BA34. Coll of Resurr Mirfield 34. **d** 36 **p** 37. V Haverhill *St E* 46-81; RD Clare 72-81; rtd 82; Perm to Offic *St E* from 82. *20 Saxon Rise, Bury St Edmunds, Suffolk IP33 3LF* Bury St Edmunds (0284) 764497

GRAVES, Jonathan Mark. b 57. BEd. St Steph Ho Ox. **d** 84 **p** 85. C St Leonards Ch Ch and St Mary *Chich* 84-88; C-in-c N Langley CD from 88. *The Vicarage, Culver Close, Eastbourne, E Sussex BN23 8EA* Eastbourne (0323) 764473

GRAVES, Peter. b 33. E Midl Min Tr Course 78. **d** 81 **p** 82. NSM Roughey (or Roffey) *Chich* from 81; NSM Itchingfield w Slinfold from 89. *2 Coniston Close, Roffey, Horsham, W Sussex RH12 4GU* Horsham (0403) 58363

GRAY, Alan. b 25. LRAM52 DCEd75. Qu Coll Birm 51. **d** 54 **p** 55. R Callander *St And* 66-74; R Alloa 74-77; Community Educn Officer 76-85; Lic to Offic 77-85; R Alyth 85-90; R Blairgowrie 85-90; R Coupar Angus 85-90; rtd 90. *Ach-na-Coile, Ancaster Road, Callander, Perthshire FK17 8EL* Callander (0877) 30158

GRAY, Alan Eric. b 18. Lich Th Coll 38. **d** 41 **p** 42. Africa 47-60; V Lower Breeding *Chich* 61-70; rtd 83. *Appletree Cottage, 81 Belmont Road, Malvern, Worcs WR14 1PN* Malvern (0684) 572453

GRAY, Angela Margery. b 46. St D Coll Lamp DipTh73. **dss** 73 **d** 80. Abth *St D* 73-80; Par Dn Dafen and Llwynhendy 80-90; Dn-in-c from 90. *71 Trallwm Road, Llwynhendy, Llanelli, Dyfed SA14 9ER* Llanelli (0554) 774213

GRAY, Charles Malcolm. b 38. Lich Th Coll 67. **d** 69 **p** 70. C St-Geo-in-the-East St Mary *Lon* 69-72; C Bush Hill Park St Mark 72-75; V Winchmore Hill H Trin from 75. *Holy Trinity Vicarage, King's Avenue, London N21 3NA* 081-360 2947

GRAY, Ms Christine Angela. b 46. Nottm Univ BA67 CertEd68 Dur Univ DipTh73. Cranmer Hall Dur 71. **dss** 80 **d** 87. Rawthorpe *Wakef* 74-81; Chapl Nottm Univ *S'well* 81-88; Par Dn Rushmere *St E* from 88. *5 The Limes, Rushmere, Ipswich IP5 7EA* Ipswich (0473) 713690

GRAY, Cyril Samuel. b 08. AKC40. **d** 40 **p** 41. V Plymouth St Jas Ham *Ex* 63-74; rtd 74. *16 Lockyer Terrace, Saltash, Cornwall PL12 6DF* Saltash (0752) 846393

GRAY, David Bryan. b 28. RD77. Roch Th Coll 59. **d** 61 **p** 62. C Linc St Giles *Linc* 61-65; V Thurlby 65-67; P-in-c Ropsley 67-75; P-in-c Sapperton w Braceby 67-75; P-in-c Somerby w Humby 67-75; R Trimley *St E* 75-82; R Orford w Sudbourne, Chillesford, Butley and Iken from 82. *The Rectory, Orford, Woodbridge, Suffolk IP12 2NN* Orford (0394) 450336

GRAY, David Kenneth. b 22. Sarum Th Coll 53. **d** 55 **p** 56. V Hounslow Heath St Paul *Lon* 65-88; rtd 88. *12 Dart Close, Oadby, Leicester LE2 4JA* Leicester (0533) 716357

GRAY, Canon Donald Cecil. b 24. K Coll Lon 46. Linc Th Coll 49. **d** 50 **p** 51. Chapl Cobgates Hosp and Farnham Hosp Guildf 67-89; R Farnham *Guildf* 67-89; RD Farnham 69-74; Hon Can Guildf Cathl 71-89; rtd 89. *13 Benenden Green, Alresford, Hants SO24 9PE* Alresford (0962) 734234

GRAY, Canon Donald Clifford. b 30. TD70. FRHistS88 Liv Univ MPhil80 Man Univ PhD85. AKC55. **d** 56 **p** 57. C Leigh St Mary *Man* 56-60; CF (TA) 58-67; V Westleigh St Pet *Man* 60-67; V Elton All SS 67-74; CF (TAVR) 67-77; QHC 74-77; R Liv Our Lady and St Nic w St Anne *Liv* 74-87; RD Liv 75-81; Hon Can Liv Cathl 82-87; Chapl to HM The Queen from 82; Can Westmr Abbey from 87; R Westmr St Marg from 87; Chapl to Speaker of Ho of Commons from 87. *1 Little Cloister, Westminster Abbey, London SW1P 3PL* 071-222 4027 or 222 5152

GRAY, Evan William. b 43. Oak Hill Th Coll 86. **d** 88 **p** 89. C Street w Walton *B & W* from 88. *54 Green Lane Avenue, Street, Somerset BA16 0QU* Street (0458) 42430

GRAY, Frank Harold Castell. b 14. ALCD41. **d** 41 **p** 42. V Watford St Luke *St Alb* 66-79; rtd 79; Perm to Offic *B & W* from 80. *9 Southwell Close, Trull, Taunton, Somerset TA3 7EU* Taunton (0823) 282567

GRAY, Canon Geoffrey Thomas. b 23. Oak Hill Th Coll 40 and 46. **d** 46 **p** 47. V Gillingham St Mary *Roch* 66-75; RD Gillingham 66-75; Perm to Offic 75-80; V Strood St Nic w St Mary 80-87; Hon Can Roch Cathl 82-87; Chapl Huggens' Coll Northfleet from 87; Hon Bp's Chapl *Roch* from 87; rtd 88. *Deanery Lodge, The Precinct, Rochester, Kent ME1 1TG* Gravesend (0474) 352428

GRAY, George Francis Selby. b 03. Trin Coll Cam BA25 MA29. Westcott Ho Cam 25. **d** 27 **p** 28. V Over *Ely* 69-79; rtd 79; Perm to Offic *Chelmsf* and *Ely* from 79. *2 Bishop Wynn Close, Ely, Cambs CB7 4BH* Ely (0353) 663032

GRAY, George Samuel. b 03. Worc Ord Coll 60. **d** 62 **p** 63. Chapl HM Pris Dorchester 69-78; rtd 73. *53 Glenferness Avenue, Bournemouth BH3 7EU* Bournemouth (0202) 765875

GRAY, Ven Hugh Henry James. b 21. TCD BA48 Div Test49 MA64. **d** 49 **p** 50. C Enniscorthy *C & O* 49-51; I Fenagh w Myshall 51-60; I Clonenagh w Roskelton 60-80; RD Baltinglass from 80; Preb Ossory

& Leighlin Cathls 70-78; Treas 78-80; Chan 80-83; I Clonenagh w Offerlane, Borris-in-Ossory etc from 80; Adn Ossory and Leighlin from 83. *St Peter's Rectory, Mountrath, Portlaoise, Co Laois, Irish Republic* Portlaoise (502) 32146

GRAY, John. ARCM. **d** 89 **p** 90. NSM Tenbury St Mich *Heref* from 89. *Flat 3, Castlemead, Burford, Tenbury Wells, Worcs WR15 8AH* Tenbury Wells (0584) 810959

GRAY, John David Norman. b 38. Oak Hill Th Coll DipHE86. **d** 86 **p** 87. C Portsdown *Portsm* 86-88; C Worthing St Geo *Chich* 88-91; TV Swanborough *Sarum* from 91. *The Vicarage, Wilcot, Pewsey, Wilts SN9 5NS* Marlborough (0672) 62282

GRAY, John Howard. b 39. St Aid Birkenhead 61. **d** 65 **p** 66. C Old Trafford St Cuth *Man* 65-68; C Urmston 68-74; V Oldham Moorside from 74. *The Vicarage, 1 Glebe Lane, Moorside, Oldham, Lancs OL1 4SJ* 061-652 6452

GRAY, Mrs Joy Dora. b 24. SRN46 SCM48 HVCert. Gilmore Ho 79. **dss** 81 **d** 87. Newick *Chich* 81-87; Hon Par Dn from 87. *10 High Hurst Close, Newick, Lewes, E Sussex BN8 4NJ* Newick (082572) 2965

GRAY, Julian Francis. b 64. Univ of Wales (Lamp) BA86. Coll of Resurr Mirfield 86. **d** 88 **p** 89. C Newport St Woolos *Mon* 88-91; Min Can St Woolos Cathl 88-91; C Bassaleg from 91. *99 The Uplands, Rogerstone, Newport, Gwent NP1 9FE* Newport (0633) 893357

GRAY, Kenneth Amphlett. b 11. St Jo Coll Dur BA34 MA37 DipTh37. **d** 35 **p** 36. Dorset and Wilts Distr Sec BFBS 62-75; rtd 75; Perm to Offic *Nor* from 81. *Windwhistle, Triple Plea Road, Woodton, Bungay, Suffolk NR35 2NS* Woodton (050844) 395

GRAY, Martin Clifford. b 44. Westcott Ho Cam 78. **d** 80 **p** 81. C Gaywood, Bawsey and Mintlyn *Nor* 80-84; V Sheringham from 84. *The Vicarage, 10 North Street, Sheringham, Norfolk NR26 8LW* Sheringham (0263) 822089

GRAY, Maurice William Halcro. b 27. Hertf Coll Ox BA48 MA60. Coll of Resurr Mirfield. **d** 60 **p** 61. C Cricklade w Latton *Bris* 60-63; Chapl Ellesmere Coll Shropshire from 63; Lic to Offic *Lich* from 63. *Ellesmere College, Ellesmere, Shropshire SY12 9AB* Ellesmere (069171) 2321

GRAY, Melvyn Dixon. b 38. Lon Univ BD86 Dur Univ MA89. NE Ord Course 84. **d** 87 **p** 88. C Richmond w Hudswell *Ripon* 87-90; P-in-c Downholme and Marske 88-90; P-in-c Forcett and Stanwick w Aldbrough 90; P-in-c Forcett and Aldbrough and Melsonby 90-91; R from 91. *The Vicarage, 1 Appleby Close, Aldbrough St John, Richmond, N Yorkshire DL11 7TT* Darlington (0325) 374634

GRAY, Michael Frederick Henry. b 36. Southn Univ CQSW78. Lich Th Coll 62. **d** 65 **p** 66. C Victoria Docks Ascension *Chelmsf* 65-67; C Plaistow St Mary 67-70; Chapl RN 70-72; Hon C Whyke w Rumboldswhyke and Portfield *Chich* 84-88; TV Crawley from 88. *St Richard's House, Crossways, Crawley, W Sussex RH10 1QF* Crawley (0293) 533727

GRAY, Neil Kenneth. b 48. Kelham Th Coll 67. **d** 71 **p** 72. C Chorley St Laur *Blackb* 71-74; C S Shore H Trin 74-78; P-in-c Preston St Oswald 78-83; C Blackpool St Steph 83-87; Chapl Co-ord Bolton HA from 87; Chapl Bolton Gen Hosp from 87. *The Chaplain's Office, Bolton General Hospital, Farnworth, Bolton BL4 0JR* Bolton (0204) 22444

GRAY, Neil Ralph. b 53. MA. St Steph Ho Ox. **d** 82 **p** 83. C Kennington St Jo w St Jas *S'wark* 82-85; C Somers Town St Mary *Lon* 85-88. *3 Parsonage Close, High Wycombe, Bucks HP13 6DT* High Wycombe (0494) 31875

GRAY, Paul Alfred. b 41. BA. Sarum & Wells Th Coll. **d** 82 **p** 83. C Harpenden St Jo *St Alb* 82-85; TV Lynton, Brendon, Countisbury, Lynmouth etc *Ex* 85-86. *Address temp unknown*

GRAY, Penelope Jane. b 63. SS Hild & Bede Coll Dur BA85 Em Coll Cam MPhil88. Westcott Ho Cam 86. **d** 89. Par Dn Evington *Leic* from 89. *51 St Denys Road, Leicester LE5 6DS* Leicester (0533) 736445

GRAY, Percy. b 28. TD71. Lon Univ BA53 St Cath Soc Ox BA55 MA59. Oak Hill Th Coll 50. **d** 55 **p** 56. C Sutton *Liv* 55-58; C Chelsea Ch Ch *Lon* 58-59; V Bermondsey St Crispin w Ch Ch *S'wark* from 59; CF (TA) 59-67; CF (TAVR) from 67; CF (ACF) from 76. *St Crispin's Vicarage, Southwark Park Road, London SE16 2HU* 071-237 5567

GRAY, Philip Thomas. b 41. Lon Univ BA65. Chich Th Coll 66. **d** 68 **p** 69. C Leigh St Clem *Chelmsf* 68-74; V Mendlesham *St E* from 74; P-in-c Wickham Skeith from

86. *The Vicarage, Mendlesham, Stowmarket, Suffolk IP14 5RS* Stowmarket (0449) 766359

GRAY, Sidney Patrick. b 19. Worc Ord Coll. **d** 63 **p** 63. V Dunholme *Linc* 65-71; R Cliffe at Hoo w Cooling *Roch* 72-78; V Gillingham St Aug 78-84; rtd 84; Perm to Offic *Roch & Cant* from 84. *September Cottage, 168 Loose Road, Maidstone, Kent ME15 7UD* Maidstone (0622) 65053

GRAY-STACK, Martha Mary. QUB BA57. **d** 90 **p** 91. NSM Limerick City *L & K* from 90. *6 Villiers Square, Church Street, Limerick, Irish Republic* Limerick (61) 48761

GRAYSHON, Matthew Richard. b 47. St Jo Coll Nottm BTh81. **d** 81 **p** 82. C Beverley Minster *York* 81-85; V Hallwood *Ches* from 85. *The Vicarage, 6 Kirkstone Crescent, Runcorn, Cheshire WA7 3JQ* Runcorn (0928) 713101

GRAYSHON, Paul Nicholas Walton. b 50. St Jo Coll Dur 81. **d** 83 **p** 84. C Walkden Moor *Man* 83-87; V Radcliffe St Andr from 87. *St Andrew's Vicarage, St Andrew's View, Radcliffe, Manchester M26 0HE* 061-723 2427

GRAYSON, Canon Robert William. b 24. Worc Coll Ox BA48 MA49 DipTh50. Wycliffe Hall Ox 49. **d** 50 **p** 51. V Stanwix *Carl* 66-79; RD Carl 71-79; Hon Can Carl Cathl from 76; V Appleby 79-89; R Ormside 81-89; rtd 89. *Panorama, North End, Burgh-by-Sands, Carlisle CA5 6BD* Burgh-by-Sands (022876) 863

GRAZEBROOK, Lt-Col Francis Michael. b 08. Ch Ch Ox BA30 MA56. St Aug Coll Cant 56. **d** 57 **p** 58. V Wolverley *Worc* 61-71; Hon C Tenbury *Heref* 72-80; rtd 75; Perm to Offic *Ox* from 83. *Arundel, Wash Hill, Wooburn Green, Bucks HP10 0JA* Bourne End (06285) 22205

GREADY, Andrew John. b 63. Univ Coll Lon BSc84. St Jo Coll Nottm DPS89. **d** 89 **p** 90. C Monkwearmouth St Andr *Dur* from 89. *10 Ashleigh Grove, Sunderland SR6 9EF* 091-548 7112

GREADY, Leslie. b 33. Southn Univ BA54 Sheff Univ MEd81. Wells Th Coll 54. **d** 56 **p** 57. C Walton St Mary *Liv* 56-59; S Africa 59-65; Rhodesia 65-73; Adn Bembesi 66-69; Adn Matabeleland 69-73; Can Res Sheff Cathl *Sheff* 73-82; Dioc Dir of Ords 81-82; V Darlington St Cuth *Dur* from 82; RD Darlington from 84. *26 Upsall Drive, Darlington, Co Durham DL3 8RB* Darlington (0325) 58911 or 482417

GREANY, Richard Andrew Hugh. b 44. Qu Coll Ox BA67 MA83. Coll of Resurr Mirfield 67. **d** 69 **p** 70. C Hartlepool St Oswald *Dur* 69-72; C Clifton All SS *Bris* 72-75; Tutor Coll of Resurr Mirfield 75-78; V Whitworth w Spennymoor *Dur* 78-83; P-in-c Byers Green 78-79; Asst Prin St Alb Minl Tr Scheme 83-88; V Flamstead *St Alb* 83-88; V Hessle *York* from 88. *The Vicarage, 4 Chestnut Avenue, Hessle, N Humberside HU13 0RH* Hull (0482) 648555

GREASLEY, James Kenneth. b 39. K Coll Lon BD AKC66. **d** 67 **p** 68. C Stoke upon Trent *Lich* 67-70; Zambia 70-76; Chapl HM Borstal Gaynes Hall 76-81; V Gt Staughton *Ely* 76-81; V Melbourn from 81; V Meldreth from 81; RD Shingay from 82. *The Vicarage, Melbourn, Royston, Herts SG8 6DY* Royston (0763) 60295

GREATBATCH, John Charles. b 56. BA. Coll of Resurr Mirfield. **d** 83 **p** 84. C Wednesbury St Paul Wood Green *Lich* 83-88; C Codsall from 88. *Church House, Bilbrook, Wolverhampton WV8 1EU* Codsall (09074) 2912

GREATHEAD, Canon Edwin Bateson. b 24. Man Univ BA49. Wycliffe Hall Ox 49. **d** 51 **p** 52. V Hatf *Sheff* 61-78; Chapl HM Borstal Hatf 75-78; V Frodingham *Linc* 78-89; Can and Preb Linc Cathl from 87; rtd 89. *17 Bakersfield, Wrawby, Brigg, S Humberside DN20 8SZ* Brigg (0652) 58603

GREATREX, Warren Robert. b 21. Qu Univ Kingston Ontario BCom41. Trin Coll Toronto LTh50 BD51. **d** 50 **p** 51. Canada 50-75; Perm to Offic *Heref* from 78. *The Highlands, Symonds Yat, Ross-on-Wye, Herefordshire HR9 6DY* Symonds Yat (0600) 890318

GREAVES, Arthur Roy Hurst. b 15. Man Univ BA38. Ridley Hall Cam 38. **d** 40 **p** 41. V Diseworth *Leic* 69-78; R Long Whatton and Diseworth 78-82; rtd 82. *Unit 103, 20 Excelsior Street, Shenton Park, W Australia 6008*

GREAVES, David Reginald. b 19. ALCD49. **d** 49 **p** 50. V Billericay St Mary *Chelmsf* 62-77; RD Brentwood 69-76; TR Billericay and Lt Burstead 77-79; P-in-c Langdon Hills 79-84; R 84-87; rtd 87. *69 Reymead Close, West Mersea, Colchester CO6 8DN* Colchester (0206) 383106

GREAVES, John Neville. b 29. AAAI56 Lon Univ DipTh60. St Aid Birkenhead 58. **d** 61 **p** 62. C Pendleton St Ambrose *Man* 61-63; C Benchill 63-65; C-in-c All SS Peel Hall (Wythenshawe) CD 65-66; C-in-c St Rich Peel

Hall (Wythenshawe) CD 66-69; Min-in-c St Rich Peel Hall w St Wythenshawe St Rich 71-73; R Sadberge *Dur* 73-78; V Dur St Cuth from 78; Chapl New Coll Dur from 78; Chapl Dur Fire Brigade from 85; RD Dur from 80. *St Cuthbert's Vicarage, Aykley Court, Durham DH1 4NW* 091-386 4526

GREED, Frederick John. b 44. Trin Coll Bris 79. **d** 81 **p** 82. C Yateley *Win* 81-85; R Ore *Chich* from 85. *St Helen's Rectory, 266 Elphinstone Road, Hastings, E Sussex TN34 2AG* Hastings (0424) 425172

GREEDY, Tegryd Joseph. b 31. St D Coll Lamp 59. **d** 61 **p** 62. C Newbridge *Mon* 61-64; C Bassaleg 64-66; V Newport St Teilo 66-74; Hon C Newport St Mark 80-83; V Goldcliffe and Whiston and Nash 83-90; Ind Chapl 83-90; V Marshfield and Peterstone Wentloog etc from 90. *The Vicarage, Church Lane, Marshfield, Cardiff CF3 8UF* Castleton (0633) 680257

GREEN, Alan John Enrique. b 56. Worc Coll Ox BTh77, Linc Th Coll 83. **d** 85 **p** 86. C Kirkby *Liv* 85-88; TV from 88. *St Martin's House, Peatwood Avenue, Kirkby, Merseyside L32 7PR* 051-546 2387

GREEN, Canon Alan Thomas. b 21. Launde Abbey. **d** 64 **p** 65. V Oaks (Charnwood Forest) *Leic* 67-70; R Braunstone 70-74; P-in-c Loddington 74-83; Hon Can Leic Cathl 78-87; P-in-c Knossington and Cold Overton 81-83; P-in-c Owston and Withcote 81-83; V Enderby w Lubbesthorpe and Thurlaston 83-87; rtd 87. *8 Halcroft Rise, Wigston Magna, Leicester LE8 2HS* Leicester (0533) 811605

GREEN, Alfred. b 06. St Aid Birkenhead 47. **d** 48 **p** 49. V Holme-in-Cliviger *Blackb* 66-73; rtd 73; Lic to Offic *Blackb* from 75. *40 Richmond Avenue, Cliviger, Burnley, Lancs BB10 4JL* Burnley (0282) 38429

GREEN, Arthur Edward. b 27. Chich Th Coll 58. **d** 59 **p** 60. C Malden St Jas *S'wark* 59-62; C Caterham 62-67; R Burgh Parva w Briston *Nor* 67-75; V Middleton 75-76; V Middleton w E Winch 76-84; R Neatishead w Irstead 84-90; V Barton Turf 84-90; R Neatishead, Barton Turf and Irstead from 90. *The Rectory, Neatishead, Norwich NR12 8BT* Horning (0692) 630645

GREEN, Barrie. b 51. SS Coll Cam BA72 MA76. Wycliffe Hall Ox 75. **d** 78 **p** 79. C Castle Vale *Birm* 78-81; V W Heath from 81; RD Kings Norton from 87. *St Anne's Vicarage, Lilley Lane, Birmingham B31 3JT* 021-475 5587

GREEN, Brian Robert. b 31. Bris Univ BA55. Tyndale Hall Bris 52. **d** 56 **p** 57. C Toxteth Park St Philemon *Liv* 56-58; V Toxteth Park St Philemon w St Silas 58-69; P-in-c Toxteth Park St Gabr 64-69; P-in-c Toxteth Park St Jo and St Thos 64-69; P-in-c Toxteth Park St Jas and St Matt 68-69; V Elsenham *Chelmsf* 69-85; V Henham 69-85; P-in-c Ugley 84-85; V Henham and Elsenham w Ugley 85-89; RD Newport and Stansted 87-89; Perm to Offic *Ex* 90-91; V Tidenham w Beachley and Lancaut *Glouc* from 91. *Tidenham Vicarage, Gloucester Road, Tutshill, Chepstow, Gwent NP6 7DH* Chepstow (0291) 622442

GREEN, Canon Bryan Stuart Westmacott. b 01. Lon Univ BD22 Winnipeg Univ Hon DD61. Lambeth DD85 Lon Coll of Div 19. **d** 24 **p** 25. R Birm St Martin *Birm* 48-70; Hon Can Birm Cathl 50-70; rtd 70; Hon C Thame w Towersey *Ox* from 71. *Westfield, 68 Southern Road, Thame, Oxon OX9 2DZ* Thame (084421) 2026

GREEN, Canon Cecil Frederick. b 08. MBE56. St Jo Coll Dur LTh31 BA33 MA36 BD. Lambeth DD82. **d** 33 **p** 35. Chapl Casablanca *Eur* 34-83; Hon Can All SS Cathl Cairo 73-83; rtd 83; Perm to Offic *St E* from 83. *25 Gainsborough Road, Felixstowe, Suffolk IP11 7HT* Felixstowe (0394) 284616

GREEN, Charles Clisby. b 11. St Aid Birkenhead 46. **d** 48 **p** 49. R Eling *Win* 68-73; R Testwood 68-73; V Marchwood 68-73; TR Eling, Testwood and Marchwood 73-75; rtd 75; Perm to Offic *Man* 77-79; Win from 79. *Fosbrooke House, 8 Clifton Drive, Lytham, Lancs FY8 5RE* Lytham (0253) 738189

GREEN, Christopher Frederick. b 46. Nottm Univ BTh75 Birm Univ DipEd85. Bp Otter Coll CertEd69 Linc Th Coll 71. **d** 75 **p** 76. C Hodge Hill *Birm* 75-77; C S Lafford *Linc* 77-79; P-in-c Worc St Mich *Worc* 79-82; Hd of Relig Studies & Lib RNIB New Coll Worc from 82. *Darenth, Walkers Lane, Whittington, Worcester WR5 2RE* Worcester (0905) 355714

GREEN, Christopher Martyn. b 58. Edin Univ BD. Cranmer Hall Dur. **d** 83 **p** 84. C Virginia Water *Guildf* 83-87; C Bromley Ch Ch *Roch* from 87. *68 Warren Avenue, Bromley BR1 4BS* 081-460 1174

GREEN, Mrs Clare Noreen. b 30. SW Minl Tr Course 84. **d** 88. NSM Bideford *Ex* 88-90; Perm to Offic from 90. *2 Lane Field Road, Londonderry Farm, Bideford, Devon EX39 3QY* Bideford (0237) 472960

GREEN, Clifford. b 28. Leeds Univ BA51. Coll of Resurr Mirfield 51. **d** 53 **p** 54. C Solihull *Birm* 53-56; CR from 58; Lic to Offic *Wakef* 59-62 and from 67; S Africa 63-66; Lic to Offic *Ripon* 75-76. *House of the Resurrection, Mirfield, W Yorkshire WF14 0BN* Mirfield (0924) 494318

GREEN, David John. b 32. K Alfred's Coll Win 51 CPC84. Sarum Th Coll 63. **d** 64 **p** 65. C Trowbridge H Trin *Sarum* 64-68; Hd of RE Trowbridge Boys' High Sch 64-68; V Bournemouth St Fran *Win* 68-70; V Weymouth St Paul *Sarum* from 70; Chapl S Dorset Tech Coll Weymouth 80-85; Weymouth Coll from 85. *St Paul's Vicarage, 58 Abbotsbury Road, Weymouth, Dorset DT4 0BJ* Weymouth (0305) 771217

GREEN, David John. b 54. DCR, MU. SW Minl Tr Course 82. **d** 85 **p** 86. C St Marychurch *Ex* 85-89; C Laira 89-90; V Maughold *S & M* from 90. *The Vicarage, Maughold, Ramsey, Isle of Man* Ramsey (0624) 812070

GREEN, David Norman. b 37. Magd Coll Cam BA60. Clifton Th Coll 60. **d** 62 **p** 63. SSF from 55; C Islington St Mary *Lon* 62-65; C Burley *Ripon* 65-68; Kenya 69-80; P-in-c Brimscombe *Glouc* from 81; P-in-c Woodchester from 90. *The Vicarage, Brimscombe, Stroud, Glos GL5 2PA* Brimscombe (0453) 882204

GREEN, David William. b 53. CertEd75 Nottm Univ BCombStuds84. Linc Th Coll 81. **d** 84 **p** 85. C S Merstham *S'wark* 84-88; C Walton-on-Thames *Guildf* from 88. *1 Egmont Road, Walton-on-Thames, Surrey KT12 2NW* Walton-on-Thames (0932) 229621

GREEN, Canon Dennis John. b 45. Lich Th Coll 69. **d** 72 **p** 73. C Hampton All SS *Lon* 72-74; P-in-c Leverington *Ely* 75-76; R 76-80; Can Res Ely Cathl from 80; Vice-Dean and Treas from 84; Dioc Development Officer for Par from 80; Dioc Development Consultant from 84. *The Black Hostelry, The College, Ely, Cambs CB7 4DL* Ely (0353) 2612

GREEN, Canon Derek George Wilson. b 27. Bris Univ BA53 MA58. Tyndale Hall Bris 48. **d** 53 **p** 54. C Weymouth St Mary *Sarum* 53-55; Chapl RAF 55-58; R N Pickenham w Houghton on the Hill *Nor* 58-89; R S Pickenham 58-89; Hon Can Nor Cathl from 78; E Region Co-ord Scripture Union from 80; R N Pickenham w S Pickenham etc from 89. *The Rectory, South Pickenham, Swaffham, Norfolk PE37 8DS* Great Cressingham (07606) 292

GREEN, Donald Henry. b 31. Selw Coll Cam BA54. Qu Coll Birm 81. **d** 83 **p** 84. C Dudley Holly Hall St Aug *Worc* 83-85; V Dudley St Barn 85-90. *The Cuckoo's Nest, 12 Mill Green, Knighton, Powys LD7 1EE* Knighton (0547) 528289

GREEN, Donald Pentney (Brother Donald). b 25. Leeds Univ BA50. Coll of Resurr Mirfield 50. **d** 52 **p** 53. C Ardwick St Benedict *Man* 52-55; SSF from 55; Sec for Miss SSF from 78; Lic to Offic *Chelmsf* 69-72 and 58-60; Papua New Guinea 60-63; Chapl HM Pris Kingston Portsm 72-76; Lic to Offic *Edin* 76-77; Org Sec Catholic Renewal 77; Lic to Offic *Lich* from 78. *42 Balaam Street, London E13 8AQ* 071-474 5863

GREEN, Mrs Dorothy Mary. b 36. Westf Coll Lon BA58. Selly Oak Coll 60. **dss** 83 **d** 87. Ryde All SS *Portsm* 83-87; C 87-91; Hon C Hempnall *Nor* from 91. *The Rectory, Hempnall, Norwich NR15 2AD* Hempnall (050842) 8157

GREEN, Douglas Edward. b 17. Sarum Th Coll 47. **d** 50 **p** 51. V Bosbury *Heref* 58-78; R Coddington 59-79; V Wellington Heath 59-79; Hon C Minsterley 78-80; rtd 82; Perm to Offic *Worc* from 83. *St Agnes, Lower Dingle, West Malvern, Worcs WR14 4BQ*

GREEN, Duncan Jamie. b 52. Sarum & Wells Th Coll 82. **d** 84 **p** 85. C Uckfield *Chich* 84-87; Youth Chapl *Chelmsf* from 87. *25 Roxwell Road, Chelmsford CM1 2LY* Chelmsford (0245) 264187

GREEN, Edward John. b 35. Lich Th Coll. **d** 59 **p** 60. C Longford *Cov* 59-61; C Wigston Magna *Leic* 61-65; V from 73; V Ellistown 65-73. *The Vicarage, Bushloe End, Wigston Magna, Leicester LE8 2BA* Leicester (0533) 883419

GREEN, Canon Prof Edward Michael Bankes. b 30. Ex Coll Ox BA53 MA53 Qu Coll Cam BA57 MA57 BD69. Ridley Hall Cam 55. **d** 57 **p** 58. C Eastbourne H Trin *Chich* 57-60; Tutor Lon Coll of Div 60-69; Prin St Jo Coll Nottm 69-75; Can Th Cov Cathl *Cov* 70-78; R Ox St Aldate w H Trin *Ox* 75-82; R Ox St Aldate w St Matt 82-86; Canada from 87; Prof Evang Regent Coll Vancouver from 87. *5800 University Boulevard, Vancouver, British Columbia, Canada, V6T 2E4* Vancouver (604) 224-3245

283

GREEN, Edward Wallace. b 11. K Coll Lon BA32 AKC33. Ripon Hall Ox 33. **d** 35 **p** 36. Chapl Oakham Sch Leics 54-58; Perm to Offic *Chelmsf* 61-79; rtd 79; Perm to Offic *Win* from 81. *Day House, Alma Road, Romsey, Hants SO51 8EB*

GREEN, Mrs Elizabeth Pauline Anne. b 29. Lon Coll of Div DipRK70. **dss** 76 **d** 87. Chorleywood Ch Ch *St Alb* 76-87; Par Dn 87-90; C Chipping Sodbury and Old Sodbury *Glouc* from 90; Asst Dioc Missr from 90. *The Old House, Parks Farm, Old Sodbury, Bristol BS17 6PX* Chipping Sodbury (0454) 311936

GREEN, Eric Kenneth. b 18. Tyndale Hall Bris 40. **d** 45 **p** 47. R All Cannings w Etchilhampton *Sarum* 63-75; V Over Kellet *Blackb* 75-83; rtd 83. *1 Hill Crescent, Burley in Wharfedale, Ilkley, W Yorkshire LS29 7QG* Burley-in-Wharfedale (0943) 864538

GREEN, Ernest James. b 31. Pemb Coll Cam BA55 MA62. Linc Th Coll 55. **d** 57 **p** 58. C Rawmarsh w Parkgate *Sheff* 57-60; Sec Th Colls Dept SCM 60-62; Prec and Sacr Bris Cathl *Bris* 62-65; Min Can 62-65; V Churchill *B & W* 65-78; RD Locking 72-78; V Burrington and Churchill 78-82; Preb Wells Cathl 81-82; V Ryde All SS *Portsm* 82-91; P-in-c Ryde H Trin 82-86; RD E Wight 83-88; TR Hempnall *Nor* from 91. *The Rectory, Hempnall, Norwich NR15 2NL* Hempnall (050842) 8157

GREEN, Ernest Swinfen. b 12. Wells Th Coll 66. **d** 67 **p** 67. V Lower Beeding *Chich* 70-77; rtd 77. *9 Barleycroft, Cowfold, Horsham, W Sussex RH13 8DP* Horsham (0403) 864352

GREEN, Frank Gilbert. b 23. Kelham Th Coll 46. **d** 50 **p** 51. C Sheff Parson Cross St Cecilia *Sheff* 50-56; SSM from 52; C Nottm St Geo w St Jo *S'well* 56-58; Basutoland 59-62; S Africa 62-69 and 84-88; Lesotho 69-84; Lic to Offic *Ox* from 88. *SSM Priory, Willen, Milton Keynes MK15 9AA* Newport Pagnell (0908) 663749

GREEN, Frederick George. b 40. Nottm Univ BA62 MA67. Linc Th Coll 64. **d** 66 **p** 67. C Warsop *S'well* 66-70; R 76-89; V Clipstone 70-76; P-in-c Norton Cuckney 85-89; TR Hucknall Torkard from 89. *The Rectory, Annesley Road, Hucknall, Nottingham NG15 7DE* Nottingham (0602) 632033

GREEN, George Henry Langston. b 12. St Aug Coll Cant 38. **d** 41 **p** 42. V Frodsham *Ches* 55-78; rtd 78; Perm to Offic *Ches* from 78. *River View, Gwespyr, Holywell, Clwyd* Prestatyn (0745) 857489

GREEN, George James. b 26. Cuddesdon Coll 69. **d** 69 **p** 70. C Handsworth St Mary *Birm* 69-76; R Croughton w Evenley *Pet* 76-88; R Aynho and Croughton w Evenley from 88. *The Rectory, Croughton Road, Aynho, Banbury, Oxon OX17 3BG* Croughton (0869) 810903

GREEN, Gordon Sydney. b 33. Ridley Hall Cam 77. **d** 79 **p** 80. C Ipswich St Marg *St E* 79-83; TV Barton Mills, Beck Row w Kenny Hill etc 83-85; V Mildenhall 85-86; Perm to Offic *Pet* from 87; rtd 88. *1 Highcliffe Close, High Street, Thornton, Bradford, W Yorkshire BD13 3EH* Bradford (0274) 835001

GREEN, Graham Herbert. b 53. City Univ BSc74. Westcott Ho Cam 75. **d** 78 **p** 79. C Hatcham St Cath *S'wark* 78-82; C S Ashford Ch Ch *Cant* 82-88; V Cheriton All So w Newington from 88. *All Souls' Vicarage, 1 Ashley Avenue, Cheriton, Folkestone, Kent CT19 4PX* Folkestone (0303) 275483

GREEN, Graham Reginald. b 48. Sarum & Wells Th Coll 71. **d** 74 **p** 75. C Chorley St Laur *Blackb* 74-76; C Padiham 76-79; V Osmondthorpe St Phil *Ripon* from 79. *St Philip's Vicarage, 68 Osmondthorpe Lane, Leeds LS9 9EF* Leeds (0532) 497371

GREEN, Canon Harry George. b 04. Lon Univ BA25 AKC27. Wells Th Coll 28. **d** 29 **p** 30. V Abbotsbury *Sarum* 65-71; rtd 71. *9 Cross Oak Road, Berkhamsted, Herts HP4 3EH* Berkhamsted (0442) 866350

GREEN, Humphrey Christian (Brother Benedict). b 24. Mert Coll Ox BA49 MA52. Cuddesdon Coll 50. **d** 51 **p** 52. C Northolt St Mary *Lon* 51-56; Lect Th K Coll Lon 56-60; Lic to Offic *Wakef* from 61; CR from 62; Vice-Prin Coll of Resurr Mirfield 65-75; Prin 75-84. *House of the Resurrection, Mirfield, W Yorkshire WF14 0BN* Mirfield (0924) 494318

GREEN, James Hardman. b 19. Open Univ BA74. **d** 52 **p** 53. R Morcott w S Luffenham *Pet* 65-75; V E Boldon *Dur* 77-84; rtd 84. *1 Netherwindings, Towthorpe Road, Haxby, York YO3 8FB* York (0904) 764364

GREEN, James Manton. b 33. E Midl Min Tr Course 82. **d** 85 **p** 86. Hon C Kirby Muxloe *Leic* from 85; Asst Chapl Leic Gen Hosp from 89. *83 Oakcroft Avenue, Kirby Muxloe, Leicester LE9 9DH* Leicester (0533) 393126

GREEN, Miss Jennifer Mary. b 55. SEN78 SRN81 RM84. Trin Coll Bris DipHE88 ADPS89. **d** 90. C Tong *Bradf* from 90. *St Christopher's Vicarage, 207 Broadstone Way, Bradford BD4 9BT* Bradford (0274) 685256

GREEN, Jeremy Nigel. b 52. St Andr Univ MA Nottm Univ DipTh. St Jo Coll Nottm 80. **d** 83 **p** 84. C Dorridge *Birm* 83-86; V Scrooby *S'well* from 86. *The Vicarage, 7 Arundel Drive, Ranskill, Retford, Notts DN22 8PG* Retford (0777) 818470

GREEN, John. b 28. AKC54. **d** 55 **p** 56. V Inskip *Blackb* 63-75; V Fairhaven 75-87; rtd 87; Perm to Offic *Blackb* from 87. *42 Westwood Road, Lytham, Lytham St Annes, Lancs FY8 5NX* Lytham (0253) 739288

GREEN, John. b 53. Nottm Univ BCombStuds83. Linc Th Coll 80. **d** 83 **p** 84. C Watford St Mich *St Alb* 83-86; C St Alb St Steph 86-91; Chapl RN from 91. *c/o MOD, Lacon House, Theobald's Road, London WC1X 8RY* 071-430 7268

GREEN, John David. b 29. Lon Univ BD66. Roch Th Coll 63. **d** 66 **p** 66. C Roch St Pet w St Marg *Roch* 66-72; V Oxshott *Guildf* 72-85; R Weybridge from 85. *The Rectory, 3 Churchfields Avenue, Weybridge, Surrey KT13 9YA* Weybridge (0932) 842566

GREEN, John Henry. b 44. K Coll Lon BD72 AKC. **d** 73 **p** 74. C Tupsley *Heref* 73-77; Asst Chapl Newc Univ *Newc* 77-79; V Stevenage St Hugh Chells *St Alb* 79-85; V St Jo in Bedwardine *Worc* from 85. *St John's Vicarage, 143 Malvern Road, Worcester WR2 4LN* Worcester (0905) 422327

GREEN, John Herbert Gardner-Waterman. b 21. Trin Hall Cam BA48 MA58. Wells Th Coll 58. **d** 59 **p** 60. R Sandhurst w Newenden *Cant* 68-90; RD W Charing 74-81; rtd 90. *Littlefield House, Rolvenden Layne, Cranbrook, Kent TN17 4NS* Cranbrook (0580) 241579

GREEN, Preb John Stanley. b 12. Keble Coll Ox BA33 MA37. Wells Th Coll 33. **d** 35 **p** 36. R Ex St Jas *Ex* 49-77; Preb Ex Cathl 69-84; rtd 77; Perm to Offic *Ex* from 84. *2 Whiteway Drive, Heavitree, Exeter EX1 3AN* Exeter (0392) 37291

GREEN, Joseph Hudson. b 28. TD76. Dur Univ TCert73. Kelham Th Coll 48. **d** 53 **p** 54. C Norton St Mich *Dur* 53-56; C Heworth St Mary 56-62; V Harton Colliery 62-69; Chapl S Shields Gen Hosp 62-69; CF (TA) 63-67; CF (TAVR) 67-77; V Leadgate *Dur* 69-78; V Dudleston Lich 78-85; V Criftins 78-85; R Hodnet w Weston under Redcastle from 85; RD Hodnet from 86; Chapl to High Sheriff of Shropshire from 87. *The Rectory, Hodnet, Market Drayton, Shropshire TF9 3NT* Hodnet (063084) 491

GREEN, Julia Ann. b 58. Nottm Univ BA80. Linc Th Coll 84. **dss** 86 **d** 87. Asst Chapl HM Pris Morton Hall 85-90; Linc St Jo *Linc* 86-87; Hon C 87-88; Hon C Bardney from 88; Chapl Linc Co and St Geo Hosps Linc from 90. *The Rectory, 10 Church Lane, Bardney, Lincoln LN3 5TZ* Bardney (0526) 398595

GREEN, Karina Beverley. b 61. Ripon Coll Cuddesdon 87. **d** 90. C Lee-on-the-Solent *Portsm* from 90. *85 Seymour Road, Lee-on-the-Solent, Hants PO13 9EQ* Lee-on-the-Solent (0705) 552108

GREEN, Laurence Alexander. b 45. K Coll Lon BD68 AKC68. DMin82 NY Th Sem STM69 St Aug Coll Cant 70. **d** 70 **p** 71. C Kingstanding St Mark *Birm* 70-73; V Erdington St Chad 73-83; Prin Aston Tr Scheme 83-89; Hon C Birchfield *Birm* 84-89; TR Poplar *Lon* from 89. *Poplar Rectory, Newby Place, London E14 0EY* 071-987 3133 or 538 9198

GREEN, Leslie James. b 31. K Coll Lon BD53 AKC54. **d** 56 **p** 57. C Catford St Andr *S'wark* 56-60; R Glas St Oswald *Glas* 60-70; Lic to Offic *Dur* 71-73; V Oxclose 73-82; TR Sheff Manor *Sheff* 82-85; V Nether w Upper Poppleton *York* from 85. *The Vicarage, 15 Nether Way, Upper Poppleton, York YO2 6JQ* York (0904) 794744

GREEN, Mrs Margaret Elizabeth. b 34. DipYL65. St Mich Ho Ox 60. **dss** 84 **d** 87. Ecclesall *Sheff* 84-87; Par Dn 87-90; Par Dn Doncaster St Jas from 90. *91 Littlemoor Lane, Doncaster, S Yorkshire DN4 0LQ* Doncaster (0302) 365884

✠**GREEN, Rt Rev Mark.** b 17. MC45. Linc Coll Ox BA40 MA44 Aston Univ Hon DSc80. Cuddesdon Coll 40. **d** 40 **p** 41 **c** 72. C Glouc St Cath *Glouc* 40-42; CF (EC) 43-46; V Newland St Jo *York* 48-53; CF 53-56; V S Bank *York* 56-58; R Cottingham 58-64; Can and Preb York Minster 63-72; Hon Chapl to Abp York 64-72; V Bishopthorpe 64-72; V Acaster Malbis 64-72; RD Ainsty 64-68; Suff Bp Aston *Birm* 72-82; Dioc Dir of Ords 80-82; rtd 82; Asst Bp Chich from 82. *13 Archery Court, Archery Road, St Leonards-on-Sea, E Sussex TN38 0HZ* Hastings (0424) 444649

GREEN, Martin Charles. b 59. Bris Univ BA81 MPhil86. Wycliffe Hall Ox 82. d 84 p 85. C Margate H Trin *Cant* 84-88; V Kingston upon Hull Southcoates St Aid *York* from 88. *St Aidan's Vicarage, 139 Southcoates Avenue, Hull HU9 3HF* Hull (0482) 74403

GREEN, Martyn. b 41. FCA. Ridley Hall Cam 78. d 80 p 81. C Wetherby *Ripon* 80-83; V Leeds St Cypr Harehills 83-90; V Ossett cum Gawthorpe *Wakef* from 90. *The Vicarage, Fearnley Avenue, Ossett, W Yorkshire WF5 9ET* Wakefield (0924) 274068

GREEN, Canon Maurice Paul. b 34. MCIMA60. Wells Th Coll 68. d 70 p 71. C Eaton *Nor* 70-74; R N w S Wootton 74-90; RD Lynn 83-89; Hon Can Nor Cathl from 88; V Swaffham from 90. *The Vicarage, White Cross Road, Swaffham, Norfolk PE37 8QY* Swaffham (0760) 721373

GREEN, Neil Howard. b 57. New Coll Ox BA80 PGCE81. Wycliffe Hall Ox 87. d 90 p 91. C Finchley St Paul and St Luke *Lon* from 90. *Church House, Howes Close, London N3 3BX* 081-346 0563

GREEN, Nicholas Eliot. b 54. Leeds Univ BA76 Lon Univ BD78 AKC. Westcott Ho Cam 78. d 79 p 80. C Southgate Ch Ch *Lon* 79-82; Chapl Brooklands Tech Coll 82-86; C Weybridge *Guildf* 82-86; V Hilton *Ely* from 86; V Fenstanton from 86. *The Vicarage, 16 Church Street, Fenstanton, Huntingdon, Cambs PE18 9JL* St Ives (0480) 63334

GREEN, Paul. b 25. RD. Sarum & Wells Th Coll 72. d 74 p 75. C Pinhoe *Ex* 74-77; P-in-c *Ex* 79-85; P-in-c Bishopsteignton 85-88; P-in-c Ideford, Luton and Ashcombe 85-88; rtd 88; Perm to Offic *Ex* from 88. *58 Maudlin Drive, Teignmouth, Devon TQ14 8SB* Teignmouth (0626) 777312

GREEN, Paul Francis. b 48. Cranmer Hall Dur BA78. d 79 p 80. C Cirencester *Glouc* 79-82; C Lydney w Aylburton 82-85; V Westbury-on-Severn w Flaxley and Blaisdon 85-90; Chapl Leics Mental Health Service Unit and Carlton Hayes Hosp from 90. *Carlton Hayes Hospital, Narborough, Leics LE9 5ES* Leicester (0533) 863481

GREEN, Paul John. b 48. Sarum & Wells Th Coll 72. d 73 p 74. C Tuffley *Glouc* 73-76; C Prestbury 76-82; P-in-c Highnam w Lassington and Rudford 82-83; P-in-c Tibberton w Taynton 82-83; R Highnam, Lassington, Rudford, Tibberton etc from 84. *The Rectory, 13 Maidenhall, Highnam, Gloucester GL2 8DJ* Gloucester (0452) 25567

GREEN, Peter. b 38. Ex Univ BSc59. Sarum Th Coll 59. d 61 p 62. C Romford St Edw *Chelmsf* 61-66; Ceylon 66-70; V Darnall H Trin *Sheff* 71-80; TV Stantonbury *Ox* 80-87; TV Stantonbury and Willen 87-91; Dep Chapl HM Pris Belmarsh from 91. *The Chaplain's Office, HM Prison Belmarsh, Western Way, London SE28 0EB* 081-317 2436

GREEN, Canon Peter Edwin. b 33. Lich Th Coll. d 62 p 63. C Sprowston *Nor* 62-65; C-in-c Heartsease St Fran CD 65-73; V Loddon w Sisland from 73; Hon Can Nor Cathl from 86. *The Vicarage, 4 Market Place, Loddon, Norwich NR14 6LT* Loddon (0508) 20251

GREEN, Peter Geoffrey. b 59. St Andr Univ MA83. Coll of Resurr Mirfield 85. d 88 p 89. C Pershore w Pinvin, Wick and Birlingham *Worc* 88-91; V Dudley St Barn from 91. *St Barnabas's Vicarage, Middlepark Road, Dudley, W Midlands DY1 2LD* Dudley (0384) 56680

GREEN, Canon Philip Harry. b 19. ALCD50. d 50 p 51. V Shipley St Paul *Bradf* 64-77; Hon Can Bradf Cathl 77-82; V Gargrave 77-82; rtd 82; Perm to Offic *Carl & Bradf* from 82. *102 Kentsford Road, Grange-over-Sands, Cumbria LA11 7BB* Grange-over-Sands (05395) 32950

GREEN, Richard Charles. b 49. K Coll Lon 68 St Aug Coll Cant 73. d 74 p 75. C Broseley w Benthall *Heref* 74-79; TV Heref St Martin w St Fran (S Wye Team Min) from 80. *Flat 3, St Martin's Parish Centre, Ross Road, Hereford HR2 7RJ* Hereford (0432) 354588 or 353717

GREEN, Robert Henry. b 57. K Coll Lon BD79. Wycliffe Hall Ox 81. d 83 p 84. C Norbury *Ches* 83-86 and from 91; C Knutsford St Jo and Toft 86-88; rtd 88. *122 Cavendish Road, Hazel Grove, Stockport, Cheshire SK7 6JH* Poynton (0625) 877042

GREEN, Robert Leonard. b 44. Sarum & Wells Th Coll. d 84 p 85. C Battersea St Luke *S'wark* 84-89; CF from 89. *c/o MOD (Army), Bagshot Park, Bagshot, Surrey GU19 5PL* Bagshot (0276) 71717

GREEN, Robert Stanley. b 42. Dur Univ BA65. Wells Th Coll 65. d 67 p 68. C Ashford *Cant* 67-73; R Otham 73-80; V Bethersden w High Halden 80-87; R Winterbourne Stickland and Turnworth etc *Sarum* from 87. *The Rectory, Winterbourne Stickland, Blandford Forum, Dorset DT11 0NL* Milton Abbas (0258) 880482

GREEN, Robin Christopher William. b 43. Leeds Univ BA64 Fitzw Ho Cam BA67. Ridley Hall Cam 65. d 68 p 69. C S'wark H Trin *S'wark* 68-71; C Englefield Green *Guildf* 71-73; Chapl Whitelands Coll of HE *S'wark* 73-78; Team Ldr Dioc Lay Tr Team 78-84; V W Brompton St Mary w St Pet *Lon* 84-87; USPG 87-90; Perm to Offic *S'wark* 88-90; NSM from 91. *2 Church Path, Mitcham, Surrey CR4 3BN* 081-543 0519

GREEN, Roger Thomas. b 43. Oak Hill Th Coll DipHE79. d 79 p 80. C Paddock Wood *Roch* 79-83; R High Halstow w All Hallows and Hoo St Mary 83-89; Chapl HM Pris Brixton 89-90; Chapl HM Pris Standford Hill from 90. *HM Prison Standford Hill, Church Road, Eastchurch, Sheerness, Kent ME12 4AA* Sheerness (0795) 880441

GREEN, Preb Ronald Henry. b 27. Lambeth MA86 Bps' Coll Cheshunt 53. d 55 p 56. RE Adv *Lon* 63-73; V Hampstead St Steph 64-73; RD N Camden (Hampstead) 67-73; V Heston 73-80; Preb St Paul's Cathl 75-83; Jt Dir Lon and S'wark Bd of Educn 79-83; Dir of Educn *Sarum* 83-86; R Chiddingfold *Guildf* 86-91; rtd 91; Perm to Offic *Nor* from 91. *Whitestones, The Buttlands, Wells-next-the-Sea, Norfolk NR23 1EZ* Fakenham (0328) 711813

GREEN, Ruth Valerie. b 56. Ex Univ CertEd77. Ox NSM Course 87. d 90. NSM Stantonbury and Willen *Ox* from 90. *4 Granes End, Great Linford, Milton Keynes, Bucks MK14 5DY* Milton Keynes (0908) 605422

GREEN, Stephen Keith. b 48. Ex Coll Ox BA69 Mass Inst of Tech MSc75. N Ord Course 84. d 87 p 88. Hong Kong from 87. *402 Tavistock, 10 Tregunter Path, May Road, Hong Kong* Hong Kong (852) 524-6772

GREEN, Steven Douglas. b 57. Univ of Wales (Ban) DipTh81. Sarum & Wells Th Coll 81. d 82 p 83. C Hawarden *St As* 82-86; V Mostyn from 86; V Ffynnongroew from 86; Miss to Seamen from 86. *The Vicarage, Hafod y Ddol Lane, Mostyn, Holywell, Clwyd CH8 9EJ* Mostyn (0745) 560513

GREEN, Stuart. b 57. Nottm Univ BA79. Linc Th Coll 83. d 85 p 86. C Boultham *Linc* 85-88; R Bardney from 88. *The Rectory, 10 Church Lane, Bardney, Lincoln LN3 5TZ* Bardney (0526) 398595

GREEN, Trevor Geoffrey Nash. b 45. BA. Oak Hill Th Coll 81. d 84 p 85. C Stalybridge H Trin and Ch Ch *Ches* 84-89; V from 89. *The Vicarage, Hough Hill Road, Stalybridge, Cheshire SK15 2HB* 061-303 1984

GREEN, Trevor Howard. b 37. Sarum & Wells Th Coll 72. d 74 p 75. C Bloxwich *Lich* 74-77; C Willenhall St Steph 77-79; P-in-c 79-80; V 80-82; V Essington 82-90; V Brewood from 90; V Bishopswood from 90. *The Vicarage, Sandy Lane, Brewood, Stafford ST19 9ET* Brewood (0902) 850368

GREEN, Vivian Hubert Howard. b 15. DD58. d 39 p 40. Chapl Linc Coll Ox 51-79; Rector Linc Coll Ox 83-87; rtd 87. *Calendars, Sheep Street, Burford, Oxford* Burford (099382) 3214

GREEN, William. b 44. Newc Univ BA66 DipEd67 MA77. N Ord Course 87. d 90 p 91. NSM Utley *Bradf* from 90. *105 Shann Lane, Keighley, W Yorkshire BD20 6DY* Keighley (0535) 605102

GREEN, William John. b 23. Birm Univ BSc43. Roch Th Coll 64. d 66 p 67. C Standish w Hardwicke and Haresfield *Glouc* 68-70; R Eastington and Frocester 70-80; P-in-c S Cerney w Cerney Wick 80-84; V S Cerney w Cerney Wick and Down Ampney 84-87; P-in-c Maisemore 87-90; rtd 90. *36 Fairfield, Upavon, Wilts SN9 6DZ* Stonehenge (0980) 630798

GREEN, William Lewis. b 12. St Cath Coll Cam BA34 MA39. Cuddesdon Coll 34. d 35 p 36. Benin 70-76; Nigeria 76-78; Zanzibar and Tanga 79-82; rtd 82; Perm to Offic *Ches* from 82. *20 Dunkirk Drive, Ellesmere Port, South Wirral L65 6QH* 051-355 5456

GREENACRE, Canon Roger Tagent. b 30. Clare Coll Cam BA52 MA56. Coll of Resurr Mirfield 52. d 54 p 55. C Hanworth All SS *Lon* 54-59; Chapl Ely Th Coll 59-60; Chapl Summer Fields Sch Ox 60-61; C N Audley Street St Mark *Lon* 62-63; Chapl Liddon Ho Lon 63-65; Chapl Paris St Geo *Eur* 65-75; RD France 70-75; Dioc Ecum Officer *Chich* 75-88; Lect Chich Th Coll 75-89; Can Res and Chan Chich Cathl *Chich* from 75; Chmn Chich Dioc Eur Ecum Cttee from 89. *4 Vicars' Close, Canon Lane, Chichester, W Sussex PO19 1PT* Chichester (0243) 784244

GREENALL, Ronald Gilbert. b 41. St Aid Birkenhead 61. d 64 p 65. C Adlington *Blackb* 64-67; C Ribbleton 67-69; R Coppull St Jo 69-84; V Garstang St Thos from 84; RD Garstang from 89. *The Vicarage, Church Street, Garstang, Preston PR3 1PA* Garstang (0995) 602162

GREENE, Colin John David. b 50. QUB BA73 Fitzw Coll Cam MA75 Nottm Univ PhD. St Jo Coll Nottm 78. d 80

p 81. Hon C Sandiacre *Derby* 80-81; C Loughb Em *Leic* 81-84; V Dishley and Thorpe Acre 84-89; Evang Tr Consultant Bible Soc 89-91; Tutor Trin Coll Bris from 91. *Dorema, 18 Cross Hayes, Malmesbury, Wilts SN16 9BG* Malmesbury (0666) 823879

GREENE, David Arthur Kirsopp. b 36. St Pet Coll Ox BA60 MA64 FETC81. Tyndale Hall Bris 61. **d** 63 **p** 64. C Southgate *Chich* 63-66; C Kirby Grindalythe *York* 66-69; C N Grimston w Wharram Percy and Wharram-le-Street 66-69; R Folke, N Wootton and Haydon w Long Burton *Sarum* 69-75; R Long Burton, Folke, N Wootton, Haydon etc 75-80; P-in-c Thornford w Beer Hackett 80-84; P-in-c High Stoy 81-84; R Bradf Abbas and Thornford w Beer Hackett from 84. *The Rectory, Church Road, Thornford, Sherborne, Dorset DT9 6QE* Yetminster (0935) 872382

GREENE, John Howe. b 22. K Coll Lon AKC48 BD49. **d** 49 **p** 50. R Burwash *Chich* 69-75; R Petworth 75-88; RD Petworth 76-88; P-in-c Egdean 76-80; R 80-88; rtd 88; Perm to Offic *Chich* from 88. *37 Wilderness Road, Hurstpierpoint, Hassocks, W Sussex BN6 9XD* Hurstpierpoint (0273) 833651

GREENER, John Desmond Francis. b 61. Trin Coll Cam BA83 MA87. Coll of Resurr Mirfield 89. **d** 91. C S'wark H Trin w St Matt *S'wark* from 91. *224 Ashenden, Deacon Way, London SE17 1UB* 071-703 6406

GREENFIELD, Canon Martin Richard. b 54. Em Coll Cam MA75. Wycliffe Hall Ox MA78. **d** 79 **p** 80. C Enfield Ch Ch Trent Park *Lon* 79-83; CMS from 84; Nigeria from 85; Hon Can Aba from 89. *c/o Trinity College, PO Box 97, Umuahia, Imo State, Nigeria*

GREENFIELD, Norman John Charles. b 27. Leeds Univ BA51. Chich Th Coll 51. **d** 53 **p** 54. C Portsea St Cuth *Portsm* 53-56; C Whitley Ch Ch *Ox* 56-60; V Moorends *Sheff* 60-65; V Littleworth *Ox* 65-71; Asst Stewardship Adv 65-70; V New Marston 71-79; Dioc Stewardship Adv *Chich* 79-88; P-in-c Amberley w N Stoke 79-83; R Guestling and Pett from 88. *The Rectory, Pett, Hastings, E Sussex TN35 4HG* Hastings (0424) 813234

GREENFIELD, Canon Walter. b 16. TD67. Selw Coll Cam BA49 MA53. Ridley Hall Cam 48. **d** 50 **p** 51. V Willingdon *Chich* 63-72; V Hove All SS 72-78; Can and Preb Chich Cathl 74-85; V W Wittering 78-85; rtd 85; Perm to Offic *B & W* from 85. *3 Hinton Close, Hinton St George, Somerset TA17 8SH* Crewkerne (0460) 73846

GREENHALGH, David Murray. b 13. Jes Coll Cam BA34 MA38 Lon Univ BD47. Ridley Hall Cam 34. **d** 36 **p** 37. V Shirley *Win* 59-78; rtd 78; Perm to Offic *Pet* from 84. *3 Cricket Lawns, Oakham, Leics LE15 6HT* Oakham (0572) 757238

GREENHALGH, Eric. b 20. Tyndale Hall Bris. **d** 63 **p** 64. V Preston St Mary *Blackb* 68-72; V Partington and Carrington *Ches* 72-81; V Inskip *Blackb* 81-85; rtd 85; Perm to Offic *Carl & Blackb* from 85. *37 Fairgarth Drive, Kirkby Lonsdale, Carnforth, Lancs LA6 2DT* Kirkby Lonsdale (05242) 72122

GREENHALGH, Eric. b 26. St Jo Coll Dur BA51 DipTh53. **d** 53 **p** 54. V Rhodes *Man* 56-89; V Birch St Mary 63-88; rtd 89; Perm to Offic *Sarum* from 89. *Church View, Hill Farm Lane, Lytchett Minster, Poole, Dorset BH16 6JF* Lytchett Minster (0202) 631495

GREENHALGH, Ian Frank. b 49. Wycliffe Hall Ox 74. **d** 77 **p** 78. C Parr *Liv* 77-80; V Wigan St Barn Marsh Green 80-84; Chapl RAF from 84. *c/o MOD, Adastral House, Theobald's Road, London WC1X 8RU* 071-430 7268

GREENHALGH, Philip Adrian. b 52. Wycliffe Hall Ox 76. **d** 79 **p** 80. C Gt Clacton *Chelmsf* 79-82; P-in-c Stalmine *Blackb* 82-86; Perm to Offic Carl and Ely from 86; Rep Leprosy Miss E Anglia from 86. *58 Lantree Crescent, Trumpington, Cambridge CB2 2NJ* Cambridge (0223) 842608

GREENHALGH, Stephen. b 53. Trin Coll Bris 77 Lon Bible Coll BA80. **d** 81 **p** 82. C Horwich H Trin *Man* 81-84; C Horwich 84-85; Chapl RAF from 85. *c/o MOD, Adastral House, Theobald's Road, London WC1X 8RU* 071-430 7268

GREENHILL, Anthony David. b 39. Bris Univ BSc59. Tyndale Hall Bris 61. **d** 63 **p** 64. C Southsea St Jude *Portsm* 63-65; India 65-78; C Kinson *Sarum* 78-81; V Girlington *Bradf* from 81. *The Vicarage, 27 Baslow Grove, Bradford, W Yorkshire BD9 5JA* Bradford (0274) 544987

GREENHOUGH, Alan Kenneth. b 40. St D Coll Lamp DipTh66. **d** 66 **p** 67. C Allestree *Derby* w C Ilkeston St Mary 70-73; V Bradwell 73-85; R Twyford w Guist w Bintry w Themelthorpe etc *Nor* from 85. *The Vicarage, Guist, Dereham, Norfolk NR20 5LU* Foulsham (036284) 255

GREENHOUGH, Arthur George. b 30. Fitzw Ho Cam BA52 MA56. Tyndale Hall Bris 55. **d** 57 **p** 58. C Wakef St Andr *Wakef* 57-63; R Birkin w Haddlesey *York* 63-85; RD Selby 77-84; P-in-c Hambleton 84-85; R Haddlesey w Hambleton and Birkin from 85. *The Rectory, Chapel Haddlesey, Selby, N Yorkshire YO8 8QF* Selby (0757) 270245

GREENHOUGH, Geoffrey Herman. b 36. Sheff Univ BA57 Lon Univ BD71. St Jo Coll Nottm 74. **d** 75 **p** 76. C Cheadle Hulme St Andr *Ches* 75-78; R Tilston and Shocklach 78-82; V Hyde St Geo 82-87; V Pott Shrigley from 87. *The Vicarage, Spuley Lane, Pott Shrigley, Macclesfield, Cheshire SK10 5RS* Bollington (0625) 573316

GREENING, Nigella May. b 21. Gilmore Ho 62. **d** 87. C Glouc St Geo w Whaddon *Glouc* 87-89; rtd 89. *Fairfield, Minsterworth, Gloucester GL2 8JG* Minsterworth (045275) 243

GREENISH, Dr Brian Vivian Isitt. b 20. LRCP MRCS Lon Univ MB BSc. **d** 89 **p** 89. NSM Bedf St Pet w St Cuth *St Alb* from 89. *69 Chaucer Road, Bedford MK40 2AW* Bedford (0234) 52498

GREENLAND, Clifford James Gomm. b 09. Clifton Th Coll 63. **d** 64 **p** 65. V Wiggenhall St Mary Magd *Ely* 67-75; rtd 75. *6 Sunset Avenue, Woodford Green, Essex IG8 0ST* 081-505 8858

GREENLAND, Robin Anthony Clive. b 31. Dur Univ BA53. Linc Th Coll 59. **d** 61 **p** 62. C Marsden *Wakef* 61-63; C Cleethorpes *Linc* 63-65; V Holton-le-Clay 65-70; V Tetney 65-70; V Embsay w Eastby *Bradf* 70-78; V Earby 78-83; V Firbank, Howgill and Killington from 83; Hon C Sedbergh, Cautley and Garsdale from 83. *The Lune Vicarage, 5 Highfield Road, Sedbergh, Cumbria LA10 5DH* Sedbergh (05396) 20670

GREENLAND, Roy Wilfrid. b 37. St Steph Ho Ox 71. **d** 73 **p** 74. C Wanstead St Mary *Chelmsf* 73-76; V Harlow St Mary Magd 76-83; P-in-c Huntingdon All SS w St Jo *Ely* 83-84; P-in-c Huntingdon St Barn 83-84; P-in-c Huntingdon St Mary w St Benedict 83-84; Bermuda 84-89; V Northn St Alb *Pet* from 89. *St Alban's Vicarage, Broadmead Avenue, Northampton NN3 2RA* Northampton (0604) 407074

GREENLEES, Geoffrey Ian Loudon. b 20. Sarum Th Coll 70. **d** 71 **p** 72. C Wilton w Netherhampton and Fugglestone *Sarum* 71-74; R Woodchurch *Cant* 75-85; rtd 85; Perm to Offic *Cant* from 85. *8 Martin's Close, Tenterden, Kent TN30 7AJ* Tenterden (05806) 2586

GREENMAN, David John. b 35. Lon Univ BA59. Oak Hill Th Coll 57. **d** 61 **p** 62. C Wandsworth St Steph *S'wark* 61-63; C Bishopwearmouth St Gabr *Dur* 63-66; C-in-c Bedgrove CD *Ox* 66-74; P-in-c Macclesfield Ch Ch *Ches* 74-77; V 77-81; P-in-c Glouc All SS *Glouc* 81-85; V Glouc St Jas 81-85; V Bare *Blackb* from 85. *St Christopher's Vicarage, 12 Elm Grove, Morecambe, Lancs LA4 6AT* Morecambe (0524) 411363

GREENSIDES, Leonard. b 17. Kelham Th Coll 38. **d** 43 **p** 44. V Yateley *Win* 66-70; V Abbotskerswell *Ex* 70-82; rtd 82; Lic to Offic Ex from 82; York from 90. *10 St John's Court, Howden, Goole, N Humberside DN14 7BE* Howden (0430) 432092

GREENSLADE, Keith James Inglis. b 27. St Mich Coll Llan 60. **d** 62 **p** 63. C Bishopsworth *Bris* 62-65; C Chippenham St Paul w Langley Burrell 65-68; V Upper Stratton from 68. *The Vicarage, Beechcroft Road, Swindon SN2 6RE* Swindon (0793) 723095

GREENSLADE, Peter Michael. b 37. Bp Burgess Hall Lamp 69. **d** 71 **p** 72. C Llanwnda w Goodwick and Manorowen *St D* 71-73; C Lydiate *Liv* 73-75; V Wigan St Cath 75-76; Chapl Gen Hosp Liv 76-78; C Knotty Ash St Jo *Liv* 76-78; C Lache cum Saltney *Ches* 78-80; V Barnton 80-84; C Warburton 85-86; Warden Petroc Chr Guest Ho 86-90; rtd 90. *c/o The Vicarage, Camrose, Haverfordwest, Dyfed SA62 6JE* Camrose (0437) 710501

GREENUP, Basil William. b 08. St Jo Coll Cam BA30 MA37. Bps' Coll Cheshunt 38. **d** 39 **p** 39. Conduct Eton Coll and Master of Choristers 40-64; rtd 69. *Barton Cottage, Coburg Road, Sidmouth, Devon EX10 8NG* Sidmouth (0395) 578586

GREENWAY, John. b 32. Bps' Coll Cheshunt 68 Qu Coll Birm 69. **d** 69 **p** 70. C Luton Ch Ch *St Alb* 69-74; C Pulloxhill w Flitton 75-76; P-in-c Marston Moretaine 76-79; P-in-c Lidlington 77-79; P-in-c Marston Morteyne w Lidlington 80-81; R from 81. *The Vicarage, Lidlington, Bedford MK43 0RN* Ampthill (0525) 403687

GREENWAY, John Waller Harry Kelynge. b 07. Cuddesdon Coll. **d** 49 **p** 50. R Itchen Abbas cum Avington *Win* 63-72; rtd 72; Perm to Offic *Win* from

72. *16 Bereweeke Way, Winchester, Hants SO22 6BJ* Winchester (0962) 63200
GREENWAY, Margaret Hester. b 26. d 87. Downend *Bris* 75-79; Oldland 79-82; Stratton St Margaret w S Marston etc 82-86; rtd 86. *5 Weston Lodge, Lower Bristol Road, Weston-super-Mare BS23 2PJ* Weston-super-Mare (0934) 623561
GREENWELL, Christopher. b 49. Linc Th Coll 79. d 81 p 82. C Scarborough St Martin *York* 81-84; V S Bank 84-89; R Bolton by Bowland w Grindleton *Bradf* from 89. *The Rectory, Sawley Road, Grindleton, Clitheroe, Lancs BB7 4QS* Clitheroe (0200) 41154
GREENWELL, Paul. b 60. Magd Coll Ox BA81 MA85. St Steph Ho Ox 82. d 85 p 86. C Hendon and Sunderland *Dur* 85-88; Chapl Univ Coll of Ripon & York St Jo from 88; Min Can and Prec Ripon Cathl *Ripon* from 88. *17 High St Agnesgate, Ripon, N Yorkshire HG4 1QR* Ripon (0765) 2609
GREENWOOD, Canon Gerald. b 33. Leeds Univ BA57 Sheff Poly MSc83. Linc Th Coll 57. d 59 p 60. C Rotherham *Sheff* 59-62; V Elsecar 62-69; V Wales 70-77; P-in-c Thorpe Salvin 74-77; Dioc Sch Officer 77-84; P-in-c Bramley and Ravenfield 77-78; P-in-c Hooton Roberts 77-78; R 78-84; Hon Can Sheff Cathl 80-84; Dioc Dir of Educn 81-84; Hon Can S'wark Cathl S'wark from 84; Dir of Educn from 84. *15C Paveley Drive, Morgan's Walk, London SW11 3TP* 071-585 1731
GREENWOOD, Gordon Edwin. b 44. Trin Coll Bris 78. d 80 p 81. C Bootle St Matt *Liv* 80-83; V Hunts Cross from 83. *The Vicarage, 7 Kingsmead Drive, Liverpool L25 0NG* 051-486 1220
GREENWOOD, Hilary Peter Frank. b 29. Nottm Univ BA57. Kelham Th Coll 50. d 57 p 58. SSM from 54; Warden Kelham Th Coll 70-74; Asst Chapl Madrid *Eur* 74-76; Lic to Offic Blackb 76-80; Man 80-82; R Longsight St Jo w St Cypr *Man* 82-89; rtd 89. *The Rectory, St John's Road, Longsight, Manchester M13 0WU* 061-224 2744
GREENWOOD, James Peter. b 61. RIBA87 Univ Coll Lon BSc83 DipArch86 St Jo Coll Dur BA90. Cranmer Hall Dur 88. d 91. C Belper *Derby* from 91. *St Swithun's House, Holbrook Road, Belper, Derby DE5 1PA* Belper (0773) 825026
GREENWOOD, John Newton. b 44. St Chad's Coll Dur BA69 DipTh70. d 70 p 71. C Hartlepool H Trin *Dur* 70-72; Lic to Offic from 72; Hd Master Archibald Primary Sch Cleveland from 84. *1 Brae Head, Eaglescliffe, Stockton-on-Tees, Cleveland TS16 9HP* Eaglescliffe (0642) 783200
GREENWOOD, Leslie. b 37. Dur Univ BA59 DipTh61. St Jo Coll Dur. d 61 p 62. C Birstall *Wakef* 61-63; C Illingworth 64-70; Chapl H Trin Sch Halifax 64-89; V Charlestown from 70. *St Thomas's Vicarage, Claremount, Halifax, W Yorkshire HX3 6AP* Halifax (0422) 365508
GREENWOOD, Michael Eric. b 44. Oak Hill Th Coll 78. d 80 p 81. C Clubmoor *Liv* 80-83; V Pemberton St Mark Newtown from 83. *The Vicarage, Victoria Street, Newtown, Wigan, Lancs WN5 9BN* Wigan (0942) 43611
GREENWOOD, Norman David. b 52. Edin Univ BMus74 Lon Univ BD78 Nottm Univ MPhil90. Oak Hill Th Coll 76. d 78 p 79. C Gorleston St Andr *Nor* 78-81; SAMS 81-83; C Cromer *Nor* 83-84; R Appleby Magna and Swepstone w Snarestone *Leic* from 84. *The Rectory, Appleby Magna, Burton-on-Trent, Staffs DE12 7BQ* Measham (0530) 70482
GREENWOOD, Robert John Teale. b 28. Leeds Univ BA53. Coll of Resurr Mirfield 53. d 55 p 56. Chapl HM Pris Holloway 69-70; Man 71-77; Styal 77-88; Lic to Offic *Ches* from 77; rtd 88; Perm to Offic St As & Ban from 89. *1 Glan y Wern, Pentrefoelas, Betws y Coed, Gwynedd LL24 0LG* Pentrefoelas (06905) 313
GREENWOOD, Canon Robin Patrick. b 47. St Chad's Coll Dur BA68 DipTh69 MA71. d 70 p 71. C Adel *Ripon* 70-73; Min Can and Succ Ripon Cathl 73-78; V Leeds Halton St Wilfrid 78-86; Dioc Can Res Glouc Cathl *Glouc* from 86; Dioc Missr, Dir Lay Tr and Dir Post-Ord Tr from 86. *9 College Green, Gloucester GL1 2LX* Gloucester (0452) 507002
GREENWOOD, Roy Douglas. b 27. Tyndale Hall Bris 58. d 60 p 61. C Ox St Matt *Ox* 60-62; V Ulpha *Carl* 62-63; V Seathwaite w Ulpha 63-72; P-in-c Haverthwaite 72-74; C Ulverston St Mary w H Trin 74-78; V Egton w Newland 78-86; Assoc Chapl Palma de Mallorca and Balearic Is *Eur* from 86. *c/o Oficina de Correos, Pollensa, Palma de Mallorca, Spain* Palma de Mallorca (71) 531845
GREER, John Edmund. b 32. QUB BSc53 BAgr54 PhD56 TCD BD65 NUU MPhil72. Bps' Coll Cheshunt 56. d 58 p 59. C Belf St Paul *Conn* 58-61; Tutor Bps' Coll

Cheshunt 61-64; Chapl 64; Ch of Ireland Educn Org 65-68; Chapl NUU 68-72; Lect 72-84; Reader from 84. *6 Beech Hill, Ballymoney, Co Antrim BT53 6DB* Ballymoney (02656) 62368
GREER, Canon Robert Ferguson. b 34. TCD BA56 MA59. d 60 p 61. C Dundela *D & D* 60-65; I Castlewellan 65-78; I Castlewellan w Kilcoo from 78; RD Kilmegan from 89; Can Dromore Cathl from 90. *The Rectory, 58 Mill Hill, Castlewellan, Co Down BT31 9NB* Castlewellan (03967) 78306
GREETHAM, Canon William Frederick. b 40. Bede Coll Dur CertEd. Cranmer Hall Dur 63. d 66 p 67. C St Annes *Blackb* 66-69; C Ashton-on-Ribble St Andr 69-71; Chapl Aysgarth Sch N Yorkshire 71-81; C Bedale *Ripon* 72-75; V Crakehall 75-82; V Hornby 75-82; V Patrick Brompton and Hunton 75-82; V Kirkby Stephen *Carl* 82-90; RD Appleby from 86; Hon Can Carl Cathl from 89; R Kirkby Stephen w Mallerstang etc from 90. *The Vicarage, Vicarage Lane, Kirkby Stephen, Cumbria CA17 4QX* Kirkby Stephen (07683) 71204
GREG, John Kennedy. b 24. Trin Coll Cam BA46 MA61. Chich Th Coll 46. d 49 p 50. V Cumwhitton *Carl* 62-75; C Carl St Barn 75; TV 75-80; Chapl Strathclyde Ho Hosp Carl 80-85; TV Carl H Trin and St Barn *Carl* 80-85; rtd 85; Perm to Offic *Carl* from 86. *113 Wigton Road, Carlisle CA2 7EL* Carlisle (0228) 38837
GREGG, David William Austin. b 37. Lon Univ BD66 Bris Univ MA69. Tyndale Hall Bris 63. d 68 p 69. C Barrow St Mark *Carl* 68-71; P-in-c Lindal w Marton 71-75; Communications Sec Gen Syn Bd for Miss and Unity 76-81; Prin Romsey Ho Coll Cam 81-88; V Haddenham w Cuddington, Kingsey etc *Ox* from 88. *The Vicarage, 27A The Gables, Haddenham, Aylesbury, Bucks HP17 8AD* Haddenham (0844) 291244
GREGORY, Alan Paul Roy. b 55. K Coll Lon BD77 MTh78 AKC. Ripon Coll Cuddesdon 78. d 79 p 80. C Walton-on-Thames *Guildf* 79-82; Tutor and Dir of Studies Sarum & Wells Th Coll 82-88; USA from 88. *4862 Cambridge Drive, Dunwoody, Atlanta, Georgia 30338, USA*
GREGORY, Brian. b 43. Trin Coll Bris. d 82 p 83. C Burscough Bridge *Liv* 82-85; V Platt Bridge from 85. *The Vicarage, Ridyard Street, Platt Bridge, Wigan, Lancs WN2 3TD* Wigan (0942) 866269
GREGORY, Clive Malcolm. b 61. Lanc Univ BA84 Qu Coll Cam BA87 MA89. Westcott Ho Cam 85. d 88 p 89. C Margate St Jo *Cant* from 88. *173 Ramsgate Road, Margate, Kent CT9 4EY* Thanet (0843) 294621
GREGORY, Father Superior. *See* DUDDING, Edward Leslie
GREGORY, Graham. b 36. Open Univ BA78 Lon Univ DipTh65. Tyndale Hall Bris 63. d 66 p 67. C Wandsworth St Mich *S'wark* 66-71; C Hastings Em and St Mary in the Castle *Chich* 71-75; V Douglas St Ninian *S & M* 75-91; Dioc Youth Officer 78-88; Chapl HM Pris Douglas 82-86; RD Douglas *S & M* 86-91; V Wollaton Park *S'well* from 91; V Lenton Abbey from 91. *St Mary's Vicarage, Wollaton Park, Nottingham NG8 1AF* Nottingham (0602) 786988
GREGORY, Ian Peter. b 45. Open Univ BA. Chich Th Coll 67. d 70 p 71. C Tettenhall Regis *Lich* 70-73; C Shrewsbury H Cross 73-76; P-in-c Walsall St Mary and All SS Palfrey 76-80; R Petrockstowe, Petersmarland, Merton, Meeth etc *Ex* 80-87; TV Ex St Thos and Em 87-91. *3 Antonine Crescent, Redhills, Exeter*
GREGORY, Ivan Henry. b 31. Leeds Univ BA52. Ely Th Coll 58. d 60 p 60. C Stoke Newington St Faith, St Matthias and All SS *Lon* 60-63; C Withycombe Raleigh *Ex* 63-67; V Braunton 67-77; V Tintagel *Truro* from 77; RD Trigg Minor 84-86. *The Vicarage, Tintagel, Cornwall PL34 0DJ* Camelford (0840) 770315
GREGORY, John Edwin. b 15. Birm Univ BSc37 PhD49. d 77 p 77. NSM Maney *Birm* from 77. *5 Silvermead Road, Sutton Coldfield, W Midlands B73 5SR* 021-354 3263
GREGORY, John Frederick. b 33. Glouc Sch of Min 75. d 78 p 78. NSM S Cerney w Cerney Wick *Glouc* 78-81; NSM Coates, Rodmarton and Sapperton etc 81-88; P-in-c Kempsford w Welford from 88. *The Parsonage, Kempsford, Fairford, Glos GL7 4ET* Kempsford (0285) 810241
GREGORY, Miss Pauline Beatrice Joan (Paula). b 20. SRN43. K Coll Lon 47. dss 54 d 87. CSA 49-57; Jamaica 58-69; Victoria Docks Ascension *Chelmsf* 70-80; Canning Town St Cedd 80-84; Colchester St Botolph w H Trin and St Giles 84-87; Hon Par Dn from 87. *51 St John's Green, Colchester CO2 7EZ* Colchester (0206) 43138
GREGORY, Peter. b 35. Cranmer Hall Dur 59. d 62 p 63. C Pennington *Man* 62-65; C N Ferriby *York* 65-68; V Tonge Fold *Man* 68-72; V Hollym w Welwick and

Holmpton *York* 72-77; P-in-c Foston w Flaxton 77-80; P-in-c Crambe w Whitwell and Huttons Ambo 77-80; R Whitwell w Crambe, Flaxton, Foston etc from 81. *The Rectory, Crambe, York YO6 7JR* Whitwell-on-the-Hill (065381) 647

GREGORY, Richard. b 11. Lich Th Coll 39. **d** 43 **p** 44. R Lydford-on-Fosse *B & W* 65-76; R Alford w Hornblotton 65-76; rtd 76; Hon C St Marychurch *Ex* from 81. *Top Flat, Lane Entrance, 18 Rathmore Road, Torquay TQ2 6NY* Torquay (0803) 27467

GREGORY, Richard Branson. b 33. Fitzw Ho Cam BA58 MA62. Sarum Th Coll 58 Ridley Hall Cam 59. **d** 60 **p** 61. C Sheff St Cuth *Sheff* 60-62; Asst Chapl Leeds Univ *Ripon* 62-64; V Yeadon St Jo *Bradf* 64-71; R Keighley 71-74; TR Keighley St Andr 74-82; Hon Can Bradf Cathl 71-82; RD S Craven 71-73 and 78-82; P-in-c Broadmayne, W Knighton, Owermoigne etc *Sarum* 82-85; R from 85. *The Rectory, Broadmayne, Dorchester, Dorset DT2 8EB* Warmwell (0305) 852435

GREGORY, Stephen Simpson. b 40. Nottm Univ BA62 CertEd63. St Steph Ho Ox. **d** 68 **p** 69. C Aldershot St Mich *Guildf* 68-71; Chapl St Mary's Sch Wantage 71-74; R Edgefield *Nor* 74-88; R Holt from 74; RD Holt 79-84. *The Rectory, Holt, Norfolk NR25 6BB* Holt (0263) 712048

GREGORY-SMITH, Thomas Gregory. b 08. St Jo Coll Cam BA30 MA34. Lon Coll of Div 33. **d** 34 **p** 35. C-in-c Wimbledon Em Ridgway Prop Chpl *S'wark* 71-76; rtd 76. *46 Sea Road, Barton-on-Sea, New Milton, Hants BH25 7NG* New Milton (0425) 610942

GREGSON, Ernest. b 06. St Aid Birkenhead 50. **d** 52 **p** 53. V Chesterfield Ch Ch *Derby* 56-71; rtd 71; Lic to Offic *Blackb* from 81. *31 Highfield Road South, Chorley, Lancs PR7 1RH* Chorley (02572) 76403

GREGSON, Peter John. b 36. Univ Coll Dur BSc61. Ripon Hall Ox 61. **d** 63 **p** 64. C Radcliffe St Thos *Man* 63-65; C Baguley 65-67; Chapl RN 68-91; V Ashburton w Buckland in the Moor and Bickington *Ex* from 91. *The Vicarage, West Street, Ashburton, Newton Abbot, Devon TQ13 7DT* Ashburton (0364) 52506

GREIG, George Malcolm. b 28. Local NSM Course 74. **d** 81 **p** 82. NSM Dundee St Mary Magd *Bre* 81-84; NSM Dundee St Jo 82-84; P-in-c Dundee St Ninian 84; Hon Chapl St Paul's Cathl Dundee from 85; NSM Dundee St Paul from 85. *61 Charleston Drive, Dundee DD2 2HE* Dundee (0382) 66709

GREIG, John Kenneth. b 38. Natal Univ BA57. St Paul's Grahamstown LTh60. **d** 61 **p** 62. S Africa 61-66 and 71-78; C Friern Barnet St Jas *Lon* 66-69; C Kenton 69-71; Chapl Whitelands Coll of HE *S'wark* 78-84; Area Ecum Officer (Croydon) from 84; V Purley St Swithun from 84. *Windsor Lodge, Purley Rise, Purley, Surrey CR8 3AW* 081-660 3744

GREIG, Martin David Sandford. b 45. Bris Univ BSc67. St Jo Coll Nottm 72. **d** 75 **p** 76. C Keresley and Coundon *Cov* 75-79; C Rugby St Andr 79-83; TV 83-86; V Cov St Geo from 86. *St George's Vicarage, 101 Moseley Avenue, Coventry CV6 1HR* Coventry (0203) 591994

GRELLIER, Brian Rodolph. b 45. AKC61. **d** 62 **p** 63. C Wandsworth St Paul *S'wark* 62-66; Japan 66-72; Miss to Seamen 72-76; V Freiston w Butterwick *Linc* from 76; Chapl HM Pris N Sea Camp from 89. *Pinchbeck House, Butterwick, Boston, Lincs PE22 0HZ* Boston (0205) 760550

GRESHAM, Eric Clifford. b 15. Lon Univ BA37 Hull Univ Coll DipEd40. K Coll Lon 59. **d** 60 **p** 60. S Rhodesia 60-65; Rhodesia 73-77; V Bamber Bridge St Aid *Blackb* 65-71; S Africa 71-73; Min Keele *Lich* 78-82; Assoc Chapl Keele Univ 78-82; rtd 82; Perm to Offic *Lich* from 82. *1 Alton Close, Silverdale, Newcastle, Staffs ST5 6RT* Newcastle-under-Lyme (0782) 635323

GRESSWELL, George Gilbert. b 03. Lon Univ BA38. Hartley Victoria Coll. **d** 43 **p** 44. V Laxey *S & M* 59-70; rtd 70; Perm to Offic *S & M* from 70. *Knock Rushen, Ballafesson, Port Erin, Isle of Man* Port Erin (0624) 832079

GRETTON, Tony Butler. b 29. St Jo Coll Dur BA53. **d** 54 **p** 55. R Norton Fitzwarren *B & W* 57-68; rtd 68; Chapl Glouc Docks Mariners' Ch *Glouc* from 73; P-in-c Brookthorpe w Whaddon and Harescombe 79-82; Hon C The Edge, Pitchcombe, Harescombe and Brookthorpe 82-89. *26 Lansdown Road, Gloucester GL1 3JD* Gloucester (0452) 304813

GREW, Richard Lewis. b 32. Clare Coll Cam BA54 MA58. Wycliffe Hall Ox 67. **d** 68 **p** 70. C Repton *Derby* 68-73; Asst Chapl Repton Sch *Derby* from 68; Lic to Offic *Derby* from 73. *36 The Pastures, Repton, Derby DE6 6GG* Burton-on-Trent (0283) 703307

GREWCOCK, Peter Joseph. b 28. Sarum Th Coll. **d** 58 **p** 59. C Mitcham St Barn *S'wark* 58-60; C Kingswood 60-62; V Howe Bridge *Man* 62-72; P-in-c Werrington, St Giles in the Heath and Virginstow *Truro* 72-73; V Leic St Chad *Leic* 73-76; P-in-c Trotton w Chithurst *Chich* 76-80; C Broadstone *Sarum* 80-84; TV Gillingham 84-88; P-in-c Milborne St Andrew w Dewlish from 88. *The Vicarage, Blandford Hill, Milborne St Andrew, Blandford Forum, Dorset DT11 0JA* Milborne St Andrew (025487) 227

GREY, Canon Edward Alwyn. b 23. Univ of Wales (Swansea) BA48. St D Coll Lamp. **d** 50 **p** 51. R Flint *St As* 69-89; RD Holywell 73-89; Can St As Cathl 76-89; rtd 89. *6 Mostyn Avenue, Prestatyn, Clwyd* Prestatyn (0745) 855302

GREY, Edwin Charles. b 03. Wycliffe Coll Toronto 46. **d** 49 **p** 50. Canada 49-70; C Bowdon *Ches* 70-76; Asst Chapl Santa Cruz *Eur* 77-78; Perm to Offic *Glouc* from 78. *Pyke's Cottage, 166 Ewen Road, Kemble, Cirencester, Glos GL7 6BT* Cirencester (0285) 770595

GREY, Eric Myrddin. b 16. St D Coll Lamp BA40 Lich Th Coll. **d** 47 **p** 48. R Brechfa w Abergorlech etc *St D* 60-83; rtd 83. *Llystyn Cottage, Brechfa, Carmarthen, Dyfed* Brechfa (0267) 202201

GREY, Richard Thomas. b 50. St D Coll Lamp BA73 Ripon Hall Ox 73. **d** 75 **p** 76. C Blaenavon w Capel Newydd *Mon* 75-77; Ind Chapl from 77; C Newport St Paul 77-80; CF(TA) from 78; Chapl Aberbargoed Hosp from 80; V Bedwellty *Mon* 80-88; R Llanwenarth Ultra from 88. *The Rectory, Govilon, Abergavenny, Gwent NP7 9PT* Gilwern (0873) 830342

GREY, Canon Roger Derrick Masson. b 38. AKC61. **d** 62 **p** 63. C Darlington H Trin *Dur* 62-63; C Bishopwearmouth St Mich 63-67; V Mabe *Truro* 67-70; Dioc Youth Chapl 67-70; Youth Chapl *Glouc* 70-77; V Stroud H Trin 77-82; Dioc Can Res Glouc Cathl from 82; Dir of Educn from 82. *7 College Court, Gloucester GL1 2NJ* Gloucester (0452) 411483

GREY, Stephen Bernard. b 56. Linc Th Coll 86. **d** 88 **p** 89. C Worsley *Man* from 88. *63 Ellenbrook Road, Worsley, Manchester M28 4FS* 061-799 4985

GREY, Canon Thomas Hilton. b 18. St D Coll Lamp BA39 Keble Coll Ox BA41 MA46. St Mich Coll Llan 41. **d** 42 **p** 43. R Haverfordwest St Thos and Haroldston E St Issell *St D* 64-77; Can St D Cathl 72-84; RD Roose 74-84; R Haverfordwest St Mary and St Thos w Haroldston 77-84; Treas St D Cathl 80-84; rtd 85. *3 Gwscum Park, Burry Port, Dyfed SA16 0DX* Burry Port (05546) 3629

GRIBBEN, John Gibson. b 44. Lon Univ DipTh73 K Coll Lon BD75 QUB MTh81. CITC 73. **d** 75 **p** 76. C Dunmurry *Conn* 75-78; CR from 81; Lic to Offic *Wakef* from 83. *College of the Resurrection, Mirfield, W Yorkshire WF14 0BW* Mirfield (0924) 490441

GRIBBIN, Canon Bernard Byron. b 35. Bradf Univ DipHP76 MPhil84. St Aid Birkenhead 58. **d** 60 **p** 61. C Maghull *Liv* 60-63; C Prescot 63-65; V Denholme Gate *Bradf* 65-71; V Bankfoot 71-79; Dioc Stewardship Adv 79-86; Prec and Chapl Choral Ches Cathl *Ches* 86-91; V Ringway from 91; Hon Can Ches Cathl from 91; Dioc Tourism Officer from 91. *Ringway Vicarage, Halebarns, Altrincham, Cheshire WA15 0HQ* 061-980 3955

GRIBBLE, Canon Arthur Stanley. b 04. Qu Coll Cam BA27 MA31. Westcott Ho Cam 27. **d** 30 **p** 31. Can Res Pet Cathl *Pet* 67-79; rtd 79; Perm to Offic *Pet* from 79; *Linc* from 80. *2 Princes Road, Stamford, Lincs PE9 1QT* Stamford (0780) 55838

GRIBBLE, Howard Frank. b 27. Magd Coll Cam BA50 MA56. Ely Th Coll 50. **d** 52 **p** 53. V Harlow St Mary Magd *Chelmsf* 62-70; R Lawhitton *Truro* 70-81; R Lezant 70-81; RD Trigg Major 75-79; P-in-c S Petherwin w Trewen 77-79; Chapl R Cornwall Hosp Truro 81-84; rtd 84. *Westerlies, Marine Drive, Widemouth Bay, Bude, Cornwall EX23 0AQ* Bude (0288) 361528

GRIBBLE, Malcolm George. b 44. Chu Coll Cam BA67 MA71. Linc Th Coll 79. **d** 81 **p** 82. C Farnborough *Roch* 81-84; V Bostall Heath 84-90; V Bexleyheath Ch Ch from 90. *The Vicarage, 113 Upton Road, Bexleyheath, Kent DA6 8LS* 081-303 3260

GRICE, Charles. b 24. MBE83. **d** 58 **p** 59. Ind Chapl *Sheff* 69-76; V Tinsley 69-73; V Oughtibridge 73-76; Gen Sec Ch Lads' and Ch Girls' Brigade 77-91; R Braithwell w Bramley *Sheff* 88-91; rtd 89. *57 Deepdale Road, Rotherham, S Yorkshire S61 2NR* Rotherham (0709) 557551

GRICE, David Richard. b 32. Keble Coll Ox BA55 MA59. St Steph Ho Ox 55. **d** 57 **p** 58. C Leeds St Aid *Ripon* 57-61; C Middleton St Mary 61-62; V Woodlesford 62-69; V Leeds St Wilfrid 69-78; TR Seacroft from 78.

The Rectory, 47 St James Approach, Seacroft, Leeds LS14 6JJ Leeds (0532) 732390

GRICE-HUTCHINSON, Canon George Arthur Claude. b 12. Bps' Coll Cheshunt 39. **d** 39 **p** 40. V Benwell St Aid *Newc* 63-74; V N Sunderland 74-79; Hon Can Newc Cathl 77-79; rtd 80. *17 Westacres Crescent, Newcastle upon Tyne NE15 7NY* 091-274 7975

GRIERSON, Peter Stanley. b 42. Lon Univ BD68 Leeds Univ MPhil74. Linc Th Coll 68. **d** 69 **p** 70. C Clitheroe St Mary *Blackb* 69-71; C Aston cum Aughton *Sheff* 72-75; V Preston St Jude w St Paul *Blackb* 75-81; V Blackb St Luke w St Phil from 89; RD Blackb from 91. *St Luke's Vicarage, Lansdowne Street, Blackburn BB2 1UU* Blackburn (0254) 581402

GRIEVE, David Campbell. b 51. St Jo Coll Dur BA74. Wycliffe Hall Ox 74. **d** 76 **p** 77. C Upton (or Overchurch) *Ches* 76-80; C Selston S'well 80-82; V Pelton *Dur* 82-89; rtd 89. *7 Abbey Road, Durham DH1 5DQ* 091-384 1268

GRIEVE, Robert Andrew Cameron. b 33. ACP65. Edin Th Coll 69. **d** 71 **p** 72. C Leigh St Mary *Man* 71-73; Hon C Chedburgh w Depden and Rede *St E* 73-75; Lic to Offic 75-77; P-in-c Newton 77-79; V Assington 77-79; R Fraserburgh w New Pitsligo *Ab* 79-83; R Corringham *Linc* 83-91; Perm to Offic from 91; V Lunsdon *Sheff* from 91. *Hill farm, Old Skellow, Doncaster, S Yorkshire DN6 8JS* Doncaster (0302) 337101

GRIEVES, Anthony Michael. b 47. St Alb Minl Tr Scheme 81. **d** 84 **p** 85. NSM Stevenage St Mary Shephall *St Alb* 84-86; NSM Stevenage St Mary Sheppall w Aston from 86. *27 Falcon Close, Stevenage, Herts SG2 9PG* Stevenage (0438) 727204

GRIEVES, Ian Leslie. b 56. Bede Coll Dur CertEd77 BEd78. Chich Th Coll 82. **d** 84 **p** 85. C Darlington St Mark w St Paul *Dur* 84-87; C Whickham 87-89; V Darlington St Jas from 89. *St James's Vicarage, Vicarage Road, Darlington, Co Durham DL1 1JW* Darlington (0325) 465980

GRIFFIN, Dr Alan Howard Foster. b 44. TCD BA66 MA69 Peterho Cam PhD71. Sarum & Wells Th Coll 75. **d** 78 **p** 79. Asst to Lazenby Chapl and Lect Ex Univ from 78; Warden from 81; Sen Warden from 84. *Duryard Halls, Lower Argyll Road, Exeter EX4 4RG* Exeter (0392) 55498 or 264203

GRIFFIN, Christopher Donald. b 59. Reading Univ BA80 CertEd81. Wycliffe Hall Ox DipTh85. **d** 85 **p** 86. C Gerrards Cross *Ox* 85-88; Chapl Felsted Sch Essex from 88. *Felsted School, Dunmow, Essex* Great Dunmow (0371) 820258

GRIFFIN, Dennis Gordon. b 24. Worc Ord Coll 66. **d** 68 **p** 69. V Rainbow Hill St Barn *Worc* 69-74; R Broughton *Man* 74-79; V Pendlebury Ch Ch 79-86; rtd 89. *Trevean, Goldsithney, Penzance, Cornwall TR20 9JZ* Penzance (0736) 711320

GRIFFIN, Gerald Albert Francis. b 31. Qu Coll Birm 74. **d** 77 **p** 78. NSM Bushbury *Lich* 77-83; Ind Chapl *Dur* 83-88; Chapl HM Pris Man 88-89; Hon C HM Pris Featherstone from 89. *HM Prison Featherstone, New Road, Wolverhampton WV10 7PU* Wolverhampton (0902) 790991

GRIFFIN, Harold Rodan Bristow. b 12. Jes Coll Cam BA33 LLB34 MA43. Ridley Hall Cam 43. **d** 45 **p** 46. V Framsden *St E* 61-71; R Helmingham 61-71; rtd 72. *Flat 48, Gretton Court, Girton, Cambridge CB3 0QN* Cambridge (0223) 276842

GRIFFIN, Canon John Henry Hugh. b 13. St Cath Coll Cam BA35 MA39. Linc Th Coll 35. **d** 38 **p** 39. R Stratford St Mary *St E* 46-72; C Hadleigh w Layham and Shelley 72-73; P-in-c Gt and Lt Glemham 73-79; P-in-c Blaxhall w Stratford St Andrew and Farnham 73-79; Hon Can St E Cathl 78-79; rtd 79; Perm to Offic *St E* from 79. *3 Church Street, Hadleigh, Ipswich IP7 5DT* Hadleigh (0473) 823100

GRIFFIN, Joseph William. b 48. Univ of Wales (Cardiff) DipTh73 DPS74. St Mich Coll Llan 70. **d** 74 **p** 75. C Killay *S & B* 74-78; C Swansea St Thos and Kilvey 78-81; V Troedrhiwgarth *Llan* 81-91; V Llanrhidian w Llanmadoc and Cheriton *S & B* from 91. *The Vicarage, Llanrhidian, Swansea SA3 1EH* Swansea (0792) 390144

GRIFFIN, Kenneth Francis. b 21. Lon Univ BSc64. St Jo Coll Nottm 72. **d** 73 **p** 74. C Bexleyheath Ch Ch *Roch* 73-77; R Kingsdown 77-82; rtd 86. *14 Hazelden Close, West Kingsdown, Sevenoaks, Kent*

GRIFFIN, Malcolm Neil. b 36. Leeds Univ BA57. Coll of Resurr Mirfield 57. **d** 59 **p** 60. C Cheadle *Lich* 59-61; C Bloxwich 61-64; P-in-c Willenhall St Anne 64-69; V Stretton w Claymills 69-75; V Baswich (or Berkswich) 75-85; V Madeley from 85. *The Vicarage, Madeley, Crewe CW3 9PX* Stoke-on-Trent (0782) 750205

GRIFFIN, Malcolm Roger. b 46. Open Univ BA DipRS83 DM90. S'wark Ord Course. **d** 83 **p** 84. NSM Romford St Andr *Chelmsf* 83-87; Hon C Romford St Jo 87-90; Hon C Gt Ilford St Alb from 90. *35 Oak Street, Romford RM7 7BA* Romford (0708) 741089

GRIFFIN, Canon Michael Richard. b 19. CD78. Trin Coll Bris 43. **d** 44 **p** 44. C Tonbridge St Steph *Roch* 44-45; C Tunbridge Wells H Trin 45-47; V Hindley St Pet *Liv* 47-51; Canada from 51; Can Huron from 64; CStJ from 78. *68 Caledonia Street, Stratford, Ontario, Canada, N5A 5W6*

GRIFFIN, Niall Paul. b 37. TCD BA61 Div Test61. **d** 61 **p** 62. C Newtownards *D & D* 61-63; C Arm St Mark *Arm* 63-64; Jamaica 64-66; C Lurgan Ch Ch *D & D* 66-69; Chapl RAF 69-84; Missr Chr Renewal Cen *D & D* 84-89; Ireland and Scotland Network Ldr SOMA from 89. *7 Cloughmore Park, Rostrevor, Newry, Co Down BT34 3AX* Rostrevor (06937) 38959

GRIFFIN, Nigel Charles. b 48. Leic Univ BSc71 Ox Univ DipTh73. Cuddesdon Coll 71. **d** 74 **p** 75. C Wandsworth St Anne *S'wark* 74-77; V Tadworth 77-84; Chapl Gt Ormond Street Hosp for Sick Children Lon 78-84; V Whitworth w Spennymoor *Dur* from 84. *The Vicarage, Horswell Gardens, Spennymoor, Co Durham DL16 7AA* Spennymoor (0388) 814522

GRIFFIN, Nigel Robert. b 50. Univ of Wales (Lamp) BA71. Ripon Hall Ox 71. **d** 73 **p** 74. C Burry Port and Pwll *St D* 73-77; C Carmarthen St Pet 77-79; Youth Chapl from 79; V Whitland and Kiffig 80-89; Warden of Ords from 86; V Llangunnor and Cwmffrwd from 89; RD Carmarthen from 91. *The Vicarage, Llangynnwr, Carmarthen, Dyfed SA31 2HY* Carmarthen (0267) 236435

GRIFFIN, Philip Jarvis. b 64. Ch Ch Ox BA86. St Steph Ho Ox BA88. **d** 89 **p** 90. C Earley St Nic *Ox* from 89. *84 Chilcombe Way, Reading RG6 3DB* Reading (0734) 664525

GRIFFIN, Robert Maurice. b 13. Tyndale Hall Bris 52. **d** 54 **p** 55. N Area Sec BCMS 70-75; V Withnell *Blackb* 75-79; rtd 79; Lic to Offic *Blackb* from 79. *86 Runshaw Lane, Euxton, Chorley, Lancs PR7 6AX* Chorley (02572) 62025

GRIFFIN, Canon Roger Thomas Kynaston. b 14. ALCD41. **d** 41 **p** 42. V W Ham *Chelmsf* 61-82; P-in-c Plaistow St Mary 71-72; Chmn RADD 73-86; Hon Can Chelmsf Cathl 80-82; rtd 82; Perm to Offic *B & W* from 83. *Warrenhurst, Church Street, Minehead, Somerset TA24 5JU* Minehead (0643) 706166

GRIFFIN, Canon Rutland Basil. b 16. ALCD41. **d** 41 **p** 42. V Dartford H Trin *Roch* 61-84; RD Dartford 64-84; Hon Can Roch Cathl 70-84; rtd 84; Perm to Offic Roch and Cant from 84. *21 The Crescent, Canterbury, Kent CT2 7AQ* Canterbury (0227) 761091

GRIFFIN, Very Rev Victor Gilbert Benjamin. b 24. TCD BA46 MA57. CITC 47. **d** 47 **p** 48. Dean St Patr Cathl Dub 68-91; rtd 91. *The Deanery, St Patrick's Close, Dublin 8, Irish Republic* Dublin (1) 543428

GRIFFIN, William George. b 13. St Pet Hall Ox BA36 MA45. Wycliffe Hall Ox 36. **d** 37 **p** 38. V Church Broughton w Barton and Sutton on the Hill *Derby* 66-72; R Brington w Whilton *Pet* 72-78; rtd 78; Perm to Offic *Pet* from 86. *6 Riverside Drive, Weedon, Northampton NN7 4RT* Weedon (0327) 41585

GRIFFITH, Brian Vann. b 34. Univ Sch Th Abth & Lamp DipTh82 BTh91. **d** 82 **p** 83. NSM Abth *St D* 82-87; NSM Llanfihangel-y-Creuddyn, Llanafan w Llanwnnws 87-88; NSM Llanbadarn Fawr w Capel Bangor from 88. *14 Ystwyth Close, Penparcau, Aberystwyth, Dyfed SY23 3RU*

GRIFFITH, David Vaughan. b 36. Univ of Wales (Lamp) BA60. Lich Th Coll 60. **d** 62 **p** 63. C Llanfairfechan *Ban* 62-66; C Dolgellau 66-70; R Llanfair Talhaiarn *St As* 70-82; P-in-c Llangernyw, Gwytherin and Llanddewi 77-85; R Llanfairtalhaiarn and Llansannan 82-85; V Colwyn from 85; Warden of Readers from 91. *The Vicarage, 28 Bodelwyddan Avenue, Old Colwyn, Colwyn Bay, Clwyd LL29 9NP* Colwyn Bay (0492) 518394

GRIFFITH, Canon Dermot George Wallace. b 13. TCD BA35. **d** 36 **p** 37. I Killyman *Arm* 47-86; RD Dungannon 67-86; Can Arm Cathl 73-86; Treas Arm Cathl 83-86; rtd 86. *The Cottage, 38 Drumkee Road, Dungannon, Co Tyrone BT71 6JA* Coalisland (08687) 48629

GRIFFITH, Donald Bennet. b 17. Dur Univ LTh40. St Aid Birkenhead 36. **d** 40 **p** 41. R Lawford *Chelmsf* 66-73; R Theydon Garnon 73-77; P-in-c Bradfield 77-82; rtd 82. *Porto Cristo, Mill Lane, Thorpe-le-Soken, Clacton-on-Sea, Essex CO16 0ED* Clacton-on-Sea (0225) 861766

GRIFFITH, Frank Michael. b 24. Bris Univ BSc50 Lon Univ DipTh60. St Aid Birkenhead 58. **d** 60 **p** 61. V Rounds Green *Birm* 67-70; R Barford *Cov* 70-78; V Wasperton 70-78; RD Stratford 77-79; R Barford w Wasperton and Sherbourne 78-89; RD Fosse 79-87; rtd 90. *3 Fighting Close, Kineton, Warwick CV35 0LS* Kineton (0926) 641751

GRIFFITH, Canon Geoffrey Grenville. b 17. Linc Coll Ox BA48 MA56. Chich Th Coll 48. **d** 50 **p** 51. V Chapel-en-le-Frith *Derby* 66-84; RD Buxton 71-78; Hon Can Derby Cathl 80-84; rtd 84; Perm to Offic *Derby* 84-90; Chapl HM Pris Morton Hall 85-90; Chapl St Barn Hospice Linc from 91. *292 Hykenham Road, Lincoln LN6 8BJ* Lincoln (0522) 695683

GRIFFITH, Glyn Keble Gethin. b 37. St D Coll Lamp BA59 Ridley Hall Cam 67. **d** 69 **p** 70. C Derby St Aug *Derby* 69-72; C Coity w Nolton *Llan* 72-75; P-in-c Heage *Derby* 75-81; V Allestree St Nic from 81. *The Vicarage, 4 Lawn Avenue, Allestree, Derby DE3 2PE* Derby (0332) 550224

GRIFFITH, Canon Hugh Emrys. b 24. St D Coll Lamp BA53. **d** 54 **p** 55. C Welshpool *St As* 54-56; C Abergele 56-58; R Llanfair Talhaiarn 58-61; R Newborough w Llangeinwen *Ban* 61-75; R Llanllyfni 75-81; R Amlwch from 81; RD Twrcelyn from 82; Can Ban Cathl from 89. *The Rectory, Amlwch, Gwynedd LL68 9EA* Amlwch (0407) 830740

GRIFFITH, John Rodney. b 40. **d** 66 **p** 67. C Stormont *D & D* 66-69; C Carrickfergus *Conn* 69-71; CF 71-85. *Address temp unknown*

GRIFFITH, Canon John Vaughan. b 33. LTh73. St D Coll Lamp 53. **d** 58 **p** 59. C Holyhead w Rhoscolyn *Ban* 58-63; R Maentwrog w Trawsfynydd 63-68; Chapl RAF 68-72; V Winnington *Ches* 72-76; V Northwich St Luke and H Trin 76-81; V Sandiway from 81; Dioc Communications Officer 84-86; Ed Ches Dioc News from 84; Hon Can Ches Cathl from 89. *The Vicarage, Sandiway, Northwich, Cheshire CW8 2JU* Sandiway (0606) 883286

GRIFFITH, Steven Ellsworth. b 63. St Steph Ho Ox. **d** 87 **p** 88. C Holyhead w Rhoscolyn w Llanfair-yn-Neubwll *Ban* 87-90; CF from 90. *c/o MOD (Army), Bagshot Park, Bagshot, Surrey GU19 5PL* Bagshot (0276) 71717

GRIFFITH, William Stephen. b 50. Univ of Wales (Ban) BA71. Westcott Ho Cam 71. **d** 73 **p** 74. C Llandudno *Ban* 73-76; C Calne and Blackland *Sarum* 76-78; P-in-c Broadwindsor w Burstock and Seaborough 78-79; TV Beaminster Area 79-81; Lic to Offic 81-83; Chapl St Pet Sch York 83-87; C Leeds St Pet *Ripon* 87; Chapl Bearwood Coll Wokingham from 87. *Bearwood College, Wokingham, Berks RG11 5BG* Wokingham (0734) 786915

GRIFFITH-JONES, Robin. b 56. New Coll Ox 74. Westcott Ho Cam 86. **d** 89 **p** 90. C Cantril Farm *Liv* from 89. *56 Denecliff, Stockbridge Village, Liverpool L28 5RE* 051-220 4524

GRIFFITHS, Alan Charles. b 46. Dur Univ BA67 DipTh69. Cranmer Hall Dur 66. **d** 69 **p** 70. C Leic H Apostles *Leic* 69-72; Lic to Offic *York* 73-77; V Lea Hall *Birm* 77-87; Asst Dir of Educn *Sheff* from 87. *9 Horbury End, Todwick, Sheffield S31 0HH* Worksop (0909) 771176

GRIFFITHS, Alec. b 42. St Chad's Coll Dur BA63 DipTh65. **d** 65 **p** 66. C Glas St Ninian *Glas* 65-68; C Greenock 68-72; R Glas H Cross 72-79; V Birchencliffe *Wakef* 79-83; Chapl Tolworth Hosp Surbiton and Kingston Hosp Surrey from 83. *107 Hook Rise South Tolworth, Surbiton, Surrey KT6 7NA* 081-397 1577

GRIFFITHS, Arthur Evan. b 27. ACP66. St Deiniol's Hawarden. **d** 69 **p** 70. Hon C Cleobury Mortimer w Hopton Wafers *Heref* 69-83; C 84-86; P-in-c Coreley w Doddington 86-88; P-in-c Knowbury 86-88; rtd 89. *Maryn Catherton Road, Cleobury Mortimer, Kidderminster Worcs DY14 8EB* Cleobury Mortimer (0299) 270489

GRIFFITHS, Beatrice Mary. b 29. Chelsea Coll Lon DipPE50 CertEd60 Lon Univ CertRK60. Westcott Ho Cam 85. **dss** 86 **d** 87. W Bridgford *S'well* 86-87; Hon Par Dn 87; Hon Par Dn Wilford Hill from 87. *7 Stella Avenue, Tollerton, Nottingham NG12 4EX* Plumtree (06077) 4155

GRIFFITHS, Caroline (Heidi) Ann. b 66. Ex Univ BA88. Linc Th Coll CMM90. **d** 90. C Newport St Woolos *Mon* from 90. *Hebron, 9 Clifton Road, Newport, Gwent NP9 4EW* Newport (0633) 267191

GRIFFITHS, David. b 38. Llan St Mich DipTh67. **d** 67 **p** 68. C Llangollen *St As* 67-71; C Rhyl 71-74; V Kerry 74-77; V Kerry and Llanmerewig 77-82; R Caerwys and Bodfari 82-87; V Gresford from 87. *The Vicarage,*

Gresford, Wrexham, Clwyd LL12 8RG Gresford (0978) 852236

GRIFFITHS, David Bruce. b 44. Sussex Univ BA69 Hull Univ MA83. Linc Th Coll. **d** 82 **p** 83. C Springfield All SS *Chelmsf* 82-84; TV Horwich *Man* from 84. *St Catherine's House, Richmond Street, Horwich, Bolton BL6 5QT* Horwich (0204) 697162

GRIFFITHS, David Mark. b 59. Kent Univ BA80. Chich Th Coll 81. **d** 83 **p** 84. C Clydach *S & B* 83-84; C Llwynderw 84-88; V Swansea St Nic from 88. *St Nicholas' Vicarage, 58A Dyfed Avenue, Townhill, Swansea SA1 6NG* Swansea (0792) 654272

GRIFFITHS, Ven David Nigel. b 27. RD77. FSA Worc Coll Ox BA52 MA56. Linc Th Coll 56. **d** 58 **p** 59. C Northn St Matt *Pet* 58-61; SPCK HQ Staff 61-67; Chapl RNR 63-77; Hon C Bromley St Andr *Roch* 65-67; V Linc St Mich *Linc* 67-73; R Linc St Mary Magd w St Paul 67-73; Vice Chan and Lib Linc Cathl 67-73; TR New Windsor *Ox* 73-87; RD Maidenhead 77-82 and 84-87; Chapl to HM The Queen from 77; Hon Can Ch Ch *Ox* 83-87; Adn Berks from 87. *21 Wilderness Road, Reading RG6 2RU* Reading (0734) 663459

GRIFFITHS, David Percy Douglas. b 25. St Mich Coll Llan. **d** 78 **p** 79. C Bettws St Dav *St D* 78-80; V Llanarth w Mydroilyn, Capel Cynon, Talgarreg etc 80-84; V Llanarth and Capel Cynon w Talgarreg etc 84-86; V Newc Emlyn w Llandyfriog and Troedyraur from 86. *The Vicarage, Newcastle Emlyn, Dyfed SA38 9LL* Newcastle Emlyn (0239) 710385

GRIFFITHS, David Wynne. b 47. Univ of Wales (Cardiff) BD73. St Mich Coll Llan 69. **d** 73 **p** 74. Hon C Gabalfa *Llan* 73-76; Lic to Offic 77-79; Hon C Tonypandy w Clydach Vale 79-80; Hon C Pontypridd St Cath 80-87; Perm to Offic from 87. *2 Brynheulog, Porth, M Glam CF39 9YB* Porth (0443) 684649

GRIFFITHS, Evan David. b 32. DEdin Cert86 Open Univ BA77 BA78. St D Coll Lamp 64. **d** 66 **p** 67. C Bettws St Dav *St D* 66-72; V Newchurch and Merthyr 72-80; V Llanybyther and Llanwenog w Llanwnnen from 80; RD Lamp and Ultra Aeron from 86. *The Vicarage, Llanybydder, Dyfed SA40 9QE* Llanybydder (0570) 480483

GRIFFITHS, Frank Wall Griffith. b 07. St Cath Coll Cam BA29 MA33. Coll of Resurr Mirfield 33. **d** 35 **p** 36. V Padbury w Adstock *Ox* 65-72; rtd 72. *Parkfield, Golf Links Road, Builth Wells, Powys* Builth Wells (0982) 553751

GRIFFITHS, Frederick Cyril Aubrey Comber. b 10. St Boniface Warminster 39. **d** 41 **p** 42. Clerical Org Sec CECS 62-67; rtd 69; Perm to Offic *Sarum* from 69. *4 Boundary View, Blandford Forum, Dorset DT11 7JT*

GRIFFITHS, Garrie Charles. b 53. St Jo Coll Nottm LTh77. **d** 77 **p** 78. Canada 77-78; C Stalybridge H Trin and Ch *Ches* 78-81; C Moreton 81-84; V Godley cum Newton Green 84-89; V Bayston Hill *Lich* from 89. *42 Eric Lock Road West, Bayston Hill, Shrewsbury SY3 0QA* Bayston Hill (074372) 2164

GRIFFITHS, Geoffrey Ernest. b 28. AKC52. **d** 53 **p** 54. C Shirehampton *Bris* 53-59; SCM Sec (W England Schs) 58-61; Lic to Offic *Bris* 59-63; Chapl Colston's Sch Bris 59-75; Chapl St Brandon's Sch Clevedon 60-63; V Atworth *Sarum* 63-72; Chapl Stonar Sch Melksham 63-66; P-in-c Shaw and Whitley *Sarum* 69-72; V Atworth w Shaw and Whitley from 72. *The Vicarage, 104 Church Street, Atworth, Melksham, Wilts SN12 8JA* Melksham (0225) 703357

GRIFFITHS, George Brian. b 25. Kelham Th Coll 46. **d** 51 **p** 52. S Africa 51-60; Basutoland 60-63; C Amersham *Ox* 64-65; C-in-c Amersham St Mich CD 66-73; V Amersham on the Hill from 73. *The Vicarage, 70 Sycamore Road, Amersham, Bucks HP6 5DR* Amersham (0494) 727553 or 726680

GRIFFITHS, Canon George Francis. b 09. Edin Th Coll 41. **d** 42 **p** 43. R Weldon w Deene *Pet* 67-77; Can Pet Cathl 74-77; rtd 77; Perm to Offic *S'wark* from 84. *90 Maryon Road, London SE7 8DJ* 081-317 7467

GRIFFITHS, Gerald Lewis. b 38. Qu Coll Birm. **d** 88 **p** 89. C Wrexham *St As* from 88. *St Mark's House, 7 Conway Drive, Wrexham, Clwyd LL13 9HR* Wrexham (0978) 356647

GRIFFITHS, Gordon John. b 31. Univ of Wales (Cardiff) BA53. S'wark Ord Course 72. **d** 75 **p** 76. NSM Sutton St Nic *S'wark* 75-78; Asst Chapl Eastbourne Coll E Sussex 78-81; NSM Willingdon *Chich* from 81; Lic to Offic 81. *15 Buckhurst Close, Willingdon, Eastbourne, E Sussex BN20 9EF* Eastbourne (0323) 505547

GRIFFITHS, Harvey Stephen. b 35. Linc Coll Ox BA58 MA62. Linc Th Coll 60. **d** 62 **p** 63. C Frodingham *Linc* 62-65; P-in-c Darlington St Cuth *Dur* 65-70;

Chapl RN from 70. *c/o MOD, Lacon House, Theobald's Road, London WC1X 8RY* 071-430 6847

GRIFFITHS, Jack. b 16. St D Coll Lamp BA39. **d** 42 **p** 43. V Ward End *Birm* 60-81; rtd 81; Perm to Offic *Birm* from 81. *21 Dunston Court, 52 Wheeleys Road, Birmingham B15 2LL* 021-440 5141

GRIFFITHS, John Alan. b 48. CPsychol AFBPsS Univ of Wales BSc72 Cape Town Univ MSc76. St Mich Coll Llan 87. **d** 89 **p** 90. C Neath w Llantwit *Llan* from 89. *Brierley, 136 Old Road, Neath, W Glam SA11 2DE* Neath (0639) 631111

GRIFFITHS, John Gareth. b 44. Lich Th Coll 68. **d** 71 **p** 72. C Shotton *St As* 71-73; C Rhyl w Rhyl St Ann 73-76; V Llanasa from 76; RD Holywell from 89. *The Vicarage, Llanasa Road, Gronant, Prestatyn, Clwyd LL19 9TL* Prestatyn (0745) 853512

GRIFFITHS, John Medwyn. b 20. Leeds Univ BA50. Coll of Resurr Mirfield 50. **d** 52 **p** 53. C Llanelly St Paul *St D* 52-55; Lic to Offic *Wakef* 57-62; CR 58-74; Lic to Offic *Lon* 62-63 and 71-75; *Ripon* 63-66; *Win* 75-81; P-in-c Halifax H Trin *Wakef* 81-82; TV Halifax 83-88; C Badsworth from 88. *Macrina, Field Lane, Upton, Pontefract, W Yorkshire WF9 1BH* Pontefract (0977) 640529

GRIFFITHS, John Whitmore. b 13. FRSA FPhS PhD. AKC38. **d** 38 **p** 39. R Bow w Bromley St Leon *Lon* 66-72; Chapl W Park Hosp Epsom 72-77; Perm to Offic *Ex* from 77; rtd 78. *3 Kerri House, The Square, North Tawton, Devon EX20 2ER* North Tawton (0837) 82530

GRIFFITHS, Leonard Lewis Rees. b 09. Univ Coll of Div 27 St Jo Coll Dur BA31 LTh31 MA43. **d** 32 **p** 33. Chapl RN Sch Haslemere 67-75; Antigua 75-76; rtd 76; Perm to Offic *Guildf* from 76. *9 Rosemary Court, Church Road, Haslemere, Surrey GU27 1BH* Haslemere (0428) 61391

GRIFFITHS, Lewis Eric Holroyd. b 05. Univ Coll Dur BA29. **d** 29 **p** 30. R Tendring *Chelmsf* 59-70; rtd 70. *12 The Cedars, Adelaide Road, Teddington, Middx TW11 0AX* 081-977 6643

GRIFFITHS, Malcolm. b 47. St Alb Minl Tr Scheme. **d** 82 **p** 83. NSM Hemel Hempstead *St Alb* 82-86; C 86-87; TV Liskeard, St Keyne, St Pinnock, Morval etc *Truro* from 87. *The Parsonage, Tremadden Lane, Liskeard, Cornwall PL14 3DS* Liskeard (0579) 46236

GRIFFITHS, Mrs Margarett. b 29. ATCL47 LRAM48. CA Tr Coll 50. **dss** 81 **d** 87. Hackington *Cant* 81-83; Ashford 84-87; Par Dn 87-89; rtd 89. *Blackford House, Haugh-of-Urr, Castle Douglas, Kirkcudbrightshire DG7 3LE* Castle Douglas (0556) 66256

GRIFFITHS, Martyn Robert. b 51. Nottm Univ BTh74 St Martin's Coll Lanc PGCE75. Kelham Th Coll 70. **d** 74 **p** 75. C Kings Heath *Birm* 74-77; C-in-c Elmdon Heath CD 77-79; TV Solihull 79-81; Asst Admin Shrine of Our Lady of Walsingham 81-85; V Oldham St Steph and All Martyrs *Man* 85-89; TR Swinton and Pendlebury from 89. *The Rectory, Vicarage Road, Swinton, Manchester M27 3WA* 061-794 1578

GRIFFITHS, Matthew Morgan. b 15. St D Coll Lamp BA37. **d** 38 **p** 39. Chapl Sandbach Sch Cheshire 67-73; R Newport w Cilgwyn *St D* 73-85; rtd 85. *Gleywa Heli, Traeth-y-De, Aberaeron, Dyfed SA46 0BE* Aberaeron (0545) 570895

GRIFFITHS, Meirion. b 38. Clifton Th Coll 63. **d** 66 **p** 67. C Upper Holloway St Pet *Lon* 66-68; C Taunton St Jas *B & W* 68-70; C Radipole *Sarum* 70-74; R Chich St Pancras and St Jo *Chich* 74-82; RD Edeyrnion *St As* 82-88; R Corwen and Llangar 82-88; Australia from 88. *87 Wittenoom Street, Collie, W Australia 6225* Collie (97) 341049

GRIFFITHS, Mervyn Harrington. b 15. Ripon Hall Ox 53. **d** 54 **p** 55. R Bighton *Win* 59-78; V Bishop's Sutton 59-78; rtd 80; Perm to Offic *Ex* from 80. *Kimberley, Clapps Lane, Beer, Seaton, Devon EX12 3HQ* Seaton (0297) 22382

GRIFFITHS, Morgan Emlyn. b 17. St D Coll Lamp BA38 St Mich Coll Llan 39. **d** 43 **p** 44. R (Llanfihangel) Cwmdu and Tretower *S & B* 60-78; V Crickhowell w Cwmdu and Tretower 78-83; rtd 83. *10 St John's, Pendre Close, Brecon, Powys LD3 9ED* Brecon (0874) 611125

GRIFFITHS, Neville. b 39. Univ of Wales BA63. St D Coll Lamp LTh66. **d** 66 **p** 67. C Newport St Mark *Mon* 66-68; C Cardiff St Jo *Llan* 68-70; Chapl Greystoke Th Tr Coll 70-76; C Greystoke w Matterdale *Carl* 70-75; TV Greystoke, Matterdale and Mungrisdale 75-76; Chapl Grey Coll Dur 76-81; C Croxdale *Dur* 76-81; R Didsbury Ch Ch *Man* 81-83; P-in-c Lowther and Askham *Carl* 83-84; R 84-88; V Guernsey St Matt *Win* from 88. *St Matthew's Vicarage, Cobo, Guernsey, Channel Islands* Guernsey (0481) 56447

GRIFFITHS, Norman. b 12. St D Coll Lamp BA36. **d** 36 **p** 37. R Penarth w Lavernock *Llan* 64-77; rtd 77; Perm to Offic *Llan* from 79. *52 Coed Mawr, Highlight Park, Barry, S Glam* Barry (0446) 743778

GRIFFITHS, Paul Edward. b 48. St Jo Coll Nottm 86. **d** 88 **p** 89. C Ipswich St Andr *St E* from 88. *16 Sandpit Close, Rushmere, Ipswich IP4 5UP* Ipswich (0473) 271323

GRIFFITHS, Richard Barre Maw. b 43. CCC Ox BA65 MA69. Cranmer Hall Dur DipTh71 BA71. **d** 71 **p** 72. C Fulwood *Sheff* 71-74; Hon C Sheff St Jo 74-76; Fell Dept of Bibl Studies Sheff Univ 74-76; C Fulham St Matt *Lon* 76-78; P-in-c 78-83; R Chich St Pancras and St Jo *Chich* from 83. *St Pancras's Rectory, 9 St John Street, Chichester, W Sussex PO19 1UR* Chichester (0243) 782124

GRIFFITHS, Robert Fred. b 20. St Aid Birkenhead 47. **d** 50 **p** 51. C-in-c Fairfield St Rich CD *Worc* 69-76; rtd 85. *56 Heathfield Road, Norton, Evesham, Worcs WR11 4TQ* Evesham (0386) 870198

GRIFFITHS, Robert Herbert. b 53. Univ of Wales (Ban) DipTh75. Chich Th Coll 75. **d** 76 **p** 77. C Holywell *St As* 76-80; CF (TA) from 79; V Llanfair D C *St As* 80-84; P-in-c Gyffylliog 80-84; Asst Dioc Youth Chapl 81-86; V Llanfair D C, Derwen, Llanelidan and Efenechtyd 84-88; Dioc Youth Chapl 86-90; V St As and Tremeirchion from 88; R Cefn from 88. *The Vicarage, 1 Llys Trewithan, Mount Road, St Asaph, Clwyd LL17 0DF* St Asaph (0745) 583264

GRIFFITHS, Robert James. b 52. Nottm Univ BTh82. St Jo Coll Nottm 79. **d** 82 **p** 83. C Kettering St Andr *Pet* 82-85; C Collier Row St Jas *Chelmsf* 85; C Collier Row St Jas and Havering-atte-Bower 86-89; R High Ongar w Norton Mandeville from 89. *The Rectory, The Street, High Ongar, Essex CM5 9NQ* Ongar (0277) 362593

GRIFFITHS, Roger. b 46. Trin Coll Bris 70. **d** 74 **p** 75. C Normanton *Derby* 74-77; C Bucknall and Bagnall *Lich* 77-80; TV 80-83; TV Abth *St D* 83-86; R Letterston w Llanfair Nant-y-Gof etc from 86. *The Rectory, Letterston, Haverfordwest, Dyfed SA62 5ST* Letterston (0348) 840336

GRIFFITHS, Roger Michael. b 47. Wycliffe Hall Ox 83. **d** 86 **p** 87. Min Can St D Cathl *St D* 86-88; V Penboyr from 88. *Penboyr Vicarage, Felindre, Llandyssul, Dyfed SA44 5XG* Velindre (0559) 370425

GRIFFITHS, Russell Howard. b 22. Glouc Th Course 75. **d** 77 **p** 78. NSM Fownhope w Fawley *Heref* 77-80; NSM Brockhampton 77-80; P-in-c Bridstow w Peterstow 80-81; TV Ross w Brampton Abbotts, Bridstow and Peterstow 81-87; rtd 87. *Green Gables, 239 Ledbury Road, Tupsley, Hereford HR1 1QN* Hereford (0432) 265362

GRIFFITHS, Shirley Thelma. b 48. Open Univ BA83. St Deiniol's Hawarden 79. **d** 82. NSM Dyserth and Trelawnyd and Cwm *St As* from 82; RE Officer from 89. *The Home Farm, Golden Grove, Llanasa, Holywell, Clwyd CH8 9NE* Prestatyn (0745) 889757

GRIFFITHS, Simon Mark. b 62. Ch Ch Coll Cant BA84. Chich Th Coll. **d** 87 **p** 88. C Cardiff St Jo *Llan* from 87; Sub-Chapl HM Pris Cardiff from 87. *17 Brithdir Street, Cardiff CF2 4LE* Cardiff (0222) 390703

GRIFFITHS, Canon Stanley Arthur. b 17. Lon Univ BSc38. Cuddesdon Coll 46. **d** 47 **p** 48. V St Neots *Ely* 65-77; RD St Neots 76-82; Hon Can Ely Cathl 76-82; V Buckden 77-82; rtd 82; Perm to Offic *Ely* and *York* from 82. *17 York Road, Malton, N Yorkshire YO17 0AX* Malton (0653) 697324

GRIFFITHS, Miss Sylvia Joy. b 50. Gipsy Hill Coll of Educn CertEd71. St Jo Coll Nottm 85. **dss** 86 **d** 87. Woodthorpe *S'well* 86-87; Par Dn 87-90; TM Bestwood from 90; Min Bestwood/Rise Park LEP from 90. *The Vicarage, 81 Cherry Orchard Mount, Bestwood, Nottingham NG5 5TJ* Nottingham (0602) 202928

GRIFFITHS, Thomas. b 31. AKC57. **d** 58 **p** 59. C Cheadle Hulme All SS *Ches* 58-61; C Oxton 61-63; V Micklehurst 63-72; V Ringway 73-91; V Liscard St Mary w St Columba from 91. *St Mary's Vicarage, 107 Manor Road, Wallasey, Merseyside L45 7LU* 051-639 1553

GRIFFITHS, Ven Thomas Elwyn. b 12. Univ of Wales BA35 Or Coll Ox BA38 MA45. St Steph Ho Ox 37. **d** 38 **p** 39. Adn Brecon *S & B* 69-78; rtd 78. *27 Parc Pendre, Brecon, Powys* Brecon (0874) 5756

GRIFFITHS, Thomas Wailes. b 02. Wadh Coll Ox BA25 MA33. St D Coll Lamp. **d** 25 **p** 26. V Gt w Lt Tew *Ox* 57-68; P-in-c Over w Nether Worton 58-67; P-in-c Innerleithen *Edin* 68-71; rtd 69; P-in-c Lerwick *Ab* 78-79; P-in-c Burravoe 78-79. *Shire House, Sidmouth Road, Lyme Regis, Dorset DT7 5ES* Lyme Regis (02974) 2055

GRIFFITHS, Trefor Idris. b 51. Univ of Wales (Cardiff) BA73 CertEd76 DPS86. St Mich Coll Llan 84. **d** 86 **p** 87. C Aberdare *Llan* 86-89; V Port Talbot St Agnes w Oakwood from 89. *St Agnes Vicarage, 29 Ynys Street, Port Talbot, W Glam SA13 1YW*   Port Talbot (0639) 883630

GRIFFITHS, Tudor Francis Lloyd. b 54. Jes Coll Ox BA76 MA81. Wycliffe Hall Ox 76. **d** 79 **p** 80. C Brecon w Battle *S & B* 79-81; Min Can Brecon Cathl 79-81; C Swansea St Mary w H Trin 81-83; V Llangattock and Llangyndir 83-88; CMS from 89; Uganda from 89. *Bishop Tucker Theological College, PO Box 4, Mukono, Uganda*

GRIFFITHS, Vyrnach Morgan. b 24. Univ of Wales (Lamp) BA50. St Mich Coll Llan 52. **d** 54 **p** 55. V Dinas w Penygraig *Llan* 69-74; R Llanddulas *St As* 74-80; R Llanddulas and Llysfaen 80-89; rtd 89. *27 Wynnstay Road, Old Colwyn, Colwyn Bay, Clwyd LL29 9DS* Colwyn Bay (0492) 512232

GRIFFITHS, William Bevan. b 13. AKC37. **d** 37 **p** 38. R Braunston *Pet* 59-79; rtd 79. *73 Glannant Way, Cimla, Neath, W Glam SA11 3YP*   Neath (0639) 635697

GRIFFITHS, William David Aled. b 52. Univ of Wales (Abth) BA74 Man Univ AHA77. Llan St Mich DipTh83. **d** 83 **p** 84. C Carmarthen St Pet *St D* 83-87; Asst Warden of Ords from 84; V Llansadwrn w Llanwrda and Manordeilo from 87. *The Vicarage, Llanwrda, Dyfed SA19 8HD*   Llangadog (0550) 777343

GRIFFITHS, William David Maldwyn. b 23. St D Coll Lamp BA47. **d** 50 **p** 51. V Llanfihangel Geneu'r Glyn *St D* 67-89; RD Llanbadarn Fawr 87-89; rtd 89. *Bro Enlli, Lower Regent Street, Aberaeron, Dyfed SA46 0HZ* Aberaeron (0545) 570176

GRIFFITHS, William Thomas Gordon. b 48. York Univ BA70 Fitzw Coll Cam BA79. Ridley Hall Cam 78. **d** 80 **p** 81. C Dulwich St Barn *S'wark* 80-83; C Egglescliffe *Dur* 83-85; Ind Chapl 85-90; V Stockton St Jas from 90. *243 Darlington Lane, Stockton-on-Tees, Cleveland TS19 8AA*   Stockton-on-Tees (0642) 676323

GRIGG, Simon James. b 61. Warw Univ BA82 MA83 Southn Univ BTh90. Chich Th Coll 87. **d** 90 **p** 91. C Cowley St Jas *Ox* from 90. *Benson Cottage, Beauchamp Lane, Cowley, Oxford OX4 3LF*   Oxford (0865) 778821

GRIGG, Canon Terence George. b 34. Kelham Th Coll 54. **d** 59 **p** 60. C Highgate Rise St Anne Brookfield *Lon* 59-62; Chapl Lee Abbey 63-69; Chapl and Lect St Luke's Coll Ex 66-70; V Stainton-in-Cleveland *York* 70-83; R Cottingham from 83; Hon Can Koforidua from 84; Can York Minster *York* from 90. *The Rectory, Hallgate, Cottingham, N Humberside HU16 4DD*   Hull (0482) 847668

GRIGG, William John Frank. b 27. SSC. Ripon Hall Ox. **d** 66 **p** 67. C Fenton *Lich* 69-74; C St Stephen by Saltash *Truro* 74-76; TV Redruth 76-79; TV Laneast w St Clether and Tresmere 79-81; P-in-c Wendron 81-85; TV Helston and Wendron 85-91; rtd 91. *St Germoe, 23 Dunheved Fields, Launceston, Cornwall PL15 7HS* Launceston (0566) 772878

GRIGGS, Canon Alan Sheward. b 33. Trin Hall Cam BA56 MA60. Westcott Ho Cam 58. **d** 60 **p** 61. C Arnold *S'well* 60-63; Succ S'wark Cathl *S'wark* 63-66; Ind Chapl 66-71; C Leeds H Trin *Ripon* 71-81; V 81-91; Soc and Ind Adv 71-81; Hon Can Ripon Cathl from 84; Soc Resp Officer from 91. *33 Harrowby Road, Leeds LS16 5HZ*   Leeds (0532) 758100 or 454268

GRIGGS, Frederick John. b 20. Peterho Cam BA48 MA53. Linc Th Coll. **d** 50 **p** 51. R Colne Engaine *Chelmsf* 62-80; P-in-c Frating w Thorrington 80-83; rtd 85. *6 Church View, Holton, Halesworth, Suffolk IP19 8PB* Halesworth (0986) 875298

✠**GRIGGS, Rt Rev Ian Macdonald.** b 28. Trin Hall Cam BA52 MA56. Westcott Ho Cam. **d** 54 **p** 55 **c** 87. C Portsea St Cuth *Portsm* 54-59; Youth Chapl *Sheff* 59-64; Bp's Dom Chapl 59-64; V Sheff St Cuth 64-71; V Kidderminster St Mary *Worc* 71-82; Hon Can Worc Cathl 77-84; TR Kidderminster St Mary and All SS etc 82-84; Preb Heref Cathl *Heref* from 84; Adn Ludlow 84-87; P-in-c Tenbury St Mich 84-87; Suff Bp Ludlow from 87. *Bishop's House, Halford, Craven Arms, Shropshire SY7 9BT*   Craven Arms (0588) 673571

GRIGGS, Kenneth Courtenay. b 13. Worc Ord Coll 56. **d** 58 **p** 59. V Dodford *Worc* 64-79; rtd 79; Perm to Offic Worc from 79; Glouc from 82. *81 Golden Vale, Churchdown, Gloucester GL3 2LX*   Churchdown (0452) 856285

GRIGOR, David Alexander. b 29. Lon Univ DipTh54. St Aid Birkenhead 51. **d** 54 **p** 55. C Hengrove *Bris* 54-57; C Marshfield w Cold Ashton 57-60; V Newport *Ex* 60-67; V Paignton St Paul Preston 67-73; Brazil 73-74;

Hon C Heavitree *Ex* 74-77; Chapl Ex Sch 74-77; Chapl Brighton Coll E Sussex 77-89; Chapl Warminster Sch Wilts from 89. *30 Church Street, Warminster, Wilts BA12 8PJ*   Warminster (0985) 215088

GRIGSBY, Peter Edward. b 31. Magd Coll Cam MA56 CertEd56. NE Ord Course 85. **d** 88 **p** 89. NSM Haxby w Wigginton *York* 88-90; C Brayton from 90. *St Francis's Vicarage, 25 Fox Lane, Thorpe Willoughby, Selby, N Yorkshire YO8 9NA*   Selby (0757) 703742

GRIGSON, Richard John Stephen. b 60. Man Univ BA83. Qu Coll Birm 86. **d** 88 **p** 89. C W Bromwich St Fran *Lich* from 88. *207 Hydes Road, West Bromwich, W Midlands B71 2EF*   021-556 0713

GRIMASON, Alistair John. b 57. CITC 76. **d** 79 **p** 80. C Belf H Trin *Conn* 79-82; C Dub Drumcondra w N Strand *D & G* 82-84; I Navan w Kentstown, Tara, Slane, Painestown etc *M & K* from 84; Dioc Youth Officer (Meath) from 90. *The Rectory, Boyne Road, Navan, Co Meath, Irish Republic*   Navan (46) 21172

GRIME, Arthur Michael. b 28. Kelham Th Coll 48. **d** 52 **p** 53. V Chiswick St Paul Grove Park *Lon* 66-88; rtd 89. *26 Madehurst Close, Brighton BN2 2YR*

GRIME, William John Peter. b 38. St Jo Coll Ox BA60 MA66. Cuddesdon Coll 69. **d** 70 **p** 71. C Blackb St Jas *Blackb* 70-74; Chapl St Martin's Coll of Educn 74-77; V Seascale *Carl* 77-78; P-in-c Irton w Drigg 77-78; V Seascale and Drigg from 78. *The Vicarage, The Banks, Seascale, Cumbria CA20 1QT*   Seascale (09467) 28217

GRIMES, William Geoffrey. b 33. Cranmer Hall Dur 59. **d** 62 **p** 63. C Preston St Jo *Blackb* 62-65; C Ribbleton 65-68; V New Longton 68-76; Adv on Services for the Deaf Sefton 77-89; Lic to Offic 80-89; Perm to Offic *Liv* 86-89; P-in-c Ingol *Blackb* 89-90; C Ashton-on-Ribble St Mich 90; P-in-c from 90. *20 South Avenue, New Longton, Preston PR4 4BB*   Longton (0772) 616849

GRIMLEY, Robert William. b 43. Ch Coll Cam BA66 MA70 Wadh Coll Ox BA68 MA76. Ripon Hall Ox 66. **d** 68 **p** 69. C Radlett *St Alb* 68-72; Hon C Moseley St Mary *Birm* 72-84; Chapl K Edw Sch Birm 72-84; V Edgbaston St Geo *Birm* from 84. *St George's Vicarage, 3 Westbourne Road, Birmingham B15 3TH*   021-454 2303

GRIMSBY, Suffragan Bishop of. See TUSTIN, Rt Rev David

GRIMSDALE, Mrs Margaret. b 24. STDip48 Lon Univ STD55. Gilmore Course 80. **dss** 82 **d** 87. Stoke Poges *Ox* 82-87; Hon Par Dn 87-88; Hon Par Dn Burrington and Churchill *B & W* 88-90; rtd 90; Perm to Offic *B & W* from 90. *6 Chapel Close, Castle Cary, Somerset BA7 7AX* Castle Cary (0963) 50866

GRIMSHAW, Canon Eric Fenton Hall. b 34. Bris Univ BA57. Tyndale Hall Bris 54. **d** 58 **p** 59. C Moss Side St Jas *Man* 58-61; C Leyland St Andr *Blackb* 61-64; V Preston St Mark 64-72; V Mirehouse *Carl* from 72; Hon Can Carl Cathl from 86. *The Vicarage, Hollins Close, Whitehaven, Cumbria CA28 8EX*   Whitehaven (0946) 693565

GRIMSTER, Barry John. b 49. Ex Univ BA70. Trin Coll Bris 72. **d** 74 **p** 75. C S Lambeth St Steph *S'wark* 74-77; C New Malden and Coombe 77-82; P-in-c Deptford St Jo 82-84; V Deptford St Jo w H Trin 84-89; V Woking St Pet *Guildf* from 89. *St Peter's Vicarage, 28 High Street, Old Woking, Surrey GU22 9ER*   Woking (0483) 762707

GRIMWADE, Eric Peter. b 14. AKC37. **d** 37 **p** 38. Chapl Cane Hill Hosp Coulsdon 69-78; C Lee-on-the-Solent *Portsm* 78-79; Hon C 79-81; rtd 79; Perm to Offic *Chich* from 82. *50 Brookway, Lindfield, Haywards Heath, W Sussex RH16 2BP*   Haywards Heath (0444) 414761

GRIMWADE, Canon John Girling. b 20. Keble Coll Ox BA48 MA52. Cuddesdon Coll 48. **d** 50 **p** 51. R Caversham *Ox* 62-81; Hon Can Ch Ch 73-90; Chapl to HM The Queen 80-90; R Caversham and Mapledurham *Ox* 81-83; P-in-c Stonesfield 83-89; rtd 89; Perm to Offic Ox and Glouc from 89. *88 Alexander Drive, Cirencester, Glos GL7 1UJ*   Cirencester (0285) 885767

GRIMWADE, Leslie Frank. b 24. FBIM60. Trin Coll Bris 74. **d** 77 **p** 78. C Taunton St Jas *B & W* 77-80; C Polegate *Chich* 80-83; R Swainsthorpe w Newton Flotman *Nor* 83-90; rtd 90; Hon Min Malmesbury Abbey *Bris* from 90; Chapl Malmesbury Hosp from 90. *Drimal, Common Road, Malmesbury, Wilts SN16 0HN*   Malmesbury (0666) 823541

GRIMWOOD, David Walter. b 48. Lon Univ BA70 K Coll Lon BD73 AKC73. **d** 74 **p** 75. C Newc St Geo *Newc* 74-78; C Whorlton 78-80; TV Totton *Win* from 80. *The Vicarage, Eling Hill, Totton, Southampton SO4 4HF* Southampton (0703) 866426

GRIMWOOD, William. b 11. St Cath Soc Ox BA36 MA39. Ripon Hall Ox 35. **d** 36 **p** 37. R Burbage w Aston Flamville *Leic* 56-85; rtd 86. *32 Forresters Road, Burbage, Leics LE10 2RX* Hinckley (0455) 39280

GRINDELL, James Mark. b 43. Nottm Univ BA66 Bris Univ MA69. Wells Th Coll 66. **d** 68 **p** 69. C Bushey Heath *St Alb* 68-72; C Ex St Dav *Ex* 72-74; Chapl St Audries Sch W Quantoxhead B & W 74-83; Chapl Berkhamsted Sch Herts 83-86; Chapl Denstone Coll Uttoxeter from 86. *The Chaplain's Office, Denstone College, Uttoxeter, Staffs ST14 5HN* Rocester (0889) 590372

✠**GRINDROD, Rt Rev John Basil.** b 19. KBE. Qu Coll Ox BA(Theol)49 MA53. Linc Th Coll 49. **d** 51 **p** 52 **c** 66. C Hulme St Mich *Man* 51-54; R Ancoats All SS 56-60; Australia from 60; Bp Riverina 66-71; Bp Rockhampton 71-80; Abp Brisbane 80-90; rtd 90. *14B Thomas Street, Murwillumbah, NSW, Australia 2484*

GRINHAM, Garth Clews. b 36. Oak Hill Th Coll 61. **d** 64 **p** 65. C Beckenham Ch Ch *Roch* 64-68; C Wallington H Trin *S'wark* 68-71; V Erith St Paul *Roch* 71-76; Asst Sec CPAS 76-81; Hon C Knockholt *Roch* 76-81; V Southport Ch Ch *Liv* from 81. *The Vicarage, 12 Gloucester Road, Southport, Merseyside PR8 2AU* Southport (0704) 65120

GRINHAM, Julian Clive. b 39. Lon Univ BA65. Oak Hill Th Coll 79. **d** 81 **p** 82. C Blackb Ch Ch w St Matt *Blackb* 81-83; Nat Sec Pathfinders, CPAS 83-88; Hd of CYPECS from 88. *c/o CPAS, Athena Drive, Tachbrook Park, Warwick CV34 6NG* Warwick (0926) 334342

GRINSTED, Richard Anthony. b 43. Leic Univ BSc65. Oak Hill Th Coll 67. **d** 70 **p** 71. C Egham *Guildf* 70-73; C Woodford Wells *Chelmsf* 73-76; P-in-c Havering-atte-Bower 76-84; R Ditton *Roch* from 84. *The Rectory, 2 The Stream, Ditton, Maidstone, Kent ME20 6AG* West Malling (0732) 842027

GRISCOME, David. b 47. Oak Hill Th Coll BA88 TCD Div Sch 89. **d** 89 **p** 90. C Glendermott *D & R* 89-91; I Clondehorkey w Cashel from 91; I Mevagh w Glenalla from 91. *Ballymore Rectory, Ballymore, Letterkenny, Co Donegal, Irish Republic* Letterkenny (74) 36185

GRIST, Anthony John. b 51. Kent Univ BA72. Westcott Ho Cam 73. **d** 76 **p** 77. C Wythenshawe St Martin *Man* 76-79; C Reddish 79-82; V Royton St Anne 82-86. *32 Manchester Road, Mossley, Ashton-under-Lyne, Lancs*

GRITTEN, Desmond Digby. b 17. ALCD54. **d** 54 **p** 55. V Kenilworth St Jo *Cov* 58-87; RD Kenilworth 63-73; rtd 87; Perm to Offic *Cant* from 87. *Arcadia, 3 Victoria Parade, Broadstairs, Kent CT10 1QS* Thanet (0843) 63062

GROSE, Reginald Ewart. b 06. Lich Th Coll 58. **d** 58 **p** 59. V Thornham St Jas *Man* 60-71; rtd 71. *The Grange, Manor Road, Goring, Reading RG8 9DY* Henley-on-Thames (0491) 3130

GROSSCURTH, Stephen. b 55. Sarum & Wells Th Coll 81. **d** 84 **p** 85. C Southport H Trin *Liv* 84-87; C Amblecote *Worc* 87-89; V Walton St Jo *Liv* from 89. *St John's Vicarage, Rice Lane, Liverpool L9 2BW* 051-525 3458

GROSSE, Anthony Charles Bain. b 30. Oak Hill Th Coll 58. **d** 61 **p** 62. C Chislehurst Ch Ch *Roch* 61-65; C Washfield *Ex* 65-71; TV Washfield, Stoodleigh, Withleigh etc 71-73; R Hemyock 73-86; P-in-c Clayhidon 76-86; R Hemyock w Culm Davy and Clayhidon from 87. *The Rectory, Hemyock, Cullompton, Devon EX15 3RQ* Hemyock (0823) 680244

GROSSE, Richard William. b 52. Solicitor 77 M Essex Tech Coll LLB73. Ridley Hall Cam 86. **d** 88 **p** 89. C Soham *Ely* 88-91; C Bedale *Ripon* from 91; C-in-c Thornton Watlass w Thornton Steward from 91. *The Rectory, Thornton Watcass, Ripon, N Yorkshire HG4 4AH* Bedale (0677) 22737

GROSVENOR, Royston Johannes Martin. b 47. K Coll Lon BD70 AKC. **d** 71 **p** 72. C Pontesbury I and II *Heref* 71-75; C Bishopston *Bris* 75-79; P-in-c Croydon St Pet S End *Cant* 79-81; V Croydon St Pet 81-84; V Croydon St Pet *S'wark* 85-87; R Merstham and Gatton from 87. *The Rectory, Gatton Bottom, Merstham, Redhill RH1 3BH* Merstham (0737) 643755

GROVE, Canon John Montgomery. b 13. Magd Coll Cam BA35 MA39. Westcott Ho Cam 39. **d** 39 **p** 40. Chapl Clifton Coll Bris 43-57; Hd Master Chorister Sch Dur 57-78; rtd 78; Hon Can Dur Cathl *Dur* from 74. *22 South Street, Durham DH1 4OP* 091-384 4787

GROVE, Ronald Edward. b 32. Oak Hill Th Coll 60. **d** 63 **p** 64. C Bromley St Jo *Roch* 63-66; V Stratford New Town St Paul *Chelmsf* from 66. *The Vicarage, 65 Maryland Road, London E15 1JL* 081-534 3640

GROVER, Wilfrid John. b 29. Lich Th Coll 55. **d** 58 **p** 59. V Cookham *Ox* 65-85; RD Maidenhead 82-85; Warden Christchurch Retreat Ho *Glouc* from 85; Perm to Offic from 85; rtd 89. *The Old Vicarage, Christchurch, Coleford, Glos GL16 7NS* Dean (0594) 35330

GROVES, James Alan. b 32. CCC Cam BA58 MA62. Wells Th Coll 58. **d** 60 **p** 61. C Milton next Gravesend Ch Ch *Roch* 60-64; C Beckenham St Jas 64-66; V Orpington St Andr from 66. *St Andrew's Vicarage, Anglesea Road, Orpington, Kent BR5 4AN* Orpington (0689) 23775

GROVES, Philip Neil. b 62. Man Univ BA84. St Jo Coll Nottm 86. **d** 88 **p** 89. C Holbeck *Ripon* 88-91; CMS from 91. *CMS Training College, Crowther Hall, Weoley Park Road, Selly Oak, Birmingham B29 6QT* 021-472 4228

GROVES, Robert John. b 42. Trin Coll Bris 74. **d** 76 **p** 77. C Norwood *S'wark* 76-79; P-in-c Clapham Park All SS 79-86; V Anerley *Roch* from 86. *The Vicarage, 234 Anerley Road, London SE20 8TJ* 081-778 4800

GROVES, Stephen James Andrew. b 60. Newc Univ BA82. Coll of Resurr Mirfield 83. **d** 86 **p** 87. C Brighton Resurr *Chich* 86-91; Sen AP St Leonards Ch Ch and St Mary from 91. *31 Alfred Street, St Leonards-on-Sea, E Sussex TN38 0HD* Hastings (0424) 443956

GROWNS, John Huntley. b 28. Chich Th Coll 57. **d** 60 **p** 61. C Hayes St Mary *Lon* 60-64; C Addlestone *Guildf* 64-67; C-in-c Kempston Transfiguration CD *St Alb* 67-74; R Stevenage St Geo 74-82; R Felpham w Middleton *Chich* 82-88; P-in-c Westmill w Gt Munden *St Alb* 88-89; Dioc Stewardship Adv from 88; P-in-c Westmill from 89. *The Rectory, Westmill, Buntingford, Herts SG9 9LL* Royston (0763) 71389

GRUBB, Greville Alexander. b 36. St Jo Coll Nottm 72. **d** 74 **p** 75. C Rushden w Newton Bromswold *Pet* 74-77; Chapl St D Coll Llandudno 77-89; Chapl Casterton Sch Cumbria from 90. *Beckside, Casterton, Carnforth, Lancs LA6 2SB* Kirkby Lonsdale (05242) 71737

GRUNDY, Anthony Brian. b 36. Pemb Coll Cam BA62 MA87. Ridley Hall Cam 61. **d** 63 **p** 64. C Hatcham St Jas *S'wark* 63-66; C Margate H Trin *Cant* 66-68; C Brixton Hill St Sav *S'wark* 68-70; V Assington *St E* 70-76; TV Much Wenlock w Bourton *Heref* 76-81; TV Wenlock 81-82; TR 82-88; RD Condover 86-88; R Burghfield *Ox* from 88. *The Rectory, Burghfield Common, Reading RG7 3BH* Burghfield Common (0734) 834433

GRUNDY, Christopher John. b 49. Trin Coll Bris 74. **d** 77 **p** 78. C Maidstone St Luke *Cant* 77-81; Argentina 81-82; Chile 82-84; Perm to Offic *Guildf* from 84. *The Lyttons, Seale, Farnham, Surrey GU10 1HR* Runfold (02518) 2071

GRUNDY, Jocelyn Pratchitt. b 22. Trin Coll Cam MA. Westcott Ho Cam 64. **d** 66 **p** 67. R Shere *Guildf* 68-73; V Fleet 73-83; C Aldershot St Mich 83-87; rtd 87. *Richmond Cottage, School Hill, Seale, Farnham, Surrey GU10 1HY* Runfold (02518) 2238

GRUNDY, Julian David. b 60. St Andr Univ MA83. Trin Coll Bris BA88. **d** 89 **p** 90. C Lanc St Thos *Blackb* from 89. *77 Ulster Road, Lancaster LA1 4AH* Lancaster (0524) 381510

GRUNDY, Canon Malcolm Leslie. b 44. AKC68 Open Univ BA76. **d** 69 **p** 70. C Doncaster St Geo *Sheff* 69-72; Ind Chapl 72-80; Dir of Educn *Lon* 80-86; P-in-c Huntingdon St Mary w St Benedict *Ely* 86; P-in-c Huntingdon All SS w St Jo 86; P-in-c Huntingdon St Barn 86; TR Huntingdon from 87; Hon Can Ely Cathl from 88. *The Rectory, 1 The Walks East, Huntingdon, Cambs PE18 6AP* Huntingdon (0480) 412674

GRUNDY, Paul. b 55. BD77 AKC. Linc Th Coll 79. **d** 80 **p** 81. C Ryhope *Dur* 80-82; C Ferryhill 82-85; TV Cramlington *Newc* 85-87; TV Swinton and Pendlebury *Man* 87-90; V Wingate Grange *Dur* from 90. *The Vicarage, Wingate, Co Durham TS28 5BW* Wellfield (0429) 838338

GRUNEBERG, Alan Conrad. b 13. Lon Univ BSc34. Oak Hill Th Coll 67. **d** 68 **p** 69. C Penn Fields *Lich* 68-73; R Aythorpe w High and Leaden Roding *Chelmsf* 73-79; rtd 79; Perm to Offic *St E* from 80. *3 Manor Park Road, Southwold, Suffolk IP18 6AF* Southwold (0502) 723347

GRYLLS, Michael John. b 38. Qu Coll Cam BA62 MA66. Linc Th Coll 62. **d** 64 **p** 65. C Shrewsbury St Silas *Sheff* 64-67; C-in-c Dunscroft CD 67-70; V Herringthorpe 70-78; RV Amport, Grateley, Monxton and Quarley *Win* 78-89; RD Andover 85-89; V Whitchurch w Tufton and Litchfield from 89. *The Vicarage, Church Street, Whitchurch, Hants RG28 7AS* Whitchurch (0256) 892535

GUDGEON, Michael John. b 40. Qu Coll Cam BA63 MA67. Chich Th Coll 65. **d** 66 **p** 67. C Kings

Heath *Birm* 66-72; Asst Chapl K Edw Sch Birm 69-72; Tutor Cuddesdon Coll 72-75; V Hawley H Trin *Guildf* 75-80; V Minley 75-80; Adult Educn Adv *Chich* 80-87; Can Res Portsm Cathl *Portsm* 87-90; Dioc Dir of Educn 87-90; V Hove St Thos *Chich* from 90. *St Thomas's Vicarage, 18 Nizells Avenue, Hove, E Sussex BN3 1PL* Brighton (0273) 736389

GUERNSEY, Dean of. *See* FENWICK, Very Rev Jeffrey Robert

GUEST, David. b 41. Dur Univ BA62. Coll of Resurr Mirfield 70. **d** 72 **p** 73. C Horsforth *Ripon* 72-75; C Richmond 75-76; C Richmond w Hudswell 76-78; R Middleham 78-81; R Middleham and Coverham w Horsehouse 81-86; R W Rainton *Dur* from 86; V E Rainton from 86. *The Rectory, West Rainton, Houghton le Spring, Tyne & Wear DH4 6PA* 091-584 3263

GUEST, Ven Frederick William. b 07. St Aug Coll Cant 27. **d** 32 **p** 33. C Tilbury Docks *Chelmsf* 32-34; Australia from 34; Can Perth 51-73; Adn Canning 61-67; Adn Perth 67-73. *203 Riley House, 20 Excelsior Street, Shenton Park, W Australia 6008* Perth (9) 381-7052

GUEST, John. b 36. Trin Coll Bris 59. **d** 61 **p** 62. C Barton Hill St Luke w Ch Ch *Bris* 61-64; C Liv St Sav *Liv* 65-66; USA from 66. *RD 5 Camp Meeting Road, Sewickley, Pennsylvania 15143, USA*

GUEST, John Andrew Kenneth. b 55. Univ of Wales (Lamp) BA78. Wycliffe Hall Ox 78. **d** 80 **p** 81. C Eastwood *S'well* 80-84; TV Toxteth St Philemon w St Gabr and St Cleopas *Liv* 84-89; C Cranham Park *Chelmsf* from 89. *72 Marlborough Gardens, Upminster, Essex RM14 1SG* Upminster (04022) 25604

GUEST, Leslie Leonard. b 15. Ripon Hall Ox 62. **d** 63 **p** 64. V Norton and Lenchwick *Worc* 66-77; R Inkberrow w Cookhill and Kington w Dormston 77-84; rtd 84; Perm to Offic *Worc* from 84. *35 Husum Way, Kidderminster, Worcs DY10 3QJ* Kidderminster (0562) 745722

GUEST, Simon Llewelyn. b 56. Univ of Wales (Lamp) BA78 CertEd79 DipTh85. St Mich Coll Llan 83. **d** 85 **p** 86. C Bassaleg *Mon* 85-88; C Cwmbran 88-89; R 89-90; V Raglan w Llandenny and Bryngwyn from 90. *The Vicarage, Primrose Green, Raglan, Gwent NP5 2DU* Raglan (0291) 690330

GUILDFORD, Bishop of. *See* ADIE, Rt Rev Michael Edgar

GUILDFORD, Dean of. *See* WEDDERSPOON, Very Rev Alexander Gillan

GUILLAN, Miss Barbara Doris. b 19. S'wark Ord Course 45. **d** 87. NSM St Stythians w Perranarworthal and Gwennap *Truro* 87-89; rtd 89; Perm to Offic *Truro* from 89. *Hillside, Perranwell Station, Truro, Cornwall TR3 7PU* Truro (0872) 865991

GUILLE, John Arthur. b 49. Southn Univ BTh79. Sarum & Wells Th Coll 73. **d** 76 **p** 77. C Chandler's Ford *Win* 76-80; P-in-c Bournemouth St Jo 80-84; P-in-c Bournemouth St Mich 83-84; V Bournemouth St Jo w St Mich 84-89; R Guernsey St Andr from 89. *The Rectory, rue des Morts, St Andrew, Guernsey, Channel Islands* Guernsey (0481) 38568

GUILLEBAUD, Miss Margaret Jean. b 43. Edin Univ BSc66. All Nations Chr Coll DipRS79 Cranmer Hall Dur 79. **dss** 80 **d** 87. New Malden and Coombe *S'wark* 80-84; Carlton Colville w Mutford and Rushmere *Nor* 84-87; C 87-91; Par Dn Rodbourne Cheney *Bris* from 91. *21 Newland Road, Swindon, Wilts SN2 3BP* Swindon (0793) 613734

GUILLOTEAU, Claude. b 32. Ripon Coll Cuddesdon 77. **d** 57 **p** 57. In RC Ch 57-76; C Warmsworth *Sheff* 78-80; C Goole 80-86; C Hatf 86-88; C Ecclesall from 88. *64 Glenorchy Road, Sheffield S7 2EN* Sheffield (0742) 584685

GUINNESS, Christopher Paul. b 43. Lon Coll of Div 64. **d** 67 **p** 68. C Farnborough *Guildf* 67-70; C Tulse Hill H Trin *S'wark* 70-74; C Worting *Win* 74-78; P-in-c S Lambeth St Steph *S'wark* 78-89; V from 89; RD Lambeth 86-90. *The Vicarage, St Stephen's Terrace, London SW8 1DH* 071-735 8461

GUINNESS, Garry Grattan. b 40. Em Coll Cam BA64 MA68. Ridley Hall Cam 64. **d** 66 **p** 67. C Wallington H Trin *S'wark* 66-69; C St Marylebone All So w SS Pet and Jo *Lon* 69-72; P-in-c Clifton H Trin, St Andr and St Pet *Bris* 72-79; V Watford St Luke *St Alb* 79-90; TR Worthing Ch the King *Chich* from 90. *4 Shakespeare Road, Worthing, W Sussex BN11 4AL* Worthing (0903) 205185

GUINNESS, Graham Alexander. b 60. Edin Univ LTh85. Edin Th Coll 82. **d** 85 **p** 86. Dioc Youth Chapl *Mor* 85-88; C Elgin w Lossiemouth 85-88; P-in-c Glas St Ninian *Glas* 88-90; R Tighnabruaich *Arg* 90-91; R

Dunoon from 90. *The Rectory, Kilbride Road, Dunoon, Argyll PA23 7LN* Dunoon (0369) 2444

GUINNESS, Peter Grattan. b 49. Man Univ BSc71 CertEd73 Nottm Univ DipTh81. St Jo Coll Nottm 80. **d** 82 **p** 83. C Normanton *Wakef* 82-87; V Fletchamstead *Cov* from 87. *St James's Vicarage, 395 Tile Hill Lane, Coventry CV4 9DP* Coventry (0203) 466262

GUINNESS, Robert Desmond. b 05. Ch Coll Cam BA27 MA30. Ridley Hall Cam. **d** 28 **p** 29. V Laleham *Lon* 52-76; rtd 76; P-in-c Laleham *Lon* 76-77. *10 Eckling Grange, Dereham, Norfolk* Dereham (0362) 691337

GUINNESS, Robin Gordon. b 38. St Jo Coll Cam MA61. Ridley Hall Cam 63. **d** 63 **p** 64. C Bedworth *Cov* 63-66; CMS 66-68; Canada from 68. *47 Prospect Street, Westmount, Quebec, Canada, H3Z 1W5* Westmount (514) 931-6796

GUISE, John Christopher. b 29. MRPharmS FRSH. W Midl Minl Tr Course 80. **d** 83 **p** 84. NSM Alfrick, Lulsley, Suckley, Leigh and Bransford *Worc* from 83. *Marsh Cottage, Leigh, Worcs WR6 5LE* Leigh Sinton (0886) 32336

GUISE, Stephen. b 48. Win Sch of Arts BA75. Chich Th Coll 85. **d** 87 **p** 88. C Bexhill St Pet *Chich* 87-90; TV Haywards Heath St Wilfrid from 90. *The Vicarage, 1 Sandy Vale, Haywards Heath, W Sussex RH16 4JH* Haywards Heath (0444) 450173

GUITE, Ayodeji Malcolm. b 57. Pemb Coll Cam BA80 MA84 Newc Poly PGCE82. Ridley Hall Cam 88. **d** 90 **p** 91. Par Dn Ely from 90. *2 Houghton Gardens, Ely, Cambs CB7 4JN* Ely (0353) 665654

GUITE, Mrs Margaret Ann. b 53. Girton Coll Cam BA74 MA78 St Jo Coll Dur PhD81. Cranmer Hall Dur 75. **dss** 79 **d** 87. Warlingham w Chelsham and Farleigh *S'wark* 79-82; Tutor Westcott Ho Cam 82-90; Cherry Hinton St Jo *Ely* 82-86; Tutor Wesley Ho Cam 87-90; Hon Par Dn Ely from 90; Hon Par Dn Chettisham from 90; Hon Par Dn Prickwillow from 90. *2 Houghton Gardens, Ely, Cambridge CB7 4JN* Ely (0353) 665654

GUIVER, Paul Alfred (Brother George). b 45. St Chad's Coll Dur BA68. Cuddesdon Coll 71. **d** 73 **p** 74. C Mill End and Heronsgate w W Hyde *St Alb* 73-76; P-in-c Bishop's Frome *Heref* 76-82; P-in-c Castle Frome 76-82; P-in-c Acton Beauchamp and Evesbatch w Stanford Bishop 76-82; CR from 85. *House of the Resurrection, Mirfield, W Yorkshire WF14 0BN* Mirfield (0924) 494318

GUIVER, Roger William Antony. b 53. Edin Univ MA75 St Chad's Coll Dur BA78. Coll of Resurr Mirfield. **d** 82 **p** 83. C Rekendyke *Dur* 82-85; Chapl Middlesb Gen Hosp from 85; P-in-c Middlesb St Columba w St Paul *York* from 85. *115 Cambridge Road, Middlesbrough, Cleveland TS5 5HF* Middlesbrough (0642) 824779

GULL, William John. b 42. Ripon Hall Ox 63. **d** 65 **p** 66. C Worksop Priory *S'well* 65-69; C Newark St Mary 69-71; P-in-c Mansf St Lawr 71-77; V 77-78; Chapl HM Young Offender Inst Lowdham Grange 78-90; R Lambley *S'well* 78-91; Chmn Dioc Bd Soc Resp from 86; V Sneinton St Cypr from 91. *St Cyprian's Vicarage, Marston Road, Nottingham NG3 7AN* Nottingham (0602) 873425

GULLAND, John Robertson. b 46. ACIB Avery Hill Coll CertEd70 Open Univ BA76 Chelsea Coll Lon MA82. Oak Hill Th Coll 88. **d** 90 **p** 91. NSM Woodside Park St Barn Lon from 90. *80 Woodlands Avenue, London N3 2NR* 081-346 6513

GULLEY, Hubert Edward Raymond. b 06. Bris Univ BA27. Sarum Th Coll 27. **d** 29 **p** 30. P-in-c Dalry *Glas* 57-75; rtd 75; Perm to Offic *Chich* from 84. *College of St Barnabas, Blackberry Lane, Lingfield, Surrey RH7 6NJ* Dormans Park (034287) 430

GULVIN, Philip Christopher. b 53. BSc76. St Jo Coll Nottm 82. **d** 85 **p** 86. C Northwood H Trin *Lon* 85-89; TV Sanderstead All SS *S'wark* from 89. *4 Mitchley Avenue, Purley, Surrey CR8 1EA* 081-660 8123

GUMBEL, Nicholas Glyn Paul. b 55. Trin Coll Cam MA76 BA85. Wycliffe Hall Ox 83. **d** 86 **p** 87. C Brompton H Trin w Onslow Square St Paul *Lon* from 86. *13 Macaulay Road, London SW4 0QP* 071-720 3538

GUMMER, Dudley Harrison. b 28. Roch Th Coll 61. **d** 63 **p** 64. C Deptford St Paul *S'wark* 63-65; C Melton Mowbray w Thorpe Arnold *Leic* 65-68; C-in-c E Goscote CD 68-75; V E Goscote 75-78; V Luton St Anne *St Alb* 78-88; R Albury w St Martha *Guildf* from 88. *Yeoman's Acre, Farley Green, Albury, Guildford, Surrey GU5 9DN* Shere (048641) 2465

GUMMER, Selwyn. b 07. Univ of Wales BA34. Wycliffe Hall Ox 39. **d** 39 **p** 40. V Brighton St Pet w Chpl Royal and St Jo *Chich* 65-70; rtd 71. *Winston Grange,*

Debenham, Stowmarket, Suffolk Debenham (0728) 860522

GUNN, Eric James. b 24. Hull Univ BTh83 MA90. Kelham Th Coll 47. **d** 52 **p** 53. R Eckington *Derby* 69-74; P-in-c Ridgeway 72-74; TR Eckington w Handley and Ridgeway 74-78; V Hornsea w Atwick *York* 78-89; rtd 89; Perm to Offic *Linc* from 89. *1 Station Road, Morton, Bourne, Lincs* Morton (0778) 37814

GUNN, Frederick George. b 11. **d** 51 **p** 51. R Witton w Brundall and Braydeston *Nor* 64-79; RD Blofield 74-79; rtd 80; Perm to Offic *Nor* from 80. *18 Thirlby Road, North Walsham, Norfolk NR28 9BA* North Walsham (0692) 403948

GUNN, Geoffrey Charles. b 12. Kelham Th Coll 28. **d** 36 **p** 37. V Shotesham *Nor* 56-77; rtd 77; Min Can Nor Cathl *Nor* from 85. *Shepherd's Close, Priory Lane, Shotesham, Norwich* Brooke (0508) 50285

GUNN, Jeffrey Thomas. b 47. St Chad's Coll Dur BA77. Coll of Resurr Mirfield 77. **d** 79 **p** 80. C Prestbury *Glouc* 79-82; P-in-c Coldham *Ely* 82-87; P-in-c Elm 82-87; P-in-c Friday Bridge 82-87; V Larkfield *Roch* from 87; P-in-c Leybourne from 87. *The Vicarage, 206 New Hythe Lane, Larkfield, Maidstone, Kent ME20 6PT* West Malling (0732) 843349

GUNN, Robert. b 35. Oak Hill Th Coll 59. **d** 62 **p** 63. C Upper Holloway St Jo *Lon* 62-66; C Woking St Jo *Guildf* 66-69; Scripture Union 69-71; R Necton w Holme Hale *Nor* 71-77; V Tottenham St Jo *Lon* 77-81; V Gt Cam Road St Jo and St Jas 82-85; V Luton St Fran *St Alb* 85-90; Chapl Luton Airport from 90. *103 Edgewood Drive, Stopsley, Luton, Beds LU2 8ER* Luton (0582) 416151

GUNN-JOHNSON, David Allan. b 49. Lambeth STh85 St Steph Ho Ox 79. **d** 81 **p** 82. C Oxhey St Matt *St Alb* 81-84; C Cheshunt 84-88; TR Colyton, Southleigh, Offwell, Widworthy etc *Ex* from 88; RD Honiton from 90. *The Vicarage, Colyton, Devon EX13 6LJ* Colyton (0297) 52307

GUNNER, Laurence Francois Pascal. b 36. Keble Coll Ox BA59 MA63. Wells Th Coll 59. **d** 61 **p** 62. C Charlton Kings St Mary *Glouc* 61-65; C Hemel Hempstead *St Alb* 65-69; Chapl Bloxham Sch Oxon 69-86; Sen Chapl Marlborough Coll Wilts from 86. *Marlborough College, Marlborough, Wilts SN8 1PA* Marlborough (0672) 512648

GUNNING, George Peter. b 36. Harper Adams Agric Coll NDA58. E Midl Min Tr Course 78. **d** 85 **p** 86. C Winterton Gp *Linc* 85-88; V Alkborough from 88. *The Vicarage, Alkborough, Scunthorpe, S Humberside DN15 9JJ* Scunthorpe (0724) 720341

GUNSTONE, Canon John Thomas Arthur. b 27. St Chad's Coll Dur BA48 MA55. Coll of Resurr Mirfield 50. **d** 52 **p** 53. C Walthamstow St Sav *Chelmsf* 52-53; C Forest Gate St John 53-58; C-in-c Rush Green St Aug CD 58-71; Chapl Barn Fellowship Winterborne Whitechurch 71-75; Tutor Sarum & Wells Th Coll 71-75; Sec Gtr Man Co Ecum Coun from 75; Lic to Offic *Man* 75-80; Hon Can Man Cathl from 80. *12 Deneford Road, Manchester M20 8TD* 061-434 8351 or 273 5508

GUNTER, Timothy Wilson. b 37. Leeds Univ BA59 St Jo Coll Cam BA62 MA66. Ridley Hall Cam 59. **d** 62 **p** 63. C Beverley Minster *York* 62-65; C Hornsea and Goxhill 65-70; V Silsden *Bradf* 70-80; V Sunninghill *Ox* from 80. *Sunninghill Vicarage, Church Lane, Ascot, Berks SL5 7DD* Ascot (0344) 20727

GUNTER, Canon William Aston. b 05. Wycliffe Hall Ox. **d** 41 **p** 42. V Manningham St Luke *Bradf* 63-66; Lic to Offic *Ches* 67-71; rtd 71; Perm to Offic *Derby* from 71. *3 Lyme Park, Chinley, Stockport, Cheshire SK12 6AG* Chinley (0663) 50651

GUNYON, Stephen Francis. b 14. Selw Coll Cam BA38 MA48. Linc Th Coll 38. **d** 40 **p** 41. V Hindhead *Guildf* 71-80; rtd 80; Perm to Offic *Pet* from 80. *18 Waverley Road, Kettering, Northants NN15 6NT* Kettering (0536) 83885

GUPPY, Kenneth Henry Stanley. b 29. Univ of Wales (Lamp) BA54. St Mich Coll Llan 54. **d** 56 **p** 57. V Llangwm Uchaf w Llangwm Isaf w Gwernesney etc *Mon* 63-85; rtd 85; Lic to Offic *Ox* from 88. *Cedar Cottage, Frieth, Henley-on-Thames, Oxon RG9 6NN*

GURD, Brian Charles (Simon). b 44. Sarum & Wells Th Coll 72. **d** 74 **p** 75. OSP from 67; Lic to Offic *Win* 74-82; Prior Alton Abbey 79-82; C Shepherd's Bush St Steph w St Thos *Lon* 82-84; NSM Willesborough *Cant* 85-87; V Bethersden w High Halden from 87. *The Vicarage, Bull Lane, Bethersden, Ashford, Kent TN26 3HA* Bethersden (023382) 266

GURDON, Mrs June Mary. b 38. Sarum Th Coll 83. **dss** 86 **d** 87. Jersey St Sav *Win* 85-86; Jersey St Mary 86-87;

Hon Par Dn 87-88; Hon Par Dn Jersey St Brelade from 88. *The Glade, St Mary, Jersey, Channel Islands* Jersey (0534) 64282

GURNEY, Miss Ann. b 27. Lon Univ DipTh48. Gilmore Ho 45. **dss** 54 **d** 87. Prin Gilmore Ho 59-70; Hd Dss (Dios Roch and S'wark) 59-70; Dio Lon 70-87; Bp's Adv for Lay Min 70-87; rtd 87; Hon Par Dn St Botolph Aldgate w H Trin Minories *Lon* from 87. *35 Archery Road, London SE9 1HF* 081-850 4083

GURNEY, Dennis Albert John. b 31. Lon Coll of Div. **d** 67 **p** 68. C Boscombe St Jo *Win* 67-69; V Hurstbourne Tarrant and Faccombe 70-77; R Jersey St Ouen w St Geo 77-84; Chapl Intercon Ch Soc from 84; Hon Chapl Miss to Seamen from 84; UAE from 84. *PO Box 7415, Dubai, United Arab Emirates* Dubai (4) 374947

GURNEY, Canon Richmond Harptree. b 24. Worc Coll Ox BA48 MA48. Cuddesdon Coll 48. **d** 50 **p** 51. R Gateshead St Mary *Dur* 66-72; TR Gateshead 72-75; P-in-c Eskdale, Irton, Muncaster and Waberthwaite *Carl* 75-78; V 78-82; Sec Dioc Past and Redundant Chs Uses Cttees 82-87; R Asby 82-89; V Bolton 82-89; V Crosby Ravensworth 82-89; Hon Can Carl Cathl from 84; rtd 89. *Dunelm, Gelt Road, Brampton, Cumbria CA8 1QH* Brampton (06977) 2516

GURR, Ralph Sydney. b 27. AKC55. **d** 57 **p** 58. C Lewisham St Mary *S'wark* 57-63; Chapl Lewisham Hosp 61-63; C Cheam *S'wark* 63-69; V Wyke *Bradf* 69-72; V Edmonton St Mich *Lon* 72-79; R Fordingbridge w Ibsley *Win* 79-82; V Fordingbridge 82-84; P-in-c N Stoneham from 84. *11 Field Close, Bassett Green Road, Southampton SO2 3DY* Southampton (0703) 554565

GUSH, Laurence Langley. b 23. CChem CEng MICE52 ACGI MRIC Lon Univ BSc44. NW Ord Course 73. **d** 76 **p** 77. NSM Sheff St Matt *Sheff* 76-82; NSM Aston cum Aughton 82-84; NSM Aston cum Aughton and Ulley 84-89; rtd 89. *86 Nursery Crescent, Anston, Sheffield S31 7BR* Dinnington (0909) 567081

GUSSMAN, Robert William Spencer Lockhart. b 50. Ch Ch Ox BA72 MA76. Coll of Resurr Mirfield BA74. **d** 75 **p** 76. C Pinner *Lon* 75-79; C Northolt W End St Jos 79-81; P-in-c Sutton *Ely* 81-82; V 82-89; P-in-c Witcham w Mepal 81-82; R 82-89; RD Ely 86-89; V Alton St Lawr *Win* from 89. *St Lawrence's Vicarage, Alton, Hants GU34 2BW* Alton (0420) 83234

GUSTERSON, Preb Charles John. b 10. AKC37. Cuddesdon Coll 37. **d** 38 **p** 39. V Stokesay *Heref* 62-75; Dioc Dir of Educn 64-76; Preb Heref Cathl 66-76; P-in-c Acton Scott 73-75; Hon C 75-86; rtd 76. *45 Back Lane, Onibury, Craven Arms, Shropshire SY7 9AT* Bromfield (058477) 77389

GUTCH, John Pitt. b 14. St Edm Hall Ox BA36 MA42. Cuddesdon Coll 38. **d** 38 **p** 39. R Elton *Ely* 67-80; RD Yaxley 72-80; P-in-c Stibbington 75-80; P-in-c Water Newton 76-80; rtd 80. *27 Manor Gardens, Warminster, Wilts BA12 8PN* Warminster (0985) 212128

GUTHRIE, Arthur. b 12. MC44. TCD BA38 MA41. **d** 39 **p** 40. I Killead w Gartree *Conn* 48-82; rtd 82; Lic to Offic *Conn* from 90. *114 Belfast Road, Antrim BT41 2AB* Antrim (08494) 66494

GUTHRIE, Donald Angus. b 31. **d** 58 **p** 59. C Rugeley *Lich* 58-61; C Penn 61-63; R Selkirk *Edin* 63-69; Vice Prin Edin Th Coll 69-74; P-in-c Whitburn *Dur* 74-76; USA from 76. *655 West Mountain View Drive, Missoula, Montana 59802, USA*

GUTHRIE, George Alexander. b 08. TCD BA32 MA41. **d** 33 **p** 34. I Ardmore *D & D* 40-77; rtd 77. *9 Manor Drive, Hillsborough Road, Lisburn, Co Antrim* Lisburn (0846) 607130

GUTHRIE, Nigel. b 60. LRAM78 ARCO80 ARCM81 Bris Univ BA82 Ox Univ BA87. Ripon Coll Cuddesdon 85. **d** 88 **p** 89. C Cov St Jo *Cov* 88-91; Chapl Cov Cathl from 91. *157 Leamington Road, Coventry* Coventry (0203) 415859

GUTSELL, Preb David Leonard Nicholas. b 35. Sheff Univ BA59 LTh74. ALCD61. **d** 61 **p** 62. C Clapham Common St Barn *S'wark* 61-65; V Upper Tulse Hill St Matthias 65-76; RD Clapham and Brixton 74-75; V Patcham *Chich* from 76; Can and Preb Chich Cathl from 89. *The Vicarage, Church Hill, Patcham, Brighton, E Sussex BN1 8YE* Brighton (0273) 552157

GUTSELL, Eric Leslie. b 44. Golds Coll Lon TCert65 Ox Univ SDES87. Ox NSM Course. **d** 82 **p** 83. NSM Gt Faringdon w Lt Coxwell *Ox* 82-88; Lic to Offic from 88. *54 Folly View Road, Faringdon, Oxford SN7 7DH* Faringdon (0367) 240886

GUTTERIDGE, David Frank. b 39. Man Univ BSc Lon Univ MSc. W Midl Minl Tr Course 82. **d** 85 **p** 87. NSM Droitwich *Worc* 85-87; NSM Droitwich Spa from 87.

97 The Holloway, Droitwich, Worcs WR9 7AS
Droitwich (0905) 773327

GUTTERIDGE, John. b 34. Oak Hill Th Coll 60. **d** 63 **p** 64. C Deptford St Luke *S'wark* 63-66; C Southgate *Chich* 66-70; P-in-c Brixton Rd Ch Ch *S'wark* 70-73; P-in-c Manuden w Berden *Chelmsf* 73-76; Distr Sec (N Lon, Herts and Essex) BFBS 76-82; Hon C Walthamstow St Gabr 79-82; V from 82; Chapl Thorpe Coombe Psycho-Geriatric Hosp from 83. *St Gabriel's Vicarage, 17 Shernhall Street, London E17 3EU* 081-520 3411

GUTTERIDGE, John Philip. b 52. QUB BA74. Chich Th Coll 75. **d** 78 **p** 79. C Leeds St Aid *Ripon* 78-82; C Manston 82-85; P-in-c Beeston Hill H Spirit from 85. *Holy Spirit Vicarage, 114 Stratford Street, Leeds LS11 7EQ* Leeds (0532) 710390

GUTTERIDGE, Richard Joseph Cooke. b 11. Trin Hall Cam BA32 MA36 BD78. Wells Th Coll 34. **d** 35 **p** 36. C Edgbaston St Bart *Birm* 35-38; Tutor Qu Coll Birm 35-37; Lect Qu Coll Birm 37-38; C Bexhill St Pet *Chich* 38-40; C Temple Balsall *Birm* 40-41; Prin Blue Coat Sch Birm 41-45; R Brampton *Ely* 45-52; Chapl RAF 52-68; Fell Ox Univ 69-72; P-in-c Longstowe *Ely* 72-73; Lic to Offic from 73. *1 Croftgate, Fulbrooke Road, Cambridge CB3 9EG* Cambridge (0223) 352626

GUTTRIDGE, John Arthur. b 26. Trin Hall Cam BA51 MA55. Westcott Ho Cam 51. **d** 53 **p** 54. Dir of Further Tr *Dur* 68-74; Dir of Studies Sarum & Wells Th Coll 74-78; C Bilston St Leon *Lich* 78-79; TV Bilston 80-84; V Wall 84-90; V Stonnall 84-90; rtd 91. *15 St George's Lane North, Worcester WR1 1RD* Worcester (0905) 22175

GUY, Canon Francis George. b 10. TCD BA32 MA46. **d** 33 **p** 34. I Dunluce *Conn* 49-82; Chan Conn Cathl 78-82; rtd 82. *11 Priestland Road, Bushmills, Co Antrim BT57 8QP* Bushmills (02657) 32057

GUY, Dr Ian Towers. b 47. MRCGP MB BS MSc. NE Ord Course. **d** 83 **p** 84. NSM Saltburn-by-the-Sea *York* 83-88; NSM Skelton w Upleatham from 88. *14 North Terrace, Skelton-in-Cleveland, Saltburn-by-the-Sea TS12 2ES* Guisborough (0287) 50309

GUY, John Richard. b 44. FRHistS80 FRSM81. St D Coll Lamp BA65 PhD85 St Steph Ho Ox 65. **d** 67 **p** 68. C Canton St Cath *Llan* 67-68; C Roath St Sav 68-70; C Machen and Rudry *Mon* 71-74; R Wolvesnewton w Kilgwrrwg and Devauden 74-80; Perm to Offic *B & W* from 80. *Selden End, Ash, Martock, Somerset TA12 6NS* Martock (0935) 823457

GUY, Kate Anne. b 26. Local NSM Course 87. **d** 88. NSM Welton *Linc* from 88. *2 Eastfield Close, Welton, Lincoln LN2 3NB* Welton (0673) 60285

GUY, Simon Edward Walrond. b 39. St Andr Univ MA61. St D Coll Lamp LTh67. **d** 67 **p** 68. C Bris St Mary Redcliffe w Temple etc *Bris* 67-68; C Knowle St Martin 68-71; C Bishopston 71-75; V Westwood *Sarum* 75-81; TV Melksham 81-82; TV Wednesfield *Lich* 82-90; R Heaton Moor *Man* from 90. *St Paul's Rectory, 42 Lea Road, Stockport, Cheshire SK4 4JU* 061-432 1227

GUY, Walter. b 19. Man Univ BA52 St Cath Soc Ox BA54 MA58. Wycliffe Hall Ox 52. **d** 54 **p** 55. C Withington St Paul *Man* 54-58; R Newton Heath St Anne 58-68; V Ellel *Blackb* from 68. *The Vicarage, Ellel, Lancaster LA2 0PW* Galgate (0524) 751254

GUYMER, Raymond John. b 41. AKC64. **d** 65 **p** 66. C W Bromwich All SS *Lich* 65-70; Chapl HM Borstal Portland 70-78; Chapl HM Youth Cust Cen Hollesley Bay Colony 78-84; Chapl HM Pris Wormwood Scrubs from 84; Lic to Offic *Lon* from 84. *HM Prison Wormwood Scrubs, PO Box 757, Du Cane Road, London W12 0AE* 081-743 0311

GWILLIAM, Christopher. b 44. St Chad's Coll Dur BA65 DipTh67. **d** 67 **p** 68. C Chepstow *Mon* 67-70; C Risca 70-72; V Cwmtillery 72-75; V Hartlepool St Oswald *Dur* 75-82; Relig Progr Producer Radio Tees 80-87; C Stockton w St Jo 82-83; R Longnewton w Elton 83-87; Relig Progr Producer Radio Nottm *S'well* from 87. *39 Birchfield Road, Arnold, Nottingham NG5 8BJ* Nottingham (0602) 415161

GWILLIAM, Canon Oswald Neol. b 03. St Chad's Coll Dur BA24. **d** 26 **p** 27. R Houghton le Spring *Dur* 48-71; Hon Can Dur Cathl 53-71; rtd 71. *Head Farm Caravan, Fenton Lane, How Hill, Carlisle*

GWILLIM, Allan John. b 51. Coll of Resurr Mirfield 87. **d** 89 **p** 90. C Skerton St Luke *Blackb* from 89. *St Luke's House, 2 Oxford Place, Lancaster LA1 2NE* Lancaster (0524) 33488

GWINN, Brian Harvey. b 35. MIQA75. St Alb Minl Tr Scheme 83. **d** 86 **p** 87. NSM Wheathampstead *St Alb* 86-88; Ind Chapl from 88. *46 Woods Avenue, Hatfield, Hertfordshire AL10 8NA* Hatfield (0707) 272365

GWYNN, Phillip John. b 57. Univ of Wales BA87 Univ of Wales (Cardiff) DPS89. St Mich Coll Llan 87. **d** 89 **p** 90. C Clydach *S & B* from 89. *The Parsonage, 37 Kelvin Road, Clydach, Swansea SA6 5JP* Swansea (0792) 845397

GWYNNE, Robert Durham. b 44. Birm Univ DipTh70. Qu Coll Birm 67. **d** 70 **p** 72. C N Hammersmith St Kath *Lon* 70-75; C Ramsey *Ely* 76-78; TV Old Brumby *Linc* 78-81; C Scartho 81; P-in-c Goxhill 81-83; P-in-c Thornton Curtis 81-83; C Edmonton All SS w St Mich *Lon* 83-84; rtd 86. *Highfield, Station Road, Legbourne, Louth, Lincs*

GWYTHER, Geoffrey David. b 51. St D Coll Lamp DipTh73. **d** 74 **p** 75. C Pemb Dock *St D* 74-77; C Milford Haven 77-81; V Llawhaden w Bletherston and Llan-y-cefn 81-88; R Prendergast w Rudbaxton from 88. *Prendergast Rectory, 5 Cherry Grove, Haverfordwest, Dyfed SA61 2NT* Haverfordwest (0437) 762625

GWYTHER, Ronald Lloyd. b 23. Lon Univ BA85. St Fran Coll Brisbane ThL47. **d** 47 **p** 48. R Pinxton *Derby* 60-73; V Swanley St Mary *Roch* 73-89; rtd 89. *20 Maylings Farm Road, Fareham, Hants PO16 7QU* Fareham (0329) 230990

GYTON, Robert Wilfred. b 21. N Ord Course. **d** 78 **p** 79. NSM Repps *Nor* 78-79; C Trunch 79-83; TV 83-88; rtd 88; Perm to Offic *Nor* from 88. *Yamato, 47 Fir Park, Ashill, Thetford, Norfolk IP25 7DE* Holme Hale (0760) 440305

H

HABBERTON, Benjamin Walter. b 12. Qu Coll Birm 46. **d** 48 **p** 49. V Springfield *Birm* 67-81; rtd 81; Perm to Offic *Ex* from 81. *The Rectory, Western Road, Zeal Monachorum, Crediton, Devon EX17 6DG* Bow (0363) 82342

HABERMEHL, Canon Kenneth Charles. b 22. Em Coll Cam BA46 MA48. Chich Th Coll 47. **d** 49 **p** 50. V Kempston *St Alb* 65-87; Hon Can St Alb 81-87; rtd 87; Perm to Offic *St Alb* from 87. *34 Bedford Road, Aspley Guise, Milton Keynes MK17 8DH* Milton Keynes (0908) 584710

HABERSHON, Kenneth Willoughby. b 35. New Coll Ox BA57 DipTh58 MA60. Wycliffe Hall Ox 57. **d** 59 **p** 60. C Finchley Ch Ch *Lon* 59-66; Sec CYFA 66-74; CPAS Staff 74-90; Hon C Slaugham *Chich* from 84; Ldr Limpsfield CYFA & Sec Ch Patr Trust from 90. *Truckers Ghyll, Horsham Road, Handcross, Haywards Heath, W Sussex RH17 6DT* Handcross (0444) 400274

HABGOOD, John Gerald Peace. b 18. St Cath Soc Ox BA40 MA45. Cuddesdon Coll 45. **d** 47 **p** 48. R Lewes St Thos and All SS *Chich* 68-75; TR Lewes All SS, St Anne, St Mich and St Thos 75-84; rtd 84; Perm to Offic *Chich* from 84. *3 Court Leet, Steyne Road, Seaford, E Sussex BN25 1QT* Seaford (0323) 896832

✠**HABGOOD, Most Rev and Rt Hon John Stapylton.** b 27. PC83. K Coll Cam BA48 MA51 PhD52 Dur Univ Hon DD75. Cuddesdon Coll 53. **d** 54 **p** 55 **c** 73. C Kensington St Mary Abbots w St Geo *Lon* 54-56; Vice-Prin Westcott Ho Cam 56-62; R Jedburgh *Edin* 62-67; Prin Qu Coll Birm 67-73; Hon Can Birm Cathl Birm 71-73; Bp Dur 73-83; Abp York from 83. *Bishopthorpe, York YO2 1QE* York (0904) 707021 or 707022

HABGOOD, Simon. b 60. Nottm Univ BTh88. St Jo Coll Nottm 85. **d** 88 **p** 89. C Holbeach *Linc* 88-90; C Alford w Rigsby 90-91; R Rattlesden w Thorpe Morieux and Brettenham *St E* from 91. *The Rectory, High Street, Rattlesden, Bury St Edmunds, Suffolk IP30 0RA* Rattlesden (04493) 7993

HABGOOD, Stephen Roy. b 52. Univ of Wales DipTh77. **d** 77 **p** 78. C Eglwyswen and Llanfair Nant-gwyn *St D* 77-81; Perm to Offic *Worc* from 85. *Oak Thatch, 76 Main Street, Bretforton, Evesham, Worcs WR11 5JJ* Evesham (0386) 830323

HACK, Ms Alison Ruth. b 53. RGN75 RSCN75 RHV80. Sarum & Wells Th Coll 89. **d** 91. Par Dn St Marylebone, St Paul *Lon* from 91. *St Paul's House, 9A Rossmore Road, London NW1 6NJ*

HACK, Canon Rex Hereward. b 28. ACA56 FCA67 Pemb Coll Cam BA50 MA56. Ripon Hall Ox 58. **d** 59 **p** 60. C Ashton on Mersey St Mary *Ches* 59-62; C Ellesmere Port 62-65; V Norton Cuckney *S'well* 65-69; V Bramhall *Ches* from 69; RD Cheadle from 87; Hon Can Ches

Cathl from 90. *The Vicarage, Robin's Lane, Bramhall, Stockport, Cheshire SK7 2PE* 061-439 2254

✠**HACKER, Rt Rev George Lanyon.** b 28. Ex Coll Ox BA52 MA56. Cuddesdon Coll 52. **d** 54 **p** 55 **c** 79. C Bris St Mary Redcliffe w Temple *Bris* 54-59; Chapl St Boniface Coll Warminster 59-64; V Bishopwearmouth Gd Shep *Dur* 64-71; R Tilehurst St Mich *Ox* 71-79; Hon Can Carl Cathl *Carl* from 79; Suff Bp Penrith from 79; Episc Adv for the Angl Young People's Assn from 87. *The Rectory, Great Salkeld, Penrith, Cumbria CA11 9NA* Lazonby (076883) 273

HACKETT, Frank James. b 33. AMIMechE68 MBIM72 MIIM79 HNC54 DMS72 Birm Univ MA77. Bps' Coll Cheshunt 62. **d** 64 **p** 65. C Feltham *Lon* 64-69; Ind Chapl *Lich* 69-73; Ind Chapl to Port of Lon from 73; P-in-c N Ockendon *Chelmsf* from 79. *11 Fairfield Avenue, Upminster, Essex RM14 3AZ* Upminster (04022) 21461

HACKETT, John. b 38. Selw Coll Cam BA60 MA65 Heidelberg Univ 62. Linc Th Coll 61. **d** 63 **p** 64. C Newton Heath All SS *Man* 63-64; C Mert St Mary S'wark 64-70; Hon C Redhill St Matt 70-74; Tutor S'wark Ord Course 72-75; V Sutton Ch Ch *S'wark* 74-85; Chapl Sutton Gen Hosp 74-85; TR Clapham Old Town *S'wark* 85-87; TR Clapham Team Min from 87; RD Clapham and Brixton from 88. *The Rectory, 20 North Side, London SW4 0RQ* 071-622 7505 or 627 0941

HACKETT, John Nigel. b 32. Trin Hall Cam BA55 MA59. Ely Th Coll. **d** 59 **p** 60. C Handsworth St Mary *Birm* 59-66; V Handsworth St Jas 66-82; P-in-c Balsall Common 82-83; V from 83. *St Peter's House, Balsall Common, Coventry CV7 7EA* Berkswell (0676) 32721

HACKETT, Peter Edward. b 25. Magd Coll Ox BA48 MA51 ALCD60. **d** 60 **p** 61. R Acton Beauchamp and Evesbatch w Stanford Bishop *Heref* 67-71; VC Heref Cathl 72-76; P-in-c St Weonards w Orcop 76-79; P-in-c Tretire w Michaelchurch and Pencoyd 76-79; P-in-c Garway 76-79; P-in-c Welsh Newton w Llanrothal 77-79; V Rounds Green *Birm* 79-87; C Sutton Coldfield H Trin 87-90; rtd 90. *32 Fairmile Road, Halesowen, W Midlands B63 3QJ* 021-550 5907

HACKETT, Ronald Glyndwr. b 47. Hatf Coll Dur BA70. Cuddesdon Coll 70. **d** 72 **p** 73. C Pemb St Mary and St Mich *St D* 72-75; C Bassaleg *Mon* 75-78; V Blaenavon w Capel Newydd 78-84; Chapl Gwent R Hosp from 84; V Newport St Paul *Mon* 84-90; V Christ Church from 90. *The Vicarage, Christchurch, Newport, Gwent NP6 1JJ* Newport (0633) 420701

HACKING, Philip Henry. b 31. St Pet Hall Ox BA53 MA57. Oak Hill Th Coll 53. **d** 55 **p** 56. C St Helens St Helen *Liv* 55-58; C-in-c Edin St Thos *Edin* 59-68; V Fulwood *Sheff* from 68. *The Vicarage, 2 Chorley Drive, Sheffield S10 3RR* Sheffield (0742) 301911

HACKING, Rodney Douglas. b 53. K Coll Lon BD74 AKC74 Man Univ MA83. St Aug Coll Cant 75. **d** 76 **p** 78. C Byker St Mich *Newc* 76-77; C Eltham St Jo *S'wark* 77-79; Ind Chapl *Ripon* 80-85; R Upwell St Pet *Ely* 85-88; R Outwell 85-88; Asst Dir S Dios Minl Tr Scheme from 89. *The Theological College, 19 The Close, Salisbury SP1 2EE* Salisbury (0722) 332235

HACKING, Stuart Peter. b 60. St Pet Coll Ox BA82 MA. Oak Hill Th Coll 83. **d** 85 **p** 86. C Shipley St Pet *Bradf* 85-88; C Darfield *Sheff* from 88. *5 Church Street, Great Houghton, Barnsley, S Yorkshire S72 0BL* Barnsley (0226) 752320

HACKNEY, Bryan William George. b 41. Hull Univ MA80. Linc Th Coll 65. **d** 68 **p** 69. C Baildon *Bradf* 68-71; R Gt and Lt Casterton w Pickworth and Tickencote *Pet* 71-74; Lic to Offic *Linc* 74-77; V Barnetby le Wold 77-81; P-in-c Somerby w Humby 77-81; P-in-c Bigby 77-81; Bp's Ind Adv *Derby* 81-85; R Morton and Stonebroom 85-91; V Mackworth St Fran from 91. *St Francis's Vicarage, Collingham Gardens, Mackworth Estate, Derby DE3 4FQ* Derby (0332) 47690

HACKNEY, Archdeacon of. See SHARPLEY, Ven Roger Ernest Dion

HACKSHALL, Brian Leonard. b 33. K Coll Lon BD53 AKC53. **d** 57 **p** 58. C Portsea St Mary *Portsm* 57-62; C Westbury-on-Trym St Alb *Bris* 62-64; V Avonmouth St Andr 64-71; Miss to Seamen 71-79; C Crawley *Chich* 79; TV from 79; Ind Chapl from 89. *35 Turnpike Place, Crawley, W Sussex RH11 7UA* Crawley (0293) 513264

HACKWOOD, Paul Colin. b 61. Bradf Coll of Educn DSocStuds82 Huddersfield Poly BSc84 Birm Univ DipTh88. Qu Coll Birm 86. **d** 89 **p** 90. C Horton *Bradf* from 89. *8 Oakley House, Park Lane, Bradford BD5 7PH* Bradford (0274) 307947

HADDELSEY, Charles Vincent Bernard. b 03. Lich Th Coll 22. **d** 26 **p** 27. Warden Launde Abbey 68-74; P-in-c

Loddington *Leic* 68-74; rtd 74; Perm to Offic *Pet* from 74; *Leic* from 84. *6 Shepherds Way, Uppingham, Oakham, Leics LE15 9PW* Uppingham (0572) 823698

HADDELSEY, Stephen Andrew. b 36. Societas Liturgica Ch Ch Ox BA58 MA62. Coll of Resurr Mirfield 60. **d** 62 **p** 63. C Pinner *Lon* 62-66; C S Ascot *Ox* 66-68; New Zealand 68-70; C Oakham *Pet* 70; V Stocking Farm *Leic* 70-78; W Germany 78-80; Lic to Offic *Eur* 78-80; R Claybrooke cum Wibtoft and Frolesworth *Leic* from 80. *The Rectory, Claybrooke Parva, Lutterworth, Leics LE17 5AE* Leire (0455) 209277

HADDEN, Geoffrey Paddock. b 05. Kelham Th Coll 26. **d** 31 **p** 32. R Horsted Keynes *Chich* 65-73; rtd 73; Perm to Offic *Cov* 73-84; Chich from 84. *63 Wealden Way, Haywards Heath, W Sussex RH16 4DD* Haywards Heath (0444) 456657

HADDLETON, Peter Gordon. b 53. UEA BA74 Southn Univ BTh80. Sarum & Wells Th Coll 76. **d** 79 **p** 80. C Thamesmead *S'wark* 79-83; TV Bridgnorth, Tasley, Astley Abbotts, Oldbury etc *Heref* 83-91; TV Heref St Martin w St Fran (S Wye Team Min) from 91. *The Vicarage, 1 Holme Lacy Road, Hereford HR2 6DP* Hereford (0432) 277234

HADDOCK, Malcolm George. b 27. Univ of Wales (Cardiff) DipTh53 BA56 CertEd73. St Deiniol's Hawarden 87. **d** 80 **p** 81. NSM Christ Church *Mon* 80-85; NSM Risca 85-87; C 87-89; C Caerleon from 89. *48 Cambria Close, Caerleon, Newport, Gwent NP6 1LF* Caerleon (0633) 422960

HADDOCK, Canon Norman. b 19. St D Coll Lamp BA41 BD51. **d** 42 **p** 43. V Cheltenham St Luke and St Jo *Glouc* 67-84; Hon Can Glouc Cathl from 74; RD Cheltenham 77-84; rtd 84. *Parkways, Wellington Square, Cheltenham, Glos GL50 4JZ* Cheltenham (0242) 526393

HADFIELD, Douglas. b 22. K Coll Cam BA44 MA49. St Jo Coll Nottm 84. **d** 88 **p** 89. Hon C Lenzie *Glas* from 88. *Fingarry, Milton of Campsie, Glasgow G65 8EH* Lennoxtown (0360) 311215

HADFIELD, Graham Francis. b 48. Bris Univ BSc69 St Jo Coll Dur DipTh71. **d** 73 **p** 74. C Blackpool St Thos *Blackb* 73-76; CF from 76. *c/o MOD (Army), Bagshot Park, Bagshot, Surrey GU19 5PL* Bagshot (0276) 71717

HADFIELD, Ven John Collingwood. b 12. Jes Coll Cam BA34 MA38. Wells Th Coll 34. **d** 35 **p** 36. C Ladybarn *Man* 35-40; P-in-c 40-44; V Bolton St Mark 44-50; V Belfield 50-62; R Rothesay *Arg* 62-64; Itinerant Priest 64-77; I Can St Jo Cathl Oban 65-77; Dioc RE Adv 66-77; Syn Clerk 73-77; Adn Caithness *Mor* from 77; P-in-c Thurso from 77; R Wick from 77. *4 Sir Archibald Road, Thurso, Caithness KW14 8HN* Thurso (0847) 62047

HADFIELD, Jonathan Benedict Philip John. b 43. Lon Univ BA64 Jes Coll Cam BA67 MA72. Edin Th Coll 66. **d** 68 **p** 69. C Fort William *Arg* 68-70; Chapl K Sch Glouc from 70. *Dulverton House, King's School, Pitt Street, Gloucester GL1 2BE* Gloucester (0452) 25993

HADFIELD, Norman. b 39. Doncaster Coll of Educn TEng78 Univ of Wales (Cardiff) DPS90. St Mich Coll Llan 89 Llan Dioc Tr Scheme 83. **d** 86 **p** 87. NSM Ferndale w Maerdy *Llan* 86-90; C Llanblethian w Cowbridge and Llandough etc from 90. *12 Grey's Walk, Cowbridge, S Glam CF7 7BQ* Cowbridge (0446) 773062

HADLEY, Charles Adrian. b 50. Trin Coll Cam BA71 MA75. Cuddesdon Coll 73. **d** 75 **p** 76. C Hadleigh w Layham and Shelley *St E* 75-78; C Bracknell *Ox* 78-82; R Blagdon w Compton Martin and Ubley *B & W* from 82; RD Chew Magna from 88. *The Rectory, High Street, Blagdon, Bristol BS18 6TA* Blagdon (0761) 62495

HADLEY, Donald Thomas. b 30. Lich Th Coll 55. **d** 58 **p** 59. V S Yardley St Mich *Birm* 66-70; V Tonge Moor *Man* 70-84; C Selly Oak St Mary *Birm* 85-90; rtd 90. *83 Grosvenor Road, Birmingham B17 9AL* 021-426 4450

HADLEY, Miss Elizabeth Ann. b 33. DipTh83. St Jo Coll Nottm 80. **dss** 81 **d** 87. Aspley *S'well* 81-85; Stone St Mich w Aston St Sav *Lich* 85-87; Par Dn from 87. *10 Beechwood Drive, Stone, Staffs ST15 0EH* Stone (0785) 815021

HADLEY, John Spencer Fairfax. b 47. Ch Ch Ox BA70 MA73. Coll of Resurr Mirfield BA72. **d** 73 **p** 74. C Stoke Newington St Mary *Lon* 73-77; C High Wycombe *Ox* 77-81; TV 82-87; Chapl Bris Univ *Bris* from 87; P-in-c Clifton St Paul from 87. *67 Waverley Road, Bristol BS6 6ET* Bristol (0272) 244261 or 466142

HADLEY, Stuart James. b 55. K Coll Lon BD76 AKC76. St Steph Ho Ox 77. **d** 78 **p** 79. C Mansf St Mark *S'well* 78-82; V Cowbit *Linc* 82-86; Perm to Offic 86-88; NSM W w E Allington and Sedgebrook from 88; NSM

Woolsthorpe from 88. *21 Truro Close, Grantham, Lincs NG31 8PH* Grantham (0476) 75854

HADWIN, Alfred. b 34. N Ord Course 85. **d** 88 **p** 89. NSM Lower Darwen St Jas *Blackb* from 88. *7 Sunny Bank Road, Blackburn BB2 3ND* Blackburn (0254) 64108

HAGAN, Kenneth Raymond. b 40. St Jo Coll Morpeth 62 ACT ThDip64. **d** 64 **p** 65. C Charlestown *Man* 64-69; Australia 69-75 and from 89; C Portsea St Mary *Portsm* 75-78; P-in-c Wolvey, Burton Hastings and Stretton Baskerville *Cov* 78-81; OCF 78-81; P-in-c Withybrook w Copston Magna *Cov* 78-81; P-in-c Shilton w Ansty 78-81; Perm to Offic *Leic* 81-83; Perm to Offic *Lon* 82-89. *PO Box 467, Hamilton, NSW, Australia 2303* Hamilton (49) 611980

HAGGAN, David Anthony. b 25. Barrister-at-Law 70 QUB LLB43. S'wark Ord Course 87. **d** 89 **p** 90. NSM Reigate St Mary *S'wark* from 89. *136 Croydon Road, Reigate, Surrey RH2 0NQ* Reigate (0737) 246197

HAGGAR, Keith Ivan. b 38. MRPharmS61. Cant Sch of Min 87. **d** 90. NSM Woodnesborough w Worth and Staple *Cant* from 90. *Burtree Cottage, The Street, Worth, Deal, Kent CT14 0DE* Sandwich (0304) 613599

HAGGARD, Amyand Richard. b 21. Jes Coll Ox MA57. Ripon Hall Ox 56. **d** 58 **p** 59. V Battersea St Phil *S'wark* 61-68; rtd 86. *78 Eland Road, London SW11 5LA* 071-228 8166

✠**HAGGART, Rt Rev Alastair Iain Macdonald.** b 15. Dur Univ LTh41 BA42 MA45 Dundee Univ Hon LLD70. Edin Th Coll 38. **d** 41 **p** 42 **c** 75. C Glas St Mary *Glas* 41-45; C Hendon St Mary *Lon* 45-48; Prec St Ninian's Cathl Perth *St And* 48-51; R Glas St Oswald *Glas* 51-59; P-in-c Glas St Martin 53-58; Can St Mary's Cathl 58-59; Syn Clerk 58-59; Provost St Paul's Cathl Dundee *Bre* 59-71; R Dundee St Paul 59-71; Prin Edin Th Coll 71-75; Can St Mary's Cathl *Edin* 71-75; Bp Edin 75-85; Primus 77-85; rtd 86. *19 Eglinton Crescent, Edinburgh EH12 5BY* 031-337 8948

HAGGIS, Timothy Robin. b 52. New Coll Ox BA75 MA79. St Jo Coll Nottm DipTh. **d** 82 **p** 83. C Chilwell *S'well* 82-86; TV Hucknall Torkard from 86. *The Vicarage, Ruffs Drive, Hucknall, Nottingham NG15 6JG* Nottingham (0602) 633640

HAGON, Roger Charles. b 58. Nottm Univ BA80. St Steph Ho Ox 82. **d** 85 **p** 86. C Charlton St Luke w H Trin *S'wark* 85-88; C St Helier from 88. *Bishop Andrewes' House, Wigmore Road, Carshalton, Surrey SM5 1RG* 081-644 9203

HAGUE, Eric. b 13. Lon Univ BA52. St Aid Birkenhead 36. **d** 39 **p** 40. R Lt Shelford w Newton *Ely* 69-76; P-in-c Parr Mt *Liv* 76-77; V 77-79; rtd 79. *Guilin, 51 High Street, Oakington, Cambridge CB4 5AG* Cambridge (0223) 233273

HAIG, Very Rev Alistair Matthew. b 39. K Coll Lon BD63 AKC63. **d** 64 **p** 65. C Forest Gate St Edm *Chelmsf* 64-67; C Laindon w Basildon 67-71; V S Woodham Ferrers 71-78; P-in-c Bath H Trin *B & W* 78-83; R 83-89; R Bocking St Mary *Chelmsf* from 89; Dean Bocking from 89. *The Deanery, Bocking, Braintree, Essex CM7 5SR* Braintree (0376) 24887 or 553092

HAIG, Andrew Livingstone. b 45. Keble Coll Ox BA67. Coll of Resurr Mirfield 67. **d** 69 **p** 70. C Elton All SS *Man* 69-75; R Brantham *St E* 75-76; R Brantham w Stutton 76-82; RD Samford 81-82; P-in-c Haverhill 82; TR Haverhill w Withersfield, the Wrattings etc 82-90; RD Clare 84-87; Chapl Qu Eliz Hosp K Lynn from 90. *The Chaplain's Office, Queen Elizabeth Hospital, King's Lynn, Norfolk* King's Lynn (0553) 766266

HAIG, Murray Nigel Francis. b 39. Univ of Wales (Lamp) BA62. Kelham Th Coll 62. **d** 66 **p** 67. C Felixstowe St Jo *St E* 66-72; C Morpeth *Newc* 72-74; V Byker St Mich 74-79; V Byker St Mich w St Lawr 79-81; V Benwell St Jas 81-85; TR Benwell Team 85-91; TR Cramlington from 91. *33 Twyford Close, Parkside Grange, Cramlington, Northd NE23 9PH* Cramlington (0670) 712259

HAIGH, Alan Bernard. b 42. NE Ord Course 87. **d** 90 **p** 91. NSM Thorner *Ripon* from 90. *4 The Paddock, Thorner, Leeds LS14 3JB* Leeds (0532) 892870

HAIGH, Colin. b 15. St Chad's Coll Dur BA40 DipTh41 MA43. **d** 41 **p** 42. V Romford St Alb *Chelmsf* 68-80; rtd 80. *93 Egremont Street, Glemsford, Sudbury, Suffolk CO10 7SG* Glemsford (0787) 281173

HAIGH, Gordon Thomas. b 07. Dur Univ LTh33 BA34 MA40 MLitt44. Qu Coll Birm 30. **d** 34 **p** 35. V Castle Morton *Worc* 59-72; rtd 72; Lic to Offic *Worc* from 74. *Church Road, Castlemorton, Malvern, Worcs WR13 6BE*

HAIGH, John Gibson. b 47. Chich Th Coll 88. **d** 90 **p** 91. C Swinton and Pendlebury *Man* from 90. *Christ Church*

House, Pendlebury Road, Swinton, Manchester M27 1AZ* 061-794 2962

HAIGH, Maurice. b 22. St Cath Coll Cam BA46 MA48 Lon Univ BD60. **d** 60 **p** 61. NSM Marton *Blackb* 60-88; rtd 88; Perm to Offic *Blackb* from 88. *20 Doncaster Road, Blackpool, Lancs FY3 9SQ* Blackpool (0253) 63897

HAIGH, Norman. b 02. Dorchester Miss Coll 27. **d** 30 **p** 31. R Aston Somerville *Glouc* 62-72; V Childswyckham 62-72; rtd 72. *Ramsay Hall, Byron Road, Worthing, W Sussex BN11 3HW* Worthing (0903) 36880

HAIGH, Owen Quentin. b 15. St Chad's Coll Dur BA43 MA46. **d** 43 **p** 44. R Wiston *Chich* 55-75; R Ashington 55-75; P-in-c Stedham w Iping 75-83; P-in-c Trotton w Chithurst 80-81; rtd 83; Perm to Offic *Chich* from 84. *Chantonbury, Smuggler's Way, Fairlight, Hastings, E Sussex TN35 4DG* Hastings (0424) 812826

HAIGH, Richard Michael Fisher. b 30. Dur Univ BA57 Birm Univ DPS71. Cranmer Hall Dur DipTh59. **d** 59 **p** 60. C Stanwix *Carl* 59-62; India 63-67 and 68-70; R Salford St Clem w St Cypr Ordsall *Man* 71-75; R Holcombe 75-85; V Unsworth from 85. *St George's Vicarage, Hollins Lane, Bury, Lancs BL9 8JJ* 061-766 2429

HAILES, Derek Arthur. b 38. Coll of Resurr Mirfield. **d** 82 **p** 83. C Sneinton St Cypr *S'well* 82-84; V Kneesall w Laxton 84-85; P-in-c Wellow 84-85; V Kneesall w Laxton and Wellow 85-88; V Sneinton St Steph w St Alb from 88. *The Vicarage, Windmill Lane, Sneinton, Notts NG2 4QB* Nottingham (0602) 580508

HAILS, Brian. b 33. JP71. ACMA62 FCMA76. NE Ord Course 77. **d** 81 **p** 82. NSM Harton *Dur* 81-87; Ind Chapl from 87. *Inhurst, 5 Hepscott Terrace, South Shields, Tyne & Wear NE33 4TH* 091-456 3490

HAILSTONE, Miss Kitty. b 22. St Andr Ho Portsm 49. dss 81 **d** 87. W Acklam *York* 60-82; rtd 82; Beverley St Mary *York* 82-87; Hon Par Dn from 87. *26 Corporation Road, Beverley, N Humberside HU17 9HG* Hull (0482) 860223

HAINES, Andrew Philip. b 47. LSE BSc68. Oak Hill Th Coll 84. **d** 87 **p** 88. C Enfield Ch Ch Trent Park *Lon* 87-91; V Hillmorton *Cov* from 91. *The Vicarage, Hoskyn Close, Hillmorton, Rugby, Warks CV21 4EL* Rugby (0788) 576279

HAINES, Daniel Hugo. b 43. TD89. Lon Univ BDS68 MRCS73 DRCOG78 Witwatersrand Univ 78. **d** 79 **p** 84. Swaziland 79-80; Falkland Is 80-82; Hon C Hatcham St Cath *S'wark* from 84. *56 Vesta Road, London SE4 2NH* 071-635 0305

HAINES, Robert Melvin. b 31. Coll of Resurr Mirfield 71. **d** 73 **p** 74. C Derringham Bank *York* 73-76; C Howden 76-79; TV Howden Team Min 80-82; R Banff *Ab* from 82; R Turriff from 82; R Cuminestown from 82. *The Rectory, Deveron Road, Turriff, Aberdeenshire AB5 7BB* Turriff (0888) 63238

HAINES, Robert Melvin. b 57. Leeds Univ BA79. St Steph Ho Ox 79. **d** 81 **p** 82. C Rushall *Lich* 81-85; Zambia 85-88; Project Ldr CARE *Liv* from 89. *Flat 2, 32 Princes Avenue, Liverpool L8 2UP*

HAINES, Stephen Decatur. b 42. Freiburg Univ MA68 Fitzw Coll Cam BA70 MA74. **d** 71 **p** 72. C Fulham St Dionis Parson's Green *Lon* 71-76; C Finchley St Mary 76-78; Hon C Clapham Old Town *S'wark* 83-87; Hon C Clapham Team Min 87-88; Hon C Camberwell St Giles w St Matt from 88. *3 Lyndhurst Square, London SE15 5AR* 071-703 4239

HAIR, James Eric. b 48. Lon Univ BA69. St Steph Ho Ox 69. **d** 72 **p** 73. C Fishponds St Jo *Bris* 72-75; C Bushey *St Alb* 75-79; P-in-c Lake *Portsm* 79-82; V 82-89; P-in-c Shanklin St Sav 79-82; V 82-89; TV Totton *Win* from 89. *The Vicarage, Cooks Lane, Calmore, Southampton SO4 2RU* Southampton (0703) 812702

HAKE, Andrew Augustus Gordon. b 25. Trin Coll Cam BA49 MA54. Wells Th Coll 50. **d** 51 **p** 52. Kenya 57-69; Perm to Offic *Bris* from 70; rtd 90. *Providence House, 12A South Street, Swindon SN1 3LA* Swindon (0793) 535772

HAKES, Leslie John. b 25. CEng MRAeS MBIM. Roch Th Coll 60. **d** 62 **p** 63. C Swansea St Pet *S & B* 62-67; V Griffin *Blackb* 67-71; V Dolphinholme 71-74; V Dolphinholme w Quernmore from 74. *The Vicarage, Dolphinholme, Lancaster LA2 9AH* Forton (0524) 791300

HALAHAN, Maxwell Crosby. b 30. Lon Univ BSc52 Southn Univ CertEd78 W Sussex Inst of HE ACertEd83. Westcott Ho Cam 54. **d** 56 **p** 57. C-in-c Cowes St Faith CD *Portsm* 66-70; V Cowes St Faith 70-77; Hon C Portsea St Sav from 77; rtd 84. *11 Bertie Road, Southsea, Hants PO4 8JX* Portsmouth (0705) 737980

HALDANE-STEVENSON, James Patrick. b 10. TD50. St Cath Soc Ox BA33 MA41. Bps' Coll Cheshunt 35. d 35 p 37. C Lambeth St Mary the Less *S'wark* 35-38; CF (TA) 37-45; C Pokesdown St Jas *Win* 38-39; R Hillington *Nor* 39-46; CF 45-55; Australia from 55; Perm to Offic *Chich* 77-78. *43 Clyde Street, Box Hill North, Victoria, Australia 3129* Box Hill North (3) 898-4993

HALE, Antony Jolyon. b 56. MRTPI89 Newc Univ BA79. Sarum & Wells Th Coll 86. d 88 p 89. C Monkseaton St Mary *Newc* from 88. *89 Queen's Road, Monkseaton, Whitley Bay, Tyne & Wear NE26 3AS* 091-252 7769

HALE, Dennis Ernest. b 26. Southn Univ MA(Ed)66. Sarum & Wells Th Coll 74. d 77 p 78. NSM N Stoneham *Win* 77-86; Assoc Chapl Southn Univ from 86. *12 Field Close, Southampton SO2 3DY* Southampton (0703) 554538

HALE, Elsie Amelia. Gilmore Ho 53. dss 58 d 87. R Devon and Ex Hosps 64-84; Heavitree w Ex St Paul *Ex* 84-88; Perm to Offic from 88. *13 Riverside Court, Colleton Crescent, Exeter EX2 4BZ*

HALE, John. b 37. Ban Coll DBS60 Trin Coll Carmarthen CertEd59. St D Coll Lamp DipTh66. d 66 p 67. C Tenby and Gumfreston *St D* 66-71; R Burton 71-78; R Burton and Rosemarket from 78. *The Rectory, Burton, Milford Haven, Dyfed SA73 1NX* Neyland (0646) 600275

HALE, John Frederick. b 29. Fitzw Ho Cam BA54 MA58. Tyndale Hall Bris. d 55 p 56. C Heigham H Trin *Nor* 55-58; C Paddington St Jas *Lon* 58-61; V St Leonards St Ethelburga *Chich* 61-79; C Prestonville St Luke 79-90; R Rotherfield w Mark Cross from 90. *The Rectory, Rotherfield, Crowborough, E Sussex TN6 3LU* Rotherfield (089285) 2536

HALE, Keith John Edward. b 53. Sheff Poly BSc75. St Jo Coll Nottm DipTh91. d 91. C Greasbrough *Sheff* from 91. *18 Coach Road, Rotherham, S Yorkshire S61 4ED* Rotherham (0709) 562378

HALE, Peter Raymond Latham. b 30. St Pet Hall Ox BA54 MA58. Linc Th Coll 54. d 56 p 57. C Old Brumby *Linc* 56-59; Prec and Chapl Gib Cathl *Eur* 59-62; V New Cleethorpes *Linc* 62-67; Chapl Sebright Sch Wolverley 67-70; V Dudley St Jas *Worc* 70-76; V Crowthorne *Ox* 76-86; RD Sonning 81-86; P-in-c Cookham 86-90; V Lacey Green from 90. *The Vicarage, Church Lane, Lacey Green, Aylesbury, Bucks HP17 0PL* Princes Risborough (08444) 7741

HALE, Richard Laurence. b 13. Jes Coll Cam BA35 MA39. Westcott Ho Cam 42. d 43 p 44. V Gt Shelford *Ely* 61-78; rtd 78; Perm to Offic *Nor* from 78. *5 Hare Road, Great Plumstead, Norwich NR13 5DD* Norwich (0603) 721062

HALE, Roger Anthony. b 41. MIH85. Brasted Th Coll 68 Oak Hill Th Coll 70. d 72 p 73. C Blackb Sav *Blackb* 72-75; C Burnley St Pet 75-77; Chapl Burnley Gen Hosp 75-77; V Fence in Pendle *Blackb* 77-82; Chapl Lancs Ind Miss 77-82; NSM Tottenham St Mary *Lon* 88-91; R Cheddington w Mentmore and Marsworth *Ox* from 91. *The Rectory, 29 Mentmore Road, Cheddington, Leighton Buzzard, Beds LU7 0SD* Cheddington (0296) 661358

HALFORD, Harry William. b 20. Qu Coll Birm 47. d 50 p 51. V Kimberworth *Sheff* 60-85; rtd 85. *14 Londesborough Way, Metheringham, Lincoln LN4 3HL* Metheringham (0526) 22217

HALFPENNY, Ven Brian Norman. b 36. CB90. St Jo Coll Ox BA60 MA64. Wells Th Coll 60. d 62 p 63. C Melksham *Sarum* 62-65; Chapl RAF 65-83; Asst Chapl-in-Chief RAF 83-88; Chapl-in-Chief RAF 88-91; QHC from 85; Can and Preb Linc Cathl *Linc* from 89. *c/o MOD, Adastral House, Theobald's Road, London WC1X 8RU* 071-430 7268

HALIFAX, Archdeacon of. See HALLATT, Ven David Marrison

HALKES, John Stanley. b 39. SW Minl Tr Course 87. d 90 p 91. NSM St Buryan, St Levan and Sennen *Truro* from 90. *The Garden House, Sancreed, Penzance, Cornwall TR20 8QS* Penzance (0736) 810839

HALL, Alan Maurice Frank. b 28. FCCA. Sarum & Wells Th Coll 86. d 89 p 90. NSM Winterbourne Stickland and Turnworth etc *Sarum* from 89. *4 The Knapp, Winterborne Houghton, Blandford Forum, Dorset DT11 0PD* Milton Abbas (0258) 880985

✠HALL, Rt Rev Albert Peter. b 30. St Jo Coll Cam BA53 MA56. Ridley Hall Cam 53. d 55 p 56 c 84. C Birm St Martin *Birm* 55-60; S Rhodesia 61-65; Rhodesia 65-70; R Birm St Martin *Birm* 71-84; Hon Can Birm Cathl 75-84; Suff Bp Woolwich *S'wark* 84-91; Area Bp Woolwich from 91; Chmn Abp's Cttee on UPA from 90. *8B Hillyfields Crescent, London SE4 1QA* 081-469 0013

HALL, Canon Alfred Christopher. b 35. Trin Coll Ox BA58 MA61. Westcott Ho Cam 58. d 61 p 62. C Frecheville *Derby* 61-64; C Dronfield 64-67; V Smethwick St Matt *Birm* 67-70; V Smethwick St Matt w St Chad 70-75; Can Res Man Cathl *Man* 75-83; Hon Can from 83; Dioc Adult Educn Officer 75-83; Dioc World Development Officer 76-88; V Bolton St Pet 83-90; Chr Concern for One World from 90. *The Knowle, Deddington, Banbury, Oxon OX15 0TB* Deddington (0869) 38225

HALL, Mrs Ann Addington. b 34. Ex Univ CertEd71. SW Minl Tr Course 82. dss 85 d 87. Ex St Mark *Ex* 85-87; Hon Par Dn 87-90; Perm to Offic from 90. *33 Union Road, Exeter EX4 6HU* Exeter (0392) 78717

HALL, Arthur John. b 23. Bris Univ BSc48. Sarum & Wells Th Coll 74. d 76 p 77. Hon C Portishead *B & W* 76-88; Chapl St Brandon's Sch Clevedon from 86. *34 Beechwood Road, Portishead, Bristol BS20 8EP* Portishead (0272) 842603

HALL, Barry George. b 38. Solicitor 62. Oak Hill Th Coll 78. d 81 p 82. NSM Stock Harvard *Chelmsf* 81-90; NSM W Hanningfield from 90. *Harvard Cottage, Swan Lane, Stock, Ingatestone, Essex CM4 9BQ* Stock (0277) 840387

HALL, Basil. b 15. PhD70 Hon DD85. d 70 p 71. Hon C Bramhall *Ches* 70-75; Dean St Jo Coll Cam 75-80; rtd 80; Perm to Offic *Ex* from 86. *2 Newton House, Newton St Cyres, Exeter EX5 5BL* Exeter (0392) 851584

HALL, Brian Arthur. b 48. Ex Univ BEd70. Cuddesdon Coll 73. d 75 p 76. C Hobs Moat *Birm* 75-79; V Smethwick from 79. *The Vicarage, Church Road, Smethwick, Warley, W Midlands B67 6EE* 021-558 1763

HALL, Charles Bryan. b 37. Liv Univ BA59. St Mich Coll Llan 59. d 62 p 63. C Prestatyn *St As* 62-64; C Cardiff St Mary *Llan* 64-67; V 73-75; C Hawarden *St As* 67-72; TV 72-73 and 84-86; P-in-c Cardiff St Steph *Llan* 73-75; V Cardiff St Mary w St Steph 75-81; V Penycae *St As* 81-84; R Llandegla and Bryneglwys and Llanarmon-yn-Ial 86-87; R Llandegla and Llanarmon yn Ial from 87. *The Rectory, Llandegla, Wrexham, Clwyd LL11 3AW* Llandegla (097888) 362

HALL, Charles John. b 40. JP. Lon Coll of Div ALCD68 LTh74. d 68 p 69. C Upton (or Overchurch) *Ches* 68-72; C Morden *S'wark* 72-76; V Hyson Green *S'well* 76-84; V Stapleford from 84; RD Beeston from 90. *The Vicarage, 61 Church Street, Stapleford, Nottingham NG9 8GA* Sandiacre (0602) 397333

HALL, Christine Mary. b 45. K Coll Lon BD67 MPhil86. d 87. NSM Bickley *Roch* from 87. *Mayfield Cottage, 25 Southborough Road, Bromley, Kent BR1 2EA* 081-467 0482

HALL, David Anthony. b 43. Reading Univ BA66. Qu Coll Birm 79. d 81 p 82. C Norton *St Alb* 81-85; TV Hitchin from 85. *Holy Saviour Vicarage, St Anne's Road, Hitchin, Herts SG5 1QB* Hitchin (0462) 456140

HALL, Denis. b 43. Lon Coll of Div 65. d 69 p 70. C Netherton *Liv* 69-71; C Roby 72-75; V Wigan St Steph 75-90; V Newton-le-Willows from 90. *The Vicarage, 243 Crow Lane East, Newton-le-Willows, Merseyside WA12 9TS* Newton-le-Willows (0925) 224869

HALL, Derek Guy. b 26. Tyndale Hall Bris 50. d 51 p 52. R Fazakerley Em *Liv* 67-74; TR 74-81; V Langdale *Carl* 81-86; rtd 86; Perm to Offic *Carl* from 86. *14 Gale Park, Ambleside, Cumbria LA22 0BN* Ambleside (05394) 33144

HALL, Desmond. b 27. St Cuth Soc Dur BSc54 PhD58. NE Ord Course 78. d 81 p 82. NSM Bishopwearmouth St Mich w St Hilda *Dur* 81-82; C Bishopwearmouth St Mary V w St Pet CD 82-85; V Leadgate from 85. *The Vicarage, Watling Road, Leadgate, Consett, Co Durham DH8 7SN* Consett (0207) 503918

HALL, Edwin George. b 40. Sarum & Wells Th Coll 88. d 91. NSM Purton *Bris* from 91. *17 Linley Cottages, Church Path, Purton, Swindon, Wilts SN5 9DR* Swindon (0793) 770520

HALL, Ernest. b 10. AKC36. d 36 p 37. V Osmotherley *York* 69-75; rtd 75. *Dulverton Hall, St Martin's Square, Scarborough YO11 2DB* Scarborough (0723) 373082

HALL, Francis Henry. b 14. Leeds Univ BA36. Coll of Resurr Mirfield 36. d 38 p 39. V Castle Cary w Ansford *B & W* 70-79; RD Cary 71-79; rtd 79. *52 Goetre Fawr Road, Dunvant, Swansea SA2 7QU* Swansea (0792) 298907

HALL, Geoffrey Hedley. b 33. Bris Univ BA55. St Steph Ho Ox 63. d 65 p 66. C Taunton H Trin *B & W* 65-67; CF 67-80; Sen CF 80-86; P-in-c Ambrosden w Arncot and Blackthorn *Ox* 72-75; V Barnsley St Edw *Wakef* from 86. *186 Racecommon Road, Barnsley, S Yorkshire S70 6JY* Barnsley (0226) 203919

HALL, George Richard Wyndham. b 49. Ex Univ LLB71. Wycliffe Hall Ox BA74 MA78. **d** 75 **p** 76. C Walton H Trin *Ox* 75-79; C Farnborough *Guildf* 79-84; Bp's Chapl *Nor* 84-87; R Saltford w Corston and Newton St Loe *B & W* from 87. *The Rectory, 12 Beech Road, Saltford, Bristol BS18 3BE* Saltford (0225) 872275

HALL, Canon George Rumney. b 37. Westcott Ho Cam 60. **d** 62 **p** 63. C Camberwell St Phil *S'wark* 62-65; C Waltham Cross *St Alb* 65-67; R Buckenham w Hassingham and Strumpshaw *Nor* 67-74; Chapl St Andr Hosp Thorpe 67-72; Chapl HM Pris *Nor* 72-74; V Wymondham *Nor* 74-87; RD Humbleyard 86-87; R Sandringham w W Newton from 87; P-in-c Castle Rising from 87; P-in-c Flitcham from 87; P-in-c Hillington from 87; P-in-c Wolferton w Babingley from 87; Dom Chapl to HM The Queen 87-89; Hon Can Nor Cathl *Nor* from 87; RD Heacham and Rising from 89; QHC from 89. *The Rectory, Sandringham, King's Lynn, Norfolk PE35 6EH* Dersingham (0485) 540587

HALL, Mrs Gillian Louise. b 45. N Ord Course 87. **d** 90. NSM Earby *Bradf* from 90. *244 Colne Road, Earby, Colne, Lancs BB8 6TD* Earby (0282) 842593

HALL, Godfrey Charles. b 43. Linc Coll Ox BA66 MA72. Cuddesdon Coll 66. **d** 68 **p** 69. C St Helier *S'wark* 68-72; Asst Chapl Ch Hosp Horsham 72-82; Hd Master Prebendal Sch Chich from 82. *53 West Street, Chichester, W Sussex PO19 1RT* Chichester (0243) 782026

HALL, Halsey Charles. b 31. Lon Univ BSc53 MSc57. Sarum & Wells Th Coll 76. **d** 78 **p** 79. C Southn Thornhill St Chris *Win* 78-81; TV Southn (City Cen) 81-91; R King's Worthy from 91. *The Rectory, Campion Way, King's Worthy, Winchester, Hants SO23 7QP* Winchester (0962) 882166

HALL, Harold Henry Stanley Lawson. b 23. Qu Coll Birm 56. **d** 58 **p** 59. V Newton Aycliffe *Dur* 69-76; R Whitburn 76-89; rtd 89. *9 Balmoral Terrace, East Herrington, Sunderland SR3 3PR* 091-528 0108

HALL, Harry. b 41. Chich Th Coll 89. **d** 91. C Boston *Linc* from 91. *23 Church Street, Boston, Lincs PE21 6NN* Boston (0205) 357193

HALL, Herbert Alexander. b 05. **d** 61 **p** 62. R Sigglesthorne *York* 70-74; R Sigglesthorne and Rise w Nunkeeling and Bewholme 74-76; rtd 76; Hon C Beverley St Mary *York* from 81. *19 Manor Close, Manor Road, Beverley, N Humberside HU17 7BP* Hull (0482) 867889

HALL, Canon Hubert William Peter. b 35. Ely Th Coll 58. **d** 60 **p** 61. C Louth w Welton-le-Wold *Linc* 60-62; C Gt Grimsby St Jas 62-69; C Gt Grimsby St Mary and St Jas 69-71; Hon Chapl Miss to Seamen from 71; V Immingham *Linc* from 71; RD Haverstoe from 86; Hon Can Linc Cathl from 89. *The Vicarage, 344 Pelham Road, Immingham, Grimsby DN40 1PU* Immingham (0469) 572560

HALL, Ian Michael. b 48. Mansf Coll Ox MA70 Leeds Univ CertEd71. Carl Dioc Tr Course 85. **d** 88 **p** 89. NSM Eskdale, Irton, Muncaster and Waberthwaite *Carl* from 88. *Fisherground Farm, Eskdale, Cumbria CA19 1TF* Eskdale (09403) 319

HALL, James. b 28. Wollongong Univ BA78. CITC 53. **d** 56 **p** 57. C Belf St Mich *Conn* 56-59; I Cleenish *Clogh* 59-62; R Openshaw *Man* 63-68; Australia 68-89; R Morley w Deopham, Hackford, Wicklewood etc *Nor* from 89. *The Rectory, Morley, Wymondham, Norfolk NR18 9DA* Wymondham (0953) 606332

HALL, Canon James Robert. b 24. TCD BA48 MA54. **d** 49 **p** 50. I Finaghy *Conn* 66-89; Can Belf Cathl 82-89; RD S Belf *Conn* 83-89; rtd 89. *3 Coachman's Way, Hillsborough, Co Down BT26 6HQ* Hillsborough (0846) 689678

HALL, Jean Margaret. b 38. Bris Univ CertEd59 DipRE59 ACertEd73. Bris Sch of Min 84. **d** 88. Hon C Bris St Andr w St Bart *Bris* 88; Hon C E Bris from 88. *25 Glebe Road, Bristol BS5 8JJ* Bristol (0272) 557208

HALL, Jeffrey Ernest. b 42. Linc Th Coll 73. **d** 75 **p** 76. C Brampton St Thos *Derby* 75-78; C New Whittington 78-81; C Whittington 78-81; TV Riverside *Ox* 81-90; R Anstey *Leic* from 90. *The Rectory, 1 Hurd's Close, Groby Road, Anstey, Leicester LE7 7FN* Leicester (0533) 362176

HALL, John Barrie. b 41. Sarum & Wells Th Coll 82. **d** 84 **p** 85. Chapl St Edward's Hosp Cheddleton 84-88; C Cheddleton *Lich* 84-88; V Rocester from 88; RD Uttoxeter from 91. *The Vicarage, Church Lane, Rocester, Uttoxeter, Staffs ST14 5JZ* Uttoxeter (0889) 590424

HALL, John Bellamy. b 10. Ridley Hall Cam 55. **d** 57 **p** 57. R Daglingworth w the Duntisbournes and Winstone *Glouc* 66-74; P-in-c Kempley w Oxenhall 74-77; rtd 77; Perm to Offic Chich from 78; St E from 83. *14 Riverside, Dunmow, Essex CM6 3AR*

HALL, Dr John Bruce. b 33. St Louis Covenant Th Sem MTh80 DMin85 Lon Coll of Div ALCD60 LTh74. **d** 60 **p** 61. C Kingston upon Hull H Trin *York* 60-67; C Beverley Minster 67-68; V Clapham Park St Steph *S'wark* 68-76; R Tooting Graveney St Nic from 76. *The Rectory, 20A Rectory Lane, London SW17 9QJ* 081-672 7691

HALL, John Charles. b 46. Hull Univ BA71. Ridley Hall Cam 71. **d** 73 **p** 74. C Bromley Common St Aug *Roch* 73-77; C Westbury-on-Trym St Alb *Bris* 78-80; Oman 80-82; C-in-c Bishop Auckland Woodhouse Close CD *Dur* 82-90; P-in-c Gt and Lt Glemham, Blaxhall etc *St E* 90-91; P-in-c Rodney Stoke w Draycott *B & W* from 91; Dioc Ecum Officer from 91. *The Vicarage, Vicarage Lane, Draycott, Cheddar, Somerset BS27 3SH* Cheddar (0934) 742315

HALL, John Curtis. b 39. CEng73 MIMechE73. Coll of Resurr Mirfield 80. **d** 82 **p** 83. C Pet Ch Carpenter *Pet* 82-86; TV Heavitree w Ex St Paul Ex from 86. *St Paul's Vicarage, Milton Road, Exeter EX2 6BL* Exeter (0392) 54783

HALL, Canon John Derek. b 25. St Cuth Soc Dur BA50. Linc Th Coll 50. **d** 52 **p** 53. V York St Chad *York* 68-90; Can and Preb York Minster from 85; rtd 90; Chapl Castle Howard York from 90. *Chanting Hill Farm, Welburn, York YO6 7EF* Whitwell-on-the-Hill (065381) 345

HALL, John Edmund. b 49. Birm Poly CQSW76 Open Univ BA84. Trin Coll Bris BA89. **d** 89 **p** 90. C Winchmore Hill St Paul *Lon* from 89. *St Paul's Lodge, 58 Church Hill, London N21 1JA* 081-882 3298

HALL, Canon John Kenneth. b 32. Qu Coll Birm 61. **d** 63 **p** 64. C Ilminster w Whitelackington *B & W* 63-66; P-in-c Mackworth St Fran *Derby* 66-69; V Blackford *B & W* 69-76; R Chapel Allerton 69-76; New Zealand from 77; Can St Pet Cathl Waikato from 85. *St Mark's Vicarage, 7 Kenrick Street, Te Aroha, New Zealand* Te Aroha (7) 884-8728

HALL, Dr John MacNicol. b 44. MRCGP75 Glas Univ BSc65 MB, ChB69 St Jo Coll Cam BA73 MA76 Nottm Univ MTh88. Westcott Ho Cam 71. **d** 86 **p** 86. NSM Knighton St Jo *Leic* 86; NSM Clarendon Park St Jo w Knighton St Mich 86-89; Perm to Offic *Ely* from 89; *St Alb* from 90. *9 Laxton Close, Eaton Ford, St Neots, Huntingdon, Cambs PE19 3AR*

HALL, John Michael. b 47. BD. Oak Hill Th Coll 68. **d** 73 **p** 74. C Walthamstow St Mary w St Steph *Chelmsf* 73-76; C Rainham 76-79; P-in-c Woodham Mortimer w Hazeleigh from 79; P-in-c Woodham Walter from 79; Ind Chapl from 79. *The Rectory, Maldon Road, Woodham Mortimer, Maldon, Essex CM9 6SN* Maldon (0621) 853778

HALL, John Michael. b 62. Leeds Univ BA. Coll of Resurr Mirfield 83. **d** 86 **p** 87. C Ribbleton *Blackb* 86-89; C Carnforth from 89. *22 Coppice Brow, Carnforth, Lancs LA5 9XG* Carnforth (0524) 734930

HALL, John Redvers. b 25. Dur Univ BA59 DipTh62 Man Univ CertEd74. **d** 61 **p** 62. C Lutterworth w Cotesbach *Leic* 61-63; C Loughb Em 63-66; Lic to Offic *Leic* 66-70; Blackb 70-81; P-in-c Ingoldmells w Addlethorpe *Linc* 81-83; V Cholsey *Ox* from 83. *The Vicarage, Church Road, Cholsey, Wallingford, Oxon OX10 9PP* Cholsey (0491) 651216

HALL, John Robert. b 49. St Chad's Coll Dur BA71. Cuddesdon Coll 73. **d** 75 **p** 76. C Kennington St Jo *S'wark* 75-78; P-in-c S Wimbledon All SS 78-84; V Streatham St Pet from 84. *St Peter's Vicarage, 113 Leigham Court Road, London SW16 2NX* 081-769 2922

HALL, John Wintour. b 17. Leeds Univ BA39. Coll of Resurr Mirfield 39. **d** 41 **p** 41. Chapl Merchant Taylors' Sch Northwood 56-82; rtd 82. *15 Carlton Place, Porthcawl, M Glam CF36 3ET* Porthcawl (065671) 2580

HALL, Dr Joseph Hayes. b 30. TD71. FGS53 St Jo Coll Dur BSc53 DipTh55 Liv Univ MA73 ThD90. Wycliffe Hall Ox 55. **d** 55 **p** 56. C Wallasey St Hilary *Ches* 55-59; C Macclesfield St Mich 59-60; CF (TA) 59-72; V Barnton *Ches* 60-67; V New Brighton All SS 67-81; V Woodford from 81. *The Vicarage, Wilmslow Road, Woodford, Stockport, Cheshire SK7 1RH* 061-439 2286

HALL, Leslie. b 37. Man Univ BSc59. E Midl Min Tr Course 83. **d** 86 **p** 87. NSM Freiston w Butterwick *Linc* from 86. *Vine Lodge, Butterwick, Boston, Lincs PE22 0EX* Boston (0205) 760375

HALL, Mrs Margaret Mercia. b 39. Bedf Coll Lon BA61 Cam Univ DipRS78. Gilmore Ho 73. **dss** 80 **d** 87. Gt Chesham *Ox* 81-87; Par Dn from 87. *19 Stanley*

Avenue, Chesham, Bucks HP5 2JG Chesham (0494) 784479

HALL, Mrs Marigold Josephine. b 29. Linc Th Coll 81. dss 83 **d** 87. Chapl Asst Hellesdon Hosp Nor from 83; Nor St Pet Parmentergate w St Jo *Nor* 83-87; C from 87; rtd 90. *8 Bracondale Court, Norwich NR1 2AS*

HALL, Michael Edward. b 32. Fitzw Ho Cam BA57 MA61. Ridley Hall Cam 68. **d** 69 **p** 70. C Aspley *S'well* 69-73; P-in-c Bulwell St Jo 73-75; V 75-81; P-in-c Tylers Green *Ox* 81-90; V from 90. *The Vicarage, Tyler's Green, High Wycombe, Bucks HP10 8HB* Penn (049481) 3367

HALL, Michael John. b 59. Jes Coll Cam MA. St Jo Coll Nottm. **d** 84 **p** 85. C Bradley *Wakef* 84-87; C Halifax 87-89; V Halifax St Anne Southowram from 89. *St Anne's Vicarage, Church Lane, Southowram, Halifax, W Yorkshire HX3 9TD* Halifax (0422) 365229

HALL, Murray. b 34. K Coll Lon. **d** 61 **p** 62. C Eaton *Nor* 61-64; C Shalford *Guildf* 64-67; V Oxshott 67-72; P-in-c Runham *Nor* 72-80; P-in-c Stokesby w Herringby 72-80; R Filby w Thrigby w Mautby 72-80; R Filby w Thrigby, Mautby, Stokesby, Herringby etc from 80. *Filby Rectory, Great Yarmouth, Norfolk NR29 3HS* Great Yarmouth (0493) 369237

HALL, Nicholas Charles. b 56. **d** 86 **p** 87. C Hyde St Geo *Ches* 86-89; C Cheadle from 89. *1 Warren Avenue, Cheadle, Cheshire SK8 1NB* 061-428 3001

HALL, Nigel David. b 46. Univ of Wales (Cardiff) BA67 BD76 Lon Univ CertEd68. St Mich Coll Llan 73. **d** 76 **p** 77. C Cardiff St Jo *Llan* 76-81; R Llanbadarn Fawr, Llandegley and Llanfihangel etc *S & B* from 81; RD Maelienydd from 89. *The Rectory, Llanbadarn Fawr, Crossgates, Llandrindod Wells LD1 5TT* Penybont (059787) 204

HALL, Philip Edward Robin. b 36. Oak Hill Th Coll 64. **d** 67 **p** 68. C Ware Ch Ch *St Alb* 67-70; C Rayleigh *Chelmsf* 70-73; R Leven w Catwick *York* 73-85; P-in-c Mayfield *Lich* from 85; P-in-c Ilam w Blore Ray and Okeover from 89. *The Vicarage, Mayfield, Ashbourne, Derbyshire DE6 2JR* Ashbourne (0335) 42855

HALL, Robert Arthur. b 35. Lon Univ BSc66. NW Ord Course 74. **d** 77 **p** 78. C York St Paul *York* 77-79; R Elvington w Sutton on Derwent and E Cottingwith 79-82; Chapl Tiffield Sch Northants 82-84; V Bessingby *York* 84-88; V Carnaby 84-88; V Fulford from 88. *The Vicarage, 1 Fulford Park, Fulford, York YO1 4QE* York (0904) 633261

HALL, Roger John. b 53. Linc Th Coll. **d** 84 **p** 85. C Shrewsbury St Giles w Sutton and Atcham *Lich* 84-87; CF from 87. *c/o MOD (Army), Bagshot Park, Bagshot, Surrey GU19 5PL* Bagshot (0276) 71717

HALL, Ronald Cecil. b 20. St Aid Birkenhead 63. **d** 65 **p** 66. R Talke *Lich* 69-74; V Birstwith *Ripon* 74-90; P-in-c Thornthwaite w Thruscross and Darley 76-77; rtd 90. *1 Pannal Ash Grove, Harrogate, N Yorkshire HG2 0HY* Harrogate (0423) 567379

HALL, Stephen Clarence. b 23. Kelham Th Coll 46. **d** 51 **p** 52. C Killingworth *Newc* 51-53; C Newc H Cross 53-56; S Rhodesia 56-65; Rhodesia 65-80; Zimbabwe from 80; S Africa from 77. *PO Box 10685, Meer-en-See, Zululand, 3901 South Africa* Richards Bay (351) 32713

HALL, Stephen Philip. b 56. Ripon Coll Cuddesdon. **d** 84 **p** 85. C Camberwell St Giles *S'wark* from 88; Chapl Brighton Poly *Chich* from 88. *20 Hanover Street, Brighton BN2 2ST* Brighton (0273) 570538

HALL, Prof Stuart George. b 28. New Coll Ox BA52 MA BD73. Ripon Hall Ox 53. **d** 54 **p** 55. C Newark w Coddington *S'well* 54-58; Tutor Qu Coll Birm 58-62; Lect Th Nottm Univ 62-73; Sen Lect 73-78; Prof Ecclesiastical Hist Lon Univ 78-90; Perm to Offic *St Alb* 80-86; *S'wark* 86-90; P-in-c Pittenweem *St And* from 90; P-in-c Elie and Earlsferry from 90. *Hopedene, 15 High Street, Elie, Leven, Fife KY9 1BY* Leven (0333) 330145

HALL, Timothy Robert. b 52. Dur Univ BA74. St Jo Coll Nottm LTh87. **d** 87 **p** 88. C Hawarden *St As* 87-89; Chapl St D Coll Llandudno from 90. *St David's College, Llandudno, Gwynedd LL30 1RD* Llandudno (0492) 581224

HALL, Walter Kenneth. b 19. Wycliffe Hall Ox 64. **d** 66 **p** 67. C Marton-in-Cleveland *York* 68-70; C Filey 70-71; P-in-c Middlesb St Cuth 71-78; V Glaisdale 78-84; rtd 84. *47 Virginia Gardens, Brookfield, Middlesbrough, Cleveland TS5 8DD* Middlesbrough (0642) 594412

HALL, Canon William Cameron. b 40. K Coll Lon 60. **d** 65 **p** 66. C Thornaby on Tees St Paul *York* 65-68; Chapl to Arts and Recreation *Dur* from 68; V Grindon 71-80; Hon Can Dur Cathl from 84; Sen Chapl Actors' Ch Union from 89. *59 Western Hill, Durham DH1 4RJ* 091-386 3177

HALL, William Nawton Sinclair. b 17. Kelham Th Coll 35. **d** 41 **p** 42. R Witton Gilbert *Dur* 55-61; R Lowther w Askham *Carl* 61-84; rtd 83; Perm to Offic *Carl* from 84. *41 Briar Rigg, Keswick, Cumbria CA12 4NN* Keswick (07687) 74103

HALL, William Norman. b 30. ARIC74 TCD BA52 MA64 BD65. TCD Div Sch Div Test54. **d** 54 **p** 55. C Dundela *D & D* 54-58; C Holywood 58-63; I Drumgooland 63-66; Chapl St Jas Choir Sch Grimsby 66-70; Asst Master Hautlieu Sch Jersey 70-73; V Jersey St Mark *Win* from 73. *The Vicarage, Springfield Road, St Helier, Jersey, Channel Islands JE2 7LE* Jersey (0534) 20595

HALL CARPENTER, Leslie Thomas Frank. b 19. Lich Th Coll 55. **d** 57 **p** 58. R Lochgilphead *Arg* 69-70; Area Sec USPG (York) 70-73; P-in-c Well *Ripon* 73-74; V Kirk Hammerton 74-75; R Hunsingore w Cowthorpe 74-75; V Nun Monkton 74-75; R Kirk Hammerton w Nun Monkton and Hunsingore 75-77; P-in-c Hackness w Harwood Dale *York* 77-79; V Melbecks and Muker *Ripon* 79-82; R Twyford w Guist w Bintry w Themelthorpe etc *Nor* 82-84; rtd 84; Perm to Offic *Nor* from 90. *Little Cogden, 6 Old Hall Drive, Dersingham, Norfolk PE31 6JT* Dersingham (0485) 542271

HALL-MATTHEWS, Preb John Cuthbert Berners. b 33. Queensland Univ BA55 K Coll Lon PGCE65. Coll of Resurr Mirfield 58. **d** 60 **p** 61. C Woodley *Ox* 60-63; C Is of Dogs Ch Ch and St Jo w St Luke *Lon* 63-65; Asst Chapl Ch Hosp Horsham 65-72; Chapl R Hosp Sch Ipswich 72-75; V Tupsley *Heref* 75-90; P-in-c Hampton Bishop and Mordiford w Dormington 77-90; RD Heref City 84-90; Preb Heref Cathl 85-90; TR Wolv *Lich* from 90. *St Peter's Rectory, 42 Park Road East, Wolverhampton WV1 4QA* Wolverhampton (0902) 23140 or 28491

HALL-THOMPSON, Colin. b 51. TCD DipTh. **d** 84 **p** 85. C Dub Rathfarnham *D & G* 84-86; Bp's C Clonmel Union *C, C & R* 86-91; I Kilbride *Conn* from 91; Hon Chapl Miss to Seamen from 91. *Kilbride Rectory, 1 Rectory Road, Doagh, Co Antrim BT39 0PT* Ballyclare (09603) 40225

HALLAM, Graham. b 53. BTh. Sarum & Wells Th Coll 79. **d** 82 **p** 83. C Witton *Ches* 82-85; C Oxton 85-87; V Stockport St Matt from 87. *St Matthew's Vicarage, Grenville Street, Stockport, Cheshire SK3 9ET* 061-480 5515

HALLAM, Lawrence Gordon. b 31. Lich Th Coll 61. **d** 63 **p** 64. R Cocking w Bepton *Chich* 68-71; V Eastbourne Ch Ch 71-84; V Bexhill St Barn 84-87; rtd 87; Perm to Offic *Chich* from 87. *170 Latimer Road, Eastbourne, E Sussex BN22 7JD* Eastbourne (0323) 410671

HALLAM, Dr Nicholas Francis. b 48. Univ Coll Ox BA71 MA81 Glas Univ PhD76 MB, ChB81. Ox NSM Course 84. **d** 87 **p** 88. NSM Ox St Clem *Ox* from 87. *56 Weldon Road, Marston, Oxford OX3 0HP* Oxford (0865) 726180

HALLAM, Peter Hubert. b 33. Trin Hall Cam BA56 MA60. Westcott Ho Cam 56. **d** 58 **p** 59. C St Annes *Blackb* 58-62; Asst Chapl and Tutor St Bede Coll Dur 62-67; V Briercliffe *Blackb* from 67. *St James's Vicarage, Briercliffe, Burnley, Lancs BB10 2HU* Burnley (0282) 23700

HALLAM, Stanley Bywater. b 16. Wells Th Coll 71. **d** 71 **p** 72. C Haughton le Skerne *Dur* 72-74; R Stanhope 74-82; rtd 82. *8 Low Well Park, Wheldrake, York YO4 6DS* Wheldrake (090489) 8803

HALLATT, Ven David Marrison. b 37. Southn Univ BA59 St Cath Coll Ox BA62 MA66. Wycliffe Hall Ox 59. **d** 63 **p** 64. C Maghull *Liv* 63-67; V Totley *Derby* 67-75; R Didsbury St Jas *Man* 75-80; R Barlow Moor 76-80; TR Didsbury St Jas and Em 80-89; Adn Halifax *Wakef* from 89. *9 Healey Wood Gardens, Brighouse, W Yorkshire HD6 3SQ* Brighouse (0484) 714553

HALLATT, John Leighton. b 34. St Pet Coll Ox BA58 MA62. Wycliffe Hall Ox 58. **d** 60 **p** 61. C Ipswich St Jo *St E* 60-63; C Warrington St Paul *Liv* 63-66; V Wadsley *Sheff* 66-72; V Hindley St Pet *Liv* 72-75; Area Sec (Scotland and Dios Newc and Dur) CMS 75-83; N Sec CMS 78-83; TR Cramlington *Newc* 83-90; V Monkseaton St Mary from 90. *The Vicarage, 77 Holywell Avenue, Whitley Bay, Tyne & Wear NE26 3AG* 091-252 2484

HALLETT, Howard Adrian. b 43. Man Univ MPhil90. Oak Hill Th Coll BA81. **d** 81 **p** 82. C Walshaw Ch Ch *Man* 81-84; V Stoke sub Hamdon *B & W* from 84; RD Ilchester from 91. *The Vicarage, 1 East Stoke, Stoke-sub-Hamdon, Somerset TA14 6RQ* Martock (0935) 822529

HALLETT, Keith Philip. b 37. Tyndale Hall Bris 61. **d** 64 **p** 65. C Higher Openshaw *Man* 64-68; C Bushbury *Lich* 68-71; P-in-c Drayton Bassett 71-72; R 72-90; V Fazeley

71-90; P-in-c Hints 78-83; V 83-90; C-in-c Canwell CD 78-83; V Canwell 83-90; RD Tamworth 81-90; P-in-c Buckhurst Hill *Chelmsf* from 90. *St John's Rectory, High Road, Buckhurst Hill, Essex IG9 5RX* 081-504-1931

HALLETT, Peter. b 49. Bath Univ BSc72. Oak Hill Th Coll DPS. **d** 76 **p** 77. C Brinsworth w Catcliffe *Sheff* 76-79; P-in-c Doncaster St Jas 80-81; V 81-86; R Henstridge and Charlton Horethorne w Stowell *B & W* from 86. *The Vicarage, Henstridge, Templecombe, Somerset BA8 0QE* Stalbridge (0963) 62266

HALLETT, Peter Duncan. b 43. CCC Cam BA66 MA68. Westcott Ho Cam 69. **d** 71 **p** 72. C Sawston *Ely* 71-73; C Lyndhurst and Emery Down *Win* 73-78; C Skegness and Winthorpe *Linc* 78-80; P-in-c Samlesbury *Blackb* 80-91; Asst Dir RE from 80; C Leyland St Ambrose from 91. *31 Spring Meadow, Clayton-le-Woods, Leyland, Preston PR5 2UR* Preston (0772) 432903

HALLETT, Raymond. b 44. E Midl Min Tr Course 85. **d** 88 **p** 89. NSM Hucknall Torkard *S'well* from 88. *26 Nursery Close, Hucknall, Nottingham NG15 6DQ* Nottingham (0602) 633360

HALLETT, Ronald Walter. b 13. Lon Univ BD36. **d** 36 **p** 37. USA 64-80; rtd 80; Chapl Community of St Denys Warminster from 80; Perm to Offic *Lich* from 83; P-in-c N Cerney w Bagendon *Glouc* 85-86. *c/o St Gabriel's Vicarage, Walstead Road, Walsall, W Midlands WS1 1LU* Walsall (0922) 22583

HALLETT, Canon Roy. b 17. St D Coll Lamp BA48. **d** 49 **p** 50. V Caldicot *Mon* 58-71; V Rumney 71-87; RD Bassaleg 82-87; Can St Woolos Cathl 86-87; rtd 87. *247 Llantarnam Road, Cwmbran, Gwent NP44 3BQ* Cwmbran (0633) 874128

HALLIBURTON, Canon Robert John. b 35. Selw Coll Cam BA56 MA60 Keble Coll Ox BA58 DPhil61 MA71. St Steph Ho Ox 58. **d** 61 **p** 62. C Stepney St Dunstan and All SS *Lon* 61-67; Lect St Steph Ho Ox 67-71; Vice-Prin 71-75; Lect Linc Coll Ox 73-75; Prin Chich Th Coll 75-82; Can and Preb Chich Cathl *Chich* 76-82; Wightring Preb and Th Lect 88-90; P-in-c St Margarets on Thames *Lon* 82-90; Can Res St Paul's Cathl from 90. *8B Amen Court, London EC4M 7BU* 071-248 3314

HALLIDAY, Christopher Norton Robert. b 48. N Ord Course 82. **d** 85 **p** 86. C Davyhulme St Mary *Man* 85-87; Lect Bolton St Pet 87-90; I Rathdrum w Glenealy, Derralossary and Laragh *D & G* from 90. *The Rectory, Rathdrum, Co Wicklow, Irish Republic* Rathdrum (404) 46160

HALLIDAY, Edwin James. b 35. NW Ord Course 70. **d** 73 **p** 74. C New Bury *Man* 73-76; V Bolton St Phil 76-82; Dioc Communications Officer 82-88; V Radcliffe St Thos and St Jo 82-90; R Gt Lever from 90. *St Michael's Rectory, 130 Green Lane, Bolton BL3 2HX* Bolton (0204) 26510

✠**HALLIDAY, Rt Rev Robert Taylor.** b 32. Glas Univ MA54 BD57. Edin Th Coll 55. **d** 57 **p** 58 **c** 90. C St Andrews St Andr *St And* 57-60; R 83-90; C Glas St Marg *Glas* 60-63; Lect NT Edin Th Coll 63-74; R Edin H Cross *Edin* 63-83; Tutor Edin Univ 69-71; Can St Mary's Cathl *Edin* 73-83; Tutor St Andr Univ *St And* 84-90; Bp Bre from 90. *St Paul's Cathedral, Castlehill, Dundee DD1 1TD or, 35 Carlogie Road, Carnoustie, Angus DD7 6ER* Dundee (0382) 29230 or (0241) 55781

HALLIDIE SMITH, Andrew. b 31. Pemb Coll Cam BA54 MA58. Ely Th Coll 55. **d** 56 **p** 57. Canada 67-70 and 79-81 and from 91; R Alresford *Chelmsf* 70-79; V Elsecar *Sheff* 81-91; rtd 91. *PO Box 765, Big River, Saskatchewan, Canada, S0J 0E0*

HALLING, William Laurence. b 43. Linc Coll Ox BA64 DipTh66 MA68 Lon Univ BD68. Tyndale Hall Bris 66. **d** 68 **p** 69. C Beckenham St Jo *Roch* 68-72; C Walton H Trin *Ox* 72-78; V Barrow St Mark *Carl* 78-86; R Kirkheaton *Wakef* from 86; Chapl Mill Hill Hosp Huddersfield from 86. *The Rectory, Church Lane, Kirkheaton, Huddersfield HD5 0JR* Huddersfield (0484) 532410

HALLIWELL, Christopher Eigil. b 57. Newc Univ BA78. Trin Coll Bris DipHE91. **d** 91. C Mildenhall *St E* from 91. *The Vicarage, 8 Church Walk, Mildenhall, Suffolk IP28 7ED* Mildenhall (0638) 712128

HALLIWELL, Ivor George. b 33. St Cath Coll Cam BA57 MA60. Wells Th Coll 58. **d** 60 **p** 60. C Hanworth St Geo *Lon* 60-62; C Willenhall *Cov* 62-65; C-in-c Whitley St Jas CD 65-68; V Whitley 68-72; V Corton *Nor* 72-77; P-in-c Hopton 72-74; V 74-77; Asst Chapl HM Pris Pentonville 77; Chapl HM Pris Ex 77-83; Wakef 83-85; P-in-c Bickington *Ex* 85-87; P-in-c Ashburton w Buckland-in-the-Moor 85-87; V Ashburton w Buckland in the Moor and Bickington 87-90; Chapl HM Pris Channings Wood from 90; Lic to Offic *Ex* from 90.

HM Prison Channing Wood, Denbury, Newton Abbot, Devon TQ12 6DW Ipplepen (0803) 812361

HALLIWELL, Michael Arthur. b 28. St Edm Hall Ox BA50 MA53. Ely Th Coll 52. **d** 54 **p** 55. C Welling *S'wark* 54-57; C Bournemouth St Alb *Win* 57-59; Asst Gen Sec C of E Coun on Foreign Relns 59-62; C St Dunstan in the West *Lon* 60-62; Chapl Bonn w Cologne *Eur* 62-67; Chapl RAF 66-67; V Croydon St Andr *Cant* 67-71; R Jersey St Brelade *Win* from 71; Chapl HM Pris Jersey 75-80; Vice-Dean Jersey *Win* from 85. *The Rectory, La Marquanderie, St Brelade, Jersey, Channel Islands JE3 8EP* Jersey (0534) 42302

HALLS, Peter Ernest. b 38. Bris Univ BA62. Tyndale Hall Bris 59. **d** 64 **p** 65. C Blackb St Barn *Blackb* 64-67; C Bromley Ch Ch *Roch* 67-70; V Halvergate w Tunstall *Nor* 70-79; V Freethorpe w Wickhampton 71-79; P-in-c Beighton and Moulton 77-79; V Tuckswood 79-90; RD Nor S 86-90; R Brooke, Kirstead, Mundham w Seething and Thwaite from 90; RD Depwade from 91. *The Vicarage, Brooke, Norwich NR15 1JV* Brooke (0508) 50378

HALMSHAW, Stella Mary. b 36. TCert57. St Alb Minl Tr Scheme 81. dss 84 **d** 87. Radlett *St Alb* 84-87; NSM 87-89; Par Dn from 90. *13 The Crosspath, Radlett, Herts WD7 8HR* Radlett (0923) 854314

HALSALL, James Campbell. b 13. FCP73 Bede Coll Dur. NW Ord Course 76. **d** 79 **p** 80. NSM Manningham St Paul and St Jude *Bradf* 79-84; NSM Manningham from 84. *School House, Low Moor, Bradford, W Yorkshire BD12 0HL* Bradford (0274) 677095

HALSALL, Michael John. b 61. Salford Univ BSc83. Wycliffe Hall Ox 88. **d** 91. C Cowley St Jo *Ox* from 91. *58 Magdalen Road, Oxford OX4 1RB* Oxford (0865) 249860

HALSE, Raymond Stafford. b 19. Lon Univ BA49. Oak Hill Th Coll 46. **d** 50 **p** 51. V Ramsgate St Luke *Cant* 68-85; P-in-c Ramsgate Ch Ch 85; rtd 85; Hon C Hordle *Win* from 86. *58 Brunel Drive, Preston, Weymouth, Dorset* Weymouth (0305) 833048

HALSEY, Anthony Michael James. b 35. Solicitor 64 K Coll Cam BA56 MA62. St Jo Coll Nottm 73. **d** 75 **p** 76. C Derby St Werburgh *Derby* 75-77; Chapl Canford Sch Wimborne 78-87; TV Sanderstead All SS *S'wark* 87-89. *Woodlands, South Road, Liphook, Hants GU30 7HS* Liphook (0428) 724459

HALSEY, George John. b 16. Lon Univ BSc36. Wycliffe Hall Ox 38. **d** 39 **p** 40. V Shelford *S'well* 66-68; V Radcliffe-on-Trent 66-68; Lic to Offic *S'wark* 73-81; rtd 81; Perm to Offic *Guildf* from 81. *70 Ashcombe Road, Dorking, Surrey RH4 1NA* Dorking (0306) 886469

✠**HALSEY, Rt Rev Henry David.** b 19. K Coll Lon BA38. Sarum Th Coll 40. **d** 42 **p** 43 **c** 68. C Petersfield w Sheet *Portsm* 42-45; Chapl RN 46-47; C Plymouth St Andr *Ex* 47-50; V Netheravon w Fittleton *Sarum* 50-53; C-in-c Chatham St Steph CD *Roch* 53-59; V Chatham St Steph 59-62; V Bromley SS Pet and Paul 62-68; Chapl Bromley Hosp 62-68; Hon Can Roch Cathl *Roch* 64-68; RD Bromley 65-66; Adn Bromley 66-68; Suff Bp Tonbridge 68-72; Bp Carl 72-89; rtd 89. *Bramblecross, Gully Road, Seaview, Isle of Wight PO34 5BY* Isle of Wight (0983) 613583

HALSEY, Brother John Walter Brooke. b 33. Cam Univ BA57 Edin Univ DPT67. Westcott Ho Cam 61. **d** 61 **p** 62. C Stocksbridge *Sheff* 61-65; Community of the Transfiguration Midlothian from 65; Ind Chapl Edin 65-69. *Monastery of the Transfiguration, 23 Manse Road, Roslin, Midlothian EH25 9LF*

HALSON, Bryan Richard. b 32. Jes Coll Cam BA56 MA60 Liv Univ MA72. Ridley Hall Cam. **d** 59 **p** 60. C Coulsdon St Andr *S'wark* 59-62; Lic to Offic *Ches* from 63; Tutor St Aid Birkenhead 63-65; Sen Tutor 65-68; Vice-Prin 68-69; Lect Alsager Coll of Educn 69-74; Prin Lect Crewe and Alsager Coll of HE from 74. *11 Winston Avenue, Alsager, Stoke-on-Trent* Alsager (0270) 3998

HALSTEAD, Leonard. b 13. St Andr Coll Pampisford 44. **d** 46 **p** 47. V Markington and S Stainley *Ripon* 69-73; V Bishop Thornton 72-73; V Halifax St Anne Southowram *Wakef* 73-78; rtd 78. *3 Aln Court, Hauxton Road, Cambridge CB2 2LH* Cambridge (0223) 840306

✠**HAMBIDGE, Most Rev Douglas Walter.** b 27. Lon Univ BD58 DD70. ALCD53. **d** 53 **p** 54 **c** 69. C Dalston St Mark w St Bart *Lon* 53-56; Canada from 56; Bp BC 69-81; Abp BC from 81. *814 Richards Street, Vancouver, British Columbia, Canada, V6B 3A7* Vancouver (604) 684-6306 or 263-3464

HAMBIDGE, John Robert. b 29. Sarum Th Coll. **d** 55 **p** 56. C Tynemouth H Trin W Town *Newc* 55-57; C Middlesb St Jo the Ev *York* 58-63; C Clerkenwell H Redeemer w St Phil *Lon* 63-64; C Richmond St Jo

S'wark 64-66; V 66-76; R Swanscombe *Roch* 76-84; V Aberedw w Llandilo Graban and Llanbadarn etc *S & B* from 84. *The Rectory, Aberedw, Builth Wells, Powys LD2 3UW* Builth Wells (0982) 560359

HAMBLEN, John William Frederick. b 24. Sarum Th Coll 64. **d** 65 **p** 66. C Marlborough *Sarum* 68-70; V Chardstock 70-77; P-in-c Lytchett Matravers 77-83; P-in-c Burpham *Chich* 83-89; Dioc Stewardship Adv 83-89; rtd 89; Perm to Offic *Ex* from 89. *29 Morningside, Dawlish, Devon EX7 9SL* Dawlish (0626) 866825

HAMBLETON, Ronald Dalzell. b 27. Ripon Hall Ox 61. **d** 62 **p** 63. C Stokesay *Heref* 62-65; V Knowbury 65-75; P-in-c Weston under Penyard 75-79; P-in-c Hope Mansell 75-79; R Weston-under-Penyard w Hope Mansel and the Lea from 79. *The Rectory, Weston under Penyard, Ross-on-Wye, Herefordshire HR9 7QA* Ross-on-Wye (0989) 62926

HAMBLIN, John Talbot. b 38. St Steph Ho Ox 64. **d** 66 **p** 67. C Newc St Jo *Newc* 66-70; C Covent Garden St Paul *Lon* 70-71; C St Marylebone Ch Ch w St Barn 71-72; C St Marylebone Ch Ch w St Paul 72-73; C Hendon St Mary 73-76; P-in-c Hornsey St Pet 76-77; V Tottenham Ch Ch W Green 76-77; V W Green Ch Ch w St Pet from 77. *Christ Church Vicarage, Waldeck Road, London N15 3EP* 081-889 9677

HAMBLIN, Roger Noel. b 42. Ripon Hall Ox 67. **d** 70 **p** 71. C Scotforth *Blackb* 70-73; C Altham w Clayton le Moors 73-76; V Cockerham w Winmarleigh 76-87; V Cockerham w Winmarleigh and Glasson from 87. *The Vicarage, 5 Lancaster Road, Cockerham, Lancaster LA2 0EB* Forton (0524) 791390

HAMBORG, Graham Richard. b 52. Bris Univ BSc73 Nottm Univ BA76 MTh77. St Jo Coll Nottm 74. **d** 77 **p** 78. C Tile Cross *Birm* 77-80; C Upton cum Chalvey *Ox* 80-82; TV 82-86; V Ruscombe and Twyford from 86. *The Vicarage, Ruscombe, Reading RG10 9UD* Twyford (0734) 341685

HAMBREY, Canon Frank Bernard. b 14. Leeds Univ BA42. Coll of Resurr Mirfield 43. **d** 44 **p** 45. Can Res Bermuda 70-75; Perm to Offic *Carl* from 77; rtd 79. *Bully Cottage, Embleton, Cockermouth, Cumbria CA13 9YA* Bassenthwaite Lake (07687) 76379

HAMBREY, Frederick Charles. b 19. Leeds Univ BA41. Coll of Resurr Mirfield 41. **d** 43 **p** 45. V Hanbury *Lich* 59-70; V Colton *Carl* 70-71; V Satterthwaite and Rusland 70-71; V Colton w Satterthwaite and Rusland 71-84; rtd 84; Perm to Offic *Carl* from 85. *Underknott, Blease Road, Threlkeld, Keswick, Cumbria CA12 4RY* Threlkeld (07687) 79604

HAMEL COOKE, Christopher Kingston. b 21. CCC Ox BA49 MA52 Birm Univ DPS67. Cuddesdon Coll 49. **d** 50 **p** 51. V Bedf St Andr *St Alb* 69-79; P-in-c Bedf St Mary 70-75; R St Marylebone w H Trin *Lon* 79-89; rtd 90; Perm to Offic *Cov* from 90. *The Malt House, Halford, Shipston-on-Stour, Warks CV36 5BT* Stratford-upon-Avon (0789) 740615

HAMER, Andrew Frank. b 07. Wycliffe Hall Ox 65. **d** 66 **p** 67. V Wethersfield *Chelmsf* 71-77; rtd 77; Perm to Offic *B & W* from 81. *9 High Green, Easton, Wells, Somerset BA5 1EG* Wells (0749) 870378

HAMER, David Handel. b 41. Cape Town Univ BA61 Trin Coll Ox BA66. Coll of Resurr Mirfield 62. **d** 66 **p** 67. S Africa 66-73; Chapl Blundell's Sch Tiverton from 73. *Mayfield House, 2 Tidcombe Lane, Tiverton, Devon EX16 4DZ* Tiverton (0884) 253098

HAMER, Irving David. b 59. **d** 84 **p** 85. C Newton Nottage *Llan* 84-88; C Roath St Marg 88-90; V Llansawel w Briton Ferry from 90; Miss to Seamen from 90. *The Vicarage, 251 Neath Road, Briton Ferry, W Glam SA11 2SL* Neath (0639) 812200

HAMER, Roderick John Andrew. b 44. K Coll Lon 64. Ridley Hall Cam 67. **d** 68 **p** 69. C Timperley *Ches* 68-72; C Brewood *Lich* 72-74; V Chesterton 74-80; C S Gillingham *Roch* 80-83; Adv Cant and Roch Coun for Soc Resp 83-90; Hon C S Gillingham 83-90; Perm to Offic *Cant* 84-90; ACUPA Link Officer (Dio Roch) 87-90; TR Southend *Chelmsf* from 90. *The Rectory, Burdett Avenue, Westcliff-on-Sea, Essex SS0 7JW* Southend-on-Sea (0702) 342687

HAMER, Canon Thomas. b 15. Univ of Wales BA37. St Mich Coll Llan 37. **d** 38 **p** 39. V Maenclochog w Llandeilo, Llanycefn, Henry's Moat *St D* 47-80; Hon Can St D Cathl from 79; V Maenclochog w Henry's Moat and Mynachlogddu etc 79-80; rtd 80. *Bryngwyn, The Crescent, Narberth, Dyfed* Narberth (0834) 860455

HAMER, Mrs Valerie Margaret. b 52. Leeds Univ BA74. S'wark Ord Course 83. **dss** 86 **d** 87. Walringham w Chelsham and Farleigh *S'wark* 86-87; Par Dn 87-88; Par Dn Caterham from 88. *The Parsonage, 43 Banstead*

Road, Caterham, Surrey CR3 5QG Caterham (0883) 342422

HAMERTON, Thomas Patrick. b 13. St Edm Hall Ox BA35 DipTh36 MA50. Cuddesdon Coll 37. **d** 38 **p** 39. R Abington *Pet* 63-76; V Welton w Ashby St Ledgers 76-83; rtd 83; Perm to Offic *Glouc* from 83. *Orchard Cottage, Paxford, Chipping Campden, Glos GL55 6XD* Paxford (038678) 305

HAMEY, Geoffrey Allan. b 25. Lon Univ BSc47. S'wark Ord Course 75. **d** 78 **p** 79. NSM Pinner *Lon* 78-83; P-in-c Fincham *Ely* 83-84; P-in-c Marham 83-84; P-in-c Shouldham 83-84; P-in-c Shouldham Thorpe 83-84; V 84-88; rtd 88; Hon C Winkleigh *Ex* from 88. *4 East Park Close, Winkleigh, Devon EX19 8LG* Winkleigh (0837) 83455

HAMILL-STEWART, Simon Francis. b 32. Pemb Coll Cam BA56. N Ord Course 77. **d** 80 **p** 81. NSM Neston *Ches* 80-83; C 83-86; V Over St Jo from 86. *St John's Vicarage, Delamere Street, Winsford, Cheshire CW7 2LY* Winsford (0606) 594651

✠**HAMILTON, Rt Rev Alexander Kenneth.** b 15. Trin Hall Cam BA37 MA41. Westcott Ho Cam 37. **d** 39 **p** 40 **c** 65. C Birstall *Leic* 39-41; C Whitworth w Spennymoor *Dur* 41-45; Chapl RNVR 45-47; V Bedminster St Fran *Bris* 47-58; V Newc St Jo *Newc* 58-65; RD Newc Cen 62-65; Suff Bp Jarrow *Dur* 65-80; rtd 80; Asst Bp B & W from 80. *3 Ash Tree Road, Burnham-on-Sea, Somerset TA8 2LB* Burnham (0628) 783823

HAMILTON, Canon Edgar Reid. b 27. TCD BA49 MA52. CITC 51. **d** 51 **p** 52. C Belf St Donard *D & D* 51-55; Dean's V Belf Cathl 55-59; C-in-c Stormont *D & D* 60-64; I from 64; RD Dundonald from 77; Can Belf Cathl from 85; Preb Wicklow St Patr Cathl Dub from 90. *64 Wandsworth Road, Belfast BT4 3LU* Belfast (0232) 657667

HAMILTON, Gerald Murray Percival. b 14. Ch Coll Cam BA37 MA41. Ridley Hall Cam 37. **d** 39 **p** 40. Prin Lect Coll of Ripon & York St Jo 67-79; R Crayke w Brandsby and Yearsley *York* 78-82; rtd 82. *Tanglewood Cottage, Newton-on-Ouse, York YO6 2BN* Linton-on-Ouse (03474) 219

HAMILTON, Henry Fowler Hew. b 08. ACA34 FCA40. Ripon Hall Ox 54. **d** 55 **p** 56. R Horsmonden *Roch* 61-66; rtd 75. *59 Sutton Lane, Tarleton, Preston, Lancs PR4 6UY* Preston (0772) 813434

HAMILTON, Canon James. b 09. TCD BA31 MA35. **d** 32 **p** 33. I Ban Abbey *D & D* 41-79; Prec Down Cathl 68-79; rtd 79. *31 Bayview Road, Bangor, Co Down BT19 2AR* Bangor (0247) 465976

HAMILTON, Canon James. b 22. Dur Univ LTh48. Tyndale Hall Bris 41. **d** 49 **p** 50. V Eccleston Ch Ch *Liv* 66-87; Hon Can Liv Cathl from 76; rtd 87. *6 Freckleton Road, St Helens, Merseyside WA10 3AW* St Helens (0744) 57716

HAMILTON, James Davy. b 20. Hatf Coll Dur 38. Edin Th Coll 40. **d** 43 **p** 45. R Sandford w Upton Hellions *Ex* 62-79; P-in-c Ashprington 79-81; P-in-c Cornworthy 79-81; R Ashprington, Cornworthy and Dittisham 81-83; C Weymouth St Paul *Sarum* 83-85; rtd 85; Perm to Offic *Ex* from 85. *21 Langaton Lane, Pinhoe, Exeter EX1 3SP* Exeter (0392) 66747

HAMILTON, John Frederick. b 57. Leeds Univ BA78. Edin Th Coll 78. **d** 80 **p** 81. C Whitkirk *Ripon* 80-83; C Leeds Belle Is St Jo and St Barn 83-86; V Oulton w Woodlesford from 86. *The Vicarage, 46 Holmsley Lane, Woodlesford, Leeds LS26 8RY* Leeds (0532) 820411

HAMILTON, John Hans Patrick. b 44. MBIM86 BD66 AKC67 DipAdEd76 DMS85. K Coll Lon 66. **d** 67 **p** 68. C Cleobury Mortimer w Hopton Wafers *Heref* 67-69; C Sanderstead All SS *S'wark* 69-73; V Battersea St Mary-le-Park 73-75; Dir of Educn *Derby* from 90. *31 Rectory Lane, Breadsall Village, Derby* Derby (0332) 831663

HAMILTON, John Nicholas. b 49. Trin Coll Cam BA71 MA75. Ridley Hall Cam 72. **d** 75 **p** 76. C Ealing Dean St Jo *Lon* 75-79; C Stoughton *Guildf* 79-83; R Denton St Lawr *Man* 83-88; R The Sherbornes w Pamber Win from 88. *The Rectory, Sherborne St John, Basingstoke, Hants RG24 9HX* Basingstoke (0256) 850434

HAMILTON, Canon Noble Ridgeway. b 23. TD66. TCD BA45 MA49. **d** 47 **p** 48. I Seapatrick *D & D* 61-89; RD Aghaderg 64-88; Can Dromore Cathl 66-89; Prec 75-84; Chan 84-89; rtd 89; Lic to Offic *D & D* from 90. *67 Meadowvale, Waringstown, Co Armagh, Irish Republic BT66 7RL* Waringstown (0762) 882064

HAMILTON, O'Brien. b 13. Pemb Coll Ox BA37 MA40. Cuddesdon Coll 37. **d** 39 **p** 40. V Paddington St Sav *Lon* 58-77; rtd 78; Hon C Nice *Eur* 85-90. *Domaine de* la Jansonne, 52 avenue Henri-Matisse, Les Pins, 248, 6200 Nice, France   France (33) 93 71 45 95

HAMILTON, Richard Alexander. b 46. Pemb Coll Cam BA67 MA87. S Dios Minl Tr Scheme 82. **d** 85 **p** 86. NSM Guernsey St Sampson Win 85-89; C Highgate St Mich Lon from 89. 17 Bisham Gardens, London N6 6DJ 081-340 7363

HAMILTON, Robert Hair. b 26. Oak Hill Th Coll 75. **d** 76 **p** 77. C Bootle St Matt Liv 76-78; C Horwich H Trin Man 78-81; R Whalley Range St Mary 81-86; Perm to Offic Ches from 86; rtd 91. The Leaves, 47 Statham Road, Birkenhead, Merseyside L43 7XS   051-653 7110

HAMILTON, Samuel Derek. b 34. Bris Univ BA58. Tyndale Hall Bris 54. **d** 59 **p** 60. Bp's C Sallaghy Clogh 79-83; rtd 83. 12 Cairnshill Court, Saintfield Road, Belfast BT8 4TX

HAMILTON, Stephen Heysham. b 10. **d** 48 **p** 49. R Awliscombe Ex 56-83; Chapl Honiton Hosp 60-83; rtd 83; Perm to Offic Ex from 84. 4 Rose Cottages, East Ogwell, Newton Abbot TQ13 6JL or, 130 High Street, Honiton, Devon EX14 8JR   Honiton (0404) 41221

HAMILTON-BROWN, James John. b 35. Lon Univ BSc59. Trin Coll Bris ADipTh90 Ridley Hall Cam 59. **d** 61 **p** 62. V Bramcote S'well 67-76; Research & Development Officer Abps' Coun Evang 76-79; Lic to Offic Sarum 76-81; TR Dorchester 81-91; rtd 91. The Old Mill, Blandford Forum, Dorset DT11 9DF   Blandford (0258) 453939

HAMILTON-MANON, Phillip Robert Christian. b 49. BA88. St Steph Ho Ox 89. **d** 90 **p** 91. C Norton St Mary Dur from 90. 33 Chingford Grove, Stockton-on-Tees, Cleveland TS19 0UD   Stockton-on-Tees (0642) 361300

HAMLET, Paul Manning. b 42. MCollP Open Univ BA81. Lambeth STh84 Kelham Th Coll 61. **d** 66 **p** 67. C Rumboldswyke Chich 66-69; C Ely 69-73; Hon C Ipswich St Bart St E 73-84; Chapl Wellington Sch Somerset from 84; CF(TAVR) from 88. 30 John Grinter Way, Wellington, Somerset TA21 9AR   Wellington (0823) 476425

HAMLYN, Canon Eric Crawford. b 37. Dur Univ BA60 MA91. Cranmer Hall Dur DipTh62. **d** 62 **p** 63. C Bushbury Lich 62-64; C Whitchurch 64-67; V Burslem St Paul 67-72; V Stafford St Paul Forebridge 72-77; V Trentham 77-85; TR Mildenhall St E 85-89; P-in-c Boxford from 89; Clergy Tr Officer from 89; Hon Can St E Cathl from 91. The Rectory, Boxford, Colchester CO6 5JT   Boxford (0787) 210191

HAMMER, Canon Raymond Jack. b 20. St Pet Hall Ox BA42 DipTh43 MA45 Lon Univ BD45 MTh55 PhD61. Wycliffe Hall Ox 42. **d** 43 **p** 44. Hon Can Kobe Japan from 64; Lect Th Birm Univ 65-77; Lic to Offic Birm 65-77; Lon 77-85; Dir W Midl NSM Course 71-76; Dir BRF 77-85; rtd 85; Perm to Offic Lon and Worc from 85; Cov from 89. 22 Midsummer Meadow, Inkberrow, Worcs WR7 4HD   Inkberrow (0386) 792883

HAMMERSLEY, John Goodwin. b 34. Keble Coll Ox BA57 MA60. Westcott Ho Cam 57. **d** 60 **p** 61. C Sheff St Swithun Sheff 60-67; Sec Par and People 67-70; P-in-c Linc St Mary-le-Wigford w St Benedict etc Linc 70-78; C Tettenhall Regis Lich 78-80; TV 80-87; Preb Lich Cathl 81-87; Chapl Metro Cen Gateshead Dur from 87; RD Gateshead W from 88. 1 West Lane, Blaydon-on-Tyne NE21 6PQ   091-414 8892

HAMMERSLEY, Peter. b 41. Lon Univ BD78 Birm Univ MEd87. Kelham Th Coll 60. **d** 65 **p** 66. C Oadby Leic 65-69; Jamaica 70-77; Min Can Worc Cathl Worc 77-84; Chapl and Hd RE K Sch Worc 77-84; V Foley Park 84-90; TV Kidderminster St Jo and H Innocents 90-91; Vice-Prin Aston Tr Scheme from 91; Warden of Readers Worc from 91. 52 Hanbury Road, Droitwich, Worcs WR9 8PD   Droitwich (0905) 776197

HAMMERSLEY, Peter Angus Ragsdale. b 35. Linc Th Coll 74. **d** 76 **p** 77. C Stafford Lich 76-79; P-in-c W Bromwich St Andr 79-83; V 83-88; P-in-c W Bromwich Ch Ch 85-88; V Streetly from 88; RD Walsall from 90. The Vicarage, Foley Church Close, Sutton Coldfield, W Midlands B74 3JX   021-353 2292

HAMMERTON, Canon Howard Jaggar. b 14. Man Univ BA36 Leeds Univ MA44. Ridley Hall Cam 36. **d** 38 **p** 39. V Leeds H Trin Ripon 65-81; rtd 81. Flat 4, Bramhope Manor, Moor Road, Bramhope, Leeds L16   Leeds (0532) 842142

HAMMETT, Barry Keith. b 47. Magd Coll Ox BA71 MA74. St Steph Ho Ox 72. **d** 74 **p** 75. C Plymouth St Pet Ex 74-77; Chapl RN 77-86; Staff Chapl to Chapl of The Fleet from 86. c/o MOD, Lacon House, Theobald's Road, London WC1X 8RY   071-430 6847

HAMMOND, Mrs Betty Marian. b 27. Gilmore Ho. **dss** 84 **d** 87. Gosport Ch Ch Portsm 84-87; C from 87.

10 Alvara Road, Gosport, Hants PO12 2HY   Gosport (0705) 583068

HAMMOND, Canon Brian Leonard. b 31. Bris Univ BSc54. Wells Th Coll 56. **d** 58 **p** 59. C Clapham H Trin S'wark 58-62; V Walworth All SS and St Steph 62-72; V S Merstham 72-87; RD Reigate 80-86; Hon Can S'wark Cathl from 83; V Spring Park All SS from 87. All Saints' Vicarage, 1 Farm Drive, Shirley, Croydon CR0 8HX   081-777 4447

HAMMOND, Eric Penharwood. b 08. St Chad's Coll Dur BA31 DipTh32 MA47. **d** 32 **p** 33. V Mickleton Glouc 52-74; rtd 74. St Francis, Outlands Lane, Curdridge, Southampton SO3 2HD   Botley (0489) 783324

HAMMOND, Frank. b 49. **d** 77 **p** 78. C Sutton Liv 77-79; C Blundellsands St Nic 80-83. 13 Leicester Avenue, Crosby, Liverpool L22 2BA

HAMMOND, James Francis. b 48. CITC 69. **d** 72 **p** 73. C Dub St Bart w Ch Ch Leeson Park D & G 72-76; C Monkstown 76-79; I Dunboyne w Kilcock, Maynooth, Moyglare etc M & K 79-87; I Holmpatrick w Balbriggan and Kenure D & G from 87. Holmpatrick Rectory, Millers Lane, Skerries, Co Dublin, Irish Republic Dublin (1) 492247

HAMMOND, Lindsay John. b 57. Southn Univ BA83. Sarum & Wells Th Coll 84. **d** 86 **p** 87. C Ashford Cant 86-90; V Appledore w Brookland, Fairfield, Brenzett etc from 90. The Vicarage, Appledore, Ashford, Kent TN26 2DB   Ashford (0233) 83250

HAMMOND, Mary. b 15. St Aid Coll Dur BA51 Maria Grey Coll Lon CertEd52. Roch and S'wark Dss Ho 40. **dss** 43 **d** 87. Australia 68-73; Abp Langton Sch Beare Green 73-75; rtd 75; Perm to Offic Linc 75-87; Win 87-89. The Close, Vicarage Road, Staines, Middx TW18 4YG   Staines (0784) 452094

HAMMOND, Canon Peter. b 21. Mert Coll Ox BA48 MA53 Salonica Univ 48. Cuddesdon Coll 50. **d** 51 **p** 52. R Bagendon Glouc 56-61; Lic to Offic York 62-83; Perm to Offic Linc from 83; Can and Preb Linc Cathl 87; rtd 90. Flat 2, 2 Greestone Place, Lincoln LN2 1PP   Lincoln (0522) 543047

HAMMOND, Peter Clark. b 27. Linc Coll Ox BA49 MA53. Wells Th Coll 51. **d** 52 **p** 53. V Walmer Cant 66-85; V Rolvenden 85-89; rtd 89. 19 Hardwick Street, Cambridge CB3 9JA   Cambridge (0223) 467425

HAMMOND, Richard John. b 45. Clare Coll Cam BA67 MA80. St Steph Ho Ox 70. **d** 74 **p** 75. C Ex St Dav Ex 74-78; V Docking Nor 79-82; C Harton Dur 82-83; Chapl RAD 84-89; C Acton Green Lon 89-91; P-in-c St Margarets on Thames from 91. The Vicarage, 30 Ailsa Road, Twickenham TW1 1QW   081-892 4171

HAMNETT, Herbert Arnold. b 22. K Coll Lon BSc49. Qu Coll Birm 49. **d** 51 **p** 52. R Yapton w Ford Chich 60-87; rtd 87; Perm to Offic St E from 87. Clarence House, Stradbrooke Road, Fressingfield, Eye, Suffolk IP21 5PP

HAMPSON, Claude Eric. b 25. Rhodes Univ Grahamstown BA49. St Paul's Grahamstown LTh50. **d** 50 **p** 51. Australia 67-74 and from 77; Vietnam 74-75; V Kilburn St Aug w St Jo Lon 75-77; rtd 85. Box 107, Edgecliff, NSW, Australia 2027   Sydney (2) 327-8215

HAMPSON, David. b 46. Chich Th Coll 69. **d** 72 **p** 73. C Penrith Carl 72-78; V Crosscrake from 78. The Vicarage, Shyreakes Lane, Crosscrake, Kendal, Cumbria LA8 0AB   Sedgwick (05395) 60333

HAMPSON, Michael John. b 67. Jes Coll Ox BA88. Ripon Coll Cuddesdon 88. **d** 91. C W Burnley Blackb from 91. 76 Wellfield Drive, Burnley, Lancs BB12 0HZ   Burnley (0282) 416092

HAMPSTEAD, Archdeacon of. See COOGAN, Ven Robert Arthur William

HAMPTON, Cyril Herbert. b 97. Bible Churchmen's Coll. **d** 49 **p** 50. R Piddlehinton Sarum 64-70; rtd 70. 17 Westerngate, The Avenue, Branksome Park, Poole, Dorset BH13 6BB   Bournemouth (0202) 767272

HAMPTON, John Stanley. b 13. St Aug Coll Cant 39 Chich Th Coll 46. **d** 48 **p** 49. V Manningham St Mary and Bradf St Mich Bradf 56-79; V Healaugh w Wighill and Bilbrough York 79-81; rtd 81. 34 Moorside, Boston Spa, Wetherby, W Yorkshire LS23 6PD   Boston Spa (0937) 843948

HAMPTON, Canon John Waller. b 28. Linc Coll Ox BA51 MA58. Westcott Ho Cam 51. **d** 53 **p** 54. C Rugby St Andr Cov 53-56; Chapl St Paul's Sch Hammersmith 56-65; Chapl St Paul's Girls Sch Hammersmith 60-65; V Gaydon w Chadshunt Cov 65-69; Asst Dir RE 65-70; C-in-c Warw St Nic 69-75; Fell Qu Coll Birm 75-76; P-in-c Wetton Lich 76-82; P-in-c Alstonfield 76-82; P-in-c Sheen 76-80; RD Alstonfield 80-82; P-in-c Butterton 80-82; P-in-c Warslow and Elkstones 80-82; P-in-c Broadway Worc 82-91; V from 91; RD Evesham from

87; Hon Can Worc Cathl from 88. *The Vicarage, 4 Lifford Gardens, Broadway, Worcs WR12 7DA* Broadway (0386) 852352

HAMPTON, Terence Alastair Godfrey Macpherson. b 38. Bris Univ PGCE73. Lon Coll of Div ALCD63 BD68. **d** 64 **p** 65. C Clifton Ch Ch w Em *Bris* 64-66; C Ickenham *Lon* 66-67; C Patchway *Bris* 67-73; TV Jersey St Brelade *Win* 73-83; R Jersey Grouville from 83. *The Rectory, Grouville, Jersey, Channel Islands* Jersey (0534) 53073

HAMPTON-SMITH, David Charles. b 22. Ch Ch Ox BA48 MA48. Cuddesdon Coll 48. **d** 50 **p** 51. V Howe Bridge *Man* 56-62; Australia from 65; rtd 87. *139 Esplanade, Port Noarlunga South, S Australia 5167* Adelaide (8) 386-1284

HANCOCK, Alfred John. b 28. Lon Univ BSc52. Ex & Truro NSM Scheme 74. **d** 77 **p** 78. NSM Phillack w Gwithian and Gwinear *Truro* 77-78 and from 86; NSM Camborne 78-86. *Redlands, Rosewarne Downs, Camborne, Cornwall TR14 0BD* Camborne (0209) 713527

HANCOCK, Bernard. b 13. Wycliffe Hall Ox 61. **d** 62 **p** 63. R Peopleton *Worc* 65-70; R Hagley 70-76; rtd 78. *The Old Post Office, Birlingham, Pershore, Worcs WR10 3AB* Evesham (0386) 750641

HANCOCK, Christopher David. b 54. Qu Coll Ox MA Dur Univ PhD. Cranmer Hall Dur BA. **d** 82 **p** 83. C Leic H Trin w St Jo *Leic* 82-85; Chapl Magd Coll Cam 85-88; USA from 88. *Virginia Theological Seminary, Seminary Road, Alexandria, Virginia 22304, USA*

HANCOCK, David Richard. b 48. Chich Th Coll. **d** 89 **p** 90. C Maidstone All SS and St Phil w Tovil *Cant* from 89; CF from 90. *85 Loose Road, Maidstone, Kent ME15 7DA* Maidstone (0622) 678679

HANCOCK, Douglas. b 25. S'wark Ord Course 63. **d** 67 **p** 68. C Hounslow St Steph *Lon* 67-70; C Highcliffe w Hinton Admiral *Win* 70-72; R Newton *Ely* 72-78; P-in-c Gorefield 72-74; V 74-78; R Tydd St Giles 74-78; P-in-c Chirton, Marden, Patney, Charlton and Wilsford *Sarum* 78-79; V 79-90; rtd 90; Perm to Offic *Ex* from 90. *6 Joan Spry Close, Witheridge, Tiverton EX16 5AU* Tiverton (0884) 860140

HANCOCK, Douglas Charles. b 16. Lon Univ BSc39 PhD52. Wycliffe Hall Ox 59. **d** 60 **p** 61. R Baughurst w Ramsdale *Win* 64-70; V Bournemouth St Andr 70-79; RD Alresford 79-84; R Hinton Ampner w Bramdean and Kilmeston 79-84; rtd 84; Perm to Offic Win from 84; Sarum from 86. *Flat 40, Fairhaven Court, 32/34 Sea Road, Bournemouth BH5 1DG* Bournemouth (0202) 301942

HANCOCK, Mrs Frances Margaret. b 34. LMH Ox BA56. Gilmore Course 78. **dss** 81 **d** 87. Isleworth All SS *Lon* 81-87; TM Ross w Brampton Abbotts, Bridstow and Peterstow *Heref* from 87. *The Vicarage, Bridstow, Ross-on-Wye, Hereford HR9 6QE* Ross-on-Wye (0989) 65805

HANCOCK, Ivor Michael. b 31. Lon Univ BD60. Linc Th Coll 65. **d** 66 **p** 67. C Havant *Portsm* 66-69; V Gosport Ch Ch 69-76; P-in-c Southend St Alb *Chelmsf* 76-80; V Hawley H Trin *Guildf* from 80; V Minley from 80; RD Aldershot 83-88. *The Vicarage, Hawley, Blackwater, Camberley, Surrey GU17 9BN* Camberley (0276) 35287

HANCOCK, John Clayton. b 36. Dur Univ BA58. Cranmer Hall Dur DipTh60. **d** 60 **p** 61. C Newbarns w Hawcoat *Carl* 60-65; V Church Coniston 65-76; R Torver 66-76; P-in-c Heversham 76-77; V from 77. *The Vicarage, Woodhouse Lane, Heversham, Milnthorpe, Cumbria LA7 7EW* Milnthorpe (05395) 63125

HANCOCK, John King. b 46. St Steph Ho Ox 79. **d** 81 **p** 82. C Tipton St Jo *Lich* 81-85; P-in-c Snibston *Leic* 85-86; TV Hugglescote w Donington, Ellistown and Snibston 86-90; V Stocking Farm from 90. *97 Halifax Drive, Stocking Farm, Leicester LE4 2DP* Leicester (0533) 353206

HANCOCK, Canon John Mervyn. b 38. St Jo Coll Dur BA61 DipTh64 MA70 Hertf Coll Ox BA63 MA66. Cranmer Hall Dur 63. **d** 64 **p** 65. C Bishopwearmouth St Gabr *Dur* 64-67; V Hebburn St Jo 67-87; RD Jarrow from 83; V S Westoe from 87; Hon Can Dur Cathl from 88. *St Michael's Vicarage, Westoe Road, South Shields, Tyne & Wear NE33 3PJ* 091-455 2132

HANCOCK, John Raymond. b 11. FBOA32. **d** 62 **p** 63. R Guernsey St Michel du Valle *Win* 65-79; rtd 79; Perm to Offic *Portsm* from 82. *Kingsomborne, The Broadway, Totland Bay, Isle of Wight PO39 0BL* Isle of Wight (0983) 754321

HANCOCK, Leonard George Edward. b 28. Open Univ BA81 Leic Univ MEd84. ALCD52. **d** 52 **p** 56. C Bilston St Leon *Lich* 52-53; C Sheff St Swithun *Sheff* 56-58; C Ecclesfield 58; C-in-c Ecclesfield St Paul CD 58-63; V

Sheff St Mary w St Simon w St Matthias 63-72; V Michael *S & M* 72-76; R Loughb All SS *Leic* 76-83; R Loughb All SS and H Trin from 83. *The Rectory, Steeple Row, Loughborough, Leics LE11 1UX* Loughborough (0509) 212780

HANCOCK, Malcolm James. b 50. AGSM70. Sarum & Wells Th Coll 85. **d** 87 **p** 88. C Sandhurst *Ox* 87-90; TV Bradbourne and Brassington *Derby* from 90. *Brassington Vicarage, Derby DE4 4DA* Carsington (062985) 281

HANCOCK, Michael. b 26. Ex Coll Ox BA50 MA54. Sarum Th Coll 50. **d** 52 **p** 53. C Bideford *Ex* 52-56; C S Molton w Nymet St George 56-59; C Withycombe Raleigh 59-61; V Culmstock from 61. *The Vicarage, Culmstock, Cullompton, Devon EX15 3LA* Craddock (0884) 840214

HANCOCK, Michael John. b 33. Lich Th Coll 55. **d** 58 **p** 59. C Romsey *Win* 69-72; C Moordown *72-75*; C Christchurch 75-78; V Guernsey St Jo 78-89; rtd 89. *10 la rue du Tertre, Vale, Guernsey, Channel Islands* Guernsey (0481) 48887

HANCOCK, Nigel John. b 35. K Coll Cam BA63 MA67. E Anglian Minl Tr Course 86. **d** 89. NSM Cam St Mary Less *Ely* from 89. *5 Atherton Close, Cambridge CB4 2BE* Cambridge (0223) 355828

HANCOCK, Paul. b 43. AKC66. **d** 67 **p** 68. C Wednesbury St Paul Wood Green *Lich* 67-70; C Rugeley 70-73; V Rickerscote 73-75; R Blisland w St Breward *Truro* 75-78; V Mansf St Lawr *S'well* 78-82; P-in-c Charleton *Ex* 82-83; P-in-c E Portlemouth, S Pool and Chivelstone 82-83; R Charleton w Buckland Tout Saints etc from 83; RD Woodleigh from 88. *The Rectory, West Charleton, Kingsbridge, Devon TQ7 2AJ* Frogmore (0548) 531211

HANCOCK, Paul Byron. b 51. **d** 75 **p** 76. C Croydon *Cant* 75-78; USA from 78; Hd Episc High Sch Baton Rouge from 78. *3200 Woodland Ridge Boulevard, Baton Rouge, Louisiana 70816, USA*

HANCOCK, Peter. b 55. Selw Coll Cam BA76 MA79. Oak Hill Th Coll BA80. **d** 80 **p** 81. C Portsdown *Portsm* 80-83; C Radipole and Melcombe Regis *Sarum* 83-87; V Cowplain *Portsm* from 87. *The Vicarage, Padnell Road, Cowplain, Portsmouth PO8 8DZ* Waterlooville (0705) 262295

HANCOCK, Peter Ernest. b 33. Man Univ BA54. Qu Coll Birm 54. **d** 56 **p** 57. C Wigston Magna *Leic* 56-59; C Hucknall Torkard *S'well* 59-61; V Sutton in Ashfield St Mich 61-65; Dioc Youth Officer *Portsm* 65-73; R Broughton Astley *Leic* 73-86; Dioc Adv for Min of Health and Healing *B & W* from 86. *9 Henley Lodge, Yatton, Bristol BS19 4JQ* Yatton (0934) 838920

HANCOCK, Peter Thompson. b 31. G&C Coll Cam BA54 MA58. Ridley Hall Cam 54. **d** 56 **p** 57. C Beckenham Ch Ch *Roch* 56-59; Chapl St Lawr Coll Ramsgate 59-62; Chapl Stowe Sch Bucks 62-67; Asst Chapl and Lect Emb Ch Paris *Eur* 67-70; V Walton H Trin *Ox* 70-80; Canada 80-84; V Northwood H Trin *Lon* from 84. *Holy Trinity Vicarage, Gateway Close, Northwood, Middx HA6 2RW* Northwood (09274) 25732

HANCOCK, Reginald Legassicke. b 28. Trin Coll Cam BA51 MA57. Clifton Th Coll 60. **d** 61 **p** 62. C Finchley Ch Ch *Lon* 61-63; CF 63-82; R Quantoxhead *B & W* from 82. *The New Rectory, Kilve, Bridgwater, Somerset TA5 1DZ* Holford (027874) 536

HANCOCK, Ronald Edward. b 24. MRCS49 LRCP49. **d** 78 **p** 79. Hon C Highbury Ch Ch *Lon* 78; Hon C Highbury Ch Ch w St Jo 79-82; R Puddletown and Tolpuddle *Sarum* 82-90; rtd 90. *9 Churchward Avenue, Weymouth, Dorset DT3 6NZ* Preston (0305) 832558

HANCOCK, William Russell. b 07. Lich Th Coll 29. **d** 31 **p** 32. V Prestwich St Gabr *Man* 64-72; rtd 72; Perm to Offic *Man* 73-88. *16 Bedern Bank, Ripon, N Yorkshire HG4 1PE* Ripon (0765) 707179

HANCOCKS, Graeme. b 58. Univ of Wales (Ban) BD79. Linc Th Coll 79. **d** 81 **p** 82. C Denbigh and Nantglyn *St As* 81-84; Asst Chapl Oslo St Edm *Eur* 84-90; Chapl Gothenburg w Halmstad, Jonkoping etc from 90. *Residence Norra Liden 15, 411-18 Gothenberg, Sweden* Gothenburg (31) 111915

HANCOX, Granville Leonard. b 32. Lich Th Coll 67. **d** 70 **p** 71. C Caverswall *Lich* 70-73; C Norton in the Moors 73-76; P-in-c Leek St Luke 76-79; TV Leek 79-83; V Priors Lee and St Georges from 83. *The Vicarage, Ashley Road, Telford, Shropshire TF2 9LF* Telford (0952) 612923

HAND, Canon Charles. b 08. Birm Univ BA29. Wycliffe Hall Ox 42. **d** 43 **p** 44. R Upton-upon-Severn *Worc* 64-73; rtd 73. *23 Scafell Close, Warndon, Worcester WR14 9BZ* Worcester (0905) 23371

✠**HAND, Most Rev Geoffrey David.** b 18. CBE75. **d** 42
p 43 **c** 50. C Heckmondwike *Wakef* 42-46; Papua New
Guinea 46-83; Bp Coadjutor New Guinea 50-63; Adn N
New Guinea 50-63; Bp Papua New Guinea 63-77; Abp
Papua New Guinea 77-83; Bp Port Moresby 77-83; rtd
83; P-in-c E w W Rudham *Nor* 83-85; P-in-c Houghton
83-85. *121 Brackenbury Road, London W6 0BQ*

HAND, Nigel Arthur. b 54. St Jo Coll Nottm. **d** 84 **p** 85. C
Birm St Luke *Birm* 84-88; C Walton H Trin *Ox*
88-89; TV from 89. *24 Como Road, Aylesbury, Bucks
HP20 1NR* Aylesbury (0296) 85990

HAND, Peter Michael. b 42. Univ Coll Ox BA63 Lon Univ
BSc75. Sarum & Wells Th Coll 77. **d** 80 **p** 81. NSM
Shaston *Sarum* 80-81; C Tisbury 81-83; C Glastonbury
St Jo w Godney *B & W* 83-84; C Glastonbury w Meare,
W Pennard and Godney 84-87; V High Littleton from
87. *The Vicarage, High Littleton, Bristol BS18 5HG*
Timsbury (0761) 72097

✠**HANDFORD, Rt Rev George Clive.** b 37. Hatf Coll Dur
BA61. Qu Coll Birm DipTh63. **d** 63 **p** 64 **c** 90. C Mansf
St Pet *S'well* 63-67; Lebanon 67-74; Dean Jerusalem
74-78; UAE 78-83; Adn Gulf 78-83; RD Tuxford and
Norwell *S'well* 83-84; V Kneesall w Laxton 83-84; P-in-c
Wellow 83-84; Adn Nottm 84-90; Suff Bp Warw *Cov*
from 90. *Warwick House, 139 Kenilworth Road,
Coventry CV4 7AF* Coventry (0203) 416200

HANDFORD, John Richard. b 32. Sydney Univ BSc52
Univ Coll Lon MSc58 Surrey Univ MA84 Lon Univ
DipTh67. Lon Coll of Div 68. **d** 69 **p** 70. Asst Chapl
Wellington Coll Berks 69-80; Hon C Windlesham *Guildf*
from 87. *Desiderata, 33 Chertsey Road, Windlesham,
Surrey GU20 6EW* Bagshot (0276) 72397

HANDFORD, Maurice. b 25. Oak Hill Th Coll 48. **d** 52
p 53. C-in-c Buxton Trin Prop Chpl *Derby* 58-87; I
Clondevaddock w Portsalon and Leatbeg *D & R* 87-90;
Dom Chapl to Bp 88-90; rtd 90; Perm to Offic *Ches*
from 90. *9 Birtlespool Road, Cheadle Hulme, Cheadle,
Cheshire SK8 5JZ* 061-485 3134

HANDFORTH, Richard Brereton. b 31. St Pet Coll Ox
BA55 MA60. Westcott Ho Cam 63. **d** 64 **p** 65. C
Hornchurch St Andr *Chelmsf* 64-65; Hong Kong 65-73;
Chapl CMS Fellowship Ho Chislehurst 73-75; Hon C
Chislehurst St Nic *Roch* 73-75; Home Educn Sec CMS
75-83; Lic to Offic *Roch* 76-83; V Biggin Hill 83-88;
Inter-change Adv CMS from 88. *67 Murray Avenue,
Bromley BR1 3DJ* 081-460 0238

HANDLEY, Ven Anthony Michael. b 36. Selw Coll Cam
BA60 MA64. Chich Th Coll 60. **d** 62 **p** 63. C Thorpe
Nor 62-66; C Gaywood, Bawsey and Mintlyn 66-72; V
Hellesdon 72-81; RD Nor N 80-81; Adn Nor from 81.
40 Heigham Road, Norwich NR2 3AU Norwich (0603)
611808

HANDLEY, Dennis Francis. b 57. MIE79 TEng(CEI)80.
Coll of Resurr Mirfield 82. **d** 85 **p** 86. C Headingley
Ripon 85-88; C Rothwell from 88. *6 Sandy Grove,
Rothwell, Leeds LS26 0TB* Leeds (0532) 827237

HANDLEY, Harold. b 14. ACIS42 AACCA44 ACWA48.
Bps' Coll Cheshunt 62. **d** 63 **p** 64. V Totternhoe *St Alb*
65-79; C Ringwood *Win* 79-80; rtd 79; Perm to Offic
Win from 80. *Risdene, 16 Barton Court Avenue, New
Milton, Hants BH25 7HD* New Milton (0425) 611771

HANDLEY, John. b 38. Oak Hill Th Coll. **d** 83 **p** 84. C
Witton w Brundall and Braydeston *Nor* 83-86; R
Reedham w Cantley w Limpenhoe and Southwood from
86. *The Rectory, Church Road, Reedham, Norwich
NR13 3TZ* Great Yarmouth (0493) 700268

HANDLEY, Neil. b 40. St Aid Birkenhead 64. **d** 67 **p** 68.
C Ashton Ch Ch *Man* 64-70; C Stretford All SS 70-73;
C Tonge 73; C-in-c Bolton St Jo Breightmet CD 74-79;
V Bolton St Jo 79-80; R Broughton 80-87; Perm to Offic
Eur from 90. *La Taire du Grel, 24250 Domme, France*
France (33) 53 28 23 42

HANDLEY, Terence Anthony. b 55. Trent Poly HNC
Open Univ BA89. Trin Coll Bris 85. **d** 87 **p** 88. C Meole
Brace *Lich* 87-91; V Stafford St Paul Forebridge from
91. *St Paul's Vicarage, 31 The Oval, Stafford ST17 4LQ*
Stafford (0785) 51683

HANDS, Graeme. b 35. Cranmer Hall Dur. **d** 61 **p** 62.
C Atherstone *Cov* 61-63; Chapl Aldwickbury Sch
Harpenden 63-66; C Cov St Alb *Cov* 66-68; P-in-c Warw
St Paul 68-80; V Radford from 80; RD Cov N from 87.
The Vicarage, 21 Tulliver Street, Coventry CV6 3BY
Coventry (0203) 598449

HANDSCOMBE, Canon Richard John. b 23. Cuddesdon
Coll 58. **d** 60 **p** 61. C Shrub End *Chelmsf* 60-63;
V Fingringhoe 63-86; P-in-c E Donyland 75-77; R
Fingringhoe w E Donyland from 86; Hon Can Chelmsf
Cathl from 89; R Abberton w Langenhoe from 89. *The*
Rectory, Fingringhoe, Colchester CO5 7BN Rowhedge
(020628) 383

HANDY, Maurice Arthur. b 04. TCD BA26 MA34. **d** 27
p 28. Can Ch Ch Cathl Dub *D & G* 63-72; Warden of
Ch's Min of Healing in Ireland 65-72; I Hacketstown
C & O 72-76; rtd 76. *55 Marley Avenue, Grange Road,
Rathfarnham, Dublin 16, Irish Republic* Dublin (1)
946041

HANFORD, Canon William Richard. b 38. Keble Coll Ox
BA60 MA64 Lon Univ BD66. St Steph Ho Ox 60. **d** 63
p 64. C Roath St Martin *Llan* 63-66; C Llantwit Major
67-68; PV Llan Cathl 68-72; Chapl RN 72-76; Lic to
Offic *Eur* 74-76; Hon C Eastbourne St Sav and St Pet
Chich 76-77; C Brighton St Pet 77-78; Can Res and Prec
Guildf Cathl *Guildf* 78-83; V Ewell from 83. *St Mary's*
*Vicarage, 14 Church Street, Ewell, Epsom, Surrey
KT17 2AQ* 081-393 2643

HANKEY, Miss Dorothy Mary. b 38. CertEd65. Trin Coll
Bris 75. **dss** 78 **d** 87. Wigan St Jas w St Thos *Liv* 78-84;
Middleton *Man* 84-85; Litherland Ch Ch *Liv* 85-87; Par
Dn 87-89; Par Dn Blackpool St Mark *Blackb* from 89.
2 St Mark's Place, Blackpool FY3 7HR Blackpool
(0253) 37735

HANKEY, Rupert. b 60. **d** 91. C Basildon St Andr w H
Cross *Chelmsf* from 91. *34 Falkenham Rise, Basildon,
Essex SS1 2JG* Basildon (0268) 282463

HANKEY, Simon. b 26. CCC Cam BA48 MA53.
Cuddesdon Coll 48. **d** 50 **p** 51. C Wellingborough All
Hallows *Pet* 50-52; C Cam St Giles w St Pet *Ely* 52-54;
C-in-c Middlesbrough Berwick Hills CD *York* 54-60; V
Scarborough St Sav w All SS 60-71; V Long Wittenham
w Lt Wittenham *Ox* 71-81; R Ashingdon w S Fambridge
Chelmsf from 81. *The Rectory, Church Road, Rochford,
Essex SS4 3HY* Southend-on-Sea (0702) 544327

HANKINS, Clifford James. b 24. Chich Th Coll 70. **d** 72
p 73. C Henfield *Chich* 72-76; V Fernhurst 76-84; V
Mithian w Mt Hawke *Truro* 84-89; rtd 89. *2 Kestrel
Close, East Wittering, Chichester, W Sussex PO20 8PQ*
Bracklesham Bay (0243) 672164

HANMER, Richard John. b 38. Peterho Cam BA61 MA65.
Linc Th Coll 62. **d** 64 **p** 65. C Sheff St Swithun *Sheff*
64-69; Bp's Chapl *Nor* 69-73; V Cinderhill *S'well* 73-81;
V Eaton *Nor* from 81. *The Vicarage, 210 Newmarket
Road, Norwich NR4 7LA* Norwich (0603) 52837

HANNA, Desmond Haldane. b 41. TCD BA63 MA67.
CITC 64. **d** 64 **p** 65. C Lurgan Ch Ch *D & D* 64-70; C
Cregagh 70-72; I Belf St Chris 72-80; I Belvoir 80-83; I
Ballywalter w Inishargie 83-90; I Dromore *Clogh* from
90. *The Rectory, 15 Galbally Road, Dromore, Omagh,
Co Tyrone BT8 3EE* Dromore (0662) 898300

HANNA, John. b 44. Trin Coll Bris DipHE82 Lon Bible
Coll BA83 Westcott Ho Cam 86. **d** 87 **p** 88. C Denton
Ch Ch *Man* from 87. *8 Browning Road, Reddish,
Stockport SK5 6JN* 061-336 3455

HANNA, Peter Thomas. b 45. ACII66 GIFireE75. CITC
85. **d** 88 **p** 89. NSM Cork St Fin Barre's Union *C, C & R*
from 88. *Mount Windsor, Farnahoe, Inishannon, Co
Cork, Irish Republic* Cork (21) 775470

HANNA, Canon Robert Charles. b 49. Oak Hill Th Coll
75. **d** 77 **p** 78. C Coleraine *Conn* 77-82; I Convoy w
Monellan and Donaghmore *D & R* from 82; Can Raphoe
Cathl from 88. *Convoy Rectory, Main Street, Convoy,
Lifford, Co Donegal, Irish Republic* Convoy (74) 47164

HANNAFORD, Robert. b 53. Ex Univ BEd76
MA78 PhD87. St Steph Ho Ox 78. **d** 80 **p** 81. C Ex St
Jas *Ex* 80-83; Chapl Ex Univ 83-88; Tutor St Steph Ho
Ox from 89. *St Stephen's House, 16 Marston Street,
Oxford OX4 1JX* Oxford (0865) 247874 or 247643

HANNAH, John Douglas. b 39. St Paul's Grahamstown
DipTh71. **d** 71 **p** 72. S Africa 71-85; C Finchley St Mary
Lon from 85. *28 Hendon Lane, London N3 1TR*
081-346 7573

HANNAH, Richard. b 24. CCC Ox BA49 MA53. St Mich
Coll Llan 49. **d** 51 **p** 52. R Shenington and Alkerton
w Shutford *Ox* 69-79; RD Deddington 78-84; P-in-c
Deddington w Clifton and Hempton 79-80; V
Deddington w Barford, Clifton and Hempton 81-89; rtd
89. *Cwm Brynnau, 4 Riverside, Llyswen, Brecon, Powys
LD3 1XX* Llyswen (0874) 754716

HANNAM, Duncan Chisholm. b 18. Dur Univ
BA42 MA45. Linc Th Coll 45. **d** 45 **p** 46. C Camberwell
St Giles *S'wark* 64-76; P-in-c Eldon *Dur* 76-81; V 81-85;
rtd 85; Perm to Offic *Bris* from 85. *2 Holway Cottages,
Swindon, Wilts SN1 4JB* Swindon (0793) 610038

HANNAY, Robert Fleming. b 23. Ch Ch Ox MA49.
Cuddesdon Coll 63. **d** 65 **p** 66. R Garsington *Ox* 69-79;
R The Claydons 79-85; rtd 88. *The Old Rectory,
Yatesbury, Calne, Wilts SN11 8YE* Calne (0249) 81731

✠**HANNON, Rt Rev Brian Desmond Anthony.** b 36. TCD BA59 MA63. CITC Div Test61. **d** 61 **p** 62 **c** 86. C Clooney *D & R* 61-64; I Desertmartin 64-69; I Londonderry Ch Ch 69-82; RD Londonderry 77-82; I Enniskillen *Clogh* 82-86; Preb Clogh Cathl 82-84; Dean Clogh 85-86; Bp Clogh from 86. *The See House, Fivemiletown, Co Tyrone BT75 0QP* Fivemiletown (03655) 21265

HANSCOMBE, Derek George. b 33. Chich Th Coll 60. **d** 62 **p** 63. C Illingworth *Wakef* 62-68; Youth Chapl *Lich* 68-74; V Coseley St Chad 74-78; USPG from 78. *c/o USPG, Partnership House, 157 Waterloo Road, London SE1 8XA* 071-928 8681

HANSEN, Harold Percy. b 05. St Chad's Coll Dur BA29 DipTh30 MA32. **d** 30 **p** 31. V Shefford *St Alb* 66-70; R Campton 66-70; rtd 70. *Moorlands, Cotherstone, Barnard Castle, Co Durham DL12 9PH* Staindrop (0833) 50726

HANSEN, James Edwin. b 41. Concordia Coll (USA) BSc64 San Jose State Univ MA71. Ch Div Sch of the Pacific (USA) MDiv86. **d** 86 **p** 87. C Swansea St Pet *S & B* 86-87; C Sketty 87-89; C Hornchurch St Andr *Chelmsf* 89-91; P-in-c Chelmsf St Andr from 91. *The Vicarage, 88 Chignall Road, Chelmsford CM1 2JB* Chelmsford (0245) 496722

HANSEN, Mrs Moira Jacqueline. b 55. K Coll Lon BSc76. Oak Hill Th Coll BA88. **d** 88. Par Dn Finchley Ch Ch *Lon* 88-91; Par Dn Broadwater St Mary *Chich* from 91. *23 Kingsland Road, Worthing, W Sussex BN14 9EB* Worthing (0903) 212153

HANSFORD, Gordon John. b 40. Southn Univ BSc61. Trin Coll Bris 77. **d** 79 **p** 80. C Ex St Leon w H Trin *Ex* 79-82; C Shirley *Win* 82-87; R Landcross, Littleham, Monkleigh etc *Ex* from 87. *The Rectory, Weare Giffard, Bideford, Devon EX39 4QP* Bideford (0237) 472017

HANSON, Christopher. b 48. Birm Bible Inst DipMin75 Wycliffe Hall Ox 87. **d** 89 **p** 90. C Heref St Pet w St Owen and St Jas *Heref* from 89. *6 Ledbury Road, Hereford HR1 2SY* Hereford (0432) 269944

HANSON, Dale Robert. b 57. Fitzw Coll Cam BA78 MA81 Univ of BC MA80. Ridley Hall Cam 81. **d** 84 **p** 85. C Much Woolton *Liv* 84-87; Hong Kong 87-91; TV Billingham St Aid *Dur* from 91. *17 Shadforth Drive, Billingham, Cleveland TS23 3PW* Stockton-on-Tees (0642) 561870

HANSON, Canon John Westland. b 19. OBE74. St Jo Coll Dur BA41 DipTh43 MA44. **d** 43 **p** 44. Chapl and Lect RAF Flying Coll Manby 50-76; R Grimoldby w Manby *Linc* 50-76; Chief Examiner Relig Studies Cam Univ 66-82; Can and Preb Linc Cathl from 67; RD Louthesk 68-77; V Woodhall Spa and Kirkstead 76-88; P-in-c Langton w Woodhall 76-88; rtd 88. *Brookfield, 28 Tor-o-Moor Road, Woodhall Spa, Lincs LN10 6TD* Woodhall Spa (0526) 52554

HANSON, Michael Beaumont. b 49. Ox Univ MA. N Ord Course. **d** 84 **p** 85. NSM Leeds St Geo *Ripon* from 84; Chapl Leeds Gr Sch from 84. *9 North Grange Mews, Leeds LS6 2EW* Leeds (0532) 785370

HANSON, Peter Richard. b 45. ARCM. Chich Th Coll 72. **d** 75 **p** 76. C Forest Gate St Edm *Chelmsf* 75-79; C Chingford SS Pet and Paul 79-81; V Leytonstone H Trin Harrow Green 81-86; Dep Chapl HM Pris Wandsworth 86-88; Chapl HM Pris Lewes 88-91; rtd 91. *Flat 2, 39 St Anne's Crescent, Lewes, E Sussex BN7 1SB* Brighton (0273) 471714

HANSON, Richard. b 14. Wells Th Coll 40. **d** 42 **p** 43. Chapl Milan *Eur* 67-72; V Harrow Weald All SS *Lon* 72-77; P-in-c Alfrick w Lulsley and Suckley *Worc* 77-78; P-in-c Leigh w Bransford 77-78; P-in-c Alfrick, Lulsley, Suckley, Leigh and Bransford 78; R 78-82; rtd 82; Perm to Offic *Linc* from 82. *The Rectory Bungalow, Horsington, Lincoln LN3 5EX* Horsington (052685) 696

HANSON, Robert Arthur. b 35. Keele Univ BA57. St Steph Ho Ox 57 Llan St Mich 59. **d** 60 **p** 61. C Longton St Mary and St Chad *Lich* 60-65; Chapl St Mary's Cathl *Edin* 65-69; R Glas St Matt *Glas* 69-79; R Paisley H Trin 79-87; V Walsall St Andr *Lich* from 87. *St Andrew's Vicarage, 28 Bentley New Drive, Walsall WS2 8SB* Walsall (0922) 721581

HANSON, Victor Emmanuel. TCD. **d** 80 **p** 82. NSM Killowen *D & R* from 82. *9 Somerset Drive, Coleraine, Co Londonderry BT51 3DQ* Coleraine (0265) 43392

HAPGOOD-STRICKLAND, Peter Russell. b 57. BA. St Steph Ho Ox. **d** 83 **p** 84. C Ashford *Cant* 83-86; C Sheerness H Trin w St Paul 86-90; V Blackb St Thos w St Jude *Blackb* from 90. *St Jude's Vicarage, 197 Burnley Road, Blackburn BB1 3HW* Blackburn (0254) 52958

HARBIDGE, Adrian Guy. b 48. St Jo Coll Dur BA70. Cuddesdon Coll 73. **d** 75 **p** 76. C Romsey *Win* 75-80; V Bournemouth St Andr 80-86; V Chandler's Ford from 86. *The Vicarage, Hursley Road, Eastleigh, Hants SO5 2FT* Chandler's Ford (0703) 252597

HARBORD, Paul Geoffrey. b 56. Keble Coll Ox BA78 MA86. Chich Th Coll 81. **d** 83 **p** 84. C Rawmarsh w Parkgate *Sheff* 83-86; C Doncaster St Geo 86-90; C-in-c St Edm Anchorage Lane CD from 90. *St Edmund's House, Anchorage Lane, Sprotborough, Doncaster, S Yorkshire DN5 8DT* Doncaster (0302) 781986

HARBORD, Philip James. b 56. St Cath Coll Ox BA77. Cranmer Hall Dur 78. **d** 80 **p** 81. C Enfield St Andr *Lon* 80-83; CMS 84-88; Pakistan 84-88; C Clay Hill St Jo and St Luke *Lon* 88-91; Chapl Wexham Park and Upton Hosps Slough from 91. *The School House, Church Road, Farnham Royal, Slough, Bucks SL2 3AW* Slough (0753) 643233

HARBOTTLE, Anthony Hall Harrison. b 25. LVO79. Ch Coll Cam BA50 MA53. Wycliffe Hall Ox 50. **d** 52 **p** 53. C Boxley *Cant* 52-54; C St Peter-in-Thanet 54-60; R Sandhurst w Newenden 60-68; Chapl R Chpl Windsor Gt Park 68-81; Chapl to HM The Queen from 68; R E Dean w Friston and Jevington *Chich* from 81. *The Rectory, East Dean, Eastbourne, E Sussex BN20 0DL* East Dean (0323) 423266

HARCOURT, Giles Sidford. b 36. Westcott Ho Cam 68. **d** 71 **p** 72. C Bishopwearmouth St Mich w St Hilda *Dur* 71-73; C Fishponds St Mary *Bris* 73-75; Bp's Dom Chapl *S'wark* 75-78; Lic to Offic 78-79; V S Wimbledon H Trin and St Pet 79-88; V Greenwich St Alfege w St Pet and St Paul from 88; Chapl RN Coll Greenwich from 89. *The Vicarage, Park Vista, London SE10 9LZ* 081-858 6828

HARCUS, Arthur Reginald. b 38. Lon Univ BD71 MPhil78. Kelham Th Coll 58. **d** 63 **p** 64. C Old Charlton *S'wark* 63-69; C Felpham w Middleton *Chich* 78-80; P-in-c Donnington 80-85; V Fernhurst 85-91; V Bolney from 91. *The Vicarage, Bolney, Haywards Heath, W Sussex RH17 5QR* Bolney (0444) 881301

HARD, Laurence John Hereward. b 13. TD51. Jes Coll Cam BA35 MA45. Westcott Ho Cam 35. **d** 36 **p** 37. V Cam All SS *Ely* 45-73; Perm to Offic from 73; rtd 78. *58 Jesus Lane, Cambridge CB5 8BS* Cambridge (0223) 355292

HARDAKER, Canon Ian Alexander. b 32. K Coll Lon BD59 AKC59. **d** 60 **p** 61. C Beckenham St Geo *Roch* 60-65; R Eynsford w Lullingstone 65-70; V Chatham St Steph 70-85; RD Roch 78-85; Hon Can Roch Cathl from 83; Clergy Appts Adv from 86. *Fielden House, Little College Street, London SW1P 3SH* 071-222 9544/5

HARDAKER, Leonard. b 24. AKC54 St Boniface Warminster. **d** 54 **p** 55. V Bolney *Chich* 68-81; R Ninfield 81-89; V Hooe 81-89; rtd 89. *7 Dale View, Silsden, Keighley, W Yorkshire BD20 0JP* Keighley (0535) 653871

HARDAKER, Stephen. b 58. Kent Univ BA79 Southn Univ BTh89. Chich Th Coll 86. **d** 89 **p** 90. C Banstead *Guildf* from 89. *14 Glenfield Road, Banstead, Surrey SM7 2DG* Burgh Heath (0737) 353938

HARDCASTLE, Frank Rata. b 05. Lon Univ BA24 BD30 AKC30. **d** 30 **p** 31. C Welwyn Garden City *St Alb* 69-71; rtd 71; Perm to Offic *Ex* from 72. *The Cottage, 30 Ashleigh Road, Exmouth, Devon EX8 2JY* Exmouth (0395) 264491

HARDCASTLE, Nigel John. b 47. Reading Univ BSc68. Qu Coll Birm DipTh71. **d** 72 **p** 73. C Weoley Castle *Birm* 72-75; C Handsworth St Andr 75-78; V Garretts Green 78-86; Exec Sec Ch Computer Project BCC 86-89; R Emmer Green *Ox* from 89. *20 St Barnabas Road, Emmer Green, Reading RG4 8LG* Reading (0734) 478239

HARDCASTLE, Richard. b 08. Leeds Univ BA29 MA31. Coll of Resurr Mirfield 26. **d** 35 **p** 36. V Bilsdale Midcable *York* 60-75; V Bilsdale 60-75; C-in-c Hawnby w Old Byland 63-75; rtd 74. *56 St John's Street, York* York (0904) 652111

HARDCASTLE, Roger Clive. b 52. Southn Univ BSc73. Qu Coll Birm DipTh77. **d** 78 **p** 79. C Walton St Mary *Liv* 78-82; V Pemberton St Fran Kitt Green from 82. *The Vicarage, 42 Sherbourne Road, Kitt Green, Wigan, Lancs WN5 0JA* Wigan (0942) 213227

HARDIE, Ven Archibald George. b 08. Trin Coll Cam BA30 MA35. Westcott Ho Cam 30. **d** 34 **p** 35. Adn W Cumberland *Carl* 70-79; V Haile 71-80; rtd 80. *Grasslees Cottage, Swindon Sharperton, Morpeth, Northd NE65 7AU* Rothbury (0669) 40274

HARDIE, John Blair. b 16. MBE46. LDS FDS MRCS38 MRCSE66. Edin Th Coll 73. **d** 76 **p** 76. Chapl St Paul's Cathl Dundee *Bre* 76-86; rtd 86; Hon C Carnoustie *Bre*

307

from 86. *4 Lammerton Terrace, Dundee DD4 7BW* Dundee (0382) 44147

HARDIE, Stephen. b 41. AKC67. **d** 68 **p** 69. C Roxbourne St Andr *Lon* 68-73; C Colchester St Mary V *Chelmsf* 73-76; R Wivenhoe from 76. *The Rectory, 44 Belle Vue Road, Wivenhoe, Colchester CO7 9LD* Wivenhoe (020682) 5174

HARDING, Alec James. b 61. St Andr Univ MA83 DTh. Cranmer Hall Dur 86. **d** 89 **p** 90. C Thirsk *York* from 89. *73 Hambleton Avenue, Thirsk, N Yorkshire YO7 1EG* Thirsk (0845) 523767

HARDING, Brian Edward. b 38. ALCD65. **d** 65 **p** 66. C Chislehurst Ch Ch *Roch* 65-68; P-in-c Baxenden *Blackb* 68-70; V 70-88; V Douglas from 88. *The Vicarage, 5 Tan House Lane, Parbold, Wigan, Lancs WN8 7HG* Parbold (0257) 462350

HARDING, Clifford Maurice. b 22. Leeds Univ BA47. Coll of Resurr Mirfield 46. **d** 48 **p** 49. V Oldham St Jo *Man* 59-65; Lic to Offic *Blackb* from 65; rtd 87. *31 Riley Avenue, St Annes, Lytham St Annes, Lancs FY8 1HZ* St Annes (0253) 725138

HARDING, David Anthony. b 30. St Edm Hall Ox BA54 MA58 Dur Univ MPhil85. Ely Th Coll 54. **d** 56 **p** 57. C Fulham All SS *Lon* 56-59; Lect Armenian Sem Istanbul 59-62; Chapl K Sch Cant 63-68; Westmr Sch 68-74; St Bede Coll Dur 74-75; SS Hild and Bede Coll 75-80; Lic to Offic *S'well* from 80; Asst Chapl Worksop Coll Notts 80-82; Chapl from 82. *Worksop College, Worksop, Notts S80 3AP* Worksop (0909) 472286

HARDING, Miss Eileen Thelma. b 18. St Mich Ho Ox 58. dss 60 **d** 87. Sec Dioc Bd for Women's Min *Chich* 63-77; Hd Dss 68-81; Dioc Lay Min Adv 77-81; rtd 81; Broadwater St Mary *Chich* 84-87; Hon Par Dn from 87. *199 King Edward Avenue, Worthing, W Sussex BN14 8DW* Worthing (0903) 39867

HARDING, Frederick Arthur. b 16. S'wark Ord Course 75. **d** 77 **p** 78. NSM Oxted *S'wark* from 77. *33 Crabwood, 13 Blue House Lane, Oxted, Surrey RH8 0UA* Oxted (0883) 716454

HARDING, Geoffrey Clarence. b 09. MC44. St Jo Coll Ox BA31 MA35. Bps' Coll Cheshunt 32. **d** 32 **p** 33. Sec and Dir Ch's Coun of Health and Healing 59-74; C St Mich Cornhill w St Pet le Poer etc *Lon* 70-74; V St Mary Woolnoth 74-83; rtd 83; Hon C St Mary Woolnoth *Lon* 83-87. *1 Oakwood Road, London NW11 6QU* 081-458 5126

HARDING, Herbert Collison. b 95. **d** 51 **p** 51. V Leamington Priors St Mary *Cov* 55-64; rtd 64; Perm to Offic *St E* from 82. *Room 10, Shaftesbury House, 5 Cowper Street, Ipswich IP4 5JD* Ipswich (0473) 719182

HARDING, John James. b 08. BEM. Worc Ord Coll 60. **d** 62 **p** 63. V Stourpaine *Sarum* 66-71; P-in-c Bockleton w Leysters *Heref* 71-76; rtd 76. *Flat 4, Trafalgar Court, 2 Richmond Road, Southsea, Hants PO5 2NU* Portsmouth (0705) 839195

HARDING, John Stuart Michael. b 45. St Jo Coll Nottm 79. **d** 81 **p** 82. C Clifton *S'well* 81-87; V Broxtowe from 87. *The Vicarage, Frinton Road, Broxtowe Estate, Nottingham NG8 6GR* Nottingham (0602) 278837

HARDING, John William Christopher. b 31. St Jo Coll Dur BA55. **d** 58 **p** 59. C Wigan St Cath *Liv* 58-60; C Much Woolton 60-63; V Whiston 63-73; V Birkdale St Jo from 73. *St John's Vicarage, 17 Kirkstall Road, Southport, Merseyside PR8 4RA* Southport (0704) 68318

HARDING, Mrs Marion. b 33. Gilmore Course 75. dss 85 **d** 87. Hertf St Andr *St Alb* 85-87; Par Dn from 87. *41 Calton Avenue, Hertford SG14 2ER* Hertford (0992) 587348

HARDING, Michael Anthony John. b 37. Brasted Th Coll 67 Sarum Th Coll 68. **d** 71 **p** 72. C Forest Hill Ch Ch *S'wark* 71-72; C Catford St Laur 72-74; C Leominster *Heref* 74-77; V Ditton Priors 77-86; R Neenton 77-86; P-in-c Aston Botterell w Wheathill and Loughton 77-86; P-in-c Burwarton w N Cleobury 77-86; R Ditton Priors w Neenton, Burwarton etc from 86. *The Vicarage, Ditton Priors, Bridgnorth, Shropshire WV16 6SQ* Ditton Priors (074634) 636

HARDING, Preb Michael David. b 38. Man Univ BA61. Lich Th Coll 61. **d** 63 **p** 64. C Hednesford *Lich* 63-67; C Blurton 67-70; V Newc St Paul from 70; RD Newc from 87; Preb Lich Cathl from 89. *St Paul's Vicarage, Hawkstone Close, Newcastle, Staffs ST5 1HT* Newcastle-under-Lyme (0782) 617913

HARDING, Peter Edward. b 39. Univ Coll Ox BA61 MA69. Wycliffe Hall Ox 62. **d** 64 **p** 65. C Westlands St Andr CD *Lich* 64-67; C Hinckley H Trin *Leic* 67-69; R Sutton cum Duckmanton *Derby* 69-75; P-in-c Elvaston

and Shardlow from 75. *The Vicarage, Elvaston, Thulston, Derby DE7 3EQ* Derby (0332) 71790

HARDING, Peter Gordon. b 45. **d** 79 **p** 80. C Kirkheaton *Wakef* 79-82; NSM New Sleaford *Linc* from 90. *67 The Drove, Sleaford, Lincs NG34 7AS* Sleaford (0529) 303849

HARDING, Peter Richard. b 46. AKC69. St Aug Coll Cant 69. **d** 70 **p** 71. C Chorley St Pet *Blackb* 70-73; C Ribbleton 73-74; C St Marylebone w H Trin *Lon* 74-80; P-in-c St Marylebone St Cypr 80-82; V from 82; AD Westmr St Marylebone from 83; Sub-Warden Guild of St Raphael from 88. *St Cyprian's Vicarage, 16 Clarence Gate Gardens, London NW1 6AY* 071-402 6979

HARDING, Richard Michael. b 42. St Alb Minl Tr Scheme. **d** 83 **p** 84. C Pershore w Pinvin, Wick and Birlingham *Worc* 83-86; V Longdon, Castlemorton, Bushley, Queenhill etc from 86. *The Vicarage, Longdon, Tewkesbury, Glos GL20 6AT* Birtsmorton (068481) 256

HARDING, Rolf John. b 22. Oak Hill Th Coll 44 Lon Coll of Div 46. **d** 49 **p** 50. C Sydenham H Trin *S'wark* 49-52; C Harold Wood *Chelmsf* 52-53; Min Harold Hill St Paul CD 53-61; V Coopersale from 61; Chapl St Marg Hosp Epping from 73; Chapl W Essex HA from 86. *The Vicarage, Coopersale Common, Epping, Essex CM16 7QT* Epping (0378) 72188

HARDING, Miss Sylvia. b 23. St Mich Ho Ox 55. dss 64 **d** 87. Midl Area Sec CPAS 66-71; Patchway *Bris* 71-78; Sec Coun of Women's Min *Bris* 77-84; rtd 84; Westbury-on-Trym St Alb *Bris* 86-87; Hon Par Dn from 87. *24 Woodhill Road, Portishead, Bristol BS20 9EU* Bristol (0272) 848638

HARDINGHAM, Paul David. b 52. Lon Univ BSc74 Fitzw Coll Cam BA77. Ridley Hall Cam 75. **d** 78 **p** 79. C Cam St Martin *Ely* 78-81; C Jesmond Clayton Memorial *Newc* 81-88; C Harborne Heath *Birm* from 88. *60 Station Road, Birmingham B17 9LP* 021-427 6907

HARDMAN, Mrs Christine Elizabeth. b 51. Lon Univ BSc(Econ)73. St Alb Minl Tr Scheme 81. dss 84 **d** 87. Markyate Street *St Alb* 84-87; Par Dn 87-88; Tutor St Alb Minl Tr Scheme 88-91; Course Dir St Alb Minl Tr Scheme from 91. *Cell View, High Street, Markyate, St Albans, Herts AL3 8PD* Luton (0582) 840285

HARDMAN, Edward Foster. b 02. St Chad's Coll Dur BA23 DipTh24 MA27. **d** 26 **p** 28. Chapl All SS Convent Colney 65-68; rtd 68. *c/o B W Bradbury Esq, 7 Bath Street, Lytham, Lancs FY8 5ES* Lytham (0253) 736670

HARDMAN, Geoffrey James. b 41. Birm Univ BA63. N Ord Course 77. **d** 80 **p** 81. NSM Latchford St Jas *Ches* from 80. *48 Denbury Avenue, Stockton Heath, Warrington WA4 2BW* Warrington (0925) 64064

HARDMAN, Harry. b 10. Man Egerton Hall 36. **d** 38 **p** 39. V Fence in Pendle *Blackb* 68-75; rtd 75. *22 Ardleigh Court, Shenfield, Brentwood, Essex CM15 8LZ* Brentwood (0277) 226739

HARDMAN, Canon Peter George. b 35. Man Univ BSc56. Ridley Hall Cam 58. **d** 60 **p** 61. C Oldham St Paul *Man* 60-63; Lic to Offic 63-67; NW England Area Sec SCM 63-64; NW England Area Sec CEM 64-67; Asst Chapl Marlborough Coll Wilts 67-72; Chapl 72-79; P-in-c Wareham *Sarum* 79-80; TR from 80; Can and Preb Sarum Cathl from 87; RD Purbeck from 89. *The Rectory, Wareham, Dorset BH20 4LQ* Wareham (0929) 552684

HARDWICK, Dennis Egerton. b 26. St Deiniol's Hawarden. **d** 82 **p** 83. NSM Lache cum Saltney *Ches* 82-85; P-in-c Backford 85-88; P-in-c Capenhurst 87-88; R Backford and Capenhurst from 88. *The Vicarage, Grove Road, Mollington, Chester CH2 4DG* Great Mollington (0244) 851071

HARDWICK, Graham John. b 42. Qu Coll Birm 68. **d** 70 **p** 71. C Watford St Mich *St Alb* 70-73; C N Mymms 73-75; Youth Officer Cov Cathl *Cov* 75-81; Chapl Lanchester Poly 76-81; V Nuneaton St Nic from 81. *61 Ambleside Way, Nuneaton, Warks CV11 6AU* Nuneaton (0203) 346900

HARDWICK, John Audley. b 28. Em Coll Cam BA51 MA55. Westcott Ho Cam 51. **d** 53 **p** 54. Chapl St Edm Sch Hindhead 63-86; Asst Hd 72-90; Lic to Offic *Guildf* 63-90; rtd 90. *Hillcroft, Kettle Lane, Audlem, Crewe CW3 0DR* Audlem (0270) 811545

HARDWICK, Mrs Susan Frances. b 44. Warw Univ BA81. Qu Coll Birm 82. dss 85 **d** 87. Chilvers Coton w Astley *Cov* 85-87; C from 87. *61 Ambleside Way, Nuneaton, Warks CV11 6AU* Nuneaton (0203) 346900

HARDWICK, Canon William George. b 14. Lich Th Coll 40. **d** 44 **p** 45. C Northn Ch Ch *Pet* 44-46; C Leic St Paul *Leic* 46-49; Basutoland 49-52; S Africa 52-78 and from 79; V Brigstock w Stanion *Pet* 78-79. *24 Lyndhurst Place, Widenham, Umkomaas, 4170 South Africa* Scottburgh (323) 31623

HARDWICKE, Paul Anthony. b 49. Linc Th Coll 74. **d** 77 **p** 78. C Rickerscote *Lich* 77-79; C Tamworth 79-84; Res Min 84-86; V Brereton from 86. *The Vicarage, Brereton, Rugeley, Staffs WS15 1DU* Rugeley (0889) 582466

HARDY, Anthony. **d** 86 **p** 87. Hon C Malden St Jas *S'wark* from 86. *48 Blake's Lane, New Malden, Surrey KT3 6NR* 081-949 0703

HARDY, Anthony William. b 56. Man Univ BEd79 MEd86. St Jo Coll Nottm LTh88. **d** 88 **p** 89. C Pennington *Man* from 88. *11 Ruby Grove, Leigh, Lancs WN7 4JW* Leigh (0942) 602246

HARDY, Bertram Frank. b 08. Lich Th Coll 51. **d** 52 **p** 52. C-in-c Lovington *B & W* 69-74; C-in-c N w S Barrow 69-74; rtd 74; Perm to Offic *B & W* from 74. *7 Churchill Avenue, Wells, Somerset BA5 3JE* Wells (0749) 74696

HARDY, Very Rev Brian Albert. b 31. St Jo Coll Ox BA51 DipTh55 MA58. Westcott Ho Cam 55. **d** 57 **p** 58 C Rugeley *Lich* 57-62; Chapl Down Coll Cam 62-66; C-in-c Livingston Miss *Edin* 66-74; Preb Heref Cathl *Heref* 74-78; Ch Planning Officer Telford 74-78; RD Telford Severn Gorge 75-78; Chapl Edin Th Coll 78-82; Chapl Edin R Infirmary 82-86; R Edin St Columba *Edin* from 82; Dean Edin from 86. *2/2 Boswell's Court, 352 Castlehill, Edinburgh EH1 2NF* 031-225 1634

HARDY, Christopher Richard. b 52. R Holloway Coll Lon BMus77 Southn Univ BTh90. Chich Th Coll 87. **d** 90 **p** 91. C Kenton *Lon* from 90. *Holy Spirit House, 660 Kenton Road, Kenton, Middx HA3 9QN* 081-204 1446

HARDY, Prof Daniel Wayne. b 30. Haverford Coll (USA) BA52. Gen Th Sem (NY) STB55 STM63. **d** 55 **p** 56. USA 55-61 and from 90; Fell and Tutor Gen Th Sem 59-61; Lic to Offic *Ox* 61-65; Lect Modern Th Thought Birm Univ 65-75; Sen Lect 75-86; Hon C Londonderry *Birm* 67-90; Van Mildert Prof Div Dur Univ 86-90; Can Res Dur Cathl *Dur* 86-90; Dir Cen Th Inquiry from 90. *Center of Theological Inquiry, Princeton, New Jersey 08540, USA* Princeton (609) 683-4797

HARDY, Miss Janet Frances. b 59. Newc Univ BA81 CertEd82. Trin Coll Bris 87. **d** 89. Par Dn Sheff St Paul Wordsworth Avenue *Sheff* from 89. *19 Lytton Drive, Sheffield S5 8AZ* Sheffield (0742) 320409

HARDY, John Charles. b 22. Sheff Univ BA48 DipEd49 Lon Univ DipTh53. St Deiniol's Hawarden 66. **d** 67 **p** 68. Hon C Chorley St Laur *Blackb* 67-87; rtd 87. *4 Glamis Drive, Chorley, Lancs PR7 1LX* Chorley (02572) 65743

HARDY, John Lewis Daniel. b 26. St Chad's Coll Dur BA51 DipTh52. **d** 52 **p** 53. C Hucknall Torkard *S'well* 52-58; V Harworth 58-65; V Sutton in Ashfield St Mary 65-85; R Keyworth from 85; P-in-c Stanton-on-the-Wolds from 85; RD Bingham S from 91. *The Rectory, Keyworth, Nottingham NG12 5FD* Plumtree (06077) 2017

HARDY, Michael Frederick Bryan. b 36. Selw Coll Cam BA60 MA64. Linc Th Coll 60. **d** 62 **p** 63. C Pontefract St Giles *Wakef* 62-66; V Lightcliffe 66-69; V Hightown 69-78; V Birkby 78-85; C Boultham *Linc* 88-89; V Misterton and W Stockwith *S'well* from 89. *The Vicarage, 5 Minster Road, Misterton, Doncaster, S Yorkshire DN10 4AP* Gainsborough (0427) 890270

HARDY, Michael Henry. b 33. Qu Coll Birm 85. **d** 86 **p** 87. C Leic St Jas *Leic* 86-88; R Arnesby w Shearsby and Bruntingthorpe from 88. *The Vicarage, Meadow Court, Fenny Lane, Shearsby, Lutterworth, Leics LE1 7PL* Leicester (0533) 478371

HARDY, Michael John. b 35. Keble Coll Ox BA58 MA66. Cuddesdon Coll 59. **d** 61 **p** 62. C Dalton-in-Furness *Carl* 61-64; C Harborne St Pet *Birm* 64-68; Min Can Ripon Cathl *Ripon* 68-73; Appt and Tr Sec USPG 73-80; R Stretford St Pet *Man* 80-91; P-in-c Newton Hall *Dur* from 91. *31 York Crescent, Durham DH1 5PT* 091-386 8049

HARDY, Michael Wilfred. b 27. St Chad's Coll Dur BA52. Coll of Resurr Mirfield. **d** 54 **p** 55. C Cullercoats St Geo *Newc* 54-57; Africa 58-62; C Ponteland 63; C Seaton Hirst 63-66; C Gosforth All SS 66-69; Australia from 69. *37 Railway Road, Collinsville, Queensland, Australia 4804* Collinsville (77) 855255

HARDY, Paul Richard. b 30. **d** 59 **p** 60. C Corringham *Chelmsf* 59-61; C Prittlewell All SS 61-64; Tanzania from 64. *PO Box 2184, Dar-es-Salaam, Tanzania*

HARDY, Pauline. b 41. CertEd. Linc Th Coll 85. **d** 87. Par Dn Walsall Wood *Lich* 87-89; Par Dn Buckm *Ox* from 89. *Church House, 5 Chandos Close, Buckingham MK18 1AW* Buckingham (0280) 812160

✠**HARDY, Rt Rev Robert Maynard.** b 36. Clare Coll Cam BA60 MA64. Cuddesdon Coll 60. **d** 62 **p** 63 **c** 80. C Langley St Aid CD *Man* 62-64; C Langley All SS and

Martyrs 64-65; Chapl and Lect Th Selw Coll Cam 65-72; V Boreham Wood All SS *St Alb* 72-75; Dir St Alb Minl Tr Scheme 75-80; P-in-c Aspley Guise *St Alb* 75-79; P-in-c Husborne Crawley w Ridgmont 76-79; R Aspley Guise w Husborne Crawley and Ridgmont 80; Suff Bp Maidstone *Cant* 80-87; Bp HM Pris from 85; Bp Linc from 87. *Bishop's House, Eastgate, Lincoln LN2 1QQ* Lincoln (0522) 534701

HARDY, Thomas Woodburn. b 26. Bp's Univ Lennoxville BA48. **d** 49 **p** 50. P-in-c Fulham St Aug *Lon* 68-73; V 73-91; rtd 91. *58 Boston Gardens, Brentford, Middx TW8 9LP* 081-847 4533

HARDY, Wallis Bertrand. b 03. Lon Univ BSc24. St Steph Ho Ox 53. **d** 54 **p** 55. Chapl Community of St Denys Warminster 64-75; rtd 75. *Ingram House, Whiteley Village, Walton-on-Thames, Surrey KT12 4EJ* Walton-on-Thames (0932) 856315

HARDY, William Marshall Conyers. b 25. Linc Th Coll 55. **d** 56 **p** 57. V Belford *Newc* 62-77; RD Bamburgh and Glendale 71-77; V Riding Mill 77-90; RD Corbridge 82-88; Hon Can Newc Cathl 88-91; rtd 90. *5 Riding Dene, Mickley, Stocksfield, Northd NE43 7DG* Hexham (0434) 682009

HARE, David (Brother David Columba). b 46. Qu Coll Birm. **d** 83 **p** 83. SSF from 83; Bp's Dom Chapl *Birm* 83-87; V Handsworth St Mich from 87. *St Michael's Vicarage, Soho Avenue, Birmingham B18 5LB*

HARE, Frank Richard Knight. b 22. Trin Hall Cam BA46 MA48. Cuddesdon Coll 46. **d** 48 **p** 49. V Steyning *Chich* 62-70; R Ashurst 62-70; TV Raveningham *Nor* 70-71; TR Barnham Broom 71-79; V Buxton w Oxnead 79-86; R Lammas w Lt Hautbois 79-86; rtd 86; Perm to Offic *St E* from 86. *14 Lee Road, Aldeburgh, Suffolk IP15 5HG* Aldeburgh (0728) 453372

HARE, Stanley Thomas. b 23. Roch Th Coll. **d** 62 **p** 63. V Sheff St Barn *Sheff* 69-73; Chapl Farnborough and Orpington Hosps 73-85; rtd 85. *15 Marshmallan Road, Mount Hawke, Truro, Cornwall TR4 8DL*

✠**HARE, Rt Rev Thomas Richard.** b 22. Trin Coll Ox BA48 MA53. Westcott Ho Cam 48. **d** 50 **p** 51 **c** 71. C Haltwhistle *Newc* 50-52; Bp's Dom Chapl *Man* 52-59; Can Res Carl Cathl *Carl* 59-65; R Barrow St Geo w St Luke 65-69; Adn Westmorland and Furness 65-71; Hon Can Carl Cathl 65-71; V Winster 69-71; Suff Bp Pontefract *Wakef* from 71. *Highfield, 306 Barnsley Road, Wakefield, W Yorkshire WF2 6AX* Wakefield (0924) 256935

✠**HARE DUKE, Rt Rev Michael Geoffrey.** b 25. Trin Coll Ox BA49 MA51. Westcott Ho Cam 50. **d** 52 **p** 53 **c** 69. C St Jo Wood *Lon* 52-56; V Bury St Mark *Man* 56-62; Past Dir Clinical Th Assn Nottm 62-64; Past Consultant 64-69; V Daybrook *S'well* 64-69; Bp St Andr *St And* from 69. *Bishop's House, Fairmount Road, Perth PH2 7AP* Perth (0738) 21580

HARES, David Ronald Walter. b 40. Qu Coll Cam BA63 MA67 CertEd. Westcott Ho Cam 64. **d** 66 **p** 67. C Cannock *Lich* 66-69; Chapl Peterho Cam 69-72; Asst Master Chesterton Sch Cam 72-74; V Kesgrave *St E* from 74. *The Vicarage, Kesgrave, Ipswich IP5 7JQ* Ipswich (0473) 622181

HAREWOOD, John Rupert. b 24. Man Univ BA48. Sarum & Wells Th Coll 76. **d** 79 **p** 80. NSM Taunton St Jas *B & W* 79-82; TV Camelot Par 82-89; rtd 89. *The Vicarage, Kenton, Exeter EX6 8NG* Starcross (0626) 890214

HARFIELD, William Charles. b 04. **d** 36 **p** 36. R Stedham w Iping *Chich* 68-75; rtd 75; Perm to Offic *Chich* from 78. *Briarwood, Vanzell Road, Easebourne, Midhurst, W Sussex GU29 9BA* Midhurst (073081) 3810

HARFORD, Julian Gray. b 29. Univ Coll Ox BA52 MA59 Lon Univ DipGCE58. Qu Coll Birm DipTh64. **d** 64 **p** 65. C W End *Win* 64-67; C Chearsley w Nether Winchendon *Ox* 67-77; C Chilton All SS 72-77; R Westbury w Turweston, Shalstone and Biddlesden 77-86; C Chenies and Lt Chalfont 86-87; C Chenies and Lt Chalfont, Latimer and Flaunden from 87. *The Rectory, Latimer, Chesham, Bucks HP5 1UA* Little Chalfont (0494) 762281

HARFORD, Michael Rivers Dundas. b 26. Trin Coll Cam BA49 MA51. Westcott Ho Cam 50. **d** 52 **p** 53. V Childwall St Dav *Liv* 66-71; Australia from 71; Adn Albany 76-79; Adn Swan 86-89; Adn Mitchell 90-91; rtd 91. *219 James Street, Guildford, W Australia 6055* Guildford (69) 279-1141

HARFORD, Timothy William. b 58. Nottm Univ BTh89. Linc Th Coll 86. **d** 89 **p** 90. C Minehead *B & W* from 89. *75 Summerland Avenue, Minehead, Somerset TA24 5BW* Minehead (0643) 702868

HARGER, Robin Charles Nicholas. b 49. BTh. Sarum & Wells Th Coll 78. **d** 81 **p** 82. C Charlton Kings St Mary *Glouc* 81-85; C Folkestone St Mary and St Eanswythe *Cant* 85-89; TV Langley and Parkfield *Man* from 89. *Holy Trinity Vicarage, 5 Wentworth Close, Middleton, Manchester M24 4AE* 061-653 1386

HARGRAVE, Alan Lewis. b 50. Birm Univ BSc73 PhD77. Ridley Hall Cam 87. **d** 89 **p** 90. C Cam H Trin w St Andr Gt *Ely* from 89. *42 Pretoria Road, Cambridge CB4 1HE* Cambridge (0223) 311144

HARGRAVE, William Stallard Lawrence. b 01. G&C Coll Cam BA27 MA31. **d** 42 **p** 42. R Bincombe w Broadwey *Sarum* 55-66; rtd 66. *2 King Street, Wilton, Salisbury* Salisbury (0722) 742257

HARGREAVE, James David. b 44. ALCM89 LTCL90 Lon Univ BA66 CertEd68. Coll of Resurr Mirfield DipTh72. **d** 73 **p** 74. C Houghton le Spring *Dur* 73-77; C Gateshead St Cuth w St Paul 77-79; V Trimdon 79-87; C-in-c Stockton Green Vale H Trin CD from 87. *4 Greymouth Close, Hartburn, Stockton-on-Tees, Cleveland TS18 5LF* Stockton-on-Tees (0642) 585749

HARGREAVES, Arthur Cecil Monsarrat. b 19. Trin Hall Cam BA42 MA46. Westcott Ho Cam 47. **d** 49 **p** 50. India 70-76; Gen Sec Conf of Br Miss Socs 76-79; Hon C Croydon St Aug *Cant* 79-81; V Marden 81-86; rtd 86. *Windrush Cottage, 87 Downscourt Road, Purley, Surrey CR8 1BJ* 081-668 8871

HARGREAVES, Dr Arthur Walsh. b 34. FRCSE FRCS Man Univ MB, ChB. St Deiniol's Hawarden. **d** 90. NSM Baguley *Man* from 90. *Greenways, Woodbourne Road, Sale, Chesire M33 3SX* 091-973 7674

HARGREAVES, John. b 43. St Jo Coll Nottm 86. **d** 88 **p** 89. C Werneth *Man* 88-91; TV Rochdale from 91. *St Peter's Vicarage, Church Road, Rochdale, Lancs OL16 5NW* Rochdale (0706) 522291

HARGREAVES, Canon John Henry Monsarrat. b 11. Trin Coll Cam BA33 MA37. Westcott Ho Cam 35. **d** 37 **p** 38. CMS (Nigeria) 43-57 and 59-63; SPCK 65-90; C in c Sevenoaks St Luke CD *Roch* 65-83; RD Sevenoaks 74-79; Hon Can Roch Cathl 81-83; rtd 83. *20 St Pauls Road West, Dorking, Surrey RH4 2HU* Dorking (0306) 888648

HARGREAVES, John Rodney. b 36. Open Univ BA74. St Deiniol's Hawarden 74. **d** 75 **p** 75. C Pontypool *Mon* 75-77; C Llanedeyrn 77-79; Chapl HM Pris Aylesbury 79-83; Stafford 83-88; Asst Chapl Gen of Pris (N) 88-90; Asst Chapl Gen of Pris from 90. *c/o Home Office, Calthorpe House, Hagley Road, Birmingham B16 8QR* 021-455 9855

HARGREAVES, John Wilson. b 46. Aber Univ BScFor67 Birm Poly DipVG73. Westcott Ho Cam 84. **d** 86 **p** 87. C Rugby St Andr *Cov* 86-90; TV Daventry *Pet* from 90; P-in-c Welton w Ashby St Ledgers from 90. *The Vicarage, Welton, Daventry, Northants NN11 5JP* Daventry (0327) 705563

HARGREAVES, Raymond. Open Univ BA79. Ripon Hall Ox 72. **d** 73 **p** 74. C Stanwix *Carl* 73-78; Chapl St Olave's Sch York from 78. *21 Oak Tree Lane, Haxby, York YO3 8YL* York (0904) 763127

HARGREAVES-STEAD, Terence Desmond. b 32. Edin Th Coll 61. **d** 63 **p** 64. C Walney Is *Carl* 63-66; Chapl Withington Univ Hosp Man 66-72; V Westleigh St Paul *Man* from 72. *St Paul's Vicarage, Westleigh Lane, Leigh, Lancs WN7 5NW* Atherton (0942) 882883

HARINGTON, Roger John Urquhart. b 48. Trin Hall Cam BA70 MA71. Coll of Resurr Mirfield 72. **d** 75 **p** 76. C Liv Our Lady and St Nic w St Anne *Liv* 75-78; Asst Chapl Leeds Univ and Poly *Ripon* 78-81; C Moor Allerton 81; TV 81-86; Dioc Drama Adv (Jabbok Theatre Co) from 86. *13 Moorfields, Leeds LS13 3JZ* Leeds (0532) 552557

HARKER, Harold Aidan. b 35. **d** 82 **p** 83. OSB from 53; C Reading St Giles *Ox* 82-83; Lic to Offic 83-87; C Halstead St Andr w H Trin and Greenstead Green *Chelmsf* 87-89; P-in-c Belchamp St Paul from 89. *The Vicarage, Belchamp St Paul, Sudbury CO10 7BT* Clare (0787) 277210

HARKER, Dr John Hadlett. b 37. CEng FIChemE MInstE CChem MRSC Dur Univ BSc59 Newc Univ PhD67. NE Ord Course 81. **d** 84 **p** 85. C Earsdon *Newc* 84-87; P-in-c Longhorsley 87-91; V Bassenthwaite, Isel and Setmurthy *Carl* from 91. *The Vicarage, Bassenthwaite, Keswick, Cumbria CA12 4QG* Bassenthwaite Lake (07687) 76410

HARKER, Stephan John. b 47. Em Coll Cam BA68 MA72. Westcott Ho Cam 70. **d** 72 **p** 73. C Marton *Blackb* 72-76; C Preston St Matt 76-79; C Fleetwood 79-80; Chapl Charterhouse Godalming from 81. *Lower Oakhurst,*

Frith Hill Road, Godalming, Surrey GU7 2ED Godalming (0483) 422155

HARKIN, John Patrick. b 53. Oak Hill Th Coll DipHE89. **d** 89 **p** 90. C Wisley w Pyrford *Guildf* from 89. *33 Engliff Lane, Woking, Surrey GU22 8SU* Byfleet (0932) 351070

HARKNESS, Verney Austin Barnett. b 19. Lon Univ BA40 DipTh63. Ridley Hall Cam 46. **d** 47 **p** 48. R Stoke next Guildf St Jo *Guildf* 63-72; Sri Lanka 73-77; P-in-c Walkington *York* 78-79; P-in-c Bishop Burton 78-79; R Bishop Burton w Walkington 79-84; rtd 85. *20 Wylies Road, Beverley, N Humberside HU17 7AP* Hull (0482) 881924

HARLAND, Albert Henry. b 17. Oak Hill Th Coll 57. **d** 59 **p** 61. V Renhold *St Alb* 69-80; rtd 80; Perm to Offic *St Alb* from 80. *123 Putnoe Lane, Bedford MK41 8LB* Bedford (0234) 45831

HARLAND, Harold William James. b 35. Hertf Coll Ox BA59 MA63. Clifton Th Coll 59. **d** 61 **p** 62. C Reigate St Mary *S'wark* 61-64; C Farnborough *Guildf* 64-68; V Walmley *Birm* 68-74; V Bromley Ch Ch *Roch* 74-86; V Foord St Jo *Cant* from 86. *St John's Vicarage, 4 Cornwallis Avenue, Folkestone, Kent CT19 5JA* Folkestone (0303) 53732

✠**HARLAND, Rt Rev Ian.** b 32. Peterho Cam BA56 MA60. Wycliffe Hall Ox 58. **d** 60 **p** 61 **c** 85. C Melton Mowbray w Thorpe Arnold *Leic* 60-63; V Oughtibridge *Sheff* 63-72; V Sheff St Cuth 72-75; P-in-c Brightside All SS 72-75; RD Ecclesfield 73-75; V Rotherham 75-79; RD Rotherham 76-79; Adn Doncaster 79-85; P-in-c Dunscroft 81-83; Hon Can Blackb Cathl *Blackb* 85-89; Suff Bp Lanc 85-89; Bp Carl from 89. *Rose Castle, Dalston, Carlisle CA5 7BZ* Raughton Head (06996) 274

HARLEY, Dr Anne Marion. b 39. St Hugh's Coll Ox MA64 DPhil65. Sarum & Wells Th Coll 85. **d** 88. Par Dn Isleworth St Jo *Lon* 88-91; Chapl Asst St Thos Hosp Lon from 91. *12 Canterbury House, Royal Street, London SE1 7LN*

HARLEY, Canon Brian Nigel. b 30. Clare Coll Cam BA53 MA57. Cuddesdon Coll 53. **d** 55 **p** 56. C Basingstoke *Win* 55-60; TV 71-73; TR 73-80; C W End 60-61; C-in-c Southn St Chris Thornhill CD 61-71; Hon Can Win Cathl from 75; V Eastleigh from 80; RD Eastleigh from 85. *The Vicarage, 1 Cedar Road, Eastleigh, Hants SO5 5DB* Eastleigh (0703) 612073

HARLEY, Christopher David. b 41. Selw Coll Cam BA63 MA69 Bris Univ PGCE64. Clifton Th Coll 64. **d** 66 **p** 67. C Finchley Ch Ch *Lon* 66-69; Hon C 75-78; Ethiopia 70-75; Hd of UK Miss CMJ 75-78; Lect All Nations Chr Coll Ware 78-85; Prin from 85; Chmn Lon Inst of Contemporary Christianity from 88; Chmn CMJ from 89; Lic to Offic *St Alb* from 79. *All Nations Christian College, Easneye, Ware, Herts SG12 8LX* Ware (0920) 461243

HARLEY, David Bertram. b 22. Down Coll Cam BA50 MA55. Westcott Ho Cam 55. **d** 56 **p** 58. Chapl Stamford Sch Lincs 58-87; Lic to Offic *Linc* from 59; Confrater Browne's Hosp Stamford from 87; rtd 87. *Beggars' Roost, Priory Road, Stamford, Lincs PE9 2ES* Stamford (0780) 63403

HARLEY, Michael. b 50. AKC73 Ch Ch Coll Cant DipEd74. St Aug Coll Cant 75. **d** 75 **p** 76. C Chatham St Wm *Roch* 75-78; C-in-c Weeke *Win* 78-81; V Southn St Mary Extra 81-86; V Hurstbourne Tarrant, Faccombe, Vernham Dean etc from 86. *The Vicarage, Hurstbourne Tarrant, Andover, Hants SP11 0AH* Hurstbourne Tarrant (026476) 222

HARLEY, Robert Peter. b 59. Leic Univ BA81. Sarum & Wells Th Coll 86. **d** 89 **p** 90. C Thornbury *Glouc* from 89. *50 Park Road, Thornbury, Bristol BS12 1HR* Thornbury (0454) 412656

HARLEY, Roger Newcomb. b 38. Ely Th Coll 61. **d** 64 **p** 65. C Plymouth St Pet *Ex* 64-66; C Heston *Lon* 66-69; C Maidstone All SS w St Phil and H Trin *Cant* 69-73; R Temple Ewell w Lydden 73-79; P-in-c Shirley St Geo 79-81; V 81-84; V Croydon H Sav *S'wark* from 85. *Holy Saviour Vicarage, 96 Lodge Road, Croydon CR0 2PF* 081-684 2526

HARLEY, William Ernest. b 08. St Pet Coll Ox BA32 MA37. Wycliffe Hall Ox 32. **d** 33 **p** 34. PC Oakridge *Glouc* 60-69; V 69-72; V Leck *Blackb* 72-75; rtd 75; Perm to Offic *Bris* 86-87. *Wing 6, St Monica Home, Cote Lane, Westbury-on-Trym, Bristol BS9 3UN* Bristol (0272) 622590

HARLOW, Antony Francis. b 24. Pemb Coll Cam BA50 MA55. Oak Hill Th Coll 84. **d** 85 **p** 86. NSM Watford St Luke *St Alb* 85-86; CMS 86-91; Uganda 86-91; Perm to Offic *St Alb* from 90. *23 Elizabeth Court,*

Hampstead Road, Watford WD1 3LR Watford (0923) 39111

HARLOW, Canon Derrick Peter. b 30. St Jo Coll Cam BA53 MA57. Ridley Hall Cam 53. **d** 55 **p** 56. C Barking St Marg *Chelmsf* 55-58; V Leyton Em 58-63; V Goodmayes All SS 63-75; R Thundersley 76-83; TR Saffron Walden w Wendens Ambo and Littlebury from 83; Hon Can Chelmsf Cathl from 84. *The Rectory, 17 Borough Lane, Saffron Walden, Essex CB11 4AG* Saffron Walden (0799) 23130

HARLOW-TRIGG, Richard John St Clair. b 63. Cam Univ BA85 MA88. Cranmer Hall Dur 87. **d** 89 **p** 90. C Hyson Green *S'well* 89-91; C Basford w Hyson Green from 91. *8 Austen Avenue, Nottingham NG7 6PE* Nottingham (0602) 785541

HARMAN, Preb John Gordon Kitchener. b 14. Qu Coll Cam BA36 MA40. Lon Coll of Div 36. **d** 37 **p** 38. R Edgware *Lon* 60-75; C-in-c Westbourne Ch Ch Prop Chpl *Win* 75-81; rtd 79; Perm to Offic *Leic* from 82; Lon from 84. *32 Lansdowne Road, Shepshed, Leics LE12 9RS* Shepshed (0509) 502865

HARMAN, Leslie Davies. b 46. Nottm Univ BTh76. St Jo Coll Nottm LTh75. **d** 76 **p** 77. C Wandsworth All SS *S'wark* 76-78; C Godstone 78-82; V Thorncombe w Winsham and Cricket St Thomas *B & W* 82-87; TV Hitchin *St Alb* from 87. *The Vicarage, St Mark's Close, Hitchin, Herts SG5 1UR* Hitchin (0462) 434686

HARMAN, Leslie Wallace. b 10. FRHistS St Cath Soc Ox 29. **d** 43 **p** 44. V Hardingstone *Pet* 69-75; Dioc Development Officer 69-75; Chs' Community Development Consultancy 69-75; rtd 75. *72 Westmount Road, London SE9 1JE* 081-850 2116

HARMAN, Michael John. b 48. Chich Th Coll 71. **d** 74 **p** 75. C Blackpool St Steph *Blackb* 74-79; Chapl RN from 79. *c/o MOD, Lacon House, Theobald's Road, London WC1X 8RY* 071-430 6847

HARMAN, Canon Robert Desmond. b 41. TCD BA65 MA71. CITC 67. **d** 67 **p** 68. C Taney Ch Ch *D & G* 67-73; I Dub Santry w Glasnevin 73-86; I Dub Sandford w Milltown from 86; Can Ch Ch Cathl Dub from 91. *The Rectory, Sandford Close, Ranelagh, Dublin 6, Irish Republic* Dublin (1) 972983

HARMAN, Theodore Allan. b 27. Linc Coll Ox BA52 MA56. Wells Th Coll 52. **d** 54 **p** 55. C Hawkshead and Low Wray *Carl* 54-55; C Kirkby Stephen w Mallerstang 55-57; Lic to Offic *Bradf* from 57; Asst Chapl Sedbergh Sch Cumbria 57-84; Chapl 84-87; Res Coll Tutor Haft Coll Dur from 87. *Gatehouse Flat, Hatfield College, Durham DH1 3RQ* 091-374 3176

HARMER, Canon Gerald William Sinden. b 04. Reading Univ DipEd23. Sarum Th Coll 26. **d** 28 **p** 29. Hon Can Truro Cathl *Truro* 45-71; V Bodmin 46-71; Chapl E Cornwall Hosp Bodmin 48-72; rtd 71. *Lanhydrock House, Bodmin, Cornwall PL30 5AD* Bodmin (0208) 72767

HARONSKI, Boleslaw. b 46. Pemb Coll Ox BA68 MA72 DPhil73. St Mich Coll Llan 80 Westcott Ho Cam 82. **d** 82 **p** 83. C Newport Maindee St Jo Ev *Mon* 82-85; V Llanishen w Trellech Grange and Llanfihangel etc 85-89; V Blackwood from 89. *The Vicarage, South View Road, Blackwood, Gwent NP6 6QL* Blackwood (0495) 224214

HARPER, Preb Alan Edwin Thomas. b 44. Leeds Univ BA65. CITC 75. **d** 78 **p** 79. C Ballywillan *Conn* 78-80; I Moville w Greencastle, Upper Moville etc *D & R* 80-82; I Londonderry Ch Ch 82-86; I Belf Malone (St Jo) *Conn* from 86; RD S Belf from 89; Preb St Audoen St Patr Cathl Dub from 90. *St John's Rectory, 86 Maryville Park, Belfast BT9 6LQ* Belfast (0232) 666644

HARPER, Alan Peter. b 50. FCA83 Man Univ BA73. Ripon Coll Cuddesdon 86. **d** 88 **p** 89. C Newport w Longford and Chetwynd *Lich* 88-91; P-in-c Wilnecote from 91. *The Vicarage, Glascote Lane, Wilnecote, Tamworth, Staffs B77 2PH* Tamworth (0827) 280806

HARPER, Brian John. b 61. Liv Univ BA82 TCD DipTh85. **d** 85 **p** 86. C Portadown St Columba *Arm* 85-88; C Drumglass 88-89; I Errigle Keerogue w Ballygawley and Killeshil from 89; Dioc Info Officer from 90. *Richmond Rectory, 24 Old Omagh Road, Ballygawley, Co Tyrone BT70 2AA* Ballygawley (06625) 68670

HARPER, Clive Stewart. b 35. FCIS71. Ridley Hall Cam 80. **d** 82 **p** 83. C Bromyard *Heref* 82-85; P-in-c Bredenbury and Wacton w Grendon Bishop 85-89; P-in-c Edwyn Ralph and Collington w Thornbury 85-89; P-in-c Pencombe w Marston Stannett and Lt Cowarne 85-89; R Bredenbury w Grendon Bishop and Wacton etc from 89. *The Rectory, Bredenbury, Bromyard, Herefordshire HR7 4TF* Bromyard (0885) 482236

HARPER, David Laurence. b 51. Qu Coll Cam BA73 MA77 PhD78. Wycliffe Hall Ox BA80. **d** 80 **p** 81.

C Mansf St Pet *S'well* 80-84; C Wollaton 84-87; V Brinsley w Underwood from 87. *102A Church Lane, Brinsley, Nottingham NG16 5AB* Langley Mill (0773) 713978

HARPER, Donald Morrison. b 10. MBE91. Qu Coll Cam BA36 MA41. Ridley Hall Cam 36. **d** 38 **p** 39. P-in-c Brighton St Geo *Chich* 65-70; Nigeria 70-72; Chapl Madeira *Eur* 72-76; rtd 75; Chapl Costa del Sol W *Eur* 76-84; Chapl Tangier 84-85; Chapl Palermo w Taormina 85-90. *Bishop's House, Lansdowne Crescent, Worcester WR3 8JH* Worcester (0905) 723972

HARPER, Geoffrey. b 32. Hertf Coll Ox BA55 MA59. Coll of Resurr Mirfield. **d** 57 **p** 58. C Cov St Pet *Cov* 57-60; C Handsworth St Mich *Birm* 60-62; C-in-c Kingstanding St Mark CD 62-71; V Kingstanding St Mark 71-73; R Sheviock *Truro* 73-80; R Antony w Sheviock 80-82; V Paul from 82; Dioc Development Rep from 86. *The Vicarage, Paul, Penzance, Cornwall TR20 8TY* Penzance (0736) 731261

HARPER, Geoffrey Roger. b 57. Jes Coll Cam BA MA DipTh. St Jo Coll Nottm 81. **d** 84 **p** 85. C Belper *Derby* 84-87; C Birstall and Wanlip *Leic* 87-90; TV Tettenhall Regis *Lich* from 90. *St Paul's Vicarage, 1 Talaton Close, Pendeford, Wolverhampton WV9 5LS* Wolverhampton (0902) 787199

HARPER, Gordon. b 32. Oak Hill Th Coll 64. **d** 66 **p** 67. C Halliwell St Pet *Man* 66-71 and from 84; P-in-c Brinsworth *Sheff* 71-75; V Brinsworth w Catcliffe 76-84. *54 Redcar Road, Bolton BL1 6LL* Bolton (0204) 849413

HARPER, Dr Gordon William Robert. b 48. Wellington Univ (NZ) BA70 St Chad's Coll Dur BA74 Nottm Univ PhD89. Coll of Resurr Mirfield 74. **d** 75 **p** 76. C Battyeford *Wakef* 75-76; New Zealand 76-80; P-in-c Byers Green *Dur* 80-83; V Evenwood 83-89; R Wolviston from 89. *The Rectory, 1 Clifton Avenue, Billingham, Cleveland TS22 5DE* Stockton-on-Tees (0642) 551666

HARPER, Horace Frederic. b 37. Lich Th Coll 58. **d** 60 **p** 61. C Stoke upon Trent *Lich* 60-63; C Fenton 63-66; V Coseley Ch Ch 66-75; V Trent Vale 75-88; P-in-c Dresden 88-89; V from 89. *Dresden Vicarage, 22 Red Bank, Longton, Stoke-on-Trent ST3 4EY* Stoke-on-Trent (0782) 321257

HARPER, Ian. b 54. AKC78. Oak Hill Th Coll 79. **d** 80 **p** 81. C Sidcup St Jo *Roch* 80-83; C Bushey *St Alb* 83-87; TV Thamesmead *S'wark* from 87. *15 Camelot Close, London SE28 0ES* 081-316 6996

HARPER, James. b 35. St Luke's Coll Ex TDip57. SW Minl Tr Course DipTh89. **d** 90 **p** 91. NSM Pendeen w Morvah *Truro* from 90. *11 Carrallack Terrace, St Just, Penzance, Cornwall TR19 7LW* Penzance (0736) 788574

HARPER, John Anthony. b 46. AKC69. **d** 70 **p** 71. C Pet St Mary *Pet* 70-73; C Abington 73-75; V Grendon w Castle Ashby 75-82; Asst Dioc Youth Chapl 75-82; R Castor w Sutton and Upton from 82. *The Rectory, 5 Church Hill, Castor, Peterborough PE5 7AU* Peterborough (0733) 380244

HARPER, John Hugh. b 34. ALAM62 Hertf Coll Ox BA57 MA61. Wells Th Coll 57. **d** 59 **p** 60. C Twerton *B & W* 59-62; R Chapel Allerton 62-69; V Blackford 62-69; V Halsetown *Truro* 69-91; RD Penwith 84-88; P-in-c S Brent *Ex* from 91. *The Vicarage, South Brent, Devon TQ10 9AN* South Brent (0364) 72774

HARPER, Joseph Frank. b 38. Hull Univ BA60 MA86. Linc Th Coll 80. **d** 81 **p** 82. C Preston St Cuth *Blackb* 81-83; C Lanc St Mary 83-87; V Bamber Bridge St Aid from 87. *St Aidan's Vicarage, Longworth Street, Bamber Bridge, Preston, Lancs PR5 5GN* Preston (0772) 35310

HARPER, Malcolm Barry. b 37. Dur Univ BSc59. Wycliffe Hall Ox 59. **d** 61 **p** 62. C Harold Wood *Chelmsf* 61-65; C Madeley *Heref* 65-68; V Slaithwaite w E Scammonden *Wakef* 68-75; V Walmley *Birm* from 75. *The Vicarage, 2 Walmley Road, Sutton Coldfield, W Midlands B76 8QN* 021-351 1030

HARPER, Martin Nigel. b 48. FRICS88. S Dios Minl Tr Scheme. **d** 85 **p** 86. NSM St Leonards Ch Ch and St Mary *Chich* from 85. *6 St Matthew's Drive, St Leonards-on-Sea, E Sussex TN38 0TR* Hastings (0424) 713631

HARPER, Canon Maurice. b 20. St Steph Ho Ox 60. **d** 62 **p** 63. V Gt Ilford St Mary *Chelmsf* 67-71; R Upminster 71-85; RD Havering 80-85; Hon Can Chelmsf Cathl 84-85; rtd 85; Perm to Offic Chelmsf & Nor from 85; St E from 87. *1 Pine Close, Harleston, Norfolk IP20 9DZ* Harleston (0379) 853401

HARPER, Canon Michael Claude. b 31. Em Coll Cam BA54 MA57. Ridley Hall Cam 53. **d** 55 **p** 56. C Clapham Common St Barn *S'wark* 58-58; Chapl Ox St Stores 58-64; C St Marylebone All So w SS Pet and Jo *Lon* 58-64; Gen Sec Fountain Trust 64-72; Dir 72-75; Hon C Hounslow H Trin *Lon* 75-80; Lic to Offic *Chich* from

81; Exec Dir SOMA from 84; Can and Preb Chich Cathl from 84. *27 Muster Green, Haywards Heath, W Sussex RH16 4AL*   Haywards Heath (0444) 417007

HARPER, Michael Sydney. b 36. Portsm Dioc Tr Course 86. **d** 87. NSM Leigh Park St Clare CD *Portsm* 87-88; NSM Warren Park St Clare from 88. *17 Hampage Green, Warren Park, Havant, Hants PO9 4HJ*   Havant (0705) 454275

HARPER, Paul. b 11. Pemb Coll Ox BA34 MA38. Clifton Th Coll 35. **d** 35 **p** 36. Hd Master Colston Prep Sch Bris 61-68; rtd 76. *2 Dawbourne House, Ashford Road, St Michaels, Tenterden, Kent*   Tenterden (05806) 2751

HARPER, Richard Michael. b 53. Lon Univ BSc75 Univ of Wales PhD78. St Steph Ho Ox BA80. **d** 81 **p** 82. C Holt *Nor* 81-84; C-in-c Grahame Park St Aug CD *Lon* 84-88; Sub-Warden & Dir of Studies St Mich Llan from 88; Lect Ch Hist Univ of Wales (Cardiff) from 88. *Sub-Warden's Flat, St Michael's College Llandaff, Cardiff CF5 2YJ*   Cardiff (0222) 563379

HARPER, Robert. b 08. Lon Coll of Div 46. **d** 46 **p** 47. R St Florence and Redberth *St D* 70-78; rtd 78. *South Hill, Talbenny, Haverfordwest, Dyfed SA62 3XA*   Broad Haven (0437) 781338

HARPER, Roger. FCA BSc. **d** 87 **p** 88. NSM Onchan *S & M* from 87. *Ballahowin House, St Mark's, Ballasalla, Isle of Man*   Douglas (0624) 851251

HARPER, Thomas Reginald. b 31. Dur Univ BA57 MA67. **d** 58 **p** 59. C Corbridge w Halton *Newc* 58-60; C Byker St Mich 60-62; V Ushaw Moor *Dur* 62-67; Asst Chapl HM Pris Dur 62-67; N Sec CMS 71-74; V Thornthwaite *Carl* 74-75; V Thornthwaite cum Braithwaite and Newlands 76-90; TV Bellingham/Otterburn Gp *Newc* from 90. *Bellingham Rectory, Hexham, Northd NE48 2JS*   Hexham (0434) 220019

HARPER, Timothy James Lincoln. b 54. LRAM Lon Univ BMus76 CertEd DipP&C. Wycliffe Hall Ox 84. **d** 86 **p** 87. C Morden *S'wark* 86-90; V Deptford St Pet from 90. *St Peter's Vicarage, Wickham Road, London SE4 1LT*   081-691 3334

HARPER, Victor Selkirk. b 12. Cranmer Hall Dur 64. **d** 65 **p** 66. R Asby w Ormside *Carl* 68-72; V Blawith w Lowick 72-77; rtd 77; Perm to Offic *York* from 87. *30 Linwood Avenue, Stokesley, Middlesbrough, Cleveland TS9 5HT*   Stokesley (0642) 710560

HARRAP, William Charles. b 32. BEM86. **d** 72 **p** 74. Hon C Bethnal Green St Jas Less *Lon* from 72. *12 Wedgewood House, Morpeth Street, London E2 0PZ*   081-980 6887

HARRATT, Philip David. b 56. Magd Coll Ox BA79 MA83. Ripon Coll Cuddesdon 82. **d** 85 **p** 86. C Ewyas Harold w Dulas, Kenderchurch etc *Heref* 85-88; V Chirbury from 88; V Trelystan from 88. *The Vicarage, Chirbury, Montgomery, Powys SY15 6BN*   Chirbury (093872) 218

HARRE, Kenneth Michael. b 25. MA. E Anglian Minl Tr Course. **d** 84 **p** 85. NSM N Walsham w Antingham *Nor* 84-87; P-in-c Nor St Helen from 87. *65 Yarmouth Road, North Walsham, Norfolk NR28 9AU*   North Walsham (0692) 403362

HARREX, David Brian. b 54. DipHE89. Trin Coll Bris 87. **d** 89 **p** 90. C Bedminster St Mich *Bris* from 89. *16 Elvaston Road, Bristol BS3 4QJ*   Bristol (0272) 667099

HARRIES, Gwilym David. b 41. Univ of Wales (Lamp) BA63. St Mich Coll Llan 63. **d** 65 **p** 66. C Llanguicke *S & B* 65-68; C Llangyfelach and Morriston 68-71; TV Abth *St D* 71-76; R Hubberston 76-82; R Hubberston w Herbrandston and Hasguard etc 82-84; V Burry Port and Pwll from 84. *The Vicarage, 134 Pencoed Road, Burry Port, Dyfed SA16 0SB*   Burry Port (05546) 2936

HARRIES, Henry Rayner Mackintosh. b 30. MBE67. Chich Th Coll 53. **d** 55 **p** 56. C Hastings H Trin *Chich* 55-58; Chapl RAF 58-79; Asst Chapl-in-Chief RAF 79-84; QHC 83-84; P-in-c Gt Brickhill w Bow Brickhill and Lt Brickhill *Ox* 84-86; R from 86; RD Mursley from 91. *The Rectory, Rushmere Close, Bow Brickhill, Milton Keynes MK17 9JB*   Milton Keynes (0908) 642086

HARRIES, Canon Lewis John. b 27. Univ of Wales BA52. St Mich Coll Llan 51. **d** 53 **p** 54. C Newport Maindee St Jo Ev *Mon* 53-58; V Goldcliffe and Whiston and Nash 58-64; V Tredegar St Geo from 64; RD Bedwellty from 78; Can St Woolos Cathl from 82. *St George's Vicarage, Tredegar, Gwent NP2 3DU*   Tredegar (0495) 252672

✠**HARRIES, Rt Rev Richard Douglas.** b 36. Selw Coll Cam BA61 MA65. Cuddesdon Coll 61. **d** 63 **p** 64 **c** 87. C Hampstead St Jo *Lon* 63-69; Chapl Westf Coll Lon 67-69; Tutor Wells Th Coll 69-71; Warden Sarum & Wells Th Coll 71-72; V Fulham All SS *Lon* 72-81; Dean K Coll Lon 81-87; FKC from 83; Consultant to Abps

Cant & York on Inter-Faith Relns from 86; Bp Ox from 87. *Bishop's House, 27 Linton Road, Oxford OX2 6UL*   Oxford (0865) 244566

HARRINGTON, Charles William. b 04. Linc Th Coll. **d** 42 **p** 43. V Letcombe Regis w Letcombe Bassett *Ox* 70-73; rtd 73; Perm to Offic *Cant* from 74. *Broadleas Retirement Home, 9 Eldorado Road, Cheltenham, Glos GL50 2PU*   Cheltenham (0242) 583232

HARRINGTON, Graham Anthony. b 20. Linc Coll Ox BA48 MA52. Wells Th Coll 48. **d** 49 **p** 50. V Blundellsands St Mich *Liv* 68-85; rtd 85. *2 Broadbridge Close, London SE3 7AD*   081-858 0966

HARRINGTON, John Christopher Thomas. b 43. Conf Catholic Colls CertRE63. Qu Coll Birm 71. **d** 74 **p** 75. C Northn St Mich *Pet* 74-76; CF (TA) 75-85; C Paston *Pet* 76-79; Chapl Doddington Co Hosp 79-83; R Benwick St Mary *Ely* 79-82; R Doddington 79-82; R Doddington w Benwick 82-83; V Eastbourne St Mich *Chich* from 83. *The Vicarage, 15 Long Acre Close, Eastbourne, E Sussex BN21 1UF*   Eastbourne (0323) 645740

HARRINGTON, Peter Anthony Saunders. b 30. Fitzw Ho Cam BA52 MA58. Ely Th Coll 53. **d** 55 **p** 56. C Croydon St Mich *Cant* 55-59; Australia 59-62; C W Wycombe *Ox* 63-66; Lic to Offic *Ox* 67-78; St Alb from 78. *5 Linfields, Little Chalfont, Amersham, Bucks HP7 9QH*   Little Chalfont (0494) 763471

HARRINGTON, William Harry. b 33. AKC57. **d** 58 **p** 59. C Childwall All SS *Liv* 58-60; C Sutton 60-64; V Ditton St Mich 64-76; V Mossley Hill St Barn 76-83; V Highfield from 83. *St Matthew's Vicarage, Highfield, Wigan, Lancs WN3 6BL*   Wigan (0942) 222121

HARRIS, Arthur Emlyn Dawson. b 27. Ex Univ BSc47 Lon Univ DipRS86. S'wark Ord Course 83. **d** 86 **p** 87. NSM Frant w Eridge *Chich* 86-87; P-in-c Withyham St Mich from 87. *The Rectory, Withyham, Hartfield, E Sussex TN7 4BA*   Hartfield (0892) 770241

HARRIS, Basil George. b 17. St Mich Coll Llan 59. **d** 61 **p** 62. Perm to Offic *Llan* 65-71; C St Alb St Sav *St Alb* 71-74; V Middleton St Cross *Ripon* 74-79; R Helpringham w Hale *Linc* 79-83; rtd 83. *12 Blounts Court, Potterne, Devizes, Wilts SN10 5QA*   Devizes (0380) 724570

HARRIS, Bernard Malcolm. b 29. Leeds Univ BA54. Coll of Resurr Mirfield 54. **d** 56 **p** 57. C Shrewsbury St Chad *Lich* 56-60; C Porthill 60-61; V Birches Head 61-66; V W Bromwich St Jas 66-78; V Sedgley All SS from 78. *All Saints' Vicarage, Vicar Street, Sedgley, Dudley, W Midlands DY3 3SD*   Sedgley (0902) 883255

HARRIS, Brian. b 33. Man Univ BSc. Qu Coll Birm 79. **d** 80 **p** 81. C Lich St Chad *Lich* 80-81; Perm to Offic *Ches* 81-87; NSM Warburton 87-88; P-in-c from 88. *The Rectory, Bent Lane, Warburton, Lymm, Cheshire WA13 9TQ*   Lymm (092575) 4716

HARRIS, Brian William. b 38. K Coll Lon BD61 AKC61. St Boniface Warminster 61. **d** 62 **p** 63. C Liversedge *Wakef* 62-65; C Kirkby *Liv* 65-70; V Dalton 70-79; V Aberford w Saxton *York* from 79. *The Vicarage, Greystones Park, Aberford, Leeds LS25 3AS*   Leeds (0532) 813623

HARRIS, Cedric Herbert. b 13. AKC37. Wycliffe Hall Ox 37. **d** 37 **p** 38. V Thornes St Jas w Ch Ch *Wakef* 57-73; V Shepley 73-78; rtd 78. *44 Rayner Street, Horbury, Wakefield, W Yorkshire WF4 5BD*   Wakefield (0924) 272297

HARRIS, Charles Edward. b 20. Roch Th Coll 63. **d** 65 **p** 66. C Hertf St Andr *St Alb* 65-71; R Syerwell w Overstone *Pet* 71-90; rtd 90. *College of St Barnabas, Blackberry Lane, Lingfield, Surrey RH7 6NJ*   Dormans Park (034287) 607

HARRIS, Charles Edwin Laurence. b 96. Ridley Hall Cam 46. **d** 47 **p** 48. V Burbage *Sarum* 50-65; rtd 65. *Church House, Sutton, Dover, Kent CT15 5DF*   Deal (0304) 374809

HARRIS, Claude Anthony. b 16. Dur Univ LTh39. Oak Hill Th Coll 36. **d** 39 **p** 40. R Stone St Mich *Lich* 60-82; V Aston 60-82; rtd 82. *Hardwick Cottage, 51 Stafford Road, Stone, Staffs ST15 0HE*   Stone (0785) 815100

HARRIS, Cyril Evans. b 30. Linc Th Coll 61. **d** 63 **p** 64. C Beaconsfield *Ox* 63-68; V Stoke Poges from 68. *The Vicarage, Park Road, Stoke Poges, Slough SL2 4PE*   Farnham Common (02814) 4177

HARRIS, David. b 52. AKC76. St Steph Ho Ox 76. **d** 77 **p** 79. C Wimbledon *S'wark* 77-80; C Coalbrookdale, Iron-Bridge and Lt Wenlock *Heref* 80-82; V Highters Heath *Birm* 82-84; Perm to Offic *Lon* from 85. *35 Paddonswick Road, London W6 0UA*   081-748 5195

HARRIS, David Rowland. b 46. Ch Ch Ox BA69 DipTh71 MA72. Wycliffe Hall Ox 70. **d** 73 **p** 74. C Virginia Water *Guildf* 73-76; C Clifton Ch Ch w Em *Bris* 76-79;

Scripture Union 79-85; V Bedf Ch Ch *St Alb* from 85. *Christ Church Vicarage, 115 Denmark Street, Bedford MK40 3TJ* Bedford (0234) 359342

HARRIS, Derrick William. b 21. **d** 63 **p** 64. V Billinge *Liv* 67-81; V Walton *Ches* 81-87; rtd 88. *3 Melrose Avenue, Southport, Merseyside PR9 9UY* Southport (0704) 213828

HARRIS, Donald Bertram. b 04. K Coll Cam BA25 MA29. Cuddesdon Coll 26. **d** 27 **p** 28. V Wilton Place St Paul *Lon* 55-77; rtd 78. *105 Marsham Court, Marsham Street, London SW1P 4LU* 071-828 1132

HARRIS, Ernest John. b 46. Lon Univ DipTh74 QUB BD75. **d** 75 **p** 76. C Lisburn Ch Ch *Conn* 75-78; C Coleraine 78-83; I Belf St Kath 83-90; I Ballinderry from 90. *The Rectory, 124 Ballinderry Road, Ballinderry Upper, Lisburn, Co Antrim BT28 2NL* Aghalee (0846) 651310

HARRIS, Evan Rufus. b 21. Univ of Wales (Lamp) BA49. Bp Burgess Hall Lamp. **d** 50 **p** 51. R Barrowby *Linc* 57-86; RD Grantham 69-78; Chapl RAF 70-76; rtd 86. *Cariad, 65 Queen Alexandra Road, Salisbury SP2 9LL* Salisbury (0722) 324456

HARRIS, Frank Edward. b 33. ACT ThL69 St Fran Coll Brisbane 65. **d** 68 **p** 69. Australia 68-71 and 73-76; C Plymstock *Ex* 71-72; C E Acton St Dunstan w St Thos *Lon* 72-73; C Bodmin *Truro* 76-77; P-in-c Menheniot 77-79; V Winton *Man* 79-87; Guinea 87-89; R Blisland w St Breward *Truro* from 90. *The Rectory, Blisland, Bodmin, Cornwall PL30 4JE* Bodmin (0208) 851020

HARRIS, Frederick John. b 17. Worc Ord Coll 67. **d** 68 **p** 70. C Sheff St Nath *Sheff* 69-71; C Aston SS Pet and Paul *Birm* 71-73; New Zealand 73-75; S Africa 75-76; C Portsea St Mary *Portsm* 77; C Clun w Chapel Lawn *Heref* 77-78; C Hartlepool St Aid *Dur* 78-80; V Trimdon Station 80-87; rtd 87. *College of St Barnabas, Blackberry Lane, Lingfield, Surrey RH7 6NJ* Dormans Park (034287) 260

HARRIS, Geoffrey Daryl. b 39. Lon Univ DipTh66 Open Univ BA83. St Aid Birkenhead 63. **d** 66 **p** 67. C Eston *York* 66-70; C Iffley *Ox* 70-75; V Bubwith *York* 75-78; V Bubwith w Ellerton and Aughton 78-79; P-in-c Stillingfleet w Naburn 79-80; R Escrick and Stillingfleet w Naburn from 80. *The Rectory, Escrick, York YO4 6EX* Escrick (090487) 406

HARRIS, George. b 36. Sarum Th Coll 66. **d** 68 **p** 69. C Shildon *Dur* 68-70; CF 70-74; P-in-c Doddington *Ely* 74-75; R 75-78; R Benwick St Mary 74-78; V Shotton *Dur* 78-86; V Stockton St Mark 86-87; V Chilton Moor from 87. *St Andrew's Vicarage, Houghton le Spring, Tyne & Wear DH4 6LU* 091-385 2468

HARRIS, Gerald Alfred. b 29. Qu Coll Birm 80. **d** 84 **p** 85. NSM Pedmore *Worc* 84-86; C Christchurch *Win* from 86. *St George's House, Jumpers Road, Christchurch, Dorset BH23 2JR* Christchurch (0202) 486248

HARRIS, Jack. b 49. Barrister-at-Law (Lincoln's Inn) 72 St Cath Coll Ox BA70 MA74 Fitzw Coll Cam BA85 MA89. Westcott Ho Cam 83. **d** 86 **p** 87. C Doncaster Ch Ch *Sheff* from 86. *Frazer House, 30 Welbeck Road, Doncaster DN4 5EY* Doncaster (0302) 349684

HARRIS, James Nigel Kingsley. b 37. St D Coll Lamp BA60. Sarum Th Coll. **d** 62 **p** 63. C Painswick *Glouc* 62-65; C Glouc St Paul 65-67; V Slad 67-77; V Cam 77-78; P-in-c Stinchcombe 77-78; V Cam w Stinchcombe 78-82; V Stonehouse from 82. *The Vicarage, Elms Road, Stonehouse, Glos GL10 2NP* Stonehouse (0453) 822332

HARRIS, James Philip. b 59. Westf Coll Lon BA82. Llan St Mich BD86. **d** 86 **p** 87. C Newport St Paul *Mon* 86-89; C Bedwellty 89-91; V Newport St Matt from 91. *St Matthew's Vicarage, 124 Caerleon Road, Newport, Gwent NP9 7GS* Newport (0633) 262377

HARRIS, Canon John. b 32. Univ of Wales (Lamp) BA55. Sarum Th Coll 55. **d** 57 **p** 58. V Pontnewynydd *Mon* 57-60; C Bassaleg 60-63; V Penmaen 63-69; V Newport St Paul 69-84; RD Newport from 77; V Newport Maindee St Jo Ev from 84; Can St Woolos Cathl from 84. *The Vicarage, St John's Road, Maindee, Newport, Gwent NP9 8GR* Newport (0633) 277009

HARRIS, John. b 45. St Steph Ho Ox 72. **d** 75 **p** 76. C Wanstead St Mary *Chelmsf* 75-84; V Penponds *Truro* 84-91; V St Gluvias from 91. *The Vicarage, St Gluvias, Penryn, Cornwall TR10 9LQ* Falmouth (0326) 73356

HARRIS, John. b 54. Leeds Univ BSc75. St Jo Coll Nottm LTh86. **d** 86 **p** 87. C S Ossett *Wakef* 86-90; V Moldgreen from 90. *The Vicarage, 35 Church Street, Moldgreen, Huddersfield HD5 9DL* Huddersfield (0484) 424432

HARRIS, John Brian. b 53. Hertf Coll Ox BA76. Ripon Coll Cuddesdon 87. **d** 89 **p** 90. C Witton *Ches* from 89. *162 Middlewich Road, Rudheath, Northwich, Cheshire CW9 7DX* Northwich (0606) 41965

HARRIS, John Peter. b 33. St D Coll Lamp BA57. **d** 58 **p** 59. Chapl St Woolos Hosp Newport 58-63; C Newport St Woolos *Mon* 58-60; Chapl St Woolos Cathl 60-63; CF (TA) 59-63; CF 63-82; V Chepstow *Mon* from 82; RD Chepstow from 85. *The Vicarage, 25 Mount Way, Chepstow, Gwent NP6 5NF* Chepstow (02912) 70980

HARRIS, John Stuart. b 29. Hertf Coll Ox BA52 MA56. Wells Th Coll 52. **d** 54 **p** 55. C Epsom St Martin *Guildf* 54-58; C Guildf H Trin w St Mary 58-63; R Bentley 63-72; V Milford 72-87; R Walton-on-the-Hill from 87; Dioc Ecum Officer from 87. *St Peter's Rectory, Walton-on-the-Hill, Tadworth, Surrey KT20 7SO* Tadworth (0737) 812105

HARRIS, Mrs Judith Helen. b 42. Chelsea Coll Lon CertEd64. St Alb Minl Tr Scheme 83. **dss** 86 **d** 87. Leagrave St Alb 86-87; Hon Par Dn from 87. *1 Liston Close, Leagrave, Luton, Beds LU4 9IIA* Luton (0582) 507611

HARRIS, Kenneth. b 28. NW Ord Course 70. **d** 72 **p** 73. NSM Upton Ascension *Ches* 72-77; NSM Eccleston and Pulford 77-80; P-in-c Hargrave 80-81; V from 81; Exec Officer Dioc Bd for Soc Resp from 84. *The Vicarage, Hargrave, Chester CH3 7RN* Huxley (082924) 378

HARRIS, Lawrence Rex Rowland. b 35. St Cath Coll Cam BA59 MA63. Ely Th Coll. **d** 61 **p** 62. C Carrington *S'well* 61-63; Chapl Rampton Hosp Retford 63-66; V Sturton w Littleborough *S'well* 66-71; V Bole w Saundby 66-71; R Clowne *Derby* from 71; RD Bolsover and Staveley 81-86. *The Rectory, Rectory Road, Clowne, Chesterfield, Derbyshire S43 4BH* Chesterfield (0246) 810387

HARRIS, Leslie Ernest. b 08. Kelham Th Coll 31. **d** 31 **p** 32. V Swinton *Sheff* 65-76; rtd 76; Perm to Offic *Sheff* from 87. *12 Hesley Grove, Chapeltown, Sheffield S30 4TX* Sheffield (0742) 469319

HARRIS, Canon Leslie Owen. b 29. UEA BA. St Mich Coll Llan 61. **d** 63 **p** 64. C Horfield H Trin *Bris* 63-71; R Winterton w E Somerton *Nor* 71-83; P-in-c Horsey 77-83; R Winterton w E and W Somerton and Horsey 83; R Kessingland 83; R Kessingland w Gisleham from 83; RD Lothingland from 86; Hon Can Nor Cathl from 90. *The Rectory, 1 Wash Lane, Kessingland, Lowestoft, Suffolk NR33 7QZ* Lowestoft (0502) 740256

HARRIS, Martin John. b 54. Trin Coll Cam BA76 MA. Wycliffe Hall Ox 82. **d** 85 **p** 86. C Lindfield *Chich* 85-88; C Galleywood Common *Chelmsf* 88-91; V Southchurch Ch Ch from 91. *Christ Church Vicarage, Warwick Road, Southend-on-Sea SS1 3BN* Southend-on-Sea (0702) 582585

HARRIS, Michael Andrew. b 53. Ian Ramsey Coll 74 Trin Coll Bris 75. **d** 78 **p** 79. C St Paul's Cray St Barn *Roch* 78-82; C Church Stretton *Heref* 82-87; Res Min Penkridge w Stretton *Lich* 87-90; Res Min Penkridge Team from 90. *31 Saxon Road, Penkridge, Stafford ST19 5EP* Penkridge (078571) 3489

HARRIS, Nicholas Bryan. b 60. Down Coll Cam BA81 MA85. Ridley Hall Cam 82. **d** 85 **p** 86. C Walney Is *Carl* 85-88; C S'wark Ch Ch *S'wark* from 88. *30A Dolben Street, London SE1 0UQ* 071-620 1374

✠**HARRIS, Rt Rev Patrick Burnet.** b 34. Keble Coll Ox BA58 MA63. Clifton Th Coll 58. **d** 60 **p** 61 **c** 73. C Ox St Ebbe w St Pet *Ox* 60-63; SAMS 63-81; Adn N Argentina 70-73; Bp 73-80; R Kirkheaton *Wakef* 81-85; Asst Bp Wakef 81-85; Sec C of E Partnership for World Miss 86-88; Asst Bp Ox 86-88; Bp S'well from 88. *Bishop's Manor, Southwell, Notts NG25 0JR* Southwell (0636) 812112

HARRIS, Paul. b 55. BEd79 DipHE84. Oak Hill Th Coll 82. **d** 84 **p** 85. C Billericay and Lt Burstead *Chelmsf* 84-87; TV Cheltenham St Mary, St Matt, St Paul and H Trin *Glouc* from 87. *100 Hewlett Road, Cheltenham, Glos GL52 6AR* Cheltenham (0242) 523920

HARRIS, Paul Ian. b 45. MSc. Qu Coll Birm. **d** 82 **p** 83. C The Quinton *Birm* 82-86; V Atherstone *Cov* from 86. *40 Holte Road, Atherstone, Warks CV9 1HN* Atherstone (0827) 713200

HARRIS, Peter Malcolm. b 52. Em Coll Cam BA74 MA79. Trin Coll Bris DipHE80. **d** 80 **p** 81. C Upton (or Overchurch) *Ches* 80-83; BCMS from 83; Portugal from 83. *Arocha, Cruzinha, Mexilhoeira Grande, 8500 Portimao, Portugal* Portimao (82) 96380

HARRIS, Raymond. b 36. Nottm Univ BA58. Lich Th Coll 58. **d** 60 **p** 61. C Clifton St Fran *S'well* 60-63; C Davyhulme St Mary *Man* 63-66; V Bacup Ch Ch 66-82; R Dunsby w Dowsby *Linc* 82-87; R Rippingale 82-87; R Rippingale Gp from 87. *The Rectory, Rippingale, Bourne, Lincs PE10 0SR* Bourne (0778) 440380

HARRIS, Canon Raymond John. b 29. Leeds Univ BA51. Coll of Resurr Mirfield 51. **d** 53 **p** 54. C Workington St Mich *Carl* 53-59; V New Swindon St Barn Gorse Hill

Bris from 59; Hon Can Bris Cathl from 80; RD Cricklade 82-88. *St Barnabas' Vicarage, 2 Ferndale Road, Swindon SN2 1EX* Swindon (0793) 523648

HARRIS, Miss Rebecca. *See* SWYER, Mrs Rebecca Jane

HARRIS, Ven Reginald Brian. b 34. Ch Coll Cam BA58 MA61. Ridley Hall Cam. **d** 59 **p** 60. C Wednesbury St Bart *Lich* 59-61; C Uttoxeter w Bramshall 61-64; V Bury St Pet *Man* 64-70; V Walmsley 70-80; RD Walmsley 70-80; Adn Man from 80; Can Res Man Cathl from 80. *4 Victoria Avenue, Eccles, Manchester M30 9HA* 061-707 6444

HARRIS, Robert Douglas. b 57. BEd. Chich Th Coll 80. **d** 82 **p** 83. C Portsea St Mary *Portsm* 82-87; V Clevedon St Jo *B & W* from 87. *St John's Vicarage, 1 St John's Road, Clevedon, Avon BS21 7TG* Clevedon (0272) 872410

HARRIS, Robert James. b 45. ALCD73. St Jo Coll Nottm 69. **d** 72 **p** 73. C Sheff St Jo *Sheff* 72-76; C Goole 76-78; V Bramley and Ravenfield 78-91; P-in-c Boulton *Derby* from 91. *The Vicarage, 1 St Mayry's Close, Boulton Lane, Alvaston, Derby DE2 0FE* Derby (0332) 571296

HARRIS, Robert William. b 26. Roch Th Coll 64. **d** 66 **p** 67. C Herne Bay Ch Ch *Cant* 66-70 and 77-84; V Nonington 70-73; V Nonington w Barfreystone 73-77; P-in-c Sark *Win* 84-91; rtd 91. *16 Sandown Lees, Sandwich, Kent CT13 9NZ* Sandwich (0304) 613746

HARRIS, Seymour David. b 40. S'wark Ord Course 73. **d** 75 **p** 76. NSM Hampton Hill *Lon* 75-80; P-in-c Fulwell St Mich and St Geo 80-85; C 85-86; R Wittersham w Stone-in-Oxney and Ebony *Cant* from 86. *The Rectory, Wittersham, Tenterden, Kent TN30 7EA* Wittersham (0797) 270227

HARRIS, Thomas William. b 54. AKC76. Linc Th Coll 77. **d** 78 **p** 79. C Norton Woodseats St Chad *Sheff* 78-81; V Barnby Dun from 81; P-in-c Kirk Bramwith 81-86; P-in-c Fenwick 81-86. *The Vicarage, Stainforth Road, Barnby Dun, Doncaster, S Yorkshire DN3 1AA* Doncaster (0302) 882835

HARRIS, William Edric Mackenzie. b 46. Sarum & Wells Th Coll 72. **d** 75 **p** 76. C Langney *Chich* 75-79; C Moulsecoomb 80-81; TV 81-85; R W Grinstead from 85. *The Rectory, West Grinstead, Horsham, W Sussex RH13 8LR* Partridge Green (0403) 710339

HARRIS, Canon William Ernest. b 21. TCD BA48 MA57. **d** 48 **p** 49. I Belf St Pet *Conn* 63-90; Preb St Audoen St Patr Cathl Dub 83-90; rtd 90. *87 Sunnylands Avenue, Carrickfergus, Co Antrim BT38 8JY* Carrickfergus (09603) 68470

HARRIS, William Fergus. b 36. CCC Cam BA59 MA63 Edin Univ DipEd70. Yale Div Sch 59 Westcott Ho Cam 60. **d** 62 **p** 63. C St Andrews St Andr *St And* 62-64; Chapl Edin Univ *Edin* 64-71; R Edin St Pet 71-83; R Perth St Jo *St And* 83-90; Hon C from 90. *c/o St John's Rectory, 6 Dupplin Terrace, Perth PH2 7DG* Perth (0738) 21379

HARRIS, William Joseph Kenneth. b 10. Sarum Th Coll 31. **d** 33 **p** 34. V Mullion *Truro* 52-75; rtd 75; Perm to Offic *Ex* from 75. *1 Beacon Court, 4 Louisa Terrace, Exmouth, Devon EX8 2AQ* Exmouth (0395) 266460

HARRIS-DOUGLAS, John Douglas. b 34. Ripon Hall Ox 65. **d** 66 **p** 67. C Ringwood *Win* 66-67; C Baswich (or Berkswich) *Lich* 67-71; R St Tudy *Truro* 71-74; R St Tudy w Michaelstow 74-76; Adv in Children's Work and Asst Dir Educn 71-76; R Fiskerton *Linc* 76-79; Dir of Educn and Adv RE 76-79; P-in-c Thormanby *York* 79-84; V Brafferton w Pilmoor and Myton on Swale 79-84; V Brafferton w Pilmoor, Myton on Swale etc from 84. *The Vicarage, Brafferton, York YO6 2QB* Boroughbridge (0423) 360244

HARRIS-EVANS, Canon Francis Douglas Harris. b 07. Keble Coll Ox BA32 MA39. Linc Th Coll 32. **d** 35 **p** 36. V Newtown Linford *Leic* 68-74; rtd 74; Perm to Offic Leic and Pet from 74. *5 Mayflower Mews, Uppingham, Leics LE15 9ZZ* Uppingham (0572) 823699

HARRIS-EVANS, William Giles. b 46. AKC68. Bangalore Th Coll DipTh70. **d** 70 **p** 71. C Clapham H Trin *S'wark* 70-74; Sri Lanka 75-78; V Benhilton *S'wark* 78-86; TR Cov E *Cov* from 86. *St Peter's Rectory, Charles Street, Coventry CV1 5NP* Coventry (0203) 225907

HARRISON, Alan George. b 20. Leeds Univ BA49. Coll of Resurr Mirfield 49. **d** 51 **p** 52. V Eastleigh *Win* 68-72; Chapl Guild of Health Lon 72-76; Chapl St Mich Convent Ham 73-86; Sec Coun for Relig Communities 76-86; rtd 86. *10 The Quadrangle, Morden College, London SE3 0PW*

HARRISON, Alan William. b 16. Lich Th Coll 38. **d** 41 **p** 42. V Somerby, Burrough on the Hill and Pickwell *Leic* 55-72; R Boxford *St E* 72-82; rtd 82; Perm to

Offic *St E* from 82. *10 Meadowlands, Woolpit, Bury St Edmunds, Suffolk IP30 9SE* Elmswell (0359) 41614

HARRISON, Albert Arthur. b 01. FCIT. **d** 63 **p** 64. Chapl Aske Chapelry 65-85; NSM Rokeby w Brignall *Ripon* 67-89; rtd 89. *16 Ronaldshay Drive, Richmond, N Yorkshire DL10 5BN* Richmond (0748) 3072

HARRISON, Alfred Tuke Priestman. b 21. Ch Ch Ox BA43 MA47. Wells Th Coll DipTh49. **d** 49 **p** 50. C Rowbarton *B & W* 49-55; C-in-c Lyngford St Pet CD 55-58; V Lyngford 58; Trinidad and Tobago 59-66 and 69-73; USA 67-68; Dean Port of Spain 69-73; V Leesfield *Man* from 73. *St Thomas's Vicarage, Wild Street, Lees, Oldham OL4 5AD* 061-624 3731

HARRISON, Mrs Alison Edwina. b 53. Newc Univ BEd75. Linc Th Coll 84. **dss** 86 **d** 87. Loughb Em *Leic* 86-87; Par Dn 87-89; C Stockton *Dur* from 89. *8 Fairfield Road, Stockton-on-Tees, Cleveland TS19 7AJ* Stockton-on-Tees (0642) 585948

HARRISON, Alistair Lee. b 22. ALCD51. **d** 51 **p** 52. C Stoke Damerel *Ex* 51-54; Chapl RAF 54-67; Asst Chapl Miss to Seamen 67-77; Lic to Offic *D & G & M & K* 77-83; C Dub St Ann w St Mark and St Steph *D & G* from 83. *8 Grosvenor Place, Rathgar, Dublin 6, Irish Republic* Dublin (1) 976053

HARRISON, Barbara Ann. b 41. Man Univ BA63 Leic Univ CertEd64. E Midl Min Tr Course 85. **d** 88. C Immingham *Linc* from 88. *2 Anglesey Drive, Immingham, Grimsby DN40 1RE* Immingham (0469) 573578

HARRISON, Mrs Barbara Anne. b 34. Westf Coll Lon BA56 CertEd57 Hull Univ MA85. Linc Th Coll 76. **dss** 79 **d** 87. Lakenham St Jo *Nor* 79-80; Chapl York Univ *York* 80-88; TM Sheff Manor *Sheff* from 88. *The Vicarage, 195 Harborough Avenue, Sheffield S2 1QT* Sheffield (0742) 398202

HARRISON, Bernard Charles. b 37. St Mich Coll Llan 61. **d** 64 **p** 65. C Toxteth Park St Marg *Liv* 64-69; C Hindley All SS 69-71; V Wigan St Geo from 71. *St George's Vicarage, 6 Wrightington Street, Wigan, Lancs WN1 2BX* Wigan (0942) 44500

HARRISON, Brian John. b 35. FCP. Glouc Sch of Min 83. **d** 86 **p** 89. NSM Broseley w Benthall *Heref* from 86. *17 Hafren Road, Little Dawley, Telford, Shropshire TF4 3HJ* Telford (0952) 591891

HARRISON, Bruce. b 49. Linc Th Coll 86. **d** 88 **p** 89. C Syston *Leic* 88-90; C Whitby *York* from 90. *Little Whitehall, Spital Bridge, Whitby, N Yorkshire YO22 4EG* Whitby (0947) 601341

HARRISON, Bruce Mountford. b 49. AKC71. **d** 72 **p** 73. C Hebburn St Cuth *Dur* 72-75; C Bethnal Green St Jo w St Simon *Lon* 75-77; P-in-c Bethnal Green St Bart 77-78; TV Bethnal Green St Jo w St Bart 78-80; C-in-c Pennywell St Thos and Grindon St Oswald CD *Dur* 80-85; V Sunderland Pennywell St Thos 85-90; V Gateshead St Helen from 90. *The Vicarage, 7 Carlton Terrace, Gateshead, Tyne & Wear NE9 6DE* 091-487 6510

HARRISON, Christopher Dennis. b 57. Clare Coll Cam BA79 BA86. Westcott Ho Cam 84. **d** 87 **p** 88. C Camberwell St Geo *S'wark* from 87. *131 Coleman Road, London SE5 7TF* 071-703 2704

HARRISON, Christopher Joseph. b 38. AKC61 Bris Univ BEd75. **d** 62 **p** 63. C Bottesford *Linc* 62-67; C Elloughton *York* 67-68; P-in-c Farmington *Glouc* 69-74; C Tredington w Stoke Orchard and Hardwicke 74-86. *Appledore, 93 Stoke Road, Bishops Cleeve, Cheltenham, Glos GL52 4RP* Cheltenham (0242) 673452

HARRISON, Colin Charles. b 32. Nottm Univ BA59. Ripon Hall Ox 59. **d** 61 **p** 62. C Everton St Chad w Ch Ch *Liv* 61-64; Japan 64-66; P-in-c Glas St Gabr *Glas* 66-71; R Clarkston 71-74; Area Sec (Inner Lon) Chr Aid 74-84; Hon C St Nic Cole Abbey *Lon* 74-78; Hon C St Botolph without Bishopsgate 78-84; Miss to Seamen from 85; Nigeria 85-86; S Africa 87-88; Korea 88-91; Trinidad and Tobago from 91. *Mariners' Club, Wrightson Road, PO Box 561, Port of Spain, Trinidad* Trinidad (1809) 625-4826 or 627-4873

HARRISON, David Henry. b 40. Lon Univ DipTh67. Tyndale Hall Bris 65. **d** 68 **p** 69. C Bolton St Paul *Man* 68-72; V Bircle 72-83; V Southport SS Simon and Jude *Liv* 83-91; TR Fazakerley Em from 91. *The Rectory, Higher Lane, Liverpool L9 9DJ* 051-525 2689

HARRISON, David Robert. b 31. Bris Univ BSc52 CertEd55. Oak Hill Th Coll 56. **d** 58 **p** 59. C Brixton Hill St Sav *S'wark* 58-60; C Harpurhey Ch Ch *Man* 60-62; Singapore 62-67; V Greenfield *Man* 67-78; V Tonge Fold 78-90; R Tasburgh w Tharston, Forncett and Flordon *Nor* from 90. *The Rectory, Tasburgh, Norwich NR15 1NB* Swainsthorpe (0508) 470656

HARRISON, David Samuel. b 44. Univ of Wales (Ban) BSc67. St Mich Coll Llan 67. d 70 p 71. C Canton St Jo Llan 70-74; C Witton Ches 74-78; V Sutton St Geo from 78. St George's Vicarage, 88 Byrons Lane, Macclesfield, Cheshire Macclesfield (0625) 23209

HARRISON, Ernest Wilfrid. b 17. Ox Univ MA Toronto Univ MA. Sarum Th Coll. d 40 p 41. C Roby Liv 40-43; C-in-c St D Huyton w Roby 43-45; C Coulsdon St Jo S'wark 45-47; Asst Dioc Missr 48-52; Canada from 52. 72 Shippigan Crescent, Willowdale, Ontario, Canada, M2J 2G2 Toronto (416) 493-1502

HARRISON, Francis Russell. b 20. E Anglian Minl Tr Course. d 82 p 83. NSM Felixstowe St Jo St E 82-85; Asst Chapl Ipswich Hosp 85-87; rtd 87; Perm to Offic St E from 87. The Strands, London Road, Copdock, Ipswich IP8 3JF Copdock (047386) 292

HARRISON, Fred. b 08. St Aid Birkenhead. d 59 p 60. V Litherland St Andr Liv 62-75; rtd 75; Lic to Offic Blackb from 81. 6 Windgate, Much Hoole, Preston PR4 4GR Longton (0772) 616336

HARRISON, Fred Graham. b 41. Lon Univ BSc62. Ridley Hall Cam 80. d 82 p 83. C Lenton S'well 82-85; V Ruddington from 85. The Vicarage, 62 Musters Road, Ruddington, Nottingham NG11 6HW Nottingham (0602) 211505

HARRISON, Herbert Gerald. b 29. Oak Hill Th Coll 53. d 56 p 57. C Chesterfield H Trin Derby 56-59; C Cam St Andr Less Ely 59-64; Miss to Seamen 64-74; Kenya 64-68; Port Chapl Ipswich 68-74; V Ipswich All SS St E 74-81; P-in-c Elmsett w Aldham 81-88; P-in-c Kersey w Lindsey 81-88; R Horringer cum Ickworth from 88. The Rectory, Manor Lane, Horringer, Bury St Edmunds, Suffolk IP29 5PY Horringer (0284) 735206

HARRISON, Ian Wetherby. b 39. Kelham Th Coll 59. d 64 p 65. C Kennington Park St Agnes S'wark 64-67; C E Ham w Upton Park Chelmsf 67-71; V Walthamstow St Mich 71-78; Dioc Ecum Officer Wakef 78-87; P-in-c Upper Hopton 78-87; P-in-c Mirfield Eastthorpe St Paul 82-87; Min and Succ St D Cathl St D 87-90; P-in-c Leic Ascension Leic from 90. St Anne's Vicarage, 76 Letchworth Road, Leicester LE3 6FH Leicester (0533) 858452

HARRISON, Jack. b 08. Ripon Hall Ox 64. d 65 p 66. V Downe Roch 69-76; rtd 76; Perm to Offic Chich from 76. Jolly Cottage, Langham Road, Robertsbridge, E Sussex TN32 5DY Robertsbridge (0580) 880374

HARRISON, John. b 49. Fitzw Coll Cam BA71 MA74. Westcott Ho Cam 74. d 77 p 78. C Nunthorpe York 77-81; C Acomb St Steph 81-83; C-in-c St Aid 81-83; V Heptonstall Wakef 83-91; R Stamford Bridge Gp of Par York from 91. The Rectory, 8 Viking Road, Stamford Bridge, York YO4 1BR Stamford Bridge 71353

HARRISON, Canon John Gordon. b 13. Wadh Coll Ox BA48 MA52. Trin Coll Bris 32. d 36 p 38. V Gerrards Cross Ox 52-84; RD Amersham 70-79; Hon Can Ch Ch from 75; rtd 84. Hope Cottage, 18 Austen Way, Chalfont St Peter, Gerrards Cross, Bucks SL6 8NW Gerrards Cross (0753) 884077

HARRISON, John Northcott. b 31. St Jo Coll Cam BA54. Westcott Ho Cam 54. d 56 p 57. C Moor Allerton Ripon 56-59; C Bedale 59-61; V Hudswell w Downholme 61-64; Youth Chapl Dur 64-68; V Auckland St Andr and St Anne 68-76; Community Chapl Stockton-on-Tees 76-83; TR Southn (City Cen) Win 83-88; V Bris Ch the Servant Stockwood Bris from 88; RD Brislington from 89. The Vicarage, Goslet Road, Bristol BS14 8SP Bristol (0272) 832633

HARRISON, Joseph Benson. b 11. OBE74. Didsbury Meth Coll. d 49 p 50. Gen Sec C of E Coun for Soc Aid 55-75; rtd 76. 50A Sedlescombe Road South, St Leonards-on-Sea, E Sussex TN38 0TJ Hastings (0424) 446241

HARRISON, Leslie John. b 12. LSE 33 Lon Univ DipEd34. Wells Th Coll 63. d 64 p 65. V Greenbank Bris 67-73; V Caxton Ely 73-80; R Longstowe 74-80; rtd 80. 55 Long Lane, Willingham, Cambridge CB4 5LD Willingham (0954) 60859

HARRISON, Martin. b 58. DCR78 BA89. Trin Coll Bris 86. d 89 p 90. C Heworth York from 89. 7 Woodlands Grove, Stockton Lane, Heworth, York YO3 0DP York (0904) 426306

HARRISON, Mary Furley. b 21. MBE63. Westf Coll Lon BA42. Moray Ho Edin CertEd43 Edin Dioc NSM Course 79. dss 83 d 86. Edin H Cross Edin 83-86; NSM from 86. Barnhill, 33 Barnton Avenue, Edinburgh EH4 6JJ 031-336 2226

HARRISON, Matthew Henry. b 64. Univ Coll Dur BA85. St Steph Ho Ox BA88. d 89 p 90. C Whickham Dur from 89. St Mary's House, 7A Coalway Drive, Whickham, Newcastle upon Tyne NE16 4BT 091-488 3015

HARRISON, Michael Burt (Brother Crispin). b 36. Leeds Univ BA59 Trin Coll Ox BA62 MA66. Coll of Resurr Mirfield 62. d 63 p 64. C W Hartlepool St Aid Dur 63-64; C Middlesb All SS York 64-66; Lic to Offic Wakef 67-69 and 78-87; CR from 68; S Africa 69-77 and from 87; Registrar Coll of the Resurr Mirfield 78-84; Vice-Prin 84-87. St Peter's Priory, PO Box 991, Southdale, 2135 South Africa Johannesburg (11) 434-2504

HARRISON, Michael Robert. b 63. Selw Coll Cam BA84 MSc85. Ripon Coll Cuddesdon BA89 Union Th Sem (NY) STM90. d 90 p 91. C S Lambeth St Anne and All SS S'wark from 90. 11 Wilkinson Street, London SW8 071-582 5154

HARRISON, Canon Noel Milburn. b 27. Lon Univ DipTh56 Leeds Univ MPhil75 PhD80. St Aid Birkenhead 54. d 57 p 58. C Doncaster St Jas Sheff 57-60; Chapl Yorkshire Res Sch for Deaf Doncaster 60-68; C Woodlands Sheff 60-62; Chapl to the Deaf 60-68; Hd Master Elmete Hall Sch Leeds 68-84; Hon C Whitgift w Adlingfleet and Eastoft 83-84; Hon C Abbeydale St Jo 84-86; Dioc Dir of Educn from 84; R Tankersley from 86; Hon Can Sheff Cathl from 88. The Rectory, Chapel Road, Barnsley, S Yorkshire S75 3AR Barnsley (0226) 744140

HARRISON, Miss Patricia Mary. b 35. CertEd65 DPEd70 Open Univ BA74. St Mich Ho Ox 57. dss 85 d 87. Nunthorpe York 85-87; NSM from 87. 22 Lamonby Close, Nunthorpe, Middlesbrough, Cleveland TS7 0QG Middlesbrough (0642) 313524

HARRISON, Paul Graham. b 53. Sarum & Wells Th Coll 76. d 79 p 80. C Brixham w Churston Ferrers Ex 79-82; C Portsea N End St Mark Portsm 82-87; V Tiverton St Andr Ex from 87. The Vicarage, 49 Tidcombe Lane, Tiverton, Devon EX16 4EQ Tiverton (0884) 257865

HARRISON, Canon Peter George Stanley. b 22. St Jo Coll Dur BA49 DipTh50. d 50 p 51. P-in-c Routh York 68-91; V Beverley Minster 68-91; RD Beverley 73-85; Can and Preb York Minster from 83; rtd 91. 19 Orchard Way, Pocklington, York YO4 2EH Pocklington (0759) 304112

HARRISON, Peter Graham. b 12. Ch Ch Ox BA34 MA38. Westcott Ho Cam 34. d 35 p 36. V Gt Torrington Ex 58-78; R Lt Torrington 59-78; rtd 78; C-in-c Holne Ex 78-85. The Vicarage, Holne, Newton Abbot, Devon TQ13 7ST Poundsgate (03643) 382

HARRISON, Peter Keith. b 44. Open Univ BA85. St Aid Birkenhead. d 68 p 69. C Higher Bebington Ches 68-71; C Walmsley Man 71-74; V Lumb in Rossendale 74-79; V Heywood St Marg 79-87; V Hey from 87. The Vicarage, 2 Lower Cross Bank, Lees, Oldham OL4 3NP 061-624 1182

HARRISON, Peter Reginald Wallace. b 39. Selw Coll Cam BA62. Ridley Hall Cam 62. d 64 p 65. C Barton Hill St Luke w Ch Ch Bris 64-69; Chapl Greenhouse Trust 69-77; Dir Northorpe Hall Trust 77-84; Lic to Offic Wakef 77-84; TR Drypool York from 84; AD W Hull Deanery from 88. The Vicarage, 139 Laburnum Avenue, Hull HU8 8PA Hull (0482) 74257

HARRISON, Philip Hubert. b 37. Sarum & Wells Th Coll 77. d 79 p 80. C Wymondham Nor 79-83; V Watton w Carbrooke and Ovington from 83. The Vicarage, Norwich Road, Watton, Thetford, Norfolk 1P25 6DB Watton (0953) 881439

HARRISON, Raymond Harold. b 16. Keble Coll Ox BA41 MA45. St Aug Coll Cant. d 42 p 43. R Fen Ditton Ely 56-75; V W Wratting 75-82; R Weston Colville 76-82; rtd 82. 2 Guntons Close, Soham, Ely, Cambs CB7 5DN Ely (0353) 720774

HARRISON, Richard Crispin. b 57. Plymouth Poly BSc79. Trin Coll Bris 82. d 85 p 86. C Southway Ex 85-89; TV Kinson Sarum from 89. The Vicarage, 41 Moore Avenue, Kinson, Bournemouth BH11 8AT Bournemouth (0202) 581135

HARRISON, Richard Kingswood. b 61. Linc Coll Ox BA83 MA88 Leeds Univ BA90. d 91. C Reading St Giles Ox from 91. 31 Holybrook Road, Reading, Berks RG1 6DG Reading (0734) 595280

HARRISON, Robert Peter. b 28. Chich Th Coll. d 60 p 61. C Ealing Ch the Sav Lon 60-64; C Hammersmith SS Mich and Geo White City Estate CD 64-66; P-in-c Fulham St Pet 66-73; V from 73. St Peter's Vicarage, 2 St Peter's Terrace, London SW6 7JS 071-385 2045

HARRISON, Robert William. b 62. Mansf Coll Ox BA84. Qu Coll Birm 87. d 89 p 90. C Sholing Win from 89. 93 Spring Road, Southampton SO2 7QH Southampton (0703) 420371

HARRISON, Prof Roland Kenneth. b 20. Lon Univ BD43 MTh47 PhD52 Huron Coll DD63. ALCD43. d 43 p 44. C Preston St Mark Blackb 43-45; C Marple All SS Ches 45-47; Chapl Clifton Th Coll 47-49; Canada from

49; Prof OT Huron Coll 49-60; Wycliffe Coll 60-86; Toronto Sch Th 69-86. *41 Cuthbert Crescent, Toronto, Ontario, Canada, M4S 2G9*   Toronto (416) 481-7808

HARRISON, Rosemary Jane. b 53. Bradf Coll of Educn CertEd76. Trin Coll Bris DipHE85. **d** 87. NSM Southway *Ex* 87-89; NSM Kinson *Sarum* from 89. *The Vicarage, 41 Moore Avenue, Kinson, Bournemouth BH11 8AT*   Bournemouth (0202) 581135

HARRISON, Steven John. b 47. FRMetS74 Univ of Wales (Abth) BSc68 PhD74. St And Dioc Tr Course 87. **d** 90 **p** 91. C Alloa *St And* from 90. *46 Westerlea Drive, Bridge of Allan, Stirling FK9 4DQ*   Stirling (0786) 833482

HARRISON, Thomas David Coleman. b 07. St Chad's Coll Regina 38. **d** 38 **p** 39. R Pulford *Ches* 52-73; rtd 73. *5 Hollyfield, Gresford, Wrexham, Clwyd LL12 8EU*   Gresford (0978) 852688

HARRISON, Walter Edward. b 1900. Em Coll Saskatoon. **d** 26 **p** 26. V Mossley *Man* 64-68; rtd 68; Perm to Offic *Man* from 68. *Axford, Ford Lane, Northenden, Manchester*   061-998 2550

HARRISON, Walter William. b 28. St Jo Coll Nottm. **d** 71 **p** 72. C Lenton *S'well* 71-74; R Carlton-in-the-Willows from 74. *St Paul's Rectory, Church Street, Nottingham NG4 1BJ*   Nottingham (0602) 616169

HARRISON, William Roy. b 34. Dur Univ BA58 DipTh59. Cranmer Hall Dur 57. **d** 59 **p** 60. C Kingswood *Bris* 59-62; Kenya 62-65; P-in-c Gt Somerford *Bris* 66; V Soundwell from 66. *The Vicarage, 46 Sweets Road, Bristol BS15 1XQ*   Bristol (0272) 671511

HARRISSON, John Anthony Lomax. b 47. Ex Univ BA72 DipTh85. Qu Coll Birm 72. **d** 74 **p** 75. C Loughton St Jo *Chelmsf* 74-81; V Chingford St Anne from 81. *St Anne's Vicarage, 200A Larkhall Road, London E4 6NP*   081-529 4740

HARROD, Victor Ralph. b 33. Oak Hill Th Coll 76. **d** 79 **p** 80. Hon C Latchingdon w Mundon and N Fambridge *Chelmsf* 79; Hon C Creeksea w Althorne, Latchingdon and N Fambridge 79-83; C Tilbury Docks 83-86; R Orsett 86-90; P-in-c Bulphan 86-90; Chapl Orsett Hosp from 86; R Orsett and Bulphan *Chelmsf* from 90. *The Rectory, Orsett, Grays, Essex RM16 3JT*   Grays Thurrock (0375) 891254

HARROLD, Jeremy Robin. b 31. Hertf Coll Ox BA54 BSc56 MA58 DipTh59. Wycliffe Hall Ox. **d** 59 **p** 60. C Rushden *Pet* 59-61; Bp's Dom Chapl *Lon* 61-64; Australia 64-67; V Harlesden St Mark *Lon* 67-72; V Hendon St Paul Mill Hill 72-84; V Stowmarket *St E* from 84; RD Stowmarket from 90. *The Vicarage, 31 Ipswich Road, Stowmarket, Suffolk IP14 1BD*   Stowmarket (0449) 613576

HARRON, James Alexander. b 37. GIMechE61 HNC59 St Aid Coll Dur 63. **d** 65 **p** 66. C Willowfield *D & D* 65-69; I Desertmartin *D & R* 69-80; Dep Sec BCMS (Ireland) 80-84; I Aghalee *D & D* from 84. *39 Soldierstown Road, Aghalee, Craigavon, Co Armagh BT67 0ES*   Aghalee (0846) 651233

HARROP, Douglas. b 21. St Aid Birkenhead 62. **d** 64 **p** 65. C Doncaster St Leon and St Jude *Sheff* 67-70; R S Witham *Linc* 70-76; R N Witham 70-76; RD Beltisloe 72-76; V Kirkdale *York* 76-85; rtd 85; Perm to Offic *Linc* from 85. *13 Dovecote, Middle Rasen, Market Rasen, Lincs LN8 3UD*   Market Rasen (0673) 843675

HARROP, Joseph Blakemore. b 17. Saltley Tr Coll Birm TCert39. Qu Coll Birm 51. **d** 53 **p** 56. CMS 53-55; Sudan 53-55; C Stoke upon Trent *Lich* 56-58; V Foxt w Whiston from 58; P-in-c Oakamoor w Cotton 78-85. *Foxt-Whiston Vicarage, Foxt, Stoke-on-Trent ST10 2HN*   Ipstones (0538) 266315

HARROP, Philip. b 65. Bretton Hall Coll BEd87. Coll of Resurr Mirfield 87. **d** 90 **p** 91. C Athersley *Wakef* from 90. *49 Laithes Lane, Barnsley, S Yorkshire*   Barnsley (0226) 202543

HARROP, Stephen Douglas. b 48. Leeds Univ CertEd74 Man Univ DSPT85 DASAE90. Edin Th Coll 77. **d** 79 **p** 82. C Middlesb St Martin *York* 79-80; C N Hull St Mich 80; C Cayton w Eastfield 80-81; C Oldham *Man* 82-84; V Oldham St Barn 84-89; Hong Kong from 89. *Flat 2-A, Marden Wing, St John's College, 82 Pokfulam Road, Hong Kong*   Hong Kong (852) 817-4189

HARRY, Bruce David. b 40. JP77. Culham Coll Ox CertEd60. N Ord Course 83. **d** 86 **p** 87. NSM Liscard St Thos *Ches* from 86. *21 Sandymount Drive, Wallasey, Merseyside L45 0LJ*   051-639 7232

HART, Allen Sydney George. b 38. Chich Th Coll 64. **d** 67 **p** 68. C N Wembley St Cuth *Lon* 67-71; C W Bromwich All SS *Lich* 71-74; TV Hucknall Torkard *S'well* 74-80; V Annesley Our Lady and All SS 80-86; V Bilborough St Jo from 86. *St John's Vicarage, Graylands Road, Nottingham NG8 4FD*   Nottingham (0602) 293320

HART, Andre Hendrik. b 62. Cape Town Univ BA86. St Steph Ho Ox 89. **d** 91. C Newbold and Dunston *Derby* from 91. *Church House, 27 Willowgarth Road, Chesterfield S41 8BL*   Chesterfield (0246) 275236

HART, Anthony. b 35. St Mich Coll Llan 77. **d** 79 **p** 80. NSM Jersey St Helier *Win* 79-81; C Heref All SS *Heref* 81-82; C Kingstone 82-84; C Eaton Bishop 82-84; C Clehonger 82-84; R Sutton St Nicholas w Sutton St Michael 84-88; R Withington w Westhide 84-88; R Jersey St Mary *Win* from 88. *St Mary's Rectory, Jersey, Channel Islands JE3 3DB*   Jersey (0534) 81410

HART, Arthur Tindal. b 08. Em Coll Cam BA31 MA36 BD44 DD52. Ripon Hall Ox 31. **d** 32 **p** 33. V Selmeston w Alciston *Chich* 66-73; rtd 73. *Flat 2, Wood House, College of St Barnabas, Lingfield, Surrey RH7 6NJ*   Dormans Park (034287) 714

HART, Colin Edwin. b 45. Leeds Univ BA66 PGCE67 Fitzw Coll Cam BA73 MA77 K Coll Lon MTh76 Leeds Univ MPhil89. Trin Coll Bris 74. **d** 74 **p** 75. C Ware Ch Ch *St Alb* 74-78; TV Sheff Manor *Sheff* 78-80; V Wombridge *Lich* 80-87; Lect in Past Th St Jo Coll Nottm from 87. *St John's College, Chilwell Lane, Bramcote, Nottingham NG9 3DS*   Nottingham (0602) 251114

HART, David Alan. b 48. Sarum & Wells Th Coll. **d** 83 **p** 84. C Fawley *Win* 83-85; CF 85-90; P-in-c Gt Warley w Childerditch and Ingrave *Chelmsf* from 90. *The Vicarage, Thorndon Gate, Ingrave, Brentwood, Essex CM13 3RG*   Brentwood (0277) 810238

HART, David Alan. b 54. Keble Coll Ox BA75 MPhil78. Union Th Sem (NY) STM79 Westcott Ho Cam 83. **d** 83 **p** 84. Asst Chapl Gresham's Sch Holt 83-84; Chapl K Edw VI Sch Nor 84-85; Chapl Shrewsbury Sch 85-87; Chapl St Jo Coll Sch Cam 87-88; C Camberwell St Giles w St Matt *S'wark* 88-90; Chapl Loughb Univ *Leic* from 90. *1 Holywell Drive, Loughborough, Leics LE11 3JU*   Loughborough (0509) 232790 or 263171

HART, David John. b 58. K Coll Lon BD80. St Mich Coll Llan. **d** 85 **p** 86. C Denbigh and Nantglyn *St As* 85-88; Chapl RAF 88-89; C Llanrhos *St As* 89-91; V Rhosllanerchrugog from 91. *1 Gerddi, Hall Street, Rhosllanerchrugog, Wrexham, Clwyd LL14 2LG*   Rhosllanerchrugog (0978) 840065

HART, David Leonard. b 42. Ripon Hall Ox 68. **d** 71 **p** 72. C Castle Vale *Birm* 71-73; Chapl All SS Hosp Birm from 73. *12 Dorchester Drive, Birmingham B17 0SW*   021-427 7828 or 523 5151

HART, David Maurice. b 35. Univ Coll Dur BSc57. Clifton Th Coll 59. **d** 61 **p** 62. C Bolton St Paul *Man* 61-64; C Hamworthy *Sarum* 64-70; R W Dean w E Grimstead 70-81; R Farley w Pitton and W Dean w E Grimstead 81-90; V Steeple Ashton w Semington and Keevil from 90. *The Vicarage, Vicarage Lane, Steeple Ashton, Trowbridge, Wilts BA14 6HH*   Devizes (0380) 870344

HART, Canon Dennis Daniel. b 22. Linc Th Coll 45. **d** 48 **p** 49. C Abbots Langley *St Alb* 48-49; C Bedf St Paul 49-53; CF 53-55; V St Alb St Sav *St Alb* from 55; Hon Can St Alb from 74; RD St Alb 84-90. *St Saviour's Vicarage, 25 Sandpit Lane, St Albans, Herts*   St Albans (0727) 51526

HART, Dennis William. b 30. JP. Open Univ BA. Oak Hill Th Coll 75. **d** 78 **p** 79. Hon C Clacton St Paul *Chelmsf* from 78. *Ogilvie School, Holland Road, Clacton-on-Sea, Essex CO15 6NG*   Clacton-on-Sea (0225) 423057

HART, Edwin Joseph. b 21. Oak Hill Th Coll 56. **d** 58 **p** 59. V Cranham Park *Chelmsf* 69-71; R Markfield *Leic* 71-89; rtd 89. *135 Grace Dieu Road, Thringstone, Leicester LE6 4AP*   Coalville (0530) 222767

HART, Canon Geoffrey William. b 27. Ex Coll Ox BA51 MA55. Ridley Hall Cam 51. **d** 54 **p** 55. C Islington St Mary *Lon* 54-58; C Leeds St Geo *Ripon* 58-59; V Harold Wood *Chelmsf* 59-65; V Southport Ch Ch *Liv* 65-73; R Cheltenham St Mary *Glouc* 73-76; TR Cheltenham St Mary, St Matt, St Paul and H Trin from 76; Hon Can Glouc Cathl from 78. *The Rectory, 18 Park Place, Cheltenham, Glos GL50 2QT*   Cheltenham (0242) 512208

HART, Graham Cooper. b 36. S Dios Minl Tr Scheme 88. **d** 91. NSM Filton *Bris* from 91. *The Old Post Office, Hambrook, Bristol, Avon BS16 1RF*   Bristol (0272) 565300

HART, Canon Graham Merril. b 23. **d** 77 **p** 77. Tanzania 77-84; Chapl Ostend w Knokke and Bruges *Eur* from 84; Miss to Seamen from 84. *Van Iseghemlaan 83, BUS 2, 8400 Ostend, Belgium*   Ostend (59) 702859

HART, Henry St John. b 12. St Jo Coll Cam BA34 Qu Coll Cam MA38 BD54. **d** 36 **p** 37. Chapl Qu Coll Cam 36-50; Dean 40-50 and 55-72; Fell from 36; Vice Pres 78-79;

Reader in Hebrew Cam Univ 72-79; rtd 80; Lic to Offic *Nor* 80-86; Perm to Offic from 86. *The Retreat, Felbrigg Hall, Norwich NR11 8PR*   West Runton (026375) 652

HART, James. b 53. MIL84 Dur Univ BA75 DipEd76 DipHE88. Oak Hill Th Coll 86. **d** 88 **p** 89. C Starbeck *Ripon* 88-90; SAMS from 90. *c/o SAMS, Allen Gardner House, Pembury Road, Tunbridge Wells, Kent TN2 3QU* Tunbridge Wells (0892) 38647

HART, John Charles. b 11. Worc Coll Ox BA34 MA40. Wycliffe Hall Ox 34. **d** 36 **p** 38. V Rudgwick *Chich* 66-77; rtd 77. *68 The Sheeplands, Sherborne, Dorset DT9 4BS* Sherborne (0935) 813921

HART, John Peter. b 39. Bris Sch of Min 80. **d** 84 **p** 85. NSM Malmesbury w Westport and Brokenborough *Bris* 84-88; C Yatton Moor *B & W* 89-90; V Bridgwater H Trin from 90. *Holy Trinity Vicarage, Hamp Street, Bridgwater, Somerset TA6 6AR* Bridgwater (0278) 422610

HART, John Richard. b 16. Ox NSM Course 72. **d** 75 **p** 76. NSM Reading St Matt *Ox* 75-77; NSM Grazeley and Beech Hill 77-88; NSM Spencer's Wood 77-88; NSM Beech Hill, Grazeley and Spencers Wood 88-89; Lic to Offic *Portsm* from 89. *Springvale Hotel, Springvale, Seaview, Isle of Wight PO34 5AN* Isle of Wight (0983) 612533

HART, Michael Anthony. b 50. AKC71. St Aug Coll Cant 72. **d** 73 **p** 74. C Southwick St Columba *Dur* 73-76; C Hendon St Alphage *Lon* 76-78; P-in-c Eltham Park St Luke *S'wark* 78-83; V 83-85; R Newington St Mary from 85; P-in-c Camberwell St Mich w All So w Em from 85. *The Rectory, 57 Kennington Park Road, London SE11 4JQ* 071-735 1894

HART, Canon Michael Stuart. b 39. Univ of Wales (Lamp) BA61 Lanc Univ MA72. Wycliffe Hall Ox 61. **d** 63 **p** 64. C W Bromwich St Jas *Lich* 63-66; C Tarrington w Stoke Edith *Heref* 66-67; C Putney St Mary *S'wark* 67-70; V Accrington St Mary *Blackb* 70-82; RD Accrington 76-82; Hon Can Blackb Cathl 81-91; V Walton-le-Dale 82-91; P-in-c Samlesbury 91; TR Heavitree w Ex St Paul *Ex* from 91. *The Rectory, 10 Sherwood Close, Heavitree, Exeter EX2 5DX* Exeter (0392) 74489

HART, Peter William. b 60. Liv Univ BA82 Universite de Haute Normandie MesL84. Sarum & Wells Th Coll 86. **d** 88 **p** 89. C Llansamlet *S & B* 88-89; C Sketty from 89. *10 Sketty Park Close, Sketty, Swansea SA2 8LR* Swansea (0792) 204086

HART, Richard. b 49. Or Coll Ox MPhil84. St D Coll Lamp BA82 Qu Coll Birm 84. **d** 85 **p** 86. C Sketty *S & B* 85-87; P-in-c Llanbister and Llanbadarn Fynydd w Llananno 87-88; V from 88. *The Vicarage, Llanbister, Llandrindod Wells, Powys LD1 6TN* Llandrindod Wells (0597) 83333

HART, Ronald George. b 46. BSc Bris Univ DSA72 Lon Univ DASS77 CQSW77. Sarum & Wells Th Coll. **d** 85 **p** 86. C Sittingbourne St Mich *Cant* 85-88; C Walton H Trin *Ox* 88-89; TV from 89. *60 Grenville Road, Southcourt, Aylesbury HP21 8EY* Aylesbury (0296) 24175

HART, Canon Tony. b 36. CCC Cam BA59 MA63. Cuddesdon Coll 59. **d** 61 **p** 62. C Middlesb All SS *York* 61-64; Bp's Dom Chapl *Dur* 64-67; C Owton Manor CD 67-70; V Harton Colliery 70-82; TR S Shields All SS 82-83; RD Jarrow 77-83; Can Res Dur Cathl from 83. *6A The College, Durham DH1 3EQ* 091-384 5489

HART, Dr Trevor Andrew. b 61. St Jo Coll Dur BA82 Aber Univ PhD89. **d** 88 **p** 88. Lect Aber Univ from 86; NSM Bieldside *Ab* from 88. *66 Tillydrone Avenue, Aberdeen AB2 2TN* Aberdeen (0224) 483433

HARTE, Frederick George. b 25. AKC53. **d** 54 **p** 55. V Bellingham St Dunstan *S'wark* 60-73; V Plumstead St Nic 73-84; V Sutton Bridge *Linc* 84-90; rtd 90; Master St Jo Hosp Bath and P-in-c of Chpl from 90. *The Master's Lodge, St John's Hospital, Chapel Court, Bath BA1 1SL* Bath (0225) 464972

HARTE, Ven Matthew Scott. b 46. TCD BA70 MA74. CITC 71. **d** 71 **p** 72. C Ban Abbey *D & D* 71-74; C Ballynafeigh St Jude 74-76; I Ardara w Glencolumbkille, Inniskeel etc *D & R* from 76; Adn Raphoe from 83. *The Rectory, Ardara, Lifford, Co Donegal, Irish Republic* Ardara (75) 41124

HARTIN, Canon James. b 30. TCD BA52 MA60. **d** 54 **p** 55. C Derriaghy *Conn* 54-56; C Finaghy 56-59; C Dundela *D & D* 59-60; I Knocknagoney 60-62; Sub-Warden CITC 63-80; Prin Lect in Ch Hist TCD from 64; Prof of Past Th TCD 80-89; Prec St Patr Cathl Dub 80-89; I Castlemacadam w Ballinaclash, Aughrim etc *D & G* from 89; RD Rathdrum from 90. *The Rectory, Avoca, Co Wicklow, Irish Republic* Avoca (402) 35127

HARTLAND, David Robson. b 33. Qu Coll Birm 64. **d** 66 **p** 67. C Brierley Hill *Lich* 66-71; V Hartshill 71-76; V Moxley 76-85; V Willenhall St Steph from 85. *St Stephen's Vicarage, Wolverhampton Street, Willenhall, W Midlands WV13 2PS* Willenhall (0902) 605239

HARTLAND, Ian Charles. b 49. K Coll Lon CertEd BD72 AKC72 MTh76. Sarum & Wells Th Coll 83. **d** 84 **p** 85. C Orpington All SS *Roch* 84-87; Lect Ch Ch Coll Cant from 87. *10 Cromwell Road, Canterbury, Kent CT1 3LD* Canterbury (0227) 760789

HARTLESS, Gordon Frederick James. b 13. LRAM40 LTCL42. Worc Ord Coll 54. **d** 55 **p** 56. P-in-c Hawnby w Old Byland *York* 69-78; P-in-c Bilsdale Midcable 75-78; R Scawton w Cold Kirby 69-78; rtd 78; Perm to Offic *York* from 78. *11 Beechfields, High Hawsker, Whitby, N Yorkshire YO22 4LQ* Whitby (0947) 880707

HARTLEY, Brian. b 41. N Ord Course 82. **d** 85 **p** 86. NSM Royton St Paul *Man* from 85. *76 Turf Lane, Royton, Oldham OL2 6JB* Shaw (0706) 843008

HARTLEY, Cyril Seymour. b 08. St Boniface Warminster 57. **d** 58 **p** 59. V Woolley *Wakef* 61-78; rtd 78. *18 Hatchfields, Great Waltham, Chelmsford, Essex CM3 1AJ* Chelmsford (0245) 360631

HARTLEY, David Michael. b 59. RGN85 Edin Univ BD81. St Steph Ho Ox 87. **d** 89 **p** 90. C Kingswinford St Mary *Lich* from 89. *4 The Village, Kingswinford, W Midlands DY6 8AY* Kingswinford (0384) 273397

HARTLEY, Godfrey. b 37. Man Univ. Cuddesdon Coll 64. **d** 64 **p** 65. C Balderton *S'well* 64-67; Miss to Seamen from 67; Portuguese E Africa 67-73; Sen Chapl and Sec for Scotland 74-89; P-in-c Glas St Gabr *Glas* 74-89; Chapl RNR from 74; Chapl Cornwall Miss to Seamen from 89. *Sandoes Gate, Feock, Truro, Cornwall TR3 6QN* Truro (0872) 865863

HARTLEY, Graham William Harrington. b 21. Ripon Hall Ox 61. **d** 62 **p** 63. V Knowsley *Liv* 66-72; V Langdale *Carl* 72-81; TV Egremont and Haile 81-85; TV Whitehaven 85-88; rtd 88; Perm to Offic *Carl* from 88. *14 Thrang Brow, Chapel Stile, Ambleside, Cumbria LA22 9JN* Langdale (09667) 322

HARTLEY, Harold Aitken. b 21. Whitaker Sch of Th. **d** 84 **p** 85. USA 84-89; NSM Fulford *York* from 89. *10 Godwins Way, Stamford Bridge, York YO4 1DB* Stamford Bridge (0759) 72552

HARTLEY, Canon Harry. b 02. Birm Univ BSc28 Open Univ BA76. St Steph Ho Ox 28. **d** 30 **p** 31. R Solihull *Birm* 53-70; Perm to Offic *Glouc* from 70; rtd 71. *Flat 1, Capel Court, The Burgage, Prestbury, Cheltenham, Glos GL52 3EL* Cheltenham (0242) 244426

HARTLEY, Herbert. b 28. AKC52. **d** 53 **p** 54. C Blackpool H Cross *Blackb* 53-55; C Reading St Giles *Ox* 55-58; V Ruscombe and Twyford 58-66; Chapl RN 66-73; C Langley Marish *Ox* 73-77; R Hedsor and Bourne End from 77. *The Rectory, 1 Wharf Lane, Bourne End, Bucks SL8 5RS* Bourne End (06285) 23046

HARTLEY, Dr John Peter. b 56. Cam Univ BA78 Leeds Univ PhD82 Dur Univ BA84. Cranmer Hall Dur 82. **d** 85 **p** 86. C Spring Grove St Mary *Lon* 85-88; C Bexleyheath St Pet *Roch* from 88. *46 Berkeley Avenue, Bexleyheath, Kent DA7 4UA* 081-301 3278

HARTLEY, John William. b 47. St Jo Coll Dur BA69. Linc Th Coll 70. **d** 72 **p** 73. C Poulton-le-Fylde *Blackb* 72-76; C Lanc St Mary 76-79; V Barrowford 79-87; V Salesbury from 87. *St Peter's Vicarage, 49A Ribchester Road, Blackburn BB1 9HU* Blackburn (0254) 48072

HARTLEY, Julian John. b 57. Oak Hill Th Coll BA85. **d** 85 **p** 86. C Eccleston Ch Ch *Liv* 85-89; V Goose Green from 89. *St Paul's Vicarage, Warrington Road, Wigan, Lancs WN1 6QB* Wigan (0942) 42984

HARTLEY, Michael Leslie. b 56. Leeds Univ BSc77. Ripon Coll Cuddesdon 87. **d** 89 **p** 90. C Standish *Blackb* from 89. *St Wilfrid's House, 7 Rectory Lane, Standish, Wigan, Lancs WN6 0XA* Standish (0257) 425806

HARTLEY, Nigel John. b 48. Portsm Poly BA. St Jo Coll Nottm. **d** 83 **p** 84. C Ipswich St Marg *St E* 83-86; P-in-c Hintlesham w Chattisham from 86; Dioc Radio Officer from 86. *The Rectory, Hintlesham, Ipswich IP8 3PT* Hintlesham (047387) 258

HARTLEY, Nigel Rogers. b 65. Mansf Coll Ox BA86 MA90. Chich Th Coll 87. **d** 89 **p** 90. C Borehamwood *St Alb* from 89. *16 Bullhead Road, Borehamwood, Herts WD6 1HS* 081-953 9788

HARTLEY, Paul. b 51. Nottm Univ BTh88. Linc Th Coll 85. **d** 88 **p** 89. C Clitheroe St Mary *Blackb* from 88. *24 Kirkmoor Road, Clitheroe, Lancs BB7 2DU* Clitheroe (0200) 28446

HARTLEY, Peter. b 44. St Cath Coll Cam BA66 MA69. Avery Hill Coll PGCE67 Ox Univ DipRE74. Sarum & Wells Th Coll 77. **d** 78 **p** 79. Hon C Freemantle *Win*

78-79; Chr Educn Officer *Pet* 79-81; Dir of Educn 81-90; Dir Coun of Educn and Tr *Chelmsf* from 90. *St Clare, Links Drive, Chelmsford, Essex CM2 9AW* Chelmsford (0245) 251461

HARTLEY, Canon Peter Goodwin. b 19. Keble Coll Ox BA48 MA52. Wells Th Coll 49. **d** 50 **p** 51. V Elstow *St Alb* 53-76; Can Res Bermuda 76-85; rtd 85; Perm to Offic *Ely* from 85. *53 Money Bank, Wisbech, Cambs PE13 2JG* Wisbech (0945) 61023

HARTLEY, Ven Peter Harold Trahair. b 09. Lon Univ BSc35 Qu Coll Ox MA48. Cuddesdon Coll 52. **d** 53 **p** 54. R Badingham w Bruisyard and Cransford *St E* 65-70; P-in-c Dennington 68-70; Adn Suffolk 70-75; rtd 75; P-in-c Badingham w Bruisyard and Cransford *St E* 75-85; P-in-c Dennington 75-85; Perm to Offic from 85. *26 Double Street, Framlingham, Woodbridge, Suffolk IP13 9BN* Framlingham (0728) 723604

HARTLEY, Peter Mellodew. b 41. MA MSc. S'wark Ord Course. **d** 83 **p** 84. NSM Salfords S'wark from 83. *60 Deerings Road, Reigate, Surrey RH2 0PN* Reigate (0737) 247940

HARTLEY, Stephen William Mark. b 50. St Chad's Coll Dur BA71. Westcott Ho Cam 72. **d** 74 **p** 75. C Holbrooks *Cov* 74-76; C Styvechale 76-79; P-in-c Snitterfield w Bearley 79-81; V 81-83; V Exhall 83-88; V Tilehurst St Cath *Ox* from 88. *The Vicarage, Wittenham Avenue, Tilehurst, Reading RG3 5LN* Reading (0734) 427786

HARTLEY, Stewart John Ridley. b 47. St Jo Coll Nottm 78. **d** 80 **p** 81. C Altham w Clayton le Moors *Blackb* 80-84; P-in-c Nelson St Phil 84-91; V from 91. *15 Thursby Road, Nelson, Lancs BB9 8LR* Nelson (0282) 698161

HARTLEY, Canon William Reginald. b 19. CCC Cam BA41 MA45. Linc Th Coll 41. **d** 42 **p** 43. R Birch St Jas *Man* 59-74; V Atherton 74-86; Hon Can Man Cathl 76-86; AD Leigh 79-85; rtd 86; Perm to Offic *Bradf* from 86. *21 Easby Close, Ilkley, W Yorkshire LS29 9DJ* Ilkley (0943) 609005

HARTNELL, Bruce John. b 42. Ex Univ BA64 Linacre Coll Ox BA66 MA. Ripon Hall Ox 64. **d** 66 **p** 67. C S Stoneham *Win* 66-69; Chapl and Tutor Ripon Hall Ox 69-74; V Knowl Hill w Littlewick *Ox* 74-78; Chapl Southn Univ *Win* 78-83; V Sholing from 83. *The Vicarage, 41 Station Road, Southampton SO2 8FN* Southampton (0703) 448337

HARVEY, Alan Douglas. b 25. FRSH82. Melbourne Coll of Div 78. **d** 79 **p** 81. Australia 79-86; Perm to Offic *Ely* 86-87; V Wiggenhall St Germans and Islington from 88; V Wiggenhall St Mary Magd from 88. *The Vicarage, 30 Lynn Road, St Germans, King's Lynn, Norfolk PE34 3EY* St Germans (055385) 371

HARVEY, Ven Anthony Ernest. b 30. Worc Coll Ox BA53 MA56 DD83. Westcott Ho Cam 56. **d** 58 **p** 59. C Chelsea Ch Ch *Lon* 58-62; Ch Ch Ox 62-69; Warden St Aug Coll Cant 69-75; Lect Th Ox Univ 76-82; Chapl Qu Coll Ox 77-82; Can and Lib Westmr Abbey from 82; Adn Westmr from 87; Sub-Dean Westmr from 87. *3 Little Cloister, Westminster Abbey, London SW1P 3PL* 071-222 4174

HARVEY, Anthony Peter. b 42. Birm Univ BSc63 MSc64. Wycliffe Hall Ox 79. **d** 81 **p** 82. C Stoke Damerel *Ex* 81-84; Canada 84-90; Chapl HM Young Offender Inst Deerbolt from 91. *HM Young Offender Institute, Bowes Road, Barnard Castle, Co Durham DL12 9BG* Teesdale (0833) 37561

HARVEY, Arthur Ernest. b 30. Lon Univ DipTh58 MSc80. Oak Hill Th Coll 54. **d** 57 **p** 58. C Rayleigh *Chelmsf* 57-60; C Morpeth *Newc* 60-63; R Pitsea *Chelmsf* 63-74; Ind Officer to Bp Chelmsf 73-80; R Bobbingworth 74-81; Chapl Bordeaux w Riberac, Cahors, Duras etc *Eur* 82-86; V Barnsbury St Andr and H Trin w All SS *Lon* 86-90; TR Barnsbury from 90. *5 Huntingdon Street, London N1 1BU* 071-607 6895 or 607 4552

HARVEY, Very Rev Brian. b 16. TCD BA38 BD41. TCD Div Sch Div Test39. **d** 40 **p** 41. Can Th Belf Cathl 63-70; I Kilkenny w Aghour and Kilmanagh *C & O* 70-91; Preb Leighlin Cathl from 70; Dean Ossory 70-91; rtd 91. *Alton, Kilbrittain, Co Cork, Irish Republic* Clonakilty (23) 49686

HARVEY, Charles Alma West. b 07. Glas Univ MA29. Edin Th Coll 29. **d** 31 **p** 32. R Gullane *Edin* 57-75; rtd 75. *17 Yewlands Crescent, Edinburgh EH16 6TB* 031-664 3089

HARVEY, Christopher John Alfred. b 41. S'wark Ord Course 66. **d** 69 **p** 70. C Grays Thurrock *Chelmsf* 69-73; C Gt Baddow 73-75; V Berechurch St Marg w St Mich from 75. *The Vicarage, 348 Mersea Road, Colchester CO2 8RA* Colchester (0206) 576859

HARVEY, Canon Cyril John. b 30. Univ of Wales (Lamp) BA51. Coll of Resurr Mirfield 51. **d** 53 **p** 54. C Caerau

w Ely *Llan* 53-57; C Milford Haven *St D* 57-61; V Castlemartin and Warren 61-65; R Begelly w Kilgetty 65-73; V Haverfordwest St Martin w Lambston 73-88; Can St D Cathl from 85; R Tenby from 88. *The Rectory, Church Park, Tenby, Dyfed SA70 7EE* Tenby (0834) 2068

HARVEY, Dennis William. TCD BA44 Div Test45 MA48. **d** 46 **p** 47. C Portarlington D,G & K 46-48; C Dub Santry, Glasnevin and Coolock *D & G* 48-49; Chapl RN 49-53; C Seagoe *D & D* 53-59; C Belf St Phil *Conn* 60; R Claverton *B & W* from 60. *Claverton Rectory, 93 Hantone Hill, Warminster Road, Bath BA2 6XE* Bath (0225) 466841

HARVEY, Frank Chivas. b 12. Edin Th Coll. **d** 49 **p** 50. Dioc Chapl *St And* 69-79; Chapl HM Pris Perth 69-79; Can St Ninian's Cathl Perth *St And* 77-79; rtd 79. *10 Pitcullen Terrace, Perth PH2 7EQ* Perth (0738) 28885

HARVEY, John. b 30. S'wark Ord Course. **d** 65 **p** 66. C Lewisham St Jo Southend S'wark 65-73; V Bellingham St Dunstan 73-78; TV Bourne Valley *Sarum* 78-81; TR 81-87; R Kilkhampton w Morwenstow *Truro* 87-90; rtd 90. *3 Riverside, The Bickerley, Ringwood, Hants BH24 1EJ*

HARVEY, John Christopher. b 65. Univ of Wales BA86 Nottm Univ BTh89. Linc Th Coll 89. **d** 89 **p** 90. C Penmaenmawr *Ban* from 89. *Glanfa, Glan-yr-Afon Road, Dwygyfylchi, Penmaenmawr, Gwynedd LL34 6UD* Penmaenmawr (0492) 622758

HARVEY, John Coburn. b 07. Trin Coll Cam BA28 MA33. **d** 36 **p** 37. W Midl Regional Sec BFBS 61-72; rtd 72; Perm to Offic *Wakef* from 72. *28 Thorpe Lane, Almondbury, Huddersfield HD5 8TA* Huddersfield (0484) 424675

HARVEY, John Wilfred. b 05. Lon Coll of Div 37. **d** 39 **p** 40. C-in-c Sheviock *Truro* 71-72; rtd 73; P-in-c St Martin by Looe *Truro* 71-72. *Chy Morvah, Marine Drive, Looe, Cornwall PL13 2DJ* Looe (05036) 3327

HARVEY, Lance Sydney Crockford. b 25. Ridley Hall Cam 67. **d** 69 **p** 70. C Mortlake w E Sheen *S'wark* 69-74; P-in-c Woolwich St Thos 75-86; V Lee Gd Shep w St Pet from 86; RD E Lewisham from 87. *The Vicarage, 47 Handen Road, London SE12 8NR* 081-852 5270

HARVEY, Leslie Francis. b 02. Birm Univ MSc22 Ball Coll Ox BA25 MA31. Westcott Ho Cam. **d** 30 **p** 32. Chapl and Hd Master The King's Sch Ches 47-64; rtd 68; Lic to Offic *Derby* from 87. *c/o Leeanda House, 19 Station Road, Borrowash, Derby DE7 3LG* Derby (0332) 675856

HARVEY, Margaret Claire. b 41. Univ of Wales (Abth) BA62 DipEd63 Lon Univ BD68. Dalton Ho Bris 66. **dss** d 80. Flint *St As* 68-74; Lect Trin Coll Bris 74-80; Connah's Quay *St As* 79-80; C 80-86; Bp's Adv for Continuing Clerical Educn from 86; Hon C Corwen and Llangar 86-87; Dn-in-c Bryneglwys from 87. *Coleg y Groes, The College, Corwen, Clwyd LL21 0AU* Corwen (0490) 2169

HARVEY, Maurice. b 31. **d** 70 **p** 71. C Lisburn St Paul *Conn* 70-72; C Ballymacarrett St Patr *D & D* 72-77; I Ballyphilip w Ardquin 77-79; I Ardmore w Craigavon 79-87; I Killyman *Arm* from 87. *St Andrew's Rectory, 85 Dungorman Road, Dungannon, Co Tyrone BT71 6SE* Dungannon (08687) 22500

HARVEY, Norman Roy. b 43. Nottm Univ DipAE86. Wycliffe Hall Ox 66. **d** 69 **p** 70. C Clay Cross *Derby* 69-72; C Dronfield 72-76; TV 76-79; Dioc Youth Officer 79-83; P-in-c Rowsley 79-89; Dioc Adv in Adult and Youth Educn 83-89; TR Eckington w Handley and Ridgeway from 89. *The Rectory, Eckington, Sheffield S31 9BG* Eckington (0246) 432196

HARVEY, Oliver Douglas. b 01. Magd Coll Ox BA25 MA45. Wells Th Coll 25. **d** 25 **p** 26. R Puddletown w Athelhampton and Burleston *Sarum* 62-69; rtd 69; Perm to Offic *Roch* from 86. *15 Old Parsonage Court, Water Lane, West Malling, Maidstone, Kent ME19 6NZ* West Malling (0732) 841117

HARVEY, Oliver Paul. b 33. Magd Coll Ox BA55 MA59. Cuddesdon Coll 57. **d** 59 **p** 60. C S Norwood St Mark *Cant* 59-61; C Hythe 61-64; Zambia 64-71; Chapl Cant Coll of Tech 71-77; Hon C Cant St Martin and St Paul *Cant* 73-77; Chapl K Sch Roch 77-88; C Roch 88-90; V Gillingham St Mary from 90. *The Vicarage, 27 Gillingham Green, Gillingham, Kent ME7 1SS* Medway (0634) 850529

HARVEY, Miss Pamela Betty. b 33. Dalton Ho Bris 57. **dss** 86 d 87. Nottm St Ann S'well 68-72; Bestwood St Matt 72-76; Consultant for NE England and Scotland from 76. *61 Upland Avenue, Leeds LS8 2SY* Leeds (0532) 400882

HARVEY, Patricia Ann. b 45. Qu Coll Birm. **dss** 82 **d** 87. Gospel Lane St Mich *Birm* 82-85; Exhall *Cov* 85-87; C 87-89; TM Droitwich Spa *Worc* from 89. *The Vicarage, 29 Old Coach Road, Droitwich Spa, Worcester WR9 8BB* Droitwich (0905) 771516

HARVEY, Patrick Arnold. b 58. TCD BA DipTh. **d** 85 **p** 86. C Bandon Union *C, C & R* 85-88; I Limerick St Mich *L & K* 88-90; Dioc Info Officer (Limerick and Killaloe) 88-90; I Abbeyleix w Old Church, Ballyroan etc *C & O* from 90. *The Rectory, Abbeyleix, Portlaoise, Co Laois, Irish Republic* Portlaoise (502) 31243

HARVEY, Canon Peter Harold Noel. b 16. Univ of Wales BA44. St Aug Coll Cant 39. **d** 40 **p** 41. Ed Ch Illustrated Publications 55-70; V Udimore *Chich* 69-76; P-in-c Brede 75-76; R Brede w Udimore 76-83; Can and Preb Chich Cathl 76-89; rtd 83. *Prebenden, 1 Smugglers' Way, Fairlight Cove, Hastings, E Sussex TN35 4DG* Hastings (0424) 813185

HARVEY, Reginald Darwin. b 28. E Anglian Minl Tr Course. **d** 82 **p** 83. NSM Gillingham w Geldeston, Stockton, Ellingham etc *Nor* from 82; Perm to Offic *St E* from 86. *Blaenwern, Mill Road, Ellingham, Bungay, Suffolk NR35 2PY* Kirby Cane (050845) 663

HARVEY, Robert Martin. b 30. S'wark Ord Course 69. **d** 70 **p** 71. C Sutton New Town St Barn *S'wark* 70-75; C Leatherhead *Guildf* 76-78; V Wadworth w Loversall *Sheff* from 78. *The Vicarage, Vicarage Drive, Wadworth, Doncaster, S Yorkshire DN11 9BW* Doncaster (0302) 851974

HARVEY, Robin Grant. b 43. Clare Coll Cam BA64 MA68 Univ of NSW PhD74. Linc Th Coll 85. **d** 87 **p** 88. C Keynsham *B & W* 87-91; R E w W Harptree and Hinton Blewett from 91. *The Rectory, Church Lane, East Harptree, Bristol BS18 6BD* West Harptree (0761) 221239

HARVEY, Stephen George Kay. b 06. Lon Univ BD39 Ridley Coll Melbourne 32. ACT ThL33. **d** 33 **p** 34. R Wath *Ripon* 60-72; rtd 72. *11 Hannams Close, Lytchett Matravers, Poole, Dorset BH16 6DN* Lytchett Minster (0202) 623481

HARVEY, Steven Charles. b 58. Reading Univ BA79 Ox Univ BA83 MA88. Ripon Coll Cuddesdon 81. **d** 84 **p** 85. C Oldham *Man* 84-87; Hd of RE and Chapl St Pet Sch York from 87. *St Peter's School, York YO3 6AB* York (0904) 623213 or 658332

HARVEY, Trevor John. b 43. Sheff Univ BA64. Coll of Resurr Mirfield 64. **d** 66 **p** 67. C Kingswinford St Mary *Lich* 66-72; V Upper Gornal 72-77; V Meir 77-86; Chapl St Geo Choir Sch Windsor from 86; Min Can Windsor from 86. *12 The Cloisters, Windsor Castle, Windsor, Berks SL4 1NJ* Windsor (0753) 842086

HARVEY, Victor Llewellyn Tucker. b 16. Ch Coll Cam BA38 MA42. Ridley Hall Cam 38. **d** 39 **p** 40. Hon CF from 46; R St Marylebone St Mary *Lon* 64-82; rtd 82; Perm to Offic *St E* from 82; P-in-c Hasketon 83-89. *The Boot, Great Bealings, Woodbridge, Suffolk IP13 6PQ* Grundisburgh (047335) 382

HARVEY, William Thomas. b 03. **d** 61 **p** 61. V Arnesby w Shearsby *Leic* 63-73; rtd 73. *Chypons Residential Home, Newlyn, Penzance, Cornwall TR18 5BU* Penzance (0736) 62492

HARVIE, Paul Johnston. b 36. ARCO74 FTCL73 Melbourne Univ BMusEd80 MMus83. St Mich Th Coll Crafers 58 Trin Coll Melbourne LTh61 ACT ThL. **d** 62 **p** 63. Australia 62-64 and 66-89; C Penton Street St Silas w All SS *Lon* 64-66; Vice-Provost St Paul's Cathl Dundee *Bre* from 89; R Dundee St Paul from 89. *7 Paradise Road, Dundee DD1 1JB* Dundee (0382) 21785

HARWOOD, Frederick Ronald. b 21. Wells Th Coll 61. **d** 63 **p** 64. V Hessenford *Truro* 66-71; V Hayle 71-87; rtd 87; Hon C Madron *Truro* from 88. *Ferncliffe, 5 Harbour View, Hayle, Cornwall TR27 4LB* Hayle (0736) 753690

HARWOOD, Canon John Rossiter. b 26. Selw Coll Cam BA51 MA55. Wycliffe Hall Ox 51. **d** 53 **p** 54. Home Educn Sec CMS 67-75; V Cheltenham Ch Ch *Glouc* 75-91; RD Cheltenham 84-89; Hon Can Glouc Cathl from 85; rtd 91. *29 Clarence Hill, Dartmouth, Devon TQ6 9NY* Dartmouth (0803) 835827

HARWOOD, Leslie Thomas Bromser. b 03. Trin Hall Cam BA25 MA30. Westcott Ho Cam 25. **d** 26 **p** 27. R Hickling *S'well* 52-78; V Kinoulton 52-78; rtd 78; Perm to Offic *S'well* from 78. *Glebe Farm Cottage, Hickling, Melton Mowbray, Leics* Melton Mowbray (0664) 822267

HARWOOD, Thomas Smith. b 10. St Jo Coll Dur 38. **d** 41 **p** 41. V Middleton St Mary *Ripon* 62-75; V E Winch *Nor* 62-75; rtd 75; Perm to Offic *Nor* from 75.

8 Beechwood Close, Watlington, King's Lynn, Norfolk PE33 0HP King's Lynn (0553) 811463

HASELDEN, Canon Eugene John Charles. b 17. Em Coll Cam BA40 MA44. Ridley Hall Cam 40. **d** 42 **p** 43. V Leamington Priors H Trin *Cov* 58-75; RD Leamington 69-75; V Lymington *Win* 75-83; RD Lyndhurst 78-82; rtd 83; Perm to Offic *Win* from 83. *1 Ashley Meadows, Romsey, Hants SO51 7LT* Romsey (0794) 522688

HASELOCK, Jeremy Matthew. b 51. York Univ BA73 BPhil74. St Steph Ho Ox BA82 MA86. **d** 83 **p** 84. C Pimlico St Gabr *Lon* 83-86; C Paddington St Jas 86-88; Bp's Dom Chapl *Chich* from 88. *Monk's Cottage, Palace Yard, Canon Lane, Chichester, W Sussex PO19 1PX* Chichester (0243) 780982

HASKINS, Thomas. b 41. TCD BA72. CITC 71. **d** 73 **p** 74. C Larne and Inver *Conn* 73-78; C Antrim All SS 78-83; I Belf St Mark 83-90; RD M Belf 89-90; I Dub Clontarf *D & G* from 90. *15 Seafield Road West, Clontarf, Dublin 3, Irish Republic* Dublin (1) 331181

HASLAM, Andrew James. b 57. Univ Coll Dur BSc78 Coll of Ripon & York St Jo PGCE79. Lambeth STh84 Trin Coll Bris 80. **d** 83 **p** 84. C Leyland St Andr *Blackb* 83-86; C Hartford *Ches* 86-88; V Grimsargh *Blackb* from 88. *St Michael's Vicarage, Preston Road, Grimsargh, Preston, Lancs PR2 5SD* Preston (0772) 653283

HASLAM, Canon David. b 31. St Chad's Coll Dur BA57. Wells Th Coll 57. **d** 59 **p** 60. C Manston *Ripon* 59-62; C Bournemouth St Pet *Win* 62-65; V E and W Worldham, Hartley Mauditt w Kingsley etc 65-71; V Boscombe St Andr from 71; RD Bournemouth 80-90; Hon Can Win Cathl from 84. *St Andrew's Vicarage, 3 Wilfred Road, Bournemouth BH5 1NB* Bournemouth (0202) 394575

HASLAM, Canon Frank. b 26. Bris Univ BA50. Tyndale Hall Bris 49. **d** 51 **p** 52. V Blackpool Ch Ch *Blackb* 65-70; V Macclesfield St Mich *Ches* 71-80; Dir of Resources 80-91; Hon Can Ches Cathl from 81; rtd 91. *Brackendale, Chester Road, Buckley, Clwyd CH7 3AH* Buckley (0244) 294544

HASLAM, James Robert. b 31. Open Univ BA74. Bps' Coll Cheshunt 55. **d** 57 **p** 58. C Penwortham St Mary *Blackb* 57-63; V Cockerham 63-74; V Cockerham w Winmarleigh 74-76; V Gt Harwood St Bart 76-88; V Fairhaven from 88. *83 Clifton Drive, Fairhaven, Lytham St Annes, Lancs FY8 1BZ* Lytham (0253) 734562

HASLAM, John Gordon. b 32. Birm Univ LLB53. Qu Coll Birm 75. **d** 77 **p** 77. Hon C Bartley Green *Birm* 77-79; Hon C Moseley St Mary from 79; Chapl to HM The Queen from 89. *34 Amesbury Road, Birmingham B13 8LE* 021-449 3394

HASLAM, Robert John Alexander. b 34. CCC Cam BA58. Coll of Resurr Mirfield 58. **d** 60 **p** 61. C Rawmarsh w Parkgate *Sheff* 60-66; Perm to Offic *Edin* 66-73; Carl 73-77; P-in-c Peebles *Edin* 77-81; V Darnall H Trin *Sheff* 81-85; Hon C Bermondsey St Hugh CD *S'wark* 86-88; R Clydebank *Glas* from 88. *21 Downam Street, Clydebank, Dunbartonshire G81 1RL* 041-952 0298

HASLAM-JONES, Christopher John. b 28. ALCD53. **d** 53 **p** 54. C Walthamstow St Jo *Chelmsf* 53-57; C High Wycombe All SS *Ox* 57-62; V Parkfield in Middleton *Man* 62-68; V Radcliffe St Andr 68-86; R Colchester Ch Ch w St Mary V *Chelmsf* from 86. *The Rectory, 21 Cambridge Road, Colchester CO3 3NS* Colchester (0206) 560175

HASLER, John Joseph. b 45. Qu Coll Birm 89. **d** 90 **p** 91. C Horfield H Trin *Bris* from 90. *40 Bishopthorpe Road, Bristol BS10 5AD* Bristol (0272) 426576

HASSALL, William Edwin. b 41. St Jo Coll Nottm 75. **d** 77 **p** 78. C Wellington w Eyton *Lich* 77-80; C Farewell 80-82; V from 82; C Gentleshaw 80-82; V from 82. *The Vicarage, Budds Road, Cannock Wood, Rugeley, Staffs WS15 4NB* Burntwood (0543) 684329

HASSELL, David Edwin. b 38. W Midl Minl Tr Course 87. **d** 90 **p** 91. NSM Worc SE *Worc* from 90. *14 Napleon Lane, Kempsey, Worcester WR5 3PT* Worcester (0905) 821381

HASSELL, John Charles. b 44. FCA. Sarum & Wells Th Coll 81. **d** 83 **p** 84. C Tottenham St Paul *Lon* 83-86; C Fingringhoe w E Donyland *Chelmsf* 86-90; V Moulsham St Jo from 90. *St John's Vicarage, Vicarage Road, Moulsham, Chelmsford, Essex CM2 9PH* Chelmsford (0245) 352344

HASSEN, Edward William. b 27. TCD. **d** 56 **p** 57. C Larne *Conn* 56-59; C Derriaghy 59-61; Chapl RAF 61-64; C-in-c Muckamore *Conn* 64-67; I from 67; RD Antrim from 74; Dioc Stewardship Adv from 91. *The Rectory, 5 Ballycraigy Road, Muckamore, Co Antrim* Antrim (08494) 62073

HASTE, Rowland Herbert. b 96. Tyndale Hall Bris 26. **d** 47 **p** 48. R Holton St Mary w Gt Wenham *St E* 51-69;

R Raydon 51-69; rtd 69. *Cloud End, Windermere Crescent, Weymouth, Dorset* Weymouth (0305) 782232

HASTED, Canon John Arthur Ord. b 28. Keble Coll Ox BA50 MA54. Wells Th Coll 51. **d** 53 **p** 54. V Sibton *St E* 64-78; V Yoxford 64-79; RD Saxmundham 75-79; rtd 79; Perm to Offic *St Alb* from 82. *1 Eton Court, Pemberley Avenue, Bedford MK40 2LH* Bedford (0234) 341402

HASTEY, Erle. b 44. St Mich Coll Llan 66. **d** 68 **p** 69. C Pontefract St Giles *Wakef* 68-71; C Almondbury 71-74; R Purlwell 74-79; P-in-c Batley Carr 76-79; V Ynyshir *Llan* 79-86; V Tylorstown w Ynyshir 86-87; V Tonyrefail w Gilfach Goch from 87. *The Vicarage, High Street, Tonyrefail, M Glam CF39 8PL* Tonyrefail (0443) 670330

HASTIE-SMITH, Ruthven Carruthers. b 13. St Edm Hall Ox BA36. Westcott Ho Cam 36. **d** 39 **p** 40. R Forfar *St And* 68-72; R Strathtay 72-75; Dioc Supernumerary 75-78; rtd 78. *Millside, Nurses Lane, Comrie, Crieff, Perthshire PH6 2DZ* Comrie (0764) 70510

HASTIE-SMITH, Timothy Maybury. b 62. Magd Coll Cam MA84. Wycliffe Hall Ox 85. **d** 88 **p** 89. C Ox St Ebbe w H Trin and St Pet *Ox* 88-91; Chapl Stowe Sch from 91. *New Field House, Stowe School, Buckingham MK18 5DF* Buckingham (0280) 812446

HASTINGS, David Kerr. b 40. St Luke's Coll Ex CertEd63. Ox NSM Course 84. **d** 87 **p** 88. Hd Master St Edburg's Sch Bicester from 82; Asst Chapl HM Pris Grendon and Spring Hill 87-89; NSM Bicester w Bucknell, Caversfield and Launton *Ox* 87-89; Chapl HM Pris Reading from 90. *18 Ridge Hall Close, Caversham, Reading RG4 7EP* Reading (0734) 461545

HASTINGS, Patrick John Alan. b 45. ACIB68 CertEd75 Sussex Univ BEd82. S Dios Minl Tr Scheme 83. **d** 86 **p** 87. NSM Whyke w Rumboldswhyke and Portfield *Chich* 86-87; C Weybridge *Guildf* 87-89; C Verwood *Sarum* from 89. *1 Broadmead Road, Three Legged Cross, Wimborne, Dorset BH21 6SA* Verwood (0202) 824447

HASTROP, Paul. b 39. Wells Th Coll 70. **d** 72 **p** 73. C Parkstone St Osmund *Sarum* 72-76; C Penzance St Mary w St Paul *Truro* 76-79; V St Blazey 79-87; TV Bournemouth St Pet w St Swithun, St Steph etc *Win* from 87. *St Stephen's Vicarage, St Stephen's Way, Bournemouth BH2 6JZ* Bournemouth (0202) 554355

HASTWELL, James Sydney. b 37. Roch Th Coll 67. **d** 69 **p** 70. C Croydon St Aug *Cant* 69-73; C Hurstpierpoint *Chich* 73-75; P-in-c Twineham 76; P-in-c Sayers Common 76; P-in-c Albourne 76; R Albourne w Sayers Common and Twineham 76-88; V Forest Row from 88. *The Vicarage, Forest Row, E Sussex RH18 5AH* Forest Row (034282) 2595

HATCH, Canon George Andrew. b 29. Leeds Univ BA. Coll of Resurr Mirfield. **d** 53 **p** 54. C S Farnborough *Guildf* 53-55; Windward Is 55-63; Barbados from 63; Assoc Dir Chr Action Development in Caribbean 73-83. *St James, Barbados* Barbados (1809) 432-1580

HATCH, Canon George William. b 12. Lon Univ BA33. Clifton Th Coll 32. **d** 35 **p** 36. R Rayleigh *Chelmsf* 56-82; Chapl HM Youth Cust Cen Bullwood Hall 75-82; Hon Can Chelmsf Cathl *Chelmsf* 76-82; RD Rochford 79-84; rtd 82. *76 Moor Park Gardens, Leigh-on-Sea, Essex SS9 4PY* Southend-on-Sea (0702) 521266

HATCH, Richard Francis. b 36. Qu Coll Cam BA60 MA64. Cuddesdon Coll 60. **d** 62 **p** 63. C Leigh St Mary *Man* 62-66; V Peel Green 66-71; V Barton w Peel Green 71-75; Dioc Broadcasting Officer 73-85; R Birch St Jas 75-78; R Fallowfield 75-78. *24 Denison Road, Victoria Park, Manchester M14 5RY* 061-225 0799

HATCHETT, Michael John. b 49. Enfield Coll BSc72 K Coll Lon BD77 AKC77. Linc Th Coll 77. **d** 78 **p** 79. C Halstead St Andr *Chelmsf* 78-79; C Halstead St Andr w H Trin and Greenstead Green 79-81; C Greenstead juxta Colchester 81-85; V Gt Totham from 85. *The Vicarage, 1 Hall Road, Great Totham, Maldon, Essex CM9 8NN* Maldon (0621) 893150

HATCHLEY, Canon Walter John. b 24. Lon Univ BA65. Coll of Resurr Mirfield 64. **d** 66 **p** 67. C Monkseaton St Pet *Newc* 66-69; C Gosforth All SS 69-72; C Cullercoats St Geo 72; TV 72-78; V Newc St Fran from 78; RD Newc E from 83; Hon Can Newc Cathl from 90. *St Francis's Vicarage, Cleveland Gardens, Newcastle upon Tyne NE7 7RE* 091-266 1071

HATCHMAN, Hugh Alleyne. b 28. Qu Coll Cam BA52 MA56. Ridley Hall Cam 52. **d** 54 **p** 55. C E Twickenham St James *Lon* 54-56; C Morden *S'wark* 56-59; Area Sec (E Midl) CPAS 59-63; V New Catton St Luke *Nor* 63-79; Chapl Bexley Hosp Kent from 79. *Bexley Hospital, Old Bexley Lane, Bexley, Kent DA5 2BW* Crayford (0322) 526282

HATCLIFFE, Charles John William Coombes. b 26. St Aid Birkenhead 59. **d** 61 **p** 62. V Stubbins *Man* 64-71; P-in-c Clifton Green 71-74; V 74-82; P-in-c Acton Burnell w Pitchford *Heref* 82-83; P-in-c Condover 82-83; P-in-c Frodesley 82-83; V Bentley *Lich* 83-89; rtd 89. *18 Silverlow Road, Nailsea, Bristol BS19 2AD* Nailsea (0272) 858597

HATFULL, Ronald Stanley. b 22. CChem42 MChemA48 FRSC48 FRSH65. Qu Coll Birm 79. **d** 82 **p** 83. NSM Castle Church *Lich* 82-89; Kingsmead Hosp Stafford 82-89; rtd 89. *Ridge House, Ridgeway Close, Hyde Lea, Stafford ST18 9BE* Stafford (0785) 52992

HATHAWAY, David Alfred Gerald. b 48. DipTh72. St Mich Coll Llan 69. **d** 72 **p** 73. C Newport St Julian *Mon* 72-74; P-in-c Oakham w Hambleton and Egleton *Pet* 74-77; V Newport St Matt *Mon* 77-83; V Abertillery 83-88; V Rumney from 88. *The Vicarage, 702 Newport Road, Rumney, Cardiff CF3 8DF* Cardiff (0222) 797882

HATHAWAY, John Albert. b 24. Sarum Th Coll 59. **d** 60 **p** 61. V Holmwood *Guildf* 66-71; R Westborough 71-74; V Newmarket All SS *St E* 74-82; V Acton w Gt Waldingfield 82-85; R W Downland *Sarum* 85-90; rtd 90. *20 Baymead Lane, North Petherton, Bridgewater, Somerset* North Petherton (0278) 663365

HATHERLEY, Peter Graham. b 46. Univ of Wales (Cardiff) BSc67 PhD70. St Mich Coll Llan 70. **d** 72 **p** 73. C Ystrad Mynach *Llan* 72-75; Hon C Tonyrefail 75-88; Perm to Offic from 88. *3 West Farm Close, Ogmore-by-Sea, Bridgend, M Glam CF32 0PT* Southerndown (0656) 880323

HATHERLEY, Victor Charles. b 17. St Aug Coll Cant 63. **d** 64 **p** 64. R E Harptree *B & W* 68-73; R E w W Harptree 73-76; R E w W Harptree and Hinton Blewett 76-82; rtd 82; Perm to Offic *B & W* from 83. *10 Fairview Road, Broadstone, Dorset BH18 9AX* Broadstone (0202) 699371

HATHWAY, Richard Peter. b 17. Kelham Th Coll 34. **d** 41 **p** 42. Chapl Highgate Sch Lon 66-81; rtd 81; Perm to Offic *Nor* from 81; *St E* from 82. *10 Station Road, Harleston, Norfolk IP20 9ES* Harleston (0379) 853590

HATHWAY, Ross Arthur. b 56. DATh87. Moore Th Coll Sydney BTh86. **d** 86 **p** 87. Australia 87-88; C Corby St Columba *Pet* from 89. *22 Portree Walk, Corby, Northants NN17 2QY* Corby (0536) 61737

HATT, Michael John. b 34. Sarum Th Coll 67. **d** 69 **p** 70. Hon C Ex St Mary Arches *Ex* 70-73; Hon C Cen Ex from 73. *133 Topsham Road, Exeter EX2 4RE* Exeter (0392) 71165

HATTAN, Jeffrey William Rowland. b 49. Cranmer Hall Dur 83. **d** 85 **p** 86. C Eston w Normanby *York* 85-89; TV from 89. *465 Normanby Road, Normanby, Middlesbrough, Cleveland TS6 0EA* Eston Grange (0642) 461288

HATTER, Canon David George. b 21. Lich Th Coll. **d** 57 **p** 58. V Mansf St Mark *S'well* 67-81; V Sutton w Carlton and Normanton upon Trent etc 81-86; P-in-c Caunton 84-86; Hon Can S'well Minster 84-86; RD Tuxford and Norwell 84-86; rtd 86; Perm to Offic *S'well* from 86. *1 North End, Farndon, Newark, Notts NG24 3SX* Newark (0636) 76960

HATTON, George Ockleston. b 08. St Aid Birkenhead 45. **d** 48 **p** 49. V Lt Leigh and Lower Whitley *Ches* 60-73; RD Gt Budworth 61-71; Perm to Offic *Heref* from 76; rtd 86. *Clatterbrune Farm House, Presteigne, Powys* Presteigne (0544) 267461

HATTON, Jeffrey Charles. b 49. K Coll Lon BD70 Bris Univ MA72. Westcott Ho Cam 73 Episc Th Sch Cam Mass 74. **d** 74 **p** 75. C Nor St Pet Mancroft *Nor* 74-78; C Earlham St Anne 78-79; Relig Broadcasting Asst IBA 79-82; Hon C Kensington St Barn *Lon* 79-84; Hon C Fulham All SS 85-89; R Win All SS w Chilcomb and Chesil *Win* from 89; Dioc Communications Officer from 89. *All Saints' Rectory, 19 Petersfield Road, Winchester, Hants SO23 8JD* Winchester (0962) 853777

HATTON, Michael Samuel. b 44. St Jo Coll Dur BA72 DipTh74. **d** 74 **p** 75. C Dudley St Jas *Worc* 74-75; C N Lynn w St Marg and St Nic *Nor* 75-77; C Walsall Wood *Lich* 78-79; Min Shelfield St Mark CD 79-89; V Middleton St Cross *Ripon* from 89. *St Cross Vicarage, Middleton Park Avenue, Leeds LS10 4HT* Leeds (0532) 716398

HATTON, Trevor. b 55. Oak Hill Th Coll BA86. **d** 86 **p** 87. C Chilwell *S'well* 86-90; R Trowell from 90. *The Rectory, Nottingham Road, Trowell, Nottingham NG9 3PF* Ilkeston (0602) 321474

HATWELL, Timothy Rex. b 53. Oak Hill Th Coll BA85. **d** 85 **p** 86. C Tonbridge St Steph *Roch* 85-90; V Cudham and Downe from 90. *The Vicarage, Cudham Lane South,*

Cudham, Sevenoaks, Kent TN14 7QA Biggin Hill (0959) 72445

HAUGHAN, John Francis. b 28. Tyndale Hall Bris 56. **d** 60 **p** 61. C Tonbridge St Steph *Roch* 60-63; C Cheltenham St Mark *Glouc* 63-67; V Tewkesbury H Trin from 67. *Holy Trinity Vicarage, 49 Barton Street, Tewkesbury, Glos GL20 5PU* Tewkesbury (0684) 293233

HAUGHTON, Peter Steele. b 57. K Coll Lon BD84 MA90 Fitzw Coll Cam DipTh85. Westcott Ho Cam 84. **d** 86 **p** 87. C Cheam Common St Phil *S'wark* 86-90; Chapl Medical Schs from 90. *St Mary le Park Vicarage, 48 Parksgate Road, London SW11 4NT* 071-228 4818

HAUGHTON, Canon Thomas George. b 08. MBE53. **d** 53 **p** 54. I Belf Upper Falls *Conn* 61-79; Can Belf Cathl 77-79; rtd 79. *47 Abbey Drive, Bangor, Co Down BT20 2DA* Bangor (0247) 461994

HAVARD, Alan Ernest. b 27. Qu Coll Birm 79. **d** 81 **p** 82. NSM Rugby St Matt *Cov* 81-84; C Portishead *B & W* 84-86; V Mickleover All SS *Derby* from 86. *All Saints' Vicarage, Etwall Road, Mickleover, Derby DE3 5DL* Derby (0332) 513793

HAVARD, David William. b 56. Man Univ BA84. Qu Coll Birm 84. **d** 85. C Man Clayton St Cross w St Paul *Man* 85-88; Canada from 88. *6661 Elwell Street, Burnaby, British Columbia, Canada, V5E 1J9*

HAVELL, Edward Michael. b 38. Dur Univ BA65. Ridley Hall Cam 66. **d** 68 **p** 69. C Ecclesall *Sheff* 68-71; C Roch St Justus *Roch* 71-74; P-in-c Holbeach Hurn *Linc* 74-75; C Hollington St Jo *Chich* 75-85; TV Rye from 85. *The Vicarage, Lydd Road, Camber, Rye, E Sussex TN31 7RN* Rye (0797) 225386

HAVENS, Mrs Anita Sue. b 44. Mass Univ BSEd67 Clark Univ (USA) MA72 Hughes Hall Cam BA79. Cranmer Hall Dur MA83. **dss** 84 **d** 87. Gateshead Hosps 84-87; Par Dn Cen Telford *Lich* 87-90; Ind Chapl 87-90; Ind Chapl *Liv* from 90. *36 Heathfield Road, Wavertree, Liverpool L15 9EZ* 051-722 0342

HAVERGAL, Donald Ernest. b 03. St Edm Hall Ox BA25 MA29. Linc Th Coll 40. **d** 40 **p** 41. R Wilby *Pet* 62-78; rtd 78. *91 Claverham Road, Yatton, Bristol BS19 4LE* Yatton (0934) 834752

HAVILAND, Edmund Selwyn. b 24. K Coll Cam BA49 MA51. Wells Th Coll 49. **d** 51 **p** 52. V E Peckham *Roch* 68-73; R E Peckham and Nettlestead 73-84; S Africa 84-85; Dep Chapl HM Pris Brixton 85-89; rtd 89; Perm to Offic *Guildf* from 89. *Hill Farm, Thursley, Godalming, Surrey GU8 6QQ* Farnham (0252) 702115

HAWES, Andrew Thomas. b 54. Sheff Univ BA77 Em Coll Cam MA79. Westcott Ho Cam 77. **d** 80 **p** 81. C Gt Grimsby St Mary and St Jas *Linc* 80-84; P-in-c Gedney Drove End 84-86; P-in-c Sutton St Nicholas 84-86; V Lutton w Gedney Drove End, Dawsmere 86-89; V Edenham w Witham-on-the-Hill from 89. *The Vicarage, Edenham, Bourne, Lincs PE10 0LS* Edenham (077832) 358

HAWES, Canon Arthur John. b 43. UEA BA Birm Univ DPS DipL&A. Chich Th Coll 65. **d** 68 **p** 69. C Kidderminster St Jo *Worc* 68-72; P-in-c Droitwich 72-76; R Alderford w Attlebridge and Swannington *Nor* from 76; Chapl Hellesdon Hosp Nor from 76; RD Sparham *Nor* from 81; Mental Health Act Commr from 86; Hon Can Nor Cathl *Nor* from 88. *The Rectory, Attlebridge, Norwich NR9 5SU* Norwich (0603) 860644 or 424222

HAWES, Clive. b 37. Univ of Wales BSc59. Coll of Resurr Mirfield 61. **d** 63 **p** 64. C Ynyshir *Llan* 63-65; C Roath St Marg 65-72; V Llanddewi Rhondda w Bryn Eirw 72-75; Chapl Ch Coll Brecon from 75. *Christ's College, Brecon, Powys LD3 8AF* Brecon (0874) 2786

HAWES, George Walter. b 10. Lon Coll of Div 39. **d** 41 **p** 42. R Rowner *Portsm* 60-78; rtd 78. *90 Kiln Road, Fareham, Hants* Fareham (0329) 286309

HAWES, Joseph Patricius. b 65. St Chad's Coll Dur BA87. St Steph Ho Ox 88. **d** 91. C Clapham Team Min *S'wark* from 91. *The Glebe House, 6 Rectory Grove, London SW4 0DZ* 071-720 3370

HAWES, Michael Rowell. b 31. AKC61. **d** 62 **p** 63. C Epsom St Martin *Guildf* 62-65; Chapl RAF 65-86; R Newnham w Nately Scures w Mapledurwell etc *Win* from 86. *The Rectory, Up Nately, Basingstoke, Hants RG27 9PL* Hook (0256) 762021

HAWKEN, Andrew Robert. b 58. K Coll Lon BD81 AKC81. St Steph Ho Ox 83. **d** 85 **p** 86. C Ex St Dav *Ex* 85-88; TV Witney *Ox* from 88. *The Vicarage, 292 Thorney Leys, Witney, Oxon OX8 7YW* Witney (0993) 773281

HAWKEN, Michael Vaughan. b 50. Lon Univ CertEd71 Open Univ BA76. Trin Coll Bris DipHE81 Trin Episc Sch for Min Ambridge Penn 81. **d** 82 **p** 83. C Roxeth Ch

Ch and Harrow St Pet *Lon* 82-86; C Ealing St Paul 86-89; P-in-c from 89. *St Paul's Vicarage, 102 Elers Road, London W13 9QE* 081-567 4628

HAWKER, Canon Alan Fort. b 44. Hull Univ BA65 Lon Univ DipTh68. Clifton Th Coll 65. **d** 68 **p** 69. C Bootle St Leon *Liv* 68-71; C Fazakerley Em 71-73; V Goose Green 73-81; TR Southgate *Chich* from 81; Can and Preb Chich Cathl from 91. *The Rectory, Forester Road, Crawley, W Sussex RH10 6EH* Crawley (0293) 523463

HAWKER, Alan John. b 53. BD76 AKC76. Sarum & Wells Th Coll 77. **d** 78 **p** 79. C Coleford w Staunton *Glouc* 78-81; C Up Hatherley 81-84; V Plymouth St Jas Ham *Ex* from 84. *St James's Vicarage, Ham Drive, Plymouth, Devon PL2 2NJ* Plymouth (0752) 362485

HAWKER, Brian Henry. b 34. AKC61. **d** 62 **p** 63. C Hemel Hempstead *St Alb* 62-66; Chapl St Jo Hosp Stone 66-69; R Stone w Hartwell w Bishopstone *Ox* 66-69; V W Wycombe 69-72; Past Consultant Clinical Th Assn 72-80, Perm to Offic *S'well* 73-75; Lic from 75; Perm *B & W* 76-84; Truro 84-90. *97 Frederick Street, Loughborough, Leics LE11 3BH* Loughborough (0509) 263542

✠**HAWKER, Rt Rev Dennis Gascoyne.** b 21. Qu Coll Cam BA48 MA53. Cuddesdon Coll 48. **d** 50 **p** 51 **c** 72. C Folkestone St Mary and St Eanswythe *Cant* 50-55; V S Norwood St Mark 55-60; Lic to Offic *Linc* 60-65; Can and Preb Linc Cathl 64-87; V Gt Grimsby St Mary and St Jas 65-72; Suff Bp Grantham 72-87; Dean Stamford 73-87; Chapl RNR from 78; rtd 87. *Pickwick Cottage, Hall Close, Heacham, King's Lynn, Norfolk PE31 7JT* Heacham (0485) 70450

HAWKER, Canon Peter Charles. b 17. FSA67 Ch Coll Cam BA39 MA43 Univ of W Aus MA43. St Barn Coll Adelaide ThL41. **d** 43 **p** 44. Sec Gen Confraternity of the Blessed Sacrament 56-85; V Linc St Botolph by Bargate *Linc* 69-85; Can and Preb Linc Cathl from 77; rtd 85. *20 Middleton's Field, Lincoln LN2 1QP* Lincoln (0522) 544337

HAWKER, Ven Peter John. b 37. Ex Univ BA59. Wycliffe Hall Ox 69. **d** 70 **p** 71. Chapl Bern w Neuchatel *Eur* 70-89; Adn Switzerland from 86; Chapl Zurich w St Gallen and Winterthur from 90. *Promenadengasse 9, 8001 Zurich, Switzerland* Zurich (1) 261-2241 or 252-6024

HAWKES, Mrs Elisabeth Anne. b 56. GRNCM78 CertEd80. Linc Th Coll 86. **d** 88. Hon Par Dn Finham *Cov* 88-90; Hon Par Dn Bexhill St Pet *Chich* from 90. *St Michael's House, Glassenbury Drive, Bexhill-on-Sea, E Sussex TN40 2NY* Bexhill-on-Sea (0424) 219937

HAWKES, Keith Andrew. b 28. Oak Hill Th Coll 72. **d** 74 **p** 75. C Gt Yarmouth *Nor* 74-77; C-in-c Bowthorpe CD 77; Chapl Dusseldorf *Eur* 77-83; TV Quidenham *Nor* 83-88; TR 88-90; RD Thetford and Rockland 86-90; R Wickmere w Lt Barningham, Itteringham etc from 90; Dioc Rural Officer from 90. *The Rectory, Itteringham, Norwich NR11 7AX* Saxthorpe (026387) 4262

HAWKES, Ronald Linton. b 54. York Univ CertEd75 Leeds Univ BEd76. Linc Th Coll 85. **d** 87. C Finham *Cov* 87-90; C Bexhill St Pet *Chich* 90; TV from 91. *St Michael's House, Glassenbury Drive, Bexhill-on-Sea TN40 2NY* Bexhill-on-Sea (0424) 219937

HAWKETT, Graham Kenneth. b 20. Bps' Coll Cheshunt 61. **d** 63 **p** 64. V Wyke *Guildf* 67-85; rtd 85; Perm to Offic *Guildf* from 85. *Bede House, Beech Road, Haslemere, Surrey GU27 2BX* Haslemere (0428) 656430

HAWKINGS, Timothy Denison. b 55. Ex Univ BA78 Nottm Univ BA80. St Jo Coll Nottm 78. **d** 81 **p** 82. C Penn *Lich* 81-85; C Stafford 85; TV from 85. *The Vicarage, Victoria Terrace, Stafford ST16 3HA* Stafford (0785) 52523

HAWKINS, Alec Borman. b 07. **d** 68 **p** 69. C Boldmere *Birm* 68-79; Perm to Offic from 79. *2 Wrekin Court, Vesey Close, Sutton Coldfield, W Midlands* 021-308 4625

HAWKINS, Alfred Pryse. b 29. St Mich Coll Llan 57. **d** 59 **p** 60. C Dowlais *Llan* 59-62; C Caerau w Ely 62-66; V Aberaman and Abercwmboi 66-77; R Ebbw Vale *Mon* 77-82; P-in-c Paddington St Dav Welsh Ch *Lon* from 82; V St Benet Paul's Wharf from 82; P-in-c St Jas Garlickhythe w St Mich Queenhithe 85-86. *St David's Vicarage, St Mary's Terrace, London W2 1SJ* 071-723 3104

HAWKINS, Allan Raeburn Giles. b 34. Selw Coll Cam BA58 MA62. Cuddesdon Coll 58. **d** 60 **p** 61. C Wellingborough All Hallows *Pet* 60-63; C Stevenage St Geo *St Alb* 63-71; R 71-74; V Swindon New Town *Bris* 74-80; USA from 80. *2212 Crooked Oak Court, Arlington, Texas 76012, USA*

HAWKINS, Alun John. b 44. BA66 AKC Univ of Wales (Ban) BD81. St Deiniol's Hawarden 78. **d** 81 **p** 82. C Penmaenmawr *Ban* 81-84; R Llanberis 84-89; Tutor Ban Dioc NSM Course 85-90; Dir of Ords *Ban* 86-90; V Knighton and Norton *S & B* from 89; Chapl Knighton Hosp from 89. *The Vicarage, Church Street, Knighton, Powys LD7 1AG* Knighton (0547) 528566

HAWKINS, Andrew Robert. b 40. St Andr Univ BSc64 Dur Univ BA68 DipTh69. St Chad's Coll Dur 65. **d** 69 **p** 70. C Sutton St Nic *S'wark* 69-73; C Wimbledon 73-77; TV Cramlington *Newc* 77-81; R Clutton w Cameley *B & W* 81-89; Chapl City of Bath Coll of FE from 90. *18 Wallycourt Road, Chew Stoke, Bristol BS18 8XN* Bristol (0272) 332422

HAWKINS, Canon Arthur Herbert. b 06. Lon Univ BD33. Lon Coll of Div 27. **d** 33 **p** 34. R Leven w Catwick *York* 68-73; Can and Preb York Minster 68-73; rtd 73. *Dulverton Hall, St Martin's Square, Scarborough YO11 2DB* Scarborough (0723) 378514

HAWKINS, Bruce Alexander. b 44. Qu Coll Ox BA66 MA71. Sarum Th Coll 66. **d** 68 **p** 69. C Epsom St Martin *Guildf* 68-71; Dioc Youth Chapl *Cant* 72-81; Hon Min Can Cant Cathl from 75; Dep Dir of Educn 81-86; V Walmer from 86. *The Vicarage, St Mary's Road, Deal, Kent CT14 7NQ* Deal (0304) 374645

HAWKINS, Clive Ladbrook. b 53. AHA79 St Pet Coll Ox BA76 MA79 DipTh82. Trin Coll Bris 80. **d** 82 **p** 83. C Win Ch Ch *Win* 82-86; R Eastrop from 86. *The Rectory, Goat Lane, Eastrop, Basingstoke, Hants RG21 1PZ* Basingstoke (0256) 464249

HAWKINS, David Frederick Cox. b 17. Clare Coll Cam BA38 MA45. Westcott Ho Cam 46. **d** 48 **p** 49. C Leckhampton SS Phil and Jas *Glouc* 49-73; R Clifford Chambers w Marston Sicca 73-79; R Welford w Weston and Clifford Chambers 79-82; rtd 82; Perm to Offic *B & W* from 83. *Orchard Rise, Back Street, Bradford-on-Tone, Taunton, Somerset TA4 1HH* Bradford-on-Tone (0823) 461331

HAWKINS, Canon David John Leader. b 49. Nottm Univ BTh73 LTh. St Jo Coll Nottm 69 ALCD73. **d** 73 **p** 74. C Bebington *Ches* 73-76; Nigeria 76-82; C Ox St Aldate w St Matt *Ox* 83-86; V Leeds St Geo *Ripon* from 86. *St George's Vicarage, 208 Kirkstall Lane, Leeds LS5 2AB* Leeds (0532) 756556

HAWKINS, David Kenneth Beaumont. b 36. LTh. Em Coll Saskatoon 63. **d** 63 **p** 64. Canada 63-85; C St Alb St Paul *St Alb* 85-87; C Hednesford *Lich* from 87. *554 Littleworth Road, Rawnsley, Cannock, Staffs WS12 5JD* Hednesford (0543) 879686

HAWKINS, David Sewell. b 33. Bps' Coll Cheshunt. **d** 58 **p** 59. C Chingford St Anne *Chelmsf* 58-59; C Bridlington Quay Ch Ch *York* 59-63; V Rudston, Grindale and Ergham w Boynton 63-64; P-in-c Boynton 63-64; V Rudston w Boynton 64-68; Chapl RADD 68-77; R Burton Agnes w Harpham *York* 77-80; P-in-c Lowthorpe w Ruston Parva 77-80; P-in-c Kilham 77-80; R Burton Agnes w Harpham, Kilham, Lowthorpe etc 80-85; R Burton Agnes w Harpham and Lowthorpe etc from 85. *The Rectory, Burton Agnes, Driffield, N Humberside* Burton Agnes (026289) 293

HAWKINS, Donald John. b 39. K Coll Lon BD62 AKC62. St Boniface Warminster 62. **d** 63 **p** 64. C Winlaton *Dur* 63-66; C Gateshead St Mary 66-69; C Ryhope 69-71; R Cockfield 71-79; Chapl N Staffs R Infirmary Stoke-on-Trent 79-89; Chapl Stoke-on-Trent City Hosp from 89. *The City General Hospital, Newcastle Road, Stoke-on-Trent ST4 6QG* Stoke-on-Trent (0782) 621133

HAWKINS, Mrs Eileen Susan Kirkland. b 45. LCST66. Lon Bible Coll DipTh71 Cranmer Hall Dur 77. **dss** 83 **d** 86. Kilmarnock *Glas* 84-86; Par Dn Heanor *Derby* from 87. *20 The Nook, Loscoe, Derby DE7 7LQ* Langley Mill (0773) 760220

HAWKINS, Canon Francis John. b 36. Ex Coll Ox BA61 MA63. Chich Th Coll 59. **d** 61 **p** 62. C Tavistock and Gulworthy *Ex* 61-64; Lect Chich Th Coll 64-73; Vice-Prin 73-75; V E Grinstead St Mary *Chich* 75-81; Min Can Chich Cathl from 81; Treas from 81; V Sidlesham 81-89; Dir of Ords from 89. *12 St Martin's Square, Chichester, W Sussex PO19 1NR* Chichester (0243) 783509

HAWKINS, Ian Clinton. b 27. Roch Th Coll 63. **d** 65 **p** 66. C Boulton *Derby* 65-68; V Cotmanhay 68-77; V Ospringe *Cant* 77-85; P-in-c Eastling 77-85; P-in-c Goodnestone H Cross w Chillenden and Knowlton 85; P-in-c Womenswold 85; V Nonington w Wymynswold and Goodnestone etc from 85. *The Vicarage, Nonington, Dover, Kent CT15 4JT* Nonington (0304) 840271

HAWKINS, James Reginald. b 39. Ex Univ BA61. Westcott Ho Cam 61. **d** 63 **p** 64. C Cannock *Lich* 63-66; C Wem 66-67; C Cheddleton 67-69; R Yoxall 69-77; R The Quinton *Birm* 77-84; V Bosbury w Wellington Heath etc *Heref* from 84. *The Vicarage, Bosbury, Ledbury, Herefordshire HR8 1QA* Ledbury (0531) 86225

HAWKINS, John. b 27. Ox Poly DipArch52 FASI73. S'wark Ord Course 84. **d** 87 **p** 88. Hon C Carshalton Beeches *S'wark* 87-89; Perm to Offic from 89. *44 Castlemaine Avenue, South Croydon, Surrey CR2 7HR* 081-688 9685

HAWKINS, John Arthur. b 45. Lon Univ DipTh69. Kelham Th Coll 64. **d** 69 **p** 70. C Cov St Alb *Cov* 70-73; C Fletchamstead 73-77; V Whitley 77-81; TV Northn Em *Pet* 81-90; TV Gt Chesham *Ox* from 90. *Christ Church Vicarage, 95 Latimer Road, Chesham, Bucks HP5 1QQ* Chesham (0494) 773318

HAWKINS, John Charles Lacey. b 18. Linc Th Coll 40. **d** 42 **p** 43. R Stockton-on-the-Forest w Holtby and Warthill *York* 60-77; R Sigglesthorne and Rise w Nunkeeling and Bewholme 77-83; rtd 83. *Woodlea, 26 Limekiln Lane, Bridlington, N Humberside YO16 5TH* Bridlington (0262) 601760

HAWKINS, John Edward Inskipp. b 63. K Coll Lon BD85. Qu Coll Birm 86. **d** 88 **p** 89. C Birchfield *Birm* from 88. *9 Leonard Avenue, Birmingham B19 1LX* 021-554 9150

HAWKINS, Canon John Henry. b 13. TCD BA35 BD51. CITC 37. **d** 37 **p** 38. I Agherton *Conn* 67-78; Can Conn Cathl 76-78; rtd 78. *11 Carnreagh Avenue, Hillsborough, Co Down* Hillsborough (0846) 682565

HAWKINS, Noel. b 46. St Jo Coll Nottm 82. **d** 84 **p** 85. C Worksop St Jo *S'well* 84-86; C Wollaton Park 86-89; TV Billericay and Lt Burstead *Chelmsf* from 89. *The Rectory, Rectory Road, Little Burstead, Billericay, Essex CM12 9TP* Billericay (0277) 656509

HAWKINS, Paul Henry Whishaw. b 46. Ex Coll Ox BA68 MA74 SS Coll Cam MA84. St Steph Ho Ox 70. **d** 72 **p** 73. C Fawley *Win* 72-75; C Ealing St Steph Castle Hill *Lon* 75-77; P-in-c Dorney *Ox* 77-78; TV Riverside 78-81; Lic to Offic *Ely* 82-87; Chapl SS Coll Cam 82-87; V Plymstock *Ex* from 87; RD Plymouth Sutton from 91. *The Vicarage, Plymstock, Plymouth PL9 9BQ* Plymouth (0752) 403126

HAWKINS, Peter Edward. b 35. Leeds Univ BA60. Coll of Resurr Mirfield 60. **d** 62 **p** 63. C Forest Gate St Edm *Chelmsf* 62-65; C Sevenoaks St Jo *Roch* 65-68; Chapl Metrop Police Cadet Corps Tr Sch 68-73; P-in-c Knowle H Nativity *Bris* 73; TV Knowle 73-79; V Westbury-on-Trym H Trin 79-87; TR Solihull *Birm* from 87. *The Rectory, Church Hill Road, Solihull, W Midlands B91 3RQ* 021-705 0069 or 705 5350

HAWKINS, Peter Michael. b 38. Kelham Th Coll 58. **d** 63 **p** 64. India 63-69; C Manningham St Paul and St Jude *Bradf* 70-72; C Bradf Cathl 72-75; V Allerton 75-90; V Pet H Spirit Bretton *Pet* from 90; P-in-c Marholm from 90. *23 Westhawe, Bretton, Peterborough PE3 8BE* Peterborough (0733) 264418

✠**HAWKINS, Rt Rev Richard Stephen.** b 39. Ex Coll Ox BA61 MA65 Ex Univ BPhil76. St Steph Ho Ox 61. **d** 63 **p** 64 **c** 88. C Ex St Thos *Ex* 63-66; C Clyst St Mary 66-75; TV Clyst St George, Aylesbeare, Clyst Honiton etc 75-78; Bp's Officer for Min 78-81; Jt Dir Ex & Truro NSM Scheme 78-81; TV Cen Ex 78-81; Dioc Dir of Ords 79-81; Adn Totnes 81-88; P-in-c Oldridge 81-87; P-in-c Whitestone 81-87; Suff Bp Plymouth from 88. *31 Riverside Walk, Tamerton Foliot, Plymouth PL5 4AQ* Plymouth (0752) 769836

HAWKINS, Roger David William. b 33. K Coll Lon BD58 AKC58. **d** 59 **p** 60. C Twickenham St Mary *Lon* 59-61; C Heston 61-64; C Dorking w Ranmore *Guildf* 64-65; V Mitcham St Mark *S'wark* 65-74; V Redhill St Matt from 74. *St Matthew's Vicarage, 27 Ridgeway Road, Redhill RH1 6PQ* Redhill (0737) 761568

HAWKINS, Roger Julian. b 32. Ripon Hall Ox 59. **d** 61 **p** 62. C-in-c Newall Green CD *Man* 61-63; Chapl RAF 63-67; R Mawgan in Pyder *Truro* 67-75; R Lanteglos by Camelford w Advent 75-78; R Newmarket St Mary w Exning St Agnes *St E* 78-85; P-in-c Coltishall w Gt Hautbois *Nor* 85-87; R Coltishall w Gt Hautbois and Horstead 87-90; Chapl Whiteley Village *Guildf* from 90. *The Chaplaincy, Whiteley Village, Walton-on-Thames KT12 4EJ* Walton-on-Thames (0932) 848260

HAWKINS, Timothy St John. b 59. CCC Ox BA82. Trin Coll Bris BA87. **d** 87 **p** 88. C Cheltenham St Mary, St Matt, St Paul and H Trin *Glouc* 87-90; C Cowplain *Portsm* from 90. *24 Wincanton Way, Cowplain, Hants* Waterlooville (0705) 257915

HAWKINS, William Arthur. b 18. Clifton Th Coll 50. **d** 53 **p** 54. R Ashill w Broadway *B & W* 58-74; R Herstmonceux *Chich* 74-83; rtd 83; Perm to Offic *Chich* from 84. *Three Gables, 17 Heighton Road, Newhaven, E Sussex BN9 0RB* Newhaven (0273) 513694

HAWKSBEE, Canon Derek John. b 28. Lon Univ BSc49. S'wark Ord Course 70. **d** 71 **p** 72. C Norbiton *S'wark* 71-75; Cand and S Area Sec SAMS 71-79; Overseas Sec 73-79; Hon Can Paraguay from 73; Hon C Tunbridge Wells St Jo *Roch* 75-79; USA 79-87; R Ravendale Gp *Linc* from 88. *The Rectory, Post Office Lane, Ashby-cum-Fenby, Grimsby, S Humberside DN37 0QS* Grimsby (0472) 822980

HAWKSWORTH, Maldwyn Harry. b 45. Aston Univ CertEd74. St Jo Coll Nottm 87. **d** 89 **p** 90. C Penn *Lich* from 89. *105 Brenton Road, Penn, Wolverhampton WV4 5NS* Wolverhampton (0902) 335439

HAWKSWORTH, Peter John Dallas. b 54. Solicitor 79 St Jo Coll Ox BA75 MA79. Sarum & Wells Th Coll 89. **d** 91. C Warminster St Denys, Upton Scudamore etc *Sarum* from 91. *39 Manor Gardens, Warminster, Wilts BA12 8PN* Warminster (0985) 214953

HAWLEY, Anthony Broughton. b 41. St Pet Coll Ox BA67 MA71. Westcott Ho Cam 67. **d** 69 **p** 70. C Wolv St Pet *Lich* 69-72; C-in-c Bermondsey St Hugh CD *S'wark* 73-84; Hon PV S'wark Cathl 83-84; TR Kirkby *Liv* from 84. *The Rectory, Mill Lane, Kirkby, Liverpool L32 2AX* 051-547 2155

HAWLEY, John Andrew. b 50. K Coll Lon BD71 AKC71. Wycliffe Hall Ox 72. **d** 74 **p** 75. C Kingston upon Hull H Trin *York* 74-77; C Bradf Cathl Par *Bradf* 77-80; V Woodlands *Sheff* 80-91; TR Dewsbury *Wakef* from 91. *The Rectory, 16A Oxford Road, Dewsbury, W Yorkshire WF13 4JT* Wakefield (0924) 465491

HAWLEY, Nigel David. b 51. Coll of Resurr Mirfield 77. **d** 80 **p** 81. C Birch w Fallowfield *Man* 80-84; P-in-c Moston St Jo 84-85; R from 85. *St John's Rectory, Railton Terrace, Moston, Manchester M9 1WW* 061-205 4967

HAWNT, John Charles Frederick. b 30. St Paul's Cheltenham. Selly Oak Coll 52 Westwood Cen Zimbabwe 72. **d** 75 **p** 76. Rhodesia 75-80; Zimbabwe 80-81; C Rugby St Andr *Cov* 81-85; R Lydeard St Lawrence w Brompton Ralph etc *B & W* from 85. *The Rectory, Lydeard St Lawrence, Taunton, Somerset TA4 3SF* Lydeard St Lawrence (09847) 220

HAWORTH, Mrs Betsy Ellen. b 24. Wm Temple Coll Rugby 80. **dss** 80 **d** 89. Walkden Moor *Man* 81-87; Third Ch Estates Commr 81-88; Lic to Offic 88-89; NSM Astley Bridge from 89. *14 Sharples Hall Fold, Bolton BL1 7EH* Bolton (0204) 591588

HAWORTH, John Luttrell. b 28. **d** 67 **p** 68. C Kilcommick *K, E & A* 67-70; C Ballymacelligott *L & K* 70-71; TV Tralee w Ballymacelligott, Kilnaughtin etc 71-72; I Kinneigh w Ballymoney *C, C & R* 72-76; I Easkey w Kilglass *T, K & A* 77-83; I Monasterevan w Nurney and Rathdaire *M & K* 83-87; I Kiltegan w Hacketstown, Clonmore and Moyne *C & O* from 87. *The Rectory, Kiltegan, Baltinglass, Co Wicklow, Irish Republic* Kiltegan (508) 73117

HAWORTH, Mark Newby. b 50. MICFor81 Aber Univ BSc73. Westcott Ho Cam 88. **d** 90 **p** 91. C Cherry Hinton St Andr *Ely* from 90. *28 Hayster Drive, Cherry Hinton, Cambridge CB1 4PB* Cambridge (0223) 412305

HAWORTH, Paul. b 47. G&C Coll Cam BA68 MA72. Westcott Ho Cam 75. **d** 78 **p** 79. C Hornchurch St Andr *Chelmsf* 78-81; C Loughton St Mary and St Mich 81-88; C Waltham H Cross 88; TV from 88. *The Vicarage, Church Road, High Beach, Loughton, Essex IG10 4AJ* 081-508 1791

HAWORTH, Stanley Robert. b 48. St Jo Coll Dur BA69. Sarum & Wells Th Coll 71. **d** 73 **p** 74. C Skipton H Trin *Bradf* 73-76; C Bradf Cathl 76-78; C Grantham *Linc* 78; TV 78-82; V Deeping St James from 82. *The Vicarage, 16 Church Street, Deeping St James, Peterborough PE6 8HD* Market Deeping (0778) 347995

HAWTHORN, Ven Christopher John. b 36. Qu Coll Cam BA60 MA64. Ripon Hall Ox 60. **d** 62 **p** 63. C Sutton St Jas *York* 62-66; V Kingston upon Hull St Nic 66-72; V Coatham 72-79; V Scarborough St Martin 79-91; RD Scarborough 82-91; Can and Preb York Minster 86-91; Adn Cleveland from 91. *Park House, Rose Hill, Great Ayton, Middlesbrough TS9 6BH* Great Ayton (0642) 723221

HAWTHORN, David. b 63. Chich Th Coll 87. **d** 90 **p** 91. C Hartlepool H Trin *Dur* from 90. *43 Alderwood Close, Hartlepool, Cleveland* Hartlepool (0429) 234787

HAWTHORN, John Christopher. b 03. G&C Coll Cam BA25 MA29. Westcott Ho Cam 25. **d** 26 **p** 27. V Chatteris *Ely* 38-73; rtd 73. *Park House, Rose Hill, Great Ayton, Middlesbrough TS9 6BH* Great Ayton (0642) 723221

HAWTHORNE, John William. b 32. St Aug Coll Cant 74. **d** 77 **p** 78. C Boxley *Cant* 77-80; P-in-c Langley 80-82; P-in-c Otham 80-82; R Otham w Langley 82-83; TR Preston w Sutton Poyntz and Osmington w Poxwell *Sarum* 83-87; V Tetbury w Beverston *Glouc* from 87. *The Vicarage, The Green, Tetbury, Glos GL8 8DN* Tetbury (0666) 502333

HAWTHORNE, Noel David. b 30. BNC Ox BA53 MA58. Ridley Hall Cam 53. **d** 55 **p** 56. V Idle H Trin *Bradf* 61-70; R Colne St Bart *Blackb* 70-91; RD Pendle 85-91; rtd 91. *56 Barrowford Road, Colne, Lancs BB8 9QE* Colne (0282) 869110

HAWTHORNE, William James. b 46. TCD 66. **d** 69 **p** 70. C Gilnahirk *D & D* 69-72; Asst Chapl Miss to Seamen 72-76; Lic to Offic *Win* 73-76; C Boultham *Linc* 76-78; C Bracebridge Heath 78-90; Dioc Adv for Relig Broadcasting 80-90; Chapl Palma de Mallorca and Balearic Is *Eur* from 90. *Nunez de Balboa 6, Son Armadans, 07014 Palma de Mallorca, Spain* Palma de Mallorca (71) 237279

HAWTIN, David Christopher. b 43. Keble Coll Ox BA65 MA70. Wm Temple Coll Rugby 65 Cuddesdon Coll 66. **d** 67 **p** 68. C Pennywell St Thos and Grindon St Oswald CD *Dur* 67-71; C Stockton St Pet 71-74; C-in-c Leam Lane CD 74-79; R Washington 79-88; Dioc Ecum Officer from 88. *2 Thornhill Terrace, Sunderland SR2 7JL* 091-510 8267

HAY, David Frederick. b 38. MA67. Qu Coll Birm 82. **d** 84 **p** 85. C Prenton *Ches* 84-88; V Stockport St Sav from 88. *St Saviour's Vicarage, 22 St Saviour's Road, Great Moor, Stockport, Cheshire SK2 7QE* 061-483 2633

HAY, Ian Gordon. b 52. Dundee Univ MA73 Edin Univ BD76 CertEd84. Edin Th Coll 73. **d** 76 **p** 77. C Dumfries *Glas* 76-79; Dioc Chapl *Bre* 79-81; R Bre 81-85; Asst Chapl H Trin Sch Halifax 85-88; Dioc Youth Officer *Carl* from 89. *2 Linden Walk, Stainburn, Workington, Cumbria CA14 4UW* Workington (0900) 603213

HAY, Jack Barr. b 31. Bps' Coll Cheshunt 57. **d** 60 **p** 61. C Byker St Ant *Newc* 60-63; C Killingworth 63-68; V Cowgate 68-77; V Woodhorn w Newbiggin from 77. *The Vicarage, 34A Front Street, Newbiggin-by-the-Sea, Northd NE64 6PS* Ashington (0670) 817220

HAY, John. b 43. St D Coll Lamp 63. **d** 67 **p** 68. C Ynyshir *Llan* 67-70; C Cardiff St Mary and St Steph w St Dyfrig etc 70-74; V Llanwynno 74-78; P-in-c Weston-super-Mare All SS *B & W* 78-80; TV Weston-super-Mare Cen Par 80-85; P-in-c Handsworth St Mich *Birm* 85-86; NSM Eastbourne St Sav and St Pet *Chich* from 88. *c/o The Vicarage, Spencer Road, Eastbourne BN21 4PA* Eastbourne (0323) 22317

HAY, John. b 45. CITC 77. **d** 79 **p** 80. C Newtownards *D & D* 79-81; I Galloon w Drummully *Clogh* 81-89; I Donacavey w Barr from 89. *Maranatha, The Rectory, Fintona, Co Tyrone BT78 2DA* Fintona (0662) 841644

HAY, Kenneth Gordon. b 14. TD50. Worc Ord Coll 63. **d** 65 **p** 66. CF (TA) 66-79; R Kelvedon Hatch *Chelmsf* 68-73; P-in-c Prittlewell St Steph 73-78; V 78-79; rtd 79. *26 Warwick Road, Thorpe Bay, Southend-on-Sea SS1 3BN* Southend-on-Sea (0702) 586496

HAY, Nicholas John. b 56. Sheff Poly BSc85 DPS88. St Jo Coll Nottm 85. **d** 88 **p** 89. C Blackb Redeemer *Blackb* from 88. *21 Skye Crescent, Blackburn BB1 2JN* Blackburn (0254) 665734

HAY, Raymond. b 38. QUB BSc60 TCD BD68. Cranmer Hall Dur 60. **d** 62 **p** 63. C Ban 62-67; Tutor St Jo Coll Dur 68-83; Lic to Offic *Dur* 68-76; P-in-c Bearpark 76-80; Asst Chapl HM Rem Cen Low Newton 83-90; P-in-c Kimblesworth *Dur* 83-87; P-in-c Sacriston and Kimblesworth 87-90. *42 Hastings Avenue, Durham DH1 3QQ* 091-386 5196

HAYBALL, Douglas Reginald. b 18. Oak Hill Th Coll 66. **d** 68 **p** 69. C Ilkley All SS *Bradf* 68-72; V Parr Mt *Liv* 72-75; P-in-c Sheepey w Ratcliffe Culey *Leic* 75-76; R Sibson w Sheepy and Ratcliffe Culey 76-86; rtd 86; Perm to Offic *B & W* from 86. *57 Parklands Way, Somerton, Somerset TA11 6JG* Somerton (0458) 73312

HAYCRAFT, Roger Brian Norman. b 43. Oak Hill Th Coll 69. **d** 73 **p** 74. C Belsize Park *Lon* 73-76; C Yardley St Edburgha *Birm* 76-79; V Hornchurch H Cross *Chelmsf* from 79. *The Vicarage, 260 Hornchurch Road, Hornchurch, Essex RM11 1PX* Hornchurch (04024) 47976

HAYDAY, Alan Geoffrey David. b 46. Kelham Th Coll 65. **d** 69 **p** 70. C Evington *Leic* 69-72; C Spalding *Linc* 72-78; V Cherry Willingham w Greetwell 78-86; RD Lawres 84-86; TR Old Brumby from 86. *St Hugh's Rectory, 114 Ashby Road, Scunthorpe, S Humberside DN16 2AG* Scunthorpe (0724) 843064

HAYDEN, David Frank. b 47. Lon Univ DipTh69 BD71. Tyndale Hall Bris 67. **d** 71 **p** 72. C Silverhill St Matt *Chich* 71-75; C Galleywood Common *Chelmsf* 75-79; R Redgrave cum Botesdale w Rickinghall *St E* 79-84; RD Hartismere 81-84; Chapl Cromer and Distr Hosp Norfolk from 84; V Cromer *Nor* from 84; P-in-c Gresham from 84; Chapl Fletcher Hosp Norfolk from 85. *The Vicarage, 30 Cromwell Road, Cromer, Norfolk NR27 0BE* Cromer (0263) 512000

HAYDEN, Eric Henry Ashmore. b 26. ACII65. Sarum & Wells Th Coll 71. **d** 73 **p** 74. C Horsham *Chich* 73-78; V Cuckfield from 78. *The Vicarage, Broad Street, Cuckfield, Haywards Heath, W Sussex RH17 5LL* Haywards Heath (0444) 454007

HAYDEN, Canon John Donald. b 40. Lon Univ BD62. Tyndale Hall Bris 63. **d** 65 **p** 66. C Macclesfield Ch Ch *Ches* 65-68; Tanzania 68-77; Home Sec USCL 77-83; TV Ipswich St Mary at Stoke w St Pet & St Mary Quay *St E* from 83. *The Church House, Stoke Park Drive, Ipswich IP2 9TH* Ipswich (0473) 687513

HAYDOCK, Canon Alan. b 41. Kelham Th Coll 60. **d** 65 **p** 66. C Rainworth *S'well* 65-68; C Hucknall Torkard 68-71; TV 71-74; V Bilborough St Jo 74-80; R E Bridgford 80-82; R E Bridgford and Kneeton from 82; RD Bingham from 84; Hon Can S'well Minster from 86. *The Rectory, Kirk Hill, East Bridgford, Nottingham NG13 8PE* East Bridgford (0949) 20218

HAYDON, Keith Frank. b 46. Cuddesdon Coll 73. **d** 75 **p** 76. C De Beauvoir Town St Pet *Lon* 75-77; C Wells St Thos w Horrington *B & W* 77-80; TV Weston-super-Mare Cen Par 80-84; TV Cowley St Jas *Ox* 84-87; TR from 87. *St James's House, Beauchamp Lane, Cowley, Oxford OX4 3LF* Oxford (0865) 779262

HAYES, Brian Richard Walker. b 33. Qu Coll Birm 81. **d** 83 **p** 84. C Cheadle Hulme All SS *Ches* 83-87; C Sheff Parson Cross St Cecilia *Sheff* 87-88; C Sheff Norwood St Leon 88-91; V Gazeley w Dalham, Moulton and Kentford *St E* from 91. *The Vicarage, Gazeley, Newmarket, Suffolk CB8 8RB* Newmarket (0638) 750719

HAYES, David Malcolm Hollingworth. b 42. K Coll Lon BD68 AKC68. **d** 69 **p** 70. C Upper Teddington SS Pet and Paul *Lon* 69-70; C Ruislip St Martin 70-75; P-in-c Ludford *Heref* 75-80; P-in-c Ashford Carbonell w Ashford Bowdler 75-80; V Eastcote St Lawr *Lon* 80-90; R Cant St Pet w St Alphege and St Marg etc *Cant* from 90. *The Master's Lodge, 58 St Peter's Street, Canterbury, Kent CT1 2BE* Canterbury (0227) 462395

HAYES, David Roland Payton. b 37. Hertf Coll Ox BA62 MA66. Coll of Resurr Mirfield 62. **d** 64 **p** 65. C Woodley *Ox* 64-67; C Emscote *Cov* 67-69; C Farnham Royal *Ox* 69-75; P-in-c 75-78; P-in-c Lathbury 78-79; P-in-c Newport Pagnell 78-79; R Newport Pagnell w Lathbury 79-85; RD Newport 80-85; Chapl Renny Lodge Hosp 85-87; R Newport Pagnell w Lathbury and Moulsoe *Ox* 85-86; P-in-c 86-87; P-in-c Bucknell w Buckton, Llanfair Waterdine and Stowe *Heref* 87-91; V Bucknell w Chapel Lawn, Llanfair Waterdine etc from 91; RD Clun Forest from 91. *The Vicarage, Bucknell, Shropshire SY7 0AD* Bucknell (05474) 340

HAYES, John Henry Andrew. b 52. BSc. Wycliffe Hall Ox 82. **d** 84 **p** 85. C Moreton *Ches* 84-87; R Barrow from 87; Bp's Chapl from 87. *The Rectory, Mill Lane, Great Barrow, Chester CH3 7JF* Tarvin (0829) 40263

HAYES, John Philip. b 52. RMN76. Chich Th Coll 79. **d** 82 **p** 84. C Wigston Magna *Leic* 82-83; C Thurmaston 83-85; TV Shirley *Birm* 85-91; V Lee St Aug *S'wark* from 91. *St Augustine's Vicarage, 336 Baring Road, London SE12 0DU* 081-857 4941

HAYES, Michael Gordon William. b 48. St Cath Coll Cam BA69 MA73 PhD73. Ridley Hall Cam 73. **d** 75 **p** 76. C Combe Down w Monkton Combe *B & W* 75-78; C Cam H Trin *Ely* 78-81; V Bathampton *B & W* 81-88; V Clevedon St Andr and Ch Ch from 88. *The Vicarage, 10 Coleridge Road, Clevedon, Avon BS21 7TB* Clevedon (0272) 872982

HAYES, Michael John. b 52. Lanc Univ BA73. Coll of Resurr Mirfield 75. **d** 78 **p** 79. C Notting Hill *Lon* 78-81; C-in-c Hammersmith SS Mich and Geo White City Estate CD 81-88. *7 Argyll Court, 82 Lexham Gardens, London W8* 071-373 0948

HAYES, Reginald Brian Michael. b 40. Univ of Wales (Cardiff) DipTh71. St Mich Coll Llan 67. **d** 71 **p** 72. C Roath St Martin *Llan* 71-77; V Brynmawr *S & B* 77-80; CF (TA) 79-87; Chapl RN 80-87; P-in-c Porthleven *Truro* 80-81; V Porthleven w Sithney 81-87; RD Kerrier 86-87; V Westmr St Matt *Lon* from 87; PV Westmr Abbey from 88. *St Matthew's Clergy House, 20 Great Peter Street, London SW1P 2BU* 071-222 3704

HAYES, Richard. b 39. K Coll Lon BD68 AKC68. **d** 69 **p** 70. C Dartford H Trin *Roch* 69-72; C S Kensington St Steph *Lon* 72-76; V Ruislip Manor St Paul 76-82; V Ealing St Pet Mt Park 82-91; R St Edm the King and St Mary Woolnoth etc from 91. *24 Cinnamon Street, London E1 9NJ* 071-481 9699

HAYES, Timothy James. b 62. **d** 89 **p** 90. C Lache cum Saltney *Ches* from 89. *69 Sandy Lane, Saltney, Chester CH4 8UB* Chester (0244) 673225

HAYLES, Graham David. b 39. Lon Univ DipTh66. Clifton Th Coll 64. **d** 67 **p** 68. C Gipsy Hill Ch Ch *S'wark* 67-70; C Heatherlands St Jo *Sarum* 70-74; V W Streatham St Jas *S'wark* 74-90; TR Hinckley H Trin *Leic* from 90. *Holy Trinity Vicarage, 1 Cleveland Road, Hinckley, Leics LE10 0AJ* Hinckley (0455) 635711

HAYLETT, Stephen John. b 57. Lanc Univ BA84. Ripon Coll Cuddesdon 84. **d** 87 **p** 88. C Dartford St Alb *Roch* 87-89; C Sevenoaks St Jo from 89. *The Clergy House, 62 Quakers Hall Lane, Sevenoaks, Kent TN13 3TX* Sevenoaks (0732) 451710

HAYLLAR, Bruce Sherwill. b 23. Trin Hall Cam BA47 MA53. Cuddesdon Coll 48. **d** 50 **p** 51. V Peacehaven *Chich* 63-72; Zambia 72-75; V Moulsecoomb *Chich* 76-81; TR 81-83; R Rotherfield w Mark Cross 83-90; RD Rotherfield 87-90; rtd 90. *Moses Farm Cottage, Piltdown, Uckfield, E Sussex TN22 3XN* Newick (082572) 2006

HAYMAN, Canon Perceval Ecroyd Cobham. b 15. St Jo Coll Cam BA37 MA41. Linc Th Coll 48. **d** 50 **p** 51. V Rogate *Chich* 63-81; R Terwick 63-81; RD Midhurst 72-81; Can and Preb Chich Cathl from 77; rtd 81. *Fiddlers Green, Bell Lane, Cocking, Midhurst, W Sussex GU29 0HU* Midhurst (073081) 3198

HAYMAN, Canon Robert Fleming. b 31. Princeton Univ BA53. Gen Th Sem (NY) MDiv56. **d** 56 **p** 56. USA 56-88; I Drumcliffe w Lissadell and Munninane *K, E & A* from 88; Preb Elphin Cathl from 88. *The Rectory, Drumcliffe, Sligo, Irish Republic* Sligo (71) 63125

HAYMAN, Canon William Samuel. b 03. St Jo Coll Ox BA25 MA28. Sarum Th Coll 25. **d** 26 **p** 27. R Cheam *S'wark* 38-72; Adn Lewisham 60-72; Chapl to HM The Queen 61-73; rtd 72; Perm to Offic *Glouc* from 82. *8 Black Jack Mews, Cirencester, Glos GL7 2AA* Cirencester (0285) 655024

HAYNE, Raymond Guy. b 32. Chich Th Coll 57. **d** 60 **p** 61. C Kings Heath *Birm* 60-63; C Clewer St Andr *Ox* 63-67; V Grimsbury 67-76; P-in-c Wardington 71-74; R Brightwell w Sotwell 76-85; RD Wallingford 81-85; R St Breoke and Egloshayle *Truro* 85-90; RD Trigg Minor and Bodmin 88-90; V Reading St Mark *Ox* from 90. *St Mark's Vicarage, 88 Connaught Road, Reading RG3 2UF* Reading (0734) 587400

HAYNES, Clifford. b 33. Cam Univ MA60. Linc Th Coll 80. **d** 82 **p** 83. C Lightcliffe *Wakef* 82-85; V Bradshaw from 85. *The Vicarage, Pavement Lane, Bradshaw, Halifax, W Yorkshire HX2 9JJ* Halifax (0422) 244330

HAYNES, Cyril Michael. b 26. Univ of Wales BEd64. **d** 84 **p** 85. NSM Wenlock *Heref* from 84. *8 Forester Avenue, Much Wenlock, Shropshire TF13 6EX* Much Wenlock (0952) 727263

HAYNES, Donald Irwin. b 28. Birm Univ BA51. Ripon Hall Ox 59. **d** 59 **p** 60. C Chatham St Mary w St Jo *Roch* 59-66; Hon C Gillingham St Mary 66-71; Lic to Offic *Birm* 71-81; P-in-c Whittington *Derby* 82-85; R 85-90; C Kinver and Enville *Lich* from 90. *The Vicarage, The Close, Enville, Stourbridge, W Midlands DY7 5JB* Stourbridge (0384) 877709

HAYNES, Frederick Charles Ronald. b 22. St D Coll Lamp BA50. **d** 51 **p** 52. C Ipswich St Bart *St E* 51-55; CR from 55; Lic to Offic *Wakef* from 55; S Africa 61-66. *House of the Resurrection, Mirfield, W Yorkshire WF14 0BN* Mirfield (0924) 494318

HAYNES, Canon John Richard. b 35. Ely Th Coll 60. **d** 63 **p** 64. C Bollington St Jo *Ches* 63-67; C Ches St Jo 67-68; C Davenham 68-70; Rhodesia 70-80; Zimbabwe 80-90; Sub-Dean Bulawayo Cathl 78-83; Hon Can Matabeleland from 90; R Bishop's Stortford *St Alb* from 90. *69 Havers Lane, Bishop's Stortford, Herts CM23 3PA* Bishop's Stortford (0279) 656546

HAYNES, John Stanley. b 30. W Midl Minl Tr Course. **d** 82 **p** 83. NSM Westwood *Cov* 82-84; C Radford Semele and Ufton 84-85; V from 85. *The Vicarage, Radford Semele, Leamington Spa, Warks CV31 1TA* Leamington Spa (0926) 27374

HAYNES, Kenneth Gordon. b 09. Worc Ord Coll. **d** 56 **p** 57. R Feltwell *Ely* 70-75; rtd 75; Hon C Steeton *Bradf* 75-79. *73 Carlbury Avenue, Acklam, Middlesbrough, Cleveland TS5 8SY* Middlesbrough (0642) 828080

HAYNES, Leonard Thomas. b 17. d 69 p 70. C Lutterworth w Cotesbach *Leic* 69-73; C-in-c Swinford w Catthorpe, Shawell and Stanford 73-74; V 74-83; rtd 83; Perm to Offic *Leic* from 83. *Milltop House, Leicester Road, Measham, Burton-on-Trent, Staffs DE12 7HF* Measham (0530) 72962

HAYNES, Canon Michael Thomas Avery. b 32. AKC61. St Boniface Warminster 61. d 62 p 63. C Hebden Bridge *Wakef* 62-64; C Elland 64-68; V Thornhill Lees 68-82; Hon Can Wakef Cathl from 82; V Lindley from 82. *The Vicarage, The Clock Tower, Lindley, Huddersfield HD3 3JB* Huddersfield (0484) 650996

HAYNES, Very Rev Peter. b 25. Selw Coll Cam BA49 MA54. Cuddesdon Coll 50. d 52 p 53. C Stokesley *York* 52-54; C Hessle 54-58; V Drypool St Jo 58-63; Asst Dir RE *B & W* 63-70; Youth Chapl 63-70; V Glastonbury St Jo 70-72; V Glastonbury St Jo w Godney 72-74; Adn Wells, Can Res and Preb Wells Cathl 74-82; V Heref St Jo *Heref* from 82; Dean Heref from 82. *The Deanery, The Cloisters, Hereford HR1 2NG* Hereford (0432) 59880

HAYNES, Peter Nigel Stafford. b 39. Hertf Coll Ox BA62 MA66. Cuddesdon Coll 62. d 64 p 65. C Norwood All SS *Cant* 64-68; C Portsea N End St Mark *Portsm* 68-72; Asst Chapl Brussels *Eur* 72-76; TV Banbury *Ox* 76-80; Asst Sec (Internat Affairs) Gen Syn Bd Soc Resp 80-85; P-in-c E Peckham and Nettlestead *Roch* from 85. *The Rectory, Bush Road, East Peckham, Tonbridge, Kent TN12 5LL* East Peckham (0622) 871278

HAYNES, Philip Mayo. b 25. St Edm Hall Ox BA50 MA50. Cuddesdon Coll 50. d 54 p 55. C Limpsfield and Titsey *S'wark* 63-70; V Purley St Mark Woodcote 70-82; R Sherington w Chicheley, N Crawley, Astwood etc *Ox* 82-90; rtd 90. *1 Ridgemont Close, Woodstock Road, Oxford OX2 7PJ* Oxford (0865) 58116

HAYTER, Canon John Charles Edwin. b 15. St Edm Hall Ox BA37 MA46. Westcott Ho Cam 37. d 38 p 39. V Boldre *Win* 55-82; rtd 82; Perm to Offic *Win* from 82. *4 St Thomas Park, Lymington, Hants SO4 9NF* Lymington (0590) 678587

HAYTER, Canon Michael George. b 18. Ch Ch Ox BA39 MA43. Cuddesdon Coll 40. d 41 p 42. R Steeple Aston *Ox* 46-83; P-in-c Tackley 76-77; rtd 83; Perm to Offic *Pet* from 84. *Felden House, Charlton, Banbury, Oxon OX17 3DL* Banbury (0295) 811426

HAYTER, Miss Mary Elizabeth. *See* BARR, Dr Mary Elizabeth

HAYTER, Raymond William. b 48. Oak Hill Th Coll 74. d 77 p 78. C Bermondsey St Jas w Ch Ch *S'wark* 77-80; C Sydenham H Trin 81-83; Asst Chapl HM Pris Brixton 83-84; Chapl HM Youth Cust Cen Stoke Heath 84-88; HM Pris Maidstone 88-91; CF from 91. *c/o MOD (Army), Bagshot Park, Bagshot, Surrey GU19 5PL* Bagshot (0276) 71717

HAYTER, Ronald William Joseph. b 19. Keble Coll Ox BA40 MA44. Wells Th Coll 40. d 42 p 43. V Wear St Luke *Ex* 55-87; rtd 87. *38C Station Road, Haddenham, Ely, Cambs CB6 3XD* Ely (0353) 740206

HAYTER, Mrs Sandra. b 46. S Dios Minl Tr Scheme 82. dss 85 d 87. Catherington and Clanfield *Portsm* 85-86; Lee-on-the-Solent 86-87; C 87-89; Par Dn Burnham w Dropmore, Hitcham and Taplow *Ox* from 89. *12 Hatchgate Gardens, Burnham, Slough SL1 8DD* Burnham (0628) 662739

HAYTER, Thomas Hugh Osman. b 1900. St Cath Coll Cam BA22 MA26. Ridley Hall Cam 21. d 23 p 24. V Somerton *B & W* 45-68; rtd 68; Perm to Offic *Bris* from 73. *Privet Cottage, Hartham, Corsham, Wilts SN13 0PZ* Corsham (0249) 713285

HAYTHORNTHWAITE, Alfred Parker. b 10. Wycliffe Hall Ox 29. d 35 p 36. V Allithwaite *Carl* 67-76; rtd 76; Perm to Offic *Carl* from 80. *St Mary's Cottage, Vicarage Lane, Kirkby Lonsdale, Cumbria LA6 2BA* Kirkby Lonsdale (05242) 71525

HAYTHORNTHWAITE, Robert Brendan. b 31. Solicitor 59 TCD BA53 LLB56 MA64 QUB DipEd71. Edin Th Coll 63. d 64 p 65. C Belf St Jo Laganbank w Orangefield *D & D* 64-66; C Belf St Thos *Conn* 66-68; Lic to Offic 68-75; C Belf Malone (St Jo) 75-89; I Shinrone w Aghancon etc *L & K* from 89; Dom Chapl to Bp of Killaloe and Clonfert from 89. *St Mary's Rectory, Shinrone, Birr, Co Offaly, Irish Republic* Roscrea (505) 47164

HAYTHORNTHWAITE, William. b 97. MBE55. K Coll Lon 59. d 59 p 60. C Christchurch *Win* 67-75; rtd 75; Perm to Offic *Win* from 75. *1 Glebe Cottage, Church Lane, New Milton, Hants BH25 6QL* New Milton (0425) 610354

HAYTON, Mark William. b 59. St Steph Ho Ox 85. d 88 p 89. C Sittingbourne St Mich *Cant* 88-91; C Kennington from 91. *158 Canterbury Road, Kennington, Ashford, Kent* Ashford (0233) 638085

HAYTON, Norman Joseph Patrick. b 32. ARICS57. Sarum Th Coll 69. d 71 p 72. C Lytham St Cuth *Blackb* 71-74; V Wesham 74-79; V Chorley St Geo 79-80; NSM Kells *Carl* 84-85; P-in-c Flimby 85-90; V Barrow St Jas from 90. *St James's Vicarage, Barrow-in-Furness, Cumbria LA14 5SS* Barrow-in-Furness (0229) 21475

HAYWARD, Canon Alan Richard. b 25. Open Univ BA72. Wycliffe Hall Ox 54. d 56 p 57. V Wollescote *Worc* 65-85; Hon Can Worc Cathl from 85; R Alvechurch 85-91; rtd 91. *2 St Kenelm's Court, St Kenelm's Road, Romsley, Halesowen, W Midlands* Romsley (0562) 710749

HAYWARD, Alfred Ross. b 20. Clifton Th Coll 52. d 54 p 55. V Woodborough *S'well* 65-70; Warden Bradwaite Gospel Tr Stathern 73-77; V Tugby and E Norton w Skeffington *Leic* 77-81; R Beeston Regis *Nor* 81-83; rtd 83. *4 Somersby Road, Nottingham NG3 5QY* Nottingham (0602) 201406

HAYWARD, Canon Christopher Joseph. b 38. TCD BA63 MA67. Ridley Hall Cam 63. d 65 p 66. C Hatcham St Jas *S'wark* 65-69; Warden Lee Abbey Internat Students' Club Kensington 69-74; Chapl Chelmsf Cathl *Chelmsf* 74-77; P-in-c Darlaston All SS *Lich* 77-83; Ind Chapl 77-83; Can Res Bradf Cathl *Bradf* from 83; Sec Bd Miss from 83. *2 Cathedral Close, Bradford, W Yorkshire BD1 4EG* Bradford (0274) 727806

HAYWARD, Clifford. b 08. St Paul's Grahamstown 51. d 52 p 53. S Africa 57-73; C Lewisham St Mary *S'wark* 73-78; rtd 78. *The Charterhouse, Charterhouse Square, London EC1M 6AN* 071-251 6357

HAYWARD, Preb Edwin Calland. b 11. ATCL30 Lon Univ BSc32 Leeds Univ DipEd44. Linc Th Coll 35. d 36 p 37. RD Tutbury *Lich* 69-81; V Burton St Modwen 69-81; Preb Lich Cathl 72-81; P-in-c Burton Ch Ch 76-81; rtd 81; Perm to Offic *Derby & Lich* from 81. *19 Henhurst Hill, Burton-on-Trent, Staffs DE13 9TB* Burton-on-Trent (0283) 48735

HAYWARD, Jeffrey Kenneth. b 47. Nottm Univ BTh74. St Jo Coll Nottm LTh74. d 74 p 75. C Stambermill *Worc* 74-77; C Woking St Jo *Guildf* 77-83; V Springfield H Trin *Chelmsf* from 83; Chapl HM Pris Chelmsf from 86; Area RD Chelmsf 86-88; RD Chelmsf from 88. *The Vicarage, 61 Hill Road, Chelmsford CM2 6HW* Chelmsford (0245) 353389

HAYWARD, Mrs Jennifer Dawn. b 38. W Midl Minl Tr Course 85. d 88. NSM Gt Malvern St Mary *Worc* 88-90; NSM Gt Malvern Ch Ch 88-90; Par Dn from 90. *St Mary's House, 137 Madresfield Road, Malvern, Worcs WR14 2HD* Malvern (0684) 575994

HAYWARD, John Andrew. b 63. MHCIMA83 Nottm Univ BTh89. Linc Th Coll 86. d 89 p 90. C Seaford w Sutton *Chich* from 89. *29 Stafford Road, Seaford, E Sussex BN25 1UE* Seaford (0323) 891831

HAYWARD, John David. b 40. AKC63. d 65 p 66. C Westleigh St Pet *Man* 65-68; C Elton All SS 68-72; R Moston St Chad 72-77; TV Stantonbury *Ox* 74-87; TV Stantonbury and Willen 87-89; P-in-c N Springfield *Chelmsf* from 89. *The Vicarage, 32 Oak Lodge Tye, Chelmsford CM1 5GZ* Chelmsford (0245) 466160

HAYWARD, Ven John Derek Risdon. b 23. Trin Coll Cam BA56 MA64. Westcott Ho Cam 56. d 57 p 58. C Sheff St Mary w St Simon w St Matthias *Sheff* 57-59; V Sheff St Silas 59-63; V Isleworth All SS *Lon* from 64; Adn Middx 74-75; Gen Sec Lon Dioc from 75. *All Saints' Vicarage, 61 Church Street, Old Isleworth, Middx TW7 6BE* 081-560 6602 or 071-821 9351

HAYWARD, Preb John Talbot. b 28. Selw Coll Cam BA52 MA56. Wells Th Coll 52. d 54 p 55. C S Lyncombe *B & W* 54-58; R Lamyatt 58-71; V Bruton w Wyke Champflower and Redlynch 58-71; RD Bruton 62-71; R Weston-super-Mare St Jo 71-75; Preb Wells Cathl from 73; TR Weston-super-Mare Cen Par from 75. *The Rectory, 71 Upper Church Road, Weston-super-Mare, Avon BS23 2HX* Weston-super-Mare (0934) 625360

HAYWARD, Ms Pamela Jane. b 52. RGN82. Westcott Ho Cam 84. d 87. Par Dn Northn St Mary *Pet* 87-90; Par Dn Bris St Mary Redcliffe w Temple etc *Bris* from 90. *1B Colston Parade, Bristol BS1 6RA* Bristol (0272) 262491

HAYWARD, Peter Noel. b 26. Leeds Univ BA48 BD78. Coll of Resurr Mirfield 48. d 50 p 51. C S Elmsall *Wakef* 50-56; C Sheldon *Birm* 56-60; C-in-c Garretts Green CD 60-69; V Garretts Green 69-70; R Hotham *York* from 70; V N Cave w Cliffe from 70; RD Howden

78-86. *The Vicarage, North Cave, Brough, N Humberside HU15 2LJ* North Cave (04302) 2398

HAYWARD, Roynon Albert Oscar James. b 25. d 67 p 68. Hon C Glouc St Paul *Glouc* 67-89; rtd 89. *37 Forest View Road, Gloucester GL4 0BX* Gloucester (0452) 21104

HAYWOOD, Frank. b 19. St Cath Soc Ox BA40 MA44. Cuddesdon Coll 40. d 42 p 43. V Challock w Molash *Cant* 62-87; rtd 87. *36A St Leonard's Road, Hythe, Kent CT21 6ER* Hythe (0303) 265356

HAYWOOD, James William. b 36. Chich Th Coll 69. d 73 p 74. C Leeds Halton St Wilfrid *Ripon* 73-76; C Workington St Jo *Carl* 76-78; V Clifton 78-84; P-in-c Barrow St Jas 84-85; V 85-89; V Crosby Ravensworth from 89; R Asby from 89; V Bolton from 89. *The Vicarage, Crosby Ravensworth, Penrith, Cumbria CA10 3JJ* Ravensworth (09315) 226

HAYWOOD, Keith Roderick. b 48. Oak Hill Th Coll 84. d 86 p 87. C Fazeley *Lich* 86-90; TV Leek and Meerbrook from 90. *St Luke's Vicarage, Novi Lane, Leek, Staffs ST13 6NR* Leek (0538) 373306

HAZEL, Sister. *See* SMITH, Hazel Ferguson Waide

HAZELGROVE, Trevor John. b 42. S'wark Ord Course 71. d 74 p 75. C Hackbridge and N Beddington *S'wark* 74-78; Ind Chapl 78-83; P-in-c Mert St Jo 78-83; V Ham St Rich 83-88. *The Flat, Spex Hall, Salisbury SP2 0QD*

HAZELL, Ven Frederick Roy. b 30. Fitzw Ho Cam BA53 MA59. Cuddesdon Coll 54. d 56 p 57. C Ilkeston St Mary *Derby* 56-59; C Heanor 59-62; V Marlpool 62-63; Chapl Univ of W Indies 63-66; C St Martin-in-the-Fields *Lon* 66-68; V Croydon H Sav *Cant* 68-84; RD Croydon 72-78; Hon Can Cant Cathl 73-84; P-in-c Croydon H Trin 77-80; Adn Croydon 84; Adn Croydon S'wark from 85. *246 Pampisford Road, South Croydon, Surrey CR2 6DD* 081-681 5496

HAZELTON, Edwin Geoffrey. b 08. OBE45. St Geo Windsor 50. d 51 p 52. R Wylye, Stockton and Fisherton Delamere *Sarum* 69-73; R Wylye, Fisherton Delamere and the Langfords 73-76; rtd 76. *Flat 7, St Nicholas's Hospital, Salisbury SP1 2SW* Salisbury (0722) 332247

HAZELTON, John. b 35. St Cath Coll Cam BA56 MA60 Bris Univ MLitt74 Newc Univ BPhil80. Wells Th Coll 59. d 61 p 62. C Twerton *B & W* 61-65; V Pitcombe w Shepton Montague 65-72; Lect SS Hild & Bede Dur 72-79; Lic to Offic *Dur* from 74; Dame Allan's Schs Newc 79-89; Chapl from 89; Lic to Offic *Newc* from 89. *36 Orchard Drive, Durham DH1 1LA* 091-384 6606

HAZELTON, Robert Henry Peter. b 22. Wells Th Coll 65. d 67 p 68. C Milton *B & W* 69-76; V Peasedown St John 76-80; V Peasedown St John w Wellow 80-89; rtd 90. *37 High Meadows, Midsomer Norton, Bath BA3 2RY* Midsomer Norton (0761) 419675

HAZELWOOD, Ms Jillian. b 32. Bp Otter Coll CertEd52 St Alb Minl Tr Scheme 82. d 87. NSM Wheathampstead *St Alb* from 87. *14 Butterfield Road, Wheathampstead, St Albans, Herts AL4 8PU* Wheathampstead (058283) 3146

HAZLEDINE, Basil William. b 18. St Pet Hall Ox BA42 MA45. Wycliffe Hall Ox 42. d 43 p 44. V Stoughton *Guildf* 60-70; V Westlands St Andr *Lich* 70-77; P-in-c Whatfield w Semer *St E* 77-78; R 78-81; P-in-c Nedging w Naughton 77-81; R Whatfield w Semer, Nedging and Naughton 81-84; rtd 84. *14 Willis Close, Epsom, Surrey KT18 7SS* Epsom (0372) 726615

HAZLEHURST, Anthony Robin. b 43. Man Univ BSc64. Tyndale Hall Bris 65. d 68 p 69. C Macclesfield Ch Ch *Ches* 68-71; C Bushbury *Lich* 71-75; P-in-c New Clee *Linc* 75-85; TV Deane *Man* from 85. *St Andrew's Vicarage, Crescent Avenue, Bolton BL5 1EN* Bolton (0204) 651851

HAZLEHURST, David. b 32. Liv Univ BSc54. St Steph Ho Ox 55. d 57 p 58. C Sheff Arbourthorne *Sheff* 57-59; C Doncaster Ch Ch 59-61; C W Wycombe *Ox* 61-63; P-in-c Collyhurst St Jas *Man* 66-67; V Blackrod 67-79; V Halliwell St Marg 79-84; R Sutton St Nic *S'wark* from 84. *The Rectory, 34 Robin Hood Lane, Sutton, Surrey SM1 2RG* 081-642 3499

HAZLETT, Stephen David. b 56. TCD BTh88. CITC. d 88 p 89. C Ballywillan *Conn* 88-90; I Rathcoole from 90. *St Comgall's Rectory, 3 Strathmore Park, Belfast BT15 5HQ* Belfast (0232) 776085 or 853251

HAZLEWOOD, Andrew Lord. b 54. BSc. Wycliffe Hall Ox. d 82 p 83. C Leckhampton SS Phil and Jas w Cheltenham St Jas *Glouc* 82-85; C Waltham H Cross *Chelmsf* 85-89; R Pedmore *Worc* from 89. *The Rectory, Pedmore Lane, Stourbridge, W Midlands DY9 0SW* Hagley (0562) 884856

HAZLEWOOD, Dr David Paul. b 47. Sheff Univ MB, ChB70 Campion Hall Ox BA72 MA77. Wycliffe

Hall Ox 70. d 73 p 74. C Chapeltown *Sheff* 73-75; Singapore 76; Indonesia 76-88; R Ipswich St Helen *St E* from 88. *St Helen's Rectory, 35 Warwick Road, Ipswich IP4 2QE* Ipswich (0473) 232898

HAZLEWOOD, Canon George Ian. b 28. St Fran Coll Brisbane 52. d 55 p 56. Australia 55-56; C Poplar All SS w St Frideswide *Lon* 56-62; Bp's Youth Chapl *St Alb* 62-67; V Yeovil H Trin *B & W* 67-74; RD Merston 72-74; V Prestbury *Glouc* from 74; Hon Can Glouc Cathl from 88; Hon Can Wangaratta from 88. *The Vicarage, Prestbury, Cheltenham, Glos GL52 3DQ* Cheltenham (0242) 244373

✠**HAZLEWOOD, Rt Rev John.** b 24. K Coll Cam BA48 MA52. Cuddesdon Coll 48. d 49 p 50 c 75. C Camberwell St Mich *S'wark* 49-50; Australia 50-53 and from 55; C Camberwell St Mich w All So *S'wark* 53-55; Vice Prin St Fran Th Coll Brisbane 55-60; Dean Rockhampton 61-68; Perth 68-75; Bp Ballarat from 75. *PO Box 89, Ballarat, Victoria, Australia 3350* Ballarat (53) 311183

HEAD, David Nicholas. b 55. Pemb Coll Cam BA77 MA81. Westcott Ho Cam 78. d 81 p 82. C Surbiton St Andr and St Mark *S'wark* 81-84; C St Marylebone w H Trin *Lon* 84-89; TV Clapham Team Min *S'wark* from 89. *49 Voltaire Road, London SW4 6DD* 071-978 1774

HEAD, Canon Derek Leonard Hamilton. b 34. ALCD58. d 58 p 59. C Bexleyheath Ch Ch *Roch* 58-61; C Wisley w Pyrford *Guildf* 61-66; C-in-c Ewell St Paul Howell Hill CD 66-73; R Headley All SS 73-81; TR 81-82; RD Farnham 80-82; V Chertsey from 82; Hon Can Guildf Cathl from 83; RD Runnymede from 88; Dir Post-Ord Tr from 90. *The Vicarage, London Street, Chertsey, Surrey KT16 8AA* Chertsey (0932) 563141

HEAD, John Leslie. b 06. Dur Univ LTh31. Sarum Th Coll 29. d 31 p 32. R Leigh St Clem *Chelmsf* 50-72; rtd 72. *21 Selwyn Road, Southend-on-Sea SS2 4DR* Southend-on-Sea (0702) 610736

HEAD, William Peter. b 18. St Edm Hall Ox BA46 MA51. Cuddesdon Coll 46. d 48 p 49. Chapl Highfield Sch Liphook 61-74; rtd 83. *3 Ferndale Road, Chichester, W Sussex PO19 4QJ* Chichester (0243) 527075

HEADING, Richard Vaughan. b 43. ARCS65 Lon Univ BSc65. Coll of Resurr Mirfield 66. d 68 p 69. C Heref St Martin *Heref* 68-75; P-in-c Birches Head *Lich* 75-77; P-in-c Northwood 75-77; TV Hanley H Ev 77-82; V Heref H Trin *Heref* from 82. *Holy Trinity Vicarage, Whitecross Road, Hereford HR4 0DH* Hereford (0432) 273086

HEADLAND, James Frederick. b 20. Clifton Th Coll 51. d 53 p 54. P-in-c Smethcott w Woolstaston *Heref* 65-81; R Church Pulverbatch 65-81; P-in-c Cantley w Limpenhoe and Southwood *Nor* 81; R Reedham 81; Reedham w Cantley w Limpenhoe and Southwood 81-86; Perm to Offic Heref from 86; Lich from 88. *3 Ashford Avenue, Pontesbury, Shrewsbury SY5 0QN* Shrewsbury (0743) 790565

HEADLEY, Carolyn Jane. b 50. MCSP71 GDipP71. Lon Bible Coll DipTh76 Oak Hill Th Coll BA. dss 83 d 87. Harlesden St Mark *Lon* 83-86; Kensal Rise St Mark and St Martin 86-87; Par Dn 87; Par Dn Uxbridge St Andr w St Jo 87-88; Par Dn Uxbridge 88-90; TM from 90; Warden of Readers (Willesden Episc Area) from 88. *St Margaret's Vicarage, 72 Harefield Road, Uxbridge, Middx UB8 1PL* Uxbridge (0895) 70759

HEADLEY, Lewis Victor. b 06. OBE50. St D Coll Lamp BA28 Ripon Hall Ox 28. d 29 p 30. R E Tisted w Colmer *Win* 67-82; rtd 82; Perm to Offic *Win* from 83. *Colonnade, Rotherfield Park, East Tisted, Alton, Hants GU34 3QM* Tisted (042058) 412

HEADS, Canon William Dobson. b 28. Bps' Coll Cheshunt. d 61 p 62. C Beamish *Dur* 61-64; C Monkwearmouth St Andr 64-65; C Stockton St Chad 65-68; V 68-76; Chapl N Tees Hosp Stockton-on-Tees from 76; Lic to Offic *Dur* 76-87; Hon Can Dur Cathl from 87. *123 The Glebe, Norton, Stockton-on-Tees, Cleveland TS20 1RD* Stockton-on-Tees (0642) 553032

HEAGERTY, Alistair John. b 42. MBE87. Or Coll Ox BA63 MA67. Lon Coll of Div BD68. d 68 p 69. C Margate H Trin *Cant* 68-72; CF from 72. *c/o MOD (Army), Bagshot Park, Bagshot, Surrey GU19 5PL* Bagshot (0276) 71717

HEAL, David Walter. b 37. Ox Univ MA63 Trin Coll Carmarthen 87. d 90 p 91. NSM Henfynyw w Aberaeron and Llanddewi Aber-arth *St D* from 90. *Caegwair Bach, Llanon, Cardigan, Dyfed SY23 5LZ* Llanon (0974) 202596

HEAL, Geoffrey. b 28. Linc Th Coll 54. d 56 p 57. V Peckham St Jo *S'wark* 62-75; V Southfields St Barn 75-88; rtd 88; Perm to Offic *Ex* from 89. *Digby*

Cottage, 5 Hind Street, Ottery St Mary, Devon EX11 1BW Ottery St Mary (0404) 814729

HEALE, Walter James Grenville. b 40. Wycliffe Hall Ox 77. **d** 79 **p** 80. C Walsall *Lich* 79-82; TV Marfleet *York* 82-89; TR from 89. *St George's Rectory, Carden Avenue, Hull HU9 4RT* Hull (0482) 791291

HEALES, John. b 48. K Coll Lon BD71 AKC71 PGCE72 DPS76. St Mich Coll Llan 75. **d** 76 **p** 77. C Cwmbran *Mon* 76-78; Chapl Rendcomb Coll Cirencester 78-82; Perm to Offic *Mon* 85-88; V Penhow, St Brides Netherwent w Llandavenny etc from 88. *Flat 1, The Rectory, Llanfaches, Newport, Gwent NP6 3AY* Penhow (0633) 400901

HEALEY, Francis John. b 14. Wells Th Coll 64. **d** 65 **p** 65. R Cucklington w Stoke Trister and Bayford *B & W* 68-79; rtd 79; Perm to Offic *Win* from 79. *3A Rushton Crescent, Bournemouth BH3 7AF* Bournemouth (0202) 552229

HEALEY, James Christopher. b 44. Linc Th Coll 84. **d** 86 **p** 87. C Boultham *Linc* 86-90; TV Gt Grimsby St Mary and St Jas 90-91; I Narraghmore w Timolin, Castledermot and Kinneagh *D & G* from 91. *Urglin Glebe, Rutland, Carlow, Irish Republic* Carlow (503) 40144

HEANEY, James Roland. b 59. DipTh85. **d** 85 **p** 86. C Ballynafeigh St Jude *D & D* 85-88; C Lisburn Ch Ch Cathl *Conn* 88-90; I Dunganstown w Redcross and Conary *D & G* from 90. *The Rectory, Redcross, Co Wicklow, Irish Republic* Wicklow (404) 41637

HEANEY, Michael Roger. b 43. TCD BA66 HDipEd67 MA69 DCG83. CITC 74. **d** 76 **p** 77. Chapl St Columba's Coll Dub from 76. *Montana, Scholarstown Road, Templeogue, Dublin 16, Irish Republic* Dublin (1) 931167

HEAP, David Leonard. b 58. Man Univ BA79. Cranmer Hall Dur 82. **d** 85 **p** 86. C Clitheroe St Jas *Blackb* 85-88; C Blackb St Gabr from 88. *100 Highbank, Blackburn BB1 8SX* Blackburn (0254) 662818

HEAP, Lt-Col Edward Jocelyne Fortrey. b 07. OBE49. RMA. St Geo Windsor 53. **d** 54 **p** 55. V Horton and Chalbury *Sarum* 63-68; rtd 68. *2 Magnolia Court, 11 Portland Avenue, Exmouth, Devon EX8 2BS* Exmouth (0395) 279894

HEAP, Simon Robin Fortrey. b 36. AKC59. St Boniface Warminster 59. **d** 60 **p** 61. C Gillingham *Sarum* 60-64; C Littleham w Exmouth *Ex* 71-77. *Little Rolleston, 11 Maer Road, Exmouth, Devon EX8 2DA* Exmouth (0395) 275050

HEAPS, Richard Peter. b 35. Qu Coll Birm 58. **d** 61 **p** 62. C Castle Bromwich SS Mary and Marg *Birm* 61-65; C-in-c Erdington St Chad CD 65-70; V Nechells 70-81; RD Aston 75-81; V Marston Green 81-86; P-in-c Shrawley and Witley w Astley *Worc* from 86. *The Rectory, Shrawley, Worcester WR6 6TS* Worcester (0905) 620489

HEAPS, William Henry. b 20. St Deiniol's Hawarden 81. **d** 83 **p** 84. NSM Tranmere St Cath *Ches* from 83; NSM Prenton from 86. *7 St Stephen's Court, Prenton Lane, Birkenhead, Merseyside L42 8QD* 051-608 4253

HEARD, Charles. b 19. S'wark Ord Course 62. **d** 65 **p** 66. C Plumstead St Nic *S'wark* 65-71; C Blackheath All SS 71-72; V Barnes H Trin 72-84; rtd 84; Hon C E Wickham *S'wark* from 84. *Flat 5, Elmfield Court, Wickham Street, Welling, Kent DA16 3DF* 081-855 9809

HEARD, Ross McPherson. b 11. Clifton Th Coll 38. **d** 41 **p** 42. R Hatch Beauchamp w Beercrocombe *B & W* 58-76; V W Hatch 62-76; rtd 76. *235 Queen Edith's Way, Cambridge CB1 4NJ* Cambridge (0223) 212252

HEARN, John. b 49. Trin Coll Bris. **d** 82 **p** 83. C Epsom Common Ch Ch *Guildf* 82-85; C Ringwood *Win* 85-88; Chapl Basingstoke Distr Hosp from 88. *The Lodge, Basingstoke and District Hospital, Basingstoke, Hants* Basingstoke (0256) 473202

HEARN, Jonathan. b 58. GradIPM85 Leeds Univ BA81. Westcott Ho Cam 89. **d** 91. C Tuffley *Glouc* from 91. *155 Tuffley Lane, Gloucester GL4 0DT* Gloucester (0452) 423104

HEARN, Peter Brian. b 31. St Jo Coll Dur 52. **d** 55 **p** 56. C Frodingham *Linc* 55-59; R Belton SS Pet and Paul 59-64; V Manthorpe w Londonthorpe 59-64; V Billingborough 64-73; V Sempringham w Pointon and Birthorpe 64-73; V Flixborough w Burton upon Stather from 73; RD Manlake from 87. *The Vicarage, Burton-upon-Stather, Scunthorpe DN15 9DZ* Scunthorpe (0724) 720276

HEARN, Thomas Michael. b 12. Oak Hill Th Coll 55. **d** 57 **p** 58. V Tushingham *Ches* 65-79; P-in-c Whitewell 73-79; R Tushingham and Whitewell 79-83; Chapl High Sheriff Cheshire 68-69; Clwyd 74-75; rtd 83; Perm to Offic *Ches*

from 83. *27 Eaton Mews, Handbridge, Chester CH4 7EJ* Chester (0244) 674834

HEARN, Thomas Peter. b 18. Selw Coll Cam BA40 MA45. Linc Th Coll 40. **d** 42 **p** 43. R Stratton w Baunton *Glouc* 62-75; V France Lynch 75-83; rtd 84; Perm to Offic *Glouc* from 84. *9 Cotswold Close, Cirencester, Glos GL7 1XP* Cirencester (0285) 655627

HEARN, Trevor. b 36. Sarum Th Coll 61. **d** 64 **p** 65. C Hounslow St Steph *Lon* 64-67; Miss to Seamen from 67; Lic to Offic *St E* 74-80; *Bris* from 80. *4 Penlea Court, Bristol BS11 0BY* Avonmouth (0272) 826107 or 822335

HEARNE, Derrick Kenneth. b 32. FBCS69 K Coll Lon BA68 AKC68. St Mich Coll Llan DMinlStuds. **d** 90 **p** 91. C Llanbadarn Fawr w Capel Bangor *St D* from 90. *60 Maesceinion, Aberystwyth, Dyfed SY23 3QQ* Aberystwyth (0970) 612899

HEARTFIELD, Canon Peter Reginald. b 27. Chich Th Coll 61. **d** 63 **p** 64. C Hurstpierpoint *Chich* 63-67; V Brighton St Alb Preston 67-73; Chapl Kent and Cant Hosp and Nunnery Fields Hosp Cant from 73; Six Preacher Cant Cathl *Cant* 79-84; Hon Can Cant Cathl from 84. *7 Lime Kiln Road, Canterbury, Kent CT1 3QH* Canterbury (0227) 765454 or 766877

HEASLIP, William John. b 44. TCD BA66. CITC 79. **d** 80 **p** 81. Chapl Mt Temple Sch Dub 80-86; Bp's C Aughaval w Burrishoole, Knappagh and Louisburgh *T, K & A* 86-88; I Aughaval w Achill, Knappagh, Dugort etc from 88; Radio Officer (Tuam) from 90. *The Rectory, Newport Road, Westport, Co Mayo, Irish Republic* Westport (98) 25127

HEATH, Frank William. b 10. Liv Univ BA36. Tyndale Hall Bris 36. **d** 38 **p** 39. R Heref St Nic *Heref* 61-79; rtd 79; Perm to Offic *Carl* from 81. *28 Derwent Drive, Hereford HR4 0QN* Hereford (0432) 352454

HEATH, Henry. b 40. FCII77. Oak Hill Th Coll 77. **d** 80 **p** 81. Hon C Lexden *Chelmsf* from 80; Hon C Halstead St Andr w H Trin and Greenstead Green from 86. *Pete Hall, Langenhoe, Colchester CO5 7NL* Colchester (0206) 35202 or 35650

HEATH, John Henry. b 41. Chich Th Coll 69. **d** 71 **p** 72. C Crediton *Ex* 71-74; C Tavistock and Gulworthy 74-76; C Brixham 76-77; C Brixham w Churston Ferrers 77-79; R Bere Ferrers 79-85; P-in-c Moretonhampstead, N Bovey and Manaton 85-88; R from 88. *The Rectory, Moretonhampstead, Newton Abbot, Devon TQ13 8NB* Moretonhampstead (0647) 40977

HEATH, Canon Peter Henry. b 24. Kelham Th Coll 40. **d** 47 **p** 48. C Derby St Anne *Derby* 47-49; C Staveley 49-52; C Brampton St Thos 52-54; C-in-c Brampton St Mark CD 54-59; V New Whittington 59-66; V Glossop from 66; RD Glossop 83-89; Hon Can Derby Cathl from 84. *The Vicarage, Old Glossop, Derbyshire SK13 9RU* Glossop (0457) 852146

HEATH, Raymond Walker. b 19. Cuddesdon Coll 46. **d** 47 **p** 48. V Rolvenden *Cant* 66-75; Perm to Offic *Glouc* from 79; rtd 84. *High Rudge, Kineton, Guiting Power, Cheltenham, Glos GL54 5UG* Guiting Power (0451) 850440

HEATH, William Walter. b 11. St Jo Coll Ox BA32. **d** 72 **p** 73. Hon C Petworth *Chich* 72-90; Perm to Offic from 90. *Malthouse, Lurgashall, Petworth, W Sussex GU28 9ET* Northchapel (042878) 212

HEATHCOTE, Edgar. b 15. Linc Th Coll 62. **d** 63 **p** 64. R Ashbrittle *B & W* 69-72; R Ashbrittle w Bathealton, Stawley and Kittisford 72-78; Lic to Offic 78-80; rtd 80; Perm to Offic *B & W* from 80. *Willow Cottage, 23 Bath Place, Taunton, Somerset TA1 4ER* Taunton (0823) 271794

HEATLEY, David Henry. b 50. Kent Univ BA72. Qu Coll Birm 86. **d** 88 **p** 89. C Liss *Portsm* from 88. *The Vicarage, Newchurch, Sandown, Isle of Wight PO36 0NN* Isle of Wight (0983) 865504

HEATLEY, Henry David. b 24. CITC 66. **d** 68 **p** 69. C Belf St Matt *Conn* 68-72; C-in-c Layde 72-78; C Belf St Mary 78-80; I Belf St Barn from 80. *102 Salisbury Avenue, Belfast BT15 5ED* Belfast (0232) 779405

HEATLEY, William Cecil. b 39. QUB BA61. Ridley Hall Cam 62. **d** 64 **p** 65. C Ballymacarrett St Patr *D & D* 64-69; C Herne Hill St Paul *S'wark* 69-74; TV Sanderstead All SS 75-82; P-in-c Peckham St Sav 82-87; V from 87. *173 Choumert Road, London SE15 4AW* 071-639 5072 or 732 3435

HEATLIE, James Welsh. b 09. Edin Univ MA30. Coates Hall Edin 30. **d** 32 **p** 33. V Stockport St Pet *Ches* 65-78; rtd 78. *5 Buchlyvie Road, Ralston, Paisley, Renfrewshire PA1 3AD*

HEATON, Alan. b 36. K Coll Lon BD64 AKC64 Nottm Univ MTh76. **d** 65 **p** 66. C Stockton St Chad *Dur* 65-68; C Englefield Green *Guildf* 68-70; C Winlaton *Dur* 70-74;

Chapl Derby Lonsdale Coll *Derby* 74-79; V Alfreton 79-87; RD Alfreton 81-86; TR Clifton *S'well* from 87. *St Mary's Rectory, 58 Village Road, Clifton, Nottingham NG11 8NE* Nottingham (0602) 211856

HEATON, Very Rev Eric William. b 20. Ch Coll Cam BA44 MA46. Lambeth DD91. **d** 44 **p** 45. Chapl St Jo Coll Ox 60-74; Sen Tutor 66-73; Dean Dur 74-79; Dean Ch Ch *Ox* from 79; rtd 90. *The Deanery, Christ Church, Oxford OX1 1DP* Oxford (0865) 276162

HEATON, Julian Roger. b 62. LSE BSc(Econ)83 Ox Univ BA86. St Steph Ho Ox 84. **d** 87 **p** 88. C Stockport St Thos w St Pet *Ches* 87-90; Asst Chapl Qu Medical Cen and Univ Hosp Nottm from 90. *The Chaplaincy Centre, D Floor, East Block, Queen's Medical Centre, Nottingham NG7 2UH* Nottingham (0602) 421421

HEATON-RENSHAW, Canon Squire Heaton. b 09. TD50. Selw Coll Cam BA30 MusB30 MA34. Westcott Ho Cam 34. **d** 35 **p** 36. V Mert St Mary *S'wark* 52-75; Perm to Offic *Win* from 75; rtd 76. *Paddock Cottage, Bentworth, Alton, Hants GU34 5RB* Alton (0420) 63512

✠**HEAVENER, Rt Rev Robert William.** b 05. TCD BA28. CITC 29. **d** 29 **p** 30 **c** 73. C Clones *Clogh* 29-31; Dioc Curate 31-32; C-in-c Lack 32-38; I Derryvullen N 38-46; R Monaghan w Tyholland 46-51; R Monaghan 46-73; R Monaghan w Tydavnet 51-73; Can St Patr Cathl Dub 62-68; Adn Clogh 68-73; Bp Clogh 73-80; rtd 80. *12 Church Avenue, Newtownabbey, Co Antrim BT37 0PJ* Belfast (0232) 863242

HEAVER, Derek Cyril. b 47. St Jo Coll Nottm BTh73. **d** 73 **p** 74. C Win Ch Ch *Win* 73-77; CF from 77. *c/o MOD (Army), Bagshot Park, Bagshot, Surrey GU19 5PL* Bagshot (0276) 71717

HEAVISIDES, Neil Cameron. b 50. Selw Coll Cam BA72 MA76 Ox Univ BA74 MA85. Ripon Hall Ox 72. **d** 75 **p** 76. C Stockton St Pet *Dur* 75-78; Succ S'wark Cathl *S'wark* 78-81; V Seaham w Seaham Harbour *Dur* 81-88; P-in-c Edington and Imber, Erlestoke and E Coulston *Sarum* 88-89; R from 89. *The Vicarage, Edington, Westbury, Wilts BA13 4PX* Bratton (0380) 830010

HEAWOOD, Canon Alan Richard. b 32. G&C Coll Cam BA54 MA58. Union Th Sem (NY) BD56 Ripon Hall Ox 56. **d** 57 **p** 58. C Horwich H Trin *Man* 57-59; C Weaste 59-60; C Beverley Minster *York* 60-62; Chapl and Lect St Pet Coll Saltley 62-65; R Hockwold w Wilton *Ely* 65-72; R Weeting 65-72; V Melbourn 72-80; V Meldreth 72-80; Hon Can Ely Cathl from 80; P-in-c Teversham 80-90; Adult Educn Sec 80-89; Dir of Educn from 80. *The Rectory, 30 Church Road, Teversham, Cambs CB1 5AW* Teversham (02205) 2220

HEAWOOD, Raymond Garth. b 02. G&C Coll Cam BA27 MA30. Ridley Hall Cam 27. **d** 28 **p** 29. V Dore *Derby* 59-67; rtd 67; Perm to Offic *Carl* from 77. *Cookson's Garth, Clappersgate, Ambleside, Cumbria LA22 9ND* Ambleside (05394) 33109

HEBBLETHWAITE, Canon Brian Leslie. b 39. Magd Coll Ox BA61 MA67 Magd Coll Cam BA63 MA68 BD84. Westcott Ho Cam 62. **d** 65 **p** 66. C Elton All SS *Man* 65-68; Chapl and Dean of Chpl Qu Coll Cam from 69; Lic to Offic *Ely* from 69; Asst Lect Cam Univ 73-77; Lect from 77; Can Th Leic Cathl *Leic* from 82. *Queen's College, Cambridge CB3 9ET* Cambridge (0223) 335511

HEBBORN, Roy Valentine Charles. S Dios Minl Tr Scheme 83. **d** 86 **p** 87. NSM Lewes All SS, St Anne, St Mich and St Thos *Chich* from 86. *3 St Anne's Terrace, Western Road, Lewes, E Sussex BN7 1RH* Lewes (0273) 474063

HEBDEN, John Percy. b 18. St Aid Birkenhead 58. **d** 60 **p** 60. V Laxey *S & M* 70-83; V Lonan 80-83; rtd 84; Hon C Douglas St Geo and St Barn *S & M* from 84. *Begra, Clayhead Road, Baldrine, Douglas, Isle of Man* Laxey (0624) 781296

HEBER-PERCY, Christopher John. b 41. St Jo Coll Cam BA64 MA68. Wells Th Coll 66. **d** 68 **p** 69. C Leigh St Mary *Man* 68-71; Asst Ind Chapl 71-80; P-in-c Oldham St Andr 75-78; TV Oldham 78-80; Ind Chapl *Win* 80-90; N Humberside Ind Chapl *York* from 90. *19 Bellfield Avenue, Hull HU8 9DS* Hull (0482) 7022033

HECKINGBOTTOM, John Michael. b 33. Leeds Univ BA55. St Steph Ho Ox 55. **d** 57 **p** 58. C Wigan All SS *Liv* 57-59; Min Can and Succ Ripon Cathl *Ripon* 59-63; P-in-c Seacroft 63-66; V Menston w Woodhead *Bradf* 66-82; P-in-c Bishop Monkton and Burton Leonard *Ripon* 82-88; Chapl Scotton Banks Hosp Knaresborough 86-88; V Collingham w Harewood *Ripon* from 88. *The Vicarage, Church Lane, Collingham, Wetherby, W Yorkshire LS22 5AU* Collingham Bridge (0937) 73975

HECTOR, Noel Antony. b 61. Barrister-at-Law 84 Sheff Univ LLB83. Oak Hill Th Coll BA91. **d** 91. C Rodbourne

Cheney *Bris* from 91. *11 Bourne Road, Swindon, Wilts SN2 2JH* Swindon (0793) 531389

HEDDLE, Dr Duncan. b 34. Wadh Coll Ox BA57 MA61 DPhil64. **d** 86 **p** 86. Chapl Aber Univ *Ab* from 86; P-in-c Bucksburn from 90. *2 Douglas Place, High Street, Aberdeen AB2 3EA* Aberdeen (0224) 485975

HEDGCOCK, Dr Walter Paul. b 09. FRCGP Lon Univ MB, BS32 MD34. S'wark Ord Course 69. **d** 72 **p** 73. C Blakeney w Lt Langham *Nor* 72-73; P-in-c Field Dalling w Saxlingham 73-76; Bp's Scientific Resp Adv 76-83; Hon C Wallingford w Crowmarsh Gifford etc *Ox* from 84. *3 Cherwell Close, Wallingford, Oxon OX10 0HF* Wallingford (0491) 37684

HEDGER, Graham. b 57. Lon Bible Coll BA Ridley Hall Cam. **d** 83 **p** 84. C Walton *St E* 83-86; TV Mildenhall 86-91; R Swainsthorpe w Newton Flotman *Nor* from 91; Dioc Evang Officer from 91. *The Rectory, Church Road, Newton Flotman, Norwich NR15 1QB* Swainsthorpe (0508) 470762

HEDGES, Mrs Anne Violet. b 53. Ripon Coll Cuddesdon 87. **d** 89. C Thetford *Nor* from 89. *23 Canon's Close, Thetford, Norfolk IP24 3PW* Thetford (0842) 752338

HEDGES, Dennis Walter. b 29. Sarum Th Coll. **d** 62 **p** 63. C Walton-on-Thames *Guildf* 62-66; C Westborough 66-69; V Blackheath and Chilworth 69-79; R Farncombe from 79; RD Godalming 84-89. *The Rectory, 38 Farncombe Hill, Godalming, Surrey GU7 2AU* Godalming (0483) 416091

HEDGES, Ian Charles. b 55. Sarum & Wells Th Coll 79. **d** 82 **p** 83. C Chessington *Guildf* 82-85; C Fleet 85-90; V S Farnborough from 90. *The Vicarage, 1 St Mark's Close, Farnborough, Hants GU14 6PP* Farnborough (0252) 544711

HEDGES, Mrs Jane Barbara. b 55. St Jo Coll Dur BA78. Cranmer Hall Dur 78. **dss** 80 **d** 87. Fareham H Trin *Portsm* 80-83; Southn (City Cen) *Win* 83-87; Par Dn 87-88; Dioc Stewardship Adv *Portsm* from 88. *10 Mallow Close, Waterlooville, Portsmouth PO7 8EF* Portsmouth (0705) 250520

HEDGES, Mrs Jane Rosemary. b 44. RGN65. S Dios Minl Tr Scheme 86. **d** 89. NSM Gillingham *Sarum* from 89. *Dene Hollow, Wyke, Gillingham, Dorset SP8 4NG* Gillingham (0747) 822812

HEDGES, John Michael Peter. b 34. Leeds Univ BA60. Ripon Hall Ox 60. **d** 61 **p** 62. C Weaste *Man* 61-65; V Ashton St Pet 65-74; C Easthampstead *Ox* 74-85; V Tilehurst St Geo 85-91; C Thatcham from 91. *22 Ashman Road, Newbury, Berks RG13 4WD* Newbury (0635) 69940

HEDGES, Leslie Norman. b 26. Bris Univ BA51 Lon Univ BD56. Clifton Th Coll 48. **d** 53 **p** 54. V Clapham Park All SS *S'wark* 59-70; V Findern *Derby* 70-82; V Willington 70-82; V Trowbridge St Thos and W Ashton *Sarum* 82-91; rtd 91. *16 Penwerris Road, Truro, Cornwall TR1 3QS* Truro (0872) 79858

HEDLEY, Dr Charles John Wykeham. b 47. R Holloway Coll Lon BSc69 PhD73 Fitzw Coll Cam BA75 MA79. Westcott Ho Cam 73. **d** 76 **p** 77. C Chingford St Anne *Chelmsf* 76-79; C St Martin-in-the-Fields *Lon* 79-84 and 85-86; P-in-c 84-85; Chapl Ch Coll Cam 86-90; TR Gleadless *Sheff* from 90. *The Rectory, 243 Hollinsend Road, Sheffield S12 2EE* Sheffield (0742) 390757

HEDLEY, Henry. b 10. St Edm Hall Ox BA32 MA43. Linc Th Coll 33. **d** 34 **p** 35. R Bletchley *Ox* 63-79; rtd 79. *6 Caldersyde, The Banks, Seascale, Cumbria* Seascale (09467) 28985

HEDLEY, William Clifford. b 35. Tyndale Hall Bris 65. **d** 67 **p** 68. C Hensingham *Carl* 67-69; C Rainhill *Liv* 69-71; C St Helens St Helen 71-73; V Low Elswick *Newc* 73-81; V Kingston upon Hull Southcoates St Aid *York* 81-87; TV Heworth from 87. *The Vicarage, 6 Forest Way, Stockton Lane, York YO3 0BJ* York (0904) 425678

HEFFER, William John Gambrell. b 30. AKC55. **d** 56 **p** 57. C Biggleswade *St Alb* 56-59; C Clacton St Jas *Chelmsf* 59-61; V Langford *St Alb* 61-67; V Luton All SS 67-73; P-in-c Eaton Socon 73-75; V 75-77; Lic to Offic 78-81; R Wingrave w Rowsham, Aston Abbotts and Cublington *Ox* 81-88; R Wilden w Colmworth and Ravensden *St Alb* from 88. *The Rectory, Wilden, Bedford MK44 2PB* Bedford (0234) 771434

HEGARTY, Gerald. b 52. QUB BA74 BD81. Union Th Coll Belf 78. **d** 86 **p** 87. NSM Leic H Trin w St Jo *Leic* 86-87; P-in-c Sibson w Sheepy and Ratcliffe Culey 87-90; Chapl St Edm Hall Ox from 90. *St Edmund Hall, Queen's Lane, Oxford OX1 4AR* Oxford (0865) 279000 or 274214

HEGGS, Thomas James. b 40. Inter-American Univ Puerto Rico BA65. Linc Th Coll 75. **d** 77 **p** 78. C Newark St

Mary *S'well* 77-80; C Newark w Hawton, Cotham and Shelton 80; R Barwell w Potters Marston and Stapleton *Leic* 80-89; R Upwell St Pet *Ely* from 89; R Outwell from 89. *The Rectory, 5 New Road, Upwell, Wisbech, Cambs PE14 9AB* Wisbech (0945) 772213

HEIDT, John Harrison. b 32. Yale Univ BA54 Ox Univ BLitt67 DPhil75. Nashotah Ho BD57 MDiv69. **d** 56 **p** 57. USA 56-75; C Ox St Mary Magd *Ox* 75-80; V Up Hatherley *Glouc* from 80; P-in-c Cheltenham St Steph from 89. *The Vicarage, Hatherley Road, Cheltenham, Glos GL51 6HX* Cheltenham (0242) 516445

HEIDT, Michael Lewis. b 65. K Coll Lon BD86. St Steph Ho Ox 88. **d** 90 **p** 91. C Reading St Luke w St Bart *Ox* from 90. *5 Denmark Street, Reading RG1 5PA* Reading (0734) 862694

HEIGHWAY, Canon Thomas John Francis. b 20. Univ of Wales (Lamp) BA47 BD65 Lanc Univ MA81 PhD87. **d** 48 **p** 49. V Blackb St Silas *Blackb* 69-88; RD Blackb 79-86; Hon Can Blackb Cathl from 86; rtd 88; Perm to Offic *S & B* from 89. *61 Mynydd Garnlwyd Road, Morriston, Swansea SA6 7PB* Swansea (0792) 799416

HEIL, Miss Janet. b 53. Liv Univ BEd75 St Jo Coll Dur BA84. Cranmer Hall Dur. **dss** 85 **d** 87. Ashton Ch Ch *Man* 85-87; Par Dn from 87. *33 Taunton Road, Ashton-under-Lyne, Lancs OL7 9DP* 061-339 6128

HEINZE, Rudolph William. b 31. Concordia Coll (USA) BSc56 CertEd56 De Paul Univ (USA) MA59 Univ of Iowa PhD65. **d** 86 **p** 87. NSM Colney St Pet *St Alb* from 86; Lect Oak Hill Th Coll from 86; Sen Tutor Oak Hill Th Coll from 88. *3 Farm Lane, London N14 4PP* 081-449 5969

HELEY, John. b 28. Lon Univ BA72. Bps' Coll Cheshunt 54. **d** 56 **p** 57. Lic to Offic *Ox* 69-72; R E w W Rudham *Nor* 72-75; P-in-c Houghton 72-74; V 74-75; V Hunstanton St Edm 75-82; V Hunstanton St Edm w Ringstead 82-83; rtd 88. *Meadow Cottage, Cradle Hall Farm, Burnham Market, Kings Lynn, Norfolk PE31 8JX* Docking (04858) 686

HELFT, Gunter. b 23. Lon Univ BA48. Ely Th Coll 46. **d** 48 **p** 49. Hd Master Abp Temple's Sch Lambeth 67-71; Hd Master Don Valley High Sch S Yorkshire 71-80; rtd 80; Perm to Offic *Worc* from 87. *19 Kenwood Avenue, Worcester WR4 9BD* Worcester (0905) 29797

HELLABY, Victor Richard Douglas. b 10. TD50. Ely Th Coll 45. **d** 46 **p** 47. R Brightling *Chich* 69-76; R Dallington 69-76; R Brightling w Dallington 76-82; RD Dallington 77-82; rtd 82; Perm to Offic *Chich* from 84. *39 Salisbury Road, Seaford, E Sussex BN25 2DB* Seaford (0323) 892409

HELLARD, Dawn Yvonne Lorraine. b 47. **d** 91. C Llantwit Major *Llan* from 91. *8 St Illtyd's Avenue, Llantwit Major, S Glam CF6 8TG* Llantwit Major (0446) 792476

HELLICAR, Hugh Christopher. b 37. Qu Coll Birm 69. **d** 70 **p** 71. C Bromyard *Heref* 70-73; C Bishop's Castle w Mainstone 73-75; Perm to Offic *S'wark* 77-85; Chich from 85. *14 Lewes Crescent, Brighton BN2 1FH*

HELLIER, Jeremy Peter. b 53. K Coll Lon BD75 AKC75. St Aug Coll Cant 75. **d** 76 **p** 77. C Walton *St E* 76-79; C Ipswich St Fran 79-80; C Wolborough w Newton Abbot *Ex* 80-82; CF 82-84; R Pendine w Llanmiloe and Eglwys Gymyn w Marros *St D* 84-89; TR Widecombe-in-the-Moor, Leusdon, Princetown etc *Ex* from 89; CF (TAVR) from 90; RD Moreton *Ex* from 91. *The Rectory, Widecombe-in-the-Moor, Newton Abbot, Devon TQ13 7TB* Widecombe-in-the-Moor (03642) 231

HELLIWELL, Christopher John Guiscard. b 60. Hatf Coll Dur BA82 Fitzw Coll Cam BA86. Westcott Ho Cam 84. **d** 87 **p** 88. C Norton St Mary *Dur* from 87. *Glebe Cottage, Norton, Stockton-on-Tees, Cleveland TS20 1EL* Stockton-on-Tees (0642) 557776

HELLYER, Stephen John. b 56. St Cath Coll Cam BA77 MA81. Wycliffe Hall Ox 82. **d** 84 **p** 85. C Plymouth St Andr w St Paul and St Geo *Ex* 84-88; Chapl Lee Abbey 88-89; Lon and SE Co-ord CPAS from 90. *8 Napoleon Road, Twickenham, Middx TW1 3EP* 081-891 1762

HELM, Alistair Thomas. b 53. Aston Univ BSc75. E Anglian Minl Tr Course 88. **d** 91. NSM Leic St Jas *Leic* from 91. *8 Byway Road, Stoneygate, Leicester LE5 5TF* Leicester (0533) 738398

HELM, Nicholas. b 57. Surrey Univ BSc81. St Jo Coll Nottm 85. **d** 88 **p** 89. C Old Ford St Paul w St Steph and St Mark *Lon* from 88. *37 Ellesmere Road, London E3 5QU* 081-980 6771

HELMS, David Clarke. b 50. Boston Univ AB72. Yale Div Sch MDiv77. **d** 77 **p** 77. USA 77-88; Ind Chapl *Worc* from 88. *1 Marlborough Avenue, Bromsgrove, Worcs B60 2PG* Bromsgrove (0527) 72110

HELYER, Patrick Joseph Peter. b 15. FRGS83. ALCD39 Wycliffe Hall Ox 38. **d** 38 **p** 39. Falkland Is 71-75; R Streat w Westmeston *Chich* 75-78; Tristan da Cunha 78-81; rtd 81; Hon C Malborough w S Huish, W Alvington and Churchstow *Ex* 81-84; Perm to Offic Heref and Glouc from 84. *Tristan, 4 Gorse Lane, Sling, Coleford, Glos GL16 8JH* Dean (0594) 34990

HEMINGWAY, Peter. b 32. S'wark Ord Course 72. **d** 75 **p** 76. NSM Belmont *S'wark* 75-79; C Herne Hill St Paul 79-81; V Headstone St Geo *Lon* from 81; V N Harrow St Alb from 87. *St Alban's Vicarage, Church Drive, Harrow, Middx HA2 7NS* 081-868 6567

HEMMING, Terry Edward. b 47. S Wales Bible Coll DipTh70 Calvin Coll Michigan MA84 S Dios Minl Tr Scheme 88. **d** 90 **p** 91. Hon C Win All SS w Chilcomb and Chesil *Win* from 90. *15 Gordon Avenue, Winchester, Hants SO23 8QE* Winchester (0962) 855701

HEMMING CLARK, Stanley Charles. b 29. Peterho Cam BA52 MA56. Ridley Hall Cam 52. **d** 54 **p** 55. C Redhill H Trin *S'wark* 54-56; C Woking St Jo *Guildf* 56-59; V Crockenhill All So *Roch* from 59. *The Vicarage, Eynsford Road, Swanley, Kent BR8 8JS* Swanley (0322) 662157

HEMMINGS, Jonathan Allen. b 52. BA. St Steph Ho Ox. **d** 82 **p** 83. NSM Wolv *Lich* 82-84; Asst Chapl St Pet Colleg Sch Wolv 82-84; C Codsall *Lich* 85-87; Chapl R Gr Sch Lanc from 88; P-in-c Over Wyresdale *Blackb* from 90. *The Vicarage, Abbeystead, Lancaster LA2 9BE* Lancaster (0524) 791394

HEMMINGS, Roy Anthony. b 48. Wolv Poly HND69 Univ of Wales (Cardiff) BD85 DPS86. St Mich Coll Llan 82. **d** 86 **p** 87. C Rhyl w Rhyl St Ann *St As* 86-90; CF from 90. *c/o MOD (Army), Bagshot Park, Bagshot, Surrey GU19 5PL* Bagshot (0276) 71717

HEMMONS, Laurence John. b 19. Worc Ord Coll 64. **d** 66 **p** 66. R Churchstanton *Ex* 69-70; P-in-c Otterford *B & W* 69-70; R Churchstanton w Otterford 70-82; R Churchstanton, Buckland St Mary and Otterford 80-84; rtd 84; Perm to Offic *Ex* from 88. *7 Westview Close, Whimple, Exeter* Whimple (0404) 822783

HEMPENSTALL, John Albert. b 43. CITC 64. **d** 67 **p** 68. C Carlow w Urglin and Staplestown *C & O* 67-70; Chapl RN from 70. *c/o MOD, Lacon House, Theobald's Road, London WC1X 8RY* 071-430 6847

HEMPHILL, John James. b 44. TCD BA68 MA72. Oak Hill Th Coll 71. **d** 73 **p** 74. C Dundonald *D & D* 73-78; I Balteagh w Carrick *D & R* from 78. *115 Drumsurn Road, Limavady, Co Londonderry BT49 0PD* Limavady (05047) 63069

HEMS, Richard Brian. b 30. K Coll Lon BD58. St Aug Coll Cant. **d** 59 **p** 60. C Whitnash *Cov* 59-63; C-in-c Tuckswood CD *Nor* 63-69; V Tuckswood 69-78; R Framingham Earl from 78; R Gt w Lt Poringland and Howe from 78. *The Rectory, Poringland, Norwich NR14 7SH* Framingham Earl (05086) 2215

HEMSLEY, David Ridgway. b 36. AKC61. **d** 61 **p** 62. C Penhill *Bris* 61-64; C Highworth w Sevenhampton and Inglesham etc 64-66; C Surbiton St Andr *S'wark* 67-70; P-in-c Tingewick w Water Stratford *Ox* 71-75; P-in-c Radclive 72-75; PM N Marston w Granborough etc 75-81; P-in-c Quainton 75-81; TV Schorne 81-90; P-in-c Lt Missenden from 90. *The Vicarage, Little Missenden, Amersham, Bucks HP7 0RA* Great Missenden (02406) 2008

HEMSTOCK, Julian. b 51. MIProdE CEng Trent Poly BSc74. Sarum & Wells Th Coll 89. **d** 91. C Carrington *S'well* from 91. *St John's House, 65 Osborne Grove, Sherwood, Nottingham NG5 2HE* Nottingham (0602) 856980

HEMSTOCK, Pat. b 51. Sarum & Wells Th Coll 89. **d** 91. Par Dn Carrington *S'well* from 91. *St John's House, 65 Osborne Grove, Nottingham NG5 2HE* Nottingham (0602) 856980

HENCHER, John Bredon. b 31. Lich Th Coll 58. **d** 60 **p** 61. C Pershore w Wick *Worc* 60-62; Bp's Dom Chapl 63-64; V Amblecote 64-70; Perm to Offic *Glouc* 72-74; Dioc RE Adv *Heref* 74-80; Perm to Offic *Heref* from 80; *Mon* from 87; Asst Chapl Mon Sch from 87. *The Tank House, Weston, Pembridge, Herefordshire HR6 9JE* Pembridge (05447) 540

HENCKEN, Alfred David. b 15. AKC42. **d** 42 **p** 43. V S Mymms K Chas *Lon* 68-80; rtd 80. *St Denis Lodge, Salisbury Road, Shaftesbury, Dorset SP7 8BS* Shaftesbury (0747) 54576

HENDERSON, Canon Alastair Roy. b 27. BNC Ox BA51 MA54. Ridley Hall Cam 52. **d** 54 **p** 55. C Ex St Leon w H Trin *Ex* 54-57; Travelling Sec IVF 57-60; C St Mary le Bow w St Pancras Soper Lane etc *Lon* 58-60; V Barton Hill St Luke w Ch Ch *Bris* 60-68; P-in-c Bris St Phil and St Jacob w Em 67-68; V Stoke Bishop from

68; Lect Clifton Th Coll 69-71; Lect Trin Coll Bris 71-73; RD Westbury and Severnside *Bris* 73-79; Hon Can Bris Cathl from 80. *The Vicarage, Mariner's Drive, Bristol BS9 1QJ* Bristol (0272) 681858

HENDERSON, Andrew Douglas. b 36. MBASW Trin Coll Cam BA60 MA64 Ox Univ DipPSA63 Liv Univ DASS65. Cuddesdon Coll 60. **d** 62 **p** 63. C Newington St Paul *S'wark* 62-64; Hon C Camberwell St Luke 65-80; Perm to Offic *Lon* from 85. *178 Lancaster Road, London W11 1QU* 071-229 6790

HENDERSON, David. b 35. Oak Hill NSM Course. **d** 83 **p** 84. NSM Rush Green *Chelmsf* from 83. *196 Marlborough Road, Romford RM7 8AL* Romford (0708) 765955

HENDERSON, Ven Edward Chance. b 16. Lon Univ BD39. ALCD39. **d** 39 **p** 40. Adn Pontefract *Wakef* 68-81; rtd 81; Perm to Offic Wakef from 81; Sheff from 82. *12 Park Lane, Balne, Goole, N Humberside DN14 0EP* Goole (0405) 861934

HENDERSON, Euan Russell Milne. b 42. St Steph Ho Ox 75. **d** 80 **p** 81. NSM Hambleden Valley *Ox* 80-83; C Reading All SS 83-84; C Maidenhead St Luke 84-86; NSM Swyncombe w Britwell Salome from 87. *The Old Forge, Stonor, Henley-on-Thames, Oxon RG9 6HE* Turville Heath (049163) 566

HENDERSON, Francis Colin. b 35. St Cath Coll Cam BA59 MA63. Cuddesdon Coll 60. **d** 62 **p** 63. C Croydon *Cant* 62-67; V Westwood *Cov* 67-75; V Chilvers Coton w Astley 75-80; P-in-c Wolston 80; P-in-c Church Lawford w Newnham Regis 80; V Wolston and Church Lawford 80-85; USA from 85. *1364 Katella Street, Laguna Beach, California 92651, USA* Laguna Beach (714) 497-2239

HENDERSON, George. b 07. ALCD32. **d** 32 **p** 33. V Farlam *Carl* 55-71; rtd 71; Perm to Offic *Carl* from 77. *Holme Eden Abbey, Warwick Bridge, Carlisle CA4 8RD* Wetheral (0228) 61806

✠**HENDERSON, Most Rev George Kennedy Buchanan.** b 21. MBE74 JP63. St Chad's Coll Dur LTh43 BA47. Edin Th Coll 40. **d** 43 **p** 45 **c** 77. C Glas Ch Ch *Glas* 43-48; Bp's Dom Chapl *Arg* 48-50; P-in-c Kinlochleven 48-50; P-in-c Nether Lochaber 48-50; R Fort William 50-77; Can St Jo Cathl Oban 60-77; Syn Clerk 64-73; Dean Arg 73-77; Bp Arg from 77; Primus from 90. *Benvoulin, 7 Achnalea, Onich, Fort William, Invernessshire PH33 6SA* Fort William (0397) 4230

HENDERSON, Ian Robert. b 29. S'wark Ord Course 64. **d** 67 **p** 69. C Ealing St Pet Mt Park *Lon* 67-72; Hon C N Acton St Gabr 72-74; V Ealing Ascension Hanger Hill 74-88; P-in-c W Twyford 85-88; V Hanger Hill Ascension and W Twyford St Mary 88-90; rtd 90. *27 Ridgeway Road, Oxford OX2 0DS* Oxford (0865) 68077

HENDERSON, James. b 22. Chich Th Coll 51. **d** 54 **p** 55. V Bolton St Geo *Man* 64-70; V Newhey 70-87; rtd 87; Perm to Offic *Man* from 87. *17 Swift Road, Rochdale, Lancs OL11 5RF* Rochdale (0706) 522228

HENDERSON, Canon James Edward. b 28. TCD BA58 MA62. **d** 59 **p** 60. C Dub Drumcondra *D & G* 59-62; C Monkstown 62-65; I Donagh w Cloncha and Culdaff *D & R* 65-85; I Stranorlar w Meenglas and Kiltevvogue from 85. *The Rectory, Stranorlar, Co Donegal, Irish Republic* Ballybofey (74) 31081

HENDERSON, Miss Janet. b 57. St Jo Coll Dur BA88 RGN82. Cranmer Hall Dur 85. **d** 88. Par Dn Wisbech SS Pet and Paul *Ely* 88-90; Par Dn Bestwood *S'well* from 90. *17 Harvest Close, Old Farm Road, Top Valley, Nottingham NG5 9BW* Nottingham (0602) 271909

HENDERSON, John William. b 13. AKC38. **d** 38 **p** 39. V Wateringbury *Roch* 63-78; rtd 78. *Cumloden, The Triangle, Somerton, Somerset TA11 6QJ* Somerton (0458) 73424

HENDERSON, Judith Ann. b 37. **d** 89. NSM Sheringham *Nor* from 89. *22 Holway Road, Sheringham, Norfolk NR26 8HR* Sheringham (0263) 823446

HENDERSON, Julian Tudor. b 54. Keble Coll Ox BA76 MA81. Ridley Hall Cam 77. **d** 79 **p** 80. C Islington St Mary *Lon* 79-83; V Hastings Em and St Mary in the Castle *Chich* from 83. *The Vicarage, Vicarage Road, Hastings, E Sussex TN34 3NA* Hastings (0424) 421543

HENDERSON, Nicholas Paul. b 48. Selw Coll Cam BA73 MA77. Ripon Hall Ox 73. **d** 75 **p** 76. C St Alb St Steph *St Alb* 75-78; Warden J F Kennedy Ho Cov Cathl 78-79; C Bow w Bromley St Leon *Lon* 79-85; P-in-c W Acton St Martin from 85; P-in-c Ealing All SS from 89. *St Martin's Vicarage, 25 Birch Grove, London W3 9SP* 081-992 2333

HENDERSON, Patrick James. b 57. R Holloway Coll Lon BA78. St Steph Ho Ox 83. **d** 86 **p** 87. C Hornsey St

Mary w St Geo *Lon* 86-90; V Whetstone St Jo from 90. *St John's Vicarage, 1163 High Road, London N20 0PG* 081-445 4569

HENDERSON, Richard Crosbie Aitken. b 57. Magd Coll Ox MA84 DPhil84. St Jo Coll Nottm 83. **d** 86 **p** 87. C Chinnor w Emmington and Sydenham etc *Ox* 86-89; I Abbeystrewry Union *C, C & R* from 89. *The Rectory, Cork Road, Skibbereen, Co Cork, Irish Republic* Skibbereen (28) 21234

HENDERSON, Robert. b 43. TCD 66 Ulster Univ DipG&C87. **d** 69 **p** 70. C Drumglass *Arm* 69-72; Chapl Miss to Seamen 72-78; Kenya 77-78; I Mostrim w Granard, Clonbroney, Killoe etc *K, E & A* 78-82; I Belf St Matt *Conn* from 82; RD M Belf from 90. *Shankill Rectory, 51 Ballygomartin Road, Belfast BT13 3LA* Belfast (0232) 714325

HENDERSON, Samuel James Noel. b 16. Hertf Coll Ox BA39 MA42. **d** 42 **p** 43. V Hickling *Nor* 65-82; rtd 82; Perm to Offic *Nor* from 82. *96 Church Lane, Beeston Regis, Sheringham, Norfolk NR26 8EY* Sheringham (0263) 825686

HENDERSON, Terry James. b 45. St Deiniol's Hawarden 76. **d** 77 **p** 77. C Wrexham *St As* 77-79; CA Wilson Carlile Coll of Evang 79-81; TV Langtree *Ox* 81-87; P-in-c Aston Cantlow and Wilmcote w Billesley *Cov* 87-90; V from 90. *The Vicarage, Wilmcote, Stratford-upon-Avon, Warks CV37 9XD* Stratford-upon-Avon (0789) 292376

HENDERSON, William Desmond. b 27. TCD BA56 MA64. **d** 56 **p** 57. I Achonry w Tubbercurry and Kilmactigue *T, K & A* 66-75; rtd 75. *8 Kingston College, Mitchelstown, Co Cork, Irish Republic*

HENDERSON, William Ernest. b 53. CEng81 MICE81 Southn Univ BSc75. St Jo Coll Nottm 87. **d** 89 **p** 90. C Win Ch Ch *Win* from 89. *18 Sparkford Close, Winchester, Hants SO22 4NH* Winchester (0962) 865051

HENDERSON, William Ralph. b 32. Oak Hill Th Coll 65. **d** 67 **p** 68. C Littleover *Derby* 67-68; C Nottm St Sav *S'well* 68-74; V Alne *York* from 75; Chapl York Distr Hosp from 86. *The Vicarage, Alne, York YO6 2HY* Tollerton (03473) 450

HENDERSON-BEGG, Robert John. b 11. Edin Univ MA32. Westcott Ho Cam 32 Qu Coll Birm 37. **d** 37 **p** 39. Asst Master Beds LEA 57-76; Perm to Offic (& Chapter Clerk) Newport Deanery *Ox* from 73; Perm to Offic *St Alb* from 73; rtd 76. Stone Cottage, High Street, Carlton, Bedford MK43 7LA* Bedford (0234) 720366

HENDEY, Clifford. b 30. K Coll Lon BD53 AKC53. **d** 54 **p** 55. C S Wimbledon All SS *S'wark* 54-58; Trinidad and Tobago 58-71 and 81-82; V Spratton *Pet* 72-77; V Leeds All So *Ripon* 77-80; R Corringham *Linc* 80-81; V Alkham w Capel le Ferne and Hougham *Cant* from 82. *20 Alexandra Road, Capel-le-Ferne, Folkestone, Kent CT18 7LD* Folkestone (0303) 50252

HENDRICKSE, Clarence David. b 41. CEng MIMechE71 Nottm Univ PGCE73. St Jo Coll Nottm 71. **d** 74 **p** 75. C St Helens St Helen *Liv* 74-76; C Netherley Ch Ch CD 76-77; TV 78-87; V Liv Ch Ch Norris Green from 87. *Christ Church Vicarage, Norris Green, 36 Sedgemoor Road, Liverpool L11 3BR* 051-226 1774

HENDRY, Leonard John. b 34. St D Coll Lamp DipTh68. **d** 68 **p** 69. C Minchinhampton *Glouc* 68-71; C Bishop's Cleeve 71-74; V Cheltenham St Mich 74-78; V Horsley and Newington Bagpath w Kingscote 78-82; Chapl Salonika *Eur* from 82. *Sebilles 5, Tsinari, Ano Poli, Salonika 546.33, Greece* Salonika (31) 281193

HENDRY, Philip David. b 48. K Coll Lon BD72 AKC72. St Aug Coll Cant 72. **d** 73 **p** 74. C Benhilton *S'wark* 73-78; TV Catford (Southend) and Downham 78-85; Chapl St Andr Sch Croydon from 85; P-in-c Croydon St Andr *S'wark* 85-86; V from 86. *St Andrew's Vicarage, 6 St Peter's Road, Croydon CR0 1HD* 081-688 6011

HENDY, Graham Alfred. b 45. St Jo Coll Dur BA67 MA75 Fitzw Coll Cam CertEd. Sarum Th Coll 67. **d** 70 **p** 71. C High Wycombe *Ox* 70-75; TV 75-78; R Upton cum Chalvey 78-83; TR 83-90; R S Walsham and Upton *Nor* from 90; Dioc Lay Tr Officer from 90. *The Rectory, The Street, South Walsham, Norfolk NR13 6DQ* South Walsham (060549) 455

HENEY, Ven William Butler. b 22. CITC. **d** 60 **p** 61. C Seagoe *D & D* 60-63; I Carrickmacross *Clogh* 64-73; I Newbridge w Carnalway and Kilcullen *M & K* from 73; Treas Kildare Cathl 81-86; Adn Kildare from 86. *The Rectory, Newbridge, Co Kildare, Irish Republic* Newbridge (45) 31306

HENLEY, Claud Michael. b 31. Keble Coll Ox BA55 MA59. Chich Th Coll 55. **d** 57 **p** 58. C Cowley St Jas *Ox* 57-60; C Wetherby *Ripon* 60-63; C Brighton St Pet *Chich* 63-69; V Brighton St Jo 69-75; V New

Groombridge from 75. *The Vicarage, Groombridge, Tunbridge Wells, Kent TN3 9SE* Langton (0892) 864265

HENLEY, David Edward. b 44. Sarum & Wells Th Coll 69. **d** 72 **p** 73. C Fareham H Trin *Portsm* 72-76; C-in-c Leigh Park St Clare CD 76-78; R Freshwater 78-87; RD W Wight 83-87; R Meonstoke w Corhampton cum Exton from 87; R Droxford from 87. *The Rectory, Meonstoke, Southampton SO3 1NF* Droxford (0489) 877512

HENLEY, John Francis Hugh. b 48. SS Mark & Jo Coll Chelsea CertEd69. St Mich Coll Llan DipTh82. **d** 82 **p** 83. C Griffithstown *Mon* 82-85; V St Hilary Greenway 85-90; V Fulham St Etheldreda w St Clem *Lon* from 90. *St Etheldreda's Vicarage, Doneraile Street, London SW6 6EL* 071-736 3809

HENLEY, Ven Michael Harry George. b 38. CB91. Lon Coll of Div LTh60. **d** 61 **p** 62. C St Marylebone w H Trin *Lon* 61-64; Chapl RN 64-68 and 74-89; Chapl of the Fleet and Adn for the RN from 89; Chapl St Andr Univ *St And* 68-72; Chapl R Hosp Sch Holbrook 72-74; QHC from 89; Hon Can Gib Cathl *Eur* from 89. *c/o MOD, Lacon House, Theobald's Road, London WC1X 8RY* 071-430 6847

HENLY, Francis Michael. b 25. Sarum Th Coll. **d** 67 **p** 68. C E w W Harnham *Sarum* 67-70; P-in-c Stour Provost w Todbere 70-75; P-in-c Rowde 75-79; V 79-83; R Poulshot 79-83; V Bishop's Cannings, All Cannings etc from 83. *The Vicarage, The Street, Bishop's Cannings, Devizes, Wilts SN10 2LD* Cannings (038086) 650

HENNELL, Canon Michael Murray. b 18. St Edm Hall Ox BA40 DipTh41 MA44 Qu Coll Cam MA49. Wycliffe Hall Ox 40. **d** 42 **p** 43. Prin Ridley Hall Cam 63-70; Can Res Man Cathl *Man* 70-84; rtd 84; Perm to Offic *Ches* from 84. *53 Cleveley Road, Meols, South Wirral L47 8XN* 051-632 4328

HENNESSEY, David Brian. b 44. FCIS69. NW Ord Course 76. **d** 79 **p** 88. Hon C Skipton Ch Ch *Bradf* 79-80; Dioc Sec *St E* 80-90; NSM Ipswich St Matt 88-90; C from 90. *127 Lavenham Road, Ipswich, Suffolk IP2 0LD* Ipswich (0473) 256542

HENNING, Mrs Judy. b 49. S Dios Minl Tr Scheme 85. **d** 88. C Catherington and Clanfield *Portsm* 88-91; C Leigh Park from 91. *The Clergy House, 32 Hursley Road, Havant, Hants PO9 4RF* Havant (0705) 475528

HENRY, Very Rev Bryan George. b 30. St D Coll Lamp BA51 St Mich Coll Llan 51. **d** 53 **p** 54. C Aberdare St Fagan *Llan* 53-57; C Penarth All SS 57-63; Chapl RAF 63-81; Provost Nicosia and Adn Cyprus 81-90; Prov Sec Jerusalem and Middle E 84-90; Exec Officer Ch in Wales from 90. *39 Cathedral Road, Cardiff CF1 9XF* Cardiff (0222) 231638

HENRY, Miss Jacqueline Margaret. b 40. Open Univ BA82. Trin Coll Bris DipHE79. dss 83 **d** 87. Deptford St Jo *S'wark* 79-82; Catshill and Dodford *Worc* 83-86; The Lye and Stambermill 86-87; Par Dn 87-89; Educn Chapl from 89. *46 Cemetry Road, Lye, Stourbridge, W Midlands DY9 7EF* Stourbridge (0384) 895263

HENRY, Canon Maurice James Birks. b 14. Dorchester Miss Coll 34. **d** 38 **p** 39. V Chelford w Lower Withington *Ches* 65-81; RD Knutsford 73-80; Hon Can Ches Cathl 76-81; rtd 81; Perm to Offic *Ches* from 81. *Norlands, 56 Holly Tree Road, Plumley, Knutsford, Cheshire WA16 0UJ* Lower Peover (0565) 722721

HENRY, Peter. b 49. BTh. St Jo Coll Nottm. **d** 84 **p** 85. C Sinfin Moor *Derby* 84-89; C Blagreaves St Andr CD 84-89; V Guernsey St Jo *Win* from 89. *St John's Vicarage, Les Amballes, St Peter Port, Guernsey, Channel Islands* Guernsey (0481) 20879

HENRY, Stephen Kenelm Malim. b 37. Bps' Coll Cheshunt 60. **d** 62 **p** 63. C Leic St Phil *Leic* 62-67; CF 67-70; V Woodhouse *Wakef* from 70. *Christ Church Vicarage, 79 Woodhouse Hill, Huddersfield HD2 1DH* Huddersfield (0484) 424669

HENRY, Trevor. b 09. St Aid Birkenhead 52. **d** 54 **p** 55. V Cookley *Worc* 63-73; rtd 73; Perm to Offic *Heref* from 85. *Northwood, Shatterford, Bewdley, Worcs DY12 1RL* Arley (02997) 249

✠**HENSHALL, Rt Rev Michael.** b 28. St Chad's Coll Dur BA54 DipTh56. **d** 56 **p** 57 **c** 76. C Sewerby w Marton *York* 56-59; C Bridlington Quay H Trin 56-59; C-in-c Micklehurst CD *Ches* 59-62; V Micklehurst 62-63; V Altrincham St Geo 63-76; Hon Can Ches Cathl 72-76; Suff Bp Warrington *Liv* from 76. *Martinsfield, Elm Avenue, Great Crosby, Liverpool L23 2SX* 051-924 7004 or 709 9722

HENSHALL, Nicholas James. b 62. Wadh Coll Ox BA84 MA88. Ripon Coll Cuddesdon 85. **d** 88 **p** 89. C Blyth St Mary *Newc* from 88. *74 Marine Terrace, Blyth, Northd NE24 2LR* Blyth (0670) 365552

HENSHALL, Ronald Keith. b 54. Loughb Coll of Educn CertEd76. Chich Th Coll 87. **d** 89 **p** 90. C Ribbleton *Blackb* from 89. *4 Farringdon Lane, Ribbleton, Preston, Lancs PR2 6LX* Preston (0772) 791373

HENSHAW, George William. b 21. St Edm Hall Ox BA48 MA48. Qu Coll Birm 48. **d** 49 **p** 50. R Man St Paul New Cross *Man* 64-70; rtd 86; Perm to Offic *Man* 86-87. *45 Highfield Terrace, Leamington Spa, Warks CV32 6EE* Leamington Spa (0926) 330801

HENSHAW, Nicholas Newell. b 49. Rhodes Univ Grahamstown BA72. Cuddesdon Coll 73. **d** 75 **p** 76. C Beaconsfield *Ox* 75-78; Chapl Wellington Coll Berks 78-80; C Pimlico St Pet w Westmr Ch Ch *Lon* 80-82; Chapl Sevenoaks Sch Kent from 82; Hon C Sevenoaks St Nic *Roch* from 82. *Orchards, Solefields Road, Sevenoaks, Kent TN13 1PF* Sevenoaks (0732) 456710

HENSON, Ms Carolyn. b 44. Solicitor 75 Bedf Coll Lon BA65 Nottm Univ MTh88 E Midl Min Tr Course 82. dss 85 **d** 87. Braunstone *Leic* 85-87; Hon Par Dn 87; Par Dn 88; Adult Educn and Tr Officer *Ely* from 89. *170 Main Street, Witchford, Ely, Cambs CB6 2HT* Ely (0353) 66741

HENSON, John Richard. b 40. Selw Coll Cam BA62 MA66. Ridley Hall Cam 62. **d** 65 **p** 66. C Ollerton *S'well* 65-68; Univs Sec CMS 68-73; Chapl Scargill Ho N Yorkshire 73-78; V Shipley St Paul *Bradf* 78-83; TR Shipley St Paul and Frizinghall from 83. *The Rectory, 47 Kirkgate, Shipley, W Yorkshire BD18 3EH* Bradford (0274) 583652

HENSON, Richard Clive. b 41. Univ of Wales (Cardiff) BSc63 PhD66. S'wark Ord Course 77. **d** 88 **p** 89. Hon C Lee St Mildred *S'wark* from 88. *122 Manor Park, London SE13 5RH* 081-852 4137

HENSTRIDGE, Edward John. b 31. FIPM AFBPsS Ex Coll Ox BA55 MA59. Wells Th Coll 55. **d** 57 **p** 58. C Milton *Portsm* 57-62; V Soberton w Newtown 62-69; Lic to Offic *Derby* 69-71; Perm *Guildf* 72-84; Lic from 84. *The White House, Thursley Road, Elstead, Godalming, Surrey GU8 6LW* Elstead (0252) 702272

HENTHORNE, Thomas Roger. b 30. E Anglian Minl Tr Course. **d** 79 **p** 80. Hd Master St Mary's Sch St Neots from 79; Hon C St Neots *Ely* from 79. *7 Chesnut Grove, Eynesbury, St Neots, Huntingdon, Cambs PE19 2DW* Huntingdon (0480) 72548

HENTON, John Martin. b 48. AKC71. **d** 74 **p** 75. C Woolwich St Mary w H Trin *S'wark* 74-77; C Cotham St Mary *Bris* 77-78; C Cotham St Sav w St Mary 78-80; R Filton 80-87; Chapl Ex Sch from 87; Chapl St Marg Sch Ex from 87. *Becket Cottage, Thorverton, Exeter EX5 5NT* Exeter (0392) 861134

HENWOOD, John Henry. b 08. Lich Th Coll 30. **d** 32 **p** 33. V Dukinfield St Luke *Ches* 56-73; rtd 73; Perm to Offic *Ex* from 83. *Eddworth Residential Home, 24 Victoria Road, Exmouth EX8 1DW* Exmouth (0395) 278250

HENWOOD, Martin John. b 58. Glas Univ BD81. Ripon Coll Cuddesdon. **d** 85 **p** 86. C Dartford H Trin *Roch* 85-88; C St Martin-in-the-Fields *Lon* from 88. *5 St Martin's Place, London WC2N 4JJ* 071-930 1862

HENWOOD, Canon Peter Richard. b 32. St Edm Hall Ox BA55 MA69. Cuddesdon Coll 56. **d** 57 **p** 58. C Rugby St Andr *Cov* 57-62; C-in-c Gleadless Valley CD *Sheff* 62-71; V Plaistow St Mary *Roch* from 71; RD Bromley from 79; Hon Can Roch Cathl from 88. *St Mary's Vicarage, 74 London Lane, Bromley BR1 4HE* 081-460 1827

HEPPLE, Gordon. b 32. Edin Th Coll. **d** 63 **p** 68. C Billingham St Cuth *Dur* 63-64; C Ryhope 64; Perm to Offic 66-68; C Wingate Grange 68-69; C Heworth St Mary 69; C Gateshead St Mary 69-71; P-in-c Low Team 71-72; R Lyons 72-79; V Basford St Aid *S'well* 79-84; V Blackhill *Dur* from 84. *St Aidan's Vicarage, 6 Laburnum Avenue, Blackhill, Consett, Co Durham DH8 5TB* Consett (0207) 502155

HEPWORTH, Ernest John Peter. b 42. K Coll Lon BD65 AKC65 Hull Univ MA87. **d** 66 **p** 67. C Headingley *Ripon* 66-69; Asst Chapl St Geo Hosp Gp Lon 69-71; C Gt Grimsby St Mary and St Jas *Linc* 71-72; TV 72-74; V Crosby 74-80; V Barton upon Humber from 80; RD Yarborough from 86. *The Vicarage, Beck Hill, Barton-on-Humber, S Humberside DN18 5EY* Barton-on-Humber (0652) 32202

HEPWORTH, James Stanley. b 09. ALCD31. **d** 32 **p** 33. V Tonbridge St Steph *Roch* 66-73; rtd 73; Perm to Offic Sheff 73-86; Blackb from 86. *9 Chelsea Mews, 46 Bispham Road, Blackpool FY2 0SX* Blackpool (0253) 58121

HEPWORTH, Michael David Albert. b 37. Em Coll Cam BA59 MA63 Lon Inst of Educn CertEd60. Ridley Hall Cam 65. **d** 67 **p** 68. C Eastbourne All SS *Chich* 67-69;

Asst Chapl Bedf Sch 69-72; Chapl 72-83; Hd Master Birkdale Sch from 83; Perm to Offic *Sheff* from 83; *Derby* from 84. *Birkdale School, Oakholme Road, Sheffield S10 3DH* Sheffield (0742) 668408

HEPWORTH, Michael Edward. b 29. Leeds Univ BA51. NW Ord Course 74. **d** 77 **p** 78. Hon C Timperley *Ches* from 77. *56 Ridgway Road, Timperley, Altrincham, Cheshire WA15 7HD* 061-980 5104

HERBERT, Alan. b 33. FPhS62 Open Univ BA80. Paton Congr Coll Nottm 54 Coll of Resurr Mirfield 67. **d** 68 **p** 68. C Cockermouth All SS w Ch Ch *Carl* 68-71; V Clifton 71-77; V Westf St Mary 77-87; R Long Marton w Dufton and w Milburn from 87. *The Rectory, Long Marton, Appleby-in-Westmorland, Cumbria CA16 6BN* Kirkby Thore (07683) 61269

HERBERT, Anthony. b 19. Bris Univ. Qu Coll Birm 46. **d** 48 **p** 49. V Dur St Cuth *Dur* 64-78; V Barrow upon Soar *Leic* 78-83; R Barrow upon Soar w Walton le Wolds 83-84; rtd 84; Perm to Offic *B & W* from 85. *12 Valley View, Clutton, Bristol BS18 4SN* Temple Cloud (0761) 52494

HERBERT, Canon Charles Vernon. b 18. St Jo Coll Dur BA42 DipTh43 MA45. **d** 43 **p** 44. V Portsdown *Portsm* 61-79; RD Havant 72-77; V Hambledon 79-84; rtd 84; Perm to Offic *Portsm* from 84. *6 Farmhouse Way, Horndean, Hants PO8 9LF* Horndean (0705) 571129

HERBERT, Christopher John. b 37. Dur Univ BA60 DipTh62. Cranmer Hall Dur 60. **d** 62 **p** 63. C Huyton Quarry *Liv* 62-65; C Rainford 65-68; V Impington *Ely* 68-78; RD N Stowe 76-78; V Gt Shelford from 78; RD Shelford 80-85. *The Vicarage, 12 Church Street, Great Shelford, Cambridge CB2 5EL* Cambridge (0223) 843274

HERBERT, Ven Christopher William. b 44. Univ of Wales (Lamp) BA65. Wells Th Coll 65. **d** 67 **p** 68. C Tupsley *Heref* 67-71; Dioc RE Adv 71-76; Dioc Dir RE 76-81; Preb Heref Cathl 76-81; V Bourne *Guildf* 81-90; Hon Can Guildf Cathl from 85; Adn Dorking from 90. *Littlecroft, Heathside Road, Woking, Surrey GU22 7EZ* Woking (0483) 772713

HERBERT, Clair Geoffrey Thomas. b 36. Tyndale Hall Bris 61. **d** 64 **p** 65. C Nottm St Sav *S'well* 64-67; C Harwell *Ox* 67-70; C Chilton All SS 67-70; V Bucklebury w Marlston 70-80; Chapl Brighton Coll Jun Sch 80-83; Hon C Upton (or Overchurch) *Ches* 85-86; C 86-88; V Collier Row St Jas and Havering-atte-Bower *Chelmsf* from 88. *St James's Vicarage, 24 Lower Bedfords Road, Romford RM1 4DG* Romford (0708) 749891

HERBERT, Clare. b 54. **d** 87. Hon Par Dn Bris St Mary Redcliffe w Temple etc *Bris* from 87. *c/o The Vicarage, 10 Redcliffe Parade West, Bristol BS1 6SP* Bristol (0272) 291962

HERBERT, David Alexander Sellars. b 39. Bris Univ BA60. St Steph Ho Ox 65. **d** 67 **p** 68. C St Leonards Ch Ch *Chich* 67-80; C St Leonards Ch Ch and St Mary 81; V Bickley *Roch* from 81. *The Vicarage, Bickley Park Road, Bromley BR1 2BE* 081-467 3809

HERBERT, David Roy. b 51. K Coll Lon BD73 AKC73. **d** 74 **p** 75. C Sheff St Aid w St Luke *Sheff* 74-76; C Sheff Manor 76-78; TV Gleadless Valley 78-83; TV Ellesmere Port *Ches* from 83. *195 Stanney Lane, Ellesmere Port, South Wirral L65 9AN* 051-335 5661

HERBERT, Geoffrey William. b 38. Ox Univ MA62 Birm Univ PhD72. Qu Coll Birm DipTh62. **d** 82 **p** 83. C Hall Green Ascension *Birm* 82-85; R Sheldon from 85. *The Rectory, 165 Church Road, Birmingham B26 3TT* 021-743 2033

HERBERT, Graham Paul. b 54. Birm Univ BA75. Wycliffe Hall Ox BA80 MA. **d** 81 **p** 82. C Crowborough *Chich* 81-85; Chapl Monkton Combe Sch Bath from 85. *Croft House, The Croft, Monkton Combe, Bath BA2 7HG* Bath (0225) 721127

HERBERT, John William. b 42. Sarum & Wells Th Coll 74. **d** 77 **p** 78. C Dudley St Thos and St Luke *Worc* 77-79; TV Malvern Link w Cowleigh 79-83; R Alfrick, Lulsley, Suckley, Leigh and Bransford from 83; RD Martley and Worc W from 91. *The Rectory, Leigh, Worcester WR6 5LE* Leigh Sinton (0886) 32355

HERBERT, Jonathan Patrick. b 62. Bris Univ BA86. Linc Th Coll 86. **d** 88 **p** 89. C Kirkby *Liv* from 88. *St Andrew's Vicarage, 9 Redwood Way, Kirkby, Liverpool L33 4DU* 051-548 7969

HERBERT, Kenneth Cyril. b 20. Univ of Wales (Abth) BA41. St D Coll Lamp LTh43. **d** 43 **p** 44. V Llangorwen *St D* 56-89; RD Llanbadarn Fawr 80-86; rtd 89. *68 Gery-llan, Penrhyncoch, Aberystwyth, Dyfed SY23 3DU* Aberystwyth (0970) 828207

HERBERT, Malcolm Francis. b 53. K Coll Lon BD74 AKC74 St Mary's Cheltenham CertEd75. Trin

Coll Bris 76. **d** 77 **p** 78. C Wotton-under-Edge w Ozleworth *Glouc* 77; C Wotton-under-Edge w Ozleworth and N Nibley 77-79; C Milton *B & W* 79-80; C Worle 80-85; V Woking Ch Ch *Guildf* from 86. *Christ Church Vicarage, 10 Russetts Close, Woking, Surrey GU21 4BH* Woking (0483) 762100

HERBERT, Michael. b 35. Nottm Univ BA57. St D Coll Lamp 59. **d** 61 **p** 62. C Paston *Pet* 61-65; C Northn All SS w St Kath 65-67; R Sutton w Upton 67-72; Asst Youth Chapl 67-72; Ind Chapl 72-84; P-in-c Pitsford 79-84; Ind Chapl *Worc* from 84; TV Redditch, The Ridge from 84. *The Parsonage, Church Road, Webheath, Redditch, Worcs B97 5PD* Redditch (0527) 402404

HERBERT, Ronald. b 53. Worc Coll Ox BA75 MA80 Lon Univ BD78 W Kentucky Univ MA79. Oak Hill Th Coll 75. **d** 79 **p** 80. C Welling *Roch* 79-89; V Falconwood, Bp Ridley 89-90; V Becontree St Mary *Chelmsf* from 90. *The Vicarage, 191 Valence Wood Road, Dagenham, Essex RM8 3AH* 081-592 2822

HERBERT, Mrs Rosemary. b 44. Westf Coll Lon BSc65. Qu Coll Birm 81. **dss** 85 **d** 87. Malvern Link w Cowleigh *Worc* 85-87; Hon Par Dn from 87. *4 Cedar Avenue, Malvern Link, Worcs WR14 2SG* Malvern (0684) 572497

HERBERT, Timothy David. b 57. Man Univ BA78 MPhil88. Ridley Hall Cam 79. **d** 81 **p** 82. C Macclesfield St Mich *Ches* 81-85; V Wharton from 85; Asst Continuing Minl Educn Officer from 90. *The Vicarage, 165 Crook Lane, Winsford, Cheshire CW7 3DR* Winsford (0606) 3215

✠**HERD, Rt Rev William Brian.** b 31. Clifton Th Coll 55. **d** 58 **p** 59 **c** 76. C Wolv St Luke *Lich* 58-61; Uganda 61-77; Adn Karamoja 70-75; Bp Karamoja 76-77; Deputation Sec (Ireland) BCMS 77-89; C Harrow H Trin St Mich *Lon* from 89. *74 Bishop Ken Road, Harrow, Middx HA3 7HR* 081-861 1710

HEREFORD, Archdeacon of. Vacant

HEREFORD, Bishop of. *See* OLIVER, Rt Rev John Keith

HEREFORD, Dean of. *See* HAYNES, Very Rev Peter

HEREWARD, Dr John Owen. b 53. FRCSE82 Lon Univ MB, BS77. Ridley Hall Cam 89. **d** 91. C W Ealing St Jo w St Jas *Lon* from 91. *13 Kirchen Road, London W13 0TY* 081-566 3458

HERITAGE, Barry. b 35. Clifton Th Coll 59. **d** 61 **p** 62. C Wolv St Jude *Lich* 61-65; C Chaddesden St Mary *Derby* 65-67; V Kidsgrove *Lich* 67-76; Area Sec (NE) CPAS 76-89; Perm to Offic *Newc* 76-89; Lic to Offic *York* 76-89; V Elloughton and Brough w Brantingham from 89. *The Vicarage, Church Lane, Elloughton, Brough, N Humberside HU15 1HN* Hull (0482) 667431

HERITAGE, Canon Thomas Charles. b 08. St Edm Hall Ox BA29 MA44 AMusTCL31. **d** 34 **p** 38. Can Res Portsm Cathl *Portsm* 64-76; rtd 76. *117 The Close, Salisbury SP1 2EY* Salisbury (0722) 29104

HERKLOTS, Canon John Radu. b 31. Trin Hall Cam BA53 MA61. Westcott Ho Cam 54. **d** 55 **p** 56. C Attercliffe w Carbrook *Sheff* 55-60; C Stoke Damerel *Ex* 60-65; V Devonport St Bart 65-72; V Denmead *Portsm* from 72; RD Havant 82-87; Hon Can Portsm Cathl from 86. *The Vicarage, Denmead, Portsmouth PO7 6NN* Waterlooville (0705) 55490

HERNIMAN, Ven Ronald George. b 23. Birkb Coll Lon BA51. Oak Hill Th Coll. **d** 54 **p** 55. R Washfield *Ex* 61-72; P-in-c Withleigh 61-72; P-in-c Calverleigh 61-72; R Stoodleigh 62-72; P-in-c Oakford 63-72; P-in-c Morebath 63-72; P-in-c Rackenford 65-72; P-in-c Templeton w Loxbeare 66-72; Adn Barnstaple 70-88; R Shirwell w Loxhore 72-82; rtd 89. *Castleland House, Oakford, Tiverton, Devon EX16 9JA*

HERON, Alexander Francis. b 28. **d** 52 **p** 53. C Bush Hill Park St Mark *Lon* 52-53; C Beckenham St Barn *Roch* 54-55; Canada 55-62 and from 77; Chapl RAF 62-77. *Apartment 5, 1917 Kaltasin Road, Sooke, British Columbia, Canada, V0S 1N0*

HERON, David George. b 49. AKC72. **d** 73 **p** 74. C Stockton St Chad *Dur* 73-77; C Beamish 77-81; R Willington and Sunnybrow from 81. *The Rectory, Willington, Crook, Co Durham DL15 0DE* Bishop Auckland (0388) 746242

HERON, George Dobson. b 34. TD. Cranmer Hall Dur 58. **d** 61 **p** 62. C Benfieldside *Dur* 61-65; C Winlaton 65-68; V Dunston St Nic 68-77; P-in-c Dunston Ch Ch 74-77; V Dunston 77-82; V Gateshead St Helen 82-89. *36 Woodlands Road, Shotley Bridge, Consett, Co Durham DH8 0DE* Consett (0207) 507733

HERON, Nicholas Peter. b 60. Man Univ BA81 Southn Univ BTh86. Sarum & Wells Th Coll. **d** 84 **p** 85. C Brinnington w Portwood *Ches* 84-87; Chapl RAF from

87. c/o MOD, Adastral House, Theobald's Road, London WC1X 8RU   071-430 7268

HERRETT, Graham. b 40. Sarum & Wells Th Coll 75. **d** 77 **p** 78. C Ilkeston St Mary Derby 77-80; TV Hucknall Torkard S'well 80-84; C Bulwell St Mary 84-87; Chapl HM Pris Nottm 84-87; Aldington 87-88; Cant 87-90; Chapl HM Pris Belmarsh from 91. The Chaplain's Office, HM Prison Belmarsh, Western Way, London SE28 0EB 081-317 2436

HERRICK, Andrew Frederick. b 58. Univ of Wales (Lamp) BA80. Wycliffe Hall Ox 80. **d** 82 **p** 83. C Abth St D 82-85; P-in-c Llangeitho and Blaenpennal w Bettws Leiki etc 85-86; R 86-88; Youth Chapl 86-88; R Aberporth w Tre-main and Blaen-porth from 88. The Rectory, Aberporth, Cardigan, Dyfed SA43 2BX   Aberporth (0239) 810556

HERRICK, David William. b 52. Middx Poly BSc73. St Jo Coll Nottm DipTh80. **d** 82 **p** 83. C Ipswich St Matt St E 82-85; C Nor St Pet Mancroft w St Jo Maddermarket Nor 85-88; V Bury St Edmunds St Geo St E from 88. The Vicarage, Acacia Avenue, Bury St Edmunds, Suffolk IP32 6HN   Bury St Edmunds (0284) 750321

HERRING, George Gilbert. b 04. Chich Th Coll. **d** 61 **p** 64. C Midhurst Chich 61-64; C Easebourne 64-72; Perm to offic Chich 72-82; Guildf from 82. 11 Derby Road, Haslemere, Surrey GU27 1BF   Haslemere (0428) 2275

HERRINGTON, Wilfrid Spencer. b 17. Chich Th Coll 72. **d** 72 **p** 72. C Bedhampton Portsm 72-77; P-in-c Holton St Mary w Gt Wenham St E 77-86; P-in-c Raydon 77-86; rtd 86; Perm to Offic Chich from 86. 1 Roffrey Avenue, Eastbourne, E Sussex BN22 0AE   Eastbourne (0323) 503212

HERRON, Robert Gordon John. b 36. MIPM75. Wycliffe Hall Ox 65. **d** 77 **p** 78. C Ditton St Mich Liv 77-80; C W Kirby St Bridget Ches 80-82; R Gorton Our Lady and St Thos Man from 82. Our Lady and St Thomas Rectory, 195B Mount Road, Gorton, Manchester M18 7GG 061-223 0421

HERTFORD, Suffragan Bishop of. See SMITH, Rt Rev Robin Jonathan Norman

HERVE, Charles. b 08. AKC31. St Steph Ho Ox 31. **d** 31 **p** 32. V Selly Oak St Wulstan Birm 60-78; rtd 78; P-in-c Kingsbury Birm 78-81; Chapl Berkeley's Hosp Worc from 83; Perm to Offic Worc from 83. 76 Melton Road, Kings Heath, Birmingham B14 7ES   021-444 6989

HERVE, John Anthony. b 49. Open Univ BA81 Birm Univ DPS85. Lich Th Coll 70. **d** 73 **p** 74. C Middlesb All SS York 73-76; CF 76-81; P-in-c Handsworth St Andr Birm 81-86; Hon C Cowley St Jo Ox 86-90; Tutor St Steph Ho Ox 86-90; V Sparkbrook St Agatha w Balsall Heath St Barn Birm from 90. St Agatha's Presbytery, 25 Merton Road, Birmingham B13 9BX 021-449 2790

HERYET, Dudley. b 18. AKC42. **d** 42 **p** 43. V Blean Cant 62-73; V Kennington 73-83; rtd 83; Perm to Offic Cant from 83. 4 Chantry Hall, Dane John, Canterbury, Kent CT1 2QS   Canterbury (0227) 451511

HESELTINE, Mrs Barbara Joan. b 42. Keele Univ BA65. S'wark Ord Course 85. **d** 88. Hon Par Dn Addington Ox 88-91; Hon Par Dn Winslow w Gt Horwood and Addington from 91. Little Manor, Manor Park, The Avenue, Whyteleafe, Surrey CR3 0AQ   081-668 0476

HESELTON, Peter Rodolphus. b 30. Em Coll Cam BA53 MA57 CertEd72. Qu Coll Birm 53. **d** 55 **p** 56. C Walsall St Matt Lich 55-59; V Moxley 59-64; V Castle Church 64-72; Hd of RE Taunton Manor Sch Surrey 72-74; Chapl Blue Coat Comp Sch Walsall 74-78; Hd of RE Sherbrook Sch Cannock 78-85; Perm to Offic Birm 78-85; Chapl Dame Allan's Schs Newc 85-88; NSM Killingworth Newc 87-88; V Widdrington from 88; V Ulgham from 88. The Vicarage, Grangemoor Road, Widdrington, Morpeth, Northd NE61 5PU   Morpeth (0670) 790389

HESELWOOD, Eric Harold. b 43. Oak Hill Th Coll 84. **d** 86 **p** 87. C Farnborough Roch 86-88; V Biggin Hill from 88. St Mark's Vicarage, 10 Church Road, Biggin Hill, Westerham, Kent TN16 3LB   Biggin Hill (0959) 72312

HESELWOOD, Mrs Hilda. b 39. CA Tr Coll 61. **dss** 85 **d** 87. Bromley Common St Luke Roch 85-87; Par Dn from 87. St Mark's Vicarage, Church Road, Biggin Hill, Kent TN16 3LB   Biggin Hill (0959) 72312

HESKETH, Canon Douglas Campbell. b 09. St Pet Hall Ox BA37 MA44. Wycliffe Hall Ox 37. **d** 38 **p** 39. V Mossley Hill St Barn Liv 53-75; Hon Can Liv Cathl 73-75; rtd 75; Hon C Southport All SS Liv 75-88. 52 Skipton Avenue, Crossens, Southport, Merseyside PR9 8JP   Southport (0704) 29584

HESKETH, John Arthur. b 14. Lich Th Coll 54. **d** 56 **p** 57. V Millbrook Ches 60-75; C Birkenhead St Jas w St Bede 75-84; rtd 84. 25 Danefield Road, Greasby, South Wirral L49 3PB   051-606 0570

HESKETH, Robin Adams Lempriere. b 18. St Cath Soc Ox BA43 MA47. St Steph Ho Ox 43. **d** 45 **p** 46. V S Petherwin w Trewen Truro 61-72; V Lewannick 62-71; P-in-c Penponds 72-73; V 73-83; rtd 84. Camelview, Marshall Road, Nanstallon, Bodmin, Cornwall PL30 5LD   Lanivet (0208) 831892

HESKETH, Ronald David. b 47. Bede Coll Dur BA68. St Mich Coll Llan 69 Ridley Hall Cam. **d** 71 **p** 72. C Southport H Trin Liv 71-74; Asst Chapl Miss to Seamen 74-75; Chapl RAF from 75. c/o MOD, Adastral House, Theobald's Road, London WC1X 8RU   071-430 7268

HESKETH, William Ritchie Harrison. b 08. Chich Th Coll 43. **d** 44 **p** 45. R Weeford Lich 71-77; V Hints 72-77; C Newborough w Ch Ch on Needwood 77-79; rtd 79. 14 Stour Close, Church Farm, Burntwood, Walsall

HESKINS, Mrs Georgiana Mary. b 48. K Coll Lon BD81 AKC81. Westcott Ho Cam 81. **dss** 83 **d** 87. Cobbold Road St Sav w St Mary Lon 83-85; St Botolph Aldgate w H Trin Minories 85-87; Par Dn 87. St Nicholas's Vicarage, 66A Whetstone Road, London SE3 8PZ   081-856 6317

HESKINS, Jeffrey George. b 55. AKC78. Chich Th Coll 80. **d** 81 **p** 82. C Primrose Hill St Mary w Avenue Road St Paul Lon 81-85; Enfield Deanery Youth Officer 85-88; C Enfield Chase St Mary 85-88; TV Kidbrooke St Jas S'wark from 88. St Nicholas's Vicarage, 66A Whetstone Road, London SE3 8PZ   081-856 6317

HESLOP, David Anthony. b 45. BSc DipEd DipTh MTh. St Jo Coll Nottm 81. **d** 83 **p** 84. C Willenhall H Trin Lich 83-86; V Gresley Derby from 86. The Vicarage, Church Street, Church Gresley, Burton-on-Trent DE11 9NR   Burton-on-Trent (0283) 223983

HESLOP, Harold William. b 40. Leeds Univ BA62 Open Univ BA72. Ox NSM Course. **d** 78 **p** 79. NSM Stoke Mandeville Ox 78-91; NSM Wendover from 82; NSM Ellesborough, The Kimbles and Stoke Mandeville from 91. 7 Chiltern Road, Wendover, Aylesbury, Bucks HP22 6DB   Wendover (0296) 624812

HESLOP, James Alan. b 37. Codrington Coll Barbados 61. **d** 64 **p** 65. Br Guiana 64-66; Guyana 66-68; Bahamas 68-72; C Haxby w Wigginton York 72-74; TV 74-76; V York St Olave w St Giles 76-87; V Northn All SS w St Kath Pet 87-88; R Felpham w Middleton Chich from 88. The Rectory, 24 Limmer Lane, Felpham, Bognor Regis, W Sussex PO22 7ET   Bognor Regis (0243) 821155

HESLOP, Michael Andrew. b 47. Trin Coll Bris 73. **d** 76 **p** 77. C Burmantofts St Steph and St Agnes Ripon 76-80; V Thorpe Edge Bradf 80-87; TV Penrith w Newton Reigny and Plumpton Wall Carl from 87. The Vicarage, 18 Skinburness Road, Silloth, Carlisle CA5 4QF   Silloth (06973) 31413

HESSELGREAVES, Canon Arthur. b 16. Univ Coll Dur BA38 DipTh40 MA41. Qu Coll Birm 39. **d** 40 **p** 41. R Cumberworth Wakef 65-80; RD Kirkburton 71-80; Hon Can Wakef Cathl 74-81; rtd 81; Perm to Offic Wakef from 81. 1 Park Avenue, Thornes, Wakefield, W Yorkshire WF2 8DS   Wakefield (0924) 381104

HESTER, Canon John Frear. b 27. St Edm Hall Ox BA48 MA52. Cuddesdon Coll 51. **d** 52 **p** 53. C Southall St Geo Lon 52-55; C Clerkenwell H Redeemer w St Phil 55-58; Sec Actors' Ch Union 58-63; Sen Chapl 70-75; Chapl Soc of Sisters of Bethany Lloyd Square 59-62; Dep Min Can St Paul's Cathl 62-75; R Soho St Anne w St Thos and St Pet 63-75; P-in-c Covent Garden St Paul 69-75; P-in-c Brighton St Jo Chich 75-80; V Brighton St Pet 75-78; Can and Preb Chich Cathl 76-85; RD Brighton 76-85; RD Kemp Town 76-83; RD Preston 76-83; P-in-c Brighton Chpl Royal 77-78; V Brighton St Pet w Chpl Royal 78-80; V Brighton St Pet w Chpl Royal and St Jo 80-85; Chapl to HM The Queen from 84; P-in-c Brighton St Nic Chich 84-85; Can Res and Prec Chich Cathl from 85. The Residentiary, Canon Lane, Chichester, W Sussex PO19 1PX   Chichester (0243) 782961

HETHERINGTON, Andrew. b 50. Sheff Univ BSc71. Wycliffe Hall Ox 71. **d** 74 **p** 75. C Leic H Trin w St Jo Leic 74-78; C Leic H Apostles 78-82; V Bootle St Mary w St Paul Liv from 82. The Vicarage, 70 Merton Road, Bootle, Merseyside L20 7AT   051-922 1315

HETHERINGTON, Dermot Hugh. b 42. Worc Coll of Educn BSc SRN63 RMN65 RM72. **d** 78 **p** 79. Hon C Raveningham Nor 78-90; Perm to Offic from 90. 1 Whiteways, Wheatacre, Beccles, Suffolk NR34 0AU   Aldeby (050277) 467

HETHERINGTON, John Carl. b 52. Linc Th Coll. **d** 84
p 85. C Crosby *Linc* 84-88; TV Cleethorpes from 88.
*St Aidan's Vicarage, Hart Street, Cleethorpes, Lincs
DN36 7RQ* Cleethorpes (0472) 692989
HETHERINGTON, John Edward. b 10. Sarum & Wells
Th Coll 75. **d** 76 **p** 77. NSM Owermoigne w Warmwell
Sarum 76-78; Chapl Torbay Hosp Torquay from 78.
Lawes Bridge, Torquay TQ2 7AA Torquay (0803)
64567
HETLING, William Maurice. b 37. AKC61. **d** 62 **p** 63. C
Eltham St Barn *S'wark* 62-66; C Horley 66-71; Jamaica
71-75; C-in-c Farnham Royal S CD *Ox* 75-78; TV W
Slough 78-80; TR 80-88; TV from 88. *St Michael's
House, Whitby Road, Slough SL1 3DW* Slough (0753)
21785
HEWAT, Patrick Duxbury. b 13. CCC Cam BA35 MA55.
K Coll Lon 48. **d** 49 **p** 50. V Grantchester *Ely* 55-70; Perm
to Offic from 70; rtd 78. *19 High Street, Bassingbourn,
Royston, Herts SG8 5NE* Royston (0763) 247611
HEWER, Sidney Eric. b 24. Nor Ord Course. **d** 78 **p** 79.
NSM Grimston w Congham *Nor* 78-91; NSM Grimston,
Congham and Roydon from 91. *42 Vong Lane, Pott Row,
Grimston, King's Lynn, Norfolk PE32 1BW* Hillington
(0485) 600635
HEWES, John. b 29. Nottm Univ BA50. Chich Th Coll
79. **d** 81 **p** 82. C Buckland in Dover w Buckland Valley
Cant 81-84; P-in-c Elmsted w Hastingleigh 84-89; P-in-c
Crundale w Godmersham 84-89; RD W Bridge 88-89; R
Lydd from 89; RD S Lympne from 89. *All Saints'
Rectory, Park Street, Lydd, Romney Marsh, Kent
TN29 9AY* Lydd (0679) 20345
HEWETSON, Christopher. b 37. Trin Coll Ox
BA60 MA64. Chich Th Coll 67. **d** 69 **p** 70. C
Leckhampton St Pet *Glouc* 69-71; C Wokingham All SS
Ox 71-73; V Didcot St Pet 73-82; R Ascot Heath 82-90;
RD Bracknell 86-90; P-in-c Headington Quarry from
90. *The Vicarage, Headington Quarry, Oxford OX3 8NU*
Oxford (0865) 62931
HEWETSON, David Geoffrey. b 31. S'wark Ord Course
71. **d** 74 **p** 75. NSM Brighton St Mich *Chich* from 74.
Flat 1, 166 Dyke Road, Brighton BN1 5PU Brighton
(0273) 564483
HEWETSON, Robin Jervis. b 39. AKC63. **d** 64 **p** 65. C
Thorpe *Nor* 64-67; C E Dereham w Hoe 67-69; TV
Mattishall w Mattishall Burgh 69-72; R Ingham w Sutton
72-78; R Catfield 75-78; R Taverham w Ringland 78-89;
P-in-c Marsham from 89; Dioc Ecum Officer from 89;
Exec Officer Norfolk Ecum Coun from 89. *The Rectory,
Marsham, Norwich NR10 5PP* Aylsham (0263) 3249
HEWETSON, Valerie Patricia. b 44. St Mary's Coll Dur
BSc66 MSc70 Leeds Univ MA75. Linc Th Coll 89. **d** 91.
Par Dn Kingston upon Hull St Nic *York* from 91.
21 Hampshire Street, Hessle High Road, Hull HU4 6PZ
Hull (0482) 504528
HEWETT, Andrew David. b 63. Univ of Wales (Lamp)
BA. Chich Th Coll 84. **d** 86 **p** 87. C Caldicot *Mon*
86-90; Chapl RAF from 90. *c/o MOD, Adastral House,
Theobald's Road, London WC1X 8RY* 071-430 7268
HEWETT, Maurice Gordon. b 28. Lon Univ BA53. Oak
Hill Th Coll 49. **d** 54 **p** 55. C Gipsy Hill Ch Ch *S'wark*
54-57; C Maidstone St Faith *Cant* 57-60; R Chevening
Roch from 60. *The Rectory, Chevening, Sevenoaks, Kent
TN13 2RU* Sevenoaks (0732) 453555
HEWISON, Alan Stuart. b 30. SS Mark & Jo Coll
Plymouth BEd82. K Coll Lon. **d** 57 **p** 58. C S Mymms K
Chas *Lon* 57-60; C Bourne *Guildf* 60-63; Chapl RN
63-79; Perm to Offic *Ex* from 79. *8 Hazelwood Crescent,
Elburton, Plymouth PL9 8BL*
HEWITT, Brian. b 29. Liv Univ BSc51. Westcott Ho Cam
53. **d** 55 **p** 56. C Roby *Liv* 55-60; V Dukinfield St Jo
Ches from 60. *St John's Vicarage, Dukinfield, Cheshire*
061-338 2306
HEWITT, Charles David. b 38. Or Coll Ox BA60 MA63.
Clifton Th Coll 63. **d** 66 **p** 67. C Southport SS Simon
and Jude *Liv* 66-70; C Bethnal Green St Jas Less w
Victoria Park *Lon* 70-76; Hon C Old Ford St Paul w St
Steph 76-82; Ldr Bridge Ho Chr Cen Shaftesbury Soc
76-90; Hon C Old Ford St Paul w St Steph and St Mark
82-90; V Homerton St Luke from 90. *St Luke's Vicarage,
23 Cassland Road, London E9 7AL* 081-985 2263
HEWITT, Colin Edward. b 52. Man Poly BA80 Em Coll
Cam BA82 MA86. Westcott Ho Cam 80. **d** 83 **p** 84. C
Radcliffe St Thos and St Jo *Man* 83-84; C Langley and
Parkfield 84-86; R Byfield w Boddington *Pet* 86-91;
Chapl RAF from 91. *c/o MOD, Adastral House,
Theobald's Road, London WC1X 8RU* 071-430 7268
HEWITT, David John. b 40. Wells Th Coll 65. **d** 68 **p** 69.
C Southsea H Spirit *Portsm* 68-70; C Bramshott 70-72;
C Much Wenlock w Bourton *Heref* 72-74; CF 74-78 and

83-87; P-in-c Hadzor w Oddingley and Tibberton w
Bredicot *Worc* 78-83; P-in-c Chew Magna w Dundry
B & W 87-88; V from 88. *The Vicarage, 24 High Street,
Chew Magna, Bristol BS18 8PW* Bristol (0272) 332199
HEWITT, David Warner. b 33. Selw Coll Cam
BA56 MA60. Wells Th Coll 57. **d** 59 **p** 60. C Longbridge
Birm 59-61; C Sheldon 61-64; V Smethwick Old Ch
64-70; V Smethwick 70-78; P-in-c Littlehampton St Jas
Chich 78-85; P-in-c Wick 78-85; V Littlehampton St
Mary 78-85; TR Littlehampton and Wick 86-89. *31A St
George's Road, London E10 5RH*
HEWITT, Francis John Adam. b 42. St Chad's Coll Dur
BA64 DipTh66. **d** 66 **p** 67. C Dewsbury Moor *Wakef*
66-69; C Huddersfield St Jo 69-73; V King Cross 73-81;
V Lastingham *York* 81; P-in-c Appleton-le-Moors 81; V
Lastingham w Appleton-le-Moors 81-84; P-in-c Rosedale
83-84; V Lastingham w Appleton-le-Moors and Rosedale
84-86; RD Helmsley from 85; V Lastingham w Appleton-
le-Moors, Rosedale etc from 86. *The Vicarage,
Lastingham, York YO6 6TN* Lastingham (07515) 344
HEWITT, Geoffrey Williams. b 48. Leeds Univ BA69.
Wells Th Coll 70. **d** 72 **p** 73. C Heywood St Luke *Man*
72-74; Ind Chapl 74-77; P-in-c Hulme St Geo 74-77; V
Mamhilad and Pontymoile *Mon* 77-80; Ind Chapl 77-80;
V Arthog w Fairbourne *Ban* 80-89; R Llangelynnin w
Rhoslefain 87-89; TV Ban from 89; Dioc Dir of Soc
Resp from 89. *St David's Vicarage, 1 Belmont Road,
Bangor, Gwynedd LL57 2LL* Bangor (0248) 353405
HEWITT, Canon George Henry Gordon. b 12. BNC Ox
BA34 DipTh35 MA38. Wycliffe Hall Ox 34. **d** 36 **p** 37.
Can Res Chelmsf Cathl *Chelmsf* 64-78; Chapl to
HM The Queen 69-82; rtd 78. *8 Rainsford Avenue,
Chelmsford CM1 2PJ* Chelmsford (0245) 259836
HEWITT, Harold William. b 12. Fitzw Ho Cam
BA35 MA39. Wycliffe Hall Ox 36. **d** 38 **p** 39. V Gt
Bowden w Welham *Leic* 66-77; rtd 77; Perm to Offic
Ches from 77. *20 Percyvale Close, Bowling Green Court,
Nantwich, Cheshire CW5 5SW* Nantwich (0270) 626660
HEWITT, Canon Henry Thomas Maxwell. b 20. TCD
BA44 MA63. **d** 44 **p** 45. V Paddington Em Harrow Road
Lon 61-72; I Abbeyleix w Old Church, Ballyroan etc
C & O 72-90; Chan Leighlin Cathl 83-89; Chan Ossory
Cathl 83-89; rtd 90. *St James's Rectory, Stradbally, Co
Waterford, Irish Republic* Stradbally (51) 93129
HEWITT, James Herbert. b 17. Ch Coll Cam BA39 MA42.
Ridley Hall Cam 40. **d** 41 **p** 42. V New Beckenham St
Paul *Roch* 65-71; R Mereworth w W Peckham 71-75;
V Bradf St Aug Undercliffe *Bradf* 75-82; rtd 82.
73 Georgetown Road, Dumfries DG1 4DG Dumfries
(0387) 63973
HEWITT, John Kaffrell. b 34. St Aid Birkenhead 60. **d** 63
p 64. C Woking Ch Ch *Guildf* 63-66; P-in-c Sudbury w
Ballingdon and Brundon *St E* 66-70; V 70-80; V
Portsdown *Portsm* from 80. *Portsdown Vicarage,
Portsdown Hill Road, Cosham, Portsmouth PO6 1BE*
Cosham (0705) 375360
HEWITT, Kenneth Victor. b 30. Lon Univ BSc49 CertEd51
MSc53. Cuddesdon Coll 60. **d** 62 **p** 63. C Maidstone St
Martin *Cant* 62-64; C Croydon St Mich 64-67; P-in-c S
Kensington St Aug *Lon* 67-73; V from 73; Asst Chapl
Lon Univ 67-73. *St Augustine's Vicarage, 117 Queen's
Gate, London SW7 5LW* 071-581 1877
HEWITT, Michael David. b 49. K Coll Lon BD79 AKC79
CertEd. Qu Coll Birm 79. **d** 80 **p** 81. C Bexleyheath Ch
Ch *Roch* 80-84; C Buckland in Dover w Buckland Valley
Cant 84-89; R Ridgewell w Ashen, Birdbrook and
Sturmer *Chelmsf* from 89. *The Rectory, Church Lane,
Ridgewell, Halstead, Essex CO9 4SA* Ridgewell
(044085) 355
HEWITT, Norman Leslie. b 09. **d** 56 **p** 57. R Broughton
Astley *Leic* 63-73; rtd 73; Lic to Offic *Leic* 73-81; Perm
to Offic from 81. *The Spinneys, Lawyers Lane, Oadby,
Leicester* Leicester (0533) 719207
HEWITT, Paul Stephen Patrick. b 59. BA DipTh. **d** 86
p 87. C Ballymacash *Conn* 86-89; Bp's C Ballymena w
Ballyclug 89-91; I Glencraig *D & D* from 91. *Glencraig
Vicarage, 3 Seahill Road, Craigavad, Holywood, Co
Down BT18 0DA* Holywood (02317) 2225
HEWITT, Robert Samuel. b 51. QUB BSc73. CITC 77.
d 80 **p** 81. C Dundela *D & D* 80-84; I Donaghadee from
84. *3 The Trees, New Road, Donaghadee, Co Down*
Donaghadee (0247) 882594
HEWITT, Stephen Wilkes. b 49. Fitzw Coll Cam BA71.
St Jo Coll Nottm DipTh90. **d** 90 **p** 91. C Eaton *Nor* from
90. *347 Unthank Road, Norwich NR4 7QG* Norwich
(0603) 506590
HEWITT, Thomas Peter James. b 24. St Andr Univ MA50.
St Steph Ho Ox 50. **d** 52 **p** 53. C Ellesmere Port *Ches*
52-56; C Leytonstone St Marg w St Columba *Chelmsf*

56-60; V Barlby *York* 60-65; V Godshill *Portsm* from 65. *The Vicarage, Godshill, Ventnor, Isle of Wight PO38 3HY* Isle of Wight (0983) 840272

HEWITT, Timothy James. St D Coll Lamp BD. Ripon Coll Cuddesdon. **d** 91. C Milford Haven *St D* from 91. *St Peter's House, 2 Starbuck Road, Milford Haven, Dyfed SA73 2BA*

HEWITT, William. b 07. Open Univ BA73. Bible Churchmen's Coll 42. **d** 44 **p** 45. V Wavertree St Thos *Liv* 50-83; rtd 83; Perm to Offic *Liv* from 83. *7 Stuart Avenue, Liverpool L25 0NH* 051-486 0086

HEWITT, William Patrick. b 48. Nottm Univ BTh79. Linc Th Coll 75. **d** 79 **p** 80. C Workington St Jo *Carl* 79-83; V Flookburgh 83-87; V Barrow St Matt 87-90; P-in-c Lowick and Kyloe w Ancroft *Newc* from 90; P-in-c Ford from 90. *The Vicarage, 1 Main Street, Lowick, Berwick-upon-Tweed TD15 2UD* Berwick-upon-Tweed (0289) 88229

HEWLETT, David Bryan. b 49. Bris Univ BEd72. Qu Coll Birm 77. **d** 79 **p** 80. C Ludlow *Heref* 79-81; TV 81-84; V Marden w Amberley and Wisteston from 84; Field Officer for Lay Min 84-91; Continuing Minl Educn Adv from 86; Dir Post-Ord Tr from 91. *The Vicarage, Marden, Hereford HR1 3EN* Sutton St Nicholas (0432) 880256

HEWLETT, David Jonathon Peter. b 57. Dur Univ BA79 PhD83. Ridley Hall Cam 82. **d** 83 **p** 84. C New Barnet St Jas *St Alb* 83-86; Lect CITC 86-91; P-in-c Feock *Truro* from 91; Jt Dir SW Minl Tr Course from 91; Adv Local Ord Min from 91. *The Vicarage, Feock, Truro, Cornwall TR3 6SD* Truro (0872) 862044

HEWLETT, Michael Edward. b 16. Mert Coll Ox BA39 MA46. Qu Coll Birm 46. **d** 48 **p** 49. C Woolfardisworthy w Kennerleigh *Ex* 69-72; TV Cheriton Fitzpaine, Woolfardisworthy etc 72-76; TV N Creedy 76-86; rtd 86; Perm to Offic *Ex* from 86; *St Alb* from 87. *Jasmine Cottage, 3 The Green, Sarratt, Rickmansworth, Herts WD3 6AY* Rickmansworth (0923) 263803

HEWSON, Thomas Robert. b 45. Man Univ BA66. S'wark Ord Course 85. **d** 89 **p** 90. C Chinnor w Emmington and Sydenham etc *Ox* from 89. *44 Cowleaze, Chinnor, Oxford OX9 4TB* Kingston Blount (0844) 53763

HEYDON, Francis Garland William Woodard. b 10. AKC36. **d** 36 **p** 37. R Nuthurst *Chich* 62-78; rtd 78. *Flat 26, Bromley College, London Road, Bromley BR1 1PE* 081-290 1731

HEYGATE, Jack Lincoln. b 11. CCC Cam BA33 MA36. Cuddesdon Coll 35. **d** 36 **p** 37. R Warbleton *Chich* 65-69; rtd 76. *Windrush, Leafield, Oxford OX8 5NP* Asthall Leigh (099387) 659

HEYGATE, Dr Stephen Beaumont. b 48. Loughb Univ BSc71 CQSW73 PhD89. St Jo Coll Nottm LTh88. **d** 88 **p** 89. C Aylestone St Andr w St Jas *Leic* 88-90; V Cosby from 90. *Cosby Vicarage, Cosby, Leicester LE9 5UU* Leicester (0533) 862313

HEYHOE, Jonathan Peter. b 53. Man Univ BA75. Trin Coll Bris 77. **d** 80 **p** 81. C Woking St Pet *Guildf* 80-83; C Heatherlands St Jo *Sarum* 83-91; Chr Renewal Cen Newry from 91. *Christian Renewal Centre, Shore Road, Rostrevor, Newry, Co Down BT34 3ET* Rostrevor (06937) 38492

HEYS, Miss Sylvia. St Chris Coll Blackheath 46. **dss** 61 **d** 87. Adv in RE *Blackb* 50-68; Lytham St Jo 68-72; Blackpool St Steph 72-82; Lytham St Cuth 82-87; Hon Par Dn from 87. *6A Fairlawn Road, Lytham St Annes, Lancs FY8 5PT* Lytham (0253) 738600

HEYWOOD, David Stephen. b 55. Selw Coll Cam BA76 MA80 SS Hild & Bede Coll Dur PhD89. St Jo Coll Dur 80. **d** 86 **p** 87. C Cheltenham St Luke and St Jo *Glouc* 86-90; TV Sanderstead All SS *S'wark* from 90. *35 Audley Drive, Warlingham, Surrey CR6 9AH* 081-657 5505

HEYWOOD, Geoffrey Thomas. b 26. St Mich Coll Llan 60. **d** 62 **p** 63. V Caerhun w Llangelynnin *Ban* 67-74; Asst Chapl HM Pris Liv 74-75; Chapl HM Pris Ex 75-77; Wakef 77-79; HM Young Offender Inst Eastwood Pk 79-90; HM Pris Leyhill 79-90; rtd 90. *5 Meadow Road, Leyhill, Wotton-under-Edge, Glos GL12 8HW*

HEYWOOD, John. b 06. Man Egerton Hall 35. **d** 35 **p** 36. V Dunham Massey St Marg *Ches* 53-75; rtd 76; Perm to Offic *Ches* from 76. *Flat 6, Hillcar, St Margaret's Road, Altrincham, Cheshire WA14 2BE* 061-928 2054

HEYWOOD, Michael Herbert. b 41. Liv Univ BSc63. Clifton Th Coll 63. **d** 65 **p** 66. C Low Elswick *Newc* 65-68; C St Helens St Mark *Liv* 68-75; Lic to Offic *Dur* 75-85; Leprosy Miss Area Org NE & Cumbria 75-85; S Lon, Surrey and Berks from 85; Lic to Offic *S'wark* from 85. *3 Valerie Court, 33 Worcester Road, Sutton, Surrey SM2 6PU* 081-643 4896

HEYWOOD, Canon Peter. b 29. AKC54. **d** 55 **p** 56. C Tynemouth Ch Ch *Newc* 55-59; C Seaton Hirst 59-63; V Sleekburn 63-71; V Wallsend St Luke 71-89; V Belford from 89; Hon Can Newc Cathl from 90. *St Mary's Vicarage, Belford, Northd NE70 7LT* Belford (06683) 213545

HEYWOOD, Peter. b 46. Cranmer Hall Dur 72. **d** 75 **p** 76. C Blackley St Andr *Man* 75-78; C Denton Ch Ch 78-80; V Constable Lee from 80. *St Paul's Vicarage, Hollin Lane, Rawtenstall, Rossendale, Lancs BB4 8HT* Rossendale (0706) 228634

HEYWOOD, Samuel Frank Bruce. b 30. ACA51 FCA61. Oak Hill Th Coll 79. **d** 81 **p** 82. C Chenies and Lt Chalfont *Ox* 81-84; R Nash w Thornton, Beachampton and Thornborough 84-89; RD Buckm 88-89; P-in-c Ellesborough 89-91; P-in-c Stoke Mandeville 89-91; R Ellesborough, The Kimbles and Stoke Mandeville from 91. *The Rectory, Ellesborough, Butler's Cross, Aylesbury, Bucks HP17 0XA* Wendover (0296) 622110

HEYWOOD-WADDINGTON, Roger. b 23. Bps' Coll Cheshunt 58. **d** 58 **p** 59. V Neen Savage w Kinlet *Heref* 61-89; rtd 89. *Brook House, St Michaels, Tenbury Wells, Worcs WR15 8TG* Tenbury Wells (0584) 811116

HEZEL, Adrian. b 43. Chelsea Coll Lon BSc64 PhD67. N Ord Course 78. **d** 81 **p** 82. NSM Mirfield *Wakef* 81-89; C 89-90; V Shelley and Shepley from 90. *6 Stonecroft Gardens, Shepley, Huddersfield HD8 8EX* Huddersfield (0484) 602640

HIBBERD, Brian Jeffery. b 35. MA. **d** 60 **p** 61. C Cam H Trin *Ely* 60-63; C Doncaster St Mary *Sheff* 63-66; Asst Master Price's Sch Fareham 66-69; Warblington Sch Havant 69-73; Carisbrooke High Sch 73-91; Perm to Offic *Portsm* 82-91. *Address temp unknown*

HIBBERD, John. b 60. Wadh Coll Ox MA82. Trin Coll Bris BA89. **d** 89 **p** 90. C Northolt St Mary *Lon* from 89. *St Richard's Church House, Sussex Crescent, Northolt, Middx UB5 4DR* 081-864 3447

HIBBERD, John Charles. b 38. Chich Th Coll 63. **d** 66 **p** 67. C W Drayton *Lon* 66-70; C Noel Park St Mark 70-72; C Ealing St Steph Castle Hill 72-75; V Gunnersbury St Jas 75-84; V Whitton SS Phil and Jas 84-86; Finance and Trust Sec Lon Dioc Fund from 87; Perm to Offic from 87. *London Diocesan House, 30 Causton Street, London SW1P 4AU* 071-821 9351

HIBBERT, Miss Anne Mary Elizabeth. b 59. Southn Univ BA81. Trin Coll Bris 81. **dss** 83 **d** 87. Muswell Hill St Jas w St Matt *Lon* 83-86; Leic H Trin w St Jo *Leic* 86-87; Par Dn 87-90; Evang Co-ord and Adv CPAS from 90. *c/o CPAS, Athena Drive, Tachbrook Park, Warwick CV34 6NG* Warwick (0926) 334242

HIBBERT, Charles Dennis. b 24. Linc Th Coll 69. **d** 70 **p** 71. C Radcliffe-on-Trent *S'well* 70-73; P-in-c Ladybrook 73-77; V 77-79; V Boughton 79-85; V Ollerton 79-85; R Nuthall 85-89; rtd 89. *27 Nottingham Road, Kimberley, Nottingham NG16 2NB* Nottingham (0602) 386302

HIBBERT, James Raymond. b 10. St Pet Coll Ox BA32 MA36. Wycliffe Hall Ox 32. **d** 34 **p** 35. V Fulwood Ch Ch *Blackb* 45-75; rtd 75; Lic to Offic *Blackb* from 75. *39 Harrison Road, Fulwood, Preston, Lancs PR2 4QJ* Preston (0772) 719113

HIBBERT, Peter John. b 43. Hull Univ BA71 Lon Univ CertEd72 MA79. Sarum & Wells Th Coll 85. **d** 88 **p** 89. C Newsome and Armitage Bridge *Wakef* from 88. *6 Berry View, Huddersfield HD4 6LQ* Huddersfield (0484) 549133

HIBBERT, Preb Roy Trevor. b 30. AKC54. **d** 55 **p** 56. C W Bromwich St Fran *Lich* 55-58; C Cannock 58-60; C-in-c Sneyd Green CD 60-62; V Sneyd Green 62-67; V Harlescott 67-81; R Newport w Longford and Chetwynd from 81; RD Edgmond from 82; P-in-c Forton from 84; Preb Lich Cathl from 87. *The Rectory, High Street, Newport, Shropshire TF10 7BH* Newport (0952) 810500

HIBBINS, Neil Lance. b 60. St Anne's Coll Ox BA82 MA87 Univ of Wales (Cardiff) DPS85. St Mich Coll Llan 83. **d** 85 **p** 86. C Griffithstown *Mon* 85-87; C Pontypool 87-88; TV Pontypool from 88. *St Matthew's House, Victoria Road, Pontypool, Gwent NP4 5JU* Pontypool (0495) 753508

HIBBS, Canon Lawrence Winston. b 14. Kelham Th Coll 31. **d** 37 **p** 38. V Chandler's Ford *Win* 68-75; R Jersey Grouville 75-83; rtd 83; Perm to Offic *Win* from 83. *13 Rectory Close, St Clement, Jersey, Channel Islands JE2 6RF* Jersey (0534) 51394

HICHENS, Anthony. b 29. AKC59. **d** 60 **p** 61. C Ashford St Hilda *Lon* 60-64; C Leeds St Wilfrid *Ripon* 64-66; Guyana 67-75; P-in-c Stratton Audley w Godington *Ox* 76-83; P-in-c Finmere w Mixbury 76-78; P-in-c Fringford w Hethe and Newton Purcell 76-83; R Stratton Audley and Godington, Fringford etc from 83. *The Rectory, Mill Road, Stratton Audley, Bicester, Oxon OX6 9BJ* Stratton Audley (08697) 238

HICHENS, Thomas Sikes. b 11. Wells Th Coll 48. **d** 50 **p** 51. R Stoke Climsland *Truro* 69-76; rtd 76. *Perch Cottage, Lamorna, Penzance, Cornwall TR19 6XL* Penzance (0736) 731395

HICK, Geoffrey Lockwood Allanson. b 07. Qu Coll Cam BA31 MA35. Wycliffe Hall Ox 31. **d** 33 **p** 34. R Bre 53-78; rtd 78. *Balloch View, Church Street, Edzell, Brechin, Angus DD9 7TQ* Edzell (03564) 219

HICKES, Roy Edward. b 31. Lon Univ DipTh60. St Aid Birkenhead 56. **d** 59 **p** 60. C New Bury *Man* 59-63; C Wyther Ven Bede *Ripon* 63-65; R Oldham St Andr *Man* 65-69; V Smallbridge 69-79; R Winford *B & W* 79-81; R Winford w Felton Common Hill 81-88; RD Chew Magna 85-88; Chapl Costa Blanca *Eur* from 88. *Buzon 3, La Cometa 18, Senija (Benisa), Alicante, Spain* Senija (65) 732465

HICKEY, Canon Francis Joseph. b 20. AKC49. **d** 50 **p** 51. V Tilbury Docks *Chelmsf* 58-87; RD Orsett and Grays 70-83; Hon Can Chelmsf Cathl 79-87; rtd 87. *202 Parkside House, Clarendon Gardens, Malvern Road, Southsea, Hants PO5 2LD* Portsmouth (0705) 750301

HICKFORD, Michael Francis. b 53. Edin Th Coll 84. **d** 86 **p** 87. Chapl St Jo Cathl Oban *Arg* 86-89; R Alexandria *Glas* from 89. *The Rectory, Queen Street, Alexandria, Dunbartonshire G83 0AS* Alexandria (0389) 52633

HICKIN, Canon Leonard Charles. b 05. Magd Coll Cam BA26 MA30. Ridley Hall Cam 26. **d** 28 **p** 29. R Chesham Bois *Ox* 64-73; rtd 72. *7 Nelson Close, Winchmore Hill, Amersham, Bucks HP7 0PB* Amersham (0494) 725004

HICKIN, Maurice Whitehouse. b 09. St Cath Coll Cam BA32 MA38 Bonn Univ DPhil33. Ely Th Coll 33. **d** 34 **p** 35. R Runwell *Chelmsf* 61-75; rtd 75. *Calle De Murillo 6, Benidoleig, Alicante 03759, Spain* Alicante (6) 558-3266

HICKLEY, Peter Michael. b 28. Ely Th Coll 56. **d** 59 **p** 60. C Shepherd's Bush St Steph *Lon* 59-62; C Lee Gd Shep w St Pet *S'wark* 62-66; V Carlton *Wakef* 66-68; C Is of Dogs Ch Ch and St Jo w St Luke *Lon* 68-70; R S Hackney St Jo w Ch Ch 70-77; R Euston w Barnham and Fakenham *St E* 77-80; TR Fenny Stratford and Water Eaton *Ox* 80-88; R Benington w Walkern *St Alb* from 88. *The Rectory, Church End, Walkern, Stevenage, Herts SG2 7PB* Walkern (043886) 322

HICKLING, Canon Colin John Anderson. b 31. K Coll Cam BA53 MA57. Chich Th Coll 56. **d** 57 **p** 58. C Pallion *Dur* 57-61; Asst Tutor Chich Th Coll 61-65; Asst Lect K Coll Lon 65-68; Lect 68-84; Hon C Munster Square St Mary Magd *Lon* 68-69; Dep Min Can St Paul's Cathl 69-78; Hon C E Dulwich St Jo *S'wark* 70-84; Dep P-in-O to HM The Queen 71-74; P-in-O 74-84; Can Th Leic Cathl *Leic* from 81; Tutor Qu Coll Birm 84-85; Lect Linc Th Coll 85-86; Hon Lect Bibl Studies Sheff Univ from 86; V Arksey *Sheff* from 86. *The Vicarage, Station Road, Arksey, Doncaster, S Yorkshire DN5 0SP* Doncaster (0302) 874445

HICKLING, John. b 34. Launde Abbey. **d** 69 **p** 70. C Melton Mowbray w Thorpe Arnold *Leic* 69-71; TV 71-75; R Waltham on the Wolds w Stonesby and Saltby 75-84; R Aylestone St Andr w St Jas from 84. *The Rectory, Old Church Street, Leicester LE2 8ND* Leicester (0533) 832458

HICKMAN, George May. b 11. AKC33. **d** 35 **p** 36. R Withycombe *B & W* 68-84; rtd 84; Perm to Offic *B & W* from 85. *1 The Causeway, Withycombe, Minehead, Somerset TA24 6PZ* Watchet (0984) 40227

HICKS, Miss Barbara. b 42. Cranmer Hall Dur BA71. **dss** 85 **d** 87. Norton Woodseats St Paul *Sheff* 85-87; Par Dn Sheff St Jo from 87. *15 Benson Road, Sheffield S2 5EU* Sheffield (0742) 759997

HICKS, Francis Fuller. b 28. Sarum & Wells Th Coll 71. **d** 74 **p** 75. C Broadstone *Sarum* 74-78; P-in-c Kington Magna and Buckhorn Weston 78-79; TV Gillingham 79-86; P-in-c Portland St Jo 86-89; V from 89. *St John's Vicarage, Ventnor Road, Portland, Dorset DT5 1JE* Portland (0305) 820103

HICKS, Herbert. b 10. Bede Coll Dur BA32 MA47. Ridley Hall Cam 34. **d** 36 **p** 37. V Bramhope *Ripon* 55-74; rtd 74. *2 Larkfield Drive, Harrogate, N Yorkshire HG2 0BX* Harrogate (0423) 58675

HICKS, Joan Rosemary. b 60. Homerton Coll Cam BEd83. Westcott Ho Cam 87. **d** 90. Par Dn Wendover *Ox* from 90. *1 Icknield Close, Wendover, Aylesbury, Bucks HP22 6HG* Aylesbury (0296) 623503

HICKS, Richard Barry. b 32. Dur Univ BA55. Sarum Th Coll 59. **d** 61 **p** 62. C Wallsend St Luke *Newc* 61-64; C Tynemouth Ch Ch 64-69; V Tynemouth St Jo 69-75; V

Prudhoe 75-82; TV Swanborough *Sarum* 82-86; R Hilperton w Whaddon and Staverton etc from 86. *The Rectory, Hilperton, Trowbridge, Wilts BA14 7RL* Trowbridge (0225) 752804

HICKS, Stuart Knox. b 34. Univ of W Ontario BA56 Huron Coll LTh59 Ox Univ DipEd67. **d** 58 **p** 60. Canada 58-65; C Allerton *Liv* 65-66; Hon C Rye Park St Cuth *St Alb* 68-72; Lic to Offic *B & W* 72-87 and from 88; Chapl Magdalen Chpl Bath 80-86; Chapl Partis Coll Bath from 88. *Folly Orchard, The Folly, Saltford, Bristol BS18 3JW* Saltford (0225) 873391

HICKS, Mrs Valerie Joy. b 47. SRN69 HVCert70. Cant Sch of Min 82. **dss** 85 **d** 87. Roch 85-87; Hon Par Dn 87-89; Par Dn Thatcham *Ox* from 89. *28 Masefield Road, Newbury, Berks RG13 4AS* Newbury (0635) 72004

HICKS, William Trevor. b 45. Hull Univ BA68 Fitzw Coll Cam BA70 MA74. Westcott Ho Cam 68. **d** 70 **p** 71. C Cottingham *York* 70-73; C Elland *Wakef* 73-76; V Walsden 76-81; V Knottingley from 81. *The Vicarage, Chapel Street, Knottingley, W Yorkshire WF11 9AN* Pontefract (0977) 672267

HIDER, David Arthur. b 46. Lon Univ BSc67. Sarum & Wells Th Coll 86. **d** 89 **p** 90. NSM Southbourne w W Thorney *Chich* from 89. *253 Main Road, Southbourne, Emsworth, Hants PO10 8JD* Emsworth (0243) 374924

HIGDON, Lewis George. b 36. Dur Univ BA58. Cranmer Hall Dur DipTh60. **d** 60 **p** 61. C Leeds St Pet *Ripon* 60-65; C Shipley St Paul *Bradf* 65-66; V Esholt 67-75; V Kirkstall *Ripon* 75-79; V Stanwix *Carl* 79-87; V Ambleside w Brathay from 87. *The Vicarage, Millans Park, Ambleside, Cumbria LA22 9AD* Ambleside (05394) 33205

HIGGINBOTTOM, Richard. b 48. Oak Hill Th Coll DipTh72 BD74. **d** 74 **p** 75. C Kenilworth St Jo *Cov* 74-77; C Finham 77-79; P-in-c Attleborough 79-81; V 81-84; Asst Chapl HM Pris Brixton 84-85; Chapl HM Pris Roch from 85. *HM Prison, Rochester, Kent ME1 3QS* Medway (0634) 830300

HIGGINBOTTOM, Richard William. b 51. Man Univ BA73 MA75. Edin Th Coll 83. **d** 85 **p** 86. C Knighton St Mary Magd *Leic* 85-87; C Northleach w Hampnett and Farmington *Glouc* 87-89; V Hayfield *Derby* from 89. *The Vicarage, 7 Station Road, Birch Vale, Stockport, Cheshire SK12 5BP* New Mills (0663) 743350

HIGGINS, Dr Bernard. b 42. MRPharmS68 Leic Poly BPharm63 PhD66. St Jo Coll Nottm 89. **d** 91. C Stockport St Geo *Ches* from 91. *40 Beachfield Road, Stockport, Cheshire SK3 8SF* 061-483 3350

HIGGINS, Bernard George. b 27. Wycliffe Hall Ox 68. **d** 70 **p** 72. C Surbiton St Matt *S'wark* 70-72; C Battersea St Mary 72-76; C Warblington and Emsworth *Portsm* 76-81; C Milton from 81. *14 Priory Crescent, Southsea, Hants PO4 8RL* Portsmouth (0705) 830085

HIGGINS, Frank Roylance. b 34. Open Univ BA74 MEd83. Bps' Coll Cheshunt 59. **d** 62 **p** 63. C Sunderland *Dur* 62-64; C S Westoe 64-66; P-in-c Smethwick St Mich *Birm* 66-67; V 67-70; V Garretts Green 70-75; Lic to Offic *Worc* 76-80; Perm to Offic *Birm* 81-87; Hon C Feckenham w Bradley *Worc* 84-87; R Ripple, Earls Croome w Hill Croome and Strensham from 87. *The Rectory, The Cross, Ripple, Tewkesbury, Glos GL20 6HA* Upton-upon-Severn (06846) 2655

HIGGINS, Geoffrey Minta. b 27. New Coll Ox BA52 MA56. Cuddesdon Coll 52. **d** 54 **p** 55. C Pet St Mary *Pet* 54-56; CF 56-77; Hong Kong from 77. *12-C Far East Consortium Building, Main Road, Yuen Long, New Territories, Hong Kong* Hong Kong (852) 479-9374

HIGGINS, Godfrey. b 39. St Chad's Coll Dur BA61 DipTh62 DipEd63. **d** 63 **p** 64. C Brighouse *Wakef* 63-66; C Huddersfield St Jo 66-68; R High Hoyland w Clayton W 68-75; V Marsden 75-84; V Pontefract St Giles from 84. *The Vicarage, The Mount, Pontefract, W Yorkshire WF8 1NE* Pontefract (0977) 706803

HIGGINS, John. b 44. Trin Coll Bris 71. **d** 73 **p** 74. C Clapham St Jas *S'wark* 73-74; C Ruskin Park St Sav and St Matt 74-77; C Hamworthy *Sarum* 77-80; V Bordesley St Andr *Birm* 80-83; V Bishop Sutton and Stanton Drew and Stowey *B & W* from 83. *The Vicarage, Bishop Sutton, Bristol BS18 4UR* Chew Magna (0272) 333385

HIGGINS, John Leslie. b 43. BA CQSW Birm Univ MEd89. Lich Th Coll 64. **d** 66 **p** 67. C Sale St Anne *Ches* 66-69; C Bredbury St Mark 69-72; V Wharton 72-74; Hon C Annan *Glas* 75-79; Hon C Lockerbie 75-79; V Coseley Ch Ch *Lich* 79-89; R Arthuret *Carl* from 89. *The Rectory, 14 Netherby Road, Longtown, Carlisle CA6 5NT* Longtown (0228) 791338

HIGGINS, Canon John Norman. b 14. Em Coll Cam BA36 MA40. Wells Th Coll 39. **d** 40 **p** 41. R Sutton St

Nic *S'wark* 67-77; R Limpsfield and Titsey 77-82; rtd 82; Perm to Offic *B & W* from 84. *Robin House, 28 College Road, Wells, Somerset BA5 2TE* Wells (0749) 76416

HIGGINS, Leslie. b 07. **d** 65 **p** 66. V Lostock Gralam *Ches* 68-75; rtd 75; C Over St Chad *Ches* 75-81; Perm to Offic from 81. *170 Middlewich Road, Winsford, Cheshire CW7 3NN* Winsford (0606) 594357

HIGGINS, Very Rev Michael John. b 35. Birm Univ LLB57 G&C Coll Cam LLB59 PhD62. Ridley Hall Cam 63. **d** 65 **p** 65. C Ormskirk *Liv* 65-67; Selection Sec ACCM 67-74; Hon C St Marylebone St Mark w St Luke *Lon* 69-74; P-in-c Woodlands *B & W* 74-80; V Frome St Jo 74-80; TR Preston St Jo *Blackb* 80-91; Dean Ely from 91. *The Deanery, Ely, Cambs CB7 4DN* Ely (0353) 667735

HIGGINS, Richard Ellis. b 63. Univ of Wales BA84. St Mich Coll Llan DipTh88 DPS89. **d** 89 **p** 90. C Bargoed and Deri w Brithdir *Llan* from 89. *61 Park Road, Bargoed, M Glam CF8 8SR* Bargoed (0443) 821386

HIGGINS, Rupert Anthony. b 59. Man Univ BA80. Wycliffe Hall Ox 82. **d** 85 **p** 86. C Plymouth St Andr w St Paul and St Geo *Ex* 85-90; C Clifton Ch Ch w Em *Bris* from 90. *62 Clifton Park Road, Bristol BS8 3HN* Bristol (0272) 739640

HIGGINS, Timothy John. b 45. Bris Univ BEd70 Lanc Univ MA74 St Jo Coll Dur DipTh79. **d** 79 **p** 80. C Northn All SS w St Kath *Pet* 79-82; V Whitton St Aug *Lon* 82-90; AD Hampton 86-90; TR Aylesbury w Bierton and Hulcott *Ox* from 90. *The Vicarage, Parson's Fee, Aylesbury, Bucks HP20 2QZ* Aylesbury (0296) 24276

HIGGINSON, Arthur Rothwell. b 14. Edin Th Coll 48. **d** 51 **p** 52. V Northn Ch Ch *Pet* 64-74; V Whitewell *Blackb* 74-79; P-in-c Hurst Green and Mitton *Bradf* 76-79; rtd 79; Lic to Offic *Blackb* from 80. *24 Moorlands, Garstang Road, Preston, Lancs PR1 1NN* Preston (0772) 51660

HIGGINSON, Gerald Scott. b 29. Keele Univ BA54 Birm Univ PhD57. NW Ord Course 73. **d** 76 **p** 77. NSM York St Mary Bishophill Junior w All SS *York* 76-84; P-in-c 84-86; P-in-c York H Trin w St Jo Micklegate and St Martin 84-86; R Micklegate H Trin and Bishophill Junior St Mary from 86. *Holy Trinity Rectory, York YO1 1LE* York (0904) 623798

HIGGINSON, Richard Edwin. b 15. St Jo Coll Dur BA39 MA42 Lon Univ BD51. Tyndale Hall Bris 35. **d** 39 **p** 40. V S Croydon Em *Cant* 69-78; P-in-c Weeton *Blackb* 78-80; rtd 80; Lic to Offic *Blackb* from 81. *30 Pennine Way, Great Eccleston, Preston PR3 0YS* Great Eccleston (0995) 70634

HIGGS, Allan Herbert Morris. b 22. St Jo Coll Dur BA48 DipTh50. **d** 50 **p** 51. V Fenham St Jas and St Basil *Newc* 61-75; Adult Educn Adv *Linc* 75-80; V Stamfordham w Matfen *Newc* 80-88; rtd 88; Perm to Offic *Bradf* from 88. *3 Southfield Lane, Addingham, Ilkley, W Yorkshire LS29 0NX* Addingham (0943) 830167

HIGGS, Andrew Richard Bowen. b 53. Man Univ BSc75. St Jo Coll Nottm 81. **d** 85 **p** 86. C Droylsden St Mary *Man* 85-88; C Harlow New Town w Lt Parndon *Chelmsf* from 88. *4A The Drive, Netteswell, Harlow, Essex CM20 3QD* Harlow (0279) 437717

✠**HIGGS, Rt Rev Hubert Lawrence.** b 11. Ch Coll Cam BA34 MA37. Ridley Hall Cam 34. **d** 35 **p** 36 **c** 65. C Richmond H Trin *S'wark* 35-36; C S Kensington St Luke *Lon* 36-38; C Boscombe St Jo *Win* 38-39; V Aldershot H Trin *Guildf* 39-45; Ed Sec CMS 45-52; V Woking St Jo 52-57; RD Woking 56-57; Adn Bradf 57-65; Suff Bp Hull *York* 65-76; RD Hull 72-76; Perm to Offic *St E* from 76; rtd 77. *The Farmstead, Chediston, Halesworth, Suffolk* Halesworth (09867) 2621

HIGGS, Michael John. b 53. Sarum & Wells Th Coll 76. **d** 80 **p** 81. C Cant St Martin and St Paul *Cant* 80-84; C Maidstone St Martin 84-88; R Egerton w Pluckley from 88. *St James's Vicarage, Egerton, Ashford, Kent TN27 9DH* Egerton (023376) 224

HIGH, Gordon Maurice Verdun. b 16. Keble Coll Ox BA48 MA52. St Steph Ho Ox 48. **d** 50 **p** 51. R Charwelton w Fawsley and Preston Capes *Pet* 61-81; rtd 81; Lic to Offic *Pet* 83-86; Perm to Offic from 86. *2 Spring Close, Daventry, Northants NN11 6YT* Daventry (0327) 77749

HIGHAM, Gerald Norman. b 40. St Aid Birkenhead 64. **d** 68 **p** 69. C Garston *Liv* 68-71; C Blundellsands St Nic 71-73; V Bolton All So w St Jas *Man* 73-78; V Tonge w Alkrington 78-84; P-in-c Edenfield 84-86; P-in-c Stubbins 84-86; V Edenfield and Stubbins from 86. *St Philip's Vicarage, Chatterton Road, Ramsbottom, Bury, Lancs BL0 0PQ* Ramsbottom (0706) 822079

HIGHAM, Canon Jack. b 33. Linc Coll Ox BA56 MA60 Birm Univ DipTh59. Union Th Sem (NY) STM61 Qu Coll Birm 58. **d** 60 **p** 61. C Handsworth *Sheff* 60-64; V Handsworth Woodhouse 64-70; USA 70-78; R Stoke Bruerne w Grafton Regis and Alderton *Pet* 78-83; RD Towcester 82-83; Can Res, Chan and Lib Pet Cathl from 83. *Canonry House, Minster Precincts, Peterborough PE1 1XX* Peterborough (0733) 62125

HIGHAM, John Leonard. b 39. Liv Univ DipSocSc71. Wycliffe Hall Ox 62. **d** 65 **p** 66. C Prescot *Liv* 65-71; V Hollinfare 71-74; Adult and Youth Service Adv Knowsley 74-76; TV Padgate 76-84; V Farnworth 84-89; TR Sutton from 89. *Sutton Rectory, Eaves Lane, St Helens, Merseyside WA9 3UB* Marshalls Cross (0744) 812347

HIGHAM (nee ANNS), Mrs Pauline Mary. b 49. Bris Univ BEd71. E Midl Min Tr Course 87. **d** 90. Par Dn Wirksworth w Alderwasley, Carsington etc *Derby* from 90. *26 Yokecliffe Crescent, Wirksworth, Derbys DE4 4ER* Wirksworth (0629) 824291

HIGHTON, William James. b 31. St Deiniol's Hawarden. **d** 82 **p** 83. NSM Thornton Hough *Ches* 82-84; C Cheadle 84-88; V Walton from 88. *St John's Vicarage, Chester Road, Higher Walton, Warrington WA4 6TJ* Warrington (0925) 62939

HIGTON, Anthony Raymond. b 42. Lon Univ BD65. Oak Hill Th Coll 65. **d** 67 **p** 68. C Newark Ch Ch *S'well* 67-69; C Cheltenham St Mark *Glouc* 70-75; R Hawkwell *Chelmsf* from 75. *The Rectory, Ironwell Lane, Hawkwell, Hockley, Essex SS5 4JY* Southend-on-Sea (0702) 203870

HILARY, Brother. See BEASLEY, William Isaac

HILARY, Sister. See HOPKINS, Hilda

HILARY, Sister. See JORDINSON, Vera

HILDAGE, James Francis. b 18. Univ of Wales BA44. Coll of Resurr Mirfield 44. **d** 46 **p** 47. V Earl Sterndale and Monyash *Derby* 56-87; Lect Matlock Coll of HE 66-83; rtd 87; Perm to Offic *Ban* from 88. *Llangwyfan Isaf, Ty Croes, Anglesey, Gwynedd LL63 5YP* Rhosneigr (0407) 810756

HILDRED, David. b 61. Bath Univ BSc83 CertEd83. Wycliffe Hall Ox 86. **d** 89 **p** 90. C Westcliff St Mich *Chelmsf* from 89. *35 Fernleigh Drive, Leigh-on-Sea, Essex SS9 1LG* Southend-on-Sea (0702) 72386

HILES, Douglas Arthur. b 18. St Deiniol's Hawarden 78. **d** 80 **p** 81. C Heaton Ch Ch *Man* 80-83; rtd 86; Hon C Harwood *Man* from 90. *413 Hough Fold Way, Bolton BL2 3PY* Bolton (0204) 24548

HILES, John Michael. b 32. Qu Coll Cam BA57 MA61. Sarum Th Coll 57. **d** 59 **p** 60. C Clifton St Jas *Sheff* 59-62; V Bramley St Fran 62-69; Hon C Holmfirth *Wakef* 69-89; Hon C Upper Holme Valley from 89. *Rosehill, Parkhead Lane, Holmfirth, Huddersfield HD7 1LB* Holmfirth (0484) 683045

HILL, Bridget Ann. b 54. Open Univ BA82 CertEd75. E Midl Min Tr Course 83. **dss** 86 **d** 87. Gt and Lt Coates w Bradley *Linc* 86-87; NSM 87-88; Par Dn Louth 88-91; TM from 91; Chapl Louth Co Hosp from 89. *Holy Trinity Vicarage, 24 Grosvenor Road, Louth, Lincs LN11 0BB* Louth (0507) 607991

HILL, Charles Merrick. b 52. Strathclyde Univ BA74. Qu Coll Birm DipTh79. **d** 80 **p** 81. C Silksworth *Dur* 80-83; C Stockton St Pet 83-85; TV Southn (City Cen) *Win* 85-87; V Portsea St Geo *Portsm* from 87. *8 Queen Street, Portsmouth PO1 3HL* Portsmouth (0705) 812215

HILL, Canon Christopher John. b 45. K Coll Lon BD67 AKC67 MTh68. **d** 69 **p** 70. C Tividale *Lich* 69-73; C Codsall 73-74; Abp's Asst Chapl on Foreign Relns *Cant* 74-81; ARCIC from 74; Sec 74-90; Hon Can Cant Cathl *Cant* 82-89; Abp's Sec for Ecum Affairs 82-89; Chapl to HM The Queen from 87; Can Res and Prec St Paul's Cathl *Lon* from 89; Select Preacher Ox Univ from 90. *3 Amen Court, London EC4M 7BU* 071-236 4532

HILL, Preb Dr Colin. b 42. Leic Univ BSc64 Open Univ PhD88. Ripon Hall Ox 64. **d** 66 **p** 67. C Leic Martyrs *Leic* 66-69; C Braunstone 69-71; Lect Ecum Inst Thornaby Teesside 71-72; V Worsbrough St Thos and St Jas *Sheff* 72-78; Telford Planning Officer *Lich* from 78; RD Telford from 80; RD Telford Severn Gorge *Heref* from 80; Preb Heref Cathl from 83. *Parkfield, Park Avenue, Madeley, Telford, Shropshire TF7 5AB* Telford (0952) 585731

HILL, Canon Colin Arnold Clifford. b 29. Bris Univ 52. Ripon Hall Ox 55. **d** 57 **p** 58. C Rotherham *Sheff* 57-61; V Brightside St Thos 61-64; R Easthampstead *Ox* 64-73; Chapl RAF Coll Bracknell 68-73; V Croydon *Cant* 73-84; Chapl Abp Jo Whitgift Foundn from 73; Hon Can Cant Cathl 75-84; V Croydon St Jo *S'wark* from 85; Hon Can S'wark Cathl from 85; Chapl to HM The

Queen from 90. *Croydon Vicarage, 22 Bramley Hill, Croydon, Surrey CR2 6LT* 081-688 1387 or 688 8104

HILL, Canon David. b 25. AKC54. **d** 55 **p** 56. V Battersea St Mich *S'wark* 62-89; RD Battersea 69-76; Hon Can S'wark Cathl 74-89; rtd 89. *70 Gloucester Avenue, Maldon, Essex CM9 6LA* Maldon (0621) 855384

HILL, David Rowland. b 34. Lon Univ BSc55. Qu Coll Birm. **d** 59 **p** 60. C Upper Tooting H Trin *S'wark* 59-61; C Cheam 61-63; C Richmond St Mary 63-68; V Sutton St Nicholas *Linc* 68-82; V Pinchbeck from 82. *The Vicarage, Spalding Road, Pinchbeck, Spalding, Lincs PE11 3ND* Spalding (0775) 768710

HILL, Canon Derek Ingram. b 12. FSA74 Trin Coll Ox BA34 MA38 Kent Univ Hon DD83. Wells Th Coll 34. **d** 35 **p** 36. R Cant St Pet and St Alphege w St Marg *Cant* 65-74; P-in-c Cant St Mildred w St Mary de Castro 72-74; R Cant St Pet w St Alphege and St Marg etc 74-76; Can Res Cant Cathl 76-83; rtd 83. *2 St John's House, 40 Northgate, Canterbury, Kent CT1 1BE* Canterbury (0227) 761954

HILL, Derek Stanley. b 28. AKC53. **d** 53 **p** 54. C Rushmere *St E* 53-55; S Africa 55-57; C Boreham Wood All SS *St Alb* 57-59; V Crowfield *St E* 59-67; P-in-c Stonham Aspal 59-61; R 61-67; V Bury St Edmunds St Geo 67-73; P-in-c Ampton w Lt Livermere and Ingham 68-73; V Gazeley w Dalham 73-75; P-in-c Lidgate w Ousden 73-74; P-in-c Gt Bradley 74-78; V Gazeley w Dalham and Moulton 75-78; V Gt Barton 78-86; V Bury St Edmunds All SS from 86. *59 Bennett Avenue, Bury St Edmunds, Suffolk IP33 3JJ* Bury St Edmunds (0284) 701063

HILL, Dudley Joseph. b 13. ARCO34 Leeds Univ BA35 MA40. Coll of Resurr Mirfield 35. **d** 37 **p** 38. V Fulford *York* 68-78; rtd 78. *Flat 11, Somerset House, Knapp Road, Cheltenham, Glos GL50 3QQ* Cheltenham (0242) 577046

HILL, Miss Elizabeth Jayne Louise. *See* DAVENPORT, Ms Elizabeth Jayne Louise

HILL, Eugene Mark. b 48. Univ of Wales (Lamp) BA71. Sarum Th Coll 71. **d** 73 **p** 74. C Sutton St Nic *S'wark* 73-77; Hon C 77-80; Asst Chapl Em Sch Wandsworth 77-87; Chapl from 87; Hon C St Helier *S'wark* 83-84; Hon C Caterham from 84; Dir Chr Studies Course from 85. *The Rectory, 5 Whyteleafe Road, Caterham, Surrey CR3 5EG* Caterham (0883) 42062

HILL, Frederick Ashton. b 13. Ch Coll Cam BA34 MA38. Chich Th Coll 36. **d** 38 **p** 39. C Beckenham St Barn *Roch* 38-44; C Swindon New Town *Bris* 44-50; R Letchworth *St Alb* 50-69; R Gt and Lt Ryburgh w Gateley and Testerton *Nor* from 69; R Stibbard from 69. *The Rectory, Great Ryburgh, Fakenham, Norfolk NR21 0EB* Great Ryburgh (032878) 234

HILL, Geoffrey Dennison. b 31. **d** 56 **p** 57. C Denton Holme *Carl* 56-59; R Asby w Ormside 59-63; R Arthuret 63-71; V Arnside 71-76; P-in-c Torver 76-79. *Address temp unknown*

HILL, George Ernest. b 25. St Jo Coll Nottm. **d** 85 **p** 87. NSM Selston *S'well* from 85. *105 Main Road, Jacksdale, Nottingham NG16 5HR* Leabrooks (0773) 603446

HILL, Mrs Gillian Beryl. b 53. Open Univ BA86. S Dios Minl Tr Scheme 87. **d** 90. NSM Southsea St Jude *Portsm* from 90. *27 Inglis Road, Southsea, Hants PO5 1PB* Portsmouth (0705) 811233

HILL, Harold Gordon Haynes. b 15. Tyndale Hall Bris 36. **d** 39 **p** 40. R Reymerston *Nor* 48-81; R Whinburgh w Westf 48-81; P-in-c Cranworth w Letton and Southbergh 78-79; rtd 81. *34 Morley Road, Sheringham, Norfolk NR26 8JE* Sheringham (0263) 824965

HILL, Henry Baxter. b 19. St Alb Minl Tr Scheme 76. **d** 79 **p** 80. Hon C Mill End and Heronsgate w W Hyde *St Alb* 79-84; Asst Chapl Amersham Hosp from 79; Perm to Offic from 84. *Stelling, 66 Quickley Lane, Chorleywood, Rickmansworth, Herts WD3 5AF* Chorleywood (0923) 282309

HILL, James Arthur. b 47. Ulster Univ BEd85. CITC. **d** 72 **p** 73. C Ballymena w Ballyclug *Conn* 72-74; C Arm St Mark w Aghavilly *Arm* 74-78; C Derg w Termonamongan *D & R* 78-79; I Inver w Mountcharles, Killaghtee and Killybegs 79-87. *53 Dufferin Avenue, Bangor, Co Down BT20 3AB* Bangor (0247) 469090

HILL, James Reginald. b 06. Man Univ BA29. S'wark Ord Course 67. **d** 69 **p** 70. C Purley Ch Ch *S'wark* 69-77; Perm to Offic Chich 77-82 and from 88; St Alb 82-88. *Bethany, Rosemary Avenue, Steyning, W Sussex BN44 3YS* Steyning (0903) 816102

HILL, John. b 56. S'wark Ord Course. **d** 89 **p** 90. NSM Upper Norwood St Jo *S'wark* from 89. *88 Sylvan Road, London SE19 2RZ* 081-653 4185

HILL, John Michael. b 34. FCA. Oak Hill NSM Course 81. **d** 85 **p** 86. NSM Rayleigh *Chelmsf* from 85; Perm to Offic *Lon* from 86. *8 High Road, Hockley, Essex SS5 4SX* Southend-on-Sea (0702) 203287

HILL, Kenneth. b 27. Wycliffe Coll Toronto LTh. **d** 58 **p** 59. Canada 58-61; C Newc St Matt w St Mary *Newc* 61-62; SSF 62-64; C Burslem St Werburgh *Lich* 64-67; C Walsall St Gabr Fullbrook 67-70; P-in-c Hanley St Jude 70-79; P-in-c Chacewater *Truro* from 79. *The Vicarage, Chacewater, Truro, Cornwall TR4 8PZ* Truro (0872) 560225

HILL, Kenneth James. b 43. Leic Univ BA64 Lon Univ BD68. Oak Hill Th Coll 65. **d** 69 **p** 70. C Southall Green St Jo *Lon* 69-72; C Blackheath Park St Mich *S'wark* 72-75; C Bath Abbey w St Jas *B & W* 75-83; P-in-c Bath St Mich w St Paul 75-82; R 82-83; R Huntspill 83-91; Omega Order from 91. *The Omega Order, Winford Manor, Winford, Bristol BS18 8DW* Nailsea (0272) 472262

HILL, Laurence Bruce. b 43. AKC67. **d** 69 **p** 70. C Feltham *Lon* 69-72; C-in-c Hampstead St Steph 72-77; V Finchley H Trin from 77. *Holy Trinity Vicarage, 91 Church Lane, London N2 0TH* 081-883 8720

HILL, Leslie Hugh. b 23. Westcott Ho Cam 73. **d** 73 **p** 74. NSM Holbrook and Lt Eaton *Derby* 73-79; NSM Loscoe 79-85; P-in-c Denby 85-88; P-in-c Horsley Woodhouse 87-88; rtd 88; Perm to Offic *Derby* from 88. *1 Hunter Drive, Kilburn, Derby DE5 0ND* Derby (0332) 881081

HILL, Malcolm Crawford. b 43. Lon Univ DipTh70. Oak Hill Th Coll 68. **d** 71 **p** 72. C Maidstone St Luke *Cant* 71-74; C Longfleet *Sarum* 74-79; V Bexleyheath St Pet *Roch* 79-90; V Lee St Mildred *S'wark* from 90. *The Vicarage, 1A Helder Grove, London SE12 0RB* 081-857 5205

HILL, Malcolm John. b 26. OStJ. Bps' Coll Cheshunt 64. **d** 65 **p** 66. C Luton Ch Ch *St Alb* 65-70; V Wilshamstead 70-78; P-in-c Westoning w Tingrith 78-80; V from 80. *The Vicarage, Church Road, Westoning, Bedford MK45 5JW* Flitwick (0525) 713703

HILL, Michael. b 32. TD77. AKC55. **d** 56 **p** 57. C Tynemouth Cullercoats St Paul *Newc* 56-59; C Drayton in Hales *Lich* 59-61; V Milton 61-64; V Preston Gubbals 64-73; V Leaton 64-76; CF (TA) 65-67; CF (TAVR) 67-87; V Oswestry St Oswald *Lich* 76-87; P-in-c Trefonen 80-83; V Sunningdale *Ox* from 87. *The Vicarage, Sidbury Close, Sunningdale, Ascot, Berks SL5 0PD* Ascot (0344) 20061

HILL, Michael Arthur. b 49. Ridley Hall Cam 74. **d** 77 **p** 78. C Addiscombe St Mary *Cant* 77-81; C Slough *Ox* 81-83; P-in-c Chesham Bois 83-90; R from 90; RD Amersham from 89. *The Rectory, Glebe Way, Chesham Bois, Amersham, Bucks HP6 5ND* Amersham (0494) 726139

HILL, Michael John (Brother Giles). b 43. OSB. S Dios Minl Tr Scheme 82. **d** 84 **p** 86. Perm to Offic *Win* from 84. *Alton Abbey, Abbey Road, Beech, Alton, Hants GU34 4AP* Alton (0420) 62145

HILL, Norman. b 20. St Chad's Coll Dur LTh48. Linc Th Coll 45. **d** 49 **p** 50. V Mosborough *Sheff* 59-72; P-in-c Codnor and Loscoe *Derby* 73-79; V 79-85; rtd 85. *6 Egmere Road, Walsingham, Norfolk NR22 6DB*

HILL, Norman William. b 14. Ch Coll Cam BA36 MA40. Linc Th Coll 43. **d** 45 **p** 46. V Rickmansworth *St Alb* 60-74; P-in-c Northill 74-78; P-in-c Moggerhanger 74-78; P-in-c Northill w Moggerhanger 78-79; RD Biggleswade 75-79; rtd 80. *West Sillywrea, Langley-on-Tyne, Hexham, Northd NE47 5NE* Hexham (0434) 684635

HILL, Canon Peter. b 36. AKC60. St Boniface Warminster 60. **d** 61 **p** 62. C Gt Berkhamsted *St Alb* 61-67; R Bedf St Mary 67-69; P-in-c 69-70; V Goldington 69-79; V Biggleswade 79-90; RD Biggleswade 80-85; Hon Can St Alb 85-90; V Holbeach *Linc* from 90. *The Vicarage, Holbeach, Spalding, Lincs PE12 7DT* Holbeach (0406) 22185

HILL, Peter. b 50. Man Univ BSc71 Nottm Univ MTh90. Wycliffe Hall Ox 81. **d** 83 **p** 84. C Porchester *S'well* 83-86; V Huthwaite from 86. *The Vicarage, Blackwell Road, Huthwaite, Sutton-in-Ashfield NG17 2QT* Mansfield (0623) 555053

HILL, Ralph Jasper. b 15. Tyndale Hall Bris 38. **d** 41 **p** 42. Asst Master Hove Gr Sch 65-78; rtd 80; Perm to Offic Chich from 82. *29 Gorham Way, Telscombe Cliffs, Newhaven, E Sussex BN9 7BA* Peacehaven (0273) 583729

HILL, Raymond John Walter. b 09. AKC34. **d** 34 **p** 35. V Westbury and Turweston *Ox* 65-77; C-in-c Shalstone w

Biddlesden 68-77; rtd 77; Perm to Offic *Glouc* from 78. *15 Shepherds Way, Stow on the Wold, Cheltenham, Glos GL54 1EA* Cotswold (0451) 31028

HILL, Raymond William. b 17. S'wark Ord Course. **d** 63 **p** 64. V Oulton Broad *Nor* 69-84; rtd 84; Perm to Offic *Chich* from 85. *30 The Dene, Uckfield, E Sussex TN22 1LB* Uckfield (0825) 764488

HILL, Richard Brian. b 47. Dur Univ BA68 DipTh70. Cranmer Hall Dur 68 Westcott Ho Cam 70. **d** 71 **p** 72. C Cockermouth All SS w Ch Ch *Carl* 71-74; C Barrow St Geo w St Luke 74-76; V Walney Is 76-83; Dir of Clergy Tr 83-90; P-in-c Westward, Rosley-w-Woodside and Welton 83-90; V Gosforth All SS *Newc* from 90. *All Saints' Vicarage, 33 Brackenfield Road, Newcastle upon Tyne NE3 4DX* 091-285 6345

HILL, Preb Richard Hebert. b 11. Linc Th Coll 34. **d** 36 **p** 37. C-in-c Pencombe w Marston Stannett and Lt Cowarne *Heref* 69-72; R Ledbury 72-78; RD Ledbury 72-78; P-in-c Eastnor 73-78; rtd 78; Perm to Offic *Heref* from 79. *4 Old School, Henley Road, Ludlow, Shropshire SY8 1RA* Ludlow (0584) 874332

HILL, Richard Hugh Oldham. b 52. CCC Ox BA74 BA77 MA78. Wycliffe Hall Ox 75. **d** 78 **p** 79. C Harold Wood *Chelmsf* 78-81; C Hampreston *Sarum* 81-86; TV N Ferriby *York* from 86. *St Barnabas House, 36 Dower Rise, Swanland, N Humberside HU14 3QT* Hull (0482) 631271

HILL, Richard Owen. b 40. Liv Univ BA63 MA65. Cuddesdon Coll 65. **d** 68 **p** 69. C Reading St Luke *Ox* 68-72; C Towcester w Easton Neston *Pet* 72-73; C Cowley St Jo *Ox* 73-75; C Walker *Newc* 75-78; P-in-c Tynemouth H Trin W Town 78-82; C Wallsend St Luke 82-83; C Didcot St Pet *Ox* 84-88; rtd 88. *44 Blewbury Road, East Hagbourne, Oxford OX11 9LF* Didcot (0235) 813073

HILL, Robert Joseph. b 45. Oak Hill Th Coll BA81. **d** 81 **p** 82. C W Derby St Luke *Liv* 81-84; P-in-c Devonport St Mich *Ex* from 84. *St Michael's Vicarage, 41 Albert Road, Plymouth PL2 1AB* Plymouth (0752) 562967

HILL, Robin. b 35. Cranmer Hall Dur 59. **d** 62 **p** 63. C Aspley *S'well* 62-65; V Mansf St Aug 65-71; R Hulland, Atlow and Bradley *Derby* 71-76; Australia 76-86; P-in-c Alkmonton, Cubley, Marston, Montgomery etc *Derby* from 86. *The Vicarage, Cubley, Ashbourne, Derby DE6 3DL* Ashbourne (0335) 330680

HILL, Roger Anthony John. b 45. Liv Univ BA67 Linacre Coll Ox BA69 MA. Ripon Hall Ox 67. **d** 70 **p** 71. C St Helier *S'wark* 70-74; C Dawley Parva *Lich* 74-75; C Cen Telford 76-77; TV 77-81; TR 81-88; TR Newark w Hawton, Cotham and Shelton *S'well* 88-89; TR Newark-upon-Trent from 89; RD Newark from 90. *The Rectory, 6 Bede House Lane, Newark, Notts NG24 1PY* Newark (0636) 704513

HILL, Sidney John. b 16. MBE45. Oak Hill Th Coll 46. **d** 48 **p** 49. V Wembdon *B & W* 63-74; Chapl Chantilly w Rouen and Le Havre *Eur* 74-78; R Gressenhall w Longham and Bittering Parva *Nor* 78-81; rtd 81. *1 Jarvis Close, Stalbridge, Sturminster Newton, Dorset DT10 2PQ* Stalbridge (0963) 62728

HILL, Simon George. b 53. Reading Univ BSc75 MSc78 Lon Univ DipRS82. S'wark Ord Course 80. **d** 83 **p** 84. Hon C Croydon St Aug *Cant* 83; Swaziland 84-86; Hon C Croydon St Aug *S'wark* from 88. *20 Tirlemont Road, South Croydon, Surrey CR2 6DS* 081-680 2570

HILL, Canon Thomas Henry. b 19. Univ of Wales BA41 BD45. **d** 66 **p** 67. R Glyncorrwg w Afan Vale and Cymmer Afan *Llan* 71-74; V Pemb St Mary and St Mich *St D* 74-84; Can St D Cathl 80-84; rtd 84. *29 Mortimer Hill, Tring, Herts HP23 5JB* Tring (044282) 6558

HILL, Trevor Walton. b 30. Leeds Univ BA57. Coll of Resurr Mirfield. **d** 59 **p** 60. C Bollington St Jo *Ches* 59-62; C Woodchurch 62-64; V Addingham *Carl* 64-67; V Carl H Trin 67-71; R Wetheral w Warw 71-80; P-in-c Doddington w Wychling *Cant* 80-82; P-in-c Newnham 80-82. *Address temp unknown*

HILL, William Henry George. b 21. S'wark Ord Course 66. **d** 69 **p** 70. C Welling *S'wark* 69-73; C Reigate St Luke S Park 73-76; V Lynsted w Kingsdown *Cant* 76-87; R Norton 76-87; rtd 87. *Little Orchard, 15 Bramley Hill, Bridport, Dorset DT6 3DP* Bridport (0308) 23915

HILL, William James. b 13. Ripon Hall Ox 60. **d** 61 **p** 62. V Chinley w Buxworth *Derby* 68-74; R Whitwell 74-77; P-in-c Denby 77-79; rtd 79; Perm to Offic *Derby* from 79. *Greenstile, 15 Harewood Road, Allestree, Derby DE3 2JP* Derby (0332) 556135

HILL-TOUT, Mark Laurence. b 50. AKC73. **d** 74 **p** 75. C Brighton Resurr *Chich* 74-77; C New Shoreham 77-79; C Old Shoreham 77-79; Dioc Stewardship Adv Lewes

and Hastings 79-84; P-in-c Stonegate 79-83; R Horsted Keynes 84-89; V St Helens *Portsm* from 89; V Sea View from 89. *The Vicarage, Eddington Road, St Helens, Ryde, Isle of Wight PO33 1XT* Isle of Wight (0983) 875190

HILLARY, Leslie Tyrone James. b 59. Cranmer Hall Dur 84. **d** 87 **p** 88. C Middlesb All SS *York* 87-89; C Stainton-in-Cleveland from 89. *4 Barwick Close, Stockton-on-Tees, Cleveland TS17 0RH* Stockton-on-Tees (0642) 766033

HILLEBRAND, Frank David. b 46. AKC68. St Boniface Warminster 68. **d** 69 **p** 70. C Wood Green St Mich *Lon* 69-72; C Evesham *Worc* 72-75; V Worc H Trin 75-80; P-in-c Kidderminster St Jo 80-81; V 81-90; TR Kidderminster St Jo and H Innocents 90-91; TV High Wycombe *Ox* from 91. *The Vicarage, Priory Avenue, High Wycombe, Bucks HP13 6SH* High Wycombe (0494) 25602

HILLIARD, David. b 57. BTh. **d** 91. C Holywood *D & D* from 91. *51 Princess Gardens, Holywood, Co Down BT18 0PN* Holywood (02317) 4554

HILLIARD, Canon Dennis Robert Coote. b 11. TCD BA34 MA44. **d** 35 **p** 36. I Can Kildare Cathl *M & K* 71-80; I Geashill 71-80; rtd 80. *37 New Court Road, Bray, Co Wicklow, Irish Republic* Dublin (1) 868739

HILLIARD, Very Rev George Percival St John. b 45. TCD BA67. **d** 69 **p** 70. C Seapatrick *D & D* 69-73; C Carrickfergus *Conn* 73-76; I Fanlobbus Union *C, C & R* 76-85; Prec Cork Cathl from 85; I Cloyne Union from 85; Dean Cloyne from 85. *The Deanery, Dungourney Road, Midleton, Co Cork, Irish Republic* Cork (21) 631449

HILLIARD, John William Richard. b 19. St Jo Coll Morpeth 54. **d** 55 **p** 56. I Carbury *M & K* 68-72; C W Bridgford *S'well* 72-78; V Mansf St Aug 78-84; P-in-c Everton and Mattersey w Clayworth 84-87; rtd 87. *Flat 4, Spencer Court, Merton Road, Southsea, Hants PO5 2AJ* Portsmouth (0705) 293918

HILLIARD, Robert Godfrey. b 52. Univ of Wales DipTh75. St Mich Coll Llan. **d** 75 **p** 76. C Whitchurch *Llan* 75-80; Chapl RN from 80. *c/o MOD, Lacon House, Theobald's Road, London WC1X 8RY* 071-430 6847

HILLIER, Derek John. b 30. Sarum Th Coll 61. **d** 63 **p** 64. C Salisbury St Mark *Sarum* 63-65; C Weymouth H Trin 65-66; R Caundle Bishop w Caundle Marsh and Holwell 66-75; P-in-c Pulham 70-78; R The Caundles and Holwell 75-81; R The Caundles w Folke and Holwell from 81. *The Rectory, Bishops Caundle, Sherborne, Dorset DT9 5ND* Bishops Caundle (0963) 23243

HILLMAN, Jesse James. b 22. S'wark Ord Course 83. **d** 86 **p** 87. Communications Sec CMS 86; NSM Kidbrooke St Jas *S'wark* 86; NSM Peterchurch w Vowchurch, Turnastone and Dorstone *Heref* from 86. *Wesley Place, Peterchurch, Hereford HR2 0RY* Peterchurch (0981) 550609

HILLMAN, John Anthony. b 32. St Chad's Coll Dur BA53. St Mich Coll Llan 54. **d** 55 **p** 56. C Llangollen *St As* 56-60; S Africa 60-86; TV Wolstanton *Lich* from 86. *The Vicarage, 14 Dorrington Grove, Newcastle, Staffs ST5 0HY* Newcastle-under-Lyme (0782) 635709

HILLS, John Bucknell. b 21. Glouc Sch of Min. **d** 89 **p** 89. NSM Moreton-in-Marsh w Batsford, Todenham etc *Glouc* from 89. *1 Corders Lane, Moreton-in-Marsh, Glos GL56 0BU* Moreton-in-Marsh (0608) 51507

HILLS, Mervyn Hyde. b 19. Ch Coll Cam BA40 MA44. Westcott Ho Cam 40. **d** 42 **p** 43. V Bourn *Ely* 53-86; R Kingston 53-86; rtd 86; Perm to Offic *Ely* from 87. *13 Bakers' Close, Comberton, Cambridge* Cambridge (0223) 262993

HILLS, Michael John. b 58. BA82. Westcott Ho Cam 87. **d** 88 **p** 89. C Workington St Jo *Carl* 88-91; C Gosforth All SS *Newc* from 91. *All Saints' Clergy House, West Avenue, Gosforth, Newcastle upon Tyne NE3 4ES* 091-285 7864

HILLS, Michael William John. b 54. Univ of Wales (Lamp) BA84. Westcott Ho Cam 85. **d** 87 **p** 88. C Reddish *Man* 87-91; V Bolton St Phil from 91. *St Philip's Vicarage, 453 Bridgeman Street, Bolton BL3 6TH* Bolton (0204) 61533

HILLS, Richard Leslie. b 36. FMA83 Qu Coll Cam MA63 DIC64 Man Univ PhD68. St Deiniol's Hawarden 85. **d** 87 **p** 88. C Urmston *Man* 87-89; C Gt Yarmouth *Nor* 89-90; NSM Mottram in Longdendale w Woodhead *Ches* from 90. *Stamford Cottage, 47 Old Road, Mottram, Hyde, Cheshire SK14 6LW* Mottram (0457) 763104

HILLS, Roger Malcolm. b 42. Oak Hill Th Coll 83. **d** 86 **p** 87. Hon C Mill Hill Jo Keble Ch *Lon* from 86; NSM Mill Hill St Mich from 86. *22 Sefton Avenue, London NW7 3QD* 081-959 1931

HILLS, Rowland Jonathan. b 12. Selw Coll Cam BA35 MA39. Cuddesdon Coll 36. **d** 37 **p** 38. R Iffley *Ox* 59-75; rtd 75; Perm to Offic *Ox* from 76; Chapl Venice w Trieste *Eur* 79-80; Chapl San Remo w Bordighera 81. *19 Church Way, Iffley, Oxford OX4 4DY* Oxford (0865) 771059

HILLS-HARROP, George Douglas. b 16. Trin Hall Cam BA37 MA41 Birm Univ DipEd38. Sarum Th Coll 50. **d** 51 **p** 52. V Higher Bebington *Ches* 58-61; Perm to Offic *Ex* 65-79 and from 86; *Heref & S&B* 79-86; rtd 81. *12 Highfield, Lapford, Crediton, Devon EX17 6PY* Crediton (0363) 22272

HILLYER, Charles Norman. b 21. Lon Univ BD48. Lambeth STh67 ALCD48. **d** 48 **p** 49. V Ponsbourne *St Alb* 59-70; Chapl Tolmers Park Hosp 59-70; Lib Tyndale Ho Cam 70-73; Org Ed UCCF 73-79; Sec Tyndale Fellowship Bibl Research Cam 73-75; P-in-c Hatherleigh *Ex* 79-81; V 81-86; rtd 86; Perm to Offic *Sarum* from 89. *Charters, The Avenue, Sherborne, Dorset DT9 3AJ* Sherborne (0935) 813357

HILTON, Clive. b 30. K Coll Lon 54. **d** 58 **p** 59. C Wythenshawe Wm Temple Ch CD *Man* 58-61; C Newton Heath All SS 61-62; C-in-c Oldham St Chad Limeside CD 62-65; V Oldham St Chad Limeside 65-70; P-in-c Gravesend H Family *Roch* 70-71; R Killamarsh *Derby* 71-88; R Broughton w Loddington and Cransley etc *Pet* from 88. *The Rectory, Gate Lane, Broughton, Kettering, Northants NN14 1ND* Kettering (0536) 790235

HILTON, Ian Anthony. b 57. St Jo Coll Nottm 83. **d** 86 **p** 87. C Nottm St Sav *S'well* 86-90; C Aspley from 90. *13 Hilcot Drive, Aspley, Nottingham NG8 5HR* Nottingham (0602) 784990

HILTON, John. b 49. Ex Univ BA70. Cuddesdon Coll 71. **d** 73 **p** 74. C W Derby (or Tuebrook) St Jo *Liv* 73-79; V Orford St Andr from 79. *St Andrew's Vicarage, Poplars Avenue, Orford, Warrington WA2 9UE* Warrington (0925) 31903

HILTON, John Read. b 41. Lon Univ BD63 AKC65 LSE BSc73. **d** 65 **p** 66. C Cov H Trin *Cov* 65-69; C Hemel Hempstead *St Alb* 69-70; Hon C Catford St Andr *S'wark* 70-81. *89 Arngask Road, Catford, London SE6 1XZ* 081-698 1965

HILTON-TURVEY, Geoffrey Michael. b 34. Oak Hill Th Coll 80. **d** 81 **p** 82. C Bispham *Blackb* 81-85; V Inskip from 85. *St Peter's Vicarage, Inskip, Preston PR4 0TT* Catforth (0772) 690316

HINCHEY, Peter John. b 30. **d** 58 **p** 59. C Malden St Jo *S'wark* 58-61; V Rosherville *Roch* 61-67; V Gillingham St Aug 67-72; V Bromley St Andr 72-74; Hon Chapl to Bp 74-78; Hon C Lamorbey H Redeemer 76-78; R Foots Cray 78-81. *Address temp unknown*

HINCHLIFF, George Victor. b 19. TCD BA41. CITC Div Test42. **d** 42 **p** 43. I Clonfeacle w Derrygortreavy *Arm* 64-85; rtd 85. *7 Montague Villas, Tandragee, Craigavon, Co Armagh BT62 2ES* Craigavon (0762) 841301

HINCHLIFF, Canon Peter Bingham. b 29. Rhodes Univ Grahamstown BA48 PhD58 Trin Coll Ox BA50 MA54 BD62 DD64. St Paul's Grahamstown 51. **d** 52 **p** 53. S Africa 52-69; Can Grahamstown Cathl 64-69; Hon Can Grahamstown from 69; Sec Ch Assembly Miss and Ecum Coun 69-72; Fell and Tutor Ball Coll Ox from 72; Chapl 72-87; Can Th Cov Cathl *Cov* from 72. *Balliol College, Oxford OX1 3BJ* Oxford (0865) 277731

✠**HIND, Rt Rev John William.** b 45. Leeds Univ BA66. Cuddesdon Coll 70. **d** 72 **p** 73 **c** 91. C Catford (Southend) and Downham *S'wark* 72-76; V Forest Hill Ch Ch 76-82; P-in-c Forest Hill St Paul 81-82; Wiccamical Preb Chich Cathl *Chich* 82-91; Prin Chich Th Coll 82-91; Suff Bp Horsham *Chich* from 91. *Bishop's Lodge, Worth, Crawley, W Sussex RH10 4RT* Crawley (0293) 883051

HIND, Canon Stanley Maurice. b 29. AKC53. **d** 54 **p** 55. C Haydock St Jas *Liv* 54-57; C Elland *Wakef* 57-60; V Mirfield Eastthorpe St Paul 60-67; V Carleton 67-78; V E Hardwick 72-78; V Morley St Pet w Churwell 78-86; V Womersley 86-87; P-in-c Kirk Smeaton 86-87; V Womersley and Kirk Smeaton from 87; Hon Can Wakef Cathl from 89. *The Vicarage, Womersley, Doncaster, S Yorkshire DN6 9BG* Pontefract (0977) 620436

HINDE, Richard Standish Elphinstone. b 12. Peterho Cam BA34 MA38 St Pet Hall Ox MA39 BLitt48 MLitt79 TCD MA62. Wycliffe Hall Ox 34. **d** 35 **p** 36. Perm to Offic *Lon* 69-72; CV Ch Ch Cathl Dub *D & G* 74-82; rtd 82. *28 Seaview, Kilcoole, Co Wicklow, Irish Republic* Dublin (1) 287-6923

HINDLE, Miss Penelope Jane Bowyn. b 45. Trin Coll Bris 76. dss 84 **d** 87. Stoneycroft All SS *Liv* 84-87; Par Dn 87-89; Asst Chapl R Free Hosp Lon from 89. *The*

Garden Flat, 40 College Crescent, London NW3 5LB 071-586 7384

HINDLEY, Andrew David. b 59. Univ of Wales (Lamp) BA. Sarum & Wells Th Coll. **d** 82 **p** 83. C Huddersfield St Pet *Wakef* 82-84; C Huddersfield St Pet and All SS 84-86; P-in-c Holmfield 86-91; R Ribchester w Stidd *Blackb* from 91; Bp's Adv for Leisure and Tourism from 91; Chapl Ribchester Hosp from 91. *The Rectory, Riverside, Ribchester, Preston PR3 3XS* Ribchester (0254) 989352

HINDLEY, Anthony Talbot. b 41. Bernard Gilpin Soc Dur 61 Oak Hill Th Coll 62. **d** 66 **p** 67. C Stoke next Guildf St Jo *Guildf* 66-69; Kenya 70-78; C Redhill H Trin *S'wark* 78-79; P-in-c Eastbourne All So *Chich* 79-83; V 83-86; V S Malling from 86. *The Vicarage, Church Lane, South Malling, Lewes, E Sussex BN7 2JA* Lewes (0273) 474387

HINDLEY, Dr Godfrey Talbot. b 09. Ch Coll Cam BChir34 MB35 MA46. **d** 66 **p** 67. Tanzania 66-70; Kenya 70-75; Perm to Offic *Ex* from 81. *21 Delves House West, Ringmer, Lewes, E Sussex BN8 5JW* Lewes (0273) 813597

HINDLEY, John. b 32. UWIST BSc71. **d** 84 **p** 85. NSM Llantilio Crossenny w Penrhos, Llanvetherine etc *Mon* 85-88; P-in-c Tilbrook *Ely* from 88; P-in-c Covington from 88; P-in-c Keyston and Bythorn from 88; P-in-c Catworth Magna from 88; RD Leightonstone from 89. *The Rectory, Church Lane, Tilbrook, Huntingdon, Cambs PE18 0JS* Huntingdon (0480) 860147

HINDLEY, Roger Dennis. b 48. Birm Univ BA70 Ox Univ BA77 MA83. Ripon Coll Cuddesdon 75 Qu Coll Birm 77. **d** 78 **p** 79. C Rubery *Birm* 78-81; C Henbury *Bris* 81-83; V Erdington St Chad *Birm* 83-89; V Hill from 89. *61 Mere Green Road, Sutton Coldfield, W Midlands B75 5BW* 021-308 0074

HINDLEY, Thomas Richard. b 31. ARIBA54 Sheff Univ BA53 Lon Univ BD66. Clifton Th Coll 61. **d** 63 **p** 64. C Kenilworth St Jo *Cov* 63-67; C Cheadle *Ches* 67-70; R Harpurhey Ch Ch *Man* from 70; R Harpurhey St Steph from 72. *Christ Church Rectory, Church Lane, Manchester M9 1BG* 061-205 4020

HINDS, Kenneth Arthur Lancelot. b 30. Bps' Coll Cheshunt. **d** 64 **p** 65. C Sawbridgeworth *St Alb* 64-67; C Gt Berkhamsted 67-71; V Boreham Wood St Mich 71-75; Trinidad and Tobago 75-79; P-in-c Gt Ilford St Luke *Chelmsf* 79-81; V from 81. *St Luke's Vicarage, Baxter Road, Ilford, Essex IG1 2HN* 081-478 1104

HINDS, Paul Anthony. b 62. **d** 88 **p** 89. C Skewen *Llan* 88-90; C Roath St Marg from 90. *St Anne's House, 3 Snipe Street, Roath, Cardiff CF2 3RB* Cardiff (0222) 884103

HINE, Canon John Timothy Matusch. b 27. TCD BA51 MA54. Linc Th Coll 53. **d** 55 **p** 56. C Boston *Linc* 55-57; PV, Sacr and Succ Lin Cathl 57-60; C Bray and Braywood *Ox* 60-61; Min Can Windsor 60-62; V Laneast w St Clether *Truro* 62-65; V Tresmere 62-65; V Fareham H Trin *Portsm* 65-67; V Asthall and Swinbrook w Widford *Ox* from 67; RD Witney 76-81 and 87-89; Hon Can Ch Ch from 88. *The Vicarage, Swinbrook, Oxford OX8 4DY* Burford (099382) 3200

HINE, John Victor. b 36. Open Univ BA82. Carl Dioc Tr Course 85. **d** 88 **p** 89. NSM Dean *Carl* from 88; NSM Clifton from 88. *Woodbank, Ullock, Workington, Cumbria CA14 4TP* Lamplugh (0946) 861752

HINE, Keith Ernest. b 50. Bradf Univ BA Leeds Univ CertEd. Nor Ord Course 89. **d** 89 **p** 90. C Wilmslow *Ches* from 89. *25 Stanneylands Road, Wilmslow, Cheshire SK9 4EJ* Wilmslow (0625) 533397

HINES, Canon Frank. b 13. Tyndale Hall Bris 36. **d** 39 **p** 40. V Claybrooke w Wibtoft *Leic* 71-78; rtd 78. *28 Overdale Road, Bayston Hill, Shrewsbury SY3 0LG* Bayston Hill (074372) 2617

HINES, Dr Richard Arthur. b 49. MSc PhD K Coll Lon MTh89. Oak Hill Th Coll 82. **d** 84 **p** 85. C Mile Cross *Nor* 84-87; Lect Oak Hill Th Coll from 87. *2 Farm Lane, Chase Side, London N14 4PP* 081-441 0568

HINEY, Thomas Bernard Felix. b 35. MC61. Ridley Hall Cam 67. **d** 69 **p** 70. C Edgbaston St Aug *Birm* 69-71; CF from 71. *c/o MOD (Army), Bagshot Park, Bagshot, Surrey GU19 5PL* Bagshot (0276) 71717

HINGE, Canon David Gerald Francis. b 30. FRSA57. Wells Th Coll 64. **d** 66 **p** 67. C Highgate Rise St Anne Brookfield *Lon* 66-69; C N Greenford All Hallows 69-71; V Winton *Man* 71-78; R Etherley *Dur* from 78; Hon Can Dur Cathl from 90. *The Rectory, Etherley, Bishop Auckland, Co Durham DL14 0HN* Bishop Auckland (0388) 832350

HINGE, Derek Colin. b 36. CChem60 MRSC60 Imp Coll Lon BSc58. St Alb Minl Tr Scheme 84. **d** 88 **p** 89. NSM

Bishop's Stortford St Mich *St Alb* from 88. *12 Avenue Road, Bishop's Stortford, Herts CM23 5NU* Bishop's Stortford (0279) 652173

HINGLEY, Bernadette. b 48. Lon Univ BSc70 York Univ CertEd73. St Jo Coll Nottm DPS77 DipTh78. **dss** 81 **d** 87. Ripon Coll Cuddesdon 81-83; W Slough *Ox* 81-83; Chapl Qu Eliz Hosp Birm 84-88; NSM Balsall Heath St Paul *Birm* 84-90; Perm to Offic from 90. *23 Woodview Drive, Edgbaston, Birmingham B15 2JF* 021-440 6343

HINGLEY, Christopher James Howard. b 48. Trin Coll Ox BA69 MA71. Wycliffe Hall Ox 81. **d** 80 **p** 81. Zimbabwe 80-81; Lic to Offic *Ox* 85-87. *Wycliffe Hall, Oxford 0X2 6PW* Oxford (0865) 274200

HINGLEY, Robert Charles. b 46. Ball Coll Ox BA69 MA74 Birm Univ CertEd73. Qu Coll Birm DipTh72. **d** 73 **p** 74. C Old Charlton *S'wark* 73-76; Asst Warden Iona Abbey 76-77; TV Langley Marish *Ox* 77-83; V Balsall Heath St Paul *Birm* 83-90; Perm to Offic from 90. *23 Woodview Drive, Edgbaston, Birmingham B15 2JF* 021-440 6343

HINGLEY, Roderick Stanley Plant. b 51. St Chad's Coll Dur BA72. St Steph Ho Ox 74. **d** 75 **p** 76. C Lower Gornal *Lich* 75-79; C Tividale 79-82; C Broseiey w Benthall *Heref* 82-84; C Wanstead St Mary *Chelmsf* from 84. *13 Wanstead Place, London E11 2SW* 081-530-4970

HINKES, Sidney George Stuart. b 25. Lon Univ BA50 BD70. St Steph Ho Ox 50. **d** 52 **p** 53. C-in-c Bayswater St Mary *CD* Ox 66-82; V Headington St Mary 83-90; rtd 90; Perm to Offic *B & W* 90-91. *c/o Mrs M Mander, 38 McLeod Street, Upper Hutt, New Zealand*

HINKLEY, Canon William Taylor. b 12. St Jo Coll Dur BA34 MA38. **d** 35 **p** 36. RD Alnwick *Newc* 67-81; V Alnwick St Mich 66-74; V Alnwick w Edlingham and Bolton Chpl 74-80; rtd 88. *Woodlea, Denwick, Alnwick, Northd NE66 3RE* Alnwick (0665) 602237

HINKSMAN, Barrie Lawrence John. b 41. K Coll Lon BD64 AKC64 Lon Gestalt Cen GDipP77. St Boniface Warminster 61. **d** 65 **p** 66. C Crosby *Linc* 65-67; Ecum Development Officer Scunthorpe Coun of Chs 67-69; C Chelmsley Wood *Birm* 69-72; TV 72-75; P-in-c Offchurch *Cov* 75-79; Dioc Tr Officer 79-91; Perm to Offic 89-90; Lic to Offic from 90. *South Bank House, 67 Cubbington Road, Lillington, Leamington Spa, Warks CV32 7AQ* Leamington Spa (0926) 882393

HINTON, David Hugh. b 31. Tyndale Hall Bris. **d** 63 **p** 64. C Bowling St Steph *Bradf* 67-71; V Denholme Gate 71-79; P-in-c Morton St Luke 79-85; V 85-86; rtd 86; Perm to Offic *Bradf* from 86. *11 Irwell Street, Bradford BD4 7EQ* Bradford (0274) 722858

HINTON, John Dorsett Owen. b 21. Wells Th Coll 59. **d** 61 **p** 62. V Pucklechurch and Abson w Dyrham *Bris* 67-86; rtd 86; Perm to Offic *Bris* from 86. *Tower House, Clifton Down Road, Bristol BS8 4AG* Bristol (0272) 739298

HINTON, Michael Ernest. b 33. K Coll Lon. **d** 57 **p** 58. C Babbacombe *Ex* 57-60; S Africa 60-66; P-in-c Limehouse St Pet *Lon* 66-68; R Felmingham *Nor* 68-72; R Suffield 68-72; P-in-c Colby w Banningham and Tuttington 68-72; Bahamas 72-76; P-in-c Mylor w Flushing *Truro* 76-77; V 77-80; R The Deverills *Sarum* 82-87; Bermuda from 87. *Address temp unknown*

HINTON, Michael George. b 27. Mert Coll Ox BA48 MA51 Reading Univ PhD59. S Dios Minl Tr Scheme 81. **d** 83 **p** 84. NSM Weston-super-Mare St Paul *B & W* 83-85; NSM Sibertswold w Coldred *Cant* 85-87; NSM Eythorne and Elvington w Waldershare etc from 87. *The Vicarage, Shepherdswell, Dover, Kent CT15 7LF* Dover (0304) 830245

HINTON, Roger Amos. b 33. Keble Coll Ox BA56 MA60. Ridley Hall Cam 56. **d** 58 **p** 59. C Drypool St Columba *York* 58-61; CMS 62-76; India 62-67; Tutor CMS Tr Coll Chislehurst 67-69; Pakistan 69-76; V Coalville *Leic* 76-78; V Coalville and Bardon Hill 78-85; RD Akeley S (Coalville) 81-84; TR Bushbury *Lich* from 85. *The Rectory, Bushbury Lane, Bushbury, Wolverhampton WV10 8JP* Wolverhampton (0902) 782226

HIPKINS, John Malcolm. b 33. MInstM. Qu Coll Birm 78. **d** 80 **p** 81. C Clayton *Lich* 80; C Derby St Luke *Derby* 81-84; V Chaddesden St Phil 84-88; rtd 88. *1 Kensington Close, Penrhyd, Amlwch, Gwynedd LL68 0RR* Amlwch (0407) 830082

HIPKINS, Leslie Michael. b 35. ACIS60 Univ Coll Dur BA57. Westcott Ho Cam 89 Oak Hill Th Coll 78. **d** 81 **p** 82. NSM Halstead St Andr w H Trin and Greenstead Green *Chelmsf* from 84; C Tolleshunt Knights w Tiptree and Gt Braxted 87-89; P-in-c Cratfield w Heveningham and Ubbeston etc *St E* from 89. *The Vicarage, Cratfield, Halesworth, Suffolk IP19 0BU* Ubbeston (098683) 564

HIPWELL, Canon Trevor Senior. b 23. TCD BA47. **d** 47 **p** 48. C Limerick St Mary *L & K* 47-49; Min Can St Patr

Cathl Dub 49-54 and 64-75; C Taney Ch Ch *D & G* 49-56; I Dub Mt Merrion from 56; Chapl Univ Coll Dub from 75; Preb Monmohenock St Patr Cathl Dub from 75. *Foster Avenue, Mount Merrion, Blackrock, Co Dublin, Irish Republic* Dublin (1) 288-0268

HIRONS, Malcolm Percy. b 36. Or Coll Ox BA59 MA62. Wycliffe Hall Ox 59. **d** 61 **p** 62. C Edgbaston St Aug *Birm* 61-64; Chapl Warw Sch 64-65; C Beverley Minster *York* 65-69; V Barnby upon Don *Sheff* 69-80; P-in-c Kirk Bramwith 75-80; P-in-c Fenwick 75-80; V Norton Woodseats St Paul from 80. *St Paul's Vicarage, 52 Norton Lees Lane, Sheffield S8 9BD* Sheffield (0742) 551945

HIRST, Alan. b 44. Leeds Univ CQSW74. Linc Th Coll 79. **d** 81 **p** 82. C Newton Heath All SS *Man* 81-84; Chapl to the Deaf 84-88; V Oldham St Chad Limeside 88-91; Dep Chapl HM Pris Liv from 91. *The Chaplain's Office, HM Prison, 68 Hornby Road, Liverpool L9 3DP* 051-525 5971

HIRST, Anthony Melville. b 50. Keele Univ BA73. Cuddesdon Coll 74. **d** 77 **p** 78. C S Gillingham *Roch* 77-80; C Coity w Nolton *Llan* 80-83; OSB from 81; R Hallaton w Horninghold, Allexton, Tugby etc *Leic* 83-90; V Arthog w Fairbourne w Llangelynin w Rhoslefain *Ban* from 90. *The Rectory, Fairbourne, Gwynedd LL37 2JB* Fairbourne (0341) 250919

HIRST, David William. b 37. Man Univ BA78. Brasted Th Coll 59 St Aid Birkenhead 61. **d** 63 **p** 64. C Clayton *Man* 63-64; C Bury St Jo 64-66; C Wythenshawe Wm Temple Ch 67-70; V Oldham St Chad Limeside 70-79; V Friezland from 79. *The Vicarage, Church Road, Friezland, Greenfield, Oldham OL3 7LQ* Saddleworth (0457) 872507

HIRST, Douglas. b 33. Oak Hill Th Coll 89. **d** 91. NSM Thorley *St Alb* from 91. *Axholme, 68 Cannons Close, Bishop's Stortford, Herts CM23 2BQ* Bishop's Stortford (0279) 651345

HIRST, Canon Godfrey Ian. b 41. MBIM Univ of Wales (Lamp) BA63. Chich Th Coll 63. **d** 65 **p** 66. C Brierfield *Blackb* 65-68; Ind Chapl *Liv* 68-71; TV Kirkby 71-75; Ind Chapl *Blackb* from 75; P-in-c Treales 75-87; Hon Can Blackb Cathl 83-87; Can Res Blackb Cathl from 87. *24 Bosburn Drive, Mellor Brook, Blackburn BB2 7PA* Blackburn (0254) 813544

HIRST, John Adrian. b 49. St Jo Coll Nottm BTh78. **d** 78 **p** 79. C Cheltenham St Mark *Glouc* 78-84; TV 84-85; TV Swan *Ox* 85-89; R Denham from 89. *The Rectory, Ashmead Lane, Denham, Uxbridge, Middx UB9 5BB* Denham (0895) 832771

HIRST, Peter Thornton. b 34. Leeds Univ BA59. Ely Th Coll 59. **d** 61 **p** 62. C Brierley Hill *Lich* 61-64; C Wednesfield St Thos 64-66; R Salford St Bart *Man* 66-71; V Sedgley St Mary *Lich* 71-77; TR Billingham St Aid *Dur* 77-86; TR Elland *Wakef* 86-90. *197 Bradley Road, Bradley Grange, Huddersfield HD2 1QF* Huddersfield (0484) 530260

HIRST, Reginald Arnold Archer. b 36. St Paul's Grahamstown. **d** 60 **p** 61. S Africa 60-88; R Wickham *Portsm* from 88. *The Rectory, Southwick Road, Wickham, Fareham, Hants PO17 6HR* Fareham (0329) 832134

HIRST, Roland Geoffrey. b 42. St Cath Coll Cam BA63 MA68. NW Ord Course 74. **d** 77 **p** 78. C Beverley St Mary *York* 77-80; P-in-C Flamborough and Bempton 80-83; V 83-86; R Bolton Abbey *Bradf* from 86. *The Beeches, Bolton Abbey, Skipton, N Yorkshire BD26 6EX* Bolton Abbey (075671) 326 or 238

HIRST, Wilfrid. b 11. Roch Th Coll 65. **d** 66 **p** 67. C Shere *Guildf* 69-71; R Kelly w Bradstone *Ex* 71-74; R Exbourne w Jacobstowe 74-77; rtd 77; Perm to Offic *Chich* from 77. *3 Park Drive, Felpham, Bognor Regis, W Sussex PO22 7RD* Middleton-on-Sea (0243) 584058

HISCOCK, David Alan. b 52. Sarum & Wells Th Coll. **d** 85 **p** 86. C Charlton Kings St Mary *Glouc* 85-89; TV Swan *Ox* from 89. *The Rectory, Marsh Gibbon, Bicester, Oxon OX6 0HJ* Bicester (0869) 7297

HISCOCK, Gary Edward. b 43. DipDrama68 Lon Univ DipRS88. Oak Hill Th Coll BA90. **d** 90 **p** 91. C Cheltenham St Luke and St Jo *Glouc* from 90. *18 Eldon Road, Cheltenham, Glos GL52 6TU* Cheltenham (0242) 528567

HISCOCK, Peter George Harold. b 31. Wadh Coll Ox BA54 MA66. Ely Th Coll 54. **d** 58 **p** 59. C Edge Hill St Dunstan *Liv* 58-61; C Kirkby 61-64; C Southport St Luke 64-66; Asst Dean of Residence TCD 66-68; Dean of Residence TCD 68-73; India 73-76; TV Jarrow *Dur* 77-82; Chapl Univ Coll Dur 82-87; RD Newc Cen *Newc* from 87; P-in-c Dinnington 87-88; TV Ch the King in the Dio of Newc from 88. *The Vicarage, 2 East Acres,*

Dinnington, Newcastle upon Tyne NE13 7NA
Ponteland (0661) 71377

HISCOX, Edward. b 23. Univ of Wales (Lamp) BA54. Wells Th Coll 54. **d** 56 **p** 57. C Swansea St Gabr *S & B* 56-59; C Llanguicke 59-64; V Drypool St Columba w St Andr and St Pet *York* 64-75; R Daglingworth w the Duntisbournes and Winstone *Glouc* from 75. *The Rectory, Daglingworth, Cirencester, Glos GL7 7AL* Cirencester (0285) 4561

HISCOX, Jonathan Ronald James. b 64. Univ of Wales (Cardiff) DipTh85. Qu Coll Birm 87. **d** 89 **p** 90. C Wiveliscombe *B & W* from 89. *18 Spring Gardens, Wiveliscombe, Taunton, Somerset TA4 2LQ* Wiveliscombe (0984) 23186

HITCH, Kim William. b 54. Leic Univ BSc75. Trin Coll Bris 76. **d** 78 **p** 79. C Becontree St Mary *Chelmsf* 78-80; C Huyton Quarry *Liv* 80-83; V Hatcham St Jas *S'wark* 83-91; TR Kidbrooke St Jas from 91. *Kidbrooke Rectory, 62 Kidbrooke Park Road, London SE3 0DU* 081-856 3438

HITCHCOCK, David. b 37. S'wark Ord Course 70. **d** 73 **p** 74. NSM Milton next Gravesend Ch Ch *Roch* from 73. *148 Old Road East, Gravesend, Kent* Gravesend (0474) 361091

HITCHINSON, Preb William Henry. b 12. Chich Th Coll 51. **d** 53 **p** 54. V Eastcote St Lawr *Lon* 56-80; Preb St Paul's Cathl 76-80; rtd 80. *66 Waller Drive, Northwood, Middx HA6 1BW* Northwood (09274) 29778

HITCHMOUGH, William. b 30. N Ord Course. **d** 81 **p** 82. NSM Penketh *Liv* 81-83; Chapl Warrington Distr Gen Hosp from 83. *15 Beecroft Close, Warrington WA5 5QX* Warrington (0925) 50541

HIZA, Douglas William. b 38. Richmond Univ Virginia BA60 MDiv63 Mankato State Univ MS70. Virginia Th Sem 60. **d** 63 **p** 64. USA 63-79; Chapl Hackney Hosp Gp *Lon* from 80; Chapl Homerton Hosp *Lon* from 80. *Homerton Hospital, Homerton Row, London E9 6SR* 081-985 5555

HJORTH, Rolf Gunnar Leer. b 25. AMICE St Jo Coll Ox BA46 MA50. Wycliffe Hall Ox 61. **d** 62 **p** 63. V Oulton *Lich* 69-78; Chapl Ostend w Knokke and Bruges *Eur* 78-84; Chapl Dusseldorf 85-90; rtd 90. *SA Fontana 104, Begur, 17255 Gerona, Spain* Gerona (72) 622915

HOAR, George Stanley. b 20. Chich Th Coll 47. **d** 50 **p** 53. V Leake *Linc* 60-71; V Castle Bytham 71-91; R Careby w Holywell and Aunby 73-91; R Lt Bytham 73-91; rtd 91. *1 Sulthorpe Road, Ketton, Stamford, Lincs* Stamford (0780) 720817

HOARE, Carol. b 46. Lon Univ BA68 Birm Univ CertEd69. Qu Coll Birm 86 W Midl Minl Tr Course 86. **d** 91. NSM Curdworth *Birm* from 91. *14 Elms Road, Sutton Coldfield, W Midlands B72 1JF* 021-354 1117

HOARE, David Marlyn. b 33. Bps' Coll Cheshunt 60. **d** 63 **p** 64. C Ampthill w Millbrook and Steppingley *St Alb* 63-67; C Bushey 67-70; V Harlington 70-76; V Oxhey All SS 76-81; V Hellesdon *Nor* from 81. *The Vicarage, Broom Avenue, Hellesdon, Norwich NR6 6LG* Norwich (0603) 426902

HOARE, Patrick Reginald Andrew Reid (Toddy). b 47. TD80 and Bars 88. Hull Univ MA90. Wycliffe Hall Ox 77. **d** 80 **p** 81. C Guisborough *York* 80-83; CF (TA) from 82; P-in-c Felixkirk w Boltby *York* from 83; P-in-c Kirby Knowle from 83; P-in-c Leake w Over and Nether Silton and Kepwick from 83; P-in-c Cowesby from 83. *The Vicarage, Knayton, Thirsk, N Yorkshire YO7 4AZ* Thirsk (0845) 537277

HOARE, Roger John. b 38. Tyndale Hall Bris 63. **d** 66 **p** 67. C Stoughton *Guildf* 66-70; C Chesham St Mary *Ox* 70-73; V Bath St Bart *B & W* 73-83; V Gt Faringdon w Lt Coxwell *Ox* 83-89; Deputation Appeals Org (NE Lon) Children's Soc from 89. *7 Field Close, Abridge, Romford RM4 1DL*

HOARE, Rupert William Noel. b 40. Trin Coll Ox BA61 MA66 Fitzw Ho Cam BA64 MA84 Birm Univ PhD73. Westcott Ho Cam 62. **d** 64 **p** 65. C Oldham St Mary w St Pet *Man* 64-67; Lect Qu Coll Birm 68-72; Can Th Cov Cathl *Cov* 70-76; R Man Resurr *Man* 72-78; Can Res Birm Cathl *Birm* 78-81; Prin Westcott Ho Cam from 81. *Westcott House, Jesus Lane, Cambridge CB5 8BP* Cambridge (0223) 350074

HOARE, Canon Simon Gerard. b 37. AKC61. **d** 62 **p** 63. C Headingley *Ripon* 62-65; C Adel 65-68; R Spofforth 68-71; R Spofforth w Kirk Deighton 71-77; V Rawdon *Bradf* 77-85; Hon Can Bradf Cathl from 85; R Carleton and Lothersdale from 85; Dioc Ecum Officer from 85. *The Rectory, Carleton, Skipton, N Yorkshire BD23 3BY* Skipton (0756) 792789

HOBBS, Antony Ewan Talbot. b 25. Ripon Hall Ox 58. **d** 60 **p** 61. V Staplefield Common *Chich* 64-89; rtd 89.

Chippers, Chalvington, Hailsham, E Sussex BN27 3TE Ripe (032183) 243

HOBBS, Basil Ernest William. b 22. St Chad's Coll Dur BA49 DipTh50. **d** 51 **p** 52. Hon C Paddington H Trin w St Paul *Lon* 69-72; Asst Chapl St Mary's Hosp (Praed Street) Paddington 69-72; Past Consultant Clinical Th Assn 73-84; Lic to Offic *S'well* 74-83; Chapl HM Pris Nottm 81-84; Hon C Nottm St Andr *S'well* 83-84; C 84-86; TV Clifton 86-87; rtd 87. *10 New Vale Road, Nottingham NG4 2LB* Nottingham (0602) 870460

HOBBS, Christopher John Pearson. b 60. Sydney Univ BA82 K Coll Lon BD89 AKC89. Wycliffe Hall Ox 89. **d** 91. C S Mimms Ch Ch *Lon* from 91. *c/o Christ Church Vicarage, St Albans Road, Barnet, Herts EN5 4LA* 081-449 0832

HOBBS, David Stanley. b 20. St D Coll Lamp BA44 LTh44. **d** 44 **p** 45. R Crunwere and Amroth *St D* 70-78; rtd 78. *Hilltop, St Bride's Lane, Saundersfoot, Dyfed SA69 9HL* Saundersfoot (0834) 813085

HOBBS, James. b 42. K Alfred's Coll Win CertEd64 C of E Bd Educn RTC 64 Open Univ BA89. Linc Th Coll 66. **d** 68 **p** 69. C Moseley St Mary *Birm* 68-73; V Kingstanding St Mark 73-77; R Rushbrooke *St E* 77-78; R Bradfield St Geo 77-80; P-in-c Bradfield St Clare 77-80; P-in-c Felsham w Gedding 77-80; R Bradfield St George w Bradfield St Clare etc 80-84; P-in-c Gt and Lt Whelnetham 84-85; R Gt and Lt Whelnetham w Bradfield St George 85-90; Chapl for Educn *Linc* from 90; Grimsby Colls of H&FE from 90. *13 Westward Ho!, Grimsby, S Humberside DN34 5AF* Grimsby (0472) 77079

HOBBS, John Antony. b 36. S Dios Minl Tr Scheme. **d** 87 **p** 88. NSM Crowborough *Chich* from 87. *May Cottage, Alice Bright Lane, Crowborough, E Sussex TN6 3SQ* Crowborough (0892) 653909

HOBBS, Ven Keith. b 25. Ex Coll Ox BA46 MA51. Wells Th Coll 56. **d** 58 **p** 59. C Clewer St Steph *Ox* 58-60; C Soho St Anne w St Thos and St Pet *Lon* 60-62; Hon C S Kensington St Steph 62-71; C 71-78; Acting Gen Sec Ch Union 78; Bp's Dom Chapl *Chich* 78-81; Adn Chich from 81. *4 Canon Lane, Chichester, W Sussex PO19 1PX* Chichester (0243) 784260

HOBBS, Kenneth Ian. b 50. Oak Hill Th Coll 74. **d** 77 **p** 78. C Southborough St Pet w Ch Ch and St Matt *Roch* 77-80; C Hoole *Ches* 80-84; V Barnston from 84. *The Vicarage, Barnston, Wirral, Merseyside L61 1BW* 051-648 1776

HOBBS, Michael Bedo. b 30. Fitzw Ho Cam BA58 MA62. Clifton Th Coll 58. **d** 60 **p** 61. C Southsea St Jude *Portsm* 60-63; Paraguay 63-65; Argentina 65-67; V Potters Green *Cov* 68-75; Distr Sec BFBS 75-82; R Plaxtol *Roch* from 82; Dioc Miss Audits Consultant from 90. *The Rectory, Plaxtol, Sevenoaks, Kent TN15 0QF* Plaxtol (0732) 810319

HOBBS, Canon Philip Bertram. b 20. MBE81. Wells Th Coll 46. **d** 48 **p** 49. C Glouc Ch Ch *Glouc* 48-51; R Boxwell w Leighterton 51-60; P-in-c Ozleworth 58-60; P-in-c Newington Bagpath w Kingscote 58-60; V Glouc St Jas 60-74; Chapl HM Pris Glouc 61-82; V Sevenhampton w Charlton Abbots and Hawling *Glouc* 74-75; P-in-c Whittington 74-75; V Sevenhampton w Charlton Abbotts and Hawling etc from 75; Hon Can Glouc Cathl from 77. *The Vicarage, Sevenhampton, Cheltenham, Glos GL54 5SW* Cheltenham (0242) 820246

HOBBS, Simon John. b 59. Ox Univ MA82. St Steph Ho Ox 80. **d** 83 **p** 84. C Middlesb Ascension *York* 83-85; C Stainton-in-Cleveland 85-88; C St Marylebone All SS *Lon* 88-90; P-in-c Paddington St Pet from 90. *St Peter's Vicarage, 59 Elgin Avenue, London W9 2DB* 071-289 2011

HOBDAY, Walter William Henry. b 10. Ely Th Coll 56. **d** 57 **p** 58. R Perivale *Lon* 59-72; P-in-c Lichborough w Maidford *Pet* 72-74; R 74-76; R Lichborough w Maidford and Farthingstone 76-79; rtd 79; Lic to Offic *Pet* 80-86; Perm from 86; St Alb from 88. *Hardwicke Cottage, 13 The Green, Bromham, Bedford MK43 8JS* Oakley (02302) 4542

HOBDEN, Brian Charles. b 38. **d** 66 **p** 67. C S Lambeth St Steph *S'wark* 66-70; C Cheadle *Ches* 70-76; USA from 76. *3215 Lilac, Portsmouth, Virginia 23703, USA*

HOBDEN, Christopher Martin. b 49. Lon Univ BSc71. Oak Hill Th Coll 80. **d** 87 **p** 88. NSM St Marylebone All So w SS Pet and Jo *Lon* 87-88; NSM Langham Place All So from 88. *24 St Mark's Crescent, London NW1 7TU* 071-482 5129

HOBDEN, David Nicholas. b 54. K Coll Lon BD76 AKC76 Cam Univ PGCE. Ripon Coll Cuddesdon 77. **d** 78 **p** 79. C Marlborough *Sarum* 78-80; C Salisbury St Thos and

St Edm 81-85; V Shalford *Guildf* from 85. *The Vicarage, East Shalford Lane, Shalford, Guildford, Surrey GU48AE* Guildford (0483) 62396

HOBDEN, Geoffrey William. b 46. DipTh. Trin Coll Bris 80. **d** 82 **p** 83. C Ex St Leon w H Trin *Ex* 82-86; V Weston-super-Mare Ch Ch *B & W* from 86. *Christ Church Vicarage, 18 Montpelier, Weston-super-Mare, Avon BS23 2RH* Weston-super-Mare (0934) 624376

HOBSON, Anthony John. b 42. Univ of Wales (Abth) BSc64 Birm Univ MSc65. Qu Coll Birm 79. **d** 81 **p** 82. NSM Bilton *Cov* from 81; P-in-c Grandborough w Willoughby and Flecknoe from 88. *4 Juliet Drive, Rugby, Warks CV22 6LY* Rugby (0788) 810416

HOBSON, Anthony Peter. b 53. St Jo Coll Cam BA74. St Jo Coll Nottm 75. **d** 77 **p** 78. C Brunswick *Man* 77-82; R Stretford St Bride from 82. *30 Stamford Street, Old Trafford, Manchester M16 9JQ* 061-872 8402

HOBSON, Herbert Leslie. b 09. St Aid Birkenhead 37. **d** 39 **p** 40. V Heath *Derby* 68-75, rtd 75, Perm to Offic *Derby* and *S'well* from 75. *40 High Tor, Skegby, Sutton-in-Ashfield, Notts NG17 3EX* Mansfield (0623) 557083

HOBSON, John Philip Hilary. b 20. FRSA56 Keble Coll Ox BA42 MA46. Ripon Hall Ox 42. **d** 43 **p** 44. Hd Master St Mary's Choir Sch Reigate 50-84; rtd 84; Perm to Offic *Linc* from 84. *19 Arnhem Way, Woodhall Spa, Lincs LN10 6TJ* Woodhall Spa (0526) 53125

HOBSON, Patrick John Bogan. b 33. MC53. Magd Coll Cam BA56 MA60. S'wark Ord Course 75 Qu Coll Birm 77. **d** 79 **p** 80. C St Jo in Bedwardine *Worc* 79-81; R Clifton-on-Teme, Lower Sapey and the Shelsleys 81-88; TR Waltham H Cross *Chelmsf* from 88. *The Rectory, Highbridge Street, Waltham Abbey, Essex EN9 1DG* Lea Valley (0992) 712115

HOCKEY, Paul Henry. b 49. Oak Hill Th Coll BA86. **d** 86 **p** 87. C Dalton-in-Furness *Carl* 86-89; R Clifton, Brougham and Cliburn from 89. *The Rectory, Clifton, Penrith, Cumbria CA10 2EA* Penrith (0768) 64766

HOCKING, Canon Hugh Michael Warwick. b 12. VRD54. Ch Coll Cam BA34 MA38. Westcott Ho Cam 34. **d** 36 **p** 37. R Guildf H Trin w St Mary *Guildf* 62-77; Chapl St Luke's Hosp Guildf 63-77; rtd 77; Chapl W Cornwall Hosp Penzance from 78. *2 Clarence Place, Penzance, Cornwall TR18 2QA* Penzance (0736) 63229

HOCKING, John Theodore. b 28. Oak Hill Th Coll 61. **d** 63 **p** 64. N Area Sec BCMS 67-71; Hon C Preston All SS *Blackb* 67-71; V Hoghton 71-78; V Blawith w Lowick *Carl* 78-86; rtd 86. *161 Watling Street Road, Fulwood, Preston, Lancs PR2 4AE* Preston (0772) 795058

HOCKING, Paul Frederick. b 43. Chich Th Coll 84. **d** 86 **p** 87. C Whitton and Thurleston w Akenham *St E* 86-89; V Ipswich All Hallows from 89. *All Hallows' Vicarage, Reynolds Road, Ipswich IP3 0JH* Ipswich (0473) 727467

HOCKLEY, Paul William. b 47. Chu Coll Cam BA68 MA72 Nottm Univ BA73. St Jo Coll Nottm 71. **d** 74 **p** 75. C Chatham St Phil and St Jas *Roch* 74-78; C Tunbridge Wells St Jo 78-81; V Penketh *Liv* from 81. *6 Poplar Avenue, Penketh, Warrington WA5 2EH* Penketh (092572) 3492

HOCKLEY, Canon Raymond Alan. b 29. LRAM53 Em Coll Cam MA71. Westcott Ho Cam 56. **d** 58 **p** 59. C Endcliffe *Sheff* 58-61; P-in-c Wicker w Neepsend 61-63; Chapl Westcott Ho Cam 63-68; Chapl Em Coll Cam 68-76; Can Res and Prec York Minster *York* from 76. *2 Minster Court, York YO1 2JJ* York (0904) 624965

HOCKRIDGE, Joan. b 25. Girton Coll Cam BA47 MA50. St Steph Ho Ox 82. dss 83 **d** 87. Ealing Ascension Hanger Hill *Lon* 83-87; Hon C 87-88; Hon C Hanger Hill Ascension and W Twyford St Mary from 88. *7 Heathcroft, London W5 3BY* 081-997 7763

HODDER, John Kenneth. b 45. Edin Univ MA68. Cuddesdon Coll 71. **d** 73 **p** 74. C Kibworth Beauchamp *Leic* 73-76; C Whittlesey *Ely* 76-80; P-in-c Coveney 80-81; R 81-87; R Downham 80-87; R Nunney and Witham Friary, Marston Bigot etc *B & W* from 87. *The Rectory, High Street, Nunney, Frome, Somerset BA11 4LZ* Frome (0373) 836732

HODDER, Trevor Valentine. b 31. Bps' Coll Cheshunt 65. **d** 67 **p** 68. C Oxhey All SS *St Alb* 67-70; C Digswell 70-73; V Colchester St Anne *Chelmsf* from 74. *St Anne's Vicarage, Compton Road, Colchester CO4 4BQ* Colchester (0206) 860931

HODGE, Albert. b 40. N Ord Course 84. **d** 87 **p** 88. C Huyton St Geo *Liv* 87-89; P-in-c Widnes St Paul from 89. *St Paul's Vicarage, Victoria Square, Widnes WA8 7QU* 051-424 2221

HODGE, Anthony Charles. b 43. AKC66. **d** 67 **p** 68. C Carrington *S'well* 67-69; C Bawtry w Austerfield 69-72; C Misson 69-72; Grenada 72-74; Trinidad and Tobago 74-76; V Tuckingmill *Truro* 76-78; V Worksop St Paul

S'well 78-81; P-in-c Patrington w Hollym, Welwick and Winestead *York* 81-86; R 86-88; V York St Olave w St Giles from 88. *St Olave's Vicarage, 52 Bootham, York YO3 7BZ* York (0904) 625186

HODGE, Colin. b 39. Sarum & Wells Th Coll. **d** 83 **p** 84. NSM Wareham *Sarum* 84-87; C Parkstone St Pet w Branksea and St Osmund 87-89; V Lilliput from 89. *The Vicarage, 55 Lilliput Road, Poole, Dorset BH14 8JX* Poole (0202) 708567

HODGE, Dr Denis Ian. b 32. Bris Univ MB, ChB56. Cuddesdon Coll 68. **d** 69 **p** 70. C Westbury *B & W* 69-72; V Alcombe 72-76; New Zealand from 76. *Address temp unknown*

HODGE, Dr Graham Anthony. b 49. Univ of Wales MA PhD86. Lambeth STh Linc Th Coll 79. **d** 80 **p** 81. C Hale *Guildf* 80-82; C Christchurch *Win* 82-86; R Chawton and Farringdon from 86. *The Rectory, Farringdon, Alton, Hants GU34 3EE* Tisted (042058) 398

HODGE, John Shaw. b 30. Chich Th Coll 78. **d** 80 **p** 81. C Furze Platt *Ox* 80-83; V Kirkwhelpington, Kirkharle, Kirkheaton and Cambo *Newc* 83-84; TV Langley Marish *Ox* 84-87; rtd 87; Perm to Offic *Cant* from 87. *St Peter's, 15 The Street, Ash, Canterbury, Kent CT3 2HH* Canterbury (0227) 813347

HODGE, Sister Marilyn Elizabeth. b 52. Wilson Carlile Coll IDC82 Carl Dioc Tr Course. **d** 89. CA from 82; Par Dn Millom *Carl* from 89. *39 Settle Street, Millom, Cumbria LA18 5AR* Millom (0229) 772843

HODGE, Canon Michael Robert. b 34. Pemb Coll Cam BA57 MA61. Ridley Hall Cam 57. **d** 59 **p** 60. C Harpurhey Ch Ch *Man* 59; C Blackpool St Mark *Blackb* 59-62; V Stalybridge Old St Geo *Man* 62-67; R Cobham w Luddesdowne and Dode *Roch* 67-81; Hon Can Roch Cathl from 81; R Bidborough from 81. *The Rectory, Rectory Drive, Bidborough, Tunbridge Wells, Kent TN3 0UL* Tunbridge Wells (0892) 528081

HODGE, Nigel John. b 61. BTh83 Univ of Wales DPS85. St Mich Coll Llan 83. **d** 85 **p** 86. C Mynyddislwyn *Mon* 85-87; C Machen 87-89; TV Ebbw Vale from 89. *177 Badminton Grove, Ebbw Vale, Gwent NP3 5UN* Ebbw Vale (0495) 304516

HODGES, Canon Dudley Alban. b 09. Selw Coll Cam BA30 MA34. Cuddesdon Coll 30. **d** 32 **p** 33. Can Res and Prec Lich Cathl *Lich* 65-76; rtd 76; Can and Preb Sarum Cathl *Sarum* 80-89. *31 The Close, Salisbury SP1 2EJ* Salisbury (0722) 320041

HODGES, Eric Henry. b 16. AKC39. **d** 39 **p** 40. CF (TA) 53-86; R Landewednack *Truro* 56-86; rtd 86. *61 Coronation Avenue, Yeovil, Somerset BA21 3DZ* Yeovil (0935) 71247

HODGES, Francis Reginald. b 26. Selw Coll Cam BA48 MA61. Chich Th Coll 48. **d** 50 **p** 51. R St Breoke *Truro* 61-76; rtd 76; C St Kew *Truro* 77-78; P-in-c 78-80. *Tregellist Cottage, St Kew, Bodmin, Cornwall PL30 3HG* Bodmin (0208) 880083

HODGES, Keith Michael. b 53. Southn Univ BTh82. Chich Th Coll 77. **d** 80 **p** 81. C Sydenham St Phil *S'wark* 80-84; Perm to Offic 85; C Leatherhead *Guildf* 86-89; V Aldershot St Aug from 89. *St Augustine's Vicarage, Holly Road, Aldershot, Hants GU12 4SE* Aldershot (0252) 20840

HODGES, Murray Knowles. b 02. K Coll Cam BA24 MA29. Ridley Hall Cam. **d** 25 **p** 26. V Muncaster w Waberthwaite *Carl* 57-75; rtd 75; Perm to Offic *Carl* from 77. *Eskside, Ravenglass, Cumbria CA18 1SF* Ravenglass (0229) 717259

HODGETTS, Alan Paul. b 54. BSc78. St Steph Ho Ox 79. **d** 82 **p** 83. C Perry Barr *Birm* 82-85; C Broseley w Benthall *Heref* 85-87; V Effingham w Lt Bookham *Guildf* from 87. *The Vicarage, Lower Road, Effingham, Leatherhead, Surrey KT24 5JR* Bookham (0372) 458314

HODGETTS, Colin William. b 40. St D Coll Lamp BA61 Ripon Hall Ox 61. **d** 63 **p** 64. C Hackney St Jo *Lon* 63-66; Hon C St Martin-in-the-Fields 70-76; C Creeksea w Althorne *Chelmsf* 76-79; Perm to Offic *Ex* from 84. *The Small School, Fore Street, Hartland, Bideford, Devon EX39 6AB* Hartland (0237) 441672

HODGETTS, Harry Samuel. b 30. Chich Th Coll 63. **d** 65 **p** 66. C Harton Colliery *Dur* 65-68; C Penzance St Mary *Truro* 68-70; V Penwerris 70-79; V Kettering St Mary *Pet* from 79. *St Mary's Vicarage, 179 Stamford Road, Kettering, Northants NN16 9SU* Kettering (0536) 512736

HODGINS, George Eric. b 12. ALCD39. **d** 39 **p** 40. R Lt Easton *Chelmsf* 63-73; R Alphamstone w Lamarsh and Pebmarsh 74-77; rtd 77. *Candles, 23 Church Street, Colne Engaine, Colchester CO6 2EX* Earls Colne (0787) 223776

HODGINS, John Henry. b 21. TCD BA43 BD48. TCD Div Sch Div Test44. **d** 45 **p** 46. Educn Org Ch of Ireland 69-71; Can Th Belf Cathl 71-76; Dean Killala *T, K & A* 76-79; Area Sec (Dios Ripon and York) CMS 79-83; C Acomb St Steph *York* 83-86; rtd 86. *57 Sandhurst Drive, Belfast BT9 5AZ* Belfast (0232) 668990

HODGINS, Ven Michael Minden. b 12. Lambeth Hon MA60 Cuddesdon Coll 38. **d** 39 **p** 40. Adn Hackney *Lon* 51-71; rtd 77. *Flat 5, Up The Quadrangle, Morden College, London SE3 0PU* 081-858 4762

HODGINS, Philip Arthur. b 57. Lanc Univ BA78 Nottm Univ DipTh83 Bradf Univ MBA90 GradIPM91. Linc Th Coll 82. **d** 85 **p** 86. C Norton *Ches* 85-88; C Whitkirk *Ripon* 88-89; Perm to Offic Bradf 89-90; Chich from 91; Jo Grooms Assn for Disabled People from 91. *Little Becks, Batts Bridge Road, Maresfield, Uckfield, E Sussex TN22 2HJ* Uckfield (0825) 762767

HODGKINSON, Canon Arthur Edward. b 13. Dur Univ LTh42. Edin Th Coll 36. **d** 39 **p** 40. Provost St Andr Cathl *Ab* 65-78; Hon Can Ch Ch Cathl Connecticut 65-78; Area Sec (S Wales) USPG 78-82; Hon Can St Andr Cathl *Ab* from 81; rtd 82; Hon C Eyemouth *Edin* 82-86; Perm to Offic *Llan* 86-89. *36 Forbes Road, Edinburgh EH10 4ED* 031-229 7593

HODGKINSON, Frank Cyril. b 18. Lon Univ BA50. Oak Hill Th Coll 46. **d** 51 **p** 52. V Barkby *Leic* 68-74; V Leic St Chris 74-77; V Ryhall w Essendine *Pet* 77-83; rtd 83; Perm to Offic *Nor* from 84. *16 Waveney Close, Wells-next-the-Sea, Norfolk NR23 1HU*

HODGKINSON, Canon John. b 27. Trin Hall Cam BA51 MA55. Linc Th Coll 51. **d** 53 **p** 54. R Old Brumby *Linc* 66-71; V Kendal H Trin *Carl* 71-90; Hon Can Carl Cathl from 84; rtd 90. *Boxtree Barn, Levens, Kendal, Cumbria LA8 8NZ* Sedgwick (05395) 60806

HODGKINSON, John David. b 09. Fitzw Coll Cam BA31 MA35. Bps' Coll Cheshunt 38. **d** 38 **p** 39. C St Vedast w St Mich-le-Querne etc *Lon* 52-54; rtd 74. *106 Earls Court Road, London W8 6EG* 071-937 4916

HODGKINSON, John David. b 57. Birm Univ BA78 Edin Univ BD89. Edin Th Coll 86. **d** 89 **p** 90. C Briercliffe *Blackb* from 89. *31 Sutcliffe Street, Briercliffe, Burnley, Lancs BB10 2JW* Burnley (0282) 56541

HODGKINSON, Oswald Merchant. b 21. Qu Coll Birm 68. **d** 69 **p** 70. C Shard End *Birm* 69-74; V 74-80; TV Wrexham *St As* 80-86; rtd 86; Perm to Offic St As & Ban from 86. *Heddwch, 24 Water Street, Abergynolwyn, Tywyn, Gwynedd LL36 9YB* Tywyn (0654) 782204

HODGSON, Andrew. b 13. TD63. Mert Coll Ox BA36 MA45. Westcott Ho Cam 45. **d** 47 **p** 48. V Honingham w E Tuddenham *Nor* 58-81; rtd 81; Perm to Offic *Derby* from 81. *10 Brook Street, Heage, Derby DE5 2AG* Ambergate (077385) 2759

HODGSON, Anthony Owen Langlois. b 35. Ripon Hall Ox 60. **d** 62 **p** 63. C Blakeney w Lt Langham *Nor* 62-65; C Stiffkey w Morston 62-65; C Paddington Ch Ch *Lon* 66-70; Area Sec (Beds & Cambs) Chr Aid 70-74; (Herts and Hunts) 70-73; (Rutland and Northants) 73-74; V Gt w Lt Gidding and Steeple Gidding *Ely* 77-81; Warden Dovedale Ho 81-89; P-in-c Ilam w Blore Ray and Okeover *Lich* 81-89; Dir Chr Rural Cen 89-91; C Uttoxeter w Bramshall from 91; C Checkley from 91; C Stramshall from 91. *The New Rectory, Church Lane, Checkley, Stoke-on-Trent* Tean (0538) 722732

HODGSON, Anthony William. b 35. Dur Univ BSc56. Wells Th Coll 58. **d** 60 **p** 61. C Gateshead St Mary *Dur* 60-62; C Leeds All SS *Ripon* 62-66; V Hartlepool St Oswald *Dur* 66-75; C-in-c Stockton St Jas CD 75-81; V Easington Colliery 81-89; V Eighton Banks from 89. *St Thomas's Vicarage, 4 Southland, Eighton Banks, Gateshead, Tyne & Wear NE9 7BR* 091-487 6927

HODGSON, Canon Charles. b 16. St Aid Coll Dur LTh42 St Jo Coll Dur BA43 MA45. St Aid Birkenhead 39. **d** 43 **p** 44. V Middleton *Birm* 60-70; R Wishaw 60-70; Dioc Adult Educn Officer 60-70; Dioc Missr and Tr Officer Ox 70-82; Hon Can Ch Ch *Ox* 81; RD Witney 81-86; rtd 82. *40 Wykeham Way, Haddenham, Aylesbury, Bucks HP17 8BX* Haddenham (0844) 292593

HODGSON, Christopher. b 24. Or Coll Ox BA49 MA54. Qu Coll Birm 50. **d** 52 **p** 53. C Cheltenham Ch Ch *Glouc* 52-55; C Liv Our Lady and St Nic *Liv* 55-57; V Anfield St Columba 57-64; V Pembury *Roch* 64-82; Chapl Pembury Hosp Tunbridge Wells 66-82; R Aynho w Newbottle and Charlton *Pet* 82-85; Chapl Burrswood Cen for Divine Healing from 85; C Castle Bromwich St Clem *Birm* from 86. *144 Lanchester Way, Birmingham B36 9LE* 021-747 4491

HODGSON, David George. b 54. Coll of Resurr Mirfield. **d** 82 **p** 83. C Stainton-in-Cleveland *York* 82-87; R Loftus 87; P-in-c Carlin How w Skinningrove 87; R Loftus and

Carlin How w Skinningrove from 87. *The Rectory, Loftus, Saltburn-by-the-Sea, Cleveland TS13 4JY* Castleton (0287) 40738

HODGSON, David Peter. b 56. Fitzw Coll Cam BA77 MA81 Nottm Univ BA82 MTh85. St Jo Coll Nottm 80. **d** 83 **p** 84. C Guiseley w Esholt *Bradf* 83-86; Asst Chapl Loughb Univ *Leic* 86-89; P-in-c Bush End *Chelmsf* 89-90; P-in-c Hatf Broad Oak 89-90; P-in-c Hatf Broad Oak and Bush End from 90; Ind Chapl from 89. *The Vicarage, Feathers Hill, Hatfield Broad Oak, Bishop's Stortford CM22 7HD* Bishop's Stortford (0279) 70274

HODGSON, Derek Cyril. b 29. Hatf Coll Dur BA50 St Chad's Coll Dur DipTh54. **d** 54 **p** 55. C Lindley *Wakef* 54-58; C-in-c Mixenden CD 58-62; V Thurlstone 62-75; V Mytholmroyd from 75. *The Vicarage, Brier Hey Lane, Mytholmroyd, Hebden Bridge HX7 5PJ* Halifax (0422) 883130

HODGSON, George. b 36. Qu Coll Birm 75. **d** 78 **p** 79. NSM Wordsley *Lich* from 78; Perm to Offic *Worc* from 84. *1 Newfield Drive, Kingswinford, W Midlands DY6 8HY* Kingswinford (0384) 292543

HODGSON, John. b 35. St Jo Coll Cam MA62 Lon Univ BD61. St Deiniol's Hawarden 80. **d** 81 **p** 82. Hon C Padiham *Blackb* 81-84; C W Burnley 85-87; V from 87. *The Vicarage, Padiham Road, Burnley, Lancs BB12 6PA* Padiham (0282) 75629

HODGSON, Ven John Derek. b 31. St Jo Coll Dur BA53. Cranmer Hall Dur DipTh59. **d** 59 **p** 60. C Stranton *Dur* 59-62; C Monkwearmouth St Andr 62-64; V Stillington 64-66; V Consett 66-75; TR Gateshead 75-83; RD Gateshead 76-83; Hon Can Dur Cathl 78-83; Can Res from 83; Adn Auckland from 83. *15 The College, Durham DH1 3EQ* 091-384 7534

HODGSON, Matthew William. b 13. Lich Th Coll 40. **d** 44 **p** 45. V Woodhorn w Newbiggin *Newc* 71-77; rtd 77. *4 Woodthorne Road, Jesmond, Newcastle upon Tyne NE2 3PB* 091-284 6441

HODGSON, Peter Richard. b 23. Dur Univ BA50. Bps' Coll Cheshunt 49. **d** 52 **p** 53. V Bolsterstone *Sheff* 61-80; V Kirton in Holland *Linc* 80-86; rtd 86. *Omega, Littlemoor Lane, Sibsey, Boston, Lincs PE22 0TU* Boston (0205) 750167

HODGSON, Robert Edward Stephen. b 14. St Aid Birkenhead 38. **d** 39 **p** 40. V Shuttleworth *Man* 71-79; rtd 79; Perm to Offic Ches and St As from 79. *17 Simpson's Way, Broughton, Chester CH4 0RA* Hawarden (0244) 536217

HODGSON, Roger Vaughan. b 27. Magd Coll Cam BA49 MA54. Cuddesdon Coll 55. **d** 56 **p** 57. C Westmr St Matt *Lon* 56-59; C Pimlico St Pet w Westmr Ch Ch 59-65; R Lt Hadham *St Alb* 65-78; Chapl Porto (or Oporto) *Eur* 78-80; Chapl and Lect St Deiniol's Lib Hawarden 81-82; V Coldwaltham *Chich* from 82. *The Vicarage, Coldwaltham, Pulborough, W Sussex RH20 1LF* Pulborough (07982) 2146

HODGSON, Ven Thomas Richard Burnham. b 26. FRMetS88. Lon Coll of Div BD52 ALCD52. **d** 52 **p** 53. V Raughton Head w Gatesgill *Carl* 67-73; Bp's Dom Chapl 67-73; Dir of Ords 70-74; Hon Can Carl Cathl from 72; V Grange-over-Sands 73-79; RD Windermere 76-79; P-in-c Mosser 79; V 79-83; Adn W Cumberland 79-91; rtd 91. *58 Greenacres, Wetheral, Carlisle CA14 8LD* Wetheral (0228) 61159

HODGSON, Vernon Charles. b 34. MRPharmS58 Lon Univ BPharm58 Univ of Wales (Cardiff) DPS91. St Mich Coll Llan 90 Llan Dioc Tr Scheme 83. **d** 86 **p** 87. NSM Roath St Marg *Llan* 86-91; C Caerphilly from 91. *St Andrew's House, Troed y Bryn, Penyrheol, Caerphilly, M Glam CF8 2PX* Caerphilly (0222) 884103

HODKIN, Canon Hedley. b 02. Sheff Univ MA23 Ch Coll Cam BA25 MA31. Westcott Ho Cam 35. **d** 35 **p** 36. Can Res Man Cathl *Man* 57-70; Sub-Dean 66-70; rtd 70; Perm to Offic Derby from 70; Lic to Offic *Sheff* 72-87. *Dulverton Hall, St Martin's Square, Scarborough YO11 2DB* Scarborough (0723) 363064

HODKINSON, George Leslie. b 48. Qu Coll Birm 86. **d** 88 **p** 89. C Hall Green St Pet *Birm* 88-91; TV Solihull from 91. *St Helen's House, 6 St Helen's Road, Solihull, W Midlands B91 2DA* 021-704 2878

HODSON, Gordon George. b 35. St Chad's Coll Dur BA59 DipTh60. **d** 60 **p** 61. C Tettenhall Regis *Lich* 60-64; C Rugeley 64-68; V Shrewsbury St Mich 68-74; V Kinnerley w Melverley 74-87; P-in-c Knockin w Maesbrook 75-87; P-in-c Chebsey from 87; P-in-c Seighford, Derrington and Cresswell from 87. *The Vicarage, Seighford, Stafford ST18 9PQ* Seighford (0785) 282829

HODSON, Keith. b 53. Hatf Coll Dur BA74. Wycliffe Hall Ox 77. **d** 80 **p** 81. C Ashton on Mersey St Mary *Ches* 80-84; C Polegate *Chich* from 84. *St Wilfrid's House, 90 Broad Road, Eastbourne, E Sussex BN20 9RA* Polegate (03212) 2088

HODSON, Margaret Christina. b 39. Linc Th Coll 88. **d** 90. Par Dn Old Trafford St Jo *Man* from 90. *115 Northumberland Road, Manchester M16 9BQ* 061-876 5055

HODSON, Raymond Leslie. b 42. St Chad's Coll Dur BSc64 DipTh66. **d** 66 **p** 67. C Adlington *Blackb* 66-68; C Cleveleys 68-72; V Ewood 72-77; V Nazeing *Chelmsf* 77-84; R Ampthill w Millbrook and Steppingley *St Alb* from 84. *The Rectory, Ampthill, Bedford MK45 2EL* Ampthill (0525) 402320

HODSON, William. b 42. Man Univ BA. Cranmer Hall Dur 81. **d** 82 **p** 83. C Ashton St Mich *Man* 82-86; V Tintwistle *Ches* from 86. *The Vicarage, Tintwistle, Hadfield, Hyde, Cheshire SK14 7JR* Glossop (0457) 852575

HOEY, David Paul. b 57. QUB BD79. CITC 79. **d** 81 **p** 82. C Belf Whiterock *Conn* 81-83; C Portadown St Mark *Arm* 83-84; I Cleenish w Mullaghdun *Clogh* 84-90; I Magheracross from 90; Dir of Ords from 91. *The Rectory, Ballinamallard, Co Fermanagh BT94 2BT* Ballinamallard (036581) 238

HOEY, Raymond George. b 46. TCD BA70 MA. **d** 72 **p** 73. C Arm St Mark *Arm* 72-78; I Camlough w Mullaglass from 78; Dom Chapl to Abp Arm from 86; RD Mullabrack from 88. *2 Maytown Road, Bessbrook, Newry, Co Down BT35 7LY* Bessbrook (0693) 830301

HOEY, Thomas Kenneth (Brother Augustine). b 15. St Edm Hall Ox BA38 MA44. Cuddesdon Coll 39. **d** 40 **p** 41. CR from 50; Master R Foundn of St Kath in Ratcliffe 68-72; Lic to Offic *Man* 73-76; Perm to Offic *Lon* from 84; rtd 85. *House of the Resurrection, Mirfield, W Yorkshire WF14 0BN* Mirfield (0924) 494318

HOEY, William Thomas. b 32. CITC 64. **d** 66 **p** 67. C Belf St Mary *Conn* 66-68; C Lisburn Ch Ch 69-72; I Ballinderry 72-78; I Belf St Simon w St Phil from 78. *St Simon's Rectory, 106 Upper Lisburn Road, Belfast BT10 0BB* Belfast (0232) 617562

HOFFMAN, George Conrad. b 33. OBE89. Bris Univ BA59. Tyndale Hall Bris. **d** 61 **p** 62. C Wimbledon St Luke *S'wark* 61-66; C Edgware *Lon* 66-68; Asst Sec Evang Alliance 68-70; Dir TEAR Fund 70-89; Exec Chmn Samaritan Internat from 89. *27 St Stephen's Gardens, Twickenham, Middx TW1 2LT* 081-891 2298

HOFFMAN, Canon Stanley Harold. b 17. St Edm Hall Ox BA39 MA43 Kent Univ MA82. Linc Th Coll 40. **d** 41 **p** 42. Dir of Educn *Roch* 65-80; Warden of Readers 73-80; Chapl to HM The Queen from 76; rtd 82; Perm to Offic *Guildf* from 82. *Cedarwood, Holly Close, Headley Down, Bordon, Hants GU35 8JN* Headley Down (0428) 713128

HOFMEESTER, Adrian Sidney. b 13. TCD BA50 MA53. **d** 51 **p** 52. I Conn w Antrim St Patr *Conn* 61-84; RD Ballymena 74-84; rtd 84. *Elstow, 11 Upper Knockbreda Road, Belfast BT6 9QH* Belfast (0232) 792040

HOGAN, Edward James Martin. b 46. Trin Coll Bris. **d** 85 **p** 86. C St Austell *Truro* 85-88; V Gt Broughton and Broughton Moor *Carl* from 88. *The Vicarage, The Green, Little Broughton, Cockermouth, Cumbria CA13 0YG* Cockermouth (0900) 825317

HOGAN, John James. b 24. St Edm Hall Ox BA51 MA56. Wells Th Coll 51. **d** 53 **p** 54. V Woore *Lich* 58-84; P-in-c Norton in Hales 82-84; V Woore and Norton in Hales 84-89; rtd 89. *Wrekin Prospect, Audlem Road, Woore, Crewe, Cheshire CW3 9SD* Pipe Gate (063081) 677

HOGAN, William Riddell. b 22. Qu Coll Birm 48. **d** 51 **p** 52. V Greetland *Wakef* 59-73; V Greetland and W Vale 73-80; V Kellington w Whitley 80-87; rtd 87. *15 The Pastures, Carlton, Goole, N Humberside DN14 9QF* Goole (0405) 862233

HOGARTH, Alan Francis. b 58. Oak Hill Th Coll BA89. **d** 89 **p** 90. C Felixstowe SS Pet and Paul *St E* from 89. *156 Colneis Road, Felixstowe, Suffolk IP11 9LQ* Felixstowe (0394) 272932

HOGARTH, Foley James Myddelton. b 16. Ch Ch Ox BA38 MA42. Wells Th Coll 38. **d** 39 **p** 40. C Rainbow Hill St Barn *Worc* 39-41; C Charlton Kings H Apostles *Glouc* 41-42; CF 42-46; V Fordcombe *Roch* 47-52; Asst Hd Master Holmewood Ho Sch Kent 52-53; Australia from 53. *77 Beulah Road, Norwood, S Australia 5068* Adelaide (8) 316318

HOGARTH, Joseph. b 32. Edin Th Coll 65. **d** 67 **p** 67. C Walney Is *Carl* 67-71; V Whitehaven St Jas 71-76; V Millom H Trin w Thwaites 76-82; V Maryport 82-91; V

Consett *Dur* from 91. *The Vicarage, 10 Aynsley Terrace, Consett, Co Durham DH8 5NF* Consett (0207) 502235

HOGBEN, Ven Peter Graham. b 25. Bps' Coll Cheshunt 60. **d** 61 **p** 62. R Westborough *Guildf* 64-71; V Ewell 71-82; Hon Can Guildf Cathl from 79; RD Epsom 80-82; Adn Dorking 82-90; rtd 90. *3 School Road, Rowledge, Farnham, Surrey GU10 4EJ* Frensham (025125) 3533

HOGG, Anthony. b 42. Univ of Wales (Lamp) BA63. Linc Th Coll 64 Chich Th Coll 78. **d** 78 **p** 79. NSM Ridgeway *Ox* 78-86; C 90-91; NSM W w E Hanney 86-88; Hd Master New Coll Sch Ox 88-89; P-in-c E Challow *Ox* from 91; P-in-c W w E Hanney from 91; P-in-c Denchworth from 91. *8 Belmont, Wantage, Oxon OX12 9AS* Wantage (02357) 65537

HOGG, Ven George Smith. b 10. TCD BA32. **d** 33 **p** 34. I Tipperary *C & O* 47-80; Adn Cashel 66-80; rtd 80. *Sunnyhome, Love Lane, Tramore, Co Waterford, Irish Republic* Waterford (51) 81494

HOGG, Neil Richard. b 46. BSc69. Ridley Hall Cam 82. **d** 84 **p** 85. C Bingham *S'well* 84-87; TV Bushbury *Lich* from 87. *The Vicarage, 17 Goodyear Avenue, Low Hill, Wolverhampton WV10 9JX* Wolverhampton (0902) 731713

HOGG, Peter Stuart. b 42. Ch Coll Cam BA65 MA68. NW Ord Course 74. **d** 77 **p** 78. NSM Bollington St Jo *Ches* 77-88; Chapl Wells Cathl Sch from 88. *18 Vicars' Close, Wells, Somerset BA5 2UJ* Wells (0749) 74527

HOGG, Robert Bell. b 08. **d** 89. NSM Edin St Mary *Edin* from 89. *141 Broughton Road, Edinburgh EH7 4JJ* 031-557 3350

HOGG, William John. b 49. New Coll Ox MA71 Lon Univ CertEd72 Crewe & Alsager Coll MSc88. Edin Th Coll 86. **d** 88 **p** 89. C Oxton *Ches* from 88. *12 Silverdale Road, Birkenhead, Merseyside L43 2JR* 051-653 8493

HOGG, William Ritson. b 47. Leeds Univ BSc69. Qu Coll Birm DipTh71. **d** 72 **p** 73. C Bordesley St Oswald *Birm* 72-76; TV Seacroft *Ripon* 76-82; V Hunslet St Mary 82-88; V Catterick from 88. *The Vicarage, Catterick, Richmond, N Yorkshire DL10 7LN* Richmond (0748) 811462

HOGGARD, Mrs Jean Margaret. b 36. NW Ord Course 76. dss 79 **d** 87. Northowram *Wakef* 79-87; Par Dn from 87. *13 Joseph Avenue, Northowram, Halifax, W Yorkshire HX3 7HJ* Halifax (0422) 201475

HOGGETT, Robert William John. b 13. Worc Ord Coll 65. **d** 67 **p** 68. C Bromsgrove St Jo *Worc* 67-71; V Keelby *Linc* 71-87; V Riby 74-87; V Aylesby 77-87; RD Haverstoe 81-86; rtd 87; Perm to Offic *Linc* from 88. *Lauriston, North Halls, Binbrook, Lincoln* Binbrook (047283) 8157

HOGWOOD, Brian Roy. b 38. Bps' Coll Cheshunt. **d** 65. NSM Thetford *Nor* from 91. *31 Byron Walk, Thetford, Norfolk IP24 1JX* Thetford (0842) 763579

HOLBROOK, Colin Eric Basford. b 42. St Steph Ho Ox 73. **d** 75 **p** 76. C Dovecot *Liv* 75-79; V Hollinfare 79-83; CMS from 83. *c/o CMS, 157 Waterloo Road, London SE1 8UU* 071-928 8681

HOLBROOK, John Edward. b 62. St Pet Coll Ox BA83 MA87. Ridley Hall Cam 82. **d** 86 **p** 87. C Barnes St Mary *S'wark* 86-89; C Bletchley *Ox* from 89. *1 Ashburnham Close, Bletchley, Milton Keynes MK3 7TR* Milton Keynes (0908) 371373

HOLBROOKE-JONES, Stanley Charles. b 27. Dur Univ BA58 DipTh60 MA77. Cranmer Hall Dur 58. **d** 60 **p** 61. C Gravesend St Jas *Roch* 60-63; C Streatham Immanuel w St Anselm *S'wark* 63-66; V W Bromwich H Trin *Lich* 66-79; V W Exe *Ex* 79-88; R Poole *Sarum* from 88; Miss to Seamen from 88. *The Rectory, 10 Poplar Close, Poole, Dorset BH15 1LP* Poole (0202) 672694

HOLCOMBE, Graham William Arthur. b 50. ARCM69. St Mich Coll Llan DipTh80. **d** 80 **p** 81. C Neath w Llantwit *Llan* 80-84; Asst Youth Chapl 81-84; PV Llan Cathl 84-86; V Pentyrch from 86. *The Vicarage, Pentyrch, Cardiff CF4 8QF* Cardiff (0222) 890318

HOLDAWAY, Graham Michael. b 51. Southn Univ BSc73. Sarum & Wells Th Coll 74. **d** 77 **p** 78. C Walton-on-Thames *Guildf* 77-81; TV Westborough 81-86. *49 Woodbridge Road, Guildford, Surrey GU2 6JW*

HOLDAWAY, Dr Simon Douglas. b 47. Lanc Univ BA73 Sheff Univ PhD81. N Ord Course 78. **d** 81 **p** 82. NSM Gleadless *Sheff* from 81; Sen Lect in Sociology Sheff Univ from 81. *136 Totley Brook Road, Sheffield S17 3QU* Sheffield (0742) 363711

HOLDAWAY, Stephen Douglas. b 45. Hull Univ BA67. Ridley Hall Cam 67. **d** 70 **p** 71. C Southn Thornhill St Chris *Win* 70-73; C Tardebigge *Worc* 73-78; Ind Chapl 73-78; Ind Chapl *Linc* from 78; Co-ord City Cen Group Min from 81. *The Rectory, Station Road, Potterhanworth, Lincoln LN4 2DX* Lincoln (0522) 791320

HOLDCROFT, Ian Thomas. b 46. St Jo Coll Cam BA68 MA71. Westcott Ho Cam 72. **d** 73 **p** 74. C Bris St Mary Redcliffe w Temple etc *Bris* 73-76; Th Educn Sec Chr Aid 76-80; Exec Sec 80-82; Hon C Battersea St Mary *S'wark* 81-86; Dep Sec Gen Syn Bd for Miss and Unity 82-86; V Whitchurch *Bris* from 86. *The Vicarage, 780 Whitchurch Lane, Bristol BS14 0EU* Whitchurch (0272) 832380

HOLDEN, Canon Arthur Stuart James. b 23. ALCD51. **d** 51 **p** 52. V Earls Colne *Chelmsf* 61-82; V White Colne 68-82; Hon Can Chelmsf Cathl from 80; V Earls Colne and White Colne 82-88; rtd 88. *10 Wroxham Close, Colchester CO3 3RQ* Colchester (0206) 560845

HOLDEN, Geoffrey. b 26. FCII54. Oak Hill Th Coll 57. **d** 59 **p** 60. R Bath St Mich w St Paul *B & W* 66-73; Chapl Bath Gp Hosps 73-91; rtd 91. *10 Marlborough Lane, Bath BA1 2NQ* Bath (0225) 427933

HOLDEN, Geoffrey Ralph. b 25. Ripon Hall Ox 64. **d** 65 **p** 66. C Walsall *Lich* 68-71; R Longton St Jas 71-75; rtd 90. *Aberscethin, Talybont, Gwynedd LL43 2AR* Dyffryn (03417) 538

HOLDEN, Hyla Rose. b 02. Sarum Th Coll. **d** 30 **p** 31. R Upminster *Chelmsf* 44-70; rtd 71. *15 Ashdown Crescent, Hadleigh, Essex SS7 2LJ* Southend-on-Sea (0702) 559525

HOLDEN, Jack Crawford (Brother Simon). b 30. Leeds Univ BA59. Coll of Resurr Mirfield 59. **d** 61 **p** 61. C Middlesb All SS *York* 61-64; Lic to Offic *Wakef* 65-69; CR from 67; Asst Chapl Univ Coll *Lon* 69-74; Lic to Offic 70-74. *House of the Resurrection, Mirfield, W Yorkshire WF14 0BN* Mirfield (0924) 494318

HOLDEN, Canon Jack Hatherley. b 12. MBE65. St Aug Coll Cant. **d** 41 **p** 42. V Stoke Newington St Andr *Lon* 65-79; rtd 79; P-in-c Islington St Pet *Lon* 80-82; P-in-c Islington St Jas w St Phil 81-82; C St Ethelburga Bishopgate 86-88. *Charterhouse, London EC1M 6AH* 071-490 0245

HOLDEN, Canon John. b 33. MBE76. Selly Oak Coll 71 Ridley Hall Cam 65. **d** 67 **p** 68. C Flixton St Jo CD *Man* 67-71; Uganda 71-75; V Aston SS Pet and Paul *Birm* 75-87; RD Aston 86-87; Hon Can Birm Cathl 86-87; R Ulverston St Mary w H Trin *Carl* from 87; RD Furness from 90. *The Rectory, Ford Park, Ulverston, Cumbria LA12 7JR* Ulverston (0229) 54331

HOLDEN, John Worrall. b 44. K Coll Lon AKC67 DPS. **d** 70 **p** 71. C Derby St Bart *Derby* 70-72; Lic to Offic 72-74; Hon C St Helier *S'wark* 74-77; Hon C St Marylebone All SS *Lon* 80-83; Hon C St Botolph Aldgate w H Trin Minories from 84. *St Botolph's Vestry, London EC3N 1AB* 071-283 1670

HOLDEN, Paul Edward. b 53. CEng79 MIM MIBF BSc75 DipHE84. Trin Coll Bris 82. **d** 86 **p** 87. C Harpurhey Ch Ch *Man* 86-88; C Harpurhey St Steph from 88; Min Harpurhey LEP from 88. *The Hollies, 6 Kingscliffe Street, Moston, Manchester M9 1NL* 061-205 1387

HOLDEN, Richard Davis. b 03. St Aid Birkenhead 33. **d** 36 **p** 37. R Sidbury *Ex* 60-70; rtd 70. *Greystones, Harpford, Sidmouth, Devon EX10 0NJ* Colaton Raleigh (0395) 68534

HOLDER, Frank. b 13. Dur Univ BA35 MA45. **d** 45 **p** 46. Chapl Miss for Deaf *Dur* 45-80; rtd 80. *3 Ash Tree Garth, Barkston Ash, Tadcaster, N Yorkshire LS24 9ET* Barkston Ash (0937) 557715

HOLDER, John William. b 41. Chester Coll CertEd61 Open Univ BA73 Bath Univ MEd85. Trin Coll Bris 85. **d** 87 **p** 88. C Brockworth *Glouc* 87-91; P-in-c Avening w Cherington from 91. *The Rectory, Avening, Tetbury, Glos GL8 8NF* Nailsworth (045383) 2098

HOLDER, Kenneth William. b 29. Sarum Th Coll 60. **d** 61 **p** 62. C Crawley *Chich* 61-65; C-in-c Wick CD 65-73; V Hangleton 73-79; R Rotherfield 79-81; R Rotherfield w Mark Cross 81-83; Chapl Eastbourne Coll E Sussex 83-84; C Farnborough *Roch* 85; TV Mildenhall *St E* from 87. *The Vicarage, Worlington, Bury St Edmunds IP28 8RU* Mildenhall (0638) 713510

HOLDING, Kenneth George Frank. b 27. Sarum & Wells Th Coll 75. **d** 77 **p** 78. C Bexley St Mary *Roch* 77-80; Min Joydens Wood St Barn CD 80-85; R Mereworth w W Peckham from 85. *The Rectory, The Street, Mereworth, Maidstone, Kent ME18 5NA* Maidstone (0622) 812214

HOLDRIDGE, Bernard Lee. b 35. Lich Th Coll 64. **d** 67 **p** 68. C Swinton *Sheff* 67-71; V Doncaster St Jude 71-81; R Rawmarsh w Parkgate 81-88; RD Rotherham 86-88; V Worksop Priory *S'well* from 88. *The Vicarage, Cheapside, Worksop, Notts S80 2HX* Worksop (0909) 472180

HOLDROYD, James Malcolm. b 35. Lon Univ LLB56 LLM58. Cuddesdon Coll 58. **d** 60 **p** 61. C Brighouse *Wakef* 60-66; V Staincross 66-72; V Marsden 72-75; V

Brighton St Bart *Chich* from 75. *16 Richmond Terrace, Brighton BN2 2NA* Brighton (0273) 685142

HOLDSTOCK, Godfrey. b 48. St Jo Coll Cam BA69 MA72 Ox Univ BA77 MA81. St Steph Ho Ox 76. **d** 78 **p** 79. C Chislehurst Annunciation *Roch* 78-81; Hon C Richmond St Mary w St Matthias and St Jo *S'wark* 82-85; V Billesdon and Skeffington *Leic* 85-89; TV High Wycombe *Ox* from 89. *The Vicarage, Rutland Avenue, High Wycombe, Bucks HP12 3XA*

HOLDSWORTH, Ian Scott. b 52. Sheff Poly BA75. Oak Hill Th Coll BA81. **d** 81 **p** 82. C Denham *Ox* 81-84; P-in-c S Leigh 84-89; P-in-c Cogges 84-88; V 88-89. *24 Church Lane, Middle Barton, Oxford* Oxford (0865) 47130

HOLDSWORTH, John Ivor. b 49. Univ of Wales (Abth) BA70 Univ of Wales (Cardiff) BD73 MTh75. St Mich Coll Llan 70. **d** 73 **p** 74. C Newport St Paul *Mon* 73-77; CF (TAVR) 75-90; V Abercrave and Callwen *S & B* 77-86; Bp's Chapl for Th Educn from 80; V Gorseinon from 86; Hon Lect Th Univ of Wales (Swansea) from 88. *The Vicarage, 42 Princess Street, Gorseinon, Swansea SA4 2US* Gorseinon (0792) 892849

HOLE, Canon Derek Norman. b 33. Linc Th Coll 57. **d** 60 **p** 61. C Knighton St Mary Magd *Leic* 60-62; S Africa 62-64; C Kenilworth St Nic *Cov* 64-67; R Burton Latimer *Pet* 67-73; V Leic St Jas *Leic* from 73; Hon Can Leic Cathl from 83; RD Christianity (Leic) S from 83; Chapl to HM The Queen from 85. *The Vicarage, 216 London Road, Leicester LE2 1NE* Leicester (0533) 542111

HOLEHOUSE, Ernest William. b 15. St Aid Birkenhead 38. **d** 41 **p** 42. C Wickenby w Friesthorpe *Linc* 71-80; C Faldingworth w Buslingthorpe 73-80; rtd 80. *Ramsay Hall, Byron Road, Worthing, W Sussex BN11 3HW* Worthing (0903) 36880

HOLFORD, Andrew Peter. b 62. Nottm Univ BSc84. Cranmer Hall Dur 87. **d** 90 **p** 91. C Waltham Cross *St Alb* from 90. *103 Northfield Road, Waltham Cross, Herts EN8 7RD* Waltham Cross (0992) 27246

HOLFORD, John Alexander. b 40. Chich Th Coll 65. **d** 67 **p** 68. C Cottingley *Bradf* 67-71; C Baildon 71-73; P-in-c Bingley H Trin 73-74; V 74-86; V Woodhall from 86. *St James's Vicarage, Galloway Lane, Pudsey, W Yorkshire LS28 8JR* Bradford (0274) 662735

✠**HOLLAND, Rt Rev Alfred Charles.** b 27. St Chad's Coll Dur BA50 DipTh52. **d** 52 **p** 53 **c** 70. C W Hackney St Barn *Lon* 52-54; Australia from 54; Asst Bp Perth 70-77; Bp Newc 78. *Bishopscourt, Brown Street, Newcastle, NSW, Australia 2300* Newcastle (49) 262767 or 263733

✠**HOLLAND, Rt Rev Edward.** b 36. AKC64. **d** 65 **p** 66 **c** 86. C Dartford H Trin *Roch* 65-69; C Mill Hill Jo Keble Ch *Lon* 69-72; Prec Gib Cathl *Eur* 72-74; Chapl Naples Ch 74-79; Chapl Bromley Hosp 79-86; V Bromley St Mark *Roch* 79-86; Suff Bp Eur from 86; Dean Brussels from 86. *11 Lanark Road, London W9 1DD* 071-286 3335

HOLLAND, Glyn. b 59. Hull Univ BA Bris Univ CertEd. Coll of Resurr Mirfield 83. **d** 85 **p** 86. C Brighouse *Wakef* 85-89; V Ferrybridge from 89; Chapl Pontefract Gen Infirmary Wakef from 89. *St Andrew's Vicarage, 5 Pontefract Road, Ferrybridge, Knottingley, W Yorkshire WF11 8PN* Pontefract (0977) 672772

HOLLAND, Dr Henry Bowlby Tristram. b 11. Edin Univ MB, ChB34. Edin Th Coll 52. **d** 66 **p** 67. Pakistan 66-71; C Edin SS Phil and Jas *Edin* 71-77; C W Linton from 77; C Penicuik from 77. *Cuaig, Linton Bank Drive, West Linton, Peeblesshire EH46 7DT* West Linton (0968) 60454

HOLLAND, Jack Newton Charles. b 08. OBE57. St Edm Hall Ox BA30 MA47. Westcott Ho Cam. **d** 31 **p** 32. R St Mabyn *Truro* 59-74; C-in-c Helland 69-74; rtd 74; Perm to Offic *B & W* from 75. *9 Playfield Close, Riverside Gardens, Henstridge, Templecombe, Somerset BA8 0QW* Stalbridge (0963) 62128

HOLLAND, John Stuart. b 52. Sarum & Wells Th Coll 77. **d** 80 **p** 81. C Wylde Green *Birm* 80-83; C Swanage and Studland *Sarum* 83-85; P-in-c Hawkley w Gussage St Andrew and Pentridge 85-88; TV Preston w Sutton Poyntz and Osmington w Poxwell from 88. *The Vicarage, 58 Littlemoor Road, Preston, Weymouth, Dorset DT3 6AA* Weymouth (0305) 833704

HOLLAND, Laurence Frederick Alfred. b 21. Sarum & Wells Th Coll. **d** 87 **p** 88. NSM Beaminster Area *Sarum* from 87. *18 St Mary Well Street, Beaminster, Dorset DT8 3BB* Beaminster (0308) 862426

HOLLAND, Matthew Francis. b 52. Lon Univ BA73. Qu Coll Birm DipTh78. **d** 79 **p** 80. C Ecclesall *Sheff* 79-83; TV Gleadless Valley 83-86; TR 86-88; V Sheff St Silas from 88. *St Silas's Vicarage, 40 Hanover Street, Sheffield S3 7WT* Sheffield (0742) 725300

HOLLAND, Paul William. b 55. Coll of Resurr Mirfield 78. **d** 80 **p** 81. C Parkstone St Pet w Branksea and St Osmund *Sarum* 80-83; CR from 85. *House of the Resurrection, Mirfield, W Yorkshire WF14 8BN* Mirfield (0924) 494318

HOLLAND, Peter Christie. b 36. St Andr Univ BSc60 Dur Univ DipTh62. Cranmer Hall Dur 60. **d** 62 **p** 63. C Darlington St Jo *Dur* 62-64; C Bishopwearmouth Ch Ch 64-69; V Tudhoe 69-77; V New Seaham 77-89; V Totternhoe, Stanbridge and Tilsworth *St Alb* from 89. *The Vicarage, Mill Road, Stanbridge, Leighton Buzzard, Beds LU7 9HX* Leighton Buzzard (0525) 210253

HOLLAND, Simon Geoffrey. b 63. MHCIMA83 Dorset Inst of HE OND81. Trin Coll Bris DipHE90. **d** 91. C Reigate St Mary *S'wark* from 91. *3 St Clair Close, Reigate, Surrey RH2 0QB* Reigate (0737) 242391

HOLLAND, Simon Paul. b 56. Univ Coll Lon LLB77 Qu Coll Cam BA80 MA84. Westcott Ho Cam 79. **d** 81 **p** 82. C Uckfield *Chich* 81-84; TV Lewes All SS, St Anne, St Mich and St Thos 84-88; TR 88-91; R Glas St Matt *Glas* from 91. *42 Hillhead Street, Glasgow G12 8PZ*

HOLLAND, Thomas Reginald. b 13. Reading Univ BA37 MA49. **d** 78 **p** 79. NSM Haddenham *Ely* 78-81; NSM Sutton from 81. *59 High Street, Sutton, Ely, Cambs CB6 2RA* Ely (0353) 778579

HOLLAND, William Geoffrey Bretton. b 36. Magd Coll Cam BA59 MA63. Westcott Ho Cam 61. **d** 63 **p** 64. C Cannock *Lich* 63-66; C Paddington Ch Ch *Lon* 66-69; Chapl Magd Coll Cam 69-73; V Twyford *Win* 74-78; V Twyford and Owslebury and Morestead 78-84; Chapl Twyford Sch Win from 84. *Twyford School, Searles Hill, Twyford, Winchester, Hants*

HOLLAND, William Michael Tristram. b 26. Jes Coll Cam BA50 MA52. St Steph Ho Ox 79. **d** 81 **p** 82. C High Wycombe *Ox* 81-84; R Steeple Aston w N Aston and Tackley from 84. *The Rectory, Fir Lane, Steeple Aston, Oxford OX5 3SF* Steeple Aston (0869) 47793

HOLLANDS, Albert William. b 17. Roch Th Coll 60. **d** 62 **p** 63. R Syderstone *Nor* 66-77; R Tattersett 67-83; P-in-c Tatterford 76-83; R Syderstone w Barmer 77-79; R Syderstone w Barmer and Bagthorpe 79-83; rtd 83; Perm to Offic *Nor* from 84. *25 Renwick Park East, West Runton, Cromer, Norfolk NR27 9LY* West Runton (026375) 352

HOLLANDS, Derek Gordon. b 45. Chich Th Coll 72. **d** 74 **p** 75. C Banstead *Guildf* 74-77; C Cranleigh 77-79; C Haywards Heath St Wilfrid *Chich* 79-80; TV 80-82; Chapl Hillingdon Area HA 82-86; Chapl W Suffolk Hosp Bury St Edm from 86. *West Suffolk Hospital, Hardwick Lane, Bury St Edmunds IP33 2QZ* Bury St Edmunds (0284) 763131

HOLLANDS, Percival Edwin Macaulay. b 36. Edin Th Coll 57. **d** 60 **p** 61. C Greenock *Glas* 60-64; C Aber St Mary *Ab* 64-65; P-in-c Aber St Clem 65-68; R Cruden 68-70; CF 70-82; C Ribbleton *Blackb* 82-83; TV 83-88; C Longton 88; C Penwortham St Mary from 88. *53 Beech Way, Penwortham, Preston, Lancs PR1 0XS* Preston (0772) 742069

HOLLANDS, Ray Leonard. b 42. S'wark Ord Course 68. **d** 71 **p** 72. NSM Hanworth All SS *Lon* 71-77 and 85-90; NSM Hanworth St Geo 77-85; NSM Marshwood Vale Team Min *Sarum* from 81. *Yew Tree Cottage, Marshwood, Bridport, Dorset DT6 5QF* Hawkchurch (02977) 566

HOLLETT, Miss Catherine Elaine. See DAKIN, Mrs Catherine Elaine

HOLLEY, Canon Geoffrey Raymond. b 28. AKC51. **d** 52 **p** 53. C Gt Ilford St Clem *Chelmsf* 52-53; C Gt Burstead 53-56; V 56-75; Bp's Ecum Officer 71-82; R Loughton St Jo from 75; Dioc Can Chelmsf Cathl from 78; RD Epping Forest from 82. *The Rectory, Church Lane, Loughton, Essex IG10 1PD* 081-508 1224

HOLLEY, Preb Graham Frank. b 29. Sarum Th Coll 60. **d** 61 **p** 62. C Heref All SS *Heref* 61-63; C W Wycombe *Ox* 63-67; V Much Marcle *Heref* from 67; P-in-c Lt Marcle 84-86; RD Ledbury 87-90; Preb Heref Cathl from 87. *The Vicarage, Dymock Road, Much Marcle, Ledbury, Herefordshire HR8 2NL* Much Marcle (053184) 643

HOLLIDAY, Arthur. b 22. St Jo Coll Dur 80. **d** 81 **p** 82. Hon C Allerton *Bradf* 81-84; Hon C Thornton St Jas from 84. *9 Alston Close, Bradford, W Yorkshire BD9 6AN* Bradford (0274) 487331

HOLLIDAY, Eric Hedley. b 13. ARCS34 Lon Univ BSc35. Ridley Hall Cam 35. **d** 37 **p** 38. V Islington St Paul Ball's Pond *Lon* 55-78; rtd 78; Perm to Offic *Ely* from 78. *4 George Place, Eynesbury, St Neots, Huntingdon, Cambs PE19 2QG* Huntingdon (0480) 215703

HOLLIDAY, Peter Leslie. b 48. FCA BCom70. Qu Coll Birm 81. **d** 83 **p** 84. C Burton *Lich* 83-87; P-in-c Longdon from 87; PV and Subchanter Lich Cath from 87. *The Vicarage, Longdon, Rugeley, Staffs WS15 4PS* Armitage (0543) 490307

HOLLIDAY, William. b 33. Qu Coll Cam BA56 MA60 McGill Univ Montreal BD58 LTh58. Montreal Dioc Th Coll 56 Linc Th Coll 58. **d** 58 **p** 59. C Stanningley St Thos *Ripon* 58-63; C Romaldkirk 63-64; India 64-77; V Thwaites Brow *Bradf* 77-86; RD S Craven 82-86; P-in-c Horton from 86. *Faith Sawrey's House, 41 Little Horton Green, Bradford BD5 0NG* Bradford (0274) 727976

HOLLIMAN, John James. b 44. St D Coll Lamp BA66. **d** 67 **p** 68. C Tideswell *Derby* 67-71; CF from 71. *c/o MOD (Army), Bagshot Park, Bagshot, Surrey GU19 5PL* Bagshot (0276) 71717

HOLLIN, Ian. b 40. Open Univ BA76. Sarum Th Coll 67. **d** 70 **p** 71. C Lanc Ch Ch *Blackb* 70-72; C S Shore H Trin 72-75; V Morecambe St Lawr 75-78; V Blackpool St Mary 78-83; PV and Succ Ex Cathl *Ex* 83-87. *Dowrich House Cottage, Crediton, Devon EX17 4EQ*

HOLLINGDALE, Derek Leslie. b 32. Ex & Truro NSM Scheme. **d** 83 **p** 84. NSM Tuckingmill *Truro* 83-85; NSM Illogan from 85. *11 Atlantic Terrace, Camborne, Cornwall TR14 7AW* Camborne (0209) 717404

HOLLINGHURST, Stephen. b 59. Univ of Wales DipTh. St Jo Coll Nottm 81. **d** 83 **p** 84. C Hyde St Geo *Ches* 83-86; C Cropwell Bishop w Colston Bassett, Granby etc *S'well* 86-90; R Pembridge w Moorcourt, Shobdon, Staunton etc *Heref* from 90. *The Rectory, Pembridge, Leominster, Herefordshire HR6 9EB* Pembridge (05447) 8998

HOLLINGS, Miss Patricia Mary. b 39. CertEd59. S'wark Ord Course 84. **d** 87. Par Dn Wyke *Bradf* from 87. *1 Greenacre Way, Wyke, Bradford, W Yorkshire BD12 9DJ* Bradford (0274) 677439

HOLLINGSHURST, Robert Peter. b 38. Ridley Hall Cam 64. **d** 67 **p** 68. C Roxeth Ch Ch *Lon* 67-70; C Attenborough w Chilwell *S'well* 70-73; C Ramsgate St Luke *Cant* 74-75; Chapl to the Deaf 78-80; TV Louth *Linc* 80-84; Chapl to the Deaf *Sarum* 84-87; P-in-c Odstock w Nunton and Bodenham from 84; P-in-c Britford from 89; P-in-c Charlton All Saints from 89. *The Rectory, Nunton, Salisbury SP5 4HP* Salisbury (0722) 330628

HOLLINGSWORTH, Geoffrey. b 53. MIPM85 Leeds Poly 74. N Ord Course 86. **d** 86 **p** 87. C Thorne *Sheff* 86-89; V Rawcliffe from 89. *The Vicarage, 5 The Green, Rawcliffe, Goole, N Humberside DN14 8QE* Goole (0405) 83298

HOLLINGSWORTH, Canon Gerald Frank Lee. b 26. Lon Univ BA53. Oak Hill Th Coll 49. **d** 54 **p** 55. Bp's Ind Adv *St E* 64-75; V Ipswich H Trin 64-72; R Ipswich St Clem w H Trin 72-75; R Gt and Lt Bealings w Playford and Culpho 75-90; RD Woodbridge 76-84; Hon Can St E Cathl from 76; rtd 90; Perm to Offic *St E* from 90. *The Conifers, Ipswich Road, Grundisburgh, Woodbridge, Suffolk IP13 6TJ* Grundisburgh (047335) 232

HOLLINGSWORTH, Paula Marion. b 62. Van Mildert Coll Dur BSc83. Trin Coll Bris BA91. **d** 91. C Keynsham *B & W* from 91. *88 Chandag Road, Keynsham, Bristol BS18 1QE* Bristol (0272) 861056

HOLLINGWORTH, Martin Douglas. b 50. **d** 77 **p** 78. C Hartford *Ches* 77-78; C Knowle *Birm* 79-81; S Africa from 81. *37 Greenfield Road, Kenilworth, Cape Town, 7700 South Africa*

HOLLINS, John Edgar. b 35. St Jo Coll Cam BA58 MA62. Oak Hill Th Coll 58. **d** 60 **p** 61. C St Alb St Paul *St Alb* 66-71; Hon C Halliwell St Paul *Man* 71-72; C Ravenhill St Jo 72-73; Perm to Offic *Birm* 79-81; V Millbrook *Ches* 81-89; rtd 89. *Tresuan, Meadway, Looe, Cornwall PL13 1JT* Looe (05036) 4062

HOLLINS, Peter Charles. b 31. **d** 62 **p** 63. C Eyres Monsell CD *Leic* 62-65; C Westwood *Sarum* 65-67; Lic to Offic *Roch* 72-77; Perm to Offic *Worc* from 79. *Ladykey, Holly Green, Upton-upon-Severn, Worcester* Upton-upon-Severn (06846) 2508

HOLLINSHEAD, Cyril Wyndham. b 09. Linc Th Coll 45. **d** 47 **p** 48. V Peasedown St John *B & W* 54-76; rtd 76. *65 Ridgeway, Sherborne, Dorset DT9 6DA* Sherborne (0935) 814232

HOLLIS, Christopher Barnsley. b 28. Clare Coll Cam BA52 MA59. Wells Th Coll 60. **d** 62 **p** 63. C Baildon *Bradf* 62-64; V Esholt 64-66; V Heaton St Barn 66-85; RD Airedale 73-82; Hon Can Bradf Cathl 77-85; Chapl HM Young Offender Inst Medomsley 85-90; V Medomsley *Dur* 85-90; P-in-c Denholme Gate *Bradf* from 90. *The Vicarage, Denholme, Bradford BD13 4EN* Bradford (0274) 832813

HOLLIS, Derek. b 60. Loughb Univ BA82. Cranmer Hall Dur 83. **d** 86 **p** 87. C Evington *Leic* 86-89; C Arnold *S'well* from 89. *15 Houldsworth Rise, Arnold, Nottingham NG5 8HZ* Nottingham (0602) 202843

HOLLIS, Douglas John. b 32. S Dios Minl Tr Scheme. **d** 84 **p** 85. NSM Haywards Heath St Wilfrid *Chich* from 84. *2 Northlands Avenue, Haywards Heath, W Sussex RH16 3RT* Haywards Heath (0444) 453688

HOLLIS, Canon Gerald. b 19. Ch Ch Ox BA42 MA45. Wells Th Coll 45. **d** 47 **p** 48. V Rotherham *Sheff* 60-74; Adn Birm 74-84; rtd 84; Perm to Offic *Sarum* from 87. *68 Britford Lane, Salisbury SP2 8AH* Salisbury (0722) 338154

HOLLIS, Howard Charles. b 16. Melbourne Univ MusBac40. Trin Coll Melbourne ThL43. **d** 45 **p** 46. V Primrose Hill St Mary w Avenue Road St Paul *Lon* 65-76; Australia from 76; rtd 83. *18 Maud Street, North Balwyn, Victoria, Australia 3104*

HOLLIS, Jeffrey Norman. b 30. Qu Coll Birm 71. **d** 74 **p** 75. C Inkberrow *Worc* 74-76; C Eastleigh *Win* 76-79; V Jersey St Jas 79-85; V Jersey St Luke 79-85; R Jersey St Sav 85-91; rtd 91. *12 Hill Farm, Stonepit Lane, Inkberrow, Worcester WR7 4EX* Inkberrow (0386) 793334

HOLLIS, Peter. b 20. Jes Coll Cam BA49. Wells Th Coll 49. **d** 51 **p** 52. R Sudbury St Greg and St Pet *St E* 67-81; R Sudbury and Chilton 81-86; rtd 86. *1 New Cottages, Brundon, Sudbury, Suffolk CO10 6XS* Sudbury (0787) 70447

HOLLIS, Timothy Knowles. b 28. St Steph Ho Ox 54. **d** 58 **p** 59. C Oatlands *Guildf* 58-60; C Crawley *Chich* 60-63; C Sotterley w Willingham *St E* 63-69; R Sotterley, Willingham, Shadingfield, Ellough etc 69-76; Perm to Offic from 77. *L'Arche, 14 London Road, Beccles, Suffolk NR34 9NH* Beccles (0502) 715329

HOLLOWAY, Canon Alan James. b 23. FPhS64 Lon Univ BD58 MTh67. Oak Hill Th Coll 53. **d** 56 **p** 57. Chapl and Lect St Paul's Coll Cheltenham 69-73; V Maisemore *Glouc* 73-76; Dir of Educn 74-82; Can Res Glouc Cathl 74-82; R Glouc St Mary de Crypt w St Jo and Ch Ch 82-88; rtd 88; Bp's Personal Asst *Glouc* from 88. *Bethany, Sandhurst Lane, Sandhurst, Gloucester GL2 9NP* Gloucester (0452) 730447

HOLLOWAY, David Dennis. b 43. Lich Th Coll 65. **d** 68 **p** 69. C Cricklade w Latton *Bris* 68-71; C Bris St Agnes w St Simon 71-72; C Bris St Agnes and St Simon w St Werburgh 72-74; V Bitton 74-78; TV E Bris 78-80; P-in-c Tormarton w W Littleton 80-83; Dioc Ecum Officer from 83. *17 Downs Park East, Bristol BS6 7QF* Bristol (0272) 623771

HOLLOWAY, David Ronald James. b 39. Univ Coll Ox BA62 MA66. Ridley Hall Cam 65. **d** 67 **p** 68. C Leeds St Geo *Ripon* 67-71; Tutor Wycliffe Hall Ox 71-72; V Jesmond Clayton Memorial *Newc* from 73. *The Vicarage, 7 Otterburn Terrace, Jesmond, Newcastle upon Tyne NE2 3AP* 091-281 2001

HOLLOWAY, Graham Edward. b 45. Chich Th Coll 69. **d** 72 **p** 73. C W Drayton *Lon* 72-75; P-in-c Hawton *S'well* 75-80; TV Newark w Hawton, Cotham and Shelton 80; V Ladybrook 80-85; P-in-c Babworth 85-87; R Babworth w Sutton-cum-Lound from 87; RD Retford from 88. *The Rectory, Babworth, Retford, Notts DN22 8ET* Retford (0777) 703253

HOLLOWAY, Howard Robinett. b 06. Keble Coll Ox BA27 MA31. Wells Th Coll 27. **d** 29 **p** 30. R Perranuthnoe *Truro* 70-72; rtd 72. *33 Aldersgate Street, Oxley, Brisbane, Queensland, Australia 4075*

HOLLOWAY, Keith Graham. b 45. Linc Coll Ox BA67 St Jo Coll Dur DipTh72. **d** 73 **p** 74. C Gt Ilford St Andr *Chelmsf* 73-78; Hon C Squirrels Heath 78-80; Min Chelmer Village CD 80-87; V E Springfield 87-89; P-in-c Gt Dunmow from 89. *3 The Charters, Church End, Dunmow, Essex CM6 2SJ* Great Dunmow (0371) 872504

✠**HOLLOWAY, Rt Rev Richard Frederick.** b 33. Lon Univ BD63. NY Th Sem STM68 Edin Th Coll 58. **d** 59 **p** 60 **c** 86. C Glas St Ninian *Glas* 59-63; P-in-c Glas St Marg 63-68; R Edin Old St Paul *Edin* 68-80; USA 80-84; V Ox St Mary Magd *Ox* 84-86; Bp Edin from 86. *The Diocesan Centre, Walpole Hall, Chester Street, Edinburgh EH3 7EN* 031-226 3359

HOLLOWAY, Roger Graham. b 33. Selw Coll Cam BA58 MA61. S'wark Ord Course 74. **d** 78 **p** 80. Hong Kong 78-80 and 85-88; Japan 80-84; PV Westmr St Marg from 88; Lic to Offic *S'wark* from 90; Nat Dir Ind Chr Fellowship from 91. *65 Fentiman Road, London SW8 1LH* 071-582 3417

HOLLOWAY, Simon Anthony. b 50. Sussex Univ BSc72. Trin Coll Bris 76. **d** 79 **p** 81. C Bushbury *Lich* 79-81; C

Castle Church 81-84; P-in-c Sparkbrook Ch Ch *Birm* from 84. *Christ Church Vicarage, 34 Grantham Road, Birmingham B11 1LU* 021-772 6558

HOLLOWOOD, Christopher George. b 54. K Alfred's Coll Win BEd76. Ripon Coll Cuddesdon 83. **d** 86 **p** 87. C Tupsley *Heref* 86-89; R Much Birch w Lt Birch, Much Dewchurch etc from 89. *The Rectory, Much Birch, Hereford HR2 8HT* Golden Valley (0981) 540558

HOLLOWOOD, Lewis William Rye. b 17. **d** 40 **p** 41. V Hadlow Down *Chich* 67-74; R Buxted St Marg 72-74; V Bexhill St Barn 75-81; Chapl Community Servants of the Cross Lindfield from 81; Dioc Communications Officer & Dir Soc Resp *Chich* 81-82; rtd 82. *Convent of the Holy Rood, Lindfield, Haywards Heath, W Sussex RH16 2QY* Lindfield (04447) 2090

HOLMAN, Francis Noel. b 37. DSPT90. Sarum Th Coll 62. **d** 65 **p** 66. C Weston Favell *Pet* 65-68; C Eckington *Derby* 68-71; Asst Chapl St Thos Hosp Lon 72-77; Chapl Hope Hosp Salford from 77; Chapl Man and Salford Skin Hosp from 88. *90 Rocky Lane, Monton, Eccles, Manchester M30 9LY* 061-787 5167 or 789 7373

HOLMAN, Geoffrey Gladstone. b 32. AKC56. **d** 57 **p** 58. C Eltham St Barn *S'wark* 57-60; CF 60-73; Dep Asst Chapl Gen 73-80; Asst Chapl Gen 80-84; QHC 82-84; V Wetwang and Garton-on-the-Wolds w Kirkburn *York* from 84; RD Harthill from 87. *The Vicarage, Wetwang, Driffield, N Humberside YO25 9XT* Driffield (0377) 86410

HOLME, Thomas Edmund. b 49. Selw Coll Cam BA71 MA75. Coll of Resurr Mirfield 71. **d** 73 **p** 74. C Wyther Ven Bede *Ripon* 73-76; C Wimbledon *S'wark* 76-78; TV 78-79; V Bermondsey St Anne 79-81; V Stamford Baron *Pet* 83-89; P-in-c Tinwell 83-89; Hon Min Can Pet Cathl 84-89; Prec Worc Cathl *Worc* from 89. *280 Bath Road, Worcester WR5 3ET* Worcester (0905) 353762

HOLMES, Alan Stewart. b 57. MInstPkg88 St Andr Univ BSc80. Ox NSM Course 85. **d** 88 **p** 89. NSM Shinfield *Ox* from 88. *21 Alandale Close, Reading RG2 8JP* Reading (0734) 313641

HOLMES, Anthony David Robert. b 38. Oak Hill Th Coll 75. **d** 77 **p** 78. C Iver *Ox* 77-81; V Bucklebury w Marlston from 81. *The Vicarage, Bucklebury, Reading RG7 6PL* Woolhampton (0734) 713193

HOLMES, Canon Charles Derek. b 25. Lon Bible Coll DipTh52 Wycliffe Hall Ox 63. **d** 65 **p** 66. C Downend *Bris* 67-70; Australia from 70; rtd 90. *27 Cremorne Avenue, Cremorne, Tasmania, Australia 7024* Cremorne (2) 489259

HOLMES, Clive Horace. b 31. Ox NSM Course. **d** 83 **p** 84. NSM Cumnor *Ox* from 83. *62 Westminster Way, Oxford OX2 0LW* Oxford (0865) 249640

HOLMES, David Roy. b 34. FIPM75. Ox NSM Course 81. **d** 84 **p** 85. NSM Ox SS Phil and Jas w St Marg *Ox* 84-85; NSM Ox St Giles and SS Phil and Jas w St Marg from 85. *48 Charlbury Road, Oxford OX2 6UX* Oxford (0865) 510061

HOLMES, Frank. b 22. NW Ord Course 75. **d** 78 **p** 79. NSM Hyde St Geo *Ches* 78-81; C Poynton 81-87; rtd 87; Perm to Offic *Ches* from 87. *277 Stockport Road, Marple, Stockport, Cheshire SK6 6ES* 061-449 9289

HOLMES, Frederick William. b 03. ACP38 AKC32. Lich Th Coll 26. **d** 38 **p** 39. R Cheddington w Mentmore *Ox* 63-68; rtd 68. *Parklea, 3 Linden Avenue, Whitchurch, Shropshire SY13 1JU* Whitchurch (0948) 2714

HOLMES, George Henry. b 07. ATCL34. **d** 42 **p** 44. V N Kelsey *Linc* 50-63; rtd 63. *Lupin Cottage, Withern, Alford, Lincs LN13 0NB* Withern (0507) 450585

HOLMES, Grant Wenlock. b 54. St Steph Ho Ox BA78 MA83. **d** 79 **p** 80. C Benhilton *S'wark* 79-82; C-in-c S Kenton Annunciation CD *Lon* 82-86; Tutor Chich Th Coll 86-87; Bp's Dom Chapl *Chich* 86-88; V Mayfield from 88. *The Vicarage, High Street, Mayfield, E Sussex TN20 6AB* Mayfield (0435) 873180

HOLMES, Canon John Robin. b 42. Leeds Univ BA64. Linc Th Coll 64. **d** 66 **p** 67. C Wyther Ven Bede *Ripon* 66-69; C Adel 69-73; V Beeston Hill St Luke 73-76; V Holbeck 76-86; RD Armley 82-86; V Manston 86; Hon Can Ripon Cathl from 89. *Manston Vicarage, Church Lane, Leeds LS15 8JB* Leeds (0532) 645530

HOLMES, Jonathan Michael. b 49. MRCVS73 Qu Coll Cam BA70 VetMB73 MA74 PhD78. Ridley Hall Cam 87. **d** 88 **p** 89. Chapl Qu Coll Cam from 88. *58 Devonshire Road, Cambridge CB1 2BL* Cambridge (0223) 312774

HOLMES, Dr Nigel Ernest Hartley. b 37. Em Coll Cam BA58 MA64 Lon Hosp BChir61 MB62. Ridley Hall Cam 62. **d** 64 **p** 65. C Cam St Phil *Ely* 64-68; I Jersey St Paul Prop Chpl *Win* 68-77; C Cam H Sepulchre w All SS *Ely* 78-80; Perm to Offic *St E* and *Ely* 80-86; P-in-c

Brinkley, Burrough Green and Carlton from 86; P-in-c Westley Waterless from 86. *The Rectory, Brinkley, Newmarket, Suffolk CB8 0SE*   Stetchworth (063876) 263

HOLMES, Nigel Peter. b 48. Nottm Univ BTh72 Lanc Univ CertEd72 Lon Univ BD76 Sheff Univ MEd84. Kelham Th Coll. **d** 72 **p** 73. C Barrow St Matt *Carl* 72-75; C Derby St Bart *Derby* 75-78; P-in-c Barlow 78-84; V Carl St Herbert w St Steph *Carl* 84-91; V Keswick St Jo from 91. *St John's Vicarage, St John's Terrace, Keswick, Cumbria CA12 4DN*   Keswick (07687) 72998

HOLMES, Peter Anthony. b 55. Univ of Wales (Ban) BA77 Brighton Poly CertEd78. Trin Coll Bris DipHE. **d** 88 **p** 89. C Croydon Ch Ch *S'wark* from 88. *15 Chatfield Road, Croydon CR0 3LA*   081-688 8635

HOLMES, Dr Peter Geoffrey. b 32. Bris Univ BSc59 MSc69 Leic Univ PhD74. St Deiniol's Hawarden 74. **d** 76 **p** 77. NSM Glen Parva and S Wigston *Leic* from 76; Prof Nottm Poly from 85. *19 Windsor Avenue, Glen Parva, Leicester LE2 9JQ*   Leicester (0533) 774534

HOLMES, Robert James. b 12. Kelham Th Coll 29. **d** 36 **p** 37. PC Breamore *Win* 67-69; V 69-71; Chapl Porto (or Oporto) *Eur* 71-74; Chapl Antwerp St Boniface 74-77; rtd 77; Perm to Offic *Chich* from 87. *8 Mount Drive, Saltdean, Brighton BN2 8QA*   Brighton (0273) 34324

HOLMES, Robert John Geoffrey. b 28. TCD BA53 MA57. Ely Th Coll 56. **d** 57 **p** 58. C Whitton St Aug CD *Lon* 57-59; C St Pancras w St Jas and Ch Ch 59-63; C Stepney St Dunstan and All SS 63-66; Chapl The Lon Hosp (Whitechapel) 63-68; C Stepney St Aug w St Phil *Lon* 66-68; S Africa 68-74; Perm to Offic *Ely* 74; *Chich* 74-76; R Telscombe w Piddinghoe and Southease *Chich* from 76. *28 Rustic Park, Telscombe Cliffs, Newhaven, E Sussex BN10 7SW*   Peacehaven (0273) 588323

HOLMES, Roger Cockburn. b 46. Jes Coll Ox BA70 MA84 Edin Univ BD76. Edin Th Coll 73. **d** 84 **p** 85. Canada 84-88; R Ditchingham w Pirnough *Nor* 88-90; R Hedenham 88-90; R Broome 88-90; R Ditchingham, Hedenham and Broome from 90. *The Rectory, Ditchingham, Bungay, Suffolk NR35 2JS*   Bungay (0986) 892716

HOLMES, Roy Grant. b 37. Ox NSM Course 83. **d** 86 **p** 87. NSM Wokingham St Paul *Ox* from 86. *58 Copse Drive, Wokingham, Berks RG11 1LX*   Wokingham (0734) 784141

HOLMES, Stanley Thomas. b 11. Selw Coll Cam BA34 MA46. St Steph Ho Ox 34. **d** 36 **p** 37. V Goring *Ox* 48-84; rtd 84; Perm to Offic *Ox* from 84. *Lower Farm, 8 Dunstan Road, Old Headington, Oxford OX3 9BY*   Oxford (0865) 62657

HOLMES, Stephen. b 54. St Andr Univ MTh84. Chich Th Coll 84. **d** 86 **p** 87. C Croydon St Jo *S'wark* 86-89; C Tewkesbury w Walton Cardiff *Glouc* from 89. *83 York Road, Tewkesbury, Glos GL20 5HB*   Tewkesbury (0684) 294756

HOLMES, Stephen John. b 50. CertEd72 DipHE83. Trin Coll Bris 81 Sarum & Wells Th Coll 88. **d** 89 **p** 90. C Skegness and Winthorpe *Linc* from 89. *55 St Andrew's Drive, Skegness, Lincs PE25 1DJ*   Skegness (0754) 68617

HOLNESS, Edwin Geoffrey Nicholas. b 39. RGN BTA. Sarum Th Coll 68. **d** 71 **p** 72. C Upper Beeding *Chich* 71-74; C Bramber w Botolphs 71-74; C Munster Square St Mary Magd *Lon* 74-75; Perm to Offic *Chich* 75-76; C Brighton Annunciation 76-77; Chapl Brighton Hosp Gp from 77; Chapl R Sussex Co Hosp Brighton from 77; Lic to Offic *Chich* from 77. *Royal Sussex County Hospital, Eastern Road, Brighton BN2 5BE*   Brighton (0273) 696955

HOLROYD, Gordon Eric. b 31. SSM. **d** 75 **p** 76. Asst Chapl St Martin's Coll Lanc 76-77; Chapl 77-78; Hon C Sheff St Matt *Sheff* 78-80; Lic to Offic *Man* 80-81; P-in-c Willen *Ox* 81-84; Perm to Offic *Blackb* from 84; NSM Middlesb All SS *York* from 89. *112 Tower Green, Middlesbrough, Cleveland TS2 1RD*   Middlesbrough (0642) 241633

HOLROYD, John Richard. b 54. Liv Univ BA75 PGCE77. Wycliffe Hall Ox 78. **d** 81 **p** 82. C Gt Stanmore *Lon* 81-84; Min Can, VC and Prec St E Cathl *St E* 84-89; TV Wolverton *Ox* from 89. *28 Harvester Close, Greenleys, Milton Keynes MK12 6LE*   Milton Keynes (0908) 222802

HOLROYD, Stephen Charles. b 56. UEA BA79. St Jo Coll Nottm 84. **d** 87 **p** 88. C Barton Seagrave w Warkton *Pet* 87-91; V Eye from 91. *The Vicarage, 4 Fountains Place, Eye, Peterborough PE6 7UN*   Peterborough (0733) 222334

HOLROYD, Thomas Arthur Wulstan. b 13. **d** 51 **p** 52. V E Acton St Dunstan *Lon* 67-78; rtd 78; Perm to Offic *Nor* from 78. *20 Hale Road, Bradenham, Thetford, Norfolk IP25 7RA*

HOLT, Alan Leonard. b 12. Dur Univ LTh42. Edin Th Coll 39. **d** 42 **p** 43. V Streetly *Lich* 50-77; rtd 77. *Old Vicarage, Rectory Way, Lympsham, Weston-super-Mare, Avon BS24 0EW*   Edingworth (0934) 527

HOLT, Brian. b 30. BMin73. Huron Coll Ontario. **d** 70 **p** 71. Canada 70-78; V Glodwick *Man* 78-83; TV E Farnworth and Kearsley 83-87; R Abbey Hey from 87. *St George's Rectory, 10 Redacre Road, Abbey Hey, Manchester M18 8RD*   061-223 1624

HOLT, David. b 44. St Jo Coll Dur BSc67 DipTh69. **d** 70 **p** 71. C Blackley St Pet *Man* 70-73; C Radcliffe St Thos 73-74; C Radcliffe St Thos and St Jo 74-75; V Ashton St Pet 75-79; Dioc Youth Officer *Guildf* 80-85; V Bagshot from 85. *The Vicarage, 43 Church Road, Bagshot, Surrey GU19 5EQ*   Bagshot (0276) 73348

HOLT, Douglas Robert. b 49. MA. Ridley Hall Cam. **d** 82 **p** 83. C Cam St Barn *Ely* 82-84; P-in-c 84-86; V 86-91; V Ealing St Mary *Lon* from 91. *Ealing Vicarage, 11 Church Place, London W5 4HN*   081-567 0414 or 579 7134

HOLT, Francis Thomas. b 38. Edin Th Coll 79. **d** 81 **p** 82. C Cullercoats St Geo *Newc* 81-83; C Ponteland 83-86; Chapl Worc Coll of HE 86-89; R Worc St Clem *Worc* from 86. *St Clement's Rectory, 124 Laugherne Road, Worcester WR2 5LT*   Worcester (0905) 422675

HOLT, Harold. b 20. **d** 52 **p** 52. V Haslingden St Jo Stonefold *Blackb* 60-72; V Blackb St Aid 72-85; rtd 85; Perm to Offic *Blackb* from 85. *24 Scott Avenue, Baxenden, Accrington, Lancs BB5 2XA*   Accrington (0254) 396474

HOLT, Jack Derek. b 38. Trin Coll Bris 71. **d** 73 **p** 74. C Daubhill *Man* 73-76; P-in-c Thornham w Gravel Hole 76-79; V 79-83; R Talke *Lich* from 83. *The Rectory, Crown Bank, Talke, Stoke-on-Trent ST7 1PU*   Stoke-on-Trent (0782) 782348

HOLT, Keith. b 37. S'wark Ord Course. **d** 82 **p** 83. NSM Selsdon St Jo w St Fran *Cant* 82-84; NSM Selsdon St Jo w St Fran *S'wark* from 85; Dean for Croydon NSMs from 90. *12 Ridge Langley, South Croydon, Surrey CR2 0AR*   081-651 1815

HOLT, Michael. b 38. Univ of Wales (Lamp) BA61 DipTh63. **d** 63 **p** 64. C Stand *Man* 63-69; V Bacup St Jo from 69. *St John's Vicarage, Bankside Lane, Bacup, Lancs OL13 8HG*   Bacup (0706) 873275

HOLT, Norman Botterill. b 16. Worc Ord Coll 60. **d** 60 **p** 61. R Earls Croome w Hill Croome and Strensham *Worc* 62-83; rtd 83. *19 Nelson Road, Sheringham, Norfolk*   Sheringham (0263) 822624

HOLT, Paul William Charles. b 53. St Jo Coll Dur BA75. Oak Hill Th Coll 75 Ridley Hall Cam 76. **d** 77 **p** 78. C Bexleyheath Ch Ch *Roch* 77-80; C Frimley *Guildf* 80-84; P-in-c Badshot Lea CD from 84. *8 Badshot Park, Badshot Lea, Farnham, Surrey GU9 9JZ*   Aldershot (0252) 331370

HOLT, Stuart Henry. b 57. Bath Univ BEd78. Ridley Hall Cam 84. **d** 87 **p** 88. C Locks Heath *Portsm* 87-90; Chapl RAF from 89. *c/o MOD, Adastral House, Theobald's Road, London WC1X 8RU*   071-430 7268

HOLTAM, Nicholas Roderick. b 54. Collingwood Coll Dur BA75 K Coll Lon BD78 AKC78 Dur Univ MA89. Westcott Ho Cam 78. **d** 79 **p** 80. C Stepney St Dunstan and All SS *Lon* 79-83; Tutor Linc Th Coll 83-88; V Is of Dogs Ch Ch and St Jo w St Luke *Lon* from 88. *Christ Church Vicarage, Manchester Road, London E14 3BN*   071-987 1915

HOLTAM, Canon Ralph. b 16. Univ of Wales BA40. St Mich Coll Llan 40. **d** 42 **p** 43. V Roath St Marg *Llan* 65-76; R Sully 76-85; Can Llan Cathl from 81; rtd 85. *19 Windsor Road, Barry, S Glam CF6 8AW*   Barry (0446) 741567

HOLTBY, Very Rev Robert Tinsley. b 21. FSA St Edm Hall Ox BA43 MA46 BD57 K Coll Cam BA47 MA52. Cuddesdon Coll 43 Westcott Ho Cam 44. **d** 46 **p** 47. Sec C of E Schs Coun 67-74; Gen Sec Nat Soc 67-77; Lic to Offic *S'wark* 68-77; Gen Sec Gen Syn Bd of Educn 74-77; Dean Chich 77-89; rtd 89. *4 Hutton Hall, Huttons Ambo, York YO6 7HW*   Malton (0653) 696366

HOLTH, Oystein Johan. b 31. Open Univ BA75. AKC54. **d** 54 **p** 55. C Greenford H Cross *Lon* 54-56; Malaya 56-63; Malaysia 63-67; Chapl St Hilda's Priory Sneaton, Whitby 67-75; Chapl St Hilda's Sch Whitby 67-75; P-in-c Pimlico St Barn *Lon* from 75; Ind Chapl from 75. *St Barnabas Clergy House, St Barnabas Street, London SW1W 8PF*   071-730 5054

HOLYER, Vincent Alfred Douglas. b 28. Ex Univ BA54. Oak Hill Th Coll 54. **d** 56 **p** 57. C Bethnal Green St Jas Less *Lon* 56-58; C Braintree *Chelmsf* 58-61; V Islington All SS *Lon* 61-65; R St Ruan w St Grade *Truro* 65-85; V Constantine from 85. *The Vicarage, Chalbury Heights, Constantine, Falmouth, Cornwall TR11 5AN* Falmouth (0326) 40259

HOLYHEAD, Rex Noel Humphrey. b 32. **d** 68 **p** 69. C Glouc St Mary de Lode and St Nic *Glouc* 68-70; C Christchurch *Win* 70-77; V Win St Jo cum Winnall 77-81; P-in-c Millbrook 81-82; R from 82. *The Rectory, 115 Regents Park Road, Southampton SO1 3NZ* Southampton (0703) 773417

HOLZAPFEL, Peter Rudolph. b 51. St Jo Coll Nottm 84. **d** 86 **p** 87. C St Jo in Bedwardine *Worc* 86-89; V Worc St Mich from 89. *St Michael's Vicarage, Burleigh Road, Worcester WR2 5QT* Worcester (0905) 421986

HOMAN, Richard Arthur. b 18. Em Coll Cam BA40 MA44. Ridley Hall Cam 40. **d** 42 **p** 43. Chapl Birkenhead Sch Merseyside 54-83; rtd 83; Perm to Offic *Ches* from 83. *58 Claremount Road, Wallasey, Merseyside L45 6UD* 051-638 6770

HOMER, Alan Fellows. b 30. Ridley Hall Cam 61. **d** 63 **p** 64. C Heref St Jas *Heref* 63-66; Dep Chapl HM Pris Brixton 66-70; V Brixton Hill St Sav *S'wark* 66-73; CF (TA) 70-73; CF 73-75; V Heeley *Sheff* 75-87; R Cheveley *Ely* from 87; R Ashley w Silverley from 87; V Wood Ditton w Saxon Street from 87; V Kirtling from 87. *The Rectory, 130 High Street, Cheveley, Newmarket, Suffolk CB8 9DG* Newmarket (0638) 730770

HOMEWOOD, Michael John. b 33. Wells Th Coll 69. **d** 71 **p** 72. C Ilfracombe H Trin *Ex* 71-72; C Ilfracombe, Lee and W Down 72-75; P-in-c Woolacombe 76-78; TV Ilfracombe, Lee, W Down, Woolacombe and Bittadon 78-82; TR S Molton, Nymet St George, High Bray etc 82-86; P-in-c Chittlehampton 85-86; TR S Molton w Nymet St George, High Bray etc from 86. *The Rectory, South Molton, Devon EX36 3AX* South Molton (07695) 2356

HOMFRAY, John Bax Tayler. b 29. Keble Coll Ox BA52 MA. Ridley Hall Cam 52. **d** 54 **p** 55. C Kingswood *Bris* 54-57; C Leckhampton St Pet *Glouc* 57-64; V Staverton w Boddington 64-86; V Staverton w Boddington and Tredington etc from 87. *The Vicarage, Staverton, Cheltenham, Glos GL51 0TW* Cheltenham (0242) 680307

HONE, Canon Frank Leslie. b 11. Kelham Th Coll 32. **d** 38 **p** 39. V Frodingham *Linc* 66-78; Can and Preb Linc Cathl 72-78; rtd 78. *Morcote, Roseala Avenue, Welton, Lincoln LN2 3RT* Welton (0673) 61548

HONES, Simon Anthony. b 54. Sussex Univ BSc75. Qu Coll Birm DipTh78. **d** 79 **p** 80. C Win Ch *Win* 79-82; C Basing 82-88; Min Chineham CD 88-90; V Surbiton St Matt *S'wark* from 90. *St Matthew's Vicarage, 20 Kingsdowne Road, Surbiton, Surrey KT6 6JZ* 081-399 4853

HONEY, Canon Frederick Bernard. b 22. Selw Coll Cam BA48 MA72. Wells Th Coll 48. **d** 50 **p** 51. V Wollaston *Worc* 55-87; RD Stourbridge 72-83; Hon Can Worc Cathl 75-87; rtd 87. *38 Park Farm, Bourton-on-the-Water, Cheltenham, Glos GL54 2YF* Cotswold (0451) 22218

HONEY, Thomas David. b 56. Lon Univ BA78. Ripon Coll Cuddesdon 80. **d** 83 **p** 84. C Mill End and Heronsgate w W Hyde *St Alb* 83-86; C Stepney St Dunstan and All SS *Lon* 86-89; TV High Wycombe *Ox* from 89. *The Vicarage, Micklefield Road, High Wycombe, Bucks HP13 7HU* High Wycombe (0494) 31141

HONEYBALL, Mark George. b 56. Ch Coll Cam BA78 MA82. Westcott Ho Cam 79. **d** 81 **p** 82. C Witham *Chelmsf* 81-84; C Bath Abbey w St Jas *B & W* 84-86; Chapl Fitzw Coll and New Hall Cam 86-90; Chapl & Hd Relig Studies Oundle Sch Pet from 90. *The School, Oundle, Peterborough PE8 4EN* Oundle (0832) 272338

HONNER, Canon Robert Ralph. b 15. St Chad's Coll Dur BA37 DipTh38 MA40. **d** 38 **p** 39. V Melbourne *Derby* 54-72; V Beeley and Edensor 72-80; rtd 80; Perm to Offic *Derby* from 80. *5 Castle Mews, Blackwell Lane, Melbourne, Derby DE7 1LW* Melbourne (0332) 864356

HONNOR, Mrs Marjorie Rochefort. b 27. Birm Univ BA48. Cranmer Hall Dur 79. **dss** 81 **d** 87. Church Oakley and Wootton St Lawrence *Win* 81-87; Par Dn 87-89; rtd 89. *33C Surrey Road, Bournemouth, Hants BH4 9BJ* Bournemouth (0202) 761021

HONOUR, Colin Reginald. b 44. Lanc Univ CertEd69 Man Univ DipAdEd75 Newc Univ MEd80. Nor Ord Course 88. **d** 91. C Walmsley *Man* from 91. *29 Shorefield Mount, Dunscar, Bolton BL7 9EL* Bolton (0204) 56424

HONOUR, Derek. b 59. Bath Univ BSc84. St Jo Coll Nottm. **d** 89 **p** 90. C High Wycombe *Ox* from 89. *21 The Haystacks, High Wycombe, Bucks HP13 6PY* High Wycombe (0494) 451202

HONOUR, Joanna. b 61. Westmr Coll Ox BEd83. St Jo Coll Nottm. **d** 89. Par Dn High Wycombe *Ox* from 89. *21 The Haystacks, High Wycombe, Bucks HP13 6PY* High Wycombe (0494) 451202

HOOD, Kenneth Ernest. b 14. Lon Univ BSc33 Em Coll Cam BA36 MA41. Westcott Ho Cam 36. **d** 38 **p** 38. V Kingsbury *Birm* 68-80; rtd 80; Perm to Offic *Birm* from 80. *78 Goodere Drive, Polesworth, Tamworth, Staffs B78 1BZ* Tamworth (0827) 894676

HOOD, Leslie. b 23. NE Ord Course. **d** 85 **p** 85. NSM Seaham w Seaham Harbour *Dur* from 85; NSM Dalton le Dale from 90; NSM Hawthorn from 90. *3 Queen Street, Seaham, Co Durham SR7 7SR* 091-581 2658

HOOD, Peter Michael. b 47. Sheff Univ BSc68 St Pet Coll Ox DipTh72. Wycliffe Hall Ox 70. **d** 73 **p** 74. C Soundwell *Bris* 73-76; P-in-c Walcot St Andr CD 76-77; TV Swindon St Jo and St Andr 77-80; V Esh *Dur* 80-88; V Hamsteels 80-88; V Stockton St Paul from 88. *65 Bishopton Road, Stockton-on-Tees, Cleveland TS18 4PE* Stockton-on-Tees (0642) 617869

HOOD, Robert Ernest Nathaniel. b 12. TCD BA34 MA42. **d** 37 **p** 38. V Holloway Em w Hornsey Road St Barn *Lon* 57-77; rtd 77; Perm to Offic *Cant* from 79. *Bromley College, London Road, Bromley BR1 1PE* Herne Bay (0227) 366317

HOOD, Canon Thomas Henry Havelock. b 24. Chich Th Coll 51. **d** 54 **p** 55. C Stella *Dur* 54-57; Australia from 57; Hon Can Brisbane from 88. *St Matthew's Rectory, 66 Quarry Road, Sherwood, Brisbane, Queensland, Australia 4075* Brisbane (7) 379-9472

HOOGERWERF, John Constant. b 50. MIH86 Bris Poly BA85. Oscott Coll (RC) 68. **d** 73 **p** 74. In RC Ch 73-84; Hon C Davyhulme Ch Ch *Man* from 84. *9 Lincoln Avenue, Stretford, Manchester M32 9TU* 061-747 4811

HOOK, Ronald Arthur. b 10. Or Coll Ox BA33 MA46. Sarum Th Coll 33. **d** 34 **p** 35. R Hurstpierpoint *Chich* 65-75; R Albourne 71-75; rtd 75; Perm to Offic *Chich* from 76. *Bramleys, 35 Manor Gardens, Hurstpierpoint, W Sussex BN6 9UG* Hurstpierpoint (0273) 832092

✠**HOOK, Rt Rev Ross Sydney.** b 17. MC45. Peterho Cam BA39 MA43 Bradf Univ DLitt81. Ridley Hall Cam 39. **d** 41 **p** 42 **c** 65. C Milton *Win* 41-43; Chapl RNVR 43-46; Chapl Ridley Hall Cam 46-48; R Chorlton-cum-Hardy St Clem *Man* 48-52; R Chelsea St Luke *Lon* 52-61; RD Chelsea 52-61; Dir Post Ord Tr *Roch* 61-65; Can Res Roch Cathl 61-65; Suff Bp Grantham *Linc* 65-72; Can and Preb Linc Cathl 66-72; Dean Stamford 72; Bp Bradf 72-80; Chief of Staff to Abp Cant 80-84; Asst Bp Cant from 80; rtd 84. *Millrock, New Rents, Newchurch, Romney Marsh, Kent TN29 0DN* Dymchurch (0303) 873115

HOOKER, Canon Roger Hardham. b 34. St Edm Hall Ox BA58 Ox Univ DipTh59. Wycliffe Hall Ox 58. **d** 60 **p** 61. C Stockton *Dur* 60-63; India 65-78; Miss Partner CMS from 79; Tutor Crowther Hall CMS Tr Coll Selly Oak 79-82; Dioc Missr *Birm* from 82; Hon Can Birm Cathl from 89. *30 Little Moor Hill, Smethwick, W Midlands B67 7BG* 021-558 3386

HOOLE, Charles. b 33. St Aid Birkenhead 61. **d** 63 **p** 64. C Skerton St Luke *Blackb* 63-65; P-in-c Preston St Jas 65-69; V Lostock Hall 69-73; Chapl HM Pris Eastchurch 74-75; V St Annes St Marg *Blackb* 75-81; V S Shore St Pet from 81. *St Peter's Vicarage, 19 Windermere Road, Blackpool FY4 2BX* Blackpool (0253) 41231

HOOLEY, John Philip. b 45. Hartley Victoria Coll 69 St Deiniol's Hawarden 78. **d** 79 **p** 79. In Meth Ch 73-78; C Heref St Martin *Heref* 79-81; CF from 81. *c/o MOD (Army), Bagshot Park, Bagshot, Surrey GU19 5PL* Bagshot (0276) 71717

HOOPER, Catherine Margaret. b 58. Leic Univ BSc81 St Jo Coll Dur BA84. **dss** 85 **d** 87. Houghton le Spring *Dur* 85-87; Par Dn 87-88; C Millfield St Mark from 88. *Church House, St Mark's Terrace, Sunderland SR4 7BN* 091-567 7750

HOOPER, Canon Charles. b 24. Witwatersrand Univ BA46. Coll of Resurr Mirfield 49. **d** 51 **p** 52. S Africa 51-68; Swaziland 68-86; Can Swaziland 71-86; CR from 89. *House of the Resurrection, Mirfield, W Yorkshire WF14 0BN* Mirfield (0924) 494318

HOOPER, Ven Charles German. b 11. Linc Coll Ox BA32 MA49. St Aug Coll Cant. **d** 34 **p** 35. Adn Ipswich *St E* 65-76; P-in-c Kelsale w Carlton 74-76; rtd 76; Perm to Offic *St E* from 76. *East Green Cottage, Kelsale, Saxmundham, Suffolk* Saxmundham (0728) 2702

HOOPER, Derek Royston. b 33. St Edm Hall Ox BA57 MA65. Cuddesdon Coll 57. **d** 59 **p** 60. C Gt Walsingham *Nor* 59-62; C Townstall w Dartmouth *Ex* 62-65; V Lynton and Brendon 65-69; C Littleham w Exmouth 70-72; TV 72-79; R Wrington w Butcombe *B & W* from 79. *The Rectory, High Street, Wrington, Bristol BS18 7QD* Wrington (0934) 862201

HOOPER, Geoffrey Michael. b 39. K Coll Lon 61. **d** 66 **p** 67. C Chesterfield All SS *Derby* 66-69; Chapl RAF 69-74; P-in-c Hook Norton w Swerford and Wigginton *Ox* 74-80; P-in-c Gt Rollright 75-80; R Hook Norton w Gt Rollright, Swerford etc 80-82; Warden Mansf Ho Univ Settlement Plaistow from 82; Dir from 86. *Mansfield House, 30 Avenons Road, London E13 8HT* 071-476 2375 or 476 1505

HOOPER, Ian. b 44. St Jo Coll York CertEd67. Trin Coll Bris DipHE88. **d** 88 **p** 89. C Martlesham w Brightwell *St E* from 88. *4 Saddlers Place, Martlesham Heath, Ipswich IP5 7SS* Ipswich (0473) 625433

HOOPER, Kevin John. b 56. St Cath Coll Cam BA77 MA81. Coll of Resurr Mirfield 78. **d** 80 **p** 81. C Holbrooks *Cov* 80-85; V Eyres Monsell *Leic* from 85. *St Hugh's Vicarage, Pasley Road, Leicester LE2 9BU* Leicester (0533) 782954

HOOPER, Preb Michael Wrenford. b 41. Univ of Wales (Lamp) BA63. St Steph Ho Ox 63. **d** 65 **p** 66. C Bridgnorth St Mary *Heref* 65-70; P-in-c Habberley 70-78; R 78-81; V Minsterley 70-81; RD Pontesbury 75-80; Preb Heref Cathl from 81; V Leominster 81-85; TR Leominster from 85; P-in-c Eyton 81-85; RD Leominster from 81. *The Rectory, Church Street, Leominster, Herefordshire HR6 8NH* Leominster (0568) 612124

HOOPER, Paul Denis Gregory. b 52. Man Univ BA75 Ox Univ BA80 MA87. Wycliffe Hall Ox 78. **d** 81 **p** 82. C Leeds St Geo *Ripon* 81-84; Dioc Youth Officer 84-87; Bp's Dom Chapl from 87; Dioc Communications Officer from 87. *18 Cathedral Close, Ripon, N Yorkshire HG4 1ND* Ripon (0765) 4518

HOOPER, Peter Guy. b 30. K Coll Lon 51. **d** 55 **p** 56. C Huddersfield SS Pet and Paul *Wakef* 55-60; C Brompton H Trin *Lon* 60-67; R Hazelbury Bryan w Stoke Wake etc *Sarum* 72-84; R Yetminster w Ryme Intrinseca and High Stoy from 84; RD Sherborne 87-91. *The Rectory, Church Street, Yetminster, Sherborne, Dorset DT9 6LG* Yetminster (0935) 872237

HOOPER, Sydney Paul. b 46. Lanc Univ BA68 CertEd69 QUB. **d** 85 **p** 87. NSM Killaney w Carryduff *D & D* 85-91; Lic to Offic from 91. *14 Briar Hill, Rossdale Road, Belfast* Belfast (0232) 790907

HOOPER, Mrs Valerie Lilian. b 31. Ex & Truro NSM Scheme 79. **dss** 82 **d** 87. Ex St Mark *Ex* 82-85; Cofton w Starcross 85-87; Hon Par Dn 87-89. *1 Cofton Hill, Cockwood, Starcross, Exeter EX6 8RB* Starcross (0626) 890046

HOOPER, William Gilbert. b 38. Ex Univ BA60. Llan St Mich DipTh82. **d** 82 **p** 83. C Hubberston w Herbrandston and Hasguard etc *St D* 82-85; R Llangwm and Freystrop from 85. *The Rectory, Llangwm, Haverfordwest, Dyfed SA62 4JP* Johnston (0437) 891317

HOOTON, Arthur Russell. b 23. Moore Th Coll Sydney ACT ThL51. **d** 52 **p** 52. V Stockingford *Cov* 65-89; rtd 89. *18 Chetwynd Drive, Nuneaton, Warks CV11 4TF* Nuneaton (0203) 343281

HOOTON, David James. b 50. St Kath Coll Liv CertEd73 DipRE81. N Ord Course 83. **d** 86 **p** 87. NSM Pemberton St Mark Newtown *Liv* 86-89; C Ashton-in-Makerfield St Thos from 89. *79 Greenfields Crescent, Ashton-in-Makerfield, Wigan, Lancs WN4 8QY* Wigan (0942) 716426

HOPCRAFT, Jonathan Richard. b 34. Or Coll Ox BA55 DipEd66 MA66. Westcott Ho Cam 57. **d** 59 **p** 60. C Cannock *Lich* 59-63; N Rhodesia 63-64; S Rhodesia 64-65; Hon C Olton *Birm* 66-68; Antigua 68-72; C Gt Grimsby St Mary and St Jas *Linc* 72; TV 72-76; P-in-c E Stockwith 76-84; V Blyton w Pilham 76-84; P-in-c Laughton w Wildsworth 76-84; TV Bilston *Lich* 84-90; P-in-c Wolv St Jo from 90. *31 Lea Road, Wolverhampton WV3 0LU* Wolverhampton (0902) 713041

HOPE, Charles Henry. b 64. FRGS89 Regent's Park Coll Ox BA87 MA90. St Jo Coll Dur BA90. **d** 90 **p** 91. C Tynemouth St Jo *Newc* from 90. *19 St Stephen's Way, North Shields, Tyne & Wear NE29 6JF* 091-258 7247

HOPE, Colin Frederick. b 49. St Mich Coll Llan 73. **d** 76 **p** 77. C Warrington St Elphin *Liv* 76-80; V Newton-le-Willows 80-84; CSWG from 84. *The Monastery, Crawley Down, Crawley, W Sussex RH10 4LH* Copthorne (0342) 712074

HOPE, Cyril Sackett. b 24. St Edm Hall Ox BA49 MA54. Ely Th Coll 50. **d** 51 **p** 52. R Dunchideock and

Shillingford *Ex* 63-77; Asst Dir of Educn from 73; P-in-c Stockland w Dalwood 77-79; V 79-90; rtd 90; Perm to Offic *Ex* from 90. *Verbena, Hind Street, Ottery St Mary, Devon EX11 1BW* Ottery St Mary (0404) 815028

✠**HOPE, Rt Rev and Rt Hon David Michael.** b 40. PC91. Nottm Univ BA62 Linacre Ho Ox DPhil65. St Steph Ho Ox 62. **d** 65 **p** 66 **c** 85. C W Derby (or Tuebrook) St Jo *Liv* 65-67 and 68-70; Chapl Bucharest *Eur* 67-68; V Orford St Andr *Liv* 70-74; Prin St Steph Ho Ox 74-82; V St Marylebone All SS *Lon* 82-85; Bp Wakef 85-91; Bp Lon from 91; Dean of the Chpls Royal and Prelate of OBE from 91. *London House, 8 Barton Street, London SW1P 3NE* 071-222 8661

HOPE, Miss Edith. b 43. SRN64 SCM66 HVCert72 Lanc Univ MA86. Wycliffe Hall Ox 89. **d** 91. Par Dn Droylsden St Mary *Man* from 91. *266 Fairfield Road, Droylsden, Manchester M35 6AN* 061-301 5422

HOPE, Robert. b 36. Dur Univ BSc61. Clifton Th Coll 61. **d** 63 **p** 64. C Woking St Mary *Guildf* 63-66, C Surbiton Hill Ch Ch *S'wark* 66-68; Th Students' Sec IVF 68-71; Hon C Wallington H Trin *S'wark* 69-71; C Ox St Ebbe w St Pet *Ox* 71-74; V Walshaw Ch Ch *Man* 74-87; TR Radipole and Melcombe Regis *Sarum* from 87. *The Rectory, 42 Melcombe Avenue, Weymouth, Dorset DT4 7TF* Weymouth (0305) 785553

HOPE, Miss Susan. b 49. St Jo Coll Dur BA83. Cranmer Hall Dur 80. **dss** 83 **d** 87. Boston Spa *York* 83-86; Brightside w Wincobank *Sheff* 86-87; Par Dn 87-89; Dn-in-c from 89. *The Vicarage, 24 Beacon Road, Sheffield S9 1AD* Sheffield (0742) 433640

HOPE, William. b 08. St Chad's Coll Dur BA30 MA34. **d** 31 **p** 32. V Euxton *Blackb* 47-73; rtd 73; Lic to Offic *Blackb* from 73. *45 Church Walk, Euxton, Chorley, Lancs PR7 6HL* Chorley (02572) 73178

HOPES, Preb Alan Stephen. b 44. K Coll Lon BD AKC66. **d** 67 **p** 68. C E Finchley All SS *Lon* 67-72; C Hendon St Alphage 72-78; V Tottenham St Paul from 78; AD E Haringey 81-86; Preb St Paul's Cathl from 87. *St Paul's Vicarage, 60 Park Lane, London N17 0JR* 081-808 7297

HOPEWELL, Jeffery Stewart. b 52. ACA79 Leic Univ BA75. E Midl Min Tr Course 82. **d** 85 **p** 86. NSM Houghton on the Hill w Keyham *Leic* 85-88; NSM Houghton-on-the-Hill, Keyham and Hungarton from 88. *33 Scotland Lane, Houghton-on-the-Hill, Leicester LE7 9GH* Leicester (0533) 415995

HOPKIN, Gerallt. b 12. Univ of Wales BA36. Sarum Th Coll 37. **d** 38 **p** 39. R St Fagans w Michaelston-s-Ely *Llan* 68-77; rtd 77; Perm to Offic *Llan* from 79. *25 Tangmere Drive, Fairwood Chase, Cardiff CF5 2PP* Cardiff (0222) 553985

HOPKINS, Aubrey Lionel Evan. b 06. Jes Coll Cam BA28 MA32. Ridley Hall Cam 28. **d** 30 **p** 31. V Folkestone H Trin w Ch Ch *Cant* 62-74; rtd 74; Perm to Offic *Roch* from 83. *Wonston, South View Road, Crowborough, E Sussex TN6 1HW* Crowborough (0892) 667471

HOPKINS, Miss Barbara Agnes. b 28. Lon Univ BSc60 Imp Coll Lon DIC66 MPhil67 DipRS80. St Alb Minl Tr Scheme 82. **dss** 85 **d** 87. Bedf All SS *St Alb* 85-86; Chapl Asst Bedf Gen Hosp 86-88; Bedf St Mich *St Alb* 86-87; Hon Par Dn 87-88; Asst Chapl Community Mental Health Linc from 89. *14 Woburn Avenue, Lincoln LN1 3HJ* Lincoln (0522) 530943

HOPKINS, Christopher Freeman. b 41. Dur Univ BA63. Wells Th Coll 63. **d** 65 **p** 66. C Spring Park *Cant* 65-69; S Africa 69-78; Botswana 78-81; R Beckley and Peasmarsh *Chich* from 81. *The Rectory, School Lane, Peasmarsh, Rye, E Sussex TN31 6UW* Peasmarsh (079721) 255

HOPKINS, Canon Douglass. b 04. Keble Coll Ox BA25 DipTh26 MA30. Wycliffe Hall Ox 25. **d** 27 **p** 28. V Ketton *Pet* 62-73; Can Pet Cathl 67-73; rtd 73. *The Spring Cottage, Dunsby, Bourne, Lincs* Dowsby (077835) 319

HOPKINS, Ernest. b 16. Tyndale Hall Bris 68. **d** 69 **p** 70. C Walton Breck *Liv* 69-70; P-in-c Everton St Chrys 70-74; P-in-c Everton St Jo 70-74; P-in-c Everton Em 70-74; V Everton St Chrys 74-79; RD Walton 76-79; V Eccleston St Luke 79-83; rtd 83; Perm to Offic *St As* from 84; *Ches* from 88. *12 Shetland Drive, Bromborough, Wirral, Merseyside L62 7JZ* 051-334 4044

HOPKINS, Henry Charles. Edin Th Coll 66. **d** 71 **p** 72. C Dundee St Martin *Bre* 71-74; R Monifieth 74-78; Miss to Seamen from 78; Kenya 78-85; Singapore from 85. *291 River Valley Road, Singapore 0923* Singapore (65) 737-2880

HOPKINS, Hilda (Sister Hilary). dss 33 **d** 87. CSA from 49. *c/o St Andrew's House, 2 Tavistock Road, Westbourne Park, London W11 1BA* 071-229 2662

HOPKINS, Hugh. b 33. TCD BA. **d** 62 **p** 63. C Ballymena *Conn* 62-64; C Belf Ch Ch 64-67; I Ballintoy 67-72; I Belf St Ninian 72-81; I Mossley 81-86; I Ballywillan from 86; Miss to Seamen from 86. *The Rectory, 10 Coleraine Road, Portrush, Co Antrim BT56 8EA* Portrush (0265) 824298

HOPKINS, Canon Hugh Alexander Evan. b 07. OBE55. Em Coll Cam BA30 MA34. Ridley Hall Cam 30. **d** 31 **p** 32. R Cheltenham St Mary *Glouc* 58-73; rtd 73. *138 Thornton Road, Cambridge CB3 0ND* Cambridge (0223) 276478

HOPKINS, Canon Hugh Graham Beynon. b 18. Jes Coll Ox BA40 MA45. St Mich Coll Llan 40. **d** 42 **p** 43. V Aberavon *Llan* 59-86; Can Llan Cathl from 81; RD Margam 81-85; rtd 86. *25B Mary Street, Porthcawl, M Glam* Porthcawl (0656) 771651

HOPKINS, John Alun. b 33. Univ of Wales (Lamp) BA55. St Steph Ho Ox 55. **d** 57 **p** 58. C Abth St Mich *St D* 57-59; C Llanelly St Paul 59-62; V from 76; R Eglwys Gymyn and Marros 62-76. *Church House, Paddock Street, Llanelli, Dyfed SA15 2RU* Llanelli (0554) 773865

HOPKINS, John Dawson. b 39. Chich Th Coll 85. **d** 87 **p** 88. C Walker *Newc* 87-89; C Newc St Fran from 89. *St Francis's House, 18 Cotswold Gardens, Newcastle upon Tyne NE7 7AE* 091-281 2147

HOPKINS, John Edgar Alexander. b 19. TD65. Jes Coll Cam BA46 MA48. Wells Th Coll 46. **d** 48 **p** 49. V Holdenhurst *Win* 65-71; C-in-c Holdenhurst St Barn CD 65-71; Chapl Stonar Sch Melksham 71-80; P-in-c Clyffe Pypard and Tockenham *Sarum* 80-81; P-in-c Broad Town 80-81; R Broad Town, Clyffe Pypard and Tockenham 81-85; rtd 85. *17 Coxstalls, Wootton Bassett, Swindon SN4 7AW* Swindon (0793) 854091

HOPKINS, Canon John Howard Edgar Beynon. b 14. Univ Coll Ox BA36 MA39. St Mich Coll Llan 36. **d** 37 **p** 38. R Bridge of Weir *Glas* 62-75; R Glas St Marg 75-84; Can St Mary's Cathl 79-84; rtd 84; Hon Can St Mary's Cathl *Glas* from 84. *156 Drymen Road, Bearsden, Glasgow G61 3RE* 041-942 6013

HOPKINS, Dr Kenneth Victor John. b 45. Univ Coll Lon BA66 Lon Univ BD69 Hull Univ PhD84. Tyndale Hall Bris 66. **d** 69 **p** 70. C S Mimms Ch Ch *Lon* 69-72; C Parkstone St Luke *Sarum* 72-76; P-in-c Trowbridge St Thos 76; V 76-81; R Wingfield w Rowley 76-81; Chapl and Lect NE Surrey Coll of Tech Ewell 81-84; Hd Student Services Essex Inst of HE 84-88; Kingston Poly from 88. *Kingston Polytechnic, Penrhyn Road, Kingston-upon-Thames, Surrey KT1 2EE* 081-549 1366

HOPKINS, Lionel. b 48. Open Univ BA82. St D Coll Lamp DipTh70. **d** 71 **p** 72. C Llandilo Talybont *S & B* 71-74; C Morriston 74-78; P-in-c Waunarllwydd 78-80; V 80-86; Youth Chapl 84-86; V Llangyfelach from 86. *The Vicarage, 64 Heol Pentre Felin, Morriston, Swansea SA6 6BY* Swansea (0792) 774120

HOPKINS, Miss Patricia Mary. b 46. Kingston Poly BEd78. Trin Coll Bris 83. **dss** 85 **d** 87. Gorleston St Andr *Nor* 85-87; C 87-88; C Woking St Jo *Guildf* 88-90; TM Barnham Broom *Nor* from 90. *The Rectory, Garveston, Norwich NR9 4QR* Dereham (0362) 858377

HOPKINS, Peter. b 54. Nottm Univ BSc75 Imp Coll Lon MSc79. Oak Hill Th Coll BA86. **d** 86 **p** 87. C Gee Cross *Ches* 86-90; R Gt Gonerby *Linc* from 90. *The Rectory, Great Gonerby, Grantham, Lincs NG31 8LN* Grantham (0476) 65737

HOPKINS, Reginald Evan. b 10. Jes Coll Cam BA33 MA43. Wycliffe Hall Ox 46. **d** 47 **p** 48. V Billingshurst *Chich* 57-73; V Compton w Up Marden 73-79; R E Marden 73-79; R N Marden 73-79; V Compton, the Mardens, Stoughton and Racton 79-81; rtd 81; Perm to Offic *Chich* from 81. *Mardens, Myrtle Road, Crowborough, E Sussex TN6 1EY* Crowborough (0892) 63631

HOPKINS, Robert James Gardner. b 42. St Alb Minl Tr Scheme. **d** 79 **p** 80. NSM Chorleywood Ch Ch *St Alb* 79-83; NSM Parr Mt *Liv* from 83. *38 Lascelles Street, St Helens, Merseyside WA9 1BA* St Helens (0744) 58886

HOPKINS, Thomas Clifford Millward. b 15. St Cath Coll Cam BA37 MA41. St Mich Coll Llan 37. **d** 38 **p** 41. V Hanmer and Bronington *St As* 66-80; V Hanmer, Bronington and Bettisfield 80-83; rtd 83; Perm to Offic *Lich* from 87. *53 Lowe Hill Gardens, Wem, Shrewsbury*

HOPKINSON, Preb Alfred Stephan. b 08. Wadh Coll Ox BA30 MA35. Linc Th Coll 34. **d** 35 **p** 36. R Bobbingworth *Chelmsf* 63-73; rtd 73; Asst Chapl Win Coll 73-90; Hon C Cam Gt St Mary w St Mich *Ely* from 90. *39 Madingley Road, Cambridge CB3 0EL* Cambridge (0223) 355285

HOPKINSON, Ven Barnabas John. b 39. Trin Coll Cam BA63 MA67. Linc Th Coll 63. **d** 65 **p** 66. C Langley All SS and Martyrs *Man* 65-67; C Cam Gt St Mary w St Mich *Ely* 67-71; Asst Chapl Charterhouse Godalming 71-75; P-in-c Preshute *Sarum* 75-76; TV Marlborough 76-81; RD Marlborough 77-81; TR Wimborne Minster and Holt 81-86; Can and Preb Sarum Cathl from 83; RD Wimborne 85-86; Adn Sarum from 86; P-in-c Stratford sub Castle from 87. *Russell House, Stratford sub Castle, Salisbury SP1 3LG* Salisbury (0722) 328756

HOPKINSON, Benjamin Alaric. b 36. Trin Coll Ox BA59. Chich Th Coll 59. **d** 61 **p** 62. C Pallion *Dur* 61-66; Rhodesia 66-67; Botswana 67-74; Hon C Sherwood *S'well* 74-77; Hon C Carrington 74-77; V Lowdham 77-85; R Whitby *York* from 85; Miss to Seamen from 85. *The Rectory, Chubb Hill Road, Whitby, N Yorkshire YO21 2JP* Whitby (0947) 602590

HOPKINSON, Colin Edward. b 57. BA LLB. Ridley Hall Cam. **d** 84 **p** 85. C Chadwell *Chelmsf* 84-87; C Canvey Is 87-90; P-in-c E Springfield from 90. *The Vicarage, Ashton Place, Chelmsford CM2 6ST* Chelmsford (0245) 469316

HOPKINSON, David John. b 47. Ox NSM Course. **d** 79 **p** 80. NSM Wardington *Ox* 79-80; Hon C Didcot St Pet 80-83; C Headingley *Ripon* 83-87; P-in-c Leeds All So 87-91; R Middleton Tyas w Croft and Eryholme from 91. *The Vicarage, Middleton Tyas, Richmond, N Yorkshire DL10 6SB* Darlington (0325) 377562

HOPKINSON, William Humphrey. b 48. ARIC73 Lon Univ BSc69 Dur Univ MA78 Nottm Univ MPhil84 Man Poly MSc90. St Jo Coll Dur DipTh76. **d** 77 **p** 78. C Normanton *Derby* 77-80; C Sawley 80-82; V Birtles *Ches* 82-87; Dir Past Studies N Ord Course from 82; Dir of Course Development from 90; Continuing Minl Educn Officer *Ches* from 87. *Thorn House, Appleton Thorn, Warrington WA4 5NS* Warrington (0925) 63434

HOPLEY, David. b 37. Wells Th Coll 62. **d** 65 **p** 66. C Frome St Mary *B & W* 65-68; R Staunton-on-Arrow w Byton and Kinsham *Heref* 68-81; P-in-c Lingen 68-81; P-in-c Aymestrey and Leinthall Earles w Wigmore etc 72-81; R Dungeon Hill *Sarum* from 81. *The Rectory, Buckland Newton, Dorchester, Dorset DT2 7BY* Buckland Newton (03005) 456

HOPLEY, Gilbert. b 40. Univ of Wales (Ban) BA62. St D Coll Lamp LTh65. **d** 65 **p** 66. C St As and Tremeirchion *St As* 65-73; Warden Ch Hostel Bangor 73-76; Chapl Univ of Wales (Ban) 73-76; V Meifod and Llangynyw *St As* 76-79; Chapl St Marg Sch Bushey 79-87; Hd Master St Paul's Cathl Choir Sch from 87. *The Headmaster's House, St Paul's Choir School, London EC4M 9AD* 071-248 5156

HOPLEY, William James Christopher. b 50. AKC74. St Aug Coll Cant 74. **d** 75 **p** 76. C Kidderminster St Jo *Worc* 75-78; Ind Chapl 78-85; Co-ord Ind Chapl from 85; TV Worc St Martin w St Pet, St Mark etc 85-86; TV Worc SE from 86. *The Vicarage, Walkers Lane, Whittington, Worcester WR5 2RE* Worcester (0905) 355989

HOPPER, Bernard. b 20. Leeds Univ BA42. Coll of Resurr Mirfield. **d** 44 **p** 45. V Brighton St Mich *Chich* 67-85; rtd 85; Perm to Offic *Chich* from 85. *64 Warren Drive, Lewes, E Sussex BN7 1HD* Lewes (0273) 475303

HOPPER, Peter John. b 37. Hull Univ Coll Dur BSc59 Lon Univ PGCE60. Nor Ord Course 89. **d** 91. C Aston cum Aughton and Ulley *Sheff* from 91. *36 Stanley Grove, Aston, Sheffield S31 0DN* Sheffield (0742) 876793

HOPPER, Robert Keith. b 45. St Jo Coll Dur 74. **d** 77 **p** 78. C Oxclose *Dur* 77-80; C Hebburn St Jo 80-82; V Lobley Hill from 82. *The Vicarage, Rowanwood Gardens, Gateshead, Tyne & Wear NE11 0DB* 091-460 4409

HOPPERTON, Thomas. b 33. Chich Th Coll 71. **d** 73 **p** 74. C Cheam *S'wark* 73-76; P-in-c 76-89; P-in-c Rotherhithe St Kath w St Barn from 89; P-in-c S Bermondsey St Bart from 91. *The Vicarage, Eugenia Road, London SE16 2RA* 071-237 3679

HOPWOOD, Adrian Patrick. b 37. CBiol MIBiol MIWEM N Lon Poly BSc61. Ox Min Course 87. **d** 90. NSM Chesham Bois *Ox* from 90. *74 Woodside Road, Amersham, Bucks HP6 6AN* High Wycombe (0494) 726209

✠**HORAN, Rt Rev Forbes Trevor.** b 05. Trin Hall Cam BA32 MA36. Westcott Ho Cam 33. **d** 33 **p** 34 **c** 60. C Newc St Luke *Newc* 33-36; C Newc St Geo 36-38; C-in-c Balkwell CD 38-40; Chapl RNVR 40-45; V Shrewsbury St Chad *Lich* 45-52; I Huddersfield *Wakef* 52-60; RD 52-60; Hon Can Wakef Cathl 55-60; Suff Bp Tewkesbury *Glouc* 60-73; rtd 73; Asst Bp Glouc from 75. *3 Silverthorne Close, Shurdington Road, Cheltenham GL53 0JF* Cheltenham (0242) 527133

HORBURY, William. b 42. Or Coll Ox BA64 MA67 Clare Coll Cam BA66 PhD71. Westcott Ho Cam 64. **d** 69 **p** 70.

Fell Clare Coll Cam 68-72; CCC Cam from 78; Lic to Offic *Ely* 69-72 and 78-90; R Gt w Lt Gransden 72-78; Lect Div Cam Univ from 84; NSM Cam St Botolph *Ely* from 90. *Corpus Christi College, Cambridge CB2 1RH* Cambridge (0223) 338000

HORDERN, Peter John Calveley. b 35. **d** 61 **p** 62. C Billingham St Aid *Dur* 61-65; Canada from 65. *346 Aberdeen Avenue, Brandon, Manitoba, Canada, R7A 1N4*

HORE, Michael John. b 50. Man Univ BSc71. Linc Th Coll 75. **d** 78 **p** 79. C Maidstone St Martin *Cant* 78-81; C St Peter-in-Thanet 81-83; R Storrington *Chich* from 83; RD Storrington from 90. *The Rectory, Storrington, Pulborough, W Sussex RH20 4EF* Storrington (09066) 2888

HORLESTON, Kenneth William. b 50. BA86. Oak Hill Th Coll 84. **d** 86 **p** 87. C Wednesfield Heath *Lich* 86-89; V Blagreaves *Derby* from 89. *St Andrew's Vicarage, 5 Greenburn Close, Littleover, Derby DE3 7FF* Derby (0332) 773877

HORLOCK, Very Rev Brian William. b 31. OBE78. Univ of Wales (Lamp) BA55. Chich Th Coll 55. **d** 57 **p** 58. C Chiswick St Nic w St Mary *Lon* 57-61; C Witney *Ox* 61-62; V N Acton St Gabr *Lon* 62-68; Chapl Oslo w Bergen, Trondheim and Stavanger *Eur* 68-89; RD Scandinavia 75-79; Adn 80-89; Hon Can Brussels Cathl 80-89; Dean Gib from 89; Chapl Gib from 89. *The Deanery, Gibraltar* Gibraltar (350) 78377 or 75745

HORN, Colin Clive. b 39. CEng MIMechE. Cant Sch of Min. **d** 83 **p** 84. NSM Yalding w Collier Street *Roch* 83-91; V Kemsing w Woodlands from 91. *The Vicarage, High Street, Kemsing, Sevenoaks, Kent TN15 6PY* Sevenoaks (0732) 61351

HORN, David Henry. b 47. Nottm Univ BA69 CQSW71. Qu Coll Birm. **d** 82 **p** 83. C Hamstead St Paul *Birm* 82-84; V Aston St Jas from 84. *The Vicarage, 215 Albert Road, Aston, Birmingham B6 5NA* 021-327 3230

HORNBY, John Hulme. b 24. AKC47. Qu Coll Birm 48. **d** 49 **p** 50. R Stretham w Thetford *Ely* 66-74; P-in-c Bratton Fleming *Ex* 74-89; P-in-c Stoke Rivers 74-89; P-in-c Challacombe 75-89; RD Shirwell 77-80; rtd 89; Perm to Offic *Ex* from 89. *6 Barbican Terrace, Barnstaple, Devon EX32 9HQ* Barnstaple (0271) 75463

HORNBY, Raymond Sefton. b 98. **d** 21 **p** 23. R Hinton Ampner w Bramdean *Win* 57-68; rtd 68; Perm to Offic *Win* from 70. *5 Pearmain, Avalon Park, La Grande Route de la Cote, Jersey, Channel Islands JE2 6LX* Jersey (0534) 59173

HORNE, Anthony Cedric. b 26. MIMechE61 MIEEE67. **d** 77 **p** 78. NSM Kingsdown *Bris* 77-83; C Soundwell 83-85; P-in-c Bris St Andr w St Bart from 85. *The Vicarage, Walsingham Road, Bristol BS6 5BT* Bristol (0272) 48683

HORNE, Brian Lawrence. b 39. FRSA Natal Univ BA60 Dur Univ DipTh62 MLitt68 Lon Univ PhD71. Gen Th Sem (NY) MDiv63 St Chad's Coll Dur 60. **d** 62 **p** 63. Tutor St Chad's Coll Dur 63-66; Lect K Coll Lon from 66. *King's College, Strand, London WC2R 2LS* 071-274 6222

HORNE, Jack Kenneth. b 20. Linc Th Coll 68. **d** 70 **p** 71. C Danbury *Chelmsf* 70-75; V Frampton *Linc* 75-85; rtd 85. *154 Kenilworth Road, Grantham, Lincs NG31 9UH* Grantham (0476) 78867

HORNE, Roger Harry. b 30. ACP52. Cuddesdon Coll 65. **d** 67 **p** 68. Chapl Cottesmore Sch Crawley 69-75; Lic to Offic *Chich* 69-75; Ex 76-77; Chapl Tawstock Sch Barnstaple 76-77; Chapl Br Emb Ankara *Eur* 77-80; Chapl Strasbourg w Stuttgart and Heidelberg 80-82; Chapl Palermo w Taormina 82-85; V Santan *S & M* 85-88; V Braddan 85-88; rtd 88; Perm to Offic *S & M* from 88. *34 Saddle Mews, Douglas, Isle of Man* Douglas (0624) 629322

HORNER, Eric. b 43. E Midl Min Tr Course 87. **d** 90. C Boultham *Linc* from 90. *35 Park Avenue, Boultham, Lincoln LN6 0BY* Lincoln (0522) 691247

HORNER, John Henry. b 40. Leeds Univ BA62 Lon Univ DipRS74 Middx Poly MA87. Oak Hill Th Coll 76. **d** 79 **p** 80. Hon C Datchworth w Tewin *St Alb* 79-85; Hon C Ware St Mary from 85. *41 St Leonard's Road, Hertford* Hertford (0992) 551696

HORNER, Peter Francis. b 27. Jes Coll Ox BA51 MA55. Kelham Th Coll 52. **d** 54 **p** 55. Tutor Kelham Th Coll 54-73; Chapl 58-73; C Averham w Kelham *S'well* 54-56; Lic to Offic 56-73; SSM from 58; Lic to Offic *Ox* 74-87; Australia from 87. *14 St John's Priory, Adelaide, Australia 5000* Adelaide (8) 223-2348

HORNER, Philip David Forster. b 30. Tyndale Hall Bris BDip67. **d** 67 **p** 68. C Ulverston St Mary w H Trin *Carl* 67-71; C Princes Risborough w Ilmer *Ox* 71-76; C

Wendover 76-89; P-in-c Ellesborough 76-89; P-in-c Gt and Lt Kimble 82-89; C Walton H Trin from 89. *49 Manor Road, Aylesbury, Bucks HP20 1JB* Aylesbury (0296) 415260

HORNER, Robert William. b 17. RD. St Pet Hall Ox MA46 DipEd. Ripon Hall Ox 56. **d** 57 **p** 58. Chapl RNR 63-74; R Chinnor *Ox* 66-73; R Emmington 66-73; V Sydenham 66-73; R Chinnor w Emmington and Sydenham 73-84; rtd 84; Perm to Offic *Ex* from 84. *29 Lammas Lane, Paignton, Devon TQ3 1PS* Paignton (0803) 528426

HORNSBY, Edgar. b 23. AKC50. **d** 51 **p** 52. Chapl St Mary's Hall and Brighton Coll 69-74; Chapl St Swithun's Sch Win 74-88; rtd 88. *1 Gough Way, Cambridge CB3 9LN* Cambridge (0223) 350899

HOROBIN, Hector Stanley. b 09. Kelham Th Coll 30 Edin Th Coll 46. **d** 46 **p** 47. V Petts Wood *Roch* 62-88; rtd 88. *23 Wentworth Close, Wentworth Close, Lyminge, Folkestone, Kent CT18 8HL* Folkestone (0303) 863095

HORROCKS, Mrs Judith Anne. b 53. Calgary Univ BSc76. St Jo Coll Nottm DPS82. dss 82 **d** 87. Denton Ch Ch *Man* 82-85; Whalley Range St Edm 85-87; Par Dn from 87; Chapl Man R Infirmary 88-90. *1 Range Road, Whalley Range, Manchester M16 8FS* 061-226 1291

HORROCKS, Oliver John. b 30. Clare Coll Cam BA53 MA57. Westcott Ho Cam 53. **d** 55 **p** 56. C Moss Side Ch Ch *Man* 55-58; C Arnold *S'well* 58-60; R Ancoats *Man* 60-67; R Barthomley *Ches* from 67. *Barthomley Rectory, Crewe, Cheshire CW2 2PE* Alsager (0270) 872479

HORROCKS, Robert James. b 56. Grey Coll Dur BSc78. St Jo Coll Nottm DipTh80 DPS82. **d** 82 **p** 83. C Denton Ch Ch *Man* 82-85; R Whalley Range St Edm from 85. *St Edmund's Rectory, 1 Range Road, Whalley Range, Manchester M16 8FS* 061-226 1291

HORROCKS, Stanley. b 22. Man Univ BA76. Coll of Resurr Mirfield 77. **d** 78 **p** 79. Hon C Man Miles Platting *Man* 78-81; Hon C Lower Broughton St Clem w St Matthias 81-87; rtd 87; NSM Higher Broughton *Man* from 87. *80 Northumberland Street, Salford M7 0DG* 061-792 1037

HORSEMAN, Christopher Michael. b 54. Bris Sch of Min 84 Trin Coll Bris 87. **d** 88 **p** 89. C Weston-super-Mare Cen Par *B & W* from 88. *St John's House, 71 Upper Church Road, Weston-super-Mare, Avon BS23 2HX* Weston-super-Mare (0934) 631606

HORSEMAN, Colin. b 46. Lon Coll of Div ALCD69 BD70 STh75. **d** 70 **p** 71. C Higher Openshaw *Man* 70-74; C Darfield *Sheff* 75-78; V Stainforth 78-88; V Heeley from 88. *The Vicarage, 151 Gleadless Road, Sheffield S2 3AE* Sheffield (0742) 557718

HORSEY, Maurice Alfred. b 30. AIB. S'wark Ord Course 61. **d** 64 **p** 65. C Oxhey All SS *St Alb* 64-67; C Coulsdon St Jo *S'wark* 67-71; P-in-c Champion Hill St Sav 71-76; Hon C Lewisham St Swithun 84-86; P-in-c Woolwich St Thos 86-90; R from 90. *St Thomas's Rectory, 80 Maryon Road, London SE7 8DL* 081-854 1828

HORSEY, Stanley Desmond. b 20. Ely Th Coll 46. **d** 49 **p** 50. V Hove St Barn *Chich* 67-77; V Hove St Barn and St Agnes 77-85; rtd 85; Perm to Offic *Chich* from 85. *27A Amesbury Crescent, Hove, E Sussex BN3 5RD* Brighton (0273) 732081

HORSFALL, David John. b 55. Bris Poly BA77. Trin Coll Bris DipHE82 St Jo Coll Nottm DPS89. **d** 89 **p** 90. C Chaddesden St Mary *Derby* from 89. *24 Ordish Avenue, Derby DE2 6QF* Derby (0332) 662420

HORSFALL, Keith. b 39. Tyndale Hall Bris 62. **d** 65 **p** 66. C Walton Breck *Liv* 65-68; C Fazakerley Em 68-70; C Mile Cross *Nor* 70-73; V Gayton 73-80; TR Parr *Liv* 80-90; V Leyland St Andr *Blackb* from 90. *St Andrew's Vicarage, Crocus Field, Leyland, Preston, Lancs PR5 2DY* Preston (0772) 621645

HORSFIELD, Allan. b 48. **d** 72 **p** 73. C Airedale w Fryston *Wakef* 72-74; C Howden *York* 75-76; P-in-c Rudston w Boynton 77-82. *Address temp unknown*

HORSFIELD, Robert Alan. b 38. Leeds Univ BA60 MA66. Coll of Resurr Mirfield 61. **d** 63 **p** 64. C Lower Gornal *Lich* 63-66; C Bridlington Quay H Trin *York* 66-68; C Sewerby w Marton 66-68; C-in-c Gt Grimsby St Matt Fairfield CD *Linc* 68-73; R Scartho 73-79; R Cleobury Mortimer w Hopton Wafers *Heref* from 79; P-in-c Neen Sollars w Milson from 81; P-in-c Knowbury 84-86; P-in-c Coreley w Doddington 84-86; RD Ludlow from 89. *The Vicarage, The Hurst, Cleobury Mortimer, Kidderminster, Worcs DY14 8EG* Kidderminster (0562) 270264

HORSHAM, Archdeacon of. See FILBY, Ven William Charles Leonard

HORSHAM, Suffragan Bishop of. See HIND, Rt Rev John William

HORSINGTON, Timothy Frederick. b 44. Dur Univ BA66. Wycliffe Hall Ox 67. **d** 69 **p** 70. C Halewood *Liv* 69-72; C Farnworth 72-75; P-in-c Llangarron w Llangrove *Heref* 75-82; P-in-c Whitchurch w Ganarew 77-82; R Llangarron w Llangrove, Whitchurch and Ganarew 83-84; R Highclere and Ashmansworth w Crux Easton *Win* from 84. *The Rectory, 2 Flexford Close, Highclere, Newbury, Berks RG15 9PE* Highclere (0635) 253991

HORSLEY, Very Rev Alan Avery. b 36. St Chad's Coll Dur BA58 Pacific State Univ MA84 PhD85. Qu Coll Birm 58. **d** 60 **p** 61. C Daventry *Pet* 60-63; C Reading St Giles *Ox* 63-64; C Wokingham St Paul 64-66; V Yeadon St Andr *Bradf* 66-71; R Heyford w Stowe Nine Churches *Pet* 71-78; RD Daventry 76-78; V Oakham w Hambleton and Egleton 78-81; Can Pet Cathl 79-86; V Oakham, Hambleton, Egleton, Braunston and Brooke 81-86; V Lanteglos by Fowey *Truro* 86-88; Provost St Andr Cathl Inverness *Mor* from 88; R Inverness St Andr from 88; P-in-c Culloden St Mary-in-the-Fields from 88; P-in-c Strathnairn St Paul from 88. *The Cathedral Rectory, 15 Ardross Street, Inverness IV3 5NS* Inverness (0463) 233535

HORSLEY, Hugh Reginald. b 10. Knutsford Test Sch 32 Bps' Coll Cheshunt 33. **d** 37 **p** 38. Area Sec (Dio Chich) USPG 66-78; rtd 78; Perm to Offic *Chich* from 78. *11 Charmandean Road, Worthing, W Sussex BN14 9LQ* Worthing (0903) 36901

HORSMAN, Andrew Alan. b 49. Otago Univ BA70 Man Univ MA72 PhD75. St Steph Ho Ox BA80 MA87. **d** 81 **p** 82. C Hillingdon All SS *Lon* 81-84; C Lt Stanmore St Lawr 84-87; TV Haxby w Wigginton *York* from 87. *The Vicarage, 5 Back Lane, Wigginton, York YO3 8ZH* York (0904) 768178

HORSWELL, Kevin George. b 55. Jes Coll Cam BA77 MA81 Nottm Univ BA81. St Jo Coll Nottm. **d** 82 **p** 83. C Bootle Ch Ch *Liv* 82-86; Chapl LMH Ox from 86; C Ox St Giles and SS Phil and Jas w St Marg *Ox* from 86. *Lady Margaret Hall, Oxford OX2 6QA or, 19 Hayfield Road, Oxford OX2 6TX* Oxford (0865) 274386 or 56802

HORTON, Andrew Charles. b 50. Ex Univ BA71. Sarum Th Coll 71. **d** 73 **p** 74. C Westbury-on-Trym St Alb *Bris* 73-76; USA 76-90; P-in-c Battersea St Mich *S'wark* from 90. *St Michael's Vicarage, 93 Bolingbroke Grove, London SW11 6HA* 071-228 1990

HORTON, Canon Christopher Peter. b 26. Leeds Univ BA49. Coll of Resurr Mirfield 49. **d** 51 **p** 52. C Blyth St Mary *Newc* 51-55; C Delaval 55-59; V Grangetown *York* from 59; Can and Preb York Minster from 85. *The Vicarage, Clynes Road, Grangetown, Middlesbrough, Cleveland TS6 7LY* Eston Grange (0642) 453704

HORTON, David Harold. b 49. St Jo Coll Dur BA72. NE Ord Course 82. **d** 86 **p** 87. C Enfield St Jas *Lon* 86-90; Min Joydens Wood St Barn CD *Roch* from 90. *St Barnabas' Church House, 6 Tile Kiln Lane, Bexley, Kent DA5 2BD* Dartford (0322) 528923

HORTON, Jeremy Nicholas Orkney. b 44. Cranmer Hall Dur 64. **d** 68 **p** 69. C Dalton-in-Furness *Carl* 68-70; C Penrith 70-73; V Hudswell w Downholme and Marske *Ripon* 73-75; R Middleton Tyas and Melsonby 75-81; P-in-c Croft 78-81; P-in-c Eryholme 78-81; V Wortley de Leeds from 81. *The Vicarage, Dixon Lane Road, Leeds LS12 4RU* Leeds (0532) 638867

HORTON, John Ward. b 27. Leeds Univ BA50. Coll of Resurr Mirfield 50. **d** 52 **p** 53. C Balkwell CD *Newc* 52-55; C Coatham *York* 55-58; C-in-c Acomb Moor CD 58-71; V Acomb Moor from 71. *The Vicarage, Thanet Road, Dringhouses, York YO2 2PE* York (0904) 706047

HORTON, Michael John. b 56. St Jo Coll Cam BA80 MA83 CertEd83 Ox Univ BA88. Wycliffe Hall Ox 86. **d** 89 **p** 90. C Northallerton w Kirby Sigston *York* from 89. *37 Ainderby Road, Northallerton, N Yorkshire DL7 8HF* Northallerton (0609) 773431

HORTON, Ralph Edward. b 41. S'wark Ord Course 75. **d** 78 **p** 79. C Streatham St Leon *S'wark* 78-81; TV Catford (Southend) and Downham 81-88; V Ashford St Matt *Lon* from 88. *The Vicarage, 99 Church Road, Ashford, Middx TW15 2NY* Ashford (0784) 52459

HORTON, Ms Roberta Anne. b 44. Leic Univ BSc66 CertEd67 Nottm Univ BCombStuds82. Linc Th Coll 79. **dss** 82 **d** 87. Cam St Jas *Ely* 82-86; Beaumont Leys *Leic* 86-87; Par Dn 87-91; Dioc Dir of Tr from 91. *8B Copeland Road, Birstall, Leicester LE4 3AA* Leicester (0533) 673462

HORWOOD, Graham Frederick. b 34. Univ of Wales (Cardiff) BA55. Coll of Resurr Mirfield 55. **d** 57 **p** 58. C Llantrisant *Llan* 57-61; C Roath St Sav 61-62; C Roath St Marg 62-66; V Clydach *S & B* 66-77; V Canton St Luke *Llan* from 77. *St Luke's Vicarage, 12 Thompson Avenue, Cardiff CF5 1EY* Cardiff (0222) 562022

HORWOOD, Thomas Gilbert. b 15. Man Univ BA41. Westcott Ho Cam 45. **d** 46 **p** 47. V Brompton w Snainton *York* 68-80; Master St Jo Hosp Bath 85-90; Min Bath St Mich Chpl *B & W* 85-90; rtd 90; Perm to Offic *Chich* from 90. *Flat 5, Bramwell Lodge, Woodmancote, Henfield, W Sussex BN5 9SX* Henfield (0273) 492570

HOSIE, David Graham. b 37. AKC62. **d** 62 **p** 63. C-in-c Winterbourne St Martin and Monkton *Sarum* 70-71; V 71-75; R The Winterbournes and Compton Valence 75-82; rtd 82. *Ellens, Broad Oak, Sturminster Newton, Dorset DT10 2HD* Sturminster Newton (0258) 72495

HOSKIN, David William. b 49. Hatf Coll Dur BSc71. Wycliffe Hall Ox 72. **d** 75 **p** 76. C Bridlington Priory *York* 75-78; C Rodbourne Cheney *Bris* 78-79; C Bebington *Ches* 79-82; R Lockington and Lund and Scorborough w Leconfield *York* 82-88; V Beverley St Mary from 88. *The Vicarage, 15 Molescroft Road, Beverley, N Humberside HU17 7DX* Hull (0482) 881437

HOSKIN, Canon Eric James. b 28. St Chad's Coll Dur BA50 DipTh52. **d** 52 **p** 53. C Coney Hill *Glouc* 52-54; C Stroud 54-57; R Ruardean 57-63; P-in-c Lydbrook 61-63; V Cheltenham Em 63-70; R Dursley 70-86; RD Dursley 77-85; Hon Can Glouc Cathl 81-86; R Easington w Liverton *York* from 86. *The Rectory, Easington, Saltburn-by-the-Sea, Cleveland TS13 4NT* Guisborough (0287) 641348

HOSKIN, Henry Brian. b 32. NW Ord Course 72. **d** 75 **p** 76. NSM Chesterfield St Aug *Derby* 75-79; NSM Bolsover 79-83; NSM Old Brampton and Loundsley Green 83-88; P-in-c Barlow from 88. *The Vicarage, Barlow, Sheffield S18 5TR* Sheffield (0742) 890269

HOSKING, Canon Harold Ernest. b 19. Lich Th Coll 51. **d** 53 **p** 54. V Newquay *Truro* 69-74; TR Redruth 74-80; R Redruth w Lanner 80-84; Hon Can Truro Cathl 78-84; rtd 84; Perm to Offic *Ex* from 84. *9 Rondle Road, Newton Abbot, Devon TQ12 2PJ* Newton Abbot (0626) 69306

HOSKINS, Hugh George. b 46. S Dios Minl Tr Scheme. **d** 84 **p** 85. NSM Hilperton w Whaddon and Staverton etc *Sarum* 84-87; C Calne and Blackland 87-90; R W Lavington and the Cheverells from 90. *The Vicarage, White Street, West Lavington, Devizes, Wilts SN10 4LW* Devizes (0380) 818388

HOSKINS, Ian David. b 41. St Chad's Coll Dur BA63 DipTh65 Dur Univ MA88. **d** 65 **p** 66. C Southwick St Cuth CD *Dur* 65-68; C Beamish 68-72; V S Moor 72-77; Asst Chapl HM Pris Dur 76-80; R Witton Gilbert *Dur* 77-88; Chapl Earl's Ho Hosp Dur from 79; R Dur St Marg *Dur* from 88; Chapl St Cuth Hospice Dur from 88. *St Margaret's Rectory, South Street, Durham DH1 4QP* 091-384 3623

HOSKINS, Canon James Paul. b 07. Lon Univ BA27. Wells Th Coll 30. **d** 31 **p** 32. V Malborough w S Huish *Ex* 67-77; rtd 77; Lic to Offic *Ex* from 77. *Brigadoon Church Road, Colaton Raleigh, Sidmouth, Devon EX10 0LW* Colaton Raleigh (0395) 68643

HOSKYNS, John Algernon Peyton. b 20. Pemb Coll Cam BA41 MA45. Westcott Ho Cam 47. **d** 49 **p** 50. R Worplesdon *Guildf* 62-72; V St Weonards w Orcop *Heref* 73-76; P-in-c Linton w Upton Bishop 76-78; P-in-c How Caple w Sollers Hope 76-85; P-in-c Sellack and King's Caple w Foy 81-85; rtd 85; Perm to Offic *Heref* from 85. *Riverknoll, Hoarwithy, Hereford HR2 6QF* Carey (0432) 840282

HOSSENT, George William Thomas. b 14. Wycliffe Hall Ox 61. **d** 63 **p** 64. V Sheff St Bart Langsett Road *Sheff* 67-75; V Arksey 75-80; rtd 80; Perm to Offic *Sheff* from 80. *19 Sunnyvale Avenue, Sheffield S17 4FD* Sheffield (0742) 363676

HOST, Mrs Charmaine Anne. b 54. W Midl Minl Tr Course 87. **d** 90. C Westwood *Cov* from 90. *60 Cannon Park Road, Coventry CV4 7AY* Coventry (0203) 692438

HOTCHEN, Stephen Jeffrie. b 50. Linc Th Coll 85. **d** 87 **p** 88. C Morpeth *Newc* 87-90; TV High Wycombe *Ox* 90-91; R Dingwall *Mor* from 91; R Strathpeffer from 91. *The Parsonage, Dingwall, Ross-shire IV15 9HU* Dingwall (0349) 62204

HOTCHIN, Hilary Moya. b 52. Birm Univ CertEd73. W Midl Minl Tr Course 85. **d** 88. NSM Redditch St Steph *Worc* from 88. *81 Bilbury Close, Redditch, Worcs B97 5XW* Redditch (0527) 403062

HOUGH, Miss Carole Elizabeth. b 59. Lon Hosp SRN81. St Jo Coll Nottm DipMin91. **d** 91. Par Dn Beoley *Worc* from 91. *4 Marshfield Close, Church Hill North, Beoley, Redditch, Worcs B98 8RW* Redditch (0527) 64246

HOUGH, Edward Lewis. b 38. Univ of Wales (Lamp) BA60. St Mich Coll Llan 60. **d** 62 **p** 63. C Baglan *Llan* 62-69; Ind Chapl *York* 69-72; R Cilybebyll *Llan* from 72; RD Neath 84-89. *The Rectory, 7 Cwmnantllyd Road, Pontardawe, W Glam SA8 3DT* Pontardawe (0792) 862118

HOUGH, Canon John Francis. b 06. St Jo Coll Ox BA29 MA32. Westcott Ho Cam 29. **d** 30 **p** 31. V Tenterden St Mildred w Smallhythe *Cant* 66-74; rtd 74; Perm to Offic *Cant* 74-88; *Chich* 75-88; *Ely* from 88. *51 Millfield Court, Brampton Road, Huntingdon, Cambs PE18 6TT* Huntingdon (0480) 413149

HOUGH, Michael. b 49. Man Univ. St Jo Coll Nottm. **d** 84 **p** 85. C Newbottle *Dur* 84-87; V Felling from 87. *The Vicarage, Carlisle Street, Felling, Gateshead, Tyne & Wear NE10 0HQ* 091-469 2440

HOUGH, Peter George. b 40. Dur Univ BA62. Wells Th Coll 62. **d** 64 **p** 65. C Stocking Farm *CD Leic* 64-68; V Leic St Aid 68-76; V Knutton *Lich* from 76. *The Vicarage, Church Lane, Knutton, Newcastle, Staffs ST5 6DU* Newcastle-under-Lyme (0782) 624282

HOUGH, Sidney Stephen Valentine. b 27. G&C Coll Cam BA50 MA54. Ripon Hall Ox 55. **d** 57 **p** 58. V Messing *Chelmsf* 62-72; R Inworth 62-72; V Messing w Inworth 72-77; Chapl Warley Hosp Brentwood 78-79; R Alphamstone w Lamarsh and Pebmarsh *Chelmsf* 79-88; rtd 88. *27 Weavers Court, Weavers Lane, Sudbury, Suffolk CO10 6HY* Sudbury (0787) 74812

HOUGHTBY, Frank. b 12. Chich Th Coll 41. **d** 41 **p** 42. R N Runcton w Hardwick and Setchey *Nor* 60-91; rtd 91. *29 Lodge Way, Grantham, Lincs* Grantham (0476) 592282

HOUGHTON, Canon Alfred Thomas. b 96. Univ Coll Dur LTh22 BA23 MA29. Lon Coll of Div. **d** 21 **p** 22. Gen Sec BCMS 45-66; rtd 66. *14 Alston Court, St Albans Road, Barnet, Herts EN5 4LJ* 081-449 1741

HOUGHTON, Bernard Frank. b 15. Linc Coll Ox BA37 MA73. Cuddesdon Coll 40. **d** 41 **p** 42. V Lacey Green *Ox* 61-81; rtd 81; Perm to Offic *Glouc* from 81. *19 Bathurst Road, Chesterton, Cirencester, Glos GL7 1SA* Cirencester (0285) 658538

HOUGHTON, Christopher Guy. b 64. W Surrey Coll of Art & Design BA86. Oak Hill Th Coll DipHE88 BA89. **d** 89 **p** 90. C Mossley Hill St Matt and St Jas *Liv* from 89. *Moss Lake Lodge, Rose Lane, Mossley Hill, Liverpool L18 8DB* 051-724 3753

HOUGHTON, David John. b 47. Edin Univ BSc(Econ)68. Cuddesdon Coll 69. **d** 71 **p** 72. C Prestbury *Glouc* 71-74; Prec Gib Cathl *Eur* 74-76; Chapl Madrid 76-78; C Croydon *Cant* 78-80; Chapl Warw Sch 80-85; P-in-c Isleworth St Fran *Lon* 85-90; SSJE from 90; USA 90-91; C Fulham All SS *Lon* 91; Chapl Gordonstoun Sch 91; TV Clapham Team Min *S'wark* from 91. *15 Elms Road, London SW4 9ER* 071-622 8703

HOUGHTON, Edward Johnson. b 23. Keble Coll Ox BA48 MA48. Linc Th Coll 48. **d** 50 **p** 51. CF (TA) 56-62; Chapl Hellingly and Amberstone Hosps 61-90; rtd 88. *1 Nursery Close, Osborne Park, Hailsham, E Sussex BN27 2PX* Hailsham (0323) 442126

HOUGHTON, Geoffrey John. b 59. Ridley Hall Cam 87. **d** 90 **p** 91. C Sholing *Win* from 90. *St Francis House, 75 Montague Avenue, Sholing, Southampton SO2 8QB* Southampton (0703) 443733

HOUGHTON, Ian David. b 50. Lanc Univ BA71 Newc Univ CertEd74 Man Univ CertRS90. Sarum & Wells Th Coll 80. **d** 82 **p** 83. C Newc St Geo *Newc* 82-85; Chapl Newc Poly from 85; Master Newc St Thos Prop Chpl from 90. *9 Chester Crescent, Newcastle upon Tyne NE2 1DH* 091-232 9789

HOUGHTON, James Robert. b 44. AKC67. **d** 68 **p** 69. C Herrington *Dur* 68-70; Asst Dioc Youth Chapl *Bris* 70-72; Perm to Offic *Ex* 73-74; C Heavitree *Ex* 78; Perm to Offic *Lon* 78-80 and from 83; C Heavitree w Ex St Paul *Ex* 78; Hon C W Drayton *Lon* 80-83; Chapl Greycoat Hosp Sch 83-88; Chapl Stonar Sch Melksham from 88. *Stonar School, Atworth, Melksham, Wilts SN12 8NT* Melksham (0225) 702309

HOUGHTON, Canon John Caswell. b 16. Dur Univ BA38 LTh38. St Boniface Warminster 34. **d** 39 **p** 40. Zambia 64-74; Promotions Sec Feed the Minds 74-81; rtd 81; Perm to Offic *Ox* from 82. *18 Cornelia Close, Bletchley, Milton Keynes MK2 3LX* Milton Keynes (0908) 370526

HOUGHTON, Michael Alan. b 49. Lanc Univ BA70 Dur Univ PGCE71 Southn Univ BTh83. Chich Th Coll 78. **d** 80 **p** 81. C Wellingborough All Hallows *Pet* 80-84; C St Helena 84-89; Tutor Coll of Ascension Selly Oak 90; V Folkestone St Pet *Cant* from 90. *St Peter's Vicarage, Folkestone, Kent CT19 6AL* Folkestone (0303) 54472

HOUGHTON, Ven Michael Richard. b 29. CCC Cam BA52 MA56. Cuddesdon Coll 52. **d** 54 **p** 55. C Portsea N End St Mark *Portsm* 54-57; New Zealand from 57; Adn Tamaki 77-81. *47 Tiri Road, Oneroa, Waiheke Island, New Zealand* Auckland (9) 728250

HOUGHTON, Peter Graham. b 51. St Jo Coll Nottm. **d** 87 **p** 88. C Toxteth Park St Clem *Liv* 87-91; Chapl Winwick Hosp Warrington from 91. *Chaplain's Office, Winwick Hospital, Warrington, Cheshire WA2 8RR* Warrington (0925) 555221

HOUGHTON, Reginald Leighton. b 10. St Chad's Coll Dur BA33 DipTh34 MA36. **d** 34 **p** 35. V Bartley Green *Birm* 60-75; rtd 75; Perm to Offic *Lich* from 75. *50 Washford Road, Meole Brace, Shrewsbury SY3 9HP* Shrewsbury (0743) 246482

HOUGHTON, Thomas. b 17. NW Ord Course 71. **d** 74 **p** 75. NSM Newc w Butterton *Lich* 74-82; Perm to Offic from 82. *Fernyhough, Crewe, Cheshire CW3 9JT* Stoke-on-Trent (0782) 750275

HOULDEN, Prof James Leslie. b 29. Qu Coll Ox BA52 MA56. Cuddesdon Coll 53. **d** 55 **p** 56. C Hunslet St Mary and Stourton *Ripon* 55-58; Tutor Chich Th Coll 58-59; Chapl 59-60; Chapl Trin Coll Ox 60-70; Prin Cuddesdon Coll 70-75; V Cuddesdon *Ox* 70-77; Prin Ripon Coll Cuddesdon 75-77; Hon Can Ch Ch *Ox* 76-77; Sen Lect NT Studies K Coll Lon 77-87; Prof Th K Coll Lon from 87. *33 Raleigh Court, Lymer Avenue, London SE19 1LS* 081-670 6648

HOULDEN, Kenneth Harry. b 10. Ridley Hall Cam 53. **d** 55 **p** 56. V Bramley *Win* 67-75; rtd 75; Perm to Offic *Win* from 75. *3 Kingfisher Court, Highfield Road, Southampton SO2 1UN* Southampton (0703) 554199

HOULDING, David Nigel Christopher. b 53. AKC76. **d** 77 **p** 78. C Hillingdon All SS *Lon* 77-81; C Holborn St Alb w Saffron Hill St Pet 81-85; V Hampstead St Steph w All Hallows from 85. *All Hallows' House, 52 Courthope Road, London NW3 2LD* 071-267 7833

HOULDSWORTH, Raymond Clifford. b 30. Bps' Coll Cheshunt 64. **d** 66 **p** 67. C Egham Hythe *Guildf* 66-70; C Cranbrook *Cant* 70-76; V Hernhill 76-82; V Minster w Monkton from 82. *The Vicarage, St Mildred's Road, Minster, Ramsgate, Kent CT12 4DE* Thanet (0843) 821250

HOULT, Roy Anthony. b 35. AKC58. **d** 59 **p** 60. C Walton St Mary *Liv* 59-63; Canada from 63; Hon Can Koot 75-79. *381 Huron Street, Toronto, Ontario, Canada, M5S 2G5*

HOUNSFIELD, Thomas Paul. b 15. Lon Coll of Div 46. **d** 47 **p** 48. R Donington *Lich* 61-80; rtd 80; Perm to Offic *Win* from 81. *10 Widden Close, Sway, Lymington, Hants SO41 6AX* Lymington (0590) 682399

HOUNSOME, Allan George. b 32. S'wark Ord Course 70. **d** 72 **p** 73. C New Eltham All SS *S'wark* 72-75; C Goldthorpe *Sheff* 75-77; C Goldthorpe w Hickleton 77-78; V Thurnscoe St Hilda from 78. *The Vicarage, Hanover Street, Thurnscoe, Rotherham, S Yorkshire S63 0HJ* Rotherham (0709) 893259

HOUSE, Ven Francis Harry. b 08. OBE55. Wadh Coll Ox BA30 MA34. Cuddesdon Coll 34. **d** 35 **p** 36. R Gawsworth *Ches* 67-78; Adn Macclesfield 67-78; rtd 78. *11 Drummond Court, Drummond Avenue, Leeds LS16 5QE* Leeds (0532) 783646

HOUSE, Graham Ivor. b 44. BA80. Oak Hill Th Coll 77. **d** 80 **p** 81. C Ipswich St Jo *St E* 80-84; V Ipswich St Andr from 84. *286 Britannia Road, Ipswich* Ipswich (0473) 728204

HOUSE, Jack Francis. b 35. Bris Univ BEd70 Lon Univ MA80. Bris & Glouc Tr Course 69. **d** 80 **p** 81. NSM Bedminster *Bris* from 80. *48 Hendre Road, Bristol BS3 2LR* Bristol (0272) 661144

HOUSE, Simon Hutchinson. b 30. Peterho Cam BA65 MA67. Cuddesdon Coll 61. **d** 64 **p** 65. V Allestree St Nic *Derby* 69-81; RD Duffield 74-81; V Bitterne Park *Win* 81-91; rtd 91. *22 Stanley Street, Southsea, Hants PO5 2DS* Portsmouth (0705) 838592

HOUSE, Vickery Willis. b 45. MA. Kelham Th Coll. **d** 69 **p** 70. C Crediton *Ex* 69-76; TV Sampford Peverell, Uplowman, Holcombe Rogus etc 76-81; R Berwick w Selmeston and Alciston *Chich* 81-90; Chapl Ardingly Coll Haywards Heath from 90. *Standgrove Cottage, College Road, Ardingley, Haywards Heath, W Sussex* Haywards Heath (0444) 892656

HOUSMAN, Arthur Martin Rowand. b 53. MA CertEd. Trin Coll Bris 81. **d** 83 **p** 84. C Croydon Ch Ch Broad Green *Cant* 83-84; C Croydon Ch Ch *S'wark* 85-87; TV Stratton St Margaret w S Marston etc *Bris* from 87. *The Vicarage, South Marston, Swindon SN3 4SR* Swindon (0793) 827021

HOUSTON, Arthur James. b 54. Trin Coll Bris BA87. d 87 p 88. C Chatham St Phil and St Jas *Roch* 87-91; I Carrigaline Union *C, C & R* from 91. *19 Windsor Court, Waterpark, Carrigaline, Co Cork, Irish Republic* Cork (21) 372224

HOUSTON, Edward Davison. b 31. TCD BA56. d 57 p 58. C Conwall Union *D & R* 57-59; India 59-88; V Whittlebury w Paulerspury *Pet* from 89. *The Rectory, Tews End Lane, Paulerspury, Towcester, Northants NN12 7NQ* Paulerspury (032733) 670

HOUSTON, Michael Alexander. b 46. Linc Th Coll 86. d 88 p 89. C Longton *Blackb* 88-91; C Woughton *Ox* from 91. *2 Braunston, Woughton Park, Milton Keynes MK6 3AU* Milton Keynes (0908) 674742

HOUSTON, Samuel Kenneth. b 43. FIMA73 QUB BSc64 PhD67. CITC 81. d 85 p 86. NSM Belf St Jas w St Silas *Conn* 85-91; NSM Belf St Andr from 91. *29 North Circular Road, Belfast* Belfast (0232) 771830

HOUSTON, William Paul. b 54. QUB BSSc76 TCD BTh78. CITC 78. d 81 p 82. C Carrickfergus *Conn* 81-83; C Ban St Comgall *D & D* 83-86; I Gilford 86-90; I Carnalea from 90. *St Gall's Rectory, 171 Crawfordsburn Road, Bangor, Co Down BT19 1BT* Helens Bay (0247) 853366

HOVENDEN, Gerald Eric. b 53. York Univ BA75 Ox Univ MA85. Wycliffe Hall Ox 78. d 81 p 82. C Pitsmoor w Ellesmere *Sheff* 81-85; Chapl Lyon w Grenoble and St Etienne *Eur* 85-90; TV S Gillingham *Roch* from 90. *26 Pear Tree Lane, Hempstead, Gillingham, Kent ME7 3PT* Medway (0634) 387892

HOVIL, Richard Guy. b 29. Ex Coll Ox BA51 MA57. Ridley Hall Cam. d 55 p 56. C Finchley Ch Ch *Lon* 55-58; Staff Worker Scripture Union 58-71; Chapl Monkton Combe Sch Bath 71-83; V Fremington *Ex* from 83. *The Vicarage, Fremington, Barnstaple, Devon EX31 2NX* Barnstaple (0271) 73879

HOW, Canon John Maxloe. b 15. Magd Coll Cam BA37 MA49. Westcott Ho Cam 39. d 39 p 40. V Barton w Pooley Bridge *Carl* 59-73; RD Penrith 61-73; V Kirkby Lonsdale w Mansergh 73-76; TR Kirkby Lonsdale 76-81; rtd 81; Perm to Offic *Carl* from 81. *4 Kilmidyke Drive, Grange-over-Sands, Cumbria LA11 7AL* Grange-over-Sands (04484) 4117

HOW, Lewis Henry. b 51. MBTI Acadia Univ (NS) BA75 BEd75 Lanc Univ MA88. Atlantic Sch of Th Halifax (NS) MDiv82. d 82 p 83. Canada 82-87; C Heysham *Blackb* from 91. *11 Heysham Mossgate Road, Heysham, Morecambe, Lancs LA3 2RN* Heysham (0524) 53846

HOWARD, Alan James. b 45. Bris Univ BA69. Clifton Th Coll. d 71 p 72. C Welling *Roch* 71-74; C Cromer *Nor* 74-78; V Sidcup St Andr *Roch* 78-86; V Leyton St Cath *Chelmsf* from 86. *St Catherine's Vicarage, Fairlop Road, London E11 1BL* 081-539 6361

HOWARD, Alban Caldicott Morton. b 13. Keble Coll Ox BA35 MA43. Ely Th Coll 36. d 37 p 38. R York St Mary Bishophill Junior w All SS *York* 60-81; rtd 82. *The Old Rectory, Tanner Row, York YO1 1JB* York (0904) 654316

HOWARD, Charles William Wykeham. b 52. Southn Univ BTh81. Sarum & Wells Th Coll 76. d 79 p 80. C St Mary-at-Latton *Chelmsf* 79-82; Chapl RN from 82. *c/o MOD, Lacon House, Theobald's Road, London WC1X 8RY* 071-430 6847

HOWARD, David John. b 51. Lon Univ BSc73. Oak Hill Th Coll 74. d 77 p 78. C Radipole and Melcombe Regis *Sarum* 77-83; R Tredington and Darlingscott w Newbold on Stour *Cov* 83-90; P-in-c Binley from 90. *8 Royston Close, Binley, Coventry CV3 2SR* Coventry (0203) 636334

HOWARD, David William. b 43. d 67 p 68. C Skegness *Linc* 67-69; C Gainsborough All SS 69-72; Jamaica from 72. *St Michael, Kew Park, Jamaica, West Indies*

HOWARD, Very Rev Donald. b 27. K Coll Lon BD58 AKC58. d 59 p 60. S Africa 62-71; R Haddington *Edin* 72-78; Can St Andr Cathl *Ab* from 78; Provost St Andr Cathl 78-91; R Aber St Andr 78-91; Chapl Aber Univ 78-82; P-in-c Aber St Ninian 80-91; Angl Adv Grampian TV 84-88; rtd 91. *c/o 15 Morningfield Road, Aberdeen AB2 4AP* Aberdeen (0224) 314765

HOWARD, Mrs Erika Kathryn. b 49. SRN70 SCM72. S Dios Minl Tr Scheme 88. d 91. NSM New Shoreham *Chich* from 91; NSM Old Shoreham from 91. *207 Upper Shoreham Road, Shoreham-by-Sea, W Sussex BN43 6BE* Shoreham-by-Sea (0273) 464451

HOWARD, Francis Curzon. b 27. d 57 p 58. C Claughton cum Grange *Ches* 57-60; C Cheltenham St Paul *Glouc* 60-62; V Sheff St Barn *Sheff* 62-65; Bermuda 65-71;

USA from 71. *Trinity Church, Church Street, Tariffville, Connecticut 06081, USA*

HOWARD, Frank Thomas. b 36. Lon Univ BSc57. Bps' Coll Cheshunt 59. d 61 p 62. C Macclesfield St Mich *Ches* 61-64; C Claughton cum Grange 64-66; V Lache cum Saltney 66-76; R Stanton *St E* from 76; RD Ixworth 79-85. *The Rectory, The Street, Stanton, Bury St Edmunds, Suffolk IP31 2DQ* Stanton (0359) 50239

HOWARD, Geoffrey. b 30. Barrister-at-Law 83 Lon Univ LLB77. E Midl Min Tr Course. d 85 p 86. NSM Barton Ely 85-87; NSM Coton 85-87; C W Walton from 87. *Cornerways, 53 School Road, West Walton, Wisbech, Cambs* Wisbech (0945) 584631

HOWARD, Geoffrey. b 45. St Jo Coll Dur BA68 DipTh70. Cranmer Hall Dur 67. d 71 p 72. C Cheetham Hill *Man* 71-74; C Denton Ch Ch 75-77; V Pendleton St Ambrose 77-91; AD Salford from 86; TR Pendleton St Thos w Charlestown from 91. *The Vicarage, 14 Eccles Old Road, Pendleton, Salford M6 7AF* 061-737 2107

HOWARD, George Granville. b 47. Trin Coll Bris. d 88 p 89. C Downend *Bris* from 88. *30 Aintree Drive, Bristol BS16 6SY* Bristol (0272) 565015

HOWARD, Jeremy Clive. b 55. Keble Coll Ox MA78. St Steph Ho Ox 80. d 82 p 83. C Reading St Giles *Ox* 82-85; USPG from 85; Zimbabwe from 86. *c/o USPG, Partnership House, 157 Waterloo Road, London SE1 8XA* 071-928 8681

HOWARD, John. b 61. Nottm Univ BTh90. Aston Tr Scheme 85 Linc Th Coll 87. d 90 p 91. C Bracknell *Ox* from 90. *15 Oakwood Road, Bracknell, Berks RG12 2SP* Bracknell (0344) 411841

HOWARD, John Alexander. b 27. Coll of Resurr Mirfield 66. d 67 p 68. C Almondbury *Wakef* 67-71; C Skelmanthorpe 71-81; R Fortrose *Mor* from 81; R Cromarty from 81; R Arpafeelie from 81. *1 Dean's Road, Fortrose, Ross-shire IV10 8TJ* Fortrose (0381) 20255

HOWARD, John Liddon. b 13. AKC36 G&C Coll Cam BA48 MA56. Wells Th Coll 36. d 37 p 38. V Westward, Rosley-w-Woodside and Welton *Carl* 63-79; rtd 79; Perm to Offic *Carl* from 80. *1 Eastwoodside Cottages, East Woodside, Rosley, Wigton, Cumbria CA7 8BD* Dalston (0228) 711430

HOWARD, John Robert. b 60. NUI BA HDipEd TCD DipTh. d 84 p 85. C Donaghcloney w Waringstown *D & D* 84-88; I Belf St Ninian *Conn* from 88; Bp's Dom Chapl from 88; Chapl Ulster Univ from 88. *St Ninian's Rectory, 33 Vaddegan Road, Newtownabbey, Co Antrim BT36 7SW* Glengormley (0232) 841630

HOWARD, Keith. b 55. Univ of Wales (Ban) DipTh81. St Jo Coll Nottm 81. d 84 p 85. C Llanidloes w Llangurig *Ban* 84-87; R Llansantffraid Glan Conway and Eglwysfach *St As* from 87. *The Rectory, Glan Conway, Colwyn Bay, Clwyd LL29 5ST* Colwyn Bay (0492) 580279

HOWARD, Malcolm. b 29. St Deiniol's Hawarden. d 73 p 74. NSM Birstall *Leic* 73-82; NSM Birstall and Wanlip 82-90; Chapl Leics Hospice 89-90; rtd 90. *65 Fielding Road, Birstall, Leicester LE4 3AH* Leicester (0533) 673046

HOWARD, Canon Michael Charles. b 35. Selw Coll Cam BA58 MA63. Wycliffe Hall Ox 58. d 60 p 61. C Stowmarket *St E* 60-64; Nigeria 64-71; Hon Can Ondo 70-71; Hon C Southborough St Pet w Ch Ch and St Matt *Roch* 72-73; Lic to Offic *Ox* from 73. *17 Milton Road, Bloxham, Banbury, Oxon OX15 4JD*

HOWARD, Michael Paul Penrose. b 40. Keele Univ BA62 Lon Univ BD69. Lon Coll of Div 66. d 69 p 70. C Nottm St Nic S'well 69-72; C Ox St Aldate w H Trin *Ox* 72-77; Chapl CCC Ox 75-77; V Dartford Ch Ch *Roch* 77-90; Chapl W Hill Hosp Dartford 77-90; P-in-c Cobham w Luddesdowne and Dode *Roch* from 90; Dioc Adv on Evang from 90. *The Vicarage, Battle Street, Cobham, Gravesend, Kent DA12 3DB* Meopham (0474) 814332

HOWARD, Paul David. b 47. Lanchester Poly BA69. St Jo Coll Nottm 74. d 77 p 78. C Bedworth *Cov* 77-83; V Newchapel *Lich* from 83. *The Vicarage, 32 Pennyfield Road, Newchapel, Stoke-on-Trent ST7 4PN* Kidsgrove (0782) 782837

HOWARD, Peter Leslie. b 48. Nottm Univ BTh77 Birm Univ MA80. St Jo Coll Nottm LTh77. d 77 p 78. C Gospel Lane St Mich *Birm* 77-81; P-in-c Nechells 81-85; V Stanley *Wakef* from 85. *The Vicarage, 379 Aberford Road, Stanley, Wakefield, W Yorkshire WF3 4HE* Wakefield (0924) 822143

HOWARD, Reginald James. b 33. AKC60. d 61 p 62. C Shildon *Dur* 61-64; C Hurworth 64-66; V Morley St Paul *Wakef* 66-75; V Westgate Common from 75.

41 Oakleigh Avenue, Wakefield, W Yorkshire WF2 9DF
Wakefield (0924) 373020

HOWARD, Richard Leonard. b 03. St Paul's Coll Burgh 26. **d** 30 **p** 31. V Markyate Street *St Alb* 68-73; rtd 86; Perm to Offic *Chich* from 86. *College of St Barnabas, Blackberry Lane, Lingfield, Surrey RH7 6NJ* Dormans Park (034287) 731

HOWARD, Canon Robert Weston. b 28. Pemb Coll Cam BA49 MA53. Westcott Ho Cam 51. **d** 53 **p** 54. C Bishopwearmouth St Mich *Dur* 53-56; C Cam Gt St Mary w St Mich *Ely* 56-60; Hong Kong 60-66; V Prenton *Ches* 66-75; RD Frodsham 74-82; P-in-c Dunham-on-the-Hill 75-77; V Helsby and Ince 75-77; V Helsby and Dunham-on-the-Hill 77-82; Hon Can Ches Cathl 78-82; V Moseley St Mary *Birm* 82-88; V Chalke Valley W *Sarum* from 88. *The Vicarage, Broad Chalke, Salisbury SP5 5DS* Salisbury (0722) 780262

HOWARD, Ronald. b 40. AMIBF65 EngTech91. Cranmer Hall Dur 86. **d** 88 **p** 89. C Baildon *Bradf* from 88. *9 Coach Road, Baildon, Shipley, W Yorkshire BD17 5JE* Bradford (0274) 593441

HOWARD, Canon Ronald Claude. b 02. SS Coll Cam BA24 MA28. Westcott Ho Cam 24. **d** 26 **p** 27. Hd Master Hurstpierpoint Coll Hassocks 45-64; Can and Preb Chich Cathl *Chich* 57-69; rtd 64. *52 Wilbury Road, Hove, E Sussex* Brighton (0273) 822142

HOWARD, Canon Ronald Trevor. b 19. Pemb Coll Cam BA41 MA45. Wells Th Coll 52. **d** 54 **p** 55. C Moulsham St Jo *Chelmsf* 54-59; R Belchamp Otten w Belchamp Walter and Bulmer from 59; RD Belchamp 75-90; Hon Can Chelmsf Cathl from 79. *The Rectory, Belchamp Otten, Sudbury, Suffolk CO10 7BG* Clare (0787) 277318

HOWARD, Stanley Reginald Kekewich. b 10. St Pet Hall Ox BA31 MA35. Ridley Hall Cam 31. **d** 33 **p** 34. V Cheltenham St Paul *Glouc* 51-76; Chapl Cheltenham Maternity and St Paul's Hosps 61-76; rtd 76; Perm to Offic *Win* from 81. *Selah, 3 Montague Road, Bournemouth BH5 2EW* Bournemouth (0202) 427376

HOWARD, Ms Susan. b 65. Lanc Univ BA86. Ripon Coll Cuddesdon 88. **d** 91. C Ditton St Mich *Liv* from 91. *24 Crown Avenue, Widnes, Cheshire WA8 8AT* 051-423 5134

HOWARD, Thomas Norman. b 40. St Aid Birkenhead 64. **d** 67 **p** 68. C Farnworth and Kearsley *Man* 67-70; C Prestwich St Marg 70-73; V Heyside 73-85; Warden Lamplugh Ho Angl Conf Cen Thwing 85-90; Hon C Langtoft w Foxholes, Butterwick, Cottam etc *York* 85-87; C 87-90; V Fence and Newchurch-in-Pendle *Blackb* from 90; Dioc Ecum Officer from 90. *The Vicarage, 12 Wheatcroft Avenue, Fence, Burnley, Lancs BB12 9QL* Nelson (0282) 67316

HOWARD, William Alfred. b 47. St Jo Coll Dur BA69. Wycliffe Hall Ox 74. **d** 77 **p** 79. C Norbiton *S'wark* 77-80; C Mile Cross *Nor* 80-84; R Grimston w Congham 84-91; R Grimston, Congham and Roydon from 91. *The Rectory, Grimston, King's Lynn, Norfolk PE32 1BQ* Hillington (0485) 600335

HOWARD JONES, Preb Raymond Vernon. b 31. AKC54. **d** 55 **p** 56. C Hutton *Chelmsf* 55-58; CF 58-62; V Walpole St Andrew *Ely* 62-64; Chapl St Crispin's Hosp Northn 64-70; V Brockhampton w Fawley *Heref* 70-86; V Fownhope from 86; RD Heref Rural 77-81; Preb Heref Cathl from 81; Communications Adv and Bp's Staff Officer from 86. *The Rectory, Stretton Sugwas, Hereford HR4 7PT* Hereford (0432) 279371

HOWARTH, Arthur. b 14. **d** 37 **p** 38. C Aylesbury *Ox* 37-40; C W Wycombe 40-42; C Acton Vale St Thos *Lon* 42-43; C Fulham All SS 43-44; C Hornsey St Mary 44-46; St Vincent 46-51; Perm to Offic Ox 51-54; Guildf 54; Nigeria from 55. *Bishop Lasbrey College Irete, PO Box 68, Owerri, Nigeria*

HOWARTH, Benjamin Wrigley. b 20. AKC43. **d** 43 **p** 44. Dep Asst Chapl Gen 67-70 and 73-75; Warden RAChD Cen 70-73; Chapl to HM The Queen 73-78; Asst Chapl Gen 75-78; R Chew Stoke w Nempnett Thrubwell *B & W* 78-85; R Norton Malreward 78-85; rtd 86; Perm to Offic *B & W* from 86. *6 Kings Road, Wells, Somerset BA5 3LU* Wells (0749) 74294

HOWARTH, Christopher. b 47. S Dios Minl Tr Scheme. **d** 83 **p** 84. NSM Uckfield *Chich* from 83. *137 Rocks Park Road, Uckfield, E Sussex TN22 2BD* Uckfield (0825) 5352

HOWARTH, Geoffrey Gifford. b 21. Oak Hill Th Coll 65. **d** 66 **p** 67. P-in-c Bootle St Mary w St Jo *Liv* 69-73; V Newburn *Newc* 73-86; rtd 86. *Beeches, Pickering Road East, Snainton, Scarborough, N Yorkshire YO13 9AF* Scarborough (0723) 859148

HOWARTH, Canon Gerald Simeon. b 10. AKC35. **d** 35 **p** 36. V Milford *Win* 55-75; rtd 75; Perm to Offic *Guildf* from 81. *12 Langton Avenue, Ewell, Epsom, Surrey KT17 1LD* 081-393 4421

HOWARTH, Jack Raymond. b 13. Leeds Univ BSc34. Coll of Resurr Mirfield 34. **d** 36 **p** 37. R Elland *Wakef* 63-75; V Halifax St Jo Cragg Vale 75-78; rtd 78; Hon C Haydock St Jas *Liv* 78-86; Chapl Wigan R Infirmary 86-88. *13/4 Ladywell Road, Edinburgh EH12 7TA* 031-334 0594

HOWARTH, Leslie John. b 22. MIEH MRSH. Sarum & Wells Th Coll 75. **d** 78 **p** 79. NSM Plymouth St Gabr *Ex* from 78. *1 Wardlow Gardens, Trevannion Park, Plymouth PL6 5PU* Plymouth (0752) 773641

HOWARTH, Robert Francis Harvey. b 31. S'wark Ord Course 71. **d** 72 **p** 73. C St Marylebone All So w SS Pet and Jo *Lon* 72-73; C St Helen Bishopsgate w St Martin Outwich 73-78; V Harlow St Mary V *Chelmsf* 78-88; P-in-c Victoria Docks Ascension from 88. *23 Burley Road, London E16 3JU* 071-474 9757

HOWARTH, Canon Ronald. b 26. TCD BA51 MA54. Linc Th Coll 50. **d** 52 **p** 53. Nigeria 55-89; rtd 91. *4 Kingston Court, Walton Street, Oxford OX2 6ES* Oxford (0865) 53046

HOWAT, Jeremy Noel Thomas. b 35. Em Coll Cam BA59 MA. Ridley Hall Cam 59. **d** 63 **p** 64. C Sutton *Liv* 63-65; C Kirk Ella *York* 65-66; C Bridlington Quay Ch Ch 66-69; R Wheldrake 69-78; Dioc Youth Officer 70-74; Argentina 78-81 and from 89; P-in-c Newton upon Ouse *York* 81-82; V Shipton w Overton 81-82; P-in-c Skelton by York 81-82; R Skelton w Shipton and Newton on Ouse 82-89; SAMS from 89. *San Bartolome, Paraguay 482, Rosario, Argentina*

HOWDEN, Canon Arthur Travis. b 11. Clare Coll Cam BA33 MA37. Wycliffe Hall Ox 33. **d** 34 **p** 35. R Wortham *St E* 71-72; P-in-c Redgrave w Botesdale 71-72; R Redgrave w Botesdale and Wortham 72-76; rtd 76; Perm to Offic *St E* from 76. *Little Thatch, Oak Lane, Rougham, Bury St Edmunds, Suffolk IP30 9JX* Beyton (0359) 70704

HOWDEN, John Travis. b 40. RIBA62. Sarum Th Coll 66. **d** 69 **p** 70. C S Gillingham *Roch* 69-72; C Banbury *Ox* 72-73; Lic to Offic *York* 73-74; Hon C Hull Newland St Jo 74-81; Hon C Stock Harvard *Chelmsf* 82-86; R Doddinghurst and Mountnessing from 86. *The Rectory, Church Lane, Doddinghurst, Brentwood, Essex CM15 0NJ* Brentwood (0277) 821366

HOWE, Alan Raymond. b 52. Nottm Univ BTh79. St Jo Coll Nottm 76. **d** 80 **p** 81. C Southsea St Simon *Portsm* 80-83; C Bexleyheath St Pet *Roch* 83-86; TV Camberley St Paul *Guildf* from 86. *St Mary's House, 37 Park Road, Camberley, Surrey GU15 2SP* Camberley (0276) 22085

HOWE, Alfred William. b 10. St D Coll Lamp BA32. **d** 33 **p** 34. V Forthampton w Chaceley *Glouc* 59-79; rtd 79; Perm to Offic *Glouc* from 80. *1 Masons Court, Barton Street, Tewkesbury, Glos GL20 5PY* Tewkesbury (0684) 296442

HOWE, Canon Charles. b 30. Lon Univ BD65 Open Univ BA79. Tyndale Hall Bris 55. **d** 58 **p** 59. C Willowfield *D & D* 58-60; C Derryloran *Arm* 60-64; C Belf St Bart Conn 64-65; I Tullyaughnish w Kilmacrennan and Killygarvan *D & R* 65-72; I Londonderry St Aug from 73; Can Derry Cathl from 85. *St Augustine's Rectory, 4 Bridgewater, Caw, Londonderry BT47 1YA* Londonderry (0504) 47532

HOWE, Canon David Randall. b 24. St Jo Coll Cam BA51 MA55. Wells Th Coll 51. **d** 53 **p** 54. V Rotherwick, Hook and Greywell *Win* 59-70; R Bossington w Broughton 70-81; R Broughton w Bossington and Mottisfont 81-86; R Broughton, Bossington, Houghton and Mottisfont 86-89; Hon Can Win Cathl from 87; rtd 89. *Little Orchard, Hilldrop Lane, Ramsbury, Marlborough, Wilts SN8 2RB* Marlborough (0672) 20326

HOWE, Miss Frances Ruth. b 28. ACIB67. Cranmer Hall Dur 78. dss 80 **d** 87. Chapl Asst R Victoria Infirmary Newc 80-87; Chapl Wylam and Fleming Ch Hosp 82-87; Chapl St Oswald's Hospice Newc from 86; C Newc Epiphany Newc 87-90. *18 Mason Avenue, Whitley Bay, Tyne & Wear NE26 1AQ* 091-285 0063

HOWE, George Alexander. b 52. St Jo Coll Dur BA73. Westcott Ho Cam 73. **d** 75 **p** 76. C Peterlee *Dur* 75-79; C Norton St Mary 79-81; V Hart w Elwick Hall 81-85; R Sedgefield 85-91; RD Sedgefield 89-91; V Kendal H Trin *Carl* from 91. *Holy Trinity Vicarage, 2 Lynngarth Drive, Kendal, Cumbria LA9 4JA* Kendal (0539) 721541 or 721248

HOWE, Canon George Reginald. b 13. TCD BA37 MA51. **d** 39 **p** 40. I Rossory *Clogh* 57-80; Chan Clogh Cathl

79-80; rtd 80. *22 Breandrum Court, Tempo Road, Enniskillen, Co Fermanagh* Enniskillen (0365) 22389

HOWE, Harry Norman. b 10. United Th Coll Limuru. **d** 73 **p** 74. Kenya 74-75; C Fringford w Hethe and Newton Purcell *Ox* 75-76; rtd 76; Perm to Offic York 76-80; Lich from 80; Wakef from 84. *28 Vernon Avenue, Huddersfield HD1 5QD* Huddersfield (0484) 516549

HOWE, Canon John. b 36. Ex Coll Ox BA58 MA63. St Steph Ho Ox 58. **d** 61 **p** 62. C Horninglow *Lich* 61-64; C Sedgley All SS 64-66; V Ocker Hill 66-73; V Gnosall 73-79; P-in-c Hoar Cross 79-82; Preb Lich Cathl from 83; V Hoar Cross w Newchurch 83-88; Can Res Lich Cathl from 88. *20 The Close, Lichfield, Staffs WS13 7LD* Lichfield (0543) 268777

✠**HOWE, Rt Rev John William Alexander.** b 20. St Chad's Coll Dur BA43 MA48 BD48. Gen Th Sem (NY) Hon DST74 Lambeth DD78. **d** 43 **p** 44 **c** 55. C Scarborough All SS 43-46; Ghana 46-50; Vice-Prin Edin Th Coll 50-55; Hon Chapl St Mary's Cathl *Edin* 51-55; Bp St Andr *St And* 55-69; Exec Officer Angl Communion 69-71; Hon Can St Mary's Cathl *Glas* from 69; Sec Gen ACC 71-82; Research Fell 83-85; rtd 85; Asst Bp Ripon from 85. *31 Scotton Drive, Knaresborough, N Yorkshire HG5 9HG* Harrogate (0423) 866224

HOWE, Nicholas Simon. b 60. Man Univ BA81 K Coll Lon MTh85. Ridley Hall Cam 86. **d** 88 **p** 89. C Lich St Chad *Lich* from 88. *38 St Chad's Road, Lichfield, Staffs WS13 7ND* Lichfield (0543) 251009

HOWE, Canon Rex Alan. b 29. Ch Coll Cam BA53 MA57. Coll of Resurr Mirfield 53. **d** 55 **p** 56. C Barnsley St Pet *Wakef* 55-57; C Helmsley *York* 57-60; V Middlesb St Martin 60-67; V Redcar 67-73; V Kirkleatham 67-73; RD Guisborough 67-73; Dean Hong Kong 73-76; Adn 75-76; TR Grantham *Linc* 77-85; RD Grantham 78-85; Can and Preb Linc Cathl 81-85; V Canford Cliffs and Sandbanks *Sarum* from 85. *The Vicarage, 14 Flaghead Road, Poole, Dorset BH13 7JW* Canford Cliffs (0202) 700341

HOWE, Ronald Douglas. b 38. K Coll Lon BD62 AKC62 LSE DSA63. **d** 64 **p** 65. C Hendon All SS Childs Hill *Lon* 64-67; C Northn St Mary *Pet* 67-69; V Potterspury w Furtho and Yardley Gobion 69-81; R Corby Epiphany w St Jo 81-86; RD Corby 81-90; V Brigstock w Stanion from 86. *The Vicarage, Brigstock, Kettering, Northants NN14 3EX* Brigstock (0536) 373371

HOWE, Roy William. b 38. ALCD67. **d** 66 **p** 67. C Bradf Cathl *Bradf* 66-70; C Barnoldswick w Bracewell 70-72; V Yeadon St Jo 72-79; P-in-c Bainton *York* 79-86; P-in-c Middleton-on-the-Wolds 79-86; P-in-c N Dalton 79-86; RD Harthill 81-87; C Watton w Beswick and Kilnwick 82-86; R Bainton w N Dalton, Middleton-on-the-Wolds etc 86-87; TV Penrith w Newton Reigny and Plumpton Wall *Carl* from 87; Dioc Chapl to Agric and Rural Life from 87. *The Vicarage, Plumpton, Penrith, Cumbria CA11 9PA* Plumpton (076884) 273

HOWE, William Ernest. b 25. ARICS51. Westcott Ho Cam 68. **d** 70 **p** 71. C Anston *Sheff* 70-73; V from 84; C Woodsetts 70-73; V Greasbrough 73-84. *The Vicarage, 17 Rackford Road, Anston, Sheffield S31 7DE* Dinnington (0909) 563447

HOWELL, Alfred. b 32. Wells Th Coll 57. **d** 59 **p** 60. V Sparkbrook Ch Ch *Birm* 66-73; Lic to Offic *Chelmsf* 73-83; P-in-c Brentwood St Geo 83-88; rtd 88. *Windy Corner, Grove Lane, Iden, Rye, E Sussex* Iden (07978) 564

HOWELL, Andrew John. b 44. Clifton Th Coll 68. **d** 71 **p** 72. C Halliwell St Pet *Man* 71-77; V Facit from 77. *The Vicarage, Facit, Rochdale, Lancs OL12 8LT* Whitworth (070685) 3931

HOWELL, Canon Basil Rayson. b 20. St Pet Hall Ox BA49 MA53. Wycliffe Hall Ox 49. **d** 51 **p** 52. V Blundellsands St Nic *Liv* 61-81; RD Bootle 69-78; rtd 81; Perm to Offic *Cov* from 81. *9 Arlington Court, Arlington Avenue, Leamington Spa CV32 5HR* Leamington Spa (0926) 314746

HOWELL, David. b 29. Clifton Th Coll 56. **d** 59 **p** 60. V W Bromwich St Paul Golds Hill *Lich* 62-71; V Deptford St Jo *S'wark* 71-81; Dir and Chapl Home of Divine Healing Crowhurst 81-89; rtd 90. *38 Lyttelton Road, Droitwich, Worcester WR9 7AB* Worcester (0905) 773385

HOWELL, Garnet Hughes. b 16. St D Coll Lamp BA37. **d** 39 **p** 40. C Aberdare *Llan* 39-41; C Penydarren 41-43; C Llansantffraed-juxta-Usk *S & B* 43-44; C Llanddetty 43-44. *16 College Street, Lampeter, Dyfed SA48 7DY*

HOWELL, Geoffrey Peter. b 52. LTCL82 Selw Coll Cam BA75 MA78. Cranmer Hall Dur 85. **d** 87 **p** 88. C Hartlepool St Luke *Dur* 87-90; TV Burford II w Greete and Hope Bagot *Heref* from 90; TV Burford III w Lt

Heref from 90; TV Tenbury from 90. *The Rectory, Burford, Tenbury Wells, Worcs WR15 8HG* Tenbury Wells (0584) 810678

HOWELL, John Anthony Neil Belville. b 39. Man Univ BA64. St Deiniol's Hawarden 77. **d** 79 **p** 81. C Wistaston *Ches* 79-82; P-in-c Derry Hill *Sarum* 82-83; V Clayton *Bradf* from 83. *The Vicarage, Clayton Lane, Clayton, Bradford, W Yorkshire BD14 6AX* Bradford (0274) 880373

✠**HOWELL, Rt Rev Kenneth Walter.** b 09. St Pet Hall Ox BA32 MA36. Wycliffe Hall Ox 32. **d** 33 **p** 34 **c** 63. C Peckham St Mary *S'wark* 33-37; Paraguay 37-38; Chile 38-47; I Wandsworth *S'wark* 48-63; RD 57-63; Bp Chile, Bolivia and Peru 63-71; C-in-c Hampstead St Jo Downshire Hill Prop Chpl *Lon* 72-79; rtd 75; Asst Bp Lon 76-79. *96 Colney Hatch Lane, London N10 1EA* 081-444 6223

HOWELL, Martin John Hope. b 38. Bris Univ BA62. Tyndale Hall Bris 59. **d** 64 **p** 65. C Bolton St Paul *Man* 64-67; C Bishopsworth *Bris* 67-70; V Swindon St Aug 70-81; TR Stratton St Margaret w S Marston etc from 81; RD Cricklade 88; RD Highworth from 88. *The Rectory, Kenwin Close, Swindon SN3 4NB* Swindon (0793) 822793

HOWELL, Roger Brian. b 43. ALCD67. **d** 67 **p** 68. C Battersea Park St Sav *S'wark* 67-71; C Southgate *Chich* 71-76; V Pendeen *Truro* 76-81; P-in-c Sancreed 76-81; V Bedgrove *Ox* 81-91; R Purley from 91. *The Rectory, 1 Westridge Avenue, Purley, Reading RG8 2DA* Reading (0734) 21003

HOWELL, Ronald William Fullerton. b 51. Man Univ BA72 CertEd Ox Univ BA78 MA. Ripon Coll Cuddesdon 76. **d** 79 **p** 80. C Newc St Fran *Newc* 79-81; C Warmsworth *Sheff* 81-82; Dioc Educn Officer 82-85; V Millhouses H Trin from 85. *Holy Trinity Vicarage, 80 Millhouses Lane, Sheffield S7 2HB* Sheffield (0742) 362838

HOWELL, Preb Walter Ernest. b 17. St D Coll Lamp BA49. **d** 50 **p** 51. V Kentish Town St Benet and All SS *Lon* 68-79; V Alexandra Park St Sav 79-84; rtd 84. *6 Wattlers Close, Copmanthorpe, York YO2 3XR* York (0904) 702615

HOWELL-EVERSON, Douglas Norman. b 19. TD53. Ripon Hall Ox 59. **d** 60 **p** 61. V Stanton-in-Peak *Derby* 62-75; R Bamford 75-85; rtd 85; Perm to Offic *Derby* and *Sheff* from 85. *25 Conway Drive, Carlton-in-Lindrick, Worksop, Notts S81 9DG* Worksop (0909) 731499

HOWELLS, Alun. b 24. St D Coll Lamp 62. **d** 64 **p** 65. C Carmarthen St Dav *St D* 64-70; V Llandyssilio and Egremont 70-71; V Llanboidy and Meidrim 71-81; V Meidrim and Llanboidy and Merthyr 81-88; rtd 88. *9 Llys Flynon, Fountain Hall Terrace, Carmarthen, Dyfed* Carmarthen (0267) 233244

HOWELLS, Canon Arthur Glyn. b 32. Univ of Wales (Lamp) BA54. St Mich Coll Llan 54. **d** 56 **p** 57. C Oystermouth *S & B* 56-58; C Llangyfelach and Morriston 58-64; V Llandefalle and Llyswen w Boughrood etc 64-69; Youth Chapl 67-71; V Landore 70-80; Dioc Missr 80-89; Can Brecon Cathl 80-89; Dir St Mary's Coll Swansea from 82; V Swansea St Jas *S & B* from 89. *St James's Vicarage, 55 Eaton Crescent, Uplands, Swansea SA1 4QN* Swansea (0792) 470532

HOWELLS, David. b 55. Grey Coll Dur BA78. Ripon Coll Cuddesdon 79. **d** 81 **p** 82. C Birtley *Dur* 81-84; Canada from 84. *17 Foster Avenue, Guelph, Ontario, Canada, N1H 3B2* Guelph (519) 823-8924

HOWELLS, David Morgan. b 24. Qu Coll Birm 72. **d** 75 **p** 76. NSM Radford *Cov* 75-87; rtd 87; Perm to Offic *Cov* from 87. *21 Banks Road, Coventry CV6 1JT* Coventry (0203) 598118

HOWELLS, Canon Donald Lockwood. b 20. Lon Univ BA43. Oak Hill Th Coll 39. **d** 43 **p** 44. R Tring *St Alb* 66-80; P-in-c Aldbury 78-80; P-in-c Puttenham w Long Marston 79-80; Hon Can St Alb 80-85; RD Berkhamsted 80-85; TR Tring 80-85; rtd 85; Perm to Offic *Cant* from 85. *10 Cadram Close, Canterbury, Kent CT2 7SD* Canterbury (0227) 462835

HOWELLS, Garfield Edwin. b 18. Man Univ. **d** 54 **p** 55. C Sanderstead All SS *S'wark* 54-57; CF 57-60; R Kingsdown *Roch* 60-64; Australia from 64. *137 Fendam Street, Warnbro, W Australia 6169* Perth (9) 593-1819

HOWELLS, Gordon. b 39. Univ of Wales (Cardiff) BSc61 DipEd62. Ripon Coll Cuddesdon 86. **d** 88 **p** 89. C Atherstone *Cov* 88-89; C Lillington from 89. *34 Lime Avenue, Leamington Spa, Warks CV32 7DF* Leamington Spa (0926) 337710

HOWELLS, Lucinda Jane Reid. b 57. Dur Univ BA78. Ripon Coll Cuddesdon 79. dss 81 **d** 85 **p** 85. Birtley *Dur*

81-84; Canada from 84. *17 Foster Avenue, Guelph, Ontario, Canada, N1H 3B2*

HOWELLS, Neil. b 23. Qu Mary Coll Lon BSc48. Bps' Coll Cheshunt 48. **d** 50 **p** 51. R Welford w Wickham *Ox* 68-73; R Welford w Wickham and Gt Shefford 73-77; RD Newbury 73-77; V Bray and Braywood 77-84; rtd 84; Perm to Offic *Sarum* from 85. *19 Loders, Bridport, Dorset DT6 3SA* Bridport (0308) 56490

HOWELLS, William Gordon. b 26. **d** 61 **p** 62. C Aberdare *Llan* 61-64; C Coity w Nolton 64-67; C Northam *Ex* 67-71; V Bishops Tawton 71-76; V Cofton w Starcross 76-80; R Aveton Gifford 80-86; V Modbury 80-86; TV Lynton, Brendon, Countisbury, Lynmouth etc from 86. *Church House, Barbrook, Lynton, Devon EX35 6PD* Lynton (0598) 52408

HOWES, Alan. b 49. Chich Th Coll 76. **d** 79 **p** 80. C Bilborough St Jo *S'well* 79-82; TV Newark w Hawton, Cotham and Shelton 82-89; TV Newark-upon-Trent from 89. *St Leonard's Vicarage, Lincoln Road, Newark, Notts NG24 2DQ* Newark (0636) 703691

HOWES, David. b 30. Open Univ BA75. Roch Th Coll 62. **d** 64 **p** 65. C Highweek *Ex* 64-67; C Clyst St George 67-71; P-in-c Woolfardisworthy w Kennerleigh 71-72; P-in-c Washford Pyne w Puddington 71-72; TR N Creedy 72-73; Perm to Offic 74-77; C Walworth *S'wark* 77-78; C-in-c Roundshaw CD 78-83; R S'wark St Geo 83-90; P-in-c S'wark St Jude 84-90; P-in-c Risley *Derby* from 90; Bp's Ind Adv from 90. *The Rectory, 80 Derby Road, Risley, Derby DE7 3SU* Sandiacre (0602) 398557

HOWES, Judith Elizabeth. b 44. SRN RSCN. Cuddesdon 88. **d** 89. Par Dn Ex St Sidwell and St Matt *Ex* from 89. *3 St James Close, Exeter EX4 6QZ* Exeter (0392) 436032

HOWES, Michael John Norton. b 43. Hull Univ BA66. Linc Th Coll 66. **d** 68 **p** 69. C Gt Berkhamsted *St Alb* 68-71; C Ampthill w Millbrook and Steppingley 71-72; Chapl RAF 72-88; V Thurlby w Carlby *Linc* from 88. *The Vicarage, Thurlby, Bourne, Lincs PE10 0EH* Bourne (0778) 422475

HOWES, Canon Norman Vincent. b 36. AKC61. **d** 62 **p** 63. C Radford *Cov* 62-66; V Napton on the Hill 66-72; V Exhall 72-83; R Walton D'Eiville from 83; V Wellesbourne from 83; RD Fosse from 87; Hon Can Cov Cathl from 89. *The Vicarage, Wellesbourne, Warwick CV35 9LS* Stratford-upon-Avon (0789) 840262

✠**HOWES, Rt Rev Peter Henry Herbert.** b 11. OBE61 PBS63. Kelham Th Coll 29. **d** 34 **p** 35 **c** 76. C Norton St Mich *Dur* 34-37; Malaya 37-63; Malaysia 63-81; Can Borneo 55-62; Adn Sarawak 61-62; Adn Kuching 62-65; Can Kuching 62-71; Adn Brunei and N Sarawak 65-71; Asst Bp Kuching 76-81; rtd 81. *7 Tower Place, York YO1 1RZ* York (0904) 638050

HOWES, Canon Roger Hylton. b 24. TD. Linc Th Coll 56. **d** 58 **p** 59. C Kidderminster St Mary *Worc* 58-60; Ind Chapl 60-64; Bp's Ind Adv 64-70; Hon Can Worc Cathl from 69; Dir of Worc Ind Miss 70-79; V Eckington from 79; V Defford w Besford from 79. *The Vicarage, Eckington, Pershore, Worcs WR10 3BN* Evesham (0386) 750203

HOWITT, Canon Alan John. b 26. ARCM49 Leeds Univ BA50. Coll of Resurr Mirfield 50. **d** 53 **p** 54. C Wanstead St Mary *Chelmsf* 53-57; Chapl Tiffield Sch Northants 57-64; V Northn St Mary *Pet* 64-75; RD Wootton 70-74; Chapl Pet Distr Hosp 75-88; Can Pet Cathl *Pet* from 75; V Pet St Jo from 75; RD Pet 76-87. *The Vicarage, 55 Thorpe Road, Peterborough PE3 6AN* Peterborough (0733) 64899

HOWITT, Ivan Richard. b 56. Kent Univ BA81. Sarum & Wells Th Coll 83. **d** 85 **p** 86. C Herne Bay Ch Ch *Cant* 85-87; C St Laurence in Thanet 87-90; R Owmby and Normanby w Glentham *Linc* from 90; P-in-c Spridlington w Saxby and Firsby from 90. *The Rectory, Owmby, Lincoln LN2 3HL* Normanby-by-Spital (06737) 275

HOWITT, John Leslie. b 28. Lon Coll of Div 60. **d** 62 **p** 63. C Attenborough w Bramcote *S'well* 62-66; Chapl Rampton Hosp Retford 66-71; P-in-c Treswell and Cottam *S'well* 68-71; Chapl HM Pris Cardiff 71-75; Dartmoor 79-83; Cant 83-87; Chapl HM Youth Cust Cen Dover 75-79; Chapl HM Det Cen Aldington 83-87; Perm to Offic *Cant* from 87; V Shobnall *Lich* from 88. *114 Shobnall Road, Burton-on-Trent, Staffs DE14 2BB* Burton-on-Trent (0283) 30910

HOWLAND, Miss Ada Lilian. b 08. St Andr Ho Portsm 47. **dss** 50 **d** 87. Australia 52-59; Southsea St Pet *Portsm* 60-74; rtd 74; Portsm Cathl *Portsm* 74-87; Hon Par Dn from 87. *38 Portsmouth Town Court, 115 High Street, Portsmouth PO1 2SX* Portsmouth (0705) 829352

HOWLAND, Ms Pamela Isobel. b 29. Lady Mabel Coll CertEd71. Qu Coll Birm 79. **dss** 82 **d** 87. Thorpe Edge *Bradf* 82-87; Par Dn 87-89; rtd 89. *308 Moorview Way, Skipton, N Yorkshire BD23 2TW* Skipton (0756) 700725

HOWLDEN, Paul Wilfrid. b 41. Trin Coll Cam BA63 MA67. Cuddesdon Coll 64. **d** 66 **p** 67. C Paulsgrove *Portsm* 66-73; Hon C Ealing Ascension Hanger Hill *Lon* 75-87; R Bishops Waltham *Portsm* 87-88; Perm to Offic from 89. *33 Chamberlain Grove, Fareham, Hants PO14 1HH* Fareham (0329) 233035

HOWSON, David James. b 34. Kelham Th Coll 54. **d** 58 **p** 59. C Morecambe St Barn *Blackb* 58-61; C Burnley St Pet 61-63; C-in-c Penwortham St Leon CD 63-65; Bp's Youth Officer *Ox* 65-67; V Whitworth *Man* 67-71; R Rufford *Blackb* 71-78; V Mellor 78-83; Lic to Offic *Ox* 83-87; Area Sec (Dio Ox) USPG 83-87; R Cherbury *Ox* from 87; RD Vale of White Horse from 91. *The Rectory, Longworth, Abingdon, Oxon OX13 5DX* Longworth (0865) 820213

HOWSON, Canon George Webster. b 15. Man Univ BA46. Sarum Th Coll 47. **d** 49 **p** 50. V Over St Chad *Ches* 60-80; RD Middlewich 74-80; rtd 80; Perm to Offic *Ches* from 80. *58 Mount Drive, Nantwich, Cheshire CW5 6JQ* Nantwich (0270) 627870

HOY, Michael John. b 30. Reading Univ BSc52. Oak Hill Th Coll 57. **d** 59 **p** 60. C Worthing St Geo *Chich* 59-62; C Tulse Hill H Trin *S'wark* 62-66; R Danby Wiske w Yafforth and Hutton Bonville *Ripon* 66-76; V Camelsdale *Chich* 76-87; V Gt Marsden *Blackb* from 87. *St John's Vicarage, Barkerhouse Road, Nelson, Lancs BB9 9JS* Nelson (0282) 63824

HOYAL, Richard Dunstan. b 47. Ch Ch Ox BA67 MA71 BA78. Ripon Coll Cuddesdon 76. **d** 79 **p** 80. C Stevenage St Geo *St Alb* 79-83; V Monk Bretton *Wakef* 83-89; V Ilkley St Marg *Bradf* from 89. *St Margaret's Vicarage, 14 Queen's Road, Ilkley, W Yorkshire LS29 9QJ* Ilkley (0943) 607015

HOYE, Reginald George. b 16. Tyndale Hall Bris 58. **d** 60 **p** 61. V Nottm St Sav *S'well* 62-82; rtd 82; Perm to Offic *S'well* from 82. *1 White Acre, Burton Joyce, Nottingham NG14 5BU* Nottingham (0602) 312485

HOYLAND, John Gregory. b 50. Sussex Univ BEd73. Wycliffe Hall Ox 75. **d** 78 **p** 79. C Pudsey St Lawr *Bradf* 78-81; P-in-c Long Preston 81-84; P-in-c Long Preston w Tosside 84; V 84; CPAS Staff 85-87; Chapl Univ Coll of Ripon & York St Jo from 87. *College of Ripon and York, Lord Mayor's Walk, York YO3 7EX* York (0904) 56771

HOYLE, David Michael. b 57. CCC Cam BA80 MA83. Ripon Coll Cuddesdon 84. **d** 86 **p** 87. C Chesterton Gd Shep *Ely* 86-88; Chapl Magd Coll Cam from 88. *Magdalene College, Cambridge CB3 0AG* Cambridge (0223) 332100

HOYLE, Ven Frederick James. b 18. St Jo Coll Dur BA47 DipTh49 MA58. **d** 49 **p** 50. Vice-Chmn and Exec Officer Dioc Past Cttee 65-85; Hon Can Man Cathl *Man* 67-85; V Rochdale 71-78; TR Rochdale 78-82; RD Rochdale 71-82; Adn Bolton 82-85; TV E Farnworth and Kearsley 82-85; rtd 85; Perm to Offic *Blackb & Man* from 85. *37 Toll Bar Crescent, Scotforth, Lancaster LA1 4NR* Lancaster (0524) 37883

HOYLE, Lawrence. b 27. St Aid Birkenhead 52. **d** 55 **p** 56. V Wrose *Bradf* 66-70; R Thwing *York* 70-81; V Wold Newton 71-81; Warden Lamplugh Ho Conf Cen 72-85; Dir Angl Renewal Min 81-89; Hon C Starbeck *Ripon* 87-89; rtd 89. *The Cottage, Lamplugh House, Thwing, Driffield, N Humberside YO25 0DY* Thwing (026287) 536

HOYLE, Miss Pamela Margaret. b 61. Nottm Univ BA82. St Jo Coll Nottm 84. **d** 87. Par Dn Bulwell St Jo *S'well* 87-91; Par Dn Cam H Trin w St Andr Gt *Ely* from 91; Cambridge Pastorate Chapl from 91. *4 Parsonage Street, Cambridge CB5 8DN* Cambridge (0223) 321144

HOYLE, Stephen Jonathan. b 64. Leeds Univ BA87. Ripon Coll Cuddesdon 88. **d** 90 **p** 91. C Lt Stanmore St Lawr *Lon* from 90. *18 Milford Gardens, Edgware, Middx HA8 6EY* 081-951 3662

HOYLE, Thomas Oldland. b 22. St Edm Hall Ox BA49 MA53. Chich Th Coll 49. **d** 50 **p** 51. V Calverton *S'well* 56-86; rtd 86. *20 Washford Gardens, Clacton-on-Sea, Essex CO15 1XA*

HRYZIUK, Petro. b 57. Lanc Univ BEd80. St Jo Coll Nottm DipTh89. **d** 90 **p** 91. C Huyton St Geo *Liv* from 90. *31 Endmoor Road, Huyton, Liverpool L36 3UH* 051-489 4086

HUARD, Ven Geoffrey Robert. b 43. Lon Univ DipTh71. Clifton Th Coll 64. **d** 70 **p** 71. C Barking St Marg *Chelmsf* 70-73; C Everton St Ambrose w St Tim *Liv* 73-74; C

Everton St Pet 74-76; Australia from 76; Adn Sydney and Cumberland from 89. *St Andrew's House, PO Box Q190, Queen Victoria Building, Sydney, NSW, Australia 2000* Sydney (2) 265-1524

HUBAND, Eric Bob. b 27. Bris Univ BSc50. Sarum Th Coll 50. **d** 52 **p** 53. C Lockleaze St Fran CD *Bris* 52-56; C Bishopsworth 56-60; V Greenbank 60-67; V Hengrove 67-77; R E Horsley *Guildf* from 77. *The Rectory, Ockham Road South, East Horsley, Leatherhead, Surrey KT24 6RL* East Horsley (04865) 2359

HUBAND, Richard William. b 39. Trin Coll Cam BA62 MA66. Qu Coll Birm 76. **d** 78 **p** 79. C Norton *St Alb* 78-81; R Aspley Guise w Husborne Crawley and Ridgmont 81-91; V Elstow from 91. *The Abbey Vicarage, Elstow, Bedford MK42 9XT* Bedford (0234) 261477

HUBBARD, Christopher Maurice. b 25. Trin Coll Cam BA49 MA69. Chich Th Coll 51. **d** 53 **p** 54. V Wymeswold *Leic* 65-72; R Lambley *S'well* 72-77; Chapl HM Youth Cust Cen Lowdham Grange 74-77; P-in-c Chilbolton cum Wherwell *Win* 77-79; R 79-90; rtd 90. *2 Wessex Mews, High Street, Stockbridge, Hants SO20 6HE* Andover (0264) 810302

HUBBARD, David Harris. b 33. St Pet Hall Ox BA57 MA61 K Coll Lon MTh88. Ridley Hall Cam 59. **d** 60 **p** 61. C Dalston St Mark w St Bart *Lon* 60-63; C Stoke Newington St Olave 63-67; Hon C 67-68; Hon C Hornsey Ch Ch 69-70; V 70-82; AD W Haringey 78-85; V Highgate All SS from 82. *All Saints' Vicarage, Church Road, London N6 4QH* 081-340 1123

HUBBARD, Mrs Elisabeth Ann. b 41. E Anglian Minl Tr Course 82. dss 85 **d** 87. Cam H Trin w St Andr Gt *Ely* 85-86; Cherry Hinton St Jo 86-87; Par Dn from 87. *8 Lilac Close, Haslingfield, Cambridge CB3 7JS* Cambridge (0223) 871255

HUBBARD, Ian Maxwell. b 43. FCollP83 ACP83 Surrey Univ BEd84 Golds Coll Lon MA86. Sarum & Wells Th Coll 69. **d** 73 **p** 74. Hon C S'wark H Trin w St Matt *S'wark* 73-78; Hon C Camberwell St Mich w All So w Em 78-87; Hon C Dulwich St Barn 87-90; C Battersea St Mary 90-91; C Battersea St Mary from 91. *22 Urlwin Street, London SE5 0NF* 071-701 1718

HUBBARD, Ms Judith Frances. *See* JONES, Ms Judith Frances

HUBBARD, Julian Richard Hawes. b 55. Em Coll Cam BA76 MA80. Wycliffe Hall Ox BA80 MA85. **d** 81 **p** 82. C Fulham St Dionis Parson's Green *Lon* 81-84; Chapl Jes Coll Ox 84-89; Tutor Wycliffe Hall Ox 84-89; Perm to Offic *Guildf* from 89; Selection Sec ACCM 89-91; Sen Selection Sec ABM from 91. *102 The Street, Shalford, Guildford, Surrey GU4 8BN* Guildford (0483) 61633

HUBBARD, Laurence Arthur. b 36. Qu Coll Cam BA60 MA64. Wycliffe Hall Ox 60. **d** 62 **p** 63. C Widcombe *B & W* 62-65; Kenya 66-73; V Pype Hayes *Birm* 73-79; P-in-c Norwich-over-the-Water Colegate St Geo *Nor* 79-85; P-in-c Nor St Aug w St Mary 79-85; Area Sec (Dios Cant and Roch) CMS from 85; Perm to Offic *Cant* from 85. *473 Tonbridge Road, Maidstone, Kent ME16 9LH* Maidstone (0622) 726666

HUBBARD, Roy Oswald. b 32. Lich Th Coll 62. **d** 64 **p** 65. C Baswich (or Berkswich) *Lich* 64-68; P-in-c Ash 68-70; V Stevenage St Pet Broadwater *St Alb* 71-78; V Flitwick 78-90; RD Ampthill 87-90; R Sharnbrook and Knotting w Souldrop from 90. *The Rectory, 81 High Street, Sharnbrook, Bedford MK44 1PE* Bedford (0234) 781444

HUBBLE, Raymond Carr. b 30. Wm Temple Coll Rugby 60. **d** 61 **p** 62. C Newbold and Dunston *Derby* 61-64; Chapl RAF 64-80; Asst Chapl-in-Chief RAF 80-85; QHC 84-85; P-in-c Odiham w S Warnborough and Long Sutton *Win* 85; P-in-c Odiham 85-86; V from 86; RD Odiham from 88. *The Vicarage, Odiham, Basingstoke, Hants RG25 1LZ* Odiham (0256) 703395

HUBBLE, Trevor Ernest. b 46. Chich Th Coll 70. **d** 76 **p** 77. C Eltham St Barn *S'wark* 76-79; Lesotho 80-87; Adn of the South 84-87; S Africa from 87. *PO Box 33, Matatiele, 4730 South Africa* Matatiele (373) 3589

HUBERT, Brother. *See* COPINGER, Stephen Hubert Augustine

HUCKETT, Andrew William. b 50. AKC72. St Aug Coll Cant 72. **d** 73 **p** 74. C Chipping Sodbury and Old Sodbury *Glouc* 73-76; Chapl Flushing Miss to Seamen *Eur* 76-79; Teesside 79-82; Chapl and Hon Sec Milford Haven from 86; Perm to Offic *St D* from 86. *The Missions to Seamen, 7A Castle Pill Road, Steynton, Milford Haven, Dyfed SA73 1HE* Milford Haven (0646) 697572

HUCKLE, John Walford. b 39. E Midl Min Tr Course. **d** 89 **p** 90. Nottm St Pet and St Jas *S'well* from 89.

16 Cropwell Road, Radcliffe-on-Trent, Nottingham NG12 2FS Radcliffe-on-Trent (0602) 332278

HUCKLE, Stephen Leslie. b 48. Ch Ch Ox BA70 BA72 MA74. Coll of Resurr Mirfield 73. **d** 75 **p** 76. C Wednesbury St Paul Wood Green *Lich* 75-78; C Aylesbury *Ox* 78-85; C Farnham Royal w Hedgerley 85-88; V Fenny Stratford from 88. *The Vicarage, Manor Road, Fenny Stratford, Milton Keynes MK2 2HW* Milton Keynes (0908) 372825

HUCKLE, Sydney George. b 16. Oak Hill Th Coll 76. **d** 79 **p** 80. Hon C Wakes Colne w Chappel *Chelmsf* 79-80; Hon C Aldham 80-81; Hon C Marks Tey 80-81; Hon C Marks Tey w Aldham and Lt Tey from 81. *Pippins, Gallows Green, Aldham, Colchester CO6 3PR* Colchester (0206) 210451

HUDDLESON, Robert Roulston. b 32. QUB BA55 TCD Div Test57. **d** 57 **p** 58. C Ballymena *Conn* 57-59; C Belf St Jas 59-63; Ethiopia 65-69; Exec Asst WCC Geneva 69-75; Dep Sec Gen Syn Bd for Miss and Unity 75-81; Admin Sec *Dur* 81-86; Lic to Offic 81-86; Dioc Sec *Ex* from 86; Lic to Offic from 86. *c/o Diocesan House, Palace Gate, Exeter EX1 1HX* Exeter (0392) 72686

✠**HUDDLESTON, Most Rev Ernest Urban Trevor.** b 13. Ch Ch Ox BA34 MA38 Aber Univ Hon DD56. Wells Th Coll 35. **d** 36 **p** 37 **c** 60. C Swindon St Mark *Bris* 36-39; CR from 41; Novice Guardian CR 56-58; Prior Lon Ho 58-60; S Africa 43-56; Bp Masasi 60-68; Suff Bp Stepney *Lon* 68-78; Bp Mauritius 78-83; Abp Indian Ocean 78-83; rtd 83. *House of the Resurrection, Mirfield, W Yorkshire WF14 0BN* Mirfield (0924) 494318

HUDDLESTON, Geoffrey Roger. b 36. TCD BA63 MA67. Ridley Hall Cam 63. **d** 65 **p** 66. C Tonbridge SS Pet and Paul *Roch* 65-69; Chapl RAF 69-85; V Lyonsdown H Trin *St Alb* from 85. *Holy Trinity Vicarage, 18 Lyonsdown Road, Barnet, Herts EN5 1JE* 081-449 0382

HUDGHTON, John Francis. b 56. BA. Cranmer Hall Dur 81. **d** 83 **p** 84. C Stockport St Geo *Ches* 83-85; C Witton 85-87; C Stockport St Alb Hall Street 87-90; V Thornton le Moors w Ince and Elton from 90. *The Vicarage, Ince Lane, Elton, Chester CH2 4QB* Helsby (0928) 724028

HUDSON, Anthony George. b 39. N Ord Course. **d** 84 **p** 85. C Harrogate St Mark *Ripon* 84-87; P-in-c Hampsthwaite from 87; P-in-c Killinghall from 87. *The Vicarage, Church Lane, Hampsthwaite, Harrogate, N Yorkshire HG3 2HB* Harrogate (0423) 770337

HUDSON, Brainerd Peter de Wirtz Goodwin. b 34. K Coll Lon BD57 AKC57. Westcott Ho Cam 57. **d** 59 **p** 60. C Morden *S'wark* 59-60; Australia 61-65; Asst Sec CCCS 65-68; Lic to Offic *Lon* 65-68; *Cant* 68-74; Chapl St Lawr Coll Ramsgate 68-74; Chapl Repton Sch Derby from 74; Lic to Offic *Derby* from 74. *11 The Cross, Repton, Derbyshire DE6 6FH* Burton-on-Trent (0283) 703250

HUDSON, Christopher John. b 45. Lon Univ BSc68 MIH73. Cranmer Hall Dur DipTh77. **d** 77 **p** 78. C Bath Weston St Jo *B & W* 77-80; P-in-c Baltonsborough w Butleigh and W Bradley 80-84; V 84-87; P-in-c Shirwell w Loxhore *Ex* 87-89; P-in-c Kentisbury, Trentishoe, E Down and Arlington 88-89; RD Shirwell from 88; TR Shirwell, Loxhore, Kentisbury, Arlington, etc from 90; P-in-c Trentishoe from 90. *The Rectory, Shirwell, Barnstaple, Devon EX31 4JR* Shirwell (0271) 850436

HUDSON, Edmund John. b 21. Qu Coll Cam BA46 MA48. Cuddesdon Coll 47. **d** 49 **p** 50. V York St Hilda *York* 56-86; rtd 86. *37 Elmfield Avenue, York YO3 9LX* York (0904) 426164

HUDSON, Canon Gerald Ernest. b 20. Ex Coll Ox BA42 MA46. Westcott Ho Cam 42. **d** 43 **p** 44. V Roehampton H Trin *S'wark* 60-71; Hon Can S'wark Cathl 68-80; Prin S'wark Ord Course 71-80; R St Mary le Bow w St Pancras Soper Lane etc *Lon* 80-85; rtd 85; Dir of Post-Ord Tr *Cant* 86-88. *10 Medina Avenue, Whitstable, Kent CT5 4EN* Whitstable (0227) 276548

HUDSON, Harold Paige. b 05. New Coll Ox BA28 MA32. Westcott Ho Cam 32. **d** 34 **p** 35. R Kirby Muxloe *Leic* 45-50; rtd 75. *La Mouette, Pontac, St Clement, Jersey, Channel Islands JE2 6SE* Jersey (0534) 51684

HUDSON, John. b 47. FRSA CSocStuds. Linc Th Coll. **d** 83 **p** 84. C Mert St Mary *S'wark* 83-86; C Kirk Ella *York* 86-88; P-in-c Lenborough *Ox* from 88; P-in-c Tingewick w Water Stratford, Radclive etc from 89. *The Vicarage, Gawcott, Buckingham MK18 4HY* Buckingham (0280) 813162

HUDSON, John. b 51. Oak Hill Th Coll 84. **d** 86 **p** 87. C Leyland St Andr *Blackb* 86-89; V Coppull from 89. *The Vicarage, Chapel Lane, Coppull, Chorley, Lancs PR7 4NA* Coppull (0257) 791218

HUDSON, Canon John Cecil. b 22. Selw Coll Cam BA46 MA48. Qu Coll Birm BD51. **d** 48 **p** 49. V Padiham *Blackb* 57-68; RD Whalley 68-83; V Clitheroe St Mary 68-85; Hon Can Blackb Cathl 79-85; rtd 85; Perm to Offic Blackb & Bradf from 85. *29 Eastfield Drive, West Bradford, Clitheroe, Lancs BB7 4TQ* Clitheroe (0200) 23531

HUDSON, John Leonard. b 44. AKC66. **d** 67 **p** 68. C Dodworth *Wakef* 67-70; Prec Wakef Cathl 70-73; V Ravensthorpe 73-80; V Royston from 80; P-in-c Carlton from 90. *The Clergy House, Church Street, Royston, Barnsley, S Yorkshire S71 4QZ* Barnsley (0226) 722410

HUDSON, John Peter. b 42. AKC64. St Boniface Warminster 64. **d** 65 **p** 66. C S Shields St Hilda w St Thos *Dur* 65-68; Chapl RN 68-84; V Mellor *Blackb* from 84. *The Vicarage, Church Lane, Mellor, Blackburn BB2 7JL* Mellor (025481) ?3?4

HUDSON, John Stephen Anthony. b 49. S Dios Minl Tr Scheme 85 Chich Th Coll 86. **d** 88 **p** 89. C Horsham *Chich* 88-91; TV Littlehampton and Wick from 91. *The Vicarage, 40 Beaconsfield Road, Wick, Littlehampton, W Sussex BN17 6LN* Littlehampton (0903) 724990

HUDSON, Leslie William George. b 11. Em Coll Saskatoon 34. **d** 39 **p** 40. V Frampton *Sarum* 69-77; V Sydling St Nic 69-77; Perm to Offic B & W, Ex and Sarum from 77; rtd 77. *Cricket House, Cricket St Thomas, Chard, Somerset TA20 4DA* Winsham (046030) 351

HUDSON, Mrs Mary Gertrude. b 29. Univ Coll Lon BA51 CertEd52. Qu Coll Birm 82. dss 85 **d** 87. Kings Norton *Birm* 85-87; Hon Par Dn from 87. *67 Wychall Lane, Birmingham B38 8TB* 021-458 3128

HUDSON, Philip Howard. b 50. St Steph Ho Ox 89. **d** 91. C Poulton-le-Fylde *Blackb* from 91. *29 Mossbourne Road, Poulton-le-Fylde, Blackpool FY6 7DU* Blackpool (0253) 884298

HUDSON, Thomas Bernard. b 16. Ch Coll Cam BA38 MA42. Chich Th Coll 38. **d** 40 **p** 41. Madagascar 50-76; C Owton Manor CD *Dur* 77-81; rtd 81; Hon C Lavender Hill Ascension *S'wark* 81-88. *College of St Barnabas, Blackberry Lane, Lingfield, Surrey RH7 6NJ* Dormans Park (034287) 260

HUDSON, Canon Thomas George. b 32. TCD BA54. CITC Div Test54. **d** 55 **p** 56. C Belf St Matt *Conn* 55-58; C Belf Ch Ch 58-60; C Carlow *C & O* 60-61; I Hacketstown 61-69; I Kinneigh Union *C, C & R* 69-72; I Monasterevan *M & K* 72-83; I Mostrim w Granard, Clonbroney, Killoe etc *K, E & A* from 83; Preb Elphin Cathl from 86. *The Rectory, Edgeworthstown, Co Longford, Irish Republic* Longford (43) 71172

HUDSON, Trevor. b 32. Dur Univ BA56. Cranmer Hall Dur DipTh. **d** 58 **p** 59. C Doncaster St Mary *Sheff* 58-62; C Attercliffe 62-64; V Stannington 64-79; V Abbeydale St Jo 79-88; V Worsbrough from 88. *St Mary's Vicarage, Church Lane, Worsbrough Village, Barnsley, S Yorkshire S70 5LU* Barnsley (0226) 203113

HUDSON, Wilfred. b 23. St Jo Coll Dur BA49 DipTh. **d** 51 **p** 52. V Anston *Sheff* 64-74; V Woodsetts 64-74; V Sheff Sharrow 74-88; rtd 88. *128 Totley Brook Road, Sheffield S17 3QU* Sheffield (0742) 365558

HUDSON, Canon Wilfrid. b 14. St Jo Coll Dur BA36 DipTh37 MA39. **d** 37 **p** 39. Hon Can Sheff Cathl *Sheff* 67-79; RD Snaith 67-79; V Goole 67-79; rtd 79. *11 Dale Grove, Leyburn, N Yorkshire DL8 5JG* Wensleydale (0969) 23466

HUDSON, Wilfrid Reginald. b 17. Clifton Th Coll 48 St Aid Birkenhead 49. **d** 51 **p** 52. V Scarisbrick *Liv* 63-78; New Hall Hosp Scarisbrick 63-78; P-in-c Creacombe *Ex* 78; P-in-c Meshaw 78; P-in-c Thelbridge 78; P-in-c W w E Worlington 78; P-in-c Witheridge 78; P-in-c Witheridge, Thelbridge, Creacombe, Meshaw etc 79; V 79-86; rtd 86. *19 Beech Hill, Wellington, Somerset TA21 8ER* Wellington (0823) 662642

HUDSON-WILKIN (formerly HUDSON), Rose Josephine. b 61. W Midl Minl Tr Course 89. **d** 91. Par Dn Wolv St Matt *Lich* from 91. *3 Westland Gardens, Wolverhampton WV3 9NU* Wolverhampton (0902) 23739

HUDSPITH, Mrs Susan Mary. b 49. St Alb Minl Tr Scheme 79. dss 83 **d** 87. Luton St Chris Round Green *St Alb* 82-87; Par Dn 87-88; NSM from 88. *171 Hart Lane, Luton LU2 0JH* Luton (0582) 34948

HUELIN, Dr Gordon. b 19. Lon Univ BD42 MTh47 PhD55. **d** 42 **p** 43. Lect K Coll Lon 59-84; FKC from 78; V St Marg Pattens *Lon* 63-84; rtd 84; Assoc Prof Univ of Notre Dame (Indiana USA) from 84. *36 Newbiggin Street, Thaxted, Dunmow, Essex CM6 2QR* Thaxted (0371) 830779

HUETT, Basil George Pringle. b 19. Lon Univ BA39 Man Univ BD42. Roch Th Coll. **d** 62 **p** 62. Ind Chapl *Roch* 62-72; C Erith St Jo 62-72; rtd 84; Perm to Offic

Roch from 84. *Hazelcroft, Stonehouse Road, Halstead, Sevenoaks, Kent TN14 7HN* Farnborough (0689) 55471

HUGGETT, David John. b 34. Lon Univ BSc56 Southn Univ PhD59. Clifton Th Coll 64. **d** 67 **p** 68. C Heatherlands St Jo *Sarum* 67-70; C Cam St Sepulchre *Ely* 70-73; R Nottm St Nic *S'well* from 73. *18 Lenton Road, Nottingham NG7 1DU* Nottingham (0602) 411383

HUGGETT, John Victor James. b 39. Dur Univ BA64. Tyndale Hall Bris 64. **d** 66 **p** 67. C Worthing St Geo *Chich* 69-71; C Woking St Pet *Guildf* 71-73; C Buckhurst Hill *Chelmsf* 73-76; V Meltham Mills *Wakef* 76-78; V Wilshaw 76-78; rtd 79; Ldr Breath Fellowship from 79; Perm to Offic *Wakef* from 79. *Allen Gardiner House, Pembury Road, Tunbridge Wells, Kent TN2 3QU*

HUGGETT, Michael George. b 38. Bris Univ BA60 Birm Univ CertEd61 Nottm Univ DCE83. E Midl Min Tr Course 85. **d** 88 **p** 89. C Sawley *Derby* from 88. *681 Tamworth Road, Long Eaton, Nottingham NG10 3AB* Nottingham (0602) 720241

HUGGILL, Cyril Howard. b 20. St Cath Soc Ox BA42 MA46 AKC44. **d** 44 **p** 45. Chapl and Lect Bp Lonsdale Coll Derby 66-70; V Biggin *Derby* 70-76; V Hartington 70-76; V Goostrey *Ches* 76-85; rtd 85. *The Granary, Silver Street, Kirkby Stephen, Cumbria* Kirkby Stephen (07683) 71068

HUGGINS, John Henry William. b 24. Wadh Coll Ox MA. Cuddesdon Coll 49. **d** 51 **p** 52. R Esher *Guildf* 55-57; rtd 90. *2 Town Place Cottages, Scaynes Hill, Haywards Heath, W Sussex RH17 7NP* Dane Hill (0825) 790580

HUGHES, Adrian John. b 57. Newc Univ BA78 Dur Univ BA82. Cranmer Hall Dur 80. **d** 83 **p** 84. C Shard End *Birm* 83-86; TV Solihull 86-90; TV Glendale Gp *Newc* from 90. *St Gregory's House, 20 Ryecroft Way, Wooler, Northd NE71 6BP* Wooler (0668) 81495

HUGHES, Alan. b 34. St D Coll Lamp BA54 St Mich Coll Llan 58. **d** 60 **p** 61. C Aberavon *Llan* 60-62; Chapl RAF 62-66; CF 66-76; USA from 76. *612 Brookfield Avenue, Cumberland, Maryland 21502, USA*

HUGHES, Alan. b 46. TD. Edin Th Coll 71. **d** 74 **p** 75. C Edin St Cuth *Edin* 74-76; P-in-c Edin St Luke 76-78; C Marske in Cleveland *York* 78-81; V New Marske 81-84; V Kirkbymoorside w Gillamoor, Farndale & Bransdale from 84; CF from 84. *The Vicarage, Kirkbymoorside, York YO6 6AZ* Kirkbymoorside (0751) 31452

HUGHES, Albert Ashbden. b 10. Univ of Wales BA37. St Mich Coll Llan 38. **d** 39 **p** 40. V Goostrey *Ches* 64-76; rtd 76; Perm to Offic *Ches* from 76. *50 Preston Road, Lytham, Lytham St Annes, Lancs FY8 5AA* Lytham (0253) 795108

HUGHES, Andrew Terrell. b 29. Bris Univ BA56 DipEd. Coll of Resurr Mirfield 64. **d** 66 **p** 67. C Weston-super-Mare St Sav *B & W* 66-70; C Yeovil St Jo w Preston Plucknett 70-73; TV Yeovil 73-83; R Wincanton 83-88; rtd 89. *2 Cove Street, Weymouth, Dorset DT4 8TS* Weymouth (0305) 778639

HUGHES, Arthur Lewis. b 36. St Deiniol's Hawarden 65. **d** 68 **p** 69. C Holywell *St As* 68-71; Lect St Mary Watford 71-75; V Thornton in Lonsdale w Burton in Lonsdale *Bradf* 75-84; V Daubhill *Man* 84-89; V Castle Town *Lich* from 89. *St Thomas's Vicarage, Doxey, Stafford ST16 1EQ* Stafford (0785) 58796

HUGHES, Arthur William Ronald. b 14. Ch Coll Cam BA36 MA40. St Mich Coll Llan 37. **d** 39 **p** 41. V Arthog w Fairbourne *Ban* 67-74; R Machynlleth and Llanwrin 74-77; rtd 77. *4 Clos y Drindod, Buarth Road, Aberystwyth, Dyfed SY23 1LR* Aberystwyth (0970) 623779

HUGHES, Bernard Patrick. b 35. DipTh64. Oak Hill Th Coll 62. **d** 65 **p** 66. C Fulham St Matt *Lon* 65-69; Chapl St Steph Hosp Lon 69-89; Chapl St Mary Abbots Hosp Lon from 69; Chapl Westmr Hosp Lon from 89. *9 Walham Grove, London SW6* 071-385 1348

HUGHES, Bertram Arthur Edwin. b 23. Clifton Th Coll 64. **d** 66 **p** 67. C Ramsgate St Luke *Cant* 68-70; Australia 70-76; P-in-c Swanton Abbott w Skeyton *Nor* 76-80; P-in-c Scottow 76-80; Australia 80-83; R Reymerston w Cranworth, Letton, Southburgh etc *Nor* 83-84; rtd 84; Perm to Offic *Ex* from 90. *88 Winslade Road, Sidmouth, Devon* Sidmouth (0395) 512452

HUGHES, Christopher. b 45. CQSW81. Sarum & Wells Th Coll 86. **d** 88 **p** 89. C Handsworth *Sheff* 88-91; TV Wombourne w Trysull and Bobbington *Lich* from 91. *59 Six Ashes Road, Bobbington, Stourbridge, W Midlands DY7 5DD* Bobbington (038488) 580

HUGHES, Christopher Clarke. b 40. Lon Coll of Div ALCD65 LTh. **d** 65 **p** 66. C Broadclyst *Ex* 65-68; C

Chenies and Lt Chalfont *Ox* 68-70; TV Lydford w Bridestowe and Sourton *Ex* 70-72; TV Lydford, Brent Tor, Bridestowe and Sourton 72-74; V Buckland Monachorum 74-83; R Ashtead *Guildf* from 83. *The Rectory, Dene Road, Ashtead, Surrey KT21 1ED* Ashtead (0372) 272135

HUGHES, David Anthony. b 25. Trin Coll Cam BA48 MA55. Linc Th Coll 74. **d** 76 **p** 77. C Boston *Linc* 76-78; V Graffoe 78-90; rtd 90. *27 St Clement's Road, Ruskington, Sleaford, Lincs NG34 9AF* Ruskington (0526) 832618

HUGHES, David Harwood. b 09. Univ of Wales BA30. St Mich Coll Llan 31. **d** 32 **p** 33. V Thorncombe *Sarum* 69-75; rtd 75; Perm to Offic *Win* from 75. *54 Newstead Road, Bournemouth BH6 3HL* Bournemouth (0202) 428794

HUGHES, David Howard. b 55. **d** 79 **p** 80. C Llanrhos *St As* 79-82; C Eckington w Handley and Ridgeway *Derby* 82-83; C Staveley and Barrow Hill 83-85; TV 85-89; V Whitworth *Man* from 89. *St Bartholomew's House, 1 Beech Close, Whitworth, Rochdale, Lancs OL12 8AR* Rochdale (0706) 853551

HUGHES, David Michael. b 41. Oak Hill Th Coll BD67. **d** 68 **p** 69. C Tunbridge Wells St Jo *Roch* 68-73; C Crookes St Thos *Sheff* 73-81; V Normanton *Wakef* 81-90; TR Didsbury St Jas and Em *Man* from 90. *St James's Rectory, 9 Didsbury Park, Manchester M20 0LH* 061-434 2178

HUGHES, Miss Debbie Ann. b 62. SS Hild & Bede Coll Dur BA83 St Jo Coll Dur BA89. Cranmer Hall Dur 87. **d** 90. C Edin Old St Paul *Edin* from 90. *41 Jeffrey Street, Edinburgh EH1 1DH* 031-556 9035

HUGHES, Douglas. b 25. Lon Coll of Div BD54 ALCD54. **d** 54 **p** 55. C Ravenhead *Liv* 54-57; C Bunbury *Ches* 57-60; V Cotmanhay *Derby* 60-68; R Risley 68-77; P-in-c Horsley 77-87; P-in-c Kirk Langley from 87; P-in-c Mackworth All SS from 87; P-in-c Mugginton and Kedleston from 89. *The Rectory, 4 Church Lane, Kirk Langley, Derby DE6 4NG* Derby (0332) 824412

HUGHES, Edward Marshall. b 13. PhD. **d** 36 **p** 37. V Croydon St Aug *Cant* 65-71; V Dover St Mary 71-84; RD Dover 74-81; rtd 84; Perm to Offic *Cant* from 84. *Woodlands, Sandwich Road, Woodnesborough, Sandwich, Kent CT13 0LZ* Sandwich (0304) 617098

HUGHES, Elfed. b 53. St Mich Coll Llan BD75. **d** 77 **p** 78. C Skewen Llan 77-80; TV Ystradyfodwg w Gelli, Rhigos and Tonpentre 80-81; P-in-c Pentre CD 81-85; V Pentre 85-87; Chapl Poly of Wales 87-91; V Llantrisant *Llan* from 91. *The Vicarage, Llantrisant, M Glam CF7 8EL* Llantrisant (0443) 223356

HUGHES, Canon Elias Edgar. b 22. Univ of Wales BA49. Coll of Resurr Mirfield 49. **d** 51 **p** 52. R Llanfair Mathafarneithaf w Llanbedrgoch *Ban* 64-76; Youth Chapl 67-72; R Dolgelly w Llanfachreth and Brithdir etc 76-87; Can Ban Cathl 78-87; RD Ystumaner 81-87; rtd 87. *Bryn Siriol, 54 Bryn Tyddyn, Pentrefelin, Criccieth, Gwynedd LL52 0PE* Criccieth (0766) 522338

HUGHES, Mrs Elizabeth Jane. b 58. K Coll Lon BD81 AKC81. Ripon Coll Cuddesdon 81. **dss** 83 **d** 87. Chipping Barnet w Arkley *St Alb* 83-86; Dunstable 86-87; Hon Par Dn from 87. *The Vicarage, 83 Half Moon Lane, Dunstable, Beds LU5 4AE* Dunstable (0582) 668019

HUGHES, Ms Eunice Nesta. b 14. K Coll Lon 38 CertEd51. Lambeth DipTh40 St Chris Coll Blackheath 34. **dss** 61 **d** 87. RE Teacher Darley Gate 62-64; Cheltenham Ladies' Coll 65-74; Cant St Martin and St Paul *Cant* 76-80; Westgate-on-Sea St Sav 80-87; Hon Par Dn from 87. *Flat 1, 4 Cedric Road, Westgate-on-Sea, Kent CT8 8NZ* Thanet (0843) 31746

HUGHES, Ven Evan Arthur Bertram. b 25. St D Coll Lamp BA48 LTh50. **d** 50 **p** 51. C Llanstadwell *St D* 70-73; Pakistan 73-74; R Johnston w Steynton *St D* 74-80; Can St D Cathl 80-85; V Newc Emlyn 80-81; V Newc Emlyn w Llandyfriog and Troedyraur 81-86; Adn Carmarthen 85-91; V Llanegwad w Llanfynydd 86-88; V Cynwil Elfed and Newchurch 88-91; rtd 91. *104 Bromwydd Road, Carmarthen, Dyfed SA31 2AW*

HUGHES, Evan Thomas. b 08. FCII36 Lon Univ BD50. **d** 47 **p** 48. Chapl St Mary's Coll Cheltenham 64-70; rtd 70; Perm to Offic *Derby* from 73. *197 Allestree Lane, Derby DE3 2PF* Derby (0332) 556602

HUGHES, Ms Evelyn. b 31. Gilmore Ho 73. **dss** 79 **d** 87. Fetcham *Guildf* 79-82; Dioc Adv Lay Min 82-86; Farnborough 83-87; C from 87; Bp's Adv for Women's Min from 87. *The Parsonage, 45 Sandhill, Farnborough, Hants GU14 8ER* Farnborough (0252) 543789

HUGHES, Canon Geraint Morgan Hugh. b 34. Keble Coll Ox BA58 MA63. St Mich Coll Llan 58. **d** 59 **p** 60.

C Gorseinon *S & B* 59-63; C Oystermouth 63-68; R Llanbadarn Fawr, Llandegley and Llanfihangel R'n 68-76; R Llandrindod w Cefnllys 76-87; R Llandrindod w Cefnllys and Disserth from 87; Can Brecon Cathl from 89. *The Rectory, Broadway, Llandrindod Wells, Powys LD1 5HT* Llandrindod Wells (0597) 822043

HUGHES, Canon Gerald Thomas. b 30. Lon Univ BD63 MTh. Qu Coll Birm 72. **d** 72 **p** 73. Lic to Offic *Cov* 72-80; P-in-c Birdingbury 80-81; P-in-c Leamington Hastings 80-81; V Leamington Hastings and Birdingbury 81-82; V Dunchurch 82-89; RD Rugby 85-89; Can Res Cov Cathl from 89. *18 Belvedere Road, Coventry CV5 6PF* Coventry (0203) 673527

HUGHES, Gwilym Berw. b 42. St Mich Coll Llan DipTh. **d** 68 **p** 69. C Conwy w Gyffin *Ban* 68-71; V Llandinorwig w Penisarwaun and Llanddeiniolen 71-75; TV Llandudno 75-80; V Penmaenmawr from 80; RD Arllechwedd from 88. *The Vicarage, Church Road, Penmaenmawr, Gwynedd LL34 6BN* Penmaenmawr (0492) 623300

HUGHES, Gwyndaf Morris. b 36. Univ of Wales (Lamp) BA57. St Steph Ho Ox 58 St Mich Coll Llan 59. **d** 59 **p** 60. C Glanogwen *Ban* 59-62; Chapl RN 62-78; R Llanfairpwll w Penmynydd *Ban* 78-90; RD Tindaethwy from 88; R Beaumaris from 90. *The Rectory, Beaumaris, Gwynedd LL58 8BN* Beaumaris (0248) 811402

HUGHES, Harold John. b 55. St Jo Coll Nottm LTh86. **d** 86 **p** 87. C Man Miles Platting *Man* 86-87; C Man Apostles w Miles Platting 87-89; V Roughtown from 89. *The Vicarage, Carrhill Road, Mossley, Ashton-under-Lyne, Lancs OL5 0BL* Mossley (0457) 832250

HUGHES, Canon Harold Mervyn. b 13. St D Coll Lamp BA34. **d** 37 **p** 38. V Hucclecote *Glouc* 46-78; rtd 78; Perm to Offic *Glouc* from 83. *13 Woodland Green, Upton St Leonards, Gloucester GL4 8DB* Gloucester (0452) 618301

HUGHES, Hazel. b 45. St Jo Coll Dur 75. **dss** 78 **d** 87. Lower Mitton *Worc* 78-81; Worc St Martin w St Pet, St Mark etc 82-87; Par Dn Worc SE 87-88; Dn-in-c Wribbenhall from 88. *Wribbenhall Vicarage, Trimpley Lane, Bewdley, Worcs DY12 1JJ* Bewdley (0299) 402196

HUGHES, Canon Henry. b 18. Kelham Th Coll 35. **d** 41 **p** 42. V Holbrooks *Cov* 50-89; Hon Can Cov Cathl 73-89; rtd 89; P-in-c Hoar Cross w Newchurch *Lich* from 89. *The Vicarage, Hoar Cross, Burton-on-Trent, Staffs DE13 8QR* Hoar Cross (028375) 263

HUGHES, Henry Charles William. b 30. K Coll Lon 58. Roch Th Coll 59. **d** 61 **p** 62. C Forest Gate Em w Upton Cross *Chelmsf* 61-64; C Woodford St Barn 64-72; Lic to Offic from 72. *99 St Anthony's Drive, Chelmsford CM2 9EH* Chelmsford (0245) 265230

HUGHES, Hugh. b 13. St D Coll Lamp BA35 St Mich Coll Llan 35. **d** 36 **p** 37. R Llaneugrad w Llanallgo and Penrhosligwy etc *Ban* 73-82; RD Twrcelyn 80-82; rtd 82; Perm to Offic *Ban* from 86. *50 Craig-y-Don, Tyn-y-Gongl, Gwynedd LL74 8SN* Tyn-y-Gongl (0248) 853500

HUGHES, Chan Hywel Maldwyn. b 20. Univ of Wales (Swansea) BA42. St Mich Coll Llan 42. **d** 44 **p** 45. V Killay *S & B* 68-87; RD Clyne 79-87; Can Brecon Cathl 81-87; Treas Brecon Cathl 81-83; Chan 83-87; rtd 88. *6 Heaseland Place, Killay, Swansea SA2 7EQ* Swansea (0792) 202021

HUGHES, Ivor Gordon. b 45. Ripon Coll Cuddesdon 75. **d** 77 **p** 78. C Newport w Longford *Lich* 77-79; Children's Educn Adv CMS 79-82; V Gt and Lt Bedwyn and Savernake Forest *Sarum* 82-86; P-in-c Urchfont w Stert 86-90; TR Redhorn from 90. *The Rectory, Urchfont, Devizes, Wilts SN10 4QP* Devizes (0380) 84672

HUGHES, Jack Griffiths. b 15. St Jo Coll Dur BA37. Oak Hill Th Coll 33. **d** 38 **p** 39. R Heaton Mersey *Man* 67-80; rtd 81; Perm to Offic *Man* from 81. *73 Derby Road, Heaton Moor, Stockport, Cheshire* 061-431 3753

HUGHES, Miss Jacqueline Monica. b 36. Lon Univ TCert56. Dalton Ho Bris 59. **dss** 77 **d** 88. Redditch St Steph *Worc* 77-79; Worc H Trin 79-82; Worc R Infirmary 82-88; Chapl Asst from 88. *38 Cockshute Hill, Droitwich, Worcs WR9 7QP* Worcester (0905) 775153

HUGHES, Canon James Edmund Crowden. b 11. St D Coll Lamp BA32 St Mich Coll Llan 33. **d** 35 **p** 36. V Oystermouth *S & B* 54-80; Can Brecon Cathl 72-80; rtd 80. *6 Myrtle Terrace, Mumbles, Swansea SA3 4DT* Swansea (0792) 366710

HUGHES, John Chester. b 24. St Jo Coll Dur BA48 DipTh50 MA51. **d** 50 **p** 51. Provost Leic 63-78; ChStJ from 74; V Bringhurst w Gt Easton *Leic* 78-87; rtd 87. *29 High Street, Hallaton, Market Harborough, Leics LE16 8UD* Hallaton (085889) 622

✛**HUGHES, Rt Rev John George.** b 35. Qu Coll Cam BA57 MA60 Leeds Univ PhD79. Cuddesdon Coll 58. **d** 60 **p** 61 **c** 87. C Brighouse *Wakef* 60-63; V Clifton 63-70; Sec Day Schs Exec 68-70; Acting Dir Educn 70; Selection Sec ACCM 70-73; Sen Selection Sec 73-76; Warden St Mich Coll Llan 76-87; Lect Ch Hist Univ of Wales 76-87; Dean Faculty of Th Univ of Wales (Cardiff) 84-87; Hon Can Llan Cathl *Llan* 80-87; Area Bp Kensington *Lon* from 87. *19 Campden Hill Square, London W8 7JY* 071-727 9818

HUGHES, Canon John Herbert Vivian. b 28. St D Coll Lamp BA51 LTh53. **d** 53 **p** 54. V Newchurch and Merthyr *St D* 62-71; V Abergwili w Llanfihangel-uwch-Gwili etc 71-89; RD Carmarthen 82-88; Can St D Cathl 87-89; rtd 89. *Deri Deg, 104 Bronwydd Road, Carmarthen, Dyfed SA31 2AR* Carmarthen (0267) 237155

HUGHES, John Malcolm. b 47. Man Univ BSc68 Leeds Univ DipTh70. Coll of Resurr Mirfield 68. **d** 71 **p** 72. C Newton Nottage *Llan* 71-78; V Llanwynno from 78. *The Vicarage, 9 Heol-y-Plwyf, Ynysybwl, Pontypridd, M Glam CF37 3HU* Ynysybwl (0443) 790340

HUGHES, John Patrick. b 41. Oak Hill Th Coll DipTh66. **d** 67 **p** 68. C Chorleywood St Andr *St Alb* 67-71; C E Twickenham St Steph *Lon* 71-76; TV High Wycombe *Ox* from 77; Chapl Wycombe Hosp 77-83. *St Andrew's House, Hatters Lane, High Wycombe, Bucks HP13 1NJ* High Wycombe (0494) 29668

HUGHES, John Richard Dutton. b 40. Fitzw Ho Cam BA61 MA66. Linc Th Coll 62. **d** 64 **p** 65. C Tye Green w Netteswell *Chelmsf* 64-67; Lic to Offic Liv 68-70; Ches 71-86; C Farnworth *Liv* 70-71; Hon C Sandbach *Ches* 73-82; P-in-c Harthill and Burwardsley 86-87; P-in-c from 87. *The Vicarage, Harthill Road, Tattenhall, Chester CH3 9NU* Tattenhall (0829) 70067

HUGHES, John Stunt Dickson. b 01. Keble Coll Ox BA25 MA48. Cuddesdon Coll 25. **d** 26 **p** 27. V Washington *Chich* 42-70; rtd 70. *3 Wye House, Down View Road, Worthing, W Sussex BN11 4QS* Worthing (0903) 36287

✛**HUGHES, Rt Rev John Taylor.** b 08. CBE75. Bede Coll Dur BA31 DipTh32 MA35. **d** 31 **p** 32 **c** 56. Asst Chapl and Tutor St Bede Coll Dur 31-34; Lect 34-35; C Shildon *Dur* 34-37; V Hartlepool St Jas 37-48; Warden S'wark Dioc Ho Blackheath and St Sav Coll 48-56; Can Miss S'wark Cathl 48-56; Suff Bp Croydon *Cant* 56-77; Bp HM Forces 66-75; Adn Croydon *Cant* 67-77; rtd 77; Asst Bp Cant 77-86; Asst Bp S'wark from 86. *Hospital of the Holy Trinity, North End, Croydon CR0 1UB* 081-686 8313

HUGHES, John Tudor. b 59. Nottm Univ BSc81 Univ of Wales (Cardiff) BD84. St Mich Coll Llan 81. **d** 84 **p** 85. C Mold *St As* 84-88; Asst Dioc Youth Chapl from 86; Min Can St As Cathl 88-90; Min St As and Tremeirchion 88-90; V Holt from 90. *The Vicarage, 5 Smithfield Drive, Holt, Wrexham, Clwyd LL13 9AJ* Farndon (0829) 270001

HUGHES, John William George. b 48. St Mich Coll Llan DipTh72. **d** 72 **p** 73. C Swansea St Pet *S & B* 72-76; V Cwmdduddwr w St Harmon's and Llanwrthwl 76-79; P-in-c Caereithin 79; V 80-86; Chapl RAF from 86. *c/o MOD, Adastral House, Theobald's Road, London WC1X 8RU* 071-430 7268

HUGHES, Canon Llewelyn. b 06. Univ of Wales BA26. Linc Th Coll 28. **d** 29 **p** 30. Can Res St As Cathl *St As* 69-74; rtd 74. *21 Monmouth Road, Borras Park, Wrexham, Clwyd* Wrexham (0978) 352453

HUGHES, Martin Conway. b 40. Ex Coll Ox BA61 MA67. Chich Th Coll. **d** 63 **p** 64. C Roehampton H Trin *S'wark* 63-67; C Addlestone *Guildf* 67-71; V Burpham 71-88; V Shamley Green from 88; RD Cranleigh from 90. *The Vicarage, Shamley Green, Guildford, Surrey GU5 0UD* Guildford (0483) 892030

HUGHES, Martyn Lawrence. b 19. Magd Coll Cam BA42 MA46 K Coll Cam BA43 MA52. Westcott Ho Cam. **d** 44 **p** 45. Chapl Harrow Sch Middx 61-73; Perm to Offic *Chich* from 73; Hd Relig Studies Rich Collyer Coll Horsham 73-84; rtd 84. *Spindleberry, Broomers, Hill Lane, Pulborough, W Sussex RH20 2DU* Pulborough (07982) 3786

HUGHES, Matthew James. b 66. K Coll Lon BD88. Westcott Ho Cam 89. **d** 91. C Heston *Lon* from 91. *147A Heston Road, Hounslow, Middx TW5 0RD* 081-570 9272

HUGHES, Dr Michael John Minto. b 50. Liv Univ MB, ChB74 DRCOG87. Wycliffe Hall Ox 76. **d** 79 **p** 80. C Stranton *Dur* 79-82; Peru 82-86; Hon C Gosforth w Nether Wasdale and Wasdale Head *Carl* 87-89; TV Thetford *Nor* from 89. *44 Nunsgate, Thetford, Norfolk IP24 3EL* Thetford (0842) 752075

HUGHES, Neville Joseph. b 52. NUU BA79. **d** 91. NSM Mullabrack w Markethill and Kilcluney *Arm* from 91. *109 Markethill Road, Portadown, Co Armagh* Portadown (0762) 841500

HUGHES, Owen. b 17. Univ of Wales BA39. St Mich Coll Llan 39. **d** 40 **p** 41. V Wesham *Blackb* 62-70; R Llanbeulan w Llanfaelog and Talyllyn *Ban* 70-71; R Church Kirk *Blackb* 71-74; V Oswaldtwistle All SS 74-82; rtd 82; Lic to Offic *Blackb* from 82. *57 Blackburn Road, Rishton, Blackburn BB1 4EU* Great Harwood (0254) 884165

HUGHES, Paul Vernon. b 53. Ripon Coll Cuddesdon 79. **d** 82 **p** 83. C Chipping Barnet w Arkley *St Alb* 82-86; TV Dunstable from 86. *The Vicarage, 83 Half Moon Lane, Dunstable, Beds LU5 4AE* Dunstable (0582) 668019 or 661645

HUGHES, Peter John. b 43. Melbourne Univ BA67 Ch Ch Ox BPhil77. Trin Coll Melbourne 64 ACT 70. **d** 70 **p** 70. Australia 70-74 and from 84, Perm to Offic *Ox* 75-77; Lic to Offic 77-79; Chapl Lon Univ *Lon* 79-84. *173 King Street, Sydney, NSW, Australia 2000* Sydney (2) 232-3022

HUGHES, Peter Knowles. b 61. Sarum & Wells Th Coll 87. **d** 90 **p** 91. C Whitchurch *Bris* from 90. *127 Bristol Road, Bristol BS14 0PU* Bristol (0272) 834992

HUGHES, Philip. b 47. St Jo Coll Nottm 79. **d** 81 **p** 82. C Dolgelly w Llanfachreth and Brithdir etc *Ban* 81-83; Youth Chapl 82-83; R Llaneugrad w Llanallgo and Penrhosligwy etc from 83. *The Rectory, Moelfre, Anglesey, Gwynedd LL72 8HE* Moelfre (024888) 654

HUGHES, Philip Geoffrey John. b 60. Nottm Univ BCombStuds82 Birm Univ DipTh88. Aston Tr Scheme 84 Qu Coll Birm 86. **d** 89 **p** 90. C Sedgley All SS *Lich* from 89. *13 The Priory, Sedgley, Dudley, W Midlands DY3 3UB* Sedgley (0902) 672541

HUGHES, Philip Stephen. b 34. Dur Univ BA59. Coll of Resurr Mirfield 59. **d** 62 **p** 63. C Horfield St Greg *Bris* 62-66; C Bedminster St Mich 66-69; P-in-c Chippenham St Pet 69-71; V 71-83; TR Bedminster 83-91; V Ashton Keynes, Leigh and Minety from 91. *The Vicarage, 23 Richmond Court, Ashton Keynes, Swindon SN6 6PP* Cirencester (0285) 861566

HUGHES, Richard Jeffrey. b 47. Trin Coll Carmarthen CertEd68. St Mich Coll Llan 74. **d** 76 **p** 77. C Llanbeblig w Caernarfon and Betws Garmon etc *Ban* 76-78; Dioc Youth Chapl 78-82; TV Holyhead w Rhoscolyn w Llanfair-yn-Neubwll 78-83; R Llanfachraeth from 83. *The Rectory, Valley, Anglesey, Gwynedd LL65 3DP* Valley (0407) 740230

HUGHES, Richard Millree. b 33. Univ of Wales BA56 MA79. St Mich Coll Llan 56. **d** 58 **p** 59. C Mold *St As* 58-61; VC St As Cathl 61-64; V Towyn 64-67; Asst Master Marlborough Sch Woodstock 77-79; R Whitchurch St Mary *Ox* from 79. *The Rectory, Whitchurch, Reading RG8 7DF* Pangbourne (0734) 843219

HUGHES, Robert Elistan-Glodrydd. b 32. Trin Coll Ox BA54 MA58 Birm Univ MLitt85. Westcott Ho Cam 55. **d** 57 **p** 58. C Stoke *Cov* 57-61; Ind Chapl *S'wark* 61-64; Birm Univ *Birm* 64-87; Chapl 64-69; Lodgings Warden and Student Welfare Adv 69-87; Dir Housing Study Overseas Students Trust from 88; Perm to Offic *Ban* from 88. *Clogwyn Melyn, Talsarnau, Gwynedd LL47 6TP* Harlech (0766) 0257

HUGHES, Rodney Thomas. b 39. Dur Univ BA60 St Cath Coll Ox DipTh61. Wycliffe Hall Ox 60. **d** 62 **p** 63. C Edin St Thos *Edin* 62-65; C Harlow New Town w Lt Parndon *Chelmsf* 65-67; R Haworth *Bradf* 67-74; R W Knighton w Broadmayne *Sarum* 74-77; R Broadmayne, W Knighton, Owermoigne etc 77-82; V Crosthwaite Keswick *Carl* from 82. *Crosthwaite Vicarage, Vicarage Hill, Keswick, Cumbria CA12 5QB* Keswick (07687) 72509

HUGHES, Steven Philip. b 52. BA St Jo Coll Dur. Ridley Hall Cam. **d** 82 **p** 83. C Chilvers Coton w Astley *Cov* 82-86; TV Kings Norton *Birm* from 86. *372 Shannon Road, Birmingham B38 9TR* 021-458 1182

HUGHES, Timothy Griffith Richard. b 18. AKC42. **d** 42 **p** 43. V Longhorsley *Newc* 67-81; Perm to Offic from 81; rtd 83. *1 Sedbergh Road, Marden Estate, North Shields, Tyne & Wear NE30 3BB* 091-251 1052

HUGHES, Ms Valerie Elizabeth. b 53. Birm Univ BA75 CertEd76. Wycliffe Hall Ox DipTh86. **d** 87. C Hallwood *Ches* 87-90; Chapl Liv Univ *Liv* from 90; Par Dn Garston from 90. *8 Stanley Street, Garston, Liverpool L19 8LP* 051-494 0613

HUGHES, William Roger. Trin Coll Carmarthen. **d** 91. NSM Llan-non *St D* from 91. *Ystowden Uchaf Farm, Mynydd Sylen, Llanelli, Dyfed SA15 5NL*

HUGHES, Canon William Rowland. b 10. St D Coll Lamp BA35. **d** 35 **p** 36. RD Twrcelyn *Ban* 73-80; Hon Can Ban Cathl 78-80; R Amlwch w Rhosybol, Llandyfrydog etc 78-80; rtd 80. *66 Craig-y-Don, Tyn-y-Gongl, Gwynedd LL74 8UB* Tyn-y-Gongl (0248) 3452

HUGHMAN, Dr June Alison. b 58. Kingston Poly BSc81 Southn Univ PhD84. Trin Coll Bris DipHE88. **d** 89. Par Dn Penge St Jo *Roch* from 89. *19 Cottingham Road, London SE20 7PU* 081-676 9992

HUGO, Canon Keith Alan. b 41. Nottm Univ BA62. Chich Th Coll 62. **d** 64 **p** 65. C Pontefract St Giles *Wakef* 64-68; C Chesterfield All SS *Derby* 68-71; V Allenton and Shelton Lock 71-77; Dioc Communications Officer *Sarum* 77-89; V Worton 77-84; V Potterne 77-84; Can and Preb Sarum Cathl from 84; V Potterne w Worton and Marston 84-89; R Wyke Regis from 89. *The Rectory, 1 Portland Road, Weymouth, Dorset DT4 9ES* Weymouth (0305) 784649

HUITSON, Christopher Philip. b 45. Keble Coll Ox BA66 MA70. Cuddesdon Coll 67. **d** 69 **p** 70. C Croydon St Sav *Cant* 69-71; Soc Service Unit St Martin-in-the-Fields Lon 71-73; C St Alb St Pet *St Alb* 73-77; V Cople 77-78; P-in-c Willington 77-78; V Cople w Willington 78-89; V Leavesden All SS from 89. *All Saints' Vicarage, Horseshoe Lane, Garston, Watford WD2 7HJ* Garston (0923) 672375

HULBERT, Charles Donald. b 09. Linc Th Coll 37. **d** 38 **p** 39. R Plaxtol *Roch* 62-74; Perm to Offic *Nor* from 74; rtd 74. *31 Holt Road, Weybourne, Holt, Norfolk NR25 7SU* Weybourne (026370) 384

HULBERT, Hugh Forfar. b 22. Bris Univ BA49. Tyndale Hall Bris 46. **d** 50 **p** 51. V Portsea St Luke *Portsm* 63-75; V Worthing H Trin *Chich* 75-81; C-in-c Hove H Trin CD 81-85; C Hailsham 86-87; rtd 87; Perm to Offic *Chich* from 87. *6 Ilex Green, Hailsham, E Sussex BN27 1TR* Hailsham (0323) 842215

HULBERT, Canon John Anthony Lovett. b 40. Trin Coll Cam BA63 MA67. Wells Th Coll 64. **d** 66 **p** 67. C Fareham H Trin *Portsm* 66-70; R Wickham 70-79; RD Bishops Waltham 74-79; V Bedf St Andr *St Alb* from 79; RD Bedf from 87; Hon Can St Alb from 91. *St Andrew's Vicarage, 1 St Edmond Road, Bedford MK40 2NQ* Bedford (0234) 354234

HULBERT, Canon Martin Francis Harrington. b 37. Dur Univ BSc58 MA62. Ripon Hall Ox 58. **d** 60 **p** 61. C Buxton *Derby* 60-63; C Eglingham *Newc* 63-67; C-in-c Loundsley Green Ascension CD *Derby* 67-71; P-in-c Frecheville 71-73; R Frecheville and Hackenthorpe *Sheff* 73-77; P-in-c Hathersage *Derby* 77-83; V 83-90; RD Bakewell and Eyam 81-90; Hon Can Derby Cathl from 89; R Brailsford w Shirley and Osmaston w Edlaston from 90. *The Rectory, Church Lane, Brailsford, Derby DE6 3BX* Ashbourne (0335) 60362

HULBURD, Ivan Mitchell. b 13. Worc Coll Ox MA38. **d** 54 **p** 55. R Hindlip w Martin Hussingtree *Worc* 67-78; rtd 78; Perm to Offic *Worc* from 78. *5 The Lodge, Wrington, Bristol BS18 7NA*

HULETT, Mrs Janet Elizabeth Mary. b 48. **d** 91. NSM Broadwater St Mary *Chich* from 91. *76 Broomfield Avenue, Worthing, W Sussex BN14 7SB* Worthing (0903) 30975

HULETT, Peter. b 31. CEng MIMechE62 Leeds Coll of Educn CertEd74. Wycliffe Hall Ox 75. **d** 77 **p** 78. C Eastwood *S'well* 77-80; C Granby w Elton 80-83; V Gilling and Kirkby Ravensworth *Ripon* 83-90; P-in-c Bishop Monkton and Burton Leonard from 90. *The Vicarage, Knaresborough Road, Bishop Monkton, Harrogate* Ripon (0765) 87372

HULL, David John. b 44. Linc Th Coll 88. **d** 90 **p** 91. C Mansf Woodhouse *S'well* from 90. *13 Church Hill Avenue, Mansfield Woodhouse, Mansfield, Notts NG19 9JU* Mansfield (0623) 20803

HULL, John Hammond. b 36. Sarum Th Coll 60. **d** 61 **p** 62. C Gt Clacton *Chelmsf* 61-66; Lic to Offic 66-75; Area Chapl (E Anglia) Toc H 66-70; (Midl Region) 70-75; Lic to Offic *Ox* from 75; Chapl Toc H HQ 75-82. *66 Grenville Avenue, Wendover, Aylesbury, Bucks HP22 6AL* Wendover (0296) 624487

HULL, Theodore James Nesbitt. b 57. Southn Univ BTh84. Sarum & Wells Th Coll 80. **d** 82 **p** 83. C Plumstead St Mark and St Marg *S'wark* 82-84; C Surbiton St Andr and St Mark 84-87; V Balham St Mary and St Jo from 87. *35 Elmfield Road, London SW17 8AG* 081-673 2231

HULL, Timothy David. b 60. Lon Bible Coll 87. St Jo Coll Nottm BTh90. **d** 90 **p** 91. C Leyton St Mary w St Edw *Chelmsf* from 90. *29 Brewster Road, London E10 6RG* 081-556 5134

HULL, Bishop Suffragan of. See SNELGROVE, Rt Rev Donald George

HULLAH, Peter Fearnley. b 49. K Coll Lon BD71 AKC71. Cuddesdon Coll 73. **d** 74 **p** 75. Asst Chapl St Edw Sch Ox 74-77; C Summertown *Ox* 74-76; C Wolvercote w Summertown 76-77; Chapl Sevenoaks Sch Kent 77-82; Hon C Sevenoaks St Nic *Roch* 77-82; Hon C Kippington 82-87; Sen Chapl K Sch Cant from 87; Hon Min Can Cant Cathl *Cant* from 87. *The King's School, Canterbury, Kent* Canterbury (0227) 475554

HULLETT, Frederick Graham. b 32. St Jo Coll York CertEd53 Leeds Univ BA58. Coll of Resurr Mirfield 58. **d** 60 **p** 61. P-in-c Haggerston St Aug w St Steph *Lon* 69-73; Lic to Offic 73-84; Perm to Offic *Linc* from 84; rtd 91. *2 Ryland Road, Welton, Lincoln LN2 3LU* Welton (0673) 60839

HULME, Alan John. b 60. Birm Univ BSc81. Wycliffe Hall Ox BA90. **d** 91. C Chilwell *S'well* from 91. *10 College Road, Chilwell, Nottingham NG9 4AS* Nottingham (0602) 256501

HULME, Norman. b 31. Kelham Th Coll 50. **d** 54 **p** 55. C Blackb St Pet *Blackb* 54-57; C Blakenall Heath *Lich* 57-59; V Gannow *Blackb* 59-64; V Anwick *Linc* 64-74; V S Kyme 64-74; V Moulton 74-83; V Earl Shilton w Elmesthorpe *Leic* 83-88; Chapl Harperbury Hosp Radlett from 88. *Harperbury Hospital, Shenley, Radlett, Herts* Radlett (0923) 854861

HULME, Suffragan Bishop of. See SCOTT, Rt Rev Colin John Fraser

HULSE, William John. b 42. Dur Univ BA65. Linc Th Coll 65. **d** 67 **p** 68. C S Westoe *Dur* 67-70; Lic to Offic *Newc* 70-72; C Far Headingley St Chad *Ripon* 72-76; R Swillington 76-88; V Shadwell from 88. *Shadwell Vicarage, 2 Church Farm Garth, Leeds LS17 8HD* Leeds (0532) 737035

HUM, Walter. b 08. MRST31 Lon Univ BSc(Econ)33. Bps' Coll Cheshunt 34. **d** 35 **p** 36. V Leeds All SS *Ripon* 54-74; rtd 74; Perm to Offic *Nor* 74-77 and from 79; P-in-c Gt Ringstead 77-79. *35 Cleaves Drive, Walsingham, Norfolk NR22 6EQ* Walsingham (0328) 820598

HUMBLE, Joseph Francis. b 24. Univ Coll Ox BA53 MA57. Cuddesdon Coll 53. **d** 55 **p** 56. V Lillington *Cov* 65-76; Chapl Miss to Seamen 76-85; Hong Kong and Singapore 76-80; Argentina 80-85; Hon C Regents Park St Mark *Lon* from 85; rtd 87. *407 Carole House, 80 Regents Park Road, London NW1 8UE* 071-483 1418

HUME, Ernest. b 45. Linc Th Coll 77. **d** 79 **p** 80. C Ilkeston St Mary *Derby* 79-81; C Sheff Manor *Sheff* 81-82; TV 82-88; V Norton Woodseats St Chad from 88. *The Vicarage, 9 Linden Avenue, Norton Woodseats, Sheffield S8 0GA* Sheffield (0742) 745086

HUME, Leslie Paul. b 09. Kelham Th Coll 27. **d** 32 **p** 33. SSM from 32; C Liv St Nic *Liv* 32-37; Chapl Kelham Th Coll 37-41; C Nottm St Geo w St Jo *S'well* 41-43; S Africa 43-49 and 51-52 and 66-76; Basutoland 50-51 and 62-66; Dir SSM 52-62; Lic to Offic *S'well* 52-62; Perm to Offic *Ox* from 76. *SSM Priory, Willen, Milton Keynes MK15 9AA* Milton Keynes (0908) 663749

HUME, Martin. b 54. Grimsby Coll of Tech HND75. Coll of Resurr Mirfield 89. **d** 91. C Brentwood St Thos *Chelmsf* from 91. *Stokes House, 25 St Thomas' Road, Brentwood, Essex CM14 4DF* Brentwood (0277) 210323

HUMMERSTONE, Jeremy David. Mert Coll Ox BA65 MA70. Wells Th Coll 70. **d** 72 **p** 73. C Helmsley *York* 72-75; C Pockley cum E Moors 72-75; P-in-c Manningford Bruce w Manningford Abbots *Sarum* 75; TV Swanborough 75-80; P-in-c Frithelstock *Ex* 80-81; P-in-c Gt Torrington 80-81; P-in-c Lt Torrington 80-81; V Gt and Lt Torrington and Frithelstock from 81. *The Vicarage, Torrington, Devon EX38 8EA* Torrington (0805) 22166

HUMPHREY, Betty. b 37. St Mich Ho Ox 59. **d** 90. C Hardwicke, Quedgeley and Elmore w Longney *Glouc* from 90. *Church House, Cornfield Drive, Hardwicke, Gloucester GL2 6QJ*

HUMPHREY, David Lane. b 57. Maine Univ BA79. St Jo Coll Nottm 84. **d** 88 **p** 89. C Springfield All SS *Chelmsf* 88-91; C Thundersley from 91. *14 Grangeway, Benfleet, Essex SS7 3RP* Rayleigh (0268) 773462

HUMPHREY, Derek Hollis. b 37. Chich Th Coll 69. **d** 72 **p** 73. C Havant *Portsm* 72-75; C Southsea H Spirit 75-78; V Finsbury Park St Thos *Lon* 78-88; V S Patcham *Chich* from 88. *10 Church Close, Brighton BN1 8HS* Brighton (0273) 502385

HUMPHREY, George William. b 38. Lon Univ BD61. Oak Hill Th Coll. **d** 62 **p** 63. C Heigham H Trin *Nor* 62-64; P-in-c Buckenham w Hassingham and Strumpshaw 64-67; Asst Master Mexborough Gr Sch 67-69; Hon C Cheadle Hulme St Andr *Ches* 70-76; Perm to Offic *Wakef* 77-78; P-in-c Kellington w Whitley 78-80; RE

Adv *Glouc* from 80. *Church House, Cornfield Drive, Hardwicke, Gloucester GL2 6QJ* Gloucester (0452) 721832

HUMPHREY, Heather Mary. b 46. CertEd68. W Midl Minl Tr Course 87. **d** 90. NSM Overbury w Teddington, Alstone etc *Worc* from 90. *2/3 Saunders Cottages, Kinsham, Tewkesbury, Glos GL20 8HP* Bredon (0684) 72816

HUMPHREY, Timothy Martin. b 62. Ex Univ BA83. St Jo Coll Nottm DipTh87. **d** 89 **p** 90. C Wallington H Trin *S'wark* from 89. *14 Harcourt Field, Wallington, Surrey SM6 8BA* 081-647 3410

HUMPHREYS, Brian Leonard. d 87 **p** 88. NSM Maughold *S & M* from 87. *Lewaigue Lodge, Port Lewaigue, Maughold, Isle of Man* Ramsey (0624) 813694

HUMPHREYS, George Bernard. b 10. AKC36. **d** 36 **p** 37. R Fobbing *Chelmsf* 65-78; rtd 78. Perm to Offic *Ex* from 78. *Prestercot, Butts Lane, Christow, Exeter EX6 7NN* Christow (0647) 52595

HUMPHREYS, James Graham. b 36. Liv Univ BEng57 PhD60. Trin Coll Bris 61. **d** 63 **p** 64. C Denton Holme *Carl* 63-66; C St Helens St Mark *Liv* 66-68; V Houghton *Carl* 68-79; V Bramcote *S'well* from 79; RD Beeston 85-90. *The Vicarage, Moss Drive, Beeston, Nottingham NG9 3HH* Nottingham (0602) 254306

HUMPHREYS, Canon John Elwyn Price. b 15. OBE77. Univ of Wales BA37. St Mich Coll Llan 38. **d** 39 **p** 41. Chapl Estoril *Eur* 57-80; Can Gib Cathl 67-80; rtd 80. *Casa Contente, Monte Estoril, Estoril, Portugal 2765* Lisbon (1) 468-3238

HUMPHREYS, John Louis. b 51. Jes Coll Cam BA72 MA76 Nottm Univ BA75. St Jo Coll Nottm 73. **d** 76 **p** 77. C W Bromwich Gd Shep w St Jo *Lich* 76-79; C Woodford Wells *Chelmsf* 79-83; V Werrington *Lich* from 83; Chapl HM Young Offender Inst Werrington from 83. *The Vicarage, 360 Ash Bank Road, Werrington, Stoke-on-Trent ST9 0JS* Ash Bank (078130) 2441

HUMPHREYS, John Robin. b 46. Lon Univ BScEng68. St Steph Ho Ox 73. **d** 76 **p** 77. C Bath Bathwick St Mary *B & W* 76-78; C Elland *Wakef* 78-81; V Doncaster St Jude *Sheff* 81-91; CF from 82; Ind Chapl *Sheff* 87-91; V Milton *Portsm* from 91. *St James's Vicarage, 287 Milton Road, Southsea, Hants PO4 8PG* Portsmouth (0705) 732786

HUMPHREYS, Canon Kenneth Glyn. b 28. Bps' Coll Cheshunt 64. **d** 66 **p** 67. C New Windsor St Jo *Ox* 66-67; C Whitley Ch Ch 67-70; V Compton 70-74; V Compton w E Ilsley 74-75; R E Ilsley 74; C Wokingham All SS 75-77; Chapl Lucas Hosp Wokingham 77-81; V California *Ox* from 81; RD Sonning 86-88; Hon Can Ch Ch from 91. *The Vicarage, Vicarage Close, Billing Avenue, Wokingham, Berks RG11 4JW* Eversley (0734) 730030

HUMPHREYS, Canon Neil Edgar. b 20. St Pet Hall Ox BA48 MA52. Linc Th Coll 48. **d** 50 **p** 51. Asst Chapl Liv Univ *Liv* 69-78; Dioc Planning Officer 72-78; Bp's Planning Adv 78-79; Hon Can Liv Cathl from 78; TV W Derby St Mary 79-89; rtd 89. *109 Thingwall Road, Wavertree, Liverpool L15 7JX* 051-722 4114

HUMPHREYS, Owen Gwilym. b 11. St D Coll Lamp BA33. St Mich Coll Llan 33. **d** 35 **p** 36. V Chilton-s-Polden w Edington *B & W* 59-76; C-in-c Catcott 75-76; rtd 76; Perm to Offic *Mon* from 77. *31 Fairfield Road, Caerleon, Newport, Gwent NP6 1DQ*

HUMPHREYS, Philip Noel. b 34. Bps' Coll Cheshunt 62. **d** 64 **p** 65. C Plymouth St Andr *Ex* 64-68; Chapl Lee Abbey 68-73; V Porchester *S'well* 73-82; RD Bingham W 82-87; P-in-c W Leake w Kingston-on-Soar etc 82-87; R W Bridgford from 82. *The Rectory, Church Drive, West Bridgford, Nottingham NG2 6AY* Nottingham (0602) 811112

HUMPHREYS, Roger John. b 45. CertEd66 Open Univ BA76. Wycliffe Hall Ox 81. **d** 83 **p** 84. Chapl Dragon Sch Ox 83-87; C Ox St Andr *Ox* 83-87; V Carterton from 87. *St John's Vicarage, Burford Road, Carterton, Oxford OX8 3AA* Carterton (0993) 842429

HUMPHREYS, Stephen Robert Beresford. b 52. K Coll Lon 74. **d** 76 **p** 77. C Northwood Hills St Edm *Lon* 76-79; C Manningham St Mary and Bradf St Mich *Bradf* 79-81; C Manningham St Paul and St Jude 82; Chapl Bradf R Infirmary 82-86; C Leeds St Pet *Ripon* 87-90. *Stowey Farm, Timberscombe, Minehead, Somerset TA24 7BW*

HUMPHREYS, William Alfred. b 18. Lich Th Coll 54. **d** 56 **p** 57. V Prees *Lich* 65-83; P-in-c Fauls 66-70; V 70-83; RD Wem and Whitchurch 80-83; rtd 83; Perm to Offic *Heref* from 83. *Bryncroft, 4 Seabridge Meadow, Bucknell, Shropshire S77 0AP* Bucknell (05474) 597

HUMPHREYS, William Haydn. b 09. AKC36. St D Coll Lamp 29. **d** 36 **p** 37. V Dewsbury St Mark *Wakef* 48-78;

Chapl Dewsbury Gen Hosp 50-78; rtd 78. *Flat 24, Marion Court, Lisvane Road, Cardiff CF4 5RZ* Cardiff (0222) 757158

HUMPHRIES, Benjamin Paul. b 56. FRGS Man Univ BA Birm Univ DipTh. Qu Coll Birm 82. **d** 85 **p** 86. C Hall Green Ascension *Birm* 85-88; P-in-c Belmont *Man* from 88. *St Peter's Vicarage, High Street, Belmont, Bolton BL7 8AF* Belmont Village (020481) 221

HUMPHRIES, Miss Catherine Elizabeth. b 53. Trin Coll Bris BA87. **d** 87. C Bath Twerton-on-Avon *B & W* 87-90; Tear Fund Overseas Personnel Dept 90-91; Hon Par Dn Norbiton *S'wark* from 91. *31 Glamorgan Road, Kingston upon Thames, Surrey KT1 4HS* 081-977 8338

HUMPHRIES, Christopher William. b 52. St Jo Coll Cam BA73 MA77 CertEd DipTh. St Jo Coll Nottm 76. **d** 79 **p** 80. C Eccleshill *Bradf* 79-82; Chapl Scargill Ho N Yorkshire 82-86; TV Guiseley w Esholt *Bradf* 86-91; V Filey *York* from 91. *The Vicarage, Filey, N Yorkshire YO14 9AD* Scarborough (0723) 512745

HUMPHRIES, David Graham. b 48. Univ of Wales (Cardiff) DipTh70. St Mich Coll Llan 67. **d** 71 **p** 72. C Neath w Llantwit *Llan* 71-72; C Bishop's Cleeve *Glouc* 81-83; C Cirencester 83-87; V Glouc St Steph from 87. *St Stephen's Vicarage, Frampton Road, Gloucester GL1 5QB* Gloucester (0452) 24694

HUMPHRIES, David John. b 51. BSc CertEd BD. Edin Th Coll. **d** 84 **p** 85. C Styvechale *Cov* 84-88; V Greetland and W Vale *Wakef* from 88. *The Vicarage, 2 Goldfields Way, Greetland, Halifax, W Yorkshire HX4 8LA* Halifax (0422) 372802

HUMPHRIES, Donald. b 43. Bris Univ BA66. Clifton Th Coll 66. **d** 68 **p** 69. C Selly Hill St Steph *Birm* 68-74; Chapl Warw Univ *Cov* 74-79; V Bedf Ch Ch *St Alb* 79-85; V Cam H Trin w St Andr Gt *Ely* from 85. *Holy Trinity Vicarage, 1 Selwyn Gardens, Cambridge CB3 9AX* Cambridge (0223) 355397

HUMPHRIES, Miss Dorothy Maud. b 22. Bedf Coll Lon BA44 Lon Univ DipEd45 Cam Univ DipTh50. Gilmore Course 85. **dss** 79 **d** 87. NSM Kidderminster Deanery from 79. *26 Linden Avenue, Kidderminster, Worcs DY10 3AB* Kidderminster (0562) 824459

HUMPHRIES, Frank Charles. b 40. St Chad's Coll Dur BA61 DipTh63. **d** 63 **p** 64. C Tottenham All Hallows *Lon* 63-66; C S Harrow St Paul 66-71; V Hillingdon All SS 71-80; V Preston Ascension from 80; Dir of Ords from 86. *The Vicarage, 319 Preston Road, Harrow, Middx HA3 0QQ* 081-904 4062

HUMPHRIES, Grahame Leslie. b 44. Lon Coll of Div ALCD70 LTh. **d** 71 **p** 72. C Wandsworth St Mich *S'wark* 71-74; C Slough *Ox* 74-77; P-in-c Arley *Cov* 77-82; R 82-84; Norfolk Churches' Radio Officer *Nor* from 84; P-in-c Bawdeswell w Foxley from 84. *The Rectory, Foxley, Dereham, Norfolk NR20 4QJ* Bawdeswell (036288) 397

HUMPHRIES, Harold Joseph. b 14. MIEE52. S'wark Ord Course 70. **d** 70 **p** 71. C Mert St Mary *S'wark* 70-71; C Glouc All SS *Glouc* 71-75; Hon C 78-82; C Glouc St Jas 75-77; Hon Min Can Glouc Cathl from 77. *Monument House, St Mary's Street, Gloucester GL1 2QR* Gloucester (0452) 20449

HUMPHRIES, John. b 49. Univ of Wales (Cardiff) DipTh70. St Mich Coll Llan 73. **d** 76 **p** 77. C Pontnewynydd *Mon* 76-78; C Ebbw Vale 78-81; V Pet Ch Carpenter *Pet* 81-86; P-in-c Kings Cliffe 86-87; R King's Cliffe w Apethorpe from 87. *The Rectory, Kings Cliffe, Peterborough PE8 6XQ* Kings Cliffe (0780) 87314

HUMPHRIES, Miss Marion Betty. b 29. K Coll Lon DipTh50 Open Univ BA84. Selly Oak Coll 51. **dss** 80 **d** 87. Newmarket St Mary w Exning St Agnes *St E* 80-82; Acomb St Steph *York* 83-86; Scarborough St Martin 86-87; Par Dn from 87. *136 Filey Road, Scarborough, N Yorkshire YO11 3AA* Scarborough (0723) 378105

HUMPHRIES, Canon Reginald Norton. b 14. AKC43. **d** 43 **p** 44. V Newport *Chelmsf* 49-84; V Ugley 55-83; RD Newport and Stansted 61-87; Hon Can Chelmsf Cathl 75-87; P-in-c Widdington 84; V Newport w Widdington 84-87; rtd 87; Perm to Offic *Linc* from 88. *The Cedars, 97 High Street, Coningsby, Lincoln LN4 4RF* Coningsby (0526) 52012

HUMPHRIES, William David. b 57. QUB BEd DipTh. **d** 86 **p** 87. C Ballyholme *D & D* 86-90; Min Can Belf Cathl 89-90; VC Belf Cathl from 90; C Belf St Anne Conn from 90. *The Vicarage, 57 Sunningdale Park, Belfast BT14 6RX* Belfast (0232) 716232

HUMPHRIS, Bernard. b 44. Sarum & Wells Th Coll 69. **d** 72 **p** 73. C Cheltenham St Luke and St Jo *Glouc* 72-77; C Lydney w Aylburton 77-82; Chapl RAF 82-84; TV Kippax w Allerton Bywater *Ripon* from 85. *The Vicarage,*

134 Leeds Road, Allerton Bywater, Castleford, W Yorkshire WF10 2HB Leeds (0532) 869415

HUMPHRISS, Canon Reginald George. b 36. Kelham Th Coll 56. **d** 61 **p** 62. C Londonderry *Birm* 61-63; Asst Dir RE *Cant* 63-66; Dioc Youth Chapl 63-66; V Preston next Faversham 66-72; P-in-c Goodnestone St Bart and Graveney 71-72; V Spring Park 72-76; R Cant St Martin and St Paul 76-90; RD Cant 82-88; Hon Can Cant Cathl from 85; R Saltwood from 90. *The Rectory, Saltwood, Hythe, Kent CT21 4QA* Hythe (0303) 266932

HUMPLEBY, Peter. b 40. Open Univ BA76 Hull Univ DipTh82. Linc Th Coll 75. **d** 77 **p** 78. C Todmorden *Wakef* 77-80; V Bruntcliffe 80-88; R Aldingham and Dendron and Rampside *Carl* from 88. *The New Rectory, Aldingham, Ulverston, Cumbria LA12 9RT* Bardsea (022988) 305

HUNDLEBY, Alan. b 41. Local NSM Course 86. **d** 86 **p** 87. NSM Fotherby *Linc* from 86. *35 Cheapside, Waltham, Grimsby, S Humberside DN37 0HE* Grimsby (0472) 827159

HUNG, Frank Yu-Chi. b 45. Birm Univ BSc68 BA75 Liv Univ MSc71 Ox Univ DipTh77. Wycliffe Hall Ox 76. **d** 78 **p** 79. C Walton H Trin *Ox* 78-82; C Spring Grove St Mary *Lon* 82-85; TV Wexcombe *Sarum* from 85. *The Rectory, Collingbourne Ducis, Marlborough, Wilts SN8 3EL* Collingbourne Ducis (0264) 850279

HUNGERFORD, Robin Nicholas. b 47. CertEd74. Trin Coll Bris DipHE88. **d** 88 **p** 89. C Swindon Dorcan *Bris* from 88. *18 Larksfield, Swindon SN3 5AD* Swindon (0793) 520139

HUNNISETT, John Bernard. b 47. AKC73. **d** 73 **p** 74. C Charlton Kings St Mary *Glouc* 73-77; C Portsea St Mary *Portsm* 77-80; V Badgeworth w Shurdington *Glouc* 80-87; R Dursley from 87. *The Rectory, The Broadwell, Dursley, Glos GL11 4JE* Dursley (0453) 542053

HUNNYBUN, Martin Wilfrid. b 44. Oak Hill Th Coll 67. **d** 70 **p** 71. C Ware Ch Ch *St Alb* 70-74; C Washfield, Stoodleigh, Withleigh etc *Ex* 74-75; TV Washfield, Stoodleigh, Withleigh etc 75-80; R Braunston *Pet* 80-85; Australia from 85. *66 Princess Street, Berry, NSW, Australia 2535* Berry (44) 641058

HUNT, Alan. b 31. St Mich Coll Llan 65. **d** 67 **p** 68. C Standish *Blackb* 67-72; V Clitheroe St Paul Low Moor 72-77; Lic to Offic from 77. *68 Coniston Drive, Walton-le-Dale, Preston, Lancs PR5 4RQ* Preston (0772) 39554

HUNT, Canon Andrew Horton Colin. b 14. Ball Coll Ox BA36. Westcott Ho Cam 38. **d** 39 **p** 40. S Rhodesia 53-65; Rhodesia 65-80; Zimbabwe 80-85; Perm to Offic *St Alb* from 85; rtd 86. *Middlepits Cottage, Turvey, Bedford MK43 8BB* Turvey (023064) 418

HUNT, Ashley Stephen. b 50. St Jo Coll Nottm. **d** 83 **p** 84. C Southchurch H Trin *Chelmsf* 83-86; TV Droitwich *Worc* 86-87; USA from 88. *Apartment 2, 3161 NE 17th Avenue, Fort Lauderdale, Florida 33334, USA*

HUNT, Bruce Allan. b 32. Nottm Univ BA54 DipEd55 Leic Univ CCouns90. ALCD59. **d** 61 **p** 62. C Watford St Mary *St Alb* 61-64; C Rayleigh *Chelmsf* 64-69; V Lepton *Wakef* 69-81; V Worksop St Jo *S'well* from 81. *St John's Vicarage, Shepherd's Avenue, Worksop, Notts S81 0JD* Worksop (0909) 478214

HUNT, Charles Evans. b 13. Dur Univ LTh44. ALCD37. **d** 37 **p** 38. V Masbrough St Paul *Sheff* 49-73; P-in-c Masbrough St Jo 56-73; V Wentworth 73-79; rtd 79; Lic to Offic *Ely* from 79. *1 Vicarage Lane, Whittlesford, Cambridge CB2 4NA* Cambridge (0223) 833402

HUNT, Mrs Christina. b 24. Qu Mary Coll Lon BSc45. S Dios Minl Tr Scheme 78. **dss** 81 **d** 87. Alderbury and W Grimstead *Sarum* 81-87; Hon Par Dn 87-91; Hon Par Dn Alderbury Team from 91. *The Heather, Southampton Road, Alderbury, Salisbury SP5 3AF* Salisbury (0722) 710601

HUNT, Christopher Paul Colin. b 38. Ch Coll Cam BA62 MA62. Clifton Th Coll 63. **d** 65 **p** 66. C Widnes St Paul *Liv* 65-68; Singapore 68-70; Malaysia 70-71; Hon C Foord St Jo *Cant* 72-73; Iran 74-80; Overseas Service Adv CMS 81-91; Lic to Offic *S'wark* 81-91; P-in-c Claverdon w Preston Bagot *Cov* from 91. *The Vicarage, Church Road, Claverdon, Warks CV35 8PD* Claverdon (0926) 842256

HUNT, David John. b 35. Kelham Th Coll 60. **d** 65 **p** 66. C Bethnal Green St Jo w St Simon *Lon* 65-69; C Mill Hill St Mich 69-73; R Staple Fitzpaine, Orchard Portman, Thurlbear etc *B & W* 73-79; P-in-c E Coker w Sutton Bingham 79-88; V E Coker w Sutton Bingham and Closworth from 88; RD Merston from 85. *The Vicarage, East Coker, Yeovil, Somerset BA22 9JG* West Coker (093586) 2125

HUNT, Derek Henry. b 38. ALCD61. **d** 62 **p** 63. C Roxeth Ch Ch *Lon* 62-66; C Radipole *Sarum* 66-70; P-in-c

Shalbourne w Ham 70-72; V Burbage 72-73; V Burbage and Savernake Ch Ch 73-78; P-in-c Hulcote w Salford *St Alb* 78-88; R Cranfield 78-88; R Cranfield and Hulcote w Salford from 88. *The Rectory, Court Road, Cranfield, Bedford MK43 0DR* Bedford (0234) 750214

HUNT, Edward Trebble. b 31. St Mich Coll Llan 56. **d** 58 **p** 59. C Swansea St Thos *S & B* 58-62; C Swansea St Mary and H Trin 62-65; P-in-c Glantawe 65-72; V 72-76; V Swansea Ch Ch from 76; Chapl HM Pris Swansea from 76. *The Vicarage, 226 Oystermouth Road, Swansea SA2 3UH* Swansea (0792) 652606

HUNT, Ernest William. b 09. St Jo Coll Dur BA31 MA34 Birm Univ BD46 St Cath Soc Ox BLitt51 Ox Univ MLitt90. St Jo Coll Dur DipTh32. **d** 32 **p** 33. Prof St D Coll Lamp 57-69; rtd 76. *16 Peachcroft Road, Abingdon, Oxon OX14 2NA* Abingdon (0235) 21549

HUNT, Giles Butler. b 28. Trin Hall Cam BA51 MA55. Cuddesdon Coll 51. **d** 53 **p** 54. C N Evington *Leic* 53-56; C Northolt St Mary *Lon* 56-58; Bp's Dom Chapl *Portsm* 58-59; Bp's Chapl *Nor* 59-62; R Holt 62-67; R Kelling w Salthouse 63-67; C Pimlico St Pet w Westmr Ch Ch *Lon* 67-72; V Barkway w Reed and Buckland *St Alb* 72-79; V Preston next Faversham, Goodnestone and Graveney *Cant* from 79. *The Vicarage, Preston Lane, Faversham, Kent ME13 8LG* Faversham (0795) 536801

HUNT, Canon Ian Carter. b 34. Chich Th Coll 61. **d** 64 **p** 65. C Plymouth St Pet *Ex* 64-67; C Daventry *Pet* 67-70; V Northn St Paul 70-91; Can Pet Cathl from 81; V Wellingborough All Hallows from 91. *The Vicarage, Church Street, Wellingborough, Northants NN8 3PA* Wellingborough (0933) 222002

HUNT, Jeremy Mark Nicholas. b 46. FRGS70 Open Univ BA73 Bris Univ DipEd. Ridley Hall Cam 83. **d** 85 **p** 86. C Leckhampton SS Phil and Jas w Cheltenham St Jas *Glouc* 85-87; Asst Chapl Vevey w Chateau d'Oex and Villars *Eur* 87-90; Asst Chapl Chapl Bern w Neuchatel 89-90. *c/o 98 Oxford Road, Cambridge CB4 3PL*

HUNT, Jessie. b 15. R Holloway Coll Lon BSc37. St Chris Coll Blackheath 44. **dss** 77 **d** 87. Westcliff St Andr *Chelmsf* 77-78; Southend 78-87; Par Dn 87-90; Chapl Asst Southend Gen Hosp from 87; Perm to Offic from 90. *22 Westminster Drive, Westcliff-on-Sea, Essex SS0 9SL* Southend-on-Sea (0702) 343632

HUNT, John Barry. b 46. Lich Th Coll 70 Qu Coll Birm 72. **d** 73 **p** 74. C Auckland St Andr and St Anne *Dur* 73-77; C Consett 77-79; R Lyons 79-89; P-in-c Hebburn St Cuth from 89. *St Cuthbert's Vicarage, Cosserat Place, Hebburn, Tyne & Wear NE31 1RD* 091-483 2038

HUNT, John Edwin. b 38. ARCO Dur Univ BA60 DipEd. E Midl Min Tr Course 78. **d** 81 **p** 82. NSM Newbold and Dunston *Derby* from 81. *4 Ardsley Road, Ashgate, Chesterfield, Derbyshire S40 4DG* Chesterfield (0246) 275141

HUNT, John Stewart. b 37. Nor Ord Course 75. **d** 78 **p** 79. NSM Hunstanton St Edm *Nor* 78-81; NSM Hunstanton St Mary w Ringstead Parva, Holme etc 81-86; NSM Sedgeford w Southmere 84-86; C Lowestoft and Kirkley 86-89; R Blundeston w Flixton and Lound from 89. *The Rectory, Market Lane, Blundeston, Lowestoft, Suffolk NR32 5AP* Lowestoft (0502) 730638

HUNT, Dr Judith Mary. b 57. MRCVS80 Bris Univ BVSc80 Lon Univ PhD85 Fitzw Coll Cam BA90. Ridley Hall Cam 88. **d** 91. Par Dn Heswall *Ches* from 91. *15 Castle Drive, Heswall, Wirral, Merseyside L60 4RJ* 051-342 5946

HUNT, Kevin. b 59. St Jo Coll Dur BA80 Ox Univ BA84 MA88. St Steph Ho Ox 81. **d** 84 **p** 85. C Mansf St Mark *S'well* 84-85; C Hendon and Sunderland *Dur* 85-88; V Sunderland Springwell w Thorney Close from 88. *The Clergy House, Springwell Road, Sunderland SR3 4DY* 091-528 3754

HUNT, Canon Michael Francis. b 26. Wadh Coll Ox BA49 MA50. St Steph Ho Ox 49. **d** 51 **p** 52. C E Clevedon All SS *B & W* 51-55; C-in-c Broxtowe CD *S'well* 56-62; R Auchterarder *St And* 62-66; R Dumfries *Glas* 66-73; R Arbroath *Bre* 73-78; R Inverness St Mich *Mor* 78-80; R Inverness St Jo 78-80; Papua New Guinea from 80; Hon Can St Jo Cathl Port Moresby from 89; Hon Prov Can from 90. *Newton Theological College, PO Box 162, Popondetta, Papua New Guinea*

HUNT, Montague Laban. b 97. Leeds Clergy Sch 20. **d** 23 **p** 24. Hon CF from 47; R S Ferriby *Linc* 53-66; V Horkstow 57-66; rtd 66. *186 Nettleham Road, Lincoln LN2 4DQ* Lincoln (0522) 528551

HUNT, Paul Firth. b 62. Ox Univ MA89 Edin Univ BD89. Edin Th Coll 86. **d** 89 **p** 90. C Leeds Halton St Wilfrid *Ripon* from 89. *67 Morritt Drive, Leeds LS15 7HZ* Leeds (0532) 609498

HUNT, Peter John. b 35. AKC58. St Boniface Warminster. **d** 59 **p** 60. C Chesterfield All SS *Derby* 59-61; C Matlock and Tansley 61-63; Chapl Matlock Hosp 61-63; Lect Matlock Teacher Tr Coll 61-63; V Tottington *Man* 63-69; CF (TA) 65-67 and from 75; V Bollington St Jo *Ches* 69-76; R Wilmslow from 76. *The Rectory, 12 Broadway, Wilmslow, Cheshire SK9 1NB* Wilmslow (0625) 523127 or 520309

HUNT, Philip Lacey Winter. b 09. St Steph Ho Ox. **d** 68 **p** 69. Chapl to the Deaf *Ox* 68-75; Hon Chapl from 75. *13 Wingfield Court, Glebe Street, Oxford OX4 1DG* Oxford (0865) 248385

HUNT, Richard William. b 46. G&C Coll Cam BA67 MA71. Westcott Ho Cam 68. **d** 72 **p** 73. C Bris St Agnes and St Simon w St Werburgh *Bris* 72-77; Chapl Selw Coll Cam 77-84; V Birchfield *Birm* from 84. *Holy Trinity Vicarage, 213 Birchfield Road, Birmingham B20 3DG* 021-356 4241

HUNT, Ms Rosalind. b 55. Man Univ BA76. St Steph Ho Ox 86. **d** 88. Chapl Jes Coll Cam from 88. *Jesus College, Cambridge CB5 8BL* Cambridge (0223) 68611

HUNT, Roy Charles Podmore. b 13. Tyndale Hall Bris 38. **d** 42 **p** 43. R Langar *S'well* 60-65; rtd 78. *14 Pound Close, Burwell, Cambridge* Newmarket (0638) 742708

HUNT, Canon Russell Barrett. b 35. NY Univ Virginia Univ Fitzw Ho Cam. Westcott Ho Cam 73. **d** 75 **p** 76. C Leic St Mary *Leic* 75-78; V Leic St Gabr 78-82; Chapl Leic Gen Hosp from 82; Hon Can Leic Cathl *Leic* from 88. *The Chaplain's Office, Leicester General Hospital, Gwendolen Road, Leicester LE5 4PW* Leicester (0533) 490490

HUNT, Simon John. b 60. Pemb Coll Ox BA81 MA85. St Jo Coll Nottm 87. **d** 90 **p** 91. C Stalybridge St Paul *Ches* from 90. *69 Fistral Crescent, Stalybridge, Cheshire SK15 3HN* 061-303 7894

HUNT, Vera Susan Henrietta. b 33. S Dios Minl Tr Scheme 88. **d** 91. Hon Chapl RAD from 91. *27 Redriff Close, Maidenhead, Berks SL6 4DJ* Maidenhead (0628) 23909

✠**HUNT, Rt Rev William Warren.** b 09. Keble Coll Ox BA31 MA35. Cuddesdon Coll 31. **d** 32 **p** 33 **c** 65. C Kendal *Carl* 32-35; C St Martin-in-the-Fields *Lon* 35-40; CF (EC) 40-44; V Radford *Cov* 44-48; V Leamington Priors H Trin 48-57; RD Leamington 53-57; V Croydon *Cant* 57-65; RD Croydon 57-65; Hon Can Cant Cathl 57-65; Suff Bp Repton *Derby* 65-77; rtd 77; Asst Bp Portsm from 77; Asst Bp Chich from 78. *15 Lynch Down, Funtington, Chichester, W Sussex PO18 9LR* Bosham (0243) 575536

HUNTER, Allan Davies. b 36. Univ of Wales (Lamp) BA57. Coll of Resurr Mirfield 57. **d** 59 **p** 60. C Cardiff St Jo *Llan* 59-68; V Llansawel 68-76; Youth Chapl 71-77; V Llansawel w Briton Ferry 76-79; V Canton St Cath from 79. *The Vicarage, 22A Romilly Crescent, Canton, Cardiff CF1 9NR* Cardiff (0222) 382796

✠**HUNTER, Rt Rev Anthony George Weaver.** b 16. Leeds Univ BA39. Coll of Resurr Mirfield 39. **d** 41 **p** 42 **c** 68. C Newc St Geo *Newc* 41-43 and 48-49; S Africa 43-48; V Ashington *Newc* 49-60; V Huddersfield SS Pet and Paul *Wakef* 60-68; RD Huddersfield 60-68; Hon Can Wakef Cathl 62-68; Bp Swaziland 68-75; R Hexham *Newc* 75-79; Asst Bp Newc 76-81; rtd 81. *Hillside, Main Street, Sheriff Hutton, York YO6 1PS* Sheriff Hutton (03477) 226

HUNTER, Cyril Stanley Maurice. b 18. Worc Ord Coll 67. **d** 69 **p** 70. C Guisborough *York* 69-72; C Northallerton w Kirby Sigston 72-75; P-in-c Thornton-le-Street w Thornton-le-Moor etc 75-79; R Thornton le Street w N Otterington etc 79-85; rtd 85. *Linden, Upsall Road, South Kilvington, Thirsk, N Yorkshire YO7 2NQ* Thirsk (0845) 522829

HUNTER, David. b 30. Edin Th Coll 60. **d** 64 **p** 65. C Glas Ch Ch *Glas* 64-67; R 67-70 and 75-78; R Coatbridge 70-73; Chapl HM Pris Glas (Barlinnie) 72-84; P-in-c Glas H Trin *Glas* 73-84; R Glas All SS from 84. *12 Woodend Drive, Glasgow G13 1QS* 041-959 3730

HUNTER, David Matheson. b 46. K Coll Lon BD69 AKC69. **d** 76 **p** 77. C Paignton St Jo *Ex* 76-80; C Plymstock 80-82; Jerusalem 82-84; P-in-c Brinkley, Burrough Green and Carlton *Ely* 84-86; P-in-c Westley Waterless 84-86; R Bressingham w N and S Lopham and Fersfield *Nor* from 87. *The Rectory, Bressingham, Diss, Norfolk IP22 2AT* Bressingham (037988) 8267

HUNTER, Canon Frank Geoffrey. b 34. Keble Coll Ox BA56 MA60 Fitzw Coll Cam BA58 MA62. Ridley Hall Cam 57. **d** 59 **p** 60. C Bircle *Man* 59-62; C Jarrow Grange *Dur* 62-65; V Kingston upon Hull St Martin *York* 65-72; V Linthorpe 72-76; V Heslington from 76; RD Derwent from 77; Can and Preb York Minster from 85. *The*

Rectory, Heslington, York YO1 5EE York (0904) 410389

HUNTER, Harold Hamilton. b 23. Dur Univ BSc48. NE Ord Course 76. **d** 79 **p** 80. NSM Corbridge w Halton *Newc* 79-82; NSM Corbridge w Halton and Newton Hall from 82. *15 Carham Close, Corbridge, Northd NE45 5NA* Hexham (0434) 632748

HUNTER, Henry. b 07. Tyndale Hall Bris 32. **d** 45 **p** 46. R Burlingham St Edmund, St Andr, St Pet etc *Nor* 62-73; rtd 73. *Silverthorn, 27 Mundesley Road, Trimingham, Norwich NR11 8ED*

HUNTER, Ian Paton. b 20. Em Coll Cam BA46 MA50. Tyndale Hall Bris 40. **d** 43 **p** 47. R Plumpton *Chich* 67-77; V Burwash Weald 77-83; P-in-c Stonegate 83-85; rtd 85; Perm to Offic *Chich* from 86. *Edzell, 15 Harrow Close, Seaford, E Sussex BN5 3PE* Seaford (0323) 899871

HUNTER, Canon John Gaunt. b 21. St Jo Coll Dur BA49. Ridley Hall Cam 49. **d** 51 **p** 52. C Bradf Cathl *Bradf* 51-54; C Compton Gifford *Ex* 54-56; V Bootle St Matt *Liv* 56-62; Uganda 62-65; Prin Bp Tucker Coll 62-65; Dioc Missr *Liv* 65-71; V Altcar 65-78; Abp York's Adv in Miss 71-78; Hon Can Liv Cathl 71-78; R Buckhurst Hill *Chelmsf* 78-79; TR 79-89; Dioc Adv in Evang *Bradf* from 89. *Cathedral House, 1A Barkerend Road, Bradford, W Yorkshire BD3 9AF* Bradford (0274) 724586

HUNTER, Lionel Lawledge Gleave. b 24. Liv Coll of Art NDD50. ALCD53. **d** 53 **p** 54. Chile 61-72; R Diddlebury w Bouldon and Munslow *Heref* 72-75; P-in-c Abdon w Clee St Margaret 73-75; P-in-c Holdgate w Tugford 73-75; Canada 75-85; V N Elmham w Billingford *Nor* 85-89; R N Elmham w Billingford and Worthing 89-90; rtd 90. *Araucana, Wyson Lane, Brimfield, Ludlow, Shropshire SY8 4AN* Brimfield (058472) 463

HUNTER, Dr Michael John. b 45. CCC Cam BA67 MA71 PhD71 Ox Univ BA75. Wycliffe Hall Ox 73. **d** 76 **p** 77. C Partington and Carrington *Ches* 76-79; CMS 80-90; Uganda 80-89; C Penn Fields *Lich* from 90. *100 Bellencroft Gardens, Merry Hill, Wolverhampton WV3 8DU* Wolverhampton (0902) 763603

HUNTER, Canon Michael Oram. b 40. K Coll Lon BD64 AKC64. **d** 65 **p** 66. C Tividale *Lich* 65-68; C Harrogate St Wilfrid *Ripon* 68-70; V Hawksworth Wood 70-78; V Whitkirk 78-86; TR Gt Grimsby St Mary and St Jas *Linc* from 86; Hon Can Linc Cathl from 89. *49 Park Drive, Grimsby, S Humberside DN32 0EG* Grimsby (0472) 342933

HUNTER, Paul. b 55. Huddersfield Poly BEd82. Chich Th Coll 86. **d** 88 **p** 90. C Weymouth H Trin *Sarum* from 88. *151 Chickerell Road, Weymouth, Dorset DT4 0BP* Weymouth (0305) 771675

HUNTER, Peter Wells. b 52. Bris Univ BSc73. Trin Coll Bris BA91. **d** 91. C New Boro and Leigh *Sarum* from 91. *7 Ethelbert Road, Wimborne, Dorset BH21 1BH* Wimborne (0202) 889405

HUNTER, Robert. b 36. **d** 63 **p** 64. C Chadderton Ch Ch *Man* 63-65; C Balderstone 65-69; C Newburn *Newc* 69-73; TV Sutton St Jas and Wawne *York* 73-81; V Bilton St Pet 81-82; Hon C N Hull St Mich from 82. *32 Park Avenue, Hull HU5 3ER* Hull (0482) 42071

HUNTER, Robert Clifford. b 09. St Pet Coll Jamaica 38. **d** 42 **p** 43. Hon CF from 51; V Lower Nutfield *S'wark* 60-72; C Gt Ness *Lich* 73-77; rtd 77. *Diamond Cottage, Motcombe, Shaftesbury, Dorset SP7 9PF* Shaftesbury (0747) 54029

HUNTER, Rodney Squire. b 33. Ox Univ BA56 MA61. Coll of Resurr Mirfield 56. **d** 58 **p** 59. C Forest Gate St Edm *Chelmsf* 58-61; Lib Pusey Ho Ox 61-65; Zambia 65-74; Malawi from 74. *Box 130, Zomba, Malawi* Malawi (265) 522419

HUNTER-BAILEY, James Ralph. b 11. Ripon Hall Ox 55. **d** 56 **p** 57. R Wychbold and Upton Warren *Worc* 64-71; Lic to Offic *Sarum* 71-78; rtd 76; Perm to Offic *Win* from 78. *46 Erica Drive, Corfe Mullen, Wimborne, Dorset BH21 3TQ* Broadstone (0202) 602260

HUNTER SMART, Ian Douglas. b 60. St Jo Coll Dur BA83. Edin Th Coll 83. **d** 85 **p** 86. C Cockerton *Dur* 85-89; TV Jarrow from 89. *12 High Back Close, Monkton Village, Jarrow, Tyne & Wear NE32 5PA* 091-489 0645

HUNTINGDON, Archdeacon of. See SLEDGE, Ven Richard Kitson

HUNTINGDON, Suffragan Bishop of. See ROE, Rt Rev William Gordon

HUNTLEY, Denis Anthony. b 56. Qu Coll Birm 77. **d** 80 **p** 81. C Llanblethian w Cowbridge and Llandough etc *Llan* 80-83; TV Glyncorrwg w Afan Vale and Cymmer Afan 83-86; R 86-89; Chapl Asst Walsgrave Hosp Cov from 89. *Walsgrave Hospital, Clifford Bridge Road, Coventry CV2 2LX* Coventry (0203) 602020

HUNTRESS, Franklin Elias. b 33. d 62 p 63. USA 62-65 and from 78; C Ches St Mary *Ches* 65-67; C Waltham Abbey *Chelmsf* 67-74; V Leic St Gabr *Leic* 75-78. *136 Rivet, New Bedford, Massachusetts 02744, USA*

HUNTRISS, John Charles. b 49. Worc Coll Ox BA71 MA74. St Steph Ho Ox 71. d 74 p 75. C Badgeworth w Shurdington *Glouc* 74-77; Asst Chapl Univ of Wales (Cardiff) *Llan* 77-79; P-in-c Mickleton *Glouc* 79-90; V from 90. *The Vicarage, Mickleton, Chipping Campden, Glos GL55 6RX* Mickleton (0386) 438279

HUNWICKE, John William. b 41. Hertf Coll Ox BA64 MA67. St Steph Ho Ox. d 67 p 68. C Beaconsfield *Ox* 67-70; C Newington St Paul *S'wark* 70-73; Chapl Lancing Coll Sussex from 73. *Hoe Court House, Lancing, W Sussex BN15 0QX* Lancing (0903) 752145

HURCOMBE, Thomas William. b 45. BD74 AKC76. d 76 p 77. C Hampstead All So *Lon* 76-79; C Is of Dogs Ch Ch and St Jo w St Luke 79-83; C Bromley All Hallows 83-89; C E Greenwich Ch Ch w St Andr and St Mich *S'wark* from 89; Ind Chapl from 89; Dioc Urban Missr from 90. *81 Charlton Road, London SE3 8TH* 081-858 9521

HURD, Alun John. b 52. Avery Hill Coll DipHE83. Trin Coll Bris BA86. d 86 p 87. C Chertsey *Guildf* 86-90; Chapl St Pet Hosp Chertsey 86-90; V W Ewell *Guildf* from 90. *All Saints' Vicarage, Church Road, West Ewell, Epsom, Surrey KT19 9QY* 081-393 4357

HURD, Arthur Edward Stanley. b 12. St Jo Coll Dur LTh41 BA42 MA45. Tyndale Hall Bris 38. d 42 p 43. R Southover *Chich* 63-77; rtd 77; Perm to Offic Chich and B & W from 77. *9 Wiltons, Wrington, Bristol BS18 7LS* Wrington (0934) 862382

HURD, John Patrick. b 37. CertEd65 Open Univ BA73. Chich Th Coll 77. d 80 p 81. NSM Billingshurst *Chich* 80-83; NSM Itchingfield w Slinfold from 83. *Groomsland Cottage, Parbrook, Billingshurst, W Sussex RH14 9EU* Billingshurst (0403) 782167

HURDLE, Canon Thomas Vivian. b 15. St Cath Coll Cam BA37 MA40. Ely Th Coll 38. d 39 p 40. Dir of Educn *Ely* 65-80; Hon Can Ely Cathl 67-80; V Madingley 70-79; rtd 80. *4 West Wratting Road, Balsham, Cambridge CB1 6DX* Cambridge (0223) 894011

HURDMAN, William Richard. b 40. AKC66 Hull Univ MA84. d 67 p 72. C Portsea St Mary *Portsm* 67-68; C N Walsham w Antingham *Nor* 71-74; V Friskney *Linc* 74-81; TR Bottesford w Ashby 81-88; TR Hackney *Lon* from 88. *The Rectory, 356 Mare Street, London E8 1HR* 081-985 5374

HURFORD, Colin Osborne. b 33. Qu Coll Ox BA55 MA59. Wells Th Coll 55. d 57 p 58. C Barnoldswick w Bracewell *Bradf* 57-61; C Warrington St Elphin *Liv* 61-63; Malaysia 63-70; P-in-c Annscroft *Heref* 71-79; P-in-c Pontesbury Hamlet of Longden 71-79; P-in-c Pontesbury III 71-79; R Longden and Annscroft 79-85; P-in-c Church Pulverbatch 81-85; R Longden and Annscroft w Pulverbatch 85-86; Tanzania 86-87; TR Billingham St Aid *Dur* from 87. *The Rectory, 12A Tintern Avenue, Billingham, Cleveland TS23 2DE* Stockton-on-Tees (0642) 531740

HURFORD, Ven Richard Warwick. b 44. d 69 p 70. Australia 69-71 and from 78; P-in-c Tisbury *Sarum* 71-73; R 73-75; R Tisbury and Swallowcliffe w Ansty 75-76; P-in-c Chilmark 76-78; TR Tisbury 76-78. *PO Box 4, Grafton, NSW, Australia 2460* Grafton (66) 424122

HURLE, Anthony Rowland. b 54. Lon Univ BSc Em Coll Cam PGCE. Wycliffe Hall Ox 80. d 83 p 84. C Ipswich St Mary at Stoke w St Pet & St Mary Quay *St E* 83-87; TV Barking St Marg w St Patr *Chelmsf* from 87. *The Vicarage, 79 Sparsholt Road, Barking, Essex IG11 7YG* 081-594 0220

HURLEY, Daniel Timothy. b 37. St Mich Coll Llan 68. d 70 p 71. C Llanfabon *Llan* 70-73; CF 73-79; R W Walton *Ely* 79-86; V Cwmddauddwr w St Harmon's and Llanwrthwl *S & B* from 86. *The Vicarage, Cwmdeuddwr, Rhayader, Powys LD6 5AP* Rhayader (0597) 810574

HURLEY, Mark Tristan. b 57. Trin Coll Bris DipHE88 BA89 Sarum & Wells Th Coll 89. d 91. C Gainsborough All SS *Linc* from 91. *4 Chestnut Avenue, Gainsborough, Lincs DN21 1EU* Gainsborough (0427) 611648

HURLEY, Patrick Norman. b 15. d 47 p 48. C Hartlepool H Trin *Dur* 61-82; rtd 82. *Fourways, Nether Compton, Sherborne, Dorset DT9 4QE* Sherborne (0935) 813319

HURLEY, Robert. b 64. Univ of Wales (Cardiff) BD86. Ridley Hall Cam 88. d 90 p 91. C Dagenham *Chelmsf* from 90. *15 Felhurst Crescent, Dagenham, Essex RM10 7XT*

HURLOCK, Ronald James. b 31. BSc PhD. St Deiniol's Hawarden. d 83 p 84. C Oxton *Ches* 83-87; Chapl Asst

Man R Infirmary from 87. *Manchester Royal Infirmary, Oxford Raod, Manchester M13 9WL* 061-276 1234

HURLOW, Canon Winston Gordon. b 14. Univ of Wales BA35 St Jo Coll Ox BA37 MA47. St Mich Coll Llan 37. d 38 p 39. R Ches St Mary *Ches* 65-82; rtd 82; Perm to Offic *Ches* from 82; Lich from 83. *20 The Firs, Chester Road, Whitchurch, Shropshire SY13 1NL* Whitchurch (0948) 4144

HURLSTON, Ronald Wilcox. b 30. St Deiniol's Hawarden 84. d 86 p 87. NSM Timperley *Ches* 86-90; C from 90. *97 Park Road, Timperley, Altrincham, Cheshire WA15 6QG* 061-962 3017

HURN, Mrs June Barbara. b 32. Birm Univ CertEd53. Cant Sch of Min 87. d 90. NSM Chislehurst St Nic *Roch* from 90. *Sandy Ridge, 64 Lubbock Road, Chislehurst, Kent BR7 5JX* 081-467 2320

HURRELL, John William. b 25. Ripon Hall Ox 65. d 66 p 67. C Glouc St Geo *Glouc* 68-70; C Thornbury 70-73; V Glouc St Steph 73-86; V Deerhurst, Apperley w Forthampton and Chaceley 86-90; rtd 90. *1 Church View, Porlock, Minehead, Somerset TA24 8NA* Minehead (0643) 862488

HURRELL, Lionel Rex. b 41. Southn Univ BA64. Coll of Resurr Mirfield 64. d 66 p 67. C St Marychurch *Ex* 66-69; C Dawlish 69-71; Dioc Youth Officer *Cov* 71-75; V Porthleven *Truro* 75-80; RD Kerrier 78-80; P-in-c Sithney 78-80; V Swindon New Town *Bris* 80-88; TR from 88. *St Mark's Rectory, Church Place, Swindon, Wilts SN1 5EH* Swindon (0793) 522546

HURST, Alaric Desmond St John. b 24. New Coll Ox BA50 MA70. Wells Th Coll 48. d 51 p 53. V Writtle *Chelmsf* 63-69; rtd 89. *9 Ganderton Court, Pershore, Worcs WR10 1AW* Worcester (0905) 840939

HURST, Antony. b 38. MA MSc. S'wark Ord Course 79. d 83 p 84. NSM S'wark H Trin w St Matt *S'wark* 83-89; NSM S'wark Ch Ch from 89. *33 Hugh Street, London SW1V 1QT* 071-828 2844

HURST, Brian Charles. b 58. Nottm Univ BA. Ripon Coll Cuddesdon 82. d 84 p 85. C Cullercoats St Geo *Newc* 84-87; C Prudhoe 87-88; TV Willington Team from 88. *The Vicarage, Berwick Drive, Newcastle upon Tyne NE28 9ED* 091-262 7518

HURST, Colin. b 49. Linc Th Coll 88. d 90 p 91. C Wavertree H Trin *Liv* from 90. *66 Grant Avenue, Wavertree, Liverpool L15 5AY* 051-733 6733

HURST, Geoffrey. b 30. St Aid Birkenhead 59. d 64 p 65. C Sheff Parson Cross St Cecilia *Sheff* 64-69; V Wellingborough St Mark *Pet* 69-77; P-in-c Leic St Mark *Leic* 77-82; TV Leic Resurr 82-83; V Willenhall St Steph *Lich* 83-85; V Nether Hoyland St Andr *Sheff* from 85. *The Vicarage, Market Street, Hoyland, Barnsley, S Yorkshire S74 0ET* Barnsley (0226) 742126

HURST, George Herbert. b 07. St Jo Coll Dur BA33 MA37. d 33 p 34. R Brooke w Kirstead *Nor* 67-72; rtd 72; Perm to Offic *Nor* from 72. *17 Breck Farm Close, Taverham, Norwich NR8 6LS* Norwich (0603) 867507

HURST, Jeremy Richard. b 40. FCP Trin Coll Cam BA61 MA MPhil. Linc Th Coll 62. d 64 p 65. C Woolwich St Mary w H Trin *S'wark* 64-69; Perm to Offic *Ex* 69-76; Ox 76-84; TV Langley Marish *Ox* 84-85; TR from 85. *The Rectory, 3 St Mary's Road, Langley, Berks SL3 7EN* Slough (0753) 42068

HURST, John. b 31. NW Ord Course 76. d 79 p 80. C Flixton St Jo *Man* 79-82; P-in-c Hindsford 82-86; V 86-88; V Halliwell St Paul from 88. *St Paul's Vicarage, Vicarage Lane, Halliwell Road, Bolton BL1 8BP* Bolton (0204) 495038

HURST, John Cecil. b 08. Trin Coll Cam BA30 MA37. Westcott Ho Cam 31. d 32 p 33. R W Meon and Warnford *Portsm* 63-73; rtd 73. *Middle Butts, Rectory Lane, Meonstoke, Southampton SO3 1NF* Droxford (0489) 877309

HURST, John Wilton. b 22. Kent Univ DipTh80. Tyndale Hall Bris 45. d 48 p 49. V Tunbridge Wells St Pet *Roch* 59-91; Chapl Pembury Hosp Tunbridge Wells 60-65; rtd 91. *Oaklands, Chapel Lane, Corfe Mullen, Wimborne, Dorset BH21 3SL* Wimborne (0202) 691935

HURST, Joseph Bennett. b 28. Man Univ BA54. Ripon Hall Ox 54. d 56 p 57. C New Bury *Man* 56-59; C Whitfield *Derby* 59-61; R Sawley 61-69; V Dethick, Lea and Holloway 69-82; R Tansley, Dethick, Lea and Holloway from 82. *Lea Vicarage, Matlock, Derbyshire DE4 5JP* Dethick (0629) 534275

HURST-BANNISTER, Michael Barnabas St Leger. b 19. Dorchester Miss Coll 41. d 44 p 45. CECS Clerical Org Sec Dios Win, Sarum and Portsm 67-78; Sen Chapl Actor's Ch Union 75-89; P-in-c Soho St Anne w St Thos and St Pet *Lon* 78-84; rtd 84. *Barford Lodge, West*

Street, Barford St Martin, Salisbury SP3 4AS Salisbury (0722) 742630

HURT, Arnold Herbert. b 04. Man Univ BSc24. Cuddesdon Coll 28. **d** 28 **p** 29. V Scunthorpe Resurr *Linc* 69-71; rtd 71; P-in-c Innerleithen *Edin* 73-77 and from 82. *St Andrew's Parsonage, Damside, Innerleithen, Peeblesshire EH44 6HR* Innerleithen (0896) 830447

HUSBAND, Terence. b 26. NW Ord Course 72. **d** 75 **p** 76. C Weaste *Man* 75-78; R Gorton St Phil 78-81; V Belford *Newc* 81-88; Lic to Offic from 88. *11 Carham Close, Corbridge, Northd NE45 5NA* Hexham (0434) 633274

HUSBANDS, Canon Norman. b 03. AKC32. St Steph Ho Ox 32. **d** 32 **p** 33. V Roade *Pet* 41-76; Can Pet Cathl 67-76; rtd 76; Lic to Offic *Pet* 76-86; Perm to Offic from 86. *47 Ridge Way, Weston Favell, Northampton NN3 3AP* Northampton (0604) 408024

HUSSELL, Thomas Stanley. b 13. Univ of Wales BSc34. Sarum Th Coll 35. **d** 37 **p** 38. V Wragby *Wakef* 61-71; Lic to Offic from 71; rtd 78. *22 St John's Grove, Wakefield, W Yorkshire WF1 3SA* Wakefield (0924) 377891

HUSSEY, William Kenneth Alfred. b 27. St Jo Coll Ox BA48 DipEd49 MA52. Wycliffe Hall Ox 51. **d** 52 **p** 53. Chapl Ipswich Sch 60-72; Hd Master Ches Cathl Choir Sch 72-74; Chapl Rendcomb Coll Cirencester 74-78; P-in-c Rendcomb *Glouc* 74-78; Chapl Berkhamsted Sch Herts 78-83; TV Redruth w Lanner *Truro* 83-84; V St Goran w St Mich Caerhays 84-89; rtd 89. *20 Albany Road, Falmouth, Cornwall TR11 3RW* Falmouth (0326) 312343

HUTCHIN, David William. b 37. LRAM ARCM LTCL Man Univ MusB58 CertEd59 DipEd59. Glouc Sch of Min 85. **d** 88 **p** 89. NSM Northleach w Hampnett and Farmington *Glouc* from 88; NSM Cold Aston w Notgrove and Turkdean from 88. *Cotswold Pharmacy, Market Place, Northleach, Cheltenham, Glos GL54 3EG* Cotswold (0451) 60295

HUTCHINGS, Colin Michael. b 36. Clifton Th Coll 66. **d** 68 **p** 69. C Worksop St Jo *S'well* 68-71; C Hampreston *Sarum* 71-76; TV Tisbury 76-82; R Waddesdon w Over Winchendon and Fleet Marston *Ox* from 82. *The Rectory, Waddesdon, Aylesbury, Bucks HP18 0JQ* Aylesbury (0296) 651312

HUTCHINGS, Ian James. b 49. Lon Univ DipTh72. Clifton Th Coll 69 Trin Coll Bris 72. **d** 73 **p** 74. C Parr *Liv* 73-77; C Timperley *Ches* 77-81; V Partington and Carrington from 81. *St Mary's Vicarage, Manchester Road, Partington, Urmston, Manchester M31 4FB* 061-775 3542

HUTCHINGS, John Denis Arthur. b 29. Keble Coll Ox BA53 MA59 MSc59. Chich Th Coll 58. **d** 60 **p** 61. C St Pancras w St Jas and Ch Ch *Lon* 60-63; Asst Chapl Denstone Coll Uttoxeter 63-67 and 79-83; C Stepney St Dunstan and All SS *Lon* 67-78; V Devonport St Boniface *Ex* 83-86; TR Devonport St Boniface and St Phil from 86. *St Boniface Vicarage, 1 Normandy Way, Plymouth PL5 1SW* Plymouth (0752) 361137

HUTCHINGS, Leslie Bloom. b 10. OBE51. Magd Coll Cam BA32 MA36 Birm Univ DipTh59. **d** 60 **p** 61. V Modbury *Ex* 67-79; R Aveton Gifford 77-79; rtd 80. *Flat 9, Homepalms House, Brunswick Square, Torquay, Devon TQ1 4UT* Torquay (0803) 299432

HUTCHINGS, Norman Leslie. b 09. MVI. Wycliffe Hall Ox 42. **d** 43 **p** 43. V Ore Ch Ch *Chich* 62-77; rtd 77; Perm to Offic Chich and Roch from 77. *6 Sunnyside Road, Rusthall, Tunbridge Wells, Kent TN4 8RB* Tunbridge Wells (0892) 33264

HUTCHINGS, Robert Henry. b 45. Nottm Univ DTPS88. E Midl Min Tr Course 85. **d** 88 **p** 89. NSM Kibworth and Smeeton Westerby and Saddington *Leic* from 88; NSM Swinford w Catthorpe, Shawell and Stanford from 90. *16 Highcroft, Husbands Bosworth, Lutterworth, Leics LE17 6LF* Market Harborough (0858) 880131

HUTCHINS, Charles Henry. b 37. FRSA87 Leeds Univ BA60 BD67. Lambeth STh84 Ridley Hall Cam 60. **d** 62 **p** 63. C Kirkheaton *Wakef* 62-65; R Arthingworth w Kelmarsh and Harrington *Pet* 65-68; V Longner Armley *Ripon* 68-79; RD Armley 75-79; Prin CA Wilson Carlile Coll of Evang 79-88; Dir Tr CA 86-88; V Kingswood *Bris* 88-89; TR from 89. *Holy Trinity Vicarage, High Street, Kingswood, Bristol BS15 4AD* Bristol (0272) 673627

HUTCHINSON, Andrew Charles. b 63. Univ of Wales (Ban) BA84. Aston Tr Scheme 85 Chich Th Coll 87. **d** 89 **p** 90. C Burnley St Cath w St Alb and St Paul *Blackb* from 89. *St Alban's House, 472 Brunshaw Road, Burnley, Lancs BB10 3JB* Burnley (0282) 27670

HUTCHINSON, Charles William Aldersey. b 10. SS Coll Cam BA32 MA37. Ely Th Coll 33. **d** 33 **p** 34. R

Washingborough w Heighington *Linc* 37-86; Chapl RNVR 43-46; rtd 86. *Minard, Archentore Road, Fort William, Inverness-shire* Fort William (0397) 702616

HUTCHINSON, Canon Cyril Peter. b 37. Dur Univ BA61. Wm Temple Coll Rugby 61. **d** 63 **p** 64. C Birm St Paul *Birm* 63-67; Prin Community Relns Officer 66-69; Perm to Offic *Birm* 67-69; *Bradf* 69-75; Dir Bradf SHARE 69-76; Hon C Manningham 75-76; V Clayton *Bradf* 76-83; RD Bowling and Horton 80-83; TR Keighley St Andr from 83; Hon Can Bradf Cathl from 84. *The Rectory, Woodville Road, Keighley, W Yorkshire BD20 6JB* Keighley (0535) 607001

HUTCHINSON, David Bamford. b 29. QUB BSc53 TCD Div Test55 QUB DipEd57. **d** 55 **p** 56. C Lisburn Ch Ch *Conn* 55-57; Uganda 57-65; I Kilkeel *D & D* 66-75; I Willowfield 75-82; V Longfleet *Sarum* from 82. *32 Alverton Avenue, Poole, Dorset BH15 2QG* Poole (0202) 723359

HUTCHINSON, Harold. b 36. NE Ord Course. **d** 84 **p** 85. C Auckland St Andr and St Anne *Dur* 84-87; V Coundon from 87. *2 Collingwood Street, Coundon, Bishop Auckland, Co Durham DH14 8LG* Bishop Auckland (0388) 603312

HUTCHINSON, Hugh Edward. b 27. CEng FICE. Bps' Coll Cheshunt. **d** 61 **p** 62. C Limehouse St Anne *Lon* 61-64; C Townstall w Dartmouth *Ex* 64-67; V Ex St Mark 67-75; P-in-c Foston on the Wolds *York* 75-77; P-in-c N Frodingham 75-77; R Beeford w Lissett 75-77; R Beeford w Frodingham and Foston 77-80; RD N Holderness 79-80; P-in-c Appleton Roebuck w Acaster Selby 80-84; P-in-c Etton w Dalton Holme from 84. *The Rectory, Etton, Beverley, N Humberside HU17 7PQ* Market Weighton (0430) 810684

HUTCHINSON, Jeremy Olpherts. b 32. Or Coll Ox BA55 MA60 St Jo Coll Dur DipTh57. **d** 57 **p** 58. C Shoreditch St Leon *Lon* 57-60; V Hoxton St Jo w Ch Ch 60-78; Hon C Hackney 78-85; C Highbury Ch Ch w St Jo and St Sav Lon 85-91; P-in-c Hanley Road St Sav w St Paul from 91. *97 Corbyn Street, London N4 3BX*

HUTCHINSON, John Charles. b 44. K Coll Lon 64. **d** 69 **p** 70. C Portsea All SS *Portsm* 69-73; TV Fareham H Trin 73-78; P-in-c Pangbourne *Ox* 78-86; P-in-c Tidmarsh w Sulham 84-86; R Pangbourne w Tidmarsh and Sulham from 86. *The Rectory, St James's Close, Pangbourne, Reading RG8 7AP* Pangbourne (0734) 842928

HUTCHINSON, Ven John Desmond. b 17. TCD BA39 MA46 Lon Univ BD48 MTh56. CITC 39. **d** 40 **p** 41. Adn Cork *C, C & R* 67-86; w Ross 72-86; w Cloyne 73-86; I Moviddy Union 75-86; rtd 86. *23 Brampton Court, Bishopstown, Cork, Irish Republic* Cork (21) 342095

HUTCHINSON, Jonathan Mark. b 45. Cant Sch of Min 85. **d** 89 **p** 90. NSM Wickham Market w Pettistree and Easton *St E* from 89. *72 Westfield Road, Ipswich IP4 2XN* Ipswich (0473) 258021

HUTCHINSON, Keith. b 40. Keble Coll Ox BA63 MA68. St Steph Ho Ox 63. **d** 66 **p** 67. C Brighouse *Wakef* 66-72; R Workington St Mich *Carl* 72-83; V Mexborough *Sheff* from 83. *The Vicarage, Church Street, Mexborough, S Yorkshire S64 0ER* Mexborough (0709) 582321

HUTCHINSON, Paul Edward. b 33. K Coll Lon. **d** 59 **p** 60. C Bromley St Mich *Lon* 59-63; C Mill Hill St Mich 63-66; C Sandridge *St Alb* 66-73; V St Alb St Mary Marshalswick 73-80; V Tunstall *Lich* 80-91; RD Stoke N 82-91; V Lower Gornal from 91. *The Vicarage, Church Street, Lower Gornal, Dudley, W Midlands DY3 2PF* Sedgley (0902) 882023

HUTCHINSON, Pauline. b 49. St Jo Coll Nottm 88. **d** 90. Par Dn Sherwood *S'well* from 90. *56 Edwinstowe Drive, Sherwood, Nottingham NG5 3EP* Nottingham (0602) 620899

HUTCHINSON, Peter Francis. b 52. Portsm Poly HND74. Sarum & Wells Th Coll 87. **d** 89 **p** 90. C Honiton, Gittisham, Combe Raleigh, Monkton etc *Ex* from 89. *31 Milldale Crescent, Honiton, Devon EX14 8RB* Honiton (0404) 44371

HUTCHINSON, Raymond John. b 51. Liv Univ BSc73. Westcott Ho Cam 73. **d** 76 **p** 77. C Peckham St Jo *S'wark* 76-78; C Peckham St Jo w St Andr 78-79; C Prescot *Liv* 79-81; V Edge Hill St Dunstan 81-87; P-in-c Waterloo Park 87-89; P-in-c Litherland Ch Ch 87-89; V Waterloo Ch Ch and St Mary from 90. *Christ Church Vicarage, 22 Crosby Road South, Liverpool L22 1RQ* 051-920 7791

HUTCHINSON, Roland Louis. b 29. TCD BA51 MA61. **d** 52 **p** 53. C Mullabrack w Kilcluney *Arm* 52-54; C Dromore Cathl *D & D* 54-62; C-in-c Rathmullan w Tyrella 62-65; I 65-74; I Magheralin w Dollingstown from 74; Treas Dromore Cathl 86-90; Prec Dromore Cathl from 90. *New Forge Road, Mageralin, Co Armagh* Moira (0846) 611273

HUTCHINSON, Canon Stephen. b 38. St Chad's Coll Dur BA60 DipTh62. **d** 62 **p** 63. C Tividale *Lich* 62-68; V Walsall St Andr 68-73; R Headless Cross *Worc* 73-81; TR Redditch, The Ridge 81-91; RD Bromsgrove 85-91; Hon Can Worc Cathl from 88; V Stourbridge St Thos from 91. *St Thomas's Vicarage, 34 South Road, Stourbridge, W Midlands DY8 3TB* Stourbridge (0384) 2401

HUTCHINSON, Stephen Theodore. b 04. Keble Coll Ox BA29 MA31. **d** 72 **p** 72. C Arbroath *Bre* 72-75; C Dundee St Salvador 75-77; P-in-c Muchalls 77-82; rtd 82. *3 Yeaman Street, Carnoustie, Angus DD7 7AU* Carnoustie (0241) 54002

HUTCHINSON, Canon William David. b 27. Wycliffe Hall Ox 55. **d** 57 **p** 58. C Ipswich St Jo *St E* 57-60; R Combs 60-65; V Ipswich St Aug 65-76; R Ewhurst *Guildf* 76-81; V Aldeburgh w Hazlewood *St E* from 81; RD Saxmundham 83-88; Hon Can St E Cathl from 87. *The Vicarage, Church Walk, Aldeburgh, Suffolk IP15 5DU* Aldeburgh (0728) 452223

HUTCHINSON-CERVANTES, Ian Charles. b 62. Cant Univ (NZ) BSc84 Reading Univ MSc86 Jes Coll Cam BA89. Westcott Ho Cam 86. **d** 89 **p** 90. C Iffley *Ox* from 89. *Church House, The Oval, Oxford OX4 4SE* Oxford (0865) 718600

HUTCHISON, Geoffrey John. b 52. Trin Hall Cam MA76 Lon Univ CertEd76. Ridley Hall Cam 77. **d** 79 **p** 80. C Harold Wood *Chelmsf* 79-83; CF 83-89; Warden Viney Hill Chr Adventure Cen from 89; P-in-c Viney Hill *Glouc* from 89. *The Vicarage, Viney Hill, Lydney, Glos GL15 4NA* Dean (0594) 516162

HUTCHISON, Henry Peter. b 20. FIChemE CCC Ox MA49 TCD MA52 SS Coll Cam MA55. Linc Th Coll 80. **d** 81 **p** 82. Hon C Cam St Barn *Ely* 81-83; Hon C Ashley w Silverley 83-85; P-in-c Abbots Ripton w Wood Walton 85-90; P-in-c Kings Ripton 85-90; rtd 90. *Meadow Lodge, Church Farm Lane, Scarning, Dereham, Norfolk NR19 2NN* Dereham (0362) 698860

HUTT, Colin Villette. b 32. FCA. Glouc Sch of Min. **d** 89 **p** 90. NSM Ludlow *Heref* from 89. *Old Yew Tree Farmhouse, Ashton Bowdler, Ludlow, Shropshire SY8 4DJ* Ludlow (0584) 74513

HUTT, David Handley. b 38. AKC68. **d** 69 **p** 70. C Bedf Park *Lon* 69-70; C Westmr St Matt 70-73; PV and Succ S'wark Cathl *S'wark* 73-78; Chapl K Coll Taunton 78-82; V Bordesley SS Alb and Patr *Birm* 82-86; V St Marylebone All SS *Lon* from 86. *All Saints' Vicarage, 7 Margaret Street, London W1N 8JQ* 071-636 1788 or 636 9961

HUTTON, Brian Allan. b 40. Bps' Coll Cheshunt. **d** 69 **p** 70. C Newc St Matt w St Mary *Newc* 69-72; C Blyth St Mary 72-75; V Sheff St Cath Richmond Road *Sheff* 75-85; R Paisley St Barn *Glas* from 85; R Paisley H Trin from 87. *11 Tantallon Drive, Paisley, Renfrewshire PA2 9JT* 041-889 6498

HUTTON, David. b 61. Hull Univ BA82 CertEd83. Coll of Resurr Mirfield 85. **d** 87 **p** 88. C Adlington *Blackb* 87-90; C Hartlepool St Oswald *Dur* from 90. *St Oswald's Clergy House, Brougham Terrace, Hartlepool, Cleveland TS24 8EU* Hartlepool (0429) 273201

HUTTON, Canon David James. b 40. Dur Univ BA64 Kent Univ MA79. Coll of Resurr Mirfield 64. **d** 66 **p** 67. C Kirkby *Liv* 66-70; Asst Chapl Kent Univ *Cant* 70-73; Chapl 73-78; Six Preacher Cant Cathl 74-80; Chapl The Lon Hosp (Whitechapel) 78-83; Can Res and Chan Liv Cathl *Liv* from 83. *4 Cathedral Close, Liverpool L1 7BR* 051-709 6271 or 708 0938

HUTTON, Griffith Arthur Jeremy. b 31. Trin Hall Cam BA56 MA59. Linc Th Coll 56. **d** 58 **p** 59. C Hexham *Newc* 58-60; C Gosforth All SS 60-65; V Whitegate *Ches* 65-71; V Whitegate w Lt Budworth 71-78; R Dowdeswell and Andoversford w the Shiptons etc *Glouc* 78-91; V Newnham w Awre and Blakeney from 91. *The Vicarage, Unlawater Lane, Newnham, Glos GL14 1BL* Dean (0594) 516648

HUTTON, Henry John. b 12. **d** 71 **p** 72. Swaziland 71-75; C Ellesmere Port *Ches* 75-79; TV 79-82; rtd 82; Perm to Offic *Liv* and *Ches* from 82. *20 Ryland Park, Heswall, Wirral, Merseyside L61 9QJ* 051-648 4375

HUTTON, John Alexander. b 26. **d** 77 **p** 78. Hon C Edin St Mary *Edin* 77-89; NSM Glenurquhart *Mor* from 89; Dioc Chapl from 89. *St Ninian's House, Glenurquhart, Inverness IV3 6TN* Glenurquhart (04564) 264

HUTTON, Joseph Charles. b 21. DFC41. Westcott Ho Cam 63. **d** 65 **p** 66. V Warborough *Ox* 67-70; V Earley St Pet 70-75; R Ludgvan *Truro* 75-79; rtd 79. *2 Baines*

Close, Bourton-on-the-Water, Cheltenham, Glos GL54 2PU

HUTTON, Patrick George. b 41. Open Univ BA87. Chich Th Coll 65. **d** 68 **p** 69. C Palmers Green St Jo *Lon* 68-71; Guyana 71-80; P-in-c Stow Bardolph w Wimbotsham and Stow Bridge *Ely* 80-88; P-in-c Nordelph 80-88; V E Bedfont *Lon* from 88. *St Mary's Vicarage, 9 Hatton Road, Feltham, Middx TW14 8JR* 081-751 0088

HUTTON, Canon Stanley Peart. b 15. St Jo Coll Dur BA37 DipTh38 MA40. **d** 38 **p** 39. R Knotting w Souldrop *St Alb* 69-80; V Sharnbrook 69-80; rtd 80; Perm to Offic *Ex* from 80. *Flat 2, Coly House, Rosemary Lane, Colyton, Devon EX13 6LS* Colyton (0297) 52744

HUXHAM, Hector Hubert. b 29. Bris Univ BA55. Tyndale Hall Bris. **d** 56 **p** 57. C Eccleston St Luke *Liv* 56-58; C Heworth H Trin *York* 59-60; V Burley *Ripon* 61-66; Chapl St Jas Univ Hosp Leeds from 67. *3 Oakwell Oval, Leeds LS8 4AL* Leeds (0532) 668851

HUXHAM, Canon Peter Richard. b 38. Worc Coll Ox BA61 MA74. St Steph Ho Ox 61. **d** 63 **p** 64. C Gillingham *Sarum* 63-67; C Osmondthorpe St Phil *Ripon* 67-70; V Parkstone St Osmund *Sarum* 70-75; TR Parkstone St Pet w Branksea and St Osmund from 75; RD Poole from 85; Can and Preb Sarum Cathl from 85. *The Rectory, 19 Springfield Road, Poole, Dorset BH14 0LG* Parkstone (0202) 748860

HUXLEY, Keith. b 33. Ch Coll Cam BA57 MA61. Cuddesdon Coll 57. **d** 59 **p** 60. C Bowdon *Ches* 59-61; C Crewe Ch Ch 61-62; C Ches St Pet 62-64; Youth Chapl 62-68; Asst Chapl Ches Cathl 65-68; V Grange St Andr 68-73; TR E Runcorn w Halton 73-77; Home Sec Gen Syn Bd for Miss and Unity 77-83; Chapl to HM The Queen from 81; TR Gateshead *Dur* from 83; RD Gateshead from 88. *The Rectory, 91 Old Durham Road, Gateshead, Tyne & Wear NE8 4BS* 091-477 3990

HUXLEY, Canon Stephen Scott. b 30. Linc Th Coll 53. **d** 56 **p** 57. C Cullercoats St Geo *Newc* 56-59; C Eglingham 59-60; C N Gosforth 60-63; V Hartburn and Meldon 63-65; V Netherwitton 63-65; V Tynemouth Priory 65-74; V Warkworth and Acklington 74-78; P-in-c Tynemouth St Jo 78-81; V 81-87; Hon Can Newc Cathl from 82; V Wylam from 87. *The Vicarage, Wylam, Northd NE41 8AT* Wylam (0661) 853254

HUXLEY, William Thomas. b 31. Oak Hill Th Coll 60. **d** 63 **p** 64. C Rainham *Chelmsf* 63-66; C Heworth w Peasholme St Cuth *York* 66-67; R The Chignals w Mashbury *Chelmsf* 67-82; V Kirby le Soken 82-86; R Kirby-le-Soken w Gt Holland 86-87. *The Vicarage, 18 Thorpe Road, Kirby Cross, Frinton-on-Sea, Essex CO13 0LT* Frinton-on-Sea (0255) 5997

HUXTABLE, Michael George. b 29. St Jo Coll Cam BA50 MA54. S Dios Minl Tr Scheme 87. **d** 90 **p** 91. NSM Fisherton Anger *Sarum* from 90. *124 Bouverie Avenue South, Salisbury, Wilts SP2 8EA* Salisbury (0722) 334364

HUYTON, Stuart. b 37. St D Coll Lamp BA62 DipTh63. **d** 63 **p** 64. C Kingswinford H Trin *Lich* 63-66; C Leek St Edw 66-69; V Wigginton 69-76; V Wombourne 76-89; RD Trysull 79-84; P-in-c Bobbington 85-89; TR Wombourne w Trysull and Bobbington from 89. *The Vicarage, School Road, Wombourne, Wolverhampton WV5 9ED* Wolverhampton (0902) 892234

HUYTON, Susan Mary. b 57. Birm Univ BA79 DipTh86. Qu Coll Birm 83. **d** 86. C Connah's Quay *St As* 86-89; C Wrexham 89-90; Dn-in-c 90-91; TM from 91. *The Vicarage, 55 Princess Street, Wrexham, Clwyd LL13 7US* Wrexham (0978) 266145

HUZZEY, Peter George. b 48. Trin Coll Bris 74. **d** 76 **p** 77. C Bishopsworth *Bris* 76-79; V from 86; C Downend 79-80; TV Kings Norton *Birm* 80-86. *St Peter's Vicarage, 61 Fernsteed Road, Bristol BS13 8HE* Bristol (0272) 642734

HYATT, Robert Keith. b 34. Em Coll Cam BA59 MA63. Ridley Hall Cam 58. **d** 60 **p** 61. C Cheltenham St Mary *Glouc* 60-63; Asst Chapl K Edw Sch Witley 63-65; C Godalming *Guildf* 65-69; Hong Kong 69-78; V Claygate *Guildf* 78-91; TV Whitton *Sarum* from 91. *The Rectory, Back Lane, Ramsbury, Marlborough, Wilts SN8 2QH* Marlborough (0672) 202253

HYDE, Alan. b 09. Lon Univ BSc33. St Aid Birkenhead 46. **d** 48 **p** 51. V Satley *Dur* 70-77; rtd 77. *1 Farbridge Crescent, Consett, Co Durham DH8 0QA* Ebchester (0207) 562279

HYDE, Dennis Hugh. b 23. Leeds Univ BA56. Sarum Th Coll 60. **d** 60 **p** 61. V Shottermill *Guildf* 65-74; Past Consultant Clinical Th Assn 74-80; rtd 80. *32 Amis Avenue, New Haw, Weybridge, Surrey KT15 3ET* Weybridge (0932) 345526

HYDE, Edgar Bonsor. b 29. Clifton Th Coll 59. **d** 61 **p** 62. C Weston-super-Mare Ch Ch *B & W* 61-66; C Chipping Campden *Glouc* 66-70; R Longborough w Condicote and Sezincote 70-78; R Longborough, Sezincote, Condicote and the Swells from 78. *The Rectory, Longborough, Moreton-in-the-Marsh, Glos GL56 0QF* Cotswold (0451) 30447

HYDE, Vyvian Donald Wingfield. b 10. Dur Univ LTh33. Sarum Th Coll 30. **d** 33 **p** 34. V Charlton-by-Dover St Bart *Cant* 56-68; rtd 68; Lic to Offic *Cant* from 68. *30 Warren Drive, St Peters, Broadstairs, Kent CT10 2RS* Thanet (0843) 64120

HYDE-DUNN, Keith Frederick. b 43. Sarum Th Coll. **d** 69 **p** 70. Rhodesia 69-72; C Horsham *Chich* 73-77; P-in-c Fittleworth 77-86; P-in-c Graffham w Woolavington from 86. *The Rectory, Graffham, Petworth, W Sussex GU28 0NL* Graffham (07986) 247

HYDER, Geoffrey Frank. b 28. St Jo Coll Dur 49. **d** 53 **p** 54. C Kingston upon Hull H Trin *York* 53-56; C Southend St Sav Westcliff *Chelmsf* 56-59; V Haggerston All SS *Lon* 59-65; V Southwick St Pet *Chich* 65-68; Regional Org (Gtr Lon) Chr Aid 68-74; R Keston *Roch* 74-83; R Speldhurst w Groombridge and Ashurst from 83; RD Tunbridge Wells 86-91. *The Rectory, Southfield Road, Speldhurst, Tunbridge Wells, Kent TN3 0PD* Langton (0892) 862821

HYDER-SMITH, Brian John. b 45. MBIM MInstAM. E Anglian Minl Tr Course 84. **d** 87 **p** 88. NSM Huntingdon *Ely* 87-90; P-in-c Abbots Ripton w Wood Walton from 90; P-in-c Kings Ripton from 90. *Abbots Ripton, Huntingdon, Cambs PE17 2LE* Abbots Ripton (04873) 260

HYDON, Ms Veronica Weldon. b 52. N Lon Poly BA73 Maria Grey Coll Lon CertEd74. Aston Tr Scheme 87 Westcott Ho Cam 89. **d** 91. Par Dn Poplar *Lon* from 91. *11 Montague Place, London E14 0EX* 071-515 2487

HYLAND, Canon Cecil George. b 38. TCD BA62 MA78. **d** 63 **p** 64. C Belf St Nic *Conn* 63-66; C Monkstown *D & G* 66-68; Ch of Ireland Youth Officer 68-73; Chapl TCD 73-79; I Tullow *D & G* 79-90; RD Killiney from 86; I Howth from 90; Dir of Ords (Dub) from 91; Can Ch Ch Cathl Dub from 91. *The Rectory, Howth Road, Dublin 13, Irish Republic* Dublin (1) 323019

HYMAS, John Thomas. b 09. St Andr Coll Pampisford 46. **d** 47 **p** 48. V Sowerby *York* 58-77; rtd 77. *Hampden Nursing Home, 120 Duchy Road, Harrogate, N Yorkshire HG1 2HE* Harrogate (0423) 565804

HYSLOP, James Stott Davidson. b 09. Edin Th Coll 60. **d** 62 **p** 63. R Galashiels *Edin* 69-76; rtd 76. *22/6 Ferry Road Avenue, Edinburgh EH4 4BL* 031-332 9277

HYSLOP, Thomas James. b 54. St Andr Univ BD76. Edin Th Coll 76. **d** 78 **p** 79. C Whitehaven *Carl* 78-81; C Walney Is 81-83; P-in-c Gt Broughton and Broughton Moor 83-85; V 85-88; V Kells from 88. *St Peter's Vicarage, Cliff Road, Whitehaven, Cumbria CA28 9ET* Whitehaven (0946) 692496

HYSON, Peter Raymond. b 51. Open Univ BA80 BA87. Oak Hill Th Coll 85. **d** 87 **p** 88. C Billericay and Lt Burstead *Chelmsf* from 87. *25 Kelvedon Road, Billericay, Essex CM12 2DP* Billericay (0277) 658853

I

IBALL, Canon Charles Herbert. b 12. Leeds Univ BA34. Coll of Resurr Mirfield 34. **d** 36 **p** 37. R Curdworth *Birm* 70-77; rtd 77; Perm to Offic *Ches* from 77. *Flat 12, Manormead Home, Tilford Road, Hindhead, Surrey GU26 6RA* Hindhead (042873) 6696

IBALL, Charles Martin John. b 40. Lich Th Coll 67. **d** 69 **p** 70. C Dudley St Edm *Worc* 69-73; C W Bromwich St Jas *Lich* 73-76; V Oxley 76-80; Hon C Whittington w Weeford from 86. *75 Carlcroft, Stoneydelph, Tamworth, Staffs B77 4DW* Tamworth (0827) 896644

IBALL, Glyn. b 41. Univ of Wales BSc63. St Mich Coll Llan 63. **d** 65 **p** 66. C Ruabon *St As* 65-71; Hon C Bedf Park *Lon* from 71; Chapl Latymer Upper Sch Hammersmith from 71. *106 Woodstock Road, London W4 1EG* 081-994 4351

IBBOTSON, Alick. b 09. St Aid Birkenhead 49. **d** 51 **p** 52. V Bishop Monkton and Burton Leonard *Ripon* 56-81; rtd 81. *The Old Chapel, Oldstead, York YO6 4BL* Coxwold (03476) 596

ICELY, Lawrence Valentine. b 07. Cuddesdon Coll 40. **d** 40 **p** 41. V Hargrave *Ches* 56-74; rtd 74; Perm to Offic

Ches from 74. *61 Oxford Road, Runcorn, Cheshire WA7 4NU* Runcorn (09285) 77147

IDDON, Roy Edward. b 40. TCert61 Lanc Univ MA88. N Ord Course 83. **d** 83 **p** 84. Hd Teacher St Andr Primary Sch Blackb from 83; NSM Bolton St Matt w St Barn *Man* 83-88; Lic to AD Walmesley from 88. *28 New Briggs Fold, Egerton, Bolton BL7 9UL* Bolton (0204) 56589

IDLE, Christopher Martin. b 38. St Pet Coll Ox BA62. Clifton Th Coll 62. **d** 65 **p** 66. C Barrow St Mark *Carl* 65-68; C Camberwell Ch Ch *S'wark* 68-71; P-in-c Poplar St Matthias *Lon* 71-76; R Limehouse 76-89; P-in-c Palgrave w Wortham and Burgate *St E* 89; P-in-c Thrandeston, Stuston and Brome w Oakley 89; R N Hartismere from 89. *The Rectory, Oakley, Suffolk IP21 4AV* Diss (0379) 740322

IENT, Peter. b 25. Leeds Univ BA49. Coll of Resurr Mirfield 49. **d** 51 **p** 52. Chapl HM Rem Cen Warrington 69-74; HM Pris Albany 74-79; Birm 80-84; Coldingley 84-88; rtd 88. *61 Whites Road, Farnborough, Hants GU14 6PB*

IEVINS, Peter Valdis. b 54. Solicitor 79 St Jo Coll Ox BA75 MA81. Westcott Ho Cam 86. **d** 88 **p** 89. C Sawston *Ely* 88-91; C Babraham 88-91. *23 Teversham Way, Sawston, Cambridge CB2 4DF* Cambridge (0223) 832955

IKIN, Gordon Mitchell. b 30. AKC57. **d** 58 **p** 59. C Leigh St Mary *Man* 58-61; V Westleigh St Paul 61-72; V Thornham St Jas from 72. *St James's Vicarage, 120 Shaw Road, Thornham, Rochdale, Lancs OL16 4SQ* Rochdale (0706) 45256

ILES, Canon Paul Robert. b 37. FRCO65 Fitzw Coll Cam BA59 MA64 St Edm Hall Ox MA80. Sarum Th Coll 59. **d** 61 **p** 62. Chapl Bp Wordsworth Sch Salisbury 61-67; C Salisbury St Mich *Sarum* 61-64; Min Can Sarum Cathl 64-67; C Bournemouth St Pet *Win* 67-72; R Filton *Bris* 72-79; V Ox SS Phil and Jas w St Marg *Ox* 79-83; Can Res and Prec Heref Cathl *Heref* from 83. *The Canon's House, The Close, Hereford HR1 2NG* Hereford (0432) 266193

ILIFF, Hugh Graham. b 07. Trin Hall Cam BA31 MA35. **d** 32 **p** 33. India 60-72; rtd 72; Chapl Le Touquet *Eur* 73-76; Perm to Offic *Roch* from 77. *Flat 24, Bromley College, Bromley BR1 1PE* 081-290 1439

ILIFFE, Walter Richard. b 17. ALCD41. **d** 44 **p** 45. R Broome *Worc* 68-87; rtd 87. *Flat 11, The Quadrangle, Beauchamp Community, Newland, Malvern, Worcs WR13 5AX* Malvern (0684) 568921

ILLING, Eric James. b 33. Kelham Th Coll 54 Chich Th Coll 55. **d** 57 **p** 58. C Leeds St Aid *Ripon* 57-60; C Leeds All SS 60-62; C E Grinstead St Swithun *Chich* 62-65; V Middleton St Mary *Ripon* 65-74; R Felpham w Middleton *Chich* 74-81; Chapl R Devon and Ex Hosp (Wonford) from 81; TR Heavitree w Ex St Paul *Ex* 81-91; R Bradninch and Clyst Hydon from 91. *The Rectory, West End Road, Bradninch, Exeter EX5 4QS* Exeter (0392) 881264

ILLINGWORTH, John Patrick Paul. b 34. New Coll Ox BA59 DipTh61 MA63. Chich Th Coll 61. **d** 63 **p** 64. C Brighouse *Wakef* 63-66; C Willesden St Andr *Lon* 66-70; Chapl Gothenburg w Halmstad and Jonkoping *Eur* 70-74; Perm to Offic *Chich* 74; V Ryhill *Wakef* 74-82; R Weston Longville w Morton and the Withinghams *Nor* from 82. *The Rectory, Weston Longville, Norwich NR9 5JU* Norwich (0603) 880163

ILLINGWORTH, William. b 23. E Midl Min Tr Course 78. **d** 81 **p** 82. NSM Allestree *Derby* 81-84; NSM Charlesworth 84-87; NSM Dinting Vale 84-87; NSM Charlesworth and Dinting Vale from 87. *19 Werneth Road, Simmondley, Glossop, Derbyshire SK13 9NF* Glossop (0457) 853866

ILOTT, Philip Edwin. b 36. Roch Th Coll 66. **d** 68 **p** 69. C Leavesden All SS *St Alb* 68-71; C-in-c Godshill CD *Portsm* 71-77; V Mayfield *Chich* 77-81; V Bexhill St Barn 81-84; Perm to Offic *Chich* from 85. *Albany House, 11 Albany Road, Bexhill-on-Sea, E Sussex TN40 1BY*

ILSON, John Robert. b 37. Leeds Univ BSc59 Lon Univ BD64 CertEd65. ALCD63. **d** 64 **p** 65. C Kennington St Mark *S'wark* 64-67; C Sydenham H Trin 67-70; Asst Dir RE *Sheff* 70-77; R Hooton Roberts 70-75; R Hooton Roberts w Ravenfield 75-77; P-in-c Kidderminster St Geo *Worc* 77-81; TR 81-85; P-in-c Powyke from 85. *The Vicarage, 31 The Greenway, Powick, Worcester WR2 4RZ* Worcester (0905) 830270

IMMS, William George Law. b 11. Lich Th Coll 64. **d** 64 **p** 65. C Swindon New Town *Bris* 69-76; Hon C Cricklade w Latton 76-81; rtd 77. *29 Trewartha Park, Weston-super-Mare, Avon BS23 2RR* Weston-super-Mare (0934) 627586

IMPEY, Miss Joan Mary. b 35. Lon Univ CertRK69. Dalton Ho Bris 65. **dss** 74 **d** 87. Kennington St Mark *S'wark* 67-75; Barking St Marg w St Patr *Chelmsf* 75-81; Harwell w Chilton *Ox* 81-87; Par Dn from 87. *31 Crafts End, Chilton, Didcot, Oxon OX11 0SA* Abingdon (0235) 832366

IMPEY, Patricia Irene. b 45. Birm Univ BA67. Carl Dioc Tr Course 88. **d** 90. Par Dn Blackpool St Paul *Blackb* from 90. *St John's Vicarage, 19 Leamington Road, Blackpool FY1 4HD* Blackpool (0253) 20626

IMPEY, Canon Richard. b 41. Em Coll Cam BA63 MA67. Harvard Univ ThM67. Ridley Hall Cam 67. **d** 68 **p** 69. C Birm St Martin *Birm* 68-72; Dir of Tr *B & W* 72-79; Dir of Ords 76-79; V Blackpool St Jo *Blackb* from 79; RD Blackpool 84-90; Hon Can Blackb Cathl from 89. *St John's Vicarage, 19 Leamington Road, Blackpool FY1 4HD* Blackpool (0253) 20626

INCE, Preb Edgar Kenelm Peter. b 16. DFC45. Wells Th Coll 54. **d** 56 **p** 57. R Ashwater *Ex* 66-73; R Ashwater w Halwill and Beaworthy 73-86; RD Holsworthy 74-80; Preb Ex Cathl from 85; rtd 86. *Prispen, Longmeadow Road, Lympstone, Exmouth, Devon EX8 5LF* Exmouth (0395) 266597

INCE, Peter Reginald. b 26. Bp's Coll Calcutta 48. **d** 51 **p** 52. India 51-55; C Leek St Luke *Lich* 55-57; C Milton 57-59; C Lewisham St Jo Southend *S'wark* 59-62; R Loddington w Cransley *Pet* 62-75; V Snibston *Leic* 75-79; R Mickleham *Guildf* from 79. *The Rectory, Mickleham, Dorking, Surrey RH5 6EB* Leatherhead (0372) 378335

IND, Dominic Mark. b 63. Lanc Univ BA87. Ridley Hall Cam 87. **d** 90 **p** 91. C Birch w Fallowfield *Man* from 90. *13 Cawdor Road, Fallowfield, Manchester M14 6LG* 061-224 4077

IND, Philip William David. b 35. K Coll Lon BD82. Wycliffe Hall Ox 74 Cranmer Hall Dur 59. **d** 65 **p** 66. C Ipswich St Jo *St E* 65-67; C Charlton Kings St Mary *Glouc* 67-71; R Woolstone w Gotherington and Oxenton 71-74; Chapl Alleyn's Sch Dulwich 76-81; C Beckenham St Geo *Roch* 83-85; V Bromley St Jo 85-87; Perm to Offic *Ox* 88-91; P-in-c Hurley from 91; P-in-c Stubbings from 91. *The Vicarage, Hurley, Maidenhead, Berks SL6 5LT* Littlewick Green (062882) 4892

✠**IND, Rt Rev William.** b 42. Leeds Univ BA64. Coll of Resurr Mirfield 64. **d** 66 **p** 67 **c** 87. C Feltham *Lon* 66-71; C Northolt St Mary 71-73; TV Basingstoke *Win* 73-87; Vice-Prin Aston Tr Scheme 79-82; Dioc Dir of Ords *Win* 82-87; Hon Can Win Cathl from 84; Suff Bp Grantham *Linc* from 87; Dean Stamford from 87. *Fairacre, 243 Barrowby Road, Grantham, Lincs NG31 8NP* Grantham (0476) 64722

INDER, Patrick John. b 30. K Coll Lon BD54 AKC54. St Boniface Warminster. **d** 55 **p** 56. V Hanwell St Mellitus *Lon* 61-77; R Rawmarsh w Parkgate *Sheff* 77-80; rtd 80; Hon C Sheff St Matt *Sheff* 82-88; Perm to Offic *Win* from 90. *61 Lea Lane, Netherton, Huddersfield HD4 7DP* Huddersfield (0484) 633179

INDER, Robert William Jack. b 15. AKC38. **d** 38 **p** 39. C Drypool St Andr and St Pet *York* 38-42; C Carl St Jo *Carl* 42-43; R Stapleton 43-51; V Sinnington *York* from 51. *The Vicarage, Sinnington, York YO6 6SE* Kirkbymoorside (0751) 31422

INESON, David Antony. b 36. DPS. ALCD62. **d** 62 **p** 63. C Sandal St Helen *Wakef* 62-65; C Birm St Geo *Birm* 66-71; V Horton *Bradf* 71-80; RD Bowling and Horton 78-80; V Sedbergh, Cautley and Garsdale 80-86; C Firbank, Howgill and Killington 81-86; TV Langley and Parkfield *Man* 86-88. *Address temp unknown*

INGALL, Heber Doveton. b 18. ALCD43. **d** 43 **p** 44. R Benefield *Pet* 56-70; P-in-c Stoke Doyle 63-67; rtd 70. *Pilgrims Lodge, Pilgrims Way, Canterbury, Kent*

INGAMELLS, Harold Frankish. b 34. Codrington Coll Barbados. **d** 59 **p** 60. Barbados 59-66; P-in-c Horbury Bridge *Wakef* 66-68; V Horbury Junction 68-75; V Monk Bretton 75-83; P-in-c Hoyland Swaine 83-84; V Thurlstone 83-84; Chapl Community of St Pet Woking from 84. *70 Sandy Lane, Woking, Surrey GU22 8BH* Woking (0483) 26267

INGAMELLS, Ronald Sidney. b 32. MITD. AKC56. **d** 57 **p** 58. C Leeds Gipton Epiphany *Ripon* 57-59; C Gt Yarmouth *Nor* 59-64; Dioc Youth Officer 64-79; Hon C Nor St Pet Mancroft 64-79; Sec Tr Development and Chr Educn Nat Coun YMCAs from 79; P-in-c Lemsford *St Alb* from 79. *7 High Oaks Road, Welwyn Garden City, Herts AL8 7BJ* Welwyn Garden (0707) 322621

INGE, John Geoffrey. b 55. St Chad's Coll Dur BSc77 Keble Coll Ox PGCE79. Coll of Resurr Mirfield. **d** 84

p 85. Asst Chapl Lancing Coll Sussex 84-86; Jun Chapl Harrow Sch Middx 86-89; Sen Chapl 89-90; V Wallsend St Luke *Newc* from 90. *St Luke's Vicarage, 148 Park Road, Wallsend, Tyne & Wear NE28 7QS* 091-262 3723

INGE, Lawrence Gane. b 05. St Aid Birkenhead 48. **d** 48 **p** 49. V Purse Caundle w Stourton Caundle *Sarum* 65-72; rtd 72; Chapl Westmr Memorial Hosp Shaftesbury 78-84; Perm to Offic *Chich* from 85. *Rochester House, College of St Barnabas, Lingfield, Surrey RH7 6NJ* Dormans Park (034287) 288

INGHAM, John Edmund. b 34. Reading Univ BA56. Clifton Th Coll 58. **d** 60 **p** 61. C Rodbourne Cheney *Bris* 60-63; C Tunbridge Wells St Jo *Roch* 63-67; V Sevenoaks Weald 67-82; V Farrington Gurney *B & W* from 82; V Paulton from 82; RD Midsomer Norton from 88. *The Vicarage, Church Street, Paulton, Bristol BS18 5LG* Midsomer Norton (0761) 416581

INGHAM, Russell Edward. b 39. Glas Univ MA61 Keble Coll Ox BA63 MA67. Cuddesdon Coll 63. **d** 64 **p** 65. Chapl St Mary's Cathl *Glas* 64-69; Warden St John's Youth Cen Tuebrook Liv 69-71; R Port Glas 71-77; R St Andrews All SS *St And* from 77. *All Saints' Rectory, North Street, St Andrews, Fife KY16 9AQ* St Andrews (0334) 73193

INGHAM, Stephen Charles. b 49. S'wark Ord Course 75. **d** 78 **p** 79. C Lee St Aug *S'wark* 78-82; R Gt w Lt Yeldham *Chelmsf* 82-84; TV Rye *Chich* 84-90; V Alderney *Win* from 90. *The Vicarage, Alderney, Guernsey, Channel Islands* Alderney (048182) 822335

INGLEBY, Anthony Richard. b 48. Keele Univ BA72. Trin Coll Bris. **d** 83 **p** 84. C Plymouth St Jude *Ex* 83-88; R Lanreath *Truro* from 88; V Pelynt from 88. *The Rectory, Lanreath, Looe, Cornwall PL13 2NU* Lanreath (0503) 20310

INGLEDEW, Peter David Gordon. b 48. AKC77. St Steph Ho Ox 77. **d** 78 **p** 79. C Whorlton *Newc* 78-81; C Poplar *Lon* 81-83; TV 83-85; V Tottenham H Trin 85-90. *Flat 3, 18 Chesham Place, Kemptown, Brighton, E Sussex*

INGLESBY, Eric Vredenburg (Paul). b 15. Qu Coll Ox BA46 MA63. Wycliffe Hall Ox 63. **d** 64 **p** 64. R Caythorpe *Linc* 66-70; C Scilly Is *Truro* 70-73; C Plymouth St Andr w St Paul and St Geo *Ex* 73-76; rtd 76. *St Helen's House, 7 Magdalene Street, Glastonbury, Somerset BA6 9EW* Glastonbury (0458) 31596 or 31678

INGLESBY, Richard Eric. b 47. Birm Univ BSc69 Bris Univ CertEd74. Wycliffe Hall Ox 85. **d** 87 **p** 88. C Cheltenham Ch Ch *Glouc* from 87. *1 Kensington Avenue, Cheltenham, Glos GL50 2NQ* Cheltenham (0242) 515915

INGLIS, Canon Angus. b 08. TD46. St Jo Coll Ox BA30 MA34. Westcott Ho Cam 30. **d** 31 **p** 32. R Nottm St Pet and St Jas *S'well* 48-79; Hon Can S'well Minster 55-79; rtd 79. *The Old Rectory, Belton, Grantham, Lincs NG32 2LW* Grantham (0476) 74545

INGRAM, Bernard Richard. b 40. Lon Coll of Div 66. **d** 66 **p** 67. C Bromley Common St Aug *Roch* 66-70; C Gravesend St Geo 70-74; Chapl Joyce Green Hosp Dartford 75-83; V Dartford St Edm *Roch* 75-83; C Strood St Fran from 83. *St Francis's Vicarage, Galahad Avenue, Strood, Rochester, Kent ME2 2YS* Medway (0634) 717162

INGRAM, Miss Emmeline Jessica Anne. b 26. Gilmore Ho 53. **dss** 54 **d** 87. Ind Chapl *Chelmsf* 68-82; rtd 86; Leigh-on-Sea St Jas *Chelmsf* 86-87; Hon Par Dn from 87. *68 Suffolk Avenue, Leigh-on-Sea, Essex SS9 3HF* Southend-on-Sea (0702) 773680

INGRAM, Gary Simon. b 58. K Coll Lon BD AKC. Ripon Coll Cuddesdon. **d** 83 **p** 84. C Spalding *Linc* 83-87; C Heaton Ch Ch *Man* 87-89; V Colne H Trin *Blackb* from 89. *Holy Trinity Vicarage, 49 Penrith Crescent, Colne, Lancs BB8 8JS* Colne (0282) 863431

INGRAM, Michael. b 28. St Jo Coll Dur 49. **d** 53 **p** 54. Chapl RAF 60-76; P-in-c St Enoder *Truro* 76-79; rtd 90. *1 Bracewood Gardens, Croydon CR0 5JL*

INGRAM, Peter Anthony. b 53. N Ord Course 83. **d** 86 **p** 87. C Maltby *Sheff* 86-89; TV Gt Snaith from 89. *31 Saffron Drive, Snaith, Goole, N Humberside DN14 9LH* Goole (0405) 860843

INGRAMS, Peter Douglas. b 56. Wheaton Coll Illinois BA77 Ox Univ BA80. Wycliffe Hall Ox 78. **d** 83 **p** 84. C Rowner *Portsm* 83-86; C Petersfield w Sheet 86-90; V Sheet from 90. *Sheet Vicarage, 2 Pulens Lane, Petersfield, Hants GU31 4DB* Petersfield (0730) 63673

INKPEN, Richard John. b 28. AKC56. **d** 58 **p** 59. C Willesden St Mary *Lon* 58-61; C Hendon St Mary 61-66; C-in-c S Kenton Annunciation CD 66-69; Chapl Montreux w Gstaad *Eur* 69-70; V Blackmoor *Portsm* from 70; RD Petersfield 80-85. *The Vicarage, Blackmoor, Liss, Hants GU33 6BN* Bordon (0420) 473548

INKPIN, David Leonard. b 32. CChem MRSC55 Liv Univ BSc54. E Midl Min Tr Course 83. **d** 86 **p** 87. NSM Market Rasen *Linc* from 86. *Weelsby House, Legsby Road, Market Rasen, Lincs LN8 3DY* Market Rasen (0673) 843360

INKPIN, Jonathan David Francis. b 60. Mert Coll Ox MA81. Ripon Coll Cuddesdon BA85. **d** 86 **p** 87. C Hackney *Lon* 86-88; Tutor Ripon Coll Cuddesdon 88-90; C Cuddesdon *Ox* 88-90; TV Gateshead *Dur* from 90. *3 Wordsworth Street, Gateshead, Tyne & Wear NE8 3HE* 091-478 2730

INMAN, John Phillip. b 12. St Jo Coll Dur BA35 DipTh36 MA38. **d** 36 **p** 37. V Grindon *Dur* 56-60; Lic to Offic *Carl* 60-77; rtd 77; Perm to Offic *Carl* from 77. *16 Collingwood Close, Coniston, Cumbria LA21 8DZ* Coniston (05394) 41629

INMAN, Malcolm Gordon. b 33. Edin Th Coll 58. **d** 60 **p** 61. C Lundwood *Wakef* 60-63; C Heckmondwike 63-70; V Wrenthorpe 70-75; V Cleckheaton St Jo from 75. *St John's Vicarage, 33 Ashbourne Avenue, Cleckheaton, W Yorkshire BD19 5JH* Cleckheaton (0274) 874896

INMAN, Mark Henry. b 31. Lon Univ BSc53. E Anglian Minl Tr Course 80. **d** 83 **p** 84. Chapl HM Young Offender Inst Hollesley Bay Colony 83-90; Hon C Orford w Sudbourne, Chillesford, Butley and Iken *St E* 83-85; Hon C Alderton w Ramsholt and Bawdsey from 85. *Green Knowe, School Lane, Hollesley, Woodbridge, Suffolk IP12 3RE* Shottisham (0394) 411667

INMAN, Martin. b 50. K Coll Lon BD72 AKC73. St Aug Coll Cant 72. **d** 73 **p** 74. C Bridgnorth St Mary *Heref* 73-77; C Parkstone St Pet w Branksea and St Osmund *Sarum* 77-79; V Willenhall St Anne *Lich* 79-85; Chapl Yeovil Distr Gen Hosp 85-91; TV Yeovil *B & W* 85-88; R Barwick 88-91; Chapl Jersey Gp of Hosps from 91. *Old Rectory, St Lawrence, Jersey, Channel Islands*

INMAN, Paul Stuart. b 60. R Agric Coll Cirencester HND82 DipAI83 Nottm Univ BTh90. Linc Th Coll 87. **d** 90 **p** 91. C Hulme Ascension *Man* from 90. *The Arnott Centre, 2 Tarnbrook Walk, Manchester M15 6NL* 061-226 4694

INMAN, Thomas Jeremy. b 45. Rhodes Univ Grahamstown BA67. St Steph Ho Ox 67. **d** 69 **p** 70. C Deptford St Paul *S'wark* 69-72; S Africa 72-76; P-in-c Donnington *Chich* 76-80; V Hangleton 80-86; V Bosham from 86. *The Vicarage, Bosham, Chichester, W Sussex PO18 8HX* Bosham (0243) 573228

INNES, Donald John. b 32. St Jo Coll Ox BA54 MA. Westcott Ho Cam 56. **d** 56 **p** 57. C St Marylebone St Mark Hamilton Terrace *Lon* 56-58; C Walton-on-Thames *Guildf* 58-67; Chapl Moor Park Coll Farnham 67-76; P-in-c Tilford *Guildf* from 76. *The Vicarage, Tilford, Farnham, Surrey GU10 2DA* Frensham (025125) 2333

INNES, Donald Keith. b 33. St Jo Coll Ox BA56 MA60 Lon Univ BD58. Clifton Th Coll 56. **d** 58 **p** 59. C Harold Hill St Paul *Chelmsf* 58-61; C Ealing Dean St Jo *Lon* 61-65; V Westacre *Nor* 65-70; R Gayton Thorpe w E Walton 65-70; V Woking St Paul *Guildf* 70-78; R Alfold and Loxwood 78-88; V Doddington w Wychling *Cant* 88-90; V Newnham 88-90; V Doddington, Newnham and Wychling from 90. *The Vicarage, The Street, Doddington, Sittingbourne, Kent ME9 0BH* Doddington (079586) 265

INNES, James Michael. b 32. Lon Univ BA56 BD59. Clifton Th Coll 59. **d** 59 **p** 60. C Blackpool St Thos *Blackb* 59-62; Tutor Clifton Th Coll 62-65; V Burton All SS *Lich* 65-73; V Ashton on Mersey St Mary *Ches* 73-90; P-in-c Brereton w Swettenham 90-91; R from 91. *The Rectory, Brereton, Sandbach, Cheshire CW11 9RY* Holmes Chapel (0477) 33263

INSLEY, Michael George Pitron. b 47. Trin Coll Ox BA69 MA70 Nottm Univ MPhil85. Wycliffe Hall Ox 69. **d** 72 **p** 73. C Beckenham Ch Ch *Roch* 72-76; P-in-c Cowden 76-79; Lect St Jo Coll Nottm 79-85; Lic to Offic *S'well* 79-85; V Tidebrook *Chich* from 85; V Wadhurst from 85. *The Vicarage, Wadhurst, E Sussex TN5 6AA* Wadhurst (089288) 2083

INVERNESS, Provost of. See HORSLEY, Very Rev Alan Avery

INWOOD, Preb Richard Neil. b 46. Univ Coll Ox BSc70 MA73 Nottm Univ BA73. St Jo Coll Nottm 71. **d** 74 **p** 75. C Fulwood *Sheff* 74-78; C St Marylebone All So w SS Pet and Jo *Lon* 78-81; V Bath St Luke *B & W* 81-89; R Yeovil w Kingston Pitney from 89; Preb Wells Cathl from 90. *The Rectory, 5 West Park, Yeovil, Somerset BA20 1DE* Yeovil (0935) 75396

ION, Robert Henry. b 18. Pemb Coll Ox BA41 MA44 BD47. Ripon Hall Ox 41. **d** 42 **p** 49. Hd Div Crewe Coll

of Educn 56-65; Sen Lect 65-73; R Church Lawton *Ches* 73-78; rtd 78. *25 Leachfield Road, Galgate, Lancaster LA2 0NX* Lancaster (0524) 751653

IORNS, Derrick John. b 11. AKC33. **d** 34 **p** 35. V Maldon All SS w St Pet *Chelmsf* 53-71; R Gt Warley St Mary 71-72; P-in-c Childerditch w Lt Warley 71-72; R Gt Warley w Childerditch 72-81; P-in-c Ingrave 79-81; rtd 81. *45 South Drive, Brentwood, Essex CM1 4DL* Brentwood (0277) 220777

IPGRAVE, Michael Geoffrey. b 58. Or Coll Ox BA78. Ripon Coll Cuddesdon 79. **d** 82 **p** 83. C Oakham, Hambleton, Egleton, Braunston and Brooke *Pet* 82-85; Japan 85-87; TV Leic Ascension *Leic* 87-90; Dioc Chapl Relns w People of Other Faiths from 91; AP Leic H Trin w St Jo from 91. *27 Tudor Road, Leicester* Leicester (0533) 622628

IPSWICH, Archdeacon of. See GIBSON, Ven Terence Allen

IREDALE, Simon Peter. b 56. Cam Univ BA78 MPhil80. Wycliffe Hall Ox 83. **d** 86 **p** 87. C Thirsk *York* 86-89; Asst Chapl Norfolk and Nor Hosp 89-90; P-in-c Kexby w Wilberfoss *York* from 90; Sub-Chapl HM Pris Full Sutton from 90. *The Vicarage, Wilberfoss, York YO4 5NG* Wilberfoss (07595) 426

IRELAND, David Arthur. b 45. MICFRM87 Mert Coll Ox BA67 MA71. Cuddesdon Coll 67. **d** 69 **p** 70. C Chapel Allerton *Ripon* 69-72; C Hampstead St Nic *St Alb* 72-76; R Clifton 76-84. *43 Harefield Avenue, Cheam, Surrey SM2 7ND* 081-642 3781

IRELAND, Leslie Sydney. b 55. York Univ BA76. St Jo Coll Nottm 83. **d** 86 **p** 87. C Harwood *Man* 86-89; C Davyhulme St Mary 89-90; V Bardsley from 90. *The Vicarage, Byrth Road, Oldham, Lancs OL8 2TJ* 061-624 9004

IRELAND, Mrs Lucy Annabel. b 53. Univ of Zimbabwe BSc74. St Jo Coll Nottm 81. **dss** 85 **d** 87. Mansf St Jo *S'well* 85-87; Hon Par Dn Harwood *Man* 87-89; Hon Par Dn Bardsley from 90. *The Vicarage, Byrth Road, Oldham OL8 2TJ* 061-624 9004

IRELAND, Mark Campbell. b 60. St Andr Univ MTh81. Wycliffe Hall Ox 82. **d** 84 **p** 85. C Blackb St Gabr *Blackb* 84-87; C Lanc St Mary 87-89; Chapl HM Pris Lanc 87-89; V Baxenden *Blackb* from 89. *The Vicarage, Langford Street, Baxenden, Accrington, Lancs BB5 2RF* Accrington (0254) 232471

IRESON, Arthur Stanley. b 05. St Cath Coll Cam BA30 MA34. Ridley Hall Cam 29 Lich Th Coll 30. **d** 30 **p** 31. C Radford *Cov* 30-32; C Hatf *St Alb* 32-36; V Watford St Jas 36-42; Chapl Watford Hosps 36-45; Chapl RAFVR 40-46; Can Res Cov Cathl *Cov* 46-50; Bp's Dom Chapl 46-47; Relig Adv Nat Assn Boys' Clubs 47-69; Teacher Wyggeston Boys' Sch Leic 55-72; Lic to Offic *Leic* 69-72; Hon C Leic St Jas from 72; Hd Master Laurels Coll Leic 72-79. *348 Victoria Park Road, Leicester LE2 1FX* Leicester (0533) 704715

IRESON, Ms Gillian Dorothy. b 39. Gilmore Ho 67. **dss** 72 **d** 87. Stepney St Dunstan and All SS *Lon* 72-87; Par Dn from 87. *St Faith's House, Shandy Street, London E1 4ST* 071-790 4194

IRESON, Canon Gordon Worley. b 06. Hatf Coll Dur LTh32 BA33. Edin Th Coll 29. **d** 33 **p** 34. Can Res St Alb 58-73; rtd 73. *College of St Barnabas, Blackberry Lane, Lingfield, Surrey RH7 6NJ* Lingfield (0342) 87710

IRESON, Philip. b 52. Newc Univ BSc73. St Jo Coll Nottm LTh84. **d** 84 **p** 85. C Owlerton *Sheff* 84-87; V The Marshland from 87; Perm to Offic *Linc* from 90; Chapl HM Young Offender Inst Hatf from 91. *The Vicarage, Swinefleet, Goole, N Humberside DN14 8DH* Reedness (040584) 643

IRESON, Richard Henry. b 46. Linc Th Coll 69. **d** 71 **p** 72. C Spilsby w Hundleby *Linc* 71-74; TV Grantham w Manthorpe 74-76; R Claypole 76-79; P-in-c Westborough w Dry Doddington and Stubton 76-77; R 77-79; R Bratoft w Irby-in-the-Marsh 79-86; V Burgh le Marsh 79-86; V Orby 79-86; R Welton-le-Marsh w Gunby 79-86; R Wyberton from 86. *The Rectory, Wyberton, Boston, Lincs PE21 7AF* Boston (0205) 622096

IRETON, Robert John. b 56. Bris Univ BEd. Oak Hill Th Coll BA. **d** 84 **p** 85. C Bromley Ch Ch *Roch* 84-87; TV Greystoke, Matterdale, Mungrisdale & W'millock *Carl* 87-90; V Falconwood, Bp Ridley *Roch* from 90. *The Vicarage, The Green, Welling, Kent DA16 2PG* 081-298 0065

IRONS, Barry. b 39. Wilson Carlile Coll 57 Coll of Resurr Mirfield 82. **d** 83 **p** 84. CA from 57; C Willersey, Saintbury, Weston-sub-Edge etc *Glouc* 83-85; R Scalford w Goadby Marwood and Wycombe etc *Leic* 85-88; P-in-c Clun w Chapel Lawn, Bettws-y-Crwyn and Newc *Heref* 88-91; Bp's Officer for Evang from 91; P-in-c Breinton from 91. *The Vicarage, Breinton, Hereford HR4 7PG* Hereford (0432) 273447

IRONSIDE, John Edmund. b 31. Peterho Cam BA55 MA59. Qu Coll Birm 55. **d** 57 **p** 58. C Spring Park *Cant* 57-60; C Guernsey St Sampson *Win* 60-63; Thailand 63-66; V Guernsey St Jo *Win* 66-72; V Sholing 72-82; R Guernsey St Sampson from 82; Miss to Seamen from 82. *The Rectory, Grandes Maisons Road, St Sampson, Guernsey, Channel Islands* Guernsey (0481) 44710

IRVINE, Christopher Paul. b 51. Nottm Univ BTh75 Lanc Univ MA76. Kelham Th Coll 73. **d** 76 **p** 76. Chapl Lanc Univ *Blackb* 76-77; C Stoke Newington St Mary *Lon* 77-80; Chapl Sheff Univ *Sheff* 80-85; Chapl St Edm Hall Ox from 85; Tutor St Steph Ho Ox 85-90; Vice-Prin St Steph Ho Ox from 91. *7 Warwick Street, Oxford* Oxford (0865) 245511 or 279021

IRVINE, Gerard Philip. b 30. QUB BA52. Edin Th Coll 56. **d** 56 **p** 57. Chapl St Andr Cathl *Ab* 56-58; Prec St Andr Cathl 58-59; C Belf Malone (St Jo) *Conn* 61-66; Chapl Community of St Jo Ev Dublin 67-77; C Dub Sandymount *D & G* from 77. *Flat 32, Mitchel House, Appian Way, Dublin 6, Irish Republic* Dublin (1) 760450

IRVINE, James Clyde. b 35. QUB BA57 NUU BPhil(Ed)83. CITC 59. **d** 59 **p** 60. C Belf St Luke *Conn* 59-62; C Lisburn Ch Ch Cathl 62-65; R Duneane w Ballyscullion 65-69; I Kilbride 69-74; Chapl Ballyclare High Sch from 73. *1A Rathmena Avenue, Ballyclare, Co Antrim BT39 9HX* Ballyclare (09603) 22933

IRVINE, John Dudley. b 49. Sussex Univ BA70. Wycliffe Hall Ox BA80. **d** 81 **p** 82. C Brompton H Trin w Onslow Square St Paul *Lon* 81-85; P-in-c Kensington St Barn from 85. *St Barnabas's Vicarage, 23 Addison Road, London W14 8LH* 071-602 6518

IRVINE, Preb John Graham Gerard Charles. b 20. Mert Coll Ox BA42 MA46. St Steph Ho Ox 42. **d** 45 **p** 46. V Westmr St Matt *Lon* 69-86; Preb St Paul's Cathl 82-86; rtd 86. *42 Montpelier Road, Brighton, E Sussex BN1 3BA* Brighton (0273) 730039

IRVINE, Very Rev John Murray. b 24. Magd Coll Cam BA45 MA49. Ely Th Coll 46. **d** 48 **p** 49. Can Res and Chan Heref Cathl *Heref* 65-78; Dir of Ords 65-78; Provost S'well 78-91; P-in-c Edingley w Halam 78-91; P-in-c Rolleston w Fiskerton, Morton and Upton 90-91; rtd 91. *9 Salston Barton, Strawberry Lane, Ottery St Mary, Devon EX11 1RG* Ottery St Mary (0404) 815901

IRVINE, Stanley. b 35. TCD DipTh83. **d** 83 **p** 84. C Arm St Mark w Aghavilly *Arm* 83-85; I Kilmoremoy w Castleconnor, Easkey, Kilglass etc *T, K & A* from 85; Dom Chapl to Bp of Tuam from 88. *The Rectory, Ballina, Co Mayo, Irish Republic* Ballina (96) 21654

IRVINE, William Barry. b 48. QUB BD75. St Jo Coll Nottm 75. **d** 76 **p** 77. C Belf St Mich *Conn* 76-80; C Mansf St Pet S'well 80-84; V Chapel-en-le-Frith *Derby* 84-90; Chapl Cheltenham Gen and Delancey Hosps from 90. *29 Brookway Drive, Charlton Kings, Cheltenham, Glos GL53 8AJ* Cheltenham (0242) 581649

IRVINE, Yvonne Patricia. b 41. Sarum & Wells Th Coll 89. **d** 90. C Walton *St E* from 90. *27 Treetops, Walton, Felixstowe, Suffolk* Felixstowe (0394) 282654

IRVING, Canon Richard. b 27. **d** 65 **p** 66. C Benwell St Jas *Newc* 65-69; C Langley Marish *Ox* 69-73; V Moulsford 73-81; Canada from 81. *1606-12141 Jasper Avenue, Edmonton, Alberta, Canada, T5N 3X8*

IRVING, Christopher. b 55. Coll of Resurr Mirfield. **d** 83 **p** 84. C Newc H Cross *Newc* 83-87; TV Willington Team 87-91; V Monk Bretton *Wakef* from 91. *St Paul's Vicarage, Monk Bretton, Barnsley, S Yorkshire S71 2HQ* Barnsley (0226) 205338

IRVING, Canon Donald Richard. b 31. Lon Univ BSc55. Lon Coll of Div 66. **d** 68 **p** 69. C Leic H Trin *Leic* 68-71; Chapl Leic Poly 70; Travel Sec CPAS 71-75; Sec Ch Soc 75-82; Sec C of E Evang Coun 76-81; Perm to Offic *Chich* 77-84; Gen Sec Intercon Ch Soc from 82; Hon Can Brussels Cathl *Eur* from 83. *10 Nevill Avenue, Hove, E Sussex* Brighton (0273) 779858

IRVING, Leslie. b 09. Keble Coll Ox BA30 DipTh31 MA46. Wycliffe Hall Ox 30. **d** 32 **p** 33. Chapl St Cath Sch Bramley 67-74; rtd 74; Perm to Offic *Chich* 74-83; *Nor* 83-88. *2 Capel Court, The Burgage, Prestbury, Cheltenham, Glos GL52 3EL* Cheltenham (0242) 576426

IRVING, Michael John Derek. b 43. BEd80. Qu Coll Birm 80. **d** 81 **p** 82. C Coleford w Staunton *Glouc* 81-84; V Dean Forest H Trin 84-91; RD Forest S 88-91; P-in-c Hempsted from 91; Dir of Ords from 91. *The Rectory, Hempsted, Gloucester GL2 6LW* Gloucester (0452) 24550

IRWIN, Albert Samuel. b 14. TCD BA38 MA44. CITC 38. **d** 38 **p** 39. V Stamford Baron *Pet* 61-81; P-in-c Tinwell 77-81; rtd 81; Lic to Offic *Pet* 81-85; Perm to Offic *Pet* from 85; *Linc* from 91. *19 Water Street, St Martins, Stamford, Lincs PE9 2NJ*

IRWIN, Alexander John. b 14. Westcott Ho Cam 71. **d** 71 **p** 72. C S Weald *Chelmsf* 71-75; P-in-c Shalford 76-77; V Wethersfield w Shalford 77-86; rtd 86. *90 The Phelps, Kidlington, Oxford OX5 1TL* Kidlington (08675) 2426

IRWIN, David John. b 44. AKC66. St Boniface Warminster 66. **d** 67 **p** 68. C Sydenham All SS *S'wark* 67-70; C Ealing Ch the Sav *Lon* 70-76; P-in-c Willesden St Andr 76-83; V Gladstone Park St Fran 76-83; V Willesden Green St Andr and St Fran of Assisi from 83. *The Clergy House, St Andrew's Road, London NW10 2QS* 081-459 2670

IRWIN, Francis William. b 29. St Chad's Coll Dur BA52 DipTh54 MA56. **d** 54 **p** 55. C Warrington St Elphin *Liv* 54-58; V Staincross *Wakef* 58-66; R Aldborough w Thurgarton *Nor* 66-80; P-in-c Gunton St Andr w Hanworth 66-80; P-in-c Gresham w Bessingham 75-80; R Aldborough w Thurgarton, Bessingham, Gunton etc 80; R Shipdham 80-81; P-in-c E w W Bradenham 80-81; R Shipdham w E and W Bradenham from 81. *The Rectory, Shipdham, Thetford, Norfolk 1P25 7LX* Dereham (0362) 820234

IRWIN, John Nesbitt Cottier. b 27. SEN79 Mert Coll Ox BA50 MA53. SW Minl Tr Course 86. **d** 87 **p** 88. NSM Buckfastleigh w Dean Prior *Ex* from 87. *56 Plymouth Road, Buckfastleigh, Devon TQ11 0DH* Buckfastleigh (0364) 43044

IRWIN, Patrick Alexander. b 55. BNC Ox BA77 MA81 Edin Univ BD81. Edin Th Coll 77 Liturgisches Inst Trier 79. **d** 81 **p** 82. Hon C Cam St Botolph *Ely* 81-84; Chapl BNC Ox from 84; Lect Th from 86; Lic to Offic *Ox* from 85; *B & W* & Perm *D & G* from 87. *Brasenose College, Oxford OX1 4AJ* Oxford (0865) 277854

IRWIN, Stewart. b 53. Sarum & Wells Th Coll 80. **d** 83 **p** 84. C Brighouse *Wakef* 83-87; V Stockton St Jo *Dur* from 87. *168 Durham Road, Stockton-on-Tees, Cleveland TS19 0DE* Stockton-on-Tees (0642) 674119

IRWIN, Miss Susan Elizabeth. b 47. Cam Univ DipRS79. St Jo Coll Dur 77. **dss** 79 **d** 87. Harborne St Faith and St Laur *Birm* 79-82; Caterham *S'wark* 82-87; Par Dn 87-88; Par Dn Kidlington w Hampton Poyle *Ox* from 88. *29 Anderson's Close, Kidlington, Oxford OX5 1ST* Kidlington (08675) 71716

IRWIN, Victor. b 32. Lon Coll of Div 64. **d** 66 **p** 67. C Leic H Trin *Leic* 66-68; CF 68-72; V Quarry Bank *Lich* 72-81; P-in-c Hopesay w Edgton *Heref* 81-85; V Lydbury N 81-85; R Wickenby Gp *Linc* 85-88; R Gartcosh *Glas* 88-91; R Airdrie 88-91; I Garrison w Slavin and Belleek *Clogh* from 91. *The Rectory, Garrison, Co Fermanagh* Belleek (036565) 372

IRWIN, William George. b 53. QUB BSc77. CITC 80. **d** 80 **p** 81. C Lisburn St Paul *Conn* 80-83; C Seagoe *D & D* 83-85; C Newtownards w Movilla Abbey 85-88; I Ballymacash *Conn* from 88; RD Lisburn from 91. *St Mark's Rectory, 97 Antrim Road, Lisburn, Co Antrim BT28 3EA* Lisburn (0846) 662393

IRWIN-CLARK, Peter Elliot. b 49. Univ Coll Lon LLB71 St Jo Coll Dur BA81. Cranmer Hall Dur 81. **d** 81 **p** 82. C Kirkheaton *Wakef* 81-86; V Shirley *Win* from 86. *The Vicarage, Wordsworth Road, Shirley, Southampton S01 5LX* Southampton (0703) 771755

ISAAC, Arthur Kenneth. b 12. St Aug Coll Cant. **d** 62 **p** 63. R Rode, Rode Hill and Woolverton *B & W* 65-72; R Hutton 72-77; rtd 77; Perm to Offic *Ex* 77-86; Chich from 86. *Bungalow No 2, Terry's Cross, Woodmancote, Henfield, W Sussex BN5 9SX* Henfield (0273) 493006

ISAAC, Bryan Raymund. b 09. MBE46. Ch Coll Cam BA31 MA35. Wycliffe Hall Ox 31. **d** 33 **p** 34. V Cudham *Roch* 62-73; rtd 74. *44 Coneygar Lane, Bridport, Dorset DT6 3AT* Bridport (0308) 56273

ISAAC, Canon David Thomas. b 43. Univ of Wales BA65. Cuddesdon Coll 65. **d** 67 **p** 68. C Llan w Capel Llanilterne *Llan* 67-71; P-in-c Swansea St Jas *S & B* 71-73; Chapl Ch in Wales Youth Coun 73-77; V Llanguicke *S & B* 77-79; Dioc Youth Officer *Ripon* 79-83; Nat Officer for Youth Work Gen Syn Bd of Educn 83-90; Dioc Dir of Educn *Portsm* from 90; Can Res Portsm Cathl from 90. *1 Pembroke Close, Portsmouth PO1 2NX* Portsmouth (0705) 818107

ISAAC, Edward Henry. b 20. Qu Coll Cam BA42 MA46. Ridley Hall Cam 45. **d** 47 **p** 48. V Millom St Geo *Carl* 66-85; rtd 85; Perm to Offic *Carl* from 86. *31 Lowther Road, Millom, Cumbria LA18 4PE* Millom (0229) 772332

ISAAC, Canon Philip Davies. b 16. Univ of Wales (Lamp) BA37. Chich Th Coll 38. **d** 42 **p** 43. R Ellon *Ab* 64-72; P-in-c Stornoway *Arg* 72-74 and 78-81; R Dunoon 75-78; Can St Jo Cathl Oban 78-81; rtd 81; Hon Can Cumbrae *Arg* from 81. *Newtonville, Crescent Road, Nairn IV12 4NB* Nairn (0667) 52794

ISAACS, John Kenneth. b 36. Cam Univ MA. E Anglian Minl Tr Course. **d** 82 **p** 83. NSM Ely 82-85; Chapl K Sch Ely from 85; Lic to Offic *Ely* from 85. *18 Barton Road, Ely, Cambs CB7 4DE* Ely (0353) 662221

ISAACSON, Cecil James. b 17. Sarum Th Coll. **d** 53 **p** 54. R Burnham Thorpe w Burnham Overy *Nor* 62-85; R Burnham Sutton w Burnham Ulph etc 69-85; rtd 85; Perm to Offic *Nor* from 85. *7 Golds Pightle, Ringstead, Hunstanton, Norfolk PE36 5LD* Holme (048525) 522

ISAM, Miss Margaret Myra Elizabeth. b 35. Nottm Univ BEd73. E Midl Min Tr Course 78. **dss** 81 **d** 87. Humberston *Linc* 81-84; Gt Grimsby St Andr and St Luke 85-87; Dn-in-c from 87. *St Luke's Vicarage, 17 Heneage Road, Grimsby, S Humberside DN32 9DZ*

ISBISTER, Charles. b 27. Chich Th Coll 58. **d** 60 **p** 61. C Tynemouth Ch Ch *Newc* 60-64; C Boyne Hill *Ox* 64-67; V Cookridge H Trin *Ripon* from 67. *Holy Trinity Vicarage, 53 Green Lane, Cookridge, Leeds LS16 7LW* Leeds (0532) 674921

ISDELL-CARPENTER, Philip Wynn Howard. b 11. St Jo Coll Ox BA33 MA37. Westcott Ho Cam 35. **d** 36 **p** 37. R Frimley *Guildf* 60-72; rtd 76; Perm to Offic *B & W* from 86. *3 Church Path, Crewkerne, Somerset TA18 7HX* Crewkerne (0460) 74075

ISHERWOOD, David Owen. b 46. BA68 MPhil72. Ridley Hall Cam 76. **d** 78 **p** 79. C Sanderstead All SS *S'wark* 78-82; C Horley 82-84; TV 84-88; P-in-c Streatham Immanuel w St Anselm 88; P-in-c Streatham Immanuel and St Andr 88-89; V from 89. *Immanuel Vicarage, 19 Streatham Common South, London SW16 3BU* 081-764 5103

ISHERWOOD, Samuel Peter. b 34. Lon Coll of Div ALCD62 LTh74. **d** 62 **p** 63. C Bacup St Sav *Man* 62-65; C Man Albert Memorial Ch 65-67; V Livesey *Blackb* 67-79; V Handforth *Ches* from 79. *The Vicarage, 36 Sagars Road, Handforth, Wilmslow, Cheshire SK9 3EE* Wilmslow (0625) 524119

ISIORHO, Father The Chief David John Phillip. b 58. Liv Poly BA80 Wolv Poly DipPSych89. Westcott Ho Cam 87. **d** 90 **p** 91. C Nuneaton St Mary *Cov* from 90. *11 Northumberland Avenue, Nuneaton, Warks CV10 8JE* Nuneaton (0203) 345455

ISITT, Canon David Edgar Reid. b 28. K Coll Cam BA49 MA53. Wells Th Coll 51. **d** 53 **p** 54. C Westbury-on-Trym H Trin *Bris* 53-56; Chapl K Coll Cam 56-60; V Haslingfield *Ely* 60-68; R Harlton 60-68; Chapl Trin Hall Cam 68-77; Can Res Bris Cathl *Bris* 77-87; P-in-c Bris Ch Ch w St Ewen and All SS 80-82; Dir Bris Sch of Min 81-87; Dioc Dir of Ords *Bris* 81-87; Lic to Offic *Ely* from 87; Chapl Fitzw Coll Cam from 90. *41 Fulbrooke Road, Cambridge CB3 9EE* Cambridge (0223) 358522

ISITT, Norman. b 34. Dur Univ BA56. Cranmer Hall Dur DipTh59. **d** 59 **p** 60. C Loughton St Mary *Chelmsf* 59-62; C Moulsham St Jo 62-64; Billericay Co Sch 64-65; Squirrels Heath Sch Romford 65-66; Althorpe and Keadby Co Sch from 66. *21 Cambridge Avenue, Bottesford, Scunthorpe, S Humberside DN16 3LT* Scunthorpe (0724) 851489

ISLE OF WIGHT, Archdeacon of. See TURNER, Ven Antony Hubert Michael

ISON, David John. b 54. Leic Univ BA76 Nottm Univ BA78 K Coll Lon PhD85. St Jo Coll Nottm 76. **d** 79 **p** 80. C Deptford St Nic and St Luke *S'wark* 79-85; Lect CA Tr Coll Blackheath 85-88; V Potters Green *Cov* from 88. *St Philip's Vicarage, Ringwood Highway, Coventry CV2 2GF* Coventry (0203) 617568

ISON, Hilary Margaret. b 55. Leic Univ BA76 Nottm Univ DipTh78. Gilmore Course 77 St Jo Coll Nottm DPS79. **d** 87. NSM Deptford St Nic and St Luke *S'wark* 87-88; NSM Potters Green *Cov* 88-90; C Rugby St Andr from 90. *St Philip's Vicarage, Ringwood Highway, Coventry CV2 2GF* Coventry (0203) 617568

ISON, John. **d** 81 **p** 82. NSM Stockton St Jo CD *Dur* 81-83; NSM Hawthorn 83-87; rtd 87; Perm to Offic *Dur* from 87. *32 Limbrick Port, Fairfield, Stockton-on-Tees, Cleveland TS19 7QF* Stockton-on-Tees (0642) 588525

ISRAEL, Dr Martin Spencer. b 27. Witwatersrand Univ MB49 MRCP52. **d** 74 **p** 75. Hon C St Mich Cornhill w St Pet le Poer etc *Lon* 74-77; Hon C S Kensington H Trin w All SS 77-82; P-in-c from 83. *Flat 2, 26 Tregunter Road, London SW10 9LS* 071-370 5160

ISSBERNER, Cllr Norman Gunther Erich. b 34. Fitzw Ho Cam BA58 MA61. Clifton Th Coll 57. **d** 59 **p** 60. C

Croydon Ch Ch Broad Green *Cant* 59-61; C Surbiton Hill Ch Ch *S'wark* 61-66; V Egham *Guildf* 66-75; V Wallington H Trin *S'wark* 75-86; UK Chmn Africa Inland Miss from 77; Adv on Miss and Evang *Chelmsf* from 86. *The Rectory, Church Lane, Sheering, Bishop's Stortford, Herts CM22 7NR* Sheering (027989) 524

ITALY, Archdeacon of. See WESTWELL, Ven George Leslie Cedric

IVE (nee KNOTT), Pamela Frances. b 58. BEd79. Wycliffe Hall Ox 88. **d** 90. Par Dn Ivybridge w Harford *Ex* from 90. *5 Orchard Court, Ivybridge, Devon PL21 9UB* Plymouth (0752) 893208

IVELL, Robert William. b 45. Lon Univ BSc71 Liv Univ CertEd Sheff Univ DBS83. Ridley Hall Cam 83. **d** 85 **p** 86. C Wadsley *Sheff* 85-88; V Laughton w Throapham from 88. *The Vicarage, Laughton, Sheffield S31 7YB* Dinnington (0909) 562300

IVENS, Edmund Masters. b 11. Edin Th Coll 37. **d** 37 **p** 38. R Dunbar *Edin* 52-79; rtd 79. *28 Kingsburgh Gardens, East Linton, East Lothian EH40 3BZ* East Linton (0620) 860283

IVES, John Edward. b 49. K Coll Lon BD74 AKC75 MTh76. Chich Th Coll 78. **d** 79 **p** 80. C Northwood Hills St Edm *Lon* 79-81; C Hillingdon St Andr 81-83; C Uxbridge St Andr w St Jo 83-87; C W Twyford 87-88; C Hanger Hill Ascension and W Twyford St Mary 88-89; Chapl Cen Middx Hosp 88-89; P-in-c Gt Ilford St Clem *Chelmsf* 89-90; TV Gt Ilford SS Clem and Marg from 90. *25 Valentines Road, Ilford, Essex IG1 4RZ* 081-518 3982

IVESON, Mrs Patricia Jill. b 35. Cam Univ CertEd55 K Coll Lon DipTh70 BD76 AKC76. **dss** 81 **d** 87. Wilmington *Roch* 81-87; Hon Par Dn from 87. *Branksome, Church Hill, Wilmington, Dartford DA2 7EH* Dartford (0322) 79100

IVIN, Miss Maureen. b 34. Gilmore Ho 60. **dss** 85 **d** 87. Grays Thurrock *Chelmsf* 85-87; Par Dn from 87. *Wendover, College Avenue, Grays, Essex RM17 5UW* Grays Thurrock (0375) 373468

IVISON, Norman William. b 54. Hull Univ BA75 DipEd76. Trin Coll Bris DipHE81 DipTh82. **d** 82 **p** 83. Ecum Liaison Officer BBC Radio Furness 82-85; C Barrow St Mark *Carl* 82-85; Chapl Barrow Sixth Form Coll 83-85; Dioc Broadcasting Officer *Lich* from 85; Relig Progr Producer BBC Radio Stoke from 85. *8 Strand Close, Stoke-on-Trent ST2 9PG* Stoke-on-Trent (0782) 219716

IVORY, Christopher James. b 54. Reading Univ BSc76. Qu Coll Birm DipTh80. **d** 81 **p** 82. C Waltham Cross *St Alb* 81-84; C Is of Dogs Ch Ch and St Jo w St Luke *Lon* 84-88; V Streatham Ch Ch *S'wark* from 88; Lambeth Adnry Ecum Officer from 90. *Christ Church Vicarage, 3 Christchurch Road, London SW2 3ET* 081-674 5723

IZZARD, Susan Amanda. b 59. Hatf Poly BA82. Trin Coll Bris BA86. **dss** 86 **d** 87. Birm St Martin w Bordesley St Andr *Birm* 86-87; Par Dn 87-89; C Handsworth St Jas 89-91; Asst Chapl Qu Eliz Hosp Birm from 90. *122 Station Road, Birmingham B21 0EX* 021-551 0206

J

JACK, Alexander Richard. b 30. Leeds Univ BSc55 MSc66. Oak Hill Th Coll 69. **d** 71 **p** 72. C Penn Fields *Lich* 71-78; P-in-c 78-83; R Barnston and Lt Dunmow *Chelmsf* from 83; RD Dunmow from 88. *The Rectory, 3 Hylands Close, Barnston, Dunmow, Essex CM6 1LG* Great Dunmow (0371) 875237

JACK, Canon Henry Graham. b 21. K Coll Lon AKC48 BD49. **d** 49 **p** 50. Chile 65-74; Hon Can Chile 66-74; R Trowbridge St Jas *Sarum* 74-87; Can and Preb Sarum Cathl 83-87; rtd 87. *285A The Common, Holt, Trowbridge, Wilts BA14 6QJ* Trowbridge (0225) 782776

JACK, Paul Pembroke. b 19. SS Coll Cam BA41. Linc Th Coll 41. **d** 42 **p** 43. V Primrose Hill St Mary *Lon* 55-57; rtd 84. *39 Warren Hill Road, Woodbridge, Suffolk IP12 4DY* Woodbridge (03943) 6562

JACK, Robin Watson. b 43. Westcott Ho Cam. **d** 90 **p** 91. C Debenham w Aspall and Kenton *St E* from 90. *Bastings Hall, Framsden, Stowmarket, Suffolk IP14 6HX*

JACKLIN, John Frederick. b 30. Oak Hill Th Coll 72. **d** 72 **p** 72. Chile 72-75; C Roxeth Ch Ch *Lon* 75-78; V Selston *S'well* from 78. *The Vicarage, Church Lane, Selston, Nottingham NG16 6EW* Ripley (0773) 810247

JACKS, David. b 59. Nottm Univ BTh87. Linc Th Coll 84. **d** 87 **p** 88. C Oakham, Hambleton, Egleton,

Braunston and Brooke *Pet* 87-90; V Weedon Bec w Everdon from 90. *The Vicarage, Church Street, Weedon, Northampton NN7 4PL* Weedon (0327) 40359

JACKSON, Alan. b 44. Newc Univ BA67 DipEd68 MEd79. NE Ord Course 79. **d** 81 **p** 82. NSM Jesmond H Trin *Newc* 81-82; Chapl Bp Wand's Sch Sunbury-on-Thames 82-89; V Hanworth St Rich *Lon* from 89. *St Richard's Vicarage, 35 Forge Lane, Hanworth, Middx TW13 6UN* 081-898 0241

JACKSON, Arthur Malcolm. b 31. TCD BA54 MA60. CITC 54. **d** 54 **p** 55. C Templecorran Union *Conn* 54-57; C Dub Santry Union *D & G* 57-58; Bp's V and Registrar *C & O* 58-61; I Monasterevan *M & K* 61-68; I Narraghmore w Fontstown and Timolin *D & G* 68-88; I Narraghmore w Timolin, Castledermot and Kinneagh 88-91; I Killanne w Killegney, Rossdroit and Templeshanbo *C & O* from 91. *The Rectory, Clonroche, Enniscorthy, Co Wexford, Irish Republic* Enniscorthy (54) 44180

JACKSON, Barry. b 30. St Jo Coll Cam BA53 DipEd54 MA57. Westcott Ho Cam 63. **d** 65 **p** 66. C Stockport St Geo *Ches* 65-68; C Bridgwater St Mary, Chilton Trinity and Durleigh *B & W* 68-70; P-in-c Thurloxton 70-75; Chapl Wycliffe Coll Stonehouse Glos 75-88; V Heathfield *Chich* from 88. *The Vicarage, Old Heathfield, Heathfield, E Sussex TN21 9AB* Heathfield (04352) 2457

JACKSON, Very Rev Dr Brandon Donald. b 34. Liv Univ LLB56 Bradf Univ Hon DLitt90. Wycliffe Hall Ox DipTh59. **d** 58 **p** 59. C New Malden and Coombe *S'wark* 58-61; C Leeds St Geo *Ripon* 61-65; V Shipley St Pet *Bradf* 65-77; Relig Adv Yorkshire TV 69-79; Provost Bradf 77-89; Dean Linc from 89. *The Deanery, 23 Minster Yard, Eastgate, Lincoln LN2 1QG* Lincoln (0522) 523608

JACKSON, Canon Cecil Thomas. b 09. TCD BA30 MA37. CITC 31. **d** 32 **p** 33. I Ballywalter *D & D* 37-74; Can Down Cathl 68-74; rtd 74. *22 Lisbane Road, Kircubbin, Newtownards, Co Down BT22 1AN* Kircubbin (02477) 1449

JACKSON, Christopher John Wilson. b 45. St Pet Coll Ox BA67 MA87. Ridley Hall Cam 69. **d** 72 **p** 73. C Putney St Marg *S'wark* 72-76; C Battersea St Pet and St Paul 76-79; TV Preston St Jo *Blackb* 79-87; P-in-c Sandal St Cath *Wakef* 87-90; V Shenley Green *Birm* from 90. *St David's Vicarage, 49 Shenley Green, Birmingham B29 4HH* 021-475 4874

JACKSON, Christopher William. b 47. AKC69. St Aug Coll Cant 69. **d** 70 **p** 71. C Newton Aycliffe *Dur* 70-73; C Owton Manor *CD* 73-76; CGA 76-77; TV Harton Colliery *Dur* 77-79; R Hemsworth *Wakef* 79-89; V Hartlepool St Oswald *Dur* from 89. *St Oswald's Clergy House, Brougham Terrace, Hartlepool, Cleveland TS24 8EU* Hartlepool (0429) 273201

JACKSON, Canon David. b 33. Leeds Univ BA60. Coll of Resurr Mirfield 60. **d** 62 **p** 63. C Lewisham St Steph *S'wark* 62-65; P-in-c New Charlton H Trin 65-69; C Old Charlton 69-72; Sen Tutor Coll of the Resurr Mirfield 72-75; R Clapham H Trin 75-78; P-in-c Clapham St Pet 76-78; TR Clapham Old Town 78-84; Hon Can S'wark Cathl from 80; V Battersea St Mary-le-Park 84-89; V Surbiton St Andr and St Mark from 89. *St Mark's Vicarage, 1 Church Hill Road, Surbiton, Surrey KT6 4UG* 081-399 6053

JACKSON, David Reginald Estcourt. b 25. OBE. Qu Coll Cam BA45 MA49. St Jo Coll Dur 80. **d** 81 **p** 82. Hon C Douglas *Blackb* 81-82; C 82-87; rtd 90. *64 The Common, Parbold, Wigan, Lancs WN8 7EA* Parbold (0257) 462671

JACKSON, David Robert. b 51. Lon Univ BDS. Linc Th Coll 81. **d** 83 **p** 84. C Hatcham St Cath *S'wark* 83-87; V Sydenham St Bart from 87. *St Bartholomew's Vicarage, 4 Westwood Hill, London SE26 6QR* 081-778 5290

JACKSON, Canon Derek. b 26. Ex Coll Ox BA51 MA55. Westcott Ho Cam 51. **d** 53 **p** 54. C Radcliffe-on-Trent *S'well* 53-56; C Frome St Jo *B & W* 56-57; V Eaton Socon *St Alb* 57-63; V Boxmoor St Jo 63-74; V Bishop's Stortford St Mich 74-85; Hon Can St Alb 82-85; Bermuda 85-89; P-in-c Cerne Abbas w Godmanstone and Minterne Magna *Sarum* from 89. *The Vicarage, Cerne Abbas, Dorchester, Dorset DT2 7LW* Cerne Abbas (03003) 251

JACKSON, Canon Derek Reginald. b 49. K Coll Lon BD72 AKC72. **d** 73 **p** 74. C Westhoughton *Man* 73-75; C Kendal H Trin *Carl* 75-78; V Pennington w Lindal and Marton 78-83; Warden of Readers from 82; V Kendal St Geo from 83; Hon Can Carl Cathl from 89. *St George's Vicarage, 3 Firbank, Sedbergh Road, Kendal, Cumbria LA9 6BE* Kendal (0539) 723039

JACKSON, Derrick Raymond. b 20. ALAM. Worc Ord Coll 63. **d** 65 **p** 66. C Headless Cross *Worc* 68-70; R Mamble w Bayton 70; TV Steeple Morden *Ely* 71-80; V Hunningham *Cov* 80-85; V Wappenbury w Weston under Wetherley 80-85; rtd 85; Perm to Offic *Ex* from 85. *Brookside, Longmeadow Road, Lympstone, Devon* Exmouth (0395) 264293

JACKSON, Doreen May. S Dios Minl Tr Scheme. **d** 88. NSM Fareham H Trin *Portsm* from 88. *134 Oak Road, Fareham, Hants PO15 5HR* Titchfield (0329) 41429

JACKSON, Mrs Frances Anne (Peggy). b 51. FCA81 ACA76 Somerville Coll Ox BA72 MA76. Ripon Coll Cuddesdon 85. **d** 87. C Ilkeston St Mary *Derby* 87-90; TM Hemel Hempstead *St Alb* from 90. *St Paul's Vicarage, 23 Saturn Way, Hemel Hempsted, Herts HP2 5NY* Hemel Hempstead (0442) 255023

JACKSON, Frank James. b 48. ACIS76 Man Univ CertEd77 Open Univ BA88. E Anglian Minl Tr Course 88. **d** 91. NSM Coggeshall w Markshall *Chelmsf* from 91. *41 Tilkey Road, Coggeshall, Colchester, Essex CO6 1PQ* Coggeshall (0376) 562910

JACKSON, Frederick George. b 43. Leeds Univ BA70. Cuddesdon Coll 70. **d** 72 **p** 73. C Cirencester *Glouc* 72-74; C Kilburn St Aug w St Jo *Lon* 74-77; C Pimlico St Mary Graham Terrace 77-81; Bp's Dom Chapl *Chich* 81-86; V Brighton St Mich from 86. *6 Montpelier Villas, Brighton BN1 3AH* Brighton (0273) 727362

JACKSON, Frederick John. b 13. AKC37. **d** 37 **p** 38. Chapl R W Sussex Hosp Chich 54-80; V Chich St Paul and St Bart *Chich* 59-80; rtd 80; Perm to Offic *Chich* from 80. *c/o S F Jackson Esq, 4A Oakdene Close, Leatherhead, Surrey KT23 4PT*

JACKSON, George. b 10. St Jo Coll Dur LTh33 BA35 MA39. St Aid Birkenhead 30. **d** 35 **p** 36. V Woodplumpton *Blackb* 53-74; C Broughton 74-77; rtd 75. *Fosbrooke House, 8 Clifton Drive, Lytham St Annes FY8 5RE* Lytham (0253) 737680

JACKSON, Harry Francis. b 30. FBOA FSMC FBCO K Coll Lon BD61 AKC61. Sarum Th Coll 61. **d** 62 **p** 62. Bermuda 62-65; C Cobham *Guildf* 65-69; R Ash from 69; Chapl RAF Farnborough from 80. *The Rectory, Church Road, Ash, Aldershot, Hants GU12 6LU* Aldershot (0252) 21517

JACKSON, Hilary Walton. b 17. St Chad's Coll Dur BA40 MA48. **d** 46 **p** 47. V Heighington *Dur* 66-82; rtd 82. *127 Bates Avenue, Darlington, Co Durham DL3 0UE* Darlington (0325) 482746

JACKSON, Hubert Edwyn Alston. b 08. MIEE67. Ripon Hall Ox DipTh56. **d** 58 **p** 59. V Ilton *B & W* 61-79; V Isle Abbots 62-79; rtd 79. *6 Ash Court, Stanway Close, Greenway Road, Taunton, Somerset TA2 6NJ* Taunton (0823) 284510

JACKSON, Ian. b 53. Jes Coll Ox BA75. Linc Th Coll 76. **d** 78 **p** 79. C Holbeach *Linc* 78-82; V Newsome *Wakef* 82-85; V Newsome and Armitage Bridge from 85. *The Vicarage, Newsome, Huddersfield HD4 6QU* Huddersfield (0484) 20664

JACKSON, John. b 20. G&C Coll Cam MA48 Lon Univ BD58. St Aug Coll Cant 57. **d** 57 **p** 58. C Burnley St Pet *Blackb* 57-60; Lic to Offic 60-67; Perm to Offic *Bradf* 67-82; *Blackb* from 82. *18 Hawthorne Avenue, Garstang, Preston PR3 1FP* Garstang (0995) 605803

JACKSON, John Edward. b 29. K Coll Lon BD57 AKC57. **d** 58 **p** 59. C Crofton Park St Hilda w St Cypr *S'wark* 58-61; V Bremhill w Foxham *Sarum* 61-69; V Netheravon w Fittleton 69-73; V Netheravon w Fittleton and Enford 73-85; V Salisbury St Mark from 85. *St Mark's Vicarage, 62 Barrington Road, Salisbury SP1 3JD* Salisbury (0722) 323767

JACKSON, John Reginald. b 25. Selw Coll Cam BA45 MA49. Ridley Hall Cam 45. **d** 48 **p** 49. R Georgeham *Ex* 67-73; V Abbotsley *Ely* 73-79; V Everton w Tetworth 73-79; V Waresley 73-79; P-in-c Garway *Heref* 79-85; P-in-c St Weonards w Orcop 79-85; P-in-c Tretire w Michaelchurch and Pencoyd 79-85; P-in-c Welsh Newton w Llanrothal 79-85; rtd 85; Perm to Offic *Heref* from 85. *4 Rosemary Gardens, Hereford HR1 1UP* Hereford (0432) 270271

JACKSON, Preb John Wilson. b 14. St Jo Coll Dur BA38. Wycliffe Hall Ox 38. **d** 40 **p** 41. RD Walsall *Lich* 68-81; V Walsall 68-81; Preb Lich Cathl 72-81; rtd 81; Perm to Offic *Birm* from 82. *6 Arnold Grove, Shirley, Solihull, W Midlands B90 3JR* 021-744 1288

JACKSON, Kathryn Dianne. b 64. Leeds Univ BA87. St Steph Ho Ox 87. **d** 90. Par Dn Headingley *Ripon* from 90. *5 Derwentwater Grove, Leeds LS6 3EN* Leeds (0532) 758937

JACKSON, Kenneth Evans. b 30. Kelham Th Coll 50. **d** 54 **p** 55. C Coppenhall *Ches* 54-57; C Stockport St

Alb Hall Street 57-60; CF 60-67; R Lewtrenchard w Thrushelton *Ex* 67-77; P-in-c Stowford 73-77; P-in-c Malborough w S Huish 77-83; P-in-c W Alvington w S Milton 82-83; V Malborough w S Huish, W Alvington and Churchstow 83-86; P-in-c Lustleigh from 86. *The Rectory, Lustleigh, Newton Abbot, Devon TQ13 9TE* Lustleigh (06477) 304

JACKSON, Kenneth William. b 30. MCSP53. Chich Th Coll 70. **d** 72 **p** 73. C Eastney *Portsm* 72-74; C Portchester 75-79; V Elson from 79. *St Thomas's Vicarage, 21 Elson Road, Gosport, Hants PO12 4BL* Gosport (0705) 582824

JACKSON, Very Rev Lawrence. b 26. AKC50. **d** 51 **p** 52. C Leic St Marg *Leic* 51-55; V Wymeswold 55-59; V Leic St Jas 59-65; V Cov H Trin *Cov* 65-73; Hon Can Cov Cathl 67-73; RD Cov N 68-73; Provost Blackb from 73. *The Provost's House, Preston New Road, Blackburn BB2 6PS* Blackburn (0254) 52502

JACKSON, Mrs Margaret Elizabeth. b 47. Mon Dioc Tr Scheme. **d** 87. C Chepstow *Mon* 87-90; C Exhall *Cov* from 90. *St Giles's House, 222 Coventry Road, Exhall, Coventry CV7 9BH* Bedworth (0203) 313975

JACKSON, Mark Harding. b 51. Open Univ BA87. Sarum & Wells Th Coll 76. **d** 79 **p** 80. C Hobs Moat *Birm* 79-83; Chapl RN from 83. *c/o MOD, Lacon House, Theobald's Road, London WC1X 8RY* 071-430 6847

JACKSON, Martin. b 56. Clare Coll Cam BA77 MA81. Cranmer Hall Dur BA80. **d** 81 **p** 82. C Houghton le Spring *Dur* 81-84; C Bishopwearmouth St Mich w St Hilda 84-86; TV Winlaton 86; V High Spen and Rowlands Gill from 86. *St Patrick's Vicarage, High Spen, Rowlands Gill, Tyne & Wear NE39 2AA* Rowlands Gill (0207) 542815

JACKSON, Michael Geoffrey St Aubyn. b 56. TCD BA79 MA82 St Jo Coll Cam BA81 MA85 PhD86 Ch Ch Ox MA89 DPhil89. CITC 86. **d** 86 **p** 87. C Dub Zion Ch *D & G* 86-89; Chapl Ch Ch Ox from 89. *Christ Church, Oxford OX1 1DP* Oxford (0865) 276236

JACKSON, Canon Michael James. b 25. Trin Hall Cam BA50 MA58. Wells Th Coll 51. **d** 55 **p** 57. V Doncaster St Geo *Sheff* 69-73; Hon Can Sheff Cathl 71-73; RD Nottm S'well 73-90; City Dean 86-91; Hon Can S'well Minster 73-91; V Nottm St Mary 73-78; P-in-c Nottm St Cath 75-78; P-in-c N Wilford St Faith 76-83; V Nottm St Mary and St Cath 78-91; rtd 91. *10 Church End, Nether Broughton, Melton Mowbray, Leics LE14 3ET* Melton Mowbray (0664) 822923

JACKSON, Michael James. b 44. CEng69 MICE69 Liv Univ BEng65 Newc Univ PhD84. NE Ord Course 82. **d** 84 **p** 85. C Houghton le Spring *Dur* 84-87; V Millfield St Mark from 87. *The Vicarage, Hylton Road, Sunderland SR4 7BN* 091-565 6372

JACKSON, Michael Richard. b 31. Selw Coll Cam BA54 MA58. Westcott Ho Cam 54. **d** 56 **p** 57. C Gosforth All SS *Newc* 56-62; R Dinnington *Sheff* 62-76; V Swinton from 76. *50 Golden Smithies Lane, Swinton, Mexborough, S Yorkshire S64 8DL* Mexborough (0709) 582259

JACKSON, Neil Lawrence. b 35. ACII Lon Univ BD71. Lon Coll of Div 68 St Jo Coll Nottm 70. **d** 71 **p** 72. C Wealdstone H Trin *Lon* 71-75; C Worthing H Trin *Chich* 75-78; V Bowling St Steph *Bradf* 78-87; RD Bowling and Horton 83-87; V Kensal Rise St Mark and St Martin *Lon* from 87. *Kensal Rise Vicarage, 93 College Road, London NW10 5EU* 081-969 4598

JACKSON, Canon Noel Benjamin. b 26. TCD BA50 MA55. **d** 51 **p** 52. C Conwall Union *D & R* 51-55; I Laghey 55-59; I Dromore *Clogh* 59-66; I Belf Upper Malone (Epiphany) *Conn* 66-82; RD S Belf 79-82; I Carnmoney from 82; Preb Castleknock St Patr Cathl Dub from 86. *Coole Glebe, 20 Glebe Road, Carnmoney, Newtownabbey, Co Antrim BT36 6UW* Glengormley (0232) 844981

JACKSON, Norman. b 14. St Jo Coll Dur BA39 DipTh40 MA42. **d** 40 **p** 41. R St Mewan *Truro* 69-79; rtd 80; Perm to Offic *Carl* from 82. *23 Riverbank Road, Kent Park, Kendal, Cumbria LA9 5JS*

JACKSON, Norman. b 20. CEng MIMechE53. S'wark Ord Course 74. **d** 77 **p** 78. NSM Erith Ch Ch *Roch* 77-82; Hon C Bishopstoke *Win* from 82. *7 Otter Close, Bishopstoke, Eastleigh, Hants SO5 6NF* Southampton (0703) 695045

JACKSON, Peter. b 39. Open Univ BA81. St Jo Coll Nottm LTh85. **d** 85 **p** 86. C Clifton *York* 85-88; Chapl Clifton Hosp N Yorkshire 85-88; TV Moor Allerton *Ripon* from 88. *73 The Avenue, Leeds LS17 7NP* Leeds (0532) 678487

JACKSON, Peter Jonathan Edward. b 53. St Pet Coll Ox BA74 MA78 PGCE78. St Steph Ho Ox 79. **d** 79 **p** 80. C

Malvern Link w Cowleigh *Worc* 79-82; Hon C Ox St Mich w St Martin and All SS *Ox* 79-80; Chapl Aldenham Sch Herts 82-90; Chapl and Hd of RE Harrow Sch from 90. *Field House South, West Street, Harrow on the Hill, Middx HA1 3ER* 081-869 1225

JACKSON, Peter Lewis. b 34. Bps' Coll Cheshunt 63. **d** 66 **p** 67. C Stockingford *Cov* 66-67; C Kenilworth St Nic 67-72; P-in-c Napton on the Hill 72-75; V 75-89; V Lower Shuckburgh 75-89; R Napton-on-the-Hill, Lower Shuckburgh etc from 89. *The Vicarage, Napton, Rugby, Warks CV23 8NE* Southam (092681) 2413

JACKSON, Peter William. b 35. Sarum Th Coll 67. **d** 68 **p** 69. C Skelton in Cleveland *York* 68-69; C Upleatham 68-70; Chapl RN from 70. *c/o MOD, Lacon House, Theobald's Road, London WC1X 8RY* 071-430 6847

JACKSON, Reginald. b 05. Lon Coll of Div 44. **d** 45 **p** 46. V Sissinghurst *Cant* 58-70; rtd 70; Master St Jo Hosp Bath 70-75. *10 The Meads, Milborne Port, Sherbourne, Dorset DT9 5DS* Milborne Port (0963) 250279

JACKSON, Reginald Grant. b 03. Birm Univ BA29. Ripon Hall Ox 28. **d** 29 **p** 30. C Bordesley St Andr *Birm* 29-31; C Moseley St Mary 31-32; C Keston *Roch* 32-35; I Saul *D & D* 35-37; I Saul w Whitminster 37-43; V Painswick *Glouc* 43-54; Canada from 62. *200 Main Street, Ailsa Craig, Ontario, N0M 1A0, Canada*

JACKSON, Robert Brandon. b 61. Lanchester Poly BA86 Ox Univ BA88. Wycliffe Hall Ox 86. **d** 89 **p** 90. C Bromley Common St Aug *Roch* from 89. *24 Mayfield Road, Bromley BR1 2HD* 081-467 3877

JACKSON, Robert Fielden. b 35. St D Coll Lamp BA57. Sarum Th Coll 57. **d** 59 **p** 60. C Altham w Clayton le Moors *Blackb* 59-62; C Lytham St Cuth 62-64; V Skerton St Chad 64-69; V Preesall 69-90; RD Garstang 85-89; V Wray w Tatham and Tatham Fells from 90. *The Vicarage, Wray, Lancaster LA2 8QF* Hornby (05242) 21030

JACKSON, Ven Robert Stewart. b 29. ALCM48 TCD BA53 MA56. CITC 54. **d** 54 **p** 55. C Aghalee *D & D* 54-57; I Derrybrusk *Clogh* 57-61; I Magheracross 61-68; I Lisnaskea 68-91; Preb Clogh Cathl 79-85; Preb Donaghmore St Patr Cathl Dub 85-91; Dioc Registrar *Clogh* 89-91; I Templemichael w Clongish, Clooncumber etc *K, E & A* from 91; Adn Elphin and Ardagh from 91. *The Rectory, Battery Road, Longford, Irish Republic* Longford (43) 46442

JACKSON, Robert William. b 49. K Coll Cam MA73 Man Univ MA. St Jo Coll Nottm 78. **d** 81 **p** 82. C Fulwood *Sheff* 81-84; V Grenoside from 84; Chapl Grenoside Hosp Sheff from 84. *St Mark's Vicarage, 19 Graven Close, Grenoside, Sheffield S30 3QT* Sheffield (0742) 467513

JACKSON, Roger. b 57. Chich Th Coll 85. **d** 88 **p** 89. C Hale *Guildf* from 88. *3 South Avenue, Farnham, Surrey GU9 0QY* Farnham (0252) 715695

JACKSON, Canon Roger Brumby. b 31. Dur Univ BSc53 DipEd54. Ridley Hall Cam 57. **d** 59 **p** 60. C Rowner *Portsm* 59-61; C Drypool St Columba w St Andr and St Pet *York* 61-64; Asst Chapl HM Pris Hull 61-64; V Plumstead St Jas w St Jo S'wark 65-68; P-in-c Plumstead St Paul 65-68; V Plumstead St Jo w St Jas and St Paul 68-74; Sub-Dean of Woolwich 71-74; Chapl Hulton Hosp Bolton from 74; V Deane *Man* 74-80; TR from 80; AD Deane 80-85; Hon Can Man Cathl from 90. *Deane Rectory, 234 Wigan Road, Bolton, Lancs BL3 5QE* Bolton (0204) 61819

JACKSON, Preb Roland Francis. b 20. Univ of Wales (Lamp) BA42. St Mich Coll Llan 42. **d** 44 **p** 45. V Stafford St Paul Forebridge *Lich* 61-72; RD Eccleshall 72-82; Chapl HM Pris Drake Hall 75-85; V Eccleshall *Lich* 72-85; Preb Lich Cathl 82-85; rtd 85; Perm to Offic *Lich* from 85. *Treginnis, 29 Meadow Drive, Haughton, Stafford ST18 9HQ* Stafford (0785) 780571

JACKSON, Ronald William. b 37. ALCD. **d** 69 **p** 70. C Crofton *Portsm* 69-74; V Wolv St Matt *Lich* 74-85; V Bloxwich 85-89; C Tamworth from 89. *The Vicarage, Church Drive, Hopwas, Tamworth, Staffs B78 3AL*

JACKSON, Canon Stanley. b 21. St Cath Soc Ox BA48 MA52. Linc Th Coll 48. **d** 49 **p** 50. R Lt Coates *Linc* 68-77; R Bradley 75-77; TR Gt and Lt Coates w Bradley 78; R Ruskington 78-86; V Dorrington 78-82; Can and Preb Linc Cathl from 79; rtd 86. *73A Lincoln Road, Ruskington, Sleaford, Lincs NG34 9AR* Ruskington (0526) 832821

JACKSON, Canon Stephen Alexander. b 18. Keble Coll Ox BA40 MA44. Cuddesdon Coll 40. **d** 42 **p** 43. R Aylestone *Leic* 65-83; RD Christianity (Leic) S 74-81; Hon Can Leic Cathl 74-81; rtd 83; Perm to Offic *Leic* from 83. *34 Bradgate Drive, Wigston Fields, Leicester LE8 1HA* Leicester (0533) 881564

JACKSON, Thomas Peter. b 27. Univ of Wales (Lamp) BA50. St Mich Coll Llan 50. **d** 52 **p** 53. C Swansea St Mary and H Trin *S & B* 52-58; Area Sec (S Midl and S Wales) UMCA 58-60; V Glouc St Steph *Glouc* 60-73; R Upton St Leonards from 73; RD Glouc N from 82. *The Rectory, Upton St Leonards, Gloucester GL4 8AG* Gloucester (0452) 66171

JACKSON, William Stafford. b 48. Sunderland Poly DCYW83. Linc Th Coll. **d** 89 **p** 90. C Heworth St Mary *Dur* from 89. *1 High Lanes, Heworth, Gateshead, Tyne & Wear NE10 9XH* 091-469 6048

JACKSON, Canon William Stanley Peter. b 39. Univ of Wales DipTh66. St Mich Coll Llan 63. **d** 66 **p** 67. C Llandrindod w Cefnllys *S & B* 66-69; C Gowerton w Waunarlwydd 69-73; V Crickadarn w Gwenddwr and Alltmawr 73-79; V Llanveigan and Llanthetty and Glyncollwng etc from 79; Dioc GFS Chapl from 84; Can Res Brecon Cathl from 90. *The Rectory, Talybont-on-Usk, Brecon, Powys LD3 7UX* Talybont-on-Usk (087487) 243

JACKSON-STEVENS, Nigel. b 42. St Steph Ho Ox. **d** 68 **p** 69. C Babbacombe *Ex* 68-73; P-in-c W Buckland 73-75; V Swimbridge 73-75; V Swimbridge and W Buckland 75-84; P-in-c Mortehoe 84-85; P-in-c Ilfracombe, Lee, W Down, Woolacombe and Bittadon 84-85; TR Ilfracombe, Lee, Woolacombe, Bittadon etc from 85. *The Vicarage, St Brannock's Road, Ilfracombe, Devon EX34 8EG* Ilfracombe (0271) 863467

JACOB, Ven Bernard Victor. b 21. St Pet Hall Ox BA48 MA52. Wycliffe Hall Ox 49. **d** 50 **p** 51. R Mortlake w E Sheen *S'wark* 68-76; TR 76-77; RD Richmond and Barnes 75-76; Adn Kingston 76-86; Adn Reigate 86-88; rtd 88. *4 The Peacheries, Chichester, W Sussex PO19 2NP*

JACOB, John Lionel Andrew. b 26. Selw Coll Cam BA50 MA54. Westcott Ho Cam 50. **d** 52 **p** 53. C Brightside St Thos *Sheff* 52-55; C Maltby 55-58; V Doncaster Intake 58-67; V Sheff St Aid w St Luke 67-75; TR Sheff Manor 75-82; R Waddington *Linc* from 82. *The Rectory, Waddington, Lincoln LN5 9RS* Lincoln (0522) 720323

JACOB, Joseph. b 38. CITC 65. **d** 68 **p** 69. C Belf St Aid *Conn* 68-70; Bp's Dom Chapl 70-71; I Kilscoran *C & O* 71-80; I Geashill *M & K* 80-83; Asst Warden Ch's Min of Healing from 83; Gen Sec (Ireland) CMJ 87-91; I Ardamine w Kiltennel, Glascarrig etc *C & O* from 91. *Ardamine Rectory, Courtown Harbour, Gorey, Co Wexford, Irish Republic* Gorey (55) 25423

JACOB, Canon William Mungo. b 44. Hull Univ LLB66 Linacre Coll Ox BA69 MA73 Ex Univ PhD. St Steph Ho Ox 70. **d** 70 **p** 71. C Wymondham *Nor* 70-73; Asst Chapl Ex Univ *Ex* 73-75; Dir Past Studies Sarum & Wells Th Coll 75-80; Vice-Prin 77-80; Selection Sec and Sec Cttee for Th Educn ACCM 80-86; Warden Linc Th Coll from 85; Can Linc Cathl *Linc* from 86; Hon C Linc Minster Gp from 88. *Warden's House, Lincoln Theological College, Drury Lane, Lincoln LN1 3BP* Lincoln (0522) 538883

JACOBS, Adrian John. b 44. Reading Univ BA65 K Coll Lon MTh72 St Chad's Coll Dur BA68 DipTh69. **d** 69 **p** 70. C Upper Norwood St Jo *Cant* 69-72; C Addington 72-76; C St Botolph without Bishopgate *Lon* 77-79; P-in-c Heydour w Culverthorpe and Welby *Linc* 79; P-in-c N w S Rauceby 79; P-in-c Wilsford w Kelby 79; P-in-c Wilsford 79; R 79-88; P-in-c Merrington *Dur* 88-90; R S, E w W Raynham, Helhoughton, etc *Nor* from 90. *The Rectory, West Raynham, Fakenham, Norfolk NR21 7HH* Weasenham St Peter (032874) 385

JACOBS, Michael David. b 41. Ex Coll Ox BA63 MA67. Chich Th Coll 63. **d** 65 **p** 66. C Walthamstow St Pet *Chelmsf* 65-68; Chapl Sussex Univ *Chich* 68-72; Perm to Offic *Leic* from 81; Lect Leic Univ from 84; Lic to Offic *Linc* from 84. *c/o The University of Leicester, University Road, Leicester LE1 7RH* Leicester (0533) 554455

JACOBS, Neville Robertson Eynesford. b 32. Lon Coll of Div ALCD59 LTh74. **d** 59 **p** 60. C Chesham St Mary *Ox* 59-62; CMS 62-67; C Keynsham *B & W* 67-71; R Croscombe and Dinder 72-80; R Pilton w Croscombe, N Wootton and Dinder 80-83; V Biddenham *St Alb* 83-89; V Chipping Sodbury and Old Sodbury *Glouc* from 89. *The Vicarage, Chipping Sodbury, Bristol BS17 6ET* Chipping Sodbury (0454) 313159

JACOBSON, William Walter. b 24. Cant Univ (NZ) LTh51. **d** 51 **p** 52. V Shiphay Collaton *Ex* 59-77; TV Clyst St George, Aylesbeare, Clyst Honiton etc 77-78 and 80-84; R Clyst St Mary, Clyst St George etc 85-89; C Ottery St Mary 79-80; Dioc Communications Officer 83-89; rtd 89; Perm to Offic *Ex* from 89. *5 Clyst Valley Road, Clyst St Mary, Exeter EX5 1DD* Topsham (0392) 874304

JACQUES, Humphrey James Kynaston. b 12. MBE45 TD57. Wells Th Coll 46. **d** 47 **p** 48. V Portesham w Langton Herring *Sarum* 53-80; P-in-c Abbotsbury 78-80; V Abbotsbury, Portesham and Langton Herring 80-81; rtd 81; Perm to Offic *B & W* from 83. *The Vine House, Buckhorn Weston, Gillingham, Dorset SP8 5HS* Templecombe (0963) 70474

JACQUET, Trevor Graham. b 56. Man Univ BSc77. Oak Hill Th Coll BA88. **d** 88 **p** 89. C Deptford St Nic and St Luke *S'wark* from 88. *11 Evelyn Street, London SE8 5RT* 071-237 1504

JACSON, Edward Shallcross Owen. b 38. St Steph Ho Ox 61. **d** 64 **p** 65. C Yate *Glouc* 64-67; C Churchdown 67-71; P-in-c Sandhurst 71-75; V Sherborne w Windrush and the Barringtons 75-76; V Sherborne, Windrush, the Barringtons etc 76-80; TV Shaston *Sarum* 80-87; Perm to Offic from 88. *Grove Farm, Melbury Abbas, Shaftesbury, Dorset* Shaftesbury (0747) 53688

JAGER, George. b 10. SS Coll Cam BA32 MA36. Westcott Ho Cam 37. **d** 38 **p** 39. V Sutton Courtenay w Appleford *Ox* 68-75; rtd 75; Perm to Offic *Leic* from 75. *The Dixons, Welford Road, South Kilworth, Lutterworth, Leics LE17 6DY* Welford (0858) 575475

JAGGER, Ian. b 55. K Coll Cam BA77 MA81 St Jo Coll Dur BA80 MA87. Cranmer Hall Dur 78. **d** 82 **p** 83. C Twickenham St Mary *Lon* 82-85; P-in-c Willen *Ox* 85-87; TV Stantonbury and Willen from 87. *The Vicarage, 2 Hooper Gate, Willen, Milton Keynes MK15 9JR* Milton Keynes (0908) 662092

JAGGER, Dr Peter John. b 38. FRHistS78 Leeds Univ MPhil76 PhD87. Lambeth MA71 Coll of Resurr Mirfield 67. **d** 68 **p** 69. C Leeds All SS *Ripon* 68-71; V Bolton w Redmire 71-77; Dir of Self Supporting Min from 77; Perm to Offic *Ches* from 77; Warden and Chief Lib St Deiniol's Lib Hawarden from 77. *St Deiniol's Library, Hawarden, Deeside, Clwyd CH5 3DF* Hawarden (0244) 532350

JAGO, Alfred Douglas James. b 08. Leeds Univ BA30. Coll of Resurr Mirfield 30. **d** 32 **p** 33. R St Stephen in Brannel *Truro* 65-76; RD St Austell 71-76; rtd 76; Hon C Charlestown *Truro* from 77. *22 Fairbourne Road, St Austell, Cornwall PL25 4NR* St Austell (0726) 75208

JAKEMAN, Francis David. b 47. Leeds Univ BSc69 Ealing Coll of Educn DMS81. Cuddesdon Coll 71. **d** 74 **p** 75. C Gt Grimsby St Mary and St Jas *Linc* 74-77; Ind Chapl *Lon* 77-88; V Harrow Weald All SS from 88. *The Vicarage, 175 Uxbridge Road, Harrow Weald, Middx HA3 6TP* 081-954 0247

JALLAND, Hilary Gervase Alexander. b 50. FRSA Ex Univ BA72. Coll of Resurr Mirfield 74. **d** 76 **p** 77. C Ex St Thos *Ex* 76-80; C Ex St Thos and Em 80; C Portsea St Mary *Portsm* 80-86; V Hempton and Pudding Norton *Nor* 86-90; TV Hawarden *St As* from 90. *The Vicarage, 1 Meadowside, Ewloe, Deeside, Clwyd CH5 2SQ* Hawarden (0244) 520778

JAMAL, Canon Khalil Sany Shukry. b 15. American Univ of Beirut BA36. Near E Sch of Th 36 Wycliffe Hall Ox 38. **d** 39 **p** 40. R Fletton *Ely* 65-88; Hon Can Jerusalem from 83; rtd 88. *1 Bishop Wynn Close, Ely, Cambs CB7 4BH* Ely (0353) 668689

JAMES, Alan Frederick. b 20. Coll of Resurr Mirfield. **d** 50 **p** 51. V Horton *Newc* 58-86; rtd 86. *38 Morwick Road, Warkworth, Morpeth, Northd NE65 0TD* Alnwick (0665) 711280

JAMES, Alan Raymond. b 30. Roch Th Coll 65. **d** 66 **p** 67. C Ex St Matt *Ex* 66-70; V Kirkswell w Coffinswell 70-88; rtd 88. *13 Hillside, Appleby Magna, Burton-on-Trent, Staffs DE12 7AB* Measham (0530) 70917

JAMES, Andrew Nicholas. b 54. BSc76. Trin Coll Bris 77. **d** 80 **p** 81. C Prescot *Liv* 80-83; C Upholland 83-85; V Hindley Green 85-91; V Dean Forest H Trin *Glouc* from 91. *Holy Trinity Vicarage, Harrow Hill, Drybrook, Glos GL17 9JX* Dean (0594) 542232

JAMES, Anne Loraine. **d** 90. NSM Ellon *Ab* from 90; NSM Cruden from 90. *Millhouse, Nethermill, Hatton, Peterhead, Aberdeenshire AB4 7SN* Cruden Bay (0779) 812609

JAMES, Arthur Kenneth. b 14. St Chad's Coll Dur BA35 DipTh35 MA38. **d** 37 **p** 38. V Marshfield and Peterstone Wentloog etc *Mon* 64-79; rtd 79. *3 Ellis Avenue, Onslow Village, Guildford, Surrey* Guildford (0483) 38582

JAMES, Barry Paul. b 49. BSc. Sarum & Wells Th Coll. **d** 82 **p** 83. C Bitterne Park *Win* 82-86; V Southn St Mary Extra from 86. *The Vicarage, 65 Peartree Avenue, Southampton SO2 7JN* Southampton (0703) 448353

JAMES, Billie. b 24. St D Coll Lamp BA50 LTh52. **d** 52 **p** 53. V Scrooby *S'well* 61-74; P-in-c Kneesall 74-82; P-in-c Ossington 74-82; V Norwell 74-82; P-in-c Laxton

77-78; V Norwell w Ossington and Cromwell 82-89; rtd 89; Lic to Offic *Heref* from 89. *2 Danum Road, Tudor Park, Ross-on-Wye, Herefordshire HR9 5UG* Ross-on-Wye (0989) 765542

JAMES, Brian Percival Harold. b 26. Southn Univ BSc53. Wycliffe Hall Ox 62. **d** 64 **p** 65. C Hartley Wintney and Elvetham *Win* 64-66; C Shelf *Bradf* 66-71; V Oldham St Ambrose *Man* from 71. *The Vicarage, Prince Charlie Street, Oldham OL1 4HJ* 061-624 7122

JAMES, Brother. *See* PICKEN, James Hugh

JAMES, Miss Carolyn Anne. b 65. Coll of Ripon & York St Jo BA87 Nottm Univ BTh91. Linc Th Coll 88. **d** 91. Par Dn Middleton St Mary *Ripon* from 91. *40 Manor Farm Gardens, Leeds LS10 3RA* Leeds (0532) 775276

✠**JAMES, Rt Rev Colin Clement Walter.** b 26. K Coll Cam BA49 MA51. Cuddesdon Coll 50. **d** 52 **p** 53 **c** 73. C Stepney St Dunstan and All SS *Lon* 52-55; Asst Chapl Stowe Sch Bucks 55-56; Chapl 56-59; Asst in Relig Broadcasting BBC 59-60; Relig Broadcasting Org W Region BBC 60-67; V Bournemouth St Pet *Win* 67-73; P-in-c Bournemouth St Steph 70-73; Dir of Tr 72-77; Can Res Win Cathl 73-77; Suff Bp Basingstoke 73-77; Bp Wakef 77-85; Bp Win from 85. *Wolvesey, Winchester SO23 9ND* Winchester (0962) 854050

JAMES, Colin Robert. b 34. IPFA. St Deiniol's Hawarden 84. **d** 87 **p** 88. NSM Llanwnda w Llanfaglan *Ban* 87-88; NSM Arfon Deanery 88-90; NSM Bistre *St As* 90-91. *1 Lea Drive, Buckley, Clwyd CH7 2BQ* Buckley (0244) 544392

JAMES, Cyril George. b 06. St D Coll Lamp BA27. **d** 29 **p** 30. V Crickhowell *S & B* 57-76; rtd 76; Lic to Offic S & B & Mon 76-82; Perm to Offic *Mon* from 82. *Bank House, Crickhowell, Powys* Crickhowell (0873) 810314

JAMES, David. b 38. Southn Univ BEd74. **d** 77 **p** 78. NSM Headbourne Worthy *Win* 77-85; NSM King's Worthy 77-85; Asst Chapl K Alfred's Coll Win 85-89; Chapl St Pet High Sch Ex from 89; Lic to Offic *Ex* from 89. *10 Barley Down Drive, Badger Farm, Winchester, Hants SO22 4LS* Winchester (0962) 63262

JAMES, Canon David Brian. b 30. FCA52 Univ of Wales (Swansea) BA63. St Mich Coll Llan 55. **d** 57 **p** 58. C Llandilo Talybont *S & B* 57-59; C Christ Church *Mon* 59-63; V Bryngwyn and Newchurch and Llanbedr etc *S & B* 63-70; V Llanveigan and Llanthetty and Glyncollwng etc 70-79; V Ilston w Pennard from 79; Hon Can Brecon Cathl 87-89; RD W Gower 89; Can Brecon Cathl from 89. *The Vicarage, 88 Pennard Road, Pennard, Swansea SA3 2AD* Bishopston (044128) 2928

JAMES, David Charles. b 45. Ex Univ BSc66 PhD71. St Jo Coll Nottm BA73. **d** 73 **p** 74. C Portswood Ch Ch *Win* 73-76; V from 90; C Goring-by-Sea *Chich* 76-78; Chapl UEA *Nor* 78-82; V Ecclesfield *Sheff* 82-90; Proctor in Convocation Sheff Cathl 85-90; RD Ecclesfield 87-90. *The Vicarage, 36 Brookvale Road, Southampton S02 1QR* Southampton (0703) 554277

JAMES, David Clive. b 40. Bris Univ BA61 K Coll Lon DipEd87. St Steph Ho Ox 64. **d** 65 **p** 66. C Portslade St Nic *Chich* 65-68; C Haywards Heath St Wilfrid 68-71; Chapl Brighton Poly 71-76; Lic to Offic from 76. *22 Bradford Road, Lewes, E Sussex BN7 1RB* Brighton (0273) 471851

JAMES, David Howard. b 47. Ex Univ BA70 MA73 Pemb Coll Cam CertEd72. Linc Th Coll 81. **d** 83 **p** 84. C Tavistock and Gulworthy *Ex* 83-86; C E Teignmouth 86-88; C W Teignmouth 86-88; P-in-c Bishopsteignton 88-89; P-in-c Ideford, Luton and Ashcombe 88-89; TV Teignmouth, Ideford w Luton, Ashcombe etc from 90. *The Vicarage, 3 Moors Park, Bishopsteignton, Teignmouth, Devon TQ14 9RH* Teignmouth (0626) 775247

JAMES, Canon David Walter Skyrme. b 36. Nottm Univ BA61. Wells Th Coll 61. **d** 63 **p** 64. C Sneinton St Cypr *S'well* 63-66; C Newark St Mary 66-69; R Kirkby in Ashfield St Thos 69-77; P-in-c Rempstone 76-84; P-in-c Costock 76-84; P-in-c Stanford on Soar 76-84; R E Leake 77-84; R Wollaton from 84; Hon Can S'well Minster from 88; AD Nottm W 90-91. *St Leonard's Rectory, Russell Drive, Nottingham NG8 2BD* Nottingham (0602) 281798

JAMES, David William. b 55. CA Tr Coll CertRS77 Coll of Resurr Mirfield 86. **d** 88 **p** 88. C New Rossington *Sheff* 88-90; V Yardley Wood *Birm* from 90. *Christ Church Vicarage, School Road, Birmingham B14 4EP* 021-474 2012

JAMES, Derek George. b 27. Sarum & Wells Th Coll 72. **d** 74 **p** 75. C Petersfield w Sheet *Portsm* 74-77; P-in-c Gosport Ch Ch 77-81; V from 81; RD Gosport from 90. *Christ Church Vicarage, 7 Elmhurst Road, Gosport, Hants PO12 1PG* Gosport (0705) 581609

JAMES, Dewi Hirwaun. b 41. Llan St Mich 66 Lich Th Coll 67. **d** 70. C Porthmadog St Jo w Borth-y-Gest and Tremadog *Ban* 70-73; C Llanbeblig w Caernarfon and Betws Garmon etc 83-85; C Ban 88-89 and from 90; C Sneff Parson Cross St Cecilia *Sheff* 89-90; Min Can Ban Cathl *Ban* from 90. *Caplandy, Glanrafan, Bangor, Gwynedd* Bangor (0248) 352466

JAMES, Ven Douglas Gordon. b 22. Univ of Wales (Abth) BA47. Qu Coll Birm 74. **d** 75 **p** 76. C Cwmbach *Llan* 75-77; C Aberdare 77-82; V from 82; Hon Can Llan Cathl from 87; Adn Margam from 88. *31 Abernant Road, Aberdare, M Glam CF44 0PY* Aberdare (0685) 872559

JAMES, Edmund Pollard. b 10. MBE70. St D Coll Lamp LDiv37. **d** 37 **p** 38. R Pyworthy w Pancraswyke *Ex* 46-77; Preb Ex Cathl 60-77; rtd 77. *St Agnes, All Saints' Lane, Clevedon, Avon BS21 6AU* Clevedon (0272) 873470

JAMES, Canon Eric Arthur. b 25. K Coll Lon AKC50 BD51 Trin Coll Cam MA55. **d** 51 **p** 52. Can Res and Prec S'wark Cathl *S'wark* 66-73; Dioc Missr *St Alb* 73-83; Can Res St Alb 73-83; Hon Can 83-90; FKC from 78; Preacher Gray's Inn from 78; Dir Chr Action 79-90; Hon Dir from 90; Chapl to HM The Queen from 84; rtd 90. *11 Denny Crescent, London SE11 4UY or, St Peter's House, 308 Kennington Lane, London SE11 5HY* 071-582 3068 or 735 2372

JAMES, Gareth Hugh. b 40. St D Coll Lamp DipTh66. **d** 66 **p** 67. C Llan N *Llan* 66-68; C Whitchurch 68-71; Chapl Llan Cathl Sch from 71. *The Cathedral School, Llandaff, Cardiff* Cardiff (0222) 563179

JAMES, George Gwynfryn. b 09. Lon Coll of Div 56. **d** 58 **p** 59. V Kinnerley w Melverley *Lich* 63-74; rtd 74. *39 Hazel Grove, The Paddocks, Oswestry, Shropshire SY11 2XB* Oswestry (0691) 659182

JAMES, Godfrey Walter. b 36. Univ of Wales (Lamp) BA58 Univ of Wales (Cardiff) MA60 St Pet Coll Ox DipEd61 BA63 MA67. St Mich Coll Llan 63. **d** 64 **p** 65. C Canton St Jo *Llan* 64-71; V Williamstown 71-85; V Kenfig Hill from 85. *The Vicarage, Kenfig Hill, Bridgend, M Glam CF33 6DR* Bridgend (0656) 740856

JAMES, Gordon Cecil. b 35. Sarum Th Coll 66. **d** 67 **p** 68. C Kew *S'wark* 67-72; P-in-c Weston Longville w Morton and the Witchinghams *Nor* 72-81; R Diss from 81. *The Rectory, 26 Mount Street, Diss, Norfolk IP22 3QG* Diss (0379) 642072

JAMES, Canon Graham Richard. b 51. Lanc Univ BA72 Ox Univ DipTh74. Cuddesdon Coll 72. **d** 75 **p** 76. C Pet Ch Carpenter *Pet* 75-79; C Digswell *St Alb* 79-82; TV Digswell and Panshanger 82-83; Lic to Offic from 83; Sen Selection Sec and Sec Cand Cttee ACCM 83-87; Abp's Chapl *Cant* from 87; Hon Can Dallas from 89. *7 The Cottages, Lambeth Palace, London SE1 7JU* 071-928 8282

JAMES, Henley George. b 31. Sarum & Wells Th Coll 79. **d** 81 **p** 82. C Tottenham H Trin *Lon* 81-85; C Cricklewood St Pet 85-88; P-in-c 88-89; V Bearwood *Birm* from 89. *St Mary's Vicarage, 27 Poplar Avenue, Birmingham B17 8EG* 021-429 2165

JAMES, Henry Anthony. b 14. St Pet Hall Ox BA36 MA43. St Mich Coll Llan 36. **d** 37 **p** 38. V St Brides Major *Llan* 49-79; rtd 79. *Bryn Fro, Lon-yr-Eglwys, St Brides Major, Bridgend, M Glam* Southerndown (0656) 880377

JAMES, Henry Glyn. b 26. Keble Coll Ox BA50 DipTh51 MA62 Toronto Univ MEd74. Wycliffe Hall Ox 50. **d** 52 **p** 53. Canada 68-73; Hon C Kidmore End *Ox* 74-77; K Jas Coll of Henley 74-87; Hon C Remenham *Ox* 77-88; Chapl The Henley Coll 87-88; Chapl Toulouse *Eur* 88-91; rtd 91. *Address temp unknown*

JAMES, Herbert Royston Joseph. b 22. Sarum Th Coll 65. **d** 67 **p** 68. C Whipton *Ex* 67-75; V Shaugh Prior 75-83; V Ipplepen w Torbryan 83-87; rtd 87; Perm to Offic *Ex* from 90. *188 Hamlin Lane, Exeter EX1 2SH*

JAMES, Howard. b 19. Chich Th Coll. **d** 87. Hon C Whitton St Aug *Lon* from 87. *95 Lyndhurst Avenue, Twickenham TW2 6BH* 081-898 1190

JAMES, Idris Frank. b 20. MISM69 AMBIM70. St D Coll Lamp 52. **d** 55 **p** 59. V Dunton *Chelmsf* 62-79; R Bulphan 64-77; rtd 85. *39 Cae Fardre, Church Village, Pontypridd, M Glam CF38 1DS* Newtown Llantwit (0443) 202834

JAMES, Jeremy Richard. b 52. Jes Coll Cam BA73 MA77 York Univ CertEd77. St Jo Coll Dur 86. **d** 88 **p** 89. C Broxbourne w Wormley *St Alb* from 88. *15 Trafalgar Avenue, Broxbourne, Herts EN10 7DJ* Hoddesdon (0992) 441524

JAMES, John Charles. b 37. **d** 70 **p** 71. C S Shields St Hilda w St Thos *Dur* 70-77; P-in-c Jarrow Docks 77-78; Seychelles from 78; C Rekendyke *Dur* 78. *c/o USPG, 15 Tufton Street, London SW1P 3QQ*

JAMES, John David. b 23. CCC Cam MA. Wells Th Coll. **d** 50 **p** 51. V Stansted Mountfitchet *Chelmsf* 61-71; V

Clacton St Jas 71-84; R Poulshot *Sarum* 84; V Rowde 84; R Rowde and Poulshot 84-88; rtd 88. *15 Beaconsfield Park, Ludlow, Shropshire* Ludlow (0584) 873754

JAMES, John Frank. b 33. Madras Univ MA57. Coll of Resurr Mirfield 60. **d** 62 **p** 63. C Portsea N End St Mark *Portsm* 62-64; C Bris St Andr Hartcliffe *Bris* 64-65; C Bris St Agnes w St Simon 65-68; V Portsea St Sav *Portsm* 68-74; Youth Sec USPG 74-82; India 82-85; Chapl HM Youth Cust Cen Glen Parva 85-87; Chapl HM Pris Grendon and HM Pris Spring Hill from 87. *HM Prison Grendon, Aylesbury, Bucks HP18 0TL* Grendon Underwood (029677) 301

JAMES, John Hugh Alexander. b 56. St Jo Coll Dur BA78 Univ of Wales DipTh81. St Mich Coll Llan. **d** 81 **p** 82. C Newton Nottage *Llan* 81-84; Prov Youth and Children's Officer Ch in Wales from 84. *Church in Wales Centre, Woodland Place, Penarth, S Glam CF6 2EX* Penarth (0222) 705278

JAMES, John Morgan. b 21. Lon Univ BD43 MTh45. ALCD43. **d** 44 **p** 45. V Sunbury *Lon* 67-77; Dir Coll of Preachers 77-85; rtd 85. *Fair Winds, 126 Pagham Road, Pagham, Bognor Regis, W Sussex PO21 4NN* Pagham (0243) 264250

JAMES, John Paul. b 30. **d** 60 **p** 61. C Milton *Portsm* 60-65; C Stanmer w Falmer and Moulsecoomb *Chich* 65-69; PC Brighton H Trin 69-71; Canada from 71. *10 Church Hill, Westmount, Quebec, Canada, H3Y 2Z9*

JAMES, Joshua James Gerwyn. b 31. St D Coll Lamp BA52. **d** 54 **p** 55. C Haverfordwest St Mary w St Thos *St D* 54-56; C Llanaber w Caerdeon *Ban* 56-57; CF 57-76; V Tidenham w Beachley and Lancaut *Glouc* 76-80; R Aberdovey *Ban* 80-82; V Quinton w Marston Sicca *Glouc* 82-90; RD Campden 88-90; P-in-c Upper Chelsea St Simon *Lon* from 90. *The Vicarage, 34 Milner Street, London SW3 2QF* 071-589 5747

JAMES, Keith Edwin Arthur. b 38. Sarum & Wells Th Coll 85. **d** 87 **p** 88. C Hempnall *Nor* from 87. *The Vicarage, Triple Plea Road, Woodton, Bungay, Suffolk NR35 2NS* Woodton (050844) 397

JAMES, Lewis John. b 20. St D Coll Lamp BA42. **d** 48 **p** 49. V Smalley *Derby* 60-85; P-in-c Morley 72-81; rtd 85; Perm to Offic *Derby* 85-87. *78 Waun Daniel, Rhos, Pontardawe, Swansea SA8 5HR* Swansea (0792) 830796

JAMES, Lionel Dennis. b 07. Qu Coll Birm. **d** 62 **p** 63. V Weedon Bec *Pet* 65-74; R Dodford w Brockhall 66-74; rtd 74. *7 Springfield Park, Mylor Bridge, Falmouth, Cornwall* Falmouth (0326) 73743

JAMES, Malcolm. b 37. CEng MICE MIStructE. N Ord Course. **d** 83 **p** 84. NSM Ripponden *Wakef* from 83. *Lower Stones, Bar Lane, Rishworth, Sowerby Bridge, W Yorkshire HX6 4EY* Halifax (0422) 822483

JAMES, Dr Martyn Howard. b 48. FRCS71 Bris Univ MB, ChB71. Coll of Resurr Mirfield 85. **d** 87 **p** 88. C Torquay St Martin Barton *Ex* from 87. *45 Isaacs Road, Barton, Torquay, Devon TQ2 8NA* Torquay (0803) 34112

JAMES, Canon Maurice. b 10. St Chad's Coll Dur LTh37 BA38. St Aug Coll Cant 34. **d** 38 **p** 39. Basutoland 41-66; Lesotho 66-73; S Africa 73-78; Perm to Offic *Ex* 78-84; *Worc* from 84; rtd 86. *Flat A, Warden's Lodge, Beauchamp Community, Newland, Malvern, Worcs WR13 5AX* Malvern (0684) 566403

JAMES, Noel Beddoe Walters. b 39. St Mich Coll Llan DipTh68. **d** 68 **p** 69. C Swansea St Nic *S & B* 68-70; C Swansea St Pet 70-72; Chapl RAF from 72. c/o MOD, *Adastral House, Theobald's Road, London WC1X 8RU* 071-430 7268

JAMES, Paul Dominic Denis. b 48. AKC71 Westmr Coll Ox DipApTh90. **d** 72 **p** 73. C Leytonstone St Marg w St Columba *Chelmsf* 72-74; C Leigh-on-Sea St Marg 74-79; V Walthamstow St Sav from 79. *St Saviour's Vicarage, 210 Markhouse Road, London E17 8EP* 081-520 2036

JAMES, Paul Maynard. b 31. Univ of Wales (Ban) BA52 Fitzw Ho Cam BA54 MA58. Ridley Hall Cam 56. **d** 57 **p** 58. C Newhaven *Chich* 57-60; Kenya 60-65; SW Area Sec CCCS 65-68; V Shrewsbury St Julian *Lich* 68-76; V Shrewsbury H Trin w St Julian 76-90; P-in-c Woore and Norton in Hales from 90; Adn's Adv Evang from 90. *The Vicarage, Woore, Crewe CW3 9SA* Pipe Gate (063081) 316

JAMES, Peter David. b 42. Keble Coll Ox BA63 Lon Univ BD67. Tyndale Hall Bris 64. **d** 67 **p** 68. C Haydock St Mark *Liv* 67-69; C Ashton-in-Makerfield St Thos 69-74; V Whiston 74-80; V Harlech and Llanfair-juxta-Harlech etc *Ban* from 80. *The Vicarage, Harlech, Gwynedd LL46 2PR* Harlech (0766) 780383

JAMES, Peter Heppell. b 19. Tyndale Hall Bris 39. **d** 42 **p** 43. R Lt Leighs *Chelmsf* 60-70; rtd 84. *57 Tynedale*

Road, Loughborough, Leics LE11 3TA Loughborough (0509) 266940

JAMES, Raymond John. b 36. Linc Th Coll 85. **d** 87 **p** 88. C Cov E *Cov* 87-91; V Wolvey w Burton Hastings, Copston Magna etc from 91. *St John's Vicarage, School Lane, Wolvey, Hinckley, Leics LE10 3LH* Hinckley (0455) 220385

JAMES, Richard Andrew. b 44. Mert Coll Ox BA67 MA70. Tyndale Hall Bris DipTh69. **d** 70 **p** 71. C Bebington *Ches* 70-73; C Histon *Ely* 73-77; Chapl Guildf Coll of Tech 77-80; C Guildf St Sav w Stoke-next-Guildf 77-80; Chapl Bedf Coll of HE *St Alb* 81-83; TV Ipsley *Worc* 84-89; R Mulbarton w Kenningham *Nor* from 89. *The Rectory, Mulbarton, Norwich NR14 8JS* Mulbarton (0508) 70296

JAMES, Richard David. b 45. Lon Coll of Div 67. **d** 70 **p** 71. C Boultham *Linc* 70-74; C Waltham 74-77; C New Waltham 74-77; P-in-c New Cleethorpes 77; TV Cleethorpes 77-87; TR E Bris from 87. *St Ambrose Vicarage, Stretford Avenue, Bristol BS5 7AN* Bristol (0272) 517299

JAMES, Richard William. b 47. St D Coll Lamp DipTh75. **d** 75 **p** 76. C Hubberston *St D* 75-78; R Pendine w Llanmiloe and Eglwys Gymyn w Marros 78-83; V Caerwent w Dinham and Llanfair Discoed etc *Mon* 83-84; Chapl Gothenburg w Halmstad, Jonkoping etc *Eur* 84-89; P-in-c Shooters Hill Ch Ch *S'wark* from 89. *Christ Church Vicarage, 1 Craigholm, London SE18 3RR* 081-856 5858

JAMES, Roger Michael. b 44. K Coll Lon BD66 AKC66. **d** 69 **p** 70. C Frindsbury w Upnor *Roch* 69-72; Lic to Offic *St Alb* 73-78; C Digswell 78-81; R Knebworth from 81. *The Rectory, 15 St Martin's Road, Knebworth, Herts SG3 6ER* Stevenage (0438) 812101

JAMES, Stephen Lynn. b 53. Middx Poly BA86. Oak Hill Th Coll 83. **d** 86 **p** 87. C Heigham H Trin *Nor* 86-89; Canada from 89. *St John's (Shaughnessy), 1490 Nanton Avenue, Vancouver, British Columbia, Canada, V6H 2E2* Vancouver (604) 731-4966

JAMES, William Arthur. b 10. Univ of Wales BA40. St Mich Coll Llan 40. **d** 42 **p** 43. R Bedwas *Mon* 54-77; rtd 77. *9 Trapwell Road, Caerphilly, M Glam CF8 3DU*

JAMES, William Glynne George. b 39. Trin Coll Carmarthen 82. **d** 85 **p** 86. NSM Gorseinon *S & B* from 85. *23 Cecil Road, Gowerton, Swansea SA4 3DF* Swansea (0792) 872363

JAMESON, David Kingsbury. b 28. Mert Coll Ox BA50 MA55. Qu Coll Birm 50. **d** 53 **p** 54. V Portsea St Cuth *Portsm* 65-70; V Enfield Jes Chpl *Lon* 70-74; RD Nuneaton *Cov* 74-79; V Nuneaton St Nic 74-80; Org Sec (Leics and Northants) CECS 80-82; Lic to Offic *Leic* 80-82; Perm to Offic *Pet* 80-82; P-in-c Forty Hill Jes Ch *Lon* 82-87; V 87-91; rtd 91. *St Bridget's Vicarage, Bridestowe, Okehampton, Devon EX20 2ER*

JAMESON, Canon Dermot Christopher Ledgard. b 27. TCD BA49 MA54. CITC 49. **d** 50 **p** 51. C Seagoe *D & D* 50-53; C Holywood 53-57; I Kilkeel 57-62; I Donaghcloney w Waringstown 62-79; Can Dromore Cathl from 77; I Kilbroney from 79; Treas Dromore Cathl 81-83; Prec Dromore Cathl 83-90; Chan Dromore Cathl from 90. *The Vicarage, 15 Kilbroney Road, Rostrevor, Co Down* Rostrevor (06937) 38293

JAMESON, Geoffrey Vaughan. b 27. Culham Coll Ox CertEd51 St Luke's Coll Ex ACertEd52. Wycliffe Hall Ox 68. **d** 70 **p** 71. C Buckm *Ox* 70-73; R Exton w Whitwell *Pet* 73-86; V Marystowe, Coryton, Stowford, Lewtrenchard etc *Ex* 86-90; rtd 90; Perm to Offic *Portsm* from 91. *18 Eglantine Walk, Cowplain, Waterlooville, Hants PO8 9BG* Horndean (0705) 571112

JAMESON, Canon John Edward. b 16. Kelham Th Coll 34. **d** 39 **p** 40. V Gosforth All SS *Newc* 62-76; Hon Can Newc Cathl 72-83; R Rothbury 76-83; rtd 83. *29 Magdalene Fields, Warkworth, Morpeth, Northd NE65 0UF* Alnwick (0665) 712510

JAMESON, Peter. b 31. Trin Coll Cam BA54 MA60. Linc Th Coll. **d** 62 **p** 63. C Earl's Court St Cuth w St Matthias *Lon* 62-68; C Notting Hill St Clem 68-72; C Notting Hill St Clem and St Mark 72-74; TV Notting Hill 74-77; V Stoke Newington St Olave from 77. *St Olave's Vicarage, Woodberry Down, London N4 2TW* 081-800 1374

JAMIESON, Hugh Gollan. b 20. TCD BA49. CITC 49. **d** 49 **p** 50. I Mothel *C & O* 69-76; I Badoney Lower *D & R* 76-78; I Donagh w Tyholland and Errigal Truagh *Clogh* 78-82; I Killeshandra w Killegar and Derrylane *K, E & A* 82-87; rtd 87. *Rose Cottage, Killyboley, Glaslough, Monaghan, Irish Republic* Monaghan (47) 88231

JAMIESON, Kenneth Euan Oram. b 24. Lon Univ DipTh68. Roch Th Coll 60. **d** 62 **p** 63. R Colchester St Mary Magd *Chelmsf* 66-71; V Bexleyheath St Pet *Roch* 71-78; P-in-c Maidstone St Faith *Cant* 78-83; P-in-c Maidstone St Paul 78-83; Ind Chapl *St Alb* 83-89; rtd 89; Lic to Offic *B & W* from 89. *4 Ashley Road, Taunton, Somerset TA1 5BP* Taunton (0823) 289367

JAMIESON, Marilyn. b 52. **d** 91. Par Dn Gateshead St Cuth w St Paul *Dur* 91; Par Dn Bensham from 91. *St Cuthbert's Vicarage, 56 Rectory Road, Gateshead, Tyne & Wear NE8 1XL* 091-477 8522

JAMIESON, Rosalind Heather. b 49. CertEd71. St Jo Coll Dur 79. **dss** 81 **d** 87. Queensbury All SS *Lon* 81-85; Richmond H Trin and Ch Ch *S'wark* 85-87; Par Dn from 87. *24 Pagoda Avenue, Richmond, Surrey TW9 2HF* 081-940 1532

JAMIESON, Thomas Lindsay. b 53. N Lon Poly BSc74. Cranmer Hall Dur DipTh76. **d** 77 **p** 78. C Gateshead Fell *Dur* 77-80; C Gateshead 80-84; TV 84-90; P-in-c Gateshead St Cuth w St Paul 90-91; TV Bensham from 91. *St Cuthbert's Vicarage, 56 Rectory Road, Gateshead, Tyne & Wear NE8 1XL* 091-477 8522

JAMIESON, William Douglas. b 38. Oak Hill Th Coll 63. **d** 66 **p** 67. C Shrewsbury St Julian *Lich* 66-68; C Bucknall and Bagnall 68-70; C Otley *Bradf* 70-74; TV Keighley 74-81; V Utley from 81. *St Mark's Vicarage, Greenhead Road, Keighley, W Yorkshire BD20 6ED* Keighley (0535) 607003

JANES, David Edward. b 40. Lon Univ BSc67. Glouc Sch of Min 86. **d** 89 **p** 90. NSM Church Stretton *Heref* from 89. *15 Watling Street South, Church Stretton, Shropshire SY6 7BG* Church Stretton (0694) 722253

JANICKER, Laurence Norman. b 47. SS Mark & Jo Coll Chelsea DipEd69. Ridley Coll Melbourne 77 St Jo Coll Nottm 83. **d** 85 **p** 86. C Beverley Minster *York* 85-89; R Lockington and Lund and Scorborough w Leconfield from 89. *The Rectory, Lockington, Driffield, N Humberside YO25 9SU* Market Weighton (0430) 810604

JANSMA, Henry Peter. b 57. NE Bible Coll (USA) BA79. Westmr Th Sem (USA) MA85. **d** 91. C Spalding *Linc* from 91. *The Chantry, 7 Church Street, Spalding, Lincs PE11 2PB* Spalding (0775) 722631

JANVIER, Philip Harold. b 57. Trin Coll Bris BA87. **d** 87 **p** 88. C Much Woolton *Liv* 87-90; TV Toxteth St Philemon w St Gabr and St Cleopas from 90. *St Gabriel's Vicarage, 2 Steble Street, Liverpool L8 6QH* 051-708 7751

JAQUET, Peter Michael. b 23. ARIBA51. Wells Th Coll 56. **d** 57 **p** 58. V Sellindge w Monks Horton and Stowting *Cant* 60-78; C Drypool St Columba w St Andr and St Pet *York* 78-80; TV Drypool 80-86; rtd 86. *20 Harthill Avenue, Leconfield, Beverley, N Humberside HU17 7LN* Hornsea (0964) 550108

JARDIN, Kenneth. b 35. TCD 67. Chapl R Sch Arm 67-72; C Arm St Mark *Arm* 69-72; Chapl RAF 72-78; V Barlings *Linc* 78-83; P-in-c Stainton-by-Langworth 78; P-in-c Scothern w Sudbrooke 78; Chapl Monte Carlo *Eur* 83-87; P-in-c Sudbury and Somersal Herbert *Derby* from 87; Dep Chapl HM Open Pris Foston Hall and Sudbury from 87. *The Rectory, Sudbury, Derby DE6 5HS* Sudbury (0283) 585302

JARDINE, Anthony. b 38. Lon Univ DipTh70. Qu Coll Birm 64. **d** 67 **p** 68. C Baldock w Bygrave and Clothall *St Alb* 67-71; C N Stoneham *Win* 71-73; P-in-c Ecchinswell cum Sydmonton 73-79; P-in-c Burghclere w Newtown 78-79; R Burghclere w Newtown and Ecchinswell w Sydmonton 79-87; P-in-c Wonston 87; R Wonston and Stoke Charity w Hunton from 87. *The Rectory, Wonston, Sutton Scotney, Winchester, Hants SO21 3PA* Winchester (0962) 760240

JARDINE, David Eric Cranswick. b 30. CCC Ox BA53 DipTh54 MA57. Wycliffe Hall Ox 53. **d** 55 **p** 56. C Wavertree St Mary *Liv* 55-58; C Liv All So Springwood 58-62; C Horley *S'wark* 62-65; V Mitcham Ch Ch 65-72; V Iford *Win* 72-89; R Smannell w Enham Alamein from 89. *The Rectory, Dunhills Lane, Enham Alamein, Andover, Hants SP11 6HU* Andover (0264) 352827

JARDINE, David John (Brother David). b 42. QUB BA65. CITC 67. **d** 67 **p** 68. C Ballymacarrett St Patr *D & D* 67-70; Asst Chapl QUB 70-73; SSF from 73; Asst Chapl HM Pris Belf (Crumlin Road) 75-79; Chapl 79-85; USA 85-88; Sen Asst Warden Ch of Ireland Min of Healing from 88. *c/o The Friary, 75 Deerpark Road, Belfast BT14 7PW* Belfast (0232) 351480

JARDINE, Norman. b 47. QUB BSc72. Trin Coll Bris 74. **d** 76 **p** 77. C Magherafelt *D & D* 76-78; C Dundonald 78-80; Bp's C Ballybeen 80-88; I Willowfield from 88.

The Rectory, 149 My Lady's Road, Belfast BT6 8FE Belfast (0232) 457654

JARDINE, Thomas Parker. b 44. Oak Hill Th Coll BA87. **d** 87 **p** 88. C Crowborough *Chich* 87-91; R Dersingham w Anmer and Shernborne *Nor* from 91. *The Vicarage, Dersingham, King's Lynn, Norfolk PE31 6JA* Dersingham (0485) 40214

JARMAN, Christopher. b 38. QUB BA63. Wells Th Coll 69. **d** 71 **p** 72. C Leckhampton SS Phil and Jas *Glouc* 71-73; Chapl RN from 73. *c/o MOD, Lacon House, Theobald's Road, London WC1X 8RY* 071-430 6847

JARMAN, John Geoffrey. b 31. IEng. S'wark Ord Course 75. **d** 78 **p** 79. NSM Chigwell *Chelmsf* 78-81; NSM Leytonstone St Marg w St Columba 81-87; C Walthamstow St Sav 87-89; V Gt Bentley from 89; P-in-c Frating w Thorrington from 89. *The Vicarage, Moors Close, Great Bentley, Colchester CO7 8QL* Great Bentley (0206) 250476

JARMY, David Michael. b 49. Cam Univ PGCE90. Chich Th Coll 76. **d** 79 **p** 80. C St Leonards Ch Ch *Chich* 79-80; C St Leonards Ch Ch and St Mary 81-82; C St Leonards SS Pet and Paul 82-85; V Sidley 85-89; Perm to Offic *Pet* 89-90; Lt Gidding Community 89-90; NSM Oundle *Pet* from 90. *13 Kings Road, Oundle, Peterborough PE8 4AX* Oundle (0832) 272916

JARRATT, Robert Michael. b 39. K Coll Lon BD62 AKC62. NY Th Sem DMin85. **d** 63 **p** 64. C Corby St Columba *Pet* 63-67; Lay Tr Officer *Sheff* 67-71; Ind Chapl *S'wark* 72-80; P-in-c Betchworth 76-80; V Ranmoor *Sheff* from 80; RD Hallam from 87. *The Vicarage, 389A Fulwood Road, Sheffield S10 3GA* Sheffield (0742) 301671 or 301199

JARRATT, Stephen. b 51. Edin Univ BD76 St Kath Coll Liv CertEd77. **d** 78 **p** 79. C Horsforth *Ripon* 78-81; C Stanningley St Thos 81-84; P-in-c Fishponds St Jo *Bris* 84-85; V from 85. *St John's Vicarage, Mayfield Park, Bristol BS16 3NW* Bristol (0272) 654130

JARRETT, Martyn William. b 44. K Coll Lon BD67 AKC67 Hull Univ MPhil91. St Boniface Warminster 64. **d** 68 **p** 69. C Bris St Geo *Bris* 68-70; C Swindon New Town 70-74; C Northolt St Mary *Lon* 74-76; V Northolt W End St Jos 76-81; V Hillingdon St Andr 81-83; P-in-c Uxbridge Moor 82-83; V Uxbridge St Andr w St Jo 83-85; Lic to Offic 85-91; Selection Sec ACCM 85-88; Sen Selection Sec 89-91; V Chesterfield All SS *Derby* from 91. *28 Cromwell Road, Chesterfield, Derbyshire S40 4TH* Chesterfield (0246) 232937 or 206506

JARRETT-KERR, William Robert (Brother Martin). b 12. BNC Ox BA34 DipTh35 MA38. Westcott Ho Cam 35. **d** 36 **p** 37. CR from 40; S Africa 52-59; Lic to Offic *Ripon* 67-76; *Wakef* from 76; rtd 82. *House of the Resurrection, Mirfield, W Yorkshire WF14 0BN* Mirfield (0924) 494318

JARROW, Suffragan Bishop of. See SMITHSON, Rt Rev Alan

JARVIE, Alexander Michael Milne. b 40. Em Coll Cam BA63 MA66. Linc Th Coll 63. **d** 65 **p** 66. C Leeds St Aid *Ripon* 65-68; C Fleetwood *Blackb* 68-70; C N Gosforth *Newc* 70-73; P-in-c Copley *Wakef* 73-76; Chapl Derby City Hosp 76-84; Chapl Bris R Infirmary from 84. *5 Downs Road, Westbury-on-Trym, Bristol BS9 3TX* Bristol (0272) 621433 or 230000

JARVIS, David Thomas. b 15. St D Coll Lamp BA36. **d** 38 **p** 39. Jerusalem 69-71; V Turnham Green Ch Ch *Lon* 72-85; rtd 85; Perm to Offic *Heref* from 85. *28 Penn Grove Road, Hereford HR1 2BH* Hereford (0432) 270196

JARVIS, Canon Eric Thomas Noel. b 24. Qu Coll Cam BA52 MA54. Ridley Hall Cam 52. **d** 54 **p** 55. V Roundhay St Edm *Ripon* 68-86; RD Allerton 79-84; Hon Can Ripon Cathl 81-86; R St Olave Hart Street w All Hallows Staining etc *Lon* 86-90; V St Marg Pattens 86-90; rtd 90. *38 Dogget Road, Cherry Hinton, Cambridge CB1 4LF* Cambridge (0223) 213387

JARVIS, Geoffrey Thomas Henry. b 21. Bps' Coll Cheshunt 61. **d** 62 **p** 63. C Abbots Langley *St Alb* 68-70; Chapl to the Deaf 70-86; P-in-c Sandridge 76-79; V 79-86; rtd 86; Perm to Offic *Nor* from 88. *Two Gables, 56 Hempstead Road, Holt, Norfolk NR25 6DG* Holt (0263) 711051

JARVIS, Graham Michael. b 60. Golds Coll Lon BMus81 PGCE83. Trin Coll Bris BA91. **d** 91. C St Keverne *Truro* from 91. *Church House, Coverack, Helston, Cornwall TR12 6TA* St Keverne (0326) 280277

JARVIS, Ian Frederick Rodger. b 38. Bris Univ BA60. Tyndale Hall Bris 61. **d** 63 **p** 64. C Penge Ch Ch w H Trin *Roch* 63-67; C Bilston St Leon *Lich* 67-71; V Lozells St Silas *Birm* 71-76; V Chaddesden St Mary

Derby from 76. *The Vicarage, 133 Chaddesden Lane, Chaddesden, Derby DE2 6LL* Derby (0332) 672336

JARVIS, Jeffrey Wallace. b 45. d 75 p 76. C Cherry Hinton St Andr *Ely* 76-77; C Nottm St Mary *S'well* 77-78; C Nottm St Mary and St Cath 78; Australia from 78. *59 Kensington Terrace, Toowong, Queensland, Australia 4066* Brisbane (7) 371-9977

JARVIS, Kenneth Eric. b 06. AKC33. d 33 p 35. V Beaulieu *Win* 60-77; rtd 77; Perm to Offic *Chich* from 77. *4 Bramwell Lodge, Terry's Cross, Henfield, W Sussex EN5 9SX* Henfield (0273) 492735

JARVIS, Miss Mary. b 35. Leeds Univ BA57 Lon Univ CertEd59. Cranmer Hall Dur 78. dss 80 d 87. Low Harrogate St Mary *Ripon* 80-84; Wortley de Leeds 84-87; C 87-88; C Upper Armley from 88. *71 Burnsall Croft, Leeds LS12 3LH* Leeds (0532) 797832

JARVIS, Wilfrid Harry. b 20. Leeds Univ BA43. Coll of Resurr Mirfield 43. d 45 p 46. C Ox St Marg *Ox* 45-48; Chapl Summer Fields Sch Ox 49-58; C Worksop Priory *S'well* 60-64; C S'well Minster 64-65; V New Basford 65-89; V Basford St Aid from 89. *St Augustine's Vicarage, 14 Claremont Road, Nottingham NG5 1BH* Nottingham (0602) 605427

JARVIS, William Arthur Walter. b 16. St Edm Hall Ox BA38 MA42. Sarum Th Coll 38. d 40 p 41. R Allington w Boscombe *Sarum* 63-72; C Thatcham *Ox* 72-81; rtd 81; Perm to Offic *Ox* from 81. *14 The Green, Charlbury, Oxford OX7 3QA* Charlbury (0608) 810147

JARVIS, William Grantham. b 13. d 66 p 67. C Binley *Cov* 67-71; V Clifton upon Dunsmore w Brownsover 71-83; P-in-c 83; rtd 83; Perm to Offic *Chich* from 84. *12 Heathlands, Westfield, Hastings, E Sussex TN35 4QZ* Hastings (0424) 753595

JASPER, Arthur Thomas McLean. b 15. Open Univ BA. Oak Hill Th Coll 36. d 39 p 40. V Gulval *Truro* 67-73; Lic to Offic 73-80; Perm to Offic *Ex* from 78; *Ely* from 87; rtd 87. *21 Long Furlong, Over, Cambridge CB4 5PG* Swavesey (0954) 31090

JASPER, David. b 51. Jes Coll Cam BA72 MA76 Keble Coll Ox BD80 Dur Univ PhD83. St Steph Ho Ox BA75 MA79. d 76 p 77. C Buckm *Ox* 76-79; C Dur St Oswald *Dur* 80; Chapl Hatf Coll Dur 81-88; Dir Cen Study of Lit and Th Dur from 88; Prin St Chad's Coll Dur from 88. *69 Birkdale Gardens, Cheveley Green, Belmont, Durham DH1 2UL* 091-384 2353 or 374 3362

JASPER, David Julian McLean. b 44. Dur Univ BA66 Nottm Univ DipTh68. Linc Th Coll 66. d 68 p 69. C Redruth *Truro* 68-72; R 72-74; TV 74-75; V St Just in Penwith 75-86; P-in-c Sancreed 82-86. *Dumplings, 28 Kelsey Avenue, Finchampstead, Wokingham, Berks RG11 4TZ* Wokingham (0734) 730243

JASPER, James Roland. b 52. CA Tr Coll 56 NE Ord Course 82. d 84 p 84. C Newburn *Newc* 84-86; V Ansley *Cov* from 86. *The Vicarage, Ansley, Nuneaton, Warks CV10 9PS* Chapel End (0203) 396403

JASPER, Jonathan Ernest Farley. b 50. AKC72 DPMSA85. St Aug Coll Cant 73. d 73 p 74. C Cheshunt *St Alb* 73-75; C Bedf St Paul 75-77; C Bedf St Pet w St Cuth 75-77; Chapl Southn Univ *Win* 77-80; Chapl Lon Univ Medical Students *Lon* 80-86; PV Chich Cathl *Chich* 86-89; P-in-c Earls Colne and White Colne *Chelmsf* from 89; P-in-c Colne Engaine from 89. *The Vicarage, 5 Shut Lane, Earls Colne, Colchester CO6 2RE* Earls Colne (0787) 222262

JAUNDRILL, John Warwick. b 47. d 88 p 89. C Bistre *St As* 88-91; P-in-c Towyn and St George from 91. *The Vicarage, 11 Chester Avenue, Kinmel Bay, Rhyl, Clwyd LL18 5LA* Rhyl (0745) 350119

JAY, Colin. b 62. Keble Coll Ox BA85 St Jo Coll Dur BA89. Cranmer Hall Dur 87. d 90 p 91. C Bishopwearmouth St Gabr *Dur* from 90. *112 Cleveland Road, Sunderland SR4 7JT* 091-528 5470

JAY, Edmund Arthur. b 41. St Chad's Coll Dur BA63. d 65 p 66. C Southwick St Columba *Dur* 69-70; Hon C Westbury-on-Trym H Trin *Bris* 72-73; P-in-c S Shields St Fran *Dur* 73-76; C S Shields St Hilda w St Thos 76-79; Chapl S Shields Gen Hosp 79-85; rtd 88. *8 St Chad's Crescent, Sunderland SR3 3TR* 091-522 6938

JAY, Ms Nicola Mary. b 37. SRN58 ONC61. NE Ord Course 88. d 91. Par Dn Whitburn *Dur* from 91. *105 Wenlock Road, South Shields, Tyne & Wear NE34 9BD* 091-455 8233

JAY, Richard Hylton Michael. b 31. Bris Univ BEd75. Sarum & Wells Th Coll 77. d 79 p 80. NSM Bath St Barn w Englishcombe *B & W* 79-81; NSM Saltford w Corston and Newton St Loe 81-88; R Hatch Beauchamp w Beercrocombe, Curry Mallet etc from 89. *The Rectory, Hatch Beauchamp, Taunton, Somerset TA3 6AB* Hatch Beauchamp (0823) 480220

JAYNE, Martin Philip. b 49. MRTPI73 Man Univ BA71 Preston Poly DMS80. Carl Dioc Tr Course 87. d 90 p 91. NSM Natland *Carl* from 90. *12 Longmeadow Lane, Natland, Kendal, Cumbria LA9 7QZ* Sedgwick (05395) 60942

JEANES, Gordon Paul. b 55. Ox Univ BA79 MA82 BD90. St Steph Ho Ox 80. d 82 p 83. C S Wimbledon H Trin and St Pet *S'wark* 82-85; C Surbiton St Andr and St Mark 85-90; Chapl St Chad's Coll Dur from 90. *St Chad's College, 18 North Bailey, Durham DH1 3RH* 091-374 3367

JEANS, Alan Paul. b 58. MIAAS84 MIBCO84 Southn Univ BTh89. Sarum & Wells Th Coll 86. d 89 p 90. C Parkstone St Pet w Branksea and St Osmund *Sarum* from 89. *79 Church Road, Poole, Dorset BH14 0NS* Parkstone (0202) 743016

JEANS, David Bockley. b 48. Mert Coll Ox BA71 MA80 PGCE73. Trin Coll Bris DipHE85. d 85 p 86. C Clevedon St Andr and Ch Ch *B & W* 85-88; V Wadsley *Sheff* from 88. *The Vicarage, 91 Airedale Road, Sheffield S6 4AW* Sheffield (0742) 348481

JEAVONS, Maurice. b 32. Ely Th Coll 60. d 62 p 63. C Longton St Jo *Lich* 62-68; V Wednesfield St Greg 68-81; V Lower Gornal 81-90. *42 Sanbeds Road, Willenhall, W Midlands WV12 4EY* Willenhall (0902) 631831

JEE, Colin Scott. b 32. Worc Coll Ox BA55 MA59. Clifton Th Coll 55. d 57 p 58. C Spitalfields Ch Ch w All SS *Lon* 57-62; C New Malden and Coombe *S'wark* 62-66; R Ludgershall *Ox* 66-78; P-in-c Oakley 73-82; RD Waddesdon 73-78; R Ludgershall w Wotton Underwood and Ashendon from 78. *The Rectory, Ludgershall, Aylesbury, Bucks HP18 9PG* Brill (0844) 238335

JEE, Jonathan Noel. b 63. BNC Ox BA84 MA88. Wycliffe Hall Ox 85. d 88 p 89. C Brampton St Thos *Derby* from 88. *1 Rhodesia Road, Chesterfield, Derbyshire S40 3AL* Chesterfield (0246) 231089

JEFF, Gordon Henry. b 32. St Edm Hall Ox BA56 MA60. Wells Th Coll 59. d 61 p 62. C Sydenham St Bart *S'wark* 61-64; C Kidbrooke St Jas 64-66; V Clapham St Paul 66-72; V Raynes Park St Sav 73-79; RD Merton 77-79; V Carshalton Beeches 79-86; P-in-c Petersham 86-90; Chapl St Mich Convent from 90. *43 Ham Common Road, Richmond, Surrey TW10 7JG* 081-948 0775

JEFFERIES, Cecil Arthur. b 11. Glouc Th Course 68. d 69 p 70. Hon C Rodborough *Glouc* 69-78; Hon C Cainscross w Selsley 78-89; rtd 89. *Daytona, 29 Upper Church Road, Cainscross, Stroud, Glos GL5 4JF* Stroud (0453) 758287

JEFFERIES, Michael Lewis. b 45. St Jo Coll Nottm. d 87 p 88. C Pudsey St Lawr and St Paul *Bradf* from 87. *18 West Park, Pudsey, W Yorkshire LS28 7SN* Pudsey (0532) 574582

JEFFERIES, Phillip John. b 42. St Chad's Coll Dur BA65 DipTh67. d 67 p 68. C Tunstall Ch Ch *Lich* 67-71; C Wolv St Pet 71-74; P-in-c Oakengates 74-80; V 80-82; P-in-c Ketley 78-82; V Horninglow from 82. *Horninglow Vicarage, Rolleston Road, Burton-on-Trent DE13 0JZ* Burton-on-Trent (0283) 68613

JEFFERSON, Charles Dudley. b 55. St Pet Coll Ox BA78 MA81. Ridley Hall Cam 79. d 81 p 82. C Chadkirk *Ches* 81-84; C Macclesfield St Pet 84-85; C 'Macclesfield Team Par 85-89; R Elworth and Warmingham from 89. *The Rectory, 38 Roman Way, Sandbach, Cheshire CW11 9EW* Crewe (0270) 762415

JEFFERSON, David Charles. b 33. Leeds Univ BA57. Coll of Resurr Mirfield 57. d 59 p 60. C Kennington Cross St Anselm *S'wark* 59-62; C Richmond St Mary 62-64; Lic to Offic from 64; Chapl Wilson's Gr Sch Camberwell 64-74; Chapl Wilson's Sch Wallington from 74. *15 Sandown Drive, Carshalton, Surrey SM5 4LN* 081-669 0640 or 773 2931

JEFFERY, Alfred Stephen. b 91. St Steph Ho Ox 31. d 31 p 32. R E Allington *Ex* 56-61; rtd 61. *Rest Haven, Gussiford Lane, Exmouth, Devon EX8 2SD* Exmouth (0395) 6761

JEFFERY, Arthur Francis. b 11. St D Coll Lamp BA33 St Mich Coll Llan 33. d 35 p 36. V Rhydymwyn *St As* 68-78; rtd 78; Perm to Offic *St As* from 78. *36 Llys Alyn, Rhydymwyn, Mold, Clwyd CH7 5HW* Mold (0352) 741435

JEFFERY, Graham. b 35. Qu Coll Cam BA58. Wells Th Coll 58. d 60 p 61. C Southn Maybush St Pet *Win* 60-63; Australia 63-66; C E Grinstead St Swithun *Chich* 66-68; C-in-c Hydneye CD 68-74; V Wick 74-76; C Hove 76-78; P-in-c Newtimber w Pyecombe 78-82; R Poynings w Edburton, Newtimber and Pyecombe from 82. *The Rectory, Poynings, Brighton BN45 7AQ* Poynings (0273) 857375

JEFFERY, Kenneth Charles. b 40. Univ of Wales BA64 Linacre Coll Ox BA67 MA70. St Steph Ho Ox 64. **d** 67 **p** 68. C Swindon New Town *Bris* 67-68; C Summertown *Ox* 68-71; C Brighton St Pet *Chich* 71-77; V Ditchling from 77. *The Vicarage, Ditchling, Hassocks, W Sussex BN6 8TS* Hassocks (07918) 3165

JEFFERY, Michael Frank. b 48. Linc Th Coll 74. **d** 76 **p** 77. C Caterham Valley *S'wark* 76-79; C Tupsley *Heref* 79-82; P-in-c Stretton Sugwas 82-84; P-in-c Bishopstone 83-84; P-in-c Kenchester and Bridge Sollers 83-84; V Whiteshill *Glouc* from 84. *The Vicarage, Farmhill Lane, Stroud, Glos GL5 4DD* Stroud (0453) 764757

JEFFERY, Norman. b 42. Bps' Coll Cheshunt. **d** 67 **p** 68. C Putney St Marg *S'wark* 67-71; C Hoddesdon *St Alb* 71-74; P-in-c Roxton w Gt Barford 74-79; V 79-86; V Woburn Sands from 86. *The Vicarage, Church Road, Woburn Sands, Milton Keynes MK17 8TR* Milton Keynes (0908) 582581

JEFFERY, Peter James. b 41. Leeds Univ BSc63 Oak Hill Th Coll 64. **d** 66 **p** 67. C Streatham Park St Alb *S'wark* 66-70; C Northn St Giles *Pet* 70-73; C Rushden St Pet 73-76; C Rushden w Newton Bromswold 77-78; V Siddal *Wakef* 78-85; V Sowerby Bridge w Norland from 85. *The Vicarage, Park Road, Sowerby Bridge, W Yorkshire HX6 2PG* Halifax (0422) 831253

JEFFERY, Peter Noel. b 37. Pemb Coll Ox BA60 MA64. Linc Th Coll 60. **d** 62 **p** 63. C W Smethwick *Birm* 62-64; P-in-c Bordesley St Andr 64-69; R Turvey *St Alb* from 69; P-in-c Stevington from 79. *The Rectory, Turvey, Bedford* Turvey (023064) 210

JEFFERY, Richard William Christopher. b 43. Ex Univ BA65. Coll of Resurr Mirfield 66. **d** 68 **p** 69. C Wembley w Wymering *Portsm* 68-71; C Salisbury St Mich *Sarum* 71-74; TV Ridgeway 74-80; V Stanford in the Vale w Goosey and Hatford *Ox* 80-89; V Topsham *Ex* from 89. *The Vicarage, Globefield, Exeter EX3 0EZ* Exeter (0392) 876120

JEFFERY, Very Rev Robert Martin Colquhoun. b 35. K Coll Lon BD58 AKC58. **d** 59 **p** 60. C Grangetown *Dur* 59-61; C Barnes St Mary *S'wark* 61-63; Asst Sec Miss and Ecum Coun Ch Assembly 64-68; Sec Dept Miss and Unity BCC 68-71; V Headington *Ox* 71-78; RD Cowley 73-78; P-in-c Tong *Lich* 78-83; V 83-87; Dioc Missr 78-80; Hon Can Lich Cathl 80-87; Adn Salop 80-87; Dean Worc from 87. *The Deanery, 10 College Green, Worcester WR1 2LH* Worcester (0905) 27821

JEFFERY, Canon Robert Michael. b 17. Selw Coll Cam BA39 MA43. Westcott Ho Cam 39. **d** 41 **p** 42. S Africa 46-76; Chapl Prestfelde Sch Shrewsbury 76-85; rtd 83. *23 St Nicholas Hospital, Salisbury, Wilts SP1 2SW* Salisbury (0722) 21737

JEFFERYES, June Ann. b 37. Dur Univ BA58. W Midl Minl Tr Course 87. **d** 90. NSM Caverswall *Lich* from 90. *8 Vicarage Crescent, Caverswall, Stoke-on-Trent ST11 9EW* Blythe Bridge (0782) 393309

JEFFERYES, Neil. b 37. St Andr Univ BSc60 Lon Univ BD62. Tyndale Hall Bris 60. **d** 63 **p** 64. C St Helens St Helen *Liv* 63-68; V Barrow St Mark *Carl* 68-77; RD Furness 74-77; P-in-c Tetsworth *Ox* 77-81; P-in-c Adwell w S Weston 77-81; P-in-c Stoke Talmage w Wheatfield 77-81; R Aston 81-85; R Tetsworth, Adwell w S Weston, Lewknor etc 81-86; V Caverswall *Lich* from 86; P-in-c Dilhorne from 86; RD Cheadle from 91. *8 Vicarage Crescent, Caverswall, Stoke-on-Trent ST11 9EW* Blythe Bridge (0782) 393309

JEFFORD, Brian Harrison. b 30. S Dios Minl Tr Scheme 79. **d** 81 **p** 82. NSM Eastbourne St Jo *Chich* from 81. *20 Derwent Road, Eastbourne, E Sussex BN20 7PH* Eastbourne (0323) 30265

JEFFORD, Peter Ernest. b 29. AKC53. **d** 54 **p** 55. C Berkeley *Glouc* 54-57; C Petersfield w Sheet *Portsm* 57-61; R Rollesby w Burgh w Billockby *Nor* 62-71; V Watton 71-81; V Watton w Carbrooke and Ovington 81-82; P-in-c Brampford Speke *Ex* 82-83; P-in-c Cadbury 82-83; P-in-c Thorverton 82-83; P-in-c Upton Pyne 82-83; TR Thorverton, Cadbury, Upton Pyne etc from 83. *The Vicarage, Thorverton, Exeter EX5 5NP* Exeter (0392) 860332

JEFFORD, Ronald. b 46. **d** 91. C Ebbw Vale *Mon* from 91. *St John's Vicarage, 10 The Crescent, Ebbw Vale, Gwent NP3 6EG* Ebbw Vale (0495) 306203

JEFFREE, Robin. b 29. AKC54. **d** 55 **p** 56. C N Harrow St Alb *Lon* 55-59; C Hendon St Mary 59-62; V Manea *Ely* 62-67; V Hartford 67-83; P-in-c Denver *Ely* 83; R from 83; P-in-c Ryston w Roxham 83; V from 83; V W Dereham from 83. *The Rectory, Denver, Downham Market, Norfolk PE38 0DP* Downham Market (0366) 387727

JEFFREYS, Timothy John. b 58. Man Univ BSc79. Cranmer Hall Dur 82. **d** 86 **p** 87. C Goodmayes All SS *Chelmsf* 86-88. *5 Herbert House, 312 Kennington Lane, London SE11 5HY*

JEFFRIES, Canon Peter George Charles. b 28. Qu Coll Birm 54. **d** 56 **p** 57. C Slad *Glouc* 56-59; C Tuffley 59-62; V Clearwell 62-69; R The Ampneys w Driffield and Poulton from 69; RD Fairford from 86; Hon Can Glouc Cathl from 89. *The Rectory, Ampney St Peter, Cirencester, Glos GL7 5SH* Cirencester (0285) 851240

JELBART, Alexander Parismas. b 21. Oak Hill Th Coll DipTh53. **d** 53 **p** 54. TR Chell *Lich* 62-70; V Madeley *Heref* 70-78; V St Helens St Mark *Liv* 78-86; rtd 86; Perm to Offic *Leic* from 86. *12 Greenacres Drive, Lutterworth, Leics LE17 4TG* Lutterworth (0455) 556355

JELF, Pauline Margaret. b 55. Chich Th Coll 88. **d** 90. Par Dn Clayton *Lich* from 90. *285 Clayton Road, Newcastle-under-Lyme, Staffs ST5 3EU* Newcastle-under-Lyme (0782) 635057

JELLEY, David. b 25. St Deiniol's Hawarden 86. **d** 87 **p** 88. NSM Evington *Leic* from 87. *117A Gartree Road, Oadby, Leicester* Leicester (0533) 703759

JELLEY, James Dudley. b 46. Linc Th Coll 78. **d** 80 **p** 81. C Stockwell Green St Andr *S'wark* 80-85; P-in-c Camberwell St Phil and St Mark 85-90; V from 91. *St Philip's Vicarage, Avondale Square, London SE1 5PD* 071-237 3239

JELLY, James Hugh. b 08. Selw Coll Cam BA31 MA36. Wells Th Coll 31. **d** 32 **p** 33. R S Petherton *B & W* 58-74; rtd 74; Hon C Malborough w S Huish *Ex* 74-78; Perm to Offic *B & W* from 79. *53 Hillview Road, Minehead, Somerset TA24 8EF* Minehead (0643) 2041

JENKIN, Hon Charles Alexander Graham. b 54. BScEng. Westcott Ho Cam 81. **d** 84 **p** 85. C Binley *Cov* 84-88; TV Canvey Is *Chelmsf* from 88. *51 St Anne's Road, Canvey Island, Essex SS8 7LS* Canvey Island (0268) 696200

JENKIN, Christopher Cameron. b 36. BNC Ox BA61 MA64. Clifton Th Coll 61. **d** 63 **p** 64. C Walthamstow St Mary *Chelmsf* 63-68; C Surbiton Hill Ch Ch *S'wark* 68-78; V Newport St Jo *Portsm* 78-88; R Newbarns w Hawcoat *Carl* from 88. *St Paul's Rectory, 353 Abbey Road, Barrow-in-Furness LA13 9JY* Barrow-in-Furness (0229) 821546

JENKINS, Allan Kenneth. b 40. Lon Univ BD63 AKC63 MTh69 PhD85. St Mich Coll Llan 63. **d** 64 **p** 65. C Llanblethian w Cowbridge *Llan* 64-70; India 70-76; R Llanarth w Clytha, Llansantffraed and Bryngwyn *Mon* 76-78; Dir of Studies Chich Th Coll 78-83; P-in-c Fowlmere *Ely* 83-87; P-in-c Thriplow 83-87; Sen Tutor E Anglian Minl Tr Course 83-87; Sen Chapl Cardiff Colls from 87; Dioc Dir Post-Ord Tr *Llan* from 88. *The Anglican Chaplaincy, 61 Park Place, Cardiff CF1 3AT* Cardiff (0222) 232550

JENKINS, Anne Christina. b 47. Birm Univ BA70 Hull Univ CertEd71 St Jo Coll Dur BA77 DipTh78. Cranmer Hall Dur 75. **dss** 78 **d** 87. Coatham *York* 78-81; OHP 81-87; Perm to Offic *York* 81-87; Ghana 87-88; Par Dn Beeston *Ripon* from 88. *38 Beechcroft View, Leeds LS11 0LN* Leeds (0532) 702109

JENKINS, Clifford Thomas. b 38. IEng MIEIecIE. Sarum & Wells Th Coll. **d** 77 **p** 78. Chapl Yeovil Coll from 77; Hon C Yeovil *B & W* 77-87; Chs FE Liason Officer (Dios B & W, Bris & Glouc) from 87; FE Adv Gen Syn Bd of Educn & Meth Div from 90. *Bethany, 10 Grove Avenue, Yeovil, Somerset BA20 2BB* Yeovil (0935) 75043

JENKINS, Clive Ronald. b 57. Ripon Coll Cuddesdon 81. **d** 84 **p** 85. C E Grinstead St Swithun *Chich* 84-87; C Horsham 87-88; TV 88-90; Dioc Youth Chapl from 90. *34 Glebelands, Pulborough, W Sussex RH20 2JJ* Pulborough (07982) 3462

JENKINS, Cyril. b 27. Univ of Wales (Lamp) BA53. Wells Th Coll 53. **d** 55 **p** 56. V Gnosall *Lich* 69-72; Chapl St Alb Sch Chorley 72-79; Lic to Offic *Blackb* from 73; Hd of Relig Studies Runshaw Coll 74-84; Lect Runshaw Tertiary Coll 84-86; rtd 86. *55 Church Walk, Euxton, Chorley, Lancs PR7 6HL* Chorley (02572) 63973

JENKINS, David Charles. b 04. St Mich Coll Llan 55. **d** 56 **p** 57. R Cemmaes *Ban* 61-70; R Llangristiolus w Cerrigceinwen and Trewalchmai 70-73; R Garthbeibio and Llanerfyl and Llangadfan *St As* 73-75; rtd 75. *Rhosilly, Newtown Road, Machynlleth, Powys* Machynlleth (0654) 2533

✠**JENKINS, Rt Rev David Edward.** b 25. Qu Coll Ox BA51 MA54 Dur Univ DD87. Linc Th Coll 52. **d** 53 **p** 54 **c** 84. C Birm Cathl *Birm* 53-54; Lect Qu Coll Birm

53-54; Chapl Qu Coll Ox 54-69; Lect Th Ox Univ 55-69; Can Th Leic Cathl *Leic* 66-82; Dir WCC Humanum Studies 69-73; Dir Wm Temple Foundn Man 73-78; Jt Dir Wm Temple Foundn from 79; Prof Th and Relig Studies Leeds Univ 79-84; Bp Dur from 84. *Auckland Castle, Bishop Auckland, Co Durham DL14 7NR* Bishop Auckland (0388) 602576

JENKINS, David Harold. b 61. SS Coll Cam BA84 MA87 Ox Univ BA88. Ripon Coll Cuddesdon 86. **d** 89 **p** 90. C Chesterton Gd Shep *Ely* 89-91; C Earley St Pet *Ox* from 91. *33 Clevdon Drive, Reading RG6 2XF* Reading (0734) 871396

JENKINS, Canon David Myrddin. b 30. Univ of Wales BEd76. St Mich Coll Llan 59. **d** 61 **p** 62. C Haverfordwest St Mary w St Thos *St D* 61-63; C Pemb Dock 63-67; Japan 67-69; Miss to Seamen 69-71; V Llansteffan and Llan-y-bri etc *St D* 71-78; R Llantwit Major *Llan* from 78; Can Llan Cathl from 89. *The Rectory, LLantwit Major, S Glam CF6 9SS* Llantwit Major (0446) 792324

JENKINS, David Noble. b 25. CCC Cam BA47 MA50. Cuddesdon Coll 48. **d** 50 **p** 51. Chapl Eastbourne Coll E Sussex 66-74; V Jarvis Brook *Chich* 75-90; rtd 90; USA from 90. *c/o 41 Brook Close, Tisbury, Salisbury, Wilts SP3 6PW*

JENKINS, David Roland. b 32. Kelham Th Coll 55. **d** 59 **p** 60. C Middlesb St Jo the Ev *York* 59-60; C Kingston upon Hull St Alb 60-64; C Roehampton H Trin *S'wark* 64-68; V Dawley St Jerome *Lon* 68-73; R Harlington from 73. *The Rectory, St Peter's Way, Hayes, Middx UB3 5AB* 081-759 9569

JENKINS, David Thomas. b 43. RIBA70 Lon Univ DipTh79. S'wark Ord Course 76. **d** 79 **p** 80. NSM Merthyr Tydfil and Cyfarthfa *Llan* 79-86; NSM Brecon St David w Llanspyddid and Llanilltyd *S & B* 86-91; P-in-c Llanguicke from 91. *The Vicarage, 10 Uplands, Pontardawe, Swansea SA5 9PA* Swansea (0792) 862003

JENKINS, Canon David Thomas Ivor. b 28. Birm Univ MA63 K Coll Lon BD52 AKC52. **d** 53 **p** 54. C Bilton *Cov* 53-56; V Wolston 56-61; Asst Dir RE *Carl* 61-63; V Carl St Barn 63-72; V Carl St Cuth 72-76; P-in-c Carl St Mary w St Paul 72-76; Hon Can Carl Cathl from 76; V Carl St Cuth w St Mary from 76; Dioc Sec from 84. *St Cuthbert's Vicarage, West Walls, Carlisle CA3 8UF* Carlisle (0228) 21982

JENKINS, Canon Eric Neil. b 23. Univ of Wales BSc43 MSc47. Wycliffe Hall Ox 60. **d** 62 **p** 63. V Hale *Liv* 65-73; Bp's Adv on Soc and Scientific Affairs 73-88; V Hightown 73-88; Hon Can Liv Cathl 83-89; rtd 89. *51 Oulton Road, Liverpool L16 8NP* 051-722 5515

JENKINS, Ernest Dennis. b 28. S Dios Minl Tr Scheme 80. **d** 83 **p** 84. NSM Lancing St Mich *Chich* 83-86; C E Grinstead St Swithun 86-89; C Portslade St Nic and St Andr from 89. *75 Vale Road, Portslade, Brighton BN14 1GD* Brighton (0273) 414888

JENKINS, Very Rev Frank Graham. b 23. St D Coll Lamp BA47 Jes Coll Ox BA49 MA53. St Mich Coll Llan 49. **d** 50 **p** 51. V Risca *Mon* 64-75; Can St Woolos Cathl 67-76; V Caerleon 75-76; Dean Mon 76-90; rtd 90. *Rivendell, 209 Christchurch Road, Newport, Gwent NP9 7QL* Newport (0633) 255278

JENKINS, Frederick Llewellyn. b 14. St D Coll Lamp BA35 St Mich Coll Llan 36. **d** 37 **p** 38. Chapl R Masonic Sch Bushey 64-77; rtd 77; Perm to Offic *Lich* from 77. *Plas Uchaf, Trefonen, Oswestry, Shropshire SY10 9DT* Oswestry (0691) 653918

JENKINS, Garry Frederick. b 48. Southn Univ BTh79. Chich Th Coll 75. **d** 79 **p** 80. C Kingsbury St Andr *Lon* 79-84; C Leigh St Clem *Chelmsf* 84-88; P-in-c Brentwood St Geo from 88. *The Vicarage, 28 Robin Hood Road, Brentwood, Essex CM15 9EN* Brentwood (0277) 213618

JENKINS, Gary John. b 59. York Univ BA80 CertEd81. Oak Hill Th Coll BA89. **d** 89 **p** 90. C Norwood *S'wark* from 89. *12 Chestnut Road, London SE27 9LF* 081-670 2400

JENKINS, Canon George Patrick. b 36. Univ of Wales (Lamp) BA61. Lich Th Coll 61. **d** 63 **p** 64. C Dursley *Glouc* 63-66; C Stroud H Trin 66-69; V Churcham w Bulley 69-81; RD Forest N from 79; V Churcham w Bulley and Minsterworth from 81; Hon Can Glouc Cathl from 90. *Churcham Vicarage, Gloucester GL2 8AF* Minsterworth (045275) 252

JENKINS, Graham Llewelyn. b 21. Llan Dioc Tr Scheme 79. **d** 82 **p** 83. NSM Llansawel w Briton Ferry *Llan* 82-85; Perm to Offic from 85. *14 Dyfed Road, Neath, W Glam SA11 3AP* Neath (0639) 2989

JENKINS, Huw Martin. b 56. **d** 88 **p** 89. C Bettws St Dav *St D* from 88. *44 Maes-y-Coed, Ammanford, Dyfed SA18 2JB* Ammanford (0269) 591035

JENKINS, Canon Illtyd Stephen. b 93. Qu Coll Ox BA16 MA18. Cuddesdon Coll 19. **d** 20 **p** 21. V St Ives *Truro* 36-63; rtd 63. *32 Cavell Road, Oxford OX4 4AS* Oxford (0865) 770571

JENKINS, Islwyn. b 12. Univ of Wales BA37 DipEd49 MA57. St Mich Coll Llan 37. **d** 38 **p** 39. Sen Lect Trin Coll Carmarthen 66-77; Lic to Offic *St D* from 66; rtd 77. *15 Courtlands Park, Carmarthen, Dyfed SA31 1EH* Carmarthen (0267) 237432

JENKINS, Jeanette. b 42. St Jo Coll Nottm 83. **dss** 84 **d** 86. NSM Kilmarnock *Glas* from 84; NSM Irvine St Andr LEP from 84; NSM Ardrossan from 84. *4 Gleneagles Avenue, Kilwinning, Ayrshire KA13 6RD* Kilwinning (0294) 53383

JENKINS, John Alfred Morgan. b 36. Univ of Wales (Lamp) BA58 St Cath Coll Ox BA60 MA64. Wycliffe Hall Ox. **d** 61 **p** 62. C Sketty *S & B* 61-69; Br Honduras 69-72; V W Byfleet *Guildf* 73-89; R Monken Hadley *Lon* from 89. *The Rectory, Hadley Common, Barnet, Herts EN5 5QD* 081-449 2414

JENKINS, John Francis. b 46. Ripon Hall Ox 77 Ripon Coll Cuddesdon 75. **d** 77 **p** 78. C Filton *Bris* 77-79; C Bris St Andr Hartcliffe 79-84; P-in-c Bris H Cross Inns Court 84-85; V from 85. *Holy Cross Vicarage, Inns Court Green, Bristol BS4 1TF* Bristol (0272) 664123

JENKINS, John Howard David. b 51. Birm Univ BA72. St Steph Ho Ox 72. **d** 74 **p** 75. C Milford Haven *St D* 74-77; PV Llan Cathl *Llan* 77-81; Chapl Lowther Coll St As 81-84; VC St As Cathl *St As* 81-84; C Neath w Llantwit *Llan* 84-86; Chapl Colston's Sch Bris 86-91; Chapl Blue Coat Sch Birm from 91. *Blue Coat School, Metchley Lane, Harborne, Birmingham B17 0HR* 021-454 1452

JENKINS, John Morgan. b 33. Mon Dioc Tr Scheme 82. **d** 85 **p** 86. NSM Cwmbran *Mon* from 85. *5 Ridgeway Avenue, Newport, Gwent NP9 5AF* Newport (0633) 259979

JENKINS, John Raymond. b 26. K Coll Lon 52. **d** 53 **p** 54. C Wrexham *St As* 53-56; Hon C 77-82; C Welshpool 56-57; V Mochdre 57-65; V Llandyssul *St D* 65-67; V Llanfair Caereinion w Llanllugan *St As* 67-70; V Llanychaiarn w Llanddeiniol *St D* from 82. *The Vicarage, Llanfarian, Aberystwyth, Dyfed SY23 4BX* Aberystwyth (0970) 617100

JENKINS, Kenneth Thomas. b 15. St D Coll Lamp BA36 Ripon Hall Ox 36. **d** 38 **p** 39. Chapl R Masonic Sch Bushey 57-59; rtd 80. *Le Terme de Ferrand, 24480 Alles sur Dordogne, France*

JENKINS, Lawrence Clifford. b 45. AKC70 Open Univ BA77. St Aug Coll Cant. **d** 71 **p** 72. C Osmondthorpe St Phil *Ripon* 71-74; C Monkseaton St Mary *Newc* 75-78; V Shiremoor 78-84; V Wheatley Hills *Sheff* from 84. *The Vicarage, Central Boulevard, Wheatley Hills, Doncaster, S Yorkshire DN2 5PE* Doncaster (0302) 342047

JENKINS, Paul Morgan. b 44. Sussex Univ BEd68 Fitzw Coll Cam BA73 MA76. Westcott Ho Cam 71. **d** 74 **p** 75. C Forest Gate St Edm *Chelmsf* 74-77; P-in-c Stourpaine, Durweston and Bryanston *Sarum* 77-83; Perm to Offic 83-85; Chapl Bryanston Sch Blandford 77-85; Lic to Offic *Derby* 84-91; Asst Chapl and Housemaster Repton Sch Derby 84-89; Dean of Chpl 89-91; R Singleton *Chich* from 91; V E Dean from 91. *The Rectory, Singleton, Chichester, W Sussex PO18 0EZ* Singleton (024363) 213

JENKINS, Ven Raymond Gordon Finney. b 98. TCD BA23 MA32 BD36. CITC 28 TCD Div Sch Div Test28. **d** 30 **p** 31. I Dub Grangegorman *D & G* 39-76; Lect TCD 39-70; Chan St Patr Cathl Dub 62-76; Adn Dub *D & G* 61-74; rtd 76; Hon CV Ch Ch Cathl Dub *D & G* from 76. *4 Damer Court, Upper Wellington Street, Dublin 7, Irish Republic* Dublin (1) 301156

JENKINS, Richard David. b 33. Magd Coll Cam BA58 MA. Westcott Ho Cam 59. **d** 61 **p** 62. C Staveley *Derby* 61-64; C Billingham St Aid *Dur* 64-68; V Walsall Pleck and Bescot *Lich* 68-73; R Whitchurch from 73; RD Wem and Whitchurch from 85. *The Rectory, Church Street, Whitchurch, Shropshire SY13 1LB* Whitchurch (0948) 892342

JENKINS, Richard Morvan. b 44. St Mich Coll Llan DipTh68 DPS69. **d** 69 **p** 70. C Tenby *St D* 69-73; V Llanrhian w Llanhywel and Carnhedryn 73-77; V Llanrhian w Llanhywel and Carnhedryn etc 77-80; R Johnston w Steynton from 80. *The Vicarage, Steynton, Milford Haven, Dyfed SA73 1AW* Milford Haven (0646) 692867

JENKINS, Canon Robert Francis. b 33. BNC Ox BA57 MA59. Wycliffe Hall Ox 57. **d** 59 **p** 60. C Hall Green Ascension *Birm* 59-63; V Dosthill and Wood End

63-71; V Brandwood 71-85; V Sutton Coldfield St Columba from 85; Hon Can S Malawi from 87. *280 Chester Road North, Sutton Coldfield, W Midlands B73 6RR* 021-354 5873

JENKINS, Very Rev Thomas Edward. b 02. St D Coll Lamp BA22 BD32. Wycliffe Hall Ox 24. d 25 p 26. Dean St D 57-72; rtd 72. *18 North Road, Cardigan, Dyfed* Cardigan (0239) 613355

JENKINS, Thomas Glennard Owen. b 22. St Jo Coll Ox BA48 MA52. Wells Th Coll 49 Wycliffe Hall Ox 50. d 50 p 51. V Hailey w Crawley *Ox* 60-79; V Penbryn and Betws Ifan w Bryngwyn *St D* 79-87; rtd 87. *24 Anwylfan, Aberporth, Cardigan, Dyfed SA43 2EL* Cardigan (0239) 811402

JENKINS, Thomas William. b 14. Univ of Wales BA40. St Mich Coll Llan 40. d 42 p 43. V Shrewsbury H Trin w St Julian *Lich* 67-75; V Ruyton 75-80; rtd 80; Perm to Offic *Lich* from 80. *4 Larkhill Road, Park Hall, Oswestry, Shropshire SY11 4AW* Oswestry (0691) 659304

JENKINS, Timothy David. b 52. Pemb Coll Ox BA73 MLitt77 MA82 St Edm Ho Cam BA84. Ridley Hall Cam 82. d 85 p 86. C Kingswood *Bris* 85-87; Sen Chapl Nottm Univ *S'well* from 88. *Lenton Lodge, Derby Road, Nottingham NG7 2QA* Nottingham (0602) 255143

JENKINS, Canon Trefor Illtyd. b 03. Chich Th Coll 26. d 27 p 29. V Swansea St Gabr *S & B* 49-73; rtd 73. *5 Ffynone Close, Swansea* Swansea (0792) 472799

JENKINS, William David. b 42. Birm Univ BA63. St D Coll Lamp LTh65. d 65 p 66. C Gorseinon *S & B* 65-67; C Llanelli *St D* 67-72; V Clydach *S & B* 72-82; Chapl Llandudno Gen Hosp from 82; V Llanrhos *St As* from 82; RD Llanrwst from 84. *Llanrhos Vicarage, 2 Vicarage Road, Llandudno, Gwynedd LL30 1PT* Llandudno (0492) 76152

JENKINS, William Frederick. b 08. St Jo Coll Dur BA33 MA38. d 35 p 36. V Histon *Ely* 60-75; rtd 75; Lic to Offic *Blackb* from 75. *6 Warwick Drive, Clitheroe, Lancs BB7 3LJ* Clitheroe (0200) 22460

JENKYNS, Preb Henry Derrik George. b 30. Sarum Th Coll 57. d 60 p 61. C Kettering SS Pet and Paul *Pet* 60-64; V Shrewsbury St Geo *Lich* 64-71; V Wednesbury St Paul Wood Green 71-76; V Stokesay *Heref* 76-86; P-in-c Acton Scott 76-86; RD Condover 80-86; Preb Heref Cathl from 83; R Kington w Huntington, Old Radnor, Kinnerton etc from 86. *The Vicarage, Kington, Herefordshire HR5 3AG* Kington (0544) 230525

JENKYNS, John Thomas William Basil. b 30. Univ of Wales (Lamp) BA54 St Cath Coll Ox BA57 MA62. Wycliffe Hall Ox 54. d 57 p 58. C Neasden cum Kingsbury St Cath *Lon* 57-60; C S Lyncombe *B & W* 60-64; V Gt Harwood St Bart *Blackb* 64-66; R Colne St Bart 66-69; V Chard St Mary *B & W* 69-87; Preb Wells Cathl 87; V Swaffham *Nor* 87-89; V Overbury w Teddington, Alstone etc *Worc* from 89. *The Vicarage, Station Road, Beckford, Tewkesbury, Glos GL20 7AD* Evesham (0386) 881380

JENKYNS, Thomas John Blackwell. b 31. St D Coll Lamp BA52. d 54 p 55. C Llanelly St Paul *St D* 54-58; C New Windsor St Jo *Ox* 58-64; Chapl RAF 64-85; P-in-c Herriard w Winslade and Long Sutton etc *Win* 85-86; V from 86. *The Vicarage, Upton Grey, Basingstoke, Hants RG25 2RB* Basingstoke (0256) 862469

JENNER, Brenda Ann. b 54. Culham Coll Ox BEd80. St Jo Coll Nottm DPS88. d 88. Par Dn Leigh St Mary *Man* from 88. *13 Jaffrey Street, Leigh, Lancs WN7 1XX* Leigh (0942) 679090

JENNER, Michael Albert. b 37. Oak Hill Th Coll 75. d 77 p 78. C Mile Cross *Nor* 77-80; P-in-c Easton *Ely* 80-86; P-in-c Ellington 80-86; P-in-c Grafham 80-86; P-in-c Spaldwick w Barham and Woolley 80-86. *Hope Cottage, 12 Main Street, Greetham, Leics LE15 7NL* Oakham (0572) 813415

JENNER, Dr Peter John. b 56. Chu Coll Cam BA77 PhD80 MA81. St Jo Coll Nottm 82. d 85 p 86. C Upperby St Jo *Carl* 85-88; Chapl Reading Univ *Ox* from 88. *30 Shinfield Road, Reading RG2 7BW* Reading (0734) 871495

JENNETT, Maurice Arthur. b 34. St Jo Coll Dur BA60. Cranmer Hall Dur 60. d 62 p 63. C Marple All SS *Ches* 62-67; V Withnell *Blackb* 67-75; V Stranton *Dur* from 75. *The Vicarage, Westbourne Road, Hartlepool, Cleveland TS25 5RE* Hartlepool (0429) 263190

JENNINGS, Miss Anne. b 41. CertEd63 STh Cam Univ CertRK67. Gilmore Ho 65. dss 71 d 87. Barton w Peel Green *Man* 71-76; Wythenshawe Wm Temple Ch 76-79; Rochdale 79-83; Chapl Rochdale Colls of FE 79-83; Hillock *Man* 83-87; Dn-in-c 87-88; Wakef Cathl *Wakef* from 88. *2 Cathedral Close, Margaret Street, Wakefield, W Yorkshire WF1 2DQ* Wakefield (0924) 378179

JENNINGS, Canon David Willfred Michael. b 44. AKC66. d 67 p 68. C Walton St Mary *Liv* 67-69; C Christchurch *Win* 69-73; V Hythe 73-80; V Romford St Edw *Chelmsf* from 80; RD Havering from 85; Hon Can Chelmsf Cathl from 87. *St Edward's Vicarage, 15 Oaklands Avenue, Romford RM1 4DB* Romford (0708) 740385

JENNINGS, Francis Kingston. b 16. TCD BA39. d 41 p 41. I Ardee w Charlestown and Collon *Arm* 57-90; RD Creggan and Louth 74-90; rtd 90. *The Rectory, Ardee, Co Louth, Irish Republic* Ardee (41) 53320

JENNINGS, Frederick David. b 48. K Coll Lon BD73 AKC73. St Aug Coll Cant 73. d 74 p 75. C Halesowen *Worc* 74-77; Perm to Offic Birm 78-80; Leic 78-80 and 85-87; P-in-c Snibston *Leic* 80-85; Community Relns Officer 81-84; P-in-c Burbage w Aston Flamville 87-91; R from 91. *The Rectory, Burbage, Hinckley, Leicester LE10 2AW* Hinckley (0455) 230512

JENNINGS, George. b 20. Lon Univ BD64. Lambeth STh89 Oak Hill Th Coll 46. d 51 p 52. V Haydock St Mark *Liv* 66-77; V Newburgh 77-89; rtd 89. *97 Watling Street South, Church Stretton, Shropshire SY6 7BH* Church Stretton (0694) 722145

JENNINGS, Harold Andrew. b 15. ATCL35 LTCL36 FTCL37 MRST39 LRAM39. St Deiniol's Hawarden 63. d 63 p 64. R Aberedw w Llandeilo Graban etc *S & B* 67-79; V Knighton and Norton 79-85; Hon C Llanbister and Llanbadarn Fynydd w Llananno 85-87; rtd 87. *Finsbury, Beaufort Road, Llandrindod Wells, Powys* Llandrindod Wells (0597) 824892

JENNINGS, Janet. b 38. SCM71 SRN74. Oak Hill Th Coll BA87. d 88. Par Dn Stevenage St Pet Broadwater *St Alb* 88-90. *Pound House, Forden, Welshpool, Powys SY21 8NU* Welshpool (0938) 76400

JENNINGS, Jonathan Peter. b 61. Lon Univ BD. Westcott Ho Cam. d 86 p 87. C Peterlee *Dur* 86-89; C Darlington St Cuth from 89. *65 Carmel Road South, Darlington, Co Durham DL3 8DS* Darlington (0325) 354503

JENNINGS, Very Rev Kenneth Neal. b 30. CCC Cam BA54 MA58. Cuddesdon Coll 54. d 56 p 57. C Ramsgate H Trin *Cant* 56-59; India 59-66; Vice-Prin Cuddesdon Coll 67-73; V Hitchin St Mary *St Alb* 73-76; TR Hitchin 77-83; Dean Glouc from 83. *The Deanery, Miller's Green, Gloucester GL1 2BP* Gloucester (0452) 24167

JENNINGS, Mervyn. b 39. Sarum & Wells Th Coll 83. d 85 p 86. C Knowle *Bris* 85-89; P-in-c Cressing *Chelmsf* from 89; Rural Youth Development Officer from 89. *The Rectory, 18 Wright's Avenue, Tye Green, Braintree, Essex CM7 8JG* Braintree (0376) 43740

JENNINGS, Paul Warwick. b 55. Birm Univ BSc77. Coll of Resurr Mirfield 77. d 80 p 81. C Dudley St Jas *Worc* 80-83; TV Halesowen 83-87; Chapl St Marg Hosp Birm from 88. *The Chaplain's Office, St Margaret's Hospital, Birmingham* 021-360 7777

JENNINGS, Peter James. b 28. St D Coll Lamp BA56 LTh57. d 57 p 58. C Dudley St Jo *Worc* 57-60; C Dudley St Thos 61-64; Chapl HM Borstal Portland 64-66; HM Pris Wakef 66-70; Liv 70-76; RD Walton *Liv* 75-76; Chapl HM Pris Styal 76-77 and from 88; Asst Chapl Gen (N) 77-89; Perm to Offic *Man* from 77; *Ches* from 79. *The Chaplain's Office, HM Prison Styal, Wilmslow, Cheshire SK9 4HR* Wilmslow (0625) 532141

JENNINGS, Robert Charles. b 31. St Edm Hall Ox BA56. St Steph Ho Ox 55. d 57 p 58. C Longton St Mary and St Chad *Lich* 57-60; C Ascot Heath *Ox* 60-62; C S Mymms K Chas *Lon* 62-64; P-in-c Tottenham St Jo 64-70; Chapl to Suff Bp Willesden 66-73; P-in-c Perivale 73; R Letchworth *St Alb* 73-78; R Hayes St Mary *Lon* from 78. *The Rectory, 170 Church Road, Hayes, Middx UB3 2LR* 081-573 2470

JENNINGS, Robert Henry. b 46. St Jo Coll Dur BA69 MA79. Qu Coll Birm DipTh71. d 72 p 73. C Dursley *Glouc* 72-74; C Coleford w Staunton 75-78; TV Bottesford w Ashby *Linc* 78-83; TV Witney *Ox* 83-89; V Lane End w Cadmore End from 89. *The Vicarage, 7 Lammas Way, Lane End, High Wycombe, Bucks HP14 3EX* High Wycombe (0494) 881913

JENNINGS, Canon Ronald Osmund. b 18. Leeds Univ BA42 Lon Univ BD56. Bps' Coll Cheshunt 42. d 44 p 45. V St Ives *Ely* 63-82; rtd 82; Perm to Offic *Ely* from 83; Linc from 84; Pet from 87. *3 Viceroy Drive, Pinchbeck, Spalding, Lincs PE11 3TS* Spalding (0775) 723883

JENNINGS, Thomas Robert. b 24. TCD BA47 MA51. d 48 p 49. C Drumragh *D & R* 48-51; CF 51-67; I Killeshandra *K, E & A* 67-70; I Newc w Newtownmountkennedy and Calary *D & G* from 70; Can Ch Ch Cathl Dub from 88. *Newcastle, Greystones, Co Wicklow, Irish Republic* Dublin (1) 281-9300

JENNINGS, Walter James. b 37. Birm Univ BMus60 MA90. Qu Coll Birm 77. **d** 80 **p** 81. Hon C Hampton in Arden *Birm* 80-84; Chapl St Alb Aided Sch Highgate Birm 84-86; C Wotton-under-Edge w Ozleworth and N Nibley *Glouc* 86-89; V Pittville from 89. *All Saints' Vicarage, 66 All Saints Road, Cheltenham, Glos GL52 2HA* Cheltenham (0242) 523341

JENNISON, Ronald Bernard. b 27. Chich Th Coll 57. **d** 59 **p** 60. C Thornaby on Tees St Paul *York* 59-62; V N Hull St Mich 62-69; V Bridlington Quay H Trin 69-77; V Sewerby w Marton 69-77; V Bridlington H Trin and Sewerby w Marton 77-79; Chapl Marseille w St Raphael Aix-en-Provence etc *Eur* 79-82; R Finmere w Mixbury, Cottisford, Hardwick etc *Ox* from 84; RD Bicester and Islip from 85. *The Rectory, Finmere, Buckingham MK18 4AT* Finmere (0280) 847184

JENNO, Charles Henry. b 25. Wells Th Coll 65. **d** 66 **p** 67. C Fishponds St Mary *Bris* 69-73; V Thornes St Jas w Ch Ch *Wakef* 73-78; V Carleton 78-82; V E Hardwick 78-82; rtd 82; Perm to Offic *Wakef* from 82. *32 Tower Avenue, Upton, Pontefract, W Yorkshire WF9 1EE* Pontefract (0977) 640925

JENSON, Philip Peter. b 56. Ex Coll Ox BA78 MA82 Down Coll Cam BA80 MA86 PhD88. Ridley Hall Cam 80. **d** 87 **p** 88. C Gt Warley Ch Ch *Chelmsf* 87-89; Lect Trin Coll Bris from 89. *77 Reedley Road, Bristol BS9 3TB* Bristol (0272) 682880

JEPHSON, Douglas Ronald Shipstone. b 17. St Jo Coll Dur BA38 MA43. **d** 40 **p** 41. R Tysoe w Compton Winyates and Oxhill *Cov* 70-81; R Whatcote 76-81; V Tysoe w Oxhill and Whatcote 81-82; rtd 82. *The Old School House, 42 The Village, Thorp Arch, Wetherby, W Yorkshire* Boston Spa (0937) 845955

JEPPS, Philip Anthony. b 34. BNC Ox BA58 MA68. Wycliffe Hall Ox 58. **d** 60 **p** 73. C Elton All SS *Man* 60; Perm to Offic *Pet* 70-73; R Church w Chapel Brampton 74-80; P-in-c Harlestone 79-80; V Kettering St Andr from 80. *St Andrew's Vicarage, Kettering, Northants NN16 8RG* Kettering (0536) 512754

JERMAN, Cecil Maldwyn. b 13. St D Coll Lamp BA34 St Mich Coll Llan 34. **d** 36 **p** 37. V New Brighton St Jas *Ches* 55-74; Lic to Offic *Ban* from 75; rtd 78. *Bryn Haul, Llaneilian, Amlwch, Gwynedd LL68 9LR* Amlwch (0407) 830977

JERMAN, Edward David. b 40. Trin Coll Carmarthen CertEd61. **d** 87 **p** 88. NSM Llandrygarn w Bodwrog and Heneglwys etc *Ban* from 87. *Tryfan, Trefor, Holyhead, Gwynedd LL65 3YT* Gwalchmai (0407) 720856

JERMY, Jack. b 22. ACP65. Ripon Hall Ox 64. **d** 65 **p** 66. Hd Master SS Simon and Jude Primary Sch Bolton 62-80; C Bolton SS Simon and Jude *Man* 65-74; P-in-c Rivington from 74. *8 Mill Lane, Horwich, Bolton BL6 6AT* Horwich (0204) 696198

JEROME, Canon Charles Stephen. b 17. Linc Th Coll 48. **d** 50 **p** 51. Dioc Dir of Chr Stewardship *Derby* 67-71; V Denby 68-71; Dioc Dir of Chr Stewardship *Ely* 71-83; P-in-c Holywell w Needingworth 71-78; V Impington 78-84; Hon Can Ely Cathl 82-84; rtd 84; Perm to Offic *Ely* from 84. *31 Greengarth, St Ives, Huntingdon, Cambs PE17 4QS* St Ives (0480) 493133

JERSEY, Dean of. *See* O'FERRALL, Very Rev Basil Arthur

JERUSALEM, Bishop of. *See* KAFITY, Rt Rev Samir

JERUSALEM, Dean of. *See* CROOKS, Very Rev Peter James

JERVIS, Christopher. b 53. BEd Cam Univ DipTh. Wycliffe Hall Ox. **d** 82 **p** 83. C Woodford Wells *Chelmsf* 82-85; Chapl Felsted Sch Essex 85-87; Chapl Canford Sch Wimborne from 87. *Merryvale, Canford Magna, Wimborne BH21 2AF* Wimborne (0202) 887722

JERVIS, Clement Frank Cooper. b 16. St Jo Coll Dur LTh39 BA40 MA45. St Aid Birkenhead 36. **d** 40 **p** 41. V Pensnett *Lich* 56-81; rtd 81; Perm to Offic *Lich* from 81; *Ches* from 83. *12 Park Avenue, Kidsgrove, Stoke-on-Trent ST7 1BG* Kidsgrove (0782) 782713

JERVIS, Preb Horace Roland. b 14. St Jo Coll Dur LTh38 BA39. St Aid Birkenhead 35. **d** 39 **p** 40. V Donnington Wood *Lich* 49-79; Preb Lich Cathl 77-79; rtd 79; Perm to Offic *Lich* from 79. *62 Rowan Road, Market Drayton, Shropshire TF9 1RR* Market Drayton (0630) 2438

JERVIS, William Edward. b 47. ARICS74. Linc Th Coll 74. **d** 77 **p** 78. C W Bromwich All SS *Lich* 77-80; C Horsham *Chich* 80-86; R W Tarring from 86. *West Tarring Rectory, Glebe Road, Worthing, W Sussex BN14 7PF* Worthing (0903) 35043

JESSETT, David Charles. b 55. K Coll Lon BD77 AKC77 MTh. Westcott Ho Cam 78. **d** 79 **p** 80. C Aveley *Chelmsf* 79-82; C Walthamstow St Pet 82-85; P-in-c Hunningham

Cov from 85; P-in-c Wappenbury w Weston under Wetherley from 85; Progr Dir Exploring Chr Min Scheme from 85; Dir CME 87-90. *The Vicarage, Hunningham, Leamington Spa, Warks CV33 9DS* Marton (0926) 632382

JESSIMAN, Timothy Edward. b 58. Oak Hill Th Coll DipHE91. **d** 91. C Baldock w Bygrave *St Alb* from 91. *60 The Tene, Baldock, Herts SG7 6DQ* Baldock (0462) 891375

JESSON, Alan Francis. b 47. MBIM82 Ealing Coll of Educn ALA70 Loughb Univ MLS77 Cam Univ MA87. E Anglian Minl Tr Course 88. **d** 91. NSM Swavesey *Ely* from 91. *25 Market Street, Swavesey, Cambridge CB4 5QG* Swavesey (0954) 30337

JESSUP, Gordon Ernest. b 36. Lon Univ BA59. Oak Hill Th Coll 57. **d** 61 **p** 62. C Barnehurst *Roch* 61-64; C Rushden St Pet 64-67; SE Sec CMJ 67-72; Youth Sec CMJ 68-78; Tr Officer CMJ 78-83; Hon C Woodside Park St Barn *Lon* 78-83; TV Bramerton w Surlingham *Nor* 83-88; P-in-c Framingham Pigot 88; P-in-c Bergh Apton w Yelverton 88; P-in-c Ashby w Thurton, Claxton and Carleton 88; R Thurton from 88. *The Rectory, 29 Ashby Road, Thurton, Norwich NR14 6AX* Thurton (050843) 738

JESSUP, William Roy. b 27. Lon Univ BSc48 CertEd. Ridley Hall Cam 59. **d** 61 **p** 62. C Walton *St E* 61-64; R Tuddenham St Mary w Cavenham 64-83; P-in-c Eriswell 75-78; Assoc Min Ipswich All SS 83-85; R Toppesfield and Stambourne *Chelmsf* from 85. *The Rectory, Park Lane, Toppesfield, Halstead, Essex CO9 4DQ* Great Yeldham (0787) 237924

JESTY, Miss Helen Margaret. b 51. York Univ BA72. Cranmer Hall Dur BA81. **dss** 82 **d** 87. S Lambeth St Steph *S'wark* 82-86; Norbiton 86-87; Par Dn 87-91; Hon Par Dn from 91. *5 Homersham Road, Kingston-upon-Thames, Surrey KT1 3PL* 081-546 5756

JEVONS, Alan Neil. b 56. Ex Univ BA77 Selw Coll Cam BA80 MA84. Ridley Hall Cam. **d** 81 **p** 82. C Halesowen *Worc* 81-84; C Heywood St Luke w All So *Man* 84-87; TV Heref St Martin w St Fran (S Wye Team Min) *Heref* from 87. *1 Prinknash Close, Belmont, Hereford HR2 7XA* Hereford (0432) 277364

JEWELL, Alan David John. b 59. St Cath Coll Ox MA86. Wycliffe Hall Ox 83. **d** 86 **p** 87. C Walton H Trin *Ox* 86-91; TV Sutton *Liv* from 91. *St Michael's Vicarage, Gartons Lane, Sutton Manor, St Helens, Merseyside WA9 4RB* St Helens (0744) 813738

JEWELL, Charles John. b 15. Bps' Coll Cheshunt 46. **d** 49 **p** 50. Tristan da Cunha 71-74; Area Sec (Dios Ex and Truro) USPG 69-71; S Africa 74-87; rtd 87; Perm to Offic *Ex* from 87. *13 Fairfield Avenue, Peverell, Plymouth PL2 3QF*

JEWELL, Mrs Maureen Ann. b 34. Chich Th Coll 90. **d** 91. NSM Parklands St Wilfrid CD *Chich* from 91. *Puck's Corner, West Way, Chichester, W Sussex PO19 3PW* Chichester (0243) 785822

JEWITT, Martin Paul Noel. b 44. AKC69. St Aug Coll Cant. **d** 70 **p** 71. C Usworth *Dur* 70-74; TV 77-78; Papua New Guinea 74-77; V Balham Hill Ascension *S'wark* from 78. *Ascension Vicarage, 22 Malwood Road, London SW12 8EN* 081-673 7666

JEYNES, Anthony James. b 44. AKC68. **d** 69 **p** 70. C Ellesmere Port *Ches* 69-73; C Birkenhead St Pet w St Matt 73-75; R Oughtrington 75-80; C Timperley 80-85; C Eastham 85-89; V New Brighton St Jas from 89. *St James's Vicarage, Victoria Road, Wallasey, Merseyside L45 9LD* 051-639 5844

JIGNASU, Nallinkumar Hiralal. b 28. Bombay Univ BA48. Bp Tucker Coll Mukono 68. **d** 68 **p** 69. Uganda 68-73; C Leamington Priors St Mary *Cov* 73-75; Nigeria 75-79; P-in-c New Humberstone *Leic* from 80. *St Barnabas' Vicarage, 32 St Barnabas' Road, Leicester LE5 4BD* Leicester (0533) 766054

JINMAN, Cecil Alfred Keith. b 20. Keble Coll Ox BA48 MA51. Wycliffe Hall Ox 48. **d** 50 **p** 51. V Claines St Geo *Worc* 59-76; rtd 76; Perm to Offic *Worc* from 76. *11 Diglis Avenue, Worcester WR1 2NS* Worcester (0905) 351736

JOANNA, Sister. *See* DAVIES, Joan Margaret

JOB, Canon Evan Roger Gould. b 36. ARCM55 Magd Coll Ox BA60 MA64. Cuddesdon Coll 60. **d** 62 **p** 63. C Liv Our Lady and St Nic *Liv* 62-65; V New Springs 65-70; Min Can and Prec Man Cathl *Man* 70-74; Prec and Sacr Westmr Abbey 74-79; Can Res, Prec and Sacr Win Cathl *Win* from 79; Vice-Dean Win from 91. *8 The Close, Winchester, Hants SO23 9LS* Winchester (0962) 854771

JOBBER, Barry William. b 38. **d** 75 **p** 76. C Fenton *Lich* 76-79; V Goldenhill 79-80. *Address temp unknown*

JOBLING, Raymond. b 23. Oak Hill Th Coll 67. **d** 67 **p** 68. C Southall H Trin *Lon* 67-70; C Beeston *Ripon* 70-72; C Felixstowe SS Pet and Paul *St E* 72-75; R Thorndon w Rishangles 75-80; Chapl Kerrison Sch 75-80; P-in-c Bedingfield w Southolt 75-80; R Gt and Lt Glemham, Blaxhall etc 80-88; rtd 88; Perm to Offic *Bradf* from 88. *Hermosa, Cragg Hill Road, Horton-in-Ribblesdale, Settle, N Yorkshire BD24 0HN* Horton-in-Ribblesdale (07296) 343

JOBSON, Clifford Hedley. b 31. St Jo Coll Dur BA54 DipTh56 MA81. **d** 56 **p** 57. C Hall Green Ascension *Birm* 56-59; C Ambleside w Rydal *Carl* 59-60; R Arthuret 60-62; CF 62-73; Dep Asst Chapl Gen 73-78; Asst Chapl Gen 78-84; QHC from 80; V Fleet *Guildf* from 84. *The Vicarage, Branksomewood Road, Fleet, Aldershot, Hants GU13 8JU* Fleet (0252) 616361

JOBSON, Canon Paul. b 39. Wells Th Coll 62. **d** 65 **p** 66. C Woolwich St Mary w H Trin *S'wark* 65-68; Chapl Culham Coll Abingdon 68-72; P-in-c Walworth St Pet *S'wark* 72-75; P-in-c Walworth All SS and St Steph 73-75; TR Walworth 75-89; Hon Can S'wark Cathl from 83; RD S'wark and Newington 85-88; V Seaham w Seaham Harbour *Dur* from 89; Hon Chapl Miss to Seamen from 89. *The Vicarage, Seaham, Co Durham SR7 7SN* 091-581 3385

JOHN, Andrew Thomas Griffith. b 64. Univ of Wales LLB. St Jo Coll Nottm BA DPS. **d** 89 **p** 90. C Cardigan and Mount and Verwick *St D* 89-91; C Abth from 91. *Ael-y-Bryn, 25 High Street, Aberystwyth, Dyfed SY23 1JG*

JOHN, Canon Arthur Gwynne. b 06. St D Coll Lamp BA31. **d** 31 **p** 32. V Morley St Pet w Churwell *Wakef* 46-76; Hon Can Wakef Cathl 72-76; rtd 76; Perm to Offic *Wakef* from 76. *37 Bradford Road, Drighlington, Bradford, W Yorkshire BD11 1AS* Leeds (0532) 852676

JOHN, Barbara. b 34. Cam Univ DipTh67. Gilmore Ho. **dss** 67 **d** 80. Merthyr Tydfil *Llan* 67-71; Loughton St Jo *Chelmsf* 71-73; Newport St Woolos *Mon* 73-78; Asst Chapl Univ Hosp of Wales Cardiff 78-85; C Radyr *Llan* from 85. *14 Pace Close, Danescourt, Llandaff, Cardiff CF5 2QZ* Cardiff (0222) 552989

JOHN, Beverley Hayes. b 49. Qu Coll Birm 83. **d** 85 **p** 86. C Oystermouth *S & B* 85-87; C Morriston 87-88; V Cefn Coed and Capel Nantddu w Vaynor etc from 88. *The Vicarage, Somerset Lane, Cefn Coed, Merthyr Tydfil, M Glam CF48 2PA* Merthyr Tydfil (0685) 74253

JOHN, Caroline Victoria. b 64. Cam Univ BA86 MA90. St Jo Coll Nottm DPS90. **d** 90. NSM Cardigan and Mount and Verwick *St D* 90-91; NSM Abth from 91. *Ael-y-Bryn, 25 High Street, Aberystwyth, Dyfed SY23 1JG*

JOHN, Daniel Francis. b 09. AKC36. **d** 36 **p** 37. R Stoke Lacy w Much Cowarne and Morton Jeffries *Heref* 53-76; P-in-c Pencombe w Marston Stannett and Lt Cowarne 68-76; rtd 76; Perm to Offic *Heref* from 76. *Winslow Croft, Bromyard, Herefordshire HR7 4SE* Pencombe (08855) 270

JOHN, Canon David Michael. b 36. Univ of Wales (Lamp) BA57. St Mich Coll Llan 57. **d** 59 **p** 60. C Pontypool *Mon* 59-61; C Roath St Marg *Llan* 61-66; Asst Chapl HM Pris Liv 66-67; Chapl HM Pris Ex 67-68; V Ystrad Rhondda *Llan* 68-76; V Pontyclun w Talygarn 76-84; R Newton Nottage from 84; Can Llan Cathl from 85. *The Rectory, 64 Victoria Avenue, Porthcawl, M Glam CF36 3HE* Porthcawl (0656) 712042

JOHN, Canon Elwyn Crebey. b 36. Univ of Wales (Lamp) BA57. St Mich Coll Llan 57. **d** 59 **p** 60. C Llanguicke *S & B* 59-62; C Llandrindod w Cefnllys 62-66; V Beguildy and Heyope 66-79; Youth Chapl 72-79; Chapl Agric & Rural Soc from 77; V Builth and Llanddewi'r Cwm w Llangynog etc from 79; Can Brecon Cathl from 88. *The Vicarage, 1 North Road, Builth Wells, Powys LD2 3BT* Builth Wells (0982) 552355

JOHN, Canon Islwyn David. b 33. St D Coll Lamp BA56. **d** 58 **p** 59. C Brynamman *St D* 58-61; C Carmarthen St Dav 61-64; V from 83; V Penbryn and Blaenporth 64-68; V Llandyssul 68-83; Can St D Cathl from 88. *St David's Vicarage, 4 Penllwyn Park, Carmarthen, Dyfed SA31 3BU* Carmarthen (0267) 234183

JOHN, Canon James Richard. b 21. Ch Coll Cam BA47 MA49. Cuddesdon Coll 47. **d** 49 **p** 50. V Bolton St Jas w St Chrys *Bradf* 66-78; R Guiseley 78-83; RD Otley 80-86; P-in-c Esholt 82-83; TR Guiseley w Esholt 83-87; Hon Can Bradf Cathl 83-87; rtd 87; Perm to Offic *Bradf* from 87. *37 Croft House Drive, Otley, W Yorkshire LS21 2ER* Otley (0943) 461998

JOHN, Dr Jeffrey Philip Hywel. b 53. Hertf Coll Ox BA75 MA78 Ox Univ DPhil84. St Steph Ho Ox 75. **d** 78 **p** 79. C Penarth w Lavernock *Llan* 78-80; Lic to Offic

from 80; Asst Chapl Magd Coll Ox 80-82; Chapl BNC Ox 82-84; Lic to Offic *Ox* from 83; Fell and Dean of Div Magd Coll Ox from 84. *Magdalen College, Oxford OX1 4AU* Oxford (0865) 276027

JOHN, Mark Christopher. b 61. SS Mark & Jo Coll Plymouth BA83. St Steph Ho Ox 84. **d** 87 **p** 88. C Treboeth *S & B* 87-90; V Swansea St Mark and St Jo from 90. *St Mark and St John Vicarage, 27 Bowen Road, Swansea SA1 2NA* Swansea (0792) 465074

JOHN, Meurig Hywel. b 46. St D Coll Lamp 67. **d** 71 **p** 72. C Llanelly Ch Ch *St D* 71-74; V Penrhyncoch and Elerch 74-79; V Llanfihangel Aberbythych 79-81; R Cilgerran w Bridell and Llantwyd 81-83; V Gwaun-cae-Gurwen 83-89; V Llanfihangel Genau'r-glyn and Llangorwen from 89. *The Vicarage, Maes y Garn, Bow Street, Aberystwyth SY24 1XX* Aberystwyth (0970) 828638

JOHN, Nigel. Univ of Wales (Cardiff) BA Selw Coll Cam MPhil. Westcott Ho Cam. **d** 91. C Carmarthen St Pet *St D* from 91. *St Peter's Clergy House, 10A The Parade, Carmarthen, Dyfed SA31 1LY* Carmarthen (0267) 237303

JOHN, Robert Michael. b 46. Edin Univ BSc67 Man Univ MSc68 PhD70 Otago Univ BD78. St Jo Coll Auckland 76. **d** 78 **p** 79. New Zealand 78-87 and from 88; C Swansea St Jas *S & B* 87-88. *16 Seaview Road, Otumoetai, Tauranga, New Zealand* Tauranga (75) 66617

JOHN, Sidney Arthur Charles Bernard. b 13. Jes Coll Ox BA35 MA39. **d** 38 **p** 39. V Barlow *Derby* 65-78; rtd 78; Perm to Offic *Ox* from 87. *2 Willow Road, Chinnor, Oxford OX9 4RA* Kingston Blount (0844) 52321

JOHN, Stephen Michael. b 63. Univ of Wales BA85. Coll of Resurr Mirfield 87. **d** 89 **p** 90. C Coity w Nolton *Llan* 89-91; C Merthyr Dyfan from 91. *9 Marloes Close, Lundy Park, Barry, S Glam CF63EL* Barry (0446) 744207

JOHN, William Glyndwr. b 21. Roch Th Coll 60. **d** 60 **p** 61. V Frizinghall *Bradf* 69-73; V Long Preston 73-80; V Sutton 80-84; rtd 84; Perm to Offic *Bradf* from 84. *Room 6, Woodlands, Woodlands Drive, Skipton, N Yorkshire BD25 1QU* Skipton (0756) 793003

JOHN-CHARLES, Brother. See VOCKLER, Rt Rev John Charles

JOHNS, Adam Aubrey. b 34. TCD BA57 MA76 NUU BA75. CITC 58. **d** 58 **p** 59. C Aghalee *D & D* 58-61; C Derriaghy *Conn* 61-63; I Billy 63-77; I Billy w Derrykeighan from 77. *Derrykeighan Rectory, Dervock, Ballymoney, Co Antrim* Dervock (02657) 41241

JOHNS, Bernard Thomas. b 36. Birm Univ BSc58. St Mich Coll Llan 61. **d** 63 **p** 64. C Aberavon *Llan* 63-65; C St Andrew's Major and Michaelston-le-Pit 65-70; V Cardiff St Andr and St Teilo 70-76; Asst Dioc Dir of Educn from 72; V Roath St Marg 76-88; R Wenvoe and St Lythans from 88. *The Rectory, Wenvoe, Cardiff CF5 6AN* Cardiff (0222) 593392

JOHNS, James Dudley. b 09. Selw Coll Cam BA34 MA38. Ridley Hall Cam 34. **d** 36 **p** 37. R Gt w Lt Wymondley *St Alb* 70-80; R Gt and Lt Wymondley w Graveley and Chivesfield 80-81; rtd 81; Perm to Offic *Nor* from 82. *Appletree Cottage, Hales Street, Tivetshall St Margaret, Norwich NR15 2EE* Tivetshall (037977) 357

JOHNS, Mrs Patricia Holly (Pat). b 33. Girton Coll Cam BA56 MA60 Hughes Hall Cam PGCE57. Ox NSM Course 87. **d** 90. NSM Wantage *Ox* from 90. *3 Post Office Lane, Wantage, Oxon OX12 8DR* Wantage (02357) 68749

JOHNS, Canon Ronald Charles. b 37. TD. Dur Univ BA59. Wells Th Coll 59. **d** 61 **p** 62. C Wigan All SS *Liv* 61-66; TV Kirkby 66-75; Ho Master Ruffwood Sch Kirkby 70-75; TV Maghull 75-79; Dep Hd Master Maghull Old Hall High Sch 75-79; P-in-c Borrowdale *Carl* 79-84; V 84-89; RD Derwent 81-89; Hon Can Carl Cathl 87-89; Can Res Carl Cathl from 89. *3 The Abbey, Carlisle CA3 8TZ* Carlisle (0228) 21834

JOHNS, Thomas Morton. b 43. Oak Hill Th Coll 67. **d** 70 **p** 71. C N Meols *Liv* 70-73; C Farnborough *Guildf* 73-76; P-in-c Badshot Lea CD 76-83; Lic to Offic Pet 83-90; Cov from 90; Chapl HM Youth Cust Cen Wellingborough 83-88; Chapl HM Young Offender Inst Swinfen Hall 88-90; Chapl Tr Officer from 88; Chapl HM Pris Service Coll from 90. *HM Prison Service College, Newbold Revel, Rugby, Warks CV23 0TN* Rugby (0788) 832666

JOHNS, Trevor Charles. b 33. St D Coll Lamp BA58. **d** 58 **p** 59. C Pemb St Mary and St Mich *St D* 58-61; R Walwyn's Castle w Robeston W 61-67; CF 67-75; V Spittal and Treffgarne *St D* 75-79; C Tring *St Alb* 79-80; TV Tring 80-85; V Knighton and Norton *S & B* 85-86; V Merthyr Cynog and Dyffryn Honddu etc from 86.

The Vicarage, Lower Chapel, Brecon, Powys   Brecon (0874) 89238

JOHNS, Canon Vernon. b 12. St D Coll Lamp BA33 St Mich Coll Llan 34. **d** 35 **p** 36. R Prendergast w Rudbaxton *St D* 67-72; Can St D Cathl 70-78; R Tenby 72-78; rtd 78. *78 Laws Street, Pembroke Dock, Dyfed SA72 6DQ* Pembroke (0646) 686149

JOHNS, William Price. b 28. Keble Coll Ox BA51 DipTh52 MA56. St Mich Coll Llan 52. **d** 53 **p** 54. C Whitchurch *Llan* 53-56; C Pontypridd St Cath 56-59; Min Can Brecon Cathl *S & B* 59-62; V Wellington *Heref* 62-78; R Wellington w Pipe-cum-Lyde and Moreton-on-Lugg from 78; P-in-c Ford 63-69. *The Vicarage, Wellington, Hereford HR4 8AU* Canon Pyon (043271) 228

JOHNSON, Alban Ernest Mackenzie. b 09. Keble Coll Ox BA31 MA62. Ely Th Coll 31. **d** 32 **p** 33. R Toft w Caldecote *Ely* 57-62; R Faldingworth w Buslingthorpe *Linc* 57-62; Bahamas 63-80; rtd 74. *The Old Rectory, Staverton, Trowbridge, Wilts BA14 6NX*

JOHNSON, Canon Alfred Henry. b 08. Hatf Coll Dur BA34. Ely Th Coll 34. **d** 35 **p** 36. V Dovercourt *Chelmsf* 49-75; Chapl Harwich Hosp 57-75; Hon Can Chelmsf Cathl 65-75; rtd 75. *20 Fronks Road, Dovercourt, Harwich, Essex* Harwich (0255) 507973

JOHNSON, Miss Annie. b 26. Trin Coll Bris 70. **dss** 75 **d** 87. Barnsbury St Andr *Lon* 75-78; Newark Ch Ch *S'well* 79-80; Newark w Hawton, Cotham and Shelton 80-87; Par Dn 87-88; rtd 88. *1 Carswell Close, Newark, Notts NG24 4HW* Newark (0636) 704299

JOHNSON, Anthony Arthur Derry. b 15. Kelham Th Coll 31. **d** 39 **p** 40. V Mill Hill St Mich *Lon* 60-73; R Chalfont St Giles *Ox* 73-80; rtd 80. *Garden Close, Long Street, Sherborne, Dorset DT9 3DD* Sherborne (0935) 3469

JOHNSON, Anthony Peter. b 45. Lon Univ DipTh71 AKC76 BD76 MTh79. Wells Th Coll 67. **d** 70 **p** 71. C Goldington *St Alb* 70-73; C Hainault *Chelmsf* 73-76; TV Loughton St Mary 76-81; V Scunthorpe All SS *Linc* 81-85; V Alkborough 85-87; Chapl Man Univ *Man* from 87; TV Man Whitworth from 87. *354 Wilbraham Road, Chorlton-cum-Hardy, Manchester M21 1UX* 061-881 7688 or 273 1465

JOHNSON, Canon Anthony Trevor. b 27. CCC Ox BA51 MA55. Cuddesdon Coll 51. **d** 53 **p** 54. C Wareham w Arne *Sarum* 53-57; C Melksham 57-60; R Tarrant Gunville, Tarrant Hinton etc 60-67; R Upton Scudamore 67-85; V Warminster St Denys 67-85; RD Heytesbury 71-76; Can and Preb Sarum Cathl from 75; P-in-c Horningsham 76-85; P-in-c Semley and Sedgehill 85-86; R E Knoyle, Semley and Sedgehill from 86. *The Rectory, Semley, Shaftesbury, Dorset SP7 9AU* East Knoyle (0747) 830362

JOHNSON, Anthony Warrington. b 40. Golds Coll Lon CertEd60. St Jo Coll Nottm 86. **d** 88 **p** 89. C Lutterworth w Cotesbach *Leic* from 88. *3 Poplar Avenue, Lutterworth, Leics LE17 4TH* Lutterworth (0455) 552443

JOHNSON, Arthur Victor. b 19. St Aid Birkenhead 62. **d** 64 **p** 65. V Oswaldtwistle All SS *Blackb* 69-73; V Lanc St Jo w St Anne 73-79; V Out Rawcliffe 79-84; rtd 84; Perm to Offic *Blackb* from 84. *25 Heysham Park, Morecambe, Lancs LA3 2UD* Heysham (0524) 52794

JOHNSON, Beverley Charles. b 35. Bp Gray Coll Cape Town 59. **d** 61 **p** 62. S Africa 61-67 and from 91; C Southsea St Pet *Portsm* 68-69; C Southwick St Cuth CD *Dur* 70-71; P-in-c Waterhouses 71-80; R Burnmoor 80-85; V Brandon 85-89; Australia 89-91. *Address temp unknown*

JOHNSON, Brian. b 42. DipRS87. S'wark Ord Course 84. **d** 87 **p** 88. NSM Dulwich St Barn *S'wark* from 87. *182 Turney Road, London SE21 7JL* 071-733 8341

JOHNSON, Brian Braithwaite. b 08. St Aug Coll Cant 65. **d** 66 **p** 67. V Baldersby *York* 69-76; V Skipton Bridge 69-76; rtd 76. *Westfield, Baldersby St James, Thirsk, N Yorkshire YO7 4PT* Melmerby (076584) 471

JOHNSON, Brian Robert. b 18. ARIBA48 Lon Univ DipArch48. **d** 67 **p** 69. Chapl Kingston Coll Mitchelstown 67-83; C Brigown *C, C & R* 67-83; rtd 83. *The Old School, Newton, Rosscarbery, Co Cork, Irish Republic* Bandon (23) 48325

JOHNSON, Canon Charles Edmund. b 15. Em Coll Cam BA40 MA42. Ridley Hall Cam 40. **d** 42 **p** 43. C Woking Ch Ch *Guildf* 42-44; Hd Master Seaford Coll Sussex 44-90; Provost from 90; Can and Preb Chich Cathl *Chich* 84-85. *Seaford College, Lavington Park, Petworth, W Sussex GU28 0NB* Graffham (07986) 392

JOHNSON, Christopher Dudley. b 26. Worc Coll Ox BA44 MA51. Cuddesdon Coll 53. **d** 56 **p** 57. V Eton w Eton Wick and Boveney *Ox* 67-88; rtd 91. *91 Edgar Road, Winchester SO23 9TW* Winchester (0962) 867441

JOHNSON, Christopher Frederick. b 43. ARICS67. Ripon Hall Ox 71. **d** 74 **p** 75. C Chatham St Steph *Roch* 74-78; V Slade Green 78-85; V Wilmington from 85. *The Vicarage, Church Hill, Wilmington, Dartford, Kent DA2 7EH* Dartford (0322) 220561

JOHNSON, Christopher Paul. b 47. St Jo Coll Nottm BTh74. **d** 74 **p** 75. C Normanton *Wakef* 74-78; P-in-c Dewsbury St Mark 78-82; V Harden and Wilsden *Bradf* 82-88; P-in-c Holbeck *Ripon* from 88. *St Luke's Vicarage, Malvern View, Leeds LS11 8SG* Leeds (0532) 717996

JOHNSON, Christopher Robert. b 43. Lon Coll of Div 66. **d** 70 **p** 71. C Everton St Geo *Liv* 70-71; C Childwall All SS 71-75; TV Gateacre 75-76; TV Bushbury *Lich* 76-87; R Burslem from 87. *The Rectory, 16 Heyburn Crescent, Burslem, Stoke-on-Trent ST6 4DL* Stoke-on-Trent (0782) 88932

JOHNSON, Canon Colin Gawman. b 32. Leeds Univ BA59. Coll of Resurr Mirfield 59. **d** 61 **p** 62. C Barrow St Matt *Carl* 61-67; V from 90; V Addingham 67-71; V Carl H Trin 71-80; V Wigton 80-90; Hon Can Carl Cathl from 85. *The Vicarage, Highfield Road, Barrow-in-Furness, Cumbria LA14 5NZ* Barrow-in-Furness (0229) 823569

JOHNSON, Cyril Francis. b 22. St Cath Coll Cam BA49 MA54. Ely Th Coll 50. **d** 52 **p** 53. R Harpole *Pet* 61-87; rtd 87. *16 Blake's Way, Eastbourne, E Sussex BN23 6EW* Eastbourne (0323) 23491

JOHNSON, David Alan. b 43. Lon Univ BSc63 PhD67. Trin Coll Bris 78. **d** 80 **p** 81. C Watford *St Alb* 80-85; V Idle H Trin *Bradf* from 85. *The Vicarage, 470 Leeds Road, Thackley, Bradford, W Yorkshire BD10 9AA* Bradford (0274) 613300

JOHNSON, David Bryan Alfred. b 36. Kelham Th Coll 56. **d** 61 **p** 62. C Streatham St Paul *S'wark* 61-63; Malaysia 63-71; V Worc St Mich *Worc* 71-74; Warden Lee Abbey Internat Students' Club Kensington 74-77; V Plumstead St Mark and St Marg *S'wark* 77-86; Chapl W Park Hosp Epsom from 86. *23 Bramblewood Close, Carshalton, Surrey SM5 1PQ* 081-669 2663 or Epsom (0372) 727811

JOHNSON, David Clark. b 15. Tyndale Hall Bris 61. **d** 62 **p** 63. V Bishopsworth *Bris* 65-74; V Stratton St Margaret 75-78; TR Stratton St Margaret w S Marston etc 78-80; rtd 80; Perm to Offic *Bris* from 80. *13 High Kingsdown, Bristol BS2 8EN* Bristol (0272) 298894

JOHNSON, David Francis. b 32. Univ Coll Ox BA55 MA59. Westcott Ho Cam 55. **d** 57 **p** 58. C Earlsdon *Cov* 57-59; C Willenhall 59-61; C Attenborough w Bramcote *S'well* 61-62; V Ravenstone w Weston Underwood *Ox* 62-66; V Crewe Ch Ch *Ches* 66-70; P-in-c Crewe St Pet 67-70; V Thornton w Allerthorpe *York* 70-79; V N Hull St Mich 79-81; V Leyburn w Bellerby *Ripon* 81-88; V Coxwold and Husthwaite *York* from 88. *The Vicarage, Coxwold, York YO6 4AD* Coxwold (03476) 301

JOHNSON, David John. b 49. Lanc Univ BA72. Linc Th Coll 78. **d** 81 **p** 82. C Stockport St Thos *Ches* 81-84; OGS from 83; C Stockton Heath *Ches* 84-88; V Tranmere St Paul w St Luke from 88. *St Paul's Vicarage, Old Chester Road, Birkenhead, Merseyside L42 3XD* 051-645 3547

JOHNSON, David William. b 40. Lon Univ BD64. Oak Hill Th Coll 60. **d** 65 **p** 66. C Tunbridge Wells St Jas *Roch* 65-68; C Kirby Muxloe *Leic* 68-72; V Burton Joyce w Bulcote *S'well* 72-83; Chapl Northgate Mental Handicap Unit Morpeth 83-87; V Mitford *Newc* 83-87; Asst Chapl R Victoria Infirmary Newc 87-89; Chapl R Shrewsbury Hosp from 89. *The Chaplaincy, Royal Shrewsbury Hospital, Shrewsbury SY3 8XF* Shrewsbury (0743) 231122

JOHNSON, David William. b 53. Selw Coll Cam BA76. Ripon Coll Cuddesdon 76. **d** 78 **p** 79. C Fulham St Etheldreda w St Clem *Lon* 78-82; Communications Sec Gen Syn Bd for Miss and Unity 82-87; PV Westmr Abbey 85-87; R Gilmorton w Peatling Parva and Kimcote etc *Leic* 87-91; R Cogenhoe *Pet* from 91. *The Rectory, Cogenhoe, Northampton NN7 1LS* Northampton (0604) 890338

JOHNSON, Preb Derek John. b 36. St Aid Birkenhead 65. **d** 68 **p** 69. C Eccleshall *Lich* 68-73; C Stafford St Mary 73-75; Chapl New Cross Hosp Wolv from 75; Preb Lich Cathl *Lich* from 83. *The Chaplain's House, New Cross Hospital, Wolverhampton WV10 0QP* Wolverhampton (0902) 732255

JOHNSON, Donald Arnold. b 28. Linc Coll Ox BA51 MA59. Cuddesdon Coll 51. **d** 53 **p** 54. C Henfield *Chich* 53-55; C Horsham 55-59; V Oving w Merston 59-68; Bp's Dom Chapl 59-69; V Hellingly 68-78; V Upper Dicker 68-78; R W Stoke from 78; V Funtington and Sennicotts from 78. *The Vicarage, Funtington, Chichester, W Sussex PO19 0LH* Bosham (0243) 575257

JOHNSON, Mrs Dorothy. SRN BSc NDN80. Qu Coll Birm. **d** 87. Bp's Asst Officer for Soc Resp *Cov* from 87; Planning Officer S Warks HA from 87. *The Firs, Stoneleigh Road, Bubbenhall, Coventry CV8 3BS* Coventry (0203) 303712

JOHNSON, Douglas Leonard. b 45. Trin Coll Bris 70. **d** 73 **p** 74. C New Malden and Coombe *S'wark* 73-76; P-in-c Upper Tulse Hill St Matthias 76-82; CPAS Staff 82-88; Hon C Wimbledon Em Ridgway Prop Chpl *S'wark* from 83; Lect and Tutor CA Coll from 88. *11 Preston Road, London SW20 0SS* 081-946 2136

JOHNSON, Edward Anthony. b 32. Univ of Wales (Swansea) BSc54. St Steph Ho Ox 79. **d** 81 **p** 82. C Wolvercote w Summertown *Ox* 81-84; P-in-c Ramsden 84-87; P-in-c Finstock and Fawler 84-87; P-in-c Wilcote 84-87; V Ramsden, Finstock and Fawler, Leafield etc from 87. *Carvers, Skippett Lane, Ramsden, Oxford OX7 3AP* Ramsden (099386) 687

JOHNSON, Mrs Elizabeth. b 47. St Hilda's Coll Ox MA69. Wycliffe Hall Ox 84. **dss** 86 **d** 87. NSM Ox St Aldate w St Matt *Ox* from 86. *29 Templar Road, Oxford OX2 8LR* Oxford (0865) 515991

JOHNSON, Eric. b 38. MIBiol66 Nottm Univ BSc60 CertEd65 Leeds Univ DipEd72. Qu Coll Birm 74. **d** 77 **p** 78. Sen Lect Cov Tech Coll from 66; NSM Earlsdon *Cov* 77-81; NSM Wolston and Church Lawford 81-86; NSM Stoneleigh w Ashow and Baginton from 90. *The Firs, Stoneleigh Road, Bubbenhall, Coventry CV8 3BS* Coventry (0203) 303712

JOHNSON, Geoffrey Kemble. b 22. RD71. Roch Th Coll 62. **d** 64 **p** 65. R Worlingham *St E* 68-84; rtd 84; Perm to Offic Nor and St E from 84. *53 St Walstans Road, Taverham, Norwich NR8 6NG* Norwich (0603) 860626

JOHNSON, Geoffrey Stuart. b 39. ALCD65 Wolv Poly DipEd. **d** 65 **p** 66. C Worksop St Jo *S'well* 65-68; Taiwan 68-71; Singapore 71-76; Aber Univ *Ab* 76-78; Perm to Offic *Heref* 78-82; P-in-c Hoarwithy, Hentland and Sellack 82-84; Chapl Horton Hosp Epsom 84-90; Chapl Brighton HA from 90. *7 Bramble Mead, Balcombe, Haywards Heath, W Sussex RH17 6HU* Balcombe (0444) 811515

JOHNSON, Gordon. b 20. **d** 43 **p** 44. R Horseheath *Ely* 64-71; R Bartlow 65-71; Hon C S Kensington St Aug *Lon* from 79; rtd 85. *Rosemary Topping, English Bicknor, Coleford, Glos* Dean (0594) 61181

JOHNSON, Gordon Edward. b 27. Oak Hill Th Coll 76. **d** 77 **p** 78. C Scarborough St Mary w Ch Ch and H Apostles *York* 77-82; V Hutton Cranswick w Skerne 82-86; P-in-c Watton w Beswick and Kilnwick 82-86; V Hutton Cranswick w Skerne, Watton and Beswick 86-88; V Bubwith w Skipwith from 88. *The Vicarage, North Duffield, Selby, N Yorkshire YO8 7RR* Selby (0757) 288079

JOHNSON, Graham. b 37. Westcott Ho Cam 66. **d** 68 **p** 69. C Stafford St Mary *Lich* 68-71; C Wombourne 71-74; Youth Chapl 74-77; P-in-c Tong 76-77; Res Min Wednesfield St Thos 77-78; TV 79-82; P-in-c Gayton w Fradswell 84-88; P-in-c Milwich 82-88; P-in-c Weston upon Trent 82-88; V Fradswell, Gayton, Milwich and Weston 88-90; TV Wolstanton from 90. *St Barnabas's Vicarage, Old Castle Avenue, Newcastle, Staffs ST5 8OG* Newcastle-under-Lyme (0782) 635978

JOHNSON, Graham James. b 43. Leeds Univ BA67. Coll of Resurr Mirfield DipTh69. **d** 70 **p** 71. C Heckmondwike *Wakef* 70-73; C Pet St Jude *Pet* 73-76; V Gt w Lt Harrowden and Orlingbury 76-83; Chapl Danetre Hosp from 83; R Daventry *Pet* from 83; RD Daventry from 88. *The Rectory, Daventry, Northants NN11 5PE* Daventry (0327) 702638

JOHNSON, Harold Barnett. b 10. Ex Coll Ox BA34 MA37. Cuddesdon Coll 34. **d** 35 **p** 36. R Waldron *Chich* 60-75; rtd 75; Hon C Eastbourne St Sav and St Pet *Chich* 75-83; Perm to Offic from 83. *Flat 1, Morley House, College of St Barnabas, Lingfield, Surrey RH7 6NJ* Dormans Park (034287) 440

JOHNSON, Harold Everard. b 14. TCD BA36 MA40 BD46. **d** 38 **p** 39. V Eccles St Andr *Man* 58-79; rtd 79; Perm to Offic *Man* from 80. *368 New Church Road, Bacup, Lancs OL13 0LD* Bacup (0706) 874922

JOHNSON, Harriet Etta. LRAM DipEd40. Trin Coll Bris. **dss** 76 **d** 87. Burundi 76-80; Ipplepen w Torbryan *Ex* 81-87; Hon Par Dn 87-90; Perm to Offic from 90. *10 Fairfield West, Huxtable Hill, Torquay TQ2 6RN* Torquay (0803) 690115

JOHNSON, Ven Hayman. b 12. New Coll Ox BA34 MA38. Bps' Coll Cheshunt 35. **d** 36 **p** 37. Adn Sheff 63-78; Chapl to HM The Queen 69-83; Can Res Sheff Cathl

Sheff 75-78; rtd 78; Perm to Offic Chich from 82; Roch from 84. *1 Parklands, Kibbles Lane, Southborough, Tunbridge Wells, Kent TN4 0LQ* Tunbridge Wells (0892) 39004

JOHNSON, Canon Hedley Wilson. b 10. Peterho Cam BA32 MA36. **d** 40 **p** 41. R Witnesham w Swilland and Ashbocking *St E* 61-78; Hon Can St E Cathl 75-78; rtd 78; Perm to Offic *St E* from 79. *45 Aldeburgh Road, Leiston, Suffolk IP16 4PN* Leiston (0728) 830884

JOHNSON, Mrs Hilary Ann. b 51. RGN72 RHV74 DipRS85. S'wark Ord Course 82. **dss** 85 **d** 87. Hon Par Dn Salfords *S'wark* 85-90; Chapl St Geo Hosp Gp Lon from 90. *11 West Avenue, Redhill, Surrey RH1 5BA* Redhill (0737) 766549

JOHNSON, Ian Lawrence. b 44. Wells Th Coll 68. **d** 71 **p** 72. C Benhilton *S'wark* 71-73; C Weymouth H Trin *Sarum* 73-76; R Pewsey 76-81; R Compton Abbas W w Wynford Eagle etc 81; P-in-c Maiden Newton w Frome Vauchurch 81; R Maiden Newton and Valleys 81-83; Sherborne Episc Area Youth Officer 81-83; Dioc Youth Officer 83-88; TR Langley and Parkfield *Man* from 88. *The Rectory, Wood Street, Middleton, Manchester M24 3GL* 061-643 5013

✠**JOHNSON, Rt Rev James Nathaniel.** b 32. Wells Th Coll 63. **d** 64 **p** 65 **c** 85. C Lawrence Weston *Bris* 64-66; St Helena 66-72; Area Sec (Dios Ex and Truro) USPG 72-74; R Combe Martin *Ex* 74-80; V Thorpe Bay *Chelmsf* 80-85; Bp St Helena 85-91; R Byfield w Boddington *Pet* from 91. *The Rectory, Church Street, Byfield, Daventry, Northants NN11 6XN* Byfield (0327) 60204

JOHNSON, John Alan. b 51. Ripon Coll Cuddesdon 75. **d** 77 **p** 78. C Boreham Wood All SS *St Alb* 77-79; C Borehamwood 79-80; TV Dunstable 80-85; Toc H from 85; Nat Chapl from 89. *Carreg-y-Saeth, 40 Lionel Avenue, Wendover, Aylesbury, Bucks HP22 6LP* Wendover (0296) 696431

JOHNSON, Canon John Anthony. b 18. Selw Coll Cam BA48 MA53 St Jo Coll Dur DipTh51. **d** 51 **p** 52. V Mansf Woodhouse *S'well* 60-70; V Beeston 70-85; RD Beeston 81-85; Hon Can S'well Minster 82-85; rtd 86. *7 The Spinney, Cranwell Avenue, Lancaster LA1 4JQ* Lancaster (0524) 65137

JOHNSON, John Cecil. b 23. Peterho Cam BA48. Ely Th Coll 57. **d** 59 **p** 60. C Whitton SS Phil and Jas *Lon* 59-70; P-in-c Fulham St Andr Fulham Fields 70-73; V 73-88; rtd 88. *13 Selkirk Drive, Telford, Shropshire TF7 4JE* Telford (0952) 588407

JOHNSON, John David. b 38. St Deiniol's Hawarden 71. **d** 71 **p** 72. C Heref St Martin *Heref* 71-73; P-in-c Ewyas Harold w Dulas 73-79; P-in-c Kilpeck 73-79; P-in-c St Devereux w Wormbridge 73-79; P-in-c Kenderchurch 73-79; P-in-c Bacton 78-79; TR Ewyas Harold w Dulas, Kenderchurch etc 79-81; R Kentchurch w Llangua, Rowlestone, Llancillo etc 79-81; Lic to Offic *St Alb* from 81; Chapl Napsbury Hosp St Alb from 81. *Napsbury Hospital, Napsbury, St Albans, Herts* Bowmansgreen (0727) 23333

JOHNSON, Joseph. b 11. Lon Coll of Div 43. **d** 45 **p** 46. V Alperton *Lon* 61-79; rtd 79; Perm to Offic *Derby* 87-90. *101 Vestry Road, Oakwood, Derby DE2 2NB* Derby (0332) 834161

JOHNSON, Joseph Clarke. b 10. Bps' Coll Cheshunt 46. **d** 48 **p** 49. V Beckermet St Bridget w Ponsonby *Carl* 57-78; rtd 78; Perm to Offic *Carl* from 78. *High Moss, Calderbridge, Seascale, Cumbria CH20 1DQ* Beckermet (094684) 289

JOHNSON, Keith Winton Thomas William. b 37. K Coll Lon BD63 AKC63. **d** 64 **p** 65. C Dartford H Trin *Roch* 64-69; Kuwait 69-73; V Erith St Jo *Roch* 73-80; V Bexley St Jo 80-91; V Royston *St Alb* from 91. *The Vicarage, 31 Baldock Road, Royston, Herts SG8 5BJ* Royston (0763) 243145

JOHNSON, Kenneth Reginald. b 06. Leeds Univ BA27. Coll of Resurr Mirfield 24. **d** 29 **p** 30. V Newtown St Luke *Win* 60-71; rtd 71. *Hilton Cottage, Church Street, Mere, Warminster, Wilts BA12 6DS* Mere (0747) 860609

JOHNSON, Malcolm Arthur. b 36. Univ Coll Dur BA60 MA64. Cuddesdon Coll 60. **d** 62 **p** 63. C Portsea N End St Mark *Portsm* 62-67; Chapl Qu Mary Coll *Lon* 67-74; V St Botolph Aldgate w H Trin Minories from 74; P-in-c St Ethelburga Bishopgate 85-89; AD The City 85-90. *St Botolph's Vestry, Aldgate, London EC3N 1AB* 071-283 1670

JOHNSON, Malcolm Stuart. b 35. AKC60. **d** 61 **p** 62. C Catford St Laur *S'wark* 61-64; Hon C Hatcham St Cath 66-76; P-in-c Kingstanding St Luke *Birm* 76-77; V 77-82; P-in-c Peckham St Jo w St Andr *S'wark* from 82. *St*

John's Vicarage, 10A Meeting House Lane, London SE15 2UN 071-639 0084

JOHNSON, Michael. b 42. Birm Univ BSc63. S'wark Ord Course 68. **d** 71 **p** 72. C Kidbrooke St Jas *S'wark* 71-74; Hon C Eynsford w Farningham and Lullingstone *Roch* 74-90; Hon C Selling w Throwley, Sheldwich w Badlesmere etc *Cant* from 90. *1 Halke Cottages, North Street, Sheldwich, Faversham, Kent ME13 0LR* Faversham (0795) 536583

JOHNSON, Michael Anthony. b 51. Ex Univ BA76. Ripon Coll Cuddesdon 76 Ch Div Sch of the Pacific (USA) 78. **d** 78 **p** 79. C Primrose Hill St Mary w Avenue Road St Paul *Lon* 78-81; C Hampstead St Jo 81-85; TV Mortlake w E Sheen *S'wark* from 85. *All Saints' Vicarage, 86 East Sheen Avenue, London SW14 8AU* 081-876 4201

JOHNSON, Michael Colin. b 37. Lon Univ DipRS80. S'wark Ord Course 77. **d** 80 **p** 81. NSM New Eltham All SS *S'wark* 80-84; NSM Woldingham from 84. *The Rectory, Station Road, Woldingham, Caterham, Surrey CR3 7DB* Woldingham (0883) 652192

JOHNSON, Michael Gordon. b 45. Lon Univ DipTh68. Kelham Th Coll 64. **d** 68 **p** 69. C Holbrooks *Cov* 68-72; C Cannock *Lich* 72-75; V Coseley Ch Ch 75-79; P-in-c Sneyd 79-82; R Longton 82-88; Chapl Pilgrim Hosp Boston from 88. *The Chaplain's Office, Pilgrim Hospital, Boston, Lincs PE21 9QS* Boston (0205) 364801 or 366217

JOHNSON, Nigel Edwin. b 41. AKC64. **d** 65 **p** 66. C Poulton-le-Sands *Blackb* 65-68; Chapl RN from 68. *c/o MOD, Lacon House, Theobald's Road, London WC1X 8RY* 071-430 6847

JOHNSON, Nigel Victor. b 48. ARCM68 LTCL75 Cam Univ DipEd69. Linc Th Coll 80. **d** 82 **p** 83. C Lindley *Wakef* 82-85; P-in-c Upperthong 85-87; Perm to Offic *Derby* 88-89; NSM Calow and Sutton cum Duckmanton 89-90; R from 90. *The Rectory, Top Road, Calow, Chesterfield S44 5AF* Chesterfield (0246) 273486

JOHNSON, Paul Anthony. b 56. Leeds Univ BA77 DCG81. Linc Th Coll 85. **d** 88 **p** 89. C Glouc St Jas and All SS *Glouc* 88-91; C Leckhampton SS Phil and Jas w Cheltenham St Jas from 91. *Flat A, Church House, 60 Painswick Road, Cheltenham, Glos GL50 2ER* Cheltenham (0242) 516362

JOHNSON, Paul Henry. b 08. Ch Coll Cam BA36 MA40. Wycliffe Hall Ox 36. **d** 38 **p** 38. V Newc St Geo *Lich* 63-72; C Welwyn Garden City *St Alb* 72-75; Hon C 75-85; rtd 75; Perm to Offic *St Alb* from 85. *39 High Oaks Road, Welwyn Garden City, Herts AL8 7BT* Welwyn Garden (0707) 326457

JOHNSON, Canon Peter Frederick. b 41. Melbourne Univ BA63 Ch Ch Ox BA68 MA72. St Steph Ho Ox 68. **d** 69 **p** 70. C Banbury *Ox* 69-71; Tutor St Steph Ho Ox 71-74; Chapl St Chad's Coll Dur 74-80; Vice-Prin 78-80; Chapl K Sch Cant 80-90; Perm to Offic *Cant* 80-81; Hon Min Can Cant Cathl 81-90; Can Res Bris Cathl *Bris* from 90. *41 Salisbury Road, Redland, Bristol BS6 7AR* Bristol (0272) 444464

JOHNSON, Richard Le Bas. b 22. TCD BA50 MA58. Sarum Th Coll 50. **d** 52 **p** 53. S Rhodesia 62-65; Rhodesia 65-72; C King's Worthy *Win* 72-74; R Crawley w Littleton 74-84; R Crawley and Littleton and Sparsholt w Lainston 84-90; rtd 90. *13 Anders Road, South Wonston, Winchester SO21 3EL* Winchester (0962) 884355

JOHNSON, Richard Miles. b 59. Bris Univ BSc82. St Jo Coll Nottm 87. **d** 90 **p** 91. C Bromley SS Pet and Paul *Roch* from 90. *13 Rochester Avenue, Bromley, Kent BR1 3DB* 081-464 9532

JOHNSON, Canon Robert Dunmore. b 18. Pemb Coll Ox BA45 MA45. Westcott Ho Cam 46. **d** 48 **p** 48. V Langton Green *Roch* 59-73; R Sundridge w Ide Hill 73-83; Hon Can Roch Cathl 81-83; rtd 83; Perm to Offic Roch, Cant and Chich from 83. *15 Acres Rise, Ticehurst, E Sussex TN5 7DD* Ticehurst (0580) 200796

JOHNSON, Robert Kenneth. b 48. N Ord Course 83. **d** 86 **p** 87. C Hattersley *Ches* 86-88; C Brinnington w Portwood 88-90; V Gospel Lane St Mich *Birm* from 90. *St Michael's Vicarage, 237 Lakey Lane, Birmingham B28 8QT* 021-777 6132 or 777 8443

JOHNSON, Ronald. b 40. Wycliffe Hall Ox 69. **d** 72 **p** 73. C Deane *Man* 72-74; C N Meols *Liv* 74-75; Chapl St Jo Sch Tiffield Northants 75-82; Warden Eton Coll Dorney

Project 82-84; Asst Chapl Eton Coll Windsor 82-84; TV Riverside *Ox* 82-84; Chapl Eastbourne Coll from 85. *14 Grange Road, Eastbourne, E Sussex BN21 4HJ* Eastbourne (0323) 34329

JOHNSON, Ronald Alan. b 32. MITSA. Ox NSM Course 84. **d** 86 **p** 87. NSM Beaconsfield *Ox* from 86. *7 Northcroft, Wooburn Green, High Wycombe, Bucks HP10 0BP* Bourne End (06285) 27141

JOHNSON, Ronald George. b 33. Chich Th Coll 75. **d** 76 **p** 77. Hon C Shipley *Chich* 76-79; C Brighton St Matthias 79-82; P-in-c Barlavington 82; P-in-c Burton w Coates 82; P-in-c Sutton w Bignor 82; R Barlavington, Burton w Coates, Sutton and Bignor from 82. *The Rectory, Sutton, Pulborough, W Sussex RH20 1PS* Sutton (07987) 220

JOHNSON, Very Rev Samuel Hugh Akinsope. b 30. K Coll Lon BD61. Linc Th Coll 52. **d** 55 **p** 56. C Whitechapel St Paul w St Mark *Lon* 55-58; C Sunbury 58-59; C Lisson Grove w St Marylebone St Matt w Em 59-60; C St Martin-in-the-Fields 60-62; Nigeria from 63; Provost Lagos Cathl from 70. *The Provost's Lodge, 2A Odunlami Street, PO Box 726, Lagos, Nigeria*

JOHNSON, Stanley. b 42. QUB BSc63 TCD BTh89. CITC 86. **d** 89 **p** 90. C Kilmore w Ballintemple, Kildallon etc *K, E & A* from 89. *Kildallon Rectory, Ballyconnell, Belturbet, Co Cavan, Irish Republic* Cavan (49) 26259

JOHNSON, Terence John. b 44. Cov Poly BA89. Lon Coll of Div ALCD70 LTh74. **d** 69 **p** 70. C Woodside *Ripon* 69-72; C Leeds St Geo 72-76; C Heworth *York* 76-81; V Budbrooke *Cov* from 81. *The Vicarage, Budbrooke, Warwick CV35 8QL* Warwick (0926) 494002

JOHNSON, Thomas Bernard. b 44. BA CertEd. Oak Hill Th Coll. **d** 84 **p** 85. C Birkenhead St Jas w St Bede *Ches* 84-88; R Ashover and Brackenfield *Derby* from 88; Hon Chapl Derbyshire St Jo Ambulance from 91. *The Rectory, Ashover, Chesterfield S45 0AU* Chesterfield (0246) 590246

JOHNSON, Canon Thomas Wyndham Page. b 11. BNC Ox BA33. Cuddesdon Coll 34. **d** 36 **p** 37. V Kilndown *Cant* 45-83; Hon Can Cant Cathl 79-83; rtd 83; Perm to Offic *Cant* from 83. *Little Park Cottage, Hook Green, Lamberhurst, Kent TN3 8LN* Lamberhurst (0892) 890391

JOHNSON, Victor Edward. b 45. Linc Th Coll 83. **d** 85 **p** 86. C Garforth *Ripon* 85-90; Dioc Video Officer from 90. *51 St James's Approach, Leeds LS14 6JJ* Leeds (0532) 731396

JOHNSON, Walter. b 21. St Aid Birkenhead. **d** 59 **p** 60. V Bracebridge *Linc* 62-73; R Weston sub Edge and Aston sub Edge *Glouc* 73-77; R Willersey, Saintbury, Weston-sub-Edge etc 77-86; rtd 86; Perm to Offic *Win* from 87. *15 Beechey Road, Bournemouth BH8 8LL* Bournemouth (0202) 557063

JOHNSTON, Alan Beere. b 14. Leeds Univ BA36. Coll of Resurr Mirfield 36. **d** 38 **p** 39. V Kingston upon Hull St Mary *York* 62-68; rtd 79. *6 Arlington Close, Goring-by-Sea, Worthing, W Sussex BN12 4ST* Worthing (0903) 46590

JOHNSTON, Canon Albert Richard. b 06. K Coll Lon 37. **d** 41 **p** 42. V Dedham *Chelmsf* 50-75; Hon Can Chelmsf Cathl 64-75; rtd 75; Perm to Offic *St E* from 76. *6 Yew Tree Court, Bury St Edmunds IP33 2JF* Bury St Edmunds (0284) 769464

JOHNSTON, Alexander Irvine. b 47. LRAM Keele Univ BA70. St Alb Minl Tr Scheme 77. **d** 80 **p** 81. NSM Hockerill *St Alb* from 80. *48 Newtown Road, Bishop's Stortford, Herts CM23 3SD* Bishop's Stortford (0279) 657479

JOHNSTON, Charles Walter. b 38. **d** 64 **p** 65. C Tollington Park St Mark w St Anne *Lon* 64-68; Argentina from 68. *Centro Anglicano, Casilla 19, Ing Juarez, Prov de Formosa, Argentina*

JOHNSTON, David Charles. b 39. TCD BA62 BD69 MA70. **d** 62 **p** 63. C Dub St Cath w St Jas *D & G* 63-68; Hon CV Ch Ch Cathl Dub 64-71; C Dub Donnybrook 68-71; Asst Master Ban Gr Sch Co Down 71-72; K Sch Pet 72-76; Ashton Sch Dunstable 76-81; Lic to Offic *St Alb* 77-81; Asst Chapl Highgate Sch Lon 81-85; C Gt Yarmouth *Nor* 85-89; P-in-c Bootle Ch Ch *Liv* from 89. *1 Breeze Hill, Bootle, Merseyside L20 9EY* 051-525 2565

JOHNSTON, Edith Violet Nicholl. b 28. **d** 87. Par Dn Bentley *Sheff* 87-88; rtd 88. *32 Tennyson Avenue, Mexborough, S Yorkshire S64 0AX* Mexborough (0709) 570189

JOHNSTON, Elizabeth Margaret. b 37. QUB BD87. **dss** 81 **d** 87. BCMS from 81; India from 81. *Union Biblical Seminary Bibwewadi, Pune 411037, MS, India*

JOHNSTON, Very Rev Frederick Mervyn Kieran. b 11. TCD BA33 MA52. **d** 34 **p** 36. Dean Cork *C, C & R* 66-71; rtd 71. *24 Lapps Court, Hartlands Avenue, Cork, Irish Republic*

JOHNSTON, Geoffrey Stanley. b 44. Aston Univ MBA81 Lon Univ DipTh68 Birm Univ CertEd78. Kelham Th Coll 64. **d** 68 **p** 69. C Blakenall Heath *Lich* 68-72 and 73-75; C St Buryan, St Levan and Sennen *Truro* 72-73; P-in-c Willenhall St Steph *Lich* 75-76; C W Bromwich All SS 76-77; Lect W Bromwich Coll of Commerce and Tech 78-82; Ind Chapl *Worc* from 82; TV Halesowen from 82. *47 Waxland Road, Halesowen, W Midlands B63 3DN* 021-550 9311

JOHNSTON, George Ralph Harden. b 23. TCD BA44 MA47. CITC 45. **d** 45 **p** 47. I Greenisland *Conn* 64-88; Can Belf Cathl 83-88; rtd 88. *183 Holywood Road, Belfast BT4 2DG* Belfast (0232) 654968

JOHNSTON, James. b 19. FCIB70. Carl Dioc Tr Course. **d** 82 **p** 83. NSM Kendal St Geo *Carl* 82-89; Perm to Offic from 89. *8 Sedbergh Drive, Kendal, Cumbria LA9 6BJ* Kendal (0539) 725422

JOHNSTON, Preb Rauceby Peter Pope. b 10. Oak Hill Th Coll 32. **d** 35 **p** 36. V Islington St Mary *Lon* 62-80; RD Islington 67-79; Preb St Paul's Cathl 70-80; P-in-c Islington St Jas w St Phil 71-80; rtd 80; Perm to Offic *Sarum* from 89. *The Rectory, 51 Millham's Road, Kinson, Bournemouth BH10 7LJ* Bournemouth (0202) 571996

JOHNSTON, Canon Robert John. b 31. Oak Hill Th Coll 64. **d** 64 **p** 65. C Bebington *Ches* 64-68; I Lack *Clogh* from 68; RD Kesh from 87; Can Clogh Cathl from 89. *The Rectory, Lack, Co Fermanagh* Kesh (03656) 360

JOHNSTON, Thomas Cosbey. b 15. Em Coll Cam BA40 MA44. Ridley Hall Cam 40. **d** 42 **p** 43. C Handsworth St Mary *Birm* 42-48; New Zealand from 48. *254 Main Road, Moncks Bay, Christchurch 8, New Zealand* Christchurch (3) 841224

JOHNSTON, Dr Walter Barr. b 09. Lon Univ MRCS32 LRCP32 MB, BS33. Oak Hill Th Coll. **d** 67 **p** 68. C Dagenham *Chelmsf* 67-70; P-in-c Burton Fleming w Fordon *York* 70; V 71-84; V Grindale and Ergham 71-84; P-in-c Wold Newton 82-84; rtd 84. *34 Almond Avenue, Leamington Spa, Warks CV32 6QD* Leamington Spa (0926) 330832

JOHNSTON, Wilfred Brian. b 44. TCD BA67 MA70. **d** 68 **p** 70. C Seagoe *D & D* 68-73; I Inniskeel *D & R* 73-82; I Castlerock w Dunboe and Fermoyle from 82; Dioc Registrar *D & D* from 89; RD Dungiven and Limavady from 91. *The Rectory, 52 Main Street, Castlerock, Coleraine, Co Londonerry BT51 4RA* Castlerock (0265) 848242

JOHNSTON, Ven William Derek. b 40. CITC 68. **d** 68 **p** 69. VC Derry Cathl *D & R* 68-70; I Swanlinbar w Templeport *K, E & A* 70-73; I Billis Union 73-84; Glebes Sec (Kilmore) from 77; I Annagh w Drumaloor and Cloverhill 84-87; Preb Kilmore Cathl 85-89; I Annagh w Drumgoon, Ashfield etc from 87; Adn Kilmore from 89. *The Rectory, Belturbet, Co Cavan, Irish Republic* Cavan (49) 22142

JOHNSTON, William Francis. b 30. CB83. TCD BA55 MA69. **d** 55 **p** 56. C Orangefield *D & D* 55-59; CF 59-77; Asst Chapl Gen 77-80; Chapl Gen 80-87; P-in-c Winslow *Ox* 87-91; RD Claydon from 89; R Winslow w Gt Horwood and Addington from 91. *The Vicarage, Winslow, Buckingham MK18 3BT* Winslow (029671) 2564

JOHNSTON, William John. b 35. Lon Univ DipTh72 BA85 MA90. CITC 67. **d** 70 **p** 71. C Belf St Donard *D & D* 70-72; C Derg *D & R* 72-78; I Drumclamph w Lower and Upper Langfield 78-91; I Kilskeery w Trillick *Clogh* from 91. *The Rectory, Kilskeery, Omagh, Co Tyrone* Trillick (036555) 228

JOHNSTON-HUBBOLD, Clifford Johnston. b 19. Lon Univ BA76 BD80. St Aid Birkenhead 49. **d** 52 **p** 53. C Stanwix *Carl* 52-55; V Gt Broughton 55-59; R Sedgeberrow *Worc* 59-73; P-in-c Hinton-on-the-Green 72-73; R Sedgeberrow w Hinton-on-the-Green from 73. *The Rectory, Sedgeberrow, Evesham, Worcs WR11 6UE* Evesham (0386) 881291

JOHNSTONE, Canon Frederic St George Harden. b 12. TCD BA34 MA43. **d** 35 **p** 36. I Templemore w Kilfithmone, Thurles and Loughmoe *C & O* 65-87; Can Cashel Cathl 75-87; rtd 87. *Stoneen, Thomastown, Co Kilkenny, Irish Republic* Thomastown (56) 24379

JOHNSTONE, Ian Douglas. b 42. St Jo Coll Morpeth 57. **d** 70 **p** 70. Australia 70-88; V Morley St Paul *Wakef* from 88. *2 Bridge Court, Bridge Street, Morley, Leeds LS27 0BD* Morley (0532) 529300

JOHNSTONE, Leslie William. b 20. ALCD49. **d** 49 **p** 50. R Bexhill St Mark *Chich* 56-85; rtd 85; Perm to Offic

Chich from 86. *4 Fitzgerald Park, Seaford, E Sussex BN25 1AX* Seaford (0323) 899708

JOHNSTONE, Peter Verney Lovett. b 37. Trin Coll Cam BA61 MA65. Cuddesdon Coll 61. **d** 63 **p** 64. C Kennington St Jo *S'wark* 63-66; Asst Chapl Southn Univ *Win* 66-70; P-in-c Earlsfield St Jo *S'wark* 70-79; V Eltham St Jo from 79. *The Vicarage, Sowerby Close, London SE9 6HB* 081-850 2731 or 859 1242

JOHNSTONE, William John Richard. b 13. Leeds Univ BA48. Coll of Resurr Mirfield. **d** 50 **p** 51. V St Neot *Truro* 63-71; V Ruislip Manor St Paul *Lon* 71-76; C Honicknowle *Ex* 76-77; rtd 78; Perm to Offic *Ex* from 82. *19 Trelawney Road, Peverell, Plymouth PL3 4JT* Plymouth (0752) 229328

JOINT, Capt Michael John. b 39. Sarum & Wells Th Coll 79. **d** 79 **p** 79. CA from 61; Hon C Chandler's Ford *Win* 79-83; Youth Chapl 79-83; V Lymington from 83. *The Vicarage, Grove Road, Lymington, Hants SO41 9RF* Lymington (0590) 673847

JOLLY, Leslie Alfred Walter. b 16. AKC40. **d** 40 **p** 41. R Chaldon *S'wark* 57-85; rtd 85; Perm to Offic S'wark and York from 85. *62 Wharfedale, Filey, N Yorkshire YO14 0DP* Scarborough (0723) 514591

JONAS, Ian Robert. b 54. St Jo Coll Nottm BTh80. **d** 80 **p** 81. C Portadown St Mark *Arm* 80-82; C Cregagh *D & D* 82-85; BCMS Sec *D & G* 85-90; V Langley Mill *Derby* from 90. *The Vicarage, 214 Cromford Road, Langley Mill, Nottingham NG16 4HB* Langley Mill (0773) 712441

JONATHAN, Brother. See EWER, Edward Sydney John

JONES, Adrian Alfred Burkett. b 37. St Aid Birkenhead 61. **d** 64 **p** 65. C Derby St Aug *Derby* 64-68; Chapl RAF 68-87; R Worlingham w Barnby and N Cove *St E* from 87. *The Rectory, Worlingham, Beccles, Suffolk NR34 7DZ* Beccles (0502) 715403

JONES, Alan David. b 32. Lon Coll of Div ALCD58 DipTh70 LTh74. **d** 58 **p** 59. C Ipswich All SS *St E* 58-60; C Southend St Jo *Chelmsf* 60-64; CF (TA) 60-62; CF (TA - R of O) 62-67; V Leyton St Cath *Chelmsf* 64-70; V Hatf Broad Oak 70-77; P-in-c Bush End 77-79; V Theydon Bois 77-88; P-in-c Finchingfield and Cornish Hall End from 88. *The Vicarage, Finchingfield, Braintree, Essex CM7 4JR* Braintree (0376) 810309

JONES, Alan John. b 47. Nottm Univ BA71. Coll of Resurr Mirfield 71. **d** 73 **p** 74. C Sedgley St Mary *Lich* 73-76; C Cov St Jo *Cov* 76-78; V W Bromwich St Fran *Lich* from 78. *Friar Park Vicarage, Wednesbury, W Midlands WS10 0HJ* 021-556 5823

JONES, Alban Vaughan. b 24. St D Coll Lamp BA51. **d** 52 **p** 53. Area Sec (Dios Ches, Ban, St As and S & M) CMS 65-72; V Ventnor H Trin *Portsm* 72-79; V Ventnor St Cath 72-79; V Marshfield and Peterstone Wentloog etc *Mon* 79-90; RD Bassaleg 87-90; rtd 90. *40 St Hilary Drive, Killay, Swansea SA2 7EH* Swansea (0792) 208178

JONES, Albert. b 97. MRST38. **d** 56 **p** 57. Chapl Qu Eliz Hosp for Children *Lon* 63-67; P-in-c Bethnal Green St Pet w St Thos *Lon* 63-67; rtd 67; Hon C Pimlico St Gabr *Lon* 68-72. *Penryn, Sedbury Lane, Tutshill, Chepstow, Gwent NP6 7EJ*

JONES, Albert. b 13. K Coll Lon 37. **d** 41 **p** 42. R Stifford *Chelmsf* 66-72; P-in-c Stondon Massey 72-79; R Doddinghurst 72-79; rtd 79. *29 Seaview Road, Brightlingsea, Colchester CO7 0PP* Brightlingsea (0206) 303994

JONES, Alfred Albert. b 36. St D Coll Lamp BA59. **d** 61 **p** 62. C Treherbert *Llan* 61-64; C Horsham *Chich* 64-82; V Shipley 82-86; Chapl Hillingdon Hosp & Mt Vernon Hosp Uxbridge 86-87. *Chantry House, Nuthurst Road, Monks Gate, Horsham, W Sussex RH13 6LG* Horsham (0403) 891218

JONES, Alwyn Humphrey Griffith. b 30. Leeds Univ BSc51. Coll of Resurr Mirfield 53. **d** 55 **p** 56. C W Hackney St Barn *Lon* 55-58; E Pakistan 58-64; India 65-73; P-in-c Bedminster St Fran *Bris* 73-75; TR Bedminster 75-83; TV Langport Area Chs *B & W* 83-85; Dep Chapl HM Pris Nor 85; Chapl HM Pris Preston 85-89; Ashwell 89-91; C Acton Green *Lon* from 91. *276 Osborne Road, London W3 8SR* 081-993 3237

✠JONES, Rt Rev Alwyn Rice. b 34. Univ of Wales (Lamp) BA55 Fitzw Ho Cam BA57 MA61. St Mich Coll Llan 57. **d** 58 **p** 59 **c** 82. C Llanfairisgaer *Ban* 58-62; N Wales Sec SCM 60-62; Staff Sec SCM 62-65; Chapl St Winifred's Sch Llanfairfechan 65-68; Dir RE *Ban* 65-75; Dioc Youth Officer *Ban* 73-76; Dir of Ords 70-75; Asst Tutor Univ of Wales (Ban) 73-76; V Porthmadog *Ban* 75-79; Hon Can Ban Cathl 75-78; Preb 78-79; Dean Brecon *S & B* 79-82; V Brecon w Battle 79-82; Bp St As from 82.

Esgobty, St Asaph, Clwyd LL17 0TW   St Asaph (0745) 583503

JONES, Miss Alyson Elizabeth. *See* DAVIE, Mrs Alyson Elizabeth

JONES, Andrea Margaret. b 46. Qu Coll Birm 88. **d** 90. Par Dn Kidderminster St Geo *Worc* from 90. *6 Forester Way, Kidderminster, Worcs DY10 1NT*   Kidderminster (0562) 745996

JONES, Andrew. b 61. Univ of Wales (Ban) BD82 CertEd83 TCD BTh85. CITC 85. **d** 85 **p** 86. Min Can Ban Cathl *Ban* 85-88; C Ban Cathl Par 85-88; R Dolgelly w Llanfachreth and Brithdir etc from 88. *The Rectory, Dolgellau, Gwynedd LL40 3YW*   Dolgellau (0341) 422225

JONES, Andrew Christopher. b 47. Southn Univ BA69 PhD75. Ridley Hall Cam 78. **d** 80 **p** 81. C Wareham *Sarum* 80-83; P-in-c Symondsbury 83; P-in-c Chideock 83; R Symondsbury and Chideock from 84. *The Rectory, Symondsbury, Bridport, Dorset DT6 6HF*   Bridport (0308) 22145

JONES, Andrew Collins. b 62. Univ Coll Dur BA83 MA84. St Steph Ho Ox 88. **d** 90 **p** 91. C Llangefni w Tregaian and Llangristiolus etc *Ban* from 90. *Flat 1, Cefni Fruit Market, Fford yr Efail, Llangefni, Gwynedd LL77 7LT*   Bangor (0248) 722851

JONES, Preb Andrew Theodore Hugh. b 22. St Cath Soc Ox BA49 MA53. St Steph Ho Ox. **d** 50 **p** 51. V Witheridge *Ex* 66-77; V Creacombe 67-77; R Thelbridge 67-77; R W w E Worlington 67-77; P-in-c Meshaw 69-77; RD S Molton 72-74; P-in-c Limington *B & W* 77-78; P-in-c Ilchester w Northover 77-78; P-in-c Yeovilton 78; R Ilchester w Northover, Limington, Yeovilton etc 78-80; V Bishops Tawton *Ex* 80-85; V Newport 80-85; RD Barnstaple 81-83; Preb Ex Cathl 82-87; TR Newport, Bishops Tawton and Tawstock 85-87; rtd 87; Perm to Offic *Ex* from 87. *Belmont House, King Street, Combe Martin, Ilfracombe, Devon EX34 0AH*   Combe Martin (027188) 3135

JONES, Canon Anthony Spacie. b 34. AKC58. **d** 59 **p** 60. C Bedf St Martin *St Alb* 59-63; Br Guiana 63-66; Guyana 66-71; V Ipswich All Hallows *St E* 72-80; RD Ipswich 78-86; Bp's Dom Chapl 80-82; V Rushmere 82-91; Hon Can St E Cathl from 83; R Brantham w Stutton from 91. *The Rectory, Rectory Lane, Brantham, Manningtree, Essex CO11 1PZ*   Colchester (0206) 392646

JONES, Canon Arthur Alexander. b 10. Birm Univ BA35 MA48 Lon Univ BD45 PhD53. **d** 52 **p** 53. Prin Lect RE Avery Hill Coll 62-75; Hon C Eltham St Sav *S'wark* 71-75; Chapl RAEC Wilton Park 75-80; rtd 75; Tutor K Coll Lon 75-80. *16 Heath Road, Beaconsfield, Bucks HP9 1DD*   Beaconsfield (0494) 676746

JONES, Arthur Howard Glyn. b 07. Ripon Hall Ox 53. **d** 55 **p** 56. R Drewsteignton *Ex* 68-76; V Hittisleigh 73-76; V Spreyton 73-76; rtd 76; Hon C Blackawton and Stoke Fleming *Ex* 76-81. *15 Fore Street, Bradninch, Exeter EX5 4NN*   Exeter (0392) 881383

JONES, Arthur Kenneth Hughes. b 14. Ch Coll Cam BA36 MA46. Wycliffe Hall Ox. **d** 53 **p** 54. V Furze Platt *Ox* 68-79; rtd 79. *107 Farm Road, Maidenhead, Berks SL6 5JQ*   Maidenhead (0628) 31909

JONES, Arthur Leslie. b 12. Univ of Wales BA36. Qu Coll Birm 36. **d** 38 **p** 39. R Upwey *Sarum* 60-80; R Buckland Ripers 75-80; rtd 80. *4 St George's Close, Harnham, Salisbury SP2 8HA*   Salisbury (0722) 336653

JONES, Barry Mervyn. b 46. St Chad's Coll Dur BA68 DipTh69. **d** 70 **p** 71. C Bloxwich *Lich* 70-72; C Norwood All SS *Cant* 72-76; C New Addington 76-78; Chapl Mayday Hosp Thornton Heath and Qu and St Mary's Hosps Croydon 78-86; Chapl Bromsgrove and Redditch DHA from 86; Chapl Alexandra Hosp Redditch from 86. *The Alexandra Hospital, Woodrow Drive, Redditch, Worcs B98 7UB*   Redditch (0527) 503030

JONES, Canon Basil Henry. b 26. Bps' Coll Cheshunt 63. **d** 64 **p** 65. C Gt Berkhamsted *St Alb* 64-67; V Leagrave 68-74; RD Luton 71-74; P-in-c Bedf St Paul 74-75; V Wigginton from 75; Hon Can St Alb from 82. *The Vicarage, Wigginton, Tring, Herts HP23 6DZ*   Tring (044282) 3273

JONES, Ven Benjamin Jenkin Hywel. b 39. Univ of Wales BA61. St Mich Coll Llan 61. **d** 64 **p** 65. C Carmarthen St Pet *St D* 64-70; V Conwil Caio w Llansawel and Talley 70-79; R Llanbadarn Fawr 79-82; V Llanbadarn Fawr w Capel Bangor from 82; Can St D Cathl 86-90; RD Llanbadarn Fawr 89-90; Adn Cardigan from 90. *The Vicarage, Llanbadarn Fawr, Aberystwyth, Dyfed SY23 3QU*   Aberystwyth (0970) 623368

JONES, Benjamin Tecwyn. b 17. Univ of Wales BA38. K Coll Lon 38. **d** 40 **p** 41. Hd Master and Chapl St

Mary's Sch Bexhill-on-Sea 69-71; V Blackb St Luke *Blackb* 71-72; P-in-c Griffin 71-72; V Blackb St Luke w St Phil 72-83; rtd 83; Lic to Offic *Blackb* from 83. *527A Livesey Branch Road, Feniscowles, Blackburn BB2 5DB*   Blackburn (0254) 209206

JONES, Canon Brian Howell. b 35. St Mich Coll Llan DipTh61. **d** 61 **p** 62. C Llanguicke *S & B* 61-63; C Swansea St Mary and H Trin 63-70; R New Radnor w Llanfihangel Nantmelan etc 70-75; V Llansamlet 75-89; Dioc Dir of Stewardship 82-89; P-in-c Capel Coelbren from 89; Dioc Missr from 89; Can Res Brecon Cathl from 89; RD Cwmtawe from 89. *The Vicarage, Capel Coelbren, Neath, W Glam SA10 9PE*   Neath (0639) 701059

JONES, Brian Michael. b 34. **d** 84. CMS from 82; Sierra Leone from 83. *PO Box 89, Segbwema, Eastern Province, Sierra Leone*

JONES, Canon Brian Noel. b 32. Edin Th Coll 59. **d** 62 **p** 63. C Monkseaton St Mary *Newc* 62-65; C Saffron Walden *Chelmsf* 65-69; P-in-c Swaffham Bulbeck *Ely* 69-75; Dioc Youth Officer 69-75; RD St Ives 75-83 and 87-89; V Ramsey 75-89; V Upwood w Gt and Lt Raveley 75-89; P-in-c Ramsey St Mary's 82-89; Hon Can Ely Cathl from 85; V Cherry Hinton St Jo from 89. *St John's Vicarage, 9 Luard Road, Cambridge CB2 2PJ*   Cambridge (0223) 247451

JONES, Brinley Morgan. b 13. St D Coll Lamp BA37. **d** 40 **p** 41. V Pwllgwaun *Llan* 54-71; R Eglwysbrewis and St Athan 71-78; rtd 78. *St Jude's, 228 New Road, Porthcawl, M Glam CF36 5BA*   Porthcawl (065671) 6123

JONES, Bryan Maldwyn. b 32. St Mich Coll Llan DipTh62. **d** 62 **p** 63. C Swansea St Barn *S & B* 62-69; V Trallwng and Betws Penpont 69-75; V Trallwng, Bettws Penpont w Aberyskir etc from 75; RD Brecon II from 80. *The Vicarage, Trallwng, Brecon, Powys LD3 8HP*   Sennybridge (0874) 636549

JONES, Bryan William. b 30. Selw Coll Cam BA53 MA57. Linc Th Coll 53. **d** 55 **p** 56. C Bedminster Down *Bris* 55-58; C Filton 58-62; P-in-c Bedminster St Mich 62-65; V 65-72; P-in-c Moorfields 72-75; TV E Bris from 75. *St Matthew's Vicarage, Victoria Avenue, Redfield, Bristol BS5 9NH*   Bristol (0272) 557350

JONES, Bryon. b 34. Open Univ BA84. St D Coll Lamp 61. **d** 64 **p** 65. C Port Talbot St Theodore *Llan* 64-67; C Aberdare 68-69; C Up Hatherley *Glouc* 69-71; C Oystermouth *S & B* 71-74; V Camrose *St D* 74-77; V Camrose and St Lawrence w Ford and Haycastle from 77. *The Vicarage, Camrose, Haverfordwest, Dyfed SA62 6JE*   Camrose (0437) 710501

JONES, Charles Derek. b 37. K Coll Lon BD60 AKC60. **d** 61 **p** 62. C Stockton St Chad *Dur* 61-64; C Becontree St Eliz *Chelmsf* 64-66; C S Beddington St Mich *S'wark* 66-73; Lic to Offic *Ex* 73-77; Perm to Offic *Liv* from 77. *8 Millfield Close, Barton Park, Farndon, Chester*   Farndon (0829) 270554

JONES, Charles Emerson Glynne. b 08. **d** 31 **p** 32. R Middleton Cheney w Chacombe *Pet* 52-75; rtd 75; Hon C N Huish *Ex* 75-83. *31 Y Berllan, Dunvant, Swansea SA2 8RD*   Swansea (0792) 201886

JONES, Charles Eurwyn. b 27. Univ of Wales BSc48 DipEd51. St Mich Coll Llan 53. **d** 55 **p** 56. C Brecon St Dav *S & B* 55-57; C Carmarthen St Dav *St D* 57-61; Tutor Old Cath Sem Bonn 61-64; Tutor Bps' Coll Cheshunt 64-67; V Carlton *S'well* 67-75; P-in-c Colwick 69-75; V Bunny w Bradmore from 75. *The Vicarage, 10 Moor Lane, Bunny, Nottingham NG11 6QX*   Nottingham (0602) 217805

JONES, Charles Harold Lloyd. b 08. St D Coll Lamp DipTh59. **d** 59 **p** 60. R Llanfairorllwyn and Llangynllo *St D* 61-70; V Llanllawddog w Capel-y-Groes 70-79; rtd 79. *15 Bro Nantlais, Gwyddgrug, Pencader, Dyfed SA39 9BQ*   Pencader (0559) 384884

JONES, Charles John Llewelyn. b 11. Jes Coll Cam BA32 MA36. St Aug Coll Cant 56. **d** 56 **p** 57. V Whittlesford *Ely* 65-84; rtd 84; Perm to Offic *Ely* from 86. *4 Bishop Wynn Close, Ely, Cambs CB7 4BH*   Ely (0353) 665230

JONES, Christopher Howell. b 50. FCCA BA. Oak Hill Th Coll 80. **d** 83 **p** 84. C Leyton St Mary w St Edw *Chelmsf* 83-86; C Becontree St Mary 86-90; P-in-c Bootle St Matt *Liv* from 90. *St Matthew's Vicarage, 418 Stanley Road, Bootle, Merseyside L20 5AE*   051-922 3316

JONES, Christopher John Stark. b 39. Lon Univ BA60 AKC60. Wells Th Coll 63. **d** 65 **p** 66. C Stanmore *Win* 65-67; C Bournemouth St Pet 67-71; C W Wycombe *Ox* 71-75; TV High Wycombe 75-77; V Wokingham St Sebastian 77-84; R Didsbury Ch Ch *Man* from 84. *Christ Church Rectory, 35 Darley Avenue, Manchester M20 8ZD*   061-445 4152

JONES, Christopher Mark. b 54. St Pet Coll Ox BA75 DipTh77 MA79 Selw Coll Cam MPhil80. Ridley Hall Cam 77. **d** 80 **p** 81. C Putney St Marg *S'wark* 80-83; C Ham St Andr 83-86; Chapl HM Rem Cen Latchmere Ho 83-86; Chapl St Jo Coll Dur from 87; Tutor Cranmer Hall Dur from 87. *8 Carlisle Road, Newton Hall, Durham DH1 5XE* 091-386 4013

JONES, Christopher Mark. b 56. St Jo Coll Cam BA78 MA82 Ox Univ BA81 MA85. Wycliffe Hall Ox 79. **d** 82 **p** 83. C Walsall *Lich* 82-84; Chapl St Jo Coll Cam 84-89; Chapl Eton Coll Windsor from 89. *Eton College, Windsor, Berks SL4 6DW* Windsor (0753) 866439

JONES, Clifford Albert. b 20. Edin Th Coll 54. **d** 56 **p** 57. V Bradf *B & W* 69-74; V Bridgwater St Jo 74-78; RD Bridgwater 76-80; R Bridgwater St Jo w Chedzoy 78-80; P-in-c Timsbury 80-85; R Timsbury and Priston 85; rtd 85; P-in-c Nor St Geo Tombland *Nor* 85-90; Hon C St Marylebone All SS *Lon* from 90. *8 Margaret Street, London W1N 8JQ*

JONES, Clive. b 51. BA82. Oak Hill Th Coll 79. **d** 82 **p** 83. C Brunswick *Man* 82-85; V Pendlebury St Jo from 85. *St John's Vicarage, 27 Bolton Road, Swinton, Manchester M27 2XS* 061-736 2176

JONES, Clive Morlais Peter. b 40. LTCL71 Univ of Wales (Cardiff) BA63 CertEd64. Chich Th Coll 64. **d** 66 **p** 67. C Llanfabon *Llan* 66-70; PV Llan Cathl 70-75; R Gellygaer 75-85; Prec and Can Llan Cathl 84-85; R Tilehurst St Mich *Ox* from 85. *The Rectory, Routh Lane, Reading RG3 4JY* Reading (0734) 427331

JONES, Colin Stuart. b 56. Southn Univ LLB77. Coll of Resurr Mirfield 81. **d** 84 **p** 85. C Mountain Ash *Llan* 84-86; C Castle Bromwich SS Mary and Marg *Birm* 86-89; V Kingshurst from 89. *St Barnabas's Vicarage, 51 Overgreen Drive, Birmingham B37 6EY* 021-770 3972

JONES, Cyril. b 27. Linc Th Coll 67. **d** 69 **p** 70. C Milnrow *Man* 69-71; C Chorlton-cum-Hardy St Werburgh 71-73; V Chadderton St Mark 73-75; R Didsbury Ch Ch 75-81; V Farlam and Nether Denton *Carl* 81-85; P-in-c Kirkbride w Newton Arlosh 85-89; rtd 89. *29 Wood Lane, Weaverham, Northwich, Cheshire CW8 3BU* Weaverham (0606) 852677

JONES, Cyril Ernest. b 29. St D Coll Lamp BA54. **d** 56 **p** 57. C Llanedy *St D* 56-60; C Llanelly 60-63; V Mydroilyn w Dihewyd 63-66; V Llanybydder 66-73; V Llanybyther and Llanwenog w Llanwnnen 73-78; V Bettws St Dav 78-81; V Conwil Caio w Llansawel and Talley from 81. *The Vicarage, Talley, Llandeilo, Dyfed SA19 7YP* Talley (0558) 685229

JONES, Cyril Maurice. b 16. **d** 39 **p** 40. C Aylesbury *Ox* 50-56; rtd 56. *Pinewood Home, Manford Way, Ilford, Essex* 081-500 8498

JONES, Canon Daniel William Ellis. b 10. Qu Coll Cam BA32 MA36. Ridley Hall Cam 32. **d** 34 **p** 36. R Trimley *St E* 62-74; Hon Can St E Cathl 73-74; rtd 75; Perm to Offic *St E* from 78. *St Martin's Cottage, Old Kirton Road, Trimley, Ipswich IP10 0QH* Felixstowe (0394) 275233

JONES, David. b 55. St Steph Ho Ox. **d** 85 **p** 86. C Fleur-de-Lis *Mon* 85-87; C Ynysddu 87; V from 87. *The Vicarage, Commercial Road, Cwmfelinfach, Ynysddu, Newport, Gwent NP1 7HW* Blackwood (0495) 200257

JONES, David Arthur. b 44. Liv Univ BA66 Sussex Univ MA68. St D Coll Lamp LTh74. **d** 74 **p** 75. C Tenby *St D* 74-76; C Chepstow *Mon* 76-78; P-in-c Teversal *S'well* 78-81; R from 81; Chapl Sutton Cen 78-89. *The Parsonage, Fackley Road, Sutton-in-Ashfield, Notts NG17 3JA* Mansfield (0623) 550730 or 554554

JONES, Ven David Elidyr Morgan Glynne. b 07. St Edm Hall Ox BA30 MA34. St Mich Coll Llan 29. **d** 30 **p** 31. Adn Montgomery *St As* 66-76; rtd 76. *Tyn-y-Coed Lodge, Berriew, Welshpool, Powys* Berriew (068685) 514

JONES, David Emrys. b 21. Lon Univ BD69 Univ of Wales MA74. St D Coll Lamp BA42. **d** 47 **p** 48. V Beddgelert *Ban* 57-72; R Llangystenyn *St As* 72-91; rtd 91. *The Rectory, Llanfor, Bala, Gwynedd* Bala (0678) 520080

JONES, David Emrys. b 24. St D Coll Lamp BA49. **d** 51 **p** 52. R Llangrannog *St D* 57-73; R Llangrannog and Llandysiliogogo 73-84; V Llanarthney and Llanddarog 84-91; rtd 91. *12 Cae Person, Llanddarog, Carmarthen, Dyfed*

JONES, Chan David Frederick Donald. b 19. Univ of Wales (Abth) BA41. Westcott Ho Cam 41. **d** 43 **p** 44. Lect Bp Burgess Th Hall Lamp 59-72; V Bettws St Dav *St D* 64-78; RD Dyffryn Aman 72-78; Can St D Cathl 75-88; V Felinfoel 78-88; Chan St D Cathl 83-88; rtd

88. *93 Nun Street, St Davids, Haverfordwest, Dyfed SA62 6NU* St Davids (0437) 720359

JONES, David Hugh. b 34. St D Coll Lamp BA56. St Mich Coll Llan 58. **d** 58 **p** 59. C Swansea St Mary and H Trin *S & B* 58-61; Inter-Colleg Sec SCM (Liverpool) 61-63; Hon Chapl Liv Univ 61-63; C Swansea St Pet *S & B* 63-69; V Llanddewi Ystradenni and Abbey Cwmhir 69-75; V Port Eynon w Rhosili and Llanddewi and Knelston 75-83; V Swansea St Barn from 83. *St Barnabas' Vicarage, 57 Sketty Road, Swansea SA2 0EN* Swansea (0792) 298601

JONES, Very Rev David Huw. b 34. Univ of Wales (Ban) BA55 Univ Coll Ox BA58 MA62. St Mich Coll Llan 58. **d** 59 **p** 60. C Aberdare *Llan* 59-61; C Neath w Llantwit 61-65; V Crynant 65-69; V Cwmavon 69-73; Lect Th Univ of Wales (Cardiff) 74-78; Sub-Warden St Mich Coll Llan 74-78; V Prestatyn *St As* 78-82; Dioc Ecum Officer 79-82; V Brecon w Battle *S & B* 82-83; V Brecon St Mary and Battle w Llanddew from 83; Dean Brecon from 82. *Blackstone, 25 Pendre, Brecon, Powys LD3 9EF* Brecon (0874) 624876

JONES, David Ian Stewart. b 34. Selw Coll Cam BA57 MA61. Westcott Ho Cam 57. **d** 59 **p** 60. C Oldham *Man* 59-63; V Elton All SS 63-66; Chapl Eton Coll Windsor 66-70; Sen Chapl 70-74; Hd Master Bryanston Sch Blandford 74-82; P-in-c Bris Ch Ch w St Ewen and All SS *Bris* 82-84; P-in-c Bris St Steph w St Nic and St Leon 82-84; P-in-c City of Bris 84; Soc Resp Adv 84-85; Dir Lambeth Endowed Charities from 85; Hon PV S'wark Cathl *S'wark* from 85. *127 Kennington Road, London SE11 6SF* 071-735 2531 or 735 1925

JONES, David James Hammond. b 45. **d** 70 **p** 70. C Cheadle *Lich* 70-73; Hon C W Bromwich All SS 78-83. *60 Hembs Crescent, Great Barr, Birmingham*

JONES, David John. b 06. St D Coll Lamp 55. **d** 57 **p** 58. V Brawdy w Haycastle and Llandeloy *St D* 59-71; RD Dewisland and Fishguard 68-71; V Llangyndeyrn 71-76; rtd 76. *73 Heol Marlais, Trimsaran, Kidwelly, Dyfed* Trimsaran (0554) 810611

JONES, Canon David John. b 18. St D Coll Lamp BA51. **d** 52 **p** 53. V Blaenpennal and Llangeitho *St D* 60-72; R Llanllwchaiarn 72-79; V Llanfihangel Ystrad w Cribyn and Cilcennin 79-82; Can St D Cathl 82-89; V Llanfihangel Ystrad and Cilcennin w Trefilan etc 82-89; RD Glyn Aeron 85-89; Chan St D Cathl 88-89; rtd 89. *Y Bwthyn, Cribyn, Lampeter, Dyfed SA48 7NF* Lampeter (0570) 470842

JONES, David Jonathan. b 04. St D Coll Lamp BA34. **d** 34 **p** 35. R Nefyn w Pistyll *Ban* 60-73; rtd 73. *Cae'r Onnen, Llangristiolus, Bodorgan, Gwynedd LL62 5PR* Llangefni (0248) 750162

JONES, David Michael. b 48. Chich Th Coll 75. **d** 78 **p** 79. C Yeovil *B & W* 78-84; C Barwick 81-84; V Cleeve w Chelvey and Brockley from 84. *The Vicarage, 106 Main Road, Cleeve, Bristol BS19 4PN* Yatton (0934) 833161

JONES, David Noel. b 29. St Deiniol's Hawarden 69. **d** 71 **p** 72. C Llandegfan w Beaumaris and Llanfaes *Ban* 71-74; TV Amlwch, Rhosybol, Llandyfrydog etc 74-77; R Llanfair Mathafarneithaf w Llanbedrgoch 77-82; V Porthmadog 82-84; V Ynyscyhaiarn w Penmorfa and Portmadoc 84-86; R Llanllyfni from 86; RD Arfon from 89. *The Rectory, 2 Mor Awel, Penygroes, Caernarfon, Gwynedd LL54 6RA* Penygroes (0286) 881124

JONES, David Raymond. b 34. Univ of Wales (Lamp) BA54 St Cath Coll Ox BA57 MA61. Wycliffe Hall Ox 58. **d** 58 **p** 59. C Ex St Dav *Ex* 58-60; C Bideford 60-63; Chapl Grenville Coll Bideford 63-66; Chapl RN 66-89; Chapl to HM The Queen from 84; Warden and Dir Ch Min of Healing Crowhurst from 89. *The Old Rectory, Crowhurst, Battle, E Sussex TN33 9AD* Crowhurst (042483) 204

JONES, David Robert. b 37. MBIM83 Dur Univ BA59 QUB MA83. Cranmer Hall Dur DipTh69. **d** 69 **p** 70. C Middleton *Man* 69-72; CF from 72. *c/o MOD (Army), Bagshot Park, Bagshot, Surrey GU19 5PL* Bagshot (0276) 71717

JONES, David Robert Deverell. b 50. Sarum & Wells Th Coll 72. **d** 75 **p** 78. C Altrincham St Geo *Ches* 75-76; C Clayton *Lich* 77-80; Carriacou 80-81; P-in-c Baschurch *Lich* 81-83; R Baschurch and Weston Lullingfield w Hordley from 83; RD Ellesmere from 85. *The Rectory, Baschurch, Shrewsbury SY4 2EB* Baschurch (0939) 260305

JONES, David Roy. b 47. **d** 80 **p** 81. C New Bury *Man* 80-83. *2 Banker Street, Darcy Lever, Bolton BL3 1RY*

JONES, David Sebastian. b 43. St Cath Coll Cam BA67 MA73. Linc Th Coll 66. **d** 68 **p** 69. C Baguley *Man* 68-71; C Bray and Braywood *Ox* 71-73; V S Ascot from 73; Chapl Heatherwood Hosp E Berks from 81.

The Vicarage, Vicarage Gardens, Ascot, Berks SL5 9DX Ascot (0344) 22388

JONES, David Vernon. b 19. St D Coll Lamp BA48. **d** 49 **p** 50. V Wolverton St Geo *Ox* 62-73; R Wolverton 73-85; rtd 85; Perm to Offic *Llan* from 85. *40 Lime Tree Way, Porthcawl, M Glam CF36 5AU* Porthcawl (0656) 771890

JONES, David Victor. b 37. Dur Univ BA59. Cranmer Hall Dur DipTh60. **d** 62 **p** 63. C Farnworth *Liv* 62-65; CF 65-68; Asst Master Hutton Gr Sch Preston from 68; Lic to Offic *Blackb* from 70. *10 Houghton Close, Penwortham, Preston PR1 9HT* Preston (0772) 745306

JONES, David Vincent. b 99. **d** 28 **p** 29. V Alvaston *Derby* 42-63; rtd 63. *The Anchorage, Looe, Cornwall* Looe (05036) 2716

JONES, Capt Derek John. b 43. CA Tr Coll 64 Sarum & Wells Th Coll 82. **d** 83 **p** 84. CA from 66; C Fleur-de-Lis *Mon* 83-85; V Rhymney from 85. *The Vicarage, Lawn Terrace, Rhymney, Gwent NP2 5LL* Rhymney (0685) 840500

JONES, Miss Diana. b 46. Qu Coll Birm 89. **d** 91. Par Dn Harnham *Sarum* from 91. *87 Netherhampton Road, Salisbury, Wilts SP2 8NA* Salisbury (0722) 23259

JONES, Preb Dick Heath Remi. b 32. Jes Coll Cam BA56. Linc Th Coll 56. **d** 58 **p** 59. C Ipswich St Thos *St E* 58-61; C Putney St Mary *S'wark* 61-65; P-in-c Dawley Parva *Lich* 65-75; P-in-c Lawley 65-75; RD Wrockwardine 70-72; P-in-c Malins Lee 72-75; RD Telford 72-80; P-in-c Stirchley 74-75; TR Cen Telford 75-80; Preb Lich Cathl 76-80; TR Bournemouth St Pet w St Swithun, St Steph etc *Win* from 80; RD Bournemouth from 90. *St Peter's Rectory, 18 Wimborne Road, Bournemouth BH2 6NT* Bournemouth (0202) 554058

JONES, Donald. b 50. BA BSc. St Jo Coll Nottm 79. **d** 82 **p** 83. C Hutton *Chelmsf* 82-86; C E Ham w Upton Park 86-88; TV from 88. *15 Greenwich Crescent, London E6 4TU* 071-476 0618

JONES, Canon Douglas Rawlinson. b 19. St Edm Hall Ox BA41 MA45. Lambeth DD Wycliffe Hall Ox 41. **d** 42 **p** 43. Lect Th Dur Univ 51-64; Prof Div 64-85; Can Res Dur Cathl *Dur* 64-85; rtd 85; Lic to Offic *Edin* from 85. *Whitefriars, King's Road, Longniddry, E Lothian EH32 0NN* Longniddry (0875) 53425

JONES, Edgar John. b 30. Univ of Wales (Lamp) BA53. St Mich Coll Llan 53. **d** 55 **p** 56. C Holyhead w Rhoscolyn w Llanfair-yn-Neubwll *Ban* 55-61; R Bodedern and Llechcynfarwy 61-70; V Bodedern, Llechcynfarwy, Llechylched etc 70-73; Perm to Offic from 73. *5 Glan Llyn, Llanfachraeth, Holyhead, Gwynedd* Holyhead (0407) 742322

JONES, Edgar Joseph Basil. b 14. Univ of Wales LLB37 St Jo Coll Ox BA40 MA43. Ripon Hall Ox 40. **d** 41 **p** 42. V Sandiway *Ches* 61-80; rtd 80; Perm to Offic *Ches* from 80. *Fron, 29 Church Walk, Llandudno, Gwynedd LL30 2HL* Llandudno (0492) 76125

JONES, Edward. b 36. Dur Univ BA60. Ely Th Coll 60. **d** 62 **p** 63. C S Shields St Hilda w St Thos *Dur* 62-65; C Cleadon Park 65-68; V Hebburn St Cuth 68-79; R Winlaton from 79. *The Rectory, Winlaton, Tyne & Wear NE21 6PL* 091-414 3165

JONES, Edward Gareth. b 36. St D Coll Lamp BA59. **d** 61 **p** 62. C Llanbadarn Fawr *St D* 61-66; V Mydroilyn w Dihewyd 66-69; Missr to the Deaf *Mon* 69-70; V Tregaron *St D* 70-75; Chapl to the Deaf (Dios Llan and Mon) 75-83; V Llanilar w Rhostie and Llangwyryfon etc *St D* from 83; RD Llanbadarn Fawr from 90. *The Vicarage, Llanilar, Aberystwyth, Dyfed SY23 4PD* Llanilar (09747) 659

JONES, Edward Graham. b 25. St Deiniol's Hawarden 62. **d** 64 **p** 65. C Bargoed w Brithdir *Llan* 64-70; V Caerau St Cynfelin from 70. *The Vicarage, Cymmer Road, Caerau, Maesteg, Bridgend, M Glam CF34 0YR* Maesteg (0656) 734223

JONES, Edward Harries. b 16. St D Coll Lamp BA38. Ely Th Coll 38. **d** 39 **p** 40. V Ffynnongroew *St As* 52-81; rtd 81. *16 Coed Pella Road, Colwyn Bay, Clwyd* Colwyn Bay (0492) 2997

JONES, Edward Melville Royds. b 99. ACGI20 DIC21 MICE24 Lon Univ BSc20. Coll of Resurr Mirfield 30. **d** 32 **p** 33. C Locks Heath *Portsm* 64-69; rtd 69; Perm to Offic *Portsm* from 82. *Grove House, Grove Road, Fareham, Hants* Fareham (0329) 232323

JONES, Edward Wynne. b 45. Univ of Wales (Abth) LLB71. St Mich Coll Llan 72. **d** 74 **p** 75. C Llandegfan w Beaumaris and Llanfaes *Ban* 74-76; V Aberffraw and Llangwyfan w Llangadwaladr 76-78; Chapl RN from 78. *c/o MOD, Lacon House, Theobald's Road, London WC1X 8RY* 071-430 6847

JONES, Mrs Elaine Joan. b 50. Oak Hill Th Coll. **d** 87. Par Dn Tottenham H Trin *Lon* from 87. *53 Woodside Gardens, London N17 6UN* 081-808 4514

JONES, Elidyr Price. b 26. St D Coll Lamp BA51. **d** 53 **p** 54. Chapl Kelly Coll Tavistock 65-86; rtd 86; Perm to Offic *St D* from 86. *Bronderi, Pontrhydfendigaid, Ystrad Meurig, Dyfed SY25 6EN* Pontrhydfendigaid (09745) 313

JONES, Mrs Elizabeth Mary. b 48. QUB BA69. Nor Ord Course 88. **d** 91. Par Dn Kippax w Allerton Bywater *Ripon* from 91. *32 Ebor Mount, Kippax, Leeds LS25 7PA* Leeds (0532) 861111

JONES, Elizabeth Somerset. b 49. **d** 88. NSM Duns *Edin* from 88; NSM Selkirk from 89. *Ellem Lodge, Duns, Berwickshire TD11 3SG* Duns (0361) 316

JONES, Elwyn. b 09. Univ of Wales BA35. St Mich Coll Llan 35. **d** 36 **p** 37. V Meliden and Gwaenysgor *St As* 72-77; rtd 77. *2 Vicarage Close, Bodelwyddan, Rhyl, Clwyd* St Asaph (0745) 583010

JONES, Emmanuel Thomas. b 19. S Dios Minl Tr Scheme. **d** 81 **p** 82. NSM Fareham H Trin *Portsm* from 81; rtd 89; Perm to Offic *Portsm* from 89. *24 Maylings Farm Road, Fareham, Hants PO16 7QU* Fareham (0329) 281387

JONES, Eric Alexander. b 19. TCD BA40 MA45 BD45. **d** 42 **p** 43. RD N Belf *Conn* 65-70; I Carnmoney 68-76; V Hensall *Sheff* 76-84; RD Snaith and Hatf 79-84; rtd 84. *2 Wilson Crescent, Mount Merrion, Blackrock, Co Dublin, Irish Republic* Dublin (1) 288-0136

JONES, Canon Eric Vernon. b 26. Ely Th Coll 57. **d** 59 **p** 60. C S Shore H Trin *Blackb* 59-63; V Preston St Matt 64-77; R Chorley St Laur from 77; Hon Can Blackb Cathl from 81. *The Rectory, Chorley, Lancs PR7 1QW* Chorley (02572) 63114

JONES, Eric Walter Nathaniel. b 26. Wells Th Coll. **d** 61 **p** 62. C Buckfastleigh w Dean Prior *Ex* 61-64; Warden Trin Youth Cen *Ex* 64-67; PV *Ex* Cathl *Ex* 64-67; Lic to Offic from 67. *Mar-y-Vela, 20A Wallaford Road, Buckfastleigh, Devon TQ11 0AR* Buckfastleigh (0364) 43260

JONES, Canon Eric Wilfred. b 22. Linc Coll Ox BA48 MA53. Cuddesdon Coll 48. **d** 50 **p** 51. Solomon Is 69-74; V Binley *Cov* 74-82; Hon Can Cov Cathl 80-87; RD Cov E 80-82; V Hatton w Haseley and Rowington w Lowsonford 82-87; P-in-c Honiley 85-87; R Hatton w Haseley, Rowington w Lowsonford etc 87; rtd 87; Perm to Offic *Bradf* from 87. *13 Park Avenue, Skipton, N Yorkshire BD23 1PN* Skipton (0756) 793302

JONES, Ernest Edward Stephen. b 39. Lon Univ BD76. St D Coll Lamp DipTh66. **d** 66 **p** 67. C N Meols *Liv* 66-69; C Kirkby 69-71; V Farnworth All SS *Man* 71-75; P-in-c Bempton *York* 75-78; R Rufford *Blackb* 78-84; V Cropredy w Gt Bourton and Wardington *Ox* 84-90; R York St Clem w St Mary Bishophill Senior *York* from 90; P-in-c York All SS N Street from 90. *St Clement's Rectory, 13 Nunthorpe Avenue, York YO2 1PF* York (0904) 624425

JONES, Evan Hopkins. b 38. St Mich Coll Llan 65. **d** 67 **p** 68. C Churston Ferrers w Goodrington *Ex* 67-70; C Tavistock and Gulworthy 70-73; R Ashprington 73-78; V Cornworthy 73-78; R S Hackney St Jo w Ch Ch *Lon* from 78; AD Hackney 84-89. *The Rectory, Church Crescent, London E9 7DH* 081-985 5145

JONES, Evan Trefor. b 32. Univ of Wales (Ban) BA54 HospCC82. Coll of Resurr Mirfield 54. **d** 56 **p** 57. C Ban St Mary *Ban* 56-62; V Llandinorwic 62-71; TV Llanbeblig w Caernarfon and Betws Garmon etc 71-84; Ed Link Dioc Magazine 79-89; R Llanfairfechan w Aber from 84. *The Rectory, Aber Road, Llanfairfechan, Gwynedd LL33 0HN* Llanfairfechan (0248) 680591

JONES, Canon Evan Trevor. b 18. Univ of Wales BA40. St Mich Coll Llan 40. **d** 42 **p** 43. V Nevern, Bayvil, Moelgrove and Monington *St D* 69-77; V Nevern and Bayvil w Eglwyswrw and Meline 77-83; RD Cemais and Sub-Aeron 80-87; V Nevern and Y Beifil w Eglwyswrw and Meline etc 83-87; Can St D Cathl 86-87; rtd 87. *Nyfer, 73 Pontwillem, Brecon, Powys* Brecon (0874) 2353

JONES, Frank Llewellyn. b 12. St Pet Hall Ox BA36 MA42. Wycliffe Hall Ox DipTh37. **d** 37 **p** 38. V Widnes St Paul *Liv* 69-77; rtd 77; Perm to Offic *Nor* from 77. *14 Stigands Gate, East Dereham, Norfolk NR19 2HF* Dereham (0362) 693304

JONES, Canon Fred Leslie. b 12. Univ of Wales (Lamp) BA34. St Mich Coll Llan 34. **d** 35 **p** 36. Can St Woolos Cathl *Mon* 67-79; V Newport St Mark 67-77; rtd 77. *4 Stirling Court, 20 Portarlington Road, Bournemouth BH4 8BY* Bournemouth (0202) 768185

JONES, Frederick. b 33. FRHistS76 Man Univ BA54 Selw Coll Cam PhD72 LSE MSc82. St Steph Ho Ox 56. **d** 58 **p** 59. C Belfield *Man* 58-59; C Westmr St Matt *Lon* 59-60; Hon C Cam St Mary Less *Ely* 71-72; Perm to Offic *Win* 72-74; Lic to Offic 74-89. *Casa Renate, Carrer del Pinsa 86, Port de Pollença, Mallorca, Spain*

JONES, Frederick John. b 32. Wells Th Coll 57. **d** 60 **p** 61. C Tottington *Man* 60-63; C Horwich H Trin 63-65; R Heaton Norris All SS 65-76; R Heaton Norris Ch w All SS 76-77; V Castleton Moor 77-88; C Greenfield from 88. *69 Manchester Road, Greenfield, Oldham OL3 7SE* Saddleworth (0457) 873954

JONES, Frederick Morgan. b 19. Univ of Wales (Lamp) BA40 BD49. St Mich Coll Llan 42. **d** 42 **p** 43. R Llanbedrog and Penrhos *Ban* 61-74; R Llanbedrog w Llannor w Llanfihangel etc 74-84; C Llangefni w Tregaian and Llangristiolus etc 84-85; rtd 85; Perm to Offic *Ban* from 85. *15 Ponc-y-Fron, Llangefni, Gwynedd LL77 7NY* Llangefni (0248) 722850

JONES, Gareth. b 35. St Aid Birkenhead 59. **d** 61 **p** 62. C Doncaster Ch Ch *Sheff* 61-65; Min Can Ripon Cathl *Ripon* 65-68; Chapl RAF 68-85; Hong Kong 85-89; R Spofforth w Kirk Deighton *Ripon* from 89. *The Rectory, Spofforth, Harrogate, N Yorkshire HG3 1AF* Spofforth (093782) 251

JONES, Gareth Lewis. b 42. K Coll Lon BD64 AKC64. **d** 65 **p** 66. C Risca *Mon* 65-70; Perm to Offic *Win* 70-74; Newc 74-75; Sarum 75; C Pontesbury I and II *Heref* 75-77; P-in-c Presteigne w Discoed 77-79; TV Hemel Hempstead *St Alb* 79-86; R Longden and Annscroft w Pulverbatch *Heref* from 86. *The Rectory, Longden, Shrewsbury SY5 8ET* Shrewsbury (0743) 860245

JONES, Chan Gareth Lloyd. b 38. Univ of Wales BA61 Selw Coll Cam BA63 MA67 Yale Univ STM69 TCD BD70 Lon Univ PhD75. Episc Sem Austin Texas Hon DD90 Westcott Ho Cam 62. **d** 65 **p** 66. C Holyhead w Rhoscolyn *Ban* 65-68; USA 68-70; P-in-c Mert *Ox* 70-72; Tutor Ripon Hall Ox 72; Sen Tutor 73-75; Lect Ex Coll Ox 73-77; Tutor and Lib Ripon Coll Cuddesdon 75-77; Lect Th Univ of Wales (Ban) 77-89; Sen Lect from 89; Sub-Dean Faculty of Th 80-89; Dean from 89; Chan Ban Cathl *Ban* from 90; Select Preacher Ox Univ 89. *Nettuno, Mount Street, Menai Bridge, Gwynedd LL59 5BW* Menai Bridge (0248) 712786

JONES, Gareth Thomas. b 14. Open Univ BA75. Clifton Th Coll 32. **d** 37 **p** 38. V Grewelthorpe *Ripon* 56-82; V Mickley 56-82; P-in-c N Stainley 77-82; rtd 82. *15 Bishopton Lane, Ripon, N Yorkshire HG4 2QN* Ripon (0765) 5643

JONES, Glyn Evan. b 44. Lon Coll of Div ALCD67 LTh. **d** 67 **p** 68. C Gt Horton *Bradf* 67-70; SAMS 71-78; Argentina 71-78; V Idle H Trin *Bradf* 78-84; V Hyson Green *S'well* 84-87; V Nottm St Steph 84-87; V Hyson Green St Paul w St Steph 87-89; V Hyson Green 89-91; V Basford w Hyson Green from 91. *The Vicarage, 18 Russell Road, Forest Fields, Nottingham NG7 6HB* Nottingham (0602) 787473

JONES, Preb Glyn Owen. b 16. St D Coll Lamp BA37 St Mich Coll Llan 38. **d** 39 **p** 40. V Hengoed *Lich* 53-75; Preb Lich Cathl 73-81; V Baschurch 75-81; rtd 81; Perm to Offic *Lich* from 81. *6 Larkhill Road, Park Hall, Oswestry, Shropshire SY11 4AW* Oswestry (0691) 662739

JONES, Canon Glyndwr. b 35. St Mich Coll Llan DipTh62. **d** 62 **p** 63. C Clydach *S & B* 62-64; C Llangyfelach 64-67; C Sketty 67-70; V Bryngwyn and Newchurch and Llanbedr etc 70-72; Miss to Seamen from 72; Aux Min Sec from 81; Asst Gen Sec 85-90; Gen Sec from 90; Hon Can Kobe Japan from 88; Chapl to HM The Queen from 90. *5 The Close, Grays, Essex RM16 2XU or, c/o St Michael Paternoster Royal, College Hill, London EC4R 2RL* Grays Thurrock (0375) 5053

JONES, Godfrey Caine. b 36. Dur Univ BA59 Lon Univ CertEd60 Birm Univ MEd71. St Deiniol's Hawarden 76. **d** 78 **p** 79. NSM Ruthin w Llanrhydd *St As* 78-81; C 83-84; Lic to Offic *Derby* 81-83; P-in-c Llanfwrog and Clocaenog and Gyffylliog *St As* 84-85; R from 85. *The Rectory, Mwrog Street, Ruthin, Clwyd LL15 1EL* Ruthin (08242) 4866

JONES, Gordon Howlett. b 26. G&C Coll Cam BA47 MA51. Westcott Ho Cam 49. **d** 51 **p** 52. C Milton *Win* 51-54; Study Sec SCM 54-58; C St Helen Bishopsgate w St Martin Outwich *Lon* 54-58; V Claremont H Angels *Man* 58-63; R Northenden 63-79; P-in-c Hilmarton and Highway *Sarum* 79-83; V Bremhill w Foxham and Hilmarton from 83; RD Calne 84-88. *The Vicarage, Hilmarton, Calne, Wilts SN11 8SB* Hilmarton (024976) 675

JONES, Gordon Michael Campbell. b 33. St D Coll Lamp BA56. St Jo Coll Dur 56. **d** 58 **p** 59. C Newport Maindee St Jo Ev *Mon* 58-60; C Penhow, St Brides Netherwent w Llandavenny etc 60-63; V Magor w Redwick and Undy 63-68; Australia 68-71; R Kirkby Thore w Temple Sowerby *Carl* 72-73; R Kirkby Thore w Temple Sowerby and w Newbiggin 73-79; P-in-c Accrington St Jas *Blackb* 79-81; P-in-c Accrington St Andr 81-83; Kuwait 83-91; R Swardeston w E Carleton, Intwood, Keswick etc *Nor* from 91. *The Vicarage, The Common, Swardeston, Norwich NR14 8DN* Mulbarton (0508) 70550

JONES, Canon Gordon Rowland. b 24. Oak Hill Th Coll 56. **d** 58 **p** 59. R Bath Walcot *B & W* 63-70; Dir Ext Studies St Jo Coll Nottm 70-73; V Orpington Ch Ch *Roch* 73-78; Sec for Chr Educn Tr 78-85; CPAS Evang 78-85; Hon C Southborough St Pet w Ch Ch and St Matt *Roch* 81-85; Hon Can Leic Cathl *Leic* 83-90; Zimbabwe 85-89; C Leic H Trin w St Jo *Leic* 89-90; rtd 91. *58 Queens Road, Tunbridge Wells, Kent TN4 9JU* Tunbridge Wells (0892) 31336

JONES, Graham Frederick. b 37. Leeds Univ BA60 GradIPM63. ALCD66. **d** 66 **p** 67. C Chesterfield H Trin *Derby* 66-70; C Leeds St Geo *Ripon* 70-73; P-in-c Newc St Geo *Lich* 73-83; New Zealand 83-87; P-in-c Westcote w Icomb and Bledington *Glouc* from 89. *The Vicarage, Chapel Street, Bledington, Oxford OX7 6UR* Kingham (0608) 658102

JONES, Griffith Bernard. b 20. Univ of Wales (Lamp) BA42. St Mich Coll Llan 42. **d** 44 **p** 45. Perm to Offic Pet 64-82; St Alb 74-82; R Llanfallteg w Clunderwen and Castell Dwyran etc *St D* 82-88; rtd 88. *17 Heol Ceirios, Llandybie, Ammanford, Dyfed SA18 2SR* Llandybie (0269) 851060

JONES, Griffith Trevor. b 56. BSc MPS Univ of Wales BD. **d** 87 **p** 88. C Llandrygarn w Bodwrog and Heneglwys etc *Ban* 87-89; R Llangefni w Tregaian and Llangristiolus etc from 89. *The Rectory, Llangefni, Gwynedd LL77 7EA* Llangefni (0248) 723104

JONES, Preb Griffith Walter Hywyn. b 24. St Mich Coll Llan 47. **d** 50 **p** 51. V Bettws y Coed and Capel Curig *Ban* 70-78; R Holyhead w Rhoscolyn w Llanfair-yn-Neubwll 78-87; Can and Preb Ban Cathl 78-90; RD Llifon and Talybolion 80-85; Spiritual Dir Cursillo Cymru 81-90; V Ynyscyhaiarn w Penmorfa and Portmadoc *Ban* 87-90; rtd 90. *The Vicarage, Glyn Ceiriog, Llangollen LL20 7EH* Glyn Ceirog (069 172) 245

JONES, Canon Griffith William. b 31. St D Coll Lamp BA53 LTh55. **d** 55 **p** 56. C Llanycil w Bala and Frongoch *St As* 55-58; V Llandrillo 58-66; V Llandrillo and Llandderfel from 66; RD Penllyn from 83; Can Cursal St As Cathl from 87. *The Vicarage, Llandrillo, Corwen, Clwyd LL21 0SW* Llandrillo (049084) 224

JONES, Gwyn Harris. b 19. Univ of Wales (Lamp) BA42. K Coll Lon 42. **d** 43 **p** 44. V Burton St Chad *Lich* 56-79; V Shrewsbury St Geo 79-87; rtd 87; Perm to Offic *Lich* from 87. *18 Kenwood Gardens, Shrewsbury* Shrewsbury (0743) 351057

JONES, Gwynfryn Lloyd. b 35. Univ of Wales (Lamp) BA59. St Mich Coll Llan 59. **d** 61 **p** 62. C Rhyl w Rhyl St Ann *St As* 61-64; C Prestatyn 64-67; V Whitford 67-75; V Llay 75-83; V Northop from 83. *The Vicarage, Northop, Mold, Clwyd CH7 6BS* Northop (035286) 235

JONES, Gwynn Rees. b 32. St D Coll Lamp BA55. **d** 57 **p** 58. C Llangystenyn *St As* 57-59; C Llanrhos 59-64; R Cefn 64-68; R Llanfyllin 68-80; V Bistre 80-89; R Flint from 89. *The Rectory, Allt Goch, Flint, Clwyd CH6 5NF* Flint (03526) 3274

JONES, Gwynne Ifor. b 10. Jes Coll Ox BA36 MA38. **d** 70 **p** 71. Hon C Llangefni w Tregaian and Llangristiolus etc *Ban* 70-81; rtd 81. *Bryn Horton, Greenfield Avenue, Llangefni, Gwynedd LL77 7NU* Llangefni (0248) 723295

JONES, Canon Harold Desmond. b 22. Sarum Th Coll 52. **d** 55 **p** 56. V Thurleigh *St Alb* 64-80; V Milton Ernest 64-80; RD Sharnbrook 70-81; Hon Can St Alb 78-90; P-in-c Knotting w Souldrop 80-82; V Sharnbrook 80-82; R Sharnbrook and Knotting w Souldrop 82-90; P-in-c Felmersham 82-87; RD Sharnbrook 86-90; rtd 90. *24 Towns End Road, Sharnbrook, Bedford MK44 1HY* Bedford (0234) 782524

JONES, Harold Philip. b 49. Leeds Univ BA72 St Jo Coll Dur BA84. Cranmer Hall Dur 82. **d** 85 **p** 86. C Scartho *Linc* 85-88; V Dodworth *Wakef* from 88. *The Vicarage, Green Road, Dodworth, Barnsley, S Yorkshire S75 3RT* Barnsley (0226) 203838

JONES, Harry Gordon. b 18. Bps' Coll Cheshunt 49. **d** 52 **p** 53. V Hurley *Ox* 64-70; V Salcombe *Ex* 70-79; P-in-c Abbotsham 79-83; rtd 83; Perm to Offic *Ex* from 83.

54 Daneshay, Northam, Bideford, Devon EX39 1DG
Bideford (0237) 473277

JONES, Haydn Llewellyn. b 42. Edin Th Coll 63. **d** 65
p 66. C Towcester w Easton Neston *Pet* 65-68; C Northn
St Matt 68-72; CF from 72. *c/o MOD (Army), Bagshot
Park, Bagshot, Surrey GU19 5PL* Bagshot (0276) 71717

JONES, Haydn Price. b 17. MBE60. St D Coll Lamp
BA38 St Mich Coll Llan 39. **d** 40 **p** 41. R Horringer cum
Ickworth *St E* 65-81; rtd 81; Hon C Aberedw w Llandilo
Graban and Llanbadarn etc *S & B* 81-83; Perm to Offic
St E from 83. *20 Boon Close, Bury St Edmunds, Suffolk
IP33 2LG* Bury St Edmunds (0284) 705867

✠**JONES, Rt Rev Haydon Harold.** b 20. **d** 47 **p** 48 **c** 76. C
Heaton St Barn *Bradf* 47-49; C Tormohun *Ex* 49-51; C
Cov St Pet *Cov* 63-64; R Clutton *B & W* 64-75; R
Clutton w Cameley 75-76; Bp Venezuela 76-86; rtd 86.
Apartado 17 467, 1015-A, Caracas, Venezuela

JONES, Howell Arfon. b 31. St Deiniol's Hawarden. **d** 83
p 84. Hon C Northwich St Luke and H Trin *Ches* 83-84;
C Bromborough 84-86; C Nantwich 86-87; V Church
Minshull w Leighton and Minshull Vernon 87-89; rtd
89. *8 Marton Close, Hough, Crewe CW2 5RD* Crewe
(0270) 841389

JONES, Hugh Owen. b 14. Coates Hall Edin 45. **d** 47 **p** 48.
V Bodenham w Hope-under-Dinmore *Heref* 63-78; R
Bodenham w Hope-under-Dinmore, Felton etc 78-80;
rtd 80; Perm to Offic *Heref* from 80. *3 Old School,
Sandpits Road, Ludlow, Shropshire SY8 1HG* Ludlow
(0584) 875213

JONES, Humphrey Ingham. b 20. St Pet Coll Ox
BA42 MA46. Cuddesdon Coll 42. **d** 43 **p** 44. Tutor and
Registrar Richmond Fellowship 68-85; Hon C
Bermondsey St Mary w St Olave, St Jo etc *S'wark* 73-78;
Perm to Offic *Lon* from 79; rtd 85. *28A Granville
Gardens, London W5 3PA* 081-992 2849

JONES, Hywel Tudor. b 13. St D Coll Lamp BA38. **d** 40
p 41. V Dafen *St D* 63-73; R Aber-porth w Tre-main
and Blaen-porth 74-78; rtd 78. *Ardwyn, 27 Williams
Terrace, Burry Port, Dyfed SA16 0PG* Burry Port
(05546) 4321

JONES, Ian Andrew. b 65. Lanc Univ BA87. St Mich Coll
Llan DPS90. **d** 90 **p** 91. C Caerphilly *Llan* from 90.
71 Bartlett Street, Caerphilly, M Glam CF8 1JT
Caerphilly (0222) 882695

JONES, Idris. b 31. **d** 88. NSM Llanfihangel Ysceifog and
Llanffinan etc *Ban* from 88. *Rhoslyn, Gaerwen, Gwynedd
LL60 6HR* Gaerwen (024877) 797

JONES, Canon Idris. b 43. Univ of Wales (Lamp)
BA64 Edin Univ LTh67. NY Th Sem DMin86 Edin Th
Coll 64. **d** 67 **p** 68. C Stafford St Mary *Lich* 67-70; Prec
St Paul's Cathl Dundee *Bre* 70-73; P-in-c Gosforth All
SS *Newc* 73-80; R Montrose *Bre* 80-88; R Inverbervie
80-88; Can St Paul's Cathl Dundee from 84; Chapl Angl
Students Dundee Univ from 88; P-in-c Invergowrie from
88. *27 Errol Road, Invergowrie, Dundee DD2 5AG*
Dundee (0382) 562525

JONES, Canon Idwal. b 13. Univ of Wales BA36. St Mich
Coll Llan 36. **d** 38 **p** 39. V Leamington Priors All SS
Cov 63-79; Hon Can Cov Cathl 72-79; rtd 80; Perm
to Offic *Cov* from 80. *Leam Cottage, Main Street,
Birdingbury, Rugby, Warks CV23 8EL* Marton (0926)
632896

JONES, Ioan Wynne. b 66. **d** 91. C Llanbeblig w Caernarfon
and Betws Garmon etc *Ban* from 91. *21 Caer Berllan,
Caernarfon, Gwynedd* Caernarfon (0286) 77481

JONES, Iorwerth Owen. b 24. St D Coll Lamp BA51. **d** 53
p 55. V Tickhill w Stainton *Sheff* 68-80; R Elworth and
Warmingham *Ches* 80-89; rtd 89. *22 Kings Oak Court,
Wrexham, Clwyd LL13 8QH* Wrexham (0978) 353779

JONES, Jack Kenneth. b 23. DGA MIPM. E Anglian Minl
Tr Course 83. **d** 84 **p** 85. C Fakenham w Alethorpe *Nor*
84-88; C Gt w Lt Snoring w Kettlestone and Pensthorpe
from 84. *The Tunns, Great Snoring, Fakenham, Norfolk
NR21 0HN* Fakenham (0328) 820441

JONES, James Morgan. b 07. TD47. **d** 57 **p** 58. R
Coychurch w Llangan and St Mary Hill *Llan* 67-77; rtd
77; Perm to Offic *Llan* from 77. *4 Woodlands Rise,
Bridgend, M Glam CF31 4SW* Bridgend (0656) 662070

JONES, James Stuart. b 48. Ex Univ BA70 PGCE71.
Wycliffe Hall Ox 81. **d** 82 **p** 83. C Clifton Ch Ch w Em
Bris 82-90; V S Croydon Em *S'wark* from 90. *38 Croham
Manor Road, South Croydon, Surrey CR2 7BE* 081-668
6676

JONES, Jaqueline Dorian. b 58. K Coll Lon BD80 AKC80.
Westcott Ho Cam 84. **dss** 86 **d** 87. Epsom St Martin
Guildf 86-87; C 87-91; Chapl Chelmsf Cathl *Chelmsf* from
91. *7 Rainsford Avenue, Chelmsford, Essex CM1 2PJ*
Chelmsford (0245) 350362

JONES, Jenkin Thomas Vivian. b 12. **d** 38 **p** 39. V Orleton
Heref 51-84; rtd 84; Perm to Offic *Heref* from 85.
*Little Haven, Caswell Terrace, Leominster, Herefordshire
HR6 8BB*

JONES, Jennifer Margaret. b 49. CertEd. Cranmer Hall
Dur 87. **d** 89. C Musselburgh *Edin* from 89; C
Prestonpans from 89. *St Andrew's Church House, High
Street, Prestonpans, East Lothian EH32 9AN*
Prestonpans (0875) 810184

JONES, John Bernard. b 49. Qu Coll Birm 86. **d** 88 **p** 89.
C Mold *St As* 88-91; P-in-c Treuddyn and Nercwys and
Erryrys from 91. *The Vicarage, Treuddyn, Mold, Clwyd
CH7 4LN* Pontybodkin (0352) 770919

JONES, John Daniel. b 14. Univ of Wales (Abth) BSc36.
St Mich Coll Llan 46. **d** 48 **p** 49. R Narbeth and Mounton
w Roboston Wathen *St D* 67-74; R Narberth w Mounton
w Roboston Wathen and Crinow 74-79; rtd 79. *Bracknell,
Pelcomb Cross, Haverfordwest, Dyfed SA62 6AA*
Camrose (0437) 710786

JONES, John Douglas Mathias. b 24. Clare Coll Cam
BA49 MA51. Chich Th Coll 49. **d** 51 **p** 52. V Cross Stone
Wakef 67-76; V Hepworth 76-89; Chapl Storthes Hall
Hosp Wakef 81-89; rtd 89. *59 Luke Lane, Holmfirth,
Huddersfield HD7 2SZ* Holmfirth (0484) 681036

JONES, Canon John Francis Williams. b 26. St D Coll
Lamp 48. **d** 52 **p** 53. C Glanadda *Ban* 52-55; V
Porthmadog 55-57; V Llandrygarn w Bodwrog 57-62;
V Llandrygarn and Bodwrog w Heneglwys 62-74; V
Llandrygarn w Bodwrog and Heneglwys etc from 74;
RD Menai and Malltraeth from 75; Hon Can Ban Cathl
81-83; Can from 83; Preb from 90. *The Vicarage,
Llandrygarn, Llanerchymedd, Gwynedd LL65 3AZ*
Gwalchmai (0407) 720234

JONES, John Harries. b 11. **d** 60 **p** 61. R Llanbedr y Cennin
w Dolgarrog, Trefriw etc *Ban* 67-74; R Llanbeulan w
Llanfaelog and Talyllyn 74-81; rtd 81. *1 Cerrig-y-Gad,
Llanfairpwllgwyngyll, Gwynedd LL61 5QF*
Llanfairpwll (0248) 713756

JONES, John Hellyer. b 20. Birm Univ LDS43. Westcott
Ho Cam 65. **d** 67 **p** 68. C Haddenham *Ely* 67-70; P-in-c
Lolworth 70-79 and 81-85; P-in-c Fen Drayton w
Conington 75-79; R Houghton w Wyton 79; rtd 85;
Perm to Offic *Ely* from 85. *13 High Street, Haddenham,
Ely, Cambs CB6 3XA* Ely (0353) 740530

JONES, John Henry. b 26. Chich Th Coll. **d** 56 **p** 57. V
Thetford St Mary *Nor* 66-70; TV Thetford 70-75; R
Framingham Earl 75-78; R Gt w Lt Poringland and
Howe 75-78; V Bath Twerton-on-Avon *B & W* 78-81;
TR 81-85; R Rode Major 85-90; rtd 91. *25 Duke Street,
Kington, Herefordshire HR5 3BL* Kington (0544)
230895

JONES, John Howard. b 48. New Coll Ox BA69 MA73
K Coll Cam CertEd70. Sarum & Wells Th Coll 76. **d** 77
p 78. C Salisbury St Mark *Sarum* 77-78; C Morriston
S & B 78-80; Dir of Ords 80-83; V Gowerton 80-83; V
Swansea St Jas 85-89; Chapl Alleyn's Foundn Dulwich
from 89. *53 Gilkes Crescent, London SE21 7BP* 081-299
4826

JONES, John Idris. b 16. St D Coll Lamp BA41. **d** 43
p 44. V Llay *St As* 66-75; rtd 75. *14 Acton Park Way,
Wrexham, Clwyd LL12 7LD* Wrexham (0978) 359530

JONES, Ven John Jenkin. b 15. Univ Coll Dur
BA39 DipTh40 MA42. **d** 40 **p** 41. V Holywell *St As*
60-71; RD Holywell 69-71; Can St As Cathl 70-74; V
Llanrhos 71-76; Adn St As 74-84; V Whitford 76-80; rtd
84; Perm to Offic *St As* from 84. *Dorlan, Pentre
Llanrhaeadr, Denbigh, Clwyd LL16 4YN* Llanynys
(074578) 447

JONES, John Morgan. b 17. Univ of Wales BA39. Ely Th
Coll 39. **d** 40 **p** 41. R Adwick-le-Street *Sheff* 60-63; rtd
82; Perm to Offic *St As* from 82. *3 Heol Awel, Abergele,
Clwyd LL22 7UQ* Abergele (0745) 823515

JONES, Canon John Philip. b 09. K Coll Lon 36. **d** 39
p 40. V Newc St Aug *Newc* 48-74; Hon Can Newc Cathl
72-74; rtd 74. *Avondale Rest Home, Osborne Road,
Newcastle upon Tyne NE2 2AH* 091-281 5058

JONES, John Samuel. b 11. Univ of Wales BA36. St D
Coll Lamp 36. **d** 38 **p** 40. V Llanfair D C *St As* 72-79;
rtd 79. *51 Snowden Drive, Ty Gwyn, Wrexham, Clwyd*
Wrexham (0978) 364914

JONES, Ven John Samuel. b 16. Univ of Wales (Lamp)
BA37 BD42. St Mich Coll Llan 38. **d** 39 **p** 40. V Llanllwni
St D 49-86; RD Lampeter and Ultra Aeron 68-82; Can St D
Cathl 72-82; Chan 78-82; Adn Cardigan 82-86; rtd 86.
Bryheulwen, Bryn Road, Lampeter, Dyfed SA48 7EE
Lampeter (0570) 422378

JONES, Canon John Stephen Langton. b 89. Jes Coll Cam
BA13. Wells Th Coll 13. **d** 14 **p** 15. Can Res and Prec

Wells Cathl *B & W* 47-67; rtd 67. *St Peter's Rectory, 18 Wimborne Road, Bournemouth BH2 6NT*

JONES, John Trevor. b 14. St D Coll Lamp BA42. **d** 43 **p** 44. V Poulton *Ches* 60-81; rtd 81; Perm to Offic *Ches* from 82. *21 Sandy Lane, Wallasey, Merseyside L45 3JY* 051-639 4794

JONES (nee HUBBARD), Ms Judith Frances. b 49. St Alb Minl Tr Scheme 79. **dss** 82 **d** 87. Hemel Hempstead *St Alb* 82-86; Longden and Annscroft w Pulverbatch *Heref* 86-87; HonC from 87. *The Rectory, Longden, Shrewsbury SY5 8ET* Shrewsbury (0743) 860245

JONES, Keith Brynmor. b 44. Selw Coll Cam BA65 MA69. Cuddesdon Coll 67. **d** 69 **p** 70. C Limpsfield and Titsey *S'wark* 69-72; Dean's V St Alb Abbey *St Alb* 72-76; P-in-c Boreham Wood St Mich 76-79; TV Borehamwood 79-82; V Ipswich St Mary le Tower w St Lawr and St Steph *St E* 82-84; V Ipswich St Mary-le-Tower from 84. *St Mary le Tower Vicarage, 8 Fonnereau Road, Ipswich IP1 3JP* Ipswich (0473) 252770

JONES, Keith Bythell. b 35. ACP BA DipHE CertEd. Trin Coll Bris. **d** 83 **p** 84. C Bris St Mary Redcliffe w Temple etc *Bris* 83-86; C Filton 86-88; TV Yate New Town from 88. *The Vicarage, Shorthill Road, Westerleigh, Bristol BS17 4QN* Chipping Sodbury (0454) 312152

JONES, Keith Ellison. b 47. Wycliffe Hall Ox 72. **d** 75 **p** 76. C Everton St Chrys *Liv* 75-79; C Buckhurst Hill *Chelmsf* 79-81; TV 81-88; TR Leek and Meerbrook *Lich* from 88. *The Vicarage, 6 Church Street, Leek, Staffs ST13 6AB* Leek (0538) 382515

JONES, Kenneth Elwyn. b 32. Nottm Univ BA54 Sheff Univ CertEd55 DipEd55. Linc Th Coll 80. **d** 82 **p** 83. C Rotherham *Sheff* 82-85; R Harthill and Thorpe Salvin from 85. *The Rectory, 36 Union Street, Harthill, Sheffield S31 8YH* Worksop (0909) 770279

JONES, Kenneth John. b 26. ALCD53. **d** 53 **p** 54. V Creech St Michael *B & W* 65-91; rtd 91; Perm to Offic *B & W* from 91. *9 Thornash Close, Monkton Heathfield, Taunton, Somerset TA2 8PQ* Taunton (0823) 413209

JONES, Canon Kenneth William. b 14. TD61. St D Coll Lamp BA36 St Mich Coll Llan 36. **d** 38 **p** 39. V Hove St Jo *Chich* 66-77; R Buxted St Marg 77-81; P-in-c High Hurstwood 78-81; rtd 82; Perm to Offic *Chich* from 82. *2/13 Grange Gardens, Eastbourne, E Sussex BN20 7DA* Eastbourne (0323) 642553

JONES, Kingsley Charles. b 45. Birm Univ BSc66 Open Univ BA75. Sarum Th Coll 66. **d** 69 **p** 70. C Penwortham St Mary *Blackb* 69-72; C Broughton 72-74; P-in-c Gt Wollaston *Heref* 74-77; Chapl RAF 77-83; V Colwich w Gt Haywood *Lich* from 83. *The Vicarage, Little Haywood, Stafford ST18 0TS* Little Haywood (0889) 881262

JONES, Leonard. b 07. FRGS44. Clifton Th Coll 51. **d** 52 **p** 53. R Knodishall w Buxlow *St E* 63-73; Hon C Gt Crosby St Luke *Liv* 73-74; Hon C Bootle St Mary w St Jo 74-78; Perm to Offic from 78. *7 Stuart Avenue, Hunts Cross, Liverpool L25 0NH* 051-486 0086

JONES, Leslie Joseph. b 23. Linc Th Coll. **d** 57 **p** 58. V Bedminster St Aldhelm *Bris* 69-75; TV Bedminster 75-80; V Abbots Leigh w Leigh Woods 80-88; rtd 88; Perm to Offic *Bris* from 88. *4 Summerleaze, Bristol BS16 4ER* Bristol (0272) 653597

JONES, Leslie Lloyd. b 13. OBE. BA. **d** 39 **p** 41. CF 42-72; Chapl to Gov of Gib 68-72; V Yarcombe w Membury *Ex* 74-83; V Yarcombe w Membury and Upottery 83-84; rtd 84; Perm to Offic *Ex* from 84. *Lower Farway, Chardstock, Axminster, Devon EX13 7DD* Chard (0460) 20397

JONES, Malcolm Francis. b 44. Open Univ BA88. Chich Th Coll 67. **d** 70 **p** 71. C Prestbury *Ches* 70-73; Chapl RAF 73-81; R Heaton Reddish *Man* 81-84; CF from 84; OStJ from 84. *c/o MOD (Army), Bagshot Park, Bagshot, Surrey GU19 5PL* Bagshot (0276) 71717

JONES, Malcolm Stuart. b 41. Sheff Univ BA62. Linc Th Coll 64. **d** 66 **p** 67. C Monkseaton St Mary *Newc* 66-69; C Ponteland 69-72; Venezuela 73-75; C Hexham *Newc* 75-77; P-in-c Killingworth from 77. *The Vicarage, Killingworth, Newcastle upon Tyne NE12 0BL* 091-268 3242

JONES, Maldwyn Lloyd. b 17. St D Coll Lamp BA39. **d** 40 **p** 41. USA 68-70; Chapl Lon Nautical Sch 71-72; Lic to Offic *Ban* 72-82; rtd 82; Perm to Offic *Ban* from 82. *The Old Post Office, Tirley, Gloucester GL19 4ES*

JONES, Ms Margaret. b 28. TCD BA53 Lon Univ BD66. **d** 87. NSM Stanstead Abbots *St Alb* 87-88; NSM Grappenhall *Ches* from 89. *22 Marlborough Crescent, Grappenhall, Warrington WA4 2EE* Warrington (0925) 66866

JONES, Mark Andrew. b 60. Southn Univ BSc82 Sussex Univ PGCE83. Oak Hill Th Coll BA91. **d** 91. C Wolv St Luke *Lich* from 91. *36 Pencombe Drive, Park Hall Estate, Wolverhampton WV4 5EW* Wolverhampton (0902) 337745

JONES, Mark Vincent. b 60. Univ of Wales (Cardiff) DipTh84. St Mich Coll Llan 81. **d** 84 **p** 85. C Whitchurch *Llan* 84-89; V Pwllgwaun w Llanddewi Rhondda 89-90; CF from 90. *c/o MOD (Army), Bagshot Park, Bagshot, Surrey GU19 5PL* Bagshot (0276) 71717

JONES, Mary Nerissa Anna. b 41. Qu Mary Coll Lon BA86. Ripon Coll Cuddesdon 86. **d** 88. Par Dn St Botolph Aldgate w H Trin Minories *Lon* from 88. *32A St Petersburgh Place, London W2 4LD* 071-221 5056

JONES, Mary Valerie. b 37. Univ of Wales (Ban) BD84. St Deiniol's Hawarden 84. **d** 85. C Holyhead w Rhoscolyn w Llanfair-yn-Neubwll *Ban* 85-87; C Ynyscyhaiarn w Penmorfa and Portmadoc 87-90; Dn-in-c Llansantffraid GC and Llanarmon DC and Pontfadog *St As* from 90. *The Vicarage, Glyn Ceiriog, Llangollen, Clwyd LL20 7EH* Glyn Ceiriog (069172) 245

JONES, Maurice Hughes Rowlestone. b 06. **d** 47 **p** 48. Chapl Mt Pleasant Hosp 62-75; V Southall H Trin *Lon* 62-75; rtd 75; Perm to Offic *Glouc* from 75. *75 Medoc Close, Wymans Brook, Cheltenham, Glos GL50 4SP* Cheltenham (0242) 230328

JONES, Maurice Maxwell Hughes. b 32. Lon Univ DipTh58 Univ of Wales (Cardiff) DPS72. Clifton Th Coll 56. **d** 60 **p** 61. C Islington St Andr w St Thos and St Matthias *Lon* 60-63; Argentina 63-71; C Whitchurch *Llan* 72-73; Area Sec (NW England) SAMS 73-77; V Haydock St Mark *Liv* 78-87; V Paddington Em Harrow Road *Lon* from 87. *Emmanuel Vicarage, 28 Windermere Avenue, London NW6 6LN* 081-969 0438

JONES, Melville Kenneth. b 40. Open Univ BA82. St D Coll Lamp DipTh66. **d** 66 **p** 67. C Aberdare *Llan* 66-71; C Caerau w Ely 71-72; Chapl Pontypridd Hosps 72-89; V Graig *Llan* 72-89; P-in-c Cilfynydd 86-89; V Llantwit Fadre from 89; Chapl E Glam Hosp from 89. *Llantwit Fadre Vicarage, Church Village, Pontypridd, M Glam CF38 1EP* Pontypridd (0443) 202538

JONES, Michael. b 49. Leeds Univ BA71 Man Univ MA73. Qu Coll Birm 83. **d** 85 **p** 86. C Leigh St Mary *Man* 85-88; C-in-c Holts CD from 88. *St Hugh's Vicarage, Covert Road, Holts, Oldham OL4 5PH* 061-620 1646

JONES, Michael Denis Dyson. b 39. CCC Cam BA62 MA66 Lon Univ MSc73. Wycliffe Hall Ox DipTh75. **d** 76 **p** 77. C Plymouth St Andr w St Paul and St Geo *Ex* 76-81; V Devonport St Budeaux from 81. *The Vicarage, Agaton Road, Plymouth PL5 2EW* Plymouth (0752) 361019

JONES, Dr Michael Emlyn. b 47. MRCP75 Aber Univ MB, ChB72. **d** 79 **p** 79. Tanzania 79-82; Hon C Duns *Edin* from 83. *Ellem Lodge, Duns, Berwickshire TD11 3SG* Longformacus (03617) 316

JONES, Neil Crawford. b 42. Univ of Wales BA63 K Coll Lon BD66 AKC66. **d** 67 **p** 68. C Holywell *St As* 67-69; C Rhyl w Rhyl St Ann 69-73; C Christchurch *Win* 73-77; V Stanmore 77-84; RD Win 82-84; V Romsey from 84; RD Romsey from 89. *The Vicarage, Romsey, Hants SO51 8EP* Romsey (0794) 513125

JONES, Canon Neville Charles. b 29. Selw Coll Cam BA52 MA57. Linc Th Coll 52. **d** 54 **p** 55. C Grangetown *Dur* 54-58; C Norton St Mary 58-60; V Greenside 60-69; V Stockton H Trin 69-73; TR Cam Stockton 73-76; P-in-c Elton 75-76; R Longnewton 76; R Longnewton w Elton 76-83; RD Stockton 77-83; Hon Can Dur Cathl from 81; Chapl Camerton Hosp Hartlepool 83-85; V Heighington *Dur* 83; Hon C Norton St Mary 85-87; Bp's Dom Chapl 85-87; P-in-c Longnewton w Elton from 87. *The Rectory, 5 The Close, Longnewton, Stockton-on-Tees, Cleveland TS21 1DW* Stockton-on-Tees (0642) 581251

JONES, Neville George. b 36. Univ of Wales (Ban) BA59. St Mich Coll Llan 59. **d** 61 **p** 62. C Broughton *St As* 61-65; C Newc *Llan* 65-68; V Laleston w Tythegston and Merthyr Mawr 68-84; V Llanishen and Lisvane from 84. *The Vicarage, 2 The Rise, Llanishen, Cardiff CF4 5RA* Cardiff (0222) 752545

JONES, Nicholas Newman. b 51. K Coll Lon 71 St Aug Coll Cant 74. **d** 75 **p** 76. C Derringham Bank *York* 75-78; C Stokesley 78-81; P-in-c Kirby Misperton 81-85; R Normanby w Edston and Salton 83-85; R Kirby Misperton w Normanby, Edston and Salton 85-87; V Eskdaleside w Ugglebarnby and Sneaton from 87. *The Vicarage, 22 Eskdaleside, Sleights, Whitby, N Yorkshire YO22 5EP* Whitby (0947) 810349

JONES, Nicholas Peter. b 55. St Mich Coll Llan DipTh82. **d** 82 **p** 83. C St Andrew's Major and Michaelston-le-Pit *Llan* 82-84; C Aberdare 84-88; Youth Chapl 85-89; V

Abercynon from 88. *The Vicarage, Abercynon, Mountain Ash, M Glam CF45 3NE* Abercynon (0443) 740207

✠**JONES, Rt Rev Noel Debroy.** b 32. CB86. Univ of Wales (Lamp) BA53. Wells Th Coll 53. **d** 55 **p** 56 **c** 89. C Tredegar St Jas *Mon* 55-57; C Newport St Mark 57-60; Nigeria 60-62; Chapl RN 62-84; Chapl of the Fleet and Adn for the RN 84-89; QHC from 83; Hon Can Gib Cathl *Eur* from 86; Bp S & M from 89. *The Bishop's House, Quarterbridge Road, Douglas, Isle of Man* Douglas (0624) 622108

JONES, Norman. b 35. St Deiniol's Hawarden 83. **d** 85 **p** 86. C Brecon St Mary and Battle w Llanddew *S & B* 85-91; Min Can Brecon Cathl from 85; V Brynmawr from 91. *The Vicarage, Dumfries Place, Brynmawr, Gwent* Brynmawr (0495) 312297

JONES, Norman. b 50. BA83. Oak Hill Th Coll 83. **d** 83 **p** 84. C Ulverston St Mary w H Trin *Carl* 83-88; Hong Kong from 88. *Christ Church Vicarage, 2 Derby Road, Kowloon Tong, Hong Kong* Hong Kong (852) 338-4433

JONES, Ven Owain William. b 21. Univ of Wales (Lamp) BA46 Selw Coll Cam BA48 MA53. St Mich Coll Llan 48. **d** 49 **p** 50. V Builth and Llanddewi'r Cwm *S & B* 62-79; Can Brecon Cathl from 69; RD Builth Elwell 71-78; Prec Brecon Cathl 75-76; Treas Brecon Cathl 76-83; Adn Brecon 78-87; V Newbridge-on-Wye and Llanfihangel Brynpabuan 79-83; Adn Gower 87-89; rtd 90. *10 Golden Close, West Cross, Swansea SA3 5PE* Swansea (0792) 405648

JONES, Patrick Geoffrey Dickson. b 28. Ch Ch Ox MA55. St Deiniol's Hawarden 79. **d** 82 **p** 83. C Sandbach *Ches* 82-84; P-in-c Braemar *Ab* from 84; R Aboyne from 84; R Ballater from 84. *The Rectory, 7 Invercauld Road, Ballater, Aberdeenshire AB3 5RP* Ballater (03397) 55726

JONES, Patrick George. b 42. Lich Th Coll 69. **d** 72 **p** 73. C Chesterton St Geo *Ely* 72-75; P-in-c Waterbeach 75-78; P-in-c Landbeach 76-78; R Charlton-in-Dover *Cant* 78-90; Cautley Trust from 90. *38 Kearsney Avenue, Kearsney, Dover CT16 3BU* Dover (0304) 824987

JONES, Paul Harwood. b 20. Qu Coll Birm 51. **d** 53 **p** 54. V White Notley w Faulkbourne *Chelmsf* 68-81; P-in-c Cressing 75-80; V Finchingfield and Cornish Hall End 81-88; RD Braintree 83-87; rtd 88; Perm to Offic *Chelmsf* from 88. *83 Kenworthy Road, Braintree, Essex CM7 7JJ* Braintree (0376) 43047

JONES, Paul Terence. b 35. Dur Univ BA60. Qu Coll Birm 60. **d** 62 **p** 63. C Rainford *Liv* 62-65; C Skelmersdale St Paul 65-68; V Huyton Quarry 68-78; V Widnes St Ambrose from 78. *St Ambrose Vicarage, Hargreaves Court, Widnes, Cheshire WA8 0QA* 051-420 8044

JONES, Ms Penelope Howson. b 58. LGSM78 Girton Coll Cam BA80 MA84. Ripon Coll Cuddesdon BA85. dss 86 **d** 87. Hackney *Lon* 86-87; Par Dn 87-88; C Cuddesdon *Ox* 88-90. *3 Wordsworth Street, Gateshead, Tyne & Wear NE8 3HE* 091-478 2730

JONES, Peter Anthony Watson. b 53. AKC75. Sarum & Wells Th Coll 76. **d** 77 **p** 78. C Hessle *York* 77-81; C Stainton-in-Cleveland 81-82; P-in-c Weston Mill *Ex* 82-84; Chapl Plymouth Poly 82-90; V Gt Ayton w Easby and Newton in Cleveland *York* from 90. *The Vicarage, Great Ayton, Middlesbrough, Cleveland TS9 6NN* Great Ayton (0642) 722333

JONES, Peter Gordon Lewis. b 31. **d** 82 **p** 83. NSM Llangynwyd w Maesteg *Llan* 82-84; Deputation Appeals Org (S & M Glam) CECS 84-87; Area Appeals Manager (Wales and Glouc) from 87; NSM Pyle w Kenfig *Llan* from 89. *18 Fulmar Road, Porthcawl, M Glam CF36 3UL* Porthcawl (0656) 715455

JONES, Peter Robin. b 42. BA CertEd. E Midl Min Tr Course 79. **d** 82 **p** 83. NSM Doveridge *Derby* from 82. *4 Cross Road, Uttoxeter, Staffs ST14 7BN* Uttoxeter (0889) 565123

JONES, Peter Russell. b 48. St Jo Coll Cam BA71 MA75 Univ of Wales MTh86. Wycliffe Hall Ox DipTh72. **d** 75 **p** 76. C Northn All SS w St Kath *Pet* 75-79; C Ban Cathl Par *Ban* 79-81; Min Can Ban Cathl 79-81; R Pentraeth and Llanddyfnan 81-85; V Conwy w Gyffin from 85; Lect Univ of Wales (Ban) from 89. *The Vicarage, Conwy, Gwynedd LL32 8LD* Aberconwy (0492) 593402

JONES, Canon Philip Bryan. b 34. Llan St Mich DipTh61. **d** 61 **p** 62. C Hope *St As* 61-64; C Llanrhos 64-67; V Kerry 67-74; R Newtown w Llanllwchaiarn w Aberhafesp from 74; RD Cedewain from 76; Sec Ch in Wales Prov Evang Cttee 80-83; Hon Can St As Cathl *St As* from 86. *The Rectory, Old Kerry Road, Newtown, Powys SY16 1BP* Newtown (0686) 625795

JONES, Philip Thomas Henry. b 34. Qu Coll Birm 58. **d** 60 **p** 61. C Castle Bromwich SS Mary and Marg *Birm*

60-67; C Reading St Mary V *Ox* 67-72; C-in-c Reading All SS CD 72-75; V Reading All SS from 75. *All Saints' Vicarage, 14 Downshire Square, Reading RG1 6NH* Reading (0734) 52000

JONES, Phillip Edmund. b 56. Man Poly BA78 Fitzw Coll Cam BA84 MA88. Westcott Ho Cam 82. **d** 85 **p** 86. C Stafford St Jo and Tixall w Ingestre *Lich* 85-89; TV Redditch, The Ridge *Worc* from 89; Ind Chapl from 89. *The Vicarage, St George's Road, Redditch, Worcs B98 8EE* Redditch (0527) 63017

JONES, Raymond. b 34. RGN RMN. Chich Th Coll 64. **d** 67 **p** 68. C Ocker Hill *Lich* 67-70; C Truro St Paul *Truro* 70-71; Chapl Selly Oak Hosp Birm 71-76; Bahamas 76-77; Turks and Caicos Is 78-79; Chapl Hospice of Our Lady and St Jo Willen 80-83; St Jas Hosp Balham & Bolingbroke Hosp Lon 83-87; NSM Leamington Priors All SS *Cov* from 87; NSM Lillington from 87. *43 Wathen Road, Leamington Spa, Warks CV32 5UY* Leamington Spa (0926) 427689

JONES, Raymond Blake. b 29. K Coll Lon BD54 AKC54. **d** 55 **p** 56. C Fenny Stratford *Ox* 55-58; C Lt Brickhill 55-58; C Wooburn 58-60; C Southbourne St Kath *Win* 60-66; R Braiseworth *St E* 66-76; V Eye 66-76; P-in-c Yaxley 74-77; RD Hartismere 76-77; V Eye w Braiseworth and Yaxley 77; R Ufford 77-82; V Southbourne St Kath *Win* from 82. *St Katharine's Vicarage, 3 Wollaston Road, Bournemouth BH6 4AR* Bournemouth (0202) 423986

JONES, Raymond Powell. b 21. JP63. St D Dioc Tr Course. **d** 82 **p** 83. NSM Bettws St Dav *St D* from 82. *227 Pen-y-Banc Road, Ammanford, Dyfed SA18 3QP* Ammanford (0269) 592069

JONES, Raymond Sydney. b 35. MSERT71. Glouc Th Course 85. **d** 87 **p** 88. NSM Madley *Heref* 87-89; NSM Preston-on-Wye w Blakemere 87-89; NSM Madley w Tyberton, Preston-on-Wye and Blakemere from 89. *Birch Hill, Clehonger, Hereford HR2 9SY* Golden Valley (0981) 250452

JONES, Raymond Trevor. b 35. Linc Th Coll. **d** 82 **p** 83. C Rushmere *St E* 82-85; Bp's Dom Chapl 85-86; CF from 86. *c/o MOD (Army), Bagshot Park, Bagshot, Surrey GU19 5PL* Bagshot (0276) 71717

JONES, Richard. b 23. St Deiniol's Hawarden 74. **d** 76 **p** 77. NSM Welshpool w Castle Caereinion *St As* from 76. *Sherwood, Rhos Common, Llandrinio, Llanymynech, Powys SY22 6RN* Llanymynech (0691) 830534

JONES, Canon Richard. b 28. St D Coll Lamp 54. **d** 56 **p** 57. C Llanaber w Caerdeon *Ban* 56-61; R Aberffraw w Llangwyfan 61-74; CF (TA) 61-71; V Llanfairisgaer *Ban* 74-79; Bp's Private Chapl 78-82; V Llanfair-is-gaer and Llanddeiniolen 79-89; RD Arfon 82-89; Can Ban Cathl from 86; V Llandegfan w Llandysilio from 89. *The Vicarage, Mount Street, Menai Bridge, Gwynedd LL57 5BW* Menai Bridge (0248) 712385

JONES, Richard. b 36. Ely Th Coll 61. **d** 64 **p** 65. C Blyth St Mary *Newc* 64-67; C Wallsend St Pet 67-69; R Paisley H Trin *Glas* 69-78; R Monifieth *Bre* from 78. *The Rectory, 29 Princes Street, Monifieth, Angus DD5 4AW* Monifieth (0382) 532266

JONES, Richard. b 42. Lon Univ BSc64. Westcott Ho Cam 65. **d** 68 **p** 69. C S Ashford Ch Ch *Cant* 68-74; V Tokyngton St Mich *Lon* 74-82; R Acton St Mary from 82; AD Ealing E 87-90; AD Ealing from 90. *The Rectory, 14 Cumberland Park, London W3 6SX* 081-992 8876

JONES, Richard Eifion. b 23. St D Dioc Tr Course 80 Llan St Mich 84. **d** 82 **p** 83. NSM Llangennech and Hendy *St D* 82-84; C Llanbadarn Fawr w Capel Bangor 84-86; V Llangadog and Gwynfe w Llandeusant from 86. *The Vicarage, Llangadog, Dyfed SA19 9AE* Llangadog (0550) 777061

JONES, Richard Keith. b 40. Jes Coll Ox BA63. Wycliffe Hall Ox 61. **d** 63 **p** 64. C Blaenavon w Capel Newydd *Mon* 63-67; C Mynyddislwyn 67-71; C Pontypool 71; V Abercarn 71-81; V Penhow, St Brides Netherwent w Llandavenny etc 81-88. *3 Llanover Road Close, Blaenavon, Gwent* Penhow (0633) 400901

JONES, Richard Martin Hugh. b 31. St D Coll Lamp 56. **d** 58 **p** 59. C Swansea St Pet *S & B* 58-63; R Llangynllo and Bleddfa 63-70; R Llandefalle w Llyswen, Boughrood etc 70-83; RD Hay 81-85 and 87-90; V Llandefalle and Llyswen w Boughrood etc from 83. *The Rectory, Church Lane, Llyswen, Brecon, Powys LD3 0UU* Llyswen (0874) 754255

JONES, Robert. b 26. Lon Univ BA52 K Coll Lon BD65 Hull Univ MA82. St Deiniol's Hawarden 79. **d** 80 **p** 81. NSM Doncaster St Mary *Sheff* 80-81; C Halifax St Jo Bapt *Wakef* 81-82; C Halifax 83; P-in-c Dewsbury St Mark 83-84; TV Dewsbury from 84. *Barford Lodge,*

58 Oxford Road, Dewsbury, W Yorkshire WF13 4EH
Dewsbury (0924) 453727

JONES, Robert. b 40. **d** 80 **p** 81. C St Laurence in Thanet *Cant* 80-83. *76 Southwood Gardens, Ramsgate, Kent*

JONES, Robert. b 45. Culham Coll Ox CertEd67. St Steph Ho Ox. **d** 85 **p** 86. C High Wycombe *Ox* 85-89; V Beckenham St Barn *Roch* 89-90; C Swanley St Mary 90-91; C Edenbridge from 91. *The Vicarage, Crockham Hill, Edenbridge, Kent TN8 6RL* Edenbridge (0732) 866515

JONES, Robert Bernard. b 24. St Jo Coll Dur BA48. Wycliffe Hall Ox. **d** 50 **p** 51. V Ringwood *Win* 61-75; R N Stoneham 75-89; rtd 89. *4 Rowden Close, West Wellow, Romsey, Hants SO51 6RF* Romsey (0794) 22966

JONES, Robert Cecil. b 32. Univ of Wales (Abth) BA54 DipEd55. Qu Coll Birm 84. **d** 86 **p** 87. C Llanbadarn Fawr w Capel Bangor *St D* 86-88; R Llanllwchaearn and Llanina from 88. *The Rectory, New Quay, Dyfed SA45 9RE* New Quay (0545) 560958

JONES, Canon Robert Dwyfor. b 20. Univ of Wales (Ban) BA41. St Mich Coll Llan 46. **d** 47 **p** 48. V Conwy w Gyffin *Ban* 69-85; Can and Treas Ban Cathl 76-85; rtd 85; Perm to Offic St As & Ban from 85. *Ormlea, 12 Hywel Place, Llandudno, Gwynedd LL30 1EF* Llandudno (0492) 74390

JONES, Robert George. b 55. Hatf Coll Dur BA77 Ox Univ BA79 MA87. Ripon Coll Cuddesdon 77. **d** 80 **p** 81. C Foley Park *Worc* 80-84; V Dudley St Fran from 84. *The Vicarage, 50 Laurel Road, Dudley, W Midlands DY1 3EZ* Dudley (0384) 253123

JONES, Robert Ivan. b 33. CertEd CertRK. Westcott Ho Cam 85. **d** 85 **p** 86. NSM Wymondham *Nor* 85-86; C Epsom St Martin *Guildf* 87-89; V Hutton Cranswick w Skerne, Watton and Beswick *York* from 89. *The Vicarage, Hutton Cranswick, Driffield, N Humberside YO25 9QA* Driffield (0377) 70402

JONES, Robert William. b 55. **d** 79 **p** 80. C Seapatrick *D & D* 79; C Ban Abbey 81-83; I Drumgath w Drumgooland and Clonduff 83-89; I Finaghy *Conn* from 89. *Finaghy Rectory, 104 Upper Lisburn Road, Finaghy, Belfast BT10 0BB* Belfast (0232) 629764

JONES, Robert William Aplin. b 32. FRSC71 CChem72 Univ of Wales (Cardiff) BSc52 MSc65. St Deiniol's Hawarden 72. **d** 73 **p** 74. C Bassaleg *Mon* 73-77; V Nantyglo 77-82; Perm to Offic 82-86; R Colwinston w Llandow and Llysworney *Llan* from 86. *The Rectory, Llandow, Cowbridge, S Glam CF7 7NT* Wick (065679) 205

JONES, Canon Robin Lang Wilson. b 07. Worc Coll Ox BA28 MA33. St Mich Coll Llan 41. **d** 41 **p** 42. R Warcop w Musgrave *Carl* 59-72; Hon Can Carl Cathl 64-72; rtd 72; Perm to Offic *Carl* from 77. *10 Brunswick Square, Penrith, Cumbria CA11 7LW* Penrith (0768) 67781

JONES, Roderick. b 48. Leeds Univ BA(Theol)70. Oak Hill Th Coll 74. **d** 76 **p** 77. C Beckenham Ch Ch *Roch* 76-80; C Uphill *B & W* 80-84; R Springfield All SS *Chelmsf* 84-90; Selection Sec ABM from 91. *76 Thorkhill Road, Thames Ditton, Surrey KT7 0UQ* 081-398 1906

JONES, Roger. b 49. St Mich Coll Llan 84. **d** 86 **p** 87. C Llangynwyd w Maesteg *Llan* 86-90; V Wiston w Walton E and Clarbeston *St D* from 90. *The Vicarage, Wiston, Haverfordwest, Dyfed SA62 4PL* Clarbeston (0437) 731266

JONES, Canon Ronald Albert. b 15. Em Coll Cam BA37 MA41. Qu Coll Birm 37. **d** 39 **p** 40. R Loughb All SS *Leic* 57-76; Hon Can Leic Cathl 63-76; P-in-c Stonesfield *Ox* 76-82; RD Woodstock 80-82; rtd 82; Perm to Offic *Ox* from 82. *11 Gwendroc Close, Truro, Cornwall TR1 2BX* Truro (0872) 73064

JONES, Ronald Elvet Lewis. b 14. Bris Univ BA38. Lich Th Coll 38. **d** 40 **p** 41. V Newbridge *Mon* 64-73; R Penhow, Netherwent w Llandavenny, Llanvaches etc 73-80; rtd 80; Lic to Offic *Mon* from 80. *1 The Retreat, King's Fee, Monmouth, Gwent NP5 3DU* Monmouth (0600) 6263

JONES, Ronald Thomas. b 19. Aristotelian Soc 64 Univ of Wales BA41. Westcott Ho Cam 41. **d** 43 **p** 44. Sen Lect Keswick Hall 60-64; Prin Lect & Hd RE 64-80; Lic to Offic *Nor* 60-84; rtd 84. *Bissom Bungalow, Penryn, Cornwall TR10 9LQ* Falmouth (0326) 72205

JONES, Rupert Sugg. b 35. Selw Coll Cam BA59 MA63. Wells Th Coll 59. **d** 61 **p** 62. C Hamer *Man* 61-64; V 64-77; Hon C 82-84; Chapl HM Det Cen Buckley Hall 64-78; Lic to Offic 77-82; Chapl Rochdale Police from 78; Hon C Smallbridge 84-90; P-in-c from 90. *Watch Hall Cottage, Millgate, Rochdale, Lancs OL16 2NU* Rochdale (0706) 54912

JONES, Russell Frederick. b 55. Edin Univ BD84. Edin Th Coll 81. **d** 84 **p** 85. C Croxteth *Liv* 84-87; V Edge

Hill St Dunstan from 87. *St Dunstan's Vicarage, Earle Road, Liverpool L7 6HD* 051-733 4385

JONES, Samuel. b 44. CITC. **d** 86 **p** 87. C Agherton *Conn* 86-88; I Conn w Antrim St Patr from 88. *St Saviour's Rectory, Connor, Kells, Co Antrim BT42 3JU* Ballymena (0266) 891254

JONES, Mrs Sharon Ann. b 60. Liv Univ BA82. Cranmer Hall Dur 83. **dss** 85 **d** 87. Rubery *Birm* 85-87; Par Dn 87-89; C-in-c Chelmsley Wood St Aug CD from 89. *1 Anglesey Avenue, Chelmsley Wood, Birmingham B36 0ND* 021-788 2720

JONES, Sian Eira. b 63. Univ of Wales (Lamp) BA84 Southn Univ BTh88. Sarum & Wells Th Coll 85. **d** 88. C Llanllwch w Llangain and Llangynog *St D* from 88. *4 Towy Close, Johnstown, Carmarthen, Dyfed SA31 3PB* Carmarthen (0267) 231645

JONES, Simon. b 63. Trin Coll Bris BA89. **d** 89 **p** 90. C Hildenborough *Roch* from 89. *12 Fellowes Way, Hildenborough, Tonbridge, Kent TN11 9DG* Tonbridge (0732) 832638

JONES, Stephen Frederick. b 43. Wells Th Coll 68. **d** 71 **p** 72. C-in-c Stockton St Jas CD *Dur* 71-74; Chapl Asst St Ebba's Hosp Epsom 74-79; Chapl Warley Hosp Brentwood 79-87; R Leigh St Clem *Chelmsf* from 87. *St Clement's Rectory, 80 Leigh Hill, Leigh-on-Sea, Essex SS9 1AR* Southend-on-Sea (0702) 75305

JONES, Stephen Frederick. b 53. Magd Coll Ox BA75 MA79 Lon Univ BD89. Linc Th Coll 81. **d** 84 **p** 85. C Kingswinford St Mary *Lich* 84-86; Succ and Dean's V St Geo Chpl from 87; Min Can Windsor from 87. *14 Horseshoe Cloister, Windsor Castle, Berks SL4 1NJ* Windsor (0753) 851726

JONES, Stephen Leslie. b 59. Hull Univ BA80. Sarum & Wells Th Coll 82. **d** 85 **p** 86. C Perry Barr *Birm* 85-88; C Blackpool St Steph *Blackb* 88-90; P-in-c Greenlands 90; V from 90. *St Anne's House, Salmesbury Avenue, Blackpool FY2 0PR* Blackpool (0253) 53900

JONES, Stephen Richard. b 49. Oak Hill Th Coll 72. **d** 75 **p** 76. C Welling *Roch* 75-79; C Cheltenham St Mark *Glouc* 79-82; V Shiregreen St Jas and St Chris *Sheff* 82-86; P-in-c Harold Hill St Geo *Chelmsf* 86-88; V from 88. *St George's Vicarage, Chippenham Road, Romford RM3 8HX* Ingrebourne (04023) 43415

JONES, Stephen William. b 46. K Coll Lon BD70 AKC70. **d** 71 **p** 72. C Streatham St Pet *S'wark* 71-76; C Leeds St Pet *Ripon* 76-79; C Leeds Richmond Hill 79-85; R Gourock *Glas* 85-88; V Porthleven w Sithney *Truro* from 88; Miss to Seamen from 88. *The Vicarage, Breageside, Porthleven, Helston, Cornwall TR13 9JS* Helston (0326) 562419

JONES, Stewart William. b 57. Heriot-Watt Univ BA79 Bris Univ DSA81. Trin Coll Bris DipHE87 BA88. **d** 88 **p** 89. C Stoke Bishop *Bris* from 88. *7 Little Stoke Road, Bristol BS9 1HQ* Bristol (0272) 682077

JONES, Sydney Clarence. b 24. St Cath Soc Ox BA42 MA46 CertEd. Linc Th Coll 43. **d** 44 **p** 45. Lic to Offic *Bradf* 69-71; V Sharow *Ripon* 71-74; Chapl Dame Allan's Schs Newc 74-79; P-in-c Chollerton w Thockrington *Newc* 79-80; V Scholes *Wakef* 80-86; rtd 86. *102 Priest Lane, Ripon, N Yorkshire HG4 1LT* Ripon (0765) 3204

JONES, Tegid Owen. b 27. Univ of Wales (Abth) LLB47. St Deiniol's Hawarden. **d** 68 **p** 69. C Rhosddu *St As* 68-71; V Wrexham 71-75; R Marchwiel 75-83; R Marchwiel and Isycoed from 83; RD Ban Isycoed from 86. *The Rectory, Marchwiel, Wrexham, Clwyd LL13 0TE* Bangor-on-Dee (0978) 780319

JONES, Thomas Elias. b 08. St D Coll Lamp BA32. **d** 32 **p** 33. CF 56-63; V Tysoe w Compton Winyates *Cov* 45-56; rtd 68. *Penrhos Residential Home, Llantwit Fardre, Pontypridd, M Glam CF38 2HA* Pontypridd (0443) 206329

JONES, Canon Thomas Glover. b 09. ALCD34. **d** 33 **p** 34. V Ruskin Park St Sav and St Matt *S'wark* 56-80; Hon Can S'wark Cathl 80; rtd 80; Lic to Offic *Cant* 80-86; S'wark from 86. *155 Shirley Church Road, Croydon CR0 5AJ* 081-777 3572

JONES, Thomas Graham. b 33. St D Coll Lamp BA57. **d** 59 **p** 60. C Llanelly *St D* 59-64; V Ysbyty Cynfyn 64-69; V Ysbyty Cynfyn w Llantrisant 69-72; V Llanelly Ch Ch from 72; RD Cydweli from 89. *Christ Church Vicarage, New Dock Road, Llanelli, Dyfed SA15 2HE* Llanelli (0554) 774264

JONES, Ven Thomas Hughie. b 27. FRSA Univ of Wales BA49 Lon Univ BD53 Leic Univ MA72. St Deiniol's Hawarden. **d** 66 **p** 67. Hon C Evington *Leic* 66-76; Hon C Kirby Muxloe 76-81; Dioc Adult Educn Officer 81-85; R Church Langton w Thorpe Langton and Tur Langto 81-85; Hon Can Leic Cathl 83-86; R Church Langton w

Tur Langton, Thorpe Langton etc 85-86; Adn Loughb from 86. *The Archdeaconry, 21 Church Road, Glenfield, Leicester LE3 8DP* Leicester (0533) 311632

JONES, Thomas Jenkin. b 19. St Mich Coll Llan 46. **d** 49 **p** 50. C Canton St Luke *Llan* 49-51; C Gellygaer 51-52; CF 52-68; V Stokenham w Sherford *Ex* from 68. *The Vicarage, Stokenham, Kingsbridge, Devon TQ7 2ST* Kingsbridge (0548) 580385

JONES, Thomas John Rhidian. b 54. Univ of Wales (Abth) LLB75 BA81. Wycliffe Hall Ox 81. **d** 83 **p** 84. C St D Cathl *St D* 83-86; Min Can St D Cathl 83-86; V Llanpumsaint w Llanllawddog from 86. *The Vicarage, Llanpumsaint, Carmarthen, Dyfed SA33 6BZ* Llanpumsaint (0267) 253205

JONES, Thomas Lloyd. b 20. Univ Coll Ox BA41 MA44. Coll of Resurr Mirfield 42. **d** 44 **p** 45. V Bishop's Stortford H Trin *St Alb* 63-70; V Welwyn Garden City 70-85; rtd 85. *12 Green Dell, Welwyn Garden City, Herts AL7 4EB* Welwyn Garden (0707) 338305

JONES, Thomas Madoc. b 06. St D Coll Lamp BA27. **d** 29 **p** 30. V Kempley w Oxenhall *Glouc* 66-71; rtd 71. *16 Pontwilliam, Brecon, Powys*

JONES, Thomas Percy Norman Devonshire. b 34. St Jo Coll Ox BA58 MA61. Cuddesdon Coll 58. **d** 60 **p** 61. C Portsea St Cuth *Portsm* 60-61; C Portsea N End St Mark 61-67; Asst Chapl Portsm Tech Coll 67-70; Chapl Portsm Poly *Portsm* 70-73; USA 73-74; V Folkestone St Sav *Cant* 75-81; V Regents Park St Mark *Lon* from 81. *4 Regent's Park Road, London NW1 7TX* 071-485 3077 or 586 1694

JONES, Canon Thomas Peter. b 20. Ex Coll Ox BA43 MA46. St Mich Coll Llan 43. **d** 45 **p** 46. R Erbistock and Overton *St As* 57-83; Can St As Cathl 78-84; RD Ban Isycoed 80-86; R Overton and Erbistock and Penley 83-86; Preb and Prec St As Cathl 84-86; rtd 86; Perm to Offic *Cov* from 86. *49 Oakleigh Road, Stratford-upon-Avon, Warks CV37 0DP* Stratford-upon-Avon (0789) 269340

JONES, Canon Thomas William Warren. b 25. CITC 49. **d** 49 **p** 50. I Belf Ardoyne *Conn* 63-70; I Ballymacash 70-88; Can Belf Cathl 85-88; rtd 88. *21 Manor Drive, Lisburn, Co Antrim BT28 1JH* Lisburn (0846) 662361

JONES, Timothy Richard Nigel. b 54. Collingwood Coll Dur BSc75 Birm Univ MSc76. Trin Coll Bris DipHE86. **d** 86 **p** 87. C Hailsham *Chich* from 86. *15 Howlett Drive, Hailsham, E Sussex BN27 1QW* Hailsham (0323) 846680

JONES, Trevor Blandon. b 43. Oak Hill Th Coll 77. **d** 80 **p** 81. Hon C Homerton St Barn w St Paul *Lon* 80-83; Hon C Harlow New Town w Lt Parndon *Chelmsf* 83-90; C from 90. *81 Ram Gorse, Harlow, Essex CM20 1PZ* Harlow (0279) 427978

JONES, Trevor Charles. b 50. Oak Hill Th Coll DipHE91. **d** 91. C Goodmayes All SS *Chelmsf* from 91. *6 Abbotsford Road, Ilford, Essex IG3 9SL* 081-599 3223

JONES, Trevor Edwin. b 49. Ripon Coll Cuddesdon 74. **d** 76 **p** 77. C Cannock *Lich* 76-79; C Middlesb Ascension *York* 79-81; V Oldham St Steph and All Martyrs *Man* 81-84; V Perry Beeches *Birm* 84-90; P-in-c Saltley from 90; P-in-c Shaw Hill from 90. *The Clergy House, St Saviour's Road, Saltley, Birmingham B8 1HW* 021-327 0570

JONES, Trevor Pryce. b 48. Southn Univ BEd76 BTh79. Sarum & Wells Th Coll 73. **d** 76 **p** 77. C Glouc St Geo *Glouc* 76-79; Warden Bp Mascall Cen *Heref* 79-84; Dioc Communications Officer 81-86; TR Heref St Martin w St Fran (S Wye Team Min) from 84; R Dewsall w Callow from 84; V Holme Lacy w Dinedor from 84; V Lt Dewchurch, Aconbury w Ballingham and Bolstone from 84; V Upper and Lower Bullinghope w Grafton from 84. *The Rectory, 91 Ross Road, Hereford HR2 7RJ* Hereford (0432) 353275 or 353717

JONES, Tudor Howell. b 39. St Mich Coll Llan DipTh67 DPS68. **d** 68 **p** 69. C Clydach *S & B* 68-72; C Swansea St Pet 72-75; V Ystradfellte 75-79; V Llanguicke 79-91; V Manselton from 91. *The Vicarage, Manor Road, Manselton, Swansea SA5 9PA* Swansea (0792) 654848

JONES, Victor Harvey. b 25. St D Coll Lamp BA53 Coll of Resurr Mirfield. **d** 55 **p** 56. Chapl RN 62-80; C Portishead *B & W* 80-83; rtd 83. *Carabone Lodge, Mawgan, Helston, Cornwall TR12 6AJ* Mawgan (032622) 613

JONES, Canon Victor Howell. b 18. Univ of Wales BA41. St Mich Coll Llan 41. **d** 43 **p** 45. V Laugharne *St D* 54-72; Chapl St D Hosp Carmarthen 72-85; V Llanllwch *St D* 72-77; V Llanllwch w Llangain 77-83; Can St D Cathl 80-85; V Llanllwch w Llangain and Llangynog 83-85; rtd 85. *Ty Clyd, 13 Picton Terrace, Carmarthen, Dyfed* Carmarthen (0267) 232352

JONES, Walter. b 14. TCD 63. **d** 65 **p** 66. C Chaddesden St Mary *Derby* 71-72; C Bootle Ch Ch *Liv* 72-75; C Ashton-in-Makerfield St Thos 75-77; TV Ebbw Vale *Mon* 77-84; rtd 84. *9 Islwyn Close, Hill Top, Ebbw Vale, Gwent*

JONES, Warwick. b 29. Univ Coll of SW TDip51 Birkb Coll Lon BA54. **d** 91. NSM Saltash *Truro* from 91. *18 Hillside Road, Saltash, Cornwall PL12 6EX* Plymouth (0752) 842031

JONES, Preb Wilfred David. b 22. Keble Coll Ox BA47 MA48. St Mich Coll Llan 47. **d** 48 **p** 49. C Aberaman *Llan* 48-50; C Cardiff St Jo 50-55; Chapl Kelly Coll Tavistock 55-62; V St Decumans *B & W* 62-76; V Ilminster w Whitelackington from 76; RD Ilminster 78-87; Preb Wells Cathl from 81. *The Vicarage, Ilminster, Somerset TA19 0DU* Ilminster (0460) 52610

JONES, Wilfred Lovell. b 39. Lon Univ BD71 CertEd. St D Coll Lamp DipTh63. **d** 63 **p** 64. C Llanllyfni *Ban* 63-65; C Llanbeblig w Caernarfon 65-68; V Llanwnog w Penstrowed 68-73; V Llanwnnog and Caersws w Carno 73-75; Lic to Offic *Cant* 77-90; Asst Chapl Dover Coll Kent 77-90; Wrekin Coll Shropshire from 91. *7 Sutherland Avenue, Wellington, Telford, Shropshire TF1 3BL* Telford (0952) 48223

JONES, Canon William. b 30. Univ of Wales (Ban) DipTh54. St Mich Coll Llan 54. **d** 55 **p** 56. C Deneio w Abererch *Ban* 55-60; V Aberdaron and Bodferin 60-66; V Llandwrog St Thos w Llandwrog 66-71; R Llanstumdwy, Llangybi w Llanarmon 71-74; R Dolbenmaen w Llanystymdwy w Llangybi etc from 74; RD Eifionydd from 75; Can Ban Cathl from 84. *The Rectory, Llanystumdwy, Criccieth, Gwynedd LL52 0SS* Criccieth (0766) 712325

JONES, William Alexander. b 13. Univ of Wales BA35. **d** 69 **p** 70. Hon C Llandegfan w Beaumaris and Llanfaes *Ban* 69-75; C 75-76; P-in-c Penmon and Llangoed w Llanfihangel Dinsylwy 76-77; TV Llandegfan and Beaumaris w Llanfaes w Penmon etc 77-81; rtd 81. *Silva, 4 Coedwig Terrace, Penmon, Beaumaris, Gwynedd* Beaumaris (0248) 509

JONES, Canon William David. b 28. Univ of Wales (Lamp) BA48 Lon Univ BD57 Leeds Univ MA73. St Mich Coll Llan 49. **d** 51 **p** 52. C Risca *Mon* 51-54; C Chepstow St Arvan's w Penterry 54-55; C St Geo-in-the-East w Ch Ch w St Jo *Lon* 55-59; C Farnham Royal *Ox* 59-65; Lect Div Culham Coll 65-67; Hd of Relig Studies Doncaster Coll of Educn 67-74; Lic to Offic *Sheff* 67-74; Lect Th Dur Univ 74-88; Vice-Prin St Bede Coll Dur 74-75; Vice-Prin SS Hild & Bede Coll Dur 75-88; Lic to Offic *Dur* 74-88; Dir of Miss Ch in Wales from 88; Hon Can St D Cathl *St D* from 90. *Church in Wales Centre, Woodland Place, Penarth, S Glam CF6 2EX* Penarth (0222) 708234

JONES, William Douglas. b 28. St Fran Coll Brisbane ThL56. **d** 56 **p** 58. Australia 56-58; Papua New Guinea 58-72; C Manston *Ripon* 72-75; V Middleton St Mary 75-87; V Ireland Wood from 87. *St Paul's Vicarage, Raynel Drive, Leeds LS16 6BS* Leeds (0532) 672907

JONES, William Edward Benjamin. b 19. TCD BA43 MA53. TCD Div Sch Div Test44. **d** 44 **p** 45. V N Wembley St Cuth *Lon* 59-81; V Ripley *Guildf* 81-87; Chapl HM Pris Send 81-87; rtd 87. *37 Bircham Road, Reepham, Norfolk NR10 4NG* Norwich (0603) 870738

JONES, Canon William Glyndwr. b 17. St D Coll Lamp BA39. **d** 42 **p** 43. V Mathry w St Edren's and Grandston etc *St D* 69-86; Hon Can St D Cathl 84-86; rtd 86. *Pencraig, Sladeway, Fishguard, Dyfed SA65 9NY* Fishguard (0348) 874673

JONES, William Hugh. b 13. Univ of Wales BA35. St Mich Coll Llan 35. **d** 38 **p** 39. R Princes Risborough *Ox* 54-73; R Princes Risborough w Ilmer 73-82; RD Aylesbury 77-80; rtd 82; Perm to Offic *Ox* from 82. *64 Ramworth Way, Foxhills, Aylesbury, Bucks HP21 7EY* Aylesbury (0296) 28838

JONES, William Lincoln. b 19. St D Coll Lamp BA41 St Mich Coll Llan 41. **d** 43 **p** 44. V Winscombe *B & W* 64-71; V Bishops Lydeard 71-73; V Bishops Lydeard w Cothelstone 73-80; P-in-c Bagborough 78-80; R Bishops Lydeard w Bagborough and Cothelstone 80-84; rtd 84; Perm to Offic *Ex* from 86. *Holme Lea Well Mead, Kilmington, Axminster, Devon EX13 7SQ* Axminster (0297) 32744

JONES, William Lloyd. b 36. Univ of Wales (Lamp) BA59. Wycliffe Hall Ox 59. **d** 61 **p** 62. C Holyhead w Rhoscolyn *Ban* 61-65; C Porthmadog 65-67; R Llanfaethlu w Llanfwrog and Llanrhyddlad etc 67-74; R Llanengan and Llangian from 74; RD LLyn from 90. *The Rectory, Abersoch, Pwllheli, Gwynedd LL53 7EA* Abersoch (075881) 2871

JONES, Wynne Martin Alban. b 02. Lon Univ BA29. **d** 56 **p** 57. I Knockaney *L & K* 60-76; rtd 76. *Our Lady's Manor, Bulloch Castle, Dalkey, Co Dublin, Irish Republic* Dublin (1) 280-6993

JONES-EVANS, Thomas Dewi Theodore. b 04. MBE54 TD50. **d** 27 **p** 28. Chapl W Park Hosp Epsom 63-72; rtd 72; Lic to Offic *Mon* 72-82; Perm to Offic from 82. *Anzio, 3 Carlton Terrace, Caerleon, Gwent NP6 1AD* Caerleon (0633) 422138

JORDAN, Anthony John. Birm Univ BEd73. **d** 83 **p** 84. Asst Chapl Uppingham Sch Leics 83-86; Hon C Uppingham w Ayston and Wardley w Belton *Pet* 83-86; Sherborne Sch Dorset 86-87. *53 Wylde Green Road, Sutton Coldfield, W Midlands* 021-354 1993

JORDAN, Avril Marilyn. b 35. Lon Univ DipEd56. SW Minl Tr Course 79. **dss** 82 **d** 87. Highweek and Teigngrace *Ex* 82-87; Par Dn 87-88; Par Dn Ottery St Mary, Alfington, W Hill, Tipton etc from 88. *9 Washbrook View, Ottery St Mary, Exeter EX11 1EP* Ottery St Mary (040481) 4849

JORDAN, Mrs Elizabeth Ann. b 58. New Hall Cam MA82. St Jo Coll Nottm DipTh84. **d** 87. Par Dn Blackpool St Jo *Blackb* 87-90; Par Dn Ewood from 90. *St Bartholomew's Vicarage, Bolton Road, Blackburn BB2 4LA* Blackburn (0254) 51206

JORDAN, Canon Frederick William. b 05. St Aid Birkenhead 27. **d** 30 **p** 31. Hon Can Roch Cathl *Roch* 61-70; PV Roch Cathl 67-75; rtd 70. *Salters Corner, 106A High Street, Hastings, E Sussex TN34 3HD* Faversham (0795) 3710

JORDAN, John. b 37. CQSW81. N Ord Course 84. **d** 87 **p** 88. C Southport Em *Liv* 87-90; V Abram from 90; V Bickershaw from 90. *The Vicarage, 9 Lee Lane, Abram, Wigan, Lancs WN2 5QU*

JORDAN, Kenneth John. b 31. K Coll Lon. **d** 69 **p** 70. Guyana 69-74; C Roath St Marg *Llan* 74-76; V Nantymoel w Wyndham 76-81; V Cardiff St Mary w St Steph 81-83; V Cardiff St Mary and St Steph w St Dyfrig etc from 83; Miss to Seamen from 83. *St Mary's Clergy House, Bute Street, Cardiff CF1 5HE* Cardiff (0222) 487777

JORDAN, Peter Harry. b 42. Leeds Univ BA64. Cranmer Hall Dur 70. **d** 73 **p** 74. C Nottm St Ann w Em *S'well* 73-77; C Edgware *Lon* 77-82; V Everton St Chrys *Liv* from 82. *The Vicarage, St Chrysostom's Way, Liverpool L6 2NF* 051-263 3755

JORDAN, Richard William. b 56. Lanchester Poly BSc78. St Jo Coll Nottm DipTh84. **d** 87 **p** 88. C Blackpool St Jo *Blackb* 87-90; V Ewood from 90. *St Bartholomew's Vicarage, Bolton Road, Blackburn BB2 4LA* Blackburn (0254) 51206

JORDAN, Robert Brian. b 43. Qu Coll Birm 68. **d** 69 **p** 70. C Norton St Mich *Dur* 69-73; C Hastings St Clem and All SS *Chich* 73-74; C Carshalton *S'wark* 74-81; V Catford St Andr from 81. *The Vicarage, 135 Wellmeadow Road, London SE6 1HP* 081-697 2600

JORDAN, Ronald Henry. b 30. K Coll Lon. **d** 57 **p** 58. C Clerkenwell H Redeemer w St Phil *Lon* 57-58; C Southgate Ch Ch 58-59; C Edmonton St Mary w St Jo 62-69; Hon C from 86; V Wood Green St Mich 69-73; Hon C Finchley H Trin 80-86. *120 Church Lane, London N2 0TB* 081-883 7828

JORDAN, Thomas. b 36. NW Ord Course 76. **d** 79 **p** 80. NSM Prenton *Ches* 79-84; NSM Egremont St Jo from 84. *31 Willowbank Road, Devonshire Park, Birkenhead L42 7JU* 051-652 4212

JORDINSON, Vera (Sister Hilary). b 37. Liv Univ BA61 CertEd61. Westcott Ho Cam 88. **d** 89. CSF from 74; Lic to Offic *Heref* from 89; Perm to Offic *Lich* from 90. *Greystones St Francis, First Avenue, Porthill, Newcastle, Staffs ST5 8QX* Newcastle-under-Lyme (0782) 636839

JORY, Joseph Nicholls. b 07. Lon Univ DipTh31. St Andr Whittlesford 40. **d** 40 **p** 41. R Spennithorne *Ripon* 46-66; R Finghall 54-66; R Hauxwell 64-66; rtd 72; Perm to Offic *Ex* from 79. *Shilstone, Chagford, Newton Abbot, Devon TQ13 8JX* Whiddon Down (064723) 307

JORYSZ, Ian Herbert. b 62. Van Mildert Coll Dur BSc84 Liv Univ PhD87. Ripon Coll Cuddesdon BA89. **d** 90 **p** 91. C Houghton le Spring *Dur* from 90. *Kepier Flat, Church Street, Houghton le Spring, Tyne & Wear DH4 4DN* 091-584 8970

JOSEPH, Hugh Stephen. b 17. St Cath Coll Cam BA39 MA43. Ripon Hall Ox 39. **d** 40 **p** 41. V Elm *Ely* 62-73; R Woodston 73-82; rtd 82; Perm to Offic Pet and Ely from 82. *25 All Saints' Road, Peterborough PE1 2QT* Peterborough (0733) 54225

JOURDAIN, Canon Ernest Edward. b 16. Selw Coll Cam BA38 MA42. Wells Th Coll 38. **d** 40 **p** 41. V Frisby-on-the-Wreake w Kirby Bellars *Leic* 71-78; C Lt Hadham *St Alb* 78-79 and 79; C Braughing w Albury, Furneux Pelham etc 79; C Braughing, Lt Hadham, Albury, Furneux Pelham etc 79-82; rtd 82; Perm to Offic *St Alb* from 82. *7 Berkley Avenue, Wilstead, Bedford MK45 3ES* Bedford (0234) 740626

JOWETT, Very Rev Alfred. b 14. CBE72. St Cath Coll Cam BA35 MA59 Sheff Univ Hon DLitt82. Linc Th Coll 43. **d** 44 **p** 45. Dean Man 64-83; rtd 83; Perm to Offic *Sheff* from 84. *37 Stone Delf, Sheffield S10 3QX* Sheffield (0742) 305455

JOWETT, Hilary Anne. b 54. Hull Univ BA75. Cranmer Hall Dur IDC80. **dss** 82 **d** 87. Sheff St Jo *Sheff* 82-83; Brampton Bierlow 83-87; Par Dn 87-89; Hon Par Dn Sheff Sharrow from 89; Chapl Nether Edge Hosp Sheff from 89. *Sharrow Vicarage, 45 St Andrew's Road, Sheffield S11 9AL* Sheffield (0742) 550533

JOWETT, Nicholas Peter Alfred. b 44. St Cath Coll Cam BA66 MA Bris Univ CertEd67 Birm Univ DipTh74. Qu Coll Birm 72. **d** 75 **p** 76. C Wales *Sheff* 75-78; TV Sheff Manor 78-83; V Brampton Bierlow 83-89; V Sheff Sharrow from 89. *Sharrow Vicarage, 45 St Andrew's Road, Sheffield S11 9AL* Sheffield (0742) 550533

JOWITT, Andrew Robert Benson. b 56. Down Coll Cam BA78 MA81 PGCE79. Wycliffe Hall Ox 88. **d** 90 **p** 91. C Northn Em *Pet* from 90. *17 Brittons Drive, Billing Lane, Southfields, Northampton NN3 5DP* Northampton (0604) 494868

JOWITT, Canon David Arthur Benson. b 25. St Jo Coll Ox BA49 MA53. Sarum Th Coll 49. **d** 51 **p** 52. OGS from 65; Superior OGS 75-81; P-in-c Edin St Ninian *Edin* 69-77; Dioc Supernumerary 77-80; Chapl Edin R Infirmary 77-80; Syn Clerk *Edin* 77-90; Can St Mary's Cathl 77-90; Vice-Provost 81-86; P-in-c S Queensferry 86-90; rtd 90; Hon C Edin Old St Paul *Edin* from 91. *2 Marchmont Crescent, Edinburgh EH9 1HN* 031-331 1923

JOWITT, John Frederick Benson. b 23. Oak Hill Th Coll 57. **d** 59 **p** 59. CF 63-73; R Thrandeston, Stuston and Brome w Oakley *St E* 73-82; V Docking *Nor* 82-83; P-in-c Gt Bircham 82-83; R Docking w the Birchams 83-88; P-in-c Stanhoe w Barwick 85-88; R Docking w The Birchams and Stanhoe w Barwick 88; rtd 88; Perm to Offic *Nor* from 88; St E from 90. *White Lodge, The Street, North Cove, Beccles, Suffolk NR34 7PN* Beccles (0502) 76404

JOY, Canon Leslie John Clifton. b 09. AKC33. St Steph Ho Ox 33. **d** 33 **p** 34. V Blyth St Mary *Newc* 64-83; RD Bedlington 69-83; Hon Can Newc Cathl 70-83; rtd 83; Perm to Offic Chelmsf from 83; Newc from 86. *20 Victoria Drive, Leigh-on-Sea, Essex SS9 1SF* Southend-on-Sea (0702) 710074

JOY, Canon Matthew Osmund Clifton. b 40. St Edm Hall Ox BA62 MA66. St Steph Ho Ox 62. **d** 64 **p** 65. C Brinksway *Ches* 64-66; C Southwick St Columba *Dur* 66-69; V Hartlepool H Trin 69-85; V Rotherham Ferham Park *Sheff* 85-88; V Masbrough from 88; RD Rotherham from 88. *256 Kimberworth Road, Rotherham, S Yorkshire S61 1HG* Rotherham (0709) 557810 or 560844

JOYCE, Mrs Alison Jane. b 59. Univ of Wales (Swansea) BA81 SS Coll Cam PGCE84 Bris Univ MLitt87. Ripon Coll Cuddesdon BA87. **d** 88. Par Dn Chalgrove w Berrick Salome *Ox* 88-90; Tutor W Midl Minl Tr Course from 90; Perm to Offic *Birm* from 90. *88 Willows Road, Balsall Heath, Birmingham B12 9QD* 021-440 5171

JOYCE, Anthony Owen. b 35. Selw Coll Cam BA60 MA64. Wycliffe Hall Ox 60. **d** 62 **p** 63. C Birm St Martin *Birm* 62-67; Rhodesia 67-70; V Birm St Luke *Birm* 70-79; V Downend *Bris* from 79; RD Stapleton 83-89. *The Vicarage, 63 Downend Road, Bristol BS16 5UF* Bristol (0272) 568064

JOYCE, Ernest Thomas Chancellor. b 16. Lon Univ LLB67. Chich Th Coll 68. **d** 70 **p** 71. C Southsea H Spirit *Portsm* 70-75; V New Southgate St Paul *Lon* 75-77; Chantry Priest Chpl St Mich and H So Walsingham 77-81; Perm to Offic *Nor* from 77; rtd 81. *16 Cleaves Drive, Walsingham, Norfolk NR22 6EQ* Walsingham (0328) 820612

JOYCE, Gordon Franklin. b 51. Birm Univ BA72. St Jo Coll Nottm 86. **d** 88 **p** 89. C Didsbury St Jas and Em *Man* from 89. *54 Mellington Avenue, Didsbury Village, Manchester M20 0NH* 061-445 6010

JOYCE, Graham Leslie. b 49. Lon Univ CertEd71. Trin Coll Bris DipHE89. **d** 89 **p** 90. C Heald Green St Cath *Ches* from 89. *103 Baslow Drive, Cheadle, Cheshire SK8 3HW* 061-437 2395

JOYCE, John Barnabas Altham. b 47. St Chad's Coll Dur BA69 Lon Univ DipEd86. St Steph Ho Ox 72. **d** 74 **p** 75. C Reading St Giles *Ox* 74-77; C Cowley St Jo 77-80; Dioc Youth and Community Officer 80-87; V Hangleton *Chich* from 87. *The Vicarage, 127 Hangleton Way, Hove, E Sussex BN3 8ER* Brighton (0273) 419409

JOYCE, Kingsley Reginald. b 49. Man Univ BSc70. Cuddesdon Coll 70. **d** 73 **p** 74. C High Wycombe *Ox* 73-76; C Fingest 76-79; P-in-c 79; C Hambleden 76-79; P-in-c 79; C Medmenham 76-79; P-in-c 79; C Fawley (Bucks) 76-79; P-in-c 79; C Turville 76-79; P-in-c 79; P-in-c Hambleden Valley 79-80; R 80-87; R Friern Barnet St Jas *Lon* 87-91; CF from 91. *c/o MOD (Army), Bagshot Park, Bagshot, Surrey GU19 5PL* Bagshot (0276) 71717

JOYCE, Margaret. b 47. Oak Hill NSM Course 86. **d** 89. NSM Chadwell Heath *Chelmsf* from 89. *Blessings, 191 Somerville Road, Chadwell Heath, Romford RM6 5AU* 081-597 4228

JOYCE, Martin Ernest Chancellor. b 50. K Coll Lon 69. **d** 73 **p** 74. C Leigh Park *Portsm* 73-77; C Milton 77-83; TV Cam Ascension *Ely* 83-85; V Blackpool St Mich *Blackb* 85-87. *Address temp unknown*

JOYCE, Dr Melville Henry Bushell. b 14. MRCPsych71 St D Coll Lamp BA39 Bris Univ MB, ChB52 DPM54. Ely Th Coll 40. **d** 41 **p** 42. C Abergavenny H Trin *Mon* 41-43; C St Winnow *Truro* 43-45; C Westbury-on-Trym H Trin *Bris* 45-46; C Henleaze 46-52; Public Preacher 52-69; Perm to Offic *Lon* 55-69; Lic to Offic from 69; Lect Psychiatry Lon Univ 58-61; Surrey Univ 61-79. *7 Stanhope Terrace, London W2 2UB* 071-262 3718

JOYCE, Canon Norman. b 14. St Jo Coll Dur BA35 MA38 DipTh38. **d** 37 **p** 38. R N Wingfield *Derby* 57-73; TR N Wingfield, Pilsley and Tupton 73-80; Hon Can Derby Cathl 77-80; rtd 80; Perm to Offic *Carl* from 80. *Fell View, Thurstonfield, Carlisle CA5 6HG* Burgh-by-Sands (022876) 471

JOYCE, Raymond. b 37. Keele Univ BA60 MA67 Linc Coll Ox BA62 MA68. St Steph Ho Ox 78. **d** 80 **p** 81. NSM Normanton *Derby* 80-83; NSM Derby St Alkmund and St Werburgh 83-87; Lic to Offic from 87. *4 South Avenue, Littleover, Derby DE3 6BA* Derby (0332) 768681

JOYCE, Terence Alan. b 57. St Jo Coll Nottm BTh84. **d** 84 **p** 85. C Mansf St Pet *S'well* 84-88; V Greasley from 88. *The Vicarage, 36 Moorgreen, Newthorpe, Notts NG16 2FB* Langley Mill (0773) 712509

JUBB, William Arthur. b 21. Kelham Th Coll 39. **d** 45 **p** 46. V Monk Bretton *Wakef* 52-74; rtd 86. *5 Mauds Terrace, Barnsley, S Yorkshire S71 2EA* Barnsley (0226) 247286

JUCKES, Jonathan Sydney. b 61. St Andr Univ MA83 Selw Coll Cam BA87. Ridley Hall Cam 85. **d** 88 **p** 89. C Sevenoaks St Nic *Roch* from 88. *40 South Park, Sevenoaks, Kent TN13 1EJ* Sevenoaks (0732) 454221

JUDD, Colin Ivor. b 35. Dur Univ BA61. Ridley Hall Cam 61. **d** 63 **p** 64. C Stratford St Jo w Ch Ch *Chelmsf* 63-66; C Kimberworth *Sheff* 66-68; Area Sec (Dios Bradf and Wakef) CMS 68-80; V Bradf St Columba w St Andr *Bradf* from 80. *St Columba's Vicarage, 163 Horton Grange Road, Bradford, W Yorkshire BD7 2DN* Bradford (0274) 571975

JUDD, Eric Sinclair Alderton. b 04. **d** 43 **p** 44. V N Willingham w Legsby *Linc* 44-73; rtd 73. *5 Baildon Crescent, North Hykeham, Lincoln LN6 8HU* Lincoln (0522) 687442

JUDD, Jack Lewis. b 09. Bris Poly MA86. Glouc Sch of Min 79 Ripon Coll Cuddesdon 80. **d** 80 **p** 81. NSM Berkeley *Glouc* 80-83; NSM Berkeley w Wick, Breadstone and Newport 84-86; NSM Lower Cam w Coaley 86-90; Perm to Offic from 90. *Minus Two, Woodend Lane, Cam, Dursley, Glos GL11 5LR* Dursley (0453) 547054

JUDD, Mrs Nicola Jane. b 51. Birm Coll of Educn CertEd72. S Dioc Minl Tr Scheme 87. **d** 90. NSM Abbotts Ann and Upper and Goodworth Clatford *Win* from 90. *13 Belmont Close, Andover, Hants SP10 2DE* Andover (0264) 63364

JUDD, Peter Somerset Margesson. b 49. Trin Hall Cam BA71. Cuddesdon Coll 71. **d** 74 **p** 75. C Salford St Phil w St Steph *Man* 74-76; Chapl Clare Coll Cam 76-81; C Burnham *Ox* 81-82; TV Burnham w Dropmore, Hitcham and Taplow 82-88; R Iffley from 88. *The Rectory, Mill Lane, Iffley, Oxford OX4 4EJ* Oxford (0865) 773516

JUDGE, James Arthur. b 20. Lon Univ BD50. ALCD50. **d** 50 **p** 51. R Street *B & W* 62-77; V Banwell 77-88; rtd 88. *512 Gipps House, 270 Jersey Road, Woollahra, NSW, Australia 2025*

JUDGE, Michael Charles. b 42. Southn Univ BTh79. Chich Th Coll 71. **d** 74 **p** 75. C Eastbourne St Mary *Chich* 74-78; C Seaford w Sutton 79-81; R Hurstpierpoint 81-89; V Easebourne from 89; Chapl K Edw VII Hosp Midhurst from 89; RD Midhurst *Chich* from 90. *The Priory, Easebourne, Midhurst, W Sussex GU29 0AJ* Midhurst (073081) 3341

JUDSON, Paul Wesley. b 46. Leic Poly DipAD69 ATD71. Cranmer Hall Dur 87. **d** 89 **p** 90. C Lobley Hill *Dur* from 89. *70 Beechwood Gardens, Lobley Hill, Gateshead, Tyne & Wear NE11 0DA* 091-460 6838

JUKES, Henry Augustus Lloyd. b 13. FRHistS58 Keble Coll Ox BA37 MA41. Lambeth STh76. **d** 38 **p** 38. V Tilney All Saints w Tilney St Lawrence *Ely* 68-78; rtd 78. *1 St Mary's Court, Ely, Cambs CB7 4HQ* Ely (0353) 4972

JUKES, Keith Michael. b 54. Leeds Univ BA76. Linc Th Coll 77. **d** 78 **p** 79. C Wordsley *Lich* 78-81; C Wolv 81-83; C-in-c Stoneydelph St Martin CD 83-90; TR Glascote and Stonydelph from 90; RD Tamworth from 90. *The Parsonage, 31 Lintly, Stonydelph, Tamworth, Staffs B77 2RD* Tamworth (0827) 898600

JULIAN, Sister. *See* WALSH, Julia Christine

JUPE, Canon Derek Robert. b 26. TCD BA53 MA67. **d** 54 **p** 55. C Lurgan Ch Ch *D & D* 54-57; C Dub Harold's Cross *D & G* 57-60; I Easkey Union *T, K & A* 60-65; Deputation Sec (Ireland) BCMS 65-72; R Man St Jerome w Ardwick St Silas *Man* 72-78; V Ardsley *Sheff* 78-83; I Tempo and Clabby *Clogh* from 83; Can Clogh Cathl from 89. *The Rectory, Clabby, Fivemiletown, Co Tyrone BT75 0RD* Fivemiletown (03655) 21697

JUPE, Martin Roy. b 27. Lon Univ BD63. St Deiniol's Hawarden. **d** 61 **p** 62. C Camborne *Truro* 61-64; V Penzance St Jo from 64; RD Penwith 73-76. *St John's Vicarage, Trewartha Terrace, Penzance, Cornwall TR18 2HE* Penzance (0736) 63620

JUPP, Roger Alan. b 56. St Edm Hall Ox BA78 MA82. Chich Th Coll 79. **d** 80 **p** 81. C Newbold and Dunston *Derby* 80-83; C Cowley St Jo *Ox* 83-85; C Islington St Jas w St Phil *Lon* 85-86; V Lower Beeding *Chich* 86-90; Dom Chapl to Suff Bp Horsham 86-91; V Burgess Hill St Jo from 90. *St John's Vicarage, 68 Park Road, Burgess Hill, W Sussex RH15 8HG* Burgess Hill (0444) 232582

JUSTICE, Peter John Michael. b 37. Chich Th Coll 60. **d** 63 **p** 64. C Mill End *St Alb* 68-70; V Eaton Bray 70-73; Hon C Prestwood *Ox* 73-84; Chapl to the Deaf 84-90; rtd 90; Perm to Offic *Ox* from 90. *Michaelmas, Dodd's Lane, Chalfont St Giles, Bucks HP8 4EL* Chalfont St Giles (02407) 5244

K

KAENEL, Brian Herbert. b 19. Coll of Resurr Mirfield 57. **d** 59 **p** 60. Asst Master St Aug Sch Kilburn 69-70; Ravensbourne Sch Bromley 71-79; Perm to Offic *Roch* from 72; rtd 84. *19 Graham Court, Cooden Close, Bromley, Kent BR1 3TT* 081-290 5728

✠KAFITY, Rt Rev Samir. Beirut Univ BA57. Near E Sch of Th 57. **d** 57 **p** 58 **c** 86. Jerusalem 57-59; Jordan 59-75; Adn Beirut 74-77; Gen Sec Cen Syn of Episc Ch in JEM 77-86; Adn Jerusalem 77-86; Bp Jerusalem from 86. *St George's Close, PO Box 1248, Jerusalem 91109, Israel*

KAGGWA, Nelson Sonny. b 58. Bible Tr Inst Tennessee DipTh83 Bp Tucker Coll Mukono 77. **d** 80 **p** 80. Kenya 80-83; USA 83; Hon C Ox SS Phil and Jas w St Marg *Ox* 84-85; C W Ham *Chelmsf* 86-87; TV Walthamstow St Mary w St Steph from 87. *41 Fraser Road, London E17 9DD* 081-520 1960

KANERIA, Rajni. b 57. Bath Univ BPharm82. Wycliffe Hall Ox 83. **d** 86 **p** 87. C Hyson Green *S'well* 86-87; C Hyson Green St Paul w St Steph 87-89; C Harold Hill St Geo *Chelmsf* from 89. *18 Petersfield Avenue, Romford RM3 9PA* Romford (0708) 74776

KAO, Peter. b 19. **d** 57 **p** 59. Miss to Seamen 58-84; rtd 84. *3 Granville Court, Harvel Crescent, London SE2 0QL* 081-310 7784

KARNEY, Gilbert Henry Peter. b 09. Trin Coll Cam BA31 MA36. Cuddesdon Coll 32. **d** 34 **p** 35. V Embleton *Newc* 54-74; P-in-c Rennington w Rock 73-74; rtd 74; Perm to Offic *Newc* 86-89; C W w E Hanney 89-91. *Darden House, Snuggs Lane, East Hanney, Wantage, Oxon OX12 0HG* Abingdon (0235) 868265

KARRACH, Dr Herbert Adolf. b 24. TCD BA46 MB48 BCh48 BAO48 LSHTM DTM&H55. E Anglian Minl Tr Course 85. **d** 88 **p** 89. Hon C Snettisham w Ingoldisthorpe and Fring *Nor* from 88. *Narnia, 5 Docking Road, Fring, King's Lynn, Norfolk PE31 6SQ* Docking (04858) 346

KARUNARATNA, Charles Winston. b 28. FPhS FRSA Serampore Coll BD60 DTh84 K Coll Lon MTh66 PhD74 Lon Inst of Educn MA90. ALCD51. **d** 51 **p** 52. C Croydon St Matt *Cant* 51-53; NSM Gt Ilford St Jo *Chelmsf* from 89. *2 Lancelot Road, Ilford, Essex IG6 3BE* 081-500 4751

KASSELL, Colin George Henry. b 42. Ripon Coll Cuddesdon 76. **d** 68 **p** 69. In RC Ch 69-75; Perm to Offic *Ox* 76-77; C Denham 77-80; V Brotherton *Wakef* 80-84; Chapl St Cath Hospice Crawley from 84. *61 Broomdashers Road, Three Bridges, Crawley, W Sussex RH10 1PP* Crawley (0293) 23547

KAUNHOVEN, Anthony Peter. b 55. Leeds Univ BA78 PGCE79 Edin Univ DipMin80. Edin Th Coll 79. **d** 81 **p** 82. C Leeds St Aid *Ripon* 81-84; C Hawksworth Wood 84-89; V Upper Nidderdale from 89. *The Vicarage, Pateley Bridge, Harrogate, N Yorkshire HG3 5LQ* Harrogate (0423) 711414

KAVANAGH, Graham George. b 47. Worc Coll Ox BA73 MA78 St Cath Coll Cam MA73. Cuddesdon Coll 71. **d** 74 **p** 75. C Shepperton *Lon* 74-77; USA from 77. *Address temp unknown*

KAVANAGH, Michael Lowther. b 58. CPsychol90 MBPsS90 York Univ BA80 Newc Univ MSc82 Leeds Univ BA86. Coll of Resurr Mirfield 84. **d** 87 **p** 88. C Boston Spa *York* from 87. *8 Lea Croft, Clifford, Wetherby, W Yorkshire LS23 6EY* Boston Spa (0937) 541173

KAVANAGH, Nicholas James Marner. b 49. Ex Coll Ox MA70 K Coll Lon BD79. Westcott Ho Cam 79. **d** 80 **p** 81. C Forest Hill Ch Ch *S'wark* 80-84; C Plumstead St Nic 87; NSM Pimlico St Mary Graham Terrace *Lon* 87-88; C from 88. *St Mary's Presbytery, 30 Bourne Street, London SW1P 8JJ* 071-730 2423

KAY, Canon Cyril John. b 05. St Aid Birkenhead 44. **d** 46 **p** 47. V Welland *Worc* 54-74; rtd 74; Perm to Offic *Glouc* from 80. *16 Kayte Close, Bishop's Cleeve, Cheltenham, Glos GL52 4AX* Cheltenham (0242) 674306

KAY, George Ronald. b 24. Sarum & Wells Th Coll 74. **d** 77 **p** 78. NSM Bemerton *Sarum* 77-87; rtd 87. *1 Victoria Close, Wilton, Salisbury SP2 0ET* Salisbury (0722) 743884

KAY, Ian Geoffrey. b 46. ALA68. N Ord Course. **d** 89 **p** 90. NSM Rochdale *Man* from 89. *92 Albion Street, Castleton, Rochdale, Lancs OL11 2UL* Rochdale (0706) 39497

KAY, Ronald William. b 28. Liv Univ BEng49 MEng51. Tyndale Hall Bris 59. **d** 61 **p** 62. C Sparkbrook Ch Ch *Birm* 61-65; V Westcombe Park St Geo *S'wark* 65-76; R Doddington *Linc* 76-78; V Skellingthorpe 76-78; V Skellingthorpe w Doddington from 78. *The Vicarage, Lincoln Road, Skellingthorpe, Lincoln LN6 5UY* Lincoln (0522) 682520

KAY, Canon Thomas Kindon. b 17. Edin Th Coll 42. **d** 45 **p** 46. R Dunfermline *St And* 65-85; Can St Ninian's Cathl Perth 69-86; Dioc Supernumerary 85-86; rtd 86. *38 Woodmill Terrace, Dunfermline, Fife KY11 4SR* Dunfermline (0383) 732206

KAYE, Alistair Geoffrey. b 62. Reading Univ BSc85. St Jo Coll Nottm DPS90. **d** 90 **p** 91. C Gt Horton *Bradf* from 90. *18 Windermere Road, Great Horton, Bradford BD7 4RQ* Bradford (0274) 573261

KAYE, Bruce Norman. b 39. Lon Univ BD64 Sydney Univ BA66. Moore Th Coll Sydney ThL64. **d** 64 **p** 65. Australia 64-66 and from 83; Perm to Offic *Dur* 67-69; Tutor St Jo Coll Dur 68-75; Sen Tutor 75-83; Vice Prin 79-83. *New College Institute, Anzac Parade, Kensington, NSW, Australia 2033* Sydney (2) 697-8946

KAYE, Canon Gerald Trevor. b 32. Man Univ BSc54. Oak Hill Th Coll. **d** 56 **p** 57. C Widnes St Ambrose *Liv* 56-58; C St Helens St Mark 58-62; V Brixton Hill St Sav *S'wark* 62-65; Canada 65-85; Hon Can Keew 70-75; Adn Patricia 75-78; V Slough *Ox* from 85. *St Paul's Vicarage, 196 Stoke Road, Slough SL2 5AY* Slough (0753) 21497

KAYE, Norman. b 15. St Chad's Coll Dur BA47. **d** 49 **p** 50. R Leighton w Eaton Constantine *Lich* 68-80; P-in-c Wroxeter 68-80; rtd 80. *7 Rope Lane, Shavington, Crewe CW2 5DT* Crewe (0270) 664170

KAYE, Peter Alan. b 47. K Coll Lon BD71 AKC71. St Aug Coll Cant 71. **d** 72 **p** 73. C Fulham All SS *Lon* 72-74; Chapl Jo Conolly Hosp Birm 74-80; Rubery Hill & Jos Sheldon Hosps Birm 74-80. *Address temp unknown*

KAYE, Timothy Henry. b 52. Linc Th Coll 77. **d** 80 **p** 81. C Warsop *S'well* 80-83; C Far Headingley St Chad *Ripon* 83-86; P-in-c Birkby *Wakef* 86; TV N Huddersfield 86-91; R Stone St Mich w Aston St Sav *Lich* from 91. *St Michael's Rectory, Lichfield Road, Stone, Staffs ST15 8PG* Stone (0785) 812747

KEABLE, Geoffrey. b 1900. St Jo Coll Ox BA22 DipTh23 MA25. Cuddesdon Coll 23. **d** 24 **p** 25. V Barnham *Chich* 59-68; C Chesterton St Luke *Ely* 68-69; rtd 69; Hon C Chesterton St Luke *Ely* 69-78. *The Coach House, Mortimer Hill, Mortimer, Reading RG7 3PG* Mortimer (0734) 333390

KEANE, Chan James Goldsworthy. b 23. OBE84 JP71. Selw Coll Cam BA47 MA49. Cuddesdon Coll 47. **d** 49 **p** 50. C Penarth w Lavernock *Llan* 49-56; Org Sec Ch in Wales Prov Youth Coun 56-65; Dir Ch in Wales Publications 65-79; Gen Sec Ch in Wales Prov Educn Coun 65-79; Hon Can Llan Cathl *Llan* from 73; R St Andrew's Major and Michaelston-le-Pit from 79, Chan Llan Cathl from 90. *The Rectory, Lettons Way, Dinas Powys, S Glam CF6 4BY* Dinas Powys (0222) 512555

KEARNS, Mary Leah. b 38. **d** 87. Par Dn Morden *S'wark* 87-88; Asst Chapl HM Pris Holloway from 88. *25 Leafield Road, London SW20 9AG* 081-540 1594

KEARON, Kenneth Arthur. b 53. TCD BA76 MA79 MPhil91. CITC 78. **d** 81 **p** 82. C Raheny w Coolock *D & G* 81-84; Lect TCD 82-90; Dean of Residence TCD 84-90; I Tullow *D & G* from 90. *Tullow Rectory, Brighton Road, Carrickmines, Dublin 18, Irish Republic* Dublin (1) 289-3135

KEAST, William. b 43. Univ Coll Ox BA65 DipEd66. Local NSM Course 86. **d** 88 **p** 89. NSM Scotton w Northorpe *Linc* from 88. *4 Crapple Lane, Scotton, Gainsborough, Lincs DN21 3QT* Scunthorpe (0724) 763190

KEAT, Roger Leslie Samuel. b 39. Wells Th Coll 64. **d** 66 **p** 67. C Stockton St Chad *Dur* 66-68; C Clapham H Spirit *S'wark* 70-73; C Wimbledon 73-75; CF from 75. *c/o MOD (Army), Bagshot Park, Bagshot, Surrey GU19 5PL* Bagshot (0276) 71717

KEATES, Frederick. b 08. Ball Coll Ox BA35 MA35. Ripon Hall Ox 35. **d** 36 **p** 37. V Four Oaks *Birm* 51-72; rtd 83. *Durley, 30 Four Oaks Road, Sutton Coldfield, W Midlands B74 2TJ* 021-308 0204

KEATING, Christopher Robin. b 39. K Coll Lon BD AKC84. Sarum Th Coll 62. **d** 65 **p** 66. C Baildon *Bradf* 65-67; CF 67-72; V Thornton Heath St Paul *Cant* 72-79; C Harold Hill St Geo *Chelmsf* 85-89; V Goodmayes All SS from 89. *All Saints' Vicarage, Broomhill Road, Ilford, Essex IG3 9SJ* 081-590 1476

KEATING, Geoffrey John. b 52. Liv Poly HND79. St Steph Ho Ox 81. **d** 84 **p** 85. C Lanc Ch Ch w St Jo and St Anne *Blackb* 84-85; C Rotherham *Sheff* 85-87; C Mexborough 87; V Bentley from 87. *The Vicarage, 42 Appleton Way, Bentley, Doncaster, S Yorkshire DN5 9NF* Doncaster (0302) 875918

KEATING, Ronald Martin. b 57. Univ of Wales (Lamp) BA80. Coll of Resurr Mirfield 80. **d** 82 **p** 83. C Ban Cathl Par *Ban* 82-84; Min Can Ban Cathl 82-84; TV Llandudno 84-86; Chapl Gwynedd Hosp Ban from 86; V Penrhosgarnedd *Ban* 86-88; TV Ban from 88. *St Peter's Vicarage, Penrhosgarnedd, Bangor, Gwynedd LL57 2NS* Bangor (0248) 352388

KEATING, William Edward. b 10. Trin Coll Ox BA32. Lich Th Coll 33. **d** 33 **p** 34. Chapl Hurstwood Park Hosp Haywards Heath 63-75; St Fran Hosp Haywards Heath 63-75; rtd 75. *Manormead, Tilford Road, Hindhead, Surrey GU26 6RP* Hindhead (0428) 607539

KEAY, Alfred David. b 26. Aston Univ MSc72. Qu Coll Birm 76. **d** 79 **p** 80. Hon C Penkridge w Stretton *Lich* 79-82; C Rugeley 82-85; V Cheswardine from 85; V Hales from 85. *The Vicarage, Cheswardine, Market Drayton, Shropshire TF9 2RS* Cheswardine (063086) 204

KEDDIE, Tony. b 37. Qu Coll Birm 63. **d** 66 **p** 67. C Barnoldswick w Bracewell *Bradf* 66-69; C New Bentley *Sheff* 69-71; TV Seacroft *Ripon* 71-79; V Kippax 79-85; TR Kippax w Allerton Bywater from 85. *The Rectory, Kippax, Leeds LS25 7HF* Leeds (0532) 862710

KEE, David. b 04. Linc Th Coll 45. **d** 47 **p** 48. OGS from 55; V Podington w Farndish *St Alb* 64-73; rtd 74; Perm to Offic *St Alb* from 74; Win from 75. *6 Princess Court, St Peter Street, Winchester, Hants SO23 8DN* Winchester (0962) 52156

KEEBLE, Dorothy Deborah. b 20. **d** 87. NSM Glas H Cross *Glas* from 87. *12 Housel Avenue, Glasgow G13 3UR* 041-959 3102

KEEBLE, Stephen Robert. b 56. K Coll Lon BD84 AKC84 Selw Coll Cam DipTh86. Westcott Ho Cam 85. **d** 87

p 88. C Lt Stanmore St Lawr *Lon* 87-90; C Headstone St Geo from 90. *The Vicarage, 96 Pinner View, Harrow, Middx HA1 4RJ* 081-427 1253

KEECH, April Irene. b 54. Pennsylvania Univ BS75. Trin Coll Bris BA89. **d** 89. C Walthamstow St Luke *Chelmsf* from 89. *23 Russell Road, London E17 6QY* 081-521 3573

KEEFER, John Samuel. b 46. BA69 MDiv72 ThM79. **d** 72 **p** 73. USA 72-79; Chapl Bucharest w Sofia *Eur* 84-86; Switzerland from 86. *Muhledorfstrasse 28, CH3018, Bern, Switzerland*

KEEGAN, Ven Donald Leslie. b 37. ACII. CITC 65. **d** 68 **p** 69. C Drumragh w Mountfield *D & R* 68-72; I Birr w Lorrha, Dorrha and Lockeen *L & K* from 72; Can Killaloe Cathl 80-82; Treas 82-87; Prec Limerick and Killaloe Cathls 87-89; Adn Killaloe, Kilfenora, Clonfert etc from 89. *The Rectory, Birr, Co Offaly, Irish Republic* Birr (509) 20021

KEEGAN, Graham Brownell. b 40. Nottm Univ CertEd68. N Ord Course 81. **d** 84 **p** 85. C Highfield *Liv* 84-87; V Ince St Mary from 87. *St Mary's Vicarage, Warrington Road, Lower Ince, Wigan, Lancs WN3 4NH* Wigan (0942) 864383

KEELER, Alan. b 58. MIEE87 CEng88 City Univ BSc81. St Jo Coll Nottm DTS90. **d** 90 **p** 91. C Paddock Wood *Roch* from 90. *3 Ashcroft Road, Paddock Wood, Kent TN12 6QT* Paddock Wood (089283) 3194

KEELEY, Keith Morgan. b 12. Man Univ BA33 MA36. **d** 49 **p** 50. R Hinstock *Lich* 59-64; rtd 77. *36 College Road, Newport, Isle of Wight PO30 1HB* Isle of Wight (0983) 523465

KEELING, Brian Arnold. b 35. Coll of Resurr Mirfield. **d** 86 **p** 87. NSM Derby St Mark *Derby* from 86. *48 Hanbury Road, Chaddesden, Derby DE2 6FT* Derby (0332) 671571

KEELING, James Michael. b 33. Dur Univ BA55 MA61. Cuddesdon Coll 57. **d** 59 **p** 60. C Pallion *Dur* 59-64; V Appleton Roebuck w Acaster Selby *York* 65-69; Asst Dir WCC Ecum Inst Celigny 69-72; Lect St Andr Univ from 72. *St Mary's College, St Andrews, Fife KY16 9JU* St Monans (03337) 76161

KEELING, Michael John. b 28. Chich Th Coll 57. **d** 60 **p** 61. C Hurstpierpoint *Chich* 60-63; C Southwick 63-64; Australia 64-73; Hon C Hammersmith St Pet *Lon* 74-75; Hon C S Lambeth St Anne and All SS *S'wark* 75-76; Perm to Offic S'wark 75-84; Chich 79-82; P-in-c Kensington St Barn *Lon* 84-85; Perm to Offic from 85. *St James's Vicarage, Maxwell Road, London SW6 2HR* 071-731 8196

KEELING, Peter Frank. b 34. Kelham Th Coll. **d** 58 **p** 59. C S Elmsall *Wakef* 58-63; C Barnsley St Mary 63-67; V Ravensthorpe 67-73; V Cudworth 73-83; R Downham Market w Bexwell *Ely* from 83; RD Fincham from 83; V Crimplesham w Stradsett from 85. *The Rectory, Downham Market, Norfolk PE38 9LE* Downham Market (0366) 382187

KEEN, Charles William Ernest. b 14. Chich Th Coll 48. **d** 51 **p** 52. R Ide Hill *Roch* 66-73; Chapl Sundridge Hosp Kent 66-73; rtd 73; Perm to Offic *Cant* from 73. *4 Godwyn Road, Deal, Kent CT14 6QR* Deal (0304) 362187

KEEN, Michael Spencer. b 41. GRSM62 ARCM St Pet Coll Ox BA68 MA72 Reading Univ CertEd. Westcott Ho Cam 68. **d** 73 **p** 74. Hon C W Derby (or Tuebrook) St Jo *Liv* 73-74; Hon C Stanley 74-76; Chs Youth and Community Officer Telford *Lich* 77-82; Dioc Unemployment Officer *Sheff* 82-89; Hon C Brixton Rd Ch Ch *S'wark* from 89; Employment Development Officer from 89. *114 Lowden Road, London SE24 0BQ* 071-274 8834

KEENAN, Leslie Herbert. b 32. Cranmer Hall Dur. **d** 66 **p** 67. C Anston *Sheff* 66-70; C Woodsetts 66-70; Chapl HM Borstal Pollington 70-78; V Balne *Sheff* 70-78; V Poughill *Truro* from 78. *The Vicarage, Poughill, Bude, Cornwall EX23 9ER* Bude (0288) 55183

KEENE, Canon David Peter. b 32. Trin Hall Cam BA56 MA60. Westcott Ho Cam. **d** 58 **p** 59. C Radcliffe-on-Trent *S'well* 58-61; C Mansf St Pet 61-64; V Nottm St Cath 64-71; R Bingham 71-81; Dioc Dir of Ords 81-90; Can Res S'well Minster from 81. *2 Vicars' Court, Southwell, Notts NG25 0HP* Southwell (0636) 813188 or 812649

KEENE, Muriel Ada. b 35. **d** 87. Dioc Lay Min Adv *S'well* 87-88; Asst Dir of Ords 88-90; Dn-in-c Oxton from 90. *2 Vicar's Court, Southwell, Notts NG25 0HP* Southwell (0636) 813188

KEEP, Andrew James. b 55. Collingwood Coll Dur BA77 Yale Univ STM84. Sarum & Wells Th Coll 78. **d** 80 **p** 81. C Banstead *Guildf* 80-83; Chapl Qu Eliz Hosp

Banstead 80-83; USA 83-84; Chapl Cranleigh Sch Surrey from 84; Lic to Offic *Guildf* from 84; Perm to Offic *Win* from 84. *Cranleigh School, Cranleigh, Surrey GU6 8QQ* Cranleigh (0483) 274561

KEETON, Canon Barry. b 40. Dur Univ BA61 MA69 MLitt78 K Coll Lon BD63 AKC63. **d** 64 **p** 65. C S Bank *York* 64-67; C Middlesb St Cuth 67-69; C Kingston upon Hull St Alb 70-71; V Appleton-le-Street w Amotherby 71-74; Dioc Ecum Adv 74-81; R Ampleforth w Oswaldkirk 74-78; P-in-c Barmby on the Marsh 78-79; P-in-c Laxton w Blacktoft 78-79; P-in-c Wressell 78-79; V Howden 78-79; TR Howden Team Min 80-91; Can and Preb York Minster 85-91; RD Howden 86-91; TR Lewes All SS, St Anne, St Mich and St Thos *Chich* from 91. *The Rectory, St Anne's Crescent, Lewes, E Sussex BN7 1SD* Lewes (0273) 472545

KEFFORD, Peter Charles. b 44. Nottm Univ BTh74. Linc Th Coll 70. **d** 74 **p** 75. C W Wimbledon Ch Ch *S'wark* 74-77; C All Hallows by the Tower etc *Lon* 77-81; C-in-c Pound Hill CD *Chich* 81; TV Worth 82-83; TR from 83. *The Rectory, Worth, Crawley, W Sussex RH10 7RT* Crawley (0293) 882229

KEGG, Gordon Rutherford. b 45. Reading Univ BSc66 Imp Coll Lon PhD71 DIC71 Lon Univ CertEd74. Oak Hill Th Coll DipHE90. **d** 90 **p** 91. C Luton Lewsey St Hugh *St Alb* from 90. *2 Landrace Road, Lewsey Farm, Luton LU4 0SN* Dunstable (0582) 604719

KEIGHLEY, David John. b 48. CertEd Open Univ BA88. Sarum & Wells Th Coll 82. **d** 83 **p** 84. C Sawbridgeworth *St Alb* 83-86; TV Saltash *Truro* 86-89; V Lanlivery w Luxulyan from 89. *The Vicarage, Luxulyan, Bodmin, Cornwall PL30 5EE* St Austell (0726) 850880

KEIGHLEY, Martin Philip. b 61. Edin Univ MA83. Westcott Ho Cam 86. **d** 88 **p** 89. C Lytham St Cuth *Blackb* 88-91; C Lanc St Mary from 91. *24 Milking Stile Lane, Lancaster LA1 5QB* Lancaster (0524) 382362

KEIGHTLEY, Canon Peter Edward. b 17. Leeds Univ BA41. Coll of Resurr Mirfield 41. **d** 43 **p** 44. V Southsea H Spirit *Portsm* 67-76; Chapl St Mary's Gen Hosp Portsm 76-82; Hon Can Portsm Cathl Portsm 81-82; rtd 82; Perm to Offic *Portsm* from 83. *11 Dolphin Court, St Helen's Parade, Southsea, Hants PO4 0QL* Portsmouth (0705) 816697

KEIGHTLEY, Thomas. b 44. CITC 79. **d** 79 **p** 80. C Seagoe *D & D* 79-83; I Belvoir from 83. *3 Brerton Crescent, Belfast BT8 4QD* Belfast (0232) 643777

KEILLER, Mrs Jane Elizabeth. b 52. Westmr Coll Ox BEd74 St Jo Coll Dur DipTh78 Bangalore Univ DipTh79. Cranmer Hall Dur 76. **dss** 80 **d** 87. Cam H Trin w St Andr Gt *Ely* 80-86; Cam St Barn 86-87; Hon Par Dn from 87. *Chestnut Cottage, 38 Pierce Lane, Cambridge CB1 5DL* Cambridge (0223) 881444

KEIRLE, Michael Robert. b 62. Trin Coll Bris BA89. **d** 89 **p** 90. C Orpington Ch Ch *Roch* from 89. *43 Haileybury Road, Orpington, Kent BR6 9EZ* Orpington (0689) 823774

KEITH, Andrew James Buchanan. b 47. Qu Coll Cam BA69 MA73. Wycliffe Hall Ox 71. **d** 74 **p** 75. C Warrington St Elphin *Liv* 74-77; C Southgate *Chich* 77-80; C-in-c Broadfield CD 80-82; P-in-c Walberton w Binsted 82-85; P-in-c Aldingbourne 83-85; Chapl Oswestry Sch from 85. *Oswestry School, Oswestry, Shropshire SY11 2TL* Oswestry (0691) 655711

KEITH, John. b 25. LRAM50 LGSM50 AGSM51. Cuddesdon Coll 60. **d** 62 **p** 63. C Raynes Park St Sav *S'wark* 65-68; rtd 90. *c/o The Post Office, Tayinloan, Tarbert, Argyll PA29 6XG*

KEITH, Canon John Frederick Butterfield. b 12. Trin Coll Cam BA35 MA44. Cuddesdon Coll 36. **d** 37 **p** 38. C Greenford H Cross *Lon* 37-41; CF (EC) 40-46; R Ashwell *St Alb* 46-51; R Fakenham w Alethorpe *Nor* 51-57; New Zealand from 58; Hon Can Christchurch Cathl 71-80; Prec 81-84. *Flat 2, 76 Bishop Street, Christchurch 1, New Zealand* Christchurch (3) 651101

KELK, Michael Anthony. b 48. Sarum & Wells Th Coll. **d** 83 **p** 84. C Ross w Brampton Abbotts, Bridstow and Peterstow *Heref* 83-86; P-in-c Burghill from 86; P-in-c Stretton Sugwas from 86. *The Vicarage, Burghill, Hereford HR4 7SG* Hereford (0432) 760246

KELLAM, Miss Margaret June. b 32. Trin Coll Bris 70. **dss** 77 **d** 87. Heeley *Sheff* 77-87; Par Dn 87-89; Chapl Asst R Hallamshire Hosp Sheff from 89. *170 Westwick Road, Sheffield S8 7BX* Sheffield (0742) 376773

KELLAND, Kenneth William Jerome. b 16. S'wark Ord Course 63. **d** 66 **p** 67. C Sholing *Win* 69-74; V Weston 74-82; rtd 82; Hon C Odiham w S Warnborough and Long Sutton *Win* 82-85; Hon C Herriard w Winslade and Long Sutton etc 85-86. *50 Wooteys Way, Alton, Hants GU34 2JZ* Alton (0420) 85325

KELLEN, David. b 52. Univ of Wales (Cardiff) DipTh73. St Mich Coll Llan 70. **d** 75 **p** 76. C Mynyddislwyn *Mon* 75-77; C Risca 77-78; C Malpas 78-81; V Newport All SS 81-88; V St Mellons and Michaelston-y-Fedw from 88. *The Vicarage, Tyr Winch Road, St Mellons, Cardiff CF3 9UP* Cardiff (0222) 796560

KELLETT, Colin. b 25. Worc Ord Coll 65. **d** 67 **p** 68. C Dewsbury Moor *Wakef* 69-72; V Lundwood 72-77; V Gawber 77-88; rtd 88. *3 Black Horse Drive, Silkstone Common, Barnsley, S Yorkshire S75 4SD* Barnsley (0226) 791561

KELLETT, Neil. b 41. Bps' Coll Cheshunt 64. **d** 66 **p** 67. C Ex St Thos *Ex* 66-72; C Win H Trin *Win* 72-74; P-in-c Redditch St Geo *Worc* 74-77; Canada from 77. *39 Fox Avenue, St John's, Newfoundland, Canada, A1B 2H8* St John's (709) 726-2883

KELLEY, Neil George. b 64. Westcott Ho Cam 88. **d** 91. C E Bedfont *Lon* from 91. *77 West Road, Feltham, Middx* 081-890 1269

KELLY, Canon Albert Norman. b 21. TCD BA43 MA63. **d** 44 **p** 45. C-in-c New Haw CD *Guildf* 66-72; V New Haw 72-78; RD Chertsey 73-75; RD Runnymede 75-78; V Egham Hythe 78-86; Hon Can Guildf Cathl 80-86; rtd 86; USPG Area Sec from 88. *21 Rosetta Road, Belfast BT6 0LQ* Belfast (0232) 693921

KELLY, Brian Eugene. b 56. BA77 PGCE79. Trin Coll Bris 86. **d** 90 **p** 91. NSM Redland *Bris* from 90. *33 Maskelyne Avenue, Bristol BS10 5BY* Bristol (0272) 245755

KELLY, Canon Brian Horace. b 34. St Jo Coll Dur BA57 DipTh58 MA69. **d** 58 **p** 59. C Douglas St Geo and St Barn *S & M* 58-61; V Foxdale 61-64; V Bolton All So w St Jas *Man* 64-73; V Maughold *S & M* 73-77; Dir of Ords from 76; V German from 77; Can and Prec St German's Cathl from 80. *The Cathedral Vicarage, Albany Road, Peel, Isle of Man* Peel (0624) 842608

KELLY, Christopher Augustine. b 15. Croix de Guerre 45 TD65. Keble Coll Ox BA37. Ripon Hall Ox 37. **d** 45 **p** 46. V Bolton Breightmet St Jas *Man* 67-76; V Nelson in Lt Marsden *Blackb* 76-83; rtd 83; Perm to Offic *Bradf* from 83. *33 River Place, Gargrave, Skipton, N Yorkshire BD23 3RY* Skipton (0756) 748247

KELLY, Canon Dennis Charles. b 31. Liv Univ BA52. Lich Th Coll 54. **d** 56 **p** 57. C Tranmere St Paul *Ches* 56-59; C-in-c Grange St Andr CD 59-63; P-in-c Grange St Andr 63-65; V 65-67; R Coppenhall 67-82; R W Kirby St Andr from 82; Hon Can Ches Cathl from 86. *St Andrew's Vicarage, 2 Lingdale Road, West Kirby, Wirral, Merseyside L48 5DQ* 051-632 4728

KELLY, Desmond Norman. b 42. Oak Hill Th Coll DipHE90. **d** 90 **p** 91. C Braintree *Chelmsf* from 90. *183 Notley Road, Braintree, Essex CM7 7HG* Braintree (0376) 22578

KELLY, Canon Edward William Moncrieff. b 28. AKC57. **d** 57 **p** 58. C Petersfield w Sheet *Portsm* 57-60; Papua New Guinea 60-65; V Gosport Ch Ch *Portsm* 65-69; Hon C Eltham St Jo *S'wark* 69-87; Org Sec New Guinea Miss 69-77; Org Sec Papua New Guinea Ch Partnership 77-87; Hon Can Papua New Guinea from 78; TR Trowbridge H Trin *Sarum* from 87. *The Rectory, Stallard Street, Trowbridge, Wilts BA14 9AA* Trowbridge (0225) 753326

KELLY, James Ganly Marks. b 16. TCD BA39 MA50. CITC 39. **d** 39 **p** 40. R Siddington w Preston *Glouc* 71-81; rtd 82. *34 Henry Avenue, Rustington, Littlehampton, W Sussex BN16 2PA* Rustington (0903) 770635

KELLY, John Adrian. b 49. Qu Coll Birm 70. **d** 73 **p** 74. C Formby St Pet *Liv* 73-77; Org Sec (Dios Liv, Blackb and S & M) CECS from 77; Deputation Appeals Org (Lancs and Is of Man) from 88. *159 Forrest Drive, South Park, Lytham, Lancs FY8 4QG* Lytham (0253) 730083

KELLY, John Bernal. b 35. K Coll Cam BA57 MA61. Qu Coll Birm 58. **d** 60 **p** 61. C Huyton St Mich *Liv* 60-62; C Gateshead Fell *Dur* 64-68; R Openshaw *Man* 68-75; V Hey 75-87; V Bury St Jo w St Mark from 87. *270 Walmersley Road, Bury, Lancs BL9 6NH* 061-764 3412

KELLY, John Dickinson. b 42. Nottm Univ BA63. Ripon Hall Ox 63. **d** 65 **p** 66. C Egremont *Carl* 65-67; C Upperby St Jo 67-70; V Arlecdon 70-73; V Barrow St Aid 73-79; V Milnthorpe 79-83; V Beetham and Milnthorpe 83-85; V Camerton St Pet 85-88; P-in-c Camerton H Trin W Seaton 86-88; V Camerton, Seaton and W Seaton from 88. *The Vicarage, Ling Beck Park, Seaton, Workington, Cumbria CA14 1JQ* Workington (0900) 2162

KELLY, John Henry. b 20. Vancouver Sch of Th STh65. **d** 55 **p** 59. C Hall Green St Pet *Birm* 69-71; V Smethwick St Mich 71-78; P-in-c Smethwick St Steph 72-78; V Selly Oak St Wulstan 78-80; R Over Whitacre w Shustoke

80-86; rtd 86; Perm to Offic *Ches* from 86. *61 Hallfields Road, Tarvin, Chester CH3 8ET* Tarvin (0829) 41218

KELLY, Canon John Norman Davidson. b 09. FBA65 Glas Univ MA31 Hon DD58 Qu Coll Ox BA34 BD51 DD51. St Steph Ho Ox 33. **d** 34 **p** 35. Lic to Offic *Ox* from 35; Can and Preb Chich Cathl *Chich* from 48; Prin St Edm Hall Ox 51-79; rtd 75. *7 Crick Road, Oxford OX2 6QJ* Oxford (0865) 512907

KELLY, John Rowe. b 32. Edin Th Coll. **d** 85 **p** 86. C Blyth St Mary *Newc* 85-88; C Slaley from 88; C Healey from 88. *The Vicarage, Slaley, Hexham, Northd NE47 0AA* Hexham (0434) 673609

KELLY, Malcolm Bernard. b 46. St Mich Coll Llan 72. **d** 74 **p** 75. C Tranmere St Paul w St Luke *Ches* 74-77; Chapl Bebington Hosp from 76; C Barnston *Ches* 77-80; R Thurstaston from 80. *The Rectory, Thurstaston, Wirral, Merseyside L61 0HQ* 051-648 1816

KELLY, Martin Herbert. b 55. Cam Univ MA90. Ripon Coll Cuddesdon 80. **d** 83 **p** 84. C Clapham Old Town *S'wark* 83-87; C Clapham Team Min 87; Chapl and Fell Selw Coll Cam from 87. *Selwyn College, Cambridge CB3 9DQ* Cambridge (0223) 335846

KELLY, Nigel James. b 60. N Staffs Poly BSc83. Ripon Coll Cuddesdon 83. **d** 86 **p** 87. C Cen Telford *Lich* 86-90; TV from 90. *19 Dodmoor Grange, Telford, Shropshire TF3 2AW* Telford (0952) 597278

KELLY, Norman James. b 11. K Coll Lon BD36 AKC36. Wycliffe Hall Ox 36. **d** 36 **p** 37. C Champion Hill St Sav *S'wark* 36-39; C Newhaven *Chich* 39-40; C E Grinstead St Swithun 40-46; V Westf 46-50; New Zealand 50-57; V Canewdon w Paglesham *Chelmsf* from 57. *The Vicarage, High Street, Canewdon, Rochford, Essex SS4 3QA* Southend-on-Sea (0702) 258217

KELLY, Paul Maitland Hillyard. b 24. Ball Coll Ox BA50 MA54. Wells Th Coll 50. **d** 52 **p** 53. C Epsom St Martin *Guildf* 52-57; C-in-c New Cathl CD 57-61; R Abinger cum Coldharbour 61-67; P-in-c Preston St Pet *Blackb* 67-70; V Ottershaw *Guildf* 70-77; R Ickenham *Lon* from 77. *St Giles's Rectory, 38 Swakeley's Road, Uxbridge, Middx UB10 8BE* Ruislip (0895) 632803

KELLY, Peter Hugh. b 46. Sarum & Wells Th Coll 81. **d** 84 **p** 85. C Fareham H Trin *Portsm* 84-87; Chapl and Prec Portsm Cathl 87-90; V Eastney from 90. *St Margaret's Vicarage, 13 Cousins Grove, Southsea, Hants PO4 9RP* Portsmouth (0705) 731316

KELLY, Richard Peter. b 47. BA PhD. CITC BTh90. **d** 90 **p** 91. C Dromore Cathl *D & D* from 90. *45 Church Street, Dromore, Co Down BT25 1AA* Dromore (0846) 699789

KELLY, Stephen Paul. b 55. Keble Coll Ox BA77. Linc Th Coll 77. **d** 79 **p** 80. C Illingworth *Wakef* 79-82; C Knottingley 82-84; V Alverthorpe from 84; Dioc Ecum Officer from 88. *The Vicarage, St Paul's Drive, Alverthorpe, Wakefield, W Yorkshire WF2 0BT* Wakefield (0924) 371300

KELLY, Canon William. b 25. St Jo Coll Dur BA51. Tyndale Hall Bris 51. **d** 52 **p** 53. Chapl W Cumberland Hosp 67-84; V Hensingham *Carl* 67-90; RD Calder 75-84; Hon Can Carl Cathl 75-90; rtd 90. *15 Knowefield Avenue, Stanwix, Carlisle, Cumbria CA3 9BQ* Carlisle (0228) 44215

KELLY, Canon William. b 35. Dur Univ BA58 St Cath Coll Ox DipTh59. Lambeth STh75 Wycliffe Hall Ox 58. **d** 60 **p** 61. C Walney Is *Carl* 60-66; R Distington 66-71; V Barrow St Matt 71-81; RD Furness 77-81; Hon Can Carl Cathl from 79; Dir of Ords from 81; V Dalston from 81; RD Carl 83-88; P-in-c Raughton Head w Gatesgill from 86. *The Vicarage, Townshead Road, Dalston, Carlisle CA5 7JF* Dalston (0228) 710215

KELLY, William Edward. b 37. Univ of Wales (Lamp) BA57 St Cath Soc Ox BA59 MA63. St Steph Ho Ox 57. **d** 60 **p** 61. C S Bank *York* 60-63; C Ingoldisthorpe *Nor* 63-66; C Heacham 63-66; Chapl RAF 66-82; Chapl Woodbridge Sch Suffolk 82-88; V Newport St Paul *Mon* from 90. *11B Victoria Place, Newport, Gwent NP9 4DZ* Newport (0633) 266657

KELLY, William Frederick Paul. b 12. Ch Ch Ox BA35 MA49. Sarum Th Coll 63. **d** 64 **p** 65. R Reepham and Hackford w Whitwell and Kerdiston *Nor* 68-80; rtd 80; P-in-c Thurning w Wood Dalling *Nor* 80-81; Chapl to Rtd Clergy and Clergy Widows Officer from 81. *40 Catton Grove Road, Norwich NR3 3NW* Norwich (0603) 424961

KELLY, William Norman. b 21. St Aid Birkenhead. **d** 64 **p** 65. Miss to Seamen 64-66; C Douglas St Geo and St Barn *S & M* 66-69; V Wingates *Man* 69-75; Perm to Offic 76-84; Chapl HM Pris Liv 77-78; Chapl HM Borstal Stoke Heath 78-84; V Castletown *S & M* from 84.

The Vicarage, Arbory Road, Castletown, Isle of Man Castletown (0624) 823509

KELLY, William Ralston. b 27. TCD BA52 MA55. Lich Th Coll 52. **d** 54 **p** 55. C Ashton on Mersey St Mary *Ches* 54-60; Bablake Sch Cov from 60. *108 Duncroft Avenue, Coventry CV6 2BW* Keresley (020333) 6807

KELLY, William Robert. b 28. QUB BSc57. CITC 62. **d** 62 **p** 63. C Lurgan Ch Ch *D & D* 62-66; I Clondehorkey *D & R* 66-70; I Raheny w Coolock *D & G* 70-75; Peru 75-83; I Ballinderry *Conn* 83-89; Hon Can Peru 83; I Belf St Aid *Conn* from 89. *St Aidan's Rectory, 35 Eglantine Avenue, Belfast BT9 6DW* Belfast (0232) 666741

KELSEY, Michael Ray. b 22. FEPA57. Wycliffe Hall Ox 60. **d** 62 **p** 63. V Scarborough St Jas *York* 68-71; Asst to the Gen Sec USCL 71-74; V Blackheath St Jo *S'wark* 74-87; rtd 87; Perm to Offic *St E* from 88. *25 Prospect Place, Leiston, Suffolk IP16 4AL* Leiston (0728) 830975

KELSHAW, Terence. b 36. Lon Univ DipTh67. Oak Hill Th Coll. **d** 67 **p** 68. C Clifton Ch Ch w Em *Bris* 67-71; C Woking St Jo *Guildf* 71-73; V Bris H Trin *Bris* 73-75; P-in-c Easton St Gabr w St Laur 73-75; V Easton H Trin w St Gabr and St Lawr 75-80; P-in-c Barton Hill St Luke w Ch Ch 76-80; USA from 80. *4304 Carlisle Northeast, Albuquerque, New Mexico 87107, USA*

KELSO, Andrew John. b 47. LRAM73 Lon Univ BA70. St Jo Coll Nottm 83. **d** 85 **p** 86. C Gorleston St Mary *Nor* 85-87; C Hellesdon 87-90; TV Ipsley *Worc* from 90. *Matchborough Vicarage, Winward Road, Redditch B98 0SX* Redditch (0527) 29098

KELSO, William Thomas Proctor. b 19. TCD BA41 MA45. CITC 43. **d** 43 **p** 44. R Blendworth, Chalton and Idsworth *Portsm* 63-70; V Balham Hill Ascension *S'wark* 70-78; Perm to Offic *Chich* from 78; Chapl and Tutor Whittington Coll Felbridge 78-84; rtd 84; Perm to Offic *S'wark* from 84. *St Martin's Cottage, 20 Kew Foot Road, Richmond, Surrey TW9 2SS* 081-948 2678

KEMBALL, Eric. b 57. Mert Coll Ox BA80 PGCE81 MA84 Leeds Univ BA83. Coll of Resurr Mirfield 81. **d** 84 **p** 85. C Lich St Chad *Lich* 84-88; V Wednesfield St Greg from 88. *St Gregory's Vicarage, 112 Long Knowle Lane, Wednesfield, Wolverhampton WV11 1JQ* Wolverhampton (0902) 731677

KEMM, William St John. b 39. Birm Univ BA62 MA65. Ridley Hall Cam 62. **d** 64 **p** 65. C Kingswinford H Trin *Lich* 64-68; C Hednesford 68-71; V Hanbury 71-76; R Berrow and Breane *B & W* from 76. *The Rectory, Parsonage Road, Berrow, Burnham-on-Sea, Somerset TA8 2NJ* Burnham-on-Sea (0278) 782301

KEMP, Allan. b 43. Bps' Coll Cheshunt 65 Oak Hill Th Coll 67. **d** 68 **p** 69. C Tunbridge Wells St Jas *Roch* 68-76; V Becontree St Mary *Chelmsf* 76-90; RD Barking and Dagenham 81-86; V Gt w Lt Chesterford from 90. *The Vicarage, Great Chesterford, Saffron Walden, Essex CB10 1NP* Saffron Walden (0799) 30317

KEMP, Allan James. b 22. Fitzw Ho Cam BA48. Wells Th Coll 49. **d** 50 **p** 51. C Speke All SS *Liv* 50-54; V Askern *Sheff* 54-58; New Zealand from 58. *Branwell, 138 Bethels Road, RD 1, Henderson, New Zealand* Henderson (9) 810-9898

KEMP, Miss Audrey. b 26. MSR49. Gilmore Ho 62. **dss** 69 **d** 87. S Ockendon Hosp 70-71; N Greenford All Hallows *Lon* 71-72; Feltham 72-80; Brentford St Faith 80-83; Hanworth All SS 83-85; Hanworth St Geo 85-87; Par Dn 87-88; rtd 88; Perm to Offic *B & W* from 88; Hon Par Dn Ditcheat w E Pennard and Pylle from 89. *25 Victoria Court, Castle Cary, Somerset BA7 7BX* Castle Cary (0963) 51276

KEMP, Barry. b 48. St Edm Hall Ox BA70 MA75 Nottm Univ DipTh73 Newc Univ CertEd82. Linc Th Coll 71. **d** 74 **p** 75. C Ashton Ch Man 74-77; CF 77-81; C Dunston *Dur* 81-83; Perm to Offic *Newc* 83-87; C Monkseaton St Mary 88. *18 Balmoral Gardens, Monkseaton, Whitley Bay, Tyne & Wear NE26 3LU* 091-252 5509

KEMP, Canon Bernard Henry. b 06. St Chad's Coll Dur BA26 MA46 DipTh46. **d** 29 **p** 30. V Guernsey St Steph *Win* 63-81; rtd 81; Perm to Offic *Win* from 81. *Carrefour, La Haye du Puits, Castel, Guernsey, Channel Islands* Guernsey (0481) 56081

KEMP, Christopher Michael. b 48. K Coll Lon BD71 AKC71. St Aug Coll Cant 75. **d** 76 **p** 77. C Weaverham *Ches* 76-79; C Latchford St Jas 79-82; P-in-c Sandbach Heath 82-88; V Macclesfield St Paul 88-89; C Cheadle Hulme All SS from 89. *3 Hulme Hall Crescent, Cheadle Hulme, Cheadle, Cheshire SK8 6LG* 061-485 8935

KEMP, Clive Warren. b 36. Sheff Univ BSc60. Clifton Th Coll 62. **d** 64 **p** 65. C Wandsworth All SS *S'wark* 64-67; C Normanton *Wakef* 67-71; V Sandal St Cath 71-76; C

Chapeltown *Sheff* 85-87; V Sheff St Jo from 87. *49 Norfolk Park Avenue, Sheffield S2 2RA* Sheffield (0742) 759998

KEMP, Eric Nelson. b 05. Lich Th Coll 37. **d** 40 **p** 41. USA 68-70; C Hawksworth w Scarrington *S'well* 70-71; rtd 71; P-in-c Morley *Derby* 81-82. *29 Capel Court, The Burgage, Prestbury, Cheltenham, Glos GL52 3EL* Cheltenham (0242) 261339

✠**KEMP, Rt Rev Eric Waldram.** b 15. FRHistS51 Ex Coll Ox BA36 MA40 BD44 DD61 Sussex Univ Hon DLitt. St Steph Ho Ox 36. **d** 39 **p** 40 **c** 74. C Newtown St Luke *Win* 39-41; Lib Pusey Ho 41-46; Chapl Ch Ch Ox 43-46; Tutor and Chapl Ex Coll Ox 46-69; Can and Preb Linc Cathl *Linc* from 52; Chapl to HM The Queen 67-69; Dean Worc 69-74; Bp Chich from 74. *The Palace, Chichester, W Sussex PO19 1PY* Chichester (0243) 782161

KEMP, Geoffrey Bernard. b 20. Lon Univ BD43. ALCD42. **d** 43 **p** 44. V Hadleigh St Barn *Chelmsf* 60-79; R Kelvedon Hatch 79-86; V Navestock 79-86; rtd 86; Perm to Offic *St E* and *Chelmsf* from 86. *24 Roman Way, Felixstowe, Suffolk IP11 9NJ* Felixstowe (0394) 276691

KEMP, Jack Noel. b 14. Univ Coll Lon BA36 MA38. Wycliffe Hall Ox 55. **d** 55 **p** 56. V Four Elms Roch 68-80; rtd 80; Perm to Offic *Cant* from 81. *L'Ancresse, 16 Church Street, Whitstable, Kent CT5 1PJ* Whitstable (0227) 265379

KEMP, John Graham Edwin. b 29. Bris Univ BA51 Lon Univ BD65. Wells Th Coll 63. **d** 65 **p** 66. C Maidenhead St Luke *Ox* 65-70; V Highmore 70-78; R Rotherfield Greys 70-78; Dep Dir Tr Scheme for NSM 78-84; P-in-c Taplow 78-82; TV Burnham w Dropmore, Hitcham and Taplow 82-84; Prin E Anglian Minl Tr Course from 84. *201A Milton Road, Cambridge CB4 1XG* Cambridge (0223) 423633 or 322633

KEMP, John Robert Deverall. b 42. City Univ BSc65 BD69. Oak Hill Th Coll 66. **d** 70 **p** 71. C Fulham Ch Ch *Lon* 70-73; C Widford *Chelmsf* 73-79; P-in-c New Thundersley 79-84; V from 84; Chapl HM Pris Bullwood Hall from 79. *St George's Vicarage, 89 Rushbottom Lane, Benfleet, Essex SS7 4DN* South Benfleet (0268) 792088

KEMP, Michael Rouse. b 36. Called to the Bar (Gray's Inn) 59. Sarum & Wells Th Coll 70. **d** 72 **p** 73. C Brompton H Trin *Lon* 72-76; V Crookes St Tim *Sheff* 76-81; V Norton Woodseats St Chad 81-87; P-in-c Mottingham St Andr *S'wark* from 87. *St Andrew's Rectory, 233 Court Road, London SE9 4TQ* 081-857 1691

KEMP, William Frederick. b 13. St Aug Coll Cant 38. **d** 40 **p** 41. R Denton w Wootton and Swingfield *Cant* 64-79; rtd 79; Perm to Offic *Cant* 79-80; Hon Min Can Cant Cathl from 80. *12 Chantry Court, St Radigund's Street, Canterbury, Kent CT1 2AD* Canterbury (0227) 462261

KEMP-WELCH, Noel Henry. b 10. K Coll Cam BA33 MA37. Cuddesdon Coll 33. **d** 35 **p** 36. Chapl St Pet Sch York 56-76; rtd 76. *Moor House, Sutton Road, Wigginton, York YO3 8RB* York (0904) 769029

KEMPSTER, Robert Alec. b 29. Selw Coll Cam MA53. Coll of Resurr Mirfield 53. **d** 55 **p** 56. C-in-c S'wark All Hallows CD *S'wark* 57-70; Chapl Evelina Children's Hosp 57-70; Guy's Hosp Lon 70-81; Nat Hosp for Nervous Diseases Lon 81-89; Chapl Convent Companions Jes Gd Shep W Ogwell 89; rtd 90; Perm to Offic *Ex* from 90. *15A Seymour Road, Newton Abbot, Devon TQ12 2PT* Newton Abbot (0626) 61720

KEMPTHORNE, Renatus. b 39. Wadh Coll Ox BA60 DipTh61 MA64. Wycliffe Hall Ox 60. **d** 62 **p** 63. C Stoke *Cov* 62-65; New Zealand 65-68 and from 83; TV Wytham *Ox* 68-75; Chapl Bp Grosseteste Coll Linc 75-83. *140 Nile Street, Nelson, New Zealand* Nelson (54) 623694

KENCHINGTON (nee BALLANTYNE), Mrs Jane Elizabeth Ballantyne. b 58. Hull Univ BSc79 Cam Univ PGCE83. Westcott Ho Cam 88. **d** 90. C Winchcombe, Gretton, Sudeley Manor etc *Glouc* from 90. *St Peter's House, 12A Barksdale, Winchcombe, Cheltenham, Glos GL54 5QW* Cheltenham (0242) 604268

KENCHINGTON, Paul Henry. b 54. Worc Coll Ox MA76. St Jo Coll Nottm BA81. **d** 82 **p** 83. C Scarborough St Mary w Ch Ch and H Apostles *York* 82-85; C Caversham and Mapledurham *Ox* 85-89; V Hucclecote *Glouc* from 89. *128 Hucclecote Road, Gloucester GL3 3SB* Gloucester (0452) 610568

KENDAL, Stephen. b 35. Leeds Univ BA59. Coll of Resurr Mirfield 59. **d** 61 **p** 62. C Seaton Hirst *Newc* 61-63; C Newc St Geo 63-66; C Gosforth All SS 66-70; Ind Chapl *Llan* 70-78; Ind Chapl *Dur* 78-91; Hon C Houghton le Spring 78-90; Ind Chapl *Worc* from 91.

15 St John's Avenue, Kidderminster, Worcs DY11 6AT Kidderminster (0562) 823929

KENDALL, Alastair Geoffrey. b 55. BSc DipTh. St Jo Coll Nottm DPS. **d** 84 **p** 85. C Glouc St Aldate *Glouc* 84-87; C Sheff St Jo *Sheff* from 87. *48 Glencoe Road, Sheffield S2 2SR* Sheffield (0742) 759996

KENDALL, Canon Bartholomew John. b 09. Pemb Coll Ox BA32. Wycliffe Hall Ox 33. **d** 35 **p** 36. V S'wark St Jude *S'wark* 48-75; rtd 75. *26 Fairview Road, Hungerford, Berks RG17 0BT* Hungerford (0488) 682264

KENDALL, Canon Cosmo Norman. b 13. Keble Coll Ox BA38 MA42. Cuddesdon Coll 38. **d** 39 **p** 40. R Buxhall w Shelland *St E* 49-84; P-in-c from 84; Hon Can St E Cathl from 77; rtd 84. *The Rectory, Buxhall, Stowmarket, Suffolk IP14 3DJ* Rattlesden (0449) 736236

KENDALL, Edward Oliver Vaughan. b 33. Dur Univ BA59. Ridley Hall Cam. **d** 61 **p** 62. C Corsham *Bris* 61-64; C Portsea St Mary *Portsm* 64-67; Asst Chapl HM Pris Pentonville 67-68; Chapl HM Borstal Portland 68-71; Lic to Offic *Bradf* from 71. *Aldby House, Stackhouse, Settle, N Yorkshire BD24 0DW* Settle (07292) 3555

KENDALL, Frank. b 40. FRSA90 CCC Cam BA62 MA68. S'wark Ord Course 74. **d** 74 **p** 75. NSM Lingfield *S'wark* 74-75 and 78-82; NSM Sketty *S & B* 75-78; NSM Limpsfield and Titsey *S'wark* 82-84; Lic to Offic *Man* 84-89; Liv from 89. *Cromwell Villa, 260 Prescot Road, St Helens, Merseyside WA10 3HR* St Helens (0744) 27626

KENDALL, George Vincent. b 21. Edin Th Coll 46. **d** 48 **p** 49. P-in-c Gretna *Glas* 56-90; P-in-c Langholm 56-90; rtd 90. *9 Kestrel Hill, Gretna, Carlisle CA6 5DH* Gretna (0461) 37004

KENDALL, Gordon Sydney. b 41. **d** 72 **p** 74. Hon C Old Ford St Paul w St Steph and St Mark *Lon* 72-82; Hon C Homerton St Luke from 86; Chapl Hackney Hosp Gp Lon and Chapl Asst Homerton Hosp Lon from 87. *The Chaplain's Office, Homerton Hospital, Homerton Road, London E9 6BE* 081-985 5555

KENDALL, Miss Jacqueline Ann. b 63. Univ of Wales (Abth) BA85. Cranmer Hall Dur 88. **d** 91. Par Dn Stockport St Sav *Ches* from 91. *48 Claremont Road, Stockport, Cheshire SK2 7DQ* 061-487 1894

KENDRA, Kenneth Ernest. b 13. OBE66. Leeds Univ BA41 MA48. Linc Th Coll 40. **d** 42 **p** 43. QHC 70; RD Alverstoke *Portsm* 71-79; V Lee-on-the-Solent 71-80; rtd 80. *Highfields, Castle Hill Lane, Mere, Warminster, Wilts BA12 6JB* Mere (0747) 860823

KENDRA, Dr Neil Stuart. b 46. FITD84 Leeds Univ BA67 Univ of Wales (Swansea) DipAD72 Bradf Univ MSc80 PhD84. Linc Th Coll 67. **d** 69 **p** 70. C Allerton *Liv* 69-72; Ldr Leeds City Cen Detached Youth Work Project 73-75; Dioc Youth Officer *Ripon* 75-77; Lect Ilkley Coll 77-78; Sen Lect Bradf and Ilkley Community Coll 78-88; Hd Community & Youth Studies St Martin's Coll from 88. *St Martin's College, Lancaster LA1 3JD* Lancaster (0524) 63446

KENDREW, Geoffrey David. b 42. K Coll Lon BD66 AKC66. **d** 67 **p** 68. C Bourne *Guildf* 67-70; C Haslemere 70-76; V Derby St Barn *Derby* from 76. *St Barnabas' Vicarage, 122 Radbourne Street, Derby DE3 3BU* Derby (0332) 42553

KENDRICK, Canon Desmond Max. b 22. Leeds Univ BA47. Wycliffe Hall Ox 50. **d** 52 **p** 53. Chapl Leeds Road Hosp Bradf 54-77; V Bradf St Clem *Bradf* 54-77; RD Bradf 63-73; Hon Can Bradf Cathl 69-89; P Otley 77-89; Chapl Wharfedale Gen Hosp 77-90; rtd 89. *26 Ashtofts Mount, Guiseley, W Yorkshire LS20 9DB* Guiseley (0943) 870430

KENDRICK, Ronald Horace. b 35. Univ of Wales (Ban) BD78 DPS79. St Deiniol's Hawarden. **d** 82 **p** 83. C Wrexham *St As* 82-85; R Llanelian and Bettws-yn-Rhos from 85. *The Rectory, Rhodfa Sant Elian, Colwyn Bay, Clwyd LL29 1XX* Colwyn Bay (0492) 517274

KENNABY, Very Rev Noel Martin. b 05. Qu Coll Cam BA28 MA32. Westcott Ho Cam. **d** 29 **p** 30. Dean St Alb 64-73; rtd 73. *Delapre House, St Andrew's Road, Bridport, Dorset DT6 3BZ* Bridport (0308) 23953

KENNARD, Mark Philip Donald. b 60. Man Univ BSc82. Cranmer Hall Dur 85. **d** 88 **p** 89. C Newark w Hawton, Cotham and Shelton *S'well* 88-89; C Newark-upon-Trent 89-91; C Cropwell Bishop w Colston Bassett, Granby etc from 91. *4 Granby Hill, Granby, Nottingham NG13 9PQ* Whatton (0949) 50774

KENNARD, Ronald Malcolm. b 15. ACA39 FCA60. Chich Th Coll 74. **d** 75 **p** 76. Hon C Cuckfield *Chich* 75-79; P-in-c Elsted w Treyford and Didling 79-83; Perm to

Offic from 83. *35 Harberton Crescent, Chichester, W Sussex PO19 4NY* Chichester (0243) 528623

KENNAUGH, Canon Thomas Edward. b 17. Keble Coll Ox BA40 MA45 DipTh41. Bps' Coll Cheshunt. **d** 41 **p** 42. R Kirkby Thore w Temple Sowerby *Carl* 68-73; R Flixton St Mich *Man* 73-83; RD Stretford 77-83; rtd 84; Perm to Offic *Ches* from 84. *12 Derwent Road, Meols, Wirral, Merseyside L47 8XZ* 051-632 2590

KENNEDY, Anthony Reeves. b 32. Lon Univ DipTh67. Roch Th Coll 64. **d** 67 **p** 68. C Ross *Heref* 67-69; C Marfleet *York* 69-71; TV 72-76; V Lightwater *Guildf* 76-83; V W Ham *Chelmsf* 83-89; V Lutton w Gedney Drove End, Dawsmere *Linc* from 89. *The Vicarage, Lowgate, Lutton, Spalding, Lincs PE12 9HP* Holbeach (0406) 364199

KENNEDY, Arthur. b 57. St Pet Coll Ox BA79 MA83. St Jo Coll Nottm 83. **d** 85 **p** 86. C Nor Heartsease St Fran *Nor* 85-89; C Tadley St Pet *Win* 89-91; R Farmborough, Marksbury and Stanton Prior *B & W* from 91. *The Rectory, Church Lane, Farmborough, Bath BA3 1AN* Timsbury (0761) 70727

KENNEDY, Brian McMahon. b 11. TCD BA33 MA38. **d** 34 **p** 35. I Clonmel Union *C, C & R* 68-85; Chapl Cork Miss to Seamen & Chapl Irish Navy 68-85; rtd 85. *22 Strathearn Park, Belfast BT42GN* Belfast (0232) 768046

KENNEDY, Carolyn Ruth. b 59. Univ of Wales (Ban) BA81 PGCE85. Ripon Coll Cuddesdon BA90. **d** 91. C Frodingham *Linc* from 91. *66 Church Lane, Scunthorpe, S Humberside DN15 7AF* Scunthorpe (0724) 848171

KENNEDY, David George. b 46. Hull Univ BEd71 MA76. Linc Th Coll 77. **d** 79 **p** 80. C Linc St Faith and St Martin w St Pet *Linc* 79-82; V Bilton St Pet *York* 82-90; V New Seaham *Dur* from 90. *Christ Church Vicarage, Station Road, Seaham, Co Durham SR7 0BH* 091-581 3270

KENNEDY, David John. b 57. St Jo Coll Dur BA78 Nottm Univ MTh81. St Jo Coll Nottm 79. **d** 81 **p** 82. C Tudhoe Grange *Dur* 81-87; C Merrington 84-87; Tutor Qu Coll Birm from 88. *The Queen's College, Somerset Road, Edgbaston, Birmingham B15 2QH* 021-454 8180 or 452 1805

KENNEDY, Francis Robert Dixon. b 14. Wadh Coll Ox BA38 MA43. Wycliffe Hall Ox 43. **d** 43 **p** 44. R Caythorpe *Linc* 71-81; rtd 81; Perm to Offic *Chich* from 81. *99 Tarring Road, Worthing, W Sussex BN11 4HB* Worthing (0903) 201830

KENNEDY, James Ernest. b 20. TCD BA46 MA51. CITC 46. **d** 46 **p** 47. I Errigal w Desertoghill *D & R* 67-81; rtd 81. *38 Prospect Road, Portstewart, Co Derry BT55 7LQ* Portstewart (026583) 2052

KENNEDY, John Wilkinson. b 20. TCD BA44 LLB44 MA50. Qu Coll Birm 48. **d** 50 **p** 51. V Doncaster St Jas *Sheff* 60-70; V Anlaby St Pet *York* 70-80; V Cloughton 80-85; P-in-c Hackness w Harwood Dale 81-85; rtd 85. *37 Coxwold View, Wetherby, W Yorkshire LS22 4PU* Wetherby (0937) 64524

KENNEDY, Michael Charles. b 39. TCD BA63 MA BD79 Open Univ PhD87. CITC 63. **d** 63 **p** 64. C Drumglass *Arm* 63-66; I Lisnadill w Kildarton from 66; Warden Dioc Guild of Lay Readers from 74; Hon VC Arm Cathl from 75; Tutor for Aux Min (Arm) from 82. *Lisnadill Rectory, 60 Newtownhamilton Road, Armagh BT60 2PW* Armagh (0861) 523630

KENNEDY, Paul Joseph Alan. b 57. Sarum & Wells Th Coll. **d** 84 **p** 85. C Shildon *Dur* 84-85; C Shildon w Eldon 85-86; C Shotton *St As* 86-88; V Waterhouses *Dur* from 88. *21 The Wynds, Esh Winning, Durham DH7 9DT* 091-373 4273

KENNEDY, Ross Kenneth. b 40. Edin Th Coll 83. **d** 85 **p** 86. C Hexham *Newc* 85-89; TV Glendale Gp from 89. *Eglingham Vicarage, Alnwick, Northd NE66 2TX* Powburn (066578) 250

KENNEDY, William Edmund. b 20. QUB BA43 TCD BA45 MA48. **d** 45 **p** 46. I Ballyculter w Kilclief *D & D* 57-85; rtd 85. *Shalom, 8 Dunnanew Road, Seaforde, Downpatrick, Co Down BT30 6PJ* Seaforde (039687) 706

KENNEDY-BELL, Preb Winnington Douglas. b 15. Keble Coll Ox BA38 MA42. Wells Th Coll 38. **d** 39 **p** 40. Overseas Relig Broadcasting Org BBC 48-75; Reader of The Temple Lon from 55; Preb St Paul's Cathl *Lon* from 73; Dep P-in-O to HM The Queen from 76; rtd 80. *1 Victoria Cottages, Kew Gardens, Richmond, Surrey TW9 3NW* 081-940 5385

KENNEN, Harry. b 16. DSC45. Sheff Univ BA38. Bps' Coll Cheshunt 38. **d** 40 **p** 41. V Whitchurch *Ex* 70-77; R Highweek and Teigngrace 77-81; rtd 81; Lic to Offic

Ex from 81. *5 Trafalgar Lawn, Barnstaple, Devon EX32 9BD* Barnstaple (0271) 43234

KENNERLEY, Mrs Katherine Virginia. Somerville Coll Ox BA58 MA65 Irish Sch of Ecum DipEcum84 TCD BA86. CITC 86. **d** 88 **p** 90. Lect CITC from 88; NSM Bray *D & G* from 88. *4 Seafield Terrace, Dalkey, Co Dublin, Irish Republic* Dublin (1) 285-9595 or 975506

KENNETH, Brother. *See* PENFOLD, Kenneth Duncan

KENNETT-ORPWOOD, Jason Robert. b 55. Llan St Mich DipTh77 DPS78. **d** 78 **p** 79. Chapl St Woolos Cathl *Mon* 78-82; Chapl St Woolos Hosp Newport 79-82; Dioc Youth Chapl *Mon* 82-85; V Cwmcarn 82-85; TV Wrexham *St As* 85-89; V Bistre from 89. *Bistre Vicarage, Mold Road, Buckley, Clwyd CH7 2NH* Buckley (0244) 550947

KENNEY, Peter. b 50. Edin Univ BD75. Edin Th Coll 73. **d** 76 **p** 77. C Cullercoats St Geo *Newc* 76-81; TV Whorlton 81-88; P-in-c N Gosforth 88; TR Ch the King in the Dio of Newc from 88. *North Gosforth Vicarage, Wideopen, Newcastle upon Tyne NE13 6NH* 091-236 2280

KENNING, Michael Stephen. b 47. St Chad's Coll Dur BA68. Westcott Ho Cam 69. **d** 71 **p** 72. C Hythe *Cant* 71-75; TV Bow w Bromley St Leon *Lon* 75-77; C-in-c W Leigh CD *Portsm* 77-81; V Lee-on-the-Solent from 81. *The Vicarage, Victoria Square, Lee-on-the-Solent, Hants PO13 9NF* Lee-on-the-Solent (0705) 550269

KENNINGTON, John Paul. b 61. Collingwood Coll Dur BA85. St Steph Ho Ox BA87. **d** 88 **p** 89. C Headington *Ox* from 88. *8 Maltfield Road, Oxford OX3 9RG* Oxford (0865) 750354

KENNY, Charles John. b 39. LGSM74 QUB BA61 MEd78. CITC 69. **d** 69 **p** 70. C Belf St Paul *Conn* 69-71; Hd of RE Grosvenor High Sch from 71; Lic to Offic from 84. *45 Deramore Drive, Belfast BT9 5JS* Belfast (0232) 669632

KENNY, Frederick William Bouvier. b 28. TCD BA53 DipEd54 MA56 LTh. **d** 56 **p** 57. C Ballymacarrett St Patr *D & D* 56-58; C Blackpool St Jo *Blackb* 58-61; Chapl Preston R Hosp 61-66; V Preston St Paul *Blackb* 61-66; Youth Adv CMS (Lon) 66-70; Youth Sec (Ireland) CMS 70-75; I Belf St Clem *D & D* 75-80; V Preston St Cuth *Blackb* 80-86; TV Bushbury *Lich* 86-90; P-in-c Stambridge *Chelmsf* from 90; Chapl Rochford Hosp from 90. *The Rectory, Stambridge, Rochford, Essex SS4 2AR* Southend-on-Sea (0702) 258272

KENNY, Thomas Patrick Francis. b 49. Univ of Wales (Cardiff) DipTh76. St Mich Coll Llan 73. **d** 76 **p** 77. C Rochdale *Man* 76-80; R Abbey Hey 80-86; V Stockton Heath *Ches* from 86. *The Vicarage, 91 Walton Road, Stockton Heath, Warrington WA4 6NR* Warrington (0925) 61396

KENNY, Canon Thomas Percival Robert. b 27. TCD BA48 MA51. **d** 50 **p** 51. I Magherafelt *Arm* 66-74; I Derryloran 74-82; CMS 83-88; Nigeria 83-88; Hon Can Owerri from 84; I Cloonclare w Killasnett and Drumlease *K, E & A* 88-90; rtd 90. *26 Clanbrassil Drive, Portadown, Craigavon, Co Armagh BT63 5EH* Portadown (0762) 336479

KENRICK, Kenneth David Norman. b 44. Liv Univ RMN. Ripon Hall Ox 70 NW Ord Course 77. **d** 77 **p** 78. C Stockport St Geo *Ches* 77-83; R Stockport St Thos 83-85; R Stockport St Thos w St Pet from 86. *St Thomas's Rectory, 25 Heath Road, Stockport, Cheshire SK2 6JJ* 061-483 2483

KENSINGTON, Area Bishop of. *See* HUGHES, Rt Rev John George

KENT, Dr Christopher Alfred. b 48. CEng77 MIChemE77 Birm Univ BSc69 PhD72 Nottm Univ DipTh83. St Jo Coll Nottm 82. **d** 84 **p** 85. C Bucknall and Bagnall *Lich* 84-86; Hon C Halesowen *Worc* from 86. *40 County Park Avenue, Halesowen, W Midlands B62 8SP* 021-550 3132

KENT, David. b 44. CEng MIMechE. N Ord Course. **d** 83 **p** 84. NSM Huddersfield St Pet and All SS *Wakef* from 83. *118 Woodside Road, Huddersfield HD4 5JW* Huddersfield (0484) 654058

KENT, Frank. b 44. ARCM76 Open Univ BA82. Ridley Hall Cam. **d** 86 **p** 87. C Faversham *Cant* 86-89; R Lyminge w Paddlesworth, Stanford w Postling etc from 89. *The Rectory, Rectory Lane, Lyminge, Folkestone, Kent CT18 8EG* Lyminge (0303) 862432

KENT, Keith Meredith. b 32. Lon Univ DipTh57. St Aid Birkenhead 55. **d** 58 **p** 59. C Fulwood Ch Ch *Blackb* 58-60; C Everton St Chrys *Liv* 60-62; C Litherland St Phil 64-68; P-in-c Everton St Polycarp 68-74; V Liv All So Springwood 74-78; V Carr Mill 78-86; V Beddgelert *Ban* from 86. *St Mary's Vicarage, 15 Oberon Wood,*

Beddgelert, Caernarfon, Gwynedd LL55 4YW Beddgelert (076686) 584

KENT, Canon Michael Patrick. b 27. St Edm Hall Ox BA50 MA52. Cuddesdon Coll 50. **d** 52 **p** 53. C W Hartlepool St Aid *Dur* 52-57; C-in-c Pennywell St Thos and Grindon St Oswald CD 57-70; V Cockerton from 70; RD Darlington 79-84; Hon Can Dur Cathl from 83. *St Mary's Vicarage, Cockerton, Darlington, Co Durham DL3 9EX* Darlington (0325) 463705

KENT, Neville. b 40. Sarum & Wells Th Coll 70. **d** 72 **p** 73. C Taunton St Andr *B & W* 72-77; R Bradf w Oake, Hillfarrance and Heathfield 77-89; Adv on Soc Concerns 80-87; RD Tone 87-89; V Worle from 89. *The Vicarage, 93 Church Road, Worle, Weston-super-Mare, Avon BS22 9EA* Weston-super-Mare (0934) 510694

KENT, Richard Hugh. b 38. Worc Coll Ox BA61 MA65. Chich Th Coll 61. **d** 63 **p** 64. C Emscote *Cov* 63-66; C Finham 66-70; V Dean Forest St Paul *Glouc* 70-75; V Glouc St Aldate 75-86; Chapl and Warden Harnhill Healing Cen from 86. *Harnhill Manor, Harnhill, Cirencester, Glos GL7 5PX* Cirencester (0285) 850283

KENT, Roger Anthony Edward. b 56. Kent Univ BA78. St Steph Ho Ox 79. **d** 81 **p** 82. C Ipswich All Hallows *St E* 81-84; C Poplar *Lon* 84-88; V Newington w Hartlip and Stockbury *Cant* from 88. *The Vicarage, Church Lane, Newington, Sittingbourne, Kent ME9 7JU* Newington (0795) 844345

KENT, Ronald. b 21. St Jo Coll Dur BA43 MA46. St Steph Ho Ox 79. **d** 45 **p** 46. Chapl Univ Coll of Ripon & York St Jo 65-76; Lic to Offic *Dur* from 76; rtd 86; P-in-c Nidd *Ripon* from 88. *The Vicarage, Nidd, Harrogate, N Yorkshire HG3 3BN* Harrogate (0423) 770060

KENTIGERN-FOX, William Poyntere Kentigern. b 38. AKC63. **d** 64 **p** 65. C S Mimms St Mary and Potters Bar *Lon* 64-67; C S Tottenham 67-70; P-in-c Duddington w Tixover *Pet* 70-76; R Barrowden and Wakerley 70-76; P-in-c Morcott w S Luffenham 75-77; R Barrowden and Wakerley w S Luffenham 77-79; R Byfield w Boddington 79-86; V Northn St Mich w St Edm from 86. *St Michael's Vicarage, 19 St Michael's Avenue, Northampton NN1 4JQ* Northampton (0604) 37928

KENWARD, Roger Nelson. b 34. Selw Coll Cam BA58 MA62. Ripon Hall Ox 58. **d** 60 **p** 61. C Paddington St Jas *Lon* 60-63; Chapl RAF 64-82; Asst Chapl-in-Chief RAF 82-89; R Laughton w Ripe and Chalvington *Chich* from 90. *The Rectory, Church Lane, Laughton, Lewes, E Sussex BN8 6AH* Ripe (032183) 642

KENWAY, Ian Michael. b 52. Leeds Univ BA74 Bris Univ PhD86. Coll of Resurr Mirfield 76. **d** 76 **p** 77. C Cov E *Cov* 76-79; C Southmead *Bris* 79-81; P-in-c Shaw Hill *Birm* 82-88; Asst Sec Gen Syn Bd for Soc Resp from 88; Hon C Rotherhithe H Trin *S'wark* from 89. *c/o Church House, Great Smith Street, London SW1P 3NZ* 071-222 9011

KENWAY, Robert Andrew. b 56. Bris Univ BA78. Westcott Ho Cam 80. **d** 82 **p** 83. C Birchfield *Birm* 82-85; C Queensbury All SS *Lon* 87-89; R Birm St Geo *Birm* from 89. *St George's Rectory, 100 Bridge Street West, Newtown, Birmingham B19 2YX* 021-359 2000

KENYON, Stanley Robert. b 31. Kelham Th Coll 51. **d** 55 **p** 56. C Eckington *Derby* 55-57; C Derby St Andr 57-59; C Lullington 59-61; C Nether and Over Seale 59-61; P-in-c Grimsby St Steph *Linc* 61-71; V Habrough 71-82; V E Halton 73-82; V Killingholme 73-82; V Barnetby le Wold Gp from 82. *The Vicarage, Barnetby, S Humberside DN38 6JL* Barnetby (0652) 688182

KEOGH, Anthony. b 35. St Mich Coll Llan 63. **d** 66 **p** 67. C Aberaman and Abercwmboi *Llan* 66-70; Hon C Penarth All SS 70-76; R Jersey H Trin *Win* from 76. *Holy Trinity Rectory, Jersey, Channel Islands* Jersey (0534) 61110

KEOGH, Henry James. b 39. TCD BA61 NUI BMus65. **d** 62 **p** 63. C Cork St Fin Barre's Cathl *C, C & R* 62-65; C Belf St Luke *Conn* 65-66; C Dromore Cathl *D & D* 66-68; I Castlecomer *C & O* 68-85; I Kilscoran w Killinick and Mulrankin from 85; Hon Chapl Miss to Seamen from 85. *The Rectory, Killinick, Wexford, Irish Republic* Wexford (53) 58989

KEOGH, Robert Gordon. b 56. TCD DipTh84. **d** 84 **p** 85. C Mossley *Conn* 84-87; I Taunagh w Kilmactranny, Ballysumaghan etc *K, E & A* 87-90; I Swanlinbar w Tomregan, Kinawley, Drumlane etc from 90. *The Rectory, Swanlinbar, Co Cavan, Irish Republic* Swanlinbar (49) 23404

KER, Desmond Agar-Ellis. b 15. Wells Th Coll 58. **d** 58 **p** 59. V Bovey Tracey St Jo *Ex* 70-80; rtd 80; Perm to Offic *S'wark* from 84. *St Silvan's House, Staffhurst Wood, Oxted, Surrey RH8 0RS* Oxted (0883) 723452

KERLEY, Brian Edwin. b 36. St Jo Coll Cam BA57 MA61. Linc Th Coll 59. **d** 61 **p** 62. C Sheerness H Trin w St Paul *Cant* 61-64; C St Laurence in Thanet 64-69; C Coulsdon St Andr *S'wark* 69-76; P-in-c Fulbourn *Ely* 76-77; R from 77; RD Quy from 83; P-in-c Gt Wilbraham from 86; P-in-c Lt Wilbraham from 86. *The Rectory, Apthorpe Street, Fulbourn, Cambridge CB1 5EY* Cambridge (0223) 880337

KERLEY, Patrick Thomas Stewart. b 42. Linc Th Coll. **d** 85 **p** 86. Hon C Thorpe *Nor* 85-90; C Wymondham from 90. *76A Norwich Road, Wymondham, Norfolk NR18 0SZ* Wymondham (0953) 605552

KERR, Anthony. Sheff Univ BA64 Man Univ CertEd65. N Ord Course. **d** 85 **p** 86. NSM Greenfield *Man* 85-87; NSM Leesfield from 87. *16 Netherlees, Spring Lane, Oldham OL4 5BA* 061-620 6512

KERR, Arthur Henry. LRAM47 TCD BA48 DA65. **d** 49 **p** 50. C Templemore *D & R* 49-50; C Dub Harold's Cross *D & G* 50-57; ICM 57-60; Chapl Rotunda Hosp 60-75; Lic to Offic *Conn* from 88. *Halothane, Mountsandel Road, Coleraine, Co Londonderry* Coleraine (0265) 44940

KERR, Charles Alexander Gray. b 33. Open Univ BA75 Birm Univ MA83 MA(Theol)88. Edin Th Coll 63. **d** 67 **p** 68. C Hawick *Edin* 67-70; C Edgbaston St Geo *Birm* 70-72; Chapl Birm Skin Hosp 70-75; P-in-c Quinton Road W St Boniface *Birm* 72-79; V 79-84; R Musselburgh *Edin* 84-86; P-in-c Prestonpans 84-86; rtd 86; Reighton w Speeton *York* from 89. *The Vicarage, Reighton, Filey, N Yorkshire* Scarborough (0723) 891839

KERR, David James. b 36. TCD BA58 MA61 BD61 HDipEd. **d** 60 **p** 61. C Belf Trin Coll Miss *Conn* 60-63; Dean's V St Patr Cathl Dub 63-66; Chapl Beechwood Park Sch St Alb from 66; C Flamstead *St Alb* from 74. *Beechwood Park School, Markyate, St Albans, Herts AL3 8AW* Luton (0582) 841191

KERR, Derek Preston. b 64. TCD BTh90. Oak Hill Th Coll. **d** 90 **p** 91. C Belf St Donard *D & D* from 90. *63 Sandhill Gardens, Belfast BT5 6FF* Belfast (0232) 659325

KERR, Miss Dora (Elizabeth). b 41. QUB BA65 Southn Univ DipEd66 Nottm Univ DipTh83. St Jo Coll Nottm 82. **dss** 84 **d** 87. Becontree St Mary *Chelmsf* 84-87; Par Dn 87-88; Par Dn Rushden w Newton Bromswold *Pet* from 88. *110 Whitehouse Court, Grove Road, Rushden, Northants NN10 0JW* Rushden (0933) 313779

KERR, George Cecil. b 36. TCD BA60 MA65. CITC 60. **d** 60 **p** 61. C Coleraine *Conn* 60-63; Div Master Annandale Gr Sch Belf 63-65; Dean of Residences QUB 65-74; Lic to Offic *D & D* from 75. *Christian Renewal Centre, Shore Road, Rostrevor, Co Down BT34 3ET* Rostrevor (06937) 38492

KERR, Mrs Jean. b 46. SS Hild & Bede Coll Dur CertEd69. N Ord Course 84. **d** 87. NSM Peel *Man* from 87; Par Dn Dixon Green 88-89; Par Dn New Bury from 89. *New Bury Vicarage, 130 Highfield Road, Farnworth, Bolton BL4 0AJ* Farnworth (0204) 72334

KERR, John Maxwell. b 43. MSOSc88 Toronto Univ BSc66 Leeds Univ MSc70 Nottm Univ DipTh76. Linc Th Coll 75. **d** 77 **p** 78. C New Windsor *Ox* 77-80; Asst Chapl Cheltenham Coll 80-81; Chapl 81-82; Asst Chapl Win Coll from 82; Hon C Win St Lawr and St Maurice w St Swithun *Win* from 84. *68 Kingsgate Street, Winchester, Hants SO23 9PE* Winchester (0962) 862317

KERR, Joseph Reid. b 43. St Steph Ho Ox 70. **d** 72. C Ox SS Phil and Jas *Ox* 72-74; Jamaica from 75. *The Rectory, King Street, Kingston, Jamaica WI* Jamaica (1809) 26888

KERR, Nicholas Ian. b 46. Em Coll Cam BA68 MA72. Westcott Ho Cam 74. **d** 77 **p** 78. C Mert St Mary *S'wark* 77-80; C Rainham *Roch* 80-84; Chapl Joyce Green Hosp Dartford 84-90; V Dartford St Edm *Roch* 84-90; V Lamorbey H Redeemer from 90. *The Vicarage, 64 Day's Lane, Sidcup, Kent DA15 8JR* 081-300 1508

KERR, Nigel Arthur. b 53. Univ of Wales (Cardiff) BA76. Westcott Ho Cam 88. **d** 90 **p** 91. C Oakham, Hambleton, Egleton, Braunston and Brooke *Pet* from 90. *45 Trent Road, Oakham, Leics LE15 6HE* Oakham (0572) 756211

KERR, Paul Turner. b 47. Cranmer Hall Dur 68. **d** 71 **p** 72. C Kingston upon Hull St Martin *York* 71-72; C Linthorpe 72-76; C Cherry Hinton St Jo *Ely* 76-78; Chapl Addenbrooke's Hosp Cam 76-78; TV Rochdale *Man* 78-84; Chapl Birch Hill Hosp Rochdale 78-84; V New Bury 84-87; TR from 87. *The Vicarage, 130 Highfield Road, Farnworth, Bolton BL4 0AJ* Farnworth (0204) 72334

KERR, Peter Albert Calvin. b 09. MC40. Called to the Bar (Gray's Inn) 62 Lon Univ BD30 LLB60 St Cath Soc

Ox BA32 MA37. Qu Coll Birm 37. **d** 37 **p** 37. C Aston SS Pet and Paul *Birm* 37-39; CF (TA - R of O) 39-59; Perm to Offic *Mon* from 81. *Hillside, Llanishen, Chepstow, Gwent NP6 6QD* Trelleck (0600) 860723

KERR, Canon Robert Andrew James. b 06. TCD BA26 MA62. CITC 27. **d** 29 **p** 30. I Derryvullen N *Clogh* 46-79; Preb Clogh Cathl 66-79; rtd 79. *12 Crichton Park, Tamlaght, Enniskillen, Co Fermanagh* Enniskillen (0365) 87405

KERR, Stephen Peter. b 46. TCD BA68 Edin Univ BD71 MPhil80. **d** 71 **p** 72. C Belf H Trin *Conn* 72-76; C Ballywillan 76-78; Lect Linc Th Coll 78-87; Dioc Officer for Adult Educn and Minl Tr *Worc* from 87; P-in-c Ombersley w Doverdale from 87. *The Rectory, Ombersley, Droitwich, Worcs WR9 0EW* Droitwich (0905) 620950

KERRIDGE, Donald George. b 32. Bede Coll Dur CertEd72 Hull Univ BA84. Wesley Coll Leeds 57 Bps' Coll Cheshunt 61. **d** 62 **p** 63. C Maniston *Ripon* 62-66; C Hawksworth Wood 66-71; Asst Chapl Brentwood Sch Essex 72-74; Lic to Offic *Linc* 81-89; R Tetney, Marshchapel and N Coates 89-91; P-in-c Linc St Swithin from 91; Asst Chapl Linc Co Hosp from 91. *St Swithin's Vicarage, Croft Street, Lincoln LN2 5AZ* Lincoln (0522) 527540

KERRIN, Albert Eric. b 26. Aber Univ MA51. Edin Th Coll 51. **d** 53 **p** 54. P-in-c Portpatrick *Glas* 69-91; P-in-c Stranraer 69-91; rtd 91. *15 London Road, Stranraer, Wigtownshire DG9 8AF* Stranraer (0776) 2822

KERRISON, Mrs Anne Edmonstone. b 23. Cranmer Hall Dur 69. **dss** 77 **d** 87. Hellesdon *Nor* 77-78; Ind Miss 78-79; Lic to Offic 79-88; Perm to Offic from 88. *Sloley Lodge, Sloley, Norwich NR12 8HE* Swanton Abbott (069269) 253

KERRUISH, Canon John Robert Joughin. b 16. Magd Coll Ox BA38 DipTh39 MA43. Wycliffe Hall Ox 39. **d** 40 **p** 41. V Branksome Park All SS *Sarum* 68-86; Can and Preb Sarum Cathl 85-86; rtd 86. *178 The Close, Salisbury* Salisbury (0722) 324371

KERRY, Martin John. b 55. Ox Univ MA78 Nottm Univ BA81 MTh83. St Jo Coll Nottm 79. **d** 82 **p** 83. C Everton St Geo *Liv* 82-85; Lic to Offic *S'well* from 85; Chapl Asst Nottm City Hosp 85-89; Chapl from 89. *The Chaplains' Office, City Hospital, Hucknall Road, Nottingham NG5 1BP* Nottingham (0602) 691169

KERSHAW, John Harvey. b 51. Coll of Resurr Mirfield 84. **d** 86 **p** 87. C Hollinwood *Man* 86-89; V Audenshaw St Hilda from 89. *St Hilda's Vicarage, Denton Road, Audenshaw, Manchester M34 5BL* 061-336 2310

KERSHAW, Savile. b 37. Bernard Gilpin Soc Dur 60 Chich Th Coll 61. **d** 64 **p** 65. C Staincliffe *Wakef* 64-66; C Saltley *Birm* 66-68; C Birm St Aid Small Heath 68-72; NSM Bordesley SS Alb and Patr from 88. *74 Longmore Road, Shirley, Solihull, W Midlands B90 3EE* 021-744 3470

KERSLEY, Stuart Casburn. b 40. CEng MIEE. Trin Coll Bris. **d** 82 **p** 83. C Lancing w Coombes *Chich* 82-87; TV Littlehampton and Wick 87-90; R Kingston Buci from 90. *The Rectory, Rectory Road, Shoreham-by-Sea, W Sussex BN43 6EB* Brighton (0273) 592591

KERSWILL, Anthony John. b 39. Lambeth STh85 Linc Th Coll 72. **d** 73 **p** 73. C Boultham *Linc* 73-76; P-in-c N Kelsey 76-83; P-in-c Cadney 76-83; V Gainsborough St Geo 83-91; V Bracebridge from 91. *The Vicarage, 60 Chiltern Road, Bracebridge, Lincoln LN5 8SE* Lincoln (0522) 32636

KESLAKE, Peter Ralegh. b 33. Sarum & Wells Th Coll. **d** 83 **p** 84. C Glouc St Geo w Whaddon *Glouc* 83-86; P-in-c France Lynch from 86. *The Vicarage, Brantwood Road, Chalford Hill, Stroud, Glos GL6 8BS* Brimscombe (0453) 883154

KESSLER, Edward Scharps. b 26. Princeton Univ BA47 Chicago Univ MA51 St Chad's Coll Dur DipTh66. **d** 66 **p** 67. C Hendon St Ignatius *Dur* 68-70; Dioc Planning Officer 70-75; P-in-c Kimblesworth 74-80; Perm to Offic *Sheff* from 87; rtd 89. *44 Hinde Street, Sheffield S4 8HJ* Sheffield (0742) 446827

KESTELL-CORNISH, Geoffrey. b 03. Bp's Univ Lennox LST32. **d** 32 **p** 33. V Bishops Tawton *Ex* 48-53; rtd 53; C Ilfracombe H Trin *Ex* 57-68; Perm to Offic from 68. *Flat 13, Mill Court, Mill Road, Barnstaple, Devon EX31 1JQ* Barnstaple (0271) 42566

KESTERTON, David William. b 59. Man Univ BSc80. Cranmer Hall Dur 85. **d** 88 **p** 89. C Cheddleton *Lich* from 88. *42 Hollow Lane, Cheddleton, Leek, Staffs ST13 7HP* Churnet Side (0538) 360225

KESTON, Dr Marion. b 44. Glas Univ MB, ChB68. St And Dioc Tr Course 87. **d** 90. NSM Dunfermline *St And*

from 90. *119 Rose Street, Dunfermline, Fife KY12 0QT* Dunfermline (0383) 620314

KETLEY, Michael James. b 39. DipHE81. Oak Hill Th Coll 79. **d** 81 **p** 82. C Bedhampton *Portsm* 81-85; R St Ive w Quethiock *Truro* 85-86; C Barkingside St Cedd *Chelmsf* from 90. *10 Marston Road, Ilford, Essex IG5 0LY* 081-551 3406

KETTLE, Alan Marshall. b 51. Leeds Univ BA72. Wycliffe Hall Ox MA78. **d** 78 **p** 79. C Llantwit Fadre *Llan* 78-81; Prov RE Adv Ch in Wales 81-84; Chapl Llandovery Coll from 84; P-in-c Cilycwm and Ystradffin w Rhandirmwyn etc *St D* from 85. *The Vicarage, Cilycwm, Llandovery, Dyfed SA20 0SP* Llandovery (0550) 21011

KETTLE, Arthur John Clare. b 05. ARCM30 LTCL39. Bps' Coll Cheshunt 64. **d** 65 **p** 66. R Wing w Pilton *Pet* 69-75; R Preston and Ridlington w Wing and Pilton 75-76; rtd 76; Perm to Offic *Pet* from 85. *61 South Street, Oakham, Leics LE15 6BG* Oakham (0572) 56301

KETTLE, David John. b 47. Bris Univ BSc69 MLitt86 Fitzw Coll Cam BA75 MA79. Westcott Ho Cam 73. **d** 76 **p** 77. C Bris St Andr Hartcliffe *Bris* 76-79; C Fishponds All SS 79-80; P-in-c 81-83; Perm to Offic *St E* from 83; New Zealand from 91. *22 Goodwin Crescent, Palmerston North, New Zealand*

KETTLE, Martin Drew. b 52. New Coll Ox BA74 Selw Coll Cam BA76 Cam Univ MA85. Ridley Hall Cam 74. **d** 77 **p** 78. C Enfield St Andr *Lon* 77-80; Chapl Ridley Hall Cam 80-84; V Hendon St Paul Mill Hill *Lon* from 85; AD W Barnet from 90. *St Paul's Vicarage, Hammers Lane, London NW7 4EA* 081-959 1856

KETTLE, Mrs Patricia Mary Carole. b 41. Worc Coll of Educn CertEd61 Lon Univ DipTh68. Dalton Ho Bris 66. **d** 87. C Wonersh *Guildf* from 87. *Wakehurst Cottage, Links Road, Bramley, Surrey GU5 0AL* Guildford (0483) 898856

KETTLE, Peter. b 51. K Coll Lon BD74 AKC74. St Aug Coll Cant 74. **d** 75 **p** 76. C Angell Town St Jo *S'wark* 75-78; C Putney St Mary 78-80; V Raynes Park St Sav 80-85; Perm to Offic from 85. *46 Allenswood, Albert Drive, London SW19 6JX* 081-785 3797

KEVILL-DAVIES, Christopher Charles. b 44. AKC69. St Aug Coll Cant 70. **d** 70 **p** 71. C Folkestone St Sav *Cant* 70-75; V Yaxley *Ely* 75-78; R Chevington w Hargrave and Whepstead w Brockley *St E* 78-86; Appeals Manager Dr Barnardos 86-88; Appeals Manager St Nich Hospice Bury St Edm 88-89; Perm to Offic *St Alb* 86-89; NSM Stansted Mountfitchet *Chelmsf* 87-89; R Barkway, Reed and Buckland w Barley *St Alb* from 89. *The Rectory, 135 High Street, Barkway, Royston, Herts SG8 8ED* Barkway (076384) 8077

KEVIS, Lionel William Graham. b 55. York Univ BA. Wycliffe Hall Ox 83. **d** 86 **p** 87. C Plaistow St Mary *Roch* 86-90; R Ash from 90. *The Rectory, The Street, Ash, Sevenoaks, Kent TN15 7HA* Ash Green (0474) 872209

KEW, William Richard. b 45. Lon Univ BD69. Lon Coll of Div LTh68. **d** 69 **p** 70. C Finchley St Paul Long Lane *Lon* 69-72; C Stoke Bishop *Bris* 72-76; USA from 76. *SPCK, PO Box 879, Sewanee, Tennessee 37375, USA* Chattanooga (615) 598-1103

KEY, Christopher Halstead. b 56. St Jo Coll Dur BA77 K Coll Lon MTh78. Ridley Hall Cam 79. **d** 81 **p** 82. C Balderstone *Man* 81-84; C Wandsworth All SS *S'wark* 84-88; C-in-c W Dulwich Em CD from 88. *Emmanuel Vicarage, 94 Clive Road, London SE21 8BU* 081-670 2793

KEY, John Christopher. b 36. Pemb Coll Cam BA60 MA65. **d** 62 **p** 63. C Rugby St Andr *Cov* 62-67; Papua New Guinea 68-71; V Cov St Geo *Cov* 71-76; RD Cov N 73-76; P-in-c Redditch St Steph *Worc* 76-81; Dioc Ecum Officer 80-81; Australia from 81. *16 Dunbar Close, Normanhurst, NSW, Australia 2076* Normanhurst (612) 635-7922 or 487-3910

KEY, Robert Frederick. b 52. Bris Univ BA73. Oak Hill Th Coll 74. **d** 76 **p** 77. C Ox St Ebbe w St Pet *Ox* 76-80; C Wallington H Trin *S'wark* 80-85; P-in-c Eynsham *Ox* 85; V Eynsham and Cassington 85-91; V Ox St Andr from 91. *The Vicarage, 46 Charlbury Road, Oxford OX2 6UX or, St Andrew's Church, Linton Road, Oxford OX2 6UG* Oxford (0865) 311695 or 311212

KEY, Roderick Charles. b 57. MTh. **d** 84 **p** 85. C Up Hatherley *Glouc* 84-87; V Glouc St Paul from 87. *St Paul's Vicarage, 2 King Edward's Avenue, Gloucester GL1 5DA* Gloucester (0452) 23732

KEYES, Alfred Edward de Hault. b 18. Keble Coll Ox BA39. Lich Th Coll 40. **d** 41 **p** 42. V Goathland *York* 63-73; R Rockbourne w Whitsbury *Win* 73-83; rtd 83; Perm to Offic *Ex* from 84. *7 Seaway Gardens, Preston, Paignton, Devon TQ3 2PE* Paignton (0803) 550303

KEYES, Graham George. b 44. St Cath Coll Cam MA Lanc Univ MA Nottm Univ MTh. E Midl Min Tr Course 82. **d** 84 **p** 85. C Evington *Leic* 84-86; Vice-Prin NE Ord Course 86-89; C Monkseaton St Mary *Newc* 86-89; P-in-c Newc St Hilda from 89. *31 Lily Avenue, Jesmond, Newcastle upon Tyne NE2 2SQ* 091-281 4998

KEYES, Mrs Iris Doreen. b 28. SRN. Gilmore Ho 69. dss 76 **d** 87. Egham Hythe *Guildf* 76-78; Chapl Asst St Pet Hosp Chertsey 78-82; Addlestone 83-86; Walton-on-Thames 86-87; C 87-89; rtd 89. *36 Finlay Gardens, Addlestone, Weybridge, Surrey KT15 2XN* Weybridge (0932) 846912

KEYTE, Douglas Joseph Henry. b 18. St Jo Coll Cam BA40 MA46. Wycliffe Hall Ox 46. **d** 48 **p** 49. Asst Master Co Gr Sch for Girls Sale 61-75; Hon C Charlestown *Man* 75-89; rtd 83; Hon C Pendleton St Thos w Charlestown *Man* from 89. *26 Heathfield Close, Sale, Cheshire M33 2PQ* 061-973 2844

KHAMBATTA, Neville Holbery. b 48. St Chad's Coll Dur BA74. S'wark Ord Course 81. **d** 84 **p** 85. NSM Thornton Heath St Jude w St Aid *S'wark* 84-87; Asst Chapl Em Sch Wandsworth 84-87; Asst Warden Horstead Cen from 87; NSM Coltishall w Gt Hautbois and Horstead *Nor* from 87. *Horstead Centre, Rectory Road, Horstead, Norwich NR12 7EP* Norwich (0603) 737215

KHOO, Boon-Hor. b 31. FBCO. Llan Dioc Tr Scheme. **d** 87 **p** 88. NSM Llan w Capel Llanilterne *Llan* from 87. *8 Verlands Close, Llandaff, Cardiff CF5 2BQ* Cardiff (0222) 561478

KICHENSIDE, Mark Gregory. b 53. Nottm Univ BTh83. St Jo Coll Nottm 80. **d** 83 **p** 84. C Orpington Ch Ch *Roch* 83-86; C Bexley St Jo 86-90; V Blendon from 90. *37 Bladindon Drive, Bexley, Kent DA5 3BS* 081-301 5387

KIDD, Anthony John Eric. b 38. Solicitor. Oak Hill NSM Course. **d** 89 **p** 90. NSM Rawdon *Bradf* 89-91; C Ilkley All SS from 91. *106 Little Lane, Ilkley, W Yorkshire LS29 8JJ* Ilkley (0943) 608055

KIDD, Donald Worcester. b 16. ALCD34. **d** 39 **p** 40. C Milton next Gravesend Ch Ch *Roch* 39-40; C Dartford H Trin 40-44; CF (EC) 44-48; Canada from 48. *RR 2, Renfrew, Ontario, Canada, K7V 3Z5*

KIDD, John Alan. b 32. Pemb Coll Cam BA58 MA61. Ridley Hall Cam 57. **d** 61 **p** 62. C Onslow Square St Paul *Lon* 61-65; S Africa 65-67; Uganda 67-69; P-in-c Mayfair Ch Ch *Lon* 69-75; V 75-79; V Virginia Water *Guildf* 79-88; Lic to Offic from 88. *c/o Diocesan House, Quarry Street, Guildford, Surrey GU1 3XG*

KIDD, Maurice Edward. b 26. Lon Coll of Div ALCD54 LTh. **d** 55 **p** 56. C Wembley St Jo *Lon* 55-58; C Middleton *Man* 58-61; Chapl Pastures Hosp Derby 61-69; Chapl Guild of Health Lon 69-72; R Hanworth St Geo *Lon* 72-82; R Chartham *Cant* from 82. *The Chantry, St Nicholas' Hospital, Harbledown, Canterbury CT2 9AD* Canterbury (0227) 761655

KIDD, Timothy. b 24. St Chad's Coll Dur BA48 DipTh50 MA53 Nottm Univ MA57 MPhil71 MEd80. Lambeth STh74. **d** 50 **p** 51. Prin Lect Kesteven Coll of Educn 65-79; Hon C Harlaxton *Linc* 66-72; Hon C Lt Ponton 66-72; Hon C Stroxton 66-72; Gen Preacher Linc from 73; Visiting Lect Univ Evansville (USA) 79-86; K Sch Grantham 80-90; Perm to Offic *Leic* from 89; rtd 90. *14 Woodlands Drive, Grantham, Lincs NG31 9DJ* Grantham (0476) 63273

KIDDLE, John. b 58. Qu Coll Cam BA80 MA83. Ridley Hall Cam 79. **d** 82 **p** 83. C Ormskirk *Liv* 82-86; V Huyton Quarry from 86. *St Gabriel's Vicarage, 2 St Agnes Road, Huyton, Liverpool L36 5TA* 051-489 2688

KIDDLE, Mark Brydges. b 34. ACP61. Wycliffe Hall Ox. **d** 63 **p** 64. C Scarborough St Luke *York* 63-66; C Walthamstow St Sav *Chelmsf* 66-71; V Nelson St Bede *Blackb* 71-76; V Perry Common *Birm* 76-79; R Grayingham *Linc* 79-84; V Kirton in Lindsey 79-84; R Manton 79-84; Hon C St Botolph Aldgate w H Trin Minories *Lon* 85-91; Hon C St Clem Eastcheap w St Martin Orgar from 91. *12 Evershed House, Old Castle Street, London E1 7NU* 071-283 3678

KIDDLE, Martin John. b 42. Lon Univ DipTh75 Open Univ BA80. St Jo Coll Nottm 74. **d** 76 **p** 77. C Gt Parndon *Chelmsf* 76-80; Asst Chapl HM Pris Wakef 80-81; HM Youth Cust Cen Portland 81-88; Chapl HM Pris Cardiff from 88. *HM Prison Cardiff, Knox Road, Cardiff CF2 1UG* Cardiff (0222) 491212

KIDDLE, Canon Peter. b 22. Fitzw Ho Cam BA50 MA54. Clifton Th Coll 57. **d** 57 **p** 58. Kenya 57-72; Hon Can Nairobi Cathl 72; V Worthing St Paul *Chich* 73-87; rtd 87; P-in-c Milton Lilbourne w Easton Royal *Sarum* 87-90. *64 Damask Way, Warminster, Wilts BA12 9PP* Warminster (0985) 214572

KIDDLE, Miss Susan Elizabeth. b 44. Birm Univ BSc66 Nottm Univ CertEd67. Local NSM Course 86. **d** 89. NSM Waddington *Linc* from 89. *16 Sycamore Drive, Brant Road, Lincoln LN5 9DR* Lincoln (0522) 722010

KIDNER, Frank Derek. b 13. ARCM33 Ch Coll Cam BA40 MA44. Ridley Hall Cam 40. **d** 41 **p** 42. Warden Tyndale Ho Cam 64-78; rtd 78; Perm to Offic *Ely* from 79. *56 Manor Park, Histon, Cambridge CB4 4JT* Cambridge (0223) 232579

KIGHTLEY, David John. b 39. AKC67. **d** 68 **p** 69. C Plymouth St Andr *Ex* 68-70; C Ex St Dav 70-73; Chapl Greenwich Distr Hosp & Brook Gen Hosp Lon 73-76; P-in-c Chippenham *Ely* from 76; P-in-c Snailwell from 76; P-in-c Isleham from 76. *The Vicarage, High Street, Chippenham, Ely, Cambs CB7 5PP* Newmarket (0638) 720550

KILDARE, Archdeacon of. *See* HENEY, Ven William Butler

KILDARE, Dean of. *See* BYRNE, Very Rev Matthew

KILFORD, John Douglas. b 38. Oak Hill Th Coll 73. **d** 75 **p** 76. C Beckenham St Jo *Roch* 75-80; P-in-c Sinfin Moor *Derby* 80-83; V Penge St Jo *Roch* from 83. *The Vicarage, St John's Road, London SE20 7EQ* 081-778 6176

KILFORD, William Roy. b 38. BA. Sarum & Wells Th Coll. **d** 84 **p** 85. C Herne *Cant* 84-87; Chapl Wm Harvey Hosp Ashford from 87; R Mersham w Hinxhill *Cant* from 87; P-in-c Sevington from 87. *The Rectory, Bower Road, Mersham, Ashford, Kent TN25 6NN* Ashford (0233) 624138

KILGOUR, Richard Eifl. b 57. Edin Univ BD85. Edin Th Coll 81. **d** 85 **p** 86. C Wrexham *St As* 85-88; V Whitford from 88; Ind Chapl from 89. *The Vicarage, Upper Downing Road, Whitford, Holywell, Clwyd CH8 9AJ* Mostyn (0745) 560976

KILLALA AND ACHONRY, Archdeacon of. *See* STRATFORD, Ven Ralph Montgomery

KILLALA, Dean of. *See* ARDIS, Very Rev Edward George

KILLALOE, KILFENORA AND CLONFERT, Dean of. *See* PERDUE, Very Rev Ernon Cope Todd

KILLALOE, KILFENORA, CLONFERT AND KILMACDUAGH, Archdeacon of. *See* KEEGAN, Ven Donald Leslie

KILLE, Vivian Edwy. b 30. Tyndale Hall Bris 60. **d** 62 **p** 63. C Dub Miss Ch *D & G* 62-66; I Emlaghfad *T, K & A* 66-74; I Aghadrumsee w Clogh and Drumsnatt *Clogh* from 74. *Sunshine Rectory, 16 Dernawilt Road, Roslea, Co Fermanagh* Roslea (036575) 206

KILLICK, Brian Anthony Hugh. b 29. Sarum Th Coll 69. **d** 70 **p** 71. C Kingsbury St Andr *Lon* 70-74; C Selston *S'well* 74-76; P-in-c Scarcliffe *Derby* 76-77; P-in-c Sutton cum Duckmanton 77-80; V Stanley from 80. *The Vicarage, Stanley, Derby DE7 6FB* Ilkeston (0602) 322942

KILLINGBACK, Oliver Edwin. b 44. S'wark Ord Course 75. **d** 77 **p** 78. C Kingston All SS w St Jo *S'wark* 77-80; C Horley 80-82; NSM Weston Favell *Pet* from 87. *18 Wansford Walk, Northampton NN3 4YF*

KILLOCK, Alfred Kenneth. b 26. Cranmer Hall Dur 72. **d** 74 **p** 75. C Moor Allerton *Ripon* 74-79; Hon C Bolton St Jas w St Chrys *Bradf* 79-83; P-in-c Oakenshaw cum Woodlands 84-90; P-in-c Allerton 90-91; rtd 91. *15 Warwick Road, Bradford BD4 7RA* Bradford (0274) 394492

KILLWICK, Simon David Andrew. b 56. K Coll Lon BD80 AKC80. St Steph Ho Ox 80. **d** 81 **p** 82. C Worsley *Man* 81-84; TV from 84. *The Vicarage, 8 Landrace Drive, Boothstown, Worsley, Manchester M28 4UY* 061-799 1208

KILMORE, Archdeacon of. *See* JOHNSTON, Ven William Derek

KILMORE, Dean of. *See* COMBE, Very Rev John Charles

KILMORE, ELPHIN AND ARDAGH, Bishop of. *See* WILSON, Rt Rev William Gilbert

KILNER, Frederick James. b 43. Qu Coll Cam BA65 MA69. Ridley Hall Cam 67. **d** 70 **p** 71. C Harlow New Town w Lt Parndon *Chelmsf* 70-74; C Cam St Andr Less *Ely* 74-79; P-in-c Milton 79-88; R from 88; Min Can Ely Cathl from 89. *The Rectory, Milton, Cambridge CB4 4AB* Cambridge (0223) 861511

KILPIN, Stanley Leonard. b 09. Worc Ord Coll 67. **d** 69 **p** 70. C Littlehampton St Mary *Chich* 69-75; P-in-c Coldwaltham 75-80; rtd 80; Perm to Offic *Chich* from 80. *20 Cedar Grove, Beverley, N Humberside* Hull (0482) 875549

KILSBY, Alfred Daniel Joseph. b 29. St Chad's Coll Dur BA54 Lon Univ BA68 MSc75. Westcott Ho Cam 54. **d** 56 **p** 57. C E Wickham *S'wark* 56-58; C Upper Tooting H Trin 58-62; Lic to Offic *St E* 62-65; Lect Educn

Battersea Coll of Educn 66-76; Lic to Offic *Chich* from 68; Chapl Forest Boys' Sch Horsham 76-84; Perm to Offic *Win* from 85. *Orange Cottage, Brookley Road, Brockenhurst, Hants SO42 7RR* Lymington (0590) 23701

KILVERT, Canon Robert Wynne. b 13. Or Coll Ox BA38 MA56. Cuddesdon Coll 39. **d** 40 **p** 41. V Catherington and Clanfield *Portsm* 62-84; Hon Can Portsm Cathl 71-85; rtd 84; Perm to Offic Portsm from 85; Chich from 87. *17 Lower Heyshott, Herne Farm, Petersfield, Hants GU31 4PZ* Petersfield (0730) 67519

KIM, Albert. b 58. Pusan Coll S Korea BA82. **d** 88 **p** 89. Korea 88-90; Miss to Seamen from 90; Perm to Offic *Birm* from 91. *The College of the Ascension, Weoley Park Road, Selly Oak, Birmingham B29 6RD* 021-472 0801

KIMBER, Geoffrey Francis. b 46. Univ Coll Lon BA67 PGCE70 DipTh74. St Jo Coll Nottm 86. **d** 88 **p** 89, C Buckhurst Hill *Chelmsf* from 88. *Glebe House, High Road, Buckhurst Hill, Essex IG9 5RX* 081-504 6652

KIMBER, Mrs Gillian Margaret. b 48. Bedf Coll Lon BA70. Oak Hill Th Coll 89. **d** 91. NSM Buckhurst Hill *Chelmsf* from 91. *Glebe House, High Road, Buckhurst Hill, Essex IG9 5RX* 081-504 6652

KIMBER, John Keith. b 45. Bris Univ BSc66. St Mich Coll Llan. **d** 69 **p** 70. C Caerphilly *Llan* 69-72; Chapl Birm Univ *Birm* 72-75; TR Bris St Agnes and St Simon w St Werburgh *Bris* 75-82; P-in-c Bris St Paul w St Barn 80-82; Hon C Westbury-on-Trym H Trin 82-83; Area Sec (Wales) USPG 83-89; TR Halesowen *Worc* from 89. *The Rectory, Halesowen, W Midlands B63 4AR* 021-550 1158

KIMBER, Kenneth Arthur John. b 26. Bps' Coll Cheshunt 65. **d** 66 **p** 67. C Gt Torrington *Ex* 66-68; C Merthyr Tydfil *Llan* 68-72; Jamaica 72-74; Canada from 74. *SS2, Site 2, C-10, Kamloops, British Columbia, Canada, V2C 6C3* Kamloops (604) 828-0678

KIMBER, Stuart Francis. b 53. Lon Univ BSc74 Fitzw Coll Cam BA79 MA84. Ridley Hall Cam 77. **d** 80 **p** 81. C Edgware *Lon* 80-83; C Cheltenham St Mark *Glouc* 83-84; TV from 84. *The Silas Vicarage, Hesters Way Lane, Cheltenham, Glos GL51 0LB* Cheltenham (0242) 580496

KIMBERLEY, John Harry. b 49. Brasted Th Coll 72 St Steph Ho Ox 74. **d** 76 **p** 77. C W Tarring *Chich* 76-79; C Portslade St Nic 79-82; C-in-c Findon Valley CD 82-89; V Findon Valley 89-90; V E Preston w Kingston from 90. *The Vicarage, 33 Vicarage Lane, East Preston, Littlehampton, W Sussex BN16 2SP* Rustington (0903) 783318

KIMBERLEY, Canon Wilfred Harry. b 19. St Steph Ho Ox 51. **d** 53 **p** 54. V Marsworth *Ox* 65-72; V Buckm 72-78; TR High Wycombe 78-84; Hon Can Ch 79-84; rtd 84; Perm to Offic Glouc from 85; Ox from 86. *Rosemary Cottage, Naunton, Cheltenham, Glos GL54 3AA* Guiting Power (0451) 850711

KIME, Thomas Frederick. b 28. Linc Coll Ox BA50 MA53. Cuddesdon Coll 54. **d** 56 **p** 57. C Forest Gate St Edm *Chelmsf* 56-58; S Africa 58-74; R Ellisfield w Farleigh Wallop and Dummer *Win* 74-83; P-in-c Cliddesden 82-83; R Cliddesden, Ellisfield, Farleigh Wallop etc from 83. *The Rectory, Ellisfield, Basingstoke, Hants RG25 2QR* Herriard (025683) 217

KINAHAN, Timothy Charles. b 53. Jes Coll Cam BA75. CITC 77. **d** 78 **p** 79. C Carrickfergus *Conn* 78-81; Papua New Guinea 81-84; I Belf Whiterock *Conn* 84-90; I Gilnahirk *D & D* from 90. *237 Lower Braniel Road, Belfast BT5 7NQ* Belfast (0232) 791748

KINCHIN-SMITH, John Michael. b 52. Fitzw Coll Cam MA. Ridley Hall Cam 79. **d** 82 **p** 83. C Sanderstead All SS *S'wark* 82-87; TV Halesworth w Linstead, Chediston, Holton etc *St E* from 87. *The Vicarage, Spexhall, Halesworth, Suffolk IP19 0RQ* Halesworth (0986) 875453

KING, Andrew Bernard. b 40. Ex Coll Ox BA62 MA66. Coll of Resurr Mirfield 62. **d** 64 **p** 65. C Upton cum Chalvey *Ox* 64-68; C Reading H Trin 68-70; C Basingstoke *Win* 75-82; C Abingdon w Shippon *Ox* 82-89; TV Abingdon 89-91; TV Plaistow *Chelmsf* from 91. *The Vicarage, 11 St Mary's Road, London E13 9AE* 081-471 8775

KING, Anthony Richard. b 34. Trin Hall Cam BA58. Ely Th Coll 58 Linc Th Coll 61. **d** 62 **p** 63. C Benwell St Jas *Newc* 62-64; C Thirsk w S Kilvington *York* 64-67; V Halifax St Aug *Wakef* 67-74; R Upton-upon-Severn *Worc* from 74; RD Upton from 86. *The Rectory, Upton-upon-Severn, Worcester WR8 0JQ* Upton-upon-Severn (06846) 2148

KING, Brian Henry. b 39. Chich Th Coll 63. **d** 65 **p** 66. C Castle Bromwich SS Mary and Marg *Birm* 65-67; C Southwick *Chich* 68-70; V Southwater 70-73; C Brighton St Alb Preston 73-74; TV Brighton Resurr 74-75; V Eastbourne St Eliz from 75. *The Vicarage, 266 Victoria Drive, Eastbourne, E Sussex BN20 8QX* Eastbourne (0323) 20068

KING, Cecil John. b 46. Selw Coll Cam BA67 MA71. Coll of Resurr Mirfield 81. **d** 81 **p** 84. Zambia 81-85; Ghana 86-88; C Headstone St Geo *Lon* 88-89; SSF from 89. *29 The Ridgeway, N Harrow, Harrow, Middx HA2 7QL* 081-429 0763

KING, Charles John. b 14. CEng46 MIEE Lon Univ BSc39. Ox NSM Course 73. **d** 76 **p** 77. NSM Cuddesdon *Ox* 76-78; NSM Wantage Downs from 78. *48 Ardington, Wantage, Oxon OX12 8PY* Abingdon (0235) 833671

KING, Christopher John. b 56. Chelsea Coll Lon BSc78 CertEd79. St Jo Coll Nottm LTh87. **d** 88 **p** 89. C Wandsworth All SS *S'wark* from 88. *44 Skeena Hill, London SW18 5PL* 081-788 5531

KING, Mrs Daphne Eileen. b 37. E Midl Min Tr Course 78. **dss** 81 **d** 87. Theddlethorpe *Linc* 84-87; Dn-in-c 87-89; Saltfleetby 84-87; Dn-in-c 87-89; Dn-in-c Healing and Stallingborough from 89. *The Rectory, Healing, Grimsby, S Humberside DN37 7NA* Grimsby (0472) 883481

KING, David Charles. b 52. K Coll Lon 73 Coll of Resurr Mirfield 77. **d** 78 **p** 79. C Saltburn-by-the-Sea *York* 78-81; Youth Officer 81-85; P-in-c Crathorne 81-85; Par Educn Adv *Wakef* 85-91; Min Coulby Newham Ecum Project *York* from 91. *20 Fox Howe, Coulby Newham, Middlesbrough, Cleveland* Middlesbrough (0642) 599815

KING, David Frederick. b 32. Sarum Th Coll 59. **d** 61 **p** 72. Hon C Andover St Mich *Win* 71-83; P-in-c 83-88; V 88-90; Chapl R S Hants Hosp and Countess Mountbatten Hospice from 90. *The Chaplain's Office, Royal South Hants Hospital, Raven Road, Southampton* Southampton (0703) 634288

KING, David Russell. b 42. Univ of Wales (Lamp) BA67. St D Coll Lamp DipTh68. **d** 68 **p** 69. C Barrow St Geo w St Luke *Carl* 68-72; P-in-c Kirkland 72-74; V Edenhall w Langwathby 72-73; P-in-c Culgaith 72-73; V Edenhall w Langwathby and Culgaith 73-74; V Flookburgh 75-79; V Barrow St Jas 79-82; P-in-c Bolton w Ireby and Uldale 82-83; R 83-90; R Burgh-by-Sands and Kirkbampton w Kirkandrews etc from 90. *The Rectory, Burgh-by-Sands, Carlisle CA5 6AW* Burgh-by-Sands (022876) 324

KING, David William Anthony. b 42. Ch Ch Ox BA63 MA68. Westcott Ho Cam 63. **d** 65 **p** 66. C Cayton w Eastfield *York* 65-68; C Southbroom *Sarum* 68-71; R Hinton Parva 71-72; V Holt St Jas 71-72; V Holt St Jas and Hinton Parva 72-75; P-in-c Horton and Chalbury 73-75; R Holt St Jas, Hinton Parva, Horton and Chalbury 75-79; TV Melton Mowbray w Thorpe Arnold *Leic* 79-83; V Foxton w Gumley and Laughton and Lubenham 83-90; P-in-c Boreham *Chelmsf* from 90. *The Vicarage, Church Road, Boreham, Chelmsford CM3 3EG* Chelmsford (0245) 467281

KING, Dennis. b 31. ACA53 FCA64. E Midl Min Tr Course 73. **d** 76 **p** 77. NSM Chesterfield All SS *Derby* from 76. *Hillcrest, Stubben Edge, Ashover, Chesterfield, Derbyshire S45 0EU* Chesterfield (0246) 590279

KING, Dennis Charles. b 27. Chich Th Coll 53. **d** 55 **p** 56. C Luton Ch Ch *St Alb* 55-58 and 59-63; USA 58-59; Bahamas 63-66; Jamaica 66-77; V Bromham w Oakley *St Alb* 77-84; TR St Marylebone Ch Ch *Lon* 84-89; V Flamstead *St Alb* from 89. *The Vicarage, Flamstead, St Albans, Herts AL3 8EF* Luton (0582) 840271

KING, Dennis Keppel. b 33. Lich Th Coll 63. **d** 65 **p** 66. C Eccleston St Thos *Liv* 65-68; C W Derby St Mary 68-71; V Aintree St Giles from 71. *St Giles Vicarage, 132 Aintree Lane, Aintree, Merseyside L10 8LE* 051-526 7908

KING, Donald. b 32. Chich Th Coll. **d** 86. NSM Forton *Portsm* from 86. *8 Burnett Road, Gosport, Hants PO12 3AH* Gosport (0705) 523440

KING, Ernest Cuthbert. b 12. Univ of W Aus BA33. Wells Th Coll 35. **d** 36 **p** 37. C Northn St Jas *Pet* 36-46; CF (EC) 39-46; V Desborough *Pet* 46-49; Australia from 49. *Cottage 113, 31 Williams Road, Nedlands, W Australia 6009* Perth (9) 380-5113

KING, Fergus John. b 62. St Andr Univ MA Edin Univ BD89. Edin Th Coll 86. **d** 89 **p** 90. Chapl St Jo Cathl Oban *Arg* from 89; C Oban St Jo from 89. *7 Strathaven Terrace, Breadalbane Street, Oban PA34 5PE* Oban (0631) 62451

KING, Frederick William. b 24. CertEd74. Richmond Th Coll 46 Qu Coll Birm 49. **d** 50 **p** 51. Chapl RAF 55-70; Chapl The Leas Sch Hoylake 70-72; Chapl Wirral Gr Sch 74-75; Chapl Summer Fields Sch Ox 75; rtd 89. *Pioch Esquis, Hameau de Gourgas, 34700 Lodeve (Herault), France*

KING, George Henry. b 24. MRHS55 NDH55. St Alb Minl Tr Scheme. **d** 79 **p** 80. Hon C Flamstead *St Alb* from 79; Dioc Agric Chapl from 90. *Chad Lane Farm, Flamstead, St Albans, Herts AL3 8HW* Luton (0582) 841648

KING, Mrs Gillian Daphne. b 38. E Midl Min Tr Course 79. **dss** 83 **d** 87. Knighton St Jo *Leic* 83-85; Clarendon Park St Jo w Knighton St Mich 86-87; Par Dn 87-89; Chapl Long Grove Hosp Epsom from 89; Chapl Kingston & Esher Mental Health Services from 89. *517 Hook Road, Chessington, Surrey KT1 1QW* 081-397 1305

KING, Harry William. b 15. Oak Hill Th Coll 38. **d** 41 **p** 42. V Sandon *St Alb* 64-67; R Wallington w Rushden 64-67; Perm to Offic from 67; rtd 80. *318 Hempstead Road, Watford WD1 3NA* Watford (0923) 32360

KING, Jeffrey Douglas Wallace. b 43. AKC67. **d** 68 **p** 69. C S Harrow St Paul *Lon* 68-71; C Garforth *Ripon* 71-74; V Potternewton 74-83; TR Moor Allerton from 83; RD Allerton 85-89; Hon Can Ripon Cathl from 90. *St John's Vicarage, Fir Tree Lane, Leeds LS17 7BZ* Leeds (0532) 684598

KING, Dr Jennifer Mary. b 41. Lon Univ BDS65 MSc75 PhD. Ripon Coll Cuddesdon 86. **d** 88. Par Dn S Hackney St Mich w Haggerston St Paul *Lon* 88-91; Chapl Lon Univ Medical Students from 91. *c/o St Bennett's Chaplaincy, Queen Mary College, 327A Mile End Road, London E1 4NF* 071-975 5555

KING, Jeremy Norman. b 66. K Coll Lon BD88 AKC88. Ripon Coll Cuddesdon 88. **d** 90 **p** 91. C Ashby-de-la-Zouch St Helen w Coleorton *Leic* from 90. *38 Avenue Road, Ashby-de-la-Zouch, Leics LE6 5FE* Ashby-de-la-Zouch (0530) 411721

KING, John. b 38. S'wark Ord Course DipRS77. **d** 80 **p** 81. C S Gillingham *Roch* 80-85; Min Joydens Wood St Barn CD 85-90; V Borstal from 90; Chapl HM Pris Cookham Wood from 90; Chapl The Foord Almshouses from 90. *The Vicarage, 76 Borstal Street, Rochester, Kent ME1 3HL* Medway (0634) 845948

KING, John Andrew. b 50. Qu Coll Birm 72. **d** 75 **p** 76. C Halesowen *Worc* 75-77; C Belper Ch Ch and Milford *Derby* 78-81; Perm to Offic from 87. *11 Well Lane, Milford, Derby DE5 0QQ* Derby (0332) 841810

KING, John Charles. b 27. St Pet Hall Ox BA51 MA55. Oak Hill Th Coll 51. **d** 53 **p** 54. C Slough *Ox* 53-57; V Ware Ch Ch *St Alb* 57-60; Ed C of E Newspaper 60-68; Lic to Offic *St Alb* 60-70; Linc from 74. *6 Somersby Way, Boston, Lincs PE21 9PQ* Boston (0205) 363061

KING, John Colin. b 39. Cuddesdon Coll 69. **d** 71 **p** 72. C Cookham *Ox* 71-75; Youth Chapl *B & W* 75-80; P-in-c Merriott 76-80; P-in-c Hinton w Dinnington 79-80; R Merriott w Hinton, Dinnington and Lopen from 80. *The Vicarage, Church Street, Merriott, Somerset TA16 5PS* Crewkerne (0460) 73226

KING, John David. b 37. Univ of Wales DipTh63. St Aid Birkenhead 67. **d** 69 **p** 70. C Whitfield *Derby* 69-71; C St Laurence in Thanet *Cant* 71-76; V Alkham w Capel le Ferne and Hougham 76-82; R Deal St Andr from 82. *St Andrew's Rectory, St Andrew's Road, Deal, Kent CT14 6AS* Deal (0304) 374354

KING, Canon John Kenneth. b 25. Lon Univ BD50. ALCD50. **d** 50 **p** 51. R Irthlingborough *Pet* 65-75; RD Higham 69-74; V Pet St Mark 75-91; Can Pet Cathl 77-91; rtd 91. *27 Plough Close, Rothwell, Kettering, Northants NN14 2YF* Kettering (0536) 713048

KING, John Michael Stuart. b 22. St Edm Hall Ox BA48 MA52. Cuddesdon Coll 48. **d** 50 **p** 51. C Hinderwell w Roxby *York* 60-71; V Hibaldstow *Linc* 71-88; rtd 88; Perm to Offic *Linc* from 88. *Old School House, Church Lane, Saxby-All-Saints, Brigg, S Humberside DN20 0QE* Saxby-All-Saints (065261) 693

KING, Joseph Stephen. b 39. St Chad's Coll Dur BA62 DipTh63 MPhil83. **d** 64 **p** 65. C Lewisham St Mary *S'wark* 64-69; Hon C Milton next Gravesend Ch Ch *Roch* 70-85; V from 85. *The Vicarage, 48 Old Road East, Gravesend, Kent DA12 1NR* Gravesend (0474) 352643

KING, Mrs Katharine Mary. b 63. St Hugh's Coll Ox BA85 MA89 SS Coll Cam BA88. Ridley Hall Cam 86. **d** 89. C Ipswich St Aug *St E* from 89. *18 Fitzmaurice Road, Ipswich IP3 9AX* Ipswich (0473) 719562

KING, Kenneth Roy. b 32. Sarum Th Coll 62. **d** 64 **p** 65. C Tuffley *Glouc* 64-67; C Swanage *Sarum* 67-71; V Broadstone 71-80; R Abenhall w Mitcheldean *Glouc* from 80. *The Rectory, Mitcheldean, Glos GL17 0BS* Dean (0594) 542434

KING, Lawrence Norman. b 38. FRICS. St Deiniol's Hawarden. **d** 80 **p** 81. NSM Lt Bowden St Hugh *Leic* 80-84; NSM Fleckney and Kilby 84-89; R Scalford w Goadby Marwood and Wycombe etc from 89. *The Rectory, 16 Church Street, Scalford, Melton Mowbray, Leics LE14 4DL* Scalford (066476) 319

KING, Canon Leslie Richard. b 06. St Jo Coll Dur BA29 MA32. **d** 30 **p** 31. R Chelsfield *Roch* 58-73; rtd 73; Perm to Offic *Ex* from 85. *St Martin's, Gidcott, Holsworthy, Devon EX22 7AS* Shebbear (040928) 412

KING, Malcolm Charles. b 37. Chich Th Coll 67. **d** 70 **p** 71. C Mill End *St Alb* 70-72; Chapl RAF 72-76; R W Lynn *Nor* 76-81; V Croxley Green All SS *St Alb* 81-90; V Grimsby St Aug *Linc* from 90; Asst Local Min Officer from 90; OGS from 90. *St Augustine's Vicarage, 145 Legsby Avenue, Grimsby, S Humberside DN32 0LA* Grimsby (0472) 77109

KING, Malcolm Stewart. b 56. Sarum & Wells Th Coll 77. **d** 80 **p** 81. C Farnham *Guildf* 80-83; C Chertsey 83-86; Chapl St Pet Hosp Chertsey 83-86; V Egham Hythe *Guildf* from 86. *St Paul's Vicarage, 214 Wendover Road, Staines, Middx TW18 3DF* Staines (0784) 453625

KING, Martin Quartermain. b 39. Reading Univ BA61. Cuddesdon Coll 62. **d** 64 **p** 65. C S Shields St Hilda w St Thos *Dur* 64-66; C Newton Aycliffe 66-71; V Chilton Moor 71-78; R Middleton St Geo 78-91; R Sedgefield from 91; RD Sedgefield from 91. *The Rectory, Sedgefield, Stockton-on-Tees, Cleveland TS21 3DW* Sedgefield (0740) 20274

KING, Maurice Charles Francis. b 32. ACP58 Em Coll Cam BA55 MA59. Chich Th Coll 78. **d** 79 **p** 80. C Burnley St Cath *Blackb* 79-81; C Burnley St Cath w St Alb and St Paul 81-83; C Sheff Parson Cross St Cecilia *Sheff* 83-88; V New Bentley from 88. *The Vicarage, Victoria Road, Bentley, Doncaster, S Yorkshire DN5 0EZ* Doncaster (0302) 875266

KING, Michael Charles. Worc Coll Ox BA56 MA60. Coll of Resurr Mirfield. **d** 62 **p** 63. Hon C Hampstead All So *Lon* 62-65; C Thorpe *Nor* 66-69; Ed Sec BRF 69-90; NSM Queensbury All SS *Lon* 69-79; Hon C Lt Stanmore St Lawr 80-90; R Cawston w Haveringland, Booton and Brandiston *Nor* from 91. *The Rectory, Cawston, Norwich NR10 4AN* Norwich (0603) 871282

KING, Nicholas Bernard Paul. b 46. Wycliffe Hall Ox 72. **d** 75 **p** 76. C Pitsmoor w Wicker *Sheff* 75-78; C Erdington St Barn *Birm* 78-80; C Sutton Coldfield H Trin 80-84; V Lynesack *Dur* from 84. *Lynesack Vicarage, Butterknowle, Bishop Auckland, Co Durham DL13 5RD* Bishop Auckland (0388) 718291

KING, Noel Quinton. b 22. St Pet Hall Ox BA47 MA48 Nottm Univ PhD54. Wycliffe Hall Ox. **d** 50 **p** 51. C E Retford *S'well* 50-51; C Nottm St Pet and St Jas 51-53; Lect Ch Hist Nottm Univ 51-55; C Shelford *S'well* 53-55; Uganda from 55. *Makerere University College, PO Box 262, Kampala, Uganda*

KING, Miss Pamela. b 25. K Coll Lon BA46 AKC46 DipEd47 CertRE51. S Dios Minl Tr Scheme 78. **dss** 80 **d** 87. Chapl St Rich Hosp Chich from 80; Chich St Paul and St Pet *Chich* 80-87; Hon Par Dn from 87. *11 Downland Court, Somerstown, Chichester, W Sussex PO19 4AQ* Chichester (0243) 788364

KING, Peter Duncan. b 48. TD. K Coll Lon LLB70 AKC70 Fitzw Coll Cam BA72 MA77. Westcott Ho Cam 70. **d** 80 **p** 81. Hon C Notting Hill *Lon* 80-84; Hon C Mortlake w E Sheen *S'wark* from 84. *49 Leinster Avenue, London SW14 7JW* 081-876 8997

KING, Peter George. b 24. Lon Univ LLB52. ALCD55. **d** 55 **p** 56. V Leyton St Paul *Chelmsf* 68-85; rtd 85. *10 Barrington Mead, Sidmouth, Devon EX10 8QW* Sidmouth (0395) 578172

KING, Canon Philip David. b 35. Keble Coll Ox BA57 MA61. Tyndale Hall Bris 58. **d** 60 **p** 61. C Redhill H Trin *S'wark* 60-63; C Wallington H Trin 63-68; V Fulham Ch Ch *Lon* 68-74; Lic to Offic *S'wark* 74-86; Gen Sec SAMS 74-86; V Roxeth Ch Ch and Harrow St Pet *Lon* 86-89; Gen Sec Syn Bd for Miss and Unity 89-90; Sec Gen Syn Bd of Miss from 91. *c/o Church House, Great Smith Street, London SW1P 3NZ* 071-222 9011

KING, Rawlins Henry Pyne. b 16. ALCD42. **d** 42 **p** 43. V Hailsham *Chich* 68-81; rtd 81; Perm to Offic *Chich* from 81. *24 Nutley Crescent, Goring-by-Sea, Worthing, W Sussex BN12 4LA* Worthing (0903) 46206

KING, Richard Andrew. b 51. Linc Th Coll. **d** 84 **p** 85. C Bramhall *Ches* 84-87; V Heald Green St Cath from 87. *217 Outwood Road, Cheadle, Cheshire SK8 3JS* 061-437 4614

KING, Richard David. b 63. Oak Hill Th Coll 87. **d** 90 **p** 91. C Foord St Jo *Cant* from 90. *126 Lucy Avenue, Folkestone, Kent CT19 5TN* Folkestone (0303) 50280

KING, Canon Robert Victor. b 17. St Jo Coll Dur BA48 DipTh50. **d** 50 **p** 51. V Peckham St Mary Magd *S'wark* 60-85; RD Camberwell 70-75; Hon Can S'wark Cathl 74-85; rtd 85; Perm to Offic *S'wark* from 85. *12 Sackville Court, Fairfield Road, East Grinstead, W Sussex RH19 4HB* East Grinstead (0342) 326540

KING, Robin Lucas Colin. b 59. Dundee Univ MA81. Ridley Hall Cam 87. **d** 89 **p** 90. C Ipswich St Aug *St E* from 89. *18 Fitzmaurice Road, Ipswich IP3 9AX* Ipswich (0473) 719562

KING, Canon Stuart John Langley. b 33. Selw Coll Cam BA57 MA61. Linc Th Coll 57. **d** 59 **p** 60. C Plymouth Crownhill Ascension *Ex* 59-62; C Horsham *Chich* 62-67; V Devonport St Mark Ford *Ex* 67-77; RD Plymouth 74-77; Can Res Cov Cathl *Cov* 77-84; V Tooting All SS *S'wark* from 84. *All Saints' Vicarage, 84 Franciscan Road, London SW17 8DQ* 081-672 3706

KING, Terence Reginald. b 33. St Steph Ho Ox 58. **d** 61 **p** 62. C Thornhill Lees *Wakef* 61-65; V Glasshoughton 65-77; V W Ardsley from 77. *St Mary's Vicarage, Woodkirk, Dewsbury, W Yorkshire WF12 7JL* Batley (0924) 472375

KING, Canon Thomas George. b 10. OBE67. Univ of Wales (Lamp) BA32 Jes Coll Ox BA34 MA38. Lambeth DD79 St Steph Ho Ox 34. **d** 34 **p** 35. R Stoke Charity and Hunton *Win* 46-87; Hon Can Win Cathl 58-87; rtd 87. *33 Western Road, Winchester, Hants SO22 5AJ* Winchester (0962) 861415

KING, Thomas James Richard. b 27. LGSM64 ACP66. St Jo Coll Nottm. **d** 85 **p** 86. Hon C Enderby w Lubbesthorpe and Thurlaston *Leic* from 85. *6 Copt Oak Road, Narborough, Leicester LE9 5EF* Leicester (0533) 864250

KING, Timothy William. b 52. CertEd. Ripon Coll Cuddesdon. **d** 81 **p** 82. C Ludlow *Heref* 81-83; C Walton-on-Thames *Guildf* 83-86; C Hammersmith St Paul *Lon* 86-88; V Send *Guildf* from 88. *St Mary's Vicarage, Vicarage Lane, Send, Surrey GU23 7JN* Guildford (0483) 222193

KING, Tony Christopher. b 62. BA. Coll of Resurr Mirfield. **d** 86 **p** 87. C Stansted Mountfitchet *Chelmsf* 86-89; USPG from 89; Botswana from 90. *PO Box 89, Molepolole, Botswana*

KING, Preb Walter Raleigh. b 45. New Coll Ox BA67 MA74. Cuddesdon Coll 71. **d** 74 **p** 75. C Wisbech SS Pet and Paul *Ely* 74-77; C Barrow St Geo w St Luke *Carl* 77-79; P-in-c Clifford *Heref* 79-83; P-in-c Cusop 79-83; P-in-c Hardwick 79-83; P-in-c Whitney w Winforton 81-84; R Cusop w Clifford, Hardwicke, Bredwardine etc 83-86; R Heref St Nic from 86; Dir of Ords from 86; Preb Heref Cathl from 86. *St Nicholas's Rectory, Breinton Road, Hereford HR4 0JY* Hereford (0432) 273810

KING-SMITH, Giles Anthony Beaumont. b 53. Univ Coll Ox BA75. Trin Coll Bris DipHE88. **d** 88 **p** 89. C Gtr Corsham *Bris* from 88. *7B Lypiatt Road, Corsham, Wilts SN13 9JB* Corsham (0249) 712619

KING-SMITH, Philip Hugh (Brother Robert). b 28. CCC Cam BA52 MA56. Cuddesdon Coll 52. **d** 54 **p** 55. C Stockton St Pet *Dur* 54-59; V Bishopwearmouth Gd Shep 59-64; SSF from 64; USA from 66. *Address temp unknown*

KINGCOME, John Parken. b 18. CEng50 MIMechE50. Sarum Th Coll 65. **d** 67 **p** 68. C Melksham *Sarum* 67-70; P-in-c Woodborough w Manningford Bohun etc 70-72; R Swanborough 72-75; TR Swanborough 75-79; RD Pewsey 75-84; Custos St Jo Hosp Heytesbury 79-84; rtd 84; Perm to Offic *B & W* from 85. *1 Victoria House, Weston Road, Bath BA1 2XY* Bath (0225) 318973

KINGHAM, Derek Henry. b 29. Oak Hill Th Coll 56. **d** 58 **p** 59. C Deptford St Jo *S'wark* 58-60; C Normanton *Derby* 60-63; R Gaulby w Kings Norton and Stretton Parva *Leic* 63-73; V Bacup St Sav *Man* from 73. *St Saviour's Vicarage, 10 Park Crescent, Bacup, Lancs OL13 9RL* Bacup (0706) 873362

KINGHAM, Canon John Arthur. b 14. Ch Coll Cam BA36 MA40. Ridley Hall Cam 36. **d** 38 **p** 39. V Gt Baddow *Chelmsf* 51-82; rtd 82. *63 Tensing Gardens, Billericay, Essex CM12 9JY* Billericay (0277) 652475

KINGHAM, Mair Josephine. b 59. Univ Coll Lon BA84. Ridley Hall Cam 85. **d** 88. C Gt Yarmouth *Nor* from 88. *31 Blake Road, Great Yarmouth, Norfolk NR30 4LT* Great Yarmouth (0493) 844161

KINGHORN, Richard. b 16. CCC Cam BA38 MA42. Linc Th Coll 39. **d** 40 **p** 46. Chapl K Coll Sch Wimbledon 58-77; rtd 77; Tutor Open Univ 78-89. *5 Edge Hill, London SW19 4LR* 081-946 0393

KINGS, Graham Ralph. b 53. Hertf Coll Ox BA77 MA80 Selw Coll Cam DipTh80. Ridley Hall Cam 78. **d** 80 **p** 81.

C Harlesden St Mark *Lon* 80-84; CMS from 85; Kenya from 85; Dir Studies St Andr Inst Kabare 85-88; Vice Prin 89-91. *St Andrew's Institute, PO Box 6, Kerugoya, Kenya* Kerugoya (163) 21256

KINGS, Jean Alison. b 63. RGN85. Cranmer Hall Dur BA90. **d** 91. Chapl Bris Poly *Bris* from 91. *36 Timberdene, Trendlewood, Stapleton, Bristol BS16 1TJ* Bristol (0272) 656725

KINGS, Peter Robert. b 33. AKC61. **d** 62 **p** 63. Dep Dir of Educn *Lon* 66-70; Dep Dir of Educn *S'wark* 66-70; Lic to Offic *Nor* from 79; rtd 86. *113 Gaywood Road, King's Lynn, Norfolk PE30 2PU* King's Lynn (0553) 772404

KINGSBURY, Richard John. b 41. Lon Univ BA63. Linc Th Coll 65. **d** 67 **p** 68. C Wallsend St Luke *Newc* 67-69; C Monkseaton St Mary 69-70; Chapl K Coll Lon 70-75; V Hungerford and Denford *Ox* 75-83; R Caversham and Mapledurham from 83. *The Rectory, 20 Church Road, Reading RG4 7AD* Reading (0734) 479130 or 471703

KINGSLAND, Desmond George. b 23. Sarum Th Coll 75. **d** 78 **p** 79. Hon C Bournemouth H Epiphany *Win* from 78. *Windy Ridge, 23 Granby Road, Bournemouth BH9 3NZ* Bournemouth (0202) 526011

KINGSLEY, Brian St Clair. b 26. St Steph Ho Ox 56. **d** 59 **p** 60. C Tilehurst St Mich *Ox* 59-63; CSWG from 63; Prior from 85; Lic to Offic *Chich* from 66. *The Monastery of Christ the Saviour, 23 Cambridge Road, Hove, E Sussex BN3 1DE* Brighton (0273) 726698

KINGSLEY-SMITH, John Sydney. b 45. ARCM. Ridley Hall Cam 78. **d** 80 **p** 81. C Nailsea H Trin *B & W* 80-84; TV Whitton *Sarum* from 84. *The Vicarage, Aldbourne, Marlborough, Wilts SN8 2BP* Marlborough (0672) 40261

KINGSNORTH, Canon Eric John. b 11. FIA38. Wells Th Coll 45. **d** 47 **p** 48. R Newark St Mary *S'well* 63-74; P-in-c Bradpole *Sarum* 74-78; rtd 78; Perm to Offic *Win* from 78. *Brodsworth, 3 De Mowbray Way, Lymington, Hants SO41 9PD* Lymington (0590) 678397

KINGSNORTH, Canon John Sydney. b 15. Keble Coll Ox BA39 MA61. Cuddesdon Coll 39. **d** 40 **p** 41. Malawi 64-73; Dep Sec USPG 73-80; Zambia 67-75; Hon C Blackheath Ascension *S'wark* 75-79; rtd 80; Hon C Barnes St Mich *S'wark* 81-84. *1 St Peter's Close, Wilton, Salisbury SP2 0LH* Salisbury (0722) 742369

KINGSTON, Albert Victor. b 08. OBE. **d** 35 **p** 36. V Folkestone St Mary and St Eanswythe *Cant* 66-72; V Platt *Roch* 72-79; rtd 79; Perm to Offic Cant from 79; Roch from 83. *8 Bedford Terrace, Tunbridge Wells, Kent TN1 1YJ* Tunbridge Wells (0892) 35398

KINGSTON, Albert William (Bertie). b 47. Bernard Gilpin Soc Dur 68 Oak Hill Th Coll 69. **d** 72 **p** 73. C Walton Breck *Liv* 72-74; C Templemore *D & R* 74-76; I Kildallon w Newtowngore and Corrawallen *K, E & A* 76-82; Bp's C Ardagh w Tashinny, Shrule and Kilcommick from 82. *Tashinny Rectory, Colehill, Ballymahon, Co Longford, Irish Republic* Mullingar (44) 57434

KINGSTON, Eric. b 24. **d** 69 **p** 70. C Ballymacarrett St Patr *D & D* 69-72; C Knock 72-76; I Annahilt w Magherahamlet from 76. *2 Loughaghrey Road, Hillsborough, Co Down BT26 6DB* Baillie's Mills (0846) 638218

KINGSTON, George Mervyn. b 47. CITC 70. **d** 73 **p** 74. C Comber *D & D* 73-77; C Belf St Donard 77-80; Min Can Down Cathl 80-84; I Ardglass w Dunsford 82-84; Bp's C Belf St Andr *Conn* 84-90; I Ballymascanlan w Creggan and Rathcor *Arm* from 90. *1 Whitemill Road, Lower Faughart, Dundalk, Co Louth, Irish Republic* Dundalk (42) 71921

KINGSTON, John Desmond George. b 40. TCD BA63 MA66. CITC 64. **d** 64 **p** 65. C Arm St Mark *Arm* 64-70; Hon VC Arm Cathl 69-70; Chapl Portora R Sch Enniskillen from 70; Lic to Offic *Clogh* from 70. *Portora Royal School, Enniskillen, Co Fermanagh BT74 7HA* Enniskillen (0365) 322658

KINGSTON, Kenneth Robert. b 42. TCD BA65 MA69. **d** 66 **p** 67. C Enniscorthy *C & O* 66-69; C Ballymena *Conn* 70-72; C Drumragh w Mountfield *D & R* 72-78; I Badoney Lower w Greenan and Badoney Upper 78-84; I Desertmartin w Termoneeny from 84. *25 Dromore Road, Desertmartin, Magherafelt, Co Londonderry BT45 5JZ* Magherafelt (0648) 32455

KINGSTON, Michael Joseph. b 51. K Coll Lon BD73 AKC73. St Aug Coll Cant 73. **d** 74 **p** 75. C Reading H Trin *Ox* 74-77; C New Eltham All SS *S'wark* 77-83; V Plumstead Ascension from 83. *The Ascension Vicarage, Thornhill Avenue, London SE18 2HS* 081-854 3395

KINGSTON, Robert George. b 46. TCD BA68 Div Test69.

d 69 **p** 72. C Belf St Thos *Conn* 69-72; C Kilkenny St Canice Cathl *C & O* 72-75; I Ballinasloe w Taughmaconnell *L & K* 77-79; I Maryborough w Dysart Enos and Ballyfin *C & O* 79-85; I Lurgan w Billis, Killinkere and Munterconnaught *K, E & A* 85-88; Registrar of Kilmore from 87; I Lurgan etc w Ballymachugh, Kildrumferton etc from 88. *The Rectory, Virginia, Co Cavan, Irish Republic* Cavan (49) 47133

KINGSTON, Roy William Henry. b 31. Chich Th Coll 60. **d** 62 **p** 63. C Leeds St Aid *Ripon* 62-66; S Africa 66-73; V Bramley *Ripon* 74-81; TR Hemel Hempstead *St Alb* 81-85; TR Fareham H Trin *Portsm* from 85; RD Alverstoke 89-90; RD Fareham from 90. *The Rectory, 9 Brook Meadow, Fareham, Hants PO15 5JH* Fareham (0329) 280180

KINGSTON, Walter Henry Christopher. b 35. Man Univ BSc55. Wells Th Coll. **d** 59 **p** 60. C Ribbleton *Blackb* 59-62; C Ex St Matt *Ex* 62-65; V Chorley All SS *Blackb* 65-67; Rhodesia 67-71; V Bamber Bridge St Aid *Blackb* 71-80; V Padiham 80-85; P-in-c Feniton *Ex* 85-88; P-in-c Buckerell 85-88; R Feniton, Buckerell and Escot from 89. *The Rectory, Feniton, Honiton, Devon EX14 0ED* Honiton (0404) 850253

KINGSTON, William Ypres. b 19. TCD BA40 MA43 BD46. TCD Div Sch. **d** 43 **p** 44. V Albany Street Ch Ch *Lon* 55-80; C Weeke *Win* 80-85; rtd 85. *20 Cedar Court, Crown Street, Egham, Surrey TW20 9DB* Egham (0784) 431605

KINGSTON-UPON-THAMES, Area Bishop of. See SELBY, Rt Rev Peter Stephen Maurice

KINGTON, David Bruce. b 45. Trin Coll Bris 72. **d** 72 **p** 73. C Wellington w Eyton *Lich* 72-77; C Boscombe St Jo *Win* 77-81; R Michelmersh, Timsbury, Farley Chamberlayne etc from 81. *The Rectory, Braishfield, Romsey, Hants SO5 0PR* Braishfield (0794) 68335

KINNA, Micheal Andrew. b 46. Chich Th Coll 84. **d** 86 **p** 87. C Leominster *Heref* 86-90; TV Wenlock from 90. *The Vicarage, Harley Road, Cressage, Shrewsbury, Shropshire SY5 6DF* Cressage (095289) 355

KINNAIRD, Keith. b 42. Chich Th Coll 72. **d** 75 **p** 76. C Didcot St Pet *Ox* 75-78; C Abingdon w Shippon 78-82; Chapl Abingdon Hosp from 79; P-in-c Sunningwell *Ox* 82-90; P-in-c Radley 88-90; R Radley and Sunningwell from 90; Chapl OStJ Ox from 91. *The Vicarage, Radley, Abingdon, Oxon OX14 2JN* Abingdon (0235) 554739

KINSELLA, Nigel John Andrew. b 37. Lanc Univ BA70. Kelham Th Coll 57. **d** 62 **p** 63. SSM 62-80; C Nottm St Geo w St Jo *S'well* 62-64; Chapl St Martin's Coll of Educn Lanc 64-67 and 73-74; Lic to Offic *Blackb* 65-70; Tutor Kelham Th Coll 70-73; WCC 74-77; Sub-Warden St Deiniol's Lib Hawarden 77-80; V Bentham St Marg *Bradf* from 80; RD Ewecross from 85. *The Vicarage, Station Road, High Bentham, Lancaster LA2 7LH* Bentham (05242) 61321

KINSEY, Bruce Richard Lawrence. b 59. K Coll Lon BD81 AKC81 MTh86. Wycliffe Hall Ox. **d** 84 **p** 85. C Gt Stanmore *Lon* 84-88; C Shepherd's Bush St Steph w St Thos 88-91; Chapl Down Coll Cam from 91; Fell from 91. *Downing College, Cambridge CB2 1DQ* Cambridge (0223) 334800

KINSEY, Paul. Nottm Univ BTh89. Linc Th Coll 86. **d** 89 **p** 90. C Connah's Quay *St As* from 89. *3 Firbrook Avenue, Connah's Quay, Deeside, Clwyd CH5 4PF* Deeside (0244) 830460

KINSEY, Russell Frederick David. b 34. Sarum Th Coll 59. **d** 62 **p** 63. C Twerton *B & W* 62-66; C N Cadbury 66-76; C Yarlington 66-76; P-in-c Compton Pauncefoot w Blackford 66-76; P-in-c Maperton 66-76; P-in-c N Cheriton 66-76; TV Camelot Par 76-79; V Pill 79-82; P-in-c Easton in Gordano w Portbury and Clapton 80-82; V Pill w Easton in Gordano and Portbury from 82. *The Vicarage, 1 Station Road, Pill, Bristol BS20 0AB* Pill (0275) 372230

KINSMEN, Barry William. b 40. Chan Sch Truro. **d** 74 **p** 75. NSM Padstow *Truro* 74-78; Dioc Adv in RE from 79; P-in-c St Issey 80-81; P-in-c Lt Petherick 80-81; R St Issey w St Petroc Minor from 81. *The Rectory, St Issey, Wadebridge, Cornwall PL27 7HJ* Rumford (0841) 540314

KIRBY, Bernard William Alexander. b 39. Keble Coll Ox BA62. Coll of Resurr Mirfield 62. **d** 65 **p** 72. C Is of Dogs Ch Ch and St Jo w St Luke *Lon* 65-66; Hon C Battersea St Phil *S'wark* 72; Hon C Battersea St Phil w St Bart 73-76; Perm to Offic 76-78 and from 83. *31 Ashness Road, London SW11 6RY* 071-223 4000

KIRBY, David Anthony. b 42. Dur Univ BA64 PhD68. N Ord Course 84. **d** 87 **p** 88. NSM Crosland Moor *Wakef*

from 87. *9 Fenay Crescent, Almondbury, Huddersfield HD5 8XY* Huddersfield (0484) 533312

KIRBY, David Graham. b 58. Univ of Wales (Cardiff) BA80 Ox Univ BA85. Wycliffe Hall Ox 83. **d** 86 **p** 87. C Northallerton w Kirby Sigston *York* 86-89; C Southport Ch Ch *Liv* from 89. *10 Sefton Street, Southport, Merseyside PR8 6SL* Southport (0704) 546294

KIRBY, Mrs Joan Florence. b 32. St Hugh's Coll Ox MA57 Lon Univ BA66. St Alb Minl Tr Scheme 79. **d** 87. NSM Hemel Hempstead *St Alb* 87-90; C Blisland w St Breward *Truro* from 90. *Penrose, Tresarrett, Blisland, Bodmin, Cornwall PL30 4QY* Bodmin (0208) 851003

KIRBY, John Howard Anthony. b 60. Oak Hill Th Coll BA91. **d** 91. C Grantham *Linc* from 91. *26 Castle Gate, Grantham, Lincs NG31 6SW* Grantham (0476) 64351

KIRBY, John Patrick. b 24. Leeds Univ BA50. Coll of Resurr Mirfield 50. **d** 52 **p** 53. P-in-c Buildwas *Lich* 68-77; P-in-c Lt Wenlock *Heref* 68-77; V Coalbrookdale 68-77; C S Gillingham *Roch* 77-83; V New Brompton St Luke 83-89; rtd 89. *2 Allen Court, Hauxton Road, Cambridge CB2 2LU* Cambridge (0223) 845303

KIRBY, Maurice William Herbert. b 31. K Coll Lon DipTh CertEd AKC. **d** 55 **p** 56. C Eltham Park St Luke *S'wark* 55-56; C Horley 56-59; C Westbury *Sarum* 59-62; R Poulshot w Worton 62-66; P-in-c Gt Cheverell 65; P-in-c Burcombe 66-68; V 68-70; V Salisbury St Mich 70-73; Chapl SS Helen and Kath Sch Abingdon 73-79; Chapl Wrekin Coll Shropshire 79-84; Hd of Relig Studies 79-84; V Frensham *Guildf* from 84; Dir of Reader Tr from 84. *The Vicarage, Frensham, Farnham, Surrey GU10 3DT* Frensham (025125) 2137

KIRBY, Neville John. b 30. Bris Univ DipEd73. Lich Th Coll. **d** 59 **p** 60. C Horfield St Greg *Bris* 59-62; P-in-c Easton All Hallows 63-65; Hon C Bris St Steph w St Nic and St Leon 65-84; Dioc Educn Officer 67-74; Lic to Offic from 84. *The Red House, 1 Cossins Road, Bristol BS6 7LY* Bristol (0272) 428293

KIRBY, Paul Michael. b 51. Wycliffe Hall Ox 74. **d** 76 **p** 77. C Gateacre *Liv* 76-79; C Barton Seagrave w Warkton *Pet* 79-83; V Bidston *Ches* from 83. *The Vicarage, 6 Statham Road, Birkenhead, Merseyside L43 7XS* 051-652 4852

KIRBY, Stennett Roger. b 54. St Pet Coll Ox BA75 MA79. Sarum & Wells Th Coll 75. **d** 77 **p** 78. C Belsize Park *Lon* 77-79; NSM Plumstead St Nic *S'wark* 88; C Leic Ch Sav *Leic* from 90. *10 Welland Street, Leicester LE2 1DP*

KIRK, Gavin John. b 61. Southn Univ BTh. Chich Th Coll 83. **d** 86 **p** 87. C Seaford w Sutton *Chich* 86-89; Chapl and Succ Roch Cath *Roch* from 89; Min Can Roch Cathl from 89. *5 St Margaret's Street, Rochester, Kent ME1 1TU* Medway (0634) 841482

KIRK, Geoffrey. b 45. Keble Coll Ox BA67. Coll of Resurr Mirfield 71. **d** 72 **p** 73. C Leeds St Aid *Ripon* 72-74; C St Marylebone St Mark w St Luke *Lon* 74-76; C Kennington St Jo *S'wark* 77-79; C Kennington St Jo w St Jas 79-81; P-in-c Lewisham St Steph and St Mark 81-87; V from 87. *St Stephen's Vicarage, Cressingham Road, London SE13 5AG* 081-318 1295

KIRK, George. b 14. Kelham Th Coll 32. **d** 38 **p** 39. R Aston cum Aughton *Sheff* 56-80; V Ulley 65-80; RD Laughton 72-79; rtd 80; Chapl to Rtd Clergy and Clergy Widows Officer *Sheff* 80-86; Lic to Offic from 86. *3 Borrowdale Crescent, North Anston, Sheffield S31 7JW* Dinnington (0909) 566774

KIRK, Geraldine Mercedes. b 49. Hull Univ MA89. **d** 87. Ind Chapl *Linc* from 87. *364 Laceby Road, Grimsby, S Humberside DN34 5LU* Grimsby (0472) 73435

KIRK, John Andrew. b 37. Lon Univ BD61 AKC61 MPhil75 Fitzw Ho Cam BA63. Ridley Hall Cam 61. **d** 63 **p** 64. C Finchley Ch Ch *Lon* 63-66; Argentina 66-79; SAMS 79-81; CMS 82-90; Dean of Miss Selly Oak Coll Birm from 90. *Department of Mission, Selly Oak Colleges, Birmingham B29 6LQ* 021-472 4231

KIRK, Steven Paul. b 59. Ex Univ LLB80 Univ of Wales (Cardiff) BD87. St Mich Coll Llan 84. **d** 87 **p** 88. C Ebbw Vale *Mon* 87-89; PV Llan Cathl *Llan* 89-91; PV and Succ Llan Cathl from 91. *1 The White House, The Cathedral Green, Llandaff, Cardiff CF5 2EB* Cardiff (0222) 569521

KIRK-DUNCAN, Ven Brian Andrew Campbell. Pemb Coll Ox BA46 MA47 TCD MA59 DPhil64. Cuddesdon Coll 39. **d** 41 **p** 42. C Summertown *Ox* 41-43; Asst Chapl Dragon Sch Ox 41-43; C Headington Quarry *Ox* 43-44; V Sevenhampton w Charlton Abbots and Hawling *Glouc* 44-47; R Bredon w Bredon's Norton *Worc* 47-62; R St Mary at Hill w St Andr Hubbard etc *Lon* from 62; Prin Becket Coll Lon 63-67; Dep Min Can St Paul's Cathl

Lon from 69; Adn Guinea from 87; Perm to Offic *St E* from 91. *The Rectory, 8 St Mary-at-Hill, London EC3R 8EE* 071-626 4184

KIRK-SMITH, Harold. b 17. Sheff Univ BA39 MA46 PhD53. Lich Th Coll 39. **d** 41 **p** 42. Chapl Rossall Sch Fleetwood 65-72; Hd of Relig Instruction Qu Mary Sch Lytham 72-82; rtd 82. *20 Lowick Drive, Hardhorn, Poulton-le-Fylde, Blackpool FY6 8HB* Poulton (0285) 886709

KIRKBY, John Victor Michael. b 39. Lon Univ BScEng62 DipMaths64 BD73. Ridley Hall Cam 65. **d** 67 **p** 68. C Muswell Hill St Jas *Lon* 67-70; Chapl Hatf Poly *St Alb* 71-75; V Wootton 75-86; RD Elstow 82-86; R Byfleet *Guildf* from 86. *The Rectory, 81 Rectory Lane, Byfleet, Weybridge, Surrey KT14 7LX* Byfleet (0932) 342374

KIRKBY, Reginald Gresham. b 16. Leeds Univ BA40. Coll of Resurr Mirfield 40. **d** 42 **p** 43. C Gorton Our Lady and St Thos *Man* 42-44; C Middlesb All SS *York* 44-46; C Becontree St Pet *Chelmsf* 46-48; C Notting Hill St Mich and Ch Ch *Lon* 48-51; V Bow Common from 51. *St Paul's Vicarage, Leopold Street, London E3 4LA* 071-987 4941

KIRKE, Clive Henry. b 51. Ridley Hall Cam. **d** 83 **p** 84. C Ainsdale *Liv* 83-86; Gen Asst Bootle Deanery 86-89; P-in-c Litherland St Andr from 89. *St Andrew's Vicarage, St Andrew's Road, Bootle, Merseyside L20 5EX* 051-922 7916

KIRKER, Richard Ennis. b 51. Sarum & Wells Th Coll 72. **d** 77. C Hitchin *St Alb* 77-78; Gen Sec LGCM from 79. *c/o LGCM, Oxford House, Derbyshire Street, London E2 6HG* 071-283 5165 or 791 1802

KIRKHAM, Clifford Gerald Frank. b 34. Open Univ BA90. Sarum & Wells Th Coll 72. **d** 74 **p** 75. C Worle *B & W* 74-76; C E Preston w Kingston *Chich* 76-78; C Goring-by-Sea 78-80; C-in-c Maybridge CD 80-82; V Maybridge 82-88; R N Chapel w Ebernoe from 88; Chapl for Rural Affairs from 89. *Northchapel Rectory, Petworth, W Sussex GU28 9HP* Northchapel (042878) 373

✠**KIRKHAM, Rt Rev John Dudley Galtrey.** b 35. Trin Coll Cam BA59 MA63. Westcott Ho Cam 60. **d** 62 **p** 63 **c** 76. C Ipswich St Mary le Tower *St E* 62-65; Bp's Chapl *Nor* 65-69; P-in-c Rockland St Mary w Hellington 67-69; Papua New Guinea 69-70; C St Martin-in-the-Fields *Lon* 70-72; C Westmr St Marg 70-72; Abp's Dom Chapl *Cant* 72-76; Suff Bp Sherborne *Sarum* 76-81; Area Bp Sherborne from 81; Can and Preb Sarum Cathl from 77; Abp's Adv to the Headmasters' Conf from 90. *Little Bailie, Dullar Lane, Sturminster Marshall, Wimborne, Dorset BH21 4AD* Sturminster Marshall (0258) 857659

KIRKHAM, Michael John. b 56. ARCO Dur Univ BA78 Ox Univ MA87. Ripon Coll Cuddesdon 78 Virginia Th Sem 80. **d** 82 **p** 83. C Ilkeston St Mary *Derby* 82-87; V Whaplode *Linc* 87-91; P-in-c Holbeach Fen 87-88; V 88-91; P-in-c Belper Ch Ch and Milford *Derby* from 91. *Christ Church Vicarage, Bridge Street, Belper, Derby DE5 1BA* Belper (0773) 824974

KIRKLAND, Richard John. b 53. Leic Univ BA75. St Jo Coll Dur 76. **d** 79 **p** 80. C Knutsford St Jo and Toft *Ches* 79-82; C Bebington 82-89; V Poulton Lancelyn H Trin from 89. *49 Dibbins Hey, Bebington, Wirral, Merseyside L63 9JU* 051-334 6780

KIRKMAN, Canon Harold. b 11. Man Univ BA43 BD47. Man Egerton Hall 35. **d** 36 **p** 37. TR Oldham *Man* 55-72; RD Oldham 63-76; Perm to Offic *Wakef* from 72; rtd 76; Perm to Offic *Man* from 76. *3 Black Dyke, Mankinholes Bank, Todmorden, Lancs OL14 6JA* Todmorden (0706) 3499

KIRKMAN, Richard Marsden. b 55. Cranmer Hall Dur. **d** 87 **p** 88. C Bridlington Priory *York* 87-90; TV Thirsk from 90. *The Vicarage, Carlton Miniott, Thirsk, N Yorkshire YO7 4NJ* Thirsk (0845) 22003

KIRKPATRICK, Errol Francis. b 28. TCD. **d** 52 **p** 53. R Kentchurch w Llangua *Heref* 66-77; V Rowlestone w Llancillo 66-77; V Walterstone 66-77; RD Abbeydore 72-77; R Porlock w Stoke Pero *B & W* 77-83; R Lapworth *Birm* 83-89; R Baddesley Clinton 83-89; rtd 89. *51 Runnymede Road, Yeovil, Somerset BA21 5RY*

KIRKPATRICK, James Michael. b 46. Chich Th Coll 70. **d** 73 **p** 74. C Elgin w Lossiemouth *Mor* 73-76; C Devonport St Mark Ford *Ex* 76-77; P-in-c 77-80; TV Ilfracombe, Lee, W Down, Woolacombe and Bittadon 80-83; V Whitleigh from 83. *St Chad's Presbytery, 17 Whitleigh Green, Plymouth PL5 4DD* Plymouth (0752) 773547

KIRKPATRICK, Jonathan Richard. b 58. CA81 Lon Univ BA85. Wilson Carlile Coll S'wark Ord Course. **d** 85 **p** 85. C Lewisham St Mary *S'wark* 85-87; Chapl Lewisham Hosp 85-87; Hon C Noel Park St Mark *Lon*

from 88; Selection Sec ACCM 88-91; ABM from 91. *29B Lymington Avenue, London N22 6JF* 081-888 5541

KIRKPATRICK, Robert. b 14. TCD BA43 BD47 MA52. **d** 55 **p** 56. R Houghton *Win* 68-71; R Stockbridge 69-71; Nigeria 71-77; R Weldon w Deene *Pet* 77-84; rtd 84; Lic to Offic *Pet* 84-85; Perm to Offic Pet & Leic from 85. *5 Stockerston Crescent, Uppingham, Oakham, Leics LE15 9UA* Uppingham (0572) 822452

KIRKPATRICK, Roger James (Brother Damian). b 41. FCA. **d** 86 **p** 87. SSF from 66; Guardian Belf Friary 80-88; Birm from 89; Prov Min from 91; NSM Belf St Pet *Conn* 86-88; Chapl R Victoria Hosp Belf 86-88. *St Francis House, 113 Gillott Road, Birmingham B16 0ET* 021-455 9784

KIRKPATRICK, William John Ashley. b 27. SEN SRN RMN. Sarum Th Coll 63. **d** 68 **p** 70. NSM St Mary le Bow w St Pancras Soper Lane etc *Lon* 68-70; NSM Soho St Anne w St Thos and St Pet 70-75; SSF 76-79; NSM S Kensington St Aug *Lon* 79-80; NSM Earl's Court St Cuth w St Matthias from 80. *Flat 3B, Langham Mansions, Earl's Court Square, London SW5 9UP* 071-373 1330

KIRKUP, Nigel Norman. b 54. K Coll Lon BD79 AKC79. **d** 80 **p** 80. Hon C Catford (Southend) and Downham *S'wark* 80-83; Hon C Surbiton St Andr and St Mark 83-85; Hon C Shirley St Geo from 85. *The Vicarage, The Glade, Croydon CR0 7QJ* 081-654 8747

KIRKWOOD, Alexander David. b 58. Ex Coll Ox BA81 Dur Univ CertEd82. Linc Th Coll 83. **d** 85 **p** 86. C Linc St Faith and St Martin w St Pet *Linc* 85-88; C Farnborough *Roch* from 88. *Church House, Leamington Avenue, Orpington, Kent BR6 9BQ* Farnborough (0689) 52843

KIRKWOOD, David Christopher. b 40. Pemb Coll Ox BA63. Clifton Th Coll 63. **d** 65 **p** 66. C Wilmington *Roch* 65-68; C Green Street Green 68-72; Youth and Area Sec BCMS 72-73; Educn and Youth Sec 73-80; Hon C Sidcup Ch Ch *Roch* 74-80; V Rothley *Leic* from 80; RD Goscote II 84-88; RD Goscote 88-90. *The Vicarage, 128 Hallfields Lane, Rothley, Leicester LE7 7NG* Leicester (0533) 302241

KIRKWOOD, Jack. b 21. Worc Ord Coll 62. **d** 63 **p** 64. V Torpoint *Truro* 66-73; V Turton *Man* 73-81; P-in-c Castleton All So 81-82; Hon C Heywood St Luke 82-84; rtd 86; Perm to Offic Blackb 86-89; York from 89. *Dulverton Hall, St Martin's Square, Scarborough YO11 2DB* Scarborough (0723) 377371

KIRKWOOD, Michael Robert Russell. b 20. Ripon Hall Ox 58. **d** 60 **p** 61. Dep Dir Bris Samaritans 64-80; Perm to Offic *Bris* 68-80; rtd 80. *Flat 3, Upper Belgrave Road, Bristol* Bristol (0272) 688295

KIRTON, Canon Richard Arthur. b 43. Dur Univ BA67 MA73 DipTh68. Wycliffe Hall Ox 68. **d** 69 **p** 70. C Warsop *S'well* 69-72; C Newark St Mary 72-75; Malaysia 75-83; Dean of Studies Th Sem 79-82; P-in-c Bleasby w Halloughton *S'well* 83-89; V Thurgarton w Hoveringham 83-89; Bp's Adv on Overseas Relns from 85; Hon Can St Mary's Cathl Kuala Lumpur from 88; V Thurgarton w Hoveringham and Bleasby etc from 89. *The Vicarage, Thurgarton, Nottingham NG14 7QP* Newark (0636) 830234

KISSELL, Barrington John. b 38. Lon Coll of Div 64. **d** 67 **p** 68. C Camborne *Truro* 67-71; C Chorleywood St Andr *St Alb* from 71; Dir Faith Sharing Min from 74. *Wick Cottage, Quickley Lane, Chorleywood, Rickmansworth, Herts WD3 5AF* Chorleywood (0923) 282188

KITCHEN, Alan. b 39. Coll of Resurr Mirfield 72. **d** 74 **p** 75. C Shelf *Bradf* 74-77; P-in-c Tong 77-79; TR 79-84; TR Manningham from 84. *The Rectory, 63 St Paul's Road, Manningham, Bradford, W Yorkshire BD8 7LS* Bradford (0274) 487042

KITCHEN, Harold Malcolm. b 33. Trin Coll Cam BA57 MA61. Tyndale Hall Bris 57. **d** 59 **p** 60. C Worksop St Jo *S'well* 59-61; C Heworth H Trin *York* 61-63; Uganda 63-66; R Burythorpe, Acklam and Leavening w Westow *York* 66-71; V Wollaton Park *S'well* 71-85; P-in-c Lenton Abbey 77-85; V Thornton in Lonsdale w Burton in Lonsdale *Bradf* 85-89; P-in-c Cofton w Starcross *Ex* 89; P-in-c Kenton w Mamhead and Powderham 89; R Kenton, Mamhead, Powderham, Cofton and Starcross from 89. *The Vicarage, 1 Staplake Rise, Starcross, Exeter EX6 8SJ* Starcross (0626) 890331

KITCHEN, Leslie Wilson. b 16. Man Univ BA38 MA39. Bps' Coll Cheshunt 39. **d** 41 **p** 42. R Garforth *Ripon* 60-72; R Cockley Cley w Gooderstone *Nor* 72-78; V Didlington 75-78; R Gt and Lt Cressingham w Threxton 75-78; R Hilborough w Bodney 75-78; R Oxborough w Foulden and Caldecote 75-78; V Pool w Arthington

Ripon 78-84; rtd 84. *3 West Terrace, Burton Leonard, Harrogate, N Yorkshire HG3 3RR* Ripon (0765) 83796

KITCHEN, Canon Martin. b 47. N Lon Poly BA71 K Coll Lon BD76 AKC77 Man Univ PhD88. S'wark Ord Course 77. **d** 79 **p** 80. Lect CA Tr Coll Blackheath 79-83; Hon C Kidbrooke St Jas *S'wark* 79-83; Chapl Man Poly *Man* 83-88; TV Man Whitworth 83-86; TR 86-88; Adv In-Service Tr *S'wark* from 88; Can Res S'wark Cathl from 88. *17 Stradella Road, London SE24 9HN* 071-274 4918

KITCHENER, Christopher William. b 46. Open Univ BA. Sarum & Wells Th Coll 82. **d** 84 **p** 85. C Bexleyheath Ch Ch *Roch* 84-88; V Gravesend St Mary from 88. *The Vicarage, 57 New House Lane, Gravesend, Kent DA11 7HJ* Gravesend (0474) 352162

KITCHENER, Canon Michael Anthony. b 45. Trin Coll Cam BA67 MA70 PhD71. Cuddesdon Coll 70. **d** 71 **p** 72. C Aldwick *Chich* 71-74; C Caversham *Ox* 74-77; Tutor Coll of Resurr Mirfield 77-83; Prin NE Ord Course *Dur* 83-90; Hon Can Newc Cathl *Newc* 84-90; Can Res and Chan Blackb Cathl *Blackb* from 90. *25 Ryburn Avenue, Blackburn BB2 7AU* Blackburn (0254) 671540

KITCHIN, Kenneth. b 46. Trin Coll Bris. **d** 89 **p** 90. C Barrow St Mark *Carl* from 89. *31 Parade Street, Barrow-in-Furness, Cumbria LA14 2LN* Barrow-in-Furness (0229) 823729

KITCHING, David Monro. b 26. Ox Univ MA. Ridley Hall Cam. **d** 82 **p** 83. C Hornchurch St Andr *Chelmsf* 82-86; P-in-c Graveley w Papworth St Agnes w Yelling etc *Ely* 86-90. *The Vicarage, Eltisley, St Neots, Huntingdon, Cambs PE19 4TG* Croxton (048087) 252

KITCHING, Paul. b 53. GTCL LTCL. Coll of Resurr Mirfield 80. **d** 83 **p** 84. C Hessle *York* 83-86; Youth Officer from 86; P-in-c Crathorne from 86. *The Rectory, Crathorne, Yarm, Cleveland TS15 0BB* Middlesbrough (0642) 701158

KITELEY, Robert John. b 51. Hull Univ BSc73 Univ of Wales (Abth) MSc75 Lon Univ PhD82. Trin Coll Bris DipTh83. **d** 83 **p** 84. C Bebington *Ches* 83-88; C Hoole from 88. *44 Ullswater Crescent, Chester CH2 2PW* Chester (0244) 319677

KITLEY, David Buchan. b 53. St Jo Coll Dur BA. Trin Coll Bris 78. **d** 81 **p** 82. C Tonbridge St Steph *Roch* 81-84; C-in-c Southall Em CD *Lon* 84-91; V Dartford Ch Ch *Roch* from 91; Chapl W Hill Hosp Dartford from 91. *The Vicarage, 67 Shepherds Lane, Dartford, Kent DA1 2NS* Dartford (0322) 20036

KITNEY, Miss Joan Olive Lily. b 22. Gilmore Ho 50. dss 60 **d** 87. Hermitage and Hampstead Norreys, Cold Ash etc *Ox* 80-84; NSM Staines St Mary and St Pet *Lon* 87-89; rtd 89. *9 John Childs' Close, Newbury, Berks RG14 7PZ* Newbury (0635) 36416

KITTERINGHAM, Ian. b 35. CCC Cam BA59 MA63. Westcott Ho Cam 59. **d** 61 **p** 62. C Rotherham *Sheff* 61-64; C Eltham H Trin *S'wark* 64-66; V Battersea St Mary-le-Park 66-73; V Reigate St Mark 73-80; V Caterham Valley 80-85; RD Caterham 84-85; V Wandsworth Common St Mary from 85; RD Tooting from 88. *The Vicarage, 291 Burntwood Lane, London SW17 0AP* 081-874 4804

KITTS, Joseph. b 27. Tyndale Hall Bris 68. **d** 60 **p** 61. C Parr *Liv* 60-63; C Bootle St Leon 63-66; V Southport SS Simon and Jude 66-74; USA from 74. *10812 Scott, Fairfax, Virginia 22030, USA*

KITWOOD, Thomas Morris. b 37. K Coll Cam BA60 MA64. Wycliffe Hall Ox 62. **d** 63 **p** 64. Asst Chapl Sherborne Sch Dorset 63-69; Uganda from 69. *PO Box 14123, Kampala, Uganda*

KIVETT, Michael Stephen. b 50. Bethany Coll W Virginia BA72. Chr Th Sem Indiana MDiv76 Sarum & Wells Th Coll 76. **d** 77 **p** 78. C Harnham *Sarum* 77-80; C E Dereham *Nor* 80-83; R S Walsham 83-88; V Upton 83-88; Chapl Lt Plumstead Hosp 84-88; V Chard St Mary *B & W* from 88. *The Vicarage, Forton Road, Chard, Somerset TA20 2HJ* Chard (0460) 62320

KLIMAS, Miss Lynda. b 58. Jes Coll Cam BA89. Cranmer Hall Dur 89. **d** 90. Par Dn Sandy *St Alb* from 90. *14 Pym's Way, Sandy, Beds SG19 1BZ* Sandy (0767) 683201

✠KLYBERG, Rt Rev Charles John. b 31. ARICS57. Linc Th Coll. **d** 60 **p** 61 **c** 85. C E Dulwich St Jo *S'wark* 60-63; N Rhodesia 63-64; Zambia 64-67 and 77-85; V Battersea St Steph *S'wark* 67-71; P-in-c Battersea Ch Ch and St Steph 71-72; V 72-77; Dean Lusaka Cath 77-85; Suff Bp Fulham *Lon* from 85; Adn Charing Cross from 90. *4 Cambridge Place, London W8 5PB* 071-937 2560

KNAPMAN, Preb Hugh William Hartly. b 07. St D Coll Lamp BA33. **d** 32 **p** 33. Preb Wells Cathl *B & W* 67-87; R Charlton Adam w Charlton Mackrell 69-75; rtd

75. *Collar Cottage, Broad Street, Somerton, Somerset TA11 7NH* Somerton (0458) 73494

KNAPP, Antony Blair. b 48. Imp Coll Lon BSc68. N Ord Course 86. **d** 89 **p** 90. C Bolton St Jas w St Chrys *Bradf* from 89. *1128 Bolton Road, Bradford BD2 4HS* Bradford (0274) 634711

✠**KNAPP-FISHER, Rt Rev Edward George.** b 15. Trin Coll Ox BA36 MA40 Cam Univ MA49. Wells Th Coll 38. **d** 39 **p** 40 **c** 60. C Brighouse *Wakef* 40-42; Chapl RNVR 42-46; Chapl Cuddesdon Coll 46-49; Prin 52-60; Lic to Offic *Ely* 49-52; Chapl St Jo Coll Cam 49-52; V Cuddesdon *Ox* 52-60; RD Cuddesdon 58-60; S Africa 60-75; Bp Pretoria 60-75; Adn Westmr 75-87; Can Westmr Abbey 75-87; Asst Bp S'wark 75-87; Asst Bp Lon 76-86; Sub-Dean Westmr 82-87; rtd 87; Asst Bp Chich from 87; Custos St Mary's Hosp Chich from 87. *2 Vicars' Close, Canon Lane, Chichester, W Sussex PO19 1PT* Chichester (0243) 789219

KNAPPER, Peter Charles. b 39. Lon Univ BA61. St Steph Ho Ox 61. **d** 63 **p** 64. C Carl H Trin *Carl* 63-68; V Westf St Mary 68-76; V Bridekirk 76-83; P-in-c Blackheath Ascension *S'wark* from 83. *Ascension Vicarage, 40 Dartmouth Row, London SE10 8AP* 081-691 8884

KNARESBOROUGH, Suffragan Bishop of. *See* MENIN, Rt Rev Malcolm James

KNEEN, Michael John. b 55. Univ Coll Lon BSc76 MSc77 St Jo Coll Dur BA85. Cranmer Hall Dur 83. **d** 86 **p** 87. C Bishop's Castle w Mainstone *Heref* 86-90; TV Bridgnorth, Tasley, Astley Abbotts, Oldbury etc from 90. *41 Innage Lane, Bridgnorth, Shropshire WV16 4HS* Bridgnorth (0746) 766418

KNELL, John George. b 35. Cant Sch of Min. **d** 82 **p** 83. NSM Sheerness H Trin w St Paul *Cant* 82-87; NSM Minster in Sheppey from 87. *11 Uplands Way, Queenborough Road, Sheerness, Kent ME12 3EF* Sheerness (0795) 665945

KNELL, Canon Raymond John. b 27. Qu Coll Cam BA48 MA52. Ridley Hall Cam 50. **d** 52 **p** 53. C Bishopwearmouth St Gabr *Dur* 52-57; C S Shields St Hilda 57-58; P-in-c Hebburn St Oswald 58-67; V Castleside 67-76; V Heworth St Mary from 76; RD Gateshead 83-87; Hon Can Dur Cathl from 87. *The Vicarage, High Heworth Lane, Heworth, Gateshead, Tyne & Wear NE10 0PB* 091-469 2111

KNIBBS, Norman Vivian. b 27. Ely Th Coll 61. **d** 63 **p** 64. C Reading St Giles *Ox* 63-67; V Northn St Dav *Pet* 67-73; TV Kingsthorpe w Northn St Dav 73-79; C Brington w Whilton and Norton from 79. *The Rectory, Great Brington, Northampton NN7 4JB* Northampton (0604) 770402

KNICKERBOCKER, Driss Richard. b 39. **d** 68 **p** 69. USA 68-76 and from 85; C St Marylebone w H Trin *Lon* 78-81; C Chelsea St Luke 81-83; P-in-c Isleworth St Fran 83-85. *115 West 7th Street, Charlotte, N Carolina 28202, USA*

KNIGHT, Alan Keith. b 27. Ripon Coll Cuddesdon 75. **d** 76 **p** 77. C Swindon Ch Ch *Bris* 76-80; R Mark w Allerton *B & W* 80-83; rtd 83. *22 Chalice Way, Glastonbury, Somerset BA6 8EX* Glastonbury (0458) 31738

KNIGHT, Ven Alexander Francis. b 39. St Cath Coll Cam BA61 MA65. Wells Th Coll. **d** 63 **p** 64. C Hemel Hempstead *St Alb* 63-68; Chapl Taunton Sch Somerset 68-75; Dir Bloxham Project 75-81; Dir of Studies Aston Tr Scheme 81-83; P-in-c Easton and Martyr Worthy *Win* from 83; Adn Basingstoke from 90; Can Res Win Cathl from 91. *The Rectory, Easton, Winchester, Hants SO21 1EG* Itchen Abbas (096278) 291

KNIGHT, Andrew James. b 50. Grey Coll Dur BA72 Ox Univ BA74 MA81. Wycliffe Hall Ox 72. **d** 75 **p** 76. Min Can Brecon Cathl *S & B* 75-78; C Brecon w Battle 75-78; C Morriston 78-82; V from 89; V Llanwrtyd w Llanddulas in Tir Abad etc 82-89. *The Vicarage, Vicarage Road, Morriston, Swansea SA6 6DR* Swansea (0792) 771329

KNIGHT, Mrs Ann. b 54. Lanc Univ CertEd75. Trin Coll Bris DipHE83 DPS84. **dss** 84 **d** 87. Wigan St Jas w St Thos *Liv* 84-87; Par Dn 87-90; C Costessey *Nor* from 90. *St Helen's House, Gurney Road, New Costessey, Norwich NR5 0HH* Norwich (0603) 744285

KNIGHT, Arthur Clifford Edwin. b 42. Univ of Wales BSc64. Wells Th Coll 64. **d** 66 **p** 67. C Llangyfelach and Morriston *S & B* 66-68; C Oystermouth 68-73; Chapl RAF from 73. *c/o MOD, Adastral House, Theobald's Road, London WC1X 8RU* 071-430 7268

KNIGHT, Barnabas. b 46. St Alb Minl Tr Scheme 86. **d** 90. NSM Weston *St Alb* from 90; NSM Ardeley from 90. *12 Munts Meadow, Weston, Hitchin, Herts SG4 7AE* Weston (046279) 489

KNIGHT, Benjamin Edward. b 10. St Cath Coll Cam BA34 MA38. Wells Th Coll 34. **d** 36 **p** 37. R Symondsbury *Sarum* 65-78; V Chideock 72-78; rtd 78. *The Coach House, Bothenhampton Old Rectory, Bridport, Dorset DT6 4BT* Bridport (0308) 24909

KNIGHT, Christopher Colson. b 52. Ex Univ BSc73 Man Univ PhD77 Southn Univ BTh83 Cam Univ MA90. Sarum & Wells Th Coll 79. **d** 81 **p** 82. Chapl St Mary's Cathl *Edin* 81-84; V Chesterton *Cov* 84-87; R Lighthorne 84-87; V Newbold Pacey w Moreton Morrell 84-87; Chapl, Fellow and Dir Studies in Th SS Coll Cam from 87. *1 Kent House, Sussex Street, Cambridge CB1 1PH* Cambridge (0223) 461003

KNIGHT, David Alan. b 59. Lanc Univ BA81. Ripon Coll Cuddesdon 82. **d** 85 **p** 86. C Stretford All SS *Man* 85-88; C Charlestown 88-89; TV Pendleton St Thos w Charlestown from 89. *73A Bolton Road, Salford M6 7HN* 061-736 2955

KNIGHT, David Charles. b 32. Clare Coll Cam BA55 MA59. Tyndale Hall Bris 55. **d** 57 **p** 58. C Cam St Paul *Ely* 57-58; C St Alb Ch Ch *St Alb* 58-61; C-in-c Wimbledon Em Ridgway Prop Chpl *S'wark* 61-67; Publications Sec BCMS 67-68; Ed Asst The Christian 68-69; V Lannarth *Truro* 69-75; RD Carnmarth N 72-75; V Fremington *Ex* 75-83; C Edmonton All SS w St Mich *Lon* 83; Chapl N Middx Hosp 83. *Address temp unknown*

KNIGHT, Canon David Charles. b 45. ATCL63 Lon Univ BA66 St Edm Hall Ox BA68 MA73. St Steph Ho Ox 68. **d** 70 **p** 71. C Northwood H Trin *Lon* 70-73; C Stevenage All SS Pin Green *St Alb* 73-77; C Cippenham CD *Ox* 77-78; TV W Slough 78-83; Dep Min Can Windsor from 81; Ecum Officer to Bp Willesden 83-91; R Lt Stanmore St Lawr *Lon* 83-91; Prec and Can Res Chelmsf Cathl *Chelmsf* from 91. *16 Rainsford Avenue, Chelmsford CM1 2PJ* Chelmsford (0245) 257306

KNIGHT, David Lansley. b 33. Em Coll Cam BA58 MA61 PGCE76. Ridley Hall Cam 57. **d** 59 **p** 60. C Chatham St Steph *Roch* 59-63; C Plymouth St Andr *Ex* 63-65; V Gravesend St Aid *Roch* 65-71; V Bexley St Mary from 71. *The Vicarage, 29 Hill Crescent, Bexley, Kent DA5 2DA* Dartford (0322) 523457

KNIGHT, Donald. b 31. Bris Univ BA55 Man Univ DASE73. Tyndale Hall Bris 51 Qu Coll Birm 82. **d** 83 **p** 84. C Chell *Lich* 83-87; R St Ruan w St Grade and Landewednack *Truro* from 87. *The Rectory, Church Cove, The Lizard, Helston, Cornwall TR12 7PQ* The Lizard (0326) 290713

KNIGHT, Canon Donald Martin. b 13. Lon Univ BSc34 St Cath Soc Ox DipTh39. Wycliffe Hall Ox 38. **d** 39 **p** 41. R Harlow New Town w Lt Parndon *Chelmsf* 57-86; RD Harlow 60-73; Chapl Harlow Hosp 65-78; Hon Can Chelmsf Cathl *Chelmsf* 71-86; rtd 86; Perm to Offic *Ox* from 86. *Bethany, 18 Lollards Close, Amersham, Bucks HP6 5JL* Amersham (0494) 727138

KNIGHT, Eric Frank Walter. b 19. St Paul's Grahamstown. **d** 51 **p** 52. V Charlton All Saints *Sarum* 68-89; rtd 89. *9 Constable Way, Salisbury, Wilts SP2 8LN* Salisbury (0722) 334870

KNIGHT, Henry Christian. b 34. Lon Univ HNC57 Fitzw Ho Cam BA62 MA66. Ridley Hall Cam 62. **d** 63 **p** 64. Succ Bradf Cathl *Bradf* 63-64; Chapl 64-66; Israel 67-79; CMJ 79-86; V Allithwaite *Carl* from 86. *The Vicarage, Boarbank Lane, Allithwaite, Grange-over-Sands, Cumbria LA11 7QR* Cartmel (05395) 32437

KNIGHT, Herbert John. b 15. Univ of Wales BA38. Ely Th Coll 38. **d** 39 **p** 41. V Knaith *Linc* 58-82; R Lea 58-82; V Upton 61-82; R Gate Burton 78-82; RD Corringham 78-82; rtd 82. *2 Gainas Avenue, Gainsborough, Lincs DN21 2RD* Gainsborough (0427) 2097

KNIGHT, John Bernard. b 34. ACIS60. Oak Hill Th Coll 61. **d** 65 **p** 66. C Morden *S'wark* 65-69; USA 69-71; V Summerfield *Birm* from 71. *Christ Church Vicarage, 64 Selwyn Road, Birmingham B16 0SW* 021-454 0374

KNIGHT, John Boughton. b 09. Kelham Th Coll 30. **d** 36 **p** 37. V Bethnal Green St Jo w St Simon *Lon* 58-71; C Soho St Anne w St Thos and St Pet 72-75; P-in-c 75-78; rtd 78. *4 Bishop Street, London N1 8PH* 071-226 6672

KNIGHT, John Francis Alan MacDonald. b 36. Coll of Resurr Mirfield 59. **d** 61 **p** 62. S Rhodesia 61-65; Rhodesia 65-80; Zimbabwe 80-87; Dean Mutare 81-87; TR Northn Em *Pet* from 87; RD Northn from 88. *12 Jersey Court, Meadowfields, Northampton NN3 3TB* Northampton (0604) 414136

KNIGHT, Jonathan Morshead. b 59. Wycliffe Hall Ox 86. **d** 88 **p** 89. C Hillingdon St Jo *Lon* from 88. *St John's Cottage, 91 Harlington Road, Uxbridge, Middx UB8 3HZ* Uxbridge (0895) 34926

KNIGHT, Mrs June. b 28. Glouc Sch of Min 85. d 87. NSM Leckhampton SS Phil and Jas w Cheltenham St Jas *Glouc* from 87. *31 St Michael's Road, Woodlands, Cheltenham, Glos GL51 5RP* Cheltenham (0242) 517911

KNIGHT, Keith Kenneth. b 36. Southn Univ BSc58. Wycliffe Hall Ox 59. d 62 p 63. C Lower Darwen St Jas *Blackb* 62-64; C Leyland St Andr 64-68; P-in-c Blackb All SS 68-71; Dioc Youth Chapl 71-88; Hon C Burnley St Pet 71-74; Warden Scargill Ho from 88. *Scargill House, Kettlewell, Skipton, N Yorkshire BD23 5HU* Kettlewell (075676) 234

KNIGHT, Kenneth William. b 15. TD50. Wycliffe Hall Ox. d 61 p 62. C Paignton Ch Ch *Ex* 61-63; V Holbeton from 63. *The Vicarage, Holbeton, Plymouth PL8 1LN* Holbeton (075530) 238

KNIGHT, Mrs Margaret Owen. b 34. Oak Hill Th Coll 78. dss 80 d 87. Chorleywood St Andr *St Alb* 80-87; Par Dn from 87. *15A Blacketts Wood Drive, Chorleywood, Herts WD3 5PY* Chorleywood (0923) 283832

KNIGHT, Michael Richard. b 47. St Jo Coll Dur BA69 MA79 Fitzw Coll Cam BA73 MA78. Westcott Ho Cam 71. d 74 p 75. C Bishop's Stortford St Mich *St Alb* 74-75; C Bedf St Andr 75-79; Chapl Angl Students Glas 79-86; P-in-c Riddings *Derby* 86; P-in-c Ironville 86; V Riddings and Ironville from 86. *The Vicarage, Ironville, Nottingham NG16 5PT* Leabrooks (0773) 602241

KNIGHT, Paul James Joseph. b 50. Oak Hill Th Coll. d 84 p 85. C Broadwater St Mary *Chich* 84-87; R Itchingfield w Slinfold from 87. *Conkers, The Street, Slinfold, Horsham, W Sussex RH13 7RR* Horsham (0403) 790197

KNIGHT, Peter John. b 51. Lon Univ AKC73 CertEd77. Sarum & Wells Th Coll 79. d 80 p 81. C Greenford H Cross *Lon* 80-83; C Langley Marish *Ox* 83; NSM W Acton St Martin *Lon* 89-90; C E Acton St Dunstan w St Thos from 90. *5 Godolphin Place, Vyner Road, London W3 7LZ* 081-749 6744

KNIGHT, Philip Stephen. b 46. Oak Hill Th Coll 75. d 77 p 78. C Pennycross *Ex* 77-80; C Epsom St Martin *Guildf* 80-83; V Clay Hill St Jo *Lon* 83-86; TV Washfield, Stoodleigh, Withleigh etc *Ex* 86-90; Chapl S Warks Hosps from 90. *South Warwickshire Hospital, Lakin Road, Warks CU34 5BW* Warwick (0926) 495321

KNIGHT, Roger George. b 41. Culham Coll Ox CertEd63. Linc Th Coll 65. d 67 p 68. C Bris St Andr Hartcliffe *Bris* 67-69; Hd Master Twywell Sch Kettering 69-74; Lic to Offic *Pet* 69-74; V Naseby 74-79; P-in-c Haselbeech 74-79; R Clipston w Naseby and Haselbech 79-82; P-in-c Kelmarsh 79-82; TR Corby SS Pet and Andr w Gt and Lt Oakley 82-88; R Irthlingborough from 88; RD Higham from 89. *The Rectory, 79 Finedon Road, Irthlingborough, Wellingborough NN9 5TY* Wellingborough (0933) 650278

KNIGHT, Roger Ivan. b 54. K Coll Lon BD79 AKC79. Ripon Coll Cuddesdon 79. d 80 p 81. C Orpington All SS *Roch* 80-84; C St Laurence in Thanet *Cant* 84-87; R Cuxton and Halling *Roch* from 87. *The Rectory, Cuxton, Rochester, Kent ME2 1AF* Medway (0634) 717134

KNIGHT, Canon Sydney Frederick Harrold. b 06. Leeds Univ BA29. Coll of Resurr Mirfield 25. d 33 p 34. C Haydock St Jas *Liv* 33-37; S Africa from 37; Hon Can St John's from 86. *PO Box 334, George, 6530 South Africa* George (441) 5472

KNIGHT, Canon Terence. b 38. Lich Th Coll 60. d 63 p 64. C Portsea St Alb *Portsm* 63-67; C Basingstoke *Win* 67-72; P-in-c Birches Head *Lich* 72-75; P-in-c Northwood 72-75; V Portsea St Sav *Portsm* from 75; RD Portsm from 89; Hon Can Portsm Cathl from 90. *St Saviour's Vicarage, Twyford Avenue, Portsmouth PO2 8PB* Portsmouth (0705) 663664

KNIGHT, Thomas. b 20. OBE60. Linc Th Coll 69. d 71 p 72. C Earlsdon *Cov* 71-74; R Southam 74-77; RD Southam 77-82; R Southam w Stockton 77-82; rtd 82. *5 Cedar Vale, Kirkbymoorside, York YO6 6BU* Kirkbymoorside (0751) 31922

KNIGHT, William Lawrence. b 39. Univ Coll Lon BSc61 PhD65. Coll of Resurr Mirfield 75. d 77 p 78. C Hatf *St Alb* 77-81; Asst Chapl Brussels Cathl *Eur* 81-84; V Pet H Spirit Bretton *Pet* 84-89; P-in-c Marholm 84-89; TR Riverside *Ox* from 89. *St Mary's Vicarage, London Road, Datchet, Slough SL3 9JW* Slough (0753) 580467

KNIGHTS, Christopher Hammond. b 61. St Jo Coll Dur BA83 PhD88. Linc Th Coll 87. d 89 p 90. C Stockton St Pet *Dur* from 89. *55 Kensington Road, Stockton-on-Tees, Cleveland TS18 4DQ* Stockton-on-Tees (0642) 678400

KNIGHTS, James William. b 34. AKC66. d 67 p 68. C Kettering St Andr *Pet* 67-71; V Braunston w Brooke 71-81; V Dudley St Jo *Worc* from 81. *St John's Vicarage, 8A New Rowley Road, Dudley, W Midlands DY2 8AS* Dudley (0384) 253807

KNIGHTS, Philip Alan. b 60. Wadh Coll Ox BA83 MA87 Leeds Univ BA87. Coll of Resurr Mirfield 85. d 88 p 89. C Seaton Hirst *Newc* 88-91; C Leytonstone St Marg w St Columba *Chelmsf* from 91. *The Presbytery, 16 Terling Close, London E11 3NP* 081-519 9252

KNIGHTS, Timothy John. b 42. St Cath Coll Cam BA64 MA68. St Steph Ho Ox 64. d 66 p 67. C Swindon New Town *Bris* 66-70; C Highgate Rise St Anne Brookfield *Lon* 70-74; V Paddington St Steph w St Luke from 74. *St Stephen's Vicarage, 25 Talbot Road, London W2 5JF* 071-229 5731

KNIGHTS JOHNSON, Nigel Anthony. b 52. BA75. Wycliffe Hall Ox 78. d 80 p 81. C Beckenham Ch Ch *Roch* 80-84; CF from 84. *c/o MOD (Army), Bagshot Park, Bagshot, Surrey GU19 5PL* Bagshot (0276) 71717

KNILL-JONES, Jonathan Waring. b 58. Univ Coll Lon BSc79. St Jo Coll Nottm DTS90. d 90 p 91. C Northolt W End St Jos *Lon* from 90. *8 Wells Close, Northolt, Middx UB5 6JD* 081-845 5338

KNOCK, Andrew Henry Drysdale. b 49. Lon Univ BA71 Stirling Univ PhD78 Edin Univ BD78. Edin Th Coll 75. d 78 p 79. Chapl St Ninian's Cathl Perth *St And* 78-80; C Alloa 80-84; P-in-c from 85; Chapl Stirling Univ *Edin* 80-84; C Bridge of Allan *St And* 80-84; C Dollar 81-84. *St John's Rectory, 29 Redwell Place, Alloa FK10 2BT* Alloa (0259) 215113

KNOPP, Alexander Edward Robert. b 09. St Jo Coll Cam BA33 MA37. Ridley Hall Cam 32. d 34 p 35. R Gt Yeldham *Chelmsf* 68-73; R Gt w Lt Snoring *Nor* 73-76; rtd 76; Perm to Offic *Ely* from 77. *24 Green Street, Duxford, Cambridge CB2 4RG* Cambridge (0223) 835894

KNOTT, Christopher Rodney. b 42. Open Univ BA77. Kelham Th Coll 64. d 68 p 69. C Withycombe Raleigh *Ex* 68-72; TV Aylesbeare and Farringdon 72-75; TV Woodbury Salterton 72-75; TV Clyst St George, Aylesbeare, Clyst Honiton etc 75-76; TR Lynton, Brendon, Countisbury, Lynmouth etc 76-81; R Highweek and Teigngrace from 81. *15 Stoneleigh Close, Pitt Hill Road, Highweek, Newton Abbot, Devon TQ12 1PX* Newton Abbot (0626) 54949

KNOTT, Mrs Gladys Phoebe. b 15. Wolsey Hall DipRS64 Glouc Sch of Min 80. dss 81 d 87. Stroud H Trin *Glouc* 81-85; Minchinhampton 85-87; Hon C from 87. *7 Dr Brown's Close, Minchinhampton, Stroud, Glos GL6 9DG* Brimscombe (0453) 885259

KNOTT, Graham Keith. b 53. Oak Hill Th Coll 77. d 80 p 81. C Normanton *Derby* 80-83; C Ripley 83-87; TV Newark w Hawton, Cotham and Shelton *S'well* 87-89; TV Newark-upon-Trent from 89. *The Vicarage, Boundary Road, Newark, Notts NG24 4AJ* Newark (0636) 704969

KNOTT, John Wensley. b 51. FIA84 Fitzw Coll Cam MA75. S Dios Minl Tr Scheme 87. d 90. NSM Canford Magna *Sarum* from 90. *21 Onslow Gardens, Wimborne, Dorset BH21 2QG* Wimborne (0202) 841595

KNOTT, Montague Hardwick. b 05. Oak Hill Th Coll 54. d 55 p 56. V Blackmore *Chelmsf* 57-80; P-in-c Stondon Massey 80; V Blackmore and Stondon Massey 80-85; rtd 85. *1 Wadham Close, Ingatestone, Essex CM4 0DL* Ingatestone (0277) 352024

KNOTT, Pamela Frances. See IVE, Pamela Frances

KNOTT, Robert Michael. b 35. MCIBSE MRIPHH. Clifton Th Coll 67. d 70 p 70. C Rolleston *Lich* 70-72; C Anslow 70-72; C Uphill *B & W* 73-75; C Weston-super-Mare St Paul 77-79; P-in-c Burgate *St E* 79-82; P-in-c Palgrave 79-82; P-in-c Wortham 79-82; P-in-c Palgrave w Wortham and Burgate 82-87; rtd 88; Perm to Offic *Nor* from 91. *Oak Dene Luana, High Road, Bressingham, Diss, Norfolk IP22 2AT*

KNOWD, George Alexander. d 88 p 89. NSM Aghalurcher w Tattykeeran, Cooneen etc *Clogh* 88-91; Dioc Info Officer 89-90; NSM Ballybay w Mucknoe and Clontibret from 91. *The Rectory, Ballybay, Co Monaghan, Irish Republic* Ballybay (42) 41102

KNOWERS, Stephen John. b 49. K Coll Lon BD72 AKC72. d 73 p 74. C Hatf *St Alb* 73-77; C Cheshunt 77-81; P-in-c Barnet Vale St Mark 81-83; V 83-85; Hon PV S'wark Cathl *S'wark* from 85; Chapl S Bank Poly from 85. *110 St George's Road, London SE1 6EU* 071-633 9746 or 928 9889

KNOWLES, Andrew William Allen. b 46. St Cath Coll Cam BA68 MA72. St Jo Coll Nottm 69. d 71 p 72. C Leic H Trin *Leic* 71-74; C Cam H Trin *Ely* 74-77; C Woking St Jo *Guildf* 77-81; V Goldsworth Park from 81. *St Andrew's Vicarage, 8 Cardingham, Woking, Surrey GU21 3LN* Woking (0483) 764523

KNOWLES, Charles Howard. b 43. Sheff Univ BSc65 Fitzw Coll Cam BA69 MA73. Westcott Ho Cam 67. **d** 69 **p** 70. C Bilborough St Jo *S'well* 69-72; VC S'well Minster 72-82; V Cinderhill from 82; AD Nottm W from 91. *The Vicarage, Nuthall Road, Nottingham NG8 6AD* Nottingham (0602) 781514

KNOWLES, Clifford. b 35. Open Univ BA82. NW Ord Course 74. **d** 77 **p** 78. C Urmston *Man* 77-80; V Chadderton St Luke 80-87; V Heywood St Luke w All So from 87. *The Vicarage, York Street, Heywood, Lancs OL10 4NN* Heywood (0706) 60182

KNOWLES, Dorothy Joy. b 20. MCThA. Gilmore Ho 64. **dss** 69 **d** 89. Finham *Cov* 69-72; Canley 72-76; Styvechale 76-84; rtd 84; Asst Chapl Harnhill Cen for Chr Healing from 88. *27 Corinium Gate, Cirencester, Glos GL7 2PX* Cirencester (0285) 654852

KNOWLES, Eric Gordon. b 44. W Midl Minl Tr Course. **d** 82 **p** 83. NSM Gt Malvern St Mary *Worc* 82-83; NSM Malvern H Trin and St Jas 83-90; NSM Lt Malvern, Malvern Wells and Wyche from 90. *45 Wykewane, Malvern, Worcs WR14 2XD* Malvern (0684) 567439

KNOWLES, Frederick Bertram. b 06. **d** 55 **p** 56. R Pebworth w Dorsington *Glouc* 68-73; rtd 73; Perm to Offic *Glouc* from 73. *Flat 6, Capel Court, Prestbury, Cheltenham, Glos GL52 3EL* Cheltenham (0242) 576422

KNOWLES, Ven George Woods Atkin. b 21. TCD BA44 MA47. **d** 44 **p** 45. I Drumachose *D & R* 63-89; Can Derry Cathl 75-86; Adn Derry 86-89; rtd 89. *22 Shanreagh Park, Limavady, Co Londonderry BT49 0SF* Limavady (05047) 62839

KNOWLES, Graeme Paul. b 51. AKC73. St Aug Coll Cant 73. **d** 74 **p** 75. C St Peter-in-Thanet *Cant* 74-79; C Leeds St Pet *Ripon* 79-81; Chapl and Prec Portsm Cathl *Portsm* 81-87; Chapter Clerk 85-87; V Leigh Park from 87; RD Havant from 90. *The Vicarage, Riders Lane, Havant, Hants PO9 4QT* Havant (0705) 475276

KNOWLES, Ian James. b 62. Keble Coll Ox BA84 MA89. Coll of Resurr Mirfield 84. **d** 86 **p** 87. C Cowley St Jas *Ox* 86-89; Chapl Quainton Hall Sch Harrow from 89. *8 Radnor Road, Harrow, Middlesex HA1 1RY* 081-863 2520

KNOWLES, John. b 28. **d** 73 **p** 74. NSM Magor w Redwick and Undy *Mon* 73-81; NSM Risca 82-83; NSM Marshfield and Peterstone Wentloog etc 83-85; C St Mellons 85-86; V Tredunnoc and Llantrissent w Llanhennoc etc from 86. *The Rectory, Tredunnock, Usk, Gwent NP5 1LY* Tredunnock (063349) 231

KNOWLES, Melvin Clay. b 43. Stetson Univ (USA) BA66 Ex Univ MA73 Ox Univ DipTh76. Ripon Coll Cuddesdon 75. **d** 77 **p** 78. C Minchinhampton *Glouc* 77-80; St Helena 80-82; TV Haywards Heath St Wilfrid *Chich* 82-88; Adult Educn Adv from 88. *27 Gatesmead, Haywards Heath, W Sussex RH16 1SN* Haywards Heath (0444) 414658

KNOWLES, Canon Philip John. b 48. MA BTh. CITC 76. **d** 76 **p** 77. C Lisburn St Paul *Conn* 76-79; I Cloonclare w Killasnett and Lurganboy *K, E & A* 79-87; I Gorey w Kilnahue *C & O* from 87; Preb Ferns Cathl from 91. *Christ Church Rectory, The Avenue, Gorey, Co Wexford, Irish Republic* Gorey (55) 21283

KNOWLES, Stephen. b 56. Dur Univ BA81 Ox Univ MSc88. Coll of Resurr Mirfield. **d** 83. C Denton *Newc* 83; C Tynemouth Cullercoats St Paul 84. *53 Hotspur Road, Wallsend, Tyne and Wear NE28 9HB* 091-234 3626

KNOWLES-BROWN, Canon John Henry. b 30. AKC53. **d** 54 **p** 55. C Hertf St Andr *St Alb* 54-58; C Bushey 58-61; Chapl RAF 61-65; C-in-c Farley Hill St Jo CD *St Alb* 65-69; V Farley Hill St Jo 69-72; V Totteridge from 72; RD Barnet 79-89; Hon Can St Alb from 85. *The Vicarage, Totteridge, London N20 8PR* 081-445 6787

KNOWLING, Richard Charles. b 46. K Coll Lon BSc67 St Edm Hall Ox BA70 MA89. St Steph Ho Ox 69. **d** 71 **p** 72. C Hobs Moat *Birm* 71-75; C Shrewsbury St Mary w All SS and St Mich *Lich* 75-77; V Rough Hills 77-83; Dir Past Th Coll of Resurr Mirfield 83-90; V Palmers Green St Jo *Lon* from 90. *St John's Vicarage, 1 Bourne Hill, London N13 4DA* 081-886 1348

KNOX, Geoffrey Martin. b 44. Dur Univ BA66 DipTh67 Sheff City Coll of Educn DipEd73. St Chad's Coll Dur 63. **d** 67 **p** 68. C Newark St Mary *S'well* 67-72; Perm to Offic *Derby* 72-74; V Woodville 74-81; V Repton 79-81; V Long Eaton St Laur from 81. *The Vicarage, Regent Street, Long Eaton, Nottingham NG10 1JX* Long Eaton (0602) 733154

KNOX, Iain John Edward. b 46. TCD BA70 MA74 Hull Univ BPhil76. Irish Sch of Ecum 74 CITC 71. **d** 71 **p** 72.

C Belf Malone (St Jo) *Conn* 71-74; Bp's Dom Chapl 72-74; Perm to Offic *D & R* 74-76; I Gweedore Union 76-80; I Clonmel w Innislounagh, Tullaghmelan etc *C & O* from 80; Bp's Dom Chapl from 82; Press & Radio Officer (Cashel) from 90. *St Mary's Rectory, 2 Western Road, Clonmel, Co Tipperary, Irish Republic* Clonmel (52) 21369

KNOX, Canon Ian Carroll. b 32. St Jo Coll Dur BA54 DipTh55. **d** 55 **p** 56. C Illingworth *Wakef* 55-58; C Lightcliffe 58-60; V Rastrick St Matt 60-77; Hon Can Wakef Cathl 76-89; RD Huddersfield 77-89; V Huddersfield St Pet 77-84; V Huddersfield St Pet and All SS 84-89; Can Res Wakef Cathl from 89; Dir of Educn from 89. *5 Kingfisher Grove, Wakefield, W Yorkshire WF2 6SD*

KNOX, Thomas Anthony. b 31. BA. Ely Th Coll. **d** 56 **p** 57. C Poplar All SS w St Frideswide *Lon* 56-59; C Eastbourne St Andr *Chich* 59-61; C Welwyn *St Alb* 61-66; V Boreham Wood St Mich 66-71; R Puttenham w Long Marston 71-79; R Toddington from 79. *The Rectory, 41 Leighton Road, Toddington, Dunstable, Beds LU5 6AL* Toddington (05255) 2298

KOMOR, Michael. b 60. Univ of Wales BSc83. Chich Th Coll 83. **d** 86 **p** 87. C Mountain Ash *Llan* 86-89; C Llantwit Major 89-91; TV from 91. *The Vicarage, Trepit Road, Wick, Cowbridge, S Glam CF7 7QL* Wick (065679) 243

KONIG, Peter Montgomery. b 44. Westcott Ho Cam 80. **d** 82 **p** 83. C Oundle *Pet* 82-86; Chapl Westwood Ho Sch from 86; Lic to Offic *Pet* from 86. *Crossways, Main Street, Yarwell, Peterborough PE8 6PR* Stamford (0780) 782873

KOPSCH, Hartmut. b 41. Sheff Univ BA63 Univ of BC MA66 Lon Univ PhD70 DipHE. Trin Coll Bris 78. **d** 80 **p** 81. C Cranham Park *Chelmsf* 80-85; V Springfield *Birm* from 85. *The Vicarage, 172 Woodlands Road, Birmingham B11 4ET* 021-777 4908

KORNAHRENS, Wallace Douglas. b 43. The Citadel Charleston BA66 Gen Th Sem (NY) STB69. **d** 69 **p** 70. USA 69-72; C Potters Green *Cov* 72-75; Chapl Community of Celebration Wargrave Oxon 75-76; P-in-c Cumbrae (or Millport) *Arg* 76-78; R Grantown-on-Spey *Mor* 78-83; R Rothiemurchus 78-83; R Edin H Cross *Edin* from 83. *Holy Cross Rectory, 18 Barnton Gardens, Edinburgh EH4 6AF* 031-336 2311

KOTHARE, Jayant. b 41. Bombay Univ BA Heidelberg Univ MDiv. **d** 86 **p** 87. C Handsworth St Mich *Birm* 86-89; C Southall St Geo *Lon* from 89. *St George's Vicarage, 1 Lancaster Road, Southall, Middx UB1 1NP* 081-574 1876

KOVOOR, George Iype. b 57. Delhi Univ BA77 Serampore Univ BD80 Chr Medical Assn of India DCHospC85. Union Bibl Sem Yavatmal 78. **d** 80 **p** 80. India 80-90; Dean St Paul's Cathl Ambala 84-88; C Derby St Aug *Derby* from 90; Min Derby Asian Chr Min Project from 90. *52 Palmerston Street, Derby DE3 6PE* Derby (0332) 271368

KROLL, Dr Una Margaret Patricia. b 25. Girton Coll Cam MB51 BChir51. S'wark Ord Course 68. **d** 88. Par Dn Mon from 88. *Ty Mawr Convent, Lydent, Monmouth, Gwent NP5 4RN* Trelleck (0600) 860244

KRONENBURG, Selwyn Thomas Denzil. b 32. Univ of Wales BA54 St Cath Soc Ox BA57 MA60 Leic Univ MA73. Wycliffe Hall Ox. **d** 57 **p** 58. C Surbiton St Matt *S'wark* 57-60; C Luton w E Hyde *St Alb* 60-62; P-in-c Loscoe *Derby* 62-65; Lect RE Bulmershe Coll 65-67; Whitelands Coll from 67; Perm to Offic *Guildf* from 77. *58 Woodfield Lane, Ashtead, Surrey KT21 2BS* Ashtead (0372) 272505

KRZEMINSKI, Stefan. b 51. Nottm Univ BTh77. Linc Th Coll 74. **d** 77 **p** 78. C Sawley *Derby* 77-79; Asst Chapl Bluecoat Sch Nottm from 79; Hon C W Hallam and Mapperley *Derby* from 84; Hd of RE Nottm High Sch from 88. *12 Newbridge Close, West Hallam, Derby DE7 6LY* Ilkeston (0602) 305052

KUHRT, Ven Gordon Wilfred. b 41. Lon Univ BD63. Oak Hill Th Coll. **d** 67 **p** 68. C Illogan *Truro* 67-70; C Wallington H Trin *S'wark* 70-73; V Shenstone *Lich* 73-79; P-in-c S Croydon Em *Cant* 79-81; V S Croydon Em *S'wark* 81-89; RD Croydon *Cant* 81-86; Hon Can S'wark Cathl *S'wark* from 87; Adn Lewisham from 89. *3A Court Farm Road, London SE9 4JH* 081-857 7982

KURTI, Peter Walter. b 60. Qu Mary Coll Lon LLB82 K Coll Lon MTh89. Ripon Coll Cuddesdon 83. **d** 86 **p** 87. C Prittlewell *Chelmsf* 86-90; Chapl Derby Coll of HE *Derby* from 90; Dep Hd Relig Resource and Research Cen from 90. *Derbyshire College of Higher*

Education, Mickleover, Derby DE3 5GX Derby (0332) 47181

KYBIRD, Paul. b 49. Selw Coll Cam BA72 MA75. Qu Coll Birm 72. **d** 74 **p** 76. C Loughb Em *Leic* 74-78; Overseas 78-81; Tutor Crowther Hall CMS Tr Coll Selly Oak 82-86; P-in-c Wreay *Carl* from 86; Lay Tr Adv from 86. *The Vicarage, Wreay, Carlisle CA4 0RL* Southwaite (06974) 73463

KYLE, Laurence Arthur Nelson. b 14. S'wark Ord Course 64. **d** 67 **p** 68. R Hopton w Market Weston *St E* 70-72; P-in-c Barningham w Coney Weston 70-72; R Hopton, Market Weston, Barningham etc 72-79; RD Ixworth 73-79; rtd 79; Perm to Offic *Nor* from 79. *Flat 3, Ellesborough Manor, Butlers Cross, Aylesbury, Bucks HP17 0XF* Aylesbury (0296) 696047

KYRIACOU, Brian George. b 42. Lon Univ LLB64. Oak Hill Th Coll 79. **d** 81 **p** 82. C Becontree St Mary *Chelmsf* 81-83; C Becontree St Cedd 83-85; C Becontree W 85; TV 85-87; V Shiregreen St Jas and St Chris *Sheff* from 87. *The Vicarage, 510 Bellhouse Road, Sheffield S5 0RG* Sheffield (0742) 456526

KYRIAKIDES-YELDHAM, Anthony Paul Richard. b 48. K Coll Lon BD73 AKC73 Birkb Coll Lon BSc82 Golds Coll Lon DASS83 CQSW82 Warw Univ MSc90 CPsychol91. **d** 74 **p** 75. C Dalston H Trin w St Phil *Lon* 74-78; NSM Lon Docks St Pet w Wapping St Jo 79-81; NSM Hackney Wick St Mary of Eton w St Aug 81-85; NSM Wandsworth Common St Mary *S'wark* 85-87; Chapl Wandsworth Mental Health Unit from 87; Chapl Springfield Hosp Lon from 87. *The Mental Health Unit, c/o Springfield Hospital, 61 Glenburnie Road, London SW17 7DJ* 081-672 9911

L

LA TOUCHE, Francis William Reginald. b 51. Linc Th Coll 73. **d** 76 **p** 77. C Yate *Bris* 76-77; C Yate New Town 77-79; Chapl Vlissingen (Flushing) Miss to Seamen *Eur* 79-83; Lic to Offic *York* 83-91; Miss to Seamen 83-91; V Burstwick w Thorngumbald *York* from 91. *The Vicarage, Main Road, Thorngumbald, Hull HU12 9NA* Withernsea (0964) 626509

LABDON, John. b 32. Oak Hill Th Coll. **d** 84 **p** 85. C Formby H Trin *Liv* 84-87; P-in-c St Helens St Mark from 87. *St Mark's Vicarage, 160 North Road, St Helens, Merseyside WA10 2TZ* St Helens (0744) 23806

LACEY, Allan John. b 48. Wycliffe Hall Ox. **d** 82 **p** 83. C Greasbrough *Sheff* 82-85; R Treeton from 85. *The Rectory, Church Lane, Treeton, Rotherham, S Yorkshire S60 5QZ* Sheffield (0742) 696542

LACEY, Ven Clifford George. b 21. AKC49. **d** 50 **p** 51. V Eltham St Jo *S'wark* 66-79; Sub-Dean of Eltham 70-79; Boro Dean of Greenwich 79-85; Adn Lewisham 85-89; rtd 89; Perm to Offic *Nor* from 89; St E from 90; Bp's Officer for Rtd Clergy & Widows (Nor) from 91. *31 Kerridges, East Harling, Norwich NR16 2QA* East Harling (0953) 718458

LACEY, Eric. b 33. Cranmer Hall Dur 69. **d** 71 **p** 72. C Blackpool St Jo *Blackb* 71-75; V Whittle-le-Woods 75-88; R Heysham from 88. *St Peter's Rectory, Main Street, Morecambe, Lancs LA3 2RN* Heysham (0524) 51422

LACEY, Canon Frank Gordon. b 26. Magd Coll Cam BA47 MA51. Ely Th Coll 48. **d** 50 **p** 51. V Ockbrook *Derby* 69-73; Dir Past Studies N Ord Course 73-81; V Birtles *Ches* 73-82; Can Res Sheff Cathl *Sheff* 82-91; rtd 91. *6 Barnes Avenue, Dronfield Woodhouse, Sheffield S18 5YG* Dronfield (0246) 416589

LACEY, Graeme Alexander Warner. b 15. Wycliffe Hall Ox. **d** 63 **p** 64. V Bexley St Jo *Roch* 67-73; R Cuxton 73-76; R Cuxton and Halling 76-80; rtd 80; Perm to Offic *Chich* from 80. *122 Westminster Drive, Bognor Regis, W Sussex PO21 3RZ* Pagham (0243) 266631

LACK, Leonard James Westbrook. b 16. Ripon Hall Ox 65. **d** 66 **p** 67. C Leighton Buzzard *St Alb* 66-81; rtd 81; Perm to Offic *Bris* from 81. *104 Queen's Crescent, Chippenham, Wilts SN14 0NP* Chippenham (0249) 659878

LACK, Martin Paul. b 57. St Jo Coll Ox MA79 MSc80. Linc Th Coll 83. **d** 86 **p** 87. C E Bowbrook *Worc* 86-89; C W Bowbrook 86-89; C Bowbrook S 89-90; C Bowbrook N 89-90; R Teme Valley S from 90. *Hanley Rectory, Broadheath, Tenbury Wells, Worcs WR15 8QW* Upper Sapey (08867) 286

LACKEY, Michael Geoffrey Herbert. b 42. Oak Hill Th Coll 73. **d** 75 **p** 76. C Hatcham St Jas *S'wark* 75-81; V New Barnet St Jas *St Alb* from 81. *St James' Vicarage, 11 Park Road, Barnet, Herts EN4 9QA* 081-449 4043

LACKEY, William Terence Charles. b 32. St Mich Coll Llan 80. **d** 82 **p** 83. C Wrexham *St As* 82-85; V Gwersyllt from 85. *The Vicarage, Old Mold Road, Gwersyllt, Wrexham, Clwyd LL11 4SB* Wrexham (0978) 756391

LADD, Mrs Anne de Chair. b 56. Nottm Univ BA78 Birm Univ CQSW80 DipSocWork80. St Jo Coll Nottm LTh DPS86. dss 86 **d** 87. Bucknall and Bagnall *Lich* 86-87; Par Dn from 87. *The Vicarage, Dawlish Drive, Stoke-on-Trent ST2 0ET* Stoke-on-Trent (0782) 260876

LADD, John George Morgan. b 36. **d** 90 **p** 91. NSM Nevern and Y Beifil w Eglwyswrw and Meline etc *St D* from 90. *Pant-Hywel, Blaenffos, Boncath, Dyfed SA37 0JB* Boncath (0239) 841517

LADD, Nicholas Mark. b 57. Ex Univ BA78 Selw Coll Cam BA81. Ridley Hall Cam 79. **d** 82 **p** 83. C Aston SS Pet and Paul *Birm* 82-86; TV Bucknall and Bagnall *Lich* from 86. *The Vicarage, Dawlish Drive, Stoke-on-Trent ST2 0ET* Stoke-on-Trent (0782) 260876

LADDS, Reginald. b 25. ACP LCP. St D Coll Lamp BA50 Westcott Ho Cam 60. **d** 60 **p** 61. Chapl Can Slade Sch Bolton 60-85; C Bolton St Pet *Man* 60-62; C Bolton All So w St Jas 62-69; Hon C Farnworth and Kearsley 76-78; P-in-c Prestolee 78; C E Farnworth and Kearsley 78-84; Chapl Townleys Hosp Bolton from 87; Hon C Turton *Man* from 88. *53 Hillside Avenue, Bromley Cross, Bolton BL7 9NQ* Bolton (0204) 56271

LADDS, Robert Sidney. b 41. LRSC72 Lon Univ BEd71. Cant Sch of Min 79. **d** 80 **p** 81. C Hythe *Cant* 80-83; C Bretherton *Blackb* from 83; Chapl Bp Rawstorne Sch Croston Preston from 83; Bp's Chapl for Min and Adv Coun for Min *Blackb* from 86. *The Rectory, 156 South Road, Bretherton, Preston PR5 7AH* Croston (0772) 600206

LADIPO, Adeyemi Olalekan. b 37. Trin Coll Bris 63. **d** 66 **p** 76. C Bilston St Leon *Lich* 66-68; Nigeria 68-84; V Canonbury St Steph *Lon* 85-87; BCMS Sec for Internat Miss 87-90; Hon C Bromley SS Pet and Paul *Roch* 89-90; V Herne Hill *S'wark* from 90. *8 Ruskin Walk, London SE24 9LZ* 071-274 5741

LAIGHT, Frederick. b 04. MBE66. **d** 31 **p** 32. Miss to Seamen from 36; rtd 69. *38 Flemming Avenue, Leigh-on-Sea, Essex SS9 3AW*

LAING, Canon Alexander Burns. b 34. Edin Th Coll 57. **d** 60 **p** 61. C Falkirk *Edin* 60-62; C Edin Ch Ch 62-70; Chapl RNR 64; P-in-c Edin St Fillan *Edin* 70-74; Chapl Edin R Infirmary 74-77; Dioc Supernumerary *Edin* from 77; R Helensburgh *Glas* from 77; Can St Mary's Cathl from 87. *The Rectory, William Street, Helensburgh, Dunbartonshire G84 8BD* Helensburgh (0436) 72500

LAING, James. b 18. AKC49. **d** 50 **p** 51. V Southgate St Andr *Lon* 69-87; rtd 87; Hon C Hinxworth w Newnham and Radwell *St Alb* from 87. *The Rectory, 10 New Inn Road, Hinxworth, Baldock, Herts SG7 5HG* Baldock (0462) 742770

LAING, Canon William Sydney. b 32. TCD BA54 MA62. CITC 55. **d** 55 **p** 56. C Crumlin *Conn* 55-59; C Dub St Ann *D & G* 59-65; I Carbury *M & K* 65-68; I Dub Finglas *D & G* 68-80; I Tallaght from 80; Can Ch Ch Cathl Dub from 90. *6 Sally Park, Firhouse Road, Tallaght, Dublin 24, Irish Republic* Dublin (1) 515884

LAIRD, Canon John Charles. b 32. Sheff Univ BA53 MA54 St Cath Coll Ox BA58 MA62 Lon Univ DipEd70. Ripon Hall Ox 56. **d** 58 **p** 59. C Cheshunt *St Alb* 58-62; Chapl Bps' Coll Cheshunt 62-64; Vice-Prin 64-67; Prin 67-69; V Keysoe w Bolnhurst and Lt Staughton *St Alb* from 69; Hon Can St Alb from 87. *The Vicarage, Church Road, Keysoe, Bedford MK44 2HW* Bedford (0234) 708251

LAIRD, Robert George (Robin). b 40. TCD 58. Edin Th Coll 63. **d** 65 **p** 66. C Drumragh *D & R* 65-68; CF from 68; QHC from 91. *c/o MOD (Army), Bagshot Park, Bagshot, Surrey GU19 5PL* Bagshot (0276) 71717

LAISTER, Peter. b 27. Univ of Wales (Lamp) BA54. St Steph Ho Ox 54. **d** 56 **p** 57. C Victoria Docks Ascension *Chelmsf* 56-60; Chapl RN 60-65; C Munster Square St Mary Magd *Lon* 65-66; Chapl Middx Hosp Lon 66-70; V Clerkenwell H Redeemer w St Phil *Lon* 70-86; USA from 86. *St Clement's Clergy House, 2013 Appletree, Philadelphia, Pennsylvania 19103, USA* Philadelphia (215) 563-1876

LAKE, Canon David Eurwyn. b 17. TD60. St D Coll Lamp BA39. **d** 40 **p** 41. V Skewen *Llan* 62-84; rtd 84. *Fairwell, 42 Brecon Road, Ystradgynlais, Swansea SA9 1HF* Swansea (0792) 849541

LAKE, Miss Eileen Veronica. b 58. Sarum & Wells Th Coll 85. **d** 88. Par Dn Islington St Mary *Lon* from 88. *Flat 3, 37 College Cross, London N1 1PT* 071-609 4171

LAKE, Stephen David. b 63. Chich Th Coll 85. **d** 88 **p** 89. C Sherborne w Castleton and Lillington *Sarum* from 88. *St Mary's House, 4 Askwith Close, Sherborne, Dorset DT9 6DX* Sherborne (0935) 815043

LAKE, Vivienne Elizabeth. b 38. Lon Univ DHistA78. Westcott Ho Cam 84. **dss** 86 **d** 87. Chesterton Gd Shep *Ely* 86-87; C 87-90; NSM Bourn Deanery from 90. *The Vicarage Flat, School Lane, Barton, Cambridge CB3 7BG* Cambridge (0223) 264147

LAKELAND, William. b 05. Edin Th Coll 45. **d** 47 **p** 48. V Macclesfield St Jo *Ches* 55-74; rtd 74; Perm to Offic S'well from 74. *31 Arundel Drive, Carlton-in-Lindrick, Worksop, Notts* Worksop (0909) 731368

LAKER, Grace. b 39. SRN63. Sarum & Wells Th Coll BTh91. **d** 91. C Helston and Wendron *Truro* from 91. *18 Roskilling, Helston, Cornwall TR13 8PF* Helston (0326) 564223

LAKER, Leopold Ernest. b 38. Sarum & Wells Th Coll 77. **d** 77 **p** 78. C Rainham *Roch* 77-80; V Horton Kirby from 80. *The Vicarage, Horton Kirby, Dartford DA4 9BN* Farningham (0322) 862201

LAMB, Bruce. b 47. Keble Coll Ox BA69 MA73 Leeds Univ DipTh72. Coll of Resurr Mirfield 70. **d** 73 **p** 74. C Romford St Edw *Chelmsf* 73-76; C Canning Town St Cedd 76-79; V New Brompton St Luke *Roch* 79-83; Chapl RN 83-87; C Rugeley *Lich* 87-88; V Trent Vale from 88. *The Vicarage, Crosby Road, Stoke-on-Trent ST4 6JY* Stoke-on-Trent (0782) 48076

LAMB, Bryan John Harry. b 35. Leeds Univ BA60 Aston Univ DCouns72. Coll of Resurr Mirfield 60. **d** 62 **p** 63. C Solihull *Birm* 62-65 and 88-89; Asst Master Malvern Hall Sch Solihull 65-74; Alderbrook Sch & Hd of Light Hall Adult Ed Cen 74-88; V Wragby *Linc* 89; Dioc Dir of Readers 89. *35 Rectory Road, Solihull, W Midlands* 021-705 2489

LAMB, Dr Christopher Avon. b 39. Qu Coll Ox BA61 MA65 Birm Univ MA79 PhD87. Wycliffe Hall Ox 61. **d** 63 **p** 64. C Enfield St Andr *Lon* 63-69; Pakistan 69-75; Tutor Crowther Hall CMS Tr Coll Selly Oak 75-78; Lic to Offic *Birm* 75-87; Co-ord BCMS/CMS Other Faiths Th Project 79-87; Dioc Community Relns Officer *Cov* from 87; TV Cov Caludon from 89. *5 Waterloo Street, Coventry CV1 5JS* Coventry (0203) 257523

LAMB, Ms Jean Evelyn. b 57. Reading Univ BA79 Nottm Univ MA88. St Steph Ho Ox 81. **dss** 84 **d** 88. Leic H Spirit *Leic* 84; Beeston S'well 88; Par Dn from 88. *13 Melbourne Road, Nottingham NG2 5BG* Nottingham (0602) 812478

LAMB, John Romney. b 21. Ch Ch Ox BA48 MA53. Wells Th Coll 49. **d** 50 **p** 51. CF 55-70; V Horsell *Guildf* 70-76; V Dorking w Ranmore 76-82; P-in-c Charing Heath w Egerton *Cant* 82-83; P-in-c Pluckley w Pevington 82-83; R Egerton w Pluckley 84-87; rtd 87. *Wayside, Budds Hill, Singleton, Chichester, W Sussex PO18 0HD* Singleton (024363) 516

LAMB, Nicholas Henry. b 52. St Jo Coll Dur BA74. St Jo Coll Nottm 76. **d** 79 **p** 80. C Luton Lewsey St Hugh *St Alb* 79-84; Bethany Fellowship 84-87. *Address temp unknown*

LAMB, Peter Francis Charles. b 15. St Cath Coll Cam BA37 MA41. Wells Th Coll 37. **d** 38 **p** 39. R Mells w Vobster, Whatley and Chantry *B & W* 70-77; rtd 77. *1 North End Cottages, Martock Road, Long Sutton, Langport, Somerset TA10 9HU* Long Sutton (0458) 241481

LAMB, Canon Philip James. b 06. Magd Coll Ox BA28 MA34. Cuddesdon Coll 29. **d** 29 **p** 30. Prin St Jo Coll York 45-71; rtd 71. *37 Westbourne Avenue, Harrogate, N Yorkshire HG2 9BD* Harrogate (0423) 62273

LAMB, Philip Richard James. b 42. Sarum & Wells Th Coll. **d** 83 **p** 84. C Wotton-under-Edge w Ozleworth and N Nibley *Glouc* 83-86; TV Worc SE *Worc* 86-91; R Billingsley w Sidbury, Middleton Scriven etc *Heref* from 91. *The Rectory, Sidbury, Bridgnorth, Shropshire WV16 6PY* Bridgnorth (0746) 632625

LAMBERT, David Francis. b 40. Oak Hill Th Coll 72. **d** 74 **p** 75. C Paignton St Paul Preston *Ex* 74-77; C Woking Ch Ch *Guildf* 77-84; P-in-c Willesden Green St Gabr *Lon* from 84; P-in-c Cricklewood St Mich from 85. *156 Anson Road, London NW2 6BH* 081-452 6305

LAMBERT, David Hardy. b 44. AKC66. V from 85; V N Ormesby 73-85; RD Guisborough from 86. *The Vicarage,*

6 Windy Hill Lane, Marske-by-the-Sea, Redcar, Cleveland TS11 7BN Middlesbrough (0642) 482896

LAMBERT, David Nathaniel. b 34. Headingley Meth Coll 58 Linc Th Coll 66. **d** 66 **p** 67. In Meth Ch 58-66; C Canwick *Linc* 66-68; C-in-c Bracebridge Heath CD 68-69; R Saltfleetby All SS w St Pet 69-73; R Saltfleetby St Clem 70-73; V Skidbrooke 70-73; V Saltfleetby 73-80; R Theddlethorpe 74-80; RD Louthesk 76-82; R N Ormsby w Wyham 80; R Fotherby from 81. *The Vicarage, Peppin Lane, Fotherby, Louth, Lincs LN11 0UG* Louth (0507) 606403

LAMBERT, Donald William. b 19. Keble Coll Ox BA40 MA44. St Steph Ho Ox 40. **d** 43 **p** 44. V Acton Green St Pet *Lon* 71-77; rtd 77; Perm to Offic *Chich* from 77. *8 Christ Church House, 34 Christ Church Road, Worthing, W Sussex BN11 1JA* Worthing (0903) 206978

LAMBERT, Gordon. b 32. Univ of Wales (Lamp) BA56. Wycliffe Hall Ox 56. **d** 58 **p** 59. C Newbarns w Hawcoat *Carl* 58-63; C-in-c Barrow St Aid CD 63-67; V Barrow St Aid 67-68; R Ousby w Melmerby 68-71; V Farlam 71-76; TV Thirsk w S Kilvington and Carlton Miniott etc *York* 76-77; TV Thirsk 77-89; RD Thirsk 81-89; V Belvedere All SS *Roch* from 89. *All Saints' Vicarage, Nuxley Road, Belvedere, Kent DA17 5JE* Erith (03224) 32169

LAMBERT, Ian Anderson. b 43. Lon Univ BA72 Nottm Univ MTh87. Ridley Hall Cam 66. **d** 67 **p** 68. C Bermondsey St Mary w St Olave, St Jo etc *S'wark* 67-70; Jamaica 71-75; Chapl RAF from 75. *c/o MOD, Adastral House, Theobald's Road, London WC1X 8RY* 071-430 7268

LAMBERT, John Clement Antony. b 28. St Cath Coll Cam BA48 MA52. Cuddesdon Coll 50. **d** 52 **p** 53. C Hornsea and Goxhill *York* 52-55; C Leeds St Pet *Ripon* 55-59; R Carlton-in-Lindrick *S'well* from 59. *The Rectory, Carlton-in-Lindrick, Worksop, Notts S81 9EF* Worksop (0909) 730222

LAMBERT, Malcolm Eric. b 58. RMN84 Leic Univ BSc80 Fitzw Coll Cam BA89. Ridley Hall Cam 87. **d** 90 **p** 91. C Humberstone *Leic* from 90. *St Mary's House, 28 Cranesbill Road, Leicester LE5 1TA* Leicester (0533) 742256

LAMBERT, Michael Roy. b 25. Univ Coll Dur BSc49. Cuddesdon Coll 52. **d** 52 **p** 53. C Middlesb St Oswald *York* 52-56; C Romsey *Win* 56-59; C Cottingham *York* 59-64; Chapl Hull Univ 59-64; V Saltburn-by-the-Sea 64-72; P-in-c Shaftesbury H Trin *Sarum* 72-73; R Shaston 74-78; R Corfe Mullen from 78. *16 Pheasant Way, Cirencester, Glos GL7 1BL* Cirencester (0285) 654657

LAMBERT, Norman. b 39. ACP66 Ch Ch Coll Cant 62 Lon Inst of Educn TCert65. Chich Th Coll 67. **d** 70 **p** 71. C Ocker Hill *Lich* 70-73; C Dudley St Edm *Worc* 73-76; P-in-c Darby End 76-77; V from 77. *St Peter's Vicarage, 25 Brooksbank Drive, Gawne Lane, Cradley Heath, W Midlands B64 5QG* Cradley Heath (0384) 637662

LAMBERT, Miss Olivia Jane. b 48. Matlock Coll of Educn BEd70. Trin Coll Bris DipHE86. **dss** 86 **d** 87. York St Luke *York* 86-87; Par Dn 87-90; Chapl York Distr Hosp 86-90; Par Dn Huntington *York* from 90. *22 Park Avenue, New Earswick, York YO3 8DB* York (0904) 764306

LAMBERT, Peter George. b 29. Coll of Resurr Mirfield 86. **d** 87 **p** 88. NSM Rothwell w Orton, Rushton w Glendon and Pipewell *Pet* from 87. *4 Cogan Crescent, Rothwell, Kettering, Northants NN14 2AS* Kettering (0536) 710692

LAMBERT, Philip Charles. b 54. St Jo Coll Dur BA75 Fitzw Coll Cam BA77 MA81. Ridley Hall Cam 75. **d** 78 **p** 79. C Upper Tooting H Trin *S'wark* 78-81; C Whorlton *Newc* 81-84; P-in-c Alston cum Garrigill w Nenthead and Kirkhaugh 84-87; TV Alston Team 87-89; R Curry Rivel w Fivehead and Swell *B & W* from 89. *The Rectory, Curry Rivel, Langport, Somerset TA10 0HQ* Langport (0458) 251375

LAMBERT, Stephen Uvedale. b 49. FRICS77 Magd Coll Cam BA70 MA75. Ox NSM Course 87. **d** 90. NSM Lt Compton w Chastleton, Cornwell etc *Ox* from 90. *Harcomb, Chastleton, Moreton-in-Marsh, Glos GL56 0SU* Barton-on-the-Heath (060874) 354

LAMBERT, Sydney Thomas. b 17. Keble Coll Ox BA39 MA44. Wells Th Coll 40. **d** 41 **p** 42. R Rendcomb *Glouc* 67-73; V Colesbourne 67-73; P-in-c Cheltenham St Pet 73-78; P-in-c Todenham w Lower Lemington 78-83; P-in-c Bourton on the Hill 78-83; rtd 83; Perm to Offic Worc and Glouc from 83. *97 Elm Road, Evesham, Worcs WR11 5DR* Evesham (0386) 446725

LAMBETH, John Raymond. b 20. Keble Coll Ox BA45 MA49. St Steph Ho Ox 45. **d** 47 **p** 48. Chapl

Convent of St Mary at the Cross Edgware 64-79; C Ealing Ch the Sav *Lon* 79-80; P-in-c Portslade St Pet and St Andr *Chich* 80-84; Perm to Offic from 84; rtd 85. *40 Rutland Court, New Church Road, Hove, E Sussex BN3 4AF* Brighton (0273) 726819

LAMBETH, Archdeacon of. *See* BIRD, Ven Colin Richard Bateman

LAMBOURNE, John Brian. b 36. Chich Th Coll 62. **d** 65 **p** 66. C Cant St Greg *Cant* 65-67; C St Mary in the Marsh 67-68; C E Grinstead St Swithun *Chich* 68-70; C Storrington 70-76; C Sullington 70-76; V Salehurst from 76; CF (TA) from 87. *St Mary's Vicarage, Fair Lane, Robertsbridge, E Sussex TN32 5AR* Robertsbridge (0580) 880408

LAMBURN, Canon Roger George Patrick. b 04. MBE55. Trin Coll Cam BA26 MA61. St Steph Ho Ox 26. **d** 27 **p** 28. Tanganyika 30-64; Tanzania from 64; rtd 72. *c/o J Fletcher Esq, USPG, 157 Waterloo Road, London SE1 8XA* 071-928 8681

LAMDIN, Keith Hamilton. b 47. Bris Univ BA69. Ripon Coll Cuddesdon 86. **d** 86 **p** 87. Adult Educn Officer *Ox* from 86; Team Ldr Par Resources Dept from 88. *41 Stapleton Road, Headington, Oxford OX3 3LX* Oxford (0865) 67160

LAMMAS, Miss Diane Beverley. b 47. Trin Coll Bris 76. **dss** 79 **d** 87. Lenton Abbey *S'well* 79-84; Wollaton Park 79-84; E Regional Co-ord CPAS 84-89; Sec for Voc and Min CPAS 84-89; Hon C Cam St Paul 87-90; Voc and Min Adv CPAS from 89. *3 Riversleigh Road, Leamington Spa, Warks CV32 6BG* Leamington Spa (0926) 427637

LAMONT, Roger. b 37. Jes Coll Ox BA60 MA62. St Steph Ho Ox 59. **d** 61 **p** 62. C Northn St Alb *Pet* 61-66; V Mitcham St Olave *S'wark* 66-73; V N Sheen St Phil and All SS 73-85; P-in-c Richmond St Luke 82-85; Chapl St Lawr Hosp Caterham from 85. *St Lawrence's Hospital, Coulsdon Road, Caterham, Surrey CR3 5YA* Caterham (0883) 340803

LANCASHIRE, Allan. b 32. Birm Univ BA54. Lich Th Coll. **d** 63 **p** 64. C Birstall *Wakef* 63-67; V Wrenthorpe 67-70; P-in-c Wolverton H Trin *Ox* 70-73; TV 73-76; Educn Officer 73-76; Dioc Schs Officer *Lich* 76-85; P-in-c Drayton St Pet (Oxon) *Ox* 85-90; P-in-c Horley w Hornton 85-90; R Horley w Hornton and Hanwell, Shenington etc from 90. *The Vicarage, Horley, Banbury, Oxon OX17 6BH* Wroxton St Mary (029573) 8165

LANCASHIRE, Douglas. b 26. SOAS Lon BA50 MA58 K Coll Lon BD55. **d** 61 **p** 79. USA 61-62; Australia 62-65; New Zealand 65-81; R Boxted w Langham *Chelmsf* from 81. *The Rectory, Wick Road, Langham, Colchester CO4 5PG* Colchester (0206) 230666

LANCASTER, Frederick Charles Thomas. b 16. Bps' Coll Cheshunt 48. **d** 51 **p** 52. R Ascot Heath *Ox* 67-81; rtd 81; Perm to Offic *Ox* from 82. *21 Withington Court, Abingdon, Oxon OX14 3QA* Abingdon (0235) 525584

LANCASTER, John Rawson. b 47. BSc. N Ord Course. **d** 82 **p** 83. C Bolton St Jas w St Chrys *Bradf* 82-86; V Barnoldswick w Bracewell from 86. *The Vicarage, 131 Gisburn Road, Barnoldswick, Colne, Lancs BB8 5JU* Barnoldswick (0282) 812028

LANCASTER, Norman. b 13. Leeds Univ BA36. Coll of Resurr Mirfield 36. **d** 38 **p** 39. V Aylesby *Linc* 71-77; R Gt Coates 71-77; rtd 77; Perm to Offic *Linc* from 77. *50 Westminster Drive, Grimsby, S Humberside DN34 4TY* Grimsby (0472) 361587

LANCASTER, Ronald. b 31. FRSC St Jo Coll Dur BA53 MA56. Cuddesdon Coll 55. **d** 57 **p** 58. C Morley St Pet w Churwell *Wakef* 57-60; C High Harrogate St Pet *Ripon* 60-63; Lic to Offic *Ely* 63-88; Chapl Kimbolton Sch Cambs 63-88; Asst Chapl 88-91; Perm to Offic *Ely* from 88. *7 High Street, Kimbolton, Huntingdon, Cambs PE18 0HB* Huntingdon (0480) 860498

LANCASTER, Archdeacon of. *See* GIBBONS, Ven Kenneth Harry

LANCASTER, Suffragan Bishop of. *See* NICHOLLS, Rt Rev John

LAND, Michael Robert John. b 43. Ripon Hall Ox 70. **d** 72 **p** 73. C Newbury St Nic *Ox* 72-75; TV Chigwell *Chelmsf* 75-80; V Walthamstow St Andr from 80. *St Andrew's Vicarage, 37 Sutton Road, London E17 5QA* 081-527 3969

LANDALL, Richard. b 57. St Jo Coll Dur 85. **d** 88 **p** 89. C Nailsea H Trin *B & W* from 88. *26 St Mary's Grove, Nailsea, Bristol BS19 2NQ* Bristol (0272) 858837

LANDEN, Edgar Sydney. b 23. ARCM46 FRCO46 St Jo Coll Dur BA54 BMus55 DipTh55. **d** 55 **p** 56. C Cirencester *Glouc* 69-76; Min Can Ch Ch *Ox* 76-88; R

Wytham 76-88; rtd 88. *4 Allandale Road, Burnham-on-Sea, Somerset TA8 2HG* Burnham-on-Sea (0278) 783062

LANDMAN, Denis Cooper. b 21. MBE60 OM(Ger)80. DipEd52. St Deiniol's Hawarden 79. **d** 82 **p** 83. Hon C Tranmere St Paul w St Luke *Ches* 82-86; Australia from 86. *41 Brighton Street, Labrador, Queensland, Australia 4216* Labrador (75) 374468

LANDRETH, Canon Derek. b 20. TD63. K Coll Cam BA47 MA52. Bps' Coll Cheshunt 47. **d** 48 **p** 49. CF (TA) 51-75; V Richmond St Mary *S'wark* 59-70; Hon Can S'wark Cathl 68-76; R Sanderstead All SS 70-74; TR 74-77; Can Res S'wark Cathl 77-82; Vice-Chmn Dioc Past Cttee 77-82; Chapl to HM The Queen from 80; P-in-c Icklesham *Chich* 82-83; V 83-88; RD Rye 84-88; P-in-c Fairlight 84-86; rtd 89. *Gossamer Cottage, Slindon, Arundel, W Sussex BN18 0QT* Slindon (024365) 224

LANDRETH, Mrs Mavis Isabella. b 32. SEN81. Gilmore Ho 67. **dss** 74 **d** 87. Walthamstow St Sav *Chelmsf* 70-75; Sanderstead All SS *S'wark* 76-79; Sheff St Cuth *Sheff* 84-85; N Gen Hosp Sheff 84-85; Icklesham *Chich* 86-87; Hon Par Dn 87-89; Perm to Offic from 89. *Gossamer Cottage, Slindon, Arundel, W Sussex BN18 0QT* Slindon (024365) 224

LANE, Andrew Harry John. b 49. Lanc Univ BA71. Cuddesdon Coll 71. **d** 73 **p** 74. C Abingdon w Shippon *Ox* 73-78; Chapl Abingdon Sch 75-78; Chapl RAF from 78. *c/o MOD, Adastral House, Theobald's Road, London WC1X 8RU* 071-430 7268

LANE, Anthony James. b 29. Leeds Univ BA53. Coll of Resurr Mirfield 53. **d** 55 **p** 56. C Tilehurst St Mich *Ox* 55-60; Min Can Win Cathl *Win* 60-63; R Handley w Gussage St Andrew and Pentridge *Sarum* 64-80; V Thurmaston *Leic* 80-85; TV Bournemouth St Pet w St Swithun, St Steph etc *Win* from 85. *1 Gervis Road, Bournemouth BH1 3ED* Bournemouth (0202) 22740

LANE, Antony Kenneth. b 58. Ripon Coll Cuddesdon 84. **d** 87 **p** 88. C Crediton and Shobrooke *Ex* 87-90; C Amblecote *Worc* from 90. *2 Lakeside Court, Lakeside, Brierley Hill, West Midlands DY5 3RQ* Lye (0384) 892118

LANE, Christopher George. b 48. NDH. Sarum & Wells Th Coll 84. **d** 86 **p** 87. C Petersfield *Portsm* 86-90; P-in-c Barton from 90. *St Paul's Vicarage, Barton, Newport, Isle of Wight PO30 2HZ* Isle of Wight (0983) 522075

LANE, David John. b 35. Magd Coll Ox BA58 MA62 BD89. Coll of Resurr Mirfield 60. **d** 62 **p** 62. Barbados 61-65; C Wolvercote *Ox* 65-66; Asst Chapl Pemb Coll Ox 66-68; Lect 68-71; Tutor St Steph Ho Ox 68-71; Canada 71-83; Assoc Prof Univ of Toronto 71-83; Tutor Coll of Resurr Mirfield from 83; Dir of Studies from 84; Vice-Prin 87-90; Prin from 90. *College of the Resurrection, Mirfield, W Yorkshire WF14 0BW* Mirfield (0924) 490441

LANE, Denis John Victor. b 29. Lon Univ LLB49 BD55. Oak Hill Th Coll 50. **d** 53 **p** 54. C Deptford St Jo *S'wark* 53-56; C Cam St Steph CD *Ely* 56-59; Singapore from 59. *Overseas Missionary Fellowship, 2 Cluny Road, Singapore 1025* Singapore (65) 473-5755

LANE, Dennis Charles William. b 17. Lon Univ BD40 AKC40. **d** 40 **p** 41. V Tandridge *S'wark* 64-91; RD Godstone 71-76; rtd 91. *7 Branksome Close, New Milton, Hants* New Milton (0425) 613302

LANE, Canon Gerald. b 29. Bede Coll Dur BA52. Sarum Th Coll 52. **d** 54 **p** 55. C Camberwell St Giles *S'wark* 54-58; C Gillingham St Aug *Roch* 58-59; V 73-78; V Camberwell St Phil and St Mark *S'wark* 59-67; V Plumstead St Nic 67-73; V Hadlow *Roch* from 78; Hon Can Roch Cathl from 87. *The Vicarage, Maidstone Road, Hadlow, Tonbridge, Kent TN11 0DJ* Hadlow (0732) 850238

LANE, Canon Harold. b 09. MBE56. St Chad's Coll Dur BA33 LTh33 MA47. St Paul's Coll Burgh 27. **d** 33 **p** 35. Bahamas 67-80; rtd 80. *20 Mallard Way, Haxby, York YO3 8NG* York (0904) 763558

LANE, Iain Robert. b 61. CCC Ox BA83. Ripon Coll Cuddesdon BA86 MA88. **d** 87 **p** 88. C Rotherhithe St Mary w All SS *S'wark* 87-91; V Bierley *Bradf* from 91. *St John's Vicarage, Bierley Lane, Bierley, Bradford, W Yorkshire BD4 6AA* Bradford (0274) 681397

LANE, John Ernest. b 39. MBIM76 Cranfield Inst of Tech MSc80. Handsworth Coll Birm 58. **d** 80 **p** 80. In Meth Ch 62-80; Hon C Peckham St Jo w St Andr *S'wark* from 80; Dir St Mungo Housing Assn from 80. *24 Harcourt Road, London SE4 2AJ* 071-286 1358

LANE, Mrs Linda Mary. b 41. ACIB66 Cam Univ DipRK70 Lon Univ BD87. Gilmore Ho 67. **dss** 82 **d** 87. Hadlow *Roch* 82-87; Hon Par Dn from 87. *The Vicarage,*

Maidstone Road, Hadlow, Tonbridge, Kent TN11 0DJ Hadlow (0732) 850238

LANE, Richard Peter. b 60. Linc Th Coll 85. **d** 88 **p** 89. C Towcester w Easton Neston *Pet* 88-91; Asst Chapl Oslo w Bergen, Trondheim, Stavanger etc *Eur* from 91. *c/o The British Embassy, BFPO 50, Oslo, Norway* Oslo (2) 552400

LANE, Roy Albert. b 42. Bris Sch of Min 82. **d** 85 **p** 86. NSM Bedminster *Bris* from 85. *20 Ashton Drive, Bristol BS3 2PW* Bristol (0272) 662298

LANE, Stephen Toller. b 29. SS Coll Cam BA52 MA56. Lon Coll of Div ALCD54 LTh74. **d** 54 **p** 55. C Heworth H Trin *York* 54-57; V Everton St Cuth *Liv* 57-63; V Eccleston St Luke 63-71; R Bradfield *Ox* 71-85; R Snettisham w Ingoldisthorpe and Fring *Nor* from 85. *The Vicarage, Station Road, Snettisham, King's Lynn, Norfolk PE31 7QJ* Dersingham (0485) 541301

LANE, William Michael. b 19. BNC Ox MA47. **d** 79 **p** 80. Asst Chapl Clifton Coll Bris 79-82; P-in-c Bris St Mich *Bris* 82-88; C 88-89; rtd 89; Perm to Offic *Bris* from 89. *8 Fremantle Square, Bristol BS6 5LL* Bristol (0272) 247925

LANG, Geoffrey Wilfrid Francis. b 33. St Jo Coll Ox BA56 MA61. Cuddesdon Coll 56. **d** 58 **p** 59. C Spalding *Linc* 58-61; Asst Chapl Leeds Univ *Ripon* 61-62; C Chesterton St Luke *Ely* 62-63; C-in-c Chesterton Gd Shep CD 63-69; V Chesterton Gd Shep 69-72; V Willian *St Alb* 72-76; Dir of Educn 72-76; R N Lynn w St Marg and St Nic *Nor* 77-86; V Hammersmith St Pet *Lon* from 86. *17 Ravenscourt Road, London W6 0UH* 081-748 1781

LANG, Very Rev John Harley. b 27. Em Coll Cam MA60 K Coll Lon AKC49 BD60 Keele Univ DLitt88. **d** 52 **p** 53. C Portsea St Mary *Portsm* 52-57; PV S'wark Cathl *S'wark* 57-60; Chapl Em Coll Cam 60-64; Asst Hd Relig Broadcasting BBC 64-67; Hd 71-80; Hd of Relig Progr BBC Radio 67-71; C Sacombe *St Alb* 73-80; Chapl to HM The Queen 76-80; Dean Lich from 80. *The Deanery, The Close, Lichfield, Staffs WS13 7LD* Lichfield (0543) 262044

LANG, William David. b 51. K Coll Lon BD74 AKC74. St Aug Coll Cant 74. **d** 75 **p** 76. C Fleet *Guildf* 75-79; C Ewell St Fran 79-82; C W Ewell 79-82; V Holmwood from 82. *The Vicarage, South Holmwood, Dorking, Surrey RH5 4JX* Dorking (0306) 889118

LANG, William Peter. b 43. Lon Univ AKC67 BD68. Coll of Resurr Mirfield 67. **d** 69 **p** 70. C Primrose Hill St Mary w Avenue Road St Paul *Lon* 69-73; P-in-c St Marylebone St Mark w St Luke 73-78; TR St Marylebone Ch Ch 78-83. *Address temp unknown*

LANGAN, Mrs Eleanor Susan. b 56. Homerton Coll Cam BEd78. Ripon Coll Cuddesdon 84. **d** 87. Hon Par Dn Grays Thurrock *Chelmsf* 87-89; Lic to Offic from 89. *The Vicarage, Fambridge Road, Althorne, Chelmsford CM3 6BZ* Maldon (0621) 740250

LANGAN, Michael Leslie. b 54. Cam Univ BA PGCE. Cranmer Hall Dur. **d** 84 **p** 85. C Grays Thurrock *Chelmsf* 84-89; V Creeksea w Althorne, Latchingdon and N Fambridge from 89. *The Vicarage, Fambridge Road, Althorne, Chelmsford CM3 6BZ* Maldon (0621) 740250

LANGDON, Eric. b 07. St Chad's Coll Dur BA31 DipTh33 MA34. **d** 32 **p** 33. V Watton w Beswick and Kilnwick *York* 57-82; rtd 82. *The Old Vicarage, Watton, Driffield, N Humberside YO25 9AJ* Driffield (0377) 70285

LANGDON, John Bonsall. b 21. Linc Coll Ox BA51 MA55. Ripon Hall Ox 52. **d** 54 **p** 55. C Erith St Jo *Roch* 54-57; C Christchurch *Win* 57-60; Min Can Ripon Cathl *Ripon* 60-63; R Swillington 63-75; P-in-c Wrangthorn 75-76; V Leeds All Hallows w St Simon 75-76; V Leeds All Hallows w Wrangthorn 76-87; P-in-c Woodhouse St Mark 85-87; V Woodhouse and Wrangthorn from 87. *St Mark's Vicarage, St Mark's Avenue, Leeds LS2 9BN* Leeds (0532) 454893

LANGDON, Canon William Ancell Martin. b 14. Selw Coll Cam BA36 MA41. Wells Th Coll 36. **d** 38 **p** 39. V Charminster *Sarum* 69-81; rtd 81. *3A Bon Accord Road, Swanage, Dorset BH19 2DN* Swanage (0929) 424167

LANGFORD, David Laurence. b 51. Local NSM Course 86. **d** 88 **p** 89. NSM Scotton w Northorpe *Linc* from 88. *1 Westgate, Scotton, Gainsborough, Lincs DN21 3QX* Scunthorpe (0724) 763139

LANGFORD, Herbert Walter. b 19. Lon Univ BA50. Wells Th Coll 50. **d** 52 **p** 53. Registrar and Examinations Sec ACCM 69-71; R Winthorpe *S'well* 71-88; V Langford w Holme 72-88; rtd 88. *26 The Orchard, Durham DH1 5DA* 091-386 3268

LANGFORD, Prof Michael John. b 31. New Coll Ox BA54 MA58 Lon Univ PhD66. Westcott Ho Cam 55. **d** 56 **p** 57. C Bris St Nath w St Kath *Bris* 56-59; Chapl

Qu Coll Cam 59-63; C Hampstead St Jo *Lon* 63-67; Canada from 67; Prof Philosophy Newfoundland Univ from 82; Prof Medical Ethics from 87. *8 Dartmouth Place, St John's, Newfoundland, Canada, A1B 2W2* St John's (709) 739-5746

LANGFORD, Peter Francis. b 54. Sarum & Wells Th Coll 76. **d** 79 **p** 80. C N Ormesby *York* 79-82; Ind Chapl 83-91; V Middlesb St Chad from 91. *St Chad's Vicarage, 9 Emerson Avenue, Linthorpe, Middlesbrough TS5 7QW* Middlesbrough (0642) 819854

LANGFORD, Peter Julian. b 33. Selw Coll Cam BA58. Westcott Ho Cam 59. **d** 60 **p** 61. C E Ham St Mary *Chelmsf* 60-67; Hon C 67-71; Hon C Beccles St Mich *St E* 71-76; Warden Ringsfield Hall Suffolk 71-87; P-in-c Ringsfield w Redisham *St E* 76-80; TV Seacroft *Ripon* from 87. *St Richard's Vicarage, Ramshead Hill, Leeds LS14 1BX* Leeds (0532) 656388

LANGHAM, John Godfrey. b 22. Lon Univ DipTh60. Oak Hill Th Coll. **d** 60 **p** 61. V Burton in Kendal *Carl* 63-79; rtd 79; Perm to Offic *Ex* from 80. *61 Holmdale, Sidmouth, Devon EX10 8DN* Sidmouth (0395) 516417

LANGHAM, Paul Jonathan. b 60. Ex Univ BA81 DipTh83 Fitzw Coll Cam BA86 MA91. Ridley Hall Cam 84. **d** 87 **p** 88. C Bath Weston All SS w N Stoke *B & W* 87-91; Chapl and Fell St Cath Coll Cam from 91. *St Catharine's College, Cambridge CB2 1RL* Cambridge (0223) 338346

LANGLEY, Dr Myrtle Sarah. b 39. FRAI TCD BA61 HDipEd62 MA67 Bris Univ PhD76 Lon Univ BD66. Dalton Ho Bris 64. **d** 88. Dir Chr Development for Miss *Liv* 87-89; Dir of Tr Inst *Carl* from 90; Dioc Dir of Tr from 90. *92 Greenacres, Wetheral, Carlisle, Cumbria CA4 8LD* Wetheral (0228) 61478

LANGLEY, Canon Robert. b 37. St Cath Soc Ox BA61. St Steph Ho Ox. **d** 63 **p** 64. C Aston cum Aughton *Sheff* 63-68; Midl Area Sec Chr Educn Movement 68-71; HQ Sec Chr Educn Movement 71-74; Prin Ian Ramsey Coll Brasted 74-77; Dir St Alb Minl Tr Scheme 77-85; Can Res St Alb 77-85; Can Res Newc Cathl *Newc* from 85. *16 Towers Avenue, Newcastle upon Tyne NE2 3QE* 091-281 0714

LANGMAN, Barry Edward. b 46. Master Mariner 73. Cant Sch of Min 87. **d** 90. NSM St Margarets-at-Cliffe w Westcliffe etc *Cant* from 90. *Hillbrow, The Street, Martin, Dover, Kent CT15 5JP* Dover (0304) 852928

LANGRISH, Canon Michael Laurence. b 46. Birm Univ BSocSc67 Fitzw Coll Cam BA73 MA77. Ridley Hall Cam 71. **d** 73 **p** 74. C Stratford w Bishopton *Cov* 73-76; Chapl Rugby Sch Warks 76-81; P-in-c Offchurch *Cov* 81-87; Dioc Dir of Ords 81-87; P-in-c Rugby St Andr 87-91; Hon Can Cov Cathl from 90; TR Rugby St Andr from 91. *The Rectory, 79 Clifton Road, Rugby, Warks CV21 3QG* Rugby (0788) 2936

LANGSTAFF, James Henry. b 56. St Cath Coll Ox BA77 MA81 Nottm Univ BA80. St Jo Coll Nottm 78. **d** 81 **p** 82. C Farnborough *Guildf* 81-84; P-in-c 84-85; C 85-86; P-in-c Duddeston *Birm* 86; P-in-c Duddeston w Nechells 86; V from 87. *St Matthew's Vicarage, Duddeston Manor Road, Birmingham B7 4QD* 021-359 1609

LANGSTON, Clinton Matthew. b 62. Derby Coll of Educn BCombStuds86. Qu Coll Birm 87. **d** 90 **p** 91. C Shirley *Birm* from 90. *51 Moreton Road, Shirley, Solihull, W Midlands B90 3EH* 021-745 1325

LANGTON, Canon Kenneth. b 26. Open Univ BA76. St Aid Birkenhead 52. **d** 55 **p** 56. C Oldham St Paul *Man* 55-57; C Ashton Ch Ch 57-58; P-in-c St Stalybridge New St Geo 58-69; P-in-c Stalybridge Old St Geo 67-69; V Stalybridge 69-71; R Radcliffe St Mary 71-83; Hon Can Man Cathl from 80; V Tyldesley w Shakerley from 83. *St George's Vicarage, 203 Manchester Road, Tyldesley, Manchester M29 8WT* Atherton (0942) 882914

LANGTON, Canon Maurice Charles. b 09. Trin Coll Cam BA30 MA34. Sarum Th Coll 33. **d** 34 **p** 35. Dir RE and Tr of Ord Cand *Chich* 56-77; Can and Preb Chich Cathl 63-77; rtd 77. *3 Caithness Road, Stamford, Lincs PE9 2TE* Stamford (0780) 51004

LANGTON-DURHAM, Alaric John. b 14. Univ Coll Ox BA36 MA45. St Aid Birkenhead 39. **d** 39 **p** 40. R Fairstead w Terling *Chelmsf* 65-86; rtd 86. *2 Thomas Heskin Court, Station Road, Bishop's Stortford, Herts CM23 6EE* Bishop's Stortford (0279) 506484

LANHAM, Frederick James. b 07. Lon Univ BCom33. Wycliffe Hall Ox 33. **d** 35 **p** 36. V Glouc Ch Ch *Glouc* 61-72; rtd 72; Perm to Offic *Chich* from 73. *Willow Cottage, High Street, Burwash, Etchingham, E Sussex TN19 7EU* Burwash (0435) 882579

LANHAM, Geoffrey Peter. b 62. Cam Univ MA84 Ox Univ MPhil86. Wycliffe Hall Ox 86. **d** 89 **p** 90. C Southborough St Pet w Ch Ch and St Matt *Roch* from 89. *54 Holden Park Road, Southborough, Tunbridge Wells, Kent TN4 0EP* Tunbridge Wells (0892) 25913

LANHAM, Richard Paul White. b 42. Dur Univ BA64. Wycliffe Hall Ox 65. **d** 67 **p** 68. C Horwich H Trin *Man* 69-72; C Worsley 72-74; V Accrington St Andr *Blackb* 74-80; V Shillington *St Alb* 80-85; V Upper w Lower Gravenhurst 80-85; rtd 85; Perm to Offic *St Alb* from 85. *10 Alexander Close, Clifton, Shefford, Beds* Hitchin (0462) 813520

LANKESTER, Joseph Posford. b 17. AKC42. **d** 42 **p** 43. V Bromsgrove All SS *Worc* 59-73; Chapl Bromsgrove and Redditch Distr Gen Hosp 67-73; RD Bromsgrove *Worc* 68-73; R Stanford-on-Teme w Orleton and Stockton 73-78; P-in-c Worc St Martin-in-the-Cornmarket 78-80; rtd 80. *88 Kilbury Drive, Whittington, Worcester* Worcester (0905) 355453

LANKESTER, Preb Robin Pryor Archibald. b 14. Lon Univ BA50. Wells Th Coll 64. **d** 65 **p** 66. Warden Sussex Gardens Int Students' Club 67-70; R Priston w Englishcombe *B & W* 70-74; R Combe Hay 70-74; Chapl Bath Univ 74-79; Preb Wells Cathl 76-79; rtd 79; Chapl Karachi Cathl and Lect Sem 80-83; Perm to Offic *B & W* from 83. *8 Horn Street, Nunney, Frome, Somerset BA11 4NP* Nunney (037384) 398

LANKEY, David. b 41. CEng MBCS Southn Univ BSc62. S'wark Ord Course 79. **d** 82 **p** 83. NSM W Wimbledon Ch Ch *S'wark* from 82. *77A Lambton Road, London SW20 0LW* 081-946 8979

LANSDALE, Charles Roderick. b 38. Leeds Univ BA59. Coll of Resurr Mirfield 59. **d** 61 **p** 62. C Nunhead St Antony *S'wark* 61-65; Swaziland 65-71; V Benhilton *S'wark* 72-78; TR Catford (Southend) and Downham 78-87; TR Moulsecoomb *Chich* from 87. *St Andrew's Rectory, Hillside, Brighton BN2 4TA* Brighton (0273) 680680

LANSLEY, Paul Sanford. b 33. Trin Coll Cam BA56 MA61. St Steph Ho Ox 56. **d** 58 **p** 59. C N Acton St Gabr *Lon* 58-60; Hon C Colchester St Jas, All SS, St Nic and St Runwald *Chelmsf* from 69; Asst Chapl Colchester Hosps from 86. *24 Worcester Road, Colchester CO1 2RH* Colchester (0206) 866306

LANTSBERY, Colin. b 39. Chich Th Coll 70. **d** 72 **p** 73. C Wednesfield St Thos *Lich* 72-75; C W Bromwich All SS 75-77; V Normacot 77-84; V Longton St Mary and St Chad from 84. *SS Mary and Chad Presbytery, 269 Anchor Road, Stoke-on-Trent ST3 5DN* Stoke-on-Trent (0782) 313142

LANYON JONES, Keith. b 49. Southn Univ BTh79. Sarum & Wells Th Coll 74. **d** 77 **p** 78. C Charlton Kings St Mary *Glouc* 77-81; Sen Chapl Rugby Sch Warks from 81; Lic to Offic *Truro* from 83. *11 Horton Crescent, Rugby, Warks CV22 5DJ* Rugby (0788) 544939

LAPAGE, Michael Clement. b 23. Selw Coll Cam BA47 MA73. Clifton Th Coll 60. **d** 61 **p** 62. Kenya 61-72; Chapl Bedf Sch 73-75; Chapl Lyon w Grenoble *Eur* 76-79; V Walford w Bishopswood *Heref* 79-88; P-in-c Goodrich w Welsh Bicknor and Marstow 83-88; Perm to Offic *Ex* from 88. *Moorlands, 20 Watts Road, Tavistock, Devon PL19 8LG* Tavistock (0822) 615901

LAPAGE, Canon Peter Reginald. b 17. MC45. Selw Coll Cam BA41 MA44. Ridley Hall Cam 46. **d** 48 **p** 49. Area Sec (Dios Lon and S'wark) CMS 66-82; rtd 82; Perm to Offic *S'wark* from 82. *37A Trinity Road, London SW19 8QS* 081-542 9737

LAPHAM, Canon Fred. b 31. Univ of Wales (Lamp) BA53. Vancouver Sch of Th LTh55 BD58. **d** 55 **p** 55. V Over St Jo *Ches* 62-70; V Upton Ascension 70-82; R Grappenhall 82-91; RD Gt Budworth 85-91; Hon Can Ches Cathl 88-91; rtd 91. *1 Coppice Gate, Lyth Hill, Shrewsbury SY3 0BT* Shrewsbury (0743) 722284

LAPWOOD, Robin Rowland John. b 57. Selw Coll Cam MA. Ridley Hall Cam 80. **d** 82 **p** 83. C Bury St Edmunds St Mary *St E* 82-86; P-in-c Bentley w Tattingstone from 86. *The Vicarage, Bentley, Ipswich IP9 2BL* Great Wenham (0473) 311495

LARCOMBE, Leslie Duke. b 12. NW Ord Course 75. **d** 77 **p** 78. NSM Elton All SS *Man* 77-78; C 78-82; rtd 82; Perm to Offic *Man* from 82. *55 Tottington Road, Bury, Lancs BL9 0NU* 061-797 6676

LARGE, Preb Denis Henry. b 18. Sarum Th Coll 39. **d** 42 **p** 43. R Clyst St Mary *Ex* 61-75; R Clyst St George 61-75; Adv Chr Stewardship 64-81; V Woodbury Salterton 67-75; V Rockbeare 67-75; R Aylesbeare and Farringdon 67-75; R Clyst Honiton 67-75; R Sowton 67-75; RD Aylesbeare 73-76; TR Clyst St George, Aylesbeare, Clyst Honiton etc 75-83; rtd 83; Perm to

Offic *Ex* from 83. *30 Higher Shaeter Street, Topsham, Devon EX3 0AW* Topsham (0392) 873295

LARGE, William Roy. b 40. Dur Univ BA DipEd. Edin Th Coll 82. **d** 84 **p** 85. C Leamington Priors All SS *Cov* 84-88; V Bishop's Tachbrook from 88; Warden of Readers and Sen Tutor from 88. *The Vicarage, 24 Mallory Road, Bishop's Tachbrook, Leamington Spa CV33 9QX* Leamington Spa (0926) 426922

LARK, William Donald Starling. b 35. Keble Coll Ox BA59 MA63. Wells Th Coll 59. **d** 61 **p** 62. C Wyken *Cov* 61-64; C Christchurch *Win* 64-66; V Yeovil St Mich *B & W* 66-75; V Earley St Pet *Ox* 75-85; V Prittlewell *Chelmsf* 85-88; V Dawlish *Ex* from 88. *The Vicarage, Dawlish, Devon EX7 9EB* Dawlish (0626) 862204

LARKIN, Peter John. b 39. ALCD62. **d** 62 **p** 63. C Liskeard w St Keyne *Truro* 62-65; C Rugby St Andr *Cov* 65-67; Sec Bp Cov Call to Miss 67-68; V Kea *Truro* 68-78; P-in-c Bromsgrove St Jo *Worc* 78-81; R Torquay St Matthias, St Mark and H Trin *Ex* from 81. *The Rectory, Wellswood Avenue, Torquay TQ1 2QE* Torquay (0803) 293280

LARKINS, Mary Herve. b 14. IDC. Coll of Ascension 39. **dss** 46 **d** 87. Gt Ayton w Easby and Newton in Cleveland *York* 46-73; rtd 74; Perm to Offic Guildf 76-86; Glouc from 87. *25 Capel Court, The Burgage, Prestbury, Cheltenham, Glos GL52 3EL* Cheltenham (0242) 576460

LARNER, Gordon Edward Stanley. b 30. Oak Hill Th Coll 57. **d** 59 **p** 60. C Peckham St Mary Magd *S'wark* 59-62; C Luton w E Hyde *St Alb* 62-68; V Lower Sydenham St Mich *S'wark* 68-73; Ind Chapl 73-83; Lic to Offic *S'well* from 84; Chapl HM Pris Ranby from 84. *HM Prison, Ranby, Retford, Notts DN22 8EU* Retford (0777) 706721

LARSEN, Clive Erik. b 55. St Jo Coll Nottm LTh90. **d** 90 **p** 91. C Weaverham *Ches* from 90. *7 Heath Road, Owley Wood, Weaverham, Northwich, Cheshire CW8 3JZ* Weaverham (0606) 853944

LARTER, John William. b 29. Lon Univ BSc51. Coll of Resurr Mirfield. **d** 54 **p** 55. C Redcar *York* 54-56; C Thornaby on Tees St Paul 56-59; C Boreham Wood All SS *St Alb* 59-62; Perm to Offic *Ox* 62-65; R Middleton Stoney 65-70; P-in-c Bucknell 65-69; R 69-70; V N Hinksey 70-77; V Eye w Braiseworth and Yaxley *St E* 77-84; RD Hartismere 78-81; P-in-c Occold w Redlingfield 80-84; V Hunstanton St Edm w Ringstead *Nor* 84-91; V Wormingford, Mt Bures and Lt Horkesley *Chelmsf* from 91. *The Vicarage, Church Road, Wormingford, Colchester CO6 3AZ* Bures (0787) 227398

LASHBROOKE, John. b 28. Kelham Th Coll 49. **d** 53 **p** 54. C Kennington St Jo *S'wark* 53-57; Br Guiana 57-59; V Sydenham St Phil *S'wark* 59-69; R Corby Epiphany w St Jo *Pet* 69-80; V Rubery *Birm* 80-88; V Horam *Chich* from 88. *The Vicarage, Horebeech Lane, Horam, Heathfield, E Sussex TN21 0DT* Horam Road (04353) 2563

LASKEY, Cyril Edward. b 44. RMN71 RGN74. Llan Dioc Tr Scheme 85. **d** 88 **p** 89. NSM Troedrhiwgarth *Llan* from 88. *207 Bridgend Road, Maesteg, Bridgend, M Glam CF34 0NL* Maesteg (0656) 734639

LAST, Eric Cyril. b 30. Oak Hill Th Coll 77. **d** 79 **p** 80. C Wandsworth All SS *S'wark* 79-83; V Earlsfield St Andr 83-88; V S Merstham from 88. *The Vicarage, Battlebridge Lane, South Merstham, Redhill, Surrey RH1 3LH* Merstham (0737) 642722

LAST, Harold Wilfred. b 17. **d** 40 **p** 41. Dir of Music St Bees, St Olave's & Felstead Schs 53-73; rtd 73. *81 Dales View Road, Ipswich* Ipswich (0473) 45135

LAST, Norman Percy George. b 31. BA CertEd ATPL. Sarum & Wells Th Coll 77 Wycliffe Hall Ox 80. **d** 81 **p** 82. C Walton-on-Thames *Guildf* 81-83; C Farnham 83-87; R Monks Eleigh w Chelsworth and Brent Eleigh etc *St E* 87-90. *Lashbrook, Thornbury, Holsworthy, Devon EX22 7BA* Shebbear (040928) 287

LATHAEN, Canon William Alan. b 06. MBE TD. Dur Univ MA. **d** 31 **p** 32. Hon Can Dur Cathl *Dur* 61-86; R Shincliffe 68-77; rtd 77. *67 Woodside, Barnard Castle, Co Durham DL12 8AR* Teesdale (0833) 37570

LATHAM, Christine Elizabeth. b 46. S'wark Ord Course 87. **d** 90. Par Dn Battersea St Pet and St Paul *S'wark* from 90. *31 Plough Road, London SW11 2DE* 071-223 2311

LATHAM, John Westwood. b 31. Ely Th Coll 57. **d** 60 **p** 61. C Cleckheaton St Jo *Wakef* 60-63; C Hemel Hempstead *St Alb* 63-65; C Wakef Cathl *Wakef* 65-67; V Outwood 67-72; TV Daventry w Norton *Pet* 72-79; V Flore w Dodford and Brockhall from 79. *The Vicarage, Flore, Northampton NN7 4LZ* Weedon (0327) 40510

LATHAM, Robert Norman. b 53. Qu Coll Birm 82. d 85
p 86. C Tamworth *Lich* 85-89; TV Wordsley from
89. *25 Middleway Avenue, Wordsley, Stourbridge, W
Midlands DY8 5NH* Kingswinford (0384) 293350
LATHAM, Trevor Martin. b 56. BD84. Ripon Coll
Cuddesdon 84. d 86 p 87. C Cantril Farm *Liv* 86-89; TV
W Derby St Mary from 89. *The Vicarage, 1 Sandicroft
Road, Liverpool L12 0LX* 051-549 2202
LATHE, Canon Anthony Charles Hudson. b 36. Jes Coll
Ox BA59 MA64 UEA DipSoc68. Lich Th Coll 59. d 61
p 62. C Selby Abbey *York* 61-63; V Hempnall *Nor*
63-72; R Woodton w Bedingham 63-72; R Fritton w
Morningthorpe w Shelton and Hardwick 63-72; R
Topcroft 63-72; R Banham 72-76; TR Quidenham 76-83;
P-in-c New Buckenham 78-79; V Heigham St Thos from
83; Hon Can Nor Cathl from 87; RD Nor S from 90. *St
Thomas's Vicarage, Edinburgh Road, Norwich NR2 3RL*
Norwich (0603) 624390
LATTIMORE, Anthony Leigh. b 35. Dur Univ BA57.
Lich Th Coll 60. d 62 p 63. C Aylestone *Leic* 62-66;
C-in-c Eyres Monsell CD 66-69; V Eyres Monsell 69-73;
V Somerby, Burrough on the Hill and Pickwell 73-86;
RD Goscote I 80-86; R Glenfield from 86. *The Rectory,
Main Street, Glenfield, Leicester LE3 8DG* Leicester
(0533) 871604
LAUGHTON, Derek Basil. b 24. Worc Coll Ox
BA49 MA52. Westcott Ho Cam 49. d 51 p 52. Chapl
Wellington Sch Somerset 64-73; Chapl Ardingly Coll
Haywards Heath 73-77; R Plumpton *Chich* 77-88; Perm
to Offic *B & W* from 88; rtd 89. *13 Pyles Thorne Road,
Wellington, Somerset TA21 8DX* Wellington (0823)
667386
LAURENCE, Ven John Harvard Christopher. b 29. Trin
Hall Cam BA53 MA57. Westcott Ho Cam 53. d 55 p 56.
C Linc St Nic w St Jo Newport *Linc* 55-59; V Crosby
59-74; Can and Preb Linc Cathl 74-79 and from 85; Dioc
Missr 74-79; Bp's Dir of Clergy Tr *Lon* 80-85; Adn
Lindsey *Linc* from 85. *The Archdeaconry, 2 Greenstone
Place, Lincoln LN2 1PP* Lincoln (0522) 531444
LAURENCE, Julian Bernard Vere. b 60. Kent Univ BA82.
St Steph Ho Ox 86. d 88 p 89. C Yeovil St Mich *B & W*
from 88; Chapl Yeovil Coll from 90; Chapl Yeovil Distr
Gen Hosp from 91. *220 Goldcroft, Yeovil, Somerset
BA21 4DA* Yeovil (0935) 25621
LAURENCE, Vere Deacon. b 11. Ex Coll Ox BA33 BSc34
MA37. Sarum Th Coll 34. d 36 p 37. V Upper Sunbury
St Sav *Lon* 53-74; R Jacobstow w Warbstow and
Treneglos *Truro* 74-83; RD Stratton 77-83; rtd 83; Perm
to Offic *B & W* from 85. *12 Westbrook Road, Weston-
super-Mare, Avon BS22 8JU* Weston-super-Mare
(0934) 415143
LAURENCE, William Gregory. b 10. St Andr Whittlesford
40. d 40 p 41. R Aynho *Pet* 65-74; V Newbottle 65-74;
rtd 74. *Flat 14, Ellesborough Manor, Butlers Cross,
Aylesbury, Bucks HP17 0XF*
LAURIE, Donovan Hugh. b 40. Man Univ MSc. Oak Hill
NSM Course. d 82 p 83. NSM Cudham and Downe *Roch*
82-84; C Tunbridge Wells St Jas 84-88; P-in-c Ventnor
St Cath *Portsm* from 88; P-in-c Ventnor H Trin from
88. *The Vicarage, Park Avenue, Ventnor, Isle of Wight
PO38 1LD* Isle of Wight (0983) 852130
LAURIE, James Andrew Stewart. b 26. Selw Coll Cam
BA51 MA55. Ridley Hall Cam 51. d 53 p 54. P-in-c Ilam
w Blore Ray and Okeover *Lich* 65-71; V Wetton 65-71;
V Alstonfield 65-71; P-in-c Calton 66-71; V Charsfield
w Debach and Monewden w Hoo *St E* 83-86; V Charsfield
w Debach, Monewden, Hoo etc 86-90; rtd 90. *Four
Winds, Hollington Road, Stubwood, Uttoxeter, Staffs
ST14 7HR* Uttoxeter (0889) 591252
LAUT, Graham Peter. b 37. Chich Th Coll 63. d 67 p 68.
C Corringham *Chelmsf* 67-68; C Leytonstone St Marg w
St Columba 68-71; P-in-c Leytonstone St Andr 71-75; V
75-80; V Romford Ascension Collier Row from 80. *The
Ascension Vicarage, 68 Collier Row Road, Romford
RM5 2BA* Romford (0708) 41658
LAVENDER, Cyril Norman. b 01. St Aug Coll Cant 32.
d 35 p 35. V Warham w Wighton *Nor* 60-69; rtd 69;
P-in-c Nor St Helen *Nor* 74-84; Perm to Offic from 84.
4 Masters House, The Great Hospital, Norwich NR1 4EL
Norwich (0603) 663946
LAVERACK, John Julian. b 51. Keele Univ BA CertEd
Bris Univ BA. Bris Bapt Coll 76 Ex & Truro NSM
Scheme 81. d 82 p 83. In Bapt Ch 79-81; C Braunton *Ex*
82-84; V Ex St Mark from 84. *St Mark's Vicarage,
36 Polsloe Road, Exeter EX1 2DN* Exeter (0392) 56478
LAVERTY, Walter Joseph Robert. b 49. CITC 70 Glouc
Th Course 73. d 73 p 74. C Belf St Donard *D & D* 73-77;
C Ballymacarrett St Patr 77-82; I Kilwarlin Upper w
Kilwarlin Lower 82-86; I Orangefield w Moneyreagh

from 86; RD Dundonald from 91. *397 Castlereagh Road,
Belfast BT5 6AB* Belfast (0232) 704493
LAVERY, Edward Robinson. Lon Univ BA DipTh. St
Aid Birkenhead 65. d 67 p 68. C Belf Trin Coll Miss
Conn 67-69; C Belf St Mary Magd 69-71; CF (TA) from
70; I Belf St Phil *Conn* 71-74; I Craigs w Dunaghy and
Killagan 74-83; I Ballymoney w Finvoy and Rasharkin
from 83. *The Rectory, Queen Street, Ballymoney, Co
Antrim* Ballymoney (02656) 62149
LAVERY, Leonard. b 06. St Aid Birkenhead 49. d 50
p 51. V Kenwyn St Jo *Truro* 64-73; rtd 73. *Glan-
Mor, Falmouth Road, Truro, Cornwall TR1 2BL* Truro
(0872) 72895
LAVILLE, Jocelyn Roger. b 30. Ball Coll Ox BA53 MA62.
St Jo Coll Lon ALCD64. d 64 p 65. C Gillingham St
Mark *Roch* 64-69; C Thorpe Edge *Bradf* 69-72;
The Philippines from 72. *PO Box 464, Manila, The
Philippines 1502* Manila (2) 722-2764
LAW, Brian Charles. b 36. Aston Univ BSc67. NW Ord
Course 75. d 78 p 79. C Litherland St Jo and St Jas *Liv*
78-81; V Warrington St Ann 81-88; P-in-c Southport St
Phil and St Paul 88-89; V from 89. *St Philip's Vicarage,
Scarisbrick New Road, Southport PR8 6QF* Southport
(0704) 532886
LAW, Bryan. b 36. Leeds Univ BA59 Lon Univ BD76.
Coll of Resurr Mirfield 59. d 61 p 62. C Winshill *Derby*
61-64; R Gorton St Phil *Man* 64-70; Lic to Offic 70-71;
Perm to Offic *Ox* from 71; Hd Master Page Hill Co
Middle Sch Buckm from 81. *35 Little Meadow, Loughton,
Milton Keynes MK5 8EH* Milton Keynes (0908) 661333
LAW, Canon Donald Edward Boughton. b 22. Lon Coll of
Div 67. d 69 p 70. C Leic H Apostles *Leic* 69-73; V
Cosby 73-81; RD Guthlaxton I (Blaby) 75-81; V Melton
Mowbray w Thorpe Arnold 81-86; Hon Can Leic Cathl
from 81; RD Framland II 84-88; TR Melton Gt Framland
86-88; rtd 88; Perm to Offic *Pet* from 88. *36 Mill Grove,
Whissendine, Oakham, Leics LE15 7EY* Whissendine
(066479) 411
LAW, Geoffrey Arthur. b 04. Bps' Coll Cheshunt 37. d 39
p 40. V Whorlton *York* 59-75; rtd 75; C York St Olave
w St Giles *York* 75-80; Hon C 80-88. *c/o D McDougall
Esq., 38 Cumberland Street, Edinburgh EH3 6RG*
031-557 1931
LAW, Gordon James. b 19. Worc Ord Coll 67. d 69 p 70.
C Hillingdon St Jo *Lon* 69-72; C Brixham *Ex* 72-76; R
Drewsteignton 76-79; V Hittisleigh 76-79; V Spreyton
76-79; C Aldershot St Mich *Guildf* 79-82; rtd 82; Perm
to Offic *Ex* from 83; Ab from 89. *Speymuir, 6 Delgaty
Terrace, Turriff, Aberdeenshire AB53 7GA* Turriff
(0888) 63970
LAW, Gordon Peter. b 35. Bernard Gilpin Soc Dur
59 Chich Th Coll 60. d 64 p 65. C Walthamstow St Barn
and St Jas Gt *Chelmsf* 64-67; C Southchurch H Trin
67-68; C Plaistow St Andr 68-69; Chapl Aldersbrook
Medical Unit 69-83; P-in-c Forest Gate All SS 69-74; V
74-83; V Romford St Jo from 83. *St John's Vicarage,
Mawney Road, Romford RM7 7BH* Romford (0708)
742265
LAW, Herbert James Wentworth. b 12. Dur Univ
BA39 DipTh39 MA42. d 40 p 41. V Barton *Ely* 69-78;
rtd 78. *37 Westlands, Comberton, Cambridge CB3 7EH*
Cambridge (0223) 263406
LAW, Jeremy Thomson. b 61. Univ of Wales (Abth)
BSc82 Southn Univ BTh89. Sarum & Wells Th Coll 84.
d 87 p 88. C Wimborne Minster and Holt *Sarum* 87-90; C
Highfield *Ox* from 90. *39C New High Street, Headington,
Oxford OX3 7AL* Oxford (0865) 69004
LAW, Jim. b 20. Lon Coll of Div 49. d 52 p 53. V Gt
Singleton *Blackb* 61-87; rtd 87; Perm to Offic *Blackb*
from 87. *30 Cedar Avenue, Poulton-le-Fylde, Blackpool
FY6 8DQ* Poulton-le-Fylde (0253) 886188
LAW, John Francis. b 35. Bps' Coll Cheshunt 65. d 67
p 68. C Styvechale *Cov* 67-71; P-in-c Cov St Anne and
All SS 71-73; TV Cov E 73-77; P-in-c Fillongley 77-82;
P-in-c Corley 77-82; V Fillongley and Corley from 82;
RD Nuneaton from 90. *The Vicarage, Holbeche Crescent,
Fillongley, Coventry CV7 8ES* Fillongley (0676) 40320
LAW, John Michael. b 43. Open Univ BA79. Westcott
Ho Cam 65. d 68 p 69. C Chapel Allerton *Ripon* 68-72;
C Ryhope *Dur* 72-73; Lic to Offic *Ely* from 74; Chapl
Ida Darw and Fulbourn Hosps Cam from 74; Mental
Health Fell Bethlem R & Maudsley Hosps from 82.
1 The Maples, Fulbourn, Cambridge Cambridge (0223)
248074
LAW, Kenneth. b 16. St Jo Coll Dur LTh39 BA40 MA43. St
Aid Birkenhead 36. d 40 p 41. V Ossett cum Gawthorpe
Wakef 54-81; CF (TA) 64-81; rtd 81; Perm to Offic
Wakef from 81. *Heathdene, Cromwell Place, Ossett, W
Yorkshire WF5 9LP* Wakefield (0924) 262740

LAW, Nicholas Charles. b 58. BA89. Trin Coll Bris 86. **d** 89 **p** 90. C Goldington *St Alb* from 89. *1 Atholl Walk, Bedford MK41 0BG* Bedford (0234) 212973

LAW, Peter James. b 46. Ridley Hall Cam 85. **d** 87 **p** 88. C Bournemouth St Jo w St Mich *Win* 87-91; V Chineham from 91; Min Chineham LEP from 91. *1 Hartswood, Chineham, Basingstoke RG24 0SJ* Basingstoke (0256) 474280

LAW, Peter Leslie. b 25. Bede Coll Dur BA48 DipEd49. Qu Coll Birm 53. **d** 55 **p** 56. Chapl St Luke's Sch Southsea 69-79; Chapl Portsm Cathl *Portsm* 69-79; V Eastney 79-90; rtd 90; Perm to Offic *Portsm* from 90. *123 Hayling Avenue, Portsmouth PO3 6DY* Portsmouth (0705) 730337

LAW, Richard Lindsay. b 34. Univ Coll Ox BA58 MA62. Cuddesdon Coll 58. **d** 60 **p** 61. C Leighton Buzzard *St Alb* 60-63; Trinidad and Tobago 63-67; V Stottesdon *Heref* 67-72; P-in-c Farlow 67-72; Chapl Framlingham Coll Suffolk 72-83; V Leigh-on-Sea St Marg *Chelmsf* from 83. *St Margaret's Vicarage, 1465 London Road, Leigh-on-Sea, Essex SS9 2SB* Southend-on-Sea (0702) 76062

LAW, Robert Frederick. b 43. St Aid Birkenhead 67. **d** 69 **p** 70. C Bengeo *St Alb* 69-72; C Sandy 72-76; P-in-c St Ippolyts 76-81; Chapl Jersey Gp of Hosps 81-84; V Crowan w Godolphin *Truro* from 84; RD Kerrier from 90. *Crowan Vicarage, Trithanis Gardens, Praze, Camborne, Cornwall TR14 9NB* Praze (0209) 831009

LAW, Dr Robert James. b 31. Lon Univ MB, BS55. Ridley Hall Cam 62. **d** 64 **p** 65. C Barnehurst *Roch* 64-66; C Edgware *Lon* 66-72; V Halwell w Moreleigh *Ex* from 72; P-in-c Woodleigh and Loddiswell 76-79; R from 79. *The Vicarage, Halwell, Totnes, Devon TQ9 7JA* Blackawton (080421) 257

LAW-JONES, Peter Deniston. b 55. Newc Univ BA77 Man Univ CertEd81 Nottm Univ BTh87. Linc Th Coll 84. **d** 87 **p** 88. C Chorley St Laur *Blackb* 87-91; V Feniscliffe from 91. *The Vicarage, St Francis Road, Feniscliffe, Blackburn BB2 2TZ* Blackburn (0254) 201757

LAWES, David Alan. b 33. Lon Bible Coll BD57 PGCE58 AcDipEd66 Lon Inst of Educn MA70. Cranmer Hall Dur 90. **d** 91. NSM Shaston *Sarum* from 91. *Barton Elm, Kington Magna, Gillingham, Dorset SP8 5EH* East Stour (074785) 448

LAWES, Geoffrey Hyland. b 37. St Jo Coll Dur BA58 DipTh62 Hertf Coll Ox BA60 MA64 Newc Univ PGCE76 MEd79. Cranmer Hall Dur 61. **d** 63 **p** 64. C Millfield St Mark *Dur* 63-66; C Jarrow Grange 66-69; Hon C 69-86; Lic to Offic 86-90; V Collierley w Annfield Plain from 90. *Collierley Vicarage, Stanley, Co Durham DH9 8QS* Stanley (0207) 236254

LAWES, Stephen George. b 40. Nottm Univ PGCE75. St Jo Coll Nottm BTh74. **d** 82 **p** 83. NSM Hillmorton *Cov* 82-86; Perm to Offic *Pet* from 85. *Oak Tree Cottage, 34 Stowe Nine Churches, Northampton* Weedon (0327) 40401

LAWES, Timothy Stanley. b 57. Nottm Univ BTh88. Linc Th Coll 85. **d** 88 **p** 89. C Wymondham *Nor* from 88. *Becketswell House, Becketswell Road, Wymondham, Norfolk NR18 9PH* Wymondham (0953) 604342

LAWLEY, Peter Gerald Fitch. b 52. Chich Th Coll 77. **d** 80 **p** 81. C Pet St Jo *Pet* 80-83; C Daventry 83-87; P-in-c Syresham w Whitfield 87-90; TV Cen Telford *Lich* from 90. *15 Carwood, Stirchley, Telford TF3 1VA* Telford (0952) 595482

LAWN, Geoffrey. b 27. Jes Coll Cam BA48 MA52 Lon Univ BD56. Ripon Hall Ox 56. **d** 57 **p** 58. C Selby Abbey *York* 57-61; V Huntington 61-70; Dioc Ecum Adv 69-74; R Newton Kyme 70-74; V Doncaster St Geo *Sheff* 74-82; Hon Can Sheff Cathl 75-82; V Pickering *York* from 82. *The Vicarage, Whitby Road, Pickering, N Yorkshire YO18 7HD* Pickering (0751) 72983

LAWRANCE, David. b 26. Man Univ BA51 BD66 St Cath Soc Ox BA53 MA57. Wycliffe Hall Ox 51. **d** 53 **p** 54. V Oldham Moorside *Man* 61-73; Ind Chapl *Sheff* 74-85; C Wetherby *Ripon* 85-91; Chapl HM Young Offender Inst Wetherby from 89; rtd 91. *21 Clarence Drive, Harrogate, N Yorkshire HG1 2QE* Harrogate (0423) 504050

LAWRANCE, Hugh Norcliffe. b 49. N Riding Coll of Educn BEd79. Linc Th Coll 83. **d** 85 **p** 86. C Lindley *Wakef* 85-87; C Barkisland w W Scammonden from 87; C Ripponden from 87. *Christ Church Vicarage, Stainland Road, Barkisland, Halifax, W Yorkshire HX4 0AR* Halifax (0422) 822339

LAWRANCE, Robert William. b 63. Jes Coll Ox BA85 MA89. Ripon Coll Cuddesdon BA87. **d** 88 **p** 89. C Astley *Man* from 88-91; Lect Bolton St Pet from 91. *114 Bromwich Street, Bolton BL2 1LL* Bolton (0204) 393615

LAWRENCE, Charles Anthony Edwin. b 53. AKC75. St Aug Coll Cant 75. **d** 76 **p** 77. C Mitcham St Mark *S'wark* 76-80; C Haslemere *Guildf* 80-82; P-in-c Ashton H Trin *Man* 82-84; V from 84; AD Ashton-under-Lyne from 91. *Holy Trinity Vicarage, Ashton-under-Lyne, Lancs OL6 7HD* 061-344 0075

LAWRENCE, Charles William. b 14. Lon Coll of Div 46. **d** 48 **p** 49. V Newland w Redbrook *Glouc* 65-73; V Glouc Ch Ch 73-79; rtd 79. *2 Prospect Terrace, St Swithin's Road, Gloucester GL2 6LJ* Gloucester (0452) 415850

LAWRENCE, David Ian. b 48. AIMLS71 MIBiol76 Univ Coll Lon BSc74. Glouc Sch of Min 84 Sarum & Wells Th Coll 87. **d** 88 **p** 89. C Wotton St Mary *Glouc* 88-91; P-in-c Cheltenham St Mich from 91. *St Michael's Vicarage, Severn Road, Cheltenham, Glos GL52 5QA* Cheltenham (0242) 515500

LAWRENCE, David John. b 53. Leeds Poly BEd77. Linc Th Coll. **d** 86 **p** 87. C Gt and Lt Coates w Bradley *Linc* 86-89; P-in-c Hemingby 89-91; R from 91. *The Rectory, Hemingby, Horncastle, Lincs LN9 9QF* Grimsby (0472) 354240

LAWRENCE, George Leslie. b 11. Bp Wilson Coll 38. **d** 41 **p** 42. R Crofton *Wakef* 69-78; rtd 79; Perm to Offic *Wakef* from 79. *702 Doncaster Road, Crofton, Wakefield, W Yorkshire WF4 1PX* Wakefield (0924) 862174

LAWRENCE, Canon Harold. b 12. Univ Coll Dur LTh35 BA36. St Aug Coll Cant 31. **d** 36 **p** 37. C Gt Stanmore *Lon* 36-38; S Africa from 39; Adn Durban 61-74; Hon Can Natal from 74. *7 Chapter Close, Pietermaritzburg, 3201 South Africa* Pietermaritzburg (331) 945686

LAWRENCE, Miss Helen. b 30. St Mich Ho Ox 62. **dss** 74 **d** 87. Braintree *Chelmsf* 74-87; Par Dn 87-90; rtd 90. *6 Reynards Close, Kirby Cross, Frinton-on-Sea, Essex CO13 0RA* Frinton-on-Sea (0255) 673837

LAWRENCE, Miss Ida Eugenia Laura. b 14. Open Univ BA81. Gilmore Ho 45. **dss** 78 **d** 87. Rayleigh *Chelmsf* 78-87; Hon Par Dn from 87. *Dilkusha, Hardwick Close, Rayleigh, Essex SS6 7QP* Rayleigh (0268) 773059

LAWRENCE, James Conrad. b 62. St Jo Coll Dur BA85. Ridley Hall Cam 85. **d** 87 **p** 88. C Bar Hill LEP *Ely* from 87. *99 The Spinney, Bar Hill, Cambridge CB3 8SU* Crafts Hill (0954) 781046

LAWRENCE, John Graham Clive. b 47. ACIB. Trin Coll Bris DipTh78. **d** 78 **p** 79. C Chatham St Phil and St Jas *Roch* 78-83; V Roch St Justus from 83. *St Justus's Vicarage, 1 Binnacle Road, Rochester, Kent ME1 2XR* Medway (0634) 841183

LAWRENCE, John Shaw. b 27. W Midl Minl Tr Course. **d** 81. NSM Birm St Martin *Birm* 81-85; Chapl Coun for Soc Aid 84-89; NSM Birm St Martin w Bordesley St Andr from 85; rtd 89. *208 Hay Green Lane, Birmingham B30 1SG* 021-451 3425

LAWRENCE, Canon Leonard Roy. b 31. Keble Coll Ox BA56 MA59. Westcott Ho Cam 56. **d** 58 **p** 59. C Stockport St Geo *Ches* 58-62; V Thelwall 62-68; V Hyde St Geo 68-75; V Prenton from 75; Hon Can Ches Cathl from 86. *The Vicarage, 1 Reservoir Road, Birkenhead, Merseyside L42 8QX* 051-608 1808

LAWRENCE, Leslie. b 44. Lon Univ DipRS84. S'wark Ord Course 86. **d** 88 **p** 89. NSM Stanwell *Lon* from 88. *Whitlocke Lodge, 16 Balfour Road, Hounslow TW3 1JX* 081-572 6280

LAWRENCE, Norman. b 45. Lon Univ BEd75. S'wark Ord Course 77. **d** 80 **p** 81. NSM Hounslow H Trin *Lon* 80-88; NSM Hounslow H Trin w St Paul from 88. *89 Bulstrode Avenue, Hounslow* 081-572 6292

LAWRENCE, Patrick Henry Andrew. b 51. TCD BA81. CITC 76. **d** 81 **p** 82. C Templemore *D & R* 81-84; C Kilkenny St Canice Cathl *C & O* 84-85; I Templebreedy w Tracton and Nohoval *C, C & R* from 85. *The Rectory, Crosshaven, Cork, Irish Republic* Cork (21) 831236

LAWRENCE, Peter Anthony. b 36. Lich Th Coll 67. **d** 69 **p** 70. C Oadby *Leic* 69-74; P-in-c Northmarston and Granborough *Ox* 74-81; P-in-c Hardwick St Mary 74-81; P-in-c Quainton 76-81; P-in-c Oving w Pitchcott 76-81; TR Schorne from 81; RD Claydon 84-88. *The Vicarage, Church Street, North Marston, Buckingham MK18 3PH* North Marston (029667) 298

LAWRENCE, Peter Halliday. b 47. ALCM K Alfred's Coll Win CertEd69 Nottm Univ BTh76. St Jo Coll Nottm 72. **d** 76 **p** 77. C Birm St Luke *Birm* 76-79; V Burney Lane from 79. *Christ Church Vicarage, Burney Lane, Birmingham B8 2AS* 021-783 7455

LAWRENCE, Ralph Guy. b 55. Trin Coll Bris DipHE89. **d** 89 **p** 90. C Cotmanhay *Derby* from 89. *76 Prince Street, Ilkeston, Derbyshire DE7 8QQ* Ilkeston (0602) 301311

LAWRENCE, Timothy Hervey. b 25. Ripon Hall Ox 58. **d** 60 **p** 61. V Kentford w Higham Green *St E* 62-84; P-in-c Herringswell 78-84; rtd 84. *13 South Street, Risby,*

Bury St Edmunds, Suffolk IP28 6QU Bury St Edmunds (0284) 810083

LAWRENCE, Victor John. b 43. ACII. Oak Hill Th Coll. d 83 p 84. C Paddock Wood *Roch* 83-87; R Milton next Gravesend w Denton from 87. *The Rectory, Church Walk, Milton, Gravesend, Kent* Gravesend (0474) 533434

LAWRENCE-MARCH, David Lawrence. b 61. Univ of Wales (Lamp) BA83. Coll of Resurr Mirfield 83. d 85 p 86. C Pet St Jude *Pet* 85-89; C Kilburn St Aug w St Jo *Lon* 89-90; Chapl St Aug Sch Kilburn from 89; C Paddington St Mary *Lon* from 90. *4 Fleming Court, St Mary's Terrace, London W2 1SE* 071-402 0878

LAWRENSON, James Percival. b 12. Kelham Th Coll 30. d 36 p 37. Chapl Berkhamsted Sch Herts 56-78; rtd 78; Perm to Offic St Alb from 78; Ox from 87. *Downside, Torrington Road, Berkhamsted, Herts* Berkhamsted (0442) 865999

LAWRENSON, Michael. b 35. Leeds Univ BA60. Coll of Resurr Mirfield 60. d 74 p 74. NSM Glenrothes *St And* 74-90; Dioc Supernumerary from 90. *Hollyburn, Falkland, Cupar, Fife KY7 7BW* Falkland (0337) 5/311

LAWRENSON, Ronald David. b 41. CITC 68. d 71 p 72. C Seapatrick *D & D* 71-78; Min Can Down Cathl 78-79; VC Belf Cathl 79-86; Bp's C Tynan w Middletown *Arm* from 86; Hon VC Arm Cathl from 86. *The Rectory, Tynan, Armagh BT60 4SS* Caledon (0861) 568619

LAWRIE, Paul Edward. b 12. Freiburg Univ LLD35 St Cath Soc Ox BA48 MA53. Wycliffe Hall Ox 46. d 48 p 49. R Todwick *Sheff* 64-78; rtd 78; Chapl Rotherham Distr Hosp 78-85; Hon C Handsworth Woodhouse *Sheff* from 85. *15 Haddon Way, Aston, Sheffield S31 0EH* Sheffield (0742) 874864

LAWRIE, Peter Sinclair. b 39. Clifton Th Coll 62. d 65 p 66. C Derby St Chad *Derby* 65-68; C Toxteth Park St Philemon w St Silas *Liv* 68-71; V Ramsey St Mary's w Ponds Bridge *Ely* 71-81; V Whitwick St Jo the Bapt *Leic* from 81. *The Vicarage, North Street, Whitwick, Leicester LE6 4EB* Coalville (0530) 36904

LAWRY, Mrs Fianach Alice Moir. b 35. St And Dioc Tr Course 85. d 88. NSM Dollar *St And* from 88. *Bridge House, 14 Bridge Street, Dollar, Clackmannanshire FK14 7DE* Dollar (02594) 2874

LAWRY, Samuel John Lockhart. b 11. CCC Cam BA33 MA38. Wells Th Coll 34. d 35 p 36. V E Meon *Portsm* 57-68; Perm to Offic from 68; rtd 76. *Broadlands House, Petersfield, Hants GU31 4BA* Petersfield (0730) 62134

LAWS, Clive Loudon. b 54. UEA BEd76. Wycliffe Hall Ox 79. d 82 p 83. C Newc w Butterton *Lich* 82-85; C Gabalfa *Llan* 85-88; R Pendine w Llanmiloe and Eglwys Gymyn w Marros *St D* from 89. *The Rectory, Pendine, Camarthen, Dyfed SA33 4PD* Pendine (09945) 405

LAWS, Edwin Kingsley. b 06. LVO53 KPM39. Bps' Coll Cheshunt 56. d 57 p 58. R Milton Abbas w Winterborne Whitechurch etc *Sarum* 60-74; Custos St Jo Hosp Heytesbury 74-79; rtd 79. *9 Stoberry Crescent, Wells, Somerset BA5 2TG* Wells (0749) 73544

LAWSON, Preb Clifford John. b 21. St Cath Soc Ox BA45 MA47. Qu Coll Birm 45. d 47 p 48. V Eccleshall *Lich* 57-71; Chapl HM Pris Drake Hall 58-71; RD Eccleshall *Lich* 65-71; Preb Lich Cathl 70-86; R Stafford St Mary 72-74; P-in-c Stafford St Chad 72-74; RD Stafford 72-77; R Stafford St Mary and St Chad 74-77; RD Oswestry 77-82; R Rhydycroesau 77-86; R Selattyn 77-86; rtd 86; Perm to Offic *Lich* from 86. *The Burwains, 22 Port Hill Drive, Shrewsbury SY3 8RS* Shrewsbury (0743) 354085

LAWSON, David McKenzie. b 47. Glas Univ MA69 Edin Univ BD76. Edin Th Coll 73. d 76 p 77. C Glas St Mary *Glas* 76-82; V Keighley All SS *Bradf* 82-85; Chapl Asst Univ Coll Hosp Lon from 85; Hon C St Pancras w St Jas and Ch Ch *Lon* from 86. *c/o The Chaplain's Office, University College Hospital, London WC1E 6AU* 071-387 9300

LAWSON, David William. b 50. ACA DipHE. Linc Th Coll. d 82 p 83. C Stafford *Lich* 82-85; TV Redruth w Lanner *Truro* 85-87; Chapl Whitley and Gulson Road Hosps Cov from 87; Chapl Cov and Warks Hosp from 87; P-in-c Whitley *Cov* from 87. *St James's Vicarage, 171 Abbey Road, Whitley, Coventry CV3 4BG* Coventry (0203) 301617

LAWSON, Canon Frederick Quinney. b 45. Leic Univ BA. St Steph Ho Ox. d 83 p 84. Hon C Loughb Em *Leic* 83-86; NSM Somerby, Burrough on the Hill and Pickwell 86-87; NSM Burrough Hill Pars 87; USA 87-88; Hon Can Salt Lake City from 87; Perm to Offic *Leic* from 88. *Broceliande, Main Street, Gaddesby, Leicester LE7 8WG* Melton Mowbray (0664) 840450

LAWSON, Gary Austin. b 53. Man Univ BA80. Ripon Coll Cuddesdon 80. d 82 p 83. C Nunhead St Antony *S'wark* 82-86; Hon C Reddish *Man* 86-87; Hon C Longsight St Jo w St Cypr 87-88; V Wythenshawe St Rich from 88. *St Richard's Vicarage, 42 Lomond Road, Manchester M22 5JD* 061-499 2022

LAWSON, John Alexander. b 62. Sheff Univ BA84. St Jo Coll Nottm DPS87. d 87 p 88. C Wellington, All SS w Eyton *Lich* from 87. *11 Rushbury Road, Wellington, Telford, Shropshire TF1 3NT* Telford (0952) 641229

LAWSON, Canon John Lawrence. b 11. Univ Coll Dur BA33 DipTh34 MA36. Wycliffe Hall Ox 35. d 35 p 36. V Chilham *Cant* 61-73; rtd 74; Perm to Offic *Cant* from 74. *13 Crawford Gardens, Cliftonville, Margate, Kent CT9 2PU* Thanet (0843) 228758

LAWSON, Michael Charles. b 52. Sussex Univ BA75. Trin Coll Bris 75. d 78 p 79. C Horsham *Chich* 78-81; C St Marylebone All So w SS Pet and *Lon* Jon 81-87; V Bromley Ch Ch *Roch* from 87. *Christ Church Vicarage, 18 Highland Road, Bromley BR1 4AD* 081-460 4864

LAWTON, George. b 10. Lon Univ DipTh35 Liv Univ MA58 Nottm Univ BD64 PhD70. Richmond Th Coll 32 Qu Coll Birm 48. d 49 p 50. R Checkley *Lich* 59-77; rtd 77; Perm to Offic *Ex* from 77. *7 Taw View Terrace, Bishop's Tawton, Barnstaple, Devon EX32 0AW* Barnstaple (0271) 77733

LAWTON, Canon John Arthur. b 13. Fitzw Ho Cam BA35 MA40. Cuddesdon Coll 35. d 37 p 38. Hon Can Liv Cathl *Liv* from 63; R Winwick 69-87; Adn Warrington 70-81; rtd 88. *32 Ringwood Close, Gorse Covert, Warrington WA3 6TQ* Padgate (0925) 818561

LAWTON, Canon John Stewart. b 19. Ox Univ MA BD DPhil50. St Steph Ho Ox 40. d 42 p 43. Warden and Chief Lib St Deiniol's Lib Hawarden 62-73; V Lt Leigh and Lower Whitley *Ches* 73-75; Dir of Min 74-84; Can Res Ches Cathl 75-84; rtd 84; Perm to Offic *Ches* from 84. *7 Ormonde Road, Chester CH2 2AH* Chester (0244) 376092

LAXON, Colin John. b 44. Cant Sch of Min. d 89 p 90. C Folkestone St Mary and St Eanswythe *Cant* from 89. *6 Copthall Gardens, Folkestone, Kent CT20 1HF* Folkestone (0303) 56440

LAXTON, Joseph Henry. b 13. Leeds Univ BA36. Coll of Resurr Mirfield 36. d 38 p 39. R Tidmarsh w Sulham *Ox* 71-78; rtd 78; Perm to Offic *Heref* from 78. *27 Charlton Rise, Sheet Road, Ludlow, Shropshire SY8 1ND* Ludlow (0584) 874409

LAY, Brian Robert. b 37. Bernard Gilpin Soc Dur 59 Chich Th Coll 60. d 63 p 64. C Battyeford *Wakef* 63-66; C Belhus Park *Chelmsf* 66-73; P-in-c Sutton on Plym *Ex* 73-80; V from 80. *St John's Vicarage, 3 Alma Street, Cattedown, Plymouth PL4 0NL* Plymouth (0752) 664191

LAYBOURNE, Michael Frederick. b 37. Qu Coll Birm 81. d 83 p 84. C High Elswick St Phil *Newc* 83-85; C High Elswick St Phil and Newc St Aug 86; C Cramlington 86-87; TV from 87. *1 Cateran Way, Cramlington, Northd NE23 6EX* Cramlington (0670) 714261

LAYCOCK, Charles. b 37. Open Univ BA88. N Ord Course. d 83 p 84. C Astley Bridge *Man* 83-86; R Crumpsall from 86. *St Matthew's Rectory, Cleveland Road, Manchester M8 6QU* 061-795 4376

LAYCOCK, Lawrence. b 42. HNC. St Deiniol's Hawarden 86. d 89 p 90. C Blackpool St Mich *Blackb* from 89. *14 Adstone Avenue, Blackpool FY3 7PD* Blackpool (0253) 399201

LAYTON, Miss Norene. b 39. Trin Coll Bris DipHE86. dss 86 d 87. Lindfield *Chich* 86-87; Par Dn from 87. *2 Church Close, Francis Road, Lindfield, Haywards Heath, W Sussex RH16 2JB* Lindfield (0444) 483945

LAZONBY, Canon Alan Frederick. b 19. TD64. St Jo Coll Dur BA40 DipTh41 MA43. d 42 p 43. R Haughton le Skerne *Dur* 57-84; RD Darlington 74-78; Hon Can Dur Cathl from 75; rtd 84. *16 Loraine Crescent, Darlington, Co Durham DL1 5TF* Darlington (0325) 485876

LE CRAS, Allan. b 20. Linc Th Coll 83. d 84 p 85. Hon C Toynton All Saints w Toynton St Peter *Linc* 84-88; Hon C Marden Hill Gp 88-90; Perm to Offic from 90. *Snipe Dales Cottage, Lusby, Spilsby, Lincs PE23 4JB* Winceby (065888) 636

LE DIEU, Miss Heather Muriel. b 41. Birm Univ BA62 MA67 DipTh. St Jo Coll Dur 77. dss 79 d 87. Birchfield *Birm* 79-82; Kings Heath 82-84; Walsall Pleck and Bescot *Lich* 84-87; Par Dn 87-88; rtd 88. *8 Hubert Croft, Hubert Road, Birmingham B29 6DU* 021-471 3566

LE FEUVRE, Henry Mauger. b 21. Lich Th Coll. d 62 p 63. P-in-c Dorrington *Heref* 69-72; P-in-c Stapleton 69-72; P-in-c Cardington 69-72; R Jersey St Lawr *Win*

72-80; R Risby w Gt and Lt Saxham and Westley *St E* 80-85; rtd 85; Perm to Offic *St E* from 85. *18 Southgate Street, Bury St Edmunds, Suffolk IP33 2AF*   Bury St Edmunds (0284) 703524

LE GRICE, Elizabeth Margaret. b 53. Man Univ BA75 MA(Theol)78. Nor Bapt Coll 75 Westcott Ho Cam 87. **d** 88. In Bapt Ch 78-82; C Whitchurch *Llan* from 88. *16 St John's Crescent, Whitchurch, Cardiff CF4 7AF*   Cardiff (0222) 627441

LE GRICE, Very Rev Frederick Edwin. b 11. Qu Coll Cam BA34 MA45. Westcott Ho Cam 34. **d** 35 **p** 36. Dean Ripon 68-84; rtd 84. *The West Cottage, Markenfield Hall, Ripon, N Yorkshire HG4 3AD*   Ripon (0765) 701655

LE GRYS, Alan Arthur. b 51. K Coll Lon BD73 AKC73 MTh90. St Aug Coll Cant 73. **d** 74 **p** 75. C Harpenden St Jo *St Alb* 74-77; C Hampstead St Jo *Lon* 77-81; Chapl Westf Coll and Bedf Coll 81-84; V Stoneleigh *Guildf* 84-91; Lect Ripon Coll Cuddesdon from 91. *Flat 2, New Building, Ripon College, Cuddesdon, Oxford OX9 9EX*   Wheatley (08677) 5688

LE MARCHAND, John Lewis Mansfield. b 43. BNC Ox BA67. Sarum Th Coll 68. **d** 71 **p** 72. C Chatham St Wm CD *Roch* 71-74; C Roch St Pet w St Marg 74-76; R Burham and Wouldham 76-81; V Scopwick w Kirkby Green *Linc* 81; V Scopwick Gp 82-84; Hon C Chatham St Mary w St Jo *Roch* from 84; Chapl RAD from 84. *24 Wallace Road, Rochester, Kent ME1 2TB*   Medway (0634) 841106 or 280356

LE PAGE, Canon Dallas Arthur des Reaux. b 17. Keble Coll Ox BA49 MA53. Cuddesdon Coll 49. **d** 51 **p** 52. C Hampstead St Steph *Lon* 53-58; S Africa from 58; rtd 86. *24 Maynard Street Gardens, Cape Town, 8001 South Africa*   Cape Town (21) 452221

LE PREVOST, Carl Andrew. b 63. Sarum & Wells Th Coll 85. **d** 88 **p** 89. C Chandler's Ford *Win* 88-91; C Southn Maybush St Pet from 91. *60 Brookwood Road, Millbrook, Southampton SO1 9AJ*   Chandler's Ford (0703) 781228

LE ROSSIGNOL, Richard Lewis. b 52. Aston Univ BSc75. Oak Hill Th Coll BA79. **d** 79 **p** 80. C E Ham St Paul *Chelmsf* 79-81; C Willesborough w Hinxhill *Cant* 81-85; Perm to Offic from 85. *64 Osborne Road, Willesborough, Ashford, Kent TN24 0EF*   Ashford (0233) 625193

LE SUEUR, Paul John. b 38. Lon Univ BSc59. Wycliffe Hall Ox 60. **d** 62 **p** 63. C Mortlake w E Sheen *S'wark* 62-65; C Witney *Ox* 65-69; R Sarsden w Churchill 69-74; P-in-c Clifton Hampden 74-77; P-in-c Rotherfield Greys H Trin 77-82; V 82-90; V Blacklands Hastings Ch Ch and St Andr *Chich* from 90. *Christ Church Vicarage, 28 Laton Road, Hastings, E Sussex TN34 2ES*   Hastings (0424) 421821

LE VAY, Mrs Clare Forbes Agard Bramhall Joanna. b 41. St Anne's Coll Ox BA64 MA Univ of Wales (Abth) MSc72 PhD86. Westcott Ho Cam 86. **d** 88. Par Dn Stamford Hill St Thos *Lon* 88-89; Par Dn Hackney from 89. *91 Mildenhall Road, London E5 0RY*   081-985 3150

LEA, Ven Montague Brian. b 34. St Jo Coll Cam BA55 Lon Univ BD71. St Jo Coll Nottm 68. **d** 71 **p** 72. C Northwood Em *Lon* 71-74; Chapl Barcelona *Eur* 74-79; V Hove Bp Hannington Memorial Ch *Chich* 79-86; Adn N France *Eur* from 86; Chapl Paris St Mich from 86. *5 rue d'Aguesseau, 75008 Paris, France*   Paris (331) 47 42 70 88

LEA, Norman. b 42. Univ of Wales (Lamp) BA67. Coll of Resurr Mirfield 66. **d** 68 **p** 69. C Newton St Pet *S & B* 68-71; C Oystermouth 71-73; C Brecon w Battle 73-74; TV Cwmbran *Mon* 74-77; V Talgarth and Llanelieu *S & B* 77-84; V Port Talbot St Theodore *Llan* from 84; Hon Chapl Miss to Seamen from 84. *St Theodore's Vicarage, Talbot Road, Port Talbot, W Glam SA13 1LB*   Port Talbot (0639) 883935

LEA, Canon Richard John Rutland. b 40. Trin Hall Cam BA63 MA67. Westcott Ho Cam 63. **d** 65 **p** 66. C Edenbridge *Roch* 65-68; C Hayes 68-71; V Larkfield 71-86; P-in-c Leybourne 76-86; RD Malling 79-84; V Chatham St Steph 86-88; Can Res and Prec Roch Cathl from 88. *2 Kings Orchard, The Precinct, Rochester ME1 1TG*   Medway (0634) 841491

LEACH, Alan William Brickett. b 28. CEng FIStructE FASI FICE MSc. S'wark Ord Course. **d** 89 **p** 90. NSM Forest Row *Chich* from 89. *Hathaway, Ashdown Road, Forest Row, E Sussex RH18 5BN*   Forest Row (034282) 3778

LEACH, Gerald. b 27. Sarum & Wells Th Coll 85. **d** 73 **p** 74. NSM Cyncoed *Mon* 73-86; C 86-87; V Dingestow and Llangovan w Penyclawdd etc from 87. *The Vicarage, Dingestow, Monmouth, Gwent NP5 4DY*   Dingestow (060083) 206

LEACH, John. b 52. K Coll Lon BD79 AKC79 St Jo Coll Dur MA. **d** 81 **p** 82. C N Walsham w Antingham *Nor* 81-85; C Crookes St Thos *Sheff* 85-89; V Styvechale *Cov* from 89. *The Vicarage, 16 Armorial Road, Coventry CV3 6GJ*   Coventry (0203) 692299

LEACH, Stephen Lance. b 42. St Steph Ho Ox 66. **d** 69 **p** 70. C Higham Ferrers w Chelveston *Pet* 69-72; TV Ilfracombe H Trin *Ex* 72-74; V Barnstaple St Mary 74-77; R Goodleigh 74-77; P-in-c Barnstaple St Pet w H Trin 76-77; P-in-c Landkey 77-79; TR Barnstaple and Goodleigh 77-79; TR Barnstaple, Goodleigh and Landkey 79-82; V Paignton St Jo from 82. *The Vicarage, Palace Place, Paignton, Devon TQ3 3AQ*   Paignton (0803) 559059

LEACH, Stephen Windsor. b 47. St Chad's Coll Dur BSc70 Linacre Coll Ox BA72 MA76. Ripon Hall Ox 70. **d** 73 **p** 74. C Swinton St Pet *Man* 73-77; C Oldham St Chad Limeside 77-79; V Shaw 79-87; V St Just in Penwith *Truro* from 87; V Sancreed from 87. *The Vicarage, St Just, Penzance, Cornwall TR19 7UB*   Penzance (0736) 788672

LEACH, Timothy Edmund. b 41. Dur Univ BA63. Ridley Hall Cam 63. **d** 65 **p** 66. C Ecclesfield *Sheff* 65-68; C Stocksbridge 68-71; C-in-c Bessacarr CD 71-80; V Goole from 80; Hon Chapl Miss to Seamen from 80. *The Vicarage, 22 Clifton Gardens, Goole, N Humberside DN14 6AS*   Goole (0405) 764259

LEACH, William Howard. b 07. Em Coll Cam BA29 MA33. Ridley Hall Cam 29. **d** 31 **p** 32. V Lydney w Aylburton *Glouc* 61-75; rtd 75; Perm to Offic *Worc* from 82. *Perrins House, Moorlands Road, Malvern, Worcs WR14 2TZ*   Malvern (0684) 568173

LEADBEATER, Michael John. b 45. Nottm Univ BTh72 St Martin's Coll Lanc CertEd73. Kelham Th Coll 68. **d** 73 **p** 74. C Manston *Ripon* 73-77; C Holbrooks *Cov* 77-79; V Tipton St Jo *Lich* 79-89; V Rushall from 89. *Rushall Vicarage, 10 Tetley Avenue, Walsall WS4 2HE*   Walsall (0922) 24677

LEADBEATER, Canon Nicolas James. b 20. Univ of Wales BA43. St Steph Ho Ox 43. **d** 45 **p** 46. V Westcote *Glouc* 67-72; P-in-c Icomb 67-72; V Westcote w Icomb 72-79; V Westcote w Icomb and Bledington 79-88; Hon Can Glouc Cathl 83-88; rtd 88. *11 Pitt Street, Gloucester GL1 2BH*   Gloucester (0452) 309644

LEAFE, Maurice Stanley Damian. b 28. Chich Th Coll 72. **d** 74 **p** 75. C Allens Cross *Birm* 74-76; C Solihull 76-81; TV 81-84; V Wellingborough St Barn *Pet* 84-88; R Harpole from 88. *The Rectory, Harpole, Northampton NN7 4DR*   Northampton (0604) 830322

LEAH, William Albert. b 34. K Coll Lon BA56 AKC57 K Coll Cam MA63. Ripon Hall Ox 60. **d** 62 **p** 63. C Falmouth K Chas *Truro* 62-63; Chapl K Coll Cam 63-67; Min Can Westmr Abbey 67-74; V Hawkhurst *Cant* 74-83; Hon Min Can Cant Cathl 78-83; V St Ives *Truro* from 83. *The Parsonage, St Andrew's Street, St Ives, Cornwall TR26 1AH*   Penzance (0736) 796404

LEAHY, David Adrian. b 56. Open Univ BA90. Qu Coll Birm. **d** 85 **p** 86. C Tile Cross *Birm* 85-88; C Warley Woods 88-91; V Hobs Moat from 91. *St Mary's House, 30 Hobs Meadow, Solihull, W Midlands B92 8PN*   021-743 4955

LEAK, David. b 42. St Jo Coll Nottm 76. **d** 79 **p** 80. C Oswestry St Oswald *Lich* 79-83; R Castlemartin w Warren and Angle etc *St D* 83-90. *Address temp unknown*

LEAK, Harry Duncan. b 30. St Cath Coll Cam BA53 MA57. Ely Th Coll 53. **d** 54 **p** 55. S Africa 54-57; Portuguese E Africa 57-61; C Eccleshall *Lich* 62-64; V Normacot 64-66; C Stoke upon Trent 66-68; V Hanley All SS 68-71; R Swynnerton 71-80; Perm to Offic from 80. *15 Sutherland Road, Tittensor, Stoke-on-Trent ST12 9JQ*

LEAK, John Michael. b 42. St Jo Coll Nottm. **d** 84 **p** 85. NSM Beeston *Ripon* 84-87; C Far Headingley St Chad 87-88; Hon C 88-90; C Headingley from 90. *10 St Chad's Rise, Leeds LS6 3QE*   Leeds (0532) 758229

✠**LEAKE, Rt Rev David.** b 35. ALCD59. **d** 59 **p** 60 **c** 69. C Watford *St Alb* 59-61; Lect 61-63; Argentina 63-69; Asst Bp Paraguay 69-73; Asst Bp N Argentina 69-80; Bp 80-90; Bp Argentina from 90. *Casilla 4293, 1000 Correo Central, Buenos Aires, Argentina*   Buenos Aires (1) 344618

LEAKEY, Ian Ramond Arundell. b 24. K Coll Cam BA47 MA49. Ridley Hall Cam 48. **d** 50 **p** 51. Rwanda Miss 53-73; V Cudham *Roch* 73-76; P-in-c Downe 76; V Cudham and Downe 76-89; rtd 89. *5 Pine Close, Beech Grange, Landford, Salisbury SP5 2AW*   Romsey (0794) 390561

LEAKEY, Peter Wippell. b 39. Lon Univ BSc60. Trin Coll Bris 73. **d** 75 **p** 76. C Colne St Bart *Blackb* 75-79; V

Copp 79-85; V Pennington *Man* from 85. *The Vicarage, Schofield Street, Leigh, Lancs WN7 4HT* Leigh (0942) 673619

LEAL, Malcolm Colin. b 33. Chich Th Coll 72. **d** 75 **p** 76. Hon C Shoreham St Giles CD *Chich* 75-87; Chapl NE Surrey Coll Guildf from 87; Hon C Arundel w Tortington and S Stoke *Chich* from 88. *8 West Park Lane, Goring-by-Sea, Worthing, W Sussex BN12 4EK* Worthing (0903) 44160

LEAMING, Ralph Desmond. b 21. Ripon Coll Cuddesdon 79. **d** 81 **p** 82. C Darlington H Trin *Dur* 81-84; V Hamsterley from 84. *The Vicarage, Hamsterley, Bishop Auckland, Co Durham DL13 3PP* Witton-le-Wear (038888) 418

LEAMY, Stuart Nigel. b 46. Pemb Coll Ox BA68 MA73. Sarum Th Coll 68. **d** 70 **p** 71. Lic to Offic *Lon* 71-81; Hon C Upholland *Liv* 72-78. *28 Church Street, Hampton, Middx TW12 2EG* 081-941 3930

LEAN, David Jonathan Rees. b 52. Univ of Wales (Lamp) DipTh74. Coll of Resurr Mirfield 74. **d** 75 **p** 76. C Tenby *St D* 75-81; V Llanrhian w Llanhywel and Carnhedryn etc 81-88; V Haverfordwest St Martin w Lambston from 88. *St Martin's Vicarage, Barn Street, Haverfordwest, Dyfed SA61 1TD* Haverfordwest (0437) 762509

LEANEY, Dr Alfred Robert Clare. b 09. Hertf Coll Ox BA32 DipTh33 MA39 BD52 DD66. Ripon Hall Ox 32. **d** 33 **p** 34. Lic to Offic *S'well* 56-74; Hd of Th Dept Nottm Univ 70-74; rtd 75. *Dunelm, Pulteney Road, Bath BA2 4HA* Bath (0225) 460363

LEANING, Very Rev David. b 36. Lich Th Coll 58. **d** 60 **p** 61. C Gainsborough All SS *Linc* 60-65; R Warsop *S'well* 65-76; RD Kington and Weobley *Heref* 76-80; R Kington w Huntington 76-80; Adn Newark *S'well* 80-91; Provost S'well from 91. *The Residence, Southwell, Notts NG25 0HP* Newark (0636) 812593 or 812649

LEARMOUTH, Michael Walter. b 50. FCA. Oak Hill Th Coll 84. **d** 84 **p** 85. C Harlow St Mary V *Chelmsf* 84-89; V Hainault from 89. *St Paul's Vicarage, Arrowsmith Road, Chigwell, Essex IG7 4NZ* 081-500 3366

LEARY, Thomas Glasbrook. b 42. AKC66. **d** 67 **p** 68. C W Bromwich All SS *Lich* 67-70; TV Croydon *Cant* 70-75; C Limpsfield and Titsey *S'wark* 75-83; V Sutton New Town St Barn from 83. *St Barnabas' Vicarage, 37 St Barnabas' Road, Sutton, Surrey SM1 4NS* 081-661 9619

LEATHARD, Brian. b 56. Sussex Univ BA Cam Univ MA. Westcott Ho Cam 79. **d** 82 **p** 83. C Seaford w Sutton *Chich* 82-85; Chapl Loughb Univ *Leic* 85-89; V Hampton Hill *Lon* from 89. *The Vicarage, St James's Road, Hampton Hill, Hampton, Middx TW12 1DQ* 081-979 2069

LEATHERBARROW, Ronald. b 35. Chester Coll TCert59. NW Ord Course 71. **d** 75 **p** 76. C Eccleston Ch Ch *Liv* 75-80; C Eccleston St Thos 80-83; R Kirklinton w Hethersgill and Scaleby *Carl* 83-86; R Blackley White Moss St Mark *Man* from 86. *St Mark's Rectory, 70 Booth Hall Road, Manchester M9 2BL* 061-740 7558

LEATHERLAND, Brian. b 43. Nottm Univ BTh73 St Martin's Coll Lanc DipEd. Kelham Th Coll 69. **d** 74 **p** 75. C Higham Ferrers w Chelveston *Pet* 74-76; C Pet St Paul 76-78; V Kings Heath 78-83; V Raunds from 83. *The Vicarage, Park Street, Raunds, Wellingborough, Northants NN9 6NB* Wellingborough (0933) 625637

LEATHERS, Brian Stanley Peter. b 61. Nottm Univ BSc83. Oak Hill Th Coll BA89. **d** 89 **p** 90. C Watford *St Alb* from 89. *8A Lammas Road, Watford WD1 8BA* Watford (0923) 32979

LEATHLEY, Hubert Brian. b 28. MBE91. Linc Th Coll 79. **d** 81 **p** 82. C Basingstoke *Win* 81-83; TV 83-91; Ind Chapl 83-91; V Kingsclere from 91. *The Vicarage, Fox's Lane, Kingsclere, Newbury, Berks RG15 8SL* Kingsclere (0635) 298272

LEAVER, David Noel. b 63. Hatf Coll Dur BA85. Wycliffe Hall Ox 89. **d** 91. C Blackheath Park St Mich *S'wark* from 91. *1A Pond Road, London SE3 9JL* 081-852 9564

LEAVER, John Francis. b 31. MPS53 Lon Univ DipTh63. St Mich Coll Llan 64. **d** 66 **p** 67. C Glouc St Cath *Glouc* 66-68; Hon C Glouc St Mary de Lode and St Nic 68-69; C Matson 69-76; Hon C Glouc St Mary de Crypt w St Jo 76-79; Hon C Glouc St Mary de Crypt w St Jo and Ch Ch 79-82; Hon C Highnam, Lassington, Rudford, Tibberton etc 82-85; Perm to Offic from 85. *29 Farthing Croft, Highnam, Gloucester GL28 8EQ* Gloucester (0452) 32749

LEAVER, Robin Alan. b 39. Clifton Th Coll 62. **d** 64 **p** 65. C Gipsy Hill Ch Ch *S'wark* 64-67; C Gt Baddow *Chelmsf* 67-71; C-in-c Reading St Mary Castle Street Prop Chpl

Ox 71-77; Chapl Luckley-Oakfield Sch Wokingham 73-75; P-in-c Cogges *Ox* 77-84. *Address temp unknown*

LEAVES (nee CRAIG), Julie Elizabeth. b 63. Southn Univ BTh87. Sarum & Wells Th Coll 82. **dss** 86 **d** 87. Thatcham *Ox* 86-87; Par Dn 87-88; Hong Kong from 88. *Flat A-2, On Lee, 2 Mount Davies Road, Hong Kong* Hong Kong (852) 523-4157

LEAVES, Nigel. b 58. Keble Coll Ox MA80 K Coll Lon MA86. Sarum & Wells Th Coll 84. **d** 86 **p** 87. C Boyne Hill *Ox* 86-88; Hong Kong from 88. *Flat A-2, On Lee, 2 Mount Davies Road, Hong Kong* Hong Kong (852) 523-4157

LEAWORTHY, John Owen. b 40. Univ of Wales BSc. Oak Hill Th Coll. **d** 82 **p** 83. C Compton Gifford *Ex* 82-85; C Plymouth Em w Efford 85-86; P-in-c Marks Tey w Aldham and Lt Tey *Chelmsf* 86-88; R 88-89; Chapl HM Pris Full Sutton 89-91. *Address temp unknown*

LECKEY, Very Rev Hamilton. b 29. TCD BA58 MA58. **d** 51 **p** 52. C Ballymacarrett St Martin *D & D* 51-55; C Ban Abbey 55-60; I from 79; I Drumgooland w Kilcoo 60-62; Private Chapl to Bp of Down 62-73; Dir of Ords 62-87; I Comber 62-79; Can Down Cathl from 74; Dean Down from 87; I Down Cathl from 87. *The Abbey Rectory, 5 Downshire Road, Bangor, Co Down BT20 3TW* Bangor (0247) 460173

LEDGARD, Canon Frank William Armitage. b 24. Wells Th Coll 49. **d** 52 **p** 53. R Bedale *Ripon* 66-87; RD Wensley 79-85; Hon Can Ripon Cathl 80-89; Bp's Adv on Chr Healing 87-89; rtd 89. *Woodburn, Patrick Brompton, Bedale, N Yorkshire DL8 1JN* Bedale (0677) 50640

LEDGARD, Canon Thomas Callinan. b 16. St Jo Coll Cam BA38 MA50. Westcott Ho Cam 38. **d** 39 **p** 40. V Cartmel *Carl* 69-79; Hon Can Carl Cathl 70-82; P-in-c Warcop, Musgrave, Soulby and Crosby Garrett 79-82; rtd 82; Perm to Offic *Carl* from 83. *Tetley Cottage, Allithwaite Road, Cartmel, Grange-over-Sands, Cumbria LA11 7SB* Cartmel (05395) 36455

LEDGER, James Henry. b 23. Oak Hill Th Coll 68. **d** 70 **p** 71. C Spitalfields Ch Ch w All SS *Lon* 70-75; V Chitts Hill St Cuth 75-91; rtd 91. *27 The Avenue, Leighton Bromswold, Huntingdon, Cambs PE18 0SH*

LEDWARD, John Archibald. b 30. FRSA85 Lon Univ BD58 Man Univ DSPT78 MA81 ThD. ALCD57. **d** 58 **p** 59. C St Helens St Helen *Liv* 58-62; V Dearham *Carl* 62-66; V Mirehouse 66-71; V Daubhill *Man* 71-77; R Newc w Butterton *Lich* 77-88; P-in-c Rockland St Mary w Hellington *Nor* 88; R Rockland St Mary w Hellington, Bramerton etc from 88. *The Rectory, Rectory Lane, Rockland St Mary, Norwich NR14 7EY* Surlingham (05088) 619

LEE, Alan Charles. b 32. S'wark Ord Course 77. **d** 79 **p** 80. NSM Acton Green St Pet *Lon* 79-82; Chapl RADD 82-83; P-in-c St Magnus the Martyr w St Marg New Fish Street *Lon* 83-84; NSM Barnes St Mich *S'wark* 84-90; Perm to Offic *Lon* from 89; C Brighton St Pet and St Nic w Chpl Royal *Chich* from 90. *40 Kemp Street, Brighton BN1 4EF* Brighton (0273) 675684

LEE, Anthony Maurice. b 35. Bps' Coll Cheshunt 62. **d** 65 **p** 66. C Pinner *Lon* 65-71; Asst Youth Chapl *Glouc* 71-72; V Childswyckham 72-73; R Aston Somerville 72-73; V Childswyckham w Aston Somerville 73-91; RD Winchcombe from 86; P-in-c Buckland 88-91; P-in-c Stanton w Snowshill 88-91; R Childswyckham w Aston Somerville, Buckland etc from 91. *The Vicarage, Childswickham, Broadway, Worcs WR12 7HL* Broadway (0386) 852240

LEE, Arnold John. b 17. St Edm Hall Ox BA40 DipTh41 MA43. Wycliffe Hall Ox 40. **d** 42 **p** 43. V Ox St Andr *Ox* 69-78; V E Boldre w S Baddesley *Win* 78-82; rtd 82; Perm to Offic *Ox* from 82. *1 Queen's Close, Eynsham, Oxford OX8 1HN* Oxford (0865) 880532

LEE, Canon Arthur Gordon. b 32. Univ of Wales (Swansea) BA52. St Mich Coll Llan 53. **d** 55 **p** 56. C Brynmawr *S & B* 55-57; C Llangyfelach and Morriston 57-60; V Llanddewi Ystradenni and Abbey Cwmhir 60-69; V Swansea St Pet from 69; RD Penderi from 90; Hon Can Brecon Cathl from 91. *The Vicarage, 59 Station Road, Fforestfach, Swansea SA5 5AU* Swansea (0792) 581514

LEE, Brian. b 37. Linc Th Coll 78. **d** 80 **p** 81. C Duston *Pet* 80-84; P-in-c Spratton 84-89; V from 89; P-in-c Maidwell w Draughton, Lamport w Faxton from 89. *The Vicarage, Spratton, Northampton NN6 8HR* Northampton (0604) 847212

LEE, Brian Ernest. b 32. ACA59 FCA70. Linc Th Coll 60. **d** 62 **p** 63. C Birch St Jas *Man* 62-65; C Withington St Paul 65-66; R Abbey Hey 66-70; Hon C Gatley *Ches* 86-88; V Egremont St Jo from 88; RD Wallasey from

91. *St John's Vicarage, 7 Silverbeech Road, Wallasey, Merseyside L44 9BT*   051-638 4360

LEE, Brian John. b 51. K Coll Lon BD78 AKC78. Coll of Resurr Mirfield 78. **d** 79 **p** 80. C Ham St Rich *S'wark* 79-82; C Surbiton St Andr and St Mark 82-85; V Shirley St Geo from 85. *St George's Vicarage, The Glade, Croydon CR0 7QJ*   081-654 8747

LEE, Christopher Garfield. b 41. St Deiniol's Hawarden 80. **d** 80 **p** 81. C Swansea St Pet *S & B* 80-81; C Oystermouth 81-83; R Cromhall w Tortworth and Tytherington *Glouc* from 83. *The New Rectory, Rectory Lane, Cromhall, Wotton-under-Edge GL12 8AN* Wickwar (045424) 767

LEE, Clive Warwick. b 34. St Pet Coll Ox BA58 MA62. Coll of Resurr Mirfield 58. **d** 60 **p** 61. C W End *Win* 60-65; C Upper Norwood St Jo *Cant* 65-69; Lic to Offic *Chich* from 69; Chapl Vinehall Sch E Sussex from 69. *2 Barracks Cottages, Robertsbridge, E Sussex TN32 5JH* Robertsbridge (0580) 880675

LEE, Colin John Willmot. b 21. Wycliffe Hall Ox 57. **d** 59 **p** 59. Bp's Ind Adv *Derby* 67-91; P-in-c Stanton by Dale 69-76; V Ilkeston St Jo 76-91; rtd 91. *3 Buttermead Close, Trowell, Nottingham NG9 3QT* Sandiacre (0602) 490100

LEE, Cyril Herbert. b 16. St Jo Coll Dur BA38 DipTh39 MA41. **d** 39 **p** 40. Chapl Oakwood Hosp Maidstone 64-66; Perm to Offic *Cant* from 74; rtd 81; Chapl HM Pris Standford Hill 81-82. *80 Church Lane, Newington, Sittingbourne, Kent ME9 4JU* Newington (0795) 842704

LEE, David Hartley. b 28. St Deiniol's Hawarden 61. **d** 63 **p** 64. C Merthyr Dyfan *Llan* 63-65; C Penarth All SS 65-70; Miss to Seamen from 70; Canada 70-84 and from 90. *Anglican Rectory, RR1, Musquodoboit Harbour, Nova Scotia, Canada, B0J 2L0*

LEE, David John. b 46. Bris Univ BSc67 Lon Univ DipTh73 Fitzw Coll Cam BA76. Ridley Hall Cam 74. **d** 77 **p** 78. C Putney St Marg *S'wark* 77-80; Uganda 80-86; Tutor Crowther Hall CMS Tr Coll Selly Oak from 86; Lic to Offic *Birm* from 87. *Crowther Hall, Weoley Park Road, Birmingham B29 6QT*   021-472 4228

LEE, David John. b 49. Oak Hill Th Coll 76. **d** 79 **p** 80. C Dagenham *Chelmsf* 79-82; P-in-c Leyton Em 82-85; V 85-91; TV Southgate *Chich* from 91. *St Andrew's Vicarage, Weald Drive, Crawley, W Sussex RH10 6ND* Crawley (0293) 531828

LEE, Ven David Stanley. b 30. Univ of Wales (Cardiff) BSc51. St Mich Coll Llan 56. **d** 57 **p** 58. C Caerau w Ely *Llan* 57-60; C Port Talbot St Agnes 60-70; Ind Chapl 60-70; R Merthyr Tydfil 70-72; Chapl Merthyr Tydfil Hosp from 70; R Merthyr Tydfil and Cyfarthfa *Llan* from 72; RD Merthyr Tydfil from 84; Can Llan Cathl from 84; Adn Llan from 91. *The Rectory, Thomastown, Merthyr Tydfil, M Glam CF47 0ER*   Merthyr Tydfil (0685) 722992

LEE, David Wight Dunsmore. b 39. Wells Th Coll 61. **d** 63 **p** 64. C Middlesb St Oswald *York* 63-67; C Northallerton w Kirby Sigston 67-69; Malawi 69-75; V Newington Transfiguration *York* 76-81; P-in-c Sheriff Hutton 81-85; P-in-c Sheriff Hutton and Farlington from 85. *The Vicarage, New Lane, Sheriff Hutton, York YO6 1QU*   Sheriff Hutton (03477) 336

LEE, Donald Hugh Thomson. b 48. Bard Coll (NY) BA70 Keble Coll Ox BA73 MA78. St Steph Ho Ox 72. **d** 74 **p** 75. C Swindon New Town *Bris* 74-79; C W Hampstead St Jas *Lon* 79-83; V Haggerston St Chad from 83. *St Chad's Vicarage, Dunloe Street, London E2 8JR*   071-739 3878

LEE, Francis George. b 37. St Aid Birkenhead 62. **d** 65 **p** 66. C Wavertree H Trin *Liv* 65-69; Bahamas 69-72; V Knowsley *Liv* 72-76; Australia 76-81; Bahamas 81-84; V Middle Rasen Drax *Linc* 84-88; Miss to Seamen from 88; R Maybole *Glas* from 88; R Girvan from 88; P-in-c Pinmore from 88. *St John's Rectory, 42 Piedmont Road, Girvan, Ayrshire KA26 0DR*   Girvan (0465) 2177

LEE, Frederick Roydon. b 13. OBE69. S'wark Ord Course 76. **d** 77 **p** 78. NSM Sundridge w Ide Hill *Roch* 77-81; rtd 81; Perm to Offic *Roch* from 81. *Tranquil, Combe Bank, Sundridge, Sevenoaks, Kent TN14 6AD* Westerham (0959) 63552

LEE, Frederick William Maxwell. b 15. Dur Univ LTh40 St Pet Hall Ox BA47 MA51 Ox Univ Inst of Educn CertEd68. Lambeth STh89 St Aid Birkenhead 37. **d** 40 **p** 41. Perm to Offic *Nor* 68-70; Asst Master Thorpe Gr Sch 68-70; Hitchin Girls' Gr Sch 70-80; C St Alb St Sav *St Alb* 74-80; rtd 80; Perm to Offic *St Alb* from 80. *13 Sandpit Lane, St Albans, Herts AL1 4DY*   St Albans (0727) 57353

LEE, Harold. b 04. St Aid Birkenhead 37. **d** 39 **p** 40. V Campsall *Sheff* 65-71; rtd 71; Hon C Bakewell *Derby*

71-74; Hon C Totley *Sheff* 74-80. *2 Cherry Tree Close, Sheffield S11 9AF*   Sheffield (0742) 550233

LEE, Canon Hector. b 33. Leeds Univ CertEd60. Kelham Th Coll 53. **d** 57 **p** 58. SSM from 57; Tutor Kelham Th Coll 60-63; Basutoland 63-66; Lesotho 66-69; S Africa 69-88; Can Bloemfontein Cathl 80-88; V Burnley St Cuth *Blackb* from 88. *The Vicarage, Barbon Street, Burnley, Lancs BB10 1TS*   Burnley (0282) 24978

LEE, Henry. b 31. St Chad's Coll Dur BA53 DipTh55 CertEd. **d** 55 **p** 56. V Medomsley *Dur* 65-75; Chapl Darlington Memorial Hosp 75-79; V Darlington H Trin *Dur* 75-82; V Brompton w Deighton *York* 82-90; rtd 90. *103 Benfieldside Road, Consett, Co Durham DH8 0RS* Consett (0207) 592170

LEE, Hoe Lynley. b 52. St Jo Coll Nottm BTh89. **d** 90. C Pitsea *Chelmsf* from 90. *112 Mallgraves, Pitsea, Basildon, Essex SS13 3QE*   Basildon (0268) 551725

LEE, Hugh Gordon Cassels. b 41. St Andr Univ BSc64. Edin Th Coll 64. **d** 67 **p** 68. C Dumfries *Glas* 67-70; C Totteridge *St Alb* 70-73; R Glas St Jas *Glas* 73-80; R Bishopbriggs 80-86; R St Fillans *St And* 86-89; P-in-c Muthill 86-90; R Comrie from 86; R Crieff from 86; P-in-c Lochearnhead from 89. *Ainsdale, 10 Dollerie Terrace, Crieff, Perthshire PH7 3ED*   Crieff (0764) 3898

LEE, Miss Iris Audrey Olive. b 26. St Andr Coll Southsea 54. **dss** 76 **d** 87. N Weald Bassett *Chelmsf* 76-87; rtd 87; NSM Clacton St Jas *Chelmsf* from 87. *30 Marine Court, Marine Parade West, Clacton-on-Sea CO15 1ND* Clacton-on-Sea (0225) 423719

LEE, John Charles Hugh Mellanby. b 44. Trin Hall Cam BA66 MA69 Brunel Univ MTech71. Ox NSM Course 78. **d** 81 **p** 82. NSM Amersham on the Hill *Ox* 81-88; NSM Ox St Aldate w St Matt from 88. *12 Walton Street, Oxford OX1 2HG*   Oxford (0865) 511382

LEE, John Foden. b 34. AKC61. **d** 61 **p** 62. C Pet All SS *Pet* 61-63; C Sudbury St Andr *Lon* 63-65; C Sherborne w Castleton and Lillington *Sarum* 65-67; V Erlestoke 67-68; R Gt Cheverell 67; V Erlestoke and Gt Cheverell 68-79; V Seend and Bulkington 79-86; Ind Chapl *Derby* from 86; V Derby St Paul from 86. *St Paul's Vicarage, Chester Green, Derby DE1 3SA*   Derby (0332) 381116

LEE, John Michael Andrew. b 62. Leeds Univ BA84. Trin Coll Bris 88. **d** 90 **p** 91. C Norbiton *S'wark* from 90. *97 Gloucester Road, Kingston upon Thames, Surrey KT1 3QW*   081-546 9678

LEE, John Royden. b 47. MInstGA87 Univ of Wales (Swansea) BSc70 MSc73. Ripon Hall Ox 73. **d** 75 **p** 76. C Swansea St Pet *S & B* 75-78; C St Botolph Aldgate w H Trin Minories *Lon* 79-84; P-in-c Chiddingstone w Chiddingstone Causeway *Roch* 84-89; R from 89. *The Rectory, Chiddingstone, Edenbridge, Kent TN8 7AH* Penshurst (0892) 870478

LEE, John Samuel. b 47. Chich Th Coll 74. **d** 77 **p** 78. C Bramley *Ripon* 77-80; C Bideford *Ex* 81-84; TV Littleham w Exmouth 84-90; P-in-c Sidbury 90-91; TV Sidmouth, Woolbrook, Salcombe Regis, Sidbury etc from 91. *The Vicarage, Glendevon, Harcombe Lane, Sidford, Devon EX10 9QN*   Sidmouth (0395) 579520

LEE, Canon John William. b 27. Bris Univ BA47. Ely Th Coll 51. **d** 52 **p** 53. C Cheltenham St Steph *Glouc* 52-56; C Blackpool St Mich CD *Blackb* 56-59; V Lt Marsden from 59; RD Pendle 78-84; Hon Can Blackb Cathl from 81. *St Paul's Vicarage, Bentley Street, Nelson, Lancs BB9 0BS*   Nelson (0282) 65888

LEE, Canon Kenneth. b 13. St Jo Coll Dur BA35 MA38. **d** 36 **p** 37. R Heswall *Ches* 52-79; RD Wirral N 75-79; rtd 79; Perm to Offic *Ches* from 79. *Greeba, Neston Road, Burton, South Wirral L64 5SY*   051-336 7698

LEE, Kenneth Peter. b 45. Em Coll Cam BA67 MA71. Cuddesdon Coll 67. **d** 69 **p** 70. C Stoke Poges *Ox* 69-72; C Witton *Ches* 72-74; V Frankby w Greasby from 74. *The Vicarage, 14 Arrowe Road, Greasby, Wirral, Merseyside L49 1RA*   051-678 6155

LEE, Leslie John. b 19. Dur Univ LTh47. St Aid Birkenhead 44. **d** 47 **p** 47. V Watton *Nor* 59-70; RD Breckles 65-70; R Coltishall w Gt Hautbois 70-84; rtd 84; Perm to Offic *Nor* from 84. *15 St Michael's Way, Brundall, Norwich NR13 5PF*   Norwich (0603) 713065

LEE, Luke Gun-Hong. b 37. Univ of Yon Sei BTh62. St Jo Coll Morpeth 64. **d** 67 **p** 68. Korea 67-79; C Bloxwich *Lich* 79-83; TV Dunstable *St Alb* 83-90; V Croxley Green All SS from 90. *All Saints' Vicarage, Croxley Green, Rickmansworth, Herts WD3 3HJ*   Rickmansworth (0923) 772109

LEE, Nicholas Knyvett. b 54. MA. Cranmer Hall Dur. **d** 85 **p** 86. C Brompton H Trin w Onslow Square St Paul *Lon* from 85. *St Paul's Church House, Onslow Square, London SW7 3NX*   071-589 3933

LEE, Peter Alexander. b 44. Hull Univ BSc(Econ)65. Ex & Truro NSM Scheme 80. **d** 83 **p** 84. NSM Ex St Sidwell and St Matt *Ex* 83-89; NSM Ex St Dav from 90. *Windyridge, Beech Avenue, Exeter EX4 6HF* Exeter (0392) 54118

✠LEE, Rt Rev Peter John. b 47. St Jo Coll Cam BA69 CertEd70 MA73. Ridley Hall Cam 70 St Jo Coll Nottm 72. **d** 73 **p** 74 **c** 90. C Onslow Square St Paul *Lon* 73-76; S Africa from 76; V-Gen and Bp Ch the King from 90. *Box 37, Kliptown, 1812 South Africa, or, 22 Maureen Street, Meredale, 2091 South Africa* Johannesburg (11) 945-3142 or 942-1179

LEE, Peter Kenneth. b 44. Selw Coll Cam BA66 MA69. Cuddesdon Coll 67. **d** 69 **p** 70. C Manston *Ripon* 69-72; C Bingley All SS *Bradf* 72-77; Chapl Bingley Coll of Educn 72-77; V Cross Roads cum Lees *Bradf* 77-90; V Auckland St Pet *Dur* from 90. *St Peter's Vicarage, 39 Etherley Lane, Bishop Auckland, Co Durham DL14 7QZ* Bishop Auckland (0388) 661856

LEE, Canon Raymond John. b 30. St Edm Hall Ox BA53 MA57. Tyndale Hall Bris 54. **d** 56 **p** 57. C Tooting Graveney St Nic *S'wark* 56-59; C Muswell Hill St Jas *Lon* 59-62; V Woking St Mary *Guildf* 62-70; V Gt Crosby St Luke *Liv* 70-82; Dioc Adv NSM from 79; V Allerton from 82; Hon Can Liv Cathl from 89. *Allerton Vicarage, Harthill Road, Liverpool L18 3HU* 051-724 1561

LEE, Reginald Wilfred. b 09. Kelham Th Coll 27. **d** 32 **p** 33. C Upper Norwood All SS w St Marg *Cant* 58-71; rtd 71. *College of St Barnabas, Blackberry Lane, Lingfield, Surrey RH7 6NJ* Dormans Park (034287) 260

LEE, Richard Alexander. b 63. St Jo Coll Nottm BTh91. **d** 91. C Gt Stanmore *Lon* from 91. *St John's House, 16 The Chase, Stanmore, Middx HA7 3RY* 081-954 4616

LEE, Robert David. b 53. QUB BD75. CITC 77. **d** 77 **p** 78. C Comber *D & D* 77-83; I Mt Merrion 83-87; CMS from 89; Egypt from 89. *PO Box 87, Zamalek, Cairo, Egypt*

LEE, Robert William. b 31. Keele Univ BA54 St Cath Soc Ox BA58 MA63. Ripon Hall Ox 56. **d** 59 **p** 60. C Dawley St Jerome *Lon* 59-62; C Bromley H Trin *Roch* 62-65; R Clayton *Man* 65-70; P-in-c Man St Paul 65-70; TV Hemel Hempstead *St Alb* 70-72; TV Corby SS Pet and Andr w Gt and Lt Oakley *Pet* 72-80; R Thornhams Magna and Parva, Gislingham and Mellis *St E* from 88. *The Rectory, Orchard Close, Gislingham, Eye, Suffolk IP23 8JW* Mellis (037983) 622

LEE, Roderick James. b 50. Linc Th Coll 88. **d** 90 **p** 91. C Rushden w Newton Bromswold *Pet* from 90. *24 Lodge Road, Rushden, Northants NN10 9HA* Rushden (0933) 316834

LEE, Steven Michael. b 56. Dur Univ BA. Trin Coll Bris 80. **d** 83 **p** 84. C Beckenham St Jo *Roch* 83-86; C Leic Martyrs *Leic* 86-90; V Coalville and Bardon Hill from 90. *Christ Church Vicarage, London Road, Coalville, Leicester LE6 2JA* Coalville (0530) 38287

LEE, Terence. b 46. FCA. Ox NSM Course. **d** 83 **p** 84. NSM Calcot *Ox* 83-87; NSM Burghfield 87-88; Perm to Offic from 88. *45 Christchurch Road, Reading RG2 7AN* Reading (0734) 312512

LEE, Thomas Richard. b 52. AKC73. St Aug Coll Cant 74. **d** 75 **p** 76. C Leam Lane CD *Dur* 75-80; Chapl RAF from 80. *c/o MOD, Adastral House, Theobald's Road, London WC1X 8RU* 071-430 7268

LEE, William George. b 11. TCD BA33 MA48. **d** 34 **p** 35. V Chislehurst Ch Ch *Roch* 61-76; rtd 76. *Dale Garth, Harmby, Leyburn, N Yorkshire DL8 5PD* Wensleydale (0969) 22649

LEE WARNER, Canon Theodore John. b 22. Univ Coll Ox BA49 MA54. Wells Th Coll 50. **d** 51 **p** 52. V Darlington H Trin *Dur* 63-74; Chapl Darlington Memorial Hosp 63-74; V Norton St Mary *Dur* 74-80; RD Barnard Castle 80-87; V Gainford 80-87; R Winston 80-87; Hon Can Dur Cathl 83-87; rtd 87. *112 Cleveland Terrace, Darlington, Co Durham DL3 8JA* Darlington (0325) 467585

LEECE, Roderick Neil Stephen. b 59. ARCM85 Wadh Coll Ox BA81 MA85 Leeds Univ BA84. Coll of Resurr Mirfield 82. **d** 85 **p** 86. C Portsea St Mary *Portsm* from 85. *166 Fearn Road, Portsmouth PO1 5LS* Portsmouth (0705) 820486

LEECH, Christopher. b 16. Linc Th Coll 37. **d** 39 **p** 40. R Combe Pyne w Rousdon *Ex* 60-76; P-in-c *Ex* from 82; rtd 82; Perm to Offic *Ex* from 82. *Nestor, Hillhead, Colyton, Devon EX13 6HH* Colyton (0297) 52034

LEECH, Kenneth. b 39. Lon Univ BA61 AKC61 Trin Coll Ox BA63 MA71. St Steph Ho Ox 62. **d** 64 **p** 65. C

Hoxton H Trin w St Mary *Lon* 64-67; C Soho St Anne w St Thos and St Pet 67-71; Tutor St Aug Coll Cant 71-74; R Bethnal Green St Matt *Lon* 74-79; Field Officer Community & Race Relns Unit BCC 80; Race Relns Officer Gen Syn Bd for Soc Resp 81-87; Hon C Notting Hill St Clem and St Mark *Lon* 82-85; Hon C Notting Dale St Clem w St Mark and St Jas 85-88; Dir Runnymede Trust 87-90; St Botolph Aldgate w H Trin Minories *Lon* from 91. *St Botolph's Church, Aldgate, London EC3N 1AB* 071-283 1670

LEECH, Miss Peggy Irene. b 29. CA Tr Coll 56. dss 85 **d** 87. Oxhey All SS *St Alb* 86-87; Par Dn 87-90; rtd 91; Hon Par Dn Oxhey All SS *St Alb* from 91. *9 The Mead, Carpenders Park, Watford, Herts WD1 5BY* 081-428 6136

LEEDS, Archdeacon of. *See* COMBER, Ven Anthony James

LEEKE, Charles Browne. b 39. TCD DipTh CertEd. **d** 83 **p** 84. C Ballymoney w Finvoy and Rasharkin *Conn* 83-86; I Faughanvale *D & R* from 86. *21 Main Street, Eglinton, Londonderry BT47 3AB* Eglinton (0504) 810217

LEEKE, Stephen Owen. b 50. E Anglian Minl Tr Course 82 Ridley Hall Cam 83. **d** 84 **p** 85. C Cherry Hinton St Andr *Ely* 84-87; P-in-c Warboys from 87; P-in-c Wistow from 87; P-in-c Bury from 87. *The Rectory, 15 Church Road, Warboys, Huntingdon, Cambs PE17 2RJ* Ramsey (0487) 822237

LEEKS, Ronald Philip. b 16. MA. **d** 39 **p** 40. V S Norwood H Innocents *Cant* 67-81; rtd 81; Chapl and Warden Jes Hosp Cant from 81. *The Warden's Lodge, Jesus Hospital, Sturry Road, Canterbury, Kent CT1 1BS* Canterbury (0227) 463771

LEEMAN, John Graham. b 41. N Ord Course 78. **d** 80 **p** 81. NSM Hull Sculcoates St Mary *York* from 80. *187 Gleneagles Park, Salthouse Road, Hull HU8 9JS* Hull (0482) 703207

LEEMING, Jack. b 34. Kelham Th Coll 56. **d** 61 **p** 62. C Sydenham St Phil *S'wark* 61-64; Chapl RAF 64-84; Chapl Salisbury Gen Infirmary 84-89; R Barford St Martin, Dinton, Baverstock etc *Sarum* from 89. *The Rectory, Barford St Martin, Salisbury SP3 4AS* Salisbury (0722) 743385

LEEMING, John Maurice. b 24. CEng MIMechE MIProdE FIED. NW Ord Course 72. **d** 75 **p** 76. NSM Endcliffe *Sheff* 75-78; C Norton 78-80; V Bolsterstone 80-89; Ind Chapl 81-89; rtd 89. *Beck House, Toftdyke Lane, Clayworth, Retford, Notts DN22 9AH* Retford (0777) 817795

LEEMING, Peter. b 23. Leeds Univ BA50. Bps' Coll Cheshunt 50. **d** 52 **p** 53. C Moordown *Win* 68-71; C Hawarden *St As* 71-78; TV 78-89; rtd 89. *2 Church Cottages, Rectory Drive, Hawarden, Deeside, Clwyd CH5 3NN* Hawarden (0244) 531186

LEES, Charles Alan. b 38. W Midl Minl Tr Course 78. **d** 81 **p** 82. NSM Yardley St Cypr Hay Mill *Birm* 81-84 and 86-87; Hon C Dorridge 84-86; Chapl E Birm Hosp 85-87; Hon C Leamington Spa and Old Milverton *Cov* 89-90. *49 Gordon Street, Leamington Spa, Warks CV31 1HR*

LEES, Canon Jesse. b 99. K Coll Lon 35. **d** 36 **p** 37. V Market Lavington and Easterton *Sarum* 63-67; rtd 67. *47 Windsor Drive, Gloucester GL4 0QT* Gloucester (0452) 411687

LEES, John Raymond. b 57. Selw Coll Cam BA78 MA82. St Steph Ho Ox 89. **d** 91. C Eastbourne St Mary *Chich* from 91. *6 Bay Pond Road, Eastbourne, E Sussex BN21 1HX* Eastbourne (0323) 28680

LEES, Mrs Kathleen Marion. b 30. Birkb Coll Lon BA60 DipRS80. S'wark Ord Course 77. dss 80 **d** 87. Epping St Jo *Chelmsf* 80-86; Hon C Hunstanton St Mary w Ringstead Parva, Holme etc *Nor* 87-88; Perm to Offic from 88. *12 Cherry Tree Road, Snettisham, King's Lynn, Norfolk PE31 7NZ* Dersingham (0485) 540364

LEES, Stephen. b 55. St Jo Coll York CertEd77 BEd78. St Jo Coll Nottm 88. **d** 90 **p** 91. C Mansf St Jo *S'well* from 90. *8 Castle Street, Mansfield, Notts NG18 5PP* Mansfield (0623) 20780

LEES, Stuart Charles Roderick. b 62. **d** 89 **p** 90. C Woodford Wells *Chelmsf* from 89. *8 Firs Walk, Woodford Green, Essex IG8 0TD* 081-505 0660

LEES-SMITH, Christopher John (Brother Edward). b 21. CCC Ox BA49 MA65. Cuddesdon Coll 48. **d** 50 **p** 51. SSF from 54; Perm to Offic *Newc* 62-74; Guardian Alnmouth Friary 65-74; Chapl to the Third Order SSF 74-91; rtd 91. *42 Balaam Street, London E13 8AQ* 071-476 5189

LEESE, Arthur Selwyn Mountford. b 09. K Coll Lon BD31 AKC31 St Cath Soc Ox BA33 MA44. Ripon Hall

Ox 31. **d** 33 **p** 34. V Hawkhurst *Cant* 51-74; rtd 74; Perm to Offic Chich from 76; Cant from 77. *84 Wickham Avenue, Bexhill-on-Sea, E Sussex TN39 3ER* Bexhill-on-Sea (0424) 213137

LEESE, Frederick Henry Brooke. b 24. AKC47. **d** 47 **p** 48. V Pagham *Chich* 60-70; V Chorley *Ches* 70-82; R Rogate w Terwick and Trotton w Chithurst *Chich* 82-90; RD Midhurst 85-90; rtd 90; Perm to Offic *B & W* from 90. *Treetops, Furnham Crescent, Chard, Somerset TA20 1AZ* Chard (0460) 65524

LEESON, Bernard Alan. b 47. Bris Univ CertEd68 Open Univ BA75 Southn Univ MA78. E Midl Min Tr Course 84. **d** 87 **p** 88. Dep Hd Master Ripley Mill Hill Sch from 80; NSM Breadsall *Derby* from 87. *99 Alfreton Road, Little Eaton, Derby DE2 5DF* Derby (0332) 832816

LEESON, David Harry Stanley. b 45. Glouc Th Course 82. **d** 85 **p** 86. NSM Stratton w Baunton *Glouc* from 85; NSM N Cerney w Bagendon from 91. *83 Cheltenham Road, Stratton, Cirencester, Glos GL7 2JB* Cirencester (0285) 651186

LEESON, Ms Sally Elizabeth. b 57. Sussex Univ BA79. Westcott Ho Cam 83. **dss** 85 **d** 87. Battersea St Pet and St Paul *S'wark* 85-87; Par Dn 87-90; Par Dn Limpsfield and Titsey from 90. *St Andrew's House, Limpsfield Chart, Oxted, Surrey RH8 0TB* Oxted (0883) 723153

LEFEVER, Henry Charles. b 06. Lon Univ BA30 BD32 Tubingen Univ PhD34. **d** 65 **p** 66. Hon C Blackheath Ascension *S'wark* 69-75; rtd 75; Perm to Offic *Cant* from 76. *10 Mulberry Court, Stour Street, Canterbury, Kent CT1 2NT* Canterbury (0227) 768304

LEFFLER, Christopher. b 33. Em Coll Cam BA57 MA61. Linc Th Coll. **d** 59 **p** 60. C Bermondsey St Mary w St Olave and St Jo *S'wark* 59-60; C Herne Hill St Paul 60-63; C-in-c Canley CD *Cov* 63-67; R Gt and Lt Glemham *St E* 67-72; R Badwell Ash w Gt Ashfield, Stowlangtoft etc 72-82; R Trimley from 82. *The Rectory, Church Lane, Trimley, Ipswich IP10 0SW* Felixstowe (0394) 286188

LEFROY, Christopher John Elton. b 25. Clare Coll Cam BA46 MA49. Ridley Hall Cam 47. **d** 49 **p** 50. V Highbury Ch Ch *Lon* 65-78; V Highbury Ch Ch w St Jo 79-82; V Highbury Ch Ch w St Jo and St Sav Lon 82-90; rtd 90. *135 The Close, Salisbury SP1 2EY* Salisbury (0722) 334008

LEFROY, John Perceval. b 40. Trin Coll Cam BA62. Cuddesdon Coll 64. **d** 66 **p** 67. C Maidstone St Martin *Cant* 66-69; C St Peter-in-Thanet 69-74; V Barming Heath 74-82; V Upchurch w Lower Halstow from 82. *The Vicarage, 15 Oak Lane, Upchurch, Sittingbourne, Kent ME9 7AT* Medway (0634) 387227

LEGG, Adrian James. b 52. St Jo Coll Nottm LTh82 BTh82. **d** 82 **p** 83. C Haughton le Skerne *Dur* 82-85; C Llanishen and Lisvane *Llan* 85-89; V Llanwddyn and Llanfihangel and Llwydiarth *St As* from 89. *The Vicarage, Llanwddyn, Oswestry, Shropshire SY10 0LY* Llanwddyn (069173) 663

LEGG, Ms Joanna Susan Penberthy. b 60. Newnham Coll Cam BA81 MA85. St Jo Coll Nottm DipTh82 MTh84 St Jo Coll Dur 83. **dss** 84 **d** 87. Haughton le Skerne *Dur* 84-85; Llanishen and Lisvane *Llan* 85-87; NSM 87-89; NSM Llanwddyn and Llanfihangel and Llwydiarth *St As* from 89. *The Vicarage, Llanwddyn, Oswestry, Shropshire SY10 0LY* Llanwddyn (069173) 663

LEGG, John Andrew Douglas. b 32. Selw Coll Cam BA55 MA59. Wells Th Coll 57. **d** 59 **p** 59. Australia 59-63; Chapl Rugby Sch Warks 63-64; P-in-c Ashford w Sheldon *Derby* 64-67; Kuwait 67-69; Solomon Is 70-73; Asst Master Lt Ilford Comp Sch 73-83; P-in-c Stapleford Tawney w Theydon Mt *Chelmsf* 78-83; R Hemingby *Linc* 83-88; Greece from 88. *Prastos, Kynorias Arkadia, Greece 22006*

LEGG, Reginald John. b 26. LRAM50 TCert45. Wells Th Coll 61. **d** 63 **p** 64. C Prestbury *Glouc* 63-66; V Milnsbridge *Wakef* 66-67; Miss to Seamen 67-74; V Methwold *Ely* 74-80; RD Feltwell 75-80; P-in-c Preston *Glouc* from 80; P-in-c Dymock w Donnington and Kempley from 80. *The Rectory, Dymock, Glos GL18 2AJ* Dymock (053185) 270

LEGG, Richard. b 37. Selw Coll Cam BA62 MA66 Brunel Univ MPhil77. Coll of Resurr Mirfield 63 NY Th Sem DMin. **d** 65 **p** 66. C Ealing St Pet Mt Park *Lon* 65-68; Chapl Brunel Univ 68-78; C Chipping Barnet w Arkley *St Alb* 81-83; TV 83-85; R St Buryan, St Levan and Sennen *Truro* from 85. *The Rectory, St Buryan, Penzance, Cornwall TR19 6BB* St Buryan (0736) 810216

LEGG, Robert Richard. b 16. MBE45. Open Univ BA78. St Aug Coll Cant 36. **d** 59 **p** 60. V W w E Tytherley *Win* 62-71; V Kingsclere 71-83; rtd 83; Perm to Offic *Win*

from 83. *The Furrow, Evingar Road, Whitchurch, Hants RG28 7EU* Whitchurch (0256) 892126

LEGG, Roger Keith. b 35. Lich Th Coll 61. **d** 63 **p** 64. C Petersfield w Sheet *Portsm* 63-66; C Portsea St Mary 66-70; Rhodesia 70-75; V Clayton *Lich* from 75. *The Vicarage, Clayton Lane, Newcastle, Staffs ST5 3DW* Newcastle-under-Lyme (0782) 614500

LEGG, Miss Ruth Helen Margaret. b 52. Hull Univ BA74 Homerton Coll Cam CertEd75. Trin Coll Bris DipHE88. **d** 88. C Clevedon St Andr and Ch Ch *B & W* from 88. *28 Rippleside Road, Clevedon, Avon BS21 7JX* Clevedon (0272) 343878

LEGGATE, Colin Archibald Gunson. b 44. Bris Sch of Min 86. **d** 88 **p** 89. NSM Brislington St Luke *Bris* from 88. *118 School Road, Bristol BS4 4LZ* Bristol (0272) 714340

LEGGE, Frederick John. b 10. Ridley Hall Cam 58. **d** 59 **p** 59. R E Leake *S'well* 63-76; P-in-c Rempstone 70-76; P-in-c Costock 70-76; P-in-c Stanford on Soar 70-76; rtd 76. *Flat 11, Ellesborough Manor, Butlers Cross, Aylesbury, Bucks HP17 0XF* Aylesbury (0296) 696001

LEICESTER, Archdeacon of. *See* SILK, Ven Robert David

LEICESTER, Bishop of. *See* BUTLER, Rt Rev Thomas Frederick

LEICESTER, Provost of. *See* WARREN, Very Rev Alan Christopher

LEIGH, Mrs Alison Margaret. b 40. CertEd63 Golds Coll Lon BEd75. Sarum & Wells Th Coll 85. **d** 87. C Chessington *Guildf* 87-90; C Green Street Green *Roch* from 90. *Woodend, 9 Ringwood Avenue, Pratts Bottom, Orpington, Kent BR6 7SY* Farnborough (0689) 861742

LEIGH, Arnold Robert. b 36. AKC60. **d** 61 **p** 62. C Lewisham St Mary *S'wark* 61-66; C Stockwell Green St Andr 66-69; V 69-72; TV Withycombe Raleigh *Ex* 72-74; TR 74-80; V Devonport St Bart from 80. *St Bartholomew's Vicarage, 13 Outland Road, Plymouth PL2 3BZ* Plymouth (0752) 562623

LEIGH, Dennis Herbert. b 34. Lon Univ BSc56 DipTh68. Chich Th Coll 58. **d** 60 **p** 61. C Roehampton H Trin *S'wark* 60-62; C E Wickham 62-67; C Plumstead St Mark and St Marg 67-73; C Corby Epiphany w St Jo *Pet* 73-74; C Paston 84-86; C Aylestone St Andr w St Jas *Leic* from 86. *38 Park Hill Drive, Leicester LE2 8HR* Leicester (0533) 832003

LEIGH, Canon James Ronald. b 32. S'wark Ord Course 63. **d** 67 **p** 68. C Purley St Barn *S'wark* 67-71; Prec St Ninian's Cathl Perth *St And* 71-73; R Leven 73-78; R Kirkcaldy from 78; R Kinghorn from 81; Can St Ninian's Cathl Perth from 90. *1 Longbraes Gardens, Kirkcaldy, Fife KY2 5YJ* Kirkcaldy (0592) 263314

LEIGH, Martin Francis. b 40. Sheff Univ BSc63. Cuddesdon Coll 65. **d** 67 **p** 68. C St Mary-at-Lambeth *S'wark* 67-70; C Bakewell *Derby* 70-74; V Ockbrook 74-82; RD Ilkeston 78-82; V Baslow from 82; Bp's Ecum Officer from 82. *The Vicarage, Baslow, Bakewell, Derbyshire DE4 1RY* Baslow (024688) 3104

LEIGH, Raymond. b 37. Lon Univ BEd81. Clifton Th Coll 65. **d** 68 **p** 69. C Chadwell *Chelmsf* 68-71; Chapl RAF 71-77; NSM Hillingdon St Jo *Lon* 87-88; C Rowley Regis *Birm* 88-90; V Londonderry from 90. *The Vicarage, 15 St Mark's Road, Smethwick, Warley, W Midlands B67 6QF* 021-429 1149

LEIGH, Roy Stephen. b 28. Imp Coll Lon BSc49. S'wark Ord Course 87. **d** 90. NSM Green Street Green *Roch* from 90. *Woodend, 9 Ringwood Avenue, Pratts Bottom, Orpington, Kent BR6 7SY* Farnborough (0689) 861742

LEIGH-HUNT, Edward Christopher. b 22. Univ Coll Dur BA47. Ely Th Coll 48. **d** 50 **p** 51. Chapl Asst St Bart Hosp Lon 66-73; C St Bart Less *Lon* 66-73; Chapl Middx Hosp 73-86; rtd 86. *14 Cain Court, Castlebar Mews, London W5 1RY* 081-991 1171

LEIGH-HUNT, Nicolas Adrian. b 46. MIEx70. Qu Coll Birm 85. **d** 87 **p** 88. C Tilehurst St Geo *Ox* from 87-91; TV Wexcombe *Sarum* from 91. *The Vicarage, 5 Eastcourt, Burbage, Marlborough, Wiltshire SN8 3AG* Marlborough (0672) 810258

LEIGHLIN, Dean of. *Vacant*

LEIGHTON, Adrian Barry. b 44. LTh. Lon Coll of Div 65. **d** 69 **p** 70. C Erith St Paul *Roch* 69-72; C Ipswich St Marg *St E* 72-75; P-in-c Ipswich St Helen 75-82; R 82-88; P-in-c Holbrook w Freston and Woolverstone from 88; RD Samford from 90. *The Rectory, Holbrook, Ipswich IP9 2QZ* Holbrook (0473) 328900

LEIGHTON, Alan Granville Clyde. b 37. MInstM AMIDHE Lon Univ DipRS. S'wark Ord Course 73. **d** 76 **p** 77. C Silverhill St Matt *Chich* 76-79; C Eston *York* 79-82; V 82-84; TR Eston w Normanby from 84. *429 Normanby Road, Normanby, Middlesbrough, Cleveland TS6 0EA* Eston Grange (0642) 460613

LEIGHTON, Canon Anthony Hindess. b 23. Lon Univ BSc44. Wells Th Coll 47. **d** 49 **p** 50. R Girton *Ely* 61-88; RD N Stowe 68-76; Hon Can Ely Cathl from 82; rtd 88. *Eastleigh, Parkhall Road, Somersham, Huntingdon, Cambs PE17 3HF* Ramsey (0487) 842750

LEIGHTON, Anthony Robert. b 56. Trin Coll Bris BA88. **d** 88 **p** 89. C Harrow H Trin St Mich *Lon* from 88. *2 Earls Crescent, Harrow, Middx HA1 1XN* 081-863 2803

LEIGHTON, John Thomas. b 08. **d** 76 **p** 77. C W Derby St Mary *Liv* 76-77; Hon C Knowsley from 77; Hon C Litherland St Phil from 84. *22 Newlyn Avenue, Litherland, Liverpool L21 9LD* 051-928 1957

LEIGHTON, Mrs Susan. Bretton Hall Coll BEd80. Trin Coll Bris BA89. **d** 89. Par Dn Harrow Weald All SS *Lon* from 89. *2 Earls Crescent, Harrow, Middx HA1 1XN* 081-863 2803

LEIPER, Dr Nicholas Keith. b 34. SS Coll Cam BA55 MB58 BChir58 MA65 LTh82. St Jo Coll Nottm. **d** 84 **p** 85. C Bidston *Ches* 84-87; TV Gateacre *Liv* from 87. *St Mark's Vicarage, Cranwell Road, Liverpool L25 1NX* 051-487 9634

LEITCH, Peter William. b 36. FCA58 ATII59. Coll of Resurr Mirfield 83. **d** 85 **p** 86. C Newsome *Wakef* 85; C Newsome and Armitage Bridge 85-88; P-in-c Upper Hopton from 88; P-in-c Mirfield Eastthorpe St Paul from 88. *The Vicarage, 4 Hopton Hall Lane, Mirfield, W Yorkshire WF14 8EL* Mirfield (0924) 493569

LEMMON, Canon Rowland. b 09. Keble Coll Ox BA31 MA40. Wells Th Coll 31. **d** 32 **p** 33. R Hexham *Newc* 62-75; rtd 75; Perm to Offic *Ex* from 82. *4 Arundel Close, Alphington, Exeter EX2 8UQ* Exeter (0392) 70365

LEMPRIERE, Norman Everard. b 28. Liv Univ BEng54. Ridley Hall Cam 55. **d** 57 **p** 58. C Ware Ch Ch *St Alb* 57-61; R Lt Munden 61-64; R Sacombe 61-64; Lee Abbey 64-66; Perm to Offic *Ex* 64-66; C Witheridge 66-69; R Nymet Rowland w Coldridge 69-75; R Denton w S Heighton and Tarring Neville *Chich* 75-81; R Sullington and Thakeham w Warminghurst from 81. *The Rectory, Thakeham, Pulborough, W Sussex RH20 3EP* West Chiltington (0798) 813121

LENDON, Canon Edward Charles. b 24. Peterho Cam BA49 MA54. Ridley Hall Cam 48. **d** 50 **p** 51. V Dagenham *Chelmsf* 68-81; RD Barking and Dagenham 76-81; R Peldon w Gt and Lt Wigborough 81-89; Hon Can Chelmsf Cathl 82-89; rtd 89. *12 Strood Close, West Mersea, Colchester CO5 8JN* West Mersea (0206) 382687

LENDRUM, Canon William Henry. b 24. TCD BA50 MA62. CITC 50. **d** 50 **p** 51. I Belf St Mary Magd *Conn* 69-91; Can Conn Cathl from 87; rtd 91. *38 Lancefield Road, Belfast BT9 6LL* Belfast (0232) 665872

LENG, Bruce Edgar. b 38. St Aid Birkenhead 68. **d** 69 **p** 70. C Sheff St Swithun *Sheff* 69-74; TV Speke St Aid *Liv* 74-78; TV Yate New Town *Bris* 78-82; R Handsworth *Sheff* from 82. *The Rectory, Handsworth, Sheffield S13 9BZ* Sheffield (0742) 692403

LENNARD, Edward Stuart Churchill. b 21. Ex Coll Ox MA42. Cuddesdon Coll 47. **d** 54 **p** 55. SSJE from 54; S Africa 57-59; Lic to Offic *Ox* 59-86; Perm to Offic from 86; rtd 88. *Green Gates Nursing Home, 2 Hernes Road, Summertown, Oxford OX2 7PT* Oxford (0865) 58815

LENNARD, Elizabeth Jemima Mary Patricia. b 21. Edin Dioc NSM Course. **dss** 82 **d** 86. Falkirk *Edin* 82-86; Hon C 86-91; rtd 91. *36 Heugh Street, Falkirk FK1 5QR* Falkirk (0324) 23240

LENNARD, Thomas Jay. b 21. MBE54. Edin Dioc NSM Course. **d** 76 **p** 77. Hon C Kelso *Edin* 76-82; Hon C Falkirk 82-91; rtd 91. *36 Heugh Street, Falkirk FK1 5QR* Falkirk (0324) 23240

LENNON, Alfred Dennis. b 32. Oak Hill Th Coll 72. **d** 74 **p** 74. C Cam H Sepulchre w All SS *Ely* 74-77; P-in-c Cam St Barn 77-83; I Edin St Thos *Edin* 83-90; P-in-c Burghwallis w Skelbrooke *Sheff* from 90; Dioc Adv for Evang from 90. *St Helen's Rectory, Burghwallis, Doncaster, S Yorkshire DN6 9JL* Doncaster (0302) 700227

LENNOX, James. b 12. TCD BA36 MA40. CITC 37. **d** 38 **p** 39. V Bingley All SS *Bradf* 63-77; rtd 77; Perm to Offic *Bradf* from 77. *30 Hazel Beck, Cottingley Bridge, Bingley, W Yorkshire BD16 1LZ* Bradford (0274) 560189

LENNOX, William Ernest Michael. b 28. Selw Coll Cam BA52 MA63 Leeds Univ CertEd55. K Coll Lon 62. **d** 63 **p** 64. C Bramley *Ripon* 63-66; C Margate St Jo *Cant* 66-71; R Kingsnorth 71-73; R Shadoxhurst 71-73; R Kingsnorth w Shadoxhurst from 73. *The Rectory, Church Hill, Kingsnorth, Ashford, Kent TN23 3EG* Ashford (0233) 620433

LENON, Philip John FitzMaurice. b 24. ARIBA52 Lon Univ BD60. Wycliffe Hall Ox 55. **d** 57 **p** 58. V Crowborough *Chich* 67-89; rtd 89. *Snowhill Cottage, Dinton, Salisbury SP3 5HN* Teffont (072276) 754

LENOX-CONYNGHAM, Andrew George. b 44. Magd Coll Ox BA65 MA73 CCC Cam PhD73. Westcott Ho Cam 72. **d** 74 **p** 75. C Poplar *Lon* 74-77; TV Poplar 77-80; Chapl Heidelberg *Eur* 80-82; Chapl Ch Coll Cam 82-86; Lic to Offic *Ely* from 83; Chapl and Fell St Cath Coll Cam from 86. *St Catharine's College, Cambridge CB2 1RL* Cambridge (0223) 338346

LENS VAN RIJN, Robert Adriaan. b 47. St Jo Coll Nottm 78. **d** 80 **p** 81. C Gt Baddow *Chelmsf* 80-83; C Edgware *Lon* 83-86; C Derby St Pet and Ch Ch w H Trin *Derby* 86-90; Chapl Eindhoven *Eur* from 91. *c/o Het Pensionaat Eijkenburg Chapel, Aalsterweg 289, Eindhoven, The Netherlands*

LENTON, Colin William. b 23. CertEd. Cuddesdon Coll 80. **d** 81 **p** 81. Hon C Cowley St Jo *Ox* 81-82; Hon C Oakley 82-85; V Langtoft w Foxholes, Butterwick and Cottam *York* 85; V Langtoft w Foxholes, Butterwick, Cottam etc 85-89; rtd 89. *Flat 3, 24 South Drive, Harrogate HG2 8AU* Harrogate (0423) 564751

LENTON, Robert Vincent. b 15. Clifton Th Coll 62. **d** 63 **p** 63. V Lacock w Bowden Hill *Bris* 71-83; rtd 83; Perm to Offic *Liv* from 83. *6 Pilling Lane, Lydiate, Merseyside L31 4HF* 051-531 8561

LENYGON, Canon Herbert Edward. b 11. Lon Univ BD53. Kelham Th Coll 32. **d** 38 **p** 39. Chapl Newc United Hosps 49-74; rtd 74; Perm to Offic *Cov* from 74. *48 Foxes Way, Warwick CV34 6AY* Warwick (0926) 493954

✠**LEONARD, Rt Rev and Rt Hon Dr Graham Douglas.** b 21. PC81 KCVO91. Ball Coll Ox BA43 MA47. Episc Th Sem Kentucky Hon DD74 Westcott Ho Cam 46. **d** 47 **p** 48 **c** 64. C Chesterton St Andr *Ely* 47-49; C St Ives w Old Hurst 49-50; C Stansted Mountfitchet *Chelmsf* 50-52; V Ardleigh 52-55; Hon Can St Alb 55-57; Dir of Educn 55-58; Can Res St Alb 57-58; Sec C of E Bd of Educn Schs Coun 58-62; Gen Sec Nat Soc 58-62; Adn Hampstead *Lon* 62-64; R St Andr Undershaft w St Mary Axe 62-64; Suff Bp Willesden 64-73; Bp Truro 73-81; Bp Lon 81-91; Dean of the Chpls Royal and Prelate of OBE 81-91; rtd 91. *25 Woodlands Road, Witney, Oxon OX8 6DR*

LEONARD, John Francis. b 48. Lich Th Coll 69. **d** 72 **p** 73. C Chorley St Geo *Blackb* 72-75; C S Shore H Trin 75-80; V Marton Moss 81-89; V Kingskerswell w Coffinswell *Ex* from 89. *The Vicarage, Pound Lane, Kingskerswell, Newton Abbot, Devon TQ12 5DW* Kingskerswell (0803) 872305

LEONARD, John James. b 41. Southn Univ BSc62. Sarum Th Coll 63. **d** 65 **p** 66. C Loughb Em *Leic* 65-70; V New Humberstone 70-78; C-in-c Rushey Mead CD 78-85; V Leic St Theodore from 85. *St Theodore's House, 4 Sandfield Close, Leicester LE4 7RE* Leicester (0533) 669956

LEONARD, Peter Michael. b 47. MRTPI Portsm Poly BSc Trent Poly DipTP. Sarum & Wells Th Coll 82. **d** 84 **p** 85. C Llantwit Major *Llan* 84-88; V Cymmer and Porth from 88. *The Vicarage, Maesgwyn, Porth, M Glam CF39 9HW* Porth (0443) 682219

LEONARD, Stanley Gwyn. b 15. Univ of Wales (Lamp) BA36. Ripon Hall Ox 36. **d** 41. C Hengoed *Llan* 41; Lic to Offic *Mon* 49-84; Hon C Trevethin 84-87. *7 Victoria Road, Pontypool, Gwent NP4 5JU* Pontypool (0495) 751726

LEONARD-JOHNSON, Philip Anthony. b 35. Selw Coll Cam BA58 MA62. Linc Th Coll 63. **d** 65 **p** 66. C Wymondham *Nor* 65-68; Rhodesia 68-80; Zimbabwe 80-82; R Adderley *Lich* from 82; V Drayton in Hales from 82; P-in-c Moreton Say from 88. *St Mary's Vicarage, Market Drayton, Shropshire TF9 1AQ* Market Drayton (0630) 652527

LEONARD-WILLIAMS, David Haigh. b 15. ARIBA47. Coll of Resurr Mirfield 54. **d** 55 **p** 56. R Clifford Chambers w Marston Sicca *Glouc* 66-73; V Northleach w Hampnett and Farmington 73-80; rtd 80; Perm to Offic *Worc* from 80. *35 Bannawell Street, Tavistock, Devon PL19 0DL* Tavistock (0822) 614059

LEONARDI, Jeffrey. b 49. Warw Univ BA71 Aston Univ DCouns79. Carl Dioc Tr Course 85. **d** 88 **p** 89. C Netherton *Carl* 88-91; V Crosscanonby from 91; V Allonby from 91. *Crosscanonby Vicarage, Crosby, Maryport, Cumbria CA15 6SJ* Maryport (0900) 812146

LEPINE, Jeremy John. b 56. BA. St Jo Coll Nottm 82. d 84 p 85. C Harrow H Trin St Mich *Lon* 84-88; TV Horley *S'wark* from 88. *St Wilfrid's Vicarage, Horley Row, Horley, Surrey RH6 8DF* Horley (0293) 771869

LEPINE, Peter Gerald (Brother Peter Timothy). b 27. St Fran Coll Brisbane ThL56. d 57 p 58. Australia 57-62 and 65-67; SSF from 62; Papua New Guinea 67-76; Solomon Is 76; Perm to Offic *Conn* 76-80; P-in-c Belf H Redeemer 80-87; Lic to Offic *Newc* from 88. *The Friary, Alnmouth, Alnwick, Northd NE66 3NJ* Alnmouth (0665) 830213

LEPPARD, Miss Myra Anne. b 47. Chich Th Coll. d 90. Asst Chapl Brighton Hosp Gp from 90; Par Dn Brighton Gd Shep Preston *Chich* from 91. *17 Loder Road, Brighton BN1 6PL* Brighton (0273) 562106

LEPPINGTON, Ms Dian. b 46. Leeds Univ BA85. Cranmer Hall Dur 81. dss 83 d 87. Potternewton *Ripon* 83-87; Par Dn from 88; Ind Chapl from 88. *52 Newton Court, Leeds LS8 2PH* Leeds (0532) 485011

LERRY, Keith Doyle. b 49. Univ of Wales (Cardiff) DipTh72. St Mich Coll Llan 69. d 72 p 73. C Caerau w Ely *Llan* 72-75; C Roath St Martin 75-84; V Glyntaff from 84. *The Vicarage, Glyntaff, Pontypridd, M Glam CF37 4AS* Pontypridd (0443) 402535

LERVY, Hugh Martin. b 68. d 91. C Brecon St Mary and Battle w Llanddew *S & B* from 91. *The Clergy House, Cathedral Close, Brecon, Powys LD3 9DP* Brecon (0874) 623776

LESITER, Canon Malcolm Leslie. b 37. Selw Coll Cam BA61 MA65. Cuddesdon Coll 61. d 63 p 64. C Eastney *Portsm* 63-66; C Hemel Hempstead *St Alb* 66-71; TV 71-73; V Leavesden All SS 73-88; RD Watford 81-88; V Radlett from 88; Hon Can St Alb Abbey from 90. *The Vicarage, 13 Christchurch Crescent, Radlett, Herts WD7 8AG* Radlett (0923) 856606

LESLIE, David Rodney. b 43. AKC67. d 68 p 69. C Belmont *Lon* 68-71; C St Giles Cripplegate w St Bart Moor Lane etc 71-75; TV Kirkby *Liv* 76-84; TR Ditton St Mich from 84. *339 Ditchfield Road, Widnes, Cheshire WA8 8XR* 051-424 2502

LESLIE, Richard Charles Alan. b 46. ACIB71. d 79. Hon C Redbourn *St Alb* 79-88; Hon C Newport Pagnell w Lathbury and Moulsoe *Ox* from 88. *49 Broad Street, Newport Pagnell, Bucks MK16 0AW* Milton Keynes (0908) 612333

LESTER, Preb Geoffrey. b 16. Trin Coll Cam BA39 MA43. Wycliffe Hall Ox 41. d 42 p 43. R Bath Abbey w St Jas *B & W* 60-89; RD Bath 61-71; Preb Wells Cathl from 62; rtd 89. *29 Woodland Grove, Claverton Down, Bath BA2 7AT* Bath (0225) 469860

LESTER, Trevor Rashleigh. b 50. CITC 83. d 89 p 90. NSM Douglas Union w Frankfield *C, C & R* from 89. *The Arches, Kilnagleary, Carrigaline, Co Cork, Irish Republic* Cork (21) 372549

L'ESTRANGE, Canon Guy James Albert. b 24. TCD BA47 MA50. CITC. d 47 p 48. R Saltwood *Cant* 68-89; RD Elham 74-80; Hon Can Cant Cathl from 81; Sec to Dioc Bd of Min 86-89; rtd 89. *36 St Stephen's Hill, Canterbury, Kent CT2 7AX* Canterbury (0227) 763226

LETALL, Ronald Richard. b 29. ACII76. Linc Th Coll 82. d 84 p 85. C Scarborough St Martin *York* 84-86; C Middlesb St Thos 86-88; R Kirby Misperton w Normanby, Edston and Salton 88-90; TV Louth *Linc* from 90. *St Michael's Vicarage, Little Lane, Louth, Lincs LN11 9DU* Louth (0507) 601340

LETCHER, Canon David John. b 34. K Coll Lon 54. Chich Th Coll 56. d 58 p 59. C St Austell *Truro* 58-62; C Southbroom *Sarum* 62-64; R Odstock w Nunton and Bodenham 64-72; RD Alderbury 68-73 and 77-82; V Downton 72-85; Can and Preb Sarum Cathl from 79; TV Dorchester from 85; RD Dorchester from 89. *St George's Vicarage, High Street, Dorchester, Dorset DT1 1LB* Dorchester (0305) 262394

LETFORD, Peter Arthur. b 36. Oak Hill Th Coll 68. d 70 p 71. C Maidstone St Faith *Cant* 70-72; CF 72-75; C Ramsgate St Luke *Cant* 75-77; P-in-c Eastling 77-79; P-in-c Becontree St Eliz *Chelmsf* 79-84; P-in-c Clay Cross *Derby* 84-90; TV N Wingfield, Clay Cross and Pilsley from 90. *The Vicarage, Stretton Road, Clay Cross, Chesterfield S45 9AQ* Chesterfield (0246) 866908

LETHEREN, William Neils. b 37. Lon Univ DipTh63. St Aid Birkenhead 61. d 64 p 65. C Liv St Mich *Liv* 64-67; V 71-75; C Kirkdale St Athanasius 67-69; C Walsall Wood *Lich* 69-71; V W Derby St Jas *Liv* 75-84; R Newton in Makerfield Em 84-88; V Garston from 88. *The Vicarage, Horrocks Avenue, Garston, Liverpool L19 5NY* 051-427 7313

LETSON, Barry. b 55. Univ of Wales (Lamp) BA77. St Deiniol's Hawarden 82. d 83 p 84. C Flint *St As* 83-86;

V Llansantffraid GC and Llanarmon DC and Pontfadog 86-89; R Montgomery and Forden and Llandyssil from 89. *The Rectory, Montgomery, Powys SY16 6PT* Montgomery (0686) 668243

LETTON, Stanley Gladstone. b 17. d 82. NSM Bre from 82. *12 Latch Road, Brechin, Angus DD9 6JE* Brechin (03562) 2519

LETTS, Gerald Vincent. b 33. Univ of Wales BA63 Birm Univ DipTh65. NY Th Sem DMin Qu Coll Birm 63. d 65 p 66. C Birstall *Leic* 65-68; V Belgrave St Mich 68-75; V Sheff St Cuth *Sheff* from 75. *St Cuthbert's Vicarage, 1 Horndean Road, Sheffield S5 6UJ* Sheffield (0742) 436506

LEUNG, Dr Peter. Trin Coll Singapore BTh60 St Andr Univ PhD73. SE Asia Sch of Th MTh69. d 60 p 61. Singapore 60-76; Malaya 60-63; Malaysia 63-76; Lect Congr Coll Man 76-77; USPG 77-83; Perm to Offic *Roch* 83-89; BCC 83-90; CCBI from 90; Perm to Offic *S'wark* from 88; Hon C Shortlands *Roch* from 90; Regional Sec (S and E Asia) CMS from 91. *14 Uplands, Beckenham, Kent BR3 3NB* 081-650 4157

LEVER, Edmund Arthur. b 23. Sarum Th Coll 55. d 57 p 58. V Brentwood St Geo *Chelmsf* 64-73; Chapl S Ockendon Hosp 73-78; rtd 88. *42 Pear Tree Close, South Ockendon, Essex RM15 6PR* South Ockendon (0708) 852933

LEVER, Julian Lawrence Gerrard. b 36. Fitzw Coll Cam BA60 MA64. Sarum Th Coll 60. d 62 p 63. C Amesbury *Sarum* 62-66; R Corfe Mullen 66-78; RD Wimborne 73-75; P-in-c Wilton w Netherhampton and Fugglestone 78-82; R 82-86; R Salisbury St Martin from 86. *The Rectory, Tollgate Road, Salisbury SP1 2JJ* Salisbury (0722) 335895

LEVERIDGE, Mrs Norma Jean. b 42. St Alb Minl Tr Scheme 79. dss 85 d 87. Lyonsdown H Trin *St Alb* 85-87; Hon Par Dn from 87. *31 Highlands Road, New Barnet, Herts EN5 5AA* 081-441 1591

LEVERTON, Michael John. b 52. K Coll Lon BD76 AKC76 MTh77. Cant Sch of Min 84. d 87 p 88. NSM Elham w Denton and Wootton *Cant* from 87. *189 Field Avenue, Canterbury, Kent CT1 1TS* Canterbury (0227) 457065

LEVERTON, Peter James Austin. b 33. CEng MIMechE68 Nottm Univ BA55. Ripon Coll Cuddesdon 79. d 81 p 82. C St Jo in Bedwardine *Worc* 81-84; V Worc St Mich 84-88; TR Worc St Barn w Ch Ch from 88. *St Barnabas' Vicarage, Church Road, Worcester WR3 8NX* Worcester (0905) 23785

LEVERTON, Peter Robert. b 25. Lich Th Coll 59. d 60 p 61. C Shepshed *Leic* 60-64; Australia 64-69; V Marshchapel *Linc* 70-73; V Grainthorpe w Conisholme 70-73; R N Coates 70-73; Miss to Seamen 73-77; P-in-c Brislington St Luke *Bris* 77-84; V Avonmouth St Andr 84-87; Ind Chapl 84-87; P-in-c Ugborough *Ex* from 87; P-in-c Ermington from 88. *The Vicarage, Lutterburn Street, Ugborough, Ivybridge, Devon PL21 0NG* Plymouth (0752) 896957

LEVETT, Colin Andrew. b 13. d 69 p 71. Par Dn Hatch End St Anselm *Lon* 69-71; AP N Wembley St Cuth 71-73; P-in-c Dollis Hill St Paul 73-78; rtd 78. *19 Wilmington Court, Bath Road, Worthing, W Sussex BN11 3QN* Worthing (0903) 210744

LEVETT, Ven Howard. b 44. AKC67. d 68 p 69. C Rotherhithe St Mary w All SS *S'wark* 68-72; P-in-c Walworth St Jo 72-77; V 77-78; P-in-c Walworth Lady Marg w St Mary 78; V Walworth St Jo 78-80; RD S'wark and Newington 78-80; Adn Egypt from 80; Miss to Seamen from 80. *The Parsonage, Stanley Bay, PO Box 685, Alexandria, Egypt* Alexandria (3) 840720 or 803542

LEVEY, Colin Russell. b 35. Open Univ BA76. S'wark Ord Course 63. d 66 p 67. C Rusthall *Roch* 66-71; Youth Chapl 71-75; Hon C Riverhead 71-75; V Lamorbey H Redeemer 75-81; V Milton next Gravesend Ch Ch 81-85; P-in-c Elmley Lovett w Hampton Lovett and Elmbridge etc *Worc* from 87; P-in-c Hartlebury from 87; P-in-c Wilden from 87. *The Rectory, Elmley Lovett, Droitwich, Worcs WR9 0PU* Hartlebury (0299) 250255

LEVICK, Brian William. b 30. Westcott Ho Cam 63. d 64 p 65. C Deeping St James *Linc* 69-70; C Hemel Hempstead *St Alb* 70-71; TV 71-77; Hon C Sedbergh, Cautley and Garsdale *Bradf* 77-83; V Firbank, Howgill and Killington 77-83; V Cononley w Bradley 83-90; rtd 90; C Kettlewell w Conistone, Hubberholme etc *Bradf* from 90. *Laburnum Cottage, Starbottom, Skipton, N Yorkshire BD23 5HY* Kettlewell (075676) 823

LEVICK, Canon Frank Hemsley. b 29. Kelham Th Coll 49. d 54 p 55. V Ribbleton *Blackb* 67-80; TR 80-85; Hon Can Blackb Cathl 75-90; R Ribchester w Stidd 85-90;

rtd 90. *The Old Nurseries, Beckingham, Doncaster, S Yorkshire DN10 4PS* Saundby (042784) 668

LEVINGSTON, Peter Owen Wingfield. b 31. TCD BA58. **d** 58 **p** 59. Chapl RAF 62-78; rtd 78. *Address temp unknown*

LEVY, Christopher Charles. b 51. Southn Univ BTh82. Sarum & Wells Th Coll 79. **d** 82 **p** 83. C Rubery *Birm* 82-85; C Stratford w Bishopton *Cov* 85-87; TV Clifton *S'well* from 87. *Holy Trinity Vicarage, Nottingham NG11 9DG* Nottingham (0602) 212454

LEWERS, Very Rev Benjamin Hugh. b 32. Selw Coll Cam BA60 MA64. Linc Th Coll. **d** 62 **p** 63. C Northn St Mary *Pet* 62-65; C Hounslow Heath St Paul *Lon* 65-68; C-in-c Hounslow Gd Shep Beavers Lane CD 65-68; Chapl Heathrow Airport 68-75; R Newark St Mary *S'well* 75-80; P-in-c Averham w Kelham 79-81; TR Newark w Hawton, Cotham and Shelton 80-81; Provost Derby from 81. *Provost's House, 9 Highfield Road, Derby DE3 1GX* Derby (0332) 41201 or 42971

LEWES AND HASTINGS, Archdeacon of. See GLAISYER, Ven Hugh

LEWES, Suffragan Bishop of. See BALL, Rt Rev Peter John

LEWIN, William Donald. b 13. TCD BA37. CITC 39. **d** 39 **p** 40. R Hale w S Charford *Win* 68-82; rtd 82; Perm to Offic *Win* from 82. *15 Shady Bower Close, Salisbury SP1 2RQ* Salisbury (0722) 331904

LEWIS, Ven Albert John Francis. b 21. Univ of Wales (Swansea) BA46. St Mich Coll Llan 46. **d** 48 **p** 49. Dioc Dir RE *Llan* 60-91; V Pendoylan 61-73; RD Llan 69-81; V Pendolyn and Welsh St Donats 73-81; Can Llan Cathl 76-81; Treas 81-91; Adn Margam 81-88; Adn Llan 88-91; rtd 91. *11 Downs View Close, Aberthin, Cowbridge, S Glam CF7 7HG*

LEWIS, Canon Alexander Thomas. b 20. Univ of Wales (Ban) BA51. St Mich Coll Llan 50. **d** 52 **p** 53. V Llandegai St Ann, Bethesda w Tregarth *Ban* 56-89; RD Arllechwedd 73-89; Hon Can Ban Cathl 82-84; Can 84-89; rtd 89. *91 Wellfield Road, Culcheth, Warrington WA3 4BX* Culcheth (092576) 2899

LEWIS, Ann Theodora Rachel. b 33. Univ of Wales (Ban) BA55. Qu Coll Birm 78. **d** 80. C Swansea St Mary w H Trin *S & B* from 80; Chapl St Mary's Coll from 90. *St Mary's Vicarage, Eden Avenue, Swansea SA2 0PS* Swansea (0792) 298616

LEWIS, Canon Arthur Griffith. b 15. Univ of Wales (Lamp) BA40. **d** 47 **p** 48. V Ystalyfera *S & B* 63-87; RD Cwmtawe 79-85; Hon Can Brecon Cathl 80-89; Can 81-85; P-in-c Capel Coelbren 85-89; rtd 89. *14 Pontwillim, Brecon, Powys LD3 9BT* Brecon (0874) 2869

LEWIS, Arthur Jenkin Llewellyn. b 42. Univ of Wales (Cardiff) MPS42 BPharm. Coll of Resurr Mirfield 71. **d** 73 **p** 74. C Cardiff St Jo *Llan* 73-78; C Christchurch *Win* 78-82; R Lightbowne *Man* from 82. *St Luke's Rectory, Kenyon Lane, Manchester M10 9HS* 061-681 1308

LEWIS, Arthur Roland. b 20. St Edm Hall Ox BA41 MA45. St Steph Ho Ox 41. **d** 43 **p** 44. S Rhodesia 58-65; Rhodesia 65-80; S Africa 80-87; rtd 87; Perm to Offic *Birm* from 88. *54 Lyndon Road, Solihull, W Midlands B92 7RQ*

LEWIS, Ven Benjamin Alec. b 12. St D Coll Lamp BA34. **d** 36 **p** 37. Adn St D 70-82; Can St D Cathl 70-82; rtd 82. *Flat 1, The Treasury, St Davids, Haverfordwest, Dyfed* St Davids (0437) 720522

LEWIS, Very Rev Bertie. b 31. Univ of Wales (Lamp) BA54 St Cath Soc Ox BA57 MA60. Wycliffe Hall Ox 54. **d** 57 **p** 58. C Cwmaman *St D* 57-60; C Abth St Mich 60-62; V Llanddewi Brefi w Llanbadarn Odwyn 62-65; V Henfynyw w Aberaeron and Llanddewi Aber-arth 65-75; V Lamp 75-80; Can St D Cathl 78-86; Chapl Abth Hosps 80-88; R Abth *St D* 80-88; Adn Cardigan 86-90; V Nevern and Y Beifil w Eglwyswrw and Meline etc 88-90; V St D Cathl from 90; Dean St D from 90. *The Deanery, St David's, Dyfed SA62 6RH* St Davids (0437) 720202

LEWIS, Brian James. b 52. Cant Univ (NZ) BA75. St Jo Coll Auckland 76. **d** 78 **p** 79. New Zealand 78-80; C Shrub End *Chelmsf* 80-82; P-in-c Colchester St Barn 82-84; V 84-88; P-in-c Romford St Andr 88-90; R from 90. *St Andrew's Rectory, 119 London Road, Romford RM7 9QD* Romford (0708) 764192

LEWIS, Canon Brinley James. b 11. Univ of Wales BA40. St D Coll Lamp 39. **d** 42 **p** 42. V Stalybridge St Paul *Ches* 65-79; RD Mottram 76-79; rtd 79; Perm to Offic *Ches* from 81. *77 Dewsnap Lane, Dukinfield, Cheshire SK16 5AW* 061-330 0507

LEWIS, Canon Christopher Andrew. b 44. Bris Univ BA69 CCC Cam PhD74. Westcott Ho Cam 71. **d** 73

p 74. C Barnard Castle *Dur* 73-76; Dir Ox Inst for Ch and Soc 76-79; Tutor Ripon Coll Cuddesdon 76-79; P-in-c Aston Rowant w Crowell *Ox* 78-81; Sen Tutor Ripon Coll Cuddesdon 79-81; Vice-Prin 81-82; V Spalding *Linc* 82-87; Can Res Cant Cathl *Cant* from 87; Dir of Minl Tr from 89. *12 The Precincts, Canterbury, Kent CT1 2EH* Canterbury (0227) 463060

LEWIS, Canon Christopher Gouldson. b 42. K Coll Cam BA64 MA68. Cuddesdon Coll 65. **d** 67 **p** 68. C Gosforth All SS *Newc* 67-71; Sarawak 71-74; V Luton St Chris Round Green *St Alb* 74-80; RD Reculver *Cant* 80-86; V Whitstable All SS w St Pet 80-84; TR Whitstable from 84; Dir of Post-Ord Tr from 88; Hon Can Cant Cathl from 91. *The Vicarage, Church Street, Whitstable, Kent CT5 1PG* Canterbury (0227) 272308

LEWIS, Christopher Thomas Samuel. b 08. CCC Cam BA30 MA39. Cuddesdon Coll 30. **d** 32 **p** 33. R Cheriton Bishop *Ex* 61-74; rtd 74. *Manormead, Tilford Road, Hindhead, Surrey GU26 6RA* Hindhead (0428) 607863

LEWIS, David Antony. b 48. Dur Univ BA69 Nottm Univ MTh84. St Jo Coll Nottm 83. **d** 83 **p** 84. C Gateacre *Liv* 83-86; V Toxteth St Cypr w Ch Ch from 86. *48 John Lennon Drive, Liverpool L6 9HT* 051-260 3262

LEWIS, David Austin. b 09. St D Coll Lamp BA31. **d** 32 **p** 33. R Llanwenarth Ultra *Mon* 64-76; rtd 76; Lic to Offic *Mon* from 77. *29 Fairfield, Penperlleni, Pontypool, Gwent NP4 0AP* Nantyderry (0873) 880101

LEWIS, Very Rev David Gareth. b 31. Univ of Wales (Ban) BA52 DipEd53 Or Coll Ox BA59 MA63. St Mich Coll Llan 56. **d** 60 **p** 61. C Neath w Llantwit *Llan* 60-63; Chapl Sarum Th Coll 63-64; Vice-Prin 64-69; Dean Belize 69-78; V Newport St Mark *Mon* 78-82; Can St Woolos Cathl 81-90; Dioc Missr 81-90; Clerical Sec Governing Body Ch in Wales from 85; V Newport St Woolos from 90; Dean Mon from 90. *The Deanery, Stow Hill, Newport, Gwent NP9 4ED* Newport (0633) 263338

LEWIS, David Glyn. b 09. Univ of Wales BA36. Ripon Hall Ox 36. **d** 39 **p** 40. V Cubbington *Cov* 68-79; rtd 80; Perm to Offic *Cov* from 80. *4 St James Close, Stratford-upon-Avon, Warks CV37 7RH* Stratford-upon-Avon (0789) 205559

LEWIS, David Hugh. b 45. Oak Hill Th Coll 88. **d** 90 **p** 91. C Oakham, Hambleton, Egleton, Braunston and Brooke *Pet* from 90. *2 Chiltern Close, Oakham, Rutland LE15 6NW* Oakham (0572) 755866

LEWIS, David Islwyn. b 15. St D Coll Lamp BA37 St Mich Coll Llan 37. **d** 38 **p** 39. V Baglan *Llan* 61-82; rtd 82; Perm to Offic *Llan* from 82. *19 Broad Street, Port Talbot, W Glam* Port Talbot (0639) 882203

LEWIS, David Roy. b 18. Univ of Wales (Lamp) BA39. St Mich Coll Llan 40. **d** 40 **p** 41. V Seven Sisters *Llan* 66-77; R Colwinston w Llandow and Llysworney 77-86; rtd 86. *Rockleigh, Colwinstone, Cowbridge, S Glam CF7 7NL* Cowbridge (04463) 2797

LEWIS, David Tudor. b 61. Jes Coll Cam BA83. Trin Coll Bris BA88. **d** 88 **p** 89. C Tile Cross *Birm* from 88. *10 Kettlewell Way, Chelmsley Wood, Birmingham B37 5JD* 021-770 5756

LEWIS, David Tudor Bowes. b 63. Keele Univ BA85 Univ of Wales (Cardiff) BTh90. St Mich Coll Llan 87. **d** 90 **p** 91. C Llangollen w Trevor and Llantysilio *St As* from 90. *Home Lea, Aber Adda, Hill Street, Llangollen, Clwyd LL20 8HE* Llangollen (0978) 861768

LEWIS, David Vaughan. b 36. Trin Coll Cam BA60 MA64. Ridley Hall Cam 60. **d** 62 **p** 63. C Rugby St Matt *Cov* 62-65; Asst Chapl K Edw Sch Witley 65-71; Hon C Rainham *Chelmsf* 71-76; V Stoke Hill *Guildf* 76-87; V Wallington H Trin *S'wark* from 87. *Holy Trinity Vicarage, Maldon Road, Wallington, Surrey SM6 8BL* 081-647 7605

LEWIS, David Watkin. b 40. Univ of Wales (Lamp) BA61 Univ of Wales (Swansea) DipYL65. Wycliffe Hall Ox 61. **d** 63 **p** 64. C Skewen *Llan* 63-66; Field Tr Officer Prov Youth Coun Ch in Wales 66-68; C Gabalfa 68-71; P-in-c Marcross w Monknash and Wick 71-73; R 73-83; RD Llantwit Major and Cowbridge 81-83; V Baglan from 83. *The Vicarage, 29 Church Road, Port Talbot, W Glam SA12 8ST* Port Talbot (0639) 812199

LEWIS, Canon Donald Edward. b 30. Univ of Wales (Lamp) BA53. Wycliffe Hall Ox 53. **d** 55 **p** 56. C Wrexham *St As* 55-59; R Castle Caereinion 59-62; Area Sec (Dios Ches, Ban, St As and S & M) CMS 62-65; India 62-65; V Hale *Ches* 65-77; V Swansea St Mary and H Trin *S & B* 77-79; RD Swansea from 78; Hon Can Brecon Cathl 79-81; Can from 81; V Swansea St Mary w H Trin and St Mark 79-83; V Swansea St Mary w H Trin from 83; Prec Brecon Cathl from 90. *The*

Vicarage, Eden Avenue, Swansea SA2 0PS Swansea (0792) 298616

LEWIS, Edward John. b 15. Qu Coll Cam BA36 MA40. Ridley Hall Cam 36. **d** 38 **p** 39. V Swanwick and Pentrich *Derby* 56-74; P-in-c Longstone 74-80; rtd 80; Perm to Offic Derby and Liv from 80. *5 Old Hall Gardens, Rainford, St Helens, Merseyside* Rainford (074488) 2242

LEWIS, Edward John. b 58. Univ of Wales BEd80 BA82. Chich Th Coll 82. **d** 83 **p** 84. C Llanguicke *S & B* 83-85; C Morriston 85-87; V Tregaron w Ystrad Meurig and Strata Florida *St D* 87-89; Chapl Manor Hosp Walsall from 89; Distr Co-ord Chapl Walsall Hosps from 90. *The Chaplain's Office, Manor Hospital, Walsall WS2 9PS* Walsall (0922) 721172

LEWIS, Elinor Glenys. b 11. SRN34 SCM35. St Chris Coll Blackheath 44. **dss** 49 **d** 78 **p** 78. New Zealand from 60; rtd 71. *10A Heybridge Lane, Christchurch 2, New Zealand* Christchurch (3) 332-6808

LEWIS, Elsie Leonora. b 26. Cranmer Hall Dur 72. **dss** 78 **d** 87. S Westoe *Dur* 78-80; Ryton 80-86; rtd 86. *53 Cushy Cow Lane, Ryton, Tyne & Wear NE40 3NL* 091-413 5845

LEWIS, Canon Elvet. b 23. St D Coll Lamp BA47 St Edm Hall Ox BA50 MA54. St Mich Coll Llan 48. **d** 51 **p** 52. V Barbourne *Worc* 65-79; RD Upton 79-80; P-in-c Kempsey 79; P-in-c Severn Stoke w Croome D'Abitot 79; P-in-c Kempsey and Severn Stoke w Croome d'Abitot 79-80; rtd 80; Perm to Offic *Worc* from 80. *Rose House, 7 Rose Hill, London Road, Worcester WR5 1EY* Worcester (0905) 359210

LEWIS, Eric. b 36. Sarum & Wells Th Coll 74. **d** 77 **p** 78. NSM Oldbury *Sarum* from 77. *St James Old House, Oliver Close, Cherhill, Calne, Wilts SN11 8XU* Calne (0249) 812144

LEWIS, Evan David Dyfrig. b 17. TD67. Univ of Wales BA47. St Mich Coll Llan 47. **d** 49 **p** 50. CF (TA) from 52; R Llanmaes and Llanmihangel *Llan* 58-88; rtd 88. *5 Oak Grove, Eglwysbrewis, St Athan, Barry, S Glam* St Athan (0446) 750123

LEWIS, Evan Edgar. b 07. K Coll Cam BA31 MA35. St D Coll Lamp BA28. **d** 31 **p** 32. V Stoke St Milburgh w Heath *Heref* 57-73; R Abdon w Clee St Margaret 57-73; R Cold Weston 57-73; rtd 73; Perm to Offic *Heref* from 73. *The Granary, Stoke St Milburgh, Ludlow, Shropshire SY8 2EV*

LEWIS, Evan Thomas Derwen. b 10. Univ of Wales BA34. St D Coll Lamp 34. **d** 35 **p** 36. V Glasbury St Pet *S & B* 46-83; rtd 83. *43 Gwernyfed Avenue, Three Cocks, Brecon, Powys LD3 0RT* Glasbury (04974) 229

LEWIS, Francis Edward Walter. b 17. Univ of Wales BA40. St Mich Coll Llan 41. **d** 42 **p** 43. V Linslade *Ox* 65-73; V Maidenhead St Luke 73-81; rtd 81. *13 Courtlands Road, Shipton-under-Wychwood, Oxford* Shipton-under-Wychwood (0993) 830604

LEWIS, Frederick. b 09. FRAI40 Univ of Wales BA31. St Mich Coll Llan 30. **d** 32 **p** 33. Chapl and Tutor Whittington Coll Felbridge 55-68; rtd 68. *Flat 2, 29 High Street, Prestatyn, Clwyd LL19 9AW* Prestatyn (0745) 853240

LEWIS, Frederick Norman. b 23. Leeds Univ BA47. Coll of Resurr Mirfield 47. **d** 49 **p** 50. V Kingswinford St Mary *Lich* 69-88; rtd 88. *27 Bramblewood Drive, Finchfield, Wolverhampton WV3 9DB* Wolverhampton (0902) 334934

LEWIS, Gary. b 61. Lanc Univ BA85. Ripon Coll Cuddesdon 86. **d** 89 **p** 90. C Blackb St Mich w St Jo and H Trin *Blackb* from 89. *6 Juniper Street, Blackburn BB1 6LW* Blackburn (0254) 65457

LEWIS, Hubert Godfrey. b 33. Univ of Wales (Lamp) BA59 DipTh60. **d** 60 **p** 61. C Merthyr Tydfil *Llan* 60-64; C Caerphilly 64-66; Perm to Offic S'wark 66-76; Cant 76-82; Hon C Shirley St Jo S'wark from 82. *4 East Way, Croydon CR0 8AH* 081-777 6587

LEWIS, Dr Ian. b 33. MRCS LRCP Lon Univ MB, BS57. Oak Hill Th Coll 61. **d** 63 **p** 64. C Heatherlands St Jo *Sarum* 63-66; Ethiopia 66-73; Hon C Bath Walcot *B & W* 75-77; Lic to Offic from 78. *22C Ashley Road, Bathford, Bath* Bath (0225) 859818

LEWIS, Ian Richard. b 54. Sheff Univ BA76 Ox Univ BA83 MA87. Wycliffe Hall Ox 81. **d** 84 **p** 85. C Rusholme *Man* 84-88; C Sandal St Helen *Wakef* 88-91; V Bath St Bart *B & W* from 91. *St Bartholomew's Vicarage, 5 Oldfield Road, Bath BA2 3NB* Bath (0225) 22070

LEWIS, Jacob Brian. b 33. Univ of Wales BA54 Fitzw Ho Cam BA56 MA60. Wells Th Coll 56. **d** 57 **p** 58. C Cardiff St Mary *Llan* 57-61; S Africa 61-63; C Cowley St Jo *Ox* 63-67; V Gladstone Park St Fran *Lon* 67-76; V Compton

w E Ilsley *Ox* from 76. *The Vicarage, Compton, Newbury, Berks RG16 0RD* Compton (0635) 578256

LEWIS, James Edward. b 22. St D Coll Lamp BA50. **d** 51 **p** 52. V Brynamman *St D* 61-72; R Llangathen w Llanfihangel Cilfargen 72-82; V Llangathen w Llanfihangel Cilfargen etc 82-90; RD Llangadog and Llandeilo 85-89; rtd 90. *3 St Mary Street, Carmarthen, Dyfed SA31 1TN* Carmarthen (0267) 221660

LEWIS, Ven John. b 35. Worc Coll Ox BA58 MA62. Ridley Hall Cam 58. **d** 60 **p** 61. C Sutton *Liv* 60-63; Asst Chapl Brussels *Eur* 63-64; Chapl Montreux 64-69; Chapl The Hague w Leiden and Voorschoten 69-81; RD The Netherlands 69-75; Adn NW Eur from 81; Chan and Sen Can Brussels Cathl from 81; Chapl Brussels w Charleroi from 81. *Chatelard, 116 rue du Chateau d'Eau, 1180 Brussels, Belgium* Brussels (2) 375-6961 or 511-7183

LEWIS, Ven John Arthur. b 34. Jes Coll Ox BA56 MA60. Cuddesdon Coll 58. **d** 60 **p** 61. C Prestbury *Glouc* 60-63; C Wimborne Minster *Sarum* 63-66; R Eastington and Frocester *Glouc* 66-70; V Nailsworth 70-78; Chapl Memorial and Querns Hosp Cirencester 78-88; V Cirencester *Glouc* 78-88; RD Cirencester 84-88; Hon Can Glouc Cathl from 85; Adn Cheltenham from 88. *Westbourne, 283 Gloucester Road, Cheltenham GL51 7AD* Cheltenham (0242) 522923

LEWIS, John Burrenston. b 18. St D Coll Lamp BA35. **d** 37 **p** 38. V Llanelly St Paul *St D* 64-72; R Ludchurch w Templeton and Crunwere 73-84; rtd 84. *7 Martin's Lodge, The Norton, Tenby, Dyfed SA70 8AB*

LEWIS, John Edward. b 31. SS Mark & Jo Coll Chelsea CertEd53. Qu Coll Birm 83. **d** 85 **p** 86. C Leominster *Heref* 85-87; TV from 87. *The Vicarage, 1A School Road, Leominster, Hereford HR6 8NS* Leominster (0568) 2124

LEWIS, John Herbert. b 42. Selw Coll Cam BA64 MA68. Westcott Ho Cam 64. **d** 66 **p** 67. C Wyken *Cov* 66-70; C Bedf St Andr *St Alb* 70-73; Lib Pusey Ho 73-77; Bp's Chapl for Graduates *Ox* 73-77; TV Woughton 78-82; TV Gt Chesham 82-88; P-in-c Newport Pagnell w Lathbury and Moulsoe 88-91; R from 91. *New Rectory, 81 High Street, Newport Pagnell, Bucks MK16 8AB* Newport Pagnell (0908) 611145

LEWIS, John Horatio George. b 47. Southn Univ BEd72 MA85. Ox NSM Course 86. **d** 89 **p** 90. NSM Newbury *Ox* from 89. *36 Glendale Avenue, Newbury, Berks RG14 6RU* Newbury (0635) 34721

LEWIS, Ven John Hubert Richard. b 43. AKC66. **d** 67 **p** 68. C Hexham *Newc* 67-70; Ind Chapl 70-77; Communications Officer *Dur* 77-82; Chapl for Agric *Heref* 82-87; Adn Ludlow from 87. *Glendale House, 51 Gravel Hill, Ludlow, Shropshire SY8 1QS* Ludlow (0584) 872862

LEWIS, John Malcolm. b 41. Reading Univ BEd. Trin Coll Bris. **d** 82 **p** 83. C Kingswood *Bris* 82-85; TV Weston-super-Mare Cen Par *B & W* from 85. *The Vicarage, 5 Walliscote Road, Weston-super-Mare, Avon BS23 1XE* Weston-super-Mare (0934) 21046

LEWIS, Very Rev John Percival. b 19. TCD BA44. CITC 47. **d** 47 **p** 48. I Knappagh *T, K & A* 51-74; RD Tuam 56-91; Can Tuam Cathl from 70; I Omey w Ballynakill, Errislannan and Roundstone 73-91; Provost Tuam 73-91; rtd 91. *Albany, Pheasant Hill, Castlebar, Co Mayo, Irish Republic* Castlebar (94) 22747

LEWIS, John Thomas. b 47. Jes Coll Ox BA69 MA73 St Jo Coll Cam BA72. Westcott Ho Cam 71. **d** 73 **p** 74. C Whitchurch *Llan* 73-77; C Llanishen and Lisvane 77-80; Asst Chapl Univ of Wales (Cardiff) 80-85; Warden of Ords 81-85; V Brecon St David w Llanspyddid and Llanilltyd *S & B* 85-91; Sec Prov Selection Panel & Bd Ch in Wales from 87; V Bassaleg *Mon* from 91. *The Vicarage, Forge Lane, Bassaleg, Newport, Gwent NP1 9NF* Newport (0633) 893258

LEWIS, Kenneth Lionel. b 22. Univ of Wales (Swansea) Keble Coll Ox BA50 MA54 Ch Coll Cam CertEd52. Wycliffe Hall Ox 52. **d** 52 **p** 53. C Bromley St Jo *Roch* 52-55; C Streatham Hill St Marg *S'wark* 55-57; R Tatsfield 57-72; Lic to Offic 72-78 and from 89; Perm to Offic Cant 75-78; Roch from 83. *9 Nostle Road, Northleach, Cheltenham, Glos GL54 3PF* Cotswold (0451) 60118

LEWIS, Leslie. b 25. Qu Coll Birm 82. **d** 83 **p** 84. NSM Garretts Green *Birm* 83-88; NSM Coleshill from 88; NSM Maxstoke from 88. *54 Bellevue Road, Birmingham B26 2QA* 021-742 3662

LEWIS, Leslie. b 28. LRAM56. St Aid Birkenhead 61. **d** 63 **p** 64. C Eastham *Ches* 63-66; C W Kirby St Bridget 66-72; V Rainow w Saltersford 72-73; V Rainow w Saltersford and Forest from 73; Clergy Widows and

Retirement Officer from 88. *The Vicarage, Rainow, Macclesfield, Cheshire SK10 5TZ* Bollington (0625) 572013

LEWIS, Malcolm John. b 50. St Steph Ho Ox 75. **d** 78 **p** 79. C Sheerness H Trin w St Paul *Cant* 78-81; C Burgess Hill St Jo *Chich* 81-87; V Heathfield St Rich from 87. *St Richard's Vicarage, Hailsham Road, Heathfield, E Sussex TN21 8AF* Heathfield (04352) 2744

LEWIS, Michael Augustine Owen. b 53. Mert Coll Ox BA75 MA79. Cuddesdon Coll 75. **d** 78 **p** 79. C Salfords *S'wark* 78-80; Chapl Thames Poly 80-84; V Welling 84-91; TR Worc SE *Worc* from 91. *The Rectory, 6 St Catherine's Hill, Worcester WR5 2EA* Worcester (0905) 355119

LEWIS, Michael David Bennett. b 41. Univ of Wales DipTh68. St Mich Coll Llan 65. **d** 68 **p** 69. C Penarth w Lavernock *Llan* 68-72; Chapl RAF 72-74; C Llanishen and Lisvane *Llan* 74-77; V Penyfai w Tondu 77 82; Chapl Ardingly Coll Haywards Heath 82-90; R Merrow *Guildf* from 90. *The Rectory, 232 Epsom Road, Merrow, Guildford, Surrey GU4 7AA* Guildford (0483) 504311

LEWIS, Michael Douglas. b 35. Hertf Coll Ox BA57 MA60. Sarum Th Coll 58. **d** 59 **p** 60. C Stogursey *B & W* 59-65; V N Curry 65-86; V Taunton H Trin from 86. *Holy Trinity Vicarage, 18 Holway Avenue, Taunton, Somerset TA1 3AR* Taunton (0823) 337890

LEWIS, Michael John. b 37. LLAM86. St Aid Birkenhead 64. **d** 66 **p** 67. C Whitnash *Cov* 66-69; C Nuneaton St Nic 69-73; TV Basildon St Martin w H Cross and Laindon *Chelmsf* 73-79; V W Bromwich St Jas *Lich* 79-85; TV Buxton w Burbage and King Sterndale *Derby* from 85. *St Mary's House, 2A New Market Street, Buxton, Derbyshire SK17 6LP* Buxton (0298) 4179

LEWIS, Norman Eric. b 34. SRN55 Open Univ BA77. Roch Th Coll 59 Lich Th Coll 60. **d** 63 **p** 64. V Hindsford *Man* 67-77; V Bolton SS Simon and Jude 77-90; rtd 90. *Millbank Cottage, Kirby Misperton, Malton, N Yorkshire YO17 0XZ* Kirby Misperton (065386) 526

LEWIS, Paul Wilfred. b 37. Ch Ch Ox BA60 DipEd61 MA64 DipTh72. Chich Th Coll 62. **d** 64 **p** 65. C St Pancras H Cross w St Jude and St Pet *Lon* 64-66; C Tottenham St Jo 66-68; Barbados 68-71; Lect Sarum & Wells Th Coll 72-74; Chapl Sarum & Wells Th Coll 73-74; Chapl LSE *Lon* 74-80; Chapl St Chris Hospice Sydenham 80-86; C St Giles Cripplegate w St Bart Moor Lane etc *Lon* 86-89; Chapl Nat Hosp for Neurology & Neurosurgery Lon from 89. *23A Queen Square, London WC1N 3AY* 071-837 3611 or 278 3706

LEWIS, Peter Anthony. b 25. Sarum & Wells Th Coll 76. **d** 79 **p** 80. Hon C Southsea St Simon *Portsm* from 79. *2 Selsey Avenue, Southsea, Hants PO4 9QL* Portsmouth (0705) 732394

LEWIS, Canon Peter Goulstone. b 25. Univ of Wales (Lamp) BA48. **d** 50 **p** 51. V Tongwynlais *Llan* 66-79; V Llantrisant 79-90; Can Llan Cathl from 85; RD Pontypridd 88-90; rtd 91; Perm to Offic *Llan* from 91. *73 Pinecroft Avenue, Cwmbach, Aberdare, M Glam CF44 0NB* Aberdare (0685) 882257

LEWIS, Peter Graham. b 40. Linc Th Coll 70. **d** 81 **p** 82. C Gt and Lt Coates w Bradley *Linc* 81-85; TV 85-87; P-in-c Southoe w Hail Weston *Ely* 87-89; R 89-90; P-in-c Lt Paxton 87-89; V from 89; P-in-c Diddington 87-89; V from 89; R Southoe from 90. *The Vicarage, 24 St James's Road, Little Paxton, St Neots, Huntingdon, Cambs PE19 4QW* Huntingdon (0480) 214280

LEWIS, Peter Richard. b 40. Dur Univ BA62 Birm Univ DipTh64. Qu Coll Birm 62. **d** 64 **p** 65. C Moseley St Mary *Birm* 64-67; C Sherborne w Castleton and Lillington *Sarum* 67-71; P-in-c Bishopstone w Stratford Tony 72-80; V Amesbury from 80; Chapl RAF from 80. *The Vicarage, Church Street, Amesbury, Salisbury SP4 7EU* Amesbury (0980) 623145

LEWIS, Dr Philip Stacey. b 04. FRSC31 CChem75 Liv Univ BSc24 PhD26. **d** 44 **p** 45. V S Cerney w Cerney Wick *Glouc* 64-74; rtd 74; Perm to Offic *Glouc* 74-90. *1 Southmead Gardens, Alcester Road, Studley, Warwicks B80 7NW* Studley (052785) 2072

LEWIS, Rachel Veronica Clare. b 59. St Jo Coll Dur BA80 Man Univ CertEd81. Sarum & Wells Th Coll 86. **d** 86. C Caereithin *S & B* 86-88; Par Dn Bolton St Pet *Man* 88-91; Chapl Bolton Colls of FE 88-91; Chapl Trin Coll Carmarthen from 91. *Trinity College, Carmarthen, Dyfed SA31* Carmarthen (0267) 237971

LEWIS, Ray Arthur. b 63. Oak Hill Th Coll 87. **d** 90 **p** 91. C Holloway St Mary Magd *Lon* from 90. *59 Bride Street, London N7 8RN* 071-607 2984

LEWIS, Raymond James. Univ of Wales (Cardiff) BA Open Univ BSc. St Mich Coll Llan. **d** 91. C Llanelly *St D*

from 91. *4 Hedley Terrace, Llanelli, Dyfed SA15 3RE* Llanelli (0554) 750355

LEWIS, Very Rev Richard. b 35. Fitzw Ho Cam BA78 MA63. Ripon Hall Ox 58. **d** 60 **p** 61. C Hinckley St Mary *Leic* 60-63; C Sanderstead All SS *S'wark* 63-66; V S Merstham 67-72; V S Wimbledon H Trin 72-74; P-in-c S Wimbledon St Pet 72-74; V S Wimbledon H Trin and St Pet 74-79; V Dulwich St Barn 79-90; Chapl Alleyn's Foundn Dulwich 79-90; RD Dulwich *S'wark* 83-90; Hon Can S'wark Cathl from 87; Dean Wells *B & W* from 90; Warden of Readers from 91. *The Dean's Lodging, 25 The Liberty, Wells, Somerset BA5 2SU* Wells (0749) 72192

LEWIS, Canon Richard Charles. b 44. Lon Univ DipTh68 DipSocSc78. ALCD69. **d** 69 **p** 70. C Kendal H Trin *Carl* 69-72; C Chipping Barnet *St Alb* 72-76; V Watford Ch Ch from 76; Hon Can St Alb Abbey from 90. *Christ Church Vicarage, Leggatts Way, Watford WD2 6BQ* Garston (0923) 672240

LEWIS, Richard Martin Lister. b 03. Bps' Coll Cheshunt 28. **d** 30 **p** 31. R Chillesford w Butley and Wantisden *St E* 68-74; rtd 74; Perm to Offic St E from 75; Nor from 83. *Flint Cottage, Foulsham, Dereham, Norfolk* Foulsham (036284) 218

LEWIS, Robert. b 38. St Pet Coll Ox BA62 MA66. Cuddesdon Coll 62. **d** 64 **p** 65. C Kirkby *Liv* 64-67 and 70-71; TV 71-75; Chapl St Boniface Coll Warminster 68-69; Tutor St Aug Coll Cant 69-70; Abp's Dom Chapl *York* 76-79; TR Thirsk from 79. *The Rectory, Thirsk, N Yorkshire YO7 1PR* Thirsk (0845) 523183

LEWIS, Robert George. b 53. Lanc Univ BEd76. Ripon Coll Cuddesdon. **d** 78 **p** 79. C Liv Our Lady and St Nic w St Anne *Liv* 78-81; Asst Dir of Educn 81-88; P-in-c Newchurch 88-89; P-in-c Glazebury 88-89; R Newchurch and Glazebury from 89. *The Rectory, Newchurch, Culcheth, Warrington WA3 4DZ* Culcheth (092576) 6300

LEWIS, Canon Robert Hugh Cecil. b 25. New Coll Ox BA50 MA50. Westcott Ho Cam 50. **d** 52 **p** 53. V Poynton *Ches* 63-91; RD Stockport 72-85; Hon Can Ches Cathl from 75; RD Cheadle 85-87; Dioc Ecum Officer 87-91; Chapl to HM The Queen from 85; rtd 91. *78 Dean Drive, Wilmslow, Cheshire SK9 2EY* Wilmslow (0625) 524761

LEWIS, Roger Edward. b 24. Qu Coll Cam BA45 MA49. Ridley Hall Cam 47. **d** 49 **p** 50. V Clacton St Paul *Chelmsf* 58-71; V Surbiton St Matt *S'wark* 71-89; rtd 89; Perm to Offic *S'wark* from 89. *Rose Cottage, 40 Grove Road, Horley, Surrey RH6 8EL* Horley (0293) 771197

LEWIS, Roger Gilbert. b 49. St Jo Coll Dur BA70. Ripon Hall Ox 70. **d** 72 **p** 73. C Boldmere *Birm* 72-76; C Birm St Pet 76-77; TV Tettenhall Regis *Lich* 77-81; V Ward End *Birm* from 81. *The Vicarage, St Margaret's Avenue, Birmingham B8 2BH* 021-327 0555

LEWIS, Preb Ronald Llewellyn. b 12. Leeds Univ BSc35. Coll of Resurr Mirfield 35. **d** 37 **p** 38. V Taunton H Trin *B & W* 63-77; Preb Wells Cathl from 73; rtd 77. *Rose Cottage, 23 Burton Place, Taunton, Somerset TA1 4HE* Taunton (0823) 274778

LEWIS, Stuart William. b 54. Newc Univ BA79. Edin Th Coll. **d** 86 **p** 87. C Ledbury w Eastnor *Heref* 86-89; Chapl Malvern Coll Worcs from 89. *The Chaplain's House, College Road, Great Malvern, Worcs WR14 3DD* Malvern (0684) 892694

LEWIS, Terence Arnold. b 15. Jes Coll Ox BA37 MA41 BD51. St Mich Coll Llan 38. **d** 39 **p** 40. R Aston Clinton w Buckland and Drayton Beauchamp *Ox* 64-86; rtd 86; Perm to Offic *Ox* 86-87 and from 90. *5 Villiers Close, Moreton Grange, Buckingham MK18 1JH* Buckingham (0280) 815849

LEWIS, Thomas James. b 17. Univ of Wales BA49. St D Coll Lamp 49. **d** 51 **p** 52. V Clyro w Bettws, Llowes and Glasbury All SS *S & B* 66-73; RD Hay 66-73; V Penclawdd 73-82; rtd 82. *34 St Nicholas Court, Gower Road, Killay, Swansea* Swansea (0792) 297866

LEWIS, Thomas Peter. b 45. Selw Coll Cam BA67 MA. Ripon Hall Ox 68. **d** 70 **p** 71. C Hatf *St Alb* 70-74; C Boreham Wood All SS 74-78; Chapl Haileybury Coll Herts 78-85; Chapl Abingdon Sch from 85. *25 Park Road, Abingdon, Oxon OX14 1DA* Abingdon (0235) 26034

LEWIS, Timothy John. b 56. Univ of Wales (Swansea) BA76. Sarum & Wells Th Coll 83. **d** 86 **p** 87. C Taunton St Mary *B & W* 86-89; Chapl RN from 89. *c/o MOD, Lacon House, Theobald's Road, London WC1X 8RY* 071-430 6847

LEWIS, Timothy John. b 62. Birm Univ BMus84. St Steph Ho Ox 85. **d** 88 **p** 89. C Leigh St Clem *Chelmsf* 88-91; C

Whitleigh *Ex* from 91. *26 Derby Road, Whitleigh, Plymouth PL5 4BL* Plymouth (0752) 703526

LEWIS, Vera Elizabeth. b 45. Lon Univ BA66 Univ of Wales (Abth) DipEd67 DipLib73. St As Minl Tr Course 82. **d** 85. NSM Garthbeibio and Llanerfyl and Llangadfan *St As* 85-86; C 87-88; NSM Llanfair Caereinion w Llanllugan 85-86; C 87-88; Dn-in-c Llanrhaiadr-yn-Mochnant and Llanarmon etc from 88. *The Vicarage, Llanrhaeadr-ym-Mochnant, Oswestry, Shropshire SY10 0JZ* Llanrhaeadr (069189) 247

LEWIS, Walter Alun. b 08. St D Coll Lamp BA31. **d** 32 **p** 33. V Pontblyddyn *St As* 44-77; rtd 77. *29 Blaenwern, Gwernymynydd, Mold, Clwyd* Mold (0352) 4462

LEWIS, Walter Arnold. b 45. NUI BA68 TCD MPhil91. TCD Div Sch 71. **d** 71 **p** 72. C Belf Whiterock *Conn* 71-73; C Belf St Mark 73-80; Bp's C Belf St Andr 80-84; I Belf St Thos from 84. *St Thomas's Rectory, 1A Eglantine Avenue, Belfast BT9 6DW* Belfast (0232) 668360

LEWIS, William George. b 14. Worc Ord Coll 63. **d** 65 **p** 65. R Berrynarbor *Ex* 70-80; rtd 80; Perm to Offic *Truro* from 80. *180 Old Roselyon Road, Par, Cornwall PL24 2LN* Par (072681) 7944

LEWIS, William George Melville. b 31. Open Univ BA. S'wark Ord Course. **d** 69 **p** 70. C Coulsdon St Jo *S'wark* 69-71; C Perry Hill St Geo 71-74; V Eltham St Barn 74-80; V Reigate St Mark 80-89; V Ham St Rich from 89. *The Vicarage, Ashburnham Road, Ham, Richmond, Surrey TW10 7NL* 081-948 3758

LEWIS, William George Rees. b 35. Hertf Coll Ox BA59 MA63. Tyndale Hall Bris 61. **d** 63 **p** 64. C Tenby w Gumfreston *St D* 63-66; C Llanelly St Paul 66-69; R Letterston 69-84; R Jordanston w Llanstinan 73-78; R Punchestown and Lt Newc 78-84; R Hubberston w Herbrandston and Hasguard etc 84-90; Prov Officer for Evang and Adult Educn from 90. *42 Lake Road North, Roath, Cardiff CF2 5QN* Cardiff (0222) 756218

LEWIS, William Herbert. b 12. BNC Ox BA35 MA40 Ox Univ DipEd50. Wycliffe Hall Ox 35. **d** 40 **p** 41. V Bedwellty *Mon* 66-80; rtd 80; Lic to Offic *Mon* from 82. *34 Albany Road, Blackwood, Gwent NP2 1DZ* Blackwood (0495) 228236

LEWIS, William John. b 10. Univ of Wales BA36. Chich Th Coll 36. **d** 38 **p** 39. V Highgate Rise St Anne Brookfield *Lon* 68-76; rtd 76; Perm to Offic St Alb from 76; Ely from 77. *75 High Street, Riseley, Bedford* Bedford (0234) 708525

LEWIS, William Meredith. b 15. Univ of Wales BA37. St Mich Coll Llan 37. **d** 39 **p** 40. V Shipston-on-Stour w Tidmington *Cov* 68-80; rtd 80; Perm to Offic Cov from 80; Birm 83-91. *7 Stuart Close, Warwick CV34 6AQ* Warwick (0926) 498263

LEWIS, William Rhys. b 20. St Mich Coll Llan 53. **d** 55 **p** 56. R Ebbw Vale *Mon* 64-73; V Llangattock and Llangyndir *S & B* 73-78; V Cwmbwrla 78-85; rtd 85; Perm to Offic *Llan* from 85. *6 Beech Avenue, Llantwit Major, S Glam CF6 9RT* Llantwit Major (0446) 796741

LEWIS-NICHOLSON, Russell John. b 45. Oak Hill Th Coll 79. **d** 81 **p** 82. C Clayton *Bradf* 81-84; Australia from 84. *121 Albert Street, Geelong West, Victoria, Australia 3218* Geelong (52) 216694

LEWISHAM, Archdeacon of. See KUHRT, Ven Gordon Wilfred

LEWTHWAITE, David. b 39. K Coll Lon BD75. St Aid Birkenhead 63. **d** 65 **p** 66. C Standish *Blackb* 65-68; S Africa 68-71; P-in-c Blackb All SS *Blackb* 71-72; C Kentish Town St Jo *Lon* 72-75; P-in-c Wilden w Colmworth and Ravensden *St Alb* 75-79; V Knottingley *Wakef* 79-81; R Maulden *St Alb* from 81; RD Ampthill from 90. *The Rectory, Clophill Road, Maulden, Bedford MK45 2AA* Ampthill (0525) 403139

LEY, John Andrew. b 16. St Deiniol's Hawarden 70. **d** 72 **p** 73. Hon C Leintwardine *Heref* 72-76; Hon C Wigmore Abbey 76-77; AP Pulloxhill w Flitton *St Alb* 77-79; Lic to Offic *Blackb* 80-81; C Stoke Lacy, Moreton Jeffries w Much Cowarne etc *Heref* 81-87; rtd 87; Perm to Offic *Lich* from 87. *4 Winchester Close, Lichfield, Staffs WS13 7SL* Lichfield (0543) 255941

LEYLAND, Derek James. b 34. Lon Univ BSc55 Birm Univ DipTh60. Qu Coll Birm 58. **d** 60 **p** 61. C Ashton-on-Ribble St Andr *Blackb* 60-63; V 80-87; C Salesbury 63-65; V Preston St Oswald 65-67; V Pendleton 67-74; Dioc Youth Chapl 67-69; Ind Youth Chapl 70-74; R Brindle 74-80; V Garstang St Helen Churchtown from 87; Sec SOSc from 90. *St Helen's Vicarage, The Green, Churchtown, Preston PR3 0HS* Garstang (0995) 602294

LEYLAND, Tyrone John. b 49. Aston Univ BSc68. St Jo Coll Nottm 89. **d** 91. C Lich St Mary w St Mich *Lich* from 91. *3 Bracken Close, Lichfield, Staffs WS14 9RU* Lichfield (0543) 417179

LEYSHON, Simon. b 63. Trin Coll Carmarthen BA86 Southn Univ BTh89. Sarum & Wells Th Coll. **d** 89 **p** 90. C Tenby *St D* from 89. *Flat 2, Rest Harrow, Cresswell Street, Tenby, Dyfed SA70 7HJ* Tenby (0834) 3267

LIBBY, John Ralph. b 55. Trin Coll Cam BA(Econ)83. Ridley Hall Cam 89. **d** 91. C Enfield St Andr *Lon* from 91. *41 Fir Tree Walk, Enfield, Middx EN1 3TZ* 081-363 4491

LICHFIELD, Archdeacon of. See NINIS, Ven Richard Betts

LICHFIELD, Bishop of. See SUTTON, Rt Rev Keith Norman

LICHFIELD, Dean of. See LANG, Very Rev John Harley

LICKESS, Canon David Frederick. b 37. St Chad's Coll Dur BA63 DipTh65. **d** 65 **p** 66. C Howden *York* 65-70; V Rudby in Cleveland w Middleton from 70; Can and Preb York Minster from 90. *The Vicarage, Hutton Rudby, Yarm, Cleveland TS15 0HY* Stokesley (0642) 700223

LIDDELL, Peter Gregory. b 40. St Andr Univ MA63 Linacre Ho Ox BA65 MA70. Andover Newton Th Coll DMin75 Ripon Hall Ox 63. **d** 65 **p** 66. C Hatf *St Alb* 65-71; USA 71-76; P-in-c Kimpton w Ayot St Lawrence *St Alb* 77-83; Dir of Past Counselling from 80. *The Old Vicarage, Kimpton, Hitchin, Herts SG4 8EF* Kimpton (0438) 832266

LIDDELOW, Peter William. b 33. Oak Hill NSM Course. **d** 82 **p** 83. NSM Finchley Ch Ch *Lon* 82-84; NSM S Mimms Ch Ch from 84. *23 King's Road, Barnet, Herts EN5 4EP* 081-441 2968

LIDDLE, George. b 48. NE Ord Course 88. **d** 90 **p** 91. C Auckland St Andr and St Anne *Dur* from 90. *15 Warkworth Avenue, Bishop Auckland, Co Durham DL14 6LU* Bishop Auckland (0388) 663378

LIDDLE, Harry. b 36. Wadh Coll Ox BA57 MA61. Wycliffe Hall Ox 62. **d** 64 **p** 65. C Withington St Paul *Man* 64-68; R Broughton 68-73; V Balby *Sheff* 73-82; R Firbeck w Letwell from 82; V Woodsetts from 82. *The Rectory, Letwell, Worksop, Notts S81 8DF* Worksop (0909) 730346

LIDDLE, Stephen John. b 60. St Jo Coll Ox BA81 PGCE82. Linc Th Coll 88. **d** 91. C Morpeth *Newc* from 91. *St Aidan's Parsonage, 42 Grange Road, Stobhill, Morpeth, Northd NE61 2UF* Morpeth (0670) 513413

LIDDON, Alfred James. b 21. Lon Univ BA49. Oak Hill Th Coll 46. **d** 51 **p** 52. R Gunton St Pet *Nor* 65-77; RD Lothingland 76-80; R Bradwell 77-88; rtd 88; Perm to Offic *Nor* from 88. *6 Pennine Way, Oulton, Lowestoft, Suffolk NR32 3HD* Lowestoft (0502) 518247

LIDWILL, Mark Robert. b 57. TCD DipTh87. **d** 87 **p** 88. C Annagh w Drumgoon, Ashfield etc *K, E & A* 87-90; I Urney w Denn and Derryheen from 90. *The Rectory, Co Cavan, Irish Republic* Cavan (49) 61016

LIFTON, Norman Reginald. b 22. ALSM. Worc Ord Coll 62. **d** 64 **p** 65. C Coleford w Staunton *Glouc* 64-66; C Hersham *Guildf* 66-68; C Milford Haven *St D* 68-70; R Spexhall w Wissett *St E* 70-77; V Berkeley *Glouc* 77-84; C Malborough w S Huish, W Alvington and Churchstow *Ex* 84-87; V Ticknall, Smisby and Stanton by Bridge *Derby* from 87. *The Vicarage, 7 Church Lane, Ticknall, Derby DE7 1JU* Melbourne (0332) 862549

LIGHTFOOT, Very Rev Vernon Keith. b 34. St Jo Coll Dur BA58. Ripon Hall Ox 58. **d** 60 **p** 61. C Rainhill *Liv* 60-62; C Liv Our Lady and St Nic 62-65; V Stanley 65-75; New Zealand from 75; Dean Waikato from 86. *The Deanery, 6 Tisdall Street, Hamilton, PO Box 338, New Zealand* Hamilton (7) 839-4683

LIGHTOWLER, Joseph Trevor. b 33. **d** 79 **p** 80. Hon C Leverstock Green *St Alb* 79-80; Hon C Chambersbury (Hemel Hempstead) 80-84; C Woodmansterne *S'wark* 84-88; R Odell and Pavenham *St Alb* from 88. *The Rectory, 3 Church Lane, Odell, Bedford MK43 7AA* Bedford (0234) 720234

LIKEMAN, Canon Martin Kaye. b 34. St Mich Coll Llan 55. **d** 57 **p** 58. C Llanwnog w Penstrowed *Ban* 57-60; C Llandudno 60-64; V Llanrhian w Llanhywel and Carnhedryn *St D* 64-73; RD Dewisland and Fishguard 71-73; V Llanstadwell from 73; Can St D Cathl from 88. *The Vicarage, Llanstadwel, Milford Haven, Dyfed* Neyland (0646) 600227

LILES, Malcolm David. b 48. Nottm Univ BA69. St Steph Ho Ox 69. **d** 71 **p** 72. C Corby Epiphany w St Jo *Pet* 71-74; C New Cleethorpes *Linc* 74-76; TV Lt Coates 76-77; TV Gt and Lt Coates w Bradley 78-82; Soc Resp Sec from 82; Hon C Gt Grimsby St Mary and St Jas from 82; P-in-c Grimsby All SS from 88. *30 Park Avenue, Grimsby, S Humberside DN32 0DQ* Grimsby (0472) 70333

LILEY, Christopher Frank. b 47. Nottm Univ BEd70. Linc Th Coll 72. **d** 74 **p** 75. C Kingswinford H Trin *Lich* 74-79; TV Stafford 79-84; V Norton *St Alb* from 84; RD Hitchin from 89. *The Vicarage, 17 Norton Way North, Letchworth, Herts SG6 1BY* Letchworth (0462) 685059

LILLEY, Alan Charles. b 34. Nottm Univ BA55 MA67 St Cath Soc Ox DipTh59. Wycliffe Hall Ox 57. **d** 59 **p** 60. C Leic H Apostles *Leic* 59-63; C New Humberstone 63-65; V Copt Oak 65-78; Perm to Offic from 80; Student Counsellor Loughb Univ from 78; Dir from 88. *12 Shepherd Walk, Kegworth, Derby DE7 2HS* Loughborough (0509) 673967

LILLEY, Christopher Howard. b 51. Local NSM Course 85. **d** 85 **p** 86. NSM Skegness and Winthorpe *Linc* from 85. *42 Queen's Drive, Skegness, Lincs PE25 1RE* Skegness (0754) 66163

LILLEY, Ivan Ray. b 32. Bps' Coll Cheshunt 58. **d** 61 **p** 62. C Kettering SS Pet and Paul *Pet* 61-64; C Gt Yarmouth *Nor* 64-75; P-in-c Tottenhill w Wormegay *Ely* 76-83; P-in-c Watlington 76-83; P-in-c Holme Runcton w S Runcton and Wallington 76-83; V Tysoe w Oxhill and Whatcote *Cov* 83-86; C Langold *S'well* from 87. *St Luke's Vicarage, Langold, Worksop, Notts S81 9NW* Worksop (0909) 730398

LILLEY, John. b 36. Liv Univ DipAdEd70. **d** 81 **p** 82. NSM Holyhead w Rhoscolyn w Llanfair-yn-Neubwll *Ban* 81-84; Chapl Scargill Ho N Yorkshire 84-87; TV Beaminster Area *Sarum* from 87; RD Beaminster from 89. *The Vicarage, 20 Orchard Way, Mosterton, Beaminster, Dorset DT8 3LT* Broadwindsor (0308) 68090

LILLIAN, Rev Mother. See MORRIS, Lillian Rosina

LILLIE, Judith Virginia. See THOMPSON, Mrs Judith Virginia

LILLINGSTON, Peter John Edward. b 23. Pemb Coll Cam BA47 MA50. Cuddesdon Coll 52. **d** 54 **p** 55. V St Martin Ludgate *Lon* 70-84; Dep Min Can St Paul's Cathl 76-84; rtd 84. *Moat House, Weston-Subedge, Chipping Campden, Glos GL55 6QT* Evesham (0386) 840695

LILLINGSTON-PRICE, Michael Christopher. b 31. Em Coll Cam BA56 MA60. Ripon Hall Ox 56. **d** 58 **p** 59. C Belvedere All SS *Roch* 58-60; CF 60-83; Chapl Morden Coll Blackheath from 83. *19 St German's Place, London SE3 0PW* 081-858 3988

LILLINGTON, Brian Ray. b 36. RMN60 FRSH84 Ex Univ DSA65 Lon Univ DipMentH67. S Dioc Minl Tr Scheme 87. **d** 90 **p** 91. NSM Yateley *Win* from 90. *Kaos, Little Vigo, Yateley, Camberley, Surrey GU17 7ES* Yateley (0252) 872760

LILLISTONE, Brian David. b 38. SS Coll Cam BA61 MA65. St Steph Ho Ox 61. **d** 63 **p** 64. C Ipswich All Hallows *St E* 63-66; C Stokesay *Heref* 66-71; P-in-c Lyonshall w Titley 71-76; R Martlesham w Brightwell *St E* from 76. *The Rectory, 17 Lark Rise, Martlesham Heath, Ipswich IP5 7SA* Ipswich (0473) 622424

LIMBERT, Kenneth Edward. b 25. CEng69 MIMechE. S'wark Ord Course 72. **d** 75 **p** 76. NSM Northwood Hills St Edm *Lon* from 75. *55 York Road, Northwood, Middx HA6 1JJ* Northwood (09274) 25791

LIMBRICK, Gordon. b 36. Open Univ BA88. St Jo Coll Nottm CertCS90. **d** 87 **p** 91. NSM Troon *Glas* 87-90; NSM Yaxley *Ely* from 90. *271 Broadway, Yaxley, Peterborough PE7 3NR* Peterborough (0733) 243170

LIMERICK AND ARDFERT, Dean of. See SIRR, Very Rev John Maurice Glover

LIMERICK, Archdeacon of. See SNOW, Ven Edward Brian

LIMERICK, ARDFERT, AGHADOE, KILLALOE, KILFENORA, CLONFERT, KILMACDUAGH AND EMLY, Bishop of. See DARLING, Rt Rev Edward Fle

LINCOLN, Archdeacon of. See BRACKENBURY, Ven Michael Palmer

LINCOLN, Bishop of. See HARDY, Rt Rev Robert Maynard

LINCOLN, Dean of. See JACKSON, Very Rev Dr Brandon Donald

LIND-JACKSON, Peter Wilfrid. b 35. Leeds Univ BA67. Linc Th Coll 67. **d** 68 **p** 69. C Heref St Martin *Heref* 68-71; P-in-c Burghill 71-78; V 78-82; P-in-c Whorlton *Dur* 82-83; V Barnard Castle 82-83; V Barnard Castle w Whorlton from 83. *The Vicarage, Barnard Castle, Co Durham DL12 8NW* Teesdale (0833) 37018

LINDARS, Frank. b 23. Wycliffe Hall Ox 54. **d** 56 **p** 57. V Shadwell *Ripon* 61-80; RD Allerton 73-78; V Masham and Healey 80-88; rtd 88. *Hope Cottage, Reeth, Richmond, N Yorkshire DL11 6SF* Richmond (0748) 84685

LINDARS, Canon Prof Frederick Chevallier (Brother Barnabas). b 23. St Jo Coll Cam BA45 MA48 BD61 DD73. Westcott Ho Cam 46. **d** 48 **p** 49. Lic to Offic *Ely* 52-78; SSF from 54; Lect Div Cam Univ 66-78; Dean Jes Coll Cam 76-78; Can Th Leic Cathl *Leic* from 77; Lic to Offic *Man* 78-90; Rylands Prof Bibl Criticism Man Univ 78-90; rtd 90; Perm to Offic *Sarum* from 90. *The Friary, Hilfield, Dorchester, Dorset DT2 7BE* Cerne Abbas (0300) 341345

LINDECK, Peter Stephen. b 31. Oak Hill Th Coll 57. **d** 59 **p** 60. C Homerton St Luke *Lon* 59-62; C Salterhebble All SS *Wakef* 62-63; C Islington St Andr w St Thos and St Matthias *Lon* 64-67; V Toxteth Park St Bede *Liv* 68-74; Nigeria 74-76; C Netherton *Liv* 76-77; C Ollerton *S'well* 77-80; C Boughton 77-80; V Whitgift w Adlingfleet and Eastoft *Sheff* 80-86; P-in-c Swinefleet 81-86; V Kilnhurst from 86; Chapl Montagu Hosp Mexborough from 86. *The Vicarage, Highthorne Road, Kilnhurst, Rotherham, S Yorkshire S62 5TX* Mexborough (0709) 589674

LINDEN, Gregory. b 25. Roch Th Coll. **d** 65 **p** 66. C Roundhay St Edm *Ripon* 65-68; C Highweek *Ex* 68-72; V Brampford Speke 72-82; R Upton Pyne 72-82; R Middleton-in-Teesdale *Dur* 82-85; V Eggleston from 85; R Middleton-in-Teesdale w Forest and Frith from 85. *The Rectory, Middleton-in-Teesdale, Barnard Castle DL12 0QW* Teesdale (0833) 40267

LINDISFARNE, Archdeacon of. See BOWERING, Ven Michael Ernest

LINDLEY, Geoffrey. b 22. St Jo Coll Ox BA45 MA47. Westcott Ho Cam 47. **d** 47 **p** 48. V Ox St Marg *Ox* 56-72; P-in-c Pyrton w Shirburn 72-79; P-in-c Lewknor 72-79; P-in-c Milton-under-Wychwood 79-80; P-in-c Shipton-under-Wychwood 79-80; V Shipton-under-Wychwood w Milton-under-Wychwood 80-85; Perm to Offic from 86; rtd 87. *139 Magdalen Road, Oxford OX4 1RL* Oxford (0865) 248876

LINDLEY, Harold Thomas. b 28. St Jo Coll Ox BA51 MA73. Wells Th Coll 51. **d** 53 **p** 54. C Normanton *Wakef* 53-57; C-in-c Rawthorpe CD 57-63; P-in-c Longstone *Derby* 63-67; V 68-74; P-in-c Barrow w Twyford 74-84; V Barrow-on-Trent w Twyford and Swarkestone from 84. *The Vicarage, Barrow-on-Trent, Derby DE7 1HA* Derby (0332) 701027

LINDLEY, Ven Ralph Adrian. b 20. CBE75. St Jo Coll Dur BA51 DipTh53. **d** 53 **p** 54. Chapl RAF 55-70; UAE 70-78; Adn Gulf 70-78; Gen Sec JMECA 78-85; rtd 86. *Taffrail, Lower Road, St Briavels, Lydney, Glos GL15 6SA* Dean (0594) 530230

LINDLEY, Richard Adrian. b 44. Hull Univ BA65 Birm Univ DPS68 Man Univ MA79. Cuddesdon Coll 66. **d** 68 **p** 69. C Ingrow cum Hainworth *Bradf* 68-70; Perm to Offic *Birm* 70-74; TV Ellesmere Port *Ches* 74-79; R Westborough *Guildf* 79-80; TR 80-84; Dir of Educn *Birm* from 84. *60 Peterbrook Road, Shirley, Solihull, W Midlands B90 1ED* 021-474 2001

LINDO, Leithland Oscar. b 29. St Aug Coll Cant 57 St Pet Coll Jamaica 53. **d** 56 **p** 57. Jamaica 56-58; C Edmonton St Mary w St Jo *Lon* 58-62; C Heston 62-66; V Staines Ch Ch from 66. *Christ Church Vicarage, Kenilworth Gardens, Staines, Middx TW18 1DR* Staines (0784) 55457

LINDOP, Andrew John. b 57. Cam Univ MA. Cranmer Hall Dur 80. **d** 82 **p** 83. C Brinsworth w Catcliffe *Sheff* 82-85; C S Shoebury *Chelmsf* 85-89; V Mosley Common *Man* from 89. *St John's Vicarage, Mosley Common Road, Worsley, Manchester M28 4AN* 061-790 2957

LINDOP, Kenneth. b 45. Linc Th Coll 71. **d** 74 **p** 75. C Leic St Phil *Leic* 74-77; C Cov H Trin *Cov* 77-80; P-in-c Cubbington 80-82; V from 82; RD Warw and Leamington from 91. *The Vicarage, Rugby Road, Cubbington, Leamington Spa, Warks CV32 7JL* Leamington Spa (0926) 423056

LINDSAY, Anthony. b 38. **d** 89. CMS from 76; Sierra Leone from 88. *c/o Rt Rev M Keili, PO Box 21, BO, Sierra Leone*

LINDSAY, Cecil. b 43. Iona Coll (NY) BBA68. CITC 85. **d** 88 **p** 88. NSM Kilmore w Ballintemple, Kildallon etc *K, E & A* 88-90; Lic to Offic from 90. *Clementstown House, Cootehill, Co Cavan, Irish Republic* Cootehill (49) 52207

LINDSAY, David Macintyre. b 46. Trin Hall Cam BA68 MA72 Ox Univ DipTh70. Cuddesdon Coll 68. **d** 71 **p** 72. C Gosforth All SS *Newc* 71-74; C Keele *Lich* 74-78; Perm to Offic *St E* 79-80; Chapl Haberdashers' Aske's Sch Elstree from 80. *36 Cranbourne Drive, Harpenden, Herts* Harpenden (0582) 765660

LINDSAY, Eric Graham. b 30. Witwatersrand Univ BA51 Lon Univ DipAdEd78 MA80 Heythrop Coll Lon

DipTh82. Coll of Resurr Mirfield 55. **d** 57 **p** 59. C Stella *Dur* 57-58; C W Hartlepool St Aid 58-60; Grenada 60-61; Perm to Offic Win 61-65; Roch 65-72; Chelmsf 72-84; C Stepney St Dunstan and All SS *Lon* 84-85; R Bridge of Weir *Glas* from 85; R Kilmacolm from 85. *St Fillan's Rectory, 4 Balmore Court, Kilmacolm, Renfrewshire PA13 4LX* Kilmacolm (050587) 2961

LINDSAY, John Carruthers. b 50. Edin Univ MA72 BD82. Edin Th Coll 79. **d** 82 **p** 83. C Broughty Ferry *Bre* 82-84; C Edin St Hilda *Edin* 84-85; TV 85-88; C Edin St Fillan 84-85; TV 85-88; R N Berwick from 88; R Gullane from 88. *The Rectory, 2 May Terrace, North Terrace, East Lothian EH39 4BA* North Berwick (0620) 2154

LINDSAY, Richard John. b 46. Sarum & Wells Th Coll 74. **d** 78 **p** 79. C Aldwick *Chich* 78-81; C Almondbury *Wakef* 81-82; C Almondbury w Farnley Tyas 82-84; V Mossley *Man* from 84. *The Vicarage, Stamford Street, Mossley, Ashton-under-Lyne, Lancs OL5 0LP* Mossley (0457) 832219

LINDSAY, Canon Richard John Alan. b 24. TCD BA46 BD52. **d** 49 **p** 50. R Chich St Pancras and St Jo *Chich* 68-74; Chapl Maisons-Lafitte *Eur* 74-82; Can Brussels Cathl 81-89; Chapl The Hague w Leiden and Voorschoten 82-89; rtd 89; Perm to Offic *Heref* from 89. *Japonica Cottage, King's Acre Road, Breinton, Hereford HR4 0SG* Hereford (0432) 50230

LINDSAY, Canon Robert. b 16. St Jo Coll Dur BA37 DipTh38 MA40. **d** 39 **p** 40. RD Derwent *Carl* 70-81; V Loweswater w Buttermere 74-81; rtd 81; Perm to Offic *Ex* from 81. *58 Primley Road, Sidmouth, Devon EX10 9LF* Sidmouth (0395) 577882

LINDSAY, Robert Ashley Charles. b 43. Leeds Univ BA66 Ex Univ BPhil81. Coll of Resurr Mirfield 66. **d** 68 **p** 69. C Mill Hill Jo Keble Ch *Lon* 68-72; C Sherborne w Castleton and Lillington *Sarum* 73-78; Chapl Coldharbour Hosp Dorset 73-78; Perm to Offic *Leic* from 87. *79 Castledine Street, Loughborough, Leics LE11 2DX* Loughborough (0509) 264360

LINDSAY-PARKINSON, Michael. b 28. Edin Th Coll 66. **d** 67 **p** 68. C Edin Ch Ch *Edin* 67-70; C Helensburgh *Glas* 70-72; R Lockerbie 72-83; R Annan 72-83; S Africa 83-88; V Alsager St Mary *Ches* from 88. *St Mary's Vicarage, 37 Eaton Road, Alsager, Stoke-on-Trent ST7 2BQ* Alsager (0270) 875748

LINDSEY, Archdeacon of. See LAURENCE, Ven John Harvard Christopher

LINES, John Anthony. b 31. Man Univ BA54 MA55 Birm Univ PhD74. St Jo Sem Wonersh 80 E Midl Min Tr Course. **d** 84 **p** 85. NSM Derby St Bart *Derby* 84-87; C Market Bosworth, Cadeby w Sutton Cheney etc *Leic* 87-90; C Wigston Magna from 90. *4 Purbeck Close, Wigston Magna, Leicester* Leicester (0533) 887588

LINFORD, Preb John Kenneth. b 31. Liv Univ BA52. Chich Th Coll 54. **d** 56 **p** 57. V Tunstall Ch Ch *Lich* 61-70; V Sedgley All SS 70-78; Chapl Chase Hosp Cannock 78-91; TR Cannock *Lich* 78-91; V Hatherton 80-91; Preb Lich Cathl from 88; rtd 91. *16 School Lane, Hill Ridware, Rugeley, Staffs WS15 3QN* Armitage (0543) 492831

LING, Andrew Joyner. b 35. ACP69 St Luke's Coll Ex TCert63 Open Univ BA80. SW Minl Tr Course 83. **d** 86 **p** 87. NSM St Mellion w Pillaton *Truro* 86-87; NSM Landulph 86-87; NSM St Dominic 86-87; NSM St Dominic, Landulph and St Mellion w Pillaton 87-90; C Saltash from 90. *The Vicarage, St Stephens, Saltash, Cornwall PL12 4AB* Saltash (0752) 842323

LINGARD, Colin. b 36. Kelham Th Coll 58. **d** 63 **p** 64. C Middlesb St Martin *York* 63-66; C Stainton-in-Cleveland 66-71; V Eskdaleside w Ugglebarnby 71-77; P-in-c Redcar w Kirkleatham 77; V Kirkleatham 78-86; RD Guisborough 83-86; V Linc St Botolph by Bargate *Linc* 86-89; Dioc Dir of Readers 86-89; R Washington *Dur* from 89. *The Rectory, The Avenue, Washington, Tyne & Wear NE38 7LE* 091-416 3957 or 416 0342

LINGARD, Keith Patrick. b 30. AKC53. **d** 54 **p** 55. C Bedf Park *Lon* 54-56; C Ruislip St Martin 56-58; C Kempston *St Alb* 58-63; Metrop Area Sec UMCA 63-65; V S Farnborough *Guildf* 65-75; R Glaston w Bisbrooke *Pet* 75-76; R Morcott w Glaston and Bisbrooke from 77. *The Rectory, Glaston, Oakham, Leics LE15 9BN* Uppingham (0572) 822373

LINGS, George William. b 49. Nottm Univ BTh74 Ox Univ PGCE75. St Jo Coll Nottm 70. **d** 75 **p** 76. C Harold Wood *Chelmsf* 75-78; C Reigate St Mary *S'wark* 78-85; V Deal St Geo *Cant* from 85. *The Vicarage, 8 St George's Road, Deal, Kent CT14 6BA* Deal (0304) 372587

LINGWOOD, David Peter. b 51. Lon Univ BEd73 Southn Univ BTh80. Sarum & Wells Th Coll 75. **d** 78 **p** 79. C Ashford St Hilda *Lon* 78-81; C Astwood Bank w Crabbs

Cross *Worc* 81; TV Redditch, The Ridge 81-86; TR Blakenall Heath *Lich* from 86. *Christ Church Rectory, Blakenall Heath, Walsall WS3 1HT* Bloxwich (0922) 479593

LINN, Frederick Hugh. b 37. Em Coll Cam BA61 MA65. Ripon Hall Ox 61. **d** 63 **p** 64. C Bramhall *Ches* 63-68; V Liscard St Mary 68-71; V Liscard St Mary w St Columba 71-74; V Wybunbury 74-82; R Eccleston and Pulford from 82. *The Rectory, Eccleston, Chester CH4 9HT* Chester (0244) 674703

LINN, John David Alan. b 29. MC51. Ridley Hall Cam 73. **d** 75 **p** 76. C Ely 75-77; P-in-c Kennett 77-81; R 81-82; P-in-c Fordham St Pet 77-81; V 81-82; P-in-c Guilden Morden 82-88; P-in-c Litlington w Abington Pigotts 82-88; P-in-c Steeple Morden 82-88; P-in-c Tadlow 82-88; P-in-c Wendy w Shingay 82-88; R Fincham from 88; V Shouldham from 88; V Shouldham Thorpe from 88; V Marham from 88. *The Rectory, High Street, Fincham, King's Lynn, Norfolk PE33 9EL* Fincham (03664) 491

LINNEGAN, Canon John McCaughan. ACCS48 ACIS70 TCD BA55. **d** 57 **p** 58. I Cappagh *D & R* 59-80; I Cappagh w Lislimnaghan 80-90; Can Derry Cathl from 82; rtd 90. *46 Lisanelly Park, Omagh, Co Tyrone* Omagh (0662) 249643

LINNEGAR, George Leonard. b 33. CGA. Kelham Th Coll 63. **d** 62 **p** 63. C Wellingborough St Mary *Pet* 62-65; Lic to Offic Lich 65-69; B & W 69-80; Hon C Lewes All SS, St Anne, St Mich and St Thos *Chich* 80-86; C from 87. *20 Morris Road, Lewes, E Sussex BN27 2AT* Lewes (0273) 478145

LINNEY, Ven Gordon Charles Scott. b 39. CITC 66. **d** 69 **p** 70. C Agherton *Conn* 69-72; Min Can Down Cathl *D & D* 72-75; I Dub St Cath w St Jas *D & G* 75-80; Preb Tipperkevin St Patr Cathl Dub 77-80; I Glenageary *D & G* from 80; Adn Dub from 88. *St Paul's Vicarage, Silchester Road, Glenageary, Co Dublin, Irish Republic* Dublin (1) 280-1616

LINNING, Alexander. b 19. Birm Univ BA40 Lon Univ BD42. **d** 61 **p** 62. Hon C W Bridgford *S'well* 61-80; Lic to Offic from 80. *7 Kingston Road, Nottingham NG2 7AQ* Nottingham (0602) 88182

LINSKILL, Martin Paul Richard. b 50. Magd Coll Ox BA72 MA75. St Steph Ho Ox 73. **d** 75 **p** 76. C Pinner *Lon* 75-80; C Greenhill *Sheff* 80-82; C Penistone *Wakef* 82-83; Tutor St Steph Ho Ox 84-91; Chapl Bede Ho Staplehurst from 91. *Bede House, Staplehurst, Kent* Staplehurst (0580) 891262

LINTON, Alan Ross. b 28. Lon Univ DipTh60. St Aid Birkenhead 57. **d** 60 **p** 61. C Blundellsands St Nic *Liv* 60-62; C Southport St Phil 62-63; C Aigburth 63-66; V Glazebury 66-67; C Formby St Pet 67-69; C Douglas *Blackb* 69-71; P-in-c Appley Bridge All SS CD 71-76; P-in-c Scorton 76-85; P-in-c Calder Vale w Admarsh 76-85; R Hoole from 85. *The Rectory, Town Lane, Preston PR4 4GT* Longton (0772) 612267

LINTON, Joseph Edmund. b 19. St Andr Univ MA46. Sarum Th Coll 46. **d** 48 **p** 49. C Monkseaton St Mary *Newc* 48-53; CF (TA) 50-54; C-in-c Lynemouth St Aid CD *Newc* 53-59; V Beltingham w Henshaw from 59. *Beltingham Vicarage, Bardon Mill, Hexham, Northd NE47 7BZ* Haltwhistle (0434) 344331

LINTON, Sydney. b 07. Pemb Coll Ox BA30 MA34. Westcott Ho Cam 31. **d** 32 **p** 33. V Barnes H Trin *S'wark* 57-71; R Codford *Sarum* 71-73; R Codford, Upton Lovell and Stockton 73-77; rtd 77. *c/o Lord Harris Court, Wokingham, Berks RG11 5EA* Wokingham (0734) 787496

LINTOTT, William Ince. b 36. St Cath Coll Cam BA58. Ely Th Coll 58. **d** 60 **p** 61. C Brighton St Wilfrid *Chich* 60-62; C Chingford SS Pet and Paul *Chelmsf* 62-66; Lic to Offic *Ely* from 66; Chapl Fulbourn Hosp Cam 66-73. *7 Haverhill Road, Stapleford, Cambridge CB2 5BX* Cambridge (0223) 842008

LINZEY, Andrew. b 52. K Coll Lon BD73 AKC73 Univ of Wales (Cardiff) DPS74 PhD86. St Aug Coll Cant 75. **d** 75 **p** 76. C Charlton-by-Dover SS Pet and Paul *Cant* 75-77; Chapl and Lect NE Surrey Coll of Tech 77-81; Chapl Essex Univ *Chelmsf* from 81; Dir of Studies Cen for Study of Th from 87. *Mariners, Rectory Hill, Wivenhoe, Colchester, Essex CO7 9LB* Colchester (0206) 823549

LIPPIATT, Michael Charles. b 39. Oak Hill Th Coll BD71. **d** 71 **p** 72. C Ardsley *Sheff* 71-74; C Lenton *S'well* 74-78; V Jesmond H Trin *Newc* from 78. *Holy Trinity Vicarage, 63 Roseberry Crescent, Jesmond, Newcastle upon Tyne NE2 1EX* 091-281 1663

LIPPIETT, Dr Peter Vernon. b 47. MRCGP80 Lon Univ MB, BS73 DRCOG79. Ripon Coll Cuddesdon 86. **d** 88

p 89. C Pinner *Lon* 88-91; V Twyford and Owslebury and Morestead *Win* from 91. *The Vicarage, Twyford, Winchester, Hants SO21 1NT* Twyford (0962) 712208

LIPSCOMB, Timothy William. b 52. Chich Th Coll 82. **d** 85 **p** 86. C Sevenoaks St Jo *Roch* 85-89; C Stanningley St Thos *Ripon* from 89. *50 Lane End, Pudsey, Leeds LS28 9AD* Leeds (0532) 566535

LIPSCOMBE, Brian. b 37. Bris Univ BA62. Tyndale Hall Bris 62. **d** 64 **p** 65. C Eccleston Ch Ch *Liv* 64-66; C Halliwell St Pet *Man* 66-69; C Frogmore H Trin *St Alb* 69-72; V Richmond Ch Ch *S'wark* 72-75; TV Mortlake w E Sheen 76-80; P-in-c Streatham Vale H Redeemer 80-88; V 85-91; R Norris Bank *Man* from 91. *St Martin's Rectory, 110 Crescent Park, Stockport, Cheshire SK4 2JE* 061-432 3537

LISEMORE, Canon Frederick John Henry. b 11. St Cath Soc Ox BA37 MA38. Ripon Hall Ox 36. **d** 37 **p** 38. V Foremark *Derby* 70-77; V Repton 70-77; Perm to Offic *Lich* from 78; rtd 78. *36 Church Lane, Barton under Needwood, Burton-on-Trent, Staffs DE13 8HU* Barton under Needwood (0283) 712554

LISK, Stewart. b 62. Regent's Park Coll Ox BA84 MA88 Univ of Wales (Cardiff) DPS87. St Mich Coll Llan 86. **d** 88 **p** 89. C Glan Ely *Llan* from 88. *2 Deere Close, Ely, Cardiff CF5 4NU* Cardiff (0222) 592129

LISMORE, Dean of. *See* WEEKES, Very Rev Cecil William

LISNEY, John Arthur Reginald. b 15. Clare Coll Cam BA37 MA41. Ridley Hall Cam 37. **d** 39 **p** 40. R Witchford w Wentworth *Ely* 54-86; rtd 87; Lic to Offic *Ely* from 87. *10 Back Hill, Ely, Cambs CB7 4BZ* Ely (0353) 663096

LISTER, Anthony Galen. b 27. RIBA DipArch. NE Ord Course. **d** 83 **p** 84. Hon C Anlaby St Pet *York* 83-87. *Ballachan, Glenuig, Lochailort, Inverness-shire* Lochailort (06877) 242

LISTER, David Ian. b 26. Roch Th Coll 61. **d** 62 **p** 64. C Scarborough St Mary w Ch Ch, St Paul and St Thos *York* 62-66; C Buttershaw St Aid *Bradf* 66-68; V Tufnell Park St Geo *Lon* 68-83; V Tufnell Park St Geo and All SS from 83. *The Vicarage, 72 Crayford Road, London N7 0ND* 071-609 1645

LISTER, Edmund. b 08. AKC35. **d** 35 **p** 36. R Dunsfold *Guildf* 67-73; rtd 73; C Bladon w Woodstock *Ox* 73-75. *The Leys, Ware Lane, Lyme Regis, Dorset DT7 3EL* Lyme Regis (02974) 3060

LISTER, Frederick William. b 07. Wells Th Coll 71. **d** 71 **p** 72. Asst Chapl The Hague w Leiden *Eur* 71-75; Chapl Gothenburg w Halmstad and Jonkoping 75-78; rtd 78; Hon C High Harrogate St Pet *Ripon* 78-82. *8 Tudor Court, Prince of Wales Mansions, Harrogate, N Yorkshire* Harrogate (0423) 502162

LISTER, Very Rev John Field. b 16. Keble Coll Ox BA38 MA42. Cuddesdon Coll 38. **d** 39 **p** 41. V Brighouse *Wakef* 54-71; Adn Halifax 61-72; RD Wakef 72-80; Provost Wakef 72-82; rtd 82; Perm to Offic *Cant* from 82. *5 Larkscliff Court, The Parade, Birchington, Kent CT7 9NB* Thanet (0843) 42543

LISTER, Joseph Hugh. b 38. Tyndale Hall Bris. **d** 64 **p** 65. C Pemberton St Mark Newtown *Liv* 64-68; Hon C Braintree *Chelmsf* 68-71; Hon C Darfield *Sheff* 71-73; P-in-c Sheff St Swithun 73-76; TV Sheff Manor 76-80; P-in-c Burston *Nor* 80-81; P-in-c Tivetshall 80-81; P-in-c Gissing 80-81; TR Winfarthing w Shelfanger 80-81; R Winfarthing w Shelfanger w Burston w Gissing etc 81-88; P-in-c Sandon, Wallington and Rushden w Clothall *St Alb* 88-89; R from 89. *The Vicarage, Payne End, Sandon, Buntingford, Herts SG9 0QU* Kelshall (076387) 256

LISTER, Miss Mary Phyllis. b 28. St Andr Ho Portsm 52. dss 80 **d** 87. Inkberrow w Cookhill and Kington w Dormston *Worc* 80-82; Ancaster *Linc* 82-87; C 87-88; rtd 88; Perm to Offic *Worc* from 88. *7 Byfield Rise, Worcester WR5 1BA* Worcester (0905) 29683

LISTER, Canon Peter. b 42. Leeds Univ BA64 Newc Univ PGCE75. Coll of Resurr Mirfield 63. **d** 65 **p** 66. C Monkseaton St Pet *Newc* 65-68; C Cramlington 68-70; Hon C 71-78; C Morpeth 79-83; V Shilbottle 83-88; Asst Dioc Dir of Educn 83-88; Dir of Educn from 88; Hon Can Newc Cathl from 88. *282 Wingrove Road North, Newcastle upon Tyne NE4 9EE* 091-274 9761

LISTON, Scott Carnie. b 62. Edin Univ BD87. Edin Th Coll. **d** 88 **p** 88. C Edin St Martin *Edin* 88-91; C Edin St Luke 88-91; C Edin St Dav from 91. *c/o The Diocesan Centre, Walpole Hall, Chester Street, Edinburgh EH3 7EN*

LITHERLAND, Norman Richard. b 30. Lon Univ BA51 Man Univ MEd72. N Ord Course 78. **d** 81 **p** 82.

NSM Flixton St Mich *Man* from 81. *1 Overdale Crescent, Urmston, Manchester M31 3GR* 061-748 4243

LITTLE, Andrew. b 27. Open Univ BA83. AKC51. **d** 52 **p** 53. V Northwood *Lich* 61-72; P-in-c Hixon 72-86; V Stowe 72-86; V Hixon w Stowe-by-Chartley 86-89; rtd 89; Perm to Offic *Nor* from 89. *5 Damocles Court, Norwich NR2 1HN* Norwich (0603) 662241

LITTLE, Ms Christine. b 60. Lanc Univ BA83. St Jo Coll Nottm DTS90 DPS91. **d** 91. Par Dn Meltham *Wakef* from 91. *6 Thick Hollins Drive, Meltham, Huddersfield HD7 3DL* Huddersfield (0484) 851404

LITTLE, Denis Theodore. b 15. St Jo Coll Dur BA36 MA39. **d** 39 **p** 40. V Lythe *York* 61-72; R Dunnington 72-80; RD Bulmer 78-80; rtd 80; C Bulmer *York* 84-86; C Bulmer w Dalby, Terrington and Welburn 86. *92 The Village, Strensall, York YO3 5BX* York (0904) 490695

LITTLE, Derek Peter. b 50. St Jo Coll Dur BA72 DipTh75. Trin Coll Bris. **d** 75 **p** 76. C Bradley *Wakef* 75-78; C Kidderminster St Geo *Worc* 78-82; V Lepton *Wakef* 82-85; E Regional Sec CPAS 85-88; Lic to Offic *Ely* 86-88; V Canonbury St Steph *Lon* from 88. *St Stephen's Vicarage, 9 River Place, London N1 2DE* 071-226 7526

LITTLE, George Nelson. b 39. CITC 70. **d** 72 **p** 73. C Portadown St Mark *Arm* 72-76; I Newtownhamilton w Ballymoyer and Belleek 76-80; I Aghaderg w Donaghmore *D & D* 80-81; I Aghaderg w Donaghmore and Scarva from 81; RD Aghaderg from 88. *Aghaderg Rectory, 32 Banbridge Road, Loughbrickland BT32 3YB* Ballinaskeagh (08206) 24073

LITTLE, Harold Clifford. b 18. Lon Univ BD42. ALCD42. **d** 42 **p** 43. V S Dulwich St Steph *S'wark* 56-87; Lect Bibl and Relig Studies Lon Univ 61-87; rtd 87; Perm to Offic *Ex* from 88. *Howden Lodge, Willand Old Village, Cullompton, Devon EX15 2RJ* Cullompton (0884) 32663

LITTLE, Herbert Edwin Samuel. b 21. Lon Univ BA54 BD68. NE Ord Course 79. **d** 80 **p** 81. NSM Dur St Cuth *Dur* 80-88. *3 Whitesmocks Avenue, Durham DH1 4HP* 091-384 2897

LITTLE, Ian Arthur Langley. b 24. ARICS52. S'wark Ord Course 63. **d** 66 **p** 67. NSM Bromley St Andr *Roch* 69-77; Perm to Offic from 77; rtd 86. *23 Vale Road, Bickley, Kent BR1 2AL* 081-467 4899

LITTLE, Ian Dawtry Torrance. b 49. SW Minl Tr Course. **d** 85 **p** 86. NSM St Stythians w Perranarworthal and Gwennap *Truro* from 85. *Kernyk, Crellow Fields, Stithians, Truro, Cornwall*

LITTLE, James Harry. b 57. York Univ BA79 Birm Univ DipTh86. Qu Coll Birm 84. **d** 87 **p** 88. C Wollaton *S'well* 87-90; C N Wheatley, W Burton, Bole, Saundby, Sturton etc from 90. *St Peter's House, Springs Lane, Sturton-le-Steeple, Retford, Notts DN22 9HJ* Gainsborough (0427) 880104

LITTLE, Canon John Richardson. b 28. Magd Coll Ox BA49 MA53 DipTh50. Westcott Ho Cam 52. **d** 54 **p** 55. C Moss Side Ch Ch *Man* 54-57; C Billingham St Aid CD *Dur* 57-60; V New Springs *Liv* 60-65; V Newc H Cross *Newc* 65-77; RD Newc W 74-77; V Gosforth All SS 77-89; Hon Can Newc Cathl from 82; V Heddon-on-the-Wall from 89. *St Andrew's Vicarage, Towne Gate, Heddon-on-the-Wall, Newcastle upon Tyne NE15 0DT* Wylam (0661) 853142

LITTLE, Richard Terence. b 17. Bible Churchmen's Coll 37. **d** 40 **p** 41. Chapl Dusseldorf *Eur* 70-75; R Meonstoke w Corhampton cum Exton *Portsm* 75-78; rtd 78; Perm to Offic St Alb & Chelmsf from 81. *1 Plaistow Way, Great Chishill, Royston, Herts SG8 8SQ* Royston (0763) 838505

LITTLE, Stephen Clifford. b 47. Man Univ MEd81. AKC72. **d** 72 **p** 73. C Grange St Andr *Ches* 72-73; C E Runcorn w Halton 73-75; P-in-c Newbold *Man* 75-77; Sector Min Milton Keynes Chr Coun 77-84; P-in-c Broughton and Milton Keynes *Ox* 77-82; TR Warw Cov from 84. *The Rectory, 184 Myton Road, Warwick CV34 6PS* Warwick (0926) 492909

LITTLECHILD, William Bryant. b 02. **d** 53 **p** 54. V Sutton Courtenay w Appleford *Ox* 55-67; rtd 67; P-in-c Chaffcombe *B & W* 76-77; P-in-c Knowle St Giles w Cricket Malherbie 76-77. *Kerris Vean, Chaffcombe, Chard, Somerset TA20 4AH* Chard (0460) 62062

LITTLEFAIR, David. b 38. ACCA71 FCCA85 Lon Univ BD79. Trin Coll Bris 76. **d** 79 **p** 80. C Bursledon *Win* 79-82; V Charles w St Matthias Plymouth *Ex* 82-89; Warden Lee Abbcy Internat Students' Club Kensington from 89. *Lee Abbey International Students' Club, 57/67 Lexham Gardens, London W8 6JJ* 071-373 7242

LITTLEJOHN, Theodore Harold. b 32. Roch Th Coll 62. **d** 64 **p** 65. C Tamerton Foliot *Ex* 64-65; C Crediton

65-69; V Wavertree St Bridget *Liv* 69-72; C Honiton, Gittisham and Combe Raleigh *Ex* 73-76; P-in-c Plymouth St Aug 76-77. *Address temp unknown*

LITTLER, Eric Raymond. b 36. Lon Univ DipTh67. Roch Th Coll 65. **d** 68 **p** 69. C Hatf Hyde St Mary *St Alb* 68-73; Chapl Welwyn Garden City Hosp 70-73; TV Pemberton St Jo *Liv* 73-78; Chapl Billinge Hosp Wigan 76-81; V Pemberton St Fran Kitt Green *Liv* 78-81; V White Notley, Faulkbourne and Cressing *Chelmsf* 81-88; V Westcliff St Andr from 81; Chapl Westcliff Hosp from 88; Chapl Southend HA from 89. *St Andrew's Vicarage, 65 Electric Avenue, Westcliff-on-Sea, Essex SS0 9NN* Southend-on-Sea (0702) 342868

LITTLER, Malcolm Kenneth. b 34. Univ of Wales (Lamp) BA55. **d** 57 **p** 58. C Llanelly *St D* 57-60; C Llandeilo Fawr 60-61; R Puncheston, Lt Newc and Castle Bythe 61-64; R Lamp Velfrey 64-68; V Llanwnda w Goodwick and Manorowen 68-74; V Llanfynydd 74-78; V The Suttons w Tydd *Linc* 87-90; V Graffoe from 90. *The Vicarage, Wellingore, Lincoln LN5 0JF* Lincoln (0522) 810246

LITTLEWOOD, Jacqueline Patricia. b 52. Linc Th Coll 77. **dss** 80 **d** 87. Crayford *Roch* 80-84; Gravesend H Family w Ifield 84-87; Par Dn from 87. *74 Apsledene, Singlewell, Gravesend, Kent DA12 5EE* Gravesend (0474) 560106

LITTLEWOOD, John Edward. b 50. UEA BSc71. Ridley Hall Cam 72. **d** 75 **p** 76. C Hellesdon *Nor* 75-78; C Eaton 78-81; Hon C S Hill w Callington *Truro* 83-89; Hon C Linkinhorne 86-89; Hon C Stoke Climsland from 89. *Haye Mill, Callington, Cornwall* Liskeard (0579) 82885

LITTLEWOOD, John Richard. b 37. Ridley Hall Cam 69. **d** 72 **p** 73. C Rushden w Newton Bromswold *Pet* 72-75; Chapl Scargill Ho N Yorkshire 75-77; V Werrington *Pet* 77-91; V Highbury Ch Ch w St Jo and St Sav Lon from 91. *Christ Church Vicarage, 155 Highbury Grove, London N5 1SA* 071-226 4544

LITTLEWOOD, Philip Nigel. b 59. Sarum & Wells Th Coll 87. **d** 90 **p** 91. C Frome St Jo and St Mary *B & W* from 90. *St Mary's House, Innox Hill, Frome, Somerset BA11 2LN* Frome (0373) 63525

LITTON, Alan. b 42. Ridley Hall Cam 66. **d** 69 **p** 70. C Bolton St Bede *Man* 69-71; C Ashton St Mich 71-73; V Haslingden St Jo Stonefold *Blackb* 73-77; Ind Chapl *York* 77-81; V Crewe All SS and St Paul *Ches* 81-84; Ind Chapl *Liv* 84-89; V Spotland *Man* from 89. *Spotland Vicarage, Willbutts Lane, Rochdale, Lancs OL11 5BE* Rochdale (0706) 48972

LIVERPOOL, Archdeacon of. *See* DURANT, Ven Stanton Vincent

LIVERPOOL, Bishop of. *See* SHEPPARD, Rt Rev David Stuart

LIVERPOOL, Dean of. *See* WALTERS, Very Rev Rhys Derrick Chamberlain

LIVERSUCH, Ian Martin. b 56. St Jo Coll Dur BA79 DPS83. Wycliffe Hall Ox 79. **d** 83 **p** 84. C Newport St Mark *Mon* 83-85; C Risca 85-88; P-in-c Newport All SS 88-91; Canada from 91. *Address temp unknown*

LIVESEY, Kenneth. b 29. Codrington Coll Barbados 57. **d** 59 **p** 60. Br Guiana 59-66; Guyana 66-72 and 84-89; P-in-c Royton St Paul *Man* 72-73; V 73-81; P-in-c Bury H Trin 81-82; TR Bury Ch King w H Trin 82-84; V Oldham St Steph and All Martyrs from 89. *The Vicarage, Moorby Street, Oldham OL1 3QU* 061-678 9565

LIVINGSTON, Bertram. TCD BA56. **d** 57 **p** 58. C Enniscorthy *C & O* 57-59; I Carrickmacross *Clogh* 59-61; I Carrickmacross w Magheracloone 61-63; C-in-c Derryvolgie *Conn* 63-78; I 78-79; I Monaghan *Clogh* 79-86; I Desertlyn w Ballyeglish *Arm* from 86. *The Rectory, 24 Cookstown Road, Moneymore, Co Londonderry* Moneymore (06487) 48200

LIVINGSTON, Richard. b 46. Qu Coll Birm. **d** 83 **p** 84. C Hobs Moat *Birm* 83-87; V Droylsden St Martin *Man* from 87. *St Martin's Vicarage, Greenside Lane, Droylsden, Manchester M35 7SJ* 061-370 9833

LIVINGSTONE, Canon Francis Kenneth. b 26. TCD MA. TCD Div Sch Div Test49. **d** 49 **p** 50. C Dub Santry Union w Coolock *D & G* 49-52; C Dub St Geo 52-57; I Castledermot Union 57-62; C Arm St Mark *Arm* 62-66; Hon VC Arm Cathl from 63; I Portadown St Sav 66-83; I Donaghmore w Upper Donaghmore from 83; Preb Yagoe St Patr Cathl Dub from 85. *66 Main Street, Castlecaulfield, Dungannon, Co Tyrone BT70 3NP* Donaghmore (08687) 61214

LIVINGSTONE, Ven John Morris. b 28. Peterho Cam BA53 MA56. Cuddesdon Coll 53. **d** 55 **p** 56. C Hunslet St Mary and Stourton *Ripon* 55-60; Chapl Liddon Ho Lon 60-63; V Notting Hill St Jo *Lon* 63-74; P-in-c Notting Hill St Mark 66-73; P-in-c Notting Hill All SS w

St Columb 67-74; P-in-c Notting Hill St Clem 68-74; TR Notting Hill 74-75; Chapl Paris St Geo *Eur* 75-84; Adn N France 79-84; Adn Riviera from 84; Chapl Nice from 84. *11 rue de la Buffa, 06000 Nice, France* France (33) 93 87 19 83

LLANDAFF, Archdeacon of. *See* LEE, Ven David Stanley

LLANDAFF, Bishop of. *See* DAVIES, Rt Rev Roy Thomas

LLANDAFF, Dean of. *See* DAVIES, Very Rev Alun Radcliffe

✠**LLEWELLIN, Rt Rev John Richard Allan.** b 38. Fitzw Ho Cam BA64 MA78. Westcott Ho Cam 61. **d** 64 **p** 65 **c** 85. C Radlett *St Alb* 64-68; S Africa 68-71; V Waltham Cross *St Alb* 71-79; R Harpenden St Nic 79-85; Hon Can Truro Cathl *Truro* from 85; Suff Bp St Germans from 85. *32 Falmouth Road, Truro, Cornwall TR1 2HX* Truro (0872) 73190

LLEWELLIN DAVIES, Dr Lawrence John David. b 16. Jes Coll Ox BA39 MA43 DipEd59 Bonn Univ ThD58. Ripon Hall Ox 39. **d** 39 **p** 40. Dean Chpl & Hd Div Hall Sir Wm Herschel Gr Sch 59-80; Lic to Offic *Ox* 67-81; rtd 81; Perm to Offic *Ox* from 81. *Deans Lodge, Hollybush Hill, Stoke Poges, Slough SL2 4PZ* Fulmer (0753) 662495

LLEWELLYN, Brian Michael. b 47. ARICS73. Sarum & Wells Th Coll 78. **d** 80 **p** 81. C Farncombe *Guildf* 80-83; Chapl RAF 83-87; R Hethersett w Canteloff w Lt and Gt Melton *Nor* from 87. *The Rectory, Norwich Road, Hethersett, Norwich NR9 3AR* Norwich (0603) 810273

LLEWELLYN, Christine Ann. b 46. **d** 89. NSM Arthog w Fairbourne w Llangelynin w Rhoslefain *Ban* from 90. *16 Belgrave Road, Fairbourne, Gwynedd LL38 2AX* Fairbourne (0341) 250282

LLEWELLYN, David John Patrick. b 16. AKC40. Wells Th Coll. **d** 46 **p** 47. I Kinneigh Union *C, C & R* 76-83; rtd 83. *Anne's Cottage, Hamilton Row, Courtmacsherry, Bandon, Co Cork, Irish Republic*

LLEWELLYN, John Francis Morgan. b 21. LVO82. Pemb Coll Cam BA46 MA48. Ely Th Coll 47. **d** 49 **p** 50. Hd Master Cathl Choir Sch 58-74; Min Can St Paul's Cathl *Lon* 58-74; Sacr and Warden Coll of Min Can 68-74; Dep P-in-O to HM The Queen 68-70 and 74-91; P-in-O 70-74; Chapl Royal St Pet-ad-Vincula at HM Tower of Lon 74-89; Sen ChStJ from 74; rtd 89. *Flat 1, Lavershot Hall, London Road, Windlesham, Surrey GU20 6LE* Ascot (0344) 24773

LLEWELLYN, Neil Alexander. b 55. LWCMD78. Westcott Ho Cam 79 Sarum & Wells Th Coll 83. **d** 84 **p** 85. C Heref St Martin *Heref* 84-86; Chapl Rotterdam Miss to Seamen *Eur* 86-89; R Docking w The Birchams and Stanhoe w Barwick *Nor* from 89. *The Vicarage, Docking, King's Lynn, Norfolk PE31 8PN* Docking (04858) 247

LLEWELLYN, William David. b 22. Univ of Wales (Lamp) BA43. **d** 48 **p** 49. V Treharris *Llan* 63-70; V Penmaen *Mon* 70-77; V St Mellons 77-87; rtd 87. *262 Cardiff Road, Newport, Gwent NP9 3AH*

✠**LLEWELLYN, Rt Rev William Somers.** b 07. Ball Coll Ox BA29 DipTh34 MA37. Wycliffe Hall Ox. **d** 35 **p** 36 **c** 63. C Chiswick St Nic w St Mary *Lon* 35-37; V Badminton w Acton Turville *Glouc* 37-49; CF (EC) 40-46; CF (TA) 48-51; V Tetbury w Beverston *Glouc* 49-61; Hon C 77-85; CF (R of O) 51-62; RD Tetbury *Glouc* 56-61; Adn Lynn *Nor* 61-72; C Blakeney w Lt Langham 62-63; C Stiffkey w Morston 62-63; Suff Bp Lynn 63-72; rtd 73; P-in-c Boxwell w Leighterton *Glouc* 73-76; Asst Bp Glouc from 73. *Glebe House, Leighterton, Tetbury, Glos GL8 8UN* Leighterton (066689) 236

LLEWELYN, John Dilwyn. b 18. St D Coll Lamp BA40 AKC42. **d** 42 **p** 43. V Plymouth St Simon *Ex* 61-82; rtd 82; Perm to Offic *Ex* from 84. *25 Oakley Close, Pinhoe, Exeter EX1 3SB* Exeter (0392) 67169

LLEWELYN, Robert Charles. b 09. Pemb Coll Cam BA32 MA36. **d** 36 **p** 37. India 51-71; Adn Poona 69-71; Warden Bede Ho Staplehurst 72-75; rtd 74; Chapl Shrine of St Julian 76-90. *80A King Street, Norwich NR1 1PQ* Norwich (0603) 662600

LLEWELYN, Robert John. b 32. Keble Coll Ox BA54 MA58. Cuddesdon Coll 55. **d** 66 **p** 67. C Bedf St Andr *St Alb* 66-69; C Cheltenham St Luke and St Jo *Glouc* 69-75; V S Cerney w Cerney Wick 75-80; V Glouc St Cath from 80; P-in-c Glouc St Mark 87-89. *St Catharine's Vicarage, 29 Denmark Road, Gloucester GL1 3JQ* Gloucester (0452) 24497

LLOYD, Canon Bernard James. b 29. AKC56. **d** 57 **p** 58. C Laindon w Basildon *Chelmsf* 57-65; V E Ham St Geo 65-82; RD Newham 76-82; Hon Can Chelmsf Cathl from 82; R Danbury from 82; P-in-c Woodham Ferrers 87-90. *The Rectory, 55 Main Road, Danbury, Chelmsford CM3 4NG* Danbury (024541) 3140

LLOYD, Bertram John. b 26. DipTh83. St Mich Coll Llan. d 83 p 84. C Malpas *Mon* 83-85; V Blaenavon w Capel Newydd from 85. *The Vicarage, Church Road, Blaenavon, Gwent NP4 9AE* Blaenavon (0495) 790292

LLOYD, Ven Bertram Trevor. b 38. Hertf Coll Ox BA60 MA64. Clifton Th Coll 62. d 64 p 65. C S Mimms Ch Ch *Lon* 64-70; V Wealdstone H Trin 70-84; RD Harrow 77-82; P-in-c Harrow Weald St Mich 80-84; V Harrow H Trin St Mich 84-89; Adn Barnstaple *Ex* from 89. *Stage Cross, Whitemoor Hill, Bishops Tawton, Barnstaple, Devon EX33 0BE* Barnstaple (0271) 75475

LLOYD, Canon Charles Henry. b 13. TCD BA34. CITC 36. d 36 p 37. I New Ross *C & O* 70-82; Preb Tassagard St Patr Cathl Dub 73-82; rtd 82. *74 The Rise, Woodpark, Ballinteer, Dublin 16, Irish Republic* Dublin (1) 951181

LLOYD, Crewdson Howard. b 31. Ex Coll Ox BA54 MA64. Wells Th Coll 64. d 66 p 67. C Ex St Dav *Ex* 66-69; C Cirencester *Glouc* 69-72; Perm to Offic *Ox* from 72; Summoner of Preachers Ox Univ 81-89. *36 Thackley End, Banbury Road, Oxford OX2 6LB* Oxford (0865) 511032

LLOYD, David John. b 52. Lon Univ BD82. St D Coll Lamp DipTh76. d 76 p 77. C Pemb St Mary and St Mich *St D* 76-77; C Llanelly 77-80; V Cilycwm and Ystradffin w Rhandir-mwyn etc 80-82; Oman 82-84; R Llanllwchaearn and Llanina *St D* 84-88; V Llangennech and Hendy 88-90. *20 West End, Llanelli, Dyfed SA15 3DN*

LLOYD, David John Silk. b 37. Univ of Wales (Lamp) BA62. St Steph Ho Ox 71. d 73 p 74. C Brentwood St Thos *Chelmsf* 73-77; C Hockley 77-80; C Wickford 80-81; C Wickford and Runwell 81-83; TV 83-88; Chapl Runwell Hosp Essex 81-88; S Africa from 88; Perm to Offic *Chelmsf* from 88. *4 Argyll House, Seaforth Road, Westcliff-on-Sea, Essex SS0 7SJ*

LLOYD, Canon David Jones. b 15. St D Coll Lamp BA37. d 38 p 39. R Cilgerran and Bridell *St D* 61-81; RD Cemais and Sub-Aeron 73-80; Can St D Cathl 73-81; rtd 81. *Flat 1, Clos y Drindod, Buarth Road, Aberystwyth, Dyfed* Aberystwyth (0970) 611658

LLOYD, David Peter. b 58. Kingston Poly BA81 DipArch84. Sarum & Wells Th Coll 88. d 90 p 91. C N Dulwich St Faith *S'wark* from 90. *70 Frankfurt Road, London SE24* 071-733 6734

LLOYD, Dr Dennis John. b 46. BSc70 MSc74 PhD81. S Dios Minl Tr Scheme. d 90. C Hamworthy *Sarum* from 90. *The Parsonage, 56 Keysworth Road, Hamworthy, Poole, Dorset BH16 5BH* Poole (0202) 674366

LLOYD, Edward Gareth. b 60. K Coll Cam BA81 MA85. Ridley Hall Cam 85. d 88 p 89. C Jarrow *Dur* 88-91; C Monkwearmouth St Pet from 91. *St Peter's Vicarage, St Peter's Way, Sunderland SR6 0DY* 091-567 3726

LLOYD, Eileen. b 50. FIMLS74 Liv Poly HNC72. Nor Ord Course 88. d 91. C Heref St Martin w St Fran (S Wye Team Min) *Heref* from 91. *89 Belmont Road, Hereford HR2 7JN* Hereford (0432) 271137

LLOYD, Mrs Elizabeth Jane. b 52. CChem GRIC74 MRIC77 HND73 Nottm Univ DipTh79. Linc Th Coll 77. dss 80 d 87. Lic to Offic St Nic w St Jo Newport *Linc* 80-81; Lic to Offic *Sarum* 81-87; Chapl Poole Gen Hosp from 85; Hon Par Dn Lytchett Matravers *Sarum* from 87. *The Rectory, Jennys' Lane, Lytchett Matravers, Poole, Dorset BH16 6BP* Morden (092945) 200

LLOYD, Miss Glenys Elizabeth Barrett. b 43. CertEd67. Cranmer Hall Dur 79. dss 82 d 87. Rainham *Roch* 82-86; Cov Caludon *Cov* 86-87; TM (Dn-in-c) from 87. *St Catherine's House, 7 St Catherine's Close, Coventry CV3 1EH* Coventry (0203) 635737

LLOYD, Graham. b 36. Brasted Th Coll 62 St Aid Birkenhead 64 Glouc Sch of Min 86. d 89 p 90. NSM Churchstoke w Hyssington and Sarn *Heref* from 89. *The Pullets Cottage, Church Stoke, Montgomery, Powys SY15 6TL* Churchstoke (0588) 620285

LLOYD, Gwilym Wyn. b 50. Leic Univ BA72 Birm Univ MSc73 Lon Univ LLB78. Trin Coll Bris DipHE85. d 87 p 88. C Bexleyheath Ch Ch *Roch* 87-91; R Darlaston St Lawr *Lich* from 91. *The Rectory, Darlaston, Wednesbury, W Midlands WS10 8AA* 021-526 2240

LLOYD, Hamilton William John Marteine. b 19. Jes Coll Ox BA41 MA45. Ripon Hall Ox. d 43 p 44. V Whitchurch w Tufton and Litchfield *Win* 68-71; V Lyndhurst 71-73; V Lyndhurst and Emery Down 73-84; rtd 84; Perm to Offic *Win* from 86. *Post Office House, North Litchfield, Whitchurch, Hants RG28 7PR* Whitchurch (0256) 893507

LLOYD, Harry James. b 22. Univ of Wales (Lamp) BA50. d 51 p 52. V Kingston *Sarum* 60-83; V Worth Matravers 60-83; C Milton Abbas, Hilton w Cheselbourne etc 83-87; rtd 87. *Linden, Streetway Lane, Cheselbourne,*

Dorchester, Dorset DT2 7NU Milborne St Andrew (025887) 331

LLOYD, Very Rev Henry Morgan. b 11. DSO41 OBE59. Or Coll Ox BA33 MA37. Cuddesdon Coll 33. d 35 p 36. Dean Truro 60-81; rtd 81. *3 Hill House, The Avenue, Sherborne, Dorset DT9 3AJ* Sherborne (0935) 812037

LLOYD, Canon Herbert James. b 31. TD. St D Coll Lamp BA57. d 58 p 59. C Wrexham *St As* 58-65; TV 71-74; R Llanferres 65-67; R Llanferres, Nercwys and Eryrys 67-71; V Rhyl w Rhyl St Ann from 74; CF (TA) from 74; Can St As Cathl *St As* from 81; Prec St As Cathl from 89. *The Vicarage, Bath Street, Rhyl, Clwyd LL18 3LU* Rhyl (0745) 353732

LLOYD, James. b 04. St D Coll Lamp BA27. d 28 p 29. R Eglwysbrewis and St Athan *Llan* 56-71; rtd 71. *Brookside Care Home, Llangorse, Brecon, Powys* Llangorse (087484) 393

LLOYD, John Everard. b 27. FCMA60 LSE BSc50. St Alb Minl Tr Scheme 84. d 87 p 88. NSM Harpenden St Nic *St Alb* 87-90; Hon C Addingham *Bradf* from 90. *2 High Springs, Owler Park Road, Ilkley, W Yorkshire LS29 0BG* Ilkley (0943) 609267

LLOYD, John James. b 14. St D Coll Lamp BA36. d 37 p 38. V Cadoxton-juxta-Neath *Llan* 63-79; rtd 79. *16 Spoonbill Close, Rest Bay, Porthcawl, M Glam* Porthcawl (065671) 5470

LLOYD, John Philip. b 15. St Chad's Coll Dur BA37 DipTh38 MA40. d 38 p 39. V Bickerton *Ches* 69-77; rtd 77; Perm to Offic *Ches* from 77. *17 Wesley Close, Bowling Green Court, Nantwich, Cheshire CW5 5SN* Nantwich (0270) 626771

LLOYD, Jonathan Wilford. b 56. MBASW City of Lon Poly BSc80 Golds Coll Lon CQSW82 DASS83 N Lon Poly MA86. S'wark Ord Course 87. d 90 p 91. NSM Sydenham St Bart *S'wark* 90-91; Soc Resp Officer from 91. *19 Beaulieu Avenue, London SE26 6PN* 081-778 9376

LLOYD, Michael Francis. b 57. Down Coll Cam BA79 MA82 St Jo Coll Dur BA83. Cranmer Hall Dur 81. d 84 p 85. C Locks Heath *Portsm* 84-87; Asst Chapl Worc Coll Ox 89-90. *Christ's College, Cambridge CB2 3BU* Cambridge (0223) 334922

LLOYD, Nigel James Clifford. b 51. Nottm Univ BTh81. Lambeth STh90 Linc Th Coll 77. d 81 p 82. C Sherborne w Castleton and Lillington *Sarum* 81-84; R Lytchett Matravers from 84. *The Rectory, Jennys' Lane, Lytchett Matravers, Poole, Dorset BH16 6BP* Morden (092945) 200

LLOYD, Oscar Wynn. b 17. St D Coll Lamp BA43. d 45 p 47. V Helsby *Ches* 66-74; V Ince 66-74; R Dodleston 74-82; rtd 82; Perm to Offic *Ches* from 82. *12 Hawarden Drive, Drury, Buckley, Clwyd* Buckley (0244) 549650

LLOYD, Pamela Valpy. b 25. Gilmore Ho 48 St Aug Coll Cant 76. dss 76 d 87. Chartham *Cant* 76-78; Cant All SS 78-85; rtd 85; Chapl Asst Kent and Cant Hosp 87; Chapl Chaucer Hosp Cant 87-90; Hon Par Dn Elham w Denton and Wootton *Cant* from 87; Sub-Chapl HM Pris Cant from 88. *Cavendish House, 9 North Holmes Road, Canterbury, Kent CT1 1QJ* Canterbury (0227) 457782

LLOYD, Peter John. b 32. TD78. Leic Univ DipSocSc53. Wells Th Coll 59. d 61 p 62. C Walmer *Cant* 61-63; CF (TA) 62-73 and 77-87; C Maidstone All SS w St Phil *Cant* 63-66; V Milton next Sittingbourne 66-69; R Brinkley, Burrough Green and Carlton *Ely* 69-73; CF 73-77; V Chessington *Guildf* 77-85; RD Epsom 82-87; V Epsom St Martin from 85. *The Vicarage, 30 St Martin's Avenue, Epsom, Surrey KT18 5HZ* Epsom (0372) 723845

LLOYD, Peter Vernon James. b 36. St Jo Coll Cam BA60 MA. Ridley Hall Cam 60. d 62 p 63. C Keynsham w Queen Charlton *B & W* 62-65; Perm to Offic *Sarum* from 65; NSM Bournemouth St Jo w St Mich *Win* from 87; NSM Bournemouth St Pet w St Swithun, St Steph etc from 90. *18 Cornelia Crescent, Branksome, Poole, Dorset BH12 1LU* Bournemouth (0202) 741422

LLOYD, Raymond David (Brother Ramon). b 35. Univ of Wales (Cardiff) DipTh61 Edin Univ MPhil74. Zurich Th Sem BD69 Edin Th Coll 71. d 72 p 72. C Glas St Mary *Glas* 72-76; Chapl Glas Univ 74-76; SSF from 78. *St Mary at the Cross, Glasshampton, Shrawley, Worcester WR6 6TQ* Great Witley (0299) 896345

LLOYD, Rex Edward Ambrose. b 04. Worc Coll Ox BA26 DipTh27 MA32. Wycliffe Hall Ox 29. d 29 p 30. R Hamsey *Chich* 54-70; Chapl HM Pris Lewes 65-69; rtd 70. *8 Kingsmead Court, Redcotts Lane, Wimborne, Dorset BH21 1JX* Wimborne (0202) 841799

LLOYD, Richard Leslie Harris. b 09. Peterho Cam BA31 MA35. Mert Coll Ox BA32 MA36 BLitt36. St Steph Ho Ox 32. d 36 p 37. Chapl St Bede Coll

Dur 63-74; rtd 74. *8 Homebryth House, Front Street, Sedgefield, Stockton-on-Tees, Cleveland TS21 3BW* Sedgefield (0740) 22468

LLOYD, Robert Graham. b 42. St Jo Coll Nottm 82. **d** 84 **p** 85. C Tonyrefail *Llan* 84-87; V Martletwy w Lawrenny and Minwear and Yerbeston *St D* 87-91; V Monkton from 91. *The Vicarage, Monkton, Pembroke, Dyfed* Pembroke (0646) 682723

LLOYD, Robert James Clifford. b 18. Selw Coll Cam BA41 MA49. Linc Th Coll 46. **d** 47 **p** 48. R Chartham *Cant* 66-81; RD W Bridge 75-81; Hon C Elham w Denton and Wootton from 82; rtd 83. *Cavendish House, 9 North Holmes Road, Canterbury, Kent CT1 1QJ* Canterbury (0227) 457782

LLOYD, Roger. b 58. K Coll Lon BA. Cranmer Hall Dur. **d** 84 **p** 85. C Hornchurch St Andr *Chelmsf* 84-87; C Gt Parndon from 87. *29 Woodhill, Great Parndon, Harlow, Essex CM18 7JS* Harlow (0279) 417644

LLOYD, Ronald. b 37. St Mich Coll Llan. **d** 83 **p** 84. C Penarth All SS *Llan* 83-85; V Cwmbach from 85. *The Vicarage, Bridge Road, Cwmbach, Aberdare, M Glam CF44 0LS* Aberdare (0685) 878674

LLOYD, Ronald Henry. b 32. Univ of Wales (Lamp) BA52 LTh54. **d** 54 **p** 56. C Manselton *S & B* 54-56; C Sketty 56-59; C Swansea St Mary 59-63; CF (TA) 59-65; V Elmley Castle w Netherton and Bricklehampton *Worc* 63-69; Chapl Dragon Sch Ox 69-82; Chapl St Hugh's Coll Ox 75-80; P-in-c Ox St Marg *Ox* 75-76; Chapl Magd Coll Ox 75-82; Prec and Chapl Ch Ch *Ox* 82-87; R Alvescot w Black Bourton, Shilton, Holwell etc from 87. *The Vicarage, Shilton, Oxford OX8 4AE* Carterton (0993) 845954

LLOYD, Samuel. b 07. Univ of Wales BA48. St Deiniol's Hawarden 69. **d** 69 **p** 70. C Llangynwyd w Maesteg *Llan* 70-83; rtd 83. *9 Station Street, Maesteg, Bridgend, M Glam* Maesteg (0656) 732386

LLOYD, Mrs Sandra. b 48. Sarum & Wells Th Coll 83. **dss** 86 **d** 87. Freshwater *Portsm* 86-87; C 87-89; C Whitwell from 89; C Niton from 89. *The Rectory, Pan Lane, Niton, Ventnor, Isle of Wight PO38 2BT* Isle of Wight (0983) 755343

LLOYD, Stephen Russell. b 47. Worc Coll Ox BA69 MA77 CertEd DipTh. Oak Hill Th Coll 76. **d** 77 **p** 78. C Canonbury St Steph *Lon* 77-80; C Braintree *Chelmsf* from 80. *St Paul's Parsonage, Hay Lane, Braintree, Essex CM7 6DY* Braintree (0376) 25095

LLOYD, Stuart George Errington. b 49. TCD BA72. **d** 75 **p** 76. C Cloughfern *Conn* 75-79; C Cregagh *D & D* 79-82; I Eglantine *Conn* 82-89; I Ballymena w Ballyclug from 89. *St Patrick's Rectory, 102 Galgorm Road, Ballymena, Co Antrim* Ballymena (0266) 652253

LLOYD, Canon Thomas Rees. b 03. St D Coll Lamp BA25 BD34. **d** 26 **p** 27. V Newc Emlyn *St D* 46-68; Can St D Cathl 63-70; rtd 70. *Mount Pleasant, Stoneleigh Road, Bubbenhall, Coventry CV8 3BT* Coventry (0203) 301406

LLOYD, Timothy David Lewis. b 37. Clare Coll Cam BA58 MA62. Cuddesdon Coll 58. **d** 60 **p** 61. C Stepney St Dunstan and All SS *Lon* 60-64; C St Alb Abbey *St Alb* 64-67; Prec St Alb Abbey 67-69; V St Paul's Walden 69-78; V Braughing w Furneux Pelham and Stocking Pelham 78-79; P-in-c Lt Hadham 78-79; V Braughing, Lt Hadham, Albury, Furneux Pelham etc 79-82; V Cheshunt from 82; RD Cheshunt from 89. *The Vicarage, Churchgate, Cheshunt, Waltham Cross, Herts* Waltham Cross (0992) 23121

LLOYD, Winston. b 12. Lon Univ DipTh57 BD78. St D Coll Lamp BA52 Lich Th Coll 52. **d** 53 **p** 54. V Harringay St Paul *Lon* 71-77; rtd 77. *25 Martindale Avenue, Heatherside, Camberley, Surrey GU15 1BB* Camberley (0276) 20315

LLOYD-JAMES, John Eifion. b 39. Clifton Th Coll 63. **d** 65 **p** 66. C Burgess Hill St Andr *Chich* 65-68; C-in-c Portslade Gd Shep Mile Oak CD 68-74; V Lancing St Mich 74-88; V Billingshurst from 88. *The Vicarage, Billingshurst, W Sussex RH14 9PY* Billingshurst (0403) 782332

LLOYD JONES, Ieuan. b 31. FBIM St Cath Coll Cam BA51 MA54. Sarum & Wells Th Coll 80. **d** 83 **p** 84. Hon C Claygate *Guildf* 83-89; Perm to Offic *Ox* from 89. *11 Southcroft, Old Marston, Oxford OX3 0PF* Oxford (0865) 793098

LLOYD-RICHARDS, David Robert. b 48. Open Univ BA84 Hull Univ MA87. St D Coll Lamp DipTh70. **d** 71 **p** 72. Miss to Seamen Singapore 70-71; Southn 76-77; C Skewen *Llan* 71-73; C Neath w Llantwit 73-76; V Pontlottyn w Fochriw 77-84; R Merthyr Dyfan 84-90; Chapl Barry Neale-Kent Hosp 84-90; Tutor Open Univ from 85; Sen Chapl Univ Hosp of Wales Cardiff from

90. *The Chaplaincy Department, University Hospital of Wales, Heath Park, Cardiff CF4 4XW* Cardiff (0222) 620957 or 747747

LOAKE, David Lorne. b 22. ARCO48 Ball Coll Ox BA47 MA48. Qu Coll Birm 49. **d** 49 **p** 50. V Sutton Coldfield St Chad *Birm* 59-72; V Sibsey w Frithville *Linc* 72-80; P-in-c New Bolingbroke w Carrington 76-80; V Sibsey w Frithville 80-88; rtd 88; Asst Ecum Officer from 88. *11 Sampshill Road, Westoning, Bedford MK45 5LF* Flitwick (0525) 714391

LOASBY, Preb Edgar Harold. b 13. BNC Ox BA35 MA46. Cuddesdon Coll 35. **d** 36 **p** 37. R Chelsea St Luke *Lon* 61-82; Preb St Paul's Cathl 71-82; rtd 82; Perm to Offic *Lon* from 82. *31 Oakley Gardens, London SW3 5QH* 071-352 8828

LOAT, Andrew Graham. b 61. Aber Univ BD83. St Jo Coll Nottm DPS87. **d** 87 **p** 88. C Llangynwyd w Maesteg *Llan* 87-90; C Llansamlet *S & B* from 90. *456 Birchgrove Road, Birchgrove, Swansea SA7 9NR* Swansea (0792) 817300

LOBANOV-ROSTOVSKY, Andrew Russell. b 17. Qu Coll Ox BA38 MA55. Cuddesdon Coll 56. **d** 57 **p** 58. Chapl St Bede's Ch for the Deaf Clapham 64-75; Chapl to the Deaf *Guildf* 75-82; rtd 82; Perm to Offic Chich 86-89; Glas 89-91; Hon C Glas St Oswald *Glas* from 91. *10 Aikenhead House, Kings Park, Carmunnock Road, Glasgow G44 5HL*

LOBB, Edward Eric. b 51. Magd Coll Ox BA74 MA76. Wycliffe Hall Ox 73. **d** 76 **p** 77. C Haughton St Mary *Man* 76-80; C Rusholme 80-84; P-in-c Whitfield *Derby* 84-90; V from 90. *The Vicarage, 116 Charlestown Road, Glossop, Derbyshire SK13 8LB* Glossop (0457) 864938

LOCK, David Stephen. b 28. **d** 63 **p** 64. C Streatham Vale H Redeemer *S'wark* 63-66; C Hatcham St Jas 66-75; V Leyton All SS *Chelmsf* from 75. *All Saints' Vicarage, 47 Melbourne Road, London E10 7HF* 081-539 2170

LOCK, Graham Robert. b 39. Hertf Coll Ox BA63. Ridley Hall Cam 62. **d** 64 **p** 65. C Bexleyheath St Pet *Roch* 64-66; C Roch St Justus 66-71; C St Mary Cray and St Paul's Cray 71-75; V Chatham St Paul w All SS 75-83; R Lambourne w Abridge and Stapleford Abbotts *Chelmsf* from 83. *The Rectory, Hoe Lane, Abridge, Romford RM4 1AU* Theydon Bois (0992) 814254

LOCK, Paul Alan. b 65. St Chad's Coll Dur BA86. Coll of Resurr Mirfield 87. **d** 89 **p** 90. C Upholland *Liv* from 89. *8 Beacon View Drive, Up Holland, Skelmersdale, Lancs WN8 0HL* Up Holland (0695) 622181

LOCK, Canon Peter Harcourt D'Arcy. b 44. AKC67. **d** 68 **p** 69. C Meopham *Roch* 68-72; C Wigmore w Hempstead 72; C S Gillingham 72-77; R Hartley 77-83; R Fawkham and Hartley 83-84; V Dartford H Trin from 84; Hon Can Roch Cathl from 90. *The Vicarage, High Street, Dartford, Kent DA1 1RX* Dartford (0322) 22782

LOCKE, Brian Henry. b 38. AKC61. **d** 62 **p** 63. C Westleigh St Pet *Man* 62-65; C Marske in Cleveland *York* 65-68; V Boosbeck w Moorsholm 68-72; Perm to Offic *Man* 78-82; P-in-c Kirkholt 82-86; V from 86; Chapl HM Young Offender Inst Buckley Hall 85-89. *St Thomas's Vicarage, Cavendish Road, Rochdale, Lancs OL11 2QX* Rochdale (0706) 45962

LOCKE, Stephen John. b 60. St Chad's Coll Dur BA82. Sarum & Wells Th Coll 84. **d** 86 **p** 87. C Blackb St Mich w St Jo and H Trin *Blackb* 86-89; C Oswaldtwistle Immanuel and All SS from 89. *All Saints' Vicarage, Aspen Lane, Oswaldtwistle, Accrington, Lancs BB5 4QA* Accrington (0254) 391240

LOCKER, Dorothea Isobel Leslie. b 19. MRPharmS41 Heriot-Watt Coll PhC41. Local NSM Course 79. **dss** 85 **d** 87. NSM Edin St Pet *Edin* from 85. *4C Mayfield Gardens, Edinburgh EH9 2BU* 031-667 3509

LOCKETT, Canon Arthur Stephen. b 18. Bps' Coll Cheshunt 61. **d** 63 **p** 64. R Barley *St Alb* 66-80; rtd 80; Perm to Offic *St Alb* from 80. *50 Honey Way, Royston, Herts SG8 7EU* Royston (0763) 243939

LOCKETT, Paul. b 48. Sarum & Wells Th Coll 73. **d** 76 **p** 77. C Horninglow *Lich* 76-78; C Tewkesbury w Walton Cardiff *Glouc* 78-81; P-in-c W Bromwich St Pet *Lich* 81-90; R Norton Canes from 90; Dean's V Lich Cathl from 91. *St James's Rectory, 81 Church Road, Norton Canes, Cannock, Staffs WS11 3PQ* Heath Hayes (0543) 278969

LOCKETT, Canon William Ernest Alfred. b 16. ARCA39 ATD51 FRSA70 FIBD NRD Florence Academy. Linc Th Coll 44. **d** 45 **p** 46. Sen Lect Liv Univ 56-82; Can Liv Cathl *Liv* 72-82; rtd 82; Perm to Offic *Liv* from 82. *The Croft, Ruff Lane, Ormskirk, Lancs L39 4QZ* Ormskirk (0695) 572119

LOCKEY, Malcolm. b 45. FRSA75 Sunderland Poly BA67 Newc Univ DipEd68. NE Ord Course 87. **d** 90.

NSM Yarm *York* from 90. *26 Blackfriars, Yarm, Cleveland TS15 9HG* Eaglescliffe (0642) 782696

LOCKHART, Antony William Castleton. b 25. GIMechE. Wells Th Coll 63. **d** 65 **p** 66. C Worplesdon *Guildf* 69-73; V Weston 73-79; TV Westborough 79-84; V Shamley Green 84-87; RD Cranleigh 85-87; Dioc Widows Officer *Cant* 89-90; rtd 90. *10 Beverley Road, Canterbury, Kent CT2 7EN* Canterbury (0227) 760980

LOCKHART, Raymond William. b 37. Qu Coll Cam BA58 LLB60 MA61. St Jo Coll Nottm 72. **d** 74 **p** 75. C Aspley *S'well* 74-76; V 81-88; R Knebworth *St Alb* 76-81; Dir CMJ Stella Carmel from 88; Jerusalem from 88. *c/o CMJ, 30C Clarence Road, St Albans, Herts AL1 4JJ* St Albans (0727) 33114

LOCKHART, Very Rev Robert Joseph Norman. b 24. TCD BA46 MA53. **d** 46 **p** 48. I Belf St Donard *D & D* 62-70; I Lurgan (Shankill) 70-89; Prec Dromore Cathl 71-75; Dean Dromore 75-89; rtd 89; Lic to Offic *D & D* from 90. *30 Church Road, Newtonbreda, Belfast BT8 4AQ* Belfast (0232) 491588

LOCKLEY, Ven Harold. b 16. Lon Univ BA37 BD43 MTh49 Nottm Univ PhD55 Em Coll Cam MLitt88. Westcott Ho Cam 46. **d** 46 **p** 47. Dir of Ords *Leic* 51-79; V Leic All SS 63-78; Adn Loughb 63-86; rtd 86. *7 Dower House Gardens, Quorn, Loughborough, Leics LE12 8DE* Loughborough (0509) 412843

LOCKWOOD, David Nicholas. b 23. Birm Univ MA81. St D Coll Lamp BA51 Qu Coll Birm 51. **d** 53 **p** 54. V Hanley Castle w Hanley Swan *Worc* 64-79; V Hanley Castle, Hanley Swan and Welland 79-81; Perm to Offic *S & B* from 81; rtd 86. *Church Row, Llowes, Hereford HR3 5JB* Glasbury (04974) 664

LOCKWOOD, Wilfred Eric. b 18. Leeds Univ BA49. Coll of Resurr Mirfield 49. **d** 51 **p** 52. V Leeds Ch Ch and St Jo and St Barn Holbeck *Ripon* 62-71; R Ducklington *Ox* 71-83; rtd 83; Perm to Offic *Nor* from 83. *15A Wells Road, Walsingham, Norfolk NR22 6DL* Walsingham (0328) 820723

LOCKYER, David Ralph George. b 41. Wells Th Coll 65. **d** 67 **p** 68. C Bottesford *Linc* 67-69; C Eling *Win* 69-73; TV Eling, Testwood and Marchwood 73-77; TR Speke St Aid *Liv* 77-84; V Halifax St Jude *Wakef* from 84; Chapl Halifax R Infirmary from 84. *St Jude's Vicarage, Kensington Road, Savile Park, Halifax, W Yorkshire HX3 0HN* Halifax (0422) 354842

LOCKYER, Desmond Edward Weston. b 18. AKC49. **d** 50 **p** 51. V Eastbourne St Mich *Chich* 68-75; V Preston 75-87; rtd 87; Perm to Offic *Chich* from 87. *Pilgrims, Nep Town Road, Henfield, W Sussex BN5 9DY* Brighton (0273) 493681

LOCKYER, Maurice David. b 19. AKC43. **d** 43 **p** 44. V Huncote *Leic* 64-77; rtd 77. *Ramsay Hall, Byron Road, Worthing, W Sussex BN11 3HY* Worthing (0903) 36880

LOCKYER, Peter Weston. b 60. Linc Coll Ox BA80 MA87. St Jo Coll Nottm 84. **d** 87 **p** 88. C Rowner *Portsm* 87-90; C Beaconsfield *Ox* 90-91; TV from 91. *St Thomas's House, Mayflower Way, Beaconsfield, Bucks HP9 1UF* Beaconsfield (0494) 672750

LOCOCK, Jillian Maud. Lon Univ BSc55. N Ord Course 81. **dss** 84 **d** 87. Didsbury Ch Ch *Man* 84-86; Chapl Asst Man R Infirmary 85-87; Chapl Asst Withington Hosp 86-88; Chapl Asst RN from 88. *20C Queen Street, Helensburgh, Dunbartonshire G84 9LG* Helensburgh (0436) 71252

LODGE, Anthony William Rayner. b 26. Wadh Coll Ox BA51 MA55. Cuddesdon Coll 65. **d** 66 **p** 67. Asst Chapl Forest Sch Snaresbrook 66-68; C Walthamstow St Pet *Chelmsf* 66-68; Chapl Ripon Gr Sch from 68. *School House, Ripon Grammar School, Ripon, N Yorkshire HG4 2DG* Ripon (0765) 2647

LODGE, Canon John Alfred Ainley. b 29. Wells Th Coll 54. **d** 57 **p** 58. C Huddersfield St Jo *Wakef* 57-60; V Shepley 60-64; V Salterhebble St Jude 64-69; C-in-c Mixenden CD 69-75; V Mixenden 75-76; V Almondbury 76-79; RD Almondbury 76-79; V Warmfield 79-88; Bp's Dom Chapl 79-87; Hon Can Wakef Cathl from 85; RD Kirkburton from 88; P-in-c Emley from 88. *The Rectory, 14 Grange Drive, Emley, Huddersfield HD8 9SF* Wakefield (0924) 848301

LODGE, Michael John. b 53. Wycliffe Hall Ox 87. **d** 89 **p** 90. C Highworth w Sevenhampton and Inglesham etc *Bris* from 89. *24 Lismore Road, Highworth, Swindon, Wilts SN6 7HU* Swindon (0793) 764729

LODGE, Robin Paul. b 60. Bris Univ BA82 Ch Ch Coll Cant PGCE83. Chich Th Coll 88. **d** 90 **p** 91. C Calne and Blackland *Sarum* from 90. *5 Tyning Park, Calne, Wilts SN11 0QE* Calne (0249) 814860

LODGE, Roy Frederick. b 38. BTh Birm Univ DipSoc62. Tyndale Hall Bris 63. **d** 66 **p** 67. C Tardebigge *Worc*

66-67; Chapl and Warden Probation Hostel Redditch 67-69; Chapl RAF 69-75; C Kinson *Sarum* 76; Lic to Offic *Pet* 76-77; Asst Chapl HM Pris Stafford 77-78; Chapl HM Pris Ranby 78-84; Chapl HM Pris Long Lartin from 84. *HM Prison Long Lartin, South Littleton, Evesham, Worcs WR11 5TZ* Evesham (0386) 830101

LODWICK, Brian Martin. b 40. Leeds Univ BA61 MPhil76 Linacre Coll Ox BA63 MA67 Univ of Wales PhD87. St Steph Ho Ox 61. **d** 64 **p** 65. C Aberaman *Llan* 64-66; C Newton Nottage 66-73; R Llansannor and Llanfrynach w Penllyn etc from 73; RD Llantwit Major and Cowbridge from 83. *The Rectory, Llansannor, Cowbridge, S Glam CF7 7RW* Cowbridge (0446) 772699

LOEWENDAHL, David Jacob. b 50. SS Coll Cam BA74 MA77. Ripon Coll Cuddesdon 75. **d** 77 **p** 78. C Walworth *S'wark* 77-80; Chapl St Alb Abbey *St Alb* 80-83; Chapl St Alb Sch 80-83; Team Ldr Community Service Volunteers 84-90; Perm to Offic *Lon* 83-90; R É and W Tilbury and Linford *Chelmsf* from 90. *The Rectory, Princess Margaret Road, East Tilbury, Grays, Essex RM18 8PB* Tilbury (0375) 842220

LOFGREN, Ms Claire. b 54. Univ of California BA76. Cranmer Hall Dur 88 Ch Div Sch of the Pacific (USA) MDiv89. **d** 90. Par Dn Usworth *Dur* from 90. *51 Wellburn Road, Washington, Tyne & Wear NE37 1BZ* 091-417 9423

LOFT, Edmund Martin Boswell. b 25. St Jo Coll Cam BA49 MA55. Ely Th Coll 49. **d** 51 **p** 52. V Fillongley *Cov* 62-77; V Earlsdon 77-90; rtd 90. *10 Quarry Road, Sheffield S17 4DA* Sheffield (0742) 360759

LOFTHOUSE, Canon Alexander Francis Joseph. b 30. Keble Coll Ox BA54 MA58. St Steph Ho Ox 54. **d** 56 **p** 57. C Barrow St Jas *Carl* 56-59; C Castleford All SS *Wakef* 59-60; V Airedale w Fryston 60-70; V Maryport *Carl* 70-78; P-in-c Helsington 78; V from 78; P-in-c Underbarrow 78; V from 78; P-in-c Levens 78; V from 78; Hon Can Carl Cathl from 85. *The Vicarage, Vicarage Road, Levens, Kendal, Cumbria LA8 8PY* Sedgwick (05395) 60233

LOFTHOUSE, Miss Brenda. b 33. RGN60 RM62 RNT69. N Ord Course 84. **d** 87. Hon Par Dn Greengates *Bradf* 87-89; Par Dn Farsley from 89. *The Old Vicarage Flat, New Street, Farsley, Pudsey, W Yorkshire LS28 5DJ* Pudsey (0532) 552373

LOGAN, Kevin. b 43. Oak Hill Th Coll 73. **d** 75 **p** 76. C Blackb Sav *Blackb* 75-78; C Leyland St Andr 78-82; V Gt Harwood St Jo 82-91; V Accrington Ch Ch from 91. *Christ Church Vicarage, 3 Bentcliff Gardens, Accrington, Lancs BB5 2NX* Accrington (0254) 235089

LOGAN, Samuel Desmond. b 39. TEng. CITC 76. **d** 78 **p** 79. NSM Belvoir *D & D* 78-85; NSM Knock 85-87; NSM Belf St Brendan 87-91; Lic to Offic from 91. *8 Casaeldona Crescent, Belfast BT6 9RE* Belfast (0232) 795473

LOGUE, Edward Maurice. b 22. **d** 78 **p** 81. Hon C Largs *Glas* from 78; Miss to Seamen from 78. *31 Eastern Avenue, Largs, Ayrshire KA30 9EG* Largs (0475) 672826

LOMAS, Charles Linaker. b 05. St Andr Whittlesford 36. **d** 39 **p** 40. C Lt Ilford St Mich *Chelmsf* 39-40; CF (EC) 40-47; Canada from 47. *Twin Acres, Quatsino, British Columbia, Canada, V0N 2V0*

LOMAS, David. b 39. BA. Cranmer Hall Dur 75. **d** 78 **p** 79. C Ches le Street *Dur* 78-81; C-in-c Newton Hall LEP 81-84; Chapl Scunthorpe Distr HA from 84. *1 Highcliff Gardens, Scunthorpe, S Humberside DN15 8JF* Scunthorpe (0724) 848651

LOMAS, Paul Roy. b 54. Man Univ TCert75. N Ord Course 86. **d** 89 **p** 90. C Hollinwood *Man* from 89. *4 Wrexham Close, Hollinwood, Oldham OL8 4SQ* 061-681 5788

LOMAX, Barry Walter John. b 39. Lambeth STh Lon Coll of Div 63. **d** 66 **p** 67. C Sevenoaks St Nic *Roch* 66-71; C Southport Ch Ch *Liv* 71-73; V Bootle St Matt 73-78; P-in-c Litherland St Andr 76-78; V New Boro and Leigh *Sarum* from 78. *The Vicarage, 15 St John's Hill, Wimborne, Dorset BH21 1BX* Wimborne (0202) 883490

LOMAX, Canon Frank. b 20. Leeds Univ BA42. Coll of Resurr Mirfield 42. **d** 44 **p** 45. V Prudhoe *Newc* 64-74; Singapore from 75; Hon Can Singapore from 75; rtd 87. *142 Killiney Road, 04-146, Singapore 0923* Singapore (65) 737-8329

LONDON, Archdeacon of. See CASSIDY, Ven George Henry

LONDON, Bishop of. See HOPE, Rt Rev and Rt Hon David Michael

LONDON, Dean of (St Paul's). See EVANS, Very Rev Thomas Eric

LONG, Miss Anne Christine. b 33. Lon Univ BA56 Ox Univ DipEd57. Lon Bible Coll BD65. **dss** 80 **d** 87. Lect St Jo Coll Nottm 80-84; Acorn Chr Healing Trust from 85; Hon Par Dn Stanstead Abbots *St Alb* from 87. *Stanstead Hall, Stanstead Abbotts, Ware, Herts SG12 8AA* Ware (0920) 871647

LONG, Anthony Auguste. b 45. Linc Th Coll 79. **d** 81 **p** 82. C Kingswinford St Mary *Lich* 81-84; TV Ellesmere Port *Ches* 84-87; V Witton from 87. *The Vicarage, 61 Church Road, Northwich, Cheshire CW9 5PB* Northwich (0606) 42943

LONG, Anthony Robert. b 48. SS Mark & Jo Coll Chelsea CertEd70. Chich Th Coll 74. **d** 77 **p** 78. C Chiswick St Nic w St Mary *Lon* 77-80; C Earley St Pet *Ox* 80-85; P-in-c Worstead w Westwick and Sloley *Nor* from 85; P-in-c Tunstead w Sco' Ruston from 85. *The Vicarage, Worstead, North Walsham, Norfolk NR28 9SE* Smallburgh (0692) 536800

LONG, Christopher William. b 47. Nottm Univ BTh78 Open Univ BA80. Linc Th Coll 75. **d** 78 **p** 79. C Shiregreen St Jas and St Chris *Sheff* 78-81; V 81-82; Chapl RAF from 82; Perm to Offic *St E* from 91. *c/o MOD, Adastral House, Theobald's Road, London WC1X 8RU* 071-430 7268

LONG, Canon Colin Angus. b 17. St D Coll Lamp BA38 St Mich Coll Llan 39. **d** 40 **p** 43. V Newport Maindee St Jo Ev *Mon* 62-83; Can St Woolos Cathl 77-83; rtd 83. *18 Newport Road, New Inn, Pontypool, Gwent NP4 0NT* Pontypool (0495) 753624

LONG, David William. b 47. K Coll Lon 67. St Aug Coll Cant 70. **d** 72 **p** 73. C Stanley *Liv* 72-73; C W Derby St Luke 73-76; C Cantril Farm 76-79; V Warrington St Barn 79-81; C-in-c Westbrook St Jas CD 82; V Westbrook St Jas from 82. *The Vicarage, 302 Hood Lane, Great Sankey, Warrington WA5 1UQ* Warrington (0925) 33873

LONG, Edward Percy Eades. b 14. Liv Univ BA36 MA38. Linc Th Coll 73. **d** 73 **p** 74. C Sedbergh, Cautley and Garsdale *Bradf* 73-84; rtd 85; Perm to Offic *Bradf* from 85. *4 Derry Cottages, Sedbergh, Cumbria LA10 5SN* Sedbergh (05396) 20577

LONG, Frederick Hugh. **d** 90. NSM Grantham *Linc* from 90. *65 Barrowby Road, Grantham, Lincs* Grantham (0476) 67278

LONG, Geoffrey Lawrence. Portsm Dioc Tr Course 88. **d** 89. NSM Whippingham w E Cowes *Portsm* from 89. *10 Minerva Road, East Cowes, Isle of Wight PO32 6DH* Isle of Wight (0983) 295917

LONG, Harry. b 27. BEM. QUB DBS. **d** 79 **p** 80. NSM Carryduff *D & D* 79-86; NSM Newtownards 86; NSM Belvoir 87-91; Lic to Offic from 91. *28 Cadger Road, Carryduff, Belfast BT8 8AU* Belfast (0232) 812348

LONG, Ven John Sanderson. b 13. Qu Coll Cam BA35 MA39. Cuddesdon Coll 35. **d** 36 **p** 37. Hon Can Ely Cathl *Ely* 70-81; Adn Ely 70-81; R Cam St Botolph 70-81; rtd 81. *23 Thornton Road, Girton, Cambridge CB3 0NP* Cambridge (0223) 276421

LONG, Canon John Sydney. b 25. Lon Univ BSc49. Wycliffe Hall Ox 50. **d** 51 **p** 52. V Barnoldswick w Bracewell *Bradf* 64-85; Hon Can Bradf Cathl 77-91; RD Skipton 83-90; R Broughton, Marton and Thornton 85-91; rtd 91. *1 Church Villa, Carleton, Skipton BD23 3DQ*

LONG, Michael David Barnby. b 32. AKC55. **d** 56 **p** 57. C Whitby *York* 56-59; C Cottingham 59-61; V Elloughton 61-66; P-in-c Brantingham 61-66; V Sheff Parson Cross St Cecilia *Sheff* 66-68; V Flamborough *York* 68-73; R Litcham w Kempston w E and W Lexham *Nor* 73-75; P-in-c York St Luke *York* 75-77; V 77-80; V Hatton w Haseley and Rowington w Lowsonford *Cov* 80-82; V Derringham Bank *York* 82-85; R Southacre 85; R Castle Acre w Newton, Rougham and Southacre 85-86; TV Grantham *Linc* 86-89; V Cayton w Eastfield *York* from 89. *The Vicarage, Eastfield, Scarborough, N Yorkshire YO11 3EE* Scarborough (0723) 582428

LONG, Dr Peter Ronald. b 48. Nottm Univ BA69 Man Univ CertEd70 DPT71. Cuddesdon Coll 71. **d** 73 **p** 74. Chapl RAFVR from 74; C Bodmin *Truro* 73-75; C Newquay 75-76; Asst Youth Chapl 75-76; Dioc Youth Chapl 76-79; Perm to Offic *Eur* 76, 78-85 and from 87; P-in-c Mawgan w St Martin-in-Meneage *Truro* 76 and 79-82; Chapl Helston Meneage Geriatric Hosp from 80; Miss to Seamen from 80; P-in-c Cury w Gunwalloe *Truro* 80-82; R Cury and Gunwalloe w Mawgan from 83; Perm to Offic *Ex* from 82. *The Rectory, Mawgan, Helston, Cornwall TR12 6AD* Mawgan (032622) 293

LONG, Canon Samuel Ernest. b 18. JP68. ALCD50 MTh88 ThD90. **d** 49 **p** 50. I Dromara w Garvaghy *D & D*

56-85; Can Dromore Cathl 81-85; Treas 82-85; rtd 85. *9 Cairnshill Court, Saintfield Road, Belfast BT8 4TX* Belfast (0232) 793401

LONG, Simon Richard. b 40. Birm Univ DPS69. Bernard Gilpin Soc Dur 61 Ely Th Coll 62 Coll of Resurr Mirfield 64. **d** 65 **p** 66. C Bournemouth St Fran *Win* 65-68; Belgium 68; USA 69-88; P-in-c Medbourne cum Holt w Stockerston and Blaston *Leic* 88-89; P-in-c Bringhurst w Gt Easton 88-89; R Six Saints circa Holt from 90. *The Rectory, Rectory Lane, Medbourne, Market Harborough, Leics LE16 8DZ* Medbourne Green (085883) 419

LONG, William Thomas. b 53. TCD DipTh81 Dur Univ MA88. **d** 81 **p** 82. C Orangefield *D & D* 81-84; C Portadown St Mark *Arm* 84-86; I Dromara w Garvaghy *D & D* 86-91; I Aghalurcher w Tattykeeran, Cooneen etc *Clogh* from 91. *St Ronan's Rectory, Killarbran, Fivemiletown, Co Tyrone* Fivemiletown (03655) 3264

LONGBOTHAM, Richard Ashley. b 14. AKC36. Sarum Th Coll 37. **d** 37 **p** 38. Rhodesia and S Africa 47-80; rtd 81. *c/o Box 172, Irene, TVL, 1657 South Africa*

LONGBOTTOM, Canon Frank. b 41. Lon Univ DipTh68 Birm Univ DPS74. Ripon Hall Ox 65. **d** 68 **p** 69. C Epsom St Martin *Guildf* 68-72; Chapl Highcroft Hosp Birm from 72; Chapl Northcroft Hosp Birm from 74; Dioc Adv for Past Care of Clergy from 89; Hon Can Birm Cathl *Birm* from 91. *46 Sunnybank Road, Sutton Coldfield, W Midlands B73 5RE* 021-350 5823 or 378 2211

LONGBOTTOM, Paul Edward. b 44. AKC67. **d** 68 **p** 69. C Rainham *Roch* 68-71; C Riverhead 71-75; C Dunton Green 71-75; V Penge Lane H Trin 75-84; V Chatham St Wm from 84. *The Vicarage, Marion Close, Chatham, Kent* Medway (0634) 61975

LONGENECKER, Dwight Leigh. b 56. Wycliffe Hall Ox 79. **d** 83 **p** 84. C Bexhill St Pet *Chich* 83-87; Chapl K Coll Choir Sch Cam 87-89; R Brading w Yaverland *Portsm* from 89. *The Vicarage, Mall Road, Brading, Sandown, Isle of Wight PO36 0DE* Isle of Wight (0983) 407262

LONGFIELD, Thomas Edwin. b 29. St Jo Coll Nottm. **d** 71 **p** 72. C Leamington Priors St Mary *Cov* 71-74; V Potters Green 75-88; rtd 88. *55 North Road, Great Clacton, Clacton-on-Sea, Essex CO15 4DF*

LONGFOOT, Richard. b 46. Oak Hill Th Coll 76. **d** 78 **p** 79. C Chaddesden St Mary *Derby* 78-81; C Cam St Martin *Ely* 81-83; R Folksworth w Morborne 83-89; R Stilton w Denton and Caldecote 83-89; R Stilton w Denton and Caldecote etc from 90. *The Rectory, Stilton, Peterborough PE7 3RF* Peterborough (0733) 240282

LONGFORD, Canon Edward de Toesny Wingfield. b 25. Ch Ch Ox BA48 MA53. Wells Th Coll 49. **d** 51 **p** 52. P-in-c Everton w Tetworth *Ely* 68-71; V 71-73; R Gamlingay 68-80; P-in-c Hatley 78-80; Hon Can Ely Cathl from 79; R Gamlingay w Hatley St Geo and E Hatley 80-90; RD St Neots 82-90; rtd 90. *9 Philippa Close, Ely CB6 1BT* Ely (0353) 667495

LONGMAN, Edward. b 37. Hatf Coll Dur BSc62 Fitzw Ho Cam BA66. Clifton Th Coll 62 Ridley Hall Cam 64. **d** 66 **p** 67. C Lower Homerton St Paul *Lon* 66-72; C Parr *Liv* 72-73; TV 74-85; Perm to Offic from 86. *66 Hard Lane, Dentons Green, St Helens, Merseyside WA10 2LA* St Helens (0744) 55667

LONGMAN, Canon Edward George. b 35. St Pet Hall Ox BA58 MA62. Westcott Ho Cam 59. **d** 61 **p** 62. C Sheff Broomhall St Mark *Sheff* 61-65; V Brightside St Thos 65-74; V Yardley St Edburgha *Birm* 74-84; RD Yardley 77-84; Hon Can Birm Cathl from 81; R Sutton Coldfield H Trin from 84; Chapl Gd Hope Hosp Sutton Coldfield 84-90. *16 Coleshill Street, Sutton Coldfield, W Midlands B72 1SH* 021-354 3607

LONGRIDGE, Peter Nevile. b 12. St Edm Hall Ox BA34 MA59. Westcott Ho Cam 34. **d** 36 **p** 37. R Highweek *Ex* 59-77; rtd 77. *4 The Path, Irsha Street, Appledore, Bideford, Devon EX39 1RU* Bideford (0237) 676042

LONGRIDGE, Richard Nevile. b 15. Sarum Th Coll 46. **d** 48 **p** 49. R Spetisbury w Charlton Marshall *Sarum* 67-77; rtd 77; Perm to Offic *Ex* from 78. *27 East Avenue, Heavitree, Exeter EX1 2DX* Exeter (0392) 435866

LONGWORTH, Arthur Victor. b 24. Trin Coll Ox BA48 MA51. St Steph Ho Ox 48. **d** 49 **p** 50. CR from 54; C Rubery *Birm* 69-70; Vice-Prin Chich Th Coll 70-73; V Walsgrave on Sowe *Cov* 73-75; Dioc Dir of Ords 73-80; V Bishop's Tachbrook 75-80; V Sheff St Matt *Sheff* 80-89; Ind Chapl 80-87; rtd 89. *18 Sycamore Avenue, Garstang, Preston PR3 1FR* Garstang (0995) 603145

LONGWORTH-DAMES, Canon Francis Robert. b 12. Jes Coll Cam BA34 MA38. Westcott Ho Cam 36. **d** 37 **p** 38.

R Warlingham w Chelsham and Farleigh *S'wark* 65-73; V Catford St Andr 74-81; rtd 81. *Top Flat, 36 Evesham Road, Cheltenham, Glos GL52 2AB* Cheltenham (0242) 239830

LONSDALE, Canon Rupert Philip. b 05. Ridley Hall Cam 47. **d** 48 **p** 49. V Thornham w Titchwell *Nor* 65-70; rtd 70; Chapl Puerto de la Cruz Tenerife *Eur* 70-73. *Reepham House, Bastion Square, Mdina, Malta*

LOOKER, Clare Margaret. b 55. Liv Univ CertEd DipRE. Westcott Ho Cam 85. **d** 87. Par Dn Prestwood and Gt Hampden *Ox* 87-90; rtd 90; Hon C Olney w Emberton *Ox* from 90. *4 Oxleys, Olney, Bucks MK46 5PH* Bedford (0234) 733448

LOONE, Sean Joseph Patrick. b 60. Cov Poly BA83 Wolv Poly CertEd84 Leeds Univ BA88. Coll of Resurr Mirfield 86. **d** 89 **p** 90. C Solihull *Birm* from 89. *17 Church Hill Close, Solihull, W Midlands B91 3QR* 021-705 8923

LOPDELL-BRADSHAW, Canon Humphrey Maitland. b 32. Edin Th Coll 58. **d** 61 **p** 62. C Edin H Cross *Edin* 61-65; C Edin St Barn 65-67; P-in-c Oldbury *Birm* 67-68; V 68-72; R Edin St Hilda *Edin* 72-77; R Hawick 77-88; R Isla-Deveron Gp Moray *Mor* from 88; R Huntly from 88; R Aberchirder from 88; R Keith from 88; Can St Andr Cathl Inverness from 91. *The Rectory, Seafield Avenue, Keith, Banffshire AB55 3BS* Keith (05422) 2782

LOPEZ FERREIRO, Serafín Julio. b 35. Dur Univ BA74 DipTh71. St Jo Coll Dur. **d** 71 **p** 72. C S Lambeth St Steph *S'wark* 71-75; C Upper Tooting H Trin 76-78; P-in-c Tooting St Aug 78-83; V from 83. *St Augustine's Vicarage, 99 Broadwater Road, London SW17 0DY* 081-672 4712

LORAINE, Kenneth. b 34. Cranmer Hall Dur 63. **d** 66 **p** 67. C Hartlepool All SS Stranton *Dur* 66-69; C Darlington St Cuth 69-72; V Preston on Tees 72-79; V Staindrop 79-87; P-in-c Haynes *St Alb* from 87; Dioc Stewardship Adv from 87. *The Vicarage, 4A North Lane, Haynes, Bedford MK45 3PW* Haynes (023066) 235

LORD, Alexander. b 13. ALCD43. **d** 43 **p** 44. R Illogan *Truro* 70-81; rtd 81; C Letton w Staunton, Byford, Mansel Gamage etc *Heref* 81-84. *43 Narrow Lane, Llandudno Junction, Gwynedd LL31 9SZ* Aberconwy (0492) 584647

LORD, Charles James. b 12. Birm Univ BSc38 Trent Poly LLB85. **d** 44 **p** 45. V Hatton w Haseley *Cov* 53-71; Chapl Rampton Hosp Retford 71-81; rtd 81. *Conifers, Back Lane, Barnby-in-the-Willows, Newark, Notts NG24 2SD* Newark (0636) 626622

LORD, Canon John Fairbourne. b 19. Kelham Th Coll 38. **d** 43 **p** 44. RD Holt *Nor* 64-79; R Thornage w Brinton w Hunworth and Stody 64-84; Hon Can Nor Cathl 77-84; rtd 84; Perm to Offic *Nor* from 84. *4 London Road, Hindolveston, Dereham, Norfolk NR20 5DB* Melton Constable (0263) 860819

LORD, Kenneth Frank. b 14. Clifton Th Coll 34. **d** 38 **p** 40. V Skelton cum Newby *Ripon* 53-81; rtd 81. *The Vicarage, Skelton-on-Ure, Ripon, N Yorkshire HG4 5AJ* Boroughbridge (0423) 322864

LORD, Stuart James. b 59. K Coll Lon BD81 AKC81. Sarum & Wells Th Coll 83. **d** 85 **p** 86. C Darwen St Pet w Hoddlesden *Blackb* 85-88; C Otley *Bradf* from 88. *73 Clair Road, Otley, W Yorkshire LS21 1DE* Otley (0943) 463753

LORIMER, Eileen Jean. b 35. CertEd56. Dalton Ho Bris 62. **dss** 84 **d** 89. Chiddingstone w Chiddingstone Causeway *Roch* 84-89; NSM from 89. *Slaters Hill, Bough Beech, Edenbridge, Kent TN8 7NU* Four Elms (073270) 303

LORING, John Henry. b 06. K Coll Cam BA28 MA32. Cuddesdon Coll 29. **d** 31 **p** 32. V Soulbury w Stoke Hammond *Ox* 58-72; rtd 72. *8 Palmers, Wantage, Oxon OX12 7HB* Wantage (02357) 4254

LOSACK, Marcus Charles. b 53. Ch Coll Cam BA76 MA78. Sarum & Wells Th Coll 78. **d** 80 **p** 81. C Hattersley *Ches* 80-82; C Dub Zion Ch *D & G* 83-86; Libya 86-89; CMS from 89; Jerusalem from 89. *c/o St George's College, PO Box 1248, Jerusalem, Israel*

LOSEBY, Everitt James Carnall. b 22. Launde Abbey. **d** 66 **p** 67. C Thurmaston *Leic* 66-70; R Seagrave w Walton le Wolds 70-75; V Thurnby Lodge 75-84; V Swinford w Catthorpe, Shawell and Stanford 84-87; rtd 87; Perm to Offic *Leic* from 87. *63 Willow Road, Blaby, Leicester LE8 3BG* Leicester (0533) 771983

LOUDEN, Terence Edmund. b 48. Ch Coll Cam BA70 MA74. Sarum & Wells Th Coll 72. **d** 75 **p** 76. C Portsea N End St Mark *Portsm* 75-78; C-in-c Leigh Park St Clare CD 78-81; R Chale 81-88; R Niton 81-88; P-in-c Whitwell 82-84; V Cosham from 88. *St Philip's Vicarage,*

Hawthorn Crescent, Cosham, Portsmouth PO6 2TL Cosham (0705) 326179

LOUGHBOROUGH, Archdeacon of. See JONES, Ven Thomas Hughie

LOUGHEED, Canon Brian Frederick Britain. b 38. TCD BA60. CITC 61. **d** 61 **p** 62. C Dub St Pet w St Audoen *D & G* 61-63; C Glenageary 63-66; I Rathmolyon Union *M & K* 66-79; I Killarney w Aghadoe and Muckross *L & K* from 79; Can Limerick and Killaloe Cathls from 87; Preb Taney St Patr Cathl Dub from 89; Dioc Info Officer (Limerick) *L & K* 90-91; Radio Officer from 91. *Appartment 3, Sunday's Well, Countess Road, Killarney, Co Kerry, Irish Republic* Killarney (64) 31832

LOUGHLIN, Canon Alfred. b 10. Clifton Th Coll 37. **d** 39 **p** 40. R Kinson *Sarum* 54-81; rtd 81. *18 Donnelly Road, Bournemouth BH6 5NW* Bournemouth (0202) 422306

LOUGHLIN, George Alfred Graham. b 43. Lon Univ DipTh68. Clifton Th Coll 65. **d** 69 **p** 70. C Plumstead All SS *S'wark* 69-73; C Bromley Ch Ch *Roch* 73-76; P-in-c Bothenhampton w Walditch *Sarum* 76-79; TV Bridport 79-83; V Heatherlands St Jo from 83. *St John's Vicarage, 72 Alexandra Road, Poole, Dorset BH14 9EW* Parkstone (0202) 741276

LOUGHTON, Michael. b 34. K Coll Lon BD58 AKC58. **d** 59 **p** 60. C Chingford SS Pet and Paul *Chelmsf* 59-62; C Eastbourne St Eliz *Chich* 62-65; R Lewes St Jo sub Castro 65-74; Perm to Offic from 87. *Follers Manor, Seaford Road, Alfriston, Polegate, E Sussex BN26 5TT* Alfriston (0323) 870252

LOUIS, Peter Anthony. b 41. St Cath Coll Ox BA63 MA77 Jes Coll Cam CertEd64 Man Univ MPhil85. Wells Th Coll 66. **d** 68 **p** 70. C E Grinstead St Mary *Chich* 68-75; C Radcliffe-on-Trent *S'well* 75-80; Hd Master Blue Coat Comp Sch Cov 80-85; V Welwyn Garden City *St Alb* from 85. *The Vicarage, 48 Parkway, Welwyn Garden City, Herts AL8 6HH* Welwyn Garden (0707) 323316

LOUW, Paul Leonard. b 32. Leeds Univ BA56 Port Eliz Univ MA79. Coll of Resurr Mirfield 56. **d** 58 **p** 59. C Solihull *Birm* 58-61; S Africa from 61. *55 Main Road, Walmer, Port Elizabeth, 6070 South Africa* Port Elizabeth (41) 513588

LOVATT, Bernard James. b 31. Lich Th Coll 64. **d** 65 **p** 66. C Burford III w Lt Heref 65-67; C Cleobury Mortimer w Hopton Wafers 67-68; C Bradford-on-Avon *Sarum* 68-69; C Wootton Bassett 69-72; C Broad Town 69-72; R Bishopstrow and Boreham 72-79; P-in-c Brighton St Geo *Chich* 79-83; V Brighton St Anne 79-83; V Brighton St Geo and St Anne 83-86; P-in-c Kemp Town St Mark and St Matt 85-86; V Brighton St Geo w St Anne and St Mark from 86. *St George's Vicarage, 33 Eaton Place, Brighton BN2 1EG* Brighton (0273) 699779

LOVATT, William Robert. b 54. SS Coll Cam BA75 K Coll Lon CertEd77 MA78. Oak Hill Th Coll 85. **d** 87 **p** 88. C Devonport St Budeaux *Ex* 87-90; Asst Chapl Paris St Mich *Eur* from 90. *5 rue d'Aguesseau, 75008 Paris, France* Paris (331) 47 42 70 88

LOVE, Ms Anette. b 53. Matlock Coll of Educn CertEd74 Nottm Univ BEd75. St Jo Coll Dur 88. **d** 90. Par Dn Gresley *Derby* from 90. *126 Chiltern Road, Swadlincote, Burton-on-Trent, Staffs DE11 9SW* Burton-on-Trent (0283) 224645

LOVE, Canon Hector William. b 07. TCD BA31 MA34. CITC 31. **d** 31 **p** 32. I Ballymascanlan w Carlingford and Omeath *Arm* 66-73; rtd 73. *4 St Elizabeth's Court, Ballyregan Road, Dundonald, Belfast BT16 0HX* Belfast (0232) 481938

LOVE, Richard Angus. b 45. AKC67. **d** 68 **p** 69. C Balham Hill Ascension *S'wark* 68-71; C Amersham *Ox* 71-73; R Scotter w E Ferry *Linc* 73-79; P-in-c Petham w Waltham and Lower Hardres w Nackington *Cant* 79-85; R Petham and Waltham w Lower Hardres etc 85-90; V Sittingbourne H Trin w Bobbing from 90. *Holy Trinity Vicarage, 47 London Road, Sittingbourne, Kent ME10 1NQ* Sittingbourne (0795) 472724

LOVE, Robert. b 45. Bradf Univ BSc68 PhD74 NE Lon Poly PGCE89. Trin Coll Bris DipTh75. **d** 75 **p** 76. C Bowling St Jo *Bradf* 75-79; TV Forest Gate St Sav w W Ham St Matt *Chelmsf* 79-85; P-in-c Becontree St Eliz from 85. *St Elizabeth's Vicarage, Hewett Road, Dagenham, Essex RM8 2XT* 081-517 0355

LOVEDAY, Joseph Michael. b 54. AKC75. St Aug Coll Cant 75. **d** 78 **p** 79. C Kettering SS Pet and Paul *Pet* 78-81; C Upper Teddington SS Pet and Paul *Lon* 81-84; CF from 84. *c/o MOD (Army), Bagshot Park, Bagshot, Surrey GU19 5PL* Bagshot (0276) 71717

LOVEGROVE, Anne Maureen. b 44. DipHE90. Oak Hill Th Coll 88. **d** 90. Par Dn Thorley *St Alb* from 90.

50 Thorley Lane, Thorley, Bishop's Stortford, Herts CM23 4AD Bishop's Stortford (0279) 655631

LOVEGROVE, Walter John. b 19. Dur Univ LTh44. St Aug Coll Cant 38. **d** 42 **p** 43. S Africa 47-72 and from 83; V Chaddesden St Phil *Derby* 72-75; P-in-c Tintinhull *B & W* 75; R Tintinhull w Chilthorne Domer, Yeovil Marsh etc 75-80; RD Martock 78-80; P-in-c Norbury St Phil *Cant* 80-81; V 81-83; rtd 86. *4 The Anchorage, Palace Hill Road, Simonstown, 7995 South Africa* Simonstown (21) 863218

LOVEJOY, Geoffrey William. b 08. St Chad's Coll Dur BA31 LTh31 MA47. Dorchester Miss Coll 28. **d** 32 **p** 33. R Stoke Goldington w Gayhurst *Ox* 65-72; P-in-c Ravenstone w Weston Underwood 67-72; rtd 73; Chapl Sevenoaks Hosp 73-79; Hon C Sevenoaks St Jo *Roch* 73-88; Perm to Offic from 88. *61 Old Mill Close, Eynsford, Dartford DA4 0BN* Farningham (0322) 866186

LOVEJOY, James Allan. b 06. Jes Coll Cam BA28 MA35. Westcott Ho Cam 35. **d** 36 **p** 37. V Westleton w Dunwich *St E* 67-74; V Darsham 71-74; rtd 74; Perm to Offic *St E* from 74. *28 Pembroke Road, Framlingham, Woodbridge, Suffolk IP13 9HA* Framlingham (0728) 723214

LOVEJOY, John Geoffrey. b 35. K Coll Lon BD60 AKC60. **d** 61 **p** 62. C Byker St Laur *Newc* 61-64; C Choppington 64-66; C Usworth *Dur* 66-70; Perm to Offic *Carl* 73-77; Algeria 77-78; Australia 79-84 and 86-88; NSM Isla-Deveron Gp Moray *Mor* 85-86; Perm to Offic *S'wark* from 88. *30 Woodside Road, Sutton, Surrey SM1 3SU* 081-644 4151

LOVELAND, John Michael. b 30. Roch Th Coll 65. **d** 67 **p** 68. C Ashford St Hilda CD *Lon* 67-71; P-in-c Earley St Nic *Ox* 71-76; V 76-79; V Kennington 79-84; V Reading St Mark 84-89; P-in-c Drayton St Pet (Berks) from 89. *The Vicarage, 8 Gravel Lane, Drayton, Abingdon, Oxon OX14 4HY* Abingdon (0235) 531374

LOVELESS, Christopher Hugh. b 61. Trin Coll Ox BA84 MA91. Linc Th Coll 89. **d** 91. C Willingdon *Chich* from 91. *11 Winchester Way, Willingdon, Eastbourne, E Sussex BN22 0JP* Eastbourne (0323) 509659

LOVELESS, Kenneth Norman Joseph. b 11. MBE90 VRD61. FSA FSAScot. Chich Th Coll. **d** 49 **p** 50. Chapl RNR from 53; V Hoxton H Trin w St Mary *Lon* 54-68; RD Hackney 67-74; rtd 76; Lic to Offic *Lon* from 76. *3 Clothworkers' Cottages, Bishop Street, London N1 8PH* 071-359 9179

LOVELESS, Martin Frank. b 46. Wycliffe Hall Ox 72. **d** 75 **p** 76. C Caversham *Ox* 75-81; V Carterton 81-86; Chapl RAF from 86. *c/o MOD, Adastral House, Theobald's Road, London WC1X 8RU* 071-430 7260

LOVELESS, Robert Alfred. b 43. Birm Univ BA66. Westcott Ho Cam 66. **d** 68 **p** 69. C Kenilworth St Nic *Cov* 68-72; C Costessey *Nor* 73-75; R Colney 75-80; R Lt w Gt Melton, Marlingford and Bawburgh 75-80; V Lt and Gt Melton w Bawburgh 80-82; P-in-c Westwood *Sarum* 82-83; Chapl Stonar Sch Melksham 82-87; P-in-c Wingfield w Rowley *Sarum* 82-83; R Westwood and Wingfield 83-87; R Paston *Pet* from 87. *The Rectory, 236 Fulbridge Road, Peterborough PE4 6SN* Peterborough (0733) 71943

LOVELESS, Canon William Harry. b 21. Lon Univ BSc60. Ridley Hall Cam 61. **d** 63 **p** 64. V Cam St Mark *Ely* 67-87; RD Cam 81-84; Hon Can Ely Cathl from 81; rtd 87. *10 Barratts Close, Langworth Gate, Lincoln LN2 4AF*

LOVELL, Charles Nelson. b 34. Or Coll Ox BA57 MA61. Wycliffe Hall Ox. **d** 59 **p** 60. C Walsall St Matt *Lich* 59-63; C St Giles-in-the-Fields *Lon* 63; Argentina 64-67; C Cam H Trin *Ely* 64; V Esh *Dur* 67-75; V Hamsteels 67-75; Chapl Winterton Hosp Sedgefield 75-83; R Stanhope *Dur* 83-86; Chapl Horn Hall Hosp Weardale from 83; R Stanhope w Frosterley *Dur* from 86; V Eastgate w Rookhope from 86; RD Stanhope from 87. *The Rectory, Stanhope, Bishop Auckland, Co Durham DL13 2UE* Weardale (03885) 528308

LOVELL, David John. b 38. JP89. Univ of Tasmania BEcon86. Qu Coll Birm 60. **d** 60 **p** 62. C Glouc St Steph *Glouc* 60-64; C Lower Tuffley St Geo CD 64-67; V Lydbrook 67-73; Australia from 73. *23 Lucas Street, Kingston, Tasmania, Australia 7050* Tasmania (29) 5709

LOVELL, Frederick Arthur. b 07. Chich Th Coll 31. **d** 34 **p** 35. R Combe Martin *Ex* 53-73; rtd 74. *18 Trelawney Avenue, Poughill, Bude, Cornwall* Bude (0288) 353237

LOVELL, Canon Harold Guildford. b 90. **d** 14 **p** 15. R Essendon and Woodhill *St Alb* 52-64; rtd 64; Perm to Offic *St Alb* from 64. *1 Church Street, Hatfield, Herts AL9 5AR* Hatfield (0707) 265275

LOVELL, Keith Michael Beard. b 43. K Coll Lon 67. **d** 68 **p** 69. C Romford St Edw *Chelmsf* 68-73; P-in-c Elmstead

73-79; V Tollesbury w Salcot Virley from 79. *The Vicarage, 12 Kings Walk, Tollesbury, Maldon, Essex CM9 8XH* Maldon (0621) 869393

LOVELL, Laurence John. b 31. St D Coll Lamp BA54 Tyndale Hall Bris. **d** 56 **p** 57. C Penge Ch Ch w H Trin *Roch* 56-60; C Illogan *Truro* 60-63; V St Keverne 63-68; Australia from 68. *St Paul's Rectory, 65 Rosa Street, Oatley, NSW, Australia 2223* Sydney (2) 580-8950

LOVELUCK, Allan (Illtyd). b 30. Queensland Univ MSocWork72. St D Coll Lamp BA53 St Mich Coll Llan 53. **d** 55 **p** 56. C Dowlais *Llan* 55-58; SSF 58-79; Lic to Offic *Chelmsf* 62-64; Australia from 64. *St James's Cathedral, Townsville, Queensland, Australia 4810*

LOVELUCK, Arthur Howell. b 19. St Mich Coll Llan 46. **d** 49 **p** 50. V Williton *B & W* 63-83; rtd 84; Perm to Offic *B & W* from 84. *21 Combeland Road, Alcombe, Minehead, Somerset TA24 6BS* Minehead (0643) 704351

LOVELUCK, Graham David. b 34. CChem FRSC Univ of Wales (Abth) BSc55 PhD58. St Deiniol's Hawarden 77. **d** 78 **p** 79. Hon C Llanfair Mathafarneithaf w Llanbedrgoch *Ban* 78-87; Hon C Llaneugrad w Llanallgo and Penrhosllugwy etc from 87. *Gwenallt, Marianglas, Gwynedd LL73 8PE* Tyn-y-Gongl (0248) 853741

LOVELY, Leslie Walter. b 09. Dur Univ LTh32. **d** 32 **p** 33. C Southn St Alb *Win* 32-35; Egypt 35-43; S Africa from 43. *5 Hagen Road, Greenside, 2193 South Africa* Johannesburg (11) 646-9599

LOVERIDGE, Douglas Henry. b 52. Sarum & Wells Th Coll. **d** 84 **p** 85. C Earley St Pet *Ox* 84-88; V Hurst from 88. *The Vicarage, Hurst, Reading RG10 0SJ* Twyford (0734) 340017

LOVERING, Mrs Jennifer Mary. b 39. Eastbourne Tr Coll CertEd59. Wycliffe Hall Ox 81. **dss** 84 **d** 87. Abingdon w Shippon *Ox* 84-87; Par Dn Abingdon from 87. *54 Picklers Hill, Abingdon, Oxon OX14 2BB* Abingdon (0235) 521371

LOVERING, Martin. b 35. Imp Coll Lon BScEng57 DMS66. Wycliffe Hall Ox 82. **d** 84 **p** 85. NSM Abingdon w Shippon *Ox* 84-88; C Abingdon 88-89; TV from 89. *54 Picklers Hill, Abingdon, Oxon OX14 2BB* Abingdon (0235) 521371

LOVETT, Francis Roland. b 25. Glouc Th Course. **d** 85 **p** 86. NSM Ludlow *Heref* from 85. *7 Poyner Road, Ludlow, Shropshire SY8 1QT* Ludlow (0584) 2470

LOVETT, Ian Arthur. b 43. NE Lon Poly BSc74 Ox Poly DipTP73. Linc Th Coll 85. **d** 87 **p** 88. C Uppingham w Ayston and Wardley w Belton *Pet* from 87. *4 Johnson Road, Uppingham, Oakham, Leics LE15 9RZ* Uppingham (0572) 822640

LOVETT, Ian James. b 49. S'wark Ord Course 73. **d** 76 **p** 77. NSM Gravesend St Geo *Roch* 76-77; NSM Willesborough w Hinxhill *Cant* 77-83; Perm to Offic *Ex* 83-85; C Compton Gifford 85; C Plymouth Em w Efford 85-86; TV from 86. *1 Yeo Close, Blandford Road, Efford, Plymouth PL3 6ER* Plymouth (0752) 785576

LOVEWELL, Robert Antony. b 34. Lich Th Coll. **d** 62 **p** 63. C Endcliffe *Sheff* 62-65; Miss to Seamen 65-79; Portuguese E Africa 65-73; V Whitton York 73-79; TV Thornaby on Tees 79-81; Ind Chapl *Ex* from 81. *65 Easterdown Close, Plymstock, Plymouth, Devon PL9 8SR* Plymouth (0752) 552323 or 402103

LOVITT, Gerald Elliott. b 25. St Mich Coll Llan 59. **d** 61 **p** 62. C Aberdare *Llan* 61-66; C Whitchurch 66-71; V Grangetown 71-76; V Rockfield and Llangattock w St Maughan's *Mon* 76-83; V Rockfield and St Maughen's w Llangattock etc from 83. *The Vicarage, Rockfield, Monmouth, Gwent NP5 3QB* Monmouth (0600) 2003

LOW, David Anthony. b 42. AKC66. **d** 67 **p** 68. C Gillingham St Barn *Roch* 67-70; V 82-88; C Wallingford *Ox* 70-73; V Spencer's Wood 73-82; P-in-c Grazeley and Beech Hill 77-82; Chapl Medway Hosp Gillingham 86-88; V Hoo St Werburgh *Roch* from 88. *The Vicarage, Hoo, Rochester, Kent ME3 9BB* Medway (0634) 250291

LOW, David John. b 32. Bris Univ BA53. Wells Th Coll 55. **d** 57 **p** 58. C Bradf Ch Ch *Man* 57-59; C Benchill 59-62; V Newbold 62-75; R Moston St Mary from 75. *St Mary's Rectory, 47 Nuthurst Road, Moston, Manchester M10 0EW* 061-681 1201

LOW, David Michael. b 39. Cape Town Univ BA60. Cuddesdon Coll 61. **d** 63 **p** 64. C Portsea St Cuth *Portsm* 63-65; S Africa 65-69; C Havant *Portsm* 69-72; V St Helens 72-88; P-in-c Sea View 80-81; V 81-88; V Sandwich Ch Ch from 88. *The Vicarage, 26 Nunwell Street, Sandown, Isle of Wight PO36 9DE* Isle of Wight (0983) 402548

LOW, John Edmund. b 09. Lon Univ BA32 AKC34. **d** 34 **p** 35. V Bedf Leigh *Man* 51-77; rtd 77. *98 Collingwood Road, Chorley, Lancs PR7 2PT* Chorley (02572) 70285

LOW, Peter James. b 52. Nottm Univ BTh89. Linc Th Coll 86. **d** 89 **p** 90. C Dartford H Trin *Roch* from 89. *68 Priory Road, Dartford, Kent DA1 2BS* Dartford (0322) 278655

LOW, Stafford. b 42. N Lon Poly BSc65. Trin Coll Bris 82. **d** 85 **p** 86. C Yeovil *B & W* 85-88; C Glastonbury w Meare, W Pennard and Godney from 88. *The Parsonage, St Mary's Road, Meare, Glastonbury, Somerset BA6 9SR* Meare Heath (04586) 276

LOW, Terence John Gordon. b 37. Oak Hill Th Coll 75. **d** 77 **p** 78. C Kensal Rise St Martin *Lon* 77-79; C Longfleet *Sarum* 79-83; P-in-c Maiden Newton and Valleys 83-84; TV Melbury 84-88; TV Buckhurst Hill *Chelmsf* from 88. *10 Albert Road, Buckhurst Hill, Essex IG9 6EH* 081-504 6698

LOW, William Roberson. b 50. Pemb Coll Cam BA73 MA77. Westcott Ho Cam 76. **d** 79 **p** 80. C Poplar *Lon* 79-83; Chapl St Alb Abbey *St Alb* 83-88; V Bushey Heath from 88. *St Peter's Vicarage, 19 High Road, Bushey Heath, Watford WD2 1EA* 081-950 1424

LOWATER, Jennifer Blanche. b 34. Eastbourne Tr Coll TCert54. Sarum & Wells Th Coll 82. **dss** 85 **d** 87. Locks Heath *Portsm* 85-87; Hon C 87-88; NSM Southsea St Pet 88-91; Asst Dir of Ords from 91. *Lower Gubbles, Hook Lane, Warsash, Southampton SO3 9HH* Locks Heath (0489) 572156

LOWCOCK, Brian Walter. b 23. Man Univ LLB43. Linc Th Coll 56. **d** 57 **p** 58. Perm to Offic *Linc* 68-73; Lic to Offic *Ely* 70-74; P-in-c Holbeach Marsh *Linc* 74-81; P-in-c Witham on the Hill 81; P-in-c Edenham 81; V Edenham w Witham-on-the-Hill 82-85; rtd 85; Perm to Offic *Ely* from 86. *2 The Chase, Ely, Cambs CB6 3DS* Ely (0353) 667641

LOWE, Alison Margaret. b 56. Linc Th Coll. **dss** 84 **d** 89. Knottingley *Wakef* 84-86; Par Educn Adv 86-89; Par Dn 89-90; Par Dn Edin Ch Ch *Edin* from 90. *6 Morningside Road, Edinburgh EH10 4DD* 031-228 6553

LOWE, Anthony Richard. b 45. York Univ BA66 Birm Univ DipTh68. Qu Coll Birm 66. **d** 69 **p** 70. C Greasbrough *Sheff* 69-71; C Thrybergh 71-75; P-in-c Sheff St Mary w St Simon w St Matthias 75-78; V Shiregreen St Hilda 78-85; V Hoxne w Denham St Jo and Syleham *St E* 85-89; P-in-c Wingfield 86-89; R Hoxne w Denham, Syleham and Wingfield from 90. *The Vicarage, Church Hill, Hoxne, Eye, Suffolk IP21 5AT* Hoxne (037975) 246

LOWE, Mrs Brenda June. b 53. Cranmer Hall Dur 75. **d** 88. Chapl to Families Trin Coll and Mortimer Ho Bris from 88. *12 Ridgehill, Bristol BS9 4SB* Bristol (0272) 621047

LOWE, David Charles. b 43. Kelham Th Coll 62. **d** 67 **p** 68. C Wingerworth *Derby* 67-70; C Greenhill St Pet 70-73; TV Eckington 73-74; TV Eckington w Handley and Ridgeway 74-78; V Bury St Edmunds St Geo *St E* 78-86; V Leiston from 86; RD Saxmundham from 88. *The Vicarage, 2 King Edward Road, Leiston, Suffolk IP16 4HQ* Leiston (0728) 831059

LOWE, David Reginald. b 42. K Coll Lon BD65 AKC65. St Boniface Warminster 65. **d** 66 **p** 67. C Tupsley *Heref* 66-69; C Lewes St Anne *Chich* 69-73; C Heref H Trin *Heref* 73-77; P-in-c Lyonshall w Titley 77-88; V Lyonshall w Titley, Almeley and Kinnersley from 88. *The Vicarage, Lyonshall, Kington, Herefordshire HR5 3LN* Lyonshall (05448) 212

LOWE, Derrick. b 34. Codrington Coll Barbados 58. **d** 60 **p** 61. Br Guiana 60-64; R Kirkwall *Ab* 65-69; R Ardwick St Benedict *Man* from 69. *The Presbytery, Bennett Street, Manchester M12 5BD* 061-223 0154

LOWE, Donald. b 33. Lich Th Coll 57. **d** 60 **p** 61. C Horwich H Trin *Man* 60; C Wythenshawe St Martin CD 60-62; C Bury St Paul 62-65; S Africa 65-69 and 73-81; V Gannow *Blackb* 70-73; V Colne H Trin 81-89; TV Melbury *Sarum* from 89. *The Vicarage, Maiden Newton, Dorchester, Dorset DT2 0AT* Maiden Newton (0300) 20284

LOWE, Canon Eric. b 29. Trin Coll Ox BA50 MA54. St Steph Ho Ox 50. **d** 52 **p** 53. C Ellesmere Port *Ches* 52-55; C Hucknall Torkard *S'well* 55-56; C Solihull *Birm* 56-58; Area Sec (NW England) UMCA 58-65; Lic to Offic *Ches & Ban* 65-88; Area Sec (Dios Ches, Ban and St As) USPG 65-88; Dio Liv 73-85; Perm to Offic *Liv* from 73; V Frodsham *Ches* from 88. *The Vicarage, Frodsham, Warrington WA6 7DU* Frodsham (0928) 33378

LOWE, Canon John Bethel. b 30. TCD BA52 BD65. Ridley Hall Cam 55. **d** 55 **p** 56. C Belf St Mary Magd

Conn 55-57; Sudan 59-64; Uganda 64-74; Warden CMS Fellowship Ho Foxbury 74-76; V Kippington *Roch* from 76; Dioc Dir of Ords from 82; Hon Can Roch Cathl from 85. *The Vicarage, 59 Kippington Road, Sevenoaks, Kent TN13 2LL* Sevenoaks (0732) 452112

LOWE, John Forrester. b 39. Nottm Univ BA61. Lich Th Coll 61. **d** 64 **p** 65. C N Woolwich *Chelmsf* 64-70; V Marks Gate 70-74; V Moulsham St Jo 74-79; V N Woolwich w Silvertown 79-82; V Birm St Pet *Birm* 82-86; Gen Sec Sharing of Min Abroad from 86. *50 Wivelsfield Road, Haywards Heath, W Sussex RH16 4EW* Haywards Heath (0444) 454531

LOWE, Michael Arthur. b 46. Lon Univ BD67 Hull Univ MA85. Cranmer Hall Dur DipTh75. **d** 76 **p** 77. C Thorpe Edge *Bradf* 76-79; C N Ferriby *York* 79-84; TV 84-86; Dir Past Studies Trin Coll Bris from 86. *Trinity College, Stoke Hill, Bristol BS9 1JP* Bristol (0272) 682803

LOWE, Michael Sinclair. b 35. Open Univ BA75 AKC61. **d** 62 **p** 63. C Wythenshawe Wm Temple Ch CD *Man* 62-66; V Facit 66-70; V Bath St Barn w Englishcombe *B & W* 70-79; V Bathford 79-86; V Branksome Park All SS *Sarum* from 86. *The Vicarage, 28 Western Road, Poole, Dorset BH13 7BP* Poole (0202) 708202

LOWE, Raymond John. b 12. OBE67. St Edm Hall Ox BA34 MA38. Sarum Th Coll 34. **d** 36 **p** 37. R Padworth *Ox* 70-77; V Mortimer W End 70-77; rtd 77; Perm to Offic *Ox* from 77. *75 Conifer Crest, Newbury, Berks RG14 6RS* Newbury (0635) 44723

LOWE, Canon Reginald Kenneth William. b 09. TCD BA31. **d** 32 **p** 33. I Blessington *D & G* 65-79; Treas Ch Ch Cathl Dub 74-79; rtd 79. *Glenbride Cottage, Kilpedder, Co Wicklow, Irish Republic* Dublin (1) 281-9211

LOWE, Richard (Brother Christopher). b 23. Birm Univ BSc44. Coll of Resurr Mirfield 46. **d** 48 **p** 49. C Victoria Docks Ascension *Chelmsf* 48-51; C Swindon New Town *Bris* 51-56; R Corringham *Chelmsf* 56-65; Lic to Offic *Wakef* 66-69 and from 86; CR from 67; Lic to Offic *Lon* from 69; Master R Foundn of St Kath in Ratcliffe from 82; Warden Community of St Denys Warminster 83-87. *St Katharine's Foundation, 2 Butcher Row, London E14 8DS* 071-790 3540

LOWE, Samuel. b 35. St D Coll Lamp. **d** 65 **p** 66. C Tenby w Gumfreston *St D* 65-67; C Lower Mitton *Worc* 67-69; C Halesowen 69-72; R Droitwich St Nic w St Pet 72-73; TV Droitwich 73-77; P-in-c Claines St Geo 77-78; P-in-c Worc St Mary the Tything 77-78; P-in-c Worc St Geo w St Mary Magd 78-84; V from 84. *St George's Vicarage, Worcester WR1 1HX* Worcester (0905) 22698

LOWE, Stephen Arthur. b 49. Nottm Univ BSc71 DipTh. Cuddesdon Coll 71. **d** 74 **p** 75. C Mansf St Mark *S'well* 74-77; Papua New Guinea 77-79; V Kirkby Woodhouse *S'well* 80-86; V Beeston from 86. *The Vicarage, Middle Street, Beeston, Nottingham NG9 1GA* Nottingham (0602) 254571

LOWE, Ven Stephen Richard. b 44. Lon Univ BSc66. Ripon Hall Ox 68. **d** 68 **p** 69. C Gospel Lane St Mich *Birm* 68-72; C-in-c Woodgate Valley CD 72-75; V E Ham w Upton Park *Chelmsf* 75-76; TR 76-88; Hon Can Chelmsf Cathl 85-88; Adn Sheff from 88. *23 Hill Turrets Close, Sheffield S11 9RE* Sheffield (0742) 350191

LOWELL, Ian Russell. b 53. AKC75. St Aug Coll Cant 75. **d** 76 **p** 77. C Llwynderw *S & B* 76-79; C Swansea St Mary w H Trin and St Mark 79-81; Chapl Ox Hosps 81-83; TV Gt and Lt Coates w Bradley *Linc* 83-88; V Wellingborough St Mark *Pet* from 88. *St Mark's Vicarage, Queensway, Wellingborough, Northants NN8 3SD* Wellingborough (0933) 673893

LOWEN, David John. b 42. **d** 88 **p** 89. C Carmarthen St Pet *St D* 88-90; P-in-c Walwyn's Castle w Robeston W from 90. *The Rectory, Walwyn's Castle, Haverfordwest, Dyfed SA26 3ED* Haverfordwest (0437) 781257

LOWEN, John Michael. b 47. Nottm Univ BTh77. Linc Th Coll 73. **d** 77 **p** 78. C Beeston *S'well* 77-80; C Stratford w Bishopton *Cov* 80-82; V Monkseaton St Mary *Newc* 82-90; V Ponteland from 90. *The Vicarage, Ponteland, Newcastle upon Tyne NE20 9PZ* Ponteland (0661) 22140

LOWERSON, John Ridley. b 41. FRHistS83 Leeds Univ BA62 MA65. S Dios Minl Tr Scheme 85. **d** 88 **p** 89. NSM Ringmer *Chich* from 88. *9 Bradford Road, Lewes, E Sussex BN7 9RB* Brighton (0273) 473413

LOWLES, Martin John. b 48. Thames Poly BSc72. St Jo Coll Dur DipTh78. **d** 78 **p** 79. C Leyton St Mary w St Edw *Chelmsf* 78-81; C Waltham Abbey 81-85; V E Ham St Paul from 85; Asst AD Newham from 91. *St Paul's Vicarage, 227 Burges Road, London E6 2EU* 081-472 5531

LOWMAN, David Walter. b 48. K Coll Lon BD73 AKC73. St Aug Coll Cant 73. **d** 75 **p** 76. C Notting Hill *Lon* 75-78; C Kilburn St Aug w St Jo 78-81; Selection Sec and Voc Adv ACCM 81-86; TR Wickford and Runwell *Chelmsf* from 86. *The Rectory, 120 Southend Road, Wickford, Essex SS11 8EB* Wickford (0268) 733147

LOWNDES, Charles. b 22. MISW57 CQSW72 Rotherham Poly DDW57. **d** 87 **p** 88. NSM Hanley H Ev *Lich* from 87. *7 Beacon Rise, Stone, Staffs ST15 0AL* Stone (0785) 812698

LOWNDES, Richard Owen Lewis. b 63. Univ of Wales (Ban) BD86. Coll of Resurr Mirfield 87. **d** 89 **p** 90. C Milford Haven *St D* 89-91; C Roath St German *Llan* from 91; Chapl Cardiff R Infirmary from 91. *St Agnes, The Clergy House, Metal Street, Roath, Cardiff CF2 1LA* Cardiff (0222) 494488

LOWRIE, Kenneth Johnson. b 08. St Aid Birkenhead 39. **d** 40 **p** 41. V Ecchinswell cum Sydmonton *Win* 59-72; rtd 72. *8 Little Lane, Haxby, York* York (0904) 760444

LOWRIE, Robert Colledge. b 33. Leeds Univ DipTh57. Chich Th Coll 68. **d** 69 **p** 70. C Sidmouth St Nic *Ex* 69-73; C Sidmouth, Woolbrook and Salcombe Regis 73-74; V W Hill 74-81; RD Ottery 77-82; TR Sidmouth, Woolbrook and Salcombe Regis 81-86; V Redlynch and Morgan's Vale *Sarum* from 86. *The Vicarage, Redlynch, Salisbury SP5 2PE* Downton (0725) 20439

LOWRIE, Ronald Malcolm. b 48. Ripon Hall Ox 70. **d** 72 **p** 73. C Knowle *Birm* 72-75; C Bourton-on-the-Water w Clapton *Glouc* 75-79; R Broadwell, Evenlode, Oddington and Adlestrop 79-81; TV Trowbridge H Trin *Sarum* 81-88; P-in-c Westwood and Wingfield 88-90; R from 90. *The Rectory, Westwood, Bradford-on-Avon, Wilts BA15 2AF* Bradford-on-Avon (02216) 3109

LOWRY, Canon Christopher Somerset. TCD BA47 MA65. **d** 47 **p** 48. I Grange *Arm* 52-80; Chapl St Luke's Mental Hosp Arm 56-91; RD Tynan 71-91; Can Arm Cathl from 79; I Loughgall w Grange 80-91; Treas Arm Cathl 86-88; Prec Arm Cathl 88-91; rtd 91. *10 Mellifont Drive, Armagh BT61 9ES* Armagh (0861) 527704

LOWRY, Canon Robert Harold. b 19. TCD BA44 MA49. CITC 44. **d** 44 **p** 45. I Willowfield *D & D* 62-75; RD Hillsborough 70-75; I Lambeg *Conn* 75-89; Can Conn Cathl from 82; rtd 90; Lic to Offic *D & D* from 90. *2 Winchester Drive, Carryduff, Belfast BT8 8QD* Belfast (0232) 813927

LOWRY, Stephen Harold. QUB BSc CertEd TCD DipTh. **d** 85 **p** 86. C Coleraine *Conn* 85-88; Bp's Dom Chapl from 87; I Greenisland from 88. *109 Station Road, Greenisland, Carrickfergus, Co Antrim BT38 8UW* Whiteabbey (0232) 863421

LOWRY, William James. b 35. K Coll Lon BD69 AKC69. **d** 71 **p** 72. C Edmonton All SS *Lon* 71-73; NSM 73-81; Chapl Bp Stopford's Sch Enfield 73-87; NSM Ponders End St Matt *Lon* 81-83; P-in-c Dub Sandymount *D & G* from 87. *11 St John's, Park Avenue, Dublin 4, Irish Republic* Dublin (1) 283-8831

LOWSON, Christopher. b 53. AKC75. Berkeley Div Sch STM78 St Aug Coll Cant 76. **d** 77 **p** 78. C Richmond St Mary *S'wark* 77-79; C Richmond St Mary w St Matthias and St Jo 79-82; P-in-c Eltham H Trin 82-83; V 83-91; V Petersfield *Portsm* from 91; R Buriton from 91. *The Vicarage, Shackleford House, 12 Dragon Street, Petersfield, Hants GU31 1AB* Petersfield (0730) 64138

LOWTHER, Leslie Cyril. b 20. St Jo Coll Dur BA41 DipTh43 MA44. **d** 43 **p** 44. V Dore *Derby* 67-73; V Dore *Sheff* 74-85; rtd 85. *47 Church Avenue, Gosforth, Newcastle upon Tyne NE3 1AN* 091-285 6033

LOWTHER, Thomas. b 14. St Jo Coll Dur BA40 LTh40. St Aid Birkenhead 36. **d** 40 **p** 41. V Harraby *Carl* 67-72; V Borrowdale 72-79; rtd 79. *5 Park Avenue, Shrewsbury SY3 8JG* Shrewsbury (0743) 67572

LOWTON, Nicholas Gerard. b 53. St Jo Coll Ox BA76. Glouc Sch of Min 86. **d** 89 **p** 90. NSM Prestbury *Glouc* from 89. *Hazelwell, College Road, Cheltenham, Glos GL53 7JD* Cheltenham (0242) 522665

LOXHAM, Geoffrey Richard. b 40. Hull Univ BA62. Cranmer Hall Dur. **d** 65 **p** 66. C Darwen St Barn *Blackb* 65-68; C Leyland St Andr 68-72; V Preston St Mark 72-79; V Edgeside *Man* 79-91; P-in-c Withnell *Blackb* from 91. *1 Balmoral Drive, Brinscall, Chorley, Lancs PR6 8ST* Brinscall (0254) 832017

LOXLEY, Harold. b 43. N Ord Course 79. **d** 82 **p** 83. NSM Sheff Parson Cross St Cecilia *Sheff* 82-87; C Gleadless 87-90; V Sheff St Cath Richmond Road from 90. *St Catherine's Vicarage, 300 Hastilar Road South, Sheffield S13 8EJ* Sheffield (0742) 399598

LOXLEY, Ronald Alan Keith. b 26. St Jo Coll Ox BA51 MA55. Wm Temple Coll Rugby 66 Cuddesdon Coll 67. **d** 68 **p** 69. C Swindon Ch Ch *Bris* 68-71; Ind

Chapl *Lon* 71-83; Ind Chapl *Chelmsf* from 83; P-in-c Theydon Garnon from 83. *The Rectory, Theydon Garnon, Epping, Essex CM16 7PQ* Epping (0378) 72608

LOXTON, John Sherwood. b 29. Bris Univ BSc50 Birm Univ BA53. Handsworth Coll Birm 50 Chich Th Coll 80. **d** 80 **p** 81. In Meth Ch 50-80; C Haywards Heath St Wilfrid *Chich* 80-82; TV 82-89; V Turners Hill from 89. *The Vicarage, Turners Hill, Crawley, W Sussex RH10 4PB* Copthorne (0342) 715278

LUBBOCK, David John. b 34. S'wark Ord Course. **d** 87 **p** 88. NSM Tulse Hill H Trin and St Matthias *S'wark* from 87. *78 Claverdale Road, London SW2 2DL* 081-674 6146

LUBKOWSKI, Richard Jan. b 51. Westmr Coll Ox BEd75 Warw Univ MA79. St Jo Coll Dur 86. **d** 88 **p** 89. C Duston *Pet* 88-90; C Hellesdon *Nor* 90-91. *22 Almond Tree Avenue, Carlton, Goole, N Humberside DN14 9QQ* Goole (0405) 862558

LUCAS, Anthony Stanley. b 41. Man Univ BA62. Qu Coll Birm 63. **d** 65 **p** 66. C N Hammersmith St Kath *Lon* 65-69; C W Wimbledon Ch Ch *S'wark* 69-74; C Caterham 74-78; P-in-c Stockwell St Mich 78-86; V 86-91; P-in-c S'wark St Geo from 91. *St George's Rectory, Manciple Street, London SE1 4LW* 071-407 2796

LUCAS, Arthur Edgar. b 24. Clifton Th Coll 60. **d** 62 **p** 63. V Willoughby-on-the-Wolds w Wysall *S'well* 66-74; P-in-c Widmerpool 71-74; R Collyhurst *Man* 75-80; V Heapey *Blackb* 80-91; rtd 91. *18 Parkway, Standish, Wigan, Lancs*

LUCAS, Ven Brian Humphrey. b 40. Univ of Wales (Lamp) BA62. St Steph Ho Ox 62. **d** 64 **p** 65. C Llan w Capel Llaniltern *Llan* 64-67; C Neath w Llantwit 67-70; Chapl RAF 70-87; Asst Chapl-in-Chief RAF 87-91; Chapl-in-Chief RAF from 91; QHC from 88; Perm to Offic *Llan* from 88. *c/o MOD, Adastral House, Theobald's Road, London WC1X 8RU* 071-430 7268

LUCAS, Canon Harry McIntyre. b 11. Leeds Univ BA33. Coll of Resurr Mirfield. **d** 35 **p** 36. V E Witton *Ripon* 64-70; rtd 76. *28 Columbus Ravine, Scarborough, N Yorkshire YO12 7JT*

LUCAS, Henry Leonard Armstrong. b 18. Linc Th Coll 43. **d** 44 **p** 45. V Embleton w Wythop *Carl* 65-76; P-in-c Torpenhow 76-77; rtd 78. *Abbeyfield House, Lorton Street, Cockermouth, Cumbria CA13 9RH* Cockermouth (0900) 825161

LUCAS, Mrs Janet Rosemary. b 46. Open Univ BA76. S Dios Minl Tr Scheme 83. **dss** 86 **d** 87. N Wembley St Cuth *Lon* 86-87; Par Dn 87-88; Par Dn Northolt W End St Jos 88-90; Asst Chapl Ealing Gen Hosp from 90; Par Dn Hanwell St Mary 90-91; Par Dn Hanwell St Chris 90-91; Par Dn Hanwell St Mary w St Chris from 91. *117 Wood End Lane, Northolt, Middx UB5 4JP* 081-422 4543

LUCAS, Canon John Arthur. b 07. Keble Coll Ox BA29 MA45. Cuddesdon Coll 29. **d** 33 **p** 34. V Ox St Thos Ox 47-74; P-in-c 74-79; Hon Can Ch Ch 70-85; rtd 74; Hon C Ox St Mary V w St Cross and St Pet *Ox* 78-85; Perm to Offic from 85. *12 Lucas Place, Iffley, Oxford OX4 4HA* Oxford (0865) 774508

LUCAS, John Maxwell. b 34. TD85. Cranmer Hall Dur 59. **d** 62 **p** 63. C Lanc St Mary *Blackb* 62-65; C Lytham St Cuth 65-68; V Blackb St Aid 68-72; V Sparkhill St Jo *Birm* 72-78; CF (TA) from 73; V Edgbaston St Aug *Birm* 78-85; V Slyne w Hest *Blackb* 85-89; Chapl HM Young Offender Inst Stoke Heath from 89. *HM Young Offender Institution, Stoke Heath, Market Drayton, Shropshire TF9 2JL* Market Drayton (0630) 4231

LUCAS, Ven John Michael. b 21. Lich Th Coll 40. **d** 44 **p** 45. V Northam *Ex* 62-76; V Chudleigh Knighton 76-83; Adn Totnes 76-81; rtd 83; Perm to Offic *Ex* from 83. *Wybray House, Shobrooke, Crediton, Devon EX17 1AP* Crediton (03632) 4792

LUCAS, Kenneth Ashley. b 18. Wells Th Coll 68. **d** 69 **p** 70. C Rye *Chich* 69-73; C Rye w Rye Harbour and Playden 73; R W Chiltington 74-83; rtd 83; Perm to Offic *Chich* from 83. *12 Delves House West, Delves Close, Ringmer, Lewes, E Sussex BN8 5JW* Ringmer (0273) 813150

LUCAS, Canon Paul de Neufville. b 33. Ch Ch Ox BA59 MA59 Cam Univ MA63. Cuddesdon Coll 57. **d** 59 **p** 60. C Westmr St Steph w St Jo *Lon* 59-63; Chapl Trin Hall Cam 63-69; V Greenside *Dur* 69-73; Chapl Shrewsbury Sch 73-77; V Batheaston w St Cath *B & W* 78-88; Preb Wells Cathl from 87; Can Res and Prec from 88. *4 The Liberty, Wells, Somerset BA5 2SU* Wells (0749) 73188

LUCAS, Peter Stanley. b 21. **d** 50 **p** 51. C Gillingham *Sarum* 50-53; Min Heald Green St Cath CD *Ches* 53-58;

V Heald Green St Cath 58-62; V Egremont St Jo 62-65; Canada from 66. *Number 404, 1241 Fairfield Road, Victoria, British Columbia, Canada, V1V 3B3*

LUCAS, Raymond Charles Henry. b 15. ALCD41. **d** 41 **p** 42. R Branston *Linc* 61-76; R Parkham, Alwington and Buckland Brewer *Ex* 76-79; rtd 80. *90 Cheverell Avenue, Salisbury SP1 3HQ* Salisbury (0722) 26281

LUCAS, Preb Richard Charles. b 25. Trin Coll Cam BA49 MA57. Ridley Hall Cam. **d** 51 **p** 52. C Sevenoaks St Nic *Roch* 51-55; Cand Sec CPAS 55-61; Asst Sec 61-67; R St Helen Bishopsgate w St Martin Outwich *Lon* 61-80; P-in-c St Andr Undershaft w St Mary Axe 77-80; R St Helen Bishopsgate w St Andr Undershaft etc from 80; Preb St Paul's Cathl from 85. *The Rectory, Great St Helen's, London EC3A 6AT* 071-283 2231

LUCAS, Ronald James. b 38. St Aid Birkenhead 64. **d** 67 **p** 68. C Swindon Ch Ch *Bris* 67-71; C Knowle St Martin 71-74; V Swindon St Jo 74-77; TR Swindon St Jo and St Andr 77-81; R Wroughton 81-83; TV Liskeard w St Keyne, St Pinnock and Morval *Truro* 83-87; R St Ive w Quethiock from 87. *The Rectory, St Ive, Liskeard, Cornwall PL14 3LX* Liskeard (0579) 82327

LUCAS, Mrs Vivienne Kathleen. b 44. Sarum & Wells Th Coll 84. **d** 87. Par Dn Whitton St Aug *Lon* from 87. *224 High Street, Feltham, Middx TW13 4HX* 081-890 4482

LUCAS, William Wallace. b 29. Sarum Th Coll 56. **d** 59 **p** 60. C Stockton St Jo *Dur* 59-63; V Norton St Mich 63-81; R Broseley w Benthall *Heref* from 81; P-in-c Jackfield from 81; P-in-c Linley w Willey and Barrow from 81. *The Rectory, Broseley, Shropshire TF12 5DA* Telford (0952) 882647

LUCK, Benjamin Paul. b 53. BD. St Mich Coll Llan 80. **d** 83 **p** 84. C Blakenall Heath *Lich* 83-87; C Torpoint *Truro* 87-89; V Tuckingmill from 89. *All Saints' Vicarage, 35 Roskear, Camborne, Cornwall TR14 8DG* Camborne (0209) 712114

LUCKCUCK, Anthony Michael. b 47. Lon Univ BA70. Wycliffe Hall Ox 70. **d** 77 **p** 78. C Mansf Woodhouse *S'well* 77-79; C Beeston 79-82; V Harworth 82-85; V Carlton from 85. *St John's Vicarage, 261 Oakdale Road, Nottingham NG4 1BP* Nottingham (0602) 874882

LUCKRAFT, Christopher John. b 50. K Coll Lon BD80 AKC80. Ripon Coll Cuddesdon. **d** 81 **p** 82. C Sherborne w Castleton and Lillington *Sarum* 81-84; Bermuda 84-87; Chapl RN from 87. *c/o MOD, Lacon House, Theobald's Road, London WC1X 8RY* 071-430 6847

LUDLOW, Canon Arthur Percival. b 26. Chich Th Coll 48. **d** 51 **p** 52. C Manston *Ripon* 51-54; C Seacroft 54-58; V Stanground *Ely* 58-72; R Somersham w Pidley and Oldhurst 72-88; P-in-c Gt w Lt Stukeley from 88; Chapl Hinchingbrooke Hosp from 88; Hon Can Ely Cathl *Ely* from 89. *The Rectory, Great Stukeley, Huntingdon, Cambs PE17 5AL* Huntingdon (0480) 453016

LUDLOW, Christopher George. b 18. AKC42. **d** 42 **p** 43. Chapl K Alfred Coll *Win* 57-70; Prin Lect Relig Studies 57-76; rtd 83. *Little Tolcarne, Burras, Helston, Cornwall TR13 0HX* Praze (0209) 831631

LUDLOW, Archdeacon of. See LEWIS, Ven John Hubert Richard

LUDLOW, Suffragan Bishop of. See GRIGGS, Rt Rev Ian Macdonald

LUFF, Alan Harold Frank. b 28. ARCM77 Univ Coll Ox DipTh52 MA54. Westcott Ho Cam 54. **d** 56 **p** 57. C Stretford St Matt *Man* 56-59; C Swinton St Pet 59-61; Prec Man Cathl 61-68; V Penmaenmawr *Ban* 68-79; Sacr Westmr Abbey 79-86; Prec Westmr Abbey from 79. *7 Little Cloister, Westminster Abbey, London SW1P 3PL* 071-222 1386

LUFF, Mrs Caroline Margaret Synia. b 44. St Hild Coll Dur BA65 Bris Univ CertEd66. SW Minl Tr Course 87. **d** 90. Par Dn Teignmouth, Ideford w Luton, Ashcombe etc *Ex* from 90. *The Rectory, 30 Dawlish Road, Teignmouth, Devon TQ14 8TG* Teignmouth (0626) 774495

LUFF, Philip Garth. b 42. St Chad's Coll Dur BA63 DipTh64. **d** 65 **p** 66. C Sidmouth St Nic *Ex* 65-69; C Plymstock 69-71; Asst Chapl Worksop Coll Notts 71-74; V Gainsborough St Jo *Linc* 74-80; V E Teignmouth *Ex* 80-89; P-in-c W Teignmouth 85-89; TR Teignmouth, Ideford w Luton, Ashcombe etc from 90. *The Rectory, 30 Dawlish Road, Teignmouth, Devon TQ14 8TG* Teignmouth (0626) 774495

LUGG, Donald Arthur. b 31. St Aid Birkenhead 56. **d** 59 **p** 60. C Folkestone H Trin w Ch Ch *Cant* 59-62; V Seasalter 62-66; Iran 67-73; V Cliftonville *Cant* from 74. *St Paul's Vicarage, Northdown Road, Margate, Kent CT9 2RD* Thanet (0843) 220857

LUGG, Stuart John. b 26. Glouc Th Course 74. **d** 76 **p** 77. NSM Fairford *Glouc* 76-79; P-in-c Kempsford w Welford 80-88; Perm to Offic from 88. *Content, Station Road, South Cerney, Cirencester, Glos GL7 5UB* Cirencester (0285) 860498

LUKE, Anthony. b 58. Down Coll Cam BA MA. Ridley Hall Cam. **d** 84 **p** 85. C Allestree *Derby* 84-87; C Oakham, Hambleton, Egleton, Braunston and Brooke *Pet* 87-88; V Allenton and Shelton Lock *Derby* from 88. *St Edmund's Vicarage, Sinfin Avenue, Allenton, Derby DE2 9JA* Derby (0332) 701194

LUKE, Brother. See SMITH, Philip Sydney Bellman

LUMAN, Arthur Cecil Rowe. b 11. St Paul's Grahamstown LTh37 St Aug Coll Cant 62. **d** 37 **p** 38. R Murston *Cant* 62-80; rtd 80; Perm to Offic *Cant* from 80. *38 Headcorn Drive, Canterbury, Kent CT2 7QU* Canterbury (0227) 457831

LUMB, David Leslie. b 28. Jes Coll Cam BA52 MA56. Oak Hill Th Coll 52. **d** 54 **p** 55. C Walcot *B & W* 54-58; C Lenton *S'well* 58-60; V Handforth *Ches* 60-71; V Plymouth St Jude *Ex* 71-87; V Southminster *Chelmsf* from 87. *The Vicarage, Burnham Road, Southminster, Essex CM0 7ES* Maldon (0621) 772300

LUMB, Dennis. b 36. Oak Hill Th Coll 77. **d** 79 **p** 80. C Penn Fields *Lich* 79-84; P-in-c Tibberton, Kinnersley and Preston Wealdmoors 84-89; R Tibberton w Bolas Magna and Waters Upton 89-91; P-in-c Saltfleetby *Linc* from 91; P-in-c Theddlethorpe from 91. *The Rectory, Main Road, Saltfleetby, Louth, Lincs* Saltfleetby (0507) 338074

LUMBY, Jonathan Bertram. b 39. Em Coll Cam BA62 MA66 Lon Univ PGCE66. Ripon Hall Ox 62. **d** 64 **p** 65. C Moseley St Mary *Birm* 64-65; Asst Master Enfield Gr Sch 66-67; C Hall Green Ascension 67-70; V Melling *Liv* 70-81; P-in-c Milverton w Halse and Fitzhead *B & W* 81-82; R 82-86; P-in-c Gisburn *Bradf* from 90; Dioc Rural Adv from 90. *The Vicarage, Gisburn, Clitheroe, Lancs BB7 4HR* Clitheroe (0200) 445214

LUMGAIR, Michael Hugh Crawford. b 43. Lon Univ BD71. Oak Hill Th Coll 66. **d** 71 **p** 72. C Chorleywood Ch Ch *St Alb* 71-74; C Prestonville St Luke *Chich* 74-75; C Attenborough *S'well* 75-80; R Tollerton 80-91; V Bexleyheath St Pet *Roch* from 91. *St Peter's Vicarage, Bristow Road, Bexleyheath, Kent DA7 4QA* 081-303 8713

LUMLEY, Preb Ralph John Charles. b 05. Lich Th Coll 30. **d** 32 **p** 33. V Shrewsbury H Cross *Lich* 57-83; RD Shrewsbury 72-82; Preb Lich Cathl 65-83; rtd 83; Perm to Offic *Lich* from 83; Hon Treas' Vicar from 87. *9 The Parchments, Lichfield, Staffs WS13 7NA* Lichfield (0543) 263335

LUMLEY, William. b 22. TCD BA44 MA49 BD49 QUB PhD77. Edgehill Th Coll Belf 49. **d** 50 **p** 51. I Ballybay *Clogh* 66-73; I Derryvullen S w Garvary 73-82; I Killucan w Clonard and Castlelost *M & K* 82-88; rtd 88. *Gallows Hill, 104 Ballyquinn Road, Limavady, Co Londonderry BT49 9EY* Limavady (05047) 66174

LUMMIS, Mrs Elizabeth Howieson. b 44. LDSRCSEng68 Lon Univ BDS68. St Jo Coll Nottm. **d** 88. NSM Burravoe *Ab* from 88; NSM Lerwick from 88. *90 North Lochside, Lerwick, Shetland ZE1 0PJ* Lerwick (0595) 3248

LUMSDEN, Frank. b 20. Edin Th Coll 51. **d** 53 **p** 54. V Lynesack *Dur* 56-76; R Castle Eden w Monkhesleden 76-86; rtd 86; Perm to Offic *Dur* from 86; Ripon from 90. *Cloud High, Eggleston, Barnard Castle, Co Durham DL12 0AU* Teesdale (0833) 50644

LUMSDON, Keith. b 45. Linc Th Coll 68. **d** 71 **p** 72. C S Westoe *Dur* 71-74; C Jarrow St Paul 74-77; TV Jarrow 77-88; V Ferryhill from 88. *St Luke's Vicarage, Church Lane, Ferryhill, Co Durham DL17 8LT* Ferryhill (0740) 51438

LUND, David Peter. b 46. Nor Ord Course 88. **d** 91. C Maghull *Liv* from 91. *6 Deyes End, Maghull, Liverpool*

LUND, John Edward. b 48. St Jo Coll Dur 78. **d** 80 **p** 81. C Peterlee *Dur* 80-83; C Bishopton w Gt Stainton 83-85; C Redmarshall 83-85; C Grindon and Stillington 83-85; V Hart w Elwick Hall from 85; Hon Chapl Miss to Seamen from 85. *The Vicarage, Hart, Hartlepool, Cleveland TS27 3AP* Hartlepool (0429) 262340

LUNGLEY, John Sydney. b 41. St Pet Coll Ox BA64 MA70. St Steph Ho Ox 64. **d** 66 **p** 67. C Burslem St Werburgh *Lich* 66-70; C Codsall 70-73; V Ocker Hill 73-88; RD Wednesbury 84-88; V Kingswinford St Mary from 88. *17 Penzer Street, Kingswinford, W Midlands DY6 7AA* Kingswinford (0384) 273716

LUNN, Brooke Kingsmill. b 32. TCD BA62 MA66. Chich Th Coll 62. **d** 64 **p** 65. C Northolt Park St Barn *Lon* 64-66; C N St Pancras All Hallows 66-68; P-in-c Hornsey St Luke 68-79; V Stroud Green H Trin from 79; AD

W Haringey from 90. *The Vicarage, Granville Road, London N4 4EL* 081-340 2051

LUNN, Christopher James Edward b 34. AKC58. **d** 59 **p** 60. C Clapham H Trin *S'wark* 59-6?; C Cranleigh *Guildf* 63-64; C Ham St Andr *S'wark* 64-66; V Ham H Rich 66-75; V Coulsdon St Andr from 75. *St Andrew's Vicarage, Julien Road, Coulsdon, Surrey CR3 2LH* 081-660 0300

LUNN, David. b ... Bris Univ ... Univ BA73 Dip ... Jo Coll ... ... C Aigburth *Liv* ... C Slough *Ox* ... P-in-c Haversham w Little Linford *Ox* from ... RD Newport from 8... *The Rectory, ... Milton Keynes ...* Milton Keynes (0908) 312136

LUNN, Rt Rev David Ramsay. b 30. Qu'oll Cam BA53 MA57. Cuddesdon Coll 53 **d** 55 **c** 80. C Bingley Newc 55-59; C N Gosforth 59-63; Chapl Line Th Coll 63-66; Sub-Warden 66-70; V Cullercoats St Geo Newc 71-77; TR ... RD Tynemouth 73-80; Bp Sheffield from 98. *Bishopscroft, Snaithing Lane, Sheffield S10 3LG* Sheffield (0742) 302741

LUNN, Leonard Arthur. b 42. T...ll Bris 69. **d** 72 **p** 73. C Walthamstow St Mary w St Steph *Chelmsf* 72-75; V Collier Row St Jas 75-85; V Collier Row St Jas and Havering-Bower 86-87; Chapl St Chris Hospice *S'wark* from 87. *52 Compton Grove, London SE3 9EL* 081-779 0284

LUNN, Canon William Bell. b 21. Edin Th Coll 47. **d** 49 **p** 50. R Elgin St Mark *Mor* 49-75; Can St Mary's Cathl 68-75; R Fochabers *Mor* 75-86; ... 75-86; Can St Andr Cathl Inverness *Mor* from 86. *67 Woodside Place, Forres, Morayshire IV36 0UF* Forres (0309) ...

LUNN, Henry. b 31. ACIB57. Wyclffe Hall Ox 73. ... **p** 75. C Ipswich St Aug *St E* 74-77; P-in-c Westerfield w Tuddenham St Martin 77-83; R Westerfield and Tuddenham St Martin w Witnesham from 83. Asst Dioc Chr Stewardship Adv 78-83. *The Rectory, Westerfield, ... Suffolk IP6 9AG* Ipswich (0473) 251013

LUNNON, Robert Reginald. b 31. K Coll Lon BD55 AKC55. St Boniface Warminster 55. **d** 56 **p** 57. C Maidstone St Mich *Cant* 56-58; C Deal St Leon 58-62; V Sturry 63-68; V Norbury St Steph *S'wark* 68-77; V Orpington All SS *Roch* from 77; RD Orpington from 79. *The Vicarage, St Keswick Road, Orpington, Kent BR5 3BU* Orpington (0689) 824624

LUNT, Canon Ronald Geoffrey. b 14. MC43. Qu'oll Ox MA38 BD67. Westcott Ho Cant 37. **d** 38 **p** 39. Master K Edw VI Sch *Birm* 52-74; Hon Can Birm Cathl 69-74; Perm to Offic *Heref* from 76. *The Station House, Ledbury, ... Ledbury (0531) 3171

LUNT, Canon Ronald Sowden. b 30. Leeds Univ BA56. Ely Th ... **d** 58 **p** 59. C Stockport St Thos *Ches* 60-61; C Wilmslow Pott 61-65; V Newton in Mottram *Ches*; RD Chester from 78; TR Ches Team from 78; Hon Can Ches Cathl from 82. *The Rectory, Vicar's Lane, Chester CH1 1QX* Chester (0244) 26357

LURIE, Miss Gillian Ruth. b 42. LRAM62 GNSM63 ACertCM80. Gilmore Ho 68. **dss** 74 **d** 87. Camberwell St Phil and St Mark *S'wark* 74-76; Haddenham *Ely* 76-79; Dioc Lay Min Adv 79-86; Longthorpe *Pet* 79-81; Pet H Spirit Bretton 81-86; Bramley *Ripon* 86-87; TM from 88. *27 Hough End Lane, Bramley, Leeds LS13 4EY* Pudsey (0532) 576202

LURKINGS, Edward Henry. b 30. Lon Univ BSc68 ARCS PhD81. ... C Brookfield St Mary *Lon* 54-59; C ... wood St Pet 59-62; Ind Chapl 62-71; Hon C ... St Mary *St Alb* 72-84; V Potterspury, Furtho, Yardley Gobion and Cosgrove *Pet* from 84. *The Vicarage, Potterspury, Towcester, Northants NN12 7PU* Yardley Gobion (0908) 542428

LURY, Anthony Patrick. b 49. K Coll Lon BD71 AKC71. St Aug Coll Cant 71. **d** 72 **p** 73. C Richmond St Mary *S'wark* 72-76; P-in-c Streatham Hill St Marg 76-81; V Salfords 81-90; V Emscote *Cov* from 90. *All Saints' Vicarage, Vicarage Fields, Warwick CV34 5NJ* Warwick (0926) 492073

LURY, Denys Patrick. b 15. Dur Univ LTh48. Bps' Coll Cheshunt 36. **d** 38 **p** 39. V Maidstone St Mich *Cant* 63-72; Chapl St Monica's Home of Rest Westbury-on-Trym 72-80; rtd 80; Perm to Offic *Bris* from 80. *14 Gerrish Avenue, Bristol BS16 5PN* Bristol (0272) 567514

LUSCOMBE, John Nickels. b 45. AKC68. **d** 69 **p** 70. C Stoke Newington St Faith, St Matthias and All SS *Lon* 69-74; V Tottenham St Phil 74-81; Zimbabwe 82-86; V

Queensbury ... *Drive, ... Middx*

LUSCOMBE, Rt Rev ... NSA80 ... C ... St Marg *Glas* ... ; Provost St Paul's ... Dundee St Paul (1 ... 90. *Woodville, Kirkton of ... Tealing* (08/621) 331

...BIRD, Jack Andrew. b 5... St Steph Ho *Ox* 90. **d** 91 **p** 91. ... from 90. *... Rossendean, ... BB24RD* ...

LUSTY, Ronald Henry. b 23. Ox ... NSM Tilehurst St Mary *Ox* 91- ... Trin from 98. *St Bernard's, ... Reading, RG...* Reading (07...)

LUTHER, Richard Grenville Litton. b ... Tyndale Hall Bris 61. **d** 68 **p** 69. C Blockley 68-70; C Bishopsworth *Bris* 70-7...; TV Radipole and Melcombe Regis ...; TR Hampreston from 90. *The Rectory, Ferndown, Wimborne, Dorset BH22 ...* (0202) 87...

LUTTER, Stuart Frank. b 26. MIEE60 ... Lon Univ 76-8... Southn Univ BA88 ... **d** 89 ... C Bexhill St ... Romsey *Win* from 72. *... Road, ... East Wellow, Romsey, Hants SO51 6BN* (0794) 23...

LUTTON, Mary Theodore Dell Boyce. b ... MA48. **d** 46 **p** 49. C Wribbenhall *Worc* ... Astleworton, Stockbush and Birtsmorton ... 23 Bridgewater Road, Oswestry, Shropshire ...* Oswestry (0691) 656125

LUXMOORE, Rt Rev Christopher Charles. b ... Coll Cam BA54 MA54. Chich Th Coll 50. **d** 52 **p** ... C New ... St Jo *Newc* 52-55; C-in-c Newsham ... 55-57; V Newsham 57-58; Chaplain and ... 58-60; V Headingley *Ripon* 60-... Hon Can *Ripon* 60-81; Can Res and Prec ... Chich Cathl 81-84; Bermuda 84-89; Suff Lewes and Hastings *Chich* from ... Provost Woodard Corp (S Division) from 89; ... *40 Willowbed Avenue, Chichester, W Sussex PO19 2JB* Chichester (0243) 784680

LYALL, Canon Graham. b 34. Univ of Wales (Lamp) ... Birm Univ ... Qu Coll Birm 61. **d** 63 **p** 64. C Moseley Ascension *Birm* 63-67; C Kidderminster St Mary *Worc* 67-72; V Dudley Holly Hall St Aug 72-79; P-in-c Bartonsham 79-81; V from 81; RD Worc E 83-89; Hon Can Worc Cathl from 85. *St Stephen's Vicarage, 1 Beech Avenue, Worcester WR3 8PZ* Worcester (0905) 52169

LYDON, Mrs Barbara. b 34. Gilmore Ho 64. **dss** 72 **d** 87. Rastrick St Matt *Wakef* 72-85; Upper Hopton 85-87; Par Dn 87; P-in-c Kellington w Whitley from 87. *The Vicarage, Manor Farm Close, Kellington, Goole, Humberside WF14 9PW* Whitley Bridge (0977) 662876

LYES-WILSDON, Mrs Patricia Mary. b 49. ALA65 Open Univ BA86. Glouc Th Course 84. Qu Coll Birm 86. **d** 87. C Thornbury *Glouc* from 87. *10 Finch Close, Thornbury, Bristol BS12 1TW* Thornbury (0454) 417056

LYNAS, Norman Noel. b 55. St Andr Univ MTh78. CITC 79. **d** 80 **p** 80. C Knockbreda *D & D* 79-81; C Holywood 81-85; I Portadown St Columba *Arm* from 85; Dioc Info Officer 86-89; Tutor for Aux Min (Arm) from 88; Radio Officer (Arm) from 90. *81 Loughgall Road, Portadown, Craigavon, Co Armagh BT62 4EG* Portadown (0762) 332746

LYNAS, Stephen Brian. b 52. St Jo Coll Nottm BTh77. **d** 78 **p** 79. C Penn *Lich* 78-81; Relig Progr Org BBC Radio Stoke-on-Trent 81-84; C Hanley H Ev 81-82; C Edensor 82-84; Relig Progr Producer BBC Bris 85-88; Lic to Offic *Bris* from 85; Relig Progr Sen Producer BBC S & W England 88-91; Hd of Relig Progr TVS from 91; Perm to Offic *Cant* from 91. *c/o TVS, Vinters Park, Maidstone ME14 5NZ* Maidstone (0622) 684542

LYNCH, Preb Donald MacLeod. b 11. CBE72. Pemb Coll Cam BA34 MA37. Wycliffe Hall Ox. **d** 35 **p** 36. Chief Sec CA 60-76; Preb St Paul's Cathl *Lon* 64-76; Chapl to HM The Queen 69-81; P-in-c Seal St Lawr *Roch* 74-85; rtd 76; RD Sevenoaks *Roch* 79-84; P-in-c Underriver 80-85; Perm to Offic Chich and Roch from 86. *Flat 2, 20 Grassington Road, Eastbourne, E Sussex BN20 7BJ* Eastbourne (0323) 20849

LYNCH, James Kenrick. b 20. ACP65. Ripon Hall Ox. **d** 61 **p** 62. Chapl Whittingham Hosp 69-72; V Barton *Blackb* 72-81; rtd 81. *12 Willow Tree Avenue, Broughton, Preston*

V Heald Green St Cath 58-62; V Egremont St Jo 62-65; Canada from 66. *Number 404, 1241 Fairfield Road, Victoria, British Columbia, Canada, V1V 3B3*

LUCAS, Raymond Charles Henry. b 15. ALCD41. **d** 41 **p** 42. R Branston *Linc* 61-76; R Parkham, Alwington and Buckland Brewer *Ex* 76-79; rtd 80. *90 Cheverell Avenue, Salisbury SP1 3HQ* Salisbury (0722) 26281

LUCAS, Preb Richard Charles. b 25. Trin Coll Cam BA49 MA57. Ridley Hall Cam. **d** 51 **p** 52. C Sevenoaks St Nic *Roch* 51-55; Cand Sec CPAS 55-61; Asst Sec 61-67; R St Helen Bishopsgate w St Martin Outwich *Lon* 61-80; P-in-c Andr Undershaft w St Mary Axe 77-80; R St Helen Bishopsgate w St Andr Undershaft etc from 80; Preb St Paul's Cathl from 85. *The Rectory, Great St Helen's, London EC3A 6AT* 071-283 2231

LUCAS, Ronald James. b 38. St Aid Birkenhead 64. **d** 67 **p** 68. C Swindon Ch Ch *Bris* 67-71; C Knowle St Martin 71-74; V Swindon St Jo 74-77; TR Swindon St Jo and St Andr 77-81; R Wroughton 81-83; TV Liskeard w St Keyne, St Pinnock and Morval *Truro* 83-87; R St Ive w Quethiock from 87. *The Rectory, St Ive, Liskeard, Cornwall PL14 3LX* Liskeard (0579) 82327

LUCAS, Mrs Vivienne Kathleen. b 44. Sarum & Wells Th Coll 84. **d** 87. Par Dn Whitton St Aug *Lon* from 87. *224 High Street, Feltham, Middx TW13 4HX* 081-890 4482

LUCAS, William Wallace. b 29. Sarum Th Coll 56. **d** 59 **p** 60. C Stockton St Jo *Dur* 59-63; V Norton St Mich 63-81; R Broseley w Benthall *Heref* from 81; P-in-c Jackfield from 81; P-in-c Linley w Willey and Barrow from 81. *The Rectory, Broseley, Shropshire TF12 5DA* Telford (0952) 882647

LUCK, Benjamin Paul. b 53. BD. St Mich Coll Llan 80. **d** 83 **p** 84. C Blakenall Heath *Lich* 83-87; C Torpoint *Truro* 87-89; V Tuckingmill from 89. *All Saints' Vicarage, 35 Roskear, Camborne, Cornwall TR14 8DG* Camborne (0209) 712114

LUCKCUCK, Anthony Michael. b 47. Lon Univ BA70. Wycliffe Hall Ox 70. **d** 77 **p** 78. C Mansf Woodhouse *S'well* 77-79; C Beeston 79-82; V Harworth 82-85; V Carlton from 85. *St John's Vicarage, 261 Oakdale Road, Nottingham NG4 1BP* Nottingham (0602) 874882

LUCKRAFT, Christopher John. b 50. K Coll Lon BD80 AKC80. Ripon Coll Cuddesdon. **d** 81 **p** 82. C Sherborne w Castleton and Lillington *Sarum* 81-84; Bermuda 84-87; Chapl RN from 87. *c/o MOD, Lacon House, Theobald's Road, London WC1X 8RY* 071-430 6847

LUDLOW, Canon Arthur Percival. b 26. Chich Th Coll 48. **d** 51 **p** 52. C Manston *Ripon* 51-54; C Seacroft 54-58; V Stanground *Ely* 58-72; R Somersham w Pidley and Oldhurst 72-88; P-in-c Gt w Lt Stukeley from 88; Chapl Hinchingbrooke Hosp from 88; Hon Can Ely Cathl *Ely* from 89. *The Rectory, Great Stukeley, Huntingdon, Cambs PE17 5AL* Huntingdon (0480) 453016

LUDLOW, Christopher George. b 18. AKC42. **d** 42 **p** 43. Chapl K Alfred Coll *Win* 57-70; Prin Lect Relig Studies 57-76; rtd 83. *Little Tolcarne, Burras, Helston, Cornwall TR13 0HX* Praze (0209) 831631

LUDLOW, Archdeacon of. See LEWIS, Ven John Hubert Richard

LUDLOW, Suffragan Bishop of. See GRIGGS, Rt Rev Ian Macdonald

LUFF, Alan Harold Frank. b 28. ARCM77 Univ Coll Ox DipTh52 MA54. Westcott Ho Cam 54. **d** 56 **p** 57. C Stretford St Matt *Man* 56-59; C Swinton St Pet 59-61; Prec Man Cathl 61-68; V Penmaenmawr *Ban* 68-79; Sacr Westmr Abbey 79-86; Prec Westmr Abbey from 79. *7 Little Cloister, Westminster Abbey, London SW1P 3PL* 071-222 1386

LUFF, Mrs Caroline Margaret Synia. b 44. St Hild Coll Dur BA65 Bris Univ CertEd66. SW Minl Tr Course 87. **d** 90. Par Dn Teignmouth, Ideford w Luton, Ashcombe etc *Ex* from 90. *The Rectory, 30 Dawlish Road, Teignmouth, Devon TQ14 8TG* Teignmouth (0626) 774495

LUFF, Philip Garth. b 42. St Chad's Coll Dur BA63 DipTh64. **d** 65 **p** 66. C Sidmouth St Nic *Ex* 65-69; C Plymstock 69-71; Asst Chapl Worksop Coll Notts 71-74; V Gainsborough St Jo *Linc* 74-80; V E Teignmouth *Ex* 80-89; P-in-c W Teignmouth 85-89; TR Teignmouth, Ideford w Luton, Ashcombe etc from 90. *The Rectory, 30 Dawlish Road, Teignmouth, Devon TQ14 8TG* Teignmouth (0626) 774495

LUGG, Donald Arthur. b 31. St Aid Birkenhead 56. **d** 59 **p** 60. C Folkestone H Trin w Ch Ch *Cant* 59-62; V Seasalter 62-66; Iran 67-73; V Cliftonville *Cant* from 74. *St Paul's Vicarage, Northdown Road, Margate, Kent CT9 2RD* Thanet (0843) 220857

LUGG, Stuart John. b 26. Glouc Th Course 74. **d** 76 **p** 77. NSM Fairford *Glouc* 76-79; P-in-c Kempsford w Welford 80-88; Perm to Offic from 88. *Content, Station Road, South Cerney, Cirencester, Glos GL7 5UB* Cirencester (0285) 860498

LUKE, Anthony. b 58. Down Coll Cam BA MA. Ridley Hall Cam. **d** 84 **p** 85. C Allestree *Derby* 84-87; C Oakham, Hambleton, Egleton, Braunston and Brooke *Pet* 87-88; V Allenton and Shelton Lock *Derby* from 88. *St Edmund's Vicarage, Sinfin Avenue, Allenton, Derby DE2 9JA* Derby (0332) 701194

LUKE, Brother. See SMITH, Philip Sydney Bellman

LUMAN, Arthur Cecil Rowe. b 11. St Paul's Grahamstown LTh37 St Aug Coll Cant 62. **d** 37 **p** 38. R Murston *Cant* 62-80; rtd 80; Perm to Offic *Cant* from 80. *38 Headcorn Drive, Canterbury, Kent CT2 7QU* Canterbury (0227) 457831

LUMB, David Leslie. b 28. Jes Coll Cam BA52 MA56. Oak Hill Th Coll 52. **d** 54 **p** 55. C Walcot *B & W* 54-58; C Lenton *S'well* 58-60; V Handforth *Ches* 60-71; V Plymouth St Jude *Ex* 71-87; V Southminster *Chelmsf* from 87. *The Vicarage, Burnham Road, Southminster, Essex CM0 7ES* Maldon (0621) 772300

LUMB, Dennis. b 36. Oak Hill Th Coll 77. **d** 79 **p** 80. C Penn Fields *Lich* 79-84; P-in-c Tibberton, Kinnersley and Preston Wealdmoors 84-89; R Tibberton w Bolas Magna and Waters Upton 89-91; P-in-c Saltfleetby *Linc* from 91; P-in-c Theddlethorpe from 91. *The Rectory, Main Road, Saltfleetby, Louth, Lincs* Saltfleetby (0507) 338074

LUMBY, Jonathan Bertram. b 39. Em Coll Cam BA62 MA66 Lon Univ PGCE66. Ripon Hall Ox 62. **d** 64 **p** 65. C Moseley St Mary *Birm* 64-65; Asst Master Enfield Gr Sch 66-67; C Hall Green Ascension 67-70; V Melling *Liv* 70-81; P-in-c Milverton w Halse and Fitzhead *B & W* 81-82; R 82-86; P-in-c Gisburn *Bradf* from 90; Dioc Rural Adv from 90. *The Vicarage, Gisburn, Clitheroe, Lancs BB7 4HR* Clitheroe (0200) 445214

LUMGAIR, Michael Hugh Crawford. b 43. Lon Univ BD71. Oak Hill Th Coll 66. **d** 71 **p** 72. C Chorleywood Ch Ch *St Alb* 71-74; C Prestonville St Luke *Chich* 74-75; C Attenborough *S'well* 75-80; R Tollerton 80-91; V Bexleyheath St Pet *Roch* from 91. *St Peter's Vicarage, Bristow Road, Bexleyheath, Kent DA7 4QA* 081-303 8713

LUMLEY, Preb Ralph John Charles. b 05. Lich Th Coll 30. **d** 32 **p** 33. V Shrewsbury H Cross *Lich* 57-83; RD Shrewsbury 62-82; Preb Lich Cathl 65-83; rtd 83; Perm to Offic *Lich* from 83; Hon Treas' Vicar from 87. *9 The Parchments, Lichfield, Staffs WS13 7NA* Lichfield (0543) 263335

LUMLEY, William. b 22. TCD BA44 MA49 BD49 QUB PhD77. Edgehill Th Coll Belf 49. **d** 50 **p** 51. I Ballybay *Clogh* 66-73; I Derryvullen S w Garvary 73-82; I Killucan w Clonard and Castlelost *M & K* 82-88; rtd 88. *Gallows Hill, 104 Ballyquin Road, Limavady, Co Londonderry BT49 9EY* Limavady (05047) 66174

LUMMIS, Mrs Elizabeth Howieson. b 44. LDSRCSEng68 Lon Univ BDS68. St Jo Coll Nottm. **d** 88. NSM Burravoe *Ab* from 88; NSM Lerwick from 88. *90 North Lochside, Lerwick, Shetland ZE1 0PJ* Lerwick (0595) 3248

LUMSDEN, Frank. b 20. Edin Th Coll 51. **d** 53 **p** 54. V Lynesack *Dur* 56-76; R Castle Eden w Monkhesleden 76-86; rtd 86; Perm to Offic *Dur* from 86; Ripon from 90. *Cloud High, Eggleston, Barnard Castle, Co Durham DL12 0AU* Teesdale (0833) 50644

LUMSDON, Keith. b 45. Linc Th Coll 68. **d** 71 **p** 72. C S Westoe *Dur* 71-74; C Jarrow St Paul 74-77; TV Jarrow 77-88; V Ferryhill from 88. *St Luke's Vicarage, Church Lane, Ferryhill, Co Durham DL17 8LT* Ferryhill (0740) 51438

LUND, David Peter. b 46. Nor Ord Course 88. **d** 91. C Maghull *Liv* from 91. *6 Deyes End, Maghull, Liverpool*

LUND, John Edward. b 48. St Jo Coll Dur 78. **d** 80 **p** 81. C Peterlee *Dur* 80-83; C Bishopton w Gt Stainton 83-85; C Redmarshall 83-85; C Grindon and Stillington 83-85; V Hart w Elwick Hall from 85; Hon Chapl Miss to Seamen from 85. *The Vicarage, Hart, Hartlepool, Cleveland TS27 3AP* Hartlepool (0429) 262340

LUNGLEY, John Sydney. b 41. St Pet Coll Ox BA64 MA70. St Steph Ho Ox 64. **d** 66 **p** 67. C Burslem St Werburgh *Lich* 66-70; C Codsall 70-73; V Ocker Hill 73-88; RD Wednesbury 84-88; V Kingswinford St Mary from 88. *17 Penzer Street, Kingswinford, W Midlands DY6 7AA* Kingswinford (0384) 273716

LUNN, Brooke Kingsmill. b 32. TCD BA62 MA66. Chich Th Coll 62. **d** 64 **p** 65. C Northolt Park St Barn *Lon* 64-66; C N St Pancras All Hallows 66-68; P-in-c Hornsey St Luke 68-79; V Stroud Green H Trin from 79; AD

W Haringey from 90. *The Vicarage, Granville Road, London N4 4EL* 081-340 2051

LUNN, Christopher James Edward. b 34. AKC58. d 59 p 60. C Clapham H Trin *S'wark* 59-62; C Cranleigh *Guildf* 63-64; C Ham St Andr *S'wark* 64-66; V Ham St Rich 66-75; V Coulsdon St Andr from 75. *St Andrew's Vicarage, Julien Road, Coulsdon, Surrey CR5 2DN* 081-660 0398

LUNN, David. b 47. Bris Univ BSc69 Dur Univ BA73 DipTh74. St Jo Coll Dur 71. d 74 p 75. C Aigburth *Liv* 74-77; C Slough *Ox* 77-81; P-in-c Haversham w Lt Linford 81-84; R Haversham w Lt Linford, Tyringham w Filgrave from 84; RD Newport from 86. *The Rectory, Haversham, Milton Keynes MK19 7DT* Milton Keynes (0908) 312136

✠**LUNN, Rt Rev David Ramsay.** b 30. K Coll Cam BA53 MA57. Cuddesdon Coll 53. d 55 p 56 c 80. C Sugley *Newc* 55-59; C N Gosforth 59-63; Chapl Linc Th Coll 63-66; Sub-Warden 66-70; V Cullercoats St Geo *Newc* 71-72; TR 72-80; RD Tynemouth 75-80; Bp Sheff from 80. *Bishopscroft, Snaithing Lane, Sheffield S10 3LG* Sheffield (0742) 302170

LUNN, Leonard Arthur. b 42. Trin Coll Bris 69. d 72 p 73. C Walthamstow St Mary w St Steph *Chelmsf* 72-75; V Collier Row St Jas 75-85; V Collier Row St Jas and Havering-atte-Bower 86-87; Chapl St Chris Hospice *S'wark* from 87. *52 Longton Grove, London SE26 6QE* 081-778 0284

LUNN, Canon William Bell. b 21. Edin Th Coll 47. d 50 p 51. R Edin St Mark *Edin* 57-75; Can St Mary's Cathl 68-75; R Fochabers *Mor* 75-86; R Aberlour 75-86; Can St Andr Cathl Inverness 79-86; rtd 86; Hon Can St Andr Cathl Inverness *Mor* from 86. *67 Woodside Drive, Forres, Morayshire IV36 0UF* Forres (0309) 75208

LUNNEY, Henry. b 31. ACIB57. Wycliffe Hall Ox 73. d 74 p 75. C Ipswich St Aug *St E* 74-77; P-in-c Westerfield w Tuddenham St Martin 77-83; R Westerfield and Tuddenham St Martin w Witnesham from 83; Asst Dioc Chr Stewardship Adv 78-83. *The Rectory, Westerfield, Ipswich, Suffolk IP6 9AG* Ipswich (0473) 251073

LUNNON, Robert Reginald. b 31. K Coll Lon BD55 AKC55. St Boniface Warminster 55. d 56 p 57. C Maidstone St Mich *Cant* 56-58; C Deal St Leon 58-62; V Sturry 63-68; V Norbury St Steph 68-77; V Orpington All SS *Roch* from 77; RD Orpington from 79. *The Vicarage, 1A Keswick Road, Orpington, Kent BR6 0EU* Orpington (0689) 824624

LUNT, Canon Ronald Geoffrey. b 13. MC43. Qu Coll Ox BA35 MA38 BD67. Westcott Ho Cam 37. d 38 p 39. Master K Edw VI Sch Birm 52-74; Lic to Offic *Birm* 52-74; Hon Can Birm Cathl 69-74; P-in-c Martley *Worc* 74-78; rtd 78; Perm to Offic *Heref* from 78. *The Station House, Ledbury, Herefordshire HR8 1AR* Ledbury (0531) 3174

LUNT, Canon Ronald Sowden. b 30. Leeds Univ BA56. Ely Th Coll 56. d 58 p 59. C Stockport St Thos *Ches* 58-61; C Ellesmere Port 61-65; V Newton in Mottram 65-78; RD Ches from 78; TR Ches Team from 78; Hon Can Ches Cathl from 82. *The Rectory, 1 Vicar's Lane, Chester CH1 1QX* Chester (0244) 26357

LURIE, Miss Gillian Ruth. b 42. LRAM62 GNSM63 ACertCM80. Gilmore Ho 68. dss 74 d 87. Camberwell St Phil and St Mark *S'wark* 74-76; Haddenham *Ely* 76-79; Dioc Lay Min Adv 79-86; Longthorpe *Pet* 79-81; Pet H Spirit Bretton 81-86; Bramley *Ripon* 86-87; C 87-88; TM from 88. *27 Houghend Lane, Bramley, Leeds LS13 4EY* Pudsey (0532) 576202

LURKINGS, Edward Henry. b 28. AKC53 Lon Univ BSc68 MSc70 PhD81. d 54 p 55. C Brookfield St Mary *Lon* 54-59; C Cricklewood St Pet 59-62; Ind Chapl 62-71; Hon C Luton St Mary *St Alb* 72-84; V Potterspury, Furtho, Yardley Gobion and Cosgrove *Pet* from 84. *The Vicarage, Potterspury, Towcester, Northants NN12 7PU* Yardley Gobion (0908) 542428

LURY, Anthony Patrick. b 49. K Coll Lon BD71 AKC71. St Aug Coll Cant 71. d 72 p 73. C Richmond St Mary *S'wark* 72-76; P-in-c Streatham Hill St Marg 76-81; V Salfords 81-90; V Emscote *Cov* from 90. *All Saints' Vicarage, Vicarage Fields, Warwick CV34 5NJ* Warwick (0926) 492073

LURY, Denys Patrick. b 15. Dur Univ LTh48. Bps' Coll Cheshunt 36. d 38 p 39. V Maidstone St Mich *Cant* 63-72; Chapl St Monica's Home of Rest Westbury-on-Trym 72-80; rtd 80; Perm to Offic *Bris* from 80. *14 Gerrish Avenue, Bristol BS16 5PN* Bristol (0272) 567514

LUSCOMBE, John Nickels. b 45. AKC68. d 69 p 70. C Stoke Newington St Faith, St Matthias and All SS *Lon* 69-74; V Tottenham St Phil 74-81; Zimbabwe 82-86; V Queensbury All SS *Lon* from 86. *The Vicarage, Waltham Drive, Edgware, Middx HA8 5PQ* 081-952 4536

✠**LUSCOMBE, Rt Rev Lawrence Edward.** b 24. ACA52 FSA80 Dundee Univ LLD87. K Coll Lon 63. d 63 p 64 c 75. C Glas St Marg *Glas* 63-66; R Paisley St Barn 66-71; Provost St Paul's Cathl Dundee *Bre* 71-75; R Dundee St Paul 71-75; Bp Bre 75-90; Primus 85-90; rtd 90. *Woodville, Kirkton of Tealing, Dundee DD4 0RD* Tealing (082621) 331

LUSTED, Jack Andrew. b 58. Sussex Univ BSc79 PGCE81. St Steph Ho Ox 88. d 90 p 91. C Moulsecoomb *Chich* from 90. *204 Bevendean Crescent, Moulsecoomb, Brighton BN2 4RD* Brighton (0273) 694335

LUSTY, Ronald Henry. b 23. Ox NSM Course. d 84 p 85. NSM Tilehurst St Mary *Ox* 84-88; NSM Reading H Trin from 88. *St Benedict's, 11 Juniper Way, Tilehurst, Reading RG3 6NB* Reading (0734) 428669

LUTHER, Richard Grenville Litton. b 42. Lon Univ BD64. Tyndale Hall Bris 66. d 68 p 69. C Preston St Mary *Blackb* 68-70; C Bishopsworth *Bris* 70-71; C Radipole *Sarum* 72-76; TV Radipole and Melcombe Regis 77-90; TR Hampreston from 90. *The Rectory, 9 Pinewood Road, Ferndown, Wimborne, Dorset BH22 9RW* Wimborne (0202) 872084

LUTHER, Stuart Frank. b 26. MIEE60 CEng66 FIEE77 Lon Univ BSc57 Southn Univ BA88. Ripon Hall Ox 66. d 69 p 70. C Bexhill St Aug *Chich* 69-72; Hon C Romsey *Win* from 72. *Beech Holme, Whinwhistle Road, East Wellow, Romsey, Hants SO51 6BN* West Wellow (0794) 23322

LUTTON, Percy Theodore Bell Boyce. b 24. TCD BA45 MA48. d 46 p 48. V Wribbenhall *Worc* 61-80; R Castlemorton, Hollybush and Birtsmorton 80-89; rtd 86. *23 Bridgeman Road, Oswestry, Shropshire SY11 2JP* Oswestry (0691) 656425

✠**LUXMOORE, Rt Rev Christopher Charles.** b 26. Trin Coll Cam BA50 MA54. Chich Th Coll 50. d 52 p 53 c 84. C Newc St Jo *Newc* 52-55; C-in-c Newsham St Bede CD 55-57; V Newsham 57-58; Trinidad and Tobago 58-66; V Headingley *Ripon* 67-81; Hon Can Ripon Cathl 80-81; Can Res and Prec Chich Cathl *Chich* 81-84; Bp Bermuda 84-89; Adn Lewes and Hastings *Chich* 89-91; Provost Woodard Corp (S Division) from 89; rtd 91. *42 Willowbed Avenue, Chichester, W Sussex PO19 2JB* Chichester (0243) 784680

LYALL, Canon Graham. b 37. Univ of Wales (Lamp) BA61 Birm Univ DipTh63. Qu Coll Birm 61. d 63 p 64. C Middlesb Ascension *York* 63-67; C Kidderminster St Mary *Worc* 67-72; V Dudley Holly Hall St Aug 72-79; P-in-c Barbourne 79-81; V from 81; RD Worc E 83-89; Hon Can Worc Cathl from 85. *St Stephen's Vicarage, 1 Beech Avenue, Worcester WR3 8PZ* Worcester (0905) 52169

LYDON, Mrs Barbara. b 34. Gilmore Ho 64. dss 72 d 87. Rastrick St Matt *Wakef* 72-85; Upper Hopton 85-87; Par Dn 87; Dn-in-c Kellington w Whitley from 87. *The Vicarage, Manor Farm Close, Kellington, Goole, N Humberside WF14 9PW* Whitley Bridge (0977) 662876

LYES-WILSDON, Mrs Patricia Mary. b 45. ALA65 Open Univ BA86. Glouc Th Course 84 Qu Coll Birm 86. d 87. C Thornbury *Glouc* from 87. *16 Finch Close, Thornbury, Bristol BS12 1TD* Thornbury (0454) 417056

LYNAS, Norman Noel. b 55. St Andr Univ MTh78. CITC 78. d 79 p 80. C Knockbreda *D & D* 79-81; C Holywood 81-85; I Portadown St Columba *Arm* from 85; Dioc Info Officer 86-89; Tutor for Aux Min (Arm) from 88; Radio Officer (Arm) from 90. *81 Loughgall Road, Portadown, Craigavon, Co Armagh BT62 4EG* Portadown (0762) 332746

LYNAS, Stephen Brian. b 52. St Jo Coll Nottm BTh77. d 78 p 79. C Penn *Lich* 78-81; Relig Progr Org BBC Radio Stoke-on-Trent 81-84; C Hanley H Ev 81-82; C Edensor 82-84; Relig Progr Producer BBC Bris 85-88; Lic to Offic *Bris* from 85; Relig Progr Sen Producer BBC S & W England 88-91; Hd of Relig Progr TVS from 91; Perm to Offic *Cant* from 91. *c/o TVS, Vinters Park, Maidstone ME14 5NZ* Maidstone (0622) 684542

LYNCH, Preb Donald MacLeod. b 11. CBE72. Pemb Coll Cam BA34 MA37. Wycliffe Hall Ox. d 35 p 36. Chief Sec CA 60-76; Preb St Paul's Cathl *Lon* 64-76; Chapl to HM The Queen 69-81; P-in-c Seal St Lawr *Roch* 74-85; rtd 76; RD Sevenoaks *Roch* 79-84; P-in-c Underriver 80-85; Perm to Offic Chich and Roch from 86. *Flat 2, 20 Grassington Road, Eastbourne, E Sussex BN20 7BJ* Eastbourne (0323) 20849

LYNCH, James Kenrick. b 20. ACP65. Ripon Hall Ox. d 61 p 62. Chapl Whittingham Hosp 69-72; V Barton *Blackb* 72-81; rtd 81. *12 Willow Tree Avenue, Broughton, Preston*

LYNCH-WATSON, Graham Leslie. b 30. AKC55. d 56 p 57. C New Eltham All SS *S'wark* 56-60; C W Brompton St Mary *Lon* 60-62; V Camberwell St Bart *S'wark* 62-66; V Purley St Barn 67-77; C Caversham *Ox* 77-81; C Caversham and Mapledurham 81-85; P-in-c Warw St Paul *Cov* 85-86; V from 86. *St Paul's Vicarage, 33 Stratford Road, Warwick CV34 6AS* Warwick (0926) 492934

LYNDS, Thomas George. b 34. Lon Coll of Div ALCD62 LTh74. d 62 p 63. C Eastbourne All So *Chich* 62-65; C Edgware *Lon* 65-72; V Wimbledon St Luke *S'wark* 72-85; P-in-c Rainham *Chelmsf* from 85; P-in-c Wennington from 85. *The Vicarage, Broadway, Rainham, Essex RM13 9YW* Rainham (04027) 52752

LYNE, Peter. b 27. Sheff Univ BA51. Qu Coll Birm 51. d 53 p 54. V Elvaston and Shardlow *Derby* 69-74; P-in-c Ashbourne St Jo 74-80; P-in-c Kniveton w Hognaston 75-80; P-in-c Fenny Bentley, Thorpe and Tissington 77-78; P-in-c Osmaston w Edlaston 78-80, P-in-c Lt Eaton 80-84; P-in-c Holbrooke 80-84; V Holbrook and Lt Eaton 84-91; rtd 91. *Plot 2, Vicarage Close, High Street, Belper, Derby* Belper (0773) 829188

LYNE, Roger Howard. b 28. Mert Coll Ox BA52 MA56. Oak Hill Th Coll 52. d 54 p 55. C Bucknall and Bagnall *Lich* 76-81; Perm to Offic *Win* from 82; rtd 88. *21 Copse Road, Burley, Ringwood, Hants BH24 4EG* Burley (04253) 2232

LYNER, John Gregory. b 17. Sarum Th Coll 57. d 59 p 60. V Bringhurst w Gt Easton *Leic* 69-74; R Stoney Stanton 74-80; Perm to Offic from 80; rtd 82. *7 Croft Avenue, Leicester LE2 8LF* Leicester (0533) 831944

LYNESS, Peter Howard Thomas. b 48. Rhodes Univ Grahamstown MA71. Coll of Resurr Mirfield 82. d 84 p 85. S Africa 84-87; Asst Admin of Shrine of Our Lady of Walsingham 87-91; Lic to Offic *Nor* 87-91; V Hockley *Chelmsf* from 91. *The Vicarage, 5A High Road, Hockley, Essex SS5 4SY* Southend-on-Sea (0702) 203668

LYNETT, Anthony Martin. b 54. K Coll Lon BD75 AKC75 Darw Coll Cam PGCE76. Sarum & Wells Th Coll 77. d 78 p 79. C Swindon Ch Ch *Bris* 78-81; C Leckhampton SS Phil and Jas w Cheltenham St Jas *Glouc* 81-83; Asst Chapl HM Pris Glouc 83-88; Chapl from 91; V Coney Hill *Glouc* 83-88; Chapl HM Young Offender Inst Deerbolt 88-91; P-in-c Glouc St Mark *Glouc* from 91. *St Mark's Vicarage, Sandhurst Lane, Gloucester GL2 9AB* Gloucester (0452) 523843

LYNN, Mrs Antonia Jane. b 59. Girton Coll Cam BA80 MA84. St Steph Ho Ox 82. dss 84 d 87. Portsm Cathl Approach 84-87; Dn-in-c Camberwell St Mich w All So w Em *S'wark* 87-91; Par Dn Newington St Mary 87-91; Perm to Offic from 91; Chapl Horton Hosp Epsom from 91. *St Dunstan's Cottage, 1 Tudor Close, Cheam, Surrey SM3 8QS* Epsom (0372) 729696 or 081-641 7911

LYNN, Dixon. b 09. Ely Th Coll 46. d 47 p 48. V Birtley *Newc* 62-75; R Wark 62-75; rtd 75. *Bridge House, Newbrough, Hexham, Northd NE47 5AR* Newbrough (043474) 219

LYNN, Edward Brown. b 14. Dur Univ BA35. Lich Th Coll 37. d 37 p 38. V Market Weighton *York* 66-77; R Goodmanham 66-77; RD Weighton 68-76; V Trimdon Grange *Dur* 77-79; V Trimdon Station 77-79; rtd 80. *53 Alderside Crescent, Lanchester, Co Durham DH7 0PZ* Lanchester (0207) 521456

LYNN, Frank Trevor. b 36. Keble Coll Ox BA61 MA63. St Steph Ho Ox 61. d 63 p 64. C W Derby St Mary *Liv* 63-65; C Chorley *Ches* 65-68; V Altrincham St Jo 68-72; Chapl RN 72-88; Hon C Walworth St Jo *S'wark* 88-90; C Cheam from 90. *4 Tudor Close, Sutton, Surrey SM3 8QS* 081-641 7911

LYNN, Jeffrey. b 39. E Midl Min Tr Course 76 Moore Th Coll Sydney. d 79 p 80. C Littleover *Derby* 79-80; Hon C Allestree 80-85; Chapl HM Pris Man 85-86; Lic to Offic *Man* 85-86; Chapl HM Pris Kirkham from 86. *The Chaplain, HM Prison Kirkham, Preston, Lancashire PR4 2RA* Kirkham (0772) 684343

LYNN, John Cairns. b 40. Surrey Univ BSc63 Lon Univ MSc66. NW Ord Course 73. d 76 p 77. NSM Hunts Cross *Liv* from 76; Chapl Liv Cathl from 80. *2 Bancroft Close, Hunts Cross, Liverpool L25 0LS* 051-486 7833

LYNN, Peter Anthony. b 38. Keele Univ BA62 St Jo Coll Cam BA64 MA68 Man PhD72. Westcott Ho Cam 67. d 68 p 69. C Soham *Ely* 68-72; Min Can St Paul's Cathl *Lon* 72-78; Perm to Offic *St Alb* 78-86; Min Can and Sacr St Paul's Cathl *Lon* 86-88; C Westmr St Matt 89-91; V Glynde, W Firle and Beddingham *Chich* from 91. *The Parsonage, Firle, Lewes, E Sussex BN8 6NP* Glynde (079159) 227

LYNN, Archdeacon of. *See* FOOTTIT, Ven Anthony Charles

LYNN, Suffragan Bishop of. *See* BENTLEY, Rt Rev David Edward

LYON, Adrian David. b 55. Coll of Resurr Mirfield 84. d 87 p 88. C Crewe St Andr *Ches* 87-90; C Altrincham St Geo from 90. *18 Hawarden Road, Altrincham, Cheshire WA14 1NG* 061-928 5897

LYON, Christopher David. b 55. Strathclyde Univ LLB75 Edin Univ BD81. Edin Th Coll 78. d 81 p 82. C Dumfries *Glas* 81-84; P-in-c Alexandria 84-88; R Greenock from 88. *St John's Rectory, 24 Forsyth Street, Greenock, Renfrewshire PA16 9DZ* Greenock (0475) 20750

LYON, Dennis. b 36. Lon Univ DipTh66. Wycliffe Hall Ox 64. d 67 p 68. C Woodthorpe *S'well* 67-70; Warden Walton Cen 70-72; V W Derby Gd Shep *Liv* 72-81; V Billinge from 81; AD Wigan W from 89. *91 Newton Road East, Billinge, Wigan, Lancs WN5 7LB* Billinge (0744) 892210

LYON, Canon Donald Robert. b 20. Trin Coll Cam BA41 DipA44 MA45. Linc Th Coll 46. d 47 p 48. V Glouc St Mark *Glouc* 52-85; Hon Can Glouc Cathl 74-85; RD Glouc City 77-83; rtd 85. *12 Doverdale Drive, Longlevens, Glos GL2 0NN* Gloucester (0452) 24070

LYON, John Harry. b 51. d 89 p 90. NSM S Patcham *Chich* from 89. *52 Barnett Road, Brighton BN1 7GH* Brighton (0273) 507545

LYON, John Richard George. b 21. Em Coll Cam BA43 MA54. Linc Th Coll 44. d 45 p 46. Prin Kilworthy Ho Tavistock 62-71; TR Bickleigh (Plymouth) *Ex* 71-77; rtd 77. *4 Conder Close, Milton, Cambridge CB4 6DZ* Cambridge (0223) 440488

LYON, Stephen Paul. b 49. Univ of Wales (Swansea) BSc71. Trin Coll Bris 74. d 77 p 78. C Hull Newland St Jo *York* 77-81; Chapl Lee Abbey 81-84; V Norbiton *S'wark* from 84; RD Kingston from 88. *21 Wolsey Close, Kingston upon Thames, Surrey KT2 7ER* 081-942 8330

LYONS, Bruce Twyford. b 37. Lon Univ DipTh69. Tyndale Hall Bris 67. d 70 p 71. C Virginia Water *Guildf* 70-73; Chapl Ostend w Knokke and Bruges *Eur* 73-78; V E Ham St Paul *Chelmsf* 78-85; V St Alb Ch Ch *St Alb* from 85; Chapl St Albans City Hosp from 88. *Christ Church Vicarage, 5 High Oaks, St Albans, Herts AL3 6DJ* St Albans (0727) 57592

LYONS, Edward Charles. b 44. Nottm Univ BTh75 LTh. St Jo Coll Nottm 71. d 75 p 76. C Cam St Martin *Ely* 75-78; P-in-c Bestwood Park *S'well* 78-85; R W Hallam and Mapperley *Derby* from 85. *The Rectory, The Village, West Hallam, Derby DE7 6GR* Ilkeston (0602) 324695

LYONS, Margaret Rose Marie. b 47. Local NSM Course 89. d 89. NSM Gainsborough All SS *Linc* from 89. *7 Morley Street, Gainsborough, Lincs DN21 2NF* Gainsborough (0427) 811223

LYONS, Paul Benson. b 44. Qu Coll Birm 68. d 69 p 70. C Rugby St Andr *Cov* 69-70; C Moston St Jo *Man* 70-72; PV Llan Cathl *Llan* 73-74; C Highgate Rise St Anne Brookfield *Lon* 74-75; Perm to Offic 76-82; C Westmr St Sav and St Jas Less 82-86; V Gt Cam Road St Jo and St Jas from 86. *St John's Vicarage, 113 Creighton Road, London N17 8JS* 081-808 4077

LYONS, William. b 22. d 80 p 81. NSM Glenrothes *St And* 80-81; NSM Kirkcaldy 81-91; NSM Kinghorn 81-91. *44 Annandale Gardens, Glenrothes, Fife KY6 1JD* Glenrothes (0592) 751905

✠LYTH, Rt Rev Richard Edward. b 16. St Edm Hall Ox BA38 MA55. Oak Hill Th Coll. d 56 p 57 c 67. C Arthuret *Carl* 56-59; Uganda 59-72; Bp Kigezi 67-72; C Chorleywood St Andr *St Alb* 74-81; rtd 81. *31 Backwoods Lane, Lindfield, Haywards Heath, W Sussex RH16 2EQ* Lindfield (04447) 2500

LYTH, Canon Richard Francis. b 05. Dur Univ LTh25 BA27. Edin Th Coll 22. d 28 p 29. R Uddingston *Glas* 39-75; rtd 75; Hon Can St Mary's Cathl *Glas* from 79. *26 Gardenside Street, Uddingston, Glasgow G71 7BY* Uddingston (0698) 812536

LYTLE, Canon John Deaville. b 23. Wadh Coll Ox BA50 MA52. Wycliffe Hall Ox 50. d 51 p 52. V Bradbourne and Brassington *Derby* 59-89; RD Wirksworth 78-88; Hon Can Derby Cathl from 82; rtd 89; Perm to Offic *Derby* from 89. *14 Manor Road, Ashbourne, Derbyshire DE6 1EH* Ashbourne (0335) 46588

M

MABBS, Miss Margaret Joyce. b 24. St Hilda's Coll Ox BA45 MA47 DipEd46 DipRS82. S'wark Ord Course 79. **dss** 82 **d** 87. Eltham Park St Luke *S'wark* 82-87; Hon Par Dn from 87. *70 Westmount Road, London SE9 1JE* 081-850 4621

McADAM, Alexander William. b 15. Univ of Wales BA37 Jes Coll Ox BA40 MA43. St Mich Coll Llan 39. **d** 41 **p** 42. V Grosmont and Skenfrith *Mon* 50-85; rtd 85. *Sally Rucks, Rectory Lane, Grosmont, Abergavenny, Gwent NP7 8LW* Golden Valley (0981) 240421

McADAM, Canon Michael Anthony. b 30. K Coll Cam BA52 MA56. Westcott Ho Cam 54. **d** 56 **p** 57. C Towcester w Easton Neston *Pet* 56-59; Chapl Hurstpierpoint Coll Hassocks 60-68; Bp's Dom Chapl *Lon* 69-73; R Much Hadham *St Alb* from 73; Hon Can St Alb from 89. *The Rectory, Much Hadham, Herts SG10 6DA* Much Hadham (027984) 2609

✠**McADOO, Most Rev Henry Robert.** b 16. TCD BA38 PhD40 BD48 DD49. Seabury-Western Th Sem Hon STD62. **d** 39 **p** 40 **c** 62. C Waterford H Trin *C & O* 39-43; I Castleventry w Ardfield *C, C & R* 43-48; I Kilmocomogue 48-52; RD Glansalney W and Bere 48-52; Preb Cork Cathl 49-52; Can Cloyne Cathl 49-52; Dean Cork 52-62; Can St Patr Cathl Dub 59-62; Bp Ossory, Ferns and Leighlin 62-77; Dean Leighlin *C & O* 62-63; Abp Dub *D & G* 77-85; rtd 85. *2 The Paddocks, Dalkey, Co Dublin, Irish Republic* Dublin (1) 280-0063

McALEESE, William Henry. b 27. TCD BA53. St Aug Coll Cant 60. **d** 60 **p** 61. I Billis *K, E & A* 68-71; C W Byfleet *Guildf* 71-74; C Gt Bookham 74-77; C Epsom Common Ch Ch 77-80; C Leatherhead 80-86; rtd 86; Perm to Offic *D & D* from 87; Perm to Offic *Conn* from 90. *30 Sharman Road, Belfast BT9 5FW* Belfast (0232) 666776

McALISTER, David. b 39. St Jo Coll Nottm 83. **d** 87 **p** 88. NSM Arpafeelie *Mor* from 87; NSM Cromarty from 87; NSM Fortrose from 87. *4 Alexander Court, Fortrose, Ross-shire IV10 8TZ* Fortrose (0381) 20410

McALISTER, Kenneth Bloomer. b 25. TCD BA51. **d** 51 **p** 53. R Ripley *Ripon* 62-91; rtd 91. *31 Wetherby Road, Knaresborough, N Yorkshire HG5 8LH* Harrogate (0423) 860705

McALISTER, Randall George Leslie. b 41. TCD BA63 MA66. **d** 64 **p** 66. C Portadown St Mark *Arm* 64-67; I Keady w Armaghbreague and Derrynoose 67-74; R Kirriemuir *St And* 74-81; R Greenock *Glas* 81-87; R Forfar *St And* from 87; R Lunan Head from 87. *The Rectory, St James's Road, Forfar, Angus DD8 1LG* Forfar (0307) 63440

McALISTER, Thomas George. b 20. TCD BA42 MA47. **d** 43 **p** 44. Chapl Wispers Sch Surrey 59-79; R Haslemere *Guildf* 69-79; V Slyne w Hest *Blackb* 79-85; rtd 85; Perm to Offic Guildf from 85; Portsm from 86. *Bywoods, Bunch Lane, Haslemere, Surrey GU27 1ET* Haslemere (0428) 3516

McALLEN, James. b 38. Lon Univ BD71. Oak Hill Th Coll 63. **d** 66 **p** 67. C Blackheath St Jo *S'wark* 66-69; C Edin St Thos *Edin* 69-73; V Selby St Jas *York* 73-80; V Wistow 75-80; V Houghton *Carl* from 80. *The Vicarage, Houghton, Carlisle CA6 4HZ* Carlisle (0228) 810076

McALLEN, Robert. b 41. Bps' Coll Cheshunt 62. **d** 65 **p** 66. C Seagoe *D & D* 65-68; C Knockbreda 68-70; CF from 70. *c/o MOD (Army), Bagshot Park, Bagshot, Surrey GU19 5PL* Bagshot (0276) 71717

MACAN, Peter John Erdley. b 36. Bp Gray Coll Cape Town 58 LTh60. **d** 60 **p** 61. S Africa 60-67; C S Lambeth St Ann *S'wark* 68-71; V Nunhead St Silas 72-81; P-in-c Clapham H Spirit 81-87; TV Clapham Team Min 87-90; V Dulwich St Clem w St Pet from 90. *St Clement's Vicarage, 140 Friern Road, London SE22 0AY* 081-693 1890

McARDLE, Thomas. b 16. Edin Th Coll 47. **d** 48 **p** 49. V Pokesdown St Jas *Win* 71-77; P-in-c Bentworth cum Shalden 77-78; P-in-c Bentworth and Shalden and Lasham 78-79; R 79-81; rtd 81; Perm to Offic *Win* from 81. *17 Broadway, Southbourne, Bournemouth BH6 4EG* Bournemouth (0202) 426854

MACARTNEY, Prof Fergus James. b 40. MRCP68 FACC76 FRCP77 Qu Coll Cam BA62 MA84 St Thos Hosp Cam BCh66 MB67. E Anglian Minl Tr Course 86 SW Minl Tr Course 88. **d** 90 **p** 91. NSM Shirwell, Loxhore, Kentisbury, Arlington, etc *Ex* from 90. *Lee Abbey Fellowship, Lynton, Devon EX35 6JJ* Lynton (0598) 52621

MACARTNEY, William Horne. b 08. Qu Coll Cam BA30 MA34. Ridley Hall Cam 31. **d** 33 **p** 34. CMS 68-70; Uganda 68-73; rtd 73; Perm to Offic *Carl* from 74. *56 Crow Green Lane, Pilgrims Hatch, Brentwood, Essex CM15 9RL* Brentwood (0277) 373090

McATEER, John Alexander. b 18. TCD BA44 MA50. CITC 44. **d** 44 **p** 45. V Hammersmith H Innocents *Lon* 59-83; rtd 83; Perm to Offic *Lon* from 83. *162 Sutton Court Road, London W4 3HR* 081-995 5317

MACAULAY, John Roland. b 39. Man Univ BSc61. Wells Th Coll 61. **d** 63 **p** 64. C Padgate Ch Ch *Liv* 63-66; C Upholland 66-73; TV 73-75; V Hindley St Pet 75-81; Chapl Liv Coll from 81. *36 Glenmore Avenue, Mossley Hill, Liverpool L18 4QF* 051-724 3785 or 724 1563

MACAULAY, Kenneth Lionel. b 55. Edin Univ BD78. Edin Th Coll 74. **d** 78 **p** 79. C Glas St Ninian *Glas* 78-80; Dioc Youth Chapl 80-86; P-in-c Glas St Matt 80-86; R Glenrothes *St And* 86-89; Chapl St Mary's Cathl *Glas* from 89; Min Glas St Mary from 89. *c/o St Mary's Cathedral, Great Western Road, Glasgow G4 9JB* 041-339 6691

McAUSLAND, William James. b 36. Edin Th Coll 56. **d** 59 **p** 60. C Dundee St Mary Magd *Bre* 59-64; R 71-79; R Glas H Cross *Glas* 64-71; Chapl St Marg Old Peoples Home 79-85; R Dundee St Marg *Bre* from 79; Chapl St Mary's Sisterhood 82-87; Chapl Dundee Hosps from 85. *19 Ancrum Road, Dundee DD2 2JL* Dundee (0382) 67227

McAVOY, George Brian. b 41. MBE78. TCD BA61 MA72. **d** 63 **p** 65. C Cork St Luke w St Ann *C, C & R* 63-66; I Timoleague w Abbeymahon 66-68; Chapl RAF 68-88; Asst Chapl-in-Chief RAF from 88. *c/o MOD, Adastral House, Theobald's Road, London WC1X 8RU* 071-430 7268

McAVOY, Philip George. b 63. Imp Coll Lon BSc85 SS Coll Cam BA90. Westcott Ho Cam 88. **d** 91. C W End *Win* from 91. *1 Gatcombe Gardens, West End, Southampton, Hants SO3 3NA* Southampton (0703) 466501

McBAY, Canon Walter Ernest. b 17. St Aid Birkenhead 47. **d** 49 **p** 50. R The Shelsleys *Worc* 67-72; V Farndon *S'well* 72-78; R Thorpe 72-78; V Swinefleet *Sheff* 78-80; C Cleethorpes *Linc* 80-83; rtd 83; Perm to Offic *Ex* from 83. *Ellesborough Manor, Butlers Cross, Aylesbury, Bucks HP17 0XF*

MACBETH, Canon Colin Rowland. b 10. Keble Coll Ox BA31 MA35. Westcott Ho Cam 35. **d** 36 **p** 37. R Weeke *Win* 69-75; rtd 75; Perm to Offic Win from 75; Portsm from 82. *2 Brookside Cottages, Brighstone, Newport, Isle of Wight PO30 4DJ* Isle of Wight (0983) 740739

McBRIDE, Stephen Richard. b 61. QUB BSc84 TCD DipTh87 BTh89. CITC 84. **d** 87 **p** 88. C Antrim All SS *Conn* 87-90; I Belf St Pet from 90. *The Rectory, 697 Antrim Road, Belfast BT15 4EH* Belfast (0232) 777053

McCABE, Alan. b 37. Lon Univ BScEng61. Ridley Hall Cam 61. **d** 63 **p** 64. C Bromley SS Pet and Paul *Roch* 63-67; PV Roch Cathl 67-70; V Bromley H Trin 70-77; V Westerham 77-88; V Eastbourne St Jo *Chich* from 88. *9 Buxton Road, Eastbourne, E Sussex BN20 7LL* Eastbourne (0323) 21105

McCABE, John Trevor. b 33. RD78. Nottm Univ BA55 St Cath Soc Ox DipTh59. Wycliffe Hall Ox 57. **d** 59 **p** 60. C Compton Gifford *Ex* 59-63; P-in-c Ex St Martin, St Steph, St Laur etc 63-66; Chapl RNR from 63; Chapl Ex Sch 64-66; V Capel *Guildf* 66-71; V Scilly Is *Truro* 71-74; TR 74-81; Can Res Bris Cathl *Bris* 81-83; V Manaccan w St Anthony-in-Meneage and St Martin *Truro* from 83; RD Kerrier 87-90; Chmn Cornwall NHS Trust for Mental Handicap from 91. *The Vicarage, Manaccan, Helston, Cornwall TR12 6HA* Manaccan (032623) 261

McCABE, Terence John. b 46. Sarum Th Coll 71. **d** 74 **p** 75. C Radford *Cov* 74-77; P-in-c Bris St Paul w St Barn *Bris* 77-80; TV E Bris 80-84; USA 84-90; R Eynesbury *Ely* from 90. *The Rectory, 7 Howitt's Lane, Eynesbury, St Neots, Huntingdon, Cambs PE19 2AJ* St Ives (0480) 403884

McCABE, Thomas Stephen. b 56. TCD BSc77. St Jo Coll Nottm DTS91. **d** 91. C Broadheath *Ches* from 91. *21 Woodheys Drive, Sale, Cheshire M33 4JB* 061-973 5274

McCABE, Dr William Alexander Beck. b 27. QUB BA50 PhD65. **d** 74 **p** 74. Sec Sheff Coun of Chs 74-80; Hon C Millhouses H Trin *Sheff* 74-80; TV Sheff Manor 80-83; C Mosborough 83; C Portsea St Cuth *Portsm* 83-86; C S w N Hayling 86-87; V Mickleover St Jo

Derby from 87. *St John's Vicarage, 7 Onslow Road, Mickleover, Derby DE3 5JJ* Derby (0332) 516545

McCAFFERTY, Canon Christine Ann. b 43. FCA76. Gilmore Course 76. **dss** 79 **d** 87. Writtle *Chelmsf* 79-81; Writtle w Highwood 81-87; Par Dn from 87; NSM Officer from 88; Bp's Dom Chapl (Bradwell) from 88; Hon Can Chelmsf Cathl from 91. *12 Hornbeam Close, Chelmsford CM2 9LW* Chelmsford (0245) 259835

McCALLA, Robert Ian. b 31. AKC55. **d** 56 **p** 57. C Barrow St Jo *Carl* 56-58; C Penrith St Andr 58-61; R Greenheys St Clem *Man* 61-64; V Glodwick 64-71; R Distington *Carl* 71-73; V Howe Bridge *Man* 73-87; Chapl Atherleigh Hosp from 75; R Heaton Mersey *Man* from 87. *St John's Rectory, 15 Priestnall Road, Stockport, Cheshire SK4 3HR* 061-432 2165

MacCALLUM, Norman Donald. b 47. Edin Univ LTh70. Edin Th Coll 66. **d** 71 **p** 72. TV Livingston LEP *Edin* 71-82; P-in-c Bo'ness from 82; R Grangemouth from 82; Miss to Seamen from 82. *33 Carronflats Road, Grangemouth, Stirlingshire FK3 9DG* Grangemouth (0324) 482438

McCAMLEY, Gregor Alexander. b 42. TCD BA64 MA67. CITC 65. **d** 65 **p** 66. C Holywood *D & D* 65-68; C Ban St Comgall 68-72; I Carnalea 72-80; I Knock from 80; Stewardship Adv from 89; Can Down Cathl from 90; Dioc Registrar from 90. *The Rectory, 29 King's Road, Belfast BT5 6JG* Belfast (0232) 471514

McCAMMON, Canon John Taylor. b 42. QUB BSc65 Lon Univ BD70. Clifton Th Coll 67. **d** 71 **p** 72. C Lurgan Ch Ch *D & D* 71-75; I Kilkeel 75-82; I Lisburn Ch Ch Cathl *Conn* from 82; Can Conn Cathl from 85. *Cathedral Rectory, 2 Clonevin Park, Lisburn, Co Antrim BT28 3BL* Lisburn (0846) 662865

McCANDLESS, Archibald Wylie. b 08. AKC34. **d** 34 **p** 35. R Glenfield *Leic* 55-74; rtd 74; Lic to Offic *Leic* 74-80; Perm to Offic from 80. *2 Windrush Drive, Oadby, Leicester LE2 4GH* Leicester (0533) 716658

McCANDLESS, John Hamilton Moore. b 24. QUB BA Ulster Poly BEd. **d** 63 **p** 64. C Jordanstown *Conn* 69-70; I Ballinderry w Tamlaght and Arboe *Arm* 70-74; I Kilbarron w Rossnowlagh and Drumholm *D & R* 84-87; rtd 87. *20 Whinsmoor Park, Broughshane, Co Antrim BT42 4JG* Broughshane (0266) 861898

McCANN, David Terence. b 44. Dur Univ BA67 DipTh69. St Chad's Coll Dur 63. **d** 69 **p** 70. C Tonge Moor *Man* 69-73; C Failsworth St Jo 73-76; Sub-Chapl HM Pris Man from 76; P-in-c Cheetwood St Alb 76-82; C Higher Broughton 76-82; P-in-c Prestwich St Hilda 82-85; V from 85. *St Hilda's Vicarage, 55 Whittaker Lane, Prestwich, Manchester M25 5ET* 061-773 3378

McCANN, Michael Joseph. b 61. Man Univ BSc82 TCD BTh91. **d** 91. C Kilcolman w Kiltallagh, Killorglin, Knockane etc *L & K* from 91. *51 Oldtown Street, Cookstown, Co Tyrone BT80 8EE* Cookstown (06487) 61224

McCANN, Roland Neil. b 39. Serampore Coll BD73. Bp's Coll Calcutta DipTh70. **d** 70 **p** 73. India 70-74; C Earley St Bart *Ox* 74-77; C-in-c Harlington Ch Ch CD *Lon* from 77. *192 Waltham Avenue, Hayes, Middx UB3 1TF* 081-573 0112

✠**McCAPPIN, Rt Rev William John.** b 19. TCD BA40 MA48 BD48. **d** 42 **p** 43 **c** 81. C Arm St Mark *Arm* 42-44; CF (EC) 44-47; P-in-c Belf Ardoyne *Conn* 47-51; I Jordanstown 51-59; Chapl Stranmills Coll Belf 56-68; I Belf St Bart *Conn* 59-71; Min Can Belf Cathl 65-69; Adn Conn 69-79; I Carnmoney 76-81; Bp Conn 81-87; rtd 87. *29 Ballynahinch Road, Carryduff, Belfast BT8 8DN* Belfast (0232) 812350

McCARRAHER, Seymour. b 26. Magd Coll Cam BA48 MA55. St Steph Ho Ox. **d** 55 **p** 56. C Southwick St Columba *Dur* 55-59; Chapl RN 59-75; C Christchurch *Win* 75-81; V Darton *Wakef* from 81. *17 Beaumont Road, Darton, Barnsley, S Yorkshire S75 5JL* Barnsley (0226) 384596

McCARTHY, Brendan. QUB BD MTh TCD DipTh81. **d** 81 **p** 82. C Drumglass *Arm* 81-83; I Ardtrea w Desertcreat 83-90; I Drumragh w Mountfield *D & R* from 90. *Drumragh Rectory, 21 Church Street, Omagh, Co Tyrone BT78 1DG* Omagh (0662) 242130

McCARTHY, David William. b 63. Edin Th Coll BD88. **d** 88 **p** 89. C Edin St Paul and St Geo *Edin* 88-91; P-in-c S Queensferry from 91. *2 Bellstane, South Queensferry, West Lothian EH30 9PU* 031-331 1923

McCARTHY, Ian Christopher. b 52. Liv Univ BA73. Chich Th Coll 84. **d** 86 **p** 87. C Barbourne *Worc* 86-88; C Halesowen 88-90; V Worksop St Paul *S'well* from 90. *St Paul's Vicarage, Cavendish Road, Worksop, Notts S80 2ST* Worksop (0909) 473289

McCARTHY, Very Rev John Francis. b 38. TCD BA61 MA72. **d** 62 **p** 63. C Seapatrick *D & D* 62-66; C Seagoe 66-71; I Moira 71-75; I Dundalk *Arm* 75-86; I Enniskillen *Clogh* from 86; Dean Clogh from 89. *The Deanery, 13 Church Street, Enniskillen, Co Fermanagh BT74 7EJ* Enniskillen (0365) 22465

McCARTHY, Peter James. b 25. OBE. Cranmer Hall Dur. **d** 85 **p** 86. Hon C Farnham w Scotton, Staveley, Copgrove etc *Ripon* 85-87; V Startforth w Bowes from 87. *The Vicarage, Startforth, Barnard Castle, Co Durham DL12 9AF* Teesdale (0833) 37371

MacCARTHY, Preb Robert Brian. b 40. TCD BA63 MA66 PhD83 NUI MA65 Ox Univ MA82. Cuddesdon Coll 77. **d** 79 **p** 80. C Carlow w Urglin and Staplestown *C & O* 79-81; Lic to Offic (Cashel, Waterford and Lismore) 81-86; Lib Pusey Ho 81-82; C Bracknell *Ox* 82-83; TV 83-86; Bp's V and Lib Kilkenny Cathl *C & O* 86-88; C Kilkenny w Aghour and Kilmanagh 86-88; Chapl Kilkenny Coll 86-88; Bp's Dom Chapl 86-89; I Castlecomer w Colliery Ch, Mothel and Bilbo from 88; RD Carlow from 88; Dioc Info Officer (Ossory and Leighlin) 88-90; Preb Ossory Cathl from 90; Preb Leighlin Cathl from 90. *The Rectory, Castlecomer, Co Kilkenny, Irish Republic* Castlecomer (56) 41677

McCARTHY, Terence Arthur. b 46. Kelham Th Coll 66. **d** 70 **p** 71. C Gt Burstead *Chelmsf* 70-74; C Wickford 74-76; TV E Runcorn w Halton *Ches* 76-80; V Runcorn H Trin 80-84; Chapl HM Pris Liv 84; Chapl HM Pris Acklington from 84. *31 High Street, Amble, Morpeth, Northd NE65 0LE* Alnwick (0665) 711888

McCARTNEY, Adrian Alexander. b 57. Stranmillis Coll BEd79 TCD BTh88. St Jo Coll Nottm LTh86. **d** 88 **p** 89. C Jordanstown w Monkstown *Conn* 88-91; Bp's C Monkstown from 91. *22 Rosemount Crescent, Jordanstown, Newtownabbey, Co Antrim BT37 0NH* Belfast (0232) 865160

McCARTNEY, Dr Garfield William Crawford (Brother Garry). MRCGP QUB MB BCh BAO. CITC 88. **d** 90 **p** 91. NSM Belf St Thos *Conn* from 90. *Thornton, 10 Clonevin Park, Lisburn, Co Antrim BT28 3BL* Lisburn (0846) 675320

McCARTNEY, Robert Charles. TCD DipTh85. **d** 85 **p** 85. C Portadown St Mark *Arm* 85-88; I Errigle Keerogue w Ballygawley and Killeshil 88-89; CF from 89. *c/o MOD (Army), Bagshot Park, Bagshot, Surrey GU19 5PL* Bagshot (0276) 71717

MacCARTY, Paul Andrew. b 34. Sarum & Wells Th Coll 73. **d** 75 **p** 76. Ind Chapl *Win* 75-80; C Bournemouth St Andr 75-84; Hon C Christchurch 80-91; C from 91. *3 Douglas Avenue, Christchurch, Dorset BH23 1JT* Christchurch (0202) 483807

McCAUGHEY, Canon Robert Morley. b 07. MA35. **d** 35 **p** 36. V Wisbech SS Pet and Paul *Ely* 61-74; Hon Can Ely Cathl 72-74; rtd 74; Perm to Offic *D & R* from 76. *Ballinahone House, Knockcloughrim, Magherafelt, Co Londonderry* Magherafelt (0648) 42110

McCAUSLAND, Norman. b 58. TCD BTh89. CITC 89. **d** 89 **p** 90. C Portadown St Columba *Arm* from 89. *14 Ardmore Crescent, Portadown, Co Armagh BT62 4DU* Portadown (0762) 331916

McCAY, Alexander Wilson Michael. b 16. Keble Coll Ox BA41 MA45. Cuddesdon Coll 41. **d** 43 **p** 44. Lic to Offic *Worc* 69-78; Chapl St Mich Sch Barnstaple 78-81; rtd 81; R Peebles *Edin* 81-89. *2E, 22 Springbank Gardens, Dunblane, Perthshire FK15 9JX* Dunblane (0786) 825018

McCLATCHEY, Alfred Henry Bailey. b 20. BNC Ox BA48 MA48. **d** 67 **p** 68. V Escomb *Dur* 69-74; V Witton Park 69-74; Bp's Dom Chapl 69-74; Bp's Dom Chapl *Worc* 74-79; R Hartlebury 74-86; rtd 86; Perm to Offic *Worc* from 86. *10 Bellars Lane, Malvern, Worcs WR14 2DN* Malvern (0684) 560336

McCLATCHIE, Canon Donald William. b 40. TCD BA65. CITC 66. **d** 66 **p** 67. C Dub Clontarf *D & G* 66-68; CV Ch Ch Cathl Dub 68-71 and 75-80; P-in-c Dub St Andr 71-75; Prec Ch Ch Cathl Dub 80-89. *Luicelle, Killiney Hill Road, Killiney, Co Dublin, Irish Republic* Dublin (1) 282-6474

McCLAUGHRY, Victor Thomas. b 13. TCD BA34 MA46. **d** 36 **p** 37. V E Preston w Kingston *Chich* 70-79; rtd 79. *16 Woodland Avenue, High Salvington, Worthing, W Sussex BN13 3AF* Worthing (0903) 692971

McCLAY, David Alexander. b 59. TCD DipTh87. **d** 87 **p** 88. C Magheralin w Dollingstown *D & D* 87-90; I Kilkeel from 90. *The Rectory, 44 Manse Road, Kilkeel, Newry, Co Down BT34 4BN* Kilkeel (06937) 62300

McCLEAN, Robert Mervyn. b 38. Edgehill Th Coll Belf 57. **d** 85 **p** 88. NSM Seapatrick *D & D* 85-91; Lic to Offic from 91. *2 Kiloanin Crescent, Banbridge, Co Down BT32 4NU* Banbridge (08206) 27419

McCLELLAN, Bruce. b 44. Selw Coll Cam BA66 MA70. St Steph Ho Ox 66. **d** 68 **p** 69. C Uppingham w Ayston *Pet* 68-72; P-in-c Gt w Lt Harrowden and Orlingbury 72-76; V Hardingstone 76-81; P-in-c Horton w Piddington 79-81; V Hardingstone and Horton and Piddington 81-85; R Crofton *Wakef* from 85. *The Rectory, 5 Hare Park Lane, Crofton, Wakefield, W Yorkshire WF4 1HW* Wakefield (0924) 862373

MACCLESFIELD, Archdeacon of. See GAISFORD, Ven John Scott

McCLOGHRY, James. b 22. St Cath Soc Ox BA49 MA52 Leic Univ Hon DRSS67. Qu Coll Birm 60. **d** 61 **p** 62. R Oxendon w Marston Trussell and E Farndon *Pet* 67-82; R Arthingworth, Harrington w Oxendon and E Farndon 82-83; R Lower Windrush *Ox* 83-89; rtd 89. *6 Hill Top Court, 2 Hill Top Road, Oxford OX4 1PB* Oxford (0865) 793430

McCLOUGHLIN, Joshua. b 27. CITC 69. **d** 70 **p** 71. C Magheraculmoney *Clogh* 70-72; C Cloughfern *Conn* 73-77; I Dunfanaghy *D & R* 77-79; I Drumkeeran w Templecarne and Muckross *Clogh* 79-83; I Aghavea from 83. *Brookeborough, Co Fermanagh* Brookeborough (036553) 210

McCLURE, David Joseph. b 07. TCD BA29 MA41. CITC 29. **d** 30 **p** 31. P-in-c Gt w Lt Oakley *Pet* 68-70; rtd 70; Perm to Offic *Ex* from 85. *Bracken, Harcombe Road, Axminster, Devon EX13 5TB* Axminster (0297) 34780

McCLURE, Robert. b 30. CITC 68. **d** 70 **p** 71. C Monaghan *Clogh* 70-72; C Belf St Matt *Conn* 72-76; Chapl HM Pris Liv 76-77; Preston 77-82; V Foulridge *Blackb* 82-88; rtd 88; Perm to Offic *Liv* from 89. *4 Mill Lane Crescent, Southport, Merseyside PR9 7PF* Southport (0704) 27476

McCLURE, Timothy Elston. b 46. St Jo Coll Dur BA68. Ridley Hall Cam 68. **d** 70 **p** 71. C Kirkheaton *Wakef* 70-73; C Chorlton upon Medlock *Man* 74-79; Chapl Man Poly 74-82; TR Man Whitworth 79-82; Gen Sec SCM from 82; Perm to Offic *Birm* from 83. *SCM Central Office, 186 St Paul's Road, Balsall Heath, Birmingham B12 8LZ* 021-440 3000

McCOLLOUGH, John Keith. b 45. AKC66. **d** 68 **p** 69. C Kilburn St Aug *Lon* 68-71; C Holborn St Alb w Saffron Hill St Pet 71-74; C Kenton 74-80; V Eyres Monsell *Leic* 80-85; TR Bury Ch King w H Trin *Man* from 85. *Holy Trinity Vicarage, Spring Street, Bury, Lancs BL9 0RW* 061-764 2006

McCOLLUM, Charles James. b 41. TCD BTh89. CITC 85. **d** 89 **p** 90. C Larne and Inver *Conn* 89-91; Bp's C Belf Whiterock from 91. *St Columba's Rectory, 194 Ballygomartin Road, Belfast BT13 3NF* Belfast (0232) 721134

McCOLLUM, Canon Robert George. b 20. TCD BA43 MA60. **d** 44 **p** 45. C Dub Santry w Glasnevin *D & G* 44-48; C Taney w St Nahi 48-54; I Donabate w Lusk 54-62; I Dub Clontarf 62-89; Can Ch Ch Cathl Dub 83-89; RD Fingal 84-89; I Rathmolyon w Castlerickard, Rathcore and Agher *M & K* from 89. *The Rectory, Rathmolyon, Co Meath, Irish Republic* Enfield (405) 55267

McCOMB, Samuel. b 33. CITC 70. **d** 71 **p** 72. C Belf St Mich *Conn* 71-74; C Lisburn Ch Ch 74-79; I from 83; I Ballinderry *Arm* 79-83. *27 Hillsborough Road, Lisburn, Co Antrim BT28 1JL* Lisburn (0846) 662163

McCONACHIE, Robert Noel. b 40. Golds Coll Lon BA86. Oak Hill Th Coll 86. **d** 88 **p** 89. C Larkfield *Roch* from 88. *The Rectory, 73 Rectory Lane North, Leybourne, Maidstone, Kent ME19 5HD* West Malling (0732) 842187

McCONNELL, Brian Roy. b 46. St Paul's Grahamstown DipTh71. **d** 71 **p** 72. S Africa 71-77 and 79-85; C Prestwich St Marg *Man* 77-79; V Liscard St Mary w St Columba *Ches* 85-90; V Altrincham St Geo from 90. *St George's Vicarage, Townfield Road, Altrincham, Cheshire WA14 4DS* 061-928 1279

McCONNELL, Peter Stuart. b 54. Linc Th Coll 89. **d** 91. C N Shields *Newc* from 91. *24 Cleveland Road, North Shields, Tyne & Wear NE29 0NG* 091-258 0554

McCONNELL, Robert Mark. b 60. Oak Hill Th Coll BA88. **d** 89 **p** 90. C Bedf Ch Ch *St Alb* from 89. *161 Dudley Street, Bedford MK40 3SY* Bedford (0234) 40630

McCORMACK, David Eugene. b 34. Wells Th Coll 66. **d** 68 **p** 69. C Lillington *Cov* 68-71; C The Lickey *Birm* 71-75; V Highters Heath 75-82; V Four Oaks from 82. *The Vicarage, 2 Walsall Road, Sutton Coldfield, W Midlands B74 4QJ* 021-308 5315

McCORMACK, George Brash. b 32. ACIS65 FCIS75 Lon Univ DipRS85. S'wark Ord Course 82. **d** 85 **p** 86. Hon C

Crofton St Paul *Roch* 85-89; C Crayford 89-91; R Fawkham and Hartley from 91. *The Rectory, 3 St John's Lane, Hartley, Dartford, Kent DA3 8ET* Longfield (04747) 3819

McCORMACK, John Heddon. b 58. Chich Th Coll 85. **d** 88 **p** 89. C Cleobury Mortimer w Hopton Wafers *Heref* 88-90; C Lymington *Win* from 90. *St Thomas's House, 10 Jonathan Close, Lymington, Hants SO41 9DY* Lymington (0590) 678488

McCORMACK, Kevan Sean. b 50. Chich Th Coll 77. **d** 80 **p** 81. C Ross *Heref* 80-81; C Ross w Brampton Abbotts, Bridstow and Peterstow 81-83; C Leominster 83; TV Leominster 84-87; Chapl R Hosp Sch Holbrook from 87. *48 The Royal Hospital School, Holbrook, Ipswich IP9 2RT* Holbrook (0473) 328847

McCORMACK, Mrs Lesley Sharman. b 50. E Anglian Minl Tr Course. **d** 88. Hon Par Dn Chevington w Hargrave and Whepstead w Brockley *St E* from 88. *Stonehouse Farm, Chevington, Bury St Edmunds, Suffolk IP29 5QW* Chevington (0284) 850277

McCOUBREY, William Arthur. b 36. CEng MIMechE. Sarum & Wells Th Coll 86. **d** 89 **p** 90. C Bedhampton *Portsm* from 89. *2 Lester Avenue, Bedhampton, Havant, Hants* Havant (0705) 483624

McCOULOUGH, David. b 61. Man Univ BA84 St Jo Coll Dur BA88. Cranmer Hall Dur 86. **d** 89 **p** 90. C Man Apostles w Miles Platting *Man* from 89. *86 Stainer Street, Longsight, Manchester M12 4PB* 061-225 6942

McCOULOUGH, Thomas Alexander. b 32. AKC59. **d** 60 **p** 61. C Norton St Mich *Dur* 60-63; India 63-67; P-in-c Derby St Jas *Derby* 67-72; Ind Chapl *York* 72-82; P-in-c Sutton on the Forest from 82; Dioc Sec for Local Min 82-89; Lay Tr Officer from 89. *The Vicarage, Sutton on the Forest, York YO6 1DW* Easingwold (0347) 810251

McCREA, Basil Wolfe. b 21. QUB BA49. Wycliffe Hall Ox 51. **d** 53 **p** 54. I Cork H Trin *C, C & R* 68-72; I Carrigaline Union 72-90; rtd 90. *30 Somerville, Carrigaline, Co Cork, Irish Republic* Cork (21) 371538

McCREA, Francis. b 53. **d** 91. C Dundonald *D & D* from 91. *6 Mount-Regan Avenue, Dundonald BT16 0JA* Belfast (0232) 485557

McCREADIE, Michael Cameron. b 51. Southn Univ. Chich Th Coll 74. **d** 77 **p** 78. C St Bart Armley w St Mary New Wortley *Ripon* 77-80; C Hemsworth *Wakef* 80-83; V Carlinghow from 83. *St John's Vicarage, 8A Amber Street, Batley, W Yorkshire WF17 8HH* Batley (0924) 472576

McCREADY, Marcus Diarmuid Julian. b 63. NUU BA85 TCD BTh88. **d** 88 **p** 89. C Seagoe *D & D* 88-91; I Clonallon w Warrenpoint from 91. *Clonallon Rectory, Donaghaguy Road, Warrenpoint, Newry, Co Down BT34 3RZ* Warrenpoint (06937) 72267

McCREADY, Maurice Shaun. b 55. MA. Ripon Coll Cuddesdon. **d** 83 **p** 84. C Bridgwater St Fran *B & W* 83-86; C Walton-on-Thames *Guildf* 86-88; C Elm Park St Nic Hornchurch *Chelmsf* from 88. *39 Woodcote Avenue, Elm Park, Hornchurch, Essex RM12 4PY* Hornchurch (04024) 52740

McCREERY, Canon William Robert Desmond. b 35. QUB BD. Oak Hill Th Coll 59. **d** 62 **p** 63. C Dundonald *D & D* 62-66; C Belf St Donard 66-69; I Annalong 69-78; I Knockbreda 78-89; Can Belf Cathl from 88; I Ban St Comgall *D & D* from 89. *2 Raglan Road, Bangor, Co Down BT20 3TL* Bangor (0247) 465230

McCRORY, Canon Peter. b 34. Chich Th Coll 63. **d** 67 **p** 68. C St Marychurch *Ex* 67-72; R Kenn 72-76; R Kenn w Mamhead 76-78; Bp's Dom Chapl S'wark 78-81; V Kew from 81; RD Richmond and Barnes 84-89; Hon Can S'wark Cathl from 90. *The Vicarage, 278 Kew Road, Kew, Richmond, Surrey TW9 3EE* 081-940 4616

McCRORY, Walter Edward. b 38. TCD 66. **d** 69 **p** 70. C Carrickfergus *Conn* 69-73; C Ballywillan 73-76; I Armoy w Loughguile and Drumtullagh from 76. *181 Glenshesk Road, Ballymoney, Co Antrim* Armoy (02657) 51226

McCUBBIN, Very Rev David. b 29. AKC54. **d** 55 **p** 56. R Kirkcaldy *St And* 63-70; R Wallsend St Pet *Newc* 70-79; R Aber St Jo *Ab* 79-81; R Glas St Bride *Glas* 81-87; Provost Cumbrae Cathl *Arg* from 87; Hon Can Cumbrae from 87; Can St Jo Cathl Oban from 87; R Cumbrae (or Millport) from 87; Syn Clerk from 88; rtd 89. *The College, Millport, Isle of Cumbrae KA28 0HE* Millport (0475) 530353

McCULLAGH, John Eric. b 46. TCD BA68 BTh88 QUB DipEd70. **d** 88 **p** 89. C Stillorgan w Blackrock *D & G* 88-91; Chapl and Hd of RE Newpark Sch Dub from 90; I Clondalkin w Rathcoole from 91. *The Rectory, Monastery Road, Clondalkin, Dublin 22, Irish Republic* Dublin (1) 592160

McCULLAGH, Mervyn Alexander. b 44. TCD BA68 BEng68. CITC 79. d 79 p 80. C Larne and Inver *Conn* 79-83; C Ballymacash 83-85; C Dub St Ann w St Mark and St Steph *D & G* 85-88; I Baltinglass w Ballynure etc *C & O* from 88; Warden of Readers from 90. *The Rectory, Baltinglass, Co Wicklow, Irish Republic* Baltinglass (508) 81321

MCCULLOCH, Alistair John. b 59. Univ of Wales (Lamp) BA81 Leeds Univ BA86. Coll of Resurr Mirfield 84. d 87 p 88. C Portsm Cathl *Portsm* 87-90; C Portsea St Mary from 90. *2 Glebe Flats, Nutfield Place, Portsmouth PO1 4JF* Portsmouth (0705) 826892

MacCULLOCH, Diarmaid Ninian John. b 51. Chu Coll Cam BA72 PhD77 Ox Univ DipTh87. Ripon Coll Cuddesdon 86. d 87. NSM Clifton All SS w St Jo *Bris* 87-88. *28 William Street, Bristol BS3 4TT*

McCULLOCH, Donald. b 25. Linc Th Coll 50. d 52 p 53. V Whitleigh *Ex* 68-75; V Whipton 75-90; rtd 90; Perm to Offic *Ex* from 90. *32 Rendlesham Gardens, Plymouth PL6 8SS* Plymouth (0752) 793503

McCULLOCH, Geoffrey Kenneth. b 10. OBE57. d 64 p 65. V Kingston upon Hull St Matt w St Barn *York* 71-79; rtd 79; Perm to Offic *Lon* from 79. *5 Roy Road, Northwood, Middx HA6 1EQ* Northwood (09274) 27438

MacCULLOCH, Nigel John Howard. b 03. TD50. Edin Th Coll 29. d 31 p 32. V Haughley w Wetherden *St E* 58-72; rtd 72; Perm to Offic *St E* from 72. *3 Klondyke Cottages, Tollgate Lane, Bury St Edmunds IP32 6DB* Bury St Edmunds (0284) 5859

✠McCULLOCH, Rt Rev Nigel Simeon. b 42. Selw Coll Cam BA64 MA69. Cuddesdon Coll 64. d 66 p 67 c 86. C Ellesmere Port *Ches* 66-70; Dir Th Studies Ch Coll Cam 70-75; Chapl 70-73; Dioc Missr *Nor* 73-78; P-in-c Salisbury St Thos and St Edm *Sarum* 78-81; R 81-86; Adn Sarum 79-86; Can and Preb Sarum Cathl 79-86; Preb Wells Cathl *B & W* from 86; Suff Bp Taunton from 86. *Sherford Farm House, Sherford, Taunton, Somerset TA1 3RF* Taunton (0823) 288759

McCULLOCH, Wg Comdr Robert Lewis. b 11. St Cath Coll Cam BA35 MA40. Linc Th Coll 35. d 37 p 38. V Kingsdown *Cant* 65-71; C Worksop St Anne *S'well* 72-74; P-in-c Radford All So w Ch Ch and St Mich 74-81; rtd 81; Perm to Offic *S'well* from 81. *7 Castle Mews, Lenton Avenue, The Park, Nottingham NG7 1EA* Nottingham (0602) 475258

McCULLOCK, Patricia Ann. b 46. CertEd72. E Midl Min Tr Course 87. d 90. C Bottesford w Ashby *Linc* from 90. *43 Copse Road, Ashby, Scunthorpe, S Humberside DN16 3JA* Scunthorpe (0724) 860415

McCULLOUGH, Roy. b 46. Linc Th Coll 70. d 73 p 74. Chapl Highfield Priory Sch Lancs 73-77; C Ashton-on-Ribble St Andr *Blackb* 73-77; V Rishton 77-86; V Burnley (Habergham Eaves) St Matt w H Trin from 86; RD Burnley from 91. *11 St Matthew Court, Harriet Street, Burnley, Lancs BB11 4JH* Burnley (0282) 24849

McCULLOUGH, Sidney. b 31. QUB BA53 DipEd61 MEd74. CITC. d 89 p 91. NSM Glencraig *D & D* 89-91; Lic to Offic from 91. *Dunowen, 153 Church Road, Holywood, Co Down BT18 9BZ* Holywood (02317) 3277

McCURDY, Hugh Kyle. b 58. Portsm Poly BA Univ of Wales (Cardiff) PGCE. Trin Coll Bris. d 85 p 86. C Egham *Guildf* 85-88; C Woking St Jo 88-91; V Histon *Ely* from 91. *The Vicarage, 1 Croft Close, Histon, Cambridge CB4 4HU* Cambridge (0223) 2255

McCURRY, Preb Norman Ernest. b 19. St Edm Hall Ox BA40 MA46. Chich Th Coll 40. d 46 p 47. V Armley St Bart *Ripon* 63-72; P-in-c New Wortley St Mary w Armley Hall 67-72; V St Bart Armley w St Mary New Wortley 72; R Stepney St Dunstan and All SS *Lon* 72-85; AD Tower Hamlets 78-83; Preb St Paul's Cathl 80-85; rtd 85; Hon C Westmr St Jas *Lon* from 87. *18 Chisenhale Road, London E3 5QZ* 081-981 4655

McCUTCHEON, Miss Irene. See TEMPLETON, Irene

McDERMID, Ven Norman George Lloyd Roberts. b 27. St Edm Hall Ox BA49 MA52. Wells Th Coll 49. d 51 p 52. C Leeds St Pet *Ripon* 51-56; V Bramley 56-64; Dioc Stewardship Adv 64-76; R Kirkby Overblow 64-80; Hon Can Ripon Cathl from 72; Dioc Stewardship Adv *Wakef* 73-76; Dioc Stewardship Adv *Bradf* 73-76; RD Harrogate *Ripon* 77-83; V Knaresborough 80-83; Adn Richmond from 83. *62 Palace Road, Ripon, N Yorkshire HG4 1HA* Ripon (0765) 4342

McDERMID, Canon Richard Thomas Wright. b 29. St Jo Coll Dur BA53 DipTh55 MA81. d 55 p 56. C Seacroft *Ripon* 55-61; V Hawksworth Wood 61-70; V High Harrogate Ch Ch from 70; Chapl Harrogate Distr Hosp 75-89; Hon Can Ripon Cathl *Ripon* from 83; Chapl to

HM The Queen from 86. *Christ Church Vicarage, 11 St Hilda's Road, Harrogate, N Yorkshire HG2 8JX* Harrogate (0423) 883390

McDERMOTT, John Alexander James. b 52. Lon Univ BSc74 MSc78 K Coll Cam BA80. Westcott Ho Cam 78. d 81 p 82. C Bethnal Green St Jo w St Bart *Lon* 81-84; P-in-c Walkern *St Alb* 84-86; R Benington w Walkern 86-87. *Address temp unknown*

MACDONALD, Alan Hendry. b 49. St Steph Ho Ox 86. d 88 p 89. C Heavitree w Ex St Paul *Ex* 88-91; C Withycombe Raleigh from 91. *St John's Vicarage, 3 Diane Close, Exmouth, Devon EX8 5PG* Exmouth (0395) 270094

MACDONALD, Alastair Douglas. b 48. St Jo Coll Dur 71. d 74 p 75. C Mottingham St Andr *S'wark* 74-78; C Woolwich St Mary w St Mich 78-81; V S Wimbledon St Andr 81-89; V Brighton St Matthias *Chich* from 89. *St Matthias's Vicarage, 45 Hollingbury Park Avenue, Brighton BN1 7JQ* Brighton (0273) 508178

MACDONALD, Cameron. b 51. Open Univ BA89. Wilson Carlile Coll 76 NE Ord Course 89. d 90 p 91. CA from 76; C Nairn *Mor* from 90. *1 Clova Crescent, Nairn IV12 4TE* Nairn (0667) 52458

MACDONALD, Colin. b 47. St Jo Coll Nottm 87. d 89 p 90. C Gt Limber w Brocklesby *Linc* from 89. *The Glebe House, Church Lane, Limber, Grimsby, S Humberside DN37 8JN* Roxton (0469) 61082

MACDONALD, Derek. b 45. Lon Univ DipTh77. Oak Hill Th Coll 74. d 77 p 78. C Braunstone *Leic* 77-80; Australia from 80. *94 Armstrong Road, Wilson, W Australia 6107* Perth (9) 458-2674

MACDONALD, Donald Courtenay. b 45. Nottm Univ BTh74 St Martin's Coll Lanc CertEd75. Kelham Th Coll 70. d 75 p 76. C Clifton All SS w Tyndalls Park *Bris* 75-78; C Clifton All SS w St Jo 78-79; Chapl Derby Lonsdale Coll *Derby* 79-84; V Derby St Andr w St Osmund from 84; RD Derby S from 89; Dioc Communications Officer from 89. *St Osmund's Vicarage, London Road, Derby DE2 8UW* Derby (0332) 571329

McDONALD, Douglas Mark. b 28. Linc Coll Ox BA54 MA59. Wells Th Coll 68. d 69 p 70. C Horsham *Chich* 69-76; TV Kirkby Lonsdale *Carl* 76-79; P-in-c Tidmarsh w Sulham *Ox* 79-83; Chapl St Audries Sch W Quantoxhead *B & W* from 83. *18 Lower Park, Minehead, Somerset TA24 8AX* Minehead (0643) 703104

McDONALD, Gordon James Joseph. b 17. Wycliffe Hall Ox 50. d 52 p 53. V Pemberton St Mark Newtown *Liv* 63-80; R Easton w Letheringham *St E* 80-83; rtd 83. *91 Ridgeway, Sherborne, Dorset DT9 6DB* Sherborne (0935) 813011

MACDONALD, Henry George Warren. b 20. TCD BA42 MA46 BD46. Div Test43. d 43 p 44. C Dub St Thos w St Barn *D & G* 43-47; Chapl RNVR 47-49; Chapl RN 49-75; QHC from 74; C Fulford *York* 75-79; Perm to Offic *Ex* from 79; OCF from 87. *12 Little Ash Road, Plymouth PL5 1JT* Plymouth (0752) 361271

McDONALD, Ian Henry. b 40. St Aid Birkenhead 65. d 68 p 69. C Kingston upon Hull H Trin *York* 68-70; C Drumglass *Arm* 70-73; I Killylea 73-80; I Eglish *L & K* 73-80; I Maghera w Killelagh *D & R* 80-91; I Killowen from 91; CF (TAVR) from 91. *St John's Rectory, Laurel Hill, Coleraine, Co Derry* Coleraine (0265) 42629

McDONALD, James Stewart. b 31. St Mich Coll Llan 59. d 62 p 63. C Haslingden w Haslingden Grane *Blackb* 62-66; V Preston St Jude 66-73; V Blackpool St Wilfrid 73-85; V Blackb St Aid from 85. *St Aidan's Vicarage, St Aidan's Avenue, Blackburn BB2 4EA* Blackburn (0254) 53519

MacDONALD, John. b 16. St Cath Soc Ox BA38 MA42 BLitt58. St Steph Ho Ox 39. d 41 p 42. Chapl Burgess Hall Lamp 60-76; Sub-Warden 62-76; V Edstaston *Lich* 76-82; V Whixall 76-82; Chapl Choral Ches Cathl *Ches* 82-85; rtd 85. *47 The Links, Gwernaffield, Mold, Clwyd CH7 5DZ* Mold (0352) 740015

MACDONALD, John Alexander. b 07. Tyndale Hall Bris. d 41 p 42. V Byker St Mark *Newc* 53-80; rtd 80. *135 Bosworth Gardens, Newcastle upon Tyne NE6 5UP* 091-265 7486

McDONALD, John Richard Burleigh. b 17. TCD BA40 BD41. d 41 p 42. C Belf St Pet *Conn* 41-45; Uganda 46-61; Educn Officer Ch of Ireland 61-64; Hd of RE Stranmills Coll Belf 66-86; Dir Post-Ord Tr *Conn* from 86. *76 Osborne Drive, Belfast BT9 6LJ* Belfast (0232) 666737

McDONALD, Lawrence Ronald. b 32. St Alb Minl Tr Scheme 84. d 87 p 88. NSM Sharnbrook and Knotting w Souldrop *St Alb* 87-90; C Bromham w Oakley and Stagsden from 90. *65 Lincroft, Oakley, Bedford MK43 7SS* Oakley (02302) 6153

MACDONALD, Malcolm James. b 42. Sarum Th Coll 70. **d** 71 **p** 73. C Hounslow St Steph *Lon* 71-72; C Hammersmith St Sav 72-76; P-in-c Hammersmith St Luke 76-79; V 79-87; V Kirkby Woodhouse *S'well* from 87. *The Vicarage, 57 Skegby Road, Kirkby-in-Ashfield, Nottingham NG17 9JE* Mansfield (0623) 759094

MACDONALD, Canon Murray Somerled. b 23. Pemb Coll Cam BA46 MA49. Ely Th Coll 47. **d** 48 **p** 49. V Fenstanton *Ely* 62-70; V Hilton 62-70; RD Huntingdon 69-76; R Huntingdon All SS w St Jo 70-82; R Huntingdon St Mary w St Benedict 71-82; Hon Can Ely Cathl 72-82; Can Res 82-88; rtd 89; Perm to Offic *Linc* from 89. *4 Hacconby Lane, Morton, Bourne, Lincs PE10 0NT* Morton (0778) 37711

MACDONALD, Ranald Alexander. b 23. Fitzw Ho Cam BA50 MA55. Westmr Coll Cam 48 Lon Coll of Div 63. **d** 63 **p** 63. In Pb Ch 51-62; R Parham & Wiggonholt w Greatham *Chich* 67-83; P-in-c Bolam w Whalton *Newc* 83-86; P-in-c Hartburn and Meldon 83-86; P-in-c Netherwitton 83-88; R Bolam w Whalton and Hartburn w Meldon 86-88; rtd 88; Perm to Offic *Chich* from 88. *2 Redbarn Cottages, High Street, Henfield, W Sussex BN5 9HP* Henfield (0273) 493370

MACDONALD, Stephen Calliss. b 35. Selw Coll Cam BA58. Westcott Ho Cam 58. **d** 60 **p** 61. C Norwood All SS *Cant* 60-64; Chapl Cov Cathl *Cov* 64-68; Chr Aid 68-70. *Crossways, Breachwood Green, Hitchin, Herts SG4 8PL* Kimpton (0438) 833210

McDONALD, William Ivan Orr. b 19. TCD BA48 MA54. Qu Coll Birm 49. **d** 50 **p** 51. Dean's V Belf Cathl 62-70; V Woolhope *Heref* 70-85; rtd 85; Perm to Offic *Heref* from 85. *1 Wyeview Villas, Hereford HR2 7RA* Hereford (0432) 59133

MACDONALD-MILNE, Brian James. b 35. CCC Cam BA58 MA62 St Pet Coll Ox MA81. Cuddesdon Coll 58. **d** 60 **p** 61. C Fleetwood *Blackb* 60-63; Solomon Is 64-78; New Hebrides 78-80; Acting Chapl Trin Coll Ox 81; Acting Chapl St Pet Coll Ox 81-82; Asst Chapl HM Pris Grendon and Spring Hill 81-82; Research Fell Qu Coll Birm 82-83; Hon AP Bordesley SS Alb and Patr *Birm* 82-83; R Landbeach *Ely* 83-88; V Waterbeach 83-88; OCF 83-88; R Radwinter w Hempstead *Chelmsf* from 88; RD Saffron Walden from 91. *The Rectory, Radwinter, Saffron Walden, Essex CB10 2SW* Radwinter (0799) 599332

MACDONALD-STEELE, Arthur Henry. b 14. Selw Coll Cam BA36. Linc Th Coll 38. **d** 38 **p** 39. P-in-c N Tuddenham *Nor* 69-75; P-in-c Hockering 69-75; rtd 75. *Amble, 6 Brentwood, Greenways, Norwich NR4 6PW* Norwich (0603) 56925

MACDONNELL, Charles Leonard. b 54. Bris Univ BA76. Ripon Coll Cuddesdon 76. **d** 78 **p** 79. C Swindon New Town *Bris* 78-80; C Westbury-on-Trym H Trin 80-82; TV Redruth w Lanner *Truro* 82-87; V Hayle from 87. *S Elwyn's Vicarage, Penpol Avenue, Hayle, Cornwall TR27 4NQ* Hayle (0736) 754866

McDONOUGH, David Sean. b 55. **d** 89 **p** 90. C Moseley St Mary *Birm* from 89. *4 Woodrough Drive, Birmingham B13 9EP* 021-449 1336

McDONOUGH, Terence. b 57. St Jo Coll Nottm LTh86. **d** 89 **p** 90. C Linthorpe *York* from 89. *64 Queens Road, Middlesbrough, Cleveland TS5 6EE* Middlesbrough (0642) 819248

McDOUGALL, David Robin. b 61. Avery Hill Coll CertEd BEd84. Ridley Hall Cam 85. **d** 87 **p** 88. C Bletchley *Ox* 87-91; C High Wycombe from 91. *Greensleeves, Bassetsbury Lane, High Wycombe, Bucks HP11 1RB* High Wycombe (0494) 27992

MacDOUGALL, Iain Ferguson. b 27. OBE JP. Clare Coll Cam BA51 MA55. Sarum & Wells Th Coll 85. **d** 86 **p** 87. NSM Langport Area Chs *B & W* 86-87; NSM Sedbergh, Cautley and Garsdale *Bradf* 87-90; NSM Appleby Deanery *Carl* from 90; OCF from 90. *Sandford Lodge, Sandford, Appleby-in-Westmorland, Cumbria CA16 6NR* Appleby (07683) 52978

MacDOUGALL, Canon Iain William. b 20. TCD BA43 MA59. CITC 43. **d** 43 **p** 44. I Mullingar, Portnashangan, Moyliscar, Kilbixy etc *M & K* 58-85; Can Meath 81-85; rtd 85. *Inchacrone, Lough Ennell, Mullingar, Co Westmeath, Irish Republic* Mullingar (44) 41820

McDOUGALL, Stuart Ronald. b 28. Leeds Univ DipAdEd MEd84. Roch Th Coll 64. **d** 66 **p** 67. C Wells St Thos w Horrington *B & W* 69-70; TV Tong *Bradf* 70-73; V Cononley w Bradley 73-82; C Thornthwaite w Thruscross and Darley *Ripon* 82-83; P-in-c Dacre w Hartwith 83-86; rtd 86. *Smallbridge Cottage, Edmondsham, Wimborne, Dorset BH21 5RH* Cranborne (07254) 626

MACDOUGALL, William Duncan. b 47. Nottm Univ BTh74 LTh74. St Jo Coll Nottm 69. **d** 74 **p** 75. C Highbury New Park St Aug *Lon* 74-77; C Tunbridge Wells St Jo *Roch* 78; SAMS 77 and 78-82; Argentina 78-82; V Rashcliffe and Lockwood *Wakef* 83-87; V Tonbridge St Steph *Roch* from 87. *St Stephen's Vicarage, 6 Brook Street, Tonbridge, Kent TN9 2PJ* Tonbridge (0732) 353079

McDOWALL, Julian Thomas. b 39. CCC Cam BA62 MA67. Linc Th Coll 62. **d** 64 **p** 65. C Rugby St Andr *Cov* 64-70; C-in-c Stoke Hill CD *Guildf* 70-72; V Stoke Hill 72-76; R Elstead from 76; V Thursley from 82. *The Rectory, Thursley Road, Elstead, Godalming, Surrey GU8 6DG* Elstead (0252) 703251

McDOWALL, Robert Angus. b 39. AKC66. **d** 67 **p** 68. C Bishopwearmouth St Mich w St Hilda *Dur* 67-69; CF 69-80; Sen CF from 80; Perm to Offic *Birm* from 91. *c/o MOD (Army), Bagshot Park, Bagshot, Surrey GU19 5PL* Bagshot (0276) 71717

McDOWALL, Roger Ian. b 40. AKC64. **d** 65 **p** 66. C Peterlee *Dur* 65-68; C Weaste *Man* 68-70; C Tonge Moor 70-73; V Whitworth 73-80; TV Torre *Ex* 80-88; V Torre All SS from 88. *All Saints' Vicarage, 45 Barton Road, Torquay TQ1 4DT* Torquay (0803) 328865

McDOWELL, Charles. b 16. BEM65. Bps' Coll Cheshunt 64. **d** 66 **p** 67. C Hilborough w Bodney *Nor* 66-70; R Colkirk 70-74; P-in-c Whissonsett w Horningtoft 71-74; R Colkirk w Oxwick, Whissonsett and Horningtoft 74-77; P-in-c Harpley 77-79; R 79-81; R Gt Massingham 77-81; rtd 81; Hon C Emscote *Cov* 85-90; Clergy Widows Officer & Chapl Cov from 90. *4 Margetts Close, Kenilworth, Warwicks CV8 1EN* ' Kenilworth (0926) 58567

MACE, Alan Herbert. b 28. Lon Univ BA49. Wycliffe Hall Ox. **d** 60 **p** 61. C Disley *Ches* 60-63; C Folkestone H Trin w Ch Ch *Cant* 63-67; Lic to Offic *Win* from 67. *15 Bassett Heath Avenue, Southampton SO1 7GP* Southampton (0703) 768161

MACE, Helen Elizabeth. b 31. Ox Univ MA. Coll of Ascension. dss 74 **d** 87. Tadcaster *York* 78-83; Asst Chapl Leeds Gen Infirmary from 83. *25 Grosvenor Park Gardens, Leeds LS6 2PL* Leeds (0532) 432799

MACE, Robert Alfred Beasley. b 16. Leeds Univ BA49. Coll of Resurr Mirfield 48. **d** 50 **p** 51. V Barnsley St Pet *Wakef* 65-72; V Barnsley St Pet and St Jo 72-84; rtd 85; Perm to Offic *Wakef* from 85. *90 Blenheim Road, Barnsley, S Yorkshire S70 6AS* Barnsley (0226) 283831

McEACHRAN, Peter. b 30. **d** 75 **p** 76. Pakistan 75-79; Area Sec (Dios Ox and St Alb) CMS from 79; Hon C Haddenham w Cuddington, Kingsey etc *Ox* from 79; rtd 86. *107 Sheerstock, Haddenham, Aylesbury, Bucks HP17 8EY* Haddenham (0844) 291436

McELHINNEY, Canon Samuel Herbert. b 08. TCD BA30 MA38. **d** 31 **p** 32. I Lambeg *Conn* 59-74; Can Conn Cathl 62-74; rtd 74. *5 Girona Avenue, Portrush, Co Antrim BT56 8HJ* Portrush (0265) 822637

McENDOO, Neil Gilbert. b 50. TCD BA72. CITC 75. **d** 75 **p** 76. C Cregagh *D & D* 75-79; C Dub St Ann *D & G* 79-82; I Dub Rathmines w Harold's Cross from 82. *The Rectory, Purser Gardens, Church Avenue, Rathmines, Dublin 6, Irish Republic* Dublin (1) 971797

MCENERY, Michael Joseph. b 35. Cant Sch of Min 77. **d** 80 **p** 81. C Smarden *Cant* 80-83; P-in-c 83-85; P-in-c Biddenden 83-85; P-in-c Harrietsham 85-86; P-in-c Ulcombe 85-86; R Harrietsham w Ulcombe 86-90; R Willesborough from 90. *The Rectory, 66 Church Road, Willesborough, Ashford, Kent TN24 0JG* Ashford (0233) 624064

MACEY, Anthony Keith Frank. b 46. Univ of Wales (Cardiff) DipTh69. St Steph Ho Ox 69. **d** 71 **p** 72. C Ex St Thos *Ex* 71-76; V Wembury 76-88; RD Ivybridge from 83; V Cockington from 88. *The Vicarage, 22 Monterey Close, Torquay TQ2 6QW* Torquay (0803) 607957

MACEY, Ralph Arthur. b 14. TD63. Leeds Univ BA38. Coll of Resurr Mirfield 38. **d** 40 **p** 41. Hd of RE Newc Ch High Sch 67-80; Hon C Gosforth All SS *Newc* 67-76; Hon C Cullercoats St Geo from 76; rtd 79. *11 Trafalgar House, Oxford Street, Tynemouth, Tyne & Wear NE30 4PR* 091-257 0019

McFADDEN, Canon Ronald Bayle. b 30. TCD BA53 MA55. **d** 54 **p** 55. V Pateley Bridge and Greenhow Hill *Ripon* 64-73; V Knaresborough St Jo 73-79; P-in-c Knaresborough H Trin 78-79; Can Res Ripon Cathl 79-90; rtd 90; Chapl Qu Mary's Sch Baldersby Park from 90. *12 Ure Bank Terrace, Ripon, N Yorkshire HG4 1JG* Ripon (0765) 604043

McFADYEN, Phillip. b 44. K Coll Lon BD69 AKC69 MTh70 ATD. St Aug Coll Cant 69. **d** 71 **p** 72. C Sheff

Broomhall St Mark *Sheff* 71-74; Chapl Keswick Hall Coll Nor 74-79; V Swardeston *Nor* 79-81; P-in-c E Carleton 79-81; P-in-c Intwood w Keswick 79-81; R Swardeston w E Carleton w Intwood and Keswick 81-85; R Swardeston w E Carleton, Intwood, Keswick etc 85-90; V Ranworth w Panxworth and Woodbastwick from 90; Dioc Clergy Tr Officer from 90. *The Vicarage, Ranworth, Norwich NR13 6HT* South Walsham (060549) 263

McFARLAND, Alan Malcolm. b 24. Lon Univ BA53. Bris Sch of Min 82. d 85 p 86. NSM Westbury-on-Trym H Trin *Bris* 85-88; Bris Sch of Min 85-88; Perm to Offic *Glouc* 88-89; NSM Lechlade from 89. *3 Briary Road, Lechlade, Glos GL7 3DD* Faringdon (0367) 52974

McFARLANE, Beverly. b 50. RGN. d 87. NSM Dundee St Martin *Bre* 87-90. *c/o Edinburgh Theological College, Coates Hall, Roseberry Crescent, Edinburgh EH12 5JT* 031-337 3838

MACFARLANE, William Angus. b 17. Worc Coll Ox BA39 MA43. Wycliffe Hall Ox 39. d 40 p 41. V Bexleyheath Ch Ch *Roch* 71-79; Perm to Offic *B & W* from '79; Chapl Sandhill Park Hosp Taunton 80-87; rtd 82. *Moorlands, Blue Anchor, Minehead, Somerset TA24 6JZ* Dunster (0643) 564

McFIE, Canon James Ian. b 28. Lich Th Coll 59. d 61 p 62. C Salford St Phil w St Steph *Man* 61-65; V Hey 65-75; V Elton All SS 75-85; V Walmsley from 85; AD Walmsley from 85; Hon Can Man Cathl from 90. *Walmsley Vicarage, Egerton, Bolton BL7 9RZ* Bolton (0204) 54283

McGARAHAN, Kevin Francis. b 51. Oak Hill Th Coll BA84. d 84 p 85. C Balderstone *Man* 84-87; Sports Chapl from 86; C Stoughton *Guildf* 87-89; C Ashton St Mich *Man* from 89. *26 Beaufort Road, Ashton-under-Lyne, Lancs OL6 6PJ* 061-330 8236

McGEARY, Peter. b 59. K Coll Lon BD AKC. Chich Th Coll 84. d 86 p 87. C Brighton St Pet and St Nic w Chpl Royal *Chich* 86-90; C St Marylebone All SS *Lon* from 90. *6 Margaret Street, London W1N 7LG* 071-636 1788

McGEE, Preb Peter John. b 36. Trin Coll Cam BA60 MA. Chich Th Coll 60. d 62 p 63. C N Keyham *Ex* 62-63; C St Marychurch 63-65; C Townstall w Dartmouth 65-68; C Cockington 68-71; V Exminster 71-78; V Alfington 78-82; V Ottery St Mary 78-82; RD Ottery 82-90; Preb Ex Cathl from 82; TR Ottery St Mary, Alfington and W Hill 82-87; TR Ottery St Mary, Alfington, W Hill, Tipton etc from 87. *The Vicar's House, Ottery St Mary, Devon EX11 1DQ* Ottery St Mary (040481) 2062

McGEE, Canon Stuart Irwin. b 30. TCD BA53 MA68. d 53 p 54. C Belf St Simon *Conn* 53-55; Singapore 55-58; I Drumholm and Rossnowlagh *D & R* 58-65; CF 65-77; Dep Asst Chapl Gen 77-88; Can Achonry Cathl *T, K & A* from 89; I Achonry w Tubbercurry and Killoran from 89. *The Rectory, Tubbercurry, Co Sligo, Irish Republic* Sligo (71) 85205

MacGILLIVRAY, Canon Alexander Buchan. b 33. Edin Univ MA55 Aber Univ DipEd67. Edin Th Coll 55. d 57 p 58. Chapl St Ninian's Cathl Perth *St And* 57-59; Chapl Aberlour Orphanage 59-62; C Aberlour *Mor* 59-62; R Oldmeldrum *Ab* from 62; R Whiterashes from 62; R Fyvie from 74; R Insch from 74; Can St Andr Cathl from 78. *The Rectory, Oldmeldrum, Inverurie, Aberdeenshire AB5 0AD* Oldmeldrum (06512) 2208

MacGILLIVRAY, Jonathan Martin. b 53. Aber Univ MA75. Coll of Resurr Mirfield. d 80 p 81. C Hulme Ascension *Man* 80-84; P-in-c Birch St Agnes 84-85; R from 85. *St Agnes's Rectory, Slade Lane, Manchester M13 0GN* 061-224 2596

McGINLEY, Jack Francis. b 36. ALCD65. d 65 p 66. C Erith St Paul *Roch* 65-70; C Morden *S'wark* 70-74; V New Catton Ch Ch *Nor* from 74; RD Nor N 84-89; Hon Can Nor Cathl from 90. *Christ Church Vicarage, 65 Elm Grove Lane, Norwich NR3 3LF* Norwich (0603) 408332

McGIRR, William Eric. b 43. CITC 68. d 71 p 72. C Carrickfergus *Conn* 71-74; C M Merrion *D & D* 74-77; I Donacavey w Barr *Clogh* 77-88; RD Kilskeery 86-88; I Ballybeen *D & D* from 88. *The Rectory, 149 Comber Road, Dundonald, Belfast BT16 0BU* Dundonald (0232) 485491

McGLASHAN, Alastair Robin. b 33. MSAnPsych90 Ch Ch Ox BA57 MA58 St Jo Coll Cam BA59 MA63. Ridley Hall Cam 58. d 60 p 61. C St Helens St Helen *Liv* 60; C Ormskirk 60-62; India 63-74; USA 74-75; C Lamorbey H Redeemer *Roch* 75-77; Chapl W Park Hosp Epsom 77-85; Maudsley Hosp Lon 85-87; Perm to Offic *S'wark* from 86. *102 Westway, London SW20 9LS* 081-542 2125

McGONIGLE, Canon Thomas. b 22. TCD BA45 MA65. TCD Div Sch 43. d 46 p 47. I Magherafelt *Arm* 74-88; I Portadown St Mark 61-74; Can Arm Cathl 72-88; Treas 79-83; Chan 83-88; Prec 88; rtd 88; Lic to Offic *Arm* from 88. *91 Kernan Gardens, Portadown, Craigavon, Co Armagh BT65 5RA* Portadown (0762) 330892

McGOWAN, Anthony Charles. b 57. Jes Coll Cam BA79 MA. Coll of Resurr Mirfield. d 82 p 83. C Milford Haven *St D* 82-85; C Penistone *Wakef* 85-86; C Thurlstone 85-86; C Penistone and Thurlstone 86-88; CR from 88. *House of the Resurrection, Mirfield, W Yorkshire WF14 0BN* Mirfield (0924) 494318

McGOWAN, James Rutherford. b 30. Trin Hall Cam BA53 MA58. Ely Th Coll 53. d 55 p 56. C Portsea St Alb *Portsm* 55-58; Asst Chapl St Edw Sch Ox 58-62; Chapl Westmr Sch 62-68; Swaziland 68-69; Chapl K Sch Ely 70-73; R Duxford *Ely* 73-79; P-in-c Ickleton 78-79; V Buckland *Ox* 79-80; V Littleworth 79-80; R Pusey 79-80; R Warbleton and Bodle Street Green *Chich* from 84. *Warbleton Rectory, Rushlake Green, Heathfield, E Sussex TN21 9QJ* Rushlake Green (0435) 830421

McGOWAN, John Boby. b 11. ARCO36 FRCO56 Dur Univ LTh39 Fitzw Ho Cam BA49 MA54. Oak Hill Th Coll 36. d 39 p 41. V Thorpe-le-Soken *Chelmsf* 71-76; rtd 76. *Waymarks, 28 Hadleigh Road, Frinton-on-Sea, Essex CO13 9HU* Frinton-on-Sea (0255) 672752

McGOWAN, Michael Hugh. b 35. St Cath Coll Cam BA58 MA62. Clifton Th Coll. d 60 p 61. C Islington St Mary *Lon* 60-63; Chapl Lyon w Grenoble and Aix-les-Bains *Eur* 63-67; Chapl Chantilly, Rouen, Caen and Le Havre 63-65; Asst Chapl Chapl Paris St Mich 63-67; V Maidenhead St Andr and St Mary Magd *Ox* 68-81; V S Mimms Ch Ch *Lon* from 82; AD Cen Barnet from 91. *Christ Church Vicarage, St Albans Road, Barnet, Herts EN5 4LA* 081-449 0832

McGOWN, Robert Jackson. b 20. Keble Coll Ox BA42 MA46. Linc Th Coll 42. d 45 p 46. C W Kirby St Bridget *Ches* 64-71; Perm to Offic from 76; rtd 85. *16 Church Road, West Kirby, Wirral, Merseyside L48 0RW* 051-625 9481

McGRANAGHAN, Patrick Joseph Colum. b 46. Glas Univ BSc68 Lanc Univ MA72. St Alb Minl Tr Scheme. d 85 p 86. NSM Markyate Street *St Alb* from 85. *Clovelly Court, Glencairn Road, Kilmacolm, Renfrewshire PA13 4NR* Kilmacolm (050587) 2733

McGRATH, Alister Edgar. b 53. Wadh Coll Ox BA75 Mert Coll Ox MA78 DPhil78 BD83. Westcott Ho Cam 78. d 80 p 81. C Wollaton *S'well* 80-83; Tutor Wycliffe Hall Ox from 83; Chapl St Hilda's Coll Ox 83-87. *Wycliffe Hall, Oxford OX2 6PW* Oxford (0865) 274209 or 244658

McGRATH, Dr Gavin John. b 53. Marietta Coll (USA) BA76 Trin Episc Sch for Min MDiv81 Dur Univ PhD90. d 81 p 82. USA 81-87; C Fulwood *Sheff* from 87. *1 Silver Birch Avenue, Sheffield S10 3TA* Sheffield (0742) 630926

McGRATH, Ian Denver. b 47. Leeds Univ CertEd72. Local NSM Course 85. d 87 p 88. NSM Ancaster *Linc* 87-89; NSM Ancaster Wilsford Gp from 89. *8 Charles Avenue, Ancaster, Grantham, Lincs NG32 3QH* Loveden (0400) 30857

McGRATH, John. b 49. Salford Univ BSc78 Man Poly CertEd79. N Ord Course 82. d 85 p 86. C Horwich *Man* 85-88; P-in-c Hillock 88-89; V from 89. *St Andrew's Vicarage, Mersey Drive, Whitefield, Manchester M25 6LA* 061-766 5561

McGREEVY, Roy. b 34. Wycliffe Hall Ox 75. d 77 p 78. C Poynton *Ches* 77-79; TV E Runcorn w Halton 79-80; V Norton 80-83; V Congleton St Steph from 83. *St Stephen's Vicarage, 6 Brook Street, Congleton, Cheshire CW12 1RJ* Congleton (0260) 272994

McGREGOR, Alistair Darrant. b 45. ALCD69. d 69 p 70. C Streatham Immanuel w St Anselm *S'wark* 69-73; Bermuda 73-76; Warden St Mich Cen New Cross 76-80; C Hatcham St Jas *S'wark* 76-80; V Nor Heartsease St Fran *Nor* 80-87; TR Thetford from 87; P-in-c Kilverstone 87-90; P-in-c Croxton 87-90; RD Thetford and Rockland from 90. *The Rectory, 6 Redcastle Road, Thetford, Norfolk IP24 3NF* Thetford (0842) 762291

MacGREGOR, Colin Highmoor. b 19. Lon Univ BSc45 Magd Coll Cam BA47 MA50. Wells Th Coll 54. d 56 p 57. V Clapham St Pet *S'wark* 60-73; V Riddlesdown 73-87; rtd 87. *Flat 3, Longacre Court, 21 Mayfield Road, South Croydon, Surrey* 081-651 2615

MACGREGOR, Gregor. b 33. St Andr Univ MA64 BD67. d 77 p 77. NSM Elie and Earlsferry *St And* 77-81; NSM Pittenweem 77-81; R Glenrothes 81-86; C Cumbrae (or Millport) *Arg* 86; P-in-c Dollar *St And* 86-91; Miss Priest Wester Hailes St Luke *Edin* from 91; TV Edin St Luke from 91. *c/o 15 Ardmillan Terrace, Edinburgh EH11 2JW* 031-337 5493

MacGREGOR, Neil. b 35. Keble Coll Ox BA60 MA80. Wells Th Coll. **d** 65 **p** 66. C Bath Bathwick St Mary w Woolley *B & W* 65-70; R Oare w Culbone 70-74; P-in-c Kenn w Kingston Seymour 74-76; R 76-80; V Lee Brockhurst *Lich* from 80; R Wem from 80. *The Rectory, Ellesmere Road, Wem, Shrewsbury SY4 5TU* Wem (0939) 32550

McGREGOR, Nigel Selwyn. b 47. FCA69. Sarum & Wells Th Coll 87. **d** 89 **p** 90. C Charlton Kings St Mary *Glouc* from 89. *3 Copt Elm Road, Charlton Kings, Cheltenham, Glos GL53 8AG* Cheltenham (0242) 519095

McGUFFIE, Duncan Stuart. b 45. MA DPhil. S Dios Minl Tr Scheme. **d** 85 **p** 85. C Sholing *Win* 85-89; V Clavering w Langley and Arkesden *Chelmsf* from 89. *The Vicarage, 54 Pelham Road, Clavering, Saffron Walden, Essex CB11 4PQ* Clavering (079985) 256

McGUINNESS, Gordon Baxter. b 57. St Andr Univ BSc79 BNC Ox MSc80. Oak Hill NSM Course. **d** 89 **p** 90. NSM Loudwater *Ox* from 89. *20 Melbourne, Micklefield, High Wycombe, Bucks HP13 7HD* High Wycombe (0494) 34732

McGUIRE, Alec John. b 51. Societas Liturgica 85 MRSH86 BAC Accred90 K Coll Cam BA73 MA76. Westcott Ho Cam 74. **d** 78 **p** 79. C Hungerford and Denford *Ox* 78-81; Prec Leeds St Pet *Ripon* 81-86; Perm to Offic from 86. *34 Gledhow Wood Road, Leeds LS8 4BZ* Leeds (0532) 400336

McGUIRE, John. b 31. Oak Hill Th Coll 59. **d** 62 **p** 65. C Tooting Graveney St Nic *S'wark* 62-64; C Normanton *Derby* 64-67; N Area Sec ICM 67-71; Chapl RNR 67-81; R Biddulph Moor *Lich* from 71. *The Rectory, Hot Lane, Biddulph Moor, Stoke-on-Trent ST8 7HP* Stoke-on-Trent (0782) 513323

McHARDY, Canon Iain William Thomson Duff. b 13. St Andr Univ MA36. Ely Th Coll 37. **d** 38 **p** 39. P-in-c Invergordon *Mor* 52-74; R Fortrose 74-80; Dean Mor 77-80; rtd 80; Hon Can St Andr Cathl Inverness *Mor* from 80. *Beech Tree Cottage, Navity, Cromarty, Ross-shire IV11 8XY* Cromarty (03817) 451

MACHIN, Roy Antony. b 38. BA79. Oak Hill Th Coll 76. **d** 79 **p** 80. C Halliwell St Pet *Man* 79-83; V Eccleston St Luke *Liv* 83-91; V Kendal St Thos *Carl* from 91; V Crook from 91. *St Thomas's Vicarage, Queen's Road, Kendal, Cumbria LA9 4PL* Kendal (0539) 21509

McHUGH, Brian Robert. b 50. FSS77 AFIMA83. York Univ BA72 Keele Univ CertEd73 Southn Univ CEurStuds78 Portsm Poly CertComp84 DPSE90. S Dioc Minl Tr Scheme 79. **d** 82 **p** 83. NSM Sarisbury *Portsm* 82-86; NSM Shedfield from 86. *28 Siskin Close, Bishops Waltham, Southampton SO3 1RQ* Bishops Waltham (0489) 896658

MACINNES, Canon David Rennie. b 32. Jes Coll Cam BA55 MA59. Ridley Hall Cam 55. **d** 57 **p** 58. C Gillingham St Mark *Roch* 57-61; C St Helen Bishopsgate w St Martin Outwich *Lon* 61-67; Prec Birm Cathl *Birm* 67-78; Angl Adv ATV 67-82; Dioc Missr 79-87; Hon Can Birm Cathl 81-87; Angl Adv Cen TV from 82; R Ox St Aldate w St Matt *Ox* from 87. *St Aldate's Parish Centre, 40 Pembroke Street, Oxford OX1 1BP* Oxford (0865) 244713

MACINTOSH, Andrew Alexander. b 36. St Jo Coll Cam BA59 MA63 BD80. Ridley Hall Cam 60. **d** 62 **p** 63. C S Ormsby Gp *Linc* 62-64; Lect St D Coll Lamp 64-67; Lic to Offic *Ely* from 67; Chapl St Jo Coll Cam from 67; Asst Dean 69-79; Lect Th from 70; Dean from 79. *St John's College, Cambridge CB2 1TP* Cambridge (0223) 338600

McINTOSH, Andrew Malcolm Ashwell. b 43. Chich Th Coll 67. **d** 70 **p** 71. C Brentwood St Thos *Chelmsf* 70-74; C Chingford SS Pet and Paul 74-79; P-in-c Maldon St Mary w Mundon 79-83; R from 83. *St Mary's Rectory, Park Drive, Maldon, Essex CM9 7JG* Maldon (0621) 857191

McINTOSH, David Henry. b 45. St Jo Coll Dur BSc67 DipTh69 LTCL87. Cranmer Hall Dur 67. **d** 70 **p** 71. C Sutton *Liv* 70-74; TV 74-75; Chapl Bethany Sch Goudhurst 75-80; V Douglas St Thos *S & M* 80-87; Dir RE and Adv in Children's Work 80-87; TV Ellesmere Port *Ches* from 88. *The Vicarage, Seymour Drive, Ellesmere Port, South Wirral L66 1LZ* 051-355 3988

MacINTOSH, George Gordon. b 41. St Jo Coll Dur BA75 DipTh76. **d** 76 **p** 77. C Ecclesall *Sheff* 76-79; Hon C Sheff St Oswald 79-81; Dioc Adult Educn Officer from 81; V Crookes St Tim 81-88; V Abbeydale St Jo from 88; RD Ecclesall from 89. *St John's Vicarage, 2 Devonshire Glen, Sheffield S17 3NY* Sheffield (0742) 360786

McINTOSH, Canon Hugh. b 14. Hatf Coll Dur LTh41 BA42 MA45. Edin Th Coll 38. **d** 42 **p** 42. R Lanark *Glas* 70-83; Can St Mary's Cathl 70-83; rtd 83; Hon Can St Mary's Cathl *Glas* from 83. *2 Ridgepark Drive, Lanark ML11 7PG* Lanark (0555) 3458

MCINTOSH, Ian MacDonald. b 64. Jes Coll Cam BA86. Trin Coll Bris BA90. **d** 90 **p** 91. C Belmont *Lon* from 90. *116 Uppingham Avenue, Stanmore, Middx HA7 2JU* 081-907 8573

MCINTOSH, Nicola Ann. b 60. Trin Coll Bris DipHE89 ADPS90. **d** 90. Par Dn Queensbury All SS *Lon* from 90. *116 Uppingham Avenue, Stanmore, Middx HA7 2JU* 081-907 8573

MACINTYRE, Angus Greer. b 14. Linc Coll Ox BA36 DipTh39 MA41. Wycliffe Hall Ox 38. **d** 39 **p** 40. V Harborne St Pet *Birm* 68-76; St Helena 76-79; rtd 79; Hon C Edin Ch Ch *Edin* 79-90. *12 Inverleith Place, Edinburgh EH3 5PZ* 031-551 3287

McINTYRE, James Whitelaw. b 37. Lon Univ BD66. Edin Th Coll 59. **d** 62 **p** 63. C Dumfries *Glas* 62-66; P-in-c Cumbernauld 66-74; R Stirling *Edin* from 74. *The Rectory, 24 Cedar Avenue, Stirling FK8 2PQ* Stirling (0786) 74380

McINTYRE, Robert Marshall. b 08. Wells Th Coll. **d** 47 **p** 48. V Wells St Cuth *B & W* 63-71; V Publow w Pensford 71-75; R Publow w Pensford, Compton Dando and Chelwood 75-76; rtd 76. *1 Water Lane, Lopen, South Petherton, Somerset TA13 5JW* South Petherton (0460) 40160

MACK, Mrs Gillian Frances. b 50. SCM73. Cant Sch of Min 84. **d** 87. NSM Deal St Geo *Cant* 87-88; NSM Deal St Leon and St Rich and Sholden from 88. *91 Blenheim Road, Deal, Kent CT14 7HA* Deal (0304) 362598

McKAE, William John. b 42. Liv Univ BSc63 Bris Univ DipTh70. Wells Th Coll 68. **d** 71 **p** 72. C Tranmere St Paul w St Luke *Ches* 71-74; C Midsomer Norton *B & W* 74-75; TV Birkenhead Priory *Ches* 75-80; R Oughtrington 80-91; Asst Chapl Hope Hosp Salford and Man and Salford Skin Hosp from 91. *The Chaplain's Office, Hope Hospital, Stott Lane, Salford, Manchester M6 8HD* 061-787 5167 or 789 7373

McKAVANAGH, Dermot James. b 51. TCD BA75 MA78 K Coll Lon BD78 AKC78. **d** 78 **p** 79. C Croydon H Sav *Cant* 78-82; Asst Chapl Wellington Coll Berks 82-87; Lic to Offic *Ox* 85-87; Chapl RAF from 87. *c/o MOD, Adastral House, Theobald's Road, London WC1X 8RU* 071-430 7268

McKAY, Brian Andrew. b 39. Sarum Th Coll 69. **d** 71 **p** 72. C Walker *Newc* 71-74; C Wooler Gp 74-77; TV 77-81; V Long Benton St Mary 81-89; TV Bellingham/Otterburn Gp from 89. *The Vicarage, Otterburn, Newcastle upon Tyne NE19 1NP* Otterburn (0830) 20212

MACKAY, Canon Douglas Brysson. b 27. Edin Th Coll 56. **d** 58 **p** 59. Prec St Andr Cathl Inverness *Mor* 58-61; P-in-c Fochabers 61-70; R 70-72; Chapl Aberlour Orphanage 64-67; P-in-c Aberlour 64-72; Syn Clerk 65-72; Can St Andr Cathl Inverness 65-72; Hon Can from 72; R Carnoustie *Bre* from 72; Can St Paul's Cathl Dundee from 81; Syn Clerk from 81. *The Rectory, Carnoustie, Angus DD7 6AB* Carnoustie (0241) 52202

MACKAY, Hedley Neill. b 27. St Aid Birkenhead 53. **d** 56 **p** 57. C Beverley St Mary *York* 56-59; C Scarborough St Mary 59-60; Nigeria 61-70; C Wawne *York* 70-71; TV Sutton St Jas and Wawne 72-76; V Huntington 76-82; TR from 82. *The Rectory, Huntington, York YO3 9NU* York (0904) 768160

MACKAY, James Alexander Nigel. b 11. TCD BA38. Edin Th Coll 38. **d** 41 **p** 42. V Weasenham *Nor* 62-67; V Rougham 62-67; Perm to Offic *Lon* 72-76; rtd 76. *29 Howbury Street, Bedford MK40 3QU*

McKAY, John Andrew. b 38. HDipEd. Chich Th Coll. **d** 74 **p** 75. C Primrose Hill St Mary w Avenue Road St Paul *Lon* 74-77; V Battersea Ch Ch and St Steph *S'wark* 77-82; I Rathkeale w Askeaton and Kilcornan *L & K* 82-85; I Dub St Bart w Ch Ch Leeson Park *D & G* from 85. *12 Merlyn Road, Ballsbridge, Dublin, Irish Republic* Dublin (1) 269-4813

McKAY, John William. b 41. Aber Univ MA62 Keble Coll Ox BA64 Selw Coll Cam PhD69. Ridley Hall Cam 66. **d** 70 **p** 71. Lect Th Hull Univ 69-82; Hon C Cottingham *York* 70-79; Hon C Willerby 79-82; R Prestwick *Glas* 82-85; Dir of Studies Roffey Place Chr Tr Cen Horsham from 85. *Roffey Place Training Centre, Faygate, Horsham, W Sussex RH12 4SA* Faygate (029383) 543

McKAY, Canon Roy. b 1900. Magd Coll Ox BA23 MA26. Ripon Hall Ox 24. **d** 26 **p** 27. R St Jas Garlickhythe w St Mich Queenhithe etc *Lon* 64-70; rtd 71. *12 Torkington Gardens, West Street, Stamford, Lincs PE9 2EW* Stamford (0780) 53181

McKEARNEY, Andrew Richard. b 57. Selw Coll Cam MA. Edin Th Coll 81. **d** 82 **p** 83. Prec St Ninian's Cathl Perth *St And* 82-84; Chapl St Mary's Cathl *Edin* 84-88; R Hardwick *Ely* from 88; R Toft w Caldecote and Childerley from 88. *The Rectory, Hardwick, Cambridge CB3 7QS* Madingley (0954) 210695

McKECHNIE, John Gregg. b 30. Em Coll Cam BA54 MA57. Ridley Hall Cam 54. **d** 55 **p** 56. C Morden *S'wark* 55-57; Tutor Clifton Th Coll 57-62; R Chich St Pancras and St Jo *Chich* 62-68; V Reading St Jo *Ox* 68-85; RD Reading 83-85; V Lindfield *Chich* from 85. *The Vicarage, Lindfield, Haywards Heath, W Sussex RH16 2HR* Lindfield (0444) 482386

McKEE, Douglas John Dunstan. b 34. Univ of W Aus BA65. St Mich Th Coll Crafers 54. **d** 57 **p** 58. Australia 57-72 and from 85; SSM from 58; Lic to Offic *S'well* 73-85. *14 St John's Street, Adelaide, S Australia 5000* Adelaide (8) 223-2348

McKEE, Canon Harold Denis. b 30. TCD BA53 MA57. **d** 54 **p** 55. C Dub Donnybrook *D & G* 54-58; Treas V St Patr Cathl Dub 56-61; C Dub St Bart 58-61; Succ Sheff Cathl *Sheff* 61-65; Can Res and Prec 65-86; C Preston St Jo *Blackb* 86-87; TV from 87. *St George's Vicarage, 6 Hastings Road, Preston, Lancs PR2 1EU* Preston (0772) 729577

McKEE, William Mulholland. b 05. **d** 49 **p** 50. R Greenstead juxta Colchester *Chelmsf* 58-74; P-in-c Farnham 74-80; rtd 80; Perm to Offic *Ex* from 87. *7 Dukes Orchard, Bradninch, Devon EX5 4RA* Exeter (0392) 881929

McKEE, William Thomas. b 18. CITC 64. **d** 65 **p** 66. C Willowfield *D & D* 68-73; Bp's C Magherally w Annaclone 73-77; I 77-85; rtd 85. *7 Donaghadee Road, Bangor, Co Down BT20 5RX* Bangor (0247) 459598

McKEEMAN, David Christopher. b 36. AKC58 DipEd76. **d** 60 **p** 61. C Catford St Andr *S'wark* 60-64; P-in-c W Dulwich Em 64-69; Lic to Offic *Win* 70-82; R Silchester from 82. *The Rectory, Silchester, Reading RG7 2LU* Silchester (0734) 700322

McKEGNEY, John Wade. b 47. TCD BA70 MA81. CITC 70. **d** 72 **p** 73. C Ballynafeigh St Jude *D & D* 72-75; C Ban St Comgall 75-80; I Drumgath w Drumgooland and Clonduff 80-83; I Gilnahirk 83-90; I Arm St Mark w Aghavilly *Arm* from 90. *St Mark's Rectory, 14 Portadown Road, Armagh BT61 9EE* Armagh (0861) 522970

MACKEITH, Mrs Ann Veronica. b 35. Bris Univ BSc57 CertEd. Gilmore Course 78. **dss** 79 **d** 87. Bishopwearmouth Ch Ch *Dur* 79-83; Bishopwearmouth St Gabr 83-86; Ryhope 86-87; Par Dn 87-88; Par Dn Darlington H Trin from 88. *135 Hummersknott Avenue, Darlington, Co Durham DL3 8RR* Darlington (0325) 463481

McKELLAR, John Lorne. b 19. Sarum Th Coll 70. **d** 72 **p** 73. C Warminster St Denys *Sarum* 72-75; USA 75-79 and 81-84; P-in-c Colchester St Barn *Chelmsf* 79-81; rtd 84. *Corrie, 105A Clay Street, Crockerton, Warminster, Wilts BA12 8AG* Warminster (0985) 213161

McKELVEY, Canon Robert Samuel James Houston. b 42. QUB BA65 MA(Ed)88. CITC 67. **d** 67 **p** 68. C Dunmurry *Conn* 67-70; CF (TAVR) from 70; P-in-c Kilmakee *Conn* 70-77; I 77-81; N Ireland Educn Org from 81; Preb St Patr Cathl Dub from 89. *19 Upper Lisburn Road, Belfast BT10 0GW* Belfast (0232) 619008 or 301130

McKELVIE, Canon Alfred. b 10. TCD BA34 MA43. CITC 35. **d** 35 **p** 36. I Ballynafeigh St Jude *D & D* 56-80; Adn Down 70-75; Chan Down Cathl 75-80; rtd 80. *50 Blenheim Park, Carryduff, Belfast BT8 8NN* Belfast (0232) 812682

McKEMEY, Alfred Douglas. b 18. Tyndale Hall Bris 38. **d** 42 **p** 43. V Burgess Hill St Andr *Chich* 68-84; RD Hurst 80-84; rtd 84; Perm to Offic *Chich* from 85; P-in-c Henfield w Shermanbury and Woodmancote from 91. *45 Parsonage Road, Henfield, W Sussex BN5 9JG* Henfield (0273) 493222

McKEMEY, Canon Robert. b 15. St Aid Birkenhead 50. **d** 52 **p** 53. I Aghadowey w Kilrea *D & R* 69-73; R Meysey Hampton w Marston Meysey *Glouc* 73-81; RD Fairford 77-81; rtd 81. *3 Sevenoaks Road, Earley, Reading RG6 2NT* Reading (0734) 660501

McKENNA, Dermot William. TCD BA63 MA66. CITC 64. **d** 64 **p** 65. I Killeshin *C & O* 66-84; rtd 84. *20 Sherwood, Pollerton, Carlow, Irish Republic*

MCKENNA, Lindsay Taylor. b 62. Glas Univ MA83 Aber Univ BD86. Edin Th Coll 87. **d** 87 **p** 88. C Broughty Ferry *Bre* 87-90; C Wantage *Ox* from 90. *5 Barnard's Way, Wantage, Oxford OX12 7EA* Wantage (02357) 3309

MACKENNA, Richard William. b 49. Pemb Coll Cam BA71 MA75. Ripon Coll Cuddesdon BA77 MA81. **d** 78

p 79. C Fulham St Dionis Parson's Green *Lon* 78-81; C Paddington St Jas 81-85; Tutor Westcott Ho Cam 85-89; V Kingston All SS w St Jo *S'wark* from 90. *15 Woodbines Avenue, Kingston upon Thames, Surrey KT1 2AZ* 081-546 2644

MACKENNA, Robert Christopher Douglass. b 44. Or Coll Ox BA72 MA75 MBAP85. Cuddesdon Coll 71. **d** 73 **p** 74. C Farncombe *Guildf* 73-77; C Tattenham Corner and Burgh Heath 77-80; P-in-c Hascombe 80-90; R from 90; RD Godalming from 91. *The Rectory, Hascombe, Godalming, Surrey GU8 4JA* Hascombe (048632) 362

McKENNA, Steven. b 64. Coll of Resurr Mirfield 86. **d** 89 **p** 90. C St Leonards Ch Ch and St Mary *Chich* from 89. *Flat 6, 21 Carisbrooke Road, St Leonards-on-Sea, E Sussex TN38 0JN* Hastings (0424) 422513

MACKENZIE, Canon Alan George Kett Fairbairn. b 11. ODE81. Univ of Wales BSc32. **d** 41 **p** 42. Chapl Miss and Coun to Deaf and Dumb 41-74; P-in-c Corscombe *Sarum* 75-77; P-in-c Halstock and the Chelboroughs 77; rtd 77. *Flat 3, 70 Richmond Road, Worthing, W Sussex BN11 4AF* Worthing (0903) 39780

MACKENZIE, Alfred Arthur. b 25. Bps' Coll Cheshunt 61. **d** 61 **p** 62. C Waltham Abbey *Chelmsf* 61-64; V Barking St Erkenwald 64-72; V Broomfield 72-83; P-in-c Willerby w Ganton and Folkton *York* 83-91; R from 91. *The Vicarage, Staxton, Scarborough, N Yorkshire YO12 4SF* Sherburn (0944) 364

MACKENZIE, Andrew John Kett. b 46. Southn Univ BA68. Local NSM Course 88. **d** 91. Fullbrook Sch New Haw from 76; NSM Woodham *Guildf* from 91. *250 Albert Drive, Sheerwater, Woking, Surrey GU21 5TY* Byfleet (0932) 346712

MACKENZIE, Miss Ann. b 54. CertEd76 DipHE82 DPS86. Trin Coll Bris 82. **dss** 85 **d** 87. Normanton *Wakef* 85-87; Par Dn 87-90; Par Dn Bletchley *Ox* from 90. *13 Burns Road, Bletchley, Milton Keynes MK3 5AN* Milton Keynes (0908) 366729

McKENZIE, Barrie. b 43. Bps' Coll Cheshunt 67 Qu Coll Birm 68. **d** 70 **p** 71. C S Westoe *Dur* 70-74; C Harton Colliery 74-77; C Norton St Mich 77-79; R Penshaw 79-87; V Hartlepool St Paul from 87. *St Paul's Vicarage, 6 Hutton Avenue, Hartlepool, Cleveland TS26 9PN* Hartlepool (0429) 72934

MACKENZIE, David Stuart. b 45. Linc Th Coll 66. **d** 69 **p** 70. C Bishopwearmouth St Mary V w St Pet CD *Dur* 69-72; C Pontefract St Giles *Wakef* 72-74; Chapl RAF from 74. *c/o MOD, Adastral House, Theobald's Road, London WC1X 8RU* 071-430 7268

MACKENZIE, George. b 09. MBE46 TD50. Worc Coll Ox BA31 MA35. Wells Th Coll 32. **d** 33 **p** 34. R Sullington *Chich* 52-74; R Storrington 53-74; rtd 74; Perm to Offic *Chich* from 74. *21 The Martlets, West Chiltington, Pulborough, W Sussex RH10 2QB* West Chiltington (0798) 812771

MACKENZIE, Canon Iain MacGregor. b 37. Qu Coll Ox BA59 MA63 Edin Univ MTh69. Wycliffe Hall Ox. **d** 63 **p** 64. C Southn St Mary w H Trin *Win* 63-66; C Christchurch 66-69; R Dunoon *Arg* 69-75; V Pokesdown All SS *Win* 75-78; C Woolston 78-79; C St Giles-in-the-Fields *Lon* 79-82; R St Marylebone St Mary 82-89; Can Res Worc Cathl *Worc* from 89. *2 College Green, Worcester WR1 2LH* Worcester (0905) 25238

MACKENZIE, Jack Llewellyn. b 29. FRSH AMIEHO MAMIT. S'wark Ord Course. **d** 79 **p** 80. Hon C Stonebridge St Mich *Lon* 79-88; Hon C Willesden St Mary from 88. *2 Beckett Square, Chiltern Park, Berkhamsted, Herts HP4 1BZ* Berkhamsted (0442) 874265

MACKENZIE, Preb Lawrence Duncan. b 30. St Aid Birkenhead 52. **d** 55 **p** 56. C Blackb St Gabr *Blackb* 55-58; C Burnley St Pet 58-60; C St Giles-in-the-Fields *Lon* 60-63; V Queensbury All SS 63-85; V Hillingdon St Jo from 85; Preb St Paul's Cathl from 89. *St John's Vicarage, Royal Lane, Uxbridge, Middx UB8 3QR* Uxbridge (0895) 33932

MACKENZIE, Peter Thomas. b 44. Lon Univ LLB67 Nottm Univ DipTh68. Cuddesdon Coll 68. **d** 70 **p** 71. C Leigh Park *Portsm* 70-75; P-in-c Sittingbourne St Mary *Cant* 75-82; V Folkestone St Sav 82-90; RD Elham 89-90; R Cant St Martin and St Paul from 90. *The Rectory, 13 Ersham Road, Canterbury, Kent CT1 3AR* Canterbury (0227) 462686

MACKENZIE, Reginald James Sterling. b 11. Sarum Th Coll 55. **d** 57 **p** 58. V St Kew *Truro* 67-73; P-in-c St Hilary 73-78; P-in-c Perranuthnoe 73-78; P-in-c St Hilary w Perranuthnoe 78-81; rtd 81. *12 Churchfield Close, Ludgram, Penzance, Cornwall TR20 8ER* Penzance (0736) 740801

MACKENZIE, Richard Graham. b 49. St Aug Coll Cant 72. **d** 73 **p** 74. C Deal St Leon *Cant* 73-75; C Deal St Leon w Sholden 75-78; C Herne 78-81; Canada from 81. *46 Victoria Avenue, Petawawa, Ontario, Canada, K8H 2G6*

MACKENZIE, Simon Peter Munro. b 52. Univ Coll Ox BA74. Coll of Resurr Mirfield 82. **d** 85 **p** 86. C Tipton St Jo *Lich* 85-91; V Perry Beeches *Birm* from 91. *St Matthew's Vicarage, 313 Beeches Road, Birmingham B42 2QR* 021-360 2100

McKEON, Canon James Ernest. b 22. TCD BA45 HDipEd49 Div Test. **d** 46 **p** 47. Warden Wilson's Hosp Sch Multyfarnham 64-83; Can Kildare Cathl *M & K* 83-88; P-in-c Geashill w Killeigh and Ballycommon 83-88; Prec Kildare Cathl 87-88; rtd 88; Dioc Info Officer (Meath) *M & K* 90-91; Radio Officer from 91. *Church House, Collinstown, Mullingar, Co Westmeath, Irish Republic* Collinstown (44) 66229

McKEON, Canon Victor Edward Samuel. b 39. FCA65. CITC. **d** 68 **p** 69. C Enniskillen *Clogh* 68-72; Accountant to Conn & D & D 72-79; P-in-c Magherahamlet *D & D* 77-79; I Derryvullen N w Castlearchdale *Clogh* from 79; Dioc Treas from 83; Can Clogh Cathl 86-89; Preb from 89. *The Rectory, Irvinestown, Co Fermanagh BT94 16W* Irvinestown (03656) 21225

McKEOWN, Steven. b 45. St Jo Coll Nottm 84. **d** 86. NSM Cumbrae (or Millport) *Arg* 86-88; USA from 88. *c/o The Community of Celebration, Alliquippo, Pennsylvania, USA*

MACKERACHER, Alasdair John. b 22. Linc Th Coll 69. **d** 71 **p** 72. C Oakdale St Geo *Sarum* 71-73; C Swanage 73-78; V Alvington w S Milton *Ex* 78-81; R Ashreigney 81-85; R Broadwoodkelly 81-85; V Brushford 81-85; V Winkleigh 81-85; V Swimbridge and W Buckland 85-88; rtd 88. *10 Rockhaven Gardens, St Minver, Wadebridge, Cornwall PL27 6PJ* Wadebridge (0208) 863671

MACKEY, John. b 34. Lich Th Coll. **d** 64 **p** 65. C Kells *Carl* 64-67; C Barrow St Matt 67-70; R Clayton *Man* 70-75; V Low Marple *Ches* 75-83; R Coppenhall from 83. *The Rectory, Coppenhall, Crewe* Crewe (0270) 215151

MACKEY, William John Noel. b 07. TCD BA28 MA51. CITC 30. **d** 31 **p** 32. Ch of Ireland Ind Officer 61-74; rtd 75; Perm to Offic *D & D* from 75. *86 North Road, Belfast BT4 3DJ* Belfast (0232) 658470

McKIBBIN, Gordon. b 29. Lon Univ DipTh57. St Aid Birkenhead 55. **d** 58 **p** 59. C Dundela *D & D* 58-60; C Knotty Ash St Jo *Liv* 61-64; V Gt Sankey from 64. *The Parsonage, Parsonage Way, Great Sankey, Warrington WA5 1RP* Penketh (092572) 3235

MACKIE, Ian William. b 31. Lon Univ BSc53 Ex Univ PGCE54. Linc Th Coll 81. **d** 83 **p** 84. C Market Rasen *Linc* 83-87; V Bracebridge Heath from 87. *1 Churchill Avenue, Bracebridge Heath, Lincoln LN4 2JX* Lincoln (0522) 546451

✠McKIE, Rt Rev John David. b 09. New Coll Ox BA35 MA44. Trin Coll Melbourne BA32 Wells Th Coll 34. **d** 32 **p** 34 **c** 46. Australia 32-60; Bp Coadjutor Melbourne 46-60; Adn Melbourne 46-60; Asst Bp Cov 60-80; V Gt w Lt Packington 66-81; rtd 81. *13 Morven Street, Mornington, Victoria 3931, Australia*

McKIE, Kenyon Vincent. b 60. Aus Nat Univ BA83 Canberra Coll DipEd84. ACT BTh88 DipMin89. **d** 86 **p** 87. Australia 86-89; Hon C Coulsdon St Andr *S'wark* from 89. *23 Rickman Hill, Coulsdon, Surrey CR5 3DS* Downland (07375) 57732

McKINLEY, Arthur Horace Nelson. b 46. TCD BA69 MA79. CITC 70. **d** 70 **p** 71. C Taney Ch Ch *D & G* 71-76; I Dub Whitechurch from 76. *Whitechurch Vicarage, Whitechurch Road, Rathfarnham, Dublin 16, Irish Republic* Dublin (1) 933953

McKINLEY, George Henry. b 23. TCD BA44 MA51. **d** 46 **p** 47. R Hackney St Jo *Lon* 65-72; TR Hackney 72-77; V Painswick w Sheepscombe *Glouc* 77-83; Bp's Chapl 83-87; C Sandhurst 83-85; C Twigworth, Down Hatherley, Norton, The Leigh etc 85-87; rtd 88. *Flat 3, Aucott House, 54 Worcester Road, Malvern, Worcs WR14 4AB* Malvern (0684) 568652

McKINLEY, John Gordon. b 11. TCD BA34 BD51. **d** 35 **p** 35. I Donaghpatrick *M & K* 62-70; rtd 70. *Tithe Cottage, College Road, Castlenock, Dublin, Irish Republic* Dublin (1) 212329

McKINNEL, Nicholas Howard Paul. b 54. Qu Coll Cam BA75 MA79. Wycliffe Hall Ox BA79 MA86. **d** 80 **p** 81. C Fulham St Mary N End *Lon* 80-83; Chapl Liv Univ *Liv* 83-87; P-in-c Hatherleigh *Ex* 87-88; R Hatherleigh, Meeth, Exbourne and Jacobstowe from 88. *The Rectory, Hatherleigh, Okehampton, Devon EX20 3JY* Okehampton (0837) 810314

McKINNEY, James Alexander. b 52. Ex Univ BA74 Hull Univ MA87. Ripon Coll Cuddesdon 75. **d** 78 **p** 79. C Wath-upon-Dearne w Adwick-upon-Dearne *Sheff* 78-82; V Doncaster Intake 82-87; Ind Chapl 84-87; Chapl Bramshill Police Coll *Win* from 87. *The Police Staff College, Bramshill, Basingstoke, Hants RG27 0JW* Hartley Wintney (025126) 2931

McKINNEY, Mervyn Roy. b 48. St Jo Coll Nottm. **d** 81 **p** 82. C Tile Cross *Birm* 81-84; C Bickenhill w Elmdon 84-89; V Addiscombe St Mary *S'wark* from 89. *St Mary Magdalene Vicarage, Canning Road, Croydon CR0 6QD* 081-654 3459

McKINNEY, Ven Wilson. b 18. TCD BA44 MA47. CITC 44. **d** 44 **p** 45. I Ballyrashane w Kildollagh *Conn* 51-84; RD Coleraine 75-76; Adn Dalriada 76-84; Can Belf Cathl 76-84; rtd 84. *4 Lissanduff Avenue, Portballintrae, Bushmills, Co Antrim BT57 8RU* Bushmills (02657) 32199

McKINNON, Archibald Vincent. b 07. **d** 77 **p** 78. Hon C Tranmere St Paul w St Luke *Ches* 77-79; Hon C W Kirby St Bridget 79-88; rtd 88; Perm to Offic *Ches* from 88. *18 Newton Park Road, West Kirby, Wirral, Merseyside L48 9XF* 051-625 5998

McKINNON, Neil Alexander. b 46. Wycliffe Hall Ox 71. **d** 74 **p** 75. C Deptford St Nic w Ch Ch *S'wark* 74-76; C St Helier 76-79; Min W Dulwich All SS and Em 79-81; TV Thamesmead from 87. *5 Finchale Road, London SE2 9PG* 081-310 5614

MACKINNON, Ross Cameron. b 52. St Steph Ho Ox 86. **d** 88 **p** 89. C Monk Bretton *Wakef* from 88. *4 Cornwall Close, Barnsley, S Yorkshire S71 2ND* Barnsley (0226) 281275

MACKINTOSH, Æneas. b 27. Kelham Th Coll 44. **d** 52 **p** 53. Prec St Andr Cathl Inverness *Mor* 52-55; C Wisbech St Aug *Ely* 55-57; P-in-c Glas St Matt *Glas* 57-60; R 60-61; R Haddington *Edin* 61-65; C Edin St Jo 65-69; R 69-81; Can St Mary's Cathl 75-87; R Gullane 81-87; R North Berwick 81-87; Info Officer & Communications Adv to the Gen Syn (Scottish Episc Ch) from 87. *31 St Albans Road, Edinburgh EH9 2LT* 031-667 4160

MACKINTOSH, Robin Geoffrey James. b 46. Rhodes Univ Grahamstown BCom71 Cranfield Inst of Tech MBA78 Ox Univ BA85 MA91. Ripon Coll Cuddesdon 83. **d** 86 **p** 87. C Cuddesdon *Ox* 86; C Cannock *Lich* 86-89; R Girton *Ely* from 89. *The Rectory, 40 Church Lane, Girton, Cambridge CB3 0JP* Cambridge (0223) 276235

McKITTRICK, Douglas Henry. b 53. St Steph Ho Ox 74. **d** 77 **p** 78. C Deptford St Paul *S'wark* 77-80; C W Derby (or Tuebrook) St Jo *Liv* 80-81; TV St Luke in the City 81-89; V Toxteth Park St Agnes and St Pancras from 89. *St Agnes's Vicarage, 1 Buckingham Avenue, Liverpool L17 3BA* 051-733 1742

McKITTRICK, Noel Thomas Llewellyn. b 28. TCD BA50 MA57 BD71. **d** 51 **p** 53. C Londonderry Ch Ch *D & R* 51-52; C Belf St Aid *Conn* 52-54; C Knockbreda *D & D* 54-58; C Keynsham w Queen Charlton *B & W* 58-59; V Glastonbury St Benedict 59-82; V Weston-super-Mare St Paul from 82. *St Paul's Vicarage, 17A Clarence Road North, Weston-super-Mare BS23 4AW* Weston-super-Mare (0934) 412687

MACKLIN, Reginald John. b 29. Bris Univ BA52. Ely Th Coll 54. **d** 55 **p** 56. C W Hackney St Barn *Lon* 55-58; C E Ham St Mary *Chelmsf* 58-61; C Northolt St Mary *Lon* 61-64; Jordan 64-68; Palma de Mallorca and Balearic Is *Eur* 68-69; P-in-c Hammersmith St Matt *Lon* 69-70; V Stanwell 70-82; V Kimbolton *Ely* 82-88; V Stow Longa 82-88; RD Leightonstone 82-88; P-in-c Keyston and Bythorn 85-88; P-in-c Catworth Magna 85-88; P-in-c Tilbrook 85-88; P-in-c Covington 85-88; R Coveney from 88; R Downham from 88; RD Ely from 89. *The Rectory, Little Downham, Ely, Cambs CB6 2ST* Ely (0353) 699237

MACKNEY, John Pearson. b 17. Univ of Wales BA39 Lon Univ MA81. St D Coll Lamp 39. **d** 41 **p** 42. C Gellygaer *Llan* 41-44; CF 44-47; C Llangeinor *Llan* 47-49; P-in-c Cardiff All SS 49-58; Chapl HM Pris Cardiff 49-58; V Mountain Ash *Llan* 58-69; Hon C Streatley w Moulsford *Ox* from 81. *Merlebank, Reading Road, Moulsford, Wallingford, Oxon OX10 9JG* Cholsey (0491) 651347

McKNIGHT, John Andrew. b 49. **d** 78 **p** 79. Australia 78-89; C Eltham St Sav *S'wark* 89-90; C Catford St Laur from 91; C Bellingham St Dunstan from 91. *75 Bexhill Road, London SE4 1SJ* 081-690 2904

McKNIGHT, Thomas Raymond. b 48. QUB BEd71. CITC 74. **d** 77 **p** 78. C Lisburn Ch Ch Cathl *Conn* 77-80; C Carrickfergus 80-82; I Kilcronaghan w Draperstown and Sixtowns *D & R* 82-86; I Magheragall *Conn* 86-91; RD

Lisburn 88-91; CF from 91. *c/o MOD (Army), Bagshot Park, Bagshot, Surrey GU19 5PL* Bagshot (0276) 71717

MACKONOCHIE, Christopher. b 12. Pemb Coll Ox BA34 MA38. Cuddesdon Coll 34. **d** 36 **p** 37. V Weston *St Alb* 74-82; rtd 82; Perm to Offic *St Alb* from 82. *4 Meeting House Lane, Baldock, Herts SG7 5BP* Baldock (0462) 894558

MACLACHLAN, Michael Ronald Frederic. b 39. Wycliffe Hall Ox 75. **d** 77 **p** 78. C Mansf St Pet *S'well* 77-80; P-in-c Newark Ch Ch 80; TV Newark w Hawton, Cotham and Shelton 80-86; P-in-c Sparkhill St Jo *Birm* 86-90; P-in-c Sparkbrook Em 86-90; V Sparkhill w Greet and Sparkbrook from 90; RD Bordesley from 90. *St John's Vicarage, 15 Phipson Road, Birmingham B11 4JE* 021-449 2760

McLACHLAN, Ms Sheila Elizabeth. b 52. SRN73 Kent Univ MA89. Wycliffe Hall Ox 80. dss 83 **d** 87. Chapl Kent Univ *Cant* from 83; Dep Master Rutherford Coll from 87. *Rutherford College, University of Kent, Canterbury, Kent CT2 7NX* Canterbury (0227) 768727 or 764000

MACLAREN, Grant. b 12. St Cath Coll Cam BA37 MA41. Wycliffe Hall Ox 37. **d** 39 **p** 40. V Derby St Pet and Ch Ch w H Trin *Derby* 57-73; V Stanley 73-80; rtd 80; Perm to Offic *Derby* from 80. *21 Tennessee Road, Chaddesden, Derby DE2 6LE* Derby (0332) 661226

McLAREN, Richard Francis. b 46. Mansf Coll Ox DSocStuds69. S'wark Ord Course 72. **d** 75 **p** 76. C Charlton St Luke w H Trin *S'wark* 75-78; C Kensington St Mary Abbots w St Geo *Lon* 78-81; Hon C St Marylebone w H Trin from 82. *84 Clarence Gate Gardens, London NW1 6QR* 071-262 4586

McLAREN, Robert Ian. b 62. Bris Univ BSc84 St Jo Coll Dur BA87. Cranmer Hall Dur 85. **d** 88 **p** 89. C Birkenhead Ch Ch *Ches* 88-90; C Bebington from 90. *48 Acreville Road, Bebington, Wirral, Merseyside L63 2HY* 051-645 9584

McLAREN, Ronald. b 31. Kelham Th Coll. **d** 59 **p** 60. C Redcar *York* 59-62; C Hornsea and Goxhill 62-65; V Middlesb St Thos 65-70; Chapl RN 70-73; Australia from 73. *56 Lincoln Street, Lindisfarne, Tasmania, Australia 7015* Hobart (2) 438134

McLAREN, William Henry. b 27. Edin Th Coll 55. **d** 56 **p** 57. C Skipton H Trin *Bradf* 56-60; V Bingley H Trin 60-65; V Allerton 65-68; R Aber St Mary *Ab* 68-73; P-in-c Newland St Aug *York* 73-74; V 74-75; V Hull St Cuth 75-81; V Hedon w Paull from 81; RD S Holderness from 84. *The Vicarage, 44 New Road, Hedon, Hull HU12 8BS* Hull (0482) 897693

McLAUGHLIN, Hubert James Kenneth. **d** 88 **p** 89. NSM Donagheady *D & R* 88-89; NSM Glendermott from 89. *9 Cadogan Park, Londonderry BT47 1QW* Londonderry (0504) 48916

MACLEAN, Alexander James. b 28. CEng MIStructE53. St Aid Birkenhead 52. **d** 55 **p** 56. R Largs *Glas* 69-71; V E Crompton *Man* 71-79; V Turners Hill *Chich* 79-89; rtd 89. *22 College Road, Ardingly, Haywards Heath, W Sussex RH17 6TY* Haywards Heath (0444) 892199

MACLEAN, Very Rev Allan Murray. b 50. Edin Univ MA72. Cuddesdon Coll 72. **d** 76 **p** 77. Chapl St Mary's Cathl *Edin* 76-81; Tutor Edin Univ 77-80; R Dunoon *Arg* 81-86; R Tighnabruaich 84-86; Can and Provost St Jo Cathl Oban from 86; R Oban St Jo from 86; R Ardbrecknish from 86; R Ardchattan from 89; Miss to Seamen from 86. *The Rectory, Ardconnel Terrace, Oban, Argyll PA34 5DJ* Oban (0631) 62323

McLEAN, Dr Bradley Halstead. b 57. McMaster Univ Ontario BSc Toronto Univ MDiv MTh PhD. **d** 83 **p** 84. C Dur St Giles *Dur* 83-84; Canada from 84. *1050 Shawmarr Road, Unit 84, Mississauga, Ontario, Canada, L5H 3V1*

MACLEAN, Donald Allan Lachlan. b 05. Linc Coll Ox BA27 MA31. Linc Th Coll. **d** 28 **p** 29. R Pitlochry *St And* 63-70; rtd 70. *Hazelbrae House, Glenurquhart, Inverness IV3 6TJ* Glenurquhart (04564) 267

McLEAN, Canon Donald Stewart. b 48. TCD BA70. CITC 70. **d** 72 **p** 73. C Glendermott *D & R* 72-75; I Castledawson 75-87; Dioc Dir of Ords from 79; I Londonderry Ch Ch from 87; Can Derry Cathl from 91. *Christ Church Rectory, 80 Northland Road, Londonderry BT48 0AL* Londonderry (0504) 263279

MACLEAN, Dorothy. b 31. Dundee Coll DipEd70. **d** 86. NSM Kirriemuir *St And* from 82. *84 Slade Gardens, Kirriemuir, Angus DD8 5AG* Kirriemuir (0575) 72396

McLEAN, Canon Douglas. b 12. Selw Coll Cam BA34 MA38. Cuddesdon Coll 34. **d** 35 **p** 36. V Perry Barr *Birm* 51-72; Dioc Dir of Ords 55-80; Hon Can Birm Cathl 61-72; RD Handsworth 62-72; Can Res Birm

Cathl 72-91; rtd 91. *83 Butlers Road, Birmingham B20 2NT* 021-554 0567 or 236 4333

McLEAN, Eileen Mary. b 44. City Univ BSc67. N Ord Course 85. **d** 88. Par Dn Burley in Wharfedale *Bradf* from 88. *7 Rosebank, Burley-in-Wharfedale, Ilkley, W Yorkshire LS29 7PQ* Burley-in-Wharfedale (0943) 863403

McLEAN, Miss Frances Ellen. b 21. RGN44 SCM45. Edin Dioc NSM Course 85. **d** 88. NSM Penicuik *Edin* from 88; NSM W Linton from 88. *56 Cuikenburn, Penicuik, Midlothian EH26 0JQ* Penicuik (0968) 75029

MACLEAN, Kenneth John Forbes. b 31. St Deiniol's Hawarden 80. **d** 81 **p** 82. C Sedgley All SS *Lich* 81-85; V Shareshill 85-90; R Bicton, Montford w Shrawardine and Fitz from 90. *The Rectory, 15 Brookside, Bicton, Shrewsbury SY3 8EP* Shrewsbury (0743) 850519

MACLEAN, Lawrence Alexander Charles. b 61. K Coll Lon BD84 AKC84. Chich Th Coll 86. **d** 88 **p** 89. C Cirencester *Glouc* 88-91; C Prestbury from 91. *8 Boulton Road, Cheltenham, Glos GL50 4RZ* Cheltenham (0242) 523177

McLEAN, Miss Margaret Anne. b 62. Qu Coll Birm 88. **d** 91. Par Dn Bedf All SS *St Alb* from 91. *9 Wingfield Close, Bedford MK40 4PB* Bedford (0234) 354631

McLEAN, Canon Michael Stuart. b 32. Dur Univ BA57. Cuddesdon Coll 57. **d** 59 **p** 60. C Camberwell St Giles *S'wark* 59-61; Lic to Offic *Nor* 61-68; R Marsham 68-74; R Burgh 68-74; RD Ingworth 70-74; P-in-c Nor St Pet Parmentergate w St Jo 74-75; TV 75-78; TR 78-86; Hon Can Nor Cathl 82-86; Can Res from 86; P-in-c Nor St Mary in the Marsh from 87. *27 The Close, Norwich NR1 4DZ* Norwich (0603) 630398

McLEAN, Robert Hedley. b 47. St Jo Coll Dur BA69. Ripon Hall Ox 69. **d** 71 **p** 72. C Redhill St Jo *S'wark* 71-74; C S Beddington St Mich 74-77; C-in-c Raynes Park H Cross CD 77; P-in-c Motspur Park 77-80; V 80-84; V Tadworth from 84. *The Vicarage, The Avenue, Tadworth, Surrey KT20 5AS* Tadworth (0737) 813152

McLEAN-REID, Robert. b 43. Oak Hill Th Coll DipHE83. **d** 83 **p** 84. C Rainham *Chelmsf* 83-86; R Challoch w Newton Stewart *Glas* 86-87; R Aber St Pet *Ab* 87-90; P-in-c Aber St Clem 89-90; V Easington Colliery *Dur* from 90. *The Vicarage, Easington Colliery, Peterlee, Co Durham SR8 3PJ* 091-527 0272

MacLEAY, Angus Murdo. b 59. Solicitor 83 Univ Coll Ox BA81 MA86. Wycliffe Hall Ox 85. **d** 88 **p** 89. C Rusholme *Man* from 88. *166 Platt Lane, Manchester M14 7PY* 061-224 6776

MACLEAY, Very Rev John Henry James. b 31. St Edm Hall Ox BA54 MA60. Coll of Resurr Mirfield 55. **d** 57 **p** 58. C E Dulwich St Jo *S'wark* 57-60; C Inverness St Mich *Mor* 60-62; R 62-70; P-in-c Grantown-on-Spey 70-78; P-in-c Rothiemurchus 70-78; Can St Andr Cathl Inverness 77-78; R Fort William *Arg* from 78; Can St Jo Cathl Oban from 80; Syn Clerk 80-88; Dean Arg from 87. *St Andrew's Rectory, Fort William, Inverness-shire PH33 6BA* Fort William (0397) 702979

McLELLAN, Eric Macpherson Thompson. b 16. St Jo Coll Dur BA38 DipTh39 MA41. **d** 39 **p** 40. Chapl Br Emb Ch Paris *Eur* 70-80; Adn N France 79-80; Perm to Offic Chich and Roch from 80; rtd 81. *7 Stainer Road, Tonbridge, Kent TN10 4DS* Tonbridge (0732) 356491

MACLEOD, Alan Roderick Hugh. b 33. St Edm Hall Ox BA56 MA61 Ox Univ DipEd62 Lon Univ DipCD69. Wycliffe Hall Ox 56. **d** 58 **p** 59. C Bognor St Jo *Chich* 58-61; Chapl Wadh Coll Ox 62; Hd of RE Picardy Boys' Sch Erith 62-68; C Erith St Jo *Roch* 63-69; Dean Lonsdale Coll Lanc Univ 70-72; Lic to Offic Blackb 70-72; Win 73-84; Hd of RE K Edw VI Sch Totnes 72-73; Perm to Offic *Ex* 72-73; St Helier Boys' Sch Jersey 73-84; V Shipton Bellinger *Win* from 84. *St Peter's Vicarage, Shipton Bellinger, Tidworth, Hants SP9 7UF* Stonehenge (0980) 42244

McLEOD, Everton William. b 57. DCR78. Oak Hill Th Coll DipHE91. **d** 91. C New Ferry *Ches* from 91. *13 Graylands Road, New Ferry, Wirral, Merseyside L62 4SB* 051-644 6850

McLEOD, Kenneth. b 22. St Chad's Coll Dur BA50 DipTh52. **d** 52 **p** 53. C Holsworthy w Cookbury *Ex* 52-55; C Braunton 55-58; R Milton Damerel and Newton St Petrock etc 58-70; RD Holsworthy 66-70; V Kirkby Fleetham *Ripon* 70-89; R Langton on Swale 70-89; P-in-c Scruton 88-89; R Kirkby Fleetham w Langton on Swale and Scruton from 90. *The Rectory, Kirkby Fleetham, Northallerton, N Yorkshire DL7 0SB* Northallerton (0609) 748251

McLEOD, Canon Ronald. b 17. Lon Univ BA39 BA50 BD71 Ex Univ BA56 Man Univ MA59. Bps' Coll Cheshunt 39. **d** 41 **p** 42. Prin RAF Chapl Sch and Asst

Chapl-in-Chief 69-73; QHC from 72; R Itchen Abbas cum Avington *Win* 73-91; Hon Can Win Cathl 84-91; rtd 91. *Melfort, High Wall, Barnstaple, Devon EX31 2DP* Barnstaple (0271) 43636

MCLOUGHLIN, Ian Livingstone. b 38. CEng MICE64. Carl Dioc Tr Course 78. **d** 83 **p** 84. NSM Stanwix *Carl* 83-88; C Barrow St Geo w St Luke 88-90; R Kirkby Thore w Temple Sowerby and w Newbiggin from 90. *The Rectory, Kirkby Thore, Penrith, Cumbria CA10 1UR* Kirkby Thore (07683) 61248

McLUCKIE, John Mark. b 67. Edin Th Coll. **d** 91. C Perth St Ninian *St And* from 91. *c/o 40 Hay Street, Perth PH1 5HS* Perth (0738) 441156

MACLURE, Canon Andrew Seaton. b 15. Ch Coll Cam BA37 MA41. Lon Coll of Div 37. **d** 39 **p** 40. Uganda 41-86; Dean Mvara 69-72; rtd 86; Perm to Offic *Chich* from 87. *42 Jonas Drive, Wadhurst, E Sussex TN5 6RL* Wadhurst (089288) 2708

McMAHON, Brian Richard. b 39. ACII. Oak Hill NSM Course 84. **d** 87 **p** 88. NSM Colney Heath St Mark *St Alb* from 87. *23 Bluebridge Avenue, Brookmans Park, Hatfield, Herts AL9 7RY* Potters Bar (0707) 55351

MACMANAWAY, Launcelot. b 12. TCD BA36 MA43. Div Test. **d** 36 **p** 37. I Youghal Union *C, C & R* 67-74; Bp's C Ardglass *D & D* 74-79; rtd 79. *4 Heatherstone Road, Bangor, Co Down* Bangor (0247) 458302

McMANN, Duncan. b 34. Jes Coll Ox BA55 MA60. Clifton Th Coll. **d** 58 **p** 59. C Newburn *Newc* 58-60; C Bishopwearmouth St Gabr *Dur* 60-62; N Area Sec BCMS 62-66; Lic to Offic *Cov* 64-66; Midl Area Sec BCMS from 66; Support Co-ord from 84. *56 Cecily Road, Coventry CV3 5LA* Coventry (0203) 503691

McMANNERS, John. b 16. FRHistS73 FBA78 St Edm Hall Ox BA39 MA45 DLitt77 St Chad's Coll Dur DipTh47 Hon DLitt84. **d** 47 **p** 48. Regius Prof Ecclesiastical Hist Ox Univ 72-84; Can Res Ch Ch *Ox* 72-84; rtd 84; Chapl All So Coll Ox from 85. *All Souls' College, Oxford* Oxford (0865) 279368

McMANUS, James Robert. b 33. Man Univ DPT82. Wycliffe Hall Ox 56. **d** 58 **p** 59. C Leic H Trin *Leic* 58-60; C Aylestone 60-63; India 66-79; V Oldham St Barn *Man* 79-83; Asst Regional Sec CMS 83-85; V Wolv St Matt *Lich* from 85. *St Matthew's Vicarage, 14 Sydenham Road, Wolverhampton WV1 2NY* Wolverhampton (0902) 453300

McMASTER, James Alexander. b 43. **d** 69 **p** 70. C Dundonald *D & D* 69-73; C Antrim All SS *Conn* 73-78; I Tempo and Clabby *Clogh* 78-83; I Knocknamuckley *D & D* from 83. *30 Mossbank Road, Ballynagarrick, Portadown, Co Armagh BT63 5SL* Gilford (0762) 831227

McMASTER, Richard Ian. b 32. Edin Th Coll 57. **d** 60 **p** 61. C Carl H Trin *Carl* 60-63; Tanganyika 63-64; Tanzania 64-66; V Broughton Moor *Carl* 66-69; V Burnley St Steph *Blackb* 69-77; V New Longton 77-89; P-in-c Woodhall Spa and Kirkstead *Linc* from 89; P-in-c Langton w Woodhall from 89; P-in-c Bucknall w Tupholme from 89; P-in-c Horsington w Stixwould from 89. *The Vicarage, Alverston Avenue, Woodhall Spa, Lincs LN10 6SN* Woodhall Spa (0526) 53856

McMASTER, William Keith. b 57. TCD. **d** 82 **p** 84. C Portadown St Columba *Arm* 82-84; C Erdington St Barn *Birm* 84-87; TV Shirley from 87. *1 Mappleborough Road, Shirley, Solihull, Birmingham B90 1AG* 021-744 3123

McMICHAEL, Andrew Hamilton. b 48. Univ of Wales (Ban) BA77 Mansf Coll Ox DSocStuds74. Chich Th Coll 87. **d** 89 **p** 90. C Chorley St Geo *Blackb* from 89. *159 Pilling Lane, Chorley, Lancs PR7 3EF* Chorley (02572) 67775

MacMILLAN, John Patrick. b 18. St Aid Birkenhead. **d** 48 **p** 49. V New Brighton Em *Ches* 60-82; rtd 82; Perm to Offic *Ches* from 82. *34 Marshlands Road, Wallasey, Merseyside* 051-638 8680

McMONAGLE, William Archibald. b 36. CITC 65. **d** 68 **p** 69. C Magheralin *D & D* 68-71; C Ban Abbey 71-81; I Grey Abbey w Kircubbin from 81. *90 Newtownards Road, Greyabbey, Co Down BT22 2QJ* Greyabbey (024774) 216

✠**McMULLAN, Rt Rev Gordon.** b 34. ACIS57 QUB BSc61 PhD71 ThD88 TCD MPhil90. Ridley Hall Cam 61. **d** 62 **p** 63 **c** 80. C Ballymacarrett St Patr *D & D* 62-67; Ch Of Ireland Stewardship Adv 67-70; C Knock 70-71; I 76-80; I Belf St Brendan 71-76; Bp Clogh 80-86; Bp *D & D* from 86. *The See House, 32 Knockdene Park South, Belfast BT5 7AB* Belfast (0232) 471973

McMULLEN, Alan John. b 14. K Coll Cam BA36 MA41. Cuddesdon Coll 39. **d** 40 **p** 41. VC York Minster *York* 49-81; rtd 81. *2 Ramsey Avenue, Acaster Lane, Bishopthorpe, York YO2 1SQ* York (0904) 701121

McMULLEN, Ronald Norman. b 36. TCD BA61 MA66. Ridley Hall Cam 61. **d** 63 **p** 64. C Fulham St Mary N End *Lon* 63-66; C Cam St Sepulchre *Ely* 66-70; C Everton St Ambrose w St Tim *Liv* 70-73; York Univ 73-75; P-in-c Heanor *Derby* 75-79; V 79-88; RD Heanor 76-83; USA from 88. *Address unknown*

McMULLON, Andrew Brian. b 56. Sheff Univ BSc DipTh. St Jo Coll Nottm. **d** 83 **p** 84. C Stainforth *Sheff* 83-86; V Blackb Redeemer *Blackb* 86-90; Chapl RAF from 90. *c/o MOD, Adastral House, Theobald's Road, London WC1X 8RU* 071-430 7268

MACNAB, Kenneth Edward. b 65. LMH Ox BA87. Coll of Resurr Mirfield 89. **d** 91. C Northn All SS w St Kath *Pet* from 91. *8 York Road, Northampton NN1 5QC* Northampton (0604) 32624

McNAMARA, Michael Ian. b 59. Van Mildert Coll Dur BA81. Ridley Hall Cam 83. **d** 85 **p** 86. C Bedf Ch Ch *St Alb* 85-89; BCMS from 89. *Orchard House, The Leys, Chesham Bois, Amersham, Bucks HP6 5NP* Amersham (0494) 725767

McNAMEE, William Graham. b 38. Birm Univ BSocSc59. Cranmer Hall Dur BA74 DipTh. **d** 75 **p** 76. C Tonbridge St Steph *Roch* 75-78; C Fazeley *Lich* 78-87; Chapl Stoke Poly from 87. *19 Paragon Avenue, Westbury Park, Clayton, Newcastle, Staffs ST5 4EX* Newcastle-under-Lyme (0782) 625544

MACNAUGHTON, Alexander. b 15. SS Coll Cam BA37 MA41. Linc Th Coll 40. **d** 41 **p** 42. India 48-73; C Derby St Thos *Derby* 74-80; Chapl Derbyshire R Infirmary 75-80; rtd 80; Perm to Offic *Derby* from 80. *12 St Mark's House, 111 Radbourne Street, Derby DE3 3BW* Derby (0332) 380341

MACNAUGHTON, Canon Donald Allan. b 17. Or Coll Ox BA40 MA43. Westcott Ho Cam 40. **d** 41 **p** 42. Hon Can Newc Cathl *Newc* 71-82; V Berwick H Trin 71-82; RD Norham 71-82; rtd 82; Chapl Marseille w St Raphael Aix-en-Provence etc *Eur* 82-87. *Flat 2, 18 Fidra Road, North Berwick, East Lothian EH39 4NG* North Berwick (0620) 2841

MACNAUGHTON, James Alastair. b 54. St Jo Coll Ox BA78 Fitzw Coll Cam BA80. Ridley Hall Cam 78. **d** 81 **p** 82. C Rounds Green *Birm* 81-85; TV Bestwood Park *S'well* 85-86; TV Bestwood 86-90; V Amble *Newc* from 90. *The Vicarage, Church Street, Amble, Morpeth, Northd NE65 0DY* Alnwick (0665) 710273

McNAUGHTON, John. b 29. St Chad's Coll Dur DipTh54. **d** 54 **p** 55. C Thorney Close CD *Dur* 54-58; C-in-c E Herrington St Chad CD 58-62; V E Herrington 62-66; CF from 66. *c/o MOD (Army), Bagshot Park, Bagshot, Surrey GU19 5PL* Bagshot (0276) 71717

MACNAUGHTON, William Malcolm. b 57. Qu Coll Cam BA80. Ridley Hall Cam 79. **d** 81 **p** 82. C Haughton le Skerne *Dur* 81-85; P-in-c Newton Hall 85-90; TV Shoreditch St Leon and Hoxton St Jo *Lon* from 90. *St John's Vicarage, Crondall Street, London N1 6PT* 071-739 9823

McNEE, William Creighton. TCD DipTh Univ of Wales (Cardiff) DipPM. **d** 82 **p** 83. C Larne and Inver *Conn* 82-84; I Donaghedy *D & R* 84-91; I Kilwaughter w Cairncastle and Craigy Hill *Conn* from 91. *15 Cairncastle Road, Ballygally, Larne, Co Antrim BT40 2RB* Larne (0574) 583220

McNEICE, Alan Denor. b 34. **d** 64. C Ballymoney w Finvoy and Rasharkin *Conn* 64-67; Jamaica 67-69; C Winchmore Hill H Trin *Lon* 71-77; C Kensington St Barn 78-79. *Address temp unknown*

McNEIGHT, Herbert Frank. b 14. Chich Th Coll. **d** 79 **p** 80. Hon C Southwick *Chich* from 79; Chapl Southlands Hosp Shore by Sea from 83. *12 Mile Oak Crescent, Southwick, Brighton BN42 4QP* Brighton (0273) 592765

McNEIL, Ann. b 41. **d** 89. NSM Henfield w Shermanbury and Woodmancote *Chich* from 89. *Lancasters, West End Lane, Henfield, W Sussex BN5 9RB* Henfield (0273) 492606

McNEILL, George Edward. b 07. Wadh Coll Ox BA28 MA31. Clifton Th Coll 32. **d** 32 **p** 33. Villar Aiglon Coll Switzerland 63-65; rtd 68; Perm to Offic *Ex* from 79. *High Grove, Victoria Place, Budleigh Salterton, Devon EX9 6JP* Budleigh Salterton (03954) 3017

McNEISH, John. b 34. Edin Th Coll 58. **d** 61 **p** 62. C Kirkcaldy *St And* 61-64; Prec St Andr Cathl *Ab* 64-66; Chapl RAF 66-72; C Wootton Bassett *Sarum* 72-75; P-in-c Stour Provost w Todbere 75-79; TR Gillingham from 79; RD Blackmore Vale 81-86. *The Rectory, Gillingham, Dorset SP8 4AH* Gillingham (0747) 822435

McNIVEN, Betty. b 47. Lanc Univ BA68. N Ord Course 83. dss 86 **d** 87. Baguley *Man* 86-87; Hon Par Dn 87-88;

Par Dn Newton Heath All SS from 88. *7 Leng Road, Newton Heath, Manchester M10 6NX*   061-681 0252

McNUTT, Very Rev John Alexander Miller. b 14. QUB CertHist. Edgehill Th Coll Belf 37. **d** 47 **p** 48. Chapl to Bp of Clogh 65-73; I Magheracross 73-84; Preb Clogh Cathl 73-80; Dean Clogh 82-84; rtd 84. *32 Madigan Park, Carrickfergus, Co Antrim BT38 7JW* Carrickfergus (09603) 68578

MACONACHIE, Canon Alwyn. b 21. TCD BA43 MA47 BD47. CITC 44. **d** 44 **p** 45. N Sec (Ireland) CMS 64-70; Gen Sec (Ireland) CMS 70-74; I Glencraig *D & D* 74-91; RD Ban 78-91; Can Down Cathl 82-91; Prec 87-90; Chan 90-91; rtd 91. *16 Springhill Road, Bangor, Co Down BT20 3NR*   Bangor (0247) 466999

MACONACHIE, Canon Charles Leslie. b 27. TCD BA71 MA74 MDiv85 PhD90. Em Coll Saskatoon 47. **d** 50 **p** 51. C Clooney *D & R* 50-54; P-in-c Lower Tamlaght O'Crilly 54 61; Chapl Newsham Gen Hosp Liv 61-63; Chapl RAF 63-67; C Londonderry Ch Ch *D & R* 69-75; I Belmont 75-78; Warden for Min of Healing from 75; I Culmore w Muff and Belmont from 78; Warden Irish Internat Order of St Luke the Physician from 82; Can Derry Cathl from 85. *The Rectory, Culmore Road, Heathfield, Londonderry BT47 8JD* Londonderry (0504) 352396

MACOURT, Ven William Albany. b 19. TCD BA40 MA46. **d** 42 **p** 43. I Ballymacarrett St Patr *D & D* 64-89; Preb Swords St Patr Cathl Dub 75-89; Adn Down *D & D* 80-89; Chan Belf Cathl 85-89; rtd 89; Dioc Info Officer *D & D* from 89. *4 Barnett's Road, Belfast BT5 7BA* Belfast (0232) 794421

McPHATE, Dr Gordon Ferguson. b 50. Aber Univ MB, ChB74 Fitzw Coll Cam BA77 MA81 MD88 Surrey Univ MSc86. Westcott Ho Cam 75. **d** 78 **p** 79. Hon C Sanderstead All SS *S'wark* 78-81; Hon PV S'wark Cathl 81-86; Lect Lon Univ 81-86; Chapl and Lect St Andr Univ *St And* from 86. *68 Winram Place, St Andrews, Fife KY16 8XH*   St Andrews (0334) 76983

MacPHEE, Roger Hunter. b 43. Leeds Univ BSc65. E Anglian Minl Tr Course. **d** 86 **p** 87. NSM Trunch *Nor* from 86. *8 Lawn Close, Knapton, North Walsham, Norfolk NR28 0SD*   Mundesley (0263) 720045

McPHERSON, Andrew Lindsay. b 58. MIPM84 St Jo Coll Dur BA79. St Jo Coll Nottm DPS88. **d** 88 **p** 89. C Bitterne *Win* from 88. *4 Aberdour Close, Bitterne, Southampton SO2 5PF*   Southampton (0703) 473436

MACPHERSON, Anthony Stuart. b 56. Qu Coll Birm 77. **d** 80 **p** 81. C Morley St Pet w Churwell *Wakef* 80-84; C Penistone 84-85; P-in-c Thurlstone 85-86; TV Penistone and Thurlstone 86-88; V Grimethorpe from 88. *The Vicarage, High Street, Grimethorpe, Barnsley, S Yorkshire S72 7JB*   Barnsley (0226) 711331

MACPHERSON, Archibald McQuarrie. b 27. Edin Th Coll 50. **d** 52 **p** 53. Asst Chapl St Andr Cathl *Ab* 52-55; Prec 55-56; P-in-c Airdrie *Glas* 56-63; R Dumbarton from 63. *The Rectory, Dixon Drive, Dumbarton G82 4AR* Dumbarton (0389) 62852

MacPHERSON, David John. b 42. Lon Univ DipTh71 BD75 Open Univ BA83 Hatf Poly MSc89. Clifton Th Coll 69 Trin Coll Bris 72. **d** 72 **p** 73. C Drypool St Columba w St Andr and St Pet *York* 72-76; Asst Chapl HM Pris Hull 72-76; P-in-c Bessingby *York* 76-78; P-in-c Carnaby 76-78; Chapl RAF 78-83; P-in-c Chedgrave w Hardley and Langley *Nor* 83-87; R from 87; Chapl Langley Sch Nor from 83. *The Rectory, Chedgrave, Norwich NR14 6NE*   Loddon (0508) 20535

MACPHERSON, Ewan Alexander. b 43. Toronto Univ BA74. Wycliffe Coll Toronto MDiv78. **d** 78 **p** 79. Canada 78-86; V Westbury sub Mendip w Easton *B & W* from 86; V Priddy from 86. *The Vicarage, Westbury sub Mendip, Wells, Somerset BA5 1HL*   Wells (0749) 870293

MACPHERSON, John. b 28. Lon Univ BSc50 Ex Univ DipEd51 Univ of W Indies HDipEd65. St Alb Minl Tr Scheme 82. **d** 89 **p** 90. NSM Gt Berkhamsted *St Alb* from 89. *Southways, 5 Kingsdale Road, Berkhamsted, Herts HP4 3BS*   Berkhamsted (0442) 866262

MACPHERSON, Peter Sinclair. b 44. Lich Th Coll 68. **d** 71 **p** 72. C Honiton, Gittisham and Combe Raleigh *Ex* 71-72; C Bideford 72-74; C Devonport St Mark Ford 74-75; V Thorncombe *Sarum* 75-79; TV Dorchester 79-85; Chapl Jersey Gp of Hosps 85-90; Chapl Derriford Hosp Plymouth from 90; Lic to Offic *Ex* from 90. *Derriford Hospital, Derriford Road, Plymouth PL8 8DH* Plymouth (0752) 777111

McQUADE, William. b 09. **d** 49 **p** 50. V Allhallows *Carl* 66-76; rtd 76. *Springwell, Ballinafad, Boyle, Co Roscommon, Irish Republic*

MacQUAIDE, Arthur John Allan. b 13. TCD BA37. **d** 38 **p** 39. I Garrison w Slavin and Belleek *Clogh* 60-80; Bp

Dom Chapl 67-73; Preb Clogh Cathl 73-80; rtd 80; C Steeton *Bradf* 84-89. *11 Cambridge Park, Ballysally, Coleraine, Co Londonderry BT51 2QT*   Coleraine (0265) 58228

MACQUARRIE, Canon John. b 19. TD62. FBA84 Glas Univ MA40 BD43 PhD54 DLitt64 Hon DD69 Ox Univ MA70 DD81. **d** 65 **p** 65. USA 65-70; Lady Marg Prof of Div Ox Univ 70-86; Can Res Ch Ch *Ox* 70-86; rtd 86. *206 Headley Way, Oxford OX3 7TA*   Oxford (0865) 61889

MACQUIBAN, Gordon Alexander. b 24. Univ of Wales (Lamp) BA49 Crewe Coll of Educn CertEd72. Ely Th Coll 49. **d** 51 **p** 52. V Ches Ch Ch *Ches* 64-71; Hon C Ches H Trin 71-85; Hon C Runcorn All SS 85-87; Hon C Frodsham 87-88; rtd 88. *4 Avon Close, Hoveland Park, Taunton, Somerset TA1 4SU*   Taunton (0823) 282602

McQUILLAN, Martha. b 33. St Mich Ho Ox 66. **dss** 70 **d** 87. Barnsbury St Andr *Lon* 70-72; Nottm St Ann w Em *S'well* 72-79; Chapl Asst Univ Hosp Nottm and Nottm Gen Hosp 79-90; rtd 90. *27 Penarth Rise, Nottingham NG5 4EE*   Nottingham (0602) 621760

McQUILLEN, Brian Anthony. b 45. Ripon Hall Ox 73. **d** 75 **p** 76. C Northfield *Birm* 75-78; C Sutton Coldfield H Trin 78-80; V Bearwood 80-89; V Glouc St Geo w Whaddon *Glouc* from 89. *St George's Vicarage, Grange Road, Gloucester GL4 0PE*   Gloucester (0452) 20851

McQUINN, Wallace Steward. b 03. Lon Univ BD36 BA49. ALCD36. **d** 36 **p** 37. R Brondesbury Ch Ch *Lon* 60-71; rtd 71; Perm to Offic *Chich* from 73. *Buxshalls, Ardingly Road, Lindfield, Haywards Heath, W Sussex*

MACRAE, Charles. b 27. RD71. Edin Univ BDS62. S Dios Minl Tr Scheme 88. **d** 91. NSM Heene *Chich* from 91. *64 Stone Lane, Worthing, W Sussex BN13 2BQ* Worthing (0903) 693877

McRAE, Keith Alban. b 44. S'wark Ord Course 68. **d** 73 **p** 74. NSM Crawley *Chich* 73-78; NSM Ifield from 78. *Plough Cottage, Ifield Street, Ifield, Crawley, W Sussex RH10 0NN*   Crawley (0293) 513629

MacRAE, Mrs Rosalind Phyllis. b 41. Sarum & Wells Th Coll 81. **dss** 84 **d** 87. Feltham *Lon* 84-87; Par Dn 87; Asst Chapl R Cornwall Hosp Truro 87-88; Chapl Mt Edgcumbe Hospice, St Austell Hosp and Penrice Hosp St Austell from 88; NSM St Austell *Truro* from 88. *7 Church Lane, Mevagissey, St Austell, Cornwall PL26 6SX*   Mevagissey (0726) 842046

McREYNOLDS, Kenneth Anthony. b 48. TCD DipTh83. **d** 83 **p** 84. C Ballymena w Ballyclug *Conn* 83-86; I Rathcoole 86-90; I Lambeg from 90. *Lambeg Rectory, 58 Belfast Road, Lisburn, Co Antrim BT27 4AT* Lisburn (08462) 3872

McVEAGH, Paul Stuart. b 56. Southn Univ BA78. Oak Hill Th Coll BA88. **d** 88 **p** 89. C Bebington *Ches* from 88. *8 Rolleston Drive, Bebington, Wirral, Merseyside L63 3DB*   051-645 5026

McVEETY, Ian. b 46. N Ord Course 82. **d** 85 **p** 86. NSM Langley and Parkfield *Man* 85-86; C 87-89; V Castleton Moor from 89. *The Vicarage, Vicarage Road North, Rochdale, Lancs OL11 2TE*   Rochdale (0706) 32353

McVEIGH, Samuel. b 49. CITC 77. **d** 79 **p** 80. C Drumragh w Mountfield *D & R* 79-82; I Dromore *Clogh* 82-90; RD Kilskeery 89-90; I Drumachose *D & R* from 90. *49 Killane Road, Limavady, Co Londonderry*   Limavady (05047) 62680

MACVICAR, Miss Mary. b 23. Edin Univ MA44 Ox Univ DipEd45. Ripon Coll Cuddesdon 86. **dss** 86 **d** 87. Bishops Waltham *Portsm* 86-87; Hon C 87-89; Perm to Offic from 89. *15 Roman Row, Bank Street, Bishops Waltham, Southampton SO3 1AN*   Bishops Waltham (0489) 895955

MacWILLIAM, Very Rev Alexander Gordon. b 23. Univ of Wales BA43 Lon Univ BD47 PhD52. St Mich Coll Llan 43. **d** 45 **p** 46. Lect Trin Coll Carmarthen 58-84; Lic to Offic *St D* 60-78; Can *St D* Cathl 78-84; Prec 84-90; V *St D* Cathl 84-90; Dean *St D* 84-90; rtd 90. *Pen Parc, Smyrna Road, Llangain, Camarthen, Dyfed SA33 5AD*   Llanstephan (026783) 333

McWILLIAM, Charles Denis. b 24. Clare Coll Cam BA49 MA52. Cuddesdon Coll 49. **d** 51 **p** 52. Perm to Offic *Sarum* 67-73; Eur 73-80; V Heyhouses *Blackb* 80-88; V Sabden and Pendleton 88-89; rtd 89. *Standen Hall Farm House, Clitheroe, Lancs BB7 1PR*   Clitheroe (0200) 26442

MADDEN, Robert Willis. b 14. TCD BA36 MA40. CITC 38. **d** 39 **p** 40. R Misterton w Walcote *Leic* 66-79; rtd 79; Perm to Offic *Derby* from 79. *22A Duffield Road, Little Eaton, Derby DE2 5DS*   Derby (0332) 832388

MADDEN, Canon Sydney Richard William. b 11. TCD BA38. **d** 40 **p** 41. I Ardamine *C & O* 55-80; Chan Ferns

Cathl 79-80; rtd 80. *Cranacrowe Lodge, Ballycanew, Gorey, Wexford, Irish Republic* Gorey (55) 27208

MADDEX, Patrick John. b 31. Edin Univ BSc54. Bps' Coll Cheshunt 55. **d** 57 **p** 58. C Baldock w Bygrave and Clothall *St Alb* 57-61; C Oxhey All SS 61-64; V Codicote 64-82; R Gt and Lt Wymondley w Graveley and Chivesfield from 82. *The Rectory, Great Wymondley, Hitchin, Herts SG4 7ES* Stevenage (0438) 353305

MADDISON, Norman. b 12. St Jo Coll Dur BA34. **d** 35 **p** 36. R Wolsingham and Thornley *Dur* 64-77; rtd 77. *Whitfield Place, Wolsingham, Bishop Auckland, Co Durham DL13 3AJ* Bishop Auckland (0388) 527127

MADDOCK, Mrs Audrey. b 27. Lon Univ CertEd79 Open Univ BA80. Bris Sch of Min 81. **dss** 84 **d** 87. Stanton St Quintin, Hullavington, Grittleton etc *Bris* 84-87; Par Dn from 87. *1 Brookside, Hullavington, Chippenham, Wilts SN14 6HD* Malmesbury (0666) 837275

MADDOCK, David John Newcomb. b 36. Qu Coll Cam BA60 MA64. Oak Hill Th Coll 60. **d** 62 **p** 63. C Bispham *Blackb* 62-65; R from 82; Canada 65-70; R Walsoken *Ely* 70-77; V Ore Ch Ch *Chich* 77-82; RD Blackpool *Blackb* from 90. *The Rectory, All Hallows Road, Blackpool FY2 0AY* Blackpool (0253) 51886

MADDOCK, Eric John. b 99. Oak Hill Th Coll 54. **d** 54 **p** 55. V Preston St Mary *Blackb* 62-66; rtd 69. *The Rectory, All Hallows Road, Bispham, Blackpool FY2 0AY* Blackpool (0253) 51886

MADDOCK, Eric Rokeby. b 10. St Pet Hall Ox BA33 MA38. Wycliffe Hall Ox 37. **d** 38 **p** 39. R Kelston *B & W* 60-76; R N Stoke 60-76; rtd 76. *22 Charlton Park, Keynsham, Bristol BS18 2ND* Bristol (0272) 864151

MADDOCK, Francis James Wilson. b 14. Bris Univ BA36 Wadh Coll Ox BA38 MA42. Cuddesdon Coll 39. **d** 40 **p** 41. R Boscastle w Davidstow *Truro* 64-74; TR 74-78; P-in-c Port Isaac 78-79; rtd 79; Perm to Offic *Ex* from 87. *8 Sylvan Close, Exmouth, Devon EX8 3BQ* Exmouth (0395) 274381

MADDOCK, Nicholas Rokeby. b 47. ABSM72 Birm Coll of Educn CertEd73. Linc Th Coll 82. **d** 82 **p** 83. C Romford St Edw *Chelmsf* 82-87; V Sway *Win* from 87. *The Vicarage, Station Road, Sway, Lymington, Hants SO41 6BA* Lymington (0590) 682358

MADDOCK, Norman. b 15. St Jo Coll Dur BA38 DipTh39 MA41. **d** 39 **p** 40. V Chatburn *Blackb* 69-79; Hon C Warton St Oswald w Yealand Conyers 79-84; rtd 80. *55 Ganton Way, Willerby, Hull HU10 7UB* Hull (0482) 656587

MADDOCK, Philip Arthur Louis. b 47. Open Univ BA82. Oak Hill Th Coll 75. **d** 78 **p** 79. C New Ferry *Ches* 78-81; C Barnston 81-82; V Over St Jo 82-85; Chapl to the Deaf 85-88; V Norley 85-88; P-in-c Treales *Blackb* from 88; Chapl to the Deaf from 88. *The Vicarage, Church Road, Treales, Preston, Lancs PR4 3SH* Preston (0772) 682219

MADDOCK, Canon Philip Lawrence. b 20. Bris Univ BA42. Cuddesdon Coll 42. **d** 43 **p** 44. Chapl St Lawr Hosp Bodmin 69-76; Can Res and Treas Truro Cathl *Truro* 76-88; rtd 88. *31 Trenethick Avenue, Helston, Cornwall TR13 8LU* Helston (0326) 564909

✠**MADDOCKS, Rt Rev Morris Henry St John.** b 28. Trin Coll Cam BA52 MA56. Chich Th Coll. **d** 54 **p** 55 **c** 72. C Ealing St Pet Mt Park *Lon* 54-55; C Uxbridge St Andr w St Jo 55-58; V Weaverthorpe w Helperthorpe and Luttons *York* 58-61; V Scarborough St Martin 61-72; Suff Bp Selby 72-83; Adv Min Health and Healing to Abps Cant and York from 83; Asst Bp B & W 83-87; Asst Bp Chich from 87; Acorn Chr Healing Trust from 91. *Whitehill Chase, High Street, Bordon, Hants GU35 0AP* Bordon (0420) 478121 or 472779

MADDOX, Preb Bernard Thomas. b 31. Kelham Th Coll 48 St Steph Ho Ox 53. **d** 55 **p** 56. C Longton St Mary and St Chad *Lich* 55-60; V Burslem St Werburgh 60-74; Chapl Haywood and Stanfield Hosps Stoke-on-Trent 60-74; P-in-c Shrewsbury All SS *Lich* 74-76; P-in-c Shrewsbury St Mich 74-76; P-in-c Shrewsbury St Mary 74-76; V Shrewsbury St Mary w All SS and St Mich 76-87; V Shrewsbury All SS w St Mich from 87; RD Shrewsbury from 82; Preb Lich Cathl from 86. *5 Lingen Close, Shrewsbury SY1 2UN* Shrewsbury (0743) 58820

MADDOX, David Morgan. b 22. Univ of Wales (Lamp) BA42 Trin Coll Cam BA61 MA64. St Mich Coll Llan 42. **d** 45 **p** 46. V Trumpington *Ely* 56-90; rtd 90. *48 High Street, Barton, Cambridge CB3 7BG* Cambridge (0223) 264127

MADDOX, David Pugh. b 16. St D Coll Lamp BA39. **d** 49 **p** 50. R Cerrigydrudion, Llanfihangel Glyn Myfyr, Llangwm *St As* 62-70; V Bryneglwys and Llandegla 70-77; R Llansantffraid Glan Conway and Eglwysfach 77-81; rtd 81. *Flat 1, Maestegfryn, Bala, Gwynedd* Bala (0678) 520533

MADDOX, Edwin Joseph Crusha. b 09. Dorchester Miss Coll 38. **d** 41 **p** 42. V Walthamstow St Sav *Chelmsf* 61-71; V Leigh-on-Sea St Jas 71-77; rtd 77. *43 Barnard Road, Leigh-on-Sea, Essex SS9 3PH* Southend-on-Sea (0702) 776822

MADDOX, Goronwy Owen. b 23. Univ of Wales (Swansea) BA52 DipEd53. Sarum Th Coll 67. **d** 70 **p** 71. Hd Master H Trin Sch Calne 57-82; Hon C Calne and Blackland *Sarum* 70-82; C 82-83; V Llywel and Traianglas w Llanulid *S & B* from 83. *The Vicarage, Llywel, Brecon, Powys LD3 8UW* Sennybridge (087482) 481

MADDOX, Hugh Inglis Monteath. b 37. CCC Cam BA60. Westcott Ho Cam 61. **d** 63 **p** 64. C Attercliffe *Sheff* 63-66; C Maidstone All SS w St Phil *Cant* 66-67; C Folkestone St Mary and St Eanswythe 67-69; C St Martin-in-the-Fields *Lon* 69-73; R Sandwich *Cant* 73-81; V St Peter-in-Thanet 81-84; V Red Post *Sarum* from 84. *The Vicarage, Morden, Wareham, Dorset BH20 7DR* Morden (092945) 244

MADDY, Kevin. b 58. GRNCM79 Selw Coll Cam BA83. Westcott Ho Cam 81. **d** 85 **p** 86. C St Peter-in-Thanet *Cant* 85-88; Perm to Offic *Nor* from 88; Chapl RAF from 88. *c/o MOD, Adastral House, Theobald's Road, London WC1X 8RU* 071-430 7268

MADGE, Donald John. b 05. Worc Ord Coll 64. **d** 65 **p** 65. C Heavitree *Ex* 65-77; rtd 77; Lic to Offic *Ex* from 78. *3 Church Terrace, Exeter EX2 5DU* Exeter (0392) 73348

MADGE, Francis Sidney. b 35. AKC58. **d** 59 **p** 60. C York St Mary Bishophill Senior *York* 59-62; C Sutton St Mich 62-64; C Ex St Jas *Ex* 64-69; R Sutton by Dover w Waldershare *Cant* 69-78; P-in-c W Wickham St Mary 78-81; V 81-84; V W Wickham St Mary *S'wark* from 85. *St Mary's Vicarage, The Avenue, West Wickham, Kent BR4 0DX* 081-777 3137

MAGAHY, Canon Gerald Samuel. b 23. TCD BA45 MA61 LLD80 Univ Coll Galway HDipEd55. **d** 53 **p** 54. Dioc Chapl and Hd Master Villiers Sch Limerick 53-61; Chapl and Hd Master K Hosp Sch Dub 61-83; Treas St Patr Cathl Dub 80-89; Chan from 89. *Seacrest, Bray Head, Co Wicklow, Irish Republic* Skibbereen (28) 67231

MAGEE, Francis Malcolm. b 24. Edin Univ MA49. **d** 54 **p** 55. Lic to Offic *S'wark* 71-75; Hon C Abbey Wood 75-78; C Mottingham St Andr 79-81; C Rotherhithe St Mary w All SS 81-83; C Rotherhithe St Kath w St Barn 83-89; rtd 89. *33 Apthorpe Street, Fulbourn, Cambs CB1 5EY* Cambridge (0223) 880218

MAGEE, Frederick Hugh. b 33. Yale Univ BA57. Westcott Ho Cam 57. **d** 59 **p** 60. C Bury St Mark *Man* 59-63; USA 63-64 and from 87; Chapl St Paul's Cathl Dundee *Bre* 74-79; R St Andrews St Andr *St And* 79-83; R Lunan Head 83-87; R Forfar 83-87. *Address temp unknown*

MAGEE, John Lawrence. b 19. Lon Univ BA52. **d** 78 **p** 79. Hon C Westbury-on-Severn w Flaxley and Blaisdon *Glouc* 78-89; rtd 89. *Sharon, Blaisdon, Longhope, Glos GL17 0AL* Gloucester (0452) 831217

MAGEE, Canon Patrick Connor. b 15. K Coll Cam BA37 MA41. Westcott Ho Cam 38. **d** 39 **p** 40. Chapl Bryanston Sch Blandford 60-70; V Ryde All SS *Portsm* 70-72; Chapl Tiffin Sch Kingston-upon-Thames 72-73; V Salisbury St Mich *Sarum* 73-75; TR Bemerton 75-84; rtd 84. *16A Donaldson Road, Salisbury SP1 3AD* Salisbury (0722) 24278

MAGGS, Miss Pamela Jean. b 47. Girton Coll Cam MA76 K Coll Lon BD79 AKC79. Qu Coll Birm 79. **dss** 80 **d** 87. Tottenham H Trin *Lon* 80-84; Asst Chapl Bryanston Sch Blandford 84-87; Perm to Offic *Chich* from 87. *6 Reed's Place, London NW1 9NA* 071-267 5435

MAGILL, Waller Brian Brendan. b 20. TCD BA42 BD45. **d** 44 **p** 45. Lect Div Nottm Coll of Educn 62-75; Hd of Dept Trent Poly 75-85; Lic to Offic *S'well* from 66; rtd 85. *16 Parkcroft Road, Nottingham NG2 6FN* Nottingham (0602) 233293

MAGNESS, Anthony William John. b 37. New Coll Ox BA62 MA65. Coll of Resurr Mirfield 78. **d** 80 **p** 81. C Gt Crosby St Faith *Liv* 80-83; C Newc St Jo *Newc* 83-85; P-in-c Newc St Luke 85-88; P-in-c Newc St Andr 88; V Newc St Andr and St Luke from 89. *St Luke's Vicarage, 6 Claremont Terrace, Newcastle upon Tyne NE2 4AE* 091-232 3341

MAGOWAN, Alistair James. b 55. Leeds Univ BSc77 DipHE. Trin Coll Bris 78. **d** 81 **p** 82. C Owlerton *Sheff* 81-84; C Dur St Nic *Dur* 84-89; Chapl St Aid Coll Dur 85-89; V Egham *Guildf* from 89. *The Vicarage, Vicarage Road, Egham, Surrey TW20 9JN* Egham (0784) 32066

MAGSON, Thomas Symmons. b 09. MA. d 75 p 76. NSM Highworth w Sevenhampton and Inglesham etc *Bris* from 75. *21 Cricklade Road, Highworth, Swindon SN6 7BW* Swindon (0793) 762579

MAGUIRE, Brian William. b 33. Hull Univ BTh84 MA88. Coll of Resurr Mirfield 70. d 72 p 73. C Guisborough *York* 72-76; TV Haxby w Wigginton 76-77; TR 78-89; V Huddersfield St Pet and All SS *Wakef* from 89. *Parish House, Venn Street, Huddersfield HD1 2RL* Huddersfield (0484) 427964

MAHOOD, Canon Brian Samuel. b 12. St Jo Coll Dur BA39 MA42. d 39 p 40. V Squirrels Heath *Chelmsf* 53-79; Hon Can Chelmsf Cathl 76-79; rtd 79. *Jesmond Dene Cottages, 79 Tenterfield Road, Maldon, Essex CM9 7EN* Maldon (0621) 855366

MAIDEN, Charles Alistair Kingsley. b 60. Trent Poly BSc84. St Jo Coll Nottm LTh88. d 89 p 90. C Porchester *S'well* from 89. *127A Digby Avenue, Nottingham NG3 6DT* Nottingham (0602) 877553

MAIDMENT, Thomas John Louis. b 43. Lon Univ BSc65. St Steph Ho Ox. d 67 p 68. C Westmr St Steph w St Jo *Lon* 67-73; P-in-c Twickenham Common H Trin 73-77; V 77-80; V Heston from 80. *The Vicarage, 147 Heston Road, Hounslow TW5 0RD* 081-570 2288

MAIDSTONE, Archdeacon of. *See* EVANS, Ven Patrick Alexander Sidney

MAIDSTONE, Suffragan Bishop. *See* SMITH, Rt Rev David James

MAIN, David. b 16. Man Univ BA40 St Jo Coll Ox BA48 MA53. Cuddesdon Coll 40. d 41 p 42. R Bracon Ash w Hethel *Nor* 57-73; rtd 73. *3 Low Farm Cottages, Keswick Road, Norwich NR4 6TX* Norwich (0603) 58109

MAIN, Canon David Murray. b 28. Univ Coll Ox BA52 MA56. St Deiniol's Hawarden 73. d 73 p 74. C Glas St Marg *Glas* 73-75; R Challoch w Newton Stewart 75-79; R Kilmarnock from 79; Can St Mary's Cathl from 85. *The Parsonage, 1 Dundonald Road, Kilmarnock, Ayrshire KA1 1EQ* Kilmarnock (0563) 23577

MAINES, Trevor. b 40. Leeds Univ BSc63. Ripon Hall Ox 63. d 65 p 66. C Speke All SS *Liv* 65-70; C Stevenage St Geo *St Alb* 70-73; V Dorridge *Birm* 73-78; Org Sec (Dio Ex) CECS 79-80; Hon C Tiverton St Pet *Ex* 79-80; Org Sec (Wales) CECS 80-87; Perm to Offic *Mon* 83-87; V Arlesey w Astwick *St Alb* from 87; RD Shefford from 91. *The Vicarage, 77 Church Lane, Arlesey, Beds SG15 6XH* Hitchin (0462) 731227

MAINEY, Ian George. b 51. CertEd73. Oak Hill Th Coll DipHE86 BA87. d 87 p 88. C Denton Holme *Carl* 87-91; V Hensingham from 91. *The Vicarage, Egremont Road, Hensingham, Whitehaven, Cumbria CA28 8QW* Whitehaven (0946) 2822

MAINWARING, Islwyn Paul. b 52. Univ of Wales (Swansea) BD75 DPS79. St Mich Coll Llan 77. d 79 p 80. C Llanilid w Pencoed *Llan* 79-82; C Llanishen and Lisvane 82-85; TV Cwmbran *Mon* 85-88; V Troedyrhiw w Merthyr Vale *Llan* from 88. *The Vicarage, Merthyr Vale, Merthyr Tydfil, M Glam CF48 4RF* Ynysowen (0443) 690249

MAINWARING, William Douglas. b 26. Univ of Wales (Swansea) DipTh73. St Mich Coll Llan 72. d 74 p 75. C Aberdare St Fagan *Llan* 74-78; V Seven Sisters 78-80; rtd 80. *3 Rhiw Nant, Abernant, Aberdare, M Glam* Aberdare (0685) 878409

MAIR, Canon James Fraser. b 24. St Pet Hall Ox BA49 MA53. Wycliffe Hall Ox 49. d 51 p 52. R Bacton w Wyverstone *St E* 67-80; V Thurston 80-89; Hon Can St E Cathl 87-89; rtd 89; Perm to Offic *St E* from 90. *The Maltings, Shop Green, Bacton, Stowmarket, Suffolk IP14 4LF* Bacton (0449) 781896

MAIRS, Adrian Samuel. b 43. DipHE. Oak Hill Th Coll 76. d 78 p 79. C Rugby St Matt *Cov* 78-82; P-in-c Mancetter 82-84; V from 84. *The Vicarage, Quarry Lane, Mancetter, Atherstone, Warks CV9 1NL* Atherstone (0827) 713266

MAITIN, Ito. b 36. Lon Univ DipTh67 BA. Kelham Th Coll 63. d 68 p 69. C Longton St Jo *Lich* 68-69; C Leek St Edw 69-71; C Lich St Chad 71-74; C Tamworth 74-81; V Penkhull from 81. *The Vicarage, 214 Queen's Road, Stoke-on-Trent ST4 7LG* Stoke-on-Trent (0782) 414092

MAITLAND, Sydney Milivoge Patrick. b 51. d 86 p 87. Hon C Glas St Geo *Glas* from 87. *14 Kersland Street, Glasgow G12 8BL* 041-339 4573

MAJOR, Maurice Edward. b 23. E Anglian Minl Tr Course. d 84 p 85. NSM Field Dalling w Saxlingham *Nor* 84-87; NSM Sharrington 84-87; NSM Gunthorpe w Bale 84-87; NSM Gunthorpe w Bale w Field Dalling, Saxlingham etc 87-89; Perm to Offic *St As* from 89.

Trem-y-Goeden, Llanfyllin, Powys SY22 5AN Llanfyllin (069184) 721

MAJOR, Richard James Edward. b 54. DipTh. Trin Coll Bris 78. d 81 p 82. C Parr *Liv* 81-84; V Burton Fleming w Fordon *York* 84-85; V Grindale and Ergham 84-85; P-in-c Wold Newton 84-85; V Burton Fleming w Fordon, Grindale etc 85-91; V Bilton St Pet from 91. *The Vicarage, 116 Main Road, Bilton, Hull HU11 4AD* Hull (0482) 811441

MAKEL, Arthur. b 39. Sheff Poly DMS75. AKC63. d 64 p 65. C Beamish *Dur* 64-68; Ind Chapl *York* 68-72; P-in-c Scotton w Northorpe *Linc* 72-81; Ind Chapl 72-81; R Epworth 81-89; P-in-c Wroot 81-89; R Epworth and Wroot from 89. *St Andrew's Rectory, Belton Road, Epworth, Doncaster DN9 1JL* Epworth (0427) 872471

MAKEPEACE, David Norman Harry. b 51. Magd Coll Ox BA74. Trin Coll Bris 83. d 85 p 86. C Romford Gd Shep Collier Row *Chelmsf* 85-88; Tanzania 88-89; C York St Paul *York* 89-91; TV Radipole and Melcombe Regis *Sarum* from 91. *The Vicarage, 106 Spa Road, Weymouth, Dorset DT3 5ER* Weymouth (0305) 771938

MAKEPEACE, James Dugard. b 40. Keble Coll Ox BA63 MA67. Cuddesdon Coll 63. d 65 p 66. C Cullercoats St Geo *Newc* 65-68; Chapl Wadh Coll Ox 68-72; Lib Pusey Ho 68-72; V Romford St Edw *Chelmsf* 72-79; V Tettenhall Regis *Lich* 79-80; TR from 80; RD Trysull from 87. *The Vicarage, 2 Lloyd Road, Tettenhall, Wolverhampton WV6 9AU* Wolverhampton (0902) 751622

MAKIN, Hubert. b 18. ACP66 Open Univ BA74. NW Ord Course. d 78 p 79. Hon C Mt Pellon *Wakef* from 78. *46 Upper Highfield, Mount Tabor, Halifax, W Yorkshire HX2 0UG* Halifax (0422) 244642

MAKIN, Miss Pauline. b 45. Cranmer Hall Dur 75. dss 78 d 87. Ashton-in-Makerfield St Thos *Liv* 78-87; Par Dn 87-89; Par Dn Rainford from 89; Asst Dioc Chapl to the Deaf from 89. *23 Windermere Drive, Rainford, St Helens, Merseyside WA11 7LD* Rainford (074488) 4254

MAKIN, Mrs Valerie Diana. Lon Univ DipRS83. S'wark Ord Course. d 88. Hon Par Dn Bryanston Square St Mary w St Marylebone St Mark *Lon* from 88; Chapl St Marylebone Healing and Counselling Cen from 88. *Flat 1, 38 Nottingham Place, London W1M 3FD* 071-487 3140

MAKOWER, Malory. b 38. TCD BA61 MA68 St Jo Coll Ox MA64 DPhil64. Ridley Hall Cam 64. d 66 p 67. C Onslow Square St Paul *Lon* 66-69; Tutor Ridley Hall Cam 69-71; Sen Tutor 71-76; P-in-c Lode and Longmeadow *Ely* 76-84; Warden E Anglian Minl Tr Course 77-79; Prin 79-84; Dir of Post-Ord Tr for NSMs *Nor* 84-90; C Gt Yarmouth 84-89; TV from 89; Dioc NSM Officer from 88. *Ludham House, 55 South Beach Parade, Great Yarmouth NR30 3JP* Great Yarmouth (0493) 853622

MALAN, Victor Christian de Roubaix. b 39. Cape Town Univ BA60 Linacre Coll Ox BA63 MA68. Wycliffe Hall Ox 61. d 63 p 64. C Springfield *Birm* 63-66; P-in-c 66-67; C New Windsor *Ox* 67-69; Chapl St Jo Coll Cam 69-74; V Northn All SS w St Kath *Pet* 74-86; V Stockport St Geo *Ches* 86-89; R N Mundham w Hunston and Merston *Chich* from 89. *The Rectory, Church Lane, Hunston, Chichester, W Sussex PO20 6AJ* Chichester (0243) 782003

MALBON, John Allin. b 36. Oak Hill Th Coll 62. d 65 p 66. C Wolv St Jude *Lich* 65-68; C Hoole *Ches* 68-71; P-in-c Crewe Ch Ch 71-75; V 75-79; V Plemstall w Guilden Sutton from 79. *The Vicarage, Guilden Sutton, Chester CH3 7EL* Mickle Trafford (0244) 300306

MALCOLM, Brother. *See* FOUNTAIN, David Roy

MALCOLM, Edward. b 34. Lon Univ BA60. Tyndale Hall Bris 61. d 68 p 68. Asst Chapl Casablanca *Eur* 68-76; P-in-c Lozells St Paul *Birm* 77-81; V Lozells St Silas 77-81; V Wolv St Luke *Lich* from 81. *St Luke's Vicarage, 122 Goldthorn Hill, Wolverhampton WV2 3HQ* Wolverhampton (0902) 340261

MALCOLM, Mercia Alana. b 54. St Andr Univ MA77 Lon Univ DipRS87. S'wark Ord Course 84. d 87. C Dartford Ch Ch *Roch* from 87-91; Par Dn Stockport St Geo *Ches* from 91. *52 Oakfield Road, Davenport, Stockport, Cheshire SK3 8SG* 061-456 7142

MALE, David Edward. b 62. Southn Univ BA83. St Jo Coll Dur BA90 Cranmer Hall Dur 88. d 91. C Leic St Chris *Leic* from 91. *502 Saffron Lane, Leicester LE2 6SD* Leicester (0533) 834506

MALE, John. b 28. ACA54 FCA65. Linc Th Coll 59. d 61 p 62. Bp's Dom Chapl *Linc* 61-72; C Linc St Pet in Eastgate w St Marg 68-70; R Riseholme 70-72; S Africa 72-85; Chapl Heathfield Sch Ascot 86-87; Chapl Lucas Hosp Wokingham from 86; rtd 89. *44 Simkins Close,*

Winkfield Row, Bracknell, Berks RG12 6QS Bracknell (0344) 886026

MALINS, Peter. b 18. Down Coll Cam BA40 MA47. Ridley Hall Cam 40. **d** 42 **p** 43. CF 47-73; QHC 72-73; V Greenwich St Alfege w St Pet and St Paul *S'wark* 73-87; P-in-c Greenwich H Trin and St Paul 76-84; Sub-Dean of Greenwich 79-81; rtd 87. *12 Ridgeway Drive, Dorking, Surrey RH4 3AN* Dorking (0306) 882035

MALKINSON, Christopher Mark. b 47. Chich Th Coll 84. **d** 86 **p** 87. C Stroud and Uplands w Slad *Glouc* 86-89; V Cam w Stinchcombe from 89. *The Vicarage, Cam, Dursley, Glos GL11 5PQ* Dursley (0453) 542084

MALKINSON, Michael Stephen. b 43. St Steph Ho Ox 65. **d** 68 **p** 69. C New Addington *Cant* 68-71; C Blackpool St Steph *Blackb* 71-74; V Wainfleet St Mary *Linc* 74-81; R Wainfleet All SS w St Thos 74-81; P-in-c Croft 80-81; V Lund *Blackb* from 81. *Lund Vicarage, Clifton, Preston PR4 0ZE* Kirkham (0772) 683617

MALLESON, Michael Lawson. b 42. Univ of Wales (Swansea) BA64 Nottm Univ DipTh68. Linc Th Coll 67. **d** 70 **p** 71. C Wakef St Jo *Wakef* 70-73; C-in-c Holmfield St Andr CD 73-75; V Holmfield 75-80; V Heworth St Alb *Dur* from 80. *The Vicarage, Coldwell Park Drive, Felling, Gateshead, Tyne & Wear NE10 9BX* 091-438 1720

MALLETT, John Christopher. b 44. E Anglian Minl Tr Course. **d** 82 **p** 83. NSM Hethersett w Canteloff *Nor* 82-85; NSM Hethersett w Canteloff w Lt and Gt Melton 85-90; Chapl Wayland Hosp Norfolk from 88. *2 Bailey Close, Hethersett, Norwich NR9 3EU* Norwich (0603) 811010

MALLETT, Michael William. b 18. St Deiniol's Hawarden. **d** 69 **p** 70. C Hyde St Geo *Ches* 69-75; V Broadheath 75-84; rtd 84; Perm to Offic *Carl* from 84. *27 Drovers Terrace, Penrith, Cumbria CA11 9EN* Penrith (0768) 65459

MALLETT, Ven Peter. b 25. CB78. AKC50. **d** 51 **p** 52. Dep Asst Chapl Gen 68-72; Asst Chapl Gen 73-74; Chapl Gen 74-80; OStJ from 76; Man Dir Inter-Ch Travel 81-86; rtd 90. *Hawthorne Cottage, Hampstead Lane, Yalding, Maidstone, Kent ME18 6HJ* Maidstone (0622) 812607

MALLIN, Very Rev Stewart Adam Thomson. b 24. Edin Th Coll 59. **d** 61 **p** 62. P-in-c Thurso 66-77; R Wick 68-77; CSG from 74; Can St Andr Cathl Inverness *Mor* from 74; R Dingwall 77-91; R Strathpeffer 77-91; Syn Clerk 81-83; Dean Mor 83-91; rtd 91; Hon C Strathnairn St Paul *Mor* from 91. *c/o Cathedral Rectory, 15 Ardross Street, Inverness IV3 5NS*

MALLINSON, Ralph Edward. b 40. Or Coll Ox BA63 MA66. St Steph Ho Ox 63. **d** 66 **p** 67. C Bolton St Pet *Man* 66-68; C Elton All SS 68-72; V Bury St Thos 72-76; V Bury Ch King 76-81; P-in-c Goodshaw 81-82; V 82-84; AD Rossendale from 83; V Goodshaw and Crawshawbooth from 84. *Goodshaw Vicarage, Goodshawfold Road, Rossendale, Lancs BB4 8QN* Rossendale (0706) 213969

MALLOCH, Elizabeth Gilmour. b 10. Edin Univ MA33 DipEd34. **dss** 85 **d** 86. NSM Edin St Mary *Edin* from 85. *173/101 Comely Bank Road, Edinburgh EH4 1DH* 031-343 6100

MALLON, Allister. b 61. Sheff Univ BA83 TCD DipTh87 BTh89. CITC. **d** 87 **p** 88. C Ballymoney w Finvoy and Rasharkin *Conn* 87-90; C Belf St Mary w H Redeemer from 90. *The Curatage, 15 Westway Park, Ballygomartin Road, Belfast BT13 3NW* Belfast (0232) 710584

MALLORY, George Henry. b 14. JP. Lon Univ BSc63. St Deiniol's Hawarden. **d** 80 **p** 81. NSM Oaks in Charnwood and Copt Oak *Leic* 80-88; Perm to Offic from 88. *2 Moscow Lane, Shepshed, Loughborough, Leics LE12 9EX* Shepshed (0509) 502395

MALMESBURY, Suffragan Bishop of. *See* FIRTH, Rt Rev Peter James

MALONEY, Terence Mark. b 63. York Univ BSc84. Cranmer Hall Dur 88. **d** 91. C Blackley St Andr *Man* from 91. *54 Tweedle Hill Road, Higher Blackley, Manchester M9 3LG* 061-740 6774

MALPASS, Clive William. b 36. AKC60. **d** 61 **p** 62. C Malden St Jo *S'wark* 61-64; C Horley 64-69; Youth Chapl *Dur* 69-72; Adv in Lay Tr 72-76; V Wyther Ven Bede *Ripon* 76-82; V Askrigg w Stallingbusk from 82. *The Vicarage, Askrigg, Leyburn, N Yorkshire DL8 3HZ* Wensleydale (0969) 50301

MALSOM, Laurence Michael. b 31. Selw Coll Cam BA55 MA59. Cuddesdon Coll 55. **d** 57 **p** 58. C Crediton *Ex* 57-60; C Plymouth St Gabr 60-62; C Sidmouth St Nic 62-64; V Harberton 64-71; V Harbertonford 64-71; RD Totnes 70-75; V S Brent 71-75; V St Marychurch 75-79; P-in-c Plymouth Crownhill Ascension 79-80; V

from 80. *The Vicarage, 33 Tavistock Road, Plymouth PL5 3AF* Plymouth (0752) 783617

MALTA, Dean of. *See* SATTERTHWAITE, Rt Rev John Richard

MALTBY, Geoffrey. b 38. Leeds Univ BA62. Wells Th Coll 68. **d** 70 **p** 71. C Mansf St Mark *S'well* 70-73; V Skegby 73-78; V Carrington 78-87; C Rainworth 87-90; Chapl for People with a Mental Handicap from 90. *18 Beverley Close, Rainworth, Mansfield, Notts NG21 0LW* Mansfield (0623) 797095

MALTBY, Canon Keith Mason. b 19. Ch Coll Cam BA47 MA52 Man Univ BD52. Ridley Hall Cam 47. **d** 49 **p** 50. Prin Lect in Div Coll of Educn Alsager 69-74; Can Res, Lib and Treas Ches Cathl *Ches* 74-86; Vice-Dean 78-86; rtd 86; Perm to Offic *Heref* from 86. *Coppins, The Grove, Minsterley, Shrewsbury SY5 0AG* Shrewsbury (0743) 791485

MALTIN, Basil St Clair Aston. b 24. Qu Coll Cam BA49 MA54. Westcott Ho Cam 50. **d** 51 **p** 52. V Bishops Lydeard *B & W* 63-71; R Pulborough *Chich* 71-90; RD Storrington 84-89; rtd 90. *13 Somerstown, Chichester, W Sussex PO19 4AG* Chichester (0243) 786740

MAN, Archdeacon of. *See* WILLOUGHBY, Ven David Albert

MANCE, Herbert William. b 19. St Jo Coll Cam BA40 MA44. Oak Hill Th Coll 47. **d** 49 **p** 50. Nigeria 58-71; Can Ibadan 70-71; C Buckhurst Hill *Chelmsf* 71-75; P-in-c Roydon 75-79; V 79-85; rtd 85; Perm to Offic *Lich* from 85. *52 Redwood Avenue, Stone, Staffs ST15 0DB* Stone (0785) 816128

MANCHESTER, Canon Charles. b 28. Univ Coll Lon BD54. Oak Hill Th Coll 50. **d** 55 **p** 56. C Nottm St Nic *S'well* 55-58; C Kinson *Sarum* 58-61; R Haworth *Bradf* 61-67; V Aldershot H Trin *Guildf* 67-87; RD Aldershot 73-78; R Newdigate from 87; Hon Can Guildf Cathl from 89. *The Rectory, Newdigate, Dorking, Surrey RH5 5DL* Newdigate (030677) 469

MANCHESTER, John Charles. b 45. Lon Univ BD69. ALCD68. **d** 69 **p** 70. C Scarborough St Martin *York* 69-73; C Selby Abbey 73-76; P-in-c Old Malton 76-79; V from 79; RD Bulmer and Malton 85-91. *The Gannock House, Old Malton, Malton, N Yorkshire YO17 0HB* Malton (0653) 692121

MANCHESTER, Archdeacon of. *See* HARRIS, Ven Reginald Brian

MANCHESTER, Bishop of. *See* BOOTH-CLIBBORN, Rt Rev Stanley Eric Francis

MANCHESTER, Dean of. *See* WADDINGTON, Very Rev Robert Murray

MANDER, Dennis Stanley. b 18. Bps' Coll Cheshunt 60. **d** 62 **p** 63. S Africa 69-78; R Lanteglos by Camelford w Advent *Truro* 78-85; rtd 85. *12 Menheniot Crescent, Langore, Launceston, Cornwall PL15 8PD* Launceston (0566) 772853

MANDER, Peter John. b 52. Liv Univ BA85. Sarum & Wells Th Coll 85. **d** 87 **p** 88. C Hale and Ashley *Ches* 87-90; TV Grantham *Linc* from 90. *The Vicarage, The Grove, Grantham NG31 7PU* Grantham (0476) 71270

MANDER, Ronald Charles Ridge. b 13. Lon Univ BD50. Kelham Th Coll 32. **d** 38 **p** 39. R Rumboldswyke *Chich* 61-67; Perm to Offic from 67; rtd 75. *7 St Gabriel's Road, Billingshurst, W Sussex RH14 9TX* Billingshurst (0403) 784486

MANDER, Canon Thomas Leonard Frederick. b 33. Ely Th Coll 60. **d** 62 **p** 63. C Cov St Mary *Cov* 62-66; V Bishop's Tachbrook 66-70; V Earlsdon 70-76; V Chesterton 76-83; R Lighthorne 76-83; V Newbold Pacey w Moreton Morrell 76-83; Hon Can Cov Cathl from 80; P-in-c S Leamington St Jo 83-84; V from 84. *St John's Vicarage, Tachbrook Street, Leamington Spa CV31 3BN* Leamington Spa (0926) 422208

MANHIRE, Ashley Lewin. b 31. AKC55. **d** 56 **p** 57. C Plymouth St Gabr *Ex* 56-59; C Cockington 59-66; V Torquay St Martin Barton 66-83; RD Ipplepen 82-87; V Shaldon from 83. *The Vicarage, Torquay Road, Shaldon, Teignmouth, Devon TQ14 0AX* Shaldon (0626) 872396

MANHOOD, Mrs Phyllis. b 32. Aston Tr Scheme 78 Qu Coll Birm 79. **dss** 82 **d** 87. Harwich *Chelmsf* 82-83; Dovercourt and Parkeston 83-85; Fawley *Win* 85-87; Par Dn from 87. *15 Long Lane Close, Holbury, Southampton SO4 1LE* Fawley (0703) 891809

✠**MANKTELOW, Rt Rev Michael Richard John.** b 27. Ch Coll Cam BA48 MA52. Chich Th Coll 51. **d** 53 **p** 54 **c** 77. C Boston *Linc* 53-56; Chapl Ch Coll Cam 57-61; Chapl Linc Th Coll 61-63; Sub-Warden 64-66; V Knaresborough St Jo *Ripon* 66-73; RD Harrogate 72-77; V Harrogate St Wilfrid 73-77; P-in-c Harrogate St Luke 75-77; Hon Can Ripon Cathl 75-77; Suff Bp Basingstoke *Win* from 77; Can Res Win Cathl 77-91; Vice-Dean Win from 87;

Hon Can Win Cathl from 91. *Bishop's Lodge, Skippetts Lane West, Basingstoke, Hants RG21 3HP* Basingstoke (0256) 468193

MANLEY, Canon Gordon Russell Delpratt. b 33. Ch Coll Cam BA56 MA60. Linc Th Coll 57. **d** 59 **p** 60. C Westbury-on-Trym St Alb *Bris* 59-61; Chapl Ch Coll Cam 61-66; V Radlett *St Alb* 66-75; V Faversham *Cant* from 75; RD Ospringe 84-90; Hon Can Cant Cathl from 90. *The Vicarage, Preston Street, Faversham, Kent ME13 8PG* Faversham (0795) 532592

MANLEY, Michael Alan. b 60. SS Hild & Bede Coll Dur BA82. Trin Coll Bris DipTh86. **d** 86 **p** 87. C Accrington St Jo *Blackb* 86-89; C Huncoat 88-89; C Accrington St Jo w Huncoat 89-90; V Preston St Luke and St Oswald from 90. *The Vicarage, 60 Harewood Road, Preston PR1 6XE* Preston (0772) 795395

MANN, Lt-Comdr Anthony James. b 34. Open Univ BA76. St Jo Coll Nottm 85. **d** 88 **p** 89. NSM Helensburgh *Glas* 88-91; Dioc Supernumerary from 91. *The Anchorage, Portkil, Kilcreggan, Helensburgh, Dunbartonshire G84 0LF* Helensburgh (0436) 842623

MANN, Brian Neville. b 29. Qu Coll Birm 57. **d** 60 **p** 88. C Ipswich St Mary Stoke *St E* 60-61; C Tonge Moor *Man* 62; NSM Homerton St Barn w St Paul *Lon* 77-85; NSM Hackney Marsh from 85. *2 Watermead House, Kingsmead Estate, London E9 5RS* 081-533 2246

MANN, Mrs Charmion Anne Montgomery. b 36. Liv Univ BA57 Bris Univ CertEd62 DipEd79. Trin Coll Bris. **dss** 82 **d** 87. Bris St Nath w St Kath *Bris* 82-84; Bris St Matt and St Nath 84-85; Asst Chapl City Cen Hosps Bris 85-88; Chapl Bris Maternity Hosp, Bris Children's Hosp and Bris R Infirmary from 88. *28 St Matthew's Road, Bristol BS6 5TT* Bristol (0272) 247316

MANN, Christopher John. b 57. Glas Univ BSc79. Westcott Ho Cam 83. **d** 86 **p** 87. C Worc SE *Worc* 86-89; Min Can and Sacr St Paul's Cathl *Lon* from 89. *7A Amen Court, London EC4M 7BU* 071-236 3871

MANN, David. b 57. BA. Ridley Hall Cam. **d** 82 **p** 83. C Monkwearmouth St Andr *Dur* 82-86; Chapl Sheff Cathl *Sheff* 86-87; C Leeds St Geo *Ripon* from 87. *40 Marlborough Grange, Leeds LS1 4NE* Leeds (0532) 431321

MANN, David Peter. b 29. Ho of Sacred Miss 51. **d** 55 **p** 56. V Shieldfield Ch Ch *Newc* 59-75; V Kingsbury St Andr *Lon* 75-89; rtd 89. *14 Grove Street, Norton, Malton, N Yorkshire YO17 9BG*

MANN, Donald Leonard. b 22. Westcott Ho Cam. **d** 47 **p** 48. V Sheen *Lich* 69-76; P-in-c Calton 72-76; P-in-c Ellastone 76; rtd 76. *Bungalow No. 24, Lyme Green Settlement, Macclesfield, Cheshire* Sutton (02605) 2209

MANN, Edmund Geoffrey. b 56. Reading Univ BA78. N Ord Course 86. **d** 89 **p** 90. C Harwood *Man* from 89. *89 New Lane, Harwood, Bolton BL2 5BY* Bolton (0204) 29448

MANN, Gary. b 63. Nottm Univ BTh90. Linc Th Coll 87. **d** 90 **p** 91. C Knottingley *Wakef* from 90. *Mylor, Chapel Street, Knottingley, W Yorkshire WF11 9AN* Pontefract (0977) 677010

MANN, Ivan John. b 52. Brunel Univ BTech74 Southn Univ BTh80. Sarum & Wells Th Coll 75. **d** 78 **p** 79. C Hadleigh w Layham and Shelley *St E* 78-81; C Whitton and Thurleston w Akenham 81-83; V Leiston 83-86; Perm to Offic 86-89; R Aldringham w Thorpe, Knodishall w Buxlow etc from 89. *The Rectory, Friston, Saxmundham, Suffolk IP17 1NP* Snape (072888) 8972

MANN, John Owen. b 55. QUB BD77 MTh86. CITC 79. **d** 79 **p** 81. C Cloughfern *Conn* 79-82; C Knock *D & D* 82-85; I Ballyrashane w Kildollagh *Conn* 85-89; R Bentworth and Shalden and Lasham *Win* from 89. *The Rectory, Bentworth, Alton, Hants GU34 5RB* Alton (0420) 63218

✠**MANN, Rt Rev Michael Ashley.** b 24. KCVO89. CBIM RMA 42 Harvard Univ AMP73. Wells Th Coll 55. **d** 57 **p** 58 **c** 74. C Wolborough w Newton Abbot *Ex* 57-59; V Sparkwell 59-62; Nigeria 62-67; Home Sec Miss to Seamen 67-69; Can Res Nor Cathl *Nor* 69-74; Vice-Dean 73-74; Dioc Ind Adv 69-74; Suff Bp Dudley *Worc* 74-76; Dean of Windsor and Dom Chapl to HM the Queen 76-89; rtd 89. *Lower End Farm Cottage, Eastington, Northleach, Glos GL54 3PN* Cotswold (0451) 60767

MANN, Peter Eric. b 51. St Jo Coll Dur BA73. Westcott Ho Cam 73. **d** 75 **p** 76. C Barrow St Jo *Carl* 75-78; C Egremont 78-80; V Carl St Luke Morton 80-86; TR Egremont and Haile from 86. *The Rectory, Grove Road, Egremont, Cumbria CA22 2LU* Egremont (0946) 820268

MANN, Ralph Norman. b 27. BNC Ox BA51 MA55 DipEd52. Ox NSM Course 79. **d** 82 **p** 83. NSM Kingham

w Churchill, Daylesford and Sarsden *Ox* 82-85; S Area Sec BCMS 82-89; P-in-c Broadwell, Evenlode, Oddington and Adlestrop *Glouc* from 89. *The Rectory, Broadwell, Moreton-in-Marsh, Glos GL56 0TU* Cotswold (0451) 31866

MANN, Robert Francis Christopher Stephen. b 17. K Coll Lon BD56 PhD60. Kelham Th Coll 36. **d** 40 **p** 41. Kilmorie Sch Lon 61-65; USA from 65; rtd 82. *107 East Chase Street, Baltimore, Maryland 2102, USA* Baltimore (301) 837-7362

MANN, Robin. b 45. MRTPI73 DipTP72 Fitzw Coll Cam BA76 MA80. Ridley Hall Cam 73. **d** 77 **p** 78. C Wetherby *Ripon* 77-80; V Hipswell 80-86; V Mamble w Bayton, Rock w Heightington etc *Worc* from 86. *The Vicarage, Far Forest, Kidderminster, Worcs DY14 9TT* Rock (0299) 266580

MANN, Sydney. b 07. Ripon Hall Ox 63. **d** 64 **p** 65. V Easington w Skeffling and Kilnsea *York* 69-74; rtd 74; Perm to Offic *Cov* from 74. *19 Landor House, Crutchley Way, Whitnash, Leamington Spa CV31 2RL* Leamington Spa (0926) 421837

MANNALL, Michael John Frederick. b 37. St Mich Coll Llan 61. **d** 63 **p** 64. C-in-c Cricklewood St Pet CD *Lon* 69-73; R Broughton *Pet* 73-75; Hon C Kingston St Luke *S'wark* from 76; rtd 84. *Walsingham, 17 Hillmont Road, Hinchley Wood, Esher, Surrey KT10 9BA*

MANNERS, Kenneth. b 29. N Ord Course. **d** 84 **p** 85. NSM Brayton *York* from 84. *16 Wistow Road, Selby, N Yorkshire YO8 0LY* Selby (0757) 702129

MANNING, Canon Arthur Lionel. b 16. St Jo Coll Cam BA38 MA44. Ridley Hall Cam 38. **d** 40 **p** 41. V Woodford *Ches* 71-81; rtd 81. *Derwenfa, 2 Bro Helyg, Llandrillo, Corwen, Clwyd LL21 0TR* Llandrillo (049084) 337

MANNING, Arthur Philip. b 35. Chester Coll BEd74. St Jo Coll Nottm 88. **d** 89 **p** 90. C Eastham *Ches* 89-90. *12 Butterbache Road, Huntingdon, Chester CH3 6BZ* Chester (0244) 314432

MANNING, Brian Hawthorne. b 29. AMCT52 CEng59 MIStructE59. NW Ord Course 70. **d** 73 **p** 74. NSM Birch St Jas *Man* 73-75; NSM Prestwich St Gabr 75-80; NSM Prestwich St Mary 80-85; NSM Marple All SS *Ches* 85-88; R Cockfield w Bradfield St Clare, Felsham etc *St E* from 88. *The Rectory, Howe Lane, Cockfield, Bury St Edmunds, Suffolk IP30 0HA* Cockfield Green (0284) 828385

MANNING, David Godfrey. b 47. Trin Coll Bris 73. **d** 76 **p** 77. C Richmond H Trin and Ch Ch *S'wark* 76-79; C Anston *Sheff* 79-83; V Blackpool St Mark *Blackb* from 83. *St Mark's Vicarage, 163 Kingscote Drive, Blackpool FY3 8EH* Blackpool (0253) 32895

MANNING, Neville Alexander. b 41. Lon Univ BD68. ALCD68. **d** 68 **p** 69. C Belvedere All SS *Roch* 68-71; C Hollington St Leon *Chich* 71-73; C Hersham *Guildf* 73-77; V Dawley St Jerome *Lon* from 77. *St Jerome's Lodge, 42 Corwell Lane, Dawley, Uxbridge, Middx UB8 3DE* 081-573 2084 or 561 7393

✠**MANNING, Rt Rev William James.** b 16. TCD BA44 MA47 Or Coll Ox MA50. TCD Div Sch Div Test44. **d** 44 **p** 45 **c** 78. C Dub Donnybrook *D & G* 44-47; C Cork St Fin Barre's Cathl *C, C & R* 47-49; Chapl Thos Coram Sch Berkhamsted 49-51; Bermuda 51-64; Can Res Bermuda 53-64; Zurich *Eur* 64-66; S Africa from 67; Dean George 72-77; Bp George 78-87. *Liamslea, 10 Dalmore Road, Tokai, 7945 South Africa* Cape Town (21) 757811

MANNS, Edwin Ernest. b 30. Portsm Dioc Tr Course 84. **d** 85. C Paulsgrove *Portsm* from 85; Chapl St Mary's Gen Hosp Portsm 90-91. *17 Kelvin Grove, Portchester, Fareham, Hants PO16 8LQ* Cosham (0705) 324818

MANSBRIDGE, Ven Michael Winstanley. b 32. Southn Univ BA54. Ridley Hall Cam 56. **d** 58 **p** 59. C Ware St Mary *St Alb* 58-60; C Claverdon w Preston Bagot *Cov* 60-62; Kenya 62-65; V Chilvers Coton w Astley *Cov* 65-75; RD Nuneaton 67-74; V Leamington Priors H Trin 75-83; UAE from 83; Miss to Seamen from 83. *St Andrew's Vicarage, PO Box 262, Abu Dhabi, United Arab Emirates* Abu Dhabi (2) 461631 or 464591

MANSEL, Canon James Seymour Denis. b 07. KCVO79. **d** 41 **p** 42. Dom Chapl to HM The Queen 65-79; Sub-Dean of the Chpls Royal 65-79; Dep Clerk of the Closet and Sub-Almoner 65-79; Can and Preb Chich Cathl *Chich* 71-79; rtd 79; Chapl to HM The Queen from 79; Hon C Westmr St Marg 80-88; PV Westmr Abbey from 83. *15 Sandringham Court, Maida Vale, London W9 1UA* 071-286 3052

MANSELL, Clive Neville Ross. b 53. Solicitor 77 Leic Univ LLB74. Trin Coll Bris DipHE81. **d** 82 **p** 83. C Gt Malvern St Mary *Worc* 82-85; Min Can Ripon Cathl *Ripon* 85-89; R Kirklington w Burneston and Wath and

Pickhill from 89. *The Rectory, Kirklington, Bedale, N Yorkshire DL8 2NJ*   Thirsk (0845) 567429

MANSFIELD, Gordon Reginald. b 35. Lon Univ DipTh61 CertEd BA. Clifton Th Coll 58. **d** 63 **p** 64. C Carl St Jo *Carl* 63-65; C Westcombe Park St Geo *S'wark* 65-68; C Rashcliffe *Wakef* 68-70; V Woodlands *Sheff* 70-80; V Steeple Bumpstead and Helions Bumpstead *Chelmsf* from 80. *The Vicarage, Church Street, Steeple Bumpstead, Haverhill, Suffolk CB9 7EA*   Haverhill (0440) 730257

MANSFIELD, Julian Nicolas. b 59. K Coll Lon BD AKC. Edin Th Coll 83. **d** 85 **p** 86. C Kirkby *Liv* 85-89; TV Ditton St Mich from 89. *St Thomas's Vicarage, 154 Liverpool Road, Widnes, Cheshire WA8 7JB*   051-420 6614

MANSFIELD, Robert William. b 45. Local NSM Course 89. **d** 88 **p** 89. NSM Louth *Linc* from 88. *The Old Railway House, Stewton, Louth, Lincs LN11 8SD*   Louth (0507) 327533

MANSFIELD, Simon David. b 55. Brunel Univ BSc81. Ripon Coll Cuddesdon 88. **d** 90 **p** 91. C N Harrow St Alb *Lon* from 90. *29 The Ridgeway, Harrow, Middx HA2 7QL*   081-429 0763

MANSFIELD, Stephen McLaren. b 59. FGA DipRJ GDip. Cranmer Hall Dur 86. **d** 89 **p** 90. C Poynton *Ches* from 89. *11 Deva Close, Poynton, Stockport, Cheshire SK12 1HH*   Poynton (0625) 871958

MANSHIP, Canon David. b 27. ARCO Keble Coll Ox BA52 MA58. Qu Coll Birm 52. **d** 54 **p** 55. C Hackney St Jo *Lon* 54-58; C Preston Ascension 58-61; C St Andr Holborn 61-65; Members' Tr Officer C of E Youth Coun 65-68; Clergy Tr Officer 68-70; Dir of Educn Win 70-79; Hon Can Win Cathl 74-79; R Old Alresford 76-79; V Abingdon w Shippon *Ox* 79-89; TR Abingdon from 89; V Shippon 89; RD Abingdon 87-90. *The Rectory, St Helen's Court, Abingdon, Oxon OX14 5BS*   Abingdon (0235) 520144

MANSLEY, Colin Edward. b 56. Edin Univ MA80 BA85. Ripon Coll Cuddesdon 83. **d** 86 **p** 87. C Worle *B & W* 86-89; C Baguley *Man* from 89. *39 Dalebrook Road, Sale, Cheshire M33 3LD*   061-973 0189

MANSON-BRAILSFORD, Andrew Henry. b 64. NUU BA86. Ripon Coll Cuddesdon 87. **d** 90 **p** 91. C Warrington St Elphin *Liv* from 90. *133 Church Street, Warrington WA1 2TL*   Warrington (0925) 33940

MANTHORP, Brian Robert. b 34. Pemb Coll Ox BA55 MA59. Westcott Ho Cam. **d** 61 **p** 62. C Busbridge *Guildf* 61-62; Lic to Offic *S'wark* 62-65; Asst Master Framlingham Coll 66-68; India 68-70; Master Oakbank Sch Keighley 70-73; Hd Master H Trin Sch Halifax 73-80; Worc Coll for the Blind 80-87; RNIB New Coll Worc from 87; Perm to Offic *Worc* from 84. *RNIB New College Worcester, Whittington Road, Worcester WR5 2JX*   Worcester (0905) 763933

MANTLE, John Ambrose Cyril. b 46. St Andr Univ MTh74 CertEd75 Kent Univ MA90. Edin Th Coll 66. **d** 69 **p** 70. C Broughty Ferry *Bre* 69-71; Perm to Offic *Bre* 71-75; Edin 75-77; Chapl St Andr Univ *St And* 77-80; P-in-c Pittenweem 78-80; P-in-c Elie and Earlsferry 78-80; Chapl and Fell Fitzw Coll Cam 80-86; Tutor Cant Sch of Min from 86; C Boxley w Detling *Cant* from 86. *The Vicarage, Boxley, Maidstone, Kent ME14 3DX*   Maidstone (0622) 58606

MANTLE, Canon Rupert James. b 15. Edin Univ MA37. Edin Th Coll 38. **d** 40 **p** 41. R Aber St Pet *Ab* 67-81; Hon C 84-87; Can St Andr Cathl 78-81; rtd 81; Hon Can St Andr Cathl *Ab* from 81. *32 Craigiebuckler Terrace, Aberdeen AB1 7SS*   Aberdeen (0224) 316636

MANTON, Paul Arthur. b 45. Lon Univ DipTh75 BD77. Oak Hill Th Coll 73. **d** 77 **p** 78. C Wolv *Lich* 77-80; C Penn Fields 80; Ind Chapl *Lon* 80-87; Hon C St Marylebone All So w SS Pet and Jo 80-87. *29 Finchley Way, London N3 1AH*   081-346 6753

MANTON, Peter Geoffrey Kevitt. b 20. Wycliffe Hall Ox. **d** 61 **p** 62. R Jersey St Jo *Win* 65-85; rtd 85; Perm to Offic *Win* from 85. *9 Clos de Gouray, Gorey, Jersey, Channel Islands*   Jersey (0534) 53204

MAPLE, David Charles. b 34. Sarum Th Coll 64. **d** 66 **p** 66. C Buckland in Dover *Cant* 66-67; C St Laurence in Thanet 67-71; Chapl RAF 71-75; P-in-c Ivychurch 75-76; P-in-c Newchurch *Cant* 75-78; P-in-c Burmarsh 75-78; P-in-c St Mary in the Marsh 75-76; R Dymchurch 76-78; R Dymchurch w Burmarsh and Newchurch 78-81; Hon Min Cant Cant Cathl from 79; Abp's Dioc Chapl 81-91; Chapl St Jo Hosp Cant from 91. *St John's Hospital, Canterbury, Kent*   Canterbury (0227) 764935

MAPLE, John Philip. b 50. Chich Th Coll 71. **d** 74 **p** 79. C Notting Hill St Mich and Ch Ch *Lon* 74-75; Lic to Offic 78-79; C Barnsbury St Dav w St Clem 79-80; C Cotham St Sav w St Mary *Bris* 80-83; TV St Marylebone Ch Ch

Lon 83-91; R St Marylebone, St Paul from 91. *St Paul's House, 9 Rossmore Road, London NW1 6NJ*   071-262 9443

MAPLES, Ven Jeffrey Stanley. b 16. Down Coll Cam BA38 MA46. Chich Th Coll 39. **d** 40 **p** 41. V Milton *Portsm* 67-73; Adn Swindon *Bris* 74-82; rtd 82. *88 Exeter Street, Salisbury SP1 2SE*   Salisbury (0722) 323848

MAPLEY, Barbara Jean. b 46. Oak Hill NSM Course. **d** 89. NSM Kelvedon *Chelmsf* from 89. *2 Janmead, Witham, Essex CM8 2EN*   Witham (0376) 516872

MAPPLEBECK, Anthony. b 16. SS Coll Cam BA38 MA42. Cuddesdon Coll 39. **d** 40 **p** 41. V Mevagissey *Truro* 55-81; rtd 81. *20 Polkirt Hill, Mevagissey, St Austell, Cornwall PL26 6UR*   Mevagissey (0726) 842956

MAPPLEBECKPALMER, Richard Warwick. b 32. CCC Cam BA56 MA60. Cuddesdon Coll 56. **d** 58 **p** 59. C Redcar *York* 58-60; C Drypool St Jo 61-63; V Pendleton St Ambrose *Man* 63-77; P-in-c Piddington *Ox* 77; P-in-c Ambrosden w Arncot and Blackthorn 77; P-in-c Mert 77; V Ambrosden w Mert and Piddington 77-88; USA from 88. *1516 Fernwood Drive, Oakland, California 94611, USA*   Oakland (415) 653-9139

MAPSON, Albert. b 96. **d** 25 **p** 26. R Staple *Cant* 51-63; rtd 63; Perm to Offic *Cant* from 64. *14 Oaten Hill Place, Canterbury, Kent CT1 3HJ*   Canterbury (0227) 766281

MAPSON, Preb John Victor. b 31. Lon Univ BA60. Oak Hill Th Coll 55. **d** 60 **p** 61. C Littleover *Derby* 60-62; C Wandsworth St Mich *S'wark* 62-65; R Willand *Ex* 65-71; P-in-c Axmouth 71-72; V 72-75; V Axmouth w Musbury 75-77; RD Honiton 76-77; V Cullompton 77-89; R Kentisbeare w Blackborough 77-89; RD Cullompton 81-89; P-in-c Sidmouth All SS from 89; Preb Ex Cathl from 91. *All Saints' Vicarage, All Saints' Road, Sidmouth, Devon EX10 8ES*   Sidmouth (0395) 515963

MAPSTONE, Trevor Anthony. b 63. Lanc Univ BSc84. St Jo Coll Nottm LTh88 DPS89. **d** 89 **p** 90. C Hoole *Ches* from 89. *8 Park Drive, Hoole Village, Chester CH2 3JS*   Chester (0244) 311104

MARCER, Graham John. b 52. Ripon Coll Cuddesdon 75. **d** 78 **p** 79. C Sherborne w Castleton and Lillington *Sarum* 78-81; C Christchurch *Win* 81-84; V Southn St Jude 84-90; P-in-c Moordown 90-91; C Sheff Parson Cross St Cecilia *Sheff* from 91. *240 Halifax Road, Sheffield S6 1AA*   Sheffield (0742) 322797

MARCETTI, Alvin Julian. b 41. San Jose State Univ BA66 Santa Clara Univ MA76. Cranmer Hall Dur 85. **d** 87 **p** 88. C Stepney St Dunstan and All SS *Lon* 87-91; Chapl City of Lon Poly from 91. *1 The Crescent, London EC3N 2LY*   071-481 1749

MARCH, Charles Anthony Maclea. b 32. CCC Cam BA55 MA70. Oak Hill Th Coll 55. **d** 57 **p** 58. C S Croydon Em *Cant* 57-60; C Eastbourne H Trin *Chich* 60-63; V Whitehall Park St Andr Hornsey Lane *Lon* 63-67; V Tunbridge Wells H Trin w Ch Ch *Roch* 67-82; V Prestonville St Luke *Chich* from 82. *St Luke's Vicarage, 64 Old Shoreham Road, Brighton BN1 5DD*   Brighton (0273) 552267

MARCH, John Vale. b 39. CCC Cam BA62 MA76. Linc Th Coll 62. **d** 64 **p** 65. C Sheldon *Birm* 64-68; C Hodge Hill 68-72; TV 72-85; C Handsworth St Jas from 85. *168 Albert Road, Birmingham B21 9JT*   021-523 0317

MARCHAND, Rex Anthony Victor. b 47. K Coll Lon BD69 AKC69. St Aug Coll Cant 69. **d** 70 **p** 71. C Leigh Park *Portsm* 70-73; C Hatf *St Alb* 73-80; R Deal St Leon and St Rich and Sholden *Cant* from 80. *St Leonard's Rectory, Addelam Road, Deal, Kent CT14 9BZ*   Deal (0304) 374076

MARCHANT, Ven George John Charles. b 16. St Jo Coll Dur LTh38 BA39 MA42 BD64. Tyndale Hall Bris 35. **d** 39 **p** 40. V Dur St Nic *Dur* 54-74; RD Dur 64-74; Hon Can Dur Cathl 72-74; Adn Auckland 74-83; Can Res Dur Cathl 74-83; rtd 83; Perm to Offic *Nor* from 83. *28 Greenways, Eaton, Norwich NR4 6PE*   Norwich (0603) 58295

MARCHANT, Canon Iain William. b 26. Wells Th Coll 59. **d** 60 **p** 61. C Dalston *Carl* 60-63; V Hawkesbury *Glouc* 63-76; R Newent 76-85; Hon Can Glouc Cathl from 84; R Newent and Gorsley w Cliffords Mesne from 85. *The Rectory, Newent, Glos GL18 1JA*   Newent (0531) 820248

MARCHANT, Peter Saunders. TCD BA82 DipTh82. **d** 82 **p** 83. C Bandon *C, C & R* 82-85; Min Can Cork Cathl 85-87; Chapl Ashton Sch Cork 85-87; Chapl Belgrade w Zagreb *Eur* 87-91; Chapl Rome from 91. *All Saints, via del Babuino, Piazza di Spagna, 00187 Rome, Italy*   Rome (6) 679-4357

MARCHANT, Canon Ronald Albert. b 26. Em Coll Cam BA50 MA52 PhD57 BD64. Ridley Hall Cam 50. **d** 54 **p** 55. C Acomb St Steph *York* 54-57; C Willian *St Alb*

57-59; V Laxfield *St E* from 59; RD Hoxne 73-78; Hon Can St E Cathl from 75; P-in-c Wilby w Brundish from 86. *The Vicarage, Laxfield, Woodbridge, Suffolk IP13 8EB* Ubbeston (098683) 218

MARDEN, Peter Edgar. b 40. Univ of Wales (Lamp) BA61 Linacre Coll Ox BA64 MA68. St Steph Ho Ox 62. **d** 65 **p** 66. C Catford St Laur *S'wark* 65-70; C Mortlake w E Sheen 70-73; V Sydenham St Phil 73-75; Lic to Offic *Cant* from 76; Perm to Offic *Roch* from 81. *65 Bower Mount Road, Maidstone, Kent ME16 8AS* Maidstone (0622) 675861

MARGAM, Archdeacon of. *See* JAMES, Ven Douglas Gordon

MARINER, Aris. b 43. Alexandria Univ BSc65. St Alb Minl Tr Scheme 84. **d** 87. NSM Stevenage H Trin *St Alb* from 87. *13 Church Lane, Stevenage, Herts SG1 3QS* Stevenage (0438) 365596

MARK, Brother. *See* SHARPE, John Brebber

MARK, Timothy John. b 34. Bris Univ BA57 MLitt68 MEd71 Leeds Univ PhD79. Didsbury Meth Coll 54. **d** 59 **p** 61. India 59-64 and 65-69; Perm to Offic *Sheff* from 73. *15 Fieldhouse Road, Sprotborough, Doncaster, S Yorkshire DN5 7RN* Doncaster (0302) 853022

MARKBY, Archibald Campbell. b 15. Em Coll Cam BA37 MA41. Ridley Hall Cam 37. **d** 39 **p** 39. V Damerham *Sarum* 71-80; V Martin 71-80; rtd 80. *Mead Cottage, Martin, Fordingbridge, Hants* Martin Cross (072589) 345

MARKBY, Peter John Jenner. b 38. Em Coll Cam BA60. Clifton Th Coll 62. **d** 64 **p** 65. C Tufnell Park St Geo *Lon* 64-68; C Crowborough *Chich* 68-73; C Polegate 73-77; R Southover from 77. *The Rectory, Southover High Street, Lewes, E Sussex BN7 1HT* Lewes (0273) 472018

MARKE, Christopher Andrew Burrows. b 42. MIEIecIE BA. Oak Hill NSM Course. **d** 84 **p** 85. NSM Brighstone and Brooke w Mottistone *Portsm* 84-86; NSM Shorwell w Kingston from 85; NSM Gatcombe from 87; NSM Chale from 89. *Cranmer House, 127 Castle Road, Newport, Isle of Wight PO30 1DP* Isle of Wight (0983) 523657

MARKER, John Howard. b 11. ALCD34. **d** 34 **p** 35. R Copford w Easthorpe *Chelmsf* 68-77; rtd 77; Perm to Offic *St E* from 83. *3 Greenacres, Great Waldingfield, Sudbury, Suffolk CO10 0SB* Sudbury (0787) 311410

MARKEY, Michael John. b 42. Chich Th Coll 71. **d** 74 **p** 75. C Hillingdon All SS *Lon* 74-77; C Reading H Trin *Ox* 77-81; V Northolt W End St Jos *Lon* 81-86; P-in-c Albany Street Ch Ch 86-89; P-in-c Munster Square St Mary Magd 86-89; V Munster Square Ch Ch and St Mary Magd from 89. *The Mission House, 24 Redhill Street, London NW1 4DQ* 071-388 3095

MARKHAM, David Christopher. b 17. Clifton Th Coll 67. **d** 69 **p** 70. C Hellesdon H Trin *Chich* 69-74; R Elmswell *St E* 74-78; P-in-c Danehill *Chich* 78-83; V 83-88; rtd 88. *16 Wilmar Way, Seal, Sevenoaks, Kent TN15 0DN* Sevenoaks (0732) 62163

MARKHAM, Deryck O'Leary. b 28. Oak Hill Th Coll 66. **d** 68 **p** 69. C Purley Ch Ch *S'wark* 68-72; V E Budleigh and Bicton *Ex* from 72; RD Aylesbeare from 89. *86 Granary Lane, Budleigh Salterton, Devon EX9 6ER* Budleigh Salterton (03954) 3340

MARKHAM, Canon Gervase William. b 10. Trin Coll Cam BA32 MA36. Westcott Ho Cam 34. **d** 36 **p** 37. V Morland w Thrimby and Gt Strickland *Carl* 65-84; Hon Can Carl Cathl 72-84; rtd 84; Perm to Offic *Carl* from 84. *The Garden Flat, Morland House, Penrith, Cumbria CA10 3AZ* Morland (09314) 654

MARKHAM, John Gabriel. b 06. Linc Coll Ox BA30 MA70. Ely Th Coll 30. **d** 31 **p** 32. Chapl Reading and Distr Hosps 60-74; rtd 74. *22 Watlington Road, Benson, Oxford OX10 6LS* Wallingford (0491) 35397

MARKHAM, John William. b 12. St Aid Birkenhead 34. **d** 37 **p** 38. V Teynham *Cant* 60-75; rtd 75; Perm to Offic *Cant* from 75. *16 Oaten Hill Place, Canterbury, Kent CT1 3HJ* Canterbury (0227) 453988

MARKLAND, Vincent Hilton. b 33. Univ of Wales (Lamp) BA55 Leic Univ PGCE58. Ripon Hall Ox 67. **d** 68 **p** 69. C Worsley *Man* 68-83; V Monton from 83. *The Vicarage, 3 Egerton Road, Monton, Eccles, Manchester M30 9LR* 061-789 2420

MARKS, Alfred Howard. b 02. Qu Coll Cam BA25 MA29. Ridley Hall Cam 25. **d** 26 **p** 27. V Ipswich St Marg *St E* 59-70; rtd 70; Lic to Offic St E 70-80; Worc 81-84; Perm to Offic *Worc* from 84. *43 Hudson Close, Worcester WR2 4DP* Worcester (0905) 429921

MARKS, Anthony Alfred. b 28. AKC53. **d** 54 **p** 55. Chapl RN 83-85; QHC from 81; P-in-c Bradninch *Ex* 83-88; R Bradninch and Clyst Hydon 88-90; rtd 90.

Bryony Cottage, The Combe, Compton Martin, Bristol BS18 6JD

MARKS, Anthony Wendt. b 43. G&C Coll Cam BA63 MA67 PhD70 BNC Ox DPhil72. St Steph Ho Ox 70. **d** 72 **p** 73. C Withington St Crispin *Man* 72-75; Chapl Lon Univ Medical Students *Lon* 75-80; Warden Liddon Ho Lon from 80; C-in-c Grosvenor Chpl *Lon* from 80. *Liddon House, 24 South Audley Street, London W1Y 5DL* 071-499 1684

MARKS, David Frederick. b 14. Univ of Wales BA37 Jes Coll Ox BA40 MA45. St Mich Coll Llan 40. **d** 41 **p** 42. Sen Lect St D Coll Lamp 74-82; rtd 82. *Wyngarth, Bryn Road, Lampeter, Dyfed SA48 7EF* Lampeter (0570) 422474

MARKS, John Alexander Rishworth. b 19. TCD BA41 MA61. CITC 43. **d** 43 **p** 44. Chapl RN 46-69; rtd 69; Perm to Offic *St Alb* from 77. *1 Linten Close, Hitchin, Herts*

MARKS, Timothy John. b 45. Man Univ BA76. **d** 88 **p** 89. NSM Burton and Sopley *Win* 88-91; R Graveley w Papworth St Agnes w Yelling etc *Ely* from 91; R Croxton and Eltisley from 91. *c/o The Vicarage, Eltisley, St Neots, Huntingdon, Cambs PE19 4TG* Croxton (048087) 252

MARKWELL, Donald Stanley. b 30. Victoria Univ Wellington MA53. **d** 79 **p** 80. Hon C Kingston Hill St Paul *S'wark* 79-82; Hon C Ham St Andr from 82. *12 Albany Mews, Kingston upon Thames, Surrey KT2 5SL* 081-546 0740

MARLEY, Alan Gordon. b 59. Birm Univ BA89. **d** 89 **p** 90. C Blandford Forum and Langton Long *Sarum* from 89. *Leslie House, The Tabernacle, Blandford Forum, Dorset DT11 7DW* Blandford (0258) 451943

MARLEY, Neville William Arthur. b 24. Em Coll Cam BA46 MA51. Ridley Hall Cam 48. **d** 50 **p** 51. V Telford Park St Thos *S'wark* 56-89; CF (TA - R of O) 64-67; rtd 89. *12 The Headlands, Darlington, Co Durham DL3 8RP* Darlington (0325) 357559

MARLOW, Preb Walter Geoffrey. b 29. AKC57. **d** 57 **p** 58. C Long Eaton St Laur *Derby* 57-61; C Mackworth St Fran 61-63; R Stoke Albany w Wilbarston *Pet* 63-68; V Calow *Derby* 68-73; R Wingerworth 73-82; P-in-c Islington St Jas w St Phil *Lon* 82-87; P-in-c Islington St Pet 82-87; V Islington St Jas w St Pet from 87; AD Islington 84-90; Preb St Paul's Cathl from 87. *St James's Vicarage, Arlington Square, London N1 7DS* 071-226 4108

MARNHAM, Charles Christopher. b 51. Jes Coll Cam BA73 MA77. Cranmer Hall Dur DipTh76. **d** 77 **p** 78. C Brompton H Trin *Lon* 77-78; C Brompton H Trin w Onslow Square St Paul 78-80; C Linthorpe *York* 80-84; R Haughton le Skerne *Dur* from 84. *The Rectory, Haughton Green, Darlington, Co Durham DL1 2DD* Darlington (0325) 468142

MARR, Canon Donald Radley. b 37. K Coll Lon 57. St Aid Birkenhead 61. **d** 64 **p** 65. V Marthall *Ches* 67-72; C W Kirby St Bridget 72-76; R Waverton 76-83; R Nantwich 83-87; RD Nantwich 86-87; RD Malpas 87-91; V Bunbury 87-91; Hon Can Ches Cathl from 91; Dioc Rural Officer from 91; rtd 91. *St Boniface, 5 Hockenhull Crescent, Tarvin, Chester CH3 8LJ* Tarvin (0829) 41302

MARR, Peter. b 36. Reading Univ PhD78. Ox NSM Course 84. **d** 87 **p** 88. NSM Reading St Giles *Ox* 87-89; C Beverley Minster *York* from 90. *38 Highgate, Beverley, N Humberside HU17 0DN* Hull (0482) 862656

MARRETT, Hedley Charles Guille. b 09. St Boniface Warminster 29. **d** 34 **p** 35. V Jersey St Simon *Win* 50-77; P-in-c Jersey All SS 67-77; rtd 77. *11 Bell Meadow, Hook, Basingstoke, Hants RG27 9HG* Hook (0256) 763176

MARRIOTT, Canon David John. b 29. St Chad's Coll Dur BA54 DipTh56. **d** 56 **p** 57. C Manston *Ripon* 56-59; Asst Chapl Cranleigh Sch Surrey 59-63; Hd Master Cathl Choir Sch *Cant* 64-67; Min Can Cant Cathl *Cant* 65-67; V Wye w Brook from 67; Chapl Wye Coll Kent *Lon* from 68; Hon Can Cant Cathl *Cant* from 79; RD W Bridge 80-87 and from 89. *The Vicarage, Wye, Ashford, Kent TN25 5AS* Wye (0233) 812450

MARRIOTT, Frank Lewis. b 29. Lich Th Coll 57. **d** 60 **p** 61. C Earlsdon *Cov* 60-64; R Tysoe w Compton Winyates and Oxhill 64-70; P-in-c Cov St Marg 70-77; R Ufton 77-83; V Long Itchington 77-83; RD Southam 82-89; V Long Itchington and Marton from 83. *The Vicarage, Leamington Road, Long Itchington, Rugby, Warks CV23 8PL* Southam (0926) 812518

MARRIOTT, Canon Richard Ward. b 38. St Pet Hall Ox BA62 MA66. Linc Th Coll 62. **d** 64 **p** 65. C Wanstead St Mary *Chelmsf* 64-70; C Grantham St Wulfram *Linc* 70-72; V Barkingside St Geo *Chelmsf* 72-82; R Chingford

SS Pet and Paul from 82; Hon Can Chelmsf Cathl from 86. *2 The Green Walk, London E4 7ER*   081-529 1291

MARRIOTT, Stanley Richard. b 36. AKC60. **d** 61 **p** 62. C Coleshill *Birm* 61-64; C Maxstoke 61-64; V Ansley *Cov* 64-78; Org Sec (E Midl) CECS 79-83; P-in-c Baxterley *Birm* 83; P-in-c Merevale w Bentley 83; P-in-c Baxterley w Hurley and Wood End and Merevale etc 83-84; R 84-87; R Newton Regis w Seckington and Shuttington from 87. *The Rectory, Newton Regis, Tamworth, Staffs B79 0NA*   Tamworth (0827) 830254

MARRISON, Geoffrey Edward. b 23. Lon Univ BA48 PhD67. Bps' Coll Cheshunt 49 Kirchliche Hochschule Th Coll Berlin 50. **d** 51 **p** 52. C Wormley *St Alb* 51-52; Malaya 52-55; Singapore 55-56; C Radlett *St Alb* 56-57; C St Botolph Aldgate w H Trin Minories *Lon* 57-58; V Crookes St Tim *Sheff* 58-61; India 62-64; Perm to Offic Cant 64-69; Lic 69-82; Perm Carl from 83; Tutor Carl Dioc Tr Course from 83. *1 Ainsworth Street, Ulverston, Cumbria LA12 7EU*   Ulverston (0229) 56874

MARROW, David Edward Armfield. b 42. Nottm Univ BA65 MA. Tyndale Hall Bris 65. **d** 67 **p** 68. C Clifton Ch Ch w Em *Bris* 67-70; Ethiopia 70-75; N Area Sec BCMS 75-77; C-in-c Ryde St Jas Prop Chpl *Portsm* 77-84; V Worthing St Geo *Chich* from 84. *The Vicarage, 20 Seldon Road, Worthing, W Sussex BN11 2LN*   Worthing (0903) 203309

MARROW, Canon Peter. b 13. Magd Coll Cam BA34 MA38. Bible Churchmen's Coll 37. **d** 37 **p** 38. R Broadwater St Mary *Chich* 53-78; Can and Preb Chich Cathl from 77; rtd 78. *Easter Cottage, Aldwick Street, Bognor Regis, W Sussex PO21 3AW*   Bognor Regis (0243) 821800

MARSDEN, Andrew Philip. b 63. Keble Coll Ox BA85 MA90 Birm Univ MA86. Wycliffe Hall Ox BA(Theol)90. **d** 91. C Newport St Jo *Portsm* from 91. *7 College Road, Newport, Isle of Wight PO30 1HB*   Isle of Wight (0983) 825030

MARSDEN, Andrew Robert. b 49. AKC71. St Aug Coll Cant 68. **d** 72 **p** 73. C New Addington *Cant* 72-75; C Prudhoe *Newc* 75-77; Asst Chapl HM Pris Wakef 77; Chapl HM Borstal Portland 77-82; HM Young Offender Inst Onley 82-89; V Ulceby Gp *Linc* from 89. *The Vicarage, Church Lane, Ulceby, S Humberside DN39 6TB*   Wootton (04698) 239

MARSDEN, Carole. b 44. Nor Ord Course 88. **d** 91. NSM Saddleworth *Man* from 91. *Birch Bank, Shaw Hall, Bank Road, Greenfield, Oldham OL3 7LE*   Saddleworth (0457) 872521

MARSDEN, Geoffrey. b 26. Lon Univ CertEd50 DipTh54 Open Univ BA79. E Anglian Minl Tr Course. **d** 86 **p** 87. NSM Higham *St E* 86-89; NSM Stratford St Mary 86-89; P-in-c Polstead from 89. *Mwaiseni, 5 Upper Street, Stratford St Mary, Colchester CO7 6LR*   Colchester (0206) 322316

MARSDEN, George Henry. b 28. TCD BA57 MA60. Em Coll Saskatoon LTh51. **d** 51 **p** 52. R Berners Roding and Willingale w Shellow *Chelmsf* 61-82; rtd 82; Perm to Offic *Cant* from 82. *43 Castle Street, Canterbury, Kent CT1 2PY*   Canterbury (0227) 457917

MARSDEN, John Joseph. b 53. York Univ BA74 Nottm Univ DipTh78 MTh81 Kent Univ PhD88. St Jo Coll Nottm 77. **d** 80 **p** 81. C Leigh St Mary *Man* 80-83; Hon C Chatham St Steph *Roch* 83-91; Ind Chapl 83-91; Lect CITC from 91. *Church of Ireland Theological College, Braemor Park, Rathgar, Dublin 14, Irish Republic*   Dublin (1) 975506

MARSDEN, John Robert. b 22. Linc Coll Ox BA48 MA49. Ripon Hall Ox 57. **d** 58 **p** 59. Chapl Dur Sch 61-85; rtd 85. *Prebends, High Kilburn, York YO6 4AJ*   Coxwold (03476) 597

MARSDEN, Miss Joyce. b 47. Trin Coll Bris DipHE80. **dss** 83 **d** 87. Wavertree H Trin *Liv* 83-85; Much Woolton 85-87; Par Dn from 87. *25 Linkside Road, Woolton, Liverpool L25 9NX*   051-428 6935

MARSDEN, Michael John. b 59. St Mich Coll Llan 78. **d** 82 **p** 83. C Neath w Llantwit *Llan* 82-85; Asst Chapl Univ Hosp of Wales Cardiff 85-89; V Graig *Llan* from 89; P-in-c Cilfynydd from 89. *St John's Vicarage, Llantrisant Road, Pontypridd, M Glam CF37 1LW*   Pontypridd (0443) 402436

MARSDEN, Canon Robert William. b 24. TCD BA49 MA52. CITC 50. **d** 50 **p** 51. C Dub St Jas *D & G* 50-54; Asst Chapl Miss to Seamen 54-58; I Currin w Drum *Clogh* 58-66; I Clones w Killeevan from 66; Prec Clogh Cathl from 86. *Killeevan Rectory, Newbliss, Co Monaghan, Irish Republic*   Newbliss (42) 54052

MARSDEN, Samuel Edward. b 44. Keble Coll Ox BA66 MA85. Linc Th Coll 66. **d** 68 **p** 69. C Liskeard w

St Keyne *Truro* 68-72; R Gerrans w St Antony in Roseland 72-77; Hong Kong 77-81; P-in-c Ingrave *Chelmsf* 81-82; P-in-c Gt Warley w Childerditch 81-82; R Gt Warley w Childerditch and Ingrave 82-89; Australia from 89. *St Ambrose Rectory, PO Box 3, Gilgandra, NSW, Australia 2827*   Gilgandra (68) 472064

MARSDEN-JONES, Watkin David. b 22. Univ of Wales (Lamp) BA48. **d** 49 **p** 50. V Copthorne *Chich* 56-70; RD E Grinstead 66-70; V Bosham 70-86; rtd 86; Perm to Offic *Chich* from 86. *10 Fairfield Road, Bosham, Chichester PO18 8JH*   Bosham (0243) 575053

MARSH, Anthony David. b 29. Roch Th Coll 64. **d** 66 **p** 67. R Wrentham w Benacre and Covehithe *St E* 69-75; R Wrentham w Benacre, Covehithe, Frostenden etc 75-80; P-in-c Beyton and Hessett 80-86; C Felixstowe St Jo 86-88; rtd 88. *32 High Road, Trimley, Ipswich*   Felixstowe (0394) 271585

MARSH, Ven Bazil Roland. b 21. Leeds Univ BA42. Lambeth MLitt91 Coll of Resurr Mirfield 42. **d** 44 **p** 45. Can Pet Cathl *Pet* from 64; R Northn St Pet w Upton 64-91; Adn Northn 64-91; rtd 91. *12 Parkway, Northampton NN3 3BS*   Northampton (0604) 406644

MARSH, Ms Carol Ann. b 44. W Midl Coll of Educn BA82. W Midl Minl Tr Course 88. **d** 91. Par Dn Wednesbury St Paul Wood Green *Lich* from 91. *315 Crankhall Lane, Wednesbury, W Midlands WS10 0QQ*   021-500 5776

MARSH, Colin Arthur. b 54. St Jo Coll Nottm. **d** 82 **p** 83. C Kirkby *Liv* 82-86; TV St Luke in the City from 86. *St Michael's Vicarage, Upper Pitt Street, Liverpool L1 5DB*   051-709 7464

MARSH, David. b 32. St Jo Coll Dur BA54 DipTh57. **d** 57 **p** 58. C Bilston St Leon *Lich* 57-62; Kenya 63-66 and 70-72; Chapl Scargill Ho N Yorkshire 67-69; Adn S Maseno 70-72; V Meole Brace *Lich* 72-77; V Westlands St Andr 77-86; V Trentham from 86. *The Vicarage, Trentham Park, Stoke-on-Trent ST4 8AE*   Stoke-on-Trent (0782) 658194

MARSH, Donald. b 35. W Midl Minl Tr Course. **d** 90 **p** 91. NSM Wednesbury St Bart *Lich* from 90. *Holly Rise, 19 Trouse Lane, Wednesbury, W Midlands WS10 7HR*   021-556 0095

MARSH, Ernest Henry. b 07. Lich Th Coll 56. **d** 57 **p** 58. P-in-c Dilhorne *Lich* 70-77; rtd 77; Perm to Offic *Derby* from 77. *Church Cottage, 40 Eccles Close, Hope, Sheffield S30 2RG*   Hope Valley (0433) 20816

MARSH, Dr Francis (John). b 47. ATCL ARCM ARCO York Univ BA69 DPhil76 Selw Coll Cam 73. Oak Hill Th Coll 72. **d** 75 **p** 76. C Cam St Matt *Ely* 75-78; C Pitsmoor w Wicker *Sheff* 79; C Pitsmoor w Ellesmere 79-81; C Crookes St Thos 81-85; V S Ossett *Wakef* from 85. *The Vicarage, 36 Manor Road, Ossett, W Yorkshire WF5 0AU*   Wakefield (0924) 264818 or 263311

MARSH, Geoffrey John. b 38. K Coll Lon BD60 AKC60 Birm Univ PGCE66. **d** 61 **p** 62. C Upper Teddington SS Pet and Paul *Lon* 61-63; C Brierley Hill *Lich* 63-66; Asst Master Borough Green Sch 67-69; P-in-c Bracknell *Ox* 69-73; P-in-c Speen 73-74; P-in-c Stockcross 73-74; R Boxford w Stockcross and Speen 74-80; PV Truro Cathl *Truro* 80-82; Chapl Truro Cathl Sch 80-82; Chapl SS Mary and Anne's Sch Abbots Bromley 82-85; Chapl Heref Cathl Sch from 85. *Cathedral School, 29 Castle Street, Hereford HR1 2NN*   Hereford (0432) 273757 or 266679

MARSH, Gordon Bloxham. b 25. Cant Sch of Min 82. **d** 85 **p** 86. NSM Loose Cant 85-86; NSM New Romney w Old Romney and Midley 86-90; NSM Asst to RD S Lympne from 90. *Westleton, St John's Road, New Romney, Kent TN28 8EN*   New Romney (0679) 66506

MARSH, Harry Carter. b 14. Chich Th Coll 48. **d** 49 **p** 50. V Sholing *Win* 60-71; R Michelmersh w Eldon w Timsbury 71-74; R Michelmersh w Mottisfont, Timsbury and Eldon 74-79; Perm to Offic from 79; rtd 80; Perm to Offic *Portsm* from 82. *Rose Croft, Manor Road, Hayling Island, Hants PO11 0QR*   Hayling Island (0705) 463526

MARSH, Jack Edmund Bruce. b 08. MA. **d** 73 **p** 74. NSM Yatton Keynell *Bris* from 73; NSM Biddestone w Slaughterford from 73; NSM Castle Combe from 73; NSM W Kington from 73. *St Peter's House, The Green, Biddestone, Chippenham, Wilts SN14 7DG*   Corsham (0249) 712835

MARSH, Lawrence Allan. b 36. Sarum Th Coll 66. **d** 67 **p** 68. C Waterlooville *Portsm* 67-70; V Shedfield 70-76; R Fen Ditton *Ely* from 76; P-in-c Horningsea from 83. *The Rectory, 16 High Street, Fen Ditton, Cambridge CB5 8ST*   Teversham (02205) 3257

MARSH, Leonard Stuart Alexander. b 55. Hull Univ BA77. Linc Th Coll 77. **d** 79 **p** 80. C Eltham St Barn

S'wark 79-81; C Camberwell St Giles 81-83; Hon C Clifton St Paul *Bris* 83-86; Chapl Bris Univ 83-86; USPG from 86. *c/o USPG, Partnership House, 157 Waterloo Road, London SE1 8XA* 071-928 8681

MARSH, Mrs Margaret Ann. b 37. Nottm Univ BSc59 Ox Univ DipEd60. Carl Dioc Tr Course 86 Lambeth STh87. d 87. Asst Chapl Garlands Hosp from 87; Dn Carl Cathl *Carl* from 87. *34 Moorville Drive South, Carlisle CA3 0AW* Carlisle (0228) 45717

MARSH, Peter Derek. b 29. Em Coll Saskatoon. d 59 p 60. Lic to Offic *Lon* 64-71; P-in-c Kilburn St Mary 71-81; rtd 81; Perm to Offic *St Alb* from 87. *231 Handside Lane, Welwyn Garden City, Herts AL8 7TP* Welwyn Garden (0707) 325105

MARSH, Ralph. b 42. Chester Coll CertEd63 ACP65 Birm Univ BPhil77. St Deiniol's Hawarden 86. d 88 p 89. NSM Tranmere St Paul w St Luke *Ches* 88-90; C Guiseley w Esholt *Bradf* trom 90. *St Oswald's House, 5 Ashtofts Mount, Guiseley, Leeds LS20 9BZ* Guiseley (0943) 79658

MARSH, Richard St John Jeremy. b 60. Keble Coll Ox BA82 MA86. Coll of Resurr Mirfield 83. d 85 p 86. C Grange St Andr *Ches* 85-87; Fell and Chapl Univ Coll Dur from 87. *3 Cosins Hall, Palace Green, Durham DH1 3RL* 091-374 3878

MARSH, Robert Christopher. b 53. Ex Univ BEd76. St Steph Ho Ox 86. d 88 p 89. C St Leonards Ch Ch and St Mary *Chich* 88-91; TV Crawley from 91. *Peterhouse, Ifield Road, Crawley, W Sussex RH11 7BW*

MARSH, Roger Philip. b 44. K Coll Lon BD72 AKC72. St Aug Coll Cant 73. d 73 p 74. C Leagrave *St Alb* 73-76; Asst Youth Officer 76-77; Resources Officer 77-80; Chapl Marlborough Coll Wilts 80-86; Master Ardingly Coll Jun Sch Haywards Heath from 86. *Junior School, Ardingly College, Haywards Heath, W Sussex RH17 6SQ* Ardingly (0444) 892279

MARSH, Mrs Shelley Ann. b 54. SRN75 SCM76. St Jo Coll Nottm 84. d 89. Hon C Glas Gd Shep w Ascension *Glas* from 89. *44 Atholl Crescent, Paisley, Renfrewshire PA1 3AW* 041-883 8668

MARSH, Simon Robert. b 59. Sarum & Wells Th Coll 79. d 82 p 83. C Mottram in Longdendale w Woodhead *Ches* 82-85; Bp's Dom Chapl *Bradf* 85-87; V Ashton Hayes *Ches* 87-90; V Macclesfield St Paul from 90. *St Paul's Vicarage, Swallow Close, Lark Hall Road, Macclesfield, Cheshire SK10 1QN* Macclesfield (0625) 422910

MARSHALL, Alan John. b 48. Carl Dioc Tr Course. d 89 p 90. NSM Carl St Luke Morton *Carl* from 89. *13 Caird Avenue, St Ann's Hill, Carlisle CA3 9RR* Carlisle (0228) 20996

MARSHALL, Alexander Robert. b 43. Glouc Sch of Min 84. d 87 p 88. NSM Newtown w Llanllwchaiarn w Aberhafesp *St As* from 87. *219 Dinas, Treowen, Newtown, Powys SY16 1NW* Newtown (0686) 624791

MARSHALL, Mrs Angela. b 48. Trin Coll Bris 74. d 88. Hon Par Dn Newc St Geo *Lich* from 88. *St George's Vicarage, 28 Hempstalls Lane, Newcastle, Staffs ST5 0SS* Newcastle-under-Lyme (0782) 614641

MARSHALL, Arthur. b 25. Oak Hill Th Coll 66. d 68 p 69. C Worksop St Jo *S'well* 68-72; R Trowell 72-78; R Abbas and Templecombe w Horsington *B & W* 78-80; V Pemberton St Mark Newtown *Liv* 80-82; V Creeksea w Althorne, Latchingdon and N Fambridge *Chelmsf* 82-86; R Epperstone *S'well* 86-89; R Gonalston 86-89; P-in-c Oxton 86-89; rtd 89. *Flat 2, Coombe Court, Tadworth, Surrey KT20 5AL* Tadworth (0737) 813347

MARSHALL, Basil Eustace Edwin. b 21. OBE69. Westcott Ho Cam 71. d 73 p 74. C Edenbridge *Roch* 73-78; P-in-c Matfield 77-85; P-in-c Lamberhurst 78-85; C Farnborough 85-86; rtd 86; Hon C Speldhurst w Groombridge and Ashurst *Roch* from 86. *7 Boyne Park, Tunbridge Wells, Kent TN4 8EL* Tunbridge Wells (0892) 21664

MARSHALL, Bernard Godfrey Graham. b 35. Birm Univ BA56 DipTh59. Qu Coll Birm 58. d 60 p 61. C Hampton *Worc* 60-64; C-in-c Fairfield St Rich CD 64-65; Chapl RN from 65. *c/o MOD, Lacon House, Theobald's Road, London WC1X 8RY* 071-430 6847

MARSHALL, Bryan John. b 40. Chich Th Coll 63. d 65 p 66. C Poulton-le-Fylde *Blackb* 65-68; C S Shore H Trin 68-70; V Wesham 70-74; PV Chich Cathl *Chich* 74-82; V Boxgrove 82-91; P-in-c Tangmere 82-84; R 84-91; R Westbourne from 91. *The Rectory, Westbourne Road, Westbourne, Emsworth, Hants PO10 8UL* Emsworth (0243) 372867

MARSHALL, Christopher John. b 56. Edge Hill Coll of HE BEd79. St Alb Minl Tr Scheme 83. d 86 p 87. C Biggleswade *St Alb* 86-89; Chapl Asst S Beds Area HA

89-91; Chapl St Helier's Hosp Carshalton from 91. *1 Rosewood Grove, Sutton, Surrey SM1 3DT*

MARSHALL, Preb Christopher John Bickford. b 32. TD78. AKC56. d 57 p 58. C Leatherhead *Guildf* 57-60; C Crewkerne *B & W* 60-63; V Long Sutton 63-72; V Long Sutton w Long Load 72-76; V Wiveliscombe from 76; RD Tone 78-87; Preb Wells Cathl from 88. *The Vicarage, South Street, Wiveliscombe, Taunton, Somerset TA4 2LZ* Wiveliscombe (0984) 23309

MARSHALL, Christopher Robert. b 49. St Chad's Coll Dur BA71. Sarum & Wells Th Coll 72. d 74 p 75. C Sheff Parson Cross St Cecilia *Sheff* 74-77; C Walsall St Gabr Fullbrook *Lich* 77-78; C Upper Gornal 78-80; V Walsall St Andr 80-86; V Willenhall St Giles from 86. *St Giles's Vicarage, Walsall Street, Willenhall, W Midlands WV13 2ER* Willenhall (0902) 605722

MARSHALL, David Charles. b 52. St Chad's Coll Dur BA73. Trin Coll Bris 74. d 76 p 77. C Meole Brace *Lich* 76-78; C W Teignmouth *Ex* 78-80; C Broadwater St Mary *Chich* 80-84; V Newc St Geo *Lich* from 84. *St George's Vicarage, 28 Hempstalls Lane, Newcastle, Staffs ST5 0SS* Newcastle-under-Lyme (0782) 614641

MARSHALL, David Edward Francis. b 04. Lon Coll of Div 25. d 29 p 30. R Farmborough *B & W* 49-72; rtd 72. *Bronel, Woodview, Chilcompton, Bath BA3 4HJ* Stratton-on-the-Fosse (0761) 232685

MARSHALL, David Evelyn. b 63. New Coll Ox BA85 Birm Univ MA88. Ridley Hall Cam 88. d 90. C Roundhay St Edm *Ripon* from 90. *1 Gledhow Grange View, Leeds LS8 1PH* Leeds (0532) 668212

MARSHALL, Eric. b 20. E Midl Min Tr Course. d 82 p 83. Chapl Grimsby Distr Hosps from 82; Hon C Gt Grimsby St Mary and St Jas *Linc* from 85. *Morn Tide, Waithe Lane, Grimsby, S Humberside DN37 0RJ* Grimsby (0472) 823681

MARSHALL, Geoffrey Osborne. b 48. St Jo Coll Dur BA71. Coll of Resurr Mirfield 71. d 73 p 74. C Waltham Cross *St Alb* 73-76; C Digswell 76-78; P-in-c Belper Ch Ch and Milford *Derby* 78-86; V Spondon from 86; RD Derby N from 90. *St Werburgh's Vicarage, Gascoigne Drive, Spondon, Derby DE2 7GL* Derby (0332) 673573

MARSHALL, Mrs Gillian Kathryn. b 54. Glouc Sch of Min 84. d 87. NSM Newtown w Llanllwchaiarn w Aberhafesp *St As* from 87. *219 Dinas, Treowen, Newtown, Powys SY16 1NW* Newtown (0686) 624791

MARSHALL, Graham George. b 38. Dur Univ BA60 St Chad's Coll Dur DipTh65. d 65 p 66. C Ashton-on-Ribble St Mich *Blackb* 65-67; C Lanc St Mary 67-71; R Church Eaton *Lich* 71-75; Prec Man Cathl *Man* 75-78; R Reddish 78-85; V Chadderton St Luke from 87. *St Luke's Vicarage, Queen's Road, Chadderton, Oldham OL9 9HU* 061-624 3562

MARSHALL, Canon Hugh Phillips. b 34. SS Coll Cam BA57 MA61. Linc Th Coll 57. d 59 p 60. C Westmr St Steph w St Jo *Lon* 59-65; V Tupsley *Heref* 65-74; V Wimbledon *S'wark* 74-78; TR 78-87; RD Merton 79-86; V Mitcham SS Pet and Paul 87-90; Hon Can *S'wark* Cathl 89-90; Chief Sec ACCM 90-91; ABM from 91. *30 Woodville Road, Morden, Surrey SM4 5AF* 081-542 3962

MARSHALL, Mrs Jean. b 36. SW Minl Tr Course 84. d 87. NSM Stratton *Truro* 87-89; NSM Bodmin w Lanhydrock and Lanivet from 89. *41 Athelstan Park, Bodmin, Cornwall PL3 1DS* Bodmin (0208) 77567

MARSHALL, John. b 37. Kelham Th Coll 53. d 62 p 63. C Winshill *Derby* 62-64; C Chaddesden St Phil 64-65; Chapl HM Borstal Morton Hall 65-75; V Swinderby *Linc* 66-77; R Church Aston *Lich* 77-84; V Auckland St Andr and St Anne *Dur* from 84; P-in-c Hunwick 88-90; Chapl Bishop Auckland Gen Hosp from 84. *St Andrew's Vicarage, Park Street, Bishop Auckland, Co Durham DL14 7JS* Bishop Auckland (0388) 604397

MARSHALL, John. b 50. St Luke's Coll Ex CertEd74 W Lon Inst of HE DipEdHChild79. S'wark Ord Course 88. d 91. Hon C Brixton Hill St Sav *S'wark* from 91. *57A Kingscourt Road, London SW16 1JA* 081-769 3665

MARSHALL, John Dixon. b 17. d 43 p 44. R Fortrose *Mor* 65-74; R Baillieston *Glas* 74-82; rtd 82. *17 Mackenzie Terrace, Rosemarkie, Fortrose, Ross-shire IV10 8UH* Fortrose (0381) 20924

MARSHALL, John Linton. b 42. Worc Coll Ox BA64 MA68 Bris Univ MLitt75. Wells Th Coll 66. d 68 p 69. C Bris St Mary Redcliffe w Temple etc *Bris* 68-71; Tutor Sarum & Wells Th Coll 71-73; Perm to Offic *Pet* 74-77; Lic to Offic *S'well* 77-81; VC S'well Minster 79-81; R Ordsall 81-88; P-in-c Grove 84-88; RD Retford 84-88; V Northowram *Wakef* from 88. *The Vicarage, Back Clough, Northowram, Halifax, W Yorkshire HX3 7HH* Halifax (0422) 202551

MARSHALL, John William. b 24. St And NSM Tr Scheme. **d** 73 **p** 74. NSM Inverkeithing *St And* 73-90; NSM Lochgelly 73-90; NSM Rosyth 73-90; rtd 90. *c/o Bishop's House, Fairmount Road, Perth PH2 7AP*

MARSHALL, Lionel Alan. b 41. TEng. St Deiniol's Hawarden 84 Qu Coll Birm 86. **d** 87 **p** 88. C Llandudno *Ban* 87-90; V Rhayader and Nantmel *S & B* from 90. *The Vicarage, Dark Lane, Rhayader, Powys LD6 5DA* Rhayader (0597) 810223

MARSHALL, Canon Maurice Peter. b 23. Oak Hill Th Coll 59. **d** 61 **p** 62. V New Ferry *Ches* 64-79; V Hartford 79-89; Hon Can Ches Cathl 87-89; rtd 89. *27 East Lane, Sandiway, Northwich, Cheshire CW8 2QQ* Northwich (0606) 888591

MARSHALL, Michael David. b 51. BSc. Trin Coll Bris. **d** 84 **p** 85. C Kennington St Mark *S'wark* 84-88; V Streatham Park St Alb from 88. *St Alban's Vicarage, 5 Fayland Avenue, London SW16 1SR* 081-769 5415

✠**MARSHALL, Rt Rev Michael Eric.** b 36. Ch Coll Cam BA58 MA62. Cuddesdon Coll 58. **d** 60 **p** 61 **c** 75. C Birm St Pet *Birm* 60-62; Min Can Ely Cathl *Ely* 62-64; Tutor Ely Th Coll 62-64; Chapl Lon Univ *Lon* 64-69; V St Marylebone All SS 69-75; Suff Bp Woolwich *S'wark* 75-84; Asst Bp Lon from 84; Preb Chich Cathl *Chich* from 90. *18 Andrewes House, The Barbican, London EC2*

MARSHALL, Canon Peter Arthur. b 31. AKC58. **d** 59 **p** 60. C Hutton *Chelmsf* 59-61; C Rickmansworth *St Alb* 61-66; Chapl Orchard View and Kingsmead Court Hosps from 66; R Lexden *Chelmsf* from 66; RD Colchester from 88; Hon Can Chelmsf Cathl from 90. *Lexden Rectory, 1 Glen Avenue, Colchester Essex CO3 3RP* Colchester (0206) 578160

MARSHALL, Peter James. b 48. Qu Coll Birm 78. **d** 80 **p** 81. C Ormskirk *Liv* 80-83; V Dallam from 83. *St Mark's House, 141A Longshaw Street, Warrington WA5 5JE* Warrington (0925) 31193

MARSHALL, Canon Peter Jerome. b 40. McGill Univ Montreal. Westcott Ho Cam 61. **d** 63 **p** 64. C E Ham St Mary *Chelmsf* 63-66; C Woodford St Mary 66-71; C-in-c S Woodford 66-71; V Walthamstow St Pet 71-81; Dep Dir of Tr 81-84; Can Res Chelmsf Cathl 81-85; Dioc Dir of Tr *Ripon* from 85; Can Res Ripon Cathl from 85. *12 Clotherholme Road, Ripon, N Yorkshire HG4 2DA* Ripon (0765) 4835

MARSHALL, Peter John. b 33. K Coll Lon 56. Codrington Coll Barbados 57. **d** 61 **p** 62. CF 67-88; rtd 88. *c/o MOD (Army), Bagshot Park, Bagshot, Surrey GU19 5PL* Bagshot (0276) 71717

MARSHALL, Peter John Charles. b 35. Bris Univ BA60. Ridley Hall Cam 60. **d** 62 **p** 63. C Lindfield *Chich* 62-65; Travelling Sec Scripture Union 65-83; Hon C Nottm St Nic *S'well* 65-67; Hon C Cheadle Hulme St Andr *Ches* 67-83; V Ilkley All SS *Bradf* from 83. *The Vicarage, 58 Curly Hill, Ilkley, W Yorkshire LS29 0BA* Ilkley (0943) 607537

MARSHALL, Robert Paul. b 60. Sheff Univ BA81 Dur Univ MA85. Cranmer Hall Dur 81. **d** 83 **p** 84. C Kirkstall *Ripon* 83-85; C Otley *Bradf* 85-87; Dioc Communications Officer from 87; P-in-c Embsay w Eastby from 87. *The Vicarage, 21 Shires Lane, Skipton, N Yorkshire BD23 6SB* Skipton (0756) 792755

MARSHALL, Canon Timothy James. b 26. Barrister-at-Law (Middle Temple) 50 BNC Ox BA48 BCL49 MA53. St Steph Ho Ox DipTh51. **d** 52 **p** 53. C Staveley *Derby* 52-60; V Shirebrook from 60; Hon Can Derby Cathl from 86. *The Vicarage, Main Street, Shirebrook, Notts NG20 8DN* Mansfield (0623) 742395

MARSHALL, Timothy John. b 53. GRSM74. Oak Hill Th Coll BA79. **d** 79 **p** 80. C Muswell Hill St Jas w St Matt *Lon* 79-85; V Hammersmith St Simon from 85. *153 Blythe Road, London W14 0HL* 071-602 1043 or 603 4879

MARSHALL, Canon William John. b 35. TCD BA57 BD61 PhD75. TCD Div Sch 59. **d** 59 **p** 60. C Ballyholme *D & D* 59-61; India 62-72; Asst Dean of Residence TCD 73-76; I Rathmichael *D & G* from 76; Can Ch Ch Cathl Dub from 90; Chan from 91. *Rathmichael Rectory, Shankill, Co Dublin, Irish Republic* Dublin (1) 282-2803

MARSHALL, William Michael. b 30. Pemb Coll Ox BA53 MA57 DipEd65 Lon Univ DipTh67 Bris Univ MLitt72 PhD79 DipTh. Sarum & Wells Th Coll 79. **d** 80 **p** 81. Asst Chapl Millfield Sch Somerset from 80; Hon C Glastonbury St Jo w Godney *B & W* 80-84; Hon C Glastonbury w Meare, W Pennard and Godney from 84. *The Long House, Baltonsborough, Glastonbury, Somerset BA6 8QP* Baltonsborough (0458) 50288

MARSHALL-TAYLOR, Aubrey. b 11. Dur Univ LTh35. Tyndale Hall Bris 32. **d** 41 **p** 42. R Graveley w Chivesfield *St Alb* 55-78; rtd 78; Perm to Offic St Alb from 79; Ox

from 87. *10 Halifax House, Little Chalfont, Amersham, Bucks HP7 9NG* Little Chalfont (0494) 763749

MARSTON, David Howarth. b 48. St Jo Coll Dur BA69. Edin Th Coll 69. **d** 71 **p** 72. C Kendal H Trin *Carl* 71-75; Perm to Offic *Glas* 75-78; Hon C Barrow St Matt *Carl* from 79. *217 Rating Lane, Barrow-in-Furness, Cumbria LA13 9LQ* Barrow-in-Furness (0229) 29023

MARSTON, William Thornton. b 59. Worc Coll Ox BA81 MA85 Cam Univ CertEd83. St Steph Ho Ox BA87. **d** 88 **p** 89. C Beckenham St Geo *Roch* from 88. *37 Rectory Road, Beckenham, Kent BR3 1HL* 081-658 7005

MART, Terence Eugene. b 47. CertEd76 BA82. St Jo Coll Nottm LTh87. **d** 87 **p** 88. C Prestatyn *St As* 87-91; Chapl Theatr Clwyd Mold 87-91; R Llangystenyn from 91. *The Rectory, Glyn y Marl Road, Llandudno Junction, Gwynedd LL31 9NS* Deganwy (0492) 83579

MARTIN, Canon Albert Harold Morris. b 10. Em Coll Cam BA32 MA35 Lon Univ DipEd39. Ridley Hall Cam 31. **d** 33 **p** 34. V Betchworth *S'wark* 71-75; rtd 75. *Salara Cottage, Gill's Bridge, Outwell, Wisbech, Cambs PE14 8TQ* Wisbech (0945) 772642

MARTIN, Alexander Lewendon. b 26. Em Coll Cam BA47 MA51. Ridley Hall Cam 56. **d** 57 **p** 58. Chapl Felsted Sch Essex 64-74; Chapl Sedbergh Sch Cumbria 74-84; R Askerswell, Loders and Powerstock *Sarum* 84-89; RD Lyme Bay 86-89; rtd 89; Perm to Offic *Ex* from 89. *Thirtover, 7 Alexandra Way, Crediton, Devon EX17 2EA* Crediton (03632) 6206

MARTIN, Canon Anthony Bluett. b 29. St Jo Coll Cam BA52 MA56. Ridley Hall Cam 52. **d** 54 **p** 55. C Rushden *Pet* 54-57; C Worthing St Geo *Chich* 57-59; CSSM 59-63; Lic to Offic *Man* 59-63; V Hoole *Ches* 63-84; Hon Can Ches Cathl from 83; V Bowdon from 84. *The Vicarage, Church Brow, Bowdon, Altrincham, Cheshire WA14 2SG* 061-928 2468

MARTIN, Anthony George. b 20. Nottm Univ LTh74. ALCD42. **d** 43 **p** 45. R Ilchester w Northover *B & W* 69-72; R Limington 69-72; R Axbridge 72-74; R Axbridge w Shipham and Rowberrow 74-80; rtd 81; Perm to Offic *B & W* from 81. *35 Dodd Avenue, Wells, Somerset BA5 3JU* Wells (0749) 675739

MARTIN, Brother. See JARRETT-KERR, William Robert

MARTIN, Brother. See COOMBE, John Morrell

MARTIN, Christopher John. b 45. Ball Coll Ox BA67 MA86. Wycliffe Hall Ox 86. **d** 88 **p** 89. C Edin St Thos *Edin* 88-90; R Duns from 90. *The Bungalow, Duns Mill, Duns, Berwickshire TD11 3HT* Duns (0361) 82209

MARTIN, Christopher John Neville. b 32. Trin Coll Ox BA54 MA57. St Deiniol's Hawarden 82 S'wark Ord Course. **d** 83 **p** 84. NSM Man St Ann *Man* 83-84; NSM N Sheen St Phil and All SS *S'wark* 84-87; NSM Petersham 87-89; C Fryerning w Margaretting *Chelmsf* from 89. *The Vicarage, Pennys Lane, Margaretting, Ingatestone, Essex CM4 0HA* Brentwood (0277) 355329

MARTIN, Prof David Alfred. b 29. LSE BSc PhD. Westcott Ho Cam. **d** 83 **p** 84. Hon C Guildf Cathl *Guildf* from 83. *174 St John's Road, Woking, Surrey* Woking (0483) 762134

MARTIN, David Geoffrey. b 34. K Coll Lon BD60 AKC61. **d** 61 **p** 62. C Liv Our Lady and St Nic *Liv* 61-63; Australia 63-66; Chapl and Lect K Coll Lon 66-70; V Kennington St Jo *S'wark* 70-77; P-in-c Camberwell St Jas 76-77; Hon C Clapham Ch Ch and St Jo 77-81; Lic to Offic 81-85; V S Wimbledon All SS 85-90; V Upper Norwood St Jo from 90. *St John's Vicarage, 2 Sylvan Road, London SE19 2RX* 081-653 0378

MARTIN, David Howard. b 47. Worc Coll Ox BEd79. AKC70 St Aug Coll Cant 70. **d** 71 **p** 72. C Sedgley All SS *Lich* 71-75; Dioc Youth Chapl *Worc* 75-81; P-in-c Worc St Andr and All SS w St Helen 75-81; R Newland, Guarlford and Madresfield from 81. *The Rectory, Madresfield, Malvern, Worcs WR13 5AB* Malvern (0684) 574919

MARTIN, Donald Dales. b 30. Sarum Th Coll 53. **d** 55 **p** 56. V Manfield w Cleasby *Ripon* 60-73; V Melbecks and Muker 73-78; R Romaldkirk w Laithkirk 78-83; V Broughton and Duddon *Carl* 83-89; rtd 89; Lic to Offic *Mor* from 89. *Bishop's House, Isle of Iona PA76 6SJ* Iona (06817) 361

MARTIN, Donald Philip Ralph. b 30. Trin Coll Toronto MA55 STB55. **d** 54 **p** 55. Canada 54-57; Tutor Kelham Th Coll 57-73; SSM from 60; P-in-c Willen *Ox* 73-81; Japan 81-82; Ghana 83-89; Dir Cleveland Lay Tr Course from 89; C Middlesb All SS *York* 89-91; NSM from 91. *All Saints' Vicarage, Grange Road, Middlesbrough, Cleveland TS1 2LR* Middlesbrough (0642) 245035

MARTIN, Douglas Arthur. b 27. TD72. Chich Th Coll 53. **d** 56 **p** 57. CF (TA) 60-75; V Laverstock *Sarum* 68-75; V Acton and Worleston *Ches* 75-90; rtd 90. *50 Marriott Road, Sandbach, Cheshire CW11 9LS* Nantwich (0270) 766503

MARTIN, Edward Eldred William. b 37. Cranfield Inst of Tech MSc84. S'wark Ord Course 65. **d** 68 **p** 69. C Greenwich St Alfege w St Pet *S'wark* 68-71; C Kidbrooke St Jas 71-75; V Peckham St Jo 75-78; P-in-c Peckham St Andr w All SS 76-78; V Peckham St Jo w St Andr 78-81; Hon PV S'wark Cathl from 81; Chapl Guy's Hosp Lon 81-88. *22 Jerringham Road, London SE14 5NX* 071-639 1402

MARTIN, Edwin John. b 43. JP89. TEng MIIExE89. **d** 83 **p** 84. NSM Cwmbran *Mon* 83-85; NSM Griffithstown 85-87; NSM Cwmbran from 87. *168 Rowleaze, Greenmeadow, Cwmbran, Gwent NP44 4LG* Cwmbran (0633) 35575

MARTIN, Frank Walter. b 13. Dur Univ LTh37. Bible Churchmen's Coll 34. **d** 37 **p** 38. Chapl Bexley Hosp Kent 64-78; rtd 79; Perm to Offic Roch from 79; St E from 88. *8 Patticroft, Glemsford, Sudbury, Suffolk CO10 7UJ* Glemsford (0787) 281736

MARTIN, George Cobain. b 34. TCD BA57 MA65. **d** 57 **p** 58. C Ban St Comgall *D & D* 57-64; I Kircubbin 64-74; R Ashby by Partney *Linc* 75-78; R Partney w Dalby 75-78; V Skendleby 75-78; P-in-c Candlesby w Scremby 77-78; R Partney from 78. *The Rectory, Partney, Spilsby, Lincs PE23 4PG* Spilsby (0790) 53570

MARTIN, George Washington Leslie. b 05. ALCD40. **d** 40 **p** 41. R Cupar *St And* 69-72; rtd 72. *20 Heriot Gate, Broughty Ferry, Dundee DP5 2DY* Dundee (0382) 74409

MARTIN, Glenn. b 52. Qu Coll Birm 84. **d** 86 **p** 87. C Chatham St Wm *Roch* 86-89; Chapl Pastures and Kingsway Hosps Derby from 89. *14 Barnwood Close, Mickleover, Derbyshire DE3 5QY* Derby (0332) 510869

MARTIN, Canon Gordon Albion John. b 30. AKC54. **d** 55 **p** 56. C Enfield Chase St Mary *Lon* 55-59; C Palmers Green St Jo 59-61; V Edmonton St Martin 61-64; V Culham *Ox* 64-67; Bp's Youth Chapl *St Alb* 67-73; P-in-c Wareside 69-73; V Harpenden St Jo from 73; RD Wheathampstead 76-87; Hon Can St Alb from 85. *St John's Vicarage, 5 St John's Road, Harpenden, Herts AL5 1DJ* Harpenden (0582) 712776

MARTIN, Graham Rowland. b 39. LCP FRSA Liv Univ CertEd58 Nottm Univ DipRE65 Lon Univ DipTh BD70 Bris Univ BEd73 Bris Poly DipEdMan80. Wells Th Coll 71. **d** 71 **p** 72. Hon C Glouc St Cath *Glouc* 71-76; P-in-c Brookthorpe w Whaddon 76-78; Perm to Offic 78-80; Hon C Hucclecote 80-82; Hon C Tuffley 82-88; NSM Hardwicke, Quedgeley and Elmore w Longney 88-89; V Kemble, Poole Keynes, Somerford Keynes etc from 89. *The Vicarage, Kemble, Cirencester, Glos GL7 6AG* Cirencester (0285) 770240

MARTIN, Dr James Davidson. b 35. MA57 BD60 PhD70. **d** 89 **p** 89. NSM St Andrews St Andr *St And* from 89; Chapl St Andr Univ from 89. *22 Kilrymont Road, St Andrews, Fife KY16 8DE* St Andrews (0334) 77361

MARTIN, James Smiley. b 32. TCD 65. **d** 67 **p** 68. C Glenavy *Conn* 67-70; C Belf St Mary 70-73; I Carnmoney 73-74; I Mallusk from 74. *The Rectory, Carwood Drive, Glengormley, Newtownabbey, Co Antrim* Glengormley (0232) 833773

MARTIN, John. b 32. Roch Th Coll 61. **d** 64 **p** 65. C Barrow St Matt *Carl* 64-66; C Netherton 66; C Bishopwearmouth St Mich *Dur* 66-67; C Wigan All SS *Liv* 67-73; C-in-c Croxteth St Paul CD 73-80; C Stockport St Alb Hall Street *Ches* 80-82; P-in-c Hyde St Thos from 82. *St Thomas's Vicarage, 14 Walker Lane, Hyde, Cheshire SK14 5PL* 061-368 1406

MARTIN, John Albert. TCD DipTh85. **d** 85 **p** 86. C Drumachose *D & R* 85-88; I Cumber Upper w Learmount from 88; Dom Chapl to Bp from 91. *Alla Rectory, 87 Cumber Road, Claudy, Co Londonderry BT47 4JA* Claudy (0504) 338214

MARTIN, John Henry. b 42. St Jo Coll Dur BA73. St Jo Coll Nottm BA73. **d** 73 **p** 74. C Ecclesall *Sheff* 73-77; C Hednesford *Lich* 77-82; V Walsall Pleck and Bescot from 82. *St John's Vicarage, Vicarage Terrace, Pleck, Walsall WS2 9HB* Walsall (0922) 31989

MARTIN, John Hunter. b 42. AKC64. **d** 65 **p** 66. C Mortlake w E Sheen *S'wark* 65-69; C-in-c Bermondsey St Hugh CD 69-72; V Bermondsey St Anne 72-78; P-in-c Lt Ouse *Ely* 78; V Littleport 78-89; V Attercliffe *Sheff* 89-90; P-in-c Darnall H Trin 89-90; TR Darnall-cum-Attercliffe from 90. *The Vicarage, 25/27 Industry Road, Sheffield S9 5FP* Sheffield (0742) 562337

MARTIN, John Keith. b 32. Sarum & Wells Th Coll 76. **d** 79 **p** 80. C Bath Bathwick *B & W* 79-82; V Weston-super-Mare St Andr Bournville 82-85; V Cinderford St Jo *Glouc* from 85. *St John's Vicarage, 1 Abbots View, Cinderford, Glos GL14 3EG* Dean (0594) 825446

MARTIN, Canon John Pringle. b 24. Bris Univ BA50. Clifton Th Coll 50. **d** 52 **p** 53. V Congleton St Pet *Ches* 59-81; RD Congleton 74-85; Hon Can Ches Cathl 80-90; R Brereton w Swettenham 81-90; rtd 90. *49 Parkhouse Road, Minehead, Somerset TA24 8AD* Minehead (0643) 706769

MARTIN, John Stuart. b 11. St Jo Coll Dur BA34. Wycliffe Hall Ox. **d** 35 **p** 36. V Upottery *Ex* 65-72; TV Farway w Northleigh and Southleigh 72-73; rtd 73. *Church Villa, 8 Church Road, Bawdrip, Bridgwater, Somerset TA7 8PU* Puriton (0278) 684092

MARTIN, Canon John Tidswell. b 24. Em Coll Cam BA48 MA52. Kelham Th Coll 48. **d** 53 **p** 54. V Kingston All SS *S'wark* 68-76; V Kingston All SS w St Jo 76-89; Hon Can S'wark Cathl from 87; rtd 89. *175 Lincoln Avenue, Twickenham, Middx TW2 6NL*

MARTIN, John William. b 12. Clifton Th Coll 37. **d** 37 **p** 38. R Itchingfield *Chich* 51-82; rtd 82; Perm to Offic Win from 82. *7 Oxey Close, Lymington Road, Barton on Sea, New Milton, Hants BH25 6PP* New Milton (0425) 613090

MARTIN, Jonathan. b 55. Leic Univ BA81. Sarum & Wells Th Coll. **d** 86 **p** 87. C Southn Thornhill St Chris *Win* 86-89; Perm to Offic from 89. *140 Melbury Avenue, Branksome, Poole, Dorset BH12 4EW* Poole (0202) 732584

MARTIN, Jonathan Sean. b 64. Ex Univ BA86 Leeds Univ BA89. Coll of Resurr Mirfield 87. **d** 90 **p** 91. C Romsey *Win* from 90. *15 Mount Temple, Romsey, Hants SO51 8UW* Romsey (0794) 523840

MARTIN, Joseph Edward. b 35. NDD55. Bps' Coll Cheshunt 58. **d** 60 **p** 61. C Short Heath *Birm* 60-62; C Caterham Valley *S'wark* 63-66; R W Hallam and Mapperley *Derby* 66-70; P-in-c Mapperley 66-67; V Wykeham and Hutton Buscel *York* 71-78; Chapl HM Pris Askham Grange 78-82; V Askham Bryan w Askham Richard *York* 78-82; R Amotherby w Appleton and Barton-le-Street 82-84; C Banbury *Ox* 85-88; C Warsop *S'well* 88-90; V Tuxford w Weston and Markham Clinton from 90. *The Vicarage, Lincoln Road, Tuxford, Newark, Notts NG22 0HP* Tuxford (0777) 870497

MARTIN, Mrs Karen. b 46. Bp Grosseteste Coll CertEd68 Lon Univ BD82. Oak Hill Th Coll 86. **d** 89. Hon Par Dn Norbury *Ches* 89-90; Par Dn from 90. *27 Davenport Road, Stockport, Cheshire SK7 4HA* 061-483 6922

MARTIN, Kenneth. b 20. Univ of Wales (Lamp) BA47. **d** 48 **p** 49. C Rumney *Mon* 48-49; C Griffithstown 49-51; CF (TA) from 52. *21 Earls Court Road, Penylan, Cardiff CF3 7DE* Cardiff (0222) 493796

MARTIN, Kenneth Cyril. b 31. AIGCM53. S'wark Ord Course 71. **d** 73 **p** 74. C Hollington St Leon *Chich* 73-76; C Horsham 76-79; P-in-c Broadwaters *Worc* 79-81; V 81; P-in-c Worc H Trin 81-86; R Stoulton w Drake's Broughton and Pirton etc 86-91; rtd 91. *The Rectory, Worcester Road, Drakes Broughton, Pershore, Worcs WR10 2AQ* Worcester (0905) 840528

MARTIN, Canon Kenneth Roger. b 16. AKC40. **d** 40 **p** 41. R Wokingham All SS *Ox* 69-81; RD Sonning 78-81; rtd 81; Perm to Offic Ex and Ox from 81. *1 Indio Road, Bovey Tracey, Devon TQ13 9BT* Bovey Tracey (0626) 832605

MARTIN, Nicholas Roger. b 53. St Jo Coll Dur BA74. Ripon Coll Cuddesdon 75. **d** 77 **p** 78. C Wolvercote w Summertown *Ox* 77-80; C Kidlington 80-82; TV 82-84; V Happisburgh w Walcot *Nor* 84-85; P-in-c Hempstead w Lessingham and Eccles 84-85; R Happisburgh w Walcot, Hempstead, Lessingham etc 85-89; R Blakeney w Cley, Wiveton, Glandford etc from 89. *The Rectory, Wiveton Road, Blakeney, Holt, Norfolk NR25 7NJ* Cley (0263) 740686

MARTIN, Nicholas Worsley. b 52. Sarum & Wells Th Coll 71. **d** 75 **p** 76. C Llan w Capel Llanilterne *Llan* 75-79; C Cardiff St Jo 79; C Caerphilly 79-83; TV Hemel Hempstead *St Alb* from 83. *St Peter's Vicarage, 7 Tollpit End, Hemel Hempstead, Herts HP1 3NT* Hemel Hempstead (0442) 254061

MARTIN, Norman George. b 22. Sarum & Wells Th Coll 74. **d** 77 **p** 78. NSM Long Ashton *B & W* 77-81; NSM Walton in Gordano 81-82; NSM E Clevedon and Walton w Weston w Clapton 82-87; Chapl Barrow and Farleigh Hosps from 87. *7 Clynder Grove, Castle Road, Clevedon, Avon BS21 7DF* Clevedon (0272) 873124

MARTIN, Paul Barri. b 58. Univ of Wales (Lamp) BA79. St Steph Ho Ox 79. **d** 81 **p** 82. C Mon 81-83; C Bassaleg

83-85; Asst Sec ACS 85-89; V Newport St Teilo *Mon* from 89. *St Teilo's Vicarage, 1 Aberthaw Road, Newport, Gwent NP9 9NS*   Newport (0633) 273593

MARTIN, Paul Dexter. b 50. Wabash Coll (USA) BA72 Univ of the South (USA) MDiv75. **d** 75 **p** 76. Educn Tutor Cov Cathl 75-76; C Norbury St Phil *Cant* 76-80; USA from 80. *1107 Broadway, Minden, Louisiana 71058, USA*   Minden (318) 377-1259

MARTIN, Mrs Penelope Elizabeth. b 44. Cranmer Hall Dur 83. **dss** 86 **d** 87. Seaham w Seaham Harbour *Dur* 86-87; Par Dn 87-89; Par Dn Cassop cum Quarrington from 89. *26 Telford Close, High Shincliffe, Durham DH1 2YJ*   091-386 1742

MARTIN, Peter. b 50. MIH75. Linc Th Coll 82. **d** 84 **p** 85. C Taunton H Trin *B & W* 84-86; C Bath Bathwick 86-88; R Cannington, Otterhampton, Combwich and Stockland from 88; Chapl Somerset Coll of Agric & Horticulture from 89. *The Rectory, 27 Brook Street, Cannington, Bridgwater, Somerset TA5 2HP*   Combwich (0278) 652953

MARTIN, Philip James. b 58. Cam Univ BA. Coll of Resurr Mirfield. **d** 84 **p** 85. C Pontefract St Giles *Wakef* 84-88; C Wantage *Ox* 88-90; C Didcot All SS 90; V Alderholt *Sarum* from 90. *The Vicarage, Alderholt, Fordingbridge, Hants SP6 3DN*   Fordingbridge (0425) 653179

MARTIN, Raymond William. b 32. MBIM Lon Univ BSc66 DMA. Glouc Th Course 73. **d** 76 **p** 76. C Glouc St Mary de Lode and St Nic *Glouc* 76-77; Hon C Redmarley D'Abitot, Bromesberrow w Pauntley etc 77-84; R 84-91; P-in-c Falfield w Rockhampton from 91; P-in-c Oldbury-on-Severn from 91; Chapl HM Pris Eastwood Park from 91. *The Vicarage, Sundayshill Lane, Falfield, Wotton-under-Edge, Glos GL12 8DQ*   Falfield (0454) 260033

MARTIN, Richard. b 34. Rhodes Univ Grahamstown BA54 Em Coll Cam BA57 MA58. Wells Th Coll 57. **d** 59 **p** 60. C Portsea St Mary *Portsm* 59-60; S Africa 60-87; C Aldershot St Mich *Guildf* from 87. *Ascension House, Ayling Hill, Aldershot, Hants GU11 3LL*   Aldershot (0252) 330224

MARTIN, Richard Charles de Villeval. b 41. St Jo Coll Ox BA64 MA67. Ox Ord Course. **d** 84 **p** 85. NSM Ox St Thos w St Frideswide and Binsey *Ox* from 84; Asst Chapl Highgate Sch from 86. *11 Benson Place, Oxford OX2 6QH*

MARTIN, Richard Hugh. b 55. Dur Univ BA78. St Jo Coll Nottm BA81 DPS82. **d** 82 **p** 83. C Gateshead *Dur* 82-85; C Redmarshall 85-88; V Scarborough St Jas w H Trin *York* from 88. *St James's Vicarage, 24 Seamer Road, Scarborough, N Yorkshire YO12 4DT*   Scarborough (0723) 361469

MARTIN, Robert David Markland. b 49. FCA80 Trin Coll Cam BA71 MA74. Trin Coll Bris BA91. **d** 91. C Kingswood *Bris* from 91. *1 Downend Road, Kingswood, Bristol BS15 1RT*   Bristol (0272) 676122

MARTIN, Robert Paul Peter. b 58. Chich Th Coll. **d** 83 **p** 84. C Anfield St Columba *Liv* 83-86; C Orford St Marg 86-87; R Blackley H Trin *Man* 87-90; C Oseney Crescent St Luke *Lon* from 90. *63 Osney Street, London NW5 2BE*   071-485 0080

MARTIN, Robin Hugh. b 35. Rhodes Univ Grahamstown BA56 Birm Univ DipTh57. **d** 58 **p** 59. C Darnall H Trin *Sheff* 58-62; C-in-c Kimberworth Park 62-65; Lic to Offic Sarum 65-66; Newc 67-71; Perm Man from 79. *696 Burnley Road East, Rossendale, Lancs*

MARTIN, Roger Ivor. b 42. DMS76 MBIM. Cant Sch of Min. **d** 85 **p** 86. V Man Saltwood *Cant* 85-90; NSM Crundale w Godmersham from 90. *Court Lodge Farm, Godmersham Park, Godmersham, Canterbury, Kent CT4 7DT*   Canterbury (0227) 730925

MARTIN, Roy Ernest. b 29. FCA54. Qu Coll Birm 74. **d** 77 **p** 77. NSM Marston Green *Birm* 77-85; NSM Sheldon 85-89; Perm to Offic from 89. *34 Walcot Green, Dorridge, Solihull, W Midlands B93 8BU*   Knowle (0564) 772943

MARTIN, Rupert Gresley. b 57. Worc Coll Ox BA78. Trin Coll Bris DipHE91. **d** 91. C Yateley *Win* from 91. *37 Walnut Close, Yateley, Camberley, Surrey*   Yateley (0252) 875798

MARTIN, Russell Derek. b 47. St Jo Coll Dur 71. **d** 74 **p** 75. C Hartlepool H Trin *Dur* 74-78; C Swindon St Jo and St Andr *Bris* 78-79; V Penhill 79-91; V Haselbury Plucknett, Misterton and N Perrott *B & W* from 91. *The Rectory, North Perrott, Crewkerne, Somerset*   Crewkerne (0460) 72063

MARTIN, Mrs Sara Galloway. b 19. MCSP40. N Ord Course 71. **dss** 79 **d** 87. Ainsworth *Man* 79-82; Tottington

82-87; Par Dn 87-88; rtd 89; Perm to Offic *Man* from 89. *36 Victoria Street, Tottington, Bury, Lancs BL8 4AG*

MARTIN, Susan. b 56. Nottm Univ BA77. Edin Th Coll 86. **d** 88. C Leigh Park *Portsm* 88-91; C Sandown Ch Ch from 91. *2 Park Mews, Station Avenue, Sandown, Isle of Wight*   Isle of Wight (0983) 408096

MARTIN, Sylvia. **dss** 75 **d** 87. Par Dn Selsdon St Jo w St Fran *S'wark* from 87. *42 Upper Selsdon Road, Selsdon, Croydon, Surrey CR2 8DE*   081-657 3422

MARTIN, Terry Allan. b 64. GRSM85 DipRCM85. Chich Th Coll 85. **d** 88 **p** 89. C Hangleton *Chich* from 88. *59 Buckley Close, Hove, E Sussex BN3 8EU*   Brighton (0273) 776168

MARTIN, Thomas Robin. b 40. Bps' Coll Cheshunt 64. **d** 67 **p** 68. C Ripley *Derby* 67-70; C Ilkeston St Mary 70-74; V Chinley w Buxworth 74-83; V Knighton St Mich *Leic* 83-85; V Thurmaston from 85. *The Vicarage, 828 Melton Road, Thurmaston, Leicester LE4 8BE*   Leicester (0533) 692555

MARTIN, William Harrison. **d** 87 **p** 88. NSM Rushen *S & M* from 87. *7A High Street, Port St Mary, Isle of Man*

MARTIN, William Henry Blyth. b 10. Keble Coll Ox BA33 MA36. Cuddesdon Coll 35. **d** 36 **p** 37. V Long Eaton St Laur *Derby* 62-80; rtd 81; Perm to Offic Cov from 81; Pet from 85. *93 Crick Road, Hillmorton, Rugby, Warks CV21 4DZ*

MARTIN, William Matthew. b 28. Ch Coll Cam BA52 MA56 TCert81. Ridley Hall Cam 52. **d** 54 **p** 55. C Weaste *Man* 54-56; V 56-61; CF (TA) 58-61; CF 61-73; Dep Asst Chapl Gen 73-82; Lic to Offic *Blackb* from 82. *40 Jepps Avenue, Barton, Preston PR3 5AS*   Broughton (0772) 862166

MARTIN-DOYLE, Mrs Audrey Brenda. b 35. Cranmer Hall Dur 80. **dss** 82 **d** 87. The Lye and Stambermill *Worc* 82-86; Chapl Lee Abbey 86-88; Ldr Aston Cottage Community from 88. *121 Albert Road, Aston, Birmingham B6 5ND*   021-326 8280

MARTIN-HARVEY, Martin. b 11. DSC45. Worc Coll Ox BA34 MA38. Ridley Hall Cam 34. **d** 36 **p** 37. C Gt Malvern Ch Ch *Worc* 36-38; Asst Chapl Br Emb Paris and Versailles 38-40; Chapl RNVR 40-46; Lic to Offic *Cant* from 47; Asst Chapl St Lawr Coll Ramsgate 47-72. *St Lawrence College, Ramsgate, Kent*   Thanet (0843) 67907

MARTINDALE, Mrs Patricia Ann. b 24. Qu Coll Birm. **dss** 84 **d** 87. Rugby St Andr *Cov* 84-87; Hon Par Dn from 87. *54 Hillmorton Road, Rugby, Warks CV22 5AD*   Rugby (0788) 3038

MARTINEAU, Canon Christopher Lee. b 16. Trin Hall Cam BA38 MA70. Linc Th Coll 39. **d** 41 **p** 42. R Skipton H Trin *Bradf* 65-83; rtd 83; Perm to Offic *Bradf* from 83. *6 Greenhead Avenue, Utley, Keighley, W Yorkshire BD20 6EY*   Keighley (0535) 609247

MARTINEAU, David Richards Durani. b 36. AKC59. **d** 60 **p** 61. C Ches St Jo *Ches* 60-64; S Africa 64-69; C Jarrow St Paul *Dur* 69-72; TV 72-75; TR Jarrow 76-85; V Gildersome *Wakef* from 85. *St Peter's House, 2A Church Street, Gildersome, Leeds LS27 7AF*   Leeds (0532) 533339

MARTINEAU, Jeremy Fletcher. b 40. K Coll Lon BD65 AKC65. **d** 66 **p** 67. C Jarrow St Paul *Dur* 66-73; Bp's Ind Adv 69-73; P-in-c Raughton Head w Gatesgill *Carl* 73-80; Chapl to Agric 73-80; Ind Chapl *Bris* 80-90; Abps' Rural Officer *Cant* from 90. *14 Stonebridge Lane, Long Itchington, Rugby, Warks CV23 8PT*   Warwick (0926) 812130

✠**MARTINEAU, Rt Rev Robert Arnold Schurhoff.** b 13. Trin Hall Cam BA35 MA39. Westcott Ho Cam 36. **d** 38 **p** 39 **c** 66. C Melksham *Sarum* 38-41; Chapl RAFVR 41-46; V Ovenden *Wakef* 46-52; V Allerton *Liv* 52-66; Hon Can Liv Cathl 61-66; RD Childwall 61-66; Suff Bp Huntingdon *Ely* 66-72; Bp Blackb 72-81; rtd 81. *Gwenallt, Park Street, Denbigh, Clwyd LL16 3DB*   Denbigh (0745) 814089

MARTINSON, Peter Stephen Douglas. b 15. K Coll Lon BA42 AKC48. **d** 49 **p** 50. Area Sec (Dio Guildf) USPG 66-80; rtd 80; Perm to Offic *Portsm* from 86. *25 Yeomans Lane, Liphook, Hants GU30 7PN*   Liphook (0428) 722498

MARTLEW, Andrew Charles. b 50. Nottm Univ BTh76 Lanc Univ MA80. Linc Th Coll 72. **d** 76 **p** 77. C Poulton-le-Fylde *Blackb* 76-79; Hon C Lanc Ch Ch 79-80; Malaysia 81-83; V Golcar *Wakef* 83-89; Dioc Schs Officer from 89; V Warmfield from 89. *The Vicarage, Kirkthorpe, Wakefield, W Yorkshire WF1 5SZ*   Wakefield (0924) 893089

MARVELL, John. b 32. Lon Univ BD63 Leic Univ MEd73 PhD85. Oak Hill Th Coll 79. **d** 80 **p** 81. NSM Colchester

Ch Ch w St Mary V *Chelmsf* 80-85; Perm to Offic 85-87; P-in-c Stisted w Bradwell and Pattiswick from 87. *The Rectory, Water Lane, Stisted, Braintree, Essex CM7 8AP* Braintree (0376) 551839

MASCALL, Canon Prof Eric Lionel. b 05. FBA74 Lon Univ BSc26 Pemb Coll Cam BA27 MA31 BD43 DD58 Ox Univ MA45 BD45 DD48 St Andr Univ Hon DD67. Ely Th Coll 31. **d** 32 **p** 33. OGS from 37; Lic to Offic *Lon* from 62; Prof Hist Th Lon Univ 62-73; Can Th and Hon Can Truro Cathl *Truro* 74-84; rtd 75. *St Mary's House, King's Mead, Seaford, E Sussex BN25 2ET*

MASCALL, Mrs Margaret Ann. b 43. LRAM64 Bris Univ CertEd65 St Jo Coll Dur BA71 MA79. Cranmer Hall Dur 69. **dss** 76 **d** 87. Hertf St Andr *St Alb* 75-79; Herne Bay Ch Ch *Cant* 79-82; Seasalter 82-84; Whitstable 84-87; Par Dn 87-90. *58 Pigeon Lane, Herne Bay, Kent CT6 7ES* Canterbury (0227) 362942

MASDING, John William. b 39. Magd Coll Ox BA61 MA65 DipEd63. Ridley Hall Cam 63. **d** 65 **p** 66. C Boldmere *Birm* 65-71; V Hamstead St Paul from 71. *Hamstead Vicarage, 840 Walsall Road, Birmingham B42 1ES* 021-357 1259

MASH, Neil Beresford. b 30. FRGS FSA LTh54. Em Coll Saskatoon 50. **d** 54 **p** 55. V Swaffham *Nor* 67-77; V Catton 77-89; rtd 89. *Brewers, 9 Pit Lane, Swaffham, Norfolk PE37 7DA* Swaffham (0760) 23046

MASH, William Edward John. b 54. ARCS MCIT81 Imp Coll Lon BSc75. St Jo Coll Nottm 87. **d** 89 **p** 90. C Beverley Minster *York* from 89. *16 The Leases, Beverley, N Humberside HU17 8LG* Hull (0482) 881324

MASHEDER, Peter Timothy Charles. b 49. AKC71. St Aug Coll Cant 71. **d** 72 **p** 73. C Barkingside St Fran *Chelmsf* 72-75; C Chingford SS Pet and Paul 75-91; P-in-c High Laver w Magdalen Laver and Lt Laver etc from 91. *The Lavers Rectory, Magdalen Laver, Ongar, Essex CM5 0ES* Harlow (0279) 33311

MASHEDER, Richard. b 36. AKC59. **d** 60 **p** 61. C Preston St Matt *Blackb* 60-62; C Padiham 62-65; P-in-c Worsthorne 65; V 65-74; CF (TA) 65-67; P-in-c Blackb St Jude *Blackb* 74-78; V Blackb St Thos 76-78; V Blackb St Thos w St Jude 78-82; V Silverdale from 82. *The Vicarage, Silverdale, Carnforth, Lancs LA5 0RH* Silverdale (0524) 701268

MASKELL, John Michael. b 45. Sarum & Wells Th Coll 86. **d** 88 **p** 89. C Swanborough *Sarum* 88-91; Chapl RAF from 91. *c/o MOD, Adastral House, Theobald's Road, London WC1X 8RU* 071-430 7268

MASLEN, Stephen Henry. b 37. CCC Ox BA62 MA65. Ridley Hall Cam 62. **d** 64 **p** 65. C Keynsham w Queen Charlton *B & W* 64-67; C Cheltenham St Mary *Glouc* 67-71; P-in-c St Mary-at-Lambeth *S'wark* 72-74; TV N Lambeth 74-79; V Horley 79-84; TR from 84; RD Reigate from 86. *4 Russells Crescent, Horley, Surrey RH6 7DN* Horley (0293) 783509

MASLEN, Trevor. b 51. Chich Th Coll 77. **d** 80 **p** 81. C Harlow St Mary Magd *Chelmsf* 80-83; C Huntingdon St Barn *Ely* 83-86; P-in-c Huntingdon 86-87; TV from 87. *St Barnabas' Vicarage, Coneygear Road, Huntingdon, Cambs PE18 7RQ* Huntingdon (0480) 453717

MASON, Adrian Keith. b 54. Hatf Poly BSc77. Ripon Coll Cuddesdon 77. **d** 80 **p** 81. C Mill End and Heronsgate w W Hyde *St Alb* 80-83; P-in-c Chardstock *Ex* 83; TV Axminster, Chardstock, Combe Pyne and Rousdon 83-87; TV Halesworth w Linstead, Chediston, Holton etc *St E* 87-88; R Brandon and Santon Downham 88-91; P-in-c Glemsford 91; P-in-c Hartest w Boxted, Somerton and Stanstead 91; P-in-c Glem Valley United Benefice from 91. *The Rectory, Glemsford, Sudbury, Suffolk CO10 7RF* Glemsford (0787) 280361

MASON, Alan Hambleton. b 27. Lon Univ BD59. Wycliffe Hall Ox 56. **d** 59 **p** 60. C Norbiton *S'wark* 59-63; V Thornton St Jas *Bradf* 63-73; V Norbiton *S'wark* 73-84; V Wavertree St Thos *Liv* from 84. *St Thomas's Vicarage, 35 Ashfield, Wavertree, Liverpool L15 1EY* 051-733 7804

MASON, Charles Godfrey. b 24. CEng71 FInstE74 Open Univ BA84. CITC 85 D & D Ord Course 85. **d** 87 **p** 89. NSM Ban St Comgall *D & D* 87-90; NSM Lecale Gp 87-91; NSM Donaghadee 90-91; Lic to Offic from 91. *20 Seymour Avenue, Bangor, Co Down BT19 1BN* Bangor (0247) 465096

MASON, Charles Oliver. b 51. Jes Coll Cam BA73 St Jo Coll Dur BA79. **d** 80 **p** 81. C Cheltenham St Mary, St Matt, St Paul and H Trin *Glouc* 80-84; C Enfield Ch Ch Trent Park *Lon* 84-88; P-in-c W Hampstead St Cuth from 88. *13 Kingscroft Road, London NW2 3QE* 081-452 1913

MASON, Dr Christina. b 42. Univ of Wales BMus63 MA65 BSc(Econ)70 Dundee Univ PhD84. **dss** 82 **d** 86.

NSM Dio Bre from 82. *53 Montifieth Road, Broughty Ferry, Dundee DD5 2RW* Dundee (0382) 79367

MASON, Clive Ray. b 34. St Chad's Coll Dur BA57. Qu Coll Birm 57. **d** 59 **p** 60. C Gateshead St Mary *Dur* 59-62; C Bishopwearmouth Ch Ch 62-64; V Darlington St Jo 64-74; P-in-c Southwick H Trin 75-84; R 84-89; V Bearpark from 89. *The Vicarage, 8 Woodland Close, Bearpark, Durham DH7 7EB* 091-373 3886

MASON, David John. b 42. Sarum & Wells Th Coll 72. **d** 74 **p** 75. C S Hackney St Jo w Ch Ch *Lon* 75-78; C Haggerston All SS 78-80; V Canning Town St Cedd *Chelmsf* 80-83; Chapl Springfield Hosp Southwick 83-87; Chapl Middx Hosp Lon from 87. *Middlesex Hospital, Mortimer Street, London W1N 8AA* 071-636 8333

MASON, Dennis Wardell. b 28. Ox NSM Course 83. **d** 86 **p** 87. NSM Ox St Barn and St Paul *Ox* from 86. *26 John Lopes Road, Eynsham, Oxford OX8 1JR* Oxford (0865) 880440

MASON, Ernest Walter. b 20. S'wark Ord Course 74. **d** 77 **p** 78. NSM Clapham H Spirit *S'wark* 77-87; NSM Clapham Team Min 87-88; rtd 88; Perm to Offic *S'wark* from 88. *35 Klea Avenue, London SW4 9HG* 081-673 5575

MASON, Francis Robert Anthony. b 56. Trin Coll Bris BA90. **d** 90 **p** 91. C Denham *Ox* from 90. *St Mark's House, 80 Green Tiles Lane, Denham, Uxbridge, Middx UB9 5HT* Uxbridge (0895) 833506

MASON, Frederic. b 13. SS Coll Cam MA38 Malaya Univ LLD60. St Aug Coll Cant 60. **d** 61 **p** 62. Prin Ch Ch Coll Cant 61-75; Hon C Hackington *Cant* 61-67; Lic to Offic 67-75; Perm to Offic Ex 75-88; Sarum from 88. *Downsview House, 63 St Mark's Avenue, Salisbury SP1 3DD* Salisbury (0722) 325165

MASON, Frederick Michael Stewart. b 15. Kelham Th Coll 32. **d** 39 **p** 40. V Cov St Fran N Radford *Cov* 59-86; rtd 86; Perm to Offic *Glouc* from 86. *Brinsworth, 2 Mercia Road, Winchcombe, Cheltenham, Glos GL54 5QD* Cheltenham (0242) 602709

MASON, Geoffrey Charles. b 48. K Coll Lon BD74 AKC74. St Aug Coll Cant 74. **d** 75 **p** 76. C Hatcham Park All SS *S'wark* 75-78; V Bellingham St Dunstan 78-87; RD E Lewisham 82-87; C Catford (Southend) and Downham 87-88; Bp's Adv for Min Development from 88. *32 King's Orchard, London SE9 5TJ* 081-859 7614 or 855 9409

MASON, John Evans. b 32. RD. Linc Th Coll 57. **d** 59 **p** 60. C Putney St Mary *S'wark* 59-62; C Berry Pomeroy *Ex* 62-64; Chapl RN 64-68; V Hopton *Nor* 68-72; Chapl RNR 69-82; P-in-c Roydon St Remigius *Nor* 72-76; R Diss 72-80; Dir of YMCA Cam 80-85; Prin YMCA Dunford Coll 85-88; Perm to Offic Glouc from 88; Ox from 89. *Westerley Cottage, Burford Street, Lechlade, Glos GL7 3AP* Faringdon (0367) 52642

MASON, John Martin. b 41. UMIST BSc63. Glouc Sch of Min 80 Qu Coll Birm 82. **d** 84 **p** 85. C Tuffley *Glouc* 84-87; P-in-c Willersey, Saintbury, Weston-sub-Edge etc from 87. *The Rectory, Weston-Subedge, Chipping Campden, Glos GL55 6QH* Evesham (0386) 840292

MASON, Julia Ann. Edin Th Coll. **d** 91. NSM Troon *Glas* from 91. *2 Balcomie Crescent, Troon, Ayrshire KA10 7AR* Troon (0292) 311707

MASON, Canon Kenneth Staveley. b 31. ARCS53 Lon Univ BSc53 BD64. Wells Th Coll 56. **d** 58 **p** 59. C Kingston upon Hull St Martin *York* 58-61; C Pocklington w Yapham-cum-Meltonby, Owsthorpe etc 61-63; C Millington w Gt Givendale 61-63; V Thornton w Allerthorpe 63-69; Sub-Warden St Aug Coll Cant 69-76; Dir Cant Sch of Min 77-81; Sec to Dioc Bd of Min *Cant* 77-87; Six Preacher Cant Cathl 79-84; Prin Cant Sch of Min 81-89; Hon Can Cant Cathl 84-89; Prin Edin Th Coll from 89; Can St Mary's Cathl *Edin* from 89. *The Theological College, Rosebery Crescent, Edinburgh EH12 5JT* 031-337 3838

MASON, Peter Charles. b 45. AKC72 BD72 Birm Univ PGCE89. St Aug Coll Cant 72. **d** 73 **p** 74. C St Mary *Derby* 73-76; C Bridgnorth St Mary *Heref* 76-78; TV Bridgnorth, Tasley, Astley Abbotts, Oldbury etc 78-88; RE Teacher from 88. *4 Woodbury Close, Bridgnorth, Shropshire WV16 4PT* Bridgnorth (0746) 762235

MASON, Canon Peter Joseph. b 34. Lon Univ BA58. Coll of Resurr Mirfield 58. **d** 60 **p** 61. C Belhus Park CD *Chelmsf* 60-63; Lic to Offic *Eur* 63-64; Asst Chapl Lon Univ *Lon* 64-70; Chapl City Univ 66-70; R Stoke Newington St Mary 70-78; V Writtle *Chelmsf* 78-81; P-in-c Highwood 78-81; V Writtle w Highwood 81-86; R Shenfield from 86; Hon Can Chelmsf Cathl from 89. *The Rectory, 41 Worrin Road, Shenfield, Brentwood, Essex CM15 8DH* Brentwood (0277) 220360

MASON, Ven Richard John. b 29. Linc Th Coll 55. **d** 58 **p** 59. C Hatf *St Alb* 58-64; Bp's Dom Chapl *Lon* 64-69; V Riverhead *Roch* 69-73; P-in-c Dunton Green 69-73; V Edenbridge 73-83; Hon Can Roch Cathl from 77; Adn Tonbridge from 77; P-in-c Crockham Hill H Trin 81-83; C-in-c Sevenoaks St Luke CD from 83. *St Luke's House, 30 Eardley Road, Sevenoaks, Kent TN13 1XT* Sevenoaks (0732) 452462

MASON, Robert Herbert George. b 48. Oak Hill Th Coll 82. **d** 84 **p** 85. C Ware Ch Ch *St Alb* 84-88; V Eastbourne All So *Chich* from 88. *All Souls' Vicarage, 53 Susan's Road, Eastbourne, E Sussex BN21 3TH* Eastbourne (0323) 31366

MASON, Roger Arthur. b 41. Lon Univ BSc65 K Coll Lon BD68 AKC68. **d** 69 **p** 70. C Enfield St Andr *Lon* 69-72; P-in-c Westbury *Heref* 72-78; P-in-c Yockleton 72-78; P-in-c Gt Wollaston 77-78; V Willesden St Mary *Lon* 78-88; V Prittlewell *Chelmsf* from 88. *Prittlewell Vicarage, 489 Victoria Avenue, Southend-on-Sea SS2 6NL* Southend-on-Sea (0702) 343470

MASON, Ronald William. b 06. ALCD38. **d** 38 **p** 39. R Gt Warley St Mary *Chelmsf* 65-71; rtd 71; Perm to Offic Ely 72-80; Cant from 81. *60 Dumpton Park Drive, Broadstairs, Kent* Thanet (0843) 69992

MASON, Thomas (Edward). b 52. Bris Univ MEd80. Trin Coll Bris BA91. **d** 91. C Glouc St Jas and All SS *Glouc* from 91. *16 Derby Road, Gloucester GL1 4AE* Gloucester (0452) 308951

MASON, Thomas Henry Ambrose. b 51. BA86. **d** 86 **p** 87. C W Drayton *Lon* 86-89; Field Officer Oak Hill Ext Coll from 89. *Oak Hill College, Chase Side, London N14 4PS* 081-449 0467

MASON, Walter Cecil. b 15. Bps' Coll Cheshunt 41. **d** 43 **p** 44. R Marksbury *B & W* 61-80; R Stanton Prior 61-80; rtd 80; Perm to Offic *B & W* from 80. *19 Westfield Park South, Bath BA1 3HT* Bath (0225) 24056

MASON, William Frederick. b 48. Linc Th Coll 75. **d** 78 **p** 79. C Ipswich St Aug *St E* 78-81; TV Dronfield *Derby* 81-88; V Ellesmere St Pet *Sheff* from 88. *The Vicarage, 85 Malton Street, Sheffield S4 7EA* Sheffield (0742) 762555

MASSEY, Frederick. b 02. Univ of Wales BA30. **d** 30 **p** 31. P-in-c Saltdean *Chich* 60-66; rtd 66; Perm to Offic Chich 66-76; Derby from 77. *2A St Mary's Close, Alvaston, Derby DE2 0GF* Derby (0332) 752442

MASSEY, Frederick Michael. b 17. AKC47. **d** 47 **p** 48. V Usselby *Linc* 53-74; R Walesby 53-89; R Kirkby w Kingerby 55-74; P-in-c Stainton-le-Vale w Kirmond le Mire 74-80; P-in-c Claxby w Normanby-le-Wold 74-80; P-in-c Tealby 74-80; P-in-c N Willingham 74-80; RD W Wold 88-89; rtd 89. *Holly House, 2A Sandy Lane, Tealby, Market Rasen, Lincs LN8 3YF* Tealby (067383) 534

MASSEY, Keith John. b 46. Oak Hill Th Coll 69. **d** 72 **p** 73. C Bermondsey St Jas w Ch Ch *S'wark* 72-76; C Benchill *Man* 76-82; V Clifton Green from 82. *St Thomas's Vicarage, Delamere Avenue, Clifton, Swinton, Manchester M27 2GL* 061-794 1986

MASSEY, Nigel John. b 60. Birm Univ BA81 MA82. Wycliffe Hall Ox. **d** 87 **p** 88. C Bearwood *Birm* 87-90; C Warley Woods 90. *St Hilda's Vicarage, Smethwick, Warley, W Midlands B67 5NQ* 021-429 1384

MASSEY, William Cyril. b 32. Lich Th Coll 58. **d** 61 **p** 62. C Heref St Martin *Heref* 61-66; V Kimbolton w Middleton-on-the-Hill 66-75; V Alveley 75-83; P-in-c Quatt 81-83; R Alveley and Quatt 84-85; R Llangarron w Llangrove, Whitchurch and Ganarew from 85. *The Vicarage, Llangrove, Ross-on-Wye, Herefordshire HR9 6EZ* Llangarron (098984) 341

MASSHEDAR, John Frederick. b 50. Dur Univ BEd74. Linc Th Coll 76. **d** 78 **p** 79. C Pocklington w Yapham-cum-Meltonby, Owsthorpe etc *York* 78-81; C Middlesb Ascension 81-82; V 82-85; V Eskdaleside w Ugglebarnby and Sneaton 85-87; V Shotton *Dur* from 87. *The Vicarage, Shotton Colliery, Durham DH6 2JW* 091-526 1156

MASSHEDAR, Richard Eric. b 57. Nottm Univ BTh86. Linc Th Coll 83. **d** 86 **p** 87. C Cassop cum Quarrington *Dur* 86-89; C Ferryhill from 89. *59 Church Lane, Ferryhill, Co Durham DL17 8LT* Ferryhill (0740) 653029

MASSINGBERD-MUNDY, John. b 07. Pemb Coll Cam BA30 MA46. Cuddesdon Coll 31. **d** 32 **p** 33. V Gt Limber w Brocklesby *Linc* 65-72; V Kirmington 65-72; rtd 72. *79 Wolverton Road, Newport Pagnell, Bucks MK16 8BH* Newport Pagnell (0908) 617242

MASSINGBERD-MUNDY, Roger William Burrell. b 36. TD. Univ of Wales (Lamp) BA59. Ridley Hall Cam 59. **d** 61 **p** 62. C Benwell St Jas *Newc* 61-64; CF (TA) 63-68;

CF (TAVR) 71-83; C Whorlton *Newc* 64-72; TV 73; P-in-c Healey 73-85; Dioc Stewardship Adv 73-85; Hon Can Newc Cathl 82-85; R S Ormsby w Ketsby, Calceby and Driby *Linc* 85-86; P-in-c Harrington w Brinkhill 85-86; P-in-c Haugh 85-86; P-in-c Oxcombe 85-86; P-in-c Ruckland w Farforth and Maidenwell 85-86; P-in-c Somersby w Bag Enderby 85-86; P-in-c Tetford and Salmonby 85-86; R S Ormsby Gp from 86; RD Bolingbroke from 88. *The Rectory, South Ormsby, Louth, Lincs LN11 8QT* Louth (0507) 480236

MASSON, Philip Roy. b 52. Hertf Coll Ox BA75 Leeds Univ BA77. Coll of Resurr Mirfield 75. **d** 78 **p** 79. C Port Talbot St Theodore *Llan* 78-82; V Penyfai w Tondu from 82; Dioc Dir Post-Ord Tr 85-88; Warden of Ords from 88. *The Vicarage, Pen-y-Fai, Bridgend, M Glam CF31 4LS* Bridgend (0656) 652849

MASTERMAN, Malcolm. b 49. K Coll Lon 73. Chich Th Coll 76. **d** 77 **p** 78. C Peterlee *Dur* 77-80; Chapl Basingstoke Distr Hosp 80-85; Chapl Freeman Hosp Newc from 85. *Freeman Hospital Chaplaincy, Freeman Road, Newcastle upon Tyne NE7 7DN* 091-284 3111

MASTERMAN, Miss Patricia Hope. b 28. St Mich Ho Ox 59. **dss** 79 **d** 87. Asst CF 79-90; rtd 90. *33 Sea Lane Gardens, Ferring, Worthing, W Sussex BM12 5EQ* Worthing (0903) 45231

✠MASTERS, Rt Rev Brian John. b 32. Qu Coll Cam BA55 MA59. Cuddesdon Coll 62. **d** 64 **p** 65 **c** 82. C Stepney St Dunstan and All SS *Lon* 64-69; V Hoxton H Trin w St Mary 69-82; P-in-c Hoxton St Anne w St Sav and St Andr 69-75; P-in-c Hoxton St Anne w St Columba 75-80; Suff Bp Fulham 82-84; Area Bp Edmonton from 85. *1 Regents Park Terrace, London NW1 7EE* 071-267 4455

MASTERS, Kenneth Leslie. b 44. Leeds Univ BA68. Cuddesdon Coll 68. **d** 70 **p** 71. C Wednesbury St Paul Wood Green *Lich* 70-71; C Tettenhall Regis 71-75; TV Chelmsley Wood *Birm* 75-79; R Harting *Chich* 79-87; V Rustington from 87. *The Vicarage, Claigmar Road, Rustington, Littlehampton, W Sussex BN16 2NL* Rustington (0903) 784749

MASTERS, Leslie. b 31. Ripon Hall Ox 73. **d** 75 **p** 76. C Hanham *Bris* 75-78; TV Bris St Agnes and St Simon w St Werburgh 78-84; Asst Chapl HM Pris Man 84; Chapl HM Pris Northeye 84-88; Chapl HM Pris Littlehey from 88. *HM Prison Littlehey, Cambs* Huntingdon (0480) 812202

MASTERS, Canon Raymond (Austin). b 26. Kelham Th Coll 45. **d** 52 **p** 53. SSM from 51; S Africa 52-65; Can Bloemfontein Cathl 58-65; Perm to Offic *Blackb* 65-68; Chapl St Martin's Coll of Educn Lanc 68-70; Asst Sec Gen Syn Bd for Miss and Unity 71-77; Hon C Harrow St Pet *Lon* 72-77; TV Cen Ex 78-82; Dioc Miss and Ecum Officer 78-82; Can Res Heref Cathl *Heref* from 82; Treas from 85; Bp's Co-ord for Min from 82. *3 Castle Street, Hereford HR1 2NL* Hereford (0432) 55933

MASTERS, Stephen Michael. b 52. St Chad's Coll Dur BA75. Coll of Resurr Mirfield 85. **d** 87 **p** 88. C Primrose Hill St Mary w Avenue Road St Paul *Lon* 87-90; C Hornsey St Mary w St Geo from 90. *Holy Innocents' Vicarage, Tottenham Lane, London N8 7EL* 081-340 1930

MASTERTON, Paul Robert. b 35. Clifton Th Coll 63. **d** 66 **p** 67. C Selly Hill St Steph *Birm* 66-68; C Sutton Coldfield H Trin 68-72; C Aldridge *Lich* 72-74; C Gt Crosby St Luke *Liv* 74-76; P-in-c Manuden w Berden *Chelmsf* 76-86; R Helpringham w Hale *Linc* from 86. *2 Vicarage Lane, Helpringham, Sleaford, Lincs NG34 0RP* Swaton (052921) 435

MASTIN, Brian Arthur. b 38. Peterho Cam BA60 MA63 BD80 Mert Coll Ox MA63. Ripon Hall Ox 62. **d** 63 **p** 64. Asst Lect Hebrew Univ Coll of N Wales (Ban) 63-65; Lect Hebrew 65-82; Sen Lect from 82; Chapl Ban Cathl *Ban* 63-65; Lic to Offic from 65. *Department of Religious Studies, University College, Bangor, Gwynedd LL57 2DG* Bangor (0248) 351151

MATCHETT, Edward James Boyd. b 19. TCD BA43 MA60. **d** 43 **p** 44. C Belf St Mary *Conn* 43-45; Miss to Seamen from 45; Iraq 47-50; New Zealand 64-69; Regional Dir Miss to Seamen (E Region) 69-74; Hong Kong 74-83; Chapl Cornish Ports 83-86; Perm to Offic *Nor* from 86. *10 Southern Reach, Mulbarton, Norwich NR14 8BU* Mulbarton (0508) 70337

MATHER, Cuthbert. b 15. Tyndale Hall Bris 36. **d** 40 **p** 41. V Needham w Rushall *Nor* 57-80; rtd 80; Perm to Offic *Nor* from 80. *2 Church Close, Hunstanton, Norfolk PE36 6BE* Hunstanton (0485) 533084

MATHER, James Malcolm. b 31. Trin Coll Cam BA54 MA59. Cuddesdon Coll 54. **d** 56 **p** 57. C S Bank *York* 56-60; C Sutton St Mich 60-61; C Hanwell St Thos

Lon 61-63; V Ilkeston H Trin *Derby* 63-72; P-in-c Upper Langwith 73-77; R 77-80; P-in-c Whaley Thorns 77-80; R Upper Langwith w Langwith Bassett etc 80; P-in-c Watlington *Ox* 80-81; V Watlington w Pyrton and Shirburn 81-86; R Harome w Stonegrave, Nunnington and Pockley *York* from 86. *The Rectory, Harome, York YO6 5JS* Helmsley (0439) 70163

MATHER, James William. b 63. Sheff Univ BA86. St Steph Ho Ox 88. **d** 91. C Doncaster St Leon and St Jude *Sheff* from 91. *47 Windsor Walk, Scawsby, Doncaster, S Yorkshire DN5 8NQ* Doncaster (0302) 786293

MATHER, Stephen Albert. b 54. Qu Coll Birm 85. **d** 87 **p** 88. C Sutton *Liv* 87-90; TV from 90. *316 Reginald Road, Sutton Leach, St Helens, Merseyside WA9 4HS* St Helens (0744) 812380

MATHER, William Bernard George, b 45. St Jo Coll Nottm 77. **d** 79 **p** 80. C St Leonards St Leon *Chich* 79-82; TR Netherthorpe *Sheff* 82-90; V Littleover *Derby* from 90. *The Vicarage, Church Street, Littleover, Derby DE3 6GF* Derby (0332) 767802

MATHERS, Alan Edward. b 36. FPhS Lon Univ BA. Oak Hill Th Coll 61. **d** 64 **p** 65. C Ox St Matt *Ox* 64-66; C Bootle St Leon *Liv* 66-68; C Hampreston *Sarum* 68-70; P-in-c Damerham 70-71; V Queniborough *Leic* 71-76; USA 76-77; P-in-c Tipton St Paul *Lich* 77-84; V 85-86; V Tipton St Matt 77-86; V Sutton Ch Ch *S'wark* from 86. *Christ Church Vicarage, 14 Christchurch Park, Sutton, Surrey SM2 5TN* 081-642 2757

MATHERS, David Michael Brownlow. b 43. Em Coll Cam BA65 MA69. Clifton Th Coll 65. **d** 67 **p** 68. C Branksome St Clem *Sarum* 67-70; C Bromley Ch Ch *Roch* 70-73; V Bures *St E* 73-80; Brazil 80-82; P-in-c Old Newton w Stowupland *St E* 82-86; V 87-90; V Thurston from 90. *Thurston Vicarage, Bury St Edmunds, Suffolk IP31 3RU* Pakenham (0359) 30301

MATHERS, Derek. b 48. N Ord Course 82. **d** 85 **p** 86. C Huddersfield St Jo *Wakef* 85-86; C N Huddersfield 86-88; TV Almondbury w Farnley Tyas from 88. *The Vicarage, 150 Fleminghouse Lane, Huddersfield HD5 8UD* Huddersfield (0484) 545085

MATHESON, David Melville. b 23. McGill Univ Montreal BA55 BD61. Linc Th Coll 77. **d** 77 **p** 78. Chapl Blue Coat Sch Reading 77-85; Hon C Verwood *Sarum* 85-88; C Stratfield Mortimer *Ox* from 88. *St Mary's School House, The Street, Mortimer, Reading RG7 3PB* Mortimer (0734) 332814

MATHESON, Canon Ronald Stuart. b 29. Lon Univ BA50. Ely Th Coll 52. **d** 54 **p** 55. C Byker St Ant *Newc* 54-57; C Hedworth *Dur* 57-59; V S Hylton 59-65; P-in-c Glenrothes *St And* 65-69; R 69-73; R Dundee St Marg *Bre* 73-78; Belize 79-80; Chapl Sliema *Eur* 81-82; Chapl Costa del Sol E from 82; Hon Can Gib Cathl from 90. *Edificio Alessandra 208, Torre Blanca del Sol, 2964 Fuengirola, Spain* Malaga (52) 581192

MATHEWS, Arthur Kenneth. b 06. OBE42 DSC44. Ball Coll Ox BA32 MA36. Cuddesdon Coll 31. **d** 32 **p** 33. V Thursley *Guildf* 68-76; rtd 76; Perm to Offic *Ox* from 77. *The Tallat, Westwell, Burford, Oxon OX8 4JT* Burford (099382) 2464

MATHEWS, Richard Twitchell. b 27. Bps' Coll Cheshunt 57. **d** 59 **p** 60. V Riddlesden *Bradf* 67-74; Australia 74-78; P-in-c Medbourne cum Holt w Stockerston and Blaston *Leic* 78-82; Chapl Alassio *Eur* 82-83; Chapl San Remo 82-83; Chapl Palma and Balearic Is w Ibiza etc 83-87; P-in-c Witchford w Wentworth *Ely* 87-91; rtd 91. *19 Dorset House, Hastings Road, Bexhill-on-Sea, E Sussex TN40 2HJ*

MATHEWS, Ronald Peel Beresford. b 24. TCD DBS DipYL. **d** 64 **p** 65. C Waterford w Killea, Drumcannon and Dunhill *C & O* 64-66; I Clonbroney w Killoe *K, E & A* 66-71; I Drumgoon and Ashfield 71-74; Dep Sec Leprosy Miss 74-84; I Kinneigh Union *C, C & R* from 84. *The Rectory, Ballineen, Co Cork, Irish Republic* Clonakilty (23) 47143

MATHIAS, John Maelgwyn. b 15. St D Coll Lamp BA38 St Mich Coll Llan 40. **d** 40 **p** 41. R Cellan w Llanfair Clydogau *St D* 54-83; Lect St Jo Ch Coll Ystrad Meurig 67-77; rtd 83. *Bronallt, Capel Seion Road, Drefach, Llanelli, Dyfed SA14 4BN*

MATHIE, Patricia Jean (Sister Donella). b 22. CertEd49. **dss** 79 **d** 87. CSA from 74; Asst Superior from 82; Notting Hill St Jo *Lon* 79-80; Notting Hill St Clem and St Mark 82-84; Kensal Town St Thos w St Andr and St Phil 85-87; Hon C from 87. *St Andrew's House, 2 Tavistock Road, London W11 1BA* 071-229 2662

MATHIESON, Eric. b 25. Down Coll Cam BA47 MA52. St Steph Ho Ox 48. **d** 50 **p** 51. C Tonge Moor *Man* 50-54; V Burnley St Cath *Blackb* 54-59; V S'wark St

Alphege *S'wark* from 59. *St Alphege Clergy House, Pocock Street, London SE1 0BJ* 071-928 6158

MATHIESON, Theodore. b 13. SS Coll Cam BA35 MA39. Cuddesdon Coll 36. **d** 37 **p** 38. C Elland *Wakef* 37-42; C Greenford H Cross *Lon* 42-46; Ox Miss Calcutta from 46; Superior Brotherhood of the Epiphany (Ox Miss) from 88. *Oxford Mission, Barisha, Calcutta 700 008, India*

MATON, Oswald. b 24. St Aug Coll Cant 75. **d** 77 **p** 78. Hon C Chatham St Steph *Roch* from 77. *304 Maidstone Road, Chatham, Kent ME4 6JJ* Medway (0634) 843568

MATTEN, Derek Norman William. b 30. **d** 56 **p** 57. C Farnworth *Liv* 56-59; C Walton H Trin *Ox* 59-62; W Germany 62-90; Perm to Offic *Ex* from 90. *7 Mount Plym, Plymouth Road, Totnes TQ9 5PH* Totnes (0803) 866732

MATTHEW, Canon Andrew Foster. b 45. Oak Hill Th Coll 68. **d** 70 **p** 71. C St Alb St Paul *St Alb* 70-74; C Harwell *Ox* 74-76; C Chilton All SS 74-76; C Harwell w Chilton 76-77; V St Keverne *Truro* 77-84; RD Kerrier 81-84; V St Austell from 84; Hon Can Truro Cathl from 89. *1 Carnsmerry Crescent, St Austell, Cornwall PL25 4NA* St Austell (0726) 73839

MATTHEWS, Alan Philip John. b 58. Man Univ BA79. St Steph Ho Ox 80. **d** 83 **p** 84. C Goldthorpe w Hickleton *Sheff* 83-87; C Hemsworth *Wakef* 87-90; R from 90. *The Rectory, 3 Church Close, Hemsworth, Pontefract, W Yorkshire WF9 4SJ* Hemsworth (0977) 610507

MATTHEWS, Barry Alan. b 46. AKC68. St Boniface Warminster St Paul's Grahamstown. **d** 69 **p** 70. S Africa 69-74 and 77-83; C Leeds St Aid *Ripon* 74-77; C Shotton *St As* 83-84; Zimbabwe from 84. *St Margaret's Rectory, 2 Greenfield Square, North End, Bulawayo, Zimbabwe*

MATTHEWS, Brian. b 32. ARIC55. Cranmer Hall Dur 59. **d** 62 **p** 63. C Belgrave St Pet *Leic* 62-65; C Whitwick St Jo the B 65-69; C Kirby Muxloe 69-71; P-in-c Bardon Hill 71-78; V Thringstone St Andr from 78. *The Vicarage, 49 Loughborough Road, Thringstone, Leicester LE6 4LQ* Coalville (0530) 222380

MATTHEWS, Canon Brian Benjamin. b 14. OBE73. Ox Univ MA. Chich Th Coll 35. **d** 37 **p** 38. Chapl Monte Carlo w Beaulieu *Eur* 58-83; Can Malta Cathl from 73; Adn Riviera 76-83; rtd 83; Chapl Beaulieu-sur-Mer *Eur* from 83. *47 Boulevard Marechal Joffre, 06310 Beaulieu-sur-Mer, France* France (33) 93 01 63 46

MATTHEWS, Canon Campbell Thurlow. b 33. Lon Univ BA56 Dur Univ DipEd57. St Jo Coll Nottm 70. **d** 71 **p** 72. C Ryton *Dur* 71-74; Chapl R Victoria Infirmary Newc 74-82; V Greenside *Dur* 74-82; R Wetheral w Warw *Carl* from 82; RD Brampton from 83; P-in-c Farlam and Nether Denton from 87; P-in-c Gilsland from 87; Hon Can Carl Cathl from 87. *The Rectory, Plains Road, Wetheral, Carlisle CA4 8LE* Wetheral (0228) 60216

MATTHEWS, Celia Inger. b 30. **d** 86. Dioc Missr *St And* from 86. *24 Barossa Place, Perth PH1 5HH* Perth (0738) 23578

MATTHEWS, Charles. b 17. CEng MIMechE51 MIProdE54. Wells Th Coll 64. **d** 66 **p** 67. C Neston *Ches* 66-73; V Liscard St Thos 73-79; V Over Tabley and High Legh 79-84; rtd 84; Perm to Offic *Ches* from 84. *Ardmore House Nursing Home, Leighton Road, South Wirral L64 3SG* 051-336 2205

MATTHEWS, Preb Clarence Sydney. b 11. Lon Univ BA30 AKC32 BD38. **d** 34 **p** 35. V Ealing St Steph Castle Hill *Lon* 54-81; RD Ealing E 68-79; rtd 81; Perm to Offic Cant from 81; Lon from 84. *5 Linden Grove, Canterbury, Kent CT2 8AB* Canterbury (0227) 66078

MATTHEWS, Colin John. b 44. Jes Coll Ox BA67 MA71 Fitzw Coll Cam BA70 MA74. Ridley Hall Cam 68. **d** 71 **p** 72. C Onslow Square St Paul *Lon* 71-74; C Leic H Apostles *Leic* 74-78; Bible Use Sec Scripture Union 78-89; Dir St Sav Ch Cen Guildf from 89. *6 Manor Way, Guildford, Surrey GU2 5RN* Guildford (0483) 33412

MATTHEWS, Francilla Lacey. b 37. S'wark Ord Course 83. **dss** 86 **d** 87. Bromley St Mark *Roch* 86-87; Hon Par Dn 87-90; Par Dn Hayes from 90. *71 Hayes Road, Bromley BR2 9AE* 081-464 4083

MATTHEWS, Frederick Peter. b 45. Grey Coll Dur BA66 MA68. K Coll Lon PGCE68 Lon Univ BSc(Econ)75. Sarum & Wells Th Coll 70. **d** 72 **p** 73. C W Wickham St Jo *Cant* 72-74; C Sholing *Win* 74-77; Lic to Offic 78-79; V Woolston from 79. *St Mark's Vicarage, 117 Swift Road, Woolston, Southampton SO2 9ER* Southampton (0703) 448542

MATTHEWS, George Charles Wallace. b 27. Sarum Th Coll 58. **d** 60 **p** 61. C Coppenhall St Paul *Ches* 60-63; C Lewes St Anne *Chich* 63-67; V Wheelock *Ches* 67-76; V Mossley from 76. *The Vicarage, 79 Leek Road,*

Congleton, Cheshire CW12 3HX   Congleton (0260) 273182

MATTHEWS, Gerald Lancelot. b 31. Ripon Hall Ox 55. **d** 57 **p** 58. C The Quinton *Birm* 57-60; C Olton 60-63; V Brent Tor *Ex* 63-72; P-in-c Lydford w Bridestowe and Sourton 70-72; TR Lydford, Brent Tor, Bridestowe and Sourton 72-78; P-in-c Black Torrington, Bradf w Cookbury etc 78-90; Perm to Offic from 90. *The Larches, Black Torrington, Beaworthy, Devon EX21 5PU*   Black Torrington (040923) 228

MATTHEWS, Gilbert Brian Reeves. b 19. Keble Coll Ox BA42 MA48. St Steph Ho Ox 41. **d** 44 **p** 45. R Rushton and Glendon *Pet* 58-79; P-in-c Thorpe Malsor 76-79; R Rushton and Glendon w Thorpe Malsor 79-81; C Spondon *Derby* 81-87; rtd 87. *1 Kenilworth Road, South Wigston, Leicester LE8 2UF*   Leicester (0533) 786577

MATTHEWS, Harold James. b 46. Leeds Univ BSc68 Fitzw Coll Cam BA70 MA74. Westcott Ho Cam 68. **d** 71 **p** 72. C Mossley Hill St Matt and St Jas *Liv* 71-74; C Stanley 74-76; TV Hackney *Lon* 76-78; Chapl Forest Sch Snaresbrook 78-83; Hd Master Vernon Holme Sch Cant 83-88; Perm to Offic Cant from 83; St Alb from 88; Hd Master Heath Mt Sch Hertf from 88. *Heath Mount School, Watton at Stone, Hertford SG14 3NG*   Ware (0920) 830230 or 830541

MATTHEWS, Heather Ann. b 49. Bris Univ BA71 Lon Univ CertEd72. Trin Coll Bris 87. **d** 89. C Blagdon w Compton Martin and Ubley *B & W* from 89. *Forsythia Cottage, Grib Lane, Blagdon, Bristol BS18 6SA*   Blagdon (0761) 63109

MATTHEWS, Canon Hubert Samuel. b 09. MBE66. Ripon Hall Ox 29. **d** 34 **p** 35. Cyprus 54-74; Hon Can Jerusalem 73-75; rtd 74. *241 Crowmere Road, Shrewsbury SY2 5LD*   Shrewsbury (0743) 355702

MATTHEWS, Canon John. b 22. TD66. Trin Coll Cam BA48 MA51. Bps' Coll Cheshunt 49. **d** 51 **p** 52. CF (TA) from 53; P-in-c Lt Canfield *Chelmsf* 62-70; V Gt Dunmow 62-88; P-in-c Gt Easton 70-83; RD Dunmow 75-88; Hon Can Chelmsf Cathl 85-88; rtd 88. *Moorside Cottage, The Common, Walberswick, New Southwold, Suffolk IP18 6TE*   Southwold (0502) 722783

MATTHEWS, Lewis William. b 29. St Jo Coll Dur BA53 DipTh55 MSc76. **d** 55 **p** 56. C Eston *York* 55-57; C Wicker w Neepsend *Sheff* 57; Ind Chapl 57-61; V Copt Oak *Leic* 61-64; R Braunstone 64-70; V Thornaby on Tees St Paul *York* 70-72; TR Thornaby on Tees 72-78; Dir Dioc Bd for Soc Resp *Lon* 80-84; Perm to Offic from 84; Warden Durning Hall Chr Community Cen Forest Gate from 84. *Durning Hall, Earlham Grove, London E7 9AB*   081-555 0142

MATTHEWS, Melvyn William. b 40. St Edm Hall Ox BA63 MA67 K Coll Lon BD67 AKC67. **d** 67 **p** 68. C Enfield St Andr *Lon* 67-70; Asst Chapl Southn Univ *Win* 70-72; Kenya 73-76; V Highgate All SS *Lon* 76-79; P-in-c Clifton St Paul *Bris* 79-87; Sen Chapl Bris Univ 79-87; Dir Ammerdown Cen from 87. *55 Southlands Drive, Timsbury, Bath BA3 1HB*   Timsbury (0761) 72636

MATTHEWS, Oswald John. b 13. St Edm Hall Ox BA37 MA40. Ripon Hall Ox 35. **d** 37 **p** 38. C Beverley Minster *York* 37-41; V Drypool St Andr and St Pet 41-48; Chapl RAF 41-45; V Fridaythorpe w Fimber and Thixendale *York* 48-52; Miss to Seamen 52-64; Argentina 52-54; New Zealand from 54. *55A Jellicoe Street, Wanganui, New Zealand*   Wanganui (64) 343-9540

MATTHEWS, Canon Percival Charles Halls. b 15. Em Coll Cam BA37 MA41. Wycliffe Hall Ox 37. **d** 38 **p** 39. V Douglas St Geo and St Barn *S & M* 57-80; RD Douglas 71-80; Can St German's Cathl 75-80; rtd 80; Perm to Offic *S & M* 80-81; Hon C German St Jo from 81. *Edelweiss, Glen Lough Circle, Glen Vine, Douglas, Isle of Man*   Marown (0624) 851860

MATTHEWS, Peter Henry. b 22. Sarum Th Coll 62. **d** 64 **p** 65. R Hilperton w Whaddon *Sarum* 70-78; P-in-c Staverton 71-72; V 72-78; P-in-c Milborne St Andrew w Dewlish 78-87; rtd 87. *Holmlands, Lambrook Road, Shepton Beauchamp, Ilminster, Somerset TA19 0LZ*   South Petherton (0460) 40938

MATTHEWS, Rodney Charles. b 36. Sarum Th Coll 62. **d** 64 **p** 65. C Gt Clacton *Chelmsf* 64-68; C Loughton St Mary 68-74; TV 74-76; V Goodmayes All SS 76-87; V Woodford Bridge from 87; Hon Chapl Sail Tr Assn from 89; P-in-c Barkingside St Cedd from 90. *St Paul's Vicarage, 4 Cross Road, Woodford Green, Essex IG8 8BS*   081-504 3815

MATTHEWS, Roger Charles. b 54. MBCS82 CEng90 Man Univ BSc75 CDipAF78. Trin Coll Bris 87. **d** 89 **p** 90. C Gt Baddow *Chelmsf* from 89. *46 New Road, Great Baddow, Chelmsford CM2 7QT*   Chelmsford (0245) 75669

MATTHEWS, Canon Roy Ian John. b 27. TD71. St Cath Soc Ox BA52 MA56. St Steph Ho Ox 52. **d** 54 **p** 55. C Barnsley St Mary *Wakef* 54-58; V Staincliffe 58-65; CF (TA) from 58; V Penistone w Midhope *Wakef* 65-72; V Brighouse 72-84; Hon Can Wakef Cathl from 76; V Darrington w Wentbridge from 84; Dioc Schs Officer 84-89; Dep Dir of Educn 85-89. *The Vicarage, Darrington, Pontefract, W Yorkshire WF8 3AB*   Pontefract (0977) 704744

MATTHEWS, Royston Peter. b 39. Univ of Wales (Lamp) BA61 DipTh64. St Mich Coll Llan 61. **d** 64 **p** 65. C Fairwater CD *Llan* 64-67; C Cadoxton-juxta-Barry 67-71; V Bettws *Mon* 71-84; V Abergavenny H Trin from 84. *Holy Trinity Vicarage, Baker Street, Abergavenny, Gwent NP7 5BH*   Abergavenny (0873) 3203

MATTHEWS, Stuart James. b 37. St Jo Coll Dur BA60. Bps' Coll Cheshunt 60. **d** 62 **p** 63. C Horsham *Chich* 62-65; C Rednal *Birm* 65-67; Min Brandwood St Bede Statutory District 67-68; C Northfield 68-73; V Thurcroft *Sheff* 73-82; RD Laughton 79-82; R Sprotbrough from 82; RD Adwick 84-89. *The Rectory, 42A Spring Lane, Sprotborough, Doncaster, S Yorkshire DN5 7QG*   Doncaster (0302) 853203

MATTHEWS, Terence Leslie. b 35. Handsworth Coll Birm 55. **d** 61 **p** 62. V Horden *Dur* 64-72; R Witton Gilbert 72-77; P-in-c Grangetown 77-85; V Cleadon 85-86; V Hebburn St Cuth 86-88; rtd 88. *7 Holmlands Park South, Sunderland SR2 7SG*   091-522 6466

MATTHEWS, Canon William Andrew. b 44. Reading Univ BA65. St Steph Ho Ox 65. **d** 67 **p** 68. C Westbury-on-Trym St Alb *Bris* 67-70; C Marlborough *Sarum* 70-73; P-in-c Winsley 73-75; V 75-81; V Bradford-on-Avon from 81; RD Bradf from 84; Can and Preb Sarum Cathl from 88. *Holy Trinity Vicarage, 18A Woolley Street, Bradford-on-Avon, Wilts BA15 1AF*   Bradford-on-Avon (02216) 4444

MATTHEWS, William Temple Atkinson. b 47. E Midl Min Tr Course 86. **d** 83 **p** 83. SSF 83-86; C Brinsley w Underwood *S'well* 86-89; TV Hitchin *St Alb* from 89. *The Vicarage, 31 Meadowbank, Hitchin, Herts SG4 0HY*   Hitchin (0462) 432179

MATTHEWS-LOYDALL, Elaine. b 63. Bp Otter Coll BA85 St Jo Coll Nottm LTh89 DPS90. **d** 90. Par Dn Nottm All SS *S'well* from 90; Asst Chapl to the Deaf from 91. *Pumpkin Cottage, 54 Wilne Road, Sawley, Notts NG10 3AN*   Long Eaton (0602) 728943

MATTHIAE, David. b 40. Fitzw Ho Cam BA63 MA69. Linc Th Coll 63. **d** 65 **p** 66. C New Addington *Cant* 65-70; C Charlton-by-Dover SS Pet and Paul 70-75; V Cant All SS 75-84; P-in-c Tunstall 84-87; R Tunstall w Rodmersham from 87; RD Sittingbourne from 88. *The Rectory, Tunstall, Sittingbourne, Kent ME9 8DU*   Sittingbourne (0795) 423907

MATTHIAS, Edwin. b 23. AKC50. **d** 51 **p** 52. C Hinckley St Mary *Leic* 51-54; C Putney St Mary *S'wark* 54-58; V Bolney *Chich* 58-65; R Chailey from 65. *Chailey Rectory, Chailey Green, Lewes, E Sussex BN8 4DA*   Newick (082572) 2286

MATTHIAS, George Ronald. b 30. CertEd51. St Deiniol's Hawarden 76. **d** 78 **p** 79. NSM Broughton *St As* 78-83; NSM Wrexham 83-85; C 85-87; V Brymbo from 87. *The Vicarage, Brymbo, Wrexham, Clwyd LL11 5LF*   Wrexham (0978) 758107

MATTOCK, Colin Graham. b 38. Chich Th Coll. **d** 84 **p** 85. C Hove All SS *Chich* 84-87; C Bexhill St Pet 87-90; V Henlow *St Alb* from 90. *The Vicarage, 12 Church Road, Henlow, Beds SG16 6AN*   Hitchin (0462) 816296

MATTOCK, Donald Walter. b 26. Toronto Univ BCom49 CertEd. Ex & Truro NSM Scheme. **d** 81 **p** 82. NSM Dawlish *Ex* 81-82; C 82-84; C Plympton St Mary 84-87; Chapl Boadreach Ho Plymouth from 85. *The White House, Ideford, Newton Abbot, Devon TQ13 0BQ*   Teignmouth (0626) 775419

MATTY, Horace Anthony. b 36. Ely Th Coll 61. **d** 63 **p** 64. C Minchinhampton *Glouc* 63-66; C Hunslet St Mary and Stourton *Ripon* 66-69; TV Wendy w Shingay *Ely* 69-71; V Parson Drove 71-74; V Southea cum Murrow 71-74; V Coven *Lich* 74-82; TV Hednesford 82-85; TV Basildon, St Martin of Tours w Nevendon *Chelmsf* from 85; P-in-c Basildon St Andr w H Cross from 85. *St Andrew's Vicarage, 3 The Fremnells, Basildon, Essex SS14 2QX*   Basildon (0268) 520516

MAUCHAN, Andrew. b 44. Hertf Coll Ox BA65 MA69 Man Univ CertEd66. Oak Hill Th Coll DipHE90. **d** 90 **p** 91. C Bridlington Priory *York* from 90. *144 Marton Road, Bridlington, N Humberside YO16 5DH*   Bridlington (0262) 677450

MAUDE, Canon Alan. b 41. Lon Univ DipTh67 BD69 Newc Univ MSc90. Lambeth STh74 Oak Hill Th Coll 66. **d** 69 **p** 70. C Balderstone *Man* 69-73; Asst Chapl Crumpsall and Springfield Hosps 73-75; C Crumpsall St Matt 73-75; Chapl R Victoria Infirmary Newc from 75; Hon Can Newc Cathl *Newc* from 88. *22 The West Rig, Newcastle upon Tyne NE3 4LR* 091-284 4966

MAUDE, Ralph Henry Evelyn. b 09. St Pet Hall Ox BA33 MA37. St Steph Ho Ox 32. **d** 33 **p** 34. V Devizes St Pet *Sarum* 66-74; rtd 74. *4 Manor Court, Swan Road, Pewsey, Wilts SN9 5DW* Marlborough (0672) 63186

MAUDSLEY, Canon George Lambert. b 27. St Jo Coll Nottm 74. **d** 75 **p** 76. C Binley *Cov* 75-77; Chapl Barn Fellowship Winterborne Whitechurch 77-83; V Salford Priors *Cov* from 83; RD Alcester from 87; Hon Can Cov Cathl from 91. *The Vicarage, Salford Priors, Evesham, Worcs WR11 5UX* Bidford-on-Avon (0789) 772445

MAUDSLEY, Keith. b 51. York Univ BA72. Ripon Hall Ox 72. **d** 75 **p** 76. C Rugby St Andr *Cov* 75-79; C Cam Gt St Mary w St Mich *Ely* 79-82; Chapl Girton Coll 79-82; P-in-c Binley *Cov* 82-89; RD Cov E 87-89; P-in-c Leek Wootton 89-91; Dioc Policy Development Adv 89-91; Dioc Adv on UPA *Liv* from 91; Soc Resp Officer from 91. *8 The Parchments, Newton-le-Willows, Merseyside WA12 0DY* Newton-le-Willows (0925) 220586

MAUDSLEY, Michael Peter. b 38. St Andr Univ BSc61. Oak Hill Th Coll 65. **d** 67 **p** 68. C Blackpool St Mark *Blackb* 67-70; C Hartford *Ches* 70-72; R Balerno *Edin* 72-82; V Stapenhill w Cauldwell *Derby* 82-91; TV Edin St Paul and St Geo *Edin* from 91. *c/o 11 East Fettes Avenue, Edinburgh EH4 1DN* 031-332 3904

MAUGHAM, James Reavley. b 04. Roch Th Coll. **d** 60 **p** 61. V Gt Ilford St Jo *Chelmsf* 68-73; P-in-c Panfield 73-79; rtd 79. *4 Orchard Road, Southminster, Essex CM0 7DQ* Maldon (0621) 772895

MAUGHAN, Geoffrey Nigel. b 48. CCC Cam BA69 MA73. Oak Hill Th Coll 75. **d** 77 **p** 78. C New Malden and Coombe *S'wark* 77-81; C Abingdon w Shippon *Ox* 81-89; TV Abingdon from 89. *69 Northcourt Road, Abingdon, Oxon OX14 1NR* Abingdon (0235) 520115 or 522549

MAUGHAN, John. b 28. Keble Coll Ox BA51 MA55. Linc Th Coll 51. **d** 53 **p** 54. C Heworth St Mary *Dur* 53-56; C Winlaton 56-59; R Penshaw 59-72; V Cleadon Park from 72. *St Cuthbert's Vicarage, 218 Sunderland Road, South Shields NE34 6AT* 091-456 0091

✠**MAUND, Rt Rev John Arthur Arrowsmith.** b 09. CBE75 MC46. Leeds Univ BA31. Coll of Resurr Mirfield 31. **d** 33 **p** 34 **c** 50. C Evesham *Worc* 33-36; C Blackheath All SS *S'wark* 36-38; S Africa 39-50; Bp Basutoland 50-66; Bp Lesotho 66-76; Asst Bp St E 76-83; Asst Bp Worc from 84; rtd 86. *Flat 1, Wardens Lodge, The Quadrangle, Newland, Malvern, Worcs WR13 5AX* Malvern (0684) 568075

MAUNDER, Alan John. b 52. UWIST BSc74. Oak Hill Th Coll DipHE88. **d** 90 **p** 91. C Birkenhead Ch Ch *Ches* from 90. *24 Bessborough Road, Birkenhead, Merseyside L43 5RW* 051-652 2317

MAUNDRELL, Canon Wolseley David. b 20. New Coll Ox BA41 DipHa42 MA45. **d** 43 **p** 44. Can Res and Treas Win Cathl *Win* 61-70; Vice-Dean Win 66-70; Asst Chapl Brussels *Eur* 70-71; V Icklesham *Chich* 72-82; RD Rye 78-84; Can and Preb Chich Cathl 81-89; TR Rye 82-89; rtd 89; P-in-c Stonegate *Chich* from 89. *The Vicarage, Stonegate, Wadhurst, E Sussex TN5 7EJ* Ticehurst (0580) 200515

MAUNSELL, Colin Wray Dymock. b 33. Pemb Coll Cam BA56 Lon Univ DipTh58. Tyndale Hall Bris. **d** 58 **p** 59. C Virginia Water *Guildf* 58-60; BCMS from 60. *c/o BCMS, 251 Lewisham Way, London SE4 1XF* 081-691 6111

MAURICE, Kenneth. b 07. St D Coll Lamp BA34. **d** 33 **p** 34. R Cruwys Morchard *Ex* 57-68; rtd 68; Perm to Offic *Ex* from 85. *c/o Little Knowle, Sidmouth, Devon*

MAURICE, Peter David. b 51. St Chad's Coll Dur BA72. Coll of Resurr Mirfield. **d** 75 **p** 76. C Wandsworth St Paul *S'wark* 75-79; TV Mortlake w E Sheen 79-85; V Rotherhithe H Trin from 85; RD Bermondsey from 91. *Holy Trinity Vicarage, Bryan Road, London SE16 1HE* 071-237 3963

MAWBEY, Miss Diane. b 55. Cranmer Hall Dur. **d** 89. Par Dn Menston w Woodhead *Bradf* from 89. *10 Derry Lane, Menston, Ilkley, W Yorkshire LS29 6NH* Ilkley (0943) 76773

MAWER, David Ronald. b 32. Keble Coll Ox BA55 MA58 Dur Univ BA57 McGill Univ Montreal PhD77. Wells Th Coll 58. **d** 59 **p** 60. C Cullercoats St Geo *Newc* 59-61; Canada from 61; Co-Ord Angl Stud St Paul Univ Ottawa

from 81; Can Ottawa from 85. *281 Billings Avenue, Ottawa, Ontario, Canada, K1H 5L2*

MAWSON, Canon Arthur Cyril. b 35. St Pet Coll Ox BA56 MA61. Wycliffe Hall Ox 61. **d** 62 **p** 63. C Walsall *Lich* 62-66; V Millhouses H Trin *Sheff* 66-73; Selection Sec ACCM 73-79; Can Res and Treas Ex Cathl *Ex* from 79; Dioc Dir of Ords from 81. *9 The Close, Exeter EX1 1EZ* Exeter (0392) 79367

MAWSON, David Frank. b 44. Selw Coll Cam BA65 MA69. Linc Th Coll 79. **d** 80 **p** 81. C Tunstall *Lich* 80-83; C Blakenall Heath 83-84; TV 84-90; Chapl Goscote Hosp Walsall 87-90; V Pelsall *Lich* from 90. *The Vicarage, 39 Hall Lane, Pelsall, Walsall WS3 4JN* Pelsall (0922) 682098

MAWSON, Frank. b 18. ACIS70. NW Ord Course 74. **d** 77 **p** 78. NSM Stockport St Mary *Ches* 77-79; P-in-c Harthill and Burwardsley 79-82; rtd 82; Perm to Offic Ches & St As from 82, Lich from 88. *Morley, 3 Hall Road, Penrhyn Bay, Llandudno, Gwynedd LL30 3HE* Llandudno (0492) 49863

MAXWELL, Christopher John Moore. b 31. MRCS59 LRCP59 Qu Coll Cam MA75. Trin Coll Bris 74. **d** 75 **p** 76. Chile 75-81; C Clevedon Ch Ch *B & W* 75; Hon C Homerton St Luke *Lon* from 81. *1 Skipworth Road, London E9* 081-985 9230

MAXWELL, Ian Charles. b 17. Ch Coll Cam BA40 MA44. Ridley Hall Cam 40. **d** 42 **p** 43. R Stanhope *Dur* 61-74; R Gt w Lt Somerford and Seagry *Bris* 74-82; rtd 82; Perm to Offic *Chich* from 82. *22 Hastings Avenue, Seaford, E Sussex BN25 3LQ* Seaford (0323) 890453

MAXWELL, Marcus Howard. b 54. Liv Univ BSc76 Man Univ MPhil89. St Jo Coll Nottm BA79. **d** 80 **p** 81. C Chadderton St Matt *Man* 80-84; V Bircle from 84. *The Vicarage, 33 Castle Hill Road, Bury, Lancs BL9 7RW* 061-764 3853

MAXWELL, Ralph. b 21. **d** 86 **p** 87. NSM Belf St Mich *Conn* 86-87; Lic to Offic 87-89; NSM Belf St Jas w St Silas from 89. *69 Woodvale Road, Belfast BT13 3BN* Belfast (0232) 742421

MAXWELL, Richard Renwick. b 23. Mert Coll Ox BA49 MA49. Westcott Ho Cam 49. **d** 51 **p** 52. R Harrietsham *Cant* 67-73; V Blean 73-84; Hon C Hindhead *Guildf* 84-88; Perm to Offic *Cant* from 85; rtd 88. *4 St Birinus Road, Woodfalls, Salisbury, Wilts SP5 2LE* Downton (0725) 22037

MAY, Arthur Harry. b 10. Lon Univ BA32 St Cath Soc Ox BA47 MA63. Wycliffe Hall Ox. **d** 47 **p** 48. Sub-Warden St Deiniol's Lib Hawarden 68-73; V Middleton w Cropton *York* 73-80; RD Pickering 75-80; rtd 80; Perm to Offic *Chich* from 81. *The Old Schoolhouse, Fletching, Uckfield, E Sussex TN22 3SP* Newick (082572) 2633

MAY, Arthur John. b 16. Linc Th Coll 40. **d** 42 **p** 43. V Belhus Park *Chelmsf* 68-83; rtd 83. *19 Warriner Avenue, Hornchurch, Essex RM12 4LH* Hornchurch (04024) 58421

MAY, Charles Henry. b 29. Lon Coll of Div ALCD58 LTh74. **d** 58 **p** 59. C Bethnal Green St Jas Less *Lon* 58-61; C Woking St Pet *Guildf* 61-64; Area Sec (W Midl) CPAS 64-67; V Homerton St Luke *Lon* 67-80; Home Sec SAMS 80-84; V Fulham Ch Ch *Lon* from 84. *Christ Church Vicarage, 40 Clancarty Road, London SW6 3AA* 071-736 4261

MAY, Denis Harry. b 31. ARICS56. S'wark Ord Course. **d** 63 **p** 64. C Eltham St Jo *S'wark* 63-65; Hon C Charing w Lt Chart *Cant* 66-70; Lic to Offic from 70. *19 Malvern Road, Ashford, Kent TN24 8JA* Ashford (0233) 638816

MAY, Donald Charles Leonard. b 25. Chich Th Coll 72. **d** 73 **p** 74. C Barkingside H Trin *Chelmsf* 73-77; V Aldersbrook from 77. *St Gabriel's Vicarage, Aldersbrook Road, London E12 5HH* 081-989 0315

MAY, Ernest William Lees. b 08. Keble Coll Ox BA32 MA36. St Steph Ho Ox 32. **d** 34 **p** 35. R Ewelme *Ox* 70-75; R Britwell Salome 70-75; rtd 75. *Swallows' Rest, Bridge, Winsham, Chard, Somerset TA20 4HP* Winsham (0460) 01488

MAY, George Louis. b 27. Selw Coll Cam BA52 MA56. Ridley Hall Cam 52. **d** 54 **p** 55. C St Mary Cray and St Paul's Cray *Roch* 54-56; C St Paul's Cray St Barn CD 56-57; C-in-c Elburton CD *Ex* 57-66; Asst Master Guthlaxton Sch Wigston 67-70; Ixworth Sch 70-72; Thurston Upper Sch 73-74; Perias Sch New Alresford from 75; Hon C Ropley w Tisted *Win* 78-79; Perm to Offic from 79. *High View, Gundleton, Alresford, Hants SA24 9SW* Alresford (0962) 733887

MAY, John Alexander Cyril. b 52. K Coll Lon BD77 Ox Univ PGCE78. Linc Th Coll 79. **d** 80 **p** 81. C Tynemouth Ch Ch *Newc* 80-82; C Tynemouth Ch Ch w H Trin 82-85; C Tynemouth St Aug 82-85; TV Glendale Gp

85-90; V Wotton-under-Edge w Ozleworth and N Nibley *Glouc* from 90. *The Vicarage, Culverhay, Wotton-under-Edge, Glos GL12 7LS* Dursley (0453) 842175

MAY, Norman Gowen. b 20. AKC48. **d** 49 **p** 50. R Balcombe *Chich* 68-78; P-in-c Selham 78-81; P-in-c Lodsworth 78-81; P-in-c Lurgashall 78-81; R Lurgashall, Lodsworth and Selham 81-88; rtd 88. *26 Bourne Way, Midhurst, W Sussex GU29 9HZ* Midhurst (073081) 5710

MAY, Peter Dudfield. b 12. St Jo Coll Cam BA34 LLB35 LLM. Ripon Hall Ox 38. **d** 39 **p** 40. R Stoke Abbott *Sarum* 53-82; V Netherbury 54-82; rtd 82. *The Parsonage Farmhouse, Dinnington, Hinton St George, Somerset TA17 8SU* Ilminster (0460) 53880

MAY, Peter Richard. b 43. MICE70 St Jo Coll Cam BA64 MA68. Trin Coll Bris 77. **d** 79 **p** 80. C Lanc St Thos *Blackb* 79-85; V Darwen St Barn 85-91; Chapl Lyon w Grenoble *Eur* from 91. *38 Chemin de Taffignon, 69110 Ste Foy-les-Lyon, France* France (33) 78 59 67 06

MAY, Richard Grainger (Brother Richard). b 19. St Cath Coll Cam BA40. Linc Th Coll 41. **d** 42 **p** 69. SSF from 43; Chapl Plaistow Maternity Hosp 71-75; Lic to Offic *Chelmsf* 73-75; Lic to Offic *Newc* from 83; rtd 89. *The Friary, Alnmouth, Alnwick, Northd NE66 3NJ* Alnmouth (0665) 830213

MAY, Simon George. b 47. FCA77 Ex Univ BA69 Univ of Wales (Ban) CertEd72. Sarum & Wells Th Coll 86. **d** 88 **p** 89. C Tamworth *Lich* from 88. *The Parsonage, Masefield Drive, Tamworth, Staffs B79 8JB* Tamworth (0827) 64918

MAY, Dr Stephen Charles Arthur. b 52. Mert Coll Ox BA73 Edin Univ BD78 Aber Univ PhD86. Ridley Hall Cam 84. **d** 86 **p** 87. C Sawley *Derby* 86-88; New Zealand from 88; Lect Systematic Th St Jo Coll Auckland from 88. *179B St John's Road, Auckland 5, New Zealand* Auckland (9) 528-4078

MAYBURY, David Kaines. b 32. G&C Coll Cam BA55 MA59. Ridley Hall Cam 55. **d** 57 **p** 58. C Sydenham H Trin *S'wark* 57-60; C Rainham *Chelmsf* 60-63; R Edin St Jas *Edin* 63-75; R Jedburgh 75-84; NSM Duns 84-91; Warden Whitchester Conf Cen 84-91; Chr Guest Ho and Retreat Cen from 91; NSM Hawick *Edin* from 91. *Whitchester Christian Centre, Borthaugh, Hawick, Roxburghshire TD9 7LN* Hawick (0450) 77477

MAYBURY, Canon John Montague. b 30. G&C Coll Cam BA53 MA57. Ridley Hall Cam 53. **d** 55 **p** 56. C Allerton *Liv* 55-59; C Rowner *Portsm* 59-62; V Wroxall 62-67; V Southsea St Simon 67-78; V Crofton from 78; Hon Can Portsm Cathl from 81. *Holy Rood Church, Gosport Road, Stubbington, Fareham, Hants PO14 2AS* Stubbington (0329) 661154

MAYBURY, Paul. b 31. St Deiniol's Hawarden 87. **d** 88 **p** 90. NSM Sutton St Geo *Ches* from 88. *30 Ryles Park Road, Macclesfield, Cheshire SK11 8AH* Macclesfield (0625) 424475

MAYELL, Howard John. b 50. Bris Sch of Min 81. **d** 84 **p** 88. NSM Patchway *Bris* 84-86; NSM Weston-super-Mare Cen Par *B & W* 87-88; C N Stoneham *Win* from 88. *All Saints' Lodge, Pointout Road, Southampton SO1 7DL* Southampton (0703) 766317

MAYER, Alan John. b 46. AKC70. St Aug Coll Cant 70. **d** 71 **p** 72. C Stanningley St Thos *Ripon* 71-74; C St Helier *S'wark* 74-79; TV Wimbledon 79-85; V Reigate St Luke S Park from 85. *St Luke's Vicarage, Church Road, Reigate, Surrey RH2 8HY* Reigate (0737) 46302

MAYER, Graham Keith. b 46. St Cath Coll Ox BA68 Nottm Univ CertEd69. Linc Th Coll 78. **d** 80 **p** 81. C Paignton St Jo *Ex* from 80. *St Boniface House, Belfield Road, Paignton, Devon TQ3 3UZ* Paignton (0803) 556612

MAYER, Mrs Paula Denice. b 45. St Hilda's Coll Ox BA68 Nottm Univ CertEd69. SW Minl Tr Course 84. **d** 88. Hon Par Dn Paignton St Jo *Ex* 88-90; Par Dn from 90. *St Boniface House, Belfield Road, Paignton, Devon TQ3 3UZ* Paignton (0803) 556612

MAYERSON, Paul Strom. b 28. PhD MEd MusBac. Ridley Hall Cam 80. **d** 82 **p** 83. C New Romney w Old Romney and Midley *Cant* 82-85; P-in-c Ospringe 85; P-in-c Eastling 85; R Eastling w Ospringe and Stalisfield w Otterden 85-90; rtd 90. *79 High Street, Wingham, Canterbury, Kent CT3 1DE* Canterbury (0227) 728513

MAYES, Andrew Dennis. b 56. K Coll Lon BD79 AKC79. St Steph Ho Ox 80. **d** 81 **p** 82. C Hendon St Alphage *Lon* 81-84; C Hockley *Chelmsf* 84-87; V Kingstanding St Mark *Birm* from 87. *St Mark's Clergy House, Bandywood Crescent, Birmingham B44 9JX* 021-360 7288

MAYES, Very Rev Gilbert. b 15. TCD BA43 MA61. CITC 44. **d** 44 **p** 45. Dean Lismore *C & O* 61-87; I Lismore w Cappoquin, Kilwatermoy, Dungarvan etc 61-87; Prec Waterford Cathl 84-87; Preb Stagonil St Patr Cathl Dub 85-87; rtd 87. *Woodford, Ballybride Road, Rathmichael, Shankill, Co Dublin, Irish Republic* Dublin (1) 282-4089

MAYES, John Charles Dougan. b 44. Bps' Coll Cheshunt 63. **d** 67 **p** 68. C Portadown St Mark *Arm* 67-74; I Aghadowey w Kilrea *D & R* 74-86; USPG Area Sec from 77; I Clooney w Strathfoyle from 86. *All Saints' Rectory, 20 Limavady Road, Londonderry BT47 1JD* Londonderry (0504) 44306

MAYES, Leonard Harry. b 25. Ely Th Coll 59. **d** 61 **p** 62. V Watford St Mich *St Alb* 69-78; V Liscard St Mary w St Columba *Ches* 78-82; R Moreton and Church Eaton *Lich* 82-90; rtd 90. *11 Covert Close, Great Haywood, Stafford ST18 0RN* Little Haywood (0889) 882994

MAYES, Ven Michael Hugh Gunton. b 41. TCD BA62 Lon Univ BD85. TCD Div Sch Div Test64. **d** 64 **p** 65. C Portadown St Columba *Arm* 64-68; Japan 68-74; Area Sec (Dios Cashel, Cork, Lim and Tuam) USPG from 75; I Cork St Mich Union *C, C & R* 75-86; I Moviddy Union 86-88; Adn Cork, Cloyne and Ross from 86; I Rathcooney Union from 88. *The Rectory, Glanmire, Co Cork, Irish Republic* Cork (21) 821098

MAYES, Stephen Thomas. b 47. St Jo Coll Nottm 67. **d** 71 **p** 72. C Cullompton *Ex* 71-75; C Cheltenham St Mark *Glouc* 76-84; P-in-c Water Orton *Birm* from 84. *The Vicarage, Water Orton, Birmingham B46 1RX* 021-747 2751

✠**MAYFIELD, Rt Rev Christopher John.** b 35. G&C Coll Cam BA57 MA61 Linacre Ho Ox DipTh63 Cranfield Inst of Tech MSc83. Wycliffe Hall Ox 61. **d** 63 **p** 64 **c** 85. C Birm St Martin *Birm* 63-67; Lect 67-71; V Luton St Mary *St Alb* 71-80; RD Luton 74-80; Adn Bedf 80-85; Hon Can Lich Cathl *Lich* from 85; Suff Bp Wolv from 85. *61 Richmond Road, Wolverhampton WV3 9JH* Wolverhampton (0902) 23008

MAYFIELD, Timothy James Edward. b 60. LMH Ox BA82. Trin Coll Bris BA88. **d** 88 **p** 89. C Ovenden *Wakef* from 88. *82 Ashfield Drive, Ovenden, Halifax, W Yorkshire HX3 5PG* Halifax (0422) 353502

MAYHEW, Canon Charles. b 40. K Coll Lon BD64 AKC64. **d** 65 **p** 66. C Nottm St Mary *S'well* 65-69; R Cawston *Nor* 69-74; P-in-c Felthorpe w Haveringland 69-74; R Barnack w Ufford and Bainton *Pet* 74-86; RD Barnack 77-86; Can Pet Cathl from 83; V Oakham, Hambleton, Egleton, Braunston and Brooke from 86. *The Vicarage, Oakham, Leics LE15 6EG* Oakham (0572) 2108

MAYHEW, Peter. b 10. MBE46. Lon Univ BSc31 Ox Univ MLitt79. Ely Th Coll 34. **d** 35 **p** 36. Australia 70-74; Chapl Soc of All SS Sisters of the Poor Ox 74-84; rtd 84; Perm to Offic *Ox* from 84; C Sandford-on-Thames 87. *St John's Home, St Mary's Road, Oxford OX4 1QE* Oxford (0865) 724309

MAYLAND, Mrs Jean Mary. b 36. JP78. LMH Ox BA57 DipTh58 MA61. St Deiniol's Hawarden. **d** 91. NSM York Minster *York* from 91. *3 Minster Court, York YO1 2JJ* York (0904) 625599

MAYLAND, Canon Ralph. b 27. VRD63. Ripon Hall Ox 57. **d** 59 **p** 60. C Lambeth St Andr w St Thos *S'wark* 59-62; Chapl RNR from 61; C-in-c Worksop St Paul CD *S'well* 62-68; V Brightside St Marg *Sheff* 68-72; Ind Chapl 68-81; V Ecclesfield 72-81; Can Res and Treas York Minster *York* from 82. *3 Minster Court, York YO1 2JJ* York (0904) 25599

MAYLOR, David Charles. b 59. Lanc Univ BSc80 Edge Hill Coll of HE PGCE81. St Jo Coll Nottm 89. **d** 91. C Hindley All SS *Liv* from 91. *45 Woodlands Avenue, Wigan, Lancs WN2 4PP* Wigan (0942) 54824

MAYNARD, John William. b 37. Lon Univ BSc58. Ripon Hall Ox 60. **d** 62 **p** 63. C St Laurence in Thanet *Cant* 62-67; C S Ashford Ch Ch 67-70; V Pagham *Chich* from 70. *The Vicarage, Church lane, Pagham, Bognor Regis, W Sussex PO21 4NX* Pagham (0243) 262713

MAYNARD, Raymond. b 30. S'wark Ord Course 75 Ox Ord Course 76. **d** 77 **p** 78. NSM Hedsor and Bourne End *Ox* 77-80; C Newport Pagnell w Lathbury 80-83; P-in-c Lacey Green 83-89; V 89; Perm to Offic *Guildf* from 90. *9 Forestdale, Grayshott, Hindhead, Surrey GU26 6TA* Hindhead (0428) 604565

MAYNARD, Canon Richard Edward Buller. b 42. AKC66. **d** 67 **p** 68. C St Ives *Truro* 67-71; C Falmouth K Chas 71-74; V St Germans 74-81; V Tideford 74-84; RD E Wivelshire 81-85; Hon Can Truro Cathl from 82; V St Germans 84-85; TR Saltash from 85; Chapl St Barn Hosp Saltash from 90. *The Vicarage, 11 Higher Port View, Saltash, Cornwall PL12 4BU* Saltash (0752) 843142

MAYNARD, Robert Walter. b 38. St Alb Minl Tr Scheme. d 85 p 86. NSM Chorleywood St Andr *St Alb* from 85. *Carmel, 4 Haddon Road, Chorleywood, Rickmansworth, Herts WD3 5AN* Chorleywood (0923) 282522

MAYNE, Brian John. b 52. LTCL75 ARICS81 Univ of Wales (Cardiff) BA73. NE Ord Course 82 Coll of Resurr Mirfield 84. d 85 p 86. C Stainton-in-Cleveland *York* 85-89; P-in-c Rounton w Welbury from 89; Chapl HM Young Offender Inst Northallerton from 89. *7 Spring Hill, Northallerton, N Yorkshire DL6 2SQ* Northallerton (0609) 82401

MAYNE, Canon John Andrew Brian. b 34. QUB BA55 Lon Univ BD62. CITC 57. d 57 p 58. C Ballymoney *Conn* 57-60; C Knock *D & D* 60-62; P-in-c Knocknagoney 62-68; P-in-c Belvoir 68-71; I 71-80; Dean Waterford *C & O* 80-84; I Lecale Gp *D & D* from 84; Can Down Cathl from 87. *9 Quoile Road, Downpatrick, Co Down BT30 6SE* Downpatrick (0396) 613101

MAYNE, Very Rev Michael Clement Otway. b 29. CCC Cam BA55 MA58. Cuddesdon Coll 55. d 57 p 58. C Harpenden St Jo *St Alb* 57-59; Bp's Dom Chapl *S'wark* 59-65; V Norton *St Alb* 65-72; Hd of Relig Progr BBC Radio 72-79; Hon Can S'wark Cathl *S'wark* 75-79; V Cam Gt St Mary w St Mich *Ely* 79-86; Dean Westmr from 86. *The Deanery, Dean's Yard, London SW1P 3PA* 071-222 2953

MAYO, Canon Gordon Edwin. b 18. St Jo Coll Dur LTh42 BA45 MA61. Oak Hill Th Coll. d 42 p 43. Warden Lee Abbey Internat Students' Club Kensington 64-71; R Coulsdon St Jo *S'wark* 71-78; Dir of Chr Stewardship 78-85; Hon Can S'wark Cathl 83-85; P-in-c Limpsfield and Titsey *S'wark* 85-89; Perm to Offic *Chich* from 90. *Keepers Cottage, Hammerpond Road, Plummers Plain, Horsham, W Sussex RH13 6PE* Handcross (0444) 400479

MAYO, Inglis John. b 46. FCA. Ripon Coll Cuddesdon 74. d 77 p 78. C Bitterne Park *Win* 77-81; C Christchurch 81-86; P-in-c Sturminster Marshall *Sarum* 86-89; P-in-c Kingston Lacy and Shapwick 86-89; V Sturminster Marshall, Kingston Lacy and Shapwick from 89. *The Vicarage, Newton Road, Sturminster Marshall, Wimborne, Dorset BH21 4BT* Sturminster Marshall (0258) 857255

MAYO, Robert William. b 61. Keble Coll Ox BA83. Cranmer Hall Dur 85. d 87 p 88. C Luton Lewsey St Hugh *St Alb* 87-90; Hd Cam Univ Miss from 90; Hon C Bermondsey St Jas w Ch Ch *S'wark* from 90. *Cambridge University Mission, 43 Old Jamaica Road, London SE16 4TE* 071-237 3788

MAYOH, John Harrison. b 23. Southn Univ BA50. Wycliffe Coll Toronto 50 Wycliffe Hall Ox 52. d 53 p 54. V Bridlington Quay Ch Ch *York* 69-80; R Aythorpe w High and Leaden Roding *Chelmsf* 80-87; rtd 87. *5 Keswick Close, Chester CH2 2PP* Chester (0244) 328789

MAYOH, Margaret Evelyn. b 38. Open Univ BA87. Trin Coll Bris DipHE82. dss 82 d 87. Halliwell St Paul *Man* 82-87; Hon Par Dn 87-91; Hon Par Dn Walmersley from 91. *40 Hillside Avenue, Bromley Cross, Bolton BL7 9NJ* Bolton (0204) 55423

MAYOR, Henry William. b 39. Or Coll Ox BA62 Birm Univ DPS67. Westcott Ho Cam 62. d 64 p 65. C The Quinton *Birm* 64-66; C Dudley St Thos *Worc* 67-71; R Birch St Agnes *Man* 71-83; Community Chapl Aylesbury *Ox* 83-89; Community Chapl Aylesbury w Bierton and Hulcott 89; R Cheetham St Luke and Lower Crumpsall St Thos *Man* from 89. *26 Saltire Gardens, Off Tetlow Lane, Salford M7 0BG* 061-792 3123

MAYOSS, Anthony (Brother Aidan). b 31. Leeds Univ BA55. Coll of Resurr Mirfield 55. d 57 p 58. C Meir *Lich* 57-62; Lic to Offic *Wakef* 62-72 and from 78; CR from 64; S Africa 73-75; Asst Chapl Lon Univ *Lon* 76-78; Bursar CR 84-90. *House of the Resurrection, Mirfield, W Yorkshire WF14 0BN* Mirfield (0924) 494318

MAYOSS-HURD, Mrs Susan Patricia. b 59. Lanc Univ BA81. Cranmer Hall Dur 82. dss 84 d 87. Ribbesford w Bewdley and Dowles *Worc* 84-87; Par Dn 87-88; C W Heath *Birm* from 88. *2 Ivyhouse Road, Birmingham B38 8JD* 021-459 5327

MBALI, Escourt Zolile. b 40. Fort Hare Univ BA68 Ox Univ BA71. St Bede's Coll Umtata 62. d 71 p 72. S Africa 71-74; Botswana 74-81; V Preston on Tees *Dur* 81-83; C Knighton St Mary Magd *Leic* 84-88; P-in-c Church Langton w Tur Langton, Thorpe Langton etc from 88; Community Relns Officer from 88. *The Rectory, Church Langton, Market Harborough, Leics LE16 7SZ* Market Harborough (0858) 84740

MBITI, John Samuel. b 31. d 63 p 64. C St Alb St Mich *St Alb* 63-64; Uganda from 64. *Makerere College, Box 262, Kampala, Uganda, E Africa*

MDUMULLA, Jonas Habel. b 50. Nairobi Univ Hull Univ BTh87 MA89. St Phil Coll Kongwa DipTh74. d 74 p 75. Tanzania 74-82; C Sutton St Jas and Wawne *York* from 82. *16 College Street, Sutton-on-Hull, Hull HU7 4UP* Hull (0482) 797531

MEACHAM, John David. b 24. AKC51 Open Univ MPhil90. Lambeth STh77. d 52 p 53. V Sittingbourne St Mich *Cant* 58-74; V Brenchley *Roch* 74-83; Bp's Chapl and Research Asst 83-86; P-in-c Gt Wishford *Sarum* 83-88; P-in-c S Newton 83-88; Sec C of E Doctrine Commn 84-89; rtd 88. *20 Chiselbury Grove, Salisbury SP2 8EP* Salisbury (0722) 332217

MEAD, Arthur Hugh. b 39. K Coll Cam BA60 MA64 New Coll Ox BLitt66. St Steph Ho Ox 61. d 80 p 80. NSM Hammersmith St Jo *Lon* from 80; Chapl St Paul's Sch Barnes from 82; Dep P-in-O to HM The Queen 85-90; P-in-O from 90. *22 Spencer Road, London W4* 081-994 4112 or 748 9162

MEAD, Colin Harvey. b 26. FCA. S Dios Minl Tr Scheme. d 84 p 85. NSM Talbot Village *Sarum* from 84. *59 Alyth Road, Bournemouth BH3 7HB* Bournemouth (0202) 763647

MEAD, Canon John Harold. b 37. Wells Th Coll 69. d 71 p 72. C Charlton Kings St Mary *Glouc* 71-75; R Stratton w Baunton 75-82; R Bishop's Cleeve from 82; RD Tewkesbury from 88; Hon Can Glouc Cathl from 90. *The Rectory, Bishops Cleeve, Cheltenham, Glos GL52 4NG* Cheltenham (0242) 675103

MEAD, Nicholas Charles. b 50. Newc Univ BEd73 Reading Univ MA76. Ridley Hall Cam 83. d 85. C Bilton *Cov* 85-88; C Whittlesey *Ely* 88-89. *Address temp unknown*

MEAD, Nigel Gerrish. b 31. Tyndale Hall Bris 62. d 64 p 65. C Shirley *Win* 64-67; C Alverdiscott w Huntshaw *Ex* 67-71; C Yarnscombe 67-71; C Beaford and Roborough 67-71; C St Giles in the Wood 67-71; R Shebbear, Buckland Filleigh, Sheepwash etc 71-88; TR Shebbear, Buckland Filleigh, Sheepwash etc from 89; P-in-c Langtree 85-86; RD Torrington from 86. *The Rectory, Shebbear, Beaworthy, Devon EX21 5RU* Shebbear (040928) 424

MEADEN, Philip George William. b 40. Open Univ BA75. Lich Th Coll 64. d 66 p 67. C Aston SS Pet and Paul *Birm* 66-70; V Lozells St Paul 70-76; Asst Chapl HM Pris Brixton 76-77; Chapl HM Pris Lewes 77-84; Aylesbury 84-88; Chapl HM Pris Wandsworth from 88. *HM Prison Wandsworth, PO Box 757, Heathfield Road, London SW18 3HS* 081-874 7292

MEADER, Philip John. b 44. Oak Hill Th Coll 73. d 75 p 76. C E Ham St Paul *Chelmsf* 75-77; CMJ 77-90; TV Lowestoft and Kirkley *Nor* from 90. *51 Beresford Road, Lowestoft, Suffolk NR32 2NQ* Lowestoft (0502) 511521

MEADOWS, John Michael. b 27. St Jo Coll Cam BA50. Ridley Hall Cam 51. d 53 p 54. C Daubhill *Man* 53-55; Overseas Miss Fellowship 56-87; Malaya 57-61; Vietnam 62-75; Refugee Reception Cen Sopley *Win* 79-82; NSM Canford Magna *Sarum* 86-88; C Radipole and Melcombe Regis from 89. *14 Carlton Road North, Weymouth, Dorset DT4 7PX* Weymouth (0305) 786556

MEADOWS, Canon Roy Sidney. b 15. Lon Univ BA52. d 38 p 39. V Kimbolton *Ely* 67-82; V Stow Longa 67-82; RD Leightonstone 74-82; Hon Can Ely Cathl 75-82; rtd 82. *The White Cottage, Kimbolton, Huntingdon, Cambs PE18 0HY* Huntingdon (0480) 861559

MEADOWS, Canon Stanley Percival. b 14. TD61. St D Coll Lamp BA46. d 47 p 48. R Man St Geo w St Barn *Man* 61-72; R Man Miles Platting 72-82; RD Ardwick 77-82; rtd 82; Perm to Offic *Man* from 82. *287 Charlestown Road, Manchester M9 2BB* 061-795 9478

MEADS, William Ivan. b 35. ACIS67 ACMA75 Qu Mary Coll Lon BA56. Linc Th Coll 75. d 77 p 78. C Cheltenham St Luke and St Jo *Glouc* 77-81; Chapl HM Pris Pentonville 81-82; Preston 82-85; Wakef 85-88; P-in-c Wroxton w Balscote and Shenington w Alkerton *Ox* 88-90; R Broughton w N Newington and Shutford etc from 90. *The Rectory, Wroxton, Banbury, Oxon OX15 6QE* Banbury (0295) 730344

MEAGER, Frederick William. b 18. St Mich Coll Llan 46. d 48 p 49. V Watford St Pet *St Alb* 64-83; RD Watford 67-72; rtd 83; Perm to Offic St Alb from 83; Ely from 84. *19 Bramley Avenue, Melbourn, Royston, Herts SG8 6HG* Royston (0763) 261199

MEAKIN, Canon Anthony John. b 28. TD76. Down Coll Cam BA52 MA56. Westcott Ho Cam 52. d 54 p 55. C Gosforth All SS *Newc* 54-60; V Alnwick St Paul 60-71; V Edlingham 62-71; CF (TA) 63-83; R Whickham *Dur*

71-88; RD Gateshead W 78-88; Hon Can Dur Cathl from 83; Bp's Sen Chapl and Exec Officer for Dioc Affairs from 88. *20 Dickens Wynd, Durham DH1 3QY* 091-386 0473

MEAKIN, David John. b 61. Hull Univ BA82 Cam Univ CertEd83. Westcott Ho Cam 86. d 88 p 89. C Upminster *Chelmsf* from 88. *6 Gaynes Park Road, Upminster, Essex RM14 2HH* Upminster (04022) 26004

MEAKIN, Ven John Ernest. b 13. Kelham Th Coll 30. d 36 p 37. Singapore 51-55; Australia from 55; rtd 80. *Staddle Stones, Elder Street, Moonta Mines, S Australia 5557*

MEANLEY, Hubert Edward Sylvester. b 10. Trin Coll Cam BA32. d 34 p 35. R Settrington *York* 68-76; P-in-c Thorpe Bassett 72-76; rtd 76. *12 Stump Cross, Boroughbridge, York YO5 9HU* Boroughbridge (0423) 322571

MEARA, David Gwynne. b 47. Or Coll Ox BA70 MA73. Lambeth STh76 Cuddesdon Coll 71. d 73 p 74. C Whitley Ch Ch *Ox* 73-77; Chapl Reading Univ 77-82; V Basildon 82-87; P-in-c Aldworth and Ashampstead 85-87; V Basildon w Aldworth and Ashampstead from 87; RD Bradfield from 90. *The Vicarage, Upper Basildon, Reading RG8 8LS* Upper Basildon (0491) 671223

MEARDON, Dr Brian Henry. b 44. Reading Univ BSc66 PhD71. Oak Hill Th Coll DipHE79 MPhil84. d 79 p 80. C Reading St Jo *Ox* 79-82; V Warfield from 82. *The Vicarage, Church Lane, Warfield, Bracknell, Berks RG12 6EE* Winkfield Row (0344) 882228

MEARNS, Christopher Lee. b 30. Worc Coll Ox BA54 MA58. Ripon Hall Ox BTh56. d 57 p 58. C Greenhill St Jo *Lon* 57-60; Canada 60-62; Lect Ripon Coll of Educn 63-75; Sen Lect Coll of Ripon and York St Jo 75-85; USA 87 and 89; Tutor Ridley Hall Cam 88; Seychelles 88 and 89-90. *14 Primrose Drive, Ripon, N Yorkshire HG4 1EY* Ripon (0765) 2695

✠**MEARS, Rt Rev John Cledan.** b 22. Univ of Wales (Abth) BA43 Univ of Wales MA48. Wycliffe Hall Ox 43. d 47 p 48 c 82. C Mostyn *St As* 47-49; C Rhosllanerchrugog 49-56; V Cwm 56-59; Lic to Offic *Llan* 59-73; Chapl St Mich Coll Llan 59-67; Lect Th Univ of Wales (Cardiff) 59-73; Sub-Warden St Mich Coll Llan 67-73; V Gabalfa *Llan* 73-82; Hon Can Llan Cathl 81-82; Bp Ban from 82. *Ty'r Esgob, Bangor, Gwynedd LL57 2SS* Bangor (0248) 362895

MEARS, Phillip David. b 40. Dur Univ BA62 DipTh63. d 65 p 66. C Sandylands *Blackb* 65-68; C Chorley St Geo 68-71; V Leyland St Ambrose 71-81; Perm to Offic *Ches* from 81; Chapl Warrington Distr Gen Hosp from 81. *20 Kingsley Drive, Appleton, Warrington WA4 5AE* Warrington (0925) 64082 or 35911

MEASEY, George. b 08. Roch Th Coll 67. d 68 p 69. C Rowner *Portsm* 68-72; C Worthing St Geo *Chich* 72-78; rtd 78; Perm to Offic *Chich* from 78. *45 Orchard Avenue, Worthing, W Sussex BN14 7PY* Worthing (0903) 205683

MEATH AND KILDARE, Bishop of. See EMPEY, Most Rev Walton Newcome Francis

MEATH, Archdeacon of. See CORRIGAN, Ven Thomas George

MEATS, Alan John. b 41. Univ of Wales (Cardiff) BA62 DipEd63 Lon Univ BD70. St Mich Coll Llan 68. d 70 p 71. C Pontypridd St Cath *Llan* 70-73; TV Ystradyfodwg 73-75; Dioc Insp of Schs 73-75 and 83-89; V Llandilo Talybont *S & B* 75-83; RD Llwchwr 81-83; V Aberdare St Fagan *Llan* 83-89; V Felinfoel *St D* from 89; Asst Dioc Dir of Educn from 89. *The Vicarage, Felinfoel, Llanelli, Dyfed SA14 8BS* Llanelli (0554) 773559

MEDCALF, James Gordon. b 31. Solicitor 63. S'wark Ord Course 87. d 90 p 91. NSM Shortlands *Roch* from 90. *14B Bromley Grove, Bromley BR2 0LN* 081-464 2211

MEDCALF, John Edward. b 19. Oak Hill Th Coll 47. d 50 p 51. V Wednesfield Heath *Lich* 61-85; rtd 85; Perm to Offic *Heref* from 86. *Clee View, Bolstone, Hereford HR2 6NE* Hereford (0432) 840339

MEDCALF, William Henry. b 15. TCD BA45 MA49. CITC 46. d 46 p 47. CMJ 50-80; rtd 80. *185 Dibdin House, London W9 1QQ* 071-328 3133

MEDFORTH, Allan Hargreaves. b 27. Qu Coll Cam BA48 MA52. Westcott Ho Cam 50. d 51 p 52. C Hexham *Newc* 51-55; PV S'well Minster *S'well* 55-59; V Farnsfield 59-72; RD S'well 66-72; V St Alb St Pet *St Alb* from 72; RD St Alb 74-84. *The Vicarage, 23 Hall Place Gardens, St Albans, Herts AL1 3SB* St Albans (0727) 51464

MEDHURST, Prof Kenneth Noel. b 38. Edin Univ MA61 Man Univ MA62 PhD69. d 91. NSM Shipley St Paul and Frizinghall *Bradf* from 91. *c/o The Rectory, 47 Kirkgate, Shipley, W Yorkshire BD18 3EH* Bradford (0274) 583652

MEDHURST, Leslie John. TCD DipTh85 BTh90 Open Univ BA91. d 85 p 86. C Seapatrick *D & D* 85-90; I Belf St Mark *Conn* from 90. *St Mark's Rectory, 119 Ligoniel Road, Belfast BT14 8DN* Belfast (0232) 713151

MEDLEY, Philip Roger. b 46. Birm Univ CertEd71. SW Minl Tr Course. d 85 p 86. NSM Ottery St Mary, Alfington and W Hill *Ex* 85-86; C Linkinhorne *Truro* 86-89; V from 89. *The Vicarage, Linkinhorne, Callington, Cornwall PL17 7LY* Liskeard (0579) 62560

MEE, Colin Henry. b 36. Reading Univ BSc58. Bris Sch of Min 83. d 85 p 86. NSM Stanton St Quintin, Hullavington, Grittleton etc *Bris* 85-87; C Swindon Ch Ch 88-90; TV Washfield, Stoodleigh, Withleigh etc *Ex* from 90. *The Vicarage, Washfield, Tiverton, Devon EX16 9QZ* Tiverton (0884) 252357

MEED, Henry Robert. b 15. Ripon Hall Ox 50. d 51 p 52. P-in-c Thornborough *Ox* 69-75; R Wingrave w Rowsham, Aston Abbotts and Cublington 75-81; rtd 81; Perm to Offic *St E* from 81. *Blyth Cottage, Church Road, Felsham, Bury St Edmunds, Suffolk IP30 0PJ* Rattlesden (0449) 737818

MEEHAN, Cyril Frederick. b 52. St Jo Coll Nottm BTh80. d 80 p 81. C Keresley and Coundon *Cov* 80-83; P-in-c Linton and Castle Gresley *Derby* 83-90; P-in-c Alvaston from 90. *The Vicarage, Church Street, Alvaston, Derby DE2 0PR* Derby (0332) 571143

MEEK, Anthony William. b 45. ACIB. Ox NSM Course 80. d 83 p 84. NSM Gt Chesham *Ox* from 83. *Elmcroft, Ley Hill, Chesham, Bucks HP5 3QR* Chesham (0494) 772816

MEEK, George Edward. b 08. Leeds Univ BA30. Coll of Resurr Mirfield 26. d 32 p 33. P-in-c Newton Longville *Ox* 68-75; P-in-c Whaddon w Tattenhoe 68-75; R Newton Longville w Stoke Hammond, Whaddon etc 75-77; rtd 77; Perm to Offic *Chich* from 77. *28 Titian Road, Hove, E Sussex BN3 5QS* Brighton (0273) 773065

MEEK, John Conway. b 33. Lon Univ BSc55 AKC56 St Cath Soc Ox BA59 MA63. Wycliffe Hall Ox 57. d 59 p 60. C Streatham Immanuel w St Anselm *S'wark* 59-62; C Bilston St Leon *Lich* 63-65; Chapl Kent and Cant Hosp 65-73; V Cant St Mary Bredin *Cant* 65-82; RD Cant 76-82; Hon Can Cant Cathl 79-82; R Bridlington Priory *York* from 82; RD Bridlington from 83. *The Rectory, Bridlington, N Humberside YO16 5JX* Bridlington (0262) 672221

MEERE, Alison Elizabeth. b 44. SRN65 HVCert67. Ripon Coll Cuddesdon 85. d 87. Par Dn Hengrove *Bris* 87-88; Par Dn Winterbourne 88-91; Par Dn Southmead from 91. *79 Ullswater Road, Southmead, Bristol BS10 6DP* Bristol (0272) 593105

MEERING, Laurence Piers Ralph. b 48. Man Univ BSc70. Trin Coll Bris 79. d 81 p 82. C Downend *Bris* 81-84; C Crofton *Portsm* 84-87; V Witheridge, Thelbridge, Creacombe, Meshaw etc *Ex* from 87. *The Vicarage, Witheridge, Tiverton, Devon EX16 8AE* Tiverton (0884) 860768

MEGAHEY, Alan John. b 44. Selw Coll Cam BA65 MA69 QUB PhD69. Westcott Ho Cam 69. d 70 p 71. Asst Chapl Wrekin Coll Shropshire 70-72; Ho Master Cranleigh Sch Surrey 72-83; Zimbabwe from 83. *Peterhouse, Post Bag 3741, Marondera, Zimbabwe* Marondera (79) 4951

✠**MEHAFFEY, Rt Rev James.** b 31. TCD BA52 MA56 BD56 QUB PhD75. d 54 p 55 c 80. C Ballymacarrett St Patr *D & D* 54-56; C Deptford St Jo *S'wark* 56-58; C Down Cathl *D & D* 58-60; P-in-c Ballymacarrett St Chris 60-62; I Kilkeel 62-66; I Cregagh 66-80; Bp D & R from 80. *The See House, 112 Culmore Road, Londonderry BT48 8JF* Londonderry (0504) 351206

MEIKLE, Canon David Skene. b 39. St Cath Coll Cam BA60 MA89. Westcott Ho Cam. d 63 p 64. C Hawick *Edin* 63-67; C Edin SS Phil and Jas 67-72; C Banbury *Ox* 72-73; TV 74-78; R Ipswich St Matt *St E* 78-91; Hon Can St E Cathl from 90; TR Mildenhall from 91. *The Vicarage, Barton Mills, Bury St Edmunds IP28 6AP* Mildenhall (0638) 716044

MEIN, James Adlington. b 38. Nottm Univ BA60. Westcott Ho Cam 61. d 62 p 63. C Edin St Columba *Edin* 63-67; Bp's Dom Chapl 65-67; Malawi 67-72; R Grangemouth *Edin* 72-82; P-in-c Bo'ness 76-82; TV Livingston LEP 82-90; R Edin Ch Ch from 90; Can St Mary's Cathl from 90. *4 Morningside Road, Edinburgh EH10 4DD* 031-229 6556

MEIRION-JONES, Huw Geraint. b 39. R Agric Coll Cirencester NDA61 MRAC61 K Coll Lon AKC69 BD71 MA84. St Aug Coll Cant 69. d 70 p 71. C Harlescott *Lich* 70-73; C Worplesdon *Guildf* 73-77; V Ash Vale 77-85; Dioc Press Officer from 85; TR Westborough from 85. *Westborough Rectory,*

Beckingham Road, Guildford, Surrey GU2 6BU
Guildford (0483) 504228

MEISSNER, Canon Charles Ludwig Birbeck Hill. b 26. TCD 60. **d** 62 **p** 63. C Monaghan *Clogh* 62-64; C Kildallon *K, E & A* 64-65; I 65-71; I Kinawley w H Trin 71-85; I Mohill w Farnaught, Aughavas, Outeragh etc from 85; Preb Elphin Cathl from 87. *St Mary's Rectory, Mohill, Co Leitrim, Irish Republic* Carrick-on-Shannon (78) 31012

MELANIPHY, Miss Angela Ellen. b 55. SRN79. Cranmer Hall Dur 87. **d** 90. C Leytonstone St Jo *Chelmsf* from 90. *86 Mornington Road, London E11 3DX* 081-539 3935

MELBOURNE, Miss Thelma. b 08. Dalton Ho Bris 68. **dss** 77 **d** 87. Earlham St Anne *Nor* 77-87; Perm to Offic from 87. *333 Earlham Road, Norwich NR2 3RQ* Norwich (0603) 53008

MELHUISH, Douglas. b 12. St Pet Hall Ox BA34 MA38. Wycliffe Hall Ox 39. **d** 39 **p** 40. Asst Master Haberdashers' Aske's Sch Hampstead 37-40; St Jo Sch Leatherhead and Lic to Offic *Guildf* 40-42; Asst Master Bedford Sch 42-46; Chapl 43-46; Lic to Offic *St Alb* 42-46; Lect & Tutor Trin Coll Carmarthen 46-48; CMS 48-68; Kenya 48-68; Perm to Offic Sarum from 69; Win 70-74; P-in-c St Lawrence *Portsm* 74-79; Perm to Offic *B & W* from 85. *27 Sturford Lane, Corsley, Warminster, Wilts BA12 7QR* Chapmanslade (037388) 396

MELINSKY, Canon Michael Arthur Hugh. b 24. Ch Coll Cam BA47 MA49. Ripon Hall Ox 57. **d** 57 **p** 59. Hon Can *Nor* Cathl and Can Missr *Nor* 68-73; Chief Sec ACCM 73-78; Prin N Ord Course 78-88; rtd 88; Perm to Offic *Nor* from 88. *15 Parson's Mead, Norwich NR4 6PG* Norwich (0603) 55042

MELLING, John Cooper. b 44. ALCD73. St Jo Coll Nottm 68. **d** 72 **p** 73. C Enfield St Andr *Lon* 72-76; C Didsbury St Jas and Em *Man* 76-79; R Gt Lever 79-84; V Seamer w E Ayton *York* from 84. *The Vicarage, 57A Main Street, Seamer, Scarborough, N Yorkshire YO12 4QD* Scarborough (0723) 863102

MELLING, Canon Leonard Richard. b 13. St Aid Birkenhead 38. **d** 41 **p** 42. V Osbaldwick w Murton *York* 67-78; RD Bulmer 72-78; Malaysia 78-81; Dean Kuching 78-81; rtd 81. *12 Heslington Road, York YO1 5AT* York (0904) 627593

MELLISH, John. b 26. Cranmer Hall Dur 67. **d** 69 **p** 70. C Ulverston St Mary w H Trin *Carl* 69-72; V Bromfield 72-73; V Bromfield w Waverton 73-79; P-in-c Allonby w W Newton 77-79; V Shap w Swindale 79-86; RD Appleby 82-86; V Bassenthwaite, Isel and Setmurthy 86-90; rtd 90. *Wyndham, 3 Old Road, Longtown, Cumbria CA6 5TH* Longtown (0228) 791441

MELLISS, Laurence John Albert. b 21. DSM45 RD69. AKC52. **d** 53 **p** 54. Chapl RNR 59-76; V Littlehampton St Mary *Chich* 64-76; RD Arundel 75-76; V Findon 76-81; R Catsfield and Crowhurst 81-86; rtd 86; Perm to Offic *Cant* from 86; Dioc Widows Officer from 89. *Chanctonbury, Church Road, New Romney, Kent TN28 8EX* New Romney (0679) 63605

MELLOR, David John. b 49. Nottm Univ BTh72. Kelham Th Coll 68. **d** 72 **p** 73. C Horninglow *Lich* 72-74; C Tividale 74-77; C Stafford St Mary and St Chad 77-79; TV Stafford 79-82; Chapl Stafford Gen Infirmary 77-82; V Burslem St Werburgh from 82; Chapl Haywood and Stanfield Hosps Stoke-on-Trent from 82. *St Werburgh's Presbytery, Haywood Road, Stoke-on-Trent ST6 7AH* Stoke-on-Trent (0782) 837582

MELLOR, Miss Dorothy Lilian. b 38. Birm Univ BA61. N Ord Course 86. **d** 89. NSM Stockton Heath *Ches* from 89. *100 Bridge Lane, Appleton, Warrington, Cheshire WA4 3AL* Warrington (0925) 67683

MELLOR, Frederick Charles Walter. b 24. Oak Hill NSM Course 80. **d** 83 **p** 84. NSM Loughton St Jo *Chelmsf* from 83; Chapl Asst Whipps Cross Hosp *Lon* from 87. *4 Scotland Road, Buckhurst Hill, Essex IG9 5NR* 081-504 6203

MELLOR, Canon Kenneth Paul. b 49. Southn Univ BA71 Leeds Univ MA72. Cuddesdon Coll 72. **d** 73 **p** 74. C Cottingham *York* 73-76; C Ascot Heath *Ox* 76-80; V Tilehurst St Mary 80-85; V Menheniot *Truro* from 85; RD W Wivelshire from 88; Hon Can Truro Cathl from 90. *The Vicarage, Menheniot, Liskeard, Cornwall PL14 3SU* Liskeard (0579) 42195

MELLOR, Robert Frederick. b 14. ACIS37 Dur Univ LTh42. Tyndale Hall Bris 38. **d** 41 **p** 42. V Tranmere St Cath *Ches* 65-79; rtd 79; Perm to Offic *Ches* from 80. *5 Fleet Croft Road, Arrowe Park, Wirral, Merseyside L49 5LY* 051-678 7717

MELLOR, Steven Richard. b 55. Linc Th Coll. **d** 82 **p** 83. C Wordsley *Lich* 82-85; C Tividale 85-89; V Ocker Hill

from 89. *St Mark's Vicarage, Ocker Hill Road, Tipton, W Midlands DY4 0XE* 021-556 0678

MELLORS, Derek George. b 38. Bris Univ CertEd60 Lon Univ BSc71 Nottm Univ DipEd74 Liv Univ MEd83. N Ord Course 81. **d** 84 **p** 85. NSM Eccleston Ch Ch *Liv* from 84. *20 Millbrook Lane, Eccleston, St Helens, Merseyside WA10 4QU* St Helens (0744) 28424

MELLORS, Canon James. b 32. Kelham Th Coll 52. **d** 56 **p** 57. C Horbury *Wakef* 56-61; V Scholes 61-72; V Mirfield 72-88; Hon Can Wakef Cathl from 83; V Leyburn w Bellerby *Ripon* from 88. *The Vicarage, Bellerby Road, Leyburn, N Yorkshire DL8 5JF* Wensleydale (0969) 22251

MELLOWS, Canon Alan Frank. b 23. Qu Coll Cam BA45 MA49. Tyndale Hall Bris 47. **d** 49 **p** 50. R Mileham *Nor* 62-74; R Beeston next Mileham 66-74; P-in-c Stanfield 62-74, P-in-c Gt w Lt Dunham 70-73; R Ashill 74-79; P-in-c Saham Toney 78-79; R Ashill w Saham Toney 79-88; Hon Can Nor Cathl 82-88; rtd 88; Perm to Offic *Nor* from 88. *8 Smugglers Close, Hunstanton, Norfolk PE36 6JU* Hunstanton (0485) 534271

MELLUISH, Mark Peter. b 59. BA. Oak Hill Th Coll. **d** 89 **p** 90. C Ashtead *Guildf* from 89. *17 Loraine Gardens, Ashtead, Surrey KT21 1PD* Ashtead (0372) 273819

MELLY, Aleck Emerson. b 24. Oak Hill Th Coll 50. **d** 53 **p** 54. R Kemberton w Sutton Maddock *Lich* 68-80; P-in-c Stockton 74-80; R Kemberton, Sutton Maddock and Stockton 81-89; rtd 89. *47 Greenfields Road, Bridgnorth, Shropshire WV16 4JG* Bridgnorth (0746) 762711

MELROSE, Kenneth Mark Cecil. b 15. Ex Coll Ox BA37 DipTh38 MA41. Ripon Hall Ox 37. **d** 39 **p** 40. V Portswood St Denys *Win* 63-71; V Bovey Tracey SS Pet and Paul *Ex* 71-85; rtd 85; Perm to Offic *Cant* from 85. *88 Wells Way, Faversham, Kent ME13 7QU* Faversham (0795) 536115

MELROSE, Michael James Gervase. b 47. St Chad's Coll Dur BA69 DipTh70. **d** 71 **p** 72. C Chelmsf All SS *Chelmsf* 71-74; C Pimlico St Pet w Westmr Ch Ch *Lon* 74-80; R Man Victoria Park *Man* from 80; P-in-c Cheetwood St Alb from 85. *The Rectory, Daisy Bank Road, Manchester M14 5QH* 061-224 4152

MELTON, Anne. b 44. N Riding Coll of Educn CertEd65. St Jo Coll Dur 80. **dss** 83 **d** 87. Newton Aycliffe *Dur* 83-87; Par Dn 87-88; Par Dn Shildon w Eldon from 88; Asst Dir of Ords from 88. *4 Eldon Bank, Eldon, Bishop Auckland, Co Durham DL14 8DX* Bishop Auckland (0388) 772397

MELVILLE, Dominic. b 63. Sussex Univ BA84 Southn Univ BTh90. Sarum & Wells Th Coll 87. **d** 90 **p** 91. C Willenhall H Trin *Lich* from 90. *13 Wesley Road, Willenhall, Wolverhampton WV12 5QT* Bloxwich (0922) 405242

MELVILLE, Malcolm Charles Crompton. b 13. Ancient Soc of Coll Youths 37 Birm Univ BSc36. Lich Th Coll 37. **d** 39 **p** 40. C Heacham *Nor* 65-67; Perm to Offic *St Alb* from 67; rtd 78. *45 Beverley Crescent, Bedford MK40 4BX* Bedford (0234) 266060

MELVIN, Gordon Thomas. b 55. BA86. Sarum & Wells Th Coll 86. **d** 88 **p** 89. C Linc St Faith and St Martin w St Pet *Linc* 88-91; TV Horsham *Chich* from 91. *Trinity House, Blunts Way, Horsham, W Sussex RH12 2BL* Horsham (0403) 55401

MEMBERY, Donald Percy. b 20. K Coll Lon BSc50 DipEd51 AKC51. Ox NSM Course. **d** 79 **p** 80. NSM Aston Rowant w Crowell *Ox* 79-81; P-in-c Swyncombe 81-85; R Swyncombe w Britwell Salome 85-88; rtd 88. *11 Carr Manor Gardens, Leeds LS17 5DQ* Leeds (0532) 691578

MENDEL, Thomas Oliver. b 57. Down Coll Cam BA79 MA82. Cranmer Hall Dur 79. **d** 81 **p** 82. Lic to Offic *Ely* 81-86; Chapl Down Coll Cam 81-86; V Minsterley *Heref* from 86. *The Vicarage, Minsterley, Shrewsbury SY5 0AA* Shrewsbury (0743) 791213

MENEY, Brian James. b 42. Glas Univ MA63. Edin Th Coll 63. **d** 65 **p** 66. C Dundee St Paul *Bre* 65-69; Lic to Offic *Edin* 69-71; C Edin H Cross 71-73; Asst Sec Rep Ch Coun 73-81; P-in-c Edin St Barn 73-81; Chapl Bede Ho Staplehurst 81-82; P-in-c Plaistow SS Phil and Jas w St Andr *Chelmsf* 82-83; TR Plaistow 83-90; V Leeds Gipton Epiphany *Ripon* from 90. *The Vicarage, 154 Amberton Road, Leeds LS9 6SP* Leeds (0532) 491845

✠MENIN, Rt Rev Malcolm James. b 32. Univ Coll Ox BA55 MA59. Cuddesdon Coll 55. **d** 57 **p** 58 **c** 86. C Southsea H Spirit *Portsm* 57-59; C Fareham SS Pet and Paul 59-62; V Nor St Jas w Pockthorpe *Nor* 62-72; P-in-c Nor St Martin 62-74; P-in-c Nor St Mary Magd 68-72; V Nor St Mary Magd w St Jas 72-86; RD Nor E 81-86;

485

Hon Can Nor Cathl from 82; Suff Bp Knaresborough *Ripon* from 86. *16 Shaftesbury Avenue, Leeds LS8 1DT* Leeds (0532) 664800

MENNISS, Andrew Philip. b 49. Univ of Wales (Swansea) BSc73. Sarum & Wells Th Coll 83. **d** 85 **p** 86. C Horsell *Guildf* 85-89; V Bembridge *Portsm* from 89. *The Vicarage, Bembridge, Isle of Wight PO35 5NA*   Isle of Wight (0983) 872175

MENON, Nicholas Anthony Thotekat. b 39. Mert Coll Ox BA61 MA65 DipTh62. St Steph Ho Ox 61. **d** 63 **p** 64. C Paddington Ch Ch *Lon* 63-66; Hon C 66-70; V Thorpe *Guildf* 70-76; V Ox SS Phil and Jas w St Marg *Ox* 76-79; Chapl Surrey Univ *Guildf* 79-81; Chapl and Ho Master Cranleigh Sch Surrey from 82. *Loveday House, Cranleigh School, Cranleigh, Surrey GU6 8PZ*   Cranleigh (0483) 272510

MENTERN, Richard John. b 19. ALCD48. **d** 48 **p** 49. V Broadheath *Ches* 57-74; P-in-c Bradf Abbas w Clifton Maybank *Sarum* 74-84; rtd 84. *Cornhill House, 48 Acreman Street, Sherborne, Dorset DT9 3PQ* Sherborne (0935) 816021

MENTZEL, Kevin David. b 60. Reading Univ BSc82 Down Coll Cam BA87 MA91. Ridley Hall Cam 85. **d** 88 **p** 89. C Ditton *Roch* from 88. *Old School Cottage, 79 New Road, Ditton, Maidstone, Kent ME20 6AE* West Malling (0732) 847669

MEPHAM, Kevin Aubrey. b 55. Sarum & Wells Th Coll 85. **d** 88 **p** 89. NSM Sidley *Chich* 88-90; C Hollington St Leon from 90. *158 Old Church Road, St Leonards-on-Sea, E Sussex TN38 9HD*   Hastings (0424) 852496

MEPHAM, Stephen Richard. b 64. K Coll Lon BD85 AKC85. Linc Th Coll 87. **d** 89 **p** 90. C Newark-upon-Trent *S'well* from 89. *12 Sawyers Close, Newark, Notts NG24 2HF*   Newark (0636) 701691

MEPSTED, Leonard Charles. b 34. Leeds Univ BA61. Coll of Resurr Mirfield 61. **d** 63 **p** 64. C Goldthorpe *Sheff* 63-65; C S Shields St Hilda w St Thos *Dur* 65-69; C Woodston *Ely* 69-71; V Friday Bridge 71-72; C Moss Side Ch Ch *Man* 72-74; P-in-c Farnworth All SS 75-76; C Lawton Moor 76-78; P-in-c Falinge 78-87; R Eastchurch w Leysdown and Harty *Cant* from 87. *The Rectory, Warden Road, Eastchurch, Sheerness, Kent ME12 4EJ*   Eastchurch (0795) 880205

✠**MERCER, Rt Rev Eric Arthur John.** b 17. Kelham Th Coll. **d** 47 **p** 48 **c** 65. C Coppenhall *Ches* 47-51; C-in-c Heald Green St Cath CD 51-53; R Stockport St Thos 53-59; R Ches St Bridget w St Martin 59-65; Dioc Missr 59-65; Hon Can Ches Cathl 64-65; Suff Bp Birkenhead 65-73; Bp Ex 73-85; rtd 85; P-in-c E Knoyle, Hindon w Chicklade and Pertwood *Sarum* 85-86; P-in-c Hindon w Chicklade and Pertwood 86-88. *Frickers House, Cow Drove, Chilmark, Salisbury SP3 5AJ*   Teffont (072276) 400

MERCER, Canon John James Glendinning. b 20. TCD BA49 MA55. **d** 50 **p** 51. I Ballyholme *D & D* 55-90; Can Belf Cathl 76-88; Preb Wicklow St Patr Cathl Dub 88-90; rtd 90. *6 Hillfoot, Groomsport, Bangor, Co Down BT19 2JJ*   Bangor (0247) 472979

✠**MERCER, Rt Rev Robert William Stanley.** b 35. St Paul's Grahamstown LTh59. **d** 59 **p** 60 **c** 77. S Rhodesia 59-63; Rhodesia 70-80; Zimbabwe 80-87; CR from 65; Lic to Offic *Wakef* 64-66; Perm to Offic *Llan* 66-68; S Africa 68-70; Bp Matabeleland 77-87; Canada from 87. *225 First Avenue, Ottawa, Ontario, Canada, K1S 2G5*

MERCER, Timothy James. b 54. Fitzw Coll Cam BA76 MA80. Westcott Ho Cam 78. **d** 81 **p** 82. C Bromley SS Pet and Paul *Roch* 81-85; R Swanscombe from 85. *The Rectory, Swanscombe, Kent DA10 0JZ*   Greenhithe (0322) 843160

MERCERON, Daniel John. b 58. Lon Univ BA81. Westcott Ho Cam 88. **d** 90 **p** 91. C Clevedon St Jo *B & W* from 90. *53 Woodington Road, Clevedon, Avon BS21 5LB* Clevedon (0272) 879832

MERCHANT, David Clifford. b 17. Univ of Wales BA37 Birm Univ MA70. St Mich Coll Llan 45. **d** 46 **p** 47. Chapl Westhill Coll of HE Birm 65-82; Hon C Northfield *Birm* from 74; rtd 82. *28 Weoley Park Road, Birmingham B29 6QU*   021-472 0910 or 472 7245

MERCHANT, Canon William Moelwyn. b 13. FRSL Univ of Wales BA33 MA50 DLitt60 Wittenberg Univ Ohio Hon DHL70. **d** 40 **p** 41. Chan Sarum Cathl *Sarum* 67-70; Can and Preb Sarum Cathl 67-73; V Llanddewi Brefi w Llanbadarn Odwyn *St D* 74-78; rtd 78. *32 Willes Road, Leamington Spa, Warks CV31 1BN*   Leamington Spa (0926) 314253

MERCIER, David Cuthbert. b 10. St Pet Hall Ox BA32 MA36. Wycliffe Hall Ox 35. **d** 37 **p** 38. C Edge Hill St Mary *Liv* 37-41; C Gt Sankey 41-44; C Parr 44-49; V Langford Budville w Runnington *B & W* 49-54;

R Phillack w Gwithian *Truro* 55-59; New Zealand from 59. *44 Haumoana Road, Haumoana, Hawkes Bay, New Zealand*   Hawkes Bay (70) 875-0147

MERCURIO, Frank James. b 46. Webster Univ (USA) BA73 MA75. St Alb Minl Tr Scheme 87. **d** 89 **p** 90. C Cheshunt *St Alb* from 89. *156 Churchgate, Cheshunt, Waltham Cross, Herts EN8 9DX*   Waltham Cross (0992) 20659

MEREDITH, Claison Charles Evans. b 26. Univ of Wales (Lamp) BA51. **d** 54 **p** 55. C Bromyard *Heref* 54-56; C Weston-super-Mare St Paul *B & W* 56-59; R Norton sub Hamdon 59-68; P-in-c Chiselborough w W Chinnock 59-68; V Weston Zoyland 69-80; V Puriton and Pawlett from 80. *The Vicarage, 1 The Rye, Puriton, Bridgwater, Somerset TA7 8BZ*   Puriton (0278) 683500

MEREDITH, James Noel Michael Creed. b 17. Keble Coll Ox BA40 MA43. Westcott Ho Cam 39. **d** 40 **p** 42. R Stoke *Cov* 61-71; RD Cov E 69-71; V Hessle *York* 71-78; R Milton Abbas, Hilton w Cheselbourne etc *Sarum* 78-80; TV Llandudno *Ban* 80-84; rtd 82. *11 Pascoe Close, Poole, Dorset BH14 0NT*   Poole (0202) 737108

MEREDITH, Robert. b 21. Bps' Coll Cheshunt 56. **d** 58 **p** 59. V Kimpton *St Alb* 67-75; RD Wheathampstead 72-76; R Kimpton w Ayot St Lawrence 75-76; R Hunsdon 76-80; R Widford 76-80; R Hunsdon w Widford and Wareside 80-84; P-in-c Braughing, Lt Hadham, Albury, Furneux Pelham etc 84-88; R Braughing w Furneux Pelham and Stocking Pelham 88-90; rtd 90; Perm to Offic *St Alb* from 90. *19 Cowper Crescent, Hertford SG14 3DZ*   Hertford (0992) 558847

MEREDITH, Roland James. b 32. Trin Coll Cam BA55 MA59. Cuddesdon Coll 55. **d** 57 **p** 58. C Bishopwearmouth St Mich *Dur* 57-59; Dioc Chapl *Birm* 59-60; C Kirkby *Liv* 60-63; V Hitchin St Mary *St Alb* 63-72; V Preston St Jo *Blackb* 72-76; TR 76-79; RD Preston 72-79; Hon Can Blackb Cathl 77-79; TR Witney *Ox* from 79; P-in-c Hailey w Crawley 79-82; RD Witney from 89. *The Rectory, 13 Station Lane, Witney, Oxon OX8 6BH*   Witney (0993) 2517

MEREDITH, Ronald Duncan d'Esterre. b 09. K Coll Lon BD32 AKC32. **d** 32 **p** 33. V Seasalter *Cant* 68-76; rtd 76; Perm to Offic *Cant* from 76. *64 Beacon Road, Broadstairs, Kent*   Thanet (0843) 69883

MEREDITH-JONES, Richard. b 26. JP79. K Coll Lon 50. **d** 54 **p** 55. Ind Chapl *Wakef* 66-70; Chapl Glenside Hosp Bris from 70; CF (TAVR) from 78; rtd 91. *18 Wetlands Lane, Portishead, Bristol BS16 1DD*

MERIONETH, Archdeacon of. See MORGAN, Ven Dr Barry Cennydd

MERIVALE, Charles Christian Robert. b 44. Cranmer Hall Dur 76. **d** 78 **p** 79. C Highbury Ch Ch *Lon* 78; C Highbury Ch Ch w St Jo 79-81; P-in-c Hawes *Ripon* 81-82; P-in-c Hardrow and St Jo w Lunds 81-82; V Hawes and Hardraw 82-84; Chapl R Cornwall Hosp Truro from 85; Lic to Offic *Truro* from 85. *1 Burley Close, Truro, Cornwall TR1 2EP*   Truro (0872) 222074 or 74242

MERRETT, Jonathan Charles. b 55. Univ of Wales (Ban) BMus77 MMus78. Ripon Coll Cuddesdon 78. **d** 81 **p** 82. C Kenilworth St Nic *Cov* 81-84; C Grandborough w Willoughby and Flecknoe 84-87; Asst Dioc Educn Officer from 87. *2 Devon House, Church Road, Long Itchington, Rugby, Warks CV23 8PW*   Southam (0926) 817971

MERRICK, Charles Philip. MBE. Sarum Th Coll. **d** 84 **p** 85. NSM Swanage and Studland *Sarum* from 84. *Plaw Hatch, Swanage, Dorset BH19 1PH*   Swanage (0929) 422235

MERRINGTON, Bill. b 55. BSc. Cranmer Hall Dur. **d** 83 **p** 84. C Harborne Heath *Birm* 83-88; V Leamington Priors St Paul *Cov* from 88. *The Vicarage, 15 Lillington Road, Leamington Spa, Warks CV32 5YS*   Leamington Spa (0926) 335331

MERRY, David Thomas. b 48. St Chad's Coll Dur BA70. AKC73. **d** 74 **p** 75. C Cirencester *Glouc* 74-78; TV Bridgnorth, Tasley, Astley Abbotts and Oldbury *Heref* 78-83; P-in-c Quatford 81-83; P-in-c Stroud H Trin *Glouc* from 83; Chapl Stroud Gen Hosp from 83. *Holy Trinity Vicarage, 10 Bowbridge Lane, Stroud, Glos GL5 2JW* Stroud (0453) 764551

MERRY, Ivor John. b 28. W Midl Minl Tr Course. **d** 87 **p** 88. NSM Redditch, The Ridge *Worc* from 87. *26 Dale Road, Redditch, Worcs B98 8HJ*   Redditch (0527) 64708

MERRY, James Thomas Arthur. b 38. Toronto Univ BA58 Saskatchewan Univ LLB74. Wycliffe Coll Toronto BTh62. **d** 61 **p** 62. Canada 61-89; I Ematris w Rockcorry, Aghabog and Aughnamullan *Clogh* from 89; Dioc Registrar from 91. *The Rectory, Dartrey, Cootehill, Co Cavan, Irish Republic*   Castleblayney (42) 42484

MERRY, Rex Edwin. b 38. AKC67. **d** 68 **p** 69. C Spalding St Jo *Linc* 68-73; C Boxmoor St Jo *St Alb* 73-83; TV Hemel Hempstead from 83. *436 Warners End Road, Hemel Hempstead, Herts HP1 3QF* Hemel Hempstead (0442) 251897

MERWOOD, Raymond George. b 27. K Coll Lon. **d** 54 **p** 56. C Wareham w Arne *Sarum* 54-55; C Rawmarsh w Parkgate *Sheff* 55-58; C Thrybergh 58-62; C Brixham *Ex* 62-67; V Newton Poppleford w Harpford from 67. *The Vicarage, Newton Poppleford, Sidmouth, Devon EX10 0EL* Colaton Raleigh (0395) 68390

MESSENGER, Paul. b 38. Univ of Wales (Lamp) BA63. Coll of Resurr Mirfield 63. **d** 65 **p** 66. C Battersea St Luke *S'wark* 65-69; C Ainsdale *Liv* 69-71; V Wigan St Steph 71-74; Asst Chapl St Marg Convent E Grinstead 74-76; Chapl Kingsley St Mich Sch W Sussex 74-76; P-in-c Southwater *Chich* 76-81; V from 81. *The Vicarage, Southwater, Horsham, W Sussex RH13 7BT* Horsham (0403) 730229

MESSENGER, Canon Reginald James. b 13. Univ Coll Dur LTh38 BA39 MA57. St Aug Coll Cant 35. **d** 39 **p** 40. India 39-80; rtd 80; Perm to Offic *Chich* from 80. *58 Oakcroft Gardens, Littlehampton, W Sussex BN17 6LT* Littlehampton (0903) 715982

MESSER, Ralph Edwin. b 32. NW Ord Course 76. **d** 79 **p** 80. NSM Escrick and Stillingfleet w Naburn *York* 79-81; Area Sec (Dio York) USPG 79-81; Ind Chapl *York* from 81; P-in-c Cawood from 81; P-in-c Ryther from 81. *The Vicarage, Cawood, Selby, N Yorkshire YO8 0TP* Cawood (075786) 273

MESSOM, Alan George. b 42. St Chad's Coll Dur BA63 DipTh65. **d** 65 **p** 66. C Newc St Gabr *Newc* 65-68; Korea 69-77; V Derby St Bart *Derby* from 78. *St Bartholomew's Vicarage, Addison Road, Derby DE2 8FH* Derby (0332) 47709

METCALF, Preb Michael Ralph. b 37. Clare Coll Cam BA61 MA65 Birm Univ MA80. Ridley Hall Cam 63. **d** 64 **p** 65. C Downend *Bris* 64-67; Perm to Offic Birm 68-78; Lich 72-81; Dioc Dir of Educn *Lich* from 83; Preb Lich Cathl from 91. *67 Park Hall Road, Walsall WS5 3HL* Walsall (0922) 33546

METCALF, Canon Robert Laurence. b 35. Dur Univ BA60. Cranmer Hall Dur DipTh62. **d** 62 **p** 63. C Bootle Ch Ch *Liv* 62-65; C Farnworth 65-67; V Wigan St Cath 67-75; Chapl Blue Coat Sch Liv from 75; R Wavertree H Trin *Liv* from 75; Dir of Ords from 82; Hon Can Liv Cathl from 87. *Wavertree Rectory, Hunters Lane, Liverpool L15 8HL* 051-733 2172

METCALFE, Alan. b 22. St Aid Birkenhead 49. **d** 52 **p** 53. V Dewsbury St Matt and St Jo *Wakef* 69-71; Warden Bridgehead Hostel Cardiff 71-73; Field View Hostel Stoke Prior 73-75; McIntyre Ho Nuneaton 75-79; C Southam w Stockton *Cov* 79-84; P-in-c Kinwarton w Gt Alne and Haselor 84-87; rtd 87; Hon C Yarcombe w Membury and Upottery *Ex* from 89. *The Vicarage, Upottery, Honiton, Devon EX14 9PW* Upottery (040486) 604

METCALFE, James. b 17. St Pet Hall Ox BA39 MA44. Wycliffe Hall Ox 39. **d** 41 **p** 42. R Wickersley *Sheff* 71-82; rtd 82; Perm to Offic *Bradf* from 83. *Scar Field, The Mains, Giggleswick, Settle, N Yorkshire BD24 0AX* Settle (07292) 3983

METCALFE, Reginald Herbert. b 38. **d** 79. Hon C Aspley Guise *St Alb* 79; Hon C Aspley Guise w Husborne Crawley and Ridgmont 80-84; Hon C Bovingdon from 84. *30 Manorville Road, Aspley, Hemel Hempstead, Herts* Hemel Hempstead (0442) 42952

METCALFE, Canon Ronald. b 41. BA. Edin Th Coll 67. **d** 69 **p** 70. C Saltburn-by-the-Sea *York* 69-72; P-in-c Crathorne 73-77; Youth Officer 73-77; Dioc Adult Tr Officer 78-88; Can Res York Minster from 88; Sec for Miss and Min from 88. *5 Minster Yard, York YO1 2JE* York (0904) 642542

METCALFE, William Bernard. b 47. St Jo Coll Cam BA69 MA73 Ball Coll Ox BA71. Ripon Hall Ox 70. **d** 72 **p** 73. C Caversham *Ox* 72-75; C Aylesbury 75-79; Ind Chapl 75-79; TV Thamesmead *S'wark* 79-84; TR Totton *Win* from 84. *Testwood Rectory, 92 Salisbury Road, Totton, Southampton SO4 3JA* Southampton (0703) 865103

METCALFE, Canon William Nelson. b 15. St Jo Coll Dur BA39 MA54. St Aid Birkenhead LTh38. **d** 39 **p** 40. R Bottesford and Muston *Leic* 62-82; RD Framland I 60-80; Hon Can Leic Cathl 75-82; rtd 82. *62 Church Lane, Sutton-on-Sea, Mablethorpe, Lincs LN12 2JB* Sutton-on-Sea (0507) 442331

METHUEN, Alan Robert. b 11. Dorchester Miss Coll 37. **d** 41 **p** 42. C-in-c Dedworth CD *Ox* 57-75; P-in-c Gt Haseley, Albury and Waterstock 76-87; rtd 87.

44 Greenfield Crescent, Stonesfield, Oxford OX7 2EH Stonesfield (099389) 8166

METHUEN, John Alan Robert. b 47. BNC Ox BA69 MA74. Cuddesdon Coll 69. **d** 71 **p** 72. C Fenny Stratford *Ox* 71-73; C Fenny Stratford and Water Eaton 74; Asst Chapl Eton Coll Windsor 74-77; P-in-c Dorney *Ox* 74-77; Warden Dorney/Eton Coll Conf Cen 74-77; V Reading St Mark 77-83; R Hulme Ascension *Man* from 83. *The Ascension Rectory, Royce Road, Manchester M15 5FQ* 061-226 5568

METHVEN, Alexander George. b 26. Lon Univ BD52 Em Coll Cam BA54 MA58. ACT ThL47 Lon Coll of Div 50. **d** 52 **p** 53. V Lower Sydenham St Mich *S'wark* 60-68; Australia from 68; rtd 91. *74 Station Road, Belgrave, Victoria, Australia 3160*

METIVIER, Robert John. b 31. Lon Univ BA68. Lambeth STh61 Ch Div Sch of the Pacific (USA) BD66 MDiv69 Codrington Coll Barbados 56. **d** 60 **p** 61. Trinidad and Tobago 61-64 and 68-78; USPG 66-67; C Gt Berkhamsted *St Alb* 78-82; V Goff's Oak St Jas 82-90; V Tokyngton St Mich *Lon* from 90. *The Vicarage, St Michael's Avenue, Wembley, Middx HA9 6SL* 081-902 3290

METTERS, Anthony John Francis. b 43. AKC65. **d** 68 **p** 69. C Heavitree *Ex* 68-74; V Plymouth Crownhill Ascension 74-79; RD Plymouth 77-79; Chapl RN from 79. *c/o MOD, Lacon House, Theobald's Road, London WC1X 8RY* 071-430 6847

METTHAM, Maurice Desmond. b 20. Sarum & Wells Th Coll 73. **d** 74 **p** 75. C Guernsey St Sav *Win* 74-81; Perm to Offic from 81. *c/o La Masse Residential Home, Grande Capelles Road, St Sampsons, Guernsey* Guernsey (0481) 49334

MEUX, Kenneth John. b 07. Selw Coll Cam BA29 MA36. Westcott Ho Cam 30. **d** 31 **p** 32. R Thorpe Morieux w Preston and Brettenham *St E* 71-74; rtd 74. *38 Paradise Row, Melcombe Bingham, Dorchester, Dorset DT2 7PQ* Milton Abbas (0258) 880532

MEWIS, David William. b 47. Leeds Inst of Educn CertEd68 Leeds Poly BEd83. N Ord Course 87. **d** 90 **p** 91. C Skipton Ch Ch *Bradf* from 90. *16 Church Street, Skipton, N Yorkshire BD23 2AR* Skipton (0756) 793851

MEWS, Stuart Paul. b 44. Leeds Univ BA64 MA67 Trin Hall Cam PhD74. Westcott Ho Cam 86. **d** 87 **p** 88. Lect Lanc Univ from 68; NSM Caton w Littledale *Blackb* 87-88; Hon C Lanc St Mary from 88. *Department of Religious Studies, Lancaster University, Lancaster LA1 4YE* Lancaster (0524) 770457

✠**MEYER, Rt Rev Conrad John Eustace.** b 22. Pemb Coll Cam BA46 MA48. Westcott Ho Cam 46. **d** 48 **p** 49 **c** 79. C Bedminster St Fran *Bris* 48-51; Chapl RNVR 50-54; C Kenwyn *Truro* 51-53; C Falmouth K Chas 54-55; V Devoran 54-64; Chapl Falmouth Hosp 55; Dioc Youth Officer *Truro* 55-60; Asst Dir RE 59-60; Dioc Educn Sec 60-69; P-in-c St Wenn 64-68; Hon Can Truro Cathl 66-79; Adn Bodmin 69-79; Suff Bp Dorchester *Ox* 79-87; rtd 87; Warden of Readers *Truro* from 88; Asst Bp Truro from 90. *Hawk's Cliff, 38 Praze Road, Newquay, Cornwall TR7 3AP* Newquay (0637) 873003

MEYER, Richard Ernest. b 44. St Jo Coll Dur BA66. Coll of Resurr Mirfield 71. **d** 73 **p** 73. C Up Hatherley *Glouc* 73-74; C Wotton St Mary 74-77; V Hampton *Worc* from 77; Chapl Evesham Hosp from 90. *The Vicarage, Hampton, Evesham, Worcs WR11 6PQ* Evesham (0386) 446381

MEYER, Stuart Thomas. b 45. GLCM69 Open Univ BA85. Trin Coll Bris 76. **d** 78 **p** 79. C Heref St Pet w St Owen *Heref* 78-79; C Heref St Pet w St Owen and St Jas 79-80; Chapl K Coll Cam 80-84; Chapl Medical Schs *S'wark* 84-87; Chapl Dulwich Hosp 87-90; Chapl Camberwell Distr HA from 90; Chapl K Coll Hosp Lon from 90. *King's College Hospital, Denmark Hill, London SE5* 071-326 3522

MEYER, William John. b 46. ACIB. Cranmer Hall Dur 83. **d** 85 **p** 86. C Merrow *Guildf* 85-89; V Grayshott from 89. *The Vicarage, Grayshott, Hindhead, Surrey GU26 6NH* Hindhead (042873) 4540

MEYNELL, Andrew Francis. b 43. Westcott Ho Cam 70. **d** 73 **p** 74. C Cowley St Jas *Ox* 73-79; TV 79-81; P-in-c Halton from 81; V Wendover from 81. *The Vicarage, 34 Dobbins Lane, Wendover, Aylesbury, Bucks HP22 6DH* Wendover (0296) 622230

MEYNELL, Mrs Honor Mary. b 37. E Midl Min Tr Course 84. **d** 87. NSM Kirk Langley *Derby* from 87. *Meynell Langley, Derby DE6 4NT* Kirk Langley (033124) 207

MEYNELL, Canon Mark. b 14. Ch Ch Ox BA37 MA44. Cuddesdon Coll. **d** 40 **p** 41. V Leamington Hastings *Cov* 65-79; R Birdingbury 74-79; Can Th Cov Cathl 73-78; rtd 79; Perm to Offic *St E* from 80. *2 Double Street,*

Framlingham, Woodbridge, Suffolk IP13 9BN
Framlingham (0728) 723898

MEYRICK, Cyril Jonathan. b 52. St Jo Coll Ox BA73 MA77. Sarum & Wells Th Coll 74. **d** 76 **p** 77. C Bicester *Ox* 76-78; Bp's Dom Chapl 78-81; Barbados 81-84; TV Burnham w Dropmore, Hitcham and Taplow *Ox* 84-90; TR Tisbury *Sarum* from 90. *The Rectory, Park Road, Tisbury, Salisbury SP3 6LF* Tisbury (0747) 870312

MIALL, Peter Brian. b 30. Scawsby Coll of Educn TCert69. **d** 89 **p** 89. Hon C Bolsterstone *Sheff* from 89. *Waldershaigh Cottage, Bolsterstone, Sheffield S30 5ZH* Sheffield (0742) 885558

MICHAEL, Brother. *See* FISHER, Rt Rev Reginald Lindsay

MICHAEL, Ian MacRae. b 40. Aber Univ MA62 Hertf Coll Ox DPhil66. Westcott Ho Cam 77. **d** 79 **p** 80. C Kings Heath *Birm* 79-82; Vice-Provost St Paul's Cathl Dundee *Bre* 82-88; V Harborne St Faith and St Laur *Birm* from 88; RD Edgbaston from 91. *The Vicarage, 115 Balden Road, Birmingham B32 2EL* 021-427 2410

MICHAELS, David Albert Emmanuel. b 49. Barrister-at-Law (Inner Temple) 73 Bede Coll Dur BA72. Westcott Ho Cam 86. **d** 88 **p** 89. C Hampstead St Jo *Lon* 88-91; TV Wolvercote w Summertown *Ox* from 91. *The Vicarage, Mere Road, Wolvercote, Oxford OX2 8AN* Oxford (0865) 515640

MICHELL, David Charles Henry. b 1900. Univ of Manitoba LLB21. Clifton Th Coll 32. **d** 35 **p** 37. R Oborne w Poyntington *Sarum* 67-78; rtd 78. *Haven Manor Inc, 6411 Coburg Road, Halifax, Nova Scotia, Canada*

MICHELL, Canon Douglas Reginald. b 19. St Jo Coll Dur BA41 MA44. Westcott Ho Cam 41. **d** 43 **p** 44. V Evington *Leic* 61-80; Hon Can Leic Cathl 67-84; RD Christianity (Leic) N 74-79; V Billesdon w Goadby and Rolleston 80-82; RD Gartree I (Harborough) 81-84; V Billesdon and Skeffington 82-84; rtd 85. Perm to Offic *St Alb* from 85. *The Old Smithy, The Green, Harrold, Bedford MK43 7DB* Bedford (0234) 721063

MICHELL, Francis Richard Noel. b 42. St Cath Coll Cam BA64 MA68. Tyndale Hall Bris 64. **d** 66 **p** 67. C Northn St Giles *Pet* 66-69; C Gateacre *Liv* 69-72; V Litherland St Paul Hatton Hill 72-79; V Rainhill 79-88; V Rainford from 88. *The Vicarage, Church Road, Rainford, St Helens, Merseyside WA11 8HD* Rainford (074488) 2200

MICHELL, Canon Jocelyn Ralph Stamerham. b 21. Trin Coll Cam BA43 MA55. Ridley Hall Cam 45. **d** 51 **p** 55. V Longstock w Leckford *Win* 70-79; Nigeria 79-82; Hon Can Asaba from 81; R Hale w S Charford *Win* 83-86; rtd 86. *4 The Crescent, Darby Green Road, Camberley, Surrey GU17 0EA* Yateley (0252) 877953

MICKLETHWAITE, Peter William. b 62. Peterho Cam BA84 MA88. St Jo Coll Nottm DipTh89 DPS90. **d** 90 **p** 91. C Leatherhead *Guildf* from 90. *58 Kingscroft Road, Leatherhead, Surrey KT22 7BU* Leatherhead (0372) 379954

MIDDLEBROOK, Bryan. b 33. Dur Univ BA55 DipEd58 Newc Univ MEd74. NE Ord Course 85. **d** 88 **p** 88. NSM Dur St Cuth *Dur* from 88. *5 Fieldhouse Terrace, Durham DH1 4NA* 091-386 6665

MIDDLEDITCH, Terry Gordon. b 30. Univ of Wales (Lamp) BA62. **d** 63 **p** 64. C Poulton-le-Fylde *Blackb* 63-67; C-in-c Heysham 65-67; C Cheltenham St Pet *Glouc* 75-77; Perm to Offic 77-82; Hon C Badgeworth w Shurdington 82-87; C Poulton-le-Sands w Morecambe St Laur *Blackb* 88-91; V Stalmine from 91. *The Vicarage, Carr End Lane, Stalmine, Blackpool FY6 0LQ* Blackpool (0253) 702538

MIDDLEMISS, Fritha Leonora. b 47. Man Univ BA68 CertEd69. Glouc Sch of Min 86. **d** 89. NSM Bengeworth *Worc* from 89. *Vine Cottage, Kennel Bank, Cropthorne, Pershore, Worcs WR10 3NB* Pershore (0386) 860330

MIDDLESEX, Archdeacon of. *See* RAPHAEL, Ven Timothy John

MIDDLETON, Alan Derek. b 46. St Jo Coll Dur BA68 MA85. Qu Coll Birm DipTh71 DPS72. **d** 72 **p** 73. C Cannock *Lich* 72-76; Warden St Helen's Youth & Community Cen Bishop Auckland 76-79; V Darlington St Jo *Dur* 79-89; TR E Darlington 89-90; V Upper Norwood All SS *S'wark* from 90. *All Saints' Vicarage, 12 Beulah Hill, London SE19 3LS* 081-653 2820

MIDDLETON, Barry Glen. b 41. Lich Th Coll 68. **d** 70 **p** 71. C Westhoughton *Man* 70-73; C Prestwich St Marg 73-74; TV Buxton w Burbage and King Sterndale *Derby* 74-77; Chapl Worc R Infirmary 77-83; Fairfield Hosp Hitchin 83-85; P-in-c Erpingham w Calthorpe *Nor* 85-86; P-in-c Erpingham w Calthorpe, Ingworth, Aldborough

etc 86; R from 86. *The Rectory, Erpingham, Norwich NR11 7QX* Cromer (0263) 768073

MIDDLETON, Hugh Charles. b 50. Nottm Univ BTh77. Linc Th Coll 73. **d** 77 **p** 78. C New Sleaford *Linc* 77-81; C Grantham 81; TV 81-83; R Caythorpe from 83. *The Rectory, Gorse Hill Lane, Caythorpe, Grantham, Lincs NG32 3DU* Loveden (0400) 73114

MIDDLETON, Kenneth Frank. b 28. Keble Coll Ox BA52 MA64. St Steph Ho Ox 52. **d** 55 **p** 56. C Leic St Matt *Leic* 55-58; C W Hackney St Barn *Lon* 58-60; V Leic St Matt and St Geo *Leic* 60-82; RD Christianity (Leic) N 79-82; P-in-c Leic St Alb 80-82; Hon Can Leic Cathl 80-82; P-in-c Belgrave St Mich 81-82; TR Bridgnorth, Tasley, Astley Abbotts, Oldbury etc *Heref* 82-87; P-in-c Quatford 83; RD Bridgnorth 83-87; TR Littleham w Exmouth *Ex* from 87. *The Rectory, 1 Maer Road, Exmouth, Devon EX8 2DA* Exmouth (0395) 272227

MIDDLETON, Leonard James. b 33. Bps' Coll Cheshunt 55. **d** 58 **p** 59. C Beckenham St Geo *Roch* 58-60; C Wallingford St Mary w All Hallows and St Leon *Ox* 60-64; V Codnor and Loscoe *Derby* 64-71; P-in-c W Tilbury *Chelmsf* 71-77; V E Tilbury 71-77; R Copford w Easthorpe from 77. *The Rectory, Copford Green, Copford, Colchester CO6 1DH* Colchester (0206) 210253

MIDDLETON, Canon Michael John. b 40. Dur Univ BSc62 Fitzw Ho Cam BA66 MA70. Westcott Ho Cam 63. **d** 66 **p** 67. C Newc St Geo *Newc* 66-69; V 77-85; S Africa 69-72; Chapl K Sch Tynemouth 72-77; R Hexham *Newc* from 85; Hon Can Newc Cathl from 90. *The Rectory, Eilansgate, Hexham, Northd NE46 3EW* Hexham (0434) 602031

MIDDLETON, Rodney. b 54. St Andr Univ BD80. St Steph Ho Ox 80. **d** 82 **p** 83. C Walton St Mary *Liv* 82-87; C-in-c Kew St Fran of Assisi CD from 87. *19 Ruddington Road, Kew, Southport, Merseyside PR8 6XD* Southport (0704) 47758

MIDDLETON, Thomas Arthur. b 36. AKC61. **d** 62 **p** 63. C Sunderland *Dur* 62-63; C Auckland St Helen 63-67; C Winlaton 67-70; C-in-c Pennywell St Thos and Grindon St Oswald CD 70-79; R Boldon from 79; Adv in Stewardship Dur Adnry from 87. *Boldon Rectory, Rectory Green, West Boldon, Tyne & Wear NE36 0QD* 091-536 7370

MIDDLETON-DANSKY, Brother Serge Wladimir. b 45. Cuddesdon Coll 74. **d** 77 **p** 78. C Wisbech SS Pet and Paul *Ely* 77-79; Lic to Offic Adnry Riviera *Eur* from 80; C Ox St Giles and SS Phil and Jas w St Marg *Ox* 83-86; Perm to Offic Ox 86-88; Truro 88-90; Caim Cryst Benedictine Fraternity & Retreat Ho from 88; P-in-c Zennor *Truro* from 90; P-in-c Towednack from 90. *The Vicarage, Zennor, St Ives, Cornwall TR26 3BY* Penzance (0736) 796955

MIDDLETON, Suffragan Bishop of. *See* TYTLER, Rt Rev Donald Alexander

MIDDLEWICK, Robert James. b 44. K Alfred's Coll Win CertEd67 Lon Univ BD76. Ripon Coll Cuddesdon 75. **d** 77 **p** 78. C Bromley SS Pet and Paul *Roch* 77-81; C Belvedere All SS 81-84; P-in-c Lamberhurst 85-88; P-in-c Matfield 85-88; V Lamberhurst and Matfield from 88. *The Vicarage, Old Town Hill, Lamberhurst, Tunbridge Wells, Kent TN3 8EL* Lamberhurst (0892) 890324

MIDGLEY, Edward Graham. b 23. St Edm Hall Ox BA47 MA48 BLitt50. Cuddesdon Coll 56. **d** 56 **p** 57. Lic to Offic *Ox* from 56; Dean St Edm Hall Ox 56-78; Vice-Prin 70-78; Chapl 78-86; Chapl St Hugh's Coll Ox 86-89. *4 St Lawrence Road, South Hinksey, Oxford OX1 5AZ* Oxford (0865) 735460

MIDGLEY, George William. b 38. N Ord Course. **d** 83 **p** 84. C Penistone and Thurlstone *Wakef* 88-89; TV from 89. *The New Vicarage, Thurlstone, Sheffield* Barnsley (0226) 762871

MIDLANE, Colin John. b 50. Lon Univ BA72. Westcott Ho Cam 73 Sarum & Wells Th Coll 77. **d** 78 **p** 79. C Bethnal Green St Pet w St Thos *Lon* 78-82; P-in-c Haggerston All SS 82-88; Chapl Hengrave Hall Cen, Bury St Edmunds 88-89; Priest Counsellor St Botolph Aldgate w H Trin from 89. *St Botolph's Vestry, London EC3N 1AB* 071-283 1670 or 283 1950

MIDWINTER, Sister Josie Isabel. b 46. Melbourne Univ DipTh77 Open Univ BA84. CA Tr Coll 69 CMS Tr Coll Crowther Hall 84. **d** 87. CA from 71; CMS from 84; Uganda from 85. *Bishop Barham Divinity College, PO Box 613, Kabale, Uganda*

MIDWOOD, Peter Stanley. b 47. Linc Th Coll 80. **d** 82 **p** 83. C Garforth *Ripon* 82-85; C-in-c Grinton w Arkengarthdale, Downholme and Marske 85-86; C-in-c Melbecks and Muker 85-86; P-in-c Swaledale 86; V from 86. *The Vicarage, Reeth, Richmond, N Yorkshire DL11 6TR* Richmond (0748) 84706

MIELL, David Keith. b 57. BSc PhD BA. Westcott Ho Cam 83. **d** 86 **p** 87. C Blackbird Leys CD *Ox* 86-89; C Walton 89-90; TV Walton Milton Keynes from 90. *The Rectory, Broughton, Milton Keynes MK10 9AA* Milton Keynes (0908) 667846

MIGHALL, Robert. b 33. St Pet Coll Ox BA57 MA61. Wycliffe Hall Ox 57. **d** 58 **p** 59. C Stoke *Cov* 58-62; C Rugby St Andr 62-64; V Newbold on Avon 64-76; V Combroke w Compton Verney from 76; V Kineton from 76. *The Vicarage, Kineton, Warwick CV35 0LL* Kineton (0926) 640248

MIHILL, Dennis George. b 31. St Alb Minl Tr Scheme 78. **d** 81 **p** 82. NSM Harpenden St Nic *St Alb* 81-86; C Sawbridgeworth 86-89; V Motspur Park *S'wark* from 89. *The Vicarage, 2 Douglas Avenue, New Malden, Surrey KT3 6HT* 081-942 3117

MILBURN, John Frederick. b 56. Westmr Coll Ox BA84. Sarum & Wells Th Coll 84. **d** 86 **p** 87. C Leavesden All SS *St Alb* 86-89; C Broxbourne w Wormley from 89; CF (TA) from 90. *St Laurence's House, 11 Wharf Road, Wormley, Broxbourne, Herts EN10 6HU* Hoddesdon (0992) 442356

MILBURN, John Kenneth. b 13. St Jo Coll Dur BA39 MA42 DipTh40. **d** 40 **p** 41. V Churchstow w Kingsbridge *Ex* 56-81; RD Woodleigh 76-80; rtd 81. *3 Willows Close, Frogmore, Kingsbridge, Devon TQ7 2NY* Frogmore (0548) 531374

MILBURN, Very Rev Robert Leslie Pollington. b 07. FSA SS Coll Cam BA30 MA34. **d** 34 **p** 35. Master of the Temple (Lon) 68-80; rtd 80; Perm to Offic Heref from 81; Worc from 85. *5 St Barnabas House, Newland, Malvern, Worcs WR13 5AX* Malvern (0684) 561044

MILES, Archibald Geoffrey. b 22. New Coll Ox BA47 MA48. Chich Th Coll 49. **d** 50 **p** 51. S Rhodesia 53-59 and 63-65; Rhodesia 65-74; P-in-c Winterbourne Stoke *Sarum* 75-80; V Shrewton 75-80; V New Marston *Ox* 80-90; rtd 90. *76 London Road, Wheatley, Oxford OX9 1YQ* Wheatley (08677) 5742

MILES, Canon Charles Reginald. b 12. Tyndale Hall Bris 36. **d** 39 **p** 40. C Wolv St Luke *Lich* 39-43; C Bucknall and Bagnall 43-46; R Dibden *Win* from 46; Hon Can Win Cathl from 75. *The Rectory, Beaulieu Road, Dibden Purlieu, Southampton SO4 5PT* Hythe (0703) 843204

MILES, Frank Norman. b 07. Univ of Wales BA28 MA33 Lon Univ BD46. St Mich Coll Llan. **d** 41 **p** 42. Lic to Offic *Llan* from 47; rtd 72. *Marcross, The Avenue, The Common, Pontypridd, M Glam CF37 4DF* Pontypridd (0443) 402706

MILES, Gerald Christopher Morgan. b 36. CEng MIEE Peterho Cam BA57 MA72 Cranfield Inst of Tech MSc72. Wycliffe Hall Ox 74. **d** 76 **p** 77. C Tunbridge Wells St Jas *Roch* 76-80; V Leigh 80-90; R Addington w Trottiscliffe 90-91; P-in-c Ryarsh w Birling 90-91; R Birling, Addington, Ryarsh and Trottiscliffe from 91. *The Vicarage, Birling Road, Ryarsh, West Malling, Kent ME19 5LS* West Malling (0732) 842249

MILES, Keith Robert George. b 53. Sarum & Wells Th Coll. **d** 89 **p** 90. NSM Fishponds St Mary *Bris* from 89. *1 Highland Square, Bristol BS8 2YB*

MILES, Lawrence. b 24. St D Coll Lamp BA48. **d** 50 **p** 51. V Cwmparc *Llan* 61-89; rtd 89. *25A Mary Street, Porthcawl, M Glam CF36 3YL* Porthcawl (0656) 772329

MILES, Malcolm Robert. b 36. AKC60. **d** 61 **p** 62. C Northn St Mary *Pet* 61-63; C E Haddon 63-67; R Broughton 67-73; Asst Chapl Nottm Univ *S'well* 73-74; V Northn H Trin *Pet* 75-84; V Painswick w Sheepscombe *Glouc* from 84; RD Bisley from 90. *The Vicarage, Orchard Mead, Painswick, Glos GL6 6YD* Painswick (0452) 812334

MILES, Mrs Marion Claire. b 41. S Dios Minl Tr Scheme 86. **d** 88. Hon Par Dn Blandford Forum and Langton Long *Sarum* from 88. *20 Alexandra Street, Blandford Forum, Dorset DT11 7JE* Blandford (0258) 452010

MILES, Canon Robert William. b 27. Magd Coll Cam BA50 MA55. Westcott Ho Cam 50. **d** 52 **p** 53. C Bury St Mary *Man* 52-55; Bp's Dom Chapl *Chich* 55-58; Kenya 58-63; Provost Mombasa 58-63; R Dalmahoy *Edin* 65-70; R Batsford w Moreton-in-Marsh *Glouc* 70-77; Perm to Offic from 79. *Boilingwell, Winchcombe, Cheltenham, Glos* Cheltenham (0242) 603337

MILES, Miss Ruth Cecilia. b 11. dss 40 **d** 87. Adv in Children's RE *Linc* 60-71; rtd 71; Perm to Offic *Glouc* from 83. *The Abbeyfield House, 326 Prestbury Road, Cheltenham, Glos GL52 3DD* Cheltenham (0242) 516357

MILFORD, Mrs Catherine Helena. b 39. LMH Ox BA61 DipTh62 MA65. Gilmore Course 81. **dss** 82 **d** 87.

Heaton St Barn *Bradf* 82-87; Par Dn 87-88; Adult Educn Adv *Win* from 88. *Church House, 9 The Close, Winchester, Hants SO23 9LS* Winchester (0962) 844644

MILLAM, Peter John. b 36. Univ of Wales (Lamp) BA58. Ridley Hall Cam 58. **d** 63 **p** 64. C Cheltenham Ch Ch *Glouc* 63-66; Falkland Is 66-70; V Pulloxhill w Flitton *St Alb* 70-79; V Luton St Paul 79-89; V Chipping Campden w Ebrington *Glouc* from 89. *The Vicarage, Chipping Campden, Glos GL55 6HU* Evesham (0386) 840671

MILLAR, Alan Askwith. b 26. Qu Coll Birm 59. **d** 60 **p** 61. V Middlesb St Aid *York* 64-72; V Cayton w Eastfield 72-88; Chapl to RD of Scarborough 88-89; rtd 89; Perm to Offic *Bradf* from 89. *23 Rowan Court, Old Bridge Rise, Ilkley, W Yorkshire LS29 9HH* Ilkley (0943) 602081

MILLAR, Andrew Charles. b 48. Hull Univ BSc69. Cuddesdon Coll 71. **d** 73 **p** 74. C Rushmere *St E* 73-76; C Ipswich All Hallows 76-79; Youth Chapl *Sheff* 79-83; Youth Chapl *Win* from 83. *Holy Trinity Rectory, Upper Brook Street, Winchester, Hants SO23 8DG* Winchester (0962) 54133

MILLAR, Miss Christine. b 55. City of Lon Poly BSc76 DipCOT81. S Dios Minl Tr Scheme 84. **d** 87. NSM Kingston Buci *Chich* 87-89; Par Dn Merstham and Gatton *S'wark* from 89. *Epiphany House, Mansfield Drive, Merstham, Surrey RH1 3JP* Merstham (0737) 642628

MILLAR, Frank. b 38. Sarum Th Coll 67. **d** 69 **p** 70. C S'wark H Trin *S'wark* 69-72; C Saltdean *Chich* 72-76; P-in-c Beaumont and Moze *Chelmsf* 76-80; P-in-c Gt Oakley 76-77; P-in-c Tendring 76-80; R Tendring and Lt Bentley w Beaumont cum Moze 80-83; R Rivenhall 83-87; Chapl Palma de Mallorca w Menorca *Eur* 87-90. *Nunel de Balboa 6, Son Armadans, 07014 Palma de Mallorca, Spain* Palma de Mallorca (71) 237279

MILLAR, Gary. b 67. **d** 91. C Tonyrefail w Gilfach Goch *Llan* from 91. *St Barnabas's Vicarage, High Street, Gilfach Goch, M Glam CF39 8SN* Tonyrefail (0443) 672298

MILLAR, John Alexander Kirkpatrick. b 39. Trin Coll Cam BA62 MA66. St Jo Coll Dur 74. **d** 76 **p** 77. C Brompton H Trin *Lon* 76-78; C Brompton H Trin w Onslow Square St Paul 78-85; V from 85; AD Chelsea from 89. *Holy Trinity Vicarage, 73 Prince's Gate Mews, London SW7 2PP* 071-584 8957

MILLARD, Albert George. b 17. Chich Th Coll. **d** 64 **p** 65. V Kintbury w Avington *Ox* 71-82; rtd 82. *8 Crown Mews, 15 Clarence Road, Gosport, Hants PO12 1DH* Gosport (0705) 511934

MILLARD, Malcolm Edoric. b 38. Lon Univ BA60. AKC60. **d** 77 **p** 78. Gambia from 77; CMS from 89. *Anglican Training Centre, Farafenni, North Bank Division, Gambia*

MILLARD, Canon Murray Clinton. b 29. Ex Coll Ox BA50 DipTh52 MA58. St Steph Ho Ox 51. **d** 53 **p** 54. C Horfield St Greg *Bris* 53-55; C Guernsey St Steph *Win* 55-61; R Jersey St Mary 61-71; R Guernsey St Sampson 71-82; V Guernsey St Steph from 82; Hon Can Win Cathl from 83. *St Stephen's Vicarage, De Beauvoir, St Peter Port, Guernsey, Channel Islands* Guernsey (0481) 20268

MILLER, Anthony Talbot. b 37. Univ of Wales (Lamp) BA59. Coll of Resurr Mirfield. **d** 61 **p** 62. C Panteg w Llanddewi Fach and Llandegfeth *Mon* 61-63; C Mon 63-65; V Holme Cultram St Mary *Carl* 65-76; Lic to Offic *Lich* 76-78; P-in-c Wrockwardine Wood 78-80; R from 80. *The Rectory, Church Road, Wrockwardine, Telford, Shropshire TF2 7AH* Telford (0952) 613865

MILLER, Barry. b 42. Bede Coll Dur TCert63 Open Univ BA79 Leic Univ MEd86. Linc Th Coll 63. **d** 65 **p** 66. C Greenside *Dur* 65-68; C Auckland St Andr and St Anne 68-71; Adv in Educn *Leic* 71-77; C Leic St Nic 77-80; Asst Chapl Leic Univ 77-80; Children's Officer Gen Syn Bd of Educn 80-84; Hd of Relig Studies W Midl Coll of HE 84-89; Hd Initial Teacher Educn Wolv Poly from 89; Perm to Offic *Leic* from 90. *Kirkstone House, 48 Top Street, Appleby Magna, Burton-on-Trent, Staffs DE12 2AH* Measham (0530) 73722

MILLER, Charles Irvine. b 35. Nottm Univ BEd76. Bps' Coll Cheshunt 61. **d** 63 **p** 64. R Ingoldmells w Addlethorpe *Linc* 68-72; P-in-c Bishop Norton 72-76; V Scunthorpe St Jo 76-83; Chapl Manor Hosp Walsall 83-89; rtd 89. *22 Dudsbury Road, West Parley, Wimborne, Dorset BH22 8RE* Wimborne (0202) 873544

MILLER, David George. b 54. Or Coll Ox BA76 MA80. Ripon Coll Cuddesdon 78. **d** 81 **p** 82. C Henfield w Shermanbury and Woodmancote *Chich* 81-84; C Monk Bretton *Wakef* 84-87; V Rastrick St Jo from 87. *St*

489

John's Vicarage, 2 St John Street, Brighouse, W Yorkshire HD6 1HN Brighouse (0484) 715889

MILLER, David James Tringham. b 45. AKC70. Sarum & Wells Th Coll 76. **d** 77 **p** 78. C Abington *Pet* 77-80; TV Corby SS Pet and Andr w Gt and Lt Oakley 80-83; V Kettering All SS from 83; RD Kettering from 87. *All Saints' Vicarage, 80 Pollard Street, Kettering, Northants NN16 9RP* Kettering (0536) 513376

MILLER, David John. b 37. Louvain Univ Belgium LicScCat67. Chich Th Coll 60. **d** 62 **p** 63. C Southsea H Spirit *Portsm* 62-65; C Roehampton H Trin *S'wark* 67-68; Chapl Luxembourg *Eur* 68-72; Chapl Lausanne 72-91. *1 bis avenue de l'Eglise Anglaise, 1006 Lausanne, Switzerland* Lausanne (21) 262636

MILLER, Preb David Reginald. b 29. AKC54. **d** 55 **p** 56. C Hockerill *St Alb* 55-58; C Combe Down *B & W* 58-61; V Pill 61-70; V Wedmore 70-74; V Wedmore w Theale 74-78; RD Axbridge 77-89; P-in-c Blackford 77-78; V Wedmore w Theale and Blackford from 78; Preb Wells Cathl from 85; Warden of Readers 85-91. *The Vicarage, Cheddar Road, Wedmore, Somerset BS28 4EJ* Wedmore (0934) 712254

MILLER, David Samuel. b 31. Lich Th Coll 62. **d** 63 **p** 64. C Leek St Edw *Lich* 63-66; C Blurton 66; C Southbourne St Kath *Win* 66-71; V E and W Worldham, Hartley Mauditt w Kingsley etc 71-76; TV Buckhurst Hill *Chelmsf* 76-80; V Elm Park St Nic Hornchurch from 80. *The Vicarage, St Nicholas Avenue, Elm Park, Hornchurch, Essex RM12 4PT* Hornchurch (04024) 51451

MILLER, Derek Charles. b 47. Ridley Coll Melbourne 68. **d** 71 **p** 72. Australia 71-74; C Hammersmith St Pet *Lon* 74-76; Asst Chapl Florence *Eur* 76-77; C Portsea St Mary *Portsm* 77-80; R Bodenham w Hope-under-Dinmore, Felton etc *Heref* from 80; RD Heref Rural from 85; Bp's Dom Chapl from 86. *The Vicarage, Bodenham, Hereford HR1 3JX* Bodenham (056884) 370

MILLER, Edward Jeffery. b 24. St Jo Coll Cam BA48 MA50. Wells Th Coll 48. **d** 50 **p** 51. C S Lyncombe *B & W* 50-53; India 54-67; P-in-c Wootton Courtenay *B & W* 68-74; R 74-83; P-in-c Timberscombe 68-74; V 74-83; P-in-c Selworthy 79-83; R Selworthy and Timberscombe and Wootton Courtenay from 83; P-in-c Luccombe 86; R from 86. *The Rectory, Selworthy, Minehead, Somerset TA24 8TL* Porlock (0643) 862445

MILLER, Dr Ernest Charles. b 56. Franklin & Marshall Coll USA BA78 Michigan Univ MA79 Keble Coll Ox DPhil90. Nashotah Ho MDiv82. **d** 82 **p** 83. USA 82-84; Warden Ho of SS Greg and Macrina 84-90; Asst Chapl Keble Coll Ox 84-88; Lic to Offic *Ox* 87-91; P-in-c New Marston from 91. *New Marston Vicarage, 8 Jack Straw's Lane, Oxford OX3 0DL* Oxford (0865) 242803

MILLER, Francis Rogers. b 54. Ex Univ BA86. St Steph Ho Ox 86. **d** 88 **p** 89. C Wednesfield *Lich* from 88. *18 Duke Street, Wednesfield, Wolverhampton WV11 1TH* Wolverhampton (0902) 733501

MILLER, Geoffrey Edward. b 28. Leeds Univ BA56. Coll of Resurr Mirfield 53. **d** 57 **p** 58. R Claypole *Linc* 63-76; R Westborough w Dry Doddington and Stubton 65-76; P-in-c Bierley *Bradf* 76-78; V 78-91; rtd 91; Chantry Priest Chpl St Mich & H So Walsingham from 91; Perm to Offic *Nor* from 91. *20 Cleaves Drive, Little Walsingham, Norfolk NR22 6EQ* Walsingham (0328) 820591

MILLER, Geoffrey Vincent. b 56. BEd. St Jo Coll Nottm. **d** 83 **p** 84. C Jarrow *Dur* 83-86; TV Billingham St Aid from 86. *17 Shadforth Drive, Billingham, Cleveland TS23 3PW* Stockton-on-Tees (0642) 561870

MILLER, Ven George Charles Alexander. b 20. TCD BA45. CITC 46. **d** 46 **p** 47. I Urney w Denn and Derryheen *K, E & A* 65-89; Preb Kilmore Cathl 77-87; Adn Kilmore 87-89; rtd 89. *Wavecrest, Blenacup, Cavan, Irish Republic* Cavan (49) 61270

MILLER, Harold Creeth. b 50. TCD BA73 MA78 Nottm Univ BA75. St Jo Coll Nottm 73. **d** 76 **p** 77. C Carrickfergus *Conn* 76-79; Dir Ext Studies St Jo Coll Nottm 79-84; Chapl QUB 84-89; I Carrigrohane Union *C, C & R* from 89. *The Rectory, Carrigrohane, Co Cork, Irish Republic* Cork (21) 871106

MILLER, Harold John. b 04. AKC34. **d** 34 **p** 35. R Rochford *Chelmsf* 56-72; rtd 72; Chapl Tone Vale Hosp Somerset 72-83; Perm to Offic *B & W* from 83. *St Christopher's, Old Cleeve, Minehead, Somerset TA24 6HH* Washford (0984) 40624

MILLER, James. b 36. QUB TCert57 TCD BA63 Div Test64 MA66 Ulster Univ DipG&C76. **d** 64 **p** 65. C Londonderry Ch Ch *D & R* 64-69; I Tamlaght O'Crilly, Upper w Lower 69-83; RD Maghera and Kilrea

76-83; P-in-c Litherland St Andr *Liv* 83-85; V 85-89; Chapl Newsham Gen Hosp Liv 86-88; P-in-c Widnes St Mary *Liv* from 89; AD Widnes from 89. *St Mary's Vicarage, St Mary's Road, Widnes, Cheshire WA8 0DN* 051-424 4233

MILLER, James Ivimey. b 33. Trin Hall Cam BA55 MA59. Ridley Hall Cam 56. **d** 61 **p** 62. C Kirk Ella *York* 67-73; R Cockfield *St E* 73-78; rtd 78; Perm to Offic *St E* from 78. *3 Grosvenor Gardens, Bury St Edmunds, Suffolk IP33 2JS* Bury St Edmunds (0284) 762839

MILLER, John David. b 50. Nottm Univ BTh73 Lanc Univ CertEd74. Kelham Th Coll 68. **d** 74 **p** 75. C Horden *Dur* 74-79; C Billingham St Aid 79-80; TV 80-84; TR S Shields All SS from 84. *The Rectory, Tyne Terrace, South Shields, Tyne & Wear NE34 0NF* 091-456 1851

MILLER, John Douglas. b 24. FCA60. N Ord Course 74. **d** 77 **p** 78. C Prestbury *Ches* 77-80; V Ashton Hayes 80-87; rtd 87. *35 Branscombe Close, Colyford, Colyton, Devon EX13 6RF* Colyton (0297) 53581

MILLER, John Forster. b 32. Ox NSM Course. **d** 83 **p** 84. NSM Patcham *Chich* 83-86; NSM Radlett *St Alb* from 86. *4 Craigweil Avenue, Radlett, Herts WD7 7EU* Radlett (0923) 857148

MILLER, John Gareth. b 57. St Jo Coll Dur BA78. Ridley Hall Cam 79 Ven English Coll Rome 80. **d** 81 **p** 82. C Addiscombe St Mary *Cant* 81-84; TV Melbury *Sarum* 84-88; TR from 88. *The Vicarage, Corscombe, Dorchester, Dorset DT2 0NU* Corscombe (093589) 247

MILLER, John Selborne. b 57. Lon Univ DBS. S'wark Ord Course 64. **d** 71 **p** 72. C Kenton *Lon* 71-74; C Fulham St Etheldreda w St Clem 74-78; Asst at Convent of the Epiphany Truro 79-81; Hon C Pimlico St Sav 81-84; C Shirley *Birm* 84-86; rtd 86; Perm to Offic *Nor* from 86. *28 Knight Street, Walsingham, Norfolk NR22 6DA* Walsingham (0328) 820824

MILLER, John Stephen Corfield. b 16. Selw Coll Cam BA38 MA41. Westcott Ho Cam 39. **d** 40 **p** 41. Australia 61-78; Asst Master Bp Reindorp Sch Guildf 78-81; rtd 81. *Brierley, 8 St Omer Road, Guildford, Surrey GU1 2DB* Guildford (0483) 60359

MILLER, Kenneth Huitson. b 30. Dur Univ BA55 DipEd. Lich Th Coll 58. **d** 60 **p** 61. C Newc St Geo *Newc* 60-63; C N Gosforth 63-67; Subchanter and Sacr Lich Cathl Lich 67-75; Chapl Lich Cathl Sch 70-75; V Wolstanton Lich 75-79; RD Newc 77-87; TR Wolstanton from 79. *The Rectory, Wolstanton, Knutton Road, Newcastle, Staffs ST5 0HU* Newcastle-under-Lyme (0782) 717561

MILLER, Kenneth Leslie. b 50. Lanc Univ BEd74. N Ord Course 78. **d** 80 **p** 81. NSM Formby St Pet *Liv* from 80; Chapl St Marg High Sch from 84; NSM Anfield St Columba from 86. *9 Hampton Road, Formby, Liverpool L37 6EJ* Formby (07048) 31256

MILLER, Luke Jonathan. b 66. SS Coll Cam BA87 MA91. St Steph Ho Ox BA90. **d** 91. C Oxhey St Matt *St Alb* from 91. *6 Lime Close, Oxhey, Watford, Herts WD1 4HD* Watford (0923) 251841

MILLER, Dr Michael Daukes. b 46. MRCGP74 Qu Coll Cam MA71 Lon Univ BCh70 MB71 DRCOG DCH. Glouc Th Course 82. **d** 85. NSM Lydney w Aylburton *Glouc* from 85. *Highmead House, Blakeney, Glos GL15 4DY* Dean (0594) 42463

MILLER, Norman Alfred Leslie. b 06. Qu Coll Cam BA28 MA32. Ridley Hall Cam 28. **d** 29 **p** 30. V Titchfield *Portsm* 47-73; rtd 73. *The Bakehouse, High Street, Easterton, Devizes, Wilts SN10 4PE* Devizes (0380) 813531

MILLER, Patrick Figgis. b 33. Ch Coll Cam BA56 MA60. Cuddesdon Coll 56. **d** 58 **p** 59. C Portsea St Cuth *Portsm* 58-61; C Cam Gt St Mary w St Mich *Ely* 61-63; Hd Dept Man Gr Sch 63-69; Can Res and Lib S'wark Cathl *S'wark* 69-72; Dir of Studies Qu Mary's Coll Basingstoke 72-79; Prin Sunbury Coll 79-80; Prin Esher Coll from 81; Lic to Offic *Guildf* from 84. *31 Hare Lane, Claygate, Esher, Surrey KT10 9BT* Esher (0372) 67563

MILLER, Paul. b 49. Oak Hill Th Coll 71. **d** 74 **p** 75. C Upton *Ex* 74-77; C Farnborough *Guildf* 77-78; P-in-c Torquay St Luke *Ex* 78-81; V 81-86; V Green Street Green *Roch* from 86. *The Vicarage, 46 Worlds End Lane, Orpington, Kent BR6 6AG* Farnborough (0689) 852905

MILLER, Paul Richard. b 37. K Coll Lon BSc60 AKC60. Linc Th Coll 60. **d** 62 **p** 63. C Sheff St Geo *Sheff* 62-65; C Bottesford *Linc* 65-67; Bp's Youth Chapl 67-69; C Corringham 67-69; Dioc Youth Officer *Ripon* 69-74; Hd Youth Nat Coun of Soc Services 74-79; P-in-c Battlesden and Pottesgrove *St Alb* 79-80; P-in-c Eversholt w Milton Bryan 79-80; P-in-c Woburn 79-80; V Woburn w Eversholt, Milton Bryan, Battlesden etc from 80. *The*

Vicarage, Park Street, Woburn, Milton Keynes MK17 9PG   Woburn (0525) 290225

MILLER, Canon Paul William. b 18. Qu Coll Birm DipTh50. d 50 p 51. Can Res Derby Cathl Derby 66-83; Chapl to HM The Queen from 81; rtd 83; Perm to Offic Derby from 83. 15 Forester Street, Derby DE1 1PP Derby (0332) 44773

MILLER, Peter Tennant. b 21. Keble Coll Ox BA47 MA63. Ripon Hall Ox 62. d 63 p 64. V Worksop St Paul S'well 68-73; P-in-c Nottm St Cath 74-75; C Nottm St Mary 75-77; R Edith Weston w N Luffenham and Lyndon w Manton Pet 77-86; rtd 86; Perm to Offic Cov 86-90. Regency Cottage, 9 Cross Road, Leamington Spa, Warks CV32 5PD   Leamington Spa (0926) 314236

MILLER, Philip Harry. b 58. Leeds Univ BA79. Chich Th Coll 80. d 82 p 83. C Reddish Man 82-86; R Lower Broughton Ascension from 86; P-in-c Cheetwood St Alb from 91. Ascension Rectory, Duke Street, Salford M7 9GX   061-834 4370

MILLER, Philip Howard. b 40. Tyndale Hall Bris 67. d 72 p 73. Argentina 72-73; C Rusholme Man 73-74; Paraguay 74-77; C Toxteth St Cypr w Ch Ch Liv 78-80; V Burscough Bridge 80-85; V Woodbridge St Jo St E from 85. St John's Vicarage, St John's Hill, Woodbridge, Suffolk IP12 1HS   Woodbridge (03943) 2083

MILLER, Richard Bracebridge. b 45. Wycliffe Hall Ox 68. d 70 p 71. C Lee Gd Shep w St Pet S'wark 70-74; C Roehampton H Trin 74-77; C Earley St Pet Ox 77-80; V Aldermaston w Wasing and Brimpton from 80. The Vicarage, Aldermaston, Reading RG7 4LX   Reading (0734) 712281

MILLER, Robert George. b 15. Bris Univ BA37. Bible Churchmen's Coll 37. d 39 p 40. V Upper Edmonton St Jas Lon 47-79; Chapl N Middx Hosp 48-81; rtd 79; Perm to Offic Lon from 80. 9 Marley Court, Aspley, Brisbane, Queensland, Australia 4034   Brisbane (7) 263-8114

MILLER, Robert William Harry. b 46. MITD AKC69 CertEd74 DipTM83. St Aug Coll Cant 70. d 70 p 71. C Hayes St Mary Lon 70-73; C St Marylebone St Mary 73-75; CGA 75-76; Perm to Offic Glouc 76-81; V Elkesley w Bothamsall S'well 81-85; R Netherfield w Colwick from 85. 40 Bourne Mews, Netherfield, Nottingham NG4 2GY   Nottingham (0602) 615566

MILLER, Ronald Anthony. b 41. CEng CPA MRAeS City Univ BSc63. S'wark Ord Course 69. d 72 p 80. NSM Crookham Guildf 72-73 and 80-85; NSM New Haw from 85. Glen Anton, Horsley Road, Downside, Cobham, Surrey   Cobham (0932) 63394

MILLER, Mrs Rosslyn. b 43. St Andr Univ MA65 Ox Univ DipEd66 Cam Univ DipRK69. dss 72 d 87. Dir of Studies Inst of Chr Studies 72; St Marylebone All SS Lon 72; Adult Educn Officer 73-78; Alford w Rigsby Linc 86-87; C 87-90; Dioc Dir of Readers from 90. 120A Station Road, Waddington, Lincoln LN5 9QS   Lincoln (0522) 720819

MILLER, Roy. d 88. NSM Leic Cathl Leic from 88. Stonebridge House, Shearsby, Lutterworth, Leics LE17 6PN   Leicester (0533) 478515

MILLER, Stephen Michael. b 63. NE Lon Poly BSc86 Nottm Univ BTh91. Linc Th Coll 88. d 91. C Dudley St Fran Worc from 91. 273 The Broadway, Dudley, W Midlands DY1 3DW   Dudley (0384) 236249

MILLER, William David. b 45. Man Univ BA66. Linc Th Coll 69. d 71 p 72. C Newc St Geo Newc 71-74; C Corbridge w Halton 74-77; C N Gosforth 77-81; TV Whorlton 81-90; Chapl K Sch Tynemouth from 90. The King's School, Tynemouth, North Shields, Tyne & Wear NE13 7AR   091-258 5995

MILLETT, Canon Francis Henry Walter. b 19. AKC48. d 49 p 50. R Nor St Jo Timberhill w All SS Nor 61-75; V Nor St Jo Sepulchre 61-75; RD Nor E 70-81; TR Nor St Pet Parmentergate w St Jo 75-77; Hon Can Nor Cathl 77-86; V Nor St Giles 77-86; rtd 87; Perm to Offic Nor from 87. 203A Unthank Road, Norwich NR2 2PH Norwich (0603) 52641

MILLETT, William Hugh. b 21. AKC49. d 50 p 51. R Richard's Castle Heref 58-78; P-in-c Stoke Lacy, Moreton Jeffries w Much Cowarne etc 78-82; Perm to Offic Worc from 83; rtd 86. 151 Upper Welland Road, Malvern, Worcs WR14 4LB   Malvern (0684) 567056

MILLGATE, Victor Frederick. b 44. St Mich Coll Llan 81. d 83 p 84. C Pemb St Mary and St Mich St D 83-85; V Manobier and St Florence w Redberth from 85. The Vicarage, Manorbier, Tenby, Dyfed SA70 7TN Manorbier (0834) 871617

MILLICHAMP, Mrs Penelope Mary. b 39. CertEd60. W Midl Minl Tr Course 82. dss 85 d 87. Wednesfield Lich 85-87; Par Dn 87-90; TM from 90. 157 Stubby Lane, Wednesfield, Wolverhampton WV11 3NE Wolverhampton (0902) 732763

MILLIER, Gordon. b 28. St Aid Birkenhead 63. d 65 p 66. C Congresbury B & W 65-69; P-in-c Badgworth w Biddisham 69-76; R Weare w Badgworth and Biddisham 76-84; R Pilton w Croscombe, N Wootton and Dinder from 84. The Rectory, The Crescent, Croscombe, Wells, Somerset BA5 3QN   Shepton Mallet (0749) 342242

MILLIGAN, William Edward. b 03. TCD BA25 MA29. CITC 28. d 28 p 29. I Bright w Ballee and Killough D & D 68-73; rtd 73. 2 Blackwood Court, Helen's Bay, Bangor, Co Down BT19 1TJ   Helens Bay (0247) 852795

MILLIGAN, Canon William John. b 28. Em Coll Cam BA49. Cuddesdon Coll 53. d 55 p 56. C Portsea N End St Mark Portsm 55-62; V New Eltham All SS S'wark 62-71; V Roehampton H Trin 71-79; Can Res St Alb 79-86; Chapl Strasbourg Eur to 86; Angl Rep Eur Insts from 90. 4 rue Stoeber, 67000 Strasbourg, France France (33) 88 35 03 40

MILLINER, Llewelyn Douglas. b 14. Univ of Wales BSc35. d 38 p 39. C-in-c Chelmsf St Luke CD Chelmsf 66-69; Perm to Offic 69-80; rtd 80; Perm to Offic Ex from 80. Fordings, Weare Giffard, Bideford, Devon EX39 4QS Bideford (0237) 473729

MILLING, David Horace. b 29. Or Coll Ox BA51 MA54 Cam Univ PhD73. Cuddesdon Coll 54. d 56 p 57. Lect St D Coll Lamp 73-75; C Caversham Ox 77-81; C Mapledurham 77-81; C Caversham St Andr 81-86; TV Upper Kennett Sarum 86-88; rtd 88. 10 The Maples, Cirencester, Glos GL7 1TQ   Cirencester (0285) 650400

MILLINGTON, Robert William Ernest. b 51. Sheff Univ BA73 St Jo Coll Dur DipTh75. d 76 p 77. C Ormskirk Liv 76-79; C Litherland St Paul Hatton Hill 79-81; V Bootle Ch Ch 81-88; Chapl K Edw Sch Witley from 88. Queen's House, 3 Gurdon's Lane, Wormley, Godalming, Surrey GU8 5TF   Wormley (0428) 684298

MILLINGTON, Stuart. b 45. Lich Th Coll 67. d 70 p 71. C Boulton Derby 70-73; C Moseley St Mary Birm 73-76; TV Staveley and Barrow Hill Derby 76-82; R Wingerworth from 82; RD Chesterfield from 91. The Rectory, Longedge Lane, Wingerworth, Chesterfield, Derbyshire S42 6PU   Chesterfield (0246) 234242

MILLINS, Leslie Albert. b 20. St Paul's Grahamstown. d 53 p 54. V Old St Pancras w Bedf New Town St Matt Lon 69-76; V Edmonton St Alphege 76-89; rtd 89; Perm to Offic Chich from 90. 68 Parkstone Road, Hastings, E Sussex TN34 2NT

MILLS, Alan Francis. b 29. Ch Coll Cam BA52 MA91. Linc Th Coll 52. d 54 p 55. C Hucknall Torkard S'well 54-58; C Bath Bathwick St Jo B & W 58-70; V Drayton 70-76; V Muchelney 70-76; V Alcombe from 76. The Vicarage, Bircham Road, Alcombe, Minehead, Somerset TA24 6BE   Minehead (0643) 703285

MILLS, Alexandra. b 56. Univ of Wales (Abth) BMus78 CertEd79. Ripon Coll Cuddesdon 88. d 90. Par Dn Earlsfield St Andr S'wark from 90. 1 Glebe House, Waynflete Street, London SW18 3QG   081-946 0616

MILLS, Anthony James. b 55. Nottm Univ BA. Linc Th Coll. d 84 p 85. C Mexborough Sheff 84-86; C Howden Team Min York 86-89; V Fylingdales and Hawsker cum Stainsacre from 89. The Vicarage, Mount Pleasant South, Robin Hood's Bay, Whitby, N Yorkshire YO22 4RN Whitby (0947) 880232

MILLS, Canon Clifford James Holden. b 13. AKC39. d 39 p 40. Hon Can St E Cathl St E 63-81; V Reydon 70-78; RD Halesworth 73-81; rtd 78. 16 St Peter's Path, Holton, Halesworth, Suffolk IP19 8NB   Halesworth (0986) 872884

MILLS, David Bryn. b 49. Ox NSM Course. d 83 p 84. NSM Stantonbury Ox 83-87; NSM Stantonbury and Willen from 87. 3 Tuffnell Close, Willen, Milton Keynes MK15 9BL   Milton Keynes (0908) 605171

MILLS, David Francis. b 51. DipHE78. Oak Hill Th Coll 76. d 79 p 80. C Rodbourne Cheney Bris 79-82; C Wolv St Matt Lich 82-85; CF 85-88; TV Braunstone Leic from 88. 36 Woodcote Road, Leicester LE3 2WD   Leicester (0533) 825272

MILLS, Geoffrey Charles Malcolm. b 33. Wycliffe Hall Ox 59. d 61 p 62. C Buckhurst Hill Chelmsf 61-65; C Ecclesall Sheff 65-69; V Endcliffe 69-78; R Whiston from 78. The Rectory, Whiston, Rotherham, S Yorkshire S60 4JA   Rotherham (0709) 364430

MILLS, Glenys Christine. b 38. Open Univ BA81. Dalton Ho Bris DipTh64. d 87. Par Dn Clifton Ch Ch w Em Bris from 87. 14 St Bartholomew's Road, Bristol BS7 9BJ Bristol (0272) 245119

MILLS, Gordon Derek. b 35. Lich Th Coll 60. d 63 p 64. C W Derby St Mary Liv 63-65; C Clifton w Glapton S'well 65-67; V N Wilford St Faith 67-72; V Farnsfield

72-82; P-in-c Kirklington w Hockerton 77-82; Asst Dir of Educn *Blackb* 82-86; P-in-c Brindle 82-86; V Gt Budworth *Ches* 86-88; P-in-c Appleton Thorn and Antrobus 87-88; V Gt Budworth and Antrobus from 88. *The Vicarage, Great Budworth, Northwich, Cheshire CW9 6HF* Comberbach (0606) 891324

MILLS, Hubert Cecil. b 44. TCD BA66 MA71. CITC 67. d 67 p 68. C Dub Rathfarnham *D & G* 67-72; Min Can St Patr Cathl Dub from 69; Succ from 72; C Dub St Steph and St Ann *D & G* 72-77; I Holmpatrick w Balbriggan and Kenure 77-86; I Killiney H Trin from 86. *Holy Trinity Rectory, Killiney, Co Dublin, Irish Republic* Dublin (1) 285-2695

MILLS, Jack Herbert. b 14. d 40 p 41. New Zealand 52-56, 59-61 and from 87; Australia 57-59 and 62-73; Hd Master St Wilfrid's Sch Ex 74-79; Chapl Community of St Wilfrid 74-79; Hon C Ewhurst *Chich* 79-81; Hon C Bodiam 79-81; Perm to Offic Ex 81-85; Chich 85-87; rtd 87. *3 St Chad's Square, Selwyn Village, Point Chevalier, Auckland 2, New Zealand* Auckland (9) 892243

MILLS, Miss Jennifer Clare. b 61. Trin Hall Cam BA82 MA86. Ridley Hall Cam 88. d 91. C Busbridge *Guildf* from 91. *14 Phillips Close, Godalming, Surrey GU7 1XZ* Godalming (0483) 420639

MILLS, Canon John. b 21. Keble Coll Ox BA45 MA47 DipTh48 Lon Univ BD57. Wycliffe Hall Ox 47. d 49 p 50. V Prescot *Liv* 63-88; RD Prescot 72-84; Hon Can Liv Cathl from 74; rtd 88. *3 The Stables, Station Lane, Guilden Sutton, Chester CH3 7SY* Mickle Trafford (0244) 300027

MILLS, John Kettlewell. b 53. BA. Cranmer Hall Dur. d 84 p 85. C Ashton on Mersey St Mary *Ches* 84-87; TV Didsbury St Jas and Em *Man* from 87. *6 Barlow Moor Road, Didsbury Village, Manchester M20 0TR* 061-445 1310

MILLS, Leslie. b 17. Wycliffe Hall Ox 68. d 68 p 69. C Basingstoke *Win* 68-77; C Basing 78-80; C York Town *Guildf* 80-84; rtd 84; Perm to Offic Win from 84; Guildf from 85; Ox from 86. *21 Mill Lane, Yateley, Camberley, Surrey GU17 7TE* Yateley (0252) 870689

MILLS, Michael Henry. b 51. AKC73. St Aug Coll Cant. d 74 p 75. C Newton Aycliffe *Dur* 74-78; C Padgate *Liv* 78-79; TV from 79. *The Vicarage, 1 Briers Close, Fearnhead, Warrington WA2 0DN* Padgate (0925) 823108

MILLS, Peter John. b 52. Sarum & Wells Th Coll 87. d 89 p 90. C Chatham St Wm *Roch* from 89. *26 Ballens Road, Chatham, Kent ME5 8NT* Medway (0634) 62787

MILLS, Philip. b 43. Univ of Wales BSc65 Linacre Coll Ox BA68 MA72. Wycliffe Hall Ox 65. d 68 p 69. C Droylsden St Mary *Man* 68-70; C Bedf Leigh 70-73; V Calderbrook 73-78; V Halifax St Anne Southowram *Wakef* 78-88; R Barnsley St Mary from 88. *The Rectory, 30 Victoria Road, Barnsley, S Yorkshire S70 2BU* Barnsley (0226) 282270

MILLS, Roger Conrad. b 58. Selw Coll Cam BA79 MA83. St Jo Coll Nottm DPS85. d 85 p 86. C Jesmond H Trin *Newc* 85-88; C Alnwick St Mich and St Paul from 88. *The Old School House, Green Batt, Alnwick, Northd NE66 1TU* Alnwick (0665) 602070

MILLS, Walter Charles. b 30. Oak Hill Th Coll 82. d 85 p 86. NSM Broomfield *Chelmsf* 85-88; C Pleshey from 88. *29 Mill Lane, Broomfield, Chelmsford CM1 5BQ* Chelmsford (0245) 441117

MILLS-POWELL, Mark. b 55. Edin Th Sem Virginia. d 83 p 84. C Huyton St Mich *Liv* 83-86; USA from 86. *The Rectory, Box 253-A, Hughesville, Maryland 20637, USA*

MILLSON, Mrs Margaret Lily. b 41. CertEd61. E Midl Min Tr Course 83. dss 86 d 87. NSM Bottesford w Ashby *Linc* from 86. *65 Timberland, Bottesford, Scunthorpe, S Humberside DN16 3SH* Scunthorpe (0724) 865489

MILLWARD, Mark Anthony. b 61. Leeds Poly BSc. St Steph Ho Ox. d 86 p 87. C Sunderland Red Ho *Dur* 86-89; C Leic Ch Sav *Leic* 89-90; V Sunderland Pennywell St Thos *Dur* from 90. *St Thomas's Vicarage, Parkhurst Road, Pennywell, Sunderland SR4 9DB* 091-534 2100

MILLYARD, Alexander John. b 29. St Jo Coll Dur BA53. Qu Coll Birm 53. d 54 p 55. Chapl HM Pris Leeds 67-69; Ex 69-71; Wandsworth 72-73; V Snibston *Leic* 73-75; V Leic All So 75-79; V Blakesley and Adstone *Pet* 79-89; R Blakesley w Adstone and Maidford etc 89-91; rtd 91. *Flat 6, Gainsborough House, Eaton Gardens, Hove, E Sussex* Brighton (0273) 728722

✠**MILMINE, Rt Rev Douglas.** b 21. CBE83. St Pet Hall Ox BA46 MA46. Clifton Th Coll 47. d 47 p 48 c 73. C Ilfracombe SS Phil and Jas *Ex* 47-50; C Slough *Ox* 50-53; Chile 54-69; Adn N Chile, Bolivia and Peru 63-69;

Hon Can Chile from 69; Area Sec SAMS 69-72; Bp Paraguay 73-85; rtd 86. *1C Clive Court, 24 Grand Parade, Eastbourne, E Sussex BN21 3DD* Eastbourne (0323) 34159

MILMINE, Neil Edward Douglas. b 46. Kent Univ BSc70. Wycliffe Hall Ox 80. d 82 p 83. C Hailsham *Chich* 82-86; C Horsham 86; TV from 86. *St Mark's House, North Heath Lane, Horsham, W Sussex RH12 4PJ* Horsham (0403) 54964

MILN, Dr Peter. b 43. MBIM Univ of Wales (Swansea) BA65 Nottm Univ MTh81 PhD89. E Midl Min Tr Course 76. d 79 p 80. NSM Uttoxeter w Bramshall *Lich* 79-85; CF (TAVR) from 82. *41 Balance Street, Uttoxeter, Staffs ST14 8JQ* Uttoxeter (0889) 565110

MILNE, Alan. b 54. RMN SRN FETC. Cranmer Hall Dur 89. d 91. C Hartlepool St Luke *Dur* from 91. *4 Newquay Close, Hartlepool, Cleveland* Hartlepool (0429) 233605

MILNE, Miss Christine Helen. b 48. LTCL71 Lon Univ DipRS86. S'wark Ord Course 83. dss 86 d 87. S Lambeth St Steph *S'wark* 86-89; Par Dn 87-89; New Zealand from 89. *Elim RD2, Keri Keri, North Island, New Zealand*

MILNE, Glenn Alexander Roscoe. b 62. Or Coll Ox BA85 MA89. Westcott Ho Cam 87. d 89 p 90. C Hexham *Newc* from 89. *3 Dipton Close, Hexham, Northd NE46 1UG* Hexham (0434) 604935

MILNER, David. b 38. St Aid Birkenhead 63. d 66 p 67. C Ulverston H Trin *Carl* 66-68; C Mickleover All SS *Derby* 68-71; C Mickleover St Jo 68-71; V 71-82; P-in-c Sandiacre 82-86; P-in-c Doveridge from 86; RD Longford from 86. *The Vicarage, Church Lane, Doveridge, Derby DE6 5NN* Uttoxeter (0889) 563420

MILNER, Eric. b 10. Mert Coll Ox BA33 MA37. Linc Th Coll 35. d 36 p 37. V Bentley *Sheff* 67-80; rtd 80; Perm to Offic *Wakef* from 86. *30 Hillcrest Avenue, Ossett, W Yorkshire* Wakefield (0924) 271740

MILNER, Leslie. b 35. Birm Univ BSc57 St Jo Coll Cam BA59. Wells Th Coll 61. d 63 p 64. C Yardley St Edburgha *Birm* 63-66; C Seacroft *Ripon* 66-71; Dir St Basil's Cen Deritend from 71; Lic to Offic *Birm* 71-86. *112 London Road, Worcester* Worcester (0905) 360271

✠**MILNER, Rt Rev Ronald James.** b 27. Pemb Coll Cam BA49 MA52. Wycliffe Hall Ox 51. d 53 p 54 c 88. Succ Sheff Cathl *Sheff* 53-58; V Westwood *Cov* 58-64; V Fletchamstead 64-70; R Southn St Mary w H Trin *Win* 70-72; P-in-c Southn St Matt 70-72; Lic to Offic 72-73; TR Southn (City Cen) 73-83; Hon Can Win Cathl 75-83; Adn Linc 83-88; Can and Preb Linc Cathl 83-88; Suff Bp Burnley *Blackb* from 88. *Dean House, 449 Padiham Road, Burnley, Lancs BB12 6TE* Burnley (0282) 23564

MILNES, David Ian. b 45. Chich Th Coll 74. d 76 p 77. C Walthamstow St Sav *Chelmsf* 76-80; C Chingford SS Pet and Paul 80-83; P-in-c Gt Ilford St Alb 83-87; V from 87. *The Vicarage, 99 Albert Road, Ilford, Essex IG1 1HS* 081-478 2428

MILROY, Mrs Ethel Doreen. b 33. Bedf Coll Lon BSc54 Bris Univ PGCE69 Nottm Univ MEd79. Nor Ord Course 88. d 91. NSM Tideswell *Derby* from 91. *Barn Cottage, Parke Road, Tideswell, Buxton* Tideswell (0298) 872242

MILTON, Andrew John. b 54. BD. St Steph Ho Ox. d 83 p 84. C Highfield *Ox* 83-87; TV Banbury from 87. *St Leonard's Vicarage, Middleton Road, Banbury, Oxon OX16 8RG* Banbury (0295) 62120

MILTON, Miss Angela Daphne. b 50. Oak Hill Th Coll 84. d 87. NSM Watford *St Alb* from 87. *34 Woodhurst Avenue, Garston, Watford WD2 6RQ* Garston (0923) 671937

MILTON, Claudius James Barton. b 29. K Coll Lon BD52 AKC52. d 53 p 54. C Sudbury St Andr *Lon* 53-57; Asst Chapl Bedf Sch 57-65; Chapl Cranbrook Sch Kent 65-74; Chapl Clayesmore Sch Blandford from 74. *28 Oakwood Drive, Iwerne Minster, Blandford Forum, Dorset DT11 8QT* Fontmell Magna (0747) 792

MILTON, Derek Rees. b 45. Open Univ BA76 Lon Univ BD80. St Jo Sem Wonersh 63. d 68 p 69. In RC Ch 68-84; Hon C Luton Lewsey St Hugh *St Alb* 84-85; Hon C Houghton Regis 85-86; C 86-89; TV Brixham w Churston Ferrers and Kingswear *Ex* from 89. *All Saints' Vicarage, 16 Holwell Road, Brixham, Devon TQ5 9NE* Brixham (08045) 55549

MILTON-THOMPSON, Dr David Gerald. b 17. OBE76. MRCS LRCP42 Em Coll Cam BA39 MA MB BChir49. Lon Coll of Div 62. d 63 p 64. CMS 49-81 and 85-88; Kenya 52-81; C Chadwell *Chelmsf* 81-82; Hon C 82-85; Uganda 85-88; rtd 88; Hon C Sevenoaks St Nic *Roch* from 88. *1 The Glebe, Oak Lane, Sevenoaks, Kent TN13 1NN* Sevenoaks (0732) 462977

MILTON-THOMPSON, Jonathan Patrick. b 51. Nottm Univ BA76. Oak Hill Th Coll 86. d 88 p 89. C Bispham Blackb from 88. Church Villa, All Hallows Road, Blackpool FY2 0AY   Blackpool (0253) 53648

MILVERTON of Lagos and Clifton, Rev and Rt Hon Lord (Fraser Arthur Richard Richards). b 30. Bps' Coll Cheshunt. d 57 p 58. C Beckenham St Geo Roch 57-59; C Sevenoaks St Jo 59-60; C Gt Bookham Guildf 60-63; V Okewood 63-67; R Christian Malford w Sutton Benger etc Bris from 67. The Rectory, Christian Malford, Chippenham, Wilts SN15 4BW   Seagry (0249) 720466

MILVERTON, Frederic Jack. b 15. Lon Univ BSc37 Leeds Univ MEd40. Ripon Hall Ox 56. d 57 p 58. Lic to Offic Sarum 70-79; Hd of Educn Weymouth Coll of Educn 70-76; Dean Educn Dorset Inst of HE 76-79; TV Oakdale St Geo 79-82; rtd 82. Flat 4, Compass South, Rodwell Road, Weymouth, Dorset DT4 8QT   Weymouth (0305) 788930

MILVERTON, Mrs Ruth Erica. b 32. Open Univ BA78 Southn Univ MA82. Sarum Th Coll 83. dss 86 d 87. Weymouth H Trin Sarum 86-87; Hon Par Dn from 87. Flat 4, Compass South, Rodwell Road, Weymouth, Dorset DT4 8QT   Weymouth (0305) 788930

MILWARD, Terence George. b 23. Ripon Hall Ox 66. d 68 p 69. C Selly Oak St Mary Birm 68-70; C Edgbaston St Bart 70-75; TV Bournemouth St Pet w St Swithun, St Steph etc Win 75-81; R Smannell w Enham Alamein 81-88; rtd 88; Lic to Offic Guildf from 88. Church House Flat, Church Lane, Witley, Godalming, Surrey GU8 5PN   Wormley (0428) 685308

MINALL, Peter. b 26. Lon Univ BSc47. Bps' Coll Cheshunt 51. d 53 p 54. C Bishop's Stortford St Mich St Alb 53-57; C Luton w E Hyde 57-63; C Tuffley Glouc 63-65; Asst Youth Chapl 65-69; V Stroud 69-84; RD Bisley 78-84; P-in-c Barnwood from 84; Chapl Coney Hill Hosp Glouc from 86. The Vicarage, Barnwood Avenue, Gloucester GL4 7AB   Gloucester (0452) 613760

MINAY, Francis Arthur Rodney. b 44. Edin Coll of Art DA65. Westcott Ho Cam 66. d 68 p 69. C Edenbridge Roch 68-73; C Bromley St Mark 73-75; V Tudeley w Capel 75-79; TV Littleham w Exmouth Ex 79-82; P-in-c Bolton Percy York from 82; Asst Chapl to Arts and Recreation in the NE from 82. The Rectory, Bolton Percy, York YO5 7AL   Appleton Roebuck (090484) 213

MINCHER, John Derek Bernard. b 31. d 60 p 61. OSB 54-80; Lic to Offic Ox 60-80; Perm to Offic St E 81-87; C Halesworth w Linstead, Chediston, Holton etc 87-90; P-in-c Worlingworth, Southolt, Tannington, Bedfield etc from 90. The Rectory, Worlingworth, Woodbridge, Suffolk IP13 7NT   Worlingworth (072876) 8102

MINCHEW, Donald Patrick. b 48. Univ of Wales (Cardiff) BD76. St Mich Coll Llan 72. d 76 p 77. C Glouc St Aldate Glouc 76-80; P-in-c Sharpness CD 80-81; V Sharpness w Purton and Brookend from 81; Miss to Seamen from 81. The Vicarage, Sanigar Lane, Newtown, Berkeley, Glos GL13 9NF   Dursley (0453) 811360

MINCHIN, Anthony John. b 35. St Cath Coll Cam BA59 MA. Wells Th Coll 59. d 61 p 62. C Cheltenham St Pet Glouc 61-64; C Bushey St Alb 64-67; V Cheltenham St Mich Glouc 65-74; V Lower Cam 74-82; V Tuffley from 82. St Barnabas' Vicarage, Tuffley, Gloucester GL4 9SB   Gloucester (0452) 24173

MINCHIN, Charles Scott. b 51. Trin Coll Cam BA72 MA75. Linc Th Coll 73. d 75 p 76. C Gt Wyrley Lich 75-78; TV Wilnecote 78-82; C Tamworth 82-84; C-in-c Glascote CD 84-88; R Brierley Hill from 88. The Rectory, 2 Church Hill, Brierley Hill, W Midlands DY5 3PX   Brierley Hill (0384) 78146

MINCHIN, Canon George Reginald. b 05. TCD BA31 MA43. d 31 p 32. I Camus-juxta-Bann D & R 65-75; Can Derry Cathl 70-75; rtd 75. 4 Fortview, Portballintrae, Bushmills, Co Antrim   Bushmills (02657) 31607

MINCHIN, Canon Sidney Frederick. b 14. Lon Univ BA36. Lich Th Coll 36. d 38 p 39. R Brandeston w Kettleburgh St E 65-79; RD Loes 70-78; rtd 79; Perm to Offic B & W from 80. 24 Fore Street, Westonzoyland, Bridgwater, Somerset TA7 0EE   Weston Zoyland (0278) 606

MINGINS, Marion Elizabeth. b 52. Birm Univ BSocSc73 CQSW75. Cam DipRS78. d 87. CA from 79; NSM Battersea Park All SS S'wark 87-89; Sen Selection Sec ACCM 87-89; OHP 89-91; Min Can and Chapl St E Cathl St E from 91; Asst Dioc Dir of Ords and Voc Adv from 91. Clopton Cottage, The Churchyard, Bury St Edmunds, Suffolk IP33 1RS   Bury St Edmunds (0284) 755868

MINHINNICK, Leslie. b 18. Jes Coll Ox BA39 MA43. Wycliffe Hall Ox 40. d 41 p 42. V Lytham St Jo Blackb

66-81; rtd 83; Perm to Offic Ban from 83. The Old School House, Cemaes, Anglesey, Gwynedd LL67 0NG   Cemaes Bay (0407) 710601

MINICH, Mason Faulconer. b 38. d 66 p 67. USA 66-71 and from 81; C Alverstoke Portsm 80; C Romford Ascension Collier Row Chelmsf 80-81. 5055 Seminary Road, Apartment 1319, Alexandria, Virginia 22311, USA

MINNS, John Alfred. b 38. Oak Hill Th Coll 63. d 68 p 69. C Cheadle Hulme St Andr Ches 68-72; C Hartford 72-74; V Wharton 74-85; V Halliwell St Paul Man 85-87; C Halliwell St Pet from 87. 12 Woodburn Drive, Smithills, Bolton BL1 6NH   Bolton (0204) 849418

MINNS, John Charles. b 42. E Anglian Minl Tr Course. d 85 p 86. NSM Heigham St Barn w St Bart Nor 85-91; NSM Nor St Geo Tombland from 91. Linton House, 3 Mill Hill Road, Norwich NR23DP   Norwich (0603) 611480

MINORS, Graham Glyndwr Cavil. b 44. Glouc Sch of Min. d 79 p 79. Hon C Lower Cam Glouc 79-83; C Leckhampton SS Phil and Jas w Cheltenham St Jas 83-89; V Cainscross w Selsley from 89. The Vicarage, 58 Cashes Green Road, Stroud, Glos GL5 4RA   Stroud (0453) 755148

MINSHALL, Douglas Arthur. b 24. E Midl Min Tr Course 78. d 81 p 82. NSM Worksop Priory S'well 81-85; NSM E Retford 85-87; C 87-88; NSM W Retford 85-87; C 87-88; P-in-c Clarborough w Hayton from 88. The Vicarage, Church Lane, Clarborough, Retford, Notts DN22 9NA   Retford (0777) 704781

MINSHALL, Neville David. b 37. Wolv Poly MA86. AKC64. d 65 p 66. C Wolv St Paul Lich 65-66; C Stafford St Mary 66-68; C Rugeley 68-69; C Shrewsbury H Cross 69-73; P-in-c Wrockwardine Wood 73-77; R Brierley Hill 77-81; R Hope w Shelve Heref from 81; V Middleton from 81; R Worthen from 81. The Rectory, Worthen, Shrewsbury SY5 9HW   Worthen (0743) 891476

MINSON, Roger Graham. b 41. Leeds Univ BA64 Bris Univ DSA69. Coll of Resurr Mirfield 64. d 66 p 67. C Horfield St Greg Bris 66-70; C Southmead 70-73; V Lawrence Weston 74-81; TV Knowle from 81. St Martin's Vicarage, St Martin's Road, Bristol BS4 2NH   Bristol (0272) 776275

MINTER, Richard Arthur. b 05. Worc Coll Ox BA29 MA33 BD55. St Steph Ho Ox 29. d 32 p 33. V Stow w Quy Ely 46-85; rtd 85; P-in-c Stow w Quy Ely from 85. The Vicarage, Quy, Cambridge CB5 9AD   Cambridge (0223) 811277

MINTON, Richard Reginald. b 09. Bible Churchmen's Coll 32. d 35 p 36. R Corley Cov 65-76; rtd 76; Chapl All Hallows Sch Rousdon 78-81. Flat B, The Old Vicarage, Case Gardens, Seaton, Devon EX12 2AN   Seaton (0297) 22170

MINTY, Kenneth Desmond. b 25. Ch Ch Ox BA48 MA51. Lich Th Coll 71 Qu Coll Birm 72. d 73 p 74. Asst Chapl Wrekin Coll Shropshire 73-84; Chapl 84-86; Hon C Lawley Lich 74-75; Hon C Cen Telford 75-81; Hon C Longdon-upon-Tern, Rodington, Uppington etc 81-89; V Ercall Magna from 89; V Rowton from 89. The Vicarage, High Ercall, Telford, Shropshire TF6 6BE   Telford (0952) 770206

MINTY, Selwyn Francis. b 34. St D Coll Lamp 58. d 61 p 62. C Tonyrefail Llan 61-66; C Pontypridd St Cath 66-69; V Cilfynydd 69-84; V Crynant from 84. The Vicarage, 35 Main Road, Crynant, Neath, W Glam SA10 8NT   Neath (0639) 750226

MIR, Amene Rahman. b 58. Man Univ BA81. Coll of Resurr Mirfield 81. d 83 p 84. C Walton St Mary Liv 83-87; Perm to Offic Man from 87; Chapl Prestwich Hosp Man and Asst Chapl Hope Hosp Salford from 90. 87 Carrington Lane, Sale, Cheshire M33 5WH   061-973 1836

MITCHAM, Andrew Mark. b 66. Kent Univ BA87 Leeds Univ BA90. Coll of Resurr Mirfield 88. d 91. Par Dn Downham Market w Bexwell Ely from 91. 82 Wimbotsham Road, Downham Market, Norfolk PE38 9QB   Downham Market (0366) 386114

MITCHELL, Albert George. b 48. TCD BA48. d 88 p 89. Bp's C Skreen w Kilmacshalgan and Dromard T, K & A from 88. The Glebe, Kilglass, Co Sligo, Irish Republic   Kilglass (96) 36258

MITCHELL, Allan. b 52. Kelham Th Coll 74 Linc Th Coll 78. d 78 p 79. C Kells Carl 78-81; C Upperby St Jo 81-83; V Pennington w Lindal and Marton 83-88; V Westf St Mary from 88. St Mary's Vicarage, Salisbury Street, Workington, Cumbria CA14 3TR   Workington (0900) 3227

MITCHELL, Andrew Patrick. b 37. Ripon Coll Cuddesdon 84 English Coll Valladolid 59. d 64 p 65. In RC Ch 64-85; C Woolwich St Mary w St Mich S'wark 85-87; V E

Wickham from 87. *St Michael's Vicarage, Upper Wickham Lane, Welling, Kent DA16 3AP* 081-304 1214

MITCHELL, Cecil Robert. b 32. QUB BSc54 TCD 63. **d** 65 **p** 66. C Belf St Mary Magd *Conn* 65-68; C Belf St Mark 68-70; Dioc Sec 70-74; Dioc Sec *D & D* 70-74; I Ballywalter 74-82; V Malew *S & M* 82-84; I Bright w Ballee and Killough *D & D* 84-89; I Killyleagh from 89. *34 Inishbeg, Killyleagh, Downpatrick, Co Down BT30 9TR* Downpatrick (0396) 828231

MITCHELL, Christopher Allan. b 51. Newc Univ BA72. Oak Hill Th Coll 82. **d** 84 **p** 85. C Guisborough *York* 84-87; C Thornaby on Tees 87-88; TV from 88. *The Vicarage, 14 Whitehouse Road, Thornaby, Stockton-on-Tees, Cleveland TS17 0AJ* Stockton-on-Tees (0642) 763071

MITCHELL, Christopher Derek. b 61. Univ of Wales (Lamp) BA85 Leic Univ MA86 Qu Coll Cam BA88. Westcott Ho Cam 87. **d** 89 **p** 90. C Streetly *Lich* from 89. *2 Foley Wood Close, Sutton Coldfield, W Midlands B74 3PJ* 021-353 0523

MITCHELL, Canon David George. b 35. QUB BA56. Sarum Th Coll 59. **d** 61 **p** 62. C Westbury-on-Trym H Trin *Bris* 61-64; C Cricklade w Latton 64-68; V Fishponds St Jo 68-77; RD Stapleton 76-77; TR E Bris 77-87; Hon Can Bris Cathl from 87; R Syston from 87; V Warmley from 87; P-in-c Bitton from 87; RD Bitton from 87. *The Vicarage, Church Avenue, Warmley, Bristol BS15 5JJ* Bristol (0272) 673965

MITCHELL, Preb David Norman. b 35. Tyndale Hall Bris 64. **d** 67 **p** 68. C Marple All SS *Ches* 67-70; C St Helens St Helen *Liv* 70-72; V S Lambeth St Steph *S'wark* 72-78; P-in-c Brixton Rd Ch Ch 73-75; SE Area Sec CPAS 78-81; R Uphill *B & W* from 81; Chapl Weston-super-Mare Gen Hosp from 86; Preb Wells Cathl *B & W* from 90. *The Rectory, 3 Old Church Road, Uphill, Weston-super-Mare, Avon BS23 4UH* Weston-super-Mare (0934) 620156

MITCHELL, Edwin. b 44. St Jo Coll Nottm BTh74. **d** 74 **p** 75. C Worksop St Jo *S'well* 74-77; C Waltham Abbey *Chelmsf* 77-80; V Whiston *Liv* 80-91; R Wombwell *Sheff* from 91. *The Rectory, 1 Rectory Close, Wombwell, Barnsley, S Yorkshire S73 8EY* Barnsley (0226) 752166

MITCHELL, Eric Sidney. b 24. S Dios Minl Tr Scheme 77. **d** 80 **p** 81. NSM Portland All SS w St Pet *Sarum* 80-83; C from 88; Bermuda 83-88. *10 Underhedge Gardens, Portland, Dorset DT5 2DX* Portland (0305) 821059

MITCHELL, Frank. b 21. Ely Th Coll 49. **d** 51 **p** 52. V Scarborough St Sav *York* 62-73; V Scarborough St Sav w All SS 73-83; rtd 83. *6 Sitwell Street, Scarborough, N Yorkshire YO11 5EX* Scarborough (0723) 367948

MITCHELL, Canon Frank Leonard. b 14. St Cath Soc Ox BA39 MA47. Wycliffe Hall Ox 46. **d** 48 **p** 49. R Hayes *Roch* 66-77; C Speldhurst w Groombridge 77; C Speldhurst w Groombridge and Ashurst 77-79; rtd 79; Perm to Offic Chich from 80; Roch from 82. *10 Beechwood Close, Burwash, Etchingham, E Sussex TN19 7BS* Burwash (0435) 822301

MITCHELL, Canon George Alfred. b 23. TCD BA45 MA56. **d** 46 **p** 47. I Carrickfergus *Conn* 59-70; I Ban St Comgall *D & D* 70-88; Can Belf Cathl 78-88; rtd 88. *2 Glendun Park, Bangor, Co Down BT20 4UX* Bangor (0247) 460882

MITCHELL, Gordon Frank Henry. b 26. QFSM. FIFireE. Sarum & Wells Th Coll 74. **d** 77 **p** 78. NSM Alderbury and W Grimstead *Sarum* 77-91; NSM Alderbury Team from 91. *Seefeld, Southampton Road, Whaddon, Salisbury SP5 3EB* Salisbury (0722) 710516

MITCHELL, Graham Bell. b 40. Otago Univ BA64 MA65 Worc Coll Ox BA73 MA76. St Chad's Coll Dur 66. **d** 68 **p** 69. C Bris St Agnes w St Simon *Bris* 68-71; C Bedminster St Mich 73-76; V Auckland St Pet *Dur* 76-78; Vice-Prin Chich Th Coll 78-83; C Brighton St Pet w Chpl Royal and St Jo *Chich* 83-86; P-in-c Scaynes Hill from 86. *The Vicarage, Scaynes Hill, Haywards Heath, W Sussex RH17 7PB* Haywards Heath (0444) 831265

MITCHELL, Canon Henry Gordon. b 20. St Chad's Coll Dur BA44 DipTh45 MA47. **d** 45 **p** 46. R Fulbeck *Linc* 52-72; RD Loveden 64-72; Can and Preb Linc Cathl

67-85; P-in-c Carlton Scroop w Normanton 69-72; V New Sleaford 72-85; rtd 85; Perm to Offic *Linc* from 85. *3 Lime Grove, Caythorpe, Grantham, Lincs NG32 3DH* Loveden (0400) 73346

MITCHELL, Miss Josephine Dorothy. b 36. Dalton Ho Bris 65. **dss** 76 **d** 87. Hailsham *Chich* 75-85; Enfield St Jas *Lon* 85-87; Par Dn from 87. *170 Addison Road, Enfield, Middx EN3 5LE* 081-805 1271

MITCHELL, Keith Adrian (Brother Anthony). b 47. Kelham Th Coll 66. **d** 70 **p** 71. C Owton Manor CD *Dur* 70-73; C Middlesb St Thos *York* 73-76; SSF 76-81; C Horden *Dur* 82; V Hartlepool St Oswald 82-89; OSB from 89; C Greenhill *Sheff* from 91. *St Peter's Clergy House, Reney Avenue, Sheffield S8 7FN* Sheffield (0742) 377422

MITCHELL, Kevin. b 49. Newc Univ BSc71 Ox Univ BA83. Ripon Coll Cuddesdon 81. **d** 83 **p** 84. C Cantril Farm *Liv* 83-86; Chapl N Middx Hosp from 86; C Gt Cam Road St Jo and St Jas *Lon* 86-90; P-in-c Cricklewood St Pet from 90. *St Peter's Vicarage, 5 Farm Avenue, London NW2 2EG* 081-450 9043

MITCHELL, Leonard David. b 30. ACA56 FCA67. Wells Th Coll 60. **d** 61 **p** 62. C Hilborough w Bodney *Nor* 61-64; C Oxborough w Foulden and Caldecote 61-64; C Cockley Cley w Gooderstone 61-64; C Gt and Lt Cressingham w Threxton 61-64; V Ernesettle *Ex* 64-67; Canada from 67. *Address temp unknown*

MITCHELL, Very Rev Patrick Reynolds. b 30. FSA81 Mert Coll Ox BA52 MA56. Wells Th Coll 52. **d** 54 **p** 55. C Mansf St Mark *S'well* 54-57; Chapl Wells Th Coll 57-61; PV Wells Cathl *B & W* 57-61; V Milton *Portsm* 61-67; V Frome St Jo *B & W* 67-73; P-in-c Woodlands 67-73; Dir of Ords 70-74; Dean Wells 73-89; Dean of Windsor and Dom Chapl to HM the Queen from 89. *The Deanery, Windsor Castle, Windsor, Berks SL4 1NJ* Windsor (0753) 865561

MITCHELL, Peter Derek. b 30. Roch Th Coll 67. **d** 69 **p** 70. C Wargrave *Ox* 69-72; V Lund *Blackb* 72-80; V Badsey w Aldington and Wickhamford from 80. *The Vicarage, Badsey, Evesham, Worcs WR11 5EW* Evesham (0386) 830343

MITCHELL, Richard John Anthony. b 64. St Martin's Coll Lanc BA85 PGCE86. Sarum & Wells Th Coll 88. **d** 91. C Kendal H Trin *Carl* from 91. *7 Wattsfield Road, Kendal, Cumbria LA9 5JH* Kendal (0539) 729572

MITCHELL, Robert Hugh. b 53. MA. Ripon Coll Cuddesdon. **d** 82 **p** 83. C E Dulwich St Jo *S'wark* 82-86; C Cam Gt St Mary w St Mich *Ely* 86-90; Chapl Girton Coll Cam 86-90; Asst Chapl Win Coll from 90. *26 St Cross Road, Winchester SO23 9HX* Winchester (0962) 860051

MITCHELL, Robert McFarlane. b 50. Man Univ BA72. Wycliffe Hall Ox 73. **d** 75 **p** 76. C Tonbridge SS Pet and Paul *Roch* 75-80; CF from 80. *c/o MOD (Army), Bagshot Park, Bagshot, Surrey GU19 5PL* Bagshot (0276) 71717

MITCHELL, Roger Sulway. b 36. Chich Th Coll 70. **d** 71 **p** 71. C Sidcup St Jo *Roch* 71-74; C Pembury 74-76; Lic to Offic *Truro* from 76; Chapl St Lawr Hosp Bodmin from 76; Chapl Cornwall and Is of Scilly Mental Health Unit from 88. *12 Beacon Road, Bodmin, Cornwall PL31 1AS* Bodmin (0208) 76357 or 73281

MITCHELL, Canon Stanley. b 04. Man Egerton Hall 33. **d** 35 **p** 36. R Heaton Moor *Man* 62-71; rtd 71; Lic to Offic *Blackb* from 71. *26 The Strand, Fleetwood, Lancs FY5 2AL* Fleetwood (03917) 4497

MITCHELL, Stephen Andrew John. b 56. Ch Ch Coll Cant CertEd78 K Coll Lon AKC77 BD80. Lambeth STh90 Coll of Resurr Mirfield 80. **d** 82 **p** 83. C Chatham St Steph *Roch* 82-87; C Edenbridge 87-91; V from 91. *The Vicarage, Crockham Hill, Edenbridge, Kent TN8 6RL* Edenbridge (0732) 862258

MITCHELL, Stephen John. b 51. Ex Univ BA73 Fitzw Coll Cam BA78 MA. Ridley Hall Cam 76. **d** 79 **p** 80. C Gt Malvern St Mary *Worc* 79-81; Prec Leic Cathl *Leic* 82-85; R Barrow upon Soar w Walton le Wolds from 85. *The Rectory, 27 Cotes Road, Barrow on Soar, Loughborough, Leics LE12 8JP* Quorn (0509) 412471

MITCHELL, Steven. b 58. BTh. St Jo Coll Nottm. **d** 83 **p** 84. C Ovenden *Wakef* 83-87; V Gawthorpe and Chickenley Heath from 87. *The Vicarage, 73 Chickenley Lane, Dewsbury, W Yorkshire WF12 8QD* Wakefield (0924) 451547

MITCHELL, Stuart Ian. b 50. Wadh Coll Ox BA71 DPhil74. S'wark Ord Course 81. **d** 85 **p** 87. NSM Charlton St Luke w H Trin *S'wark* 85-86; NSM Kidbrooke St Jas 86-88; NSM Newbold and Dunston *Derby* from 88. *1 Hollens Way, Holme Hall, Chesterfield, Derbyshire S40 4XR* Chesterfield (0246) 211053

MITCHELL, Tom Good. b 21. K Coll (NS) STh62. d 63 p 64. Canada 63-81; V Misterton and W Stockwith *S'well* 81-87; rtd 87; Perm to Offic *Glouc* from 87. *Ashbury, Binyon Road, Winchcombe, Cheltenham, Glos GL54 5QQ* Cheltenham (0242) 604279

MITCHELL, Wilfred Christopher. b 15. Lich Th Coll 51. d 53 p 54. V Linc All SS *Linc* 69-81; rtd 81. *51A Downview Road, Worthing, W Sussex BN11 4QH* Worthing (0903) 502745

MITCHELL, William Blanchard. b 26. Lon Univ DipTh54. St Aid Birkenhead 53. d 55 p 56. CF 61-77; V Nicholforest and Kirkandrews on Esk *Carl* 77-84; R Kirkby Thore w Temple Sowerby and w Newbiggin 84-89; rtd 89. *Koi Hai, 23 Longlands Road, Carlisle CA3 9AD* Carlisle (0228) 42630

MITCHELL-INNES, Charles William. b 47. Pemb Coll Cam BA69 MA73. Sarum Th Coll 83. d 86 p 87. Asst Chapl Sherborne Sch Dorset 86-89; Perm to Offic *Sarum* from 86; Chapl Milton Abbey Sch Dorset from 90. *Monmouth House, Milton Abbey School, Blandford Forum, Dorset DT11 0DA* Milton Abbas (0258) 880676

MITCHELL-INNES, James Alexander. b 39. Ch Ch Ox BA64 MA66. Lon Coll of Div 65. d 67 p 68. C Cullompton *Ex* 67-71; Nigeria 71-75; P-in-c Puddletown w Athelhampton and Burleston *Sarum* 75-78; R Puddletown and Tolpuddle 78-82; V Win Ch Ch *Win* from 82. *Christ Church Vicarage, Sleepers Hill, Winchester, Hants SO22 4ND* Winchester (0962) 62414

MITCHINSON, Frank. b 37. AKC60. d 61 p 62. C Cross Heath *Lich* 61-64; C Forrabury w Minster and Trevalga *Truro* 64-68; C Harpenden St Nic *St Alb* 68-70; R Southwick *Chich* 70-83; V Billingshurst 83-88; V Preston from 88. *35 Preston Drove, Brighton BN1 6LA* Brighton (0273) 555033

MITCHINSON, Canon Ronald. b 35. Linc Th Coll 66. d 68 p 69. C Heworth St Mary *Dur* 68-72; C Banbury *Ox* 72-73; TV 73-76; New Zealand 76-82; TR Banbury *Ox* 82-86; RD Deddington 84-86; Ind Chapl from 86; Hon Can Ch Ch from 90. *20 The Glebe, Cumnor, Oxford OX2 9QA* Oxford (0865) 862535

MITFORD, Bertram William Jeremy. b 27. Wells Th Coll 62. d 64 p 65. C Hollinwood *Man* 64-67; C Atherton 67-68; C Frome St Jo *B & W* 68-71; V Cleeve 72-74; V Cleeve w Chelvey and Brockley 74-79; C Shepton Mallet 79-84; Chapl HM Pris Shepton Mallet from 79; C Shepton Mallet w Doulting *B & W* from 84. *2 Charlton Road, Shepton Mallet, Somerset BA4 5NY* Shepton Mallet (0749) 2825

MITRA, Avijit. b 53. Keble Coll Ox BA76. Ox NSM Course 84. d 88 p 89. NSM Abingdon *Ox* from 88; Asst Chapl Abingdon Sch from 88. *Waste Court, 76 Bath Street, Abingdon, Oxon OX14 1EB* Abingdon (0235) 520326

MITSON, Miss Joyce. b 37. Man Univ CertEd64. Trin Coll Bris DipHE79. dss 79 d 87. Wellington w Eyton *Lich* 79-85; Farnworth *Liv* 85-87; Par Dn from 87. *43 Hampton Drive, Cronton, Widnes, Cheshire WA8 9DA* 051-423 3900

MITTON, Michael Simon. b 53. Ex Univ BA75. St Jo Coll Nottm 76. d 78 p 79. C High Wycombe *Ox* 78-82; C Kidderminster St Geo *Worc* 82; TV 82-89; Dir Angl Renewal Min from 89; Angl Renewal Min Adv *Ripon* 90-91. *6 Scriven Road, Knaresborough, N Yorkshire HG5 9EQ* Harrogate (0423) 862034

MOAKES, Benjamin Hall. d 81 p 83. Hon C Camberwell St Mich w All So w Em *S'wark* from 81. *92 Day House, Bethwin Road, London SE5 0YE* 071-703 2907

MOATE, Gerard Grigglestone. b 54. BA. Oak Hill Th Coll 79. d 82 p 83. C Mildmay Grove St Jude and St Paul *Lon* 82-85; C Hampstead St Jo 85-88; P-in-c Pinxton *Derby* 88; V Charlesworth and Dinting Vale from 88. *The Vicarage, Marple Road, Charlesworth, Broadbottom, Hyde, Cheshire SK14 6DA* Glossop (0457) 852440 or 868740

MOATE, Phillip. b 47. SRN DN RNT. N Ord Course 87. d 90 p 91. NSM Upper Holme Valley *Wakef* from 90. *128 Slaithwaite Road, Meltham, Huddersfield HD7 3PW* Huddersfield (0484) 851205

MOATT, Richard Albert. b 54. K Coll Lon BD76 AKC76. Linc Th Coll 80. d 81 p 82. C Egremont and Haile *Carl* 81-85; V Addingham, Edenhall, Langwathby and Culgaith from 85. *The Vicarage, Langwathby, Penrith, Cumbria CA10 1LW* Langwathby (076881) 212

MOBBERLEY, Keith John. b 56. BA. Westcott Ho Cam. d 84 p 85. C Cov Caludon *Cov* 84-87; C Kenilworth St Nic from 87. *St Barnabas's House, 145 Albion Street, Kenilworth, Warks CV8 2FY* Kenilworth (0926) 53901

MOBBERLEY, Mrs Susan. b 57. Kent Univ BA79. Westcott Ho Cam 81. dss 84 d 90. Cov Caludon *Cov*

84-87; Lic to Offic from 87. *St Barnabas' House, 145 Albion Street, Kenilworth, Warks CV8 2FY* Kenilworth (0926) 53901

MOBBS, Bernard Frederick. b 26. S'wark Ord Course 71. d 72 p 73. C Purley St Barn *S'wark* 72-74; Vice-Prin S'wark Ord Course 74-80; P-in-c Sydenham St Bart *S'wark* 80-87; V Dormansland from 87. *The Vicarage, The Platt, Dormansland, Lingfield, Surrey RH7 3RA* Lingfield (0342) 832391

MOBERLY, Richard Hamilton. b 30. Trin Hall Cam BA53 MA57. Cuddesdon Coll 53. d 55 p 56. C Walton St Mary *Liv* 55-59; C Kensington St Mary Abbots w St Geo *Lon* 59-63; N Rhodesia 63-64; Zambia 64-66; V Kennington Cross St Anselm *S'wark* 73-77; TV N Lambeth 74-80; Ind Chapl from 80. *5 Atherfold Road, London SW9 9LL* 071-733 6754 or 822 3005

MOBERLY, Robert Walter Lambert. b 52. New Coll Ox MA77 Selw Coll Cam MA80 Trin Coll Cam PhD81. Ridley Hall Cam 74. d 81 p 82. C Knowle *Birm* 81-85; Lect Dur Univ from 85. *8 Princes Street, Durham DH1 4RP* 091-386 4255 or 374 2067

MOBLEY, Ronald John. b 15. Worc Ord Coll. d 62 p 63. V Eastleach w Southrop *Glouc* 68-73; V Newland w Redbrook 74-80; rtd 80; Hon C St-Mary-le-Strand w St Clem Danes *Lon* 85-86. *7 Regency Court, South Cliff, Eastbourne, E Sussex*

MOCKFORD, John Frederick. b 28. Em Coll Cam BA52 MA56. Ridley Hall Cam 52. d 54 p 55. C Ardwick St Silas *Man* 54; C Harpurhey Ch Ch 54-57; V Bootle St Leon *Liv* 57-64; CMS 65-73; Uganda 66-73; Can Missr Kampala 72-73; V Bushbury *Lich* 73-77; TR 77-84; Preb Lich Cathl 81-84; Dir Miss and Past Studies Ridley Hall Cam 84-88; V Ipswich St Marg *St E* from 88. *St Margaret's Vicarage, 32 Constable Road, Ipswich IP4 2UW* Ipswich (0473) 253906

MOCKFORD, Peter John. b 57. Nottm Univ BSc79 St Jo Coll Dur BA88. Cranmer Hall Dur 86. d 89 p 90. C Tamworth *Lich* from 89. *19 Perrycrofts Crescent, Tamworth, Staffs B79 8UA* Tamworth (0827) 69021

MOFFAT, George. b 46. Edin Univ BD77 Open Univ BA87. Edin Th Coll 67. d 72 p 73. C Falkirk *Edin* 73-76; C Edin St Pet 76-81; Chapl Edin Univ 77-81; C Heston *Lon* 81-84; V S Elmsall *Wakef* from 84. *The Vicarage, Doncaster Road, South Elmsall, Pontefract, W Yorkshire WF9 2HS* Pontefract (0977) 642861

MOFFATT, Neil Thomas. b 46. Fitzw Coll Cam BA68 MA72. Qu Coll Birm 69. d 71 p 72. C Old Charlton *S'wark* 71-74; C Walworth St Pet 74-75; C Walworth 75-77; V Dormansland 77-86; TR Padgate *Liv* from 86. *The Rectory, Padgate, Warrington WA2 0PD* Padgate (0925) 821555

MOFFATT, Canon Percy Elliott. b 15. St Aug Coll Cant 38. d 40 p 41. R Stoke *Cov* 71-75; TR Cov Caludon 76-78; Hon Can Cov Cathl 76-82; V Dunchurch 78-82; rtd 82; Perm to Offic *Cov* from 82. *49 Dalehouse Lane, Kenilworth, Warks CV8 2EP* Kenilworth (0926) 55881

MOFFETT, Mrs Marie-Louise. b 25. St Andr Univ MA46 Cam Univ DipRS76. d 87. St Andr Univ Angl Chapl Team from 87. *10 Queen's Gardens, St Andrews, Fife KY16 9TA* St Andrews (0334) 73678

MOGFORD, Canon Stanley Howard. b 13. St Pet Hall Ox BA35 DipTh36 MA39. Westcott Ho Cam 36. d 37 p 38. V Llanblethian w Cowbridge and Llandough etc *Llan* 63-80; rtd 80; Perm to Offic *Llan* from 80. *Fortis Green, 19 Plas Treoda, The Common, Cardiff* Cardiff (0222) 618839

MOIR, David William. b 38. St Aid Birkenhead 64. d 67 p 68. C Danbury *Chelmsf* 67-70; C Bollington St Jo *Ches* 70-72; V Sutton St Jas 72-81; V Prestbury from 81; RD Macclesfield from 88. *The Vicarage, Prestbury, Macclesfield, Cheshire SK10 4DG* Prestbury (0625) 829288

MOIR, Nicholas Ian. b 61. G&C Coll Cam BA82 MA86 Ox Univ BA86. Wycliffe Hall Ox 84. d 87 p 88. C Enfield St Andr *Lon* 87-91; Bp's Dom Chapl *St Alb* from 91. *6 Abbey Hill Road, St Albans, Herts* St Albans (0727) 839805

MOLE, Arthur Penton. b 10. Witwatersrand Univ BA30. Bps' Coll Cheshunt 33. d 35 p 36. R Old Alresford *Win* 71-76; rtd 76; Perm to Offic *Worc* from 76. *15 Garden Styles, Pershore, Worcs WR10 1JW* Pershore (0386) 554167

MOLE, David Eric Harton. b 33. Em Coll Cam BA54 MA58 PhD62. Ridley Hall Cam 55. d 59 p 59. C Selly Hill St Steph *Birm* 59-62; Tutor St Aid Birkenhead 62-63; Chapl Peterho Cam 63-69; Ghana 69-72; Lect Qu Coll Birm 72-76; Tutor USPG Coll of the Ascension Selly Oak 76-87; Res Min Burton *Lich* from 87; Chapl Burton Gen Hosp from 87. *St Modwen's House, Moor*

Street, Burton-on-Trent, Staffs DE143SU   Burton-on-Trent (0283) 38149

MOLE, Jennifer Vera. b 49. CertEd70. Qu Coll Birm 82. **d** 84. C Pontypool *Mon* 84-87; C Cyncoed 87-88; TV from 88. *100 Hill Rise, Llanedeyrn, Cardiff CF2 6UL* Cardiff (0222) 733915

MOLESWORTH, Canon Anthony Edward Nassau. b 23. Pemb Coll Cam BA45 MA48. Coll of Resurr Mirfield 45. **d** 46 **p** 47. Swaziland 52-71; Can 68-71; R Huish Episcopi w Pitney *B & W* 71-78; P-in-c High Ham 76-78; TR Langport Area Chs 78-84; R Charlton Musgrove, Cucklington and Stoke Trister 84-90; RD Bruton 86-90; rtd 90. *3 Barrow Hill, Stourton Caundle, Sturminster Newton, Dorset DT10 2LD* Stalbridge (0963) 62337

MOLL, Randell Tabrum. b 41. Lon Univ BD65. Wycliffe Hall Ox. **d** 66 **p** 67. C Drypool St Columba w St Andr and St Pet *York* 66-70; C Netherton *Liv* 70-72; C Sefton 70-72; Ind Chapl 70-75; P-in-c Brockmoor *Lich* 76-81; rtd 81. *Address temp unknown*

MOLLER, Canon George Brian. b 35. TCD BA60 MA64 Lon Univ BD84. **d** 61 **p** 62. C Belf St Pet *Conn* 61-64; C Larne and Inver 64-68; P-in-c Rathcoole 68-69; I 69-86; I Belf St Bart from 86; Chapl Stranmillis Coll of Educn Belf from 88; Preb Conn Cathl *Conn* from 90. *St Bartholomew's Rectory, 16 Mount Pleasant, Belfast BT9 5DS* Belfast (0232) 669995

MOLONY, Nicholas John. b 43. St Jo Coll Dur BA67 Birm Univ DipTh70 MA78. Qu Coll Birm 67. **d** 70 **p** 71. C Beaconsfield *Ox* 70-75; P-in-c Chesham Ch Ch 75-80; TV Gt Chesham 80-81; P-in-c Weston Turville 81-90; P-in-c Stoke Mandeville 87-89; P-in-c Gt Marlow from 90; P-in-c Bisham from 90. *12 Thamesfield Gardens, Marlow, Bucks SL7 1PZ* Marlow (0628) 482660

MONBERG, Ulla Stefan. b 52. BA81. Westcott Ho Cam 88. **d** 90. Par Dn Westmr St Jas *Lon* from 90. *St James's Church, 197 Piccadilly, London W1V 9LF* 071-734 4511

MONCUR, Henry Alexander. b 11. AKC43. **d** 43 **p** 44. V Stoke Golding w Dadlington *Leic* 57-79; rtd 79; Perm to Offic *Pet* from 80. *56 Beaufort Drive, Kettering, Northants NN15 6SF* Burton Latimer (0536) 725791

MONEY, Jack Humphrey. b 25. MNFSH. Sarum Th Coll 58. **d** 59 **p** 60. V Stanmer w Falmer and Moulsecoomb *Chich* 63-75; R Heene 75-84; rtd 90. *33 Eriswell Road, Worthing, W Sussex BN11 3HP* Worthing (0903) 203598

MONK, Mrs Mary. b 38. CertEd58. S'wark Ord Course 85. **d** 88. NSM Lee Gd Shep w St Pet *S'wark* from 88. *9 Horn Park Lane, London SE12 8UX* 081-318 5802

MONK, Nicholas John. b 32. Westcott Ho Cam 61. **d** 63 **p** 64. C Bris H Cross Inns Court *Bris* 63-67; C Stoke Bishop 67-69; V Swindon All SS 69-75; V Ashton Keynes w Leigh 75-87; P-in-c Minety w Oaksey 82-87; RD Malmesbury 85-88; V Ashton Keynes, Leigh and Minety 87-91; TR Swindon St Jo and St Andr from 91. *The Vicarage, Verwood Close, Swindon SN3 2LE* Swindon (0793) 611473

MONKS, John Stanley. b 12. AKC42. St D Coll Lamp 38. **d** 42 **p** 43. V Blyth St Cuth *Newc* 66-83; rtd 83. *56 West Dene Drive, North Shields, Tyne & Wear NE30 2SZ* 091-257 0157

MONKS, Roger James. b 39. G&C Coll Cam BA61. Coll of Resurr Mirfield 61. **d** 63 **p** 64. C Higham Ferrers *Pet* 63-66; C Cheshunt *St Alb* 68-70; Chapl Dartington Hall Sch 70-71. *18 Coleson Hill Road, Wrecclesham, Farnham, Surrey*

MONMOUTH, Archdeacon of. See TYTE, Ven Keith Arthur Edwin

MONMOUTH, Bishop of. See WRIGHT, Rt Rev Royston Clifford

MONMOUTH, Dean of. See LEWIS, Very Rev David Gareth

MONROE, James Allen. b 35. Stranmillis Coll TCert57. St Aid Birkenhead 63. **d** 64 **p** 65. C Belf St Mich *Conn* 64-68; C Coleraine 68-71; I 77-86; I Ballynure and Ballyeaston 71-77; I Holywood *D & D* from 86; RD Holywood from 89. *The Vicarage, 156 High Street, Holywood, Co Down* Holywood (02317) 2069

MONTAGUE, Mrs Juliet. b 52. Nottm Univ BTh82. Linc Th Coll 78. **dss** 82 **d** 87. Gainsborough All SS *Linc* 82-86; Chapl Linc Cathl from 86; Chapl Linc Colls of FE from 86. *1 Greestone Place, Lincoln LN2 1PP* Lincoln (0522) 535599

MONTAGUE, Canon William John. b 18. K Coll Cam BA40 MA44. Linc Th Coll 40. **d** 42 **p** 43. Can Missr *Wakef* 62-72; Vice-Provost Wakef Cathl 72-74; R Buckland *S'wark* 74-84; rtd 84; Perm to Offic Guildf and S'wark from 85. *24 Chapel Road, Tadworth, Surrey KT20 5SB* Tadworth (073781) 2877

MONTAGUE-YOUENS, Canon Hubert Edward. b 30. Ripon Hall Ox 55. **d** 58 **p** 59. V Kidderminster St Geo *Worc* 68-72; R Ribbesford w Bewdley and Dowles 72-81; RD Kidderminster 76-81; Hon Can Worc Cathl 78-81; TR Bridport *Sarum* 81-86; RD Lyme Bay 82-86; Chapl K Edw VII Hosp Midhurst 86-89; V Easebourne *Chich* 86-89; rtd 89. *71 Gloucester Road, Tewkesbury, Glos GL20 5SS* Tewkesbury (0684) 292363

✠**MONTEFIORE, Rt Rev Hugh William.** b 20. St Jo Coll Ox BA46 MA47 SS Coll Cam BD63 Aber Univ Hon DD77. Westcott Ho Cam 48. **d** 49 **p** 50 **c** 70. C Newc St Geo *Newc* 49-51; Chapl and Tutor Westcott Ho Cam 51-53; Vice-Prin 53-54; Dean G&C Coll Cam 54-63; Asst Lect Th Cam Univ 56-59; Lect 59-63; Can Th Cov Cathl *Cov* 59-69; V Cam Gt St Mary w St Mich *Ely* 63-70; Hon Can Ely Cathl 69-70; Suff Bp Kingston-upon-Thames *S'wark* 70-78; Bp Birm 78-87; rtd 87; Asst Bp S'wark from 87. *White Lodge, 23 Bellevue Road, London SW17 7EB* 081-672 6697

MONTGOMERIE, Andrew Simon. b 60. Keble Coll Ox BA82. Ridley Hall Cam 83. **d** 85 **p** 86. C Childwall All SS *Liv* 85-87; C Yardley St Edburgha *Birm* 87-90; TV Solihull from 90. *St Michael's House, 2 Cheltondale Road, Solihull, W Midlands B91 1EJ* 021-704 4730

MONTGOMERY, Canon Anthony Alan. b 33. Trin Hall Cam BA56. Edin Th Coll 56. **d** 58 **p** 59. C Dumfries *Glas* 58-63; P-in-c Airdrie 63-66; R 66-68; Chapl Gordonstoun Sch from 68; Can St Andr Cathl Inverness *Mor* from 81. *Easter Hillside, Mosstowie, Elgin IV30 3XE* Alves (034385) 282

MONTGOMERY, Charles George Greathead. b 08. AKC33. **d** 33 **p** 34. V Poundstock *Truro* 44-45; rtd 75. *Jasmine Cottage, Ash Cross, Bradworthy, Holsworthy, Devon EX22 7SP*

MONTGOMERY, Canon John Alexander. b 11. TCD BA34. **d** 35 **p** 36. I Ardagh w Kilcommick *K, E & A* 67-80; Preb Elphin Cathl 78-80; rtd 80; Hon C Bathgate *Edin* from 83; Hon C Linlithgow from 83. *6 Watson Place, Armadale, Bathgate, West Lothian EH48 2NJ* Armadale (0501) 31470

MONTGOMERY, Pembroke John Charles. b 24. Codrington Coll Barbados. **d** 53 **p** 55. St Vincent 55-73; Can Kingstown Cathl 63-73; P-in-c Derby St Jas *Derby* 73-74; V 74-90; rtd 90. *37 Church Street, Tetbury, Glos* Tetbury (0666) 504817

MONTGOMERY, Thomas Charles Osborne. b 59. Edin Univ BD81. Edin Th Coll 77. **d** 82 **p** 83. C Glas St Mary *Glas* 82-85; C Dumfries 85-88; R Hamilton from 88. *The Rectory, 4 Auchingramont Road, Hamilton, Lanarkshire ML3 6JT* Hamilton (0698) 429895

MONTGOMERY, Archdeacon of. See PRITCHARD, Ven Thomas William

MOODY, Aubrey Rowland. b 11. Coll of Resurr Mirfield 53. **d** 55 **p** 56. C Wanstead St Mary *Chelmsf* 55-57; V Feering from 57. *Feering Vicarage, Colchester, Essex CO5 9NL* Kelvedon (0376) 70226

MOODY, Christopher John Everard. b 51. New Coll Ox BA72 Lon Univ MSc90. Cuddesdon Coll BA74. **d** 75 **p** 76. C Fulham All SS *Lon* 75-79; C Surbiton St Andr and St Mark *S'wark* 79-82; Chapl K Coll Lon 82-87; V S Lambeth St Anne and All SS *S'wark* from 87; RD Lambeth from 90. *The Vicarage, 179 Fentiman Road, London SW8 1JY* 071-735 3191

MOODY, Colin John. b 36. Chich Th Coll 61. **d** 63 **p** 64. C Hove All SS *Chich* 63-69; C Dulwich St Barn *S'wark* 69-70; Perm to Offic Bris 70-71; Chich 72-78; Lic Ely from 78. *11 Hewitts, Henfield, W Sussex BN5 9TD* Henfield (0273) 495062

MOODY, Derek Frank. b 41. Univ of Wales BA62. Chich Th Coll 63. **d** 65 **p** 66. C Ellesmere Port *Ches* 65-69; C Lewisham St Jo Southend *S'wark* 69-73; TV Catford (Southend) and Downham 73-75; V Ham St Rich 75-83; V Catford St Laur 83-88; TV Brighton St Pet and St Nic w Chpl Royal *Chich* from 88. *5 Clifton Road, Brighton BN1 3HP* Brighton (0273) 21399

MOODY, Geoffrey Sidney. b 13. St Cath Soc Ox BA35 MA39. Worc Ord Coll. **d** 54 **p** 55. V Holly Bush w Birtsmorton *Worc* 67-78; P-in-c Castle Morton 72-78; rtd 78; Perm to Offic *Lich* 78-90. *30 Meadow Lane, Derrington, Stafford ST18 9NA* Stafford (0785) 59184

MOODY, Preb George Henry. b 27. ACIS56 ARCA68 DipPD77. Cranmer Hall Dur 69. **d** 71 **p** 72. C Marske in Cleveland *York* 71-74; Chapl to the Deaf *Lich* 74-89; Preb Lich Cathl 83-89; rtd 89. *21 Priestcrofts, Marske-by-the-Sea, Redcar, Cleveland TS11 7HW* Redcar (0642) 489660

MOODY, Ivor Robert. b 57. K Coll Lon BD AKC. Coll of Resurr Mirfield. **d** 82 **p** 83. C Leytonstone St Marg w St Columba *Chelmsf* 82-85; C Leigh-on-Sea St Marg

85-88; V Tilbury Docks from 88. *St John's Vicarage, Dock Road, Tilbury, Essex RM18 7PP* Tilbury (0375) 2417

MOOKERJI, Michael Manoje. b 45. Baring Union Coll Punjab BSc69. Ridley Hall Cam 83. **d** 85. C Heanor *Derby* from 85. *143 Ray Street, Heanor, Derbyshire DE7 7GE* Langley Mill (0773) 768554

MOON, Arthur Thomas. b 22. ACP53 LCP56 Lon Univ DipTh66. Sarum Th Coll 65. **d** 66 **p** 67. C Fulwood Ch Ch *Blackb* 66-71; Hon C Bispham 71-80; C 80-87; rtd 87; Perm to Offic *Blackb* from 87. *15 Kirkstone Drive, Blackpool FY5 1QQ* Blackpool (0253) 853521

MOON, John Charles. b 23. Sarum Th Coll 49. **d** 51 **p** 52. V Spalding St Jo *Linc* 67-82; V Spalding St Jo w Deeping St Nicholas 82-86; rtd 86. *14 Harrox Road, Moulton, Spalding, Lincs PE12 6PR* Holbeach (0406) 370111

MOON, Philip Russell. b 56. Em Coll Cam BA78 MA82 Reading Univ PGCE79. Wycliffe Hall Ox BA82. **d** 85 **p** 86. C Crowborough *Chich* 85-87; Sec of CYFA (CPAS) from 87. *10 Claremont Road, Tunbridge Wells, Kent TN1 1SZ* Tunbridge Wells (0892) 28839

MOON, Thomas Arnold. b 24. Lon Univ BA51. Oak Hill Th Coll 49. **d** 52 **p** 53. C Fazakerley Em *Liv* 52-56; V Everton St Benedict 56-70; V Formby St Luke from 70. *St Luke's Vicarage, Formby, Liverpool L37 2DE* Formby (07048) 77655

MOOR, David Drury. b 18. St Edm Hall Ox BA39 MA44. Wells Th Coll 46. **d** 48 **p** 49. V Bournemouth St Mich *Win* 69-83; rtd 83; Perm to Offic Win & Sarum from 83. *93 Western Avenue, Bournemouth BH10 6HG* Bournemouth (0202) 512455

MOOR, Maurice Albert Charles. b 03. St Paul's Coll Burgh 30. **d** 34 **p** 35. V Chute w Chute Forest *Sarum* 45-62; Lic to Offic *Ban* from 63; rtd 68. *Edensor Lodge, Llwyngwril, Gwynedd LL37 2JJ* Fairbourne (0341) 250495

MOORE, Anthony Harry. b 34. Westcott Ho Cam 88. **d** 90 **p** 91. C Eyke w Bromeswell, Rendlesham, Tunstall etc *St E* from 90. *Lark Rise, Bromeswell, Woodbridge, Suffolk IP12 3DL* Woodbridge (0394) 380894

MOORE, Anthony Richmond. b 36. Clare Coll Cam BA59 MA63. Linc Th Coll 59. **d** 61 **p** 62. C Roehampton H Trin *S'wark* 61-66; C New Eltham All SS 66-70; PM Blackbird Leys CD *Ox* 70-81; Dioc Ecum Officer from 80; TV Dorchester from 81. *The Rectory, Marsh Baldon, Oxford OX9 9LS* Nuneham Courtenay (086738) 215

MOORE, Arthur Lewis. b 33. Dur Univ BA58 PhD64. Cranmer Hall Dur DipTh59. **d** 62 **p** 63. C Stone *Roch* 62-66; C Clevedon St Andr *B & W* 66-68; Chapl Wycliffe Hall Ox 68-70; Vice-Prin 70-83; P-in-c Ampfield *Win* 83-84; V Hursley and Ampfield from 84. *The Vicarage, Ampfield, Romsey, Hants SO5 9BT* Braishfield (0794) 68291

MOORE, Arthur Robert. b 15. Sarum Th Coll 62. **d** 63 **p** 64. V Steeple Ashton w Semington *Sarum* 67-79; V Keevil 72-79; P-in-c Southwick w Boarhunt *Portsm* from 79; rtd 84. *1 High Street, Southwick, Fareham, Hants PO17 6EB* Cosham (0705) 382113

MOORE, Canon Bernard Geoffrey. b 27. New Coll Ox BA47 MA52. Ely Th Coll 49. **d** 51 **p** 52. C Chorley St Pet *Blackb* 51-54; Bp's Dom Chapl 54-55; C-in-c Blackpool St Mich CD 55-67; Chapl Victoria Hosp Blackpool 58-67; V Morecambe St Barn *Blackb* 67-81; R Standish 81-88; Hon Can Blackb Cathl from 86; RD Chorley from 86; V Charnock Richard from 88. *The Vicarage, Church Lane, Charnock Richard, Chorley, Lancs PR7 5NA* Coppull (0257) 791385

MOORE, Bernard George. b 32. Qu Coll Birm 57. **d** 60 **p** 61. C Middlesb St Columba *York* 60-62; S Africa 62-70; Chapl RN 70-74; C Milton *Portsm* 74-76; New Zealand from 76. *45 Feasegate Street, Manurewa, New Zealand* Auckland (9) 267-6924

MOORE, Preb Brian Birkett. b 24. Oak Hill Th Coll 51. **d** 53 **p** 54. V Southall Green St Jo *Lon* 67-74; RD Ealing W 72-74; Chapl Wembley Hosp 74-89; V Wembley St Jo *Lon* 74-89; RD Brent 77-82; Preb St Paul's Cathl 80-89; C Roxeth Ch Ch and Harrow St Pet 89; rtd 89. *41 Schoolfields Road, Shenstone, Lichfield, Staffs WS14 0LL* Lichfield (0543) 480748

MOORE, Brian Philip. b 51. AKC72. St Aug Coll Cant 72. **d** 74 **p** 75. C Hatf *St Alb* 74-78; C Radlett 78-81; V Eaton Bray w Edlesborough from 81; RD Dunstable 85-90. *The Vicarage, Eaton Bray, Dunstable, Beds LU6 2DN* Eaton Bray (0525) 220261

MOORE, Preb Clive Granville. b 31. St Pet Hall Ox BA54 MA58. Wycliffe Hall Ox 54. **d** 55 **p** 56. C Newbarns w Hawcoat *Carl* 55-57; CF 57-61; Chapl Joyce Green Hosp Dartford 61-69; R Stone *Roch* 61-69; R Radstock *B & W* 69-71; P-in-c Writhlington 69-71; R Radstock w

Writhlington 71-83; RD Midsomer Norton 81-83; R S Petherton w the Seavingtons from 83; RD Crewkerne from 83; Preb Wells Cathl from 90. *The Rectory, Hele Lane, South Petherton, Somerset TA13 5DY* South Petherton (0460) 40377

MOORE, Colin Frederick. b 49. CITC 66. **d** 72 **p** 73. C Drumglass w Moygashel *Arm* 72-80; I Newtownhamilton w Ballymoyer and Belleek 80-87; I Newtownhamilton w Ballymoyer and Pomeroy etc from 87; Hon VC from 85. *71 Ballymoyer Road, Whitecross, Armagh BT60 2LA* Glenanne (086157) 256

MOORE, David. b 36. Univ of Wales (Lamp) BA61 Magd Coll Cam BA63 MA68. Linc Th Coll 63. **d** 65 **p** 66. C Saltburn-by-the-Sea *York* 65-69; C Northallerton w Kirby Sigston 69-72; V Kirklevington from 72; V High and Low Worsall from 73; Chapl HM Det Cen Kirklevington 72-89; Chapl HM Young Offender Inst Kirklevington Grange from 89. *The Vicarage, Kirk Levington, Yarm, Cleveland TS15 9LQ* Eaglescliffe (0642) 782439

MOORE, David James Paton. b 60. Sheff Univ BEng82. Cranmer Hall Dur 88. **d** 91. C Pemberton St Mark Newtown *Liv* from 91. *34 Larch Avenue, Pemberton, Wigan, Lancs* Wigan (0942) 217348

MOORE, David Leonard. b 51. **d** 80 **p** 82. Hon C Brixton St Matt *S'wark* 80-82; C 82-84; TV Bris St Agnes and St Simon w St Werburgh *Bris* 84-86; Perm to Offic from 86. *St Werburgh's Vicarage, 15 St Werburgh's Park, Bristol BS2 9YD* Bristol (0272) 558863 or 551755

MOORE, Dr David Metcalfe. b 41. Hull Univ BA64 PhD69. Trin Coll Bris 76. **d** 78 **p** 79. C Marple All SS *Ches* 78-82; V Loudwater *Ox* 82-90; V Chilwell *S'well* from 90. *Christ Church Vicarage, 8 College Road, Beeston, Nottingham NG9 4AS* Nottingham (0602) 222809

MOORE, David Roy. b 39. Clare Coll Cam BA61. Ripon Hall Ox 61. **d** 63 **p** 64. C Melton Mowbray w Thorpe Arnold *Leic* 63-66; Dep Dir The Samaritans 66-73; C St Steph Walbrook and St Swithun etc *Lon* 66-73; C Daybrook *S'well* 77-80; V 80-87; V Ham St Andr *S'wark* from 87. *The Vicarage, Ham Common, Richmond, Surrey TW10 5HG* 081-940 9017

MOORE, Dr Deborah Claire Patricia. b 62. Essex Univ BSc83 Liv Univ PhD88 SS Coll Cam BA89. Ridley Hall Cam 87. **d** 90. Par Dn Hale and Ashley *Ches* from 90. *233 Ashley Road, Hale, Altrincham, Cheshire WA15 9SS* 061-941 1824

MOORE, Canon Dennis Charles. b 19. Lon Univ BD46. Tyndale Hall Bris 39. **d** 43 **p** 44. V Wellington w Eyton *Lich* 62-70; RD Wrockwardine 66-70; V Watford St Mary *St Alb* 70-73; P-in-c Watford St Jas 70-73; V Watford 73-84; RD Watford 75-81; rtd 84; Perm to Offic *Nor* from 84. *82 Greenways, Eaton, Norwich NR4 6HF* Norwich (0603) 502492

MOORE, Donald John. b 31. Chich Th Coll 86. **d** 87 **p** 88. C Uckfield *Chich* 87-88; C Southwick 89-90; Bermuda from 90. *PO Box DD188, St David's DD01, Bermuda* Bermuda (809) 297-1231

MOORE, Douglas Gregory. b 49. Bris Univ BA71 CertEd72. Coll of Resurr Mirfield 87. **d** 89 **p** 90. C Hessle *York* from 89. *60 Beverley Road, Hessle, N Humberside HU13 9BL* Hull (0482) 648349

✠**MOORE, Rt Rev Edward Francis Butler.** b 06. TCD BA28 MA40 PhD44 Hon DD59. **d** 30 **p** 31 **c** 59. C Bray *D & G* 30-32; Hon CV Ch Ch Cathl Dub 31-35; C Dub Clontarf 32-34; I Castledermot w Kinneagh 34-40; I Greystones 40-58; RD Delgany 50-58; Can Ch Ch Cathl Dub 51-58; Adn Glendalough 57-58; Bp K, E & A 59-81; rtd 81. *Drumlona, Sea Road, Kilcoole, Co Wicklow, Irish Republic* Dublin (1) 876648

MOORE, Canon Edward James. b 32. TCD BA56 MA59. **d** 56 **p** 57. C Belf St Luke *Conn* 56-59; CF 59-62; C Dunmurry *Conn* 62-64; P-in-c Kilmakee 64-70; I Belf H Trin 70-80; I Jordanstown w Monkstown 80-91; I Jordanstown from 91; RD N Belf from 88; Can Belf Cathl from 89. *120A Circular Road, Jordanstown, Co Antrim BT37 0RH* Belfast (0232) 862119

MOORE, Ernest Roy. b 21. ARIBA Man Univ MA(Theol)76. NW Ord Course 70. **d** 73 **p** 74. NSM Cheadle *Ches* 73-78; NSM Bramhall 78-90. *Orchard Cottage, 3 Thorn Road, Bramhall, Stockport, Cheshire SK7 1HG* 061-439 8173

MOORE, Canon Fred. b 11. St Jo Coll Dur LTh42 BA44. St Aid Birkenhead 39. **d** 43 **p** 44. V Camerton, Seaton and W Seaton *Carl* 54-72; RD Maryport 67-70; Hon Can Carl Cathl 70-77; RD Solway 70-77; V Gt Broughton 72-77; rtd 77; Perm to Offic *Carl* from 77. *30 Braeside, Seaton, Workington, Cumbria* Workington (0900) 62358

MOORE, Canon Henry James William. b 33. TCD BA55 MA70. **d** 56 **p** 57. C Mullabrack *Arm* 56-61; C Drumglass 61-63; I Clogherney 63-81; I Ballinderry w Tamlaght and Arboe from 81; Preb Arm Cathl from 90. *10 Brookmount Road, Coagh, Cookstown, Co Tyrone BT80 0BB* Ballyronan (064887) 255

✠**MOORE, Rt Rev Henry Wylie.** b 23. Liv Univ BCom50 Leeds Univ MA72. Wycliffe Hall Ox 50. **d** 52 **p** 53 **c** 83. C Farnworth *Liv* 52-54; C Middleton *Man* 54-56; CMS 56-60; Iran 57-60; R Burnage St Marg *Man* 60-63; R Middleton 60-74; Home Sec CMS 74-80; Exec Sec CMS 80-83; Bp Cyprus and the Gulf 83-86; Gen Sec CMS 86-90; rtd 90; Asst Bp Dur from 90. *Grosvenor House, Farnley Mount, Durham DH1 4DZ* 091-383 0698

MOORE, Herbert Alexander. b 15. Univ of Wales BA36 BD54 MA82. Tyndale Hall Bris 36. **d** 38 **p** 39. Chapl and Asst Master Hillstone Sch Malvern 71-80; rtd 80. *28 Blackmore Road, Malvern, Worcs WR14 1QT* Malvern (0684) 55661

MOORE, Preb Herbert Alfred Harold. b 17. Ex Coll Ox BA40 MA43. Cuddesdon Coll 40. **d** 41 **p** 42. V Acton Green St Pet *Lon* 64-71; V S Kensington St Steph 71-86; RD Kensington 76-84; P-in-c S Kensington H Trin w All SS 78-83; Preb St Paul's Cathl 80-86; rtd 86; Perm to Offic *Worc* from 86. *212B West Malvern Road, Malvern, Worcs WR14 4BA* Malvern (0684) 562470

MOORE, Hugh Desmond. b 37. St Cath Soc Ox BA58 MA64. St Steph Ho Ox 58. **d** 61 **p** 62. C Kingston St Luke *S'wark* 61-68; Asst Chapl Lon Univ *Lon* 68-70; Chapl Edgware Gen Hosp from 70; V Hendon St Alphage *Lon* from 70; AD W Barnet 85-90. *The Vicarage, Montrose Avenue, Edgware, Middx HA8 0DN* 081-952 4611

MOORE, Ivan. MA BTh. **d** 90 **p** 91. C Knock *D & D* from 90. *3 Sandown Park South, Knock, Belfast BT5 6HE* Belfast (0232) 653370

MOORE, Ven James Edward. b 33. TCD BA54 MA64. **d** 56 **p** 57. C Knock *D & D* 56-60; C Ban St Comgall 60-62; P-in-c Belvoir 62-68; I Groomsport 68-75; I Dundela from 75; Can Down Cathl 85-89; Treas 87-89; Adn Down from 89. *4 Sydenham Avenue, Belfast BT4 2DR* Belfast (0232) 659047

MOORE, James Frederick. b 12. Sheff Univ BSc35 MSc36. **d** 38 **p** 40. Lic to Offic *Bradf* 55-84; rtd 77. *215 Bradford Road, Riddlesden, Keighley, W Yorkshire BD20 5JR* Keighley (0535) 606094

MOORE, James Kenneth. b 37. AKC62. St Boniface Warminster 62. **d** 63 **p** 64. C W Hartlepool St Oswald *Dur* 63-66; C-in-c Manor Park CD *Sheff* 66-76; TV Sheff Manor 76-78; R Frecheville and Hackenthorpe 78-87; V Bilham from 87. *The Vicarage, Churchfield Road, Clayton, Doncaster, S Yorkshire DN5 7DH* Pontefract (0977) 643756

MOORE, John. b 22. **d** 57 **p** 58. I Templepatrick *Conn* 68-85; rtd 85. *Cuthona, 67 Prospect Road, Portstewart, Co Londonderry BT55 7NQ* Portstewart (026583) 3905

MOORE, John. b 26. Univ of Wales (Lamp) BA51. Oak Hill Th Coll 51. **d** 53 **p** 54. V Retford *S'well* 67-73; R Aspenden and Layston w Buntingford *St Alb* 73-86; V Stanstead Abbots 86-91; rtd 91. *20 Radley Road, Abingdon, Oxon OX14 3PQ* Abingdon (0235) 532518

MOORE, John Arthur. b 33. Cuddesdon Coll 70. **d** 71 **p** 72. Hon C Gt Burstead *Chelmsf* 71-74; Chapl Barnard Castle Sch from 74. *Littlemoor, Mount Eff Lane, Barnard Castle, Co Durham DL12 8UW* Teesdale (0833) 38601

MOORE, Canon John Cecil. b 37. TCD BA61 MA67 BD69. CITC 62. **d** 62 **p** 63. C Belf St Matt *Conn* 62-65; C Holywood *D & D* 65-70; I Ballyphilip w Ardquin 70-77; I Mt Merrion 77-79; I Donaghcloney w Waringstown from 79; Treas Dromore Cathl from 90. *54 Banbridge Road, Waringstown, Lurgan, Co Armagh* Waringstown (0762) 881218

MOORE, John David. b 30. St Chad's Coll Dur BA54 DipEd55 DipEd56. **d** 56 **p** 57. C Wallsend St Pet *Newc* 56-60; C Leamington Priors All SS *Cov* 60-62; V Longford 62-75; P-in-c Nuneaton St Mary 75-77; V 77-83; V St Ives *Ely* from 83. *The Vicarage, St Ives, Huntingdon, Cambs PE17 4DH* St Ives (0480) 63254

MOORE, John Ernest. b 24. Oak Hill NSM Course. **d** 84 **p** 85. NSM Hornchurch H Cross *Chelmsf* 84-86; NSM S Woodham Ferrers 86-91; NSM Canvey Is from 91. *7 Butterbur Chase, South Woodham Ferrers, Chelmsford CM3 7AG* Chelmsford (0245) 325092

MOORE, John Henry. b 35. Nottm Univ BMus56 CertEd57 MA61. E Midl Min Tr Course 87. **d** 90. NSM Gotham *S'well* from 90. *19 Hall Drive, Gotham, Nottingham NG11 0JT* Nottingham (0602) 830670

MOORE, John Keith. b 26. Sarum & Wells Th Coll 78. **d** 81 **p** 82. NSM Guildf All SS *Guildf* 81-86; NSM Guildf

H Trin w St Mary from 86; Dean of Chapter from 90. *65 Rookwood Court, Guildford, Surrey GU2 5EL* Guildford (0483) 61251

MOORE, John Michael. b 48. Em Coll Cam BA70 MA73. Cuddesdon Coll 72. **d** 74 **p** 75. C Almondbury *Wakef* 74-78; TV Basingstoke *Win* 78-88; P-in-c Southn St Alb from 88. *St Alban's Vicarage, 357 Burgess Road, Southampton SO2 3BD* Southampton (0703) 554231

MOORE, John Richard. b 35. LTh59. St Jo Coll Nottm 56. **d** 59 **p** 60. C Northwood Em *Lon* 59-63; V Burton Dassett *Cov* 63-66; Youth Chapl 63-71; Dir Lindley Lodge Educn Trust Nuneaton 71-82; TR Kinson *Sarum* 82-88; Dir CPAS from 88. *c/o CPAS, Athena Drive, Tachbrook Park, Warwick CV34 6NG* Warwick (0926) 334242

MOORE, John Richard. b 45. Linc Th Coll 80. **d** 82 **p** 83. C Gt Grimsby St Mary and St Jas *Linc* 82-86; V Skirbeck Quarter from 86; Miss to Seamen from 86. *St Thomas's Vicarage, 2 Linley Drive, Boston, Lincs PE21 7EJ* Boston (0205) 367380

MOORE, Leonard Richard. b 22. Leeds Univ BA47. Coll of Resurr Mirfield 47. **d** 49 **p** 50. Lic to Offic *St Alb* 68-70; P-in-c Bedf H Trin 70-74; rtd 87; Hon C Cardington *St Alb* from 87. *22 Dart Road, Bedford MK41 7BT* Bedford (0234) 57536

MOORE, Mrs Margaret Doreen. b 37. Westf Coll Lon BA58 CertEd59 BD63. Dalton Ho Bris 61. **dss** 85 **d** 87. Harold Hill St Paul *Chelmsf* 85-87; Hon Par C S Woodham Ferrers 87-91; C Canvey Is from 91. *14 St Peter's Road, Canvey Island, Essex SS8 9NQ* Canvey Island (0268) 690261

MOORE, Matthew Edward George. b 38. Oak Hill Th Coll 77. **d** 77 **p** 78. C Larne and Inver *Conn* 77-80; I Desertmartin *D & R* 80-84; I Milltown *Arm* from 84. *10 Derrylileagh Road, Portadown, Craigavon, Co Armagh BT62 1TQ* Annaghmore (0762) 851246

MOORE, Canon Mervyn. b 18. Leeds Univ BA40. Coll of Resurr Mirfield 40. **d** 42 **p** 43. C Middlesb St Martin *York* 42-45; C Helmsley 45-49; V Osbaldwick w Murton 49-54; S Africa from 54. *Canonsgarth, 11A Twelfth Avenue, Parktown North, 2193 South Africa* Johannesburg (11) 298724

MOORE, Canon Michael Mervlyn Hamond. b 35. Pemb Coll Ox BA60 MA63. Wells Th Coll 60. **d** 62 **p** 63. C Bethnal Green St Matt *Lon* 62-66; Chapl Bucharest w Sofia and Belgrade *Eur* 66-67; Asst Gen Sec C of E Coun on Foreign Relns 67-70; Gen Sec 70-72; Abp's Asst Chapl on Foreign Relns *Cant* 72-82; Hon C Walworth St Pet *S'wark* 73-80; Hon Can Cant Cathl *Cant* 74-90; HM Chapl Hampton Court Palace from 82. *Hampton Court Palace, East Molesey, Surrey KT8 9AU* 081-977 2762

MOORE, Norman Butler. b 25. St Jo Coll Dur BA50 DipTh52. **d** 52 **p** 53. C Aston St Jas *Birm* 52-55; V 57-59; C Gravesend St Jas *Roch* 55-57; V Warley Woods *Birm* 59-64; Bp's Youth Chapl and Asst Dir of Educn *Worc* 65-66; V Lucton w Eyton *Heref* 66-69; V Hazelwell *Birm* 69-75; V Watford St Andr *St Alb* from 75. *St Andrew's Vicarage, 18 Park Road, Watford WD1 3QN* Watford (0923) 224858

MOORE, Paul. b 59. Ball Coll Ox BA82 DPhil86. Wycliffe Hall Ox DipTh87. **d** 89 **p** 90. C Ox St Andr *Ox* from 89. *5 Squitchey Lane, Oxford OX2 7LD* Oxford (0865) 53944

MOORE, Peter. b 21. Leeds Univ BA47. Coll of Resurr Mirfield 46. **d** 48 **p** 49. R Mundford w Lynford *Nor* 65-76; P-in-c Ickburgh w Langford 65-76; P-in-c Cranwich 65-76; V Whitley *Newc* 76-86; rtd 86; Perm to Offic *Newc* from 86. *31 Glebelands, Corbridge, Northd NE45 5DS* Hexham (0434) 633207

MOORE, Very Rev Peter Clement. b 24. FSA Ch Ch Ox BA45 MA48 DPhil54. Cuddesdon Coll 45. **d** 47 **p** 48. Min Can Cant Cathl *Cant* 47-49; C Bladon w Woodstock *Ox* 49-51; Chapl New Coll Ox 49-51; V Alfrick w Lulsley *Worc* 52-59; V Pershore w Wick 59-67; RD Pershore 65-67; Can Res Ely Cathl *Ely* 67-73; Treas 69; Vice-Dean 71; Dean St Alb from 73. *The Deanery, Sumpter Yard, St Albans, Herts AL1 1BY* St Albans (0727) 52120

MOORE, Raymond. b 47. QUB BSc70. **d** 87 **p** 88. NSM Belf All SS *Conn* from 87. *14 Osborne Park, Belfast BT9 6JN* Belfast (0232) 669168

MOORE, Canon Richard Noel. b 34. TCD BA56 MA60. **d** 57 **p** 58. C Derry Cathl *D & R* 57-60; I Clondehorkey 60-66; I Stranorlar w Meenglas and Kilteevogue 66-76; I Glendermott from 76; Can Derry Cathl from 89. *Glendermott Rectory, Altnagelvin, Londonderry BT47 2LS* Londonderry (0504) 43001

MOORE, Richard Norman Theobald. b 39. St Andr Univ BSc62 Lon Univ BD66. Clifton Th Coll. **d** 66 **p** 67. C Stowmarket *St E* 66-69; C New Humberstone *Leic* 69-72; P-in-c Leic Martyrs 73; V 73-84; Chapl Manor Hosp Epsom from 84. *72 Newton Wood Road, Ashtead, Surrey* Ashtead (0372) 72525

MOORE, Robert Allen. b 32. Univ of the Pacific BA54 Boston Univ STB58 STM59. **d** 63 **p** 63. USA 63-80; V Farington *Blackb* 80-83; TV Preston St Jo 83-85; P-in-c Fleetwood 85-87; V Leyland St Jas from 87. *St James's Vicarage, 201 Slater Lane, Leyland, Preston PR5 3SH* Leyland (0772) 21034

MOORE, Canon Robert Denholm. b 23. TCD BA45. **d** 46 **p** 47. C Londonderry Ch Ch *D & R* 46-49; C Dub Clontarf *D & G* 49-53; I Clondehorkey *D & R* 53-60; RD Kilmacrenan W 59-60; I Clonleigh w Donaghmore 60-65; I Tamlaghtfinlagan w Myroc from 65; Can Derry Cathl from 80. *Finlagan Rectory, 77 Ballykelly Road, Limavady, Co Derry BT49 9DS* Limavady (05047) 62743

MOORE, Canon Robert George Chaffey. b 11. Kelham Th Coll 28. **d** 39 **p** 40. R Compton Abbas *Sarum* 49-73; Can and Preb Sarum Cathl from 72; TV Shaston 73-77; rtd 77. *48 Rectory Road, Salisbury SP2 7SD* Salisbury (0722) 335819

MOORE, Robin Hugh. b 52. CertEd BEd QUB BD TCD DipTh. **d** 84 **p** 85. C Derryloran *Arm* 84-86; C Knock *D & D* 86-89; Bp's C Belf St Steph w St Luke *Conn* from 89. *92 Lansdowne Road, Belfast BT15 4AB* Belfast (0232) 774119

MOORE, Ronald Spencer. b 09. Leeds Univ BA33. Coll of Resurr Mirfield 33. **d** 35 **p** 36. R Warburton *Ches* 63-74; rtd 74. *2 Russell Avenue, Sale, Cheshire M33 2ET* 061-973 2157

MOORE, Terry Chapple. b 47. BA BD MLitt. **d** 80 **p** 81. Canada 80-84; Chapl Stirling Univ *Edin* 85-87; C Callander *St And* 85-87; P-in-c 87-89; C Doune 85-87; P-in-c 87-89; C Aberfoyle 85-87; P-in-c 87-89; P-in-c Stratton *Truro* 89; R Stratton and Launcells from 89. *The Vicarage, Diddies Road, Stratton, Bude, Cornwall EX23 9DW* Bude (0288) 352254

MOORE, Canon Thomas Robert. b 38. TCD 65. Lambeth DipTh79 MA84. **d** 68 **p** 69. C Dub Drumcondra w N Strand *D & G* 68-70; C Portadown St Columba *Arm* 70-72; I Kilskeery w Trillick *Clogh* 72-85; RD Kilskeery 81-86; Dioc Sec from 83; I Trory w Killadeas from 85; Can Clogh Cathl 86-89; Preb from 89; Preb Donaghmore St Patr Cathl Dub from 91. *The Rectory, Rossfad, Ballinamallard, Co Fermanagh BT94 2LS* Ballinamallard (036581) 477

MOORE, William Henry. b 14. K Coll Lon 34. **d** 38 **p** 39. Perm to Offic *Nor* 62-71 and from 88; Asst Master Mildenhall Sec Sch 68-73; Heartsease Sch Nor 73-75; C Mildenhall *St E* 71-73; rtd 79. *21 Green Court, Brakestone Drive, Thorpe, Norwich NR7 0DN* Norwich (0603) 32758

MOORE, Canon William James Foster. b 26. TCD BA50. **d** 50 **p** 51. C Glenavy *Conn* 50-53; C Coleraine 53-57; I Rasharkin w Finvoy 57-66; I Broomhedge 66-83; I Dunluce from 83; Can Belf Cathl from 88. *17 Priestland Road, Bushmills, Co Antrim* Bushmills (02657) 31221

MOORE, William Morris. b 33. QUB BSc55 TCD. **d** 61 **p** 62. C Belf St Mich *Conn* 61-64; I 70-80; C Belf All SS 64-70; I Ballynafeigh St Jude *D & D* from 80. *11 Bladon Drive, Belfast BT9 5JL* Belfast (0232) 667500

MOORE, William Thomas Sewell. b 21. MRCS LRCP MA. Westcott Ho Cam. **d** 82 **p** 83. Chapl Countess Mountbatten Ho Southn 84-90; Hon C Shedfield *Portsm* from 84; rtd 90. *Crossways, Blind Lane, Wickham, Fareham, Hants PO17 5HD* Wickham (0329) 832119

MOORGAS, Geoffrey Gordon. b 30. Sarum & Wells Th Coll 80. **d** 81 **p** 82. C Brixton St Matt *S'wark* 81-84; C Clapham Old Town 84-87; C Clapham Team Min 87; Namibia from 87. *PO Box 1482, Swakopmund, 9000 Namibia* Swakopmund (641) 2418

MOORHEAD, Michael David. b 52. BSc BA. St Steph Ho Ox. **d** 83 **p** 84. C Kilburn St Aug w St Jo *Lon* 83-87; C Kenton 87-89; V Harlesden All So from 89. *All Souls' Vicarage, 3 Station Road, London NW10 4UJ* 081-965 4988

MOORHOUSE, Christine Susan. b 49. K Coll Lon BD71. W Midl Minl Tr Course. **dss** 86 **d** 87. NSM Stourbridge St Thos *Worc* from 86. *20 High Street, Stourbridge, W Midlands DY8 4NJ* Stourbridge (0384) 395381

MOORHOUSE, Humphrey John. b 18. Oak Hill Th Coll 37. **d** 41 **p** 42. R Vange *Chelmsf* 45-83; rtd 83. *12 Waverley Road, Benfleet, Essex SS7 4AZ* South Benfleet (0268) 754952

MOORHOUSE, Llewellyn Owen. b 14. Ely Th Coll 63 St Deiniol's Hawarden. **d** 64 **p** 65. V Grayrigg *Carl* 68-75; P-in-c Sawrey 75-80; rtd 80. *Regent House, 17 Church Street, Beaumaris, Gwynedd LL58 8AB* Beaumaris (0248) 810628

MOORHOUSE, Norman. b 12. Tatterford Ord Test Sch. **d** 48 **p** 49. V Rock w Heightington *Worc* 68-75; rtd 75; Perm to Offic *Nor* from 75. *Leathes Prior, 74 The Close, Norwich, Norfolk NR1 4DR* Norwich (0603) 610911

MOORHOUSE, Peter. b 42. Liv Univ BSc64 Hull Univ CertEd. Linc Th Coll 79. **d** 81 **p** 82. C Horsforth *Ripon* 81-85; R Ackworth *Wakef* from 85. *The Rectory, Ackworth, Pontefract, W Yorkshire WF7 7EJ* Pontefract (0977) 780880

MOORSE, Frank Robert. b 08. Clifton Th Coll. **d** 59 **p** 60. R Dolton *Ex* 63-78; R Iddesleigh w Dowland 68-78; R Monkokehampton 68-78; rtd 78. *11 Bryant Gardens, Clevedon, Avon BS21 5HD* Clevedon (0272) 879082

MOORSOM, Christopher Arthur Robert. b 55. Ox Univ BA. Sarum & Wells Th Coll 79. **d** 82 **p** 83. C Bradford-on-Avon *Sarum* 82-85; R Broad Town, Clyffe Pypard and Tockenham 85-89; V Banwell *B & W* from 89. *The Vicarage, 3 East Street, Banwell, Weston-super-Mare, Avon BS24 6BN* Banwell (0934) 822320

MOORSOM, Robert Coverdale. b 23. ARCM48. Cuddesdon Coll 49. **d** 50 **p** 51. V Bierley *Bradf* 65-71; C Wareham *Sarum* 71-80; TV Gillingham 80-83; R The Lulworths, Winfrith Newburgh and Chaldon 83-89; rtd 89. *4 Hodges Close, Poole, Dorset BH17 7QE* Poole (0202) 684897

MORALEE, Thomas Edward (Tony). b 33. S'wark Ord Course. **d** 82 **p** 83. NSM Wandsworth All SS *S'wark* 82-90; NSM Gt Bookham *Guildf* from 91. *71 Eastwick Park, Leatherhead, Surrey KT23 3NH* Leatherhead (0372) 454433

MORAY, ROSS AND CAITHNESS, Bishop of. *See* SESSFORD, Rt Rev George Minshull

MORAY, ROSS AND CAITHNESS, Dean of. *See* PAUL, Very Rev John Douglas

MORCOM, Canon Anthony John. b 16. Clare Coll Cam BA38 MA42. Cuddesdon Coll 38. **d** 39 **p** 40. V Cam St Mary Less *Ely* 66-73; RD Cam 71-73; Can Res Ely Cathl 74-83; rtd 84; Lic to Offic *Ely* from 84. *33 Porson Road, Cambridge CB2 2ET* Cambridge (0223) 62352

MORDECAI, Mrs Betty. b 27. Birm Univ BA48 Cam Univ CertEd49. Wycliffe Hall Ox 85. **dss** 86 **d** 87. Leamington Priors All SS *Cov* 86-87; Hon Par Dn 87-89; Par Dn Worc City St Paul and Old St Martin etc *Worc* from 89. *3 Severn Terrace, Worcester WR1 3EH* Worcester (0905) 612894

MORDECAI, Thomas Huw. b 59. Bris Univ BA81 St Jo Coll Dur BA85. Cranmer Hall Dur 83. **d** 87 **p** 88. C Gillingham St Mary *Roch* 87-90; Chapl Warw Sch from 90. *21 Calder Walk, Leamington Spa, Warks CV31 1SA* Leamington Spa (0926) 886042

MORE, Richard David Antrobus. b 48. St Jo Coll Dur BA70 DipTh71. Cranmer Hall Dur 70. **d** 72 **p** 73. C Macclesfield St Mich *Ches* 72-77; Chapl Lee Abbey 77-82; V Porchester *S'well* from 82; RD Gedling from 90. *The Vicarage, Marshall Hill Drive, Nottingham NG3 6FY* Nottingham (0602) 606185

MORECROFT, Michael William. b 40. MIBiol Man Univ MEd. W Midl Minl Tr Course. **d** 86 **p** 87. Hd Master Polesworth Sch Warks from 86; Hon C Wylde Green *Birm* 86-89; Hon C Castle Bromwich St Clem from 89. *St Clement's Vicarage, Castle Bromwich, Birmingham B36 9JG* 021-747 4460

MORELAND, John Ralph Hardwicke. b 09. ALCD34 St Jo Coll Dur LTh34 BA36 MA41. **d** 36 **p** 37. V E Budleigh and Bicton *Ex* 47-71; rtd 71. *51 Brackendale Road, Queen's Park, Bournemouth BH8 9HY* Bournemouth (0202) 33202

MORETON, Mark. b 39. Jes Coll Cam BA64 MA68. Westcott Ho Cam. **d** 65 **p** 66. C Portsea All SS *Portsm* 65-70; C St Martin-in-the-Fields *Lon* 70-72; Chapl Jes Coll Cam 72-77; R Stafford St Mary and St Chad *Lich* 77-79; P-in-c Stafford Ch Ch 77-79; P-in-c Marston w Whitgreave 77-79; TR Stafford 79-91; V W Bromwich All SS from 91. *All Saints' Vicarage, 90 Hall Green Road, West Bromwich, W Midlands B71 3LB* 021-588 2647

MORETON, Dr Michael Bernard. b 44. St Jo Coll Cam BA66 MA70 Ch Ch Ox BA66 MA69 DPhil69. St Steph Ho Ox 66. **d** 68 **p** 69. C Banstead *Guildf* 68-74; R Alburgh *Nor* 74-75; R Denton 74-75; R Middleton Cheney w Chacombe *Pet* 75-87. *Penny Royal, 19 Thorpe Road, Chacombe, Banbury, Oxon OX17 2JW* Banbury (0295) 710631

MORETON, Preb Michael Joseph. b 17. Univ Coll Lon BA40 Ch Ch Ox BA47 MA53. Wells Th Coll 47. **d** 48 **p** 49. Lect Th Ex Univ 57-86; R Ex St Mary Steps *Ex* 59-86; RD Christianity 83-89; Preb Ex Cathl from 85; rtd 86; P-in-c Ex St Mary Steps *Ex* from 86. *St Mary Steps Rectory, 10 Victoria Park Road, Exeter EX2 4NT* Exeter (0392) 77685

MORETON, Philip Norman Harley. b 28. Linc Th Coll. **d** 57 **p** 58. V Linc St Giles *Linc* 65-70; V Bracebridge Heath 71-77; V Seasalter *Cant* 77-84; TV Whitstable 84-88; rtd 88. *37 West Drive, Birmingham B20 3ST* 021-554 0976

MOREY, Preb Desmond James. b 16. Em Coll Cam BA37 MA41. Wycliffe Hall Ox 39. **d** 40 **p** 41. V Taunton St Mary *B & W* 61-81; Preb Wells Cathl 74-81; rtd 81; Perm to Offic Roch and Cant from 81. *64 Anglesey Avenue, Loose, Maidstone, Kent ME15 9SY* Maidstone (0622) 746294

✠**MORGAN, Rt Rev Alan Wyndham.** b 40. Univ of Wales (Lamp) BA62. St Mich Coll Llan 62. **d** 64 **p** 65 **c** 89. C Llangyfelach and Morriston *S & B* 64-69; C Swansea St Pet 69-72; C Cov E *Cov* 72-73; TV 73-83; Bp's Officer for Soc Resp 78-83; Adn Cov 83-89; Suff Bp Sherwood *S'well* from 89. *Sherwood House, High Oakham, Mansfield, Notts NG18 5AJ* Mansfield (0623) 657491

MORGAN, Ven Dr Barry Cennydd. b 47. Lon Univ BA69 Selw Coll Cam BA72 MA74 Univ of Wales PhD86. Westcott Ho Cam 70. **d** 72 **p** 73. Chapl Bryn-y-Don Community Sch 72-75; C St Andrew's Major and Michaelston-le-Pit *Llan* 72-75; Ed Welsh Churchman 75-82; Lect Th Univ of Wales (Cardiff) 75-77; Chapl and Lect St Mich Coll Llan 75-77; Warden Ch Hostel Ban 77-84; Chapl and Lect Th Univ of Wales (Ban) 77-84; In-Service Tr Adv *Ban* 78-84; Dir of Ords 82-84; Can Ban Cathl 83-84; R Wrexham *St As* 84-86; Adn Merioneth *Ban* from 86; R Criccieth w Treflys from 86. *The Rectory, Criccieth, Gwynedd LL52 0AG* Criccieth (0766) 523222

MORGAN, Bernard Spencer Trevor. b 32. AKC55. **d** 56 **p** 57. C Havant *Portsm* 56-62; C Yatton Keynell *Bris* 62-65; P-in-c Mutford w Rushmere *Nor* 65-67; P-in-c Gisleham 65-67; R Kessingland 65-83; RD Lothingland 71-76; R St Just in Roseland w Philleigh *Truro* 83-87; V Ludham w Potter Heigham *Nor* from 87; RD Waxham from 89. *The Vicarage, Ludham, Great Yarmouth, Norfolk NR29 5QA* Great Yarmouth (069262) 282

MORGAN, Miss Beryl. b 30. dss 63 **d** 87. Rickerscote *Lich* 63-69; Hd Dss 70-87; Dioc Lay Min Adv from 70; Willenhall H Trin 80-87; Par Dn from 87. *3 Milestone Way, Willenhall, W Midlands WV12 5YA* Bloxwich (0922) 475321

MORGAN, Brian. b 35. Lon Univ BA58. Wells Th Coll 59. **d** 61 **p** 62. C Withington St Chris *Man* 61-63; C Rochdale 63-65; Trinidad and Tobago 65-69; V Heywood St Jas *Man* 69-74; Miss to Seamen 74-80; Kenya 74-77; Chapl Pernis Miss to Seamen *Eur* 77-78; Antwerp 78-80; V Skerton St Chad *Blackb* 80-84; P-in-c Oswaldtwistle Immanuel 84-87; P-in-c Oswaldtwistle All SS 84-87; V Barrowford from 87. *The Vicarage, Wheatley Lane Road, Barrowford, Nelson, Lancs BB9 6QS* Nelson (0282) 63206

MORGAN, Chandos Clifford Hastings Mansel. b 20. CB73. Jes Coll Cam BA42 MA46. Ridley Hall Cam 42. **d** 44 **p** 45. Chapl RN 51-72; Chapl of the Fleet and Adn for the RN 72-75; Chapl Dean Close Sch Cheltenham 76-83; R St Marg Lothbury and St Steph Coleman Street etc *Lon* 83-89; rtd 89. *Westwood Farmhouse, West Lydford, Somerton, Somerset TA11 7DL* Wheathill (096324) 301

MORGAN, Christopher Basil. b 22. Hertf Coll Ox BA50 MA54. Chich Th Coll 48. **d** 51 **p** 52. R Brampton *Nor* 56-90; R Hevingham 56-90; rtd 90; NSM Icklesham Chich 90. *21 River Bank, Potter Heigham, Great Yarmouth, Norfolk NR29 5ND*

MORGAN, Christopher Heudebourck. b 47. Lon Univ DipTh70 Lanc Univ BA73. Kelham Th Coll 66. **d** 73 **p** 74. C Birstall *Leic* 73-76; Asst Chapl Brussels *Eur* 76-80; P-in-c Redditch St Geo *Worc* 80-81; TV Redditch, The Ridge 81-85; V Sonning *Ox* from 85; Prin Berks Chr Tr Scheme 85-89. *The Vicarage, Sonning, Reading RG4 0UR* Reading (0734) 693298

MORGAN, David Farnon Charles. b 43. Leeds Univ BA68. Coll of Resurr Mirfield 68. **d** 70 **p** 71. C Swinton St Pet *Man* 70-73; C Langley All SS and Martyrs 73-75; R Salford St Clem w St Cypr Ordsall 75-76; R Salford Ordsall St Clem 76-86; V Adlington *Blackb* from 86. *St Paul's Vicarage, 35 Grove Crescent, Adlington, Chorley, Lancs PR6 9RJ* Adlington (0257) 480253

MORGAN, David Joseph. b 47. Bp Burgess Hall Lamp 66 St Deiniol's Hawarden 74. **d** 74 **p** 75. C Pemb Dock

St D 74-77; C Burry Port and Pwll 77-80; Miss to Seamen from 80; Sen Chapl and Sec Welsh Coun from 85. *25 Glanmor Park Road, Sketty, Swansea SA2 0QG* Swansea (0792) 206637

MORGAN, David Watcyn. b 14. St D Coll Lamp. **d** 64 **p** 65. R Herbrandston and St Ishmael w Hasguard *St D* 70-83; rtd 83. *26 Gwscwm Park, Burry Port, Dyfed SA16 0DX* Burry Port (05546) 4951

MORGAN, Denis. b 36. Cuddesdon Coll 67. **d** 69 **p** 70. C Bush Hill Park St Steph *Lon* 69-72; C Stevenage St Nic *St Alb* 72-75; V Croxley Green St Oswald 75-85; V Shillington from 85. *All Saints' Vicarage, Shillington, Hitchin, Herts SG5 3LS* Hitchin (0462) 711240

MORGAN, Preb Dewi Lewis. b 16. Univ of Wales BA37. St Mich Coll Llan 38. **d** 39 **p** 40. R St Bride Fleet Street w Bridewell etc *Lon* 62-84; Preb St Paul's Cathl 76-84; P-in-c St Dunstan in the West 78-79; rtd 84; Perm to Offic *S'wark* from 85. *217 Rosendale Road, London SE21 8LW* 081-670 1308

MORGAN, Canon Edgar Francis Andrew. b 07. St Jo Coll Dur BA34 MA38. **d** 34 **p** 35. V Coleshill *Birm* 61-75; V Maxstoke 61-75; rtd 75; Perm to Offic *B & W* from 75. *34 Severn Avenue, Weston-super-Mare, Avon BS23 4DQ* Weston-super-Mare (0934) 21299

MORGAN, Enid Morris Roberts. b 40. St Anne's Coll Ox BA61 Univ of Wales (Ban) MA73. United Th Coll Abth BD81. **d** 84. C Llanfihangel w Llanafan and Llanwnnws etc *St D* 84-86; Dn-in-c from 86. *The Vicarage, Llanafan, Aberystwyth, Dyfed SY23 4AX* Crosswood (09743) 253

MORGAN, Evan Griffith. b 07. St D Coll Lamp BA31. **d** 32 **p** 33. R Reynoldston and Knelston w Llanddewi *S & B* 67-71; R Penrice and Reynoldston 71-77; rtd 77. *634 Gower Road, Upper Killay, Swansea SA2 7EX* Swansea (0792) 203146

MORGAN, Evan Tom Parry. b 10. St D Coll Lamp BA31 St Mich Coll Llan 32. **d** 34 **p** 35. R Llangoedmor and Llechryd *St D* 60-78; rtd 78. *Gwellfor, Rhoshill, Cardigan, Dyfed SA43 2TR* Boncath (0239) 841263

MORGAN, Frank Charles. b 14. Bps' Coll Cheshunt 53. **d** 54 **p** 55. V Cleveleys *Blackb* 65-81; rtd 81; Lic to Offic *Blackb* from 82. *27 Parkside Road, St Annes, Lytham St Annes, Lancs FY8 3SZ* St Annes (0253) 727647

MORGAN, Gareth Morison Kilby. b 33. Bris Univ BA56. Cuddesdon Coll 57 Bangalore Th Coll. **d** 61 **p** 62. C St Helier *S'wark* 61-65; Chapl Scargill Ho N Yorkshire 65-70; Dir RE *Linc* 71-74; Dir of Educn *St E* 74-81; TR Hanley H Ev *Lich* 81-89; TR Cen Telford from 89. *The Rectory, Church Road, Dawley, Telford, Shropshire TF4 2AS* Telford (0952) 501655

MORGAN, Geoffrey. b 51. AKC72. St Aug Coll Cant 73. **d** 74 **p** 75. C Hulme Ascension *Man* 74-77; C Nantwich *Ches* 77-79; C Hatf *St Alb* 79-86; Chapl S Beds HA and Luton and Dunstable Hosp from 86. *5 Thirlstone Road, Luton, Beds LU4 8QT* Luton (0582) 594948

MORGAN, Gerald. b 16. St Mich Coll Llan 46. **d** 47 **p** 48. Miss to Seamen 54-70; V Marystowe w Coryton *Ex* 70-79; P-in-c Lewtrenchard w Thrushelton 78-79; P-in-c Stowford 78-79; V Marystowe, Coryton, Stowford, Lewtrenchard etc 79-81; rtd 82; Hon C Braunton *Ex* from 82. *St Anne's Parsonage, Saunton, Braunton, Devon EX33 1LG* Braunton (0271) 812412

MORGAN, Gerallt. b 12. St Cath Soc Ox BA47 MA51. Wycliffe Hall Ox 45. **d** 47 **p** 48. R Whiston *Sheff* 65-78; rtd 78; Perm to Offic *Win* from 78. *Capel Court, The Burgage, Prestbury, Cheltenham, Glos GL52 3EL* Cheltenham (0242) 572606

MORGAN, Glyn. b 21. Oak Hill Th Coll 73. **d** 76 **p** 77. Hon C Barton Seagrave w Warkton *Pet* from 76. *St Edmund's House, Warkton, Kettering, Northants* Kettering (0536) 520610

MORGAN, Glyn. b 33. Univ of Wales (Ban) BA55 MA69. Coll of Resurr Mirfield 55. **d** 57 **p** 58. C Dolgellau *Ban* 57-60; C Conway 60-63; V Corris 63-68; Hd of RE Friars' Sch Ban 69-70; Lic to Offic 70-71; Hd of RE Oswestry Boys' Modern Sch 70-74; Hon C Oswestry H Trin *Lich* 71-79; Hd of RE Oswestry High Sch for Girls 74-79; Hd of RE Fitzalan Sch Oswestry 79-88; Perm to Offic *Lich* from 79; St As from 84; V Meifod and Llangynyw *St As* from 88; RD Caereinion from 89. *The Vicarage, Meifod, Powys SY22 6DH* Meifod (093884) 231

MORGAN, Graham. b 47. S'wark Ord Course. **d** 83 **p** 84. NSM S Kensington St Steph *Lon* 83-90; NSM Hammersmith H Innocents from 90. *24 Charleville Court, Charleville Road, London W14 9JG* 071-381 3211

MORGAN, Grenville. b 15. Leeds Univ BA40. Coll of Resurr Mirfield 40. **d** 42 **p** 43. V Drayton in Hales *Lich* 60-72; R Adderley 60-72; V Finchingfield and Cornish

Hall End *Chelmsf* 72-80; rtd 80; Perm to Offic *Cant* from 81. *12 Ramsey Close, Canterbury, Kent CT2 8DL* Canterbury (0227) 457904

MORGAN, Gwilym Howell Rowland. b 15. Univ of Wales (Cardiff) BA39. Clifton Th Coll 40. d 41 p 42. V Tidenham w Beachley and Lancaut *Glouc* 58-75; R Tibberton w Taynton 75-80; rtd 80; Perm to Offic *Glouc* from 83. *25 Horsbere Road, Gloucester GL3 3PT* Gloucester (0452) 612187

MORGAN, Canon Gwilym Owen. b 17. LSE BSc47. Westcott Ho Cam 46. d 48 p 49. Chapl Salford R Hosp 51-71; R Salford St Phil w St Steph *Man* 59-71; RD Salford 57-71; Hon Can Man Cathl 62-71; Can Res 71-85; Sub-Dean 72-85; rtd 86; Perm to Offic *Man* from 86. *20 Lyndhurst Road, Didsbury Village, Manchester M20 0AA* 061-434 2732

MORGAN, Harold Evan. b 17. St D Coll Lamp BA38 d 40 p 41. V Newc *Llan* 68-82; rtd 83; Perm to Offic *Llan* from 82. *28 Seaview Drive, Ogmore-by-Sea, Bridgend, M Glam* Southerndown (0656) 880467

MORGAN, Henry. b 45. Hertf Coll Ox BA68. Westcott Ho Cam 68. d 70 p 71. C Lee St Marg *S'wark* 70-73; C Newington St Paul 73-76; V Camberwell St Mich w All So w Em 76-84; V Kingswood from 84. *The Vicarage, Woodland Way, Kingswood, Tadworth, Surrey KT20 6NW* Mogador (0737) 832164

MORGAN, Ian David John. b 57. BA. Ripon Coll Cuddesdon. d 83 p 84. C Heref H Trin *Heref* 83-86; C New Shoreham *Chich* 86-88. *Address temp unknown*

MORGAN, Ian Stephen. b 50. Open Univ BA88. Sarum & Wells Th Coll 86. d 88 p 89. C Baldock w Bygrave *St Alb* 88-91; C Rumburgh w S Elmham w the Ilketshalls *St E* from 91. *The New House, The Street, St James, South Elmham, Halesworth, Suffolk*

MORGAN, James (Geoffrey) Selwyn. b 59. Ex Univ BA81 PGCE82 Dur Univ CCSk91. Cranmer Hall Dur 88. d 91. C Reading St Agnes w St Paul *Ox* from 91. *23 Blandford Road, Reading, Berks RG2 8RJ* Reading (0734) 862513

MORGAN, John Aeron. b 15. St D Coll Lamp BA37. d 40 p 41. R Harley w Kenley *Heref* 62-73; P-in-c Hughley 65-73; V Pencarreg and Llanycrwys *St D* 73-86; rtd 86. *46 Penybryn, Lampeter, Dyfed* Lampeter (0570) 422198

MORGAN, John Geoffrey Basil. b 21. Wells Th Coll 59. d 60 p 61. V Ensbury *Sarum* 69-82; C W Parley 82-86; rtd 86. *62 Shapland Avenue, Bournemouth BH11 9PX* Bournemouth (0202) 578289

MORGAN, John Roland. b 31. Birm Univ BA54. Bps' Coll Cheshunt 54. d 55 p 56. C Selly Oak St Mary *Birm* 55-57; C Yardley Wood 57-58; C Hamstead St Paul 58-61; V Smethwick St Chad 61-68; V Balsall Common 68-82; V N Leigh *Ox* from 82; RD Woodstock from 87. *The Vicarage, New Yatt Road, North Leigh, Witney, Oxon OX8 6TT* Freeland (0993) 881136

MORGAN, John William Miller. b 34. Lon Univ BSc56. Wycliffe Hall Ox 61. d 63 p 64. C St Alb Ch Ch *St Alb* 63-68; V Luton St Matt High Town 68-79; V Mangotsfield *Bris* 79-90; P-in-c Stanton St Quintin, Hullavington, Grittleton etc from 90. *The Rectory, Stanton St Quintin, Chippenham, Wilts SN14 6DE* Malmesbury (0666) 837187

MORGAN, Katharine. b 41. d 91. NSM Lougher *S & B* from 91. *68 Borough Road, Lougher, Swansea SA4 2RT*

MORGAN, Kenneth James. b 14. Selw Coll Cam BA36 MA43. Wells Th Coll 36. d 38 p 39. V Shalford *Guildf* 66-84; rtd 84; Perm to Offic *Guildf* from 85. *Greenwood, The Close, Wonersh, Guildford, Surrey GU5 0PA* Guildford (0483) 898791

MORGAN, Mark Anthony. b 58. LLB. Chich Th Coll. d 84 p 85. C Thorpe *Nor* 84-87; C Eaton 87-90; V Southtown from 90. *St Mary's Vicarage, Southtown, Great Yarmouth, Norfolk NR31 0AB* Great Yarmouth (0493) 655048

MORGAN, Martin Paul. b 46. St Steph Ho Ox 71. d 73 p 74. C Kettering St Mary *Pet* 73-76; C Fareham SS Pet and Paul *Portsm* 76-80; V Portsea Ascension from 80. *The Vicarage, 98 Kirby Road, Portsmouth PO2 0PW* Portsmouth (0705) 660123

MORGAN, Mervyn Thomas. b 24. Ch Coll Cam BA48 MA71. Chich Th Coll 79. d 80 p 81. NSM Lewes All SS, St Anne, St Mich and St Thos *Chich* 80-82; P-in-c Glynde, W Firle and Beddingham 82-84; V Burwash Weald 84-89; R Alphamstone w Lamarsh and Pebmarsh *Chelmsf* from 89. *The Rectory, Alphamstone, Bures, Suffolk CO8 5HH* Twinstead (0787) 269646

MORGAN, Michael. b 32. Lon Univ BSc67 MSc67 PhD63. d 74 p 75. NSM Portsdown *Portsm* from 74. *1 Widley Road, Cosham, Portsmouth PO6 2DS* Cosham (0705) 377442

MORGAN, Michael John. b 45. Nottm Univ BA66 MEd71. Linc Th Coll 80. d 82 p 83. C Bulkington *Cov* 82-83; C Bulkington w Shilton and Ansty 83-85; V Longford 85-89; R Norton *Sheff* from 89. *The Rectory, Norton, Sheffield S8 8JQ* Sheffield (0742) 745066

MORGAN, Morley Roland. b 47. Univ of Wales (Lamp) BA76. St Steph Ho Ox 76. d 77 p 78. C Merthyr Dyfan *Llan* 77-78; C Llantrisant 78-80; TV Cov Caludon *Cov* 80-86; Chapl N Man Gen Hosp from 86. *North Manchester General Hospital, Delaunays Road, Crumpsall, Manchester M8 6RB* 061-795 4567

MORGAN, Nicholas John. b 50. K Coll Lon BD71 AKC71 CertEd. St Aug Coll Cant 72. d 73 p 74. C Wythenshawe Wm Temple Ch *Man* 73-76; C Southam w Stockton *Cov* 76-79; V Brailes from 79; R Sutton under Brailes from 79; RD Shipston from 90. *The Vicarage, Brailes, Banbury, Oxon OX15 5HT* Brailes (060885) 230

MORGAN, Preb Peter Birkett. b 30. Ch Ch Ox BA52 MA61 BLitt61. Ripon Hall Ox 52. d 56 p 57. C St Marylebone w H Trin *Lon* 56-60; V Wealdstone H Trin 60-69; V Enfield St Andr from 69; AD Enfield 82-87; Preb St Paul's Cathl from 85. *The Vicarage, Silver Street, Enfield, Middx EN1 3EG* 081-363 8676

MORGAN, Philip. b 51. Lon Univ BSc75 Univ of Wales (Cardiff) BD78. St Mich Coll Llan 75. d 78 p 79. C Swansea St Nic *S & B* 78-81; C Morriston 81-83; C Swansea St Mary w H Trin 83-84; USA from 84. *705 Sixth, Box 374, Howe, Indiana 46746, USA*

MORGAN, Canon Philip Brendan. b 35. G&C Coll Cam BA59 MA63. Wells Th Coll 59. d 61 p 62. C Paddington Ch Ch *Lon* 61-66; C Trunch w Swafield *Nor* 66-68; P-in-c Nor St Steph 68-72; Sacr Nor Cathl 72-74; Can Res and Sub-Dean St Alb 74-81; Hon Can St Alb from 81; R Bushey from 81; RD Aldenham from 91. *The Rectory, High Street, Bushey, Watford WD2 1BD* 081-950 6408 or 950 1546

MORGAN, Canon Philip Reginald Strange. b 27. St D Coll Lamp BA51 Keble Coll Ox BA53 MA57. Wells Th Coll 57. d 57 p 58. C Fleur-de-Lis *Mon* 57-59; C Bassaleg 59-62; CF (TA) 62-74; V Dingestow and Wanastow *Mon* 62-65; V Dingestow and Penrhos 65-66; R Machen and Rudry 66-75; R Machen 75-76; V Caerleon from 76; Can St Woolos Cathl from 84. *The Vicarage, Caerleon, Newport, Gwent NP6 1AZ* Caerleon (0633) 420248

MORGAN, Philip Richard Llewelyn. b 27. Wadh Coll Ox BA50 MA52. St Steph Ho Ox 53. d 55 p 56. C Warlingham w Chelsham and Farleigh *S'wark* 55-58; Chapl Haileybury Coll Herts 58-73; Hd Master Haileybury Jun Sch Berks 73-87; R The Deverills *Sarum* from 87. *The Rectory, 6 Homefield Close, Longbridge Deverill, Warminster, Wilts BA12 7DQ* Warminster (0985) 40278

MORGAN, Canon Reginald Graham. b 25. St D Coll Lamp LTh48. d 48 p 49. C Chirk *St As* 48-50; C Llangollen and Trevor 50-55; R Llanwyddelan w Manafon 55-66; V Rhuddlan from 66; RD St As from 78; Hon Can St As Cathl 83-89; Can from 89. *The Vicarage, Rhuddlan, Rhyl, Clwyd LL18 2UE* Rhuddlan (0745) 591568

MORGAN, Reginald Graham Tharle. b 46. St Jo Coll Nottm LTh75. d 75 p 76. C Oadby *Leic* 76-79; S Africa from 80. *PO Box 112, Greytown, Natal, 3500 South Africa* Greytown (334) 32192

MORGAN, Robert Chowen. b 40. St Cath Coll Cam BA63 MA. St Chad's Coll Dur 64. d 66 p 67. C Lanc St Mary *Blackb* 66-76; Lect Lanc Univ 67-76; Lect Th Ox Univ from 76; P-in-c Sandford-on-Thames *Ox* from 87. *Lower Farm, Sandford-on-Thames, Oxford OX4 4YR* Oxford (0865) 748848

MORGAN, Robert Harman. b 28. Univ of Wales (Cardiff) BA55. Coll of Resurr Mirfield 55. d 57 p 58. C Penarth w Lavernock *Llan* 57-61; C Caerau w Ely 61-67; V Glan Ely from 67. *Church House, Grand Avenue, Ely, Cardiff CF5 4HX* Cardiff (0222) 591633

MORGAN, Robert Hugh. b 49. d 91. C Swansea St Pet *S & B* from 91. *St Illtyd's Parsonage, 18 Ystrad Road, Forestffach, Swansea SA5 4BT* Swansea (0792) 586437

MORGAN, Robert Oscar Thomas. b 05. Univ of Wales BA27. St Mich Coll Llan 30. d 30 p 31. Miss to Seamen 48-71; Chapl Dunkirk and N France *Eur* 64-71; rtd 71; Lic to Offic Eur from 71; Blackb from 74. *84 Palatine Avenue, Scotforth, Lancaster LA1 4HF* Lancaster (0524) 66777

MORGAN, Roger. b 32. Bris Univ BA59. Tyndale Hall Bris 56. d 61 p 62. C Chitts Hill St Cuth *Lon* 61-64; R Kingham *Ox* 64-69; R Kingham and Daylesford 69-78; P-in-c Sarsden w Churchill 74-78; V W Hampstead St Cuth *Lon* 78-87; P-in-c Fyfield *Chelmsf* 87-89; P-in-c Willingale w Shellow and Berners Roding 88-89; R

Fyfield and Moreton w Bobbingworth from 90. *The Rectory, Fyfield, Ongar, Essex CM5 0SD* Fyfield (0277) 899255

MORGAN, Roger William. b 40. Mert Coll Ox BA62 Cam Univ MA67. Ridley Hall Cam 80. **d** 81 **p** 82. NSM Cam St Paul *Ely* 81-84; V Corby St Columba *Pet* 84-90; V Leic H Trin w St Jo *Leic* from 90. *29 Holmfield Road, Leicester* Leicester (0533) 704986

MORGAN, Canon Samuel. b 07. St D Coll Lamp BA32. **d** 32 **p** 33. V Felinfoel *St D* 64-77; Can St D Cathl 72-79; rtd 77. *10 Ty'r Fran Avenue, Llanelli, Dyfed* Llanelli (0554) 772977

MORGAN, Simon John. b 58. Univ of Wales (Swansea) BA81 Univ of Wales (Cardiff) BD86. **d** 86 **p** 87. C Penarth All SS *Llan* 86-87; C Port Talbot St Theodore 87-89; C Gellygaer from 89. *Ty Catwg, St Mary Street, Gilfach, Bargoed, M Glam CF8 8NG* Bargoed (0443) 821803

MORGAN, Steve Shelley. b 48. Univ of Wales DipTh70. St Mich Coll Llan 67. **d** 71 **p** 72. C Llan w Capel Llanilterne *Llan* 71-74; C Llanharan w Peterston-s-Montem 71-74; C Neath w Llantwit 74-77; TV Merthyr Tydfil and Cyfarthfa from 77. *Christchurch Vicarage, Georgetown, Merthyr Tydfil, M Glam CF48 1DR* Merthyr Tydfil (0685) 71995

MORGAN, Thomas John Walford. b 16. Univ of Wales BA37. St D Coll Lamp 37. **d** 39 **p** 40. V Swallowfield *Ox* 71-81; rtd 81. *57 Felinfoel Road, Llanelli, Dyfed SA15 3JQ* Llanelli (0554) 752303

MORGAN, Trevor. b 12. Univ of Wales (Swansea) BA37. St Mich Coll Llan 44. **d** 44 **p** 45. R Pipe and Lyde w Moreton on Lugg *Heref* 66-77; rtd 77; Perm to Offic *Heref* from 77. *4 Meadow Drive, Canon Pyon, Hereford HR4 8NT* Canon Pyon (043271) 678

MORGAN, Verna Ireta. b 42. NE Ord Course. **d** 89. NSM Potternewton *Ripon* from 89. *62 Mexborough Road, Leeds LS7 3EH* Leeds (0532) 682520

MORGAN, Canon William Badham. b 40. Univ of Wales (Cardiff) BSc65. Ripon Hall Ox 69. **d** 72 **p** 73. C Merthyr Tydfil and Cyfarthfa *Llan* 72-76; P-in-c Penydarren 76-83; V from 83; Hon Can Llan Cathl from 88; RD Merthyr Tydfil from 91. *The Vicarage, Penydarren, Merthyr Tydfil, M Glam* Merthyr Tydfil (0685) 725559

MORGAN, Canon William Charles Gerwyn. b 30. Univ of Wales (Lamp) BA52. St Mich Coll Llan 52. **d** 56 **p** 57. C Hubberston *St D* 56-62; V Ambleston w St Dogwells 62-68; Miss to Seamen from 68; V Fishguard w Llanychar *St D* 68-85; V Fishguard w Llanychaer and Pontfaen w Morvil etc from 85; Can St D Cathl from 85. *The Vicarage, Fishguard, Dyfed SA65 9AU* Fishguard (0348) 872895

MORGAN, William John. b 38. Selw Coll Cam BA62 MA66. Cuddesdon Coll 62. **d** 65 **p** 66. C Cardiff St Jo *Llan* 65-68; Asst Chapl Univ of Wales (Cardiff) 68-70; Perm to Offic *Lon* 70-73; C Albany Street Ch Ch 73-78; P-in-c E Acton St Dunstan 78-80; V E Acton St Dunstan w St Thos from 80. *The Vicarage, 54 Perryn Road, London W3 7NA* 081-743 4117

MORGAN, William Stanley Timothy. b 41. Univ of Wales (Lamp) BA63. Wycliffe Hall Ox 63. **d** 66 **p** 67. C Abth St Mich *St D* 66-69; V Ambleston w St Dogwells 69-70; V Ambleston, St Dogwells, Walton E and Llysyfran 70-74; V Llan-non 74-80; V Lamp 80-87; V Lamp Pont Steffan w Silian from 87. *The Vicarage, Lampeter, Dyfed SA48 7EJ* Lampeter (0570) 422460

MORGAN-JONES, Christopher John. b 43. Bris Univ BA66 Chicago Univ MBA68 McMaster Univ Ontario MA69. Cuddesdon Coll 70. **d** 73 **p** 74. C Folkestone St Sav *Cant* 73-76; P-in-c Swalecliffe 76-82; V Addington 82-84; V Addington *S'wark* from 85; RD Croydon Addington 85-90. *Addington Vicarage, Spout Hill, Croydon CR0 5AN* Lodge Hill (0689) 842167 or 841838

MORGAN-JONES, Richard James. b 46. **d** 75 **p** 76. C Bromley St Mark *Roch* 75-77; Perm to Offic 77-84. *15 Wendover Road, Bromley, Kent*

MORGANS, Paul Hywel. b 61. LWCMD83. Chich Th Coll 86. **d** 90 **p** 91. C Johnston w Steynton *St D* from 90. *2 Burford Close, Johnston, Haverfordwest, Dyfed SA62 3EX* Haverfordwest (0437) 890106

MORISON, John Donald. b 34. ALCD60. **d** 61 **p** 62. C Rayleigh *Chelmsf* 61-64; C St Austell *Truro* 64-67; V Meltham Mills *Wakef* 67-71; Youth Chapl *Cov* 71-76; S Africa 76-82; Can Port Elizabeth 80-82; Bardsley Missr 82-86; Lic to Offic *S'wark* 82-86; Dioc Missr *Derby* from 86; V Quarndon from 86. *St Paul's Vicarage, 149 Church Road, Quarndon, Derby DE6 4JA* Derby (0332) 559333

MORLEY, Athelstan John. b 29. Linc Coll Ox BA52 MA56. Ridley Hall Cam. **d** 54 **p** 55. C Surbiton St Matt *S'wark* 54-57; Succ Chelmsf Cathl *Chelmsf* 57-60;

R Mistley w Manningtree 60-69; R Hadleigh St Jas from 69. *The Rectory, 50 Rectory Road, Benfleet, Essex SS7 2ND* Southend-on-Sea (0702) 558992

MORLEY, Frank. b 15. Worc Ord Coll 63. **d** 65 **p** 66. V Overton w Fyfield and E Kennett *Sarum* 68-73; V Urchfont w Stert 74-81; rtd 81; Perm to Offic Heref from 81; Worc from 86; C Much Birch w Lt Birch, Much Dewchurch etc *Heref* 86. *12A Cornmeadow Green, Claines, Worcester WR3 7PN* Worcester (0905) 56542

MORLEY, Miss Gillian Dorothy. b 21. Greyladies Coll 49. **dss** 70 **d** 87. Lewisham St Swithun *S'wark* 70-82; Sturry w Fordwich and Westbere w Hersden *Cant* 82-87; Perm to Offic from 87. *28 Glen Iris Avenue, Canterbury, Kent CT2 8HP* Canterbury (0227) 459992

MORLEY, John. b 43. AKC. St Deiniol's Hawarden. **d** 68 **p** 69. C Newbold on Avon *Cov* 68-73; C Solihull *Birm* 73-76; C-in-c Elmdon Heath CD 76-77; Chapl RAF from 77. *c/o MOD, Adastral House, Theobald's Road, London WC1X 8RU* 071-430 7268

MORLEY, Keith. b 44. St Chad's Coll Dur BA66 DipTh67. **d** 67 **p** 68. C S Yardley St Mich *Birm* 67-70; C Solihull 70-73; V Shaw Hill 73-77; P-in-c Burton Coggles *Linc* 77-79; P-in-c Boothby Pagnell 77-79; V Lavington w Ingoldsby 77-79; P-in-c Bassingthorpe w Bitchfield 77-79; R Ingoldsby 79-87; RD Beltisloe 84-87; P-in-c Old Dalby and Nether Broughton *Leic* from 87; RD Framland (Melton) 88-90. *The New Vicarage, Old Dalby, Melton Mowbray, Leics LE14 3LB* Melton Mowbray (0664) 822878

MORLEY, Canon Leonard. b 04. Man Egerton Hall 35. **d** 37 **p** 38. V Kingsley *Ches* 56-72; rtd 72; Perm to Offic Cant from 79; Chich from 81. *Ramsay Hall, Byron Road, Worthing, W Sussex* Worthing (0903) 214004

MORLEY, Canon Leslie James. b 45. K Coll Lon BD67 AKC67 MTh68. **d** 69 **p** 70. C Birm St Pet *Birm* 69-72; C W Brompton St Mary *Lon* 72; C W Brompton St Mary w St Pet 73-74; Chapl Nottm Univ *S'well* 74-80; Dir of Post-Ord Tr 80-85; Can Res and Vice-Provost S'well Minster 80-85; Hon Can from 85; Chapl Bluecoat Sch Nottm 85-90; R Nottm St Pet and St Jas *S'well* 85; AD Nottm Cen from 90. *3 King Charles Street, Standard Hill, Nottingham NG1 6GB* Nottingham (0602) 474891

MORLEY, Peter. b 36. St Jo Coll Nottm 81. **d** 83 **p** 84. C Sheff St Jo *Sheff* 83-87; Chapl Shrewsbury Hosp Sheff 85-87; V Worsbrough Common from 87; Chapl Mt Vernon Hosp Barnsley from 87. *The Vicarage, 9 Mount Close, Barnsley, S Yorkshire S70 4EE* Barnsley (0226) 282619

MORLEY, Terence Martin Simon. b 49. Dur Univ CertEd78. St Steph Ho Ox 71. **d** 74 **p** 75. C Kingston upon Hull St Alb *York* 74-76; C Middlesb All SS 76-77; Perm to Offic *Dur* 77-78; Hon C Worthing St Andr *Chich* 78-80; C Brighton Ch Ch 80-82; C Hove St Patr 80-82; C Ayr *Glas* 83-86; C Maybole 85-86; P-in-c Coatbridge 86-88; R from 88. *St John's Rectory, 86 Dunbeth Road, Coatbridge, Lanarkshire ML5 3ES* Coatbridge (0236) 23562

MORLEY, Trevor. b 39. MPS62 MRSH84 Man Univ BSc62. Ripon Hall Ox 65. **d** 67 **p** 68. C Compton Gifford *Ex* 67-70; Chapl Hammersmith Hosp Lon 70-83; Hon C N Hammersmith St Kath *Lon* 70-83; Chapl Univ Coll Hosp Lon from 83; Hon Chapl St Luke's Hosp for the Clergy from 89. *University College Hospital, Gower Street, London WC1E 6AU* 071-388 2195 or 387 9300

MORLEY, Very Rev William Fenton. b 12. CBE80. Or Coll Ox BA34 MA38 Lon Univ BD45. St D Coll Lamp BA32 Wycliffe Hall Ox 35. **d** 35 **p** 36. Dean Sarum 71-77; rtd 77. *7 Cavendish Place, Bath BA1 2UB* Bath (0225) 312598

MORLEY-BUNKER, John Arthur. b 27. Wells Th Coll 67. **d** 68 **p** 69. C Horfield H Trin *Bris* 68-71; P-in-c Easton All Hallows 71-75; V 75-82; RD Bris City 74-79; V Horfield St Greg from 82. *St Gregory's Vicarage, Horfield, Bristol BS7 0PD* Bristol (0272) 692839

MORLEY-PEARCE, Bridget Natalie. b 28. Gilmore Ho 52. **dss** 72 **d** 87. Is of Dogs Ch Ch and St Jo w St Luke *Lon* 72-78; Asst Chapl HM Pris Holloway 79-88; rtd 88; Lic to Offic *Carl* from 88. *3 Tindale Terrace, Tindale Fell, Brampton, Cumbria CA8 2QJ*

MORLING, David Arthur. b 45. CertEd66 Open Univ BA78. S Dios Minl Tr Scheme 83. **d** 85 **p** 86. NSM Parklands St Wilfrid CD *Chich* from 85. *52 Worcester Road, Chichester, W Sussex PO19 4DZ* Chichester (0243) 782281

MORPHET, George Thexton. b 12. ACT ThL47. **d** 38 **p** 39. Australia 53-62 and from 68; Miss to Seamen 53-77; rtd 77. *68 Spowers Street, Bribie Island, Queensland, Australia 4507*

MORPHY, George David. b 49. Lon Univ BA Birm Univ BEd. W Midl Minl Tr Course. **d** 89 **p** 90. NSM Ribbesford w Bewdley and Dowles *Worc* from 89. *41 Hallow Road, Worcester WR2 6BX* Worcester (0905) 422007

MORPHY, Michael John. b 43. Newc Univ BSc65 Dur Univ MSc66 QUB PhD73. Ripon Coll Cuddesdon 82. **d** 84 **p** 85. C Halifax *Wakef* 84-86; V Luddenden w Luddenden Foot from 86. *The Vicarage, 50 Carr Field Drive, Luddenden, Halifax, W Yorkshire HX2 6RJ* Halifax (0422) 882127

MORRELL, Geoffrey Bernard. b 45. AKC68. **d** 69 **p** 71. C W Leigh CD *Portsm* 69-76; V Shedfield from 76; RD Bishops Waltham 82-88. *The Vicarage, Church Road, Shedfield, Southampton SO3 2HY* Wickham (0329) 832162

✠**MORRELL, Rt Rev James Herbert Lloyd.** b 07. AKC30. Ely Th Coll 30. **d** 31 **p** 32 **c** 59. C Hendon St Alphage *Lon* 31-36; C Brighton St Mich *Chich* 36-40, Chapl Supt Brighton Boys' Hostel 40-41; Chapl for Work among Men and Boys 40-41; Lect C of E Moral Welfare Coun 41-44; V Roughey (or Roffey) 44-46; Adn Lewes 46-49; Suff Bp Lewes 59-77; Can and Preb Chich Cathl 59-84; FKC from 60; rtd 77; Asst Bp Chich from 77. *83 Davigdor Road, Hove, E Sussex BN3 1RA* Brighton (0273) 733971

MORRELL, Mrs Jennifer Mary. b 49. N Ord Course 84. **d** 87. Par Dn Crewe All SS and St Paul *Ches* 87-90; Par Dn Padgate *Liv* from 90. *12 Dunscar Close, Birchwood, Warrington WA3 7LS* Padgate (0925) 831475

MORRELL, Nigel Paul. b 38. S'wark Ord Course 73. **d** 76 **p** 77. C Letchworth St Paul w Willian *St Alb* 76-85; V Farley Hill St Jo from 85; RD Luton from 90. *The Vicarage, 47 Rotheram Avenue, Luton LU1 5PP* Luton (0582) 29466

MORRELL, Robin Mark George. b 29. Cuddesdon Coll 58. **d** 60 **p** 61. C Petersfield w Sheet *Portsm* 60-63; C-in-c Stockwood CD *Bris* 63-71; Lic to Offic 71-72; R Honiton, Gittisham and Combe Raleigh *Ex* 72-78; Lay Tr Officer *S'wark* 78-81; Asst Chapl HM Pris Brixton 81-85; Past Counsellor from 85; Hon C Hatcham St Cath *S'wark* from 91. *46 Erlanger Road, London SE14 5TG* 071-252 9346

MORRIS, Alan Ralph Oakden. b 29. Roch Th Coll 59. **d** 61 **p** 62. C Riverhead *Roch* 61-62; C Roch St Pet w St Marg 62-66; C Wrotham 66-74; V Biggin Hill 74-82; R Kingsdown 82-88; V Seal St Pet from 88. *The Vicarage, Church Street, Seal, Sevenoaks, Kent TN15 0AR* Sevenoaks (0732) 62955

MORRIS, Albert George. b 15. Tyndale Hall Bris 47. **d** 48 **p** 49. C-in-c Bridgemary CD *Portsm* 67-80; rtd 81; Perm to Offic *Portsm* from 82. *Cherith, 12 Woodlands Close, Sarisbury Green, Southampton SO3 6AQ* Locks Heath (0489) 573980

MORRIS, Canon Alexander Dorner. b 23. Jes Coll Cam BA48 MA53. Linc Th Coll 49. **d** 51 **p** 52. V Bexley St Mary *Roch* 63-71; V Leatherhead *Guildf* 71-89; RD Leatherhead 72-77; Hon Can Guildf Cathl 86-89; rtd 89. *9 Roses Cottages, West Street, Dorking, Surrey RH4 1QL* Dorking (0306) 882485

MORRIS, Arthur Ronald. b 17. Jes Coll Ox BA38 MA42. St Steph Ho Ox 38. **d** 40 **p** 41. V Edmonton St Mich *Lon* 66-71; Australia from 71; rtd 82. *47 Andrew Street, Lota, Queensland, Australia 4179*

MORRIS, Bernard Lyn. b 28. St Aid Birkenhead 55. **d** 58 **p** 59. C-in-c Hartcliffe St Andr CD *Bris* 58-61; C Bishopston 61-63; R Ardwick St Thos *Man* 63-69; R Aylton w Pixley, Munsley and Putley *Heref* 69-79; P-in-c Tarrington w Stoke Edith 72-77; R 77-79; P-in-c Queen Camel, Marston Magna, W Camel, Rimpton etc *B & W* 79-80; R 80-87; R Queen Camel w W Camel, Corton Denham etc from 87. *The Rectory, England's Lane, Queen Camel, Yeovil, Somerset BA22 7NN* Marston Magna (0935) 850326

MORRIS, Beti Elin. b 36. CertEd57. Sarum & Wells Th Coll 87. **d** 89. C Llangeitho and Blaenpennal w Bettws Leiki etc *St D* from 89. *Hafdir, Llanwnen Road, Lampeter, Dyfed SA48 7JP* Lampeter (0570) 422385

MORRIS, Brian Michael Charles. b 32. S Dios Minl Tr Scheme 82. **d** 85 **p** 86. NSM Denmead *Portsm* 85-89; C S w N Hayling from 89. *5 Culver Drive, Hayling Island, Hants PO11 9LX* Hayling Island (0705) 466342

MORRIS, Christopher John. b 45. K Coll Lon AKC67 BD68. **d** 68 **p** 69. C W Bromwich All SS *Lich* 68-72; C Porthill 72-74; Min Can Carl Cathl *Carl* 74-77; Ecum Liaison Officer BBC Radio Carl 74-77; Dioc Communications Officer *Carl* 77-83; V Thursby 77-83; Angl Adv Border TV from 82; V Upperby St Jo *Carl* 83-91; P-in-c Lancost w Kirkcambeck and Walton

from 91. *The Vicarage, Lanercost, Brampton, Cumbria CA8 2HQ* Brampton (06977) 2478

MORRIS, Christopher Mangan. b 47. Chich Th Coll 71. **d** 73 **p** 74. C Athersley *Wakef* 73-76; C Kippax *Ripon* 76-78; TV Seacroft 78-81; V Oulton w Woodlesford 81-86; V Hawksworth Wood from 86. *St Mary's Vicarage, Cragside Walk, Leeds LS5 3QE* Leeds (0532) 582923

MORRIS, Prof Colin. b 28. FRHistS71 Qu Coll Ox BA48 MA53. Linc Th Coll 51. **d** 53 **p** 54. Chapl Pemb Coll Ox 53-69; Prof Medieval Hist Southn Univ from 69; Lic to Offic *Win* from 69. *53 Cobbett Road, Southampton SO2 4HJ* Southampton (0703) 227258

MORRIS, Canon David Edmond. b 27. Univ of Wales (Cardiff) BA55. St D Coll Lamp 55. **d** 57 **p** 58. C Llanfihangel-ar-arth *St D* 57-59; C Ysbyty Ystwyth w Ystradmeurig 59-61; CF 61-81; QHC from 78; V Penllergaer *S & B* from 81; RD Llwchwr from 86; Can Brecon Cathl from 90. *The Vicarage, 16 Swansea Road, Penllergaer, Swansea SA4 1AQ* Gorseinon (0792) 892603

MORRIS, David Freestone (Brother Augustine). b 05. **d** 36 **p** 37. OSB from 24; Abbot 48-74; Lic to Offic *Ox* from 54; rtd 74. *Elmore Abbey, Church Lane, Speen, Newbury, Berks RG13 1SA* Newbury (0635) 33080

MORRIS, David Meeson. b 35. Trin Coll Ox BA56 MA60. Chich Th Coll 57. **d** 60 **p** 61. C Westmr St Steph w St Jo *Lon* 60-65; Lib Pusey Ho 65-68; Chapl Wadh Coll Ox 67-68; C Sheff Norwood St Leon *Sheff* 68-69; Ind Chapl 68-72; C Brightside St Marg 69-72; R Adderley *Lich* 72-82; V Drayton in Hales 72-82; RD Tutbury from 82; Chapl Burton Gen Hosp 82-90; P-in-c Burton St Modwen *Lich* 82; V Burton from 82. *The Vicarage, Rangemore Street, Burton-on-Trent, Staffs DE14 2ED* Burton-on-Trent (0283) 36235

MORRIS, David Michael. b 59. Ox Univ MA84. Sarum & Wells Th Coll 82. **d** 84 **p** 85. C Angell Town St Jo *S'wark* 84-87; C Mitcham SS Pet and Paul 87-90; V Llandygwydd and Cenarth w Cilrhedyn etc *St D* from 90. *The Vicarage, Llechryd, Cardigan, Dyfed SA43 2NE* Llechryd (023987) 552

MORRIS, David Pryce. b 39. Univ of Wales (Ban) DipTh62. Kelham Th Coll 55 St Mich Coll Llan 62. **d** 63 **p** 64. C Colwyn Bay *St As* 63-70; R St George 70-76; Dioc Children's Adv 75-87; V Bodelwyddan and St George 76-79; V Connah's Quay from 79; St As Dioc Adult Lay Tr Team from 88; Ed St As Dioc News from 89; Dioc Info Officer from 90. *The Vicarage, Church Hill, Connah's Quay, Deeside, Clwyd CH5 1AZ* Deeside (0244) 830224

MORRIS, Dennis Gordon. b 41. ALCM58 DipTh67. St D Coll Lamp 64. **d** 67 **p** 68. C Neath w Llantwit *Llan* from 67. *18 Woodland Road, Neath, W Glam SA11 3AL* Neath (0639) 635738

MORRIS, Edward. b 42. **d** 72 **p** 73. C Darlington H Trin *Dur* 72-75; Tutor St Steph Ho Ox 75-82; Sen Tutor 79-82; R Shadforth *Dur* 82-86; Chapl Qu Charlotte's and Hammersmith Hosps Lon from 86. *The Chaplain's Office, Hammersmith Hospital, Du Cane Road, London W12 0HS* 081-743 2030

MORRIS, Canon Edwin Alfred. b 32. Wells Th Coll 62. **d** 64 **p** 65. C Wood End *Cov* 64-66; Lic to Offic 66-68; Ind Chapl 68-85; P-in-c Churchover w Willey 74-85; RD Rugby 78-85; R City of Bris from 85; Hon Can Bris Cathl from 89; RD Bris City from 91. *2 Fremantle Square, Bristol BS6 5TL* Bristol (0272) 427546 or 277977

MORRIS, Mrs Elizabeth Mary. b 22. Univ Coll Lon BSc50 DipRS82. S'wark Ord Course 82. **dss** 83 **d** 87. Purley St Mark Woodcote *S'wark* 83-87; Hon Par Dn Littleham w Exmouth *Ex* from 87. *7 Strawberry Hill, Lympstone, Exmouth, Devon EX8 5JZ* Exmouth (0395) 265727

MORRIS, Canon Frank Leo. b 20. St Steph Ho Ox 50. **d** 53 **p** 54. R Wyddial *St Alb* 65-79; P-in-c 79-82; V Gt w Lt Hormead 65-79; RD Buntingford 68-75; V Gt w Lt Hormead, Anstey, Brent Pelham etc 79-82; V Hormead, Wyddial, Anstey, Brent Pelham etc 82-89; Hon Can St Alb 85-89; rtd 89. *9 Manland Avenue, Harpenden, Herts AL5 4RG* Harpenden (0582) 462348

MORRIS, Geoffrey David. b 43. Fitzw Coll Cam BA65 MA69 Westmr Coll Ox DipEd67. N Ord Course. **d** 82 **p** 83. C Man Clayton St Cross w St Paul *Man* 82-85; V Lower Kersal from 85. *St Aidan's Vicarage, Littleton Road, Salford M7 0TN* 061-792 3072

MORRIS, George Erskine. b 34. **d** 62 **p** 63. C Kidderminster St Jo *Worc* 62-66; Canada from 66. *11203-68 Street NW, Edmonton, Alberta, Canada, T5B 1N6*

MORRIS, Graham Edwin. b 60. Sarum & Wells Th Coll 83. **d** 86 **p** 87. C Coalbrookdale, Iron-Bridge and Lt Wenlock *Heref* 86-90; TV Bilston *Lich* from 90.

8 Cumberland Road, Bilston, Wolverhampton WV14 6LT Bilston (0902) 497794

MORRIS, Canon Gwilym Alun. b 09. CBE64. Qu Coll Birm 38. **d** 39 **p** 40. V Coxwold *York* 70-75; rtd 75; Hon Can Bahrain from 88. *Captain Cook's Cottage, Grape Lane, Whitby, N Yorkshire YO22 4BA* Whitby (0947) 602434

MORRIS, Henry James. b 47. Lon Univ BSc69. Wycliffe Hall Ox MA. **d** 79 **p** 80. C Woodford Wells *Chelmsf* 79-82; C Gt Baddow 82-87; R Siddington w Preston *Glouc* from 87. *The Rectory, Preston, Cirencester, Glos GL7 5PR* Cirencester (0285) 654187

MORRIS, Ian Henry. b 42. Sarum & Wells Th Coll 73. **d** 75 **p** 76. C Lawrence Weston *Bris* 75-78; C St Buryan, St Levan and Sennen *Truro* 78-81; P-in-c Lanteglos by Fowey 81-84; V 84-85; R Lanteglos by Camelford w Advent from 85. *The Rectory, Trefrew Road, Camelford, Cornwall PL32 9TQ* Camelford (0840) 212286

MORRIS, Ian James Patrick. b 43. Dur Univ BA65. Westcott Ho Cam 67. **d** 69 **p** 70. C Wisbech SS Pet and Paul *Ely* 69-72; C Gaywood, Bawsey and Mintlyn *Nor* 72-76; Asst Chapl Basingstoke Distr Hosp 76-78; Chapl Meanwood Park Hosp Gp Leeds 78-88; Chapl Addenbrooke's Hosp Cam from 88. *Addenbrooke's Hospital, Hills Road, Cambridge CB2 2QQ* Cambridge (0223) 245151

MORRIS, Ivor Leslie. b 50. Chich Th Coll 82. **d** 84 **p** 85. C Southend *Chelmsf* 84-87; C Somers Town St Mary *Lon* 87-90; P-in-c Chelmsf Ascension *Chelmsf* from 90. *The Vicarage, 57 Maltese Road, Chelmsford CM1 2PD* Chelmsford (0245) 353914

MORRIS, Canon John. b 25. Westcott Ho Cam. **d** 65 **p** 66. V Leverstock Green *St Alb* 68-80; TR Chambersbury (Hemel Hempstead) 80-82; V N Mymms 82-90; RD Hatf 83-88; Hon Can St Alb from 87; rtd 90. *2 Whetstone Close, Welwyn, Herts AL6 0QW* Welwyn (043871) 7142

MORRIS, John Derrick. b 18. MRCS43 LRCP43. Lon Coll of Div 62. **d** 64 **p** 65. V Broadway *Worc* 64-71; Hon C St Leonards St Leon *Chich* 71-83; rtd 83; Perm to Offic *Chich* from 84. *17 Pretoria Avenue, Midhurst, W Sussex GU29 9PP* Midhurst (073081) 4084

MORRIS, John Dudley. b 33. Ball Coll Ox BA57 DipTh59 MA61. Wycliffe Hall Ox 58. **d** 60 **p** 61. C Tonbridge SS Pet and Paul *Roch* 60-65; C Enfield Ch Ch Trent Park *Lon* 65-69; Chapl Elstree Sch Woolhampton 70-74; Hd Master Handcross Park Sch W Sussex 74-89; V Rudgwick *Chich* from 89. *The Vicarage, Rudgwick, Horsham, W Sussex RH12 3DD* Rudgwick (040372) 2127

MORRIS, John Edgar. b 20. Keble Coll Ox BA42 MA50. Wycliffe Hall Ox 42. **d** 44 **p** 45. V Ainsdale *Liv* 66-82; R Broadwell, Evenlode, Oddington and Adlestrop *Glouc* 82-88; rtd 89. *29 Letch Hill Drive, Bourton-on-the-Water, Cheltenham, Glos GL54 2DQ* Cotswold (0451) 20571

MORRIS, John Owen. b 56. Nottm Univ BCom82. Linc Th Coll 79. **d** 82 **p** 83. C Morriston *S & B* 82-84; C Kingstone w Clehonger and Eaton Bishop *Heref* 84-87; P-in-c Lugwardine w Bartestree and Weston Beggard from 87. *The Vicarage, Lugwardine, Hereford HR1 4AE* Hereford (0432) 850244

MORRIS, Canon John Richard. b 23. Or Coll Ox BA48 MA52. Westcott Ho Cam 48. **d** 50 **p** 51. R Sanderstead All SS *S'wark* 64-70; Warden Caius Ho Miss from 70; V Battersea St Mary 70-88; Hon Can S'wark Cathl from 76; RD Battersea 76-81; Hon C Battersea St Mary-le-Park 76-79; Hon C Battersea Park All SS 84-88; rtd 88; Master Abp Holgate Hosp Pontefract from 88. *Archbishop Holgate Hospital, Robin Lane, Hemsworth, Pontefract, W Yorkshire WF9 4PP* Hemsworth (0977) 610434

MORRIS, Kenneth Owen. b 12. Univ of Wales BA34. St Mich Coll Llan 35. **d** 37 **p** 38. V Aston w Benington *St Alb* 59-60; Lic to Offic 60-77; rtd 77. *20 Middle Mead, Hook, Basingstoke, Hants RG27 9NX* Basingstoke (0256) 762228

MORRIS, Kevin John. b 63. Westcott Ho Cam 85. **d** 88 **p** 89. C Roath St Marg *Llan* from 88. *St Philip's House, Cairnmuir Road, Tremorfa, Cardiff CF2 2RU* Cardiff (0222) 460600

MORRIS, Leslie Heber. b 26. Ox Univ MA47. Qu Coll Birm 83. **d** 84. NSM W Leigh *Portsm* 84-85; NSM Warblington and Emsworth 86-88. *3 Southbrook Road, Langstone, Havant, Hants* Portsmouth (0705) 484578

MORRIS, Lillian Rosina (Rev Mother Lillian). b 29. dss 70 **d** 87. CSA from 68; Mother Superior from 82; Sherston Magna w Easton Grey *Bris* 71-73; Notting Hill All SS w St Columb *Lon* 74-82. *St Andrew's House, 2 Tavistock Road, London W11 1BA* 071-229 2662

MORRIS, Margaret Jane. E Midl Min Tr Course 86. **d** 89. NSM Quorndon *Leic* from 89. *10 Toller Road, Quorn, Loughborough, Leics LE12 8AH* Quorn (0509) 412092

MORRIS, Martin Geoffrey Roger. b 41. Trin Coll Cam BA63 MA67. St D Coll Lamp 63. **d** 66 **p** 67. C Newport St Paul *Mon* 66-72; R Lamp Velfrey *St D* 72-74; R Lamp Velfrey and Llanddewi Velfrey from 74; RD St Clears from 83. *The Rectory, Lampeter Velfrey, Narberth, Dyfed SA67 8UH* Llanteg (083483) 241

MORRIS, Ms Mary. b 27. Birm Univ BA49 CertEd50 MA56. dss 68 **d** 87. Kinver *Lich* 83-87; Hon Par Dn Kinver and Enville from 87. *Lyndhurst, Dunsley Road, Kinver, Stourbridge, W Midlands DY7 6LN* Kinver (0384) 877245

MORRIS, Michael Alan. b 46. Jes Coll Cam BA70 MA74. Coll of Resurr Mirfield 79. **d** 81 **p** 82. C Leamington Priors All SS *Cov* 81-83; C Milton *Portsm* 83-88; R Petworth *Chich* 88-90; Chapl St Pet Hosp Chertsey from 90. *The Chaplain's Office, St Peter's Hospital, Chertsey, Surrey KT16 0PZ* Chertsey (0932) 872000

MORRIS, Norman Foster Maxwell. b 46. Ex Univ BA68 MA72 K Coll Lon MTh85 Univ of Wales (Cardiff) MA91. S'wark Ord Course 75. **d** 78 **p** 79. C Hackbridge and N Beddington *S'wark* 78-81; Chapl Tonbridge Sch Kent 81-85; Chapl Mon Sch from 85; Lic to Offic *Mon* from 87; Asst Warden Jones Almshouses Mon from 89. *The Chaplain's House (The Barn), The Burgage, Old Dixton Road, Monmouth, Gwent NP5 3DP* Monmouth (0600) 713506

MORRIS, Paul David. b 56. St Jo Coll Nottm BTh79. **d** 80 **p** 81. C Billericay and Lt Burstead *Chelmsf* 80-84; C Luton Lewsey St Hugh *St Alb* 84-89; Bp's Adv on Evang *S'well* from 89. *39 Davies Road, Nottingham NG2 5JE* Nottingham (0602) 811311

MORRIS, Peter. b 45. Leeds Univ CertEd66. Tyndale Hall Bris 68. **d** 71 **p** 72. C Southport SS Simon and Jude *Liv* 71-74; Min-in-c Ch Ch Netherley LEP 74-76; V Bryn from 76. *The Vicarage, 12 Bryn Road, Ashton-in-Makerfield, Wigan, Lancs WN4 0AA* Ashton-in-Makerfield (0942) 727114

MORRIS, Canon Peter Arthur William. b 23. Bps' Coll Cheshunt 57. **d** 58 **p** 59. V Sawbridgeworth *St Alb* 62-74; V S Gillingham *Roch* 74-79; Warden Pleshey Retreat Ho 79-85; P-in-c Pleshey *Chelmsf* 79-85; Hon Can Chelmsf Cathl 81-85; P-in-c Rumburgh w S Elmham w the Ilketshalls *St E* 85-89; rtd 89; Perm to Offic *St E* from 90. *The Cottage on the Common, Westleton, Saxmundham, Suffolk IP17 3AZ* Westleton (072873) 788

MORRIS, Canon Peter Michael Keighley. b 27. St Jo Coll Ox BA49 MA56. Westcott Ho Cam 51. **d** 54 **p** 55. Lic to Offic *St D* 55-85; Lect Univ of Wales (Lamp) 55-69; Sen Lect 69-90; Dean Faculty of Th 77-81; Can St D Cathl from 85; rtd 90. *Hafdir, Llanwnen Road, Lampeter, Dyfed SA48 7JP* Lampeter (0570) 422385

MORRIS, Philip Gregory. b 50. Leeds Univ BA71 MPhil74. Coll of Resurr Mirfield 71. **d** 73 **p** 74. C Aberdare *Llan* 74-77; C Neath w Llantwit 77-80; V Cymmer and Porth 80-88; Dioc Missr from 88; TV Llantwit Major from 88. *60 Ham Lane South, Llantwit Major, S Glam CF6 9RN* Llantwit Major (0446) 793770

MORRIS, Raymond. b 48. Open Univ HND70 BA88. N Ord Course 80. **d** 83 **p** 84. C Tonge w Alkrington *Man* 83-86; R Blackley St Paul from 86. *St Paul's Rectory, Erskine Road, Manchester M9 2RB* 061-740 1518

MORRIS, Raymond Arthur. b 62. Trin Coll Ox MA Lon Univ LLB. Clifton Th Coll 66. **d** 67 **p** 91. Perm to Offic *York* 69-91; NSM Linthorpe from 91. *3 Medina Gardens, Middlesbrough, Cleveland TS5 8BN* Middlesbrough (0642) 593726

MORRIS, Raymond John Walton. b 08. OBE69. Em Coll Cam BA33 MA37. Lon Coll of Div 33. **d** 34 **p** 35. V Brompton H Trin *Lon* 69-75; rtd 75. *12 St Edward's Court, Salisbury Street, Shaftesbury, Dorset SP7 8LZ* Shaftesbury (0747) 53422

MORRIS, Reginald Brian. b 31. St Mich Coll Llan 56. **d** 59 **p** 60. CF 62-78; V Cheswardine *Lich* 78-84; V Hales 78-84; Perm to Offic 84-86; C Cen Telford 86-89; rtd 89. *Woodside Cottage, School Lane, Prees, Whitchurch, Shropshire SY13 2BU* Whitchurch (0948) 840090

MORRIS, Richard Samuel. b 10. TCD BA35 MA39. Edgehill Th Coll Belf 31. **d** 58 **p** 59. I Kilsaran w Drumcar, Dunleer and Dunany *Arm* 69-75; rtd 75. *26 Kingsway Park, Belfast BT5 7EW* Belfast (0232) 483175

MORRIS, Robert John. b 45. Leeds Univ BA67. Coll of Resurr Mirfield 74. **d** 76 **p** 77. C Beeston Hill St Luke *Ripon* 76; C Holbeck 76-78; C Moseley St Mary *Birm* 78-83; P-in-c Handsworth St Jas 83-88; P-in-c

Handsworth St Mich 86-87; V from 88. *St James's Vicarage, Austin Road, Birmingham B21 8NU* 021-554 4151

MORRIS, Robin Edward. b 32. St Jo Coll Ox BA55 MA60. Westcott Ho Cam 55. **d** 57 **p** 58. C Halliwell St Thos *Man* 57-61; V Castleton Moor 61-71; V Stalybridge 71-80; R Heswall *Ches* from 80. *The Rectory, Heswall, Wirral, Merseyside L60 0DZ* 051-342 3471

MORRIS, Stanley James. b 35. Keble Coll Ox BA58 MA63. Chich Th Coll 59. **d** 61 **p** 62. C Tunstall Ch Ch *Lich* 61-64; C W Bromwich All SS 64-67; V Wilnecote 67-88; V Alrewas from 88. *The Vicarage, Alrewas, Burton-on-Trent, Staffs DE13 7BT* Burton-on-Trent (0283) 790486

MORRIS, Stephen Bryan. b 54. Linc Th Coll 88. **d** 90 **p** 91. C Glouc St Geo w Whaddon *Glouc* from 90. *3 Rylands, Tuffley, Gloucester GL4 0QA* Gloucester (0452) 500716

MORRIS, Stephen Francis. b 52. St Jo Coll Nottm BTh79. **d** 79 **p** 80. C N Hinksey *Ox* 79-82; C Leic H Apostles *Leic* 82-85; TV Shenley and Loughton *Ox* 85-88; TV Watling Valley from 88. *114 Blackmoor Gate, Furzton, Milton Keynes MK4 1DN* Milton Keynes (0908) 502871

MORRIS, Canon Stuart Collard. b 43. AKC66. St Boniface Warminster 66. **d** 67 **p** 68. C Hanham *Bris* 67-71; C Whitchurch 71-74; P-in-c Wapley w Codrington and Dodington 74-77; P-in-c Westerleigh 74-77; P-in-c Holdgate w Tugford *Heref* 77-82; P-in-c Abdon w Clee St Margaret 77-82; R Diddlebury w Bouldon and Munslow 77-82; P-in-c Sotterley, Willingham, Shadingfield, Ellough etc *St E* 82-87; RD Beccles and S Elmham from 83; P-in-c Westhall w Brampton and Stoven 86-88; P-in-c Flixton w Homersfield and S Elmham from 86; Hon Can St E Cathl from 87; V Bungay H Trin w St Mary from 87. *The Vicarage, 3 Trinity Gardens, Bungay, Suffolk NR35 1HH* Bungay (0986) 892110

MORRIS, Canon Thomas Ernest Gilbert. b 06. Ex Coll Ox. St D Coll Lamp BA28. **d** 30 **p** 31. Hon Can Accra from 55; V Rockfield and Llangattock w St Maughan's *Mon* 69-77; rtd 77. *3 Church Row, Llanfrynach, Brecon, Powys LD3 7BX* Llanfrynach (087486) 319

MORRIS, Thomas Gordon. b 25. CertEd48. St Mich Coll Llan 80. **d** 83 **p** 85. NSM Morriston *S & B* 83-86; C Caereithin 86-87; P-in-c 87-88; V from 88. *The Vicarage, 64 Cheriton Close, Portmead, Swansea SA5 5LA* Swansea (0792) 583646

MORRIS, Timothy David. b 48. Lon Univ BSc69 DipTh75. Trin Coll Bris 72. **d** 75 **p** 76. C Edin St Thos *Edin* 75-77; R Edin St Jas 77-83; R Troon *Glas* 83-85; R Galashiels *Edin* from 85. *The Rectory, Parsonage Road, Galashiels, Selkirkshire TD1 3HS* Galashiels (0896) 3118

MORRIS, Mrs Valerie Ruth. b 46. St Hugh's Coll Ox BA68 MA72. Qu Coll Birm 76. **dss** 78 **d** 87. Burton *Lich* 82-87; Par Dn 87-90; Hon Par Dn from 90. *The Vicarage, Rangemore Street, Burton-on-Trent, Staffs DE14 2ED* Burton-on-Trent (0283) 36235

MORRIS, William Humphrey. b 29. FRAS84 Univ of Wales BA54 MA72 Birm Univ DipTh58 Trin Coll Cam BA62 MA66 PhD75 Man Univ MEd76 PhD80 Ox Univ DPhil85 DD88. Qu Coll Birm 56. **d** 58 **p** 59. V Sandbach Heath *Ches* 65-68; Lic to Offic from 69; rtd 84. *Stonyflats Farm, Smallwood, Sandbach, Cheshire CW11 0XH*

MORRIS, William James. b 23. St Deiniol's Hawarden 72. **d** 73 **p** 74. NSM Brecon Adnry 73-78; NSM Crickhowell w Cwmdu and Tretower *S & B* from 78. *The School House, Cwmdu, Crickhowell, Powys NP8 1RU* Bwlch (0874) 730355

MORRIS, William Richard Price. b 23. FCollP82. Glouc Sch of Min. **d** 88 **p** 89. Hon C Bussage *Glouc* 88-90; Perm to Offic 90-91; Hon C France Lynch from 91. *c/o The Vicarage, Brantwood Road, Chalford Hill, Stroud, Glos GL6 8BS* Brimscombe (0453) 883154

MORRISON, Alexander Grant. b 37. St Fran Coll Brisbane ThL ACT St Columb's Hall Wangaratta. **d** 66 **p** 67. Australia 66-82; C Hayes St Mary *Lon* 83-84; R Black Notley *Chelmsf* from 84. *The Rectory, 71 Witham Road, Black Notley, Braintree, Essex CM7 8LJ* Braintree (0376) 49619

MORRISON, Andrew Leslie. b 11. TD53. Pemb Coll Ox BA33 MA37. Westcott Ho Cam 33. **d** 35 **p** 36. V Bury and Houghton *Chich* 64-76; rtd 76; Perm to Offic *Chich* from 76. *14 Guildford Place, Chichester, W Sussex PO19 4DU* Chichester (0243) 784310

MORRISON, Barry John. b 44. Pemb Coll Cam BA66 MA70. ALCD69. **d** 69 **p** 70. C Stoke Bishop *Bris* 69-72; C Edgware *Lon* 72-76; Chapl Poly of Cen Lon 76-83; Hon C Langham Place All So 76-83; P-in-c W Hampstead St Luke 83-88; V from 88; Chapl Westf Coll

from 84. *St Luke's Vicarage, 12 Kidderpore Avenue, London NW3 7SU* 071-794 2634

MORRISON, Cecil. b 10. St Chad's Coll Dur BA32 DipTh33 MA35. Cuddesdon Coll 33. **d** 34 **p** 35. V Greenwich St Alfege w St Pet *S'wark* 64-72; rtd 72; Lic to Offic *S'wark* from 72. *1 Alexander Court, Kidbrooke Grove, London SE3 0LH* 081-858 9905

MORRISON, Frederick George. b 37. Lich Th Coll 61. **d** 63 **p** 65. C Sidley *Chich* 63-66; Chapl RAF 66-82; R Gt w Lt Stukeley *Ely* 82-83; Chapl Eastbourne Hosp Gp 83-85; USA from 85. *Address temp unknown*

MORRISON, Iain Edward. b 36. St Steph Ho Ox 76. **d** 78 **p** 79. C Brighton St Aug and St Sav *Chich* 78-81; C Felpham w Middleton 81-83; P-in-c Barnham and Eastergate 83-85; R Aldingbourne, Barnham and Eastergate 85-91; V Jarvis Brook from 91. *The Vicarage, Tubwell Lane, Jarvis Brook, Crowborough, E Sussex TN6 3RH* Crowborough (0892) 652639

MORRISON, James Wilson Rennie. b 42. Aber Univ MA65. Linc Th Coll 76. **d** 78 **p** 79. C Whitley Ch Ch *Ox* 78-81; R Burghfield 81-87; CF from 87. *c/o MOD (Army), Bagshot Park, Bagshot, Surrey GU19 5PL* Bagshot (0276) 71717

MORRISON, John. b 18. **d** 76. Chapl St Paul's Cathl Dundee *Bre* 76-82; Hon C Dundee St Martin from 82. *81 Byron Street, Dundee DD3 6ER* Dundee (0382) 813344

MORRISON, Ven John Anthony. b 38. Jes Coll Cam BA60 MA64 Linc Coll Ox MA68. Chich Th Coll 61. **d** 64 **p** 65. C Birm St Pet *Birm* 64-68; C Ox St Mich *Ox* 68-71; Chapl Linc Coll Ox 68-74; C Ox St Mich w St Martin and All SS *Ox* 71-74; V Basildon 74-82; RD Bradfield 78-82; V Aylesbury 82-89; RD Aylesbury 85-89; TR Aylesbury w Bierton and Hulcott 89-90; Adn Buckm from 90. *60 Wendover Road, Aylesbury, Bucks HP21 9LW* Aylesbury (0296) 23269

MORRISON, Richard James. b 55. Sarum & Wells Th Coll 87. **d** 89 **p** 90. C Boston *Linc* from 89. *17 Witham Gardens, Boston, Lincs PE21 8PP* Boston (0205) 363772

MORRISON, Robin Victor Adair. b 45. Nottm Univ BA67. Bucharest Th Inst 67 Ripon Hall Ox 68. **d** 70 **p** 71. C Hackney St Jo *Lon* 70-73; Chapl Newc Univ *Newc* 73-76; P-in-c Teversal *S'well* 76-78; Chapl Sutton Cen 76-78; Asst Hd Deans Community St Livingston *Edin* 78-80; R Edin St Columba 80-81; Chapl Birm Univ *Birm* 81-88; Prin Soc Resp Officer *Derby* from 88. *216 Derby Road, Sandiacre, Nottingham NG10 5HE* Nottingham (0602) 392243

MORRISON, Walter Edward. b 15. ALCD41. **d** 41 **p** 42. V Bath St Luke *B & W* 66-81; rtd 81; Perm to Offic *B & W* from 81. *15 Ashley Road, Clevedon, Avon BS21 7UX* Clevedon (0272) 876088

MORRISON, Walter John Raymond. b 30. Jes Coll Cam BA55 MA58. Westcott Ho Cam 55. **d** 57 **p** 58. C Dalston St Mark w St Bart *Lon* 57-60; C Totteridge *St Alb* 60-63; V Letchworth St Paul 63-71; RD Hitchin 70-71; R Ludlow *Heref* 72-83; RD Ludlow 78-83; Preb Heref Cathl 78-83; Chapl St Thos Hosp Lon 83-86; Chapl Eastbourne Hosp Gp from 86. *Eastbourne District General Hospital, Kings Drive, Eastbourne, E Sussex BN21 2UD* Eastbourne (0323) 21351

MORRISON-WELLS, Canon John Frederick Pritchard. b 42. Univ of Wales (Lamp) BA65. Coll of Resurr Mirfield 65. **d** 67 **p** 68. C Bartley Green *Birm* 67-70; C Handsworth St Andr 70-73; V Perry Barr 73-80; RD Bordesley 80-90; V Birm St Aid Small Heath from 80; P-in-c Small Heath St Greg 83-85 and from 89; Hon Can Birm Cathl from 83; P-in-c Bordesley St Oswald from 91. *St Aidan's Clergy House, 172 Herbert Road, Birmingham B10 0PR* 021-772 0318

MORROW, David. b 63. NUU BSc86 TCD BTh89. CITC 86. **d** 89 **p** 90. C Portadown St Mark *Arm* from 89. *115 Brownstown Road, Portadown, Craigavon, Co Armgagh BT62 3PZ* Craigavon (0762) 335562

MORROW, Ven Derek James. b 15. TCD BA42 MA47. CITC 46. **d** 46 **p** 47. I Julianstown and Colpe w Drogheda and Duleek *M & K* 64-81; Adn Meath 79-81; rtd 81. *Greystones, 4 Cyprus Avenue, Belfast* Belfast (0232) 653984

MORROW, Canon Edward Sidney. b 34. **d** 74 **p** 75. Namibia 75-78, 79-87 and 89-90; C Truro St Paul *Truro* 78-79; Chapl to Namibians in Eur 87-89; C W Hackney St Barn *Lon* 87-89; Hon Can Windhoek from 87; V Stamford Hill St Thos *Lon* from 90. *The Vicarage, 37 Clapton Common, London E5 9AA* 081-806 1463

MORROW, Joseph John. b 54. JP87. Edin Univ BD79. NY Th Sem DMin87 Edin Th Coll 76. **d** 79 **p** 80. Chapl St Paul's Cathl Dundee *Bre* 79-82; P-in-c Dundee St

Martin 82-85; R 85-90; P-in-c Dundee St Jo from 85. *63 Albert Street, Dundee DD1 6NZ*   Dundee (0382) 457703

MORSE, Harry Arthur Carminowe. b 59. St Jo Coll Dur BA81 SS Paul & Mary Coll Cheltenham PGCE85. Oak Hill Th Coll BA91. **d** 91. C Summerfield *Birm* from 91. *The Flat, 74A Cavendish Road, Birmingham B16 0HS* 021-420 1263

MORSHEAD, Ivo Francis Trelawny. b 27. ACA52 FCA63. Cuddesdon Coll 61. **d** 63 **p** 64. C Wimbledon *S'wark* 68-73; V Elham *Cant* 73-78; V Whitchurch *Ex* 78-91; rtd 91. *28 Edge Street, London W8 7PN*   071-727 5975

MORSON, Dorothy Mary. b 29. Linc Th Coll 71. **d** 87. Par Dn Cen Telford *Lich* 87-89; rtd 89; Perm to Offic *Lich* from 89. *Ashleigh, Hunter Street, Shrewsbury SY3 8QN*   Shrewsbury (0743) 69225

MORSON, John. b 41. **d** 88. NSM Eyemouth *Edin* from 88; NSM Duns from 88. *Cruachan, Reston, Eyemouth, Berwickshire TD14 5JS*   Reston (08907) 61206

MORSON, Preb John Basil. b 10. OBE56 MC43 TD53. Linc Th Coll 30. **d** 33 **p** 34. V Lee Brockhurst *Lich* 62-79; R Wem 62-79; rtd 79. *Ashleigh, Hunter Street, Shrewsbury SY3 8QN*   Shrewsbury (0743) 369225

MORT, Alister. b 52. BSc BA. Oak Hill Th Coll. **d** 82 **p** 83. C Cheadle Hulme St Andr *Ches* 82-85; C Rodbourne Cheney *Bris* 86-87; TV 87-90; V New Milverton *Cov* from 90. *2 St Mark's Road, Leamington Spa, Warks CV32 6DL*   Leamington Spa (0926) 421004

MORT, Ivan Laurence. b 61. Nottm Univ BTh87. Linc Th Coll 84. **d** 87 **p** 88. C Aston cum Aughton and Ulley *Sheff* 87-90; C Greenstead juxta Colchester *Chelmsf* from 90. *1 Stour Walk, Colchester CO3 3UX*   Colchester (0206) 871757

✠**MORT, Rt Rev John Ernest Llewelyn.** b 15. CBE65. St Cath Coll Cam BA38 MA42 Ahmadu Bello Univ Zaria Hon LLD70. Westcott Ho Cam 38. **d** 40 **p** 41 **c** 52. C Dudley St Thos *Worc* 40-44; Bp's Dom Chapl 44-52; V St Jo in Bedwardine 48-52; Bp N Nigeria 52-69; Can Res and Treas Leic Cathl *Leic* 70-88; Asst Bp Leic from 72; rtd 88. *271 Forest Road, Woodhouse, Loughborough, Leics LE12 8TZ*

MORTER, Ian Charles. b 54. AKC77. Coll of Resurr Mirfield 77. **d** 78 **p** 79. C Colchester St Jas, All SS, St Nic and St Runwald *Chelmsf* 78-82; C Brixham w Churston Ferrers *Ex* 82-83; TV 84-86; TV Brixham w Churston Ferrers and Kingswear 86; TV Sidmouth, Woolbrook and Salcombe Regis 86-91; TV Sidmouth, Woolbrook, Salcombe Regis, Sidbury etc from 91. *St Francis' Vicarage, Woolbrook Road, Sidmouth, Devon EX10 9XH*   Sidmouth (0395) 514522

MORTIBOYS, John William. b 45. K Coll Lon BD69 AKC69. Sarum Th Coll 71. **d** 71 **p** 72. C Reading All SS *Ox* from 71. *All Saints' Vicarage, 14 Downshire Square, Reading RG1 6NH*   Reading (0734) 52000

MORTIMER, Anthony John. b 42. Sarum & Wells Th Coll 68. **d** 71 **p** 72. C Heref St Martin *Heref* 71-79; V Kingstone 79-85; P-in-c Clehonger 80-85; P-in-c Eaton Bishop 80-85; TR Pinhoe and Broadclyst *Ex* from 85. *The Vicarage, 15 Park Lane, Pinhoe, Exeter EX4 9HL* Exeter (0392) 67541

MORTIMER, Arthur James. b 12. Fitzw Ho Cam BA33 MA37. Coll of Resurr Mirfield 33. **d** 35 **p** 36. V Lt Thurrock St Jo *Chelmsf* 56-77; rtd 77; Perm to Offic *Nor* from 77. *2 Gateley Gardens, Norwich NR3 3TU* Norwich (0603) 429559

MORTIMER, Charles Philip. b 38. Linc Th Coll 68. **d** 70 **p** 71. C Penistone w Midhope *Wakef* 70-74; V Luddenden 74-77; P-in-c Luddenden Foot 74-77; Chapl RAF from 77. *c/o MOD, Adastral House, Theobald's Road, London WC1X 8RU*   071-430 7268

MORTIMER, Douglas Hayman. b 10. Lich Th Coll 32. **d** 35 **p** 36. V Lytchett Minster *Sarum* 54-78; rtd 78. *8 George's Mews, Corfe Mullen, Wimborne, Dorset BH21 3UF*   Wimborne (0202) 699565

MORTIMER, Very Rev Hugh Sterling. b 23. TCD BA44 MA53. **d** 46 **p** 47. Hon VC 57-85; I Arm St Mark *Arm* 66-83; Can Arm Cathl 67-72; Treas 72-73; Chan 73-75; Prec 75-83; Dean Elphin and Ardagh *K, E & A* 83-91; I Sligo w Knocknarea and Rosses Pt 83-91; rtd 91. *95 Sharman Road, Stranmillis, Belfast BT9 5HE* Belfast (0232) 669184

MORTIMER, Lawrence George. b 45. St Edm Hall Ox BA67 MA71 St Chad's Coll Dur DipTh68. **d** 70 **p** 71. C Rugby St Andr *Cov* 70-75; V Styvechale 75-89; Dioc Broadcasting Officer 80-89; Dioc Communications Officer from 89. *14 Fairlands Park, Coventry CV4 7DS* Coventry (0203) 413158

MORTIMER, William Raymond. b 31. GradIEE58 AMIEE66. St Deiniol's Hawarden 68. **d** 69 **p** 70. C Flint

St As 69-71; Lic to Offic 72-73; V Llanwddyn and Llanfihangel and Llwydiarth 73-85; RD Llanfyllin 83-84; R Llanwrst and Llanddoget and Capel Garmon from 85. *The Rectory, Llanrwst, Gwynedd LL26 0DW*   Llanrwst (0492) 640223

MORTIMER-ANDERSON (formerly ANDERSON), Robert Edwin. b 42. Leeds Univ DipTh68. Coll of Resurr Mirfield 68. **d** 70 **p** 71. C Forest Gate St Edm *Chelmsf* 70-73; Chapl RN 73-78; C Tilbury Docks *Chelmsf* 78; Chapl Belgrade w Zagreb, Bucharest and Sofia *Eur* 78-80; Chapl Bucharest w Sofia 80-81; V Romford St Alb *Chelmsf* 81-91; V Woodville *Derby* from 91. *St Stephen's Vicarage, Woodville, Swadlincote, Derbyshire DE11 8DL*   Burton-on-Trent (0283) 217278

MORTIMORE, David Jack. St Mich Coll Llan. **d** 91. C Pemb St Mary and St Mich *St D* from 91. *13 Holyland Drive, Pembroke, Dyfed SA71 4BG*   Pembroke (0646) 685544

MORTIMORE, Robert Edward. b 39. Kelham Th Coll 61 Wells Th Coll 66. **d** 69 **p** 70. C Byfleet *Guildf* 69-72; New Zealand from 72. *2 Kowhai Park Road, Whangarei, New Zealand*   Whangarei (89) 489158

MORTON, Alan McNeile. b 28. Lon Univ BD49 AKC51 MTh68 BA78. St Boniface Warminster. **d** 52 **p** 53. C Egham Hythe *Guildf* 52-55; Bp's Dom Chapl *St E* 55-58; Dioc Youth Officer 56-58; C Ipswich St Mary Stoke 58-59; V Ipswich St Fran 59-64; Perm to Offic *Ely* 68-69; Chapl Reading Sch 69-78 and 83-88; Hd Master St Sebastian's Sch Wokingham 78-83. *8 Blenheim Drive, Oxford OX2 8DG*   Oxford (0865) 56371

MORTON, Albert George. b 34. Saskatchewan Univ BA61 McGill Univ Montreal MA73. Em Coll Saskatoon 56. **d** 61 **p** 61. Canada 61-65; C Stanford-le-Hope *Chelmsf* 66-69; V Linc St Geo Swallowbeck *Linc* 69-82; R Lt Munden w Sacombe *St Alb* 82-89; R The Mundens w Sacombe from 89. *The Rectory, Little Munden, Dane End, Ware, Herts SG12 0NT*   Dane End (0920) 438766

MORTON, Alfred Bruce. b 21. TCD BA42 MA47. Linc Th Coll 43. **d** 44 **p** 45. R Northfield *Birm* 57-73; RD Kings Norton 62-73; Chapl Partis Coll Bath 73-84; C Marksbury *B & W* 81-83; P-in-c Melling w Tatham *Blackb* 84-87; rtd 87; Perm to Offic *Blackb* from 87. *6 Stanley Drive, Hornby, Lancaster LA2 8NA*   Hornby (05242) 21999

MORTON, Andrew Edward. b 51. Lon Univ BA72 BD74 AKC74. St Aug Coll Cant 75. **d** 76 **p** 77. C Feltham *Lon* 76-79; C Pontlottyn w Fochriw *Llan* 79-81; V Ferndale w Maerdy 81-88; V Tylorstown w Ynyshir from 88; Dir of Studies Llan Ord Course from 91. *The Vicarage, Graig Road, Ynyshir, Porth, M Glam CF39 0NS*   Porth (0443) 684148

MORTON, Arthur. b 15. CVO79 OBE61. **d** 38 **p** 39. Dir NSPCC 54-79; rtd 80; Perm to Offic *Portsm* from 85. *25 Cottes Way, Fareham, Hants PO14 3NF*   Stubbington (0329) 663511

MORTON, Mrs Christine Mary. b 39. Linc Th Coll 78. **dss** 80 **d** 87. Ore *Chich* 80-84; Southwick 84-85; Winchmore Hill St Paul *Lon* 85-87; Par Dn from 87. *122 Bourne Hill, London N13 4BD*   081-886 3157

MORTON, Clive Frederick. b 47. Lon Univ BA70. St Jo Coll Dur 78. **d** 80 **p** 81. C Countesthorpe w Foston *Leic* 80-83; C Glen Parva and S Wigston 83-86; V Birm St Pet *Birm* from 86. *St Peter's Vicarage, 32 George Street West, Birmingham B18 7HF*   021-523 8000

MORTON, Howard Knyvett. b 30. St Jo Coll Cam BA51 MA67. Linc Th Coll 55. **d** 57 **p** 58. C Hatf Hyde St Mary *St Alb* 57-60; Asst Master Heaton Gr Sch Newc 60-66; CMS 66-72; Lic to Offic *Newc* from 73. *North View Lodge, Bingfield, Corbridge, Northd*   Hexham (0434) 672483

MORTON, Jenny. b 50. Bedf Coll Lon BA72 Leic Univ PGCE73. E Midl Min Tr Course 87. **d** 90. C New Mills *Derby* from 90. *St George's House, 32 Church Road, New Mills, Stockport, Cheshire SK12 4NJ*   New Mills (0663) 746301

MORTON, John Francis Eric. b 17. Leeds Univ BA38. Coll of Resurr Mirfield 38. **d** 40 **p** 41. V Beeston Hill H Spirit *Ripon* 60-77; rtd 77. *1 Deanery Close, Minster Road, Ripon, N Yorkshire HG4 1LZ*   Ripon (0765) 701227

MORTON, Canon John Ivan. b 32. Linc Coll Ox BA55 MA59. Wells Th Coll. **d** 57 **p** 58. C Shrewsbury St Chad *Lich* 57-60; C Dunham Massey St Marg *Ches* 60-62; V Derby St Luke *Derby* 62-70; R W Kirby St Andr *Ches* 70-75; V Northn St Matt *Pet* from 75; RD Northn 79-88; Can Pet Cathl from 82. *St Matthew's Vicarage, St Matthew's Parade, Northampton NN2 7HF* Northampton (0604) 713615

MORTON, Canon John Peter Sargeson. b 12. Keble Coll Ox BA35 MA39. Lich Th Coll 35. **d** 36 **p** 37. V Ambleside w Rydal and Brathay *Carl* 67-78; rtd 78; Perm to Offic *Glouc* from 78. *35 Gretton Road, Winchcombe, Cheltenham, Glos GL54 5EG* Cheltenham (0242) 603384

MORTON, Sister Rita. b 34. Wilson Carlile Coll. **dss** 85 **d** 87. CA from 76; Par Dn Harlow New Town w Lt Parndon *Chelmsf* 87-89; Par Dn Harold Hill St Geo from 89. *330 Straight Road, Romford RM3 8XX* Ingrebourne (04023) 71133

MORTON, Rupert Neville. b 25. St Steph Ho Ox 51. **d** 54 **p** 55. C Aldershot St Mich *Guildf* 54-57; Prec Guildf Cathl 57-58; V Middlesb St Chad *York* 58-62; Chapl Carter Bequest Hosp Middlesb 58-62; V Bramley *Guildf* 62-79; V Grafham 62-79; R Cranleigh 71-76; R Haslemere from 79. *The Rectory, 7 Derby Road, Haslemere, Surrey GU27 2PA* Haslemere (0428) 4578

MORTON, Mrs Sheila. b 44. Sarum & Wells Th Coll 79. **dss** 84 **d** 87. HM Forces Dusseldorf 84-86; Cov St Mary *Cov* 86-87; Par Dn 87-89; Par Dn Boston Spa *York* from 89. *9 Nursery Way, Boston Spa, Wetherby, W Yorkshire LS23 6PS* Wetherby (0937) 845762

MORTON, Canon William Derek. b 28. Wells Th Coll 67. **d** 69 **p** 70. C Kibworth Beauchamp *Leic* 69-72; Ind Chapl *Nor* from 72; Hon Can Nor Cathl from 90; RD Nor E from 90. *42 Heigham Road, Norwich NR2 3AU* Norwich (0603) 625734

MORTON, William Wright. b 56. TCD BTh88. **d** 88 **p** 89. C Drumachose *D & R* 88-91; I Conwal Union w Gartan from 91. *Conwal Rectory, Magherennan, Letterkenny, Co Donegal, Irish Republic* Letterkenny (74) 22573

MOSEDALE, Hugh Alfred. b 14. AKC48. **d** 49 **p** 50. C W Derby St Mary *Liv* 49-52; C Lewisham St Mary *S'wark* 52-55; C Walton St Mary *Liv* 55-57; V Middleton Junction *Man* 57-61; R Boxworth *Ely* from 61; R Elsworth w Knapwell from 61; RD Bourn 72-81. *The Rectory, Boxworth, Cambridge CB3 8LZ* Elsworth (09547) 226

MOSELEY, Arthur William. b 27. Lich Th Coll. **d** 60 **p** 61. C Castle Church *Lich* 60-64; C Bloxwich 64-66; V Bradley St Martin 66-72; C Stoke upon Trent 73-74; V Brown Edge 74-85; V Criftins from 85; V Dudleston from 85. *The Vicarage, Criftins, Ellesmere, Shropshire SY12 9LN* Dudleston Heath (069175) 212

MOSELEY, Colin Francis. b 40. FRICS ACIArb. **d** 79 **p** 80. NSM Fishponds St Mary *Bris* 79-84; Hon C Winterbourne Down 84-86; Hon C Frenchay and Winterbourne Down from 86. *7 Prospect Close, Winterbourne Down, Bristol BS17 1BD* Winterbourne (0454) 778064

MOSELEY, David John Reading. b 30. Univ Coll Ox BA54 MA58. Wells Th Coll 54. **d** 56 **p** 57. C Farnworth and Kearsley *Man* 56-59; Trinidad and Tobago 59-63; V Bedminster St Paul *Bris* 63-75; TV Bedminster 75-78; V Kilmington w Shute *Ex* from 78; P-in-c Stockland w Dalwood 90. *The Vicarage, Kilmington, Axminster, Devon EX13 7RF* Axminster (0297) 33156

MOSELEY, Hugh Martin. b 47. St Jo Coll Dur BA70. Westcott Ho Cam 71. **d** 73 **p** 74. C Hythe *Cant* 73-77; P-in-c Eythorne w Waldershare 77-83; V Ringmer *Chich* from 83. *The Vicarage, Ringmer, Lewes, E Sussex BN8 5LA* Ringmer (0273) 812243

MOSELEY, Roger Henry. b 38. Edin Th Coll 60. **d** 63 **p** 64. C Friern Barnet All SS *Lon* 63-66; C Grantham St Wulfram *Linc* 66-69; P-in-c Swaton w Spanby 69-73; P-in-c Horbling 69-73; V Soberton w Newtown *Portsm* 73-80; V Sarisbury from 80. *The Vicarage, 149 Bridge Road, Sarisbury Green, Southampton SO3 7EN* Locks Heath (0489) 572207

MOSELING, Stephen. b 57. Chich Th Coll 83. **d** 86 **p** 87. C Burnley St Cath w St Alb and St Paul *Blackb* 86-89; C Rawmarsh w Parkgate *Sheff* 89-91; V Colindale St Matthias *Lon* from 91. *St Matthias' Vicarage, Rushgrove Avenue, London NW9 6QY* 081-205 8783

MOSES, Very Rev Dr John Henry. b 38. Nottm Univ BA59 PhD65. Linc Th Coll 62. **d** 64 **p** 65. C Bedf St Andr *St Alb* 64-70; P-in-c Cov St Pet *Cov* 70-73; P-in-c Cov St Mark 71-73; TR Cov E 73-77; RD Cov E 73-77; Adn Southend *Chelmsf* 77-82; Provost Chelmsf from 82; Chmn Coun of Cen for Th Study Essex Univ from 87. *Provost's House, 3 Harlings Grove, Waterloo Lane, Chelmsford CM1 1YQ* Chelmsford (0245) 354318

MOSES, Leslie Alan. b 49. Hull Univ BA71 Edin Univ BD76. Edin Th Coll 73. **d** 76 **p** 77. C Edin Old St Paul *Edin* 76-79; R from 86; R Leven *St And* 79-85; P-in-c Edin St Marg *Edin* from 86. *Lauder House, 39 Jeffrey Street, Edinburgh EH1 1DH* 031-556 3332

MOSES, Norman. b 12. AKC37. **d** 37 **p** 38. V Grangetown *Dur* 58-77; rtd 77. *1 Wayside, Sunderland, Tyne & Wear SR2 7QJ* 091-514 2150

MOSFORD, Denzil Huw Erasmus. b 56. St D Coll Lamp DipTh77 AKC78 Sarum & Wells Th Coll 77. **d** 79 **p** 80. C Clydach *S & B* 79-82; V from 87; Jamaica 82-85; V Ystalyfera *S & B* 85-87. *The Vicarage, 1 Woodland Park, Ynystawe, Swansea SA6 5AF* Swansea (0792) 843203

MOSFORD, Denzil Joseph. b 28. **d** 86 **p** 87. C Manselton *S & B* 86-89; V Port Eynon w Rhosili and Llanddewi and Knelston from 89. *The Rectory, Port Eynon, Swansea SA3 1NL* Swansea (0792) 390456

MOSLEY, Edward Peter. b 38. Clifton Th Coll 62. **d** 67 **p** 68. C Mirehouse *Carl* 67-69; C Newbarns w Hawcoat 69-72; R Aikton 72-77; R Orton St Giles 73-77; V Silloth 77-78; CF from 78. *c/o MOD (Army), Bagshot Park, Bagshot, Surrey GU19 5PL* Bagshot (0276) 71717

MOSS, Arthur Robinson. b 15. St D Coll Lamp BA40. **d** 40 **p** 41. V Cannington *B & W* 58-80; rtd 80; Hon C Aisholt *B & W* 80-89. *1 Withiel Drive, Cannington, Bridgwater, Somerset TA5 2LY* Combwich (0278) 652424

MOSS, Barrie. b 42. Lon Univ BD65. ALCD64. **d** 65 **p** 66. C Willesden St Matt *Lon* 65-67; C Kingsbury St Andr 67-70; C Harrow Weald All SS 70-74; P-in-c Radwinter *Chelmsf* 74-77; P-in-c Radwinter w Hempstead 77-78; R 78-80; V Beamish *Dur* 80-88; V Gateshead Harlow Green from 88. *St Ninian's Vicarage, Ivy Lane, Low Fell, Gateshead, Tyne & Wear NE9 6QD* 091-487 6685

MOSS, Very Rev Basil Stanley. b 18. Qu Coll Ox BA41 MA45. Linc Th Coll 42. **d** 43 **p** 44. Hon Can Bris Cathl *Bris* 66-73; Chief Sec ACCM 66-73; Provost Birm 73-85; rtd 85; Perm to Offic Worc from 85; Birm from 86. *25 Castle Grove, Stourbridge, W Midlands DY8 2HH* Stourbridge (0384) 378799

MOSS, Christopher Ashley. b 52. Ex Univ BA73 York Univ DSA77 Southn Univ DASS78 CQSW78. Wycliffe Hall Ox 89. **d** 91. C Malvern H Trin and St Jas *Worc* from 91. *23 Tennyson Drive, Malvern, Worcs WR14 2TQ* Ingrebourne (04023) 76917

MOSS, Clement. b 16. OBE. LSMF. **d** 48 **p** 48. Hon C Bedf St Jo and St Leon *St Alb* from 83. *22 Meadway, Harrold, Bedford MK43 7DR* Bedford (0234) 720608

MOSS, David Glyn. b 62. St Anne's Coll Ox BA83 Em Coll Cam BA89. Westcott Ho Cam 87. **d** 90 **p** 91. C Halesowen *Worc* from 90. *Alton House, 30 Tenderfields, Halesowen, W Midlands B63 3LH* 021-550 2278

MOSS, Francis Duncan. b 23. AKC43. Wells Th Coll 53. **d** 54 **p** 55. R Kemerton *Glouc* 64-80; R Mobberley *Ches* 80-86; rtd 88. *10 Bryn Mor Court, Penrhyn Bay, Llandudno, Gwynedd LL30 3PA* Llandudno (0492) 47994

MOSS, Harold George Edward. b 20. Glouc Th Course 79. **d** 80 **p** 81. NSM Cirencester *Glouc* 80-83; NSM Brimpsfield, Cranham, Elkstone and Syde 83-89; rtd 89. *57 Queen Elizabeth Road, Cirencester, Glos GL7 1DH* Cirencester (0285) 652857

MOSS, Ivan Douglas Francis. b 24. Chich Th Coll. **d** 76 **p** 77. Hon C Crawley *Chich* from 76. *14 Normanhurst Close, Three Bridges, Crawley, W Sussex RH10 1YL* Crawley (0293) 522172

MOSS, James Wilfred. b 15. Oak Hill Th Coll 75. **d** 76 **p** 77. Hon C Frogmore H Trin *St Alb* 76-78 and from 81; Hon C Watford St Luke 78-81. *8A The Rise, Park Street, St Albans, Herts AL2 2NT* St Albans (0727) 872467

MOSS, Kenneth Charles. b 37. ARCS59 Lon Univ BSc59 DIC62 PhD62. **d** 66 **p** 67. Canada 66-73; Chapl Ex Univ *Ex* 73-83; V St Marychurch from 83; RD Ipplepen from 87. *The Vicarage, Hampton Avenue, St Marychurch, Torquay TQ1 3LA* Torquay (0803) 37661 or 39054

MOSS, Canon Leonard Godfrey. b 32. K Coll Lon BD59 AKC59. **d** 60 **p** 61. C Putney St Marg *S'wark* 60-63; C Cheam 63-67; R Much Dewchurch w Llanwarne and Llandinabo *Heref* 67-72; Dioc Ecum Officer 69-83; V Marden w Amberley 72-80; Preb Heref Cathl from 79; V Marden w Amberley and Wisteston 80-84; Can Heref Cathl from 84; Dioc Soc Resp Officer from 84. *1 Carter Grove, Hereford HR1 1NT* Hereford (0432) 265465

MOSS, Peter Hextall. b 34. Clare Coll Cam BA59 MA62. Linc Th Coll 59. **d** 61 **p** 62. C Easington Colliery *Dur* 61-63; C Whickham 63-65; C-in-c Town End Farm CD 65-72; TV Mattishall *Nor* 72-75; P-in-c Welborne 75-84; P-in-c Mattishall w Mattishall Burgh 75-84; TR Hempnall 84-89. *High House Cottage, Gunn Street, Foulsham, Dereham, Norfolk NR20 5RN* Foulsham (036284) 823

MOSS, Peter John. b 41. K Coll Cam BA64 MA67. Westcott Ho Cam 63. d 84 p 85. Hon C Leighton Buzzard w Eggington, Hockliffe etc *St Alb* from 84. *84 Regent Street, Leighton Buzzard, Beds LU7 8JZ* Leighton Buzzard (0525) 372904

MOSS, Prof Rowland Percy. b 28. ACIT MSOSc Lon Univ BSc PhD. St Deiniol's Hawarden 82. d 83 p 84. NSM Cheadle Hulme St Andr *Ches* from 83. *154 Acre Lane, Cheadle Hulme, Cheadle, Cheshire SK8 7PD* 061-439 1599

MOSS, Stephen. b 51. Lon Univ BSc69. S'wark Ord Course. d 85 p 86. NSM Clapham Ch Ch and St Jo *S'wark* 85-87; NSM Clapham Team Min from 87. *59A Bromfelde Road, London SW4 6PP* 071-720 3152

MOSS, Victor Charles. b 25. Oak Hill Th Coll BD65. d 66 p 67. C Macclesfield St Mich *Ches* 66-68; C Belper *Derby* 69-71; V Chesterfield Ch Ch from 71. *Christ Church Vicarage, 89 Sheffield Road, Chesterfield, Derbyshire S41 7JH* Chesterfield (0246) 273508

MOSS, Wilfrid Maurice. b 10. St Jo Coll Dur LTh34 BA35 MA41. Tyndale Hall Bris 31. d 35 p 36. V Sidcup Ch Ch *Roch* 50-75; rtd 75; Perm to Offic *Ex* 75-85; B & W from 85. *Stonehaven, 4 West Viewclose, Middlezoy, Bridgwater, Somerset TA7 0NP* Burrowbridge (082369) 8851

MOSSE, Mrs Barbara. b 51. Open Univ BA77. CA Tr Coll IDC81 Lambeth STh83. d 90. NSM Southbourne w W Thorney *Chich* from 90. *8 Long Copse Court, Long Copse Lane, Emsworth, Hants PO10 7UW* Emsworth (0243) 376155

MOSSMAN, Preb Donald Wyndham Cremer. b 13. OBE65. Lon Coll of Div LTh39. d 39 p 40. Preb St Paul's Cathl *Lon* 60-86; RD W Haringey 67-71; C Highgate St Mich 69-71; R St Jas Garlickhythe w St Mich Queenhithe etc 71-84; Hon C Warsaw *Eur* 77-84; Hon Can Brussels Cathl from 81; rtd 84. *The Charterhouse, Charterhouse Square, London EC1M 6AN* 071-251 8002

MOSSOP, Henry Watson. b 08. Lich Th Coll 52. d 54 p 55. V Twyford w Guist *Nor* 66-73; rtd 73; Perm to Offic *Nor* from 74. *Crossing Cottage, Pond Lane, Antingham, North Walsham, Norfolk NR28 0NH* North Walsham (0692) 403561

MOSSOP, Canon Robert Owen. b 09. Peterho Cam BA30 MA35. Westcott Ho Cam 32. d 33 p 34. V Constantine *Truro* 50-73; RD Kerrier 60-73; Hon Can Truro Cathl 69-84; rtd 73. *Westwood, Carnmenellis, Redruth, Cornwall TR16 6PB* Stithians (0209) 860288

MOTE, Gregory Justin. b 60. Oak Hill Th Coll BA83. d 86 p 87. C W Ealing St Jo w St Jas *Lon* 86-90; C St Helen Bishopsgate w St A.dr Undershaft etc from 90. *64 Arbery Road, London E3 5DD* 081-983 1079

MOTH, Miss Susan. b 44. Leic Univ BA65 K Coll Lon CertEd80. Linc Th Coll 83. dss 85 d 87. Churchdown St Jo *Glouc* 85-87; C from 87. *6 Keriston Avenue, Churchdown, Gloucester GL3 2BU* Churchdown (0452) 714197

MOTHERSOLE, John Robert. b 25. Chich Th Coll. d 84 p 85. NSM Hayes St Anselm *Lon* from 84. *116 Nestles Avenue, Hayes, Middx UB3 4QD* 081-848 0626

MOTION, Alexander William. b 08. Pemb Coll Cam BA31 LLB32 MA36. K Coll Lon. d 51 p 52. V Newc St Andr *Newc* 53-77; rtd 77. *Ellesborough Manor, Butlers Cross, Aylesbury, Bucks HP17 0XF* Aylesbury (0296) 696130

MOTT, Julian Ward. b 52. Loughb Univ BSc77. Ripon Coll Cuddesdon 78. d 81 p 82. C Aylestone *Leic* 81-84; C Gt Ilford St Mary *Chelmsf* 84-88; R Chevington w Hargrave and Whepstead w Brockley *St E* from 88. *The Rectory, Chevington, Bury St Edmunds, Suffolk IP29 5QL* Chevington (0284) 850204

MOTT, Peter John. b 49. Ch Coll Cam BA70 MA75 Dundee Univ PhD73 Nottm Univ BA79. St Jo Coll Nottm 77. d 80 p 81. C Hull Newland St Jo *York* 80-83; C Selly Park St Steph and St Wulstan *Birm* 83-87; C Mosborough *Sheff* from 87. *Emmanuel House, 2 Harwood Gardens, Sheffield S19 6LE* Sheffield (0742) 489470

MOTTERSHEAD, Derek. b 39. Open Univ BA74 BEd. Chich Th Coll 65. d 69 p 70. C Walthamstow St Barn and St Jas Gt *Chelmsf* 69-72; C Chelmsf All SS 72-77; P-in-c Cold Norton w Stow Maries 77-80; V Leytonstone St Andr from 80. *St Andrew's Vicarage, 7 Forest Glade, London E11 1LU* 081-989 0942

MOTTRAM, Andrew Peter. b 53. AKC77. Ripon Coll Cuddesdon 77. d 78 p 79. C E Bedfont *Lon* 78-81; C Hatf *St Alb* 81-84; V Milton Ernest from 84; V Thurleigh from 84. *The Vicarage, Thurleigh Road, Milton Ernest, Bedford MK44 1RF* Oakley (02302) 2885

MOTYER, John Alexander. b 24. TCD BA46 MA51 BD51. Wycliffe Hall Ox 47. d 47 p 48. V W Hampstead St Luke *Lon* 65-70; Dep Prin Tyndale Hall Bris 70-71; Prin and Dean Trin Coll Bris 71-81; Min Westbourne Ch Ch Prop Chpl *Win* 81-89; rtd 89; Perm to Offic *Ex* from 90. *10 Littlefield, Bishopsteignton, Teignmouth, Devon TQ14 9SG* Teignmouth (0626) 770986

MOTYER, Stephen. b 50. Pemb Coll Cam BA73 MA77 Bris Univ MLitt79. Trin Coll Bris 73. d 76 p 77. Lect Oak Hill Th Coll 76-83; C Braughing, Lt Hadham, Albury, Furneux Pelham etc *St Alb* 83-87; Lect Lon Bible Coll from 87. *12 Lower Tail, Carpenders Park, Watford, Herts WD1 5DD* 081-428 9422

MOUGHTIN, Ross. b 48. St Cath Coll Cam BA70 St Jo Coll Dur BA75. d 76 p 77. C Litherland St Paul Hatton Hill *Liv* 76-79; C Heswall *Ches* 79-84; Chapl Edw Unit Rochdale Infirmary from 83; V Thornham w Gravel Hole *Man* from 84. *St John's Vicarage, 1177 Manchester Road, Rochdale, Lancs OL11 2XZ* Rochdale (0706) 31825

MOULD, Mrs Jacqueline. b 66. QUB BD88. d 91. C Belf St Aid *Conn* from 91. *50 Ashley Avenue, Lisburn Road, Belfast BT9 7BT* Belfast (0232) 669622

MOULD, Jeremy James. b 63. Nottm Univ BA85. d 91. C Mossley *Conn* from 91. *50 Ashley Avenue, Lisburn Road, Belfast BT9 7BT* Belfast (0232) 669622

MOULD, William Douglas Gordon. b 10. ALCD38. d 38 p 39. R Combe Hay *B & W* 63-70; rtd 70. *4 Shakespeare Avenue, Bath BA2 4RF* Bath (0225) 314309

MOULDER, Kenneth. b 53. Lon Univ BEd75. Ridley Hall Cam 78. d 81 p 82. C Harold Wood *Chelmsf* 81-84; C Darfield *Sheff* 84-88; V Walkergate *Newc* from 88; P-in-c Byker St Mark from 90. *St Oswald's Parsonage, Woodhead Road, Newcastle upon Tyne NE6 4RX* 091-263 6249

MOULE, Prof Charles Francis Digby. b 08. CBE. FBA66 Em Coll Cam BA29 MA34 St Andr Univ Hon DD58. Ridley Hall Cam 31. d 33 p 34. Lady Marg Prof Div Cam Univ 51-76; Can Th Leic Cathl *Leic* 55-76; rtd 76; Perm to Offic *Chich* from 81. *1 King's Houses, Pevensey, E Sussex BN24 5JR* Eastbourne (0323) 762436

MOULE, George William Henry. b 04. Em Coll Cam BA26 MA30. d 36 p 37. V Damerham *Sarum* 59-70; rtd 70; Perm to Offic *Carl* from 77. *Herne Cottage, Abbey Road, St Bees, Cumbria CA27 0ED*

MOULE, Kevin David. b 54. Coll of Resurr Mirfield 77. d 80 p 81. C E Finchley All SS *Lon* 80-84; C Notting Hill St Mich and Ch Ch 84-91; P-in-c Isleworth St Fran from 91. *St Francis Vicarage, 865 Great West Road, Isleworth, Middx TW7 5PD* 081-560 4839

MOULTON, Paul Oliver. b 43. BSc. N Ord Course 77. d 80 p 81. C Wilmslow *Ches* 80-85; V Knutsford St Cross from 85; Chapl Mary Dendy Hosp Knutsford from 86. *St Cross Vicarage, Mobberley Road, Knutsford, Cheshire WA16 8EL* Knutsford (0565) 2389

MOULTON, William Arthur. b 11. d 48 p 49. Asst Chapl & Sen Lect Coll SS Mark & Jo Chelsea 48-62; Prin Lect Bp Grosseteste Coll Linc 62-76; Hon PV Linc Cathl *Linc* from 76. *Bungalow 7, Terrys Cross, Woodmancote, Henfield, W Sussex BN5 9SX* Henfield (0273) 493091

MOUNSEY, William Lawrence Fraser. b 51. St Andr Univ BD75. Edin Th Coll 76. d 78 p 79. C Edin St Mark *Edin* 78-81; Chapl RAF 81-90; Chapl Heriot-Watt Univ Edin from 90; R Dalmahoy from 90. *The Rectory, Dalmahoy, Kirknewton, Midlothian EH27 8EB* 031-333 1683

MOUNSTEPHEN, Philip Ian. b 59. Southn Univ BA80 Magd Coll Ox MA87. Wycliffe Hall Ox 85. d 88 p 89. C Gerrards Cross and Fulmer *Ox* from 88. *Moss End, 24 Fulmer Drive, Gerrards Cross, Bucks SL9 7HJ* Gerrards Cross (0753) 887587

MOUNT, Miss Judith Mary. b 35. Bedf Coll Lon BA56 Lon Univ CertEd57. Ripon Coll Cuddesdon 81. dss 83 d 87. Carterton *Ox* 83-85; Charlton on Otmoor and Oddington 85-87; Dioc Lay Min Adv and Asst Dir of Ords 86-89; Par Dn Islip w Charlton on Otmoor, Oddington, Noke etc from 87; Assoc Dioc Dir Ords & Adv for Women in Ord Min from 89. *St Mary's House, High Street, Charlton-on-Otmoor, Oxford OX5 2UQ* Charlton-on-Otmoor (086733) 513

MOUNTFORD, Brian Wakling. b 45. Newc Univ BA66 Cam Univ MA73 Ox Univ MA90. Westcott Ho Cam 66. d 68 p 69. C Westmr St Steph w St Jo *Lon* 68-69; C Paddington Ch Ch 69-73; Chapl SS Coll Cam 73-78; V Southgate Ch Ch *Lon* 78-86; V Ox St Mary V w St Cross and St Pet *Ox* from 86. *12 Mansfield Road, Oxford OX1 3TA* Oxford (0865) 59676

MOUNTFORD, John. b 55. Nottm Univ BEd77 Birm Univ MA80 Ex Univ MPhil86. Linc Th Coll 73. d 78 p 79. C Wombourne *Lich* 78-80; C Upper Gornal 80-82;

C Paignton St Jo *Ex* 82-86; Papua New Guinea 86-87; Chapl Blue Coat Sch Birm 87-90; Perm to Offic *Birm* 88-90; Australia from 91. *Collegiate School of St Peter, St Peters College, Adelaide, Australia 5069* Adelaide (8) 423451

MOUNTNEY, Frederick Hugh. b 14. St Chad's Coll Dur BA36 MA39. Lich Th Coll 36. **d** 37 **p** 38. V Heref All SS *Heref* 56-75; Chapl Vic Eye Hosp Heref 56-75; Chapl Bonn w Cologne *Eur* 75-79; rtd 79; Perm to Offic Heref from 79; St E and Nor from 82; Eur from 90. *St Martin's, 44 London Road, Harleston, Norfolk IP20 9BW* Harleston (0379) 853744

MOUNTNEY, John Michael. b 47. St Chad's Coll Dur BA69 MA84. Cuddesdon Coll 69. **d** 71 **p** 72. C Morpeth *Newc* 71-75; C Longbenton St Bart 75-77; Sub-Warden Community of All Hallows Ditchingham 77-83; R Blundeston w Flixton and Lound *Nor* 83-87; TR Nor St Pet Parmentergate w St Jo from 87; Warden Julian Shrine from 87. *The Rectory, 10 Stepping Lane, Norwich NR1 1PE* Norwich (0603) 622509

MOURANT, Sidney Eric. b 39. DipTh70. Oak Hill Th Coll BD73. **d** 89 **p** 90. C Oxton *Ches* from 89. *36 Noctorum Dell, Birkenhead, Merseyside L43 9UL* 051-652 8050

MOURANT, Stephen Philip Edward. b 54. Nottm Univ BTh83. St Jo Coll Nottm. **d** 83 **p** 84. C Cropwell Bishop w Colston Bassett, Granby etc *S'well* 83-86; C Marple All SS *Ches* 86-89; P-in-c Harlow St Mary V *Chelmsf* 89-90; V from 90. *St Mary's Vicarage, 5 Staffords, Old Harlow, Essex CM17 0JR* Harlow (0279) 450633

MOVERLEY, Ruth Elaine. b 55. **d** 90. C Llangynwyd w Maesteg *Llan* from 90. *15 Yr Ysfa, Maesteg, M Glam CF31 4HP* Maesteg (0656) 738845

MOWAT, Geoffrey Scott. b 17. CCC Ox BA39 MA49. Ripon Hall Ox 58. **d** 59 **p** 60. V Coln St Aldwyn w Hatherop and Quenington *Glouc* 64-77; RD Fairford 74-77; Malaysia 77-83; rtd 83; Perm to Offic *B & W* 86-87; Min Bath St Mary Magd Holloway from 87. *106 Midford Road, Bath BA2 5RU* Bath (0225) 833310

MOWBRAY, David. b 38. Fitzw Ho Cam BA60 MA64 Lon Univ BD62. Clifton Th Coll. **d** 63 **p** 64. C Northn St Giles *Pet* 63-66; Lect Watford St Mary *St Alb* 66-70; V Broxbourne 70-77; R Broxbourne w Wormley 77-84; V Hertf All SS from 84. *All Saints' Vicarage, Churchfields, Hertford SG13 8AE* Hertford (0992) 582096

MOWBRAY, Derek David Whitfield. b 19. Lon Univ BD42 Dur Univ MLitt52 Sheff Univ PhD58 Leeds Univ PhD59. ALCD42. **d** 42 **p** 43. R Bris St Jo w St Mary-le-Port *Bris* 71-74; Perm to Offic from 75; rtd 84. *20 Glyndarwen Close, Derwen Fawr, Swansea SA2 8EQ* Swansea (0792) 208708

MOWLL, John Edward. b 12. St Edm Hall Ox BA34 MA38. Westcott Ho Cam 35. **d** 36 **p** 37. V Golcar *Wakef* 60-77; rtd 77. *21 Smith Close, Salter Street, London SE16 1PB*

MOWLL, John Kingsford. b 33. Em Coll Cam BA57 MA61 Lon Univ BD60. Clifton Th Coll 57. **d** 59 **p** 60. C Halliwell St Paul *Man* 59-62; C Cheadle *Ches* 62-66; Argentina 66-69 and 70-79; C Peckham St Mary Magd *S'wark* 69; V Buglawton *Ches* from 80. *St John's Vicarage, Buxton Road, Buglawton, Congleton, Cheshire CW12 2DT* Congleton (0260) 273294

MOWLL, John William Rutley. b 42. Sarum Th Coll 63. **d** 66 **p** 67. C Oughtibridge *Sheff* 66-69; C Hill *Birm* 69-73; Ind Chapl *Worc* 73-78; V Upper Arley 73-78; P-in-c Upton Snodsbury and Broughton Hackett etc 78-81; R 81-83; V Boughton under Blean w Dunkirk *Cant* 83-89; V Boughton under Blean w Dunkirk and Hernhill from 89. *The Vicarage, The Street, Boughton-under-Blean, Faversham, Kent ME13 9BG* Canterbury (0227) 751410

MOXLEY, Cyril Edward. b 09. Ch Coll Cam BA32 MA37. Ely Th Coll 33. **d** 35 **p** 37. V S Stoneham *Win* 65-74; rtd 74; Hon Chapl Win Cathl from 79. *2 Sutton Gardens, St Peter Street, Winchester, Hants SO23 8HP* Winchester (0962) 53575

MOXON, Canon Michael Anthony. b 42. Lon Univ BD78. Sarum Th Coll 67. **d** 70 **p** 71. C Kirkley *Nor* 70-74; Min Can St Paul's Cathl *Lon* 74-81; Sacr 77-81; Warden Coll of Min Canons 79-81; V Tewkesbury w Walton Cardiff *Glouc* 81-90; Chapl to HM The Queen from 86; Can Windsor from 90; Chapl R Chpl Windsor Gt Park from 90. *The Chaplain's Lodge, The Great Park, Windsor, Berks SL4 2HP* Egham (0784) 432434

MOXON, William James. b 25. Qu Coll Birm 68. **d** 69 **p** 70. C Letchworth St Paul *St Alb* 69-72; C-in-c N Brickhill CD 72-76; Chapl Puerto de la Cruz Tenerife *Eur* 76-78; Egypt 78-80; V Altrincham St Jo *Ches* 80-90;

rtd 90. *14 Broomlee, Bancroft, Milton Keynes MK13 0PU* Milton Keynes (0908) 322029

MOY, Mrs Joy Patricia. b 35. Cant Sch of Min 87. **d** 90. NSM Cranbrook *Cant* from 90. *1 Dobells, Cranbrook, Kent TN17 3BL* Cranbrook (0580) 713066

MOYNAGH, Dr David Kenneth. b 46. LRCP70 MRCS70 MRCGP76 Lon Univ MB, BS70. S Dios Minl Tr Scheme 88. **d** 91. NSM Ore *Chich* from 91. *Stalkhurst Farm, Ivyhouse Lane, Hastings, E Sussex TN35 4NN* Hastings (0424) 751314

MOYNAGH, Michael Digby. b 50. Southn Univ BA73 Lon Univ MA74 Aus Nat Univ PhD78 Bris Univ MA85. Trin Coll Bris DipHE84. **d** 85 **p** 86. C Northwood Em *Lon* 85-89; P-in-c Wilton *B & W* 89-90; TR from 90. *The Vicarage, Fons George, Wilton, Taunton, Somerset TA1 3JT* Taunton (0823) 284253

MOYNAN, David George. b 53. DipTh. **d** 86 **p** 87. C Seagoe *D & D* 86-88; C Taney w St Nahi *D & G* 88-89; I Arklow w Inch and Kilbride from 89; Miss to Seamen from 89. *The Rectory, Arklow, Co Wicklow, Irish Republic* Arklow (402) 32439

MOYNAN, Canon William John. b 20. TCD BA44. **d** 44 **p** 45. I Swords w Donabate and Kilsallaghan *D & G* 68-90; Can Ch Ch Cathl Dub from 83; rtd 90. *The Rectory, Church Road, Tramore, Co Waterford, Irish Republic* Tramore (51) 81301

MOYSE, Mrs Pauline Patricia. b 42. Ex Univ CertEd62. Sarum & Wells Th Coll 88. **d** 91. NSM Fleet *Guildf* from 91. *18 Fir Tree Way, Fleet, Hants GU13 9NB* Fleet (0252) 629068

MPUNZI, Nduna Ananias. b 46. Birm Univ DPS79 Glas Univ LTh84. St Pet Coll Alice 69. **d** 71 **p** 72. S Africa 71-78; C Bilston *Lich* 84-86; TV 86-90; P-in-c Caldmore from 90. *Palfrey Vicarage, Dale Street, Walsall WS1 4AN* Walsall (0922) 33451

MUDDIMAN, Ms Gillian Anne. b 55. LMH Ox BA76 CertEd77 MA80. St Jo Coll Nottm 84. **dss** 86 **d** 87. Tutor E Midl Min Tr Course from 86; Beeston *S'well* 86-87; Lect St Jo Coll Nottm from 87. *c/o St John's College, University of Nottingham, Nottingham NG7 2RD* Nottingham (0602) 506101

MUDDIMAN, John Bernard. b 47. Keble Coll Ox BA67 MA72 DPhil76 Selw Coll Cam BA71 MA75. Westcott Ho Cam 69. **d** 72 **p** 73. Hon C Ox St Giles *Ox* 72-83; Chapl New Coll Ox 72-76; Tutor St Steph Ho Ox 76-83; Vice-Prin 80-83; Lect Th Nottm Univ 83-90; Fell Mansf Coll Ox from 90; Lic to Offic *Ox* from 90. *Mansfield College, Oxford OX1 3TF* Oxford (0865) 270999

MUDGE, Frederick Alfred George. b 31. Leeds Univ BSc58 Univ of Wales BD67. St Mich Coll Llan 58. **d** 61 **p** 62. C Cwmavon *Llan* 61-64; PV Llan Cathl 64-70; R Llandough w Leckwith 70-88; V Penarth All SS from 88. *All Saints' Vicarage, 2 Lower Cwrt-y-Vil Road, Penarth, S Glam CF6 2HQ* Penarth (0222) 708952

MUGGLETON, Major George. b 25. Chich Th Coll 55. **d** 57 **p** 58. R Stisted w Bradwell and Pattiswick *Chelmsf* 69-87; rtd 87. *Curvalion House, Creech St Michael, Taunton, Somerset TA3 5QF* Henlade (0823) 443842

MUIR, David Murray. b 49. Glas Univ MA70 Nottm Univ BA72. St Jo Coll Nottm 70. **d** 76 **p** 77. C Fulham St Mary N End *Lon* 76-80; C Aspley *S'well* 80; India 81-85; Dir Ext Studies St Jo Coll Nottm from 85. *St John's College, Bramcote, Nottingham NG9 3DS* Nottingham (0602) 251117

MUIR, David Trevor. b 49. TCD MA. CITC. **d** 78 **p** 79. C Dub Clontarf *D & G* 78-80; C Monkstown w St Mary 80-83; I Kilternan from 83. *The Rectory, Kilternan, Co Dublin, Irish Republic* Dublin (1) 955603

MUIR, John Johnston. b 20. Strathclyde Univ BSc81. St Jo Coll Nottm 83. **d** 85 **p** 87. Hon C Glas St Marg *Glas* 85-91; rtd 91. *15 Merrycrest Avenue, Giffnock, Glasgow G46 6BY* 041-637 6470

MUIR, John William. b 38. Dur Univ BA59 Mansf Coll Ox MA65. Chich Th Coll 78. **d** 78 **p** 79. In Congr Ch (England & Wales) 62-70; In United Ch of Zambia 70-78; C Brighouse *Wakef* 78-80; V Northowram 80-87; V Sowerby from 87. *The Vicarage, Towngate, Sowerby, Sowerby Bridge, W Yorkshire HX6 1JJ* Halifax (0422) 31036

MULCOCK, Edward John. b 16. Leeds Univ BA37. Coll of Resurr Mirfield 37. **d** 39 **p** 40. V Fulham St Jo Walham Green *Lon* 66-76; V Fulham St Jas Moore Park 69-76; V Walham Green St Jo w St Jas 76-83; rtd 84. *Flat 2, Gardens Court, 57 Parkstone Road, Poole, Dorset BH15 2NX* Poole (0202) 673162

MULHOLLAND, Nicholas Christopher John. b 44. Chich Th Coll 77. **d** 79 **p** 80. C Thornbury *Glouc* 79-83; R Boxwell, Leighterton, Didmarton, Oldbury etc from 83.

The Rectory, Leighterton, Tetbury, Glos GL8 8UW Leighterton (0666) 890283

MULKERN, Richard Neville. b 39. S'wark Ord Course 88. **d** 91. NSM Leytonstone St Andr *Chelmsf* from 91; Min Sec and Welfare Officer Miss to Seamen from 91. *224 Hainault Road, London E11 1EP* 081-556 9800

MULLARD, George Edward. b 14. St D Coll Lamp BA38 Sarum Th Coll 38. **d** 39 **p** 40. V E Coker w Sutton Bingham *B & W* 69-79; rtd 79. *Alvington Cottage, Brympton, Yeovil, Somerset BA22 8TH* Yeovil (0935) 71752

MULLEN, Peter John. b 42. Liv Univ BA70. **d** 70 **p** 71. C Manston *Ripon* 70-72; C Stretford All SS *Man* 72-73; C Oldham St Mary w St Pet 73-74; Lic to Offic 74-77; V Tockwith and Bilton w Bickerton *York* 77-89. *16 Whin Road, Dringhouses, York YO2 2JZ*

MULLENGER, Canon Alan Edward Clement. b 15. Lon Univ BD64. Kelham Th Coll 35. **d** 40 **p** 41. SSM from 40; C Sheff Parson Cross St Cecilia *Sheff* 40-48; S Africa 48-56; Basutoland 56-61; Wycliffe Hall Ox 63-64; Perm to Offic Ox 63-64; Nor 64-65; St Aug Coll Walsingham 64-65; Ghana 65-74; Hon Can Kumasi 73-74; Lesotho from 74; Hon Can Lesotho Cathl from 88. *St John's Rectory, PO Box 270, Maseru 100, Lesotho*

MULLENGER, William. b 44. Linc Th Coll 68. **d** 69 **p** 70. C Clapham St Jo *S'wark* 69-73; C Hook 73-81; P-in-c Camberwell St Phil and St Mark 81-85; V Hackbridge and N Beddington from 85. *All Saints' Vicarage, New Road, Mitcham, Surrey CR4 4JL* 081-648 3650

MULLENS, John Langford. b 06. Selw Coll Cam BA28 MA52. Westcott Ho Cam 29. **d** 29 **p** 30. R Farthinghoe w Thenford *Pet* 54-71; rtd 71; Perm to Offic Roch, Cant and Chich from 72. *Brentwood Court, 29D Frant Road, Tunbridge Wells, Kent TN2 5JT* Tunbridge Wells (0892) 27770

MULLER, Vernon. b 40. Natal Univ BA61 St Chad's Coll Dur DipTh64. **d** 64 **p** 65. S Africa 64-76; Chapl Friern Hosp Lon 77-91; Chapl R Berks and Battle Hosps Reading from 91. *The Chaplain's Office, Royal Berkshire Hospital, London Road, Reading RG1 5AN* Reading (0734) 875111

MULLER, Wolfgang Wilhelm Bernard Heinrich Paul. b 28. ALCD54. **d** 55 **p** 56. C Tonbridge SS Pet and Paul *Roch* 55-56; C Chatham St Steph 56-59; C-in-c Wigmore w Hempstead CD 59-65; V Wigmore w Hempstead 65-72; V S Gillingham 72-73; W Germany 73-90; Germany from 90. *Lindenallee 61, 5 Koln 51, Germany*

MULLETT, John St Hilary. b 25. St Cath Coll Cam BA47 MA49. Linc Th Coll. **d** 50 **p** 51. V Oxton *Ches* 69-77; R Ashwell *St Alb* 77-90; RD Buntingford 82-88; rtd 90; Fell St Cath Coll Cam from 90. *13 Church Lane, Madingley, Cambridge CB3 8AF* Madingley (0954) 211670

MULLINEAUX, John. b 16. Man Univ BA38. Kelham Th Coll 38. **d** 41 **p** 42. V Caton w Littledale *Blackb* 67-81; rtd 81; Lic to Offic *Blackb* from 81. *10 Ashfield Avenue, Lancaster LA1 5DZ* Lancaster (0524) 36769

MULLINER, Denis Ratliffe. b 40. BNC Ox BA62 MA66. Linc Th Coll 70. **d** 72 **p** 73. C Sandhurst *Ox* 72-76; Chapl Bradfield Coll Berks from 76. *Bradfield College, Reading* Bradfield (0734) 744263

MULLINS, Joe. b 20. MC45. Trin Coll Ox BA49 MA59. Ridley Hall Cam 48. **d** 50 **p** 51. India 52-74; Australia from 74; rtd 86. *24 Bunny Street, Weston, ACT, Australia 2611* Canberra (62) 288-9973

MULLINS, Malcolm David. b 42. St Edm Hall Ox BA63. St Steph Ho Ox 63. **d** 65 **p** 66. C Lamorbey H Redeemer *Roch* 69-75; C Solihull *Birm* 75-77; rtd 77. *38 Herga Road, Harrow, Middx HA3 5AS* 081-861 2671

MULLINS, Peter Matthew. b 60. Ch Ch Ox BA82 MA86 Birm Univ DPS84 Irish Sch of Ecum MPhil90. Qu Coll Birm 82. **d** 84 **p** 85. C Caversham and Mapledurham *Ox* 84-88; Perm to Offic *D & G* 88-89; TV Old Brumby *Linc* from 89. *Westcliff Vicarage, Dorchester Road, Scunthorpe, S Humberside DN17 1YG* Scunthorpe (0724) 847671

MULLINS, Timothy Dougal. b 59. Dur Univ. Wycliffe Hall Ox 83. **d** 85 **p** 86. C Reading Greyfriars *Ox* 85-89; C Haughton le Skerne *Dur* from 89. *2 Tayside, Darlington, Co Durham DL1 3QT* Darlington (0325) 357455

MULRAINE, Miss Margaret Haskell. b 24. Birm Univ BA45 DipEd46. Sarum Th Coll 83. **dss** 86 **d** 87. Wareham *Sarum* 86-87; Hon Par Dn from 87. *5 Trinity Close, Trinity Lane, Wareham, Dorset BH20 4LL* Wareham (0929) 552523

MULRENAN, Richard John. b 12. ACA36 FCA60. Tyndale Hall Bris 37. **d** 46 **p** 47. V Braintree *Chelmsf* 66-77; rtd 77; Perm to Offic *Ox* from 83. *37A Newland, Witney, Oxon OX8 6JN* Witney (0993) 705318

MUMFORD, Albert Edward. b 47. MCIT. Qu Coll Birm 85. **d** 87 **p** 88. C Leic Ascension *Leic* 87-91; C Burbage w Aston Flamville from 91. *122 Glenfield Road, Leicester LE3 6DF* Leicester (0533) 858943

MUMFORD, Dr David Bardwell. b 49. MRCPsych86 St Cath Coll Cam BA71 MA75 Bris Univ MB, ChB81 Edin Univ MPhil89. Bp's Coll Calcutta 71 Cuddesdon Coll 73. **d** 75. C Bris St Mary Redcliffe w Temple etc *Bris* 75-76; NSM 76-82; NSM Edin St Columba *Edin* 82-86; NSM Calverley *Bradf* from 86. *3 Town Wells Drive, Calverley, W Yorkshire LS28 5NN* Leeds (0532) 574766

MUMFORD, David Christopher. b 47. Mert Coll Ox BA68 MA74 York Univ MSW CQSW81. Linc Th Coll 84. **d** 86 **p** 87. C Shiremoor *Newc* 86-89; C N Shields 89-91; V Byker St Ant from 91. *St Anthony's Vicarage, Enslin Gardens, Newcastle upon Tyne NE6 3ST* 091-265 1605

MUMFORD, Grenville Alan. b 34. Richmond Th Coll DipTh. **d** 78 **p** 78. C Witham *Chelmsf* 78-81; C-in-c Gt Ilford St Marg CD 81-85; V Gt Ilford St Marg 85-87; P-in-c Everton and Mattersey w Clayworth *S'well* 87-89; R from 89. *The Rectory, Abbey Lane, Mattersey, Doncaster, S Yorkshire DN10 5DX* Retford (0777) 817364

MUMFORD, Canon Hugh Raymond. b 24. Oak Hill Th Coll 50. **d** 53 **p** 54. V Nether Cerne *Sarum* 69-71; R Godmanstone 69-71; R Cerne Abbas w Upcerne 69-71; R Minterne Magna 69-71; V Cerne Abbas w Godmanstone and Minterne Magna 71-89; RD Dorchester 75-79; Can and Preb Sarum Cathl 77-89; rtd 89. *10 South Walks Road, Dorchester, Dorset DT1 1ED* Dorchester (0305) 264971

MUMFORD, John Alexander. b 52. St Andr Univ MTh75. Ridley Hall Cam 75. **d** 77 **p** 78. C Canford Magna *Sarum* 77-82; C Ches Square St Mich w St Phil *Lon* 82-85; USA from 85. *Address temp unknown*

MUMFORD, Mary Josephine. b 43. Lon Univ BSc64 DipVG69. W Midl Minl Tr Course 84. **d** 87. Asst Chapl Leic Poly *Leic* from 87; Par Dn Leic H Spirit from 87. *122 Glenfield Road, Leicester LE3 6DF* Leicester (0533) 858943

MUMFORD, Michael David. b 29. **d** 79 **p** 80. Chapl Lister Hosp Stevenage 79-83; C Royston *St Alb* 83-87; P-in-c Kelshall 83-88; P-in-c Therfield 83-88; C Barkway, Reed and Buckland w Barley 87-88; R Ewhurst *Chich* from 88; R Bodiam from 88; RD Rye 90-91. *The Rectory, Ewhurst Green, Robertsbridge, E Sussex TN32 5TB* Staplecross (058083) 268

✠MUMFORD, Rt Rev Peter. b 22. Univ Coll Ox BA50 MA54. Cuddesdon Coll 50. **d** 51 **p** 52 **c** 74. C Salisbury St Mark *Sarum* 51-55; C St Alb Abbey *St Alb* 55-57; V Leagrave 57-63; V Bedf St Andr 63-69; R Crawley *Chich* 69-73; Can and Preb Chich Cathl 72-73; Adn St Alb 73-74; Suff Bp Hertf 74-81; Bp Truro 81-89; rtd 89. *Greystones, Zeals, Warminster, Wilts BA12 6LZ* Bourton (0747) 840392

MUNBY, Philip James. b 52. Pemb Coll Ox BA75 MA80. St Jo Coll Nottm 76. **d** 78 **p** 79. C Gipsy Hill Ch Ch *S'wark* 78-82; C-in-c W Dulwich Em CD 82-88; V Barnsley St Geo *Wakef* from 88. *St George's Vicarage, 100 Dodworth Road, Barnsley, S Yorkshire S70 6HL* Barnsley (0226) 203870

MUNCEY, William. b 49. BA80. Oak Hill Th Coll. **d** 80 **p** 81. C Wandsworth St Mich *S'wark* 80-84; C Morden 84-88; TV from 88. *5 Willows Avenue, Morden, Surrey SM4 5SG* 081-646 2002

MUNDEN, Alan Frederick. b 43. Nottm Univ BTh74 Birm Univ MLitt80 Dur Univ PhD87. St Jo Coll Nottm LTh74. **d** 74 **p** 75. C Cheltenham St Mary *Glouc* 74-76; C Cheltenham St Mary, St Matt, St Paul and H Trin 76; Hon C Jesmond Clayton Memorial *Newc* 76-80; C 80-83; V Cheylesmore *Cov* from 83. *Christ Church Vicarage, 11 Frankpledge Road, Coventry CV3 5GT* Coventry (0203) 502770

MUNGAVIN, David Stewart. b 60. Stirling Univ BA80. Edin Th Coll 87. **d** 90 **p** 91. C Glas St Marg *Glas* from 90. *St Margaret's, 351 Kilmarnock Road, Glasgow G43 2DS* 041-636 1131

MUNGAVIN, Canon Gerald Clarence. b 27. Edin Th Coll 51. **d** 54 **p** 55. C Dunfermline *St And* 54-55; C Glas Gd Shep *Glas* 55-57; CF 57-60; C Stanwix *Carl* 60-62; Chapl RAF 62-75; R Turriff *Ab* 75-81; R Cuminestown 75-81; R Banff 75-81; R Banchory from 81; R Kincardine O'Neil from 81; Can St Andr Cathl from 89. *The Rectory, High Street, Banchory, Kincardineshire AB3 3TB* Banchory (03302) 2783

MUNN, Carole Christine. b 45. E Midl Min Tr Course 83. d 90. NSM Long Bennington w Foston *Linc* from 90. *The Rectory, Claypole, Newark, Notts NG23 5BH* Newark (0636) 626224

MUNN, George. b 44. MM72. Linc Th Coll 85. d 87 p 88. C Boston *Linc* 87-90; R Claypole from 90. *The Rectory, Claypole, Newark, Notts NG23 5BH* Newark (0636) 626224

MUNN, Richard Probyn. b 45. Selw Coll Cam BA67. Cuddesdon Coll 67. d 69 p 70. C Cirencester *Glouc* 69-72; Zambia 72-80; Adn S Zambia 80; P-in-c Kings Stanley *Glouc* 80-83; R Lezant w Lawhitton and S Petherwin w Trewen *Truro* from 84. *The Vicarage, South Petherwin, Launceston, Cornwall PL15 7JA* Launceston (0566) 3782

MUNNS, Stuart Millington. b 36. OBE77. St Cath Coll Cam BA58 MA62. Cuddesdon Coll 58. d 60 p 61. C Allenton and Shelton Lock *Derby* 60-63; C Brampton St Thos 63-65; C-in-c Loundsley Green Ascension CD 65-66; Bp's Youth Chapl 66-72; Nat Dir of Community Industry 72-77; Hon C Hornsey Ch Ch *Lon* 72-77; Dioc Missr *Liv* 77-82; V Knowsley 77-82; P-in-c Stramshall *Lich* 82-88; V Uttoxeter w Bramshall 82-88; RD Uttoxeter 82-87; P-in-c Kingstone w Gratwich 84-88; P-in-c Marchington w Marchington Woodlands 84-88; P-in-c Checkley 86-88; Perm to Offic *B & W* 88-90; NSM Wells St Thos w Horrington from 90. *39 Wheeler Grove, Wells, Somerset BA5 2GB* Wells (0749) 77343

MUNRO, Basil Henry. b 40. Ripon Hall Ox 73. d 75 p 76. C N Mymms *St Alb* 75-78; C St Alb St Steph 78-80; V 80-87; R Aston-on-Trent and Weston-on-Trent *Derby* from 87; Chapl Aston Hall Hosp Derby from 87. *The Rectory, Rectory Gardens, Aston-on-Trent, Derby DE7 2AZ* Derby (0332) 792658

MUNRO, Donald Alexander. b 08. Clifton Th Coll. d 46 p 47. V Kilmington *B & W* 69-83; rtd 84; Perm to Offic *B & W* from 84. *182 Harepath Road, Seaton, Devon EX12 2HE* Seaton (0297) 20567

MUNRO, Duncan John Studd. b 50. Magd Coll Ox BA72 MA76. Wycliffe Hall Ox 73. d 76 p 77. C Ecclesall *Sheff* 76-77; C Sheff St Barn and St Mary 78-80; Lic to Offic from 80. *70 Dobcroft Road, Sheffield S7 2LS* Sheffield (0742) 363101

MUNRO, Canon Louis Cecil Garth. b 16. Leeds Univ BA40. Coll of Resurr Mirfield 40. d 42 p 43. V Forton *Portsm* 55-81; rtd 81; Perm to Offic *Portsm* from 81. *7 St Helens Road, Alverstoke, Gosport, Hants PO12 2RL* Gosport (0705) 585494

MUNRO, Terence George. b 34. Jes Coll Cam BA56 MA60. Linc Th Coll 59. d 61 p 62. C Far Headingley St Chad *Ripon* 61-64; Jamaica 64-70; R Methley w Mickletown *Ripon* 70-79; V Hunslet Moor St Pet and St Cuth 79-85; R Barwick in Elmet from 85. *The Rectory, Barwick in Elmet, Leeds LS15 4JR* Leeds (0532) 812218

MUNT, Cyril. b 27. AKC52. d 53 p 54. C Ashford *Cant* 53-56; C Dorking w Ranmore *Guildf* 56-60; R Cheriton w Newington *Cant* 60-68; R Harbledown 68-83; R Porlock w Stoke Pero *B & W* from 83. *The Rectory, Porlock, Minehead, Somerset TA24 8QL* Porlock (0643) 862208

MUNT, Canon Donald James. b 20. ALCD53 St Jo Coll Nottm LTh74. d 53 p 54. V Deptford St Pet *S'wark* 69-76; R Litcham w Kempston w E and W Lexham *Nor* 76-83; P-in-c Mileham 81-83; P-in-c Beeston next Mileham 81-83; P-in-c Stanfield 81-83; R Litcham, Kempston, Lexham, Mileham, Beeston etc 84-87; RD Brisley and Elmham 85-87; Hon Can Nor Cathl 87-88; rtd 88; Perm to Offic *Nor* from 88. *7 Irwin Close, Reepham, Norwich NR10 4EQ* Norwich (0603) 870618

MUNT, Canon Neil. b 20. AKC43. Linc Th Coll 43. d 44 p 45. V Godmanchester *Ely* 62-74; Hon Can Ely Cathl 74-86; V Ely 74-86; V Prickwillow 76-86; V Chettisham 76-86; RD Ely 82-86; rtd 86; Perm to Offic *Ely* from 86. *8A Wood Street, Doddington, March, Cambs PE15 0SA* March (0354) 740738

MURCH, Robin Norman. b 37. Wells Th Coll. d 67 p 68. C Wisbech St Aug *Ely* 67-70; C Basingstoke *Win* 70-73; C Whitstable All SS *Cant* 73-76; V Queenborough from 76. *The Vicarage, North Road, Queenborough, Kent ME11 5ET* Sheerness (0795) 662648

MURDIN, Frank Laurence. b 11. Leeds Univ BA34. Coll of Resurr Mirfield 34. d 36 p 37. V Greetham w Stretton and Clipsham *Pet* 65-76; rtd 76. *48 Pinewood Close, Bourne, Lincs PE10 9RL* Bourne (0778) 3696

MURDOCH, Alexander Edward Duncan. b 37. Oak Hill Th Coll 68. d 71 p 72. C Kensington St Helen w H Trin *Lon* 71-72; C Kensington St Barn 73-74; CF 74-78; C W Kirby St Bridget *Ches* 78-84; V N Shoebury *Chelmsf* 84-87; V W Poldens *B & W* from 87. *The Vicarage, Holy*

Well Road, Edington, Bridgwater, Somerset TA7 9LE Bridgwater (0278) 722055

MURDOCH, David John. b 58. Birm Univ BSocSc81. Ripon Coll Cuddesdon 81. d 84 p 85. C Penwortham St Leon *Blackb* 84-87; C Wirksworth w Alderwasley, Carsington etc *Derby* 87-89; R Shirland from 89. *The Rectory, Shirland, Derby DE5 6BB* Alfreton (0773) 836003

MURFET, Edward David. b 36. Qu Coll Cam BA59 MA63. Chich Th Coll 59. d 61 p 62. C Croydon St Mich *Cant* 61-64; C Hunslet St Mary and Stourton *Ripon* 64-65; C Hackney Wick St Mary of Eton w St Aug *Lon* 65-69; Chapl Bern *Eur* 69-71; Chapl Naples 71-74; Chapl Rome 74-77; Lic to Offic *Bris* 78-81; Gen Sec CEMS 81-86; C Leeds St Pet *Ripon* 87-89; P-in-c 89-90; P-in-c Leeds City from 91. *16 Oatland Green, Leeds LS7 1SN* Leeds (0532) 441696

MURFET, Gwyn. b 44. Linc Th Coll 71. d 74 p 75. C Scalby w Ravenscar and Staintondale *York* 74-77; P-in-c S Milford 77-83; R 83-84; V Kirkby Ireleth *Carl* from 84. *The Vicarage, School Road, Kirkby-in-Furness, Cumbria LA17 7UQ* Kirkby-in-Furness (0229) 89256

MURGATROYD, Canon Eric. b 17. Open Univ BA77. Lich Th Coll 43. d 46 p 46. V Cottingley *Bradf* 66-77; Hon Can Bradf Cathl 77-83; V Woodhall 77-83; rtd 83; Perm to Offic *Bradf* from 83. *34 Ferncliffe Drive, Baildon, Shipley, W Yorkshire BD17 5AQ* Bradford (0274) 594072

MURPHY, Alexander Charles. b 28. d 55 p 56. NSM Edin St Jas *Edin* 88-90; TV Edin St Mark from 90; TV Edin St Andr and St Aid from 90. *House of St Aidan, Duddingston Park South, Edinburgh EH15 3EH* 031-669 4756

MURPHY, David. b 14. Lon Univ BA50 BD52. d 49 p 50. V Haverton Hill *Dur* 67-73; V W Pelton 73-82; rtd 82. *8 St Helier's Way, Stanley, Co Durham DH9 0UR* Stanley (0207) 230639

MURPHY, Jack. b 27. N Ord Course 83. d 86 p 87. C St Bart Armley w St Mary New Wortley *Ripon* 86-90; C Hawksworth Wood from 90. *St Andrew's House, Butcher Hill, Leeds LS16 5BG* Leeds (0532) 784560

MURPHY, Canon John Gervase Maurice Walker. b 26. LVO. TCD BA52 MA55. d 52 p 53. C Lurgan Ch Ch *D & D* 52-55; CF 55-73; Asst Chapl Gen 73-77; V Ranworth w Panxworth *Nor* 77-79; RD Blofield 79; Dom Chapl to HM The Queen 79-87; Chapl to HM The Queen from 87; R Sandringham w W Newton *Nor* 79-87; RD Heacham and Rising 85-87; Hon Can Nor Cathl 86-87; Chapl Intercon Ch Soc 87-91; Falkland Is 87-91; Miss to Seamen 87-91. *Saffron Close, 17 Ringstead Road, Heacham, King's Lynn, Norfolk PE31 7JA*

MURPHY, Maurice Vincent. b 49. Van Mildert Coll Dur BSc70. d 85 p 86. NSM Malpas *Mon* 85-86; Perm to Offic *Man* from 86. *18 Higher Ridings, Bromley Cross, Bolton BL7 9HP*

MURPHY, Peter Frederick. b 40. AKC65. d 67 p 68. C Paddington St Jo w St Mich *Lon* 67-72; P-in-c Basingstoke *Win* 72-76; TV 76-81; V Hythe from 81. *The Vicarage, 14 Atheling Road, Hythe, Southampton SO4 6BR* Hythe (0703) 842461

MURPHY, Philip John Warwick. b 65. Kent Univ BA87. Chich Th Coll 88. d 91. C Broadstone *Sarum* from 91. *1A Mission Road, Broadstone, Poole, Dorset BH18 8JJ* Broadstone (0202) 603840

MURPHY, Ronald Frederick. b 38. d 84 p 85. P-in-c N Cerney w Bagendon *Glouc* 87-90. *70 Tattershall, Toot Hill, Swindon* Swindon (0793) 694870

MURPHY, Thomas. b 20. TCD BA56 MA64 Div Test. CITC 57. d 57 p 58. I Newtownhamilton w Ballymoyer and Belleek *Arm* 63-76; Hon VC Arm Cathl from 69; I Sixmilecross w Termonmaguirke 76-90; rtd 90. *6 Wyndway Court, Windmill, Carrickfergus, Co Antrim BT38 8HX* Carrickfergus (09603) 64893

MURPHY, William Albert. b 43. Lon Univ BD73 QUB MTh78. d 73 p 74. C Lisburn Ch Ch *Conn* 73-79; Supt & Chapl Ulster Inst for the Deaf from 79; Chapl HM Pris Belf (Maze) from 82. *42 Plantation Avenue, Lisburn, Co Antrim BT27 5BL* Lisburn (0846) 677816

MURRAY, Alan. b 37. Sarum Th Coll 62. d 64 p 65. C High Elswick St Phil *Newc* 64-68; C Seaton Hirst 68-74; V Seghill from 74. *The Vicarage, Seghill, Cramlington, Northd NE23 7EA* 091-237 1601

MURRAY, Christopher James. b 49. Open Univ BA78. St Jo Coll Nottm 79. d 81 p 82. C Heatherlands St Jo *Sarum* 81-84; C Hamworthy 84-90; R Passenham *Pet* from 90. *The Rectory, Deanshanger, Milton Keynes MK19 6JP* Milton Keynes (0908) 262371

MURRAY, David McIlveen. b 36. ALCD61. d 61 p 62. C Mortlake w E Sheen *S'wark* 61-64; C Lyncombe *B & W*

64-67; C Horsham *Chich* 67-73; V Devonport St Bart *Ex* 73-79; R Chalfont St Peter *Ox* from 79; RD Amersham 86-89. *The Vicarage, 4 Austen Way, Chalfont St Peter, Gerrards Cross, Bucks SL9 8NW* Gerrards Cross (0753) 882389

MURRAY, Gordon Stewart. b 33. Birkb Coll Lon BSc72. Ripon Coll Cuddesdon 76. **d** 78 **p** 79. C Kenilworth St Nic *Cov* 78-81; V Potterspury w Furtho and Yardley Gobion *Pet* 81-83; V Potterspury, Furtho, Yardley Gobion and Cosgrove 84; TV Wolvercote w Summertown *Ox* 84-90; P-in-c Walworth *S'wark* from 90. *St Peter's Rectory, Liverpool Grove, London SE17 2HH* 071-703 3139

MURRAY, Hugh Peter William. b 13. Ox Univ MA47. Cuddesdon Coll 75. **d** 75 **p** 75. NSM Coln St Aldwyn w Hatherop and Quenington *Glouc* 75-81; Perm to Offic from 81. *Millfield, Ablington, Coln St Aldwyns, Cirencester, Glos GL7 5AN* Coln St Aldwyns (028575) 372

MURRAY, Ian Hargraves. b 48. Man Univ BSc71. St Jo Coll Nottm 79. **d** 81 **p** 82. C Erith St Paul *Roch* 81-84; C Willenhall H Trin *Lich* 84-87; TV from 87. *18 Heather Grove, Willenhall, W Midlands* Willenhall (0902) 631498

MURRAY, Ian William. b 32. Lon Univ BA53 PGCE54. Oak Hill NSM Course 80. **d** 83 **p** 84. NSM Pinner *Lon* from 83. *4 Mansard Close, West End Lane, Pinner, Middx HA5 3FQ* 081-866 2984

MURRAY, Canon John Desmond. b 16. TCD BA38 MA46. CITC 39. **d** 39 **p** 40. I Milltown *D & G* 70-82; Can Ch Ch Cathl Dub 79-82; rtd 82. *3 Adare Close, Killincarrig, Greystones, Co Wicklow, Irish Republic* Dublin (1) 287-6359

MURRAY, John Douglas. b 16. Keble Coll Ox BA38 MA46. Bps' Coll Cheshunt 38. **d** 40 **p** 41. Tutor St Pet Coll of Educn Birm 50-78; Lic to Offic *Birm* 50-79; P-in-c Streat w Westmeston *Chich* 79-86; rtd 81; Perm to Offic *Birm* from 87. *104 Sunnybank Road, Sutton Coldfield, W Midlands B73 5RL* 021-354 9488

MURRAY, Canon John Grainger. b 45. CITC 67. **d** 70 **p** 71. C Carlow *C & O* 70-72; C Limerick St Mary *L & K* 72-77; I Rathdowney w Castlefleming, Donaghmore etc *C & O* from 77; Preb Leighlin Cathl 83-88; Chan 89-90; Prec from 90; Preb Ossory Cathl 83-88; Chan 89-90; Prec from 90. *Rathdowney, Portlaoise, Co Laois, Irish Republic* Rathdowney (505) 46311

MURRAY, John Louis. b 47. Keble Coll Ox BA67 MA69. **d** 82 **p** 83. Asst Chapl Strasbourg *Eur* from 82. *c/o Eglise des Peres Dominicains, rue de l'Universite, 67000 Strasbourg, France* France (33) 88 36 12 25

MURRAY, John Thomas. b 33. Edin Th Coll 63. **d** 66 **p** 67. C Golcar *Wakef* 66-70; Guyana 70-74; Hon C Paddington St Mary Magd *Lon* 80-82; Asst Chapl Athens St Paul w Kyfissia *Eur* 82-83; Chapl Br Emb Ankara 83-85; R Johnstone *Glas* from 86. *St John's Rectory, Floors Street, Johnstone, Renfrewshire PA5 8QS* Johnstone (0505) 20623

MURRAY, Mrs Margaret Janice. b 46. Carl Dioc Tr Course. **dss** 86 **d** 87. Walney Is *Carl* 86-87; Hon Par Dn 87-89; Par Dn Carl H Trin and St Barn from 89. *Sandsfield Vicarage, 104 Housesteads Road, Carlisle CA2 7XG* Carlisle (0228) 36710

MURRAY, Paul Ridsdale. b 55. BEd. St Steph Ho Ox. **d** 83 **p** 84. C Hartlepool St Oswald *Dur* 83-86; C S Shields All SS 86-88; V Sacriston and Kimblesworth from 88. *The Vicarage, 1A Church Parade, Sacriston, Durham DH7 6AD* 091-371 1853

MURRAY, William Robert Craufurd. b 44. St Chad's Coll Dur BA66 DipTh68. **d** 68 **p** 69. C Workington St Mich *Carl* 68-71; C Harrogate St Wilfrid *Ripon* 71-74; P-in-c Sawley 74; V Winksley cum Grantley and Aldfield w Studley 74; R Fountains 74-81; New Zealand from 81. *St Barnabas's Vicarage, 7 Makora Street, Fendalton, Christchurch 4, New Zealand* Christchurch (3) 351-7064

MURRAY-LESLIE, Adrian John Gervase. b 46. Lich Th Coll 67. **d** 69 **p** 70. C Sheff St Cuth *Sheff* 69-73; C Mosborough 73-75; C-in-c Mosborough CD 75-80; Warden Champion Ho Youth Cen Edale from 80; P-in-c Edale *Derby* from 80. *The Vicarage, Edale, Sheffield S30 2ZA* Hope Valley (0433) 70254

MURRAY-STONE, Albert Edmund Angus. b 14. Immanuel Coll Ibadan 58. **d** 68 **p** 68. P-in-c Boscastle w Davidstow *Truro* 78-81; V Falmouth All SS 81-83; rtd 83. *23 Golden Park Avenue, Barton, Torquay* Torquay (0803) 315312

MURRELL, Canon John Edmund. b 28. Westcott Ho Cam. **d** 66 **p** 67. C Ivychurch w Old Romney and Midley *Cant* 66-70; R Bardwell *St E* 70-75; Perm to Offic *Ely* 75-77; V Wenhaston w Thorington and Bramfield w Walpole *St E* 77-86; V Thorington w Wenhaston and

Bramfield from 86; P-in-c Walberswick w Blythburgh from 86; RD Halesworth 85-90; Hon Can St E Cathl from 89. *The Vicarage, Walberswick, Southwold, Suffolk IP18 6UN* Southwold (0502) 722118

MURRIE, Clive Robert. b 44. Ripon Coll Cuddesdon. **d** 79 **p** 80. C Kenton Ascension *Newc* 79-80; C Prudhoe 80-83; V Burnopfield *Dur* 83-87; R Stella from 87. *The Rectory, Shibdon Road, Blaydon-on-Tyne, Tyne & Wear NE21 5AE* 091-414 2720

MURSELL, Alfred Gordon. b 49. ARCM75 BNC Ox BA70 MA73 BD87. Cuddesdon Coll 71. **d** 73 **p** 74. C Walton St Mary *Liv* 73-77; V E Dulwich St Jo *S'wark* 77-86; Tutor Sarum Th Coll from 87. *68A The Close, Salisbury SP1 2EN* Salisbury (0722) 330125

MUSGRAVE, Canon James Robert Lord. b 20. TCD BA43 MA51. **d** 44 **p** 45. C Belf St Andr *Conn* 44-46; C Derriaghy 46-51; R Duneane w Ballyscullion 51-54; I Belf St Steph 54-64; I Magheragall 64-85; Can Conn Cathl 82-85; Bp's C Killead w Gartree from 87. *61 Crumlin Road, Aldergrove, Crumlin, Co Antrim BT29 4AQ* Crumlin (08494) 53532

MUSGRAVE-BROWN, Canon Christopher Taylor Musgrave. b 99. Em Coll Cam BA21 MA27. Wycliffe Hall Ox 25. **d** 27 **p** 28. R Hasketon *St E* 60-69; rtd 69; Lic to Offic *St E* from 69; Chapl W Suffolk Hosp 70-79. *58 Rembrandt Way, Bury St Edmunds, Suffolk IP33 2LT* Bury St Edmunds (0284) 753710

MUSHEN, Canon Francis John. b 34. Birm Univ BA60. Ripon Hall Ox 60. **d** 62 **p** 63. C Foleshill St Laur *Cov* 62-65; C Halesowen *Worc* 65-69; V Stourbridge Norton St Mich 69-81; Hon Can Worc Cathl from 81; P-in-c Bromsgrove St Jo 81-87; V from 87. *The Vicarage, 12 Kidderminster Road, Bromsgrove, Worcs B61 7LW* Bromsgrove (0527) 76517

MUSK, Dr Bill Andrew. b 49. Ox Univ BA70 MA75 Univ of S Africa D Litt et Phil84 Lon Univ DipTh73. Fuller Th Sem California ThM80 Trin Coll Bris DipTh81. **d** 81 **p** 82. Egypt 81-86; CMS 88-89; TV Maghull *Liv* from 89. *1 St Peter's Row, Moorhey Road, Liverpool L31 5LU* 051-526 3434

MUSKETT, David John. b 63. Southn Univ BA85. Ripon Coll Cuddesdon 87. **d** 90 **p** 91. C Kempston Transfiguration *St Alb* from 90. *16 Rosedale Way, Kempston, Bedford MK42 8JE* Bedford (0234) 854861

MUSPRATT, Oscar. b 06. Ridley Coll Melbourne ThL29. **d** 29 **p** 30. V Penn *Ox* 45-89; rtd 90. *2 Penn Mead, Church Road, Penn, High Wycombe, Bucks HP10 8NY* Penn (049481) 6031

MUSSELWHITE, Edward Charles. b 15. **d** 64 **p** 65. V Bream *Glouc* 66-75; R Dowdeswell and Andoversford w the Shiptons etc 75-77; rtd 78; Perm to Offic *B & W* from 80. *13 Channel Heights, Bleadon, Weston-super-Mare, Avon BS24 9LX* Bleadon (0934) 812566

MUSSON, David John. b 46. Open Univ BA86. Linc Th Coll 70. **d** 73 **p** 74. C New Sleaford *Linc* 73-76; C Morton 76-80; P-in-c Thurlby 80-86; P-in-c Silk Willoughby from 86; R Quarrington w Old Sleaford from 86. *The Rectory, 77 Grantham Road, Quarrington, Sleaford, Lincs NG34 7NP* Sleaford (0529) 306776

MUSSON, Dr John Keith. b 39. CEng MIMechE Nottm Univ BSc61 PhD66. St As Minl Tr Course 85. **d** 88 **p** 89. Assoc Prin NE Wales Inst of HE from 80; Hon C Holywell *St As* from 88. *29 The Beeches, Holywell, Clwyd CH8 7SW* Holywell (0352) 713894

MUSSON, William (John). b 58. UMIST BSc80. St Jo Coll Nottm 88. **d** 91. C Nantwich *Ches* from 91. *22 Beatty Road, Nantwich, Cheshire CW5 5JP* Nantwich (0270) 623620

MUST, Albert Henry. b 27. Clifton Th Coll 61. **d** 63 **p** 64. C Becontree St Mary *Chelmsf* 63-68; V Highbury Vale St Jo *Lon* 68-78; V Highbury New Park St Aug 78-84; V Walthamstow St Jo *Chelmsf* from 84. *St John's Vicarage, Brookscroft Road, London E17 4LH* 081-527 3262

MUST, Mrs Shirley Ann. b 35. St Mich Ho Ox 61. **dss** 82 **d** 87. Highbury New Park St Aug *Lon* 82-84; Walthamstow St Jo *Chelmsf* 84-87; Hon Par Dn from 87. *St John's Vicarage, Brookscroft Road, London E17 4LH* 081-527 3262

MUSTOE, Alan Andrew. b 52. Man Univ BA74. Qu Coll Birm DipTh77. **d** 78 **p** 79. C Chatham St Wm *Roch* 78-82; R Burham and Wouldham 82-88; Dioc Info Officer 83-88; V Strood St Nic w St Mary from 88. *The Vicarage, 3 Central Road, Strood, Rochester, Kent ME2 3HF* Medway (0634) 719052

MUSTON, David Alan. b 33. Nottm Univ BA60. Ridley Hall Cam 62. **d** 64 **p** 65. C Tankersley *Sheff* 64-67; C Goole 67-70; Sec Ind Cttee of Gen Syn Bd for Soc Resp 70-76; Ind Chapl *Win* 77-79; V Leigh St Mary *Man*

79-83; R Otham w Langley *Cant* from 83. *The Rectory, Church Road, Otham, Maidstone, Kent ME15 8SB* Maidstone (0622) 861470

MUTCH, Miss Sylvia Edna. b 36. St Mich Ho Ox 57. **dss** 79 **d** 87. Clifton *York* 79-87; Par Dn from 87. *5 Manor Park Close, Shipton Road, York YO3 6UZ* York (0904) 24241

MUXLOW, Canon George. b 19. Qu Coll Birm. **d** 55 **p** 56. R Oakdale St Geo *Sarum* 63-82; TR 82-84; rtd 84. *9 Cuthburga Road, Wimborne, Dorset BH21 1LH* Wimborne (0202) 887940

MYATT, Andrew William Gilchrist. b 62. Wycliffe Hall Ox 85. **d** 88 **p** 89. C Cogges *Ox* 88-91; C S Leigh 88-91; Vineyard Ministries from 91. *53 Dupont Road, London SW20 8EH* 081-543 6907

MYATT, Edwin Henry. b 54. MA. Ripon Coll Cuddesdon. **d** 84 **p** 85. C W Bromwich St Fran *Lich* 84-88; C Sedgley All SS from 88. *16 Browning Road, The Straits, Lower Gornal, Dudley, W Midlands* Sedgley (09073) 77451

MYATT, Philip Bryan. b 29. Wycliffe Hall Ox 54. **d** 57 **p** 58. C Fareham St Jo *Portsm* 57-61; C Westgate St Jas *Cant* 61-64; R Woodchester *Glouc* 64-70; R Bath Walcot *B & W* 70-91; R The Edge, Pitchcombe, Harescombe and Brookthorpe *Glouc* from 91. *The Rectory, Edge, Stroud, Glos GL6 6PF* Painswick (0452) 812319

MYCOCK, Geoffrey John Arthur. b 22. Open Univ BA76. St Deiniol's Hawarden 76. **d** 77 **p** 78. Hon C Ches H Trin *Ches* 77-79; Bp's Dom Chapl 79-80; P-in-c Hargrave 79-80; V Sandbach Heath 80-82; Chapl and Lect St Deiniol's Lib Hawarden 82-85; V Holt *St As* 85-90; rtd 90. *20 Eaton Close, Broughton, Chester CH4 0RF* Chester (0244) 531214

MYERS, Canon Arnold George. b 23. Keble Coll Ox BA44 DipTh46 MA48. St Steph Ho Ox. **d** 47 **p** 48. R W Derby St Mary *Liv* 62-79; TR 79-84; RD W Derby 71-78; rtd 84; Perm to Offic *Liv* from 84. *10 Surrey Drive, West Kirby, Wirral, Merseyside L48 2HP* 051-625 2250

MYERS, Duncan Frank. b 57. Warw Univ BSc. St Jo Coll Nottm. **d** 84 **p** 85. C Upton cum Chalvey *Ox* 84-86; C Farnborough *Guildf* 86-90; Chapl Nottm Poly *S'well* from 90. *3 Carisbrooke Drive, Mapperley, Nottingham NG3 5DS* Nottingham (0602) 605447

MYERS, John Bulmer. b 19. Worc Ord Coll 64. **d** 66 **p** 67. NSM Huddersfield St Jo *Wakef* 74-76; C 76-79; V Cornholme 79-88; rtd 88. *284 Burnley Road, Todmorden, Lancs OL14 8EW* Todmorden (0706) 812224

MYERS, Paul Henry. b 49. ALA72. Qu Coll Birm 74. **d** 77 **p** 78. C Baildon *Bradf* 77-80; C W Bromwich All SS *Lich* 80-83; Chapl RAF 83-86; V Milton *Lich* from 87. *The Vicarage, Baddeley Green Lane, Milton, Stoke-on-Trent ST2 7EY* Stoke-on-Trent (0782) 534062

MYERS, Peter John. b 60. St Jo Coll Dur BA81. Linc Th Coll CMM84. **d** 84 **p** 85. C Bulwell St Mary *S'well* 84-88; C Shrewsbury H Cross *Lich* from 88. *52 Canon Street, Cherry Orchard, Shrewsbury SY2 5HQ* Shrewsbury (0743) 69692

MYERSCOUGH, Robin Nigel. b 44. K Coll Lon BD69. Coll of Resurr Mirfield. **d** 81 **p** 82. Hon C Diss *Nor* 81-84; Asst Chapl Sedbergh Sch Cumbria 84-85; Chapl Dur Sch from 85. *7 Pimlico, Durham DH1 4QW* 091-384 3664

MYHILL, Christopher John. b 47. Oak Hill Th Coll DipHE79. **d** 79 **p** 80. C Stanford-le-Hope w Mucking *Chelmsf* 79-82; C Leyton St Luke 82-87; V Chatteris *Ely* from 87. *The Vicarage, Church Lane, Chatteris, Cambs PE16 6JA* Chatteris (03543) 2173

MYLES, Peter Rodney. b 42. K Coll Lon 61 St Aug Coll Cant 70. **d** 71 **p** 72. C Tideswell *Derby* 71-74; C W Brompton St Mary w St Pet *Lon* 74-79; P-in-c Notting Hill St Pet 79-82; Chapl to Bp Kensington 82-87; C Kensington St Mary Abbots w St Geo from 82; P-in-c St Geo Campden Hill from 82. *25 Campden Hill Square, London W8 7JY* 071-727 9486

MYLNE, Canon Angus Fletcher. b 99. CCC Ox BA22 MA30. Westcott Ho Cam 25. **d** 27 **p** 28. C Petersfield w Sheet *Portsm* 27-30; S Africa from 30; Hon Can Natal from 66. *18 Taylor Road, Scottsville, Pietermaritzburg, 3201 South Africa* Pietermaritzburg (331) 460718

MYLNE, Denis Colin. b 31. Jordan Hill Coll Glas CYCW75. Kelham Th Coll 69. **d** 71. Perm to Offic Glas 74-84; Ab 84-88; C Bedf All SS *St Alb* 88-91; C Harpenden St Jo from 91. *2 Linwood Road, Harpenden, Herts AL5 1RR* Harpenden (0582) 767551

MYNETT, Colin. b 25. Roch Th Coll 61. **d** 63 **p** 64. R Lifton *Ex* 66-71; R Kelly w Bradstone 66-71; TV Devonport St Aubyn 71-75; V Cinderford St Jo *Glouc* 75-84; P-in-c Pittville 84-89; rtd 89. *5 Heron Close,*

Hatherley, Cheltenham, Glos GL51 6HA Cheltenham (0242) 523341

MYNETT, John Alan. b 37. CEng MIMechE67 Bris Univ BSc59 MSc61. N Ord Course 82. **d** 85 **p** 86. NSM Poynton *Ches* 85-90; NSM Macclesfield Team Par from 90. *46 Barber Street, Macclesfield SK11 7HT* Macclesfield (0625) 614103

MYNORS, James Baskerville. b 49. Peterho Cam BA70 MA74. Ridley Hall Cam 70 St Jo Coll Nottm 77. **d** 78 **p** 80. Hon C Leic H Apostles *Leic* 78-79; C Virginia Water *Guildf* 79-83; C Patcham *Chich* 83-88; Sen Tutor E Anglian Minl Tr Course 88-90; Vice-Prin from 90; P-in-c Fowlmere *Ely* from 88; P-in-c Thriplow from 88. *The Rectory, Fowlmere, Royston, Herts SG8 7SU* Fowlmere (076382) 8195

N

NADEN, Anthony Joshua. b 38. Jes Coll Ox BA62 MA64 SOAS Lon PhD73. Wycliffe Hall Ox 60. **d** 62 **p** 63. C Rowner *Portsm* 62-66; C Fisherton Anger *Sarum* 70-72; Ghana from 72. *PO Box 3, Walewale, NR Ghana*

NADERER, Gordon Kenneth Charles Maximilian. b 14. Wycliffe Hall Ox. **d** 44 **p** 45. R Rodmell w Southease *Chich* 54-74; V Westham 74-83; rtd 83; Perm to Offic *Chich* from 83. *65 Church Lane, South Bersted, Bognor Regis, W Sussex PO22 9QA* Bognor Regis (0243) 866885

NADIN, Dennis Lloyd. b 37. St D Coll Lamp BA60 Man Univ MEd81. Ridley Hall Cam 63. **d** 64 **p** 65. C Childwall All SS *Liv* 64-67; C Seacroft *Ripon* 67-69; Project Officer Grubb Inst 69-70; Lect CA Tr Coll Blackheath 70-72; Community Educn Essex Co Coun 73-80; Public Preacher *Chelmsf* from 73. *79 Bishopsfield, Harlow, Essex CM18 6UH* Harlow (0279) 430176

NADKARNI, Edward Wasant. b 41. Trin Coll Cam BA64 MA67. Cuddesdon Coll 68. **d** 69 **p** 70. C E Ham St Mary *Chelmsf* 69-71; C Hertf St Andr *St Alb* 71-74; Chapl for Educn Bedf Deanery 74-78; Chapl Lanc Univ *Blackb* 78-83. *Address temp unknown*

NAGEL, Lawson Chase Joseph. b 49. ARHistS75 Michigan Univ BA71 K Coll Lon PhD82. Sarum & Wells Th Coll. **d** 83 **p** 84. C Chiswick St Nic w St Mary *Lon* 83-86; Sec Gen Confraternity of the Blessed Sacrament from 85; V Horsham *Chich* 86; TV 86-91; OStJ from 89; V Aldwick *Chich* from 91. *The Vicarage, 25 Gossamer Lane, Aldwick, Bognor Regis, W Sussex PO21 3AT* Pagham (0243) 262049

NAIDU, Michael Sriram. b 28. Univ of the South (USA) 81. Ridley Hall Cam 86. **d** 80 **p** 85. Acting Chapl Stuttgart *Eur* from 85. *Stiftswaldstrasse 15, 7000 Stuttgart 80, Germany* Stuttgart (711) 682849

NAIRN, Frederick William. b 43. TCD 64. Luther NW Th Sem DMin88. **d** 67 **p** 68. C Larne and Inver *Conn* 67-70; Chapl RAF 70-74; P-in-c Harmston *Linc* 75-77; V 77-84; V Coleby 78-84; USA from 84. *4900 Nathan Lane, Plymouth, Minnesota 55442, USA*

NAIRN, Stuart Robert. b 51. K Coll Lon BD75 AKC75. St Aug Coll Cant 75. **d** 76 **p** 77. C E Dereham *Nor* 76-80; TV Hempnall 80-88; V Narborough w Narford from 88; V Pentney w W Bilney from 88; RD Lynn from 91. *The Vicarage, Narborough, King's Lynn, Norfolk PE32 1TE* Narborough (0760) 338552

NAIRN-BRIGGS, George Peter. b 45. AKC69. St Aug Coll Cant 69. **d** 70 **p** 71. C Catford St Laur *S'wark* 70-73; C Raynes Park St Sav 73-75; V Salfords 75-81; V St Helier 81-87; Dioc Soc Resp Adv *Wakef* from 87. *21 Willow Park, Wakefield, W Yorkshire WF1 2JP or, Church House, Wakefield, W Yorkshire WF1 1LP* Wakefield (0924) 824393 or 371802

NAISH, Timothy James Neville. b 57. St Jo Coll Ox BA80 MA88. W Midl Minl Tr Course 86. **d** 87 **p** 88. C Cov H Trin *Cov* 87; CMS from 88; Zaire from 88. *c/o PO Box 22037, Kitwe, Zambia*

NAISMITH, Mrs Carol. b 37. St Andr Univ MA59. Edin Dioc NSM Course 85. **d** 90. NSM Edin Old St Paul *Edin* from 90. *38 Castle Avenue, Edinburgh EH12 7LB* 031-334 4486

NANCARROW, Mrs Rachel Mary. b 38. Cam Inst of Educn TCert59. E Anglian Minl Tr Course 87. **d** 90. NSM Girton *Ely* from 90. *1 Oakington Road, Girton, Cambridge CB3 0QH* Cambridge (0223) 232693

NANKIVELL, Christopher Robert Trevelyan. b 33. Jes Coll Ox BA55 MA63. Linc Th Coll 56. **d** 58 **p** 59. C

Bloxwich *Lich* 58-60; C Stafford St Mary 60-64; P-in-c Malins Lee 64-72; Soc Welfare Sector Min to Milton Keynes Chr Coun 73-76; Lect Qu Coll Birm 76-81. *424 King's Road, Birmingham B44 0UJ*   021-354 6520

NAPIER, Charles John Lenox. b 29. Univ Coll Ox BA52 MA57. Philosophical and Th Coll of Soc of Jes Louvain STL60. **d** 60 **p** 60. In RC Ch 60-63; C Illogan *Truro* 63-66; Tutor Lon Coll of Div 66-70; Tutor St Jo Coll Nottm 70-73; TV S Molton w Nymet St George *Ex* 73-75; TV S Molton, Nymet St George, High Bray etc 75-80; R Drewsteignton from 80; V Hittisleigh from 80; V Spreyton from 80. *The Rectory, Drewsteignton, Exeter EX6 6QW*   Drewsteignton (0647) 227

NAPLEY, David John. b 13. S'wark Ord Course 65. **d** 68 **p** 69. C Hurst Green *S'wark* 68-71; C Ham St Andr 71-74; TV Quidenham w Eccles and Snetterton *Nor* 74-77; P-in-c Earsham 77-79; R Earsham w Alburgh and Denton 79-83; rtd 83; Perm to Offic Nor from 84; St E 87-88. *2 Waveney Road, Ditchingham, Bungay, Suffolk NR35 2RF*   Bungay (0986) 2233

NARUSAWA, Masaki Alec. b 53. K Coll Lon BD77 AKC77. Linc Th Coll 77. **d** 78 **p** 79. C Hendon St Alphage *Lon* 78-81; C Eastcote St Lawr 81-84; V Glodwick *Man* from 84. *St Mark's Vicarage, 1 Skipton Street, Oldham OL8 2JF*   061-624 4964

NASH, Alan Frederick. b 46. Sarum & Wells Th Coll 72. **d** 75 **p** 76. C Foley Park *Worc* 75-79; P-in-c Mildenhall *Sarum* 79-82; Dioc Youth Officer 79-82; TV N Wingfield, Pilsley and Tupton *Derby* 82-85; Perm to Offic 85-87. *The Vicarage, Ankerbold Road, Tupton, Chesterfield, Derbyshire S42 6DX*   Chesterfield (0246) 862410

NASH, Brian John. b 54. St Jo Coll Dur BSc75. St Jo Coll Nottm 77. **d** 80 **p** 81. C Birm St Luke *Birm* 80-84; C Bucknall and Bagnall *Lich* 84; TV from 84. *St John's Parsonage, 28 Greasley Road, Stoke-on-Trent ST2 8JE*   Stoke-on-Trent (0782) 542861

NASH, David. b 25. K Coll Lon BD51 AKC51. **d** 52 **p** 53. R Rivenhall *Chelmsf* 66-83; P-in-c Boscastle w Davidstow *Truro* 83-85; TR 85-90; rtd 90. *9 Boscundle Avenue, Golden Bank, Falmouth TR11 5BU*

NASH, David John. b 41. Pemb Coll Ox BA64 MA70. Wells Th Coll 65. **d** 67 **p** 68. C Preston Ascension *Lon* 67-70; TV Hackney *S'well* 70-75; TV Clifton *S'well* 76-82; V Winchmore Hill St Paul *Lon* from 82; AD Enfield from 87. *St Paul's Vicarage, Church Hill, London N21 1JA*   081-886 3545

NASH, Paul Alexander. b 20. Glouc Th Course 73. **d** 76 **p** 76. NSM Coleford w Staunton *Glouc* 76-88. *16 Orchard Road, Coombs Park, Coleford, Glos GL16 8AU*   Dean (0594) 32758

NASH, Reginald Frank. b 15. **d** 66 **p** 67. P-in-c Sharpness *Glouc* 69-75; V Dymock w Donnington 75-77; R Dymock w Donnington and Kempley 77-80; rtd 80; Perm to Offic *Glouc* from 80. *31 Woodview Road, Cam, Dursley, Glos GL11 5RJ*   Dursley (0453) 546731

NASH, Richard Edward. b 10. Westcott Ho Cam 54. **d** 56 **p** 57. V Eridge Green *Chich* 68-72; R Winterborne Came *Sarum* 73-75; P-in-c Stinsford 73-75; rtd 75. *7 Herbert Terrace, Wookey Hole Road, Wells, Somerset BA5 2NN*   Wells (0749) 75306

NASH, Robin Louis. b 51. Open Univ BA87. Chich Th Coll 82. **d** 84 **p** 85. C Lymington *Win* 84-86; C Andover w Foxcott 86-90; R Kegworth *Leic* from 90. *The Rectory, 24 Nottingham Road, Kegworth, Derby DE7 2FH*   Kegworth (0509) 672349

NASH, Ven Trevor Gifford. b 30. Clare Coll Cam BA53 MA57. Cuddesdon Coll 53. **d** 55 **p** 56. C Cheshunt *St Alb* 55-57; CF (TA) 56-67; C Kingston All SS *S'wark* 57-61; C Stevenage *St Alb* 61-63; V Leagrave 63-67; Dir Luton Samaritans 66-67; Chapl St Geo Hosp Gp Lon 67-73; R Win St Lawr and St Maurice w St Swithun *Win* 73-82; Bp's Adv Min of Healing from 73; P-in-c Win H Trin 77-82; RD Win 78-82; Hon Can Win Cathl from 80; Adn Basingstoke 82-90; Acorn Trust Exec Co-ord from 90. *The Corner Stone, 50B Hyde Street, Winchester, Hants SO23 7DY*   Winchester (0962) 861759

NASH, William Henry. b 31. Oak Hill Th Coll 58. **d** 61 **p** 62. C New Milverton *Cov* 61-64; C Toxteth Park St Philemon w St Silas *Liv* 64-67; V Bryn 67-76; NW Area Sec CPAS 76-82; V Penn Fields *Lich* from 82. *St Philip's Vicarage, Church Road, Bradmore, Wolverhampton WV3 7EN*   Wolverhampton (0902) 341943

NASH, William Paul. b 48. St Mich Coll Llan 86. **d** 87 **p** 88. C Pemb Dock *St D* 87-89; P-in-c Llawhaden w Bletherston and Llan-y-cefn 89-90; V from 90. *The Vicarage, Llanwhaden, Narberth, Dyfed SA67 8DS*   Llanwhaden (09914) 225

NASH, William Warren. b 09. TCD BA35 MA58. CITC 36. **d** 36 **p** 38. I Aghadrumsee *Clogh* 51-74; rtd 74. *Strathmore, 45 Mulberry Green, Harlow, Essex CM17 0EY*

NASH-WILLIAMS, Piers le Sor Victor. b 35. Trin Hall Cam BA57 MA61. Cuddesdon Coll 59. **d** 61 **p** 62. C Milton *Win* 61-64; Asst Chapl Eton Coll Windsor 64-66; Perm to Offic *Chich* 66-68; C Furze Platt *Ox* 69-72; V Newbury St Geo Wash Common 72-73; TV Newbury 73-91; R Ascot Heath from 91. *The Rectory, Ascot Heath, Ascot, Berks SL5 8DQ*   Ascot (0344) 21200

NASON, David. b 44. ACA68 FCA78. Ripon Coll Cuddesdon 84. **d** 86 **p** 87. C Banstead *Guildf* 86-89; PV Chich Cathl *Chich* from 89; Chapl Prebendal Sch Chich from 89. *1 St Richard's Walk, Canon Lane, Chichester, W Sussex PO19 1QA*   Chichester (0243) 775615

NATERS, Charles James Reginald. b 20. Selw Coll Cam BA45 MA47. Coll of Resurr Mirfield 46. **d** 47 **p** 48. SSJE from 54; S Africa 59-68; Lic to Offic *Ox* 69-76; Lon 76-85 and from 88; Leic from 85; rtd 90; Superior Gen SSJE from 91. *St Edward's House, 22 Great College Street, London SW1P 3QA*   071-222 9234

NATHANAEL, Brother. *See* THOMPSON, Nathanael

NATHANAEL, Martin Moses. b 43. Lon Univ BEd73 K Coll Lon MTh77. Ripon Coll Cuddesdon 77. **d** 79 **p** 80. C Hampton All SS *Lon* 79-82; P-in-c Kensal Town St Thos w St Andr and St Phil 82-83; Hd of Div Bishop Stopford Sch London 83-91; TV Tring *St Alb* from 91. *The Vicarage, Watery Lane, Wilstone, Tring, Herts HP23 4PH*   Tring (044282) 3008

NATHANIEL, Ivan Wasim. Punjab Univ MA65. Bp's Coll Calcutta 59. **d** 62 **p** 64. India 62-68; C Newland St Aug *York* 68-70; Hon C Crawley *Chich* from 70; Chapl H Trin Sch Crawley from 70. *8 Lincoln Close, Tilgate, Crawley, W Sussex RH10 5ET*   Crawley (0293) 546644

NATTRASS, Michael Stuart. b 41. Man Univ BA62. Cuddesdon Coll 62. **d** 64 **p** 65. C Easington Colliery *Dur* 64-65; C Silksworth 65-68; Perm to Offic *S'well* 68-72; Lic Dur 72-76; Perm Lon 76-78; Hon C Pinner *Lon* from 78. *81 Cecil Park, Pinner, Middx HA5 5HL*   081-866 0217

NAUMANN, Canon David Sydney. b 26. Ripon Hall Ox 54. **d** 55 **p** 56. Dioc Youth Chapl *Cant* 63-70; Warden St Gabr Retreat Ho Westgate 68-70; V Littlebourne 70-82; RD E Bridge 78-82; Hon Can Cant Cathl from 81; R Sandwich 82-91; RD Sandwich 85-90; rtd 91. *2 The Forrens, The Precincts, Canterbury, Kent CT1 2ER*   Canterbury (0227) 458939

NAUNTON, Hugh Raymond. b 38. Open Univ BA75. Chich Th Coll 60. **d** 63 **p** 64. C Stanground *Ely* 63-66; Perm to Offic *S'wark* 66-78; Hon C Cheam Common St Phil from 79; Perm to Offic *Guildf* from 82. *35 Farm Way, Worcester Park, Surrey KT4 8RZ*   081-330 6303

NAYLOR, Frank. b 36. Lon Univ BA58 Liv Univ MA63. NW Ord Course 73. **d** 75 **p** 76. NSM Eccleston Ch Ch *Liv* from 75. *27 Daresbury Road, Eccleston, St Helens, Merseyside WA10 5DR*   St Helens (0744) 57034

NAYLOR, Frederick. b 11. St Aug Coll Cant 34. **d** 38 **p** 39. V Bishop Burton *York* 66-77; rtd 78. *2 York Road, Bishop Burton, Beverley, N Humberside*   Hornsea (0964) 550226

NAYLOR, Ian Frederick. b 47. AKC70. St Aug Coll Cant 70. **d** 71 **p** 72. C Camberwell St Giles *S'wark* 71-74; OSB 74-86; Chapl RN from 86. *c/o MOD, Lacon House, Theobald's Road, London WC1X 8RY*   071-430 6847

NAYLOR, James Barry. b 50. Lon Univ BSc71 St Benet's Hall Ox BA75. Wycliffe Hall Ox 72. **d** 76 **p** 76. C Catford (Southend) and Downham *S'wark* 76-79; TV 79-82; P-in-c Lewisham St Swithun 82-87; V E Dulwich St Jo from 87; RD Dulwich from 90. *St John's Vicarage, 62 East Dulwich Road, London SE22 9AU*   071-639 3807

NAYLOR, Miss Jean. b 29. Linc Th Coll 77. **dss** 79 **d** 87. Charlton St Luke w H Trin *S'wark* 79-84; Crofton Park St Hilda w St Cypr 84-87; Par Dn 87-89; rtd 89. *12 Winter Terrace, Barnsley, S Yorkshire S75 2ES*   Barnsley (0226) 204767

NAYLOR, John Watson. b 26. Trin Hall Cam BA52 MA56. Ripon Hall Ox 64. **d** 66 **p** 67. C Otterburn w Elsdon and Horsley w Byrness *Newc* 69-72; R Husborne Crawley w Ridgmont *St Alb* 72-76; Chapl Caldicott Sch Farnham Royal 76-80; P-in-c Chollerton w Thockrington *Newc* 80-82; P-in-c Birtley 82; R Chollerton w Birtley and Thockrington 82-91; rtd 91. *Abbeyfield House, Bellingham, Hexham, Northd NE48 2BS*   Hexham (0434) 220106

NAYLOR, Canon Peter Aubrey. b 33. Kelham Th Coll 54 Ely Th Coll 57. **d** 58 **p** 59. C Shepherd's Bush St Steph *Lon* 58-62; C Portsea N End St Mark *Portsm*

62-66; Chapl HM Borstal Portsm 64-66; V Foley Park *Worc* 66-74; V Maidstone All SS w St Phil and H Trin *Cant* 74-81; P-in-c Tovil 79-81; V Maidstone All SS and St Phil w Tovil 81-91; Hon Can Cant Cathl from 79; RD Sutton 80-86; R Biddenden and Smarden from 91. *The Rectory, Biddenden, Ashford, Kent TN27 8AN* Biddenden (0580) 291454

NAYLOR, Peter Edward. b 30. Linc Th Coll 58. **d** 61 **p** 62. C S Beddington St Mich *S'wark* 61-64; V S Lambeth St Ann 64-77; V Nork *Guildf* 77-90; R Ecton *Pet* from 90; Warden Ecton Ho from 90. *23 West Street, Ecton, Northampton NN6 0QE* Northampton (0604) 416322

NAYLOR, Peter Henry. b 41. MIMechE HND64. Chich Th Coll 64. **d** 67 **p** 68. C Filton *Bris* 67-70; C Brixham *Ex* 70-72; C Leckhampton St Pet *Glouc* 72-76; V Brockworth from 76; P-in-c Gt Witcombe from 91. *The Vicarage, 42 Court Road, Brockworth, Gloucester GL3 4ET* Gloucester (0452) 862725

NAYLOR, Robert James. b 42. Liv Univ CQSW66. N Ord Course 74. **d** 77 **p** 78. C Aigburth *Liv* 77-80; Soc Resp Officer *Glouc* 80-85; Leonard Cheshire Foundn (Lon) from 85. *The Hobbit, High Street, Winfrith, Newburgh, Dorchester, Dorset DT2 8JN* Warmwell (0305) 853705

NAYLOR, Russell Stephen. b 45. Leeds Univ BA70 St Chad's Coll Dur DipTh72. Ho of Resurr Mirfield 64. **d** 72 **p** 73. C Chapel Allerton *Ripon* 72-75; Ind Chapl *Liv* 75-81; P-in-c Burtonwood 81-83; V from 83. *The Vicarage, Chapel Lane, Burtonwood, Warrington WA5 4PT* Newton-le-Willows (0925) 225371

NAYLOR, Stanley. b 29. NW Ord Course 76. **d** 79 **p** 80. NSM Girlington *Bradf* 79-80; C Tong 80-83; C Ingrow cum Hainworth 83-85; P-in-c Bradf St Clem from 85. *St Clement's Vicarage, Barkerend Road, Bradford, W Yorkshire BD3 8QX* Bradford (0274) 737699

NAZER, Raymond. b 20. St Chad's Coll Dur LTh42 BA43. Edin Th Coll 39. **d** 43 **p** 44. V Ipswich All Hallows *St E* 62-72; V Castle Acre w Newton *Nor* 72-84; R Southacre 72-84; P-in-c Rougham 82-84; rtd 84; Perm to Offic *Nor* from 84. *12 Malsters Close, Mundford, Thetford, Norfolk IP26 5HJ* Thetford (0842) 878329

✠**NAZIR-ALI, Rt Rev Dr Michael James.** b 49. Karachi Univ BA70 St Edm Hall Ox BLitt74 MLitt81 Fitzw Coll Cam MLitt76. ACT PhD83 Ridley Hall Cam 70. **d** 74 **p** 76 **c** 84. Tutorial Supervisor Th Cam Univ 74-76; C Cam H Sepulchre w All SS *Ely* 74-76; Pakistan 76-86; Sen Tutor Karachi Th Coll 76-81; Provost Lahore 81-84; Bp Raiwind 84-86; Asst to Abp Cant 86-89; Co-ord of Studies and Ed Lambeth Conf 88; Hon C Ox St Giles and SS Phil and Jas w St Marg *Ox* 86-89; Hon C Limpsfield and Titsey *S'wark* from 89; Gen Sec CMS from 89; Asst Bp S'wark from 89. *c/o CMS, Partnership House, 157 Waterloo Road, London SE1 8UU* 071-928 8681

NEAL, Alan. b 27. Trin Coll Bris DipTh84. **d** 84 **p** 85. Hon C Broughty Ferry *Bre* 84-85; P-in-c Dundee St Ninian 85-86; R Annan *Glas* from 86; R Lockerbie from 86. *The Rectory, St Bryde's Terrace, Lockerbie, Dumfriesshire DG11 2EJ* Lockerbie (05762) 2484

NEAL, Anthony Terrence. b 42. BA CertEd. Chich Th Coll 65. **d** 68 **p** 69. C Cross Green St Sav and St Hilda *Ripon* 68-73; NSM Hawksworth Wood 73-78; Asst Chapl and Hd of RE Abbey Grange High Sch Leeds 73-81; NSM Farnley *Ripon* 78-81; Dioc Adv in RE *Truro* 81-85; Children's Officer 85-87; P-in-c St Erth 81-84; V from 84; Stewardship Adv 87-88. *The Vicarage, 43 School Lane, St Erth, Hayle, Cornwall TR27 6HN* Hayle (0736) 753194

NEAL, Christopher Charles. b 47. St Pet Coll Ox BA69. Ridley Hall Cam 69. **d** 72 **p** 73. C Addiscombe St Mary *Cant* 72-76; C Camberley St Paul *Guildf* 76-83; TV 83-86; V Thame w Towersey *Ox* from 86. *The Vicarage, Lashlake Lane, Thame, Oxon OX9 3AB* Thame (084421) 2225

NEAL, Geoffrey Martin. b 40. AKC63. **d** 64 **p** 65. C Wandsworth St Paul *S'wark* 64-66; USA 66-68; C Reigate St Mark *S'wark* 68-70; P-in-c Wandsworth St Faith 70-72; V 72-75; V Houghton Regis *St Alb* from 75. *The Vicarage, Bedford Road, Houghton Regis, Dunstable, Beds LU5 5DJ* Luton (0582) 867593

NEAL, John Edward. b 44. Nottm Univ BTh74. Linc Th Coll 70. **d** 74 **p** 75. C Lee St Marg *S'wark* 74-77; C Clapham St Jo 77; C Clapham Ch Ch and St Jo 77-81; P-in-c Eltham St Barn 81-83; V from 83; Sub-Dean of Eltham from 89. *St Barnabas' Vicarage, 449 Rochester Way, London SE9 6PH* 081-856 8294

NEALE, Alan James Robert. b 52. LSE BSc(Econ)73 Ox Univ BA76 MA81. Wycliffe Hall Ox 74. **d** 77 **p** 78. C Plymouth St Andr w St Paul and St Geo *Ex* 77-80; C Portswood Ch Ch *Win* 80-82; V Stansted Abbots *St Alb*

82-85; Asst Master Chelmsf Hall Sch Eastbourne 85-88; USA from 88. *34 John Street, Newport, Rhode Island 02840, USA* Newport (401) 849-3431 or 846-0660

NEALE, David. b 50. Lanchester Poly BSc72. St Mich Coll Llan BD83. **d** 83 **p** 84. Min Can St Woolos Cathl *Mon* 83-87; Chapl St Woolos Hosp Newport 85-87; R Blaina and Nantyglo *Mon* 87-91; Video Production Officer Bd of Miss from 91. *Church in Wales Centre, Woodlands Place, Penarth, S Glam CF6 2EX* Penarth (0222) 705278 or 708234

NEALE, Geoffrey Arthur. b 41. Brasted Th Coll 61 St Aid Birkenhead 63. **d** 65 **p** 66. C Stoke *Cov* 65-68; C Fareham H Trin *Portsm* 68-71; TV 71-72; R Binstead 72-77; TR Bottesford w Ashby *Linc* 77-80; V Horncastle w Low Toynton 80-90; V Glanford Bridge 90; V Brigg from 90. *The Vicarage, 10 Glanford Road, Brigg, S Humberside DN20 8DJ* Brigg (0652) 53989

NEALE, James Edward McKenzie. b 38. Selw Coll Cam BA61. Clifton Th Coll 61. **d** 63 **p** 64. C Everton St Ambrose w St Tim *Liv* 63-72; Relig Adv BBC Radio Merseyside 72-76; V Bestwood St Matt *S'well* 76-86; Dioc Urban Officer 86-91; V Nottm St Mary and St Cath from 91. *St Mary's Vicarage, Standard Hill, Nottingham NG1 6GA* Nottingham (0602) 472476

✠**NEALE, Rt Rev John Robert Geoffrey.** b 26. AKC54 St Boniface Warminster 54. **d** 55 **p** 56 **c** 74. C St Helier *S'wark* 55-58; Chapl Ardingly Coll Haywards Heath 58-62; Recruitment Sec CACTM 63-66; ACCM 66-68; Can Missr and Dir Post-Ord Tr 68-74; R Hascombe *Guildf* 68-74; Hon Can Guildf Cathl 68-74; Adn Wilts *Sarum* 74-80; Suff Bp Ramsbury 74-81; Area Bp Ramsbury 81-88; Hon Can Sarum Cathl 74-88; Sec Partnership for World Miss from 89; Asst Bp *S'wark* from 89; Asst Bp Lon from 89. *12 Ambassador Square, Cahir Street, London E14 8RL* 071-538 9841

NEALE, Martyn William. b 57. G&C Coll Cam BA78 MA82. Ripon Coll Cuddesdon 78. **d** 81 **p** 82. C Perry Hill St Geo *S'wark* 81-83; C Purley St Mark Woodcote 83-85; V Abbey Wood from 85. *The Vicarage, 1 Conference Road, London SE2 0YH* 081-311 0377

NEAUM, Canon David. b 12. Lich Th Coll 34. **d** 37 **p** 38. C Burton All SS *Lich* 37-39; C Cannock 39-43; R Kingstone w Gratwich 43-46; R Leigh 46-52; Tristan da Cunha 52-56; S Rhodesia 56-65; Rhodesia 65-80; Zimbabwe 80-81; St Helena 81-84; Australia from 84. *Holy Trinity Rectory, Ararat, Victoria, Australia 3377* Ararat (53) 521109

NEAVE, Garry Reginald. b 51. Leic Univ MA73 PGCE74. S'wark Ord Course DipRS DipPSE. **d** 82 **p** 83. Hon C Harlow St Mary Magd *Chelmsf* from 82; Chapl Harlow Tertiary Coll from 84; Hon C St Mary-at-Latton *Chelmsf* from 87. *College Street, The High, Harlow CM20 1LT* Harlow (0279) 441288

NEECH, Canon Alan Summons. b 15. Dur Univ LTh37. Tyndale Hall Bris 34. **d** 39 **p** 40. BCMS (India) 39-65; Gen Sec BCMS 66-81; Hon C Slough *Ox* 75-81; rtd 80; RD Loddon *Nor* 85-90; Perm to Offic from 90. *The Gardens Cottage, Rockland St Mary, Norwich, Norfolk NR14 7HQ* Surlingham (05088) 519

NEED, Philip Alan. b 54. AKC75. Chich Th Coll 76. **d** 77 **p** 78. C Clapham Ch Ch and St Jo *S'wark* 77-79; C Luton All SS w St Pet *St Alb* 80-83; V Harlow St Mary Magd *Chelmsf* 83-89; P-in-c Chaddesden St Phil *Derby* 89-91; Bp's Dom Chapl *Chelmsf* from 91. *Willowdene, Maldon Road, Margaretting, Ingatestone, Essex CM4 9JW* Ingatestone (0277) 352472

NEEDHAM, George Oswald. b 18. Man Univ BA49. Wycliffe Hall Ox 49. **d** 51 **p** 52. R Thurstaston *Ches* 64-79; rtd 79; Perm to Offic *Ches* from 79. *14 Gills Lane, Barnston, Wirral, Merseyside L61 1AD* 051-648 6732

NEEDHAM, John. b 09. St Jo Coll Dur BA30 MA33 DipTh33. **d** 32 **p** 33. C-in-c Hayton St Jas *Carl* 67-72; V Torpenhow 72-75; rtd 75; Perm to Offic *Carl* from 77. *Priory Close, St Bees, Cumbria CA27 0DR* Egremont (0946) 822572

NEEDHAM, Miss Patricia. b 32. **d** 87. Par Dn Warmsworth *Sheff* 87-89; Par Dn Norton Woodseats St Chad from 89. *14 Dalewood Drive, Sheffield S8 0EA* Sheffield (0742) 362688

NEEDHAM, Peter (Brother Douglas). b 56. Chich Th Coll 86. **d** 88 **p** 88. SSF from 80; C S Moor *Dur* 88-90; Chapl RN from 91. *c/o MOD, Lacon House, Theobald's Road, London WC1X 8RY* 071-430 6847

NEEDLE, Paul Robert. b 45. Lon Univ DipTh70. Oak Hill Th Coll 67. **d** 70 **p** 71. C Gt Horton *Bradf* 70-74; C Pudsey St Lawr 74-77; Chapl St Luke's Hosp Bradf 78-80; Hon C Horton *Bradf* 78-80; NSM Irthlingborough *Pet* 87-90; NSM Gt w Lt Addington from 90. *The*

Rectory, Great Addington, Kettering, Northants NN14 4BS Cranford (053678) 257

NEELY, Dr William George. b 32. Lon Univ BD62 QUB PhD. **d** 56 **p** 57. C Cregagh *D & D* 56-62; C-in-c Mt Merrion 62-68; I 68-76; Dioc Missr (Down) 70-76; Can Down Cathl 74-76; I Kilcooley w Littleton, Crohane and Killenaule *C & O* 76-84; P-in-c Fertagh 79-84; I Keady w Armaghbreague and Derrynoose *Arm* from 84; Tutor for Aux Min (Arm) from 86. *31 Crossmore Road, Keady, Armagh BT60 3JY* Keady (0861) 531230

NEEP, Edwin Phipps. b 18. St Cath Soc Ox BA50 MA54. Ripon Hall Ox 46. **d** 51 **p** 52. V Blagdon *B & W* 58-81; rtd 81. *36 Church Close, Yatton, Bristol BS19 4HG* Yatton (0934) 837225

NEIGHBOUR, William. b 17. Oak Hill Th Coll 48. **d** 50 **p** 51. V Tytherington *Glouc* 62-82; rtd 82. *Mount Pleasant Cottage, Yarcombe Hill, Stockland, Honiton, Devon EX14 9EB* Upottery (040486) 427

NEIL, Richard Wilfred. b 16. Lon Univ DipTh57. Lon Coll of Div 51. **d** 53 **p** 54. V Devonport St Mich Ex 60-81; rtd 81. *22 Park Street, Plymouth PL3 4BL* Plymouth (0752) 558974

NEIL-SMITH, John Christopher. b 20. Pemb Coll Cam BA43 MA46. Westcott Ho Cam 43. **d** 44 **p** 45. V S Hampstead St Sav *Lon* 59-91; rtd 91. *40 Madeley Road, London W5 2LH* 081-991 2971

NEILL, Charles Christopher Stanley. b 33. G&C Coll Cam BA57 MA60. Cuddesdon Coll 65. **d** 66 **p** 67. C Heref St Jo *Heref* 66-67; VC Heref Cathl and Chapl Heref Cathl Sch 67-78; Chapl Abingdon Sch 78-80; TV Wolvercote w Summertown *Ox* 80-84; Chapl St Edw Sch Ox from 80. *34 Oakthorpe Road, Oxford OX2 7BE* Oxford (0865) 58835

NEILL, Canon Erberto Mahon. b 16. TCD BA40 MA Div Test. **d** 39 **p** 40. I Castleknock w Mulhuddart, Clonsilla etc *D & G* 61-75; I Dub Harold's Cross 77-81; I Boyle Union *K, E & A* 81-87; Preb Elphin Cathl 83-87; rtd 87. *124 Avondale Road, Killiney, Co Dublin, Irish Republic* Dublin (1) 285-3707

NEILL, Very Rev Ivan Delacherois. b 12. CB63 OBE58. Jes Coll Cam BA35 MA38. Lon Coll of Div 35. **d** 36 **p** 37. Provost Sheff 66-74; Perm to Offic *Glouc* 74-86; rtd 77; Perm to Offic S'wark from 86. *Greathed Manor, Dormansland, Lingfield, Surrey RH7 6PA* Lingfield (0342) 833992

NEILL, James Purdon. b 41. Lon Univ DipTh63. Oak Hill Th Coll 60. **d** 64 **p** 65. C Kendal St Thos *Carl* 64-68; Chapl Park Hill Flats Sheff 68-71; P-in-c Mansf St Jo S'well 71-77; V Nottm St Ann w Em from 77. *St Ann's Vicarage, 17 Robin Hood Chase, Nottingham NG3 4EY* Nottingham (0602) 505471

✠**NEILL, Rt Rev John Robert Winder.** b 45. TCD BA66 MA69 Jes Coll Cam BA68 MA72. Ridley Hall Cam 67. **d** 69 **p** 70 c 86. C Glenageary *D & G* 69-71; Lect CITC 70-71 and 82-84; Bp's V, Lib and Chapter Registrar Kilkenny Cathl 71-74; Dioc Registrar (Ossory, Ferns and Leighlin) *C & O* 71-74; I Abbeystrewry *C, C & R* 74-78; I Dub St Bart w Ch Ch Leeson Park *D & G* 78-84; Dean Waterford *C & O* 84-86; Adn Waterford 84-86; Prec Lismore Cathl 84-86; I Waterford w Killea, Drumcannon and Dunhill 84-86; Bp T, K & A from 86; Dean Achonry from 86. *Bishop's House, Crossmolina, Co Mayo, Irish Republic* Ballina (96) 31317

NEILL, Robert Chapman. b 51. Lon Univ BD82. CITC 77. **d** 77 **p** 78. C Lurgan (Shankill) *D & D* 77-82; I Tullylish 82-88; I Mt Merrion from 88. *The Rectory, 122 Mount Merrion Avenue, Belfast BT6 0FS* Belfast (0232) 644308

NEILL, Ven William Barnet. b 30. TCD BA61. **d** 63 **p** 64. C Belf St Clem *D & D* 63-66; C Dundonald 66-72; I Drumgath 72-80; I Drumgooland 76-80; I Mt Merrion 80-83; I Dromore Cathl from 83; Adn Dromore from 85. *28 Church Street, Dromore, Co Down BT25 1AA* Dromore (0846) 692275

NEILL, Very Rev William Benjamin Alan. b 46. Open Univ BA76. CITC 68. **d** 71 **p** 72. C Dunmurry *Conn* 71-74; C Coleraine 75-77; C Dub St Ann w St Steph *D & G* 77-78; I Convoy w Monellan and Donaghmore *D & R* 78-81; I Faughanvale 81-86; I Waterford w Killea, Drumcannon and Dunhill *C & O* from 86; Dean Waterford from 86; Prec Lismore Cathl from 86; Prec Cashel Cathl from 87. *The Deanery, 41 Grange Park Road, Waterford, Irish Republic* Waterford (51) 74119

NEILSON, John William. b 12. AKC35. **d** 35 **p** 37. V Lympne w Hythe *Cant* 45-82; rtd 82; Perm to Offic *Cant* from 82. *Homeleigh, 6 Harman Avenue, Lympne, Kent* Hythe (0303) 268394

NELLIST, Mrs Valerie Ann. b 48. SRN69 SCM71. St And Dioc Tr Course 87. **d** 90. NSM Inverkeithing *St And* from 90. *28 Glamis Gardens, Dalgety Bay, Dunfermline, Fife KY11 5TD* Dalgety Bay (0383) 824066

NELSON, Canon Allen James. b 29. CITC 53. **d** 55 **p** 56. C Glenageary *D & G* 55-57; C Dub Clontarf 57-60; I Bailieborough w Mullagh *K, E & A* 60-75; P-in-c Knockbride 66-72; P-in-c Knockbride w Shercock 72-75; I Julianstown w Colpe *M & K* 75-81; I Julianstown and Colpe w Drogheda and Duleek from 81; Dioc Glebes Sec from 81; Can Meath from 84. *The Rectory, Eastham Road, Bettystown, Co Meath, Irish Republic* Drogheda (41) 27345

NELSON, Christopher James. b 57. Preston Poly HNC80 Nottm Univ BTh88. Aston Tr Scheme 83 St Jo Coll Nottm 85. **d** 88 **p** 89. C Blackpool St Thos *Blackb* 88-90; C Altham w Clayton le Moors from 90. *1 Oakfield Avenue, Clayton le Moors, Accrington, Lancs BB5 5XG* Accrington (0254) 231227

NELSON, Frank. b 12. Jes Coll Ox BA35 MA40 Lon Univ BSc44. Ox NSM Course. **d** 78 **p** 78. NSM Sutton Courtenay w Appleford *Ox* 78-89. *6 Tullis Close, Sutton Courtenay, Abingdon, Oxon OX14 4BD* Abingdon (0235) 848567

NELSON, Graham William. b 61. Birm Univ CYCW85. St Jo Coll Nottm BA91. **d** 91. C Pype Hayes *Birm* from 91. *11 Varley Road, Birmingham B24 0LB* 021-382 6169

NELSON, Kenneth Edmund. b 10. St Jo Coll Cam BA33 MA36. Qu Coll Birm 46. **d** 47 **p** 48. R Crayke w Brandsby and Yearsley *York* 68-78; rtd 78. *Flat 1, Holly Mount, 23B Ripon Road, Harrogate, N Yorkshire HG1 2JL* Harrogate (0423) 568460

NELSON, Michael. b 44. Lon Univ BD66. Coll of Resurr Mirfield 66. **d** 68 **p** 69. C Newbold and Dunston *Derby* 68-72; C N Gosforth *Newc* 72-77; V Seaton Hirst 77-83; V Blyth St Mary from 83; P-in-c Horton 86-87; RD Bedlington from 88. *St Mary's Vicarage, 51 Marine Terrace, Blyth, Northd NE24 2JP* Blyth (0670) 353417

NELSON, Canon Nelson John. b 21. Ripon Hall Ox 64. **d** 65 **p** 66. V W Smethwick *Birm* 68-90; RD Warley 79-86; Hon Can Birm Cathl from 83; rtd 90. *68 Pembroke Way, Stourport-on-Severn, Worcs DY13 8QZ* Stourport (02993) 2821

NELSON, Paul John. b 52. Nottm Univ BCombStuds84. Linc Th Coll 81. **d** 84 **p** 85. C Waltham Cross *St Alb* 84-87; C Sandridge 87-90; V from 90. *The Vicarage, 2 Anson Close, House Lane, Sandridge, St Albans, Herts AL4 9EN* St Albans (0727) 66089

NELSON, Ralph Archbold. b 27. St Cuth Soc Dur BA50. Bps' Coll Cheshunt 50. **d** 52 **p** 53. C Penwortham St Mary *Blackb* 52-57; C Eglingham *Newc* 57-58; V Featherstone *Wakef* 58-80; V Kirkham *Blackb* from 80; RD Kirkham 88-91. *The Vicarage, Kirkham, Preston PR4 2SE* Kirkham (0772) 683644

NELSON, Robert Gibson. b 34. ALCD61. **d** 61 **p** 62. Australia 69-72; V Guernsey St Jo *Win* 72-78; R Guernsey Ste Marie du Castel 78-86; V Guernsey St Matt 84-86; rtd 86. *Le Petit Feugre, Clos des Mielles, Castel, Guernsey, Channel Islands* Guernsey (0481) 52726

NELSON, Robert Towers. b 43. MSOSc Liv Coll of Tech BSc65. NW Ord Course 76. **d** 79 **p** 80. NSM Liv Our Lady and St Nic w St Anne *Liv* 79-83; NSM Liscard St Thos *Ches* 83-87; P-in-c from 87; Dioc Ind Missr from 87; Asst Sec SOSc from 89. *5 Sedbergh Road, Wallasey, Merseyside L44 2BR* 051-630 2830

NELSON, William. b 38. Oak Hill Th Coll 74. **d** 76 **p** 77. C Hensingham *Carl* 76-81; V Widnes St Paul *Liv* 81-89; R Higher Openshaw *Man* from 89. *St Clement's Rectory, Ashton Old Road, Manchester M11 1HJ* 061-370 1538

NENER, Dr Thomas Paul Edgar. b 42. FRCSEd71 FRCS71 Liv Univ MB, ChB. Coll of Resurr Mirfield 78. **d** 80 **p** 81. C Warrington St Elphin *Liv* 80-83; V Haydock St Jas from 83. *169 Church Road, Haydock, St Helens, Merseyside WA11 0NJ* Ashton-in-Makerfield (0942) 727956

NENO, David Edward. b 62. SS Mark & Jo Coll Plymouth BA85. Ripon Coll Cuddesdon 85. **d** 88 **p** 89. C Chapel Allerton *Ripon* 88-91; C Acton St Mary *Lon* from 91. *39 Derwent Water Road, London W3 6DF* 081-992 7514

NESBITT, Charles Howard. b 09. St Jo Coll Dur LTh34 BA35. Bp Wilson Coll 31. **d** 35 **p** 36. V Stalmine *Blackb* 68-74; rtd 75. *Sunnyside Eventide Home, 75 South Oswald Road, Edinburgh EH9 2HH* 031-667 6831

NESBITT, Charles Maurice Grillet. b 09. Univ Coll Lon BA31. St Geo Windsor. **d** 50 **p** 51. V Harlesden All So *Lon* 63-74; rtd 74; Perm to Offic *Bris* 74-81 and from

83; Hon C Bris St Paul w St Barn 81-83; Hon C Bris St Agnes and St Simon w St Werburgh 81-83. *5 Ryland Place, St Werburghs, Bristol BS2 9YZ* Bristol (0272) 555921

NESBITT, Heather Hastings. b 48. S'wark Ord Course 88. **d** 90. Par Dn Camberwell St Luke *S'wark* from 90. *122 Farnborough Way, London SE15 6HL* 071-701 4766

NESBITT, Ronald. b 58. Sheff Univ LLB TCD DipTh85. CITC 82. **d** 85 **p** 86. C Ballymena w Ballyclug *Conn* 85-88; C Holywood *D & D* 88-90; I Helen's Bay from 90. *2 Woodland Avenue, Helens Bay, Bangor, Co Down BT19 1TX* Helens Bay (0247) 853601

NESBITT, William Ralph. b 17. MBIM. Lambeth STh83 Sarum Th Coll 70. **d** 70 **p** 71. C Ilford *Win* 70-76; Hon C Southbourne St Kath from 76; Hon C Southbourne St Chris from 76; Hon C Pokesdown All SS from 76. *6 Foxholes Road, Bournemouth BH6 3AS* Bournemouth (0202) 425164

NESHAM, George Dove. b 20. ALCD50. Lon Coll of Div. **d** 50 **p** 51. V W Ardsley *Wakef* 62-77; V Ripponden 77-80; V Satley *Dur* 80-87; RD Stanhope 81-87; rtd 87. *29 Ettrick Road, Jarrow, Tyne & Wear NE32 5SL* 091-489 8071

NESHAM, Robert Harold. b 15. **d** 68 **p** 69. C Upton St Leonards *Glouc* 68-72; V Poulton 72-73; P-in-c Down Ampney 72-73; V Down Ampney w Poulton 73-84; rtd 84. *Church Cottage, Cricklande Street, Poulton, Cirencester, Glos GL7 5HX* Cirencester (0285) 851528

NETHERWOOD, Mrs Anne Christine. b 43. ARIBA68 Liv Univ BArch66. St Deiniol's Hawarden 88. **d** 91. NSM Ellesmere and Welsh Frankton *Lich* from 91. *2 White Cottage, Perthy, Ellesmere, Shropshire SY12 9HR* Ellesmere (0691) 622582

NEUDEGG, Mrs Joan Mary. b 36. Cant Sch of Min 81. **dss** 84 **d** 87. Chalk *Roch* 84-86; Hon C Dean Forest H Trin *Glouc* 87-90; Hon C Woolaston w Alvington from 90. *The Rectory, Main Road, Alvington, Lydney, Glos GL15 6AT* Netherend (059452) 387

NEUDEGG, Leslie. b 35. Lon Univ DipRS83 Open Univ BA84. S'wark Ord Course 77. **d** 80 **p** 81. Hon C Chalk *Roch* 80-86; Area Org CECS 86-89; P-in-c Woolaston w Alvington *Glouc* from 89. *The Rectory, Main Road, Alvington, Lydney, Glos GL15 6AT* Netherend (059452) 387

NEVELL, Frederick George. b 24. Lon Univ BA51. Oak Hill Th Coll 46. **d** 51 **p** 52. V W Kilburn St Luke w St Simon and St Jude *Lon* 64-73; V Clapham Common St Barn *S'wark* 73-90; rtd 90. *19 Bolton Road, Folkestone, Kent CT19 5RX* Folkestone (0303) 41428

NEVILL, James Michael. b 50. Cranmer Hall Dur. **d** 86 **p** 87. C Sowerby Bridge w Norland *Wakef* 86-91; CF from 91. *c/o MOD (Army), Bagshot Park, Bagshot, Surrey GU19 5PL* Bagshot (0276) 71717

NEVILLE, Alfred John. b 21. K Coll Lon BA40. Sarum & Wells Th Coll. **d** 83 **p** 84. NSM Weston-super-Mare St Paul *B & W* from 83. *12 Woodford Court, 21 Clarence Road North, Weston-super-Mare, Avon BS23 4AW* Weston-super-Mare (0934) 631176

NEVILLE, David Bruce. b 61. Ravensbourne Coll of Art & Design BA83. St Jo Coll Nottm LTh89. **d** 91. C Broxtowe *S'well* from 91. *33 Blandford Road, Chilwell, Nottingham NG9 4GY* Nottingham (0602) 228442

NEVILLE, Canon Graham. b 22. CCC Cam BA47 MA49 CertEd. Chich Th Coll 48. **d** 50 **p** 51. Chapl Sutton Valence Sch Kent 68-73; Six Preacher Cant Cathl *Cant* 69-78; Prin Lect Relig Studies Eastbourne Coll of Educn 73-80; Dir of Educn *Linc* 80-87; Can and Preb Linc Cathl 82-88; rtd 87; Perm to Offic *Linc* from 88. *16 Silverdale Avenue, Worcester WR5 1PY* Worcester (0905) 360319

NEVILLE, Michael Robert John. b 56. Hatf Coll Dur BA80 Cam Univ CertEd81. Wycliffe Hall Ox 82. **d** 85 **p** 86. C E Twickenham St Steph *Lon* 85-88; Proclamation Trust from 88. *11 Upper Wimpole Street, London W1M 7TD* 071-935 7158

NEVIN, Ronald. b 32. DMin88. Linc Th Coll 63. **d** 64 **p** 65. C Norton St Mary *Dur* 64-66; R Cockfield 66-70; USA from 70. *Box 96, Claymont, Delaware 19703, USA* Wilmington (302) 798-6683

NEW, David John. b 37. Lon Univ BSc58. Chich Th Coll 65. **d** 67 **p** 68. C Folkestone St Mary and St Eanswythe *Cant* 67-72; C Kings Heath *Birm* 72-74; V S Yardley St Mich 74-83; V Moseley St Agnes from 83. *St Agnes' Vicarage, 5 Colmore Crescent, Birmingham B13 9SJ* 021-449 0368

NEW, Derek. b 30. **d** 86 **p** 87. NSM Brondesbury St Anne w Kilburn H Trin *Lon* from 86. *20 Lynton Road, London NW6 6BL* 071-328 0187

NEW, John Bingley. b 29. Lon Univ BD70. Chich Th Coll 77. **d** 77 **p** 78. C Sholing CD *Win* 77-79; C Sholing 79; V Micheldever and E Stratton, Woodmancote etc 79-91; rtd 91. *Duffield, Church Road, Kings Somborne, Stockbridge, Hants SO20 6NX* Romsey (0794) 388406

NEW, Philip Harper. b 08. St Jo Coll Dur LTh32 BA33. St Aid Birkenhead 29. **d** 33 **p** 34. R Beckingham *S'well* 69-73; P-in-c Walkeringham 69-73; rtd 73; Perm to Offic *S'well* from 73. *17 Muir Avenue, Tollerton, Nottingham NG12 4EZ* Plumtree (06077) 5406

NEW, Canon Thomas Stephen. b 30. K Coll Cam BA52 MA56. Cuddesdon Coll 52. **d** 54 **p** 55. C Greenford H Cross *Lon* 54-55; C Old St Pancras w Bedf New Town St Matt 55-58; C Woodham *Guildf* 58-64; V Guildf All SS 64-72; V Banstead from 72; RD Epsom 76-80; Hon Can Guildf Cathl from 79; Sub-Chapl HM Pris Downview from 88. *The Vicarage, Court Road, Banstead, Surrey SM7 2NQ* Burgh Heath (0737) 351134

NEWALL, Arthur William. b 24. Univ of Wales (Lamp) BA49. Chich Th Coll 49. **d** 51 **p** 52. R Foots Cray *Roch* 68-78; V Henlow *St Alb* 78-89; rtd 89. *38 Fairhaven Road, Southport, Merseyside PR9 9UH* Southport (0704) 26045

NEWALL, Richard Lucas. b 43. AKC66. **d** 66 **p** 67. C Roby *Liv* 66-69; C Douglas St Geo and St Barn *S & M* 69-71; Lic to Offic *Man* 72-75; C Ban St Mary *Ban* 75-77; R Newborough w Llangeinwen from 77. *Newborough Rectory, Anglesey, Gwynedd LL61 6RP* Newborough (024879) 285

NEWARK, Archdeacon of. *Vacant*

NEWBON, Eric. b 23. Fitzw Ho Cam BA51 MA55. Ridley Hall Cam 51. **d** 53 **p** 54. V Southport All So *Liv* 65-85; rtd 85; Perm to Offic *Ches* from 86. *33 Haymakers Way, Saughall, Chester CH1 6AR* Saughall (0244) 880123

NEWBON, Kenneth. b 29. Wells Th Coll 67. **d** 69 **p** 70. C Church Stretton *Heref* 69-72; P-in-c Cressage w Sheinton 72-75; R Braunstone *Leic* 75-81; TR 81-84; P-in-c Eardisley w Bollingham and Willersley *Heref* 84-88; P-in-c Brilley w Michaelchurch on Arrow 84-88; P-in-c Whitney w Winforton 84-88; RD Kington and Weobley from 87; R Eardisley w Bollingham, Willersley, Brilley etc from 88. *The Rectory, Church Street, Eardisley, Hereford HR3 6LB* Eardisley (05446) 440

NEWBURY, Canon Robert. b 22. St D Coll Lamp BA46. **d** 48 **p** 49. V Manselton *S & B* 63-84; V Manselton w Hafod 84-90; Hon Can Brecon Cathl from 85; rtd 91. *4 Cobham Close, Gorseinon, Swansea SA4 2FA* Swansea (0792) 654848

NEWBY, Peter Gordon. b 23. **d** 64 **p** 65. R Lt Bowden St Nic *Leic* 69-72; V Jersey Gouray St Martin *Win* 72-77; Chapl Jersey Gp of Hosps 78-80; R Much Birch w Lt Birch, Much Dewchurch etc *Heref* 80-88; rtd 89; Perm to Offic *Ex* from 90. *18 Woodfields, Seaton, Devon EX12 2UX* Seaton (0297) 24562

NEWCASTLE, Bishop of. *See* GRAHAM, Rt Rev Andrew Alexander Kenny

NEWCASTLE, Provost of. *See* COULTON, Very Rev Nicholas Guy

NEWCOMBE, Kenneth Harry. b 27. Ridley Hall Cam 70. **d** 72 **p** 73. C Melton Mowbray w Thorpe Arnold *Leic* 72-78; P-in-c W Bridgford *S'well* 78-84; V Radcliffe-on-Trent 84-85; V Shelford 84-85; P-in-c Holme Pierrepont w Adbolton 84-85; R Radcliffe-on-Trent and Shelford etc from 85. *The Rectory, Radcliffe-on-Trent, Nottingham NG12 2FB* Radcliffe-on-Trent (0602) 332203

NEWCOMBE, Timothy James Grahame. b 47. AKC75. St Aug Coll Cant 75. **d** 76 **p** 77. C Heref St Martin *Heref* 76-79; C Hitchin *St Alb* 79-85; R Croft and Stoney Stanton *Leic* 85-91; P-in-c Launceston *Truro* from 91. *St Mary's Vicarage, Dunheved Road, Launceston, Cornwall PL15 9JE* Launceston (0566) 772974

NEWCOME, James William Scobie. b 53. Trin Coll Ox BA74 MA78 Selw Coll Cam BA77 MA81. Ridley Hall Cam 75. **d** 78 **p** 79. C Leavesden All SS *St Alb* 78-82; P-in-c Bar Hill LEP *Ely* from 82; Tutor Ridley Hall Cam 83-88. *108 Stonefield, Bar Hill, Cambridge CB3 8TE* Crafts Hill (0954) 81629

NEWELL, Aubrey Francis Thomas. b 20. St D Coll Lamp BA43. **d** 45 **p** 46. V Gawcott and Hillesden *Ox* 62-77; P-in-c Radclive 69-72; RD Buckm 70-76 and 82-84; P-in-c Padbury w Adstock 72-77; V Lenborough 77-87; rtd 87. *5 Church View, Steeple Claydon, Buckingham MK18 2QR* Steeple Claydon (029673) 8271

NEWELL, Christopher David. b 53. Lon Univ DipRS87. S'wark Ord Course 84. **d** 87 **p** 88. C Stockwell St Mich *S'wark* 87-90; Chapl Asst R Lon Hosp (Mile End and Whitechapel) from 90. *The Chaplain's Office, The Royal London Hospital, London E1 1BB* 071-377 7000 or 377 7385

NEWELL, Jack Ernest. b 26. CEng FIChemE ARCS BSc. Glouc Th Course 80. **d** 83 **p** 84. NSM Hempsted *Glouc* from 83. *Hempsted House, Hempsted, Gloucester GL2 6LW* Gloucester (0452) 23320

NEWELL, Kenneth Ernest. b 22. S Dios Minl Tr Scheme 77. **d** 79 **p** 80. NSM Lynton, Brendon, Countisbury, Lynmouth etc *Ex* 79-85; TR 85-89; RD Shirwell 84-89; rtd 89; Perm to Offic *Ex* from 89. *Mole End, Lydiate Lane, Lynton, Devon EX35 6HE* Lynton (0598) 53507

NEWELL, Samuel James. b 28. TCD BA53 MA63. TCD Div Sch Div Test54. **d** 54 **p** 55. C Belf St Mary *Conn* 54-57; C Derriaghy 57-60; C Reading St Mary V *Ox* 60-63; V Chesham Ch Ch 63-74; P-in-c Wraysbury 74-78; TV Riverside from 78. *St Andrew's Vicarage, 57 Welley Road, Wraysbury, Staines, Middx TW19 5ER* Wraysbury (0784) 482740

NEWELL PRICE, Dr John Charles. b 29. MRCGP64 SS Coll Cam BA50 MB, ChB53. Local NSM Course 88. **d** 91. NSM Frensham *Guildf* from 91. *Dragon Lodge, Millbridge, Frensham, Farnham, Surrey GU10 3DQ* Frensham (025125) 3317

NEWHAM, Jill. b 37. Oak Hill NSM Course. **d** 89. NSM W w E Mersea *Chelmsf* 89-91; NSM Peldon w Gt and Lt Wigborough from 91. *c/o The Rectory, Church Road, Peldon, Colchester CO5 7PT* Peldon (0206) 35303

NEWHAM, Canon Raymond George. b 14. AKC49. **d** 49 **p** 50. Ind Adv *Chich* 62-83; V Brighton St Anne 62-76; Can and Preb Chich Cathl 74-83; P-in-c Hamsey 76-83; rtd 83; Perm to Offic *Chich* from 83. *2 The Triangle, Western Road, Lancing, W Sussex BN15 8RY* Lancing (0903) 763775

NEWHOUSE, Ven Robert John Darrell. b 11. Worc Coll Ox BA35 MA38. Cuddesdon Coll 35. **d** 36 **p** 37. Adn Totnes *Ex* 66-76; Can Res Ex Cathl 66-76; Treas 70-76; rtd 76; Perm to Offic *Ex* from 76. *Pound Cottage, Northlew, Okehampton, Devon EX20 3NR* Beaworthy (0409) 221532

✠NEWING, Rt Rev Kenneth Albert. b 23. Selw Coll Cam BA53 MA57. Coll of Resurr Mirfield 53. **d** 55 **p** 56 **c** 82. C Plymstock *Ex* 55-63; R Plympton St Maurice 63-82; RD Plympton 71-76; Preb Ex Cathl 75-82; Adn Plymouth 78-82; Suff Bp Plymouth 82-88; Lic to Offic *Ox* from 88; OSB from 89. *Elmore Abbey, Church Lane, Newbury, Berks RG13 1SA* Newbury (0635) 33080

NEWING, Peter. b 33. FSAScot59 FRSA60 ACP67 MCollP86 Birm Univ CertEd55 Dur Univ BA63 Bris Univ BEd76 NY State Univ BSc85 EdD88. Cranmer Hall Dur 63. **d** 65 **p** 66. C Blockley w Aston Magna *Glouc* 65-69; P-in-c Taynton 69-75; P-in-c Tibberton 69-75; R Brimpsfield w Elkstone and Syde 75-83; R Brimpsfield, Cranham, Elkstone and Syde from 83. *The Rectory, Brimpsfield, Gloucester GL4 8LD* Gloucester (0452) 863621

NEWLANDS, Christopher William. b 57. Bris Univ BA79. Westcott Ho Cam. **d** 84 **p** 85. C Bishops Waltham *Portsm* 84-87; Hon C Upham 85-87; Prec and Sacr Dur Cathl *Dur* from 87. *8 The College, Durham DH1 3EQ* 091-386 4733

NEWLANDS, Prof George McLeod. b 41. Edin Univ MA63 Heidelberg Univ BD66 PhD70 Ch Coll Cam MA73. **d** 82 **p** 82. Lect Cam Univ 73-86; Lic to Offic *Ely* from 82; Fell and Dean Trin Hall Cam 82-86; Prof Div Glas Univ from 86; Perm to Offic *Glas* from 86. *8 Hills Avenue, Cambridge CB1 4XA or, The University, Glasgow G12 8QQ* Cambridge (0223) 248631 or 041-339 8855

NEWLYN, Canon Edwin. b 39. AKC64. **d** 65 **p** 66. C Belgrave St Mich *Leic* 65-68; Miss to Seamen 68-81; Brazil 68-69; C Glas St Gabr *Glas* 69-73; S Africa 73-76; V Fylingdales *York* 81; P-in-c Hawsker 81; V Fylingdales and Hawsker cum Stainsacre 81-88; RD Whitby from 85; P-in-c Goathland from 88; Can York Minster from 90. *The Vicarage, Goathland, Whitby, N Yorkshire YO22 5AN* Whitby (0947) 86227

NEWMAN, Adrian. b 58. Bris Univ BSc80 DipHE85 MPhil89. Trin Coll Bris 82. **d** 85 **p** 86. C Forest Gate St Mark *Chelmsf* 85-89; V Hillsborough and Wadsley Bridge *Sheff* from 89. *Christ Church Vicarage, 218 Foxhill Road, Sheffield S6 1HJ* Sheffield (0742) 311576

NEWMAN, Alan George. b 18. Lich Th Coll 41. **d** 44 **p** 45. V Bradford-on-Avon Ch Ch *Sarum* 56-76; R Monkton Farleigh w S Wraxall 76-84; rtd 84; Perm to Offic *Sarum* from 84. *14 White Horse Road, Winsley, Bradford-on-Avon, Wilts* Bradford-on-Avon (02216) 4119

NEWMAN, Alfred John Gordon. b 19. Qu Coll Birm 71. **d** 74 **p** 74. Hon C Hall Green St Pet *Birm* 74-84; Perm to Offic *St E* from 84. *Willowmere, Rectory Road, Middleton, Saxmundham, Suffolk IP17 3NW* Westleton (072873) 457

NEWMAN, Cecil Ernest. b 21. Bris Univ BA58 DipTh58. Roch Th Coll 61. **d** 62 **p** 63. Lic to Offic *Roch* 67-86; Chapl Darenth Park Hosp Dartford 67-86; rtd 86. *6 Birtrick Drive, Meopham, Kent DA13 0LR* Meopham (0474) 813678

NEWMAN, David Malcolm. b 54. FSAScot81 Aber Univ LTh BTh. St Steph Ho Ox 89. **d** 91. C St Mary-at-Latton *Chelmsf* from 91. *The Church House, 68 Fesants Croft, Harlow, Essex CM20 2JU* Harlow (0279) 435497

NEWMAN, David Maurice Frederick. b 54. Hertf Coll Ox BA75 MA79. St Jo Coll Nottm. **d** 79 **p** 80. C Orpington Ch Ch *Roch* 79-83; C Bushbury *Lich* 83-86; V Ockbrook *Derby* from 86. *The Vicarage, 265 Victoria Avenue, Ockbrook, Derby DE7 3RL* Derby (0332) 662352

NEWMAN, Dennis Gerard. b 30. Nottm Univ BA55 DipTh55 Wisconsin Univ MTh69 PhD. Roch Th Coll 60. **d** 61 **p** 61. C Hampden Park *Chich* 61-63; C Wadhurst 63-65; C Tidebrook 63-65; V Eastbourne Ch Ch 65-71; V Preston 71-74; V Hampden Park from 74. *The Vicarage, 60 Brassey Avenue, Eastbourne, E Sussex BN22 9QH* Eastbourne (0323) 53166

NEWMAN, Mrs Diana Joan. b 43. Sarum Th Coll 81. **dss** 84 **d** 87. Parkstone St Pet w Branksea and St Osmund *Sarum* 84-87; Hon Par Dn from 87. *62 Vale Road, Poole, Dorset BH14 9AU* Parkstone (0202) 745136

NEWMAN, Eric William. b 26. Vancouver Sch of Th STh65. **d** 56 **p** 57. Miss to Seamen 67-91; Chapl Newport, Gwent 68-78; Chapl Tyne & Wear 78-91; rtd 91. *1 Sunnycroft, Portskewett, Chepstow, Gwent NP6 4RY* Caldicot (0291) 420679

NEWMAN, Geoffrey Maurice. b 22. Ox NSM Course 77. **d** 80 **p** 81. NSM Binfield *Ox* 80-84; Chapl St Geo Sch Ascot 82-84; V Teynham *Cant* 84-87; rtd 87. *55 St Mildred's Road, Westgate-on-Sea, Kent CT8 8RJ* Thanet (0843) 33837

NEWMAN, Graham Anthony. b 44. Ripon Coll Cuddesdon 79. **d** 81 **p** 82. C Walker *Newc* 81-84; C Whorlton 84-87; V Warkworth and Acklington from 87. *The Vicarage, 11 Dial Place, Warkworth, Morpeth, Northd NE65 0UR* Alnwick (0665) 711217

NEWMAN, James Edwin Michael. b 59. Nottm Univ BA80 Ox Univ BA90. Wycliffe Hall Ox 88. **d** 91. C Bidston *Ches* from 91. *55 Bridle Close, Birkenhead, Merseyside L43 9UU* 051-677 8700

NEWMAN, John Humphrey. b 19. ALCD49. **d** 49 **p** 50. R Knockholt *Roch* 74-82; rtd 82; Perm to Offic *Chich* from 84. *Stonegarth, Pett Level Road, Fairlight, Hastings, E Sussex TN35 4EA* Hastings (0424) 812518

NEWMAN, Laurence Victor. b 23. Wells Th Coll. **d** 66 **p** 67. C Milton *Win* 69-71; Asst Chapl HM Pris Wandsworth 71-72; Chapl HM Rem Cen Ashford 72-77; Chapl HM Pris Win 77-88; Las Palmas *Eur* 88-89; Chapl Algarve 89-91; rtd 91. *41 Nuns Road, Winchester, Hants SO23 7EF* Winchester (0962) 867699

NEWMAN, Michael Alan. b 40. Chich Th Coll 67. **d** 70 **p** 71. C Kilburn St Aug *Lon* 70-73; C St-Geo-in-the-East St Mary 75-78. *April Cottage, Georges Lane, Storrington, Pulborough, W Sussex RH20 3JH* Storrington (0903) 744354

NEWMAN, Michael John. b 50. Leic Univ BA72 MA75 Ex Coll Ox DipTh74. Cuddesdon Coll 73. **d** 75 **p** 76. C Tettenhall Regis *Lich* 75-79; C Uttoxeter w Bramshall 79-82; R Norton Canes 82-89; TR Rugeley from 89. *The Rectory, 20 Church Street, Rugeley, Staffs WS15 2AB* Rugeley (0889) 582149

NEWMAN, Paul Anthony. b 48. Lon Univ BSc70 Leeds Univ DipTh75. Coll of Resurr Mirfield 73. **d** 76 **p** 77. C Catford St Laur *S'wark* 76-81; TV Grays All SS *Chelmsf* 81-83; TV Lt Thurrock St Mary 81-83; W Ham Adnry Youth Chapl 83-87; P-in-c Forest Gate All SS 83-89; V 89-91; Dep Chapl HM Pris Wormwood Scrubs from 91. *HM Prison Wormwood Scrubs, Du Cane Road, London W12 0AA* 081-743 0311

NEWMAN, Richard David. b 38. BNC Ox BA60 MA63. Lich Th Coll 60. **d** 62 **p** 63. C E Grinstead St Swithun *Chich* 62-66; C Gt Grimsby St Jas *Linc* 66-69; C Gt Grimsby St Mary and St Jas 69-73; TV 73-74; V St Nicholas at Wade w Sarre *Cant* 74-75; P-in-c Chislet w Hoath 74-75; V St Nicholas at Wade w Sarre and Chislet w Hoath 75-81; V S Norwood H Innocents 81-84; V S Norwood H Innocents *S'wark* from 85. *Holy Innocents' Vicarage, 192A Selhurst Road, London SE25 6XX* 081-653 2063

NEWMAN, Richard Frank. b 37. Lich Th Coll. **d** 62 **p** 63. C Kettering SS Pet and Paul *Pet* 62-65; C Foleshill St Laur *Cov* 65-69; R Kislingbury w Rotherthorpe *Pet* 69-79; V Stannington *Sheff* 79-88; V Mosborough from 88. *The Vicarage, Duke Street, Mosborough, Sheffield S19 5DG* Sheffield (0742) 486518

NEWMAN, Preb Thomas Percival. b 20. Lich Th Coll 55. d 57 p 58. V Willenhall St Giles *Lich* 65-85; Preb Lich Cathl 81-85; rtd 85; Perm to Offic *Lich* from 85. *Flat 8, Shepwell Green, Willenhall, W Midlands WV13 2QJ* Willenhall (0902) 607320

NEWNHAM, Eric Robert. b 43. Sarum & Wells Th Coll 70. d 75 p 76. Hon C Blackheath Ascension *S'wark* from 75. *27 Morden Hill, London SE13 7NN* 081-692 6507

NEWNHAM, Osmond James. b 31. TD84. Leeds Univ BA55. Coll of Resurr Mirfield 55. d 57 p 58. C Salisbury St Mark *Sarum* 57-60; CF (R of O) 59-71; C Pewsey *Sarum* 60-62; R Chickerell w Fleet from 62; CF (TA) 71-86. *The Rectory, Chickerell, Weymouth, Dorset DT3 4DS* Weymouth (0305) 784915

NEWNS, Donald Frederick. b 07. St Aid Birkenhead 34. d 37 p 38. R Litcham w Kempston w E and W Lexham *Nor* 61-72; rtd 73. *Lexham, Walkergate, Alnwick, Northd NE66 1NB* Alnwick (0665) 602872

NEWPORT, Derek James. b 39. Acadia Univ (NS) BA82 MEd84. Sarum & Wells Th Coll 74. d 76 p 77. C Tavistock and Gulworthy *Ex* 76-78; Canada 78-86; V Malborough w S Huish, W Alvington and Churchstow *Ex* from 86. *The Vicarage, Malborough, Kingsbridge, Devon TQ7 3RR* Kingsbridge (0548) 561234

NEWPORT, Archdeacon of. *See* EVANS, Ven John Barrie

NEWSAM, Bernard Hugh. b 01. Selw Coll Cam BA26 MA31. Cuddesdon Coll 27. d 28 p 29. V Baldersby *York* 50-69; V Skipton Bridge 50-69; rtd 69. *4 Herisson Close, Pickering, N Yorkshire YO18 7HB* Pickering (0751) 73077

NEWSAM, Peter William. b 62. Called to the Bar (Gray's Inn) 84 Ex Univ LLB83. St Steph Ho Ox 85. d 88 p 89. C Whitleigh *Ex* 88-91; C-in-c Middleton-on-Sea CD *Chich* from 91. *St Nicholas House, 3 Byron Close, Felpham, Bognor Regis, W Sussex PO22 6QU* Bognor Regis (0243) 586348

NEWSOME, David Ellis. b 55. St Jo Coll Dur BA77. Westcott Ho Cam 80. d 82 p 83. C Finchley St Mary *Lon* 82-85; C Fulham All SS 85-87; Bp's Dom Chapl *Birm* 87-91; V Gravelly Hill from 91. *All Saints' Vicarage, Broomfield Road, Birmingham B23 7QA* 021-373 0730

NEWSOME, John Keith. b 49. Mert Coll Ox BA73 MA76. Ripon Coll Cuddesdon 73. d 76 p 77. C Bywell St Pet *Newc* 76-78; C Berwick H Trin 78-82; Chapl Bonn w Cologne *Eur* from 86. *c/o The British Embassy, Friedrich-Ebert Allee 77, 5300 Bonn 1, Germany* Bonn (228) 234061 or 315779

NEWSON, John David. b 32. MIAAP85 MAJA85 Southn Univ BSc53 PhD57. Cuddesdon Coll 64. d 65 p 66. Hon C Cant All SS *Cant* 65-77; Lect Ch Ch Coll Cant 65-80. *124 Queen's Road, Buckhurst Hill, Essex IG9 5BJ* 081-505 7748

NEWSUM, Alfred Turner Paul. b 28. Coll of Resurr Mirfield 52. d 53 p 54. C Roath St German *Llan* 53-59; C Westmr St Matt *Lon* 59-60; C Washwood Heath *Birm* 60-68; P-in-c Small Heath St Greg 68-78; V Birm St Aid Small Heath 72-80; V Stockland Green from 80. *The Vicarage, Bleak Hill Road, Birmingham B23 7EL* 021-373 0130

NEWTH, Barry Wilfred. b 33. Bris Univ BA56. ALCD58. d 58 p 59. C Upton (or Overchurch) *Ches* 58-62; C Kimberworth *Sheff* 62-63; V Clifton *Man* 63-72; V Radcliffe St Thos 72-74; V Radcliffe St Thos and St Jo 74-81; R Heaton Mersey 81-86; V Kirkby Malham *Bradf* 86-87; P-in-c Coniston Cold 86-87; V Kirkby-in-Malhamdale w Coniston Cold from 87. *The Vicarage, Kirkby Malham, Skipton, N Yorkshire BD23 4BS* Airton (07293) 215

NEWTON, Miss Ann. b 46. Trin Coll Bris 75. d 87. Par Dn Rothley *Leic* 87-91; Par Dn Becontree St Mary *Chelmsf* from 91. *19 Bosworth Road, Dagenham, Essex RM10 7NU* 081-593 6780

NEWTON, Barrie Arthur. b 38. Dur Univ BA61. Wells Th Coll 61. d 63 p 64. C Walton St Mary *Liv* 63-67; C N Lynn w St Marg and St Nic *Nor* 67-69; Chapl Asst The Lon Hosp (Whitechapel) 69-71; Chapl K Coll Hosp Lon 72-77; P-in-c Bishops Sutton w Stowey *B & W* 77-81; P-in-c Compton Martin w Ubley 79-81; P-in-c Bridgwater St Jo w Chedzoy 81-83; Chapl St Mary's Hosp (Praed Street) Paddington from 83. *St Mary's Hospital, Praed Street, London W2 1NY* 071-725 6666 or 725 1508

NEWTON, Brian Karl. b 30. Keble Coll Ox BA55 MA59. Wells Th Coll 56. d 58 p 59. C Barrow St Geo *Carl* 58-61; Trinidad and Tobago 61-69 and 71-77; Gen Ed USPG 69-71; P-in-c Gt Coates *Linc* 77; TV Gt and Lt Coates w Bradley 78-88; V Burgh le Marsh from 88. *41 Chapman Avenue, Burgh le Marsh, Skegness, Lincs PE24 5LY* Skegness (0754) 810216

NEWTON, Canon Christopher Wynne. b 25. Trin Hall Cam BA46. Westcott Ho Cam 48. d 50 p 51. TR Hemel Hempstead *St Alb* 66-72; RD Milton Keynes *Ox* 72-77; TV Swan 78-84; RD Claydon 78-84; Dioc Ecum Officer 79-84; Hon Can Ch Ch 80-83; P-in-c Lt Gaddesden *St Alb* 84-86; rtd 86; Perm to Offic *St Alb* from 86. *9 Ashtree Way, Hemel Hempstead, Herts HP1 1QS* Hemel Hempstead (0442) 54484

NEWTON, David Ernest. b 42. Sarum & Wells Th Coll 72. d 74 p 75. C Wigan All SS *Liv* 74-80; VC York Minster *York* 80-85; R Ampleforth w Oswaldkirk 85-86; P-in-c E Gilling 85-86; R Ampleforth and Oswaldkirk and Gilling E from 86. *The Rectory, Ampleforth, York YO6 4DU* Ampleforth (04393) 264

NEWTON, Derek Lewis. b 14. K Coll Lon BA36. Wycliffe Hall Ox 54. d 55 p 56. Nigeria 58-78; C Woodford St Mary w St Phil and St Jas *Chelmsf* 78-85; rtd 85; Perm to Offic *Chelmsf* from 85. *13 Dorcester Court, Buckingham Road, London E18 2NG* 081-505 8157

NEWTON, Gerald Blamire. b 30. Lich Th Coll. d 69 p 70. C Leeds Halton St Wilfrid *Ripon* 69-73; C Gt Yarmouth *Nor* 73-74; P-in-c Cattistock w Chilfrome and Rampisham w Wraxall *Sarum* 74-77; V Coney Hill *Glouc* 77-79; V Bryneglwys and Llandegla *St As* 79-80; R Llandegla and Bryneglwys and Llanarmon-yn-Ial 80-86; P-in-c Burythorpe, Acklam and Leavening w Westow *York* from 86. *The Rectory, Burythorpe, Malton, N Yorkshire YO17 9LJ* Burythorpe (065385) 220

NEWTON, Graham Hayden. b 47. AKC69. St Aug Coll Cant 70. d 70 p 71. C St Mary-at-Lambeth *S'wark* 70-73; TV Catford (Southend) and Downham 73-78; P-in-c Porthill *Lich* 78-79; TV Wolstanton 79-86; V Stevenage H Trin *St Alb* from 86. *Holy Trinity Vicarage, 18 Letchmore Road, Stevenage, Herts SG1 3JD* Stevenage (0438) 353229

NEWTON, John. b 39. AKC65. d 66 p 67. C Whipton *Ex* 66-68; C Plympton St Mary 68-74; V Broadwoodwidger 74-81; R Kelly w Bradstone 74-81; R Lifton 74-81; Chapl All Hallows Sch Rousdon from 81. *Home Farm, Rousdon, Lyme Regis, Dorset DT7 3XT* Seaton (0297) 21606

NEWTON, John Richard. b 25. FBIM. St Jo Coll Dur 76 Cranmer Hall Dur. d 78 p 79. C Cottingham *York* 78-80; R Beeford w Frodingham and Foston 80-86; R Todwick *Sheff* from 86. *The Rectory, 136 Kiveton Lane, Todwick, Sheffield S31 0HL* Worksop (0909) 770283

NEWTON, Very Rev Keith. b 52. K Coll Lon BD73 AKC73. St Aug Coll Cant 74. d 75 p 76. C Gt Ilford St Mary *Chelmsf* 75-78; TV Wimbledon *S'wark* 78-85; Malawi from 85; Dean Blantyre from 86; Can S Malawi from 86. *St Paul's Cathedral, PO Box 326, Blantyre, Malawi* Malawi (265) 620417

NEWTON, Kenneth. b 24. Open Univ BA74 Columbia Univ MA PhD. Lambeth STh75 St Aid Birkenhead 49. d 52 p 53. R Failsworth St Jo *Man* 64-70; V Frizington and Arlecdon *Carl* 70-75; Bermuda 76-85; R Rollesby w Burgh w Billockby w Ashby w Oby etc *Nor* 85-89; rtd 89; Perm to Offic *Nor* from 89. *4 Sidney Close, Martham, Great Yarmouth, Norwich NR29 4TG* Great Yarmouth (0493) 740724

NEWTON, Nigel Ernest Hartley. b 38. St Jo Coll Nottm 85. d 89 p 90. Hon C Largs *Glas* from 89; Asst Chapl Ashbourne Home Largs from 89. *9 Kyles View, Largs, Ayrshire KA30 9ET* Largs (0475) 687014

NEWTON, Miss Pauline Dorothy. b 48. Southn Univ BA70 CertEd71 MPhil79. Sarum Th Coll 79. dss 82 d 87. Bemerton *Sarum* 82-87; Hon Par Dn from 87. *13 Highbury Avenue, Salisbury SP2 7EX* Salisbury (0722) 25707

NEWTON, Peter. b 35. Sarum & Wells Th Coll 74. d 77 p 78. Hon C Reading St Barn *Ox* 77-79; C Bracknell 79-83; TV 83-85; V Knowl Hill w Littlewick from 85. *St Peter's Vicarage, Knowl Hill, Reading RG10 9YD* Littlewick Green (062882) 2732

NEWTON, Peter. b 39. St Jo Coll Nottm 73. d 75 p 76. C Porchester *S'well* 75-79; R Wilford from 79. *The Rectory, Main Road, Wilford, Nottingham NG11 7AJ* Nottingham (0602) 815661

NEWTON, Raymond David. b 43. K Coll Lon BSc65. Linc Th Coll 65. d 67 p 68. C Ipswich St Matt *St E* 67-71; C E w W Barkwith *Linc* 71-74; R Chelmondiston w Harkstead *St E* 74-78; R Chelmondiston w Harkstead and Shotley w Erwarton from 78. *The Rectory, Chelmondiston, Ipswich, Suffolk IP9 1HY* Woolverstone (0473) 780214

NEWTON, Richard. b 47. Lon Univ DipTh72. Trin Coll Bris 72. d 73 p 74. C Fareham St Jo *Portsm* 73-76; C Cheltenham St Mark *Glouc* 76-83; P-in-c Malvern St

Andr *Worc* from 83. *48 Longridge Road, Malvern, Worcs WR14 3JB* Malvern (0684) 573912

NEWTON, Richard John Christopher. b 60. Bris Univ BSc81. Qu Coll Birm 85. d 88 p 89. C Bris Ch the Servant Stockwood *Bris* from 88. *66 Lacey Road, Bristol BS14 8LS* Whitchurch (0272) 833825

NEWTON, Robert Keith. b 61. Man Univ BA83. St Steph Ho Ox 86. d 89 p 90. C Ludlow *Heref* from 89. *St Mary's Vicarage, Ashford Carbonel, Ludlow, Shropshire SY8 4DA* Richards Castle (058474) 352

NEWTON, William. b 51. Chich Th Coll 86. d 88 p 89. C Leigh-on-Sea St Marg *Chelmsf* from 88. *45 Eaton Road, Leigh-on-Sea, Essex SS9 3PF* Southend-on-Sea (0702) 777863

NEWTON, Canon William Ronald. b 12. Birm Univ BA43. Westcott Ho Cam 41. d 43 p 44. Hon Can Truro Cathl *Truro* 71-83; V Penzance St Mary w St Paul 73-82; rtd 82; Perm to Offic *Chich* from 83. *52 Rutland Court, New Church Road, Hove, E Sussex BN3 4BB* Brighton (0273) 773422

NEY, Ven Reginald Basil. b 22. OBE78. ARCM55. Lich Th Coll 41. d 45 p 46. Chapl Madrid *Eur* 56-87; Can Gib Cathl 62-87; Adn Gib 63-87; rtd 87; Hon Can Gib Cathl *Eur* from 87. *Apartamento 24, Bloque A-3, Colonia Ducal, Playa de Gandia, Valencia, Spain*

NIAS, John Charles Somerset. b 18. Worc Coll Ox BA40 MA45 BD46. Wells Th Coll 40. d 41 p 42. V Finstock and Fawler *Ox* 56-83; V Ramsden 56-83; Dir of Studies Cen Readers' Bd 63-73; rtd 83; Perm to Offic Win and Portsm from 83; *Chich* from 88. *29 Southleigh Road, Warblington, Havant, Hants PO9 2QG* Havant (0705) 453186

NIBLETT, David John Morton. b 24. Wells Th Coll 51. d 54 p 55. V Barnstaple St Pet w H Trin *Ex* 65-75; V S Brent 75-90; rtd 90. *2 Beretun Orchard, Glastonbury, Somerset BA6 8AX* Glastonbury (0458) 33101

NICE, John Edmund. b 51. Univ of Wales (Ban) BA73. Coll of Resurr Mirfield 74. d 76 p 77. C Oxton *Ches* 76-79; C Liscard St Mary w St Columba 79-82; V Latchford St Jas from 82. *St James's Vicarage, Manx Road, Warrington WA4 6AJ* Warrington (0925) 31893

NICHOL, William David. b 58. Hull Univ BA84. Ridley Hall Cam 84. d 87 p 88. C Hull Newland St Jo *York* 87-90; C Kirk Ella from 90. *77 Carr Lane, Willerby, Hull HU10 6JS* Hull (0482) 658974

NICHOLAS, Canon Arnold Frederick. b 34. Jes Coll Cam BA58 MA62. Ely Th Coll 58. d 60 p 61. C Wisbech St Aug *Ely* 60-63; P-in-c Lt Massingham *Nor* 63-65; Youth Chapl 63-67; Chapl Bp Otter Coll Chich 67-70; R Westbourne *Chich* 70-76; V Stansted 70-76; Can and Preb Chich Cathl 76-82; RD Chich 76-80; P-in-c Chich St Pet 76-81; V Chich St Paul and St Bart 80-81; V Chich St Paul and St Pet 81-82; V Wisbech SS Pet and Paul *Ely* 82-90; RD Wisbech 82-90; V Fordham St Pet from 90; P-in-c Kennett from 90. *The Vicarage, Fordham, Ely, Cambs CB7 5NR* Newmarket (0638) 720266

NICHOLAS, Brian Arthur. b 19. St Edm Hall Ox BA47 MA53. Wycliffe Hall Ox 62. d 64 p 65. V Chudleigh Knighton *Ex* 69-76; V Ex St Mark 76-84; rtd 84; Perm to Offic *Ex* from 84. *Windyridge, 4 Little Johns Cross Hill, Exeter EX2 9PJ* Exeter (0392) 219222

NICHOLAS, Ernest Milton. b 25. ACP50 Newc Univ DipAdEd69 Lanc Univ MA78. NE Ord Course 85. d 86 p 87. NSM Hexham *Newc* from 86. *Hillside, Eilansgate, Hexham, Northd NE46 3EW* Hexham (0434) 603609

NICHOLAS, Gwynfryn Lloyd. b 16. Univ of Wales BA39. St D Coll Lamp 39. d 40 p 41. C Roath St Marg *Llan* 66-68; rtd 68. *8 Llanina Grove, Trowbridge Estate, Rumney, Cardiff* Cardiff (0222) 791598

NICHOLAS, Herbert Llewellyn. b 19. St D Coll Lamp 51. d 53 p 54. V Pontypridd St Matt *Llan* 65-89; rtd 89. *47 Meadow Crescent, Tonteg, Pontypridd, M Glam CF38 1NL* Pontypridd (0443) 206156

NICHOLAS, Malcolm Keith. b 46. FIMLS71 Open Univ BA79. S Dios Minl Tr Scheme 81. d 84 p 85. NSM Gatcombe *Portsm* from 84; NSM Shorwell w Kingston from 88. *Bunkers Cottage, Bunkers Lane, Rookley, Isle of Wight PO38 3NJ* Chillerton (0983) 721687

NICHOLAS, Maurice Lloyd. b 30. Kelham Th Coll 54. d 58 p 59. Chapl RADD 65-75; C Northolt St Mary *Lon* 75-85; rtd 85; Hon C Upper Teddington SS Pet and Paul *Lon* 85-90; Hon C Teddington SS Pet and Paul and Fulwell from 90. *58 Elton Close, Hampton Wick, Kingston-upon-Thames, Surrey KT1 4EE* 081-977 9340

NICHOLAS, Patrick. b 37. Selw Coll Cam BA60 MA65. Wells Th Coll 60. d 62 p 63. C Camberwell St Giles *S'wark* 62-63; C Warlingham w Chelsham and Farleigh 63-65; C Oxted 65-68; Hong Kong 68-74; C Portsea St Mary *Portsm* 75. *Address temp unknown*

NICHOLAS, Paul James. b 51. Univ of Wales (Lamp) DipTh73 BA. Coll of Resurr Mirfield 73. d 74 p 75. C Llanelly *St D* 74-78; C Roath St Marg *Llan* 78-84; P-in-c Leic St Pet *Leic* 84-87; V Shard End *Birm* from 87. *The Vicarage, 47 Shustoke Road, Birmingham B34 7BA* 021-747 3299

NICHOLAS, William Ronald. b 06. St D Coll Lamp BA28 Wells Th Coll 28. d 29 p 31. R Johnston w Steynton *St D* 53-74; rtd 74. *9 Milford Road, Johnston, Haverfordwest, Dyfed* Haverfordwest (0437) 890303

NICHOLL, John Hawdon. b 41. GRSM63 Ex Coll Ox BA66 MA71. Cuddesdon Coll 74. d 75 p 76. C Headingley *Ripon* 75-78; V Hawksworth Wood 78-86; V Bognor *Chich* from 86. *The Vicarage, 17 Victoria Drive, Bognor Regis, W Sussex PO21 2RH* Bognor Regis (0243) 821423

NICHOLL, Joseph Edward Chancellor. b 20. MC45. Qu Coll Cam BA46 MA48. Ridley Hall Cam. d 48 p 49. Asst Chapl Stowe Sch Bucks 62-72; Chapl 72-75; P-in-c Stowe *Ox* 75-81; R Angmering *Chich* 82-85; rtd 85; Perm to Offic *Chich* from 86. *24 Rufus Close, Lewes, E Sussex BN7 1BG* Lewes (0273) 479164

NICHOLLS, Alan Fryer. b 26. Univ Coll Ex BA50. Sarum Th Coll 50. d 52 p 53. C Wootton Bassett *Sarum* 52-55; C Chesterfield All SS *Derby* 55-56; V Ringley *Man* 56-60; Chapl Prebendal Sch Chich 60-63; PV Chich Cathl *Chich* 60-63; V Selmeston w Alciston 63-65; Chapl Woodbridge Sch Suffolk 65-66; Asst Chapl & Ho Master 66-86; TV Bruton and Distr *B & W* from 86. *The Parsonage, Batcombe, Shepton Mallet, Somerset BA4 6HF* Upton Noble (074985) 671

NICHOLLS, Prof Charles Geoffrey William. b 21. St Jo Coll Cam BA47 MA49. Wells Th Coll 51. d 52 p 53. C Wendover *Ox* 52-55; Chapl to Students in Edin 55-60; Canada from 60; Prof Relig Studies Univ of BC from 61. *3760 West 34th Avenue, Vancouver, Canada, V6N 2L1*

NICHOLLS, David Gwyn. b 36. Lon Univ BSc57 K Coll Cam PhD62 Yale Univ STM62 Ox Univ MA73. Chich Th Coll 61. d 62 p 63. C Bloomsbury St Geo w St Jo *Lon* 62-66; Trinidad and Tobago 66-73; Chapl Lect and Fell Ex Coll Ox 73-78; P-in-c Littlemore *Ox* 78-86; V from 86. *The Vicarage, St Nicholas' Road, Oxford OX4 4PP* Oxford (0865) 749939

✠**NICHOLLS, Rt Rev John.** b 43. AKC66. d 67 p 68 c 90. C Salford St Clem Ordsall *Man* 67-69; C Langley All SS and Martyrs 69-72; V 72-78; Dir Past Th Coll of Resurr Mirfield 78-83; Lic to Offic *Wakef* 79-83; Can Res Man Cathl *Man* 83-90; Suff Bp Lanc *Blackb* from 90. *Wheatfield, 7 Dallas Road, Lancaster LA1 1TN* Lancaster (0524) 32897

NICHOLLS, John Gervase. b 15. Qu Coll Cam BA38 MA42. Lon Coll of Div 38. d 39 p 40. Cyprus 67-75; R Ipswich St Clem w H Trin *St E* 75-81; rtd 81; P-in-c Wilby w Brundish *St E* 81-84; Perm to Offic *Nor* from 85; *Nor* from 88. *17 Moorfield Road, Mattishall, Dereham, Norfolk NR20 3NZ* Dereham (0362) 858501

NICHOLLS, Leonard Samuel. b 07. Ex Coll Ox BA29 MA34. Bps' Coll Cheshunt 30. d 32 p 33. R Etwall w Egginton *Derby* 68-71; rtd 71. *Old Post House, Framfield, Uckfield, E Sussex* Framfield (0825) 890311

NICHOLLS, Mark Richard. b 60. LSE BSc82 Leeds Univ MA88. Coll of Resurr Mirfield 86. d 89 p 90. C Warrington St Elphin *Liv* from 89. *18 Harbord Street, Warrington WA1 2JW* Warrington (0925) 573142

NICHOLLS, Michael Stanley. b 34. AKC59. St Boniface Warminster 59. d 60 p 61. C Torquay St Martin Barton CD *Ex* 60-63; C E Grinstead St Mary *Chich* 63-66; C-in-c Salfords CD *S'wark* 66-68; V Salfords 68-75; V Tunbridge Wells St Barn *Roch* from 75. *The Vicarage, 31 Lansdowne Road, Tunbridge Wells, Kent TN1 2NQ* Tunbridge Wells (0892) 23609

NICHOLLS, Neil David Raymond. b 65. Univ Coll Lon BA86. Wycliffe Hall Ox BA90. d 91. C Westmr St Steph w St Jo *Lon* from 91. *Flat B, Napier Hall, Hide Place, London SW1P 4NJ*

NICHOLLS, Robert William. b 10. Lon Univ BA31 AKC33. St Steph Ho Ox 33. d 33 p 34. V Barnham *Chich* 69-71; rtd 75. *Old Rectory Cottage, Worth, Crawley, W Sussex RH10 7RT* Crawley (0293) 883193

NICHOLLS, Roy Meacham. b 29. CEng MIMechE62. Glouc Sch of Min 85. d 88 p 89. NSM Pershore w Pinvin, Wick and Birlingham *Worc* from 88. *5 Paddock Close, Pershore, Worcs WR10 1HJ* Pershore (0386) 553508

NICHOLLS, Stanley Charles. b 28. St Chad's Coll Dur BA53. Bps' Coll Cheshunt 53. d 54 p 55. V Ruswarp w Sneaton *York* 68-78; V Kirkby-in-Cleveland 78-88; rtd 88. *1 Brecks Close, Wigginton, York YO3 8TW* York (0904) 765114

✠**NICHOLLS, Rt Rev Vernon Sampson.** b 17. Clifton Th Coll 38. **d** 41 **p** 41 **c** 74. C Bedminster Down *Bris* 41-42; C Liskeard w St Keyne *Truro* 42-44; CF (EC) 44-46; V Meopham *Roch* 46-56; RD Cobham 54-56; V Walsall *Lich* 56-67; RD Walsall 56-67; Chapl Walsall Gen Hosp 56-67; Preb Lich Cathl *Lich* 64-67; Adn Birm 67-74; Dean St German's Cathl *S & M* 74-83; Bp S & M 74-83; rtd 83; Asst Bp Cov from 83. *4 Winston Close, Hathaway Park, Stratford-upon-Avon, Warks CV37 9ER* Stratford-upon-Avon (0789) 294478

NICHOLS, Albert Percival. b 18. Tyndale Hall Bris. **d** 57 **p** 57. P-in-c Chiselborough w W Chinnock *B & W* 60-70; R E Chinnock 60-77; R Middle Chinnock 60-70; R Middle w W Chinnock 70-78; RD Martock 75-78; P-in-c Norton sub Hamdon w Chiselborough etc 78-86; R Norton sub Hamdon, W Chinnock, Chiselborough from 86; rtd 86; Perm to Offic B & W and Sarum from 86. *53 East Street, Beaminster, Dorset DT8 3DS* Beaminster (0308) 862871

NICHOLS, Canon Barry Edward. b 40. ACA63 FCA73. S'wark Ord Course 66. **d** 69 **p** 70. NSM Surbiton St Andr and St Mark S'wark from 69; Hon Can S'wark Cathl from 90; Dean for MSE Kingston from 90. *32 Corkran Road, Surbiton, Surrey KT6 6PN* 081-390 3032

NICHOLS, Dennis Harry. b 25. Kelham Th Coll 47. **d** 52 **p** 53. V Bury H Trin *Man* 61-81; V St Gluvias *Truro* 81-90; RD Carnmarth S 85-90; rtd 90. *11 Marlborough Crescent, Falmouth, Cornwall TR11 2RJ* Falmouth (0326) 312243

NICHOLS, Matthew William Hardwicke. b 04. St D Coll Lamp BA26 Wells Th Coll 28. **d** 28 **p** 29. V Huddersfield St Thos *Wakef* 64-75; rtd 75; Chapl St Marg Convent Aber 75-78; Perm to Offic *Worc* from 78; Chapl Beauchamp Community Malvern Link 82-84. *St Christopher's, The Quadrangle, Newland, Malvern, Worcs WR13 5AX* Malvern (0684) 565392

NICHOLS, Canon Raymond Maurice. b 22. ALCD53. **d** 53 **p** 54. Home Sec SPCK 64-71; Overseas Sec 67-73; Publisher 73-74; P-in-c Dorchester *Ox* 74-78; P-in-c Newington 77-78; TR Dorchester 78-87; V Warborough 78-87; rtd 87. *12 Abbey Court, Cerne Abbas, Dorchester, Dorset DT2 7JH* Cerne Abbas (0300) 341456

NICHOLSON, Brian Warburton. b 44. St Jo Coll Nottm 70 Lon Coll of Div ALCD73 LTh74. **d** 73 **p** 74. C Canford Magna *Sarum* 73-77; C E Twickenham St Steph *Lon* 77-80; V Colchester St Jo *Chelmsf* from 80. *St John's Vicarage, Evergreen Drive, Colchester CO4 4HU* Colchester (0206) 843232

NICHOLSON, Miss Clare. b 46. RMN80 Keele Univ BA70 CertEd70 Lon Univ DN80. St Jo Coll Nottm DPS85. **dss** 85 **d** 87. Bletchley *Ox* 85-87; Par Dn 87-89; Par Dn Milton Keynes 89-90; Par Dn Prestwood and Gt Hampden from 90. *28 St Peter's Close, Prestwood, Great Missenden, Bucks HP16 9ET* Great Missenden (02406) 6351

NICHOLSON, David. b 57. Sarum & Wells Th Coll 80. **d** 83 **p** 84. C Trevethin *Mon* 83-85; C Ebbw Vale 85-87; V Newport St Steph and H Trin from 87; Hon Chapl Miss to Seamen from 87. *St Stephen's Vicarage, Adeline Street, Newport, Gwent NP9 2HA* Newport (0633) 265192

NICHOLSON, Canon Donald. b 10. St Chad's Coll Dur BA32 DipTh34 MA35. **d** 33 **p** 34. Hon Can St Mary's Cathl *Edin* from 64; Chapl Stacklands Retreat Ho W Kingsdown 71-75; rtd 75; St Marg Convent Aber from 80; Hon Can St Andr Cathl *Ab* from 84. *St Margaret's Convent, 17 Spital, Aberdeen AB2 3HT* Aberdeen (0224) 638407

NICHOLSON, Dorothy Ann. b 40. S'wark Ord Course 81. **dss** 84 **d** 87. Carshalton Beeches S'wark 84-87; Par Dn 87-88; Par Dn Brixton Rd Ch Ch 88-89; Par Dn Malden St Jo from 89. *4 Glebe Gardens, New Malden, Surrey KT3 5RY*

NICHOLSON, Dr Ernest Wilson. b 38. TCD BA60 MA64 Glas Univ PhD64 Cam Univ BD71 DD78. Westcott Ho Cam 69. **d** 69 **p** 70. Lect Div Cam Univ 67-79; Fell Chapl and Dir of Th Studies Pemb Coll Cam 69-79; Dean 73-79; Prof of Interpr of H Scripture Or Coll Ox 79-90; Provost from 90; Lic to Offic *Ox* from 84. *Oriel College, Oxford OX1 4EW* Oxford (0865) 276533

NICHOLSON, Guy Colville. b 21. Univ of NZ BE45. Oak Hill Th Coll 51. **d** 53 **p** 54. C Beckenham Ch Ch *Roch* 53-56; V Hemswell w Harpswell *Linc* 56-63; V Glentworth 56-63; Chapl RAF 58-63; RD Aslackhoe *Linc* 60-63; New Zealand 63-84; Australia 84-87; Chapl HM Pris Northeye from 88. *HM Prison, Barnhorn Road, Bexhill-on-Sea, E Sussex TN39 4QW* Cooden (04243) 5511

NICHOLSON, John Paul. b 57. Sarum Th Coll. **d** 82 **p** 83. C Kirkby *Liv* 82-85; TV Speke St Aid from 85. *62 East Millwood Road, Speke, Liverpool L24 6SQ* 051-425 4398

NICHOLSON, Joseph. b 14. LRAM45 St Jo Coll Dur BA35 DipTh37 MA38. **d** 37 **p** 38. Asst Master Penhill Sec Sch Swindon 69-75; Perm to Offic Bris 69-75; Mon 75-77; P-in-c Blaenavon w Capel Newydd *Mon* 77-79; rtd 79. *52 Seacroft Road, Mablethorpe, Lincs LN12 2DJ* Mablethorpe (0521) 7574

NICHOLSON, Joseph Smith. b 16. St Jo Coll Dur BA40 DipTh41 MA43. **d** 41 **p** 42. Chapl HM Pris Leyhill 70-73; Styal 73-76; Dur 76-82; rtd 81. *17 Rack Close, Andover, Hants* Andover (0264) 356690

NICHOLSON, Kevin Smith. b 47. Edin Th Coll. **d** 91. C Burntisland *St And* from 91. *Lovedale Cottage, Abbotsford Road, Lochore KY5 8DT* Burntisland (0592) 861331

NICHOLSON, Nigel Patrick. b 46. Sarum & Wells Th Coll 72. **d** 75 **p** 76. C Farnham *Guildf* 75-78; C Worplesdon 78-81; P-in-c Compton 81-85; R Compton w Shackleford and Peper Harow 85-89; R Cranleigh from 89. *The Rectory, Cranleigh, Surrey GU6 8AS* Cranleigh (0483) 273620

NICHOLSON, Canon Peter Charles. b 25. Lambeth MA89 Chich Th Coll. **d** 59 **p** 60. C Sawbridgeworth *St Alb* 59-62; Min Can, Prec and Sacr Pet Cathl *Pet* 62-67; V Wroxham w Hoveton *Nor* 67-74; V Lyme Regis *Sarum* 74-80; Gen Sec St Luke's Hosp for the Clergy from 80; NSM Harlington *Lon* 80-87; Hon PV S'wark Cathl *S'wark* from 87; Can and Preb Chich Cathl *Chich* from 89. *St Luke's Cottage, 13 Brearley Close, Uxbridge, Middx UB8 1JJ* Uxbridge (0895) 233522

NICHOLSON, Peter Charles. b 44. Oak Hill Th Coll 74. **d** 76 **p** 77. C Croydon Ch Ch Broad Green *Cant* 76-80; C Gt Baddow *Chelmsf* 80-88; TV from 88. *42 Riffams Drive, Great Baddow, Chelmsford CM2 7QH* Chelmsford (0245) 71516

NICHOLSON, Rodney. b 45. Mert Coll Ox BA68 MA71. Ridley Hall Cam 69. **d** 72 **p** 73. C Colne St Bart *Blackb* 72-75; C Blackpool St Jo 75-78; V Ewood 78-90; V Clitheroe St Paul Low Moor from 90. *The Vicarage, St Paul's Street, Clitheroe, Lancs BB7 2LS* Clitheroe (0200) 22418

NICHOLSON, Roland. b 40. Sarum & Wells Th Coll 72. **d** 74 **p** 75. C Morecambe St Barn *Blackb* 74-78; V Feniscliffe 78-90; V Sabden and Pendleton from 90. *St Nicholas's Vicarage, Westley Street, Sabden, Blackburn BB6 9EH* Burnley (0282) 71384

NICHOLSON, Trevor Parry. b 35. St Edm Hall Ox BA58 MA. Wycliffe Hall Ox 58. **d** 60 **p** 61. C Eastbourne Ch Ch *Chich* 60-63; C Ifield 63-67; Asst Youth Chapl *Win* 67-73; Chapl Shoreham Gr Sch 73-78; P-in-c Capel *Guildf* 78-85; V 85-90; Chapl Qu Anne's Sch Caversham from 90. *2 Henley Road, Caversham, Reading, Berks* Reading (0734) 471582

NICHOLSON, Miss Velda Christine. b 44. CertEd65. Birm Bible Inst DipTh69 Cranmer Hall Dur 81. **dss** 82 **d** 87. Gt and Lt Driffield *York* 82-86; Newby 86-87; Par Dn 87-88; TM Cramlington *Newc* from 88. *9 Megstone Avenue, Cramlington, Northd NE23 6TU* Cramlington (0670) 732681

NICHOLSON, William Surtees. b 15. Coll of Resurr Mirfield 39. **d** 41 **p** 42. R Ashington *Chich* 61-74; V Bamburgh and Lucker *Newc* 74-81; rtd 81. *Pepperclose Cottage, The Wynding, Bamburgh, Northd NE69 7DB* Bamburgh (06684) 437

NICKALLS, Frederick William. b 13. Oak Hill Th Coll 49. **d** 51 **p** 52. R Nailsea H Trin *B & W* 67-78; rtd 78; Perm to Offic *Win* from 82. *Flat 7, Ellesborough Manor, Butlers Cross, Aylesbury, Bucks HP17 0XF* Aylesbury (0296) 696289

NICKLES, Albert Arthur. b 17. Ch Coll Cam BA38. Cuddesdon Coll 38. **d** 39 **p** 40. Ghana 53-73; Madagascar from 73; rtd 82. *St Paul's Theological College, BP 1707, Anfananaiivo, Malagasy Democratic Republic*

NICKLESS, Christopher John. b 58. Univ of Wales BA79. Coll of Resurr Mirfield 79. **d** 81 **p** 82. C Bassaleg *Mon* 81-85; TV Ebbw Vale from 85. *St Mary's Vicarage, Cwm Road, Waunlwyd, Ebbw Vale, Gwent NP3 6TR* Ebbw Vale (0495) 371258

NICKLESS, Canon Victor George. b 08. Dur Univ BA34 LTh34. Lon Coll of Div 30. **d** 34 **p** 35. R Wrotham *Roch* 63-77; rtd 77. *East Wing, Ford Place, Ford Lane, Wrotham Heath, Sevenoaks, Kent* West Malling (0732) 844172

NICKLIN, Ivor. b 41. FRSA68 BEd MTh73 PhD76 MA84. Wycliffe Hall Ox. **d** 84 **p** 85. NSM Weaverham *Ches* 84-89; P-in-c Kings Walden *St Alb* from 89; P-in-c Offley w Lilley from 89. *The Vicarage, Church Road, Kings Waldon, Hitchen, Herts SG4 8LX* Whitwell (0438) 871278

NICKOLS-RAWLE, Peter John. b 44. Sarum & Wells Th Coll 76. **d** 78 **p** 79. C Ex St Thos *Ex* 78-80; C Ex St Thos and Em 80; C Old Shoreham *Chich* 80-86; C New Shoreham 80-86; P-in-c Donnington 86-90; Chapl RAF from 90. *c/o MOD, Adastral House, Theobald's Road, London WC1X 8RU* 071-430 7268

NICOL, Ernest. b 25. S'wark Ord Course 71. **d** 74 **p** 75. NSM Hornsey Ch Ch *Lon* 74-75; NSM Hornsey St Geo 76-84; C Hendon Ch Ch 85-90; rtd 90; C Steeton *Bradf* from 90; Asst Chapl Airedale Hosp Bradf from 90. *12 Parkway, Steeton, Keighley BD20 6SX* Keighley (0535) 654270

NICOLAS, Brother. *See* STEBBING, Michael Langdale

NICOLE, Bruce. b 54. ACIB. Wycliffe Hall Ox 89. **d** 91. C Headley All SS *Guildf* from 91. *7 Windmill Drive, Bordon, Hants GU35 8AL* Headley Down (0428) 714565

NICOLL, Alexander Charles Fiennes. b 34. Lon Univ DipTh66. Lon Coll of Div 66. **d** 68 **p** 69. C Trentham *Lich* 68-71; C Hednesford 72-74; P-in-c Quarnford 74-84; V Longnor 74-84; P-in-c Sheen 80-84; V Longnor, Quarnford and Sheen from 85. *The Vicarage, Longnor, Buxton, Derbyshire* Longnor (029883) 316

NICOLL, Miss Angela Olive. b 50. Linc Th Coll 77. **dss** 79 **d** 87. Catford St Laur *S'wark* 79-83; Peckham St Jo w St Andr 83-87; Par Dn 87-88; Par Dn New Addington from 88. *78 Gascoigne Road, Croydon CR0 0NE* Lodge Hill (0689) 848123

NICOLL, George Lorimer. b 23. **d** 75. NSM Clydebank *Glas* from 75. *19 McKenzie Avenue, Clydebank, Dunbartonshire G81 2AT* 041-952 5116

NICOLSON, Paul Roderick. b 32. Cuddesdon Coll 65. **d** 67 **p** 68. C Farnham Royal *Ox* 67-70; Lic to Offic *St Alb* 70-82; C Hambleden Valley *Ox* from 82. *The Vicarage, Turville, Henley-on-Thames, Oxon RG9 6QU* Turville Heath (049163) 240

NIELD, Colin. b 35. Leeds Univ MA(Theol)69. Sarum Th Coll 58. **d** 60 **p** 61. V Laxton *S'well* 68-70; V Egmanton 69-70; R W Retford 70-84; R Elie and Earlsferry *St And* 85-89; R Pittenweem 87-89; rtd 89; Perm to Offic Ex from 89; Sarum from 91. *Gramercy, 110 West Bay Road, Bridport, Dorset DT6 4AX* Bridport (0308) 27462

NIELSEN, Ronald Marius Boniface. b 09. **d** 51 **p** 52. OSB from 46; Lic to Offic *Ox* from 51. *Elmore Abbey, Speen, Newbury, Berks RG13 1SA* Newbury (0635) 33080

NIGHTINGALE, John Brodie. b 42. Pemb Coll Ox BA64 Bris Univ DSocStuds65 Qu Coll Cam BA67. Westcott Ho Cam 65. **d** 67 **p** 68. C Wythenshawe St Martin *Man* 67-70; Nigeria 70-76; P-in-c Amberley w N Stoke *Chich* 76-79; Adult Educn Adv 76-79; Asst Home Sec Gen Syn Bd for Miss and Unity 80-84; Miss Sec 84-87; P-in-c Wolverton w Norton Lindsey and Langley *Cov* from 87; Dioc Miss Adv from 87. *The Rectory, Wolverton, Stratford-upon-Avon, Warks CV37 0HF* Stratford-upon-Avon (0789) 731278

NIGHTINGALE, William Hirst. b 11. ACCS52. St Aug Coll Cant. **d** 61 **p** 63. Ind Chapl *S'wark* 65-76; Hon C Wimbledon 70-81; rtd 82; Perm to Offic *S'wark* from 84. *14 Melbury Gardens, London SW20 0DJ* 081-946 8361

NIMMO, Alexander Emsley. b 53. Aber Univ BD76 Edin Univ MPhil83. Edin Th Coll 76. **d** 78 **p** 79. Prec St Andr Cathl Inverness *Mor* 78-81; P-in-c Stornoway *Arg* 81-84; R 84; R Edin St Mich and All SS *Edin* 84-90; R Aber St Marg *Ab* from 90. *St Margaret's Rectory, Gallowgate, Aberdeen AB1 1EA* Aberdeen (0224) 644969

NIND, Canon Anthony Lindsay. b 26. MBE86. Ball Coll Ox BA50 MA50. Cuddesdon Coll 50. **d** 52 **p** 53. R Langton Matravers *Sarum* 61-70; Brazil 70-75; Chapl Vienna Ch Ch *Eur* 75-80; Adn Switzerland 80-86; Chapl Zurich w St Gallen and Winterthur 80-86; Hon Can Brussels Cathl from 81; Dean Gib 86-89; rtd 89. *7 Trinity Close, Trinity Lane, Wareham, Dorset BH20 4LL* Wareham (0929) 553434

NIND, Robert William Hampden. b 31. Ball Coll Ox BA54 MA60. Cuddesdon Coll 54. **d** 56 **p** 57. C Spalding *Linc* 56-60; Jamaica 60-67; P-in-c Battersea St Bart *S'wark* 67-70; V Brixton St Matt 70-82; Lic to Offic 82-84 and from 89; Ind Chapl 84-89; Ind Chapl *Ox* from 89. *1 Ivy Crescent, Cippenham Lane, Slough SL1 5DA* Slough (0753) 28131

NINEHAM, Canon Prof Dennis Eric. b 21. Qu Coll Ox BA43 MA46 Cam Univ BD64 Birm Univ Hon DD72. Linc Th Coll 44. **d** 44 **p** 45. Warden Keble Coll Ox 69-79; Hon Can Bris Cathl *Bris* 80-86; Prof Th Bris Univ 80-86; rtd 86; Perm to Offic *Ox* from 87. *4 Wootten*

Drive, Iffley Turn, Oxford OX4 4DS Oxford (0865) 715941

NINHAM, Canon Cecil Ronald. b 08. Lon Univ BD31. AKC31. **d** 31 **p** 32. V Loddon w Sisland *Nor* 52-73; Hon Can Nor Cathl 59-79; rtd 73. *21 St Mary's Road, Poringland, Norwich NR14 7SR* Framingham Earl (05086) 2346

NINIS, Ven Richard Betts. b 31. Linc Coll Ox BA53 MA62. Linc Th Coll 53. **d** 55 **p** 56. C Poplar All SS w St Frideswide *Lon* 55-62; V Heref St Martin *Heref* 62-71; V Upper and Lower Bullinghope w Grafton 68-71; R Dewsall w Callow 68-71; Dioc Missr 69-74; Preb Heref Cathl 70-74; Telford Planning Officer *Lich* 70-74; Can Res and Treas Lich Cathl from 74; Adn Stafford 74-80; Adn Lich from 80. *24 The Close, Lichfield, Staffs WS13 7LD* Lichfield (0543) 258813

NIXON, Mrs Annette Rose. b 37. K Coll Lon BD58 Newc Univ CertEd73. **d** 88. Dioc Youth Officer *Ox* 84-90; Par Dn Earley St Pet from 88. *17 Wallace Close, Reading RG5 3HW* Reading (0734) 669116

NIXON, Canon Bernard Lawrence. b 26. St Jo Coll Dur BA55 DipTh56. **d** 56 **p** 57. C Goole *Sheff* 56-60; Chapl Wm Baker Tech Coll 60-67; V Silsoe *St Alb* 67-82; RD Ampthill 75-87; Hon Can St Alb from 79; V Silsoe, Pulloxhill and Flitton from 82. *The Vicarage, Silsoe, Bedford MK45 4ED* Silsoe (0525) 60438

NIXON, Canon Charles Hunter. b 07. Keble Coll Ox BA30 MA47. Dorchester Miss Coll 31. **d** 33 **p** 34. Hon Can Ely Cathl *Ely* 70-78; R Coveney 73-78; rtd 78; Perm to Offic *Nor* from 78. *23 Cleeves Drive, Walsingham, Norfolk NR22 6EQ* Walsingham (0328) 820310

NIXON, David John. b 59. St Chad's Coll Dur BA81. St Steph Ho Ox 88. **d** 91. C Plymouth St Pet *Ex* from 91. *56 Neswick Street, Plymouth PL1 5JN* Plymouth (0752) 225713

NIXON, John David. b 38. CEng70 MICE Leeds Univ BSc60. Linc Th Coll 76. **d** 78 **p** 79. C Rugby St Andr *Cov* 78-83; TV 83-86; TV Bicester w Bucknell, Caversfield and Launton *Ox* from 86. *The Vicarage, The Spinney, Launton, Bicester, Oxon OX6 0EP* Bicester (0869) 252377

NIXON, Phillip Edward. b 48. Ch Ch Ox MA73 DPhil73 Trin Coll Cam BA80. Westcott Ho Cam 78. **d** 81 **p** 82. C Leeds Halton St Wilfrid *Ripon* 81-84; V Goring *Ox* 84; V Goring w S Stoke from 84. *The Vicarage, Manor Road, Goring, Reading RG8 9DR* Goring-on-Thames (0491) 872196

NIXON, Rosemary Ann. b 45. CertEd66 Lon Univ DipTh72 BD73 Dur Univ MA83. Dalton Ho Bris 69. **dss** 73 **d** 87. W Hampstead St Luke *Lon* 73-75; Tutor St Jo Coll w Cranmer Hall Dur 75-89; Ches le Street *Dur* 78-87; NSM 87-89; TM Gateshead from 90; Dir Urban Studies Unit from 90. *St Columba House, Peterborough Close, Gateshead NE8 1RB* 091-478 5116

NIXSON, Peter. b 27. Ball Coll Ox BA51 MA59 Ex Univ PGCE67 DipEd72. Coll of Resurr Mirfield 51. **d** 53 **p** 54. C Babbacombe *Ex* 53-56; C Swindon New Town *Bris* 56-57; C Boyne Hill *Ox* 57-60; C-in-c Bayswater St Mary CD 60-66; Perm to Offic Ex 66-67 and 70-85; Lich 67-69; Hd RE Oswestry Boys' High Sch 67-69; Hon C Oswestry H Trin *Lich* 69-70; Sch Coun Tiverton 70-75; Newton Abbot 75-85; V Winkleigh *Ex* from 85; R Ashreigney from 85; R Broadwoodkelly from 85; V Brushford from 85; RD Chulmleigh from 87. *The Vicarage, Torrington Road, Winkleigh, Devon EX19 8HR* Winkleigh (0837) 83719

✠**NOAKES, Most Rev George.** b 24. Univ of Wales (Abth) BA48 Univ of Wales Hon DD90. Wycliffe Hall Ox 49. **d** 50 **p** 52 **c** 82. C Lamp *St D* 50-56; V Eglwyswrw and Meline 56-59; V Tregaron 59-67; V Cardiff Dewi Sant *Llan* 67-76; R Abth *St D* 76-80; Can St D Cathl 77-79; Adn Cardigan 79-82; V Llanychaiarn w Llanddeiniol 80-82; Bp St D 82-91; Abp Wales 87-91; rtd 91. *Hafod-Lon, Rhydargaeau, Carmarthen, Dyfed* Llanpunsaint (0267) 253302

NOAKES, Harold Isaac. b 05. St Jo Coll Cam BA28 MA31. Bps' Coll Cheshunt. **d** 31 **p** 32. R Ampton w Lt Livermere and Ingham St E 65-68; rtd 75. *Rutlands, Willows Green, Chelmsford* Chelmsford (0245) 361243

NOAKES, Preb Kenneth William. b 43. Trin Coll Ox BA65 MA68 DPhil71. Cuddesdon Coll 66. **d** 68 **p** 69. C Prestbury *Glouc* 68-71; Lib Pusey Ho 71-76; Past Tr Chapl *Truro* from 76; P-in-c Marhamchurch 77-91; R Marhamchurch w Launcells 78-87; Preb St Endellion from 85; V Torpoint from 87. *The Vicarage, 3 Grove Park, Torpoint, Cornwall PL11 2PP* Plymouth (0752) 812418

NOAKES, Ronald Alfred. b 13. LTCL MRST Open Univ BA76 Auckland Univ. St Anselm's Coll LTh. **d** 37 **p** 37. New Zealand 37-47; C S w N Hayling *Portsm* 47-48; Chapl Marseille, Hyeres and St Raphael 48-52; Mediterranean Miss to Seamen 48-52; Chapl RAF 52-62; V Whixley w Green Hammerton *Ripon* from 61. *The Vicarage, Whixley, York YO5 8AR* Boroughbridge (0423) 330269

NOBBS, John Ernest. b 35. Tyndale Hall Bris 60. **d** 63 **p** 64. C Walthamstow St Mary *Chelmsf* 63-66; C Braintree 66-69; C Wakef St Andr and St Mary *Wakef* 69-71; C Tooting Graveney St Nic *S'wark* 71-74; C Woking St Pet *Guildf* 74-77; C Worthing St Geo *Chich* 78-88; C Rayleigh *Chelmsf* from 88. *86 Lower Lambricks, Rayleigh, Essex SS6 8DB* Rayleigh (0268) 777430

NOBES, Richard Arthur. b 36. Ch Ch Ox BA58 MA65. St Steph Ho Ox 58. **d** 60 **p** 61. C Rushall *Lich* 60-63; Asst Chapl K Sch Ely 63-66; Perm to Offic *Ely* 63-64; Hon Min Can Ely Cathl 64-69; C Ely 66-69; V Cople *St Alb* 69-76; P-in-c Willington 71-76; V Thornbury *Glouc* 76-85; C Hendon St Alphage *Lon* 90; R Gamlingay w Hatley St Geo and E Hatley *Ely* from 90. *The Rectory, Gamlingay, Sandy, Beds SG19 3EU* Gamlingay (0767) 50228

NOBLE, Alexander Frederick Innes. b 30. Selw Coll Cam BA53 MA57. Lon Coll of Div 53. **d** 55 **p** 56. C Stratton St Margaret *Bris* 55-57; C Brislington St Luke 57-59; Chapl Pierrepont Sch Frensham 59-61; Asst Chapl Repton Sch Derby 61-63; Chapl 63-66; Chapl Blundell's Sch Tiverton 66-72; St Jo C of E Sch Cowley 73-76; Cranbrook Sch Kent 76-81; St Geo Sch Harpenden 81-90. *The Parsonage, Gaston Lane, South Warnborough, Basingstoke, Hants RG25 1RH* Basingstoke (0256) 862843

NOBLE, Canon Arthur. b 12. TCD BA35 MA38. TCD Div Sch Div Test. **d** 36 **p** 37. I Lisburn Ch Ch *Conn* 61-82; Preb Conn Cathl 74-79; Prec 79-82; rtd 82. *38 King's Road, Knock, Belfast BT5 6JJ* Belfast (0232) 652815

NOBLE, Christopher John Lancelot. b 58. Aston Tr Scheme 88 Oak Hill Th Coll DipHE90. **d** 90 **p** 91. C Tonbridge SS Pet and Paul *Roch* from 90. *12 Salisbury Road, Tonbridge, Kent TN10 4PB* Tonbridge (0732) 357205

NOBLE, David. b 37. S Dios Minl Tr Scheme 84. **d** 87 **p** 88. C Alverstoke *Portsm* 87-89; Australia from 90. *Anglican Rectory, Lancaster Road, PO Box 139, Jerramungup, W Australia 6337* Albany (98) 351175

NOBLE, Francis Alick. b 10. Trin Coll Cam BA33 MA37. Linc Th Coll 33. **d** 36 **p** 37. R Guiseley *Bradf* 67-78; rtd 78; Perm to Offic *St As* from 78. *16 Aberconwy Parc, Prestatyn, Clwyd LL19 9HH* Prestatyn (0745) 856820

NOBLE, Graham Edward. b 49. SS Paul & Mary Coll Cheltenham CertEd71 Open Univ BA74. E Anglian Minl Tr Course 85. **d** 88 **p** 89. C Kesgrave *St E* 88-90; P-in-c Gt and Lt Blakenham w Baylham and Nettlestead from 90. *The Rectory, Stowmarket Road, Great Blakenham, Ipswich IP6 0LS* Ipswich (0473) 623840

NOBLE, Paul Vincent. b 54. Leeds Univ BA75 PGCE76 Ox Univ BA81 MA85. St Steph Ho Ox 79. **d** 82 **p** 83. C Prestbury *Glouc* 82-85; P-in-c Avening w Cherington 85-90; V The Suttons w Tydd *Linc* from 90. *The Vicarage, Sutton St James, Spalding, Lincs PE12 0EE* Sutton St James (094585) 457

NOBLE, Peter Hirst. b 37. Lon Univ BD68 Leeds Univ MPhil72. Cranmer Hall Dur 65. **d** 68 **p** 69. C Honley *Wakef* 68-72; P-in-c Moss *Sheff* 72-81; V Askern from 72. *The Vicarage, Askern, Doncaster, S Yorkshire DN6 0PH* Doncaster (0302) 700404

NOBLE, Philip David. b 46. Glas Univ BSc67 Edin Univ BD70. Edin Th Coll 67. **d** 70 **p** 71. C Edin Ch Ch *Edin* 70-72; Papua New Guinea 72-75; R Cambuslang *Glas* 76-83; R Uddingston 76-83; Ev Prestwick 83-85; R Prestwick from 85. *56 Ayr Road, Prestwick, Ayrshire KA9 1RR* Prestwick (0292) 77108

NOBLE, Robert. b 43. TCD BA66 BD73. **d** 68 **p** 69. C Holywood *D & D* 68-71; Chapl RAF from 71. *c/o MOD, Adastral House, Theobald's Road, London WC1X 8RU* 071-430 7268

NOBLETT, William Alexander. b 53. Southn Univ BTh78. Sarum & Wells Th Coll 74. **d** 78 **p** 79. C Sholing *Win* 78-80; I Ardamine w Kiltennel, Glascarrig etc *C & O* 80-82; Chapl RAF 82-84; V Middlesb St Thos *York* 84-87; Asst Chapl HM Pris Wakef 87-89; Chapl from 89. *HM Prison, Love Lane, Wakefield, W Yorkshire WF2 9AG* Wakefield (0924) 378282

NOCK, Peter Arthur. b 15. Keble Coll Ox BA36 MA42. Bps' Coll Cheshunt 37. **d** 39 **p** 40. V Maney *Birm* 71-81;

rtd 81; Perm to Offic *Carl* from 81. *West View, Dufton, Appleby, Cumbria CA16 6DB* Appleby (07683) 51413

NOCK, Roland George William. b 62. Edin Th Coll. **d** 91. C Dunfermline *St And* from 91. *27 Victoria Terrace, Dunfermline KY12 0LY* Dunfermline (0383) 732362

NOCKELS, Donald Reginald. b 09. Leeds Univ BA32. Coll of Resurr Mirfield 32. **d** 34 **p** 35. V Cononley w Bradley *Bradf* 63-73; rtd 73. *Ellesborough Manor, Butlers Cross, Aylesbury, Bucks HP17 0XF*

NOCKELS, John Martin. b 46. Lich Th Coll Qu Coll Birm 73. **d** 73 **p** 74. C Eccleshill *Bradf* 73-76; C Fawley *Win* 76-78; V Southn St Jude 78-84; R Tadley St Pet from 84. *The Rectory, The Green, Tadley, Basingstoke, Hants RG26 6PB* Tadley (0734) 814860

NODDER, Jonathan James Colmore. b 37. Lon Univ DipTh64. Tyndale Hall Bris 63. **d** 65 **p** 66. C Bebington *Ches* 65-71; V Stockport St Mark 71-88; V Burton in Kendal *Carl* 88-90; V Burton and Holme from 90. *St James's Vicarage, Glebe Close, Burton-in-Kendal, Carnforth, Lancs LA6 1PL* Carnforth (0524) 781391

NODDER, Thomas Arthur (Brother Arnold). b 20. K Coll Lon 58. **d** 60 **p** 61. Brotherhood of the H Cross from 49; SSF from 63; Lic to Offic Newc 69-70; Birm 70-83 and 89-90; Perm from 90; Lic Sarum 83-89; rtd 90. *c/o The Provincial Bursar, 113 Gillott Road, Birmingham B16 0ET* 021-454 8302

NODDINGS, John Henry. b 39. Chich Th Coll 80. **d** 81 **p** 82. C Southborough St Pet w Ch Ch and St Matt *Roch* 81-83; C Prittlewell *Chelmsf* 83-86; V Clay Hill St Jo *Lon* 86-88; V Clay Hill St Jo and St Luke from 88; Chapl Chase Farm Hosp Enfield from 88. *St Luke's Vicarage, 92 Browning Road, Enfield, Middx EN2 0HG* 081-363 6055

NOEL, Brother. *See* ALLEN, Noel Stephen

NOEL, Canon Frank Arthur. b 20. TCD BA44 MA49. CITC 45. **d** 45 **p** 46. I Mullabrack w Kilcluney *Arm* 63-75; RD Mullabrack 75-88; I Acton w Drumbanagher 75-88; Preb Arm Cathl 86-88; rtd 88; Lic to Offic *Arm* from 90. *31 Woodford Drive, Armagh BT60 7AY* Armagh (0861) 527787

NOEL, Samuel Maurice. b 16. Oak Hill Th Coll 40. **d** 41 **p** 42. I Ballymascanlan *Arm* 74-83; rtd 83. *Creggan, Grahamville Estate, Newry, Co Down BT34 4DD* Kilkeel (06937) 64092

NOEL-COX, Edward Lovis. b 99. Bps' Coll Cheshunt 22. **d** 23 **p** 25. Chapl Qu Mary's Hosp Carshalton 51-64; rtd 64; Perm to Offic *Chich* from 66. *Flat 1B, 22 Bedford Avenue, Bexhill-on-Sea, E Sussex TN40 1NG* Bexhill-on-Sea (0424) 225157

NOISE, Robin Allan. b 31. K Coll Lon 53. **d** 57 **p** 58. C Wyken *Cov* 57-60; R Churchover w Willey 60-66; P-in-c Harborough Magna 62-66; V S Leamington St Jo 66-81; V Alveston from 81. *The Vicarage, Alveston, Stratford-upon-Avon, Warks CV37 7QB* Stratford-upon-Avon (0789) 292777

NOKES, Miss Amy Louisa Mary. b 12. dss 62 **d** 87. Hon C Portsea St Geo *Portsm* 87-89; rtd 89. *The Home of Comfort, 17 Victoria Grove, Southsea, Hants PO5 1NF*

NOKES, Peter Warwick. b 48. Leic Univ BA71. Westcott Ho Cam 79. **d** 81 **p** 82. C Northfield *Birm* 81-84; C Ludlow *Heref* 84-87; P-in-c Writtle w Highwood *Chelmsf* from 87. *The Vicarage, 19 Lodge Road, Writtle, Chelmsford CM1 3HY* Chelmsford (0245) 421282

NOKES, Robert Harvey. b 39. Keble Coll Ox BA61 MA65 Birm Univ DipTh63. Qu Coll Birm 61. **d** 63 **p** 64. C Totteridge *St Alb* 63-67; C Dunstable 67-73; V Langford 73-90; R Braughing w Furneux Pelham and Stocking Pelham from 90. *The Rectory, 7A Green End, Braughing, Ware, Herts SG11 2PG* Ware (0920) 822619

NOLAN, James Charles William. b 44. Chich Th Coll 75. **d** 77 **p** 78. C Crewe St Andr *Ches* 77-79; C Sale St Anne 79-83; R Holme Runcton w S Runcton and Wallington *Ely* from 83; V Tottenhill w Wormegay from 83; R Watlington from 83. *The Rectory, Downham Road, Watlington, King's Lynn, Norfolk PE33 0HS* King's Lynn (0553) 810305

NOLAN, James Joseph. b 16. Cranmer Hall Dur. **d** 61 **p** 62. V Heworth w Peasholme St Cuth *York* 66-72; CPAS Staff 72-74; R Bridlington Priory *York* 74-82; rtd 82. *9 Vicarage Close, Seamer, Scarborough, N Yorkshire YO12 4QS* Scarborough (0723) 862443

NOLAN, Canon John. b 25. TCD BA51 MA55. CITC 51. **d** 51 **p** 52. C Carrickfergus *Conn* 51-53; Dean's V Belf Cathl 53-55; VC 55-79; Min Can 60-88; C Belf Upper Falls *Conn* from 79; Can Belf Cathl from 88; RD Derriaghy *Conn* from 90. *38 Upper Green, Dunmurry, Belfast BT17 0EL* Belfast (0232) 610755

NOLAN, Marcus. b 54. Bris Univ BEd. Ridley Hall Cam. **d** 83 **p** 84. C Dagenham *Chelmsf* 83-86; C Finchley St

Paul and St Luke *Lon* 86-90; V W Hampstead Trin from 90. *Holy Trinity Church Office, Finchley Road, London NW3 5HT* 071-435 0083

NOON, Canon Edward Arthur. b 16. Selw Coll Cam BA38 MA42. Bps' Coll Cheshunt 38. **d** 40 **p** 41. V Horley *S'wark* 65-77; Hon Can S'wark Cathl 72-83; P-in-c Purley St Barn 77-83; rtd 83; Hon C Overbury w Teddington, Alstone etc *Worc* 83-86; Perm to Offic *Glouc* from 86. *40 Shepherds Leaze, Wotton-under-Edge, Glos GL12 7LQ* Dursley (0453) 844978

NORBURN, Very Rev Richard Evelyn Walter. b 21. Witwatersrand Univ BA44 TDip44. St Paul's Grahamstown 49. **d** 51 **p** 53. V Norbury St Phil *Cant* 65-75; V Addington 75-81; Hon Can Cant Cathl 79-81; RD Croydon Addington 81; Dean Botswana 81-88; rtd 89. *Tebogong, 2 Rectory Cottages, Middleton, Saxmundham, Suffolk IP17 3NR* Saxmundham (0728) 73721

NORBURN, Canon Richard Henry. b 32. St Edm Hall Ox BA57 DipTh58. Wycliffe Hall Ox 57. **d** 59 **p** 59. C Sudbury St Greg and St Pet *St E* 59-65; Dioc Youth Officer 65-74; P-in-c Gt Livermere 74-81; R Ampton w Lt Livermere and Ingham 74-81; RD Thingoe 78-88; Hon Can St E Cathl from 81; R Ingham w Ampton and Gt and Lt Livermere from 81. *The Rectory, Ingham, Bury St Edmunds, Suffolk IP31 1NS* Culford (028484) 430

NORFOLK, Ven Edward Matheson. b 21. Leeds Univ BA44. Coll of Resurr Mirfield 41. **d** 46 **p** 47. R Gt Berkhamsted *St Alb* 69-81; Hon Can St Alb 72-82; V Kings Langley 81-82; Adn St Alb 82-87; rtd 87; Perm to Offic *Ex* from 87. *5 Fairlawn Court, Sidmouth, Devon EX10 8UR* Sidmouth (0395) 514222

NORFOLK, Archdeacon of. *See* DAWSON, Ven Peter

✠**NORGATE, Rt Rev Cecil Richard.** b 21. St Chad's Coll Dur BA47 DipTh49. **d** 49 **p** 50 **c** 84. C Wallsend St Pet *Newc* 49-54; Tanganyika 54-64; Tanzania from 64; Can and V-Gen 57-83; Bp Masasi from 84. *Private Bag, PO Masasi, Mtwara Region, Tanzania*

NORGATE, Norman George. b 32. Qu Coll Cam BA55 MA58. Ridley Hall Cam. **d** 57 **p** 58. C Erith St Paul *Roch* 57-60; C E Twickenham St Steph *Lon* 60-63; V Bexleyheath St Pet *Roch* 63-71; V Woking St Mary *Guildf* 71-83; V Tunbridge Wells St Jas *Roch* from 83. *The Vicarage, 12 Shandon Close, Tunbridge Wells, Kent TN2 2RE* Tunbridge Wells (0892) 30687

NORKETT, Alan. b 45. Sarum & Wells Th Coll 85. **d** 87 **p** 88. C Shrewsbury St Giles w Sutton and Atcham *Lich* 87-90; V Mow Cop from 90. *The Vicarage, 5 Congleton Road, Mow Cop, Stoke-on-Trent ST7 3PJ* Stoke-on-Trent (0782) 515077

NORMAN, Andrew Herbert. b 54. K Coll Lon BD77 AKC77 PhD88. St Steph Ho Ox 77. **d** 78 **p** 79. C Deal St Leon w Sholden *Cant* 78-81; C Maidstone All SS and St Phil w Tovil 81-84; V Tenterden St Mich from 84; Chapl Benenden Hosp Kent from 86. *The Vicarage, Ashford Road, St Michael's, Tenterden, Kent TN30 6PY* Tenterden (05806) 4670

NORMAN, Arthur Leslie Frayne. b 08. Sarum Th Coll 29. **d** 31 **p** 33. Chapl HM Pris Swansea 58-75; rtd 75. *4 Malvern Terrace, Brynmill, Swansea* Swansea (0792) 59310

NORMAN, Dr Edward Robert. b 38. FRHistS72 Selw Coll Cam BA61 PhD64 MA65 BD67 DD78. Linc Th Coll 65. **d** 65 **p** 71. Fell Jes Coll Cam 64-71; Lect Cam Univ 64-88; Lic to Offic *Ely* from 65; Fell and Dean Peterho 71-88; Six Preacher Cant Cathl *Cant* 84-89; Chapl Ch Ch Coll Cant from 88. *Christ Church College, Canterbury, Kent CT1 1QU* Canterbury (0227) 762444

NORMAN, Garth. b 38. St Chad's Coll Dur BA62 DipTh63 MA68 Cam Inst of Educn PGCE68 UEA MEd84. **d** 63 **p** 64. C Wandsworth St Anne *S'wark* 63-66; C Trunch w Swafield *Nor* 66-71; R Gimingham 71-77; RD Repps 75-83; TR Trunch 77-83; Prin Chiltern Chr Tr Course *Ox* 83-87; C W Wycombe w Bledlow Ridge, Bradenham and Radnage 83-87; Dir of Tr *Roch* from 88. *18 Kings Avenue, Rochester, Kent ME1 3DS* Medway (0634) 41232

NORMAN, Jillianne Elizabeth. b 59. DCR80. Ridley Hall Cam 85. **d** 88. Par Dn Fishponds St Jo *Bris* from 88. *38 Chester Park Road, Bristol BS16 3RQ* Bristol (0272) 652184

NORMAN, Canon John Ronald. b 15. GradIT Lon Univ BA40. Linc Th Coll 40. **d** 42 **p** 43. R Dunnington *York* 61-72; R Bolton Percy 72-82; Dioc Worship Adv 72-82; Can and Preb York Minster from 77; rtd 82. *Iona, 5 Northfield Close, Pocklington, York YO4 2EG* Pocklington (0759) 303170

NORMAN, John William Leneve. b 15. Clifton Th Coll 40. **d** 42 **p** 43. V Paulton *B & W* 62-81; V Farrington Gurney 77-81; rtd 81; Perm to Offic *B & W* from 82. *4 Hill View Road, Charlcombe Lane, Bath BA1 6NX* Bath (0225) 333584

NORMAN, Linda Mary. b 48. Man Univ BSc69 CertEd70 St Jo Coll Dur BA82. **dss** 83 **d** 87. York St Mich-le-Belfrey *York* 83-87; Par Dn 87-88; rtd 88. *23 Ainsty Avenue, Dringhouses, York YO2 2HH* York (0904) 706152

NORMAN, Michael Heugh. b 18. Qu Coll Cam BA48 Kent Univ MA. Westcott Ho Cam 48. **d** 50 **p** 51. C St Peter-in-Thanet *Cant* 50-52; S Africa from 52. *5 Rosedale Cottage, Lower Nursery Road, Rosebank, 7700 South Africa* Cape Town (21) 685-3622

NORMAN, Michael John. b 59. Southn Univ LLB82. Wycliffe Hall Ox 82. **d** 85 **p** 86. C Woodley *Ox* 85-89; C Uphill *B & W* from 89. *2 Westbury Crescent, Weston-super-Mare, Avon BS23 4RB* Weston-super-Mare (0934) 623195

NORMAN, Peter John. b 59. Chich Th Coll 84. **d** 87 **p** 88. C Farncombe *Guildf* 87-91; C Cockington *Ex* from 91. *St Peter's House, Queensway, Chelston, Torquay TQ2 8BP* Torquay (0803) 606555

NORMAN, Roy Albert. b 23. **d** 65 **p** 66. C Thornbury *Glouc* 67-70; P-in-c Woolaston w Alvington 70-80; R 80-88; rtd 88. *Yew Tree Cottage, Crossways, Ruardean, Glos GL17 9XB* Dean (0594) 542503

NORMAN, Canon William Beadon. b 26. Trin Coll Cam BA49 MA55. Ridley Hall Cam 52. **d** 52 **p** 53. V Alne *York* 65-74; RD Warley *Birm* 74-79; V Blackheath 74-79; Hon Can Birm Cathl 78-91; TR Kings Norton 79-91; RD Kings Norton 82-87; Warden Dioc Readers Bd from 84; rtd 91. *37 Cloudesdale Road, London SW17 8ET*

NORMAN, William John. b 08. St Andr Whittlesford. **d** 44 **p** 45. Area Sec CMS 56-74; R Buriton *Portsm* 74-79; rtd 79. *22 Middlehill Road, Colehill, Wimborne, Dorset BH21 2SD* Wimborne (0202) 884775

NORMINGTON, Eric. b 16. S'wark Ord Course. **d** 63 **p** 64. V Bath Weston All SS *B & W* 71-78; P-in-c N Stoke 76-78; R Bath Weston All SS w N Stoke 78-81; rtd 81; Perm to Offic *Ex* from 81. *53 Higher Woolbrook Park, Sidmouth, Devon EX10 9ED* Sidmouth (0395) 512016

NORRIS, Mrs Alison. b 55. St Andr Univ MTheol77 Dur Univ CertEd78. Cant Sch of Min. **dss** 82 **d** 87. Warlingham w Chelsham and Farleigh *S'wark* 83-85; Willingham *Ely* 85-87; Hon Par Dn 87-90; Hon Par Dn Worle *B & W* from 90. *6 Rookery Close, Worle, Weston-super-Mare, Avon BS22 9LN* Weston-super-Mare (0934) 512467

NORRIS, Allan Edward. b 43. St Jo Coll Dur BA72 DipTh73. Cranmer Hall Dur 69. **d** 73 **p** 74. C Plumstead St Jo w St Jas and St Paul *S'wark* 73-78; C Battersea Park St Sav 78-82; C Battersea St Geo w St Andr 78-82; V Grain w Stoke *Roch* from 82. *The Parsonage, Isle of Grain, Rochester, Kent ME3 0BS* Medway (0634) 270263

NORRIS, Andrew David. b 54. CPsychol St Andr Univ BSc78 Lon Univ MPhil80. E Anglian Minl Tr Course 87. **d** 90. C Worle *B & W* from 90. *6 Rookery Close, Worle, Weston-super-Mare, Avon BS22 9LN* Weston-super-Mare (0934) 512467

NORRIS, Andrew Peter. b 62. Aston Univ BSc83. St Jo Coll Nottm BA86 DPS87. **d** 87 **p** 88. C Mountsorrel Ch Ch and St Pet *Leic* 87-90; C Harborne Heath *Birm* 90-91; P-in-c Edgbaston St Germain from 91. *St Germain's Vicarage, 180 Portland Road, Birmingham B16 9TD*

NORRIS, Barry John. b 46. Nottm Univ CQSW75 MTh86 Open Univ BA80. St Jo Sem Wonersh. **d** 70 **p** 71. In RC Ch 70-72; C Wisbech SS Pet and Paul *Ely* 76-78; TV E Ham w Upton Park *Chelmsf* 78-81; Chapl RAF 81-87; V N Tadley St Mary *Win* from 87. *St Mary's Vicarage, Bishopswood Road, Tadley, Basingstoke, Hants RG26 6HQ* Tadley (0734) 814435

NORRIS, Clifford Joseph. b 29. Codrington Coll Barbados. **d** 61 **p** 68. Antigua 61-62; C Penton Street St Silas w All SS *Lon* 68-70; C Stepney St Dunstan and All SS 70-73; P-in-c Bethnal Green St Jas the Gt w St Jude 73-82; V Aveley and Purfleet *Chelmsf* from 82. *The Vicarage, Mill Road, Aveley, South Ockendon, Essex RM15 4SR* Purfleet (0708) 864865

NORRIS, Canon Edward Colston. b 06. St Cath Soc Ox BA37 MA41. Ridley Hall Cam 37. **d** 38 **p** 39. Chapl Napsbury Hosp St Alb 47-81; Hon Can St Alb 69-81; rtd 81. *8 Westwick Close, Hemel Hempstead, Herts HP2 4NH* Hemel Hempstead (0442) 53018

NORRIS, Eric Richard. b 43. Ripon Hall Ox 66. **d** 69 **p** 70. C Huyton St Mich *Liv* 69-72; C Mexborough *Sheff* 72-74; V Dalton 74-78; Lic to Offic Carl from 78; Dur from 89; Org Sec (Dio Carl) CECS 78-89; Area Appeals Manager N Co from 89. *25 Hardwick Road, Sedgefield, Stockton-on-Tees, Cleveland TS21 2AL* Sedgefield (0740) 22789

NORRISS, Victor William. b 11. Lon Univ BA32. Cuddesdon Coll 38. **d** 39 **p** 40. C Ringwood *Win* 68-71; R Wonston 71-86; rtd 86. *28 Petty Close, Tadburn Gardens, Romsey, Hants SO51 8UY* Romsey (0794) 523038

NORTH, Albert. b 13. Lon Univ BA35. Sarum Th Coll 64. **d** 65 **p** 66. V Gt w Lt Saling *Chelmsf* 70-72; V St Osyth 72-81; rtd 81; Perm to Offic *B & W* from 86. *18 Nelson House, Nelson Place West, Bath BA1 2BA* Bath (0225) 330896

NORTH, Barry Albert. b 46. **d** 82 **p** 83. C Brampton St Thos *Derby* 82-84; C Chesterfield St Aug 84-88; P-in-c Derby St Mark from 88. *St Mark's Vicarage, 119 Francis Street, Derby DE2 6DE* Derby (0332) 40183

NORTH, David Roland. b 45. Lich Th Coll 70 Qu Coll Birm 72. **d** 73 **p** 74. C Salesbury *Blackb* 73-76; C Marton 76-79; V Penwortham St Leon 79-87; R Whittington St Jo *Lich* from 87. *The Rectory, Whittington, Oswestry, Shropshire SY11 4DF* Oswestry (0691) 652222

NORTH, George Lewis. b 16. AKC41. **d** 41 **p** 42. C Northn St Mary *Pet* 41-46; C Whitchurch *Lich* 46-49; V Northn Ch Ch *Pet* 49-52; Chapl LCC Res Sch Hutton 52-57; R Brington w Molesworth and Old Weston *Ely* from 57; V Leighton Bromswold from 68. *The Rectory, Brington, Huntingdon, Cambs PE18 0PU* Bythorn (08014) 305

NORTH, Robert. b 54. Lon Univ BSc77. Ripon Coll Cuddesdon 78. **d** 81 **p** 82. C Leominster *Heref* 81-86; TV Heref St Martin w St Fran (S Wye Team Min) from 86; TV Dewsall w Callow from 86; TV Holme Lacy w Dinedor from 86; TV Lt Dewchurch, Aconbury w Ballingham and Bolstone from 86; TV Upper and Lower Bullinghope w Grafton from 86. *The Vicarage, Holme Lacy, Hereford HR2 6LU* Hereford (0432) 73352

NORTH, Canon Vernon Leslie. b 26. Bps' Coll Cheshunt 61. **d** 63 **p** 64. C N Holmwood *Guildf* 63-65; C Dunstable *St Alb* 65-68; V Stotfold from 68; RD Shefford 79-91; Hon Can St Alb from 89. *The Vicarage, Church Road, Stotfold, Hitchin, Herts SG5 4NE* Hitchin (0462) 730218

NORTH WEST EUROPE, Archdeacon of. See LEWIS, Ven John

NORTHALL, Linda Barbara. b 50. Birm Univ BA72 Worc Coll of Educn PGCE75. Qu Coll Birm 88. **d** 90. C Wood End *Cov* from 90. *189 Deedmore Road, Coventry CV2 1ER* Coventry (0203) 619514

NORTHALL, Malcolm Walter. b 26. Bps' Coll Cheshunt 59 Ely Th Coll 63. **d** 64 **p** 65. C Bromsgrove St Jo *Worc* 64-67; V Blockley w Aston Magna *Glouc* 67-82; P-in-c Churchdown 82; V from 82. *The Vicarage, 5 Vicarage Close, Churchdown, Gloucester GL3 2NE* Churchdown (0452) 713203

NORTHAM, Canon Cavell Herbert James. See CAVELL-NORTHAM, Canon Cavell Herbert James

NORTHAM, Susan Jillian. b 36. Oak Hill Th Coll. **d** 89. NSM Enfield Ch Ch Trent Park *Lon* from 89. *22 Crescent East, Hadley Wood, Barnet, Herts EN4 0EN* 081-449 4483

NORTHAMPTON, Archdeacon of. See CHAPMAN, Ven Michael Robin

NORTHCOTT, Canon Geoffrey Stephen. b 21. Leeds Univ BA42. Coll of Resurr Mirfield 40. **d** 47 **p** 48. V Luton St Sav *St Alb* 68-89; Hon Can St Alb 72-89; RD Luton 82-89; rtd 89. *8 Nelson House, Nelson Place West, Bath BA1 2BA* Bath (0225) 338296

NORTHCOTT, Michael Stafford. b 55. St Chad's Coll Dur BA76 MA77 PhD. St Jo Coll Dur 80. **d** 81 **p** 82. C Chorlton-cum-Hardy St Clem *Man* 81-84; Malaysia 84-90; Lect New Coll Edin Univ from 90; NSM Edin Old St Paul *Edin* 90-91. *7 North Fort Street, Edinburgh EH6 4EY* 031-554 1651

NORTHCOTT, William Mark. b 36. Clifton Th Coll 61. **d** 64 **p** 65. C Walthamstow St Luke *Chelmsf* 64-68; C Idle H Trin *Bradf* 68-70; N Sec CMJ 70-79; V Withnell *Blackb* 79-90; R Glenrothes *St And* 90-91; Asst Dioc Supernumerary 90-91. *Address temp unknown*

NORTHERN FRANCE, Archdeacon of. See LEA, Ven Montague Brian

NORTHFIELD, Stephen Richmond. b 55. Lon Univ BSc77 Southn Univ BTh84. Sarum & Wells Th Coll 79. **d** 82 **p** 83. C Colchester St Jas, All SS, St Nic and St Runwald *Chelmsf* 82-85; C Chelmsf All SS 85-89; V Ramsey w Lt Oakley and Wrabness from 89. *The Vicarage, Ramsey*

Road, Ramsey, Harwich, Essex CO12 5EU Ramsey (0255) 880291

NORTHOLT, Archdeacon of. See SHIRRAS, Ven Edward Scott

NORTHOVER, Kevin Charles. b 57. Coll of Resurr Mirfield 89. **d** 91. C Kingston upon Hull St Alb *York* from 91. *St Alban's Clergy House, 43 Fairfield Road, Hull HU5 4QX* Hull (0482) 43642

NORTHRIDGE, Canon Herbert Aubrey Hamilton. b 16. TCD BA40 MA43. **d** 41 **p** 42. I Derg *D & R* 50-81; Can Derry Cathl 72-81; rtd 81. *Goblusk, Ballinamallard, Co Fermanagh BT94 2LW* Ballinamallard (036581) 676

NORTHUMBERLAND, Archdeacon of. See THOMAS, Ven William Jordison

NORTHWOOD, Michael Alan. b 36. Lon Univ BSc60. Wells Th Coll 62. **d** 64 **p** 65. C Eastbourne St Mary *Chich* 64-66; C Sanderstead All SS *S'wark* 66-68; P-in-c Alton Barnes w Alton Priors etc *Sarum* 69-75; Lic to Offic 76-86; Perm to Offic *Ox* from 86. *Saratoga, Long Grove, Seer Green, Beaconsfield, Bucks HP9 2QH* Beaconsfield (0494) 671127

NORTON, Anthony Bernard. b 40. Man Univ BA62. Linc Th Coll 63. **d** 65 **p** 66. C Westbury-on-Trym H Trin *Bris* 65-68; C Bris St Agnes w St Simon 68-70; P-in-c Bris St Werburgh 70-72; TV Bris St Agnes and St Simon w St Werburgh 72-77; V Lakenham St Alb *Nor* 77-85; TV Trunch from 85. *The Rectory, Clipped Hedge Lane, Southrepps, Norwich NR11 8NS* Southrepps (0263) 833404

NORTON, Harold Mercer. b 06. Lon Th Coll 28. **d** 31 **p** 32. Hon CF from 60; V Brill w Boarstall *Ox* 60-72; rtd 72. *Dulverton Hall, St Martin's Square, Scarborough YO11 2DQ* Scarborough (0723) 379549

NORTON, James Herbert Kitchener. b 37. Qu Coll Birm 78. **d** 81 **p** 82. NSM Donnington Wood *Lich* 81-83; C Matson *Glouc* 83-86; V New Mills *Derby* from 86. *St George's Vicarage, Church Lane, New Mills, Stockport SK12 4NP* New Mills (0663) 743225

NORTON, John Colin (Brother Andrew). b 25. Magd Coll Ox BA50 MA54. Cuddesdon Coll 50. **d** 52 **p** 53. C Bris St Mary Redcliffe w Temple *Bris* 52-57; C Bitterne Park *Win* 57-61; C-in-c Bishopwearmouth St Mary V w St Pet CD *Dur* 63-68; V Clifton All SS w Tyndalls Park *Bris* 68-78; Hon Can Bris Cathl 77-80; V Clifton All SS w St Jo 78-80; V Penistone *Wakef* 80-83; CR from 85. *St Peter's Priory, PO Box 991, Southdale, 2135 South Africa*

NORTON, Leslie Miles. b 10. Sarum Th Coll 46. **d** 48 **p** 49. V Dulwich Common St Pet *S'wark* 55-83; rtd 83; Perm to Offic *Bris* from 83. *46 St Dennis Road, Malmesbury, Wilts SN16 9BH* Malmesbury (0666) 824767

NORTON, Michael Clive Harcourt. b 34. Selw Coll Cam BA56 MA60 STM69 Univ of NSW MCom81. Union Th Sem (NY) 68 Wells Th Coll 56. **d** 58 **p** 59. C Gt Ilford St Jo *Chelmsf* 58-62; Australia from 62. *All Saints' Rectory, 2 Ambrose Street, Hunters Hill, Sydney, NSW, Australia 2110* Sydney (2) 817-2167

NORTON, Michael George Charles. b 34. Kelham Th Coll 55. **d** 59 **p** 60. C Sedgley All SS *Lich* 59-63; C Wombourne 63-65; C Stafford St Mary 65-68; V W Bromwich St Pet 68-76; V Wigginton from 76. *The Vicarage, Wigginton, Tamworth, Staffs B79 9DN* Tamworth (0827) 64537

NORTON, Michael James Murfin. b 42. Lich Th Coll 66. **d** 67 **p** 68. C W Bromwich St Fran *Lich* 67-70; C Wellington Ch Ch 70-72; C Norwood All SS *Cant* 72-76; V Elstow *St Alb* 76-82; Asst Chapl HM Pris Wakef 82-83; Chapl HM Pris Camp Hill 83-87; Parkhurst 87-88; Chapl HM Pris Win from 88. *HM Prison Winchester, Romsey Road, Winchester, Hants SO22 5DF* Winchester (0962) 854494

NORTON, Paul James. b 55. BA86. Oak Hill Th Coll 83. **d** 86 **p** 87. C Luton St Fran *St Alb* 86-89; C Bedworth *Cov* from 89. *St Andrew's House, Smorrall Lane, Bedworth, Nuneaton, Warks CV12 0JN* Bedworth (0203) 363322

NORTON, Peter Eric Pepler. b 38. TCD BA61 G&C Coll Cam PhD64. St Jo Coll Dur 78. **d** 80 **p** 81. C Ulverston St Mary w H Trin *Carl* 80-83; P-in-c Warcop, Musgrave, Soulby and Crosby Garrett 83-84; R 84-90; OCF 83-90; V Appleby *Carl* from 90; R Ormside from 90. *The Vicarage, Appleby-in-Westmorland, Cumbria CA16 6QW* Appleby (07683) 51461

NORTON, William Fullerton. b 23. Selw Coll Cam BA46 MA52. Wycliffe Hall Ox 46. **d** 48 **p** 49. C Tooting Graveney St Nic *S'wark* 68-71; V Hanley Road St Sav w St Paul *Lon* 71-89; rtd 89. *106 Trinity Road, London SW17 7RL* 081-672 1344

NORWICH, Archdeacon of. See HANDLEY, Ven Anthony Michael

NORWICH, Bishop of. See NOTT, Rt Rev Peter John

NORWICH, Dean of. See BURBRIDGE, Very Rev John Paul

NORWOOD, Christopher Leslie. b 46. St Chad's Coll Dur BA68. Coll of Resurr Mirfield 68. **d** 70 **p** 71. C Armley St Bart *Ripon* 70-72; C St Bart Armley w St Mary New Wortley 72-74; Chapl Tiffield Sch Northants 74-75; C-in-c Dunscroft CD *Sheff* 75-78; V Dunscroft 78-81; TV Frecheville and Hackenthorpe 81-88; V Hackenthorpe from 88. *The Vicarage, 61 Sheffield Road, Sheffield S12 4LR* Sheffield (0742) 484486

NORWOOD, Philip Geoffrey Frank. b 39. Em Coll Cam BA62 MA66. Cuddesdon Coll 63. **d** 65 **p** 66. C New Addington *Cant* 65-69; Abp's Dom Chapl 69-72; V Hollingbourne 72-78; P-in-c Wormshill 74-78; P-in-c Bredgar w Bicknor and Huckinge 74-78; P-in-c St Laurence in Thanet 78-82; V 82-88; RD Thanet 86-88; V Spalding *Linc* from 88. *The Parsonage, Spalding, Lincs PE11 2PB* Spalding (0775) 722772

NOTLEY, Michael James. b 41. St Edm Hall Ox BA63 MA68. E Midl Min Tr Course 84. **d** 87 **p** 88. Hon C Oadby *Leic* from 87. *1 Berkeley Close, Oadby, Leicester LE2 4SZ* Leicester (0533) 713872

NOTT, Michael. b 34. Ex Coll Ox BA58 MA62 Birm Univ MEd88. Coll of Resurr Mirfield. **d** 60 **p** 61. C Solihull *Birm* 60-69; Min Can Worc Cathl *Worc* 69-77; Chapl K Sch Worc 69-77; P-in-c Worc St Nic *Worc* 77-84; P-in-c Worc St Andr and All SS w St Helen 82-84; Children's Officer 84-87; Droitwich Spa 87-89; V Broadheath, Crown E and Rushwick from 89; Chapl Worc Coll of HE from 89. *The Vicarage, Crown East Lane, Rushwick, Worcester WR2 5TU* Worcester (0905) 428801

✠**NOTT, Rt Rev Peter John.** b 33. Fitzw Ho Cam BA61 MA65. Westcott Ho Cam 58. **d** 61 **p** 62 **c** 77. C Harpenden St Nic *St Alb* 61-64; Chapl Fitzw Coll Cam 64-69; Fell 66-69; Chapl New Hall Cam 66-69; R Beaconsfield *Ox* 69-76; TR 76-77; Preb Wells Cathl *B & W* 77-85; Suff Bp Taunton 77-85; Bp Nor from 85. *The Bishop's House, Norwich NR3 1SB* Norwich (0603) 629001

NOTTAGE, Terence John. b 36. Oak Hill Th Coll 62. **d** 65 **p** 66. C Finchley St Paul Long Lane *Lon* 65-68; C Edgware 68-72; V Harlesden St Mark 72-86; V Kensal Rise St Mark and St Martin 86; TR Plymouth Em w Efford *Ex* from 86; P-in-c Laira from 88. *Emmanuel Vicarage, 9 Seymour Drive, Plymouth PL3 5BG* Plymouth (0752) 663321

NOTTINGHAM, Birman. b 29. St Chad's Coll Dur BA53 MA56 MEd64 Lanc Univ PhD75. Ely Th Coll 53. **d** 55 **p** 56. C Monkwearmouth Venerable Bede *Dur* 55-58; Lic to Offic Dur 58-70; Blackb from 66. *The Senior Common Room, St Martin's College, Lancaster LA1 3JD* Lancaster (0524) 63446

NOTTINGHAM, Archdeacon of. See WALKER, Ven Thomas Overington

NOURSE, John. b 22. St Jo Coll Cam BA43 ACertCM90 St Jo Coll Cam MA47. Wells Th Coll 48. **d** 49 **p** 51. Min Can and Prec Cant Cathl *Cant* 69-73; V Charing w Lt Chart 73-83; V Charing w Charing Heath and Lt Chart 84-88; rtd 88; Perm to Offic *Ex* from 90. *High Mead, Greenhill Avenue, Lympstone, Exmouth, Devon EX8 5HW* Exmouth (0395) 264480

NOURSE, Peter. b 10. RD43. Fitzw Ho Cam BA36 MA39. Wells Th Coll 37. **d** 37 **p** 38. V Eardisland *Heref* 62-76; P-in-c Shobdon 65-76; rtd 76; Perm to Offic *Heref* from 76. *Priory End, Church Street, Leominster, Herefordshire HR6 8NJ* Leominster (0568) 3936

NOWELL, John David. b 44. AKC67. **d** 68 **p** 69. C Lindley *Wakef* 68-70; C Lightcliffe 70-72; V Wyke *Bradf* 72-80; V Silsden from 80. *The Vicarage, Briggate, Silsden, Keighley, W Yorkshire BD20 9JS* Steeton (0535) 652670

NOYCE, Colin Martley. b 45. Brasted Th Coll 73 Ridley Hall Cam 74. **d** 76 **p** 77. C Cam St Jas *Ely* 76-78; Chapl RN 78-82; R Mistley w Manningtree *Chelmsf* 82-86; Miss to Seamen 86-90; Kenya 86-89; Trinidad and Tobago 89-90; V Four Marks *Win* from 90. *The Vicarage, Lymington Bottom, Four Marks, Alton, Hants GU34 5AA* Alton (0420) 63344

NOYES, Roger. b 39. Linc Th Coll 65. **d** 67 **p** 68. C Adel *Ripon* 67-70; Chapl Aldenham Sch Herts 70-74; V Aldborough w Boroughbridge and Roecliffe *Ripon* 74-89; Rural Min Adv 89-90. *The Three Horseshoes Cottage, Norton le Clay, York* Harrogate (0423) 324547

NUDDS, Douglas John. b 24. St Aid Birkenhead 48. **d** 51 **p** 52. Chapl Leic R Infirmary 68-72; High Royds Hosp Menston 72-79; V Bradf St Wilfrid Lidget Green *Bradf* 79-84; Lic to Offic *St Alb* from 84; Chapl Shenley Hosp Radlett Herts 84-89; rtd 89; Perm to Offic *Nor* from 89.

31 Hamlet Close, North Walsham, Norfolk NR28 0DL North Walsham (0692) 404263

NUGENT, Canon Alan Hubert. b 42. Dur Univ BA65 MA78. Wycliffe Hall Ox 65 United Th Coll Bangalore DipTh66. **d** 67 **p** 68. C Mossley Hill St Matt and St Jas *Liv* 67-71; C Bridgnorth St Mary *Heref* 71-72; Chapl Dur Univ *Dur* 72-78; P-in-c Bishopwearmouth Ch Ch 78-85; P-in-c Brancepeth from 85; Dioc Dir of Educn from 85; Hon Can Dur Cathl from 86. *The Rectory, Brancepeth, Durham DH7 8EL* 091-378 0503 or 384 3692

NUGENT, Eric William. b 26. Bps' Coll Cheshunt 56. **d** 58 **p** 59. C Rochford *Chelmsf* 58-61; C Eastwood 61-62; C-in-c Eastwood St Dav CD 62-66; V Eastwood St Dav 66-79; P-in-c Weeley 79-81; V Lt Clacton 80-81; R Weeley and Lt Clacton from 81. *The Vicarage, 2 Holland Road, Little Clacton, Clacton-on-Sea, Essex CO16 9RS* Clacton-on-Sea (0225) 860241

NUNN, Andrew Peter. b 57. Leic Poly BA79 Leeds Univ BA82. Coll of Resurr Mirfield 80. **d** 83 **p** 84. C Manston *Ripon* 83-87; C Leeds Richmond Hill from 87; Chapl Agnes Stewart C of E High Sch Leeds from 87. *St Hilda's Clergy House, 70 Cross Green Lane, Leeds LS9 0DG* Leeds (0532) 481145

NUNN, Miss Christina Mary. Trin Coll Bris BA87. **d** 87. Par Dn Hilperton w Whaddon and Staverton etc *Sarum* 87-90. *Address temp unknown*

NUNN, Geoffrey William John. b 24. St Jo Coll Dur BA51. **d** 52 **p** 53. C Upminster *Chelmsf* 52-58; V Dagenham St Martin from 58. *St Martin's Vicarage, Goresbrook Road, Dagenham, Essex RM9 6UX* 081-592 0967

NUNN, Peter. b 32. Kelham Th Coll 53. **d** 57 **p** 58. Chapl Winwick Hosp Warrington 65-90; rtd 90. *1 Rylands Street, Springfield, Wigan WN6 7BL* Wigan (0942) 35407

NUNN, Canon Peter Michael. b 38. Sarum Th Coll 64. **d** 66 **p** 67. C Hornsey St Geo *Lon* 66-71; C Cleator Moor w Cleator *Carl* 71-72; V Carl St Luke Morton 72-79; V Wotton St Mary *Glouc* from 79; OCF RAF from 80; RD Glouc City *Glouc* from 88; Hon Can Glouc Cathl from 90. *Holy Trinity Vicarage, Church Road, Longlevens, Gloucester GL2 0AJ* Gloucester (0452) 24129

NUNN, Peter Rawling. b 51. Ox Univ BA73 Sheff Univ MSc74 BA85. Oak Hill Th Coll 82. **d** 85 **p** 86. C Bispham *Blackb* 85-87; C-in-c Anchorsholme 87-89; V from 89. *36 Valeway Avenue, Thornton Cleveleys, Blackpool FY5 3RN* Blackpool (0253) 856646

NUNNERLEY, William John Arthur. b 27. Univ of Wales (Lamp) BA54 St Chad's Coll Dur DipTh56. **d** 59 **p** 60. C Tredegar St Geo *Mon* 56-60; Chapl RN 60-81; QHC from 79; R Barnoldby le Beck *Linc* from 81; R Waltham from 81. *The Rectory, 95 High Street, Waltham, Grimsby, S Humberside DN37 0PN* Grimsby (0472) 822172

NURSER, Canon John Shelley. b 29. Peterho Cam BA50 MA54 PhD58. Wells Th Coll 58. **d** 58 **p** 59. C Tankersley *Sheff* 58-61; Dean Trin Hall Cam 61-68; Australia 68-74; R Freckenham w Worlington *St E* 74-76; Can Res and Chan Linc Cathl *Linc* from 76. *The Chancery, 11 Minster Yard, Lincoln LN2 1PJ* Lincoln (0522) 525610

NURTON, Robert. b 44. Univ of Wales (Lamp) BA67. Ridley Hall Cam 67. **d** 69 **p** 70. C Bris St Andr Hartcliffe *Bris* 69-73; C Ipswich St Mary at Stoke w St Pet & St Mary Quay *St E* 73-77; Chapl RN from 77. *c/o MOD, Lacon House, Theobald's Road, London WC1X 8RY* 071-430 6847

NUTTALL, George Herman. b 31. St Jo Coll Dur BA59 DipTh61. Cranmer Hall Dur 59. **d** 61 **p** 62. C Eccleshill *Bradf* 61-65; V Oldham St Barn *Man* 65-70; Area Sec (Dios Derby and Lich) CMS 70-81; V Derby St Aug *Derby* 81-84; Chapl Bournemouth and Poole Colls *Sarum* from 85; Chapl Dorset Inst of HE 85-90; Bournemouth Poly from 90. *14 Crescent Road, Poole, Dorset BH14 9AS* Poole (0202) 745806 or 52411

NUTTALL, Michael John Berkeley. b 36. AKC60. St Boniface Warminster 61. **d** 61 **p** 62. C Chapel Allerton *Ripon* 61-64; C Stanningley St Thos 64-68; V Leeds Gipton Epiphany 68-76; P-in-c Stainby w Gunby *Linc* 76-83; R N Witham 76-83; R S Witham 76-83; TV Bottesford w Ashby 83-88; I Adare w Kilpeacon and Croom *L & K* from 88. *The Rectory, Adare, Co Limerick, Irish Republic* Limerick (61) 396227

NUTTALL, Robert. b 10. FACCA. Westcott Ho Cam 73. **d** 74 **p** 75. C Gt Wakering *Chelmsf* 74-76; Chapl Southend Gen Hosp 76-82; rtd 82; Perm to Offic Ches from 82; Man from 84. *72 Edge Lane, Stretford, Manchester M32 8JP* 061-865 5340

NUTTALL, Wilfrid. b 29. ACP59 Open Univ BA82. Chich Th Coll 82. **d** 84 **p** 85. C Accrington St Jo *Blackb* 84-86; C Darwen St Cuth w Tockholes St Steph 86-89; V Foulridge from 89. *The Vicarage, Skipton Road, Foulridge, Colne, Lancs BB8 7NP* Colne (0282) 865491

NYAHWA, Stanley Musa. b 33. Gweru Coll Zimbabwe TCert52 BBC Film Sch CFTV67 Ryerson Coll Toronto ACTVR71. Edin Th Coll 62. **d** 65 **p** 66. C Leeds St Matt Lt Lon *Ripon* 65-67; Zambia 68-74; Chapl Haarlem *Eur* 76-83; Zimbabwe 81-83; C Lewisham St Mary *S'wark* from 91. *36D Clarendon Rise, London SE13 5EY* 081-690 1585

NYE, Charles Stanley. b 09. St Pet Hall Ox BA31 MA35 BD35. **d** 34 **p** 35. R Tiverton St Pet *Ex* 61-75; rtd 75. *4 Warren Court, 8 Warren Road, Liverpool L23 6UP* 051-931 4541

NYE, Canon David Charles. b 39. K Coll Lon BD65. **d** 63 **p** 64. C Charlton Kings St Mary *Glouc* 63-67; C Yeovil St Jo w Preston Plucknett *B & W* 67-70; V Lower Cam *Glouc* 70-74; Min Can Glouc Cathl 74-79; Dir of Ords 74-79; Prin Glouc Th Course 74-79; V Glouc St Mary de Lode and St Nic *Glouc* 74-76; V Maisemore 76-79; Chapl Grenville Coll Bideford 79-81; V Leckhampton SS Phil and Jas w Cheltenham St Jas *Glouc* from 81; Hon Can Glouc Cathl from 88; RD Cheltenham from 89. *St Philip's Vicarage, 80 Painswick Road, Cheltenham, Glos GL50 2EW* Cheltenham (0242) 525460

NYE, John Arthur Keith. b 04. Mert Coll Ox BA25 MA29 Man Univ BD27. Man Egerton Hall 25. **d** 27 **p** 28. V Ribby w Wrea *Blackb* 61-69; rtd 69. Lic to Offic *Blackb* from 69. *c/o Mrs J A Lee, The Croft, 7 St Clements Avenue, Blackpool FY3 8LT*

✠**NYE, Rt Rev Mark.** b 09. St Jo Coll Ox BA31 MA36. Cuddesdon Coll 32. **d** 33 **p** 34 **c** 73. C Richmond St Luke *S'wark* 33-36; S Africa from 36; Dean and R St Alb Cathl Pretoria 65-73; Adn Pretoria 65-66; Adn N Transvaal 73-77; Suff Bp Pretoria 73-83; rtd 83. *6 Leighwoods, Kenilworth Road, Kenilworth, 7700 South Africa* Cape Town (21) 616693

NYE, Ven Nathaniel Kemp. b 14. AKC36. Cuddesdon Coll 36. **d** 37 **p** 38. Tait Missr Cant 66-72; Adn Maidstone *Cant* 72-79; rtd 79. *Lees Cottage, Boughton Lees, Ashford, Kent TN25 4HX* Ashford (0233) 626175

O

OADES, Michael Anthony John. b 45. Brasted Th Coll 69 Sarum & Wells Th Coll 71. **d** 73 **p** 74. C Eltham Park St Luke *S'wark* 73-78; C Coulsdon St Andr 78-81; P-in-c Mert St Jas 81-85; V 85-87; V Benhilton from 87. *All Saints' Vicarage, All Saints' Road, Sutton, Surrey SM1 3DA* 081-644 9070

OADES, Canon Peter Robert. b 24. Fitzw Ho Cam BA47 CertEd48 MA53. **d** 67 **p** 68. VC Sarum Cathl *Sarum* 68-74; Chapl Sarum Cathl Sch 68-74; P-in-c Sturminster Newton and Hinton St Mary *Sarum* 74-75; V 75-81; R Stock and Lydlinch 75-81; RD Blackmore Vale 78-81; V Woodford Valley 81-89; Can and Preb Sarum Cathl 85-89; rtd 89; Perm to Offic *Sarum* from 89; Hon Chapl to the Deaf from 89; Perm to Offic *Win* from 89. *28 Mulberry Gardens, Fordingbridge, Hants SP6 1BP* Fordingbridge (0425) 657113

OAKE, Barry Richard. b 47. ARICS71. Ripon Coll Cuddesdon 83. **d** 85 **p** 86. C Wantage *Ox* 85-88; C Warlingham w Chelsham and Farleigh *S'wark* 88-91; R N w S Wootton *Nor* from 91. *The Rectory, Castle Rising Road, South Wootton, King's Lynn, Norfolk PE30 3JA* King's Lynn (0553) 671381

OAKES, Graham. b 42. Leeds Univ DipTh68. Chich Th Coll 68. **d** 70 **p** 71. C Hulme Ascension *Man* 70-74; C Clifton All SS w Tyndalls Park *Bris* 74-76; P-in-c Chadderton St Mark *Man* 76-78; V 78-82; V King Cross *Wakef* from 82. *The Vicarage, West Royd Avenue, Halifax, W Yorkshire HX1 3NU* Halifax (0422) 352933

OAKES, Canon Hugh Toft. b 16. Bp Wilson Coll 39. **d** 41 **p** 42. V Humberston *Linc* 54-84; Can and Preb Linc Cathl from 79; rtd 84. *26 Pearson Road, Cleethorpes, S Humberside DN35 0DT* Cleethorpes (0472) 696859

OAKES, Miss Jennifer May. b 43. Trin Coll Bris DipHE80. dss 82 **d** 87. Wilnecote *Lich* 82-85; Bentley 85-87; Par Dn 87-89; NSM Hixon w Stowe-by-Chartley from 89. *10 Meadow Glade, Hixton, Stafford ST8 0NT* Weston (0889) 271068

OAKES, Jeremy Charles. b 51. ACA75 FCA81. Westcott Ho Cam 75. **d** 78 **p** 79. C Evington *Leic* 78-81; C Ringwood *Win* 81-84; P-in-c Thurnby Lodge *Leic* 84-89; TV Oakdale St Geo *Sarum* from 89. *St Paul's Vicarage, 16 Rowbarrow Close, Poole, Dorset BH17 9EA* Poole (0202) 699807

OAKES, John Cyril. b 49. AKC71. St Aug Coll Cant 71. **d** 72 **p** 73. C Broseley w Benthall *Heref* 72-76; C Cannock *Lich* 76-79; TV 79-83; V Rough Hills from 83. *St Martin's Vicarage, Dixon Street, Wolverhampton WV2 2BG* Wolverhampton (0902) 341030

OAKES, Canon Leslie John. b 28. AKC53. **d** 54 **p** 55. C Bedf Leigh *Man* 54-58; C Walsall St Matt *Lich* 58-60; Chapl Selly Oak Hosp Birm 60-64; V Longbridge *Birm* from 64; Hon Can Birm Cathl from 84. *St John's Vicarage, 220 Longbridge Lane, Birmingham B31 4JT* 021-475 3484

OAKES, Melvin. b 36. Linc Th Coll 77. **d** 79 **p** 80. C Lt Ilford St Mich *Chelmsf* 79-82; V Highams Park All SS from 82. *All Saints' Vicarage, 12A Castle Avenue, London E4 9QD* 081-527 3269

OAKES, Robert. b 47. St Aug Coll Cant. **d** 82 **p** 83. NSM Probus, Ladock and Grampound w Creed *Truro* 82-84; TV Bodmin w Lanhydrock and Lanivet 85-88; R S Hill w Callington from 88; P-in-c Linkinhorne 88-89. *The Rectory, Liskeard Road, Callington, Cornwall PL17 7JD* Liskeard (0579) 83341

OAKES, Rowland Dalimore. b 05. St D Coll Lamp LDiv35 BA35. **d** 35 **p** 36. USA 62-71; rtd 71. *Box 239, St George, Maine 04857, USA*

OAKHAM, Archdeacon of. See FERNYHOUGH, Ven Bernard

OAKLEY, Barry Wyndham. b 32. TD72. SS Coll Cam BA53 MA57. Ridley Hall Cam 56. **d** 58 **p** 59. C Alverstoke *Portsm* 58-61; C Bermondsey St Mary w St Olave and St Jo *S'wark* 61-63; V Crofton *Portsm* 63-78; V Edmonton All SS *Lon* 78-82; P-in-c Edmonton St Mich 80-82; V Edmonton All SS w St Mich from 82. *All Saints' Vicarage, 43 All Saints' Close, London N9 9AT* 081-803 9199

OAKLEY, Hilary Robert Mark. b 53. Univ of Wales (Ban) BSc75 Ox Univ BA78. Ripon Coll Cuddesdon 76. **d** 79 **p** 80. C Birm St Pet *Birm* 79-82; C Cam Gt St Mary w St Mich *Ely* 82-86; Chapl Girton Coll Cam 82-86; Chapl Zurich w St Gallen and Winterthur *Eur* 86-88; NSM Dio Lon from 88. *19 Denman House, Lordship Road, London N16 0JD* 081-800 0032

OAKLEY, Richard John. b 46. AKC69. St Aug Coll Cant 69. **d** 70 **p** 71. C Wythenshawe Wm Temple Ch *Man* 70-75; V Ashton H Trin 75-80; CR from 82; Lic to Offic *Lon* from 88. *Royal Foundation of St Katharine, 2 Butcher Row, London E14 8DS* 071-790 3540

OAKLEY, Robert Paul. b 51. Sheff Univ BScTech72 PGCE74. St Jo Coll Nottm DipTh89. **d** 89 **p** 90. C Heatherlands St Jo *Sarum* from 89. *91 Churchill Road, Poole, Dorset BH12 2LR* Poole (0202) 748754

OAKLEY, Robin Ian. b 37. Ripon Hall Ox 68. **d** 70 **p** 71. C Leighton Buzzard *St Alb* 70-73; C Watford St Mich 73-76; R Ickleford 76-80; R Ickleford w Holwell from 80. *The Rectory, 36 Turnpike Lane, Ickleford, Hitchin, Herts SG5 3XB* Hitchin (0462) 432925

OAKLEY, Miss Susan Mary. b 55. Salford Univ BSc76. St Jo Coll Nottm LTh86 DPS87. **d** 87. Par Dn Armthorpe *Sheff* 87-91; C Howell Hill *Guildf* from 91. *18 Nonsuch Walk, Cheam, Sutton, Surrey SM2 0JY* 081-393 4019

OAKLEY, Timothy Crispin. b 45. Qu Coll Cam BA66 MA70. St Jo Coll Nottm 73. **d** 76 **p** 77. C Bromley Common St Aug *Roch* 76-79; C Fairfield *Liv* 79-81; CMS 82-90; Kenya 82-90; P-in-c Beaford, Roborough and St Giles in the Wood *Ex* from 91. *The Vicarage, Beaford, Winkleigh, Devon EX19 8NN* Beaford (08053) 213

OATES, Alan. b 32. S'wark Ord Course 79. **d** 80 **p** 81. NSM Rayleigh *Chelmsf* 80-87; TV Jarrow *Dur* from 87. *St Mark's House, Randolph Street, Jarrow, Tyne & Wear NE32 3AQ* 091-483 2092

OATES, Austin Edwin. b 17. Worc Ord Coll. **d** 63 **p** 64. V Plemstall w Guilden Sutton *Ches* 67-74; V Crowton 74-88; rtd 88. *31 Haleview Road, Helsby, Warrington, Cheshire* Helsby (0928) 723908

OATES, Canon John. b 30. Kelham Th Coll 53. **d** 57 **p** 58. C Hackney Wick St Mary of Eton w St Aug *Lon* 57-60; Development Officer C of E Youth Coun 60-64; Sec C of E Coun Commonwealth Settlement 64-65; Gen Sec 65-72; Sec C of E Cttee on Migration & Internat Affairs 68-72; V Richmond St Mary *S'wark* 70-79; P-in-c Richmond St Jo 76-79; V Richmond St Mary w St Matthias and St Jo 79-84; RD Richmond and Barnes 79-84; R St Bride Fleet Street w Bridewell etc *Lon* from

84. *St Bride's Rectory, Fleet Street, London EC4Y 8AU*
071-353 1301 or 583 0239

OATES, John Francis Titus. b 27. SSC Worc Coll Ox
BA50 MA54. Qu Coll Birm 50. **d** 52 **p** 53. C Hunslet St
Mary *Ripon* 52-56; Chapl RN 56-67; USA from 67.
RR1, Box 878, Belfast, Maine 04915, USA Belfast (207)
338-4796

OATEY, Canon Michael John. b 31. Chich Th Coll 57.
d 60 **p** 61. C W Drayton *Lon* 60-66; V Chiswick St Mich
66-74; R St Sampson *Truro* 72-74; V Tywardreath w
Tregaminion from 74; Hon Can Truro Cathl from 88.
The Vicarage, Tywardreath, Par, Cornwall PL24 2PL
Par (072681) 2998

OBAN, Provost of. See MACLEAN, Very Rev Allan
Murray

OBEE, Douglas Walter. b 18. Roch Th Coll 65. **d** 67 **p** 68.
C Beckenham St Geo *Roch* 67-71; R Whitestone *Ex*
71-75; V Oldridge 72-75; P-in-c Harford 76-87; V
Ivybridge 76-87; V Ivybridge w Harford 87; rtd 87; Perm
to Offic *Ex* from 88. *16 Kerswill Road, Devon EX4 1NY*
Exeter (0392) 439405

O'BENEY, Robin Mervyn. b 35. Ely Th Coll 61. **d** 64 **p** 65.
C Liss *Portsm* 64-65; C Portsea St Cuth 65-68; Hon C
Wymondham *Nor* 74-76; R Swainsthorpe w Newton
Flotman 76-80; NSM Sparkenhoe Deanery Leic 87-90;
V Billesdon and Skeffington *Leic* 90-91. *Tigh Na Bochd,
Bunessan, Isle of Mull*

OBERST, Simon Julian. b 57. ACA83 Trin Coll Cam
BA79 MA82. Wycliffe Hall Ox DipTh90. **d** 91. C S
Croydon Em *S'wark* from 91. *12 Hurst View Road,
South Croydon, Surrey CR2 7AG* 081-688 5861

O'BRIEN, Andrew David. b 61. Nottm Univ BTh88. Linc
Th Coll 85. **d** 88 **p** 89. C Clare w Poslingford *St E* 88-89;
C Clare w Poslingford, Cavendish etc 89-91; V Belton
All SS *Linc* from 91. *The Vicarage, Belton, Doncaster,
S Yorkshire DN9 1NS* Epworth (0427) 872207

O'BRIEN, Donogh Smith. b 34. St Pet Hall Ox
BA56 MA60. Ripon Hall Ox 56. **d** 57 **p** 58. Lic to Offic
Liv from 66; Chapl Wade Deacon Gr Sch Widnes 67-84;
rtd 84. *Fourways, 178 Lunts Heath Road, Farnworth,
Widnes, Cheshire WA8 9AZ* 051-424 0147

O'BRIEN, George Edward. b 32. Clifton Th Coll 61. **d** 64
p 65. C Denton Holme *Carl* 64-68; V Castle Town *Lich*
68-88; Chapl Kingsmead Hosp Stafford from 88; Chapl
St Geo Hosp Stafford from 88. *185 Tixall Road, Stafford
ST16 3XJ* Stafford (0785) 44261

O'BRIEN, Canon James Henry. b 10. Bps' Coll Cheshunt
42. **d** 44 **p** 45. RD Darwen *Blackb* 64-75; V Darwen St
Cuth 67-75; Hon Can Blackb Cathl 73-75; rtd 75; C
Adlington *Blackb* 75-79; Lic to Offic from 79. *21 Suffolk
Street, Blackburn BB2 4ES* Blackburn (0254) 64799

O'BRIEN, John. b 41. St Jo Coll Cam BA63 MA67. Ridley
Hall Cam 63. **d** 65 **p** 66. C Wotton St Mary *Glouc* 65-69;
Youth Chapl 67-69; Lect Coll of SS Paul and Mary
Cheltenham 69-85; V Twigworth, Down Hatherley,
Norton, The Leigh etc *Glouc* from 85. *The Rectory,
Twigworth, Gloucester GL2 9PQ* Gloucester (0452)
731483

O'BRIEN, Robert Stephen. b 36. S'wark Ord Course 67.
d 71. C Esher *Guildf* 71-73; Hon C St Lawr Jewry *Lon*
73-83. *c/o Charles Fulton & Co Ltd, 30 Cornhill, London
EC3*

O'BYRNE, Francis Michael. b 12. Tyndale Hall Bris 41.
d 44 **p** 45. I Athboy Union *M & K* 56-81; Can Meath
76-81; rtd 81. *Birch Lea, Old Connaught Avenue, Bray,
Co Wicklow, Irish Republic* Dublin (1) 282-4429

OCCOMORE, Albert Ernest. b 06. Ridley Hall Cam. **d** 64
p 65. C Gidea Park *Chelmsf* 64-76; rtd 76. *11 Sawyers
Court, Shorter Avenue, Shenfield, Brentwood, Essex
CM15 8RE* Brentwood (0277) 233875

OCKFORD, Paul Philip. b 46. St Chad's Coll Dur BA67.
St Steph Ho Ox 68. **d** 70 **p** 71. C Streatham St Pet *S'wark*
70-74; C Cheam 74-77; P-in-c Eastrington *York* 77-79;
TV Howden Team Min 80-83; R Sherburn and W and
E Heslerton w Yedingham from 83. *The Rectory,
Sherburn, Malton, N Yorkshire YO17 8PL* Sherburn
(0944) 70524

OCKWELL, Canon Herbert Grant. b 12. Kelham Th Coll
30. **d** 36 **p** 37. R Blendworth, Chalton and Idsworth
Portsm 70-81; rtd 81; Perm to Offic Portsm from 81;
Chich from 82. *72 Bowes Hill, Rowlands Castle, Hants
PO9 6BS* Rowlands Castle (0705) 412301

O'CONNELL, Miss Mary Joy. b 49. York Univ
BA71 Leeds Univ CertEd74. Chich Th Coll 84. **dss** 86
d 87. Cinderhill *S'well* 86-87; Par Dn from 87. *The
Vicarage, Nuthall Road, Nottingham NG8 6AD*
Nottingham (0602) 789000

O'CONNOR, Canon Alfred Stanley. b 20. TCD
BA43 MA60. **d** 43 **p** 44. I Drumglass *Arm* 65-85; Can

Arm Cathl 83-85; rtd 85. *Highfield, Greenhill Road,
Brookeborough, Co Fermanagh* Brookeborough
(036553) 725

O'CONNOR, Canon Brian Michael McDougal. b 42. St
Cath Coll Cam BA67 MA69. Cuddesdon Coll 67. **d** 69
p 70. C Headington *Ox* 69-71; Sec Dioc Past and
Redundant Chs Uses Cttees 72-79; P-in-c Mert 72-76; V
Rainham *Roch* from 79; RD Gillingham 81-88; Hon
Can Roch Cathl from 89. *The Vicarage, 80 Broadview
Avenue, Rainham, Kent ME8 9DE* Medway (0634)
31538

O'CONNOR, Daniel. b 33. Dur Univ BA54 MA67 St Andr
Univ PhD81. Cuddesdon Coll 56. **d** 58 **p** 59. C Stockton
St Pet *Dur* 58-62; C W Hartlepool St Aid 62-63; CMD
63-70; USPG 70-72; India 63-72; Chapl St Andr Univ
St And 72-77; R Edin Gd Shep *Edin* 77-82; Prin Coll of
the Ascension Selly Oak 82-90; Dir Scottish Chs Ho
(Chs Together in Scotland) from 90. *Scottish Churches
House, Dunblane, Perthshire FK15 0AJ* Dunblane
(0786) 823588

O'CONNOR, Edward Howard. b 32. FRSH AIMLS59.
Immanuel Coll Ibadan 76. **d** 77 **p** 79. Nigeria 77-81;
P-in-c Newchurch *Portsm* 81-83; V 83-91; P-in-c Arreton
82-83; V 83-91; Chapl HM Pris Kingston from 91.
23 Arundel Road, Ryde, Isle of Wight PO33 1BW

O'CONNOR, John Goodrich. b 34. Keble Coll Ox
BA58 MA60. Lich Th Coll. **d** 61 **p** 62. C Blackpool St
Steph *Blackb* 61-66; C Holbeck *Ripon* 66-68; C Hendon
St Mary *Lon* 68-73; TV Thornaby on Tees *York* 73-79;
TR 79-89; V Blyth St Cuth *Newc* from 89. *The Vicarage,
29 Ridley Avenue, Blyth, Northd NE24 3BA* Blyth
(0670) 352410

O'CONNOR, Nigel George. b 25. TD66. Linc Th Coll 53.
d 55 **p** 56. CF (TA) 62-71; R Ivychurch w Old Romney
and Midley *Cant* 65-74; V Brenzett w Snargate and
Snave 65-74; R Newchurch 65-74; R St Mary in the
Marsh 65-74; R Burmarsh 65-74; V Brookland w Fairfield
65-74; CF (R of O) 71-91; V S w N Hayling Portsm
74-85; V Corby Glen *Linc* 85-91; rtd 91. *Winterbourne
House, Allington, Salisbury SP4 0BZ*

O'CONNOR, Samuel John. b 18. Linc Th Coll 67. **d** 69
p 70. C Walmer *Cant* 69-72; C Faversham 72-75; P-in-c
Teynham 75; V Ringwood *Win* 75-85; rtd 85; Perm to
Offic *Win* from 85. *94 Fairview Drive, Hythe,
Southampton SO4 5GY* Hythe (0703) 843823

O'CONNOR, William Goodrich. b 04. Bps' Coll Cheshunt
36. **d** 36 **p** 38. V Holbeck *Ripon* 66-75; P-in-c Holbeck
St Edw 66-67; rtd 75; Hon C Mottram in Longdendale
w Woodhead *Ches* 75-78; Perm to Offic from 78.
*Queenscourt Residential Home, Victoria Crescent,
Chester* Chester (0244) 677313

ODDIE, Samuel. b 02. Bp Wilson Coll 27. **d** 28 **p** 29. V
Bourton *Ox* 61-70; rtd 70. *Ramsey Hall, 13 Byron Road,
Worthing, W Sussex BN11 3NH* Worthing (0903) 36880

ODDY, Canon Frederick Brian. b 29. Univ of Wales
(Lamp) BA50. Linc Th Coll 50. **d** 52 **p** 53. C Preston
Em *Blackb* 52-55; C St Annes 55-57; V Chorley St Jas
57-64; V Warton St Oswald 64-76; P-in-c Yealand
Conyers 74-76; V Warton St Oswald w Yealand Conyers
from 76; RD Tunstall 84-90; Hon Can Blackb Cathl
from 89. *St Oswald's Vicarage, Warton, Carnforth, Lancs
LA5 9PG* Carnforth (0524) 732946

ODLING-SMEE, Dr George William. b 35. FRCS68 K Coll
Dur MB, BS59. **d** 77 **p** 78. NSM Belf St Thos *Conn*
77-90; NSM Belf St Geo from 90. *10 Deramore Park
South, Belfast BT9 5JY* Belfast (0232) 669275

ODLUM, Michael Julian. b 24. DFC45. St Mich Coll Llan
55. **d** 56 **p** 57. V Sampford Arundel *B & W* 65-74;
Asst Chapl HM Pris Wandsworth 74; Chapl HM Pris
Standford Hill 74-81; Leic 82-89; rtd 89. *67A Main
Street, Kirby Muxloe, Leicester LE9 9AN* Leicester
(0533) 387900

O'DONNELL, Kevin George. b 57. Man Univ
BA78 CertEd79. St Steph Ho Ox 86. **d** 88 **p** 89. C
Tokyngton St Mich *Lon* 88-90; C Ascot Heath *Ox* from
90. *The Parsonage, King Edward's Road, Ascot, Berks
SL5 8PD* Ascot (0344) 885500

O'DONOHUE, Kevin Paul. b 22. Qu Coll Birm 54. **d** 56
p 57. C Alston w Garrigill *Newc* 56-59; P-in-c 59-60;
P-in-c Berwick H Trin 60-61; P-in-c Otterburn 61; V
Choppington 61-80; V Cumwhitton *Carl* from 80; R
Castle Carrock w Cumrew and Croglin from 80. *The
Rectory, Castle Carrock, Carlisle CA4 9LZ* Hayton
(0228) 70231

O'DONOVAN, Canon Oliver Michael Timothy. b 45. Ball
Coll Ox BA68 MA71 DPhil75. Wycliffe Hall Ox 68. **d** 72
p 73. Tutor Wycliffe Hall Ox 72-77; Canada 77-82; Can
Res Ch Ch *Ox* from 82; Regius Prof Moral and Past Th

Ox Univ from 82. *Christ Church, Oxford OX1 1DP* Oxford (0865) 276219

OEHRING, Anthony Charles. b 56. Sheff City Poly BA79 CQSW79. Ridley Hall Cam 86. **d** 88 **p** 89. C Gillingham *Sarum* 88-91; TV S Gillingham *Roch* from 91. *60 Parkwood Green, Parkwood, Rainham, Gillingham ME8 9PP* Snodland (0634) 35837

OEPPEN, John Gerard David. b 44. St D Coll Lamp DipTh67. **d** 67 **p** 68. C-in-c Cwmmer w Abercregan CD *Llan* 67-70; TV Glyncorrwg w Afan Vale and Cymmer Afan 70-71; C Whitchurch 71-74; V Aberavon H Trin 74-78; V Bargoed and Deri w Brithdir 78-86; R Barry All SS from 86. *The Rectory, 3 Park Road, Barry, M Glam CF6 8NU* Barry (0446) 734629

OESTREICHER, Canon Paul. b 31. Univ of NZ BA53 MA56 Lanchester Poly Hon DLitt91. Linc Th Coll 56. **d** 59 **p** 60. C Dalston H Trin w St Phil *Lon* 59-61; C S Mymms K Chas 61-68; Asst in Relig Broadcasting BBC 61-64; Assoc Sec Internat Affairs Dept BCC 64-69; V Blackheath Ascension *S'wark* 68-81; Dir of Tr 69-72; Hon Can S'wark Cathl 78-81; Lic to Offic 81-86; Asst Gen Sec BCC 81-86; Can Res Cov Cathl *Cov* from 86; Dir of Internat Min from 86. *20 Styvechale Avenue, Coventry CV5 6DX* Coventry (0203) 673704

O'FERRALL, Very Rev Basil Arthur. b 24. CB79. TCD BA48 MA65. TCD Div Sch Div Test48. **d** 48 **p** 49. C Coleraine *Conn* 48-51; Chapl RN 51-75; Chapl of the Fleet and Adn for the RN 75-80; QHC 75-80; Hon Can Gib Cathl *Eur* 77-80; Chapl to HM The Queen 80-85; Bp's Chapl Norfolk Broads *Nor* 80-85; V Ranworth w Panxworth and Woodbastwick 80-85; Hon Can Win Cathl *Win* from 85; R Jersey St Helier from 85; Dean Jersey from 85; Pres Jersey Miss to Seamen from 85. *The Deanery, St Helier, Jersey, Channel Islands* Jersey (0534) 20001

OFFER, Clifford Jocelyn. b 43. Ex Univ BA67. Westcott Ho Cam 67. **d** 69 **p** 70. C Bromley SS Pet and Paul *Roch* 69-74; TV Southn (City Cen) *Win* 74-83; TR Hitchin *St Alb* from 83. *The Rectory, 21 West Hill, Hitchin, Herts SG5 2HZ* Hitchin (0462) 434017

OGDEN, Cyril Newton. b 12. AKC39. **d** 39 **p** 40. V Holbeach Fen *Linc* 69-77; V Whaplode 60-77; rtd 77; Perm to Offic Linc 77-88; Glouc from 88. *1 Chapelside, Clapton Row, Bourton-on-the-Water, Cheltenham, Glos GL54 2DN* Cotswold (0451) 21440

OGDEN, Canon David Edgar Foster. b 21. St Chad's Coll Dur BA48 Dur Univ Hon MA85. Bps' Coll Cheshunt 48. **d** 50 **p** 51. Dir RE *Blackb* 66-78; Can Res Newc Cathl *Newc* 66-78; V Greatham *Dur* 78-86; Master Greatham Hosp 78-86; RD Hartlepool 78-86; rtd 86. *9 Eastwood Grange Road, Hexham, Northd NE46 1UE* Hexham (0434) 604312

OGDEN, Eric. b 34. NW Ord Course 73. **d** 76 **p** 77. NSM Lydgate St Anne *Man* from 76. *40 Burnedge Lane, Grasscroft, Oldham OL4 4EA* Saddleworth (0457) 873661

OGDEN, Canon Eric Grayson. b 06. AKC32. St Steph Ho Ox 32. **d** 32 **p** 33. R Upper St Leonards St Jo *Chich* 65-72; rtd 72; Chapl Costa del Sol E *Eur* 72-76; Chapl Malaga w Almunecar and Nerja 76-78; Hon C Worthing St Andr *Chich* from 79. *Ramsay Hall, 13 Byron Road, Worthing, W Sussex BN11 3HN* Worthing (0903) 820993

OGDEN, Harry. b 30. AKC57. **d** 58 **p** 59. C Hollinwood *Man* 58-60; C Langley St Aid CD 60-61; R Lightbowne 61-69; V Farnworth and Kearsley 69-72; V Oldham St Steph and All Martyrs 72-79; R Moss Side Ch Ch from 79. *Christ Church Rectory, Monton Street, Manchester M14 4LT* 061-226 2476

OGDEN-SWIFT, Geoffrey William. b 21. Pemb Coll Cam BA46 MA48. Cuddesdon Coll 47. **d** 49 **p** 50. V Soham *Ely* 66-80; RD Fordham 70-78; P-in-c Over 80-86; rtd 87. *40 Station Road, Fulbourn, Cambridge CB1 5ES* Cambridge (0223) 881571

OGILVIE, Gordon. b 42. Glas Univ MA64 Lon Univ BD67. ALCD66. **d** 67 **p** 68. C Ashtead *Guildf* 67-72; V New Barnet St Jas *St Alb* 72-80; Dir Past Studies Wycliffe Hall Ox 80-87; P-in-c Harlow New Town w Lt Parndon *Chelmsf* 87-89; R from 89; Chapl Princess Alexandra Hosp Harlow from 88. *The Rectory, 43 Upper Park, Harlow, Essex CM20 1TW* Harlow (0279) 424616

OGILVIE, Ian Douglas. b 37. Em Coll Cam BA59 MA63. Linc Th Coll 59. **d** 61 **p** 62. C Clapham H Trin *S'wark* 61-63; C Cam Gt St Mary w St Mich *Ely* 63-66; Chapl Sevenoaks Sch Kent 66-77; Hon C Sevenoaks St Nic *Roch* 67-77; Chapl Malvern Coll Worcs 77-84; Hd Master St Geo Sch Harpenden 84-87; Lic to Offic *St Alb* 84-87; Bp's Dom Chapl 87-89; P-in-c Aldenham 87-91; Appeals

Dir Mind 89-91. *The Vicarage, Aldenham, Watford WD2 8BE* Radlett (0923) 855905

OGLE, Ms Catherine. b 61. Leeds Univ BA82 MPhil85 Fitzw Coll Cam BA87. Westcott Ho Cam 85. **d** 88. C Middleton St Mary *Ripon* 88-91; Relig Ed Radio Leeds from 91. *27 De Lacy Mount, Kirkstall, Leeds LS5 3JF* Leeds (0532) 783702

OGLESBY, Leslie Ellis. b 46. Univ Coll Ox BA69 MA73 City Univ MPhil73 Fitzw Coll Cam BA73 MA77. Ripon Coll Cuddesdon 77. **d** 78 **p** 79. C Stevenage St Mary Shephall *St Alb* 78-80; Dir St Alb Minl Tr Scheme 80-87; V Markyate Street *St Alb* 80-87; Dir Continuing Minl Educn from 87. *41 Holywell Hill, St Albans, Herts AL1 1HE* St Albans (0727) 830802

OGLEY, John. b 40. Oak Hill Th Coll 62. **d** 65 **p** 66. C Ardsley Sheff 65-68; C Carlton-in-the-Willows *S'well* 68-71; P-in-c Tollerton 71-79; V Skegby from 79. *The Vicarage, Skegby, Sutton-in-Ashfield, Notts NG17 3ED* Mansfield (0623) 558800

O'GORMAN, Paul Anthony. b 46. Portsm Poly BSc79. Oak Hill Th Coll DipHE81. **d** 81 **p** 82. C Leyton St Mary w St Edw *Chelmsf* 81-83; C Rayleigh 83-84; CF 84-87; R Northiam *Chich* from 87. *The Rectory, Hastings Road, Northiam, Rye, E Sussex TN31 6NH* Northiam (0797) 253118

O'HANLON, Canon William Douglas. b 11. Peterho Cam BA32 MA37. Clifton Th Coll 32. **d** 37 **p** 38. Can and Preb Sarum Cathl *Sarum* from 61; R Studland 72-82; rtd 82. *Crown Hill, 14 Bon Accord Road, Swanage, Dorset BH19 2DT* Swanage (0929) 425416

OKEKE, Canon Ken Sandy Edozie. b 41. Nigeria Univ BSc67. **d** 76 **p** 76. Nigeria 76-80 and 87-89; Chapl to Nigerians in UK and Irish Republic 80-87; Hon Can Kwara from 85; C Man Whitworth *Man* from 89; Chapl Insts Higher Learning Man from 89. *296 Wilbraham Road, Chorlton-cum-Hardy, Manchester M21 1UU* 061-881 5771

OKELLO, Modicum. b 53. St Paul's Coll Limuru 78 Trin Coll Bris BA90 Wycliffe Hall Ox 89. **d** 78 **p** 79. Kenya 78-79; Uganda 80-86; NSM Goodmayes All SS *Chelmsf* from 91. *c/o All Saints' Vicarage, Broomhill Road, Ilford, Essex IG3 9SJ* 081-590 1476

OLD, Arthur Anthony George. b 36. Clifton Th Coll 69. **d** 71 **p** 72. C Clitheroe St Jas *Blackb* 71-73; C Bispham 73-77; V Haslingden St Jo Stonefold 77-81; TV Lowestoft and Kirkley *Nor* 81-83; Chapl to the Deaf *Cant* from 83; P-in-c Hernhill 83-85; C Preston next Faversham, Goodnestone and Graveney from 85. *69 Whitstable Road, Canterbury, Kent CT2 8EA* Canterbury (0227) 765816

OLDAKER, Denis McLean. b 07. Lon Univ BD33. AKC33. **d** 33 **p** 34. Hon Can Roch Cathl *Roch* 59-70; R Seale *Guildf* 70-81; rtd 81; Perm to Offic *Guildf* from 82. *1 Park Road, Farnham, Surrey GU9 9QN* Farnham (0252) 724208

OLDALE, Harry. b 17. Bps' Coll Cheshunt 51. **d** 53 **p** 54. R Edgefield *Nor* 60-71; V Weybourne w Upper Sheringham 71-76; R Kelling w Salthouse 76-83; V Weybourne w Upper Sheringham 76-83; rtd 83; Perm to Offic *Nor* from 85. *St Stephen's, 24 Station Road, Holt, Norfolk NR25 6BS* Holt (0263) 713964

OLDEN, Canon Aidan Ronald Cuming. b 17. TCD BA38 MA41. CITC 39. **d** 40 **p** 41. C Newry St Mary *D & D* 40-41; Dean's V Belf Cathl 41-42; Succ St Patr Cathl Dub 42-47; I Kingscourt *M & K* 47-60; Can Meath from 58; I Kells w Balrathboyne, Moynalty etc from 60; Preb Tipper St Patr Cathl Dub from 64; RD Clonard and Trim *M & K* from 67. *The Rectory, Kells, Co Meath, Irish Republic* Ceanannus Mor (46) 40151

OLDFIELD, Roger Fielden. b 45. Qu Coll Cam BA67 MA71 City of Lon Poly DMS69 Lon Univ BD75. Trin Coll Bris 75. **d** 75 **p** 76. C Halliwell St Pet *Man* 75-80; V from 80. *St Peter's Vicarage, 1 Sefton Road, Harpers Lane, Bolton BL1 6HT* Bolton (0204) 849412

OLDHAM, Canon Arthur Charles Godolphin. b 05. AKC33. **d** 33 **p** 34. Dir of Ords *Guildf* 58-71; Can Res Guildf Cathl 61-71; rtd 71; Perm to Offic *Guildf* from 81. *Dora Cottage, Beech Hill, Godalming, Surrey GU8 4HL* Wormley (0428) 682087

OLDHAM, Charles Harry. b 14. St D Coll Lamp BA47. **d** 48 **p** 49. V Goff's Oak St Jas *St Alb* 68-79; rtd 79. *94 Prestbury Drive, Warminster, Wilts BA12 9LE* Warminster (0985) 213678

OLDHAM, Canon John. b 19. Kelham Th Coll 38. **d** 44 **p** 45. V Derby St Barn *Derby* 64-72; V Buxton 72-74; TR Buxton w Burbage and King Sterndale 74-84; Hon Can Derby Cathl 79-85; rtd 84; Perm to Offic *Derby* from 84. *Rose Cottage, Holt Lane, Lea, Matlock, Derbyshire DE4 5GQ* Dethick (062984) 469

OLDLAND, John Leyshon. b 06. Chich Th Coll 29. d 33 p 34. Chapl Community of St Pet Horbury 71-73; rtd 73; Hon C Bethnal Green St Matt w St Jas the Gt *Lon* from 85. *17 Rapley House, Turin Street, London E2 6NH* 071-729 7610

OLDNALL, Frederick Herbert. b 16. Ripon Hall Ox 56. d 57 p 58. V Rosliston w Coton in the Elms *Derby* 62-83; rtd 83. *19 Keeling Road, Kenilworth, Coventry CY8 2JP* Kenilworth (0926) 52417

OLDROYD, Preb Colin Mitchell. b 30. Down Coll Cam BA54 MA60. Wells Th Coll 60. d 61 p 62. C Elton All SS *Man* 61-63; C Ex St Dav *Ex* 63-66; P-in-c Neen Sollars w Milson *Heref* 66-78; P-in-c Coreley w Doddington 66-78; R Cleobury Mortimer w Hopton Wafers 66-78; RD Ludlow 75-78; P-in-c Eastnor 78-81; R Ledbury 78-81; RD Ledbury 78-81; Chapl Ledbury Cottage Hosp Heref from 79; R Ledbury w Eastnor *Heref* from 81; Preb Heref Cathl from 84; P-in-c Lt Marcle from 85. *The Rectory, Ledbury, Herefordshire HR8 1PL* Ledbury (0531) 2571

OLDROYD, David Christopher Leslie. b 42. FRICS. S Dios Minl Tr Scheme. d 85 p 86. NSM Four Marks *Win* 85-90; rtd 90. *Medstead Lodge, Wield Road, Medstead, Alton, Hants GU34 5LY* Alton (0420) 62835

OLDROYD, James Healey. b 08. Worc Ord Coll. d 55 p 56. V Worc St Mark *Worc* 61-75; rtd 75; Perm to Offic *Worc* from 75. *7 Grayling Close, Worcester WR5 3HY* Worcester (0905) 355603

OLDROYD, Trevor. b 33. Hatf Coll Dur BA55 Lon Univ BD60. Wycliffe Hall Ox 60. d 61 p 62. C Barnes St Mary *S'wark* 61-65; C Wimbledon 65-68; W Germany 68-73; Chapl Dudley Sch 73-80; Asst Chapl Wellington Coll Berks 80-82; P-in-c Rendcomb *Glouc* 82-86; Chapl Rendcomb Coll 82-86; Chapl Wrekin Coll Shropshire 86-90; V Deptford St Jo w H Trin *S'wark* from 91. *St John's Vicarage, St John's Vale, London SE8 4EA* 081-692 2857

OLHAUSEN, William John. b 37. TCD BA60 MA63. Ridley Hall Cam 60. d 62 p 63. C Grassendale *Liv* 62-66; Asst Chapl Dur Univ *Dur* 66-70; Lect Dur Univ 66-70; V Hazlemere *Ox* 70-89; RD Wycombe 78-83. *One Way, New Yatt, Witney, Oxon OX8 6TF* Witney (0993) 86708

OLIVE, Dan. b 29. ARIBA54. Sarum & Wells Th Coll 79. d 82 p 83. NSM Wells St Cuth w Wookey Hole *B & W* 82-85; C Yatton Moor 86-88; R Mells w Buckland Dinham, Elm, Whatley etc from 88. *The Rectory, Mells, Frome, Somerset BA11 3PT* Mells (0373) 812320

OLIVER, Anthony Grant. b 09. OBE42. Wells Th Coll 59. d 60 p 61. C Haywards Heath St Rich *Chich* 60-68; Australia from 68; rtd 74. *Sunrise, 75 Inlet Drive, Denmark, W Australia 6333* Denmark (98) 481491

OLIVER, Arthur Norman. b 16. Worc Ord Coll 63. d 65 p 66. C W Worthing St Jo *Chich* 69-71; R Etchingham 71-85; V Hurst Green 72-85; rtd 85; Perm to Offic Ely 86-89; Chich from 89. *1 April Place, Buckhurst Road, Bexhill-on-Sea, E Sussex TN40 1UE* Bexhill-on-Sea (0424) 219838

OLIVER, Bernard John. b 31. CEng65 MIMechE. S'wark Ord Course 75. d 78 p 79. NSM Chipping Ongar *Chelmsf* 78-81; C Waltham Abbey 81-85; C High Ongar w Norton Mandeville 85-87; C Somerton w Compton Dundon, the Charltons etc *B & W* 87-88. *1 Orchard Way, Mosterton, Beaminster, Dorset DT8 3LT* Broadwindsor (0308) 68037

OLIVER, Canon David Ryland. b 34. Univ of Wales (Lampt) BA56 St Cath Coll Ox BA58 MA62. Wycliffe Hall Ox 56. d 58 p 59. C Carmarthen St Pet *St D* 58-61; C Llangyfelach and Morriston *S & B* 61-63; R Aberedw w Llandeilo Graban etc 63-66; R Llanbadarn Fawr, Llandegley and Llanfihangel 66-67; Lic to Offic Llan 68-70; Ban 70-73; V Nevin w Pistyll w Tudweiliog w Llandudwen etc *Ban* 73-74; V Abercrave and Callwen *S & B* 74-77; V Llangyfelach 77-79; R Llanllwchaearn and Llanina *St D* 79-83; V Cwmaman from 83; Hon Can St D Cathl from 90. *The Vicarage, Cwmaman, Garnant, Ammanford, Dyfed SA18 1JQ* Amman Valley (0269) 822107

OLIVER, Eric Edwin. b 08. Bp Wilson Coll 37. d 38 p 39. V Staveley w Kentmere *Carl* 68-76; rtd 76; Lic to Offic *Blackb* from 76. *96 Park Avenue, Euxton, Chorley, Lancs PR7 6JQ* Chorley (02572) 71881

OLIVER, Graham Frank. b 42. St Barn Coll Adelaide. d 68 p 69. Australia 68-86; C Ealing Ch the Sav *Lon* from 86. *The Clergy House, The Grove, London W5 5DX* 081-567 1288

OLIVER, John Andrew George. b 28. OBE. St Jo Coll Dur BA53 DipTh55. d 55 p 56. C Bermondsey St Mary w St Olave and St Jo *S'wark* 55-58; C Dulwich St Barn 58-61; Chapl RN 61-83; QHC 79-83; R Guisborough

York 83-89; Chapl and Tutor Whittington Coll Felbridge from 89. *32 Whittington College, Felbridge, East Grinstead, W Sussex RH19 2QU* East Grinstead (0342) 322790

OLIVER, Ven John Graham Wyand. b 47. Ridley Hall Cam 76. d 78 p 79. C Shortlands *Roch* 78-81; C Hammersmith St Paul *Lon* 81-85; Zambia from 85; Adn S Zambia from 89. *c/o USPG, Partnership House, 157 Waterloo Road, London SE1 8XA* 071-928 8681

✠**OLIVER, Rt Rev John Keith.** b 35. G&C Coll Cam BA59 MA63 MLitt65. Westcott Ho Cam. d 64 p 65 c 90. C Hilborough w Bodney *Nor* 64-68; Chapl Eton Coll Windsor 68-72; R S Molton w Nymet St George *Ex* 73-75; P-in-c Filleigh w E Buckland 73-75; P-in-c Warkleigh w Satterleigh and Chittlehamholt 73-75; P-in-c High Bray w Charles 73-75; RD S Molton 74-80; TR S Molton, Nymet St George, High Bray etc 75-82; P-in-c N Molton w Twitchen 77-79; TR Cen Ex 82-85; Adn Sherborne *Sarum* 85-90; P-in-c W Stafford w Frome Billet 85-90; Can Res Sarum Cathl 85-90; Bp Heref from 90. *Bishop's House, The Palace, Hereford HR4 9BN* Hereford (0432) 271355

OLIVER, Canon John Michael. b 39. Univ of Wales (Lamp) BA62. Ripon Hall Ox 62. d 64 p 65. C High Harrogate St Pet *Ripon* 64-67; C Bramley 67-72; V Low Harrogate St Mary 72-78; V Beeston from 78; RD Armley from 86; Hon Can Ripon Cathl from 87. *Beeston Vicarage, 16 Town Street, Leeds LS11 8AN* Leeds (0532) 705529

OLIVER, Paul Robert. b 41. Lon Univ DipTh65. Tyndale Hall Bris 63. d 66 p 67. C Virginia Water *Guildf* 66-70; Scripture Union (E Region) 70-74; TV Thetford *Nor* 75-83; V Earlham St Anne from 83. *The Vicarage, Bluebell Road, Norwich NR4 7LP* Norwich (0603) 52922

OLIVER, Philip Maule. b 38. Birm Univ LLB59. Wells Th Coll 62. d 64 p 65. C Chesterton *Lich* 64-67; C Tettenhall Wood 67-71; V Milton 71-78; V Ixworth and Bardwell *St E* from 78; P-in-c Honington w Sapiston and Troston from 81; RD Ixworth from 85. *The Vicarage, Ixworth, Bury St Edmunds, Suffolk IP31 2HE* Pakenham (0359) 30311

OLIVER, Roland John. b 29. Ex Univ TCert54. Lich Th Coll. d 59 p 60. C Sedgley All SS *Lich* 59-62; V Weston Rhyn 62-77; V Lt Aston from 77. *The Vicarage, 3 Walsall Road, Little Aston, Sutton Coldfield, W Midlands B74 3BD* 021-353 0356

OLIVER, Stephen John. b 48. AKC70. St Aug Coll Cant 70. d 71 p 72. C Clifton w Glapton *S'well* 71-75; P-in-c Newark Ch Ch 75-79; R Plumtree 79-85; Sen Producer BBC Relig Broadcasting Dept Lon 85-87; Chief Producer from 87; Perm to Offic *Pet* from 87. *16 Trent Close, Wellingborough, Northants NN8 3XN* Wellingborough (0933) 676083

OLIVER, Canon Terence Maule. b 07. Univ Coll Dur BA32. Linc Th Coll 31. d 36 p 37. V Shilbottle *Newc* 66-76; rtd 76; Lic to Offic *Newc* from 76; Hon Can Kuala Lumpur Cathl from 87. *Restharrow, Longhorsley, Morpeth, Northd NE65 8SY* Longhorsley (067088) 253

OLIVER, Thomas Gordon. b 48. Nottm Univ BTh72 LTh74 DipAdEd80. St Jo Coll Nottm 68 ALCD72. d 72 p 73. C Thorpe Edge *Bradf* 72-76; C Woodthorpe *S'well* 76-80; V Huthwaite 80-85; Dir Past Studies St Jo Coll Nottm from 85. *St John's College, Beeston, Nottingham NG9 3DS* Nottingham (0602) 251114

OLIVEY, Hugh Charles Tony. b 35. St Mich Coll Llan 77. d 79 p 80. C St Winnow *Truro* 79-81; C Lanhydrock 81-82; C Lostwithiel 81-82; C Lanivet 81-82; P-in-c 82-83; TV Bodmin w Lanhydrock and Lanivet 84-89; P-in-c St Neot 89-90; P-in-c Warleggan 89-90; R St Neot and Warleggan from 90. *The Vicarage, St Neot, Liskeard, Cornwall PL14 6NG* Liskeard (0579) 20472

OLLIER, Cecil Rupert. b 13. St Edm Hall Ox BA34 MA42. Ely Th Coll 34. d 36 p 37. V Fenton *Lich* 58-73; R Moreton Say 73-78; rtd 78; Hon C Kettering SS Pet and Paul *Pet* 78-80; Chapl Berkeley's Hosp Worc 80-82; Master Abp Holgate's Hosp Hemsworth from 83. *20 Ludwall Road, Normacot, Longton, Stoke-on-Trent* Stoke-on-Trent (0782) 333592

OLLIER, Timothy John Douglas. b 44. Trin Hall Cam BA66 MA69. Cuddesdon Coll 66. d 68 p 69. C Silksworth *Dur* 68-71; C St Marylebone w H Trin *Lon* 71-74; C Winlaton *Dur* 74-77; V Bishopton w St Stainton 77-88; R Redmarshall 77-88; P-in-c Grindon and Stillington 83-88; RD Barnard Castle from 88; V Gainford from 88; R Winston from 88. *The Vicarage, Gainford, Darlington, Co Durham DL2 3DS* Darlington (0325) 730261

O'LOUGHLIN, Gordon Raymond. b 32. Linc Coll Ox BA56 MA60. Wells Th Coll 56. **d** 58 **p** 59. C Bournemouth St Fran *Win* 58-62; C Tunbridge Wells St Barn *Roch* 62-65; Chapl Roch Th Coll 65-67; Sub-Warden 67-69; V Kingston upon Hull St Alb *York* 69-78; Dir of Post-Ord Tr 77-82; Can and Preb York Minster 78-81; TV York All SS Pavement w St Crux and St Martin etc 78-82; V Bromley St Andr *Roch* 82-87; P-in-c Brighton St Paul *Chich* from 87. *St Paul's Parsonage, 9 Russell Place, Brighton BN1 2RG* Brighton (0273) 739639

O'LOUGHLIN, Michael Wilfred Bryan. b 23. Ch Coll Cam BA47 MA58 PhD64. **d** 81 **p** 82. NSM Linton *Ely* from 81; Chapl Addenbrooke's Hosp Cam 84-88; NSM Shudy Camps from 84; NSM Castle Camps from 84; Chmn Dioc Bd Soc Resp from 88. *Ditches Close, 42 The Grip, Linton, Cambridge CB1 6NR* Cambridge (0223) 891357

OLSEN, Arthur Barry. b 37. Univ of NZ BA61. Melbourne Coll of Div BD73 ACT ThL64. **d** 64 **p** 64. New Zealand 64-81; C Hersham *Guildf* 81-84; P-in-c Botleys and Lyne from 84; P-in-c Long Cross from 84. *The Vicarage, Lyne, Chertsey, Surrey KT16 0AJ* Ottershaw (0932) 874405

OLUMIDE, Oluseye Abiola. b 42. Bradf Univ BA89. Clifton Th Coll 68. **d** 71 **p** 72. C Halliwell St Pet *Man* 71-72; C Collyhurst St Oswald and St Cath 71; C Salford St Phil w St Steph 72; C Wood Green St Mich *Lon* 73; P-in-c 73; C Stanmer w Falmer and Moulsecoomb *Chich* 73-76; C Moss Side St Jas w St Clem *Man* 76; C Hulme Ascension 76-77; Chapl Asst N Man Gen Hosp 77-80; Chapl St Bernard's Hosp Southall 80-86; Chapl Lynfield Mt and Chapl St Luke's Hosps Bradf from 86; Chapl Bradf R Infirmary from 86. *Bradford Royal Infirmary, Duckworth Lane, Bradford, W Yorkshire BD9 6RJ* Bradford (0274) 542200

OLYOTT, Ven Leonard Eric. b 26. Lon Univ BA50. Westcott Ho Cam 50. **d** 52 **p** 53. C Camberwell St Geo *S'wark* 52-55; C Hatf *St Alb* 55-60; V Chipperfield St Paul 60-68; V Crewkerne *B & W* 68-71; R Crewkerne w Wayford 71-77; RD Crewkerne 72-77; Preb Wells Cathl from 76; Adn Taunton from 77. *4 Westerkirk Gate, Staplegrove, Taunton, Somerset TA2 6BQ* Taunton (0823) 323838

O'MALLEY, Brian Denis Brendan. b 40. Oscott Coll (RC) Coll of Resurr Mirfield 82. **d** 77 **p** 77. In RC Ch 77-81; Warden St Greg Retreat Rhandirmwyn *St D* 81-82; Lic to Offic 82-83; Chapl and Min Can St D Cathl 83-85; V Wiston w Ambleston, St Dogwells, Walton E etc 85-89; V Wiston w Clarbeston and Walton E 89; R Walton W w Talbenny and Haroldston W from 89. *All Saints' Rectory, Walton West, Haverfordwest, Dyfed SA62 3UB* Broad Haven (0437) 781279

OMAN, Brian Malcolm. b 14. Qu Coll Cam BA36 MA46. Chich Th Coll 36. **d** 37 **p** 38. OGS from 39; R Greenford H Cross *Lon* 62-74; V Kings Sutton *Pet* 74-88; rtd 88; Perm to Offic *Pet* from 88. *The Old Post Office, Church Street, Sulgrave, Banbury, Oxon OX17 2RP* Sulgrave (029576) 8317

O'NEIL, Thomas Arthur. b 11. St Chad's Coll Dur BA32 MA50. **d** 34 **p** 35. Chapl St Steph Coll Broadstairs 63-67; Perm to Offic *Cant* from 67; rtd 76. *9 Sewell Close, Birchington, Kent CT7 0BP* Thanet (0843) 43750

O'NEILL, Christopher John. b 53. ALAM LGSM MSAPP Worc Coll Ox BA75 MA80 CertEd91 CCouns91 DipTHPsych91. Ripon Coll Cuddesdon 77. **d** 78 **p** 79. Asst Chapl Rugby Sch Warks 78-80; Chapl Charterhouse Godalming from 81. *14 Chapelfields, Charterhouse, Godalming, Surrey GU7 2BF* Godalming (0483) 414437

O'NEILL, Gary. b 57. K Coll Lon BD79 AKC79. Westcott Ho Cam 80. **d** 81 **p** 82. C Oldham *Man* 81-84; C Birch w Fallowfield 84-87; R Moston St Chad from 87. *The Rectory, 30 Hawthorn Road, New Moston, Manchester M10 0RH* 061-681 3203

O'NEILL, Very Rev Nevil. b 23. TCD BA45 MA55. **d** 46 **p** 47. I Galloon w Drummully *Clogh* 66-81; Preb Clogh Cathl 80-86; I Clogh w Errigal Portclare 81-89; Dean Clogh 86-89; rtd 89. *9 Ashgrove, Derrychara, Enniskillen, Co Fermanagh, Irish Republic*

O'NEILL, William Lloyd. b 11. TCD BA32 MA38. **d** 34 **p** 35. P-in-c Portfield *Chich* 67-79; rtd 79; Perm to Offic *Chich* from 79. *1 Fishbourne Road, Chichester, W Sussex PO19 3HS* Chichester (0243) 782603

ONIONS, Martin Giles. b 63. TC. Chich Th Coll 85. **d** 88 **p** 89. C Eastbourne St Mary *Chich* 88-91; C-in-c Hydneye CD from 91. *St Peter's House, The Hydneye, Eastbourne, E Sussex BN22 9BY* Eastbourne (0323) 504392

ONSLOW, Denzil Octavia (Sister Denzil). b 19. CertRK58. dss 61 **d** 87. CSA from 59; Novice Guardian 68-73 and

from 90; Notting Hill St Jo and St Pet *Lon* 80-87; Hon Par Dn from 87. *St Andrew's House, 2 Tavistock Road, London W11 1BA* 071-229 2662

ORAM, Canon Geoffrey William James. b 14. Em Coll Cam BA37 MA40. Ridley Hall Cam 36. **d** 38 **p** 39. V Aldeburgh w Hazlewood *St E* 64-80; rtd 80; Perm to Offic *St E* 80-81 and from 86; P-in-c Ipswich St Mich 81-86. *Pantiles, Spring Meadow, Hillfarm Road, Playford, Ipswich IP6 9ED* Ipswich (0473) 622566

ORAM, John Ernest Donald. b 34. Open Univ BA74. Tyndale Hall Bris. **d** 61 **p** 62. C Cheetham Hill *Man* 61-64; C Gt Baddow *Chelmsf* 64-67; V Blackb St Barn *Blackb* 67-72; Bp's Chapl for Soc Resp *Sheff* 72-86; Chapl Psychotherapist 79-86. *12 Montgomery Road, Sheffield S7 1LQ* Sheffield (0742) 582332 or 682883

✠**ORAM, Rt Rev Kenneth Cyril.** b 19. Lon Univ BA39 AKC41. Linc Th Coll 42. **d** 42 **p** 43 **c** 74. C Cranbrook *Cant* 42-45; S Africa 46-87; Adn Bechuanaland 53-60; Dean Kimberley 60-64; Dean and Adn Grahamstown 64-74; Bp and Asst Bp Lich from 87. *10 Sandringham Road, Stafford ST17 0AA* Stafford (0785) 53974

ORAM, Roland Martin David. b 45. Trin Coll Cam BA68. Cranmer Hall Dur DipTh78. **d** 78 **p** 79. C Aspley *S'well* 78-81; Chapl Alleyn's Sch Dulwich 81-88; Chapl Versailles w Grandchamp and Gif-sur-Yvette *Eur* from 88. *31 rue du Pont Colbert, 78000 Versailles, France* Paris (331) 39 02 79 45

ORAM, Stephen John. b 58. **d** 84 **p** 85. C Kidderminster St Jo *Worc* 84-88; Chapl RAF from 88. *c/o MOD, Adastral House, Theobald's Road, London WC1X 8RU* 071-430 7268

ORCHARD, Canon George Richard. b 41. Ex Coll Ox BA62 BA64 MA66. Ripon Hall Ox 62. **d** 65 **p** 66. C Greenhill St Pet *Derby* 65-70; Member Ecum Team Min Sinfin Moor 70-78; V Sinfin Moor 76-78; TR Dronfield 78-86; Can Res Derby Cathl from 86. *24 Kedleston Road, Derby DE3 1GU* Derby (0332) 43144

ORCHARD, Harry Frank. b 23. Roch Th Coll. **d** 63 **p** 64. V Preston *Sarum* 67-71; R Teffont Evias and Teffont Magna 71-73; V Dinton 71-73; C Fovant w Compton Chamberlayne etc 76-78; Lic to Offic 78-80 and from 82; RD Chalke 80-82; rtd 88. *Downstream, Burcombe, Salisbury SP2 0EJ* Salisbury (0722) 742322

ORCHARD, Nigel John. b 56. CertEd78. St Steph Ho Ox 82. **d** 85 **p** 86. C Tottenham St Paul *Lon* 85-89; C Is of Dogs Ch Ch and St Jo w St Luke 89-90; TV from 90. *St Luke's House, Strafford Street, London E14 8LT* 071-515 9888

ORFORD, Barry Antony. b 49. St Steph Ho Ox 71. **d** 73 **p** 74. C Mon 73-77; VC St As Cathl *St As* 77-81; C St As and Tremeirchion 77-81; CR from 83. *House of the Resurrection, Mirfield, W Yorkshire WF14 0BN* Mirfield (0924) 494318

ORFORD, Keith John. b 40. FCTT. E Midl Min Tr Course 76. **d** 79 **p** 80. NSM Matlock Bank *Derby* from 79. *27 Lums Hill Rise, Matlock, Derby DE4 3FX* Matlock (0629) 55349

ORLAND, Canon Ernest George. b 28. Lich Th Coll 61. **d** 62 **p** 63. C Northn St Mich *Pet* 62-65; R Gayton w Tiffield 65-69; R Corby SS Pet and Andr 69-72; TR Corby SS Pet and Andr w Gt and Lt Oakley 72-81; RD Corby 79-81; Can Pet Cathl from 79; V Pet All SS from 81. *All Saints' Vicarage, 208 Park Road, Peterborough PE1 2UJ* Peterborough (0733) 54130

ORME, John. b 29. Sarum Th Coll 58. **d** 60 **p** 61. C Heald Green St Cath *Ches* 60-64; C Ellesmere Port 64-67; Chapl Harperbury Hosp Radlett 67-73; P-in-c Luton All SS w St Pet *St Alb* 73-79; V 79-87; V Oxhey St Matt from 87. *The Vicarage, St Matthew's Close, Eastbury Road, Oxhey, Watford WD1 4PT* Watford (0923) 241420

ORME, John Theodore Warrington. b 16. AKC39. **d** 39 **p** 40. Perm to Offic St Alb 49-52; Lon 68-70; Ox 70-71; rtd 78. *Dunraven House, 12 Bourne Avenue, Salisbury SP1 1LP*

ORME, Martin Kitchener. b 27. K Coll Lon BD50 AKC50 Open Univ BA75. **d** 51 **p** 52. C Blackb St Pet *Blackb* 51-54; C Burnley St Cath 54-57; Chapl RN 57-78; Chapl R Hosp Sch Holbrook 78-87; P-in-c Ipswich St Mary at the Elms *St E* from 87. *The Vicarage, 68 Black Horse Lane, Ipswich IP1 2EF* Ipswich (0473) 252822

ORME, Stewart. b 22. Leeds Univ BA49 Open Univ BA75. St Steph Ho Ox 50. **d** 52 **p** 53. R Albury w St Martha *Guildf* 59-87; rtd 87. *The Spinney, Hawksford Lane West, Fernhurst, Haslemere, Surrey* Haslemere (0428) 654789

ORME, Sydney. b 27. Oak Hill Th Coll 54. **d** 58 **p** 59. C Halliwell St Pet *Man* 58-61; V Friarmere 61-73; V

Knypersley *Lich* from 73. *62 Park Lane, Knypersley, Stoke-on-Trent ST8 7AU* Stoke-on-Trent (0782) 512240

ORMEROD, Henry Lawrence. b 35. Pemb Coll Cam BA58 MA63. Qu Coll Birm DipTh59. **d** 60 **p** 61. C Chigwell *Chelmsf* 60-64; C Thundersley 64-68; C Canvey Is 68-72; V Stanground *Ely* 72-77; TR Stanground and Farcet 77-81; TR Swindon St Jo and St Andr *Bris* 81-90; TR N Wingfield, Clay Cross and Pilsley *Derby* from 90. *The Rectory, St Lawrence Road, North Wingfield, Chesterfield, Derbyshire S42 5HX* Chesterfield (0246) 851181

ORMISTON, Albert Edward. b 26. Oak Hill Th Coll 53. **d** 56 **p** 57. C Worksop St Jo *S'well* 56-58; P-in-c Everton St Polycarp *Liv* 58-59; V 59-63; Org Sec SAMS 63-67; Perm to Offic Carl, Ches, Bradf, Liv & Man 63-67; Lic Preacher *Blackb* 63-67; R Gateacre *Liv* 67-73; V Tonbridge St Steph *Roch* 73-86; V Dent w Cowgill *Bradf* from 86. *The Vicarage, Dent, Sedbergh, Cumbria LA10 5QR* Dent (05875) 226

ORMROD, Paul William. b 57. Liv Univ BA80. Westcott Ho Cam 80. **d** 83 **p** 84. C Prescot *Liv* 83-86; TV Padgate from 86. *The Vicarage, 20 Warren Lane, Woolston WA1 4ES* Padgate (0925) 813083

ORMSBY, Mrs Diana Clare. b 21. Sunderland Tr Coll CertEd. Sarum & Wells Th Coll 77. **dss** 80 **d** 87. Lydford, Brent Tor, Bridestowe and Sourton *Ex* 80-87; Hon C from 87. *Lipscliffe, Coryton, Okehampton, Devon EX20 4AB* Chillaton (082286) 344

ORMSBY, Robert Daly. b 22. CCC Ox BA42 MA48. Sarum & Wells Th Coll 77. **d** 78 **p** 79. Hon C Lydford, Brent Tor, Bridestowe and Sourton *Ex* from 78. *Lipscliffe, Coryton, Okehampton, Devon EX20 4AB* Chillaton (082286) 344

ORMSTON, Derek. b 43. Univ of Wales (Lamp) DipTh67. **d** 67 **p** 68. C Ogley Hay *Lich* 67-70; C Tettenhall Regis 70-74; P-in-c Leek All SS 74-79; TV Leek and Meerbrook 79-83; Youth Chapl *Bris* 83-87; R Brinkworth w Dauntsey from 87; Chapl New Coll Swindon from 87. *The Rectory, Brinkworth, Chippenham, Wilts SN15 5AS* Brinkworth (066641) 207

ORMSTON, Joseph. b 24. Oak Hill Th Coll 47. **d** 51 **p** 53. V Wimbledon St Luke *S'wark* 65-71; R Stamford St Geo w St Paul *Linc* 71-89; Chapl Stamford and Rutland Infirmary 71-89; rtd 89; Perm to Offic Linc, Pet and Ely from 89. *84 Fountains Place, Eye, Peterborough, Cambs PE6 7XX* Peterborough (0733) 222067

ORMSTON, Richard Jeremy. b 61. Southlands Coll Lon BA83. Oak Hill Th Coll BA87. **d** 87 **p** 88. C Rodbourne Cheney *Bris* 87-91; R Collingtree w Courteenhall and Milton Malsor *Pet* from 91. *The Rectory, Collingtree, Northampton NN4 0NF* Northampton (0604) 761895

ORPIN, Mrs Gillian. b 32. SRN53. Oak Hill Th Coll 82. **d** 87. Par Dn Passenham *Pet* from 87. *58 Ridgmont, Deanshanger, Milton Keynes MK19 6JQ* Milton Keynes (0908) 565684

ORPWOOD, Canon William Warren Coverdale Lipscomb. b 01. Pemb Coll Ox BA30 MA30. Ridley Hall Cam 24. **d** 26 **p** 27. V Alveston *Bris* 61-70; RD Almondsbury 65-70; rtd 70. *c/o M Griffiths Esq, St Nicholas House, High Street, Bristol BS1 2AW*

ORR, Very Rev David Cecil. b 33. TCD BA56 MA68. **d** 57 **p** 58. C Drumragh *D & R* 57-60; I Convoy 60-70; RD Raphoe 66-70; I Maghera 70-80; I Drumragh w Mountfield 80-84; Dean Derry from 84; I Templemore from 84; Miss to Seamen from 84. *The Deanery, 30 Bishop Street, Londonderry BT48 6PP* Londonderry (0504) 262746

ORR, Nathaniel Blair. b 13. Wycliffe Hall Ox 63. **d** 64 **p** 65. R Offord D'Arcy w Offord Cluny *Ely* 66-75; P-in-c Gt w Lt Paxton and Toseland 67-75; V Tynemouth St John Aug *Newc* 75-81; rtd 81; Perm to Offic *Liv* from 82. *16 Tinsley Avenue, Southport, Merseyside PR8 6HT* Southport (0704) 31073

ORR, Reginald Henry Pache. b 11. Qu Coll Cam BA36 MA40. Bps' Coll Cheshunt 36. **d** 38 **p** 40. V Frimley Green *Guildf* 63-74; R Peper Harow 74-79; R Shackleford 74-79; rtd 79; Perm to Offic *Guildf* from 82. *163 Stoke Road, Guildford, Surrey GU1 1EY* Guildford (0483) 61471

ORRELL, Joseph Albert. b 30. Lon Univ BD56. Lich Th Coll 60. **d** 61 **p** 62. C Orford St Marg *Liv* 61-63; V Hollinfare 63-71; V New Springs 71-76; Lic to Offic from 77. *24 Kenyon Road, Wigan, Lancs WN1 2DQ* Wigan (0942) 35285

ORTON, Richard. b 33. Keble Coll Ox BA56 MA60 Leeds Univ. Lich Th Coll 60. **d** 61 **p** 64. C Penistone w Midhope *Wakef* 61-62; Hon C Meltham 62-69; Hon C Horsforth *Ripon* 69-72; C Far Headingley St Chad 72-75; V Hellifield *Bradf* 75-80; RD Bowland 78-80; R Hutton

Chelmsf 80-87; R Wallasey St Hilary *Ches* from 87. *St Hilary's Rectory, Church Hill, Wallasey, Merseyside L45 3NH* 051-638 4771

OSBORN, David Ronald. b 42. Bris Univ BA66 Bath Univ MEd82. Clifton Th Coll 62. **d** 66 **p** 67. C Farndon *S'well* 66-69; P-in-c W Bridgford 69-72; Asst Dioc Dir Educn *Carl* 72-77; P-in-c Kirkandrews-on-Eden w Beaumont and Grinsdale 72-77; Hd RE and Chapl Dauntsey's Sch Devizes 77-83; V Southbroom *Sarum* 83-86; Consultant to Lay Tr Schemes *Ox* 86; Hd RE Bexhill High Sch 86-90. *29 St James's Avenue, Bexhill-on-Sea, E Sussex TN40 2DW* Bexhill-on-Sea (0424) 220367

OSBORN, David Thomas. b 58. PGCE80 K Coll Lon BD79 AKC79. Linc Th Coll 82. **d** 83 **p** 84. C Bearsted w Thurnham *Cant* 83-86; Chapl RAF 86-90; R Bassingham *Linc* from 90; V Aubourn w Haddington from 90; V Carlton-le-Moorland w Stapleford from 90; R Thurlby w Norton Disney from 90. *The Rectory, Torgate Lane, Bassingham, Lincoln LN5 9HF* Lincoln (0522) 788383

OSBORN, Mrs Diana Marian. b 52. R Holloway Coll Lon BSc74 CertEd75. NE Ord Course 81. **dss** 84 **d** 87. Malden St Jo *S'wark* 84-87; Par Dn 87-89; Par Dn Brampton *Ely* from 89. *30 Chestnut Close, Brampton, Huntingdon, Cambs PE18 8TP* Huntingdon (0480) 411389

OSBORN, Preb John Geoffrey Rowland. b 33. Jes Coll Cam BA55 MA59. Wells Th Coll 63. **d** 65 **p** 66. C Easthampstead *Ox* 65-68; Lic to Offic *Blackb* 68-70; Brunei 70-75; Asst Dir RE *Blackb* 75-77; V Tockholes 75-77; Dir RE *B & W* 77-83; Dir and Sec Lon Bd for Schs *Lon* from 83; Preb St Paul's Cathl from 86. *c/o London Diocesan House, 30 Causton Street, London SW1P 4AU* 071-821 9311

OSBORN, Maurice. b 25. Univ of Wales BA50. Wycliffe Hall Ox 55. **d** 55 **p** 56. Chapl Dauntsey's Sch Devizes 57-72; Asst Master 58-78; P-in-c Bishop's Lavington *Sarum* 79-83; P-in-c Lt Cheverell 82-83; P-in-c W Lavington and the Cheverells 83-90; rtd 90. *Greensand Cottage, West Lavington, Devizes, Wilts SN10 4LB* Devizes (0380) 813244

OSBORN, Reginald Richardson. b 12. Worc Coll Ox BA32 MA38 BLitt38. Ridley Hall Cam 46. **d** 47 **p** 47. V Bromley Common St Luke *Roch* 63-77; P-in-c Syresham w Whitfield *Pet* 77-86; rtd 86; Perm to Offic *Ox* from 87. *Nest Lea, 25 Pigeon House Lane, Freeland, Oxford OX7 2AG* Freeland (0993) 881269

OSBORNE, Alexander Deas. b 34. Liv Univ BSc54 PhD57. Oak Hill NSM Course 78. **d** 81 **p** 82. NSM Redbourn *St Alb* from 81. *19 Rickyard Meadow, Redbourn, St Albans, Herts AL3 7HT* Redbourn (0582) 793749

OSBORNE, Anthony Russell. b 47. Sarum & Wells Th Coll 77. **d** 79 **p** 80. C Heref St Martin *Heref* 79-81; TV 82-86; TV Hanley H Ev *Lich* from 86. *The Vicarage, 18 Cromer Road, Stoke-on-Trent ST1 6QN* Stoke-on-Trent (0782) 215499

OSBORNE, Arthur Frederick. b 09. K Coll Lon BD44 AKC44. K Coll Lon 28. **d** 33 **p** 34. Chapl and Prin Lect Kirkby Fields Coll of Educn 65-72; Chapl Northn Coll of Educn 72-75; rtd 75. *21 Pembroke Avenue, Orton Longueville, Peterborough* Peterborough (0733) 233656

OSBORNE, Brian Charles. b 38. St Andr Univ MA61 Lon Univ DipTh80. Clifton Th Coll 61. **d** 63 **p** 64. C Skirbeck H Trin *Linc* 63-68; V from 80; P-in-c New Clee 68-71; V 71-75; V Derby St Aug *Derby* 75-80; Chapl Pilgrim Hosp Boston 84-88; RD Holland E *Linc* from 85. *Holy Trinity Vicarage, 64 Spilsby Road, Boston, Lincs PE21 9NS* Boston (0205) 363657

OSBORNE, David Robert. b 50. Birm Univ BSc71 MEd86 Nottm Univ DipTh72 Bris Univ PGCE73. St Jo Coll Dur 78. **d** 80 **p** 81. C Penkridge w Stretton *Lich* 80-85; R Longdon-upon-Tern, Rodington, Uppington etc from 85. *The Vicarage, Wrockwardine, Telford, Shropshire TF6 5DD* Telford (0952) 40969

OSBORNE, David Victor. b 36. Dur Univ BA59. Cranmer Hall Dur DipTh62. **d** 62 **p** 63. C Kennington Cross St Anselm *S'wark* 62-66; C Sandal St Helen *Wakef* 66-67; R Ancoats *Man* 67-73; V Claremont H Angels 73-80; R Breedon cum Isley Walton and Worthington *Leic* 80-87; V Beaumont Leys from 87. *5 Beacon Close, Beaumont Leys, Leicester LE4 1BN* Leicester (0533) 352667

OSBORNE, Derek James. b 32. Tyndale Hall Bris 53. **d** 57 **p** 58. C Weymouth St Mary *Sarum* 57-60; C Southgate *Chich* 60-63; V Croydon Ch Ch Broad Green *Cant* 63-71; V Cromer *Nor* 71-83; P-in-c Gresham w Bessingham 71-80; Hon Can Nor Cathl 77-83; V Northwood Em *Lon* from 83. *Emmanuel Vicarage, 3 Gatehill Road, Northwood, Middx HA6 3QB* Northwood (09274) 21598

OSBORNE, Hayward John. b 48. New Coll Ox BA70 MA73. Westcott Ho Cam 71. **d** 73 **p** 74. C Bromley SS Pet and Paul *Roch* 73-77; C Halesowen *Worc* 77-80; TV 80-83; TR Worc St Barn w Ch Ch 83-88; V Moseley St Mary *Birm* from 88. *St Mary's Vicarage, 18 Oxford Road, Birmingham B13 9EH* 021-449 1459 or 449 2243

OSBORNE, June. b 53. Man Univ BA74. St Jo Coll Nottm. **dss** 80 **d** 87. Birm St Martin *Birm* 80-84; Old Ford St Paul w St Steph and St Mark *Lon* 84-87; Par Dn from 87. *36 Tredegar Square, London E3 5AE* 081-980 2839

OSBORNE, Ralph. b 38. Kent Univ DipTh80. Bernard Gilpin Soc Dur 62 Clifton Th Coll 63. **d** 66 **p** 67. C Harpurhey Ch Ch *Man* 66-68; C Chorlton on Medlock St Sav 68-71; C Wilmington *Roch* 71-74; V St Mary Cray and St Paul's Cray 74-85; P-in-c Bath St Steph *B & W* 85-88; P-in-c Charlcombe 86-88; R Charlcombe w Bath St Steph from 88. *St Stephen's Rectory, Richmond Place, Lansdown, Bath BA1 5PZ* Bath (0225) 317535

OSBORNE, Canon Robin Orbell. b 29. Leeds Univ BA54. Coll of Resurr Mirfield 52. **d** 54 **p** 55. C Wellingborough All Hallows *Pet* 54-58; C Oxhey St Matt *St Alb* 60-61; V Woburn 61-65; V Battlesden and Pottesgrove 61-65; V Cheshunt 65-82; RD Cheshunt 70-81; Hon Can St Alb 76-82; V Penzance St Mary w St Paul *Truro* 82-88; Can Res and Treas Truro Cathl from 88. *Lemon Lodge, Lemon Street, Truro, Cornwall TR1 2PE* Truro (0872) 72094

OSBOURNE, David John. b 56. Linc Th Coll 78. **d** 79 **p** 80. C Houghton le Spring *Dur* 79-82; C Spalding St Jo *Linc* 82-83; C Spalding St Jo w Deeping St Nicholas 83-84; V Swineshead from 84; RD Holland W from 86. *The Vicarage, Swineshead, Boston, Lincs PE20 3JA* Boston (0205) 820271

OSGERBY, Dr John Martin. b 34. Sheff Univ BSc56 PhD59. Linc Th Coll 75. **d** 77 **p** 78. C Rotherham *Sheff* 77-80; C-in-c W Bessacarr CD 80-84; V W Bessacarr 84-87; Warden of Readers from 86; R Fishlake w Sykehouse, Kirk Bramwith, Fenwick etc from 87. *The Vicarage, Fishlake, Doncaster, S Yorkshire DN7 5JW* Doncaster (0302) 841396

OSGOOD, Graham Dean. b 39. Lon Univ BSc62. ALCD71 St Jo Coll Nottm 71. **d** 71 **p** 72. C Bebington *Ches* 71-76; V Gee Cross from 76. *The Vicarage, Higham Lane, Hyde, Cheshire SK14 5LX* 061-368 2337

OSMAN, David Thomas. b 49. Bradf Univ BTech72. Trin Coll Bris 75. **d** 78 **p** 79. C Stranton *Dur* 78-81; C Denton Holme *Carl* 81-84; V Preston on Tees *Dur* from 84. *The Vicarage, Quarry Road, Eaglescliffe, Stockton-on-Tees, Cleveland TS16 9BD* Stockton-on-Tees (0642) 780516

OSMAN, Ernest. b 35. St Aid Birkenhead 61. **d** 64 **p** 65. C Heaton Ch Ch *Man* 64-68; V Farnworth St Pet 68-77; V St Martin's *Lich* 77-85; V Endon w Stanley from 85. *The Vicarage, Leek Road, Endon, Stoke-on-Trent ST9 9BH* Stoke-on-Trent (0782) 502166

OSMAN, Stephen William. b 53. Matlock Coll of Educn CertEd74 Teesside Poly CQSW80. St Jo Coll Dur 88. **d** 90 **p** 91. C Newbarns w Hawcoat *Carl* from 90. *50 Furness Park, Barrow-in-Furness, Cumbria LA14 5PS* Barrow-in-Furness (0229) 836953

OSMASTON, Miss Amiel Mary Ellinor. b 51. Ex Univ BA73 St Jo Coll Dur BA84. St Jo Coll Nottm DPS77 Cranmer Hall Dur 82. **dss** 84 **d** 87. Ches le Street *Dur* 84-87; Par Dn 87-88; Dir Miss and Past Studies Ridley Hall Cam from 89. *Ridley Hall, Sidgwick Avenue, Cambridge CB3 9HG* Cambridge (0223) 311672

OSMOND, David Methuen. b 38. Qu Coll Birm 75. **d** 77 **p** 78. C Yardley St Edburgha *Birm* 77-80; V Wythall 80-89; R W Coker w Hardington Mandeville, E Chinnock etc *B & W* from 89. *The Rectory, 7 Cedar Fields, West Coker, Yeovil, Somerset BA22 9DB* West Coker (093586) 2328

OSMOND, Mrs Heather Christine. b 44. ABSM64 ARCM65 Birm Poly CertEd65. Qu Coll Birm 83. **dss** 84 **d** 87. Brandwood *Birm* 84-85; Wythall 85-87; Par Dn 87-89; Perm to Offic *B & W* from 89. *The Rectory, 7 Cedar Fields, West Coker, Yeovil, Somerset BA22 9DB* West Coker (093586) 2328

OSMOND, Oliver Robert. b 44. Ch Coll Cam BA66 MA70. Cuddesdon Coll 66 Trin Coll Toronto STB69. **d** 69 **p** 70. Canada 69-81; V Mill Hill Jo Keble *Lon* from 81. *John Keble Vicarage, 142 Deans Lane, Edgware, Middx HA8 9NT* 081-959 1312

OSSORY AND LEIGHLIN, Archdeacon of. See GRAY, Ven Hugh Henry James

OSSORY, Dean of. Vacant

OSTLE, Arthur John. b 08. St Aid Birkenhead 38. **d** 38 **p** 39. C Gt Crosby St Luke *Liv* 38-40; CF (EC) 40-46; C Sefton *Liv* 46-47; V Bootle St Mary w St Jo 47-51;

Canada from 52. *311-400 Sandringham Crescent, London, Ontario, Canada, N6C 5A8*

OSWALD, John Edward Guy. b 39. Qu Coll Cam BA63 MA67. Ridley Hall Cam. **d** 68 **p** 69. C Chippenham St Paul w Langley Burrell *Bris* 68-72; C Hengrove 72-75; P-in-c Hardenhuish 75-79; P-in-c Kington 75-79; TV Chippenham St Paul w Hardenhuish etc 79-82; P-in-c Gt w Lt Somerford and Seagry 82-86; P-in-c Corston w Rodbourne 84-86; R Gt Somerford, Lt Somerford, Seagry, Corston etc from 86. *The Rectory, Frog Lane, Great Somerford, Chippenham, Wilts SN15 5JA* Seagry (0249) 720220

OSWALD, Ronald William. b 17. TCD BA38 MA53 BD57 BA59. TCD Div Sch. **d** 55 **p** 56. V Castle Hedingham *Chelmsf* 67-80; R Panfield 80-87; rtd 87. *1 Abbey Cottages, Galhampton, Castle Cary, Somerset BA22 7AQ* Castle Cary (0963) 50623

OSWIN, Frank Anthony. b 43. Chich Th Coll 69. **d** 71 **p** 72. C Radford *Cov* 71-74; C Shrub End *Chelmsf* 74-76; V Layer-de-la-Haye 76-80; V Eastwood St Dav from 80. *St David's Vicarage, 400 Rayleigh Road, Eastwood, Leigh-on-Sea, Essex SS9 5PT* Southend-on-Sea (0702) 523126

OTAGIRI, Norman Kenji. b 19. Oak Hill NSM Course. **d** 83 **p** 84. NSM Bentley Common *Chelmsf* from 83. *65 Saville Road, Chadwell Heath, Romford RM6 6DS* 081-599 2299

OTTAWAY, Bernard Wyndham. b 15. Keble Coll Ox BA38 MA43. Cuddesdon Coll 38. **d** 39 **p** 40. R Loughton St Jo *Chelmsf* 55-71; R Birdbrook w Sturmer 71-76; P-in-c Ashen w Ridgewell 74-76; R Ridgewell w Ashen, Birdbrook and Sturmer 76-81; P-in-c Farnham 81-85; rtd 85; Perm to Offic Guildf 86-89; Chelmsf from 89. *Wash Farm House, Ridgewell, Halstead, Essex CO9 4PJ* Ridgewell (044085) 593

OTTAWAY, Michael John. b 17. Mert Coll Ox BA40 MA44. Cuddesdon Coll 40. **d** 41 **p** 42. V Wolvercote *Ox* 49-76; TV Wolvercote w Summertown 76-83; rtd 83; Perm to Offic *Chich* from 84. *13 Bishopstone Road, Seaford, E Sussex BN25 2UB* Seaford (0323) 899179

OTTER, Anthony Frank. b 32. Kelham Th Coll 54. **d** 59 **p** 60. C Bethnal Green St Jo w St Simon *Lon* 59-63; C Aylesbury *Ox* 63-68; V Hanslope w Castlethorpe 68-77; P-in-c N w S Moreton 77-79; P-in-c Aston Tirrold w Aston Upthorpe 77-79; R S w N Moreton, Aston Tirrold and Aston Upthorpe from 79. *The Rectory, South Moreton, Didcot, Oxon OX11 9AF* Didcot (0235) 812042

OTTERWELL, Anthony David. b 40. **d** 89 **p** 90. NSM Brighton Resurr *Chich* from 89. *44 Havelock Road, Brighton BN1 6GF* Brighton (0273) 563196

OTTEY, John Leonard. b 34. AKC60 Nottm Univ BA70. **d** 61 **p** 62. C Grantham St Wulfram *Linc* 61-64; R Keyworth *S'well* 70-85; P-in-c Stanton-on-the-Wolds 71-85; P-in-c E Retford 85-87; V from 87; P-in-c W Retford 85-87; R from 87. *The Rectory, Rectory Road, Retford, Notts DN22 7AY* Retford (0777) 703116

OTTLEY, David Ronald. b 57. Lanc Univ BA78. Sarum & Wells Th Coll 79. **d** 81 **p** 82. C Urmston *Man* 81-85; Lect Bolton St Pet 85-87; P-in-c Halliwell St Thos 87-88; V Bolton St Thos from 88. *St Thomas's Vicarage, Cloister Street, Bolton BL1 3HA* Bolton (0204) 41731

OTTLEY, Ronald. b 28. St Deiniol's Hawarden 81. **d** 83 **p** 84. Hon C Prestbury *Ches* from 83. *The Beeches, 4 Salisbury Place, Tytherington, Macclesfield, Cheshire SK10 2HP* Macclesfield (0625) 432649

OTTO, Francis James Reeve. b 42. New Coll Ox BA64 MA68. Wells Th Coll 68. **d** 69 **p** 70. C St Stephen by Saltash *Truro* 69-72; C Newquay 72-73; V Lanteglos by Fowey 73-79; V St Goran w St Mich Caerhays 79-82; Chapl St Mary's Hall Brighton from 82. *30 Madehurst Close, Brighton BN2 2YR* Brighton (0273) 690054

OTTOSSON, Krister Alexander. b 39. Lon Univ BSc61. Wycliffe Hall Ox 62 Ch Div Sch of the Pacific (USA) MDiv65. **d** 65 **p** 66. C Ches le Street *Dur* 65-68; NW Area Sec Chr Educn Movement 68-71; Educn Sec BCC 71-76; Adv in Lay Tr *Dur* 76-81; Adult Educn Officer Gen Syn Bd of Educn 81-82; City Cen Chapl *Newc* from 82. *71 Longdean Park, Chester le Street, Co Durham DH3 4DG* 091-388 9622

OULD, Julian Charles. b 57. MHCIMA77. Coll of Resurr Mirfield 80. **d** 83 **p** 84. C Hebburn St Cuth *Dur* 83-86; C Pet H Spirit Bretton *Pet* 86-90; R Peakirk w Glinton from 90. *The Rectory, 11 Lincoln Road, Glinton, Peterborough PE6 7JR* Peterborough (0733) 252265

OULESS, John Michael. b 22. AKC49. Ridley Hall Cam 49. **d** 50 **p** 51. V Southwick w Glapthorn *Pet* 62-71; Chapl Glapthorn Road Hosp Oundle 63-71; R Cogenhoe

Pet 71-89; R Whiston 71-89; rtd 89. *2 Clos du Roncherez, St Brelade, Jersey, Channel Islands JE3 8FG*   Jersey (0534) 44916

OUTHWAITE, Stephen Anthony. b 35. Wells Th Coll 62. **d** 64 **p** 65. C Bitterne Park *Win* 64-67; C-in-c N Tadley CD 67-71; R Milton from 71; RD Christchurch 82-90. *The Rectory, New Milton, Hants BH25 6QN*   New Milton (0425) 615150

OUTRAM, David Michael. b 42. Univ of Wales (Ban) BA77 BD79. Coll of Resurr Mirfield 79. **d** 80 **p** 81. C Llandegfan and Beaumaris w Llanfaes w Penmon etc *Ban* 80-82; Chapl Prebendal Sch Chich 82-86; PV Chich Cathl *Chich* 82-86; Asst Chapl Wellington Coll Berks 86-89; Hd of Div from 87; Chapl from 89. *7 Chaucer Road, Wellington Chase, Crowthorne, Berks RG11 7QN* Crowthorne (0344) 778373 or 772262

OVENDEN, Edward Clifford Lewis. b 10. Chich Th Coll 31. **d** 33 **p** 34. V Epping St Jo *Chelmsf* 55-75; rtd 76; Perm to Offic *Chich* from 76. *1 Highlands Drive, St Leonards-on-Sea, E Sussex TN38 0HS*   Hastings (0424) 425194

OVENDEN, John Anthony. b 45. Open Univ BA80. Sarum & Wells Th Coll 71. **d** 74 **p** 75. C Handsworth *Sheff* 74-77; C Isfield *Chich* 77-80; C Uckfield 77-80; P-in-c Stuntney *Ely* 80-85; Min Can, Prec and Sacr Ely Cathl 80-85; V Primrose Hill St Mary w Avenue Road St Paul *Lon* from 85. *St Mary's Vicarage, 44 King Henry's Road, London NW3 3RP* 071-722 3062

OVENDEN, Richard Reginald. b 1900. Sarum Th Coll 24. **d** 27 **p** 28. V W Alvington *Ex* 54-69; rtd 69. *St Clare, 12 Rodney Road, Backwell, Bristol BS19 3HW*   Flax Bourton (027583) 3161

OVERELL, Alan Herbert. b 25. St Edm Hall Ox BA49 DipTh50 MA53. St Steph Ho Ox 49. **d** 51 **p** 52. R Salford Trin *Man* 65-70; P-in-c Leeds Em *Ripon* 71-89; Chapl Leeds Poly and Leeds Univ 71-89; rtd 89. *16 Orville Gardens, Leeds LS6 2BS*   Leeds (0532) 785830

OVEREND, Alan. b 53. Sheff Univ BA75. Oak Hill Th Coll 84. **d** 86 **p** 87. C Aughton St Mich *Liv* 86-89; P-in-c Eccleston Park from 89. *St James's Vicarage, 159A St Helens Road, Prescot, Merseyside L34 2QB*   051-426 6421

OVEREND, Barry Malcolm. b 49. K Coll Lon BD71 AKC71 DipMin88. St Aug Coll Cant 71. **d** 72 **p** 73. C Nailsworth *Glouc* 72-74; C High Harrogate Ch Ch *Ripon* 75-78; V Collingham w Harewood 78-87; V Far Headingley St Chad from 87. *St Chad's Vicarage, Otley Road, Leeds LS16 5JT* Leeds (0532) 752224

OVERINGTON, David Vernon. b 34. W Aus Advanced Ed Coll DipRE90. ALCD60. **d** 60 **p** 61. C Penge Ch Ch w H Trin *Roch* 60-62; C Lenton *S'well* 62-65; P-in-c Brackenfield w Wessington *Derby* 65-71; P-in-c Cubley w Marston Montgomery 71-76; Australia from 76. *Anglican Department of Education, PO Box 653, Morley, W Australia 6062* Perth (9) 377-4455

OVERTHROW, Royston John. b 45. Portsm Dioc Tr Course 84. **d** 85. NSM Portsm Cathl *Portsm* 85-91; Perm to Offic from 91. *3 Farthing Lane, Portsmouth PO1 2NP* Portsmouth (0705) 827009

OVERTHROW, Terence Reginald Charles. b 36. Glouc Th Course 76. **d** 79 **p** 79. NSM Glouc St Geo *Glouc* 79-82; NSM Hardwicke, Quedgeley and Elmore w Longney 82-87; C Twigworth w Down Hatherley 87; R Pebworth w Dorsington and Honeybourne from 87; RD Campden from 90. *The Vicarage, Honeybourne, Evesham, Worcs WR11 5PP* Evesham (0386) 830302

OVERTON, Charles Henry. b 51. CCC Ox BA74 MA77 Fitzw Coll Cam PGCE75 BA79 MA85. Ridley Hall Cam 77. **d** 80 **p** 81. C Tonbridge SS Pet and Paul *Roch* 80-84; Lic to Offic *Cant* 84-87; Asst Chapl St Lawr Coll Ramsgate 84-87; P-in-c Aythorpe w High and Leaden Roding *Chelmsf* from 88. *The Rectory, Stortford Road, Leaden Roding, Dunmow, Essex CM6 1QZ*   White Roding (0279) 876387

OVERTON, David Malcolm. b 52. Chich Th Coll. **d** 84 **p** 85. C Ches H Trin *Ches* 84-86; C Woodchurch 86-88; C Coppenhall from 88. *St Raphael, 149 Broad Street, Crewe CW1 3UD* Crewe (0270) 257003

OVERTON, Keith Charles. b 28. E Anglian Minl Tr Course 78. **d** 81 **p** 82. NSM Duxford *Ely* 81-84; NSM Whittlesford 84-88; P-in-c from 88; P-in-c Pampisford 88-90. *56 Duxford Road, Whittlesford, Cambridge CB4 4NQ* Cambridge (0223) 832336

OVERTON, Thomas Vincent Edersheim. b 34. New Coll Ox BA58 DipTh59 MA61. Wycliffe Hall Ox 58. **d** 60 **p** 61. C W Hampstead Trin *Lon* 60-63; C Leeds St Geo *Ripon* 63-67; Perm to Offic *Lon* 68-71; Thailand 71-78; R Knossington and Cold Overton *Leic* 78-81; V Owston

and Withcote 78-81; R Bedf St Jo and St Leon *St Alb* 81-90; Perm to Offic *B & W* 90-91; V Leigh *Roch* from 91. *The Vicarage, Leigh, Tonbridge, Kent TN11 8QJ* Hildenborough (0732) 833022

OVERY, Arthur William. b 19. JP. Nor Ord Course 73. **d** 76 **p** 77. NSM Lowestoft St Marg *Nor* 76-78; NSM Lowestoft and Kirkley 79-89; Perm to Offic from 89. *The Hollies, Warren Road, Lowestoft, Suffolk NR32 4QD* Lowestoft (0502) 561289

OVEY, Michael John. b 58. Ball Coll Ox BA81 BCL82. Ridley Hall Cam 88. **d** 91. C Crowborough *Chich* from 91. *2 Woodland Way, Crowborough, E Sussex TN6 3BG* Crowborough (0892) 662909

OWEN, Bryan Philip. b 47. CertEd70. Cant Sch of Min 83. **d** 86 **p** 87. NSM Deal St Geo *Cant* 86-87; C Herne 87-89; R Clarkston *Glas* from 89. *St Aidan's Rectory, 8 Golf Road, Clarkston, Glasgow G76 7LZ*   041-638 2860

OWEN, Christine Rose. b 62. Univ of Wales (Ban) BA83 PGCE84. Qu Coll Birm 86. **d** 88. C Ynyscyhaiarn w Penmorfa and Portmadoc *Ban* 88-90; Chapl Lon Univ *Lon* from 90. *14 Rokeby House, Lamb's Conduit Street, London WC1N 3LX*   071-404 0926

OWEN, Canon Cledwyn. b 15. Univ of Wales BA36. Dorchester Miss Coll 36. **d** 38 **p** 39. R Newtown w Llanllwchaiarn w Aberhafesp *St As* 67-74; V Llangollen w Trevor and Llantysilio 74-82; Chan St As Cathl 76-82; rtd 82; Perm to Offic *Lich* from 83. *14 Green Lane, Bayston Hill, Shrewsbury SY3 0NS*

OWEN, Canon David William. b 31. Down Coll Cam BA55 MA58. Linc Th Coll 55. **d** 57 **p** 58. C Salford St Phil w St Steph *Man* 57-61; C Grantham St Wulfram *Linc* 61-65; V Messingham 65-70; V Spilsby w Hundleby 70-77; R Aswardby w Sausthorpe 71-77; R Langton w Sutterby 71-77; R Halton Holgate 73-77; P-in-c Firsby w Gt Steeping 75-77; P-in-c Lt Steeping 75-77; Chapl Louth Co Hosp from 77; TR Louth *Linc* from 77; RD Louthesk 82-89; Can and Preb Linc Cathl from 85. *The Rectory, Westgate, Louth, Lincs LN11 9YE* Louth (0507) 603213

OWEN, Derek Malden. b 29. Oak Hill Th Coll 74. **d** 76 **p** 77. C Eastbourne H Trin *Chich* 76-78; C Walthamstow St Mary w St Steph *Chelmsf* 78-81; R Ditcheat w E Pennard and Pylle *B & W* 81-83. *Mirmonte, Warren Rise, New Malden, Surrey*

OWEN, Edgar. b 26. W Midl Minl Tr Course. **d** 82 **p** 83. NSM Garretts Green *Birm* 82-88; NSM Stechford from 88. *Flat 1, 41 Averill Road, Birmingham B26 2EG* 021-783 5603

OWEN, Canon Edward Goronwy. b 01. Univ of Wales BA21 Jes Coll Ox BA28 MA35. **d** 28 **p** 29. V Llanrhos *St As* 64-71; rtd 71. *3 Marston Drive, Rhos, Colwyn Bay, Clwyd LL28 4YG* Colwyn Bay (0492) 547933

✠OWEN, Rt Rev Edwin. b 10. TCD BA32 MA41. **d** 34 **p** 35. c 72. C Glenageary *D & G* 34-36; C Dub Ch Ch Leeson Park 36-38; Min Can St Patr Cathl Dub 35-36; Chan V 36-38; Succ 38-42; I Birr w Eglish *L & K* 42-57; RD Lower Ormond 46-57; Can Killaloe Cathl 54-57; Dean Killaloe 57-72; Dioc Sec (Killaloe etc) 57-72; RD Upper O'Mullod and Traderry 57-60; RD Kilfenora and Corkovasker 60-72; Bp Killaloe 72-76; Bp L & K 76-81; rtd 81. *5 Frankfort Avenue, Rathgar, Dublin 6, Irish Republic* Dublin (1) 972205

OWEN, Ethelston John Charles. b 20. St D Coll Lamp BA42. **d** 48 **p** 49. V Clehonger *Heref* 60-80; R Eaton Bishop 60-80; rtd 80; Perm to Offic *Heref* from 81. *3 Yew Tree Close, Kingstone, Hereford*   Golden Valley (0981) 250785

OWEN, Geoffrey Neill. b 55. Chich Th Coll. **d** 85 **p** 86. C Streatham St Pet *S'wark* 85-89; C Battersea Ch Ch and St Steph from 89. *Christchurch Flat, Cabul Road, London SW11 2PN* 071-350 0851

OWEN, George Charles. b 14. Linc Th Coll. **d** 52 **p** 53. V Burton Coggles *Linc* 60-75; V Aubourn w Haddington 75-79; R Bassingham 75-79; V Carlton-le-Moorland w Stapleford 75-79; R Thurlby w Norton Disney 75-79; rtd 79. *8 Byrn Howerd Terrace, Oakdale, Blackwood, Gwent NP2 0LE* Blackwood (0495) 227619

OWEN, Gerald. b 16. St D Coll Lamp BA49. **d** 50 **p** 51. V Wednesbury St Bart *Lich* 64-83; rtd 83. *35 Troon Place, Wordsley, Stourbridge, W Midlands DY8 5EN* Kingswinford (0384) 294952

OWEN, Gordon Campbell. b 41. FRMetS65 MRAeS66 Univ of Wales (Ban) BD76 PGCE77. Ban Ord Course 79. **d** 81 **p** 82. Hd RE Eirias High Sch Colwyn Bay 77-88; Chapl RAF from 81; AP Ban Cathl *Ban* 82-88; Chapl St Kath Coll and Liv Inst of HE 88-91; Dioc Liaison Officer for RE *Liv* 88-91; V Llanfair-is-gaer and Llanddeiniolen

Ban from 91; Educn Officer from 91. *The Vicarage, Port Dinorwic, Gwynedd LL56 4SQ* Bangor (0248) 671513

OWEN, Harry Dennis. b 47. Oak Hill Th Coll 73. **d** 76 **p** 77. C Fulham Ch Ch *Lon* 76-81; V Byker St Mark *Newc* 81-89; V Plumstead All SS *S'wark* from 89. *All Saints' Vicarage, 106 Herbert Road, London SE18 3PU* 081-854 2995

OWEN, Canon James. b 31. Trin Hall Cam BA53 MA58. Ely Th Coll. **d** 56 **p** 57. C W Brompton St Mary *Lon* 56-60; C Clifton All SS *Bris* 60-62; Chapl Jes Coll Cam 62-66; Chapl Repton Sch Derby 66-67; Asst Chapl Nottm Univ *S'well* 67-69; Chapl and S'well Dioc Lect 69-74; V Cam St Mary Less *Ely* from 74; OStJ from 75; Hon Can Ely Cathl *Ely* from 86. *4 Newnham Terrace, Cambridge CB3 9EX* Cambridge (0223) 350733

OWEN, James Thomas. b 48. Linc Th Coll 77. **d** 80 **p** 81. C Palmers Green St Jo *Lon* 80-84; C Timperley *Ches* 84-87; C Bramhall from 87. *33 Dawlish Close, Bramhall, Stockport, Cheshire SK7 2JD* 061-440 8415

OWEN, John Edward. b 52. Middx Poly BA75. Sarum & Wells Th Coll BTh81. **d** 81 **p** 82. C S Ashford Ch Ch *Cant* 81-85; TV Bemerton *Sarum* 85-91; V St Leonards and St Ives *Win* from 91. *The Vicarage, Pine Drive, St Leonards, Ringwood, Hants BH24 2LN* Ringwood (0425) 473406

OWEN, John Glyndwr. b 20. St D Coll Lamp BA48. **d** 49 **p** 50. R Honington w Sapiston and Troston *St E* 71-81; rtd 81. *93 Mill Lane, Sawston, Cambridge CB2 4HY* Cambridge (0223) 832458

OWEN, John Peregrine. b 19. Univ of Wales (Swansea) BA41. St Mich Coll Llan 41. **d** 43 **p** 44. R Dowlais *Llan* 59-76; RD Merthyr Tydfil 69-76; R Wenvoe and St Lythans 76-87; RD Penarth and Barry 85-87; rtd 87. *3 Pen-y-Maes, Fforest View, Morriston, Swansea SA6 9DG* Swansea (0792) 793011

OWEN, Keith Robert. b 57. Warw Univ BA Ox Univ BA MA85 Hull Univ MA(Ed)89. St Steph Ho Ox 79. **d** 82 **p** 83. C Headingley *Ripon* 82-85; Chapl Grimsby Colls of H&FE 85-90; Chapl for Educn *Linc* 85-90; P-in-c Linc St Botolph by Bargate from 90; Chapl to Caring Agencies Lin City Cen from 90. *St Botolph's Vicarage, 84 Little Bargate Street, Lincoln LN5 8JL* Lincoln (0522) 520469

OWEN, Lionel Edward Joseph. b 19. S'wark Ord Course 66. **d** 69 **p** 70. C Hythe *Cant* 69-73; C Deal St Leon 73-75; V Teynham 75-84; RD Ospringe 80-84; rtd 84; Perm to Offic *Cant* from 84. *Green Hayes, London Road, Hythe, Kent CT21 4JH* Hythe (0303) 267642

OWEN, Preb Noah. b 10. St D Coll Lamp BA34. **d** 34 **p** 35. RD Chew Magna *B & W* 71-77; R Chew Stoke w Nempnett Thrubwell 73-77; R Norton Malreward 77; rtd 77; Perm to Offic *B & W* 79-80; Preb Wells Cathl 76-77 and from 80. *West Grove, Crewkerne, Somerset TA18 7ES* Crewkerne (0460) 74023

OWEN, Owen Thomas. b 19. Liv Univ 37 Lanc Univ MA77. St Chad's Coll Dur DipTh45. **d** 45 **p** 46. R Clifton w Glapton *S'well* 60-62; Chapl and Sen Lect Nottm Coll of HE 60-62; Lic to Offic *Liv* from 62; Sen Lect Liv Coll of HE from 62; Prin from 65; rtd 84. *1 Oakwood Road, Halewood, Liverpool L26 1XD* 051-486 8672

OWEN, Peter Russell. b 35. Llan St Mich DipTh63. **d** 63 **p** 64. C Wrexham *St As* 63-64; C Connah's Quay 64-65; Asst Chapl Miss to Seamen 66-69; P-in-c Upper Norwood All SS w St Marg *Cant* 69-72; C Hawarden *St As* 72-75; V Cilcain and Nannerch 75-79; R Cilcen and Nannerch and Rhydymwyn 79-83; V Brymbo and Bwlchgwyn 83-87; R Llangynhafal and Llanbedr Dyffryn Clwyd from 87. *The Rectory, Llanbedr Dyffryn Clwyd, Ruthin, Clwyd LS15 1UP* Ruthin (08242) 4051

OWEN, Phillip Clifford. b 42. G&C Coll Cam BA65 MA69. Ridley Hall Cam 71. **d** 73 **p** 74. C Stowmarket *St E* 73-76; C Headley All SS *Guildf* 76-81; TV 81-89; R Clifton-on-Teme, Lower Sapey and the Shelsleys *Worc* from 89. *The Rectory, Clifton-on-Teme, Worcester WR6 6DJ* Shelsley Beauchamp (08865) 483

OWEN, Raymond Philip. b 37. Man Univ BScTech60 AMCT60 Teesside Poly DMS83. Chich Th Coll 65. **d** 67 **p** 68. C Elland *Wakef* 67-70; C Lindley 70-73; V Bradshaw 73-80; Ind Chapl *Dur* 80-91; TR Hanley H Ev *Lich* from 91. *The Rectory, 35 Harding Road, Stoke-on-Trent ST1 3BQ* Stoke-on-Trent (0782) 266031

OWEN, Richard Ellis. b 12. Clifton Th Coll 48. **d** 50 **p** 51. V Badminton w Acton Turville *Glouc* 61-71; V Kemble w Poole Keynes 71-73; R Pebworth w Dorsinton 73-79; R Pebworth w Dorsington and Marston Sicca 79-83; rtd 83; Perm to Offic *Glouc* from 83. *40 Ballards Close, Mickleton, Chipping Campden, Glos GL55 6TN* Mickleton (0386) 438755

OWEN, Canon Richard Llewelyn. b 27. Univ of Wales (Lamp) BA51. St Mich Coll Llan 51. **d** 53 **p** 54. C Holyhead w Rhoscolyn w Llanfair-yn-Neubwll *Ban* 53-57; C Porthmadog 57-59; R Llanfechell, Bodewryd, Rhosbeirio, Llanfflewin 59-67; Youth Chapl 66-67; V Penrhyndeudraeth and Llanfrothen 67-77; R Llangefni w Tregaian and Llangristiolus etc 77-89; Can Ban Cathl from 82; Treas from 86; Can Missr and V Bangor Cathl Par from 89. *1 Alotan Crescent, Penrhosgarnedd, Bangor, Gwynedd LL57 2NG* Bangor (0248) 355911

OWEN, Richard Matthew. b 49. Sheff Univ BA70 Leeds Univ CertEd73. N Ord Course 84. **d** 87 **p** 88. NSM Chorlton-cum-Hardy St Werburgh *Man* 87-89; C N Reddish 89-91; Perm to Offic *York* from 91. *39 Fairfax Street, York YO1 1EB* York (0904) 679989

OWEN, Robert David Glyn. b 06. Bps' Coll Cheshunt 37. **d** 39 **p** 40. V Burslem St Paul *Lich* 63-67; rtd 67. *18 Bromley College, High Street, Bromley BR1 1PE* 081-460 2570

OWEN, Robert Glynne. b 33. St Mich Coll Llan 56. **d** 58 **p** 59. C Machynlleth and Llanwrin *Ban* 58-62; C Llanbeblig w Caernarfon 62-65; V Carno and Trefeglwys 65-69; Hon C Dorking w Ranmore *Guildf* 69-75; Perm to Offic *St As* from 75. *Briar Croft, Minera Road, Ffrwd, Cefn y Bedd, Wrexham, Clwyd LL12 9TR* Wrexham (0978) 751015

OWEN, Robert Lee. b 56. Univ of Wales (Cardiff) BD79. Qu Coll Birm 79. **d** 81 **p** 82. C Holywell *St As* 81-84; Perm to Offic *Birm* from 85; Chapl Blue Coat Sch Birm 85-87; Chapl St Elphin's Sch Matlock from 87. *Devonshire House, St Elphin's School, Matlock, Derbyshire DE4 2EU* Matlock (0629) 732724

OWEN, Ronald Alfred. b 44. Sarum & Wells Th Coll 80. **d** 81 **p** 82. C Wotton St Mary *Glouc* 81-83; CF from 83. *c/o MOD (Army), Bagshot Park, Bagshot, Surrey GU19 5PL* Bagshot (0276) 71717

OWEN, Roy Meredith. b 21. Univ of Wales BA43. St Mich Coll Llan 43. **d** 45 **p** 46. V Pontyclun w Talygarn *Llan* 62-75; C Cadoxton-juxta-Barry 82-85; rtd 85; Perm to Offic *Llan* from 86. *Laurel Cottage, Brynna Road, Pencoed, Bridgend, M Glam CF35 6PA* Pencoed (0656) 862262

OWEN, Canon Stanley Alfred George. b 17. Worc Ord Coll 57. **d** 59 **p** 60. R Bickenhill w Elmdon *Birm* 60-86; rtd 86; Perm to Offic *Birm* from 86; Chmn and Sec Assn Ch Fellowships from 88. *Bickenhill House, 154 Lode Lane, Solihull, W Midlands B91 2HP* 021-704 9281

OWEN, Tuddyd. b 12. Univ of Wales (Ban) BA35. St Mich Coll Llan 36. **d** 36 **p** 37. V Tywyn *Ban* 57-77; rtd 77; Canada from 81. *120 Poplar Street, PO Box 1424, Stellarton, Novia Scotia, Canada, BOK 150* New Glasgow (902) 755-4036

OWEN, William. b 05. OBE. **d** 30 **p** 31. Kenya 54-81; rtd 81; Perm to Offic *Cant* from 81. *51 Bridge Down, Bridge, Canterbury, Kent CT4 5BA* Canterbury (0227) 830625

OWEN, William David. b 17. Univ of Wales BA39. Wycliffe Hall Ox 40. **d** 41 **p** 42. C Fishguard *St D* 41-45; C Old Swinford *Worc* 45-49; C-in-c Astwood Bank and Crabbs Cross CD 49-50; V Astwood Bank w Crabbs Cross 50-63; V Claines St Jo from 63. *The Vicarage, Claines, Worcester WR3 7RP* Worcester (0905) 51251

OWEN-JONES, Peter John. b 47. CEng84 MIMechE84 MBIM87 FPWI90 RMCS BScEng68. E Midl Min Tr Course 85. **d** 88 **p** 89. NSM Holbrook and Lt Eaton *Derby* from 88. *6 Station Road, Little Eaton, Derby DE2 5DN* Derby (0332) 831423

OWENS, Ashby. b 43. Man Univ BA65 Fitzw Ho Cam BA67 MA71. Ridley Hall Cam 65. **d** 68 **p** 69. C Chorley *Ches* 68-71; C Barnston 71-74; V Alsager St Mary 74-83; V Brinnington w Portwood from 83. *St Luke's Vicarage, Brinnington Road, Stockport, Cheshire SK5 8BS* 061-430 4164

OWENS, Christopher Lee. b 42. Coll of Ripon & York St Jo 61 Lon Inst of Educn TCert. Linc Th Coll 66. **d** 69 **p** 70. C Dalston H Trin w St Phil *Lon* 69-72; C Portsea N End St Mark *Portsm* 72-81; TV E Ham w Upton Park *Chelmsf* from 81. *147 Katherine Road, London E6 1ES* 081-472 1067

OWENS, Philip Roger. b 47. Univ of Wales (Ban) DipTh70. Wells Th Coll 71. **d** 71 **p** 72. C Colwyn Bay *St As* 71-74; C Wrexham 74-77; TV 77-80; P-in-c Yoxford *St E* 80-85; Asst Stewardship and Resources Adv 80-85; R Ban Monachorum and Worthenbury *St As* from 85; Dioc Stewardship Officer from 89. *The Rectory, 8 Ludlow Road, Bangor-on-Dee, Wrexham, Clwyd LL13 0JG* Bangor-on-Dee (0978) 780608

OWENS, Canon Rodney Stones. b 19. Lon Univ BA53. Bps' Coll Cheshunt 48. **d** 50 **p** 51. Perm to Offic *St E*

65-74; Teacher Ipswich Sch 65-74; R Coddenham 74-75; R Gosbeck 74-75; P-in-c Hemingstone w Henley 74-75; R Coddenham w Gosbeck and Hemingstone w Henley 75-84; RD Bosmere 78-84; Hon Can St E Cathl 81-84; rtd 84; Perm to Offic *St E* from 85. *10 Warren Lane, Martlesham Heath, Ipswich IP5 7SH* Ipswich (0473) 623411

OWENS, Stephen Graham Frank. b 49. Ch Coll Cam BA71 CertEd72 MA75. Qu Coll Birm 73. **d** 75 **p** 76. C Stourbridge Norton St Mich *Worc* 75-80; Tanzania 80-88; V Dudley Wood *Worc* from 88. *The Vicarage, 57 Lantern Road, Dudley, W Midlands DY2 0DL* Cradley Heath (0384) 69018

OWERS, Ian Humphrey. b 46. Em Coll Cam BA68 MA72. Westcott Ho Cam 71. **d** 73 **p** 74. C Champion Hill St Sav *S'wark* 73-77; V Peckham St Sav 77-82; P-in-c E Greenwich Ch Ch w St Andr and St Mich 82-83; V from 83; P-in-c Westcombe Park St Geo from 85. *St George's Vicarage, 89 Westcombe Park Road, London SE3 7RZ* 081-858 3006

OWST, Clifford Samuel. b 09. FCII34. Linc Th Coll 77. **d** 77 **p** 78. Hon C Mablethorpe w Stain *Linc* 77-78; Hon C Mablethorpe w Trusthorpe 78-83; New Zealand from 83. *32 Rewi Street, Torbay, Auckland 10, New Zealand*

OXBORROW, Paul Leonard. b 54. Bris Univ BA76. Coll of Resurr Mirfield 84. **d** 86 **p** 87. C Watford St Mich *St Alb* 86-89; C Royston from 89. *12 Prince Andrew's Close, Royston, Herts SG8 9DZ* Royston (0763) 243265

OXBROW, Mark. b 51. Reading Univ BSc72 Fitzw Ho Cam BA75 MA79. Ridley Hall Cam 73. **d** 76 **p** 77. C Luton Ch Ch *Roch* 76-80; TV Newc Epiphany *Newc* 80-88; Chapl Newc Mental Health Unit 80-88; Br Regional Sec CMS from 88. *63 Abbotts Drive, Wembley, Middx HA0 3SB* or, *CMS, Partnership House, 157 Waterloo Road, London SE1 8UU* 081-904 3379 or 071-928 8681

OXENFORTH, Colin Bryan. b 45. St Chad's Coll Dur BA67 DipTh69. **d** 69 **p** 70. C Bromley St Andr *Roch* 69-72; C Nunhead St Antony *S'wark* 72-76; V Toxteth St Marg *Liv* 76-89; V Brixton St Matt *S'wark* from 89. *The Vicarage, 5 St Matthew's Road, London SW2 1ND* 071-274 3553

OXFORD, Victor Thomas. b 41. Chich Th Coll 65. **d** 68 **p** 69. C Norton in the Moors *Lich* 68-73; C Norton Canes 73-75; TV Cannock 75-81; V Chesterton from 81. *The Vicarage, Church Street, Chesterton, Newcastle, Staffs ST5 7HJ* Newcastle-under-Lyme (0782) 562479

OXFORD, Archdeacon of. See WESTON, Ven Frank Valentine

OXFORD, Bishop of. See HARRIES, Rt Rev Richard Douglas

OXFORD, Dean of (Christ Church). See HEATON, Very Rev Eric William

OXLEY, Cecil Robert. b 23. Coll of Resurr Mirfield 84. **d** 84 **p** 85. NSM Derby St Luke *Derby* from 84. *46 Trowells Lane, Derby DE3 3LT* Derby (0332) 32226

OXLEY, Christopher Robert. b 51. Sheff Univ BA73 PGCE74 Ox Univ BA78 MA83. Wycliffe Hall Ox 76. **d** 79 **p** 80. C Greasbrough *Sheff* 79-82; C Doncaster St Leon and St Jude 82-84; Asst Chapl Brussels *Eur* 84-87; V Humberstone *Leic* from 87. *St Mary's Vicarage, Vicarage Lane, Humberstone, Leicester LE5 1EE* Leicester (0533) 767281

OXLEY, David William. b 63. TCD BA85 BTh89. CITC 85. **d** 89 **p** 90. C Dub Ch Ch Cathl Gp *D & G* from 89; CV Ch Ch Cathl Dub from 90. *32 Shandon Drive, Phibsborough, Dublin 7, Irish Republic* Dublin (1) 307168

OYET, Canon Julius Isotuk. b 39. Concordia Coll (USA) MA79. Immanuel Coll Ibadan DipPTh70. **d** 70 **p** 72. Nigeria 70-90; C Warblington and Emsworth *Portsm* from 91; CMS from 91. *Parish House, 41 Woodlands Avenue, Emsworth, Hants PO10 7QB* Emsworth (0243) 370115

P

PACEY, Edgar Prentice. b 29. Edin Univ MA50. Edin Th Coll 52. **d** 54 **p** 55. C Motherwell *Glas* 54-56; C Glas St Mary 56-61; R Coatbridge 61-70; Perm to Offic 70-77; Hon C Glas St Martin 77-83; P-in-c Rothesay *Arg* from 83; R Tighnabruaich from 91. *8 Auchnacloich Road, Rothesay, Isle of Bute PA20 0EB* Rothesay (0700) 2893

PACKER, James. b 21. St Mich Coll Llan 63. **d** 65 **p** 66. C-in-c Ingol St Marg CD *Blackb* 68-70; Chapl HM Pris Preston 70-73; Gartree 73-77; Wymott 77-86; rtd 86; Perm to Offic *Blackb* from 86. *52 Highfield Road South, Chorley, Lancs PR7 1RH* Chorley (02572) 67689

PACKER, Prof James Innell. b 26. CCC Ox BA48 MA52 DPhil55. Wycliffe Hall Ox 49. **d** 52 **p** 53. Lic to Offic Ox 66-69; Bris 70-79; Prin Tyndale Hall Bris 70-72; Assoc Prin Trin Coll Bris 72-79; Canada from 79; Prof Hist Th Regent Coll Vancouver 79-89; Prof Th from 89; rtd 91. *2398 West 34th Avenue, Vancouver, Canada, V6M 1G7* Vancouver (604) 266-6722

PACKER, Ven John Richard. b 46. Keble Coll Ox BA67 MA. Ripon Hall Ox 67. **d** 70 **p** 71. C St Helier *S'wark* 70-73; Chapl Abingdon St Nic *Ox* 73-77; Tutor Ripon Hall Ox 73-75; Tutor Ripon Coll Cuddesdon 75-77; V Wath-upon-Dearne w Adwick-upon-Dearne *Sheff* 77-86; RD Wath 83-86; TR Sheff Manor 86-91; RD Attercliffe 90-91; Adn W Cumberland *Carl* from 91. *Moorside, 50 Stainburn Road, Workington, Cumbria CA14 1SN* Workington (0900) 66190

PACKER, Canon John William. b 18. K Coll Lon BA40 AKC40 BD41 MTh48. **d** 41 **p** 42. Hd Master Can Slade Gr Sch Bolton 53-77; Lic to Offic *Man* 53-77; Hon Can Man Cathl 75-78; rtd 77; Perm to Offic *Cant* from 78. *Netherbury, Meadow Close, Bridge, Canterbury, Kent CT4 5AT* Canterbury (0227) 830364

PACKER, Roger Ernest John. b 37. ARCO59 Pemb Coll Cam BA60 MA64. Cuddesdon Coll 60. **d** 62 **p** 63. C Chippenham St Andr w Tytherton Lucas *Bris* 62-65; C Caversham *Ox* 65-70; R Sandhurst 70-91; V Bridgwater St Mary, Chilton Trinity and Durleigh *B & W* from 91. *The Vicarage, 7 Durleigh Road, Bridgwater, Somerset TA6 7HU* Bridgwater (0278) 422437 or 424972

PACKHAM, Ms Elizabeth Daisy. b 33. Golds Coll Lon BSc54 CertEd55. N Ord Course. **dss** 83 **d** 87. Fairfield *Derby* 83-84; Buxton w Burbage and King Sterndale 84-87; Par Dn from 87. *97 St John's Road, Buxton, Derbyshire SK17 6UT* Buxton (0298) 5697

PACKWOOD, John William. b 35. Kelham Th Coll 55. **d** 59 **p** 60. C Anfield St Marg *Liv* 59-63; C Ribbleton *Blackb* 63-65; V Accrington St Pet 65-73; Asst Chapl HM Pris Man 73; Chapl HM Pris Preston 73-77; Gartree 77-79; V Wistow w Newtown Harcourt *Leic* 79-81; V Kilby 79-82; V Glen Magna w Stretton Magna 82-84; V Gt Glen, Stretton Magna and Wistow etc 84-89; TV Leic H Spirit from 89. *St Andrew's Vicarage, 53B Jarrom Street, Leicester LE2 7DM* Leicester (0533) 549658

PADDICK, Graham. b 47. S'wark Ord Course. **d** 89 **p** 90. C St Helier *S'wark* from 89. *St Peter's House, 189 Bishopsford Road, Morden, Surrey SM4 6BH* 081-648 3792

PADDISON, Michael David William. b 41. Oak Hill Th Coll 75. **d** 77 **p** 78. C Gt Warley Ch Ch *Chelmsf* 77-80; C Rayleigh 80-83; R Scole, Brockdish, Billingford, Thorpe Abbots etc *Nor* from 83; RD Redenhall from 89. *The Rectory, Mill Lane, Norwich Road, Scole, Diss, Norfolk IP21 4DY* Diss (0379) 740250

PADDOCK, Canon Gerald Alfred. b 39. Oak Hill Th Coll 66. **d** 69 **p** 70. C Whitehall Park St Andr Hornsey Lane *Lon* 69-73; C Edgware 73-76; P-in-c Ab Kettleby w Wartnaby and Holwell *Leic* 76-81; Dioc Missr 80-87; Hon Can Leic Cathl from 80; V Oaks in Charnwood and Copt Oak from 81; Police Liaison Officer from 81; Dioc Voc Officer from 81. *The Vicarage, Oaks-in-Charnwood, Lougborough, Leics LE12 9YD* Shepshed (0509) 503246

PADDOCK, John Allan Barnes. b 51. Liv Univ BA74 Man Univ CertEd75. St Steph Ho Ox BA77 MA81. **d** 80 **p** 81. C Matson *Glouc* 80-82; Asst Chapl Madrid *Eur* 82-83; Chapl R Gr Sch Lanc 83-86; Chapl RAF 86-91. *Address temp unknown*

PADGET, William Thomas. b 19. **d** 77 **p** 78. NSM Rodbourne Cheney *Bris* 77-90; rtd 90; Perm to Offic *Bris* from 90. *45 George Tweed Gardens, Ramleaze Drive, Swindon SN5 9PX* Swindon (0793) 871760

PAGAN, Canon Keith Vivian. b 37. St Jo Coll Dur BA60 MA66. Chich Th Coll 60. **d** 62 **p** 63. C Clacton St Jas *Chelmsf* 62-64; C Wymondham *Nor* 64-70; P-in-c Guestwick 70-80; P-in-c Kettlestone 70-79; V Hindolveston 70-80; R Islay *Arg* from 80; R Campbeltown from 80; Miss to Seamen from 80; Can St Jo Cathl Oban *Arg* from 85. *The Rectory, Argyll Street, Campbeltown, Argyll PA28 6AY* Campbeltown (0586) 553846

PAGE, Canon Alan George. b 24. Em Coll Cam BA48 MA52. Wycliffe Hall Ox 49. **d** 51 **p** 52. Kenya 53-71; Hon Can Mt Kenya 71-75; Hon Can Mt Kenya S 75-84; C S Lyncombe *B & W* 71-72; R Freshford w

Limpley Stoke 72-76; R Freshford, Limpley Stoke and Hinton Charterhouse 76-84; Can Mt Kenya Cen from 84; C Fulham St Mary N End *Lon* 87-89; rtd 89. *45 Ashley Avenue, Bath BA1 3DS* Bath (0225) 310532

PAGE, Alan Richard Benjamin. b 38. Univ of Wales (Lamp) BA60 BSc. St Mich Coll Llan 60. **d** 62 **p** 63. C Cardiff St Andr and St Teilo *Llan* 62-64; C Newport St Julian *Mon* 64-67; C Hoxton H Trin w St Mary *Lon* 67-69; C Winchmore Hill H Trin 69-71; V Camden Town St Mich w All SS and St Thos from 71. *St Michael's Vicarage, 1 Bartholomew Road, London NW5* 071-485 1256

PAGE, Arthur Henry. b 21. Open Univ BA79. Sarum & Wells Th Coll. **d** 82 **p** 82. NSM Gtr Corsham *Bris* 82-87; Perm to Offic *Dur* 88; NSM Shadforth from 89. *9 Foxton Way, High Shincliffe, Durham DH1 2PJ* 091-386 2141

PAGE, David. b 48. Bris Univ BA70 Leic Univ MA74 Southn Univ PGCE74 Nottm Univ DipTh82. St Jo Coll Nottm 81. **d** 83 **p** 84. C Morden *S'wark* 83-86; V Wimbledon St Luke 86-91; P-in-c Clapham Common St Barn from 91. *St Barnabas' Vicarage, 12 Lavender Gardens, London SW11 1DL* 071-223 5953

✠**PAGE, Rt Rev Dennis Fountain.** b 19. G&C Coll Cam BA41 MA45. Linc Th Coll 41. **d** 43 **p** 44 **c** 75. C Rugby St Andr *Cov* 43-49; R Weeting *Ely* 49-65; R Hockwold w Wilton 49-65; RD Feltwell 53-65; Hon Can Ely Cathl 63-65 and 68-75; V Yaxley 65-75; Adn Huntingdon 65-75; Suff Bp Lanc *Blackb* 75-85; rtd 85; Perm to Offic *St E* from 85. *Larkrise, Hartest, Bury St Edmunds, Suffolk IP29 4ES* Bury St Edmunds (0284) 830694

PAGE, Mrs Dorothy Jean. b 29. Portsm Poly CertEd50. Ox NSM Course 84. **d** 87. NSM Wantage Downs *Ox* from 87. *11 North Street, Marcham, Abingdon, Oxon OX13 6NG* Frilford Heath (0865) 391462

PAGE, Ian George. b 62. Ex Univ BSc84 York Univ PGCE85. Edin Th Coll 87. **d** 90 **p** 91. C Blackpool St Steph *Blackb* from 90. *The Clergy House, 17 St Stephen's Avenue, Blackpool FY2 9RB* Blackpool (0253) 54273

PAGE, Mrs Irene May. b 38. Birm Univ BA58. NE Ord Course 85. **d** 87. Par Dn Cockfield *Dur* 87-90; Par Dn Waterloo St Jo w St Andr *S'wark* from 90. *21 Windmill House, Windmill Walk, London SE1 8LX* 071-928 2259

PAGE, John Jeremy. b 56. Keble Coll Ox BA79 MA83 Edin Univ BD86. Edin Th Coll 83. **d** 86 **p** 87. C Wetherby *Ripon* 86-89; TV Wrexham *St As* from 89. *The Vicarage, 160 Borras Road, Wrexham, Clwyd LL13 9ER* Wrexham (0978) 350202

PAGE, John Laurance Howard. b 40. ALCD. **d** 65 **p** 66. C Spitalfields Ch Ch w All SS *Lon* 65-69; C Win Ch Ch *Win* 69-72; C Ringwood 72-76; V Lockerley and E Dean w E and W Tytherley 76-89; RD Romsey 85-89; V Lord's Hill from 89. *1 Tangmere Drive, Lord's Hill, Southampton SO1 8GY* Southampton (0703) 731182

PAGE, Michael John. b 42. K Coll Lon BD66 AKC66. **d** 67 **p** 68. C Rawmarsh w Parkgate *Sheff* 67-72; C-in-c Gleadless Valley CD 72-74; TR Gleadless Valley 74-77; V Lechlade *Glouc* 77-86; RD Fairford 81-86; V Winchcombe, Gretton, Sudeley Manor etc from 86. *The Vicarage, Langley Road, Winchcombe, Cheltenham, Glos GL54 5QP* Cheltenham (0242) 602368

PAGE, Owen Richard. b 53. FIMLS83 Trent Poly HNC77 Derby Coll of Educn DMS85. Linc Th Coll 89. **d** 91. C Gt Bookham *Guildf* from 91. *19 The Lorne, Great Bookham, Leatherhead, Surrey KT23 4JY* Leatherhead (0372) 453729

PAGE, Canon Richard Dennis. b 23. G&C Coll Cam BA48 MA50. Ridley Hall Cam 48. **d** 50 **p** 51. V Ecclesfield *Sheff* 64-71; RD Ecclesfield 66-71; P-in-c Holkham w Egmere and Waterden *Nor* 71-78; R Wells next the Sea 71-78; RD Burnham and Walsingham 72-78; V Hemsby 78-83; P-in-c Brooke w Kirstead 83-85; P-in-c Mundham w Seething 83-85; P-in-c Thwaite 83-85; R Brooke, Kirstead, Mundham w Seething and Thwaite 85-89; Hon Can Nor Cathl 87-89; rtd 90. *The Greyhound, Back Street, Reepham, Norfolk NR10 4SJ* Norwich (0603) 870886

PAGE, Thomas William. b 57. Sarum & Wells Th Coll 84. **d** 87 **p** 88. C Caterham *S'wark* from 87. *70 Spencer Road, Caterham, Surrey CR3 5LB* Caterham (0883) 344460

PAGE, Canon Trevor Melvyn. b 41. Dur Univ BA63 Fitzw Coll Cam BA67 MA72. Westcott Ho Cam 64. **d** 67 **p** 68. C Millhouses H Trin *Sheff* 67-69; Chapl Sheff Univ 69-74; V Doncaster Intake 74-82; Dioc Dir of Ords and Dir of In-Service Tr from 82; Can Res Sheff Cathl from 82; Dioc Dir of Min from 89. *393 Fulwood Road, Sheffield S10 3GE* Sheffield (0742) 305707

PAGE, William George. b 42. Linc Th Coll 83. **d** 85 **p** 86. C Boston *Linc* 85-89; V Sibsey w Frithville from 89.

The Vicarage, Sibsey, Boston, Lincs PE22 0RT Boston (0205) 750305

PAGE, William Wilson. b 14. Wycliffe Hall Ox. **d** 59 **p** 60. C Coleshill *Birm* 68-71; C Lavington w Ingoldsby *Linc* 71-74; R Gt and Lt Casterton w Pickworth and Tickencote *Pet* 74-87; rtd 87. *21 Fane Close, Stamford, Lincs PE9 1HB* Stamford (0780) 64921

PAGE-CHESTNEY, Michael William. b 47. Linc Th Coll 80. **d** 82 **p** 83. C Barton upon Humber *Linc* 82-85; TV Gt Grimsby St Mary and St Jas 85-91; V Blyton w Pilham from 91. *The Vicarage, Blyton, Gainsborough, Lincs DN21 3JZ* Laughton (042782) 216

PAGE-TURNER, Edward Gregory Ambrose Wilford. b 31. Qu Coll Birm 57. **d** 60 **p** 61. C Helmsley *York* 60-64; C Kensington St Phil Earl's Court *Lon* 64-67; C Walton-on-Thames *Guildf* 67-70; V Seend *Sarum* 70-71; V Seend and Bulkington 71-79; R Bladon w Woodstock *Ox* 79-87; P-in-c Begbroke 80-86; P-in-c Shipton-on-Cherwell 80-86; P-in-c Hampton Gay 80-85; RD Woodstock 84-87; P-in-c Wootton by Woodstock 85-87; R Patterdale *Carl* 87-89; R Askerswell, Loders and Powerstock *Sarum* from 89. *The Vicarage, Loders, Bridport, Dorset DT6 3SA* Bridport (0308) 27175

PAGE-WOOD, Ivan Thomas. b 05. Bris Univ BA25. Sarum Th Coll 26. **d** 28 **p** 29. V Lower Cam *Glouc* 64-70; rtd 70; Perm to Offic Glouc and Bris 70-90. *34 Hollis Gardens, Cheltenham, Glos GL51 6JQ* Cheltenham (0242) 512122

PAGET, Alfred Ivor. b 24. St Aid Birkenhead 56. **d** 59 **p** 60. C Hoylake *Ches* 59-62; Hong Kong 62-63; Australia 63-64; C Hyde St Geo *Ches* 64-66; R Gt and Lt Henny w Middleton *Chelmsf* 66-74; C Gt Holland 74-79; V Holland-on-Sea from 79. *The Vicarage, 297 Frinton Road, Holland-on-Sea, Clacton-on-Sea CO15 5SP* Clacton-on-Sea (0225) 812420

PAGET, David Rolf. b 54. Worc Coll Ox BA78. St Steph Ho Ox BA80. **d** 81 **p** 82. C Sheerness H Trin w St Paul *Cant* 81-84; C E Bedfont *Lon* 84-88; P-in-c Fulham St Andr Fulham Fields 88-89; V from 89. *St Andrew's Vicarage, 10 St Andrew's Road, London W14 9SX* 071-385 5578

PAGET, Harold Leslie. b 09. St Aug Coll Cant 53. **d** 54 **p** 55. R Swalecliffe *Cant* 64-76; rtd 76; Perm to Offic *Cant* from 76. *70 Marine Parade, Tankerton, Whitstable, Kent CT5 2BB* Whitstable (0227) 272888

PAGET, Richard Campbell. b 54. Collingwood Coll Dur BA76 Rob Coll Cam BA87. Ridley Hall Cam 85. **d** 88 **p** 89. C Gipsy Hill Ch Ch *S'wark* from 88. *34 Woodland Hill, London SE19 1NY* 081-761 7924

PAGET, Robert James Innes. b 35. AKC59. **d** 60 **p** 61. C Attenborough w Bramcote *S'well* 60-63; C Cheltenham St Mark *Glouc* 63-72; P-in-c Pilsley *Derby* 72-73; TV N Wingfield, Pilsley and Tupton 73-89; R Pinxton from 89. *The Rectory, Town Street, Pinxton, Nottingham NG16 6HH* Ripley (0773) 580024

PAGET-WILKES, Ven Michael Jocelyn James. b 41. NDA64. ALCD69. **d** 69 **p** 70. C Wandsworth All SS *S'wark* 69-74; V Hatcham St Jas 74-82; V Rugby St Matt *Cov* 82-90; Adn Warw from 90. *10 Northumberland Road, Leamington Spa, Warks CV32 6HA* Leamington Spa (0926) 313337

PAGETT, Andrew Stephen. b 45. Bris & Glouc Tr Course. **d** 82 **p** 83. NSM Swindon New Town *Bris* from 82. *93 Lansdown Road, Swindon SN1 3ND* Swindon (0793) 539283

PAICE, Michael Antony. b 35. Kelham Th Coll 55. **d** 60 **p** 61. C Skegby *S'well* 60-62; C Carlton 62-66; V Misterton and W Stockwith 66-81; P-in-c Littleton on Severn w Elberton *Bris* 81-83; V Olveston 81-83; Deputation Appeals Org CECS 83-89; R Sutton St Nicholas w Sutton St Michael *Heref* from 89; R Withington w Westhide from 89. *The Rectory, Sutton St Nicholas, Hereford HR1 3BA* Hereford (0432) 72253

PAICE, William Henry. b 08. Worc Ord Coll. **d** 57 **p** 58. C-in-c Gurnard All SS CD *Portsm* 68-73; rtd 73. *Garden House, The Laurels, Church Street, Shelfanger, Diss, Norfolk IP22 2DG* Diss (0379) 61128

PAIN, Canon David Clinton. b 36. K Coll Lon 56. **d** 64 **p** 64. Benin 64-67; Ghana 67-86; Hon Can Accra 80-86; V Kemp Town St Mary *Chich* from 86. *St Mary's Vicarage, 11 West Drive, Brighton BN2 2GD* Brighton (0273) 698601

PAIN, John Holland. b 04. Wadh Coll Ox BA25 MA32. Wycliffe Hall Ox 27. **d** 27 **p** 28. V Framfield *Chich* 59-69; rtd 69. *1 Townsend Mews, Wilburton, Ely, Cambs CB6 3SQ* Ely (0353) 740450

PAIN, Lawrence Percy Bernard. b 11. Lon Univ BA32. Wells Th Coll 48. **d** 49 **p** 50. V Rowledge *Guildf* 70-81; rtd 81; Perm to Offic *Portsm* from 89. *62 Forest*

Close, Waltham Chase, Southampton SO3 2NB Bishops Waltham (0489) 894972

PAIN, Michael Broughton George. b 37. Dur Univ BA61. Wycliffe Hall Ox 61. **d** 63 **p** 64. C Downend *Bris* 63-67; C Swindon Ch Ch 67-70; V Alveston 70-78; V Guildf Ch Ch *Guildf* 78-90; TR Melksham *Sarum* from 90. *The Rectory, Canon Square, Melksham, Wilts SN12 6LX* Melksham (0225) 703262

PAIN, Richard Edward. b 56. Bris Univ BA79 Univ of Wales (Cardiff) BD84. St Mich Coll Llan 81. **d** 84 **p** 85. C Caldicot *Mon* 84-86; P-in-c Cwmtillery 86-88; V from 88; V Six Bells from 88. *St Paul's Vicarage, Cwmtillery, Abertillery, Gwent NP3 1LS* Abertillery (0495) 212364

PAINE, Dr David Stevens. b 24. St Jo Coll Cam MB47 BChir47 MA52. Ridley Hall Cam 52. **d** 54 **p** 55. C Rowner *Portsm* 54-56; C Freshwater 56-59; V S Cerney w Cerney Wick *Glouc* 59-64. *42 Newton Road, Cambridge CB1 5EF* Cambridge (0223) 353300

PAINE, Canon Ernest Liddell. b 11. Trin Coll Bris 34. **d** 37 **p** 38. P-in-c Lighthorne *Cov* 71-76; P-in-c Chesterton 71-76; RD Dassett Magna 75-76; P-in-c Newbold Pacey w Moreton Morrell 76; Hon Can Cov Cathl 76; rtd 76. *1 Abbey Court, Cerne Abbas, Dorchester, Dorset DT2 7JH* Cerne Abbas (0300) 341358

PAINE, Kevin Adrian Martin. b 56. Univ of Wales (Cardiff) DipTh81. St Mich Coll Llan. **d** 81 **p** 82. Chapl St Woolos Cathl *Mon* 81-85; Perm to Offic from 85. *35 Risca Road, Newport, Gwent* Newport (0633) 258197

PAINE, Peter Stanley. b 46. K Coll Lon BD69 AKC69. Linc Th Coll DipMin89 Cuddesdon Coll 69. **d** 71 **p** 72. C Leeds St Aid *Ripon* 71-74; C Harrogate St Wilfrid 74-78; V Beeston Hill H Spirit 78-82; TV Seacroft 82-90; V Martham w Repps w Bastwick *Nor* from 90. *St Mary's Vicarage, Martham, Great Yarmouth, Norfolk NR29 4PR* Great Yarmouth (0493) 740240

PAINE, William Barry. b 58. TCD DipTh84. CITC. **d** 84 **p** 85. C Glendermott *D & R* 84-86; C Lurgan St Jo *D & D* 86-88; I Kilbarron w Rossnowlagh and Drumholm *D & R* from 88. *The Rectory, Ballintra, Co Donegal, Irish Republic* Ballintra (73) 34025

PAINTER, Canon David Scott. b 44. LTCL65 Worc Coll Ox BA68 MA72. Cuddesdon Coll 68. **d** 70 **p** 71. C Plymouth St Andr *Ex* 70-73; Chapl Plymouth Poly 71-73; C St Marylebone All SS *Lon* 73-76; Abp's Dom Chapl *Cant* 76-80; Dir of Ords 76-80; V Roehampton H Trin *S'wark* 80-91; PV Westmr Abbey from 81; RD Wandsworth *S'wark* 85-90; Perm to Offic 91; Dioc Dir of Ords from 91; Can Res and Treas S'wark Cathl from 91. *22 Rochelle Close, Harbut Road, London SW11 2RX* 081-871 1118

PAINTER, John. b 25. Selw Coll Cam BA48 MA53. Ripon Hall Ox 48. **d** 50 **p** 51. V Sandown Ch Ch *Portsm* 66-72; R Keinton Mandeville *B & W* 72-77; P-in-c Lydford-on-Fosse 76-77; R Keinton Mandeville w Lydford on Fosse 77-90; RD Cary 81-90; RD Bruton 82-85; rtd 90. *1 Fairview Terrace, Station Road, Castle Cary, Somerset BA7 7BX* Castle Cary (0963) 50756

PAIRMAN, David Drummond. b 47. GGSM CertEd. Chich Th Coll 82. **d** 84 **p** 85. C Cowes St Mary *Portsm* 84-87; C Marshwood Vale *Sarum* 87-90; C Hawkchurch 87-90; C Marshwood Vale Team Min from 90. *The Rectory, Hawkchurch, Axminster, Devon EX13 5XD* Axminster (0297) 225

PAISEY, Gerald Herbert John. b 31. Leic Univ CertEd62 Nottm Univ DipRE68 DipAdEd70 MPhil77 Lanc Univ MA78. St Alb Minl Tr Scheme 80. **d** 88. NSM Inverbervie *Bre* 88-90; NSM Stonehaven from 90; NSM Catterline from 90. *20 St Michael's Way, Newtonhill, Stonehaven, Kincardineshire AB3 2GS* Stonehaven (0569) 30322

PAISH, Miss Muriel Dorothy. b 21. Birm Univ CertEd41. Glouc Sch of Min. **dss** 85 **d** 87. Uley w Owlpen and Nympsfield *Glouc* 85-87; Hon C from 87. *5 Woodstock Terrace, Uley, Dursley, Glos GL11 5SW* Dursley (0453) 860429

PAISLEY, James. b 05. Edin Th Coll 27. **d** 29 **p** 30. V Hampstead Norris *Ox* 47-70; V Compton 47-70; rtd 70; Perm to Offic *Ex* from 70. *15 Wilton Way, Abbotskerswell, Newton Abbot, Devon TQ12 5PG* Newton Abbot (0626) 53728

PAISLEY, John Joseph. b 17. Oak Hill Th Coll 46. **d** 49 **p** 50. V Blackpool St Mark *Blackb* 65-82; rtd 82; Perm to Offic *Carl* from 82. *16 Yetlands, Dalston, Carlisle CA5 7PB* Carlisle (0228) 710985

PAISLEY, Ronald Gordon. b 15. Clifton Th Coll 50. **d** 52 **p** 53. V Becontree St Alb *Chelmsf* 60-73; V Toxteth Park St Clem *Liv* 73-80; rtd 80; Perm to Offic *Carl* from 86. *Glen Rosa, Station Road, Brampton, Cumbria CA8 1EX* Brampton (06977) 3022

PAISLEY, Samuel Robinson. b 51. Edin Th Coll. **d** 91. C St Mary's Cathl *Glas* from 91. *42 Hillhead Street, Glasgow G12 8PZ* 041-339 8904

PAKENHAM, Charles Wilfrid. b 18. Trin Coll Ox BA40 MA52. Wycliffe Hall Ox 40. **d** 41 **p** 42. V Litherland Ch Ch *Liv* 52-84; rtd 84; P-in-c W Woodhay w Enborne, Hampstead Marshall etc *Ox* from 91. *15 Cook Road, Albourne, Marlborough, Wilts SN8 2EG* Marlborough (0672) 40531

PAKENHAM, Stephen Walter. b 29. Qu Coll Cam BA57 MA61. Linc Th Coll 57. **d** 59 **p** 60. V Donnington *Chich* 64-75; V Appledram 64-75; V Durrington 75-81; V St Mary Bourne and Woodcott *Win* 81-88; rtd 88. *The Malthouse, Frogmore, Kingsbridge, Devon TQ7 2PG* Frogmore (0548) 531703

PALFREY, Canon Claude Hugh. b 13. Linc Th Coll 44. **d** 46 **p** 47. R Nor St Jo Maddermarket *Nor* 58-81; Prec Nor Cathl 58-84; Hon Can 75-84; rtd 82; Perm to Offic *Nor* from 84. *60 The Close, Norwich NR1 4EH* Norwich (0603) 628084

PALIN, John Edward. b 47. Univ of Wales (Cardiff) DipTh70 DPS71 Open Univ BA83 Leeds Univ MA89. St Mich Coll Llan 67. **d** 71 **p** 72. C Staveley *Derby* 71-74; C Nottm St Mary *S'well* 75-77; P-in-c Thistleton 77-79; V Greetham w Stretton and Clipsham *Pet* 77-79; V Greetham and Thistleton w Stretton and Clipsham 79-83; TR Staveley and Barrow Hill *Derby* 83-87; Chapl R Hallamshire Hosp Sheff 87-88; Perm to Offic *Sheff* 88-90; C Bramley *Ripon* 90-91; TV from 91. *St Margaret's Vicarage, Newlay Lane, Leeds LS13 2AJ* Pudsey (0532) 574811

PALIN, Roy. b 34. Man Univ BA56. Ripon Hall Ox 65. **d** 67 **p** 68. C Ilkeston St Mary *Derby* 67-70; C Wollaton *S'well* 70-71; V Harby w Swinethorpe 71-79; V Thorney w Wigsley and Broadholme 71-79; P-in-c N Clifton 75-79; R Harby w Thorney and N and S Clifton 79-80; V Tuxford 80-81; P-in-c Laxton 80-81; V Markham Clinton 80-81; P-in-c Weston 80-81; V Tuxford w Weston and Markham Clinton 81-90; R Nuthall from 90. *The Rectory, 24 Watnall Road, Nuthall, Nottingham NG16 1DU* Nottingham (0602) 384987

PALK, Mrs Deirdre Elizabeth Pauline. b 41. AIL77 Reading Univ BA63 City of Lon Poly DipBS74 DipRS84. S'wark Ord Course 81. **dss** 84 **d** 87. Wanstead H Trin Hermon Hill *Chelmsf* 84-87; Hon Par Dn from 87; Hon Par Dn Walthamstow St Pet from 88. *3 Ashdon Close, Woodford Green, Essex IG8 0EF* 081-505 3547

PALLANT, Canon Roger Frank. b 35. Trin Coll Cam BA57 MA61. Wells Th Coll 57. **d** 59 **p** 60. C Stafford St Mary *Lich* 59-62; C Ipswich St Mary le Tower *St E* 62-65; Dioc Youth Chapl 62-65; Dev Officer C of E Youth Coun 65-70; Hon C Putney St Mary *S'wark* 66-71; Org Sec New Syn Gp 70-71; R Hintlesham w Chattisham *St E* 71-80; V Ipswich All Hallows 80-88; Hon Can *St E* Cathl from 85; P-in-c Sproughton w Burstall from 88; Dioc Officer for Local NSM from 88. *The Rectory, Glebe Close, Sproughton, Ipswich IP8 3BQ* Ipswich (0473) 241078

PALLETT, Ian Nigel. b 59. Leeds Univ BA80. Linc Th Coll 81. **d** 84 **p** 85. C Halesowen *Worc* 84-88; C Mansf Woodhouse *S'well* from 88. *68 Ley Lane, Mansfield Woodhouse, Mansfield, Notts NG19 8JX* Mansfield (0623) 650093

PALMER, Alister Gordon. b 46. Univ of Tasmania BA73 DipEd74. Trin Coll Bris 78 Ridley Hall Cam 80. **d** 80 **p** 81. C Patchway *Bris* 80-83; C Bushbury *Lich* 83-86; V Wednesfield Heath from 86. *Holy Trinity Vicarage, Bushbury Road, Heath Town, Wolverhampton WV10 0LY* Wolverhampton (0902) 738313

PALMER, Angus Douglas. b 40. St Chad's Coll Dur BA62 DipTh63. **d** 63 **p** 64. C Wallsend St Pet *Newc* 63-66; C Newc H Cross 66-69; C Bottesford *Linc* 69-70; R Penicuik *Edin* 70-83; R W Linton 77-83. *6 Hackworth Gardens, Wylam, Northd NE41 8EJ* Wylam (0661) 853786

PALMER, Bernard Joseph. b 20. St Cath Soc Ox BA49 MA64. Worc Ord Coll 64. **d** 66 **p** 67. R Harvington *Worc* 69-78; V Stoulton w Drakes Broughton and Pirton 78-85; rtd 85; Perm to Offic *Ex* from 85. *Jervis Cottage, Dunsford, Exeter EX6 7HD* Christow (0647) 52945

PALMER, Canon David Henry. b 33. Bris Univ BA54. Linc Th Coll 56. **d** 58 **p** 59. C E Dulwich St Jo *S'wark* 58-62; C Pet All SS *Pet* 62-68; V Northn H Trin 68-74; Chapl Br Emb Ankara *Eur* 74-77; Chapl Rome 77-84; Can Malta Cathl 79-84; Hon Can Malta Cathl from 84; V Brighton St Matthias *Chich* 84-88; P-in-c Upper Teddington SS Pet and Paul *Lon* 88-90; P-in-c Fulwell St Mich and St Geo 88-90; V Teddington SS Pet and Paul and Fulwell from 90; AD Hampton from 90.

The Vicarage, 1 Bychurch End, Teddington, Middx TW11 8PS   081-977 3330

PALMER, David Philip. b 50. Sarum & Wells Th Coll. **d** 84 **p** 85. C St Ives *Ely* 84-86; C Luton All SS w St Pet *St Alb* 86-88; V Stocksbridge *Sheff* from 88. *The Vicarage, Victoria Road, Stocksbridge, Sheffield S30 5FX* Sheffield (0742) 886964

PALMER, David Roderick. b 34. St Jo Coll Dur BA56 Birm Univ DipTh58 Trin Coll Ox. Qu Coll Birm 56. **d** 60 **p** 61. C Loughton St Jo *Chelmsf* 60-63; C Pimlico St Gabr *Lon* 63-64; Miss to Seamen 64-67; CF 67-74; Chapl Luxembourg *Eur* 74-80; P-in-c Exton and Winsford and Cutcombe w Luxborough *B & W* 80-82; P-in-c Wrington w Butcombe 82-84; Dep Dir of Tr Inst Wednesbury St Jas *Lich* 84-86; C Gt Wyrley 86-89; V Wilshamstead and Houghton Conquest *St Alb* from 90. *The Vicarage, Wilshamstead, Bedford MK45 3EU*   Bedford (0234) 740423

PALMER, Canon Derek George. b 28. Selw Coll Cam BA50 MA54. Wells Th Coll 50. **d** 52 **p** 53. C Stapleton *Bris* 52-54; C Bishopston 54-58; C-in-c Hartcliffe St Andr *CD* 58-62; V Bris St Andr Hartcliffe 62-68; V Swindon Ch Ch 68-76; Hon Can Bris Cathl 74-76; Adn Roch 77-83; Can Res Roch Cathl 77-83; Hon Can 83-87; Home Sec Gen Syn Bd for Miss and Unity 83-87; TR Dronfield *Derby* 87-90; TR Dronfield w Holmesfield from 90; Chapl to HM The Queen from 90. *The Rectory, Church Street, Dronfield, Sheffield S18 6QB*   Dronfield (0246) 412328

PALMER, Derek James. b 54. Man Univ BA77. Qu Coll Birm 77. **d** 79 **p** 80. C Leek *Lich* 79-83; CF from 83. *c/o MOD (Army), Bagshot Park, Bagshot, Surrey GU19 5PL* Bagshot (0276) 71717

PALMER, Preb Francis Harvey. b 30. Jes Coll Cam BA52 MA56. Wycliffe Hall Ox 53. **d** 55 **p** 56. V Cam H Trin *Ely* 64-71; Chapl to Cam Pastorate 64-71; Prin Ridley Hall Cam 71-72; R Worplesdon *Guildf* 72-80; Bp's Ecum Officer 74-80; P-in-c Blymhill w Weston-under-Lizard *Lich* 80-82; Dioc Missr and Sec to Bd for Miss and Unity 80-90; Preb Lich Cathl 86-89; TV Walsall 87-90; rtd 90. *The Old Vicarage, Claverley, Wolverhampton WV5 7DT*   Claverley (07466) 746

PALMER, Francis Noel. b 97. Wadh Coll Ox BA21 MA43 Drew Univ New Jersey BD25. **d** 31 **p** 32. V Bromley St Jo *Roch* 54-68; rtd 68; Perm to Offic *Cant* from 68. *44 Princess Margaret Avenue, Cliftonville, Margate, Kent CT9 3DZ* Thanet (0843) 225853

PALMER, Frank Reginald Charles. b 07. AKC30. **d** 30 **p** 31. C Lon Docks St Pet w Wapping St Jo *Lon* 56-60; rtd 60; Perm to Offic *Lon* 60-62 and from 71; Win 63; Ox 65-67. *3 Mary Wharrie House, Fellows Road, London NW3 3LX* 071-722 1709

PALMER, Canon George Henry. b 14. AKC37. **d** 37 **p** 38. V Deddington w Clifton and Hempton *Ox* 63-78; RD Deddington 65-78; Hon Can Ch Ch from 77; rtd 79. *Preston House, Preston Crowmarsh, Oxford OX10 6SL* Wallingford (0491) 38296

PALMER, Graham. b 31. Em Coll Cam BA53 MA57. Qu Coll Birm 56. **d** 58 **p** 59. C Camberwell St Giles *S'wark* 58-61; C Kilburn St Aug *Lon* 61-67; P-in-c Fulham St Alb 67-73; V from 73. *St Alban's Vicarage, 4 Margravine Road, London W6 8HJ* 071-385 0724

PALMER, Hugh. b 50. Pemb Coll Cam BA72 MA76. Ridley Hall Cam 73. **d** 76 **p** 77. C Heigham H Trin *Nor* 76-80; Bp's Chapl for Tr and Miss 80-84; C St Helen Bishopsgate w St Andr Undershaft etc *Lon* from 85. *30 Tredegar Square, London E3 5AG* 071-283 2231

PALMER, Hugh Maurice Webber. b 28. Magd Coll Cam BA51 MA55. Cuddesdon Coll 51. **d** 53 **p** 54. C Bitterne Park *Win* 53-57; N Rhodesia 57-62; V Owslebury w Morestead *Win* 62-65; Rhodesia 65-70; C Headbourne Worthy *Win* 70-71; P-in-c Stratton Strawless *Nor* 72-77; R Hainford 72-77; R Haynford w Stratton Strawless 77-80; Chapl HM Pris Stafford 80-82; Standford Hill 82-89; Sub-Chapl HM Pris Nor from 89. *2B Millfield Road, North Walsham, Norfolk NR29 0EB*   North Walsham (0692) 403664

PALMER, Ian Stanley. b 50. K Coll Lon BD71. Cranmer Hall Dur 73. **d** 75 **p** 76. C Huyton St Mich *Liv* 75-78; Chapl Dur Univ *Dur* 78-83; V Collierley w Annfield Plain 83-90; Australia from 90. *The Bishop's Registry, 48 Church Street, Newcastle, NSW, Australia 2300* Newcastle (49) 293094

PALMER, Mrs Jacqueline Merrill. b 60. Leeds Univ BA82. Cranmer Hall Dur 83. **dss** 85 **d** 87. Asst Chapl Hull Univ *York* 85-87. *60 Magnolia Road, Merry Oak, Southampton SO2 7LH* Southampton (0703) 432591

PALMER, John Michael Joseph. b 18. VRD62. **d** 61 **p** 62. Chapl RNR 62-91; V Fernhurst *Chich* 67-72; Bp's Dom

Chapl *Truro* 73-74; Lic to Offic 74-75; Perm to Offic *Win* from 82; rtd 83. *18 rue Lamennais, St Pierre de Plesguen, France*

PALMER, John Richard Henry. b 29. AKC52. **d** 53 **p** 54. C Englefield Green *Guildf* 53-57; Australia 57-62; C Wareham w Arne *Sarum* 62-63; V Derby St Jo *Derby* 63-66; Chapl Holloway Sanatorium Virginia Water 66-70; Chapl Brookwood Hosp Woking from 70. *Red Gables, Brookwood Hospital, Knaphill, Woking, Surrey GU21 2RG* Brookwood (04867) 4545

PALMER, John Russell. b 25. Birm Univ BSc46. Cuddesdon Coll 70. **d** 71 **p** 72. C Weeke *Win* 71-76; V Four Marks 76-90; rtd 90. *33 Montague Road, Bournemouth BH5 2EW* Bournemouth (0202) 426536

PALMER, Malcolm Leonard. b 46. Sarum & Wells Th Coll. **d** 82 **p** 83. C Cannock *Lich* 82-85; Chapl RAF 85-89; Asst Chapl HM Pris Dur 89-90; Chapl HM Young Offender Inst Hewell Grange and HM Rem Cen Brockhill from 90. *HM Young Offender Institute Hewell Grange, Redditch, Worcester B97 6QQ* Redditch (0527) 550843

PALMER, Marion Denise. b 42. SRN64 SCM66 Open Univ BA82. Linc Th Coll 84. **dss** 86 **d** 87. Poplar *Lon* 86-87; Par Dn 87-90; Par Dn Gillingham St Mary *Roch* from 90. *146 Woodlands Road, Gillingham, Kent ME7 2SX* Medway (0634) 571197

PALMER, Dr Maureen Florence. b 38. Qu Eliz Coll Lon BSc60 PhD64 DipRS79. Ripon Coll Cuddesdon DipTh84. **dss** 85 **d** 87. Tupsley *Heref* 85-87; C 87-88; Par Dn Talbot Village *Sarum* from 88. *18 Hillside Road, Wallisdown, Bournemouth, Dorset BH12 5DJ* Bournemouth (0202) 520251

PALMER, Michael Christopher. b 43. AKC67. **d** 68 **p** 69. C Easthampstead *Ox* 68-71; Miss to Seamen 71-73; Hong Kong 73; Lic to Offic Ox 76-79; Truro 79-83; Dioc Soc Resp Adv *Truro* from 83; Bp's Dom Chapl 85-87; V Devoran from 87. *The Vicarage, Devoran, Truro, Cornwall TR3 6PA* Truro (0872) 863116

PALMER, Norman Ernest. b 28. Lon Univ DipTh56 BD59. Roch Th Coll 66. **d** 67 **p** 67. V Bozeat w Easton Maudit *Pet* 69-90; rtd 90. *4 St Augustine's Close, Bexhill-on-Sea, E Sussex TN39 3AZ* Bexhill-on-Sea (0424) 218573

PALMER, Peter Malcolm. b 31. Chich Th Coll 56. **d** 59 **p** 60. C Leighton Buzzard *St Alb* 59-63; C Apsley End 63-65; C Hitchin H Sav 65-69; R Ickleford 69-76; V Oxhey St Matt 76-86; V Kensworth, Studham and Whipsnade from 86. *The Vicarage, Clayhall Road, Kensworth, Dunstable, Beds LU6 3RF*   Whipsnade (0582) 872223

PALMER, Peter Parsons. b 27. **d** 59 **p** 61. SSJE from 59; Canada 59-79; Perm to Offic *Leic* 80-86; Lon from 86. *SSJE Priory, 228 Iffley Road, Oxford OX4 1SE*   Oxford (0865) 242227

PALMER, Philip Edward Hitchen. b 35. St Jo Coll Cam MA61 DipAdEd74. Ridley Hall Cam 61 E Anglian Minl Tr Course 87. **d** 90 **p** 91. NSM Gt Oakley w Wix *Chelmsf* from 90. *Glebe House, Great Oakley, Harwich, Essex CO12 5BJ* Clacton-on-Sea (0255) 880737

PALMER, Robert William. b 28. DMS. Wells Th Coll 63. **d** 65 **p** 66. C Earlsdon *Cov* 65-69; P-in-c Cov St Mark 69-71; Chapl Cov and Warks Hosp 69-71; Hon C Binley *Cov* 72-76; V Sheff St Paul Wordsworth Avenue *Sheff* 76-84; V Deepcar from 84. *St John's Vicarage, 27 Carr Road, Deepcar, Sheffield S30 5PQ*   Sheffield (0742) 885138

PALMER, Canon Stephen Charles. b 47. Oak Hill Th Coll 71. **d** 74 **p** 75. C Crofton *Portsm* 74-77; Bp's Dom Chapl 77-80; Chapl RNR from 78; R Brighstone and Brooke w Mottistone *Portsm* 80-91; P-in-c Shorwell w Kingston 82-86; RD W Wight 87-91; Hon Can Portsm Cathl from 91; Falkland Is from 91. *The Deanery, Stanley, Falkland Islands* Falkland Islands (500) 100

PALMER, Terence Henry James. b 34. St Edm Hall Ox BA65 MA69. St D Coll Lamp BA55 LTh57. **d** 57 **p** 58. C Griffithstown *Mon* 57-60; Min Can and C St D Cathl *St D* 60-63; Perm to Offic Ox & B & W 63-65; C Mon 65-69; C-in-c St Hilary Greenway CD 69-72; R Roggiett w Llanfihangel Roggiett 72-80; R Portskewett and Roggiett w Llanfihangel Rogiet from 80; RD Netherwent from 89; Dir NSM Studies from 91. *The Rectory, 19 Main Road, Portskewett, Newport, Gwent NP6 4SG* Caldicot (0291) 420313

PALMER, William Frederick. b 15. Kelham Th Coll 33. **d** 40 **p** 41. R Chalfont St Giles *Ox* 68-73; V Mill Hill St Mich *Lon* 73-81; rtd 81; Perm to Offic *St Alb* from 81. *22 The Sycamores, Baldock, Herts SG7 5BJ*   Baldock (0462) 892456

PALMER, William John. b 09. St D Coll Lamp BA33. **d** 34 **p** 35. V Dinnington *Newc* 68-74; rtd 74. *Whitegates, Aydon Road, Corbridge, Northd NE45 5DR*

PALMER-PALMER-FFYNCHE, Lt-Comdr Barry Marshall. b 23. Hertf Coll Ox BA47 MA48. Westcott Ho Cam 47. **d** 49 **p** 50. Chapl Westmr Hosp Lon 66-73; V Chipping Sodbury and Old Sodbury *Glouc* 73-88; rtd 88. *Finch's Folly, Home Farm Stables, 45 Hay Street, Marshfield, Chippenham, Wilts SN14 8PF* Bath (0225) 891096

PAMMENT, Canon Gordon Charles. b 31. TCD BA54. Linc Th Coll 56. **d** 58 **p** 60. I Macroom Union *C, C & R* 65-72; I Rathcormac Union 72-78; I Fermoy Union 78-91; Preb Ross Cathl 89-91; Preb Cork Cathl 89-91; rtd 91. *5 Langford Place, Co Cork, Irish Republic*

PAMPLIN, Dr Richard Lawrence. b 46. Lon Univ BScEng68 Dur Univ BA75. NY Th Sem DMin85 Wycliffe Hall Ox 75. **d** 77 **p** 78. C Greenside *Dur* 77-80; C Sheff St Barn and St Mary *Sheff* 80-84; R Wombwell 84-90; P-in-c Madeley *Heref* from 90. *St Michael's Vicarage, Church Street, Madeley, Telford TF7 5BN* Telford (0952) 585718

PANG, Wing-On. b 43. BA67 Lon Univ MA70. Oak Hill Th Coll 87. **d** 87 **p** 88. C Pennycross *Ex* from 87. *23 Pennycross Park Road, Peverell, Plymouth PL2 3NP* Plymouth (0752) 772758

PANGBOURNE, John Godfrey. b 36. Ridley Hall Cam 82. **d** 84 **p** 85. C Ashtead *Guildf* 84-88; V Ore Ch Ch *Chich* from 88. *Christ Church Vicarage, 76 Canute Road, Ore, Hastings, E Sussex TN35 5HT* Hastings (0424) 421439

PANKHURST, Donald Araunah. b 28. Qu Coll Birm DipTh64. **d** 64 **p** 65. C Pemberton St Jo *Liv* 64-68; V Aspull 68-76; R Newchurch 76-88; R Winwick from 88. *The Rectory, Golborne Road, Winwick, Warrington WA2 8SZ* Warrington (0925) 32760

PANNELL, Roy Charles. b 45. AKC69. **d** 70 **p** 71. C Sheff Parson Cross St Cecilia *Sheff* 70-75; V New Bentley 75-82; V Greenhill from 82. *St Peter's Vicarage, Reney Avenue, Sheffield S8 7FN* Sheffield (0742) 377422

PANNETT, Philip Anthony. b 36. MPS59 AKC63. **d** 64 **p** 65. C Stanmer w Falmer and Moulsecoomb *Chich* 64-68; C Hangleton 68-72; Teacher Bodiam Manor Sch 74-76. *35 Dudley Road, Brighton BN1 7GN* Brighton (0273) 551431

PANTER, Canon Noel. b 09. Ex Coll Ox BA31 DipTh32 MA35. Wycliffe Hall Ox 31. **d** 33 **p** 34. Hon Can Worc Cathl *Worc* 66-77; V Gt Malvern Ch Ch 68-77; rtd 77; Perm to Offic Heref from 78; Glouc from 79. *2 Park View, Oatleys Road, Ledbury, Herefordshire HR8 2BN* Ledbury (0531) 2789

PANTER, Richard James Graham. b 48. Oak Hill Th Coll 73. **d** 76 **p** 77. C Rusholme *Man* 76-80; C Toxteth St Cypr w Ch Ch *Liv* 80-85; V Clubmoor from 85. *St Andrew's Vicarage, 176 Queen's Drive, Liverpool L13 0AL* 051- 226 1977

PANTER MARSHALL, Mrs Susan Lesley. b 49. Portsm Poly BSc72 Grad LI84. S Dioc Minl Tr Scheme 88. **d** 91. NSM Southover *Chich* from 91. *30 South Way, Lewes, E Sussex BN7 1LY* Lewes (0273) 474670

PANTING, John. b 36. K Coll Cam BA60 MA64. Ridley Hall Cam 60. **d** 63 **p** 63. C Woking St Pet *Guildf* 63-65; Chapl Dean Close Sch Cheltenham 65-68; Lic to Offic *York* 68-70; C Stratford w Bishopton *Cov* 70-75; TV 75-79; V Keresley and Coundon from 79. *The Vicarage, 34 Tamworth Road, Coventry CV6 2EL* Keresley (020333) 2717

PANTON, Alan Edward. b 45. K Coll Lon BD67 AKC67. **d** 68 **p** 69. C Eltham St Jo *S'wark* 68-73; C Horley 73-78; V Dallington *Pet* from 78. *The Vicarage, The Barton's Close, Dallington, Northampton NN5 7HN* Northampton (0604) 51478

PAPE, Timothy Vernon Francis. b 39. Lon Univ BSc63. Wells Th Coll 63. **d** 65 **p** 66. C Pershore w Wick *Worc* 65-69; Perm to Offic *Bris* 69-73; Hon C Southbroom *Sarum* from 75; Hd Master Chirton Primary Sch Wilts from 81. *Old Brewery House, Shaw, Melksham, Wilts SN12 8EF* Melksham (0225) 702259

PAPWORTH, John. b 21. Lon Univ BSc(Econ). **d** 75 **p** 76. Zambia 76-81; Hon C Paddington St Sav *Lon* 81-83; Hon C St Marylebone St Mark Hamilton Terrace from 85. *24 Abercorn Place, London NW8* 071-286 4366

PAPWORTH, Shirley Marjorie. b 33. **d** 88. Par Dn Hornchurch H Cross *Chelmsf* from 88. *16 Cheviot Road, Hornchurch, Essex RM11 1LP* Hornchurch (04024) 72491

PARADISE, Bryan John. b 49. Southn Univ BSc Lon Bible Coll BA. Cranmer Hall Dur. **d** 82 **p** 83. C High Harrogate Ch Ch *Ripon* 82-86; Dioc Adult Educn Officer *Guildf* from 86; P-in-c Dunsfold 86-90; R from 90. *The Rectory, Church Green, Dunsfold, Godalming, Surrey GU8 4LT* Dunsfold (048649) 207

PARE, Philip Norris. b 10. K Coll Cam BA33 MA37. Cuddesdon Coll 33. **d** 34 **p** 35. V and Provost Wakef Cathl *Wakef* 62-71; V Cholsey *Ox* 73-82; rtd 82; Perm to Offic *Heref* from 83. *73 Oakland Drive, Ledbury, Herefordshire HR8 2EX* Ledbury (0531) 3619

PARE, Stephen Charles. b 53. Sussex Univ BEd75. Llan St Mich DipTh80. **d** 80 **p** 81. C Cardiff St Jo *Llan* 80-83; P-in-c Marcross w Monknash and Wick 83; TV Llantwit Major 83-91; V Penmark w Porthkerry from 91. *The Vicarage, Penmark, Barry, S Glam CF6 9BN* Barry (0446) 711713

PARFITT, Brian John. b 49. Ex Coll Ox BA71 MA76. Wycliffe Hall Ox 71. **d** 74 **p** 75. C Newport St Mark *Mon* 74-78; R Blaina 78-83; Chapl Blaina and Distr Hosp Gwent 83-86; R Blaina and Nantyglo *Mon* 83-86; Perm to Offic B & W, Bris, Ox, St D & Win from 86; CPAS Staff from 86. *59A Downs Park East, Bristol BS6 7QG* Bristol (0272) 629928

PARFITT, Graeme Stanley. b 36. Qu Coll Birm 77. **d** 79 **p** 80. C Fishponds St Jo *Bris* 79-82; V Southmead from 82. *St Stephen's Vicarage, Wigton Crescent, Bristol BS10 6DR* Bristol (0272) 507164

PARFITT, John Arthur. b 49. St Jo Coll Nottm BTh81. **d** 81 **p** 82. C Radcliffe-on-Trent *S'well* 81-84; C Chilwell 84-86; V Awsworth w Cossall from 86. *The Vicarage, The Lane, Awsworth, Nottingham NG16 2QP* Ilkeston (0602) 321274

PARFITT, Preb John Hubert. b 29. Birm Univ DipTh66 Southn Univ MA72 BPhil. Qu Coll Birm 78. **d** 80 **p** 81. C Fladbury, Wyre Piddle and Moor *Worc* 80-82; C Malvern Link w Cowleigh 82; V Hanley Castle, Hanley Swan and Welland 82-83; Dir RE *B & W* from 84; Preb Wells Cathl from 85. *4 Oakridge Close, Sidcot, Winscombe, Avon BS25 1LY* Wells (0749) 72446

PARFITT, Keith John. b 44. K Coll Lon BD68 AKC68. St Aug Coll Cant 69. **d** 70 **p** 71. C Kettering St Andr *Pet* 70-74; Asst Soc and Ind Adv *Portsm* 74-89; RD Alverstoke 79-86; C-in-c Bridgemary CD 81-82; V Bridgemary 82-89; Dioc UPA Officer *Blackb* from 89. *37 Buncer Lane, Blackburn BB2 6SN* Blackburn (0254) 54910

PARGETER, Canon Muriel Elizabeth. b 28. St Mich Ho Ox 53. **dss** 82 **d** 87. Hd Dss *Roch* 82-87; Dioc Dir of Ords 87-90; Hon Can Roch Cathl from 87; rtd 90. *63 Pavilion Road, Worthing, W Sussex BN4 7EE* Worthing (0903) 214476

PARISH, George Richard. b 33. ACIB60 Qu Coll Cam BA56 MA60. S'wark Ord Course 85. **d** 88 **p** 89. NSM Sunninghill *Ox* from 88. *The Shieling, Heathfield Avenue, Ascot, Berks SL5 0AL* Ascot (0344) 25840

PARISH, Nicholas Anthony. b 58. Oak Hill Th Coll BA84 Ridley Hall Cam 84. **d** 86 **p** 87. C Eltham H Trin *S'wark* 86-89; C Barnes St Mary 89-91; V Streatham St Paul from 91. *St Paul's Vicarage, Chillerton Road, London SW17 9BE* 081-672 5536

PARISH, Stephen Richard. b 49. Oak Hill Th Coll DipTh77. **d** 77 **p** 78. C Chadderton Ch Ch *Man* 77-81; C Chell *Lich* 81-82; TV 82-88; V Warrington St Ann *Liv* from 88. *St Ann's Vicarage, 1A Fitzherbert Street, Warrington, Cheshire WA2 7QG* Warrington (0925) 31781

PARK, Allan. b 38. Lich Th Coll 61. **d** 64 **p** 65. C Westf St Mary *Carl* 64-67; C Lawton Moor *Man* 67-69; R Lightbowne 69-81; V Barton w Peel Green from 81. *St Michael's Vicarage, 684 Liverpool Road, Eccles, Manchester M30 7LP* 061-789 3751

PARK, Canon John Raymond. b 11. Keble Coll Ox BA33 MA37. Linc Th Coll 34. **d** 35 **p** 36. Hon Can Liv Cathl *Liv* from 66; R W Tanfield and Well w Snape *Ripon* 74-76; rtd 76. *52 Longridge Lane, Upper Poppleton, York YO2 6HA* York (0904) 794658

PARK, Robert William. b 12. Man Univ BA38. Bps' Coll Cheshunt 35. **d** 39 **p** 40. V Shackerstone and Congerstone *Leic* 62-77; rtd 77. *2 Sidmouth Close, Alvaston, Derby DE2 0QY* Derby (0332) 754112

PARK, Canon Trevor. b 38. Lon Univ BA64 Open Univ PhD90. Lambeth STh81 Linc Th Coll 64. **d** 66 **p** 67. C Crosthwaite Kendal *Carl* 66-68; Asst Chapl Solihull Sch Warks 69-71; Chapl St Bees Sch Cumbria 71-77; V St Bees *Carl* 71-77; V Dalton-in-Furness 77-84; V Natland from 84; Hon Can Carl Cathl from 86; RD Kendal from 89. *The Vicarage, Natland, Kendal, Cumbria LA9 7QQ* Sedgwick (05395) 60355

PARKE, Edmund George. b 14. JP. TCD BA37 MA47. **d** 38 **p** 39. Chapl Soc Work Dept Dundee Corp 69-75; Tayside Regional Coun 75-79; rtd 79. *9 Netherlea Place,*

Newport-on-Tay, Fife DD6 8NW Newport-on-Tay (0382) 542048

PARKE, Canon George Reginald. b 09. Linc Th Coll 40. **d** 42 **p** 43. Hon Can Newc Cathl *Newc* 70-80; V Beadnell 73-80; rtd 80. *West House, Dunstan, Alnwick, Northd NE66 3TB* Embleton (066576) 257

PARKE, Simon Frederick Fenning. b 57. MA. Wycliffe Hall Ox. **d** 84 **p** 85. C Isleworth St Jo *Lon* 84-87; C St Marylebone All So w SS Pet and Jo 87-88; C Langham Place All So from 88. *25 Fitzroy Street, London W1P 5AF* 071-580 3745 or 387 1360

PARKER, Alfred. b 20. Man Univ BA47. Wycliffe Hall Ox 41. **d** 49 **p** 50. V Belmont *Man* 65-87; rtd 87. *21 Edgeley Road, Whitchurch, Shropshire SY13 1EU*

PARKER, Angus Michael Macdonald. b 53. Bris Univ BSc74. St Jo Coll Nottm DipTh81 DPS83. **d** 83 **p** 84. C Northn St Giles *Pet* 83-86; Assoc Min Attenborough S'well from 86. *120 Seaburn Road, Beeston, Nottingham NG9 6HJ* Long Eaton (0602) 735655

PARKER, Arthur Townley. b 14. Worc Ord Coll 59. **d** 61 **p** 62. Chapl Hostel of God Clapham 71-73; rtd 74; Perm to Offic *Blackb* from 87. *30 Langdale Road, Morecambe, Lancs LA4 5XA* Morecambe (0524) 419183

PARKER, Betsee. b 51. Wellesley Coll (USA) AB82 Harvard Univ MDiv85. Harvard Univ Sch 82. **d** 88. USA 88-90; Par Dn Gleadless Valley *Sheff* from 90. *St John's Vicarage, Blackstock Close, Sheffield S14 1AE* Sheffield (0742) 398632

PARKER, Carole Maureen. b 45. N Ord Course. **d** 87. NSM Coalville and Bardon Hill *Leic* 87-90. *165 Leicester Road, Mountsorrel, Leicester LE12 7DB*

PARKER, David Anthony. b 38. St Chad's Coll Dur BA62 DipTh64. **d** 64 **p** 65. C Palmers Green St Jo *Lon* 64-65; C Kenton 65-71; C W Hyde St Thos *St Alb* 71-75; P-in-c Brinksway *Ches* 76-80; V 80-83; V Weston from 83. *All Saints' Vicarage, 13 Cemetery Road, Weston, Crewe CW2 5LQ* Crewe (0270) 582585

PARKER, David Arthur. b 48. Lon Univ DipTh71. Kelham Th Coll. **d** 71 **p** 72. C Newc Ch Ch *Newc* 71-74; C Hendon *Dur* 74-79; C-in-c Southwick St Cuth CD 79-84; V Sunderland Red Ho 84-88; rtd 88. *St Agnes Retreat House, St Agnes Avenue, Knowle, Bristol BS4 2HH* Bristol (0272) 776806

PARKER, Dr David Charles. b 53. St Andr Univ MTh75 Em Coll Cam DipTh76 Univ of Leiden DTh90. Ridley Hall Cam 75. **d** 77 **p** 78. C Hendon St Paul Mill Hill *Lon* 77-80; C Bladon w Woodstock *Ox* 80-85; C-in-c Shipton-on-Cherwell 80-85; C-in-c Begbroke 80-85; C-in-c Hampton Gay 80-85; Lect Qu Coll Birm from 85; Perm to Offic *Birm* 85-89; Lic to Offic from 89; Sen Angl Tutor Qu Coll Birm from 89. *The Queen's College, Somerset Road, Birmingham B15 2QH* 021-454 7506

PARKER, David John. b 33. St Chad's Coll Dur BA55 Hull Univ MA85. Linc Th Coll 57. **d** 59 **p** 60. C Tynemouth Ch Ch *Newc* 59-60; C Ponteland 60-63; C Byker St Mich 63-64; C-in-c Byker St Martin CD 64-69; V Whorlton 69-73; TR 73-80; Ind Chapl *Linc* 80-84; Master St Thos the Martyr Newc 84-89; C-in-c Newc St Thos Prop Chpl *Newc* 84-89; Exec Officer Dioc Bd Soc Resp *Man* from 90. *43 Acresfield Road, Salford M6 7GE* 061-737 6891

PARKER, David Louis. b 47. Lon Univ LLB70 Ox Univ MA82. Wycliffe Hall Ox BA79. **d** 80 **p** 81. C Broadwater St Mary *Chich* 80-84; TR Ifield from 84. *The Vicarage, Ifield, Crawley, W Sussex RH11 0NN* Crawley (0293) 520843

PARKER, David William. b 21. SEN CQSW MBASW. Glouc Th Course 77 Sarum & Wells Th Coll 81. **d** 81 **p** 81. Chapl HM Pris Leyhill 81-84; NSM Cromhall w Tortworth *Glouc* 81-83; NSM Wickwar w Rangeworthy 83-87; Perm to Offic from 88. *22 Durham Road, Charfield, Wotton-under-Edge, Glos GL12 8TH* Falfield (0454) 260253

PARKER, Dennis. b 22. Tyndale Hall Bris 63. **d** 64 **p** 65. C-in-c Reading St Mary Castle Street Prop Chpl *Ox* 68-70; R Newdigate *Guildf* 70-87; rtd 87. *Cleve House, Flint Hill, Dorking, Surrey RH4 2LL* Dorking (0306) 889458

PARKER, Frank Maxwell Lewis. b 12. St Deiniol's Hawarden 66. **d** 67 **p** 68. V Temple Fortune St Barn *Lon* 71-76; V Long Buckby w Watford *Pet* 76-82; rtd 82; Lic to Offic *Pet* 83-85; Perm to Offic from 85. *4 Station Road, West Haddon, Northampton NN6 7AU* West Haddon (078887) 385

PARKER, George Arthur. b 17. St Pet Hall Ox BA39 MA43. Wycliffe Hall Ox 39. **d** 40 **p** 41. Asst Master Ch Sch Bury 65-73; C Whalley *Blackb* 73-82; rtd 82; Lic to Offic *Blackb* from 83. *91 King Street, Whalley, Blackburn, Lancs BB6 9SW* Blackburn (0254) 823978

PARKER, George Jeffrey. b 24. LCP69. Cuddesdon Coll 70. **d** 70 **p** 71. Hd Master St Nic Sch Codsall 70-76; Hon C Codsall *Lich* 70-76; Hon C Lapley w Wheaton Aston 76-80; Lic to Offic 80-82; R Hepworth *St E* 82-86; P-in-c Hinderclay w Wattisfield 82-86; P-in-c Thelnetham 82-86; R Hepworth, Hinderclay, Wattisfield and Thelnetham 86-89; rtd 89. *Cranham, 42 Sheringham Covert, Beaconside, Staffs ST16 3YL* Stafford (0785) 58223

PARKER, George William. b 29. **d** 53 **p** 54. Canada 53-59 and from 78; C W Hackney St Barn *Lon* 59-61; V Haggerston St Mary w St Chad 61-68; C Portsea N End St Mark *Portsm* 73-75; V Darlington St Jo *Dur* 75-78. *RR3, Newport, Nova Scotia, Canada, B0N 2A0*

PARKER, Hugh James. b 30. ACP55 TCD MA57 NUU DASE74. **d** 63 **p** 64. Lic to Offic *Conn* 63-70; Dioc C from 70; Hd Master Larne High Sch from 81. *29 Ransevyn Drive, Whitehead, Co Antrim BT38 9NW* Whitehead (09603) 78106

PARKER, Hugh White. b 12. AKC39. **d** 39 **p** 40. R Waddesdon w Over Winchendon and Fleet Marston *Ox* 64-79; rtd 79; Perm to Offic *Ox* from 79. *4 St Mary's Close, Bicester, Oxon OX6 8BW* Bicester (0869) 42421

PARKER, John Bristo. b 26. Edin Th Coll 61. **d** 64 **p** 65. V Sledmere *York* 68-74; R Cowlam 68-74; P-in-c Wetwang 69-74; V Sledmere and Wetwang w Cowlan 74-79; V Kirkby Ireleth *Carl* 79-83; V Rillington w Scampston, Wintringham etc *York* 83-87; R Bishop Wilton w Full Sutton, Kirby Underdale etc 87-91; rtd 91. *East Lodge, Sledmere, Driffield, N Humberside*

PARKER, Canon John William. b 06. AKC34. Sarum Th Coll 34. **d** 35 **p** 36. V Coates *Linc* 62-75; R Willingham 62-75; R Stow in Lindsey 62-75; Can and Preb Linc Cathl from 74; rtd 75. *6 Minster Yard, Lincoln LN2 1PJ* Lincoln (0522) 525097

PARKER, John William. b 39. St Steph Ho Ox 76. **d** 78 **p** 79. Hd Master St Mary's Sch Penzance 78-82; Hon C Penzance St Mary w St Paul *Truro* 78-82; Hd Master Ch Ch Sch Albany St 82-83; Hon C Munster Square St Mary Magd *Lon* 82-83; V Gateshead St Cuth w St Paul *Dur* 83-89; V Hunslet St Mary *Ripon* from 89. *St Mary's Vicarage, Church Street, Leeds LS10 2QY* Leeds (0532) 719661

PARKER, Preb Joseph French. b 09. St Chad's Coll Dur BA37 DipTh38 MA40. **d** 38 **p** 39. RD W Bromwich *Lich* 61-76; V W Bromwich All SS 61-76; Preb Lich Cathl 67-76; rtd 76; Perm to Offic *Carl* from 77. *Tea Rose Cottage, Edenhall, Penrith, Cumbria CA11 8SX* Langwathby (076881) 543

PARKER, Miss Margaret. b 27. Lightfoot Ho Dur 54. **dss** 60 **d** 87. Monkwearmouth St Andr *Dur* 61-79; Adv for Accredited Lay Min 74-87; Adv for Accredited Lay Min *Newc* 79-87; Newc St Geo 79-87; C 87; rtd 87; Perm to Offic *Dur* from 87. *53 Devonshire Road, Durham DH1 2BJ* 091-386 3233

PARKER, Margaret Grace. See TORDOFF, Mrs Margaret Grace

PARKER, Matthew John. b 63. Man Univ BA85 SS Coll Cam BA88. Ridley Hall Cam 85. **d** 88 **p** 89. C Twickenham St Mary *Lon* from 88. *84 Clifden Court, Clifden Road, Twickenham TW1 4LR* 081-892 5281

PARKER, Michael John. b 54. Cam Coll of Art and Tech BA76 Lon Univ BD85. Trin Coll Bris 82. **d** 85 **p** 86. C Leic H Trin w St Jo *Leic* 85-88; P-in-c Edin Clermiston Em *Edin* 88-90; I Edin St Thos from 90. *16 Belgrave Road, Edinburgh EH12 6NF* 031-334 1309

PARKER, Michael John. b 57. BSc. Wycliffe Hall Ox 80. **d** 83 **p** 84. C Heigham H Trin *Nor* 83-86; C Muswell Hill St Jas w St Matt *Lon* 86-90; R Bedf St Jo and St Leon *St Alb* from 90. *St John's Rectory, 36 St John's Street, Bedford MK42 0DH* Bedford (0234) 354818

PARKER, Peter Edward. b 32. FRSA Edin Univ MA55 Lon Univ PGCE56. Sarum & Wells Th Coll 73. **d** 74 **p** 75. C Kirkby Lonsdale w Mansergh *Carl* 74-76; C Kingston St Jo S'wark 76; C Kingston All SS w St Jo 76-80; Chapl S Bank Poly 80-85; Ind Chapl *Chelmsf* 85-90; Chapl Chelmsf Cathl 85-90; R Mistley w Manningtree and Bradfield from 90. *The Rectory, 21 Malthouse Road, Mistley, Manningtree, Essex CO11 1BY* Colchester (0206) 392200

PARKER, Philip Vernon. b 60. Birm Univ BSc82 PGCE83. Wycliffe Hall Ox BA89. **d** 90 **p** 91. C Walkergate *Newc* from 90. *258 Westbourne Avenue, Walkergate, Newcastle upon Tyne NE6 4XU* 091-262 4875

PARKER, Ramon Lewis (Brother Raphael). b 36. Kelham Th Coll 56. **d** 61 **p** 62. C Tonge Moor *Man* 61-64; C Clerkenwell H Redeemer w St Phil *Lon* 64-65; V Prestwich St Hilda *Man* 65-71; SSF from 71; Chapl St D Univ Coll Lamp *St D* 81-86; Lic to Offic *Sarum* from

87. *The Friary, Hilfield, Dorchester, Dorset DT2 7BE*
Cerne Abbas (0300) 341345

PARKER, Reginald Boden. b 01. MRST36 Lon Univ
BSc23 DipEd24 St Cath Soc Ox BA35 MA39. Ripon
Hall Ox 32. **d** 35 **p** 36. R Bentham St Jo *Bradf* 64-72;
rtd 72. *3 Yew Tree Cottages, Sheepscombe, Stroud, Glos
GL6 7RB* Painswick (0452) 812650

PARKER, Richard Frederick. b 36. Oak Hill Th Coll
72. **d** 74 **p** 75. C Wootton *St Alb* 74-76; C Hove Bp
Hannington Memorial Ch *Chich* 76-81; R Northwood
Portsm 81-88; V W Cowes H Trin 81-88; V Aldershot
H Trin *Guildf* from 88. *2 Cranmore Lane, Aldershot,
Hants GU11 3AS* Aldershot (0252) 20618

PARKER, Robert Lawrence. b 34. ALCD59. **d** 59 **p** 60. C
Chippenham St Paul *Bris* 59-61; C Swindon Ch Ch
61-63; New Zealand 63-71; P-in-c Over Stowey w Aisholt
B & W 71-73; V Nether Stowey 71-73; V Nether Stowey
w Over Stowey from 73; RD Quantock from 87. *St
Mary's Vicarage, Nether Stowey, Bridgwater, Somerset
TA5 1LJ* Nether Stowey (0278) 732247

PARKER, Robert William. b 18. Linc Th Coll 81. **d** 81
p 82. NSM Mablethorpe w Trusthorpe *Linc* 81-83; NSM
Alford w Rigsby 83-86; NSM Alberbury w Cardeston
Heref 87-90; NSM Ford 87-90; rtd 90; Perm to Offic
Linc from 90. *17 The Glade, Sandilands, Sutton-on-Sea,
Lincs SN12 2RZ* Sutton-on-Sea (0507) 442572

PARKER, Roland John Graham. b 48. AKC72 Hull Univ
BA(Ed)83. St Aug Coll Cant 71. **d** 74 **p** 75. C Linc St
Faith and St Martin w St Pet *Linc* 74-78; V Appleby
78-84; Ind Chapl 78-84; V N Kelsey from 84; V Cadney
from 84. *The Vicarage, North Kelsey, Lincoln LN7 6EZ*
North Kelsey (06527) 205

PARKER, Russell Edward. b 48. Lon Univ DipTh77 Man
Univ BA80 Nottm Univ MTh82. St Jo Coll Nottm 80.
d 81 **p** 82. C Walmsley *Man* 81-85; V Coalville and
Bardon Hill *Leic* 85-90; Acorn Chr Healing Trust from
90. *165 Leicester Road, Mountsorrel, Loughborough,
Leicester LE12 7DB* Leicester (0533) 302790

PARKER, Thomas Henry Louis. b 16. Em Coll Cam
BA38 MA42 BD50 DD61. Lon Coll of Div 38. **d** 39 **p** 40.
V Oakington *Ely* 61-71; Lect Dur Univ 71-81; rtd 81.
72 Windsor Road, Cambridge Cambridge (0223) 312215

PARKER, Timothy Percy. b 58. Man Univ BA. St Jo Coll
Nottm DipTh. **d** 85 **p** 86. C Pitsmoor Ch Ch *Sheff* 85-87;
C Kimberworth 87-89; C Brightside w Wincobank 89-91;
C Upper Armley *Ripon* from 91. *115A Heights Drive,
Leeds LS12 3TG* Leeds (0532) 637240

PARKER, William Albert Stuart. b 26. Wells Th Coll 68.
d 70 **p** 71. C Bartley Green *Birm* 70-72; C Sutton
Coldfield H Trin 72-75; V Allens Cross 75-82; V
Lydbrook *Glouc* 82-88; V Holbeach Marsh *Linc* from
88. *The Vicarage, Holbeach Hurn, Spalding, Lincs
PE12 8JT* Holbeach (0406) 22337

PARKER, William Joseph. b 10. Man Univ BA37. Ridley
Hall Cam 35. **d** 37 **p** 38. R Barnburgh *Sheff* 66-77; rtd
77; Perm to Offic St As & Ban from 78. *23 Victoria
Park, Colwyn Bay, Clwyd* Colwyn Bay (0492) 2057

PARKES, Kevin. b 62. Trent Poly BA84. Sarum & Wells
Th Coll 85. **d** 88 **p** 89. C Wandsworth St Anne *S'wark*
from 88. *28 Aslett Street, London SW18 2BN* 081-874
3813

PARKES, Norman John. b 36. Edin Th Coll 78. **d** 76 **p** 76.
Hon C E Kilbride *Glas* 76-78; C Glas St Marg 78-80; R
from 85; R Challoch w Newton Stewart 80-85. *St
Margaret's Rectory, 22 Monreith Road, Glasgow
G43 2NY* 041-632 3292

PARKES, Robert Stephen. b 12. Selw Coll Cam
BA35 MA40. Linc Th Coll 37. **d** 38 **p** 39. R Pangbourne
Ox 65-77; rtd 78; Perm to Offic *Win* from 78. *22 Arle
Close, Alresford, Hants SO24 9BG* Alresford (0962)
4109

PARKHILL, Alan John. b 43. TCD BA66. CITC 68. **d** 67
p 68. C Knockbreda *D & D* 67-70; Asst Warden Elswick
Lodge Newc 71-72; C Ban St Comgall 73-78; Bp's C
Kilmore 78-82; I Kilmore w Inch 82-86; I Clonfeacle
w Derrygortreavy *Arm* from 86. *4 Clonfeacle Road,
Benburb, Dungannon, Co Tyrone BT71 7LQ* Benburb
(0861) 548239

PARKIN, George David. b 37. Cranmer Hall Dur
BA60 DipTh62. **d** 62 **p** 63. C Balderstone *Man* 62-65; C
Tunstead 65-67; C Gateshead Fell *Dur* 69-73; Nigeria
74-76; V Walton Breck *Liv* from 80. *Holy Trinity
Vicarage, Richmond Park, Liverpool L6 5AD* 051-263
1538

PARKIN, John Edmund. b 44. Open Univ BA73. St Jo
Coll Nottm 83. **d** 85 **p** 86. C Aberavon *Llan* 85-90; R
Eglwysilan from 90. *The Rectory, Brynhafod Road,
Aberitridwr, Caerphilly, M Glam CF8 2BH* Senghenydd
(0222) 830220

PARKIN, John Francis. b 40. Linc Th Coll 65. **d** 68 **p** 69.
C Cullercoats St Geo *Newc* 68-72; C Stony Stratford *Ox*
72-73; TV Lt Coates *Linc* 73-76; Perm to Offic from 88.
The Firs, Louth Road, Horncastle, Lincs Horncastle
(06582) 3208

PARKIN, Trevor Kinross. b 37. Cranmer Hall Dur 63.
d 66 **p** 67. C Kingston upon Hull St Martin *York* 66-69;
C Reading St Jo *Ox* 69-73; Ind Chapl *Lon* 73-80; Hon C
Langham Place All So 73-80; Ind Chapl *Ely* 80-82; V
Maidenhead St Andr and St Mary Magd *Ox* from
82. *St Mary's Vicarage, Maidenhead, Berks SL6 1QJ*
Maidenhead (0628) 24908

PARKINSON, Andrew. b 56. Keble Coll Ox BA77 MA80.
Westcott Ho Cam 78. **d** 80 **p** 81. C S Shore H Trin
Blackb 80-85; V Lea from 85. *St Christopher's Vicarage,
848 Blackpool Road, Lea, Preston PR2 1XL* Preston
(0772) 729716

PARKINSON, Arthur Norman. b 09. TCD BA32. **d** 33
p 34. I Acton w Drumbanagher *Arm* 63-75; Prec Arm
Cathl 73-75; rtd 75. *34 Old Rectory Park, Portadown,
Craigavon, Co Armagh BT62 3QH* Portadown (0762)
336491

PARKINSON, Miss Brenda. b 40. Lancs Poly CQSW.
Dalton Ho Bris 65. **dss** 74 **d** 87. Ribbleton *Blackb* 75-80;
Ingol 82-87; Par Dn 87-88; Par Dn Ashton-on-Ribble
St Mich from 88. *18 The Cloisters, Ashton-on-Ribble,
Preston PR2 2PY* Preston (0772) 735314

PARKINSON, David Thomas. b 42. Linc Th Coll 77. **d** 79
p 80. C Yate New Town *Bris* 79-82; TV Keynsham
B & W 82-88; R Bleadon from 88. *The Rectory,
Coronation Road, Bleadon, Weston-super-Mare, Avon
BS24 0PG* Bleadon (0934) 812297

PARKINSON, Derek Leslie. b 29. Ripon Hall Ox 64. **d** 66
p 67. C Guildf Ch Ch *Guildf* 66-69; P-in-c Preston St
Sav *Blackb* 69-74; P-in-c Preston St Jas 69-74; P-in-c
Fontmell Magna *Sarum* 74-81; P-in-c Ashmore 74-81;
P-in-c Kingswood w Alderley and Hillesley *Glouc* 81-82;
R from 82. *The Rectory, Kingswood, Wotton-under-
Edge, Glos GL12 8RS* Dursley (0453) 843361

PARKINSON, Edward James. b 19. TCD BA50 MA54.
d 51 **p** 52. C Belf St Mary *Conn* 51-53; C Lanc St Mary
Blackb 53-55; CF (TA) from 54; R Limehouse St Anne
Lon 55-60; V Hampton St Mary 60-69; Lic to Offic
Newc 74-80; Master of the Charterhouse Hull from 80;
AD Cen & N Hull Deanery *York* 87-89. *The
Charterhouse, Charterhouse Lane, Hull HU2 8AF* Hull
(0482) 29307

PARKINSON, Francis Wilson. b 37. Lon Univ DipTh63
Open Univ BA80. St Aid Birkenhead 59. **d** 62 **p** 63. C
Monkwearmouth St Andr *Dur* 62-64; C Speke All SS
Liv 64-67; CF from 67. *c/o MOD (Army), Bagshot
Park, Bagshot, Surrey GU19 5PL* Bagshot (0276) 71717

PARKINSON, George Stanley. b 20. St Jo Coll Dur
BA47 DipTh48. **d** 48 **p** 49. V Pennington *Man* 58-71; V
Eccles St Mary 71-80; V Churt *Guildf* 80-90; RD
Farnham 82-88; rtd 90. *12 Bevere Court, Bevere,
Worcester WR3 7RE* Worcester (0905) 57106

PARKINSON, Ian Richard. b 58. Univ Coll Dur BA79 Lon
Univ BD84. Wycliffe Hall Ox 80. **d** 83 **p** 84. C Hull
Newland St Jo *York* 83-86; C Linthorpe from 86.
23 Linden Grove, Middlesbrough, Cleveland TS5 5NF
Middlesbrough (0642) 815961

PARKINSON, Preb John Fearnley. b 30. MBE90.
ALCD54. **d** 55 **p** 56. C Plymouth St Andr *Ex* 55-59;
Metrop Sec USCL 59-62; Relig Adv Westward TV 62-81;
V Devonport St Budeaux 62-66; CF (TA) 63-77; V
Kenton *Ex* 66-75; R Kenton w Mamhead 75-79; R
Kenton w Mamhead and Powderham 79-83; Preb Ex
Cathl from 75; Relig Adv SW TV 82-83; Provost St
Chris Cathl Bahrain 83-89; CMS from 90; Hon Chapl
Br Emb Israel from 90. *c/o The British Embassy,
192 Hayarkon Street, Tel Aviv, Israel* Tel Aviv (3)
524-9171

PARKINSON, John Reginald. b 32. Qu Coll Birm 79. **d** 81
p 82. NSM Catshill *Worc* 81-85; C Knightwick w
Doddenham, Broadwas and Cotheridge 85-88; C Martley
and Wichenford 85-88; P-in-c Berrow w Pendock and
Eldersfield 88-89; R Berrow w Pendock, Eldersfield,
Hollybush etc from 89. *The Vicarage, Berrow, Malvern,
Worcs WR13 6JN* Birtsmorton (068481) 237

PARKINSON, Joseph Greenwood. b 10. Tyndale Hall Bris
30. **d** 34 **p** 36. V Onecote cum Bradnop *Lich* 58-75; rtd
75. *18 Alder Road, Market Drayton, Shropshire TF9 3HZ*
Market Drayton (0630) 653032

PARKINSON, Peter. b 23. Roch Th Coll 61. **d** 63 **p** 64. V
Newton-on-Trent *Linc* 68-73; R Kettlethorpe 68-73; V
Grainthorpe w Conisholme 74-83; V Marshchapel 74-83;
R N Coates 74-83; V Bicker 83-88; rtd 88. *11 Waltham*

Road, Doddington, Lincoln LN6 0SD   Lincoln (0522) 680604

PARKINSON, Raymond Neville. b 21. Bris Univ BA53. Tyndale Hall Bris 50. **d** 54 **p** 55. V Ashby-de-la-Zouch H Trin *Leic* 69-79; V Swannington St Geo and Coleorton 79-87; rtd 87; Perm to Offic *Leic* from 87; Linc from 88. *45 Kipling Drive, Mablethorpe, Lincs LN12 2RF* Sutton-on-Sea (0507) 441140

PARKINSON, Simon George Denis. b 39. Univ of Wales (Lamp) BA66. Westcott Ho Cam 65. **d** 67 **p** 68. C Rothwell *Ripon* 67-70; Chapl RAF 70-73; C Leeds St Pet *Ripon* 74-75; V Horbury Junction *Wakef* 76-83; V Hanging Heaton from 83. *The Vicarage, Hanging Heaton, Batley, W Yorkshire WF17 6DW* Dewsbury (0924) 461917

PARKINSON, Thomas Alan. b 40. St Jo Coll York CertEd61 DipTh62. NW Ord Course 75. **d** 78 **p** 79. NSM Shett Parson Cross St Cecilia *Sheff* 78-82; NSM Goldthorpe w Hickleton 82-90; C 90; C Cantley from 90. *10 Manse Close, Cantley, Doncaster, S Yorkshire DN4 6QX* Doncaster (0302) 539783

PARLETT, Gordon Alec. b 14. Oak Hill Th Coll 46. **d** 49 **p** 50. R Buckland in Dover *Cant* 56-72; Hon Chapl Miss to Seamen 58-72; Chapl Buckland Hosp Dover 59-72; V Loose *Cant* 72-87; rtd 87; Perm to Offic Chich & Cant from 89. *St Giles's Parsonage, Bodiam, Robertsbridge, E Sussex TN32 5UJ* Staplecross (0580) 830793

PARNELL-HOPKINSON, Clive. b 46. Sarum & Wells Th Coll 75. **d** 78 **p** 79. C Maldon All SS w St Pet *Chelmsf* 78-81; C Chandler's Ford *Win* 81-84; Chapl RAF from 84. *c/o MOD, Adastral House, Theobald's Road, London WC1X 8RU* 071-430 7268

PARR, Frank. b 35. Nottm Univ BCombStuds82 Lanc Univ MA86. Linc Th Coll 79. **d** 82 **p** 83. C Padiham *Blackb* 82-85; P-in-c Accrington St Andr 85-88; V Oswaldtwistle Immanuel and All SS from 88. *Immanuel Vicarage, New Lane, Oswaldtwistle, Accrington, Lancs BB5 3QN* Accrington (0254) 233962

PARR, George. b 12. MC45. St Jo Coll Dur BA37. **d** 38 **p** 39. V Ripon H Trin *Ripon* 59-78; rtd 78. *Pollensa, 22 South Grange Road, Ripon, N Yorkshire HG4 2NH* Ripon (0765) 4163

PARR, Canon James Edwin Cecil. b 20. TCD BA42 MA47. **d** 43 **p** 44. I Cloughfern *Conn* 59-82; Can Conn Cathl 80-82; rtd 82. *26B Feumore Road, Ballinderry Upper, Lisburn* Aghalee (0846) 651851

PARR, Dr John. b 53. St Edm Hall Ox BA74 MA87 Lon Univ BD79 Sheff Univ PhD90. Trin Coll Bris 75. **d** 79 **p** 80. C Gt Crosby St Luke *Liv* 79-82; C Walton St Mary 82-84; V Ince St Mary 84-87; Tutor and Lect Ridley Hall Cam from 87. *Dashwood House, Ridley Hall, Cambridge CB3 9HG* Cambridge (0223) 65984

PARR, William George Hossack Redmond. b 08. Kelham Th Coll 24. **d** 31 **p** 32. R Frenchay *Bris* 62-73; rtd 73; Perm to Offic *Cant* from 73. *8 Dean Close, Weston-super-Mare, Avon BS22 0YN* Weston-super-Mare (0934) 515069

PARRATT, Dennis. b 53. St Steph Ho Ox. **d** 84 **p** 85. C Cainscross w Selsley *Glouc* 84-88; C Old Shoreham *Chich* 88-91; C New Shoreham 88-91. *17 Colvill Avenue, Shoreham-by-Sea, W Sussex BN43 5WN* Shoreham-by-Sea (0273) 464528

PARRETT, Mrs Rosalind Virginia. b 43. Cant Sch of Min 84. **d** 87. NSM Selling w Throwley, Sheldwich w Badlesmere etc *Cant* 87-91; Asst Chapl Cant Hosp 87-91; Par Dn Stantonbury and Willen *Ox* from 91. *1 Stable Yard, Downs Barn, Milton Keynes MK14 7RS* Milton Keynes (0908) 663346

PARRETT, Simon Christopher. b 60. Sarum & Wells Th Coll. **d** 87 **p** 88. C Ifield *Chich* from 87. *1 Francis Edwards Way, Crawley, W Sussex RH11 8GG* Faygate (0293) 851758

PARRETT, Stanley Frederick Donald. b 24. **d** 78 **p** 79. NSM Whitchurch w Ganarew *Heref* 78-83; C Goodrich w Welsh Bicknor and Marstow 83-86; C Walford w Bishopswood 83-86; R Pembridge w Moorcourt, Shobdon, Staunton etc 86-89; rtd 89. *4 Manley Lane, Pembridge, Leominster, Herefordshire HR6 9EE*

PARRISH, Robert Carey. b 57. St Steph Ho Ox 89. **d** 91. C Abington *Pet* from 91. *21 Lime Avenue, Northampton NN3 2HA* Northampton (0604) 711264

PARROTT, David Wesley. b 58. Oak Hill Th Coll BA. **d** 84 **p** 85. C Thundersley *Chelmsf* 84-87; C Rainham 87-89; P-in-c Heydon w Gt and Lt Chishill 89-90; P-in-c Elmdon w Wendon Lofts and Strethall 89-90; P-in-c Chrishall 89-90; R Heydon, Gt and Lt Chishill, Chrishall etc from 91. *1 Hall Lane, Great Chishill, Royston, Herts SG8 8SG* Royston (0763) 838703

PARROTT, George. b 37. Leeds Univ BA61. Bps' Coll Cheshunt 61. **d** 63 **p** 64. C Lower Mitton *Worc* 63-65; C-in-c Fairfield St Rich CD 65-68; Zambia 68-70; C Cleethorpes *Linc* 70-75; R Withern 75-80; P-in-c Gayton le Marsh 76-80; P-in-c Strubby 76-80; P-in-c Authorpe w Tothill 76-80; P-in-c Belleau w Aby and Claythorpe 76-80; P-in-c N and S Reston w Castle Carlton 76-80; P-in-c Swaby w S Thoresby 76-80; R Withern 80-90; V Reston 80-90; V Messingham from 90. *The Vicarage, Messingham, Scunthorpe, S Humberside DN17 3SG* Scunthorpe (0724) 762823

PARROTT, Canon Gerald Arthur. b 32. St Cath Coll Cam BA56 MA60. Chich Th Coll. **d** 58 **p** 59. C Ashington *Newc* 58-61; C Brighton St Pet *Chich* 61-63; V Leeds St Wilfrid *Ripon* 63-68; R Lewisham St Jo Southend *S'wark* 69-73; TR Catford (Southend) and Downham 73-77; RD E Lewisham 75-77; Can Res and Prec S'wark Cathl 77-88, TR Wimbledon from 88. *Wimbledon Rectory, 14 Arthur Road, London SW19 7DZ* 081-946 2830

PARROTT, Martin William. b 57. Keele Univ BA79 Lon Univ PGCE80. Ripon Coll Cuddesdon 82. **d** 85 **p** 86. C Birchfield *Birm* 85-88; Chapl Lon Univ *Lon* from 88; P-in-c Univ Ch Ch the King Lon from 90. *11 Ormonde Mansions, 106 Southampton Row, London WC1B 4BP* 071-242 7533

PARRY, Albert Evans. b 09. Univ of Wales BA32. St Mich Coll Llan 32. **d** 33 **p** 34. R Briton Ferry *Llan* 42-76; rtd 76. *Ashgrove Bungalow, Llantwit Major, S Glam CF6 9SS* Llantwit Major (0446) 792644

PARRY, Canon Bryan Horace. b 33. St Mich Coll Llan 65. **d** 67 **p** 68. C Holyhead w Rhoscolyn w Llanfair-yn-Neubwll *Ban* 67-71; TV 71-73; P-in-c Small Heath St Greg *Birm* 73-78; V 78-80; V Perry Barr from 80; RD Handsworth from 83; P-in-c Kingstanding St Luke from 86; Hon Can Birm Cathl from 87. *St John's Vicarage, Church Road, Birmingham B42 2LB* 021-356 7998

PARRY, Brychan Vaughan. b 13. Univ of Wales DipTh37. St Andr Coll Pampisford 41. **d** 42 **p** 42. V Gt Barton *St E* 69-78; rtd 78. *64 Cuckmere Road, Seaford, E Sussex BN25 4DJ* Seaford (0323) 898273

PARRY, Christopher Hugh Foster. b 61. Univ of Wales (Ban) BTh82. Linc Th Coll 83. **d** 85 **p** 86. C Llandegfan and Beaumaris w Llanfaes w Penmon etc *Ban* 85-88; R Llanbedrog w Llannor w Llanfihangel etc from 88. *Ty'n Llan, Llanbedrog, Pwllheli, Gwynedd LL53 7TU* Pwllheli (0758) 740919

PARRY, David Thomas Newton. b 45. Selw Coll Cam BA67 MA71. Lambeth STh76 Cuddesdon Coll 67. **d** 69 **p** 70. C Oldham St Mary w St Pet *Man* 69-73; C Baguley 73-74; Tutor Sarum & Wells Th Coll 74-78; V Westleigh St Pet *Man* 78-88; TR E Farnworth and Kearsley from 88. *The Rectory, Church Street, Farnworth, Bolton BL4 8AQ* Farnworth (0204) 72819

PARRY, Denis. b 34. Sarum & Wells Th Coll 83. **d** 85 **p** 86. C Hubberston w Herbrandston and Hasguard etc *St D* 85-89; P-in-c Herbrandston and Hasguard w St Ishmael's 89-90; R from 90. *The Rectory, Herbrandston, Milford Haven, Dyfed SA73 3SJ* Milford Haven (0646) 693263

PARRY, Canon Dennis John. b 38. Univ of Wales (Lamp) BA60. St Mich Coll Llan 60. **d** 62 **p** 63. C Caerphilly *Llan* 62-64; C Aberdare St Fagan 64-67; Canada 67-69; R Gellygaer *Llan* 69-75; V Llanwnnog and Caersws w Carno *Ban* 75-89; V Llanidloes w Llangurig from 89; Hon Can Ban Cathl from 90. *The Vicarage, Llanidloes, Powys SY18 6HZ* Llanidloes (05512) 2370

PARRY, Derek Nugent Goulding. b 32. Ely Th Coll 60. **d** 63 **p** 64. C Fareham SS Pet and Paul *Portsm* 63-67; C Portsea N End St Mark 67-74; P-in-c Piddletrenthide w Plush, Alton Pancras etc *Sarum* from 74. *The Vicarage, Piddletrenthide, Dorchester, Dorset DT2 7QX* Piddletrenthide (03004) 300

PARRY, Eric Gordon. b 1900. Univ Coll Ox BA22 MA26. Ridley Hall Cam 22. **d** 23 **p** 24. V Sharow *Ripon* 58-70; RD Ripon 62-70; rtd 70. *Abbeyfield House, Church Lane, Ripon, N Yorkshire HG4 2ES* Ripon (0765) 5644

PARRY, John Idris. b 16. St D Coll Lamp BA37. **d** 52 **p** 53. Warden CMS Fellowship Ho Foxbury 68-74; V Langton Green *Roch* 74-81; rtd 81. *Abbeyfield House, 39 East Parade, Rhyl, Clwyd LL18 3AN* Rhyl (0745) 332890

PARRY, John Seth. b 22. Tyndale Hall Bris 40 and 47. **d** 48 **p** 49. V Chaddesden St Mary *Derby* 60-76; V Ravenhead *Liv* 76-87; rtd 87. *22 Thingwall Lane, Liverpool L14 7NX* 051-228 6832

PARRY, Keith Melville. b 31. ARICS65 Lon Univ DipRS83. S'wark Ord Course 80. **d** 83 **p** 84. NSM Bexley St Jo *Roch* 83-88; C Orpington All SS from 88. *12 Mosyer*

Drive, Orpington, Kent BR5 4PW   Orpington (0689) 38599

PARRY, Canon Kenneth Charles. b 34. Ripon Hall Ox 56. **d** 58 **p** 59. C Stoke *Cov* 58-61; Chapl RN 61-65; V Cradley *Worc* 65-70; V Gt Malvern H Trin 70-83; RD Malvern 74-83; Hon Can Worc Cathl 80-83; V Budleigh Salterton *Ex* 83-91; Can Res Ex Cathl from 91. *6 The Close, Exeter, Devon EX1 1EZ*   Exeter (0392) 72498

PARRY, Marilyn Marie. b 46. W Coll Ohio BA68 Man Univ MA77. Episc Th Sch Cam Mass BA68 Gilmore Ho 76. **dss** 79 **d** 87. Westleigh St Pet *Man* 79-85; Chapl Asst N Man Gen Hosp 85-90; Tutor N Ord Course from 90. *The Rectory, Church Street, Farnworth, Bolton BL4 8AQ*   Farnworth (0204) 72819

PARRY, Nicholas John Sinclair. b 56. Sarum & Wells Th Coll 82. **d** 85 **p** 86. C Hendon St Mary *Lon* 85-87; C Verwood *Sarum* 87-90; TV Witney *Ox* from 90. *The Vicarage, 17 Chestnut Avenue, Witney, Oxon OX8 6PD*   Witney (0993) 705061

PARRY, Richard Nigel. b 56. Univ of Wales (Cardiff) BD86. St Mich Coll Llan 82. **d** 86 **p** 87. C Holywell *St As* 86-89; V Berse and Southsea from 89. *The Vicarage, Smithy Lane, Southsea, Wrexham LL11 6PN*   Wrexham (0978) 750150

PARRY, Miss Violet Margaret. b 30. Selly Oak Coll 53. **dss** 82 **d** 87. W Kilburn St Luke w St Simon and St Jude *Lon* 82-83; St Marylebone St Mary 83-86; Stamford All SS w St Jo *Linc* 86-87; C 87-90; Perm to Offic *Linc* from 90. *4 Torkington Gardens, Stamford, Lincs PE9 2EW*   Stamford (0780) 52831

PARRY, William. b 10. St D Coll Lamp BA35. **d** 40 **p** 41. Chapl Exe Vale Hosp Gp 63-75; rtd 75; Lic to Offic *Ban* from 76. *24 Tyddyn Isaf, Menai Bridge, Gwynedd*   Menai Bridge (0248) 715960

PARRY, William Daniel. b 09. St Chad's Coll Dur BA31 DipTh32 MA34. **d** 32 **p** 33. V Llandinam 48-72; V Llandinam w Trefeglwys w Penstrowed *Ban* 72-78; RD Arwystli 53-73; Can Ban Cathl from 60; Chan 70-78; rtd 78. *14 Cae Mawr, Penrhyncoch, Aberystwyth, Dyfed SY23 3EJ*   Aberystwyth (0970) 828118

PARRY CHIVERS, Stanley. b 06. St Paul's Coll Burgh 25. **d** 29 **p** 30. V Brondesbury St Laur *Lon* 47-71; rtd 71; Perm to Offic *Ex* 71-73 and from 74; P-in-c Barnstaple St Mary 73-74. *The Grange Retirement Home, Aylesbury Road, Wendover, Bucks HP22 6JQ*   Wendover (0296) 622646

PARRY-JENNINGS, Christopher William. b 34. Lon Coll of Div 57. **d** 60 **p** 62. C Claughton cum Grange *Ches* 60-63; C Folkestone H Trin w Ch Ch *Cant* 63-67; New Zealand from 67. *39 Major Hornbrook Road, Mount Pleasant, Christchurch, New Zealand*   Christchurch (3) 3841-253

PARRY JONES, Leonard. b 29. Univ of Wales (Ban) BA52. St Mich Coll Llan 52. **d** 54 **p** 55. C Newtown w Llanllwchaiarn w Aberhafesp *St As* 54-58; C Abergele 58-60; V Pennant, Hirnant and Llangynog 60-65; V Llanynys w Llanychan 65-71; V Brynymaen w Trofarth from 71; RD Rhos from 77. *The Vicarage, Brynymaen, Colwyn Bay, Clwyd LL28 5EW*   Colwyn Bay (0492) 532567

PARSELLE, Stephen Paul. b 53. LTh. St Jo Coll Nottm. **d** 82 **p** 83. C Boscombe St Jo *Win* 82-86; CF from 86. *c/o MOD (Army), Bagshot Park, Bagshot, Surrey GU19 5PL*   Bagshot (0276) 71717

PARSLOW, Ven John Henry. b 18. MBE74. Qu Coll Birm 47. **d** 50 **p** 51. V Worc H Trin *Worc* 58-60; Nyasaland 60-64; Malawi from 64; rtd 84. *PO Box 30642, Chichiri, Blantyre 3, Malawi*   Malawi (265) 640489

PARSONAGE, Robert Leslie. b 20. St Aid Birkenhead 43. **d** 46 **p** 47. CF 52-74; V Bayswater *Lon* 74-83; rtd 83; Perm to Offic *Lon* 83-88; Preacher Newland Almshouses Glos from 88; Lic to Offic *Glouc* from 88. *The Lecturer's House, 11 Almshouse Road, Newland, Coleford, Glos GL16 8NL*   Dean (0594) 32441

PARSONS, Andrew David. b 53. UEA BA74 Fitzw Coll Cam BA77 MA81. Westcott Ho Cam 75. **d** 78 **p** 79. C Hellesdon *Nor* 78-82; C Eaton 82-85; P-in-c Burnham Thorpe w Burnham Overy 85-87; R Burnham Sutton w Burnham Ulph etc 85-87; R Burnham Gp of Par from 87. *The Rectory, Church Walk, Burnham Market, King's Lynn, Norfolk PE31 8UL*   Fakenham (0328) 738317

PARSONS, Arthur. b 45. St Jo Coll Nottm LTh. **d** 75 **p** 76. C Cuddington *Guildf* 75-78; C Liskeard w St Keyne and St Pinnock *Truro* 78-81; P-in-c Ludgvan 81-83; R from 83; Chapl Falmouth Fire Brigade from 91. *The Rectory, Ludgvan, Penzance, Cornwall TR20 8EZ*   Penzance (0736) 740784

PARSONS, Arthur Gordon Boyd. b 20. TD50. SSC MIPM50 MRCO83 BA. Ripon Hall Ox 54. **d** 56 **p** 57.

OCF RAF 65-73; V Friskney *Linc* 69-73; R Tansor w Cotterstock and Fotheringhay *Pet* 74-76; V Forest Town *S'well* 76-78; V Sutton cum Lound 78-85; rtd 85; Hon C Holsworthy w Hollacombe and Milton Damerel *Ex* 87-88; Hon C Bude Haven *Truro* 88-89; Hon C Bude Haven and Marhamchurch from 89. *15 Seawell Road, Bude, Cornwall EX23 8PD*   Bude (0288) 354022

PARSONS, Bernard. b 26. Ely Th Coll 60. **d** 62 **p** 63. C Bourne *Linc* 62-64; V W Pinchbeck 64-71; V Sutton Bridge 71-83; R Coningsby w Tattershall from 83. *The Rectory, Coningsby, Lincoln LN4 4RA*   Coningsby (0526) 42223

PARSONS, Christopher James Hutton. b 54. Univ of Wales (Ban) BA75 Birm Univ DipTh78. Qu Coll Birm. **d** 79 **p** 80. C Crowthorne *Ox* 79-83; V Tilehurst St Cath 83-88; P-in-c Wrentham w Benacre, Covehithe, Frostenden etc *St E* 89-91; R from 91. *The Rectory, Wrentham, Beccles, Suffolk NR34 7LX*   Wrentham (050275) 208

PARSONS, David. b 37. Qu Coll Cam BA61. Ridley Hall Cam. **d** 62 **p** 63. C Ormskirk *Liv* 62-65; C Beccles St Mich *St E* 65-68; V Woodbridge St Jo 68-73; Chapl Edgarley Hall Sch Glastonbury 73-78; Asst Master Bruton Sch for Girls from 78; Chapl Bruton Sch for Girls from 86. *13 Ivythorn Road, Street, Somerset BA16 0TE*   Street (0458) 46110

PARSONS, Derek Adrian. b 27. Clare Coll Cam BA49 MA52. Ridley Hall Cam 51. **d** 53 **p** 54. CF (TA) 55-82; Chapl K Edw Sch Witley 62-75; P-in-c Alfold *Guildf* 75-78; Perm to Offic from 78; rtd 88. *3 Rodney Way, Guildford, Surrey GU1 2NY*   Guildford (0483) 61874

PARSONS, Desmond John. b 25. Coll of Resurr Mirfield 65. **d** 66 **p** 67. C Purley St Mark Woodcote *S'wark* 66-70; V W Dulwich All SS and Em 71-83; R Limpsfield and Titsey from 83. *The Rectory, Limpsfield, Oxted, Surrey RH8 0DG*   Oxted (0883) 712512

PARSONS, Ernest Francis. b 15. Wells Th Coll. **d** 66 **p** 67. C Highworth w Sevenhampton and Inglesham etc *Bris* 67-70; V Sparkbrook Em *Birm* 71-86; rtd 86; Perm to Offic *Birm* from 86. *50 Delrene Road, Shirley, Solihull, W Midlands B90 2HJ*   021-745 7339

PARSONS, Geoffrey Fairbanks. b 35. Trin Coll Cam BA58 MA68. Ridley Hall Cam 59. **d** 61 **p** 62. C Over St Chad *Ches* 61-64; C Heswall 64-69; V Congleton St Steph 69-75; V Weaverham from 75. *The Vicarage, Weaverham, Northwich, Cheshire CW8 3NJ*   Weaverham (0606) 852110

PARSONS, George Edward. b 35. St D Coll Lamp BA60 Ripon Hall Ox 60. **d** 62 **p** 63. C Leominster *Heref* 62-66; C Bromfield 67-70; C Culmington w Onibury 67-70; C Stanton Lacy 67-70; Perm to Offic Heref 71-73; Glouc 79-82; Lic to Offic 73-77; C Caynham 78-79; Hon C Bishop's Cleeve *Glouc* from 82; Sub-Chapl HM Pris Glouc from 88. *116 Linden Avenue, Prestbury, Cheltenham, Glos GL52 3DS*   Cheltenham (0242) 242464

PARSONS, George Horace Norman. b 19. S'wark Ord Course 65. **d** 68 **p** 69. C Hatcham St Cath *S'wark* 68-72; C Horley 72-76; P-in-c S Wimbledon All SS 76-78; P-in-c Caterham 78-81; C 82-84; Chapl St Lawr Hosp Caterham 82-84; rtd 85. *8 Russell Road, Mitcham, Surrey CR4 2YS*   081-646 4386

PARSONS, Gilbert Harvey. b 20. St Pet Hall Ox BA46 MA46. Cuddesdon Coll 48. **d** 50 **p** 51. V Stokenchurch and Cadmore End *Ox* 61-72; P-in-c Ibstone w Fingest 65-72; RD Aston 66-72; V Burford w Fulbrook 72-74; V Burford w Fulbrook and Taynton 74-85; rtd 85. *Windrush, 23 Highlands Way, Whiteparish, Salisbury SP5 2SZ*   Whiteparish (0794) 884832

PARSONS, John Banham. b 43. Selw Coll Cam BA65 MA68. Ridley Hall Cam 65. **d** 67 **p** 68. C Downend *Bris* 67-71; Public Preacher Withywood LEP 71-77; P-in-c Hengrove 77-78; V 78-85; V Letchworth St Paul w Willian *St Alb* from 85. *St Paul's Vicarage, 177 Pixmore Way, Letchworth, Herts SG6 1QT*   Letchworth (0462) 683083

PARSONS, John Christopher. b 27. Keble Coll Ox BA52 MA56 CQSW77. St Steph Ho Ox 52. **d** 54 **p** 55. C Chingford SS Pet and Paul *Chelmsf* 54-57; Chapl RN 57-59; R Ingham w Sutton *Nor* 59-65; C Lowestoft St Marg 66-69; Lic to Offic Chelmsf 69-71; Truro 71-74; Chapl RADD Essex Area 69-71; Chapl to the Deaf 71-85; Perm to Offic *Ex* 73-74; P-in-c Godolphin *Truro* 74-80; P-in-c St Enoder from 80. *St Enoder Rectory, Churchtown, Summercourt, Newquay, Cornwall TR8 5DF*   St Austell (0726) 860724 or 74242

PARSONS, Laurie. b 19. Keble Coll Ox BA41. Wells Th Coll 41. **d** 43 **p** 44. V Radford Semele *Cov* 70-83; V

Radford Semele and Ufton 83-84; rtd 84; Perm to Offic Cov and Pet from 84. *86 Bull Baulk, Middleton Cheney, Banbury, Oxon OX17 2SR* Banbury (0295) 711829

PARSONS, Mrs Margaret Anne. b 31. Sheff Poly CQSW77. E Midl Min Tr Course 73. **dss** 77 **d** 87. Dronfield *Derby* 77-87; Par Dn 87-89; Par Dn Tidworth, Ludgershall and Faberstown *Sarum* from 89. *The Rectory, St George's Road, Tidworth, Hants SP9 7EW* Stonehenge (0980) 43889

PARSONS, Canon Marlene Beatrice. b 43. Wilson Carlile Coll. **dss** 76 **d** 87. Coulsdon St Jo *S'wark* 76-79; Hill *Birm* 79-86; Dioc Lay Min Adv 80-90; Vice Prin W Midl Minl Tr Course 86-90; Hon Can Birm Cathl from 89; Dioc Dir of Ords from 90; Dean of Women from 90. *257 Gillott Road, Birmingham B16 0RX* 021-454 3974

PARSONS, Martin. b 07. Qu Coll Cam BA28 MA32. Lon Coll of Div 29. **d** 30 **p** 31. Ext Sec CMJ 69-72; rtd 72. *61 Elm Tree Road, Locking, Weston-super-Mare, Avon BS24 8EL* Banwell (0934) 822090

PARSONS, Miss Mary Elizabeth. b 43. Wilson Carlile Coll 65. **dss** 78 **d** 87. Chapl Asst Chu Hosp Ox 78-89; Chapl from 89. *21 Woodlands Road, Oxford OX3 7RU* Oxford (0865) 63909 or 741841

PARSONS, Dr Michael William Semper. b 47. St Cath Coll Ox BA69 MA74 DPhil74 Selw Coll Cam BA77 MA81. Ridley Hall Cam 75. **d** 78 **p** 79. C Edmonton All SS *Lon* 78-81; Lic to Offic *Dur* 81-85; P-in-c Derby St Aug *Derby* from 85; Voc Adv from 87. *St Augustine's Vicarage, 155 Almond Street, Derby DE3 6LY* Derby (0332) 766603

PARSONS, Richard Edgar. b 46. K Coll Lon BD69 AKC69 MTh70 MPhil84. **d** 71 **p** 72. C Doncaster Intake *Sheff* 71-73; Hon C Blackheath All SS *S'wark* 73-84; Lect CA Tr Coll Blackheath 73-79; Selection Sec ACCM 79-84; V Hendon St Mary *Lon* from 84; V Hendon Ch Ch from 84; Dir of Ords from 85. *The Vicarage, Parson Street, London NW4 1QR* 081-203 2884

PARSONS, Robert Arthur Frederick. b 15. St Deiniol's Hawarden 56. **d** 57 **p** 58. R Whitton w Pilleth *S & B* 64-79; V Whitton and Pilleth and Cascob etc 79-85; rtd 85; P-in-c Llanfihangel Talyllyn w Llanywern and Llangasty *S & B* from 86. *The Vicarage, Swn-y-Cwm, Llanfihangel Talyllyn, Brecon, Powys LD3 7TG* Brecon (0874) 84374

PARSONS, Robert Martin. b 43. Qu Coll Cam BA65 MA69. ALCD68. **d** 68 **p** 69. C Chapeltown *Sheff* 68-71; C Sheff St Jo 71-75; V Swadlincote *Derby* from 75; RD Repton 81-91; P-in-c Gresley 82-86. *The Vicarage, Church Street, Swadlincote, Burton-on-Trent, Staffs DE11 8LF* Burton-on-Trent (0283) 217756

PARSONS, Roger John. b 37. Sarum Th Coll 62. **d** 65 **p** 66. C Bitterne Park *Win* 65-69; C Clerkenwell H Redeemer w St Phil *Lon* 69-72; C Willesden St Andr 72-76; C St Laurence in Thanet *Cant* 76-81; Chapl Luton and Dunstable Hosp 81-86; St Mary's Hosp Luton 81-86; C Luton All SS w St Pet *St Alb* 81-86; Trustee St Benedict's Trust from 85; TV E Dereham *Nor* 86-88; TV E Dereham and Scarning 89; Perm to Offic from 89. *40 Lawson Way, Sheringham, Norfolk NR26 8BZ* Sheringham (0263) 825849

PARSONS, Stephen Christopher. b 45. Keble Coll Ox BA67 MA72 BLitt78. Cuddesdon Coll 68. **d** 70 **p** 71. C Whitstable All SS *Cant* 70-71; C Croydon St Sav 71-74; Perm to Offic *Ox* 74-76; C St Laurence in Thanet *Cant* 76-79; V Lugwardine w Bartestree and Weston Beggard *Heref* 79-87; V Lechlade *Glouc* from 87. *The Vicarage, Sherbourne Street, Lechlade, Glos GL7 3AH* Faringdon (0367) 52262

PARSONS, Stephen Drury. b 54. Qu Mary Coll Lon BSc76 CCC Cam MSc79. Westcott Ho Cam 79. **d** 82 **p** 83. C Stretford All SS *Man* 82-85; C Newton Heath All SS 85-86; V Ashton St Jas 86-90. *8 Ripponden Street, Oldham OL1 4JG*

PARSONS, Dr Victor. b 29. RD75. FRCP72 BNC Ox MA53 MB, ChB53 DM72. Coll of Resurr Mirfield 90. **d** 91. Hon C Upper Norwood All SS *S'wark* from 91. *15 Glyn Close, London SE25 6DT* 081-653 2182

PARSONS, Wilfrid Herbert. b 09. ALCD36. **d** 36 **p** 37. V Bothenhampton w Walditch *Sarum* 70-76; rtd 76; Perm to Offic *Sarum* from 76. *Westerly, Bowhayes, Bridport, Dorset DT6 4EB* Bridport (0308) 23225

PARSONS, William George. b 20. Em Coll Cam BA47 MA50. Wells Th Coll 49. **d** 51 **p** 52. V Warmley *Bris* 68-71; V Syston 68-71; Lic to Offic 71-76; P-in-c Luckington w Alderton 76-80; C N Stoneham *Win* 80-84; Chapl St Cross Hosp Win 84-87; rtd 85; Perm to Offic *Win* from 86. *c/o J W Parsons Esq, 105 Woolsbridge Road, Ashley Heath, Ringwood, Hants BH24 2LZ* Ringwood (0425) 474829

PARTINGTON, Canon Brian Harold. b 36. St Aid Birkenhead 60. **d** 63 **p** 64. C Barlow Moor *Man* 63-66; C Deane 66-68; V Patrick *S & M* from 68; Bp's Youth Chapl 68-77; RD Peel from 76; P-in-c German St Jo 77-78; V from 78; P-in-c Foxdale 77-78; V from 78; Can St German's Cathl from 85. *The Vicarage, Patrick, Peel, Isle of Man* Peel (0624) 842637

PARTINGTON, Kenneth. b 41. Lanc Univ MA86. Ripon Hall Ox. **d** 70 **p** 71. C Atherton *Man* 70-72; C Kippax *Ripon* 72-75; V Cartmel Fell *Carl* from 75; V Crosthwaite Kendal from 75; V Witherslack from 75; V Winster from 78. *The Vicarage, Crosthwaite, Kendal, Cumbria LA8 8HT* Crosthwaite (04488) 276

PARTINGTON, Peter John. b 57. Peterho Cam MA. St Jo Coll Nottm 79. **d** 81 **p** 82. C Cov H Trin *Cov* 81-85; C Woking St Jo *Guildf* 85-87; R Busbridge from 87. *Busbridge Rectory, Godalming, Surrey GU7 1XA* Godalming (0483) 421267

PARTRIDGE, Anthony John. b 38. Univ of Wales (Lamp) BA61 Linacre Ho Ox BA63 K Coll Lon PhD77. St Steph Ho Ox 61. **d** 64 **p** 65. C Sydenham All SS *S'wark* 64-67; Hon C 68-74; Lic to Offic from 74; Prin Lect Thames Poly from 75. *Thames Polytechnic, Wellington Street, London SE18 6PF* 081-316 8973

PARTRIDGE, Canon David John Fabian. b 36. Ball Coll Ox BA60 MA. Westcott Ho Cam 60. **d** 62 **p** 63. C Halliwell St Thos *Man* 62-65; C St Martin-in-the-Fields *Lon* 65-69; R Warblington and Emsworth *Portsm* from 69; Hon Can Portsm Cathl from 84. *The Rectory, 20 Church Path, Emsworth, Hants PO10 7DP* Emsworth (0243) 2428

PARTRIDGE, Ian Starr. b 36. Linc Th Coll 87. **d** 89 **p** 90. C Barton upon Humber *Linc* from 89. *7 West Grove, Barton-on-Humber, S Humberside DN18 5AG* Barton-on-Humber (0652) 32697

PARTRIDGE, Miss Margaret Edith. b 35. Birm Univ DipTh68. Gilmore Ho 63. **dss** 85 **d** 87. Amblecote *Worc* 85-87; Par Dn 87-89; Par Dn Borehamwood *St Alb* from 89. *35 Winstre Road, Borehamwood, Herts WD6 5DR* 081-207 6603

PARTRIDGE, Martin David Waud. b 38. Ox NSM Course 86. **d** 89 **p** 90. NSM Wargrave *Ox* from 89. *Ellums, Cockpole Green, Wargrave, Reading RG10 8NE* Wargrave (0734) 403849

PARTRIDGE, Michael John. b 61. St Edm Hall Ox BA83 MA89 St Jo Coll Dur BA86. Cranmer Hall Dur 84. **d** 87 **p** 88. C Amington *Birm* 87-90; C Sutton Coldfield H Trin from 90. *1 Trinity Hill, Sutton Coldfield, W Midlands B72 1SH* 021-355 3352

PARTRIDGE, Ronald Malcolm. b 49. Lon Univ DipTh73. Cuddesdon Coll 74. **d** 75 **p** 76. C Bris St Andr Hartcliffe *Bris* 75-78; C E Bris 78-82; V Easton All Hallows 82-85; TV Brighton St Pet w Chpl Royal and St Jo *Chich* 85-86; TV Brighton St Pet and St Nic w Chpl Royal 86-88; C-in-c Bermondsey St Hugh CD *S'wark* 88-90; Asst Chapl Gt Ormond Street Hosp for Sick Children Lon from 91. *c/o Hospital for Sick Children, Great Ormond Street, London WC1N 3JH* 071-405 9200

PARTRIDGE, Canon Timothy Reeve. b 39. Lon Univ BSc60 AKC60. Wells Th Coll 60. **d** 62 **p** 63. C Glouc St Cath *Glouc* 62-65; C Sutton St Nicholas *Linc* 65-74; R Bugbrooke *Pet* from 74; RD Daventry 81-88; Can Pet Cathl from 83. *The Rectory, Bugbrooke, Northampton NN7 3PB* Northampton (0604) 830373

✠**PARTRIDGE, Rt Rev William Arthur.** b 12. Birm Univ BA33. Linc Th Coll 33. **d** 35 **p** 36 **c** 53. C The Lye *Worc* 35-38; India 39-63; Chapl RAFVR 43-46; Asst Bp Calcutta 53-63; V Ludford *Heref* 63-69; Preb Heref Cathl 63-77; Asst Bp Heref 63-75; rtd 76. *Flat 3, Capel Court, The Burgage, Prestbury, Cheltenham, Glos GL52 3EL* Cheltenham (0242) 576505

PASCHAL, Brother. *See* WORTON, David Reginald

PASCOE, Harold John. b 42. St D Coll Lamp BA65 DipTh67. **d** 67 **p** 68. C Upper Gornal *Lich* 67-70; C Walsall St Gabr Fullbrook 70-73; V Walsall St Andr 73-80; V Donnington Wood from 80. *The Vicarage, St George's Road, Donnington Wood, Telford, Shropshire TF2 7NJ* Telford (0952) 604239

PASKETT, Ms Margaret Anne. b 45. York Univ BSc81 Leeds Univ MEd83. NE Ord Course 84. **d** 87. Par Dn Marske in Cleveland *York* from 87. *5 Howard Drive, Marske-by-the-Sea, Redcar, Cleveland TS11 7JE* Redcar (0642) 474528

PASKINS, David James. b 52. Univ of Wales (Lamp) BA73 Trin Hall Cam BA76 MA81. Westcott Ho Cam 74. **d** 77 **p** 78. C St Peter-in-Thanet *Cant* 77-80; C Swanage *Sarum* 80-82; R Waldron *Chich* from 82. *The Rectory, Sheepsetting Lane, Waldron, Heathfield, E Sussex TN21 0UY* Heathfield (04352) 2816

PASLEY, Canon Charles Victor. b 19. d 58 p 59. I Skreen w Kilmacshalgan and Dromard *T, K & A* 61-87; RD Straid 66-87; Dom Chapl to Bp of Tuam 69-87; Can Achonry Cathl 75-87; rtd 87. *51 Beaumont Avenue, Churchtown, Dublin 14, Irish Republic*   Dublin (1) 988903

PASLEY, James. b 16. d 61 p 62. I Athy w Kilberry *D & G* 70-88; I Athy w Kilberry, Fontstown and Kilkea 88-91; rtd 91. *4 La Verna, Fort Road, Gorey, Co Wexford, Irish Republic*   Gorey (55) 22238

PASSANT, Keith. b 39. St Jo Coll Dur BA62 CertEd70. St Alb Minl Tr Scheme 77. d 87 p 88. C Hatf Hyde St Mary *St Alb* from 87. *Church House, Hollybush Lane, Welwyn Garden City, Herts AL7 4JS*   Welwyn Garden (0707) 323214

PASSINGHAM, Eric Albert. b 27. Wells Th Coll 69. d 70 p 71. C Chatham St Steph *Roch* 70-74; C Crawley *Chich* 74-79; TV 79-86; P-in-c Rusper from 86. *The Rectory, High Street, Rusper, Horsham, W Sussex RH12 4PX*   Rusper (0293) 871251

PASTERFIELD, Canon Dunstan Patrick. b 17. Clare Coll Cam BA49 MA53. Cuddesdon Coll 49. d 51 p 51. C Dennington *St E* 51-53; Canada from 53; Hon Can Calgary from 78. *Box 212, Arcola, Saskatchewan, Canada, S0C 0G0*   Saskatchewan (306) 455-2785

✠**PASTERFIELD, Rt Rev Philip John.** b 20. Trin Hall Cam BA49 MA53. Cuddesdon Coll 49. d 51 p 52 c 74. C Streatham St Leon *S'wark* 51-54; Chapl K Edw VII Hosp Midhurst 54-60; V W Lavington *Chich* 54-60; R Woolbeding 55-60; V Oxton *Ches* 60-68; RD Birkenhead 66-68; Can Res St Alb 68-74; RD St Alb 71-74; Suff Bp Crediton *Ex* 74-84; rtd 84; Asst Bp Ex from 84. *2 Brixton Court, Brixton, Plymouth PL8 2AH*   Plymouth (0752) 880817

PATCHING, Colin John. b 47. Linc Th Coll 84. d 86 p 87. C Farnley *Ripon* 86-89; C Didcot St Pet *Ox* from 89. *25 Sovereign Close, Didcot, Oxon OX11 8TR*   Didcot (0235) 819949

PATE, Barry Emile Charles. b 50. NE Lon Poly BA80 CQSW80. S'wark Ord Course 85. d 88 p 89. NSM E Dulwich St Jo *S'wark* from 88. *31 Hichisson Road, London SE15 3AN*   071-732 8685

PATEMAN, Donald Herbert. b 15. ALCD84. d 48 p 49. C Bethnal Green St Jas Less *Lon* 48-51; Hon Sec Soc for Relief of Distress 52-66; C Bromley All Hallows 54-56; V Dalston St Mark w St Bart from 56. *St Mark's Vicarage, Sandringham Road, London E8 2LL*   071-254 4741

PATEMAN, Edward Brian. b 29. Leeds Univ BA51. Qu Coll Birm 51. d 53 p 54. C Stockton St Pet *Dur* 53-57; Lect Bolton St Pet 57-58; V Coxhoe 58-65; V Dalton le Dale from 65; RD Houghton 72-75; R Hawthorn from 88. *The Vicarage, Church Lane, Murton, Seaham, Co Durham SR7 9RD*   091-526 2410

PATEMAN, Norman Carter. b 10. AIB31 Lon Univ BA50. d 39 p 40. Sec OMF 66-75; rtd 75; Perm to Offic *St Alb* from 83. *24 Victor Smith Court, Hunters Ride, Bricket Wood, St Albans, Herts AL2 3LZ*   St Albans (0727) 674045

PATEN, Richard Alfred. b 32. CEng MICE61 Ch Coll Cam BA56 MA60. Ripon Hall Ox 61. d 63 p 64. C Oadby *Leic* 63-67; C Pet St Mark *Pet* 67-71; Chapl Community Relns from 71; Bp's Dioc Chapl 73-85. *198 Lincoln Road, Peterborough PE1 2NQ*   Peterborough (0733) 66288

PATERNOSTER, Canon Michael Cosgrove. b 35. Pemb Coll Cam BA59 MA63. Cuddesdon Coll 59. d 61 p 62. C Surbiton St Andr *S'wark* 61-63; Chapl Qu Coll Dundee 63-68; Dioc Supernumerary *Bre* 63-68; Chapl Dundee Univ 67-68; Sec Fellowship of SS Alb and Sergius 68-71; R Dollar *St And* 71-75; R Stonehaven *Bre* 75-90; Hon Can St Paul's Cathl Dundee 81-90; R Aber St Jas *Ab* from 90. *31 Gladstone Place, Aberdeen AB1 6UX*   Aberdeen (0224) 322631

PATERSON, David. b 33. Ch Ch Ox BA55 MA58. Linc Th Coll 56. d 58 p 59. C Kidderminster St Mary *Worc* 58-60; C Wolv St Geo *Lich* 60-64; V Loughb St Pet *Leic* from 64. *St Peter's Vicarage, 129 Ashby Road, Loughborough, Leics LE11 3AB*   Loughborough (0509) 263047

PATERSON, Douglas Monro. b 30. Em Coll Cam BA54 MA57. Tyndale Hall Bris 55. d 57 p 58. C Walcot *B & W* 57-60; C Portman Square St Paul *Lon* 60-62; Lect Oak Hill Th Coll 60-62; C-in-c Hampstead St Jo Downshire Hill Prop Chpl *Lon* 62-65; Lect All Nations Chr Coll Ware 62-65; Rwanda 67-73; C Edin St Thos *Edin* 73-75; Lect Northumbria Bible Coll from 73; Perm to Offic *Edin* from 75; Lic to Offic *Newc* from 76.

Northumbria Bible College, Berwick-upon-Tweed TD15 1PA   Berwick-upon-Tweed (0289) 305681

PATERSON, Gordon Ronald. b 16. MBE57. Ripon Hall Ox 58. d 59 p 60. V Swanmore St Barn *Portsm* 62-85; RD Bishops Waltham 79-82; rtd 85; Perm to Offic Win and Portsm from 85. *28 Eastways, Bishops Waltham, Southampton SO3 1EX*   Bishops Waltham (04893) 5671

PATERSON, James Beresford. b 21. DSC42. St Andr Univ MPhil85. Westcott Ho Cam 59. d 61 p 62. R Broughty Ferry *Bre* 64-72; Dioc Supernumerary 72-75; Sec Scottish Ch Action for World Development 72-79; P-in-c Glencarse 76-84; Dioc Sec 79-84; Hon Can St Paul's Cathl Dundee 79-89; rtd 84. *67 Ipswich Road, Woodbridge, Suffolk IP12 4BT*   Woodbridge (03943) 3512

PATERSON, Mrs Jennifer Ann. b 49. S Dios Minl Tr Scheme. d 88. C Hale *Guildf* from 88. *4 St George's Close, Badshot Lea, Farnham, Surrey GU9 9LZ*   Aldershot (0252) 316775

PATERSON, Very Rev John Thomas Farquhar. b 38. TCD BA61 MA64 BD71. CITC 63. d 63 p 64. C Drumglass *Arm* 63-65; C Dub St Bart *D & G* 66-68; Min Can St Patr Cathl Dub 67-83; Asst Dean of Residence TCD 68-72; C-in-c Dub St Mark *D & G* 68-71; I Dub St Bart w Ch Ch Leeson Park 72-78; Dean Kildare *M & K* 78-89; I Kildare w Kilmeague and Curragh 78-89; Hon Sec Gen Syn 85-91; Dean Ch Ch Cathl Dub *D & G* from 89; I Dub Ch Ch Cathl Gp from 89; Radio Officer from 91. *The Deanery, St Werburgh Street, Dublin 8, Irish Republic*   Dublin (1) 679-8991 or 781385

PATERSON, Rex Douglas Trevor. b 27. AKC54. d 55 p 56. C Maidenhead St Luke *Ox* 55-58; C Littlehampton St Mary *Chich* 58-62; V Woodingdean 62-73; V Ferring from 73. *The Vicarage, 19 Grange Road, Worthing, W Sussex BN12 5LS*   Worthing (0903) 41645

PATERSON, Robert Mar Erskine. b 49. St Jo Coll Dur BA71 DipTh72 MA82. d 72 p 73. C Harpurhey St Steph *Man* 72-73; C Sketty *S & B* 73-78; V Llangattock and Llangynidr 78-83; V Gabalfa *Llan* from 83. *St Mark's Vicarage, 208 North Road, Cardiff CF4 3BL*   Cardiff (0222) 613286 or 619211

PATERSON, Robin Fergus. b 32. Moore Th Coll Sydney 83. d 87 p 89. Singapore 87-88; NSM Crieff *St And* from 88; NSM Comrie from 88. *Lake Cottage, St Fillans, Crieff, Perthshire PH6 2NF*   St Fillans (076485) 248

PATERSON, Robin Lennox Andrew. b 43. GSM62. N Ord Course 84. d 87 p 88. C Manston *Ripon* from 87. *2 Manston Avenue, Leeds LS15 8BT*   Leeds (0532) 641301

PATERSON, Canon William John McCallum. b 19. Leeds Univ BA41. Coll of Resurr Mirfield 41. d 43 p 44. R Finghall *Ripon* 69-79; R Hauxwell 69-79; R Spennithorne 69-79; Hon Can Ripon Cathl 75-84; R Kirk Hammerton w Nun Monkton and Hunsingore 79-84; rtd 84. *Dellwood, Ampleforth, York*   Ampleforth (04393) 645

PATEY, Colin Frank. b 49. SS Coll Cam BA71 MA75. St Steph Ho Ox 72. d 74 p 75. C Hedworth *Dur* 74-78; C Weymouth St Paul *Sarum* 78-81; V Grimethorpe *Wakef* 81-88; Chapl Coalville Community Hosp from 88. *The Chaplain's Office, Coalville Hospital, Broom Leys Road, Coalville, Leicester LE6 3DE*   Coalville (0530) 510510

PATEY, Very Rev Edward Henry. b 15. Liv Univ Hon LLD80. d 39 p 40. Dean Liv 64-82; rtd 82; Perm to Offic *Bris* from 82. *139 High Street, Malmesbury, Wilts SN16 9AL*   Malmesbury (0666) 822482

PATIENT, Peter Leslie. b 29. Chich Th Coll 63. d 66 p 67. C Headington *Ox* 66-69; C Stroud *Glouc* 69-72; C Welwyn *St Alb* 72-75. *28 Young's Rise, Welwyn Garden City, Herts AL8 6RU*   Welwyn Garden (0707) 328830

PATO, Luke Luscombe Lungile. b 49. Fort Hare Univ BA76 Manitoba Univ MA80. St Bede's Coll Umtata DipTh71. d 73 p 75. S Africa 73-81; Canada 81-90; Tutor Coll of the Ascension Selly Oak from 90. *College of the Ascension, Weoley Park Road, Selly Oak, Birmingham B29 6RD*   021-472 1667

PATON, Canon David Macdonald. b 13. BNC Ox BA36 MA39. d 39 p 40. Hon Can Cant Cathl *Cant* 66-80; R Glouc St Mary de Crypt w St Jo *Glouc* 69-79; Chapl to HM The Queen 72-81; R Glouc St Mary de Crypt w St Jo and Ch Ch *Glouc* 79-81; Perm to Offic *Cant* from 80; rtd 81; Perm to Offic *Glouc* from 81. *37A Cromwell Street, Gloucester GL1 1RE*   Gloucester (0452) 422051

PATON, George Hemsell. b 23. Wadh Coll Ox MA49. Oak Hill Th Coll 50. d 52 p 53. V Kemp Town St Mark and St Matt *Chich* 67-71; R Ripe w Chalvington 71-76; R Laughton w Ripe and Chalvington 77-78; V Iford w Kingston and Rodmell 78-90; rtd 90. *77 Springett Avenue, Ringmer, Lewes, E Sussex BN8 5QT*   Ringmer (0273) 812754

PATON, Ian Fisher. b 13. Leeds Univ BA36. Coll of Resurr Mirfield 36. **d** 38 **p** 39. C Blandford Forum *Sarum* 38-41; C Hanover Square St Geo *Lon* 41-44; Chapl RNVR 44-47; Chapl RN 47-57; Perm to Offic *Bris* 58-62; C St Teath *Truro* 62-67; Australia from 67. *c/o Box 271, Geraldton, W Australia 6530*

PATON, Canon Ian James. b 57. MA. Westcott Ho Cam 79. **d** 82 **p** 83. C Whitley Ch Ch *Ox* 82-84; Bp's Dom Chapl 84-86; Chapl Wadh Coll Ox 86-90; C Ox St Mary V w St Cross and St Pet *Ox* 86-90; Can and Vice-Provost St Mary's Cathl Edin from 90; R Edin St Mary from 90. *33 Manor Place, Edinburgh EH3 7EB* 031-226 3389

PATON, John David Marshall. b 47. Barrister 70. St Steph Ho Ox 81. **d** 83 **p** 84. C Bethnal Green St Matt *Lon* 83-84; C Bethnal Green St Matt w St Jas the Gt 84-86; P-in-c St-Geo-in-the-East St Mary 86-89; V from 89. *400 Commercial Road, London E1 0LB* 071-791 0772

PATON, Ven Michael John Macdonald. b 22. Magd Coll Ox BA49 MA54. Linc Th Coll 52. **d** 54 **p** 55. Sen Chapl Sheff United Hosps 67-70; Chapl Weston Park Hosp Sheff 70-78; V Sheff Broomhall St Mark *Sheff* 70-78; Adn Sheff 78-87; Can Res Sheff Cathl 78-87; rtd 88. *947 Abbeydale Road, Sheffield S7 2QD* Sheffield (0742) 366148

PATON-WILLIAMS, David Graham. b 58. Warw Univ BA81 Trin Coll Ox DipTh82 Selw Coll Cam BA86 MA90. Ridley Hall Cam 84. **d** 87 **p** 88. C S Westoe *Dur* 87-90; C Newton Aycliffe from 90. *3 Hardwick Court, Newton Aycliffe, Co Durham DL5 4RB* Aycliffe (0325) 320112

PATRICIA, Sister. *See* PERKINS, Patricia Doris

PATRICK, Hugh Joseph. b 37. TCD BA62 MA66. **d** 63 **p** 64. C Dromore Cathl *D & D* 63-66; C Lurgan Ch Ch 66-70; C Rothwell *Ripon* 70-73; V Thurnscoe St Hilda *Sheff* 73-78; V Wales from 78; P-in-c Thorpe Salvin 78-82. *The Vicarage, Manor Road, Wales, Sheffield S31 8PD* Worksop (0909) 771111

PATRICK, John Andrew. b 62. St Jo Coll Dur BA84. Ripon Coll Cuddesdon 87. **d** 89 **p** 90. C Frankby w Greasby *Ches* from 89. *5 Flail Close, Greasby, Wirral, Merseyside L49 2RN* 051-605 0735

PATRICK, John Peter. b 23. AKC. **d** 52 **p** 53. C S Westoe *Dur* 52-55; C Woodhouse *Wakef* 55-58; C Batley All SS 58-59; V Upperthong 59-75; V Slaithwaite w E Scammonden 75-80; V Donington *Linc* from 80. *The Vicarage, Donington, Spalding, Lincs PE11 4UE* Spalding (0775) 820418

PATSTON, Raymond Sidney Richard. b 26. Kelham Th Coll 47. **d** 51 **p** 52. C Hammersmith H Innocents *Lon* 51-53; C Acton Green St Pet 53-56; Area Sec E Counties UMCA 56-62; C Chesterton St Luke *Ely* 56-59; R Downham Market w Bexwell 61-71; V Clee *Linc* from 71. *Old Clee Rectory, 202 Clee Road, Grimsby, S Humberside DN32 8NG* Grimsby (0472) 691800

PATTEN, Mrs Helen Edna. b 43. St Hilda's Coll Ox BA65 Lon Univ CertEd70 DipTh75. Trin Coll Bris 73 Oak Hill Th Coll 81. **dss** 83 **d** 87. Tunbridge Wells St Jo *Roch* 82-86; Patcham *Chich* 86-87; Par Dn from 87. *70 Overhill Drive, Brighton BN1 8WJ* Brighton (0273) 554791

PATTEN, John. b 27. Qu Coll Birm 74. **d** 76 **p** 77. NSM Armitage *Lich* 76-79; NSM Lich St Mary w St Mich from 79. *31 Trent Valley Road, Lichfield, Staffs WS13 6EZ* Lichfield (0543) 268245

PATTENDEN, Henry Albert. b 11. Lich Th Coll 53. **d** 54 **p** 55. C Etruria *Lich* 67-72; C Widley w Wymering *Portsm* 72-73; rtd 76. *6 Compton Close, Lichfield Road, Stafford ST17 4PW* Stafford (0785) 47355

PATTERSON, Alfred Percy. **d** 85 **p** 87. NSM Aghalee *D & D* 85-91; C Gilford from 91. *Ashtree Hill, Trandragee, Craigavon, Co Armagh BT62 2LH* Craigavon (0762) 840363

PATTERSON, Alister John. b 22. Man Univ BA. Qu Coll Birm 84. **d** 84 **p** 85. C Gresley *Derby* 84-85; C Swadlincote 84-85; V Winshill from 85. *The Vicarage, Mill Hill Lane, Winshill, Burton-on-Trent, Staffs DE15 0BB* Burton (0524) 45043

PATTERSON, Andrew John. b 56. Master Mariner 85. Qu Coll Birm 85. **d** 88 **p** 89. C Newc St Phil and St Aug *Newc* from 88. *25 Kingsway, Newcastle upon Tyne NE4 9UH* 091-256 0624

✠**PATTERSON, Rt Rev Cecil John.** b 08. CMG58 CBE54. St Cath Coll Cam BA30 MA34. Lambeth DD63 Bps' Coll Cheshunt 30. **d** 31 **p** 32 **c** 42. C Kingsbury H Innocents *Lon* 31-34; Niger 34-69; Asst Bp Niger 42-45; Bp Niger 45; Abp W Africa 61-69; Abp's Rep for Community Relns 70-72; Asst Bp Lon 70-76; rtd 73.

6 High Park Road, Kew, Richmond, Surrey 081-876 1697

PATTERSON, Charles David Gilliat. b 40. Lon Univ DipTh74. Oak Hill Th Coll 71. **d** 74 **p** 75. C Brompton H Trin *Lon* 74-77; C Spring Grove St Mary 77-80; V Bures *St E* from 80. *The Vicarage, Bures, Suffolk CO8 5AA* Bures (0787) 227315

PATTERSON, Colin Hugh. b 52. CertEd75 St Pet Coll Ox MA77 Univ of Wales (Cardiff) MPhil90. Trin Coll Bris DipHE86. **d** 87 **p** 88. C Blackb Sav *Blackb* 87-90; C Haughton le Skerne *Dur* from 90. *1 Aviemore Court, Darlington, Co Durham DL1 2TF* Darlington (0325) 486382

PATTERSON, Mrs Diane Rosemary. b 46. W Midl Minl Tr Course 88. **d** 91. C Hill *Birm* from 91. *3 Dower Road, Sutton Coldfield, W Midlands B75 6UA* 021-308 0759

PATTERSON, Hugh John. b 38. Southn Univ MPhil76. AKC63. **d** 64 **p** 65. C Epsom St Martin *Guildf* 64-65; Chapl Ewell Coll 65-68; Asst Chapl and Lect Bp Otter Coll Chich 68-71; Lect Dudley Coll of Educn 71-77; Lect Wolv Poly from 77; Hon C Morville w Aston Eyre *Heref* from 82; Hon C Upton Cressett w Monk Hopton from 82; Hon C Acton Round from 82. *6 Victoria Road, Bridgnorth, Shropshire WV16 4LA* Bridgnorth (0746) 765298

PATTERSON, Ian Francis Riddell. b 31. TCD BA55. **d** 55 **p** 56. C Belf St Mary *Conn* 55-59; C Finaghy 59-63; I Craigs w Dunaghy and Killagan 63-66; Belf Trin Coll Miss 66-68; I Belf H Redeemer 68-80; I Kilroot 80-90; I Kilroot and Templecorran from 90. *29 Downshire Gardens, Carrickfergus, Co Antrim BT38 7LW* Carrickfergus (09603) 62387

PATTERSON, Sister Jennifer Mary. b 41. CA Tr Coll IDC65. **dss** 77 **d** 87. CA from 65; Chapl Asst HM Pris Holloway 75-79; Ho Mistress Ch Hosp Sch Hertf 78-79; Chapl Asst RAChD 80-90. *Church Army, Pipers Club, Hameln BFPO 31* Hameln (5151) 3539 or 42199

PATTERSON, John. b 27. MBIM76 Regent St Poly Lon DMS58. Bps' Coll Cheshunt 60. **d** 61 **p** 62. C Maidenhead St Luke *Ox* 61-65; Chapl RAF 65-72; V Ashton St Jas *Man* 72-78; USA 78-90; R Somercotes and Grainthorpe w Conisholme *Linc* from 90. *The Rectory, Keeling Street, North Somercotes, Louth, Lincs LN11 7QU* North Somercotes (050785) 559

PATTERSON, John Norton. b 39. TCD BA64 MA68. **d** 65 **p** 66. C Belf St Paul *Conn* 65-68; C Larne and Inver 68-72; I Ballintoy w Rathlin and Dunseverick from 72; Miss to Seamen from 72. *The Rectory, 2 Ballinlea Road, Ballintoy, Ballycastle, Co Antrim BT54 6NQ* Ballycastle (02657) 62411

PATTERSON, Norman John. b 47. Peterho Cam BA69. Lon Coll of Div ALCD DPS St Jo Coll Nottm 70. **d** 73 **p** 74. C Everton St Ambrose w St Tim *Liv* 73-74; C Everton St Pet 74-78; TV 79-84; C Aigburth from 84; Dioc Adv Past Care and Counselling from 84. *5 Burkhill Road, Liverpool L17 6AY* 051-427 9125

PATTERSON, Patric Douglas MacRae. b 51. Wycliffe Hall Ox 73. **d** 76 **p** 77. C Bebington *Ches* 76-79; Canada from 79. *156 Barrie Street, Kingston, Ontario, Canada, K7L 3J9*

PATTERSON, Philip Fredrick. b 50. Ulster Univ BSc QUB BD. **d** 82 **p** 83. C Lurgan (Shankill) *D & D* 82-86; I Carrowdore w Millisle 86-89; I Knockbreda from 89. *Knockbreda Rectory, 69 Church Road, Belfast BT8 4AN* Belfast (0232) 641493

PATTERSON, William Alfred. b 54. Wycliffe Hall Ox 77. **d** 79 **p** 80. C Partington and Carrington *Ches* 79-81; Canada from 81. *115 Norton Avenue, Kimberley, British Columbia, Canada, V1A 1X8*

PATTERSON, Canon William James. b 30. CBE91. Ball Coll Ox BA53 MA57. Ely Th Coll 53. **d** 55 **p** 56. C Newc St Jo *Newc* 55-58; Trinidad and Tobago 58-65; R Esher *Guildf* 65-72; RD Emly 68-72; R Downham *Ely* 72-80; P-in-c Coveney 78-80; Adn Wisbech 79-84; V Wisbech St Mary 80-84; Dean Ely 84-90; V Everton w Tetworth from 90; V Abbotsley from 90; V Waresley from 90; Hon Can Ely Cathl from 90. *The Vicarage, Everton, Sandy, Beds SG19 3JZ* Sandy (0767) 691827

PATTINSON, Kenneth Graham. b 24. Bp Tucker Coll Mukono. **d** 85 **p** 86. CMS from 75; Uganda 86-90; NSM Theydon Bois *Chelmsf* from 90. *16 Purlieu Way, Theydon Bois, Epping, Essex CM16 7EX* Theydon Bois (0992) 812267

PATTINSON, Sir William (Derek). b 30. Kt90. Qu Coll Ox BA52 MA56. St Deiniol's Hawarden 90. **d** 91. NSM Pimlico St Gabr *Lon* from 91. *4 Strutton Court, Great Peter Street, London SW1P 2HH* 071-222 6307

PATTISON, Anthony. b 50. MRPharmS73 Heriot-Watt Univ BSc72. Sarum & Wells Th Coll 85. **d** 87 **p** 88. C

Cullercoats St Geo *Newc* 87-89; Ind Chapl from 89; C Cramlington 89-91; TV from 91. *24 Lindsey Close, Beaconhill Glade, Cramlington, Northd NE23 8EJ* Cramlington (0670) 732735

PATTISON, George Linsley. b 50. Edin Univ MA72 BD77 Dur Univ PhD. Edin Th Coll 74. **d** 77 **p** 78. C Benwell St Jas *Newc* 77-80; P-in-c Kimblesworth *Dur* 80-83; R Badwell Ash w Gt Ashfield, Stowlangtoft etc *St E* from 83. *The Rectory, Badwell Ash, Bury St Edmunds, Suffolk IP31 3DH* Walsham-le-Willows (0359) 259575

PATTISON, Graham Bentley. b 39. Open Univ BA75. Kelham Th Coll 59. **d** 64 **p** 65. C Beamish *Dur* 64-66; C Benfieldside 66-67; C Barnsley St Mary *Wakef* 67-70; TV Tong *Bradf* 70-74; TR 74-77; Master Sherburn Hosp Dur from 77; Soc Resp Officer *Dur* from 77. *The Master's House, Sherburn Hospital, Durham DH1 2SE* 091-372 0332

PATTISON, Stephen Bewley. b 53. Selw Coll Cam BA76. Edin Th Coll 76. **d** 78 **p** 80. C Gosforth All SS *Newc* 78-79; NSM St Nic Hosp Newc 78-82; Hon C Newc St Thos Prop Chpl *Newc* 80-82; Chapl Edin Th Coll 82-83; Lect Past Studies Birm Univ 83-88; Perm to Offic *Birm* 83-86 and from 87; Hon C Moseley St Mary 86-87. *15 Forest Court, Forest Road, Birmingham B13 9DL* 021-449 4762

PATTON, Ven Desmond Hilton. b 12. TCD BA35. **d** 36 **p** 37. I Carlow w Urglin and Staplestown *C & O* 59-77; Adn Ossory and Leighlin 62-76; rtd 76; Chapl Mageough Home *D & G* from 88. *Littleholme, Delgany, Co Wicklow, Irish Republic* Dublin (1) 287-5207

PAUL, Brother. *See* SINGLETON, Ernest George

PAUL, David Brown. b 47. Keele Univ BEd70. St Steph Ho Ox 72. **d** 74 **p** 75. C Millfield St Mary *Dur* 74-79; P-in-c Romford St Andr *Chelmsf* 79-80; R 80-85; V E Finchley All SS *Lon* from 85. *All Saints' Vicarage, 1 Twyford Avenue, London N2 1NV* 081-883 9315

PAUL, Very Rev John Douglas. b 28. Edin Univ MA52. Ely Th Coll 52. **d** 54 **p** 55. C Portsea Ascension *Portsm* 54-56; Nyasaland 56-60; Portuguese E Africa 60-70; Adn Metangula 65-70; R Castle Douglas *Glas* 70-75; R Edin St Mark *Edin* 75-80; R Elgin w Lossiemouth *Mor* from 80; Syn Clerk from 89; Can St Andr Cathl Inverness from 89; Dean Mor from 91. *8 Gordon Street, Elgin, Morayshire IV30 1JQ* Elgin (0343) 547505

PAUL, John Matthew. b 61. K Coll Lon BA82 Fitzw Coll Cam BA88. Westcott Ho Cam 86. **d** 89 **p** 90. C Writtle w Highwood *Chelmsf* from 89. *20 Home Mead, Writtle, Chelmsford CM1 3LH* Chelmsford (0245) 421854

PAUL, John Wilfred. b 30. St Jo Coll Morpeth LTh52 BA82. **d** 51 **p** 52. Australia 51-57; C Mitcham Ascension *S'wark* 57-59; V Clapham St Jo 59-65; CF (TA) 60-67; V Balham St Mary *S'wark* 66-85; V Balham St Mary and St Jo 85-86; R St Andr-by-the-Wardrobe w St Ann, Blackfriars *Lon* from 86; R St Jas Garlickhythe w St Mich Queenhithe etc from 86. *St Andrew's House, St Andrew's Hill, London EC4V 5DE* 071-248 7546

PAUL, Naunihal Chand (Nihal). b 40. Allahabad Univ MA. Bangalore Th Coll BD. **d** 69 **p** 70. India 70-74; C Urmston *Man* 75-77; P-in-c Farnworth St Pet 77-80; TV E Farnworth and Kearsley 80-83; TV Laindon St Martin and St Nic w Nevendon *Chelmsf* 83-90; R Laindon w Dunton from 90. *38 Claremont Road, Laindon, Basildon, Essex SS15 5PZ* Basildon (0268) 411190

PAUL, Roger Philip. b 53. Clare Coll Cam BA74 CertEd76 MA88. Westcott Ho Cam 78. **d** 81 **p** 82. C Cov Caludon *Cov* 81-85; R Warmington w Shotteswell and Radway w Ratley from 85. *The Rectory, Warmington, Banbury, Oxon OX17 1BT* Farnborough (029589) 213

PAULEY, Denniss Franklyn. b 19. Chich Th Coll. **d** 57 **p** 58. C Pentonville St Silas w All SS and St Jas *Lon* 69-84; rtd 84; Hon C Pentonville St Silas w All SS and St Jas *Lon* from 84. *87A Richmond Avenue, London N1 0LX* 071-607 2865

PAULIN, Canon James Marmaduke. b 06. Open Univ BA73. St Andr Whittlesford 35. **d** 37 **p** 38. V Bywell St Pet *Newc* 57-71; Hon Can Newc Cathl 64-71; RD Corbridge 66-71; rtd 71. *51 Shortridge Terrace, Jesmond, Newcastle upon Tyne NE2 2JE*

PAVEY, Mrs Angela Mary. b 55. Hull Univ BA77 Nottm Univ BCombStuds84. Linc Th Coll 81. **dss** 84 **d** 87. Linc St Faith and St Martin w St Pet *Linc* 84-86; Chapl Boston Coll of FE from 87; Asst Min Officer from 89. *The Rectory, Fishtoft, Boston, Lincs PE21 0RZ* Boston (0205) 363216

PAVEY, Gordon Sidney Alfred. b 19. Lon Univ BD47 Leeds Univ MEd58. Chich Th Coll 40. **d** 42 **p** 43. V Huddersfield St Thos *Wakef* 54-64; Youth Chapl 54-57; Lic to Offic *Bris* from 68; Prin Lect Th Bris Poly

from 77; rtd 84. *2 Carey's Close, Clevedon, Avon BS21 6BA* Clevedon (0272) 872623

PAVEY, John Bertram. b 51. Keele Univ BA73 Hull Univ PGCE74. Linc Th Coll 81. **d** 83 **p** 84. C Boultham *Linc* 83-86; R Fishtoft from 86. *The Rectory, Fishtoft, Boston, Lincs PE21 0RZ* Boston (0205) 363216

PAVEY, Michael Trevor. b 32. ALCD59. **d** 59 **p** 60. C Nor St Pet Mancroft *Nor* 59-61; C N Walsham w Antingham 61-63; Chapl RAF 63-83; R Mark w Allerton *B & W* from 83. *The Rectory, Vicarage Lane, Mark, Highbridge, Somerset TA9 4NN* Mark Moor (027864) 258

PAVEY, Canon Peter John. b 29. Lon Univ BD54. ALCD54. **d** 55 **p** 56. C Bexleyheath Ch Ch *Roch* 55-58; Tutor St Aid Birkenhead 58-63; Chapl 62-63; Israel 63-66; Vice-Prin Ridley Hall Cam 66-70; Acting Prin 70-71; V Letchworth St Paul *St Alb* 71-77; RD Hitchin 74-84; P-in-c Willian 77; V Letchworth St Paul w Willian 77-84; Hon Can St Alb from 82; R Clifton from 84. *The Rectory, 8 Rectory Close, Clifton, Shefford, Beds SG17 5EL* Hitchin (0462) 812295

PAVLIBEYI, Andrew Christos. b 53. Trent Poly CertEd76. Oak Hill Th Coll BA88 Wycliffe Hall Ox 84. **d** 86 **p** 87. C Finchley Ch Ch *Lon* 86-89; Chapl Lon Univ from 89. *139C Whitfield Street, London W1P 5RY* 071-387 1016

PAWLEY, Clive. b 35. AKC59. **d** 60 **p** 61. C Lt Ilford St Barn *Chelmsf* 60-63; C Bourne *Guildf* 63-67; V Tongham from 67. *The Vicarage, Tongham, Farnham, Surrey GU10 1DU* Runfold (02518) 2224

PAWSEY, Jack Edward. b 35. Trin Coll Ox BA59 MA65. Westcott Ho Cam 64. **d** 66 **p** 67. Sec Coun Soc Aid *S'wark* 66-75; Race Relns Worker 75-78; Acting Sec Coun Soc Aid 78-82; Perm to Offic 84-86; Hon C Camberwell St Geo from 86. *20 Addington Square, London SE5 7JZ* 071-701 2769

PAWSON, Geoffrey Philip Henry (Brother Godfrey). b 04. Jes Coll Cam BA26 MA31. Wells Th Coll 26. **d** 27 **p** 28. CR from 46; Barbados 66-69; Lic to Offic *Wakef* from 69; rtd 71. *House of the Resurrection, Mirfield, W Yorkshire WF14 0BN* Mirfield (0924) 494318

PAWSON, John Walker. b 38. Kelham Th Coll 58. **d** 63 **p** 64. C N Hull St Mich *York* 63-67; C Lower Gornal *Lich* 67-70; V Tipton St Jo 70-78; V Meir Heath from 78; RD Stoke from 88. *St Francis's Vicarage, Meir Heath, Stoke-on-Trent ST3 7LH* Blythe Bridge (0782) 393189

PAXMAN, Denis James. b 24. FRMetS82 St Edm Hall Ox BA50 DipTh51 MA54. Ely Th Coll 52. **d** 53 **p** 54. Warden St Mich Coll Tenbury 65-77; V Tenbury St Mich *Heref* 65-77; Chapl Howell's Sch Denbigh 77-82; V Lakenheath *St E* 83-87; R Tain *Mor* from 87; Prin Moray Ord Course from 87; rtd 89. *St Andrew's Rectory, Tain, Ross-shire IV19 1HE* Tain (0862) 2193

PAXON, Robin Michael Cuninghame. b 46. St Jo Coll Dur BA69. Westcott Ho Cam 68. **d** 71 **p** 72. C Croydon St Pet S End *Cant* 71-77; C Saffron Walden w Wendens Ambo and Littlebury *Chelmsf* 77-80; P-in-c Plaistow St Mary 80-83; TV Plaistow 83-89; TV Dovercourt and Parkeston from 90. *St Paul's Vicarage, Station Road, Parkeston, Harwich, Essex CO12 4PZ* Harwich (0255) 502633

PAXTON, Cyril. b 14. S'wark Ord Course 64. **d** 67 **p** 68. C Riddlesdown *S'wark* 67-74; C Uckfield *Chich* 74-77; C Isfield 74-77; C S Petherton w the Seavingtons *B & W* 77-83; rtd 79; Perm to Offic *B & W* from 83. *Cobblers, Hinton St George, Somerset TA17 8SA* Crewkerne (0460) 72741

PAXTON, John Ernest. b 49. Ex Univ BA71. Westcott Ho Cam 74. **d** 74 **p** 75. C Redditch St Steph *Worc* 74-77; UAE 77-81; C Bolton St Pet *Man* from 81; Ind Missr from 81. *23 Kinloch Drive, Bolton BL1 4LZ* Bolton (0204) 493620

PAY, Norman John. b 50. St Jo Coll Dur BA72 DipTh73. Cranmer Hall Dur. **d** 74 **p** 75. C S Moor *Dur* 74-78; C Rawmarsh w Parkgate *Sheff* 78-80; C-in-c New Cantley CD 80-82; V New Cantley 82-89; V Doncaster St Leon and St Jude from 89; Asst Clergy In-Service Tr Officer from 90. *St Leonard's Vicarage, Barnsley Road, Doncaster, S Yorkshire DN5 8QE* Doncaster (0302) 784858

PAYN, Peter Richard. b 33. Moore Th Coll Sydney LTh59. **d** 60 **p** 60. Australia 60-79; C Blackb Ch Ch w St Matt *Blackb* 79-81; V Lowestoft Ch Ch *Nor* from 81. *The Vicarage, 1 Beeching Drive, Lowestoft, Suffolk NR32 4TB* Lowestoft (0502) 572444

PAYNE, Alan Frank. b 19. Bps' Coll Cheshunt 63. **d** 65 **p** 66. V Oulton w Woodlesford *Ripon* 79-80; V Thurgoland *Wakef* 80-82; rtd 82; Perm to Offic *Wakef* from 82. *6 Highfields, Hoylandswaine, Sheffield S30 6JP* Barnsley (0226) 762469

PAYNE, Arthur Edwin. b 37. K Alfred's Coll Win CertEd59 Ban Coll DipRE60 Univ of Wales (Swansea) ACertEd68. St Mich Coll Llan 86. **d** 87 **p** 88. C Swansea St Gabr *S & B* 87-90; Chapl Univ of Wales (Swansea) 89-90; V Brynmawr 90-91; TV Wickford and Runwell *Chelmsf* from 91; Chapl Runwell Hosp Essex from 91. *The Vicarage, Church End Lane, Wickford, Essex SS11 7JQ* Wickford (0268) 732068

PAYNE, Canon Charles Thomas Leonard. b 11. Kelham Th Coll 29. **d** 34 **p** 35. V Streatham Ch Ch *S'wark* 42-79; Chapl CA Hostel Streatham 48-79; RD Streatham *S'wark* 73-79; Hon Can S'wark Cathl 75-79; rtd 79; Perm to Offic *St E* from 79. *6 Cedar Walk, Acton, Sudbury, Suffolk CO10 0UN* Sudbury (0787) 76812

PAYNE, Cyril Douglas. b 16. Sarum Th Coll 46. **d** 49 **p** 50. V Wellingborough All SS *Pet* 63-82; rtd 82; Perm to Offic *Cant* from 82. *32 London Road, Canterbury, Kent CT2 8LN* Canterbury (0227) 65694

PAYNE, Cyril Gordon. b 26. Bris Univ BA53. Linc Th Coll 53. **d** 55 **p** 56. V Otterbourne *Win* 63-75; V Milford 75-90; rtd 90. *11 Oaklands, Lymington, Hants SO41 9TH* Lymington (0590) 671274

PAYNE, David James. b 31. Clare Coll Cam BA54 MA61. Wycliffe Hall Ox 60. **d** 62 **p** 63. C Gt Faringdon w Lt Coxwell *Ox* 62-63; C Guildf Ch Ch *Guildf* 63-66; R Shackleford 66-73; R Peper Harow 66-73; R Odell *St Alb* 73-78; V Pavenham 73-78; Warden Home of Divine Healing Crowhurst 78-84; R Wraxall *B & W* from 84. *The Rectory, Wraxall, Bristol BS19 1NA* Bristol (0272) 857086

PAYNE, David Ronald. b 49. DMS77 Open Univ BA87. St Mich Coll Llan. **d** 90 **p** 91. C Oystermouth *S & B* from 90. *66 Queen's Road, Mumbles, Swansea SA3 4AN* Swansea (0792) 360438

PAYNE, Canon Denis Alfred. b 22. Or Coll Ox BA50 MA53. Wells Th Coll 50. **d** 51 **p** 52. Min Sec ACCM 67-69; Sen Selection Sec 69-73; Dir Post-Ord Tr and Further Tr for Clergy *St E* 73-84; Dioc Dir of Ords 73-87; Can Res St E Cathl 73-89; rtd 89; Perm to Offic *St E* from 90. *The Crooked House, Brussels Green, Darsham, Saxmundham, Suffolk IP17 3RN* Yoxford (072877) 705

PAYNE, Francis Michael Ambrose. b 18. Keble Coll Ox BA39 MA43. Ely Th Coll 39. **d** 41 **p** 42. R Henley *Ox* 63-78; RD Henley 73-78; R Ecton *Pet* 78-83; rtd 83; Perm to Offic *Nor* from 83. *The Monastery, Happisburgh, Norwich NR12 0AB* Walcott (0692) 650076

PAYNE, Frederick Gates (Eric). b 19. Jes Coll Cam BA40 MA43. Lon Coll of Div 40. **d** 42 **p** 43. Ethiopia 48-67; SW Org Sec CMJ 68-85; rtd 84; Perm to Offic *B & W* from 85. *83 Penn Lea Road, Bath BA1 3RQ* Bath (0225) 423092

PAYNE, James John Henry. b 26. MBE69. St Pet Hall Ox BA53 MA59. Tyndale Hall Bris 48 Linc Th Coll 53. **d** 53 **p** 54. Nigeria 57-88; Hon Can Lagos 71-88; rtd 88; Perm to Offic *Ox* from 88. *1 Timberyard Cottages, Shellingford, Faringdon, Oxon SN7 7QA* Stanford in the Vale (0367) 710274

PAYNE, John. b 58. Glas Univ BSc80 Edin Univ BD84. Edin Th Coll 81. **d** 90 **p** 90. C Dur St Nic *Dur* from 90. *15 Providence Row, Durham DH1 1RS* 091-384 1065

PAYNE, John Charles. b 04. St Aid Birkenhead 50. **d** 51 **p** 52. V Preston St Sav *Blackb* 62-69; rtd 69. *Dulverton Hall, St Martin's Square, Scarborough YO11 2DB* Scarborough (0723) 373082

PAYNE, John Percival. b 49. Nottm Univ BA70. Cuddesdon Coll 70. **d** 72 **p** 73. C Tilehurst St Mich *Ox* 72-76; C Cross Green St Sav and St Hilda *Ripon* 76-79; Chapl St Hilda's Priory Sneaton, Whitby 79-83; V Leeds Belle Is St Jo and St Barn *Ripon* 83-88; Chapl St Hilda's Sch Whitby from 88. *Melrose, 41 Coach Road, Sleights, Whitby, N Yorkshire YO22 5AA* Whitby (0947) 810585

PAYNE, John Rogan. b 44. Episc Th Coll Sao Paulo. **d** 78 **p** 79. Brazil 78-86; C Ilkley All SS *Bradf* 86-88; R Elvington w Sutton on Derwent and E Cottingwith *York* from 88. *The Rectory, Church Lane, Elvington, York YO4 5AD* Elvington (090485) 462

PAYNE, Canon Joseph Marshall. b 17. TCD BA38 MA52. **d** 40 **p** 41. Asst Chapl-in-Chief RAF 65-72; V Malew *S & M* 72-82; RD Castletown 77-82; Can St German's Cathl 78-80; Can and Treas 80-84; rtd 82; Perm to Offic *S & M* from 84. *Ard-ny-Shee, 3 Viking Close, Ballakillowey, Colby, Isle of Man* Port Erin (0624) 832039

PAYNE, Kenneth Alan. b 45. Pemb Coll Ox BA68 MA71. Qu Coll Birm 71. **d** 74 **p** 74. Hon C Perry Barr *Birm* 74-78; Hon C Ruislip Manor St Paul *Lon* 78-79; C Hawksworth Wood *Ripon* 79-84; R Stanningley St Thos

from 84. *The Rectory, Stanningley Road, Stanningley, Pudsey, W Yorkshire LS28 6NB* Pudsey (0532) 573460

PAYNE, Leonard Vivian. b 20. St D Coll Lamp BA42 Lich Th Coll 42. **d** 44 **p** 46. V Weston-super-Mare St Paul *B & W* 62-81; rtd 81. *3 Ham Manor, Llantwit Major, S Glam CF6 9RT* Llantwit Major (04465) 6906

PAYNE, Michael Frederick. b 49. NE Surrey Coll of Tech HND72. St Jo Coll Nottm 81. **d** 83 **p** 84. C Hyson Green *S'well* 83-86; P-in-c Peckham St Mary Magd *S'wark* 86-90; V from 90. *St Mary's Vicarage, 22 St Mary's Road, London SE15 2DW* 071-639 4596

PAYNE, Ralfe Dudley. b 22. Lon Univ BA50. Qu Coll Birm 50. **d** 52 **p** 53. V Brockmoor *Lich* 63-75; C Kinver 76-79; R Himley 79-89; V Swindon 79-89; rtd 89. *Highfield, Dunsley, Kinver, Stourbridge, W Midlands DY7 6LY* Kinver (0384) 873612

PAYNE, Richard Derek. b 29. K Coll Lon 51. **d** 55 **p** 56. C Stevenage *St Alb* 55-58; C Clayton w Keymer *Chich* 58-60; C-in-c Coldean CD 60-63; R Telscombe w Piddinghoe 63-75; R Telscombe w Piddinghoe and Southease 75-76; Chapl Holmswood Sch Tunbridge Wells 76-78; Perm to Offic Chich from 78; Cant from 79; Org Sec (SE England) CECS from 78. *Greystones, Duddleswell, Uckfield, E Sussex TN22 3BH* Nutley (082571) 2314

PAYNE, Robert Christian. b 42. Llan St Mich DipTh65. **d** 65 **p** 66. C Charlton Kings St Mary *Glouc* 65-69; C Waltham Cross *St Alb* 69-71; V Falfield *Glouc* 71-72; P-in-c Rockhampton 71-72; V Falfield w Rockhampton 72-76; Chapl HM Det Cen Eastwood Park 71-76; HM Youth Cust Cen Everthorpe 76-79; Glen Parva 79-85; Pris Service Chapl Tr Officer 85-88; Chapl HM Pris Swinfen Hall 85-88; Asst Chapl Gen of Pris (SW) 88-90; Asst Chapl Gen of Pris from 90. *c/o Home Office, Calthorpe House, Hagley Road, Birmingham B16 8QR* 021-455 9855

PAYNE, Robert Harold Vincent. b 44. St Jo Coll Nottm 77. **d** 79 **p** 80. C Didsbury St Jas *Man* 79-80; C Didsbury St Jas and Em 80-83; V Southchurch Ch Ch *Chelmsf* 83-90; P-in-c Charles w St Matthias Plymouth *Ex* from 90. *The Vicarage, 6 St Lawrence Road, Plymouth PL4 6HN* Plymouth (0752) 665640

PAYNE, Robert Sandon. b 48. ARICS72 Reading Univ BSc69. Ripon Coll Cuddesdon 77. **d** 80 **p** 81. C Bridgnorth, Tasley, Astley Abbotts and Oldbury *Heref* 80-83; P-in-c Wistanstow from 83; P-in-c Acton Scott from 86. *The Parsonage, Wistanstow, Craven Arms, Shropshire SY7 8DQ* Craven Arms (05882) 2778

PAYNE, Victor Harold. b 27. S'wark Ord Course 82. **d** 85 **p** 86. Hon C Sanderstead All SS *S'wark* from 85. *8 Langley Oaks Avenue, Sanderstead, Surrey CR2 8DH* 081-657 5658

PAYNE, Victor John. b 45. Open Univ BA81. Llan St Mich DipTh69 DPS70. **d** 70 **p** 71. C Ystrad Mynach *Llan* 70-72; C Whitchurch 72-75; CF (TA) 74-75; CF 75-85 and from 87; V Talgarth and Llanelieu *S & B* 85-87. *c/o MOD (Army), Bagshot Park, Bagshot, Surrey GU19 5PL* Bagshot (0276) 71717

PAYNE, Walter Richard Stanley. b 29. FRSC64 Lon Univ BSc54 PhD63 DipRS78. S'wark Ord Course 75. **d** 78 **p** 79. NSM Lamorbey H Trin *Roch* 78-85; Perm to Offic from 85. *120 Hurst Road, Sidcup, Kent DA15 9AF* 081-302 0267

PAYNE, Warwick Martin. b 26. AKC51. **d** 52 **p** 53. C Mansf St Pet *S'well* 52-56; Gambia 56-58; C Winlaton *Dur* 59-62; S Africa from 63. *PO Box 20, Ugie, 5470 South Africa*

PAYNE, William George. b 96. **d** 49 **p** 50. V Middle Hendon *Dur* 61-66; rtd 66; Lic to Offic *Dur* 66-71; Hon C Bishopwearmouth Ch Ch 71-84. *Flat 5, Old School Place, North Grove, Wells, Somerset BA5 2TD*

PAYNE COOK, John Andrew Somerset. b 43. St Pet Coll Ox BA65 MA. Coll of Resurr Mirfield 65. **d** 68 **p** 69. C St Mary-at-Latton *Chelmsf* 68-71; C Gt Berkhamsted *St Alb* 71-76; C-in-c N Brickhill CD 76-82; V N Brickhill and Putnoe 83-85; TR Tring from 85. *The Rectory, Church Yard, Tring, Herts HP23 5AE* Tring (044282) 2170

PAYNTER, Stephen Denis. b 59. Bath Univ BSc82 CertEd82. Trin Coll Bris BA89. **d** 89 **p** 90. C Nailsea Ch Ch *B & W* from 89. *32 Southfield Road, Nailsea, Bristol BS19 1JB* Bristol (0272) 855789

PAYNTON, Paul Alexander. b 42. Hull Univ DipMin88. Linc Th Coll 72. **d** 74 **p** 75. C Uppingham w Ayston *Pet* 74-77; P-in-c Market Overton w Thistleton 77-79; R Teigh w Whissendine 77-79; R Teigh w Whissendine and Market Overton from 79. *The Vicarage, 3 Paddock Close, Whissendine, Oakham, Leics LE15 7HW* Whissendine (066479) 333

PAYTON, Canon Arthur Edward. b 16. Lambeth MA81. d 39 p 41. Hon C Kelvedon *Chelmsf* 69-82; Hon Can Gib Cathl *Eur* 73-84; rtd 81; P-in-c Wickmere w Lt Barningham and Itteringham *Nor* 84-88; Perm to Offic from 88. *The Grange, Sandy Lane, West Runton, Cromer, Norfolk NR27 9LT* West Runton (026375) 400

PAYTON, John Vear. b 36. Bps' Coll Cheshunt 60. d 63 p 64. C Hatf Hyde St Mary *St Alb* 63-72; V Farley Hill St Jo 72-84. *41 Trowbridge Gardens, Luton LU2 7JY* Luton (0582) 450612

PEACE, Geoffrey. b 23. S'wark Ord Course. d 68 p 69. NSM Ashford St Hilda CD *Lon* 68-73; NSM Ashford St Hilda 73-80; C Spilsby w Hundleby *Linc* 80-83; C Sandhurst *Ox* 83-85; V Owlsmoor 85-88; rtd 88. *21 Balfour Road, Bournemouth BH9 2AZ* Bournemouth (0202) 525700

PEACH, Malcolm Thompson. b 31. St Chad's Coll Dur BA56. Sarum Th Coll 56. d 58 p 59. C Beamish *Dur* 58-61; Chapl Dur Univ 61-65; NE England Sec SCM 61-65; C-in-c Stockton St Mark CD *Dur* 65-72; P-in-c Bishopwearmouth St Nic 72-81; V 81-85; V S Shields St Hilda w St Thos from 85; Hon Chapl Miss to Seamen from 85. *St Hilda's Vicarage, 40 Lawe Road, South Shields, Tyne & Wear NE33 2EU* 091-454 1414

PEACH, Sidney John Elias. b 11. St Boniface Warminster 34. d 37 p 38. P-in-c Ipswich St Mary at the Elms *St E* 68-75; rtd 75. *2 Woodbury Avenue, Wells, Somerset BA5 2XN* Wells (0749) 75496

PEACHELL, David John. b 45. Oak Hill Th Coll 85. d 86 p 87. C Prescot *Liv* 86-89; CF from 89. *c/o MOD (Army), Bagshot Park, Bagshot, Surrey GU19 5PL* Bagshot (0276) 71717

PEACOCK, David. b 39. Liv Univ BA61 Lanc Univ MA71. Westcott Ho Cam 84. d 84 p 85. Prin Lect St Martin's Coll Lanc 84-85; Hon C Lanc St Mary *Blackb* 84-85; Hon C Roehampton H Trin *S'wark* from 85; Prin Whitelands Coll of HE from 85. *Whitelands College, West Hill, London SW15 3SN* 081-788 8268

PEACOCK, David Christopher. b 57. York Univ BA78 DPhil83. Wycliffe Hall Ox 89. d 91. C Old Brumby *Linc* from 91. *32 Alvingham Road, Scunthorpe, S Humberside DN16 2HD* Scunthorpe (0724) 840616

PEACOCK, Very Rev Hubert Henry Ernest. b 13. St Edm Hall Ox BA35 MA44. Linc Th Coll 39. d 39 p 40. S Africa 56-77; Lic to Offic (Cashel, Waterford and Lismore) *C & O* 78-80; P-in-c Kilrossanty 80-83; P-in-c Stradbally 80-83; Dean Leighlin 83-88; I Leighlin w Grange Sylvae, Shankill etc 83-88; rtd 88. *Loughbrack Cottage, Dunnamaggan, Kilkenny, Irish Republic* Kilkenny (56) 28337

PEACOCK, John. b 35. ALCD60. d 60 p 61. C Addiscombe St Mary *Cant* 60-62; C Felixstowe St Jo *St E* 62-65; Chapl RAF 65-70; Australia from 71. *4A Lockerbie Road, Thornleigh, NSW, Australia 2121* Sydney (2) 816-0222

PEACOCK, Leslie John Frederick. b 11. MBE58. d 51 p 52. C-in-c Fawkenhurst *Cant* 63-73; V Newington w Bobbing and Iwade 73-77; rtd 77; Perm to Offic *Ex* 77-83; Win from 83. *14 Ashford Close, Fordingbridge, Hants SP6 1DH* Fordingbridge (0425) 52684

PEACOCK, Thomas Edward. b 35. Dur Univ BSc55 PhD58. d 64 p 65. C S'wark St Sav w All Hallows *S'wark* 64-67; Australia 67-68 and from 70; C Jarrow *Dur* 68-69. *9 Bergamot Street, Bald Hills, Queensland, Australia 4036* Brisbane (7) 261-1711

PEACOCK, William John. b 15. Worc Ord Coll 65. d 67 p 68. C Netherton St Andr *Worc* 69-74; R Ebbw Vale *Mon* 74-78; V Caerwent w Dinham and Llanfair Discoed 78-83; rtd 83; Perm to Offic *Chich* from 87. *2 Dickens Way, Eastbourne, E Sussex BN23 7TG* Eastbourne (0323) 763897

PEACOCKE, Dr Arthur Robert. b 24. Ex Coll Ox BA45 BSc47 MA48 DPhil48 DSc62 DD82 Birm Univ DipTh60 BD71. d 71 p 71. Fell and Tutor St Pet Hall Ox 65-73; Dean Clare Coll Cam 73-84; Lic to Offic Ely 73-85; Ox from 85; Dir Ian Ramsey Cen Ox 85-88; Warden SOSc from 87; Hon Chapl Ch Ch Ox from 88. *St Cross College, Oxford OX1 3LZ* Oxford (0865) 512041

✠**PEACOCKE, Rt Rev Cuthbert Irvine.** b 03. TD51. TCD BA25 MA28. d 26 p 27 c 70. C Seapatrick St Patr *D & D* 26-30; Hd Ch of Ireland Miss Belf 30-33; R Derriaghy *Conn* 33-35; I Dundela *D & D* 35-56; CF (R of O) from 38; RD Holywood *D & D* 48-50; Adn Down 50-56; Dean Belf 56-70; Bp D & R 70-75; rtd 75. *32 Lisburn Road, Hillsborough, Co Down BT26 6HW*

PEAD, Charles Henry. b 31. d 87 p 88. NSM Llanfrechfa and Llanddewi Fach w Llandegveth *Mon* from 87.

Jasmine, Caerleon Road, Llanfrechfa, Cwmbran, Gwent NP44 8DQ Cwmbran (0633) 32685

PEAKE, Charles Clifford. b 17. St Jo Coll Ox BA38 Leeds Univ MA88. Qu Coll Birm 38. d 40 p 41. V Starbeck *Ripon* 68-78; R Farnham w Scotton and Staveley and Copgrove 78-82; rtd 82. *8 Burke Street, Harrogate, N Yorkshire HG1 4NR* Harrogate (0423) 522265

PEAKE, Robert Ernest. b 27. Univ Coll Lon BSc51 FSS. Coll of Resurr Mirfield 83. d 85 p 86. C Linslade *Ox* 85-88; TV Gt Chesham 88-89; rtd 89. *Butley Cottage, Chestnut Way, Longwick, Aylesbury, Bucks HP17 9SD* Princes Risborough (08444) 4952

PEAKE, Canon Simon Jeremy Brinsley. b 30. Worc Coll Ox BA54 MA56. St Steph Ho Ox 53. d 57 p 58. C Eastbourne St Andr *Chich* 57-60; S Africa 60-69; Zambia 69-77; Chapl Athens w Kyfissia *Eur* 77-87; Chapl Vienna w Budapest and Prague 87-91; Chapl Vienna w Budapest from 91; Hon Can Malta Cathl from 87. *c/o The British Embassy, Jauresgasse 12, Vienna A-1030, Austria* Vienna (1) 712-3396 or 505-1374

PEAL, John Arthur. b 46. K Coll Lon BD70 AKC. d 71 p 72. C Portsea All SS w St Jo Rudmore *Portsm* 71-74; C Westbury *Sarum* 71-77; V Borstal *Roch* 77-82; Chapl HM Pris Cookham Wood 78-82; Chapl Erith and Distr Hosp from 82; V Erith Ch Ch *Roch* from 82; P-in-c Erith St Jo from 86. *Christ Church Vicarage, Victoria Road, Erith, Kent DA8 3AN* Erith (0322) 334729

PEAL, William John. b 26. K Coll Lon BSc47 AKC PhD52. St Jo Coll Nottm 79. d 80 p 81. C Coalville and Bardon Hill *Leic* 80-83; TV Melton Mowbray w Thorpe Arnold 83-86; TV Melton Gt Framland 86-90; rtd 90. *20 Conway Road, Knypersley, Stoke-on-Trent ST8 7AL* Stoke-on-Trent (0782) 513580

PEARCE, Alfred Edward. b 16. AKC48. d 48 p 49. R Hackington *Cant* 67-87; rtd 87. *12 Mead Way, Canterbury, Kent* Canterbury (0227) 464048

PEARCE, Mrs Angela Elizabeth. b 36. K Coll Lon BSc58 CertEd59 BD79 AKC79. dss 79 d 87. Chapl Raines Sch 79-87; Homerton St Barn w St Paul *Lon* 79-85; Upper Chelsea St Simon 85-87; Hon Par Dn 87-89; Hon Par Dn Limehouse from 89. *Limehouse Rectory, 5 Newell Street, London E14 7HP* 071-987 1502

PEARCE, Brian Edward. b 39. Kelham Th Coll 59. d 64 p 65. C Smethwick St Matt *Birm* 64-68; C Kings Norton 68-72; TV 73-80; TR Swindon Dorcan *Bris* 80-91; C-in-c Withywood CD from 91. *63 Turtlegate Avenue, Withywood, Bristol BS13 8NN* Bristol (0272) 641263

PEARCE, Clive. b 40. Univ of Wales (Lamp) BA63. St Steph Ho Ox 63. d 65 p 66. C Acton Green St Pet *Lon* 65-67; C Eastcote St Lawr 67-73; V Hatch End St Anselm from 73. *The Vicarage, 50 Cedar Drive, Pinner, Middx HA5 4DE* 081-428 4111

PEARCE, Canon Denis William Wilfrid. b 25. Bps' Coll Cheshunt 55. d 58 p 59. C Lt Ilford St Mich *Chelmsf* 58-62; C Leytonstone St Jo 62-65; C-in-c Leytonstone St Aug CD 65-74; V Leytonstone H Trin Harrow Green 65-81; P-in-c Leyton St Luke 78-81; R Capel w Lt Wenham *St E* 81-86; P-in-c Lavenham 86-89; R from 89; RD Lavenham from 87; Hon Can St E Cathl from 90. *The Rectory, Lavenham, Sudbury, Suffolk CO10 9SA* Lavenham (0787) 247244

PEARCE, Desmond. b 30. Univ of Wales (Abth) BA52. E Midl Min Tr Course 85. d 88 p 89. NSM Chellaston *Derby* 88-90; NSM Walsall St Gabr Fullbrook *Lich* 90; C Stoke Lacy, Moreton Jeffries w Much Cowarne etc *Heref* from 91. *Ocle Pychard Vicarage, Burley Gate, Hereford HR1 3QR* Hereford (0432) 820385

PEARCE, Preb Eustace Kenneth Victor. b 13. Lon Univ BSc65 Ox Univ DipAnth64. ALCD37. d 37 p 38. CF (TA) 66-81; Preb Lich Cathl *Lich* 67-81; V Audley 71-81; rtd 81; Chief Exec Hour of Revival Chr Broadcasting Assn from 83; Perm to Offic *Ches* from 85. *15 Kynnersley Avenue, Kidsgrove, Stoke-on-Trent ST7 1AP* Stoke-on-Trent (0782) 773325

PEARCE, Canon Frank. b 31. St Aid Birkenhead. d 57 p 58. C Worksop Priory *S'well* 57-61; P-in-c W Retford 61-62; R 62-70; R Kettering SS Pet and Paul *Pet* from 70; Chapl Kettering Gen and St Mary's Hosps from 70; Can Pet Cathl *Pet* from 78. *The Rectory, Market Place, Kettering, Northants* Kettering (0536) 513385

PEARCE, Canon Gerald Nettleton. b 25. St Jo Coll Dur BA49 DipTh51. d 51 p 52. R Wilford *S'well* 61-73; RD Bingham 73-84; P-in-c Holme Pierrepont w Adbolton 73-84; V Radcliffe-on-Trent 73-84; V Shelford 73-84; Hon Can S'well Minster 77-84; R Sigglesthorne and Rise w Nunkeeling and Bewholme *York* 84-91; RD N Holderness 86-90; rtd 91; Dioc Rtd Clergy & Widows Officer from 91. *Sutherland Bridge, Cropton, Pickering, N Yorkshire YO18 8EU* Lastingham (07515) 420

PEARCE, Mrs Janet Elizabeth. b 49. Somerville Coll Ox BA72 MA76 CertEd74. N Ord Course 85. d 88. Hon Par Dn Helsby and Dunham-on-the-Hill *Ches* 88-91; Par Dn from 91. *4 Fieldway, Frodsham, Warrington WA6 6RQ* Frodsham (0928) 33553

PEARCE, Preb John Frederick Dilke. b 32. Ex Coll Ox BA55 MA59. Westcott Ho Cam. d 57 p 58. C Dalston St Mark w St Bart *Lon* 57-60; C Chelsea Ch Ch 60-63; R Lower Homerton St Paul 63-81; Preb St Paul's Cathl from 70; P-in-c Clapton Park All So 72-77; V 77-84; RD Hackney 74-79; R Homerton St Barn w St Paul 81-85; TR Hackney Marsh 85; P-in-c Upper Chelsea St Simon 85-89; AD Chelsea 88-89; R Limehouse from 89. *Limehouse Rectory, 5 Newell Street, London E14 7HP* 071-987 1502

PEARCE, Jonathan. b 55. St Jo Coll Nottm BTh85. d 85 p 86. C Gt Chesham *Ox* 85-89; C Newport Pagnell w Lathbury and Moulsoe from 89. *3 Castle Meadow Close, Newport Pagnell, Bucks MK16 9EJ* Newport Pagnell (0908) 617071

PEARCE, Kenneth Jack. b 25. CIPFA. Linc Th Coll 62. d 63 p 64. V Derby St Mark *Derby* 68-87; rtd 87. *117 Oaks Cross, Stevenage, Herts SG2 8LT* Stevenage (0438) 317385

PEARCE, Michael Hawkins. b 29. Sarum Th Coll 61. d 62 p 63. C Bedminster St Aldhelm *Bris* 62-65; C Bishopston 65-68; R Jacobstow w Warbstow *Truro* 68-74; V Treneglos 68-74; V St Teath from 74. *The Vicarage, St Teath, Bodmin, Cornwall PL30 3JF* Bodmin (0208) 850292

PEARCE, Neville John Lewis. b 33. CBIM88 Leeds Univ LLB53 LLM54. Trin Coll Bris 90. d 91. NSM Bath Walcot *B & W* from 91. *Penshurst, Weston Lane, Bath, Avon BA1 4AB* Bath (0225) 426925

PEARCE, Reginald Frederic George. b 15. St Aug Coll Cant 38. d 40 p 41. V Laneast w St Clether *Truro* 68-76; V Tresmere 70-76; V Laneast w St Clether and Tresmere 76-78; P-in-c St Erth 78-80; rtd 80. *Braehead House, Auburn Road, Kenilworth, 7700 South Africa* Cape Town (21) 797-1917

PEARCE, Robert John. b 47. GLCM LLCM79. Ripon Coll Cuddesdon 79. d 82 p 83. C Broseley w Benthall *Heref* 82-83; C Kington w Huntington, Old Radnor, Kinnerton etc 83-85; R Westbury from 85; R Yockleton from 85; V Gt Wollaston from 85. *The Rectory, Westbury, Shrewsbury SY5 9QX* Shrewsbury (0743) 884216

PEARCE, Ronald Edgar John. b 21. Univ of Wales (Lamp) BA42. Lich Th Coll 42. d 44 p 45. V Warmley *Bris* 61-68; R Syston 62-68; Chapl R Wolv Sch 68-86; rtd 86. *52 Cherrington Gardens, Bramstead Avenue, Compton, Wolverhampton* Wolverhampton (0902) 756420

PEARCE, Stephen Wilson. b 34. K Coll Lon. d 62 p 63. C Chorley St Jas *Blackb* 62-64; C Sheff St Steph w St Phil and St Ann *Sheff* 64-66; C Warton St Oswald *Blackb* 66-69; V Skerton St Chad 69-77 and 78-80; Canada 77-78; C Fleetwood *Blackb* 80-81; TV Raveningham *Nor* 81-85; P-in-c Martin w Thornton *Linc* from 85; P-in-c Scrivelsby w Dalderby from 85; P-in-c Roughton w Haltham from 85; P-in-c Kirkby-on-Bain from 85; P-in-c Thimbleby from 85; RD Horncastle from 89. *The Vicarage, Main Road, Thornton, Horncastle, Lincs LN9 5JU* Horncastle (06582) 6456

PEARCE, Trevor John. b 27. Roch Th Coll 65. d 67 p 68. C Cheriton Street *Cant* 67-69; C Willesborough w Hinxhill 69-73; V Devonport St Barn *Ex* 73-79; Chapl N Devon Distr Hosp Barnstaple 79-83; V Derby St Andr w St Osmund *Derby* 83-84; Chapl Derby R Infirmary from 83; Lic to Offic *Derby* from 84. *Royal Infirmary, London Road, Derby DE1 2QY* Derby (0332) 47141

PEARCEY, Paul Alan Cyril. b 37. St Jo Coll Dur BA59. Cranmer Hall Dur DipTh61. d 61 p 62. C Deane *Man* 61-65; Chapl Red Bank Schs 65-67; C-in-c Blackley White Moss St Mark CD *Man* 67-73; R Cwmbach Llechryd and Llanelwedd w Llanfaredd *S & B* 73-79; V Llanelwedd w Llanfaredd w Llansantffraed etc from 79; RD Builth Elwell from 84. *The Rectory, Llanelwedd, Builth Wells, Powys LD2 3TY* Builth Wells (0982) 553701

PEARCY, Vernon Charles. b 23. K Coll Lon BD56 AKC56. d 56 p 57. C Belmont *S'wark* 68-70; C Wimbledon 70-76; C S w N Hayling *Portsm* 76-77; R Warbleton and Bodle Street Green *Chich* 78-83; C Cleethorpes *Linc* 83-86; rtd 88. *20 Springfield Crescent, Poole, Dorset BH14 0LL* Poole (0202) 743782

PEARE, Canon Oliver Arthur Patrick. b 17. TCD BA43 MA55. CITC 46. d 46 p 47. I Kinsale Union C, C & R 66-87; Treas Cork Cathl 84-87; Preb Tymothan

St Patr Cathl Dub 84-87; rtd 87. *High Copse, Compass Hill, Kinsale, Co Cork, Irish Republic* Cork (21) 774191

PEARKES, Nicholas Robin Clement. b 49. Ex Univ BA. Linc Th Coll. d 82 p 83. C Plymstock *Ex* 82-85; P-in-c Weston Mill 85-86; TV Devonport St Boniface and St Phil from 86. *The Vicarage, Bridwell Lane, Plymouth PL5 1AN* Plymouth (0752) 362060

PEARMAIN, Andrew Neil. b 55. K Coll Lon BD79 AKC79. Ridley Hall Cam 79. d 81 p 82. C Cranleigh *Guildf* 81-84; P-in-c Frimley 85-86; C 86-87; Chapl Frimley Park Hosp 87. *35 Cavendish Road, Bournemouth* Bournemouth (0202) 553395

PEARMAIN, Brian Albert John. b 34. Lon Univ BD68. Roch Th Coll 63. d 66 p 67. C Shirley St Jo *Cant* 66-69; C Selsdon St Jo w St Fran 69-73; P-in-c Louth H Trin *Linc* 73-75; TV Louth 75-79; R Scartho from 79; RD Grimsby and Cleethorpes from 89. *44 Waltham Road, Scartho, Grimsby DN33 2LX* Grimsby (0472) 72728

PEARS, John Barbour. b 10. Sarum Th Coll 46. d 48 p 49. Chapl N Gen Hosp Sheff 56-73; Dioc Chapl *Sheff* 73-78; Lic to Offic 78-79; rtd 79; Hon C Sheff St Cuth *Sheff* 79-86. *Dulverton Hall, St Martin's Square, Scarborough YO11 2DB* Scarborough (0723) 373082

PEARSE, Andrew George. b 46. Wycliffe Hall Ox 71. d 74 p 75. C Homerton St Luke *Lon* 74-77; C Chadderton Em *Man* 77-81; R Collyhurst 81-89; Area Sec (NE and E Midl) SAMS from 89. *9 Troutsdale Avenue, Rawcliffe, York YO3 6TR* York (0904) 655881

PEARSE, Percy George Hedley. b 13. Univ Coll Dur LTh35 BA36 MA39. ALCD35. d 36 p 37. R Doddinghurst *Chelmsf* 59-72; R Stondon Massey 59-72; R Debden 72-77; RD Saffron Walden 74-78; rtd 78; Perm to Offic *Win* from 78. *3 Chalfont Avenue, Christchurch, Dorset BH23 2SB* Christchurch (0202) 482914

PEARSE, Ronald Thomas Hennessy. b 26. AKC52. d 53 p 54. R Asfordby *Leic* 58-84; P-in-c Scalford w Wycombe and Chadwell 75-76; R Thurcaston 84-89; rtd 89; Perm to Offic *Leic* 89-90. *45 Middleton Place, Loughborough, Leics LE11 2BY* Loughborough (0509) 215478

PEARSON, Andrew George Campbell. b 41. Qu Coll Ox BA63 BA66. Wycliffe Hall Ox 63. d 71 p 72. C Gillingham St Mark *Roch* 71-72; C Billingshurst *Chich* 72-77; C Ches Square St Mich w St Phil *Lon* 77-82; Co-ord Busoga Trust from 82. *15 Chadwin Road, London E13 8ND or, 2 Elizabeth Street SW1W 9RB* 071-476 6730

PEARSON, Andrew John. b 59. Humberside Coll of Educn HND83. Westcott Ho Cam 86. d 89 p 90. C Knaresborough *Ripon* from 89. *9 Castle Yard, Knaresborough, N Yorkshire HG5 8AS* Harrogate (0423) 864678

PEARSON, Brian. b 29. LTCL53 Lon Inst of Educn CertEd54. Sarum & Wells Th Coll 71. d 73 p 74. C Rainham *Roch* 73-77; Chapl Asst Pembury Hosp Tunbridge Wells 77-80; C Pembury *Roch* 77-80; V Gravesend St Aid from 80; Chapl Gravesend and N Kent Hosp 81-83. *The Vicarage, St Gregory's Crescent, Gravesend, Kent DA12 4JL* Gravesend (0474) 352500

PEARSON, Canon Brian Robert. b 35. Leeds Univ BA59. Coll of Resurr Mirfield 59. d 61 p 62. C Chesterfield All SS *Derby* 61-66; P-in-c Derby St Jo 66-72; P-in-c Derby St Anne 66-72; R Thorpe *Nor* 72-90; Hon Can Nor Cathl 85-90; RD Nor E 86-90; V Harrogate St Wilfrid and St Luke *Ripon* from 90. *St Wilfrid's Vicarage, 51B Kent Road, Harrogate, N Yorkshire HG1 2EU* Harrogate (0423) 503259

PEARSON, Brian William. b 49. CEng MBCS FHSM Brighton Poly BSc71 City Univ MSc80. S'wark Ord Course and Clapham Ord Scheme 76. d 79 p 80. Hon C Plumstead All SS *S'wark* 79-81; Perm to Offic *Chich* 81-83; Hon C Broadwater St Mary 83-88; Bp's Research and Dioc Communications Officer *B & W* 88-90; Dioc Missr 91; Abp's Officer for Miss and Evang and Tait Missr *Cant* from 91. *20 Pilgrim's Way, Canterbury, Kent CT1 1XU or, Lambeth Palace, London SE1 7JU* Canterbury (0227) 459781

PEARSON, Christian David John (Brother Christian). b 42. Open Univ BA76 CCC Cam BA79 MA83. AKC65. d 66 p 67. C Pallion *Dur* 66-68; C Peterlee 68-71; SSF from 71; Lic to Offic *Sarum* 71-73; Tanzania 74-75; Lic to Offic *Ely* 75-90; Asst Chapl Keble Coll Ox 82-83; Chapl St Cath Coll Cam 83-86; Chapl Down Coll Cam 86-90; Lic to Offic *Lon* from 90; Dep Warden & Chapl Lon Ho Trust from 90. *William Goodenough House, Mecklenburgh Square, London WC1N 2AN* 071-837 8888

PEARSON, Christopher John. b 49. GRSM LRAM ARCM. Oak Hill NSM Course 81. d 84 p 85. NSM Barton Seagrave w Warkton *Pet* 84-86; C Kettering St

Andr 86-88; V Nassington w Yarwell and Woodnewton from 88. *The Vicarage, 46 Church Street, Nassington, Peterborough PE8 6QG* Stamford (0780) 782271

PEARSON, David. b 57. Man Poly BA78. Trin Coll Bris 85. d 88 p 89. C Shawbury *Lich* from 88; C Morton from 88; C Stanton on Hine Heath from 88. *10 Bridge Way, Shawbury, Shrewsbury SY4 4PG* Shawbury (0939) 250902

PEARSON, Edgar. b 13. Tyndale Hall Bris 37. d 41 p 42. C Handforth *Ches* 41; R Dallinghoo and Pettistree *St E* 65-83; P-in-c Bredfield w Boulge 74-86; rtd 83; P-in-c Dallinghoo and Pettistree *St E* 83-86. *Maendy House, Penrhos, Raglan, Gwent NP5 2LQ* Llantilio (060085) 398

PEARSON, Geoffrey Charles. b 49. ARCS BSc. Oak Hill Th Coll. d 82 p 83. C Foord St Jo *Cant* 82-86; V Ramsgate St Luke from 86. *St Luke's Vicarage, St Luke's Avenue, Ramsgate, Kent CT11 7JX* Thanet (0843) 592562

PEARSON, Geoffrey Seagrave. b 51. St Jo Coll Dur BA72 DipTh73. Cranmer Hall Dur 72. d 74 p 75. C Kirkheaton *Wakef* 74-77; P-in-c Blackb Ch Ch w St Matt *Blackb* 77-82; V Blackb Redeemer 82-85; Asst Home Sec Gen Syn Bd for Miss and Unity 85-89; Hon C Forty Hill Jes Ch *Lon* 85-89; Exec Sec BCC Evang Cttee 86-89; V Roby *Liv* from 89. *The Vicarage, 11 Church Road, Liverpool L36 9TL* 051-489 1438

PEARSON, George Michael. b 31. FCA FBCS MIMC. Coll of Resurr Mirfield 89 Qu Coll Birm 86. d 88 p 90. NSM Solihull *Birm* from 88. *67A Hampton Lane, Solihull, W Midlands B91 2QD* 021-705 0288

PEARSON, Harold (Brother Geoffrey). b 21. Ch Coll Cam BA43 MA46. Chich Th Coll 43. d 45 p 46. SSF from 48; Papua New Guinea 59-70; Min Gen SSF 70-85; Australia 67-70; Hon Can Win Cathl *Win* from 81; Zimbabwe from 86; rtd 91. *St Barnabas's Friary, 191 Westwood, PO Kambuzuma, Harare, Zimbabwe* Harare (4) 27307

PEARSON, Harry MacGregor. b 02. MICE ACGI Lon Univ BSc. d 64 p 65. C Canvey Is *Chelmsf* 64-69; P-in-c Overbury w Alstone, Teddington and Lt Washbourne *Worc* 69-71; rtd 71; Perm to Offic St As from 71; Lich from 81. *17 Park Drive, Oswestry, Shropshire SY11 1BN* Oswestry (0691) 655783

PEARSON, Henry Gervis. b 47. Mansf Coll Ox BA72 MA76. St Jo Coll Nottm 72. d 74 p 75. C Southgate *Chich* 74-76; TV 76-82; V Debenham w Aspall and Kenton *St E* from 82; Chapl to Suffolk Fire Service from 88; RD Loes from 89. *The Vicarage, Gracechurch Street, Debenham, Stowmarket, Suffolk IP14 6RE* Debenham (0728) 860265

PEARSON, Ian. b 49. Liv Univ BA71. S'wark Ord Course 79. d 82 p 83. NSM Lavender Hill Ascension *S'wark* 82-85; Archivist USPG 82-85; Lic to Offic *Lon* from 84; Perm to Offic S'wark 85-90; Archivist Nat Soc from 85; Hon C Westmr St Matt *Lon* 86-88. *74 Park Meadow, Old Hatfield, Herts AL9 5HB* Hatfield (0707) 274333

PEARSON, Canon James Stuart. b 28. St Jo Coll Dur BA57. Cranmer Hall Dur 57. d 58 p 59. C Halifax St Jo Bapt *Wakef* 58-63; V Alverthorpe 63-70; V Knottingley 70-78; Dioc Soc Resp Adv 78-87; V Woolley from 78; Chapl Bretton Hall Coll of Educn from 87; Hon Can Wakef Cathl from 89. *Woolley Vicarage, Wakefield, W Yorkshire WF4 2JU* Barnsley (0226) 382550

PEARSON, James William. b 20. FCA59. Qu Coll Birm 75. d 78 p 79. NSM Beoley *Worc* 78-90; Perm to Offic from 90. *Ringwood, Rowney Green, Alvechurch, Birmingham B48 7QE* Redditch (0527) 66952

PEARSON, John Alfred Fowler. b 12. AKC33. Ely Th Coll 34. d 35 p 36. V Golders Green St Mich *Lon* 61-76; Perm to Offic *Chich* from 76; rtd 77. *College of St Barnabas, Blackberry Lane, Lingfield, Surrey RH7 6NJ* Dormans Park (034287) 717

PEARSON, John Edwin. b 26. Westcott Ho Cam. d 61 p 62. C-in-c Hove St Patr *Chich* 69-74; R Lewes St Jo sub Castro 74-76; rtd 75; Perm to Offic *Chich* from 76. *Tile Cottage, Balcombe, Haywards Heath, W Sussex* Balcombe (0444) 411

PEARSON, John Nigel. b 45. CA Tr Coll IDC75 E Midl Min Tr Course 78. d 81 p 82. C Stapenhill w Cauldwell *Derby* 81-83; V Measham *Leic* from 83. *The Vicarage, High Street, Measham, Burton-on-Trent, Staffs DE12 7HZ* Measham (0530) 70354

PEARSON, Kevin. b 54. Leeds Univ BA75 Edin Univ BD79. Edin Th Coll 76. d 79 p 80. C Horden *Dur* 79-81; Chapl Leeds Univ *Ripon* 81-87; R Edin St Salvador *Edin* from 87; Dir of Ords from 90. *The Rectory, 44 Stenhouse Street West, Edinburgh EH11 3QU* 031-443 2228

PEARSON, Ms Lindsey Carole. b 61. Cov Poly BA85 CQSW85. Westcott Ho Cam 86. d 89. Par Dn High Harrogate St Pet *Ripon* from 89. *9 Castle Yard, Knaresborough, N Yorkshire HG5 8AS* Harrogate (0423) 864678

PEARSON, Michael John. b 53. Southn Univ BTh78. Sarum Th Coll 74. d 78 p 79. C Paignton St Jo *Ex* 78-82; TV Ilfracombe, Lee, W Down, Woolacombe and Bittadon 82-85; TV Ilfracombe, Lee, Woolacombe, Bittadon etc 85-86; TV Barnstaple from 86; Chapl N Devon Distr Hosp Barnstaple from 86. *The Rectory, Sowden Lane, Barnstaple, Devon EX32 8BU* Barnstaple (0271) 73837

PEARSON, Peter. b 09. Tyndale Hall Bris 32. d 35 p 36. V Fremington *Ex* 45-74; rtd 75; P-in-c Nymet Rowland w Coldridge *Ex* 75-77; P-in-c Chawleigh w Cheldon 77-78. *41 Barum Court, Litchdon Street, Barnstaple, Devon EX32 8QL* Barnstaple (0271) 73525

PEARSON, Mrs Priscilla Dawn. b 45. Oak Hill Th Coll BA90. d 90. C Stanford-le-Hope w Mucking *Chelmsf* from 90. *Glebe House, Wharf Road, Stanford-le-Hope SS17 0BY* Grays Thurrock (0375) 641210

PEARSON, Raymond Joseph. b 44. AKC71. St Aug Coll Cant 71. d 72 p 73. C Wetherby *Ripon* 72-75; C Goring-by-Sea *Chich* 75-77; C Bramley *Ripon* 77-82; V Patrick Brompton and Hunton from 82; V Crakehall from 82; V Hornby from 82; World Miss Officer from 88; Asst RD Wensley from 91. *The Vicarage, Patrick Brompton, Bedale, N Yorkshire DL8 1JN* Bedale (0677) 50439

PEARSON, Robert James Stephen. b 52. Cov Poly BA74. St Steph Ho Ox 85. d 87 p 88. C Stoke Newington St Mary *Lon* 87-90; C Haggerston All SS from 90. *All Saint's Vicarage, Livermere Road, London E8 4EZ* 071-254 0436

PEARSON, Roderick Percy. b 21. Linc Th Coll 74. d 75 p 76. C Darlington St Cuth w St Hilda *Dur* 75-80; V Bishop Middleham from 80. *The Vicarage, Bishop Middleham, Ferryhill, Co Durham DL17 9AE* Ferryhill (0740) 651360

PEARSON, Roy Barthram. b 35. K Coll Lon 56. d 60 p 61. C Brookfield St Mary *Lon* 60-64; C St Marylebone St Cypr 64-70; V Tottenham All Hallows from 70. *The Priory, Church Lane, London N17* 081-808 2470

PEARSON, Stephen. d 43 p 44. P-in-c Clapton *Pet* 69-77; R Luddington w Hemington and Thurning 69-77; rtd 77. *Address excluded by request*

PEARSON-MILES, David. b 37. St Jo Coll Nottm 74. d 76 p 77. C Hazlemere Ox 76-79; R Waddesdon w Over Winchendon and Fleet Marston 79-82; CF from 82. *c/o MOD (Army), Bagshot Park, Bagshot, Surrey GU19 5PL* Bagshot (0276) 71717

PEART, John Graham. b 36. Bps' Coll Cheshunt 65. d 68 p 69. C Cheshunt *St Alb* 68-70; C St Alb St Pet 70-73; R Hunsdon 73-76; R Widford 73-76; Ind Chapl 76-82; Chapl St Geo Hosp and Distr Gen Hosp Stafford 82-87; Qu Eliz Hosp and Bensham Hosp Gateshead 87-89; Garlands Hosp from 89; P-in-c Cotehill and Cumwhinton *Carl* from 89. *The Vicarage, Cotehill, Carlisle CA4 0DY* Carlisle (0228) 60323

PEASE, John Alfred. b 29. St Aid Birkenhead 58. d 60 p 61. C Swinton *Sheff* 60-63; C Sheff Parson Cross St Cecilia 63-65; V Bolton-upon-Dearne 65-70; V S Kirkby *Wakef* 70-81; V Bovey Tracey St Jo *Ex* 81-84; RD Moreton 83-86; P-in-c Chudleigh Knighton 83-84; V Bovey Tracey St John, Chudleigh Knighton etc from 84. *St John's Vicarage, Newton Road, Bovey Tracey, Newton Abbot, Devon TQ13 9BD* Bovey Tracey (0626) 833451

PEASTON, Canon Monroe. b 14. BNC Ox BA36 MA43 Lon Univ BD48. Union Th Sem (NY) PhD64 Montreal Dioc Th Coll Hon DD75 Wycliffe Hall Ox 36. d 38 p 39. Canada 64-84; Hon Can Montreal from 66; rtd 84; USA from 84. *333 Old Mill Road (19), Santa Barbara, California 93110, USA* Santa Barbara (805) 967-7545

PEAT, David James. b 62. Leeds Univ BA84. Cranmer Hall Dur 86. d 89 p 90. C Wetherby *Ripon* from 89. *53 Barleyfields Road, Wetherby, W Yorkshire LS22 4PT* Wetherby (0937) 63628

PEAT, David William. b 37. Clare Coll Cam BA59 PhD63. Westcott Ho Cam 72. d 75 p 76. C Chesterton St Andr *Ely* 75-77; Chapl Univ Coll of Ripon & York St Jo 77-83; V E Ardsley *Wakef* 83-87; Prin Willesden Min Tr Scheme from 87. *Glebe House, Royal Lane, Hillingdon, Middx* Uxbridge (0895) 56427

PEAT, Ven Lawrence Joseph. b 28. Linc Th Coll 55. d 58 p 59. C Bramley *Ripon* 58-61; V 65-73; R Heaton Norris All SS *Man* 61-65; P-in-c Southend St Erkenwald *Chelmsf* 73-74; TR Southend St Jo w St Mark, All SS w St Fran etc 74-79; R Skelsmergh w Selside and

Longsleddale *Carl* 79-86; RD Kendal 84-89; TV Kirkby Lonsdale 86-89; Hon Can Carl Cathl from 88; Adn Westmorland and Furness from 89. *Woodcroft, Levens, Kendal, Cumbria LA8 8NQ* Sedgwick (05395) 61281

PEATFIELD, Canon Alfred Charles Henry. b 22. New Coll Ox BA48 MA48. Ripon Hall Ox 48. **d** 51 **p** 52. C Hackney St Jo *Lon* 51-54; V Battersea St Paul *S'wark* 54-56; Malaya 56-63; Malaysia 63-70; Adn N Malaya 64-70; V Hornchurch St Andr *Chelmsf* from 70; RD Havering 76-80; Hon Can Chelmsf Cathl from 80. *222 High Street, Hornchurch, Essex RM12 6QP* Hornchurch (04024) 41571

PEATMAN, Michael Robert. b 61. Keble Coll Ox BA85 MA89 St Jo Coll Dur BA89. Cranmer Hall Dur 87. **d** 90 **p** 91. C Greasley *S'well* from 90. *2 Grantham Close, Giltbrook, Notts NG16 2WB* Nottingham (0602) 384960

PECK, David George. b 11. Jes Coll Cam BA32 MA48 Linc Coll Ox MA51. St Steph Ho Ox 32. **d** 34 **p** 35. R Shellingford *Ox* 63-83; rtd 83. *The Barn House, Chapel Road, Stanford in the Vale, Faringdon, Oxon SN7 8LE* Stanford in the Vale (0367) 710511

PECK, Trevor Paul Owen. b 47. Lich Th Coll 69. **d** 72 **p** 73. C Hatf *Sheff* 72-74; C Swinton 75-77; TV Gt Grimsby St Mary and St Jas *Linc* 77-81; P-in-c Glentworth 81-86; P-in-c Hemswell w Harpswell 81-86; V Burgh le Marsh 86-87; R Bratoft w Irby-in-the-Marsh 86-87. *5 Mellors Lodge, Robin Hood Chase, Nottingham NG3 4EY* Nottingham (0602) 411340 or 413360

PECK, William Gerard. b 18. AKC40. Lich Th Coll 40. **d** 41 **p** 42. Hon CF from 49; R Fornham All SS *St E* 63-82; rtd 83; Perm to Offic *St E* from 83. *37 Catherine Road, Woodbridge, Suffolk IP12 4JP* Woodbridge (03943) 6479

PECKETT, Desmonde Claude Brown. b 19. Ex & Truro NSM Scheme. **d** 77 **p** 78. NSM Charlestown *Truro* from 77. *Smugglers, Porthpean, St Austell, Cornwall PL26 6AY* St Austell (0726) 72768

PECKETT, John Freeman. b 20. Clifton Th Coll. **d** 74 **p** 76. Kenya 74-77; Hon C Harringay St Paul *Lon* 77-79; Hon C Palmers Green St Jo 80-85; rtd 85. *30A Finchley Road, Westcliff-on-Sea, Essex SS0 8AD* Southend-on-Sea (0702) 332667

PECKHAM, Richard Graham. b 51. Sarum & Wells Th Coll 84. **d** 86 **p** 87. C Bishop's Cleeve *Glouc* 86-89; TV Ilfracombe, Lee, Woolacombe, Bittadon etc *Ex* from 89. *The Vicarage, Springfield, Woolacombe, Devon EX34 7BX* Woolacombe (0271) 870467

PECKOVER, Cecil Raymond. b 16. Ridley Hall Cam 62. **d** 63 **p** 64. V Emneth *Ely* 65-78; R Clenchwarton 78-80; rtd 80; Perm to Offic *Nor* from 81. *The Whins, The Common, North Runcton, King's Lynn, Norfolk* King's Lynn (0553) 841539

PEDLAR, John Glanville. b 43. Ex Univ BA68. St Steph Ho Ox 68. **d** 70 **p** 71. C Tavistock and Gulworthy *Ex* 70-73; Prec Portsm Cathl *Portsm* 74-77; Prec St Alb Abbey *St Alb* 77-81; V Redbourn from 81; PV Westmr Abbey from 87. *The Vicarage, Church End, Redbourn, St Albans, Herts AL3 7DU* Redbourn (0582) 793122

PEDLEY, Miss Betty. b 49. ALCM78 Leeds Univ BEd71 Ripon Coll of Educn CertEd70 Coll of Preceptors DSpEd81. N Ord Course 85. **d** 88. Par Dn Sowerby *Wakef* from 88. *24 Towngate, Sowerby, Sowerby Bridge, W Yorkshire HX6 1HY* Halifax (0422) 834344

PEDLEY, Geoffrey Stephen. b 40. Qu Coll Cam BA64 MA67. Cuddesdon Coll 64. **d** 66 **p** 67. C Liv Our Lady and St Nic *Liv* 66-69; C Cov H Trin *Cov* 69-71; Zambia 71-77; P-in-c Stockton H Trin *Dur* 77-83; V Stockton St Pet 77-88; Chapl to HM The Queen from 84; R Whickham *Dur* from 88. *The Rectory, Church Chare, Whickham, Newcastle upon Tyne NE16 4SH* 091-488 7397

PEDLEY, Nicholas Charles. b 48. DipSocWork75 CQSW75. Qu Coll Birm 88. **d** 90 **p** 91. C Stafford St Jo and Tixall w Ingestre *Lich* from 90. *42 Longhurst Drive, Stafford ST16 3RG* Stafford (0785) 214239

PEDLOW, Henry Noel. b 37. QUB BA59. **d** 61 **p** 62. C Belf St Phil *Conn* 61-66; C Belf St Nic 66-70; I Eglantine 70-82; I Kilkeel *D & D* 82-89; I Belf St Donard from 89. *St Donard's Rectory, 421 Beersbridge Road, Belfast BT5 5DU* Belfast (0232) 652321

PEEBLES, Alexander Paterson. b 21. Westcott Ho Cam 62. **d** 63 **p** 64. P-in-c Grendon Underwood w Edgcott *Ox* 67-73; P-in-c Twyford (Bucks) 67-73; P-in-c Marsh Gibbon 67-73; P-in-c Preston Bissett, Chetwode and Barton Hartshorn 67-73; RD Claydon 71-73; R Glenrothes *St And* 73-78; Can St Ninian's Cathl Perth 78-82; Dioc Supernumerary 81-82; P-in-c Bathgate *Edin* 82-87; P-in-c Linlithgow 82-87; rtd 86; NSM Newburgh

St And from 88. *The Studio, 5 Hillside Place, Newport-on-Tay, Fife DD6 8DH* Newport-on-Tay (0382) 542530

PEEBLES, David Thomas. b 64. Bris Univ BA85 Dur Univ PGCE86. Coll of Resurr Mirfield 88. **d** 90 **p** 91. C Crewe St Andr *Ches* from 90. *48 Manor Way, Crewe CW2 6JX* Crewe (0270) 212244

PEEK, John Richard. b 51. Bris Univ BSc72 Nottm Univ BA75. St Jo Coll Nottm 73. **d** 76 **p** 77. C Hebburn St Jo *Dur* 76-78; C Dunston 78-81; R Armthorpe *Sheff* 81-86; Chapl Casterton Sch from 89. *Casterton School, Carnforth, Lancs* Carnforth (0524) 271202

PEEK, Roland Denys. b 17. Sarum Th Coll 69. **d** 70 **p** 71. C Ex St Matt *Ex* 70-74; R Moretonhampstead 74-78; R Moretonhampstead, N Bovey and Manaton 78-84; rtd 84. *The Barns, Veryan, Truro, Cornwall TR2 5QA* Truro (0872) 501752

PEEL, Basil Headley. b 26. TCD BA52 MA55. Wells Th Coll 52. **d** 54 **p** 55. C Oswestry St Oswald *Lich* 54-59; C Leek St Edw 59-62; V Chesterton 62-68; V Willenhall H Trin 68-79; V Longsdon from 79; P-in-c Rushton from 84; P-in-c Horton from 84. *The Vicarage, Longsdon, Stoke-on-Trent ST9 9QF* Leek (0538) 385318

PEEL, Mrs Christine Mary. CertEd. Portsm Dioc Tr Course. **d** 90. NSM Sheet *Portsm* from 90. *7 Crundles, Herne Farm, Petersfield, Hants GU31 4PJ* Petersfield (0730) 66926

PEEL, David Charles. b 41. AKC75. St Aug Coll Cant 75. **d** 76 **p** 77. C Tynemouth Cullercoats St Paul *Newc* 76-79; C Tynemouth St Jo 79-84; Ldr Cedarwood Project 84-88 and from 91; Warden Communicare Ho 89-91; Min Killingworth 89-91. *23 Cedarwood Avenue, North Shields, Tyne and Wear NE29 6AF*

PEEL, Derek. b 46. Chich Th Coll 69. **d** 72 **p** 73. C Ealing St Pet Mt Park *Lon* 72-74; C Westmr St Matt 75-79; V Bournemouth St Fran *Win* 79-82; R Lon Docks St Pet w Wapping St Jo *Lon* from 82. *St Peter's Clergy House, Wapping Lane, London E1 9RW* 071-481 2985

PEEL, Derrick. b 50. Open Univ BA82. Linc Th Coll 75. **d** 78 **p** 79. C Otley *Bradf* 78-82; V Shelf from 82; P-in-c Buttershaw St Aid from 89. *The Vicarage, 80 Carr House Road, Shelf, Halifax, W Yorkshire HX3 7RJ* Bradford (0274) 677413

PEEL, John Bruce. b 30. TCD BA54 MA68. Wells Th Coll 69. **d** 70 **p** 71. C Wilmslow *Ches* 70-75; V Weston 75-83; V Henbury from 83; Chapl Parkside Hosp Ches from 83. *The Vicarage, Henbury, Macclesfield, Cheshire SK11 9NN* Macclesfield (0625) 424113

PEEL, Dr Michael Jerome. b 31. Bris Univ BA55 MLitt73 St Cath Soc Ox DipTh59 Man Univ BD65 K Coll Lon PhD88. Wycliffe Hall Ox 57. **d** 59 **p** 60. C Stretford St Matt *Man* 59-61; C Chorlton upon Medlock 61-62; Chapl Man Univ 61-62; C Chorlton-cum-Hardy St Clem 62-65; V Chirbury *Heref* 65-68; P-in-c Marton 65-68; R Iver Heath *Ox* 68-87; V Linslade from 87. *The Vicarage, Vicarage Road, Linslade, Leighton Buzzard, Beds LU7 7LP* Leighton Buzzard (0525) 372149

PEELING, Mrs Pamela Mary Alberta. b 44. Oak Hill Th Coll 83. **dss** 86 **d** 87. Moulsham St Luke *Chelmsf* 86-87; Hon Par Dn 87-88; Hon Par Dn N Springfield from 88. *129 Waterhouse Lane, Chelmsford CM1 2RY* Chelmsford (0245) 259285

PEERS, John Edward. b 39. Bps' Coll Cheshunt 60. **d** 63 **p** 64. C Crayford *Roch* 63-67; C Beckenham St Jas 67-69; C Winlaton *Dur* 69-72; P-in-c Silksworth 72-81; R Lt Bowden St Nic *Leic* 81-86; P-in-c Lt Bowden St Hugh 83-86; RD Gartree I (Harborough) 84-88; R Market Harborough Transfiguration 86-88; V Skipton Ch Ch *Bradf* from 88. *Christ Church Vicarage, Carleton Road, Skipton, N Yorkshire BD23 2BE* Skipton (0756) 793612

PEERS, Michael John. b 65. SS Paul & Mary Coll Cheltenham BA86. Ripon Coll Cuddesdon 88. **d** 91. C Birstall and Wanlip *Leic* from 91. *33 Walker Road, Birstall, Leicester LE4 3BP* Leicester (0533) 677572

PEET, Derek Edwin. b 26. Sheff Univ BA51 DipEd Lon Univ DipTh57. Qu Coll Birm 66. **d** 67 **p** 68. C Hebden Bridge *Wakef* 67-70; V Darton 70-79; TR Gleadless Valley *Sheff* 79-85; V Kirk Hallam *Derby* from 85. *The Vicarage, 71 Ladywood Road, Ilkeston, Derbyshire DE7 4NF* Ilkeston (0602) 322402

PEET, John Christopher. b 56. Or Coll Ox BA80 MA83 Clare Coll Cam BA82 MA87. Ridley Hall Cam 80. **d** 83 **p** 84. C Menston w Woodhead *Bradf* 83-86; C Prenton *Ches* 86-89; V Harden and Wilsden *Bradf* from 89. *The Vicarage, Wilsden Old Road, Harden, Bingley, W Yorkshire BD16 1JD* Cullingworth (0535) 272344

PEET, John Michael. b 44. AKC67. **d** 68 **p** 72. C Battersea St Pet *S'wark* 68-69; C Sutton St Nic 69-74; C Perry Hill St Geo 74-78; TV Stepney St Dunstan and All SS *Lon* 78-81; P-in-c Stamford Hill St Bart 81-86; V 87-89; P-in-c

Mile End Old Town H Trin 89-90; P-in-c Bromley All Hallows 89-90; TR Bow H Trin and All Hallows from 90. *Holy Trinity Vicarage, 28 Coborn Street, London E3 2AB* 081-980 2074

PEGG, Brian Peter Richard. b 30. Sarum & Wells Th Coll 82. **d** 83 **p** 84. C Furze Platt *Ox* 83-85; V Ashbury, Compton Beauchamp and Longcot w Fernham from 85. *The Vicarage, Ashbury, Swindon SN6 8LN* Ashbury (079371) 231

PEGG, Charles William. b 06. ACT ThL31. **d** 31 **p** 32. V Oakengates *Lich* 58-74; rtd 74; P-in-c Gt Bircham *Nor* 74-78; Perm to Offic from 79. *140 Fearnville Road, Leeds LS8 3DZ* Leeds (0532) 400284

PEGG, Gerald Francis. b 37. FCII70. S'wark Ord Course 88. **d** 91. NSM Belmont *S'wark* from 91. *26 Wilbury Avenue, Sutton, Surrey SM2 7DU* 081-643 1396

PEGG, Stephen Roland. b 48. Linc Th Coll 72. **d** 74 **p** 75. C Mile End Old Town H Trin *Lon* 74-77; Jamaica from 77. *PO Box 98, Montego Bay, Jamaica*

PEGLER, Frederic Arthur. b 19. Selw Coll Cam BA46 MA48. Qu Coll Birm 46. **d** 47 **p** 48. Canada 63-84; rtd 84; Perm to Offic *St Alb* 84-85. *307-1060 Linden Avenue, Victoria, British Columbia, Canada, V8V 4H2*

PEIRCE, Canon John Martin. b 36. Jes Coll Cam BA59 MA65. Westcott Ho Cam 65. **d** 66 **p** 67. C Croydon *Cant* 66-70; C Fareham H Trin *Portsm* 70-71; TV 71-76; TR Langley Marish *Ox* 76-85; RD Burnham 78-82; Dir of Ords from 85; Dir of Post-Ord Tr from 85; Can Res Ch Ch from 87. *70 Yarnells Hill, Oxford OX2 9BG* Oxford (0865) 721330

PEIRSON, Peter Kenneth. b 16. Worc Coll Ox BA37 MA46 DipEd48. Lich Th Coll 53. **d** 54 **p** 55. V Edmonton St Martin *Lon* 64-77; R Preston and Ridlington w Wing and Pilton *Pet* 77-82; rtd 82; Perm to Offic *Ely* from 83. *9 Elm Drive, Offord Cluny, Huntingdon, Cambs PE18 9RN* Huntingdon (0480) 811364

PELHAM, John. b 36. New Coll Ox BA61 MA65. **d** 79 **p** 80. NSM Balerno *Edin* from 79. *2 Horsburgh Bank, Balerno, Midlothian EH14 7DA* 031-449 3934

PELL, Charles Andrew. b 54. Leeds Univ CertEd77. Aston Tr Scheme 87 St Jo Coll Nottm 87. **d** 89 **p** 90. C Mottram in Longdendale w Woodhead *Ches* 89-90; C Handforth from 90. *61 Pickmere Road, Handforth, Wilmslow, Cheshire SK9 3TB* Wilmslow (0625) 529570

PELLANT, Walter Reginald Guy. b 14. OBE79. AKC42. Cuddesdon Coll 42. **d** 43 **p** 44. Chapl RAF 48-69; Asst Chapl-in-Chief RAF 69-71; QHC from 70; Chapl Geneva *Eur* 71-80; rtd 80. *3 Fountain Court, 13 The Avenue, Poole, Dorset* Bournemouth (0202) 768521

PELLEY, John Lawless. b 34. Oak Hill Th Coll 67. **d** 69 **p** 70. C Fareham St Jo *Portsm* 69-72; C Frogmore H Trin *St Alb* 72-76; V Standon from 76; RD Bishop's Stortford from 91. *The Vicarage, Kents Lane, Standon, Ware, Herts SG11 1PJ* Ware (0920) 821390

PELLY, Raymond Blake. b 38. Worc Coll Ox BA61 MA69 Geneva Univ DTh71. Linc Th Coll. **d** 63 **p** 64. C Gosforth All SS *Newc* 63-65. *28 Collingwood Street, Freeman's Bay, Auckland 1, New Zealand* Auckland (9) 764923

PELTON, Ian Simpson. b 30. Keble Coll Ox 50. Sarum Th Coll 55. **d** 57 **p** 58. C Crook *Dur* 57-61; C Harton 61-65; V Coxhoe from 65. *St Mary's Vicarage, 16 The Avenue, Coxhoe, Durham DH6 4AD* 091-377 0222

PELTOR, Lawrence Frank. b 08. Keble Coll Ox BA33 MA37. Linc Th Coll 33. **d** 34 **p** 35. Hon CF from 45; R Willey w Barrow *Heref* 60-72; C Wybunbury *Ches* 72-73; rtd 73; Perm to Offic *Heref* from 73. *5 Cliff Gardens, Cliff Road, Bridgnorth, Shropshire WV16 4EZ* Bridgnorth (0746) 763173

PELZ, Werner. b 21. Lon Univ BA49. Linc Th Coll 50. **d** 51 **p** 52. C-in-c Lostock CD *Man* 54-63; rtd 86. *Warrina Lot 7, Mount Riddell Road, Healesville, Victoria, Australia 3777*

PEMBERTON, Anthony Thomas Christie. b 57. BA. Cranmer Hall Dur 82. **d** 84 **p** 85. C Maidstone St Luke *Cant* 84-88; Chapl Ox Pastorate from 88. *14 Walton Street, Oxford OX1 2HG* Oxford (0865) 244713

PEMBERTON, Arthur. b 48. Trin Coll Bris 76. **d** 79 **p** 80. C Harborne Heath *Birm* 79-84; R The Quinton 84-91. *Address temp unknown*

PEMBERTON, Mrs Carolyn Mary (Carrie). b 55. St Hilda's Coll Ox BA78. Cranmer Hall Dur 83 NE Ord Course 84. **dss** 86 **d** 87. NSM Leeds St Geo *Ripon* 86-87; CMS from 87; CMS Miss Partner and Dir Angl Th Inst Zaire 88-90. *18 Noster Hill, Beeston, Leeds LS11 8QE* Leeds (0532) 706240

PEMBERTON, Crispin Mark Rugman. b 59. St Andr Univ MTh83. St Steph Ho Ox 84. **d** 86 **p** 87. C Acton St Alb w All SS *Lon* 86-88; C Acton Green 88-90; C Leckhampton SS Phil and Jas w Cheltenham St Jas

Glouc from 90. *72 Salisbury Avenue, Warden Hill, Cheltenham, Glos GL51 5BU* Cheltenham (0242) 517057

PEMBERTON, David Charles. b 35. K Coll Lon 57. **d** 61 **p** 62. C Pokesdown St Jas *Win* 61-65; C W Derby St Mary *Liv* 65-67; C-in-c Cantril Farm St Jude CD 67-71; V Cantril Farm 71-74; V Devonport St Boniface *Ex* 75-83; V Stanwell *Lon* from 83. *The Vicarage, 1 Lord Knyvett Close, Staines, Middx TW19 7PQ* Ashford (0784) 252044

PEMBERTON, Jeremy Charles Baring. b 56. Mert Coll Ox MA77 Fitzw Ho Cam MA80. Ridley Hall Cam 78. **d** 81 **p** 82. C Stranton *Dur* 81-84; C Leeds St Geo *Ripon* 84-87; CMS from 87; CMS Miss Partner and Dir Angl Th Inst Zaire 87-90. *18 Noster Hill, Beeston, Leeds LS11 8QE* Leeds (0532) 706240

PEMBERTON, Thomas Warwick Winstanley. b 26. St Jo Coll Cam BA50 MA55. Cuddesdon Coll 62. **d** 63 **p** 64. V Rickerscote *Lich* 66-73; V Titchfield *Portsm* 73-91; rtd 91. *Hill Cottage, Heydon Road, Corpusty, Norwich NR11 6RU* Saxthorpe (026387) 648

PEMBERTON, Canon Wilfred Austin. b 14. Lon Univ BA39 AKC41 BD42 Nottm Univ PhD52. **d** 41 **p** 42. C Colchester St Giles *Chelmsf* 41-43; P-in-c 43-46; V Stonebroom *Derby* 46-51; Asst Bisp Hosp of Schs 48-51; Chapl Morton Hosp Derby 49-51; R Breaston *Derby* 51-61; R Wilne and Draycott w Breaston from 61; Chapl Draycott Hosp Derby 62-72; Hon Can Derby Cathl *Derby* from 80. *The Rectory, 68 Risley Lane, Breaston, Derby DE73AU* Draycott (03317) 2242

PEMBREY, Gerald Marcus. b 29. Glouc Sch of Min 89. **d** 90. NSM Bream *Glouc* from 90. *Kings Wood, The Tufts, Bream, Lydney, Glos GL15 6HW* Dean (0594) 562750

PENDLEBURY, Stephen Thomas. b 50. ACA78 Southn Univ BSc73. Ridley Hall Cam 86. **d** 88 **p** 89. C Birkenhead St Jas w St Bede *Ches* from 88. *St James Vicarage, 56 Tollemache Road, Birkenhead, Merseyside L43 8SZ* 051-652 1016

PENDLETON, David Julian. b 24. K Coll Lon BD54 AKC54. **d** 54 **p** 55. C-in-c Shenley Green CD *Birm* 65-70; V Shenley Green 70-89; rtd 89. *258 Mulberry Road, Birmingham B30 1ST* 021-475 4874

PENDLETON, George. b 39. St Deiniol's Hawarden 76. **d** 78 **p** 79. C Pemb Dock *St D* 78-80; R Llangwm and Freystrop 80-83; V Darlaston All SS *Lich* 83-88; Ind Chapl *Linc* from 88. *11 Ferndown, Great Coates, Grimsby, S Humberside DN37 9PW* Grimsby (0472) 884183

PENDLETON, John Thomas. b 12. Dorchester Miss Coll 39. **d** 41 **p** 42. V Cleckheaton St Luke *Wakef* 62-77; rtd 77; Perm to Offic *Wakef* from 77. *25 Meadow Close, Robertown, Liversedge, W Yorkshire WF15 7QE* Heckmondwike (0924) 405255

PENDLETON, Mervyn Boulton. b 13. SS Coll Cam BA35 MA42. Chich Th Coll 35. **d** 37 **p** 38. R Kimpton w Thruxton w Fyfield *Win* 71-78; rtd 78. *20 Owers Way, West Wittering, Chichester, W Sussex PO20 8HA*

PENDORF, Canon James Gordon. b 45. Drew Univ New Jersey BA67. Episc Th Sch Cam Mass BD71. **d** 71 **p** 71. USA 71-76; V Colne H Trin *Blackb* 76-80; Sen Dioc Stewardship Adv *Chelmsf* 80-83; Dioc Sec *Birm* from 83; Hon Can Birm Cathl from 90. *Kairos, 19 Medlar Close, Telford, Shropshire TF3 5EB* Telford (0952) 506778

PENFOLD, Brian Robert. b 54. Lon Univ BSc75 Bris Univ PGCE77. Oak Hill Th Coll BA84. **d** 84 **p** 85. C Norwood *S'wark* 84-88; C Rayleigh *Chelmsf* from 88. *St Michael's House, 13 Sir Walter Raleigh Drive, Rayleigh, Essex SS6 9JB* Rayleigh (0268) 785043

PENFOLD, Colin Richard. b 52. St Pet Coll Ox BA74 MA78. Ridley Hall Cam 81. **d** 84 **p** 85. C Buckhurst Hill *Chelmsf* 84-87; C Greenside *Dur* 87-90; V Cononley w Bradley *Bradf* from 90. *The Vicarage, 3 Meadow Close, Cononley, Keighley, W Yorkshire BD20 8LZ* Cross Hills (0535) 634369

PENFOLD, Kenneth Duncan (Brother Kenneth). b 32. Leeds Univ BA56 Lon Univ DipEd74. Coll of Resurr Mirfield 57. **d** 59 **p** 60. Hon C Belvedere All SS *Roch* 59-62; Lic to Offic *Glouc* 62-67; CGA from 63; Prior from 77; Lic to Offic *Pet* 67-72; Bradf 74-79; Perm to Offic Ex from 78; Glouc 78-80; P-in-c Manningham St Mary and Bradf St Mich *Bradf* 79-83; Perm to Offic *Man* from 85; Lic to Offic *Lich* from 87. *The Priory, Lawley Village, Telford, Shropshire TF4 2PD* Telford (0952) 504068

PENFOLD, Dr Susan Irene. b 52. York Univ BA73 Bris Univ PhD77 Selw Coll Cam BA83 MA87. Ridley Hall Cam 81. **dss** 84 **d** 87. Buckhurst Hill *Chelmsf* 84-87;

Hon Par Dn Greenside *Dur* 87-90; Hon C Cononley w Bradley *Bradf* from 90. *The Vicarage, 3 Meadow Close, Cononley, Keighley, W Yorkshire BD20 8LZ* Cross Hills (0535) 634369

PENGELLEY, Peter John. b 22. Sarum & Wells Th Coll 72. **d** 74 **p** 75. C Midsomer Norton *B & W* 74-78; R Stogursey w Fiddington 78-88; Ind Chapl from 80; rtd 88; Perm to Offic *B & W* from 89. *Rosslyn Cottage, Roadwater, Watchet, Somerset TA23 0RB* Washford (0984) 40798

PENGELLY, Geoffrey. b 50. Oak Hill Th Coll 86. **d** 88 **p** 89. C Redruth w Lanner and Treleigh *Truro* from 88. *37 Clinton Road, Redruth, Cornwall TR15 2LW* Redruth (0209) 212627

PENMAN, Robert George. b 42. St Jo Coll Auckland LTh66. **d** 65 **p** 66. New Zealand 65-73; C Alverstoke *Portsm* 73-74, CF 74-77; C Bridgwater St Mary w Chilton Trinity *B & W* 77-80; P-in-c Haselbury Plucknett w N Perrott 80-81; P-in-c Misterton 80-81; V Haselbury Plucknett, Misterton and N Perrott 81-89; P-in-c Appleton *Ox* from 89. *The Rectory, Oaksmere, Appleton, Abingdon, Oxon OX13 5JS* Oxford (0865) 862458

PENN, Canon Arthur William. b 22. Man Univ BA49. Wycliffe Hall Ox 49. **d** 51 **p** 52. V Brampton *Carl* 67-83; RD Brampton 74-83; P-in-c Gilsland w Nether Denton 75-81; Hon Can Carl Cathl from 78; P-in-c Gilsland 81-83; V Rockcliffe and Blackford 83-88; rtd 88. *1 Well Lane, Warton, Carnforth, Lancs LA5 9QZ* Carnforth (0524) 733079

PENN, Barry Edwin. b 46. Univ of Wales (Swansea) BA72. St Jo Coll Nottm 77. **d** 79 **p** 80. C New Barnet St Jas *St Alb* 79-83; TV Preston St Jo *Blackb* from 83. *St James's Vicarage, Larkhill Road, Preston, Lancs PR1 4HQ* Preston (0772) 54112

PENN, Christopher Francis. b 34. ACII63. Wells Th Coll 68. **d** 70 **p** 71. C Andover w Foxcott *Win* 70-72; C Odiham w S Warnborough 72-75; C Keynsham w Queen Charlton *B & W* 75; C Keynsham 75-76; TV 76-82; R Chilcompton w Downside and Stratton on the Fosse 82-87; RD Midsomer Norton 84-86; V Bathford 87-90; V Avonmouth St Andr *Bris* from 90; Ind Chapl from 90. *St Andrew's Vicarage, Bristol BS11 9ES* Bristol (0272) 822302

PENN, Clive Llewellyn. b 12. Oak Hill Th Coll 47. **d** 48 **p** 49. V Jersey Gouray St Martin *Win* 66-71; Lic to Offic 71-86; rtd 77. *Unit 21, 4 Gorge Road, Campbell Town, Adelaide, S Australia 5074*

PENNAL, David Bernard. b 37. Ripon Hall Ox 64. **d** 67 **p** 68. C Moseley St Mary *Birm* 67-71; C Bridgwater St Mary w Chilton Trinity *B & W* 71-73; P-in-c Hilton w Cheselbourne and Melcombe Horsey *Sarum* 73-76; R Milton Abbas, Hilton w Cheselbourne etc 76-78; P-in-c Spetisbury w Charlton Marshall 78-88; R Spetisbury w Charlton Marshall and Blandford St Mary from 89. *The Rectory, Spetisbury, Blandford Forum, Dorset DT11 9DF* Blandford (0258) 453153

PENNANT, David Falconer. b 51. Trin Coll Cam MA73. Trin Coll Bris BD84 PhD88. **d** 86 **p** 87. C Bramcote *S'well* 86-88; C Woking St Jo *Guildf* from 88. *St Saviour's House, 13 Heath Drive, Brookwood, Woking, Surrey GU24 0HG* Brookwood (04867) 2161

PENNANT, Philip Vivian Rogers. b 14. TD69. Trin Coll Cam BA47 MA48. St Mich Coll Llan 48. **d** 49 **p** 50. R Sutton Bonington *S'well* 65-79; P-in-c Adisham *Cant* 79-84; P-in-c Goodnestone H Cross w Chillenden and Knowlton 79-84; rtd 84. *2 Manor Close, Bradford Abbas, Sherborne, Dorset DT9 6RN* Yeovil (0935) 23059

PENNELL, Canon James Henry Leslie. b 06. TD50. Edin Th Coll 29. **d** 29 **p** 30. R Pentlow, Foxearth, Liston and Borley *Chelmsf* 65-72; Hon Can St Andr Cathl Inverness *Mor* from 66; rtd 72; Perm to Offic *St E* from 73. *The Croft, Hundon, Sudbury, Suffolk* Hundon (044086) 221

PENNEY, David Richard John. b 39. Dur Univ BA63 DipTh65. Cranmer Hall Dur 66. **d** 67 **p** 68. C Chilvers Coton w Astley *Cov* 67-70; C Styvechale 70-72; P-in-c Shilton w Ansty 72-77; P-in-c Withybrook 73-77; R Easington w Liverton *York* 77-85; Soc Resp Adv *Sarum* from 85. *Linwood, 48 Bouverie Avenue, Salisbury SP2 8DX* Salisbury (0722) 332500 or 411966

PENNEY, Herbert Richard. b 07. TCD BA33 MA45. **d** 34 **p** 35. V Plumpton Wall *Carl* 62-73; rtd 73. *21 Castle Court, Pewsey Road, Marlborough, Wilts* Marlborough (0672) 511047

PENNEY, John Edward. b 12. St Jo Coll Dur LTh33 BA34 MA37. Clifton Th Coll 30. **d** 35 **p** 36. V Wisborough Green *Chich* 51-77; rtd 77; Perm to Offic *Ex* from 77. *28 Oakleigh Road, Exmouth, Devon EX8 2LN* Exmouth (0395) 264863

PENNEY, William Affleck. b 41. K Coll Lon BD63 AKC63. **d** 66 **p** 67. C Chatham St Steph *Roch* 66-70; Ind Chapl 70-77; P-in-c Bredhurst 70-72; Hon C S Gillingham 72-74; Hon C Eynsford w Farningham and Lullingstone 74-77; Bp's Dom Chapl 74-88; Hon Ind Chapl from 77; Hon C Balham St Mary and St Jo *S'wark* from 89. *54 Foxbourne Road, London SW17 8EW* 081-672 8575

PENNIE, Canon Gibb Niven. b 09. Aber Univ MA30 BD44. Edin Th Coll 34. **d** 36 **p** 37. R Greenock *Glas* 57-77; Can St Mary's Cathl 61-77; rtd 77; Hon Can St Mary's Cathl *Glas* from 77. *111 Earlbank Avenue, Glasgow G14 9DY* 041-954 6397

PENNINGTON, Frederick William. b 11. K Coll Lon. **d** 55 **p** 56. V N Molton w Twitchen *Ex* 66-77; P-in-c Molland 68-77; rtd 77; Lic to Offic *Ex* from 77. *Sunset Cottage, West Street, Hartland, Bideford, Devon EX39 6BQ* Bideford (0237) 441206

PENNINGTON, Howard Studholme. b 48. Univ of Wales BD85. St Mich Coll Llan 82. **d** 85 **p** 86. C Westmr St Steph w St Jo *Lon* 85-88; C Brookfield St Mary from 88. *St Anne's Vicarage, 106 Highgate West Hill, London N6 6AP* 081-340 5190

PENNINGTON, John Kenneth. b 27. Man Univ LLB48. Linc Th Coll 51. **d** 52 **p** 53. C Wavertree H Trin *Liv* 52-56; C Rotherham *Sheff* 56-59; India 59-63; V Nelson St Phil *Blackb* 64-66; Area Sec USPG (Dios Derby, Leic and S'well) 66-71; (Dios Derby and Sheff) 71-75; C Nottm St Mary *S'well* 75-78; C Nottm St Mary and St Cath from 78. *3 St Jude's Avenue, Nottingham NG3 5FG* Nottingham (0602) 623420

PENNINGTON, John Michael. b 32. IEng AMIEE MIHospE Em Coll Cam BA54 MA58. Wells Th Coll 58. **d** 60 **p** 61. C Stockport St Geo *Ches* 60-64; V Congleton St Steph 64-68; Chapl Nor Sch 68-70; V Hattersley *Ches* 70-72; C-in-c Upton Priory CD 72-75; V Upton Priory 75-79; Perm to Offic *Newc* 83-87; V Tynemouth St Jo from 87. *St John's Vicarage, Percy Main, North Shields, Tyne & Wear NE29 6HS* 091-257 1819

PENNISTON, Canon Joe Cyril. b 12. Ely Th Coll 35. **d** 35 **p** 36. R Whitby *York* 65-85; RD Whitby 65-85; Can and Preb York Minster 73-90; rtd 85; Perm to Offic *York* from 90. *10 The Chase, Langton Road, Norton, Malton, N Yorkshire YO17 9AD* Malton (0653) 7856

PENNOCK, John Harding Lovell. b 16. Ripon Hall Ox 63. **d** 65 **p** 66. V Hill *Birm* 68-78; P-in-c Sculthorpe w Dunton and Doughton *Nor* 78-82; rtd 82. *12 Swallow Croft, Lichfield, Staffs WS13 7HE* Lichfield (0543) 24002

PENNY, Diana Eleanor. b 51. Open Univ BA87. Nor Ord Course 87. **d** 89. Hon C Gillingham w Geldeston, Stockton, Ellingham etc *Nor* from 89. *68 High Road, Wortwell, Harleston, Norfolk IP20 0EF* Homersfield (098686) 365

PENNY, Edwin John. b 43. Leeds Univ BA64. Coll of Resurr Mirfield 64. **d** 66 **p** 67. C Wombourne *Lich* 69-71; C Wednesbury St Paul Wood Green 71-74; V Kingshurst *Birm* 74-79; Chapl All Hallows Convent Norfolk 79-82; rtd 82; Hon Chapl Overgate Hospice Yorkshire 82-84; Hon C Raveningham *Nor* 84-90; All Hallows Hosp Nor Past Team from 90. *68 High Road, Wortwell, Harleston, Norfolk IP20 0EF* Homersfield (098686) 365

PENNY, Michael John. b 36. Linc Th Coll 78. **d** 80 **p** 81. C Knighton St Mary Magd *Leic* 80-83; TV Leic Resurr 83-85; V Blackfordby from 85; RD Akeley W (Ashby) from 88. *11 Vicarage Close, Blackfordby, Burton-on-Trent, Staffs DE11 8AZ* Burton (0524) 219445

PENNY, Wilfred Joseph. b 05. K Coll Lon. **d** 32 **p** 33. R Winford *B & W* 62-73; rtd 73. *Ormidale Lodge Nursing Home, 42 Albert Road, Clevedon, Avon BS21 7RR* Clevedon (0272) 878951

PENRITH, Bishop Suffragan of. See HACKER, Rt Rev George Lanyon

PENTLAND, Raymond Jackson. b 57. Open Univ BA90. St Jo Coll Nottm DPS88. **d** 88 **p** 89. C Nottm St Jude *S'well* 88-90; Chapl RAF Coll Cranwell from 90. *c/o MOD, Adastral House, Theobald's Road, London WC1X 8RU* 071-430 7268

PENTREATH, Canon Harvey. b 29. Wells Th Coll 54. **d** 57 **p** 58. C Bris St Ambrose Whitehall *Bris* 57-60; C Leatherhead *Guildf* 60-63; C Haslemere 63-65; R Elstead 65-72; V Cuddington 73-80; Hon Can Guildf Cathl 80; V Helston *Truro* 80-85; RD Kerrier 84-86; TR Helston and Wendron from 85; Hon Can Truro Cathl from 88. *St Michael's Rectory, Church Lane, Helston, Cornwall TR13 8PF* Helston (0326) 572516

PENWARDEN, Canon Peter Herbert. b 21. Keble Coll Ox BA42 MA46. Linc Th Coll 42. **d** 44 **p** 45. C New Eltham All SS *S'wark* 44-49; V S Wimbledon All SS

49-61; V Benhilton 61-71; Vice Provost S'wark from 71; Can Res S'wark Cathl from 71. *73 St George's Road, London SE1 6ER* 071-735 8322

PEOPLES, James Scott. b 59. TCD BA DipTh HDipEd90. **d** 85 **p** 86. C Carlow w Urglin and Staplestown *C & O* 85-90; Chapl Kilkenny Coll 90-91; I Portarlington w Cloneyhurke and Lea *M & K* from 91. *The Rectory, Portarlington, Co Laois, Irish Republic* Portarlington (502) 23144

PEPPER, Leonard Edwin. b 44. Ex Univ BA71. Ripon Hall Ox 71. **d** 73 **p** 74. C Cottingham *York* 73-76; C Kingshurst *Birm* 76-79; Dir Past Studies St Steph Ho Ox 80-89; TV Aylesbury w Bierton and Hulcott *Ox* from 89. *4 Cubb Field, Aylesbury, Bucks HP21 8SH* Aylesbury (0296) 25008

PEPPIATT, Martin Guy. b 33. Trin Coll Ox BA57 MA60. Wycliffe Hall Ox 57. **d** 59 **p** 60. C St Marylebone All So w SS Pet and Jo *Lon* 59-63; Kenya 65-69; V E Twickenham St Steph *Lon* from 69. *St Stephen's Vicarage, 21 Cambridge Park, Twickenham TW1 2JE* 081-892 5258

PERCIVAL, Brian Sydney. b 37. Univ of Wales (Ban) BA61. N Ord Course 81. **d** 84 **p** 85. NSM Norbury *Ches* 84-88; P-in-c Werneth from 88. *The Vicarage, Compstall, Stockport, Cheshire SK6 5HU* 061-427 1259

PERCIVAL, Derek Walton. b 32. N Ord Course. **d** 84 **p** 85. C Skelmersdale St Paul *Liv* 84-87; V Ashton-in-Makerfield St Thos from 87. *The Vicarage, Warrington Road, Ashton-in-Makerfield, Wigan, Lancs WN4 9PL* Ashton-in-Makerfield (0942) 727275

PERCIVAL, Geoffrey. b 46. Ridley Hall Cam 73. **d** 76 **p** 77. C Eccleshill *Bradf* 76-79; C Otley 79-82; V Windhill from 82. *The Vicarage, 300 Leeds Road, Windhill, Shipley, W Yorkshire BD18 1EZ* Bradford (0274) 581502

PERCIVAL, Martin Eric. b 45. Lon Univ BSc66 Linacre Coll Ox BA70 MA74. Wycliffe Hall Ox 67. **d** 70 **p** 71. C Anfield St Marg *Liv* 70-73; C Witney *Ox* 73-74; TV Bottesford w Ashby *Linc* 74-76; TV Grantham 76-80; R Coningsby w Tattershall 80-82; P-in-c Coleford w Holcombe *B & W* 82-83; V 83-84; Chapl Rossall Sch Fleetwood 84-88; Chapl Woodbridge Sch Suffolk from 88. *27 Haughgate Close, Woodbridge, Suffolk IP12 1LQ* Woodbridge (03943) 3997

PERCY, Donald. b 45. Kelham Th Coll 66. **d** 71 **p** 72. C Hendon St Ignatius *Dur* 71-75; C Gorton Our Lady and St Thos *Man* 75-77; C Middlesb St Thos *York* 77-82; Guyana 82-86; P-in-c S Moor *Dur* 86-90; V from 90. *St George's Vicarage, South Moor, Stanley, Co Durham DH9 7EN* Stanley (0207) 232564

PERCY, Mrs Emma Margaret. b 63. Jes Coll Cam BA85 MA89 St Jo Coll Dur BA89. Cranmer Hall Dur 87. **d** 90. C Bedf St Andr *St Alb* 90-91; Par Dn from 91. *5 St Minver Road, Bedford MK40 2NQ* Bedford (0234) 217330

PERCY, Gordon Reid. b 46. St Jo Coll Dur BA68 DipTh70. Cranmer Hall Dur 69. **d** 71 **p** 72. C Flixton St Jo *Man* 71-76; C Charlesworth *Derby* 76-77; P-in-c 77-87; P-in-c Dinting Vale 80-87; V Long Eaton St Jo from 87. *St John's Vicarage, 59 Trowell Grove, Long Eaton, Nottingham NG10 4AY* Long Eaton (0602) 734819

PERCY, Martyn William. b 62. Bris Univ BA84. Cranmer Hall Dur 88. **d** 90 **p** 91. C Bedf St Andr *St Alb* from 90. *5 St Minver Road, Bedford MK40 3DQ* Bedford (0234) 217330

PERDUE, Very Rev Ernon Cope Todd. b 30. TCD BA52 BD56 MEd73 UCD DipPsych76 MPsychSc80. TCD Div Sch 53. **d** 54 **p** 55. C Dub Drumcondra w N Strand *D & G* 54-58; C Dub Booterstown w Carysfort 58-60; Dean of Residence TCD 60-68; C-in-c Dub St Mark *D & G* 66-68; C-in-c Dub St Steph 68-69; I Rathmichael 69-76; Careers Counsellor Wicklow Voc Sch 76-82; I Limerick *L & K* 82-87; Can Limerick Cathl 82-87; Dean Killaloe, Kilfenora and Clonfert from 87; I Killaloe w Stradbally from 87. *The Deanery, Killaloe, Co Clare, Irish Republic* Killaloe (61) 376687

✠**PERDUE, Rt Rev Richard Gordon.** b 10. TCD BA31 MA38 BD38. **d** 33 **p** 34 **c** 54. C Dub Drumcondra w N Strand *D & G* 33-36; C Dub Rathmines 36-40; I Castledermot w Kinneagh 40-43; I Roscrea *L & K* 43-54; Adn Killaloe and Kilfenora 51-54; Bp Killaloe, Kilfenora, Clonfert and Kilmacduagh 54-57; Bp C, C & R 57-78; rtd 78. *Hadlow 4RD, Timaru, South Island, New Zealand* Timaru (68) 60250

PERERA, George Anthony. b 51. Edin Univ BD74. Linc Th Coll 74. **d** 76 **p** 77. Chapl Mabel Fletcher Tech Coll Liv 76-79; C Wavertree H Trin *Liv* 76-79; TV Maghull from 79; Chapl Park Lane Hosp Maghull 79-89; Asst

Chapl Ashworth Hosp from 89. *St James's Vicarage, 23 Green Link, Liverpool L31 8DW* 051-526 6626

PERFECT, Leslie Charles. b 12. Keble Coll Ox BA35 MA39. Wells Th Coll 35. **d** 36 **p** 37. V Effingham w Lt Bookham *Guildf* 71-80; rtd 81; USA 81-90. *21 Oakfield Avenue, Golborne, Warrington WA3 3QT* Ashton-in-Makerfield (0942) 727407

PERHAM, Michael Francis. b 47. Keble Coll Ox BA74 MA78. Cuddesdon Coll 74. **d** 76 **p** 77. C Addington *Cant* 76-81; Sec C of E Doctrine Commn 79-84; Bp's Dom Chapl *Win* 81-84; TR Oakdale St Geo *Sarum* from 84. *The Rectory, 99 Darby's Lane, Poole, Dorset BH15 3EU* Poole (0202) 675419

PERKIN, David Arthur. b 30. Pemb Coll Ox BA54 MA58. Linc Th Coll 54. **d** 56 **p** 57. C St Jo Wood *Lon* 56-61; Chapl Loughb Univ *Leic* 61-84; V Paddington St Jas *Lon* from 84. *The Vicarage, 6 Gloucester Terrace, London W2 3DD* 071-723 8119

PERKIN, Jonathan Guy. b 52. Westmr Coll Ox BEd76. Trin Coll Bris 89. **d** 91. C Cullompton *Ex* from 91. *19 Exeter Road, Cullompton, Devon EX15 1DX* Cullompton (0884) 33494

PERKIN, Paul John Stanley. b 50. Ch Ch Ox BA71 MA75 CertEd. Wycliffe Hall Ox 78. **d** 80 **p** 81. C Gillingham St Mark *Roch* 80-84; C Brompton H Trin w Onslow Square St Paul *Lon* 84-87; P-in-c Battersea Rise St Mark S'wark from 87. *St Mark's Vicarage, 7 Elsynge Road, London SW18 2HW* 081-874 6023

PERKINS, Alban Leslie Tate. b 08. Kelham Th Coll 28. **d** 34 **p** 35. SSM from 33; C Nottm St Geo w St Jo *S'well* 34-37 and 68-72; S Africa 37-67 and 76-80; Can Bloemfontein Cathl 52-67; Lesotho 72-76; Perm to Offic Man 81-86; Blackb from 86. *Willen Priory, Milton Keynes MK15 9AA* Milton Keynes (0908) 663749

PERKINS, Colin Blackmore. b 35. FCII65. Lon Coll of Div 68. **d** 70 **p** 71. C Hyson Green *S'well* 70-73; V Clarborough w Hayton 73-79; P-in-c Cropwell Bishop 79-84; P-in-c Colston Bassett 79-84; P-in-c Granby w Elton 79-84; P-in-c Langar 79-84; V Tithby w Cropwell Butler 79-84; V Cropwell Bishop w Colston Bassett, Granby etc from 84. *The Vicarage, 2 Dobbin Close, Cropwell Bishop, Nottingham NG12 3GR* Nottingham (0602) 893172

PERKINS, David. b 51. Sarum & Wells Th Coll. **d** 87 **p** 88. C New Mills *Derby* 87-90; V Marlpool from 90. *The Vicarage, Marlpool, Derby DE7 7BP* Langley Mill (0773) 712097

PERKINS, David John Elmslie. b 45. ATII75 Dur Univ BA66 DipTh68. Cranmer Hall Dur. **d** 69 **p** 70. C Wadsley *Sheff* 69-71; C Shortlands *Roch* 71-73; Perm to Offic Lon 76-78; B & W 78-80; Lic from 80. *Rainbow's End, Montacute Road, Stoke-sub-Hamdon, Somerset TA14 6UQ* Martock (0935) 823314

PERKINS, Douglas Brian. b 32. Or Coll Ox BA56 MA63 DipEd67. St Steph Ho Ox 56. **d** 58 **p** 60. C Burnley St Cath *Blackb* 58-59; C Teddington St Alb *Lon* 59-60; Hon C Ox St Barn *Ox* 63-64; Chapl Beechwood Park Sch St Alb 64-66; Lic to Offic St Alb 64-66; Lon 66-68; C Holborn St Alb w Saffron Hill St Pet *Lon* 69-79; V Streatham Ch Ch *S'wark* 79-87; TV Swinton and Pendlebury *Man* 87-90; C Notting Dale St Clem w St Mark and St Jas *Lon* from 90. *176 Holland Road, London W14 8AH* 071-602 5486

PERKINS, Canon Eric William. b 08. Leeds Univ BA29. Coll of Resurr Mirfield 26. **d** 31 **p** 32. R Upton cum Chalvey *Ox* 56-76; Hon Can Ch Ch 62-79; Sub Warden Community St Jo Bapt Clewer from 70; rtd 76; C Burnham w Dropmore, Hitcham and Taplow *Ox* 83-84; C Farnham Royal w Hedgerley 84-85. *St Augustine's House, 53 Hatch Lane, Windsor, Berks SL4 3QY* Windsor (0753) 863060

PERKINS, Julia Margaret. b 49. Linc Th Coll 85. **d** 87. Par Dn Owton Manor *Dur* 87-89; Par Dn Leam Lane from 89. *71 Ridgeway, Leam Lane Estate, Gateshead, Tyne & Wear NE10 8DE* 091-438 0636

PERKINS, Malcolm Bryan. b 20. SS Coll Cam BA41 MA45. Wycliffe Hall Ox 41. **d** 43 **p** 44. Chapl St Bart Hosp Roch 59-74; R Wouldham *Roch* 65-73; Chapl Medway Hosp Gillingham 65-67; Toc H Staff Padre (SE Region) 73-85; Hon C Roch 74-85; rtd 85; Perm to Offic *Roch* from 85. *Roke Cottage, 3 Belgrave Terrace, Laddingford, Maidstone, Kent ME18 6BP* East Peckham (0622) 871774

PERKINS, Patricia Doris (Sister Patricia). b 29. Gilmore Ho 60. dss 73 **d** 87. CSA from 71; Sherston Magna w Easton Grey *Bris* 73-75; Cant St Martin and St Paul *Cant* 76-78; Kilburn St Aug w St Jo *Lon* 80-84; Abbey Ho Malmesbury 84-87; Hon Par Dn Bayswater from 87; Chapl St Mary's Hosp (Praed Street) Paddington and

St Chas Hosp Ladbroke Grove 88-89; rtd 89; Dean of Women's Min *Lon* from 89; Dioc Dir of Ords from 90. *St Andrew's House, 2 Tavistock Road, London W11 1BA* 071-229 2662

PERKINSON, Neil Donald. b 46. Wycliffe Hall Ox 84. **d** 85 **p** 86. C Workington St Jo *Carl* 85-88; TV Cockermouth w Embleton and Wythop from 88. *14 Harrot Hill, Cockermouth, Cumbria CA13 0BL* Cockermouth (0900) 824383

PERKS, David Leonard Irving. b 38. Sussex Univ MA75. S Dios Minl Tr Scheme. **d** 87 **p** 88. NSM Lewes All SS, St Anne, St Mich and St Thos *Chich* from 87; Chapl HM Pris Lewes from 91. *45 Fitzjohns Road, Lewes, E Sussex BN7 1PR* Lewes (0273) 475781

PERKS, Edgar Harold Martin. b 31. Open Univ BA87. Glouc Sch of Min 85. **d** 88 **p** 89. NSM Bromfield *Heref* 88-89; NSM Culmington w Onibury 88-89; NSM Stanton Lacy 88-89; NSM Culmington w Onibury, Bromfield etc from 90. *The Oaklands, Bromfield Road, Ludlow, Shropshire SY8 1DW* Ludlow (0584) 5525

PERMAN, George Hayward. b 01. Tyndale Hall Bris 31. **d** 34 **p** 35. V Ealing St Mary *Lon* 53-68; rtd 68; Perm to Offic *Chich* from 80. *2 Wakehurst Court, St George's Road, Worthing, W Sussex BN11 2DJ* Worthing (0903) 38540

PERRENS, Eric George. b 16. Sheff Univ BA38. Lich Th Coll 38. **d** 40 **p** 41. V Rawcliffe *Sheff* 69-77; R Bradfield 77-82; rtd 82. *32 Bracken Close, Whitby, N Yorkshire* Whitby (0947) 600847

PERRENS, Everard George. b 15. St Cath Coll Cam BA37 MA42. Linc Th Coll 40. **d** 42 **p** 43. Chapl St Marg Sch Bushey 65-74; Hon C Earlsdon *Cov* 75-79; C Allesley Park 79-80; rtd 80; Hon C Earlsdon *Cov* 80-83; Perm to Offic from 83. *4 Regency Drive, Kenilworth, Warks CV8 1JE* Kenilworth (0926) 55779

PERRETT, David Thomas. b 48. Cranmer Hall Dur 80. **d** 82 **p** 83. C Stapleford *S'well* 82-86; V Ollerton 86-87; P-in-c Boughton 86-87; V Ollerton w Boughton from 87. *The Vicarage, 65 Larch Road, New Ollerton, Newark, Notts NG22 9SX* Mansfield (0623) 860323

PERRETT-JONES, Reginald James Archibald. b 04. Univ of Wales BA34. Dorchester Miss Coll 34. **d** 37 **p** 38. R Cliddesden and Winslade *Win* 61-77; R Cliddesden 77-82; rtd 82; Perm to Offic *B & W* from 83. *Clydach, 26 Bridges Mead, Dunster, Minehead, Somerset TA24 6PN* Dunster (0643) 821764

PERRIN, Ven Donald Barton Edward. b 05. TCD BA33 MA36. Div Test33. **d** 33 **p** 34. Adn Dalriada *Conn* 65-76; rtd 76. *5 Corbawn Court, Shankhill, Co Dublin, Irish Republic* Dublin (1) 821109

PERRINS, Harold. b 21. Kelham Th Coll 38. **d** 44 **p** 45. V Edingale *Lich* 69-77; R Harlaston 69-77; V Shobnall 77-86; rtd 86; Perm to Offic *Lich* from 86. *20 Meadow Rise, Barton under Needwood, Burton-on-Trent DE13 8DT* Barton under Needwood (0283) 713515

PERRIS, Anthony. b 48. Univ of Wales (Abth) BSc69 Selw Coll Cam BA76 MA79. Ridley Hall Cam 74. **d** 77 **p** 78. C Sandal St Helen *Wakef* 77-80; C Plymouth St Andr w St Paul and St Geo *Ex* 80-87; TV Yeovil *B & W* 87-88; V Preston Plucknett from 88. *97 Preston Road, Yeovil, Somerset BA20 2OW* Yeovil (0935) 29398

PERRIS, John Martin. b 44. Liv Univ BSc66 Bris Univ DipTh70. Trin Coll Bris 69. **d** 72 **p** 73. C Sevenoaks St Nic *Roch* 72-76; C Bebington *Ches* 76-79; V Redland *Bris* from 79; RD Horfield from 91. *Redland Vicarage, 151 Redland Road, Bristol BS6 6YE* Bristol (0272) 737423

PERROTT, John Alastair Croome. b 36. Univ of NZ LLB60. Clifton Th Coll 62. **d** 64 **p** 65. C Tunbridge Wells St Pet *Roch* 64-67; C Stanford-le-Hope *Chelmsf* 67-78; R Elmswell *St E* from 78. *The Rectory, Elmswell, Bury St Edmunds, Suffolk IP30 9DY* Elmswell (0359) 40512

PERROTT, Canon Joseph John. b 19. **d** 64 **p** 65. C Dub St Geo *D & G* 64-71; C Dub Drumcondra 71-72; I Drimoleague Union *C, C & R* 72-75; RD Cork City 74-80; I Mallow Union 75-78; I Ballydehob w Aghadown from 78; Can Cloyne Cathl from 85; Preb Cork Cathl from 85. *The Rectory, Ballydehob, Co Cork, Irish Republic* Ballydehob (28) 37117

PERRY, Andrew Nicholas. b 62. Westmr Coll Ox BA(Theol)86. Trin Coll Bris MA91. **d** 91. C Bath Weston All SS w N Stoke *B & W* from 91. *23 Lucklands Road, Weston, Bath BA1 4AX* Bath (0225) 421417

PERRY, Anthony Robert. b 21. Kelham Th Coll 48. **d** 52 **p** 53. SSM from 52; C Sheff Parson Cross St Cecilia *Sheff* 52-56; S Africa 56-58 and 71-88; Lesotho 59-70; Chich Th Coll 88-90; Willen Priory from 90. *Willen*

Priory, Milton Keynes MK15 9AA Milton Keynes (0908) 663749

PERRY, Canon Colin Charles. b 16. K Coll Cam BA38 MA42. Westcott Ho Cam 39. **d** 40 **p** 41. PC Salisbury St Fran *Sarum* 64-69; V 69-71; V Preston 71-81; RD Weymouth 75-79; Can and Preb Sarum Cathl 77-82; TR Preston w Sutton Poyntz and Osmington w Poxwell 81-82; rtd 82. *6 The Ridgeway, Corfe Mullen, Wimborne, Dorset BH21 3HS* Broadstone (0202) 697298

PERRY, David William. b 42. St Chad's Coll Dur BA64 DipTh66. **d** 66 **p** 67. C Middleton St Mary *Ripon* 66-69; C Bedale 69-71; C Marton-in-Cleveland *York* 71-75; V Skirlaugh w Long Riston from 75; N Humberside Ecum Officer from 75. *The Vicarage, Skirlaugh, Hull HU11 5HE* Hornsea (0964) 562259

PERRY, Edward John. b 35. AKC62. **d** 63 **p** 64. C Honicknowle *Ex* 63-65; C Ashburton w Buckland-in-the-Moor 65-70; V Cornwood from 70; Asst Dir of Educn from 71. *The Vicarage, Cornwood, Ivybridge, Devon PL21 9QH* Cornwood (075537) 237

PERRY, Geoffrey. b 33. K Coll Lon BD57 AKC57. **d** 58 **p** 59. C Falmouth K Chas *Truro* 58-63; C Fishponds St Jo *Bris* 63-66; R St Ive *Truro* 66-75; RD W Wivelshire 73-76; R St Ive w Quethiock 75-84; R St Dennis from 84. *The Rectory, Carne Hill, St Dennis, St Austell, Cornwall PL26 8AZ* St Austell (0726) 822317

PERRY, Harold George. b 31. St Aid Birkenhead 58. **d** 60 **p** 61. V Earby *Bradf* 64-68; rtd 85. *29 Circular Road, Prestwich, Manchester M25 8NR* 061-798 0609

PERRY, John. b 09. TD60. PhD50. **d** 32 **p** 33. Can St Ninian's Cathl Perth *St And* 61-77; R Comrie 65-77; rtd 77. *29 Balhousie Street, Perth PH1 5HJ* Perth (0738) 26594

✠**PERRY, Rt Rev John Freeman.** b 35. Lon Coll of Div ALCD59 LTh74 MPhil86. **d** 59 **p** 60 **c** 89. C Woking Ch Ch *Guildf* 59-62; C Chorleywood Ch Ch *St Alb* 62; Min Chorleywood St Andr CD 63-66; V Chorleywood St Andr 66-77; RD Rickmansworth 72-77; Warden Lee Abbey 77-89; RD Shirwell *Ex* 80-84; Hon Can Win Cathl *Win* from 89; Suff Bp Southn from 89. *Ham House, The Crescent, Romsey, Hants SO51 7NG* Romsey (0794) 516005

PERRY, John Neville. b 20. Leeds Univ BA41. Coll of Resurr Mirfield 41. **d** 43 **p** 44. V Feltham *Lon* 63-75; RD Hounslow 67-75; Adn Middx 75-82; R Orlestone w Snave and Ruckinge w Warehorne *Cant* 82-86; rtd 86. *73 Elizabeth Crescent, East Grinstead, W Sussex RH19 3JG* East Grinstead (0342) 315446

PERRY, John Walton Beauchamp. b 43. Ex Coll Ox BA64 Sussex Univ MA67. E Anglian Minl Tr Course 82 Westcott Ho Cam 84. **d** 85 **p** 86. C Shrewsbury St Chad w St Mary *Lich* 85-89; V Batheaston w St Cath *B & W* from 89. *The Vicarage, 34 Northend, Batheaston, Bath BA1 7ES* Bath (0225) 858192

PERRY, Jonathan Robert. b 55. St Jo Coll Nottm DipTh. **d** 82 **p** 83. C Filey *York* 82-84; C Rayleigh *Chelmsf* 84-88; Asst Chapl St Geo Hosp Linc 88-90; Chapl Qu Eliz Hosp Gateshead from 90. *The Chaplain's Office, Queen Elizabeth Hospital, Gateshead, Tyne & Wear NE9 4SX* 091-487 8989

PERRY, Mrs Lynne Janice. b 48. **d** 90. NSM Llanfair Mathafarneithaf w Llanbedrgoch *Ban* from 90. *Bryn Haul, Benllech, Anglesey, Gwynedd* Tyn-y-Gongl (0248) 853125

PERRY, Martin Herbert. b 43. Cranmer Hall Dur 66. **d** 70 **p** 71. C Millfield St Mark *Dur* 70-74; C Haughton le Skerne 74-77; V Darlington St Matt 77-79; V Darlington St Matt and St Luke 79-84; TR Oldland *Bris* 84-91; V from 91. *39 Sunnyvale Drive, Longwell Green, Bristol BS15 6YQ* Bristol (0272) 327178

PERRY, Martyn. b 57. S Wales Bapt Coll DipTh85 DPS86 Coll of Resurr Mirfield 89. **d** 90 **p** 91. In Bapt Ch 85-89; C Hornsey St Mary w St Geo *Lon* from 90. *153 Priory Road, London N8 8NA* 081-348 5873

PERRY, Michael Arnold. b 42. Lon Univ BD64 Southn Univ MPhil74. Oak Hill Th Coll 62 Ridley Hall Cam 63. **d** 65 **p** 66. C St Helens St Helen *Liv* 65-68; C Bitterne *Win* 68-72; V 72-81; R Eversley 81-89; V Tonbridge SS Pet and Paul *Roch* from 89. *The Vicarage, Church Street, Tonbridge, Kent TN9 1HD* Tonbridge (0732) 770962

PERRY, Ven Michael Charles. b 33. Trin Coll Cam BA55 MA59. Westcott Ho Cam 56. **d** 58 **p** 59. C Baswich (or Berkswich) *Lich* 58-60; Chapl Ripon Hall Ox 61-63; Chief Asst Home Publishing SPCK 63-70; Adn Dur from 70; Can Res Dur Cathl from 70. *7 The College, Durham DH1 3EQ* 091-386 1891

PERRY, Very Rev Robert Anthony. b 21. Leeds Univ BA47. Coll of Resurr Mirfield 47. **d** 49 **p** 50. Sarawak

54-63; Malaysia 63-66 and 76-80; Chapl HM Pris Gartree 70-73; P-in-c Mottingham St Edw S'wark 73-75; P-in-c Presteigne w Discoed Heref 80-83; R Presteigne w Discoed, Kinsham and Lingen 83-86; rtd 86; Perm to Offic Heref from 87. St Benedict's, Presteigne Road, Knighton, Powys LD7 1HY   Knighton (0547) 528320

PERRY, Roy John. b 28. Chich Th Coll 71. d 72 p 73. Hon C Yeovil H Trin B & W 72-76; C 76-77; TV Withycombe Raleigh Ex 77-84; TR Ex St Thos and Em 84; TV Sampford Peverell, Uplowman, Holcombe Rogus etc from 86; P-in-c Halberton 87-88. The Vicarage, Halberton, Tiverton, Devon EX16 7AU   Tiverton (0884) 821149

PERRY, Valerie Evelyn. b 39. Southn Univ CertEd59 Lon Univ DipRS85. S'wark Ord Course 82. dss 85 d 87. Romford St Edw Chelmsf 85-87; NSM 87-89; Par Dn from 89. 10 Rosemary Avenue, Romford, Essex RM1 4HB   Romford (0708) 720231

PERRY-GORE, Canon Walter Keith. b 34. Univ of Wales (Lamp) BA59. Westcott Ho Cam 60. d 61 p 62. C St Austell Truro 61-64; Barbados 64-70; Canada from 70. PO Box 239, North Hatley, Quebec, Canada, J0B 2C0   Sherbrooke (819) 842-2686

PERRYMAN, David Francis. b 42. Brunel Univ BSc64. Oak Hill Th Coll 74. d 76 p 77. C Margate H Trin Cant 76-80; R Ardingly Chich 80-90; V Bath St Luke B & W from 90. St Luke's Vicarage, Hatfield Road, Bath BA2 2BD   Bath (0225) 311904

PERRYMAN, James Edward. b 56. Lon Bible Coll BA85 Oak Hill Th Coll 86. d 88 p 89. C Gidea Park Chelmsf 88-91; C Becontree St Mary from 91. 104 Temple Avenue, Dagenham, Essex RM8 1LS   081-592 2174

PERRYMAN, John Frederick Charles. b 49. Mert Coll Ox BA71 MA74. Ridley Hall Cam 72. d 74 p 75. C Shortlands Roch 74-78; Asst Chapl St Geo Hosp Gp Lon 78-82; Chapl Withington Univ Hosp Man from 83. 24 Alan Road, Withington, Manchester M20 9WG   061-445 4769 or 445 8111

PERSSON, Matthew Stephen. b 60. Dundee Univ BSc82. Wycliffe Hall Ox 88. d 91. C Bath Twerton-on-Avon B & W from 91. Rose Cottage, 42 High Street, Bath BA2 1DB   Bath (0225) 27966

✠**PERSSON, Rt Rev William Michael Dermot.** b 27. Or Coll Ox BA51 MA55. Wycliffe Hall Ox 51. d 53 p 54 c 82. C S Croydon Em Cant 53-55; C Tunbridge Wells St Jo Roch 55-58; V S Mimms Ch Ch Lon 58-67; R Bebington Ches 67-79; V Knutsford St Jo and Toft 79-82; Suff Bp Doncaster Sheff from 82. Bishop's Lodge, Hooton Roberts, Rotherham, S Yorkshire S65 4PF   Rotherham (0709) 853370

PERTH, Provost of. See FRANZ, Very Rev Kevin Gerhard

PESCOD, John Gordon. b 44. Leeds Univ BSc70. Qu Coll Birm DipTh71. d 72 p 73. C Camberwell St Geo S'wark 72-75; Chapl R Philanthropic Soc Sch Redhill 75-80; P-in-c Nunney w Wanstrow and Cloford B & W 80-84; R Nunney and Witham Friary, Marston Bigot etc 84-87; R Milverton w Halse and Fitzhead from 87. The Vicarage, Milverton, Taunton, Somerset TA4 1LR   Milverton (0823) 400305

PESKETT, Canon Osmond Fletcher. b 12. Dur Univ LTh44. Tyndale Hall Bris. d 37 p 38. V St Keverne Truro 68-77; rtd 77. Gairloch, Hensleigh Drive, St Leonards, Exeter EX2 4NZ   Exeter (0392) 214387

PESKETT, Richard Howard. b 42. Selw Coll Cam BA64 MA67. Ridley Hall Cam 64. d 68 p 69. C Jesmond H Trin Newc 68-71; Singapore 71-91; Trin Coll Bris from 91. c/o Trinity College, Stoke Hill, Bristol, Avon BS9 1JP   Bristol (0272) 682803

PESKETT, Timothy Lewis. b 64. St Kath Coll Liv BA86. Chich Th Coll BTh90. d 90 p 91. C Verwood Sarum from 90. 33 Newtown Lane, Verwood, Wimborne, Dorset BH21 6JD   Bournemouth (0202) 827278

PETER, Brother. See ROUNDHILL, Stanley

PETER TIMOTHY, Brother. See LEPINE, Peter Gerald

PETERBOROUGH, Bishop of. See WESTWOOD, Rt Rev William John

PETERBOROUGH, Dean of. See WISE, Very Rev Randolph George

PETERKEN, Canon Peter Donald. b 28. K Coll Lon BD51 AKC51. d 52 p 53. C Swanley St Mary Roch 52-55 and 62-65; C Is of Dogs Ch Ch and St Jo w St Luke Lon 55-57; R S Perrott w Mosterton and Chedington Sarum 57-59; Br Guiana 59-62; R Killamarsh Derby 65-70; V Derby St Luke 70-90; RD Derby N 79-90; Hon Can Derby Cathl from 85; R Matlock from 90. The Rectory, Church Street, Matlock, Derbyshire DE4 3BZ   Matlock (0629) 582199

PETERS, Christopher Lind. b 56. Oak Hill Th Coll. d 82 p 83. C Knockbreda D & D 82-84; C Lisburn Ch Ch Cathl Conn 84-87; I Kilmocomogue Union C, C & R from 87. The Rectory, Durrus, Bantry, Co Cork, Irish Republic   Bantry (27) 61011

PETERS, Canon Cyril John (Bill). b 19. Fitzw Ho Cam BA42 MA45. Chich Th Coll 40. d 42 p 43. C Brighton St Mich Chich 42-45 and 47-50; CF (EC) 45-47; Hon CF from 47; Chapl Brighton Coll E Sussex 50-69; R Uckfield Chich from 69; R Isfield from 69; R Lt Horsted from 69; RD Uckfield from 73; Can and Preb Chich Cathl from 81. The Rectory, Belmont Road, Uckfield, E Sussex TN22 1BP   Uckfield (0825) 762251

PETERS, David Lewis. b 38. Ch Ch Ox BA62 MA66. Westcott Ho Cam 63. d 65 p 66. C Stand Man 70-74; P-in-c Hillock 70-74; V 74-82; V Haslingden w Haslingden Grane Blackb 82-88; rtd 88. 15 Ambleside Avenue, Rawtenstall, Rossendale, Lancs BB4 6RY   Rossendale (0706) 228913

PETERS, Geoffrey John. b 51. MInstC(Glas) BCom BSc MDiv. Gujranwala Th Sem 90 Oak Hill Th Coll 85. d 87 p 88. C Forest Gate St Sav w W Ham St Matt Chelmsf 87-90; C Wembley St Jo Lon from 90. 19 Bowrons Avenue, Wembley, Middx HA0 4QS   081-902 5997

PETERS, John Thomas. b 58. Connecticut Univ BA80 LTh. St Jo Coll Nottm 84. d 87 p 88. C Virginia Water Guildf from 87. 17 Sundon Crescent, Virginia Water, Surrey GU25 4RF   Wentworth (0344) 2473

PETERS, Canon Kenneth. b 54. Univ of Wales (Cardiff) DipTh77 Tokyo Univ MBA88. St Mich Coll Llan 74. d 77 p 78. C Mountain Ash Llan 77-80; Asst Chapl Mersey Miss to Seamen 80-82; Perm to Offic Ches from 80; Chapl Miss to Seamen from 82; Japan 82-89; Hon Can Kobe Japan from 85; Chapl Supt Mersey Miss to Seamen from 89. Colonsay House, 20 Crosby Road South, Liverpool L22 1RQ   051-920 3253

PETERS, Michael. b 41. Chich Th Coll 75. d 77 p 78. C Redruth Truro 77-79; TV 79-80; TV Redruth w Lanner 80-82; R St Mawgan w St Ervan and St Eval 82-86; Chapl HM Pris Liv 86-87; Chapl HM Pris Bris from 87. The Chaplain's Office, HM Prison, Cambridge Road, Bristol BS7 8PS   Bristol (0272) 426661

PETERS, Richard Paul. b 13. Univ Coll Ox BA35 MA39. Cuddesdon Coll 37. d 38 p 39. Warden Home of Divine Healing Crowhurst 69-78; rtd 78; Perm to Offic Chich from 79. Flat 3, Bramwell Lodge, Woodmancote, Henfield, W Sussex BN5 9SX   Henfield (0273) 493749

PETERS, Robert David. b 54. BA76. Oak Hill Th Coll 78. d 79 p 80. C Hyde St Geo Ches 79-83; C Hartford 83-86; V Lindow from 86. St John's Vicarage, 137 Knutsford Road, Wilmslow, Cheshire SK9 6EL   Alderley Edge (0625) 583251

PETERS, Stephen Eric. b 45. Westcott Ho Cam 74. d 77 p 78. C Wanstead St Mary Chelmsf 77-79; C Leigh-on-Sea St Marg 79-81; P-in-c Purleigh 81-82; P-in-c Cold Norton w Stow Maries 81-82; R Purleigh, Cold Norton and Stow Maries 83-84; V Bedf Park Lon 84-87; Perm to Offic Ex 87-88; TR Totnes and Berry Pomeroy 88-90. Vineyard Cottage, Dartington, Totnes, Devon TQ9 6HW   Totnes (0803) 867199

PETERSON, Dennis. b 25. Oak Hill Th Coll 51. d 54 p 55. C Leyton All SS Chelmsf 54-56; C Leeds St Geo Ripon 56-58; V E Brixton St Jude S'wark from 58. St Jude's Vicarage, Dulwich Road, London SE24 0PA   071-274 3183

PETFIELD, Bruce le Gay. b 34. FHA. NE Ord Course 76. d 79 p 80. NSM Morpeth Newc 79-86; C Knaresborough Ripon 86-87; V Flamborough York from 87; V Bempton from 87. The Vicarage, Church Street, Flamborough, Bridlington, N Humberside YO15 1PE   Bridlington (0262) 850336

PETIT, Andrew Michael. b 53. Solicitor. Cam Univ MA. Trin Coll Bris DipHE82. d 83 p 84. C Stoughton Guildf 83-87; C Shirley Win from 87. 16 Radway Road, Southampton SO1 2PW   Southampton (0703) 779603

PETITT, Michael David. b 53. BCombStuds. Linc Th Coll 79. d 82 p 83. C Arnold S'well 82-86; Asst Chapl HM Youth Cust Cen Glen Parva 86-87; V Blaby Leic from 87. The Rectory, Wigston Road, Blaby, Leicester LE8 3FA   Leicester (0533) 771679

PETRICHER, Georges Herbert Philippe. b 53. St Paul's Coll Mauritius. d 84 p 85. Mauritius 83-85; Hon C Tooting All SS S'wark 85-87; C Kings Heath Birm 87-90; C Hamstead St Paul from 90. 14 Yateley Avenue, Birmingham B42 1JN   021-358 0351

PETRIE, Alistair Philip. b 50. Lon Univ DipTh76. Fuller Th Sem California DMin90 Oak Hill Th Coll 73. d 76 p 77. C Eston York 76-79; P-in-c Prestwick Glas 79-81; R 81-82; Canada from 82. Brentwood Memorial Chapel, 792 Sea Drive, Brentwood Bay, British Columbia, Canada, V0S 1A0   Brentwood Bay (604) 652-3860

PETT, Douglas Ellory. b 24. Lon Univ BD46 BD48 AKC48 PhD74. K Coll Lon 48. **d** 49 **p** 50. Chapl St Mary's Hosp (Praed Street) Paddington 66-83; rtd 83. *23 Polsue Way, Tresillian, Truro, Cornwall TR2 4BE* Tresillian (087252) 573

PETTENGELL, Ernest Terence. b 43. K Coll Lon. **d** 69 **p** 70. C Chesham St Mary *Ox* 69-72; C Farnborough *Guildf* 72-75; Asst Master K Alfred Sch Burnham-on-Sea 75-78; C Bishop's Cleeve *Glouc* 78-80; Chapl Westonbirt Sch 80-85; P-in-c Shipton Moyne w Westonbirt and Lasborough *Glouc* 80-85; V Berkeley w Wick, Breadstone and Newport from 85. *The Vicarage, Berkeley, Glos GL13 9BH* Dursley (0453) 810294

PETTERSEN, Alvyn Lorang. b 51. TCD BA73 Dur Univ BA75 PhD81. Sarum & Wells Th Coll 78. **d** 81 **p** 82. Lic to Offic *Ely* 81-85; Chapl Clare Coll Cam 81-85; Fell and Chapl Ex Coll Ox from 85; Lic to Offic *Ox* from 85. *Exeter College, Oxford OX1 3DP* Oxford (0865) 279610

PETTET, Christopher Farley. b 54. Ox Univ BEd78. St Jo Coll Nottm 87. **d** 90 **p** 91. C Luton St Mary *St Alb* from 90. *34 Wychwood Avenue, Luton, Beds LU2 7HU* Luton (0582) 29902

PETTIFER, Canon Bryan George Ernest. b 32. Qu Coll Cam BA55 MA59 MEd. Wm Temple Coll Rugby 56 Ridley Hall Cam 57. **d** 59 **p** 60. C Attercliffe w Carbrook *Sheff* 59-61; C Ecclesall 61-65; Chapl City of Bath Tech Coll 65-74; Adult Educn Officer *Bris* 75-80; Dir Past Th Sarum & Wells Th Coll 80-85; Can Res St Alb from 85; Prin St Alb Minl Tr Scheme from 85. *25 Corinium Gate, St Albans, Herts AL3 4HY* St Albans (0727) 52403

PETTIFER, John Barrie. b 38. Linc Th Coll 63. **d** 65 **p** 66. C Stretford St Matt *Man* 65-67; C Stand 67-71; V Littleborough from 71. *The Vicarage, Deardon Street, Littleborough, Lancs OL15 9DZ* Littleborough (0706) 78334

PETTIFOR, David Thomas. b 42. Ripon Coll Cuddesdon 78. **d** 81. C Binley *Cov* 81-84; P-in-c Wood End 84-88; V from 88. *St Chad's Vicarage, Hillmorton Road, Coventry CV2 1FY* Coventry (0203) 612909

PETTIGREW, Miss Claire Gabrielle. b 23. St Mich Ho Ox 55. **dss** 77 **d** 87. Nor Heartsease St Fran *Nor* 77-81; Heigham H Trin 81-87; Dioc Lay Min Adv 83-87; Assoc Dioc Dir of Ords 87-89; rtd 89; Lic to Offic *Nor* from 89. *Granary Cottage, Norwich NR3 1RW* Norwich (0603) 619829

PETTIGREW, Canon Stanley. b 27. TCD BA49 MA62. **d** 50 **p** 51. C Newc *D & D* 50-53; C Dub Clontarf *D & G* 53-57; I Derralossary 57-62; Miss to Seamen from 62; I Wicklow w Killiskey *D & G* from 62; RD Delgany from 85; Can Ch Ch Cathl Dub from 87. *The Rectory, Wicklow, Irish Republic* Wicklow (404) 67132

PETTIT, Archibald Benjamin. b 06. Worc Ord Coll 63. **d** 65 **p** 66. V Whitwick St Andr *Leic* 69-77; rtd 77. *18 Rockville Drive, Embsay, Skipton, N Yorkshire BD23 6NX* Skipton (0756) 4540

PETTIT, Arthur George Lifton. b 08. Jes Coll Ox BA31 MA35. St D Coll Lamp BA29 St Steph Ho Ox 32. **d** 32 **p** 33. R Remenham *Ox* 50-73; rtd 73. *324 Cowley Mansions, Mortlake High Street, London SW14* 081-876 8671

PETTITT, Donald. b 09. Bps' Coll Cheshunt 57. **d** 57 **p** 58. V Worstead w Westwick and Sloley *Nor* 69-78; rtd 78; Perm to Offic *Nor* from 79. *15 Arbor Road, Cromer, Norfolk NR27 9DW* Cromer (0263) 512539

PETTITT, Maurice. b 13. Clare Coll Cam BA35 MA57 MusBac37. Lich Th Coll 56. **d** 57 **p** 58. V Riccall *York* 69-78; RD Escrick 73-78; rtd 78. *Holbeck House, Lastingham, York YO6 6TJ* Lastingham (07515) 517

PETTITT, Mervyn Francis. b 39. Qu Coll Birm DipTh66. **d** 66 **p** 67. C Loughton St Jo *Chelmsf* 69-72; R Downham w S Hanningfield 72-82; P-in-c W w S Hanningfield 77-78; C Leigh-on-Sea St Marg 82-85; rtd 85. *60 Suffolk Avenue, Leigh-on-Sea, Essex*

PETTITT, Robin Adrian. b 50. MRTPI79 Newc Univ BA77. St Steph Ho Ox 81. **d** 83 **p** 84. C Warrington St Elphin *Liv* 83-87; C Torrisholme *Blackb* from 87. *14 Lambrigg Close, Morecambe, Lancs LA4 4UE* Morecambe (0524) 422249

PETTITT, Simon. b 50. Nottm Univ BTh74 CertEd. Kelham Th Coll 70. **d** 75 **p** 76. C Penistone *Wakef* 75-78; Dioc Youth Officer 78-80; Dioc Schs Officer *St E* 80-86; P-in-c Hintlesham w Chattisham 80-86; V Bury St Edmunds St Jo from 86; RD Thingoe from 88. *The Vicarage, 37 Well Street, Bury St Edmunds, Suffolk IP33 1EQ* Bury St Edmunds (0284) 754335

PETTY, Brian. b 34. Man Univ BA90 Melbourne Univ DipRE. St Aid Birkenhead 59. **d** 62 **p** 63. C Meole Brace *Lich* 62-65; Chapl RAF 65-69; Australia 70-75; P-in-c

Kimbolton w Middleton-on-the-Hill *Heref* 76-79; P-in-c Pudleston-cum-Whyle w Hatfield, Docklow etc 76-79; P-in-c Haddenham *Ely* 79-80; V 80-84; V Fairfield *Derby* 84-90; Chapl St Geo Sch Ascot from 90. *The Hermitage, Ascot Priory, Priory Road, Ascot, Berks SL5 8RT* Ascot (0344) 882259

PETTY, Very Rev John Fitzmaurice. b 35. Trin Hall Cam BA59 MA65. Cuddesdon Coll 64. **d** 66 **p** 67. C Sheff St Cuth *Sheff* 66-69; C St Helier *S'wark* 69-75; V Hurst *Man* 75-88; AD Ashton-under-Lyne 83-87; Hon Can Man Cathl from 86; Provost Cov from 88. *Provost's Lodge, Priory Row, Coventry CV1 5ES* Coventry (0203) 227597

PETZSCH, Hugo Max David. b 57. Edin Univ MA79 BD83. Edin Th Coll 80. **d** 83 **p** 84. C Dollar *St And* 83-86; New Zealand 86-90; R Alyth *St And* from 90; R Blairgowrie from 90; R Coupar Angus from 90. *The Rectory, 10 Rosemount Park, Blairgowrie PH10 6TZ* Blairgowrie (0250) 4583

PEVERELL, Paul Harrison. b 57. Ripon Coll Cuddesdon. **d** 82 **p** 83. C Cottingham *York* 82-85; V Middlesb St Martin from 85. *St Martin's Vicarage, Whinney Banks, Middlesbrough, Cleveland TS5 4LA* Middlesbrough (0642) 819634

PEYTON, Nigel. b 51. JP. Edin Univ MA73 BD76. Union Th Sem (NY) STM77 Edin Th Coll 73. **d** 76 **p** 77. Chapl St Paul's Cathl Dundee *Bre* 76-82; Dioc Youth Chapl 76-85; Chapl Invergowrie 79-82; P-in-c 82-85; P-in-c Nottm All SS *S'well* 85; V from 86; Chapl Bluecoat Sch Nottm from 90. *The Vicarage, 16 All Saints' Street, Nottingham NG7 4DP* Nottingham (0602) 704197 or 786362

PEYTON JONES, Donald Lewis. b 14. DSC42. K Coll Lon 59. **d** 61 **p** 62. V Salcombe Regis *Ex* 62-72; C-in-c Lundy Is 73-78; V Appledore 73-78; rtd 79; Chapl Miss to Seamen from 79. *Fort Cottage, Cawsand, Cornwall PL10 1PA* Plymouth (0752) 822382

PEYTON JONES, Mrs Dorothy Helen. b 58. LMH Ox BA79 MPhil80. Trin Coll Bris DipTh86. **dss** 86 **d** 87. W Holl St Luke *Lon* 86-87; Par Dn 87-89; C Glas St Oswald *Glas* from 89. *43A Queen Mary Avenue, Glasgow G42 8DS* 041-424 0008

PHAIR, Edgar Nevill. b 15. TCD BA39 MA46. **d** 40 **p** 41. V Addiscombe St Mildred *Cant* 60-72; V Benenden 72-81; rtd 81; Perm to Offic *Cant* from 81; Chapl Benenden Hosp Kent from 81. *Bryn-y-Cwm Farm, Cwm Lane, Abergavenny, Gwent NP7 5NR*

PHAIR, Henry Lloyd. b 17. MBE64. TCD BA42 MA49. **d** 42 **p** 43. Chapl RAF 55-72; V Ercall Magna *Lich* 76-81; V Rowton 76-81; rtd 82; Perm to Offic *Chich* from 82. *43 Ashleigh Road, Horsham, W Sussex RH12 2LE* Horsham (0403) 51161

PHALO, Arthur. b 25. **d** 52 **p** 54. S Africa 53-76; SSJE from 60. *St Edward's House, 22 Great College Street, London SW1P 3QA* 071-222 9234

PHARAOH, Douglas William. b 18. MSHAA56. Worc Ord Coll 68. **d** 69 **p** 70. C Gt Malvern Ch Ch *Worc* 69-71; P-in-c Gateshead St Cuth *Dur* 72-73; V New Seaham 73-76; V Wymeswold *Leic* 76-78; V Wymeswold and Prestwold w Hoton 78-80; P-in-c Grandborough w Willoughby and Flecknoe *Cov* 80-81; V 81-83; rtd 83; Perm to Offic *Cov* from 83. *5 Margetts Close, Kenilworth, Warks CV8 1EN* Kenilworth (0926) 53807

PHARAOH, James. b 05. AKC22. **d** 28 **p** 29. V Headcorn *Cant* 57-71; rtd 71; Perm to Offic *Roch* from 71. *5 Springshaw Close, Sevenoaks, Kent* Sevenoaks (0732) 456542

PHEELY, William Rattray. b 35. EN(M)88. Edin Th Coll 57. **d** 60 **p** 61. C Glas St Mary *Glas* 60-63; C Salisbury St Martin *Sarum* 63-66; Guyana 66-82; V Bordesley St Oswald *Birm* 82-86; Perm to Offic from 86. *Flat 23, Frogmoor House, 571 Hob Moor Road, Birmingham B25 8XD* 021-783 1970

PHEIFFER, John Leslie. b 18. Wells Th Coll. **d** 67 **p** 68. Chapl Twickenham Prep Sch 69-71; C Chobham w Valley End *Guildf* 71-76; C Highcliffe w Hinton Admiral *Win* 77-79; V Portswood St Denys 79-85; rtd 86. *4 Haywards Close, Felpham, Bognor Regis, W Sussex PO22 8HF* Bognor Regis (0243) 828985

PHELAN, Frederick James (Lawrence). b 44. Edin Th Coll 87 Edin Dioc NSM Course 77. **d** 81 **p** 82. Hon AP Jedburgh *Edin* 82-87; Miss Priest Cove Bay *Ab* 89-90; P-in-c Cove Bay from 90; R Aber St Pet from 90. *St Mary's House, 32 Burnbutts Crescent, Cove Bay, Aberdeen AB1 4NU* Aberdeen (0224) 895033

PHELPS, Canon Arthur Charles. b 26. St Cath Coll Cam BA50 MA55. Ridley Hall Cam 51. **d** 53 **p** 54. V Collier Row St Jas *Chelmsf* 65-75; R Thorpe Morieux w Preston and Brettenham *St E* 75-84; R Rattlesden w Thorpe

Morieux and Brettenham 84-90; Hon Can St E Cathl from 89; rtd 90. *Newland, Sandy Lane, Harlyn Bay, Padstow, Cornwall PL28 8SD* Padstow (0841) 520697

PHELPS, Ian James. b 29. Oak Hill Th Coll 53. **d** 56 **p** 57. C Peckham St Mary *S'wark* 56-59; R Gaddesby w S Croxton *Leic* 59-67; R Beeby 59-67; Asst Dioc Youth Chapl and Rural Youth Adv 65-67; CF (TA) 60-67; CF (R of O) 67-84; Lic to Offic *Leic* from 67; Youth Chapl 67-85; Dioc Adult Educn Officer 85-91; Past Asst Leic Adnry from 91. *1 Weir Lane, Houghton-on-the-Hill, Leicester LE7 9GR* Leicester (0533) 416599

PHELPS, Ian Ronald. b 28. FLS58 Lon Univ BSc53 PhD57. Chich Th Coll 57. **d** 59 **p** 60. C Brighton Gd Shep Preston *Chich* 59-61; C Sullington 62-64; C Storrington 62-64; R Newtimber w Pyecombe 64-68; V Brighton St Luke 68-74; TV Brighton Resurr 74-76; V Peacehaven from 76. *41 Bramber Avenue, Peacehaven, E Sussex BN10 8HR* Peacehaven (0273) 583149

PHENNA, Peter. b 31. ALCD63. **d** 63 **p** 64. C St Marylebone All SS *Lon* 63-69; V Cam St Martin *Ely* 69-85; Lic to Offic from 85; Asst Gen Sec CPAS from 85; Dir Promotion Division from 89. *62 Newbold Terrace East, Leamington Spa, Warwickshire CV32 4EZ* Leamington Spa (0926) 424852

PHILBRICK, Gary James. b 57. Southn Univ BA78 K Alfred's Coll Win CertEd79 ACertCM84 Edin Univ BD86. Edin Th Coll 83. **d** 86 **p** 87. C Southn Maybush St Pet *Win* 86-90; R Fawley from 90. *The Rectory, 1 Sheringham Close, Southampton SO4 1SQ* Southampton (0703) 893552

PHILIPSON, John Wharton. b 05. St Jo Coll York 24. St Deiniol's Hawarden 66. **d** 66 **p** 67. Asst Dioc Dir of Educn *Newc* from 66; Hon C Gosforth St Nic 66-79. *1 Otterburn Terrace, Newcastle upon Tyne NE2 3AP* 091-281 4645

PHILLIPS, Andrew Graham. b 58. Ex Univ BSc79. Chich Th Coll 84. **d** 87 **p** 88. C Frankby w Greasby *Ches* 87-89; C Liv St Chris Norris Green *Liv* from 89. *17 Fairmead Road, Liverpool L11 5AS* 051-226 5933

PHILLIPS, Canon Dr Anthony Charles Julian. b 36. Lon Univ BD63 AKC63 G&C Coll Cam PhD67 St Jo Coll Ox MA75 DPhil80. Coll of Resurr Mirfield 66. **d** 66 **p** 67. C-in-c Chesterton Gd Shep CD *Ely* 66-69; Fell Dean and Chapl Trin Hall Cam 69-74; Chapl St Jo Coll Ox 75-85; Hd Master K Sch Cant from 85; Hon Can Cant Cathl *Cant* from 86; Can Th Truro Cathl *Truro* from 86. *The King's School, Canterbury, Kent CT1 2ES* Canterbury (0227) 475501

PHILLIPS, Benjamin Lambert Meyrick. b 64. K Coll Cam BA86 MA90. Ridley Hall Cam 87. **d** 90 **p** 91. C Wareham *Sarum* from 90. *110 Northmoor Way, Wareham, Dorset BH20 4ET* Wareham (0929) 552607

PHILLIPS, Brian Edward Dorian William. b 36. Bris Univ BA58. Ripon Hall Ox 58. **d** 60 **p** 61. C Ross *Heref* 60-64; Chapl RAF 64-68; Hon C Fringford w Hethe and Newton Purcell *Ox* 68-73; Chapl Howell's Sch Denbigh 73-76; C Cleobury Mortimer w Hopton Wafers *Heref* 76-80; V Dixton from 80. *The Vicarage, 38 Hillcrest Road, Wyesham, Monmouth, Gwent NP5 3LH* Monmouth (0600) 2565

PHILLIPS, Canon Brian Robert. b 31. Clare Coll Cam BA53 MA57. Linc Th Coll 54. **d** 56 **p** 57. V Highworth w Sevenhampton and Inglesham etc *Bris* 69-84; Hon Can Bris Cathl from 84; P-in-c Long Newnton 84-87; P-in-c Crudwell w Ashley 84-87; R Ashley, Crudwell, Hankerton, Long Newnton etc 87-90; rtd 90. *Hannington, Hospital Road, Shirrell Heath, Southampton SO3 2JR* Wickham (0329) 834547

PHILLIPS, Very Rev Christopher John. b 49. Barrington Coll Rhode Is BA73. Sarum & Wells Th Coll 73. **d** 75 **p** 76. C Southmead *Bris* 75-78; Hong Kong from 78; Dean Hong Kong from 87. *c/o St John's Cathedral, Garden Road, Hong Kong* Hong Kong (852) 523-4157

PHILLIPS, David Elwyn. b 17. St D Coll Lamp 62. **d** 64 **p** 65. C Port Talbot St Theodore *Llan* 68-70; V Abercanaid 70-87; rtd 87. *Carmel, 13 Tyleri Gardens, Abertillery, Gwent NP3 1EZ*

PHILLIPS, David Keith. b 61. New Coll Ox MA90. St Jo Coll Dur BA90. **d** 91. C Denton Holme *Carl* from 91. *118 Dalston Road, Carlisle CA2 5JP* Carlisle (0228) 22938

PHILLIPS, Duncan Laybourne. b 08. Wycliffe Hall Ox 45. **d** 47 **p** 48. P-in-c Eye, Croft w Yarpole and Lucton *Heref* 69-73; R 73-81; rtd 81; Perm to Offic *Heref* from 81. *82 Westcroft, Leominster, Herefordshire HR6 8HQ* Leominster (0568) 3564

PHILLIPS, Edward Leigh. b 12. St Edm Hall Ox BA34 MA47. Wycliffe Hall Ox 33. **d** 35 **p** 36. V Kingston w Iford *Chich* 52-75; V Iford w Kingston and Rodmell 75-78; RD Lewes 65-77; rtd 78; Perm to Offic *Glouc*

from 78. *35 Woodland Green, Upton St Leonards, Gloucester GL4 8BD* Gloucester (0452) 619894

PHILLIPS, Canon Frederick Wallace. b 12. MC43. Univ of Wales BA34. St Mich Coll Llan 34. **d** 36 **p** 37. V Margate St Jo *Cant* 64-74; Hon Can Cant Cathl 66-84; R Smarden 74-82; R Biddenden 80-82; rtd 82; Perm to Offic *Cant* from 84. *6 South Close, The Precincts, Canterbury CT1 2EJ* Canterbury (0227) 450891

PHILLIPS, Canon Geoffrey John. b 23. BNC Ox BA47 MA56. Ridley Hall Cam 54. **d** 56 **p** 57. R Gillingham w Geldeston and Stockton *Nor* 65-70; V Eaton 70-81; RD Nor S 71-81; Hon Can Nor Cathl 78-81; Chapl Vienna w Budapest and Prague *Eur* 81-87; rtd 87; Perm to Offic *Nor* from 87. *Mere Farmhouse, White Heath Road, Bergh Apton, Norwich NR15 1AY* Thurton (050843) 656

PHILLIPS, Gordon Joshua. b 14. St D Coll Lamp BA36 Ely Th Coll 36. **d** 38 **p** 39. V Isleworth St Mary *Lon* 56-85; rtd 85; Perm to Offic *Lon* from 85. *Ward MD2, West Middlesex Hospital, Twickenham Road, Isleworth, Middx TW7 6AF* 081-560 2121

PHILLIPS, Gwilym Caswallon Howell. b 07. **d** 32 **p** 33. V Evenley *Pet* 61-72; rtd 72. *1 The Glebe, Flore, Northampton NN7 4LX* Weedon (0327) 40423

PHILLIPS, Horace George. b 38. Man Univ BA60 Birm Univ DipTh62 MEd84. Qu Coll Birm 60. **d** 62 **p** 63. C Wotton St Mary *Glouc* 62-65; C Standish w Hardwicke and Haresfield 65-68; C-in-c Watermoor Holy Trin 68-74; V Churchdown St Jo 74-79; P-in-c Beckford w Ashton under Hill 79-85; P-in-c Overbury w Alstone, Teddington and Lt Washbourne *Worc* 84-85; V Overbury w Teddington, Alstone etc 85-88; P-in-c Peopleton and White Ladies Aston etc from 88; Dioc Sch Officer from 88. *The Rectory, Peopleton, Pershore, Worcs WR10 2EE* Worcester (0905) 840243

PHILLIPS, Ven Ivor Lloyd. b 04. MC45. Univ of Wales (Abth) BSc25. St Mich Coll Llan 30. **d** 31 **p** 32. Hon CF from 46; Can St Woolos Cathl *Mon* 62-73; Warden of Ords 62-73; Adn Newport 64-73; R Tredunnoc w Kemeys Inferior etc 65-73; rtd 73; Perm to Offic *St D* from 73. *2 Pier House, Crackwell Street, Tenby, Dyfed SA70 7HA* Tenby (0834) 3550

PHILLIPS, Ivor Lynn. b 44. Leeds Univ BA70. Cuddesdon Coll 69. **d** 71 **p** 72. C Bedlinog *Llan* 71-73; C Roath St Marg 73-77; TV Wolv All SS *Lich* 77-78; TV Wolv 78-81; Chapl Charing Cross Hosp Lon 81-91; Chapl Milan w Genoa and Varese *Eur* from 91. *via Solferino 17, 20121 Milan, Italy* Milan (2) 655-2258

PHILLIPS, Mrs Janet Elizabeth. b 37. Bp Grosseteste Coll CertEd57. E Midl Min Tr Course 81. **dss** 84 **d** 87. Wisbech St Aug *Ely* 84-86; Cam St Jas 86-87; Par Dn 87-91; Par Dn Wisbech SS Pet and Paul from 91. *18 Pickards Way, Wisbech, Cambs PE13 1SD* Wisbech (0945) 476149

PHILLIPS, Jeffery Llewellyn. b 32. Sarum & Wells Th Coll. **d** 87 **p** 88. C Ringwood *Win* 87-90; V Somborne w Ashley from 90. *The Vicarage, Winchester Road, Kings Somborne, Stockbridge, Hants SO20 6PF* Romsey (0794) 388223

PHILLIPS, John David. b 29. G&C Coll Cam BA50 MA54 CertEd69. SW Minl Tr Course 85. **d** 87 **p** 88. NSM St Martin w E and W Looe *Truro* 87-88; NSM St Merryn from 88. *The Vicarage, St Merryn, Padstow, Cornwall PL28 8ND* Padstow (0841) 520379

PHILLIPS, John Eldon. b 50. Univ of Wales (Cardiff) BEd85. St Mich Coll Llan. **d** 90 **p** 91. NSM Merthyr Cynog and Dyffryn Honddu etc *S & B* from 90. *Tegfan, Camden Court, Pwllgloyw, Brecon, Powys LD3 7RP* Brecon (0874) 89281

PHILLIPS, John William Burbridge. b 39. Dur Univ BSc60 Lon Univ BD68. Tyndale Hall Bris 65. **d** 68 **p** 69. C Barton Seagrave *Pet* 68-71; C Northn All SS w St Kath 71-75; R Irthlingborough 75-88; V Weedon Lois w Plumpton and Moreton Pinkney etc from 88. *The Vicarage, Weedon Lois, Towcester, Northants NN12 8PN* Blakesley (0327) 860278

PHILLIPS, Joseph Benedict. b 11. **d** 37 **p** 38. V Bradf St Andr *Bradf* 59-66; rtd 76. *100 Ruskin Avenue, Lincoln LN2 4BT* Lincoln (0522) 34411

PHILLIPS, Kenneth John. b 37. Coll of Resurr Mirfield 67. **d** 67 **p** 68. C Blackb St Jas *Blackb* 67-69; C-in-c Lea CD 70-80; V Lea 80-84; P-in-c Priors Hardwick, Priors Marston and Wormleighton *Cov* from 85; RD Southam from 89. *The Vicarage, Priors Marston, Rugby, Warks CV23 8RT* Byfield (0327) 60053

PHILLIPS, Lamont Wellington Sanderson. b 33. S'wark Ord Course 73. **d** 76 **p** 78. NSM Tottenham St Paul *Lon* 76-83; P-in-c Upper Clapton St Matt 83-88; V from 88.

St Matthew's Vicarage, 20 Moresby Road, London E5
9LF 081-806 2430

PHILLIPS, Canon Martin Nicholas. b 32. Em Coll Cam
BA57 MA61. Linc Th Coll 57. **d** 59 **p** 60. C Stocking
Farm CD Leic 59-63; V Sheff St Silas Sheff 63-71; V
Birstall Leic 72-82; R Wanlip 72-82; V Birstall and
Wanlip 82-88; R Loughb Em from 88; Hon Can
Leic Cathl from 90. The Rectory, 47 Forest Road,
Loughborough, Leics LE11 3NW   Loughborough
(0509) 263264

PHILLIPS, Michael John. b 54. Trent Poly BA77. Sarum
& Wells Th Coll 78. **d** 81 **p** 82. C Killay S & B 81-83; C
Treboeth 83-85; Hong Kong 85-89; Japan 89-91; TR
Scilly Is Truro from 91. The Chaplaincy, St Mary's, Isles
of Scilly TR21 0NA   Scillonia (0720) 22421

PHILLIPS, Michael Thomas. b 46. CQSW81. Linc Th Coll
89. **d** 90 **p** 91. C Hyson Green S'well 90-91; C Basford w
Hyson Green from 91. 47 Plantation Side, Nottingham
NG7 5NR   Nottingham (0602) 788075

PHILLIPS, Mrs Patricia. b 45. Glouc Sch of Min 83. **dss**
86 **d** 87. Newent and Gorsley w Cliffords Mesne Glouc
86-87; C from 87. 30 Knights Way, Newent, Glos
GL18 1QL   Newent (0531) 820865

PHILLIPS, Patrick Noble Stowell. b 22. Edin Univ MA50.
ALCD52. **d** 52 **p** 53. Canada 66-71; R Arthuret Carl
71-88; rtd 88. 14 Gipsy Lane, Reading RG6 2HB
Reading (0734) 64654

PHILLIPS, Percy Graham. b 26. St Aid Birkenhead 46.
d 51 **p** 52. V Stonebridge St Mich Lon 65-70; R Vernham
Dean w Linkenholt Win 70-78; C Farnham Guildf 78-82;
TV Cove St Jo 82-89; rtd 89. 22 Charts Close, Cranleigh,
Surrey GU6 8BH

PHILLIPS, Peter. b 26. Oak Hill Th Coll 63. **d** 65 **p** 66. C
St Alb St Paul St Alb 69-73; V Riseley w Bletsoe 73-84;
R Arley Cov 84-91; rtd 91. Hilford House, 10 Albert
Road, Clevedon, Avon BS21 7RP Bristol (0272) 875801

PHILLIPS, Raymond Arthur. b 29. K Coll Lon 49. **d** 53
p 54. C Stepney St Aug w St Phil Lon 53-56; N Rhodesia
56-64; Zambia 64-68; V Stoke Newington St Faith, St
Matthias and All SS Lon 68-73; Trinidad and Tobago
73-80; V Hillingdon All SS Lon from 80. All Saints'
Vicarage, Ryefield Avenue, Hillingdon, Uxbridge, Middx
UB10 9BT   Uxbridge (0895) 33991

PHILLIPS, Canon Rees William Hippesley. b 12. Jes Coll
Ox BA35 MA38. Cuddesdon Coll 36. **d** 37 **p** 38. R
Outwell Ely 64-73; Chapl Community of the Epiphany
Truro 73-77; rtd 77; Perm to Offic Ox from 77.
107 Bloxham Road, Banbury, Oxon OX16 9JT
Banbury (0295) 251765

PHILLIPS, Robin Michael. b 33. AKC58. **d** 59 **p** 60. C
Hanwell St Mellitus Lon 59-61; C St Margarets on
Thames 61-64; C Hangleton Chich 64-68; V Mellor
Derby from 68; RD Glossop from 89. The Vicarage,
Mellor, Stockport, Cheshire SK6 5LX   061-427 1203

PHILLIPS, Stephen. b 38. QUB BA60. Linc Th Coll 60.
d 62 **p** 63. C Waddington Linc 62-65; C Gt Grimsby St
Jas 65-72; V Kirmington from 72; V Gt Limber w
Brocklesby from 73; R Croxton from 82. The Vicarage,
Great Limber, Grimsby, S Humberside DN37 8JN
Roxton (0469) 60641

PHILLIPS, Thomas Wynford. b 15. Univ of Wales
BA37 BD40. St Mich Coll Llan. **d** 43 **p** 44. R Upton
Magna Lich 68-73; V Withington 68-73; R Roche Truro
73-80; R Withiel 73-80; RD St Austell 76-80; rtd 80.
Brynawelon, Wheal Quoit Avenue, St Agnes, Cornwall
TR5 0SJ   St Agnes (087255) 2862

PHILLIPS, William Ufelgwyn Maundy. b 11. St D Coll
Lamp BA. **d** 34 **p** 35. V Roath St Sav Llan 51-73; V
Margam 73-80; P-in-c Llanharry 81-83; rtd 83; Perm to
Offic Llan from 83. 1 St Paul's Court, Heol Fair,
Llandaff, Cardiff   Cardiff (0222) 553146

PHILLIPS-SMITH, Edward Charles. b 50. AKC71. **d** 73
p 74. C Wolv Lich 73-76; Chapl St Pet Colleg Sch Wolv
77-87; Hon C Wolv Lich 78-87; V Stevenage St Pet
Broadwater St Alb 87-89; Chapl Millfield Jun Sch
Somerset from 89. 1 Edgarley Cottages, Cinnamon Lane,
Glastonbury, Somerset BA6 8LB   Glastonbury (0458)
34833

PHILLIPSON, Christopher Quintin. b 14. Ch Coll Cam
BA36 MA40. Ridley Hall Cam 36. **d** 38 **p** 39. V
Aldingbourne Chich 70-81; rtd 81; Perm to Offic
Chich from 82. 91 Little Breach, Chichester, W Sussex
PO19 4TZ   Chichester (0243) 785557

PHILLIPSON-MASTERS, Miss Susan Patricia. b 52.
FIST76 ACP80 Sussex Univ CertEd73 K Alfred's Coll
Win BEd81. Trin Coll Bris DipHE88. **d** 89. C Saltford
w Corston and Newton St Loe B & W from 89.
27 Trenchard Road, Saltford, Bristol BS18 3DT   Bath
(0225) 873834

PHILLPOT, Donald John. b 27. St Jo Coll Dur
BA53 DipTh55. **d** 55 **p** 56. C Southmead Bris 55-60; C
Brislington St Luke 60-63; R Stapleton Heref 63-68; V
Dorrington 63-68; P-in-c Astley Abbotts 68-78; R
Bridgnorth w Tasley 68-78; V Lillington Cov from
78. The Vicarage, Lillington, Leamington Spa, Warks
CV32 7RH   Leamington Spa (0926) 424674

PHILPOTT, Canon John David. b 43. Leic Univ BA64.
Trin Coll Bris 69. **d** 72 **p** 73. C Knutsford St Jo Ches
72-75; C Toft 72-75; C Bickenhill w Elmdon Birm 75-79;
V Birm St Luke 79-91; RD Birm City 83-88; Hon Can
Birm Cathl 89-91; V Chilvers Coton w Astley Cov from
91. Chilvers Coton Vicarage, Coventry Road, Nuneaton,
Warks CV11 4NJ   Nuneaton (0203) 383010

PHILPOTT, John Wilfred. b 44. K Coll Lon BD67 AKC67.
d 68 **p** 69. C Norbury St Steph Cant 68-71; C Addiscombe
St Mildred 71-75; V Whitfield w Guston from 75. The
Vicarage, 45 Bewsbury Cross Lane, Whitfield, Dover
CT16 3EZ   Dover (0304) 820314

PHILPOTT, Ronald. b 38. IPFA. Cranmer Hall Dur 88.
d 89 **p** 90. NSM S Ossett Wakef from 89. 38 South Parade,
Ossett, W Yorkshire WF5 0EF   Wakefield (0924) 273052

PHILPOTT, Preb Samuel. b 41. Kelham Th Coll 60. **d** 65
p 66. C Swindon New Town Bris 65-70; C Torquay St
Martin Barton Ex 70-73; TV Withycombe Raleigh 73-76;
V Shaldon 76-78; P-in-c Plymouth St Pet 78-80; V from
80; RD Plymouth Devonport from 86; Preb Ex Cathl
from 91. St Peter's Vicarage, 23 Wyndham Square,
Plymouth PL1 5EG   Plymouth (0752) 662110

PHILPS, Mark Seymour. b 51. Worc Coll Ox BA73 MA78
Lon Univ MA75 Nottm Univ BA79. St Jo Coll Nottm
77. **d** 80 **p** 81. C Chadwell Heath Chelmsf 80-83; C
Woodford Wells 83-87; V Tipton St Matt Lich from 87.
St Matthew's Vicarage, Dudley Road, Tipton, W Midlands
DY4 8DJ   021-557 1929

PHIPPS, David John. b 46. Bris Univ BSc68. Trin Coll
Bris 75. **d** 78 **p** 79. C Madron w Morvah Truro 78-80; C
Kenilworth St Jo Cov 80-83; TV Barnstaple, Goodleigh
and Landkey Ex 83-84; TV Barnstaple from 85. The
Vicarage, Tanners Road, Landkey, Barnstaple, Devon
EX32 0NQ   Swimbridge (0271) 830083

PHIPPS, Canon Frederick George. b 30. Kelham Th Coll
50. **d** 54 **p** 55. C Staveley Derby 54-59; Korea 59-65;
Australia from 65; Can Ch Ch Cathl Ballarat from 84.
St John's Rectory, Barclay Street, Port Fairy, Victoria,
Australia 3284   Port Fairy (55) 681028

PHIPPS, John Maclean. b 14. Em Coll Cam BA38 MA50.
Cuddesdon Coll 38. **d** 39 **p** 40. V Speenhamland Ox
53-71; V Buckland 72-79; V Littleworth 72-79; R Pusey
72-79; rtd 79; Perm to Offic Chich from 84. Flat 4,
Hometye House, Grosvenor Road, Seaford, E Sussex
BN25 2BQ   Seaford (0323) 897890

✠**PHIPPS, Rt Rev Simon Wilton.** b 21. MC45. Trin Coll
Cam BA48 MA53. Westcott Ho Cam 48. **d** 50 **p** 51 **c** 68.
C Huddersfield St Pet Wakef 50-53; Chapl Trin Coll
Cam 53-58; Ind Chapl Cov 58-68; C Cov Cathl 58-68;
Hon Can Cov Cathl 65-68; Suff Bp Horsham Chich
68-75; Bp Linc 75-86; rtd 86; Asst Bp Chich from 86;
Asst Bp S'wark from 86. Sarsens, Shipley, Horsham, W
Sussex RH13 8PX   Coolham (0403) 741354

PHIZACKERLEY, Ven Gerald Robert. b 29. Univ Coll
Ox BA52 MA56. Wells Th Coll 52. **d** 54 **p** 55. C Carl St
Barn Carl 54-57; Chapl Abingdon Sch 57-64; R
Gaywood, Bawsey and Mintlyn Nor 64-78; RD Lynn
68-78; Hon Can Nor Cathl 75-78; Hon Can Derby Cathl
Derby from 78; P-in-c Ashford w Sheldon 78-91; Adn
Chesterfield from 78. The Old Parsonage, Taddington,
Buxton, Derbyshire SK17 9TW   Taddington (0298)
85607

PHYALL, Albert Thomas. b 02. AKC31. **d** 31 **p** 32. V Hayes
St Anselm Lon 44-75; rtd 75; Hon C St Marylebone
Annunciation Bryanston Street Lon 75-80; Hon C
Kensington St Jo the Bapt from 79. 33 Elsham Road,
London W14 8HB   071-603 6135

PHYPERS, David John. b 39. Leic Univ BA60 CertEd61
Lon Univ BD65. Linc Th Coll 76. **d** 78 **p** 79. NSM
Normanton Derby 78-80; NSM Sinfin 80-87; Lic to Offic
87-88; P-in-c Denby from 88; P-in-c Horsley Woodhouse
from 88. 103 Church Street, Denby Village, Derby
DE5 8PH   Derby (0332) 780730

PIACHAUD, Preb Francois Allen. b 12. Lon Univ
BA32 BD35 Selw Coll Cam BA37 MA41. Westcott Ho
Cam 37. **d** 37 **p** 38. V Chelsea Ch Ch Lon 51-86; Preb
St Paul's Cathl 61-86; RD Chelsea 74-77; rtd 86; Perm
to Offic Ox from 86. 8 Linden Avenue, Maidenhead,
Berks SL6 6HB   Maidenhead (0628) 20866

PIBWORTH, John David. b 23. OBE79. Ripon Hall Ox
59. **d** 61 **p** 62. C N Stoneham Win 61-66; V Pennington
from 66; Chapl RNVR 67-79. The Vicarage, Ramley

Road, Pennington, Lymington, Hants SO41 8LH
Lymington (0590) 672646

PICK, David. b 44. Linc Th Coll 85. **d** 87 **p** 88. C Howden Team Min *York* 87-90; P-in-c Sledmere and Cowlam w Fridaythorpe, Fimer etc from 90. *The Vicarage, Sledmere, Driffield, N Humberside YO25 0XQ* Driffield (0377) 86220

PICK, William Harry. b 23. Open Univ BA77. St Aid Birkenhead 51. **d** 54 **p** 55. V Stoneycroft All SS *Liv* 67-79; R N Meols 79-88; rtd 88. *8 Morley Road, Southport, Merseyside PR9 9JS*

PICKARD, Francis William James. b 21. Worc Ord Coll 64. **d** 66 **p** 67. V Old Warden *St Alb* 68-73; P-in-c Caldecote All SS 72-73; P-in-c Hinxworth w Newnham and Radwell 73-86; rtd 86. *58 Angerstein Close, Weeting, Brandon, Suffolk IP27 0RL* Thetford (0842) 813578

PICKARD, Canon Frank Eustace. b 31. Lon Univ BSc52 St Cath Soc Ox BA56 MA63. St Steph Ho Ox. **d** 57 **p** 58. C Haydock St Jas *Liv* 57-59; C Davenham *Ches* 59-60; Asst Master St Dunstan's Sch Lon 60-63; Min Can Pet Cathl *Pet* 63-72; P-in-c Newborough 67-68; V 68-72; R Isham w Pytchley 72-76; R Abington from 76; Can Pet Cathl from 86. *The Rectory, 5 Abington Park Crescent, Northampton NN3 3AD* Northampton (0604) 31041

PICKARD, Hedley Arthur Mitchell. b 27. Linc Th Coll 61. **d** 63 **p** 64. C Bridlington Quay H Trin *York* 63-66; V Bempton 66-71; V Lt Hulton *Man* 71-75; Chapl Palma and Balearic Is w Ibiza etc *Eur* 75-83; R Stoke Bruerne w Grafton Regis and Alderton *Pet* from 83. *The Rectory, Stoke Bruerne, Towcester, Northants NN12 7SD* Roade (0604) 862352

PICKARD, Ronald William. b 16. ALCD39. **d** 39 **p** 40. Chapl Br Emb Ankara *Eur* 70-71; rtd 81. *23 Tower Gardens, Deep Lane, Crediton, Devon EX17 2BQ* Crediton (0363) 774234

PICKARD, Stephen Kim. b 52. Newc Univ Aus BCom Dur Univ PhD. Melbourne Coll of Div BD St Jo Coll Morpeth 77. **d** 80 **p** 80. Australia 80-82 and from 91; C Dur St Cuth *Dur* 82-84; Chapl Van Mildert Coll Dur 84-90; Chapl Trev Coll Dur 84-90. *Moore Theological College, 1 King Street, Newtown, NSW, Australia 2042*

PICKARD, William Priestley. b 31. MIPM72. Clifton Th Coll 56. **d** 59 **p** 60. C Upper Tulse Hill St Matthias S'wark 59-63; Asst Warden Shaftesbury Crusade Bris from 64. *21 Rylestone Grove, Bristol BS9 3UT* Bristol (0272) 620372

PICKEN, David Anthony. b 63. Lon Univ BA84 Kent Univ PGCE85. Linc Th Coll 87. **d** 90 **p** 91. C Worth *Chich* from 90. *32 Felbridge Avenue, Crawley, W Sussex RH10 7BD* Crawley (0293) 886663

PICKEN, James Hugh (Brother James). b 51. Victoria Univ Wellington BMus75. Ripon Coll Cuddesdon BA79. **d** 80 **p** 81. C Jarrow *Dur* 80-83; SSF from 83; Perm to Offic *Sarum* from 87. *The Friary, Hilfield, Dorchester, Dorset DT2 7BE* Cerne Abbas (0300) 341345

PICKEN, William Middlewood Martin. b 06. SS Coll Cam BA28 MA32. Westcott Ho Cam 29. **d** 30 **p** 31. Hon PV Truro Cathl *Truro* from 37; R St Martin by Looe 37-71; rtd 71. *2 Stratton Terrace, Falmouth, Cornwall*

PICKERING, David Colville. b 41. Kelham Th Coll 61. **d** 66 **p** 67. C Chaddesden St Phil *Derby* 66-70; C New Mills 70-72; C Buxton 72-74; V Chesterfield St Aug 74-90; R Whittington from 90. *The Rectory, 84 Church Street North, Old Whittington, Chesterfield S41 9QW* Chesterfield (0246) 450651

PICKERING, Ven Fred. b 19. St Pet Hall Ox BA41 MA45. St Aid Birkenhead 41. **d** 43 **p** 44. V Chitts Hill St Cuth *Lon* 68-74; Adn Hampstead 74-84; rtd 84; Perm to Offic *Pet* from 84. *23 Broadgate Way, Warmington, Peterborough* Oundle (0832) 280548

PICKERING, John Alexander. b 41. TCD BA63 MA66. CITC 65. **d** 65 **p** 66. C Magheralin *D & D* 65-67; C-in-c Outeragh *K, E & A* 67; I 68-71; Deputation Sec Hibernian Bible Soc 71-74; C-in-c Drumgoon and Ashfield 74-80; I Keady w Armaghbreague and Derrynoose *Arm* 80-83; I Drumcree from 83. *78 Drumcree Road, Portadown, Craigavon, Co Armagh BT62 1PE* Portadown (0762) 333711

PICKERING, John David. b 38. **d** 86 **p** 86. NSM Ellon *Ab* 86-88; NSM Cruden 86-88; Ind Chapl *Dur* from 88. *131 Victoria Road, West Hebburn, Tyne and Wear NE31 1UU* 091-483 9142

PICKERING, John Michael Staunton. b 34. Sarum & Wells Th Coll 71. **d** 72 **p** 73. C Gaywood, Bawsey and Mintlyn *Nor* 72-77; P-in-c Foulsham 77-81; R Foulsham w Hindolveston and Guestwick 81-88; P-in-c Bacton w Edingthorpe w Witton and Ridlington from 88. *The*

Vicarage, Church Road, Bacton, Norwich NR12 0JP Walcott (0692) 650375

PICKERING, John Roger. b 28. Fitzw Ho Cam BA52 MA56. Linc Th Coll 62. **d** 63 **p** 66. C Folkestone H Trin w Ch Ch *Cant* 71-73; P-in-c Buckland Newton *Sarum* 73-77; P-in-c Wootton Glanville and Holnest 73-77; P-in-c Osmington w Poxwell 77-80; C Eston w Normanby *York* 83-84; P-in-c Swine 84-90; rtd 90. *The Bull Pens, Treworder Farm, Ruan Minor, Helston, Cornwall TR12 7JL* The Lizard (0326) 290908

PICKERING, Malcolm. b 37. Sarum Th Coll 65. **d** 68 **p** 69. C Milton *Portsm* 68-70; C Stanmer w Falmer and Moulsecoomb *Chich* 70-75; Chapl Brighton Coll of Educn 71-75; V Hooe *Chich* 75-80; R Ninfield 75-80; V Ventnor H Trin *Portsm* 80-88; V Ventnor St Cath 80-88; Chapl St Cath Sch Ventnor 87-88; V Marton *Blackb* from 88. *St Paul's Vicarage, 55 Vicarage Lane, Blackpool FY4 4EF* Blackpool (0253) 62679

PICKERING, Mark Penrhyn. b 36. Liv Univ BA59 St Cath Coll Ox BA62 MA67. Wycliffe Hall Ox 60. **d** 63 **p** 64. C Claughton cum Grange *Ches* 63-67; C Newland St Jo *York* 67-72; TV Marfleet 72-76; V Kingston upon Hull St Nic 76-85; V Elloughton and Brough w Brantingham 85-88; Chapl Hull R Infirmary from 88. *1 Nunburnholme Avenue, North Ferriby, N Humberside HU14 3AW* Hull (0482) 632425

PICKERING, Stephen Philip. b 52. Coll of Resurr Mirfield 78. **d** 79 **p** 80. C Wallsend St Luke *Newc* 79-82; Chapl RN from 82. *c/o MOD, Lacon House, Theobald's Road, London WC1X 8RY* 071-430 6847

PICKERING, Thomas. b 07. Ch Coll Cam BA28 MA32. Ely Th Coll 30. **d** 30 **p** 31. C Leic St Mary *Leic* 30-35; C Leic St Geo 35-46; Lic to Offic 46-81; Perm to Offic from 81. *10 Park Hill Drive, Leicester LE2 8HR* Leicester (0533) 831242

PICKERING, William Stuart Frederick. b 22. Manitoba Univ Hon DCL81 K Coll Lon BD49 AKC49 PhD58. **d** 50 **p** 51. Canada 56-66; Lic to Offic *Newc* 66-87; rtd 87. *37 Gough Way, Cambridge CB3 9LN* Cambridge (0223) 312537

PICKETT, Brian Laurence. b 48. Reading Univ BA70. Qu Coll Birm BA73 MA77 Ripon Coll Cuddesdon. **d** 88 **p** 88. C Highcliffe w Hinton Admiral *Win* from 88. *3 Tresillian Way, Walkford, Christchurch, Dorset BH23 5QP* Highcliffe (0425) 273546

PICKETT, Joanna Elizabeth. b 53. Leic Univ BA74 MA80. Wycliffe Hall Ox 87. **d** 89. Chapl Southn Univ *Win* from 89. *38 Chamberlain Road, Southampton SO2 1PS* Southampton (0703) 585453

PICKETT, Peter Leslie. b 28. MRCS Lon Univ LDS. S Dios Minl Tr Scheme 83. **d** 86 **p** 87. NSM Eastbourne H Trin *Chich* 86-88; P-in-c Danehill from 88. *The Vicarage, Dane Hill, Haywards Heath, W Sussex RH17 7ER* Dane Hill (0825) 790269

PICKLES, Harold. b 13. Sarum Th Coll 34. **d** 36 **p** 37. V Edwinstowe w Carburton *S'well* 57-78; rtd 78; Perm to Offic St Alb 78-84; Ripon from 84. *3 Old Deanery Close, Minster Road, Ripon, N Yorkshire HG4 1LZ* Ripon (0765) 4375

PICKLES, Mark Andrew. b 62. Edin Univ BA83. Cranmer Hall Dur 85. **d** 88 **p** 89. C Rock Ferry *Ches* 88-91; C Hartford from 91. *71 School Lane, Hartford, Northwich, Cheshire CW8 1PF* Northwich (0606) 784755

PICKSTONE, Charles Faulkner. b 55. BNC Ox BA77 MA81 Leeds Univ BA80. Coll of Resurr Mirfield 78. **d** 81 **p** 82. C Birkenhead Priory *Ches* 81-84; Chapl Paris St Geo *Eur* 84; C Camberwell St Giles w St Matt S'wark 84-89; V Catford St Laur from 89. *St Laurence's Vicarage, 31 Bromley Road, London SE6 2TS* 081-698 9706

PICKTHORN, Canon Charles Howard. b 25. Linc Coll Ox BA48 MA52. Sarum Th Coll 48. **d** 50 **p** 51. R Bourton-on-the-Water w Clapton *Glouc* 60-91; Chapl RAF 60-76; RD Stow *Glouc* 67-90; P-in-c Gt Rissington 68-81; Hon Can Glouc Cathl from 77; rtd 91. *267 Prestbury Road, Prestbury, Cheltenham, Glos GL52 2EX* Cheltenham (0242) 521447

PICKUP, Harold. b 17. St Pet Hall Ox BA39 MA46. Ridley Hall Cam 46. **d** 47 **p** 48. C Middleton *Man* 47-50; V Gravesend St Mary *Roch* 51-57; Australia from 57. *69 Haig Street, Mowbray Heights, Tasmania, Australia 7248* Launceston (3) 262820

PICTON, Arthur David. b 39. Ch Ch Ox BA62 MA67. Chich Th Coll. **d** 65 **p** 66. C Hulme St Phil *Man* 65-67; C Swinton St Pet 67-71; R Stretford St Pet 71-79; P-in-c Knights Enham *Win* 79-86; R 86-89; V Basing from 89. *The Vicarage, Old Basing, Basingstoke, Hants RG24 0DJ* Basingstoke (0256) 473762

PIDOUX, Ian George. b 32. Univ Coll Ox BA55 MA60. Coll of Resurr Mirfield 54. **d** 57 **p** 58. C Middlesb All SS *York* 57-60; C Haggerston St Aug w St Steph *Lon* 60-62; C Aylesford *Roch* 80-81; TV Rye *Chich* 81-84; P-in-c Bridgwater St Jo *B & W* 84-86; V from 86. *St John's Vicarage, Blake Place, Bridgwater, Somerset TA6 5AU* Bridgwater (0278) 422540

PIDSLEY, Christopher Thomas. b 36. ALCD61. **d** 61 **p** 62. C Enfield Ch Ch Trent Park *Lon* 61-66; C Rainham *Chelmsf* 66-70; V Chudleigh *Ex* from 70; RD Moreton 86-91. *The Vicarage, Chudleigh, Newton Abbot, Devon TQ13 0JF* Chudleigh (0626) 853241

PIERCE, Anthony Edward. b 41. Univ of Wales (Swansea) BA63 Linacre Coll Ox BA65 MA71. Ripon Hall Ox 63. **d** 65 **p** 66. C Swansea St Pet *S & B* 65-67; C Swansea St Mary and H Trin 67-74; Chapl Univ of Wales (Swansea) 71-74, V Llwynderw from 74. *Llwynderw Vicarage, Fairwood Road, West Cross, Swansea SA3 5JP* Swansea (0792) 401903

PIERCE, Brian William. b 42. St Steph Ho Ox 86. **d** 88 **p** 89. C Cudworth *Wakef* from 88. *7 Lindrick Close, Cudworth, Barnsley, S Yorkshire S72 8ET* Barnsley (0226) 716099

PIERCE, Bruce Andrew. b 58. TCD BBS80 BTh89. CITC 86. **d** 89 **p** 90. C Raheny w Coolock *D & G* from 89. *115 Ayrfield Drive, Coolock, Dublin 13, Irish Republic* Dublin (1) 473250

PIERCE, Canon Claude Anthony. b 19. OBE. Magd Coll Cam BA47 MA49 BD53. Ely Th Coll 47. **d** 48 **p** 49. C Chesterfield All SS *Derby* 48-51; Chapl Magd Coll Cam 51-56; Australia from 56. *61 Hawkestone Street, Cottesloe, W Australia 6011* Perth (9) 383-2719

PIERCE, Jeffrey Hyam. b 29. FBIM80 Chelsea Coll Lon BSc51. Ox NSM Course 86. **d** 88 **p** 89. NSM Gt Missenden w Ballinger and Lt Hampden *Ox* from 88. *The Well House, Lee Common, Great Missenden, Bucks HP16 9JX* The Lee (024020) 477

PIERCE, Keith Ernest. b 31. S Dios Minl Tr Scheme. **d** 84 **p** 85. NSM Blacklands Hastings Ch Ch and St Andr *Chich* 84-85; NSM Hollington St Jo from 85. *92 Park View, Hastings, E Sussex TN34 2PD* Hastings (0424) 426817

PIERCE, Stephen Barry. b 60. Birm Univ BA(Theol)81 MA(Theol)82. Cranmer Hall Dur. **d** 85 **p** 86. C Huyton St Mich *Liv* 85-89; V Walton Breck Ch Ch from 89. *Christ Church Vicarage, 157 Hartnup Street, Liverpool L5 1UW* 051-263 2518

PIERCE, Thomas. b 25. St Mich Coll Llan 57. **d** 59 **p** 60. C Minera *St As* 59-65; V 76-83; V Brynford and Ysceifiog 65-76; V Rossett from 83; RD Wrexham 86-90. *The Vicarage, Rossett, Wrexham, Clwyd LL12 0HE* Rossett (0244) 570498

PIERCE, William Johnston. b 32. N Ord Course. **d** 89 **p** 90. NSM Gt Crosby St Luke *Liv* from 89. *60 Kingswood Drive, Crosby, Liverpool L23 3DF* 051-924 2400

PIERCY, Henry Graham. b 05. Armstrong Coll Dur BSc27. Ridley Hall Cam 27. **d** 29 **p** 30. V Newc St Geo *Newc* 50-68; rtd 68. *24 Whitebridge Park Way, Newcastle-upon-Tyne NE3 5LU* 091-284 7999

PIERPOINT, David. **d** 86 **p** 87. NSM Athboy w Ballivor and Killallon *M & K* 86-89; NSM Narraghmore w Timolin, Castledermot and Kinneagh *D & G* from 89; Chan V St Patr Cathl Dub from 90. *57 Woodlands Road, Dun Laoghaire, Co Dublin, Irish Republic* Dublin (1) 285-5139

PIERSSENE, Jeremy Anthony Rupert. b 31. CCC Cam BA55 MA. Ridley Hall Cam 56. **d** 58 **p** 59. C Enfield Ch Ch Trent Park *Lon* 58-61; Travelling Sec Scripture Union 61-69; Chapl Rugby Sch Warks 69-76; R Windlesham *Guildf* from 76; RD Surrey Heath 84-90. *The Rectory, Windlesham, Surrey GU20 6AA* Bagshot (0276) 72363

PIGGOTT, Andrew John. b 51. Qu Mary Coll Lon BSc(Econ)72. St Jo Coll Nottm 83. **d** 86 **p** 87. C Dorridge *Birm* 86-89; TV Kidderminster St Geo *Worc* from 89. *38 Comberton Avenue, Kidderminster, Worcs DY10 3EG* Kidderminster (0562) 824490

PIGGOTT, Raymond George. b 16. Leeds Univ BA38. Coll of Resurr Mirfield 38. **d** 40 **p** 41. V Roughey (or Roffey) *Chich* 65-80; P-in-c Lynch w Iping Marsh 80-83; rtd 83; Perm to Offic *Chich* from 85. *15 Yeoman's Lane, Liphook, Hants GU30 7PN* Liphook (0428) 722976

PIGOTT, Graham John. b 44. Kingston Coll of Art NDD64 Lon Univ DipTh71 BD73 Nottm Univ MPhil84. St Jo Coll Nottm DPS81. **d** 81 **p** 82. C Beeston *S'well* 81-84; P-in-c W Bridgford 84-88; V Wilford Hill from 88. *The Parsonage, Boundary Road, West Bridgford, Notts NG2 7BD* Nottingham (0602) 233492

PIGOTT, Canon John Drummond. b 26. TCD Div Test50 BA50 MA56. **d** 51 **p** 52. C Belf St Phil *Conn* 51-54; C Jordanstown 54-56; Chapl RAF 56-59; R Upper Clatford w Goodworth Clatford *Win* 59-65; V Warley Woods *Birm* 65-74; RD Warley 72-74; V Boldmere from 74; Hon Can Birm Cathl from 81; RD Sutton Coldfield from 88. *The Vicarage, Church Road, Sutton Coldfield, W Midlands B73 5RX* 021-373 0207

PIGOTT, Nicholas John Capel. b 48. Qu Coll Birm 75. **d** 78 **p** 79. C Belmont *Dur* 78-79; C Folkestone St Sav *Cant* 79-82; C Birm St Geo *Birm* 82-85; V Stevenage St Hugh Chells *St Alb* from 85. *St Hugh's House, 4 Mobbsbury Way, Chells, Stevenage, Herts SG2 0HL* Stevenage (0438) 54307

PIGREM, Terence John. b 39. Oak Hill Th Coll 66. **d** 69 **p** 70. C Islington St Andr w St Thos and St Matthias *Lon* 69-73; C Barking St Marg w St Patr *Chelmsf* 73-75; TV 75-76; C W Holl St Luke *Lon* 76-79; V from 79. *St Luke's Vicarage, Penn Road, London N7 9RE* 071-607 1504

PIKE, David Frank. b 35. CEng MIMechE BA Lon Univ TCert. S Dios Minl Tr Scheme 82. **d** 85 **p** 86. NSM Lancing w Coombes *Chich* 85-88; R Albourne w Sayers Common and Twineham from 88. *The Rectory, 5 The Twitten, Albourne, Hassocks, W Sussex BN6 9DF* Hassocks (0273) 832129

PIKE, Eric Sydney. b 13. Lon Univ BSc52 Lon Inst of Educn DipRE67. S'wark Ord Course 78. **d** 79 **p** 80. NSM Wimbledon Em Ridgway Prop Chpl *S'wark* 79-84; NSM Iford *Win* 84-85. *31 Seaward Avenue, Bournemouth BH6 3SJ* Bournemouth (0202) 432398

PIKE, George Richard. b 38. BSc. W Midl Minl Tr Course 79. **d** 82 **p** 83. NSM Edgbaston St Bart *Birm* 82-89; NSM S Yardley St Mich from 89. *9 Star Hill, Edgbaston, Birmingham B15 2LT* 021-440 2843

PIKE, Horace Douglas. b 13. AKC48. **d** 48 **p** 49. V Baildon *Bradf* 59-71; R Burnsall 72-78; rtd 78; P-in-c Birdsall w Langton *York* 81-86. *18 Southfield Close, Rufforth, York YO2 3RE* Rufforth (090483) 418

PIKE, Canon James. b 22. TCD. **d** 68 **p** 69. C Clooney *D & K* 68-72; I Ardstraw 72-76; I Ardstraw w Baronscourt 76-86; I Ardstraw w Baronscourt, Badoney Lower etc from 76; Can Derry Cathl from 90. *2 Bunderg Road, Newtownstewart, Co Tyrone, Omagh BT78 4NQ* Newtownstewart (06626) 61342

PIKE, Paul Alfred. b 38. Wycliffe Hall Ox. **d** 84 **p** 85. C Penn Fields *Lich* 84-89; Japan from 89. *c/o Overseas Missionary Fellowship, Belmont, The Vine, Sevenoaks, Kent TN13 3TZ* Sevenoaks (0732) 450747

PIKE, Peter John. b 53. Southn Univ BTh. Sarum & Wells Th Coll 81. **d** 84 **p** 85. C Broughton *Blackb* 84-88; V Woodplumpton from 88; Asst Dir of Ords and Voc Adv from 89. *The Vicarage, Woodplumpton, Preston PR4 0RX* Catforth (0772) 690355

PIKE, Robert James. b 47. Kelham Th Coll 66. **d** 70 **p** 71. C Cov St Pet *Cov* 70-74; C Bilton 74-76; P-in-c Southall St Geo *Lon* 76-81; V S Harrow St Paul 81-86; C Hillingdon St Jo 86-88; Chapl Hillingdon Hosp & Mt Vernon Hosp Uxbridge 88-90; Perm to Offic from 91. *6 Salt Hill Close, Uxbridge, Middx UB8 1PZ* Uxbridge (0895) 235212

PIKE, Roger Walter. b 31. Roch Th Coll 65. **d** 67 **p** 68. C Wokingham St Paul *Ox* 67-70; C Whitley Ch Ch 70-76; C-in-c California CD 76-80; V Cowes St Faith *Portsm* from 80. *The Vicarage, St Faith's Roads, Cowes, Isle of Wight PO31 7HH* Isle of Wight (0983) 292656

✠**PIKE, Rt Rev St John Surridge.** b 09. TCD BA32 MA35 DD58. **d** 32 **p** 33 **c** 58. Hd of S Ch Miss Ballymacarrett *D & D* 37-47; Gambia 47-52; I Belf St Geo *Conn* 52-57; Bp Gambia and Rio Pongas 58-63; V Ewshott *Guildf* 63-71; Asst Bp Guildf 63-83; V Botleys and Lyne 71-83; V Long Cross 71-83; rtd 83; Perm to Offic *Win* from 84. *Wisteria Cottage, Old Rectory Lane, Twyford, Winchester, Hants SO21 1NS* Twyford (0962) 712253

PILDITCH, Miss Patricia Desiree. b 21. dss 82 **d** 87. Barnstaple *Ex* 82-87; Hon Par Dn from 87; Asst Chapl N Devon Distr Hosp Barnstaple from 82. *4 The Mews, Swimbridge, Barnstaple, Devon EX32 0QB* Swimbridge (0271) 830770

PILGRIM, Colin Mark. b 56. BA77 Geneva Univ CES84. Westcott Ho Cam 81. **d** 84 **p** 85. C Chorlton-cum-Hardy St Clem *Man* 84-87; C Whitchurch *Bris* 87-89; V Bedminster Down from 89. *St Oswald's Vicarage, Cheddar Grove, Bristol BS13 7EN* Bristol (0272) 642649

PILGRIM, Ms Judith Mary. b 44. Westcott Ho Cam 88. **d** 90. C Probus, Ladock and Grampound w Creed *Truro* from 90. *50 Gwell-an-Nans, Probus, Truro TR2 4ND* St Austell (0726) 882859

PILKINGTON, Charles George Willink. b 21. Trin Coll Cam BA42 MA64. Westcott Ho Cam. **d** 63 **p** 64. R Withington St Chris *Man* 68-88; rtd 88; Perm to Offic *Man* from 88. *32 Rathen Road, Withington, Manchester M20 9GH* 061-434 5365

PILKINGTON, Canon Christopher Frost. b 23. Trin Coll Cam BA50 MA60. Ridley Hall Cam 50. **d** 52 **p** 53. R Bris St Steph w St Nic and St Leon *Bris* 68-81; P-in-c 81-82; Hon Can Bris Cathl 79-82; Hon Chapl Cancer Help Cen Bris 82-89; Lic to Offic from 82; rtd 89. *North Lawn, Ston Easton, Bath BA3 4DG* Chewton Mendip (076121) 472

PILKINGTON, Edward Russell. b 39. ALCD65. **d** 65 **p** 66. C Eccleshill *Bradf* 65-68; C Billericay St Mary *Chelmsf* 68-72; V New Thundersley 72-78; R Theydon Garnon 78-82; V Gidea Park from 82. *St Michael's Vicarage, Main Road, Romford RM2 5EL* Romford (0708) 741084

PILKINGTON, John Rowan. b 32. Magd Coll Cam BA55 MA59. Ridley Hall Cam 57. **d** 59 **p** 60. C Ashtead *Guildf* 59-61; C Wimbledon *S'wark* 62-65; R Newhaven *Chich* 65-75; R Farlington *Portsm* 75-89; V Darlington St Mark w St Paul *Dur* from 89. *St Mark's Vicarage, 394 North Road, Darlington, Co Durham DL1 3BH* Darlington (0325) 382400

PILKINGTON, Canon Peter. b 33. Jes Coll Cam BA55 MA59. Westcott Ho Cam 58. **d** 59 **p** 60. C Bakewell *Derby* 59-62; Chapl Eton Coll Windsor 62-75; Hd Master K Sch Cant 75-85; Hon Can Cant Cathl *Cant* 75-90; High Master St Paul's Sch Barnes from 86. *St Paul's School, Lonsdale Road, London SW13 9JT* 081-748 8135

PILKINGTON, Timothy William. b 54. Nottm Univ BA85. Linc Th Coll 82. **d** 85 **p** 86. C Newquay *Truro* 85-88; C Cockington *Ex* 88-91; R St John w Millbrook *Truro* from 91. *The Vicarage, Millbrook, Torpoint, Cornwall PL10 1BW* Plymouth (0752) 822264

PILL, Hugh Godfrey Reginald. **d** 89 **p** 90. NSM Hugglescote w Donington, Ellistown and Snibston *Leic* 89-91; NSM Malborough w S Huish, W Alvington and Churchstow *Ex* from 91. *c/o The Vicarage, Malborough, Kingsbridge, Devon TQ7 3RR* Kingsbridge (0548) 561234

✠**PILLAR, Rt Rev Kenneth Harold.** b 24. Qu Coll Cam BA48 MA53. Ridley Hall Cam 48. **d** 50 **p** 51 **c** 82. C Childwall All SS *Liv* 50-53; Chapl Lee Abbey 53-57; V New Beckenham St Paul *Roch* 57-62; V Cant St Mary Bredin *Cant* 62-65; Warden Lee Abbey 65-70; V Waltham Abbey *Chelmsf* 70-82; RD Chigwell 76-78; RD Epping Forest 78-82; Suff Bp Hertf *St Alb* 82-89; rtd 89; Asst Bp Sheff from 89. *75 Dobcroft Road, Sheffield S7 2LS* Sheffield (0742) 367902

PILLAR, Kenneth James. b 50. St Jo Coll Nottm 70. **d** 74 **p** 75. C Wilmington *Roch* 74-79; CF 79-87 and from 89; R Curry Rivel w Fivehead and Swell *B & W* 87-89. *c/o MOD (Army), Bagshot Park, Bagshot, Surrey GU19 5PL* Bagshot (0276) 71717

PIMENTEL, Peter Eric. b 55. BA. Ridley Hall Cam. **d** 82 **p** 83. C Gt Ilford St Andr *Chelmsf* 82-85; Chapl Basingstoke Distr Hosp 85-88; TV Grays Thurrock from 88. *St Mary's Vicarage, 147 Rectory Road, Grays, Essex RM17 6AG* Grays Thurrock (0375) 373685

PIMLOTT, Stephen John. b 45. SS Coll Cam BA67 MA71 Trin Coll Ox BA73 MA79. Cuddesdon Coll 71. **d** 74 **p** 75. C Newbold and Dunston *Derby* 74-78; C Walworth St Jo *S'wark* 78-82; V Bordesley St Benedict *Birm* from 82; Chapl E Birm Hosp from 82. *St Benedict's Vicarage, 55 Hob Moor Road, Birmingham B10 9AY* 021-772 2726

PIMPERTON, Raymond Swindale. b 12. Linc Th Coll 77. **d** 77 **p** 78. Hon C Holbeach *Linc* 77-83; rtd 83; Perm to Offic *Linc* from 83. *6 Chestnut Avenue, Holbeach, Spalding, Lincs PE12 7NE* Holbeach (0406) 22458

PINCHES, Donald Antony. b 32. Pemb Coll Cam BA55 MA60 Linacre Coll Ox BA67. Wycliffe Hall Ox 64. **d** 67 **p** 68. C Aylesbury *Ox* 67-71; C Compton Gifford *Ex* 71-74; TV Lydford, Brent Tor, Bridestowe and Sourton 74-77; V Shiphay Collaton from 77. *St John's Vicarage, 83 Cadewell Lane, Torquay TQ2 7HP* Torquay (0803) 613361

PINCHIN, Antony Peter. b 57. St Jo Coll Cam BA79 MA86. Coll of Resurr Mirfield 79. **d** 81 **p** 82. C Hawley H Trin *Guildf* 81-84; Asst Admin Shrine of Our Lady of Walsingham 84-87; Lic to Offic *Nor* 85-87; V Higham and Merston *Roch* from 87. *The Vicarage, Hermitage Road, Higham, Rochester, Kent ME3 7NE* Medway (0634) 717360

PINDER, Ven Charles. b 21. AKC49. **d** 50 **p** 51. V Catford St Laur *S'wark* 60-73; Sub-Dean of S Lewisham 68-73; Boro Dean of Lambeth 73-86; Adn Lambeth 86-88; rtd 88. *22 Somerstown, Chichester, W Sussex PO19 4AG* Chichester (0243) 779708

PINDER, John Ridout. b 43. Peterho Cam BA65 MA69. Cuddesdon Coll 65. **d** 73 **p** 74. C Leavesden All SS *St Alb* 73-76; Gen Sec Melanesian Miss 77-89; P-in-c Harpsden w Bolney *Ox* 82-89; R Farlington *Portsm* from 89. *27 Farlington Avenue, Farlington, Portsmouth PO6 1DF* Cosham (0705) 375145

PINDER-PACKARD, John. b 47. Lon Univ BSc. N Ord Course 81. **d** 84 **p** 85. NSM Mosborough *Sheff* 84-85; C Norton 85-88; V New Whittington *Derby* from 88. *The Vicarage, New Whittington, Chesterfield S43 2EF* Chesterfield (0246) 455830

PINE, David Michael. b 41. Lich Th Coll 68. **d** 71 **p** 72. C Northam *Ex* 71-74; R Toft w Caldecote and Childerley *Ely* 74-80; R Hardwick 74-80; V Ipswich St Andr *St E* 80-84; P-in-c Hazelbury Bryan w Stoke Wake etc *Sarum* from 84. *The Rectory, Hazelbury Bryan, Sturminster Newton, Dorset DT10 2ED* Hazelbury Bryan (02586) 251

PINK, Canon David. b 34. Qu Coll Cam BA58 MA62. Linc Th Coll 58. **d** 60 **p** 61. V Kirton in Holland *Linc* 65-71; V Spittlegate 71-77; Ecum Officer Lincs and S Humberside 77-85; Can and Preb Linc Cathl from 77; P-in-c Canwick 77-87; R Washingborough w Heighington 87-88; R Washingborough w Heighington and Canwick 88-90; rtd 90; Perm to Offic *Linc* from 91. *The Old School, Swarby, Sleaford, Lincs NG34 8TG* Sleaford (0529) 5403

PINKERTON, Ms Patricia Edith. b 38. California Univ BA72 MA75 BTh80. Ch Div Sch of the Pacific (USA). **d** 81 **p** 82. USA 81-88; C Coleford w Staunton *Glouc* from 88. *Highfield House, New Road, Coalway, Coleford, Glos GL16 7JA* Dean (0594) 32017

PINNER, John Philip. b 37. K Coll Lon BA59. Westcott Ho Cam 69. **d** 71 **p** 72. C Dover St Mary *Cant* 71-74; Chapl Felsted Sch Essex 74-83; New Zealand from 81. *c/o Rathkeale College, Masterton, New Zealand* Masterton (59) 84395

PINNER, Terence Malcolm William. b 35. AKC59 Southn Univ MA89. **d** 60 **p** 61. C Eltham St Barn *S'wark* 60-64; S Africa 64-67 and 69-74; USPG 67-69; Sec for Home Affairs Conf of Br Miss Socs 74-76; P-in-c Hinstock *Lich* 76-79; Adult Educn Officer 76-79; Adult RE Officer 79-83; Chapl Southn Univ *Win* 83-88; Tutor S Dios Minl Tr Scheme from 88; Dioc Dir of Ords from 88. *6 The Mayflowers, Bassett Crescent East, Southampton SO2 3FN* Southampton (0703) 768472

PINNOCK, Geoffrey Gilbert. b 16. K Coll Lon 47. **d** 50 **p** 51. USA 66-72; Perm to Offic Lon 72-73; S'wark 73-74; C Battersea St Phil w St Bart *S'wark* 74-75; P-in-c Boconnoc w Bradoc *Truro* 75-81; rtd 81; Perm to Offic Ox & Lon from 81. *11 Drove Acre Road, Oxford OX4 3DF* Oxford (0865) 247355

PINSENT, Ewen Macpherson. b 30. Edin Th Coll 67. **d** 69 **p** 70. C Holt *Nor* 69-72; R Kelso *Edin* 72-82; P-in-c Blendworth, Chalton and Idsworth *Portsm* 82; R Blendworth w Chalton w Idsworth & Rowlands Castle 82-90; R Blendworth w Chalton w Idsworth from 90. *Blendworth Rectory, Portsmouth PO8 0AB* Horndean (0705) 592174

PIPE-WOLFERSTAN, Clare Rachel. b 54. Bris Univ BA75. Bris Sch of Min 84. **d** 88. NSM Bris St Mary Redcliffe w Temple etc *Bris* from 88. *14 Acramans Road, Bristol BS3 1DQ* Bristol (0272) 663430

PIPER, Andrew. b 58. Magd Coll Ox BA79 MA83. Chich Th Coll 80. **d** 83 **p** 84. C Eastbourne St Mary *Chich* 83-88; TV Lewes All SS, St Anne, St Mich and St Thos from 88. *St Michael's Rectory, St Andrew's Lane, Lewes, E Sussex BN7 1UW* Lewes (0273) 474723

PIPER, Gary Quentin David. b 42. Nottm Coll of Educn TCert65 Maria Grey Coll Lon DipEd71. Oak Hill Th Coll 75. **d** 78 **p** 79. Hon C Fulham St Matt *Lon* 78-85; V from 85; AD Hammersmith from 86. *St Matthew's Vicarage, 2 Clancarty Road, London SW6 3AB* 071-731 3272

PIPER, Graham. b 58. Chich Th Coll BTh91. **d** 91. C Horsham *Chich* from 91. *18 Queensway, Horsham, W Sussex RH13 5AY* Horsham (0403) 52986

PIPER, John Howard. b 09. St Chad's Coll Dur BA31. **d** 32 **p** 34. R Rearsby w Ratcliffe on the Wreake *Leic* 68-78; P-in-c Thrussington 77-78; R Rearsby w Ratcliffe-on-the-Wreake etc 78-82; rtd 82; Perm to Offic *Leic* from 82. *52 Avenue Road, Queniborough, Leicester LE7 8FA* Leicester (0533) 606605

PIPER, Kenneth John. b 29. St Luke's Coll Ex TCert53 Leeds Univ DipEd67. S Dios Minl Tr Scheme 79. **d** 82 **p** 83. NSM Bradf w Oake, Hillfarrance and Heathfield *B & W* 82-87; Chapl to Norway and Scandinavia Lay Tr

Officer *Eur* 87-89; R Durrington *Sarum* from 90. *The Rectory, Church Street, Durrington, Salisbury SP4 8AL* Stonehenge (0980) 52229

PIPER, Canon Leonard Arthur. b 08. Clifton Th Coll 32. **d** 35 **p** 36. R Hurworth *Dur* 39-73; OCF RAF 40-87; R Dinsdale w Sockburn *Dur* 61-73; Hon Can Dur Cathl 70-73; rtd 73. *Bridge Cottage, Over Dinsdale, Darlington, Co Durham DL2 1PW* Dinsdale (0325) 332864

PIPPEN, Brian Roy. b 50. St D Coll Lamp DipTh73. **d** 73 **p** 74. C Newport Maindee St Jo *Ev Mon* 73-77; TV Cwmbran 77-84; V Christ Church 84-90; R Pontypool from 90. *The Vicarage, Trevethin, Pontypool, Gwent NP4 8JF* Pontypool (0495) 762228

PIRIE, John Henry. b 07. Leeds Univ BA29. Coll of Resurr Mirfield 26. **d** 32 **p** 33. V Walworth St Jo *S'wark* 56-72; rtd 72; Lic to Offic *S'wark* 72-84; Perm to Offic from 84. *42 Walter's Close, Brandon Street, London SE17 1NE* 071-708 1509

PITCHER, Canon David John. b 33. Ely Th Coll 55. **d** 58 **p** 59. C Kingswinford St Mary *Lich* 58-61; C Kirkby *Liv* 61-66; R Ingham w Sutton *Nor* 66-72; V Lakenham St Jo 72-76; R Framlingham w Saxtead *St E* from 76; RD Loes 82-89; Hon Can St E Cathl from 85. *The Rectory, Framlingham, Woodbridge, Suffolk IP13 9BJ* Framlingham (0728) 723653

PITCHER, Ronald Charles Frederick. b 21. AKC50. **d** 51 **p** 52. V Newall Green *Man* 61-73; Chapl Wythenshawe Hosp Man 64-73; C-in-c Danesholme CD *Pet* 73-81; V Estover *Ex* 81-91; rtd 91. *18 East Wyld Road, Weymouth, Dorset* Weymouth (0305) 771916

PITCHES, Reginald Morgan. b 08. Keble Coll Ox BA30 MA34. Cuddesdon Coll 30. **d** 31 **p** 32. V Bridekirk *Carl* 69-76; rtd 76; Perm to Offic *Carl* from 77. *Fife Lodge, Low Lorton, Cockermouth, Cumbria* Lorton (090085) 297

PITCHFORD, Herbert John. b 34. Dur Univ BA60. Ridley Hall Cam 60. **d** 62 **p** 63. C Heref St Martin *Heref* 62-68; R Much Birch w Lt Birch 68-78; P-in-c Much Dewchurch w Llanwarne and Llandinabo 73-78; R Much Birch w Lt Birch, Much Dewchurch etc 78-80; V Grange Park St Pet *Lon* 80-91; V Wylde Green *Birm* from 91. *17 Greenhill Road, Sutton Coldfield, W Midlands B72 1DS* 021-373 8348

PITE, Miss Sheila Reinhardt. b 60. St Jo Coll Dur BA82. Oak Hill Th Coll 85. **d** 88. Par Dn Derby St Aug *Derby* from 88. *70 Violet Street, Derby DE3 8SQ* Derby (0332) 762821

PITHERS, Brian Hoyle. b 34. Chich Th Coll 63. **d** 66 **p** 67. C Wisbech SS Pet and Paul *Ely* 66-70; V Fenstanton 70-75; V Hilton 70-75; V Habergham Eaves St Matt *Blackb* 75-85; P-in-c Habergham Eaves H Trin 78-85; V Burnley (Habergham Eaves) St Matt w H Trin 85-86; TR Ribbleton from 86. *The Rectory, Ribbleton Avenue, Ribbleton, Preston, Lancs PR2 6QP* Preston (0772) 791747

PITMAN, Clifford George. b 19. St D Coll Lamp BA48. **d** 49 **p** 50. V Tonna *Llan* 60-85; rtd 85; Perm to Offic *Llan* from 85. *7 Mackworth Drive, Neath, W Glam SA11 2BR* Neath (0639) 630262

PITMAN, Ernest Charles. b 07. St Chad's Coll Regina 27. **d** 30 **p** 31. R Denton *Linc* 71-73; rtd 73. *5 Church Street, Denton, Grantham, Lincs NG32 1FL* Grantham (0476) 870676

PITT, Beatrice Anne. b 50. CertEd DipHE. Trin Coll Bris 80. **d** 82. C Rhyl w Rhyl St Ann *St As* 82-85; CMS from 87; Zaire from 88. *c/o 6 Undercliffe Road, Kendal, Cumbria LA9 4PS* Lancaster (0524) 202779

PITT, George. b 52. QUB BD79. CITC 81. **d** 81 **p** 82. C Belf St Mary *Conn* 81-86; C Hawarden *St As* 87; CMS from 87; Zaire from 88. *c/o 6 Undercliffe Road, Kendal, Cumbria LA9 4PS* Lancaster (0524) 202779

PITT, Mervyn George Mottram. b 10. Qu Coll Cam BA32 MA36. Wells Th Coll 32. **d** 34 **p** 35. R Over Wallop w Nether Wallop *Win* 62-78; rtd 78; Perm to Offic *Win* from 78. *21 Greatwell Road, Romsey, Hants* Romsey (0794) 522500

PITT, Robert Edgar. b 37. Chich Th Coll 70. **d** 73 **p** 74. C Knowle *Bris* 73-77; C Wells St Cuth w Coxley and Wookey Hole *B & W* 77-81; TV Wellington and Distr from 81. *All Saints' Vicarage, 8 Exeter Road, Wellington, Somerset TA21 9DH* Wellington (0823) 472742

PITT, Trevor. b 45. Hull Univ BA66 MA69. Linc Th Coll 68 Union Th Sem (NY) STM70. **d** 70 **p** 71. C Sheff St Geo *Sheff* 70-74; TV Gleadless Valley 74-78; TR 78-79; Vice-Prin Cant Sch of Min from 79; P-in-c Elham *Cant* 79-82; V Elham w Denton and Wootton from 82; Six Preacher Cant Cathl from 85. *The Vicarage, Elham, Canterbury, Kent CT4 6TT* Elham (0303) 840219

PITTIS, Stephen Charles. b 52. Oak Hill Th Coll DipTh75. **d** 76 **p** 77. C Win Ch Ch *Win* 76-79; Chapl Bournemouth and Poole Colls *Sarum* 79-84; V Woking St Paul *Guildf* from 84. *St Paul's Vicarage, Pembroke Road, Woking, Surrey GU22 7ED* Woking (0483) 772081

PITTOCK, John Leslie. b 10. St Aug Coll Cant. **d** 61 **p** 62. R Pluckley w Pevington *Cant* 64-78; rtd 78; Perm to Offic *Cant* from 78. *112 Sandyhurst Lane, Ashford, Kent TN25 4NT* Ashford (0233) 623700

PITTS, Eve. b 50. **d** 89. C Bartley Green *Birm* from 89. *19 Elmcroft Avenue, Birmingham B32 4LZ* 021-422 1436

PITTS, Canon Michael James. b 44. Worc Coll Ox BA67. Qu Coll Birm 67. **d** 69 **p** 70. C-in-c Pennywell St Thos and Grindon St Oswald CD *Dur* 69-72; C Darlington H Trin 72-74; Chapl Dunkerque w Lille Arras etc Miss to Seamen *Eur* 74-79; V Tudhoe *Dur* 79-81; Chapl Helsinki w Moscow *Eur* 81-85; Chapl Stockholm 85-88; Hon Can Brussels Cathl from 87; Canada from 88; Hon Chapl Miss to Seamen from 88. *1500 Avenue Docteur, Penfield, Montreal, Quebec, Canada, H3G 1B9*

PITYANA, Nyameko Barney. b 45. BA BD. Ripon Coll Cuddesdon. **d** 82 **p** 83. C Woughton *Ox* 82-85; V Highters Heath *Birm* 85-88; Dir Progr to Combat Racism WCC from 89. *59 rue de Lyon, 1203 Geneva, Switzerland* Geneva (22) 791-6202

PIX, Stephen James. b 42. Ex Coll Ox BA64 DipTh65 MA68. Clifton Th Coll 66. **d** 68 **p** 69. C St Helens St Helen *Liv* 68-71; Lic to Offic *S'wark* 71-76; Hon C Wallington H Trin 76-84; V Osmotherley w E Harlsey and Ingleby Arncliffe *York* 84-89; V Ox St Mich w St Martin and All SS *Ox* from 89. *The Vicarage, 24 St Michael's Street, Oxford OX1 2EB* Oxford (0865) 242444 or 240940

PIZZEY, Lawrence Roger. b 42. Dur Univ BA64. Westcott Ho Cam 65. **d** 67 **p** 68. C Bramford *St E* 67-71; Tutor Woodbridge Abbey 71-77; Asst Chapl Woodbridge Sch Suffolk 71-77; P-in-c Flempton w Hengrave and Lackford *St E* 77-85; R Culford, W Stow and Wordwell 77-85; P-in-c Acton w Gt Waldingfield from 85. *The Vicarage, Acton, Sudbury, Suffolk CO10 0BA* Sudbury (0787) 77287

PLACE, Donald Lee. b 37. **d** 74. C Stainton-in-Cleveland *York* 79-81; TV Loughton St Jo *Chelmsf* 81-83; Chapl Worc R Infirmary & Hosps 83-85. *51 Stephenson Road, Worcester WR1 3EB* Worcester (0905) 25328 or 27122

PLACE, Rodger Goodson. b 37. St Chad's Coll Dur BA60 DipTh62. **d** 62 **p** 63. C Pontesbury I and II *Heref* 62-65; C Heref St Martin 65-68; V Ditton Priors 68-75; R Neenton 68-75; P-in-c Aston Botterell w Wheathill and Loughton 69-75; P-in-c Burwarton w N Cleobury 69-75; P-in-c Dacre *Ripon* 75; P-in-c Dacre w Hartwith 75-76; V 76-82; V Wyther Ven Bede from 82. *The Vicarage, Houghley Lane, Leeds LS13 4AU* Leeds (0532) 631361

PLAISTER, Keith Robin. b 43. K Coll Lon BD65 AKC65. **d** 66 **p** 67. C Laindon w Basildon *Chelmsf* 66-71; V Gt Wakering 71-78; P-in-c Foulness 78; V Gt Wakering w Foulness 78-90; C Witham from 91. *153 Honeysuckle Way, Witham, Essex CM8 2YD* Witham (0376) 519017

PLAISTOWE, Ven Ronald Percy Frank. b 11. St Jo Coll Dur LTh34 BA35. Clifton Th Coll. **d** 35 **p** 36. C Bris St Ambrose Whitehall *Bris* 35-39; C St Alb Westbury Park Clifton 39-42; V Cleeve *B & W* 42-48; New Zealand from 48; Adn Timaru 53-63; Adn Sumner 63-68; Adn Christchurch 68-71. *165 Main Road, Christchurch 8, New Zealand* Christchurch (3) 849632

PLANT, Mrs Edith Winifred Irene (Ewith). b 31. Liv Univ BEd71. Cranmer Hall Dur 81. **dss** 83 **d** 87. Countesthorpe w Foston *Leic* 83-86; Loughb All SS and H Trin 86-87; Par Dn 87-90; Par Dn Thurnby Lodge from 90. *3 Rosshill Crescent, Thurnby Lodge, Leicester LE5 2RE* Leicester (0533) 431487

PLANT, John Frederick. b 61. Man Univ BA82 Birm Univ DPS. Qu Coll Birm 83. **d** 85 **p** 86. C Kersal Moor *Man* 85-88; Chapl Aston Univ *Birm* from 88. *27 Worlds End Road, Birmingham B20 2NP* 021-507 0247

PLANT, Richard. b 41. Qu Coll Birm 88. **d** 90 **p** 91. C Skelmersdale St Paul *Liv* from 90. *6 Wilcove, Skelmersdale, Lancs WN8 8NF* Skelmersdale (0695) 26491

PLANT, Richard George Nicholas. b 45. Man Univ BA67. Coll of Resurr Mirfield 68. **d** 71 **p** 72. C Cleckheaton St Jo *Wakef* 71-74; P-in-c Adel *Ripon* 74-78; V Ireland Wood 78-82; V St Bart Armley w St Mary New Wortley from 82. *Armley Vicarage, Wesley Road, Leeds LS12 1SR* Leeds (0532) 638620

PLANT, Robert David. b 28. Birm Univ BSc49. St Deiniol's Hawarden 74. **d** 76 **p** 80. NSM Llandrillo-yn-Rhos *St As*

76-79; NSM St Nicholas at Wade w Sarre and Chislet w Hoath *Cant* from 79. *4 Sandalwood Drive, St Nicholas-at-Wade, Birchington, Kent CT7 0PE* Thanet (0843) 47276

PLASTOW, Graham Henry George. b 40. St Jo Coll Nottm 68. **d** 71 **p** 72. C St Marylebone w H Trin *Lon* 71-74; C Marlborough *Sarum* 74-77; P-in-c N Shoebury *Chelmsf* 77-83; Chapl St Jo Hosp Chelmsf 83-88; P-in-c E Hanningfield *Chelmsf* from 83; P-in-c W Hanningfield 87-89. *The Rectory, 7 Abbeyfields, East Hanningfield, Chelmsford CM3 8XB* Chelmsford (0245) 400217

PLATT, Andrew Martin Robert. b 41. Oak Hill Th Coll 74. **d** 76 **p** 77. C St Alb St Paul *St Alb* 76-79; V Gazeley w Dalham and Moulton *St E* 79-85; RD Mildenhall 84-86; V Gazeley w Dalham, Moulton and Kentford 85-86; P-in-c Saxmundham 86-89; R from 89. *The Rectory, Manor Gardens, Saxmundham, Suffolk IP17 1ET* Saxmundham (0728) 604234

PLATT, Canon Ernest Wilfrid. b 10. Sheff Univ BA32. Lich Th Coll 32. **d** 34 **p** 35. V Hinckley St Mary *Leic* 56-91; RD Sparkenhoe II 60-71; Hon Can Leic Cathl from 74; rtd 91. *216 Brookside, Burbage, Hinckley, Leics LE10 2TW* Hinckley (0455) 233928

PLATT, George Herbert. b 06. Linc Th Coll 30. **d** 33 **p** 34. R Willoughby w Sloothby w Claxby *Linc* 64-71; R Ulceby w Fordington 68-71; rtd 71. *76 Wilson Street, Anlaby, Hull HU10 7AJ* Hull (0482) 653053

PLATT, Harold Geoffrey. b 27. Down Coll Cam BA50 MA52. Ridley Hall Cam 51. **d** 53 **p** 54. R Lower Broughton St Clem *Man* 57-66; P-in-c Salford St Matthias w St Simon 62-66; Lic to Offic *Man* 66-76; Worc 76-82 and from 85; Hon C Belbroughton w Fairfield and Clent *Worc* 83-90; NSM Hagley from 87; rtd 90; Co-ord for Decade of Evang from 90. *Island House, Belbroughton, Stourbridge, W Midlands DY9 0DX* Belbroughton (0562) 730616

PLATT, John Dendy. b 24. Magd Coll Cam BA49 MA55. Wells Th Coll 50. **d** 52 **p** 53. R Skelton w Hutton-in-the-Forest *Carl* 59-71; rtd 89. *Smallburgh Hill, Smallburgh, Norwich NR12 9AD* Smallburgh (0692) 536524

PLATT, Dr John Emerson. b 36. Pemb Coll Ox BA59 MA65 DPhil77 Hull Univ MTh72. Cuddesdon Coll 59. **d** 61 **p** 62. C Adlington *Blackb* 61-64; C Sutton St Mich *York* 64-68; C Ox St Giles *Ox* 68-71; Asst Chapl Pemb Coll Ox 68-69; Chapl from 69. *Pembroke College, Oxford OX1 1DW* Oxford (0865) 276426

PLATT, Mrs Katherine Mary. b 29. ARIBA51 Sheff Univ BA51. Westcott Ho Cam 76. **dss** 79 **d** 87. Chesterton Gd Shep *Ely* 78-84; Whitton St Aug *Lon* 84-86; Dean of Women's Min from 86; Hampton St Mary 86-87; Par Dn from 87. *St Mary's Lodge, Church Street, Hampton, Middx TW12 2EB* 081-979 4102

PLATT, Michael Robert. b 39. SS Coll Cam MA60 Nottm Univ PGCE61. Cuddesdon Coll 62. **d** 64. C Far Headingley St Chad *Ripon* 64-65; Asst Teacher Belmont Coll Barnstaple 65-68; Qu Coll Taunton from 68; Ho Master 72-83. *8 Court Hill, Taunton, Somerset TA1 4SX* Taunton (0823) 270687

PLATT, Ronald. b 46. Qu Coll Birm 83. **d** 85 **p** 86. C Lydney w Aylburton *Glouc* 87-88; Australia from 88. *23 Griffin Crescent, Manning, W Australia 6152* Perth (9) 450-3163

PLATT, William David. b 31. St Chad's Coll Dur BA54. Coll of Resurr Mirfield 54. **d** 56 **p** 57. C Bethnal Green St Jo w St Simon *Lon* 56-60; C Pinner 60-65; V N Hammersmith St Kath 65-72; V Woodham *Guildf* 72-88; Chapl Community of St Mary V Wantage from 88. *10 Denchworth Road, Wantage, Oxon OX12 9AU* Wantage (02357) 2289

PLATTEN, Canon Stephen George. b 47. Lon Univ BEd72 Trin Coll Ox DipTh74. Cuddesdon Coll 72. **d** 75 **p** 76. C Headington *Ox* 75-78; Linc Th Coll 78-83; Tutor 78-83; Perm to Offic *Linc* 78-83; Can Res Portsm Cathl *Portsm* 83-89; Dir of Ords 83-89; Abp's Sec for Ecum Affairs *Cant* from 90; Hon Can Cant Cathl from 90; Lic to Offic *S'wark* from 90. *3 Lambeth Palace Cottages, London SE1 7JU* 071-928 8282

PLATTS, Mrs Hilary Anne Norrie. b 60. SRN81 K Coll Lon BD85 AKC85. Ripon Coll Cuddesdon 86. **d** 88. C Moulsham St Jo *Chelmsf* 88-90; Chapl Reading Univ *Ox* from 90; C Calcot from 90. *32 Bourne Avenue, Reading, Berks RG2 0DU* Reading (0734) 872935

PLATTS, Timothy Caradoc. b 61. LMH Ox BA83 MA88 St Cross Coll Ox DPhil88. Ripon Coll Cuddesdon 87. **d** 89 **p** 90. C Whitley Ch Ch *Ox* from 89. *32 Bourne Avenue, Reading RG2 0DU* Reading (0734) 872935

PLAXTON, Ven Cecil Andrew. b 02. St Edm Hall Ox BA24 MA28. Cuddesdon Coll 25. **d** 26 **p** 27. Can and Preb Sarum Cathl *Sarum* from 48; Adn Wilts 51-74; rtd

74. *12 Castle Court, St John's Street, Devizes, Wilts SN10 1DQ* Devizes (0380) 723391

PLAXTON, Edmund John Swithun. b 36. AKC60. **d** 61 **p** 62. C Crofton Park St Hilda w St Cypr *S'wark* 61-65; C Coulsdon St Jo 65-69; V Forest Hill St Paul 69-80; V Belmont from 80. *The Vicarage, Belmont Rise, Sutton, Surrey SM2 6EA* 081-642 2363

PLEDGER, Miss Alison Frances. b 56. Univ of Wales (Cardiff) BA79 PGCE80. Linc Th Coll 89. **d** 91. Par Dn Soham *Ely* from 91. *4 Yew Trees, Soham, Ely, Cambs CB7 5BW* Ely (0353) 722975

PLIMLEY, Canon William. b 17. St Aid Birkenhead 50. **d** 52 **p** 53. V Laisterdyke *Bradf* 55-83; Hon Can Bradf Cathl 67-83; rtd 83; Perm to Offic *Bradf* from 83. *465 Bradford Road, Pudsey, W Yorkshire LS28 8ED* Bradford (0274) 664862

PLIMMER, Wayne Robert. b 64. St Chad's Coll Dur BA85. St Steph Ho Ox 86. **d** 88 **p** 89. C Cockerton Dur 88-91; C Poulton-le-Fylde *Blackb* from 91. *24 Roylen Avenue, Blackpool FY6 7PH* Blackpool (0253) 884535

PLOWMAN, Richard Robert Bindon. b 38. Solicitor 61. Ridley Hall Cam 76. **d** 78 **p** 79. C Combe Down w Monkton Combe *B & W* 78-81; C Combe Down w Monkton Combe and S Stoke 81-83; V Coxley, Henton and Wookey from 83. *The Vicarage, Vicarage Lane, Wookey, Wells, Somerset BA5 1JT* Wells (0749) 77244

PLOWRIGHT, Ernest William. b 09. Bris Univ BA29. Sarum Th Coll 28. **d** 30 **p** 31. V Muchelney *B & W* 58-70; V Drayton 58-70; rtd 70; Perm to Offic *B & W* from 70. *8 Davis Terrace, Tucker Street, Wells, Somerset BA5 2DX* Wells (0749) 73486

PLUCK, Richard. b 60. Southn Univ BTh90. Aston Tr Scheme 84 Sarum & Wells Th Coll 88. **d** 90 **p** 91. C Harpenden St Nic *St Alb* from 90. *37 St James Road, Harpenden, Herts AL5 4PB* Harpenden (0582) 761657

PLUMB, Gordon Alan. b 42. Leeds Univ BA. Sarum & Wells Th Coll. **d** 82 **p** 83. C Biggleswade *St Alb* 82-86; TV Grantham *Linc* from 86. *The Vicarage, Edinburgh Road, Harrowby, Grantham, Lincs NG31 9QR* Grantham (0476) 64781

PLUMLEY, Jack Martin. b 10. St Jo Coll Dur BA32 MLitt39 K Coll Cam MA50. **d** 33 **p** 34. R Milton *Ely* 47-57; Perm to Offic 67-80 and from 80; rtd 77; P-in-c Longstowe *Ely* 80; Chapl Pemb Coll Cam 81-82; Acting Dean 81-82. *13 Lyndewode Road, Cambridge CB1 2HL* Cambridge (0223) 350328

PLUMLEY, Paul Jonathan. b 42. St Jo Coll Nottm 71. **d** 74 **p** 75. C Mile Cross *Nor* 74-77; P-in-c Wickham Skeith *St E* 77-79; P-in-c Stoke Ash, Thwaite and Wetheringsett 77-79; Assoc Min Woodbridge St Jo 80-81; Chapl RAF 81-86; Perm to Offic *Roch* from 86. *4 Cedar Ridge, Tunbridge Wells, Kent TN2 3NX* Tunbridge Wells (0892) 21999

PLUMMER, Arthur Jasper. b 09. Keble Coll Ox BA31 MA36. Ely Th Coll 31. **d** 32 **p** 33. R Atherington and High Bickington *Ex* 57-74; rtd 74; Perm to Offic *Chich* from 84. *11 Courtney King House, 169 Eastern Road, Brighton BN2 2AP* Brighton (0273) 605530

PLUMMER, Canon Charles Henry. b 06. St Aid Birkenhead 40. **d** 40 **p** 41. RD Hingham and Mitford *Nor* 66-86; R E Dereham w Hoe 66-73; P-in-c Mattishall 70-73; P-in-c Hockering w Mattishall Burgh 70-73; P-in-c N Tuddenham 70-73; P-in-c Welborne 70-73; P-in-c Yaxham 70-73; rtd 73; Perm to Offic *Glouc* 86-88. *10 Walton House Court, Northleach, Cheltenham, Glos* Cotswold (0451) 60859

PLUMMER, Mrs Deborah Ann. b 49. St Hugh's Coll Ox BA71 MA74. St Alb Minl Tr Scheme 82. **dss** 85 **d** 87. Ickenham *Lon* 85-87; Par Dn 87-88; C Northolt St Mary from 88. *St Hugh's Church House, 22 Gosling Close, Northolt, Middx UB6 9UE* 081-575 8534

PLUMMER, Miss June Alice. b 29. Bris Univ BA50 CertEd51. Sarum & Wells Th Coll 89. **d** 89. NSM Hanham *Bris* from 89. *11 Glenwood Drive, Oldland Common, Bristol BS15 6RZ* Bristol (0272) 323044

PLUMPTON, Paul. b 50. Keble Coll Ox BA72 MA76. St Steph Ho Ox 72. **d** 74 **p** 75. C Tonge Moor *Man* 74-76; C Atherton 76-79; V Oldham St Jas from 79. *8 Rosedale Close, Oldham OL1 4BU* 061-633 4441

PLUMPTRE, John Basil. b 25. Pemb Coll Cam BA49 MA54 CertEd52. Launde Abbey 75. **d** 75 **p** 76. C Leic St Pet *Leic* 75-80; C Stanford on Soar *S'well* 81-90; C Rempstone 81-90; C Costock 81-90; C E Leake 81-90; rtd 91. *14 Outwoods Road, Loughborough, Leics* Loughborough (0509) 215452

PLUNKETT, Michael Edward. b 38. Leeds Univ BSc61. Ely Th Coll 61. **d** 63 **p** 64. C Kirkby *Liv* 63-68; Lect Stockton-on-Tees 68-72; Lic to Offic *Dur* 72-73; TV Stockton 73-75; V Cantril Farm *Liv* 75-81; Soc Resp

Officer 81-89; V Melling from 81. *The Vicarage, Tithebarn Lane, Melling, Liverpool L31 1EE* 051-526 6013

PLUNKETT, Pelham Stanley. b 12. TCD BA36 MA39. **d** 59 **p** 59. V Mile Cross *Nor* 69-81; rtd 81; Hon C Hordle *Win* 81-86; Hon C Eastbourne All SS *Chich* from 86. *Flat 3, 11 Grassington Road, Eastbourne, E Sussex BN20 7BJ* Eastbourne (0323) 648193

PLUNKETT, Peter William. b 30. Oak Hill Th Coll. **d** 61 **p** 62. C Fazakerley Em *Liv* 61-64; C St Helens St Mark 64-68; V Kirkdale St Paul N Shore 68-79; P-in-c Bootle St Mary w St Jo 77-79; V Bootle St Mary w St Paul 79-81; V Goose Green 81-89; V W Derby St Jas from 89. *St James's Vicarage, Mill Lane, Liverpool L12 7LQ* 051-256 8693

PLYMOUTH, Archdeacon of. See ELLIS, Ven Robin Gareth

PLYMOUTH, Suffragan Bishop of. See HAWKINS, Rt Rev Richard Stephen

POARCH, Canon John Chilton. b 30. Bris Univ BA54. Ridley Hall Cam 54. **d** 56 **p** 57. C Swindon Ch Ch *Bris* 56-59; C Corsham 59-61; Seychelles 61-63; V Brislington St Cuth *Bris* 63-69; Adn Seychelles 69-72; V Warmley *Bris* 72-86; R Syston 72-86; RD Bitton 79-85; P-in-c Bitton 80-86; Hon Can Bris Cathl from 82; P-in-c Langley Fitzurse from 86; Dioc Dir of Ords from 86; P-in-c Draycot Cerne from 87. *The Vicarage, Kington Langley, Chippenham, Wilts SN15 5NJ* Kington Langley (024975) 231

POCKLINGTON, Canon Eric Charles. b 12. Kelham Th Coll 28. **d** 35 **p** 36. V St Oswald in Lee w Bingfield *Newc* 70-78; RD Hexham 71-78; Hon Can Newc Cathl 74-78; rtd 78; P-in-c Eyemouth *Edin* 78-82; Perm to Offic *Heref* from 82. *71 Oakland Drive, Ledbury, Herefordshire HR8 2EX* Ledbury (0531) 3617

POCOCK, Frank Lovell. b 08. OBE59. Em Coll Cam BA32 MA36. Ridley Hall Cam 33. **d** 33 **p** 34. R Ringwould w Oxney *Cant* 67-77; P-in-c Kingsdown 74-77; rtd 77; Perm to Offic *Cant* from 79. *55 Balfour Road, Deal, Kent* Deal (0304) 372314

POCOCK, Mrs Gillian Margaret. b 35. Nottm Univ BA57. Cranmer Hall Dur 82. dss 83 **d** 87. Bearpark *Dur* 83-87; Hon Par Dn 87-88; Par Dn S Hetton w Haswell 88; Chapl St Aid Coll Dur from 89; Par Dn Esh *Dur* from 90. *11 Cooke's Wood, Broompark, Durham DH7 7RL* 091-386 1140

POCOCK, Lynn Elizabeth. b 48. Coll of Wooster Ohio BA69 CertEd71 Birm Univ DipTh75. Qu Coll Birm 73. dss 82 **d** 87. Gleadless *Sheff* 82-85; Thorpe Hesley 85-87; Par Dn from 87. *The Vicarage, 30 Barnsley Road, Thorpe Hesley, Rotherham, S Yorkshire S61 2RR* Sheffield (0742) 463487

POCOCK, Nigel John. b 47. Lon Univ BSc68 Birm Univ MA83. Lambeth STh78 Oak Hill Th Coll 69. **d** 72 **p** 73. C Tunbridge Wells St Jas *Roch* 72-75; C Heatherlands St Jo *Sarum* 75-78; V Leic St Chris *Leic* 78-83; R Camborne *Truro* from 83; RD Carnmarth N from 91. *The Rectory, Rectory Gardens, Camborne, Cornwall TR14 7DN* Camborne (0209) 713340

PODGER, Richard Philip Champeney. b 38. K Coll Cam BA61 MA66. Cuddesdon Coll 62. **d** 64 **p** 65. C Doncaster St Geo *Sheff* 64-68; C Orpington All SS *Roch* 68-74; W Germany 76-88; Chapl Kassel *Eur* 83-88; TV Whitstable *Cant* from 88. *The Rectory, Swalecliffe Court Drive, Whitstable, Kent CT5 2NF* Chestfield (022779) 2826

POGMORE, Edward Clement. b 52. Sarum & Wells Th Coll 76. **d** 79 **p** 80. C Calne and Blackland *Sarum* 79-82; TV Oakdale St Geo 82-89; Min Creekmoor LEP 82-89; Chapl Nuneaton Hosps and Geo Eliot Hosp Nuneaton from 89. *The Chaplain's Office, George Eliot Hospital, College Street, Nuneaton, Warks CV10 7DJ* Coventry (0203) 351351

POIL, Preb Ronald Wickens. b 30. AKC56. **d** 57 **p** 58. C Willesborough *Cant* 57-60; Chapl RAF 60-76; P-in-c Edith Weston w Normanton *Pet* 65-67; V Southbourne *Chich* 76-80; P-in-c W Thorney 76-80; RD Westbourne from 78; V Southbourne w W Thorney from 80; Preb Chich Cathl from 90. *The Vicarage, 273 Main Road, Southbourne, Emsworth, Hants PO10 8JE* Emsworth (0243) 372436

POINTS, John David. b 43. Qu Coll Birm 78. **d** 80 **p** 81. C Wednesbury St Paul Wood Green *Lich* 80-85; V Sedgley St Mary from 85. *St Mary's Vicarage, Hurst Hill, Sedgley, Dudley, W Midlands DY3 1LD* Sedgley (0902) 883310

POLE, David John. b 46. Bath Academy of Art BA72. Trin Coll Bris 84. **d** 86 **p** 87. C Bris St Mary Redcliffe w Temple etc *Bris* 86-90; V Alveston from 90. *The*

Vicarage, Gloucester Road, Alveston, Bristol BS12 2QT Thornbury (0454) 414810

POLE, Francis John Michael. b 42. FRSA MBIM CQSW AMInstTA. St Jo Sem Wonersh 62. **d** 67 **p** 68. In RC Ch 67-75; C Walthamstow St Pet *Chelmsf* 75; C Penge Lane H Trin *Roch* 76-77; C Shirley St Jo *Cant* 77-79; Assoc Chapl The Hague *Eur* 80-83; V Norbury St Steph and Thornton Heath *Cant* 83-84; V Norbury St Steph and Thornton Heath *S'wark* from 85. *St Stephen's Vicarage, Warwick Road, Thornton Heath, Surrey CR7 7NH* 081-684 3820

POLHILL, Arthur John Henry. b 20. Sarum Th Coll 65. **d** 67 **p** 68. C Tormohun *Ex* 67-71; V Tipton w Venn Ottery 71-87; rtd 87. *First Floor Flat, 44 Castle Road, Salisbury SP1 3RJ* Salisbury (0722) 333888

POLHILL, Mrs Christine. b 46. Nottm Coll of Educn CertEd67. St Alb Minl Tr Scheme 81. dss 84 **d** 87. St Alb St Mary Marshalswick *St Alb* 84-87; Hon Par Dn from 87. *Rivendell, 49 Jerome Drive, St Albans, Herts AL3 4LT* St Albans (0727) 53095

POLITT, Robert William. b 47. ARCM LGSM68. Oak Hill Th Coll 73. **d** 76 **p** 77. C Bexleyheath St Pet *Roch* 76-82; TV Southgate *Chich* 82-90; Chapl N Foreland Lodge Sch Basingstoke from 90. *Cottage, North Foreland Lodge School, Sherfield-on-Loddon, Basingstoke, Hants RG27 0HU* Basingstoke (0256) 880051

POLKINGHORNE, John Charlton. b 30. FRS74 Trin Coll Cam MA56 PhD55 ScD74. Westcott Ho Cam 79. **d** 81 **p** 82. NSM Chesterton St Andr *Ely* 81-82; C Bedminster St Mich *Bris* 82-84; V Blean *Cant* 84-86; Dean Trin Hall Cam 86-89; Pres Qu Coll Cam from 89. *The President's Lodge, Queen's College, Cambridge CB3 9ET* Cambridge (0223) 335532

POLL, Martin George. b 61. Kent Univ BA83. Ripon Coll Cuddesdon 84. **d** 87 **p** 88. C Mill Hill Jo Keble Ch *Lon* 87-90; Chapl RN from 90. *c/o MOD, Lacon House, Theobald's Road, London WC1X 8RY* 071-430 6847

POLLAK, Canon Peter Henry. b 18. Worc Ord Coll 67. **d** 69 **p** 70. C Claines St Jo *Worc* 69-73; R Grimley w Holt 73-88; RD Martley and Worc W 84-88; Hon Can Worc Cathl from 85; rtd 88. *2 Tweenways, Main Road, Kempsey, Worcester WR5 3JY* Worcester (0905) 820351

POLLARD, Mrs Christine Beryl. b 45. DCR DNM. Nor Ord Course 86. **d** 89. Par Dn Ingrow cum Hainworth *Bradf* from 89. *Endhlch, 2 Prospect Drive, Fell Lane, Keighley, W Yorkshire BD22 6DD* Keighley (0535) 602682

POLLARD, Canon Clifford Francis. b 20. AKC49. **d** 50 **p** 51. Dir of Educn *Cant* 69-87; Hon Can Cant Cathl from 72; rtd 87. *6 Lady Wootton's Green, Canterbury, Kent CT1 1NG* Canterbury (0227) 761674

POLLARD, David. b 55. LSE BSc77. Trin Coll Bris DipHE80. **d** 80 **p** 81. Canada 81-84; C-in-c Hillsfield and Monkspath LEP *Birm* 85-89; BCMS from 89; Spain from 89. *San Vicente De Paul 8, Casa 2, 1-A, 41010 Seville, Spain* Seville (54) 433-5176

POLLARD, David John Athey. b 44. ACP74 Culham Coll Ox CertEd69. St Jo Coll Nottm LTh88. **d** 88 **p** 89. C Illogan *Truro* 88-91; R Roche and Withiel from 91. *The Rectory, Fore Street, Roche, St Austell, Cornwall PL26 8EP* St Austell (0726) 890301

POLLARD, David Stanley. b 49. Lon Univ BD80 AKC80 Bradf Univ MA. **d** 80 **p** 81. CGA 78-89; C Manningham St Mary and Bradf St Mich *Bradf* 80-83; P-in-c 83-84; TV Manningham 84-85; C 86-87; Lic to Offic 85-89; P-in-c Sidlesham *Chich* from 89; Chapl Chich Coll of Tech from 90. *The Vicarage, Church Farm Lane, Sidlesham, Chichester, W Sussex PO20 7RE* Chichester (0243) 641237

POLLARD, Eric John. b 43. Chich Th Coll 83. **d** 85 **p** 86. C Brighton St Matthias *Chich* 85-90; C E Grinstead St Swithun from 90. *St Luke's House, Holtye Avenue, East Grinstead, W Sussex RH19 3EG* East Grinstead (0342) 323800

POLLARD, James Adrian Hunter. b 48. St Jo Coll Nottm BTh78. **d** 78 **p** 79. C Much Woolton *Liv* 78-81; CMS 81-84; V Toxteth Park Ch Ch *Liv* 85-90; CF from 90. *c/o MOD (Army), Bagshot Park, Bagshot, Surrey GU19 5PL* Bagshot (0276) 71717

POLLARD, John Edward Ralph. b 40. ALCD68. **d** 67 **p** 68. C Ollerton *S'well* 67-71; C Walton H Trin *Ox* 71-74; P-in-c Cuddington w Dinton 74-77; V Haddenham 74-77; V Kingsey 75-77; V Haddenham w Cuddington and Kingsey 77-85; RD Aylesbury 80-85; V Haddenham w Cuddington, Kingsey etc 85-87; V Furze Platt from 87. *St Peter's Vicarage, 259 Courthouse Road, Maidenhead, Berks SL6 6HF* Maidenhead (0628) 21961

POLLARD, Noel Stewart. b 28. Sydney Univ BA51 BD56 Ch Ch Ox BA58 MA63. **d** 53 **p** 53. Australia 53-56 and

61-72; Chapl Ch Ch Ox 57-58; C Cam St Sepulchre *Ely* 58-61; Lect St Jo Coll Nottm 72-88; Lect Nottm Univ 72-88; Vice-Prin Ridley Hall Cam from 88. *193 Huntingdon Road, Cambridge CB3 0DL* Cambridge (0223) 276328

POLLARD, Roger Frederick. b 32. Sheff Univ BSc52 Lanc Univ MA78. Linc Th Coll 56. **d** 58 **p** 59. C Catford St Laur *S'wark* 58-63; Ghana 63-66; C Fulford *York* 66-67; C Camberwell St Geo *S'wark* 67; Asst Master Roch Valley Sch Milnrow 68-69; S Craven Sch Cross Hills from 69; Perm to Offic *Bradf* from 70. *High Close Barn, New House Lane, Long Preston, Skipton BD23 4QU* Long Preston (07294) 627

POLLARD, William Gilbert. b 12. CCC Cam BA34. Linc Th Coll 34. **d** 36 **p** 37. Nigeria 49-78; rtd 78; Perm to Offic Roch & Chich from 80. *2 Regency Terrace, Tunbridge Wells, Kent TN2 4SD* Tunbridge Wells (0892) 34570

POLLIT, Preb Michael. b 30. Worc Coll Ox BA54 MA58. Wells Th Coll 54. **d** 56 **p** 57. C Cannock *Lich* 56-59; C Codsall 59-62; V W Bromwich St Pet 62-67; R Norton in the Moors 67-76; RD Leek 72-76; V Shrewsbury St Chad w St Mary from 76; Preb Lich Cathl from 81; P-in-c Shrewsbury St Alkmund from 91. *St Chad's Vicarage, Shrewsbury SY1 1RH* Shrewsbury (0743) 3761

POLLIT, Ruth Mary. b 65. SS Paul & Mary Coll Cheltenham BA88. St Jo Coll Nottm DPS90. **d** 90. Par Dn Caverswall *Lich* from 90. *4 Brindon Close, Stoke-on-Trent ST3 6NY* Stoke-on-Trent (0782) 321067

POLLITT, Graham Anthony. b 48. BA79. Oak Hill Th Coll 76. **d** 79 **p** 80. C Rusholme *Man* 79-82; TV Southgate *Chich* 82-83; C Burgess Hill St Andr 83-86; Chapl St Martin's Coll of Educn *Blackb* 86-90; Chapl Cheltenham Coll from 90. *The Park, Cheltenham, Gloucester GL50 2RH* Cheltenham (0242) 513836

POLLOCK, Christopher John. b 62. TCD BTh89. CITC 86. **d** 89 **p** 90. C Agherton *Conn* 89-91; C Ballymoney w Finvoy and Rasharkin from 91. *14 Queen's Avenue, Ballymoney, Co Antrim BT53 7DP* Ballymoney (02656) 64329

POLLOCK, Duncan James Morrison. b 54. QGM. Linc Th Coll BCombStuds. **d** 83 **p** 84. C Folkestone St Mary and St Eanswythe *Cant* 83-85; CF from 85. *c/o MOD (Army), Bagshot Park, Bagshot, Surrey GU19 5PL* Bagshot (0276) 71717

POLLOCK, Hugh Gillespie. b 36. Oak Hill Th Coll 61. **d** 64 **p** 65. C Maidstone St Luke *Cant* 64-68; C Washfield *Ex* 68-71; C Washfield, Stoodleigh, Withleigh etc 71-73; Chapl Lee Abbey 73-76; V Dersingham *Nor* 76-80; P-in-c Anmer 79-80; P-in-c Shernbourne 79-80; R Dersingham w Anmer and Shernborne 80-89; RD Heacham and Rising 87-89; C Barnstaple *Ex* from 89. *Holy Trinity Vicarage, Victoria Road, Barnstable EX32 9HP* Barnstaple (0271) 44321

POLLOCK, James Colin Graeme. b 53. St Chad's Coll Dur BA76. Ripon Coll Cuddesdon 77. **d** 78 **p** 79. C Hartlepool St Oswald *Dur* 78-81; C Hartlepool St Aid 81-84; V Dawdon from 84. *The Vicarage, Melbury Street, Seaham, Co Durham SR7 7NF* 091-581 2317

POLLOCK, John Charles. b 23. Trin Coll Cam BA46 MA48. Ridley Hall Cam 49. **d** 51 **p** 52. Ed The Churchman 53-58; R Horsington *B & W* 53-58; Perm to Offic *Ex* from 61; rtd 88. *Rose Ash House, South Molton, Devon EX36 4RB* Bishops Nympton (07697) 403

POLLOCK, Neil Thomas. b 38. Lon Univ DipTh68. Bernard Gilpin Soc Dur 63 Lich Th Coll 64. **d** 67 **p** 68. C Lt Stanmore St Lawr *Lon* 67-72; C-in-c Uxbridge St Marg 72-81; R Norwood St Mary 81-86; TR Ridgeway *Sarum* from 86. *The Rectory, 3 Butts Road, Chiseldon, Swindon SN4 0NN* Swindon (0793) 740369

POLLOCK, Norman Stuart. b 09. Dorchester Miss Coll 33. **d** 35 **p** 36. R Lichborough w Maidford *Pet* 65-72; Chapl St Kath Convent Parmoor 72-83; C Hambleden *Ox* 72-79; Chapl HM Borstal Finnamore Wood 73-76; rtd 74; Warden St Kath Convent Parmoor 80-83; Perm to Offic *Guildf* from 86. *34 Worplesden Road, Guildford, Surrey GU2 6RS* Guildford (0483) 503650

POMEROY, Michael James. b 26. Sarum Th Coll 64. **d** 66 **p** 67. Co Chapl ACF 69-89; Hon CF from 89; P-in-c Ibberton w Belchalwell and Woolland *Sarum* 69-72; R 72-73; R Okeford Fitzpaine, Ibberton, Belchalwell etc 73-90; rtd 90. *Brandon, Wavering Lane, Gillingham, Dorset SP8 4NR* Gillingham (0747) 822498

POMERY, David John. b 45. SS Mark & Jo Coll Chelsea CertEd67. Chich Th Coll 75. **d** 77 **p** 78. C Coseley Ch Ch *Lich* 77-79; C Stocksbridge *Sheff* 79-81; V Bentley 81-87; Radlett Prep Sch from 87. *Radlett Preparatory School, Kendall Hall, Radlett, Herts* Radlett (0923) 856812

POMFRET, Albert. b 23. Univ of Wales (Cardiff) BSc57 Lon Univ MA69. Oak Hill NSM Course 72. **d** 75 **p** 76. NSM Dartford Ch Ch *Roch* 75-80; Perm to Offic from 80. *70 Wentworth Drive, Dartford DA1 3NG* Dartford (0322) 226377

POND, Nigel Peter Hamilton. b 40. AKC65. **d** 66 **p** 67. C E Dereham w Hoe *Nor* 66-69; C Chapl RN 69-85; TR Woughton *Ox* from 85; Chapl Milton Keynes Gen Hosp from 85; RD Milton Keynes *Ox* from 90. *The Rectory, 10 Forest Rise, Milton Keynes MK6 5EU* Milton Keynes (0908) 670070

✠**PONNIAH, Rt Rev Jacob Samuel.** b 22. Bihar Univ MA59. Western Th Sem Michigan MTh64 Madras Chr Coll BA48 United Th Coll Bangalore 48. **d** 52 **p** 53 **c** 78. India 53-90; Bp Vellore 78-87; Dioc Missr *Linc* 90-91; P-in-c Fulletby w Greetham and Ashby Puerorum 90-91; P-in-c Hameringham w Scrafield and Winceby 90-91; P-in-c High Toynton 90-91; P-in-c Mareham on the Hill 90-91; P-in-c Belchford 90-91; Miss Partner CMS from 91. *c/o Rydall Hall, Ambleside, Cumbria LA22 9LX* Ambleside (05394) 32050

PONT, Gordon John Harper. b 35. Glas Univ BSc56 BD65. Edin Th Coll 56. **d** 59 **p** 60. C Dunfermline *St And* 59-62; C Motherwell *Glas* 62-65; R Largs 65-68; Dioc Supernumerary *Bre* 68-71; Chapl Dundee Univ 68-73; R Dundee St Luke 71-74; Hon Chapl St Paul's Cathl Dundee from 74; NSM Dundee St Paul from 74. *5 Westpark Road, Dundee DD2 1NU* Dundee (0382) 69883

PONT, Philip Roy. b 03. Edin Th Coll 56. **d** 56 **p** 56. R Moffat *Glas* 64-76; rtd 76. *3 Highburgh Drive, Rutherglen, Glasgow G73 3RR* 041-647 5984

PONTEFRACT, Archdeacon of. See UNWIN, Ven Kenneth

PONTEFRACT, Suffragan Bishop of. See HARE, Rt Rev Thomas Richard

PONTER, John Arthur. b 37. Univ of Wales BA61 Linacre Coll Ox BA63 MA68 UEA PhD81. Wycliffe Hall Ox 61. **d** 63 **p** 64. C Gidea Park *Chelmsf* 63-67; C-in-c Colchester St Anne CD 67-69; V Colchester St Anne 69-72; Chapl UEA *Nor* 73-78; Chelmsf Cathl *Chelmsf* 79-85; V Moulsham St Jo 79-85; Lic to Offic *Man* from 85; Dir Man Chr Inst from 85. *8 Deneway Close, Stockport, Cheshire SK4 2HX* 061-442 4092

PONTIN, Colin Henry. b 37. Trin Coll Bris. **d** 83 **p** 84. C Downend *Bris* 83-86; C Riverside *Ox* 86-88; V Eton w Eton Wick and Boveney 88-90; TV Riverside from 91. *The Vicarage, 69A Eton Wick Road, Windsor, Berks SL4 6NE* Windsor (0753) 852268

POODHUN, Lambert David. b 30. Natal Univ BA53. Edin Th Coll 54. **d** 56 **p** 57. S Africa 56-76; Adn Durban 75-76; C Upton cum Chalvey *Ox* 77-80; Chapl Kingston Hosp Surrey 80-81; Tooting Bec Hosp Lon 81-84; Chapl Hurstwood Park and St Fran Hosps Haywards Heath from 84. *8 Nursery Close, Haywards Heath, W Sussex RH16 1HP* Haywards Heath (0444) 452571

POOLE, Arthur James. b 09. Qu Coll Birm 36. **d** 38 **p** 39. V Gt Haywood *Lich* 65-78; R Tixall w Ingestre 65-78; rtd 78; Perm to Offic *Lich* from 78. *18 Balmoral Road, Stafford ST17 0AN* Stafford (0785) 40245

POOLE, Clifford George. b 36. Keble Coll Ox BA61 MA65. S'wark Ord Course 83. **d** 86 **p** 87. C W Dulwich All SS and Em *S'wark* 86-90; Chapl Luxembourg *Eur* from 90. *1 rue Ernest Beres, L-1232 Howald, Luxembourg* Luxembourg (352) 485397

POOLE, Denis Tom. b 19. St Jo Coll Dur 39. St Aid Birkenhead 41. **d** 43 **p** 44. V Biddulph *Lich* 64-85; Chapl Biddulph Grange Hosp Staffs 64-85; rtd 85; Perm to Offic *Win* from 85. *14 Curlew Drive, Hythe, Southampton SO4 6GA* Hythe (0703) 846497

POOLE, Edward John. b 53. Hull Univ BA81. St Steph Ho Ox 81. **d** 83 **p** 84. C Stevenage St Andr and St Geo *St Alb* 83-86; Madagascar 86-88; V Weston *St Alb* from 88; P-in-c Ardeley from 88. *The Vicarage, 14 Munts Meadow, Weston, Hitchin, Herts SG4 7AE* Weston (046279) 330

POOLE, Frederick Harold. b 14. Clifton Th Coll 54. **d** 56 **p** 56. R Chorlton on Medlock St Steph *Man* 60-68; rtd 79. *43 Albion Street, Wallasey, Merseyside L45 9LE* 051-638 8952

POOLE, Miss Joan Wendy. b 37. Sarum Dioc Teacher Tr Coll CertEd57 Dalton Ho Bris DipTh66 Trin Coll Bris 86. **d** 87. Par Dn Longfleet *Sarum* 87-89; Par Dn Hamworthy from 89. *35 Inglesham Way, Hamworthy, Poole, Dorset BH15 4PA* Poole (0202) 678702

POOLE, John. b 19. Peterho Cam MA44. St Alb Minl Tr Scheme 77. **d** 80 **p** 81. NSM Bedf St Andr *St Alb* 80-87;

NSM Elstow from 87. *35 Falcon Avenue, Bedford MK41 7DY* Bedford (0234) 262208

POOLE, John Denys Barlow. b 33. Qu Coll Cam BA57 MA61. Cuddesdon Coll 57. **d** 59 **p** 60. CF 57-72; C Leagrave *St Alb* 59-62; C Raynes Park St Sav *S'wark* 62-65; C Apsley End *St Alb* 65-72; R W Wickham St Jo *Cant* 73-84; V W Wickham St Jo *S'wark* from 85. *The Rectory, 30 Coney Hill Road, West Wickham, Kent BR4 9BX* 081-462 4001

POOLE, John Robert. b 46. Lon Univ BSc69 Bris Univ DipTh71. Clifton Th Coll 69. **d** 72 **p** 73. C Horton *Bradf* 72-75; C Otley 76-79; V Bankfoot from 79. *The Vicarage, Carbottom Road, Bankfoot, Bradford, W Yorkshire BD5 9AA* Bradford (0274) 726529

POOLE, Martin Bryce. b 59. Reading Univ BSc80 Nottm Univ DipTh82 DipAct85. St Jo Coll Nottm DPS84. **d** 87 **p** 88. NSM Tulse Hill H Trin and St Matthias *S'wark* from 87. *51 Ladas Road, London SE27 0UP* 081-761 3190

POOLE, Martin Ronald. b 59. Aston Univ BSc81 Leeds Univ BA86. Coll of Resurr Mirfield 84. **d** 87 **p** 88. C Sheff St Cath Richmond Road *Sheff* 87-90; C W Hampstead St Jas *Lon* from 90. *1 St James's House, 2 Sherriff Road, London NW6 2AP* 071-372 6441

POOLE, Peter William. b 35. St Pet Hall Ox BA59 MA63. Wells Th Coll 59. **d** 61 **p** 62. C Cheriton Street *Cant* 61-64; C Birchington w Acol 64-67; V Newington 67-73; P-in-c Lower Halstow 72-73; V Beacdurst 73-76; V Lane End w Cadmore End *Ox* 84-89; R Chalfont St Giles from 89. *The Rectory, 2 Deanway, Chalfont St Giles, Bucks HP8 4JH* Chalfont St Giles (02407) 2097

POOLE, Ronald John Ajax. b 10. Selw Coll Cam BA32 MA36. Wells Th Coll 32. **d** 33 **p** 35. V Tondu *Llan* 60-73; rtd 73; Perm to Offic *Llan* from 73. *20 Park Place, Canola, Bryncethin, Bridgend, M Glam* Aberkenfig (0656) 720232

POOLE, Roy John. b 26. Lon Univ BD54. St Jo Coll Lon LTh54. **d** 54 **p** 55. Regional Supervisor (S and E England) Chr Aid 68-74; Australia from 74; rtd 91. *Unit 8, 131 Hastings Street, Scarborough, W Australia 6019* Perth (9) 245-1204

POOLE, Stanley Burke-Roche. b 09. K Coll Lon BA31 MA34. Qu Coll Birm 36. **d** 38 **p** 39. V Littlebourne *Cant* 48-70; rtd 74. *13 Chaucer Court, New Dover Road, Canterbury, Kent CT1 3AU* Canterbury (0227) 51586

POOLE, Stuart. b 33. CEng65 FIEE85 Loughb Coll of Educn DLC55 Lon Univ BScEng55 Man Univ MSc76. **d** 91. NSM Cheadle *Ches* from 91. *1 Dene House, Green Pastures, Stockport, Cheshire SK4 3RB* 061-432 6426

POOLEY, Peter Owen. b 32. Kelham Th Coll 54. **d** 58 **p** 59. C Paddington St Mary Magd *Lon* 58-62; R Rockland St Mary w Hellington *Nor* 62-67; Asst Master Thos Lethaby Sch 67-70; St Phil Gr Sch Edgbaston 70-74; Lordswood Gr Sch 74-80; Hon C Edgbaston St Geo *Birm* 77-80; R Elton *Ely* from 80; P-in-c Stibbington from 80; P-in-c Water Newton from 80. *The Rectory, Elton, Peterborough PE8 6SA* Oundle (0832) 280222

POOLMAN, Alfred John. b 46. K Coll Lon BD69 AKC69 Sheff Univ DipPs83. St Aug Coll Cant 69. **d** 70 **p** 71. C Headingley *Ripon* 70-74; C Moor Allerton 75-78; C Monk Bretton *Wakef* 78-80; C Athersley 80; V Copley 80-90; Chapl Halifax Gen Hosp 80-90; R Llanfynydd *St As* from 90. *The Rectory, Llanfynydd, Wrexham, Clwyd LL11 5HH* Caergwrle (0978) 762304

POPE, Charles Guy. b 48. AKC70. St Aug Coll Cant 70. **d** 71 **p** 72. C Southgate Ch *Lon* 71-74; C N St Pancras All Hallows 74-77; C Hampstead St Steph 74-77; V New Southgate St Paul 77-86; V Brookfield St Mary from 86; P-in-c Highgate Rise St Anne Brookfield from 88. *St Mary's Vicarage, 85 Dartmouth Park Road, London NW5 1SL* 071-267 5941

POPE, Colin. b 51. Brasted Place Coll 74. Linc Th Coll 75. **d** 78 **p** 79. C W Derby Gd Shep *Liv* 78-81; C-in-c Westbrook St Phil CD 81-82; V Westbrook St Phil 82-87; V Orrell from 87; Chapl Billinge Hosp Wigan from 87. *St Luke's Vicarage, 10 Lodge Road, Orrell, Wigan, Lancs WN5 7AT* Up Holland (0695) 623410

POPE, Daniel Legh. b 23. Cuddesdon Coll 67. **d** 68 **p** 69. C Llanelly St D 68-71; V Radley *Ox* 71-88; Miss to Seamen from 88; Cyprus from 88. *St Andrew's Church, PK 171, Girne, Mersin 10, Turkey*

POPE, David Allan. b 20. Or Coll Ox BA45 MA72. Ely Th Coll 45. **d** 47 **p** 48. R Broadstairs *Cant* 65-73; P-in-c Berwick *Chich* 73-76; P-in-c Arlington 73-75; P-in-c Selmeston w Alciston 74-76; R Berwick w Selmeston and Alciston 76; P-in-c Rusper 76-79; R Colsterworth *Linc* 79-81; P-in-c Ingworth 81-85; P-in-c Alby w Thwaite *Nor* 81-85; P-in-c Erpingham w Calthorpe 81-85; P-in-c Aldborough w Thurgarton 83-85; rtd 85; Perm to Offic

Nor from 85. *Brickfield Farm, Stibbard, Fakenham, Norfolk NR21 0EE* Great Ryburgh (032878) 294

POPE, Donald Keith. b 35. Sarum & Wells Th Coll 81. **d** 76 **p** 77. Hon C Caerleon *Mon* 76-82; C 82-83; V Pontypool 83-86; R Grosmont and Skenfrith and Llangattock etc from 86. *The Rectory, Grosmont, Abergavenny, Gwent NP7 8LW* Golden Valley (0981) 240587

POPE, Michael John. b 37. Sarum Th Coll 62. **d** 65 **p** 66. C Broseley w Benthall *Heref* 65-68; C Shrewsbury St Giles *Lich* 68-71; P-in-c Shrewsbury St Geo 71-75; V 75-79; V Gnosall from 79. *The Vicarage, Gnosall, Stafford ST20 0ER* Stafford (0785) 822213

POPE, Michael Ronald. b 41. Bps' Coll Cheshunt 65. **d** 68 **p** 69. C Lyonsdown H Trin *St Alb* 68-72; C Seaford w Sutton *Chich* 72-76; R Hurstpierpoint 76-80. *Isle of Wight Cheshire Home, Popham Road, Shanklin, Isle of Wight PO37 6RG* Isle of Wight (0983) 862193

POPE, Very Rev Robert William. b 16. OBE70. Dur Univ LTh40. St Aug Coll Cant 35. **d** 39 **p** 40. Chapl RN 44-71; V Whitchurch w Tufton and Litchfield *Win* 71-77; Dean Gib *Eur* 77-82; rtd 82; Min Prov Third Order Soc of St Fran 85-87; Min Gen 87-90. *5 Wreath Green, Tatworth, Chard, Somerset TA20 2SN* Chard (0460) 20987

POPE, Rodney John. b 22. St D Coll Lamp BA48 BD67 MA71. **d** 49 **p** 50. V Eastham *Ches* 62-72; V Gt w Lt Saling *Chelmsf* 72-87; rtd 87; Perm to Offic *B & W* from 89. *4 Abbey Close, Curry Rivel, Langport, Somerset TA10 0EL* Langport (0458) 250808

POPEJOY, Wilfred. b 28. St Jo Coll Nottm 88. **d** 88. Hon C Donisthorpe and Moira w Stretton-en-le-Field *Leic* from 88. *79 Donisthorpe Lane, Moira, Burton-on-Trent, Staffs DE12 6BB* Burton-on-Trent (0283) 760476

POPP, Miss Julia Alice Gisela. b 45. Univ of BC BA71. St Jo Coll Nottm 78. **dss** 81 **d** 87. Woking St Mary *Guildf* 81-83; Hornsey Rise St Mary w St Steph *Lon* 83-87; Par Dn Hornsey Rise Whitehall Park Team 87-91; Par Dn Sutton St Nic *S'wark* from 91; Missr Sutton Town Cen from 91. *14 Strathearn Road, Sutton, Surrey SM1 2RS* 081-643 6712

POPPLE, Ven Dennis. b 31. Vancouver Sch of Th LTh72 San Francisco Th Sem DMin89 St Aid Birkenhead 59. **d** 62 **p** 63. C Walkden Moor *Man* 62-65; Canada from 65; Admin Adn from 87. *302-814 Richards Street, Vancouver, British Columbia, Canada, V6B 3A7* Vancouver (604) 684-6306

POPPLEWELL, Andrew Frederick. b 53. St Jo Coll Dur BA75. Wycliffe Hall Ox 76. **d** 78 **p** 79. C Clifton *York* 78-81; C Lich St Chad *Lich* 82-84; V Laisterdyke *Bradf* from 84. *The Vicarage, Parsonage Road, Laisterdyke, Bradford, W Yorkshire BD4 8PY* Bradford (0274) 664565

PORTEOUS, Canon Eric John. b 34. AKC58. **d** 59 **p** 60. C Wandsworth St Paul *S'wark* 59-62; C Leeds St Pet *Ripon* 62-66; V Wortley de Leeds 66-72; RD Armley 70-72; R Woolwich St Mary w H Trin *S'wark* 72-77; Sub-Dean of Woolwich 74-77; P-in-c Woolwich St Mich 75-77; R Woolwich St Mary w St Mich 77-79; Chapl Whipps Cross Hosp Lon from 79; Lic to Offic *Chelmsf* 79-86; Hon Can Chelmsf Cathl from 86. *128 Grove Hill, London E18 2HZ* 081-530 5660 or 539 5522

PORTEOUS, Michael Stanley. b 35. S'wark Ord Course 70. **d** 73 **p** 74. C Barnes St Mich *S'wark* 73-76; Chapl Greycoat Hosp Sch 76-78; C Brighton Annunciation *Chich* 78-80; Chapl Ch Hosp Horsham 80-85; TV Moulsecoomb *Chich* 85-88; R W Blatchington from 88. *St Peter's Rectory, 23 Windmill Close, Hove, E Sussex BN3 7LJ* Brighton (0273) 732459

PORTER, Anthony. b 52. Hertf Coll Ox BA74 MA78 Fitzw Ho Cam BA76 MA80. Ridley Hall Cam 74. **d** 77 **p** 78. C Edgware *Lon* 77-80; C Haughton St Mary *Man* 80-83; P-in-c Bacup Ch Ch 83-87; V 87-91; R Rusholme from 91. *27 Park Range, Victoria Park, Manchester M14 5HR* 061-224 1123

PORTER, Arthur William. b 29. St Deiniol's Hawarden 70. **d** 70 **p** 71. C Ruislip St Martin *Lon* 70-80; V Kingsbury H Innocents from 80. *The Vicarage, 54 Roe Green, London NW9 0PJ* 081-204 7531 or 205 4089

PORTER, Brian John Henry. b 33. SW Minl Tr Course 78. **d** 81 **p** 82. NSM Plymouth St Andr w St Paul and St Geo *Ex* 81-85; NSM Perm to Offic 85-87; NSM Devonport St Barn 87-90; C Brampton St Thos *Derby* from 90. *Rose Cottage, Cotton Mill Hill, Chesterfield S42 7EU* Chesterfield (0246) 569106

PORTER, David Anthony. b 34. Wycliffe Hall Ox 73. **d** 75 **p** 76. C Watford St Luke *St Alb* 75-78; C Worting *Win* 78-81; V Snettisham *Nor* 81-82; P-in-c Ingoldisthorpe 81-82; C Fring 81-82; R Snettisham w Ingoldisthorpe and Fring 82-84; Chapl Asst Colchester Gen Hosp 87-88;

Chapl Maidstone Hosp from 88. *Maidstone Hospital, Hermitage Lane, Maidstone, Kent ME16 9QQ* Maidstone (0622) 29000

✠**PORTER, Rt Rev David Brownfield.** b 06. Hertf Coll Ox BA27 DipTh29 MA31. Wycliffe Hall Ox. **d** 29 **p** 30 **c** 62. C Wrangthorn *Ripon* 29-31; Tutor Wycliffe Hall Ox 31-35; Chapl 33-35; Chapl Wadh Coll Ox 34-35; V Highfield *Ox* 35-43; V Darlington *Dur* 43-47; R Edin St Jo *Edin* 47-61; Dean Edin 54-61; Suff Bp Aston *Birm* 62-72; rtd 72; Asst Bp Glouc from 75. *Silver Leys, Brockhampton, Cheltenham, Glos GL54 5TH* Cheltenham (0242) 820431

PORTER, David Michael. b 37. Coll of Ripon & York St Jo BA88. Ely Th Coll 61. **d** 64 **p** 65. C Clun w Chapel Lawn *Heref* 64-67; C Scarborough St Mary w Ch Ch, St Paul and St Thos *York* 67-69; C Fulford 69-71; V Strensall 71-78; V Easingwold w Raskelfe from 78; Chapl Claypenny and St Monica's Hosps from 78. *The Vicarage, Easingwold, York YO6 3JT* Easingwold (0347) 21394

PORTER, Dennis Percy. b 26. K Coll Lon BSc47 AKC49 Birm Univ DipTh58. **d** 72 **p** 73. NSM Ecclesall *Sheff* 72-79; Chapl Whirlow Grange Conf Cen Sheff from 79. *75 Marsh House Road, Sheffield S11 9SQ* Sheffield (0742) 362058

PORTER, Geoffrey Ernest. b 14. AKC48. **d** 48 **p** 49. R Ingrave *Chelmsf* 53-78; rtd 79. *Beecham's View, 25 Station Road, Mursley, Milton Keynes MK17 0SA* Mursley (029672) 460

PORTER, John Dudley Dowell. b 33. St Edm Hall Ox BA60 MA61. Qu Coll Birm 57. **d** 59 **p** 60. C Londonderry *Birm* 59-62; C Tettenhall Regis *Lich* 62-65; Chapl RAF 65-69; V Wombourne *Lich* 69-75; V Rickerscote 75-81; P-in-c Chapel Chorlton 81-85; P-in-c Maer 81-85; P-in-c Whitmore 81-85; R Chapel Chorlton, Maer and Whitmore from 85. *The Rectory, Snape Hall Road, Newcastle, Staffs ST5 5HZ* Whitmore (0782) 680258

PORTER, Canon Prof Joshua Roy. b 21. Mert Coll Ox BA42 MA47. St Steph Ho Ox 42. **d** 45 **p** 46. Prof Th Ex Univ 62-86; Can and Preb Chich Cathl *Chich* from 65; rtd 86; Lic to Offic *Lon* from 87. *36 Theberton Street, London N1 0QX*

PORTER, Joy Dove. b 50. Lon Univ PGCE83 Ex Univ CPS86. Lon Bible Coll BA(Theol)81 Wycliffe Hall Ox 89. **d** 91. Par Dn Chalgrove w Berrick Salome *Ox* from 91. *1 Saw Close, Chalgrove, Oxford OX9 7TW* Stadhampton (0865) 891307

PORTER, Kenneth Wilfred. b 27. St Aid Birkenhead 58. **d** 61 **p** 62. C Queensbury *Bradf* 61-63; C Oldham St Paul *Man* 63-65; V Wardle from 65; Chapl Birch Hill Hosp from 84. *St James's Vicarage, 59 Alpine Drive, Wardle, Rochdale, Lancs OL12 9NY* Rochdale (0706) 78148

PORTER, Michael Edward. b 44. Trin Coll Bris 75. **d** 77 **p** 78. C Corby St Columba *Pet* 77-81; C Rainham *Chelmsf* 81-82; TV from 82. *St John's Parsonage, South End Road, Rainham, Essex RM13 7XT* Rainham (04027) 55260

PORTER, William Albert. b 28. Univ of NZ BA51 MA52. Coll of Resurr Mirfield 53. **d** 55 **p** 56. C Perry Barr *Birm* 55-58; New Zealand 59-62; Fiji 62-67; Can and Prec H Trin Cathl Suva 65-67; C Wimbledon *S'wark* 68; Asst Chapl HM Pris Liv 69-70; Chapl 79-87; Chapl HM Pris Brixton 70-74; Long Lartin 74-79; Nottm 87-90; P-in-c Sneinton St Matthias *S'well* from 90. *St Matthias Vicarage, Sneinton, Nottingham NG3 2FG* Nottingham (0602) 502750

PORTER, William George Ernest. b 17. Ripon Hall Ox 60. **d** 60 **p** 61. V Brinsley w Underwood *S'well* 67-82; rtd 82; Perm to Offic *S'well* from 82. *6 Ringwood Avenue, Mansfield, Notts NG18 4DA* Mansfield (0623) 21656

PORTEUS, Canon Alan Cruddas. b 12. St Chad's Coll Dur BA32 DipTh34. **d** 35 **p** 36. V Ponteland *Newc* 60-77; Hon Can Newc Cathl 72-79; P-in-c Blanchland w Hunstanworth 77-79; rtd 79. *14 Wembley Avenue, Whitley Bay, Tyne & Wear NE25 8TE* 091-251 1895

PORTEUS, James Michael. b 31. Worc Coll Ox BA55 MA58. Cuddesdon Coll. **d** 57 **p** 58. C Fleetwood *Blackb* 57-60; C Ox St Mary V *Ox* 60-62; USA 62-69 and from 86; Chapl Lon Univ *Lon* 69-74; V Hampstead Garden Suburb 74-86. *715 North Park Avenue, Tucson, Arizona 85719, USA*

PORTEUS, Matthew Thomas. b 10. TCD BA32. **d** 33 **p** 34. V W Haddon w Winwick *Pet* 56-73; rtd 73. *12 North Hill Way, Bridport, Dorset DT6 4JX* Bridport (0308) 24551

PORTEUS, Robert John Norman. b 50. TCD BA72. CITC 75. **d** 75 **p** 76. C Portadown St Mark *Arm* 75-79; I Ardtrea w Desertcreat 79-83; I Annaghmore from 83.

54 Moss Road, Portadown, Co Armagh BT62 1ND Annaghmore (0762) 851555

PORTHOUSE, John Clive. b 32. Lon Univ BD58. Tyndale Hall Bris 55 Oak Hill Th Coll 58. **d** 60 **p** 61. C Leyton All SS *Chelmsf* 60-62; C Kendal St Thos *Carl* 62-64; V Flimby 64-68; V Sidcup St Andr *Roch* 68-74; V Beckenham St Jo 74-86; RD Beckenham 80-86; V Southborough St Pet w Ch Ch and St Matt from 86. *The Vicarage, 86 Prospect Road, Southborough, Tunbridge Wells, Kent TN4 0EG* Tunbridge Wells (0892) 28534

PORTHOUSE, Roger Gordon Hargreaves. b 39. Tyndale Hall Bris 66. **d** 69 **p** 70. C Wellington w Eyton *Lich* 69-71; C Cheadle *Ches* 71-75; R Frettenham w Stanninghall *Nor* 75-81; R Spixworth w Crostwick 75-81; V Hailsham *Chich* from 81. *St Mary's Vicarage, Vicarage Road, Hailsham, E Sussex BN27 1BL* Hailsham (0323) 842381

PORTSMOUTH, Archdeacon of. See CROWDER, Ven Norman Harry

PORTSMOUTH, Bishop of. See BAVIN, Rt Rev Timothy John

PORTSMOUTH, Provost of. See STANCLIFFE, Very Rev David Staffurth

PORTWOOD, Derek. b 31. Keele Univ MA70. ALCD58. **d** 57 **p** 58. C Laisterdyke *Bradf* 57-60; C-in-c Westlands St Andr CD *Lich* 60-66; V Westlands St Andr 66-69. *49 Abbey Road, Cambridge CB5 8HH*

POST, David Charles William. b 39. Jes Coll Cam BA61 MA65. Oak Hill Th Coll 61. **d** 63 **p** 64. C Orpington Ch Ch *Roch* 63-66; C Fulwood *Sheff* 66-68; V Lathom *Liv* 68-75; V Poughill *Truro* 75-78; V Braddan *S & M* 78-79; Dioc Missr 78-79; P-in-c Santan *S* 78-79; V Sherburn in Elmet *York* 79-91; P-in-c Kirk Fenton 84-85; V Thornthwaite cum Braithwaite and Newlands *Carl* from 91. *Thornthwaite Vicarage, Braithwaite, Keswick, Cumbria CA12 5RY* Braithwaite (07687) 78243

POST, Oswald Julian. b 48. Derby Lonsdale Coll BEd79. E Midl Min Tr Course. **d** 84 **p** 85. Travelling Sec Rwanda Miss 79-89; Hon C Hulland, Atlow, Bradley and Hognaston *Derby* 84-89; V Wormhill, Peak Forest w Peak Dale and Dove Holes from 89. *The Parsonage, The Hallsteads, Dove Holes, Buxton, Derbyshire SK17 8BJ* Chapel-en-le-Frith (0298) 813344

POSTILL, John Edward. b 35. Oak Hill Th Coll 64. **d** 67 **p** 68. C Southgate *Chich* 67-70; C Bowling St Jo *Bradf* 70-74; TV Winfarthing w Shelfanger *Nor* 74-79; R Slaugham *Chich* from 79. *The Rectory, Handcross, Haywards Heath, W Sussex RH17 6BU* Handcross (0444) 400221

POSTILL, Richard Halliday. b 37. Hull Univ BSc59. Westcott Ho Cam 66. **d** 68 **p** 69. C Wylde Green *Birm* 68-72; C Kingswinford St Mary *Lich* 72-76; V Yardley Wood *Birm* 76-86; V Acocks Green from 86. *34 Dudley Park Road, Acocks Green, Birmingham B27 6QR* 021-706 9764

POSTLES, Donald. b 29. MPS51 Birm Univ DipTh59 MA65. Qu Coll Birm 56. **d** 59 **p** 60. C Southport H Trin *Liv* 59-62; C Prescot 62-63; V Wigan St Steph 63-71; V Farnworth 71-84; V Mossley Hill St Barn from 84. *St Barnabas's Vicarage, Carsdale Road, Mossley Hill, Liverpool L18 1LZ* 051-733 1432

POSTLETHWAITE, Alan James. b 38. Dur Univ BA60. Linc Th Coll 60. **d** 62 **p** 63. C Cottingham *York* 62-65; C Cockermouth All SS w Ch Ch *Carl* 65-68; V Seascale 68-77; P-in-c Irton w Drigg 75-77; P-in-c Whitehaven Ch Ch w H Trin 77; V Whitehaven 77-84; TR Kidderminster St Mary and All SS etc *Worc* 84-90; P-in-c Upper Arley 86-90; TR Kidderminster St Mary and All SS w Trimpley etc from 90; RD Kidderminster from 91. *The Vicarage, 22 Roden Avenue, Kidderminster, Worcs DY10 2RF* Kidderminster (0562) 823265

POSTON, Robert Charles. b 12. St Edm Hall Ox BA36 MA59. Bps' Coll Cheshunt 35. **d** 37 **p** 38. Hon CF from 46; V Westcliff St Andr *Chelmsf* 61-73; rtd 73; Perm to Offic Ely and Chelmsf from 73. *The Old School Cottage, Stoke by Nayland, Colchester CO6 4QY* Colchester (0206) 263651

POTHEN, Simon John. b 60. Westmr Coll Ox BA86. Ripon Coll Cuddesdon 86. **d** 88 **p** 89. C Southgate Ch Ch *Lon* 88-91; C Tottenham St Mary from 91. *The Mission House, Mitchley Road, London N17*

POTIPHER, John Malcolm Barry. b 42. St Alb Minl Tr Scheme 79. **d** 82 **p** 83. Chapl Herts Fire Brigade from 82; NSM Chambersbury (Hemel Hempstead) *St Alb* 82-84; NSM Hemel Hempstead 84-86; NSM Digswell and Panshanger from 86. *6 Pentley Close, Welwyn Garden City, Herts AL8 7SH* Welwyn Garden (0707) 320681

POTT, Canon Roger Percivall. b 09. K Coll Lon. St Steph Ho Ox. **d** 33 **p** 34. V Heacham *Nor* 45-84; R Ingoldisthorpe 46-81; Hon Can Nor Cathl from 81; rtd 84. *7 Peddars Way, Ringstead, Hunstanton, Norfolk PE36 5LF* Holme (048525) 356

POTTER, Charles Elmer. b 42. Georgetown Univ (USA) BS65 Valparaiso Univ JD73. Wycliffe Coll Toronto MDiv81. **d** 81 **p** 82. C Southport Ch Ch *Liv* 81-84; Chapl Lee Abbey 84-87; Australia from 87. *27 Pascoe Street, Westmeadows, Victoria, Australia 3049* Melbourne (3) 309-5061

POTTER, Colin Michael. b 53. Lanc Univ BA74 Birm Univ DipTh82. Qu Coll Birm 80. **d** 83 **p** 84. C Middlewich w Byley *Ches* 83-87; TV Ches Team from 87. *St Thomas of Canterbury Vicarage, 33 Abbott's Grange, Liverpool Road, Chester CH2 1AJ* Chester (0244) 371612

POTTER, Frank Higton. b 23. CEng MICE55 FIWSc70 Man Univ BScTech49 AMCT49. Sarum & Wells Th Coll 88. **d** 89 **p** 90. Lic to Offic *St E* from 89. *Iceni, Workhouse Green, Upper Road, Little Cornard, Sudbury, Suffolk CO10 0NZ* Bures (0787) 228158

POTTER, George Koszelski St John. b 22. ARCM45 Em Coll Cam BA43 MA47 St Cath Coll Ox DipTh53. Wycliffe Hall Ox 51. **d** 53 **p** 54. Hd of RE Harris C of E High Sch Rugby 68-76; Hd of RE Rock Valley Sch Rochdale 76-77; V Langcliffe w Stainforth *Bradf* 77-84; P-in-c Horton-in-Ribblesdale 80-84; V Langcliffe w Stainforth and Horton 85-87; rtd 87. *Bridge Cottage, Clapham, Lancaster LA2 8DP* Clapham (04685) 628

POTTER, Guy Anthony. b 18. St Jo Coll Cam BA40 MA44. Cuddesdon Coll 40. **d** 41 **p** 42. R Heene *Chich* 65-75; R Black Notley *Chelmsf* 75-83; rtd 83; Perm to Offic *Cov* from 83. *4 Manor Court Avenue Road, Leamington Spa, Warks CV31 3NL* Leamington Spa (0926) 35236

POTTER, Harry Drummond. b 54. Em Coll Cam BA76 MA79 MPhil81. Westcott Ho Cam 79. **d** 81 **p** 82. C Deptford St Paul *S'wark* 81-84; Chapl Selw Coll Cam 84-87; Newnham Coll Cam 84-87; Chapl HM Pris Wormwood Scrubs 87-88; Chapl HM Young Offender Inst Aylesbury from 88. *HM Young Offender Institute, Bierton Road, Aylesbury, Bucks HP20 1EH* Aylesbury (0296) 24435

POTTER, James David. b 35. AKC66. **d** 67 **p** 68. C Longbridge *Birm* 67-70; Lic to Offic 71-73; V N Harborne 73-78; V Smethwick H Trin w St Alb 78-83; V Blurton *Lich* 83-90; V Dordon *Birm* from 90. *St Leonard's Vicarage, Dordon, Tamworth, Staffs B78 1TE* Tamworth (0827) 892294

POTTER, John Ellis. b 45. Sarum & Wells Th Coll 82. **d** 84 **p** 85. C Wootton Bassett *Sarum* 84-88; TV Swindon New Town *Bris* from 88. *St Luke's House, 135 County Road, Swindon SN1 2EB* Swindon (0793) 36679

POTTER, Canon John Henry. b 26. Lon Univ BA50. Oak Hill Th Coll 50. **d** 52 **p** 53. P-in-c Ilfracombe SS Phil and Jas *Ex* 69-72; V 72-76; R Poole *Sarum* 76-87; RD Poole 80-85; Can and Preb Sarum Cathl from 83; P-in-c Charmouth and Catherston Leweston 87-91; rtd 91. *3 Millhams Close, Bournemouth BH10 7LW* Bournemouth (0202) 580269

POTTER, John Michael. b 28. ALCD56. **d** 56 **p** 57. C Addiscombe St Mary *Cant* 56-60; V Kettlewell w Conistone *Bradf* 60-79; P-in-c Arncliffe w Halton Gill 75-78; P-in-c Hubberholme 78-79; V Kettlewell w Conistone and Hubberholme 79-82; R Somersham w Flowton and Offton w Willisham *St E* from 82. *The Rectory, Somersham, Ipswich IP8 4PJ* Ipswich (0473) 831274

POTTER, Keith (Clement). b 39. Leeds Univ CSocStuds78 Bradf Univ MA81. Chich Th Coll 62. **d** 64 **p** 65. C Doncaster Ch Ch *Sheff* 64-68; C Tong *Bradf* 68-70; V Bradf St Columba w St Andr 70-79; V Yeadon St Andr from 79. *St Andrew's Vicarage, Haw Lane, Yeadon, Leeds LS19 7XQ* Leeds (0532) 503989

POTTER, Kenneth Benjamin. Lon Univ BA. NE Ord Course. **d** 87 **p** 88. NSM Ryton w Hedgefield *Dur* from 87. *Ellesmere, Peth Lane, Ryton, Tyne & Wear NE40 3PB*

POTTER, Malcolm Emmerson. b 48. Bedf Coll Lon BSc70. St Jo Coll Nottm DPS75. **d** 75 **p** 76. C Upton (or Overchurch) *Ches* 76-78; CPAS Staff 78-84; Development Officer St Jo Coll Nottm 84-86; P-in-c Wellington, All SS w Eyton *Lich* from 86. *All Saints' Vicarage, 35 Crescent Road, Wellington, Telford, Shropshire TF1 3DW* Telford (0952) 641251

POTTER, Peter Maxwell. b 46. Univ of Wales (Swansea) BA69 Univ of BC MA71. Sarum & Wells Th Coll 83. **d** 85 **p** 86. C Bradford-on-Avon *Sarum* 85-88; C Harnham 88-91; P-in-c N Bradley, Southwick and Heywood from 91. *The Vicarage, 62 Church Lane, North Bradley,* *Trowbridge, Wilts BA14 0TA* Trowbridge (0225) 752635

POTTER, Phillip. b 54. Stirling Univ BA75. Trin Coll Bris 82. **d** 84 **p** 85. C Yateley *Win* 84-88; V Haydock St Mark *Liv* from 88. *St Mark's Vicarage, 2 Stanley Bank Road, Haydock, Merseyside WA11 0UL* St Helens (0744) 23957

POTTER, Richard Antony. b 36. K Coll Cam BA60 MA64. Ridley Hall Cam 60. **d** 62 **p** 63. C Luton w E Hyde *St Alb* 62-72; V Lyonsdown H Trin 72-85; R Broxbourne w Wormley from 85. *The Vicarage, Churchfields, Broxbourne, Herts EN10 7AU* Hoddesdon (0992) 462382

POTTER, Timothy John. b 49. Bris Univ BSc71. Oak Hill Th Coll 73. **d** 76 **p** 77. C Wallington H Trin *S'wark* 76-79; C Hampreston *Sarum* 79-81; TV Stratton St Margaret w S Marston etc *Bris* 81-87; P-in-c Hatf Heath *Chelmsf* 87-89; P-in-c Sheering 87-89; R Hatf Heath and Sheering from 90. *The Vicarage, Broomfields, Hatfield Heath, Bishop's Stortford CM22 7EA* Bishop's Stortford (0279) 730288

POTTIER, Ronald William. b 36. S'wark Ord Course 73. **d** 76 **p** 77. NSM Lower Sydenham St Mich *S'wark* from 76. *12 Neiderwald Road, London SE26 4AD* 081-699 4375

POTTS, Henry Arthur. b 16. Trin Coll Cam BA48. St Steph Ho Ox 48. **d** 50 **p** 50. Chapl Dr Kerin Trust Burrswood 69-74; P-in-c Bris St Jas w St Pet *Bris* 74-77; R Balsham *Ely* 77-85; P-in-c Horseheath 84-85; P-in-c W Wickham 84-85; rtd 85; Perm to Offic *Chich* from 86. *4 Friars Road, Winchelsea, E Sussex TN36 4ED* Rye (0797) 223050

POTTS, Canon Hugh Cuthbert Miller. b 07. Linc Coll Ox BA29 MA41. St Steph Ho Ox 37. **d** 37 **p** 38. V Glouc St Cath *Glouc* 61-80; Hon Can Glouc Cathl from 69; rtd 80. *5 Hilton Close, Hempsted, Gloucester GL2 6LQ* Gloucester (0452) 305188

POTTS, James. b 30. K Coll Lon BD56 AKC56. **d** 57 **p** 58. C Brighouse *Wakef* 57-59; Tanganyika 59-64; Tanzania 64-71; C-in-c Athersley and New Lodge CD *Wakef* 71-73; V Athersley 73-77; V Madeley *Lich* 77-85; V Baswich (or Berkswich) from 85; RD Stafford from 88. *The Vicarage, 97 Baswich Lane, Stafford ST17 0BN* Stafford (0785) 51057

POTTS, Wilfrid Mark Allinson. b 11. Ch Ch Ox BA33 MA37. Cuddesdon Coll 34. **d** 36 **p** 37. V Carisbrooke St Mary *Portsm* 64-81; V Carisbrooke St Nic 64-81; rtd 81; Hon Chapl Win Cathl *Win* from 81; Perm to Offic from 81. *10 Sparkford Close, Winchester, Hants SO22 4NH* Winchester (0962) 866056

POTTS, William Gilbert. b 17. Bps' Coll Cheshunt 46. **d** 49 **p** 50. V Winshill *Derby* 64-82; rtd 82; Perm to Offic *Derby* from 82. *28 Roydon Close, Mickleover, Derby DE3 5PN* Derby (0332) 516328

POULARD, Christopher. b 39. FCA. Ridley Hall Cam 82. **d** 84 **p** 85. C N Walsham w Antingham *Nor* 84-86; C Oulton Broad 86-90; TV Raveningham from 90. *The Rectory, Rectory Road, Haddiscoe, Norwich NR14 6PG* Aldeby (050277) 774

POULTER, Alan John. b 39. St Aid Birkenhead 64. **d** 67 **p** 68. C Heswall *Ches* 67-72; V Bredbury St Mark 72-78; V Oxton from 78. *8 Wexford Road, Oxton, Birkenhead, Merseyside L43 9TB* 051-652 1194

POULTER, Joseph William. b 40. Dur Univ BA61 BA66 DipTh67. Cranmer Hall Dur 66. **d** 67 **p** 68. C Harlow New Town w Lt Parndon *Chelmsf* 67-71; C Washington *Dur* 71-77; Producer Metro Radio from 75; C-in-c Town End Farm CD 77-83; V Sunderland Town End Farm from 83. *Town End Farm House, Bootle Street, Sunderland SR5 4EY* 091-536 3823

POULTNEY, Wilfred Howard. b 25. Qu Coll Birm 71. **d** 73 **p** 74. NSM S Leamington St Jo *Cov* 73-85; NSM Holbrooks from 85. *25 Deerhurst Road, Coventry CV6 4EJ* Coventry (0203) 687192

POULTON, Arthur Leslie. b 28. K Coll Lon BA53 AKC53 BD60 Leic Univ MA85. Tyndale Hall Bris 53. **d** 55 **p** 56. C New Catton St Luke *Nor* 55-56; C Earlham St Anne 56-58; C Chorleywood Ch Ch *St Alb* 58-61; R E Barnet 61-64; Ches Coll of FE 64-87; Chapl 64-84; Sen Lect 66-87; P-in-c Gt Canfield *Chelmsf* from 87; Dir of Studies Course in Chr Studies from 87. *The Rectory, Great Canfield, Dunmow, Essex CM6 1JX* Bishop's Stortford (0279) 871300

POULTON, Ian Peter. b 60. Lon Univ BSc(Econ)83 TCD DipTh86. **d** 86 **p** 87. C Newtownards *D & D* 86-89; I Bright w Ballee and Killough from 89; Relig Adv Downtown Commercial Radio from 91. *Bright Rectory, 126 Killough Road, Downpatrick, Co Down BT30 8LL* Ardglass (0396) 842041

POULTON, Katharine Margaret. b 61. Man Univ BA83 TCD DipTh87. d 87. C Ban St Comgall *D & D* from 87. *Bright Rectory, 126 Killough Road, Downpatrick, Co Down BT30 8LL* Ardglass (0396) 842041

POUNCE, Alan Gerald. b 34. Lon Univ BSc55. Wycliffe Hall Ox 57. d 59 p 60. C Wednesfield Heath *Lich* 59-61; C Heref St Pet w St Owen *Heref* 61-63; R Gt w Lt Dunham *Nor* 63-69; Perm to Offic *Ox* from 69. *38 Longdown Road, Little Sandhurst, Camberley, Surrey GU17 8QG* Crowthorne (0344) 772870

POUNCEY, Canon Cosmo Gabriel Rivers. b 11. Qu Coll Cam BA32 MA36. Cuddesdon Coll 33. d 34 p 35. V Tewkesbury w Walton Cardiff *Glouc* 63-81; P-in-c Tredington w Stoke Orchard and Hardwicke 63-81; RD Tewkesbury 68-81; Hon Can Glouc Cathl 72-81; P-in-c Deerhurst w Apperley 74-80; rtd 81; Perm to Offic *Worc* from 81. *Gannicox, Birlingham, Pershore, Worcs WR10 3AB* Evesham (0386) 750720

POUNCY, Anthony Grenville. b 14. Qu Coll Cam BA37 MA41. Tyndale Hall Bris 37. d 38 p 39. V Woking St Pet *Guildf* 67-79; rtd 79; Perm to Offic *Portsm* from 81. *11 Amersham Court, Craneswater Park, Southsea, Hants PO4 0NX* Portsmouth (0705) 733302

POUND, Ven Keith Salisbury. b 33. St Cath Coll Cam BA54 MA58. Cuddesdon Coll. d 57 p 58. C St Helier *S'wark* 57-61; Tr Officer Hollowford Tr & Conf Cen Sheff 61-64; Warden 64-67; V S'wark H Trin 68-74; P-in-c Newington St Matt 68-74; V S'wark H Trin w St Matt 74-78; RD S'wark and Newington 73-78; TR Thamesmead 78-86; Sub-Dean of Woolwich 84-86; Hon Can S'wark Cathl from 85; RD Greenwich 85-86; Chapl Gen of Pris from 86; Chapl to HM The Queen from 88. *c/o HM Prison Service Chaplaincy, Home Office, Cleland House, Page Street, London SW1P 4LN* 071-217 6266

POUNDE, Nigel. b 46. Edin Univ MA69. Cranmer Hall Dur DipTh71. d 72 p 73. C Southsea St Simon *Portsm* 72-75; C Clayton w Keymer *Chich* 75-79; Malaysia 80-86; TV Wolv *Lich* from 87. *St Chad's Vicarage, Manlove Street, Wolverhampton WV3 0HG* Wolverhampton (0902) 26580

POUNTAIN, Eric Gordon. b 24. Sarum Th Coll 65. d 66 p 67. C New Bury *Man* 66-76; Lic to Offic *Blackb* 76-80; Chapl Lancs (Preston) Poly 80-81; P-in-c Preston St Mark 80-81; V Salesbury 81-86; rtd 86. *116 Harewood Road, Rishton, Blackburn BB1 4DZ* Blackburn (0254) 888091

POVALL, Charles Herbert. b 18. Man Univ MEd71. St Deiniol's Hawarden 75. d 76 p 77. C Norbury *Ches* 76-83; rtd 83; Perm to Offic *Ches* from 83. *3 Magda Road, Stockport, Cheshire SK2 7LX* 061-483 6713

POVEY, John Michael. b 44. St Jo Coll Nottm BTh76. d 76 p 77. USA from 76. *67 East, Pittsfield, Massachusetts 01201, USA*

POVEY, Kenneth Vincent. b 40. AKC62. d 63 p 64. C Crewe Ch Ch *Ches* 63-66; C Neston 66-69; C Kensington St Mary Abbots w St Geo *Lon* 69-72; R Ches H Trin *Ches* 72-81; Chapl Copenhagen w Aarhus *Eur* 81-86; R Gawsworth *Ches* from 86. *The Rectory, Gawsworth, Macclesfield, Cheshire SK11 9RJ* North Rode (0260) 223201

POW, Miss Joyce. b 29. RGN55 SCM57 RSCN60 RNT73. St Jo Coll Nottm. d 88. Hon Par Dn Largs *Glas* from 88. *15 Shuma Court, Skelmorlie, Ayrshire PA17 5EJ* Wemyss Bay (0475) 520289

POWDRILL, Wilfred Roy. b 23. St Aid Birkenhead 54. d 56 p 57. R Anstey *Leic* 69-75; V Glen Parva and S Wigston 75-81; rtd 81. *19 Capel Court, The Burgage, Prestbury, Cheltenham, Glos GL52 3EL* Cheltenham (0242) 568265

POWE, David James Hector. b 50. Brighton Poly CertMS86. Wycliffe Hall Ox 88. d 90 p 91. C Ventnor St Cath *Portsm* from 90. *74 Upper Gills Cliff Road, Ventnor, Isle of Wight PO38 1AD* Isle of Wight (0983) 58570

POWE, Eric James. b 23. Univ of Wales (Lamp) BA50 BD61. St Steph Ho Ox 50. d 52 p 53. C Ramsgate H Trin *Cant* 52-54; C Buckland in Dover 54-57; CF 57-73; R Broadstairs *Cant* from 73. *The Rectory, Nelson Place, Broadstairs, Kent CT10 1HQ* Thanet (0843) 62921

POWE, Roger Wayne. b 46. Lon Univ BEd70 MA78. S'wark Ord Course 73. d 76 p 77. NSM Surbiton St Andr S'wark 76-77; NSM Surbiton St Andr and St Mark 77-79; Asst Chapl Giggleswick Sch N Yorkshire 79-80; C St Marylebone All SS *Lon* 80-81; Asst Chapl Hurstpierpoint Coll Hassocks from 81. *Hurstpierpoint College, Hassocks, W Sussex* Hurstpierpoint (0273) 833636

POWELL, Anthony James. b 51. Sarum & Wells Th Coll 78. d 79 p 80. C Larkfield *Roch* 79-83; C Leybourne 79-83; V Boro Green from 83. *The Vicarage, 24 Maidstone Road, Borough Green, Sevenoaks, Kent TN15 8BD* Borough Green (0732) 882447

POWELL, Colin Arthur. b 32. Hatf Coll Dur BA53. Oak Hill Th Coll 56. d 58 p 59. C Leyland St Andr *Blackb* 58-61; C Lanc St Thos 61-64; C Tranmere St Cath *Ches* 64-65; R Cheetham Hill *Man* 65-81; TV Oldham 81-86; TV Rochdale from 86. *Good Shepherd Vicarage, 160 Entwisle Road, Rochdale OL16 2JJ* Rochdale (0706) 40130

POWELL, Mrs Diane. b 41. Ex Univ. SW Minl Tr Course 85. d 88. Hon C St Merryn *Truro* from 88. *Tredower, St Merryn, Padstow, Cornwall PL28 8PR* Padstow (0841) 520345

POWELL, Douglas Louis. b 16. Hertf Coll Ox BA38 BTh40 MA56. St Steph Ho Ox 39. d 41 p 42. Sen Lect Th Ex Univ 67-81; rtd 81. *94 Union Road, Exeter EX4 6HT* Exeter (0392) 73654

POWELL, Dudley John. b 44. Tyndale Hall Bris 65. d 69 p 70. C Blackb Sav *Blackb* 69-71; C Rodbourne Cheney *Bris* 71-74; P-in-c Kingsdown 74-79; V 79-80; V Stoke Gifford 80-90; TR from 90. *The Vicarage, Stoke Gifford, Bristol BS12 6PB* Bristol (0272) 692486

POWELL, Canon Edward. b 07. d 30 p 31. R Belchamp St Paul *Chelmsf* 42-88; R Ovington w Tilbury 43-88; RD Belchamp 48-74; Hon Can Chelmsf Cathl 80-88; rtd 88. *The Granary, Deepdale, Potton, Sandy, Beds SG19 2NH* Potton (0767) 261449

POWELL, Eleanor Ann. b 55. Gwent Coll Newport CertEd76 Univ of Wales BA82. Qu Coll Birm 82. d 83. C Caereithin *S & B* 83-86; C Bishopston 86-88; Dioc Children's Officer *Glouc* from 88. *8 Kevin Close, Barnwood, Gloucester GL4 7JA* Gloucester (0452) 614304

POWELL, Francis David Claude. b 09. Leeds Univ BA31. Coll of Resurr Mirfield 31. d 33 p 34. V Hammersmith St Matt *Lon* 70-75; rtd 75; Perm to Offic Ox and St Alb from 75. *St Martha's Lodge, Park Road, Tring, Herts HP23 6BP* Tring (044282) 3041

POWELL, Preb Frank. b 29. AKC52. d 53 p 54. C Stockingford *Cov* 53-56; C Netherton St Andr *Worc* 56-60; P-in-c W Bromwich St Jo *Lich* 60-66; C W Bromwich Gd Shep w St Jo 60-66; V 66-69; V Bilston St Leon 69-76; P-in-c Hanbury 76-82; V Hanbury w Newborough 83-86; V Basford from 86; Preb Lich Cathl from 87. *211 Basford Park Road, Basford, Newcastle, Staffs ST5 0PG* Newcastle-under-Lyme (0782) 619045

POWELL, Geoffrey Peter. b 25. Chich Th Coll 54. d 56 p 57. V Wanborough *Bris* 62-75; R Lyddington w Wanborough 75-80; V St Cleer *Truro* 80-90; rtd 91. *The Old Bakery, Oare, Marlborough, Wilts SN8 4JQ* Marlborough (0672) 62627

POWELL, John. b 44. St Luke's Coll Ex CertEd66. Glouc Sch of Min 81. d 84 p 85. NSM Stroud and Uplands w Slad *Glouc* 84-89; Chapl Eliz Coll Guernsey from 89. *c/o Elizabeth College, Guernsey, Channel Islands* Guernsey (0481) 726544

POWELL, John Hughes. b 28. Univ of Wales (Cardiff) BSc48. Llan Dioc Tr Scheme 76. d 80 p 81. NSM Llanfabon *Llan* from 80. *Cartref, 64 High Street, Nelson, Treharris, M Glam CF46 6HA* Nelson (0443) 450454

POWELL, John Reginald. b 36. Nottm Univ BA59 PGCE71 St Cath Coll Ox DipPSA60. Ripon Hall Ox 59. d 61 p 62. C Thornhill *Wakef* 61-64; C Hebden Bridge 61-64; P-in-c Halifax St Aug 64-67; Hon C Lanc Ch Ch *Blackb* 67-69; V Holland Fen *Linc* 69-73; Perm to Offic *York* 73-84; Chapl K Sch Ely 77-84; V Skerton St Chad *Blackb* 84-89; V Ashton-on-Ribble St Andr from 89. *240 Tulketh Road, Ashton-on-Ribble, Preston, Lancs PR2 1ES* Preston (0772) 726848

POWELL, Miss Katherine. b 56. Sydney Univ BSocStuds79. Wycliffe Hall Ox 84. dss 86 d 87. Broadwater St Mary *Chich* 86-87; Par Dn 87-91; Asst Chapl Ch Hosp Horsham from 91. *1 Garden Cottages, Christ's Hospital, Horsham, W Sussex RH13 7NG* Horsham (0403) 54538

POWELL, Kelvin. b 49. Wycliffe Hall Ox 71. d 74 p 75. C Prescot *Liv* 74-77; C Ainsdale 77-79; V Bickershaw 79-85; R Hesketh w Becconsall *Blackb* from 85. *All Saints' Rectory, Silverdale, Hesketh Bank, Preston, Lancs PR4 6RZ* Preston (0772) 814798

POWELL, Llewellyn. b 28. Glouc Th Course 67. d 70 p 71. C Quinton *Glouc* 70-73; P-in-c 74-76; V Church Honeybourne w Cow Honeybourne 76-83; R Pebworth w Dorsington and Honeybourne 83-87; rtd 87. *Bodathro Bungalow, Llangynin, St Clears, Carmarthen, Dyfed SA33 4LD* Llanboidy (0994) 448301

POWELL, Mark. b 57. Bath Univ BSc78 PhD81. Ripon Coll Cuddesdon BA84 MA88. **d** 85 **p** 86. C Evesham *Worc* 85-88; V Exhall *Cov* from 88. *Exhall Vicarage, Ash Green, Coventry CV7 9AA* Coventry (0203) 362997
POWELL, Ralph Dover. b 49. ARMCM70. Chich Th Coll 71. **d** 74 **p** 75. C Coppenhall *Ches* 74-77; C Heref H Trin *Heref* 77-80; V Crewe St Barn *Ches* from 80. *St Barnabas' Vicarage, West Street, Crewe, Cheshire CW1 3AX* Crewe (0270) 212418
POWELL, Raymond Leslie. b 35. AKC61. **d** 62 **p** 63. C Hendon St Mary *Lon* 62-67; C Huntingdon All SS w St Jo *Ely* 67-75; V Huntingdon St Barn 75-79; P-in-c Sawston 79-81; V from 81; P-in-c Babraham from 85; RD Shelford from 89. *The Vicarage, Church Lane, Sawston, Cambridge CB2 4JR* Cambridge (0223) 832248
POWELL, Richard Michael Wheler. b 19. St Edm Hall Ox BA45. Wells Th Coll 47. **d** 49 **p** 50. R Tarporley *Ches* 62-72, P-in-c Lt Budworth 69-70; R Overton w Laverstoke and Freefolk *Win* 73-81; P-in-c Damerham *Sarum* 81-84; P-in-c Martin 81-84; rtd 84; Perm to Offic *B & W* from 85. *2 The Lynch, Mere, Warminster, Wilts BA12 6DQ* Mere (0747) 860798
POWELL, Richard Penry. b 15. Dur Univ LTh38. St Aid Birkenhead 34. **d** 38 **p** 39. V Wrockwardine *Lich* 64-80; V Uppington 64-80; rtd 80; Perm to Offic *Lich* from 80. *34 Herbert Avenue, Wellington, Telford, Shropshire TF1 2BS* Telford (0952) 242528
POWELL, Samuel John. b 21. Qu Coll Ox BA53 MA57. **d** 47 **p** 48. Lic to Offic *Ox* 47-53 and 56-58; C Pontnewynydd *Mon* 53-55; C Ashchurch *Glouc* 55-56; Brazil from 58. *Caixa Postal 161, Campos do Jordao, Sao Paulo, Brazil*
POWELL, Stuart William. b 58. K Coll Lon BD80 AKC80. Ripon Coll Cuddesdon 86. **d** 88 **p** 89. C Horden *Dur* 88-90; C Northolt Park St Barn *Lon* from 90. *3 Vernon Rise, Greenford, Middx UB6 0EQ* 081-422 6989
POWELL, William Michael. b 33. Bps' Coll Cheshunt 58. **d** 61 **p** 62. C Golders Green St Mich *Lon* 61-64; C Hatcham St Cath *S'wark* 64-67; C Woodham *Guildf* 67-72; V Guildf All SS 72-84; RD Guildf 78-84; TR Headley All SS 84-89; V Addlestone from 89. *The Vicarage, 140 Church Road, Addlestone, Weybridge, Surrey KT15 1SJ* Weybridge (0932) 842879
POWER, Alan Edward. b 26. Worc Coll Ox BA50 MA53. Lich Th Coll. **d** 57 **p** 58. C Summerfield *Birm* 57-60; C Oldbury 60-63; V Short Heath from 63. *St Margaret's Vicarage, Somerset Road, Birmingham B23 6NQ* 021-373 6989
POWER, David Michael. b 56. BA81 BEd. Oak Hill Th Coll. **d** 81 **p** 82. C Warblington and Emsworth *Portsm* 81-84; C-in-c Hartplain CD 84-88; V Hartplain from 88. *61 Hartplain Avenue, Cowplain, Portsmouth PO8 8RG* Waterlooville (0705) 264551
POWER, Canon Ivor Jonathan. b 43. Lambeth STh87 CITC 66. **d** 69 **p** 70. C Dromore Cathl *D & D* 69-71; C Enniscorthy *C & O* 71-74; I Youghal *C, C & R* 74-78; I Youghal Union 78-81; I Athlone w Benown, Kiltoom and Forgney *M & K* from 81; RD Clonmacnoise from 86; Can Meath from 87; Dir of Ords (Meath) from 91. *The Rectory, Bonavalley, Athlone, Co Westmeath, Irish Republic* Athlone (902) 78350
POWER, James Edward. b 58. Nottm Univ BSc81 Leeds Univ BA85. Coll of Resurr Mirfield 83. **d** 86 **p** 87. C Cadoxton-juxta-Barry *Llan* 86-89; Chapl Harrow Sch Middx from 89. *16 Crown Street, Harrow, Middx HA2 0HR* 081-869 1234
POWER, Mrs Jeanette. b 57. Oak Hill Th Coll BA82. dss 82 **d** 87. Warblington and Emsworth *Portsm* 82-84; Hartplain CD 84-87; Hon C Hartplain from 87. *61 Hartplain Avenue, Cowplain, Portsmouth PO8 8RG* Waterlooville (0705) 264551
POWER, Canon Norman Sandiford. b 16. Worc Coll Ox BA38 MA42. Ripon Hall Ox 38. **d** 40 **p** 41. V Birm St Jo Ladywood *Birm* 52-88; Hon Can Birm Cathl from 65; rtd 89. *28 Park Hill Road, Birmingham B17* 021-427 2626
POWLES, Charles Anthony. b 39. E Anglian Minl Tr Course. **d** 88 **p** 89. Hon C Hemsby *Nor* from 88. *Mairin, Ormesby Road, Hemsby, Great Yarmouth, Norfolk NR29 4LA* Great Yarmouth (0493) 732493
POWLES, Michael Charles. b 34. Reading Univ BSc56. Qu Coll Birm DipTh60. **d** 60 **p** 61. C Goodmayes All SS *Chelmsf* 60-65; C Surbiton St Matt *S'wark* 65-78; Lic to Offic from 79. *Spring Cottage, 3 Rushett Close, Long Ditton, Surrey KT7 0UR* 081-398 9654
POWLEY, Robert Mallinson. b 39. Fitzw Coll Cam MA65 DPS68 DipSocWork69. Ridley Hall Cam 61. **d** 63 **p** 64. C Bermondsey St Mary w St Olave, St Jo etc

S'wark 63-67; C Moseley St Anne *Birm* 67-69; Lic to Offic *Man* 72-77; Hon C Walshaw Ch Ch 77-88; V Prestwich St Gabr from 88; Bp's Dom Chapl from 88. *St Gabriel's Vicarage, 8 Bishops Road, Prestwich, Manchester M25 8HT* 061-773 8839
POWNALL, Canon Tom Basil. b 19. Jes Coll Cam BA41 MA44. Ridley Hall Cam 41. **d** 42 **p** 43. Warden Mabledon Conf Cen Tonbridge 68-74; P-in-c Fressingfield w Weybread *St E* 74-79; P-in-c Wingfield w Syleham 76-79; P-in-c Fressingfield w Weybread and Wingfield 79-86; RD Hoxne 81-86; Hon Can St E Cathl 83-86; RD Hartismere 84-85; rtd 86; Perm to Offic Roch and Cant from 86. *2 Abingdon Road, Maidstone, Kent ME16 9DP* Maidstone (0622) 720572
POWNE, Peter Rebbeck Lamb. b 23. Sarum & Wells Th Coll 80. **d** 83 **p** 84. C Calne and Blackland *Sarum* 83-86; V Netheravon w Fittleton and Enford from 86. *The Vicarage, Netheravon, Salisbury SP4 9QP* Stonehenge (0980) 70353
POWYS, Edward Lionel Garrod. b 07. St Edm Hall Ox BA29 MA33. Wycliffe Hall Ox 29. **d** 31 **p** 32. V Lt Eaton *Derby* 55-73; rtd 73; P-in-c Mydroilyn St Dav 80-84. *16 Mentone Crescent, Edgmond, Newport, Shropshire TF10 8HR* Newport (0952) 810961
POYNER, Maurice John. b 20. St Deiniol's Hawarden. **d** 83 **p** 84. Hon C Humberstone *Leic* 83-90; Perm to Offic from 90. *127 Colchester Road, Leicester LE5 2DJ* Leicester (0533) 768372
POYNTING, Charles Robert Macvicar. b 23. Hertf Coll Ox BA48 MA48. Wells Th Coll 48. **d** 50 **p** 51. C Gt Bookham *Guildf* 50-52; C Epsom Common Ch 52-55; V Ashton H Trin *Man* 55-62; V Belfield 62-82; V Digby *Linc* from 82. *The Vicarage, Digby, Lincoln LN4 3NE* Metheringham (0526) 20235
✠**POYNTZ, Rt Rev Samuel Greenfield.** b 26. TCD BA48 MA51 BD53 PhD60. CITC 50. **d** 50 **p** 51 **c** 78. C Dub St Geo *D & G* 50-52; C Bray 52-55; C Dub St Michan w St Paul 55-59; Sec and Sch Insp Ch Educn Soc for Ireland 56-75; I Dub St Steph 59-78; I Dub St Ann 67-78; Adn Dub 74-78; Bp C, C & R 78-87; Bp Conn from 87. *Bishop's House, 22 Deramore Park, Belfast BT9 5JU* Belfast (0232) 668442
PRAGNELL, John William. b 39. Lon Univ BD65. Lambeth STh87 LTh88. **d** 65 **p** 66. C Bitterne *Win* 65-68; C Hatf Hyde St Mary *St Alb* 68-73; Kuwait 73-75; Chapl Leavesden Hosp and Abbots Langley Hosp 75-88; Watford Gen Hosp 86-88; V St Alb St Steph *St Alb* from 88; RD St Alb from 91. *St Stephen's Vicarage, 14 Watling Street, St Albans, Herts AL1 2PX* St Albans (0727) 862598
PRAGNELL, Michael John. b 40. CChem MRSC FIQA81 MSOSc88 MA PhD. Ox NSM Course 81. **d** 84 **p** 85. NSM High Wycombe *Ox* from 84. *28 Carver Hill Road, High Wycombe, Bucks HP11 2UA* High Wycombe (0494) 33056
PRAILL, David William. b 57. FRGS90 York Univ BA79. Cranmer Hall Dur 81. **d** 82 **p** 83. C Digswell and Panshanger *St Alb* 82-84; CMS 84-89; Course Dir St Geo Coll Jerusalem 85-89; Dir McCabe Educn Trust 90-91; Dir St Luke's Hospice Harrow and Wembley from 91. *1A St Ann's Crescent, London SW18 2ND* 081-870 3694
PRANCE, Frederick Charles Victor. b 15. St Aid Birkenhead 46. **d** 48 **p** 49. R Wickford *Chelmsf* 62-73; V Westcliff St Mich 73-82; rtd 82. *144 Station Road, Leigh-on-Sea, Essex SS9 3BW* Southend-on-Sea (0702) 712368
PRANCE, Robert Penrose. b 47. Southn Univ DipTh. Sarum & Wells Th Coll 69. **d** 72 **p** 73. C Gillingham and Fifehead Magdalen *Sarum* 72-76; P-in-c Edmondsham 76-80; P-in-c Woodlands 76-80; P-in-c Wimborne St Giles 76-80; P-in-c Cranborne 77-80; R Cranborne w Boveridge, Edmondsham etc 80-83; Chapl Sherborne Sch Dorset from 83. *Rosslyn House, Acreman Street, Sherborne, Dorset DT9 3NU* Sherborne (0935) 813846
PRASADAM, Goruganthula Samuel Narayanamurthy. b 34. Andhra Univ India BA57. Bangalore Th Coll BD65 Union Th Sem (NY) STM68. **d** 62 **p** 65. India 62-74; C Llanbeblig w Caernarfon and Betws Garmon etc *Ban* 75-76; C Norbury *Ches* 77-78; V Aberaman and Abercwmboi *Llan* 78-83; N Sec CMS 83-87; V Luton All SS w St Pet *St Alb* from 87. *All Saints' Vicarage, Shaftesbury Road, Luton LU4 8AH* Luton (0582) 20129
PRASADAM, Jemima. b 38. BD61 BA87. Cranmer Hall Dur 86. **d** 87. Par Dn Luton All SS w St Pet *St Alb* from 87; Miss Partner CMS from 87. *All Saints' Vicarage, Shaftesbury Road, Luton, Beds LU4 8AH* Luton (0582) 20129

PRATER, Raleigh Brandon. b 09. ALCD40. **d** 40 **p** 41. Chapl Harrow Hosp 64-75; V Roxeth Ch Ch *Lon* 64-75; rtd 75. *13 Shirley Gardens, Rusthall, Tunbridge Wells, Kent* Tunbridge Wells (0892) 21724

PRATT, Basil David. b 38. Ripon Hall Ox 64. **d** 67 **p** 68. C Lewisham St Jo Southend *S'wark* 67-68; C Caterham Valley 68-70; CF from 70. *c/o MOD (Army), Bagshot Park, Bagshot, Surrey GU19 5PL* Bagshot (0276) 71717

PRATT, Benjamin John. b 42. TCD BA63. Cuddesdon Coll 68. **d** 70 **p** 71. C Ballymoney *Conn* 70-72; C Monaghan *Clogh* 72-74; Ind Chapl Kirkby *Liv* 74-83. *Misty Heights, Garvary, Enniskillen, Co Fermanagh BT94 3BZ* Enniskillen (0365) 322603

PRATT, Canon David George. b 10. Jes Coll Ox BA34 MA38 BD50. St D Coll Lamp BA32. **d** 34 **p** 35. V Sandylands *Blackb* 53-80; Hon Can Blackb Cathl 71-81; rtd 81; Perm to Offic *Blackb* from 81. *30 Longlands Lane, Morecambe, Lancs LA3 2NS* Heysham (0524) 51363

PRATT, Edward Andrew. b 39. Clare Coll Cam BA61 MA65. Clifton Th Coll 63. **d** 66 **p** 67. C Southall Green St Jo *Lon* 66-69; C Drypool St Columba w St Andr and St Pet *York* 69-71; P-in-c Radbourne *Derby* 71-74; R Kirk Langley 71-78; V Mackworth All SS 71-78; V Southsea St Simon *Portsm* from 78. *St Simon's Vicarage, 6 Festing Road, Southsea, Hants PO4 0NG* Portsmouth (0705) 733068

PRATT, Eric. b 32. Open Univ BA83. Ridley Hall Cam. **d** 60 **p** 61. C Denton Holme *Carl* 60-63; C Cockermouth All SS w Ch Ch 63-65; C Bredbury St Mark *Ches* 66-69; V Eaton and Hulme Walfield 69-75; V Hollingworth from 75. *The Vicarage, Hollingworth, Hyde, Cheshire SK14 8HS* Mottram (0457) 62310

PRATT, Mrs Janet Margaret. b 40. Herts Coll BEd78. St Alb Minl Tr Scheme 78. **dss** 81 **d** 87. High Wych and Gilston w Eastwick *St Alb* 81-87; Hon Par Dn 87-89; Par Dn Histon *Ely* from 89; Par Dn Impington from 89. *The Vicarage, 60 Impington Lane, Impington, Cambridge CB4 4NJ* Cambridge (0223) 232826

PRATT, John Anthony. b 38. Selw Coll Cam BA61 MA65. Qu Coll Birm DipTh66. **d** 66 **p** 67. C Harrow Weald All SS *Lon* 66-69; C St Pancras w St Jas and Ch Ch 69-74; C Saffron Walden *Chelmsf* 74-75; TV Saffron Walden w Wendens Ambo and Littlebury 75-79; V St Mary-at-Latton 79-82; Chapl Princess Alexandra Hosp Harlow 82-88; RD Harlow *Chelmsf* 83-88; R Tolleshunt Knights w Tiptree and Gt Braxted from 88. *The Rectory, Rectory Road, Tiptree, Colchester CO5 0SX* Tiptree (0621) 815260

PRATT, Very Rev John Francis Isaac. b 13. Keble Coll Ox BA34 MA38. Wells Th Coll 34. **d** 36 **p** 37. Provost S'well 70-78; P-in-c Edingley w Halam 73-78; rtd 78; Perm to Offic Ox from 82; B & W from 83. *42 Bickerton Road, Oxford OX3 7LS* Oxford (0865) 63060

PRATT, Kenneth George. b 21. E Anglian Minl Tr Course 81. **d** 84 **p** 85. NSM March St Jo *Ely* 84-87; Chapl Doddington Hosp from 87; P-in-c Doddington w Benwick from 87. *The Rectory, Ingle's Lane, Doddington, March, Cambs PE15 0TE* March (0354) 740063

PRATT, Michael. b 34. MIL ACP. W Midl Minl Tr Course. **d** 83 **p** 84. NSM Bournville *Birm* 83-90; NSM Stirchley from 90. *3 Teazel Avenue, Bournville, Birmingham B30 1LZ* 021-459 5236

PRATT, Richard David. b 55. Linc Coll Ox BA77 MA81 Nottm Univ BCombStuds84. Linc Th Coll 81. **d** 84 **p** 85. C Wellingborough All Hallows *Pet* 84-87; TV Kingsthorpe w Northn St Dav from 87. *42 Fallow Walk, Northampton NN2 8DE* Northampton (0604) 846215

PRATT, Samuel Charles. b 40. Oak Hill Th Coll 69. **d** 71 **p** 72. C Upper Holloway St Jo *Lon* 71-73; C Bucknall and Bagnall *Lich* 73-76; V Liv St Mich *Liv* 76-80; Chapl Liv R Hosp from 80. *23 Caithness Road, Liverpool L8 9SJ* 051-427 4997

PRATT, Canon William Ralph. b 47. Keble Coll Ox BA69 MA73. Linc Th Coll 70. **d** 72 **p** 73. C Ifield *Chich* 72-78; TV 78; C Brighton St Pet w Chpl Royal 79-80; C Brighton St Pet w Chpl Royal and St Jo 80-83; P-in-c Hove St Jo 83-87; Dioc Communications Officer from 87; Can and Preb Chich Cathl from 90. *23 Wilbury Avenue, Hove, E Sussex BN3 6HS* Brighton (0273) 732267

PREBBLE, Ven Albert Ernest. b 08. Univ of NZ BA31 MA32 St Jo Coll Auckland 32. **d** 32 **p** 33. Perm to Offic *Pet* from 59; V Greenhill St Jo *Lon* 63-72; rtd 72. *23 Glebe Rise, Kings Sutton, Banbury, Oxon OX17 3PH* Banbury (0295) 811993

PREBBLE, Frederick John. b 25. Sarum Th Coll. **d** 56 **p** 57. V Saltley *Birm* 63-75; R Capel w Lt Wenham *St E*

75-80; rtd 80. *1B Chamberlin Road, Norwich NR3 3LZ* Norwich (0603) 402067

PRECIOUS, John Robert. b 08. St Aid Birkenhead 32. **d** 35 **p** 36. Miss to Seamen 39-73; rtd 73. *6 Parkside, Alexandra Road, Heathfield, E Sussex TN21 8EB* Heathfield (04352) 5591

PREECE, Barry Leslie. b 48. Lich Th Coll 68. **d** 71 **p** 72. C Ewell *Guildf* 71-74; C York Town 75-77; P-in-c Ripley 77-81; Chapl HM Det Cen Send 77-81; V Cuddington *Guildf* 81-88; V Cobham from 88. *The Vicarage, St Andrew's Walk, Cobham, Surrey KT11 3EQ* Cobham (0932) 62109

PREECE, Colin George. b 51. Bernard Gilpin Soc Dur 71 Chich Th Coll 72. **d** 75 **p** 76. C Upper Gornal *Lich* 75-78; C Wednesbury St Paul Wood Green 78-81; V Oxley 81-89; V Kennington *Cant* from 89. *The Vicarage, 212 Faversham Road, Kennington, Ashford, Kent TN24 9AF* Ashford (0233) 620500

PREECE, Canon James Derick. b 13. Sheff Univ MPhil86. Lich Th Coll 37. **d** 40 **p** 41. V Sheff St Matt *Sheff* 60-80; Hon Can Sheff Cathl 73-80; RD Ecclesall 74-80; rtd 80; Lic to Offic *Sheff* from 82. *113 Nursery Crescent, Anston, Sheffield S31 7BR* Dinnington (0909) 562748

PREECE, Joseph. b 23. Univ of Wales (Ban) BA50 Univ of Wales (Swansea) DipSocSc51 LSE CertCC52 Lon Univ DBRS72. NW Ord Course 73. **d** 73 **p** 74. C Claughton cum Grange *Ches* 73-74; C Barnston 74-75; R Aldford and Bruera 75-80; V Wincle and Wildboarclough 80-82; P-in-c Cleeton w Silvington *Heref* 82-86; P-in-c Farlow 82-86; V Stottesdon 82-86; R Stottesdon w Farlow, Cleeton and Silvington 86-88; rtd 88. *Lingholm, Woodhall Drive, Hanwood, Shrewsbury SY5 8JU* Shrewsbury (0743) 860946

PREECE, Mark Richard. b 61. St Paul's Cheltenham BA85. Linc Th Coll 85. **d** 87 **p** 88. C Coity w Nolton *Llan* 87-89; C Penarth w Lavernock from 89. *Church House, 153 Windsor Road, Penarth, S Glam CF6 1JF* Penarth (0222) 701144

PREECE, Robert James. b 44. RGN RMN. St Steph Ho Ox 72. **d** 75 **p** 76. C Middlesb All SS *York* 75-78; C Reading St Giles *Ox* 78-82; V Reading St Luke 82-86; P-in-c Earley St Bart 85-86; V Reading St Luke w St Bart from 86. *St Luke's Vicarage, 14 Erleigh Road, Reading RG1 5LH* Reading (0734) 62372

PREECE, Ronald Alexander. b 29. Lon Univ BD56. ALCD55. **d** 56 **p** 57. C Rusholme *Man* 56-59; Brazil 60-63; Perm to Offic *Cant* 63-70; OMF from 70; SW Regional Dir from 76; Perm to Offic *Bris* from 76. *174 Redland Road, Bristol BS6 6YG* Bristol (0272) 737490

PRENTICE, Brian. b 40. St Jo Coll Nottm 81. **d** 83 **p** 84. C W Bromwich All SS *Lich* 83-86; C Tettenhall Wood 86-89; TV 89-90; V Essington from 90. *The Vicarage, Wolverhampton Road, Essington WV11 2BX* Bloxwich (0922) 478540

PRENTICE, Michael Charles. b 35. Bps' Coll Cheshunt 59. **d** 62 **p** 63. C Lon Docks St Pet w Wapping St Jo *Lon* 62-66; C Cranford 66-70; C Bethnal Green St Jas the Gt w St Jude 70-71; C Walsingham and Houghton *Nor* 71-73; C Southall Ch Redeemer *Lon* 73; V Acton Vale St Thos 73-78; P-in-c Stow Bardolph w Wimbotsham and Stow Bridge *Ely* 78-80; R Woodford *Pet* from 80. *The Rectory, Woodford, Kettering, Northants* Thrapston (08012) 2478

PRENTICE, Walter Gordon. b 07. Nor Ord Course 73. **d** 75 **p** 76. C Swanton Morley w Worthing *Nor* 75-77; P-in-c Scarning w Wendling 77-78; rtd 78; Perm to Offic Nor 78-80; St E 80-88; Hon C Cherry Hinton St Andr *Ely* from 88. *13 St Andrew's Glebe, Cherry Hinton, Cambridge CB1 3JS* Cambridge (0223) 215285

PRENTIS, Richard Hugh. b 36. Ch Coll Cam BA60 MA64. Sarum Th Coll 69. **d** 71 **p** 72. C Bath Bathwick St Mary *B & W* 71-76; Bp's Dom Chapl *Lich* 76-80; PV Lich Cathl 76-80; V Longton St Mary and St Chad 80-84; V Shifnal from 84; P-in-c Badger 84-85; P-in-c Ryton 84-85; P-in-c Beckbury 84-85. *The Vicarage, Shifnal, Shropshire TF11 9AB* Telford (0952) 460625

PRESCOTT, Canon Anthony John. b 34. AKC59. **d** 60 **p** 61. C Swindon New Town *Bris* 60-66; P-in-c Birm St Aid Small Heath *Birm* 66-68; V 68-72; Hon C Washwood Heath from 72; Asst Sec ACS 72-74; Gen Sec from 74; Hon Can St Woolos Cathl *Mon* from 83. *264A Washwood Heath Road, Birmingham B8 2XS* 021-328 0749 or 354 9885

PRESSWELL, John Lawrence Rowley. b 28. Southn Univ BEd79. AKC51. **d** 52 **p** 53. V Battersea St Bart *S'wark* 69-71; P-in-c Newtown St Luke *Win* 71-73; C Lymington 73-79; Chapl Crookham Court Sch Newbury 79-81; Chapl Stanbridge Earls Sch Romsey 81-82; C Doncaster

St Geo *Sheff* 82-85; V Edlington 85-86; C Handsworth 86-88; C Rotherham 88-90; rtd 90. *The Cottage, Todds Lane, Burton-upon-Stather, Scunthorpe, S Humberside DN15 9DG* Scunthorpe (0724) 721266

PREST, Canon Walter. b 09. St Chad's Coll Dur BA33 DipTh34 MA36. **d** 34 **p** 35. Hon Can Truro Cathl *Truro* 61-82; Preb St Endellion 70-81; R St Endellion 70-81; rtd 81. *College of St Barnabas, Blackberry Lane, Lingfield, Surrey RH7 6NJ* Dormans Park (034287) 612

PRESTNEY, Mrs Patricia Christine Margaret. b 49. Oak Hill Th Coll 84. **d** 87. NSM Lawford *Chelmsf* from 87; Perm to Offic *St E* from 91. *Greshams Farm, Harwich Road, Great Bromley, Essex CO7 7UH* Great Bentley (0206) 250925

PRESTON, David Francis. b 50. BNC Ox BA72 MA78. St Steph Ho Ox 72. **d** 74 **p** 75. C Beckenham St Jas *Roch* 74-79; C Hockley *Chelmsf* 81-83; C Lamorbey H Redeemer *Roch* 83-89; V Gillingham St Barn from 89. *1 St Barnabas's Close, Oxford Road, Gillingham, Kent ME7 4BU* Medway (0634) 51010

PRESTON, Donald George. b 30. St Alb Minl Tr Scheme 77. **d** 80 **p** 81. NSM Elstow *St Alb* 80-87; NSM Goldington from 87. *106 Putnoe Street, Bedford MK41 8HJ* Bedford (0234) 267313

PRESTON, Preb Frederick Arnold. MBE53. Leeds Univ BA42. Coll of Resurr Mirfield 42. **d** 44 **p** 45. C Greenford H Cross *Lon* 44-51; CF 51-61; R W Hackney St Barn *Lon* from 61; Preb St Paul's Cathl from 75. *The Rectory, 306 Amhurst Road, London N16 7UE* 071-254 3235

PRESTON, Frederick John. b 32. MBE72. Oak Hill Th Coll 54 St Jo Coll Northwood LTh67. **d** 57 **p** 58. V Otterton *Ex* 69-71; CF 71-79; NSM 79-84; Chapl Intercon Ch Soc 84-89; rtd 89. *Elm Cottage, Craggs Lane, Tunstall, Richmond, N Yorkshire DL10 7RB* Richmond (0748) 832037

PRESTON, Graham Leslie. b 53. Ripon Coll Cuddesdon. **d** 82 **p** 83. C Mitcham Ascension *S'wark* 82-85; C Portsea N End St Mark *Portsm* 85-88; P-in-c Crofton Park St Hilda w St Cypr *S'wark* from 88. *St Hilda's Vicarage, Buckthorne Road, London SE4 2DG* 081-699 1277

PRESTON, James Martin. b 31. Trin Coll Cam MA55 Ch Ch Ox MA57. Virginia Th Sem 57 S'wark Ord Course 87. **d** 88 **p** 88. NSM Blackheath Ascension *S'wark* from 88. *14A Church Terrace, London SE13 5BT* 081-318 3089

PRESTON, John. b 26. St Aid Birkenhead 58. **d** 52 **p** 52. In RC Ch 50-57; C Chadderton Ch Ch *Man* 58-59; C Didsbury Ch Ch 59-63; R Cheetham St Jo from 63. *St John's Rectory, Brideoak Street, Manchester M8 7AY* 061-205 2005

PRESTON, John Baker. b 23. Lon Univ BA49. Oak Hill Th Coll 46. **d** 51 **p** 52. V Blackheath St Jo *S'wark* 57-65; Perm to Offic *Cant* from 69; rtd 88. *43 Wedgwood Drive, Lower Parkstone, Poole, Dorset BH14 8ES*

PRESTON, John Martyn. b 13. St Jo Coll Cam BA35 MA42. Qu Coll Birm 35. **d** 36 **p** 37. C Masborough St Paul w St Jo *Sheff* 68-72; C Howden *York* 73-75; C Bedf Leigh *Man* 75-76; C Ashton St Mich 76-78; rtd 78. *Top Flat, 17 Granville Road, Scarborough, N Yorkshire YO11 2RA*

PRESTON, Dr John Michael. b 40. K Coll Lon BD63 AKC63 Lon Univ BA81 Southn Univ PhD91. St Boniface Warminster. **d** 65 **p** 66. C Heston *Lon* 65-67; C Northolt St Mary 67-72; Trinidad and Tobago 72-74; P-in-c Aveley *Chelmsf* 74-78; V 78-82; C Eastleigh *Win* 82-84; C-in-c Boyatt Wood CD 84-87; V W End from 87. *The Vicarage, Elizabeth Close, West End, Southampton SO3 3BU* Southampton (0703) 472180

PRESTON, Joseph Arthur. b 11. Bps' Coll Cheshunt 60. **d** 61 **p** 62. Hd Master Newtown Sch Hatfield 52-72; Perm to Offic *Nor* 72-76 and 77-88; P-in-c Gt w Lt Snoring 76-77; rtd 77; Perm to Offic *Ex* from 88. *The Coach House, Powderham, Exeter EX6 8JJ* Dawlish (0626) 891353

PRESTON, Leonard Arthur. b 09. Leeds Univ BA32 DipEd48. Coll of Resurr Mirfield 34. **d** 34 **p** 35. Chapl Laleham Abbey 56-76; rtd 76; Perm to Offic *Cant* from 76. *Underhill, Mountain Street, Chilham, Canterbury, Kent CT4 8DG* Canterbury (0227) 730266

PRESTON, Maurice. b 25. Lon Univ DipTh69 BD77. St Aid Birkenhead. **d** 57 **p** 58. V Thorpe Hesley *Sheff* 62-84; V Rawcliffe 84-89; rtd 89. *19 Erw Goch, Abergele, Clwyd LL22 9AQ* Abergele (0745) 826952

PRESTON, Michael Christopher. b 47. Hatf Coll Dur BA68. Ripon Coll Cuddesdon 75. **d** 78 **p** 79. C Epsom St Martin *Guildf* 78-82; C Guildf H Trin w St Mary 82-86; V Epsom St Barn from 86. *St Barnabas' Vicarage, Hook Road, Epsom, Surrey KT19 8TU* Epsom (0372) 722874

PRESTON, Canon Percival Kenneth. b 16. Ch Ch Ox BA38 MA48. Cuddesdon Coll 38. **d** 40 **p** 45. V Horfield St Greg *Bris* 55-81; Hon Can Bris Cathl 74-82; RD Horfield 76-81; rtd 81; Perm to Offic Bris from 82; Glouc from 83. *56 Gloucester Road, Rudgeway, Bristol BS12 2RT* Almondsbury (0454) 612794

PRESTON, Reuben James. b 65. York Univ BSc86 MEng87. Westcott Ho Cam 88. **d** 91. C Weoley Castle *Birm* from 91. *34 Shenley Lane, Weoley Castle, Birmingham B29 5PL* 021-476 3990

PRESTON, Canon Prof Ronald Haydn. b 13. Lon Univ BSc(Econ)35 St Cath Soc Ox BA40 MA44 DD83. Ripon Hall Ox 38. **d** 40 **p** 41. Prof of Soc and Past Th Man Univ 70-80; Hon Can Man Cathl *Man* 71-80; rtd 80; Perm to Offic *Man* from 80. *161 Old Hall Lane, Manchester M14 6HJ* 061-225 3291

PRESTON, Miss Rosemary Muriel. b 23. St Mich Ho Ox DipTh. **dss** 80 **d** 87. Burundi 80-85; NSM Buckland Monachorum *Ex* from 87. *Fresh Springs, 3 Buckland Court, Crapstone, Yelverton, Devon PL20 7UE* Yelverton (0822) 854037

PRESTON, Thomas Leonard. b 27. Tyndale Hall Bris. **d** 64 **p** 65. C Moss Side St Jas *Man* 64-66; C Urmston 66-68; V Thornham w Gravel Hole 68-76; Chapl to the Deaf *Chich* 76-80; TV York All SS Pavement w St Crux and St Martin are *York* from 80; Chapl to the Deaf from 80. *Glenfield, Bull Lane, Heworth, York YO3 0TS* York (0904) 423213

PRESTON, William. b 25. St Cath Coll Cam BA46 MA50 Reading Univ MSc79. Oak Hill Th Coll 48. **d** 50 **p** 51. Cranbrook Sch Kent 69-90; Perm to Offic Cant from 64; Roch from 66; rtd 90. *29 Orchard Way, Horsmonden, Tonbridge, Kent TN12 8LA* Brenchley (089272) 2616

PRESTON-THOMAS, Canon Colin Barnabas Rashleigh. b 28. K Coll Lon 48. Edin Th Coll 51. **d** 53 **p** 54. C Edin St Dav *Edin* 53-54; Chapl St Ninian's Cathl Perth *St And* 54-55; Prec St Ninian's Cathl Perth 55-60; Chapl HM Pris Perth 55-60; P-in-c Inverkeithing *St And* 60; R 61-72; P-in-c Rosyth 60; R 61-72; Syn Clerk from 68; Can St Ninian's Cathl Perth from 68; R Forfar 72-82; Dioc Sec 80-90; R Kilmaveonaig from 82; R Pitlochry from 82. *The Parsonage, Perth Road, Pitlochry, Perthshire PH16 5DJ* Pitlochry (0796) 2176

PREVETT, Mark Norman. b 59. Univ of Wales (Cardiff) BD88. St Mich Coll Llan 85. **d** 88 **p** 89. C Brynmawr *S & B* 88-90; C Bassaleg *Mon* from 90. *St Ann's House, 2 High Cross Drive, Rogerstone, Newport, Gwent NP1 9AB* Newport (0633) 895441

PREVITE, Anthony Michael Allen. b 41. TCD DipTh88. CITC 85. **d** 88 **p** 89. C Galway w Kilcummin *T, K & A* 88-91; I Omey w Ballynakill, Errislannan and Roundstone from 91. *The Rectory, Church Hill, Clifden, Co Galway, Irish Republic* Clifden (91) 21147

PREWER, Dennis. b 30. Kelham Th Coll 50. **d** 54 **p** 55. C Stockport St Thos *Ches* 54-58; C Gt Grimsby St Mary and St Jas *Linc* 58-62; V Gt Harwood St Jo *Blackb* 62-64; V Scarcliffe *Derby* 64-70; Org Sec (Dio Ches) CECS from 70; Dios Liv, Ban and St As 70-78; Dio Man from 78; Lic to Offic *Ches* from 70; Perm to Offic *Man* from 78. *19 Alan Drive, Marple, Stockport, Cheshire SK6 6LN* 061-427 2827

PRICE, Alec John. b 32. Solicitor 58 Univ of Wales (Abth) LLB55. St Deiniol's Hawarden 77. **d** 79 **p** 80. Hon C St As 79-80; VC St As Cathl 79-83; Hon C St As and Tremeirchion 80-83; R Cilcen and Nannerch and Rhydymwyn 84-88; Min Can and PV Bre Cathl *S & B* 88-90; Perm to Offic *Lich* 90-91; Res Min Shrewsbury St Chad w St Mary and Chapl Shrewsbury Town Cen from 91. *St Alkmund's, 31 Belvidere Road, Shrewsbury SY2 5LS* Shrewsbury (0743) 344155

PRICE, Alun Huw. b 47. St D Coll Lamp DipTh70. **d** 70 **p** 71. C Carmarthen St Dav *St D* 70-73; V Bettws Evan 73-77; CF from 77. *c/o MOD (Army), Bagshot Park, Bagshot, Surrey GU19 5PL* Bagshot (0276) 71717

PRICE, Anthony Ronald. b 49. Linc Coll Ox BA71 MA83 St Jo Coll Dur BA78. **d** 79 **p** 80. C St Alb St Paul *St Alb* 79-81; C Lydiard Millicent w Lydiard Tregoz *Bris* 85-86; TV The Lydiards 86-91; V Marston *Ox* from 91. *The Vicarage, Marston, Oxford OX3 0PR* Oxford (0865) 247034

PRICE, Ven Cecil Johnston. b 25. ARCM TCD BA48 MA52. CITC 49. **d** 50 **p** 51. C Tralee *L & K* 50-53; C Cork St Ann w St Luke Shandon *C, C & R* 53-56; I Desertserges 56-58; I Limerick St Mich *L & K* 58-67; Can Limerick Cathl 63-67; I Bandon *C, C & R* 67-69; I Delgany *D & G* from 69; Adn Glendalough from 89. *The Rectory, Delgany, Co Wicklow, Irish Republic* Dublin (1) 287-4515

PRICE, Mrs Christine Janice. b 45. SW Minl Tr Course 83. **dss** 86 **d** 87. Roxbourne St Andr *Lon* 86-87; Hon Par Dn from 87. *43 Yeading Avenue, Rayners Lane, Harrow, Middx HA2 9RL* 081-866 9119

PRICE, Clive Stanley. b 42. ALCD69. **d** 69 **p** 70. C Chenies and Lt Chalfont *Ox* 69-75; R Upper Stour *Sarum* 75-79; C-in-c Panshanger CD *St Alb* 79-82; TV Digswell and Panshanger 82-86; Dioc Ecum Officer *Newc* from 86; P-in-c St Oswald in Lee w Bingfield from 86. *St Oswald's Vicarage, Wall, Hexham NE46 4DU* Hexham (0434) 81354

PRICE, David. b 27. Wycliffe Hall Ox 61. **d** 63 **p** 64. C Bucknall and Bagnall *Lich* 63-67; C Abingdon w Shippon *Ox* 67-76; Israel 76-84; V S Kensington St Luke *Lon* from 84; P-in-c S Kensington St Jude from 88. *St Luke's Vicarage, 1 Cathcart Road, London SW10 9NL* 071-352 7553

PRICE, David Rea. b 39. St Aid Birkenhead 61. **d** 63 **p** 64. C Green Street Green *Roch* 63-66; C Gillingham St Mary 66-69; C New Windsor St Jo *Ox* 69-72; V Winkfield 72-80; RD Bracknell 78-86; V Sunningdale 80-86; TR Wimborne Minster and Holt *Sarum* from 86; RD Wimborne from 88. *The Rectory, 17 King Street, Wimborne, Dorset BH21 1DZ* Wimborne (0202) 882340

PRICE, Canon David Trevor William. b 43. FRHistS79 Keble Coll Ox BA65 MA69. Sarum & Wells Th Coll 72. **d** 72 **p** 73. Lic to Offic *St D* 72-82; Lect Univ of Wales (Lamp) 72-87; Chapl from 79-80; Sen Lect from 87; Dioc Archivist *St D* from 82; P-in-c Bettws Bledrws from 86; Hon Can St D Cathl from 90. *Bodlondeb, 65 Bridge Street, Lampeter, Dyfed SA48 7AB* Lampeter (0570) 422707

PRICE, Dawson. b 31. OBE. Peterho Cam BA52. Oak Hill NSM Course 88. **d** 91. NSM Harpenden St Jo *St Alb* from 91. *1 Rye Close, Harpenden, Herts AL5 4LD* Harpenden (0582) 460380

PRICE, Canon Derek William. b 27. St Pet Hall Ox BA51 MA55. Qu Coll Birm 51. **d** 53 **p** 54. C St Marylebone St Mark Hamilton Terrace *Lon* 53-57; C Stevenage *St Alb* 57-63; Jamaica 63-67; R Bridgham and Roudham *Nor* 67-80; R E w W Harling 69-80; Hon Can Nor Cathl from 75; RD Thetford and Rockland 76-86; P-in-c Kilverstone 80-87; P-in-c Croxton 80-87; TR Thetford 80-87; R Castle Acre w Newton, Rougham and Southacre from 87. *The Vicarage, Back Lane, Castle Acre, King's Lynn, Norfolk PE32 2AR* Castle Acre (07605) 256

PRICE, Chan Desmond. b 23. St D Coll Lamp BA50. **d** 51 **p** 52. R Dinas and Llanllawer *St D* 68-72; V Llandeilo Fawr w Llandyfeisant 72-79; V Llandilo Fawr and Taliaris 79-91; Can St D Cathl from 83; Chan St D Cathl 89-91; RD Llangadog and Llandeilo 90-91; rtd 91. *24 Diana Road, Llandeilo, Dyfed SA19 6RS* Llandeilo (0558) 824039

PRICE, Canon Edward Glyn. b 35. Univ of Wales (Lamp) BA55. Ch Div Sch of the Pacific (USA) BD58. **d** 58 **p** 59. C Denbigh *St As* 58-65; V Llanasa 65-76; V Buckley 76-91; Dioc RE Adv from 77; RD Mold from 86; Can St As Cathl from 87; V Llandrillo-yn-Rhos from 91. *Llandrillo Vicarage, 36 Llandudno Road, Colwyn Bay, Clwyd LL28 4UD* Colwyn Bay (0492) 48878

PRICE, Canon Eric. b 14. Bps' Coll Cheshunt 42. **d** 44 **p** 45. V Handsworth St Mich *Birm* 61-84; rtd 85; Perm to Offic *Birm* from 85. *11 Brosil Avenue, Birmingham B20 1LB* 021-523 0414

PRICE, Frank Watkin. b 22. ALCM37 Univ of Wales (Lamp) BA45. St Mich Coll Llan 45. **d** 47 **p** 48. C Cwmaman *St D* 47-50; C Llanelly 50-52; Chapl RAF 52-68; Hd Master Amman Valley Lower Sch 68-85; R St Nicholas w Bonvilston and St George's-Ely *Llan* from 85. *The Rectory, 8 Ger-y-Llan, St Nicholas, Cardiff CF5 6SY* Peterston-super-Ely (0446) 760728

PRICE, Frederick Leslie. b 30. Oak Hill Th Coll 59. **d** 61 **p** 62. C Hougham in Dover Ch Ch *Cant* 61-64; R Plumbland and Gilcrux *Carl* from 64. *The Rectory, Gilcrux, Carlisle CA5 2QN* Aspatria (06973) 20255

PRICE, Geoffrey David. b 46. NDA NCA. Oak Hill Th Coll DipHE. **d** 83 **p** 84. C Gt Baddow *Chelmsf* 83-86; C Hampreston *Sarum* 86-88; TV from 88. *The Vicarage, 19 Canford Bottom, Wimborne, Dorset BH21 2HA* Wimborne (0202) 884796

PRICE, Canon George. b 04. FRAI36. Ripon Hall Ox 44. **d** 34 **p** 35. V Pet St Mark *Pet* 50-74; Can Pet Cathl 63-74; RD Pet 68-74; rtd 74. *15 Malton Way, York YO3 6SG* York (0904) 54128

PRICE, Gerald Andrew. b 31. NE Ord Course. **d** 84 **p** 85. C Monkseaton St Mary *Newc* 84-87; V Cowgate from

87. *St Peter's Vicarage, Druridge Drive, Newcastle upon Tyne NE5 3LP* 091-286 9913

PRICE, Very Rev Hilary Martin Connop. b 12. Qu Coll Cam BA33 MA37. Ridley Hall Cam 34. **d** 36 **p** 37. Provost Chelmsf 67-77; rtd 77. *98 St James's Street, Shaftesbury, Dorset SP7 8HF* Shaftesbury (0747) 52118

PRICE, John Francis. b 32. Qu Coll Cam BA54 MA. Ridley Hall Cam 54. **d** 56 **p** 57. C Leic H Apostles *Leic* 56-60; V Forest Gate St Mark *Chelmsf* 60-71; V Harold Hill St Geo 72-79; R Loughton St Mary 79-83; TR Loughton St Mary and St Mich 83-88; R Kirby-le-Soken w Gt Holland from 88. *The Rectory, 18 Thorpe Road, Kirby Cross, Frinton-on-Sea, Essex CO13 0LT* Frinton-on-Sea (0255) 5997

PRICE, John Newman. b 32. St Alb Minl Tr Scheme 80. **d** 83 **p** 84. NSM Bedf St Pet w St Cuth *St Alb* 83-88; C Lt Berkhamsted and Bayford, Essendon etc from 88. *The Rectory, 1 Berkhamsted Lane, Little Berkhamsted, Hertford SG13 8LU* Cuffley (0707) 875940

PRICE, Canon John Richard. b 34. Mert Coll Ox BA58 MA62. Westcott Ho Cam 58. **d** 60 **p** 61. C Man St Aid *Man* 60-63; C Bramley *Ripon* 63-67; V Leeds All Hallows w St Simon 67-74; P-in-c Wrangthorn 73-74; V Claughton cum Grange *Ches* 74-78; V Mottram in Longdendale w Woodhead 78-88; RD Mottram 79-88; Hon Can Ches Cathl from 86; R Nantwich from 88. *The Rectory, Nantwich, Cheshire CW5 5RQ* Nantwich (0270) 625268

PRICE, Joseph Roderick. b 45. St Mich Coll Llan 71. **d** 75 **p** 76. C Fleur-de-Lis *Mon* 75-79; CF from 79. *c/o MOD (Army), Bagshot Park, Bagshot, Surrey GU19 5PL* Bagshot (0276) 71717

PRICE, Lawrence Robert. b 43. LICeram71 N Staffs Poly CertCT66 MDCT74. St Jo Coll Dur 76. **d** 78 **p** 79. C Harlescott *Lich* 78-80; C Cheddleton 80-83; P-in-c Calton 83-84; P-in-c Cauldon 83-84; P-in-c Grindon 83-84; P-in-c Waterfall 83-84; R Calton, Cauldon, Grindon and Waterfall 85-88; rtd 88. *Heathcote House, 61 Hillside Road, Cheddleton, Leek, Staffs ST13 7JQ* Leek (0538) 360230

PRICE, Martin Randall Connop. b 45. Lon Univ BSc71 Fitzw Coll Cam BA75 MA79. Ridley Hall Cam 73. **d** 76 **p** 77. C Keynsham *B & W* 76-79; Ind Chapl *Sheff* 79-83; V Wortley 79-83; R Hook Norton w Gt Rollright, Swerford etc *Ox* from 83. *Hook Norton Rectory, Banbury, Oxon OX15 5QQ* Hook Norton (0608) 737223

PRICE, Michael Graham. b 62. Ex Coll Ox BA84. Linc Th Coll 84. **d** 86 **p** 87. C Salford St Phil w St Steph *Man* 86-90; R Man Gd Shep from 90. *The Rectory, 3 Campion Walk, Beswick, Manchester M11 3SB* 061-223 1724

PRICE, Canon Norman Havelock. b 28. Univ of Wales (Lamp) BA52. St Mich Coll Llan 52. **d** 54 **p** 55. C Newport Maindee St Jo Ev *Mon* 54-58; V Llantilio Crossenny and Llanfihangel Ystern etc 58-64; V Mon St Thos-over-Monnow 64-65; V Mon St Thos-over-Monnow and Wonastow 65-71; V St Thos-over-Monnow w Wonastow and Michel Troy from 71; RD Mon from 84; Can St Woolos Cathl from 91. *St Thomas's Vicarage, Overmonnow, Monmouth, Gwent NP5 3ES* Monmouth (0600) 2693

PRICE, Canon Peter Bryan. b 44. Oak Hill Th Coll 72. **d** 74 **p** 75. C Portsdown *Portsm* 74-78; Chapl Scargill Ho N Yorkshire 78-80; P-in-c Addiscombe St Mary *Cant* 80-81; V 81-84; V Addiscombe St Mary S'wark 85-88; Can Res and Chan S'wark Cathl from 88; Sec USPG from 91. *7 Temple West Mews, West Square, London SE11 4TJ* 071-735 5924

PRICE, Peter Charles. b 27. Vancouver Sch of Th DipTh61. **d** 61 **p** 62. Canada 61-66; C St Mary-at-Latton *Chelmsf* 66-68; C Bearsted *Cant* 68-74; TV Ebbw Vale *Mon* 74-77; V Llanfihangel Crucorney w Oldcastle etc 77-87; St Helena 87-90; V Llanishen w Trelleck Grange and Llanfihangel etc *Mon* from 90. *The Vicarage, Llanishen, Chepstow, Gwent NP6 6QL* Trelleck (0600) 860845

PRICE, Philip. b 24. Tyndale Hall Bris 50. **d** 55 **p** 56. Kenya 55-75; R Gt Horkesley *Chelmsf* 75-89; rtd 89. *229 Meadgate Avenue, Great Baddow, Chelmsford CM2 7NJ* Chelmsford (0245) 251499

PRICE, Philip Roger. b 09. Qu Coll Birm. **d** 57 **p** 58. C Wraxall *B & W* 68-72; V Mark 72-77; P-in-c Chapel Allerton 77; R Mark w Allerton 77-79; rtd 79; Perm to Offic *B & W* from 80. *61 Summerlands Park Avenue, Ilminster, Somerset TA19 9BU* Ilminster (0460) 53428

PRICE, Raymond Francklin. b 30. Wycliffe Hall Ox 61. **d** 62 **p** 63. C Bilston St Leon *Lich* 62-67; C Keighley *Bradf* 67-70; V Mangotsfield *Bris* 70-79; Ind Chapl *Birm* 79-86; C Birm St Martin 84-85; C Birm St Martin w

Bordesley St Andr 85-86; V Edgbaston St Aug from 86. *St Augustine's Vicarage, 44 Vernon Road, Birmingham B16 9SH* 021-454 0127

PRICE, Richard Philip. b 38. Edin Th Coll 60. d 63 p 64. C Edin St Aid Miss Niddrie Mains *Edin* 63-65; C Edin Old St Paul 65-68; R Aber St Marg *Ab* 68-77; P-in-c Edin St Ninian *Edin* 77-81; V Carnforth *Blackb* from 81; RD Tunstall from 90. *The Vicarage, North Road, Carnforth, Lancs LA5 9LJ* Carnforth (0524) 732948

PRICE, Roy Ernest. b 13. AKC38. d 38 p 39. V S Stoke w Woodcote *Ox* 59-79; rtd 79; Perm to Offic *Win* from 82. *74A London Road, Whitchurch, Hants RG28 7LY* Whitchurch (0256) 892581

PRICE, Stanley George. b 32. FRICS69. Trin Coll Bris 84. d 85 p 86. C Newport w Longford and Chetwynd *Lich* 85-88; V Ipstones w Berkhamsytch and Onecote w Bradnop from 88. *The Vicarage, Ipstones, Stoke-on-Trent ST10 2LF* Ipstones (0538) 266313

PRICE, Timothy Fry. b 51. NE Lon Poly CQSW. St Jo Coll Nottm 85. d 87 p 88. C Church Stretton *Heref* from 87. *23 Church Street, Church Stretton, Shropshire SY6 6DQ* Church Stretton (0694) 722069

PRICE, Victor John. b 35. Oak Hill Th Coll 62. d 65 p 66. C Rainham *Chelmsf* 65-70; V Dover St Martin *Cant* 70-78; V Madeley *Heref* 78-90; P-in-c Derby St Pet and Ch Ch w H Trin *Derby* from 90. *16 Farley Road, Derby DE3 6BX* Derby (0332) 47821

PRICE, William Haydn. b 20. Sarum & Wells Th Coll 77. d 80 p 81. NSM Alverstoke *Portsm* 80-85; rtd 85; Perm to Offic *Portsm* from 85. *15 Amersham Close, Alverstoke, Gosport, Hants PO12 2RU* Gosport (0705) 580965

PRICE, Canon William Kenneth. b 22. Keble Coll Ox BA44 MA48. St Mich Coll Llan 44. d 46 p 47. V Aberdare St Fagan *Llan* 65-71; V Ilston w Pennard *S & B* 71-79; V Morriston 79-89; Chapl Morriston Hosp Swansea 79-89; Can Brecon Cathl *S & B* 82-89; RD Cwmtawe 86-89; rtd 89. *40 Llantwit Road, Neath, W Glam SA11 3LB* Neath (0639) 645883

PRICE, William Norman. b 52. GRNCM73. N Ord Course 86. d 89 p 90. NSM Lower Broughton Ascension *Man* from 89. *14 Watkins Drive, Prestwich, Manchester M25 8DS* 061-720 7804

PRICE, William Trevor. b 17. Univ of Wales BA43. St Mich Coll Llan 44. d 45 p 46. V Aberdare St Fagan *Llan* 72-83; rtd 83; Perm to Offic *Llan* from 83. *147 Queen's Drive, Llantwit Fardre, Pontypridd, M Glam* Newtown Llantwit (0443) 206219

PRICE-ROBERTS, Mervyn. b 29. Trin Coll Carmarthen TCert51 Univ of Wales DipRE52 BEd79. St Mich Coll Llan 89 Ban Ord Course 84. d 87 p 88. NSM Caer Rhun w Llangelynin w Llanbedr-y-Cennin *Ban* 87-89; V Llandegai and Llandegai St Ann w Tregarth from 89. *St Ann's Vicarage, Bethesda, Bangor, Gwynedd LL57 4AX* Bethesda (0248) 602638

PRICHARD, Canon Thomas John. b 16. FRHistS82 Keele Univ PhD81 Univ of Wales (Ban) BA38 MA72. Chich Th Coll 38. d 39 p 40. Can Llan Cathl *Llan* 66-84; R Neath w Llantwit 69-84; rtd 84. *Tros-yr-Afon, Llangwnnadl, Pwllheli, Gwynedd LL53 8NS* Tudweiliog (075887) 393

PRIDAY, Gerald Nelson. b 35. Glouc Th Course. d 85 p 88. NSM Eardisland *Heref* from 85; NSM Aymestrey and Leinthall Earles w Wigmore etc from 85; NSM Kingsland from 85. *14 Boarsfield, Kingsland, Leominster, Herefordshire HR6 9SN* Kingsland (056881) 772

PRIDDIN, Mrs Maureen Anne. b 46. Leeds Univ BA67 Nottm Univ DipEd68. E Midl Min Tr Course 82. dss 85 d 87. Mickleover St Jo *Derby* 85-87; Hon Par Dn 87; Dioc World Development Officer 87-90. *7 Portland Close, Mickleover, Derby DE3 5BR* Derby (0332) 513672

PRIDDIS, Anthony Martin. b 48. CCC Cam BA69 MA73 New Coll Ox DipTh71 MA75. Cuddesdon Coll 69. d 72 p 73. C New Addington *Cant* 72-75; Chapl Ch Ch Ox 75-80; Lic to Offic *Ox* 76-80; TV High Wycombe 80-86; P-in-c Amersham 86-90; R from 90. *The Rectory, Church Street, Amersham, Bucks HP7 0DB* Amersham (0494) 729380

PRIDEAUX, Humphrey Grevile. b 36. CCC Ox BA60 MA63 Birm Univ CertEd66 Lon Univ DipEd73 Open Univ BA87. Linc Th Coll 59. d 61 p 62. C Northn St Matt *Pet* 61-62; C Milton *Portsm* 62-65; Perm to Offic *Birm* 65-66; Hd of RE Qu Mary's Gr Sch Walsall 66-69; Lic to Offic *Lich* 66-69; Lect St Martin's Coll Lanc 69-80; Lic to Offic *Blackb* 69-80; Perm to Offic *Portsm* 80-86; Hon C Fareham H Trin 86-90; Hon C Bishops Waltham from 90. *3 Wordsworth Close, Bishops Waltham, Southampton SO3 1RT* Bishops Waltham (04893) 6685

PRIDGEON, Paul Garth Walsingham. b 45. Sussex Univ BA69 CertEd. Glouc Sch of Min 87. d 87 p 88. NSM Cirencester *Glouc* from 87. *4 Abbey Way, Cirencester, Glos GL7 2DT* Cirencester (0285) 656860

PRIDHAM, Peter Arthur George Drake. b 16. Ely Th Coll 62. d 64 p 65. C Berwick H Trin *Newc* 67-71; V Sleekburn 71-76; P-in-c Otterburn w Elsdon and Horsley w Byrness 76-80; TV Bellingham/Otterburn Gp 80-84; rtd 84. *Bishop Harland Cottage, Greatham Hospital, Greatham, Hartlepool TS25 2HS* Hartlepool (0429) 870582

PRIDMORE, John Stuart. b 36. Nottm Univ BA62 MA67. Ridley Hall Cam 62. d 65 p 66. C Camborne *Truro* 65-67; Tutor Ridley Hall Cam 67-68; Chapl 68-71; Asst Chapl K Edw Sch Witley 71-75; Chapl 75-86; Tanzania 86-88; Angl Chapl Hengrave Hall Cen 88-89; C St Martin-in-the-Fields *Lon* from 89. *5 St Martin's Place, London WC2N 4JJ* 071-930 1646, 930 0089 or 930 1862

PRIEST, David. b 44. Chich Th Coll 69. d 73 p 74. C S Harrow St Paul *Lon* 73-76; C S Kensington St Steph 76-83; Perm to Offic 83-90; Hon C Pimlico St Mary Graham Terrace from 90. *78 Lupus Street, London SW1V 3EL* 071-821 0978

PRIEST, Richard Mark. b 63. Oak Hill Th Coll BA90. d 90. C Okehampton w Inwardleigh *Ex* from 90. *19 Fern Meadow, Okehampton, Devon EX20 1PB* Okehampton (0837) 54263

PRIESTLEY, Canon Alan Charles. b 41. Lon Univ BD69. Kelham Th Coll 64 Wm Temple Coll Rugby 65. d 65 p 66. C Edgbaston St Aug *Birm* 65-68; C Chelmsley Wood 68-72; TV 72-76; V Hazelwell from 76; Dioc Communications Officer from 83; Bp's Press Officer from 85; Hon Can Birm Cathl from 87. *The Vicarage, 316 Vicarage Road, Birmingham B14 7NH* 021-444 4469

PRIESTLEY, John Christopher. b 39. Trin Coll Ox BA60. Wells Th Coll 61. d 68 p 69. C Habergham All SS *Blackb* 68-70; C Padiham 70-75; V Colne Ch Ch from 75; Chapl to HM The Queen from 90; RD Pendle *Blackb* from 91. *The Vicarage, Keighley Road, Colne, Lancs BB8 7HF* Colne (0282) 863511

PRIESTMAN, John Christopher. b 22. K Coll Lon BSc51. Linc Th Coll 57. d 58 p 59. V Loose *Cant* 64-72; V S Ashford Ch Ch 72-80; TV Beaminster Area *Sarum* 80-82; RD Beaminster 81-82; P-in-c Marnhull 82-88; R 88-90; RD Blackmore Vale 86-90; rtd 90. *3 Mill Yard, Wickhambreaux, Canterbury, Kent CT3 1RQ* Canterbury (0227) 720550

PRIESTNALL, Reginald Hayward. b 22. Jes Coll Cam BA44 MA47. Ridley Hall Cam 44. d 45 p 46. V Rockingham w Caldecote *Pet* 67-71; V Northn St Mich 71-77; V Ketton 77-89; RD Barnack 86-89; rtd 89. *156 Ryeland Road, Northampton NN5 6XJ* Northampton (0604) 758502

PRIESTNER, Hugh. b 45. Nottm Univ BTh75. Linc Th Coll 71. d 75 p 76. C Seaton Hirst *Newc* 75-78; C Longbenton St Bart 78-81; P-in-c Glendale Gp 81-82; TV 83-88; Chapl Stafford Distr Gen Hosp and Stafford Distr Infirmary from 88. *Stafford District Hospital, Weston Road, Stafford ST16 3SA* Stafford (0785) 57731

PRIESTNER, James Arthur. b 14. Leeds Univ BA39. Coll of Resurr Mirfield 39. d 41 p 42. V Longhoughton w Howick *Newc* 70-79; rtd 79. *54 Cauldwell Avenue, Whitley Bay, Tyne & Wear NE25 9RW* 091-252 7226

PRIME, Geoffrey Daniel. b 12. Lich Th Coll 32. d 35 p 36. Org Sec (Dios Derby, Linc, Sheff & S'well) CECS 62-65; Perm to Offic *Derby* from 62; rtd 77. *Westside Mill Farm, Hulme End, Buxton, Derbyshire SK17 0EY* Hartington (029884) 461

PRINCE, Dennis Alan Ford. b 18. AKC48. d 48 p 49. R Slinfold *Chich* 60-73; R Sedlescombe w Whatlington 73-88; rtd 88. *7 Windmill Close, Glanfield, Portsmouth PO8 0NA*

PRINCE, Helena. b 23. Lightfoot Ho Dur. dss 66 d 87. W Derby St Mary *Liv* 65-85; rtd 85. *5 Dominic Close, Liverpool L16 1JZ* 051-722 0263

PRINCE, Hugh. b 12. St Cath Soc Ox BA34 MA38. Wycliffe Hall Ox 34. d 36 p 37. V Isel w Setmurthy *Carl* 67-72; R Bowness 72-76; rtd 77. *1 Hillside, Temple Sowerby, Penrith, Cumbria CA10 1SD* Kirkby Thore (07683) 61629

PRING, Althon Kerrigan. b 34. AKC58. d 59 p 60. C Limehouse St Anne *Lon* 59-61; C Lt Stanmore St Lawr 61-64; C Langley Marish *Ox* 64-68; P-in-c Radnage 68-72; P-in-c Ravenstone w Weston Underwood 72-75; P-in-c Stoke Goldington w Gayhurst 72-75; R Gayhurst w Ravenstone, Stoke Goldington etc 75-85; P-in-c 85-86; RD Newport 78-80; TV Woughton 86-90; P-in-c Nash w Thornton, Beachampton and Thornborough from 90.

The Rectory, Chapel Lane, Thornborough, Buckingham MK18 2DJ Buckingham (0280) 812515

PRINGLE, Ven Cecil Thomas. b 43. TCD BA65. CITC 66. **d** 66 **p** 67. C Belf St Donard *D & D* 66-69; I Cleenish *Clogh* 69-80; I Mullaghdun 78-80; I Rossory from 80; Preb Clogh Cathl 86-89; Adn Clogh from 89. *Rossory Rectory, Derryhonnelly Road, Co Fermanagh* Enniskillen (0365) 22874

PRINGLE, Miss Janyce Mary. b 32. ARCM53 LRAM54 Ex Univ DipAdEd70 MPhil85. SW Minl Tr Course 83. **dss** 86 **d** 87. Asst Chapl Torbay Hosp 86-89; Torquay St Matthias, St Mark and H Trin *Ex* 86-87; Hon Par Dn from 87. *Pendower, Wheatridge Lane, Torquay TQ2 6RA* Torquay (0803) 607136

PRINGLE, John Richard. b 55. Lon Univ AKC76 CertEd77 Open Univ BA84. Chich Th Coll 78. **d** 78 **p** 79. C Northn St Matt *Pet* 78-81; C Delaval *Newc* 81-84; V Newsham from 84. *St Bede's Vicarage, Newcastle Road, Newsham, Blyth, Northd NE24 4AS* Blyth (0670) 352391

PRINGLE, Thomas Andrew. b 36. FRMetS MRIN. Cant Sch of Min 85 Edin Th Coll 89. **d** 89 **p** 91. NSM Is of Arran *Arg* from 89; Hon Chapl Miss to Seamen from 89. *8 Torr Righe, Shiskine, Brodick, Isle of Arran KA27 8HD* Shiskine (077086) 222

PRINS, Canon Stanley Vernon. b 30. TD76. Dur Univ BSc54 MA69. Ripon Hall Ox 56. **d** 58 **p** 59. C Benwell St Jas *Newc* 58-61; Asst Chapl Newc Univ 61-65; CF (TA) from 64; C-in-c Whorlton H Nativity Chpl Ho Estate *Newc* 65-72; TV Whorlton 73-76; V Humshaugh 76-83; P-in-c Simonburn 82-83; P-in-c Wark 82-83; RD Bellingham from 83; R Humshaugh w Simonburn and Wark from 83; Hon Can Newc Cathl from 88. *The Vicarage, Humshaugh, Hexham, Northd NE46 4AA* Hexham (0434) 681304

PRINT, Norman George. b 38. Cuddesdon Coll 64. **d** 66 **p** 67. C Banbury *Ox* 66-69; C Whitley Ch Ch 69-75; P-in-c Shiplake 75-77; V Shiplake w Dunsden 77-90; R Balcombe *Chich* from 90. *The Rectory, Balcombe, Haywards Heath, W Sussex RH17 6PA* Balcombe (0444) 811249

PRIOR, Ven Christopher. b 12. CB68. Keble Coll Ox BA37 MA41. Cuddesdon Coll 37. **d** 38 **p** 39. Adn Portsm 69-77; rtd 77. *Ponies End, West Melbury, Shaftesbury, Dorset SP7 0LY* Fontmell Magna (0747) 811239

PRIOR, David Clement Lyndon. b 40. Trin Coll Ox BA63 MA66. Ridley Hall Cam 65. **d** 67 **p** 68. C Reigate St Mary *S'wark* 67-72; S Africa 72-79; Can Cape Town Cathl 76-79; C Ox St Aldate w H Trin *Ox* 79-82; C Ox St Aldate w St Matt 82-84; USA 84-85; V Ches Square St Mich w St Phil *Lon* from 85. *St Michael's Vicarage, 4 Chester Square, London SW1W 9HH* 071-730 8889

PRIOR, David Henry. b 42. Chich Th Coll 67. **d** 70 **p** 71. C S Kirkby *Wakef* 70-73; C Barnsley St Mary 73-77; V Middlestown 77-84; R Corringham *Chelmsf* from 84. *The Rectory, Church Road, Corringham, Stanford-le-Hope, Essex SS17 9AP* Stanford-le-Hope (0375) 673074

PRIOR, Ian Graham. b 44. Lon Univ BSc(Econ)71. Oak Hill Th Coll 78. **d** 80 **p** 81. C Luton Ch Ch *Roch* 80-83; TV Southgate *Chich* from 83. *Broadfield Vicarage, 10 Colonsay Road, Crawley, W Sussex RH11 9DF* Crawley (0293) 537976

PRIOR, Ian Roger Lyndon. b 46. St Jo Coll Dur BA68. Lon Coll of Div 68. **d** 70 **p** 71. C S Croydon Em *Cant* 70-73; Perm to Offic *S'wark* 73-85; Dir Overseas Personnel TEAR Fund 73-79; Dep Dir 79-83; Admin Dir CARE Trust and CARE Campaigns from 85; NSM New Malden and Coombe *S'wark* from 85. *39 Cambridge Avenue, New Malden, Surrey KT3 4LD* 081-949 0912

PRIOR, James Murray. b 39. Edin Univ BCom64. St And Dioc Tr Course 85. **d** 90 **p** 91. NSM Kirriemuir *St And* from 90; NSM Forfar from 90. *Horniehaugh, Glenquiech, Forfar, Angus DD8 3UG* Cortachy (05754) 287

PRIOR, John Gilman Leathes. b 15. Qu Coll Cam BA37 MA41. Ridley Hall Cam 37. **d** 39 **p** 40. V Camberley St Paul *Guildf* 63-74; V Crondall 75-77; V Crondall and Ewshot 77-80; rtd 80; Perm to Offic Win from 80; Guildf from 82; Portsm from 84. *River Cottage, Station Road, Bentley, Farnham, Surrey GU10 5JY* Bentley (0420) 34413

PRIOR, Preb John Miskin. b 27. Lon Univ BSc(Econ)48. Westcott Ho Cam 49. **d** 51 **p** 52. C Bedminster St Fran *Bris* 51-55; C Sherston Magna w Easton Grey 55-57; C Yatton Keynell 57-61; C Castle Combe 57-61; C Biddestone w Slaughterford 57-61; V Bishopstone w Hinton Parva 61-66; V Marshfield w Cold Ashton 66-82; P-in-c Tormarton w W Littleton 68-82; RD Bitton 73-79; R Trull w Angersleigh *B & W* from 82; RD Taunton 84-90; Preb Wells Cathl from 90. *The Rectory, Wild*

Oak Lane, Trull, Taunton, Somerset TA3 7JT Taunton (0823) 253518

PRIOR, Canon Kenneth Francis William. b 26. St Jo Coll Dur BA49. Oak Hill Th Coll 46. **d** 49 **p** 50. V Hove Bp Hannington Memorial Ch *Chich* 65-70; R Sevenoaks St Nic *Roch* 70-87; Hon Can Roch Cathl 82-87; C-in-c Hampstead St Jo Downshire Hill Prop Chpl *Lon* 87-90; rtd 89. *41 Osidge Lane, London N14 5JL* 081-368 4586

PRIOR, Canon Kenneth George William. b 17. Bris Univ BA39. Bible Churchmen's Coll 35. **d** 40 **p** 41. V Longfleet *Sarum* 55-82; RD Poole 75-80; Can and Preb Sarum Cathl 77-82; rtd 82. *5 Manor Road, Weymouth, Dorset DT3 5HR* Weymouth (0305) 788188

PRIOR, Nigel John. b 56. Bris Univ BA78. Westcott Ho Cam 79. **d** 81 **p** 82. C Langley All SS and Martyrs *Man* 81-82; C Langley and Parkfield 82-84; C Bury St Jo w St Mark 84-87; R Man Clayton St Cross w St Paul from 87. *The Rectory, 54 Clayton Hall Road, Manchester M11 4WH* 061-223 0766

PRIOR, Stephen Kenneth. b 55. Rhode Is Coll (USA) BA78. Wycliffe Hall Ox 79. **d** 82 **p** 83. C Aberavon *Llan* 82-85; P-in-c New Radnor and Llanfihangel Nantmelan etc *S & B* 85-86; V 86-90; V Llansamlet from 90. *The Vicarage, Llansamlet, Swansea SA7 9RL* Swansea (0792) 771420

PRIORY, Barry Edwin. b 44. FCIS Open Univ BA81. Qu Coll Birm 84. **d** 86 **p** 87. C Boldmere *Birm* 86-89; C Somerton w Compton Dundon, the Charltons etc *B & W* from 89. *The Parsonage, Charlton Adam, Somerton, Somerset TA11 7AS* Charlton Mackrell (045822) 3061

PRISTON, David Leslie. b 28. Lon Bible Coll 49 Oak Hill Th Coll 66. **d** 66 **p** 67. C Heref St Pet w St Owen *Heref* 66-71; R Beeby *Leic* 72-88; R Gaddesby w S Croxton 72-88; R S Croxton Gp from 88. *The Rectory, 19 Main Street, South Croxton, Leicester LE7 8RJ* Melton Mowbray (0664) 840245

PRITCHARD, Antony Robin. b 53. Van Mildert Coll Dur BSc74 SS Paul & Mary Coll Cheltenham CertEd75. St Jo Coll Nottm DipTh82 DPS84. **d** 84 **p** 85. C Desborough *Pet* 84-87; C Rushden w Newton Bromswold from 87. *45 Pytchley Road, Rushden, Northants NN10 9XB* Rushden (0933) 56398

PRITCHARD, Brian James Pallister. b 27. CCC Cam BA51 MA66. Westcott Ho Cam 51. **d** 53 **p** 54. C Attercliffe w Carbrook *Sheff* 53-58; V New Bentley 58-60; Chapl Park Hill Flats Sheff 60-67; P-in-c Sheff St Swithun *Sheff* 67-72; V Welton *Linc* from 72; RD Lawres from 86. *The Vicarage, Welton, Lincoln LN2 3JP* Welton (0673) 60264

PRITCHARD, Colin Ivor. b 44. Lon Inst of Educn TCert65. Chich Th Coll 66. **d** 69 **p** 70. C Kettering St Mary *Pet* 69-72; Chapl Clayesmore Sch Blandford 72-74; Asst Chapl Ellesmere Coll Shropshire 74-77; C Duston *Pet* 77-80; V Wellingborough St Andr 80-89; R Sedlescombe w Whatlington *Chich* from 89. *The Rectory, Church Hill, Sedlescombe, Battle, E Sussex TN33 0QP* Sedlescombe (0424) 870233

PRITCHARD, Colin Wentworth. b 38. K Coll Lon St Boniface Warminster 59. **d** 63 **p** 64. C Putney St Marg *S'wark* 63-67; C Brixton St Matt 67-70; C Milton *Portsm* 70-74; V Mitcham St Mark *S'wark* 74-82; R Long Ditton from 82. *The Rectory, 67 St Mary's Road, Surbiton, Surrey KT6 5HB* 081-398 1583

PRITCHARD, David Paul. b 47. FRCO LTCL BA. Wycliffe Hall Ox 80. **d** 82 **p** 83. C Kidlington *Ox* 82-84; P-in-c Marcham w Garford 84-85; V from 86; RD Abingdon from 91. *The Vicarage, 24 Church Street, Marcham, Abingdon, Oxon OX13 6NP* Frilford Heath (0865) 391319

PRITCHARD, Donald Oliver. b 22. Qu Coll Birm 73. **d** 75 **p** 76. Hon C Dunchurch *Cov* 75-83; P-in-c Mells w Buckland Dinham, Elm, Whatley etc *B & W* 83-84; R 84-88; rtd 88. *Moonrakers, Pengelly, Callington, Cornwall PL17 7DZ* Liskeard (0579) 84329

PRITCHARD, John Lawrence. b 48. St Pet Coll Ox BA70 DipTh70 MA73. Ridley Hall Cam 70. **d** 72 **p** 73. C Birm St Martin *Birm* 72-76; Asst Dir RE *B & W* 76-80; Youth Chapl 76-80; P-in-c Wilton 80-88; Dir Past Studies Cranmer Hall Dur from 89. *Cranmer Hall, Durham DH1 3RJ* 091-374 3568

PRITCHARD, John Richard. b 21. St D Coll Lamp. St Mich Coll Llan 46. **d** 48 **p** 49. V Lepton *Wakef* 57-69; rtd 86. *53 Hallas Road, Kirkburton, Huddersfield HD8 0QQ* Huddersfield (0484) 605747

PRITCHARD, Miss Kathryn Anne. b 60. St Cath Coll Ox MA Bradf Univ DIT. St Jo Coll Dur. **d** 87. Par Dn Addiscombe St Mary *S'wark* 87-90; CPAS Staff from 90. *16 Lindsey Crescent, Kenilworth, Warks CV8 1FL* Kenilworth (0926) 50114

PRITCHARD, Kenneth John. b 30. Liv Univ BEng51. NW Ord Course 72. **d** 74 **p** 75. C Ches Team *Ches* 74-78; Miss to Seamen 78-84; V Runcorn St Jo Weston *Ches* 78-84; V Gt Meols from 84. *St John's Vicarage, Birkenhead Road, Meols, South Wirral L47 0LF* 051-632 1661

PRITCHARD, Malcolm John. b 55. Bradf Univ BA85 CQSW85. St Jo Coll Nottm 86. **d** 88 **p** 89. C Peckham St Mary Magd *S'wark* from 88. *75 Hollydale Road, London SE15 2TE* 071-639 2742

PRITCHARD, Michael Owen. b 49. Trin Coll Carmarthen CertEd71. St Mich Coll Llan 71. **d** 73 **p** 74. C Conwy w Gyffin *Ban* 73-76; TV Dolgelly w Llanfachreth and Brithdir etc 76-78; Dioc Children's Officer 77-86; V Bettws y Coed and Capel Curig 78-83; CF (TAVR) from 79; V Bettws-y-Coed and Capel Curig w Penmachno etc *Ban* 83-86; Chapl Claybury Hosp Woodford Bridge from 86. *The Chaplain's Office, Claybury Hospital, Essex IG8 8DY* 081-504 7171

PRITCHARD, Canon Neil Lawrence. b 15. St Jo Coll Dur BA39 MA45. **d** 39 **p** 40. Hon Can Blackb Cathl *Blackb* 66-81; Dir of Ords 73-82; V Salesbury 73-80; Bp's Dom Chapl 78-83; rtd 80; Lic to Offic *Blackb* from 83. *46 Harrington Avenue, South Shore, Blackpool FY4 1QE* Blackpool (0253) 44794

PRITCHARD, Mrs Norma Kathleen. b 32. Birm Univ BA53 CertEd54. E Midl Min Tr Course 81. **dss** 84 **d** 87. Derby St Alkmund and St Werburgh *Derby* 84-87; Par Dn 87-90; Par Dn Derby St Andr w St Osmund from 90. *44 Evans Avenue, Allestree, Derby* Derby (0332) 557702

PRITCHARD, Peter Benson. b 30. FPhS60 LCP68 Univ of Wales (Lamp) BA51 St Cath Coll Ox DipTh57 Lon Univ DipEd70 Liv Univ MEd74 PhD81. Ripon Hall Ox 55. **d** 58 **p** 59. C Wavertree H Trin *Liv* 58-60; C Sefton 60-61; C-in-c Thornton CD 61-64; Chapl Liv Coll Boys' Sch 64-70; Hon C Wavertree St Bridget 70-90; Lect CF Mott Coll of Educn 70-76; Sen Lect Liv Coll of HE 76-83; Sen Lect Liv Poly 83-87; Perm to Offic Liv & Ches from 90; Tutor Open Univ from 90. *68 Gleggside, West Kirby, Wirral, Merseyside L48 6EA* 051-625 8093

PRITCHARD, Peter Humphrey. b 47. Univ of Wales (Ban) BA70 Liv Univ PGCE73 Birm Univ DipTh87. Qu Coll Birm 85. **d** 87 **p** 88. C Llanbeblig w Caernarfon and Betws Garmon etc *Ban* 87-90; R Llanberis w Llanrug from 90. *The Rectory, Llanberis, Caernarfon, Gwynedd LL55 4TF* Llanberis (0286) 870285

PRITCHARD, Robert Edmond. b 08. TCD BA38 MA44. **d** 41 **p** 42. I Dunfanaghy *D & R* 68-77; rtd 77. *5 Prince Edward Park, Stramillis, Belfast* Belfast (0232) 681786

PRITCHARD, Canon Stephen Edward. b 08. MC42 TD63. Univ Coll Dur BA32 MA35. **d** 33 **p** 34. V Slaley *Newc* 69-76; Hon Can Newc Cathl 70-76; rtd 76. *19 Redburn Crescent, Acomb, Hexham, Northd NE46 4QZ* Hexham (0434) 604931

PRITCHARD, Thomas. b 14. Ch Ch Ox BA37 MA40. Westcott Ho Cam 37. **d** 38 **p** 39. V Ex St Dav *Ex* 62-81; rtd 81; Perm to Offic *Ex* from 81. *3 Mill Cottages, Exton, Exeter EX3 0PH* Topsham (039287) 3018

PRITCHARD, Ven Thomas William. b 33. Keele Univ BA55 DipEd55. St Mich Coll Llan 55. **d** 57 **p** 58. C Holywell *St As* 57-61; C Ruabon 61-63; V 77-87; R Pontfadog 63-71; R Llanferres, Nercwys and Eryrys 71-77; Dioc Archivist from 76; Can St As Cathl from 84; RD Llangollen 86-87; Adn Montgomery from 87; V Berriew and Manafon from 87. *The Vicarage, Berriew, Welshpool, Powys SY21 8PL* Berriew (0686) 640223

PRITT, Stephen. b 06. AKC31. **d** 31 **p** 32. R Helhoughton w Raynham *Nor* 60-80; rtd 80; Perm to Offic *Glouc* from 80. *65 Manor Lane, Charfield, Wotton-under-Edge, Glos GL12 8TL* Falfield (0454) 260145

PRIVETT, Peter John. b 48. Qu Coll Birm 75. **d** 78 **p** 79. C Moseley St Agnes *Birm* 78-81; V Kingsbury 81-87; P-in-c Dilwyn and Stretford *Heref* 87-90; Dioc Children's Adv from 87; TV Leominster from 90. *33 Westgate, Leominster, Herefordshire HR6 8SA* Leominster (0568) 613176

PROBART, Raymond. b 21. Sarum Th Coll 49. **d** 51 **p** 52. V Douglas *Blackb* 60-88; rtd 88. *76 Waterside Way, Radstock, Bath BA3 3YQ* Radstock (0761) 33908

PROBERT, Christopher John Dixon. b 54. Univ of Wales (Cardiff) DipTh77 DPS78. St Mich Coll Llan 74. **d** 78 **p** 79. C Aberdare St Fagan *Llan* 78-79; C Cadoxton-juxta-Barry 79-81; R Llanfynydd *St As* 81-84; V Gosberton Clough and Quadring *Linc* 84-86; TV Cov Caludon *Cov* 86-88; V Llanrhian w Llanhowel and Carnhedryn etc *St D* 88-91; V Tregaron w Ystrad Meurig and Strata Florida from 91. *The Vicarage, Tregaron, Dyfed SY25 6HL* Tregaron (09744) 280

PROBERT, Edward Cleasby. b 58. St Cath Coll Cam BA80 MA84. Ripon Coll Cuddesdon BA84. **d** 85 **p** 86. C Esher *Guildf* 85-89; V Earlsfield St Andr *S'wark* from 89. *St Andrew's Vicarage, St Andrew's Court, London SW18 3QE* 081-946 4214

PROBETS, Canon Desmond. b 26. AKC50. **d** 51 **p** 52. C Finsbury St Clem *Lon* 51-52; C Kenton 52-62; Solomon Is 62-72; Dean Honiara Cathl 69-72; V Timperley *Ches* from 72; RD Bowdon 77-87; Hon Can Ches Cathl from 82. *The Vicarage, 12 Thorley Lane, Timperley, Altrincham, Cheshire WA14 7AZ* 061-980 4330

PROCTER, Andrew David. b 52. St Jo Coll Ox BA74 MA BA86. Trin Coll Bris 74. **d** 77 **p** 78. C Barnoldswick w Bracewell *Bradf* 77-80; P-in-c Kelbrook 80-82; V 82-87; V Heaton St Barn from 87. *The Vicarage, Parsons Road, Heaton, Bradford, W Yorkshire BD9 4AY* Bradford (0274) 496712 or 499354

PROCTOR, Herbert Oliver Hayward. b 92. St Mich Coll Llan 56. **d** 56 **p** 57. V Beguildy and Heyope *S & B* 64-66; rtd 66. *8 Grange Court, Boundary Road, Newbury, Berks RG14 7PH*

PROCTOR, Hugh Gordon. b 08. MFBA Keble Coll Ox BA30. Cuddesdon Coll 31. **d** 32 **p** 33. V Forest and Frith *Dur* 50-82; rtd 82. *4 Wrentnall Cottages, Forest in Teesdale, Barnard Castle, Co Durham DL12 0XS*

PROCTOR, Ven Jesse Heighton. b 08. Lon Univ BA29 MA32. St Andr Whittlesford 34. **d** 35 **p** 36. Adn Warw *Cov* 58-74; rtd 74; Perm to Offic *Heref* from 75. *Dilkusha, 22 Bank Crescent, Ledbury, Herefordshire HR8 1AA* Ledbury (0531) 2241

PROCTOR, Kenneth Noel. b 33. St Aid Birkenhead 61. **d** 63 **p** 64. C Oldham St Paul *Man* 63-66; C Davyhulme St Mary 66-69; V Norden w Ashworth from 69. *The Vicarage, Heap Road, Rochdale, Lancs OL12 7SN* Rochdale (0706) 41001

PROCTOR, Canon Michael Thomas. b 41. Ch Ch Ox BA65 MA67. Westcott Ho Cam 63. **d** 65 **p** 66. C Monkseaton St Mary *Newc* 65-69; Pakistan 69-72; C Willington *Newc* 72-77; TV Willington Team 77-79; Ed Sec Nat Soc 79-84; P-in-c Roxwell *Chelmsf* 79-84; Hon Can Chelmsf Cathl from 85; Dir of Miss and Unity from 85; Bp's Ecum Officer from 85. *124 Broomfield Road, Chelmsford CM1 1RN* Chelmsford (0245) 353915

PROCTOR, Noel. b 30. St Aid Birkenhead 62. **d** 64 **p** 65. C Haughton le Skerne *Dur* 64-67; R Byers Green 67-70; Chapl HM Pris Eastchurch 70-74; Dartmoor 74-79; Chapl HM Pris Man from 79. *222 Moor Lane, Salford, Manchester M7 0QH* 061-792 1284

PROCTOR, Mrs Susan Katherine. b 44. **d** 89. Par Dn Beighton *Sheff* from 89. *19 Norton Park Crescent, Sheffield S8 8GX* Sheffield (0742) 745754

PROCTOR, William Cecil Gibbon. b 03. TCD BA25 BD28 MA59. **d** 27 **p** 28. Sec Ch of Ireland Jew's Soc 65-71; rtd 72. *20 Crannagh Park, Rathfarnham, Dublin 14, Irish Republic* Dublin (1) 905821

PROFIT, David Hollingworth. b 17. Man Univ BA38. Cuddesdon Coll 40. **d** 41 **p** 42. C Kings Heath *Birm* 41-44; C Athlone *M & K* 44-48; S Africa from 48. *Braehead House, Auburn Road, Kenilworth, 7700 South Africa* Cape Town (21) 762-6041

PROPHET, Canon John Roy Henderson. b 10. Dur Univ LTh48 BA49. ALCD34. **d** 34 **p** 35. Hon Can Leic Cathl *Leic* 70-80; R Church Langton w Thorpe Langton and Tur Langto 73-80; rtd 80; Perm to Offic Leic & Pet from 80. *29 Glebe Way, Oakham, Leics LE15 6LX* Oakham (0572) 755852

PROSSER, Canon David George. b 33. Univ of Wales (Lamp) BA55. Coll of Resurr Mirfield 55 St Mich Coll Llan 59. **d** 60 **p** 61. C Caerphilly *Llan* 60-64; C Moordown Win 64-65; Chapl RN 65-81; V Morecambe St Barn *Blackb* 81-85; V Lt Paxton *Ely* 85-86; V Diddington 85-86; R Southoe w Hail Weston 85-86; Chapl Hamburg w Kiel *Eur* from 86; Miss to Seamen from 86; Hon Can Brussels Cathl *Eur* from 91. *Beim Gruenen Jaeger 16, 2000 Hamburg 36, Germany* Hamburg (40) 439-2334

PROSSER, Canon Kendall Frederick Evans. b 01. Jes Coll Ox BA24 MA37. St D Coll Lamp BA21 BD38. **d** 24 **p** 25. Hon Can Glouc Cathl *Glouc* 49-81; V Norton and the Leigh and Evington 53-81; rtd 81. *Greenlands Nursing Home, 24 Denmark Road, Gloucester GL1 3HZ*

PROSSER, Malcolm George. b 22. Univ of Wales (Lamp) BA44. St Mich Coll Llan 44. **d** 45 **p** 46. V High Littleton *B & W* 66-87; rtd 87. *141 Westway, Broadstone, Dorset BH18 9LQ* Broadstone (0202) 694280

PROSSER, Rhys. b 51. BA74. Sarum & Wells Th Coll 77. **d** 80 **p** 81. C Wimbledon *S'wark* 80-83; C St Helier 83-88; TV Gt and Lt Coates w Bradley *Linc* from 88. *St Nicholas's Vicarage, Great Coates, Grimsby, S Humberside DN37 9NS* Grimsby (0472) 882495

PROSSER, Richard Hugh Keble. b 31. Trin Coll Cam BA53 MA57 Leeds Univ PGCE63. Cuddesdon Coll 55. **d** 57 **p** 58. C Wigan All SS *Liv* 57-60; CR 62-87; S Rhodesia 64-65; Rhodesia 65-80; Zimbabwe 80-90; TR Pocklington Team *York* 90; R Pocklington and Owsthorpe and Kilnwick Percy etc from 90. *The Vicarage, 29 The Balk, Pocklington, York YO4 2QQ* Pocklington (0759) 302133

PROSSER, William Stanley. b 04. St D Coll Lamp LDiv35. **d** 35 **p** 36. V Pauntley w Upleadon *Glouc* 67-73; rtd 72; Perm to Offic *Heref* from 74. *Leecote, 23 Merrivale Lane, Ross-on-Wye, Herefordshire HR9 5JL* Ross-on-Wye (0989) 64605

PROTHERO, Brian Douglas. b 52. St Andr Univ MTh75 Dundee Univ CertEd77. Linc Th Coll 84. **d** 86 **p** 87. C Thornbury *Glouc* 86-89; V Goodrington *Ex* from 89. *Goodrington Vicarage, 16 Cliff Park Avenue, Paignton, Devon TQ4 6LT* Paignton (0803) 556476

PROTHERO, Cecil Charles. b 15. Lon Univ BSc(Econ)47 Bris Univ MEd74. **d** 68 **p** 69. C Ex St Mary Arches *Ex* 68-70; Chapl St Luke's Coll Ex 70-78; Dep PV Ex Cathl *Ex* from 78. *Les Gots, La Rochette, 16110 La Rochefoucauld, Charente, France* France (33) 45 63 98 95

PROTHERO, David John. b 43. St Pet Coll Ox BA66 MA70. St Steph Ho Ox 68. **d** 70 **p** 71. C Kirkby *Liv* 70-72; C St Marychurch *Ex* 72-74; V Marldon 74-83; Chapl HM Pris Channings Wood 78-83; V Torquay St Martin Barton *Ex* from 83. *St Martin's Vicarage, Beechfield Avenue, Barton, Torquay, Devon TQ2 8HU* Torquay (0803) 327223

PROTHERO, John Martin. b 32. Oak Hill Th Coll 64. **d** 66 **p** 67. C Tipton St Martin *Lich* 66-69; C Wednesfield Heath 69-72; Distr Sec BFBS 72-85; Lic to Offic *S'well* 73-86; Hon C Gedling 73; V Willoughby-on-the-Wolds w Wysall and Widmerpool from 86. *The Rectory, Keyworth Road, Wysall, Nottingham NG12 5QQ* Wymeswold (0509) 880269

PROTHEROE, Rhys Illtyd. b 50. St D Coll Lamp DipTh74. **d** 74 **p** 75. C Pembrey *St D* 74-76; C Carmarthen St Dav 76-78; V Llanegwad 78-79; V Llanegwad w Llanfynydd 79-82; V Gorslas from 82. *The Vicarage, Black Lion Road, Cross Hands, Llanelli, Dyfed SA14 6RU* Cross Hands (0269) 842561

PROTHEROE, Canon Robin Philip. b 33. St Chad's Coll Dur BA54 DipTh56 MA60 Nottm Univ MPhil75 Ox Univ DipEd62. **d** 57 **p** 58. C Roath St Marg *Llan* 57-60; Asst Chapl Culham Coll Abingdon 60-64; Perm to Offic *S'well* 64-66; Lic to Offic 66-84; P-in-c Barton in Fabis 70-73; P-in-c Thrumpton 70-73; Dir of Educn *Bris* from 84; Hon Can Bris Cathl from 85; Selector for ACCM 88-91; ABM from 91; Bp's Insp of Th Colls from 88. *29 Barley Croft, Bristol BS9 3TG* Bristol (0272) 683245 or 214411

PROUD, Andrew John. b 54. K Coll Lon BD79 AKC79. Linc Th Coll 79. **d** 80 **p** 81. C Stansted Mountfitchet *Chelmsf* 80-83; TV Borehamwood *St Alb* 83-90; C Hatf from 90. *Church Cottage, Church Street, Hatfield, Herts AL9 5AP* Hatfield (0707) 272119

PROUD, Clyde Douglas. b 09. St Aid Birkenhead 35. **d** 37 **p** 38. V Withernwick *York* 69-72; R Rise 69-72; C Bankfoot *Bradf* 72-79; rtd 74. *Dulverton Hall, St Martin's Square, Scarborough YO11 2DB* Scarborough (0723) 373082

PROUD, David John. b 56. Leeds Univ BA77 Dur Univ CertEd78. Ridley Hall Cam 85. **d** 88 **p** 89. C Lindfield *Chich* 88-91; TV Horsham from 91. *St John's House, Church Road, Broadbridge Heath, Horsham, W Sussex RH12 3ND* Horsham (0403) 65238

PROUDMAN, Canon Colin Leslie John. b 34. Lon Univ BD60 MTh63. Wells Th Coll 60. **d** 61 **p** 62. C Radlett *St Alb* 61-64; Canada from 64; Dean of Div Toronto Div Coll from 90. *Trinity College, 6 Hoskin Avenue, Toronto, Ontario, Canada, M5S 1H8*

PROUT, David William. b 47. FRSA Leeds Univ DipEd. St Steph Ho Ox 71. **d** 74 **p** 75. C Hanworth All SS *Lon* 74-77; Chapl Westmr City Sch 77-78; Hon C Pimlico St Pet w Westmr Ch Ch *Lon* 77-78; Chapl Roch Cathl *Roch* 78-81; C St Alb Abbey *St Alb* 81-82; Chapl St Hilda's Priory Sneaton, Whitby 82-89; P-in-c Aislaby and Ruswarp *York* from 89. *The Vicarage, Aislaby, Whitby, N Yorkshire YO21 1FU* Whitby (0947) 810350

PROUT, Hubert Douglas. b 18. St D Coll Lamp BA38. **d** 41 **p** 42. V Kirk Hallam *Derby* 58-84; rtd 84; Perm to Offic *Llan* from 85. *9 Caldy Close, Porthcawl, M Glam CF36 3QL* Porthcawl (0656) 786479

PROWSE, Mrs Barbara Bridgette Christmas. b 41. R Holloway Coll Lon BA62. **d** 91. C Kingsthorpe w Northn St Dav *Pet* from 91. *22 Tollgate Close,*

Kingsthorpe, Northampton NN2 6RP Northampton (0604) 721016

PRUDOM, William Haigh. b 26. STh79 APhS81 Hull Univ MPhil88. St D Coll Lamp 60. **d** 62 **p** 63. C Aylesford *Roch* 62-63; C Margate St Jo *Cant* 63-66; V Long Preston *Bradf* 66-73; C Darlington St Cuth *Dur* 73-75; V Ticehurst *Chich* 75-79; P-in-c Flimwell 78-79; V Ticehurst and Flimwell 79-81; R Spennithorne w Finghall and Hauxwell *Ripon* from 81. *The Rectory, Spennithorne, Leyburn, N Yorkshire DL8 4HS* Wensleydale (0969) 23010

PRUEN, Edward Binney. b 56. K Coll Lon BD77 AKC77. St Jo Coll Nottm 78. **d** 79 **p** 80. C Kidderminster St Mary *Worc* 79-82; C Woking St Jo *Guildf* 82-84; Chapl Asst R Marsden Hosp Lon and Surrey 84-86; C Stapleford *S'well* 86-88; Min Winklebury CD *Win* 88; V Winklebury from 88. *The Vicarage, Willoughby Way, Basingstoke, Hants RG23 8BD* Basingstoke (0256) 23941

PRUEN, Hugh Barrington. b 18. AKC50. **d** 50 **p** 51. R Skegness *Linc* 64-71; V Heckington w Howell 71-79; R Ashley w Weston by Welland and Sutton Bassett *Pet* 79-83; rtd 83; Perm to Offic *Linc* from 83. *Ashleigh, Church Road, Old Bolingbroke, Spilsby, Lincs PE23 4HF* East Kirkby (07903) 504

PRUEN, Hugh George. b 30. Worc Coll Ox BA53 MA62. Ely Th Coll 55. **d** 58 **p** 59. C Eastover *B & W* 58-63; Canada 63-66; P-in-c Selsey *Chich* 66-75; P-in-c Belbroughton *Worc* 75-82; V S w N Bersted *Chich* from 82. *121 Victoria Drive, Bognor Regis, W Sussex PO21 2EH* Bognor Regis (0243) 862018

PRYCE, Donald Keith. b 35. Man Univ BSc. Linc Th Coll 69. **d** 71 **p** 72. C Heywood St Jas *Man* 71-74; P-in-c 74-75; V 75-86; R Ladybarn from 86. *St Chad's Rectory, 1 St Chad's Road, Withington, Manchester M20 9WH* 061-445 1185

PRYCE, Robin Mark. b 60. Sussex Univ BA82. Westcott Ho Cam 84 United Th Coll Bangalore 85. **d** 87 **p** 88. C W Bromwich All SS *Lich* 87-90; Chapl and Fell CCC Cam from 90. *Corpus Christi College, Cambridge CB2 1RH* Cambridge (0223) 338002

PRYCE, William Robert. b 28. MBE91. **d** 79 **p** 80. Hon C Leverstock Green *St Alb* 79-80; Perm to Offic *Sheff* 80-84; Hon C Sheff St Barn and St Mary 84-90; NSM Alveley and Quatt *Heref* from 91. *28 Crooks Cross, Alveley, Bridgnorth, Shropshire WV15 6LS* Quatt (0746) 780588

PRYER, Miss Frances Margaret. b 24. Gilmore Ho 59. dss 69 **d** 87. Hornchurch St Andr *Chelmsf* 66-83; rtd 84; Hon Par Dn Leigh-on-Sea St Aid *Chelmsf* from 87. *73 Bohemia Chase, Leigh-on-Sea, Essex SS9 4PW* Southend-on-Sea (0702) 520276

PRYKE, Dr Edward John. b 20. K Coll Lon BD51 AKC51 St Cath Coll Ox BA53 MA57 BLitt63 Lon Univ PhD71. Wycliffe Hall Ox 51. **d** 53 **p** 54. Asst Chapl & Sen Lect Coll SS Mark & Jo Chelsea 62-73; Coll of SS Mark & Jo Plymouth 71-74; P-in-c S Pool w Chivelstone *Ex* 74-75; R E Portlemouth 74-76; P-in-c Gt Paxton *Ely* 76-78; V 78-84; P-in-c 85; P-in-c Offord D'Arcy w Offord Cluny 76-78; R 78-84; P-in-c 85; rtd 85; Co-ord BRF (Dio Glos) from 90. *3 Limber Hill, Wyman's Brook, Cheltenham, Glos GL50 4RJ* Cheltenham (0242) 244629

PRYKE, Jonathan Justin Speaight. b 59. Trin Coll Cam BA80 MA85. Trin Coll Bris BD85. **d** 85 **p** 86. C Corby St Columba *Pet* 85-88; C Jesmond Clayton Memorial *Newc* from 88. *15 Lily Avenue, Jesmond, Newcastle upon Tyne NE2 2SQ* 091-281 9854

PRYOR, Derek John. b 29. Lon Univ DipTh57 BD63 Birm Univ MEd74. Linc Th Coll 79 Chich Th Coll 79. **d** 80 **p** 81. Hon C Youlgreave *Derby* 80-82; Hon C Stanton-in-Peak 80-82; Hon C Ingham w Cammeringham w Fillingham *Linc* 82-87; Chapl Bp Grosseteste Coll Linc 83-84; Dioc Schs Officer *Linc* from 87. *Walnut Cottage, Chapel Lane, Fillingham, Gainsborough, Lincs DN21 5BP* Hemswell (042773) 276

PRYOR, William Lister Archibald. b 39. Trin Coll Cam BA67 MA69. Ox NSM Course 72. **d** 75 **p** 76. NSM Summertown *Ox* 75-76; NSM Wolvercote w Summertown from 76. *Elm Tree Cottage, Summer Fields, Oxford OX2 7EH* Oxford (0865) 515102

PRYS, Deiniol. b 53. Univ of Wales (Ban) DipTh82 Univ of Wales (Cardiff) DPS83. St Mich Coll Llan 82. **d** 83 **p** 84. C Llanbeblig w Caernarfon and Betws Garmon etc *Ban* 83-86; TV Amlwch 86-88; V Llanerchymedd from 89. *The Vicarage, Llanerchymedd, Anglesey, Gwynedd LL71 8EH* Llanerchymedd (0248) 470525

PRYSOR-JONES, John Glynne. b 47. JP. CQSW73 MBASW Birm Univ DPS80. Westcott Ho Cam 88. **d** 90

p 91. C Mitcham St Mark *S'wark* from 90. *7 Graham Road, Mitcham, Surrey CR4 2HB* 081-648 3284

PRYTHERCH, David. b 30. Down Coll Cam BA54 MA58 Lon Univ CertEd68 DipAdEd71. Coll of Resurr Mirfield 54. **d** 56 **p** 57. C Blackpool St Steph *Blackb* 56-61; R Matson *Glouc* 61-65; Chapl St Elphin's Sch Matlock 65-85; V Thornton-le-Fylde *Blackb* from 85; RD Poulton from 91. *The Vicarage, Meadows Avenue, Thornton Cleveleys, Blackpool FY5 2TW* Cleveleys (0253) 855099

PUCKRIN, Christopher. b 47. Oak Hill Th Coll. **d** 82 **p** 83. C Heworth *York* 82-84; C Sherburn in Elmet 84-85; P-in-c Kirkby Wharfe 85-86; P-in-c Kirk Fenton 85-86; V Kirk Fenton w Kirkby Wharfe and Ulleskelfe 86-87; C York St Mich-le-Belfrey from 87. *13 Hempland Drive, York YO3 0AY* York (0904) 422418

PUDDEFOOT, John Charles. b 52. St Pet Hall Ox BA74 Edin Univ BD78. Edin Th Coll 76. **d** 78 **p** 79. C Darlington H Trin *Dur* 78-81; Ind Chapl *Chich* 81-84; Lic to Offic *Ox* 85-87. *Eton College, Windsor, Berks* Windsor (0753) 869991

PUDDY, Kenneth Wilfred. b 15. Hatf Coll Dur BA36 DipTh38. St Aug Coll Cant 37. **d** 39 **p** 39. V Kingsbury Episcopi w E Lambrook *B & W* 55-89; RD Ilminster 59-71; rtd 90. *La Rambaudie, La Gresignac, Verteillac 24320, France* France (33) 53 91 04 07

PUGH, Canon David. b 22. Univ of Wales (Abth) BA48. St D Coll Lamp 48. **d** 50 **p** 51. C Llanllwchaiarn *St D* 50-57; R Ban Teifi w Henllan 57-70; R Ban Teifi w Henllan and Llanfairorllwyn 70-81; RD Emlyn from 73; R Ban Teifi w Henllan and Llanfairorllwyn etc from 81; Can St D Cathl from 88. *The Vicarage, Henllan, Llandyssul, Dyfed SA44 5TN* Llandyssul (0559) 370463

PUGH, Dilwyn. b 11. St D Coll Lamp BA35. **d** 35 **p** 36. V Dixton *Heref* 70-79; rtd 79; Perm to Offic *Mon* from 82. *15 The Willows, Raglan, Gwent NP5 3EB* Raglan (0291) 690227

PUGH, Ernest William. b 16. AKC41. **d** 41 **p** 42. Hd of Div Ormskirk Gr Sch 59-81; Hon C Liv St Steph w St Cath *Liv* 59-73; P-in-c 73-81; rtd 81; Hon C W Derby (or Tuebrook) St Jo *Liv* 81-89. *The Cottage, 54 Derwent Road, Liverpool L13 6QR* 051-228 4022

PUGH, Frank William. b 19. Roch Th Coll 62. **d** 64 **p** 65. R Fordington *Sarum* 70-73; TV Dorchester 73-78; R Stalbridge 78-89; rtd 89. *3 Rose Cottages, Balsam Lane, Wincanton, Somerset BA9 9HZ* Wincanton (0963) 34100

PUGH, Harry. b 48. K Coll Lon BD70 AKC71 Lanc Univ MA89. **d** 72 **p** 73. C Milnrow *Man* 72-75; P-in-c Rochdale Gd Shep 75-78; TV Rochdale 78-79; Perm to Offic *Liv* 79-82; C Darwen St Cuth *Blackb* 82-85; C Darwen St Cuth w Tockholes St Steph 85-86; V Burnley St Steph from 86. *St Stephen's Vicarage, 154 Todmorden Road, Burnley, Lancs BB11 3ER* Burnley (0282) 24733

PUGH, Canon John. b 18. St D Coll Lamp BA40. **d** 42 **p** 43. V Bagillt *St As* 61-73; RD Holywell 71-73; V Rossett 73-83; RD Wrexham 77-82; Hon Can St As Cathl from 79; rtd 83. *Benton Croft, Box Lane, Wrexham, Clwyd LL12 7RB*

PUGH, Ronald Keith. b 32. Jes Coll Ox BA54 MA57 DPhil57. Ripon Hall Ox 56. **d** 59 **p** 60. C Bournemouth St Mich *Win* 59-61; Asst Chapl Bryanston Sch Blandford 61-66; Chapl Cranleigh Sch Surrey 66-68; Lic to Offic *Win* from 68; Lect K Alfred Coll Winchester from 68. *6 Windermere Gardens, Alresford, Hants SO24 9NL* Alresford (0962) 732879

PUGH, Stephen Gregory. Southn Univ BEd77. Linc Th Coll 85. **d** 87 **p** 88. C Harpenden St Nic *St Alb* 87-90; C Stevenage All SS Pin Green from 90. *156 Durham Road, Stevenage, Herts SG1 4HZ* Stevenage (0438) 740621

PUGH, Wilfred Daniel. b 31. Lich Th Coll 63. **d** 64 **p** 66. Asst Chapl HM Pris Pentonville 69-70; Chapl HM Youth Cust Cen Dover 70-75; Chapl HM Pris Cardiff 75-78; V Ystradyfodwg *Llan* 78-79; TV Cannock *Lich* 79-84; P-in-c Newfoundpool *Leic* 84-85; TV Leic Ascension 85-86; rtd 87. *29 Summerfield Drive, Llantrisant, Pontyclun, M Glam CF7 8QF* Llantrisant (0443) 225685

PUGH, William Bryan. b 34. Man Univ. Ridley Hall Cam 59. **d** 61 **p** 62. C Oseney Crescent St Luke w Camden Square St Paul *Lon* 61-64; C N Wembley St Cuth 64-67; CF 67-88; QHC from 85; Chapl Heathfield Sch Ascot from 88. *3 College Close, Camberley, Surrey GU15 4JU* Camberley (0276) 28799

PUGMIRE, Alan. b 37. Lon Univ DipTh63. Tyndale Hall Bris 61. **d** 64 **p** 65. C Islington St Steph w St Bart and St Matt *Lon* 64-66; C St Helens St Mark *Liv* 66-71; R Stretford St Bride *Man* 71-82; R Burnage St Marg from 82; AD Heaton from 88. *St Margaret's Rectory, 250 Burnage Lane, Manchester M19 1FL* 061-432 1844

PUGSLEY, Anthony John. b 39. ACIB. Oak Hill Th Coll 89. **d** 90 **p** 91. C Chadwell *Chelmsf* from 90. *7 Cedar Road, Grays, Essex RM16 4ST* Tilbury (0375) 850877

PULESTON, Mervyn Pedley. b 35. K Coll Lon BD60 AKC60. **d** 61 **p** 62. C Gt Marlow *Ox* 61-65; C-in-c Blackbird Leys CD 65-70; R Kidlington 70-85; TR Kidlington w Hampton Poyle 85-86; Chapl Geneva *Eur* from 86. *108 Route Swiss, 1290 Versoix, Switzerland* Geneva (22) 755-4883

PULFORD, Christopher. b 59. Pemb Coll Ox BA81 MA87. Trin Coll Bris. **d** 84 **p** 85. C Parr *Liv* 84-87; Chapl Berkhamsted Sch Herts from 87. *131 High Street, Berkhamsted, Herts HP4 2DJ* Berkhamsted (0442) 873008

PULFORD, John Shirley Walter. b 31. Jes Coll Cam BA55 MA59. Cuddesdon Coll 55. **d** 57 **p** 58. C Blackpool St Steph *Blackb* 57-60; N Rhodesia 60-63; V Newington St Paul *S'wark* 63-68; C Seacroft *Ripon* 68-70; Asst Chapl HM Pris *Liv* 70-71; Chapl HM Pris *Linc* 71-73; Counsellor Linc Colls Art and Tech 73-79; Cam Univ Counselling Service from 79; Dir from 82. *14 Trumpington Street, Cambridge CB2 1QA* Cambridge (0223) 332865

PULFORD, Canon Stephen Ian. b 25. Clifton Th Coll 53. **d** 56 **p** 57. C Heref St Jas *Heref* 56-58; R Coberley w Cowley *Glouc* from 58; P-in-c Colesbourne from 75; Hon Can Glouc Cathl from 84; RD Cirencester 88-89. *The Rectory, Coberley, Cheltenham GL53 9QZ* Coberley (024287) 232

PULLAN, Ben John. b 43. MSc. **d** 77 **p** 78. NSM Westbury-on-Trym St Alb *Bris* 77-91; NSM Henleaze from 91. *52 Druid Stoke Avenue, Bristol BS9 1DQ* Bristol (0272) 682697

PULLAN, Lionel Stephen. b 37. ARCO58 FIST77 Keble Coll Ox BA58 MA62. Cuddesdon Coll 58. **d** 60 **p** 61. C Tranmere St Paul *Ches* 60-63; C Higher Bebington 63-64; Perm to Offic 64-70; Hon C Luton St Chris Round Green *St Alb* 70-72; Hon C Hitchin H Sav 72-73; Hon C Welwyn 73-75; Hon C Welwyn w Ayot St Peter 75-78; Hon C Kimpton w Ayot St Lawrence 78-82; Hon C Stevenage St Andr and St Geo 82-85; Deputation Appeals Org CECS 85-90; Perm to Offic *St Alb* 85-89; Public Preacher 89-90; V Sundon from 90. *St Mary's Vicarage, 1 Selina Close, Sundon, Luton LU3 3AW* Luton (0582) 583076 or 573236

PULLAN, Mrs Pauline Margaret. b 32. Nor Ord Course 79. **dss** 82 **d** 87. Stockport St Sav *Ches* 82-83; Wilmslow 83-87; Par Dn from 87; Sub-Chapl HM Pris Styal from 89. *12 Acacia Avenue, Wilmslow, Cheshire SK9 6AX* Wilmslow (0625) 525865

PULLEN, James Stephen. b 43. Lon Univ BSc64 Linacre Coll Ox BA68. St Steph Ho Ox 66. **d** 68 **p** 69. C Chorlton-cum-Hardy St Clem *Man* 68-72; C Doncaster St Leon and St Jude *Sheff* 72-73; Chapl St Olave and St Sav Sch Orpington 73-75; Chapl Haileybury Coll Herts from 75; Perm to Offic *St Alb* from 75. *Edmonstone, Haileybury, Hertford SG13 7NU* Hoddesdon (0992) 463384

PULLEN, Roger Christopher. b 43. Lon Univ BSc65 PGCE90. Wells Th Coll 65. **d** 67 **p** 68. C S w N Hayling *Portsm* 67-69; C Farlington 69-73; V Farington *Blackb* 73-80; V Chorley All SS 80-83; V Kingsley *Ches* from 83. *St John's Vicarage, Pike Lane, Kingsley, Warrington WA6 8EH* Kingsley (0928) 88386

PULLIN, Andrew Eric. b 47. Linc Th Coll 71. **d** 73 **p** 74. C Pershore w Wick *Worc* 73-75; C Pershore w Pinvin, Wick and Birlingham 75-77; TV Droitwich 77-80; V Woburn Sands *St Alb* 80-85; Perm to Offic *B & W* from 85. *85 Weymouth Road, Frome, Somerset* Frome (0373) 72170

PULLIN, Arthur. b 18. St Jo Coll Dur LTh39 BA40 MA45. ALCD39. **d** 41 **p** 42. V Midhurst *Chich* 65-85; R Woolbeding 65-85; RD Midhurst 81-85; rtd 85; Perm to Offic *Chich* from 85. *38 Carters Way, Wisborough Green, W Sussex RH14 0BY* Wisborough Green (0403) 700566

PULLIN, Christopher. b 56. St Chad's Coll Dur BA77. Ripon Coll Cuddesdon 79. **d** 80 **p** 81. C Tooting All SS *S'wark* 80-85; V New Eltham All SS from 85. *All Saints' Vicarage, 22 Bercta Road, London SE9 3TZ* 081-850 9894

PULLIN, Peter. MA MSc CEng. Trin Coll Bris. **d** 88 **p** 89. NSM Rugby St Andr *Cov* 88-90; NSM Aylesbeare, Rockbeare, Farringdon etc *Ex* from 90. *Applegarth, 5 Minchin Orchard, Aylesbeare, Exeter EX5 2BY* Woodbury (0395) 32877

PULMAN, Edgar James. b 17. Selw Coll Cam BA48 MA53. ALCD50. **d** 50 **p** 51. V Finchley H Trin *Lon* 63-76; C Norton sub Hamdon, W Chinnock, Chiselborough etc *B & W* 77-78; Lic to Offic from 79; rtd 82. *5 Manor*

House, Norton Sub Hamdon, Stoke-Sub-Hamdon, Somerset TA14 6SJ Chiselborough (093588) 521

PULMAN, John. b 34. Nottm Univ CTPS81. E Midl Min Tr Course 78. **d** 81 **p** 82. NSM Mansf St Pet *S'well* 81-83; C Mansf Woodhouse 83-86; V Flintham from 86; R Car Colston w Screveton from 86; Chapl HM Young Offender Inst Whatton 86-90; Chapl HM Pris Whatton from 90. *The Vicarage, Woods Lane, Flintham, Newark, Notts NG23 5LR* Newark (0636) 525750

PUMFREY, John Lawrence. b 06. Bps' Coll Cheshunt 48. **d** 49 **p** 50. V Hamstead St Paul *Birm* 62-71; rtd 71. *18 Highfield, Callow End, Worcester WR2 4TP* Worcester (0905) 830609

PUMPHREY, Norman (John) Albert. b 21. Nor Ord Course 76. **d** 77 **p** 78. NSM Aylsham *Nor* from 77; Chapl St Mich Hosp Aylsham from 88. *12 Buxton Road, Aylsham, Norwich NR11 6JD* Aylsham (0263) 733207

PUNCHARD, Herbert Oliver. b 01. **d** 34 **p** 35. V Litlington w Abington Pigotts *Ely* 48-68; V Wendy w Shingay 55-68; R Croydon w Clopton 66-68; rtd 68. *St Luke's Home, Military Hill, Cork, Irish Republic* Cork (21) 501621

PUNSHON, Keith. b 48. JP. Jes Coll Cam BA69 MA73 Birm Univ DipTh73 MA77. Qu Coll Birm 71. **d** 73 **p** 74. C Yardley St Edburgha *Birm* 73-76; Chapl Eton Coll Windsor 76-79; V Hill *Birm* 79-86; V S Yardley St Mich *Birm* from 86. *St Michael's Vicarage, 60 Yew Tree Lane, Birmingham B26 1AP* 021-705 2563

PURCELL, Stanley Thomas. b 08. AKC41. **d** 41 **p** 42. V Bushley *Worc* 66-77; Chapl to Mentally Handicapped 68-77; rtd 77; Perm to Offic *Worc* from 77. *49 Arundel Road, Tewkesbury, Glos GL20 8AU* Tewkesbury (0684) 293830

PURCELL, Canon William Ernest. b 09. Univ of Wales BA34 Keble Coll Ox BA36 MA43. Qu Coll Birm 36. **d** 37 **p** 38. Can Res Worc Cathl *Worc* 66-76; rtd 76; Perm to Offic *Ox* from 83. *14 Conifer Close, Cumnor Hill, Oxford OX2 9HP* Oxford (0865) 725233

PURCELL, Ven William Henry Samuel. b 12. Fitzw Ho Cam BA36 MA41. Westcott Ho Cam 36. **d** 37 **p** 38. Adn Dorking *Guildf* 68-82; rtd 82; Perm to Offic *Guildf* from 82. *55 Windfield, Epsom Road, Leatherhead, Surrey KT22 8UQ* Leatherhead (0372) 75708

PURCHAS, Mrs Catherine Patience Ann. b 39. St Mary's Coll Dur BA61. St Alb Minl Tr Scheme 77. **dss** 80 **d** 87. RE Resource Cen 80-81; Relig Broadcasting Chiltern Radio 81-87; Wheathampstead *St Alb* 81-87; Hon Par Dn from 87; Relig Broadcasting Beds Radio from 88. *The Rectory, Church Street, Wheathampstead, St Albans, Herts AL4 8LR* Wheathampstead (058283) 3144

PURCHAS, Thomas. b 35. Qu Coll Birm 59. **d** 62 **p** 63. C Hatf *St Alb* 62-71; R Blunham 71-78; R Blunham w Tempsford and Lt Barford 78-80; R Wheathampstead from 80. *The Rectory, Church Street, Wheathampstead, St Albans, Herts AL4 8LR* Wheathampstead (058283) 3144

PURDIE, Dr Anthony Watson. b 08. FRCOG51 FRCSGlas65 FRCPGlas68 Glas Univ MB, ChB31 K Coll Lon BD76 AKC76. **d** 76 **p** 77. NSM Waltham Abbey *Chelmsf* 76-77; NSM Goodmayes St Paul 77-80; Perm to Offic *Ex* from 82. *Shearwater, Pope's Lane, Colyford, Colyton, Devon EX13 6QR* Colyton (0297) 553206

PURDY, John David. b 44. Leeds Univ BA65 DipTh74 MPhil76. Coll of Resurr Mirfield 72. **d** 75 **p** 76. C Marske in Cleveland *York* 75-78; C Marton-in-Cleveland 78-80; V Newby 80-87; V Kirkleatham from 87. *Kirkleatham Vicarage, 130 Mersey Road, Redcar, Cleveland TS10 4DF* Redcar (0642) 482073

PURNELL, Steven. b 53. BA. Qu Coll Birm. **d** 82 **p** 83. C Worc St Barn w Ch Ch *Worc* 82-85; V Terriers *Ox* from 85. *St Francis's Vicarage, Terriers, High Wycombe, Bucks HP13 5AB* High Wycombe (0494) 20676

PURSER, Alan Gordon. b 51. Leic Univ BSc73. Wycliffe Hall Ox 74. **d** 77 **p** 78. C Beckenham Ch Ch *Roch* 77-81; TV Barking St Marg w St Patr *Chelmsf* 81-84; S Africa 84-88; C Enfield Ch Ch Trent Park *Lon* from 88; Proclamation Trust from 88. *The Parsonage, 34 Crescent East, Hadley Wood, Herts EN4 0EN* 081-449 2572

PURVEY-TYRER, Neil. b 66. Leeds Univ BA87 MA88. Westcott Ho Cam 88. **d** 90 **p** 91. C Denbigh and Nantglyn *St As* from 90. *34 Trewen, Denbigh, Clwyd LL16 3HF* Denbigh (0745) 716426

PURVIS, Canon Colin. b 19. Kelham Th Coll 37. **d** 44 **p** 45. V Heworth St Mary *Dur* 62-76; R Egglescliffe 76-84; Hon Can Dur Cathl from 83; rtd 84; Perm to Offic Newc and Ripon from 84. *15 Milbank Court, Darlington, Co Durham DL3 9PF* Darlington (0325) 355711

PURVIS, Stephen. b 48. AKC70. **d** 71 **p** 72. C Peterlee *Dur* 71-75; Dioc Recruitment Officer 75-79; V Stevenage All SS Pin Green *St Alb* 79-88; TR Borehamwood from 88. *7 Furzehill Road, Borehamwood, Herts WD6 2DG* 081-953 2554

PUSEY, Ian John. b 39. Sarum Th Coll 69. **d** 71 **p** 72. C Waltham Abbey *Chelmsf* 71-75; TV Stantonbury *Ox* 75-80; P-in-c Bletchley 80-84; R from 84. *75 Church Green Road, Bletchley, Milton Keynes MK3 6BY* Milton Keynes (0908) 373357

PUSEY, Robert Guy. b 09. St Edm Hall Ox BA36 MA51. Linc Th Coll 36. **d** 38 **p** 39. V Cowleigh *Worc* 59-73; TV Malvern Link w Cowleigh 73-75; rtd 75; Perm to Offic *Worc* from 75. *Flat 2, 3 Orchard Road, Malvern, Worcs WR14 3DA* Malvern (0684) 573716

PUTMAN, Nina Maude Elaine. b 20. dss 75 **d** 87. New Malden and Coombe *S'wark* 75-87; NSM from 87; rtd 80. *57 Alric Avenue, New Malden, Surrey KT3 4JL* 081-949 6042

PYATT, Noel Watson. b 34. AKC57. **d** 58 **p** 59. C Prenton *Ches* 58-61; C Cheadle Hulme All SS 61-63; P-in-c Hattersley 63-66; V 66-70; V Ches St Paul from 70. *St Paul's Vicarage, 10 Sandy Lane, Chester CH3 5UL* Chester (0244) 25877

PYBURN, Canon Alan. b 29. G&C Coll Cam BA51 MA55. Westcott Ho Cam 53. **d** 55 **p** 56. C Barnard Castle *Dur* 55-57; Chapl G&C Coll Cam 57-60; V Dallington *Pet* 60-72; V Ox St Giles *Ox* 72-79; P-in-c Remenham from 79; R Henley from 79; RD Henley from 84; Can Ch Ch from 90. *The Rectory, Hart Street, Henley on Thames, Oxon RG9 2AU* Henley-on-Thames (0491) 577340

PYBUS, Antony Frederick. b 54. Birm Univ BA77. St Jo Coll Dur 78. **d** 81 **p** 82. C Ches H Trin *Ches* 81-84; C W Hampstead St Jas *Lon* 84-89; V Alexandra Park St Andr from 89. *St Andrew's Vicarage, 34 Alexandra Park Road, London N10 2AB* 081-444 6898

PYE, Allan Stephen. b 56. Univ of Wales (Lamp) BA78 Lanc Univ MA85 MPhil87. Westcott Ho Cam 79. **d** 81 **p** 82. C Scotforth *Blackb* 81-85; C Oswaldtwistle All SS 85-87; Chapl Wrightington Hosp 87-91; V Wrightington *Blackb* 87-91; P-in-c Hayton St Mary *Carl* from 91. *The Vicarage, Hayton, Carlisle CA4 9HR* Hayton (022870) 248

PYE, James Timothy. b 58. Oak Hill Th Coll BA90. **d** 90 **p** 91. C Normanton *Derby* from 90. *211 Village Street, Derby DE3 8DE* Derby (0332) 767407

PYE, Joseph Terence Hardwidge. b 41. ARICS64. Trin Coll Bris 70. **d** 73 **p** 74. C Blackb Ch Ch *Blackb* 73-76; OMF 77-90; Korea 77-90; V Castle Church *Lich* from 90. *Castle Church Vicarage, Castle Bank, Stafford ST16 1DJ* Stafford (0785) 223673

PYECROFT, Eric Stanley. b 26. Hatf Coll Dur BA50 St Chad's Coll Dur DipTh53. **d** 53 **p** 54. C Belgrave St Mich *Leic* 53-54; C Leic St Paul 54-57; R Cole Orton 57-60; Area Sec (Wales, Glouc and Heref) UMCA 60-62; E Co 62-64; Chapl St Gabr Convent Sch Newbury 64-68; Perm to Offic *Glouc* 68-72; P-in-c Oakridge 72-79; P-in-c Bisley 79; P-in-c Bisley w Oakridge 79-83; P-in-c Bisley, Oakridge, Miserden and Edgeworth 83; V from 83. *Winsley Cottage, Oakridge Lynch, Stroud, Glos GL6 7NZ* Frampton Mansell (028576) 260

PYKE, Alan. b 37. Trin Coll Bris BA87. **d** 87 **p** 88. CA 58-87; C Ipswich St Mary at Stoke w St Pet & St Mary Quay *St E* 87-90; R Creeting St Mary, Creeting St Peter etc from 90. *The Rectory, Forward Green, Stowmarket, Suffolk IP14 5EF* Stowmarket (0449) 711347

PYKE, Richard Ernest. b 50. Sarum & Wells Th Coll. **d** 82 **p** 83. C Bushey *St Alb* 82-85; C Gt Berkhamsted 85-89; V St Alb St Mary Marshalswick from 89. *The Vicarage, 1 Sherwood Avenue, St Albans, Herts AL4 9QA* St Albans (0727) 51544

PYKE, Thomas Fortune. b 62. St Chad's Coll Dur BA85 Fitzw Coll Cam BA88. Ridley Hall Cam 86. **d** 89 **p** 90. C Hitchin *St Alb* from 89. *67 Whitehill Road, Hitchin, Herts SG4 9HP* Hitchin (0462) 457402

PYLE, John Alan. b 31. Qu Coll Birm. **d** 69 **p** 70. C Fenham St Jas and St Basil *Newc* 69-72; C Monkseaton St Pet 72-74; C Morpeth 74-78; R Bothal 78-83; TV Willington Team from 83. *St Mary's Vicarage, Churchill Street, Wallsend, Tyne & Wear NE28 7SX* 091-262 8208

PYM, David Pitfield. b 45. Nottm Univ BA65 Ex Coll Ox DPhil68. Ripon Hall Ox 66. **d** 68 **p** 69. C Nottm St Mary *S'well* 68-72; Chapl RN 72-76 and 79-84; Chapl Worksop Coll Notts 76-79; R Avon Dassett w Farnborough and Fenny Compton *Cov* from 84. *The Rectory, Avon Dassett, Leamington Spa, Warks CV33 0AR* Farnborough (029589) 305

PYM, Francis Victor. b 24. ARIBA52 DipArch52. St Jo Coll Dur 75. **d** 76 **p** 77. C Keighley *Bradf* 76-79; Chapl

Bethany Fellowship 79-87; Dir Joshua Chr Trust from 88; Hon C Slaugham *Chich* from 88; Research Asst House of Lords from 89. *Bolney House, Bolney, Haywards Heath, W Sussex RH17 5QR* Handcross (0444) 881877

PYM, Gordon Sydney. b 19. Worc Ord Coll 59. **d** 61 **p** 62. V Owston *Sheff* 69-72; V Hensall 72-75; rtd 75. *6 Grenoside Road, Swinton, Mexborough, S Yorkshire S64 8RP* Mexborough (0709) 586884

PYNE, Robert Leslie. b 51. Lanchester Poly BA72 Leeds Univ DipTh78. Coll of Resurr Mirfield 76. **d** 79 **p** 80. C Clifton All SS w St Jo *Bris* 79-81; Bp's Dom Chapl *Ox* 81-84; TV High Wycombe 84-90; Chapl RN from 90. *c/o MOD, Lacon House, Theobald's Road, London WC1X 8RY* 071-430 6847

✠**PYTCHES, Rt Rev George Edward David.** b 31. Bris Univ BA54 Nottm Univ MPhil84. Tyndale Hall Bris 51. **d** 55 **p** 56 **c** 70. C Ox St Ebbe *Ox* 55-58; C Wallington H Trin *S'wark* 58-59; Chile 59-77; Suff Bp Valparaiso 70-72; Bp Chile, Bolivia and Peru 72-77; V Chorleywood St Andr *St Alb* from 77. *St Andrew's Vicarage, Quickley Lane, Chorleywood, Rickmansworth, Herts WD3 5AE* Chorleywood (0923) 282391

PYTCHES, Peter Norman Lambert. b 32. Lon Univ BD57 Bris Univ MLitt67 Southn Univ PhD81. Lambeth STh74 Tyndale Hall Bris 53. **d** 57 **p** 58. C Heatherlands St Jo *Sarum* 57-61; V 71-76; C Cromer *Nor* 61-63; V Plymouth St Jude *Ex* 63-71; Dir Past Tr Oak Hill Th Coll 76-81; V Finchley Ch Ch *Lon* from 81; AD Cen Barnet 86-91. *Christ Church Vicarage, 616 High Road, London N12 0AA* 081-445 2377 or 445 2532

Q

QUANCE, John David. b 42. Kelham Th Coll 61. **d** 67 **p** 68. C Southgate Ch Ch *Lon* 67-70; C Norbury St Phil *Cant* 70-73; Asst Chapl Middx Hosp Lon 73-80; R Failsworth St Jo *Man* from 80; Australia 84-85. *St John's Rectory, Pole Lane, Failsworth, Manchester M35 9PB* 061-681 2734

QUARMBY, David John. b 43. St Jo Coll Dur BA64 Lon Univ CertEd70 Man Univ MEd89. Ridley Hall Cam 65. **d** 67 **p** 68. C Bournville *Birm* 67-71; V Erdington St Chad 71-73; Lic to Offic *Blackb* 73-83; Perm to Offic *Man* 83-90; C Oldham St Paul from 90; Counsellor Huddersfield Poly from 90. *275 Frederick Street, Oldham OL8 4HX* 061-626 2771

QUARRELL, John Beck. b 39. Hull Coll of Educn CertEd59. Chich Th Coll 67. **d** 70 **p** 71. C Horbury *Wakef* 70-71; C Sowerby 71-73; V Brotherton 74-80; Chapl Pontefract Gen Hosp 78-80; Staincliffe Hosp Wakef 82-88; V Staincliffe *Wakef* 80-88; R Farndon w Thorpe, Hawton and Cotham *S'well* from 89. *The Rectory, 3 Marsh Lane, Farndon, Newark, Notts NG24 3SS* Newark (0636) 705048

QUARTON, Robert Edward. b 43. E Midl Min Tr Course 84. **d** 87 **p** 88. C Gresley *Derby* 87-88; C Clay Cross 88-90; C N Wingfield, Clay Cross and Pilsley 90-91; R Darley from 91. *The Rectory, 15 Hall Rise, Darley Dale, Matlock, Derbyshire DE4 2FW* Matlock (0629) 734866

QUASHIE, Canon Kobina Adduah. b 34. ACIS60 Univ of Ghana LLB71 LLM74 DipTh80. **d** 78 **p** 78. Ghana 78-80; Chapl Middx Hosp Lon 80; Funding Officer USPG from 80; Hon Can Kumasi from 86; Hon Can Koforidua from 86; Hon Can Accra from 87. *32 Chandos Road, London NW2 4LU* 081-452 5721 or 071-928 8681

QUENNELL, Brian Michael. b 19. **d** 74 **p** 75. C Oakham w Hambleton and Egleton *Pet* 74-78; V Denford w Ringstead 78-87; rtd 87; Perm to Offic *Pet* from 87. *3 Crispin Cottages, Baker Street, Walgrave, Northampton NN6 9QL* Northampton (0604) 781022

QUIGLEY, John Molesworth. b 21. BNC Ox BA43 MA47. Wycliffe Hall Ox 43. **d** 44 **p** 45. C Wembley St Jo *Lon* 44-46; Hon C Ellesmere Port *Ches* 75; Hon C Bromborough 75-77 and 80-82; Hon C Prenton 77-80; Hon C Wallasey St Hilary 82-84; rtd 84; Perm to Offic *Bradf* from 85. *Flat 3, Ashbrook, 4 Grove Road, Ilkley, W Yorkshire LS29 9PE* Ilkley (0943) 609380

QUIGLEY, Thomas Molesworth. b 19. Lon Univ BD45. ALCD41. **d** 42 **p** 43. C Champion Hill St Sav *S'wark* 42-45; CF 45-58; C Upperby St Jo *Carl* 58-62; C Accrington St Jas *Blackb* 62-70; Australia from 70. *1/42 Hampden Road, Artarmon, Sydney, NSW, Australia 2064*

QUILL, John Stephen. b 51. Nottm Univ DipTh78. Linc Th Coll 76. **d** 79 **p** 80. C Sawbridgeworth *St Alb* 79-81; C Watford Ch Ch 81-85; Dioc Soc Services Adv *Worc* 85-90; Adv to Bd of Soc Resp from 90. *48 Byfield Rise, Worcester WR5 1BA* Worcester (0905) 611901

QUILL, Canon Walter Paterson. b 35. **d** 60 **p** 61. C Glendermott *D & R* 60-63; I Kilbarron 63-66; I Kilcronaghan w Ballynascreen 66-81; I Derg w Termonamongan from 81; RD Strabane from 87; Can Derry Cathl from 89; RD Newtownstewart and Omagh from 90. *The Rectory, Castlederg, Co Tyrone BT81 7HZ* Castlederg (06626) 71362

QUILLIAM, Miss Anne Eleanor Scott. b 31. Bedf Coll Lon BA54 CertEd55. Dalton Ho Bris 59. **d** 87. Par Dn Toxteth St Philemon w St Gabr and St Cleopas *Liv* from 87. *40 Madryn Street, Liverpool L8 3TT* 051-727 5899

QUIN, Canon Cosslett William Charles. b 07. TCD BA30 BD. **d** 31 **p** 32. I Dunganstown w Redcross *D & G* 65-71; rtd 71. *Spruce Cottage, 2 Church Road, Carryduff, Belfast BT8 8DT* Belfast (0232) 813768

QUIN, Eric Arthur. b 22. Magd Coll Cam BA46 MA48 Lon Univ BD56. Bps' Coll Cheshunt 46. **d** 48 **p** 49. V St Ippolyts *St Alb* 58-70; RD Hitchin 68-70; V Haynes 70-87; rtd 87. *Annabel's Cottage, The Lydiate, Lower Heswall, Merseyside L60 8PR* 051-342 8650

QUIN, John James Neil. b 31. Ox Univ MA DipEd53. Qu Coll Birm 61. **d** 63 **p** 64. C Cannock *Lich* 63-68; V Sneyd Green 68-78; V Stafford St Paul Forebridge 78-90; TV Tettenhall Regis from 90. *Church Cottage, Church Road, Tettenhall, Wolverhampton WV6 9AJ* Wolverhampton (0902) 751941

QUIN, Ven Thomas Rothwell. b 15. OBE80. TCD BA39 MA49. **d** 39 **p** 40. Asst Chapl-in-Chief RAF 63-70; Prin RAF Chapl Sch 66-70; QHC 67-70; Chapl Zurich w St Gallen and Winterthur *Eur* 70-80; Adn Switzerland 79-80; rtd 80; Perm to Offic *Sarum* from 80. *New Rushford, Walnut Close, Sutton Veny, Warminster, Wilts BA12 7BS* Warminster (0985) 40794

QUINE, Christopher Andrew. b 38. St Aid Birkenhead 61. **d** 64 **p** 65. C Hunts Cross *Liv* 64-67; C Farnworth 67-71; C-in-c Widnes St Jo 67-71; V Clubmoor 71-78; V Formby H Trin from 78. *Holy Trinity Vicarage, 2A Brows Lane, Formby, Liverpool L37 3HZ* Formby (07048) 73642

QUINE, David Anthony. b 28. Qu Coll Cam BA52 MA59. Ridley Hall Cam 53. **d** 55 **p** 56. Lic to Offic *York* 68-71; Chapl Monkton Combe Sch Bath 71-85; rtd 85; Perm to Offic *Carl* from 85. *Stickle Cottage, Dungeon Ghyll, Great Langdale, Ambleside, Cumbria LA22 9JY* Langdale (09667) 669

QUINE, Canon Ernest Kendrick Leigh. b 21. St Jo Coll Dur BA50 MA55 DipTh51 Nottm Univ DPhil68. **d** 51 **p** 52. C Grassendale *Liv* 51-52; C Shrewsbury St Almund *Lich* 52-54; C-in-c Park Estate St Chris CD *Leic* 54-61; V Belgrave St Pet from 61; Hon Can Leic Cathl from 67. *St Peter's Vicarage, Vicarage Lane, Leicester LE4 5PD* Leicester (0533) 661401

✠**QUINLAN, Rt Rev Alan Geoffrey.** b 33. Kelham Th Coll 54. **d** 58 **p** 59 **c** 88. C Bedf Leigh *Man* 58-61; S Africa from 61; Suff Bp Cen Region from 88. *Bishop's House, 79 Kildare Road, Newlands, 7700 South Africa* Cape Town (21) 642444

QUINN, Arthur Hamilton Riddel. b 37. TCD BA60 MA64 BD67. **d** 61 **p** 62. C Belf H Trin *Conn* 61-63; C Belf St Mary Magd 63-64; Chapl Hull Univ *York* 64-69; Chapl Keele Univ *Lich* 69-74; P-in-c Keele 72-74; V Shirley St Jo *Cant* 74-84; V Shirley St Jo *S'wark* from 85. *The Vicarage, 49 Shirley Church Road, Croydon CR0 5EF* 081-654 1013

QUINN, Cecil Hugh. b 24. Oak Hill Th Coll 74. **d** 76 **p** 77. C Bedf St Jo and St Leon *St Alb* 76-79; Deputation Sec Irish Ch Miss from 79; I Rathmullan w Tyrella *D & D* 80-89; rtd 89. *10 Ballydonnell Road, Downpatrick, Co Down BT30 8EN* Ballykinler (039685) 237

QUINN, Derek John. b 55. TCD BTh88. **d** 88 **p** 89. C Mossley *Conn* 88-91; I Cappagh w Lislimnaghan *D & R* from 91. *20 Gartmore Gardens, Omagh, Co Tyrone BT78 5DZ* Omagh (0662) 242273

QUINN, George Bruce. b 23. **d** 82 **p** 83. APM Douglas Deanery from 82. *85 Port-e-Chee Avenue, Douglas, Isle of Man* Douglas (0624) 674080

QUINN, Dr John James. b 46. TCD BA70 PhD76. St Jo Coll Nottm DipTh80. **d** 81 **p** 82. C Gorleston St Andr *Nor* 81-84; R Belton 84-90; R Burgh Castle 84-90; R Belton and Burgh Castle from 90. *The Rectory, Belton, Great Yarmouth, Norfolk NR31 9JQ* Great Yarmouth (0493) 780210

QUINN, Kenneth Norman. b 40. QUB BSc62 CEng MICE. CITC 80. **d** 85 **p** 86. NSM Seapatrick *D & D* 85-91; Lic to Offic from 91. *4 Knollwood, Seapatrick, Banbridge, Co Down BT32 4PE* Banbridge (08206) 23515

QUINNEY, William Elliott. b 33. Linc Th Coll 62. **d** 64 **p** 65. C Coalville *Leic* 64-68; P-in-c Ibstock 68-69; R Nailstone w Carlton 69-79; R Nailstone and Carlton w Shackerstone from 79. *The Rectory, Rectory Lane, Nailstone, Nuneaton, Warks CV13 0QQ* Ibstock (0530) 60281

R

RABAN, Canon James Peter Caplin Priaulx. b 18. TD50. Chich Th Coll 52. **d** 54 **p** 55. V Southn Maybush St Pet *Win* 66-80; RD Southn 70-83; Hon Can Win Cathl 73-83; Chapl Countess Mountbatten Ho Southn 80-83; rtd 83; Perm to Offic *Leic* from 85. *242 Welland Park Road, Market Harborough, Leics LE16 9DP* Market Harborough (0858) 465816

RABBETTS, Reginald Douglas Cyprian. b 14. AKC38. Sarum Th Coll 38. **d** 38 **p** 39. V Woodlands *Win* 50-83; rtd 83; Perm to Offic *Win* from 83. *The Lean-To, Ship Inn, Ashford Hill, Newbury, Berks RG15 8BD* Tadley (0734) 811793

RABJOHNS, Alan. b 40. Leeds Univ BA62. Coll of Resurr Mirfield 62. **d** 64 **p** 65. C Ashington *Newc* 64-67; C Upton cum Chalvey *Ox* 67-76; V Roath St Sav *Llan* from 76. *St Saviour's Vicarage, 115 Splott Road, Cardiff CF2 2BY* Cardiff (0222) 461203

RABLEN, Antony Ford. b 52. St Jo Coll Nottm. **d** 82 **p** 83. C Clifton *York* 82-85; TV Marfleet from 85. *107 Amethyst Road, Hull HU9 4JG* Hull (0482) 76208

RABY, Canon Alfred Charles. b 04. St Jo Coll Ox BA27 MA30. Wells Th Coll 27. **d** 28 **p** 29. R Clapham H Trin *S'wark* 54-74; rtd 75; Perm to Offic *St E* from 75. *134B Southgate Street, Bury St Edmunds, Suffolk IP33 2AF* Bury St Edmunds (0284) 703487

RABY, Charles John. b 17. Clifton Th Coll 40. **d** 42 **p** 43. V Claverley *Heref* 57-82; rtd 82; Perm to Offic *St D* from 82. *Clover Lea, 42 Whitlow, Saundersfoot, Dyfed SA69 9AE* Saundersfoot (0834) 813317

RABY, Malcolm Ernest. b 47. Leeds Univ BEd73. N Ord Course 81. **d** 84 **p** 85. NSM Chadkirk *Ches* 84-88; Consultant CPAS from 88. *33 Nightingale Avenue, Cambridge CB1 4SG* Cambridge (0223) 213349

RACE, Alan. b 51. Bradf Univ BTech73 Ox Univ DipTh75 Birm Univ MA82. Cuddesdon Coll 73. **d** 76 **p** 77. C Tupsley *Heref* 76-79; Asst Chapl Kent Univ *Cant* 79-84; Dir of Studies S'wark Ord Course from 84. *12 Kelmore Grove, London SE22 9BH* 081-693 3860

RACE, Christopher Keith. b 43. St Paul's Grahamstown DipTh78. **d** 78 **p** 80. S Africa 78-86; V Tanworth St Patr Salter Street *Birm* from 86. *The Vicarage, Vicarage Road, Earlswood, Solihull, W Midlands B94 6DH* 021-728 2579

RACTLIFFE, Dudley John. b 38. Man Univ BA62 Birm Univ DPS69. Ridley Hall Cam 63. **d** 66 **p** 67. C Radford *Cov* 66-68; C Haslemere *Guildf* 69-73; V Perry Beeches *Birm* 73-78; V Worle *B & W* 78-88; Dioc Ecum Officer from 88; R Dowlishwake w Kingstone, Chillington etc from 88. *The Rectory, Dowlish Wake, Ilminster, Somerset TA19 0NX* Ilminster (0460) 53374

RADCLIFFE, Canon Albert Edward. b 34. Lon Univ BD63. St Aid Birkenhead Ch Div Sch of the Pacific (USA) 61. **d** 62 **p** 63. C Knotty Ash St Jo *Liv* 62-64; C Blundellsands St Nic 64-66; Israel 66-69; V Tonge w Alkrington *Man* 69-77; R Ashton St Mich 77-91; AD Ashton-under-Lyne 87-91; Can Res Man Cathl from 91. *The Rectory, Hutton Avenue, Ashton-under-Lyne, Lancs OL6 6QY* 061-330 1172

RADCLIFFE, David Jeffrey. b 52. Linc Th Coll 77. **d** 79 **p** 80. C Poulton-le-Fylde *Blackb* 79-84; V Ingol 84-88; R Lowther and Askham *Carl* from 88. *Lilac House, Lowther, Penrith, Cumbria CA10 2HH* Hackthorpe (09312) 277

RADCLIFFE, James Warner. b 23. FICE66 FRTPI66 Liv Univ BEng43 MEng46. Cranmer Hall Dur 76. **d** 78 **p** 79. C Penrith *Carl* 78-79; C Penrith w Newton Reigny 79-81; P-in-c Barton w Pooley Bridge 81-83; P-in-c Martindale 83; V Barton, Pooley Bridge and Martindale 83-86; Perm to Offic from 86; rtd 88. *Sunny Vale, Church View, Heversham, Milnthorpe, Cumbria LA7 7EN* Milnthorpe (05395) 63572

RADCLIFFE, Mrs Rosemary. b 45. SW Minl Tr Course 87. **d** 90. NSM Devoran *Truro* from 90. *Belmont Cottage, Devoran, Truro, Cornwall TR3 6PZ* Truro (0872) 865509

RADFORD, Andrew John. b 44. Trin Coll Bris 72. **d** 74 **p** 75. C Shirehampton *Bris* 74-78; Producer Relig Progr BBC Radio Bris 78-80; V Bath St Barn w Englishcombe *B & W* 80-85; Dioc Communications Officer *Glouc* from 85. *2 High View, Hempsted, Gloucester GL2 6LN* Gloucester (0452) 424426 or 410022

RADFORD, Donald George. b 16. Lich Th Coll 55. **d** 56 **p** 57. C-in-c Stoke Hill CD *Guildf* 60-69; Perm to Offic *Glouc* from 79; rtd 81. *9 Cranham Road, Cheltenham, Glos GL52 6BQ* Cheltenham (0242) 524132

RADFORD, Leslie. b 24. Lon Univ DipTh75. Local NSM Course. **d** 85 **p** 86. NSM Scotter w E Ferry *Linc* from 85. *1 Carr Villas, Laughton, Gainsborough, Lincs DN21 3QF* Laughton (042782) 265

RADFORD, Maurice Frederick. b 06. Bps' Coll Cheshunt 60. **d** 60 **p** 61. R Glemsford *St E* 63-71; P-in-c Somerton 63-71; rtd 71; Lic to Offic *St E* from 71. *33 Harvest House, Cobbold Road, Felixstowe, Suffolk IP11 7RW* Felixstowe (0394) 285985

RADFORD, Samuel. b 17. Kelham Th Coll 40. **d** 45 **p** 46. C Barton upon Humber *Linc* 69-71; Lic to Offic *Wakef* from 71; rtd 82. *18 Caistor Road, Barton-on-Humber, S Humberside* Barton-on-Humber (0652) 635006

RADLEY, Peter. b 31. Bps' Coll Cheshunt 60. **d** 62 **p** 63. C Lillington *Cov* 62-63; C Nuneaton St Nic 63-67; P-in-c Skillington *Linc* 67-68; V Waltham *Ox* from 68. *The Vicarage, Waltham St Lawrence, Reading RG10 0JD* Twyford (0734) 343249

RADLEY, Roy Taylor. b 24. Edin Th Coll 47. **d** 50 **p** 51. Miss to Seamen 53-68; Sec (Midl Region) Leprosy Miss from 68; Perm to Offic *S'well* from 82; rtd 89. *200 Broadway, Derby DE3 1BP* Derby (0332) 43109

RADLEY, Stephen Gavin. b 62. K Coll Lon BSc83 AKC83. Cranmer Hall Dur BA87 St Jo Coll Dur 85. **d** 89 **p** 90. C Darlington St Matt and St Luke *Dur* from 89. *31 Derwent Street, Darlington, Co Durham DL3 6AU* Darlington (0325) 488316

RAFFAY, Julian Paul. b 60. Stirling Univ BSc84. Cranmer Hall Dur BA89. **d** 90 **p** 91. C Adel *Ripon* from 90. *16 Adel Vale, Leeds LS16 8LF* Leeds (0532) 610238

RAFFINGTON, Arthur Benjamin. b 19. Lon Bible Coll 75 K Coll Lon 75 Whitby Hall Ox BA83. W Indies United Th Coll 76. **d** 77 **p** 78. Jamaica 77-82; Hon C Upper Tooting H Trin *S'wark* from 82. *94 Ritherdon Road, London SW17 8QQ* 081-673 0630

RAGAN, Mrs Jennifer Mary. b 39. Linc Th Coll 71. **dss** 80 **d** 87. Hackney Lon 80-84; Hornchurch St Andr *Chelmsf* 84-87; Par Dn 87-88; Par Dn Ingrave St Steph CD 88-90; Par Dn Gt Parndon from 90. *14 Deer Park, Harlow, Essex CM19 4LD* Harlow (0279) 431133

RAGBOURNE, Miss Pamela Mary. b 27. CertEd47. Dalton Ho Bris 53. **dss** 76 **d** 87. CPAS Staff 68-79; Tottenham St Jo *Lon* 79-81; Gt Cam Road St Jo and St Jas 82-84; Camberley St Paul *Guildf* 84-86; rtd 87; Perm to Offic *Glouc* from 87. *14 Crispin Close, Winchcombe, Cheltenham, Glos GL54 5JY* Cheltenham (0242) 603469

RAGGETT, Geoffrey Francis. b 22. Lon Coll of Div 60. **d** 62 **p** 63. V E Ham St Paul *Chelmsf* 66-72; Chapl Woking Gp Min 72-76; Chapl Long Grove Hosp Epsom 76-90; rtd 90; Perm to Offic *Guildf* from 90. *5 Burnet Grove, Epsom, Surrey KT19 8HU* Epsom (0372) 722666

RAHI, Hakim Banta Singh. b 36. Union Bibl Sem Yavatmal BD71. **d** 74 **p** 74. India 74-83; In URC 83-88; Perm to Offic *Birm* from 88; Ecum Evang Asian Community from 88. *3 Hobson Close, Norton Street, Birmingham B18 5RH* 021-554 2144

RAHILLY, Philip James. b 54. Univ of Wales (Cardiff) BD86. Wycliffe Hall Ox 86. **d** 88 **p** 89. C Knightwick w Doddenham, Broadwas and Cotheridge *Worc* 88; C Martley and Wichenford, Knightwick etc 89-91; C Worc St Barn w Ch Ch from 91. *214 Tolladine Road, Worcester WR4 9AU* Worcester (0905) 724391

RAI, Miss Mary Anne. b 61. Southn Univ BTh83. Trin Coll Bris DipTh86. **dss** 86 **d** 87. Bury St Edmunds St Mary *St E* 86-87; Par Dn 87-89; Perm to Offic from 90. *4 Pippin Close, Moreton Hall, Bury St Edmunds IP33 1BR* Bury St Edmunds (0284) 706806

RAIKES, Canon Myles Kenneth. b 23. New Coll Ox BA47 MA51. Wells Th Coll 47. **d** 49 **p** 50. V Bushey Heath *St Alb* 63-70; R Digswell 70-77; Hon Can St Alb 76-77; P-in-c Meare *B & W* 77-81; P-in-c W Coker 82-83; Dioc Ecum Officer 84-88; C Ilminster w Whitelackington 84-85; C S Petherton w the Seavingtons 85-87; rtd 88.

7 West Street, South Petherton, Somerset TA13 5DQ South Petherton (0460) 41056

RAIKES, Peter. b 37. St Mich Coll Llan 78. **d** 80 **p** 81. C Roath St Marg *Llan* 80-82; V Resolven 82-86; V Resolven w Tonna from 86; RD Neath from 89. *The Vicarage, Resolven, Neath, W Glam SA11 4AN* Resolven (0639) 710354

RAIKES, Robert Laybourne. b 32. Wells Th Coll 59. **d** 61 **p** 62. C Poplar All SS w St Frideswide *Lon* 61-66; C Grendon Underwood w Edgcott *Ox* 66-68; C Swan 68-71; V Whitchurch Canonicorum and Wootton Fitzpaine *Sarum* 71-75; V Whitchurch Canonicorum w Wooton Fitzpaine etc 75-81; P-in-c Branksome St Aldhelm 81-82; V 82-91; V Pitminster w Corfe *B & W* from 91. *The Vicarage, Pitminster, Taunton, Somerset TA3 3AZ* Blagdon Hill (082342) 232

RAILTON, John Robert Henry. b 45. FCIB79 Reading Univ BSc68. S Dios Minl Tr Scheme 82. **d** 85 **p** 86. NSM Wickham *Portsm* 85-89; C Bridgemary 89-90; V from 90. *19 Morris Close, Gosport, Hants PO13 0SS* Gosport (0705) 235288

RAINBOW, Preb Gerald Anton Hayward. b 15. St Edm Hall Ox BA38 MA41. Linc Th Coll 38. **d** 39 **p** 40. V Leominster *Heref* 57-80; RD Leominster 60-80; Preb Heref Cathl from 67; P-in-c Eyton 69-80; rtd 80. *65 King's Acre Road, Hereford HR4 0QL* Hereford (0432) 66718

RAINBOW, Henry David. b 10. Ripon Hall Ox 64. **d** 65 **p** 66. Chapl HM Pris Cardiff 67-71; Pentonville 71-74; Cant 74-78; rtd 78; Perm to Offic Cant from 79; Ex from 89. *1 Upton Hill Road, Brixham, Devon TQ5 9QR* Brixham (08045) 4611

RAINE, Patrick John Wallace. b 21. DFC. Sarum & Wells Th Coll 72. **d** 74 **p** 75. C Chandler's Ford *Win* 74-76; R Highclere and Ashmansworth w Crux Easton 76-84; R Copythorne and Minstead 84-87; rtd 87. *The Flat, Guildford House, Madeira Road, Seaview, Isle of Wight PO34 5BA* Isle of Wight (0983) 615991

RAINE, Stephen James. b 49. Lanchester Poly DipAD69 Sheff Poly BA80. N Ord Course 85. **d** 86 **p** 87. C Cottingham *York* 86-90; V Dunscroft *Sheff* from 90. *The Vicarage, 162 Station Road, Dunscroft, Doncaster, S Yorkshire DN7 4JR* Doncaster (0302) 841328

RAINER, John Charles. b 54. Ex Univ BA76 DipTh78 CertEd78. St Jo Coll Nottm 86. **d** 88 **p** 89. C Fletchamstead *Cov* from 88. *2A Beech Tree Avenue, Coventry CV4 9FG* Coventry (0203) 473197

RAINES, Ms Gisela Rolanda. b 58. K Coll Lon BD83. dss 84 **d** 87. Charlton St Luke w H Trin *S'wark* 84-87; Par Dn 87; Chapl Imp Coll *Lon* 87-91. *St Jude's Vicarage, 18 Collingham Road, London SW5 0LX* 071-259 2301

RAINES, William Guy. b 46. Lon Univ BSc69 MSc70 Ox Univ BA80. Ripon Coll Cuddesdon 78. **d** 81 **p** 82. C W Drayton *Lon* 81-84; C Charlton St Luke w H Trin *S'wark* 84-87; Chapl K Coll Lon from 87; Chapl Imp Coll from 91. *St Jude's Vicarage, 18 Collingham Road, London SW5 0LX* 071-259 2301

RAINFORD, Robert Graham. b 55. Lanc Univ CertEd76 BEd77. St Steph Ho Ox 81. **d** 83 **p** 84. C Burnley St Cath w St Alb and St Paul *Blackb* 83-86; C-in-c Hawes Side St Chris CD 86-89; V Hawes Side from 89. *The Vicarage, Hawes Side Lane, Blackpool FY4 5AH* Blackpool (0253) 697937

RAINSBERRY, Edward John. b 24. TCD BA48 MA58. TCD Div Sch Div Test49. **d** 49 **p** 50. C Abbeystrewry Union *C, C & R* 49-52; Chapl RAF 52-58; V Long Compton *Cov* 58-84; R Whichford 58-84; V Long Compton, Whichford and Barton-on-the-Heath from 84. *The Vicarage, Long Compton, Shipston-on-Stour, Warks CV36 5JH* Long Compton (060884) 207

RAINSBURY, Mark James. b 56. NE Lon Poly BA79. Oak Hill Th Coll BA87. **d** 88 **p** 89. C Tonbridge St Steph *Roch* from 88. *20 Woodfield Road, Tonbridge, Kent TN9 2LQ* Tonbridge (0732) 354745

RAINSFORD, Peter John. b 31. FCP72. Qu Coll Birm 75. **d** 77 **p** 78. Hon C Lich St Chad *Lich* 77-81; C 82; C Coseley Ch Ch 82-84; V Wednesbury St Bart from 84. *The Vicarage, Little Hill, Wednesbury, W Midlands WS10 9DE* 021-556 0378

RAITH, Robert. b 31. Edin Univ MA61. Coll of Resurr Mirfield 57. **d** 59 **p** 60. C Edin St Jas *Edin* 59-61; P-in-c 76-77; Asst Prov Youth Org 61-65; C Dalmahoy 61-65; C Edin St Mark 66-76; Dioc Supernumerary 77-78; P-in-c Edin St Luke 78-79; Perm to Offic from 79; Pilsdon Community 87-90. *62 Rodwell Road, Weymouth, Dorset DT4 8QU* Weymouth (0305) 781386

RAITT, Derek. b 41. K Coll Lon BD63 AKC63. **d** 64 **p** 65. C Blackb St Jas *Blackb* 64-67; C Burnley St Pet 67-69; V Foulridge 69-74; V Euxton from 74. *The Vicarage,*

Wigan Road, Euxton, Chorley, Lancs PR7 6JH Chorley (02572) 62102

RAKE, David John. b 47. Nottm Univ BA68 PhD73. Wycliffe Hall Ox DipTh73. **d** 74 **p** 75. C Radcliffe-on-Trent *S'well* 74-77; P-in-c Upwell St Pet *Ely* 77-79; P-in-c Outwell 77-79; Chapl Warw Univ *Cov* 79-86; V Kenilworth St Nic from 86. *The Vicarage, 7 Elmbank Road, Kenilworth, Warks CV8 1AL* Kenilworth (0926) 54367

RALPH, Charles. b 15. TCD BA47 MA58. **d** 47 **p** 48. R Fordley w Middleton *St E* 64-81; R Theberton 64-81; rtd 82; Perm to Offic *St E* from 82; TV Raveningham *Nor* 82; P-in-c Rossinver *K, E & A* 85-86. *2 Gayfer Avenue, Kesgrave, Ipswich IP5 7PZ* Ipswich (0473) 624313

RALPH, Dr Richard Gale. b 51. FRSA90 Pemb Coll Ox BA73 MA78 DPhil78. S Dios Minl Tr Scheme 84. **d** 87 **p** 88. NSM St Leonards Ch Ch and St Mary *Chich* from 87; NSM St Pancras H Cross w St Jude and St Pet *Lon* from 87. *17 Duke's Road, London WC1H 9AB* 071-387 0152

RALPH-BOWMAN, Murray Peter. b 13. Qu Coll Cam BA35 MA45. Wells Th Coll 36. **d** 37 **p** 38. V Queen Camel *B & W* 57-78; R W Camel 57-78; rtd 78; P-in-c Bryngwyn and Newchurch and Llanbedr etc *S & B* from 78. *The Rectory, Rhosgoch, Builth Wells, Powys LD2 3JU* Painscastle (04975) 260

RALPHS, John Eric. b 26. MBAP66 St Cath Coll Ox BA52 MA56. Wycliffe Hall Ox 53. **d** 53 **p** 54. C Wolvercote *Ox* 53-55; Chapl Asst Radcliffe Infirmary Ox 54-62; Lic to Offic *Ox* 55-66 and from 86; Chapl Dragon Sch Ox 55-68; Asst Chapl HM Pris Ox 58-61; Jun Chapl Mert Coll Ox 59-62; Chapl St Hugh's Coll Ox 62-67; Priest-Psychotherapist from 68; Perm to Offic *Ox* 83-86. *209 Woodstock Road, Oxford OX2 7AB* Oxford (0865) 515550

RALPHS, Robert Brian. b 31. Qu Coll Birm 75. **d** 78 **p** 79. Hon C Wednesbury St Jo *Lich* 78-80; Hon C Wednesbury St Paul Wood Green 80-81; Perm to Offic from 81. *204 Bromford Lane, West Bromwich, W Midlands B70 7HX* 021-553 0119

RALPHS, Miss Sharon Ann. b 55. St Mary's Coll Dur BA77. Cranmer Hall Dur 81. dss 83 **d** 87. Caverswall *Lich* 83-87; Par Dn 87-89; Asst Dioc Officer for Minl Tr *St As* from 90. *Coleg y Groes, Corwen, Clwyd LL21 0AU* Corwen (0490) 2169

RAMELL, Arthur Lewis. b 05. Cuddesdon Coll 50. **d** 51 **p** 52. V Colerne *Bris* 56-76; P-in-c N Wraxall 68-76; rtd 76. *Woodridge House, Andover Road, Newbury, Berks RG14 6NP* Newbury (0635) 44851

RAMELL, John Edwin. b 25. Bris Univ BA55. Tyndale Hall Bris. **d** 56 **p** 57. V Wombridge *Lich* 60-70; TR Chell 70-82; V Congleton St Pet *Ches* 82-90; rtd 90. *10 Newland Close, Eynsham, Oxford OX8 1LE* Oxford (0865) 880180

RAMM, Canon Norwyn MacDonald. b 24. Linc Coll Ox BA60 MA64. St Pet Coll Jamaica 49. **d** 51 **p** 52. V Ox St Mich *Ox* 61-71; P-in-c Ox All SS w St Martin 61-71; V Ox St Mich w St Martin and All SS 71-88; Chapl HM Pris Ox 75-88; Hon Can Ch Ch *Ox* from 85; Chapl to HM The Queen from 85; rtd 88. *Fairlawn, Church Lane, Harwell, Didcot, Oxon OX11 0EZ* Abingdon (0235) 835454

RAMON, Brother. See LLOYD, Raymond David

RAMPTON, Paul Michael. b 47. St Jo Coll Dur BA69 DipTh70 MA73 K Coll Lon PhD85. Wycliffe Hall Ox 72. **d** 73 **p** 74. C Folkestone H Trin w Ch Ch *Cant* 73-77; P-in-c Kingsdown 77-79; P-in-c Ringwould w Oxney 77-79; R Ringwould w Kingsdown 79-83; V Maidstone St Paul 83-88; V Maidstone St Martin from 88. *St Martin's Vicarage, Northumberland Road, Maidstone, Kent ME15 7LP* Maidstone (0622) 676282

RAMPTON, Mrs Valerie Edith. b 41. Nottm Univ BSc63 MSc66 BA79. Gilmore Course 78. dss 82 **d** 87. Sneinton St Chris w St Phil *S'well* 80-87; Par Dn 87-88; Par Dn Stapleford from 88; Dioc Adv on Women in Min from 90. *106 Boxley Drive, Nottingham NG2 7GL* Nottingham (0602) 233257

RAMSAY, Alan Burnett. b 34. AKC62. **d** 63 **p** 64. C Clapham H Trin *S'wark* 63-67; C Warlingham w Chelsham and Farleigh 67-71; P-in-c Stockwell St Mich 71-78; V Lingfield 78-85; P-in-c Crowhurst 83-85; V Lingfield and Crowhurst from 85; RD Godstone from 88. *The Vicarage, Lingfield, Surrey RH7 6HA* Lingfield (0342) 832021

RAMSAY, Carl Anthoney St Aubyn. b 55. W Midl Minl Tr Course 88. **d** 90 **p** 91. C Wednesfield Heath *Lich* from 90. *220 Bushbury Road, Fallings Park, Wolverhampton WV10 0NT* Wolverhampton (0902) 735689

RAMSAY, Jack. b 05. ALCD33. **d** 33 **p** 34. R Easton in Gordano w Portbury and Clapton *B & W* 70-80; rtd 80; Perm to Offic *B & W* from 80. *10 Priory Gardens, Easton In Gordano, Bristol BS20 0PF* Pill (0275) 372380

RAMSAY, James Anthony. b 52. **d** 86 **p** 87. C Olney w Emberton *Ox* 86-89; V Blackbird Leys from 89. *Church House, 1 Cuddesdon Way, Oxford OX4 5JH* Oxford (0865) 778728

RAMSAY, John Leslie. b 02. LRAM. Linc Th Coll 54. **d** 56 **p** 57. V Keelby w Risby and Aylesby *Linc* 62-71; V Hogsthorpe 71-76; V Mumby 71-76; rtd 76; Perm to Offic *Linc* from 76. *61 Clive Avenue, Lincoln LN6 7UR* Lincoln (0522) 536081

RAMSAY, Kenneth William. b 18. ALCD48. **d** 52 **p** 53. Perm to Offic Portsm 69-80; Sarum 77-87; rtd 87; Hon C Burstow *S'wark* from 87. *14 Woodside Crescent, Smallfield, Horley, Surrey RH6 9ND* Smallfield (0342) 843561

RAMSAY, Max Roy MacGregor. b 34. Ball Coll Ox MA. Qu Coll Birm 82. **d** 84 **p** 85. C Hale *Ches* 84-86; Lic to Offic 86; C Nantwich 87; V Haslington w Crewe Green from 87. *The Vicarage, 163 Crewe Road, Haslington, Crewe CW1 1RL* Crewe (0270) 582388

RAMSBOTTOM, Albert Ernest. b 16. Lon Univ BD39. ALCD39. **d** 39 **p** 40. V Penge Lane H Trin *Roch* 62-75; R Mereworth w W Peckham 75-82; rtd 82; Perm to Offic *Birm* from 83. *178 Damson Lane, Solihull, W Midlands B92 9JU* 021-705 4631

RAMSBOTTOM, Julie Frances. b 54. Trevelyan Coll Dur BA(Theol)76. S'wark Ord Course 88. **d** 91. Par Dn Bray and Braywood *Ox* from 91. *63 Moor End, Holyport, Maidenhead, Berks SL6 2YJ* Maidenhead (0628) 778478

RAMSBURY, Area Bishop of. See VAUGHAN, Rt Rev Peter St George

RAMSDEN, Arthur Stuart. b 34. Kelham Th Coll 56. **d** 61 **p** 62. C Featherstone *Wakef* 61-63; C Barnsley St Pet 63-67; V Charlestown 67-70; V Middlestown 70-77; V Purston cum S Featherstone from 77. *The Vicarage, Victoria Street, Featherstone, Pontefract, W Yorkshire WF7 5EZ* Pontefract (0977) 792288

RAMSDEN, Preb Francis Samuel Lloyd. b 12. Lon Coll of Div 31. **d** 35 **p** 37. V Trentham *Lich* 58-77; C Solihull *Birm* 77-79; TV 79-80; rtd 80; Perm to Offic *Birm* from 80. *40 Orchard Croft, Barnt Green, Birmingham B45 8NJ* 021-447 7125

RAMSDEN, Peter Stockton. b 51. Univ Coll Lon BSc74 Leeds Univ DipTh76. Coll of Resurr Mirfield 74. **d** 77 **p** 78. C Houghton le Spring *Dur* 77-80; C S Shields All SS 80-83; Papua New Guinea 83-90; P-in-c Micklefield *York* from 90. *The Vicarage, Great North Road, Micklefield, Leeds LS25 4AG* Leeds (0532) 862154

RAMSDEN, Raymond Leslie. b 49. Open Univ BA86. **d** 78 **p** 79. C Greenhill St Jo *Lon* 78-85; C Staines St Mary and St Pet 85-90; V Hounslow St Steph from 90. *St Stephen's Vicarage, Parkside Road, Hounslow TW3 2BP* 081-570 3056

RAMSEY-HARDY, Stuart John Andrew. b 46. St Jo Coll Dur BA69. Wycliffe Hall Ox 69. **d** 74 **p** 75. C Stoke Newington St Mary *Lon* 74-77; C Hersham *Guildf* 78-79; Hon C Thames Ditton 79-83. *23 New Row, London WC2* 071-836 2217

RANDALL, Colin Antony. b 57. SS Paul & Mary Coll Cheltenham BEd78 Bris Univ DipHE82 Lon Univ BD84. Trin Coll Bris 80. **d** 84 **p** 85. C Denton Holme *Carl* 84-87; C Brampton RD 87-90; R Hanborough and Freeland *Ox* from 90. *The Rectory, Swan Lane, Long Hanborough, Oxford OX7 2BT* Freeland (0993) 881270

RANDALL, Colin Michael Sebastian. b 50. Aston Univ BSc72. Qu Coll Birm 72. **d** 75 **p** 76. C Tonge w Alkrington *Man* 75-78; C Elton All SS 78-82; P-in-c Bridgwater H Trin *B & W* 82-86; V 86-90; V Bishops Hull from 90. *The Vicarage, Bishops Hull, Taunton, Somerset TA1 5EB* Taunton (0823) 333032

RANDALL, David William. b 47. Sarum Th Coll 68. **d** 71 **p** 72. C Poplar *Lon* 71-75; C St Botolph Aldgate w H Trin Minories 75-77; TV Notting Hill 77-82; V Notting Hill St Clem and St Mark 82-85; V Kensington St Jas Norlands 83-85; V Notting Dale St Clem w St Mark and St Jas 85-88; Dir CARA from 88; Hon C Walham Green St Jo w St Jas *Lon* 88-89; NSM Chiswick St Nic w St Mary from 89. *64A Grove Park Road, London W4 3SB* 081-742 1017

RANDALL, Ian Neville. b 39. Or Coll Ox BA62 MA65. St Steph Ho Ox 62. **d** 65 **p** 66. C Perivale *Lon* 65-68; C Fulham St Jo Walham Green 68-73; C Cowley St Jas *Ox* 73-79; TV 79-82; V Didcot St Pet from 82. *St Peter's Vicarage, Didcot, Oxon OX11 8PN* Didcot (0235) 812114

RANDALL, James Anthony. b 36. ACIB69 Kent Univ DipTh80. Ridley Hall Cam 68. **d** 70 **p** 71. C Rusthall *Roch* 70-74; V Shorne 74-79; V Bexleyheath Ch Ch 79-89; R Stone from 89. *The Rectory, Church Road, Stone, Greenhithe, Kent DA9 9BE* Greenhithe (0322) 842076

RANDALL, John Randall. b 28. Lon Univ BD64 LTh85. ALCD60. **d** 60 **p** 61. C Woking St Jo *Guildf* 60-62; C High Wycombe All SS *Ox* 62-65; V Patchway *Bris* 65-73; P-in-c Olveston 73-80; Warden Roch Dioc Conf and Retreat Ho Chislehurst 80-84; TR Trunch *Nor* from 84. *The Rectory, Mundesley, Norwich NR11 8DG* Mundesley (0263) 720520

RANDALL, John Terence. b 29. St Cath Coll Cam BA52 MA59. Ely Th Coll 52. **d** 54 **p** 55. C Luton Ch Ch *St Alb* 54; C Dunstable 54-57; C Ely 57-60; C March St Jo 60-62; Area Sec (S Midl) UMCA 62-64; Area Sec (Dios Birm and Cov) USPG 65-76; P-in-c Avon Dassett w Farnborough *Cov* 76-78; P-in-c Fenny Compton 76-78; R Avon Dassett w Farnborough and Fenny Compton 78-84; V New Bilton from 84; RD Rugby from 89. *The Vicarage, New Street, Rugby CV22 7BE* Rugby (0788) 544011

RANDALL, Kelvin John. b 49. JP. K Coll Lon BD71 AKC71 PGCE72. St Jo Coll Nottm DPS73. **d** 74 **p** 75. C Peckham St Mary Magd *S'wark* 74-78; C Portsdown *Portsm* 78-81; C-in-c Crookhorn Ch Cen CD 81-82; R Bedhampton 82-90; RD Havant 87-89; P-in-c Bournemouth St Jo w St Mich *Win* from 90; Chapl Talbot Heath Sch Bournemouth from 90. *The Vicarage, 13 Durley Chine Road South, Bournemouth BH2 5JT* Bournemouth (0202) 761962

RANDALL, Mrs Lynda Lorraine. b 44. Sarum & Wells Th Coll 89. **d** 91. Par Dn Chesterton St Andr *Ely* from 91. *35 Pakenham Close, Chesterton, Cambridge CB4 1PW* Cambridge (0223) 315040

RANDALL, Miss Marian Sally. b 49. Trin Coll Bris 75. **dss** 80 **d** 87. Peckham St Mary Magd *S'wark* 80-83; Sutton Ch Ch 83-87; Par Dn from 87. *14A Christchurch Park, Sutton, Surrey SM2 5TN* 081-661 7130

RANDALL, Martin Trevor. b 51. St Jo Coll Dur BA74. Trin Coll Bris 74. **d** 77 **p** 78. C Ashton on Mersey St Mary *Ches* 77-80; C Everton St Sav w St Cuth *Liv* 80-82; V W Derby Gd Shep 82-91; P-in-c Toxteth Park Ch Ch from 91; P-in-c Toxteth Park St Bede from 91. *Christ Church Vicarage, 5 Linnet Lane, Liverpool L17 3BE* 051-727 2827

RANDALL, Philip Joseph. b 10. K Coll Lon 57. **d** 58 **p** 59. V Eye *Pet* 61-77; rtd 77; Perm to Offic *Pet* from 85. *104 Deerleap, Bretton, Peterborough PE3 6YD* Peterborough (0733) 266782

RANDALL, Samuel Paul. b 59. Leeds Univ MA90. Ridley Hall Cam 85. **d** 87 **p** 88. C Kingston upon Hull St Nic *York* 87-89; CF from 89. *c/o MOD (Army), Bagshot Park, Bagshot, Surrey GU19 5PL* Bagshot (0276) 71717

RANDALL, William Alfred. b 14. Lon Univ BD41 AKC41. **d** 41 **p** 42. V Aveley *Chelmsf* 61-73; R Wickford 73-79; P-in-c Runwell 75-79; rtd 79; Perm to Offic *Portsm* from 82. *43 Tunbridge Crescent, Liphook, Hants GU30 7QH* Liphook (0428) 724382

RANDELL, John Harrison. b 35. Lon Univ BD62. Chich Th Coll 77. **d** 78 **p** 78. C Ribbleton *Blackb* 78-82; V Barton from 82. *St Lawrence's Vicarage, Garstang Road, Barton, Preston PR3 5AA* Broughton (0772) 862020

RANDELL, Phillip John. b 45. Lon Univ DipTh68 BD73 CertEd. Linc Th Coll 67. **d** 68 **p** 69. C Henbury *Bris* 68-71; C Summertown *Ox* 71-73; C Liskeard w St Keyne *Truro* 73-75; Chapl Coll of St Mark and St Jo Plymouth *Ex* 75-79; Tanzania 80-82; R Alvescot w Black Bourton, Shilton, Holwell etc *Ox* 82-87; R St Gennys, Jacobstow w Warbstow and Treneglos *Truro* from 87. *The Rectory, Jacobstow, Bude, Cornwall EX23 0BR* St Gennys (08403) 206

RANDLE, Canon Howard Stanley. b 12. St Jo Coll Dur LTh34 BA35. St Aid Birkenhead 30. **d** 35 **p** 36. R Mobberley *Ches* 46-80; rtd 80; Perm to Offic *Ches* from 80. *7 Carlisle Close, Mobberley, Cheshire* Mobberley (056587) 3483

RANDOLPH, Michael Richard Spencer. b 25. FRSA62. Cant Sch of Min 88. **d** 90. C Biddenden and Smarden *Cant* from 90. *Little Smarden House, Smarden, Kent TN27 8NB* Smarden (023377) 216

RANGER, Keith Brian. b 34. Down Coll Cam BA58 MA63. Glas NSM Course 58. **d** 81 **p** 82. OMF 81-89; Hong Kong 81-89; Perm to Offic *Ches* from 89. *17 Stanhope Road, Bowden, Altrincham, Cheshire WA14 3LA* 061-928 3801

RANKEN, John Peter. b 33. Leeds Univ BA57. Coll of Resurr Mirfield. **d** 59 **p** 60. C Middlesb St Aid *York*

59-62; C Middlesb St Oswald 62-65; Ind Chapl 62-67; Zambia 68-75. *Address temp unknown*

RANKEN, Michael David. b 28. Man Univ BScTech49. S'wark Ord Course 76. **d** 79 **p** 80. Hon C Epsom St Martin *Guildf* from 79. *9 Alexandra Road, Epsom, Surrey KT17 4BH* Epsom (03727) 24823

RANKIN, Dennis. b 29. Keble Coll Ox BA53 MA62. St Steph Ho Ox 53. **d** 55 **p** 56. C Liv St Steph w St Cath *Liv* 55-57; C Boxmoor St Jo *St Alb* 57-59; C Brighton St Martin *Chich* 59-62; C-in-c Langney St Rich CD 62-69; V Hove St Thos 69-83; R Buxted and Hadlow Down 83-86; V Bexhill St Aug from 86; RD Battle and Bexhill from 90. *St Augustine's Vicarage, Bexhill-on-Sea, E Sussex TN39 3AZ* Bexhill-on-Sea (0424) 210785

RANKIN, John Cooper. b 24. Glas Univ MA44 Lon Univ BD53. Edin Th Coll 48. **d** 50 **p** 51. Prin Lect Bp Otter Coll Chich 69-84; rtd 84. *28 Worcester Road, Chichester, W Sussex PO19 4DW* Chichester (0243) 789467

RANKIN, Robert Paterson. b 11. Edin Th Coll 46. **d** 48 **p** 49. V Woodhouse Eaves *Leic* 58-86; V Woodhouse 61-86; rtd 86. *101 Leicester Road, Shepshed, Loughborough, Leics LE12 9DF* Shepshed (0509) 507130

RANKIN, William John Alexander. b 45. Van Mildert Coll Dur BA68 Fitzw Coll Cam BA73 MA77. Westcott Ho Cam 71. **d** 74 **p** 75. C St Jo Wood *Lon* 74-78; Chapl Clifton Coll Bris 78-86; P-in-c The Claydons *Ox* 86-91; R from 91. *The Rectory, Queen Catherine Road, Steeple Claydon, Buckingham MK18 2PY* Steeple Claydon (029673) 8055

RANN, Preb Harry Harvey. b 18. Sarum Th Coll 47. **d** 50 **p** 51. Dean's Chapl and PV Ex Cathl *Ex* 62-77; Sacr 65-77; Succ 73-77; V Colyton 77-84; R Colyton and Southleigh 84-86; RD Honiton 84-86; Preb Ex Cathl from 84; TR Colyton, Southleigh, Offwell, Widworthy etc 86-87; rtd 87. *4 Scattor View, Bridford, Exeter EX6 7JF* Christow (0647) 52741

RANSOM, Nigel Lester. b 60. Leeds Univ BA81. Wycliffe Hall Ox 83 SE Asia Sch of Th MTh83. **d** 85 **p** 86. C Gidea Park *Chelmsf* 85-88; C Widford from 88. *16 Wood Street, Chelmsford, Essex CM2 9AS* Chelmsford (0245) 256377

RANSOME, Arthur. b 21. St Jo Coll Nottm 71. **d** 72 **p** 72. Israel 72-76; C Virginia Water *Guildf* 76-79; P-in-c Peper Harow 79-82; P-in-c Shackleford 79-82; P-in-c Seale 82-89; rtd 89. *St Gwendron, Rock Road, Rock, Wadebridge, Cornwall PL27 6NP* Wadebridge (0208) 862825

RANSON, Arthur Frankland. b 50. St Jo Coll Dur BA73. Wycliffe Hall Ox 73. **d** 75 **p** 76. C Bare *Blackb* 75-78; C Scotforth 78-81; V Leyland St Ambrose from 81. *St Ambrose Vicarage, 61 Moss Lane, Leyland, Preston PR5 2SH* Leyland (0772) 421150

RANSON, George Sidney. b 28. Open Univ BA78. NE Ord Course 85. **d** 86 **p** 87. NSM Acomb H Redeemer *York* 86-88; C Warton St Oswald w Yealand Conyers *Blackb* 88-90; V Pilling from 90. *The Vicarage, School Lane, Pilling, Preston, Lancs PR3 6AA* Blackpool (0253) 790231

RANSON, Terence William James. b 42. AFAIM91 AKC64 MTh87 STM88. St Boniface Warminster 64. **d** 65 **p** 66. C Walton St Mary *Liv* 65-69; C Ipswich St Mary le Tower *St E* 69-71; Chapl Mersey Miss to Seamen 71-74; V N Keyham *Ex* 74-79; Australia 79-91; Sen Chapl/State Sec Fremantle Miss to Seamen 79-91; V N Mymms *St Alb* from 91. *The Vicarage, North Mymms Park, Hatfield, Herts AL9 7TN* Bowmansgreen (0727) 822062

RANYARD, Michael Taylor. b 43. Nottm Univ BTh74. Linc Th Coll 71. **d** 74 **p** 75. C Sutton in Ashfield St Mary *S'well* 74-76; Hon C Lewisham St Mary *S'wark* 76-77; C Rushmere *St E* 77-79; R Hopton, Market Weston, Barningham etc 79-83; Chr Educn and Resources Adv *Dur* from 83. *20 Norwich Road, Newton Hall, Durham DH1 5QA* 091-386 3948

RAPHAEL, Brother. See PARKER, Ramon Lewis

RAPHAEL, Ven Timothy John. b 29. Leeds Univ BA53. Coll of Resurr Mirfield. **d** 55 **p** 56. C Westmr St Steph w St Jo *Lon* 55-60; V Welling *S'wark* 60-63; New Zealand 63-72; Dean Dunedin 65-72; V St Jo Wood *Lon* 72-83; AD Westmr St Marylebone 82-83; Adn Middx from 83. *12 St Ann's Villas, London W11 4RS* 071-603 0856

RAPHOE, Archdeacon of. See HARTE, Ven Matthew Scott

RAPHOE, Dean of. See REEDE, Very Rev Samuel William

RAPKIN, Kevern. b 39. Univ of Wales (Lamp) BA62. Lich Th Coll 63. **d** 65 **p** 66. C Hanley w Hope *Lich* 65-68; C Woodchurch *Ches* 68-70; C Abbots Langley *St Alb* 70-73; Australia from 73. *The Rectory,*

195 Lesmurdie Road, Lesmurdie, W Australia 6076 Perth (9) 291-9300

RAPLEY, Frederick Arthur. b 27. Roch Th Coll 67. **d** 69 **p** 70. C Tenterden St Mildred w Smallhythe *Cant* 69-75; P-in-c Sittingbourne H Trin w Bobbing *Cant* V 85-89; rtd 89. *10 Lemsford Lane, Welwyn Garden City, Herts AL8 6YJ* Welwyn Garden (0707) 376198

RAPLEY, Joy Naomi. b 41. CertEd63 Open Univ BA73. Sarum & Wells Th Coll 87. **d** 89. Par Dn Welwyn Garden City *St Alb* from 89. *10 Lemsford Lane, Welwyn Garden City, Herts AL8 6YJ* Welwyn Garden (0707) 376198

RAPSEY, Peter Nigel. b 46. K Coll Lon BD68 AKC68. St Boniface Warminster. **d** 69 **p** 70. C Walton-on-Thames *Guildf* 69-73; C Fleet 73-77; P-in-c The Collingbournes and Everleigh *Sarum* 77-79; TV Wexcombe 79-84; R Wokingham St Paul *Ox* from 84. *St Paul's Rectory, Holt Lane, Wokingham, Berks RG11 1ED* Wokingham (0734) 780629

RASHBROOK, Alan Victor. b 42. S'wark Ord Course. **d** 75 **p** 76. Hon C Woking St Mary *Guildf* 75-83. *Hope Cottage, Robin Hood Lane, Sutton Green, Guildford GU4 7QG* Woking (0483) 762760

RASON, Frederick George. b 26. Qu Coll Birm 68. **d** 69 **p** 70. C Weymouth H Trin *Sarum* 69-72; P-in-c Yatesbury 72-73; P-in-c Cherhill 72-73; R Oldbury 73-76; R W Parley from 76. *The Rectory, 250 New Road, West Parley, Wimborne, Dorset BH22 8EW* Ferndown (0202) 873561

RASTALL, Preb Thomas Eric. b 19. St Aid Birkenhead 62. **d** 63 **p** 64. V Brown Edge *Lich* 67-74; P-in-c Croxden 74-78; V Denstone 74-81; P-in-c Ellastone 78-81; V Denstone w Ellastone and Stanton 81-91; RD Uttoxeter 87-91; Preb Lich Cathl 89-91; rtd 91. *21 Hammerton Way, Wellesbourne, Warwick CV35 9NS* Stratford-upon-Avon (0789) 842422

RATCLIFF, David William. b 37. K Coll Lon DipAdEd82. Edin Th Coll 59. **d** 62 **p** 63. C Croydon St Aug *Cant* 62-65; C Selsdon St Jo w St Fran 65-69; V Milton Regis St Mary 69-75; Hon Min Can Cant Cathl from 75; Asst Dir of Educn 75-91; Dioc Adv in Adult Educn and Lay Tr 75-91; Hon Pres Protestant Assn for Adult Educn in Eur 82-88; Germany from 91. *Sebastian-Rinz Strasse 22, D-6000 Frankfurt, Germany* Frankfurt (69) 550184

RATCLIFF, Richard Charles. b 09. Univ Coll Ox BA32. St Steph Ho Ox 33. **d** 33 **p** 34. V Boxgrove *Chich* 65-75; R Tangmere 66-75; Chapl RAF 66-75; rtd 75; P-in-c Appledram *Chich* 77-84; Perm to Offic from 84. *135 Birdham Road, Chichester, W Sussex PO20 7DY* Chichester (0243) 784870

RATCLIFFE, Michael David. b 43. Lon Univ BSc65 Southn Univ PGCE67 Lon Univ BA75 Dur Univ DipTh77 Lanc Univ MA84. Cranmer Hall Dur 75. **d** 77 **p** 78. C Blackpool St Thos *Blackb* 77-81; V Oswaldtwistle St Paul from 81. *St Paul's Vicarage, 71 Union Road, Oswaldtwistle, Accrington, Lancs BB5 3DD* Accrington (0254) 231038

RATCLIFFE, Peter William Lewis. b 30. Birm Univ BSc55 Lon Univ BD58. Tyndale Hall Bris 55. **d** 58 **p** 59. C Cam St Andr Less *Ely* 58-61; R Wistow 61-74; R Bury 61-74; V Rainham *Chelmsf* 74-85; R Wennington 75-85; V Heacham *Nor* 85-87; P-in-c Sedgeford w Southmere 85-87; V Heacham and Sedgeford from 87. *The Vicarage, Heacham, King's Lynn, Norfolk PE31 7HJ* Heacham (0485) 70268

RATHBAND, Kenneth William. b 60. Edin Univ BD86. Edin Th Coll 82. **d** 86 **p** 87. NSM Dundee St Paul *Bre* 86-88; TV Dundee St Martin 88-89; NSM Edin SS Phil and Jas *Edin* from 90. *43 Scotland Street, Edinburgh EH3 6PY* 031-557 3797

RATHBONE, Very Rev Norman Stanley. b 14. Ch Coll Cam BA35 MA39. Westcott Ho Cam 37. **d** 38 **p** 39. Dean Heref 69-82; V Heref St Jo 69-82; rtd 82; Perm to Offic *Heref* from 82. *The Daren, Newton St Margarets, Hereford* Michaelchurch (098123) 623

RATHBONE, Paul. b 36. BNC Ox BA58 MA62. Wycliffe Hall Ox 58. **d** 60 **p** 61. C Carl St Jo *Carl* 60-63; C Heworth w Peasholme St Cuth *York* 63-68; V Thorganby w Skipwith and N Duffield 68-83; V Acaster Malbis from 83; V Bishopthorpe from 83. *The Vicarage, 48 Church Lane, Bishopthorpe, York YO2 1QG* York (0904) 706476

RATHBONE, Royston George. b 27. Leeds Univ CertEd78. St D Coll Lamp 58. **d** 60 **p** 61. C Risca *Mon* 60-63; C Newport St Mark 63-65; CF (TAVR) 64-73; V Ebbw Vale St Jo *Mon* 65-68; Chapl HM Pris Coldingley 68-73; Linc 73-77; Man 77-79; HM Youth Cust Cen Everthorpe 79-86; HM Pris Lindholme 86-89; HM Young Offender Inst Everthorpe 89-91; Chapl HM Pris Everthorpe from

91. *HM Prison, Everthorpe, Brough, N Humberside HU15 1RB* Howden (0430) 422471

RATINGS, John William. b 37. St Pet Coll Ox BA62 MA71. Cuddesdon Coll 62. **d** 64 **p** 65. C Langley All SS and Martyrs *Man* 64-68; C Easthampstead *Ox* 68-71; V Wargrave from 71; RD Sonning from 88. *The Vicarage, Wargrave, Reading RG10 8EU* Wargrave (0734) 402202

RATLEDGE, Canon Ernest David. b 11. Man Univ BA32 MA33 BD52. Bps' Coll Cheshunt 33. **d** 34 **p** 35. R Prestwich St Mary *Man* 67-78; RD Radcliffe and Prestwich 67-78; rtd 78. *22 Abbot's Walk, Cerne Abbas, Dorchester, Dorset DT2 7JN* Cerne Abbas (0300) 341633

RATTERAY, Alexander Ewen. b 42. Codrington Coll Barbados 61. **d** 65 **p** 66. C S Kirkby *Wakef* 66-68; C Sowerby St Geo 68-71; V Airedale w Fryston 71-80; Bermuda from 80. *St John's Rectory, PO Box HM 544, Hamilton HM CX, Bermuda* Bermuda (1809) 292-3261

RAVALDE, Geoffrey Paul. b 54. Barrister 78 St Cuth Soc Dur BA76 SS Coll Cam BA86 MA90. Westcott Ho Cam 84. **d** 87 **p** 88. C Spalding *Linc* 87-91; P-in-c Wigton *Carl* from 91. *The Vicarage, Longthwaite Road, Wigton, Cumbria CA7 9JR* Wigton (06973) 42337

RAVEN, Barry. b 48. Sarum & Wells Th Coll 69. **d** 72 **p** 73. C Henbury *Bris* 72-76; P-in-c S Marston w Stanton Fitzwarren 76-78; TV Stratton St Margaret w S Marston etc 78-80; P-in-c Coalpit Heath 80-84; V from 84. *The Vicarage, Coalpit Heath, Bristol BS17 2RP* Winterbourne (0454) 775129

RAVEN, Charles Frank. b 58. ACIB84 Magd Coll Ox BA80 MA86 St Jo Coll Dur BA87. Cranmer Hall Dur 85. **d** 88 **p** 89. C Heckmondwike *Wakef* from 88. *2 Horton Street, Heckmondwike, W Yorkshire WF16 0LL* Heckmondwike (0924) 409400

RAVEN, Thomas Denys Milville. b 22. Lon Coll of Div 65. **d** 66 **p** 67. C Bradfield *Ox* 66-71; V Otterton *Ex* 71-74; V Tidebrook *Chich* 74-85; V Wadhurst 74-85; P-in-c Tasburgh *Nor* 85-87; P-in-c Tharston 85-87; P-in-c Forncett St Mary w St Pet 85-87; P-in-c Flordon 85-87; R Tasburgh w Tharston, Forncett and Flordon 87-89; rtd 89; Perm to Offic *St E* from 90. *Barfield, Church View, Holton, Halesworth, Suffolk IP19 8PB* Halesworth (0986) 875185

RAVENSCROFT, Ven Raymond Lockwood. b 31. Leeds Univ BA53. Coll of Resurr Mirfield 54. **d** 55 **p** 56. S Africa 55-57; S Rhodesia 57-59; Bechuanaland 59-62; C St Ives *Truro* 62-64; V Falmouth All SS 64-68; V St Stephens by Launceston 68-73; P-in-c Launceston St Thos 68-73; V Launceston St Steph w St Thos 73-74; TR Probus, Ladock and Grampound w Creed 74-88; RD Powder 77-81; Hon Can Truro Cathl 82-88; P-in-c St Erme 84-85; Adn Cornwall from 88; Can Lib Truro Cathl from 88. *Archdeacons's House, Knights Hill, Kenwyn, Truro TR1 3UY* Truro (0872) 70059

RAVENSDALE, Canon Victor Andrew Joseph. b 14. OBE73. Golds Coll Lon. CMS Tr Coll Blackheath 48 Makerere Coll Kampala 64. **d** 66 **p** 67. Uganda 66-73; Chapl Basel w Angarten and Freiburg-im-Breisgau *Eur* 73; R Stilton w Denton and Caldecote *Ely* 73-77; R Folksworth w Morborne 74-77; Chapl Lisbon *Eur* 77-84; Can Gib Cathl 81-85; rtd 84; Asst Chapl Lisbon *Eur* 84-85; Perm to Offic *Cant* from 85. *96 Church Path, Deal, Kent CT14 9TJ* Deal (0304) 360523

✠RAWCLIFFE, Rt Rev Derek Alec. b 21. OBE71. Leeds Univ BA42. Coll of Resurr Mirfield 42. **d** 44 **p** 45 **c** 74. C Claines St Geo *Worc* 44-47; Solomon Is 47-58; New Hebrides 58-80; Adn S Melanesia 59-74; Asst Bp Melanesia 74-75; Bp New Hebrides 75-80; Bp Glas 81-91; rtd 91; Asst Bp Ripon from 91. *Kitkatts, Wetherby Road, Bardsey, Leeds LS17 9BB* Collingham Bridge (0937) 72201

RAWDON-MOGG, Timothy David. b 45. St Jo Coll Dur BA76. Cuddesdon Coll 75. **d** 77 **p** 78. C Wotton St Mary *Glouc* 77-80; C Ascot Heath *Ox* 80-82; V Woodford Halse w Eydon *Pet* 82-88; V Shrivenham w Watchfield and Bourton *Ox* from 88. *St Andrew's Vicarage, Shrivenham, Swindon SN6 8AN* Swindon (0793) 782243

RAWE, Alan Charles George. b 29. ALCD56. **d** 56 **p** 57. C W Kilburn St Luke w St Simon and St Jude *Lon* 56-59; Lect Watford St Mary *St Alb* 59-61; R Ore *Chich* 61-69; R Moreton *Ches* 69-80; V Coppull *Blackb* 80-83; Miss to Seamen from 83; Felixstowe Seafarers' Cen from 88. *International Seafarers' Centre, Carr Road, Felixstowe, Suffolk IP11 8TG* Felixstowe (0394) 675944 or 673599

RAWLING, Miss Jane Elizabeth. b 51. Birm Univ BSc73 St Jo Coll York CertEd75. St Jo Coll Nottm LTh84. **dss**

84 **d** 87. Southsea St Jude *Portsm* 84-87; C 87-88; C St Paul's Cray St Barn *Roch* from 88. *50 Batchwood Green, Orpington, Kent BR5 2NF* Orpington (0689) 871467

RAWLING, Stephen Charles. b 43. Man Univ BSc64 Bris Univ MSc71 DipTh73. Sarum & Wells Th Coll 71. **d** 73 **p** 74. C Bris St Andr Hartcliffe *Bris* 73-76; C Westlands St Andr *Lich* 76-78; R Darlaston St Lawr 78-90; P-in-c Bloxwich 90; TR from 90. *All Saints' Vicarage, 3 Elmore Row, Bloxwich, Walsall WS3 2HR* Bloxwich (0922) 76598

RAWLINGS, Brenda (Susan). b 48. Sussex Univ CertEd69 DipHE81. Oak Hill Th Coll 85. **d** 87. Par Dn Green Street Green *Roch* 87-90; Par Dn Collier Row St Jas and Havering-atte-Bower *Chelmsf* from 90. *44 Highfield Road, Collier Row, Romford RM5 3RA* Romford (0708) 745620

RAWLINGS, John Dunstan Richard. b 25. Oak Hill Th Coll 62. **d** 64 **p** 65. Chapl R Aircraft Establishment Farnborough 69-80; Hon C Camberley St Paul *Guildf* 76-80; C 80; P-in-c Strethall *Chelmsf* 80-81; P-in-c Elmdon and Wendon Lofts 80-81; V Elmdon w Wendon Lofts and Strethall 81-88; rtd 88. *14 Huddington Glade, Yateley, Camberley, Surrey GU17 7FG* Yateley (0252) 875731

RAWLINGS, John Edmund Frank. b 47. AKC69. St Aug Coll Cant 69. **d** 70 **p** 71. C Rainham *Roch* 70-73; C Tattenham Corner and Burgh Heath *Guildf* 73-76; Chapl RN from 76. *c/o MOD, Lacon House, Theobald's Road, London WC1X 8RY* 071-430 6847

RAWLINGS, Philip John. b 53. St Jo Coll Nottm BTh83. **d** 83 **p** 84. C Blackley St Andr *Man* 83-87; C Halliwell St Pet from 87. *St Andrew's House, 29 Tattersall Avenue, Bolton BL1 5TE* Bolton (0204) 42444

RAWLINS, Douglas Royston. b 17. OBE68. Univ of Wales BSc39. St Steph Ho Ox 39. **d** 41 **p** 42. Malaya 50-63; Malaysia 63-80; rtd 80; Perm to Offic *Nor* from 81. *60 Pineheath Road, High Kelling, Holt, Norfolk NR25 6RH* Holt (0263) 712225

RAWLINSON, Curwen. b 32. MBE73. Leeds Univ CertEd55 Man Univ DipEd56 Open Univ BA80. Sarum Th Coll 59. **d** 61 **p** 62. C Wigan St Mich *Liv* 61-63; CF 63-78; Dep Asst Chapl Gen 78-80; Asst Chapl Gen 80-85; QHC from 83; R Uley w Owlpen and Nympsfield *Glouc* from 85; RD Dursley from 89. *The Rectory, Uley, Dursley, Glos GL11 5SN* Dursley (0453) 860249

RAWLINSON, Rowland. b 20. Liv Univ DipAdEd68 Open Univ BA74. St Deiniol's Hawarden 79. **d** 80 **p** 81. Hon C Barnston *Ches* 80-82; C 82-85; rtd 85; Hon C Higher Bebington *Ches* from 85. *18 Winston Grove, Moreton, Wirral L46 0PQ* 051-677 5641

RAWSON, Michael Graeme. b 62. York Univ BA84 Ox Univ BA88. St Steph Ho Ox 86. **d** 89 **p** 90. C Brighouse *Wakef* from 89. *34 Stanley Street, Brighouse, W Yorkshire HD6 1SX* Brighouse (0484) 718919

RAY, Mrs Joanna Zorina. b 55. AIMLS78 Qu Eliz Coll Lon BSc77 Garnett Coll Lon CertEd80. S'wark Ord Course 84. **d** 87. NSM Carshalton *S'wark* from 87. *73 Ruskin Road, Carshalton, Surrey SM5 3DD* 081-669 0529

RAY, John Mead. b 28. OBE79. St Andr Univ MA50 DipEd51. CMS Tr Coll Chislehurst 60. **d** 70 **p** 71. Miss Partner CMS from 70; C Sparkhill St Jo *Birm* 87-90; C Sparkbrook Em 87-90; C Sparkhill w Greet and Sparkbrook 90; Deanery Missr from 90. *25 Tennyson Road, Birmingham B10 0HA* 021-766 8716

RAY, Robin John. b 44. Sarum & Wells Th Coll 72. **d** 74 **p** 75. C Bourne Valley *Sarum* 74-78; P-in-c Dilton Marsh 78-82; V 82-87; V Taunton Lyngford *B & W* from 87. *St Peter's Vicarage, Eastwick Road, Taunton, Somerset TA2 7HD* Taunton (0823) 275085

RAYBOULD, Norman William. b 18. Lich Th Coll 51. **d** 54 **p** 55. V St Martin's *Lich* 67-76; V Sheriffhales w Woodcote 76-83; rtd 83; Perm to Offic *Lich* from 83. *Borrowdale, St Martin's Road, Gobowen, Oswestry, Shropshire SY11 3PH* Oswestry (0691) 652621

RAYMENT, Andrew David. b 45. Univ of Wales (Lamp) BA68 Univ of Wales (Abth) MA70. Ridley Hall Cam 78. **d** 80 **p** 81. C Costessey *Nor* 80-83; C Earlham St Anne 83-90; Missr from 86; V Catton from 90. *St Margaret's Vicarage, 1 Parkside Drive, Norwich NR6 7DP* Norwich (0603) 425615

RAYMENT-PICKARD, Hugh Douglas John. b 61. Kent Univ BA84 Em Coll Cam BA87. Westcott Ho Cam 85. **d** 88 **p** 89. C St Jo on Bethnal Green *Lon* 88-91; C Hackney from 91. *21 Blurton Road, London E5 0NL*

RAYMER, Victoria Elizabeth. b 46. Wellesley Coll (USA) BA68 MA69 JD78 Harvard Univ PhD81. St Steph Ho Ox BA86 Qu Coll Birm DPS89. **d** 89. Par Dn Bushey

St Alb from 89. *6 Farm Way, Bushey, Watford WD2 3SS* 081-950 9005

RAYMOND, Geoffrey Austin. b 23. Bris Univ BSc44. Qu Coll Birm 53. **d** 55 **p** 56. V Lupset *Wakef* 64-76; V Upavon w Rushall *Sarum* 76-88; P-in-c 88; RD Avon 80-85; rtd 88. *4 Finch Close, Shepton Mallet, Somerset BA4 5GA* Shepton Mallet (0749) 344102

RAYMOND, George William. b 07. MBE55. Wycliffe Hall Ox. **d** 67 **p** 68. Hon C W Wickham St Jo *Cant* 67-84; Hon C W Wickham St Jo *S'wark* 85-87; rtd 87. *58 Gates Green Road, West Wickham, Kent BR4 9DG* 081-462 4980

RAYNER, David. b 49. Trin Hall Cam BA72 MA75. Westcott Ho Cam 75. **d** 78 **p** 79. C Chorlton-cum-Hardy St Clem *Man* 78-81; C Cam Gt St Mary w St Mich *Ely* 81-84; Warden Trin Coll Cen Camberwell 84-88; V Camberwell St Geo *S'wark* 84-88; Warden Bp Mascall Cen *Heref* 89-90; V Smethwick II Trin w St Alb *Birm* from 90; P-in-c W Smethwick from 90. *The Vicarage, 69 South Road, Smethwick, Warley, W Midlands B67 7BP* 021-558 0373

RAYNER, Canon George Charles. b 26. Bps' Coll Cheshunt 50. **d** 52 **p** 53. R Wootton *Portsm* 69-89; Hon Can Portsm Cathl from 84; rtd 89; Perm to Offic *B & W* from 89. *Grianan, 23 Hood Close, Glastonbury, Somerset BA6 8ES* Glastonbury (0458) 33795

RAYNER, Paul Anthony. b 39. Dur Univ BA60 Lon Univ BD68 Cape Town Univ MA79. Lon Coll of Div 65. **d** 68 **p** 69. C Crookes St Thos *Sheff* 68-72; S Africa 72-79; P-in-c S Shoebury *Chelmsf* 80-84; R from 84. *The Rectory, Church Road, Shoeburyness, Essex SS3 9EU* Southend-on-Sea (0702) 292778

RAYNER, Richard Noel. b 24. Lon Univ BD51. Oak Hill Th Coll 50. **d** 52 **p** 53. V Slough *Ox* 65-72; V Heworth w Peasholme St Cuth *York* 72-75; V Heworth 75-81; V Okehampton w Inwardleigh *Ex* 81-89; RD Okehampton 87-89; rtd 89; Perm to Offic *Ex* from 90. *Dolphin Lodge, Western Road, Newton Abbot TQ13 7ED*

RAYNER, Stewart Leslie. b 39. Dur Univ BA61 DipTh66 MA73. Cranmer Hall Dur. **d** 67 **p** 68. C Whiston *Sheff* 67-70; C Doncaster St Geo 70-74; R Adwick-le-Street 74-85; V Totley 85-91; Asst Chapl Kingsway Hosp Derby from 91. *c/o The Mental Health Unit, Kingsway Hospital, Derby DE3 3LZ* Derby (0332) 362221

RAYNOR, Duncan Hope. b 58. Ex Coll Ox MA80 MA(Theol)82 Birm Univ PGCE88. Qu Coll Birm 82. **d** 84 **p** 85. C Kings Heath *Birm* 84-87; Perm to Offic from 87; Hd of RE Alderbrook Sch Solihull from 88. *134 Addison Road, Birmingham B14 7EP* 021-443 2147

RAYNOR, Eric William. b 13. Keble Coll Ox BA33. St Andr Whittlesford 34. **d** 36 **p** 37. V Saffron Walden *Chelmsf* 62-73; RD Saffron Walden 65-74; V Saffron Walden w Wendens Ambo 72-74; rtd 78. *Highlands Farmhouse, Brampton, Beccles, Suffolk NR34 8DB* Brampton (050279) 801

RAYNOR, Michael. b 53. Lanc Univ BA74 MSc75. Ripon Coll Cuddesdon BA84. **d** 85 **p** 86. C Gt Crosby St Faith *Liv* 85-88; V Warrington St Barn from 88. *St Barnabas' Vicarage, 73 Lovely Lane, Warrington WA5 1TY* Warrington (0925) 33556

RAYNOR, Robert Ernest. b 14. Lon Univ BA36 TCD BA49 MA55 BD55. CITC 49. **d** 49 **p** 50. I Drummaul w Duneane and Ballyscullion *Conn* 68-72; Lect and Chapl Stranmillis Coll Belf 72-79; C Belf St Bart 72-79; rtd 79. *4 Beechwood Grove, Beechill Road, Belfast BT8 4PT*

RAYNOR-SMITH, Charles Alfred Walter. b 12. Sarum Th Coll. **d** 55 **p** 56. V Colehill *Sarum* 62-81; rtd 81. *19 Tatnam Road, Poole, Dorset BH15 2OW* Poole (0202) 71510

RAZEY, Miss Florence Hannah. b 12. St Andr Ho Portsm 38. **dss** 43 **d** 87. Nether Hoyland St Pet *Sheff* 69-72; rtd 72; Elson *Portsm* 72-87; Hon C from 87. *2 Naish Drive, Gosport, Hants PO12 4AP* Gosport (0705) 523799

RAZZALL, Charles Humphrey. b 55. Worc Coll Ox BA76 Qu Coll Cam BA78 Worc Coll Ox MA81. Westcott Ho Cam 76. **d** 79 **p** 80. C Catford (Southend) and Downham *S'wark* 79-83; V Crofton Park St Hilda w St Cypr 83-87; UPA Field Officer from 87; TV Oldham *Man* from 87. *7 Hampton Street, Oldham OL8 1RF*

READ, Andrew Gordon. b 40. ARICS63 Nottm Univ BA69. Cuddesdon Coll 70. **d** 70 **p** 71. C E Retford *S'weil* 70-72; C Woodthorpe 72-76; P-in-c Newark St Leon 76-78; Perm to Offic *Roch* from 79. *13 Clevedon Road, London SE20 7QQ* 081-778 9545

READ, Charles William. b 60. Man Univ BA81 Man Poly CertEd82. St Jo Coll Nottm 86. **d** 88 **p** 89. C Oldham *Man* 88-90; C Urmston from 90. *157 Stretford Road, Urmston, Manchester M31 1LW* 061-748 8411

READ, Christopher Holditch. b 19. Qu Coll Birm 50. **d** 53 **p** 54. R Grangemouth *Edin* 63-72; V Parwich w Alsop en le Dale *Derby* 72-87; P-in-c Fenny Bentley, Thorpe and Tissington 77; rtd 87; Perm to Offic *Mor* 88-89. *11 Stafford Court, Stafford Road, Dornoch, Sutherland IV25 3ON* Dornoch (0862) 810059

READ, Geoffrey Philip. b 61. Bris Univ LLB82. Wycliffe Hall Ox 85. **d** 88 **p** 89. C Dorking St Paul *Guildf* from 88. *6 Falkland Road, Dorking, Surrey RH4 3AB* Dorking (0306) 889513

READ, Ian. b 34. Selw Coll Cam BA57. Linc Th Coll 57. **d** 59 **p** 60. C Shard End *Birm* 59-63; Mozambique 64-76; Dean Maciene 71-76; P-in-c Edgbaston St Germain *Birm* 76-80; V Worc St Wulstan *Worc* from 80. *St Wulstan's Vicarage, Cranham Drive, Warndon, Worcester WR4 9PA* Worcester (0905) 57806

READ, Jack. b 19. Qu Coll Birm 67. **d** 68 **p** 69. C Tong *Bradf* 68-70; C Baildon 70-72; V Queensbury 72-86; rtd 86; Perm to Offic *Bradf* from 86. *7 Silver Birch Grove, Wyke, Bradford, W Yorkshire BD12 9ET* Bradford (0274) 670737

READ, James Arthur. b 51. Nottm Coll of Educn BEd74. E Midl Min Tr Course 84. **d** 87 **p** 88. C Weoley Castle *Birm* 87-91; C W Smethwick from 91. *St Paul's Vicarage, West Park Road, Smethwick, Warley, W Midlands B67 7JH* 021-558 0470

READ, John. b 33. Worc Coll Ox BA56 MA60. Chich Th Coll 56. **d** 58 **p** 59. C Babbacombe *Ex* 58-60; C Heavitree 60-63; V Swimbridge 63-69; V Ex St Matt 69-80; P-in-c Ex St Sidwell 79-80; R Ex St Sidwell and St Matt 80-83; Chapl Warneford Hosp Leamington Spa 83-89; Chapl S Warks Hosps 83-89; Chapl Dur and Ches le Street Hosps from 89; Chapl Dryburn Hosp from 89. *48 Westcott Drive, Durham DH1 5AQ* 091-386 7590

READ, Canon John Charles. b 07. St D Coll Lamp Keble Coll Ox BA MA35. St Steph Ho Ox 29. **d** 31 **p** 32. V Canton St Luke *Llan* 43-77; Can Llan Cathl 72-77; rtd 77; Perm to Offic *Llan* from 79. *9 Granville Avenue, Cardiff CF5 1BW* Cardiff (0222) 569249

READ, John Hanson. b 17. St Jo Coll Ox BA49 MA53. Qu Coll Birm 49. **d** 50 **p** 51. R Beddington *S'wark* 61-78; RD Sutton 65-70; P-in-c Guestling *Chich* 78; P-in-c Pett 78; R Guestling and Pett 78-83; rtd 83; Perm to Offic *Chich* 84-89; RD Rye 89-90. *6 Oast House Road, Icklesham, Winchelsea, E Sussex TN36 4BN* Hastings (0424) 814440

READ, John Ronald James. b 39. Univ of Wales (Lamp) BA62 DipTh63. **d** 63 **p** 64. C Mold *St As* 63-65; Papua New Guinea 66-70; C Cheshunt *St Alb* 70-72; Chapl RAF 72-88; Chapl HM Pris Standford Hill 88-90; V Clifton *Derby* from 90; R Norbury w Snelston from 90. *The Vicarage, Clifton, Ashbourne, Derbyshire DE6 2GJ* Ashbourne (0335) 42199

READ, John Samuel. b 33. Fitzw Ho Cam BA56. Clifton Th Coll 62. **d** 64 **p** 65. C Sneinton St Chris w St Phil *S'well* 64-67; C Huyton St Geo *Liv* 67-70; Lic to Offic *Blackb* 70-72; V Moldgreen *Wakef* 72-84; V Rawtenstall St Mary *Man* 84-91; Chapl Rossendale Gen Hosp 84-91; R Earsham w Alburgh and Denton *Nor* from 91. *The Rectory, Earsham, Bungay, Suffolk NR35 2TF* Bungay (0986) 2147

READ, Robert Edgar. b 47. Kelham Th Coll 66. **d** 70 **p** 71. C Harton Colliery *Dur* 70-75; C Wilmslow *Ches* 76-80; V Gatley from 80. *St James's Vicarage, 11 Northenden Road, Cheadle, Cheshire SK8 4EN* 061-428 4764

READ, Victor. b 29. Lon Univ BD58. ALCD57. **d** 58 **p** 59. C Wimbledon *S'wark* 58-61; C Lt Marlow *Ox* 61-64; V Wootton *Linc* 64-67; R Croxton 64-67; V Ulceby 64-67; V Linc St Pet in Eastgate w St Marg 67-73; V W Wimbledon Ch Ch *S'wark* from 73. *16 Copse Hill, London SW20 0HG* 081-946 4491

READE, Canon Nicholas Stewart. b 46. Leeds Univ BA70 DipTh72. Coll of Resurr Mirfield 70. **d** 73 **p** 74. C Coseley St Chad *Lich* 73-75; C Codsall 75-78; V Upper Gornal 78-82; V Mayfield *Chich* 82-88; RD Dallington 82-88; V Eastbourne St Mary from 88; RD Eastbourne from 88; Can and Preb Chich Cathl from 90; Min Hydneye CD from 91. *The Vicarage, 2 Glebe Close, Eastbourne, E Sussex BN20 8AW* Eastbourne (0323) 20420

READER, John. b 53. Trin Coll Ox BA75 MA79 Man Univ DipTh83 MPhil87. Ripon Coll Cuddesdon 76. **d** 78 **p** 79. C Ely 78-80; C Baguley *Man* 80-83; TV Kirkby Lonsdale *Carl* 83-86; V Lydbury N *Heref* 86-89; P-in-c Hopesay w Edgton 86-89; Tutor Glouc Sch for Min 86-89; Vice-Prin Glouc Sch for Min 89-90; R Lydbury N w Hopesay and Edgton *Heref* 89-90; Dir Past Th Sarum & Wells Th Coll from 90. *11 Chiselbury Grove,*

Harnham, Salisbury, Wilts SP2 8EP Salisbury (0722) 28898

READER, Roger James. b 58. BA. St Steph Ho Ox. **d** 83 **p** 84. C Somers Town St Mary *Lon* 83-86; C Hoxton H Trin w St Mary from 86. *Holy Trinity Vicarage, 3 Bletchley Street, London N1 7QG* 071-253 4796

READER, Dr Trevor Alan John. b 46. Lon Univ BSc68 MSc70 Portsm Poly PhD72. S Dios Minl Tr Scheme 83. **d** 86 **p** 87. C Alverstoke *Portsm* 86-89; P-in-c Hook w Warsash from 89. *The Vicarage, 112 Osborne Road, Warsash, Southampton SO3 6GH* Locks Heath (0489) 572324

READER-MOORE, Anthony. b 43. Kent Univ BA80 Hull Univ MA83. Linc Th Coll. **d** 82 **p** 83. C Addiscombe St Mildred *Cant* 82-84; C Addiscombe St Mildred *S'wark* 85-86; R N Wheatley, W Burton, Bole, Saundby, Sturton etc *S'well* from 86; Rural Officer from 89. *The Rectory, Middlefield Road, North Wheatley, Retford, Notts DN22 9DA* Gainsborough (0427) 880293

READING, Albert Edward. b 16. **d** 68 **p** 69. C Newtown w Llanllwchaiarn w Aberhafesp *St As* 68-71; C Colwyn Bay 71-73; V Penycae 73-80; rtd 80. *67 Primrose Way, Maesgwyn, Wrexham, Clwyd LL11 2AT* Wrexham (0978) 365248

READING, Canon Laurence John. b 14. DSC44. Lon Univ BD39 AKC39. **d** 39 **p** 40. Sec C of E Bd of Adult Educn Cttee 65-72; Can Heref Cathl *Heref* 72-82; rtd 82. *11 Wakelin Way, Witham, Essex CM8 2TX* Witham (0376) 513251

READING, Area Bishop of. *See* BONE, Rt Rev John Frank Ewan

REAGON, Darrol Franklin. b 46. Univ of Wales (Cardiff) DipTh76. St Mich Coll Llan 74. **d** 76 **p** 77. C Llandrillo-yn-Rhos *St As* 76-78; C Hawarden 78-81; V Northwich St Luke and H Trin *Ches* 81-85; V Moulton *Linc* 85-91; V Scunthorpe Resurr from 91. *The Vicarage, Mirfield Road, Scunthorpe, S Humberside DN15 8AN* Scunthorpe (0724) 842196

REAKES-WILLIAMS, Gordon Martin. b 63. St Cath Coll Cam BA86 MA89. St Jo Coll Dur BA90. **d** 91. C Harold Wood *Chelmsf* from 91. *48 Harold Court Road, Harold Wood, Romford RM3 0YX* Ingrebourne (04023) 41348

REAKES-WILLIAMS, John Michael Reakes Andrew. b 30. St Fran Coll Brisbane 69. **d** 70 **p** 71. Australia 70-73; C Northfield *Birm* 73-74; C Penarth w Lavernock *Llan* 74-76; V Llanbradach 76-78; R Llanfabon 78-79; V Oswestry H Trin *Lich* from 79. *Holy Trinity Vicarage, Oswestry, Shropshire SY11 2RN* Oswestry (0691) 652540

REALE, Mrs Kathleen. b 38. Carl Dioc Tr Course 83. **dss** 86 **d** 87. Dalston *Carl* 86-87; Par Dn 87-90; Par Dn Westward, Rosley-w-Woodside and Welton from 87; Par Dn Thursby from 89; Dn-in-c Gt Salkeld w Lazonby from 90. *The Rectory, Lazonby, Penrith, Cumbria CA10 1BL* Lazonby (076883) 750

REANEY, Christopher Thomas. b 60. Univ of Wales (Lamp) BA82. St Mich Coll Llan DipTh85. **d** 85 **p** 86. C Newport Maindee St Jo Ev *Mon* 85-87; C Griffithstown 88-89; V Treherbert w Treorchy *Llan* from 89. *The Vicarage, John Street, Treorchy, M Glam CF46 5PS* Treorchy (0443) 772241

REANEY, Joseph Silvester. b 13. Selw Coll Cam BA35 MA42. Wells Th Coll 36. **d** 37 **p** 38. C Lewisham St Jo Southend *S'wark* 37-40; C Bellingham St Dunstan 40-42; Chapl RAFVR 42-46; V Gt Barr *Lich* from 47. *Great Barr Vicarage, Chapel Lane, Birmingham B43 7BD* 021-357 1390

REAR, Michael John. b 40. Hull Univ MA. Lich Th Coll 61. **d** 64 **p** 65. C Kingston upon Hull St Alb *York* 64-69; C Goldthorpe *Sheff* 69-73; V Thornbury *Bradf* 73-89; V Walsingham and Houghton *Nor* from 89. *The Vicarage, Walsingham, Norfolk NR22 6BL* Walsingham (0328) 820345

REARDON, Bernard Morris Garvin. b 13. Keble Coll Ox BA35 MA38. Ripon Hall Ox 35. **d** 37 **p** 38. Sen Lect, Reader, and Hd Relig Studies Newc Univ 63-78; rtd 78. *2 The Grove, Benton, Newcastle upon Tyne NE12 9PE* 091-266 1574

REARDON, Canon Martin Alan. b 32. Selw Coll Cam BA54 MA58. Cuddesdon Coll 56. **d** 58 **p** 59. C Rugby St Andr *Cov* 58-62; C Wicker w Neepsend *Sheff* 62-65; Lic to Offic 65-71; Sub-Warden Linc Th Coll 71-78; Sec Gen Syn Bd for Miss and Unity 78-89; Can and Preb Linc Cathl *Linc* from 79; Perm to Offic *Chich* from 81; R Plumpton 89-90; Gen Sec Chs Together in England from 90. *Churches Together in England, Interchurch House, 35-41 Lower Marsh, London SE1 7RL* 071-620 4444

REASON, Jack. b 28. St Alb Minl Tr Scheme 77. **d** 80 **p** 81. NSM Luton Lewsey St Hugh *St Alb* 80-85; C Bideford *Ex* 85-88; R Northlew w Ashbury from 88; R Bratton Clovelly w Germansweek from 88. *The Rectory, Northlew, Okehampton, Devon EX20 3NJ* Beaworthy (0409) 221714

REAST, Mrs Eileen Joan. b 40. E Midl Min Tr Course 81. **dss** 84 **d** 87. Linc St Mary-le-Wigford w St Benedict etc *Linc* 80-87; C 87-90; C Stamford All SS w St Jo from 90. *26 Hazel Grove, Stamford, Lincs PE9 2HJ* Stamford (0780) 56942

REAVIL, Michael Edward. b 51. Qu Coll Birm 89. **d** 91. C Cofton Hackett w Barnt Green *Birm* from 91. *41 Fiery Hill Road, Barnt Green, Birmingham B45 8JZ* 021-445 2195

REAY, John. b 08. Ely Th Coll. **d** 60 **p** 61. V Crosscrake *Carl* 62-71; V Millom H Trin w Thwaites 71-75; rtd 75; Perm to Offic *Carl* from 77. *Woodlands, Drovers' Lane, Penrith, Cumbria CA11 7RB* Penrith (0768) 65226

REBERT, Nicholas Aubrey Russell. b 47. Open Univ BA88. **d** 71 **p** 72. Ceylon 71-72; Sri Lanka 72-83; C Whitehaven *Carl* 84-88; TV from 88; Chapl W Cumberland Hosp from 88. *43 Leathwaite, Whitehaven, Cumbria CA28 7UG* Whitehaven (0946) 64891

RECORD, John. b 47. St Chad's Coll Dur BA71. Westcott Ho Cam 71. **d** 73 **p** 74. C Paddington St Jo w St Mich *Lon* 73-75; C Witney *Ox* 75-78; P-in-c Lt Compton and Chastleton 78-80; R Lt Compton w Chastleton, Cornwell etc 80-83; V Hawkhurst *Cant* from 83; RD W Charing from 89. *The Vicarage, Hawkhurst, Kent TN18 4QB* Hawkhurst (0580) 753397

RECORD, Sister Marion Eva. b 25. MRCS50 LRCP50 FFARCS57 Lon Univ BD79. **dss** 78 **d** 87. OHP from 72; Chapl Hull Univ *York* 72-78; Chapl York Univ 78-80; Lic to Offic from 80. *Martin House, Grove Road, Clifford, Wetherby, W Yorkshire LS23 6TX* Wetherby (0937) 843449

REDDING, Roger Charles. b 45. Chich Th Coll 87. **d** 89 **p** 90. C Yeovil *B & W* 89-90; C Yeovil St Mich from 90. *9 Derwent Gardens, Yeovil, Somerset* Yeovil (0935) 27988

REDDINGTON, Gerald Alfred. b 34. Lon Univ DipRS79. S'wark Ord Course 76. **d** 79 **p** 79. NSM St Vedast w St Mich-le-Querne etc *Lon* 79-85; Dir Past Support Gp Scheme 83-86; Hon C St Marylebone All SS 85-90; Perm to Offic *Portsm* from 88; V Ealing St Barn *Lon* from 90. *St Barnabas' Vicarage, 66 Woodfield Road, London W5 1SH* 081-998 0826

REDFEARN, John William Holmes. Sheff Univ BA30 MA31 DipEd31. **d** 33 **p** 34. Chapl Haberdashers' Aske's Sch Elstree 56-72; Perm to Offic *Lon* 61-76; rtd 72. *184 Cardiff Road, Llandaff, Cardiff CF5 2AD* Cardiff (0222) 567692

REDFEARN, Michael. b 42. Open Univ BA78 Hull Univ MA84 BA86. St Aid Birkenhead 64. **d** 68 **p** 69. C Bury St Pet *Man* 68-71; C Swinton St Pet 71-74; Ind Chapl *Bris* 74-81; Ind Chapl *York* 81-86; St Alb Minl Tr Scheme from 86; V Southill *St Alb* from 86. *The Vicarage, Southill, Biggleswade, Beds SG18 9LH* Hitchin (0462) 813331

REDFERN, Canon Alastair Llewellyn John. b 48. Trin Coll Cam BA74 Ch Ch Ox MA74. Qu Coll Birm 75. **d** 76 **p** 77. C Tettenhall Regis *Lich* 76-79; Tutor Ripon Coll Cuddesdon 79-87; Hon C Cuddesdon *Ox* 83-87; Can Res Bris Cathl *Bris* from 87. *Bristol Cathedral, College Green, Bristol BS1 5TJ* Bristol (0272) 421039

REDGERS, Brian. b 42. Dur Univ BA65. Westcott Ho Cam 65. **d** 67 **p** 68. C Rushmere *St E* 67-73; Lic to Offic from 73. *44 Belvedere Road, Ipswich*

REDGRAVE, Cecil Goulden. b 14. Oak Hill Th Coll 37. **d** 41 **p** 42. V New Milverton *Cov* 60-76; R Tredington and Darlingscott w Newbold on Stour 76-83; rtd 83; Perm to Offic *Cov* from 83. *30 Elmdene Road, Kenilworth, Warks CV8 2BX* Kenilworth (0926) 57118

REDGRAVE, Miss Christine Howick. b 50. AIAT73. Trin Coll Bris 75. **dss** 78 **d** 87. Watford *St Alb* 78-83; Maidenhead St Andr and St Mary Magd *Ox* 83-85; Bracknell 85-87; Par Dn from 87. *The Vicarage, 4 Micheldever Way, Bracknell, Berks RG12 3XX* Bracknell (0344) 50651

REDGRAVE, Ronald Oliver. b 18. Ox NSM Course. **d** 83 **p** 84. NSM Boyne Hill *Ox* 83-85; Perm to Offic *St E* 85-86; P-in-c Alderton w Ramsholt and Bawdsey 86-88; rtd 88. *Fair Field, Ferry Road, Bawdsey, Woodbridge, Suffolk IP12 3AW* Shottisham (0394) 411607

REDGRAVE, Susan Frances. b 55. CQSW75. St Deiniol's Hawarden 89. **d** 90. NSM Leic Resurr *Leic* 90; Par Dn

De Beauvoir Town St Pet *Lon* from 90. *46A Mortimer Road, London N1 5AP* 071-254 8430

REDHEAD, Edward. b 30. St Deiniol's Hawarden 60. **d** 63 **p** 64. C Mottram in Longdendale w Woodhead *Ches* 63-67; V Rivington *Man* 67-72; V Bloxwich *Lich* 72-75; Hon C Lich St Chad 82-84; P-in-c Bromfield w Waverton *Carl* 84-85; V 85-90; P-in-c W Newton 84-85; V 85-90; R Harrington from 90. *The Rectory, Rectory Close, Harrington, Workington, Cumbria CA14 5PN* Harrington (0946) 830215

REDHEAD, Canon Francis Edward. b 34. G&C Coll Cam BA58. Chich Th Coll 58. **d** 60 **p** 61. C Adel *Ripon* 60-69; Chapl St Geo Hosp Rothwell from 69; V Rothwell *Ripon* 69-76; P-in-c Lofthouse 74-76; V Rothwell w Lofthouse 76-86; RD Whitkirk 78-88; Hon Can Ripon Cathl from 81; V Rothwell from 86. *Holy Trinity Vicarage, Beech Grove, Rothwell, Leeds LS26 0EL* Leeds (0532) 822369

REDMAN, Canon Arthur Thomas. b 28. Dur Univ BA52. Ridley Hall Cam 62. **d** 63 **p** 64. C Heaton St Barn *Bradf* 63-66; C Hitchin St Mary *St Alb* 66-70; PM 72-75; Perm to Offic *Nor* 70-72; V Swanwick and Pentrich *Derby* 75-80; V Allestree from 80; P-in-c Morley 82-85; Hon Can Derby Cathl from 86; RD Duffield from 87. *St Edmund's Vicarage, Allestree, Derby DE3 2FN* Derby (0332) 557396

REDMAN, Douglas Stuart Raymond. b 35. MCIOB64. Roch Th Coll 66. **d** 68 **p** 69. C Shortlands *Roch* 68-71; V from 80; R Kingsdown 71-76; R Chatham St Mary w St Jo 76-80; RD Beckenham from 90. *The Vicarage, 37 Kingswood Road, Bromley BR2 0HG* 081-460 4989

REDMAYNE, John. b 12. OBE44 TD46. FCA36. Qu Coll Birm DipTh49. **d** 49 **p** 50. C Esher *Guildf* 49-51; Jamaica 51-57; R Girton *Ely* 58-60; USPG 61-70; New Zealand from 70. *15 Rawene Street, Waikanae, New Zealand* Waikanae (58) 36062

REDMOND, Ernest Wilkinson. b 10. TCD BA36. CITC 36. **d** 36 **p** 37. I Augher w Newtownsaville and Eskrahoole *Clogh* 65-73; RD Clogh 58-73; Preb Clogh Cathl 67-78; Chan 78-79; I Monaghan 73-79; rtd 79. *5 Ashbury Park, Bangor, Co Down* Bangor (0247) 58244

REDPATH, Stewart Rosbotham. b 11. TCD BA39. CITC 39. **d** 39 **p** 40. I Loughgall *Arm* 62-80; rtd 80. *22 Rosemount Park, Armagh BT60 1AX* Armagh (0861) 522698

REDRUP, Robert John. b 38. Leeds Univ BA65. Oak Hill Th Coll 65. **d** 69 **p** 70. C Maidenhead St Andr and St Mary Magd *Ox* 69-74; C St Keverne *Truro* 74-78; P-in-c Kea 78-80; V from 80; P-in-c Highertown and Baldhu 80-84. *The Vicarage, Kea, Truro, Cornwall TR3 6AE* Truro (0872) 72850

REDVERS HARRIS, Jonathan Francis. b 60. Solicitor 87 Southn Univ LLB81. Ridley Hall Cam 87. **d** 90 **p** 91. C Enfield St Jas *Lon* from 90. *Glebe House, 146 Hertford Road, Enfield, Middx EN3 5AY* 081-804 3100

REDWOOD, Canon David Leigh. b 32. Glas Univ DipSocWork78. Edin Th Coll 57. **d** 59 **p** 60. C Stirling *Edin* 59-61; C Glas Ch Ch *Glas* 61-64; P-in-c Glas Ascension 64-66; R 66-69; R Hamilton 69-74; R Callander *St And* 74-76; Hon C 76-85; R Lochearnhead 74-76; R Killin 74-76; Hon C Doune 76-85; Hon C Aberfoyle 78-85; R Dunfermline from 85; Can St Ninian's Cathl Perth from 90. *The Rectory, 17 Ardeer Place, Dunfermline, Fife KY11 4YX* Dunfermline (0383) 723901

REECE, Gp Capt Arthur. b 13. DSO44 OBE54 DFC42 AFC43. St Deiniol's Hawarden 77. **d** 79 **p** 80. Hon C Lache cum Saltney *Ches* 79-80; V Tilstone Fearnall and Wettenhall 80-90; rtd 90. *Tawelfan, Bryn Goodman, Ruthin, Clwyd LL15 1EL* Ruthin (08242) 2968

✠**REECE, Rt Rev David.** b 13. G&C Coll Cam BA34 MA38. St Mich Coll Llan 35. **d** 36 **p** 37. C Abth St Mich *St D* 36-41; C Llanelly 41-49; V Pemb St Mary and St Mich 49-56; V Port Talbot St Theodore *Llan* 56-71; RD Margam 66-71; Can Llan Cathl 69-71; Adn Margam 71-81; Asst Bp Llan 77-83; rtd 83. *16 Preswylfa Court, Merthyr Mawr Road, Bridgend, M Glam CF31 3NX* Bridgend (0656) 653115

REECE, Donald Malcolm Hayden. b 36. CCC Cam BA58 MA62. Cuddesdon Coll 58. **d** 60 **p** 61. C Latchford St Jas *Ches* 60-63; C Matlock and Tansley *Derby* 63-67; C-in-c Hackenthorpe Ch CD 67-70; Rhodesia 70-73; V Leic St Pet *Leic* 74-82; V Putney St Marg *S'wark* from 82. *St Margaret's Vicarage, 46 Luttrell Avenue, London SW15 6PE* 081-788 5522

REECE, Paul Michael. b 60. Southn Univ BA81. Coll of Resurr Mirfield 83. **d** 85 **p** 86. C Borehamwood *St Alb* 85-89; C Potters Bar from 89. *11 Otways Close, Potters Bar, Herts EN6 1TE* Potters Bar (0707) 55028

REED, Alan Ronald. b 44. Sarum Th Coll 66. **d** 68 **p** 70. C Ifield *Chich* 68-71; C Perivale *Lon* 71-72; C Ruislip St Martin 72-75; C Burgess Hill St Jo *Chich* 76-78; V Shoreham Beach 78-80; V Roughey (or Roffey) from 80; P-in-c Rusper 84-86. *Roffey Vicarage, 52 Shepherds Way, Horsham, W Sussex RH12 4LX* Horsham (0403) 6533

REED, Albert. b 36. Univ of Wales BA58 BD63. St Mich Coll Llan 58. **d** 61 **p** 62. C Rhymney *Mon* 61-64; Chapl St Woolos Cathl 64-66; R Blaina 66-67; Hon C Dudley St Edm *Worc* from 72. *21 Tanfield Road, Dudley, W Midlands DY2 8XF* Dudley (0384) 256118

REED, Allan Norman. b 31. Keble Coll Ox BA55 MA59 Man Univ CertEd72. Wycliffe Hall Ox. **d** 57 **p** 58. C Beverley Minster *York* 57-60; C Marfleet 60-64; R S Levenshulme *Man* 64-71; Lic to Offic from 71. *6 Lawton Road, Stockport, Cheshire SK4 2RG* 061-432 9806

REED, Mrs Annette Susan. b 54. Birm Univ BA76 Univ of Wales (Cardiff) CQSW78. Qu Coll Birm 84. **d** 87. C Churchover w Willey *Cov* from 89; C Clifton upon Dunsmore and Newton from 89. *18 Robertson Close, Clifton upon Dunsmore, Rugby, Warks CV23 0DJ* Rugby (0788) 569974

REED, Brian. b 43. Bris Univ BSc65 Nottm Univ DipTh76. Linc Th Coll 73. **d** 76 **p** 77. C S Ashford Ch Ch *Cant* 76-78; C Spring Park 78-83; V Barming Heath from 83. *St Andrew's Vicarage, 416 Tonbridge Road, Maidstone, Kent ME16 9LW* Maidstone (0622) 726245

REED, Bruce Douglas. b 20. Fitzw Ho Cam BA52 MA56. Lambeth MLitt90 Moore Th Coll Sydney LTh45. **d** 46 **p** 46. Chapl Fitzw Ho Cam 50-54; C Cam St Paul *Ely* 53-54; Chmn Grubb Inst from 69; rtd 85. *The Grubb Institute, Cloudesley Street, London N1 0HU* 071-278 8061

REED, Christopher John. b 42. Selw Coll Cam BA64 MA68 Dur Univ DipTh66. Cranmer Hall Dur 64. **d** 67 **p** 68. C Gt Ilford St Andr *Chelmsf* 67-70; P-in-c Bordesley St Andr *Birm* 70-72; V 72-80; V Crofton St Paul *Roch* from 80. *St Paul's Vicarage, 2 Oakwood Road, Orpington, Kent BR6 8JH* Farnborough (0689) 852939

REED, Colin Charles. b 40. LCP75 FCP85 Lon Univ DipTh70. **d** 69 **p** 70. C Weston-super-Mare Ch Ch *B & W* 69-71; Kenya 71-79; Australia from 80; Educn Sec CMS from 84. *32 Lochinvar Parade, Carlingford, NSW, Australia 2118*

REED, Canon Douglas Victor. b 19. AKC41 Middlebury Coll (USA) Hon DD51. St Steph Ho Ox 41. **d** 42 **p** 43. V Chislehurst Annunciation *Roch* 52-85; Hon Can Roch Cathl 81-85; rtd 85; Perm to Offic *Roch* from 85. *6 Crown Lane, Chislehurst, Kent BR7 5PL* 081-467-3360

REED, Duncan Esmond Bousfield. b 51. AKC74 Ch Ch Coll Cant PGCE75. St Aug Coll Cant 76. **d** 76 **p** 77. C Houghton le Spring *Dur* 76-79; C Stockton St Pet 79-83; V Darlington St Mark w St Paul 83-88; V Benfieldside from 88. *St Cuthbert's Vicarage, Church Bank, Consett, Co Durham DH8 0NW* Consett (0207) 503019

REED, Geoffrey Martin. b 51. Univ of Wales (Cardiff) BA73. Oak Hill Th Coll 73. **d** 76 **p** 77. C Swansea St Nic *S & B* 76-78; C Sketty 78-84; V Glasbury and Llowes 84-86; V Glasbury and Llowes w Clyro and Bettws from 86. *St Peter's Vicarage, Glasbury, Hereford HR3 5NU* Glasbury (04974) 657

REED, Jack. b 23. Bris Univ BA49 Lon Univ BD51. Tyndale Hall Bris. **d** 51 **p** 52. V Drypool St Columba w St Andr and St Pet *York* 66-80; TR Drypool 80-83; P-in-c Thwing 83-85; P-in-c Rudston w Boynton and Kilham 83-85; V 85-87; rtd 88. *32 Dower Rise, Swanland, North Ferriby, N Humberside HU14 3QT* Hull (0482) 632649

REED, John Peter Cyril. b 51. BD78 AKC78. Ripon Coll Cuddesdon 78. **d** 79 **p** 80. C Croydon *Cant* 79-82; Prec St Alb Abbey *St Alb* 82-86; R Timsbury and Priston *B & W* from 86; Rural Affairs Chapl from 87. *The Rectory, Timsbury, Bath BA3 1HY* Timsbury (0761) 70153

REED, Mrs Kathleen Jean Dorothy. b 29. Gilmore Ho 68. **dss** 73 **d** 87. Ashford St Matt *Lon* 69-87; Par Dn 87-90; rtd 90. *56 Stirling Avenue, New Cubbington, Leamington Spa, Warks CV32 7HR* Leamington Spa (0926) 886374

REED, Matthew Colin. b 50. Edin Univ BD82. Edin Th Coll 72. **d** 84 **p** 85. C Edin St Pet *Edin* 84-87; P-in-c Linlithgow from 87; P-in-c Bathgate 87-91. *The Parsonage, 69 Muir Road, Bathgate, West Lothian EH48 2QQ* Bathgate (0506) 52292

REED, Neil Andrew. b 62. St Chad's Coll Dur BA84. Coll of Resurr Mirfield. **d** 87 **p** 88. C Bishopwearmouth Ch Ch *Dur* 87-89; C Sunderland Springwell w Thorney Close from 89. *The Clergy House, Springwell Road, Sunderland SR3 4DY* 091-528 3754

REED, Mrs Pamela Kathleen. b 38. E Midl Min Tr Course. **dss** 84 **d** 87. Cam Ascension *Ely* 84-87; Par Dn 87-88; Par Dn Cherry Hinton St Andr 88-90; C from 91; C Teversham from 91. *39 Eland Road, Cherry Hinton, Cambridge CB1 4XZ* Cambridge (0223) 862438

REED, Richard David. Trin Coll Carmarthen. **d** 91. NSM Dale and St Brides w Marloes *St D* from 91. *Tamarisk, Glebe Lane, Marloes, Haverfordwest, Dyfed SA62 3AY* Dale (0646) 636662

REED, Robert Chase. b 47. Boston Univ BSc70 TCD HDipEd72. **d** 87 **p** 88. NSM Taney w St Nahi *D & G* from 87; Res Hd Master Wesley Coll Dub from 87. *Embury House, Wesley College, Dublin 16, Irish Republic* Dublin (1) 987066 or 987343

REED, Roger William. b 39. Wycliffe Hall Ox 65. **d** 68 **p** 69. C Portsea St Cuth *Portsm* 68-71; C Enfield St Jas *Lon* 71-74; P-in-c Becontree St Thos *Chelmsf* 74-78; R Debden and Wimbish w Thunderley from 78; RD Saffron Walden 82-91. *The Rectory, Debden, Saffron Walden, Essex CM11 3LB* Saffron Walden (0799) 40285

REED, Simon John. b 63. Trin Coll Ox BA86 MA90. Wycliffe Hall Ox BA(Theol)90. **d** 91. C Walton H Trin *Ox* from 91. *5 Bateman Drive, Brookhurst, Aylesbury, Bucks HP21 8AF* Aylesbury (0296) 82096

REED, Stanley John. b 14. Open Univ BA81. Clifton Th Coll 48. **d** 50 **p** 51. V Plymouth St Aug *Ex* 60-76; V Upottery, Luppitt and Monkton 76-81; rtd 81. *10 Lamb Park, Chagford, Newton Abbot, Devon TQ13 8DN* Chagford (0647) 433528

REED, William Harvey. b 47. K Coll Lon BD69 AKC69. St Aug Coll Cant 69. **d** 70 **p** 71. C Stockton St Mark CD *Dur* 70-72; C Billingham St Cuth 72-76; C S Westoe 76-79; V Chilton Moor 79-87; R Hutton *Chelmsf* from 87. *The Rectory, Hutton Village, Brentwood, Essex CM13 1RX* Brentwood (0277) 210495

REEDE, Very Rev Samuel William. b 24. TCD BA48 MA52 BD55. CITC 50. **d** 50 **p** 51. C Waterford Ch Ch *C & O* 50-54; C Cregagh *D & D* 54-59; Hd S Ch Miss Ballymacarrett 59-67; Chapl Stranmillis Coll Belf 64-68; Can Raphoe Cathl *D & R* from 67; I Raphoe w Raymochy 67-68; I Raphoe w Raymochy and Clonleigh from 68; Dean Raphoe from 80. *The Deanery, Raphoe, Lifford, Co Donegal, Irish Republic* Raphoe (74) 45226

REES, Anthony John. b 49. St Jo Coll Dur BA72 DipTh73 MA77 Man Univ MEd89. **d** 74 **p** 75. C Smethwick St Matt w St Chad *Birm* 74-77; C Bolton St Pet *Man* 77-80; R Cheetham St Mark 80-88; V Mottram in Longdendale w Woodhead *Ches* from 88. *The Vicarage, 29 Ashworth Lane, Mottram, Hyde, Cheshire SK14 6NT* Mottram (0457) 762268

REES, Brian. b 48. McGill Univ Montreal BA74 St Andr Univ BD76 PhD80. Montreal Dioc Th Coll 76. **d** 80 **p** 81. Canada 80-85; Chapl Bedf Sch from 85. *Pemberley House, 17 Pemberley Avenue, Bedford MK40 2LE* Bedford (0234) 268324

REES, Brynley Mervyn. b 18. Univ of Wales BA38. Lon Coll of Div 40. **d** 41 **p** 42. V St Alb Ch Ch *St Alb* 60-84; rtd 84; C Weobley w Sarnesfield and Norton Canon *Heref* from 84. *The Rectory, Staunton-on-Wye, Hereford HR4 7LW* Moccas (09817) 302

REES, Christopher John. b 40. Dur Univ BA62. Ridley Hall Cam 62. **d** 64 **p** 65. C Wilmslow *Ches* 64-70; C Birkenhead St Pet w St Matt 70-75; V Lostock Gralam 75-83; R Davenham from 83. *The Rectory, Church Street, Davenham, Northwich, Cheshire CW9 8NF* Northwich (0606) 42450

REES, Daniel Brynmor. b 07. St D Coll Lamp 59. **d** 60 **p** 61. V Brawdy w Hayscastle, Llandeloy and Llanrheithan *St D* 71-77; rtd 77. *The Croft, Treffynnon, Haverfordwest, Dyfed*

REES, David Aylwin. b 14. Univ of Wales (Lamp) BA46. **d** 47 **p** 48. V Spittal and Treffgarne *St D* 53-75; V Dale 75-77; V Dale and St Brides w Marloes 78-84; rtd 84. *Cartrefle, North Road, Aberystwyth, Dyfed SY23 2EE* Aberystwyth (0970) 615745

REES, David Elwyn. b 37. Univ of Wales (Swansea) BA60. Ripon Hall Ox 63. **d** 65 **p** 66. C Swansea St Thos and Kilvey *S & B* 65-69; V 81-87; C Sketty 69-73; V Clyro w Bettws, Llowes and Glasbury All SS 73-80; V Hay w Llanigon and Capel-y-Ffin from 87. *The Vicarage, Hay-on-Wye, Hereford HR3 5DQ* Hay-on-Wye (0497) 820612

REES, Canon David Frederick. b 21. SS Coll Cam BA48 MA52. Sarum Th Coll 48. **d** 50 **p** 51. V Penwortham St Mary *Blackb* 62-90; RD Leyland 70-84; Hon Can Blackb Cathl 79-90; rtd 90. *4 Queensdale Close, Walton-le-Dale, Preston, Lancs PR5 4JU* Preston (0772) 59010

REES, David Grenfell. b 18. St D Coll Lamp BA40 Qu Coll Birm. **d** 43 **p** 44. V Dyffryn *Llan* 60-84; Perm to Offic from 84; rtd 84. *10 Tyn-yr-Heol Road, Bryncoch, Neath, W Glam* Bryncoch (0639) 644488

REES, Dr David John. b 44. Lon Univ BD66. NY Th Sem DMin88 St Aug Coll Cant 72. **d** 73 **p** 74. C Goldington *St Alb* 73-75; Malaysia 76-80; V Milton Ernest *St Alb* 81-84; V Thurleigh 81-84; V Bedf St Martin 84-91; V Willesden St Mary *Lon* from 91. *The Vicarage, 18 Neasden Lane, London NW10 2TT* 081-459 2167

REES, David Philip Dunn Hugh. b 38. Jes Coll Ox BA60 MA64 Ox Univ DipEd67. Westcott Ho Cam 62. **d** 64 **p** 65. C Salford St Phil w St Steph *Man* 64-66; Perm to Offic St As 66-67; Derby 67-74; Chapl St Marg C of E High Sch Aigburth Liv 74-83; V Meliden and Gwaenysgor *St As* from 84; Dioc Adv for Schs from 85; Warden of Readers from 89; Warden of Ords from 91. *The Vicarage, Meliden, Prestatyn, Clwyd LL19 8HN* Prestatyn (0745) 856220

REES, David Richard. b 60. Llan St Mich DipTh84. **d** 84 **p** 85. C Llanstadwell *St D* 84-86; C Carmarthen St Dav from 86. *26 Knoll Gardens, Carmarthen, Dyfed SA31 3EJ* Carmarthen (0267) 235636

REES, Eric Vernon. b 19. St Jo Coll Dur BA41 MA44. St Andr Pampisford 43. **d** 43 **p** 44. C-in-c Enfield St Giles CD *Lon* 68-80; C Edmonton All SS 80-82; C Edmonton All SS w St Mich 82-90; rtd 90. *45 Monmouth Road, London N9 0JB* 081-807 4329

REES, Gruffydd Nicholas. b 23. Univ of Wales (Lamp) BA46. Wycliffe Hall Ox 46. **d** 48 **p** 49. V Llanbister and Llanbadarn Fynydd w Llananno *S & B* 62-75; V New Radnor and Llanfihangel Nantmelan etc 75-84; V Llangenny and Llanbedr Ystradyw w Patricio 84-88; rtd 88. *Trefilan, 26 Lakeside Avenue, Llandrindod Wells, Powys LD1 5NT* Llandrindod Wells (0597) 825451

REES, Hugh Lorimer Octavius. b 06. Magd Coll Ox BA29 MA39. St Steph Ho Ox 29. **d** 30 **p** 31. V Kensington St Mary Abbots w St Geo *Lon* 60-77; rtd 77; Perm to Offic *S'wark* from 83. *32 Inner Park Road, London SW19 6EG* 081-788 0625

REES, James Arthur. b 04. Qu Coll Newfoundland 25. **d** 28 **p** 29. R W Tarring *Chich* 58-75; rtd 75; RD Worthing *Chich* 75-80; Perm to Offic 80-84. *11 Bath Road, Worthing, W Sussex BN11 3NU* Worthing (0903) 207820

REES, John Harold. b 15. St Mich Coll Llan 53. **d** 54 **p** 55. V Llanarthney and Llanddarog *St D* 66-83; rtd 83. *Erwlon, Cwmisfael Road, Llanddarog, Carmarthen, Dyfed SA32 8NU* Llanddarog (0267) 275219

✠REES, Rt Rev John Ivor. b 26. Univ of Wales (Abth) BA50. Westcott Ho Cam 50. **d** 52 **p** 53 **c** 88. C Fishguard w Llanychar *St D* 52-55; C Llangathen w Llanfihangel Cilfargen 55-57; P-in-c Uzmaston and Boulston 57-59; V Slebech and Uzmaston w Boulston 59-65; V Llangollen and Trevor *St As* 65-74; RD Llangollen 70-74; R Wrexham 74-76; Can St As Cathl 75-76; Dean Ban 76-88; V Bangor Cathl Par 79-88; Asst Bp St D 88-91; Adn St D 88-91; Bp St D from 91. *Llys Esgob, Abergwili, Carmarthen, Dyfed SA31 2JG* Carmarthen (0267) 236597

REES, John Martin Rawlins Gore. b 30. St D Coll Lamp BA53. **d** 55 **p** 57. C Mold *St As* 55-56; C Broughton 56-59; C Newtown 59-61; V Penycae 61-73; V Northop 73-83; V Bickerton w Bickley *Ches* from 83. *The Vicarage, Bickerton, Malpas, Cheshire SY14 8AR* Broxton (0829) 782266

REES, John Philip Walford. b 41. St D Coll Lamp BA62 Linacre Coll Ox BA(Theol)64 MA(Theol)69 Univ of Wales (Cardiff) BD73. Wycliffe Hall Ox 62. **d** 64 **p** 65. C Reading St Jo *Ox* 64-67; V Patrick *S & M* 67-68; C Pontypool *Mon* 68-70; Area Sec (Dios Glouc, Heref and Worc) CMS 70-75; V Bream *Glouc* 75-91; Team Ldr Ichthus Chr Fellowship from 91. *66 College Park Close, London SE13 5HA* 081-852 8017

REES, John Tyssul. b 09. St D Coll Lamp. **d** 65 **p** 66. V Trelech a'r Betws and Abernant *St D* 72-78; rtd 78. *Overdale, 15 Parc Puw, Drefach Felindre, Llandyssul, Dyfed SA44 5UJ* Velindre (0559) 370864

REES, Ven John Wynford Joshua. b 24. Univ of Wales (Lamp) BA52. **d** 53 **p** 54. C Abth *St D* 53-60; V Llanyre w Llanfihangel Helygen, Llanwrthwl etc *S & B* 60-71; R Llanyre w Llanfihangel Helygen and Diserth 71-87; V Llanyre w Llanfihangel Helygen from 87; RD Maelienydd 74-87; Hon Can Brecon Cathl 77-79; Can Res from 79; Treas 83-87; Adn Brecon from 87. *The Vicarage, Llanyre, Llandrindod Wells, Powys LD1 6DY* Llandrindod Wells (0597) 828530

REES, Judith Margaret. b 39. Southn Univ BTh89. **dss** 86 **d** 87. Sanderstead All SS *S'wark* 86-87; Par Dn 87; Dir

Cottesloe Chr Tr Progr *Ox* from 89; Par Dn Gt Horwood 89-91; Par Dn Winslow w Gt Horwood and Addington from 91. *15 Weston Road, Great Horwood, Milton Keynes MK17 0QR* Winslow (029671) 3603

✝REES, Rt Rev Leslie Lloyd. b 19. Kelham Th Coll 36. **d** 42 **p** 43 **c** 80. C Roath St Sav *Llan* 42-45; Asst Chapl HM Pris Cardiff 42-45; Chapl HM Pris Dur 45-48; Dartmoor 48-55; Win 55-62; V Princetown *Ex* 48-55; Chapl Gen of Pris 62-80; Hon Can Cant Cathl *Cant* 66-80; Chapl to HM The Queen 71-80; Hon Can Lich Cathl *Lich* 80-86; Suff Bp Shrewsbury 80-86; rtd 86; Asst Bp Win from 87. *Kingfisher Lodge, 20 Arle Gardens, Alresford, Hants SO24 9BA* Alresford (0962) 734619

REES, Michael Lloyd. b 51. St D Coll Lamp DipTh74. **d** 74 **p** 75. C Cardigan and Mount and Verwick *St D* 74-77; Min Can St D Cathl 77-81; TV Abth 81-83; Dioc Children's Adv from 83; V Penboyr 83-88; V Henfynyw w Aberaeron and Llanddewi Aber-arth from 88. *The Vicarage, Aberaeron, Dyfed SA46 0EP* Aberaeron (0545) 570433

REES, Percival Antony Everard. b 35. Pemb Coll Ox BA56 MA59. Clifton Th Coll 58. **d** 60 **p** 61. C Heatherlands St Jo *Sarum* 60-65 and 69-70; India 65-69; V W Hampstead St Luke *Lon* 70-82; Lect Oak Hill Th Coll 82-86; V Enfield Ch Ch Trent Park *Lon* from 87. *Christ Church Vicarage, Chalk Lane, Barnet, Herts EN4 9JQ* 081-441 1230 or 449 0556

REES, Peter Frederick Ransom. b 18. Lon Univ BA47. Linc Th Coll 47. **d** 49 **p** 50. V Laneside *Blackb* 53-83; rtd 83; Lic to Offic *Blackb* from 84. *11 Rydal Road, Morecambe, Lancs LA3 1DT* Morecambe (0524) 424482

REES, Philip William Watkins. b 11. St D Coll Lamp BA33 St Steph Ho Ox 33. **d** 34 **p** 35. V Swansea St Mark *S & B* 53-78; rtd 78. *22 Ffynone Drive, Swansea SA1 6DP* Swansea (0792) 473776

REES, Canon Richard John Edward Williams. b 36. Univ of Wales (Lamp) BA58. St Mich Coll Llan 58. **d** 60 **p** 61. C St Issells *St D* 60-64; C Llanedy 64-67; V Whitchurch w Solva and St Elvis 67-77; RD Dewisland and Fishguard from 73; V Whitchurch w Solva and St Elvis w Brawdy etc from 77; Can St D Cathl from 87. *The Vicarage, Whitchurch, Solva, Haverfordwest, Dyfed* St Davids (0437) 721281

REES, Canon Richard Michael. b 35. St Pet Hall Ox BA57 MA61. Tyndale Hall Bris 57. **d** 59 **p** 60. C Crowborough *Chich* 59-62; C Clifton Ch Ch w Em *Bris* 62-64; V Clevedon Ch Ch *B & W* 64-72; V Cam H Trin *Ely* 72-84; Lic to Offic *S'wark* 84-90; Chief Sec CA 84-90; Can Res Ches Cathl and Dioc Missr *Ches* from 90. *5 Abbey Green, Chester CH1 2JH* Chester (0244) 347500

REES, Canon Sidney. b 12. St D Coll Lamp BA34 St Mich Coll Llan 35. **d** 37 **p** 38. V Whitland and Kiffig *St D* 65-79; Can St D Cathl 77-79; rtd 79. *10 Morfa Lane, Carmarthen, Dyfed SA31 3AS* Carmarthen (0267) 235757

REES, Vivian John Howard. b 51. Southn Univ LLB72 Ox Univ BA79 MA84 Leeds Univ MPhil84. Wycliffe Hall Ox 76. **d** 79 **p** 80. C Moor Allerton *Ripon* 79-82; Sierra Leone 82-86; Lic to Offic *Ox* from 86. *Oxford Diocesan Registry, 16 Beaumont Street, Oxford OX1 2LZ* Oxford (0865) 241974

REES, William David Cledwyn. b 25. FRGS54 Qu Coll Cam BA49 DipEd50 MA52 Univ of Wales MA75 PhD81. St Deiniol's Hawarden 63. **d** 65 **p** 66. Hon C Rhyl w Rhyl St Ann *St As* 65-72; Chapl and Lect St Mary's Coll Ban 72-77; Lic to Offic *Ban* 72-77; Lect Univ of Wales (Ban) from 77; Chapl Univ of Wales (Ban) *Ban* 77-84; Sec Dioc Schs Cttee 84-86. *Anwylfa, Fron Park Avenue, Llanfairfechan, Gwynedd LL33 0AS* Llanfairfechan (0248) 680054

REES, Canon William Elfyn. b 17. St D Coll Lamp BA37 Wycliffe Hall Ox 38. **d** 40 **p** 45. R Alverstoke *Portsm* 62-82; rtd 82. *28 Church Close, Llangynidr, Crickhowell, Powys* Bwlch (0874) 730125

REESE, John David. b 49. Cuddesdon Coll 73. **d** 76 **p** 77. C Kidderminster St Mary *Worc* 76-81; Malaysia 81-85; V Bishop's Castle w Mainstone *Heref* 85-91; RD Clun Forest 87-91; V Tupsley from 91; P-in-c Hampton Bishop and Mordiford w Dormington from 91. *The Vicarage, 10/ Church Road, Hereford HR1 1RT* Hereford (0432) 274490

REEVE, Brian Charles. b 36. Lon Univ BSc57 BD60. Tyndale Hall Bris 58. **d** 61 **p** 62. C Eccleston St Luke *Liv* 61-63; C Upton (or Overchurch) *Ches* 63-65; C Pemberton St Mark Newtown *Liv* 65-68; V Macclesfield Ch Ch *Ches* 68-74; V Stone Ch Ch *Lich* 74-84; RD Trentham 77-84; V Hoole *Ches* from 84; Chapl Ches

City Hosp 84-91. *All Saints' Vicarage, 2 Vicarage Road, Hoole, Chester CH2 3HZ* Chester (0244) 322056

REEVE, David Michael. b 44. St Cath Coll Cam BA67 MA71. Coll of Resurr Mirfield 68. **d** 70 **p** 71. C Willingdon *Chich* 70-73; C Hove All SS 73-76; C Moulsecoomb 76-80; R Singleton 80-90; V E Dean 80-90; V W Dean 80-90; R Hurstpierpoint from 90. *The Rectory, 21 Cuckfield Road, Hurstpierpoint, Hassocks, W Sussex BN6 9RP* Hurstpierpoint (0273) 832203

REEVE, John David Genge. b 14. Em Coll Cam BA36 MA40. Westcott Ho Cam 38. **d** 39 **p** 40. V Worth *Cant* 63-80; rtd 80; Perm to Offic *Cant* from 81. *62 Sycamore Close, Lydd, Romney Marsh, Kent TN29 9LE* Lydd (0679) 20438

REEVE, Kenneth Robert. b 23. St Cath Coll Ox BA49 MA53. Sarum Th Coll 64. **d** 68 **p** 69. Hon C Farleigh Hungerford w Tellisford *B & W* 68-71; Hon C Norton St Philip 72-74; Hon C Hinton Charterhouse 72-74; Seychelles 74-76; Perm to Offic B & W from 77; Chich 78-82. *Sundial, Hill Close, Wincanton, Somerset BA9 9NF* Wincanton (0963) 33369

REEVE, Dr Richard Noel. b 29. MB, ChB. St Deiniol's Hawarden. **d** 84 **p** 85. Hon C Norton *Ches* 84-85; C Filey *York* 85-87; TV Brayton 87-90; rtd 90; Perm to Offic *Man* from 90. *14 Kingsfield Drive, Manchester M20 0JA* 061-445 3478

REEVE, Roger Patrick. b 42. Fitzw Coll Cam BA65 MA68. Coll of Resurr Mirfield. **d** 67 **p** 68. C Barnstaple St Pet w H Trin *Ex* 67-74; V Ernesettle 74-78; V Braunton from 78; RD Barnstaple from 85. *The Vicarage, Braunton, Devon EX33 2EL* Braunton (0271) 813367

REEVE, Canon Ronald Ernest. b 22. Ox Univ BA MA BD DPhil. Wycliffe Hall Ox 48. **d** 50 **p** 51. C Bexleyheath Ch Ch *Roch* 50-52; V New Hythe 52-54; Canada 54-59 and from 63; Vice-Prin Cranmer Hall Dur 60-63; Prof K Coll NS 63-68; Prof Bp's Univ Lennoxville & Can Quebec Cathl 68-88. *1137 rue Vimont, Sillery, Quebec, Canada, G1S 3P9* Quebec City (418) 681-6511

REEVES, Christopher. b 30. Nottm Univ BA53. Wells Th Coll 53. **d** 55 **p** 56. C Rowbarton *B & W* 55-59; C Cant St Greg *Cant* 59-61; Chapl Schiedam Miss to Seamen *Eur* 61-67; V Barkingside H Trin *Chelmsf* from 67. *Barkingside Vicarage, Mossford Green, Ilford, Essex IG6 2BJ* 081-550 2669

REEVES, David Eric. b 46. Sarum Th Coll 68. **d** 71 **p** 72. C Guildf H Trin w St Mary *Guildf* 71-74; C Warmsworth *Sheff* 74-78; V Herringthorpe 78-90; V Cleveleys *Blackb* from 90. *The Vicarage, Rough Lea Road, Thornton Cleveleys, Blackpool FY5 1DP* Blackpool (0253) 852153

REEVES, Donald St John. b 34. Qu Coll Cam BA57 MA61. Cuddesdon Coll 62. **d** 63 **p** 64. C Maidstone All SS w St Phil *Cant* 63-65; Bp's Dom Chapl *S'wark* 65-68; V St Helier 69-80; R Westmr St Jas *Lon* from 80. *St James's Rectory, 197 Piccadilly, London W1V 9LF* 071-734 4511

REEVES, Mrs Elizabeth Anne. See THOMAS, Mrs Elizabeth Anne

REEVES, Gillian Patricia. b 46. S'wark Ord Course 87. **d** 90. Par Dn Shirley St Geo *S'wark* from 90. *3 Malcolm Road, London SE25 5HE* 081-654 7702

REEVES, James Lacey. b 23. FCIS58. S'wark Ord Course 60. **d** 74 **p** 75. NSM Wisborough Green *Chich* 74-81; C Horsham 81-83; R W Chiltington from 83. *The Rectory, West Chiltington, Pulborough, W Sussex RH20 2JY* West Chiltington (0798) 813117

REEVES, John Graham. b 44. Kelham Th Coll 64. **d** 69 **p** 71. C Aston cum Aughton *Sheff* 69-71; C Ribbleton *Blackb* 72-74; C Cleveleys 74-75; P-in-c Huncoat 75-77; V 77-82; V Knuxden from 82. *St Oswald's Vicarage, Bank Lane, Knuxden, Blackburn BB1 2AP* Blackburn (0254) 598321

REEVES, Canon Joseph Wilfred. b 02. Birm Univ BSc26 MSc40. Bps' Coll Cheshunt 31. **d** 33 **p** 34. V Ferring *Chich* 45-73; RD Worthing 58-71; Preb Chich Cathl 63-82; rtd 73. *6 Penland Road, Bexhill-on-Sea, E Sussex TN40 2JG* Bexhill-on-Sea (0424) 215559

REEVES, Kenneth Gordon. b 32. K Coll Lon BD53 AKC53 CertEd54. Ripon Coll Cuddesdon 86. **d** 87 **p** 88. NSM Dorchester *Ox* 87-89; V Deddington w Barford, Clifton and Hempton from 89. *The Vicarage, Earls Lane, Deddington, Banbury, Oxon OX15 0TJ* Deddington (0869) 38329

REEVES, Kenneth William. b 38. TCD 67 NUI DipSocSc76. **d** 69 **p** 70. C Killowen *D & R* 69-70; I Ardara 70-76; TV Quidenham *Nor* 76-81; V Swaffham 81-86; Chapl Nor Coll of Educn from 86; P-in-c Lakenham St Alb *Nor* from 86. *St Alban's Vicarage,*

Eleanor Road, Norwich NR1 2RE   Norwich (0603) 621843

REEVES, Nicholas John Harding. b 44. ALCD69. **d** 69 **p** 70. C Upton (or Overchurch) *Ches* 69-72; C Woodlands *Sheff* 72-74; C-in-c Cranham Park CD *Chelmsf* 74-79; V Cranham Park 79-88; R Aldridge *Lich* from 88. *The Rectory, 14 The Green, Aldridge, Walsall WS9 8NH* Aldridge (0922) 52414

REGAN, Brian. b 46. MBIM80. W Midl Minl Tr Course 88. **d** 91. C Cov St Jo *Cov* from 91. *10 Northumberland Road, Coventry CV1 3AQ*   Coventry (0203) 229166

REGAN, Philip. b 49. Qu Mary Coll Lon BSc MSc. Wycliffe Hall Ox 81. **d** 83 **p** 84. Hon C Scotforth *Blackb* 83-89; P-in-c Combe St Nicholas w Wambrook *B & W* from 89; P-in-c Whitestaunton from 89. *The Vicarage, Combe St Nicholas, Chard, Somerset TA20 3NJ* Chard (0460) 62121

REGINALD, Brother. See BOX, Reginald Gilbert

REGLAR, Canon Gerald John. b 11. Melbourne Univ BA Ox Univ BA MA. Kelham Th Coll 34. **d** 37 **p** 38. C Cowley St Jo *Ox* 37-40; Australia from 40. *13 Binnowie Street, Ingle Farm, S Australia 5098*   Adelaide (8) 263-8473

REID, Andrew John. b 47. Birm Univ BEd70 Man Univ MEd76 Lon Univ DipRS88. S'wark Ord Course 88. **d** 88 **p** 89. NSM Westerham *Roch* 88-90; Chapl Abp Tenison Gr Sch Kennington from 90. *Archbishop Tenison's School, The Oval, London SE11* 071-735 4070

REID, Canon Colin Guthrie. b 30. **d** 56 **p** 57. C Kendal St Thos *Carl* 56-59; C Crosthwaite Keswick 59-60; R Caldbeck w Castle Sowerby 60-76; RD Wigton 69-70; P-in-c Sebergham 75-76; R Caldbeck, Castle Sowerby and Sebergham from 76; Hon Can Carl Cathl from 88. *The Rectory, Caldbeck, Wigton, Cumbria CA7 8EW* Caldbeck (06998) 233

REID, Donald. b 58. Glas Univ LLB79 Pemb Coll Ox MPhil81 Edin Univ BD85. Edin Th Coll 82. **d** 85 **p** 86. C Greenock *Glas* 85-87; C Baillieston from 87; C Glas St Serf from 87. *21 Swinton Road, Baillieston, Glasgow G69 6DS* 041-771 3000

REID, Very Rev Douglas William John. b 34. Edin Th Coll 60. **d** 63 **p** 64. C Ayr *Glas* 63-68; R Glas St Jas 68-74; R Glas St Ninian from 74; Syn Clerk 79-87; Can St Mary's Cathl 79-87; Dean Glas from 87. *32 Glencairn Drive, Glasgow G41 4PW* 041-423 1247

REID, Gavin Hunter. b 34. K Coll Lon BA56. Oak Hill Th Coll 58. **d** 60 **p** 61. C E Ham St Paul *Chelmsf* 60-63; C Rainham 63-66; Publications Sec CPAS 66-71; Hon C St Paul's Cray St Barn *Roch* 68-71; Ed Sec USCL 71-74; Hon C Woking St Jo *Guildf* from 72; Sec for Evang CPAS from 74; Consultant Missr CPAS from 90; BMU Adv from 90. *138 St John's Road, Woking, Surrey GU21 1PS* Woking (0483) 715589

REID, Herbert Alan. b 31. AKC55. **d** 56 **p** 57. C Penwortham St Mary *Blackb* 56-59; C-in-c Penwortham St Leon CD 59-63; V Brierfield 63-72; V Warton St Paul 72-79; V Read in Whalley from 79. *The Vicarage, George Lane, Read, Burnley, Lancs BB12 7RQ* Padiham (0282) 71361

REID, Hugh Gamble. b 33. Roch Th Coll 63. **d** 64 **p** 64. C Martin w Thornton *Linc* 64-66; Bp's Youth Chapl 66-69; C Alford w Rigsby 66-69; Chapl HM Borstal Everthorpe 69-71; Chapl HM Pris Dur 71-74; Wakef 74-77; V Northowram *Wakef* 77-79; Chapl HM Pris Coldingley 79-81; Chapl HM Rem Cen Risley 81-85; Chapl HM Pris Holloway 85-88; C Guilden Morden *Ely* 88-89; C Shingay Gp of Par 90; R Upwell Ch Ch from 90; R Welney from 90. *Christchurch Rectory, Wisbech, Cambs PE14 9PQ*

REID, Ian Davison. b 37. Liv Univ BA61 MA63. Clifton Th Coll 63. **d** 65 **p** 66. C Edge Hill St Cath *Liv* 65-68; C Heworth *York* 68-76; V Linthorpe from 76; Can and Preb York Minster from 90. *5 Park Road South, Middlesbrough, Cleveland TS5 6LD*   Middlesbrough (0642) 817306

REID, James. b 46. Strathclyde Univ BSc69. W Midl Minl Tr Course 88. **d** 91. NSM Attleborough *Cov* from 91. *87 Shakespeare Drive, Whitestone, Nuneaton CV11 6NW* Nuneaton (0203) 341553

REID, Peter Ivor. b 30. Qu Coll Cam BA53 MA72. St Mich Coll Llan 78. **d** 80 **p** 81. C Llantwit Major and St Donat's *Llan* 80-83; C Llantwit Major 83-84; V Laleston w Tythegston 84; V Laleston w Tythegston and Merthyr Mawr 84-88; V Roath St Marg from 88. *Roath Vicarage, Waterloo Road, Cardiff CF2 5AD* Cardiff (0222) 484808

REID, Stewart Thomas. b 45. Oak Hill Th Coll 66. **d** 70 **p** 71. C Normanton *Derby* 70-73; C Leyland St Andr *Blackb* 73-78; V Halliwell St Luke *Man* from 78. *St*

Luke's Vicarage, Chorley Old Road, Bolton BL1 3BE Bolton (0204) 43060

REID, Canon William Frederick (Eric). b 22. OBE88. TCD BA45 MA53. **d** 46 **p** 47. Chapl Netherne Hosp Coulsdon 67-76; C-in-c Netherne St Luke CD *S'wark* 67-76; Lic to Offic from 76; Sec and Dir Tr Gen Syn Hosp Chapl Coun 76-87; Hon Can Newc Cathl *Newc* 79-88; rtd 88. *65 Lagham Park, South Godstone, Godstone, Surrey RH9 8EP*   South Godstone (0342) 893312

REID, William Gordon. b 43. Edin Univ MA63 Keble Coll Ox BA66 MA72. Edin Th Coll 63 Cuddesdon Coll 66. **d** 67 **p** 68. C Edin St Salvador *Edin* 67-69; Chapl and Tutor Sarum Th Coll 69-72; R Edin St Mich and All SS *Edin* 72-84; Provost St Andr Cathl Inverness *Mor* 84-87; Chapl Ankara *Eur* 87-89; Chapl Stockholm w Gavle and Vasteras from 89; Miss to Seamen from 89. *Strymansgatan 1, 114 54 Stockholm, Sweden* Stockholm (8) 663-8248

REIGATE, Archdeacon of. See COOMBS, Ven Peter Bertram

REILLY, Frederick James. b 29. CITC 70. **d** 73 **p** 74. C Agherton *Conn* 73-75; C Ballymena 75-82; I Ballyscullion *D & R* from 82. *The Rectory, 8 Ballynease Road, Bellaghy, Co Londonderry BT45 8AZ*   Bellaghy (064886) 214

REILLY, Thomas Gerard. b 38. **d** 64 **p** 64. In RC Ch 64-73; Hon C Clapton Park All So *Lon* 73-76; Hon C Haggerston All SS 76-78; C Walthamstow St Sav *Chelmsf* 79-85; P-in-c Forest Gate Em w Upton Cross 85-89; V from 89. *Emmanuel Vicarage, 2B Margery Park Road, London E7 9JY* 081-536 0244

REINDORP, David Peter Edington. b 52. Trin Coll Cam BA82 MA86 CQSW DASS. Westcott Ho Cam 79. **d** 83 **p** 84. C Chesterton Gd Shep *Ely* 83-85; C Hitchin *St Alb* 85-88; V Waterbeach *Ely* from 88; R Landbeach from 88; OCF from 88. *The Vicarage, 8 Chapel Street, Waterbeach, Cambridge CB5 9HR*   Cambridge (0223) 860353

REINDORP, Michael Christopher Julian. b 44. Trin Coll Cam BA67 MA70. Cuddesdon Coll 67 United Th Coll Bangalore 68. **d** 69 **p** 70. C Poplar *Lon* 69-74; V Chatham St Wm *Roch* 74-84; R Stantonbury *Ox* 84-87; TR Stantonbury and Willen from 87. *The Rectory, Great Linford, Milton Keynes MK14 5BD*   Milton Keynes (0908) 605892

REISS, Michael Jonathan. b 58. FIBiol90 Trin Coll Cam BA78 MA82 PhD82 PGCE83. E Anglian Minl Tr Course 87. **d** 90 **p** 91. NSM Comberton *Ely* from 90. *7 Barrons Way, Comberton, Cambridge CB3 7EQ*   Cambridge (0223) 262958

REISS, Robert Paul. b 43. Trin Coll Cam BA67 MA71. Westcott Ho Cam 67. **d** 69 **p** 70. C St Jo Wood *Lon* 69-73; Bangladesh 73; Chapl Trin Coll Cam 73-78; Selection Sec ACCM 78-85; Sen Selection Sec 83; TR Grantham *Linc* from 86. *The Rectory, Church Street, Grantham, Lincs NG31 6RR* Grantham (0476) 63710

REITH, Charles Martin. b 27. Edin Univ MA52. Edin Th Coll 55. **d** 57 **p** 58. C Edin St Cuth *Edin* 57-64; P-in-c Edin St Hilda 64-66; R 66-71; Dioc Chapl *Mor* 71-77; Hon C Stirling *Edin* 77-80; Perm to Offic Mor, Glas, Edin and St And from 80; CSG Ho Scotlandwell from 80. *Apple Grove Cottage, Well Road, Scotlandwell, Kinross KY13 7JB*

REITH, Ivor Stuart Weston. b 16. Ridley Hall Cam 65. **d** 66 **p** 67. R Angmering *Chich* 69-81; rtd 81; Perm to Offic *Chich* from 84. *10 Cross Road, Southwick, Brighton BN42 4HE* Brighton (0273) 597301

REITH, Robert Michael. b 55. Oak Hill Th Coll BA83. **d** 83 **p** 84. C Kendal St Thos *Carl* 83-87; C Leyland St Andr *Blackb* from 87. *St John's House, Leyland Lane, Leyland, Preston, Lancs PR5 3HB*   Preston (0772) 621646

REMPEY, Philip Roland. b 19. Glouc Th Course 74. **d** 76 **p** 76. NSM Charlton Kings St Mary *Glouc* 76-88; Perm to Offic from 88. *87 Ravensgate Road, Charlton Kings, Cheltenham, Glos GL53 8NS*   Cheltenham (0242) 519313

RENDALL, John Albert. b 43. Hull Univ BTh84 MA89. Ripon Hall Ox 65. **d** 68 **p** 69. C Southsea St Simon *Portsm* 68-71; C Wallington H Trin *S'wark* 71-77; P-in-c Rufforth w Moor Monkton and Hessay *York* 77-79; R from 79; P-in-c Long Marston 77-79; R from 79; RD New Ainsty from 85. *The Vicarage, Rufforth, York YO2 3QB* Rufforth (090483) 262

RENDELL, Peter Vivian. b 26. K Coll Lon 48. **d** 52 **p** 53. V Felton *Newc* 68-77; V Tynemouth Cullercoats St Paul 77-89; RD Tynemouth 83-87; rtd 89. *22 Woodburn*

Square, Whitley Bay, Tyne & Wear NE25 3JE 091-252 4916

RENFREY, Edward Donald John-Baptist. b 53. DipTh. St Barn Coll Adelaide 75. **d** 76 **p** 77. Australia 76-84; Chapl RN from 84. *c/o MOD, Lacon House, Theobald's Road, London WC1X 8RY* 071-430 6847

RENISON, Gary James. b 62. SS Hild & Bede Coll Dur BA83. Ridley Hall Cam 84. **d** 86 **p** 87. C Stapenhill w Cauldwell *Derby* 86-89; C Cheadle Hulme St Andr *Ches* from 89. *198 Bruntwood Lane, Cheadle Hulme, Cheadle, Cheshire SK8 6BE* 061-485 1154

RENNARD, Edward Lionel. b 51. Nottm Univ BTh80. Linc Th Coll 76. **d** 80 **p** 81. C Old Brumby *Linc* 80-82; C-in-c Gt Grimsby St Matt Fairfield CD 82-86; V Fairfield St Matt 86-88; V Hykeham 88-91; TR from 91. *The Vicarage, Mill Lane, North Hykeham, Lincoln LN6 9PA* Lincoln (0522) 681168

RENNARD, Margaret Rose. b 49. CertEd75. Linc Th Coll 76. **d** 87. C Fairfield St Matt *Linc* 87-88; C Hykeham from 88; Chapl HM Pris Morton Hall from 91. *The Vicarage, Mill Lane, North Hykeham, Lincoln LN6 9PA* Lincoln (0522) 681168

RENNIE, Iain Hugh. b 43. Ripon Coll Cuddesdon 88. **d** 90 **p** 91. C Poulton-le-Sands w Morecambe St Laur *Blackb* from 90. *31 Dallam Avenue, Morecambe, Lancs LA4 5BB* Morecambe (0524) 422974

RENNIE, Paul Antony. b 58. **d** 87 **p** 88. C Nairn *Mor* 87-90; C Forres 87-90; C Edin St Pet *Edin* from 90. *10 Hope Park Crescent, Edinburgh EH8 9NA* 031-668 1541

RENNISON, Walter Patrick. b 18. MBE52. TCD BA40 MA45. **d** 42 **p** 43. CF 45-73; V Milland *Chich* 73-87; rtd 87. *14 Heathfield Court, Fleet, Hants GU13 8DX* Fleet (0252) 615358

RENOUF, Peter Mark. b 30. Down Coll Cam BA55 MA59 Cam Univ DipEd56. Ridley Hall Cam. **d** 58 **p** 59. C Rainham *Chelmsf* 58-61; Asst Chapl Wellington Coll Berks 61-63; Chapl 63-69; V Eastbourne All SS *Chich* 69-78; R Farnborough *Guildf* 78-84; C Welford w Wickham and Gt Shefford *Ox* 85-86; C Welford w Wickham and Gt Shefford, Boxford etc 86-89; P-in-c Beedon and Peasemore w W Ilsley and Farnborough from 89. *The Vicarage, Beedon, Newbury, Berks RG16 8SW* East Ilsley (063528) 244

RENOUF, Canon Robert Wilson. b 28. Niagara Univ BSc51 Pacific State Univ PhD77. Claremont Sch of Th DMin81 Lambeth STh86 Selly Oak Coll CMM86 Gen Th Sem (NY) MDiv54. **d** 54 **p** 55. USA 54-56 and 58-82 and from 91; Nicaragua 56-58 and 82-85; Fell and Tutor Coll of the Ascension Selly Oak 85-86; Hon PV S'wark Cathl *S'wark* 86-91; Miss Personnel Sec USPG 86-88; Adv Decade of Evang ACC 89-91. *PO Box 41330, Tucson, Arizona 85717, USA*

RENOWDEN, Very Rev Charles Raymond. b 23. Univ of Wales (Lamp) BA44 Selw Coll Cam BA49 MA53. Ridley Hall Cam 50. **d** 51 **p** 52. C Hubberston *St D* 51-55; Lect St D Coll Lamp 55-67; Sen Lect 67-71; Dean and Lib St As Cathl *St As* from 71; P-in-c Cefn 71-88; V St As 71-80; V St As and Tremeirchion from 80. *The Deanery, St Asaph, Clwyd LL17 0RL* St Asaph (0745) 583597

RENOWDEN, Ven Glyndwr Rhys. b 29. CB87. St D Coll Lamp BA49 LTh52. **d** 52 **p** 53. C Tenby and Gumfreston *St D* 52-55; C Chepstow *Mon* 55-58; Chapl RAF 58-75; Asst Chapl-in-Chief RAF 75-83; Chapl-in-Chief RAF 83-88; QHC from 80; Can and Preb Linc Cathl *Linc* 83-88; P-in-c Llanfallteg w Clunderwen and Castell Dwyran *St D* from 90. *Red Cedars, Kenystyle, Penally, Tenby, Dyfed SA70 7PJ* Tenby (0834) 2673

RENSHAW, Anthony. b 40. McGill Univ Montreal LTh87 DipMin87. Montreal Dioc Th Coll 83. **d** 87 **p** 88. Canada 87-90; P-in-c Ainsdale *Liv* 90-91; V from 91. *The Vicarage, 708 Liverpool Road, Southport, Merseyside PR8 3QE* Southport (0704) 77760

RENSHAW, David William. b 59. Oak Hill Th Coll BA85. **d** 85 **p** 86. C Shawbury *Lich* 85-88; V Childs Ercall from 88; R Stoke upon Tern from 88. *The Vicarage, Childs Ercall, Market Drayton, Shropshire TF9 2DA* Childs Ercall (095278) 229

RENSHAW, Peter Selwyn Kay. b 29. Keble Coll Ox BA52 MA64. St Steph Ho Ox 52. **d** 64 **p** 65. Lic to Offic Ox 64-66; Chapl RN 66-70; Chapl Athens St Paul and Br Emb *Eur* 71-74; Gothenburg 74-75; Chapl RN Sch Haslemere 75-81; Costa Blanca *Eur* 81-82; R Ewelme *Ox* 83-85; R Ewelme, Brightwell Baldwin, Cuxham w Easington from 85. *The Rectory, Ewelme, Oxford OX9 6HP* Wallingford (0491) 37823

RENWICK, Colin. b 30. St Aid Birkenhead. **d** 59 **p** 60. C Drypool St Columba w St Andr and St Pet *York* 59-62; C Wigan St Cath *Liv* 62-64; Min Thornton CD 64-77; V

Thornton from 77; RD Bootle 83-89. *The Vicarage, Water Street, Liverpool L23 1TB* 051-931 4676

RENYARD, Christopher. b 52. Open Univ BA87. Coll of Resurr Mirfield 81. **d** 84 **p** 85. C Heckmondwike *Wakef* 84-88; C Harpenden St Nic *St Alb* from 88. *10 Crossway, Harpenden, Herts AL5 4RA* Harpenden (0582) 713007

RENYARD, Paul Holmwood. b 42. K Coll Lon BD65 AKC65. **d** 66 **p** 67. C Croydon St Aug *Cant* 66-69; C Farnham *Guildf* 69-72; V Capel 72-78; Asst Dir RE 72-78; Asst Dir RE *Roch* 78-83; Hon C Roch 78-83; V Holdenhurst *Win* from 83. *The Vicarage, 6 Broad Avenue, Queen's Park, Bournemouth BH8 9HG* Bournemouth (0202) 33438

REPATH, George David. b 43. Univ of Wales (Lamp) DipTh68. **d** 68 **p** 69. C Cardiff St Jo *Llan* 68-73; C Gt Stanmore *Lon* 73-77; V Stratfield Mortimer *Ox* 77-85; RD Bradfield 82-85; P-in-c Mortimer W End w Padworth 83-85; V Bray and Braywood from 85. *The Vicarage, Bray, Maidenhead, Berks SL6 2AB* Maidenhead (0628) 21527

REPATH, John Richard. b 48. Univ of Wales (Cardiff) DipTh75. St Mich Coll Llan 72. **d** 75 **p** 76. C Canton St Jo *Llan* 75-79; C Burghclere w Newtown and Ecchinswell w Sydmonton *Win* 80-83; R Bewcastle and Stapleton *Carl* 83-88; P-in-c Kirklinton w Hethersgill and Scaleby 86-88; R Bewcastle, Stapleton and Kirklinton etc from 88. *The Rectory, Stapleton, Carlisle CA6 6LD* Roadhead (06978) 660

REPTON, Suffragan Bishop of. See RICHMOND, Rt Rev Francis Henry Arthur

RESTALL, Gerald Dalton. b 22. K Coll Lon BD50 AKC50. **d** 51 **p** 52. V Becontree St Eliz *Chelmsf* 62-71; CF (R of O) 69-77; R & V Reading St Mary *Ox* 72-77; R & V Reading St Mary w St Laur 77-88; rtd 88. *20 Sudbury Avenue, Hereford HR1 1YB* Hereford (0432) 279194

RESTALL, Miss Susan Roberta. b 45. SRD. Sarum & Wells Th Coll 79. **dss** 82 **d** 87. Dorchester *Sarum* 82-84; Portland All SS w St Pet 84-87; Par Dn 87; TM Yate New Town *Bris* from 87. *67 Mountbatten Close, Yate, Bristol BS17 5TE* Chipping Sodbury (0454) 316920

REUSS, John Christopher Edward. b 1900. Lon Coll of Div 36. **d** 38 **p** 39. C Sydenham H Trin *S'wark* 38-39; Chapl RAF 39-45; R Longhope *Glouc* 45-46; Canada 46-48 and from 52; USA 48-52. *14627 Marine Drive, White Rock, British Columbia, Canada, V4B 1B8*

REVELL, Patrick Walter Millard. b 32. Wells Th Coll 65. **d** 67 **p** 68. C Leic St Jas *Leic* 67-74; V Quorndon 74-82; TR Camelot Par *B & W* 82-90; RD Cary from 90; RD Bruton from 90; V Castle Cary w Ansford from 90. *The Vicarage, Church Street, Castle Cary, Somerset BA7 7EJ* Castle Cary (0963) 51615

REVELL, Stanley. b 15. AKC38. **d** 38 **p** 39. R Elvington *York* 64-69; rtd 69. *Fairway, Syke Lane, Nawton, York YO6 5SA* Helmsley (0439) 71201

REVETT, Graham Francis. b 40. AKC63. **d** 64 **p** 65. C Pennywell St Thos and Grindon St Oswald CD *Dur* 64-68; C Hartlepool St Aid 68-71; V Shiney Row 71-80; V Herrington 73-80; RD Houghton 76-80; TR Cullercoats St Geo *Newc* from 80; RD Tynemouth from 87. *The Vicarage, Beverley Gardens, North Shields, Tyne & Wear NE30 4NS* 091-252 1817

REX, James Maxwell. b 29. TD66. CEng59 FICE73. Trin Coll Bris 88. **d** 89 **p** 90. NSM Stoke Bishop *Bris* from 89. *15 Southfield Road, Bristol BS9 3BG* Bristol (0272) 621984

REYNISH, David Stuart. b 52. Nottm Univ BEd75. Linc Th Coll 72. **d** 77 **p** 78. C Boston *Linc* 77-80; C Chalfont St Peter *Ox* 80-84; V Thursby *Carl* 84-88; R Iver Heath *Ox* from 88. *The Rectory, 2 Pinewood Close, Iver Heath, Bucks SL0 0QS* Iver (0753) 654470

REYNOLDS, Alan Martin. b 53. Sarum & Wells Th Coll 73. **d** 77 **p** 78. C Glan Ely *Llan* 77-84; V Pontyclun w Talygarn from 84. *The Vicarage, Heol Miskin, Pontyclun, M Glam CF7 9AJ* Llantrisant (0443) 225477

REYNOLDS, Alan Thomas William. b 43. Lon Univ BSc64. Linc Th Coll 64. **d** 66 **p** 67. C Leic St Pet *Leic* 66-70; C Huntington *York* 70-72; Jamaica 72-76; V Stechford *Birm* 76-83; P-in-c Hampton in Arden 83-86; V from 87; Chapl E Birm Hosp 86-88; Chapl Parkway Hosp Solihull from 88. *1 High Street, Hampton in Arden, Solihull, W Midlands B92 0AE* Hampton-in-Arden (06755) 2604

REYNOLDS, Alfred Stanley. b 18. Birm Univ BSc39 Open Univ BA88. St Deiniol's Hawarden 69. **d** 70 **p** 71. Hon C Illogan *Truro* 70-85; Hon C Trowbridge St Thos and W Ashton *Sarum* from 85. *42 Cloford Close, Trowbridge BA14 9DH* Trowbridge (0225) 763542

REYNOLDS, David Hammerton. b 39. St Jo Coll Dur BA62. Qu Coll Birm DipTh63. **d** 65 **p** 66. C N Ormesby

York 65-68; C Hessle 68-71; V Sherburn in Elmet 71-79; V Fulford 79-87; Resp for Clergy In-Service Tr York Area 82-87; C Egloskerry *Truro* 87; TV Bolventor 87-90; TR Brayton *York* from 90. *The Rectory, Doncaster Road, Brayton, Selby, N Yorkshire YO8 9HE* Selby (0757) 704707

REYNOLDS, David James. b 48. St Jo Coll Dur BA72 DipTh73 Lanc Univ MA85. Cranmer Hall Dur 69. **d** 73 **p** 74. C Formby H Trin *Liv* 73-77; P-in-c Widnes St Paul 77-80; V Southport St Paul 80-87; P-in-c Mawdesley *Blackb* 87-91; R from 91. *Mawdesley Rectory, Green Lane, Ormskirk, Lancs L40 3TH* Rufford (0704) 822203

REYNOLDS, Derrick Wilfrid. b 15. St Paul's Grahamstown LTh. **d** 49 **p** 50. V Sparkwell *Ex* 62-73; V Ilsington 73-86; rtd 86; Perm to Offic *Ex* from 86. *White Gates, 7 West Buckeridge Road, Teignmouth, Devon TQ14 8NF* Teignmouth (0626) 772165

REYNOLDS, Gordon. b 42. Sarum & Wells Th Coll 71. **d** 72 **p** 73. C Tunstall *Lich* 72-74; Zambia 75-88; C Southmead *Bris* 88-90. *c/o Hilfield Priory, Cerne Abbas, Dorset* Cerne Abbas (0300) 341345

REYNOLDS, Canon John Lionel. b 34. JP. Chich Th Coll 58. **d** 61 **p** 62. C Whitkirk *Ripon* 61-64; C Tong *Bradf* 64-68; V Chisledon and Draycot Foliatt *Sarum* 68-74; RD Marlborough 74-76; TR Ridgeway 74-76; V Calne and Blackland 76-89; RD Calne 77-84; Can and Preb Sarum Cathl from 80; V Woodford Valley from 89. *The Vicarage, Middle Woodford, Salisbury SP4 6NR* Middle Woodford (072273) 310

REYNOLDS, John Stewart. b 19. FSA81 St Edm Hall Ox BA42 MA45 BLitt50. Ridley Hall Cam 42. **d** 44 **p** 45. R Besselsleigh w Dry Sandford *Ox* 56-85; Lect Wycliffe Hall Ox 71-78; rtd 85; Perm to Offic *Ox* from 85. *Linden Lodge, 59 St Mary's Road, Oxford OX4 1PZ* Oxford (0865) 727386

REYNOLDS, Neil Francis Arthur. b 59. Southn Univ BEd83. Chich Th Coll 84. **d** 86 **p** 87. C St Mary-at-Latton *Chelmsf* 86-89; C Hockerill *St Alb* from 89. *17 Legions Way, Bishop's Stortford, Herts CM23 2AU* Bishop's Stortford (0279) 657261

REYNOLDS, Paul Andrew. b 57. BA86. Trin Coll Bris 83. **d** 86 **p** 87. C Reading St Jo *Ox* 86-90; C Dorridge *Birm* from 90. *2 Hurst Green Road, Bentley Heath, Solihull, W Midlands B93 8AE* Knowle (0564) 775494

REYNOLDS, Philip Delamere. b 53. Leeds Univ CertEd74 Nottm Univ BCombStuds82. Linc Th Coll 79. **d** 82 **p** 83. C Huddersfield St Jo *Wakef* 82-85; C Barkisland w W Scammonden 85-87; P-in-c Skelmanthorpe from 87. *St Aidan's Vicarage, Radcliffe Street, Skelmanthorpe, Huddersfield HD8 9AF* Huddersfield (0484) 863232

REYNOLDS, Raymond Ernest. b 29. Nottm Univ MPhil89. Lambeth STh84 CA Tr Coll 50 Chich Th Coll 58. **d** 60 **p** 61. C Leeds St Marg *Ripon* 60-62; C Beeston *S'well* 62-64; R Farnley *Ripon* 64-76; R Higham-on-the-Hill w Fenny Drayton *Leic* 76-81; R Higham-on-the-Hill w Fenny Drayton and Witherley 81-90; V Sutton *Ely* from 90; R Witcham w Mepal from 90. *The Vicarage, 7 Church Lane, Sutton, Ely, Cambs CB6 2RQ* Ely (0353) 778645

REYNOLDS, Richard Michael. b 42. St Steph Ho Ox 65. **d** 67 **p** 68. C Kidderminster St Mary *Worc* 67-70; Guyana 70-73; TV N Creedy *Ex* 73-80; R Holsworthy w Hollacombe 80-86; R Holsworthy w Hollacombe and Milton Damerel from 86. *The Rectory, Holsworthy, Devon EX22 6BH* Holsworthy (0409) 253435

REYNOLDS, Canon Stanley Kenneth. b 14. Bps' Coll Cheshunt 47. **d** 50 **p** 51. V Chaddesden St Phil *Derby* 64-70; V Greenhill St Pet 70-74; V Greenhill *Sheff* 74-81; P-in-c Burghwallis w Skelbrooke 81-89; Hon Can Sheff Cathl 83-89; rtd 89. *4 Burton Close, Diss, Norfolk IP22 3YJ* Diss (0379) 650562

RHAM, Canon John Theodore. b 27. Magd Coll Cam BA50 MA65. Sarum Th Coll 50. **d** 52 **p** 53. C Harborne St Pet *Birm* 52-54; C Coleshill 54-56; C Falmouth K Chas *Truro* 56-59; R St Ewe 59-68; RD St Austell 65-68; V Budock from 68; RD Carnmarth S 77-84; Hon Can Truro Cathl from 80. *St Budock Vicarage, Budock, Falmouth, Cornwall TR11 5DA* Falmouth (0326) 72227

RHODES, Adrian Michael. b 48. K Coll Lon BD71 AKC71 DPST76. Qu Coll Birm 71. **d** 72 **p** 73. C Bury St Jo *Man* 73-75; Chapl N Man Gen Hosp 75-77; C Crumpsall *Man* 75-77; Chapl Walsall Manor and Bloxwich Hosps 77-83; Chapl Walsall Gen Hosp 81-83; Chapl Man R Infirmary from 83; Chapl St Mary's Hosp Man from 83. *58 Errwood Road, Burnage, Manchester M19 2QH* 061 224 1739 or 273 1234

RHODES, Anthony John. b 27. Mert Coll Ox BA50 MA53 DipTh53. St Steph Ho Ox 52. **d** 54 **p** 55. C Northn St Alb *Pet* 54-57; C Oakham 57-60; P-in-c S Queensferry

Edin 60-74; V Mitcham St Olave *S'wark* 74-81; V Owston *Linc* from 81; V W Butterwick from 81. *The Vicarage, Church Street, Owston Ferry, Doncaster, S Yorkshire DN9 1RG* Owston Ferry (042772) 305

RHODES, Arthur. b 31. Dur Univ BA58. Cranmer Hall Dur 57. **d** 59 **p** 60. C Kirkdale St Lawr *Liv* 59-61; C Litherland St Phil 61-64; V St Helens St Matt Thatto Heath 64-67; V Samlesbury *Blackb* 67-79; Lic to Offic from 80. *88 Deborah Avenue, Fulwood, Preston, Lancs PR2 2HU* Preston (0772) 712212

RHODES, David. b 34. St Chad's Coll Dur BA60. **d** 61 **p** 62. C Dudley St Jo *Worc* 61-64; C-in-c Stourbridge St Mich Norton CD 64-68; V Astwood Bank w Crabbs Cross 69-78; Dioc Ecum Officer 73-78; TR Hackney *Lon* 78-88; R St Giles Cripplegate w St Bart Moor Lane etc from 88. *The Rectory, 4 The Postern, Wood Street, London EC2Y 8BJ* 071-606 3630

RHODES, David George. b 45. Univ of Wales (Abth) BA66. Trin Coll Bris 83. **d** 85 **p** 86. C Brinsworth w Catcliffe *Sheff* 85-89; V Mortomley from 89. *The Vicarage, Mortomley Lane, High Green, Sheffield S30 4HS* Sheffield (0742) 848231

RHODES, David Grant. b 43. Ex Univ BA66 Southn Univ Leeds Univ DipAdEd75. Sarum & Wells Th Coll 69. **d** 72 **p** 73. C Mirfield *Wakef* 72-75; V Batley St Thos 75-80; Dioc Adult Educn Officer 75-80; Hon C Huddersfield St Jo 85-86; Dir BRF 86-87; V Roberttown *Wakef* from 87. *The Vicarage, Church Road, Liversedge, W Yorkshire WF15 7PF* Heckmondwike (0924) 402064

RHODES, Geoffrey David. b 34. Birm Univ BSc55. Ridley Hall Cam 68. **d** 70 **p** 71. C Sedbergh *Bradf* 70-74; P-in-c Howgill w Firbank 73-76; P-in-c Killington 73-76; C Sedbergh, Cautley and Garsdale 74-76; R Carleton-in-Craven 76-78; P-in-c Lothersdale 76-78; R Carleton and Lothersdale 78-85; V Giggleswick and Rathmell w Wigglesworth from 85. *The Vicarage, Bankwell Road, Giggleswick, Settle, N Yorkshire BD24 0AP* Settle (0729) 822425

RHODES, Heather. b 32. **d** 88. Par Dn Purley St Mark Woodcote *S'wark* from 89. *24 Highfield Road, Purley, Surrey CR8 2JG* 081-660 1486

RHODES, Canon John Lovell. b 33. MBE81. Lon Univ BD59. St Aid Birkenhead 55. **d** 59 **p** 60. C Bradf St Clem *Bradf* 59-61; C Heeley *Sheff* 61-66; Ind Chapl *Linc* from 66; RD Grimsby and Cleethorpes 76-83; Can and Preb Linc Cathl from 77; Sen Ind Chapl from 81. *19 Augusta Close, Grimsby, S Humberside DN34 4TQ* Grimsby (0472) 343167

RHODES, Leslie Howard. b 04. St Jo Coll Dur BA27. **d** 28 **p** 29. V Urmston *Man* 57-73; rtd 73; C Much Birch w Lt Birch, Much Dewchurch etc *Heref* 73-79; Perm to Offic *Man* from 80. *84 Red Lane, Bolton, Lancs BL2 5EL* Bolton (0204) 28378

RHODES, Lois Christine. b 34. Lon Univ BSc61. Glouc Sch of Min 84. **d** 87. NSM Weobley w Sarnesfield and Norton Canon *Heref* from 87; NSM Letton w Staunton, Byford, Mansel Gamage etc from 87. *Bellbrook, Bell Square, Weobley, Hereford HR4 8SE* Weobley (0544) 318410

RHODES, Maurice Arthur. b 27. Ridley Hall Cam 67. **d** 69 **p** 70. C Skipton Ch Ch *Bradf* 69-71; C Brierley Hill *Lich* 71-74; V Walsall Wood from 74. *The Vicarage, St John's Close, Walsall Wood, Walsall WS9 9LP* Brownhills (0543) 372284

RHODES, Peter Stuart. b 26. ACP67. Coll of Resurr Mirfield 77. **d** 78 **p** 79. NSM Newbold and Dunston *Derby* from 78. *42 Westbrook Drive, Chesterfield, Derbyshire S40 3PQ* Chesterfield (0246) 566628

RHODES, Robert George. b 41. Man Univ BSc62. Ripon Hall Ox DipTh73. **d** 74 **p** 75. C Banbury *Ox* 74-77; TV Banbury 77-81; P-in-c Longhorsley *Newc* 81-86; Adult Educn Adv 81-86; R Wolverton *Ox* from 86. *The Rectory, Aylesbury Street, Wolverton, Milton Keynes MK12 5HY* Milton Keynes (0908) 312501

RHODES, Canon Trevor Martin. b 38. Kelham Th Coll 59 Qu Coll Birm 70. **d** 71 **p** 71. C Bordesley St Oswald *Birm* 71-73; Chapl St Basil's Ch Cen Birm 72-73; C Padiham *Blackb* 73-76; P-in-c Preston St Oswald 76-78; Chapl HM Borstal Hindley 78-80; V Blackhill *Dur* 80-83; V Cowgate *Newc* 83-87; Hon Can Koforidua from 86; V Wesham *Blackb* 87-90; V Danby *York* from 90. *The Vicarage, Danby, Whitby, N Yorkshire YO21 2NQ* Castleton (0287) 660388

RHODES-WRIGLEY, James. b 35. AKC59. **d** 60 **p** 61. C S Harrow St Paul *Lon* 60-66; V Hendon Ch Ch 66-71; V Northolt Park St Barn from 71. *The Vicarage, Raglan Way, Northolt, Middx UB5 4SX* 081-422 3775

RHYDDERCH, David Huw. b 48. Univ of Wales (Cardiff) DipTh73. St Mich Coll Llan 70. **d** 73 **p** 74. C Gellygaer

Llan 73-76; C Penarth All SS 76-78; V Resolven 78-81; V Ystrad Rhondda w Ynyscynon from 81; RD Rhondda from 89. *St Stephen's Vicarage, Ystrad, Pentre, M Glam CF41 7RR* Tonypandy (0443) 434426

RHYMES, Canon Douglas Alfred. b 14. Birm Univ BA39. Ripon Hall Ox 39. **d** 40 **p** 41. V Camberwell St Giles *S'wark* 68-76; Hon Can S'wark Cathl 69-84; P-in-c Woldingham 76-84; rtd 84; Perm to Offic *Chich* from 84. *7 Duke's Road, Fontwell, Arundel, W Sussex BN18 0SP* Eastergate (0243) 543268

RHYS, Canon David Edwin. b 37. Peterho Cam BA61 MA65 Lon Univ BA74. St Steph Ho Ox. **d** 63 **p** 64. C Tividale *Lich* 63-65; C Eltham St Jo *S'wark* 65-72; Hon C 75-82; Chapl and Warden LMH Settlement 72-75; P-in-c Woolwich St Mary w St Mich 82-83; R from 83; RD Greenwich 86-90; Sub-Dean of Woolwich 86-87; Hon Can S'wark Cathl from 90. *The Rectory, 43 Rectory Place, London SE18 5DA* 081-854 2302

RHYS, Trevor William. b 11. Kenyon Coll Ohio BA35. Sarum Th Coll 35. **d** 38 **p** 39. V Stogumber *B & W* 67-76; rtd 76. *4 Appleton House, 81 Ash Lane, Wells, Somerset BA5 2LW* Wells (0749) 74921

RICE, Brian Keith. b 32. Peterho Cam BA55 MA59. Seabury-Western Th Sem BD57 STM67 MDiv79 Linc Th Coll. **d** 57 **p** 58. C Winchmore Hill St Paul *Lon* 57-60; C Derby St Werburgh *Derby* 60-63; C Mackworth St Fran 63-66; Chapl Kingsway Hosp Derby 63-66; Educn Sec USPG 66-72; Dir of Educn *Birm* 72-84; Chapl St Chad's Hosp Birm 77-84; Soc Resp Officer *Dur* from 84. *39 Darlington Road, Hartburn, Stockton-on-Tees, Cleveland TS18 5ET* Stockton-on-Tees (0642) 582241

RICE, Brian Thomas. b 46. Univ of Wales (Cardiff) BD77. St Mich Coll Llan 75. **d** 77 **p** 78. C Llanelly *St D* 77-79; P-in-c Llandygwydd and Cenarth w Cilrhedyn 79-80; V 80-83; V Llandingat w Myddfai from 83; RD Llangadog and Llandeilo from 91. *The Vicarage, Llandovery, Dyfed SA20 0EH* Llandovery (0550) 20524

RICE, David. b 57. Nottm Univ BA79. Ripon Coll Cuddesdon 80. **d** 82 **p** 83. C Cirencester *Glouc* 82-86; R Theale and Englefield *Ox* from 86. *The Rectory, Theale, Reading RG7 5AS* Reading (0734) 302759

RICE, Franklin Arthur. b 20. FRICS49. St Alb Minl Tr Scheme 77. **d** 80 **p** 81. NSM Hoddesdon *St Alb* 80-84; Perm to Offic *Guildf* from 85. *1 Oatlands Court, St Mary's Road, Weybridge, Surrey KT13 9QE* Weybridge (0932) 846462

RICE, John Leslie Hale. b 38. FBIM GIMechE Lon Univ BScEng60 BD68. E Midl Min Tr Course 73. **d** 76 **p** 77. NSM Allestree St Nic *Derby* from 76; NSM Ind Specialist from 90. *14 Gisborne Crescent, Allestree, Derby DE3 2FL* Derby (0332) 557222

RICE-OXLEY, John Richard. b 44. Keble Coll Ox BA66 MA69 Dur Univ MA85. Lon Coll of Div 68. **d** 70 **p** 71. C Eastwood *S'well* 70-73; Youth Adv CMS 73-78; V Mansf St Jo *S'well* 78-82; P-in-c Thornley *Dur* 82-85; P-in-c Darlington St Matt and St Luke 85-87; V from 87. *St Matthew's Vicarage, 63A Brinkburn Road, Darlington, Co Durham DL3 6DX* Darlington (0325) 463412

RICH, Christopher Robin. b 49. Sarum & Wells Th Coll 72. **d** 74 **p** 75. C Sholing 74-76; C Southn Maybush St Pet 76-79; R Fawley 79-90; Dir Soc Resp from 90. *15 Shelley Close, Winchester SO22 5AS* Winchester (0962) 862338

RICH, Harold Reginald. b 22. Local NSM Course. **d** 79 **p** 80. NSM St Austell *Truro* 79-87; rtd 87; Perm to Offic *Truro* from 87. *106 Eastbourne Road, St Austell, Cornwall PL25 4SS* St Austell (0726) 75600

RICH, Nicholas Philip. b 49. St Cuth Soc Dur BA74 CertEd75 Coll of Ripon & York St Jo CertEd83. Linc Th Coll 86. **d** 88 **p** 89. C W Acklam *York* 88-91; Chapl St Geo Sch Harpenden from 91. *7 Stewart Road, Harpenden, Herts AL5 4QE* Harpenden (0582) 712951

RICH, Paul Michael. b 36. OBE87. Sarum Th Coll 62. **d** 65 **p** 66. C Woodbridge St Mary *St E* 65-68; C W Wycombe *Ox* 68-70; CF 70-88; Lic to Offic *S & B* 88-90; V Crondall and Ewshot *Guildf* from 91. *The Vicarage, Farm Lane, Crondall, Farnham, Surrey GU10 5QE* Aldershot (0252) 850379

RICH, Peter Geoffrey. b 45. Oak Hill Th Coll 74. **d** 77 **p** 78. C Blackheath St Jo *S'wark* 77-80; C Surbiton St Matt 80-87; V St Alb St Luke *St Alb* from 87. *St Luke's Vicarage, Cellbarnes Lane, St Albans, Herts AL1 5QJ* St Albans (0727) 65399

RICH, Thomas. b 52. St Jo Coll Nottm 86. **d** 88 **p** 89. C Netherton *Liv* from 88. *5 Emerald Close, Bootle, Merseyside L30 8RJ* 051-526 8309

RICHARD, Brother. *See* MAY, Richard Grainger

RICHARD, David Thomas. b 16. St D Coll Lamp BA39. **d** 40 **p** 41. V Darlaston St Geo *Lich* 62-70; V Mostyn *St As* 70-86; rtd 86; Perm to Offic *St D* from 86. *Ael-y-Bryn, New Quay, Dyfed* New Quay (0545) 560745

RICHARDS, Alan Grenville. b 41. Kelham Th Coll 64. **d** 69 **p** 70. C Northolt St Mary *Lon* 69-75; V Fatfield *Dur* 75-84; V Beighton *Sheff* 84-91; V Endcliffe from 91. *St Augustine's Vicarage, 31 Brocco Bank, Sheffield S11 8RQ* Sheffield (0742) 661932

RICHARDS, Albert George Granston. b 06. Lon Univ BSc30. Wycliffe Hall Ox 54. **d** 55 **p** 60. V Offley w Lilley *St Alb* 69-74; RD Hurst *Chich* 75-80; P-in-c Poynings 80-82; P-in-c Edburton 80-82; rtd 82; Perm to Offic *Chich* from 82. *East Coombe, North Bank, Hassocks, W Sussex BN6 8JG* Hassocks (07918) 2203

RICHARDS, Andrew David Thomas. b 55. St Jo Coll Dur BA76. St Steph Ho Ox 76. **d** 78 **p** 79. C Shirley *Birm* 78-80; C Cowley St Jo *Ox* 80-82. *11 Thomas Avenue, Reading, Berks*

RICHARDS, Anthony Francis. b 26. Wadh Coll Ox BA51 MA54. Ridley Hall Cam 50. **d** 52 **p** 53. C Finchley Ch Ch *Lon* 52-55; C Maidenhead St Andr and St Mary Magd *Ox* 55-59; Lect All Nations Chr Coll Ware 58-59; V High Wycombe Ch Ch *Ox* 59-63; P-in-c 63-67; V Terriers 63-73; USA 70-71; V Cinderford St Steph w Littledean *Glouc* 73-80; V Clacton St Paul *Chelmsf* from 80; New Zealand 88-89. *7 St Albans Road, Clacton-on-Sea, Essex CO15 6BA* Clacton-on-Sea (0225) 424760

RICHARDS, Mrs April. b 42. Man Univ BSc63. S Dios Minl Tr Scheme 82. **dss** 85 **d** 87. Catherington and Clanfield *Portsm* 85-87; C 87-89; C E Meon from 89; C Langrish from 89. *1A Hawthorn Road, Horndean, Portsmouth PO8 0ES* Horndean (0705) 594304

RICHARDS, Barbara May. b 53. Sarum & Wells Th Coll. **d** 88. Chapl Princess Marg Hosp Swindon from 88. *187 Redcliffe Street, Rodbourne, Malmesbury, Wilts*

RICHARDS, Basil Ernest. b 18. Lich Th Coll 51. **d** 53 **p** 54. Hon C Gt Malvern Ch Ch *Worc* 78-84; Perm to Offic from 84; Chapl Laslett's Almshouses 84-88; rtd 88. *6 Shirley Close, Malvern, Worcs WR14 2NH* Malvern (0684) 565441

RICHARDS, Brian Gordon. b 21. Sarum & Wells Th Coll 71. **d** 73 **p** 74. C Milton *Win* 73-78; P-in-c Hook w Greywell 78-83; R Hook 83-88; rtd 88. *Grenville Cottage, Main Road, Bourton, Gillingham, Dorset SP8 5ES* Gillingham (0747) 840514

RICHARDS, Canon Brian Murley. b 09. Ex Coll Ox BA32 MA35. Cuddesdon Coll 33. **d** 34 **p** 35. R Avening *Glouc* 56-74; rtd 74; Perm to Offic *Glouc* from 83. *Uplands Cottage, 99 Slad Road, Stroud, Glos GL5 1QZ* Stroud (0453) 762539

RICHARDS, Charles Dennis Vincent. b 37. AKC61. **d** 62 **p** 63. Chapl St Ninian's Cathl Perth *St And* 62-64; C Pimlico St Mary Graham Terrace *Lon* 64-66; C St Marylebone Ch Ch w St Barn 66-68; C Wood Green St Mich 68-69; C-in-c S Kenton Annunciation CD 69-77; P-in-c Wembley Park St Aug 70-73; Hon C Paddington St Jo w St Mich from 76. *48A Kendal Street, London W2 2BP* 071-262 5633

RICHARDS, Charles Edmund Nicholas. b 42. Trin Coll Cam BA64 MA68. Westcott Ho Cam 64. **d** 66 **p** 67. C Rugby St Andr *Cov* 66-72; TV Basingstoke *Win* 72-77; R Rotherhithe St Mary w All SS *S'wark* from 77; RD Bermondsey 81-91. *The Rectory, St Marychurch Street, London SE16 4JE* 071-231 2465

RICHARDS, Dr Christopher Mordaunt. b 40. New Coll Ox BA63 MA72 Bris Univ MB, ChB72. Cuddesdon Coll 63. **d** 65 **p** 81. C Bris St Mary Redcliffe w Temple etc *Bris* 65-66; Perm to Offic 66-72; Hon C Keynsham *B & W* 81-90; Perm to Offic from 90. *43 Charlton Road, Keynsham, Bristol BS18 2JG* Bristol (0272) 862844

RICHARDS, Daniel James. b 40. St D Coll Lamp DipTh66. **d** 66 **p** 67. C Kingswinford H Trin *Lich* 66-69; C Banbury *Ox* 69-71; C Aylesbury 71-73; C-in-c Stoke Poges St Jo Manor Park CD 73-78; R W Slough 78-80; R Ilchester w Northover, Limington, Yeovilton etc *B & W* 80-90; RD Ilchester 81-91; RD Martock from 89; TR Bruton and Distr from 90. *The Rectory, Bruton, Somerset BA10 0EF* Bruton (0749) 2372

RICHARDS, Canon David. b 30. Bris Univ BA52. St Mich Coll Llan 52. **d** 54 **p** 55. C Llangynwyd w Maesteg *Llan* 54-56; Iran 57-61 and 62-66; C Skewen *Llan* 61-62; V Cwmbach 66-76; Warden of Ords 71-77; R Coity w Nolton from 76; Can Llan Cathl from 88. *Nolton Rectory, 5 Merthyrmawr Road North, Bridgend, M Glam CF31 3NH* Bridgend (0656) 652247

RICHARDS, David Arnold. b 56. Wycliffe Hall Ox 76. **d** 81 **p** 82. C Skewen *Llan* 81-84; C Barking St Marg w St Patr *Chelmsf* 84-85; TV 85-90; Chapl Barking Hosp

87-88; P-in-c Stratford St Jo and Ch Ch w Forest Gate St Jas *Chelmsf* from 90. *Stratford Vicarage, Deanery Road, Stratford, London E15 4LP* 081-534 8388

RICHARDS, Canon Derek Gordon. b 31. Univ of Wales (Lamp) BA54. St Deiniol's Hawarden 68. **d** 69 **p** 70. C Neath w Llantwit *Llan* 69-73; V Llangeinor 73-77; V Arthog w Fairbourne *Ban* 77-80; R Llanaber w Caerdeon 80-83; R Llandudno from 83; Hon Can Ban Cathl from 89. *The Rectory, Church Walk, Llandudno, Gwynedd LL30 2HL* Llandudno (0492) 76624

RICHARDS, Edwin Thomas. Leeds Univ BA41. St D Coll Lamp 46. **d** 48 **p** 49. S Africa 50-86; R Llanganten, Llanafan Fawr, Llangammarch etc *S & B* 86-89; rtd 89. *The Vicarage, Maes Glas, Llangammarch Wells, Powys LD4 4AA*

RICHARDS, Eric. b 36. TD86. Ely Th Coll 62. **d** 63 **p** 64. C Fen Ditton *Ely* 63-65; C Woodston 65-68; Ceylon 68-71; Miss to Seamen 71-73; R Roos w Tunstall *York* 73-74; P-in-c Garton w Grimston and Hilston 73-74; R Roos and Garton in Holderness w Tunstall etc 74-79; CF (TAVR) 73-79; CF (TA) 79-89; Sen CF (TA) from 89; V Wykeham and Hutton Buscel *York* from 79; RD Pickering from 80; Abp's Adv on Rural Affairs from 83. *The Vicar's House, Hutton Buscel, Scarborough, N Yorkshire YO13 9LL* Scarborough (0723) 862945

RICHARDS, Gwynfryn. b 02. Univ of Wales BSc21 Jes Coll Ox BA23 MA28 Boston Univ STB28. St Mich Coll Llan 29. **d** 30 **p** 31. Dean Ban 62-71; rtd 71. *Llain Werdd, Llandegfan, Menai Bridge, Gwynedd LL59 5LY* Menai Bridge (0248) 713429

RICHARDS, Harold John Thomas. b 16. St D Coll Lamp BA39 St Mich Coll Llan 45. **d** 47 **p** 48. R Goetre *Mon* 69-82; rtd 82. *48 Longhouse Barn, Goetre, Pontypool, Gwent NP4 0BD* Nantyderry (0873) 880744

RICHARDS, Canon Iorwerth. b 20. Univ of Wales (Lamp) BA41. K Coll Lon 41. **d** 43 **p** 44. R Penmaen w Nicholaston *S & B* 60-71; RD W Gower 71-88; V Oxwich w Penmaen and Nicholaston 71-89; Hon Can Brecon Cathl 83-85; Can Brecon Cathl 85-89; rtd 89. *17 Carrick Avenue, Llanelli, Dyfed*

RICHARDS, Irving St Clair. b 40. Coll of Resurr Mirfield 72. **d** 74 **p** 75. C Wigston Magna *Leic* 74-78; P-in-c N Evington from 78. *The Vicarage, 214 East Park Road, Leicester LE5 5FD* Leicester (0533) 736752

RICHARDS, James Harcourt. b 30. Oak Hill Th Coll. **d** 63 **p** 64. C Liv Ch Ch Norris Green *Liv* 63-66; C Fazakerley Em 66-68; P-in-c Edge Hill St Cath 68-73; V St Helens St Matt Thatto Heath 73-87; R Feltwell *Ely* from 87. *The Rectory, 8 The Beck, Feltwell, Thetford, Norfolk IP26 4DB* Thetford (0842) 828631

RICHARDS, Mrs Jane Valerie. b 43. Westf Coll Lon BA64 Birm Univ CertEd65. S Dios Minl Tr Scheme 84. **d** 87. NSM Locks Heath *Portsm* from 87; Asst Chapl Qu Alexandra Hosp Portsm from 90. *16 Lodge Road, Locks Heath, Southampton SO3 6QY* Locks Heath (0489) 573891

RICHARDS, John. b 20. FSA70 Univ of Wales (Lamp) BA40 Keble Coll Ox BA42 MA46 BLitt48. Westcott Ho Cam 43. **d** 43 **p** 44. CF (TA) 62-86; Master Wellington Sch 67-82; V Hoylake *Ches* 67-86; rtd 86; Perm to Offic *Ches* from 86. *Ithaca, 56 Cleveley Road, Meols, South Wirral L47 8XR* 051-632 5135

RICHARDS, Ven John. b 33. SS Coll Cam BA55 MA59. Ely Th Coll 57. **d** 59 **p** 60. C Ex St Thos *Ex* 59-64; R Holsworthy w Cookbury 64-74; R Hollacombe 64-74; RD Holsworthy 70-74; V Heavitree 74-77; TR Heavitree w Ex St Paul 78-81; RD Christianity 78-81; Adn Ex and Can Res Ex Cathl from 81. *12 The Close, Exeter, Devon EX1 1EZ* Exeter (0392) 75745

RICHARDS, Preb John Francis. b 37. Dur Univ BA61. Wells Th Coll 61. **d** 63 **p** 64. C Sherwood *S'well* 63-67; C Bishopwearmouth St Mich *Dur* 67-69; C Egg Buckland *Ex* 69-75; V Plymouth St Jas Ham 75-83; V Plympton St Mary from 83; RD Plymouth Moorside from 88; Preb Ex Cathl from 91. *St Mary's Vicarage, 58 Plymbridge Road, Plympton, Plymouth PL7 4QG* Plymouth (0752) 336157

RICHARDS, John George. b 48. Qu Coll Birm 87. **d** 89 **p** 90. C Acocks Green *Birm* from 89. *74 Oxford Road, Acocks Green, Birmingham B27 6DT* 021-707 7596

RICHARDS, John Henry. b 34. CCC Cam BA57 MA75. Llan St Mich BD77. **d** 77 **p** 78. C Llangynwyd w Maesteg *Llan* 77-79; C Cardiff St Jo 79-82; Asst Chapl Univ of Wales (Cardiff) 79-82; V Penmark w Porthkerry 82-83; R Stackpole Elidor w St Petrox *St D* 83-85; R St Petrox w Stackpole Elidor and Bosherston etc from 85. *The Rectory, Stackpole, Pembroke, Dyfed SA71 5BZ* Lamphey (0646) 672472

RICHARDS, John Stanley. b 39. St Jo Coll Dur BA60. Ridley Hall Cam 61. **d** 64 **p** 65. C Fordingbridge w Ibsley *Win* 64-67; CF (TA) 64-68; C Bitterne Park *Win* 67-68; C Pokesdown All SS 68-70; Fell Qu Coll Birm 70-71; C Chesterton St Andr *Ely* 71-73; Asst Chapl Canford Sch Wimborne 73-77; Assoc Dir Fountain Trust 77-80; Perm to Offic *Guildf* 77-81; Dir Renewal Servicing from 81; NSM New Haw *Guildf* from 81. *Renewal Servicing, PO Box 17, Shepperton, Middx TW17 8NU*

RICHARDS, John William. b 29. Southn Univ BSc55. Sarum & Wells Th Coll 78. **d** 81 **p** 82. NSM Woking St Mary *Guildf* 81-85; C Addlestone 85-87; C S Gillingham *Roch* 87-89. *Heathside, Madeira Road, West Byfleet, Weybridge, Surrey KT14 6DE* Byfleet (0932) 346460

RICHARDS, Jonathan Berry Hillacre. b 52. DipHE86. Oak Hill Th Coll 84. **d** 86 **p** 87. C Okehampton w Inwardleigh *Ex* 86-89; C Bratton Fleming 89; TV Shirwell, Loxhore, Kentisbury, Arlington, etc from 90. *The Vicarage, 2 Barnfield, Bratton Fleming, Barnstaple, Devon EX31 4RT* Brayford (0598) 710807

RICHARDS, Julian. b 25. Wycliffe Hall Ox 71. **d** 73 **p** 74. C Hessle *York* 73-76; P-in-c Rowley 76-82; Chapl HM Pris Hull 79-82; P-in-c Boldre *Win* 82-83; P-in-c Boldre w S Baddesley 83; V from 83. *The Vicarage, Boldre, Lymington, Hants SO41 5QF* Lymington (0590) 673484

RICHARDS, Keith David. b 50. Didsbury Coll of Educn CertEd72. S'wark Ord Course 79. **d** 82 **p** 83. NSM Walworth *S'wark* 82-85; Chapl Derbyshire Coll of HE 85-87; V Rottingdean *Chich* from 87. *The Vicarage, Steyning Road, Rottingdean, Brighton BN2 7GA* Brighton (0273) 309216

RICHARDS, Kelvin. b 58. Univ of Wales (Abth) BSc80 MA88. Ripon Coll Cuddesdon BA82. **d** 83 **p** 84. C Killay *S & B* 83-86; C Morriston 86-89; V Llangattock and Llangyndir from 89. *The Rectory, Llangattock, Crickhowell, Powys NP8 1PH* Crickhowell (0873) 810270

RICHARDS, Kendrick Steven William. b 55. DMS81 Nottm Univ BTh87. St Jo Coll Nottm 84. **d** 87 **p** 88. C Belper *Derby* 87-91; V Ilkeston St Jo from 91. *St John's Vicarage, St John's Road, Ilkeston, Derbyshire DE7 5PA* Ilkeston (0602) 325446

RICHARDS, Llewelyn. b 15. St Deiniol's Hawarden 73. **d** 75 **p** 76. NSM Corwen and Llangar *St As* 75-85; Past Care Gwyddelwern 78-85; rtd 85. *120 Maesyfallen, Corwen, Clwyd LL21 9AD* Corwen (0490) 2195

RICHARDS, Mrs Mary Edith. b 33. SW Minl Tr Course 85. **d** 87. NSM Kea *Truro* 87-88; Asst Chapl Bris Poly *Bris* 88-91; C E Clevedon and Walton w Weston w Clapton *B & W* from 91. *5 Chestnut Grove, Clevedon, Avon BS21 7LA* Bristol (0272) 875244

RICHARDS, Norman John. b 47. BSc. Ridley Hall Cam. **d** 83 **p** 84. C Luton St Fran *St Alb* 83-86; R Aspenden and Layston w Buntingford from 86. *The Vicarage, Vicarage Road, Buntingford, Herts SG9 9BH* Royston (0763) 71552

RICHARDS, Peter Garth. b 30. Lon Univ BA51 St Chad's Coll Dur DipTh55. **d** 55 **p** 56. C Manston *Ripon* 55-57; C Adel 57-62; V Holbeck St Matt 62-66; C Clyst St George *Ex* 66-75; TV Clyst St George, Aylesbeare, Clyst Honiton etc 75-81. *3 Brooklands Orchard, Ottery St Mary, Devon* Ottery St Mary (0404) 814935

RICHARDS, Peter Lane Campling. b 26. St Cath Soc Ox BA51 MA55. Wells Th Coll 51. **d** 53 **p** 54. C Cheltenham St Paul *Glouc* 53-56; C Stonehouse 56-58; Tutor Bps' Coll Cheshunt 58-60; Chapl 60-61; Vice-Prin 61-64; R Marston Moretaine *St Alb* 64-75; P-in-c Sharpness *Glouc* 75-80; R Dumbleton w Wormington and Toddington 80-91; R Dumbleton w Wormington from 91; P-in-c Didbrook w Stanway and Hailes 82-91; P-in-c Toddington, Stanton, Didbrook w Hailes etc from 91. *The Rectory, Dumbleton, Evesham, Worcs WR11 6TH* Evesham (0386) 881410

RICHARDS, Robert Graham. b 42. St Jo Coll Nottm LTh. **d** 80 **p** 81. C Radipole and Melcombe Regis *Sarum* 80-83; TV Billericay and Lt Burstead *Chelmsf* 84-91; UK Dir CMJ from 91. *22 Dove Park, Chorleywood, Rickmansworth, Herts* Chorleywood (0923) 285114

RICHARDS, Ronald Jervis. b 16. St D Coll Lamp BA37. St Mich Coll Llan 38. **d** 39 **p** 40. Chapl RAF 43-71; R Quendon w Rickling *Chelmsf* 71-75; V Dedham 75-83; rtd 83. *2 Hollies Road, St Stephens, Launceston, Cornwall PL15 8HB* Launceston (0566) 776296

RICHARDS, Simon Granston. b 47. Nottm Univ BTh72. St Jo Coll Nottm 68 ALCD72. **d** 72 **p** 73. C Waltham Abbey *Chelmsf* 72-77; TV Basildon St Martin w H Cross and Laindon etc 77-80; V Grayshott *Guildf* 80-88; V Eccleston Ch Ch *Liv* from 88. *The Vicarage, Chapel*

Lane, Eccleston, St Helens, Merseyside WA10 5DA St Helens (0744) 22698

RICHARDS, Canon Thomas John Wynzie. b 25. St D Coll Lamp BA49. **d** 51 **p** 52. C Llandybie *St D* 51-53; V 71-87; C Llandegai *Ban* 53-56; R Llanymawddwy 56-57; Chapl Nat Nautical Sch Portishead 57-71; RD Dyffryn Aman *St D* 78-85; Can St D Cathl from 83; V Pencarreg and Llanycrwys from 87; Treas St D Cathl from 89. *The Vicarage, Cwmann, Lampeter, Dyfed* Lampeter (0570) 423350

RICHARDS, Trevor Thomas. b 09. Univ of Wales BSc30 MSc39. St Deiniol's Hawarden 70. **d** 70 **p** 71. Hon C Charlton w Brokenborough and Hankerton *Bris* 70-73; Lic to Offic from 73. *Mill Leaze, Upper Minety, Malmesbury, Wilts SN16 9PT* Malmesbury (0666) 860323

RICHARDS, Victor John Richard. b 12. AKC48. **d** 48 **p** 49. R Chulmleigh *Ex* 64-90; RD Chulmleigh 69-87; P-in-c Wembworthy 75-81; P-in-c Eggesford 77-81; P-in-c Chawleigh w Cheldon 77-81; R 82-90; R Wembworthy w Eggesford 82-90; rtd 90. *Willow Tree House, Rectory Road, Ogwell, Newton Abbot, Devon* Newton Abbot (0626) 332509

RICHARDS, William Antony. b 28. Ex Coll Ox BA52 MA56. St Steph Ho Ox 52. **d** 54 **p** 55. C Fenton *Lich* 54-55; C Kingswinford St Mary 55-60; V Meir 60-64; R Warmington w Shotteswell *Cov* 64-75; RD Dassett Magna 70-74; Org Sec (Dios Cov, Leic and Pet) CECS 75-81; V Bidford-on-Avon *Cov* from 81. *The Vicarage, Bidford-on-Avon, Alcester, Warks B50 4BQ* Bidford-on-Avon (0789) 772217

RICHARDS, Canon William Hughes. b 37. St D Coll Lamp BA58. **d** 60 **p** 61. C Llandyssul *St D* 60-63; C Llanelly 63-65; V Llanddewi Brefi w Llanbadarn Odwyn 65-73; V Pembrey 73-83; V Llangunnor and Cwmffrwd 83-88; V Cardigan and Mount and Verwick from 88; Can St D Cathl from 89. *The Vicarage, Napier Gardens, Cardigan, Dyfed SA43 1EG* Cardigan (0239) 612722

RICHARDS, Canon William Neal. b 38. ALCD63. **d** 63 **p** 64. C Otley *Bradf* 63-65; C Leamington Priors St Mary *Cov* 65-67; CMS 67-69; Kenya 69-74; Asst Provost and Can Res Nairobi Cathl 70-74; V Gt Malvern St Mary *Worc* 74-86; Chapl Kidderminster Health Distr 86-91; RD Kidderminster *Worc* 89-91; R Martley and Wichenford, Knightwick etc from 91. *The Rectory, Martley, Worcester WR6 6QA* Wichenford (08866) 664

RICHARDSON, Miss Anne. dss 80 **d** 87. Chapl Asst Westmr Hosp Lon 80-85; Chapl from 85. *Westminster Hospital, Dean Ryle Street, Horseferry Road, London SW1P 2AP* 081-746 8083 or 746 8000

RICHARDSON, Canon Charles. b 13. AKC35. Linc Th Coll 35. **d** 36 **p** 37. R Rawmarsh w Parkgate *Sheff* 54-76; Hon Can Sheff Cathl 75-80; R Harthill 76-80; rtd 80; Perm to Offic *Sheff* from 81. *41 Nether Green Road, Sheffield S11 7EH* Sheffield (0742) 304699

RICHARDSON, Charles Leslie. b 54. St Jo Coll Dur BA76. Coll of Resurr Mirfield 77. **d** 79 **p** 80. C Folkestone St Mary and St Eanswythe *Cant* 79-83; C Maidstone St Martin 83-86; Selection Sec and Voc Adv ACCM 86-91; ABM from 91; PV Westmr Abbey from 87. *Old Town Rectory, High Street, Hastings, E Sussex TN34 3ES* Hastings (0424) 422023

RICHARDSON, Clive John. b 57. Trin Coll Bris BA82 Oak Hill Th Coll DipHE83. **d** 83 **p** 84. C Woking St Pet *Guildf* 83-86; C Worplesdon 86-90; V Rowledge from 90. *The Vicarage, Church Lane, Rowledge, Farnham, Surrey GU10 4EN* Frensham (025125) 2402

RICHARDSON, David Anthony. b 41. Kelham Th Coll 57. **d** 66 **p** 67. C Tong *Bradf* 66-68; C Richmond St Mary S'wark 68-71; C Sanderstead All SS 71-74; TV 74-78; R Beddington from 78. *The Rectory, 18 Bloxworth Close, Wallington, Surrey SM6 7NL* 081-647 1973

RICHARDSON, David Gwynne. b 39. K Coll Lon 60. **d** 64 **p** 65. C Birtley *Dur* 64-67; Bp's Soc and Ind Adv 67-77; TV Brayton *York* from 78; Ind Chapl from 78; Chapl IMinE from 85. *20 Mayfield Drive, Brayton, Selby, N Yorkshire YO8 9JZ* Selby (0757) 706239 or 704385

RICHARDSON, David John. b 50. MA LLB. S'wark Ord Course. **d** 85 **p** 86. NSM S Croydon Em *S'wark* from 85. *20 Hurst View Road, South Croydon, Surrey CR2 7AG* 081-688 4947

RICHARDSON, Douglas Stanley. b 23. Bps' Coll Cheshunt 55. **d** 57 **p** 58. C Hampton St Mary *Lon* 57-61; V W Twyford 61-69; V Notting Hill St Pet 69-78; V Staines St Pet 78-83; P-in-c Staines St Mary 81-83; V Staines St Mary and St Pet from 83; AD Spelthorne from 83. *St Peter's Vicarage, 14 Thames Side, Staines, Middx TW18 2HA* Staines (0784) 453039

RICHARDSON, Canon Edward James Aubin. b 10. Ex Coll Ox BA33 MA39. Wycliffe Hall Ox 36. **d** 38 **p** 39. R Jersey St Ouen w St Geo *Win* 47-76; rtd 76; Perm to Offic *Heref* from 77. *The Blessing, 1 Farm Cottage, Snailbeach, Shrewsbury SY5 0LP* Shrewsbury (0743) 791489

RICHARDSON, Canon Eric Hatherley Humphrey. b 12. Qu Coll Ox BA35. Westcott Ho Cam 35. **d** 36 **p** 37. C Stoke Newington St Mary *Lon* 36-39; S Africa from 39. *44 Frere Street, Kensington B, Randburg, 2194 South Africa* Johannesburg (11) 787-7813

RICHARDSON, Geoffrey Stewart. b 47. St Jo Coll Ox BA69 MA73. St Steph Ho Ox 70. **d** 72 **p** 73. C Roxbourne St Andr *Lon* 72-75; C Woodford St Barn *Chelmsf* 75-80; V Goodmayes St Paul 80-87; P-in-c Coates *Linc* from 87; P-in-c Willingham from 87; R Stow in Lindsey from 87. *The Rectory, Normanby Road, Stow, Lincoln LN1 2DF* Gainsborough (0427) 788251

RICHARDSON, Gerald. b 24. Chich Th Coll 54. **d** 56 **p** 57. V Smethwick St Steph *Birm* 67-72; R Aylestone Park *Leic* 72-85; Perm to Offic from 85; rtd 89. *55 Stonesby Avenue, Leicester LE2 6TX* Leicester (0533) 830561

RICHARDSON, Harold. b 22. Worc Ord Coll 62. **d** 64 **p** 65. V Rockcliffe *Carl* 66-74; rtd 87. *21 St Catherine's Place, Edinburgh EH9 1NU* 031-667 8040

RICHARDSON, Canon Jack Cyril. b 11. Leeds Univ BSc36. Coll of Resurr Mirfield 35. **d** 35 **p** 36. R Upper Clatford w Goodworth Clatford *Win* 65-77; rtd 77; Perm to Offic *St Alb* from 78. *Robin Cottage, The Street, Braughing, Ware, Herts SG11 2QR* Ware (0920) 822020

RICHARDSON, James Aidan. b 28. St Chad's Coll Dur BA51 DipTh54. **d** 54 **p** 55. C Ferryhill *Dur* 54-56; C Stirling *Edin* 56-58; P-in-c Bo'ness 58-64; P-in-c Linlithgow 58-64; V Linthwaite *Wakef* 64-79; RD Blackmoorfoot 77-79; V Clifton from 79; P-in-c Hartshead 83-88. *31 Robin Hood Way, Brighouse, W Yorkshire HD6 4LA* Brighouse (0484) 713290

RICHARDSON, James Arthur. b 19. MC44. ARICS53 Lon Univ BSc51. Ridley Hall Cam 60. **d** 62 **p** 62. V Streatham Park St Alb *S'wark* 65-87; rtd 87. *18 Cranden Road, Eastbourne, E Sussex BN20 8LW* Eastbourne (0323) 37711

RICHARDSON, James Horner. b 19. Ch Coll Cam BA42 MA45. Ridley Hall Cam 41. **d** 43 **p** 44. Hon CF from 53; V Huyton St Mich *Liv* 59-70; V Ormskirk 70-80; V Giggleswick *Bradf* 80-82; P-in-c Rathmell 80-82; V Giggleswick and Rathmell w Wigglesworth 82-84; rtd 84; Hon Chapl Spennithorne Hall from 84; Hon C Aysgarth and Bolton cum Redmire *Ripon* from 84. *Mere Cottage, Redmire, Leyburn, N Yorkshire DL8 4ED* Wensleydale (0969) 23917

RICHARDSON, Canon James John. b 41. FRSA91 Hull Univ BA63 Sheff Univ DipEd64. Cuddesdon Coll 66. **d** 69 **p** 70. C Wolv St Pet *Lich* 69-72; P-in-c Hanley All SS 72-75; R Nantwich *Ches* 75-82; Hon Can Ripon Cathl *Ripon* 82-88; V Leeds St Pet 82-88; Exec Dir Coun of Chrs and Jews from 88; Lic to Offic *Pet* from 88. *27 Strawberry Hill, Wellingborough Road, Northampton NN3 5HL* Northampton (0604) 405183

RICHARDSON, John. b 15. OBE70 VRD58. St Aid Birkenhead 46. **d** 48 **p** 49. V Mitford *Newc* 66-82; rtd 82. *3 Home Farm Cottages, Seaton Burn, Newcastle upon Tyne NE13 6DB* Stannington (067089) 582

RICHARDSON, John. b 41. Qu Coll Birm 69. **d** 72 **p** 73. C Ormskirk *Liv* 72-74; C Doncaster St Geo *Sheff* 74-77; R Hemsworth *Wakef* 77-79; V Penallt *Mon* 79-85; R Amotherby w Appleton and Barton-le-Street *York* 85-89; P-in-c Hovingham 86-89; C 89; P-in-c Slingsby 86-89; TR Street Team Min 89-90; R Skelton w Shipton and Newton on Ouse from 90. *The Rectory, Church Lane, Skelton, York YO3 6XT* York (0904) 470045

RICHARDSON, John. b 47. Linc Th Coll 78. **d** 80 **p** 81. C Keighley St Andr *Bradf* 80-83; V Hugglescote w Donington *Leic* 83-84; V Hugglescote w Donington-le-Heath and Ellistown 84-86; TR Hugglescote w Donington, Ellistown and Snibston from 86; RD Akeley S (Coalville) from 87. *The Rectory, Grange Road, Hugglescote, Leicester LE6 2SQ* Coalville (0530) 32557

RICHARDSON, John. b 55. Lon Univ BEd BD. St Steph Ho Ox. **d** 83 **p** 84. C Thornbury *Glouc* 83-86; C Sheff Parson Cross St Cecilia *Sheff* 86-87; C Clacton St Jas *Chelmsf* 87-90; R Gt Tey and Wakes Colne w Chappel from 90. *The Rectory, Brook Road, Great Tey, Colchester CO6 1JF* Colchester (0206) 211481

RICHARDSON, John Hedley. b 45. Leeds Univ BA72. Qu Coll Birm 72. **d** 74 **p** 75. C Chaddesden St Phil *Derby* 74-76; Perm to Offic 76-86; TV Old Brampton and Loundsley Green 86-91; R Caston w Griston, Merton,

Thompson etc *Nor* from 91. *The Rectory, Caston, Attleborough, Norfolk NR17 1DD* Caston (095383) 222

RICHARDSON, Canon John Henry. b 37. Trin Hall Cam BA61 MA65. Cuddesdon Coll 61. **d** 63 **p** 64. C Stevenage *St Alb* 63-66; C Eastbourne St Mary *Chich* 66-68; V Chipperfield St Paul *St Alb* 68-75; V Rickmansworth 75-86; RD Rickmansworth 77-86; V Bishop's Stortford St Mich from 86; Hon Can St Alb from 87. *St Michael's Vicarage, 27 Church Street, Bishop's Stortford, Herts* Bishop's Stortford (0279) 654416

RICHARDSON, John Humphrey. b 33. Dur Univ BA57. Chich Th Coll 57. **d** 59 **p** 60. C Bexhill St Barn *Chich* 59-61; C Stanmer w Falmer and Moulscoomb 61-64; C Ifield 64-70; R Earnley and E Wittering 70-79; V Stamford All SS w St Pet *Linc* 79-81; R Stamford St Jo w St Clem 79-81; RD Aveland and Ness w Stamford 80-87; V Stamford All SS w St Jo from 81. *All Saints' Vicarage, 8 St Peter's Hill, Stamford, Lincs PE9 2PE* Stamford (0780) 62163

RICHARDSON, John Malcolm. b 39. Glas Univ MA60 BD63. Andover Newton Th Coll STM65 Edin Th Coll 84. **d** 84 **p** 85. C Edin Old St Paul *Edin* 84-86; R Leven *St And* 86-90; R Newport-on-Tay from 90; R Tayport from 90. *St Mary's Rectory, 8 High Street, Newport-on-Tay, Fife DD6 8DA* Newport-on-Tay (0382) 543311

RICHARDSON, John Paul. b 44. St Steph Ho Ox 74. **d** 76 **p** 77. C Kingsbury St Andr *Lon* 76-78; C Blackpool St Steph *Blackb* 78-79; C Marton 79-81; V Newchurch-in-Pendle 81-83; V Leigh St Jo *Man* 83-89; TR Stanley *Dur* from 89. *St Andrew's Rectory, Churchbank, Stanley, Co Durham DH9 0DU* Stanley (0207) 233936

RICHARDSON, John Peter. b 50. Keele Univ BA72. St Jo Coll Nottm 73. **d** 76 **p** 77. C Birm St Paul *Birm* 76-79; C Blackheath 79-81; P-in-c Sparkbrook Ch Ch 81-83; Chapl NE Lon Poly *Chelmsf* from 83; Hon C Stratford St Jo and Ch Ch w Forest Gate St Jas from 83. *4 Matthew's Park Avenue, London E15 4AE* 081-536 0230 or 590 7722

RICHARDSON, Very Rev John Stephen. b 50. Southn Univ BA71. St Jo Coll Nottm 72. **d** 74 **p** 75. C Bramcote *S'well* 74-77; C Radipole and Melcombe Regis *Sarum* 77-80; P-in-c Stinsford, Winterborne Came w Whitcombe etc 80-83; Asst Dioc Missr 80-83; V Nailsea Ch Ch *B & W* 83-90; Adv on Evang 86-90; Provost Bradf from 90. *The Provost's House, Cathedral Close, Bradford BD1 4EG* Bradford (0274) 732023

RICHARDSON, Prof John Stuart. b 46. Trin Coll Ox BA68 MA71 DPhil73. **d** 79 **p** 80. NSM St Andrews St Andr *St And* 79-87; Chapl St Andr Univ 80-87; Prof Classics Edin Univ from 87; TV Edin St Columba *Edin* from 87. *29 Merchiston Avenue, Edinburgh EH10 4PH* 031-228 3094

RICHARDSON, John William. b 56. Bp Otter Coll BA85. Chich Th Coll 85. **d** 87 **p** 88. C E Preston w Kingston *Chich* 87-89; C Goring-by-Sea 89-90; TV Aldrington from 91. *12 Walsingham Road, Hove, E Sussex BN3 4FF* Brighton (0273) 720373

RICHARDSON, Joseph Edmund. b 27. St Chad's Coll Dur BA49. Sarum Th Coll 51. **d** 52 **p** 53. R Davenham *Ches* 65-76; V Sale St Anne 76-84; R Delamere 84-88; rtd 88. *2 Dol Acar, Rhyd-y-Foel, Abergele, Clwyd LL22 8DX*

RICHARDSON, Maurice. b 12. **d** 66 **p** 67. V Lowdham *S'well* 69-77; rtd 77; Perm to Offic S'well from 77; Leic from 82. *Old Orchard, Granby, Nottingham NG13 9PR* Whatton (0949) 50860

RICHARDSON, Neil. b 46. Southn Univ BTh83. Sarum & Wells Th Coll 71. **d** 74 **p** 75. C Oldham St Mary w St Pet *Man* 74-77; C-in-c Holts CD 77-82; R Greenford H Cross *Lon* from 82. *The Rectory, Oldfield Lane, Greenford, Middx UB6 9JS* 081-578 1543

RICHARDSON, Paul. b 58. Univ of Wales (Cardiff) BSc80. Ridley Hall Cam 81. **d** 84 **p** 85. C Stanwix *Carl* 84-87; Ind Chapl 87-89; Staff Priest Dalton-in-Furness 87-89; V Marton Moss *Blackb* from 89. *The Vicarage, 187 Common Edge Road, Blackpool FY4 5DL* Blackpool (0253) 62658

RICHARDSON, Robert Trevor. b 34. St Mich Coll Llan 58. **d** 60 **p** 61. C Cymmer and Porth *Llan* 60-62; C Worsley *Man* 62-65; V Waterfoot from 65. *The Vicarage, Waterfoot, Rossendale, Lancs* Rossendale (0706) 215959

RICHARDSON, Ronald Eric. b 48. York Univ CertEd Leeds Univ BEd. N Ord Course. **d** 82 **p** 83. NSM Wakef St Andr and St Mary *Wakef* 82-83; C 83-90; NSM S Ossett from 90. *37 Stanley Road, Wakefield, W Yorkshire WF1 4NA* Wakefield (0924) 381047

RICHARDSON, Simon John. b 56. Univ of Wales (Ban) BA77. Ridley Hall Cam 81. **d** 84 **p** 85. C Luton St Mary

St Alb 84-88; C Middleton *Man* from 88. *206 Rochdale Road, Middleton, Manchester M24 2GH* 061-643 4913

RICHARDSON, Stephen. b 99. Worc Ord Coll 57. **d** 58 **p** 59. R Meysey Hampton w Marston Meysey *Glouc* 61-73; Perm to Offic from 73; rtd 75. *The Lee, Church Street, Meysey Hampton, Cirencester, Glos GL7 5JU* Poulton (028585) 407

RICHARDSON, Miss Susan. b 58. Cranmer Hall Dur. **d** 87. Par Dn Stokesley *York* 87-91; Par Dn Beverley St Nic from 91. *11 Cherry Garth, Beverley, N Humberside HU17 0ET* Hull (0482) 870505

RICHARDSON, Thomas Warner. b 11. St Jo Coll Dur BA38 MA44. Westcott Ho Cam 38. **d** 38 **p** 39. Hon CF from 46; V St Austell *Truro* 65-72; P-in-c Teversal *S'well* 72-76; rtd 76. *27 Woodlands Meadows, Huddersfield HD8 0XQ* Huddersfield (0484) 607433

RICHARDSON, Thomas Wood. b 16. Newc Ord Sch 61 Cranmer Hall Dur 65. **d** 66 **p** 67. C Rothbury *Newc* 66-70; C Hexham 70-75; V Chevington 75-84; rtd 84. *46 Fountain Head Bank, Seaton Sluice, Whitley Bay, Tyne & Wear NE26 4HU* 091-237 1405

RICHARDSON, Trevor Charles. b 37. Keble Coll Ox BA60 MA64. Westcott Ho Cam 78. **d** 78 **p** 79. C W Hampstead St Jas *Lon* 78-82; V St Pancras H Cross w St Jude and St Pet from 82. *47 Argyle Square, London WC1H 8AL* 071-278 5238

RICHARDSON, Canon William. b 11. Qu Coll Ox BA34 MA37 BD52. Ripon Hall Ox 35. **d** 36 **p** 37. Can and Preb York Minster *York* 70-87; TR Sutton St Jas and Wawne 71-78; rtd 78. *1 Precentor's Court, York YO1 2EJ* York (0904) 39237

RICHENS, Canon Geoffrey Roger. b 23. ALCD52. **d** 52 **p** 53. C St Helens St Helen *Liv* 52-56; V Widnes St Mary 56-80; V Skelmersdale St Paul from 80; Hon Can Liv Cathl from 89. *The Vicarage, Church Road, Skelmersdale, Lancs WN8 8ND* Skelmersdale (0695) 22087

RICHERBY, Glynn. b 51. K Coll Lon BD73 AKC73. St Aug Coll Cant 73. **d** 74 **p** 75. C Weston Favell *Pet* 74-78; Prec Leic Cathl *Leic* 78-81; V Glen Parva and S Wigston from 81; Dir Post Ord Tr from 86. *The Vicarage, 1 St Thomas's Road, Wigston, Leicester LE8 2TA* Leicester (0533) 782830

RICHES, John Kenneth. b 39. CCC Cam BA61 MA65. Westcott Ho Cam 62. **d** 65 **p** 66. C Costessey *Nor* 65-68; Chapl SS Coll Cam 68-73; Lect Glas Univ 73-86; Sen Lect from 86; Chmn Balmore Trust from 80; Lic to Offic *Glas* from 85. *Viewfield, Balmore, Glasgow G64 4AE* Balmore (0360) 20254

✠**RICHES, Rt Rev Kenneth.** b 08. CCC Cam BA31 MA35. Gen Th Sem (NY) Hon STD56 Lambeth DD57. Cuddesdon Coll 32. **d** 32 **p** 33 **c** 52. C Portsea St Mary *Portsm* 32-35; C E Dulwich St Jo *S'wark* 35-36; Chapl SS Coll Cam Bradf 36-44; Lic to Offic *Bradf* 36-44; R Bredfield w Boulge *St E* 42-44; Prin Cuddesdon Coll 44-52; V Cuddesdon *Ox* 44-52; Hon Can Portsm Cathl *Portsm* 50-52; Adn Ox and Can Res Ch Ch *Ox* 52-56; Suff Bp Dorchester 52-56; Bp Linc 56-74; rtd 74; Perm to Offic *St E* from 74. *Little Dingle, Dunwich, Saxmundham, Suffolk IP17 3EA* Westleton (072873) 316

RICHEY, Canon Robert Samuel Payne. b 23. TCD BA46. **d** 48 **p** 49. C Moy *Arm* 48-50; I Killinagh w Kiltyclogher *K, E & A* 50-60; I Killinagh w Kiltyclogher and Innismagrath 60-72; I Killinagh w Kiltyclogher, Killargue etc 72-91; I Killinagh w Kiltyclogher and Innismagrath from 91; Sec Dioc Bd Educn from 64; Dioc Sec (Kilmore) from 72; Preb Kilmore Cathl from 80; Dioc Info Officer (Kilmore) from 81. *Killinagh Rectory, Blacklion, Sligo, Irish Republic* Bundoran (72) 53010

RICHMOND, Arnold. b 19. Sarum & Wells Th Coll 77. **d** 80 **p** 81. NSM Axminster *Ex* 80-83; Dep PV Ex Cathl from 83; NSM Axminster, Chardstock, Combe Pyne and Rousdon 83-86; NSM Colyton, Southleigh, Offwell, Widworthy etc from 86. *New House Farm, Combpyne Road, Musbury, Axminster, Devon EX13 6SS* Colyton (0297) 53501

✠**RICHMOND, Rt Rev Francis Henry Arthur.** b 36. TCD BA59 MA66 Strasbourg Univ BTh60 Linacre Coll Ox MLitt64. Wycliffe Hall Ox 60. **d** 63 **p** 64 **c** 86. C Woodlands *Sheff* 63-66; Chapl Sheff Cathl 66-69; V Sheff St Geo 69-77; Chapl Sheff Univ 74-77; Warden Linc Th Coll 77-86; Can and Preb Linc Cathl *Linc* 77-86; Suff Bp Repton *Derby* from 86; Hon Can Derby Cathl from 86. *Repton House, Lea, Matlock, Derbyshire DE4 5JP* Dethick (0629) 534644

RICHMOND, Gordon Hazlewood. b 33. Launde Abbey 77. **d** 79 **p** 80. C Leic St Paul *Leic* 79-81; C Shepshed 81-84; V Ryhall w Essendine *Pet* 84-91; RD Barnack from 89; V Gretton w Rockingham and Caldecote from

91. *The Vicarage, Gretton, Corby, Northants NN17 3BY* Rockingham (0536) 770237

RICHMOND, Peter James. b 54. Writtle Agric Coll HND76. St Jo Coll Nottm LTh80. **d** 80 **p** 81. C Ogley Hay *Lich* 80-83; C Trentham 83-85; P-in-c Wolv St Jo 85-89; P-in-c Loppington w Newtown from 89; P-in-c Edstaston from 89. *The Vicarage, Loppington, Shrewsbury SY4 5ST* Wem (0939) 33388

RICHMOND, Archdeacon of. *See* McDERMID, Ven Norman George Lloyd Roberts

RICKETTS, Allan Fenn. b 46. Open Univ BA76. Cranmer Hall Dur 68. **d** 71 **p** 72. C Rowley Regis *Birm* 71-72; C The Quinton 72-74; C Brierley Hill *Lich* 74-77; TV Chelmsley Wood *Birm* 77-82; TV Ross w Brampton Abbotts, Bridstow and Peterstow *Heref* 82-88; R Linton w Upton Bishop and Aston Ingham from 88. *Linton Rectory, Ross-on-Wye, Herefordshire HR9 7RX* Ross-on-Wye (0989) 82472

RICKETTS, Miss Kathleen Mary. b 39. CertEd59 Univ of W Aus BA79. Westcott Ho Cam 81. **dss** 83 **d** 87. All Hallows by the Tower etc *Lon* 83-87; Par Dn 87-88; Par Dn Hall Green Ascension *Birm* from 88. *40 Studland Road, Hall Green, Birmingham B28 8NW* 021-777 5800

RICKETTS, Peter William. b 28. DLC53. St Alb Minl Tr Scheme 76. **d** 79 **p** 80. NSM Hertf All SS *St Alb* 79-86; R Blunham w Tempsford and Lt Barford from 86. *The Rectory, Park Lane, Blunham, Bedford MK44 3NJ* Biggleswade (0767) 40298

RIDDEL, Canon Robert John. b 37. CITC. **d** 68 **p** 69. C Derryloran *Arm* 68-74; I Keady w Armaghbreague and Derrynoose 74-80; I Mullaghdun *Clogh* 80-84; I Cleenish 80-84; I Fivemiletown from 84; RD Clogh from 85; Can Clogh Cathl from 91. *The Rectory, Fivemiletown, Co Tyrone* Fivemiletown (03655) 31030

RIDDELL, Morris Stroyan. b 34. Lon Univ DipTh59 BD69. Tyndale Hall Bris 57. **d** 60 **p** 60. R Bris St Jo w St Mary-le-Port *Bris* 67-70; Dir Bris Samaritans 67-70; Chapl HM Pris Long Lartin 71-74; Brixton 74-78; Chapl Cane Hill Hosp Coulsdon 78-85; Chapl HM Rem Cen Latchmere Ho 85-89; rtd 89. *Flat 3, 30 Montpelier Crescent, Brighton BN1 3JJ* Brighton (0273) 29229

RIDDELSDELL, Canon John Creffield. b 23. Selw Coll Cam BA47 MA52 Lon Univ BD70. Ridley Hall Cam 47. **d** 49 **p** 50. Kenya 52-77; V Gt Ilford St Andr *Chelmsf* 77-88; rtd 88. *Waverley, Mill Lane, Walton on the Naze, Essex CO14 8PE* Clacton-on-Sea (0225) 850213

RIDDING, George. b 24. Or Coll Ox BA50 MA57. Wells Th Coll 60. **d** 61 **p** 62. Hd Master W Buckland Sch Barnstaple 68-78; USPG 78-82; P-in-c Broadhembury w Payhembury *Ex* 82-83; P-in-c Plymtree 82-83; R Broadhembury, Payhembury and Plymtree 83-89; rtd 89. *Cherwell, Higher Blandford Road, Shaftesbury, Dorset SP7 8DA* Shaftesbury (0747) 51390

RIDDING, William Thomas. b 54. Southn Univ BTh. Sarum & Wells Th Coll 80. **d** 83 **p** 84. C Verwood *Sarum* 83-86; TV Gillingham from 86. *The Rectory, Buckhorn Weston, Gillingham, Dorset SP8 5HG* Templecombe (0963) 70215

RIDDLE, Kenneth Wilkinson. b 20. St Cath Soc Ox BA42 MA46. Ripon Hall Ox 42. **d** 43 **p** 44. R Lowestoft St Marg *Nor* 65-68; rtd 85. *The Old Post Office, East Lyng, Taunton, Somerset TA3 5AU* Burrowbridge (082369) 427

RIDEOUT, Preb Gordon Trevor. b 38. BA87. Lon Coll of Div 58. **d** 62 **p** 63. C Southgate *Chich* 62-65; Chapl Dr Barnardo's Barkingside & Woodford Br 65-67; CF 67-73; V Nutley *Chich* 73-79; V Eastbourne All SS from 79; Chapl Brighton Poly from 80; Preb Chich Cathl from 90. *All Saints' Vicarage, Grange Road, Eastbourne, Sussex BN21 4HE* Eastbourne (0323) 410033

RIDER, Andrew. b 62. RMN85 Nottm Univ BTh90. Aston Tr Scheme 85 St Jo Coll Nottm 87. **d** 90 **p** 91. C Luton Ch Ch *Roch* from 90. *11 Fallowfield, Chatham, Kent ME5 0DU* Medway (0634) 408246

RIDER, Canon Dennis William Austin. b 34. Lon Univ DipTh61. St Aid Birkenhead 58. **d** 61 **p** 62. C Derby St Aug *Derby* 61-64; C Sutton *Liv* 64-67; R Stiffkey w Morston, Langham Episcopi etc *Nor* 67-71; V Buxton w Oxnead 71-79; R Lammas w Lt Hautbois 72-79; R Gaywood, Bawsey and Mintlyn 79-91; RD Lynn 89-91; Hon Can Nor Cathl from 90; R E Dereham and Scarning from 91. *The Vicarage, 1 Vicarage Meadows, Dereham, Norfolk NR19 1TW* Dereham (0362) 693143

RIDER, Geoffrey Malcolm. b 29. Selw Coll Cam BA53 MA57. Coll of Resurr Mirfield 53. **d** 55 **p** 56. C S Elmsall *Wakef* 55-60; C Barnsley St Mary 60-63; V Cleckheaton St Jo 63-67; Lic to Offic S'wark from 68; *Lon* from 75. *58 Melbury Gardens, London SW20 0DJ* 081-946 5735

RIDER, Neil Wilding. b 35. St Jo Coll Dur BA59 DipTh61. Cranmer Hall Dur 59. **d** 62 **p** 63. C Blackb St Barn *Blackb* 62-64; C Chadderton Em *Man* 64-69; C Deane 69-72; V Coldhurst 72-75; Perm to Offic Ely 76-78; St D from 80; C Didsbury Ch Ch 78-80. *Caergrawnt, Cwmann, Lampeter, Dyfed SA48 8EL* Lampeter (0570) 422921

RIDGE, Aubrey. b 25. Oak Hill Th Coll 67. **d** 68 **p** 69. C Gorleston St Andr *Nor* 68-70; C Hamworthy *Sarum* 70-75; P-in-c Pitsea *Chelmsf* 75-78; R 78-81; P-in-c Stoke Ash, Thwaite and Wetheringsett *St E* 81-85; P-in-c Bedingfield and Thorndon w Rishangles 81-85; P-in-c Thorndon w Rishangles, Stoke Ash, Thwaite etc 85-86; P-in-c Risby w Gt and Lt Saxham and Westley 86-90; rtd 90. *59 Holloway Road, Dorchester, Dorset DT1 1LF* Dorchester (0305) 260180

RIDGE, Haydn Stanley. b 24. Univ of Wales (Lamp) BA51 Bris Univ CertEd52. Qu Coll Birm 56. **d** 56 **p** 57. Div Master Guernsey Gr Sch 60-75; Hon C Guernsey St Steph *Win* from 62; Dep Hd St Peter Port Sch 75-80; Hd St Sampson Sch 75-87; rtd 91. *St David, Les Cherfs, Castel, Guernsey, Channel Islands* Guernsey (0481) 56209

RIDGEWAY, David. b 59. St Chad's Coll Dur BSc80 Cam Univ CertEd81. Ripon Coll Cuddesdon 84. **d** 87 **p** 88. C Kempston Transfiguration *St Alb* 87-90; C Radlett from 90. *43 Gills Hill Lane, Radlett, Herts WD7 8DG* Radlett (0923) 855921

RIDGEWELL, Kenneth William. b 29. Lich Th Coll 56. **d** 59 **p** 60. Jerusalem 69-71; C Northwood H Trin *Lon* 71-73; Asst Chapl St Bart Hosp Lon 73-80; Chapl Herrison Hosp Dorchester 81-86; rtd 86. *Address temp unknown*

RIDGEWELL, Miss Mary Jean. b 54. Dur Univ BA76 PGCE77. Ridley Hall Cam 89. **d** 91. Par Dn Trowbridge St Jas *Sarum* from 91. *33 Gloucester Road, Trowbridge, Wilts BA14 0AA* Trowbridge (0225) 751912

RIDGWAY, David. b 28. Trin Hall Cam BA54 MA58. Westcott Ho Cam 54. **d** 56 **p** 57. C Milton *Portsm* 56-59; CF 59-63; R Gosforth *Carl* 63-70; V Walney Is 70-76; P-in-c Irthington 76-78; P-in-c Crosby-on-Eden 77-78; V Irthington, Crosby-on-Eden and Scaleby from 79. *The New Vicarage, Irthington, Carlisle CA6 4NJ* Brampton (06977) 2379

RIDGWAY, Mrs Janet Elizabeth Knight. b 40. St Alb Minl Tr Scheme. **dss** 86 **d** 87. Tring *St Alb* 86-87; Hon Par Dn from 87. *Barleycombe, Trooper Road, Aldbury, Tring, Herts HP23 4RW* Aldbury Common (044285) 303

RIDGWAY, Canon Maurice Hill. b 18. FSA St D Coll Lamp BA40. Westcott Ho Cam 40. **d** 41 **p** 42. V Bowdon *Ches* 62-83; rtd 83; Perm to Offic *Ches* and *St As* from 83; *Lich* from 84. *Milkwood Cottage, Rhydycroesau, Oswestry, Shropshire SY10 7PS* Oswestry (0691) 655330

RIDING, Pauline Alison. b 61. SEN82. Oak Hill Th Coll BA90. **d** 90. Par Dn Moor Allerton *Ripon* from 90. *409 Harrogate Road, Leeds LS17 7BY* Leeds (0532) 681900

RIDLEY, Alfred Forbes. b 34. Bps' Coll Cheshunt 62. **d** 65 **p** 66. C Prittlewell St Mary *Chelmsf* 65-69; R Paulerspury *Pet* 69-73; P-in-c Wicken 71-73; V W Haddon w Winwick 73-83; RD Brixworth 80-83; R Guernsey St Philippe de Torteval *Win* from 83; R Guernsey St Pierre du Bois from 83. *The Rectory, St Pierre du Bois, Guernsey, Channel Islands* Guernsey (0481) 63544

RIDLEY, Andrew Roy. b 55. St Pet Coll Ox BA77. Ripon Coll Cuddesdon 78. **d** 79 **p** 80. C Bollington St Jo *Ches* 79-83; V Runcorn St Mich from 83. *St Michael's Vicarage, 145 Greenway Road, Runcorn, Cheshire WA7 4NR* Runcorn (09285) 72417

RIDLEY, Derek. b 40. Newc Univ BSc74. Cranmer Hall Dur 75. **d** 78 **p** 79. C Upperby St Jo *Carl* 78-81; C Penrith w Newton Reigny 81; C Penrith w Newton Reigny and Plumpton Wall 81-82; TV 82-86; V Cadishead *Man* from 86. *St Mary's Vicarage, Penry Avenue, Cadishead, Manchester M30 5AF* 061-775 2171

RIDLEY, Jay. b 41. Birm Univ BA63. St Steph Ho Ox 63. **d** 65 **p** 66. C Woodford St Mary *Chelmsf* 65-67; C Prittlewell St Mary 67-70; C-in-c Dunscroft CD *Sheff* 70-75; Chapl HM Pris Wormwood Scrubs 75-77; HM Rem Cen Ashford 77-84; Chapl HM Young Offender Inst Feltham 84-91; Chapl HM Pris Ashwell from 91. *HM Prison Ashwell, Oakham, Leics LE15 7LS* Oakham (0572) 756075

RIDLEY, John Sidney. b 15. Trin Coll Cam BA37 MA43. Chich Th Coll 37. **d** 39 **p** 40. Chapl Emscote Lawn Sch Warw 64-72; Asst Master St Dunstan's Coll Catford

72-81; Lic to Offic *S'wark* from 72; rtd 81. *4 Morden Road, London SE3 0AA*

RIDLEY, Canon Laurence Roy. b 19. St Pet Hall Ox BA41 MA45. Wycliffe Hall Ox 41. **d** 42 **p** 43. V Higher Bebington *Ches* 69-90; RD Wirral N 79-89; Hon Can Ches Cathl 80-90; rtd 90. *6 Newtons Lane, Winterley, Sandbach, Cheshire CW11 9NL* Crewe (0270) 505929

RIDLEY, Lesley. b 46. Cranmer Hall Dur 75. **dss** 78 **d** 87. Upperby St Jo *Carl* 78-81; Penrith w Newton Reigny and Plumpton Wall 81-86; Cadishead *Man* 86-87; Par Dn from 87. *St Mary's Vicarage, Penry Avenue, Cadishead, Manchester M30 5AF* 061-775 2171

RIDLEY, Michael Edward. b 37. Ex Univ MA90. AKC62. **d** 63 **p** 64. C Chapel Allerton *Ripon* 63-67; C Epsom St Martin *Guildf* 67-70; C Claxby w Normanby-le-Wold etc *Linc* 70-72; V Leake 72-75; R Harlaxton w Wyville and Hungerton 75-80; R Stroxton 76-80; Dioc Stewardship Adv *Portsm* 80-86; P-in-c Rowlands Castle 80-82; C Blendworth w Chalton w Idsworth & Finchdean Castle 83-86; TV N Creedy *Ex* 86-90; R W Downland Sarum from 90. *The Rectory, Mill End, Damerham, Fordingbridge, Hants SP6 3HU* Rockbourne (07253) 642

RIDLEY, Michael Laurence. b 59. BA81. Ripon Coll Cuddesdon 81. **d** 83 **p** 84. C Bollington St Jo *Ches* 83-88; V Thelwall from 88. *The Vicarage, Bell Lane, Thelwall, Warrington WA4 2SX* Warrington (0925) 61166

RIDLEY, Peter John. b 39. Keble Coll Ox BA61. Tyndale Hall Bris 61. **d** 63 **p** 64. C Clifton Ch Ch w Em *Bris* 63-67; C Lambeth St Andr w St Thos *S'wark* 67-69; V W Hampstead St Cuth *Lon* 69-77; V Eynsham *Ox* 77-85; RD Woodstock 82-84; V Nicholforest and Kirkandrews on Esk *Carl* from 85. *Nicholforest Vicarage, Penton, Carlisle CA6 5QF* Nicholforest (022877) 221

RIDLEY, Stephen James. b 57. St Pet Coll Ox MA83. Ripon Coll Cuddesdon 80. **d** 82 **p** 83. C Heald Green St Cath *Ches* 82-85; Chapl Ches Coll 85-90; Dioc Press Officer 85-90; Chapl Birkenhead Sch Merseyside from 90. *1 Kingsmead Road South, Oxton, Birkenhead L43 6TA* 051-652 7495

RIDLEY, Stewart Gordon. b 47. AKC72. St Aug Coll Cant 72. **d** 73 **p** 74. C St Bart Armley w St Mary New Wortley *Ripon* 73-77; C Hawksworth Wood 77-79; C Rothwell w Lofthouse 79-81; R Whitwood *Wakef* 81-87; R Ingoldmells w Addlethorpe *Linc* from 87; RD Calcewaithe and Candleshoe from 89. *The Rectory, Ingoldmells, Skegness, Lincs PE25 1QG* Skegness (0754) 73906

RIDOUT, Christopher John. b 33. K Coll Lon BD57 AKC57. **d** 58 **p** 59. C Roxeth Ch Ch *Lon* 58-62; CMS 62-63; Kenya 63-75; C Gt Malvern St Mary *Worc* 75-79; R Bredon w Bredon's Norton from 79; RD Pershore from 91. *The Rectory, Bredon, Tewkesbury, Glos GL20 7LF* Bredon (0684) 72237

✠**RIDSDALE, Rt Rev Philip Bullen.** b 15. Trin Coll Cam BA37 MA45. Ridley Hall Cam 45. **d** 47 **p** 48 **c** 72. C St Helens St Helen *Liv* 47-49; Uganda 49-64; Adn Ruwenzori 61-64; Hon Can Ruwenzori from 63; R Bramfield w Stapleford *St Alb* 64-66; R Bramfield w Stapleford and Waterford 66-72; RD Hertf 70-72; Bp Boga-Zaire 72-80; rtd 81; Perm to Offic *Ely* from 81. *3 Pemberton Terrace, Cambridge CB2 1JA* Cambridge (0223) 62690

RIDYARD, Preb John Gordon. b 33. St Aid Birkenhead 59. **d** 62 **p** 63. C Lanc St Mary *Blackb* 62-65; C Bushbury *Lich* 65-68; V Darlaston All SS 68-76; TV Wolv St Mark 76-78; TV Wolv 78-82; Preb Lich Cathl from 82; V Bishopswood 82-89; V Brewood 82-89; RD Penkridge 83-89; R Newc w Butterton from 89. *The Rectory, Seabridge Road, Newcastle-under-Lyme, Staffs ST5 2HS* Newcastle-under-Lyme (0782) 616397

RIDYARD, Malcolm Charles. b 32. St D Coll Lamp BA54 Wycliffe Hall Ox 54. **d** 56 **p** 57. C Widnes St Paul *Liv* 56-59; C Ashton-in-Makerfield St Thos 59-61; India 62-71; Area Sec (Dios B & W, Bris and Sarum) CMS 71-80; P-in-c Church Coniston *Carl* 80-87; P-in-c Torver 80-87; R Bootle, Corney, Whicham and Whitbeck from 87. *The Rectory, Bootle, Millom, Cumbria LA19 5TH* Bootle (06578) 223

RIEM, Roland Gerardus Anthony. b 60. St Chad's Coll Dur BSc82 Kent Univ PhD86. St Jo Coll Nottm DipTh87 DPS89. **d** 89 **p** 90. C Deal St Leon and St Rich and Sholden *Cant* from 89. *327 London Road, Deal, Kent CT14 9PR* Deal (0304) 372597

RIESS, Trevor William. b 54. Down Coll Cam MA76 CertEd77. St Jo Coll Nottm 84. **d** 86 **p** 87. C Stainforth *Sheff* 86-88; Chapl St Jas Choir Sch Grimsby 89; C Lowestoft and Kirkley *Nor* 89-90; TV from 90;

Lothingland Hosp from 90. *8 Oulton Street, Lowestoft, Suffolk NR32 3BB* Lowestoft (0502) 574185

RIGBY, Francis Michael. d 90. NSM Alvescot w Black Bourton, Shilton, Holwell etc *Ox* from 90. *20 Garner Close, Carterton, Oxford OX8 3GA* Carterton (0993) 842701

RIGBY, Harold. b 34. Nottm Univ BA56 Man Poly DipEd77. Ripon Hall Ox BA58 MA62. **d** 58 **p** 59. C Barlow Moor *Man* 58-61; C Bury St Jo 61-64; C-in-c Lostock CD 64-76; C Davyhulme St Mary 76; Hon C 76-79; Lic to Offic from 79. *17 Atwood Road, Disbury, Manchester M20 0TA* 061-445 7454

RIGBY, John Basil. b 19. Sarum Th Coll 46. **d** 48 **p** 49. V Boreham Wood All SS *St Alb* 61-72; V Sandbach *Ches* 72-83; rtd 83; Perm to Offic *Ches* from 83. *6 West Way, Sandbach, Cheshire CW11 9LQ* Crewe (0270) 763615

RIGBY, Joseph. b 37. Open Univ BA72. Ox NSM Course. **d** 78 **p** 79. NSM Earley St Pet *Ox* 78-80; C Penzance St Mary w St Paul *Truro* 80-82; V Mevagissey 82-83; P-in-c St Ewe 83; R Mevagissey and St Ewe 83-90; rtd 90. *Woodville, Agar Road, Truro TR1 1JU*

RIGBY, Michael John. b 52. MA MSc. Ridley Hall Cam. **d** 82 **p** 83. C Reading St Jo *Ox* 82-86; C Wallington H Trin *S'wark* from 86. *47 Park Hill Road, Wallington, Surrey SM6 0RU* 081-647 7551

RIGBY, Ronald Robert Pierpoint. b 13. Bris Univ BA34 St Cath Soc Ox BA36 MA41. Wycliffe Hall Ox 34. **d** 36 **p** 37. V Michael *S & M* 65-72; Lic to Offic 72-76; Perm to Offic 76-90; rtd 78. *Hope Cottage, Poortown, Peel, Isle of Man* Peel (0624) 842822

RIGBY, William. b 51. Leic Univ BSc(Econ)72 Newc Poly BSc82. Cranmer Hall Dur 86. **d** 88 **p** 89. C Morpeth *Newc* from 88. *19 The Turn, Morpeth, Northd NE61 2DU* Morpeth (0670) 511662

RIGG, Arthur Neville. b 17. Lanc Univ MA69. St Aid Birkenhead 49. **d** 51 **p** 52. V Kirkby Stephen *Carl* 70-80; rtd 81; Perm to Offic *Carl* from 81. *Nab Barn, South Dyke, Penrith, Cumbria CA11 9LL* Lazonby (076883) 762

RIGG, John Foster. b 15. **d** 44 **p** 46. R Bawdrip *B & W* 69-86; rtd 86; Perm to Offic *B & W* from 86. *6 Spaxton Road, Durleigh, Bridgwater, Somerset TA5 2AP* Bridgwater (0278) 423937

RIGGS, Marcus John Ralph. b 55. Brighton Poly BA78 Southn Univ BTh82. Chich Th Coll 79. **d** 82 **p** 83. C St Leonards Ch Ch and St Mary *Chich* 82-85; C Eastbourne St Andr 85-86; C Brighton St Mich 86-88; Asst Dir Dioc Bd of Soc Resp from 88. *35 Camelford Street, Brighton BN2 1TQ* Brighton (0273) 605706

RIGGS, Sidney James. b 39. Bps' Coll Cheshunt 62. **d** 63 **p** 64. C S'wark St Geo *S'wark* 63-66; C Plymouth Crownhill Ascension *Ex* 66-69; Asst Youth Chapl *Glouc* 69-71; Hon Min Can Glouc Cathl 71-74; Min Can Glouc Cathl 74-76; V Glouc St Mary de Lode and St Nic from 76. *38 St Mary's Square, Gloucester GL1 2QT* Gloucester (0452) 412679

RIGHTON, Sidney Lawrence. b 13. Bps' Coll Cheshunt 46. **d** 48 **p** 49. V Dewsbury Moor *Wakef* 67-76; V Darrington w Wentbridge 76-79; rtd 79. *Flat 2, Hereford Court, Hereford Road, Harrogate, N Yorkshire HG1 2PX* Harrogate (0423) 507128

RIGLER, Edgar Henry (Tony). b 18. St Jo Coll Dur BA50. Wycliffe Hall Ox 48. **d** 50 **p** 51. V Ealing Dean St Jo *Lon* 67-80; P-in-c Ealing St Jas 77-80; V Portsea St Luke *Portsm* 80-88; rtd 88; Hon Bp's Adv on Evang *Portsm* 88-90. *50 John Amner Close, Chevington Park, Lynn Road, Ely, Cambs CB6 1DT* Ely (0353) 668100

RILEY, Preb Harold. b 03. Birm Univ BA24. Coll of Resurr Mirfield 25. **d** 27 **p** 28. V Kilburn St Aug w St Jo *Lon* 55-75; rtd 75; P-in-c St Mary Aldermary *Lon* 76-81; C 81-84. *49 Delaware Mansions, London W9 2LH* 071-289 3734

RILEY, Harold Collier. b 15. Selw Coll Cam BA37 MA43. Linc Th Coll 37. **d** 39 **p** 40. R Alvescot, Black Bourton and Shilton *Ox* 63-79; R Alvescot w Black Bourton, Shilton, Holwell etc 80-82; rtd 82; Perm to Offic *Win* from 82. *8 Lyster Road, Fordingbridge, Hants SP6 1QY* Fordingbridge (0425) 655326

RILEY, John Graeme. b 55. St Jo Coll Dur BA78. Trin Coll Bris 79. **d** 81 **p** 82. C Hensingham *Carl* 81-84; C Preston St Cuth *Blackb* 84-87; V Blackb Ch Ch w St Matt from 87. *The Vicarage, Brandy House Brow, Blackburn BB2 3EY* Blackburn (0254) 56292

RILEY, Canon John Martin. b 37. St D Coll Lamp BA62 DipTh63. **d** 63 **p** 64. C Conwy w Gyffin *Ban* 63-68; P-in-c Llanfachreth 68-70; TV Dolgellau, Llanfachreth, Brithdir etc 70-72; V Beddgelert 72-78; Dioc Youth Chapl 72-78; V Tywyn 78-82; V Towyn w Aberdovey from 82; RD Ystumaner from 87; Can Ban Cathl from

90. *The Vicarage, Towyn, Gwynedd LL36 9DD* Tywyn (0654) 710295

RILEY, Canon Kenneth Joseph. b 40. Univ of Wales BA61 Linacre Ho Ox BA64. Wycliffe Hall Ox 61. **d** 64 **p** 65. C Fazakerley Em *Liv* 64-66; Chapl Brasted Place Coll Westerham 66-69; Chapl Oundle Sch Pet 69-74; Chapl Liv Cathl *Liv* 74-75; Chapl Liv Univ from 74; V Mossley Hill St Matt and St Jas 75-83; RD Childwall 82-83; Can Res Liv Cathl from 83; Treas 83-87; Prec from 87. *3 Cathedral Close, Liverpool L1 7BR* 051-708 0934

RILEY, Mrs Lesley Anne. b 54. Trin Coll Bris 79. **dss** 81 **d** 87. Hensingham *Carl* 81-84; Preston St Cuth *Blackb* 84-87; Hon Par Dn Blackb Ch Ch w St Matt from 87. *The Vicarage, Brandy House Brow, Blackburn BB2 3EY* Blackburn (0254) 56292

RILEY, Martin Shaw. b 47. Selw Coll Cam BA71 Cam Univ CertEd72 MA75. Sarum & Wells Th Coll 85. **d** 87 **p** 88. C Tuffley *Glouc* from 87; Hon Min Can Glouc Cathl from 88. *18 Tuffley Lane, Gloucester GL4 0DT* Gloucester (0452) 414565

RILEY, Michael Charles. b 57. Ball Coll Ox BA79 MA83 Ex Univ CertEd80. Edin Th Coll 84. **d** 86 **p** 87. C Newc St Geo *Newc* 86-89; C Chiswick St Nic w St Mary *Lon* 89-90; V Chiswick St Paul Grove Park from 90. *St Paul's Vicarage, 64 Grove Park Road, London W4 3SB* 081-994 2163

RILEY, Patrick John. b 39. Leeds Univ BA62. Coll of Resurr Mirfield 62. **d** 64 **p** 65. C Rowbarton *B & W* 64-72; P-in-c Farleigh Hungerford w Tellisford 72-73; P-in-c Rode, Rode Hill and Woolverton 72-73; R Rode Major 73-85; RD Frome 78-85; V Glastonbury w Meare, W Pennard and Godney from 85; Preb Wells Cathl from 90. *The Vicarage, 17 Lambrook Street, Glastonbury, Somerset BA6 8BY* Glastonbury (0458) 32362

RILEY, Peter Arthur. b 23. Kelham Th Coll 40. **d** 51 **p** 52. Jamaica 62-77; V Abertillery *Mon* 77-83; R Panteg 83-88; rtd 88; Hon C Dartmouth *Ex* from 88. *6 Church Field, Dartmouth, Devon TQ6 9HH* Dartmouth (0803) 835309

RILEY, Reuben Cecil. b 17. St Pet Hall Ox BA39 MA43. Wycliffe Hall Ox. **d** 50 **p** 51. V Blackb St Luke *Blackb* 68-71; V Tunstall 71-90; P-in-c Leck 84-90; rtd 90. *Tunstall Vicarage, Carnforth, Lancs LA6 2RQ* Tunstall (046834) 228

RILEY, Sidney David. b 43. Birm Univ BA. Ridley Hall Cam 69. **d** 71 **p** 72. C Herne Bay Ch Ch *Cant* 71-74; C Croydon St Sav 74-77; C-in-c Aylesham CD 77; P-in-c Aylesham 77-78; V 78-82; V Tudeley w Capel *Roch* from 82; Asst Chapl Pembury Hosp 83-86. *The Vicarage, Sychem Lane, Five Oak Green, Tonbridge, Kent TN12 6TL* Paddock Wood (089283) 6653

RILEY, Canon William. b 24. St Aid Birkenhead 48. **d** 51 **p** 52. C Edge Hill St Dunstan *Liv* 51-53; C Halsall 53-57; V Prestolee *Man* 57-62; P-in-c Ringley 60-62; R Tarleton *Blackb* from 62; RD Leyland 84-89; Hon Can Blackb Cathl from 90. *The Rectory, Blackgate Lane, Tarleton, Preston PR4 6UT* Hesketh Bank (0772) 812614

RIMELL, Gilbert William. b 22. Llan Dioc Tr Scheme 76. **d** 81 **p** 82. NSM Laleston w Tythegston and Merthyr Mawr *Llan* from 81. *75 Bryntirion Hill, Bridgend, M Glam CF31 4BY* Bridgend (0656) 658002

RIMMER, Andrew Malcolm. b 62. Magd Coll Cam BA84 MA88. Wycliffe Hall Ox 86. **d** 88 **p** 89. C Romford Gd Shep Collier Row *Chelmsf* from 88. *15 Ferndale Road, Collier Row, Romford, Essex RM5 3ER* Romford (0708) 728720

RIMMER, Anthony Robert Walters. b 41. Hull Univ BA63. Coll of Resurr Mirfield 64. **d** 66 **p** 67. C Leeds All SS *Ripon* 66-69; C Kippax 69-72; C Preston St Jo *Blackb* 72-76; TV 76-83; P-in-c Glasson Ch Ch 83-86; Chapl Dunkerque Miss to Seamen *Eur* from 86; Sec for France from 86. *130 rue de l'Ecole Maternelle, 59140 Dunkerque, France* France (33) 28 59 04 20

RIMMER, David Henry. b 36. Ex Coll Ox BA60 MA65. Linc Th Coll 62. **d** 64 **p** 65. C Liv Our Lady and St Nic *Liv* 64-66; C Daybrook *S'well* 66-69; Chapl St Mary's Cathl *Edin* 69-71; R Kirkcaldy *St And* 71-78; R Haddington *Edin* 78-83; R Dunbar 79-83; R Edin Gd Shep from 83. *9 Upper Coltbridge Terrace, Edinburgh EH12 6AD* 031-337 2698

RIMMER, John Clive. b 25. Oak Hill Th Coll 63. **d** 65 **p** 66. C-in-c Dallam CD *Liv* 64-70; V Southport SS Simon and Jude 74-83; V Westhead 83-90; Chapl Ormskirk Hosp Liv 84-90; rtd 90. *14 Hurlston Drive, Ormskirk, Lancs L39 1LD* Ormskirk (0695) 570838

RIMMER, Paul Nathanael. b 25. Jes Coll Ox BA48 MA50. Wycliffe Hall Ox 48. **d** 50 **p** 51. V Marston *Ox* 59-90;

RD Cowley 69-73; rtd 90. *32 Ulfgar Road, Wolvercote, Oxford OX2 8AZ* Kidlington (08675) 52567

RIMMER, Roy Malcolm. b 31. Fitzw Ho Cam BA58 MA62. Tyndale Hall Bris 54. **d** 59 **p** 60. C Ox St Clem *Ox* 59-62; The Navigators 62-70; Oslo St Edm *Eur* 62-64; Public Preacher *S'wark* 64-66; Perm to Offic *Ox* 66-70; C Portman Square St Paul *Lon* 70-75; R Rougham *St E* 75-87; P-in-c Rushbrooke 78-87; P-in-c Beyton and Hessett 86-87; V Newmarket All SS from 87. *The Vicarage, 17 Cardigan Street, Newmarket, Suffolk CB8 8HZ* Newmarket (0638) 662514

RIMMINGTON, Gerald Thorneycroft. b 30. FCP66 Lon Univ BSc56 PhD64 Leic Univ MA59 Nottm Univ MEd72 PhD75. **d** 76 **p** 78. Canada 76-79; Lic to Offic *Leic* 79-80; R Paston *Pet* 81-86; V Cosby *Leic* 86-90; Dir of Continuing Minl Educn 87-90; R Barwell w Potters Marston and Stapleton from 90. *The Rectory, 14 Church Lane, Barwell, Leicester LE9 8DG* Earl Shilton (0455) 43866

RINGLAND, Tom Laurence. b 61. SS Hild & Bede Coll Dur BSc83. Trin Coll Bris BA89. **d** 89 **p** 90. C Southgate *Chich* from 89. *20 Chandler Close, Crawley, W Sussex RH10 6DF* Crawley (0293) 551217

RINGROSE, Brian Sefton. b 31. Clare Coll Cam BA54 MA58. Tyndale Hall Bris 56. **d** 58 **p** 59. C Ox St Ebbe *Ox* 58-60; C Erith St Paul *Roch* 60-61; India 61-75; P-in-c Ox St Matt *Ox* 75-78; Interserve (Scotland) from 78. *12 Elm Avenue, Lenzie, Glasgow G66 4HJ* 041-776 2943

RINGROSE, Canon Hedley Sidney. b 42. Open Univ BA79. Sarum Th Coll 65. **d** 68 **p** 69. C Bishopston *Bris* 68-71; C Easthampstead *Ox* 71-75; V Glouc St Geo w Whaddon *Glouc* 75-88; RD Glouc City 83-88; Hon Can Glouc Cathl from 86; V Cirencester from 88; RD Cirencester from 89. *Cirencester Vicarage, 1 Dollar Street, Cirencester, Glos GL7 2AJ* Cirencester (0285) 653142

RINGWOOD, Arthur George. b 07. Bris Univ BA29. AKC32. **d** 34 **p** 35. Chapl Community Sisters of Love of God Burwash 65-74; Perm to Offic *Bris* from 72; rtd 74. *Wing 1, St Monica Home, Cote Lane, Westbury-on-Trym, Bristol BS9 3UN* Bristol (0272) 621111

RIOCH, Mrs Wenda Jean. b 35. Sarum & Wells Th Coll 84. **d** 87. Par Dn Basingstoke *Win* 87-91; Par Dn Catshill and Dodford *Worc* from 91. *27 Greendale Close, Catshill, Bromsgrove, Worcs B61 0LR* Bromsgrove (0527) 35708

RIPLEY, Geoffrey Alan. b 39. Dur Univ BA62. St Aid Birkenhead. **d** 64 **p** 65. C E Herrington *Dur* 64-67; Hon C Hodge Hill CD *Birm* 68-70; Youth Chapl *Liv* 70-75; Chapl Liv Cathl 70-78; Bp's Dom Chapl 75-78; V Wavertree St Bridget 78-87; Lay Tr Adv *B & W* from 87. *35 Orchard Road, Street, Somerset BA16 0BT* Street (0458) 46435

RIPON, Bishop of. See YOUNG, Rt Rev David Nigel de Lorentz

RIPON, Dean of. See CAMPLING, Very Rev Christopher Russell

RIPPINGALE, Denis Michael. b 29. Leeds Univ BA52. Coll of Resurr Mirfield 52. **d** 54 **p** 55. C S Kirkby *Wakef* 54-58; C King Cross 58-60; C Derby St Thos *Derby* 60-63; V Altofts *Wakef* 63-71; V S Elmsall 71-84; V Marsden from 84. *The Vicarage, 20 Station Road, Marsden, Huddersfield HD7 6DG* Huddersfield (0484) 844174

RISBY, John. b 40. Lon Univ DipTh66. Lambeth STh82 Oak Hill Th Coll 64. **d** 67 **p** 68. C Fulham Ch Ch *Lon* 67-68; C Ealing St Mary 68-70; C Chitts Hill St Cuth 70-73; C Hove Bp Hannington Memorial Ch *Chich* 73-76; V Islington St Jude Mildmay Park *Lon* 76-82; P-in-c Islington St Paul Ball's Pond 78-82; V Mildmay Grove St Jude and St Paul 82-84; R Hunsdon w Widford and Wareside *St Alb* from 84. *The Rectory, Acorn Street, Hunsdon, Ware, Herts SG12 8PB* Ware (0920) 870171

RISDON, Edward Mark. b 02. Dur Univ LTh. K Coll Lon 29. **d** 29 **p** 30. C Almondbury *Wakef* 29-31; S Africa 31-33 and from 39; S Rhodesia 33-39. *La Plage, Moody Street, Umkomaas, 4170 South Africa*

RISDON, John Alexander. b 42. Lon Univ DipTh66. Clifton Th Coll 66. **d** 68 **p** 69. C Ealing Dean St Jo *Lon* 68-72; C Heref St Pet w St Owen *Heref* 72-74; Ord Cand Sec CPAS 74-77; Hon C Bromley Ch Ch *Roch* 74-77; TV Cheltenham St Mary, St Matt, St Paul and H Trin *Glouc* 77-86; R Stapleton *Bris* from 86. *The Rectory, 21 Park Road, Bristol BS16 1AZ* Bristol (0272) 583858

RISING, Sidney Frederick. b 28. E Midl Min Tr Course 73. **d** 76 **p** 77. NSM W Bridgford *S'well* 76-79; C 79-82; V Whatton w Aslockton, Hawksworth, Scarrington etc 82-87; Chapl HM Det Cen Whatton 82-87; Chapl to Notts Police from 87; Rural Officer *S'well* 87-89; P-in-c

Perlethorpe 88-90; P-in-c Norton Cuckney 89-90; P-in-c Staunton w Flawborough from 90; P-in-c Kilvington from 90. *3 Pelham Close, Newark, Notts NG24 4XL* Newark (0636) 72293

RITCHIE, Brian Albert. b 34. Open Univ BA80 Birm Univ MA84. Qu Coll Birm 60. **d** 63 **p** 64. C S Leamington St *Cov* 63-67; C-in-c Canley CD 67-70; Perm to Offic 71-80; Hon C Cov H Trin 82-88; R Hatton w Haseley, Rowington w Lowsonford etc from 88. *North Ferncumbe Rectory, Hatton Green, Warwick CV35 7LA* Haseley Knob (0926) 484332

RITCHIE, Canon David Caldwell. b 20. Ex Coll Ox BA42 MA46. Wells Th Coll 45. **d** 47 **p** 48. V Pinner *Lon* 65-73; P-in-c Bradford-on-Avon *Sarum* 73-75; V 75-81; RD Bradf 80-84; Can and Preb Sarum Cathl 81-85; V Winsley 81-84; Custos St Jo Hosp Heytesbury 84-85; rtd 85; Hon Can Papua New Guinea from 85. *Langdales, Oddford Vale, Tisbury, Salisbury SP3 6NJ* Tisbury (0747) 870270

RITCHIE, David John Rose. b 48. St Jo Coll Dur BA72 DipTh74. **d** 74 **p** 75. C Harold Wood *Chelmsf* 74-79; TV Ipsley *Worc* 79-84; Chapl Vevey w Chateau d'Oex and Villars *Eur* from 84. *La Parsonage, Champsvavaux, 1807 Blonay, Switzerland* Lausanne (21) 943-2239

RITCHIE, David Philip. b 60. Hatf Coll Dur BA85. Wycliffe Hall Ox 85. **d** 87 **p** 88. C Chadwell *Chelmsf* 87-90; C Waltham H Cross from 90. *St Lawrence House, 46 Mallion Court, Waltham Abbey, Essex EN9 3EQ* Waltham Cross (0992) 767916

RITCHIE, Miss Jean. b 30. Lon Univ CertEd51 DipCD71. Trin Coll Bris DipTh79. **dss** 79 **d** 87. Ox St Ebbe w H Trin and St Pet *Ox* 79-87; Par Dn 87-91; rtd 91; Perm to Offic *B & W* from 91. *63 Holland Road, Clevedon, Avon BS21 7YJ* Clevedon (0272) 871762

RITCHIE, John Brocket. b 12. Roch Th Coll 63. **d** 63 **p** 64. C Burnham *B & W* 68-71; R Otterhampton w Combwich and Stockland 71-83; rtd 83. *2 Kenwyn Road, Truro, Cornwall TR1 3SU* Truro (0872) 76301

RITCHIE, John Young Wylie. b 45. Aber Univ MA69 Univ of Wales (Cardiff) BD76. St Mich Coll Llan 73. **d** 76 **p** 77. C Trevethin *Mon* 76-78; C Cwmbran 78-81; TV 81-82; C Ind Chapl *York* 82-91; P-in-c Micklefield 82-88; P-in-c Aislaby and Ruswarp 88-89; C Scalby w Ravenscar and Staintondale 89-91; C Shelf *Bradf* from 91. *St Michael's House, Collinfield Rise, Bradford BD6 2SL* Bradford (0274) 607486

RITCHIE, Mrs Margaret Mary. b 35. Keele Univ BA57. W Midl Minl Tr Course 84. **d** 87. NSM Earlsdon *Cov* from 87; NSM Hatton w Haseley, Rowington w Lowsonford etc from 88. *North Ferncumbe Rectory, Hatton, Warwick CV35 7LA* Haseley Knob (0926) 484332

RITCHIE, Samuel. b 31. Lon Coll of Div 65. **d** 67 **p** 68. C Westlands St Andr *Lich* 67-70; V Springfield H Trin *Chelmsf* 70-82; Chapl HM Pris Chelmsf 70-82; Brixton 82-84; Hull 84-86; Chapl HM Pris Wymott from 86. *HM Prison Wymott, Moss Lane, Leyland, Preston, Lancs PR5 3LW* Preston (0772) 421461

RITCHIE, William James. b 62. TCD MA DipTh. **d** 86 **p** 87. C Enniscorthy w Clone, Clonmore, Monart etc *C & O* 86-89; Egypt from 89. *Address temp unknown*

RITSON, Arthur William David. b 35. AKC58. **d** 59 **p** 60. C Bishopwearmouth St Mich *Dur* 59-63; Chapl RN 63-67; C Sudbury St Greg and St Pet St *E* 67-69; R Lt Hallingbury *Chelmsf* 69-83; P-in-c Broomfield from 83. *The Vicarage, Butlers Close, Broomfield, Chelmsford CM1 5BE* Chelmsford (0245) 440318

RITSON, Canon Gerald Richard Stanley. b 35. CCC Cam BA59 MA63. Linc Th Coll 59. **d** 61 **p** 62. C Harpenden St Jo *St Alb* 61-65; C Goldington 65-69; R Clifton 69-76; Sec to Dioc Past Cttee 76-87; P-in-c Aldenham 76-87; Hon Can St Alb 80-87; Can Res St Alb from 87. *2 Sumpter Yard, St Albans, Herts AL1 1BY* St Albans (0727) 861744

RIVERS, Arthur. b 20. Oak Hill Th Coll 52. **d** 53 **p** 54. V Burscough Bridge *Liv* 60-79; V Holmesfield *Derby* 79-86; rtd 86; Hon C Warton St Oswald w Yealand Conyers *Blackb* 86-88. *Holmlea, Hale, Milnthorpe, Cumbria LA7 7BL* Milnthorpe (05395) 63588

RIVERS, David John. b 51. St Jo Coll Nottm BA84. **d** 84 **p** 85. C Woodthorpe *S'well* 84-88; C Hyson Green w St Paul w St Steph 88; Asst Chapl Colchester Gen Hosp 89-91; Chapl Leeds Gen Infirmary from 91. *Leeds General Infirmary, St George Street, Leeds LS1 3EX* Leeds (0532) 432799

RIVERS, John Arthur. b 21. E Anglian Minl Tr Course 79. **d** 81 **p** 82. NSM Blakeney w Cley, Wiveton, Glandford etc *Nor* 81-86; Hon C Cromer from 86.

28 Compit Hills, Cromer, Norfolk NR27 9LJ Cromer (0263) 513051

RIVERS, Paul Tudor. b 43. St Steph Ho Ox 70. **d** 72 **p** 73. C Croydon St Mich *Cant* 72-75; C W Bromwich Ch Ch *Lich* 75-79; V Wolv St Steph 79-87; V Kilburn St Aug w St Jo *Lon* from 87. *St Augustine's Clergy House, Kilburn Park Road, London NW6 5XB* 071-624 1637

RIVETT, Dr Andrew George. b 52. LRCP76 MRCS76 Lon Univ MB, BS76. Oak Hill Th Coll 85. **d** 87 **p** 88. C Stanford-le-Hope w Mucking *Chelmsf* 87-90; C Slough *Ox* from 90. *205 Rochfords Gardens, Slough SL2 5XD* Slough (0753) 21508

RIVETT, Leonard Stanley. b 23. MSSCLE82 MYPS90 St Jo Coll Dur BA47 DipTh49 York Univ CLHist88. **d** 49 **p** 50. V Norton *York* 62-74; Warden Wydale Hall 74-83; R Elvington w Sutton on Derwent and E Cottingwith 83-88; rtd 88; OCF RAF from 90. *47 Ryecroft Avenue, York YO2 2SD* York (0904) 705364

RIVETT, Peter John. b 42. St Jo Coll Dur BA71 DipTh72. Cranmer Hall Dur. **d** 72 **p** 73. C Newland St Jo *York* 72-76; TV Marfleet 76-82; V Oxhey All SS *St Alb* from 82. *All Saints' Vicarage, Gosforth Lane, Watford WD1 6AX* 081-428 3696

RIVETT-CARNAC, Canon Sir Thomas Nicholas, Bt. b 27. Westcott Ho Cam. **d** 63 **p** 64. C Brompton H Trin *Lon* 68-72; P-in-c Kennington St Mark *S'wark* 72-87; V 87-89; RD Lambeth 79-83; Hon Can S'wark Cathl 80-89; rtd 89. *23 Heather Close, Horsham, W Sussex RH12 4XD* Horsham (0403) 53705

RIVIERA, Archdeacon of the. See LIVINGSTONE, Ven John Morris

RIVIERE, Jonathan Byam Valentine. b 54. Cuddesdon Coll. **d** 83 **p** 84. C Wymondham *Nor* 83-88; TV Quidenham from 88. *The Vicarage, Mill Road, Old Buckenham, Attleborough, Norfolk NR17 1SG* Attleborough (0953) 860047

RIVIERE, Mrs Tanagra June. b 41. S Dios Minl Tr Scheme 88. **d** 91. NSM Medstead cum Wield *Win* from 91. *The Drey, Paice Lane, Medstead, Alton, Hants GU34 5PT* Alton (0420) 63330

RIX, Patrick George. b 30. Magd Coll Ox BA54 DipEd55 MA57. Ridley Hall Cam 58. **d** 60 **p** 61. Asst Chapl Wrekin Coll Shropshire 62-70; Asst Chapl Gresham's Sch Holt 70-80; Chapl Bloxham Sch Oxon 80-86; rtd 86; P-in-c Swanton Abbott w Skeyton *Nor* 89; Perm to Offic from 89. *5 Rye Close, North Walsham, Norfolk NR28 9EY* North Walsham (0692) 402649

ROACH, Charles Alan. b 08. SS Coll Cam BA33 MA37. Westcott Ho Cam 33. **d** 35 **p** 36. St Mich Mt 66-75; Perm to Offic *Truro* from 66; rtd 75. *Trehoward, Green Lane West, Marazion, Cornwall TR17 0HH* Penzance (0736) 710514

ROACH, Kenneth Thomas. b 43. St Andr Univ BD69 Fitzw Coll Cam BA71 MA75. Westcott Ho Cam 69. **d** 71 **p** 72. C Glas St Marg *Glas* 71-73; CF 73-76; R Johnstone *Glas* 76-85; R Milngavie from 85; R Bearsden from 85. *34 Roman Road, Bearsden, Glasgow G61 2SQ* 041-942 0386

ROAKE, Anthony Richard. b 52. Keble Coll Ox BA75 MA80. Wycliffe Hall Ox 75. **d** 77 **p** 78. C Clifton *S'well* 77-80; V Lapley w Wheaton Aston *Lich* 80-86; V Bournemouth St Andr *Win* from 86. *St Andrew's Vicarage, 53 Bennett Road, Bournemouth BH8 8QQ* Bournemouth (0202) 396022

ROAN, Canon William Forster. b 21. St Chad's Coll Dur BA47 DipTh49. **d** 49 **p** 50. V Workington St Jo *Carl* 70-86; Hon Can Carl Cathl 72-86; RD Solway 77-84; rtd 86; Perm to Offic *Carl* from 86. *41 Chiswick Street, Carlisle CA1 1HJ* Carlisle (0228) 21756

ROBB, Ian Archibald. b 48. K Coll Lon 68. **d** 72 **p** 73. C E Ham w Upton Park *Chelmsf* 72-74; C Leckhampton SS Phil and Jas w Cheltenham St Jas *Glouc* 74-79; P-in-c Cheltenham St Mich 79-90; V Lower Cam w Coaley from 90. *St Bartholomew's Vicarage, Lower Cam, Dursley, Glos GL11 5JR* Dursley (0453) 542679

ROBB, Robert Hammond Neill. b 46. Open Univ BA89 Man Univ 66. St Deiniol's Hawarden 87. **d** 87 **p** 88. C Lache cum Saltney *Ches* 87-89; V Norley and Crowton from 89. *The Vicarage, Crowton, Northwich, Cheshire CW8 2RQ* Kingsley (0928) 88110

ROBBINS, David Ronald Walter. b 47. Sarum & Wells Th Coll 85. **d** 87 **p** 88. C Meir Heath *Lich* 87-89; C Collier Row St Jas and Havering-atte-Bower *Chelmsf* from 89. *St John's House, 428 Havering Road, Romford, Essex RM1 4DF* Romford (0708) 743330

ROBBINS, Peter Tyndall. b 25. Magd Coll Ox BA46 DipTh47 MA51. Westcott Ho Cam 48. **d** 50 **p** 51. V Charing w Lt Chart *Cant* 63-73; V Basing *Win* 73-83; V Kingsclere 83-90; rtd 90; Perm to Offic *Birm* from

91. *73 Summerfield Road, Bolehall, Tamworth, Staffs B77 3BJ* Tamworth (0827) 60805

ROBBINS, Richard Harry. b 14. Lon Univ BD47 Keble Coll Ox DipTh50. ALCD41. **d** 41 **p** 42. Chile 63-86; rtd 86. *61 Richmond Wood Road, Bournemouth BH8 9DQ* Bournemouth (0202) 512247

ROBBINS, Stephen. b 53. K Coll Lon BD74 AKC74. St Aug Coll Cant 75. **d** 76 **p** 77. C Tudhoe Grange *Dur* 76-80; C-in-c Harlow Green CD 80-84; V Gateshead Harlow Green 84-87; CF from 87. *c/o MOD (Army), Bagshot Park, Bagshot, Surrey GU19 5PL* Bagshot (0276) 71717

ROBBINS, Walter. b 35. **d** 72 **p** 73. Argentina 73-82; Adn N Argentina 80-82; C Southborough St Pet w Ch Ch and St Matt *Roch* 82-86; V Sidcup St Andr from 86. *The Vicarage, St Andrew's Road, Sidcup, Kent DA14 4SA* 081-300 4712

ROBERT, Brother. See KING-SMITH, Philip Hugh

ROBERTS, Alan Moss. b 39. CEng68 MIMechE68 MIMarE68. St Jo Coll Nottm 77. **d** 79 **p** 80. C Bromsgrove St Jo *Worc* 79-83; C Edgbaston St Germain *Birm* 83-89; R Broadhembury, Payhembury and Plymtree *Ex* from 89. *The Rectory, Broadhembury, Honiton, Devon EX14 0LT* Broadhembury (040484) 240

ROBERTS, Andrew Alexander. b 49. Open Univ BA75 Bp Otter Coll CertEd70. Sarum & Wells Th Coll 76. **d** 80 **p** 81. NSM Dorchester *Sarum* 80-85; C Swanage and Studland 85-87; TV from 87. *The Vicarage, 9 Cecil Road, Swanage, Dorset BH19 1JJ* Swanage (0929) 422953

ROBERTS, Canon Arthur Clifford. b 34. Univ of Wales (Ban) BA56. Coll of Resurr Mirfield 56. **d** 58 **p** 59. C Hawarden *St As* 58-66; R Llandysilio and Penrhos and Llandrinio etc 66-74; V Shotton from 74; Dioc Adv on Spirituality and Min of Deliverance from 81; Dioc RE Adv from 82; Can St As Cathl from 82; Preb and Sacr St As Cathl from 86. *The Vicarage, Shotton, Deeside, Clwyd CH5 1QD* Deeside (0244) 812183

ROBERTS, Arthur Frederick. b 09. K Coll Lon 38. **d** 39 **p** 40. R Shipdham *Nor* 62-75; rtd 75; Perm to Offic *Nor* from 75. *Moatside, Page's Lane, Saham Toney, Thetford, Norfolk IP25 7HJ* Watton (0953) 882405

ROBERTS, Canon Arthur Stansfield. b 06. Bp Wilson Coll 35. **d** 38 **p** 39. V Carbis Bay *Truro* 48-79; Hon Can Truro Cathl from 68; rtd 79. *Stonehaven, North Perrott, Crewkerne, Somerset TA18 7SX* Crewkerne (0460) 77355

ROBERTS, Bernard John. b 21. Ox NSM Course 79. **d** 82 **p** 83. NSM Wendover *Ox* from 82. *19 The Paddocks, Wendover, Aylesbury, Bucks HP22 6HE* Wendover (0296) 623445

ROBERTS, Bryan Richard. b 55. Univ of Wales (Cardiff) DipTh78 BD80. St Mich Coll Llan 78. **d** 80 **p** 81. C Finham *Cov* 80-83; Asst Youth Officer *Nor* 83-86; R N and S Creake w Waterden from 86; P-in-c E w N and W Barsham from 86. *The New Vicarage, Front Street, South Creake, Fakenham, Norfolk NR21 9PF* South Creake (032879) 433

ROBERTS, Christopher Michael. b 39. Man Univ DipAE79. Qu Coll Birm 62. **d** 64 **p** 65. C Milton next Gravesend Ch Ch *Roch* 64-68; C Thirsk w S Kilvington *York* 68-69; V Castleton *Derby* 69-75; TV Buxton w Burbage and King Sterndale 75-79; Perm to Offic *Bath* 87-90; NSM Marple All SS *Ches* 87-90; Asst Chapl Rainhill Hosp *Liv* 90-91; Asst Chapl St Helens Hosp *Liv* 90-91; Chapl Asst Whiston Co Hosp Prescot 90-91; Chapl R United Hosp Bath from 91. *The Chaplain's Office, Royal United Hospital, Combe Park, Bath BA1 3NG* Bath (0225) 428331

ROBERTS, Colin Edward. b 50. Sarum & Wells Th Coll. **d** 83 **p** 84. C Harton *Dur* 83; C S Shields All SS 83-85; C Thamesmead *S'wark* 85-87; TV 87-89; C Streatham St Pet 89-90; Zimbabwe from 90. *c/o The Manager, Barclays Bank, 107A Plumstead High Street, London SE18 1SE* 081-670 4737

ROBERTS, Cyril. b 41. St Deiniol's Hawarden. **d** 84 **p** 85. C Maltby *Sheff* 84-86; TR Gt Snaith from 86. *The Rectory, Pontefract Road, Snaith, Goole, N Humberside DN14 9JS* Goole (0405) 860866

ROBERTS, David. b 44. Ex Univ BA65. St Steph Ho Ox 65. **d** 67 **p** 68. C Southwick St Columba *Dur* 67-72; C-in-c Southwick St Cuth CD 72-79; R Alyth *St And* 79-84; R Blairgowrie 79-84; R Coupar Angus 79-84; P-in-c Taunton St Jo *B & W* from 84. *17 Henley Road, Taunton, Somerset* Taunton (0823) 284176

ROBERTS, David Alan. b 38. Open Univ BA82. Ripon Hall Ox 71. **d** 73 **p** 74. C W Bridgford *S'well* 73-75; V Awsworth w Cossall 77-82; V Oxclose *Dur* from

82. *37 Brancepeth Road, Washington, Tyne & Wear NE38 0LA* 091-416 2561

ROBERTS, David Donald. b 21. TD69. Univ of Wales BA42. St Mich Coll Llan 42. **d** 44 **p** 45. CF (TA) 55-91; V Newton in Makerfield St Pet *Liv* 59-70; V Birkdale St Jas 70-91; rtd 91. *2 Fulwood Avenue, Southport, Merseyside*

ROBERTS, Preb David Henry. b 38. St Chad's Coll Dur BA60. Qu Coll Birm DipTh62. **d** 62 **p** 63. C Stonehouse *Glouc* 62-65; C Hemsworth *Wakef* 65-69; V Newsome 69-76; R Pontesbury I and II *Heref* from 76; RD Pontesbury from 83; Preb Heref Cathl from 85. *The Deanery, Pontesbury, Shrewsbury SY5 0PS* Shrewsbury (0743) 790316

ROBERTS, David John. b 36. Man Univ BSc58. St D Coll Lamp 65. **d** 67 **p** 68. C Rhosllanerchrugog *St As* 67-70; R Cerrigydrudion w Llanfihangel G M, Llangwm etc 70-75; R Llanrwst and Llanddoget 75-77; R Llanrwst and Llanddoget and Capel Garmon 77-84; RD Llanrwst 77-84; V Abergele from 84. *The Vicarage, Rhuddlan Road, Abergele, Clwyd LL22 7HH* Abergele (0745) 833132

ROBERTS, Derek Francis Madden. b 16. Ch Ch Ox BA46 MA48. St Steph Ho Ox 46. **d** 48 **p** 49. Canada 52-80; rtd 80; Perm to Offic *Ex* from 80. *Sunnyside, North Bovey, Newton Abbot, Devon TQ13 8QZ* Moretonhampstead (0647) 40464

ROBERTS, Dewi. b 57. LWCMD77 Cyncoed Coll CertEd78. St Mich Coll Llan DipTh84. **d** 84 **p** 85. C Clydach *S & B* 84-88; V Glantawe from 88. *The Vicarage, 122 Mansel Road, Bon-y-Maen, Swansea SA1 7JR* Swansea (0792) 652839

ROBERTS, Dilwyn Carey. b 38. St Deiniol's Hawarden 74. **d** 76 **p** 77. C Glanadda *Ban* 76-77; TV Amlwch, Rhosybol, Llandyfrydog etc 77-81; V Llanllechid 81-85; V Caerhun w Llangelynnin 85-87; V Caer Rhun w Llangelynin w Llanbedr-y-Cennin from 87. *Caerhun Vicarage, Tynygroes, Conwy, Gwynedd LL32 8UG* Tynygroes (0492) 650250

ROBERTS, Donald James. b 26. Sarum & Wells Th Coll 83. **d** 86 **p** 87. NSM Corfe Castle, Church Knowle, Kimmeridge etc *Sarum* 86-88; C Broadstone 88-91; rtd 91; NSM Corfe Castle, Church Knowle, Kimmeridge etc *Sarum* from 91. *14 Colletts Close, Corfe Castle, Wareham, Dorset BH20 5HG* Corfe Castle (0929) 480900

ROBERTS, Canon Edward Eric. b 11. St Aug Coll Cant 34. **d** 61 **p** 62. Can Res and Vice-Provost S'well Minster *S'well* 69-79; Bp's Dom Chapl 69-79; rtd 80; Perm to Offic *S'well* from 84. *24 Manor Close, Southwell, Notts NG25 0AP* Southwell (0636) 813246

ROBERTS, Edward Henry. b 06. Man Univ BA33 BD36. Ridley Hall Cam 64. **d** 65 **p** 66. R High Laver w Magdalen Laver *Chelmsf* 67-77; P-in-c Moreton w Lt Laver 73-77; rtd 77. *154 High Street, Ongar, Essex CM5 9JJ* Ongar (0277) 363066

✠**ROBERTS, Rt Rev Edward James Keymer.** b 08. CCC Cam BA30 MA35 Hon DD65. Cuddesdon Coll 30. **d** 31 **p** 32 **c** 56. C St Marylebone All SS *Lon* 31-35; Vice-Prin Cuddesdon Coll 35-39; Hon Can Portsm Cathl *Portsm* 47-49; R Brading w Yaverland 49-52; Adn Is of Wight 49-52; Adn Portsm 52-56; Suff Bp Malmesbury *Bris* 56-62; Suff Bp Kensington *Lon* 62-64; Bp Ely 64-77; rtd 77; Asst Bp Portsm from 77. *The House on the Marsh, Brading, Sandown, Isle of Wight PO36 0BD* Isle of Wight (0983) 407434

ROBERTS, Edward John Walford. b 31. Trin Coll Carmarthen CertEd. St D Dioc Tr Course. **d** 79 **p** 80. NSM Burry Port and Pwll *St D* from 79. *St Mary's Parsonage, Llwynygog, Cwm, Burry Port, Dyfed SA16 0YR* Burry Port (05546) 3652

ROBERTS, Edward Owen. b 38. K Coll Lon BD63 AKC63. **d** 64 **p** 65. C Auckland St Andr and St Anne *Dur* 64-67; C Cheltenham St Paul *Glouc* 67-68; Asst Master Colne Valley High Sch Linthwaite 69-71; V Meltham Mills *Wakef* 71-75; R Emley 75-88; RD Kirkburton 80-88; V Huddersfield H Trin from 88; RD Huddersfield from 89. *Holy Trinity Vicarage, 132 Trinity Street, Huddersfield HD1 4DT* Huddersfield (0484) 22998

ROBERTS, Edward Thomas. b 20. St D Coll Lamp BA42. **d** 44 **p** 45. V Ban St Jas *Ban* 62-85; rtd 85; Perm to Offic *Ban* from 85. *Angorfa, Carreg y Gad, Llanfairpwllgwyngyll, Gwynedd LL61 5QF* Llanfairpwll (0248) 715719

ROBERTS, Canon Elwyn. b 25. Univ of Wales (Ban) DipTh54. St Mich Coll Llan 54. **d** 55 **p** 56. C Llanfairfechan *Ban* 55-61; V Capel Curig 61-69; V Glanogwen 69-88; Hon Can Ban Cathl from 84; R Llansadwrn w Llanddona and Llaniestyn etc from 88.

The Rectory, Llansadwrn, Menai Bridge, Gwynedd LL59 5SL Beaumaris (0248) 810534

ROBERTS, Ven Elwyn. b 31. Univ of Wales (Ban) BA52 Keble Coll Ox BA54 MA59. St Mich Coll Llan 54. **d** 55 **p** 56. C Glanadda *Ban* 55-57; V 66-71; Lib and Lect St Mich Coll Llan 57-66; Dir Post-Ord Tr *Ban* 70-90; R Llandudno 71-83; Can Ban Cathl 77-78; Chan Ban Cathl 78-83; Adn Merioneth 83-86; R Criccieth w Treflys 83-86; Adn Ban from 86. *Deiniol, 31 Trefonwys, Bangor, Gwynedd LL57 2HU* Bangor (0248) 355515

✠**ROBERTS, Rt Rev Eric Matthias.** b 14. Univ of Wales BA35 St Edm Hall Ox BA37 MA41. St Mich Coll Llan 38. **d** 38 **p** 39 **c** 71. C Penmaenmawr *Ban* 38-40; Lic to Offic *Llan* 40-47; Chapl St Mich Coll Llan 40-45; Sub-Warden 45-47; V Port Talbot St Theodore *Llan* 47-56; V Roath St Marg 56-65; RD Cardiff 61-65; Adn Margam 65-71; Bp St D 71-81; rtd 81. *2 Tudor Close, Westbourne Road, Penarth, S Glam* Penarth (0222) 708591

ROBERTS, Canon Francis Frederick Claudius. b 19. Dur Univ LTh43. Oak Hill Th Coll 40. **d** 43 **p** 44. V Lt Missenden *Ox* 50-89; Hon Can Ch Ch 85-89; rtd 89. *182 Wendover Road, Stoke Mandeville, Aylesbury, Bucks*

ROBERTS, Frederick Henry. b 22. CPsychol89 AFBPsS Univ of Wales (Ban) BA49 Lon Univ MA60 PhD68. Wycliffe Hall Ox. **d** 51 **p** 52. Chapl Maudsley Hosp Lon 64-75; Perm to Offic *Chelmsf* from 76; rtd 91. *The Green, High Street, Fowlmere, Cambs SG8 7SS* Fowlmere (076382) 8864

ROBERTS, Geoffrey Thomas. b 12. ARCM33. Worc Ord Coll 64. **d** 65 **p** 66. V Edenham *Linc* 67-79; P-in-c Witham on the Hill 76-79; rtd 79; Perm to Offic *Linc* 79-89. *West Flat, The Riding School, Grimsthorpe, Bourne, Lincs PE10 0LY* Edenham (077832) 240

ROBERTS, George Nelson. b 24. Cranmer Hall Dur 83. **d** 84 **p** 85. C Netherton *Liv* 84-86; V Carr Mill from 86. *The Vicarage, Eskdale Avenue, St Helens, Merseyside WA11 7EN* St Helens (0744) 32330

ROBERTS, Glyn. b 47. Kelham Th Coll 67. **d** 72 **p** 73. C Wombourne *Lich* 72-76; C Sheff Parson Cross St Cecilia *Sheff* 76-79; C New Bentley 79-82; C Greenhill 82; C Fenton *Lich* 86-87; V Bishopweamouth Gd Shep *Dur* from 87. *The Good Shepherd Vicarage, Forest Road, Sunderland SR4 0DX* 091-565 6870

ROBERTS, Gordon Branford. b 11. **d** 83 **p** 83. NSM Prestonville St Luke *Chich* from 83. *Flat 42, Tongdean Court, London Road, Brighton BN1 6YL* Brighton (0273) 558172

ROBERTS, Harold William. b 22. Qu Coll Birm 49. **d** 51 **p** 52. V Rawtenstall St Jo *Man* 64-71; Chapl Bolton Gen Hosp 72-88; V Dixon Green *Man* 72-88; rtd 88; Perm to Offic *Man* from 88. *9 Captain Lees Gardens, Westhoughton, Bolton BL5 3YF* Westhoughton (0942) 811026

ROBERTS, Canon Harry Benjamin. b 08. Down Coll Cam BA30 MA34. Ridley Hall Cam 30. **d** 32 **p** 33. V Youlgreave *Derby* 70-77; P-in-c Stanton-in-Peak 75-77; rtd 77; Perm to Offic *Derby* from 77. *12 Lowside Close, Calver, Sheffield S30 1WZ* Hope Valley (0433) 30751

ROBERTS, Canon Henry Edward. b 28. Oak Hill Th Coll 53. **d** 56 **p** 57. C Edgware *Lon* 56-58; C Bedworth *Cov* 58-61; V Bethnal Green St Jas Less *Lon* 61-73; V Old Ford St Mark Victoria Park 61-73; V Bethnal Green St Jas Less w Victoria Park 73-78; RD Tower Hamlets 76-78; Can Res Bradf Cathl *Bradf* 78-82; Dioc Dir Soc Resp 78-82; V Bermondsey St Jas w Ch Ch *S'wark* 82-90; P-in-c Bermondsey St Anne 82-90; Hon Can S'wark Cathl from 90; Gen Adv for Inner City Min from 90. *45 Aldbridge Street, London SE17 2RG* 071-703 2893

ROBERTS, Canon Hugh Godfrey Lloyd. b 09. AKC34. St Steph Ho Ox 34. **d** 34 **p** 35. R Ashley w Weston by Welland and Sutton Bassett *Pet* 69-79; rtd 79; Perm to Offic Pet from 79; Leic from 81. *4 Victoria Avenue, Market Harborough, Leics LE16 7BQ* Market Harborough (0858) 463071

ROBERTS, Hughie Graham. b 28. St Mich Coll Llan 57. **d** 60 **p** 62. C Pontlottyn *Llan* 60-62; C Roath St German 62; C Ystrad Mynach 62-63; C Tonge w Alkrington *Man* 63-65; Chapl RN 65-69; V Goldcliffe and Whiston and Nash *Mon* 69-73; V Garndiffaith 73-78; V Monkton *St D* 78-82; V Llansteffan and Llan-y-bri etc from 82. *The Vicarage, Llanstephan, Carmarthen, Dyfed SA33 5JT* Llanstephan (026783) 293

ROBERTS, James Arthur. b 34. Lon Univ BSc56. Bps' Coll Cheshunt 58. **d** 60 **p** 61. C Upper Holloway St Steph *Lon* 60-62; C March St Jo *Ely* 62-65; V Coldham 65-70; V Friday Bridge 65-70; V Ridgeway *Derby* 70-72; P-in-c Gleadless *Sheff* 72-74; TR 74-79; P-in-c Catfield *Nor* 79-82; P-in-c Ingham w Sutton 79-82; R Aldwincle w

Thorpe Achurch, Pilton, Wadenhoe etc *Pet* from 82. *The Rectory, Aldwincle, Kettering, Northants NN14 3EL* Clopton (08015) 613

ROBERTS, James Michael Bradley. b 18. Wycliffe Hall Ox 53. **d** 55 **p** 56. V Clerkenwell St Jas and St Jo w St Pet *Lon* 62-88; rtd 88. *42 Lavender Hill, Tonbridge, Kent TN9 2AT* Tonbridge (0732) 359756

ROBERTS, Miss Janet Lynne. b 56. Trin Coll Bris 76. **dss** 82 **d** 87. Dagenham *Chelmsf* 82-86; Huyton St Mich *Liv* 86-87; Par Dn from 87. *1 Derby Terrace, Bluebell Lane, Huyton, Liverpool L36 9XJ* 051-449 3700

ROBERTS, Jeffrey David. b 25. St Cath Coll Cam BA46 MA50 Lon Univ BSc58. **d** 65 **p** 66. Hd Master Adams' Gr Sch Newport Shropshire 59-73; Hd Master St Geo Sch Gravesend 74-82. *Corner House, Keyston, Huntingdon, Cambs PE18 0RD* Bythorn (08014) 254

ROBERTS, John Anthony Duckworth. b 43. K Coll Lon BD65 AKC65. St Boniface Warminster 65. **d** 66 **p** 67. C Wythenshawe Wm Temple Ch CD *Man* 66-69; C Bradford-on-Avon *Sarum* 69-72; Chapl Dauntsey's Sch Devizes 72-73; CF 73-77; P-in-c Verwood *Sarum* 77-81; V 81-86; V Clitheroe St Mary *Blackb* from 86. *St Mary's Vicarage, Church Street, Clitheroe, Lancs BB7 2DD* Clitheroe (0200) 23317

ROBERTS, John Arthur. b 37. CEng68 MIEE68 Man Univ BScTech59. Cranmer Hall Dur DipTh71. **d** 71 **p** 72. C Wellington w Eyton *Lich* 71-75; P-in-c Newton Flowery Field *Ches* 75-80; V Dunham Massey St Marg 80-91; Chapl Countess of Ches Hosp from 91. *500 Overpool Road, Ellesmere Port, Cheshire*

ROBERTS, John Charles. b 50. Nottm Univ BA71. Westcott Ho Cam 71. **d** 73 **p** 74. C Newark St Mary S'well 73-77; Chapl RAF from 77. *c/o MOD, Adastral House, Theobald's Road, London WC1X 8RU* 071-430 7268

ROBERTS, John David. b 08. MBE. St D Coll Lamp BA33. **d** 33 **p** 34. Hon Chapl Miss to Seamen from 62; rtd 73. *2 Restmorel Terrace, Falmouth, Cornwall TR11 3HW* Falmouth (0326) 312415

ROBERTS, John Edward Meyrick. b 20. TD. Cam Univ CertEd73 Keble Coll Ox BA80 MA80. Nor Ord Course 76. **d** 80 **p** 81. NSM Mundford w Lynford *Nor* 80-83; P-in-c w Wratting *Ely* 83-88; P-in-c Weston Colville 83-88; rtd 88; Hon AP Clun w Chapel Lawn, Bettws-y-Crwyn and Newc *Heref* 89-91; Hon AP Clun w Bettws-y-Crwyn and Newc from 91. *Ford House, Clun, Craven Arms, Shropshire SY7 8LD* Clun (05884) 784

ROBERTS, Dr John Gunn. b 18. FRCS MB, ChB. Oak Hill NSM Course 82. **d** 82 **p** 82. NSM Chorleywood St Andr *St Alb* from 82. *Templar Cottage, Berks Hill, Chorleywood, Rickmansworth, Herts WD3 5AJ* Chorleywood (0923) 282061

ROBERTS, John Haywood Boyd. b 15. St Cath Soc Ox BA43 MA48. Ripon Hall Ox 40. **d** 43 **p** 44. V Crockham Hill H Trin *Roch* 69-80; rtd 80; Perm to Offic *Roch* from 81. *19 Forge Croft, Edenbridge, Kent TN8 5BW* Edenbridge (0732) 863005

ROBERTS, John Hugh. b 42. Open Univ BA75. Wells Th Coll 65. **d** 67 **p** 68. C Wareham w Arne *Sarum* 67-70; C Twyford *Win* 70-72; Perm to Offic Leic and S'well 72-73; Pet from 86; V Nassington w Yarwell *Pet* 73-77; Asst Master Sponne Sch Towcester from 78. *Pimlico House, Pimlico, Brackley, Northants NN13 5TN* Brackley (0280) 5378

ROBERTS, John Mark Arnott. b 54. K Coll Lon AKC75 CertEd76. Chich Th Coll 77. **d** 77 **p** 78. C Ashford *Cant* 77-82; V St Mary's Bay w St Mary-in-the-Marsh etc from 82; RD Sandwich from 91. *The Vicarage, Jefferstone Lane, St Mary's Bay, Romney Marsh, Kent TN29 0SW* Dymchurch (0303) 874188

ROBERTS, John Robert. b 15. Chich Th Coll 47. **d** 49 **p** 50. V Whiteshill *Glouc* 59-80; rtd 80; Perm to Offic *Glouc* from 81. *1 Fairby, Paganhill Lane, Stroud, Glos GL5 4JX* Stroud (0453) 750316

ROBERTS, John Victor. b 34. St Edm Hall Ox BA58 MA62. Tyndale Hall Bris 58. **d** 60 **p** 61. C Southport Ch Ch *Liv* 60-62; C Pemberton St Mark Newtown 62-65; V Blackb Sav *Blackb* 65-71; Chapl Blackb & Lancs R Infirmary and Park Lee Hosp 65-71; V Parr *Liv* 71-73; TR 73-80; R Much Woolton from 80; RD Childwall 84-89; AD Liv S from 89. *The Rectory, 67 Church Road, Liverpool L25 6DA* 051-428 1853

ROBERTS, John Victor. b 40. GIPE61. Qu Coll Birm 83. **d** 85 **p** 86. C Ludlow *Heref* 85-89; P-in-c Coreley w Doddington from 89; P-in-c Knowbury from 89. *The Vicarage, Clee Hill, Ludlow, Shropshire SY8 3JG* Ludlow (0584) 890181

ROBERTS, John William. b 09. ALCD38. **d** 38 **p** 39. R Grappenhall *Ches* 60-74; rtd 74. *11 Oakley Road,*

Morecambe, Lancs LA3 1NR   Morecambe (0524) 414234

ROBERTS, John William Melton. b 32. St Deiniol's Hawarden. **d** 69 **p** 70. C Rhosymedre *St As* 69-72; C Wrexham 72-74; C Llanrhos 74-76; R Montgomery and Forden 76-77; R Montgomery and Forden and Llandyssil 78-89; R Llanddulas and Llysfaen from 89; Miss to Seamen from 89. *The Rectory, 2 Rhodfa Wen, Llysfaen, Colwyn Bay, Clwyd LL29 8LE*   Colwyn Bay (0492) 516728

ROBERTS, Jonathan George Alfred. b 60. Lon Univ BD. Qu Coll Birm. **d** 84 **p** 85. C Shepshed *Leic* 84-86; C Braunstone 86-87; Dioc Youth Adv *Dur* from 88. *24 Monks Crescent, Durham DH1 1HD*   091-386 1691

ROBERTS, Joseph Aelwyn. b 18. Univ of Wales (Lamp) BA40. St Mich Coll Llan 41. **d** 42 **p** 43. V Llandegai *Ban* 52-88; Dioc Dir for Soc Work 73-88; rtd 88. *The Vicarage, Llandegai, Bangor, Gwynedd*   Bangor (0248) 353711

ROBERTS, Keith Mervyn. b 55. LGSM78 St Pet Coll Birm CertEd76. Qu Coll Birm 89. **d** 91. C Hall Green St Pet *Birm* from 91. *4 Etwall Road, Birmingham B28 0LE*   021-778 4375

ROBERTS, Canon Kenneth William Alfred. b 26. Roch Th Coll 63. **d** 65 **p** 66. C Waterlooville *Portsm* 65-67; C Honicknowle *Ex* 67-68; C Christchurch *Win* 68-69; C Shiphay Collaton *Ex* 70-71; CF 71-74; R Bassingham *Linc* 74-75; V Carlton-le-Moorland w Stapleford 74-75; R Thurlby w Norton Disney 74-75; V Aubourn w Haddington 74-75; Chapl R Hosp Sch Holbrook 75-78; P-in-c Copdock w Washbrook and Belstead *St E* 78-79; P-in-c Brandeston w Kettleburgh 79-82; Chapl Brandeston Hall Sch 79-84; Chapl Lisbon *Eur* 84-86; Can and Chan Malta Cathl 86-89; R Wimbotsham w Stow Bardolph and Stow Bridge etc *Ely* from 89. *The Rectory, Wimbotsham, King's Lynn, Norfolk PE34 3QG*   Downham Market (0366) 384279

ROBERTS, Kevin Thomas. b 55. Qu Coll Cam BA78 MA82 Nottm Univ BA82. St Jo Coll Nottm 80. **d** 83 **p** 84. C Beverley Minster *York* 83-86; C Woodley *Ox* 86-91; V Meole Brace *Lich* from 91. *The Vicarage, Meole Brace, Shrewsbury SY3 9EZ*   Shrewsbury (0743) 231744

ROBERTS, Laurence James. b 51. AMGAS86 Sussex Univ BEd73. Sarum & Wells Th Coll 75. **d** 78 **p** 79. C Rotherhithe St Mary w All SS *S'wark* 78-81; Ind Chapl 81-84; Hon Priest Nunhead St Silas 82-84; TV Plaistow *Chelmsf* 84-89; Chapl Newham Gen Hosp and Plaistow Hosp from 84; Tutor Community Nursing Services from 89; Tutor Westmr Past Foundn from 90; Perm to Offic *Chelmsf* from 90. *209 Hartsbourne Avenue, Liverpool L25 2RY*   051-487 9791

ROBERTS, Malcolm Kay. b 54. Jes Coll Ox BA76 MA82. Ripon Coll Cuddesdon 84. **d** 87 **p** 88. C Frodingham *Linc* 87-91; R Fiskerton w Reepham from 91. *The Rectory, Reepham Road, Fiskerton, Lincoln LN3 4EZ*   Lincoln (0522) 750577

ROBERTS, Martin Vincent. b 53. LRAM72 Birm Univ BA76 MA77 PhD82. Ripon Coll Cuddesdon 76. **d** 78 **p** 79. C Perry Barr *Birm* 78-81; Sen Chapl and Lect W Sussex Inst of HE 81-86; Sen Chapl Leic Poly *Leic* from 86; TV Leic H Spirit 86-89; TR from 89. *2 Sawday Street, Leicester LE2 7JW*   Leicester (0533) 552540

ROBERTS, Matthew Garnant. b 13. St D Coll Lamp BA37. **d** 37 **p** 38. C-in-c Hinton Ampner w Bramdean *Win* 68-70; R 70-74; R Hinton Ampner w Bramdean and Kilmeston 74-78; rtd 78; Lic to Offic *B & W* from 79. *The Granary, Quaperlake Street, Bruton, Somerset BA10 0NA*   Bruton (0749) 812545

ROBERTS, Matthew John. b 12. AKC37 TCD BA46 MA49 Glas Univ PhD50. **d** 37 **p** 38. C Bethnal Green St Jas Less *Lon* 37-39; Chapl RAF 39-41; R Claypole *Linc* 41-43; V Kirkoswald w Renwick *Carl* 44-48; R Castle Carrock w Cumrew and Croglin 44-48; R Harrington 48-53; V Prince's Park St Paul *Liv* 53-57; Canada from 57. *Box 13, 22 Beech Street, Uxbridge, Ontario, Canada, L0C 1K0*

ROBERTS, Michael. b 46. Sarum Th Coll 86. **d** 88 **p** 89. C Reading St Matt *Ox* 88-91; C Douglas St Geo and St Barn *S & M* from 91. *62 Ballabrooie Way, Douglas, Isle of Man*   Douglas (0624) 621547

ROBERTS, Michael Brian. b 46. Or Coll Ox BA68 MA72 St Jo Coll Dur BA73 DipTh74. Cranmer Hall Dur 71. **d** 74 **p** 75. C St Helens St Helen *Liv* 74-76; C Goose Green 76-78; C Blundellsands St Nic 78-80; V Fazakerley St Nath 80-87; V Chirk *St As* from 87. *The Vicarage, Trevor Road, Chirk, Wrexham, Clwyd LL14 5HD*   Chirk (0691) 778519

ROBERTS, Michael Graham Vernon. b 43. Keble Coll Ox BA65. Cuddesdon Coll 65 Ch Div Sch of the

Pacific (USA) MDiv67. **d** 67 **p** 68. C Littleham w Exmouth *Ex* 67-70; Chapl Clare Coll Cam 70-74; V Bromley St Mark *Roch* 74-79; Tutor Qu Coll Birm 79-85; TR High Wycombe *Ox* 85-90; Vice-Prin Westcott Ho Cam from 90. *Westcott House, Jesus Lane, Cambridge CB5 8BP*   Cambridge (0223) 350074

ROBERTS, Myrfyn Wyn. b 35. Univ of Wales (Ban) BA57 BMus60 Lon Univ DipRS77. S'wark Ord Course 74. **d** 76 **p** 77. C Stepney St Dunstan and All SS *Lon* 76-79; R Crofton *Wakef* 79-85; Chapl HM Pris Dur 85-87; Chapl HM Rem Cen Ashford 87-88; Chapl HM Young Offender Inst Dover from 88. *HM Young Offender Institute, The Citadel, Western Heights, Dover, Kent CT17 9DR*   Dover (0304) 203848

ROBERTS, Nicholas John. b 47. Lon Univ BD70 AKC70 MTh78. St Aug Coll Cant 70. **d** 71 **p** 72. C Tividale *Lich* 71-74; C St Pancras H Cross w St Jude and St Pet *Lon* 74-76; C Camberwell St Giles *S'wark* 76-78; Chapl Ch Coll Cam 78-82; V Kingstanding St Luke *Birm* 82-85; Chapl Princess Louise Hosp Lon from 85; Chapl St Chas Hosp Ladbroke Grove from 85; Chapl Paddington Community Hosp from 85. *St Charles's Hospital, Exmoor Street, London W10*   081-968 2333

ROBERTS, Oswald John Theodore. b 12. St Cath Soc Ox BA40 MA44. **d** 42 **p** 43. R Crowmarsh Gifford w Newnham Murren *Ox* 53-77; rtd 77; Perm to Offic *Worc* from 78. *Milton Lodge, 42 Bromyard Road, Worcester WR2 5BT*   Worcester (0905) 425906

ROBERTS, Paul Carlton. b 57. Worc Coll Ox BA78 MA86 CertEd. St Jo Coll Nottm 84. **d** 87 **p** 88. C Hazlemere *Ox* from 87. *Church House, George's Hill, Widmer End, High Wycombe, Bucks HP15 6BH*   High Wycombe (0494) 713848

ROBERTS, Paul John. b 60. Man Univ BA82 CertEd83. St Jo Coll Nottm 83. **d** 85 **p** 86. C Burnage St Marg *Man* 85-88; Tutor Trin Coll Bris from 88. *Trinity College, Stoke Hill, Bristol BS9 1JP*   Bristol (0272) 682803

ROBERTS, Peter. b 40. NW Ord Course 71. **d** 74 **p** 75. C Stockport St Geo *Ches* 74-77; V Bickerton 77-78; V Bickerton w Bickley 78-83; R Alderley from 83. *The Rectory, Alderley, Macclesfield, Cheshire SK10 4UB*   Alderley Edge (0625) 583134

ROBERTS, Peter Francis. b 59. N Illinois Univ BSc81 Leeds Univ BA87. Coll of Resurr Mirfield 85. **d** 88 **p** 89. C Leeds All So *Ripon* from 88; Asst Dioc Youth Chapl from 91. *31 Lovell Park Hill, Leeds LS7 1DF*   Leeds (0532) 458678

ROBERTS, Peter Gwilym. b 42. N Ord Course 78. **d** 81 **p** 82. NSM Seaforth *Liv* 81-83; TV Kirkby 83-88; Dioc Adv UPA from 88. *79 Moor Lane, Crosby, Liverpool L23 2SQ*   051-924 9106

ROBERTS, Peter Reece. b 43. Chich Th Coll 73. **d** 75 **p** 76. C Cadoxton-juxta-Barry *Llan* 75-79; C Brixham w Churston Ferrers *Ex* 79-81; C Bexhill St Pet *Chich* 81-84; R Heene from 84; RD Worthing from 89. *Heene Rectory, 4 Lansdowne Road, Worthing, W Sussex BN11 4LY*   Worthing (0903) 202312

ROBERTS, Philip Alan. b 59. Chich Th Coll 85. **d** 88 **p** 89. C Friern Barnet St Jas *Lon* from 88. *62 Larch Close, London N11 3NN*   081-361 8570

ROBERTS, Philip Anthony. b 50. St Jo Coll Dur BA73. Wycliffe Hall Ox 75. **d** 77 **p** 78. C Roby *Liv* 77-79; C Ainsdale 79-80; C Pershore w Pinvin, Wick and Birlingham *Worc* 80-83; Chapl Asst Radcliffe Infirmary Ox 83-88; John Radcliffe & Littlemore Hosps Ox 83-88; Chapl R Victoria & Bournemouth Gen Hosps 88-91; Chapl Heref Co Hosp from 91. *County Hospital, Hereford HR1 2ER*   Hereford (0432) 355444

ROBERTS, Philip John. b 20. **d** 74 **p** 75. NSM Downend *Bris* from 74. *Windrush, 190A Overndale Road, Bristol BS16 2RH*   Bristol (0272) 568753

ROBERTS, Canon Phillip. b 21. Sarum Th Coll 55. **d** 57 **p** 58. V Westbury *Sarum* 63-73; TR Dorchester 73-80; Can and Preb Sarum Cathl from 75; R Upper Chelsea H Trin w St Jude *Lon* 80-87; rtd 87; V of Close Sarum Cathl *Sarum* from 89. *112 Harnham Road, Salisbury SP2 8JW*   Salisbury (0722) 23291

ROBERTS, Ven Raymond Harcourt. b 31. CB84. St Edm Hall Ox BA54 MA58. St Mich Coll Llan 54. **d** 56 **p** 57. C Bassaleg *Mon* 56-59; Chapl RNR 58-59; Chapl RN 59-80; Chapl of the Fleet and Adn for the RN 80-84; Hon Can Gib Cathl *Eur* 80-84; QHC 80-84; Gen Sec JMECA 85-89. *13 Oast House Crescent, Farnham, Surrey GU9 0NP*   Farnham (0252) 722014

ROBERTS, Richard. b 23. Univ of Wales BA48. St Mich Coll Llan 48. **d** 50 **p** 51. R Llanrwst and Llanddoget *St As* 68-75; RD Llanrwst 73-75; V Llandrillo-yn-Rhos 75-90; rtd 91. *Ardudwy, 32 Belmont Avenue, Bangor, Gwynedd LL57 2HT*   Bangor (0248) 364899

ROBERTS, Canon Richard Stephanus Jacob. b 28. TCD BA51 MA57. **d** 51 **p** 52. C Orangefield *D & D* 51-54; Miss to Seamen from 54; Sen Chapl Ch on the High Seas from 72; Hon Can Win Cathl *Win* from 82. c/o *The Missions to Seamen, 12-14 Queen's Terrace, Southampton SO1 1BP* Southampton (0703) 333106

ROBERTS, Canon Robert David. b 12. Univ of Wales BA39. St Mich Coll Llan 40. **d** 41 **p** 42. R Llangelynnin w Rhoslefain *Ban* 69-81; Hon Can Ban Cathl 78-81; rtd 81. *1 Lon-y-Wylan, Llanfairpwllgwyngyll, Gwynedd LL61 5JU* Llanfairpwll (0248) 715451

ROBERTS, Ronald Barry. b 40. S Dios Minl Tr Scheme 80. **d** 83 **p** 85. NSM Wedmore w Theale and Blackford *B & W* 83-85; C Odd Rode *Ches* 85-87; V Eaton and Hulme Walfield from 87. *The Vicarage, Hulme Walfield, Congleton, Cheshire CW12 2JG* Congleton (0260) 279863

ROBERTS, Mrs Rosanne Elizabeth. b 51. Glouc Sch of Min 85. **d** 88. NSM Charlton Kings St Mary *Glouc* from 88. *25 Buckles Close, Charlton Kings, Cheltenham, Glos GL53 8QT* Cheltenham (0242) 525771

ROBERTS, Stephen Bradley. b 66. K Coll Lon BD90 Wycliffe Hall Ox 89. **d** 91. C W Hampstead St Jas *Lon* from 91. *42 Birchington Road, London NW6 4LJ* 071-372 1050

ROBERTS, Stephen John. b 58. BD. Westcott Ho Cam. **d** 83 **p** 84. C Riverhead w Dunton Green *Roch* 83-86; C St Martin-in-the-Fields *Lon* 86-89; Warden Trin Coll Cen Camberwell from 89; V Camberwell St Geo *S'wark* from 89. *St George's Vicarage, 115 Wells Way, London SE5 7SZ* 071-703 2895

ROBERTS, Sydney Neville Hayes. b 19. K Coll Lon 38. Cuddesdon Coll 45. **d** 47 **p** 48. R Theale w N Street *Ox* 69-76; R Theale and Englefield 76-85; rtd 85. *34 Stonebridge Road, Steventon, Abingdon, Oxon OX13 6AU* Abingdon (0235) 834777

ROBERTS, Mrs Sylvia Ann. b 40. Stockwell Coll Lon TCert60. S Dios Minl Tr Scheme 81. **dss** 84 **d** 87. Crookhorn *Portsm* 84-88; Hon Par Dn Bedhampton 88-89; Par Dn Southn (City Cen) *Win* from 89. *22 Gordon Avenue, Portswood, Southampton SO2 1BZ* Southampton (0703) 584301

ROBERTS, Tegid. b 47. **d** 87 **p** 88. Lic to Offic *Ban* from 87. *Arwel, Llanrug, Caernarfon, Gwynedd LL55 3BA* Llanberis (0286) 870760

ROBERTS, Terry Harvie. b 45. Sarum & Wells Th Coll 87. **d** 89 **p** 90. C Weymouth H Trin *Sarum* from 89. *Weldon Lodge, 65 Rodwell Road, Weymouth, Dorset DT4 8QX* Weymouth (0305) 786977

ROBERTS, Canon Thomas. b 21. Lon Coll of Div 61. **d** 63 **p** 64. C Burscough Bridge *Liv* 63-68; V St Helens St Matt Thatto Heath 68-73; Chapl Basel w Freiburg-im-Breisgau *Eur* 73-91; Can Brussels Cathl from 80. c/o *Intercontinental Church Society, 175 Tower Bridge Road, London SE1 2AQ* 071-407 4588

ROBERTS, Canon Thomas Ewart. b 17. VRD65. Liv Univ BA41. St Aid Birkenhead 39. **d** 41 **p** 42. Hon Can Cant Cathl *Cant* 67-71; V Chesterfield All SS *Derby* 71-74; Hon Can Cant Cathl *Cant* 81-84; V Tenterden St Mildred w Smallhythe 75-82; RD W Charing 81-82; rtd 82; Asst Chapl Kent and Cant Hosp from 82; Perm to Offic *Cant* from 84. *2 Lesley Avenue, Canterbury, Kent CT1 3LF* Canterbury (0227) 451072

ROBERTS, Vaughan Simon. b 59. Univ of Wales (Ban) BA80. McCormick Th Sem Chicago MA82 Westcott Ho Cam 83. **d** 85 **p** 86. C Bourne *Guildf* 85-89; Chapl Phyllis Tuckwell Hospice Farnham 88-89; Chapl Bath Univ *B & W* from 89. *The Chaplain's House, The Avenue, Bath BA2 7AX* Bath (0225) 826193 or 826458

ROBERTS, Vincent Akintunde. b 55. Kingston Poly BA(Econ)81. S'wark Ord Course. **d** 91. Hon C Brixton Rd Ch Ch *S'wark* from 91. *118 Waddon New Road, Croydon, Surrey CRO 4JE* 081-667 9322

ROBERTS, Vivian Phillip. b 35. Univ of Wales BD78. St D Coll Lamp 57. **d** 60 **p** 61. C Cwmaman *St D* 60-64; R Puncheston, Lt Newc and Castle Bythe 64-72; V Brynamman 72-77; V Brynaman w Cwmllynfell 77-83; V Pembrey from 83. *The Vicarage, Ar-y-Bryn, Burry Port, Dyfed SA16 0AJ* Burry Port (05546) 2403

ROBERTS, Wallace Lionel. b 31. Univ of Wales (Lamp) BA58. St D Coll Lamp 55. **d** 59 **p** 60. C Astley Bridge *Man* 59-61; Hon C Stand 61-66; Asst Master Stand Gr Sch 61-66; Hon C Heaton Moor *Man* 67-70; Lect Stockport Tech Coll 67-70; Hon CF BOAR 70-76; Swaziland 76-85; Chapl Porto (or Oporto) *Eur* 86-89; Chapl Hordle Ho Sch Milford-on-Sea 89-90; Hon AP Portishead *B & W* from 91. *24 St Mary's Park Road, Portishead, Bristol BS20 8QL* Bristol (0272) 848934

ROBERTS, Canon William. b 19. St Mich Coll Llan 61. **d** 62 **p** 63. R Llanfechell, Bodewryd, Rhosbeirio, Llanfflewin *Ban* 67-72; R Llanfechell w Bodewryd w Rhosbeirio etc 72-78; R Machynlleth and Llanwrin 78-86; RD Cyfeiliog and Mawddwy 78-85; Hon Can Ban Cathl 83-86; rtd 86. *Drws-y-Llan, 26 Church Walks, Llandudno, Gwynedd LL30 2HL* Llandudno (0492) 874843

ROBERTS, William Henry. b 30. Open Univ BA78. S'wark Ord Course 66. **d** 69 **p** 70. C New Beckenham St Paul *Roch* 69-72; Hd Master St Alb C of E Secondary Sch 72-77; C Solihull *Birm* 73-77; Hon C from 83; Hd Master Brentside High Sch Ealing 77-83; Hon C Ealing St Steph Castle Hill *Lon* 79-82; Hd Master Pres Kennedy Community Coll from 83. *108 Widney Manor Road, Solihull, W Midlands B91 3JJ* 021-704 1026

ROBERTS, Wynne. b 61. Ridley Hall Cam 85. **d** 87 **p** 88. C Ban Cathl Par *Ban* 87-90; Min Can Ban Cathl 87-90; V Ynyscyhaiarn w Penmorfa and Portmadoc from 90. *The Vicarage, Porthmadog, Gwynedd LL49 9PA* Porthmadog (0766) 512167

ROBERTSHAW, Jonothan Kempster Pickard Sykes. b 41. AKC65. **d** 66 **p** 67. C Perranzabuloe *Truro* 66-69; Miss to Seamen 69-76; Hong Kong 69-72; Namibia 73-76; TV Probus, Ladock and Grampound w Creed *Truro* 76-79; TV N Hill w Altarnon, Bolventor and Lewannick 79-80; P-in-c Lansallos 80-84; R from 84; P-in-c Talland 80-84; V from 84. *Talland Vicarage, 3 Claremont Falls, Looe, Cornwall PL13 2JQ* Polperro (0503) 72356

ROBERTSON, Agnes Muriel Hodgson. Edin Th Coll. **d** 91. NSM Lochgelly *St And* from 91. *164 Main Street, Lochgelly KY5 9DR* Lochgelly (0592) 782268

ROBERTSON, Canon Arthur Charles. b 16. St Jo Coll Dur BA47 DipTh49. **d** 49 **p** 50. V Ilkeston St Mary *Derby* 62-84; RD Ilkeston 66-78; P-in-c Ilkeston H Trin 72-84; rtd 84; Hon C Morley *Derby* from 85. *83 St Wilfrid's Road, West Hallam, Derby DE7 6HG* Ilkeston (0602) 308858

ROBERTSON, David John. b 54. Sheff Univ BA76. Ridley Hall Cam 77. **d** 79 **p** 80. C Downend *Bris* 79-83; C Yate New Town 83-85; TV 85-87; TV High Wycombe *Ox* from 87; RD Wycombe from 91. *199 Cressex Road, Booker, High Wycombe, Bucks HP12 4PZ* High Wycombe (0494) 30134

ROBERTSON, Canon Donald Keith. b 07. St D Coll Lamp BA36. **d** 36 **p** 37. Can Res Lich Cathl *Lich* 60-76; rtd 76; Perm to Offic *Carl* from 77. *Hempgarth, Hayton, Carlisle CA4 9HR* Hayton (022870) 293

ROBERTSON, Edward Macallan. b 28. Aber Univ MA49 Qu Coll Ox BLitt51. Coll of Resurr Mirfield 53. **d** 55 **p** 56. C Swindon New Town *Bris* 55-60; C Hawick *Edin* 60-69; R Alloa *St And* 70-73; Lic to Offic *Edin* 74-78; P-in-c Bathgate 78-82; P-in-c Linlithgow 78-82; Hon C Strathtay *St And* 82-89; R Auchterarder from 90; R Muthill from 90. *The Rectory, Auchterarder, Perthshire PH3 1AD* Auchterarder (0764) 62525

ROBERTSON, Ernest Ian. b 22. Bede Coll Dur BA49. Wycliffe Hall Ox 49. **d** 51 **p** 52. Chapl Shotley Bridge Hosp 60-81; V Benfieldside *Dur* 60-87; Chapl HM Det Cen Medomsley 61-87; rtd 87. *Flat 11, Thornley House, Sherburn House Hospital, Durham DH1 2SE* 091-372 1992

ROBERTSON, Ian Hugh. b 44. LGSM64 ARCM65 Makerere Univ Kampala DipTh83. St Mark's Dar-es-Salaam. **d** 83 **p** 83. SSF 73-82; Zimbabwe 83-87; TV Barrow St Geo w St Luke *Carl* 87-90; V Reigate St Mark *S'wark* from 90. *St Mark's Vicarage, 8 Alma Road, Reigate, Surrey RH2 0DA* Reigate (0737) 244063

ROBERTSON, James Alexander. b 46. Sarum & Wells Th Coll 72. **d** 75 **p** 76. C Monkseaton St Pet *Newc* 75-78; C Prudhoe 78-79; TV Brayton *York* 79-84; V Redcar from 84. *St Peter's Vicarage, 66 Aske Road, Redcar, Cleveland TS10 2BP* Redcar (0642) 490700

ROBERTSON, Canon James Smith. b 17. OBE84. Glas Univ MA38. Edin Th Coll 38. **d** 40 **p** 41. Sec for Ch Colls of Educn Gen Syn Bd of Educn 68-73; Sec USPG 73-83; Chapl to HM The Queen from 80; rtd 83; Perm to Offic Lon and S'wark from 83. *13 Onslow Avenue Mansions, Onslow Avenue, Richmond, Surrey TW10 6QD* 081-940 8574

ROBERTSON, John Charles. b 61. St Pet Coll Ox BA81 Trin Coll Cam BA89. Ridley Hall Cam 87. **d** 90 **p** 91. C Kenilworth St Jo *Cov* from 90. *14 Siddeley Avenue, Kenilworth, Warks CV8 1EW* Kenilworth (0926) 59992

ROBERTSON, Mrs Priscilla Biddulph. b 25. St And Dioc Tr Course 87. **d** 90. C St Andrews St Andr *St And* from 90. *111 Market Street, St Andrews, Fife KY16 9PE* St Andrews (0334) 74976

ROBERTSON, Scott. b 64. Edin Univ BD90. Edin Th Coll 86. **d** 90 **p** 91. C Glas Gd Shep w Ascension *Glas* from 90. *63 Westfield Drive, Cardonald, Glasgow G52 2SG* 041-882 4996

ROBERTSON, Stuart Lang. b 40. Glas Univ MA63. St Jo Coll Nottm DipTh74. **d** 75 **p** 76. C Litherland St Jo and St Jas *Liv* 75-78; C Edin St Thos *Edin* 78-81; C Edin St Pet 81-83; Chapl Edin Univ 81-83; R Edin St Jas from 83; Miss to Seamen from 83. *29 Dudley Gardens, Edinburgh EH6 4PU* 031-554 3520

ROBERTSON, Thomas John. b 15. Univ of Wales BA38 Lon Univ DipTh64 DipEd66. St Steph Ho Ox 38. **d** 40 **p** 41. Hd of RE Bramhall Gr Sch & Lic to Offic Man 61-74; V Taddington and Chelmorton *Derby* 74-80; rtd 80; Perm to Offic *Derby* 80-87; *Ches* and *Man* from 80, *3 Sefton Drive, Worsley, Manchester M28 4NG*

ROBERTSON-GLASGOW, John Nigel. b 13. Cuddesdon Coll 46. **d** 47 **p** 48. R Chipping Warden w Edgcote *Pet* 50-79; R Chipping Warden w Edgcote and Aston le Walls 79; rtd 79; Perm to Offic *Nor* from 80. *19 Hayes Lane, Fakenham, Norfolk NR21 9EP* Fakenham (0328) 863674

ROBIN, John Bryan Carteret. b 22. Trin Coll Ox BA48 MA55. Cuddesdon Coll 49. **d** 77 **p** 78. Chapl Rishworth Sch Ripponden 77-81; Australia from 82. *St George's Vicarage, 22 Hobson Street, Queencliff, Victoria, Australia 3225* Geelong (52) 1532

ROBIN, Peter Philip King. b 23. Trin Coll Cam BA48 MA81. Cuddesdon Coll 49. **d** 51 **p** 52. Papua New Guinea 54-75; R Elsing w Bylaugh *Nor* 76-85; R Lyng w Sparham 76-85; P-in-c Holme Cultram St Mary *Carl* 85-88; rtd 88; Perm to Offic *Carl* from 88. *191 Brampton Road, Carlisle CA3 9AX* Carlisle (0228) 45293

ROBINS, Christopher Charles. b 41. St Mich Coll Llan 66. **d** 68 **p** 69. C Bideford *Ex* 68-71; C Dawlish 71-74; V Laira 74-81; P-in-c E Allington 81; P-in-c Dodbrooke 81-83; P-in-c Churchstow w Kingsbridge 81-83; R Kingsbridge and Dodbrooke from 83. *The Rectory, Church Street, Kingsbridge, Devon TQ7 1NW* Kingsbridge (0548) 856231

ROBINS, Douglas Geoffrey. b 45. Open Univ BA90. Ex & Truro NSM Scheme. **d** 81 **p** 83. NSM Kenwyn *Truro* 81-84; Lic to Offic from 84. *4 Enys Road, Truro, Cornwall TR1 3TE* Truro (0872) 77469

ROBINS, Henry Temple. b 02. Qu Coll Cam BA24 MA29. Cuddesdon Coll 24. **d** 25 **p** 27. R Whimple *Ex* 55-72; rtd 73; Perm to Offic *Ex* from 73. *Woodhayes, 36-40 St Leonard's Road, Exeter EX2 4LR* Exeter (0392) 422539

ROBINS, Ian Donald Hall. b 28. K Coll Lon BD51 AKC51 Lanc Univ MA74. **d** 52 **p** 53. C St Annes *Blackb* 52-55; C Clitheroe St Mary 55-57; V Trawden 57-67; Hd of RE St Chris C of E Sch Accrington 67-76; P-in-c Hugill *Carl* 76-82; Asst Adv for Educn 76-82; Chapl St Martin's Coll of Educn *Blackb* 82-86; V St Annes St Marg from 86. *The Vicarage, 13 Rowsley Road, Lytham St Annes, Lancs FY8 2NS* St Annes (0253) 722648

ROBINS, Mrs Mary Katherine. b 34. FRGS Bris Univ BSc55 CertEd56. St Alb Minl Tr Scheme. **dss** 84 **d** 87. N Mymms *St Alb* 84-87; Hon Par Dn from 87. *15 Bluebridge Road, Brookmans Park, Hatfield, Herts* Potters Bar (0707) 56670

ROBINS, Roger Philip. b 44. AKC68. **d** 69 **p** 70. C Farncombe *Guildf* 69-73; C Aldershot St Mich 73-79; V New Haw 79-89; RD Runnymede 83-88; R Worplesdon from 89. *The Rectory, Perry Hill, Worplesdon, Guildford, Surrey GU3 3RB* Guildford (0483) 234616

ROBINSON, Alan Booker. b 27. Keble Coll Ox BA51 MA56. Sarum Th Coll 51. **d** 53 **p** 54. C Leeds All So *Ripon* 53-56; C Ilkley St Marg *Bradf* 57-59; V Carlton *Wakef* 59-66; V Hooe *Ex* from 66; RD Plympton 81-82; RD Plymouth Sutton 86-91. *The Vicarage, 9 St John's Drive, Plymstock, Plymouth PL9 9SD* Plymouth (0752) 403076

ROBINSON, Alan Ian Peter. b 53. Coll of Resurr Mirfield 82. **d** 85 **p** 86. C Colchester St Jas, All SS, St Nic and St Runwald *Chelmsf* 85-88; C Pimlico St Pet w Westmr Ch Ch *Lon* 88-90; P-in-c Wellingborough St Mary *Pet* from 90. *The Church House, 3 Lister Road, Wellingborough NN8 4EN* Wellingborough (0933) 225620

ROBINSON, Albert. b 15. Roch Th Coll 60. **d** 61 **p** 62. P-in-c Roydon All SS *Nor* 64-73; V Gt w Lt Plumstead 73-81; rtd 81; Perm to Offic *Glouc* from 81. *63 Marleyfield Way, Churchdown, Gloucester GL3 1JW* Gloucester (0452) 855178

ROBINSON, Andrew Nesbitt. b 43. AKC67. **d** 68 **p** 69. C Balsall Heath St Paul *Birm* 68-71; C Westmr St Steph w St Jo *Lon* 71-75; Chapl Sussex Univ *Chich* from 75; Chapl Brighton Poly from 75; P-in-c Stanmer w Falmer from 80. *St Laurence House, Park Street, Brighton BN1 9PG* Brighton (0273) 606928 or 606755

ROBINSON, Anthony William. b 56. CertEd. Sarum & Wells Th Coll. **d** 82 **p** 83. C Tottenham St Paul *Lon* 82-85; TV Leic Resurr *Leic* 85-89; TR from 89. *St Gabriels House, 20 Kerrysdale House, Leicester LE4 7GH* Leicester (0533) 661452

ROBINSON, Arthur Robert Basil. b 32. ACP67 St Jo Coll Dur BA56. Wycliffe Hall Ox 56. **d** 58 **p** 59. C Pemberton St Mark Newtown *Liv* 58-62; CF 62-65; Asst Master Colne Valley High Sch Linthwaite 65-69; Asst Chapl HM Pris Man 69; Chapl HM Borstal Roch 69-74; Peru 74-77; V Golcar *Wakef* 77-83. *Address temp unknown*

ROBINSON, Arthur William. b 35. Dur Univ BSc60. Clifton Th Coll 60. **d** 62 **p** 63. C Ox St Clem *Ox* 62-65; Chile 65-77; V Hoxton St Jo w Ch Ch *Lon* 78-88; TV Gateacre *Liv* from 88. *Christ Church House, 44 Brownbill Bank, Liverpool L27 7AE* 051-487 7759

ROBINSON, Brian. b 39. St Aid Birkenhead 62. **d** 64 **p** 65. C Knotty Ash St Jo *Liv* 64-68; C Sutton 68-72; V Hunts Cross 72-79; V Livesey *Blackb* 79-88; V Burscough Bridge *Liv* from 88. *St John's Vicarage, 253 Liverpool Road South, Ormskirk, Lancs L40 7TD* Burscough (0704) 893205

ROBINSON, Brian John Watson. b 33. St Cath Coll Cam BA56 MA60. Westcott Ho Cam 57. **d** 58 **p** 59. C Whitworth w Spennymoor *Dur* 58-62; India 62-66; P-in-c Preston St Steph *Blackb* 66-72; V Ashton-on-Ribble St Andr 72-79; Lic to Offic 79-82; V Preston St Jude w St Paul from 82; Chapl Preston R Hosp from 83. *St Jude's Vicarage, 97 Garstang Road, Preston, Lancs PR1 1LD* Preston (0772) 52987

ROBINSON, Bryan. b 32. Fitzw Ho Cam BA56. Ely Th Coll 56. **d** 58 **p** 59. C Fleetwood *Blackb* 58-65; V Burnley St Andr 65-74; V Burnley St Marg 65-74; V Burnley St Andr w St Marg from 74; RD Burnley 85-91. *St Andrew's Vicarage, 230 Barden Lane, Burnley, Lancs BB10 1JD* Burnley (0282) 23185

ROBINSON, Cedric Henry. b 17. K Coll Lon. **d** 58 **p** 59. V Norton w Whittington *Worc* 67-79; P-in-c Hanbury 79-84; R W Bowbrook 84-87; rtd 87. *7 Mortlake Drive, Martley, Worcester WR6 6QU* Wichenford (0886) 888628

ROBINSON, Christopher Gordon. b 49. Ridley Hall Cam. **d** 82 **p** 83. C Stanton *St E* 82-85; C Lawshall 85-86; C Lawshall w Shimplingthorne and Alpheton 86; P-in-c 86-89; TV Oakdale St Geo *Sarum* from 89. *The Vicarage, 25 Nuthatch Close, Poole, Dorset BH17 7XR* Broadstone (0202) 602441

ROBINSON, Daffyd Charles. b 48. Qu Coll Birm 77. **d** 80 **p** 85. C Abington *Pet* 80-82; C Immingham *Linc* 85-90; R Willoughby from 90. *The Rectory, Station Road, Willoughby, Alford, Lincs* Alford (0507) 462045

ROBINSON, David. b 42. Sarum & Wells Th Coll. **d** 82 **p** 83. C Billingham St Cuth *Dur* 82-86; V Longwood *Wakef* from 86. *St Mark's Vicarage, 313 Vicarage Road, Longwood, Huddersfield HD3 4HJ* Huddersfield (0484) 653576

ROBINSON, David Hugh. b 47. Linc Th Coll 76. **d** 79 **p** 80. C Bulkington *Cov* 79-82; P-in-c Whitley 82-87; Chapl Walsgrave Hosp Cov from 87. *8 Shirley Road, Walsgrave-on-Sowe, Coventry CV2 2EN* Coventry (0203) 614193 or 602020

ROBINSON, David Mark. b 55. Univ Coll Dur BSc76 Leic Univ MA80 CQSW80. Cranmer Hall Dur 86. **d** 88 **p** 89. C Shipley St Pet *Bradf* from 88. *43 George Street, Saltaire, Shipley, W Yorkshire BD18 4PT* Bradford (0274) 583457

ROBINSON, David Michael Wood. b 28. Glas Univ BSc50 Lon Univ BD54. **d** 57 **p** 57. C Erith St Jo *Roch* 57-58; Japan 58-71; R Holton and Waterperry *Ox* 71-88; RD Aston and Cuddesdon from 88; R Holton and Waterperry w Albury and Waterstock from 88. *The Rectory, Holton, Oxford OX9 1PR* Wheatley (08677) 2460

ROBINSON, David William Clough. b 40. Univ of Wales BA61 BD67 Jes Coll Ox BLitt71. St Mich Coll Llan 64. **d** 67 **p** 68. C Canton St Cath *Llan* 69-71; Lib and Lect St Mich Coll Llan from 72; Lect Th Univ of Wales (Cardiff) from 72; Hon C Woodside Park St Barn *Lon* 78-85. *6 Hillside Mansions, Barnet Hill, Barnet, Herts EN5 5RH*

ROBINSON, Denis. b 53. SS Mark & Jo Coll Plymouth CertEd75. Sarum & Wells Th Coll 88. **d** 91. NSM Bisley and W End *Guildf* from 91; Asst Chapl Gordon's Sch Woking from 91. *Mandarin, Gordon's School, West End, Woking, Surrey GU24 9PT* Camberley (0276) 858275

ROBINSON, Denis Hugh. b 53. BEd76. S Dios Minl Tr Scheme 88. **d** 91. NSM Bisley and W End *Guildf* from 91. *c/o The Rectory, Clews Lane, Bisley, Woking, Surrey GU24 9DY* Brookwood (04867) 3377

ROBINSON, Denis Winton. d 88. Par Dn Mullavilly *Arm* from 88. *Greenacres, 2 Black's Lane, Trandragee, Craigavon, Co Armagh BT62 2EF* Craigavon (0762) 840718

ROBINSON, Dennis Winston. b 42. QUB BSc68. CITC. **d** 88 **p** 89. NSM Mullavilly *Arm* from 88. *Greenacres, 2 Blacks Lane, Tandragee, Craigavon, Co Armagh BT62 2EF* Tandragee (0762) 840718

ROBINSON, Douglas. b 48. Nottm Univ BEd70 Lon Univ BD74. Trin Coll Bris 71 Union Th Sem Virginia MA75. **d** 75 **p** 76. C Southport Ch Ch *Liv* 75-78; V Clubmoor 78-85; Chapl Epsom Coll Surrey 85-88; Chapl Dauntsey's Sch Devizes from 89. *Dauntsey's School, West Lavington, Devizes, Wilts SN10 4HE* Devizes (0380) 812742

ROBINSON, Dugald Clifford. b 23. Qu Coll Birm 69. **d** 70 **p** 71. C Stratford w Bishopton *Cov* 70-74; V Allesley Park 74-86; Perm to Offic *Cov* from 86. *5 Wedgewoods, 34 Beechwood Avenue, Coventry CV5 6QG* Coventry (0203) 679617

ROBINSON, Ernest Yeomans. b 03. **d** 56 **p** 57. V Hensall *Sheff* 68-72; I Kilmoe Union *C, C & R* 76-78; rtd 78. *Ilen Lodge, Rath, Baltimore, Skibereen, Co Cork, Irish Republic* Skibbereen (28) 20152

ROBINSON, Francis George. b 08. Cranmer Hall Dur 68. **d** 69 **p** 70. C Haxby w Wigginton *York* 69-71; V Sherburn 71-75; V Kexby w Wilberfoss 75-77; rtd 77. *20 Little Lane, Haxby, York YO3 8QU* York (0904) 761690

ROBINSON, Geoffrey. b 28. Hartley Victoria Coll 49 Ely Th Coll 52. **d** 53 **p** 54. C Prenton *Ches* 53-58; V Gt Saughall from 58. *The Vicarage, Church Road, Saughall, Chester CH1 6EN* Saughall (0244) 880213

ROBINSON, George. b 27. MIMechE HNC59. Oak Hill Th Coll 59. **d** 61 **p** 62. C Branksome St Clem *Sarum* 61-64; Australia from 64. *24 Abingdon Road, Roseville, NSW, Australia 2069* Roseville (2) 416-4330

ROBINSON, Gordon Stanislaus. b 13. K Coll Lon BD37 AKC37. **d** 37 **p** 38. R Charlton Horethorne w Stowell *B & W* 53-78; rtd 78; Lic to Offic *B & W* from 79. *18 North Street, Stoke-sub-Hamdon, Somerset TA14 6QP* Martock (0935) 823742

ROBINSON, Canon Gordon Victor Michael. b 18. Keble Coll Ox BA40 MA46. Cuddesdon Coll 40. **d** 41 **p** 42. V Ellesmere Port *Ches* 55-71; Hon Can Ches Cathl 62-83; TR Ellesmere Port 71-73; R Tarporley 73-76; TR Birkenhead Priory 76-82; Exec Officer Bd for Soc Resp 82-83; rtd 83; Perm to Offic *Ches* from 83. *69 Marian Drive, Great Boughton, Chester CH3 5RY* Chester (0244) 315828

ROBINSON, Hugh Stanley. b 21. AKC47. **d** 47 **p** 48. V Chiddingly *Chich* 67-83; V Laughton 67-76; Asst Chapl HM Pris Northeye 83-86; rtd 86; Perm to Offic *Lich* from 86. *2 Brook Drive, Wem, Shrewsbury SY4 5HQ* Wem (0939) 34683

ROBINSON, Ian. b 57. Nottm Univ BTh87. Linc Th Coll 84. **d** 87 **p** 88. C Bottesford w Ashby *Linc* 87-90; TV from 90. *Holy Spirit Vicarage, 180 Enderby Road, Scunthorpe DN17 2JX* Scunthorpe (0724) 842083

ROBINSON, Ian Cameron. b 19. OBE72. Em Coll Cam BA40 MA44. Linc Th Coll 71. **d** 72 **p** 73. C Ipswich St Aug *St E* 72-74; V Darsham 74-84; V Westleton w Dunwich 74-84; RD Saxmundham 79-83; rtd 84; Perm to Offic *St E* from 84. *Corner House, Rectory Street, Halesworth, Suffolk IP19 8BS* Halesworth (0986) 873573

ROBINSON, James. b 23. Ridley Hall Cam 70. **d** 72 **p** 73. C Mixenden CD *Wakef* 72-73; C Carlton-in-Lindrick *S'well* 73-74; C Tuxford 75-77; C Selston 77-85; P-in-c Shireoaks from 85. *The Vicarage Bungalow, Shireoaks Road, Shireoaks, Worksop, Notts S81 8NB* Worksop (0909) 486537

ROBINSON, Mrs Jane Hippisley. b 41. Somerville Coll Ox MA66 K Coll Lon PGCE. S Dios Minl Tr Scheme 88. **d** 91. NSM Ealing St Pet Mt Park *Lon* from 91. *60 Madeley Road, London W5 2LU* 081-991 0206

ROBINSON, John Ellis. b 07. OStJ. ALCD30. **d** 30 **p** 31. V Leeds w Broomfield *Cant* 60-73; rtd 73. *27 Golf Road, Deal, Kent CT14 6PY* Deal (0304) 372620

ROBINSON, John Francis Napier. b 42. St Edm Hall Ox BA64 MA68 Lon Univ DipTh68. Clifton Th Coll 65. **d** 68 **p** 69. C Southport Ch Ch *Liv* 68-71; C Coleraine *Conn* 71-74; Deputation Sec (Ireland) BCMS 74-76; TV Marfleet *York* 76-81; V Yeadon St Jo *Bradf* from 81. *St John's Vicarage, Yeadon, Leeds LS19 7SE* Rawdon (0532) 502272

ROBINSON, John Kenneth. b 36. K Coll Lon BD61 AKC61. **d** 62 **p** 63. C Poulton-le-Fylde *Blackb* 62-65; C Lanc St Mary 65-66; Chapl HM Pris Lanc 65-66; Singapore 66-68; V Colne H Trin *Blackb* 68-71; USPG 71-74; Grenada 71-74; V Skerton St Luke *Blackb* 74-81; Area Sec (E Anglia) USPG 81-91; Min Can St E Cathl *St E* 82-91; Chapl Gtr Lisbon *Eur* from 91. *Lote 5, Rua da Ginjeira, Alcoitao, 2765 Estoril, Portugal* Lisbon (1) 269-2303

ROBINSON, John Leonard William. b 23. Lon Univ BA50. Bps' Coll Cheshunt 50. **d** 52 **p** 53. C Victoria Docks Ascension *Chelmsf* 52-55; C Kilburn St Aug *Lon* 55-63; C Westmr St Jas 63-81; V Compton, the Mardens, Stoughton and Racton *Chich* from 81; V Stansted from 85. *The Vicarage, Compton, Chichester, W Sussex PO18 9HD* Compton (0705) 631252

ROBINSON, Jonathan William Murrell. b 42. Sarum Th Coll 65. **d** 68 **p** 69. C Tooting All SS *S'wark* 68-71; C Bourne *Guildf* 71-76; Dir Grail Trust Chr Community Cen Burtle *B & W* 78-82; Hon C Willesden Green St Gabr *Lon* 78-82; V Stoke St Gregory w Burrowbridge and Lyng *B & W* 82-90; Dir Grail Retreat Cen from 90. *The Grail Retreat Centre, Tan-y-Bryn House, Tan-y-Bryn Street, Abergynolwyn, Gwynedd LL36 9YA* Abergynolwyn (0654) 782268

ROBINSON, Canon Joseph. b 27. K Coll Lon BD51 AKC51 MTh58. **d** 52 **p** 53. C Tottenham All Hallows *Lon* 52-55; Min Can St Paul's Cathl 55-68; Lect K Coll Lon 59-68; FKC from 73; Can Res Cant Cathl *Cant* 68-80; Master of the Temple from 81. *The Master's House, Temple, London EC4 7BB* 071-353 8559

ROBINSON, Keith. b 48. Lon Univ BA75 BD77 AKC77. Westcott Ho Cam 77. **d** 78 **p** 79. C Bow w Bromley St Leon *Lon* 78-81; C Leighton Buzzard w Eggington, Hockliffe etc *St Alb* 81-88; PV Westmr Abbey from 82; V Bulkington w Shilton and Ansty *Cov* from 88. *The Vicarage, School Lane, Bulkington, Nuneaton CV12 9JB* Bedworth (0203) 312396

ROBINSON, Kenneth Borwell. b 37. Lon Univ BA62. Ridley Hall Cam 68. **d** 70 **p** 71. C Walthamstow St Jo *Chelmsf* 70-74; P-in-c Becontree St Alb 74-78; P-in-c Heybridge w Langford 78-84; C Horley *S'wark* 84; TV from 84. *St Francis's House, 84 Balcombe Road, Horley, Surrey RH6 9AY* Horley (0293) 76322

ROBINSON, Kevin Peter. b 57. K Coll Lon BD79 AKC79. Coll of Resurr Mirfield 80. **d** 82 **p** 83. C Duston *Pet* 82-89; TV Catford (Southend) and Downham *S'wark* from 89. *St Barnabas's Vicarage, 1 Churchdown, Bromley BR1 5PS* 081-698 4851

ROBINSON, Leslie. b 31. St Aid Birkenhead 56. **d** 59 **p** 60. C Hugglescote w Donington *Leic* 59-61; C Greenside *Dur* 61-63; C-in-c New Cantley CD *Sheff* 63-66; VC Heref Cathl *Heref* 66-67; R Easton-on-the-Hill *Pet* 67-69; Hon Min Can Pet Cathl 68-69; C Weston-super-Mare St Jo *B & W* 69-70; V Winkleigh *Ex* 70-72; V Dishley and Thorpe Acre *Leic* 72-78; V Cloughton *York* 78-79; V Hedon w Paull 79-81; V Bywell St Pet *Newc* 81-86; V Wymeswold and Prestwold w Hoton *Leic* from 86. *The Vicarage, The Stockwell, Wymeswold, Loughborough, Leics LE12 6UF* Wymeswold (0509) 880275

ROBINSON, Miss Margaret. b 32. S'wark Ord Course 83. dss 86 **d** 87. Finsbury St Clem w St Barn and St Matt *Lon* 86-87; Par Dn St Giles Cripplegate w St Bart Moor Lane etc from 87. *St Luke's House, Roscoe Street, London EC1* 071-253 4720

ROBINSON, Michael John. b 45. Nottm Univ BA66. Linc Th Coll 78. **d** 79 **p** 80. C Aston cum Aughton *Sheff* 79-80; C Rotherham 80-82; TV Howden Team Min *York* 82-86; V Heywood St Jas *Man* from 86. *St James's Vicarage, 46 Bury Old Road, Heywood, Lancs OL10 3JD* Heywood (0706) 69754

ROBINSON, Dr Neal Sydney. b 48. Worc Coll Ox BA70 MA75 Birm Univ PhD77. Qu Coll Birm 74. **d** 76 **p** 77. C Folkestone St Sav *Cant* 76-79; Chapl Bradf Univ *Bradf* 79-87; Perm to Offic *Glouc* from 87; Lect Coll of SS Mary and Paul Cheltenham 87-88; Sen Lect 88-90; Sen Lect Cheltenham & Glouc Coll of HE from 90. *Cheltenham & Gloucester College of Higher Education, Cheltenham, Glos GL50 2RH* Cheltenham (0242) 513836

ROBINSON, Ven Neil. b 29. St Jo Coll Dur BA52 DipTh54. **d** 54 **p** 55. C Kingston upon Hull H Trin *York* 54-58; V Glen Parva and S Wigston *Leic* 58-68; Hon Can Leic Cathl 68-83; RD Sparkenhoe I 69-83; R Market Bosworth w Shenton 69-83; Can Res Worc Cathl *Worc* 83-87; Adn Suffolk *St E* from 87. *38 Saxmundham Road, Aldeburgh, Suffolk IP15 5JE* Aldeburgh (0728) 454034

ROBINSON, Norman Leslie. b 50. Liv Univ BSc71. Lon Bible Coll BA78 Wycliffe Hall Ox 78. **d** 80 **p** 81. C

Bebington *Ches* 80-83; C St Helens St Helen *Liv* 83-90; P-in-c Westward, Rosley-w-Woodside and Welton *Carl* from 90. *The Vicarage, Rosley, Wigton, Cumbria CA7 8AU* Wigton (06973) 43723

ROBINSON, Paul Leslie. b 46. Dur Univ BA67 Nottm Univ DipTh73. Linc Th Coll 71. **d** 74 **p** 75. C Poynton *Ches* 74-76; C Prenton 76-78; V Seacombe 78-88; V Stalybridge St Paul from 88. *St Paul's Vicarage, Huddersfield Road, Stalybridge, Cheshire SK15 2PT* 061-338 2514

ROBINSON, Peter. b 42. Univ of Wales (Lamp) BA63 DipEd64 Univ of Wales (Cardiff) BD71. N Ord Course 78. **d** 81 **p** 82. NSM Rochdale *Man* 81-83; C Rochdale 83-86; V Shore from 86; Chapl for Readers from 90. *St Barnabas's Vicarage, Littleborough, Lancs OL15 8EZ* Littleborough (0706) 78356

ROBINSON, Peter Charles. b 53. Open Univ BA83. Oak Hill Th Coll 85. **d** 87 **p** 88. C Nottm St Ann w Em *S'well* 87-89; C Worksop St Anne from 89. *6 Meadow Drive, Hawkswood Estate, Worksop, Notts S80 3QF* Worksop (0909) 501287

ROBINSON, Peter Edward Barron. b 40. Sarum & Wells Th Coll 76. **d** 78 **p** 79. C Petersfield w Sheet *Portsm* 78-82; R Bentworth and Shalden and Lasham *Win* 82-88; R W Horsley *Guildf* from 88. *The Rectory, 80 East Lane, West Horsley, Leatherhead, Surrey KT24 6LQ* East Horsley (04865) 2173

ROBINSON, Peter McCall. b 24. Worc Coll Ox BA48 MA50. Wells Th Coll 48. **d** 50 **p** 51. S Africa 57-71 and 81-82; V Payhembury *Ex* 71-79; R Cheriton w Tichborne and Beauworth *Win* 79-81; V Marystowe, Coryton, Stowford, Lewtrenchard etc *Ex* 82-85; V Blackawton and Stoke Fleming 85-88; rtd 88; Perm to Offic *Ex* from 89. *8 Malden Road, Sidmouth, Devon EX10 9LS* Sidmouth (0395) 514494

ROBINSON, Peter Stanley. b 20. Lon Univ BD49 Nottm Univ MA55. Qu Coll Birm 53. **d** 53 **p** 54. C Poplar All SS w St Frideswide *Lon* 69-71; TV 71-73; V Owston *Linc* 73-81; V W Butterwick 73-81; R Earl Soham w Cretingham and Ashfield cum Thorpe *St E* 81-84; V Whaplode Drove *Linc* 84-86; V Gedney Hill 84-86; rtd 86. *Unit 217, St Francis Court, 34 Robinson Road, Inglewood, W Australia 6052*

ROBINSON, Philip. b 38. JP79. MIPM74. S Dios Minl Tr Scheme 88. **d** 91. NSM Ickenham *Lon* from 91. *30 Grove Farm Park, Northwood, Middx HA6 2BQ* Northwood (09274) 26389

ROBINSON, Raymonde Robin. b 43. St Jo Coll Dur BA66. Chich Th Coll 67. **d** 70 **p** 71. C Ealing St Barn *Lon* 70-72; C Pinner 72-75; C Clerkenwell H Redeemer w St Phil 75-80; TV Kingsthorpe w Northn St Dav *Pet* 80-89; R Letchworth *St Alb* from 89. *The Rectory, 39 South View, Letchworth, Herts SG6 3JJ* Letchworth (0462) 684822

ROBINSON, Richard Albert. b 14. TCD BA36. **d** 38 **p** 39. I Taunagh w Kilmactranny, Ballysumaghan etc *K, E & A* 60-85; rtd 85. *c/o St John's Hospital, Co Sligo, Irish Republic*

ROBINSON, Richard Hugh. b 35. St Jo Coll Cam BA58 MA62. Ridley Hall Cam 58. **d** 60 **p** 81. C Cheadle Hulme St Andr *Ches* 60-62; Hon C Alvanley 62-64; Perm to Offic *York* 64-80; Hon C Elloughton and Brough w Brantingham 80-86; C 86-87; Ext Dir CMJ 87-88. *Old Hall, Doomgate, Appleby, Cumbria CA16 6RB* Appleby (07683) 52802

ROBINSON, Canon Richard Malcolm. b 20. Ex Coll Ox BA42 DipTh43 MA46. Wycliffe Hall Ox 42. **d** 44 **p** 45. R Edin Ch Ch *Edin* 64-76; V Dent w Cowgill *Bradf* 76-85; RD Ewecross 80-85; Hon Can Bradf Cathl 83-85; rtd 85; Perm to Offic *Bradf* from 85. *Hollinwood, 15 Raikeswood Road, Skipton, N Yorkshire BD23 1NB* Skipton (0756) 791577

ROBINSON, Canon Roger George. b 24. Qu Coll Cam BA46 MA50. Ridley Hall Cam 46. **d** 48 **p** 49. C Gorleston St Andr *Nor* 48-51; C Drypool St Andr and St Pet *York* 51-54; P-in-c Kingston upon Hull Southcoates St Aid 54-55; V 55-60; V Clifton 60-70; Chapl Clifton Hosp N Yorkshire 61-70; V Far Headingley St Chad *Ripon* 70-81; RD Headingley 72-81; Hon Can Ripon Cathl 81; R Drayton w Felthorpe *Nor* from 81. *The Rectory, Drayton, Norwich NR8 6EF* Norwich (0603) 868749

ROBINSON, Ronald Frederick. b 46. Brasted Place Coll 72. Oak Hill Th Coll 74. **d** 76 **p** 77. C Pennington *Man* 76-77; C Bedhampton *Portsm* 77-79; C Portsea N End St Mark 79-82; V from 90; R Rowner 82-90. *The Vicarage, 3A Wadham Road, Portsmouth PO2 9ED* Portsmouth (0705) 662500

ROBINSON, Roy David. b 35. AKC59. **d** 60 **p** 61. C Acocks Green *Birm* 60-62; C Shirley 62-65; C Haslemere *Guildf*

65-70; R Headley w Box Hill 70-85; V Hinchley Wood from 85. *The Vicarage, 98 Manor Road, Esher, Surrey KT10 0AE* 081-398 4443

ROBINSON, Simon John. b 51. Edin Univ MA72 DSA73 PhD89 Ox Univ BA77. Wycliffe Hall Ox 75. **d** 78 **p** 79. C Haughton le Skerne *Dur* 78-81; Chapl Asst N Tees Hosp Stockton-on-Tees 81-83; C Norton St Mary *Dur* 81-83; Chapl Heriot-Watt Univ *Edin* 83-90; R Dalmahoy 83-90; Chapl Leeds Univ *Ripon* from 90. *14 Parkside Green, Meanwood, Leeds LS6 4NY* Leeds (0532) 746297

ROBINSON, Stuart. b 39. N Ord Course. **d** 87 **p** 88. C Hull St Martin w Transfiguration *York* 87-90; P-in-c Preston and Sproatley in Holderness from 90. *The Rectory, Preston, Hull HU12 8TB* Hull (0482) 898375

ROBINSON, Canon Thomas Fisher. b 20. St Jo Coll Dur BA49. **d** 50 **p** 51. V Garston *Liv* 67-88; Hon Can Liv Cathl from 85; rtd 88. *208 Mather Avenue, Liverpool L18 9TG* 051-427 7055

ROBINSON, Thomas Hugh. b 34. CBE89. TCD BA55 MA71. **d** 57 **p** 58. C Belf St Clem *D & D* 57-60; Kenya 61-64; I Youghal *C, C & R* 64-66; CF 66-89; Dep Chapl Gen 86-89; TR Cleethorpes *Linc* from 90. *42 Queens Parade, Cleethorpes, S Humberside DN35 0DG* Cleethorpes (0472) 693234

ROBINSON, Thomas Irven. b 10. TCD BA34 MA45. **d** 34 **p** 35. Dhahran 69-71; P-in-c Stourpaine, Durweston and Bryanston *Sarum* 71-77; rtd 77; Perm to Offic *Ox* from 77. *1 Avon Court, Cressex Close, Binfield, Bracknell, Berks RG12 5DR* Bracknell (0344) 51136

ROBINSON, Timothy James. b 59. Middx Poly BA84. St Steph Ho Ox 88. **d** 91. C Burythorpe, Acklam and Leavening w Westow *York* from 91. *41 Ambleside Grove, Acklam, Middlesbrough ST5 5DQ* Middlesbrough (0642) 820264

ROBINSON, Ven William David. b 31. Univ Coll Dur BA54 DipTh58 MA62. Cranmer Hall Dur. **d** 58 **p** 59. C Standish *Blackb* 58-61; C Lanc St Mary 61-63; V Blackb St Jas 63-73; P-in-c Shireshead 73-86; Hon Can Blackb Cathl from 75; Adn Blackb from 86; V Balderstone 86-87. *7 Billinge Close, Blackburn BB2 6SB* Blackburn (0254) 53442

ROBINSON, William Pitchford. b 50. Nottm Univ BTh75. Kelham Th Coll 71. **d** 75 **p** 76. C Bow w Bromley St Leon *Lon* 75-79; Hon C Barkingside St Geo *Chelmsf* 79-82; Chapl Claybury Hosp Woodford Bridge 79-85; Hon C Barkingside St Fran *Chelmsf* 82-85; Australia from 86. *The Rectory, 18 Walter Road, Bassendean, W Australia 6054* Bassendean (9) 325-6644

ROBLIN, Ven Graham Henry. b 37. OBE. AKC61. **d** 62 **p** 63. C St Helier *S'wark* 62-66; CF 66-87; Warden RAChD Cen Bagshot 83-86; Sen CF (BAOR) 87-89; Dep Chapl Gen from 89; Adn of the Army from 90; QHC from 88. *c/o MOD (Army), Bagshot Park, Bagshot, Surrey GU19 5PL* Bagshot (0276) 71717

ROBOTHAM, Eric William. b 07. Ex Coll Ox BA30 BTh32 MA35. Wycliffe Hall Ox 30. **d** 32 **p** 33. Australia from 53; Adn Goldfields 56-60; rtd 77. *38 North Street, Bassendean, W Australia 6054* Bassendean (9) 279-8393

ROBOTTOM, David Leonard Douglas. b 40. Qu Coll Birm 80 Sarum & Wells Th Coll 81. **d** 83 **p** 84. C Uppingham w Ayston and Wardley w Belton *Pet* 83-87; TV Sidmouth, Woolbrook and Salcombe Regis *Ex* 87-91; TV Sidmouth, Woolbrook, Salcombe Regis, Sidbury etc from 91. *5 Meadow View Close, Salcombe Heights, Sidmouth, Devon EX10 9AP* Sidmouth (0395) 577620

ROBSON, Andrew. b 13. K Coll Lon 37. **d** 41 **p** 42. V Lowick and Kyloe *Newc* 61-79; rtd 79. *22 Horsdonside, Wooler, Northd NE71 6PE* Wooler (0668) 81588

ROBSON, Angus William. b 13. Kelham Th Coll 32. **d** 38 **p** 39. V Jersey St Jas *Win* 50-75; Chapl HM Pris Jersey 60-75; rtd 78. *Flat 1, La Petite Carriere, Wellington Road, St Helier, Jersey, Channel Islands* Jersey (0534) 31656

ROBSON, Bernard John. b 33. Ch Ch Ox BA56 MA60. Tyndale Hall Bris 57. **d** 60 **p** 61. C Walmley *Birm* 60-64; C Stapenhill w Cauldwell *Derby* 64-68; Area Sec (SE) CPAS 68-71; E Region Co-ord 71-84; Perm to Offic *Nor* 71-84; P-in-c Tolleshunt D'Arcy w Tolleshunt Major *Chelmsf* 84-90; C Chadwell from 90. *31 Ruskin Road, Grays, Essex RM16 4HB* Tilbury (0375) 842777

ROBSON, Featherstone. b 30. Southn Univ CertEd52 Nottm Univ DipEd74. Oak Hill Th Coll 55. **d** 58 **p** 59. Teacher Larkmead Sch Abingdon 68-71; Dorking Gr Sch 71-76; Ho Master Scarisbrook Hall Sch Ormskirk 77-78; Chapl Dean Close Jr Sch Cheltenham 78-79; Asst Chapl K Edward Sch Witley 79-81; Deputation Sec for England Irish Ch Miss 82-86; Perm to Offic *Ox* from 86; rtd 86. *71 Springfield Drive, Abingdon, Oxon OX14 1JF* Abingdon (0235) 33421

ROBSON, George. b 34. AKC58. **d** 59 **p** 60. C Chorley St Geo *Blackb* 59-62; Chapl RAF 62-87; R Raithby *Linc* from 87; R Lt Steeping from 87; V Spilsby w Hundleby from 87; R Aswardby w Sausthorpe from 87; R Langton w Sutterby from 87; R Halton Holgate from 87; R Firsby w Gt Steeping from 87. *The Vicarage, Spilsby, Lincs PE23 5DU* Spilsby (0790) 52526

ROBSON, Gilbert Alan. b 30. St Pet Hall Ox BA53 MA57. Linc Th Coll 56. **d** 57 **p** 58. C Chatham St Mary w St Jo *Roch* 57-59; Sub Warden Roch Th Coll 59-62; Min Can Roch Cathl *Roch* 59-62; Bp's Dom Chapl 61-64; Chapl Roch Th Coll 62-64; R Wouldham *Roch* 62-64; Chapl Nor Coll of Educn 65-68; Sen Lect in Div 68-72; Dir of Ords *Ches* 72-74; V Shotwick 72-74; Bp's Dom Chapl 72-74; Chapl Eton Coll Windsor 74-89; R Wrotham *Roch* from 89. *The Rectory, Wrotham, Sevenoaks, Kent TN15 7RA* Borough Green (0732) 882211

ROBSON, Ian Leonard. b 32. Bps' Coll Cheshunt 61. **d** 63 **p** 64. C Croxley Green All SS *St Alb* 63-65; C Harpenden St Nic 65-68; V Redbourn 68-72; V Ashford St Matt *Lon* 72-77; V Kensington St Mary Abbots w St Geo from 77. *St Mary Abbots Vicarage, Vicarage Gate, London W8 4HN* 071-937 6032 or 937 9490

ROBSON, Irwin. b 20. **d** 63 **p** 64. C-in-c Byker St Martin CD *Newc* 69-74; V Willington 74-76; TR Willington Team 76-83; V Ulgham 83-87; V Widdrington 83-87; rtd 88; Perm to Offic *Newc* from 88. *8 Brinkburn Place, Amble, Morpeth, Northd NE65 0BJ* Alnwick (0665) 710765

ROBSON, John Phillips. b 32. St Edm Hall Ox. AKC58. **d** 59 **p** 60. C Huddersfield SS Pet and Paul *Wakef* 59-62; Asst Chapl Ch Hosp Horsham 62-65; Chapl 65-80; Chapl Wellington Coll Berks 80-89; Lic to Offic *Ox* 80-89; Chapl R Victorian Order from 89; Chapl to Qu Chpl of the Savoy from 89. *Queen's Chapel of the Savoy, Savoy Hill, Strand, London WC2R 0DA* 071-379 8088

ROBSON, Patricia Anne. b 40. CertEd60. SW Minl Tr Course 85. **d** 87. Dioc Youth Officer *Truro* from 87; Hon C Paul from 87; Hon C Kenwyn St Geo from 88. *1 Penair View, Truro, Cornwall TR1 1XR* Truro (0872) 70617

ROBSON, Paul Coutt. b 37. Leeds Univ BA60. Coll of Resurr Mirfield 63. **d** 64 **p** 65. C Stokesay *Heref* 64-66; S Africa 66-69; Chapl HM Pris Man 70-71; HM Borstal Feltham 71-74; Hollesley 74-78; HM Pris Grendon and Spring Hill 79-87; Chapl HM Pris Nor from 87. *Chaplain's Office, HM Prison, Norwich NR1 4LU* Norwich (0603) 37531

ROBSON, Peter Cole. b 45. Clare Coll Cam BA66 MA70 Or Coll Ox BLitt69 MLitt70. Coll of Resurr Mirfield 70. **d** 71 **p** 72. C Gt Grimsby St Mary and St Jas *Linc* 71-73; Chapl BNC Ox 73-76; R Timsbury *B & W* 76-79; P-in-c Blanchland w Hunstanworth *Newc* 80-83; rtd 87. *The Elms, 17 Eden Terrace, Durham DH1 2HJ* 091-384 7159

ROBSON, Stephen Thomas. b 54. Chich Th Coll 84. **d** 86 **p** 87. C Newc St Fran *Newc* 86-89; C Gateshead St Cuth w St Paul *Dur* 89-91; TV Stanley from 91. *St Stephen's House, Holly Hill Gardens East, Stanley, Co Durham DH9 6NN*

ROBSON, Thomas George Harry. b 11. Jes Coll Ox BA34 MA41. Wells Th Coll 35. **d** 36 **p** 37. Rhodesia 68-79; Hon C E Grinstead St Swithun *Chich* 79-81; rtd 86. *1/2 Sackville College, East Grinstead, E Sussex RH19 3BX* East Grinstead (0342) 21835

ROBSON, William. b 34. FCIS66 FCCA80. Sarum & Wells Th Coll 77. **d** 79 **p** 80. C Lymington *Win* 79-81; CF from 81. *c/o MOD (Army), Bagshot Park, Bagshot, Surrey GU19 5PL* Bagshot (0276) 71717

ROBUS, Keith Adrian. b 59. Chich Th Coll 85. **d** 88 **p** 89. C Greenhill St Jo *Lon* from 88. *20 Manor Court, Bonnersfield Lane, Harrow, Middx HA1 2LD* 081-861 1237

ROBY, Richard James. b 33. Imp Coll Lon BSc54. St Alb Minl Tr Scheme 82. **d** 85 **p** 86. NSM Bushey *St Alb* from 85. *53 Kingsfield Road, Oxhey, Watford WD1 4PP* Watford (0923) 229346

ROCHDALE, Archdeacon of. *See* DALBY, Ven Dr John Mark Meredith

ROCHE, Barry Robert Francis. b 40. Lon Univ BD66 Dur Univ DipTh67. Clifton Th Coll 63. **d** 68 **p** 69. C Beckenham Ch Ch *Roch* 68-72; C Ches le Street *Dur* 72-74; C-in-c N Bletchley CD *Ox* 74-78; Chapl All SS Hosp Chatham from 78; R Luton Ch Ch *Roch* from 78. *Luton Rectory, Capstone Road, Chatham, Kent ME5 7PN* Medway (0634) 43780

ROCHE, Harold John. b 24. Ripon Hall Ox 54. **d** 54 **p** 55. C Southport St Phil *Liv* 54-57; V Wigan St Steph 57-63; R Sutcombe *Ex* from 63; R W w E Putford 64-71;

V Putford from 71; P-in-c Bradworthy 71-72; RD Holsworthy from 80. *The Rectory, Sutcombe, Holsworthy, Devon EX22 7PU* Bradworthy (040924) 298

ROCHESTER, Thomas Robson. b 33. NE Ord Course 85. **d** 90. NSM Glendale Gp *Newc* from 90. *Yearle House, Wooler, Northd NE71 6RB* Wooler (0668) 81314

ROCHESTER, Archdeacon of. *See* WARREN, Ven Norman Leonard

ROCHESTER, Bishop of. *See* TURNBULL, Rt Rev Michael

ROCHESTER, Dean of. *See* SHOTTER, Very Rev Edward Frank

ROCK, Mrs Jean. b 37. Gilmore Course. **dss** 79 **d** 87. Douglas St Matt *S & M* 79-81; Marown 81-83; Chapl Asst Oswestry and Distr Hosp 83-90; Oswestry St Oswald *Lich* 83-87; Par Dn 87-90; Cl-in-c Pont Robert and Pont Dolanog *St As* from 90. *Ty'r Eglwys, Pont Robert, Meifod, Powys* Meifod (093884) 454

ROCKALL, Miss Valerie Jane. b 42. City of Cov Coll CertEd63. St Alb Minl Tr Scheme 78. **dss** 81 **d** 87. Asst Hd Wigginton Sch Tring 73-90; Boxmoor St Jo *St Alb* 81-87; NSM Hemel Hempstead 87-90; Par Dn Ampthill w Millbrook and Steppingley from 90. *18 Russell Drive, Ampthill, Beds MK45 2UA* Ampthill (0525) 405812

ROCKLEY, Canon Thomas Alfred. b 06. Leeds Univ BA29. Coll of Resurr Mirfield 24. **d** 31 **p** 32. Can Res and Chan Blackb Cathl *Blackb* 64-75; rtd 75; Lic to Offic *Blackb* from 75. *32 Rutland Street, Blackburn BB2 1UY* Blackburn (0254) 670897

RODDA, William Reginald. b 09. Clifton Th Coll 35. **d** 36 **p** 37. R Leigh w Batcombe *Sarum* 71-73; rtd 74. *2 Cuthburga Road, Wimborne, Dorset BH21 1LH* Wimborne (0202) 883285

RODEN, Cyril John. b 20. E Anglian Minl Tr Course 79. **d** 81 **p** 82. NSM Clenchwarton *Ely* 81-89; rtd 89; Perm to Offic Nor & Ely from 89. *52 Jubilee Bank, Clenchwarton, King's Lynn, Norfolk PE34 4BW* King's Lynn (0553) 773826

RODEN, John Michael. b 37. St Jo Coll York CertEd64 Open Univ BA82. Ripon Hall Ox 71. **d** 73 **p** 74. C Saltburn-by-the-Sea *York* 73-77; Chapl St Pet Sch York 77-82; Warden Marrick Priory *Ripon* 83; Hon C Appleton Roebuck w Acaster Selby *York* 84-85; P-in-c 86; P-in-c from 86; Youth Officer from 86. *All Saints' Vicarage, Appleton Roebuck, York YO5 7DG* Appleton Roebuck (090484) 327

RODEN, Michael Adrian Holland. b 60. Ripon Coll Cuddesdon 82. **d** 85 **p** 86. C S Lambeth St Anne and All SS *S'wark* 85-88; C Wandsworth St Paul 88-90; C Ox St Mary V w St Cross and St Pet *Ox* from 90; Chapl Wadh Coll Ox from 90. *22 Stratford Street, Oxford OX4 1SN* Oxford (0865) 247592

RODERICK, Bertram David. b 22. S'wark Ord Course 63. **d** 66 **p** 67. C Horley *S'wark* 69-72; V Sutton New Town St Barn 73-82; R Burstow 82-89; rtd 89. *April Cottage, 2 Church Lane, Henfield, W Sussex BN5 9NY* Henfield (0273) 493797

RODERICK, Charles Edward Morys. b 10. Trin Coll Ox BA32 MA51. Ripon Hall Ox 38. **d** 39 **p** 40. V Ches Square St Mich w St Phil *Lon* 53-71; Chapl to HM The Queen 62-80; V Longparish w Hurstbourne Priors *Win* 71-80; rtd 80; Perm to Offic *Win* from 80. *135 Little Ann, Andover, Hants SP11 7NW* Andover (0264) 710229

RODERICK, John Howard. b 12. St D Coll Lamp BA33. St Mich Coll Llan 33. **d** 35 **p** 36. V Wotton St Mary *Glouc* 60-73; R Bromsberrow 73-77; rtd 78; Perm to Offic *Glouc* from 79. *24 Biddulph Way, Ledbury, Herefordshire HR8 2HN* Ledbury (0531) 4474

RODERICK, Philip David. b 49. Univ of Wales (Swansea) BA70 Univ of Wales (Abth) BD77 Lon Univ CertEd71. Linc Th Coll 79. **d** 80 **p** 81. C Llanfair-is-gaer and Llanddeiniolen *Ban* 80-82; TV Holyhead w Rhoscolyn w Llanfair-yn-Neubwll 82-84; Warden Angl Chapl Cen 84-88; Chapl and Lect Th Univ of Wales (Ban) 84-88; Dir Chiltern Chr Tr Course *Ox* from 88; Prin Buckm Adnry Chr Tr Scheme from 88. *18 Sunter's Wood Close, Booker, High Wycombe, Bucks HP12 4DZ* High Wycombe (0494) 21605

RODFORD, Brian George. b 50. Hatf Poly BEd84. **d** 79 **p** 80. Hon C St Alb St Steph *St Alb* 79-85; Hon C Hendon St Mary *Lon* 85-90; Hon C Winchmore Hill H Trin from 90. *177 Winchmore Hill Road, London N21 1QN* 081-882 1195

✠**RODGER, Rt Rev Patrick Campbell.** b 20. Ch Ch Ox BA43 MA47. Westcott Ho Cam 47. **d** 49 **p** 50 **c** 70. C Edin St Jo *Edin* 49-51; Chapl Edin Univ 51-55; C Woodside Park St Barn *Lon* 55-58; Study Sec SCM 55-58; R Kilmacolm *Glas* 58-61; R Bridge of Weir 58-61;

Exec Sec of Faith & Order Dept WCC 61-66; R Edin St Mary *Edin* 66-70; Vice-Provost St Mary's Cathl 66-67; Provost 67-70; Bp Man 70-78; Bp Ox 78-86; rtd 86; Asst Bp *Edin* from 86. *12 Warrender Park Terrace, Edinburgh EH9 1EG*   031-229 5075

RODGER, Canon Raymond. b 39. Westmr Coll Ox DipApTh91. Bps' Coll Cheshunt 62. **d** 63 **p** 64. C Frodingham *Linc* 63-66; Asst Chapl St Geo Hosp Gp Lon 66-69; C Waltham *Linc* 69-73; V Nocton 73-86; P-in-c Potter Hanworth 74-86; P-in-c Dunston 77-86; RD Graffoe from 81; Can and Preb Linc Cathl from 85; V Nocton w Dunston and Potterhanworth from 86. *The Vicarage, Nocton, Lincoln LN4 2BJ*   Metheringham (0526) 20296

RODGERS, Arthur Harold. b 07. Bp's Coll Calcutta. **d** 39 **p** 41. R Trotton w Chithurst *Chich* 57-72; rtd 72; Perm to Offic *Chich* from 73. *8 Beresford Road, Goudhurst, Cranbrook, Kent TN17 1DN*   Goudhurst (0580) 211874

RODGERS, Canon Cyril George Hooper. b 20. Qu Coll Birm 50. **d** 52 **p** 53. CF (TA - R of O) 62-87; V Wiggenhall St Germans and Islington *Ely* 66-76; RD Lynn Marshland 68-76; R Woolpit *St E* 76-84; RD Lavenham 78-87; Hon Can St E Cathl 84-87; R Woolpit w Drinkstone 84-87; rtd 87. *Fox Farm, Wetherden, Stowmarket, Suffolk* Elmswell (0359) 40364

RODGERS, David. b 26. Sarum Th Coll 63. **d** 65 **p** 66. V Leigh Woods *B & W* 68-76; R Wellow w Foxcote and Shoscombe 76-79; C Wells St Cuth w Coxley and Wookey Hole 79-82; P-in-c Wookey w Henton 79-82; V Ercall Magna *Lich* 82-89; V Rowton 82-89; RD Wrockwardine 84-88; rtd 89. *8 Crabtree Lane, Wem, Shrewsbury SY4 5AJ*

RODGERS, Frank. b 27. Linc Th Coll 69. **d** 71 **p** 72. C Alford w Rigsby *Linc* 71-75; P-in-c Quadring 75-80; P-in-c Gosberton Clough 75-80; V Gosberton Clough and Quadring 80-84; R S Kelsey 80-84; P-in-c Usselby 80-84; P-in-c Kirkby w Kingerby 80-84; P-in-c N Owersby w Thornton le Moor 80-84; R S Kelsey Gp 84-86; V Cranwell from 86; R Leasingham from 86. *The Rectory, 3 Moor Lane, Leasingham, Sleaford, Lincs NG34 8JN* Sleaford (0529) 306756

RODGERS, Frank Ernest. b 46. Tyndale Hall Bris 68. **d** 71 **p** 72. C Madeley *Heref* 71-74; C Littleover *Derby* 74-77; V Clodock and Longtown w Craswell and Llanveyno *Heref* 77-79; P-in-c St Margaret's w Michaelchurch Eskley and Newton 77-79; V Clodock and Longtown w Craswall, Llanveynoe etc from 79; RD Abbeydore from 90. *The Vicarage, Longtown, Hereford HR2 0LD*   Longtown Castle (087387) 289

RODGERS, John Terence Roche. b 28. TCD BA53 MA57. Bps' Coll Cheshunt. **d** 57 **p** 58. C Templecorran *Conn* 57-60; C Derriaghy 60-61; C Antrim All SS 61-64; I Belf St Steph 64-79; I Dunmurry from 79. *27 Church Avenue, Dunmurry, Belfast BT17 9RS*   Belfast (0232) 610984

RODGERS, Dr Richard Thomas Boycott. b 47. FRCS81 Lon Univ MB, BS70. St Jo Coll Nottm DipTh77. **d** 77 **p** 78. C Littleover *Derby* 77-80; C Birm St Martin w Bordesley St Andr *Birm* 89-90; Lect from 89; Perm to Offic from 90. *63 Meadow Brook Road, Birmingham B31 1ND*   021-476 0789

RODLEY, Ian Tony. b 48. Qu Coll Birm 77. **d** 80 **p** 81. Dioc Children's Adv *Bradf* 80-85; C Baildon 80-85; V Bradf St Wilfrid Lidget Green 85-90; Chapl to the Deaf from 88; V Otley from 90. *The Vicarage, Otley, W Yorkshire LS21 3HR*   Otley (0943) 462240

RODRIGUEZ-VEGLIO, Francis Bonny. b 33. Sarum Th Coll 62. **d** 64 **p** 65. C Alnwick St Paul *Newc* 64-68; V Horton w Piddington *Pet* 68-79; P-in-c Preston Deanery 68-79; Chapl ACF 75-82; TV Scilly Is *Truro* 79-82; Hon Chapl Miss to Seamen 79-82; Perm to Offic *Pet* 86-88; C Leic Ch Sav *Leic* 88-91; V Kirkwhelpington, Kirkharle, Kirkheaton and Cambo *Newc* from 91. *The Vicarage, Kirkwhelpington, Newcastle upon Tyne NE19 2RT* Otterburn (0830) 40260

RODWELL, Barry John. b 39. Birm Univ CertEd59 Cam Univ DipAdEd77. Ridley Hall Cam 67. **d** 70 **p** 71. C Sudbury St Greg and St Pet *St E* 70-73; Hd of RE Hedingham Sch 73-80; R Sible Hedingham *Chelmsf* 80-85; RE Adv from 85. *Gimbals, 9 Greenways, Gosfield, Halstead, Essex CO9 1TW*   Halstead (0787) 472257

RODWELL, John Stanley. b 46. Leeds Univ BSc68 Ox Univ DipTh73 Southn Univ PhD74. Cuddesdon Coll 71. **d** 74 **p** 75. Hon C Horfield H Trin *Bris* 74-75; Hon C Skerton St Luke *Blackb* 75-77; Lic to Offic from 77. *7 Derwent Road, Lancaster LA1 3ES*   Lancaster (0524) 62726

ROE, Alan Arthur. b 26. Kelham Th Coll 43. **d** 51 **p** 52. V Walsingham and Houghton *Nor* 69-77; rtd 77; Perm to

Offic *Nor* from 77. *26 Cleaves Drive, Walsingham, Norfolk NR22 6EQ*   Walsingham (0328) 820107

ROE, Mrs Caroline Ruth. b 57. Birm Univ BA80. Wycliffe Hall Ox 81. **dss** 84 **d** 87. Olveston *Bris* 84-87; Par Dn 87-88; NSM Alveley and Quatt *Heref* from 88; Bp's Voc Officer from 90. *31 Bridge Road, Alveley, Bridgnorth, Shropshire WV15 6JN*   Bridgnorth (0746) 780977

ROE, Frank Ronald. b 31. Brasted Th Coll Westcott Ho Cam 55. **d** 57 **p** 58. C S w N Hayling *Portsm* 57-61; Hong Kong 61-77; Sen Chapl St Jo Cathl 61-66; Asst Chapl 77; Sen Chapl Miss to Seamen 66-69; Australia from 77; Hon Chapl Miss to Seamen from 77. *29 Andrew Street, PO Box 810, Esperance, W Australia 6450* Esperance (90) 713661

ROE, George Henry Edward Talbot. b 07. Selw Coll Cam BA30 MA35. Sarum Th Coll 30. **d** 32 **p** 33. R Wheathampstead *St Alb* 46-79; rtd 79. *1 Owlstone Road, Cambridge CB3 9JH*   Cambridge (0223) 311213

ROE, Canon Joseph Thorley. b 22. AKC49 DipAdEd Hull Univ PhD90. K Coll Lon 46. **d** 50 **p** 51. Prin Lect & Sen Couns Bretton Hall Coll Wakef 67-74; Sec for Miss and Unity *Ripon* 74-78; Dioc Missr and Bp's Dom Chapl 75-78; Can Res Carl Cathl *Carl* 78-82; Dioc Dir of Tr 78-82; Dioc Adult Educn Officer *Wakef* 82-88; Hon Can Wakef Cathl from 83; Dir of Educn 85-88; rtd 88. *29 Milnthorpe Drive, Wakefield, W Yorkshire WF2 7HU* Wakefield (0924) 256938

ROE, Peter Harold. b 37. K Coll Lon BD62 AKC62. **d** 63 **p** 64. C Knowle St Barn *Bris* 63-65; C Leckhampton St Pet *Glouc* 65-68; V Shaw Hill *Birm* 68-73; V Hobs Moat 73-90; V Packwood w Hockley Heath from 90. *The Vicarage, Nuthurst Lane, Hockley Heath, Solihull, W Midlands B94 5RP*   Knowle (0564) 783121

ROE, Robert Henry. b 22. LCP57. Westcott Ho Cam 72. **d** 74 **p** 75. Hd Master St Mary's Primary Sch Saffron Walden 74-83; NSM Saffron Walden w Wendens Ambo *Chelmsf* 74-75; NSM Saffron Walden w Wendens Ambo and Littlebury 75-87; NSM Blakeney w Cley, Wiveton, Glandford etc *Nor* from 87. *Larchmount, High Street, Cley, Holt, Norfolk NR25 7RG*   Cley (0263) 740369

ROE, Robin. b 28. CBE MC68. TCD BA52 MA55. **d** 53 **p** 54. CF 55-81; QHC 77-81; R Merrow *Guildf* 81-89; rtd 89. *Lansdowne, 6 Mitchells Close, Shalford, Guildford, Surrey GU4 8HY*   Guildford (0483) 63852

✠**ROE, Rt Rev William Gordon.** b 32. Jes Coll Ox BA55 MA57 DipTh57 DPhil62. St Steph Ho Ox 56. **d** 58 **p** 59 **c** 80. C Bournemouth St Pet *Win* 58-61; C Abingdon w Shippon *Ox* 61-69; Vice-Prin St Chad's Coll Dur 69-74; V Dur St Oswald *Dur* 74-80; RD Dur 74-80; Hon Can Dur Cathl 79-80; Suff Bp Huntingdon *Ely* from 80; Can Res Ely Cathl 80-89. *14 Lynn Road, Ely, Cambs CB6 1DA*   Ely (0353) 662137

ROEBUCK, Austin Vincent. b 06. Lich Th Coll 40. **d** 43 **p** 44. V Lyddington w Stoke Dry and Seaton *Pet* 66-71; rtd 71. *Dulverton Hall, St Martin's Square, Scarborough YO11 2DB*   Scarborough (0723) 373082

ROEBUCK, John William. b 11. Keble Coll Ox BA34. Cuddesdon Coll 45. **d** 47 **p** 48. R Kirkwall *Ab* 69-77; rtd 77; Perm to Offic *Derby* from 77. *55 Stone Street, Llandovery, Dyfed SA20 0DQ*   Llandovery (0550) 21132

ROEMMELE, Michael Patrick. b 49. TCD BA72 MA76. **d** 73 **p** 74. C Portadown St Columba *Arm* 73-77; C Drumachose *D & R* 77-80; Bahrain 79-83; Cyprus 79-83; Chapl RAF from 83. *c/o MOD, Adastral House, Theobald's Road, London WC1X 8RU*   071-430 7268

ROESCHLAUB, Robert Friedrich. b 39. Purdue Univ BSc63. Berkeley Div Sch MDiv66. **d** 66 **p** 66. USA 66-77; Hon C Tilehurst St Cath *Ox* 78-79; Hon C Tilehurst St Mich 79-82; P-in-c Millom H Trin w Thwaites *Carl* 82-85; P-in-c Millom 85-89; R Dunstall w Rangemore and Tatenhill *Lich* from 89. *The Vicarage, Church Road, Rangemore, Burton-on-Trent, Staffs DE13 9RW* Barton-under-Needwood (0283) 712509

ROFF, Andrew Martin. b 42. Bede Coll Dur BSc65. Westcott Ho Cam 65. **d** 70 **p** 71. C Ches St Mary *Ches* 70-73; Min Can Blackb Cathl *Blackb* 73-76; P-in-c Blackb St Jo 74-75; V Longton 76-81; Chapl Trin Coll Glenalmond 82-83; R Allendale w Whitfield *Newc* from 83. *The Rectory, Allendale, Hexham, Northd NE47 9AS* Hexham (0434) 683336

ROFF, John Michael. b 47. St Chad's Coll Dur BSc69. Westcott Ho Cam 70. **d** 72 **p** 73. C Lanc St Mary *Blackb* 72-75; C Dronfield *Derby* 75-76; TV 76-80; TR N Wingfield, Pilsley and Tupton 80-85; V Ilkeston St Mary 85-90; V Stockport St Geo *Ches* from 90. *St George's Vicarage, 28 Buxton Road, Stockport, Cheshire SK2 6NU* 061-480 2453

ROGAN, Canon John. b 28. St Jo Coll Dur BA49 MA51 DipTh54 Open Univ BPhil81. **d** 54 **p** 55. C Ashton St Mich *Man* 54-57; C Sheff Sharrow *Sheff* 57-61; Ind Chapl 57-61; Sec C of E Ind Cttee 61-66; V Leigh St Mary *Man* 66-78; RD Leigh 71-78; Hon Can Man Cathl 75-78; Provost St Paul's Cathl Dundee *Bre* 78-83; R Dundee St Paul 78-83; Soc Resp Adv *Bris* from 83; Can Res Bris Cathl from 83. *84 Concorde Drive, Bristol BS10 6PX*   Bristol (0272) 505803

ROGERS, Alan Chad John. b 33. Selw Coll Cam BA56 MA60. Bps' Coll Cheshunt 58. **d** 60 **p** 61. C Sudbury St Andr *Lon* 60-62; Mauritius 62-66; V Edmonton St Alphege *Lon* 66-71; V Enfield St Geo from 71. *St George's Vicarage, 706 Hertford Road, Enfield, Middx EN3 6NR*   Lea Valley (0992) 762581

ROGERS, Canon Alan David. b 24. K Coll Cam BA47 MA50. Cuddesdon Coll 50. **d** 52 **p** 53. Lect Div Weymouth Coll 67-73; Lic to Offic *Sarum* from 69; Hd of Relig and Th Depts Dorset Inst of Educn 73-82; Hon Can Antananarivo from 84; rtd 89. *4 Fossett Way, Weymouth, Dorset DT4 9HD*   Weymouth (0305) 779942

✠**ROGERS, Rt Rev Alan Francis Bright.** b 07. Lambeth MA59. Bps' Coll Cheshunt 28. **d** 30 **p** 31 **c** 59. C Shepherd's Bush St Steph *Lon* 30-32; C Twickenham Common H Trin 32-34; Mauritius 34-49; Adn 46-49; Bp 59-66; Hon Can St Jas Cathl 44-59; V Twickenham St Mary *Lon* 49-54; Hon C from 85; V Hampstead St Jo 54-59; RD Hampstead 55-59; Suff Bp Fulham 66-70; Suff Bp Edmonton 70-75; rtd 75; Asst Bp Pet 75-84; P-in-c Wappenham w Abthorpe and Slapton 77-80; C Abthorpe w Slapton 81-83; Asst Bp Lon from 85. *20 River Way, Twickenham, Middx TW2 5JP*   081-894 2031

ROGERS, Brian Robert. b 36. Open Univ BA80. St Jo Coll Nottm 70. **d** 72 **p** 73. C Ealing St Mary *Lon* 72-74; C Greenside *Dur* 74-75; Lic to Offic 75-85; Perm to Offic *Lich* from 85. *23 New Road, Uttoxeter, Staffs*   Uttoxeter (0889) 563515

ROGERS, Brian Victor. b 50. Trin Coll Bris 75. **d** 78 **p** 79. C Plumstead St Jo w St Jas and St Paul *S'wark* 78-83; P-in-c Gayton *Nor* 83-85; P-in-c Gayton Thorpe w E Walton 83-85; P-in-c Westacre 83-85; P-in-c Ashwicken w Leziate 83-85; R Gayton Gp of Par 85-91; R Rackheath and Salhouse from 91. *The Rectory, Rackheath, Norwich NR13 6NG*   Norwich (0603) 720097

ROGERS, Cecil George. b 05. St D Coll Lamp BA28. **d** 28 **p** 29. R W Horsley *Guildf* 43-53; rtd 53; Perm to Offic *Lon* from 82. *Peasmarsh Place, Peasmarsh, Rye, E Sussex TN31 6XE*   Peasmarsh (079721) 633

ROGERS, Charles Murray. b 17. Qu Coll Cam BA38 MA40 Lon Univ DipEd43. Westcott Ho Cam 38. **d** 40 **p** 41. India 46-71; Jerusalem 71-80; Hong Kong 80-89; rtd 82; Canada from 89. *Box 683, 103 Brant Street, Deseronto, Ontario, Canada, K0K 1XO*

ROGERS, Christopher Antony. b 47. N Ord Course 79. **d** 81 **p** 82. C Chesterfield St Aug *Derby* 81-84; C Chaddesden St Phil 84-86; R Whitwell from 86. *The Rectory, Whitwell, Worksop, Notts S80 4RE*   Worksop (0909) 720220

ROGERS, Christopher John. b 47. Bp Lonsdale Coll CertEd Nottm Univ DipEd. E Midl Min Tr Course. **d** 84 **p** 85. NSM Ockbrook *Derby* 84-91; P-in-c Risby w Gt and Lt Saxham and Westley *St E* from 91. *The Rectory, Risby, Bury St Edmunds, Suffolk IP28 6RQ*   Bury St Edmunds (0284) 810416

ROGERS, Clive William. b 62. Selw Coll Cam BA83 MA87 Southn Univ BTh90. Chich Th Coll 87. **d** 90 **p** 91. C Leic Ascension *Leic* from 90. *26 Chevin Avenue, Braunstone Frith, Leicester LE3 6PX*   Leicester (0533) 872558

ROGERS, Cyril David. b 55. Birm Univ BA76 BTh. Sarum & Wells Th Coll 80. **d** 83 **p** 84. C Leagrave *St Alb* 83-87; TV Langtree *Ox* from 87. *The Vicarage, Reading Road, Woodcote, Reading RG8 0QZ*   Checkendon (0491) 680979

ROGERS, David. b 48. Univ of Wales (Ban) BA69. Westcott Ho Cam 70. **d** 72 **p** 73. C Rainbow Hill St Barn *Worc* 72-75; C Tolladine 72-75; C Astwood Bank w Crabbs Cross 75-79; V Cradley 79-90; V Beoley from 90. *The Vicarage, Church Hill, Beoley, Redditch, Worcs B98 9AR*   Redditch (0527) 63976

ROGERS, David Alan. b 55. MCIT82 City of Lon Poly BA77. Linc Th Coll 88. **d** 90 **p** 91. C Kingston upon Hull St Nic *York* from 90. *242 Anlaby Park Road South, Hull HU4 7BZ*   Hull (0482) 641329

ROGERS, Ven David Arthur. b 21. Ch Coll Cam BA47 MA52. Ridley Hall Cam 47. **d** 49 **p** 50. V Sedbergh *Bradf* 59-74; RD Sedbergh 59-73; V Garsdale 60-74; V Cautley w Dowbiggin 60-74; Hon Can Bradf Cathl 67-77; P-in-c Firbank, Howgill and Killington 73-77; RD Ewecross 73-77; V Sedbergh, Cautley and Garsdale 74-79; Adn Craven 77-86; rtd 86; Perm to Offic Bradf from 86; Blackb from 87; Carl from 89. *Borrens Farm, Leck, Carnforth, Lancs LA6 2JG*   Kirkby Lonsdale (05242) 71616

ROGERS, David Eland. b 17. Wycliffe Hall Ox 49. **d** 51 **p** 52. V Hanworth All SS *Lon* 61-72; Chapl Whiteley Village Walton-on-Thames 72-82; rtd 82. *29 Chalkpit Terrace, Dorking, Surrey*   Dorking (0306) 888509

ROGERS, David Martyn. b 56. Univ of Wales (Lamp) BA77 K Coll Lon BD79 AKC79 St Kath Coll Liv DipEd86. Chich Th Coll 79. **d** 80 **p** 81. C Hockerill *St Alb* 80-85; Perm to Offic *St As* 85-87; C W Hampstead St Jas *Lon* 87; C Kilburn St Mary 87-90; V New Longton *Blackb* from 90; Chapl to Lancs Constabulary from 90. *All Saints' Vicarage, Station Road, New Longton, Preston, Lancs PR4 4LN*   Preston (0772) 613347

ROGERS, Canon Donovan Charles Edgar. b 08. Clifton Th Coll 32. **d** 35 **p** 36. C Leyton Em *Chelmsf* 35-37; C N Woolwich 37-38; Chapl RAF 38-41; CF 41-46; S Africa from 47. *The Cottage, Beach Road, Noordhoek, 7985 South Africa*   Cape Town (21) 891117

ROGERS, Edward Lyon Beresford Cheselden. b 22. VRD65. Keble Coll Ox BA48 MA51. Wells Th Coll 48. **d** 49 **p** 50. Chapl RNR 58-74; R St Giles Cripplegate w St Bart Moor Lane etc *Lon* 66-87; rtd 87; Perm to Offic *Chelmsf* from 87. *Windy Ridge, Wethersfield Road, Finchingfield, Braintree, Essex CM7 4NS*   Great Dunmow (0371) 810741

ROGERS, Henry Richard. b 04. Trin Coll Cam BA26 MA30. Westcott Ho Cam 25. **d** 27 **p** 28. R Liddington *Bris* 63-68; rtd 69. *Cove, Achahoish, Lochgilphead, Argyll*   Ormsary (08803) 266

ROGERS, Canon John. b 34. Univ of Wales (Lamp) BA55 Or Coll Ox BA58 MA61. St Steph Ho Ox 57. **d** 59 **p** 60. C Roath St Martin *Llan* 59-63; Br Guiana 63-66; Guyana 66-71; V Caldicot *Mon* 71-77; V Mon 77-84; RD Mon 81-84; R Ebbw Vale from 84; RD Blaenau Gwent from 86; Can St Woolos Cathl from 88. *The Rectory, Eureka Place, Ebbw Vale, Gwent NP3 6PN*   Ebbw Vale (0495) 301723

ROGERS, Preb John Arnold. b 34. Univ of Wales (Lamp) BA57. **d** 59 **p** 60. C Blaenavon w Capel Newydd *Mon* 59-62; C Bassaleg 62-67; C Old Ford St Paul w St Steph *Lon* 67-73; P-in-c 73-75; V 75-79; V Hampton St Mary from 79; AD Hampton 82-86; Preb St Paul's Cathl from 86; Dir of Ords from 87. *St Mary's Vicarage, Church Street, Hampton, Middx TW12 2EB*   081-979 3071

ROGERS, John Iorwerth. b 17. Univ of Wales (Lamp) BA39. Ripon Hall Ox 39. **d** 41 **p** 42. Lic to Offic *Derby* from 59; Hd Master Normanton Sch Buxton 71-86; rtd 87. *15 Plas Hen, Llanddaniel, Gaerwen, Gwynedd LL60 6HW*   Gaerwen (024877) 812

ROGERS, John Robin. b 36. St Alb Minl Tr Scheme 78. **d** 81 **p** 82. NSM Digswell and Panshanger *St Alb* 81-84; C Welwyn w Ayot St Peter from 85. *St Michael's House, 3 London Road, Woolmer Green, Knebworth, Herts SG3 6JU*   Stevenage (0438) 813043

ROGERS, John William Trevor. b 28. Qu Coll Birm. **d** 85 **p** 86. NSM Dunchurch *Cov* from 85. *15 Hillyard Road, Southam, Leamington Spa, Warks CV33 0LD*   Southam (092681) 3469

ROGERS, Keith Frederick. b 10. Keble Coll Ox BA33 MA37. Chich Th Coll 34. **d** 36 **p** 37. R Chilthorne Domer, Yeovil Marsh and Thorne Coffin *B & W* 71-75; rtd 75. *Oliver House, Priory Street, York YO11 1ES*

ROGERS, Canon Kenneth. b 33. Cuddesdon Coll 68. **d** 69 **p** 70. C Perranzabuloe *Truro* 69-71; C Truro St Paul 71-74; P-in-c Kenwyn St Geo 74-87; RD Powder 81-88; Hon Can Truro Cathl from 87; TR Bodmin w Lanhydrock and Lanivet from 87; RD Trigg Minor and Bodmin from 89. *The Rectory, Bodmin, Cornwall PL31 2AB*   Bodmin (0208) 73867

ROGERS, Llewelyn. Univ of Wales (Lamp) BA59. St Mich Coll Llan. **d** 61 **p** 62. C Holywell *St As* 61-64; C Hawarden 64-70; R Bodfari 70-73; V Rhosymedre 73-77; V Llansantffraid-ym-Mechain 77-83; V Llansantffraid-ym-Mechain and Llanfechain from 83; RD Llanfyllin from 84. *The Vicarage, Llansantffraid-ym-Mechain, Powys SY22 6TZ*   Llansantffraid (0691) 828244

ROGERS, Malcolm Dawson. b 63. SS Hild & Bede Coll Dur BA84 Selw Coll Cam BA88. Ridley Hall Cam 86. **d** 89 **p** 90. C Ipswich St Jo *St E* from 89. *2A Norbury Road, Ipswich IP4 4RQ*   Ipswich (0473) 710025

ROGERS, Mark James. b 64. Univ of Wales (Lamp) BA. Qu Coll Birm. **d** 89 **p** 90. C Dudley Holly Hall St Aug *Worc* from 89. *218 Stourbridge Road, Holly Hall, Dudley, W Midlands*   Brierley Hill (0384) 261026

ROGERS, Martin Stephen. b 28. St Edm Hall Ox BA50 MA54. Cuddesdon Coll 50. **d** 52 **p** 53. C Reading St Mary V *Ox* 52-54; C Buxton *Derby* 54-57; Australia 58-64; Lect Cuddesdon Coll 65-73; Chapl Littlemore Hosp Ox 65-74; Dept of Educn Cam Univ 73-76; Chapl Univ Coll of Ripon & York St Jo from 76; Postgraduate Medical Educn Adv Leeds Univ from 90. *The College, College Road, Ripon, N Yorkshire HG4 2QX* Ripon (0765) 2691

ROGERS, Maurice George Walden. b 23. AKC51. **d** 52 **p** 53. V Gt Ilford St Luke *Chelmsf* 61-72; V Woodford St Barn 72-89; rtd 89. *The Coach House, 13 Bodorgan Road, Bournemouth BH2 6NQ*

ROGERS, Michael Ernest. b 34. Sarum & Wells Th Coll 83. **d** 85 **p** 86. C Roehampton H Trin *S'wark* 85-88; V Ryhill *Wakef* from 88. *The Vicarage, 20 School Lane, Ryhill, Wakefield, W Yorkshire WF4 2DW* Barnsley (0226) 722363

ROGERS, Michael Hugh Walton. b 52. K Coll Lon BD73 AKC73. St Aug Coll Cant 74. **d** 75 **p** 76. C Eastbourne St Andr *Chich* 75-78; C Uppingham w Ayston *Pet* 78-82; V Eye 82-90; R Cottesmore and Barrow w Ashwell and Burley from 90. *The Rectory, Cottesmore, Oakham, Leics LE15 7DJ* Oakham (0572) 812202

ROGERS, Canon Noel Desmond. b 26. TD71. Univ of Wales (Lamp) BA51. **d** 53 **p** 54. C Rhyl w Rhyl St Ann *St As* 53-58; V Everton St Geo *Liv* 58-64; CF (TA) 59-75; R Newton in Makerfield Em *Liv* 64-74; V Rostherne w Bollington *Ches* from 74; CF (R of O) 75-81; RD Knutsford *Ches* from 85; Hon Can Ches Cathl from 87. *The Vicarage, Rostherne, Knutsford, Cheshire WA16 6RY* Bucklow Hill (0565) 830595

ROGERS, Mrs Patricia Anne. b 54. Lon Univ BD. Trin Coll Bris. **d** 87. Hon C Gayton Gp of Par *Nor* 87-91; Hon C Rackheath and Salhouse from 91; Chapl to the Deaf from 91. *The Rectory, Stonehill, Rackheath, Norwich NR13 6NG* Norwich (0603) 720097

ROGERS, Percival Hallewell. b 12. MBE45. St Edm Hall Ox BA35 MA46. Bps' Coll Cheshunt. **d** 46 **p** 47. Hd Master Portora R Sch Enniskillen 54-73; Chapl Gresham's Sch Holt 74-75; USA 76-80; Warden Lay Readers and Ords *Clogh* 81-84; C Sandford-on-Thames *Ox* 85-87; rtd 87; Perm to Offic *Ox* from 87. *7 Eyot Place, Oxford OX4 1SA* Oxford (0865) 244976

ROGERS, Philip Gordon. b 31. Lich Th Coll 62. **d** 64 **p** 65. C Morecambe St Barn *Blackb* 64-67; C Bingley All SS *Bradf* 67-71; V Cross Roads cum Lees 71-76; V Heaton St Martin from 76. *St Martin's Vicarage, Haworth Road, Bradford, W Yorkshire BD9 6LL* Bradford (0274) 543004

ROGERS, Philip John. b 52. Univ of Wales CertEd74 Nottm Univ BTh79. St Jo Coll Nottm 76. **d** 79 **p** 80. C Stretford St Bride *Man* 79-84; P-in-c Plumstead St Jo w St Jas and St Paul *S'wark* 84-85; V from 85. *St John's Vicarage, 176 Griffin Road, London SE18 7QA* 081-855 1827

ROGERS, Richard Anthony. b 46. Ex Coll Ox BA69 Birm Univ DipTh70. Qu Coll Birm 70. **d** 71 **p** 72. C Shirley *Birm* 71-74; Chapl Solihull Sch W Midl 74-78; Hon C Cotteridge *Birm* 78-84; Hon C Hill from 84. *169 Clarence Road, Sutton Coldfield, W Midlands B74 4LB* 021-308 0310

ROGERS, Richard George. b 21. **d** 88 **p** 88. NSM Eythorne and Elvington w Waldershare etc *Cant* from 88. *Maydeken, Church Road, Coldred, Dover, Kent CT15 5AQ* Shepherdswell (0304) 830157

ROGERS, Robert. b 42. Bernard Gilpin Soc Dur 66 St Aid Birkenhead 67 Ridley Hall Cam 69. **d** 70 **p** 71. C Childwall St Dav *Liv* 70-73; C Huntington *York* 73-76; TR Brayton 76-89; RD Selby 84-89; V New Malton from 89. *The Vicarage, 17 The Mount, Malton, York YO17 0ND* Malton (0653) 692089

ROGERS, Robert Charles. b 55. St Pet Coll Birm CertEd77. St Jo Coll Nottm 87. **d** 89 **p** 90. C Wellesbourne *Cov* from 89. *4 Loxley Close, Wellesbourne, Warwick CV35 9RU* Stratford-upon-Avon (0789) 842348

ROGERS, Ronald James. b 31. Bris Univ BA56 St Cath Soc Ox BA58 MA65. Wycliffe Hall Ox 56. **d** 58 **p** 59. C Gt Yarmouth *Nor* 58-62; C Newington St Mary *S'wark* 67-69; C Liv Our Lady and St Nic w St Anne *Liv* 78-83; C Pimlico St Pet w Westmr Ch Ch *Lon* 83-85; Chapl Westmr City Sch 85-87; P-in-c Westmr St Sav and St Jas Less *Lon* from 87. *59 Aylesford Street, London SW1V 3RY* 071-821 9865

ROGERS, Sally Jean. b 54. Univ of Wales (Lamp) BA77 Nottm Univ BTh87. Linc Th Coll 84. **d** 87. Par Dn Bris St Mary Redcliffe w Temple etc *Bris* 87-90; Par

Dn Greenford H Cross *Lon* from 90. *177 Costons Lane, Greenford, Middx UB6 9AD* 081-578 1596

ROGERS, Thomas More Fitzgerald. b 13. **d** 62 **p** 63. Chapl to the Deaf *Guildf* 69-72; Chapl to the Deaf *Cant* 72-77; rtd 77. *417 Sedlescombe Road North, St Leonards-on-Sea, E Sussex TN37 7PD* Hastings (0424) 751913

ROGERS, Vernon Donald. b 12. Keble Coll Ox BA34 MA40. Ely Th Coll 35. **d** 36 **p** 37. R Stoke-in-Teignhead and Combe-in-Teignhead *Ex* 71-77; rtd 77; Perm to Offic *B & W* from 77. *2 Stoberry Cresent, Wells, Somerset BA5 2TG* Wells (0749) 77701

ROGERS, Vivian Francis Edward. b 27. Oak Hill Th Coll 61. **d** 63 **p** 64. C Iver *Ox* 63-68; R Norton Fitzwarren *B & W* 68-77; V Grassendale *Liv* 77-84; R Swainswick w Langridge *B & W* from 84. *The Rectory, Upper Swainswick, Bath BA1 8BX* Bath (0225) 852239

ROGERS, William Arthur. b 41. Lon Univ BA64 CertEd, Chich Th Coll 79. **d** 81 **p** 82. C Chandler's Ford *Win* 81-84; R Bentley and Binsted from 84. *The Vicarage, Binsted, Alton, Hunts GU34 4NX* Bentley (0420) 22174

✠**ROGERSON, Rt Rev Barry.** b 36. Leeds Univ BA60. Wells Th Coll 60. **d** 62 **p** 63 **c** 79. C S Shields St Hilda w St Thos *Dur* 62-65; C Bishopwearmouth St Nic 65-67; Lect Lich Th Coll 67-71; Vice-Prin 71-72; Lect Sarum & Wells Th Coll 72-74; V Wednesfield St Thos *Lich* 75-79; TR Wednesfield 79; Hon Can Lich Cathl 79-85; Suff Bp Wolv 79-85; Bp Bris from 85. *Bishop's House, Clifton Hill, Bristol BS8 1BW* Bristol (0272) 730222

ROGERSON, Colin Scott. b 30. St Andr Univ MA55. Edin Th Coll. **d** 57 **p** 58. C Byker St Ant *Newc* 57-59; C Newc St Geo 59-63; C Wooler 63-67; V Tynemouth St Aug 67-75; C Dur St Marg *Dur* 75-88; P-in-c Hebburn St Jo from 88. *St John's Vicarage, 23 St John's Avenue, Hebburn, Tyne & Wear NE31 2TZ* 091-483 2054

ROGERSON, David George. b 38. St Chad's Coll Dur BA60 DipTh63 Newc Univ DipEd67. **d** 63 **p** 64. C Wallsend St Luke *Newc* 63-67; C Delaval 67-70; V Long Benton St Mary 70-81; V N Sunderland from 81; Warden Seahouses Dioc Hostel from 81. *The Vicarage, South Lane, North Sunderland, Seahouses, Northd NE68 7TU* Seahouses (0665) 720202

ROGERSON, Derek Russell. b 23. Lon Univ BA51. Sarum Th Coll 51. **d** 53 **p** 54. R Harpurhey St Steph *Man* 64-70; V Rochdale Gd Shep 70-74; Asst Chapl HM Pris Man 74-76; Chapl HM Pris Kirkham 76-83; Haverigg 84-88; rtd 88. *26 Market Street, Millom, Cumbria LA18 4AH* Millom (0229) 775261

ROGERSON, Ian Matthew. b 45. Bede Coll Dur CertEd67 Open Univ BA76. Oak Hill Th Coll DipHE81. **d** 83 **p** 84. C Haughton St Mary *Man* 83-86; V Ramsbottom St Andr from 86. *St Andrew's Vicarage, Henwick Hall Ave, Ramsbottom, Bury, Lancs BL0 9YH* Ramsbottom (0706) 826482

ROGERSON, Canon Prof John William. b 35. Man Univ BD61 DD75 Linacre Ho Ox BA63 MA67. Ripon Hall Ox 61. **d** 64 **p** 66. C Dur St Oswald *Dur* 64-67; Lect Th Dur Univ 64-75; Sen Lect 75-79; Lic to Offic Dur 67-79; Sheff 79-82; Prof Bibl Studies Sheff Univ from 79; Hon Can Sheff Cathl *Sheff* from 82. *60 Marlborough Road, Sheffield S10 1DB* Sheffield (0742) 681426

ROLAND, Andrew Osborne. b 45. Mert Coll Ox BA66 DPM69. Cranmer Hall Dur BA84. **d** 84 **p** 85. C Streatham St Leon *S'wark* 84-87; C Kingston All SS w St Jo from 87. *St John's House, 15 Springfield Road, Kingston upon Thames KT1 2SA* 081-546 3096

ROLAND-SHRUBB, David John. b 38. Roch Th Coll 68. **d** 70 **p** 71. C Corringham *Chelmsf* 70-72; C Burgh le Marsh *Linc* 72-74; CF 74-78; Hon Min Can Ripon Cathl *Ripon* 77-78; P-in-c Mirfield Eastthorpe St Paul *Wakef* 78-81; R Caister *Nor* 81-83; Hon Min Can Nor Cathl 81-83; Perm to Offic *Linc* from 90. *Strawberry Farm, Bicker, Boston, Lincs PE20 3BW* Spalding (0775) 820451

ROLFE, Charles Edward. b 34. Wells Th Coll 68. **d** 70 **p** 71. C Bath Twerton-on-Avon *B & W* 70-79; TV Wellington and Distr 79-85; P-in-c Frome Ch Ch 85-89; V from 89; Chapl Victoria Hosp Frome from 85; Chapl St Adhelm's Hosp Frome from 88. *73 Weymouth Road, Frome, Somerset BA11 1HJ* Frome (0373) 73249

ROLFE, Joseph William. b 37. Qu Coll Birm 78. **d** 81 **p** 82. NSM Tredington and Darlingscott w Newbold on Stour *Cov* 81-91; NSM Brailes from 91; NSM Sutton under Brailes from 91; NSM Shipston Deanery from 91. *35 Manor Lane, Shipston-on-Stour, Warks CV36 4EF* Shipston-on-Stour (0608) 61737

ROLL, Sir James William Cecil, Bt. b 12. Chich Th Coll 34. **d** 37 **p** 38. V Becontree St Jo *Chelmsf* 58-83; rtd 83. *82 Leighcliff Road, Leigh-on-Sea, Essex SS9 1DN*

ROLLETT, Robert Henry. b 39. Leeds Univ BA61 Leic Univ CertEd62. Linc Th Coll 77. **d** 79 **p** 80. C Littleport *Ely* 79-82; P-in-c Manea 82-83; V 83-85; P-in-c Wimblington 82-83; R 83-85; V Thorney Abbey from 85. *The Abbey Vicarage, The Green, Thorney, Peterborough PE6 0QD* Peterborough (0733) 270388

ROLLINSON, Frederick Mark. b 24. **d** 71 **p** 72. C Bow w Bromley St Leon *Lon* 71-76; P-in-c Bethnal Green St Barn from 76. *11 Vivian Road, London E3 5RE* 081-980 3568 or 981 6511

ROLLINSON, Canon John Knighton. b 14. FRCO34 Sheff Univ BMus36 AKC48. **d** 49 **p** 50. R Whittington *Derby* 64-81; P-in-c New Whittington 78-81; rtd 81; Perm to Offic *Derby* from 81. *75 Yew Tree Drive, Somersall, Chesterfield, Derbyshire S40 3NB* Chesterfield (0246) 568647

ROLLS, Peter. b 40. HNC Leeds Inst of Educn CertEd. N Ord Course. **d** 83 **p** 84. NSM Meltham *Wakef* from 83. *14 Heather Road, Meltham, Huddersfield HD7 3EY* Huddersfield (0484) 850389

ROLPH, Pauline Gladys. b 30. SRN51 SCM53 HVCert65. Oak Hill Th Coll 88. **d** 90. Hon C Chingford St Anne *Chelmsf* from 90. *150 Station Road, Chingford, London E4 6AN* 081-529 8134

ROLPH, Reginald Lewis George. b 29. Open Univ BA74. Bps' Coll Cheshunt 55. **d** 58 **p** 59. C Perivale *Lon* 58-61; C Wokingham St Paul *Ox* 61-63; C Letchworth *St Alb* 63-78; Perm to Offic from 78. *22 Souberie Avenue, Letchworth, Herts SG6 3JA* Letchworth (0462) 684596

ROLSTON, Cyril Willis Matthias. b 29. CITC 66. **d** 68 **p** 69. C Portadown St Mark *Arm* 68-71; I Loughgilly w Clare 71-81; Dir of Ords from 72; I Moy w Charlemont from 81. *St James's Rectory, 37 The Square, Moy, Dungannon, Co Tyrone BT71 7SG* Moy (08687) 84312

ROLSTON, Ven John Ormsby. b 28. TCD BA51 MA59 BD63. CITC 51. **d** 51 **p** 52. C Belf St Mary Magd *Conn* 51-55; C Knock *D & D* 55-59; P-in-c Gilnahirk 59-63; I 63-66; I Belf St Jas *Conn* 66-79; RD N Belf 71-88; I Belf St Jas w St Silas from 79; Can Belf Cathl from 82; Adn Conn from 88. *St James's Rectory, 33 Fortwilliam Park, Belfast BT15 4AP* Belfast (0232) 779442

ROLT, Canon Eric Wilfrid. b 17. Pemb Coll Cam BA39 MA45. Ely Th Coll 39. **d** 40 **p** 41. R Campsey Ashe and Marlesford *St E* 69-83; P-in-c Parham w Hacheston 70-83; RD Loes 78-82; rtd 83; Perm to Offic *St E* from 83. *2 Great Back Lane, Debenham, Stowmarket, Suffolk 1P14 6RD* Debenham (0728) 860525

ROLTON, Patrick Hugh. b 49. Sarum & Wells Th Coll 72. **d** 74 **p** 75. C Roch 74-79; C Edenbridge 79-81; R N Cray w Ruxley from 81. *St James's Rectory, 2 St James Way, Sidcup, Kent DA14 5ER* 081-300 1655

ROM, Hugh. b 22. S'wark Ord Course 77. **d** 80 **p** 81. NSM Ealing Ascension Hanger Hill *Lon* 80-82; P-in-c St Kath Cree from 82. *86 Leadenhall Street, London EC3A 3DH* 071-283 5733

ROM, Norman Charles. b 24. S'wark Ord Course 63. **d** 66 **p** 67. C Leatherhead *Guildf* 66-71; Chapl HM Pris Cant 71-74; Pentonville 74-85; Stocken 85-87; P-in-c Empingham *Pet* 85-87; R Empingham and Exton w Horn w Whitwell from 87. *The Rectory, 5 Nook Lane, Empingham, Oakham, Leics LE15 8PT* Empingham (078086) 215

ROMANES, William. b 11. Magd Coll Cam BA35 MA39. Ripon Hall Ox 35. **d** 36 **p** 37. R Ringsfield w Redisham *St E* 71-76; rtd 76; Hon C Bordesley St Benedict *Birm* from 76. *10 Shireland Close, Birmingham B20 1AN* 021-523 7572

ROMANIS, Adam John Aidan. b 57. Pemb Coll Ox BA78 MA83. Westcott Ho Cam 81. **d** 84 **p** 85. C Northfield *Birm* 84-88; TV Seaton Hirst *Newc* from 88. *St Andrew's Vicarage, Hawthorn Road, Ashington, Northd NE63 9AU* Ashington (0670) 818691

RONAYNE, Peter Henry. b 34. FCA68. Oak Hill Th Coll 64. **d** 66 **p** 67. C Chesham St Mary *Ox* 66-69; C Worthing H Trin *Chich* 69-74; V Shoreditch St Leon w St Mich *Lon* 74-82; P-in-c Norwood S'wark 82-85; V from 85; RD Streatham from 87. *The Vicarage, 6 Chatsworth Way, London SE27 9HR* 081-670 2706

RONCHETTI, Quentin Marcus. b 56. Ripon Coll Cuddesdon 79. **d** 80 **p** 81. C Eastbourne St Mary *Chich* 80-83; C Moulsecoomb 83-85; TV 85-90; V Findon Valley from 90. *The Vicarage, 29 Central Avenue, Findon, Worthing, W Sussex BN14 0DS* Findon (0903) 872900

RONE, Canon James. b 35. St Steph Ho Ox 79. **d** 80 **p** 81. C Stony Stratford *Ox* 80-82; P-in-c Fordham St Pet *Ely* 82-83; V 83-89; P-in-c Kennett 82-83; R 83-89; Can Res

Ely Cathl from 89. *Powchers Hall, The College, Ely, Cambs CB7 4DL* Ely (0353) 662909

ROOKE, George William Emmanuel. b 12. Lon Univ BA33 BD34 AKC34. **d** 35 **p** 36. R Worc St Martin-in-the-Cornmarket *Worc* 66-77; rtd 77; Perm to Offic *Heref* from 77. *106 Church Road, Tupsley, Hereford HR1 1RT* Hereford (0432) 266915

ROOKE, Henry John Warburton. b 10. Ch Ch Ox BA32 MA45. Wycliffe Hall Ox 34. **d** 35 **p** 36. V Weobley w Sarnesfield *Heref* 51-69; rtd 69. *Flat 22, Manormead, Tilford Road, Hindhead, Surrey GU26 6RA* Hindhead (0428) 605082

ROOKE, James Templeman. b 43. E Midl Min Tr Course 79. **d** 84 **p** 85. NSM Bassingham *Linc* from 84; NSM Hykeham from 89. *The Chestnuts, Main Street, Norton Disney, Lincoln LN6 9JU* Lincoln (0522) 788315

ROOKE, John George Michael. b 47. St Jo Coll Dur BA72 DipTh74. Cranmer Hall Dur 71. **d** 74 **p** 75. C Skelmersdale St Paul *Liv* 74-78; TV Speke St Aid 78-81; Ind Chapl 81-85; V Knotty Ash St Jo from 85. *St John's Vicarage, Thomas Lane, Liverpool L14 5NR* 051-228 2396

ROOKE, Patrick William. b 55. Open Univ BA85. Sarum & Wells Th Coll 75. **d** 78 **p** 79. C Mossley *Conn* 78-81; C Ballywillan 81-83; I Craigs w Dunaghy and Killagan 83-88; I Ballymore *Arm* from 88. *Glebe Hill Road, Tandragee, Craigavon, Co Armagh BT62 2EP* Tandragee (0762) 840234

ROOKWOOD, Colin John. b 40. TCD BA64 MA68 Lon Univ PGCE67 DipTh69. Clifton Th Coll 67. **d** 70 **p** 71. C Eccleston Ch Ch *Liv* 70-75; V Penge St Jo *Roch* 75-82; V Childwall All SS *Liv* from 82. *Childwall Vicarage, Childwall Abbey Road, Liverpool L16 0JW* 051-722 3147

ROOM, Canon Frederick John. b 24. St Jo Coll Ox BA49 MA53. Wells Th Coll 49. **d** 51 **p** 52. C-in-c Farnham Royal S CD *Ox* 58-70; TV Thetford *Nor* 70-89; Sen Ind Missr 75-89; Hon Can Nor Cathl from 77; rtd 89. *61 Beechwood Drive, Thorpe St Andrew, Norwich NR7 0LN* Norwich (0603) 35877

ROOME, Colin Timothy. b 53. Lon Univ BSc Bris Univ MA. Trin Coll Bris 79. **d** 82 **p** 83. C Romford Gd Shep Collier Row *Chelmsf* 82-85; C Chasetown *Lich* 85-86; Min Chase Terrace St Jo Distr Ch from 86. *7 Hill Lane, Chase Terrace, Burntwood, Walsall WS7 8LS* Burntwood (0543) 684124

ROOMS, Nigel James. b 60. CEng86 MIChemE86 Leeds Univ BSc81. St Jo Coll Nottm DipTh89. **d** 90 **p** 91. C Chell *Lich* from 90. *2 Silverstone Crescent, Chell, Stoke on Trent ST6 6XA* Stoke-on-Trent (0782) 839334

ROONEY, James. b 31. TCD BA58. **d** 58 **p** 59. C Belf St Matt *Conn* 58-60; I 74-82; C Coleraine 60-61; I Ballintoy 61-66; P-in-c Rathlin 62-66; I Craigs w Dunaghy and Killagan 67-74; RD M Belf 80-82; I Cloughfern from 82; Can Belf Cathl from 90. *126 Doagh Road, Newtownabbey, Co Antrim BT37 9QR* Belfast (0232) 862437

ROONEY, Leslie Francis. b 16. Lon Univ BSc36 BD40 AKC40. **d** 40 **p** 41. Chapl Hostel of God S'wark 66-71; Chapl Ex Cathl Sch 72-81; Dep PV Ex Cathl *Ex* from 73; rtd 81. *1A Tuns Lane, Silverton, Exeter EX5 4HY* Exeter (0392) 860137

ROOSE-EVANS, James Humphrey. b 27. St Benet's Hall Ox BA52 MA56. **d** 81 **p** 81. Lic to Offic *Heref* from 81; Lon from 89. *The Old Rectory, Bleddfa, Knighton, Powys LD7 1PA*

ROOSE FRANCIS, Leslie. See FRANCIS, Leslie

ROOT, Canon Prof Howard Eugene. b 26. St Cath Soc Ox BA51 Magd Coll Cam MA53 Magd Coll Ox MA70. Ripon Hall Ox 49. **d** 53 **p** 54. Asst Lect Div Cam Univ 53-57; C Trumpington *Ely* 53; Chapl Em Coll Cam 54-56; Dean Em Coll Cam 56-66; Lect Div Cam Univ 57-66; Prof Th Southn Univ 66-81; Can Th Win Cathl *Win* 67-80; St Aug Can Cant Cathl *Cant* 80-91; Dir Angl Cen Rome from 81; Abp Cant Counsellor on Vatican Affairs from 81; Prof Pontifical Gregorian Univ Rome from 84. *Centro Anglicano, Palazzo Doria, Via del Corso 303, 00186 Roma, Italy* Rome (6) 678-0302

ROOT, John Brereton. b 41. Lon Univ BA64 Em Coll Cam BA66 MA. Ridley Hall Cam 64. **d** 68 **p** 69. C Harlesden St Mark *Lon* 68-73; C Lower Homerton St Paul 73-76; Chapl Ridley Hall Cam 76; Vice-Prin 76-79; V Alperton *Lon* from 79. *34 Stanley Avenue, Wembley, Middx HA0 4JB* 081-902 1729

ROOTES, William Brian. Edin Th Coll. **d** 91. NSM Auchterarder *St And* from 91. *Belhie, Aberuthven, Auchterarder PH3 1EH* Auchterarder (0764) 63259

ROPER, Timothy Hamilton. b 34. Qu Coll Cam BA57 MA61. Sarum Th Coll 57. **d** 59 **p** 60. C Kingsthorpe

Pet 59-62; C Kirkby *Liv* 62-65; Chapl Rossall Sch Fleetwood 65-84; R Arthingworth, Harrington w Oxendon and E Farndon *Pet* from 84; RD Brixworth from 89. *35 Main Street, Great Oxendon, Market Harborough, Leics LE16 8NE* Market Harborough (0858) 462052

ROPER, Preb William Lionel. b 17. Leeds Univ BA39. Coll of Resurr Mirfield 39. **d** 41 **p** 42. R S Molton w Nymet St George *Ex* 61-71; R High Bray w Charles 61-71; V Paignton St Jo 72-82; Preb Ex Cathl from 77; rtd 82. *12 Exeter Gate, South Molton, Devon EX36 4AN* South Molton (07695) 2147

ROSAMOND, Derek William. b 49. Linc Th Coll 87. **d** 89 **p** 90. C Cov Caludon *Cov* from 89. *111 Momus Boulevard, Coventry CV2 5NB* Coventry (0203) 457727

ROSCAMP, Alan Nicholas Harrison. b 12. Dur Univ LTh37 BA39 MA42. St Aid Birkenhead 32. **d** 36 **p** 37. V Wadhurst *Chich* 51-63; V Tidebrook 52-63; Perm to Offic *Cant* from 63; rtd 78. *Horton Green, Ruckinge, Ashford, Kent TN26 2PF* Ham Street (023373) 2491

ROSE, Andrew David. b 45. BA81. Oak Hill Th Coll 78. **d** 81 **p** 82. C Northwood Em *Lon* 81-86; V Iver *Ox* from 86. *The Vicarage, Widecroft Road, Iver, Bucks SL0 9JY* Iver (0753) 653131

ROSE, Anthony James. b 47. Trin Coll Bris BD72. **d** 73 **p** 74. C Halliwell St Pet *Man* 73-76; CF from 76. *c/o MOD (Army), Bagshot Park, Bagshot, Surrey GU19 5PL* Bagshot (0276) 71717

ROSE, Anthony John. b 53. Birm Univ BA79 DipHE86. Trin Coll Bris 84. **d** 86 **p** 87. C The Quinton *Birm* 86-90; R Abbas and Templecombe w Horsington *B & W* from 90. *The Rectory, 8 Church Hill, Templecombe, Somerset BA8 0HG* Templecombe (0963) 70302

ROSE, Barry Ernest. b 35. Chich Th Coll 58. **d** 61 **p** 62. C Forest Gate St Edm *Chelmsf* 61-64; Antigua 64-66; Dominica 66-69; V St Mary-at-Latton *Chelmsf* 69-79; V Stansted Mountfitchet 79-88; V Halstead St Andr w H Trin and Greenstead Green from 88; RD Halstead and Coggeshall from 91. *The Vicarage, Parsonage Street, Halstead, Essex CO9 2LD* Halstead (0787) 472171

ROSE, Miss Geraldine Susan. b 47. Trin Coll Bris DipTh76 BD78. **dss** 78 **d** 87. Tonbridge St Steph *Roch* 78-80; Littleover *Derby* 80-87; Par Dn 87-88; Par Dn Wombwell *Sheff* from 88. *5 Church Street, Jump, Barnsley, S Yorkshire S74 0HZ* Barnsley (0226) 749139

ROSE, Glyn Clee. b 16. Jes Coll Ox BA39 MA42. Bps' Coll Cheshunt 49. **d** 51 **p** 52. Miss to Seamen 66-73; R Millbrook *Win* 73-81; rtd 81; Perm to Offic *Win* from 81. *11 Collins Lane, Hursley, Winchester, Hants SO21 2JX* Hursley (0962) 75403

ROSE, Canon Gordon Henry. b 23. St Cath Soc Ox BA48 MA53. Wells Th Coll 49. **d** 50 **p** 51. C Bournemouth St Andr *Win* 50-55; R Bishopstoke from 55; Hon Can Win Cathl from 82. *The Rectory, 10 Stoke Park Road, Bishopstoke, Eastleigh, Hants SO5 6DA* Eastleigh (0703) 612192

ROSE, Ingrid Elizabeth. b 57. Univ of Wales (Abth) BA78 DipEd79. St D Coll Lamp 84. **d** 87. NSM Ysbyty Cynfyn w Llantrisant and Eglwys Newydd *St D* 87-90. *Ystwyth Villa, Pontrhydygroes, Ystrad Meurig, Dyfed* Pontrhydygroes (097422) 311

ROSE, James Edward. b 50. Selw Coll Cam BA75. Trin Coll Bris 73. **d** 75 **p** 76. C Easton H Trin w St Gabr and St Lawr *Bris* 75-77; Dir Greenhouse Trust 77-82; Hon C Gipsy Hill Ch Ch *S'wark* 82-86. *Address temp unknown*

ROSE, John Clement Wansey. b 46. New Coll Ox BA71 MA72. Ripon Hall Ox 70. **d** 72 **p** 73. C Harborne St Pet *Birm* 72-76; TV Kings Norton 76-81; V Maney from 81. *The Vicarage, Maney Hill Road, Sutton Coldfield, W Midlands B72 1JJ* 021-354 2426

ROSE, John Spencer. b 20. Univ of Wales (Cardiff) BA42. St Mich Coll Llan 42. **d** 44 **p** 45. V Crickadarn w Gwenddwr and Alltmawr *S & B* 65-73; V Lougher 73-85; rtd 85. *58 Gladys Street, Dowlais, Merthyr Tydfil, M Glam CF48 2AU* Merthyr Tydfil (0685) 73376

ROSE, Mrs Judith Anne. b 36. Newnham Coll Cam BA57 MA65 Ox Univ DipTh87. Ripon Coll Cuddesdon 86. **d** 87. Par Dn Kettering All SS *Pet* from 87. *The Vicarage, Squires Hill, Rothwell, Kettering, Northants NN14 2BQ* Kettering (0536) 710268

ROSE, Miss Kathleen Judith. b 37. Lon Univ DipTh66 Lon Bible Coll BD73 St Mich Ho Ox 64. **dss** 76 **d** 87. Leeds St Geo *Ripon* 76-81; Bradf Cathl *Bradf* 81-85; S Gillingham *Roch* 85-87; Par Dn 87-90; Gillingham 88-90; Bp's Dom Chapl from 90; Asst Dir of Ords from 90. *Bishopscourt Flat, 24 St Margaret's Street, Rochester, Kent ME1 1TS* Medway (0634) 842721

ROSE, Lionel Stafford. b 38. Wells Th Coll 69. **d** 71 **p** 72. C Minchinhampton *Glouc* 71-73; C Thornbury 73-75; R Ruardean 75-80; V Whiteshill 80-84; CF from 84. *c/o MOD (Army), Bagshot Park, Bagshot, Surrey GU19 5PL* Bagshot (0276) 71717

ROSE, Mrs Lynda Kathryn. b 51. Called to the Bar (Gray's Inn) 81 Ex Univ BA73 Ox Univ BA86. Wycliffe Hall Ox 86. **d** 87. C Highfield *Ox* 87-88; C Ox St Clem from 89. *95 Staunton Road, Oxford OX3 7TR* Oxford (0865) 68774

ROSE, Paul Rosamond. b 32. Trin Hall Cam BA56 MA60. Westcott Ho Cam 56. **d** 59 **p** 60. C Wandsworth St Anne *S'wark* 59-61; C Tormohun *Ex* 61-64; S Rhodesia 64-65; Rhodesia 65-67; Min Can, Prec and Sacr Pet Cathl *Pet* 67-72; V Paddington St Jo w St Mich *Lon* 72-79; PV Westmr Abbey 74-79; Min Can and Prec Cant Cathl *Cant* 79-84; V Rothwell w Orton *Pet* 84-87; R Rothwell w Orton, Rushton w Glendon and Pipewell from 87. *The Vicarage, Squire's Hill, Rothwell, Kettering, Northants NN14 2BQ* Kettering (0536) 710268

ROSE, Peter Charles. b 30. St Aug Coll Cant 70. **d** 72 **p** 73. C St Martin-in-the-Fields *Lon* 72-76; C St Buryan, St Levan and Sennen *Truro* 76-78; V Feock 78-82; TV Gt Grimsby St Mary and St Jas *Linc* 82-84; rtd 84. *25 Quai du Hable, 76200 Dieppe, France* France (33) 35 84 51 06

ROSE, Robert Alec Lewis. b 41. Man Univ BSc64. Wycliffe Hall Ox 85. **d** 87 **p** 88. C Vange *Chelmsf* 87-91; C Langdon Hills from 91. *197 Great Berry Lane, Langdon Hills, Basildon, Essex SS16 6BS* Basildon (0268) 531668

ROSE, Roy. b 11. Worc Ord Coll 63. **d** 64 **p** 65. R Hale *Linc* 68-77; V Helpringham 68-77; P-in-c Scredington 73-77; rtd 77; Perm to Offic *Linc* from 77. *72 Lincoln Road, Ruskington, Sleaford, Lincs NG34 9AB* Ruskington (0526) 832669

ROSE, Miss Susan Mary. b 36. Lon Univ DipTh70. Dalton Ho Bris 68 Trin Coll Bris 74. **dss** 81 **d** 87. Brinsworth w Catcliffe *Sheff* 75-77; Scargill Ho N Yorkshire 77-83; Netherthorpe *Sheff* 83-87; Trin Coll Bris from 87. *63 Highbury Road, Horfield, Bristol BS7 0DA*

ROSE, Westmoreland Charles Edward. b 32. St Jo Coll Nottm 85. **d** 87 **p** 88. C Fairfield *Derby* 87-90; P-in-c Linton and Castle Gresley from 90. *The Vicarage, 40 Main Street, Linton, Burton-on-Trent, Staffs DE12 6PZ* Burton-on-Trent (0283) 76144

ROSE-CASEMORE, John. b 27. Chich Th Coll. **d** 55 **p** 56. C Epsom Common Ch Ch *Guildf* 55-58; C Hednesford *Lich* 58-60; V Dawley 60-65; R Puttenham and Wanborough *Guildf* 65-72; R Frimley 72-83; RD Surrey Heath 76-81; R Ludgershall and Faberstown *Sarum* 83-86; R Tidworth, Ludgershall and Faberstown from 86. *The Rectory, Ludgershall, Andover, Hants SP11 9QF* Andover (0264) 770393

ROSE-CASEMORE, Penelope Jane. b 56. Bris Univ CertEd77 BEd78. Westcott Ho Cam DipRS82. **dss** 85 **d** 87. Waterloo St Jo w St Andr *S'wark* 85-87; Par Dn 87-88; Asst Chapl Gt Ormond Street Hosp for Sick Children Lon 88-90; Par Dn Balham St Mary and St Jo *S'wark* from 90; Par Dn Upper Tooting H Trin from 90. *29 Avoca Road, London SW17 8SL* 081-767 2308

ROSENTHALL, Henry David. b 08. QUB BA30 TCD 30. **d** 32 **p** 33. R Bolingbroke w Hareby *Linc* 66-72; R Ulceby w Fordington 72-76; R Willoughby w Sloothby w Claxby 72-76; rtd 76; P-in-c Salle *Nor* 78-80; Perm to Offic from 80. *Station Road, Reepham, Norwich NR10 4LJ* Norwich (0603) 870202

ROSEWEIR, Clifford John. b 43. MIPM Glas Univ MA64. S'wark Ord Course 84. **d** 85 **p** 86. NSM Redhill H Trin *S'wark* 85-89; P-in-c Croydon St Martin from 89. *1 New Ballards, Royal Rusell School, Coombe Lane, Croydon CR9 5BX* 081-760 5891

ROSHEUVEL, Siegfried Winslow Patrick. b 39. Lon Univ BA86. Codrington Coll Barbados 64. **d** 68 **p** 68. Guyana 68-75; C Worksop Priory *S'well* 75-78; Area Sec (Dios Chelmsf and St Alb) USPG 78-89; (Dio Lon) from 89. *22 Old Park Road, London N13 4RE* 081-886 9862

ROSKELLY, James Hereward Emmanuel. b 57. BSc ACSM80. Cranmer Hall Dur 83. **d** 86 **p** 87. C Dunster, Carhampton and Withycombe w Rodhuish *B & W* 86-90; C Ealing St Mary *Lon* from 90. *38 Airedale Road, London W5 4SD* 081-567 6926

ROSKILLY, Dr John Noel. b 33. DRCOG60 MRCGP62 Man Univ MB, ChB58. St Deiniol's Hawarden 74. **d** 75 **p** 76. NSM Bramhall *Ches* 75-86; V Capesthorne w Siddington and Marton 86-91; Bp's Officer for NSM from 91; Dioc Dir of Counselling from 91. *North View, Hawkins Lane, Rainow, Macclesfield, Cheshire SK10 5TL* Macclesfield (0625) 501014

ROSKROW, Neil. b 27. St Alb Minl Tr Scheme. **d** 85 **p** 86. NSM Digswell and Panshanger *St Alb* 85-90; P-in-c Gt Gaddesden from 90. *The Vicarage, Pipers Hill, Great*

Gaddesden, Hemel Hempstead, Herts HP1 3BY Hemel Hempstead (0442) 252672

ROSKROW, Mrs Pamela Mary. b 25. St Alb Minl Tr Scheme. **dss** 85 **d** 87. Digswell and Panshanger *St Alb* 85-87; Hon Par Dn 87-90; Hon Par Dn Gt Gaddesden from 90. *The Vicarage, Pipers Hill, Great Gaddesden, Hemel Hempstead, Herts HP1 3BY* Hemel Hempstead (0442) 252672

ROSS, Alastair Alexander. b 54. CCC Ox BA75. St Jo Coll Nottm 76. **d** 79 **p** 80. C Huyton St Mich *Liv* 79-82; C-in-c Halewood St Mary CD 82-83; TV Halewood 83-87; V Netherton from 87. *The Vicarage, 183 St Oswald's Lane, Bootle, Merseyside L30 5QF* 051-525 1882

ROSS, Anthony McPherson. b 38. OBE. Univ of Wales (Lamp) BA60 Lon Univ BD63. St Mich Coll Llan 60. **d** 61 **p** 62. C Gabalfa *Llan* 61-65; Chapl RN from 65. *c/o MOD, Lacon House, Theobald's Road, London WC1X 8RY* 071-430 6847

ROSS, David Alexander. b 46. Lon Univ DipTh73. Oak Hill Th Coll 73. **d** 75 **p** 76. C Northwood Em *Lon* 75-80; R Eastrop *Win* 80-86; V Hove Bp Hannington Memorial Ch *Chich* from 86. *82 Holmes Avenue, Hove, E Sussex BN3 7LD* Brighton (0273) 732821

ROSS, Derek Leighton. b 11. St Cath Coll Ox BA34 MA38. Wycliffe Hall Ox 34. **d** 36 **p** 37. Hd Master Felsted Sch 51-71; Asst Chapl 54-71; V Lindsell *Chelmsf* 71-73; V Stebbing 71-73; V Stebbing w Lindsell 73-78; rtd 78; Perm to Offic *Chich* from 78. *66 Palmeira Avenue, Hove, E Sussex BN3 3GF* Brighton (0273) 777821

ROSS, Duncan Gilbert. b 48. Lon Univ BSc70. Westcott Ho Cam 75. **d** 78 **p** 79. C Stepney St Dunstan and All SS *Lon* 78-84; V Hackney Wick St Mary of Eton w St Aug from 84. *St Mary's House, Eastway, London E9 5JA* 081-986 8159

ROSS, Frederic Ian. b 34. Man Univ BSc56. Westcott Ho Cam 58 Episc Th Sem Mass DipTh61. **d** 62 **p** 63. C Oldham *Man* 62-65; Sec Th Colls Dept SCM 65-69; Teacher Man Gr Sch 69-84; Lic to Offic *Man* 69-84; V Shrewsbury H Cross *Lich* from 84. *131 Underdale Road, Shrewsbury SY2 5EG* Shrewsbury (0743) 248859

ROSS, Frederick. b 36. Qu Coll Birm. **d** 64 **p** 65. C Hessle *York* 64-68; V Marlpool *Derby* 68-73; P-in-c Norbury w Snelston 73-74; R 74-81; P-in-c Clifton 73-74; V 74-81; RD Ashbourne 78-81; V Melbourne from 81; RD Melbourne 81-86 and from 90. *The Vicarage, Church Square, Melbourne, Derby DE7 1EN* Melbourne (0332) 862347

ROSS, George Douglas William. b 15. Linc Th Coll 76. **d** 76 **p** 77. NSM Barton upon Humber *Linc* 76-81; Perm to Offic from 81. *45 York Road, Brigg, S Humberside DN20 8DX* Brigg (0652) 57137

ROSS, Henry Ernest. b 40. NW Ord Course 70. **d** 73 **p** 74. NSM Litherland St Phil *Liv* 73-75; C Newton-le-Willows 75-77; P-in-c Walton St Luke 77-79; V from 79; RD Walton 84-89. *St Luke's Vicarage, 136 Southport Road, Bootle, Merseyside L20 9EH* 051-523 5460

ROSS, John Colin. b 50. Oak Hill Th Coll 84. **d** 86 **p** 87. C Stowmarket *St E* 86-89; C Wakef St Andr and St Mary *Wakef* 89-91; R Gt and Lt Whelnetham w Bradfield St George *St E* from 91. *The Rectory, Little Whelnetham, Bury St Edmunds, Suffolk IP30 0DA* Sicklesmere (028486) 332

ROSS, John Paton. b 29. Or Coll Ox BA52 MA55 Edin Univ PhD73. Wycliffe Hall Ox 54. **d** 57 **p** 58. C Hornchurch St Andr *Chelmsf* 57-59; Tutor Ridley Hall Cam 59-62; Chapl 62-63; Asst Lect Th Cam Univ 62-67; Sen Admin Officer Univ of Edin 67-81; Asst Sec 81-90; Hon C Edin St Mary *Edin* from 78. *1A Suffolk Road, Edinburgh EH16 5NR* 031-667 2403

ROSS, Malcolm Hargrave. b 37. Dur Univ BSc58. Westcott Ho Cam 63. **d** 64 **p** 65. C Armley St Bart *Ripon* 64-67; USPG 67-75; Trinidad and Tobago 67-71; V New Rossington *Sheff* 71-75; Bp's Missr in E Lon 75-82; P-in-c Haggerston All SS 75-82; V Bedf Leigh *Man* 82-85; Area Sec (Dios Bris and Glouc) USPG 85-90; Bp's Officer for Miss and Evang *Bris* from 90; P-in-c Lacock w Bowden Hill from 90. *The Vicarage, Folly Lane, Lacock, Chippenham, Wilts SN15 2LL* Lacock (024973) 272

ROSS, Oliver Charles Milligan. b 58. Lon Univ BA80 St Edm Ho Cam BA85. Ridley Hall Cam 84. **d** 87 **p** 88. C Preston St Cuth *Blackb* 87-90; C Paddington St Jo w St Mich *Lon* from 90. *12 Connaught Street, London W2 2AF* 071-724 7302 or 262 1732

ROSS, Canon Philip James. b 18. St Jo Coll Cam BA40 MA44. Ridley Hall Cam 40. **d** 41 **p** 42. Sierra Leone 69-83; rtd 83; Perm to Offic *Heref* from 84.

36 Westcroft, Leominster, Herefordshire HR6 8HF Leominster (0568) 4258

ROSS, Canon Raymond John. b 28. Trin Coll Cam BA52 MA57. St Steph Ho Ox 52. **d** 54 **p** 55. C Clifton All SS *Bris* 54-58; C Solihull *Birm* 58-66; C-in-c Hobs Moat CD 66-67; V Hobs Moat 67-72; R Newbold and Dunston *Derby* from 72; RD Chesterfield 78-91; Hon Can Derby Cathl from 86. *Newbold Rectory, St John's Road, Chesterfield, Derbyshire S41 8QN* Chesterfield (0246) 450374

ROSS, Vernon. b 57. RGN86 Portsm Poly BSc79. Trin Coll Bris DipHE91. **d** 91. C Fareham St Jo *Portsm* from 91. *7A Upper St Michael's Grove, Fareham, Hants PO14 1DN* Fareham (0329) 825420

ROSS, Dean of. *See* TOWNLEY, Very Rev Robert Keith

ROSSDALE, David Douglas James. b 53. Westmr Coll Ox DipApTh90. K Coll Lon 72 Chich Th Coll 80. **d** 81 **p** 82. C Upminster *Chelmsf* 81-86; V Moulsham St Luke 86-90; V Cookham *Ox* from 90. *The Vicarage, Church Gate, Cookham, Maidenhead, Berks SL6 9SP* Bourne End (06285) 23969

ROSSETER, Miss Susan Mary. b 46. Man Univ BA67 Edin Univ DASS71. St Jo Coll Nottm LTh84. **d** 87. Par Dn Bromley Common St Aug *Roch* 87-88; Par Dn Pudsey St Lawr and St Paul *Bradf* from 88. *34 The Lanes, Pudsey, W Yorkshire LS28 7AQ* Pudsey (0532) 551080

ROSSITER, Donald William Frank. b 30. **d** 80 **p** 81. NSM Abergavenny St Mary w Llanwenarth Citra *Mon* from 80. *10 Meadow Lane, Abergavenny, Gwent NP7 7AY* Abergavenny (0873) 5648

ROSSITER, Raymond Stephen David. b 22. St Deiniol's Hawarden 75. **d** 76 **p** 77. NSM Sale St Anne *Ches* 76-90; rtd 90; Perm to Offic *Ches* from 90. *75 Temple Road, Sale, Cheshire M33 2FQ* 061-962 3240

ROSTRON, Derek. b 34. St Mich Coll Llan 65. **d** 67 **p** 68. C Morecambe St Barn *Blackb* 67-70; C Ribbleton 70-72; V Chorley All SS 72-79; C Woodchurch *Ches* 79-80; V Audlem from 80; RD Nantwich from 88. *St James's Vicarage, 66 Heathfield Road, Audlem, Crewe CW3 0HG* Audlem (0270) 811543

ROTHERHAM, Eric. b 36. Clifton Th Coll 63. **d** 67 **p** 68. C Gt Crosby St Luke *Liv* 67-69; C Sutton 69-71; V Warrington St Paul 72-79; Lic to Offic 79-80. *7 Paul Street, Warrington WA2 7LE* Warrington (0925) 33048

ROTHERY, Cecil Ivor. b 24. St Jo Coll Winnipeg 50. **d** 53 **p** 54. Canada 53-72; C Gainsborough All SS *Linc* 72-74; R Fleet 74-79; P-in-c Wrawby 79-80; C Glanford Bridge 79-80; rtd 80; Perm to Offic *S'well* 80-83; *Sheff* from 83. *129 Queen Street, Retford, Notts DN22 7DA* Retford (0777) 701551

ROTHERY, Robert Frederick. b 34. Lon Coll of Div 67. **d** 69 **p** 70. C Burscough Bridge *Liv* 69-72; C Chipping Campden *Glouc* 72-75; P-in-c Didmarton w Oldbury-on-the-Hill and Sopworth 75-77; R Boxwell, Leighterton, Didmarton, Oldbury etc 77-83; R Stow on the Wold from 83; RD Stow from 90. *The Rectory, Stow on the Wold, Cheltenham, Glos GL54 1AA* Cotswold (0451) 30607

ROTHWELL, Bryan. b 60. St Edm Hall Ox BA81 MA85. Trin Coll Bris. **d** 85 **p** 86. C Carl St Jo *Carl* 85-88; C Ulverston St Mary w H Trin 88-90; P-in-c Preston St Mary *Blackb* from 90. *St Mary's Vicarage, St Mary's Close, Preston PR1 4XN* Preston (0772) 794222

ROTHWELL, Edwin John. b 53. Lanc Univ BA74 PhD79. Sarum & Wells Th Coll 88. **d** 90 **p** 91. C Malvern Link w Cowleigh *Worc* from 90. *17 Bosbury Road, Malvern, Worcs WR14 1TR* Malvern (0684) 569890

ROTHWELL, Canon Eric. b 12. Man Univ BA35. Lich Th Coll 35. **d** 37 **p** 38. Hon Can Blackb Cathl *Blackb* 61-77; R Chorley St Laur 63-77; rtd 77; Perm to Offic *Blackb* and *Carl* from 79. *The Coach House, 7 Wood Broughton Hall, Cartmel, Cumbria LA11 7SH* Cartmel (05395) 36574

ROTHWELL, Harold. b 34. AKC58. K Coll Lon St Boniface Warminster. **d** 59 **p** 60. C Old Brumby *Linc* 59-62; P-in-c Sheff St Steph w St Phil and St Ann *Sheff* 62-64; V Caistor w Holton le Moor and Clixby *Linc* 67-77; Chapl Caistor Hosp 67-77; Org Sec (Dios Ex and B & W) CECS 77-81; P-in-c Deeping Fen *Linc* 78-81; C Boston 86-88; C Spilsby w Hundleby from 88. *48 Boston Road, Spilsby, Lincs PE23 5HQ* Spilsby (0790) 53441

ROTHWELL, Michael John Hereward. b 46. Chich Th Coll 74. **d** 78 **p** 79. C Chelmsf All SS *Chelmsf* 78-82; C Clacton St Jas 82-85; V Thorpe *Guildf* from 85. *The Vicarage, Church Approach, Coldharbour Lane, Thorpe, Egham, Surrey TW20 8TQ* Chertsey (0932) 565986

ROTHWELL-JACKSON, Christopher Patrick. b 32. St Cath Soc Ox BA58 MA62. St Steph Ho Ox 55. **d** 59 **p** 60. C E Clevedon All SS *B & W* 59-62; C Midsomer

Norton 62-65; Teacher St Pet Primary Sch Portishead 65-68; Lic to Offic 68-75; Hd Master Bp Pursglove Sch Tideswell from 75; Lic to Offic *Derby* from 76. *Hardy House, Tideswell, Buxton, Derbyshire SK17 8HL* Tideswell (0298) 871468

ROUCH, David Vaughan. b 36. Oak Hill Th Coll 67. **d** 69 **p** 70. C Denton Holme *Carl* 69-74; V Litherland St Jo and St Jas *Liv* from 74. *The New Vicarage, 175 Linacre Lane, Bootle, Merseyside L20 6AB* 051-922 3612

ROULSTON, Joseph Ernest. b 52. FRSC86 BNC Ox BA74 MA78 Lon Univ PhD81. **d** 86 **p** 87. C Edin St Hilda *Edin* 86-88; C Edin St Fillan 86-88; NSM Edin St Mich and All SS from 88. *106 Gilmore Place, Edinburgh EH3 9PP* 031-228 3862

ROUND, Keith Leonard. b 49. Sarum & Wells Th Coll 88. **d** 90 **p** 91. C Meir *Lich* from 90. *11 Melrose Avenue, Meir Heath, Stoke-on-Trent ST3 7LY* Stoke-on-Trent (0782) 399690

ROUND, Malcolm John Harrison. b 56. Lon Univ BSc77 BA. Oak Hill Th Coll. **d** 81 **p** 82. C Guildf St Sav w Stoke-next-Guildf 81-85; C Hawkwell *Chelmsf* 85-88; R Balerno *Edin* from 88. *53 Marchbank Drive, Balerno, Midlothian EH14 7ER* 031-449 4127

ROUNDHILL, Canon Jack. b 22. TCD BA44 MA47 BD47. **d** 45 **p** 46. V Dorking w Ranmore *Guildf* 63-76; RD Dorking 70-75; Hon Can Guildf Cathl 76-89; R Cranleigh 76-89; rtd 89; Perm to Offic *Bris, Sarum* and *Ox* from 89. *2 River Park, Marlborough, Wilts SN8 1NH* Marlborough (0672) 516312

ROUNDHILL, Stanley (Brother Peter). b 14. Chich Th Coll 46. **d** 49 **p** 50. OSP from 39; rtd 84. *The Abbey, Alton, Hants GU34 4AP* Alton (0420) 62145

ROUNDS, Canon Philip Rigby. b 21. Wells Th Coll 49. **d** 52 **p** 53. R Wyke Regis *Sarum* 67-89; Can and Preb Sarum Cathl 77-89; rtd 89. *8 Rodwell Lodge, Rodwell Road, Weymouth, Dorset DT4 8QT* Weymouth (0305) 781373

ROUNDTREE, Ven Samuel William. b 19. TCD BA42 MA54. CITC 43. **d** 43 **p** 44. Treas Leighlin Cathl *C & O* 62-78; RD Maryborough 62-82; Preb Ossory Cathl 62-78; I Dunleckney 62-82; Chan Ossory and Leighlin Cathls 78-80; Prec 80-82; I New Ross w Old Ross, Whitechurch, Fethard etc 82-88; Adn Ferns 86-88; rtd 88. *7 Bellevue Cottages, Delgany, Greystones, Co Wicklow, Irish Republic*

ROUNTREE, Canon Cecil John. b 19. TCD BA41 MA50. CITC 42. **d** 42 **p** 43. I Templeharry w Borrisnafarney *L & K* 61-79; Can Killaloe Cathl 67-76; Treas Killaloe Cathl 76-79; I Creagh Union 79-80; Chan Killaloe Cathl 79-80; I Achonry w Tubbercurry and Killoran *T, K & A* 80-89; Can Tuam Cathl 84-89; rtd 89. *Greenaun, Dromahair, Co Leitrim, Irish Republic* Sligo (71) 64132

ROUNTREE, Richard Benjamin. b 52. NUI BA73. CITC 76. **d** 76 **p** 77. C Orangefield *D & D* 76-80; C Dub Zion Ch *D & G* 80-83; I Dalkey St Patr from 83; Dioc Dir Decade of Evang from 90. *The Rectory, Church Road, Dalkey, Co Dublin, Irish Republic* Dublin (1) 280-3369

ROUTH, Mrs Eileen Rosemary. b 41. Cant Sch of Min 82. **dss** 85 **d** 87. Par Dn St Sav *Cant* 85-87; C Par Dn 87-90; Par Dn Woodnesborough w Worth and Staple 90-91; Dn-in-c from 91. *The Vicarage, Woodnesborough, Sandwich, Kent CT13 0NF* Sandwich (0304) 613056

ROWBERRY, Michael James. b 46. Sussex Univ BA74. St Steph Ho Ox. **d** 87 **p** 88. C Wolvercote w Summertown *Ox* 87-88. *St Oswald's Vicarage, Jardine Crescent, Tile Hill, Coventry CV4 9PL* Coventry (0203) 465072

ROWCROFT, Kenneth George Caulfeild. b 19. **d** 50 **p** 51. V Monkton Wyld *Sarum* 67-74; rtd 76. *Colway Rise, Colway Lane, Lyme Regis, Dorset* Lyme Regis (02974) 3349

ROWDON, John Michael Hooker. b 27. Witwatersrand Univ BA52. Ridley Hall Cam 52. **d** 54 **p** 55. C Broadwater St Mary *Chich* 54-56; C Streatham Immanuel w St Anselm *S'wark* 56-59; Nigeria 60-62; C All Hallows Lon Wall *Lon* 62-66; Warden Toc H Tower Hill 64-66; Australia from 66. *Rottnest Island, W Australia 6161* Perth (9) 292-5047

ROWE, Andrew Gidleigh Bruce. b 37. AKC62. St Boniface Warminster. **d** 63 **p** 64. C Midsomer Norton *B & W* 63-68; Chapl RN 68-84; Hon C Winkfield and Cranbourne *Ox* 84-86; Chapl Heathfield Sch 84-86; TV Wellington and Distr *B & W* from 86. *22 Dyers Close, West Buckland, Wellington, Somerset TA21 9JU* Wellington (0823) 664925

ROWE, Canon Antony Silvester Buckingham. b 26. St Jo Coll Dur 53. **d** 55 **p** 56. C Holbrooks *Cov* 55-59; V Cov St Mary 59-83; RD Cov S 72-82; Hon Can Cov Cathl from 76; R Harbury and Ladbroke from 83. *The Rectory,*

2 Vicarage Lane, Harbury, Leamington Spa, Warks CV33 9HA Harbury (0926) 612377

ROWE, Arthur John. b 35. TCD 73. **d** 76 **p** 77. C Ban Abbey *D & D* 76-78; I Kilbarron *D & R* 78-79; I Kilbarron w Rossnowlagh 79-82; P-in-c Hockering *Nor* 82-85; P-in-c Honingham w E Tuddenham 82-85; P-in-c N Tuddenham 82-85; R Hockwold w Wilton *Ely* from 85; R Weeting from 85. *The Rectory, Hockwold, Thetford, Norfolk IP26 4JG* Thetford (0842) 828271

ROWE, Bryan. b 50. Carl Dioc Tr Course 87. **d** 90 **p** 91. C Kells *Carl* from 90. *165 High Road, Kells, Whitehaven, Cumbria CA28 9HA* Whitehaven (0946) 65965

ROWE, Cecil Leonard. b 16. AKC48. **d** 48 **p** 49. R Girvan *Glas* 68-72; R Stratford St Mary *St E* 72-83; P-in-c Higham 72-83; rtd 83. *15 Bristol Road, Colchester CO1 2YU* Colchester (0206) 866411

ROWE, Mrs Christine Elizabeth. b 55. Southn Univ BEd77. Ripon Hall Ox 83. **dss** 86 **d** 87. Denham *Ox* 86-87; Par Dn 87-89; Par Dn Aylesbury 89; Par Dn Aylesbury w Bierton and Hulcott from 89. *18 Bronte Close, Haydon Hill, Aylesbury, Bucks HP19 3LF* Aylesbury (0296) 432677

ROWE, Cyril Ashton. b 38. AKC62. **d** 63 **p** 64. C Bethnal Green St Matt *Lon* 63-68; P-in-c 68-74; V Stoke Newington St Faith, St Matthias and All SS from 74. *St Matthias Vicarage, Wordsworth Road, London N16 8DD* 071-254 5063

ROWE, David Brian. b 58. Trin Coll Bris DipHE83. **d** 83 **p** 84. C Radipole and Melcombe Regis *Sarum* 83-86; C Cranham Park *Chelmsf* 86-88; NSM Eastrop *Win* from 88. *19 Beaulieu Court, Basingstoke, Hants RG21 2DQ* Basingstoke (0256) 468046

ROWE, Edward Nelson. b 05. TCD BA29 MA40. Bps' Coll Cheshunt. **d** 62 **p** 63. I Currin w Drum and Newbliss *Clogh* 66-76; RD Clones 72-76; rtd 76. *22 Old Rossory Road, Enniskillen, Co Fermanagh BT74 7LE* Enniskillen (0365) 24333

ROWE, Everhard James. b 05. Bps' Coll Cheshunt 28. **d** 28 **p** 29. V Bath Weston All SS *B & W* 47-70; rtd 70; Perm to Offic *Ex* from 82. *13 The Avenue, Tiverton, Devon EX16 4HP* Tiverton (0884) 257152

ROWE, Geoffrey Lewis. b 44. Univ of Wales (Lamp) BA. Ripon Coll Cuddesdon 80. **d** 82 **p** 83. C Milber *Ex* 82-84; TV Withycombe Raleigh 84-90; R Clyst St Mary, Clyst St George etc from 90. *The Rectory, 40 Clyst Valley Road, Clyst St Mary, Exeter EX5 1DD* Exeter (0392) 874363

ROWE, Joan Patricia. b 54. Trin Coll Bris BA87. **d** 88. C Radstock w Writhlington *B & W* from 88. *18 Birch Road, Radstock, Bath BA3 3TP* Radstock (0761) 37926

ROWE, John Goring. b 23. McGill Univ Montreal BA48 BD51 Selw Coll Cam BA53. Montreal Dioc Th Coll LTh51. **d** 51 **p** 52. C Trumpington *Ely* 51-53; Hon C Bow Common *Lon* 53-84; rtd 88. *10 Cordelia Street, London E14 6DZ* 071-515 4681

ROWE, John Nigel. b 24. Ball Coll Ox MA52 BD53 Leeds Univ PhD82. Ely Th Coll 49. **d** 54 **p** 55. V Newchurch-in-Pendle *Blackb* 60-80; V Denholme Gate *Bradf* 80-89; rtd 89. *2 St Cynidr Villas, Glasbury, Hereford HR3 5NN* Glasbury (04974) 7802

ROWE, Leslie Vernon. b 25. Oak Hill Th Coll 62. **d** 65 **p** 66. P-in-c Lt Burstead *Chelmsf* 69-74; R Frinton 74-84; CMJ 84-90; Jerusalem 84-85; SW Area Sec CMJ 85-90; rtd 90. *5 Lodge Lane, Upton, Gainsborough, Lincs DN21 5NW* Corringham (042783) 546

ROWE, Peter Farquharson. b 19. Selw Coll Cam BA41. Westcott Ho Cam 41. **d** 43 **p** 44. V Eltham Park St Luke *S'wark* 65-77; V Ravensthorpe w E Haddon and Holdenby *Pet* 77-84; rtd 84; Perm to Offic *Ex* and *Sarum* from 84. *3 Fishweir Terrace, Fishweir Lane, Bridport, Dorset DT6 3HW* Bridport (0308) 56538

ROWE, Philip William. b 57. Southn Univ BSc78. Lambeth STh86 Trin Coll Bris 82. **d** 85 **p** 86. C Tooting Graveney St Nic *S'wark* 85-89; V Abbots Leigh w Leigh Woods *Bris* from 89. *The Vicarage, Church Road, Abbots Leigh, Bristol BS8 3QU* Pill (0275) 37996

ROWE, Richard Nigel. b 41. St Pet Coll Saltley DipEd64. St Steph Ho Ox 67. **d** 70 **p** 71. C Acton Green St Pet *Lon* 70-74; C Leigh St Clem *Chelmsf* 74-80; V Leytonstone St Marg w St Columba 80-89; RD Waltham Forest 86-89; V Thaxted from 89. *The Vicarage, Watling Lane, Thaxted, Essex CM6 2QY* Thaxted (0371) 830221

ROWE, Samuel Ernest Allen. b 16. TCD BA39 MA44. **d** 40 **p** 41. I Monart w Ballycarney and Templescobin *C & O* 72-83; rtd 83. *Chestnut Lodge, Bloomfield, Enniscorthy, Co Wexford, Irish Republic*

ROWE, Stanley Hamilton. b 18. St Pet Hall Ox BA48 MA52. ALCD50. **d** 50 **p** 51. Hd of RE Jo Hampden Sch High Wycombe 67-83; Perm to Offic *Ox*

67-84 and from 86; rtd 83; Hon C Aston Rowant w Crowell *Ox* 84-86. *37 Greenwood Avenue, Chinnor, Oxford OX9 4HW*   Kingston Blount (0844) 51278

ROWE, Stephen Mark Buckingham. b 59. SS Mark & Jo Coll Plymouth BA81. Ripon Coll Cuddesdon 83. **d** 86 **p** 87. C Denham *Ox* 86-89; C Aylesbury w Bierton and Hulcott 89-90; TV from 90. *18 Bronte Close, Haydon Hill, Aylesbury, Bucks HP19 3LF*   Aylesbury (0296) 432677

ROWE, William Alfred. b 11. Open Univ BA72. Bps' Coll Cheshunt 50. **d** 52 **p** 53. V Ermington *Ex* 62-72; R Bratton Clovelly w Germansweek 72-76; rtd 76; Lic to Offic *Ex* from 76. *Grangelea, 38 Preston Down Road, Paignton, Devon TQ3 2RL*   Paignton (0803) 556124

ROWELL, Alan. b 50. Lon Univ BSc71 AKC71. Trin Coll Bris DipTh75. **d** 75 **p** 76. C W Hampstead St Cuth *Lon* 75-78; C Camborne *Truro* 78-81; V Pendeen w Morvah from 81. *The Vicarage, Pendeen, Penzance, Cornwall TR19 7SE*   Penzance (0736) 788777

ROWELL, Canon Douglas Geoffrey. b 43. CCC Cam BA64 MA68 PhD68. Cuddesdon Coll. **d** 68 **p** 69. Lic to Offic *Ox* from 68; Asst Chapl New Coll Ox 68-72; Chapl Keble Coll Ox from 72; Wiccamical Preb Chich Cathl *Chich* from 81. *Keble College, Oxford OX1 3PG*   Oxford (0865) 272787

ROWELL, Frank. b 22. Chich Th Coll 50. **d** 52 **p** 53. R Otley *St E* 65-83; R Clopton 65-83; R Clopton w Otley, Swilland and Ashbocking 83-88; rtd 88; Perm to Offic *St E* from 90. *37 Riverview, Melton, Woodbridge, Suffolk IP12 1QU*   Woodbridge (0394) 385449

ROWELL, William Kevin. b 51. Reading Univ BSc71. Linc Th Coll 78. **d** 80 **p** 81. C Cannock *Lich* 80-83; Ind Chapl 83-86; C Ketley and Oakengates 83-86; R Norton in the Moors from 86. *The New Rectory, Norton Lane, Stoke-on-Trent ST6 8BY*   Stoke-on-Trent (0782) 534622

ROWETT, David Peter. b 55. Univ Coll Dur BA76. Ripon Coll Cuddesdon 82. **d** 84 **p** 85. C Yeovil *B & W* 84-88; C Yeovil St Mich 88-89; V Fairfield St Matt *Linc* from 89. *St Matthew's Vicarage, Thirlmere Avenue, Fairfield, Grimsby, S Humberside DN33 3AE*   Grimsby (0472) 821183

ROWETT, Mrs Margaret Pettigrew Coupar. b 33. Sarum & Wells Th Coll 84. **dss** 86 **d** 87. Widley w Wymering *Portsm* 86-87; C 87-88; Par Dn Plympton St Mary *Ex* 88-91; rtd 91. *27 Pinewood Close, Plympton, Plymouth, Devon PL7 3DW*   Plymouth (0752) 336393

ROWETT, William Berkeley. b 09. ADipR58 Lon Univ BA61. Westcott Ho Cam 62. **d** 62 **p** 63. Chapl Scilly Is and V St Mary's *Truro* 66-71; V Madron w Morvah 71-80; rtd 80; Perm to Offic *Guildf* from 80; *Lon* and *S'wark* from 81. *Three Ducks, 30 The Island, Thames Ditton, Surrey KT7 0SQ*   081-398 7196

ROWLAND, Christopher Charles. b 47. Ch Coll Cam BA69 MA73 PhD75. Ridley Hall Cam 72. **d** 75 **p** 76. Hon C Benwell St Jas *Newc* 75-78; Hon C Gosforth All SS 78-79; Dean Jes Coll Cam 79-91; Lic to Offic *Ely* from 79; Prof of Exegesis of H Scripture Ox Univ from 91. *Queen's College, Oxford*   Oxford (0865) 279121

ROWLAND, Ms Dawn Jeannette. b 38. RSCN61 RGN63. S'wark Ord Course. **dss** 84 **d** 87. Par Dn Croydon H Sav *S'wark* 84-89; Par Dn Riddlesdown from 89. *9 Hartley Hill, Purley, Surrey CR8 4EP*   081-660 6270

ROWLAND, Derek John. b 47. St Jo Coll Nottm 84. **d** 86 **p** 87. C Porchester *S'well* 86-89; V Fairfield *Liv* from 89. *St John's Vicarage, 19 Lockerby Road, Liverpool L7 0HG*   051-263 4001

ROWLAND, Derrick Edward. b 31. Univ of Wales (Lamp) BA55 St Cath Soc Ox BA57. Wycliffe Hall Ox. **d** 57 **p** 58. C Reading St Jo *Ox* 57-61; V Smethwick St Matt *Birm* 61-67; V Turnditch *Derby* 67-74; Dir of Educn 74-83; Lic to Offic 83-85; Adult Educn Officer Gen Syn Bd of Educn from 85. *c/o Church House, Great Smith Street, London SW1P 3NZ*   071-222 9011

ROWLAND, Eric Edward James. b 35. Leeds Univ BA62. Coll of Resurr Mirfield 61. **d** 63 **p** 64. C S Kirkby *Wakef* 63-65; C Headingley *Ripon* 65-70; V Osmondthorpe St Phil 70-79; R Sandy *St Alb* from 79; RD Biggleswade from 85. *The Rectory, Sandy, Beds SG19 1AQ*   Sandy (0767) 680512

ROWLAND, Geoffrey Watson. b 17. **d** 55 **p** 56. C Blackheath Park St Mich *S'wark* 65-71; V W Bromwich St Paul Golds Hill *Lich* 71-76; Chapl Community Relns *Lon* 77-83; C Southall Green St Jo 83; rtd 83; Perm to Offic *Lon* from 83. *3 Amber Court, Longford Avenue, Southall, Middx UB1 3QR*   081-574 3442

ROWLAND, Henry Rees. b 03. Lon Coll of Div ALCD32 LTh74. **d** 32 **p** 33. V Bournemouth St Mich *Win* 50-69; Chapl Bournemouth and Distr Hosp 51-73; rtd 69; Perm

to Offic *St Alb* from 76. *5 The Green, Welwyn, Herts AL6 9EA*   Welwyn (043871) 5372

ROWLAND, Robert William. b 51. Birm Univ BA72 Univ of Wales (Cardiff) DPS73. St Mich Coll Llan 72. **d** 74 **p** 75. C Connah's Quay *St As* 74; C Shotton 74-76; C Llanrhos 76-81; V Dyserth and Trelawnyd and Cwm from 81. *The Vicarage, Dyserth, Rhyl, Clwyd LL18 6DB*   Dyserth (0745) 570750

ROWLAND, Mrs Rosemary Katrine. b 38. Nottm Univ BA60 PGCE61 Lon Univ CertRS91. S'wark Ord Course 88. **d** 91. NSM W Acton St Martin *Lon* from 91. *32 Glencairn Drive, London W5 1RT*   081-997 8915

ROWLAND-SMITH, Albert. b 07. **d** 57 **p** 58. V Exhall *Cov* 66-71; rtd 71. *Manormead Nursing Home, Tilford Road, Hindhead, Surrey GU26 6RA*   Hindhead (042873) 5082

ROWLANDS, Very Rev Daniel John. b 25. Pemb Coll Cam BA49 MA54. Bps' Coll Cheshunt 49. **d** 51 **p** 52. Miss to Seamen 53-75; Asst Gen Sec Miss to Seamen Paternoster Royal 69-75; R Woodbridge St Mary *St E* 75-82; Dean Gib *Eur* 82-86; Perm to Offic *St D* 86-88; P-in-c Llangrannog and Llandysiliogogo from 88; RD Glyn Aeron from 89; rtd 90. *Glyn Coed, Dolwen, Aberporth, Dyfed SA43 2DE*   Aberporth (0239) 811042

ROWLANDS, Edward. b 18. DipFL90. Kelham Th Coll 37. **d** 44 **p** 44. R Pemberton St Jo *Liv* 64-75; V Haigh 75-83; rtd 83; Perm to Offic *Liv* from 83. *24 Hallbridge Gardens, Up Holland, Skelmersdale, Lancs WN8 0ER*   Up Holland (0695) 624362

ROWLANDS, Emyr Wyn. b 42. Univ of Wales (Ban) DipTh70. St Mich Coll Llan 69. **d** 70 **p** 71. C Holyhead w Rhoscolyn *Ban* 70-74; V Bodedern, Llechcynfarwy, Llechylched etc 74-88; R Machynlleth and Llanwrin from 88. *The Rectory, Machynlleth, Powys SY20 8HE*   Machynlleth (0654) 2261

ROWLANDS, Forrest John. b 25. LSE BSc(Econ)51. Chich Th Coll 54. **d** 56 **p** 57. R Kingston by Sea *Chich* 62-74; rtd 90. *16 Glebeside Avenue, Worthing, W Sussex BN14 7PR*   Worthing (0903) 823465

ROWLANDS, Frank Wilson. b 29. LCP58 Lon Univ BA61. St Deiniol's Hawarden 78. **d** 81. Hon C Weston *Ches* 81-82. *20 Springfield Drive, Wistaston, Crewe CW2 2RA*

ROWLANDS, Graeme Charles. b 53. K Coll Lon BD74 AKC74. St Aug Coll Cant 75. **d** 76 **p** 77. C Higham Ferrers w Chelveston *Pet* 76-79; C Gorton Our Lady and St Thos *Man* 79-81; C Reading H Trin *Ox* 81-89; P-in-c Kentish Town St Silas *Lon* from 89. *St Silas Presbytery, 11 St Silas Place, London NW5 3QP*   071-485 3727

ROWLANDS, Canon John Henry Lewis. b 47. Univ of Wales (Lamp) BA68 Magd Coll Cam BA70 MA74 Dur Univ MLitt86. Westcott Ho Cam 70. **d** 72 **p** 73. C Abth *St D* 72-76; Chapl St D Coll Lamp 76-79; Youth Chapl *St D* 76-79; Lect Th Univ of Wales (Cardiff) from 79; Dean Faculty of Th Univ of Wales from 91; Dir of Academic Studies St Mich Coll Llan 79-84; Warden of Ords *Llan* 85-88; Sub-Warden St Mich Coll Llan 84-88; Warden from 88; Hon Can Llan Cathl from 90. *St Michael's College, Llandaff, Cardiff CF5 2YJ*   Cardiff (0222) 563116 or 563379

ROWLANDS, Canon John Llewellyn. b 13. TD55. Th Chad's Coll Dur BA35. **d** 36 **p** 37. R Ryton *Dur* 62-74; RD Ches le Street 64-74; Hon Can Dur Cathl 72-78; V Kelloe 74-78; rtd 78; Perm to Offic *Dur* and *Newc* from 78. *7 Glebelands, Corbridge, Northd NE45 5DS*   Corbridge (0434) 632390

ROWLANDS, Canon Joseph Haydn. b 36. Univ of Wales (Lamp) BA61 DipTh63. **d** 63 **p** 64. C Llanfairisgaer *Ban* 63-68; R Maentwrog w Trawsfynydd 68-75; V Henfynyw w Aberaeron and Llanddewi Aber-arth *St D* 75-80; R Trefdraeth *Ban* 80-84; V Llandyssul *St D* from 84; Hon Can St D Cathl 88-90; Res Can St D Cathl from 90. *The Vicarage, Llandyssul, Dyfed SA44 6BU*   Llandyssul (0559) 322277

ROWLANDS, Kenneth Albert. b 41. MA DipAE. NW Ord Course 70. **d** 73 **p** 74. NSM Hoylake *Ches* 73-80; NSM Oxton 80-82; Perm to Offic from 82. *77 Queen's Avenue, Meols, South Wirral L47 0LL*   051-632 3033

ROWLANDS, Mark. b 56. Cranmer Hall Dur 86. **d** 88 **p** 89. C Hattersley *Ches* 88-90; C Stockport St Alb Hall Street from 91. *11 Martham Drive, Offerton, Stockport, Cheshire SK2 5XZ*   061-487 2861

ROWLANDS, Michael Huw. b 62. Birm Univ BA85 Univ of Wales (Cardiff) BD88. St Mich Coll Llan 85. **d** 88 **p** 89. C Penarth All SS *Llan* from 88. *84 Coleridge Avenue, Penarth, S Glam CF6 1SR*   Penarth (0222) 708044

ROWLANDS, Richard. b 34. St Mich Coll Llan 59. d 62 p 63. C Tywyn *Ban* 62-65; C Penmaenmawr 65-69; V Carno and Trefeglwys 69-71; CF 71-83. *Rhyd Casadog, Ty'n Lon Po, Holyhead, Gwynedd* Gwalchmai (0407) 720843

ROWLANDS, Robert. b 31. Roch Th Coll. d 68 p 69. C Hooton *Ches* 68-71; V Stretton 71-88; P-in-c Appleton Thorn and Antrobus 87-88; V Stretton and Appleton Thorn from 88. *The Vicarage, Stretton, Warrington WA4 4NT* Warrington (0925) 73276

ROWLANDSON, Gary Clyde. b 50. Lon Univ CertEd72 BA85. Oak Hill Th Coll 82. d 85 p 86. C Muswell Hill St Jas w St Matt *Lon* 85-89; C Northwood Em from 89. *64 Chester Road, Northwood, Middx HA6 1BH* Northwood (09274) 25019

ROWLEY, Christopher Francis Elmes. b 48. St Jo Coll Dur BA70 St Luke's Coll Ex PGCE71. St Steph Ho Ox 76. d 78 p 79. C Parkstone St Pet w Branksea and St Osmund *Sarum* 78-81; TV 82-85; P-in-c Chard Gd Shep Furnham *B & W* 85-89; P-in-c Dowlishwake w Chaffcombe, Knowle St Giles etc 88-89; R Chard, Furnham w Chaffcombe, Knowle St Giles etc 89-91; V Stoke St Gregory w Burrowbridge and Lyng from 91. *The Vicarage, Stoke St Gregory, Taunton, Somerset TA3 6EG* North Curry (0823) 490247

ROWLEY, David Michael. b 39. N Ord Course 87. d 90 p 91. C Stainland *Wakef* from 90. *18 Burcote Drive, Outlane, Huddersfield HD3 3FY* Huddersfield (0484) 375458

ROWLEY, Edward Patrick. b 29. Dur Univ BSc52. Coll of Resurr Mirfield 55. d 57 p 58. R Ampleforth w Oswaldkirk *York* 63-73; Chapl Yorkshire Res Sch for Deaf Doncaster 74-84; R Finningley *S'well* 84-85; P-in-c Elkesley w Bothamsall 87-91; P-in-c Gamston w Eaton and W Drayton 88-91; rtd 91. *116 Lincoln Road, Tuxford, Newark, Notts NG22 0HS*

ROWLEY, Canon William George. b 12. Chich Th Coll 53. d 55 p 56. V Allington *Sarum* 64-73; RD Lyme Bay 71-76; P-in-c Powerstock w W Milton, Witherstone and N Poorton 73-78; rtd 78. *Hatton, Court Close, Bradpole, Bridport, Dorset DT6 3EA* Bridport (0308) 56265

ROWLING, Catherine. b 55. Man Poly BEd77. Westcott Ho Cam 83 NE Ord Course 85. dss 86 d 87. Gt Ayton w Easby and Newton in Cleveland *York* 86-87; Par Dn 87-89; Chapl Teesside Poly from 89. *10 Allendale Tee, New Marske, Redcar, Cleveland TS11 8HN* Redcar (0642) 484833

ROWLING, Richard Francis. b 56. BA. Westcott Ho Cam. d 84 p 85. C Stokesley *York* 84-87; C Stainton-in-Cleveland 87-90; V New Marske from 90. *10 Allendale Tee, New Marske, Redcar, Cleveland TS11 8HN* Redcar (0642) 484833

ROWNTREE, Peter. b 47. St D Coll Lamp BA68 Univ of Wales (Cardiff) MA70. St Steph Ho Ox 70. d 72 p 73. C Stanwell *Lon* 72-75; C Northolt St Mary 75-79; Chapl Ealing Gen Hosp 79-83 and from 87; Chapl Cherry Knowle Hosp Sunderland 83-87; Chapl Ryhope Hosp Sunderland 83-87. *Ealing Hospital, Uxbridge Road, Southall, Middx UB1 3HW* 081-574 2444

ROWSELL, Canon John Bishop. b 25. Jes Coll Cam BA49 MA55. Ely Th Coll 49. d 51 p 52. C Hackney Wick St Mary of Eton w St Aug *Lon* 51-55; C Is of Dogs Ch Ch and St Jo w St Luke 55-56; C Reading St Mary V *Ox* 56-59; V Hightown *Wakef* 59-69; R Harlton *Ely* 69-81; V Haslingfield 69-81; V Methwold from 81; RD Feltwell from 81; R Northwold from 82; Hon Can Ely Cathl from 84. *The Vicarage, Globe Street, Methwold, Thetford, Norfolk IP26 4PQ* Methwold (0366) 728892

ROWSON, Frank. b 40. CEng67 MIStructE67. Sarum & Wells Th Coll 87. d 90 p 91. NSM Ore Ch Ch *Chich* from 90. *149 Priory Road, Hastings, E Sussex TN34 3JD* Hastings (0424) 439802

ROWSTON, Geoffrey. b 34. Sarum Th Coll 59. d 62 p 63. C Ashburton w Buckland-in-the-Moor *Ex* 62-65; C Basingstoke *Win* 65-68; V Netley 68-78; V W End 78-87; R Alderbury and W Grimstead *Sarum* 87-91; P-in-c Whiteparish 89-91; TR Alderbury Team from 91. *The Rectory, 5 The Copse, Alderbury, Salisbury SP5 3BL* Salisbury (0722) 710229

✠ROWTHORN, Rt Rev Jeffery William. b 34. Societas Liturgica MNAAL MHSA MHSGBI Ch Coll Cam BA57 MA62 Or Coll Ox BLitt72. Cuddesdon Coll 61 Union Th Sem (NY) BD61 Berkeley Div Sch DD87. d 62 p 63 c 87. C Woolwich St Mary w H Trin *S'wark* 62-65; R Garsington *Ox* 65-68; USA from 68; Chapl and Dean Union Th Sem NY 68-73; Assoc Prof Past Th Yale and Berkeley Div Schs 73-87; Suff Bp Connecticut from 87. *337 Main, Portland, Connecticut 06480, USA* New Haven (203) 342-0298

✠ROXBURGH, Rt Rev James William. b 21. St Cath Coll Cam BA42 MA46. Wycliffe Hall Ox 42. d 44 p 45 c 83. C Folkestone H Trin w Ch Ch *Cant* 44-47; C Handsworth St Mary *Birm* 47-50; V Bootle St Matt *Liv* 50-56; V Drypool St Columba w St Andr and St Pet *York* 56-65; V Barking St Marg *Chelmsf* 65-73; P-in-c Barking St Patr 65-73; Hon Can Chelmsf Cathl 72-77; V Barking St Marg w St Patr 73-75; TR 75-77; Adn Colchester 77-83; Suff Bp Barking 83-84; Area Bp Barking 84-90; rtd 90; Asst Bp Liv from 91. *53 Preston Road, Southport, Merseyside PR9 9EE* Southport (0704) 542927

ROXBY, Gordon George. b 39. Lon Univ BSc61. Coll of Resurr Mirfield 61. d 63 p 64. C Fleetwood *Blackb* 65-66; C Kirkham 66-68; V Runcorn St Jo Weston *Ches* 68-78; R Moston St Chad *Man* 78-86; V Bury St Pet from 86; AD Bury from 86. *St Peter's Vicarage, St Peter's Road, Bury, Lancs BL9 9QZ* 061-764 1187

ROY, David Brian. b 25. MIAAS ARIBA Leeds Univ DipArch50. d 88 p 89. Hon C Framland Deanery 88; 90-91; Hon C Burrough Hill Pars *Leic* 88-90; TV Melton Gt Framland from 91. *16 Somerby Road, Pickwell, Melton Mowbray, Leics LE14 2RA* Somerby (066477) 775

ROYALL, Preb Arthur Robert. b 19. Lambeth MA. Qu Coll Birm 51. d 53 p 54. P-in-c Bromley St Mich *Lon* 64-71; R Poplar All SS w St Frideswide 64-71; P-in-c Poplar St Sav w St Gabr and St Steph 68-71; RD Tower Hamlets 68-76; R Poplar 71-73; P-in-c Mile End Old Town H Trin 73-76; P-in-c Bethnal Green St Barn 73-75; Preb St Paul's Cathl 73-86; R Bow w Bromley St Leon 73-76; Clergy Appts Adv 76-85; Perm to Offic *Nor* from 77; *Ely* from 78; rtd 86; Perm to Offic *Lon* from 86. *Carmelite House, 10 Pit Lane, Swaffham, Norfolk PE37 7DA* Swaffham (0760) 23300

ROYCROFT, James Gordon Benjamin. b 26. CITC. d 56 p 57. I Drung w Castleterra *K, E & A* 67-83; I Larah and Lavey 67-83; I Drumkeeran w Templecarne and Muckross *Clogh* 83-91; rtd 91. *Boa Island, Kesh, Co Fermanagh*

ROYDEN, Charles. b 60. Wycliffe Hall Ox BA86. d 87 p 88. C Bidston *Ches* 87-91; V N Brickhill and Putnoe *St Alb* from 91. *The Vicarage, Calder Rise, North Brickhill, Bedford MK41 7UY* Bedford (0234) 58699

ROYDEN, Eric Ramsay. b 29. St Deiniol's Hawarden 75. d 77 p 78. Hon C Tranmere St Paul w St Luke *Ches* 77-81; C Eastham 81; V New Brighton All SS from 81. *All Saints' Vicarage, 2 Zetland Road, Wallasey, Merseyside L45 0JX* 051-639 2748

ROYDEN, Ross Eric. b 55. Nottm Univ MTh82 Lon Bible Coll BA77. Wycliffe Hall Ox 79. d 81 p 82. C Moreton *Ches* 81-84; Chapl Bedf Coll of HE *St Alb* from 84. *4 Bradgate Road, Bedford MK40 3DE* Bedford (0234) 51671 or 212465

ROYDS, John Caress. b 20. Qu Coll Cam BA47 MA52. d 74 p 75. C Kettering St Andr *Pet* 74-76; P-in-c Loddington w Cransley 76; R 76-81; Dir of Educn 76-81; V Northn St Jas 81-85; CMS 85-86; Pakistan 85-86; rtd 87. *16B Donaldson Road, Salisbury SP1 3AD* Salisbury (0722) 332293

ROYLE, Antony Kevan. b 50. FIA76 Lon Univ BSc71. Trin Coll Bris 76. d 79 p 80. C Chell *Lich* 79-82; C Leyland St Andr *Blackb* 82-86; V Blackb Sav from 86; Chapl Blackb R Infirmary & Park Lee Hosp from 86; Chapl E Lancs Hospice from 86. *The Vicarage, Onchan Road, Blackburn BB2 3NT* Blackburn (0254) 55344

ROYLE, Preb Edward. b 04. St Edm Hall Ox BA26 MA30. Westcott Ho Cam 27. d 28 p 29. V Heavitree *Ex* 54-73; Preb Ex Cathl from 64; rtd 73. *Speedwell, 11 Lower South View, Farnham, Surrey GU9 7LB* Farnham (0252) 724830

ROYLE, Frank Peace. b 08. Man Egerton Hall 35. d 36 p 37. V Perranzabuloe *Truro* 60-77; rtd 77; Perm to Offic *Truro* from 77. *3 Droskyn Way, Perranporth, Cornwall TR6 0DS* Truro (0872) 572671

ROYLE, Michael Arthur. b 38. Univ of Wales (Ban) BSc61 Lon Univ DipTh63. St Jo Coll Nottm 81. d 82 p 83. C Boulton *Derby* 82-85; C Belper 85-87; P-in-c Smalley from 86; P-in-c Morley from 87; RD Heanor from 89. *The Vicarage, Main Road, Smalley, Derby DE7 6EF* Derby (0332) 880380

ROYLE, Peter Sydney George. b 34. K Coll Lon BD57 AKC57. d 58 p 59. C St Helier *S'wark* 58-62; Australia 62-68; P-in-c Sydenham St Phil *S'wark* 69-72; V Leigh Park *Portsm* 72-85; RD Havant 77-82; V S w N Hayling from 85. *The Vicarage, 5 Havant Road, Hayling Island, Hants PO11 0PR* Hayling Island (0705) 462914

ROYLE, Roger Michael. b 39. AKC61. d 62 p 63. C Portsea St Mary *Portsm* 62-65; C St Helier *S'wark* 65-68; PV and Succ S'wark Cathl 68-71; P-in-c Dorney *Ox*

71-74; Chapl Eton Coll Windsor 74-82; Lic to Offic *S'wark* from 82; Hon C Froyle and Holybourne *Win* from 90. *Address excluded by request*

ROYLE, Canon Stanley Michael. b 43. K Coll Lon BD69 AKC69 Man Univ MA75. St Aug Coll Cant 71. **d** 72 **p** 73. C Timperley *Ches* 72-76; Perm to Offic 76-81; R Milton Abbas, Hilton w Cheselbourne etc *Sarum* 81-86; Dir of Ords from 86; Adv on Continuing Minl Educn from 86; Can and Preb Sarum Cathl from 89. *Three Firs, Blandford Road, Sturminster Marshall, Wimborne, Dorset* Sturminster Marshall (0258) 857326

ROYSTON-BALL, Peter. b 38. St Mich Coll Llan 61. **d** 65 **p** 66. C Dartford St Alb *Roch* 65-67; C Chislehurst Annunciation 67-69; C St Marylebone Ch Ch w St Paul *Lon* 69-75; Hon C New Windsor *Ox* 75-78; Perm to Offic *S'wark* 75-88; C Leic St Eliz Nether Hall *Leic* from 88. *St Elizabeth House, Austin Rise, Nether Hall, Leicester LE5 1HJ* Leicester (0533) 415812

RUBIO, Angel. b 08. Madras Univ BA42. **d** 39 **p** 40. R Water Newton *Ely* 68-75; R Stibbington 68-75; rtd 75; Asst Chapl Palma de Mallorca and Balearic Is *Eur* from 80. *Calle Son Oliva 2-9-2A, 07014 Palma de Mallorca, Spain* Palma de Mallorca (71) 203283

RUCK, John. b 47. Bris Univ BSc68. **d** 80 **p** 83. Indonesia 80-86 and from 87; Perm to Offic *Birm* 86-87. *Address temp unknown*

RUCK, William. b 28. Qu Coll Birm. **d** 58 **p** 59. C Kells *Carl* 58-61; Australia 61-64; V Ingleton w Chapel le Dale *Bradf* 64-80; RD Ewecross 78-80; Chapl High Royds Hosp Menston from 80. *18 Hall Drive, Burley-in-Wharfedale, Ilkley, W Yorkshire LS29 7LL* Burley-in-Wharfedale (0943) 863017

RUDD, Canon Charles Robert Jordeson. b 34. TCD BA56 MA65 BD65. **d** 57 **p** 58. C Lurgan Redeemer *D & D* 57-61; C Lisburn Ch Ch Cathl *Conn* 61-62; C Willowfield *D & D* 62-66; I Drumgooland w Kilcoo 66-75; I Moira from 75; Can Belf Cathl from 90. *The Rectory, 1 Main Street, Moira, Craigavon, Co Armagh BT67 0LE* Moira (0846) 611268

RUDD, Colin Richard. b 41. AKC64. **d** 65 **p** 66. C N Stoneham *Win* 65-70; V Rotherwick, Hook and Greywell 70-74; R Hook w Greywell 74-78; Toc H 78-89; Lic to Offic *Ox* 83-89; V Buckland from 89. *The Vicarage, Buckland, Faringdon, Oxon SN7 8QN* Buckland (036787) 618

RUDD, Canon Julian Douglas Raymond. b 19. Leeds Univ BA40. Coll of Resurr Mirfield 40. **d** 42 **p** 43. R Old Alresford *Win* 60-70; RD Alresford 60-70; V Warw St Mary *Cov* 70-76; V Warw St Mary w St Nic 76-83; TR Warw 83-84; RD Warw 77-79; rtd 84. *East Close, Church Walk, Penny Street, Sturminster Newton, Dorset DT10 1DF* Sturminster Newton (0258) 73283

RUDD, Robert Arthur. b 33. ALCD60. **d** 60 **p** 61. C Blackb Sav *Blackb* 60-63; C Huyton St Geo *Liv* 63-65; V Bickershaw 65-72; Asst Chapl HM Pris Liv 72-73; Chapl HM Pris Brim 73-78; Parkhurst 78-86; Chapl HM Pris Camp Hill from 86. *The Chaplain, HM Prison Camphill, Newport, Isle of Wight PO30 5PB* Isle of Wight (0983) 527661

RUDDELL, Ven Joseph Frith William. b 06. TCD BA29 MA34. CITC 30. **d** 30 **p** 31. I Killanne Union *C & O* 48-72; Adn Ferns 59-71; rtd 72. *Lyre, Milehouse, Enniscorthy, Co Wexford, Irish Republic* Enniscorthy (54) 33754

RUDDLE, Canon Donald Arthur. b 31. Linc Th Coll 64. **d** 66 **p** 67. C Kettering SS Pet and Paul *Pet* 66-70; V Earlham St Anne *Nor* 70-79; V E Malling *Roch* from 79; RD Malling from 84; Hon Can Roch Cathl from 88. *The Vicarage, 21 High Street, East Malling, Maidstone, Kent ME19 6AJ* West Malling (0732) 843282

RUDDOCK, Brian John. b 45. Dur Univ BA66. Westcott Ho Cam 67. **d** 69 **p** 70. C Ross *Heref* 69-72; C Kettering SS Pet and Paul *Pet* 72-75; P-in-c Colchester St Steph *Chelmsf* 75-77; R Colchester St Leon, St Mary Magd and St Steph 77-84; R March St Pet *Ely* 84-89; R March St Mary 84-89; RD March 87-89; Dioc Unemployment Officer *Sheff* from 89. *36 Sandygate, Wath-upon-Dearne, Rotherham, S Yorkshire S63 7LW* Rotherham (0709) 873254

RUDDOCK, Canon Charles Cecil. b 28. TCD DBS. TCD Div Sch. **d** 57 **p** 58. C Belf St Mary *Conn* 57-59; C Carnmoney 59-61; C Belf St Aid 61-63; I Kiltegan w Rathvilly *C & O* 63-69; C Newtownards *D & D* 69-72; Australia 72-83; I Mallow Union *C, C & R* 83-89; I Fenagh w Myshall, Aghade and Ardoyne *C & O* from 89; Preb Ossory Cathl from 91; Preb Leighlin Cathl from 91. *The Glebe House, Ballon, Co Carlow, Irish Republic* Ballon (503) 59367

RUDDOCK, Edgar Chapman. b 48. St Jo Coll Dur BA70 DipTh73 MA77. **d** 74 **p** 75. C Birm St Geo *Birm* 74-78; R 78-83; Swaziland from 83. *PO Box 1751, Mbabane, Swaziland*

RUDDOCK, Canon Kenneth Edward. b 30. TCD BA52 QUB MTh79. CITC53 Div Test. **d** 53 **p** 54. C Ballymena *Conn* 53-56; C Belf St Thos 56-60; I Tomregan w Drumlane *K, E & A* 60-68; I Belf St Luke *Conn* 68-80; Miss to Seamen from 80; I Whitehead w Islandmagee *Conn* from 80; Can Lisburn Cathl from 90; RD Carrickfergus from 90; Dioc Info Officer from 90. *The Rectory, 74 Cable Road, Whitehead, Carrickfergus, Co Antrim BT38 9SJ* Whitehead (09603) 73300

RUDDOCK, Norman Trevor. b 35. TCD BA57 MA60 HDipEd62. TCD Div Sch 58. **d** 58 **p** 59. C Belf St Steph *Conn* 58-60; C Dub Ch Ch Leeson Park *D & G* 60-63; Perm to Offic 63-73; USA 70-72; I Killanne *C & O* 73-81; I Castlepollard and Oldcastle w Loughcrew etc *M & K* from 84. *St Michael's Rectory, Castlepollard, Mullingar, Irish Republic* Mullingar (44) 61123

RUDDOCK, Reginald Arthur. b 07. Oak Hill Th Coll 61. **d** 62 **p** 63. R Holton w Bratton St Maur *B & W* 70-76; C Camelot Par 76; R Holton 76-77; rtd 77. *Freshford, Horsington, Templecombe, Somerset BA8 0EF* Templecombe (0963) 70511

RUDDOCK, Reginald Bruce. b 55. AGSM77. Chich Th Coll. **d** 83 **p** 84. C Felpham w Middleton *Chich* 83-86; C Portsea St Mary *Portsm* 86-88; P-in-c Barnes St Mich *S'wark* from 88. *St Michael's Vicarage, 39 Elm Bank Gardens, London SW13 0NX* 081-876 5230

RUDDY, Canon Denys Henry. b 22. Jes Coll Ox BA48 MA53. Linc Th Coll 48. **d** 50 **p** 51. R Longworth and Hinton Waldrist *Ox* 58-77; RD Vale of White Horse 68-75; Warden of Readers 70-87; Chapl Abingdon St Nic 77-87; Hon Can Ch Ch 79-87; RD Abingdon 79-80; rtd 87; Perm to Offic *Ox* from 87. *32 Coberley Close, Downhead Park, Milton Keynes MK15 9BJ* Milton Keynes (0908) 604719

RUDGE, Percy William Humble. b 18. St Jo Coll Dur BA40 DipTh41 MA43. **d** 41 **p** 42. V Gosforth St Nic *Newc* 70-82; Hon Chapl to Bp from 82; rtd 83. *315 Heaton Road, Newcastle upon Tyne NE6 5QD* 091-265 8727

RUDKIN, Simon David. b 51. Bradf Univ BA74 K Coll Lon BD77 AKC72. Coll of Resurr Mirfield 77. **d** 78 **p** 79. C Flixton St Mich *Man* 78-81; C Atherton 81-84; V Lever Bridge 84-91; P-in-c Pennington w Lindal and Marton *Carl* from 91. *The Vicarage, Main Road, Swarthmoor, Ulverston, Cumbria LA12 0SE* Ulverston (0229) 53174

RUDLAND, Patrick Ivor. b 20. ACP62 Lon Univ CertEd62. Tyndale Hall Bris 56. **d** 59 **p** 60. C Tunbridge Wells St Jas *Roch* 59-62; Lic to Offic 62-66; Hon C Sevenoaks St Nic 66-69; Hon C Tonbridge SS Pet and Paul 69-85; Hon C Shipbourne from 85. *Flat 4, 12 Dry Hill Road, Tonbridge, Kent TN9 1LX* Tonbridge (0732) 351694

RUDMAN, David Walter Thomas. b 48. Lon Univ DipTh70 BD72. Oak Hill Th Coll 68. **d** 72 **p** 73. C Plymouth St Jude *Ex* 72-75; C Radipole *Sarum* 76-77; Warden of St Geo Ho Braunton from 77; R Georgeham *Ex* from 88. *The Rectory, Georgeham, Devon EX33 1JS* Croyde (0271) 890809

RUDMAN, Thomas Peter William. b 22. Oak Hill Th Coll 60. **d** 62 **p** 63. V Lowestoft Ch Ch *Nor* 67-73; V Stapenhill w Cauldwell *Derby* 73-81; V Sutton le Marsh *Linc* 81-87; RD Calcewaithe and Candleshoe 85-87; rtd 87; Perm to Offic *Win* from 87. *1 Morley Close, Burton, Christchurch, Dorset BH23 7LA* Christchurch (0202) 476255

RUEHORN, Eric Arthur. b 33. St Aid Birkenhead 58. **d** 61 **p** 62. C Harpurhey Ch Ch *Man* 61-65; V Roughtown 65-74; V Hawkshaw Lane from 74. *St Mary's Vicarage, Bolton Road, Hawkshaw, Bury, Lancs BL8 4JN* Tottington (0204) 882955

RUFF, Brian Chisholm. b 36. FCA70 Lon Univ BD66. Oak Hill Th Coll 63. **d** 67 **p** 68. C Cheadle *Ches* 67-71; Educn and Youth Sec CPAS 72-76; V New Milverton *Cov* 76-90; Min Westbourne Ch Ch CD *Win* from 90. *43 Branksome Dene Road, Bournemouth BH4 8JW* Bournemouth (0202) 762164

RUFF, Michael Ronald. b 49. K Coll Lon BD72 AKC72. St Aug Coll Cant 72. **d** 73 **p** 74. C Old Shoreham *Chich* 73-76; Chapl Ellesmere Coll Shropshire 77-81; Chapl Grenville Coll Bideford 81-87; Chapl Stamford Sch Lincs from 87. *Stamford School, Stamford, Lincs* Stamford (0780) 62171

RUFFLE, John Leslie. b 43. ALCD66. **d** 66 **p** 67. C Eastwood *S'well* 66-70; C Keynsham w Queen Charlton *B & W* 70-75; P-in-c Weston-super-Mare Em 75; TV Weston-super-Mare Cen Par 75-84; V Yatton Moor

84-91; TR from 91. *The Rectory, 1 Well Lane, Yatton, Bristol BS19 4HT* Yatton (0934) 832184

RUFFLE, Leslie Norman. b 12. Tyndale Hall Bris 49. **d** 50 **p** 51. R Chawleigh w Cheldon *Ex* 70-77; R Eggesford 70-77; rtd 77; Perm to Offic *Ex* from 86. *16 Fairfield, Sampford Peverell, Tiverton, Devon EX16 7TD*

RUFFLE, Peter Cousins. b 19. Lon Univ BD42. ALCD42. **d** 42 **p** 43. Prin CA Wilson Carlile Coll of Evang 66-74; Can Res Blackb Cathl *Blackb* 74-78; V Meole Brace *Lich* 78-85; rtd 85; Perm to Offic *Win* and *Portsm* from 85. *84 Queen's Crescent, Stubbington, Fareham, Hants PO14 2QQ* Stubbington (0329) 663791

RUFLI, Alan John. b 63. TCD BA89. **d** 91. C Donaghcloney w Waringstown *D & D* from 91. *St Patrick's Church House, 51 Main Street, Donaghcloney, Co Armagh* Waringstown (0762) 882326

RUGG, Andrew Philip. b 47. Kent Univ BA82. Sarum & Wells Th Coll 83. **d** 85 **p** 86. C Harlesden All So *Lon* 85-90; TV Benwell Team *Newc* from 90. *56 Dunholme Road, Newcastle upon Tyne NE4 6XE* 091-273 5356

RUMALSHAH, Inayat. b 14. **d** 37 **p** 38. India 37-73; C Hazlemere *Ox* 74-76; C Wooburn 76-79; rtd 79. *40 Highfield Road, Bourne End, Bucks SL8 5BG* Bourne End (06285) 25186

RUMALSHAH, Munawar Kenneth. b 41. Punjab Univ BSc60 Serampore Coll BD65 Karachi Univ MA68 Cam Univ CertEd86. Bp's Coll Calcutta 62. **d** 65 **p** 66. Pakistan 65-70 and from 89; C Roundhay St Edm *Ripon* 70-73; Area Sec (Dios Ripon and York) CMS 73-74; Asst Home Sec N Province 74-78; Educn Sec BCC 78-81; P-in-c Southall St Geo *Lon* 81-88. *c/o USPG, 157 Waterloo Road, London SE1 8XA* 071-928 8681

RUMBALL, Frank Thomas. b 43. Sarum & Wells Th Coll 72. **d** 74 **p** 75. C Bromyard *Heref* 74-78; TV Ewyas Harold w Dulas 78-79; TV Ewyas Harold w Dulas, Kenderchurch etc 79-81; C Minsterley 81-82; P-in-c Eye, Croft w Yarpole and Lucton from 82. *The Vicarage, Eye, Leominster, Herefordshire HR6 0DP* Yarpole (056885) 229

RUMBALL, William Michael. b 41. Birm Univ BSc63 PhD66 BA75. Wycliffe Hall Ox 78. **d** 80 **p** 81. C S Molton, Nymet St George, High Bray etc *Ex* 80-83; V S Hetton w Haswell *Dur* 83-90; V S Wingfield and Wessington *Derby* from 90. *The Vicarage, South Wingfield, Derby DE5 7LJ* Alfreton (0773) 832484

RUMBLE, Miss Alison Merle. b 49. Surrey Univ BSc71. Trin Coll Bris BA89. **d** 89. Par Dn Willesden Green St Gabr *Lon* from 89. *31 Olive Road, London NW2 6TY* 081-450 8707

RUMBOLD, Bernard John. b 43. **d** 73 **p** 75. Papua New Guinea 73-76; C Gt Burstead *Chelmsf* 76-77; Chapl RAF from 77. *c/o MOD, Adastral House, Theobald's Road, London WC1X 8RU* 071-430 7268

RUMBOLD, Graham Charles. b 44. Open Univ BA79. S Dios Minl Tr Scheme 76. **d** 79 **p** 80. NSM Widley w Wymering *Portsm* from 79; Chapl Cynthia Spencer Unit Manfield Hosp from 82; Lic to Offic *Pet* from 82. *3 Calstock Close, Favell Green, Northampton* Northampton (0604) 27389

RUMENS, Canon John Henry. b 21. AKC49. **d** 50 **p** 51. R Salisbury St Edm *Sarum* 59-72; RD Salisbury 69-72; Can and Preb Sarum Cathl 72-85; R Trowbridge H Trin 72-79; P-in-c Sturminster Marshall 79-83; V 83-85; rtd 85. *20 Constable Way, Salisbury SP2 8LN* Salisbury (0722) 334716

RUMING, Canon Gordon William. b 27. Kelham Th Coll 45. **d** 52 **p** 53. C Baildon *Bradf* 52-55; C Prestbury *Glouc* 55-60; C Penzance St Mary *Truro* 60-61; R Calstock from 61; Hon Can Truro Cathl from 79; RD E Wivelshire 85-91. *The Rectory, Sand Lane, Calstock, Cornwall PL18 9QX* Tavistock (0822) 832518

RUMSEY, Ian Mark. b 58. Van Mildert Coll Dur BSc79 St Jo Coll Dur BA89. Cranmer Hall Dur 87. **d** 90 **p** 91. C Dalston *Carl* from 90. *2 Yetlands, Dalston, Carlisle CA5 7PB* Dalston (0228) 710379

RUMSEY, Canon Philip Charles. b 21. Bps' Coll Cheshunt 59. **d** 61 **p** 62. R Knebworth *St Alb* 66-76; V Luton Lewsey St Hugh 76-81; Hon Can St Alb 81-87; R High Wych and Gilston w Eastwick 81-87; rtd 87. *1 Folly Drive, Tupsley, Hereford HR1 1NE* Hereford (0432) 279987

RUMSEY, Thomas Philip. b 14. Selw Coll Cam BA37 MA41. St Aug Coll Cant 33. **d** 38 **p** 39. R Skelsmergh w Selside and Longsleddale *Carl* 70-79; rtd 79; Perm to Offic *Carl* from 79. *The Old School*

Cottage, Heversham, Milnthorpe, Cumbria LA7 7ER Milnthorpe (05395) 63634

✠**RUNCIE, Rt Rev and Rt Hon Lord (Robert Alexander Kennedy of Cuddesdon,).** b 21. MC45 PC80. BNC Ox BA48 MA48 Hon DD80. Westcott Ho Cam 48. **d** 50 **p** 51 **c** 70. C Gosforth All SS *Newc* 50-52; Chapl Westcott Ho Cam 53-54; Vice-Prin 54-56; Dean Trin Hall Cam 56-60; V Cuddesdon *Ox* 60-70; Prin Cuddesdon Coll 60-70; Can and Preb Linc Cathl *Linc* 69-70; Bp St Alb 70-80; Hon Fell BNC Ox from 78; Abp Cant 80-91; rtd 91; Asst Bp St Alb from 91. *26A Jennings Road, St Albans, Herts AL1 4PD* St Albans (0727) 48021

RUNCORN, David Charles. b 54. BA77 Ox Poly DipPsych88. St Jo Coll Nottm 77. **d** 79 **p** 80. C Wealdstone H Trin *Lon* 79-82; Chapl Lee Abbey 82-89; C Ealing St Steph Castle Hill *Lon* 89-90; V from 90. *St Stephen's Vicarage, St Stephen's Road, London W13 8HD* 081-998 1708

RUNCORN, Canon Dennis Brookes. b 22. Ch Coll Cam BA47 MA52. Ridley Hall Cam 47. **d** 49 **p** 50. V Shortlands *Roch* 67-80; RD Beckenham 73-80; Hon Can Roch Cathl from 78; V Shorne 80-87; rtd 87; Perm to Offic *Derby* from 87. *14 Hollowood Avenue, Littleover, Derby DE3 6JD* Derby (0332) 765859

RUNDELL, Canon Geoffrey Edmund. b 21. St Jo Coll Dur BA48 DipTh49. **d** 49 **p** 50. V Tarvin *Ches* 67-86; rtd 86; Hon Can Ches Cathl *Ches* 86; Perm to Offic from 86. *22 Oaklands Crescent, Tattenhall, Chester CH3 9QT* Tattenhall (0829) 70685

RUNDLE, Mrs Beryl Rosemary. b 28. Bris Univ BA49. S Dios Minl Tr Scheme 83. **dss** 86 **d** 87. Tangmere *Chich* 86-87; Hon Par Dn from 87; Boxgrove 86-87; Hon Par Dn from 87. *1 Caedwalla Drive, Tangmere, Chichester, W Sussex PO20 6HJ* Chichester (0243) 778214

RUNDLE, Nicholas John. b 59. Southn Univ BA80. St Steph Ho Ox. **d** 84 **p** 85. C E Preston w Kingston *Chich* 84-87; Chapl RAF 87-91; Australia from 91. *Address temp unknown*

RUNDLE, Penelope Anne. b 36. St Hugh's Coll Ox MA59 Lon Univ DAA64. S Dios Minl Tr Scheme 85. **d** 88. Hon Par Dn Mere w W Knoyle and Maiden Bradley *Sarum* from 88. *14 Church Street, Maiden Bradley, Warminster, Wilts BA12 7HW* Maiden Bradley (09853) 610

RUPP, Ernest Walter. b 25. Westmr Coll Lon CertEd55. St Jo Coll Nottm 84. **d** 85 **p** 86. NSM Leic Ascension *Leic* 85-89; Chapl Glenfield Hosp *Leic* 86-89; R Barkestone w Plungar, Redmile and Stathern *Leic* from 89. *The Rectory, Church Lane, Redmile, Nottingham NG13 0GE* Bottesford (0949) 43729

RUSBY, Frank Edward. b 31. St Edm Hall Ox BA54 MA58. Linc Th Coll 54. **d** 56 **p** 57. C Louth w Welton-le-Wold *Linc* 56-59; R Kingston Bagpuize *Ox* 59-61; V Fyfield w Tubney 59-61; V Fyfield w Tubney and Kingston Bagpuize 61-78; R Sutton St Nic *S'wark* 78-84; R Horne 84-88; P-in-c Outwood 84-88; V Croydon St Pet from 88. *23 Whitgift Avenue, South Croydon, Surrey CR2 6AZ* 081-688 4715

RUSCOE, John. b 12. Man Univ BA35. Lich Th Coll 35. **d** 37 **p** 38. R Redruth *Truro* 57-70; R Mawnan 70-84; rtd 84. *34 Tregenver Road, Falmouth, Cornwall TR11 2QW* Falmouth (0326) 315300

RUSCOE, Canon John Ernest. b 32. Dur Univ BA57. Qu Coll Birm 57. **d** 59 **p** 60. C Jarrow St Paul *Dur* 59-63; C Whitburn 63-65; V S Hylton from 65; Hon Can Dur Cathl from 85. *The Vicarage, South Hylton, Sunderland SR4 0QB* 091-534 2325

RUSHER, James Victor Francis. b 28. Ridley Hall Cam 58. **d** 60 **p** 61. C Kensington St Helen w H Trin *Lon* 60-63; C Edgbaston St Bart *Birm* 63-66; V Summerfield 66-71; V Knowle 71-82; Perm to Offic from 82; Chapl Parkway Hosp Solihull from 85. *4 Froxmere Close, Solihull, W Midlands B91 3XG* 021-705 4514

RUSHFORD, Harold Tilney. b 08. Qu Coll Birm 55. **d** 56 **p** 57. V Dawdon *Dur* 59-83; rtd 84. *Dalden, 18 Windsor Drive, Houghton le Spring, Tyne & Wear DH5 8JS* 091-584 9682

RUSHFORTH, Colin Stephen. b 53. Chich Th Coll 74. **d** 77 **p** 78. C Moulsecoomb *Chich* 77-79; C Rumboldswyke 79-81; C Whyke w Rumboldswhyke and Portfield 81-82; V Friskney *Linc* 82-84; P-in-c Thorpe St Peter 82-84; TV Leic H Spirit *Leic* 84-87; Chapl Leic R Infirmary from 87. *Leicester Royal Infirmary, Infirmary Square, Leicester LE1 5WW* Leicester (0533) 541414

RUSHFORTH, Richard Hamblin. b 40. Keble Coll Ox BA62 MA71. Chich Th Coll 62. **d** 64 **p** 65. C St Leonards Ch Ch *Chich* 64-79; Org Sec Fellowship of St Nic 79-81; V Portslade St Nic and St Andr from 81; Min Portslade Gd Shep Mile Oak CD 88-89. *The Vicarage, South*

Street, Portslade, Brighton BN4 2LE   Brighton (0273) 418090

RUSHTON, James David. b 39. Dur Univ BA61. Cranmer Hall Dur DipTh64. **d** 64 **p** 65. C Upper Armley *Ripon* 64-67; C Blackpool Ch Ch *Blackb* 67-70; V Preston St Cuth 70-79; V Denton Holme *Carl* from 79. *St James's Vicarage, Goschen Road, Carlisle CA2 5PF*   Carlisle (0228) 515639

RUSHTON, Malcolm Leslie. b 47. Bris Univ BSc69 Birm Univ PhD72 Fitzw Coll Cam BA74. Ridley Hall Cam 72. **d** 75 **p** 76. C Cullompton *Ex* 75-79; Chapl Univ Coll *Lon* 79-87; Chapl R Veterinary Coll Sch of Pharmacy 87-90; Chapl R Free Medical Sch 87-90. *191A Kentish Town Road, London NW5*   071-482 4077

RUSHTON, Philip William. b 38. Open Univ BA87. Clifton Th Coll 62. **d** 65 **p** 66. C Brixton St Paul *S'wark* 65-67; C Aldridge *Lich* 67-69; C Bushbury 69-71; Chapl Nat Nautical Sch Portishead 71-72; Chapl RAF 72-79; P-in-c Bolton on Swale *Ripon* 79-87; P-in-c The Cowtons 80-82; V 82-89; CF (TA) from 88; R Litcham, Kempston, Lexham, Mileham, Beeston etc *Nor* from 89. *The Rectory, Litcham, King's Lynn, Norfolk PE32 2QR* Fakenham (0328) 701223

RUSHTON, Mrs Susan Elizabeth. b 44. Univ of Wales (Cardiff) BA65. Bris Sch of Min 83. dss 86 **d** 87. Westbury-on-Trym H Trin *Bris* 86-87; Hon Par Dn 87-91; C Wotton St Mary *Glouc* from 91. *102 Lavington Drive, Gloucester GL2 0HT*   Gloucester (0452) 504252

RUSHTON, Mrs Valerie Elizabeth Wendy. b 40. Birm Univ BSocSc62 DPS87. W Midl Minl Tr Course 86. **d** 89. C Nuneaton St Nic *Cov* from 89. *113 St Nicholas Park Drive, Nuneaton, Warks CV11 6EF*   Nuneaton (0203) 375830

RUSK, Canon Frederick John. b 28. QUB BA50. **d** 53 **p** 54. C Ballymoney *Conn* 53-56; C Belf St Nic 56-59; I Broomhedge 59-65; RE Insp 64-66; I Belf St Simon 65-78; I Ballymena w Ballyclug 78-84; Preb Conn Cathl 84-86; Treas Conn Cathl 86-90; I Belf St Nic from 88; Prec Conn Cathl 90; Chan Conn Cathl from 90. *15 Harberton Park, Belfast BT9 6TW*   Belfast (0232) 667753

RUSK, Michael Frederick. b 58. Cam Univ BA MA. Westcott Ho Cam 81. **d** 84 **p** 85. C Altrincham St Geo *Ches* 84-87; Chapl Collingwood and Grey Coll Dur 87-90; Chapl Collingwood Coll Dur from 90; C-in-c Neville's Cross St Jo CD from 90. *St John's Vicarage, The Avenue, Durham DH1 4DX*   091-384 4260

RUSS, Timothy John. b 41. AKC64. Sarum Th Coll 66. **d** 66 **p** 67. C Walthamstow St Pet *Chelmsf* 66-70; C Epping St Jo 70-73; C Stepney St Dunstan and All SS *Lon* 73-75; Youth Officer 75-79; Tutor YMCA Nat Coll Walthamstow 79-84; Hon C St Botolph Aldgate w H Trin Minories *Lon* 82-89; Selection Sec ACCM 84-89; Dir Healing and Counselling Cen from 89; Gen Sec Inst of Religion and Medicine from 89; Hon C Hoxton St Anne w St Columba *Lon* from 90. *3 Gloucester Square, London E2 8RS*   071-729 4326 or 935 6374

RUSSELL, Adrian Camper. b 45. Chich Th Coll 79. **d** 81 **p** 82. C Marton *Blackb* 81-84; C Haslemere *Guildf* 84-85; V Hartlepool H Trin *Dur* 85-89; P-in-c Cornforth from 89. *Cornforth Vicarage, 1 Broadoak, Bishop Middleham, Ferryhill, Co Durham DL17 9BW*   Ferryhill (0740) 654591

✠**RUSSELL, Rt Rev Anthony John.** b 43. St Chad's Coll Dur BA65 Trin Coll Ox DPhil71. Cuddesdon Coll 65. **d** 70 **p** 71 **c** 88. C Hilborough w Bodney *Nor* 70-73; P-in-c Preston-on-Stour w Whitchurch *Cov* 73-76; P-in-c Atherstone on Stour 73-76; V Preston on Stour and Whitchurch w Atherstone 77-88; Can Th Cov Cathl 77-88; Chapl Arthur Rank Cen 73-82; Dir 83-88; Chapl to HM The Queen 83-88; Area Bp Dorchester *Ox* from 88. *Holmby House, Sibford Ferris, Banbury, Oxon OX15 5RG*

RUSSELL, Brian Kenneth. b 50. Trin Hall Cam BA73 MA76 Birm Univ MA77 PhD83. Cuddesdon Coll 74. **d** 76 **p** 77. C Redhill St Matt *S'wark* 76-79; Dir of Studies NE Ord Course 79-83; P-in-c Merrington *Dur* 79-83; Dir of Studies and Lect Linc Th Coll 83-86; Perm to Offic *S'wark* from 86; Selection Sec and Sec Cttee for Th Educn ACCM 86-91; ABM from 91. *9 Furze Close, Redhill, Surrey RH1 1DN*   Redhill (0737) 765290

RUSSELL, Brian Robert. b 61. QUB BA TCD DipTh85. **d** 85 **p** 86. C Dub Drumcondra w N Strand *D & G* 85-87; C Carrickfergus *Conn* 87-90; I Kilmegan w Maghera *D & D* from 90. *7B Moneylane Road, Dundrum, Newcastle, Co Down BT33 0NR*   Dundrum (039675) 225

RUSSELL, Canon Derek John. b 30. St Pet Hall Ox BA54 MA58. Qu Coll Birm 54. **d** 56 **p** 57. Chapl HM

Pris Wormwood Scrubs 63-65 and 71-89; Stafford 65-69; Pentonville 70; SE Regional Chapl 74-81; Chapl HM Rem Cen Latchmere Ho 74-77; Asst Chapl Gen of Pris 81-83; Dep 83-90; Hon Can Cant Cathl *Cant* 86-90; rtd 90. *25 Piers Avenue, Whitstable, Kent CT5 2HQ* Canterbury (0227) 276654

RUSSELL, Eric. b 19. Dur Univ LTh42 BA48 MA53 Man Univ BD52 Nottm Univ MPhil87. Oak Hill Th Coll 38. **d** 42 **p** 43. Hd of Relig Studies Sheff Coll of Educn 67-78; Lic to Offic *Sheff* 67-78; Lect Liv Bible Coll 78-88; rtd 88. *16A St Paul's Street, Southport, Merseyside PR8 1LZ*   Southport (0704) 534797

RUSSELL, Eric Watson. b 39. FCA73. Clifton Th Coll 66. **d** 69 **p** 70. C Kinson *Sarum* 69-73; C Peckham St Mary Magd *S'wark* 73-77; TV Barking St Marg w St Patr *Chelmsf* 77-82; V Lozells St Paul and St Silas *Birm* from 82; RD Aston from 89. *St Silas's Vicarage, 103 Heathfield Road, Handsworth, Birmingham B19 1HE* 021-523 5645

RUSSELL, George Frederick Robert. b 29. S'wark Ord Course 62. **d** 65 **p** 66. C Catford St Laur *S'wark* 65-67; C Malden St Jo 67-70; V Wandsworth St Paul 70-79; V Hurst Green from 79. *Hurst Green Vicarage, Church Way, Oxted, Surrey RH8 9EA*   Oxted (0883) 712674

RUSSELL, Dr George Lawrence. b 09. Edin Univ MB, ChB32. Westcott Ho Cam 34. **d** 35 **p** 36. R Bentley *Guildf* 72-79; rtd 79. *47 Church Street, Fontmell Magna, Shaftesbury, Dorset SP7 0NY*   Fontmell Magna (0747) 811397

RUSSELL, Ven Harold Ian Lyle. b 34. Lon Coll of Div ALCD59 BD60. **d** 60 **p** 61. C Iver *Ox* 60-63; C Fulwood *Sheff* 63-67; V Chapeltown 67-75; RD Tankersley 73-75; V Nottm St Jude *S'well* 75-89; Hon Can S'well Minster from 88; Adn Cov from 89. *9 Armorial Road, Coventry CV3 6GH*   Coventry (0203) 417750

RUSSELL, Herbert Mark. b 12. Dur Univ LTh38. Trin Coll Bris 35. **d** 38 **p** 39. V Danehill *Chich* 67-77; rtd 77; Hon C Glynde, W Firle and Beddingham *Chich* 77-80; Perm to Offic from 80. *Pelham House, London Road, Cuckfield, Haywards Heath, W Sussex RH17 5EU* Haywards Heath (0444) 417954

RUSSELL, Mrs Isabel. b 31. Lightfoot Ho Dur 58. dss 71 **d** 87. Gt Barr *Lich* 71-74; E Farleigh and Coxheath *Roch* 75-84; Ogwell and Denbury *Ex* 85-87; Hon Par Dn from 87; Sub-Chapl HM Pris Dartmoor from 89. *Church Cottage, Manaton Green, Newton Abbot, Devon TQ13 9UJ*   Manaton (064722) 297

RUSSELL, John Arthur. b 29. AKC62. **d** 63 **p** 64. C Fareham H Trin *Portsm* 63-67; R Greatham w Empshott 67-79; V Ham St Andr *S'wark* 79-87; P-in-c Battersea St Luke from 87. *52 Thurleigh Road, London SW12 8UD* 081-673 6506

RUSSELL, John Graham. b 35. G&C Coll Cam BA58 MA62. Westcott Ho Cam 59. **d** 61 **p** 62. C Durleigh *B & W* 61-66; C Bridgwater St Mary w Chilton Trinity 61-66; C Far Headingley St Chad *Ripon* 66-72; P-in-c Leeds St Matt Lt Lon 72-79; V Rowley Regis *Birm* 79-84; V Hall Green Ascension from 84. *The Vicarage, 592 Fox Hollies Road, Birmingham B28 9DX*   021-777 3689

RUSSELL, Jonathan Vincent Harman. b 43. K Coll Lon 68. **d** 69 **p** 70. C Addington *Cant* 69-73; C Buckland in Dover w Buckland Valley 73-76; P-in-c Selling 76-85; P-in-c Throwley w Stalisfield and Otterden 79-85; R Selling w Throwley, Sheldwich w Badlesmere etc from 85; Hon Min Can Cant Cathl from 83; RD Ospringe from 90. *The Rectory, Selling, Faversham, Kent ME13 9RD* Canterbury (0227) 752221

RUSSELL, Jonathan Wingate. b 55. BSc BA DMS DIM. St Jo Coll Nottm 81. **d** 84 **p** 85. C Southsea St Jude *Portsm* 84-87; P-in-c Shorwell w Kingston from 87; P-in-c Gatcombe from 87; P-in-c Chale from 89. *The Vicarage, 5 Northcourt Close, Shorwell, Isle of Wight PO30 3LD* Isle of Wight (0983) 741044

RUSSELL, Lloyd George Winkler. b 19. Hatf Coll Dur LTh45 BA49. **d** 45 **p** 46. Perm to Offic *Roch* 58-81 and from 85; Jamaica 82-85; rtd 85; Perm to Offic *S'wark* from 85. *39 Pembroke Road, Bromley, Kent BR1 2RT* 081-460 1498

RUSSELL, Martin Christopher. b 48. St Jo Coll Dur BA70. Coll of Resurr Mirfield 72. **d** 74 **p** 75. C Huddersfield SS Pet and Paul *Wakef* 74-75; C Huddersfield St Pet 75-77; Trinidad and Tobago 78-85; V S Crosland *Wakef* from 85; P-in-c Helme from 85. *The Vicarage, South Crosland, Huddersfield HD4 7DB*   Huddersfield (0484) 661080

RUSSELL, Michael John. b 38. Clifton Th Coll 66. **d** 68 **p** 69. C Cranham Park CD *Chelmsf* 68-70; C Bucknall and Bagnall *Lich* 70-77; P-in-c Tintwistle *Ches* 77-79; V

79-86; New Zealand from 86. *201 Cambridge Avenue, Ashurst, New Zealand*   Ashurst (63) 268543

RUSSELL, Morris Charles. b 14. AKC36. **d** 37 **p** 38. C Tottenham St Phil *Lon* 37-39; C Winchmore Hill H Trin 39-41; CF (EC) 41-46; V Thornham w Titchwell *Nor* 46-51; R Newmarket St Mary *St E* 51-59; R Ipswich St Matt 59-66; New Zealand from 67. *19 Paisley Street, Howick, New Zealand*   Auckland (9) 534-3116

RUSSELL, Neil. b 47. Nottm Univ CPS81. E Midl Min Tr Course 78. **d** 81 **p** 82. NSM Wyberton *Linc* 81-84; C 84-85; V Frampton from 85; Agric Chapl and Countryside Officer from 88. *The Vicarage, Frampton, Boston, Lincs PE20 1AE*   Boston (0205) 722294

RUSSELL, Mrs Noreen Margaret. b 39. Man Univ BA60 Lon Univ PGCE61 BD66. W Midl Minl Tr Course 90. **d** 91. NSM Swynnerton and Tittensor *Lich* from 91. *40 Old Road, Barlaston, Stoke-on-Trent, Staffs ST12 9EQ*   Barlaston (078139) 2992

RUSSELL, Norman Atkinson. b 43. Chu Coll Cam BA65 MA69 Lon Univ BD70. Lon Coll of Div 67. **d** 70 **p** 71. C Clifton Ch Ch w Em *Bris* 70-74; C Enfield Ch Ch Trent Park *Lon* 74-77; R Harwell w Chilton *Ox* 77-84; P-in-c Gerrards Cross 84-88; P-in-c Fulmer 85-88; R Gerrards Cross and Fulmer from 88. *The Rectory, Oxford Road, Gerrards Cross, Bucks SL9 7DJ*   Gerrards Cross (0753) 883301

RUSSELL, Miss Pamela. b 34. SRN SCM. Coll of Resurr Mirfield 85. **dss** 86 **d** 87. Barnburgh w Melton on the Hill *Sheff* 86-87; Hon Par Dn from 87. *94 Melton Mill Lane, High Melton, Doncaster, S Yorkshire DN5 7TF*   Mexborough (0709) 582703

RUSSELL, Paul Selwyn. b 38. ALCD61. **d** 61 **p** 62. C Gillingham St Mark *Roch* 61-64; SAMS in Chile, Peru and Bolivia 64-84; V Brinsworth w Catcliffe *Sheff* 84-91; R Brinklow *Cov* from 91; R Harborough Magna from 91; V Monks Kirby w Pailton and Stretton-under-Fosse from 91. *The Rectory, 31 Coventry Road, Brinklow, Rugby, Warks CV23 0NE*   Rugby (0788) 832274

RUSSELL, Philip John Seymour. b 1900. Wells Th Coll 22. **d** 23 **p** 24. rtd 67; Perm to Offic *Glas* from 68. *High Portling, Dalbeattie, Kirkcudbrightshire DG5 4PZ*   Rockcliffe (055663) 359

RUSSELL, Ralph Geoffrey Major. b 19. St Aug Coll Cant 47 Sarum Th Coll 48. **d** 50 **p** 51. V New Bradwell w Stantonbury *Ox* 62-73; P-in-c Linslade 74-75; V 75-87; rtd 87; Perm to Offic *Ox* from 87; Pet from 89. *60 Cheneys Walk, Bletchley, Milton Keynes MK3 6JY*   Milton Keynes (0908) 641998

RUSSELL, Richard Alexander. b 44. Univ of Wales (Abth) BA65 McMaster Univ Ontario MA67 Bris Univ MA73 PGCE74 MEd76. Trin Coll Bris DipHE81. **d** 82 **p** 83. C Hartlepool St Paul *Dur* 82-85; P-in-c Bath Widcombe *B & W* 85-88; V from 88. *Widcombe Vicarage, 65 Prior Park Road, Bath BA2 4NL*   Bath (0225) 310580

RUSSELL, Roger Geoffrey. b 47. Worc Coll Ox BA69 MA73. Cuddesdon Coll 70. **d** 72 **p** 73. C Anlaby Common St Mark *York* 72-75; C Wilton Place St Paul *Lon* 75-86; R Lancing w Coombes *Chich* from 86. *The Vicarage, 63 Manor Road, Lancing, W Sussex BN15 0EY*   Lancing (0903) 753212

RUSSELL, Ronald Albert. b 20. K Coll Lon AKC49 BD50. **d** 50 **p** 51. Kenya 63-84; Chapl Convent Companions Jes Gd Shep W Ogwell 84-88; Chapl HM Pris Channings Wood 88-91; rtd 91. *Church Cottage, Manaton, Newton Abbot, Devon TQ13 9UJ*   Manaton (064722) 297

RUSSELL, Stephen Waldemar. b 25. Lon Univ BA48 DipEd48. Coll of Resurr Mirfield 48. **d** 50 **p** 51. Perm to Offic *S'wark* 70; Oman 70-75; C Havant *Portsm* 75-76; rtd 89. *15 Eaton Hall, Eaton Gardens, Hove, E Sussex BN3 3TZ*   Brighton (0273) 207491

RUSSELL, William Douglas. b 16. LCP72 Open Univ BA73. Worc Ord Coll 57. **d** 59 **p** 60. V Stanton Drew *B & W* 61-82; rtd 82; Perm to Offic *B & W* from 82. *42 Keward Avenue, Wells, Somerset BA5 1TS*   Wells (0749) 77203

RUSSELL, William Warren. b 52. QUB BSocSc74. CITC 74. **d** 77 **p** 78. C Agherton *Conn* 77-79; C Lisburn Ch Ch Cathl 79-83; I Magheradroll *D & D* from 83. *18 Church Road, Ballynahinch, Co Down*   Ballynahinch (0238) 562289

RUSSELL-SMITH, Joy Dorothea. b 29. St Anne's Coll Ox BA52 MA55 K Coll Lon BD67. Ridley Hall Cam 83. **dss** 85 **d** 87. Witney *Ox* 85-87; Par Dn 87-88; NSM Saffron Walden w Wendens Ambo and Littlebury *Chelmsf* from 88. *1 The Meadow, Littlebury Green, Saffron Walden CB11 4XE*   Royston (0763) 838856

RUSSELL-SMITH, Mark Raymond. b 46. St Jo Coll Dur BA71. Cranmer Hall Dur DipTh72. **d** 72 **p** 73. C Upton (or Overchurch) *Ches* 72-75; C Deane *Man* 76-77; UCCF

Travelling Sec 77-80; Lic to Offic *York* 78-81; BCMS from 81; Kenya from 81. *Box 18, Kapsabet, Kenya*

RUSSON, Joseph Kenneth. b 21. St Aid Birkenhead 56. **d** 59 **p** 60. C Haslingden w Haslingden Grane *Blackb* 59-62; C Preston St Matt 62-65; V Burnley St Jas from 65; Chapl Burnley Gen Hosp from 65. *St James's Vicarage, March Street, Burnley, Lancs BB12 0BT*   Burnley (0282) 24758

RUSTED, Very Rev Edward Charles William. b 19. OBE60. Dur Univ BA41 MA44 Lon Univ PGCE54. K Coll (NS) Hon DD87 St Boniface Warminster LTh40. **d** 42 **p** 43. C Bounds Green *Lon* 42-44; Chapl RNVR 44-47; C N Audley Street St Mark *Lon* 47-49; Kennington St Jo *S'wark* 49-50; USPG 50-68; V Norbury St Oswald *Cant* 68-77; Canada from 77. *10 Gibbs Place, St John's, Newfoundland, Canada, A1B 1L2*   St John's (709) 579-5871

✠**RUSTON, Rt Rev John Harry Gerald.** b 29. SS Coll Cam BA52 MA56. Ely Th Coll 52. **d** 54 **p** 55 **c** 83. C Leic St Andr *Leic* 54-57; OGS from 55; Tutor Cuddesdon Coll 57-61; C Cuddesdon *Ox* 57-61; S Africa 62-91; Suff Bp Pretoria 83-91; Bp St Helena from 91. *Bishopsholme, PO Box 62, St Helena*   St Helena (290) 4471

RUTHERFORD, Anthony Richard. b 37. Culham Coll Ox TCert62 Lon Univ DipAdEd68 Sussex Univ MA77. S'wark Ord Course 83. **d** 86 **p** 87. Hon C Tunbridge Wells St Luke *Roch* 86-88; C Bromley SS Pet and Paul 88-90; V Wragby *Linc* from 90; Asst Min Officer from 90. *The Vicarage, Louth Road, Wragby, Lincoln LN3 5QX*   Wragby (0673) 858368

RUTHERFORD, Daniel Fergus Peter. b 65. Hatf Coll Dur BA86 CertEd87. Ridley Hall Cam 88. **d** 90 **p** 91. C Harold Wood *Chelmsf* from 90. *22 Gubbins Lane, Harold Wood, Romford, Essex RM3 0QA*   Ingrebourne (04023) 44397

RUTHERFORD, Graeme Stanley. b 43. Cranmer Hall Dur BA77 MA78. ACT 66. **d** 66 **p** 67. Australia 66-73 and from 77; C Holborn St Geo w H Trin and St Bart *Lon* 73-74; C Dur St Nic *Dur* 74-77. *552 Burke Road, Camberwell, Victoria, Australia 3124*   Camberwell (882) 4851

RUTHERFORD, Ian William. b 46. Univ of Wales (Lamp) BA68. Cuddesdon Coll 68. **d** 70 **p** 71. C Gosforth All SS *Newc* 70-73; C Prestbury *Glouc* 73-76; Chapl RN from 76. *c/o MOD, Lacon House, Theobald's Road, London WC1X 8RY*   071-430 6847

RUTHERFORD, Janet Elizabeth. b 37. S'wark Ord Course 86. **d** 89. NSM Plaistow St Mary *Roch* 89-90; Lic to Offic *Linc* from 91. *The Vicarage, Louth Road, Wragby, Lincoln LN3 5QX*   Wragby (0673) 858368

RUTHERFORD, Canon John Allarton Edge. b 10. SS Coll Cam BA32 MA36. Westcott Ho Cam 32. **d** 33 **p** 34. V Walsham le Willows *St E* 70-83; P-in-c 83-85; Hon Can St E Cathl 82-85; rtd 84; Perm to Offic *St E* from 85. *Jalla Halli, Hinderclay, Diss, Norfolk IP22 1HN*   Diss (0379) 898948

RUTHERFORD, Canon John Bilton. b 23. Qu Coll Birm 49. **d** 52 **p** 53. V Walker *Newc* 66-74; V Benwell St Jas 74-81; Hon Can Newc Cathl 80-90; V Lesbury w Alnmouth 81-90; RD Alnwick 86-89; rtd 90. *68 Worcester Way, Woodlands Park, Wideopen, Newcastle upon Tyne NE4 5JE*   091-236 4785

RUTHERFORD, Peter George. b 34. Nor Ord Course 73. **d** 76 **p** 77. NSM New Catton Ch Ch *Nor* 76-79; NSM Eaton 79-80; NSM Nor St Steph from 81. *30 The Close, Norwich NR1 4DZ*   Norwich (0603) 624386

RUTHERFORD, Peter Marshall. b 57. St Andr Univ MTheol81. CITC 83. **d** 83 **p** 84. C Stormont *D & D* 83-85; CF from 85. *c/o MOD (Army), Bagshot Park, Bagshot, Surrey GU18 5PL*   Bagshot (0276) 71717

RUTHERFORD, Thomas Thompson. b 13. Qu Coll Birm 75. **d** 76 **p** 77. NSM Southam *Cov* 76-77; NSM Southam w Stockton 77-86; Perm to Offic from 86. *17 Elan Close, Leamington Spa, Warks CV32 7BX*   Leamington Spa (0926) 429688

RUTLEDGE, Christopher John Francis. b 44. Lon Univ BSc67. Sarum Th Coll 67. **d** 70 **p** 71. C Birm St Pet *Birm* 70-73; C Calne and Blackland *Sarum* 73-76; P-in-c Derry Hill 76-78; V 78-81; P-in-c Talbot Village 81-82; V from 82. *The Vicarage, 20 Alton Road, Talbot Village, Bournemouth BH10 4AE*   Bournemouth (0202) 529349

RUTLEDGE, Francis George. b 62. DipTh Ulster Poly BA83 TCD BTh90. **d** 86 **p** 87. C Holywood *D & D* 86-89; C Willowfield 89-91; I Kilmakee *Conn* from 91. *Kilmakee Rectory, 60 Killeaton Park, Dunmurry, Belfast BT17 9HE*   Belfast (0232) 610505

✠**RUTT, Rt Rev Cecil Richard.** b 25. CBE73. Pemb Coll Cam BA54 MA58 Seoul Confucian Univ Hon DLitt74. Kelham Th Coll 47. **d** 51 **p** 52 **c** 66. C Chesterton St Geo

Ely 51-54; Korea 54-74; Adn W Seoul 65-66; Asst Bp Taejon 66-68; Bp Taejon 68-74; Hon Can Truro Cathl *Truro* 74-79; Suff Bp St Germans 74-79; Bp Leic 79-90; rtd 90. *3 Marlborough Court, Falmouth, Cornwall TR11 2QU*   Falmouth (0326) 312276

RUTT, Canon Denis Frederic John. b 17. Kelham Th Coll 34. **d** 41 **p** 42. R Kirkley *Nor* 61-71; RD Lothingland 65-71; R N Lynn w St Marg and St Nic 71-76; Can Res and Prec Lich Cathl *Lich* 76-83; rtd 83; Perm to Offic *Bradf* from 83. *28 St Philip's Way, Burley in Wharfedale, Ilkley, W Yorkshire LS29 7EW*   Burley (04253) 863778

RUTT-FIELD, Benjamin John. b 48. Chich Th Coll. **d** 90 **p** 91. C Wickford and Runwell *Chelmsf* from 90. *8 Honington Close, Shotgate, Wickford, Essex SS11 8XB*   Wickford (0268) 561044

RUTTER, Canon Allen Edward Henry. b 28. Qu Coll Cam BA52 Cam Univ DipAgr53 Qu Coll Cam MA56. Cranmer Hall Dur DipTh58. **d** 59 **p** 60. C Bath Abbey w St Jas *B & W* 59-60; C E Dereham w Hoe *Nor* 60-64; R Cawston 64-69; Chapl Cawston Coll 64-69; P-in-c Felthorpe w Haveringland 64-69; S Africa 69-73; P-in-c Over and Nether Compton, Trent etc *Sarum* 73-80; RD Sherborne 77-87; P-in-c Oborne w Poyntington 79-80; P-in-c Queen Thorne from 80; Can and Preb Sarum Cathl from 86. *The Rectory, Trent, Sherborne, Dorset DT9 4SL*   Marston Magna (0935) 851049

RUTTER, Martin Charles. b 54. Wolv Poly BSc75 Southn Univ BTh81. Sarum & Wells Th Coll 76. **d** 79 **p** 80. C Cannock *Lich* 79-82; C Uttoxeter w Bramshall 82-86; V W Bromwich St Jas from 86; P-in-c W Bromwich St Paul Golds Hill from 89. *St James's Vicarage, 151A Hill Top, West Bromwich, W Midlands B70 0SB*   021-556 0805

RUTTER, William Ralph. b 94. **d** 58 **p** 59. R Hardwick *Pet* 60-69; rtd 69; Lic to Offic *Pet* 70-79; Perm to Offic *Ox* from 87. *Manormead Nursing Home, Tilford Road, Hindhead, Surrey GU26 6RA*   Hindhead (0428) 604780

RYALL, John Francis Robert. b 30. New Coll Ox BA52 MA57. Westcott Ho Cam 52. **d** 54 **p** 55. C Petersfield w Sheet *Portsm* 54-56; C Portsea St Mary 56-62; C Warblington and Emsworth 62-65; C Freshwater 65-67; R Frating w Thorrington *Chelmsf* 67-73; R Gt Yeldham 74-76; P-in-c Lt Yeldham 75-76; R Gt w Lt Yeldham 76-80; P-in-c Thorley *Portsm* 80-82; P-in-c Shalfleet 80-82; V from 82; V Calbourne w Newtown from 82. *The Vicarage, Shalfleet, Newport, Isle of Wight PO30 4NF*   Calbourne (0983) 238

RYALL, Michael Richard. b 36. TCD BA58 MA65 HDipEd66. TCD Div Sch Div Test58. **d** 58 **p** 59. C Dub St Geo *D & G* 58-62; CF 62-65 and 68-90; CF (TAVR) 67-68; C Dub Rathmines *D & G* 65-66; Dungannon Sec Sch 66-68; R Yardley Hastings, Denton and Grendon etc *Pet* from 90. *The Rectory, Yardley Hastings, Northampton NN7 1EL*   Yardley Hastings (060129) 223

RYAN, James Francis. b 47. Surrey Univ BSc. Trin Coll Bris DipHE84. St Jo Coll Nottm. **d** 83 **p** 84. C Littleover *Derby* 83-86; C Chipping Sodbury and Old Sodbury *Glouc* 86-89; V Pype Hayes *Birm* from 89. *St Mary's Vicarage, 1162 Tyburn Road, Birmingham B24 0TB*   021-373 3534

RYAN, Michael Dennis George Conybeare. b 15. Qu Coll Birm 54. **d** 56 **p** 57. V Greenhead *Newc* 64-74; V Branxton 74-80; V Cornhill w Carham 74-80; rtd 80; P-in-c Coldstream *Edin* 80-87; NSM from 87. *Crooks Cottage, Hirsel, Coldstream, Berwickshire TD12 4LR*   Coldstream (0890) 2358

RYAN, Roger John. b 47. Lon Bible Coll BA79 Oak Hill Th Coll 79. **d** 80 **p** 81. C Luton St Fran *St Alb* 80-83; R Laceby *Linc* 83-88; V Summerstown *S'wark* from 88. *St Mary's Vicarage, 46 Wimbledon Road, London SW17 0UQ*   081-946 9853

RYAN, Stephen John. b 49. Univ of Wales (Swansea) BA70 Bris Univ DipTh73. Sarum & Wells Th Coll 70. **d** 73 **p** 74. C Llantrisant *Llan* 73-77; V Treherbert w Treorchy 77-89; Youth Chapl 80-85; RD Rhondda 84-89; V Aberdare St Fagan from 89. *St Fagan's Vicarage, Trecynon, Aberdare, M Glam CF44 8LL*   Aberdare (0685) 881435

RYCROFT, Stanley. b 30. Bris Univ MEd81 Open Univ BA84. Sarum Th Coll 56. **d** 59 **p** 60. C Earley St Bart *Ox* 59-62; Chapl Whittlebury Sch Towcester 62-63; C Christchurch *Win* 63-67; Chapl Durlston Court Sch Barton on Sea 67-71; Chapl Millfield Jun Sch Somerset 71-75; Chapl Wellington Sch Somerset 75-83; V Silksworth *Dur* from 84. *St Matthew's Vicarage, Silksworth Road, Sunderland SR3 2AA*   091-521 1167

RYDER, Derek Michael. b 36. St Cath Coll Cam BA60 MA64. Tyndale Hall Bris 61. **d** 63 **p** 64. C Hampreston *Sarum* 63-66; Asst Chapl Brentwood Sch

Essex 66-72; Chapl Ipswich Sch 72-77; Home Sec CMJ 77-87; TR Wexcombe *Sarum* from 87; RD Pewsey from 89. *The Vicarage, Shalbourne, Marlborough, Wilts SN8 3QH*   Marlborough (0672) 870421

RYDER, Canon Lisle Robert Dudley. b 43. Selw Coll Cam BA68 MA72 Birm Univ DPS76. Sarum Th Coll 69. **d** 71 **p** 72. C Lowestoft St Marg *Nor* 71-75; Chapl Asst Oxon Area HA 76-79; C Littlehampton St Jas *Chich* 79-85; C Wick 79-85; C Littlehampton St Mary 79-85; Chapl Worc R Infirmary from 85; Hon Can Worc Cathl *Worc* from 89. *1 Holywell Hill, Henwick Road, Worcester WR2 5NZ*   Worcester (0905) 426202

RYDER, Canon Vivian Charles. b 14. OBE76. Qu Coll Birm 63. **d** 64 **p** 65. Argentina 65-81; Can and Sub-Dean Buenos Aires 74-81; P-in-c Horseheath *Ely* 81-84; rtd 83; Lic to Offic *Ely* from 85. *The Rectory, West Wickham Road, Horseheath, Cambridge CB1 6QA*   Cambridge (0223) 892530

RYDER-JONES, Preb William Henry. b 16. St D Coll Lamp BA38 Ridley Hall Cam 39. **d** 40 **p** 41. V Torquay St Luke *Ex* 49-77; rtd 78. *19 Stourwood Avenue, Southbourne, Bournemouth BH6 3PW*

RYDINGS, Donald. b 33. Jes Coll Ox BA57 MA61. Linc Th Coll 57. **d** 59 **p** 60. C Poulton-le-Fylde *Blackb* 59-62; Staff Sec SCM Ox 62-66; C Ox St Mary V *Ox* 62-66; C-in-c Bourne End St Mark CD 66-74; R Hedsor and Bourne End 74-76; P-in-c Gt Missenden w Ballinger and Lt Hampden from 76; RD Wendover 79-89. *The Vicarage, 2 Walnut Close, Great Missenden, Bucks HP16 9AA*   Great Missenden (02406) 2470

RYE, David Ralph. b 33. AKC59. **d** 60 **p** 61. C Rushmere *St E* 60-64; C Barnham Broom w Kimberley, Bixton etc *Nor* 64-76; TV Barnham Broom 76-82; TR from 82; P-in-c Reymerston w Cranworth, Letton, Southburgh etc from 85. *The Vicarage, Barnham Broom, Norwich NR9 4DB*   Barnham Broom (060545) 204

RYE, Peter Harry. b 29. AKC52. **d** 53 **p** 54. C Grantham St Wulfram *Linc* 53-58; C Lowestoft St Marg *Nor* 58-60; V Martham 60-68; V W Somerton 60-68; Chapl to the Deaf *Ox* 68-73; V Brize Norton and Carterton 73-80; V Carterton 80-81; V Freeland and Cassington 81-84; V N Hinksey 84-89; R N Hinksey and Wytham from 90. *The Vicarage, 81 West Way, Oxford OX2 9JY*   Oxford (0865) 242345

RYECART, John Reginald. b 07. AKC32. St Steph Ho Ox 32. **d** 33 **p** 34. V Gt Sampford w Hempstead *Chelmsf* 60-74; rtd 74. *100 Fronks Road, Dovercourt, Essex CO12 3RY*   Harwich (0255) 507370

RYELAND, John. b 58. K Coll Lon BD80 AKC80. Linc Th Coll 80. **d** 81 **p** 82. C Enfield St Jas *Lon* 81-84; C Coulsdon St Andr *S'wark* 84-87; C-in-c Ingrave St Steph CD *Chelmsf* from 87. *St Stephen's House, St Stephen's Crescent, Ingrave, Essex CM13 2AT*   Brentwood (0277) 214623

RYLAND, Colin William. b 16. TD52. MRCVS. St Steph Ho Ox 61. **d** 62 **p** 63. R Church w Chapel Brampton *Pet* 66-73; V Wellingborough St Barn 73-83; rtd 83. *13 St John's Road, Durham DH1 4NU*   091-386 9638

RYLANDS, Mrs Amanda Craig. b 52. CertEd75. All Nations Chr Coll DipMiss82 Trin Coll Bris DipHE85. **dss** 85 **d** 87. Chippenham St Andr w Tytherton Lucas *Bris* 85-87; Par Dn Stockport St Geo *Ches* 87; NSM 88-91; Par Dn Acton and Worleston from 91. *St Mary's Vicarage, Chester Road, Acton, Nantwich, Cheshire CW5 8LG*   Nantwich (0270) 628864

RYLANDS, Mark James. b 61. SS Hild & Bede Coll Dur BA83. Trin Coll Bris BA87. **d** 87 **p** 88. C Stockport St Geo *Ches* 87-91; V Acton and Worleston from 91. *St Mary's Vicarage, Chester Road, Acton, Nantwich, Cheshire CW5 8LG*   Nantwich (0270) 628864

RYLANDS, Canon Thomas Michael. b 18. CCC Cam BA39 MA46. Wells Th Coll. **d** 47 **p** 48. R Malpas and Threapwood *Ches* 68-85; RD Malpas 70-84; Hon Can Ches Cathl 72-85; rtd 85; Perm to Offic Ches from 85. *Haughton Thorn, Tarporley, Cheshire CW6 9RN*   Tarporley (0829) 260215

RYLE, Denis Maurice. b 16. OBE70. St Aid Birkenhead 35. **d** 39 **p** 40. Dep Asst Chapl Gen 65-73; P-in-c Latimer w Flaunden *Ox* 73-85; rtd 85. *5 Church Close, Wheldrake, York YO4 6DP*   York (0904) 898124

RYLEY, Canon Patrick Macpherson. b 30. Pemb Coll Ox BA54 Lon Univ BD56. Clifton Th Coll 54. **d** 56 **p** 57. C Ox St Clem *Ox* 56-59; Burma 60-66; Kenya 68-75; V Lynn St Jo *Nor* from 76; RD Lynn 78-83; Hon Can Nor Cathl from 90. *St John's Vicarage, Blackfriars Road, King's Lynn, Norfolk PE30 1NT*   King's Lynn (0553) 773034

RYMER, David John Talbot. b 37. Chich Th Coll 63. **d** 66 **p** 67. C Tuffley *Glouc* 66-69; Rhodesia 69-79; P-in-c S

Kensington St Jude *Lon* 79-82; V 82-88; P-in-c Ambergate *Derby* from 88; P-in-c Heage from 88. *The Vicarage, 65 Derby Road, Ambergate, Derby DE5 2GD* Ambergate (0773) 852072

RYRIE, Alexander Crawford. b 30. Edin Univ MA52 BD55 Glas Univ MLitt75. Union Th Sem (NY) STM56. **d** 83 **p** 83. Hon C Edin St Mary *Edin* 83-85; R Jedburgh from 85. *The Rectory, 46 Castlegate, Jedburgh, Roxburghshire TD8 6BB* Jedburgh (0835) 63892

RYRIE, Mrs Isabel. b 31. ABPsS73 CPsychol88 Edin Univ MA51 Glas Univ MEd70. Moray Ho Edin DipRE52. **d** 89. Bp's Dn Jedburgh *Edin* 89-91; NSM Edin St Mary from 91. *The Rectory, 46 Castlegate, Jedburgh, Roxburghshire TD8 6BB* Jedburgh (0835) 63892

S

SABELL, Michael Harold. b 42. Open Univ BA78 Surrey Univ MSc. Sarum & Wells Th Coll 77. **d** 80 **p** 81. NSM Shirley *Win* 80-82; Chapl to the Deaf 81-82; NSM Finham *Cov* 82-85; Chapl to the Deaf 82-85; Chapl to the Deaf *Sheff* 85-89; Chapl to the Deaf *Lich* from 89. *55 Bustleholme Lane, West Bromwich, W Midlands B71 3BD* 021-588 6417

SABOURIN, Robert. b 21. TCD. **d** 52 **p** 53. Public Preacher (Dio *Win*) 60-80; Perm to Offic *Win* 80-86; rtd 86; Chapl Rouen and Le Havre *Eur* 86-87; Chapl Menton 87-90; Lic to Offic from 90. *Batiment 2, Appartment 63, Residence Grand Gaillon, 27600 Gaillon, France* France (33) 32 53 94 31

SACKEY, Victor Raymond Kofi. b 43. Southlands Coll Lon CertEd75. Kelham Th Coll 68 Sarum Th Coll 70. **d** 77 **p** 89. Ghana 77-81; Nigeria 82-85; C Willesden Green St Andr and St Fran of Assisi *Lon* 86-89; C Ruislip St Martin from 89. *5 North Drive, Ruislip, Middx HA4 8HA* Ruislip (0895) 633788

SADDINGTON, Peter David. b 42. Cranmer Hall Dur. **d** 84 **p** 85. C Tudhoe Grange *Dur* 84-86; C Monkwearmouth St Andr 86-88; V Burnopfield from 88. *The Vicarage, Burnopfield, Newcastle upon Tyne NE16 6HQ* Burnopfield (0207) 70261

SADGROVE, Canon Michael. b 50. Ball Coll Ox BA71 MA75. Trin Coll Bris 72. **d** 75 **p** 76. Lic to Offic *Ox* 75-77; Tutor Sarum & Wells Th Coll 77-82; Vice-Prin 80-82; V Alnwick St Mich and St Paul *Newc* 82-87; Prec Cov Cathl *Cov* from 87; Vice-Provost Cov Cathl from 87; Can Res Cov Cathl from 87. *35 Morningside, Coventry CV5 6PD* Coventry (0203) 675446

SADLER, Preb Anthony Graham. b 36. Qu Coll Ox BA60 MA64. Lich Th Coll 60. **d** 62 **p** 63. C Burton St Chad *Lich* 62-65; V Rangemore 65-72; V Dunstall 65-72; V Abbots Bromley 72-79; V Pelsall 79-90; RD Walsall 82-90; Preb Lich Cathl from 87; P-in-c Uttoxeter w Bramshall from 90; P-in-c Stramshall from 90; P-in-c Kingstone w Gratwich from 90; P-in-c Checkley from 90; P-in-c Marchington w Marchington Woodlands from 90. *The Vicarage, 12 Orchard Close, Uttoxeter ST14 7DZ* Uttoxeter (0889) 563651

SADLER, John Ernest. b 45. Nottm Univ BTh78. Linc Th Coll 74. **d** 78 **p** 79. C Brampton St Thos *Derby* 78-81; TV Cov Caludon *Cov* 81-85; P-in-c High Elswick St Phil *Newc* 85; P-in-c Newc St Aug 85; V Newc St Phil and St Aug from 86. *The Vicarage, St Philip's Close, Newcastle upon Tyne NE4 5JE* 091-273 7407

SADLER, John Harvey. b 33. K Coll Lon AKC57 BD66 Warw Univ MEd78 Birm Univ PhD83. St Boniface Warminster 57. **d** 58 **p** 59. C Addlestone *Guildf* 58-60; C Hemel Hempstead *St Alb* 60-62; S Africa 62-66; C Frimley *Guildf* 67-69; V Ewell 69-71; Hd of Relig Studies Dyson Perrins High Sch from 78; NSM Malvern Link w Cowleigh *Worc* from 80; Perm to Offic *Heref* from 82. *Little Queenswood, Stone Drive, Colwall, Malvern, Worcs WR13 6QL* Colwall (0684) 40047

SADLER, Michael Stuart. b 57. Wycliffe Hall Ox 78. **d** 81 **p** 82. C Henfynyw w Aberaeron and Llanddewi Aber-arth *St D* 81-88; V Llanddewi Rhydderch w Llangattock-juxta-Usk etc *Mon* 88-90; V Llanddewi Rhydderch and Llangattock etc from 90. *The Vicarage, Llanddewi Rhydderch, Abergavenny, Gwent NP7 9TS* Abergavenny (0873) 840373

SAGAR, Brian. b 39. Sarum & Wells Th Coll 78. **d** 80 **p** 81. C Radcliffe St Thos and St Jo *Man* 80-82; P-in-c Charlestown 82-85; R Gt Lever 85-89; Chapl Cov Ch Housing Assn *Cov* from 89. *20 Mapperley Close,*

Walsgrave on Sowe, Coventry CV2 2SE Coventry (0203) 616700

SAGE, Andrew George. b 58. Chich Th Coll 83. **d** 85 **p** 86. C Rawmarsh w Parkgate *Sheff* 85-87; C Fareham SS Pet and Paul *Portsm* 87-89; C Southsea H Spirit from 89. *219 Fawcett Road, Southsea, Hants PO4 0DH* Portsmouth (0705) 812128

SAGE, Canon Jesse. b 35. Trin Hall Cam BA61 MA65. Chich Th Coll 61. **d** 63 **p** 64. C Feltham *Lon* 63-67; S Africa 67-72; R Abbas and Temple Combe *B & W* 72-75; R Abbas and Templecombe w Horsington 76-77; Chapl Agric and Rural Soc in Kent *Cant* from 78; Hon Can Cant Cathl from 90. *The Rectory, Pluckley, Ashford, Kent TN27 0QT* Pluckley (023384) 232

SAGE, John Arthur. b 32. MInstP Lon Univ BSc54. St Alb Minl Tr Scheme 78. **d** 81 **p** 82. NSM Stevenage St Mary Shephall *St Alb* 81-86; NSM Stevenage St Mary Sheppall w Aston 86-87; C St Peter-in-Thanet *Cant* from 87. *St Andrew's House, 29 Reading Street, Broadstairs, Kent CT10 3AZ* Thanet (0843) 68923

SAGOVSKY, Nicholas. b 47. CCC Ox BA69 St Edm Ho Cam PhD81. St Jo Coll Nottm BA73. **d** 74 **p** 75. C Newc St Gabr *Newc* 74-77; C Cam Gt St Mary w St Mich *Ely* 81; Vice-Prin Edin Th Coll 82-86; Dean of Chpl Clare Coll Cam from 86. *Clare College, Cambridge CB2 1TL* Cambridge (0223) 333240

✠**SAINSBURY, Rt Rev Roger Frederick.** b 36. Jes Coll Cam BA58 MA62. Clifton Th Coll. **d** 60 **p** 61 **c** 91. C Spitalfields Ch Ch w All SS *Lon* 60-63; Missr Shrewsbury Ho Everton 63-74; P-in-c Everton St Ambrose w St Tim *Liv* 67-74; Warden Mayflower Family Cen Canning Town *Chelmsf* 74-81; P-in-c Victoria Docks St Luke 78-81; V Walsall *Lich* 81-87; TR 87-88; Adn W Ham *Chelmsf* 88-91; Area Bp Barking from 91. *15 Wallenger Avenue, Romford, Essex RM2 6EP* Romford (0708) 21866

SAINT, Arthur James Maxwell. b 10. St Jo Coll Ox BA31 MA35. Cuddesdon Coll 34. **d** 35 **p** 36. V Ox SS Phil and Jas *Ox* 65-76; rtd 76. *65 Ramsay Road, Oxford OX3 8AY* Oxford (0865) 61241

SAINT, David Gerald. b 45. Sarum & Wells Th Coll 72. **d** 75 **p** 76. C Wellingborough All Hallows *Pet* 75-79; R Kislingbury w Rothersthorpe 79-83; V Kings Heath 83-85; Relig Progr Producer BBC Radio Northn from 85; Perm to Offic *Pet* from 86. *49 Colwyn Road, Northampton NN1 3PZ* Northampton (0604) 239100

ST ALBANS, Archdeacon of. See DAVIES, Ven Philip Bertram

ST ALBANS, Bishop of. See TAYLOR, Rt Rev John Bernard

ST ALBANS, Dean of. See MOORE, Very Rev Peter Clement

ST ANDREWS, DUNKELD AND DUNBLANE, Bishop of. See HARE DUKE, Rt Rev Michael Geoffrey

ST ANDREWS, DUNKELD AND DUNBLANE, Dean of. See WATT, Very Rev Alfred Ian

ST ASAPH, Archdeacon of. See DAVIES, Ven John Stewart

ST ASAPH, Bishop of. See JONES, Rt Rev Alwyn Rice

ST ASAPH, Dean of. See RENOWDEN, Very Rev Charles Raymond

ST DAVIDS, Archdeacon of. Vacant

ST DAVIDS, Bishop of. See REES, Rt Rev John Ivor

ST DAVIDS, Dean of. See LEWIS, Very Rev Bertie

ST EDMUNDSBURY AND IPSWICH, Bishop of. See DENNIS, Rt Rev John

ST EDMUNDSBURY AND IPSWICH, Provost of. See FURNELL, Very Rev Raymond

ST GERMANS, Suffragan Bishop of. See LLEWELLIN, Rt Rev John Richard Allan

ST JOHN, Ferdinand Richard John. b 08. Ely Th Coll. **d** 47 **p** 48. R Ashton w Hartwell *Pet* 70-74; R Tinwell 74-77; rtd 77; Perm to Offic *Pet* from 86. *40 St Anne's Close, Oakham, Leics* Oakham (0572) 755622

ST JOHN-CHANNELL, Michael Alister Morrell. b 53. Bris Univ BEd76. Ripon Coll Cuddesdon 76. **d** 78 **p** 79. C Portsea St Mary *Portsm* 78-81; PV Linc Cathl *Linc* 82-85; P-in-c Linc St Mary-le-Wigford w St Benedict etc 82-85; R Cranford *Lon* from 85. *The Rectory, 34 High Street, Cranford, Hounslow TW5 9RG* 081-897 8836

ST JOHN NICOLLE, Michael George. b 29. St Jo Coll Dur BA52 DipEd. **d** 70 **p** 71. C Lt Bowden St Nic *Leic* 70; C Knighton St Jo 71-74; R Desford 74-81; R Tarrant Valley *Sarum* 81-85; R Jersey St Jo *Win* from 85. *St John's Rectory, Jersey, Channel Islands* Jersey (0534) 61677

ST LEGER, Canon Robert Joseph. b 21. TCD BA44 MA54. **d** 45 **p** 46. C Willowfield *D & D* 45-50; C-in-c Sallaghy *Clogh* 50-58; I Lisbellaw from 58; Preb Clogh Cathl 78-88;

Chan Clogh Cathl from 88. *The Rectory, Lisbellaw, Enniskillen, Co Fermanagh* Lisbellaw (0365) 87219

SAKER, Sidney William. b 08. Dur Univ 32. ALCD35. **d** 35 **p** 36. Perm to Offic *Leic* from 46; Lic to Offic *S'wark* 64-73; Area Sec (SW Lon) Leprosy Miss 71-73; rtd 73. *397 Uppingham Road, Leicester LE5 4DP* Leicester (0533) 760855

SALENIUS, Richard Mark. b 57. K Coll Lon BD79 AKC79. Linc Th Coll 79. **d** 80 **p** 81. C St Marylebone w H Trin *Lon* 80-84; C Sale St Anne *Ches* 84-87; V Macclesfield St Jo from 87. *St John's Vicarage, 47 Ivy Lane, Macclesfield, Cheshire SK11 8NU* Macclesfield (0625) 424185

SALES, Patrick David. b 43. K Coll Lon AKC68 BD74. **d** 69 **p** 70. C Maidstone All SS w St Phil *Cant* 69-72; C Chart next Sutton Valence 72-74; C Birchington w Acol 75-77; V Boughton under Blean w Dunkirk 77-83; Hon Min Can Cant Cathl from 83; V Herne from 83; RD Reculver from 86. *The Vicarage, Herne, Herne Bay, Kent CT6 7HE* Herne Bay (0227) 374328

SALISBURY, Miss Anne Ruth. b 37. Bible Churchmen's Coll. **d** 87. Par Dn Harrow H Trin St Mich *Lon* from 87. *1A Headstone Drive, Harrow, Middx HA3 5QX* 081-427 1129

SALISBURY, George Malcolm Owen. b 11. Bp's Coll Calcutta 40. **d** 43 **p** 44. R Shenley *St Alb* 68-81; rtd 81; Chapl St Alb City Hosp 81-87. *33 Elizabeth Court, Jersey Farm, St Albans, Herts AL4 9JB* St Albans (0727) 834568

SALISBURY, Harold Gareth. b 21. St Pet Hall Ox BA42 MA46. Wycliffe Hall Ox 42. **d** 44 **p** 45. V Duddo *Newc* 63-70; V Norham 63-70; V Norham and Duddo 70-78; V Snaith *Sheff* 78-86; P-in-c Cowick 78-86; TR Gt Snaith 86; rtd 86; Perm to Offic *Pet* from 87. *33 Nightingale Drive, Towcester, Northants NN12 7RA* Towcester (0327) 53674

SALISBURY, John Forbes. b 16. St Jo Coll Dur 46. **d** 50 **p** 51. V Tosside *Bradf* 67-79; Lic to Offic 80-84; rtd 81; Perm to Offic *Bradf* from 84. *14 Victoria Mill, Belmont Wharf, Skipton, N Yorkshire BD23 1RL* Skipton (0756) 701411

SALISBURY, Roger John. b 44. Lon Univ BD67. Lon Coll of Div 66. **d** 68 **p** 69. C Harold Wood *Chelmsf* 68-73; V Dorking St Paul *Guildf* 73-82; R Rusholme *Man* 82-90; TR Gt Chesham *Ox* from 90. *The Rectory, Church Street, Chesham, Bucks HP5 1HY* Chesham (0494) 783629

SALISBURY, Tobias. b 33. Em Coll Cam BA60. Ripon Hall Ox 60. **d** 62 **p** 63. C Putney St Mary *S'wark* 62-65; C Churchdown St Jo *Glouc* 65-67; V Urchfont w Stert *Sarum* 67-73; R Burton Bradstock w Shipton Gorge and Chilcombe 73-79; P-in-c Long Bredy w Lt Bredy and Kingston Russell 75-79; TR Bride Valley 79-86; V Gt and Lt Bedwyn and Savernake Forest from 86. *The Vicarage, Great Bedwyn, Marlborough, Wilts SN8 3PF* Marlborough (0672) 870779

SALISBURY, Archdeacon of. See HOPKINSON, Ven Barnabas John

SALISBURY, Bishop of. See BAKER, Rt Rev John Austin

SALISBURY, Dean of. See DICKINSON, Very Rev the Hon Hugh Geoffrey

SALMON, Alan Clive. b 63. Bris Univ BA84 Univ of Wales (Cardiff) DPS85. St Mich Coll Llan 84. **d** 86 **p** 87. C Llanelly *St D* 86-88; C Roath St German *Llan* 88-90; V Nevern and Y Beifil w Eglwyswrw and Meline etc *St D* from 90. *The Vicarage, Nevern, Newport, Dyfed SY42 0NF* Newport (0239) 820427

SALMON, Andrew Ian. b 61. St Jo Coll Nottm BTh88. **d** 88 **p** 89. C Collyhurst *Man* from 88. *7 Redbrook Avenue, Miles Platting, Manchester M10 8GJ* 061-205 5105

SALMON, Andrew Meredith Bryant. b 30. Jes Coll Cam BA54 MA58. Ridley Hall Cam 54. **d** 56 **p** 57. C Enfield Ch Ch Trent Park *Lon* 56-58; Chapl Monkton Combe Sch Bath 58-71; Chapl Milton Abbey Sch Dorset 71-89; TV Bride Valley *Sarum* from 89. *The Vicarage, Litton Cheney, Dorchester, Dorset DT2 9AG* Long Bredy (0308) 482302

SALMON, Anthony James Heygate. b 30. CCC Ox BA53 DipTh54 MA57. Cuddesdon Coll 54. **d** 56 **p** 57. C S Norwood St Mark *Cant* 56-59; S Africa 59-69; Chapl USPG Coll of the Ascension Selly Oak 69-74; P-in-c Frinsted 74-78; R Harrietsham *Cant* 74-85; P-in-c Ulcombe 81-85; V Chobham w Valley End *Guildf* from 85. *The Vicarage, Bagshot Road, Chobham, Woking, Surrey GU24 8BY* Chobham (0276) 858197

SALMON, Bernard Bryant. b 24. Trin Hall Cam BA50 MA54. Wells Th Coll 50. **d** 52 **p** 53. C Stockton St Pet *Dur* 52-55; C Longbenton St Bart *Newc* 55-58; R

Cramlington 58-71; V Winscombe *B & W* from 71; RD Locking 78-86. *The Vicarage, Winscombe Hill, Winscombe, Avon BS25 1DE* Winscombe (093484) 3164

SALMON, Mrs Constance Hazel. Gilmore Course. **dss** 80 **d** 87. Sidcup St Andr *Roch* 80-87; Hon Par Dn 87-88; rtd 88. *43 Old Mill Close, Eynsford, Dartford DA4 0BN* Dartford (0322) 866034

SALMON, Mrs Margaret. b 37. Leeds Univ BA59 CertEd60. SW Minl Tr Course 85. **d** 88. NSM Yelverton, Meavy, Sheepstor and Walkhampton *Ex* from 88. *Hinnies, Leg-o-Mutton Corner, Yelverton, Devon PL20 6DJ* Yelverton (0822) 853310

SALMON, Richard Harold. b 35. Fitzw Ho Cam BA57. Clifton Th Coll 57. **d** 59 **p** 60. C Blackheath Park St Mich *S'wark* 59-62; C St Alb St Paul *St Alb* 62-64; OMF 64-66; Malaysia 66-75; P-in-c March St Wendreda *Ely* 75-76; R 76-85; V Congresbury w Puxton and Hewish St Ann *B & W* from 85. *The Vicarage, Station Road, Congresbury, Bristol BS19 5DX* Yatton (0934) 833126

SALMON, Very Rev Thomas Noel Desmond Cornwall. b 13. TCD BA35 BD42 MA49. CITC 36. **d** 37 **p** 38. Lect TCD 45-89; Dean Ch Ch Cathl Dub *D & G* 67-89; I Dub Ch Ch Cathl 76-89; rtd 89. *3 Glengeary Terrace, Dun Laoghaire, Co Dublin, Irish Republic* Dublin (1) 280-0101

SALMON, William John. b 50. Lon Univ BSc72. St Jo Coll Dur 77. **d** 79 **p** 80. C Summerstown *S'wark* 79-81; C Hampreston *Sarum* 81-86; V Sundon *St Alb* 86-90; Dep Chapl HM Young Offender Inst Glen Parva 90-91; Chapl HM Pris Whitemoor from 91. *HM Prison Whitemoor, Longhill Road, March, Cambs PE15 0PR* March (0354) 660653

SALONIA, Ivan. b 38. CQSW78 Open Univ BA81 N Lon Poly MA85. Milan Th Coll (RC). **d** 63 **p** 64. In RC Ch (Hong Kong) 64-73; Hon C Woolwich St Thos *S'wark* 89-91; C Greenwich St Alfege w St Pet and St Paul from 91. *48 Crookston Road, London SE9 1YB* 081-850 0529

SALOP, Archdeacon of. See FROST, Ven George

SALSBURY, Harry. b 31. Lon Univ TCert62. **d** 60 **p** 61. NSM Bexhill St Pet *Chich* 83-84; Chapl Brighton Coll Jun Sch E Sussex from 84. *39 Croxden Way, Eastbourne, E Sussex BN22 0UH* Eastbourne (0323) 507091

SALT, David Christopher. b 37. Univ of Wales (Lamp) BA59. Sarum Th Coll 59. **d** 61 **p** 62. C Kidderminster St Mary *Worc* 61-66; Ind Chapl 66-72; R Knightwick w Doddenham, Broadwas and Cotheridge 72-82; Chapl Worc Coll of HE 72-82; V Redditch St Steph from 82; P-in-c Tardebigge 84-88; RD Bromsgrove from 91. *St Stephen's Vicarage, 248 Birchfield Road, Redditch, Worcs B97 4LZ* Redditch (0527) 541738

SALT, David Thomas Whitehorn. b 32. K Coll Lon AKC56 BD57. **d** 57 **p** 58. New Hebrides 57-63; Solomon Is 63-66; C Hawley H Trin *Guildf* 66-68; V Shelf *Bradf* 68-73; R Checkendon *Ox* 73-81; RD Henley 78-84; TR Langtree 81-84; Chapl Hungerford Hosp 84-89; V Hungerford and Denford *Ox* 84-89; P-in-c Harpsden w Bolney from 89; Gen Sec Melanesian Miss from 89. *The Rectory, 2 Harpsden Way, Henley-on-Thames, Oxon RG9 1NL* Henley-on-Thames (0491) 573401

SALT, Very Rev John William. b 41. Kelham Th Coll 61. **d** 66 **p** 67. C Barrow St Matt *Carl* 66-70; S Africa from 70; Adn S Zululand and Dean Eshowe Cath from 89. *PO Box 207, Eshowe, 3815 South Africa* Eshowe (354) 41215

SALT, Leslie. b 29. Linc Th Coll 68. **d** 69 **p** 69. C Alford w Rigsby *Linc* 69-75; V Torksey from 75; R Kettlethorpe from 77; P-in-c Marton 77; V from 77; P-in-c Newton-on-Trent 77; V from 77. *The Vicarage, Torksey, Lincoln LN1 2EE* Torksey (042771) 249

SALT, Neil. b 64. Univ of Wales (Ban) BA85 Edin Univ BD89. Edin Th Coll 86. **d** 89 **p** 90. C Stretford All SS *Man* from 89. *29 Lomond Avenue, Stretford, Manchester M32 0DT* 061-865 1580

SALTER, Arthur Thomas John. b 34. TD88. AKC60. **d** 61 **p** 62. C Ealing St Pet Mt Park *Lon* 61-65; C Shepherd's Bush St Steph w St Thos 65-66; C Holborn St Alb w Saffron Hill St Pet 66-70; P-in-c Barnsbury St Clem 70-77; P-in-c Islington St Mich 70-77; V Pentonville St Silas w All SS and St Jas from 70; CF (TAVR) from 75; Gen Sec Angl and E Chs Assn from 76; Chmn from 90; P-in-c St Dunstan in the West *Lon* from 79. *The Vicarage, 87 Richmond Avenue, London N1 0LX* 071-607 2865 or 405 1929

SALTER, Canon George Alfred. b 25. TCD BA47 MA. CITC 49. **d** 49 **p** 50. C Rathdowney *C & O* 49-51; C Cork St Luke *C, C & R* 51-53; I Fermoy Union 53-55; I Cork St Luke w St Ann 55-73; Preb Ross Cathl 69-88;

Preb Cork Cathl 69-88; I Cork St Luke Union from 73; Preb St Patr Cathl Dub from 88; Treas Cork Cathl *C, C & R* from 88. *The Rectory, Mahony's Avenue, St Luke's, Cork, Irish Republic* Cork (21) 501672

SALTER, John Frank. b 37. Dur Univ BA62 DipTh64. Cranmer Hall Dur 62. **d** 64 **p** 65. C Bridlington Priory *York* 64-67; Travelling Sec IVF 67-70; V Stoughton *Guildf* from 70; RD Guildf from 89. *The Vicarage, 3 Shepherd's Lane, Guildford, Surrey GU2 6SJ* Guildford (0483) 61603

SALTER, John Leslie. b 51. AKC76. Coll of Resurr Mirfield 77. **d** 78 **p** 79. C Tottenham St Paul *Lon* 78-82; P-in-c Castle Vale *Birm* 82-83; TV Curdworth w Castle Vale 83-90; R St Cuth of Lindisfarne, Castle Vale from 90. *St Cuthbert's Vicarage, Reed Square, Castle Vale, Birmingham B35 7PS* 021-747 4041

SALTER, Nigel Christopher Murray. b 46. Loughb Univ BTech. Ripon Coll Cuddesdon 79. **d** 81 **p** 82. C Glouc St Aldate *Glouc* 81-84; C Solihull *Birm* 84-88; V Highters Heath from 88. *Immanuel Vicarage, Pickenham Road, Hollywood, Birmingham B14 4TG* 021-430 7578

SALTER, Richard. b 24. Edin Th Coll 46. **d** 48 **p** 49. C Dundee St Salvador *Bre* 48-51; C Watford St Andr *St Alb* 51-54; C Oxhey St Matt 54-58; V Roberttown *Wakef* 58-62; V Watford St Jo *St Alb* from 62. *St John's Vicarage, 9 Monmouth Road, Watford WD1 1QW* Watford (0923) 36174

SALTER, Roger John. b 45. Trin Coll Bris 75. **d** 79 **p** 80. C Bedminster St Mich *Bris* 79-82; C Swindon Ch Ch 82-84; V Bedminster Down 84-89; P-in-c Northwood *Portsm* from 89. *The Rectory, Northwood, Cowes, Isle of Wight PO31 8PR* Isle of Wight (0983) 292544

SALTER, Samuel. b 22. St Edm Hall Ox BA49 MA53. St Steph Ho Ox 49. **d** 50 **p** 51. Chapl Cheltenham Coll 65-81; TV Grantham *Linc* 81-87; rtd 87; Perm to Offic *Linc* from 87. *6 Gladstone Terrace, Grantham, Lincs NG31 8BW* Grantham (0476) 60249

SALWAY, Canon Donald Macleay. b 31. St Pet Hall Ox BA54 MA59. Oak Hill Th Coll 54. **d** 56 **p** 57. C Holloway St Mary w St Jas *Lon* 56-67; V Cam St Phil *Ely* 67-81; V Mile Cross *Nor* from 81; RD Nor N from 89; Hon Can Nor Cathl from 91. *St Catherine's Vicarage, Aylsham Road, Mile Cross, Norwich NR3 2RJ* Norwich (0603) 426767

SAMBELL, David John. b 31. St Aid Birkenhead 60. **d** 63 **p** 64. C Sutton St Geo *Ches* 63-67; C Alsager St Mary 67-71; V Crewe St Pet 71-81; V Upton Priory from 81. *The Vicarage, Churchway, Upton Priory, Macclesfield, Cheshire SK10 3HT* Macclesfield (0625) 827761

SAMBROOK, Ernest. b 16. Kelham Th Coll 36. **d** 42 **p** 43. V Stockport St Sav *Ches* 58-76; V Brinnington w Portwood 76-82; rtd 82; Perm to Offic *Ches* from 86. *189 Overdale Road, Stockport, Cheshire SK6 3EN* 061-494 1614

SAMMAN, Peter Bryan. b 27. TCD BA53. Coll of Resurr Mirfield 53. **d** 55 **p** 56. V Lanc Ch Ch *Blackb* 67-74; V Lostock Hall 74-85; V Morecambe St Barn 85-91; rtd 91. *14 Wentworth Crescent, Morecambe, Lancs LA3 3NX* Morecambe (0524) 419015

SAMME, Raymond Charles. b 50. Trent Poly MIBiol80. Oak Hill Th Coll 85. **d** 87 **p** 88. C Holmer w Huntington *Heref* 87-90; C Derby St Alkmund and St Werburgh *Derby* from 90. *54 Park Grove, Derby DE3 1HG* Derby (0332) 372408

SAMMONS, John Trevor. b 22. Birm Univ BA48. Ripon Hall Ox. **d** 50 **p** 51. V Birm St Luke *Birm* 55-70; Chapl Birm Skin Hosp 56-70; P-in-c Nomans Heath *Lich* 70-82; R Newton Regis w Seckington and Shuttington *Birm* 70-86; rtd 87; Perm to Offic *Birm* from 87. *39 Kurtus, Dosthill, Tamworth, Staffs B77 1NX* Tamworth (0827) 283875

SAMPFORD, John Alfred. b 36. Lich Th Coll 58. **d** 61 **p** 62. C Lambeth St Phil *S'wark* 61-65; C Beddington 65-69; V Hampstead Ch Ch *Lon* 69-79; V Enfield Chase St Mary from 79. *St Mary Magdalene Vicarage, 30 The Ridgeway, Enfield, Middx EN2 8QH* 081-363 1875

SAMPSON, Clive. b 38. St Jo Coll Cam BA61 MA64. Ridley Hall Cam 63. **d** 65 **p** 66. C Tunbridge Wells St Jo *Roch* 65-69; Travelling Sec Scripture Union 69-79; V Maidstone St Luke *Cant* from 79. *The Vicarage, 24 Park Avenue, Maidstone, Kent ME14 5HN* Maidstone (0622) 754856

SAMPSON, Desmond William John. b 25. FRICS60. Roch Th Coll 63. **d** 65 **p** 66. C Hythe *Cant* 65-70; V Alkham w Capel le Ferne and Hougham 70-76; V Wingham w Elmstone and Preston w Stourmouth 76-86; RD E Bridge 81-86; C Hythe 86-91; rtd 91. *25 Albert Road, Hythe, Kent CT21 6BP* Hythe (0303) 268457

SAMPSON, Preb Everard Archbold. b 12. Keble Coll Ox BA33 MA47. Linc Th Coll 33. **d** 35 **p** 36. V Holcombe Burnell *Ex* 49-77; Preb Ex Cathl from 60; rtd 77; Sub-Dean Ex Cathl *Ex* from 84. *11 Arundel Close, Alphington, Exeter EX2 8UG* Exeter (0392) 438389

SAMPSON, Canon Frank. b 11. Keble Coll Ox BA38 MA46. Cuddesdon Coll 38. **d** 39 **p** 40. C Anfield St Columba *Liv* 39-43; C S Kensington St Aug *Lon* 43-46; V W Derby (or Tuebrook) St Jo *Liv* from 46; Chapl Park Hosp Liv from 54; Hon Can Liv Cathl from 69. *St John's Vicarage, Tuebrook, Liverpool L13 7EA* 051-228 2023

SAMPSON, Jeremy John Egerton. b 23. Dur Univ BSc45. Wells Th Coll 46. **d** 48 **p** 49. V Killingworth *Newc* 62-76; V Consett *Dur* 76-90; RD Lanchester 80-85; rtd 90. *6 Kilkenny Road, Guisborough, Cleveland TS14 7LE* Guisborough (0287) 632734

SAMPSON, Canon Terence Harold Morris. b 41. ACA64 FCA75. Bps' Coll Cheshunt 64. **d** 67 **p** 68. C Penrith St Andr *Carl* 67-72; V Carl St Barn 72-80; TR Carl H Trin and St Barn 80-84; Chapl Cumberland Infirmary 83-84; R Workington St Mich *Carl* from 84; Hon Can Carl Cathl from 89; RD Solway from 90. *St Michael's Rectory, Dora Crescent, Workington, Cumbria CA14 2EZ* Workington (0900) 602311

SAMS, Michael Charles. b 34. Ox NSM Course 81. **d** 84 **p** 85. NSM Abingdon *Ox* from 84. *13 Hound Close, Abingdon, Oxon OX14 2LU* Abingdon (0235) 529084

SAMS, Brother. *See* DOUBLE, Richard Sydney

SAMUEL, David Norman. b 30. Univ of Wales DipTh54 BA58 Hull Univ MA74 PhD83. Edin Th Coll 60. **d** 61 **p** 62. C Bishop's Stortford St Mich *St Alb* 61-65; C Bedf St Jo 65-68; R Ashby w Fenby and Brigsley *Linc* 68-83; R Beelsby 68-83; V E and W Ravendale w Hatcliffe 68-83; Dir Ch Soc 83-91; Min Reading St Mary Castle Street Prop Chpl *Ox* from 91. *1 Downshire Square, Reading RG1 6NJ* Reading (0734) 595131

SAMUEL, Canon James Louis. b 30. Birm Poly CQSW72 Open Univ BA77. Sarum Th Coll 59. **d** 61 **p** 62. C Dursley *Glouc* 61-63; C Matson 63-65; C Leckhampton SS Phil and Jas 65-66; C Blakenall Heath *Lich* 67-69; P-in-c Dudley Holly Hall St Aug *Worc* 81-86; V from 86; RD Dudley from 87; Hon Can Worc Cathl from 88. *St Augustine's Vicarage, 1 Hallchurch Road, Dudley, W Midlands DY2 0TG* Brierley Hill (0384) 261026

SAMUEL, Stuart. b 48. AKC70. St Aug Coll Cant 70. **d** 71 **p** 72. C Golcar *Wakef* 71-77; V Brampton St Mark *Derby* 77-79; P-in-c Hathern *Leic* 79-83; R Hathern, Long Whatton and Diseworth 83-90; R Hathern, Long Whatton and Diseworth w Belton etc from 90. *The Rectory, Hathern, Loughborough, Leics LE12 5LA* Loughborough (0509) 842259

SAMUEL, Theophilus. b 34. BScTech59. Oak Hill Th Coll 70. **d** 72 **p** 73. C Slough *Ox* 72-73; Chapl Community Relns 73-78; Chapl Brunel Univ *Lon* 78-85; V W Drayton from 85. *The Vicarage, 191 Station Road, West Drayton, Middx UB7 7NQ* West Drayton (0895) 442194

SAMUELS, Ann Elizabeth. b 51. Birm Univ BA73 CertEd74. Trin Coll Bris 85. **d** 87. Par Dn Moreton *Ches* 87-91; Par Dn Halton from 91. *The Vicarage, Halton, Runcorn, Cheshire WA7 2BE* Runcorn (0928) 563636

SAMUELS, Christopher William John. b 42. AKC66. **d** 67 **p** 68. C Kirkholt *Man* 67-72; C-in-c Houghton Regis St Thos CD *St Alb* 72-76; R Tarporley *Ches* 76-83; R Ches St Mary from 83. *The Rectory, St Mary-without-the-Walls, Chester CH4 7HL* Chester (0244) 671202

SAMUELS, Peter. b 34. Open Univ BA79. Kelham Th Coll 57. **d** 61 **p** 62. C Whitton St Aug *Lon* 61-65; C Milton next Gravesend Ch Ch *Roch* 65-67; P-in-c Stand Lane St Jo *Man* 67-69; V 69-72; R Droylsden St Andr 72-83; R Haughton St Anne from 83. *St Anne's Rectory, St Anne's Drive, Denton, Manchester M34 3EB* 061-336 2374

SAMUELS, Raymond John. b 49. Qu Mary Coll Lon BSc73 Essex Univ CertEd74. Trin Coll Bris 85. **d** 87 **p** 88. C Moreton *Ches* 87-91; V Halton from 91. *The Vicarage, Halton, Runcorn, Cheshire WA7 2BE* Runcorn (0928) 563636

SAMUELS, Sheila Mary. b 57. St Andr Univ MA79 Wolfs Coll Ox MLitt82 CertEd83. Trin Coll Bris BA89. **d** 89. C Skirbeck H Trin *Linc* from 89. *43 Spilsby Road, Boston, Lincs PE21 9NX* Boston (0205) 368721

SAMWAYS, Denis Robert. b 37. Leeds Univ BA62. Coll of Resurr Mirfield 62. **d** 64 **p** 65. C Clun w Chapel Lawn *Heref* 64-69; C Pocklington w Yapham-cum-Meltonby, Owsthorpe etc *York* 69-71; C Millington w Gt Givendale 69-71; R Hinderwell w Roxby 71-76; Hon C 80-91; Hon C Loftus 76-80; V Boosbeck w Moorsholm from 91.

The Vicarage, Boosbeck, Saltburn-by-the-Sea, Cleveland TS12 3AY Guisborough (0287) 51728

SAMWAYS, John Feverel. b 44. BA DipTh. Trin Coll Bris 81. **d** 83 **p** 84. C Patcham *Chich* 83-86; C Ox St Aldate w St Matt *Ox* from 86. *60 Abingdon Road, Oxford OX1 4PE* Oxford (0865) 243434

✠**SANANA, Rt Rev Rhynold Ewaruba.** b 39. St Barn Coll Adelaide. **d** 67 **p** 67 **c** 76. Papua New Guinea 67-72 and 73-90; Asst Bp New Guinea 76-90; Bp Dogura 77-88; Australia 72-73; Lakenham St Mark *Nor* from 90. *9 Duverlin Close, Greenways, Norwich NR4 6HS* Norwich (0603) 54078

SANDAY, Robert Ward. b 55. Sarum & Wells Th Coll 89. **d** 91. C Swindon Ch Ch *Bris* from 91. *58 Upham Road, Swindon SN3 1DN* Swindon (0793) 521296

SANDBERG, Peter John. b 37. Lon Univ LLB59. Lon Coll of Div 67. **d** 69 **p** 70. C Hailsham *Chich* 69-72; C Billericay St Mary *Chelmsf* 72-77; TV Billericay and Lt Burstead 77-83; P-in-c Thundersley 83; R from 83; RD Hadleigh from 90. *St Peter's Rectory, 390 Church Road, Thundersley, Benfleet, Essex SS7 3HG* South Benfleet (0268) 792235

SANDEMAN, Arthur Alastair Malcolm. b 14. Chich Th Coll 37. **d** 39 **p** 40. V Cressing *Chelmsf* 61-75; rtd 75; Perm to Offic *Ex* from 75. *20 Orient Road, Paignton, Devon TQ3 2PB* Paignton (0803) 521385

SANDERCOMBE, Percy Oliver. b 07. St Boniface Warminster 35. **d** 38 **p** 39. V Burton and Sopley *Win* 67-73; rtd 73. *71 South Street, Warminster, Wiltshire BA12 8ED* Warminster (0985) 213005

SANDERS, Allan Cameron Ebblewhite. b 34. CCC Ox MA59 Univ of E Africa MEd69. Ox NSM Course 82. **d** 85 **p** 86. Hd Master Reading Blue Coat Sch from 74; Hon C Sonning *Ox* from 85. *Headmaster's House, Reading Blue Coat School, Sonning, Reading RG4 0SU* Reading (0734) 693200

SANDERS, Colin Anthony Wakefield. b 26. Wadh Coll Ox MA55. Ox NSM Course 89. **d** 90. NSM Eynsham and Cassington *Ox* from 90. *Little Firs, 41 Bladon Road, Woodstock, Oxford OX7 1QD* Woodstock (0993) 813357

SANDERS, Frederick Alvin Oliver. b 06. CCC Cam BA28 MA37. Coll of Resurr Mirfield. **d** 30 **p** 31. CF (TA) from 50; R Stalbridge *Sarum* 59-78; rtd 78; Lic to Offic *L & K* from 78. *Skehanagh Point, Coolbawn, Nenagh, Co Tipperary, Irish Republic* Nenagh (67) 28007

SANDERS, Graham Laughton. b 32. Kelham Th Coll 52. **d** 56 **p** 57. C Glouc St Paul *Glouc* 56-60; India 61-68; V Heaton St Martin *Bradf* 68-76; V Gt Waltham *Chelmsf* 76-79; Sec Dioc Liturg Cttee 78-87; P-in-c Ford End 79; V Gt Waltham w Ford End 79-87; TR Guiseley w Esholt *Bradf* from 87. *The Rectory, The Green, Guiseley, Leeds LS20 9BT* Guiseley (0943) 74321

SANDERS, Henry William. b 36. **d** 62 **p** 64. C Nottm St Ann *S'well* 62-65; C Dagenham *Chelmsf* 65-67; C W Thurrock 67-73; C W Ham 73-78. *20 Vale Road, London E7*

SANDERS, Herbert. b 21. Clifton Th Coll 51. **d** 53 **p** 54. V Oxenhope *Bradf* 59-66; Lic to Offic *Linc* 66-81; rtd 81. *The Vicarage, Low Toynton, Horncastle, Lincs* Horncastle (0507) 523410

SANDERS, Mrs Hilary Clare. b 57. Hull Univ BA79 UEA CertEd81. E Anglian Minl Tr Course 83. **dss** 85 **d** 87. Haverhill w Withersfield, the Wrattings etc *St E* 85-87; Hon Par Dn Melton from 87; Dioc Schs Officer from 88. *The Rectory, 7 Norman Close, Melton, Woodbridge, Suffolk IP12 1JT* Woodbridge (0394) 380279

SANDERS, Mark. b 57. Hull Univ BA79 Cam Univ BA82. Westcott Ho Cam 80. **d** 83 **p** 84. C Haverhill w Withersfield, the Wrattings etc *St E* 83-87; P-in-c Melton from 87. *The Rectory, 7 Norman Close, Melton, Woodbridge, Suffolk IP12 1JT* Woodbridge (0394) 380279

SANDERS, Michael Barry. b 45. Fitzw Coll Cam BA67 MA71 Lon Univ BD71. St Jo Coll Nottm 68 Lon Coll of Div. **d** 71 **p** 72. C Ashtead *Guildf* 71-74; Chapl St Jo Coll Cam 75-79; V Dorridge *Birm* 79-89; TR Walsall *Lich* from 89. *The Vicarage, 48 Jesson Road, Walsall WS1 3AX* Walsall (0922) 24012

SANDERS, Mrs Nora Irene. b 29. Lon Univ BA50 CertEd51. W Midl Minl Tr Course 74. **dss** 78 **d** 87. Dorridge *Birm* 78-87; Par Dn 87-90; rtd 90. *4 Barston Lane, Solihull, W Midlands B91 2SS* Solihull (021-705 2391

SANDERS, Raymond Joseph. b 20. Lon Univ BA40 BD49. Qu Coll Birm 65. **d** 65 **p** 65. R Headless Cross *Worc* 67-73; R Dunsfold *Guildf* 73-85; rtd 85; Perm to Offic *Chich* from 85. *The Brambles, Maple Leaf, Coldwaltham, Pulborough, W Sussex RH20 1LN* Pulborough (07982) 2878

SANDERS, Roderick David Scott. b 58. Southn Univ BA80 CertEd81. Cranmer Hall Dur 85. **d** 88 **p** 89. C Luton St Mary *St Alb* from 88. *72 Crawley Green Road, Luton LU2 0QU* Luton (0582) 35548

SANDERS, Mrs Susan Rachel. b 61. St Mary's Coll Dur BA83. Cranmer Hall Dur 85. **d** 88. Par Dn Luton St Mary *St Alb* from 88. *72 Crawley Green Road, Luton LU2 0QU* Luton (0582) 35548

SANDERS, Wendy Elizabeth. b 49. Carl Dioc Tr Course 87. **d** 90. NSM Bampton w Mardale *Carl* from 90. *The Vicarage, Bampton Grange, Penrith, Cumbria CA10 2QR* Bampton (09313) 239

SANDERS, William John. b 48. Liv Inst of Educn BA80. Wycliffe Hall Ox 81. **d** 83 **p** 84. C Netherton *Liv* 83-87; P-in-c Wavertree St Bridget from 87. *St Bridget's Vicarage, 93 Salisbury Road, Watertree, Liverpool L15 2HU* 051-733 1117

SANDERSON, Colin James. b 54. SEN SRN. St Mich Coll Llan 85. **d** 87 **p** 88. C Merthyr Dyfan *Llan* 87-90; C Cadoxton-juxta-Barry 90-91; V Llangeinor from 91. *The Vicarage, Corbett Street, Ogmore Vale, Bridgend, M Glam* Bridgend (0656) 842565

SANDERSON, Daniel. b 40. AKC66. **d** 67 **p** 68. C Upperby St Jo *Carl* 67-72; V Addingham 72-75; V Ireleth w Askam from 75. *St Peter's Vicarage, Duke Street, Askham-in-Furness, Cumbria LA16 7AD* Dalton-in-Furness (0229) 62647

SANDERSON, Miss Gillian. b 47. Cranmer Hall Dur 80. **dss** 82 **d** 87. Allesley *Cov* 82-86; Warw 86-87; Par Dn from 87. *The Vicarage, 25 Sutherland Close, Warwick CV34 5UJ* Warwick (0926) 492097

SANDERSON, Harold. b 26. St Aid Birkenhead. **d** 61 **p** 62. V Warrington St Ann *Liv* 64-73; P-in-c Warrington St Pet 70-73; V Orrell 73-79; V Scarisbrick 79-91; rtd 91. *29 Green Lane, Ormskirk, Lancs L39 1ND*

SANDERSON, Howard Walter. b 08. FRGS57. St Andr Coll Pampisford 44 Truine Sem (USA). **d** 45 **p** 46. V Barling w Lt Wakering *Chelmsf* 66-72; rtd 72; Hon Chapl Sliema *Eur* 78-80; Hon Chapl Alassio 81-82; Hon C Genoa w Alassio from 82. *Filanla Court E71, Makarios Avenue, Larnaca, Cyprus* Larnaca (41) 631888

SANDERSON, Very Rev Peter Oliver. b 29. St Chad's Coll Dur BA52 DipTh54. **d** 54 **p** 55. C Houghton le Spring *Dur* 54-59; Jamaica 59-63; Chapl RAF 63-67; P-in-c Winksley cum Grantley and Aldfield w Studley *Ripon* 67-68; V 68-74; V Leeds St Aid 74-84; Can St Paul's Cathl Dundee *Bre* from 84; Provost St Paul's Cathl Dundee from 84; R Dundee St Paul from 84. *St Paul's Cathedral Rectory, 4 Richmond Terrace, Dundee DD2 1BQ* Dundee (0382) 68548

SANDERSON, Peter Richard Fallowfield. b 18. St Cath Soc Ox BA41 MA46. Chich Th Coll 41. **d** 42 **p** 44. V Poundstock *Truro* 56-74; P-in-c Hove St Patr *Chich* 74-79; P-in-c Buxted St Mary 79-82; P-in-c Hadlow Down 79-82; P-in-c Buxted and Hadlow Down 82-83; rtd 83; Perm to Offic *Chich* from 83. *Nova Scotia, 48 Parklands Road, Hassocks, W Sussex BN6 8JZ* Hassocks (07918) 3117

SANDERSON, Scott. b 42. Oak Hill Th Coll DipHE. **d** 82 **p** 83. C Galleywood Common *Chelmsf* 82-88; P-in-c Newport w Widdington from 88. *The Vicarage, Newport, Saffron Walden, Essex CB11 3RB* Saffron Walden (0799) 40339

SANDES, Denis Lindsay. **d** 89. C Bandon Union *C, C & R* from 89. *Oldchapel, Bandon, Co Cork, Irish Republic* Cork (21) 41053

SANDFORD of Banbury, Rev and Rt Hon Lord (John Cyril Edmondson). b 20. DSC43. Dartmouth RN Coll. Westcott Ho Cam 56. **d** 58 **p** 60. Perm to Offic *St Alb* from 63; Chapl for Miss and Ecum St Alb 63-66; Chmn Redundant Chs Cttee Ch Commrs 82-88; rtd 85. *27 Ashley Gardens, Ambrosden Avenue, London SW1P 1QD* 071-834 5722

SANDFORD, Edward Noel Teulon. b 17. St Pet Hall Ox BA43 MA44. Wycliffe Hall Ox. **d** 43 **p** 44. SW Regional Sec BFBS 66-82; Perm to Offic *B & W, Bris, Sarum & Glos* from 72; rtd 82. *3 Madeira Road, Clevedon, Avon BS21 7TJ* Clevedon (0272) 874035

SANDFORD, Jack. b 11. Ripon Hall Ox. **d** 60 **p** 61. V Barkingside St Laur *Chelmsf* 67-77; rtd 77. *15 Lyndhurst Road, Holland-on-Sea, Clacton-on-Sea CO15 5HT* Clacton-on-Sea (0225) 815294

SANDFORD, Nicholas Robert. b 63. Kent Univ BA84 Univ of Wales (Cardiff) BD87. St Mich Coll Llan 84. **d** 87 **p** 88. C Neath w Llantwit *Llan* 87-90; C Cardiff St Jo from 90. *41 Colum Road, Cardiff CF1 3EE* Cardiff (0222) 224036

SANDFORD, Paul Richard. b 47. Em Coll Cam BA69 MA73. Wycliffe Hall Ox 72. **d** 75 **p** 76. C Upper Holloway St Pet *Lon* 75-77; C Finchley St Paul Long Lane 77-81; Ind Chapl *Newc* 81-88; TV Cramlington 81-88; TV Dronfield *Derby* 88-90; TV Dronfield w Holmesfield from 90. *St Philip's Vicarage, 43 Firthwood Road, Dronfield, Sheffield S18 6BW* Dronfield (0246) 413893

SANDHAM, Stephen McCourt. b 41. K Coll *Lon* BD65 AKC65. **d** 66 **p** 67. C Stockton St Pet *Dur* 66-69; C Bishopwearmouth Gd Shep 69-71; C Bishopwearmouth St Mich w St Hilda 71-75; V Darlington St Mark w St Paul 75-82; P-in-c Sunderland St Chad 82-87; R Shincliffe from 87. *The Rectory, Shincliffe, Durham DH1 2NJ* 091-386 2142

SANDS, Colin Robert. b 38. JP84. Chester Coll CertEd64. N Ord Course 82. **d** 85 **p** 86. Hd Master Magull Primary Sch from 80; NSM Bootle Ch Ch *Liv* from 85. *16 Strafford Drive, Bootle, Merseyside L20 9JW* 051-525 8709 or 526 1378

SANDS, Frederick William. b 25. St Deiniol's Hawarden 86. **d** 87 **p** 88. Chapl Asst Leic Gen Hosp 87-89; Chapl from 89. *Cobblestones, Laughton, Lutterworth, Leics LE17 6QE* Leicester (0533) 403163

SANDS, Nigel Colin. b 39. Dur Univ BA64 MA68. Oak Hill Th Coll 65. **d** 67 **p** 68. C Skelmersdale St Paul *Liv* 67-71; C Childwall All SS 71-72; V Wavertree St Bridget 72-78; P-in-c Welford w Wickham and Gt Shefford *Ox* 78-86; P-in-c Boxford w Stockcross and Speen 84-86; R Welford w Wickham and Gt Shefford, Boxford etc from 86. *The Rectory, Wickham, Newbury, Berks RG16 8HD* Boxford (048838) 244

SANDS, Percy. b 01. Fitzw Hall Cam BA23 MA27. Ridley Hall Cam 23. **d** 29 **p** 30. R Upton *Ex* 52-66; rtd 66. *31 Lloyd Avenue, Torquay TQ2 7DH* Torquay (0803) 613464

SANDS, William James. b 55. St Jo Coll Nottm LTh. **d** 83 **p** 84. C St Mary-at-Latton *Chelmsf* 83-86; Zimbabwe 86-87; C Woodford St Mary w St Phil and St Jas *Chelmsf* 87-89; C-in-c Barkingside St Cedd 87-89; P-in-c Elmsett w Aldham *St E* from 89; P-in-c Kersey w Lindsey from 89. *The Rectory, Hadleigh Road, Elmsett, Ipswich IP7 6ND* Offton (047333) 219

SANFORD, William Henry Steward (Brother Gabriel). b 14. AKC36 Lon Univ BD37. Westcott Ho Cam 37. **d** 37 **p** 38. P-in-c Bermondsey St Paul *S'wark* 48-54; CR from 57; rtd 84. *House of the Resurrection, Mirfield, W Yorkshire WF14 0BN* Mirfield (0924) 494318

SANGER, Reginald Stephen John. b 15. Wycliffe Hall Ox. **d** 57 **p** 58. V Lee St Mildred *S'wark* 62-83; rtd 83; Perm to Offic *Chich* from 87. *62 Quantock Road, Durrington, Worthing, W Sussex BN13 2HQ* Worthing (0903) 692905

SANGSTER, Andrew. b 45. K Coll Lon BD67 AKC67 BA71 MA84. **d** 69 **p** 70. C Aylesford *Roch* 69-72; C Shirley *Win* 73-76; V Woolston 76-79; Prov Youth Chapl Ch in Wales 79-82; New Zealand 82-89; Chapl Eton Coll Windsor from 89. *Eton College, Windsor, Berks SL4 6AX* Windsor (0753) 841042

SANKEY, Julian. b 52. Qu Coll Ox BA74 MA79. St Jo Coll Nottm 84. **d** 86 **p** 87. C New Barnet St Jas *St Alb* 86-89; C Mansf St Pet *S'well* from 89. *85 Delamere Drive, Mansfield, Notts NG18 4DD* Mansfield (0623) 649119

SANKEY, Terence Arthur Melville. b 51. CertTS. Trin Coll Bris 87. **d** 89 **p** 90. C Chalke Valley W *Sarum* from 89. *The Vicarage, Ebbesbourne Wake, Salisbury SP5 5JL* Salisbury (0722) 780774

SANSBURY, Christopher John. b 34. Peterho Cam BA57 MA. Westcott Ho Cam 58. **d** 59 **p** 60. C Portsea N End St Mark *Portsm* 59-63; C Weeke *Win* 63-71; V N Eling St Mary 71-78; R Long Melford *St E* from 78. *The Rectory, Long Melford, Sudbury, Suffolk CO10 9DL* Sudbury (0787) 310845

✠**SANSBURY, Rt Rev Cyril Kenneth.** b 05. Peterho Cam BA27 MA31 Trin Coll Toronto Hon DD54. Westcott Ho Cam 27. **d** 28 **p** 29 **c** 61. C Dulwich Common St Pet *S'wark* 28-31; Hon C Wimbledon 31-32; Japan 32-41; Canada 41-45; Warden Linc Th Coll 45-52; Can and Preb Linc Cathl *Linc* 48-53; Warden St Aug Coll Cant 52-61; Hon Can Cant Cathl *Cant* 53-61; Bp Singapore 61-66; Asst Bp Lon 66-73; Gen Sec BCC 64-73; rtd 73; P-in-c Nor St Mary in the Marsh *Nor* 73-84; Hon Min Can Nor Cathl from 73. *20 The Close, Norwich NR1 4DZ* Norwich (0603) 664516

SANSOM, John Reginald. b 40. St Jo Coll Nottm 73. **d** 75 **p** 76. C Ipswich St Marg *St E* 75-79; P-in-c Emneth *Ely* 79-85; P-in-c Hartford 85-86; TV Huntingdon from 86.

The Vicarage, Longstaff Way, Hartford, Huntingdon, Cambs PE18 7XT Huntingdon (0480) 52086

SANSOM, Canon Michael Charles. b 44. Bris Univ BA66 St Jo Coll Dur PhD74. Cranmer Hall Dur 68. **d** 72 **p** 73. C Ecclesall *Sheff* 72-76; Lic to Offic *Ely* 76-88; Dir of Studies Ridley Hall Cam 76-88; Vice-Prin 79-88; Dir of Ords *St Alb* from 88; Can Res St Alb from 88. *4D Harpenden Road, St Albans, Herts AL3 5AB* St Albans (0727) 833777

SANSOM, Robert Arthur. b 29. St Aid Birkenhead 60. **d** 62 **p** 63. C Sutton in Ashfield St Mary *S'well* 62-65; V Holbrooke *Derby* 65-70; Canada from 70. *2254 Amherst Avenue, Sidney, British Columbia, Canada, V8L 2G7*

SANSOME, Geoffrey Hubert. b 29. Man Univ BA53. Qu Coll Birm DipTh62. **d** 62 **p** 63. C Prenton *Ches* 62-68; P-in-c Liscard St Thos 68-72; V Kingsley 72-83; V Wybunbury w Doddington 83-91; V Marbury from 91. *The Vicarage, Marbury, Whitchurch, Shropshire SY13 4LN* Whitchurch (0948) 3758

SANSUM, David Henry. b 31. Bris Univ BA52 MA63. St Aid Birkenhead 54. **d** 56 **p** 57. C Henleaze *Bris* 56-59; C Stratton St Margaret 59-60; C Stoke Bishop 60-64; V Stechford *Birm* 64-76; V Ashbourne w Mapleton *Derby* from 76; V Ashbourne St Jo from 81; RD Ashbourne from 91. *The Vicarage, Belle Vue Road, Ashbourne, Derbyshire DE6 1AT* Ashbourne (0335) 43129

✠**SANTER, Rt Rev Mark.** b 36. Qu Coll Cam BA60 MA64. Westcott Ho Cam. **d** 63 **p** 64 **c** 81. Tutor Cuddesdon Coll 63-67; C Cuddesdon *Ox* 63-67; Fell and Dean Clare Coll Cam 67-72; Tutor 68-72; Prin Westcott Ho Cam 73-81; Hon Can Win Cathl *Win* 78-81; Area Bp Kensington *Lon* 81-87; Bp Birm from 87. *Bishop's Croft, Old Church Road, Birmingham B17 0BG* 021-427 1163 or 427 2062

SANTRAM, Philip James. b 27. **d** 52 **p** 54. India 52-66; Ethiopia 66-68; C Horton *Bradf* 68-71; C Whitley Ch Ch *Ox* 71-72; V Tilehurst St Mary 76-78; Canada from 78. *3544 du Souvenir, Laval, Quebec, Canada, H7V 1X2*

SAPSFORD, John Garnet. b 38. **d** 76 **p** 76. C Whiteshill *Glouc* 76-81; Australia from 81. *105 Echuca Road, Mooroopna, Victoria, Australia 3629* Bendigo (54) 434711

SARALIS, Preb Christopher Herbert. b 34. Univ of Wales BA54 St Cath Coll Ox BA56 MA60. Wycliffe Hall Ox. **d** 57 **p** 58. C Abergavenny St Mary w Llanwenarth Citra *Mon* 57-61; C Bridgwater St Mary w Chilton Trinity *B & W* 61-65; V Berrow 65-72; RD Burnham 72-76; R Berrow and Breane 72-76; V Minehead from 76; RD Exmoor 80-86; Preb Wells Cathl from 84. *The Vicarage, 7 Paganel Road, Minehead, Somerset TA24 5ET* Minehead (0643) 3530

SARAPUK, Susan. b 59. Lon Univ BA80 Univ of Wales PGCE81. St Mich Coll Llan DPS90. **d** 90. C Morriston *S & B* from 90. *8 Heol Rhosyn, Morriston, Swansea SA6 6EJ* Swansea (0792) 771866

SARGAN, Miss Phyllis Elsie. b 24. TCert44 Lon Univ DSocStuds67. Gilmore Ho IDC51. **d** 88. Hon C Bawtry w Austerfield and Misson *S'well* from 88; rtd 90. *Pilgrim House, 1 Highfield Road, Bawtry, Doncaster DN10 6QN* Doncaster (0302) 710587

SARGANT, John Raymond. b 38. CCC Cam BA61 MA70. Westcott Ho Cam 64 Harvard Div Sch 66. **d** 67 **p** 68. C Croydon *Cant* 67-72; Zambia 72-75; P-in-c Bradford-on-Avon Ch Ch *Sarum* 76-81; V 81-90; TV Marlborough from 90; Adv on Inter-Faith Relns from 90. *Preshute Vicarage, 7 Golding Avenue, Marlborough, Wilts SN8 1TH* Marlborough (0672) 513408

✠**SARGEANT, Rt Rev Frank Pilkington.** b 32. St Jo Coll Dur BA55 DipTh58 Nottm Univ DipAdEd73. Cranmer Hall Dur 57. **d** 58 **p** 59 **c** 84. C Gainsborough All SS *Linc* 58-62; C Gt Grimsby St Jas 62-66; V Hykeham 66-73; Dir In-Service Tr and Adult Educn *Bradf* 73-84; Can Res Bradf Cathl 73-77; Adn Bradf 77-84; Suff Bp Stockport *Ches* from 84. *32 Park Gates Drive, Cheadle Hulme, Cheadle, Cheshire SK8 7DF* 061-486 9715

SARGEANT, George Henry. b 19. Bps' Coll Cheshunt 60. **d** 62 **p** 63. C-in-c Gt w Lt Wratting *St E* 69-70; R 70-77; C-in-c Barnardiston 69-70; R 71-77; rtd 84. *1 Belgrave Gardens, Dereham, Norfolk NR19 1PZ* Dereham (0362) 693020

SARGEANT, Kenneth Stanley. b 19. Lon Coll of Div 68. **d** 70 **p** 71. C E Ham St Paul *Chelmsf* 70-73; C Southborough St Pet w Ch Ch and St Matt *Roch* 73-77; Chapl Joyce Green Hosp Dartford 77-88; R Greenhithe St Mary *Roch* 77-88; rtd 88. *2 Westfield Close, Polegate, E Sussex BN26 6EF* Polegate (03212) 8153

SARGEANTSON, Kenneth William. b 30. **d** 90 **p** 91. NSM The Marshland *Sheff* from 90; Perm to Offic *Linc* from 90. *81 Oxford Road, Goole, N Humberside DN14 6NY* Goole (0405) 767453

SARGENT, John Philip Hugh. b 34. Or Coll Ox BA55 MA63. Chich Th Coll 55. **d** 57 **p** 58. C Kington w Huntington *Heref* 57-59; C Bridgnorth St Mary 59-63; C Leighton Buzzard *St Alb* 63-64; V Stonebroom *Derby* 64-73; Chapl Southn Gen Hosp from 74. *General Hospital, Tremona Road, Southampton SO9 4XY* Southampton (0703) 796745

SARGENT, Preb Richard Henry. b 24. Man Univ BA50. Ridley Hall Cam 50. **d** 52 **p** 53. V Bushbury *Lich* 67-73; V Castle Church 73-89; RD Stafford 81-88; Preb Lich Cathl 87-89; rtd 89. *6 Kingcup Road, Moss Pit, Stafford ST17 9JQ* Stafford (0785) 223582

SARGISSON, Conrad Ralph. b 24. Keble Coll Ox BA46 MA50. Wells Th Coll 48. **d** 50 **p** 51. V Penzance St Mary *Truro* 62-73; RD Penwith 72-73; V Westbury-on-Trym H Trin *Bris* 73-79; P-in-c Blisland w St Breward *Truro* 79-83; V Mylor w Flushing 83-91; rtd 91. *Lugg View, Aymestry, Leominster, Herefordshire HR6 9ST* Leominster (0568) 81289

SARKIES, Col John Walter Robert Courtney. b 12. Lon Univ MRCS36 LRCP36 DOMS48. Cuddesdon Coll 57. **d** 59 **p** 60. C Bearsted *Cant* 59-61; S Africa 61-67; Mauritius 67-69; Hon C Douglas St Matt *S & M* from 69. *2 Westminster Terrace, Douglas, Isle of Man* Douglas (0624) 74835

SASADA, Benjamin John. b 33. MA. E Anglian Minl Tr Course. **d** 82 **p** 83. NSM Dickleburgh, Langmere, Shimpling, Thelveton etc *Nor* from 82; Perm to Offic St E from 84; NSM Diss *Nor* from 88. *The Grange, Walcott Green, Diss, Norfolk IP22 3SS* Diss (0379) 642174

SATTERFORD, Douglas Leigh. b 18. DSC42. Ripon Hall Ox 59. **d** 60 **p** 61. V Lyminster *Chich* 65-85; V Poling 66-85; rtd 85; Perm to Offic Chich from 85; St E from 90. *24 Wheatfields, Whatfield, Ipswich IP7 6RB*

SATTERLY, Gerald Albert. b 34. Lon Univ BA56 Ex Univ Hon BA. Wycliffe Hall Ox 58. **d** 60 **p** 61. C Southborough St Pet *Roch* 60-63; C S Lyncombe *B & W* 63-66; V Sheff St Barn *Sheff* 66-69; R Adwick-le-Street 69-73; V Awre and Blakeney *Glouc* 73-82; P-in-c Newnham 80-82; V Newnham w Awre and Blakeney 82-90; R Instow *Ex* from 90; V Westleigh from 90. *The Rectory, Quay Lane, Instow, Bideford, Devon EX39 4JR* Instow (0271) 860346

✠**SATTERTHWAITE, Rt Rev John Richard.** b 25. CMG91. Leeds Univ BA46. Coll of Resurr Mirfield 48. **d** 50 **p** 51 **c** 70. C Carl St Barn *Carl* 50-53; C Carl St Aid and Ch Ch 53-55; Asst Gen Sec C of E Coun on Foreign Relns 55-59; C St Mich Paternoster Royal *Lon* 55-59; P-in-c 59-65; Gen Sec C of E Coun on Foreign Relns 59-70; V St Dunstan in the West *Lon* 59-70; Hon Can Cant Cathl *Cant* 63-70; Gen Sec Abp's Commn on RC Relns 65-70; Suff Bp Fulham *Lon* 70-80; Bp Gib 70-80; Dean Malta *Eur* from 70; Bp Eur from 80. *5A Gregory Place, London W8 4NG* 071-937 2796

SAUL, Norman Stanley. b 30. St Aid Birkenhead 51. **d** 54 **p** 55. V Barton *Blackb* 68-72; V Foxdale *S & M* 72-77; V Maughold 77-90; CF (ACF) 80-86; rtd 90. *15 Croft Meadow, Bamber Bridge, Preston PR5 8HX* Preston (0772) 314475

SAUNDERS, Andrew Vivian. b 44. Leeds Univ BA65. Coll of Resurr Mirfield 66. **d** 68 **p** 69. C Goodmayes St Paul *Chelmsf* 68-71; C Horfield H Trin *Bris* 71-75; C Oldland 75-77; Ind Chapl *B & W* 77-80; P-in-c Buckland Dinham w Elm, Orchardleigh etc 77-78; P-in-c Buckland Dinham 78-80; V Westf 80-90; R Clutton w Cameley from 90. *The Rectory, Main Road, Temple Cloud, Bristol BS18 5DA* Temple Cloud (0761) 52296

SAUNDERS, Brian Gerald. b 28. Pemb Coll Cam BA49 MA53. Cuddesdon Coll 63. **d** 66 **p** 67. NSM Gt Berkhamsted *St Alb* 66-87; P-in-c Lt Gaddesden from 87. *The Rectory, Little Gaddesden, Berkhamsted, Herts HP4 1PA*

SAUNDERS, Bruce Alexander. b 47. St Cath Coll Cam BA68 MA72 Ox Univ DipTh70. Cuddesdon Coll 68. **d** 71 **p** 72. C Westbury-on-Trym H Trin *Bris* 71-74; Hon C Clifton St Paul 74-78; Asst Chapl Bris Univ 74-78; TV Fareham H Trin *Portsm* 78-84; TR Mortlake w E Sheen *S'wark* from 84; RD Richmond and Barnes from 89. *The Rectory, 170 Sheen Lane, London SW14 8LZ* 081-876 4816

SAUNDERS, David. b 28. Keble Coll Ox BA50 DipTh51 MA59. Cuddesdon Coll 51. **d** 53 **p** 54. C Mexborough *Sheff* 53-56; C Sheff St Cuth 56-60; V New Bentley 60-67; V Grimsby All SS *Linc* 67-78; V Caistor w Clixby 78-88; P-in-c Grasby from 78; Chapl Caistor Hosp from 78; P-in-c Searby w Owmby *Linc* from 79; V Dunholme from 88. *The Vicarage, Holmes Lane, Dunholme, Lincoln LN2 3QT* Welton (0673) 60132

SAUNDERS, David Anthony. b 48. Trin Coll Bris 76. **d** 78 **p** 79. C Bath Walcot *B & W* 78-80; Asst Dir RE 80-90; Youth Chapl 80-82; C Long Ashton 83-84; V Bath St Bart 84-90; V Cullompton *Ex* from 90; R Kentisbeare w Blackborough from 90; Chapl RN from 90. *The Vicarage, Gravel Walk, Cullompton, Devon EX15 1DA* Cullompton (0884) 33249

SAUNDERS, Edward George Humphrey. b 23. St Jo Coll Cam BA48 MA50. Ridley Hall Cam. **d** 50 **p** 51. Lic to Offic *Leic* 69-71; V Ches Square St Mich w St Phil *Lon* 71-84; P-in-c Mayfair Ch Ch 80-84; Hon C Ox St Andr *Ox* from 84; rtd 88. *The Hensol, Shire Lane, Chorleywood, Rickmansworth, Herts WD3 5NH* Chorleywood (0923) 284816

SAUNDERS, George Arthur. b 18. Kelham Th Coll 35. **d** 41 **p** 42. V Plumstead Ascension *S'wark* 57-82; rtd 82. *69 Estuary Park, Combwich, Bridgwater, Somerset TA5 2RF* Combwich (0278) 653091

SAUNDERS, Graham Howard. b 53. Hatf Poly BSc77. Trin Coll Bris BA86. **d** 86 **p** 87. C Birm St Martin w Bordesley St Andr *Birm* 86-89; C Olton from 89. *35 Marsden Close, Solihull, W Midlands B92 7JR* 021-707 3559

SAUNDERS, Guy. b 27. AKC51. **d** 52 **p** 53. P-in-c Burton w Coates *Chich* 69-81; P-in-c Up Waltham 69-81; P-in-c Duncton 69-81; P-in-c Bolney 81-83; V 83-91; rtd 91. *3 April Close, Horsham, W Sussex RH12 2LL* Horsham (0403) 40867

SAUNDERS, Henry Wilfred. b 19. St Steph Ho Ox 48. **d** 51 **p** 52. R St Tudy *Truro* 60-70; RD Bodmin 68-70; Chapl HM Pris Holloway 71-76; Haverigg 76-84; rtd 84. *6 Argyll Street, Ryde, Isle of Wight PO33 3BZ* Isle of Wight (0983) 64406

SAUNDERS, John Barry. b 40. Chich Th Coll. **d** 83 **p** 84. C St Breoke *Truro* 83-84; C St Breoke and Egloshayle 84-87; V Treverbyn from 87; RD St Austell from 91. *The Vicarage, Treverbyn Road, Stenalees, St Austell, Cornwall PL26 8TL* St Austell (0726) 850335

SAUNDERS, Kenneth John. b 35. Linc Th Coll 73. **d** 75 **p** 76. C Boultham *Linc* 75-79; V Swinderby 79-87; V Cherry Willingham w Greetwell from 87. *The Vicarage, 14 Church Lane, Cherry Willingham, Lincoln LN3 4AB* Lincoln (0522) 750356

SAUNDERS, Malcolm Walter Mackenzie. b 34. Em Coll Cam BA58 MA62. Wycliffe Hall Ox 58. **d** 60 **p** 61. C Northn St Giles *Pet* 60-63; C Northn St Alb 63-66; V Corby St Columba 66-84; Nat Dir Evang Explosion 84-91; Lic to Offic *Pet* 84-91; V Ketton from 91. *The Vicarage, 4 Edmonds Drive, Ketton, Stamford, Lincs PE9 3TH* Stamford (0780) 720228

SAUNDERS, Mrs Margaret Rose. b 49. Newnham Coll Cam BA71 St Jo Coll York CertEd72. St Alb Minl Tr Scheme 85. **d** 88. Hon Par Dn Gt Berkhamsted *St Alb* 88-90; Hon Chapl Asst Gt Berkhamsted St Hosp Lon 88-90; Asst Chapl Aylesbury Vale HA (Priority Care Unit) and Stoke Mandeville Hosp from 90; and Chapl St Jo Hosp Aylesbury from 90. *9 North Road, Berkhamsted, Herts HP4 3DU* Berkhamsted (0442) 873608

SAUNDERS, Martin Paul. b 54. K Coll Lon BD76 AKC76. Westcott Ho Cam 77. **d** 78 **p** 79. C Seaton Hirst *Newc* 78-81; Hong Kong 81; C Egglescliffe *Dur* 81-82; Chapl to Arts and Recreation 81-84; C Jarrow 82-84; TV 84-88; V Southwick St Columba from 88. *St Columba's Vicarage, Southwick, Sunderland SR5 1RU* 091-516 0244 or 548 1646

SAUNDERS, Michael. b 35. AKC61. **d** 61 **p** 62. C Leigh Park *Portsm* 61-66; V Weston *Guildf* 66-73; C St Alb Abbey *St Alb* 73-76; P-in-c Eversholt w Milton Bryan 76-79; C 79-80; P-in-c Old Alresford *Win* 80; R Old Alresford and Bighton 80-82; Perm to Offic *Win* from 82; *Portsm* from 83. *11 Perins Close, Alresford, Hants* Alresford (0962) 733496

SAUNDERS, Dr Michael. b 38. FRCP MSOSc MB, BS. NE Ord Course 82. **d** 84 **p** 85. Lic to Offic *York* from 84; Tutor NE Ord Course from 84. *Anandgiri, Cuddy Shaw Plantations, Thorpe Underwood, York YO5 9ST* Harrogate (0423) 330688

SAUNDERS, Michael Walter. b 58. CChem MRSC84 Grey Coll Dur BSc79. Wycliffe Hall Ox 86. **d** 89 **p** 90. C Deane *Man* from 89. *281 Deane Church Lane, Bolton BL3 4ES* Bolton (0204) 64313

SAUNDERS, Reginald Frederick. b 15. **d** 79 **p** 80. NSM Perth St Ninian *St And* from 79; NSM Stanley from 79. *31 Muirend Road, Perth PH1 1JU* Perth (0738) 26217

SAUNDERS, Canon Richard Charles Hebblethwaite. b 17. Qu Coll Ox BA40 DipTh41 MA42. Westcott Ho Cam 41. **d** 42 **p** 43. V Bris St Ambrose Whitehall *Bris* 62-75; TR E Bris 75-77; P-in-c Colerne 77-82; P-in-c N Wraxall 77-82; RD Chippenham 80-82; rtd 82; Hon C Honiton,

Gittisham, Combe Raleigh, Monkton etc *Ex* from 85. *St Michael's Cottage, Gittisham, Honiton, Devon EX14 0AH* Honiton (0404) 850634

SAUNDERS, Richard George. b 54. BNC Ox BA76 MA81. St Jo Coll Nottm 82. **d** 85 **p** 86. C Barrow St Mark *Carl* 85-89; C Cranham Park *Chelmsf* from 89. *226 Moor Lane, Upminster, Essex RM14 1HN* Upminster (04022) 21711

SAUNDERS, Ronald. b 37. ACP67 CertEd62 Columbia Univ MA82. Sarum Th Coll 69. **d** 68 **p** 70. Malawi 68-72; C Kensington St Mary Abbots w St Geo *Lon* 72-73; C Bournemouth St Fran *Win* 73-77; Canada 77-81; C Gt Marlow *Ox* 81-82; Area Org Leprosy Miss 82-85; V Penycae *St As* 85-87; TV Wrexham 87-88. *Address temp unknown*

SAUNT, James Peter Robert. b 36. Chich Th Coll 73. **d** 75 **p** 76. C Portland All SS w St Pet *Sarum* 75-78; P-in-c Bratton 78-81; V from 81; Chapl HM Young Offender Inst Erlestoke from 81. *The Vicarage, Bratton, Westbury, Wilts BA13 4SN* Bratton (0380) 830374

SAUSBY, John Michael. b 39. AKC. **d** 63 **p** 64. C Crosland Moor *Wakef* 63-65; C Halifax St Jo *Rapt* 65-67; V Birkby 67-77; V Holmfirth 77-89; TR Upper Holme Valley from 89. *2 Rosegarth Avenue, Newmill Road, Holmfirth, Huddersfield HD7 2TE* Holmfirth (0484) 683285

SAVAGE, Christopher Marius. b 46. Bps' Coll Cheshunt Qu Coll Birm 68. **d** 70 **p** 71. C Battersea St Luke *S'wark* 70-75; TV Newbury *Ox* 75-80; R Lich St Mary w St Mich *Lich* 80-85; V Chessington *Guildf* from 85. *The Vicarage, Garrison Lane, Chessington, Surrey KT9 2LB* 081-397 3016

SAVAGE, Leslie Walter. b 15. Cranmer Hall Dur 63. **d** 65 **p** 66. V Bolton w Cliburn *Carl* 69-74; V Holme-in-Cliviger *Blackb* 74-81; rtd 81; Perm to Offic *Chich* from 81. *42 Wilton Road, Bexhill-on-Sea, E Sussex TN40 1HX* Bexhill-on-Sea (0424) 223829

SAVAGE, Mark David John. b 55. Birm Univ BA76 Dur Univ BA82 Newc Univ MLitt83. Cranmer Hall Dur 80. **d** 83 **p** 84. C Newc St Gabr *Newc* 83-86; Adult Educn Adv from 86. *119 Brighton Grove, Newcastle upon Tyne NE4 5NT* 091-272 3019

SAVAGE, Michael Atkinson. b 33. St Pet Hall Ox BA57 MA61. Tyndale Hall Bris 57. **d** 59 **p** 60. C Rugby St Matt *Cov* 59-62; C Welling *Roch* 62-66; V Bowling St Steph *Bradf* 66-73; V Ben Rhydding from 73; RD Otley from 87. *The Vicarage, Ben Rhydding, Ilkley, W Yorkshire LS29 8PT* Ilkley (0943) 607363

SAVAGE, Paul James. b 58. Liv Univ BA81. Wycliffe Hall Ox 88. **d** 91. C Litherland St Phil *Liv* from 91. *3 Harrington Road, Litherland, Liverpool L21* 051-928 7879

SAVAGE, William Humphrey. b 15. Worc Ord Coll 63. **d** 65 **p** 66. V Thorverton *Ex* 68-73; V Cadbury 68-73; R Alphington 73-79; C Ex St Matt 79-80; C Ex St Sidwell and St Matt 80-84; rtd 84; Perm to Offic *Ex* from 84. *1A Welsford Avenue, Wells, Somerset BA5 2HX* Wells (0749) 75659

SAVIGE, John Sydney. b 24. Launde Abbey. **d** 73 **p** 74. C Leic St Pet *Leic* 73-75; P-in-c Harby 76-77; P-in-c Stathern 76-77; R Harby w Stathern 77-83; RD Framland I 80-88; R Harby, Long Clawson and Hose 83-89; rtd 89. *43 Kingston Way, Seaford, E Sussex BN25 4NG* Seaford (0323) 490572

SAVILE, Canon Ian Keith Wrey. b 26. Trin Hall Cam BA51 MA52. Ridley Hall Cam 51. **d** 53 **p** 54. C Bootle St Matt *Liv* 53-56; C Birkdale St Jo 56-57; V Barrow St Mark *Carl* 57-64; V Wandsworth All SS *S'wark* 64-74; RD Wandsworth 69-74; V S'well H Trin 74-81; V Canford Magna *Sarum* 81-88; TR 88; RD Wimborne 86-88; Can and Preb Sarum Cathl 86-88; Perm to Offic *Cov* from 88; Patr Sec CPAS from 88. *22 Whitefield Close, Coventry CV4 8GY* Coventry (0203) 462874

SAVILL, David. b 27. TD69 and Bar 75. Em Coll Cam BA49 MA52. Ridley Hall Cam 50. **d** 52 **p** 53. V Heston *Lon* 67-73; Hon C Mettingham w Ilketshall St John *St E* 73-79; Hon C Mettingham 79-80; Chapl Felixstowe Coll 80-90; rtd 90. *Sancroft, 210 Park View, Crewkerne, Somerset TA18 8JL* Crewkerne (0460) 77298

SAVILLE, David James. b 39. Ch Ch Ox BA60 MA64. Clifton Th Coll 61. **d** 63 **p** 64. C Guildf St Sav 63-66; C St Leonards St Leon *Chich* 66-68; Cand Sec CPAS 69-74; V Taunton St Jas *B & W* 74-80; RD Taunton N 78-80; V Chorleywood Ch St Alb 80-90; RD Rickmansworth 86-90; Adv for Evang Edmonton *Lon* from 91. *9 Twyford Avenue, London N2 9NU* 081-442 1442

SAVILLE, Edward Andrew. b 47. Leeds Univ CertEd70 Open Univ BA75. Carl Dioc Tr Inst. **d** 90. C Accrington

St Jo w Huncoat *Blackb* from 90. *21 Ambleside Close, Huncoat, Accrington, Lancs BB5 6HY* Blackburn (0254) 393994

SAVILLE, George Edward. b 15. **d** 42 **p** 43. V Ilkeston H Trin *Derby* 56-63; rtd 80. *Fernecumbe House, Kings Coughton, Alcester, Warks* Alcester (0789) 762960

SAVILLE, Jeremy David. b 35. Or Coll Ox BA59 MA62. Chich Th Coll 58. **d** 60 **p** 61. C Tynemouth Cullercoats St Paul *Newc* 60-63; C Hexham 63-65; Lic to Offic *Ox* 65-68; Chapl Cuddesdon Coll 65-68; R Holt *Nor* 68-73; P-in-c Kelling w Salthouse 68-71; R Edgefield 71-73; R Hoe 73-78; R E Dereham w Hoe 73-80; V E Dereham 80-81; R Scarning w Wendling 78-81; R Beckenham St Geo *Roch* 81-89; Hon Can Roch Cathl 86-89; R Ashdon w Hadstock *Chelmsf* from 89. *The Rectory, Ashdon, Saffron Walden, Essex CB10 2HP* Ashdon (079984) 897

SAVILLE-DEANE, Marcus. b 58. Imp Coll Lon BSc80. Wycliffe Hall Ox 83. **d** 87 **p** 88. C Spring Grove St Mary *Lon* from 87. *c/o The Bishop of Kensington, 19 Campden Hill Square, London W8 7JY*

SAVINS, Thomas George. b 13. Bris Univ BA36. St Boniface Warminster. **d** 38 **p** 39. V Halton in Hastings St Clem *Chich* 66-70; R Hastings St Clem and All SS 70-81; rtd 81; Perm to Offic *Chich* from 82. *33 Park Lane, Eastbourne, E Sussex BN21 2UY* Eastbourne (0323) 58983

SAWARD, Canon Michael John. b 32. Bris Univ BA55. Tyndale Hall Bris. **d** 56 **p** 57. C Croydon Ch Ch Broad Green *Cant* 56-59; C Edgware *Lon* 59-64; Sec Liv Coun of Chs 64-67; Radio and TV Officer CIO 67-72; Hon C Beckenham St Jo *Roch* 70-72; V Fulham St Matt *Lon* 72-78; V Ealing St Mary 78-91; AD Ealing E 79-84; Preb St Paul's Cathl 85-91; P-in-c Ealing St Paul 86-89; Can Res and Treas St Paul's Cathl from 91. *6 Amen Court, London EC4M 7BU* 071-248 8572

SAWLE, Martin. b 49. Solicitor 74 Dundee Univ LLB70. N Ord Course 87. **d** 90 **p** 91. NSM Longton *Blackb* from 90. *30 Fossdale Moss, Leyland, Preston, Lancs PR5 3WT* Preston (0772) 452936

SAWLE, Ralph Burford. b 14. Lich Th Coll 34. **d** 37 **p** 38. V St Giles on the Heath w Virginstow *Truro* 68-72; V Werrington 68-72; V St Neot 72-79; rtd 79; Perm to Offic *Win* from 79. *32 Cavendish Close, Romsey, Hants SO51 7HT* Romsey (0794) 516132

SAWLE, William John. b 16. Lon Univ BD39. Tyndale Hall Bris 34. **d** 39 **p** 40. V Leyland St Andr *Blackb* 57-81; rtd 81. *8 Queensdale Close, Walton-le-Dale, Preston PR5 4JU* Preston (0772) 821213

SAWREY, Harold. b 14. Edin Th Coll 58. **d** 60 **p** 61. R Orton All SS *Carl* 63-80; P-in-c Tebay 77-80; rtd 80; Perm to Offic *Carl* from 81. *8 Atkinson Court, Newby Bridge, Ulverston, Cumbria LA12 8NW* Newby Bridge (05395) 31314

SAWYER, Alfred. b 48. Univ of Georgia 71. Episc Th Sem Kentucky 78. **d** 78 **p** 79. C Finchley St Luke *Lon* 81-83; Israel from 83. *Christ Church, Jaffa Gate, PO Box 14037, Jerusalem, Israel* Jerusalem (2) 289234 or 282678

SAWYER, Andrew William. b 49. AKC71. St Aug Coll Cant 71. **d** 72 **p** 73. C Farnham *Guildf* 72-75; C Dawlish *Ex* 75-78; R Colkirk w Oxwick, Whissonsett and Horningtoft *Nor* 78-82; R Colkirk w Oxwick w Pattesley, Whissonsett etc 82-90; V Hungerford and Denford *Ox* from 90. *The Vicarage, Hungerford, Berks RG17 0JB* Hungerford (0488) 82844

SAWYER, Derek Claude. b 33. ALCD58. **d** 58 **p** 59. C Kirby Muxloe *Leic* 58-60; C Braunstone 60-65; Mauritius 65-68; V Knighton St Mich *Leic* 68-82; Chapl Kifissia *Eur* 82; Lic to Offic *Glouc* 85-87; V Glouc St Aldate from 87. *St Aldate's Vicarage, Finlay Road, Gloucester GL4 9TN* Gloucester (0452) 23906

SAWYERS, Thomas Adam Barton. b 21. **d** 61 **p** 62. I Lissan *Arm* 69-82; rtd 82. *82 Coleraine Road, Portrush, Co Antrim* Portrush (0265) 823441

SAXBEE, Preb John Charles. b 46. Bris Univ BA68. Cranmer Hall Dur DipTh69 PhD74. **d** 72 **p** 73. C Compton Gifford *Ex* 72-77; P-in-c Weston Mill 77-80; V 80-81; TV Cen Ex 81-87; Jt Dir SW Min Tr Course from 81; Preb Ex Cathl from 88. *32 Barnfield Road, Exeter EX1 1RX* Exeter (0392) 72091

SAXBY, Harold. b 11. St Chad's Coll Dur BA37 MA40. **d** 38 **p** 39. R Jarrow St Paul *Dur* 69-76; rtd 76; Hon C Wrington w Butcombe *B & W* 79-84. *The Post House, Ryme Intrinseca, Sherborne, Dorset DT9 6JX* Sherborne (0935) 872345

SAXBY, Martin Peter. b 52. St Jo Coll Dur BA77 DipTh78. Cranmer Hall Dur 74. **d** 78 **p** 79. C Peckham St Mary Magd *S'wark* 78-81; C Ramsey *Ely* 81-84; P-in-c Yaxham

Nor 84-89; P-in-c Welborne 84-89; P-in-c Mattishall w Mattishall Burgh 84-89; R Mattishall w Mattishall Burgh, Welborne etc 89-90; V Rugby St Matt *Cov* from 90. *St Matthew's Vicarage, 7 Vicarage Road, Rugby, Warks CV22 7AJ* Rugby (0788) 560572

SAXON, Miss Doreen Harold Graham. b 29. Qu Coll Birm 77. **dss** 80 **d** 87. Wolv *Lich* 86-87; Par Dn 87-89; rtd 89. *20 Chequerfield Drive, Penn Fields, Wolverhampton WV3 7DH* Wolverhampton (0902) 342432

SAXON, Canon Eric. b 14. Man Univ BA35 MA80 Lon Univ BD40. ALCD40. **d** 40 **p** 41. R Man St Ann *Man* 51-82; Chapl to HM The Queen 67-84; OStJ from 73; rtd 82; Perm to Offic *Ches* from 83. *27 Padstow Drive, Bramhall, Stockport, Cheshire SK7 2HU* 061-439 7233

SAXTON, James. b 54. Lanc Univ BEd77 Hull Univ MEd85. Linc Th Coll 84. **d** 86 **p** 87. C Moor Allerton *Ripon* 86-90; C Knaresborough from 90. *39 Birkdale Avenue, Knaresborough, N Yorkshire HG5 0LS* Harrogate (0423) 864484

✠**SAY, Rt Rev Richard David.** b 14. KCVO88. Ch Coll Cam BA38 MA41 Kent Univ Hon DCL87. Lambeth DD61 Ridley Hall Cam 38. **d** 40 **c** 61. C Croydon *Cant* 39-43; C St Martin-in-the-Fields *Lon* 43-50; Asst Sec C of E Youth Coun 42-44; Gen Sec 44-47; Gen Sec BCC 47-55; R Hatf *St Alb* 55-61; Hon Can St Alb 57-61; Bp Roch 61-88; ChStJ from 61; Ld High Almoner to HM The Queen 70-88; rtd 88; Asst Bp Cant from 88. *23 Chequers Park, Wye, Ashford, Kent TN25 5BB* Wye (0233) 812720

SAYER, Cecil Albert. b 12. Leeds Univ BA34. Coll of Resurr Mirfield 34. **d** 36 **p** 37. C-in-c Clifton All SS *Bris* 66-73; Asst Master Qu Eliz Gr Sch Ashbourne 73-77; rtd 77; Perm to Offic *Wakef* from 87. *58 Hope Bank, Honley, Huddersfield HD7 2PR*

SAYER, Derek John. b 32. St Steph Ho Ox 55. **d** 58 **p** 58. C Tottenham All Hallows *Lon* 58-61; C Letchworth *St Alb* 61-63; Chapl RADD 63-64 and 66-82; C Lancing St Mich *Chich* 64-66; C Dorking w Ranmore *Guildf* from 89. *79 Ashcombe Road, Dorking, Surrey RH4 1LX* Dorking (0306) 882065

SAYER, Harold John. b 15. CCC Cam BA36. **d** 67 **p** 68. C Churchdown St Jo *Glouc* 67-71; C-in-c Wapley w Codrington and Dodington *Bris* 71-73; R Highnam w Lassington and Rudford *Glouc* 73-81; rtd 81; Perm to Offic *Glouc* from 81; *Ox* from 83. *27 Woolstrop Way, Quedgeley, Gloucester GL2 6NL* Gloucester (0452) 502091

SAYER, John Martin. b 35. Bris Univ BA57. Clifton Th Coll 59. **d** 61 **p** 62. C Hamworthy *Sarum* 61-64; Area Sec (N England, Glas, Edin and S & M) CMJ 64-66; Canada 66-78; USA from 78. *Box 968, Grapeland, Texas 75844, USA*

SAYER, William Anthony John. b 37. St Mich Coll Llan 60. **d** 64 **p** 65. C Gorleston St Andr *Nor* 64-67; P-in-c Witton w Ridlington 67-71; P-in-c Honing w Crostwight 67-71; V Bacton w Edingthorpe 67-71; CF 71-84; Miss to Seamen from 84; R Holkham w Egmere w Warham, Wells and Wighton *Nor* from 84; RD Burnham and Walsingham from 87. *The Rectory, Wells-next-the-Sea, Norfolk NR23 1JB* Fakenham (0328) 710107

SAYERS, Guy Anthony. b 10. Ex Coll Ox BA35 MA37. Ely Th Coll 34. **d** 36 **p** 37. R Empingham *Pet* 68-81; rtd 81; Perm to Offic *Pet* from 82. *57 Radcliffe Road, Stamford, Lincs PE9 1AU* Stamford (0780) 55191

SAYERS, Simon Philip. b 59. Cam Univ MA81. Oak Hill Th Coll 83. **d** 85 **p** 86. C Alperton *Lon* 85-89; C Hornsey Rise Whitehall Park Team 89-90; TV from 90. *43 Dresden Road, London N19 3BG* 071-281 8775

SAYWELL, Philip. b 33. Linc Th Coll 58. **d** 60 **p** 61. C Stepney St Dunstan and All SS *Lon* 60-63; C Calstock *Truro* 63-66; V Lanteglos by Fowey 66-73; Iran 73-77; R Cockley Cley w Gooderstone *Nor* 78-81; V Didlington 78-81; R Gt and Lt Cressingham w Threxton 78-81; R Hilborough w Bodney 78-81; R Oxborough w Foulden and Caldecote 78-81; UAE 81-84; Perm to Offic *Chich* 84-88. *Little Ashott, Exford, Minehead, Somerset TA24 7NG* Exford (064383) 619

SCAIFE, Andrew. b 50. Ex Coll Ox BA73 MA76. Wycliffe Hall Ox. **d** 77 **p** 78. C Everton St Geo *Liv* 77-81; P-in-c Liv St Mich 81; TV St Luke in the City 81-86; V Litherland St Phil from 86. *St Philip's Vicarage, Orrell Road, Litherland, Liverpool L21 8NG* 051-928 3902

SCALES, Barbara Marion. b 24. S'wark Ord Course. **dss** 82 **d** 87. St Helier *S'wark* 82-87; Hon Par Dn 87-89; Chapl Asst St Helier's Hosp Carshalton 82-88; Par Dn Cheam Common St Phil *S'wark* from 89. *51 Tonfield Road, Sutton, Surrey SM3 9JP* 081-644 3712

SCAMMELL, Frank. b 56. Cam Univ MA. St Jo Coll Nottm BA83. **d** 82 **p** 83. C Stapenhill w Cauldwell *Derby*

82-86; TV Swanage and Studland *Sarum* from 86. *The Vicarage, Studland, Swanage, Dorset BH19 3AJ* Studland (092944) 441

SCAMMELL, Canon John James Frank. b 07. AKC32. St Paul's Coll Burgh 32. **d** 32 **p** 33. V Leighton Buzzard *St Alb* 54-80; V Eggington 54-80; P-in-c Billington 65-80; rtd 80; Perm to Offic *St Alb* from 80. *49 Heath Court, Plantation Road, Leighton Buzzard LU7 7JR* Leighton Buzzard (0525) 381380

SCAMMELL, John Richard Lyn. b 18. TD50. Bris Univ LLB45. Wycliffe Hall Ox 46. **d** 48 **p** 49. RAChD 53-73; P-in-c Bicknoller *B & W* 73-78; P-in-c Crowcombe 55-78; R Bicknoller w Crowcombe and Sampford Brett 78-81; rtd 83; Perm to Offic *Guildf* from 84. *4 Pine Ridge Drive, Lower Bourne, Farnham, Surrey GU10 3JW* Farnham (0252) 713100

SCANDINAVIA, Archdeacon of. See BROWN, Ven Gerald Arthur Charles

SCANLON, Geoffrey Edward Leyshon. b 44. Coll of Resurr Mirfield. **d** 76 **p** 77. C Beamish *Dur* 76-79; C-in-c Bishopwearmouth St Mary V w St Pet CD 79-81; USA from 81. *1226 North Vermilion, Danville, Illinois 61832, USA* Illinois (217) 442-1677

SCARBOROUGH, John Richard Derek. b 32. Lon Univ BA54. Cuddesdon Coll. **d** 69 **p** 70. C Fulbeck *Linc* 69-72; C Bassingham 73-74; Lic to Offic 74-76 and from 78; R Boothby Graffoe 76-77; R Navenby 76-77; V Wellingore w Temple Bruer 76-77; V Graffoe 77-78. *Hales Cottage, 47 High Street, Navenby, Lincoln LN5 0DZ* Lincoln (0522) 811031

SCARGILL, Christopher Morris. b 57. UEA BA79 York Univ MA81 Leeds Univ CertEd81 Nottm Univ BTh89. Linc Th Coll 86. **d** 89 **p** 90. C Desborough *Pet* from 89. *5 Cromwell Close, Desborough, Northants NN14 2PJ* Kettering (0536) 761809

SCARTH, John Robert. b 34. Leeds Univ BSc55 CertEd St Jo Coll Dur DipTh65. Cranmer Hall Dur 63. **d** 65 **p** 66. C Dewsbury All SS *Wakef* 65-68; V Shepley 68-72; Asst Master Kingston-upon-Hull Gr Sch 72-78; St Mary's C of E Sch Hendon 78-81; V Ossett cum Gawthorpe 81-88; R Tarrington w Stoke Edith, Aylton, Pixley etc *Heref* from 88. *The Rectory, Tarrington, Hereford HR1 4EU* Hereford (0432) 890314

SCARTH, Maurice John. b 31. MInstPS. St Deiniol's Hawarden 81. **d** 83 **p** 84. C Llandrillo-yn-Rhos *St As* 83-87; V Rhosymedre from 87. *The Vicarage, Church Street, Rhosymedre, Wrexham, Clwyd LL14 3EA* Ruabon (0978) 810125

SCATTERGOOD, William Henry. b 26. **d** 56 **p** 57. Australia 56-84; V Lonan *S & M* from 84; V Laxey from 84. *The New Vicarage, South Cape, Laxey, Isle of Man* Laxey (0624) 781666

SCEATS, David Douglas. b 46. Ch Coll Cam BA68 MA72 Bris Univ MA71. Clifton Th Coll 68. **d** 71 **p** 72. C Cam St Paul *Ely* 71-74; Lect Trin Coll Bris 74-83; V Shenstone *Lich* 83-86; Dioc Tr Officer 86-91; P-in-c Colton 86-90; Dioc Dir of Local Min Development from 91; Warden of Readers from 91. *Diocesan Local Ministry Office, The Old Registry, The Close, Lichfield WS13 7LD* Lichfield (0543) 254435

SCHARF, Ulrich Eduard Erich Julian. b 35. Melbourne Univ BA59 MA67 Linacre Coll Ox BA67 MA72 Lon Univ PhD81. Ripon Hall Ox 65. **d** 67 **p** 68. C Hackney St Jo *Lon* 68-71; Lic to Offic 71-75; Chapl to Bp Stepney 71-75; P-in-c Shadwell St Paul w Ratcliffe St Jas 75-90; R St-Geo-in-the-East w St Paul 79-86; P-in-c W Ham *Chelmsf* from 90. *The Vicarage, Devenay Road, London E15 4AZ* 081-519 0955

SCHAUFELBERGER, Johan Henry. b 16. Lon Univ BA38. Coll of Resurr Mirfield 38. **d** 40 **p** 41. V Wantage *Ox* 61-83; rtd 84. *The Vicarage, Kennington, Oxford OX1 5PG*

SCHERFF, Gijsbertus. b 47. Ridley Hall Cam 85. **d** 87 **p** 88. C Luton Ch Ch *Roch* 87-89; CMS from 89; Syria from 89. *c/o Church of the Redeemer, PO Box 598, Amman, Jordan*

SCHIBILD, Nigel Edmund David Shields. b 47. BA81. Oak Hill Th Coll 78. **d** 81 **p** 82. C Eccleston Ch Ch *Liv* 81-85; P-in-c Sydenham H Trin *S'wark* 85-87; V from 87; Asst Chapl Mildmay Miss Hosp from 91. *Holy Trinity Vicarage, 1 Sydenham Park Road, London SE26 4DY* 081-699 5303

SCHIFF, Canon Leonard Maro. b 08. Ex Coll Ox BA29 MA34. Westcott Ho Cam 32. **d** 32 **p** 33. Chapl to Overseas Peoples *Birm* 69-75; Hon Can Birm Cathl 69-75; Chapl Aston Univ 72-75; rtd 75; Perm to Offic *Carl* from 77. *9 Hoad Terrace, Ulverston, Cumbria LA12 7AS* Ulverston (0229) 57032

SCHOFIELD, Andrew Thomas. b 47. K Coll L...
BD70 AKC71 PGCE72. St Aug Coll Cant 70. **d** 81 **p** 82.
C Whittlesey *Ely* 81-84; C Ramsey 84-87; P-in-c Ellington
from 87; P-in-c Grafham from 87; P-in-c Spaldwick w
Barham and Woolley from 87; P-in-c Easton from 87.
*The Vicarage, Parsons Drive, Ellington, Huntingdon,
Cambs PE18 0AU* Huntingdon (0480) 890485

SCHOFIELD, David. b 43. Linc Th Coll 74. **d** 75 **p** 76. C
Gainsborough All SS *Linc* 75-78; R Bolingbroke w
Hareby 78-79; P-in-c Hagnaby 78-79; P-in-c
Hagworthingham w Asgarby and Lusby 78-79; P-in-c
Mavis Enderby w Raithby 78-79; P-in-c E Kirkby w
Miningsby 78-79; R Bolingbroke 79-81; C-in-c Stamford
Ch Ch CD 81-90; V Crowle from 90. *The Vicarage,
Crowle, Scunthorpe DN17 4LE* Scunthorpe (0724)
710268

SCHOFIELD, Edward Denis. b 20. **d** 61 **p** 62. V Boughton
under Blean *Cant* 66-75; P-in-c Dunkirk 73-75; V
Boughton under Blean w Dunkirk 75-76; V Sandgate
St Paul 76-85; rtd 85. *58 Fruitlands, Malvern, Worcs
WR14 4XA* Malvern (0684) 567252

SCHOFIELD, John Martin. b 47. Selw Coll Cam
BA69 MA73. St Steph Ho Ox 70. **d** 72 **p** 73. C Palmers
Green St Jo *Lon* 72-75; C Friern Barnet St Jas 75-80; V
Luton St Aug Limbury *St Alb* 80-89; V Biddenham from
89; Dir Continuing Minl Educn from 89. *The Vicarage,
57 Church End, Biddenham, Bedford MK40 4AS*
Bedford (0234) 54433

SCHOFIELD, John Verity. b 29. Jes Coll Ox
BA52 DipTh53 MA56. Cuddesdon Coll 53. **d** 55 **p** 56. C
Cirencester *Glouc* 55-59; R Stella *Dur* 59-67; Kenya
67-69; Asst Chapl St Paul's Sch Barnes 69-70; Chapl
71-80; Australia 81-83; Gen Sec Friends of Elderly &
Gentlefolk's Help from 83. *42 Ebury Street, London
SW1W 0LZ* 071-730 1458

SCHOFIELD, Nigel Timothy. b 54. FRCO Dur Univ
BA76 Nottm Univ BCombStuds83. Linc Th Coll 80.
d 83 **p** 84. C Cheshunt *St Alb* 83-86; TV Colyton,
Southleigh, Offwell, Widworthy etc *Ex* from 86. *The
Rectory, Offwell, Honiton, Devon EX14 9SB*
Wilmington (040483) 480

SCHOFIELD, Richard Wyndham. b 09. Or Coll Ox
BA32 MA38. Ripon Hall Ox 36. **d** 37 **p** 38. R
Grundisburgh w Burgh *St E* 58-82; rtd 82; Perm to Offic
St E from 82. *5 Constable Road, Ipswich* Ipswich (0473)
56340

SCHOFIELD, Preb Rodney. b 44. St Jo Coll Cam
BA64 MA67 St Pet Hall Ox BA70 MA73. St Steph Ho
Ox 68. **d** 71 **p** 72. C Northn St Mary *Pet* 71-76; V
Irchester 76-84; Lesotho 84-86; R W Monkton *B & W*
from 86; Asst Dir of Ords 87-89; Dir of Ords from 89;
Preb Wells Cathl from 90. *The Rectory, West Monkton,
Taunton, Somerset TA2 8QT* West Monkton (0823)
412226

SCHOLEFIELD, John. b 27. Leeds Univ BSc50. Wells
Th Coll 51. **d** 53 **p** 54. C Ossett cum Gawthorpe *Wakef*
53-56; C Hebden Bridge 56-58; V Sowerby St Geo 58-64;
V Darton 64-70; V Stoke Gabriel *Ex* 70-84; P-in-c
Collaton St Mary 82-84; V Stoke Gabriel and Collaton
St Mary from 84. *The Vicarage, Stoke Gabriel, Totnes,
Devon TQ9 6QX* Stoke Gabriel (080428) 307

SCHOLER, Douglas William. b 23. Chich Th Coll 47. **d** 50
p 51. V W Pennard w W Bradley *B & W* 70-81; P-in-c
Bleadon 81-82; R 82-87; rtd 87. *Rose Cottage, Middle
Road, Cossington, Bridgwater, Somerset TA7 8LH*
Bridgwater (0278) 722778

SCHOLEY, Donald. b 38. Leeds Univ CertEd60. Lich Th
Coll 69. **d** 72 **p** 73. C Blaby *Leic* 72-75; TV Daventry w
Norton *Pet* 75-78; R Wootton w Quinton and Preston
Deanery from 78. *The Rectory, Water Lane, Wootton,
Northampton NN4 0LG* Northampton (0604) 761891

SCHOLFIELD, Peter. b 35. Sarum Th Coll 64. **d** 66 **p** 67.
P-in-c Carlton *Wakef* 69-90; rtd 90. *31 Springhill Avenue,
Crofton, Wakefield, W Yorkshire* Wakefield (0924)
863430

SCHUNEMANN, Bernhard ... Down Coll Cam BA49 MA
Lon BD86 AKC86. Ripon Coll C... MD67. Oak Hill NSM
C Kirkby *Liv* from 90. *14 Wingate Road,* ... Ch S'wark
Liverpool L33 6UQ 051-546 1504 ... CR0 6XF ... Coll

SCHWABACHER, Kurt Frederick. b 12. Chich Th Coll
36. **d** 39 **p** 40. V Forest Hill St Paul *S'wark* 63-68; Perm
to Offic *Roch* from 68; rtd 77. *1 Raleigh Court, 21A The
Avenue, Beckenham, Kent BR3 2DL* 081-650 8670

SCLATER, John Edward. b 46. Nottm Univ BA68 St Edm
Hall Ox CertEd71. Cuddesdon Coll 69. **d** 71 **p** 72. C
Bris St Mary Redcliffe w Temple etc *Bris* 71-75; Chapl
Bede Ho Staplehurst 75-79; Chapl Warw Sch 79; P-in-c
Offchurch *Cov* 79-80; Belgium 81-89; Willen Priory
89-91; C Linslade *Ox* from 91. *75 Grange Close, Leighton
Buzzard, Beds LU7 7PP* Leighton Buzzard (0525)
383082

SCOBIE, Geoffrey Edward Winsor. b 39. AFBPsS Bris
Univ BSc62 MSc68 Birm Univ MA70 Glas Univ PhD78.
Tyndale Hall Bris 62. **d** 65 **p** 66. C Summerfield *Birm*
65-66; C Moseley St Anne 66-67; Lect Psychology Glas
Univ from 67; Hon C Glas St Silas *Glas* 70-83; P-in-c
83-84; Hon R 84-85; TR 85-86; Team Chapl 86-88; Asst
Team Chapl from 88. *3 Norfolk Crescent, Bishopbriggs,
Glasgow G64 3BA* 041-722 2907

SCOONES, Roger Philip. b 48. DipTh. Trin Coll Bris.
d 82 **p** 83. C Childwall All SS *Liv* 82-85; Bradf Cathl
Bradf 85-90; V Congleton St Pet *Ches* from 90. *St Peter's
Vicarage, Chapel Street, Congleton, Cheshire CW12 4AB*
Congleton (0260) 273212

SCORER, John Robson. b 47. Westcott Ho Cam 73. **d** 75
p 76. C Silksworth *Dur* 75-78; C Newton Aycliffe 78-82;
V Sherburn 82-83; V Sherburn w Pittington 83-89; P-in-c
Croxdale from 89; Chapl to Dur Police from 89.
*The Rectory, Sunderland Bridge, Croxdale, Durham
DH6 5HB* 091-378 0273

SCOTLAND, Nigel Adrian Douglas. b 42. McGill Univ
Montreal MA71 Aber Univ PhD75 CertEd75 Bris Univ
MLitt. Gordon-Conwell Th Sem MDiv70 Lon Coll of
Div ALCD66 LTh74. **d** 66 **p** 67. C Harold Wood *Chelmsf*
66-69; USA 69-70; Canada 70-72; Lic to Offic *Ab* 72-75;
Chapl and Lect St Mary's Coll Cheltenham 75-79; Sen
Lect 77-79; Chapl and Sen Lect Coll of SS Paul and
Mary 79-84; NSM Cheltenham St Mark *Glouc* from 85;
Sen Lect Chelt & Glouc Coll of HE from 89. *67 Hall
Road, Leckhampton, Cheltenham GL53 0HP*
Cheltenham (0242) 529167

SCOTLAND, Primus of the Episcopal Church in. *See*
HENDERSON, Most Rev George Kennedy Buchanan

SCOTT, Adam. b 47. TD78. Barrister 72 CEng81 MIEE81
Ch Ch Ox BA68 MA72 City Univ MSc79. S'wark Ord
Course 73. **d** 75 **p** 76. NSM Blackheath Park St Mich
S'wark from 75; Dean for MSE, Woolwich from 90.
19 Blackheath Park, London SE3 9RW 081-852 3286

SCOTT, Alfred Thomas. b 19. St Steph Ho Ox 78. **d** 81
p 82. NSM S Ascot *Ox* 81-85; NSM Bridport *Sarum*
85-89; Perm to Offic 89-90; rtd 90. *22 Castle Hill Court,
Cross Lane, Bodmin, Cornwall PL31 2DY*

SCOTT, Preb Allan George. b 39. Man Univ BA61. Coll
of Resurr Mirfield 61. **d** 63 **p** 64. C Bradf cum Beswick
Man 63-66; P-in-c 66-72; Hon C Bramhall *Ches* 72-74;
Hon C Tottenham St Jo *Lon* 74-76; Hon C Bush Hill
Park St Steph 76-79; R Stoke Newington St Mary from
79; Preb St Paul's Cathl from 91. *The Rectory, Stoke
Newington Church Street, London N16 9ES* 071-254
6072

SCOTT, Andrew Charles Graham. b 28. Mert Coll Ox
BA57 MA. Wells Th Coll 57. **d** 59 **p** 60. C Rugby St
Andr *Cov* 59-64; Chapl RN 64-68; C Prenton *Ches*
68-71; V Tow Law *Dur* 71-81; RD Stanhope 77-81; V
Bampton w Clanfield *Ox* from 81. *5 Deanery Court,
Broad Street, Bampton, Oxford OX8 2LY* Bampton
Castle (0993) 851222

SCOTT, Basil John Morley. b 34. Qu Coll
BA59 Banaras Hindu Univ MA65. Ridley Hall C
d 60 p 61. C Woking St Pet Guildf 60-63; In
TR Kirby Muxloe Leic 83-89; Asian Outr...
(Leicester Martyrs) from 89. 16 Eastleigh... Carl
LE3 0DB Leicester (0533) 542476
SCOTT, Bernard de Sausmarez. b ..., Perm to Offic
BA12 MA55. Ely Th Coll 12. Queens 7-in-c Theddingworth
58-64; rtd 65. 61 Queens 7-in-c Theddingworth
Dorchester (0305) 26644Asst Chapl Oundle Sch Pet
SCOTT, Brian. b 35. and Wakerley w S Luffenham Pet
Mirfield 59. d 61 and Wakerley w S Luffenham Pet
61-62; Asst M Rectory, Barrowden, Oakham, Leics
Leic 65-62... Morcott (057287) 248
71-78... Morcott (057287) 248

SCOTT, Charles Geoffrey. b 32. St Jo Coll Cam
BA54 MA58. Cuddesdon Coll 56. d 58 p 59. C Brighouse
Wakef 58-61; C Bathwick w Woolley B & W 61-64; V
Frome Ch Ch 64-78; R Winchelsea Chich from 78.
The Rectory, St Thomas Street, Winchelsea, E Sussex
TN36 4EB Rye (0797) 226254

SCOTT, Christopher John Fairfax. b 45. Magd Coll Cam
BA67 MA71. Westcott Ho Cam 68. d 70 p 71. C Nor St
Pet Mancroft Nor 70-73; Chapl Magd Coll Cam 73-79;
V Hampstead Ch Ch Lon from 79. Christ Church
Vicarage, 10 Cannon Place, London NW3 1EJ 071-435
6784

SCOTT, Christopher Michael. b 44. SS Coll Cam
BA66 MA70. Cuddesdon Coll 66. d 68 p 69. C New
Addington Cant 68-73; C Westmr St Steph w St Jo Lon
73-78; V Enfield St Mich 78-81; V Effingham w Lt
Bookham Guildf 81-87; R Esher from 87; RD Emly
from 91. The Rectory, Esher Place Avenue, Esher,
Surrey KT10 8PY Esher (0372) 462611

SCOTT, Christopher Stuart. b 48. Sarum & Wells Th Coll
79. d 81 p 82. C Enfield Chase St Mary Lon 81-82; C
Coalbrookdale, Iron-Bridge and Lt Wenlock Heref
82-86; P-in-c Breinton 86-89; Chapl Hickeys Alms
Houses Richmond from 89. Hickeys Alms Houses,
164 Sheen Road, Richmond, Surrey TW9 1XD 081-940
6568

SCOTT, Clifford Wentworth. b 04. Lon Univ BSc25.
Ridley Hall Cam 25. d 27 p 28. R Sapcote Leic 64-72;
rtd 72. 4 Egerton Road, Padstow, Cornwall PL28 8DJ
Padstow (0841) 532649

SCOTT, Colin. b 32. Dur Univ BA54. Coll of Resurr
Mirfield 58. d 60 p 61. C Wallsend St Pet Newc 60-64; C
Seaton Hirst 64-68; C Longbenton St Bart 68-70; V
Benwell St Aid 70-77; V Sleekburn 77-89; P-in-c
Cambois 77-88; V Longhoughton w Howick from 89. The
Vicarage, 3 South End, Longhoughton, Alnwick, Northd
NE66 3AW Longhoughton (0665) 577305

✠SCOTT, Rt Rev Colin John Fraser. b 33. Qu Coll Cam
BA56 MA60. Ridley Hall Cam 56. d 58 p 59 c 84. C
Clapham Common St Barn S'wark 58-61; C Hatcham St
Jas 61-64; V Kennington St Mark 64-71; RD Lambeth
68-71; Vice-Chmn Dioc Past Cttee 71-77; Hon Can
S'wark Cathl 73-84; TR Sanderstead All SS 77-84; Suff
Bp Hulme Man from 84. 1 Raynham Avenue, Didsbury,
Manchester M20 0BW 061-445 5922

SCOTT, Cuthbert Le Messurier. b 13. Wells Th Coll 60.
d 61 p 62. V Paddington St Jo w St Mich Lon 64-72; V
Shamley Green Guildf 72-83; rtd 83; Perm to Offic
Chich from 84; Chapl St Dunstans from 88. Flat 10,
6 Sussex Square, Brighton, Sussex BN2 1FJ Brighton
(0273) 689832

SCOTT, Ven David. b 24. Trin Hall Cam BA50 MA54.
Cuddesdon Coll 50. d 52 p 53. V Boston Linc 66-75;
Can and Preb Linc Cathl 71-89; RD Holland E 71-75;
Adn Stow 75-89; V Hackthorn w Cold Hanworth 75-89;
P-in-c N w S Carlton 78-89; Chapl to HM The Queen
from 84; rtd 89. 4 Honing Drive, Southwell, Notts
NG25 0LB Southwell (0636) 813900

SCOTT, David Lamplough. b 21. Selw Coll Cam
BA42 MA48. Ripon Hall Ox 42. d 44 p 45. R Rippingale
Linc 55-74; R Dunsby w Dowsby 63-74; V Hale Liv
74-86; rtd 86. 8 Langwith Drive, Holbeach, Spalding,
Lincs PE12 7HQ Holbeach (0406) 25268

SCOTT, David Lloyd Thomas. b 31. FCA Jes Coll Cam
BA76 MA80. Ridley Hall Cam 73. d 76 p 77. C Swindon
Ch Ch Bris 76-79; R Ripple Worc 79-82; V Broadheath,
Crown E and Rushwick 82-88; V Lenton S'well from 88.
The Vicarage, 35A Church Street, Nottingham NG7 2FH
Nottingham (0602) 701059

SCOTT, David Victor. b 47. St Chad's Coll Dur BA69.
Cuddesdon Coll 69. d 71 p 72. C St Mary-at-Latton

b 12. Linc Th Coll 76. d 76 p 76.
...ombwell Sheff 76-90; rtd 90. 17 Wood Walk,
...ombwell, Barnsley, S Yorkshire S73 0LZ Barnsley
(0226) 753020

SCOTT, Canon Eric Walter. b 16. St Jo Coll Cam
BA38 MA43. Ridley Hall Cam 38. d 40 p 41. C Reading
St Jo Ox 40-43; C Cam H Trin Ely 43-45; C-in-c Tilehurst
St Mary CD Ox 45-49; V Brimpton w Wasing 49-53;
Canada 53-87 and 89-90; Perm to Offic Nor 87-89.
4 Allen Court, Hauxton Road, Trumpington, Cambridge
CB2 2LU Cambridge (0223) 841015

SCOTT, Gary James. b 61. Edin Univ BD87. Edin Th
Coll 85. d 87 p 88. C Edin St Cuth Edin 87-90; R Peebles
from 90. St Peter's Rectory, 36 Wemyss Place, Peebles
EH45 8JT Peebles (0721) 20571

SCOTT, Canon Gordon. b 30. Man Univ BA51. St Jo
Coll Dur 51. d 53 p 54. C Monkwearmouth St Andr Dur
53-55; C Stranton 55-56; C Ches le Street 56-59; V
Marley Hill 59-62; Chapl Forest Sch Snaresbrook 62-66;
Chapl Dunrobin Sch Sutherland 66-72; Chapl
Pocklington Sch York 72-74; V Barton w Pooley Bridge
Carl 74-80; RD Penrith 79-82; P-in-c Lazonby 80; R Gt
Salkeld w Lazonby 80-90; Hon Can Carl Cathl from 83;
P-in-c Patterdale from 90. The Rectory, Patterdale,
Penrith, Cumbria CA11 0NL Glenridding (08532) 209

SCOTT, Harold James. b 05. Dur Univ LTh30. St Aug
Coll Cant 26. d 30 p 31. V Swavesey Ely 61-71; rtd 71.
44 Partridge Drive, Bar Hill, Cambridge CB3 8EN
Crafts Hill (0954) 780242

SCOTT, Hedley. b 36. Coll of Resurr Mirfield 68. d 70
p 71. C High Elswick St Phil Newc 70-73; C Sleekburn
73-76; V Shilbottle 76-82; V Scotswood from 82. St
Margaret's Vicarage, 14 Heighley Street, Newcastle upon
Tyne NE15 6AR 091-274 6322

SCOTT, Ian Michael. b 25. Bris Univ BA50 Leic Univ
DipEd51. Bps' Coll Cheshunt 52. d 53 p 54. C
Rotherhithe St Mary w All SS S'wark 53-55; C Lavender
Hill Ascension 55-59; C Camberwell St Mich w All So
w Em 59-60; C Kettering St Mary Pet 60-63; V
Haverstock Hill H Trin w Kentish Town St Barn Lon
from 63. Holy Trinity Vicarage, 70 Haverstock Hill,
London NW3 2BE 071-485 3791

SCOTT, Mrs Inez Margaret Gillette. b 26. St Alb Minl Tr
Scheme 76. dss 79 d 87. Preston w Sutton Poyntz and
Osmington w Poxwell Sarum 83-86; Dorchester 86-87;
Par Dn 87-88; NSM from 88; rtd 88. 14 Came View
Road, Dorchester, Dorset DT1 2AE Dorchester (0305)
267547

SCOTT, James Alexander Gilchrist. b 32. Linc Coll Ox
BA56 DipTh57 MA60. Wycliffe Hall Ox 56. d 58 p 59.
C Shipley St Paul Bradf 58-61; Abp's Dom Chapl York
61-65; Brazil 65-68; V Grassendale Liv 68-77; V Thorp
Arch York 77; P-in-c Walton 77; V Thorp Arch w
Walton 77-89; Chapl HM Pris Rudgate 77-82; Askham
Grange 82-87; RD Tadcaster 78-86; V Kirk Ella from
89. The Vicarage, School Lane, Kirk Ella, Hull
HU10 7NR Hull (0482) 653040

SCOTT, James McIntosh. b 12. Hertf Coll Ox BA34 MA38.
Wycliffe Hall Ox 34. d 37 p 38. V Disley Ches 66-77; rtd
77. 23 College Road, Buxton, Derbyshire Buxton (0298)
77824

SCOTT, James William. b 39. S Dios Minl Tr Scheme 84.
d 88 p 89. NSM Bremhill w Foxham and Hilmarton
Sarum from 88. 14 Bremhill, Calne, Wilts SN11 9LA
Calne (0249) 813114

SCOTT, John. b 54. QUB BD79. CITC 80. d 81 p 82. C
Willowfield D & D 81-83; C Newtownards 83-85; I
Kilskeery w Trillick Clogh 85-90; rtd 90; Lic to Offic
D & D from 90. 60 Lismore Road, Ardglass, Co Down
BT30 7SY Downpatrick (0396) 841958

SCOTT, John David. b 52. St Jo Coll Ox BA74 MA78
Leeds Univ BA78. Coll of Resurr Mirfield 76. d 78 p 79.
C Oundle Pet 78-81; C Dalston H Trin w St Phil Lon
81-85; V Ponders End St Matt from 85. St Matthew's
House, Church Road, Enfield, Middx EN3 4NT 081-443
2255

SCOTT, John Eric. b 16. FSA St Cath Coll Ox
BA38 MA42. Ripon Hall Ox 39. d 40 p 41. Ho Master
Forest Sch Snaresbrook 55-81; P-in-c St Mich Cornhill
w St Pet le Poer etc Lon 81-85; rtd 85. 17 Harman
Avenue, Woodford Green, Essex IG8 9DS 081-505
7093

SCOTT, John Gabriel. b 16. OBE68. St Chad's Coll Dur LTh45. St Aug Coll Cant 39. **d** 44 **p** 45. Chapl RN 46-71 and 74-75; QHC 68-71; R Hindon w Chicklade w Pertwood *Sarum* 71-73; C Widley w Wymering *Portsm* 76-81; rtd 81; Perm to Offic *Portsm* from 82. *278 Northern Parade, Hilsea, Portsmouth PO2 9RD* Portsmouth (0705) 690377

SCOTT, Preb John Gilbert Mortimer. b 25. St Edm Hall Ox BA49 MA52. Bps' Coll Cheshunt. **d** 51 **p** 52. C Ex St Thos *Ex* 51-54; C Wolborough w Newton Abbot 54-58; V Clawton 58-66; R Tetcott w Luffincott 58-66; RD Holsworthy 65-66; V Newton St Cyres 66-84; RD Cadbury 81-84; Preb Ex Cathl from 84; P-in-c Bampton 84; P-in-c Clayhanger 84; P-in-c Petton 84; V Bampton, Morebath, Clayhanger and Petton from 84. *The Vicarage, Bampton, Tiverton, Devon EX16 9NG* Bampton (0398) 331385

SCOTT, John Harold. b 46. Univ of Wales (Cardiff) BSc69. St Steph Ho Ox 69. **d** 72 **p** 73. C Skewen *Llan* 72-74; C Port Talbot St Theodore 74-77; P-in-c Bedlinog 77-78; V 78-85; R Penderin w Ystradfellte and Pontneathvaughan *S & B* from 85. *The Vicarage, Ystradfellte, Aberdare, M Glam CF44 9JE* Glyn Neath (0639) 720405

SCOTT, John Peter. b 47. Open Univ BA80. Lambeth STh81 K Coll Lon 69 St Aug Coll Cant 74. **d** 75 **p** 76. C Dartford St Alb *Roch* 75-78; C-in-c Goring-by-Sea *Chich* 78-81; Chapl Wells and Meare Manor Hosps 81-86; CF (TAVR) 82-90; Chapl Pangbourne Coll Berks 86-90; C-in-c Reigate St Phil CD *S'wark* 90; Min from 90; Chapl St Bede's Ecum Sch Redhill from 90. *The Parsonage, 102A Nutley Lane, Reigate, Surrey RH2 9HA* Reigate (0737) 244542

SCOTT, Keith Brounton de Salve. b 55. **d** 83 **p** 84. C Belf St Matt *Conn* 83-87; I Ardclinis and Tickmacrevan w Layde and Cushendun from 87. *76 Largy Road, Carnlough, Ballymena, Co Antrim BT44 0JJ* Carnlough (0574) 885618

SCOTT, Kenneth James. b 46. Bris Univ BA68. Trin Coll Bris 71. **d** 73 **p** 74. C Illogan *Truro* 73-76; C Camberley St Paul *Guildf* 76-81; R Bradf Peverell, Stratton, Frampton etc *Sarum* from 81. *The Rectory, Frampton, Dorchester, Dorset DT2 9NL* Maiden Newton (0300) 20429

SCOTT, Kevin Francis. b 51. GRSC Peterho Cam MA Mert Coll Ox DPhil. Wycliffe Hall Ox. **d** 83 **p** 84. C Ox St Ebbe w H Trin and St Pet *Ox* 83-86; P-in-c Prestonpans *Edin* from 86; R Musselburgh from 86. *The Rectory, 12 Windsor Gardens, Musselburgh, Midlothian EH21 7LP* 031-665 2925

SCOTT, Canon Malcolm Kenneth Merrett. b 30. ACA53 FCA64. Clifton Th Coll. **d** 58 **p** 59. C Plymouth St Gabr Th Ch *Lon* 58-60; CMS 60-61; Uganda 61-74; V Sunnyside w Bourne End *St Alb* 74-90; V Clapham from 90. *The Vicarage, Green Lane, Clapham, Bedford MK41 6ER* Bedford (0234) 52814

SCOTT, Michael Bernard Campion. b 29. Or Coll Ox BA52 MA56 DTh. Edin Th Coll 52. **d** 54 **p** 55. C Reading St Mary V *Ox* 66-72; C-in-c Reading St Mark CD 72-76; C-in-c Orton Malborne CD *Ely* 76-91; Chapl Glouc Cen for Mentally Handicapped Orton 77-91; rtd 91. *13 Mill Street, Puddletown, Dorchester, Dorset* Puddletown (0305) 848030

SCOTT, Patrick Henry Fowlis. b 25. Jes Coll Cam BA51 MA55. Wells Th Coll 51. **d** 53 **p** 54. CF 57-70; Dep Asst Chapl Gen 70-71 and 74-80; Sen CF 72-74; P-in-c Fridaythorpe w Fimber and Thixendale *York* 80-83; P-in-c Sledmere and Wetwang w Cowlan 80-83; V Sledmere and Cowlam w Fridaythorpe, Fimer etc 84-90; rtd 90. *3 Appleby Glade, Haxby, York YO3 8YW* York (0904) 769258

SCOTT, Peter Crawford. b 35. Ch Ch Ox BA56 MA61. Cuddesdon Coll 60. **d** 62 **p** 63. C Broseley w Benthall *Heref* 62-66; P-in-c Hughenden *Ox* 66-71; C Hykeham *Linc* 71-73; P-in-c Stottesdon *Heref* 73-76; Australia from 76. *St Andrew's Rectory, Alvie, Victoria, Australia 3253* Geelong (52) 348232

SCOTT, Peter James Douglas Sefton. b 59. Edin Univ BD83. Edin Th Coll 81. **d** 83 **p** 84. C Helensburgh *Glas* 83-86; C-in-c Glas St Oswald 86-89; R from 89. *1 King's Park Avenue, Glasgow G44 4UW* 041-632 1852

SCOTT, Peter Lawrence. b 20. St Cath Coll Cam BA43 MA46. Ely Th Coll. **d** 47 **p** 48. R Withyham St Mich *Chich* 53-86; rtd 86. *Richmond House, 2 Chamberlain Street, Wells, Somerset BA5 2PF* Wells (0749) 76636

SCOTT, Peter Lindsay. b 29. Keble Coll Ox BA54 MA58. Linc Th Coll 54. **d** 56 **p** 57. C Weston-super-Mare St Sav *B & W* 56-59; C Knowle H Nativity *Bris* 59-61; P-in-c

Glas St Pet *Glas* 61-63; V Heap Bridge *Man* 63-73; V Rochdale St Geo w St Alb 73-86; R Droylsden St Andr from 86. *St Andrew's Rectory, Merton Drive, Droylsden, Manchester M35 6BH* 061-370 3242

SCOTT, Simon James. b 65. Ch Ch Ox BA87 MA91. Wycliffe Hall Ox 88. **d** 91. C Cheadle All Hallows *Ches* from 91. *26 Kelsall Road, Cheadle, Cheshire SK8 2NE* 061-491 2204

SCOTT, Terence. b 56. QUB BSc77. CITC 77. **d** 80 **p** 81. C Ballymena *Conn* 80-83; C Antrim All SS 83-85; P-in-c Conn w Antrim St Patr 85-88; I Magherafelt Arm from 88. *St Swithin's Rectory, 1 Churchwell Lane, Magherafelt, Co Londonderry BT45 6AL* Magherafelt (0648) 32365

SCOTT, Timothy Charles Nairne. b 61. Ex Univ BA83. Westcott Ho Cam 84. **d** 87 **p** 88. C Romford St Edw *Chelmsf* 87-89; CP from 89. *58B Howard Road, London E17 4SJ* 081-521 7016

SCOTT, Vernon Malcolm. b 30. TCD BA57 MA60. TCD Div Sch Div Test56 Ridley Hall Cam 58. **d** 58 **p** 59. C Limehouse St Anne *Lon* 58-62; C N St Pancras All Hallows 62-66; V Enfield St Mich 66-77; R Tansor w Cotterstock and Fotheringhay *Pet* 77-81; R Barby w Onley 81-83; V Kilsby 81-83; R Barby w Kilsby 83-90; R Coxford Gp *Nor* from 90. *The Rectory, Broomsthorpe Road, East Rudham, King's Lynn, Norfolk PE31 8RG* East Rudham (048522) 756

SCOTT, Walter David Craig. b 22. Selw Coll Cam BA49 MA53. Sarum Th Coll 49. **d** 51 **p** 52. V Cleadon Park *Dur* 67-71; V Bulkington *Cov* 72-83; RD Bedworth 76-79; V Bulkington w Shilton and Ansty 83-87; rtd 87; Perm to Offic *Cov* from 87. *8 Osprey Close, Nuneaton, Warks CV11 6TF* Nuneaton (0203) 345561

SCOTT, William. b 20. Coll of Resurr Mirfield. **d** 60 **p** 61. C Wolborough w Newton Abbot *Ex* 60-63; Chapl St Cath Sch Bramley 63-66; Chapl SS Mary and Anne's Sch Abbots Bromley 72-76; Perm to Offic *Cant* from 79; Chapl Boulogne-sur-Mer w Calais and Lille *Eur* from 90. *42 Westgate Court Avenue, Canterbury, Kent CT2 8JR* Canterbury (0227) 56277

SCOTT, William John. b 46. TCD BA70. CITC. **d** 71 **p** 72. C Ban St Comgall *D & D* 71-74; C Holywood 74-80; I Carnalea 80-90; I Seapatrick from 90. *The Rectory, 63 Lurgan Road, Banbridge, Co Down BT32 4LY* Banbridge (08206) 22612

SCOTT, William Sievwright. b 46. Edin Th Coll 67. **d** 70 **p** 71. C Glas St Ninian *Glas* 70-73; C Bridgwater St Fran *B & W* 73-77; R Shepton Beauchamp w Barrington, Stocklinch etc 77-81; P-in-c Cossington 82-84; P-in-c Woolavington 82-84; Chapl Community of All Hallows Ditchingham 84-91; V Pimlico St Mary Graham Terrace *Lon* from 91. *St Mary's Presbytery, 30 Bourne Street, London SW1W 8JJ* 071-730 2423

SCOTT-DEMPSTER, Canon Colin Thomas. b 37. Em Coll Cam BA65 MA68. Cuddesdon Coll 64. **d** 66 **p** 67. C Caversham Ox 66-69; Chapl Coll of SS Mark and Jo Chelsea 69-73; V Chieveley w Winterbourne and Oare *Ox* from 73; RD Newbury from 77; Can Ch Ch from 90. *Chieveley Vicarage, Newbury, Berks RG16 8UT* Chieveley (0635) 248341

✠SCOTT-JOYNT, Rt Rev Michael Charles. b 43. K Coll Cam BA65 MA68. Cuddesdon Coll 65. **d** 67 **p** 68 **c** 87. Tutor Cuddesdon Coll 67-71; Chapl 71-72; C Cuddesdon *Ox* 67-70; TV Newbury St Nic 72-75; P-in-c Caversfield 75-79; P-in-c Bicester 75-79; RD Bicester and Islip 76-81; P-in-c Bucknell 76-79; TR Bicester w Bucknell, Caversfield and Launton 79-81; Can Res St Alb 82-87; Dir of Ords and Post-Ord Tr 82-87; Hon Can Lich Cathl *Lich* from 87; Suff Bp Stafford from 87. *Ash Garth, Broughton Cres, Barlaston, Stoke-on-Trent ST12 9DD* Barlaston (078139) 3108

SCOTT-OLDFIELD, Ivor Erroll Lindsay. b 21. Univ Coll Dur BA49. Sarum Th Coll 49. **d** 51 **p** 52. Dir Gen RADD 68-87; rtd 87. *11E Prior Bolton Street, London N1 2NX*

SCOTT-THOMPSON, Ian Mackenzie. b 57. Ch Ch Ox BA78. St Jo Coll Nottm BA82. **d** 83 **p** 84. C Hartley Wintney, Elvetham, Winchfield etc *Win* 83-85; C Bitterne 85-89; V Iford from 89. *St Saviour's Vicarage, Colemore Road, Iford, Bournemouth BH7 6RZ* Bournemouth (0202) 425978

SCRACE, David Peter. b 46. Sarum & Wells Th Coll 79. **d** 81 **p** 82. C Abbots Langley *St Alb* 81-85; TV Chippenham St Paul w Hardenhuish etc *Bris* 85-91; P-in-c Harnham *Sarum* from 91. *The Vicarage, Old Blandford Road, Harnham, Salisbury SP2 8DQ* Salisbury (0722) 333564

SCREECH, Royden. b 53. K Coll Lon BD74 AKC74. St Aug Coll Cant 75. **d** 76 **p** 77. C Hatcham St Cath *S'wark* 76-80; V Nunhead St Antony 80-87; P-in-c Nunhead St

Silas 82-87; RD Camberwell 83-87; V New Addington from 87. *St Edward's Vicarage, Cleves Crescent, Croydon CR0 0DL* Lodge Hill (0689) 845588

SCRINE, Ralph. b 19. Bris Univ BA40 Fitzw Ho Cam BA46 MA60 Lon Univ MPhil81. Westcott Ho Cam 45. **d** 46 **p** 47. Chapl Ch Ch Coll Cant 68-75; Sen Lect Ch Ch Coll Cant 68-84; rtd 84; Perm to Offic *Cant* from 84. *Little Henny, Stone Street, Petham, Canterbury, Kent CT4 5PP* Petham (022770) 725

SCRIVEN, Henry William. b 51. Sheff Univ BA72. St Jo Coll Nottm 73. **d** 75 **p** 76. C Wealdstone H Trin *Lon* 75-79; SAMS (Argentina) 79-82; USA 82-83; SAMS (Spain) 84-90; Chapl Madrid w Bilbao *Eur* from 90. *c/o British Embassy, Fernando el Santo 16, 28010 Madrid, Spain* Madrid (1) 319-0200 or 576-5109

SCRIVEN, Hugh Alexander. b 59. Trin Coll Cam BA80. Cranmer Hall Dur 81. **d** 84 **p** 85. C Pudsey St Lawr and St Paul *Bradf* 84-87; C Madeley *Heref* from 87. *1 Spencer Drive, Sutton Hill, Telford, Shropshire TF7 4JY* Telford (0952) 680004

SCRIVEN, Paul Michael. b 51. Bris Univ BSc72 Lon Univ CertEd74. S Dios Minl Tr Scheme 84. **d** 87 **p** 88. NSM Redmarley D'Abitot, Bromesberrow w Pauntley etc *Glouc* 87-90; Lic to Offic *Heref* from 90. *The Grove, Llangrove, Ross-on-Wye, Herefordshire HR9 6EN* Llangarron (098984) 733

SCRIVEN, Stanley William. b 10. ALCD41. **d** 41 **p** 42. C Whitton and Thurleston w Akenham *St E* 71-76; rtd 76. *22 Southlands Road, Weymouth, Dorset DT4 9LQ* Weymouth (0305) 788607

SCRIVENER, Robert Allan. b 54. Nottm Univ BEd78. Linc Th Coll 79. **d** 80 **p** 81. C Sherwood *S'well* 80-83; C Burghclere w Newtown and Ecchinswell w Sydmonton *Win* 83-86; TV Hemel Hempstead *St Alb* from 86. *St Barnabas' Vicarage, Everest Way, Adeyfield, Hemel Hempstead HP2 4HY* Hemel Hempstead (0442) 53681

SCRIVENS, Ernest. b 25. Lon Univ DipTh53. **d** 62 **p** 63. Miss to Seamen W Australia 69-79; V Yeadon St Jo *Bradf* 79-80; Australia from 81; rtd 88. *111 Bamboo Avenue, Benowa, Queensland, Australia 4217* Benowa (75) 971805

SCRUBY, Ven Ronald Victor. b 19. Trin Hall Cam BA48 MA52. Cuddesdon Coll 48. **d** 50 **p** 51. Adn Is of Wight *Portsm* 65-77; Adn Portsm 77-85; rtd 85; Perm to Offic *Portsm & Chich* from 85. *The Dower House, Rogate, Petersfield, Hants GU31 5EG* Rogate (0730) 821325

SCUFFHAM, Canon Frank Leslie. b 30. AKC56 DSRS68. **d** 57 **p** 58. C Kettering SS Pet and Paul *Pet* 57-59; Ind Chapl *Sheff* 60-61; Ind Chapl *Pet* from 61; Can Pet Cathl from 72; RD Corby 76-79; P-in-c Stoke Albany w Wilbarston 79; R from 79. *The Rectory, Stoke Albany, Market Harborough, Leics LE16 8PZ* Dingley (085885) 213

SCUPHOLME, Albert Cooper. b 11. Em Coll Cam BA33 MA37. Coll of Resurr Mirfield 33. **d** 35 **p** 36. R Thurcaston *Leic* 68-76; rtd 76; Perm to Offic *Nor* from 76. *5 Town Close, Holt, Norfolk NR25 6JN* Holt (0263) 2676

SCUTT, John Melville. b 07. St Edm Hall Ox BA29 DipTh30 MA33. Wycliffe Hall Ox 29. **d** 31 **p** 32. V Woodford Wells *Chelmsf* 60-72; rtd 72; C Colney Heath St Mark *St Alb* 72-73; P-in-c Elvedon *St E* 75-77; Perm to Offic *St Alb* from 77. *25 Gravenhurst Road, Campton, Shefford, Beds SG17 5NY* Hitchin (0462) 813031

SCUTTER, James Edward. b 36. **d** 60 **p** 61. C Tilbury Docks *Chelmsf* 60-63; S Rhodesia 63-65; Rhodesia 65-80; Zimbabwe from 80. *c/o 46 Park Road, PO Box 2422, Bulawayo, Zimbabwe*

SEABROOK, Alan Geoffrey. b 43. ALCD65. **d** 66 **p** 67. C Bethnal Green St Jas Less *Lon* 66-70; C Madeley *Heref* 70-73; V Girlington *Bradf* 74-80; P-in-c Abdon w Clee St Margaret *Heref* 80-83; R Bitterley 80-83; P-in-c Cold Weston 80-83; P-in-c Hopton Cangeford 80-83; P-in-c Stoke St Milburgh w Heath 80-83; R Bitterley w Middleton, Stoke St Milborough etc from 83. *The Rectory, Bitterley, Ludlow, Shropshire SY8 3HJ* Ludlow (0584) 890239

SEABROOK, Geoffrey Barry. b 45. Open Univ BA77 DipEd Lon Univ MA(Ed)84. Chich Th Coll 66. **d** 69 **p** 70. C Tottenham All Hallows *Lon* 69-72; C Winchmore Hill H Trin 72-74; V Hornsey St Geo 74-82; P-in-c Hornsey St Mary 80-82; R Hornsey St Mary w St Geo from 82; P-in-c Hornsey H Innocents from 84. *Hornsey Rectory, 140 Cranley Gardens, London N10 3AH* 081-883 6846

SEAFORD, John Nicholas. b 39. Dur Univ BA67 DipTh68. St Chad's Coll Dur 68. **d** 68 **p** 69. C Bush Hill Park St

Mark *Lon* 68-71; C Stanmore *Win* 71-73; V N Baddesley 73-76; V Chilworth w N Baddesley 76-78; V Highcliffe w Hinton Admiral from 78; RD Christchurch from 90. *The Vicarage, 33 Nea Road, Christchurch, Dorset BH23 4NB* Highcliffe (0425) 272767

SEAGER, Roland Douglas. b 08. St Boniface Warminster 32. **d** 33 **p** 34. P-in-c Nottm St Cath *S'well* 71-73; rtd 74; Perm to Offic *S'well* from 74. *22 Willow Road, Carlton, Nottingham NG4 3BH*

SEAGO, Canon Jesse Edward Charles. b 06. ALCD37. **d** 37 **p** 38. Hon Can Chelmsf Cathl *Chelmsf* 66-74; V Southend St Sav Westcliff 67-74; rtd 74. *3 Priams Way, Stapleford, Cambridge CB2 5DT* Cambridge (0223) 841715

SEAL, Edward Hugh. b 10. ARCM31 Lon Univ BMus36. Wells Th Coll 46. **d** 48 **p** 49. R Poulton-le-Sands *Blackb* 63-78; rtd 78; Lic to Offic *Blackb* from 79. *3 Fern Bank, Scotforth, Lancaster LA1 4TT* Lancaster (0524) 67078

SEAL, Nicholas Peter. b 57. Ex Univ BA. Linc Th Coll 81. **d** 83 **p** 84. C Wareham *Sarum* 83-87; Chapl K Alfred Coll *Win* 87-91; V Stanmore from 91. *St Luke's Vicarage, Mildmay Street, Stanmore, Winchester, Hants SO22 4BX* Winchester (0962) 865240

SEAL, Philip Trevor. b 32. AKC55. **d** 56 **p** 57. C Godalming *Guildf* 56-60; C Tamworth *Lich* 60-61; R Lich St Chad 61-73; Chapl HM Youth Cust Cen Swinfen Hall 66-73; R Shere *Guildf* 74-88; RD Cranleigh 76-81; V Abbotsbury, Portesham and Langton Herring *Sarum* from 88. *The Vicarage, Portesham, Weymouth, Dorset DT3 4HB* Abbotsbury (0305) 217

SEAL, Ronald Frederick. b 28. Lich Th Coll. **d** 61 **p** 62. C Bedhampton *Portsm* 61-65; R N and S Kilworth *Leic* 65-71; R Barwell w Potters Marston and Stapleton 71-80; P-in-c Upper Stour *Sarum* 80-83; R Upper Stour 84-90; RD Heytesbury 87-89; Bermuda from 90; Miss to Seamen from 90. *St Peter's Rectory, PO Box GE85, St George's, Bermuda* Bermuda (1809) 297-0216

SEAL, William Christopher Houston. b 50. Occidental Coll (USA) BA72. Ch Div Sch of the Pacific (USA) MDiv81. **d** 81 **p** 82. USA 81-88; R Etton w Helpston *Pet* from 88. *The Rectory, Helpston, Peterborough PE6 7DW* Peterborough (0733) 253456

SEAL, William George. b 27. Lon Univ DipTh71. Oak Hill Th Coll 67. **d** 70 **p** 71. C Plumstead St Jo w St Jas and St Paul *S'wark* 70-73; C Camberwell All SS 73-80; V Luton St Matt High Town *St Alb* from 80. *St Matthew's Vicarage, Wenlock Street, Luton LU2 0NQ* Luton (0582) 32320

SEALE, Daisy Elaine. b 09. Gilmore Ho 55. **dss** 62 **d** 87. Clapham H Trin *S'wark* 62-69; rtd 69; W Cheshire Hosp *Ches* 69-75; Uffculme *Ex* 75-87; Hon Par Dn from 87. *The Fold, 2 Grantlands, Uffculme, Cullompton, Devon EX15 3ED* Craddock (0884) 840517

SEALE, William Arthur. b 62. NUI BA84 TCD DipTh87. **d** 87 **p** 88. C Drumragh w Mountfield *D & R* 87-90; I Drumgath w Drumgooland and Clonduff *D & D* from 90. *The Rectory, 29 Cross Road, Hilltown, Newry, Co Down BT34 5TF* Rathfriland (08206) 30304

SEALY, Daniel O'Neill. b 21. Oak Hill Th Coll 62. **d** 64 **p** 65. Chapl RN 67-73; Nigeria 73-79; Libya 79-82; Tunisia 82-86; rtd 86; I Kilgariffe Union *C, C & R* from 87. *The Rectory, Gallanes, Clonakilty, Co Cork, Irish Republic* Clonakilty (23) 33357

SEALY, Canon Gordon William Hugh. b 27. Leeds Univ BA53 MA64. Coll of Resurr Mirfield 53. **d** 55 **p** 56. C Greenford H Cross *Lon* 55-58; Br Honduras 58-68; R Tarrant Gunville, Tarrant Hinton etc *Sarum* 68-74; V Leic St Paul *Leic* from 74; Hon Can Leic Cathl from 86. *St Paul's Vicarage, Kirby Road, Leicester LE3 6BD* Leicester (0533) 28062

SEALY, Stephen. b 52. K Coll Lon BD86 AKC86. Linc Th Coll 86. **d** 88 **p** 89. C Botley *Portsm* 88-91; Prec Cant Cathl *Cant* from 91. *c/o Cathedral House, The Precincts, Canterbury, Kent CT1 2EH*

SEAMAN, Canon Arthur Roland Mostyn. b 32. TCD BA55 DipEd56 Div Test56 MA58. Westcott Ho Cam 58. **d** 58 **p** 59. C Blackley St Pet *Man* 58-61; C Sanderstead All SS *S'wark* 61-62; V Heywood St Luke *Man* 62-70; Dir of Educn 70-85; Hon Can Man Cathl from 74; R Chorlton-cum-Hardy St Werburgh from 85. *St Werburgh's Rectory, Wilbraham Road, Manchester M21 1ST* 061-881 1642

SEAMAN, Canon Brian Edward. b 35. Dur Univ BA59. Cranmer Hall Dur. **d** 61 **p** 62. C Burnage St Marg *Man* 61-65; Chapl Mayflower Family Cen Canning Town *Chelmsf* 65-75; V High Elswick St Paul *Newc* from 75; Hon Can Newc Cathl from 82. *St Paul's Vicarage, Park Close, Newcastle upon Tyne NE4 6SB* 091-273 4705

SEAMAN, Paul Robert. b 61. Bp Grosseteste Coll BEd82. Chich Th Coll 83. **d** 86 **p** 87. C Tilehurst St Mich *Ox* 86-91; TV Moulsecoomb *Chich* from 91. *Coldean Vicarage, Selham Drive, Coldean, Brighton BN1 9EL* Brighton (0273) 601854

SEAMAN, Robert John. b 44. ACP DipEd. E Anglian Minl Tr Course. **d** 84 **p** 85. NSM Downham Market w Bexwell *Ely* 84-90; V Southea w Murrow and Parson Drove from 90; V Guyhirn w Ring's End from 90. *Southea Vicarage, Main Road, Parson Drove, Wisbech, Cambs PE13 4JA* Wisbech (0945) 700426

SEAMER, Stephen James George. b 50. AKC73. Ridley Hall Cam 74. **d** 75 **p** 76. C Rustington *Chich* 75-78; C Bulwell St Jo *S'well* 78-79; P-in-c Camber and E Guldeford *Chich* 79-80; TV Rye 80-83; V Knowle *Birm* 83-87; Assoc Chapl Brussels Cathl *Eur* 87-90; P-in-c Tervuren w Liege from 90. *Smisstraat 8, 3080 Vossem-Tervuren, Belgium* Brussels (2) 767-3435

SEAR, Peter Lionel. b 49. Ex Univ BA72. Linc Th Coll 72. **d** 74 **p** 75. C Sheldon *Birm* 74-77; C Caversham *Ox* 77-81; C Caversham and Mapledurham 81-85; V Thatcham from 85. *The Vicarage, 17 Church Gate, Newbury, Berks RG13 4PJ* Thatcham (0635) 62616

SEAR, Terence Frank. b 39. LDSRCSEng62 Univ Coll Lon BDS63. Portsm Dioc Tr Course 88. **d** 89. NSM Ryde H Trin *Portsm* from 89; NSM Swanmore St Mich w Havenstreet from 89. *Glebe Cottage, Wray Street, Ryde, Isle of Wight PO33 3ED* Isle of Wight (0983) 615856

SEARIGHT, Mervyn Warren. b 26. TCD DBS. **d** 59 **p** 60. C Dub Crumlin *D & G* 59-63; C Dub Grangegorman 63-65; India 65-66; C Dub St Steph *D & G* 67-68; I Killermogh *C & O* 68-77; I Aughaval *T, K & A* 77-79; I Kiltegan w Hacketstown, Clonmore and Moyne *C & O* 79-86; C Dub St Geo w St Thos, Finglas and Free Ch *D & G* from 86. *The Rectory, Cappagh Road, Finglas, Dublin 11, Irish Republic* Dublin (1) 341015

SEARLE, Charles Peter. b 20. Selw Coll Cam BA48 MA53. Ridley Hall Cam. **d** 50 **p** 51. V Weston-super-Mare Ch Ch *B & W* 60-70; V Woking Ch Ch *Guildf* 70-85; rtd 85; Perm to Offic *Ex* from 85. *Old Chimes, 14 Gravel Walk, Cullompton, Devon EX15 1DA* Cullompton (0884) 33386

SEARLE, Capt Francis Robert. b 52. IDC74. CA Tr Coll 72 St Steph Ho Ox 88. **d** 90 **p** 91. CA from 72; C Lancing w Coombes *Chich* from 90. *30 Greenoaks, Lancing, W Sussex BN15 0HE* Lancing (0903) 767077

SEARLE, Hugh Douglas. b 35. St Cath Coll Cam BA59 MA63 Cranfield Inst of Tech MSc85. Oak Hill Th Coll 59. **d** 61 **p** 62. C Islington H Trin Cloudesley Square *Lon* 61-64; Chapl HM Pris Lewes 64-65; HM Borstal Roch 65-69; HM Youth Cust Cen Hollesley Bay Colony 70-74; Parkhurst 74-78; P-in-c Barton *Ely* 78-84; V from 84; P-in-c Coton 78-84; R from 84; RD Bourn from 81. *The Vicarage, Barton, Cambridge CB3 7BG* Cambridge (0223) 262218

SEARLE, Michael Owen. b 26. Sarum & Wells Th Coll 76. **d** 78 **p** 79. C Stanmore *Win* 78-82; TV Seacroft *Ripon* 82-83; rtd 91. *73 Beaconfield Road, Beacon Park, Plymouth PL2 3LF* Plymouth (0752) 776832

SEARLE, Michael Westran. b 47. Leeds Univ LLB68 Nottm Univ DipTh69. Cuddesdon Coll 69. **d** 71 **p** 72. C Norton St Mary *Dur* 71-74; C Westbury-on-Trym H Trin *Bris* 74-77; V Bedminster Down 77-84; V Bris Ch the Servant Stockwood 84-88; Dir of Tr *York* from 88. *Cavalino, Back Lane, Allerthorpe, York YO4 4RP* Pocklington (0759) 302544

SEARLE, Ralph Alan. b 57. Cam Univ MA. Coll of Resurr Mirfield 81. **d** 83 **p** 84. C Cockerton *Dur* 83-86; C S Shields All SS 86-88; TV from 88. *79 Chesterton Road, South Shields, Tyne & Wear NE34 9TL* 091-536 1831

SEARLE-BARNES, Albert Victor. b 28. Sheff Univ BA48 Lon Univ BD53. ALCD53. **d** 53 **p** 54. C Iver *Ox* 53-55; C Attenborough w Bramcote *S'well* 55-59; C Bramcote 55-59; R Cratfield w Heveningham and Ubbeston *St E* 59-64; R Wick w Doynton *Bris* 64-70; Perm to Offic 70-72; V Downend 73-78; V Market Rasen *Linc* 78-86; R Linwood 79-86; V Legsby 79-86; R Green's Norton w Bradden *Pet* 86-88; V Hambledon *Portsm* from 88. *The Vicarage, Church Lane, Hambledon, Portsmouth PO7 6RT* Hambledon (070132) 717

SEARS, Derek Lynford. b 25. St Jo Coll Cam BA49 MA53. Wycliffe Hall Ox 49. **d** 51 **p** 52. V Freckleton *Blackb* 66-74; Jamaica 74-78; V Ashton-on-Ribble St Mich *Blackb* 78-90; P-in-c Preston St Mark 82-90; rtd 90. *61 Greencroft, Penwortham, Preston, Lancs PR1 9LB* Preston (0772) 740190

SEARS, Frank. b 29. Wycliffe Hall Ox 62. **d** 64 **p** 65. C Ashtead *Guildf* 64-72; V Finchley St Luke *Lon* 72-82; P-in-c Finchley St Paul Long Lane 76-82; TR Whitton *Sarum* 82-90. *The Rectory, 118 Lower Road, Salisbury SP2 9NW* Salisbury (0722) 334632

SEATON, Canon James Bradbury. b 29. Ch Coll Cam BA53 MA57. Westcott Ho Cam 53. **d** 55 **p** 56. C Derby St Werburgh *Derby* 55-58; C Darlington St Cuth *Dur* 58-64; V Preston on Tees 64-72; TV Stockton H Trin 72-73; TV Cen Stockton 73-75; R Anstey *Leic* 75-89; RD Sparkenhoe III 81-89; Hon Can Leic Cathl from 87; R Market Harborough Transfiguration from 89. *The Rectory, Rectory Lane, Little Bowden, Market Harborough, Leics LE16 8AS* Market Harborough (0858) 462926

SEBER, Derek Morgan. b 43. Man Univ CertRS79 Man Poly CTUS83 MA88. Oak Hill Th Coll 71. **d** 73 **p** 74. C Collyhurst *Man* 73-76; C Radcliffe St Thos and St Jo 76-77; Ind Missr 77-89; P-in-c Hulme St Geo 77-83; Hon C Moss Side St Jas w St Clem from 83; Project Officer Linking Up from 89. *56 Alness Road, Whalley Range, Manchester M16 8HW* 061-861 0360 or 832 5208

SECCOMBE, Marcus John. b 34. Oak Hill Th Coll 60. **d** 63 **p** 64. C Woodthorpe *S'well* 63-67; C Doncaster St Mary *Sheff* 67-72; V Owston 72-90; R Rossington from 90. *The Rectory, Sheep Bridge Lane, Rossington, Doncaster, S Yorkshire DN11 0EZ* Doncaster (0302) 867597

SECKER, Brian. b 34. Qu Coll Birm 62. **d** 65 **p** 66. C Goldthorpe *Sheff* 65-68; V New Bentley 68-75; P-in-c Pet St Barn *Pet* 75-80; V Pet St Paul from 75. *St Paul's Vicarage, Peterborough PE1 2PA* Peterborough (0733) 43746

SECOMBE, Preb Frederick Thomas. b 18. St D Coll Lamp BA40 St Mich Coll Llan 40. **d** 42 **p** 43. R Hanwell St Mary *Lon* 69-83; AD Ealing W 78-82; rtd 83. *30 Westville Road, Penylan, Cardiff CF2 5AG* Cardiff (0222) 483978

SECRETAN, Mrs Jenny Ruth. b 54. St Aid Coll Dur BA76 Ex Univ CertEd77 Nottm Univ DipTh82. Linc Th Coll 81. **dss** 84 **d** 87. Asst Chapl Newc Poly *Newc* 84-86; Sunderland St Chad *Dur* 84-86; Bordesley St Oswald *Birm* 86-87; Par Dn 87-91. *St Oswald's Clergy House, 11 St Oswald's Road, Birmingham B10 9RB* 021-772 2674

SECRETAN, Paul Lawrence. b 49. Linc Th Coll. **d** 83 **p** 84. C Sunderland St Chad *Dur* 83-86; V Bordesley St Oswald *Birm* 86-91; Chapl Miss to Seamen from 91. *c/o The Missions to Seamen, Mill Dam, South Shields, Tyne and Wear NE33 1EF* 091-456 0878

SECRETAN, Philip Buckley. b 09. TD50. FLAS46 FRICS70 Pemb Coll Ox BA32 MA46. Roch Th Coll 62. **d** 63 **p** 64. R Folkington *Chich* 66-79; V Wilmington 66-79; rtd 79; Perm to Offic *Chich* from 79. *70 Newick Drive, Newick, Lewes, E Sussex BN8 4PB* Newick (082572) 2857

SECRETT, Ian Russell. b 27. Clare Coll Cam BA48 MA52. Westcott Ho Cam 73. **d** 73 **p** 74. C Bris St Andr w St Bart *Bris* 73-75; P-in-c Burwell *Ely* 75-76; V from 76; P-in-c Swaffham Bulbeck from 88; P-in-c Swaffham Prior from 88. *The Vicarage, Burwell, Cambridge CB5 0HB* Newmarket (0638) 741262

SEDDON, Ernest Geoffrey. b 26. ARIBA51 Man Univ DipArch50 DipTh83 MA85. St Deiniol's Hawarden 80. **d** 80 **p** 81. C Dunham Massey St Marg *Ches* 80-83; P-in-c Warburton 82-87; P-in-c Dunham Massey St Mark 85-86; V from 86. *The Vicarage, Back Lane, Dunham Massey, Altrincham, Cheshire WA14 4SG* 061-928 5611

SEDDON, Philip James. b 45. Jes Coll Cam BA68 MA71. Ridley Hall Cam 67. **d** 70 **p** 71. C Tonge w Alkrington *Man* 70-74; Nigeria 74-78; Lect St Jo Coll Nottm 78-79; Lic to Offic *Ely* 79-85; Chapl Magd Coll Cam 79-85; Lect Bibl Studies Selly Oak Colls from 86; Lic to Offic *Birm* from 87. *Central House, Selly Oak Colleges, Birmingham B29 6QT* 021-472 4231

SEDEN, Martin Roy. b 47. Man Univ MSc Salford Univ PhD. E Midl Min Tr Course. **d** 82 **p** 83. NSM Knighton St Mary Magd *Leic* from 82. *139 Shanklin Drive, Leicester LE2 3QG* Leicester (0533) 702128

SEDGLEY, Canon Timothy John. b 42. St Jo Coll Ox BA63 DipTh64 MA68. Westcott Ho Cam 64. **d** 66 **p** 67. C Nor St Pet Mancroft *Nor* 66-70; V Costessey 70-79; RD Nor N 75-79; V Walton-on-Thames *Guildf* from 79; Hon Can Guildf Cathl from 86; RD Emly 86-91. *The Vicarage, Ashley Park Avenue, Walton-on-Thames, Surrey KT12 1EV* Walton-on-Thames (0932) 227184

SEDGMORE, Evan. b 09. St D Coll Lamp 47. **d** 50 **p** 51. V Llanbradach *Llan* 71-76; rtd 76; Perm to Offic *Llan* from 76. *52 Hockland Road, Newton, Porthcawl, M Glam CF36 5SG* Porthcawl (065671) 8991

SEDGWICK, Jonathan Maurice William. b 63. BNC Ox BA85 MA89 Leeds Univ BA88. Coll of Resurr Mirfield 86. **d** 89 **p** 90. C Chich St Paul and St Pet *Chich* from 89. *37 Somerstown, Chichester, W Sussex PO19 4AL* Chichester (0243) 775199

SEDGWICK, Peter Humphrey. b 48. Trin Hall Cam BA70 Dur Univ PhD83. Westcott Ho Cam 71. **d** 74 **p** 75. C Stepney St Dunstan and All SS *Lon* 74-77; P-in-c Pittington *Dur* 77-79; Lect Th Birm Univ 79-82; Hon C The Lickey *Birm* 79-82; Th Consultant for NE Ecum Gp *Dur* 82-88; Abp's Adv on Ind Issues *York* from 88; Lect Th Hull Univ from 88. *Kingston, 21 Southwood Road, Cottingham, N Humberside HU16 5AE* Hull (0482) 847151

SEED, Richard Edward. b 55. S Africa Univ BTh86. Kalk Bay Bible Inst S Africa DipTh79. **d** 80 **p** 81. S Africa 80-85 and 87-89; Zimbabwe 85-87; Asst Chapl Kingham Hill Sch 89-90; C Beckenham Ch Ch *Roch* from 90. *78 The Drive, Beckenham, Kent BR3 1EG* 081-650 7669

SEED, Richard Murray Crosland. b 49. Edin Th Coll 69. **d** 72 **p** 73. C Skipton Ch Ch *Bradf* 72-75; C Baildon 75-77; Chapl HM Det Cen Kidlington 77-80; TV Kidlington *Ox* 77-80; V Boston Spa *York* from 80; P-in-c Newton Kyme 84-85; P-in-c Clifford from 89. *The Vicarage, Boston Spa, Wetherby, W Yorkshire LS23 5EA* Boston Spa (0937) 842454 or 844402

SEEDS, Colin Wilfred. b 39. Man Univ BSc60 Linacre Coll Ox BA67 MA. Ripon Hall Ox 65. **d** 67 **p** 68. C Frecheville *Derby* 67-70; Lic to Offic 71-75 and 76-82; P-in-c Milford 75-76; P-in-c Bridge Hill 75-76; V Mickleover St Jo 82-87; V Alfreton from 87. *The Vicarage, Church Street, Alfreton, Derby DE5 7AH* Alfreton (0773) 833280

SEELEY, John Frederick. b 36. AKC61. **d** 62 **p** 63. C Lower Broughton Ascension *Man* 62-64; C Chiswick St Paul Grove Park *Lon* 64-66; C Ruislip St Mary 66-67; C Hampstead Garden Suburb 67-69; P-in-c St Jo Wood All SS 69-71; C Stamford Hill St Bart 74-80; P-in-c Harringay St Paul 80-84; V from 84. *St Paul's Vicarage, Wightman Road, London N4 1RW* 081-340 5299

SEELEY, Martin Alan. b 54. Jes Coll Cam BA76 MA79. Union Th Sem (NY) STM78. **d** 78 **p** 79. C Bottesford w Ashby *Linc* 78-80; USA from 80; Selection Sec ACCM 90-91; ABM from 91. *6942 Dartmouth Road, St Louis, Missouri 63130, USA*

SEFTON, Thomas Albert. b 21. Kelham Th Coll 38. **d** 45 **p** 46. C Deptford St Paul *S'wark* 45-47; C Lewisham St Jo Southend 47-48; CF 48-55; V Tottenham St Paul *Lon* 55-58; Australia from 58. *29 Ella Gladstone Drive, Eagle Bay, W Australia 6281* Dunsborough (97) 553192

SEGAL, Michael Bertram. b 20. Lon Univ BA44. Cuddesdon Coll 46. **d** 48 **p** 49. V S Wimbledon St Pet *S'wark* 61-71; V Crofton Park St Hilda w St Cypr 72-82; P-in-c Grendon w Castle Ashby *Pet* 82-85; V Gt Doddington 82-85; rtd 85; Perm to Offic *Cant* from 85. *9 Glebe Gardens, Lenham, Maidstone, Kent ME17 2QA* Maidstone (0622) 858033

SEIGNIOR, James Frederick. b 97. TD46. Univ Coll Lon ALA28. St Deiniol's Hawarden 45. **d** 46 **p** 47. V Bruera *Ches* 49-69; rtd 69; Australia 69-79; Perm to Offic *Glouc* 79-80; *Guildf* from 80. *64 Roof of the World, Boxhill Road, Tadworth, Surrey KT20 7JR* Betchworth (073784) 4520

SELBY, George Raymond. b 22. Nottm Univ BA53 Lon Univ PhD67. Wells Th Coll 56. **d** 57 **p** 58. Chapl Leeds Univ *Ripon* 67-70; C Leeds Em 67-70; Prin NW Ord Course 70-77; Hon Can Man Cathl *Man* 70-79; Can Res St As Cathl *St As* 79-81; USA 81-85; C Kenilworth St Nic *Cov* 85-86; Perm to Offic *B & W* from 86; rtd 87. *The Old Cider House, Jubilee Gardens, Milverton, Taunton, Somerset TA4 1JU* Taunton (0823) 400029

✠**SELBY, Rt Rev Peter Stephen Maurice.** b 41. St Jo Coll Ox BA64 MA67 K Coll Lon PhD75. Episc Th Sch Cam Mass BD66 Bps' Coll Cheshunt 66. **d** 66 **p** 67 **c** 84. C Queensbury All SS *Lon* 66-69; C Limpsfield and Titsey *S'wark* 69-77; Assoc Dir of Tr 69-73; Vice-Prin *S'wark* Ord Course 70-72; Asst Dioc Missr *S'wark* 73-77; Dioc Missr *Newc* 77-84; Can Res Newc Cathl 77-84; Suff Bp Kingston-upon-Thames *S'wark* 84-91; Area Bp Kingston-upon-Thames from 91. *24 Albert Drive, London SW19 6LS or, Episcopal Area Office, Whitelands Cottage, London SW15 3SN* 081-789 3218 or 780 2308

SELBY, Ḏ..ꞏꞏꞏp Sydney Arthur. b 17. K Coll Lon 41. **d** 48 **p** 49. V Kild̶w̶i̶c̶k̶ Ḏꞏꞏꞏḏf 53-74; RD S Craven 73-74; Hon Can Bradf Cathl 73-82; V G..ꞏꞏꞏ rꞏ 74-82; RD Bowland 80-81; rtd 82; Perm to Offic *Bradf* from 8... *The Readers House, Slaidburn Road, Waddington, Clitheroe, Lancs BB7 3JG*

SELBY, Suffragan Bishop of. *See* TAYLOR, Rt Rev Humphrey Vincent

SELF, David Christopher. b 41. Toronto Univ BSc62 MA64 K Coll Lon BD68 AKC68. **d** 69 **p** 70. C Tupsley *Heref* 69-73; Chapl Dur Univ *Dur* 73-78; TV Southn (City Cen) *Win* 78-84; TR Dunstable *St Alb* from 84; RD Dunstable from 90. *The Rectory, 8 Furness Avenue, Dunstable, Beds LU6 3BN* Dunstable (0582) 64467 or 69725

SELF, John Andrew. **d** 81. CMS from 77; Pakistan from 77. *c/o Amberley, 3 Tyning End, Widcombe, Bath BA2 6AN*

SELF, Peter Allen. b 41. S Dios Minl Tr Scheme 84. **d** 87 **p** 87. NSM Wilton *B & W* 87-91; NSM Taunton Lyngford from 91. *20 Dyers Close, West Buckland, Wellington, Somerset TA21 9JU* Wellington (0823) 473408

SELL, John Lewis. b 10. Univ Coll Dur LTh37 BA40 New Coll Ox BA43 MA47. St Boniface Warminster 30. **d** 35 **p** 36. R Coln St Denys w Coln Rogers *Glouc* 50-75; V Sandhurst 75-80; rtd 81; Perm to Offic *Glouc* from 81. *79 Calton Road, Gloucester GL1 5DT* Gloucester (0452) 416906

SELL, Noel Lightfoot. b 15. St Cath Coll Cam BA38 MA44. Wycliffe Hall Ox. **d** 41 **p** 42. V Broomfield *B & W* 64-77; V Kingston St Mary 64-77; rtd 77. *32 Saxon Way, Saffron Walden, Essex CB11 4EG* Saffron Walden (0799) 26165

SELLARS, Charles Harold. b 18. Leeds Univ BA40. Coll of Resurr Mirfield 37. **d** 42 **p** 44. Chapl Qu Sch Rheindahlen Germany *Eur* 61-70; V Hampton St Mary *Lon* 70-78; R Nuthurst *Chich* 78-83; P-in-c Lynch w Iping Marsh 83-86; rtd 86; Perm to Offic *Chich* from 87. *50 Rewhams Road, Horsham, W Sussex RH12 2NZ* Horsham (0403) 60641

SELLER, James Stoddart. b 16. TD64. St Jo Coll Dur LTh45. Tyndale Hall Bris 40. **d** 44 **p** 45. R Burnby *York* 60-89; R Londesborough 60-89; R Nunburnholme 60-89; P-in-c Shiptonthorpe w Hayton 79-89; rtd 89. *7 Wilton Road, Hornsea, N Humberside HU18 1QU* Hornsea (0964) 533160

SELLER, Dr Mary Joan. b 40. Qu Mary Coll Lon BSc61 Lon Univ PhD64 DSc82. S'wark Ord Course. **d** 91. NSM Hurst Green *S'wark* from 91. *11 Home Park, Oxted, Surrey RH8 0JS* Oxted (0883) 715675

SELLERS, Anthony. b 48. Southn Univ BSc71 PhD76. Wycliffe Hall Ox 84. **d** 86 **p** 87. C Luton St Mary *St Alb* 86-90; V Luton St Paul from 90. *5 Blaydon Road, Luton LU2 0RP* Luton (0582) 481796

SELLERS, George William. b 35. N Ord Course. **d** 89 **p** 90. NSM Rothwell *Ripon* from 89. *16 Thornegrove, Rothwell, Leeds LS26 0HP* Leeds (0532) 823522

SELLERS, Warren John. b 43. K Coll Lon 63. Sarum Th Coll 65. **d** 68 **p** 69. C Guildf H Trin w St Mary *Guildf* 68-72; C Chich St Paul and St Pet *Chich* 72-73; C Epping St Jo *Chelmsf* 73-76; Hon C Pulborough *Chich* 76-90; Hon C Fleet *Guildf* from 90; Hd Master St Pet Sch Farnborough from 90. *7 Camden Walk, Fleet, Aldershot, Hants GU13 9EW* Fleet (0252) 629413

SELLGREN, Eric Alfred. b 33. AKC61. **d** 62 **p** 63. C Ditton St Mich *Liv* 62-66; V Hindley Green 66-72; V Southport St Paul 72-80; Warden Barn Fellowship Winterborne Whitchurch 80-86; V The Iwernes, Sutton Waldron and Fontmell Magna *Sarum* from 86. *The Vicarage, Iwerne Minster, Blandford Forum, Dorset DT11 8NF* Fontmell Magna (0747) 811291

SELLIX, Martin Gordon. b 45. Ridley Hall Cam 74. **d** 76 **p** 77. C Crofton St Paul *Roch* 76-80; Ind Chapl *Chelmsf* from 80; R Rayne 80-86; V Blackmore and Stondon Massey from 86; RD Ongar from 89. *The Vicarage, Church Street, Blackmore, Ingatestone, Essex CM4 0RN* Ingatestone (0277) 821464

SELLORS, Michael Harry. b 36. K Coll Lon 60 St Boniface Warminster 61. **d** 61 **p** 62. C Willesden St Mary *Lon* 61-64; C Aldershot St Mich *Guildf* 64-67; V Hale 67-84; P-in-c E w W Beckham *Nor* 84-85; P-in-c Bodham 84-85; V Weybourne w Upper Sheringham 84-85; R Kelling w Salthouse 84-85; R Weybourne Gp from 85. *The Rectory, Weybourne, Holt, Norfolk NR25 7SY* Weybourne (026370) 268

SELMAN, Cyril Allen. b 25. Wycliffe Hall Ox 64. **d** 65 **p** 65. V Beedon *Ox* 69-87; R Peasemore 69-87; rtd 88. *10 Griffin Terrace, Penrhyndeudraeth, Gwynedd LL48 6LR*

SELMAN, Michael Richard. b 47. Sussex Univ BA68 Bris Univ MA70. Coll of Resurr Mirfield 71. **d** 73 **p** 74. C Hove All SS *Chich* 73-74; C Horfield H Trin *Bris* 74-78; P-in-c Landkey *Ex* 78-79; C Barnstaple and Goodleigh 78-79; TV Barnstaple, Goodleigh and Landkey 79-82; TR 82-84; RD Barnstaple 83-85; P-in-c Sticklepath 85-..; TR Barnstaple 85; TR Cen Ex from 85. *The*

Rectory, 3 Spicer Road, Exeter EX1 1SX Exeter (0392) 72450

SELMES, Brian. b 48. Nottm Univ BTh74. Linc Th Coll 70. **d** 74 **p** 75. C Padgate *Liv* 74-77; C Sydenham St Bart *S'wark* 77-80; Chapl Aycliffe Hosp Darlington from 80; Chapl Darlington Memorial Hosp from 80. *56 West Crescent, Darlington, Co Durham DL3 7PR* Darlington (0325) 359688 or 380100

SELVEY, Canon John Brian. b 33. Dur Univ BA54. Cuddesdon Coll 56. **d** 58 **p** 59. C Lanc St Mary *Blackb* 58-61; C Blackb Cathl 61-65; Cathl Chapl 64-65; V Foulridge 65-69; V Walton-le-Dale 69-82; V Cleveleys 82-89; Hon Can Bloemfontein Cathl from 88; V Slyne w Hest *Blackb* from 89. *The Vicarage, Summerfield Drive, Slyne, Lancaster LA2 6AQ* Hest Bank (0524) 822128

SELVINI, John Claude Gaston. b 46. ESC (Paris) 68. St Steph Ho Ox 72. **d** 75 **p** 76. C Derby St Luke *Derby* 75-78; C Bordesley St Oswald *Birm* 78-80; C Shrewsbury All SS w St Mich *Lich* 80-88; V Goldenhill from 88. *St John's Vicarage, Drummond Street, Stoke-on-Trent ST6 5RF* Stoke-on-Trent (0782) 782736

SELWOOD, Robin. b 37. ALCD61. **d** 61 **p** 62. C Lenton *S'well* 61-63; C Norbury *Ches* 63-66; V Newton Flowery Field 66-75; V Kelsall 75-89; V Sale St Paul from 89. *St Paul's Vicarage, 15 Springfield Road, Sale, Cheshire M33 1XG* 061-973 1042

SELWOOD, Timothy John. b 45. Lon Univ LLB66. Sarum Th Coll. **d** 83 **p** 84. NSM Colbury *Win* 83-85; NSM Copythorne and Minstead from 85. *Forest Cottage, Seamans Lane, Minstead, Lyndhurst, Hants SO43 7FT* Southampton (0703) 812873

SELWYN, David Gordon. b 38. MEHS Clare Coll Cam BA62 MA66 New Coll Ox MA66. Ripon Hall Ox 62. **d** 64 **p** 65. C Ecclesall *Sheff* 64-65; Asst Chapl New Coll Ox 65-68; Lect St D Univ Coll Lamp *St D* from 68. *19 Penhryn, Lampeter, Dyfed SA48 7EU* Lampeter (0570) 422748

SEMEONOFF, Mrs Jean Mary Agnes. b 36. BSc56 Leic Univ CertEd57. E Midl Min Tr Course 84. **d** 87. Par Dn Leic H Spirit *Leic* 87 and from 89; Chapl to the Deaf *Derby* 87-89; Chapl to the Deaf *Leic* from 89. *107 Letchworth Road, Leicester LE3 6FN* Leicester (0533) 858854

SEMEONOFF, Dr Robert. b 40. Edin Univ PhD67 BSc62. E Midl Min Tr Course 81. **d** 84 **p** 85. NSM Leic H Spirit *Leic* 84-88; Hon C from 89; NSM Loughb Gd Shep 88-89; Chapl Leic Univ from 89. *107 Letchworth Road, Leicester LE3 6FN* Leicester (0533) 858854

SEMPER, Cecil Michael. b 29. LLCM St D Coll Lamp BA51 Fitzw Ho Cam BA53 MA57 Lanc Univ PGCE. St Mich Coll Llan 53. **d** 54 **p** 55. C Hawarden *St As* 54-60; R Montgomery 60-66; RD Pool 65-76; R Montgomery and Forden 66-76; V Gresford 76-87; R Claypole *Linc* 87-89; V Stoke by Nayland w Leavenheath *St E* from 89. *The Vicarage, Stoke by Nayland, Colchester CO6 4QH* Nayland (0206) 262248

SEMPER, Very Rev Colin Douglas. b 38. Keble Coll Ox BA62. Westcott Ho Cam 61. **d** 63 **p** 64. C Guildf H Trin w St Mary *Guildf* 63-66; Hon C 66-82; Sec ACCM 67-69; Producer Relig Broadcasting Dept BBC 69-75; Overseas Relig Broadcasting Org BBC 75-79; Hd of Relig Progr BBC Radio 79-82; Hon Can Guildf Cathl *Guildf* 80-82; Provost Cov 82-87; Can, Treas and Steward Westmr Abbey from 87. *8 Little Cloister, Westminster Abbey, London SW1P 3PL* 071-222 5791

SEMPLE, Henry Michael. b 40. FIMA FBIM FRSA K Coll Lon BSc62 Birkb Coll Lon PhD67. S Dios Minl Tr Scheme. **d** 87 **p** 88. Dep-Prin Guildf Coll of Tech from 87; NSM Steyning *Chich* from 87; Perm to Offic *Guildf* from 87. *Tilings, Goring Road, Steyning, W Sussex BN44 3GF* Steyning (0903) 813677

SEMPLE, Patrick William. b 45. Sussex Univ BA66 Bris Univ DipTh70. Sarum & Wells Th Coll 68. **d** 72 **p** 73. C Paddington Ch *Lon* 72-75; Ind Chapl *Nor* 75-79; P-in-c Woodbastwick 76-79; V Kensington St Barn *Lon* 79-83; V Coleford w Staunton *Glouc* from 83; P-in-c Forest of Dean Ch Ch w English Bicknor 84-89. *The Vicarage, 40 Boxbush Road, Coleford, Glos GL16 8DN* Dean (0594) 33379

SEMPLE, Studdert Patrick. b 39. TCD BA66. CITC 67. **d** 67 **p** 68. C Orangefield *D & D* 67-70; I Stradbally *C & O* 71-82; Ch of Ireland Adult Educn Officer 82-88; I Donoughmore and Donard w Dunlavin *D & G* from 88. *The Rectory, Donard, Dunlavin, Co Wicklow, Irish Republic* Naas (45) 54631

SENAR, Canon Howard. b 15. FSA. St Chad's Coll Dur BA37 DipTh38 MA40 Lon Univ BD58. **d** 38 **p** 39. Chapl Ashridge Management Coll 62-82; R Lt Gaddesden

St Alb 62-82; Dir of Ords 63-76; Hon Can St Alb 68-82; NSM Aylesbeare, Rockbeare, Farringdon etc *Ex* 82-87; rtd 87; Perm to Offic *Ex* from 87. *Dunholm, Down St Mary, Crediton, Devon EX17 6EF* Copplestone (0363) 84878

SENIOR, Canon David Geoffrey Christopher Murray. b 16. Magd Coll Ox BA40 MA42. Westcott Ho Cam 40. **d** 41 **p** 42. C Nunhead St Antony *S'wark* 41-44; C Eltham St Jo 44-48; C York St Mich-le-Belfrey *York* 48-55; V Helmsley from 55; V Pockley cum E Moors 55-77; RD Helmsley 75-85; Can and Preb York Minster from 83. *Canons Garth, Helmsley, York YO6 5AQ* Helmsley (0439) 70236

SENIOR, David John. b 47. Oak Hill Th Coll. **d** 82 **p** 83. C Market Harborough *Leic* 82-85; TV Marfleet *York* from 85. *St Giles's Vicarage, Church Lane, Hull HU9 5RL* Hull (0482) 783690

SENIOR, George. b 36. Open Univ BA83. E Midl Min Tr Course 82. **d** 86 **p** 87. NSM Spratton *Pet* 86-90; NSM Cottesbrooke w Gt Creaton and Thornby 86-90; C Darwen St Pet w Hoddlesden *Blackb* from 90. *8 Stansfield Street, Darwen, Lancs BB3 2NR* Darwen (0254) 703796

SENIOR, John Peter. b 23. Lon Univ BSc48. Edin Th Coll 63. **d** 65 **p** 66. C Heysham *Blackb* 68-71; V Blackpool St Mich 71-79; V Heddon-on-the-Wall *Newc* 79-88; rtd 88. *56 Thorpe Lane, Huddersfield HD5 8TA* Huddersfield (0484) 530466

SENNITT, Nicholas David. b 43. St Steph Ho Ox. **d** 83 **p** 84. C Dalton *Sheff* 83-86; V Moorends from 86. *The Vicarage, West Road, Moorends, Doncaster, S Yorkshire DN8 4LH* Thorne (0405) 812237

SENTAMU, John Mugabi. b 47. MA DD. **d** 79 **p** 79. Chapl HM Rem Cen Latchmere Ho 79-82; C Ham St Andr *S'wark* 79-82; C Herne Hill St Paul 82-83; P-in-c Tulse Hill H Trin 83-84; V Upper Tulse Hill St Matthias 83-84; V Tulse Hill H Trin and St Matthias from 85; P-in-c Brixton Hill St Sav 87-89. *The Vicarage, 49 Trinity Rise, London SW2 2QP* 081-674 6721

SENTANCE, Cecil Leslie. b 23. Lon Univ BSc58. S'wark Ord Course 64. **d** 67 **p** 68. C Finchley St Mary *Lon* 67-73; V Friern Barnet St Pet le Poer 73-75; V Feltham 75-82; Bursar Chich Th Coll and Custos St Mary's Hosp 82-86; rtd 86. *Bryn Gosal, Eglwysbach, Colwyn Bay, Clwyd LL28 5UN* Tynygroes (0492) 650768

SEPPALA, Christopher James. b 59. St Jo Coll Dur BA82. Chich Th Coll 83. **d** 85 **p** 86. C Whitstable *Cant* 85-88; C S Ashford Ch Ch 88-91. *9 Newton Road, Whitstable, Kent CT5 2JD* Whitstable (0227) 266411

SERCOMBE, Theodore Friend. b 27. Ch Coll Cam BA47 MA51 Ox Univ DipTh70. Wycliffe Hall Ox 68. **d** 70 **p** 71. C Plymouth St Andr *Ex* 70-73; New Zealand from 73. *46 Invergarry Road, Taupo, New Zealand* Taupo (74) 83372

SERGEANT, John Middlemore. b 13. Wadh Coll Ox BA34 DipTh35 MA38. Wycliffe Hall Ox 34. **d** 36 **p** 37. R Fringford w Hethe and Newton Purcell *Ox* 68-78; P-in-c Cottisford 68-78; P-in-c Hardwick w Tusmore 68-78; rtd 78; Hon C Glympton *Ox* from 82. *37 Rectory Crescent, Middle Barton, Oxford OX5 4BP* Steeple Aston (0869) 40622

SERGEL, Canon Clement Stuart. b 13. Clare Coll Cam BA35 MA52. Wycliffe Hall Ox 35. **d** 37 **p** 38. C Oatlands *Guildf* 37-39; C Hornsey Ch Ch *Lon* 39-41; S Rhodesia 41-52 and 55-62; Dean Bulawayo 55-62; S Africa 41-55 and from 62; Prec Cape Town 52-55; Hon Can St John's 87-90. *c/o St Stephen's Rectory, Central Square, Pinelands, 7405 South Africa* Cape Town (21) 531-4255 or 531-3350

SERJEANT, John Frederick. b 33. K Coll Lon 55. **d** 56 **p** 57. C Over St Chad *Ches* 56-59; C-in-c Brinnington St Luke CD 59-63; V Brinnington 63-69; V Gatley 69-79; TV Halesworth w Linstead and Chediston *St E* 79-80; TV Halesworth w Linstead, Chediston, Holton etc 80-82; C Chesterfield All SS *Derby* 82-88; Chapl Chesterfield R Hosp 82-88; Chapl Chesterfield and N Derby R Hosp from 88. *188 Queen Victoria Road, New Tupton, Chesterfield, Derbyshire S42 6DW* Chesterfield (0246) 863395

SERJEANTSON, Eric William. b 09. St Jo Coll Ox BA32 MA40. St Boniface Warminster 30. **d** 32 **p** 33. V Leebotwood w Longnor *Heref* 54-74; P-in-c Stapleton 72-74; P-in-c Dorrington 72-74; rtd 74; Perm to Offic *Heref* 74-90. *6 Chartwell Close, Church Stretton, Shropshire SY6 6ES* Church Stretton (0694) 723244

SEROCOLD, Ralph Edward Pearce. b 16. ERD54. Trin Coll Cam BA38 MA45. Bps' Coll Cheshunt 57. **d** 58 **p** 59. R N Stoneham *Win* 69-75; V Hamble le Rice 75-82; rtd 82; Perm to Offic *Portsm* from 82. *Pleasant*

House, West Street, Hambledon, Waterlooville, Hants PO7 4RW Hambledon (070132) 626

SERTIN, John Francis. b 22. Fitzw Ho Cam BA50 MA54. Tyndale Hall Bris. **d** 45 **p** 46. C Sidcup Ch Ch *Roch* 45-47; Chapl Fitzw Ho Cam 47-50; C-in-c St Paul's Cray St Barn CD *Roch* 50-59; V Chitts Hill St Cuth *Lon* 59-62; Sec Ch Soc 62-67; P-in-c Woburn Square Ch Ch *Lon* 67-77; R Holborn St Geo w H Trin and St Bart 67-80; R Donyatt w Horton, Broadway and Ashill *B & W* from 80. *The Rectory, Broadway, Ilminster, Somerset TA19 9RE* Ilminster (0460) 2559

SERTIN, Canon Peter Frank. b 27. Fitzw Ho Cam BA50 MA55. Ridley Hall Cam 50. **d** 52 **p** 53. C Beckenham Ch Ch *Roch* 52-55; Chapl K Edw Sch Witley 55-62; V Woking St Paul *Guildf* 62-69; V Chorleywood Ch Ch *St Alb* 69-80; Chapl Paris St Mich *Eur* 80-85; Adn N France 84-85; R Hambledon *Guildf* 85-89; TR Canford Magna *Sarum* from 89. *The Rectory, Canford Magna, Wimborne, Dorset BH21 3AF* Wimborne (0202) 883382

SERVANT, Ms Alma Joan. b 51. Nottm Univ BA76 DipLib79. Westcott Ho Cam 83. **dss** 85 **d** 87. Ordsall *S'well* 85-87; Par Dn 87-88; Par Dn Man Whitworth *Man* from 88; Chapl Man Poly from 88. *11 Mardale Avenue, Withington, Manchester M20 9TU* 061-434 4071

SERVANTE, Kenneth Edward. b 29. AKC55. **d** 56 **p** 57. C Chaddesden St Phil *Derby* 56-58; C Brampton St Thos 58-61; C Whitfield 61-63; V Derby St Paul 63-70; V Elmton 70-81; P-in-c Winster 81-82; P-in-c Elton 81-82; R S Darley, Elton and Winster from 82. *The Vicarage, Winster, Matlock, Derbyshire DE4 2DH* Winster (062988) 256

SERVICE, Donald Thomas McKinlay. b 26. Trin Coll Cam BA51 MA53. Ridley Hall Cam 51. **d** 53 **p** 54. C Ealing Dean St Jo *Lon* 53-57; C Farnborough *Guildf* 57-61; Asst Chapl Kingham Hill Sch Ox 62-77; Chapl 77-79; V Mayfield *Lich* 79-84; P-in-c Weare w Badgworth and Biddisham *B & W* 84-85; P-in-c Compton Bishop w Loxton and Christon 84-85; R Crook Peak from 85. *The Rectory, Sparrow Hill Way, Weare, Axbridge, Somerset BS26 2LE* Axbridge (0934) 733140

SESSFORD, Alan. b 34. Bps' Coll Cheshunt 65. **d** 66 **p** 67. C Highcliffe w Hinton Admiral *Win* 66-69; C Minehead *B & W* 70; C Chandler's Ford *Win* 70-73; V Burton and Sopley from 73. *The Vicarage, Burton, Christchurch, Dorset BH23 7JU* Christchurch (0202) 484471

✠SESSFORD, Rt Rev George Minshull. b 28. St Andr Univ MA51. Linc Th Coll 51. **d** 53 **p** 54 **c** 70. C Glas St Mary *Glas* 53-58; Chapl Glas Univ 55-58; P-in-c Cumbernauld 58-66; R Forres *Mor* 66-70; Bp Mor from 70. *Spynie House, 96 Fairfield Road, Inverness IV3 5LL* Inverness (0463) 231059

SETTIMBA, John Henry. b 52. Pan Africa Chr Coll BA. **d** 78 **p** 80. Kenya 78-81; Uganda 81-85; C Allerton *Bradf* 86-87; C W Ham *Chelmsf* from 87. *St Thomas House, 29A Mortham Street, London E15 3LS* 081-519 0653

SEVILLE, Christopher John. b 57. Trin Hall Cam MA80. Coll of Resurr Mirfield 87. **d** 89 **p** 90. C Knowle *Bris* from 89. *41 Bayham Road, Bristol BS4 2DR* Bristol (0272) 719333

SEWARD, Jolyon Frantom. b 57. Univ of Wales (Cardiff) BA81. Chich Th Coll 83. **d** 86 **p** 87. C Llanblethian w Cowbridge and Llandough etc *Llan* 86-88; C Newton Nottage from 88. *5B West End Avenue, Porthcawl, M Glam CF36 3NE* Porthcawl (0656) 713762

SEWELL, Godfrey John. St D Coll Lamp BA59. **d** 60 **p** 61. C Llangattock J Caerleon and Llanhennog *Mon* 60-63; W Indies 63-90; Dep Chapl HM Pris Liv 90-91; Chapl HM Pris Brinsford from 91. *HM Prison Brinsford, New Road, Featherstone, Wolverhampton WV10 7PY* Wolverhampton (0902) 791118

SEWELL, John. b 10. MBE46. Tyndale Hall Bris 60. **d** 61 **p** 62. R Yelvertoft w Clay Coton and Lilbourne *Pet* 69-74; rtd 75. *Flat 4, 75 Chatsworth Gardens, Eastbourne, E Sussex BN20 7JP* Eastbourne (0323) 640980

SEWELL, Jonathan William. b 60. Lanc Univ BA82 BTh86. Linc Th Coll 83. **d** 86 **p** 87. C Ilkeston St Mary *Derby* 86-89; C Enfield Chase St Mary *Lon* from 89. *8 Comreddy Close, Enfield, Middx EN2 8RL* 081-363 3640

SEWELL, Robin Warwick. b 42. Trin Coll Bris. **d** 82 **p** 83. C Hinckley H Trin *Leic* 82-85; C Broadwater St Mary *Chich* 85-89; Chapl Barcelona *Eur* from 89. *Calle San Juan dela Salle 41, Horacio 38, 08022 Barcelona, Spain* Barcelona (3) 417-8867

SEWELL, Miss Sarah Frances. b 61. Wycliffe Hall Ox 87. **d** 91. C Binley *Cov* from 91. *3 Tysoe Croft, Coventry CV3 2FF* Coventry (0203) 636335

SEXTON, Canon Michael Bowers. b 28. SS Coll Cam BA52 MA56. Wells Th Coll 52. **d** 54 **p** 55. C Miles Platting St Luke *Man* 54-57; C Bradf cum Beswick 57-58; C-in-c Oldham St Chad Limeside CD 58-62; R Filby w Thrigby w Mautby *Nor* 62-72; P-in-c Runham 67-72; P-in-c Stokesby w Herringby 68-72; R Hethersett w Canteloff 72-85; V Ketteringham 73-84; RD Humbleyard 81-86; Hon Can Nor Cathl from 85; R Hethersett w Canteloff w Lt and Gt Melton 85-86; V Hunstanton St Mary w Ringstead Parva, Holme etc from 86. *St Mary's Vicarage, Hunstanton, Norfolk PE36 6JS* Hunstanton (0485) 532169

SEYMOUR, David. b 43. Kelham Th Coll 60. **d** 68 **p** 69. C Cowley St Jas *Ox* 68-73; TV Lynton, Brendon, Countisbury, Lynmouth etc *Ex* 73-77; C-in-c Luton (Princes Park) CD *Roch* 78-79; V Rosherville 79-90; rtd 90. *4 Swinburne Drive, Lowry Hill, Carlisle CA3 0PY* Carlisle (0228) 818246

SEYMOUR, David Raymond Russell. b 56. Keble Coll Ox BA79 MA88. St Steph Ho Ox 79. **d** 81 **p** 82. C Tilehurst St Mich *Ox* 81-85; TV Parkstone St Pet w Branksea and St Osmund *Sarum* 85-91; V Bradford-on-Avon Ch Ch from 91. *Christ Church Vicarage, 3D Mount Pleasant, Bradford-on-Avon, Wilts BA15 1SJ* Bradford-on-Avon (02216) 7656

SEYMOUR, Canon John Charles. b 30. Oak Hill Th Coll 51 and 55 Wycliffe Coll Toronto 54. **d** 57 **p** 58. C Islington St Andr w St Thos and St Matthias *Lon* 57-60; C Worthing St Geo *Chich* 60-63; V Thornton *Leic* 63-70; R Kirby Muxloe 70-81; TR 81-83; Hon Can Leic Cathl from 82; RD Sparkenhoe I 83-88; R Market Bosworth w Shenton 83-87; TR Market Bosworth, Cadeby w Sutton Cheney etc from 87; RD Sparkenhoe W (Hinkley & Bosworth) from 89. *The Rectory, Park Street, Market Bosworth, Nuneaton, Warks CV13 0LL* Market Bosworth (0455) 290239

SEYMOUR, Ralph. b 05. Cuddesdon Coll 73. **d** 73 **p** 73. Hon C Tring *St Alb* 73-80; Perm to Offic from 80. *6 Regal Court, Tring, Herts HP23 4PT* Tring (044282) 2223

SEYMOUR-WHITELEY, Richard Dudley. b 59. Leic Poly BSc80. Linc Th Coll 82. **d** 85 **p** 86. C Bushey *St Alb* 85-89; C Stevenage St Mary Sheppall w Aston from 89. *31 Harefield, Shephall, Stevenage, Herts SG2 9NG* Stevenage (0438) 365714

SHACKELL, Kenneth Norman. b 26. S'wark Ord Course. **d** 69 **p** 70. NSM Greenwich St Alfege w St Pet and St Paul *S'wark* from 69. *48 Crooms Hill, London SE10 8HD* 081-858 3458

SHACKLEFORD, Richard Neal. b 40. Univ of Denver BA64 Univ of N Colorado MA74. St Steph Ho Ox 84. **d** 86 **p** 87. C Poulton-le-Fylde *Blackb* 86-88; USA from 88. *565 South Olive Way, Denver, Colorado 80224, USA*

SHACKLETON, Canon Alan. b 31. Sheff Univ BA53. Wells Th Coll 54. **d** 56 **p** 57. C Ladybarn *Man* 56-58; C Bolton St Pet 58-61; V Middleton Junction 61-70; V Heywood St Luke 70-84; AD Rochdale from 82; Hon Can Man Cathl from 84; V Heywood St Luke w All So 85-86; TV Rochdale from 86. *The Vicarage, Sparrow Hill, Rochdale OL16 1QT* Rochdale (0706) 45014

SHACKLETON, Arnold. b 08. BA31. Chich Th Coll 75. **d** 75 **p** 76. Hon C Chislehurst Annunciation *Roch* 75-83; Perm to Offic from 83. *54 High Street, Chislehurst, Kent* 081-467 6759

SHACKLETON, Bernard. b 35. Lon Univ BD65 St Chad's Coll Dur BA58 DipTh60. **d** 60 **p** 61. C Chislehurst Annunciation *Roch* 60-67; V Higham and Merston 67-87; V N Curry *B & W* from 87. *The Vicarage, North Curry, Taunton, Somerset TA3 6JU* North Curry (0823) 490255

SHACKLETON, Ian Roderick. b 40. St Fran Coll Brisbane 69 ACT ThL71. **d** 72 **p** 72. Australia 72-78; C Birch St Agnes *Man* 79-80; P-in-c Newton Heath St Wilfrid and St Anne 80-87; NSM W Derby (or Tuebrook) St Jo *Liv* 87-90; C from 90. *12 Green Lane, Liverpool L13 7EA* 051-259 5002

SHACKLOCK, David Peter Riley. b 36. CCC Cam BA60 MA64. Ridley Hall Cam 60. **d** 62 **p** 63. C Park Estate St Chris CD *Leic* 62-66; CF 66-71; R Redhill *Chich* 71-80; V Fulham St Mary N End *Lon* 80-87; V Redhill H Trin *S'wark* from 87. *Holy Trinity Vicarage, 2 Carlton Road, Redhill RH1 2BX* Redhill (0737) 766604

SHAFEE, Kenneth Harold. b 30. ALA64. Ex & Truro NSM Scheme 78. **d** 81 **p** 82. NSM Littleham w Exmouth *Ex* 81-85; Custos St Jo Hosp Heytesbury 85-89; NSM Lydford, Brent Tor, Bridestowe and Sourton *Ex* 89-90; rtd 90; Perm to Offic *Ex* from 90. *The Firs, Exeter Road, Dawlish, Devon EX7 0LX* Dawlish (0626) 888326

SHAIL, Canon William Frederick. b 15. Kelham Th Coll. **d** 41 **p** 42. V Bournemouth St Alb *Win* 68-78; V Burley

Ville 78-84; rtd 84; Perm to Offic *Win* from 84. *19 Halton Close, Bransgore, Christchurch, Dorset BH23 8HZ* Bransgore (0425) 73064

SHAKESPEARE, Daniel. b 19. E Anglian Minl Tr Course 79. **d** 81 **p** 82. NSM Hethersett w Canteloff *Nor* 81-85; NSM Hethersett w Canteloff w Lt and Gt Melton from 85. *23 Central Crescent, Hethersett, Norwich NR9 3EP* Norwich (0603) 810727

SHALLCROSS, Martin Anthony. b 37. FRICS70. Sarum & Wells Th Coll 75. **d** 78 **p** 79. NSM Landford w Plaitford *Sarum* 78-81; NSM Bramshaw 78-81; NSM Tisbury from 81. *Wallmead Farm, Tisbury, Salisbury SP3 6RB* Tisbury (0747) 870208

SHAMASH, Albert Saul. b 11. Bp's Coll Calcutta DipTh42. **d** 41 **p** 43. V Brackenfield w Wessington *Derby* 71-76; rtd 76; Perm to Offic *Derby* from 76. *The Coppice, 70 Broadway, Swanwick, Derby DE55 1AJ* Leabrooks (0773) 605547

SHAMBROOK, Roger William. b 46. Sarum & Wells Th Coll 78. **d** 83 **p** 84. OSP 76-82; C Southbourne St Kath *Win* 83-86; TV Bridport *Sarum* from 86. *The Vicarage, Parsonage Road, Bridport, Dorset DT6 5ET* Bridport (0308) 23458

SHAND, Dr Brian Martin. b 53. Univ Coll Lon BA76 PhD82. St Steph Ho Ox 85. **d** 87 **p** 88. C Uxbridge St Marg *Lon* 87-88; C Uxbridge 88-90; C Worplesdon *Guildf* from 90; Relig Affairs Producer BBC Radio Surrey from 90. *St Albans House, 96 Oak Hill, Wood Street Village, Guildford, Surrey GU3 3ES* Guildford (0483) 235136

SHAND, John. b 06. Aber Univ MA27. Edin Th Coll 32. **d** 34 **p** 35. R Buckie *Ab* 69-71; rtd 71. *7 Albany Court, Dennyduff Road, Fraserburgh, Aberdeenshire AB43 5NG* Fraserburgh (0346) 27948

SHANKS, Robert Andrew Gulval. b 54. Ball Coll Ox BA75 G&C Coll Cam BA79. Westcott Ho Cam 77. **d** 80 **p** 81. C Potternewton *Ripon* 80-83; C Stanningley St Thos 84-87. *52 Newton Court, Leeds LS8 2PH* Leeds (0532) 485011

SHANNON, Brian James. b 35. St Chad's Coll Dur BA59 DipTh61. **d** 61 **p** 62. C Palmers Green St Jo *Lon* 61-65; C Kenton 65-70; V Roxbourne St Andr 70-81; V Thorpe-le-Soken *Chelmsf* from 81. *The Vicarage, Mill Lane, Thorpe-le-Soken, Clacton-on-Sea CO16 0ED* Clacton-on-Sea (0225) 861234

SHANNON, Canon Francis Thomas. b 16. TCD BA39 MA. CITC. **d** 39 **p** 40. I Carnew w Kilrush *C & O* 61-91; RD Wexford 68-91; Preb Ferns Cathl from 71; Treas 80-81; Chan 81-85; Prec from 85; rtd 91. *The Rectory, Carnew, Co Wicklow, Irish Republic* Gorey (55) 26207

SHANNON, Ven Malcolm James Douglas. b 49. TCD BA72 MA75. CITC 75. **d** 75 **p** 76. C Clooney *D & R* 75-78; I Kilcolman w Kiltallagh, Killorglin, Knockane etc *L & K* from 78; Adn Ardfert and Aghadoe from 88; Dir of Ords from 91. *Kilcolman Rectory, Miltown, Killarney, Co Kerry, Irish Republic* Tralee (66) 67302

SHANNON, Trevor Haslam. b 33. Selw Coll Cam BA57 MA61 Lon Univ BD69. Westcott Ho Cam 57. **d** 59 **p** 60. C Moss Side Ch Ch *Man* 59-62; V Woolfold 62-66; Chapl Forest Sch Snaresbrook 66-80 and 87-88; V Gt Ilford St Marg *Chelmsf* 88-90; RD Redbridge from 90; TR Gt Ilford SS Clem and Marg from 90. *70 Brisbane Road, Ilford, Essex IG1 4SL* 081-554 7542

SHANNON, Canon William Patrick. b 09. ARCO34 Glas Univ MA31. Edin Th Coll 31. **d** 33 **p** 34. R Kington w Huntington *Heref* 65-75; RD Kington and Weobley 72-75; Preb Heref Cathl 74-75; rtd 75; Hon Can St Andr Cathl *Ab* from 76; Perm to Offic *Glouc* from 76. *1 Abbey Cottage, Gloucester Road, Tewkesbury, Glos GL20 5SR* Tewkesbury (0684) 295330

SHAPLAND, David Edward. b 26. Cuddesdon Coll 51. **d** 53 **p** 54. Warden Llanerchwen Trust 70-91; Lic to Offic *S & B* 70-79; *Chich* from 79; rtd 91. *Boundary House, Udimore, Rye, E Sussex TN31 6BG* Brede (0424) 882127

SHARE, David James. b 30. Sarum Th Coll 56. **d** 58 **p** 59. C Whipton *Ex* 58-63; Min Tiverton St Andr Statutory Distr 63-69; RD Tiverton 67-74; V Tiverton St Andr 69-79; P-in-c Ex St Thos 79-80; TR Ex St Thos and Em 80-83; V Woodbury from 83. *The Vicarage, Woodbury, Exeter EX5 1EF* Woodbury (0395) 32315

SHARLAND, Canon Charles Thomas. b 08. Wycliffe Hall Ox 45. **d** 45 **p** 46. R Heigham H Trin *Nor* 61-75; Hon Can Nor Cathl 73-85; rtd 75; Perm to Offic *Nor* from 75. *101 Trafford Road, Norwich NR1 2QT* Norwich (0603) 626817

SHARLAND, Mrs Marilyn. b 40. City of Birm Coll CertEd61. Oak Hill Th Coll 84. **dss** 86 **d** 87. Barkingside St Laur *Chelmsf* 86-87; Hon Par Dn 87-88; Hon Par

Dn Hucclecote *Glouc* 88-89; C Coney Hill from 89. *58 Bullfinch Road, Gloucester GL4 8LX* Gloucester (0452) 416788

SHARMAN, Herbert Leslie John. b 27. St Aid Birkenhead 60. **d** 62 **p** 63. C Stanwix *Carl* 62-66; C Brandon and Santon Downham *St E* 66-87; Perm to Offic from 87. *18 Princes Close, Brandon, Suffolk IP27 0LH* Thetford (0842) 811163

SHARMAN, Hilary John. b 32. Leeds Univ BA58. Coll of Resurr Mirfield 58. **d** 60 **p** 61. C Hertf St Andr *St Alb* 60-64; C Harpenden St Nic 64-72; V High Cross from 72; V Thundridge from 72. *7 Ducketts Wood, Thundridge, Ware, Herts SG12 0SR* Ware (0920) 465561

SHARP, Alfred James Frederick. b 30. Oak Hill Th Coll 62. **d** 64 **p** 65. C Hanley Road St Sav w St Paul *Lon* 64-68; P-in-c Leverton *Linc* 68-84; Chapl Pilgrim Hosp Boston 76-84; P-in-c Benington w Leverton *Linc* 84; V Ch Broughton w Boylestone & Sutton on the Hill *Derby* 84-89; R Ch Broughton w Barton Blount, Boylestone etc from 89. *The Vicarage, Chapel Lane, Church Broughton, Derby DE6 5BB* Sudbury (028378) 296

SHARP, Andrew Timothy. b 58. K Alfred's Coll Win BA79. Wycliffe Hall Ox 82. **d** 85 **p** 86. C Scarborough St Mary w Ch Ch and H Apostles *York* 85-89; C Luton St Fran *St Alb* 89-90; V from 90. *The Vicarage, 145 Hollybush Road, Luton LU2 9HQ* Luton (0582) 28030

SHARP, Bernard. b 03. AKC30. **d** 30 **p** 31. R Gleadless *Sheff* 34-71; rtd 71. *80 Ecclesall Road South, Sheffield S11 9PG* Sheffield (0742) 361447

SHARP, Bernard Harold. b 40. Linc Th Coll 64. **d** 67 **p** 68. C Newton Aycliffe *Dur* 67-69; C Leam Lane CD 69-71; Malawi 72-75; P-in-c Blakenall Heath *Lich* 75-77; TV Gateshead *Dur* 77-79; C Warmsworth *Sheff* 84; C Caerau w Ely *Llan* from 85. *92 Bishopston Road, Ely, Cardiff CF5 5DZ* Cardiff (0222) 566297

SHARP, Brian Phillip. b 48. Cant Sch of Min 85. **d** 88 **p** 89. C S Ashford Ch Ch *Cant* from 88. *38 Bond Road, Ashford, Kent TN23 1UG* Ashford (0233) 631644

SHARP, Cyril Harry. b 07. MBE63. St Aug Coll Cant 38. **d** 39 **p** 40. V Hanwell St Thos *Lon* 64-75; rtd 75. *The Grange, 20 Church Street, Highbridge, Somerset TA9 3AF*

SHARP, Canon David Malcolm. b 33. Hertf Coll Ox BA56 MA59. Cuddesdon Coll 56. **d** 58 **p** 59. C Bris St Mary Redcliffe w Temple *Bris* 58-65; V Henleaze 65-75; V Nor St Pet Mancroft *Nor* 75-82; R Nor St Pet Mancroft w St Jo Maddermarket from 82; Hon Can Nor Cathl from 86. *The Chantry, Chantry Road, Norwich NR2 1QZ* Norwich (0603) 610443 or 627816

SHARP, Kenneth Granville. b 12. Selw Coll Cam BA34 MA38. Westcott Ho Cam 34. **d** 35 **p** 36. India 40-82; Adn Delhi 68-70; rtd 82. *The Brotherhood House, 7 Court Lane, New Delhi 110054, India* New Delhi (11) 251-8515

SHARP, Michael William Hamilton. Ch Ch Ox BA49 MA52. Qu Coll Birm 50. **d** 52 **p** 53. C Greenhill St Jo *Lon* 52-55; Chapl Ripon Hall Ox 55-58; V Brockley Hill St Sav *S'wark* 58-64; R Kidbrooke St Jas 64-72; R Streatham St Leon 73-81; Hon C Ufford *St E* 81-83; P-in-c Stratford St Mary 84-91; P-in-c Higham 84-91; P-in-c Raydon 87-91; Perm to Offic from 91. *Tunstall Old School, School Road, Tunstall, Woodbridge, Suffolk IP12 2JZ* Colchester (0206) 322128

SHARP, Canon Nevill Maurice Granville. b 02. Selw Coll Cam BA24 MA29. Westcott Ho Cam 24. **d** 25 **p** 26. Hon Can Cant Cathl *Cant* 54-79; V Ashford 55-72; RD E Charing 55-72; rtd 72; Perm to Offic *Cant* from 79. *4 Kings Avenue, Birchington, Kent* Thanet (0843) 41324

SHARP, Ralph Norman. b 96. Qu Coll Cam BA21 MA24. Ridley Hall Cam 21. **d** 22 **p** 23. Iran 24-67; rtd 67; Perm to Offic *Bris* from 68. *7 Hungerford Road, Chippenham, Wilts SN15 1QW* Chippenham (0249) 652659

SHARP, Canon Reuben Thomas George. b 27. ALCD57. **d** 57 **p** 58. C Pudsey St Lawr *Bradf* 57-60; V Cononley w Bradley 60-63; Dioc Youth Chapl 60-63; Dioc Youth Officer *Wakef* 63-68; V Dewsbury All SS 68-84; RD Dewsbury 68-90; Hon Can Wakef Cathl from 76; TR Dewsbury 84-90; V Cawthorne from 90. *The Vicarage, 5 Church Lane, Cawthorne, Barnsley, S Yorkshire S75 4DW* Barnsley (0226) 790235

SHARP, Preb Robert. b 36. FLCM58. St Aid Birkenhead 64. **d** 67 **p** 68. C Shipley St Paul *Bradf* 67-70; C-in-c Thwaites Brow CD 70-74; V Thwaites Brow 74-77; P-in-c Alberbury w Cardeston *Heref* 77-78; V 78-87; V Ford 77-87; V Claverley w Tuckhill from 87; RD Bridgnorth from 89; Preb Heref Cathl from 91. *The*

Vicarage, Claverley, Wolverhampton WV5 7DP Claverley (07466) 268

SHARPE, Alan Brian. b 39. Lich Th Coll 64. **d** 67 **p** 68. C Croydon Woodside *Cant* 67-70; C Portsea St Mary *Portsm* 70-75; V Sheerness H Trin w St Paul *Cant* 75-83; V Hove St Patr w Ch Ch and St Andr *Chich* 83-90; V Hove St Patr from 90. *St Patrick's Vicarage, 30 Cambridge Road, Hove, E Sussex BN3 1DF* Brighton (0273) 733151

SHARPE, Bruce Warrington. b 41. JP88. DMS85 MBIM85. Ely Th Coll 62 St Steph Ho Ox 64. **d** 65 **p** 66. C Streatham St Pet *S'wark* 65-67; St Lucia 67-68; Hon C Leic St Matt and St Geo *Leic* 68-69; Hon C Catford St Laur *S'wark* 69-70; Hon C Deptford St Paul 70-75; Hon C Lamorbey H Redeemer *Roch* 76-83; Perm to Offic 83-88; Hon C Sidcup St Andr from 88. *72 Faraday Avenue, Sidcup, Kent DA14 4JF* 081-300 0695

SHARPE, Cecil Frederick. b 23. Edin Th Coll 52. **d** 54 **p** 55. V Wythall *Birm* 58-80; Perm to Offic from 80; rtd 88. *35 Shirley Park Road, Shirley, Solihull, W Midlands B90 2BZ* 021-745 6905

SHARPE, David Francis. b 32. Ex Coll Ox BA56 MA59. St Steph Ho Ox 57. **d** 60 **p** 61. C Hunslet St Mary and Stourton *Ripon* 60-63; C Notting Hill St Jo *Lon* 63-68; V Haggerston St Mary w St Chad 68-78; P-in-c Haggerston St Aug w St Steph 73-78; V Haggerston St Chad 78-83; V Mill Hill St Mich from 83. *St Michael's Vicarage, 9 Flower Lane, London NW7 2JA* 081-959 1449

SHARPE, David Robert Scott. b 31. Keble Coll Ox BA54 MA66. Ely Th Coll 54. **d** 56 **p** 57. C Bethnal Green St Jo w St Simon *Lon* 56-59; C St Ives *Truro* 59-61; V Pencoys w Carnmenellis 61-65; V Penwerris 65-69; Lic to Offic *Portsm* from 73. *16 Privett Place, Gosport, Hants PO12 3SQ* Gosport (0705) 589248

SHARPE, Derek Martin Brereton. b 29. Birkb Coll Lon BA60. NE Ord Course 87. **d** 90 **p** 91. NSM Scarborough St Luke *York* from 90; Asst Chapl Scarborough Distr Hosp from 90. *Low Farm House, Allerston, Pickering, N Yorkshire YO18 7PG* Scarborough (0723) 859271

SHARPE, Gerard John. b 23. Westcott Ho Cam. **d** 64 **p** 65. C Thetford St Cuth w H Trin *Nor* 64-70; V Holme *Ely* 70-76; R Conington 70-76; R Glatton from 74; V Holme w Conington from 76; RD Yaxley 82-88. *The Vicarage, Holme, Peterborough PE7 3PH* Ramsey (0487) 830622

SHARPE, Harold Dudley. b 18. Ch Coll Cam BA40. St Andr Whittlesford. **d** 41 **p** 42. Chapl RN 46-73; rtd 73; Perm to Offic *B & W* from 75. *44 Kingsdon, Somerton, Somerset TA11 7JX* Ilchester (0935) 384

SHARPE, Miss Joan Valerie. b 33. E Midl Min Tr Course 73. **d** 88. Hon Par Dn Warsop *S'well* from 88. *1 Forest Court, Eakring Road, Mansfield, Notts NG18 3DP* Mansfield (0623) 631505

SHARPE, John Brebber (Brother Mark). b 14. **d** 85. CSWG from 82; Lic to Offic *Chich* from 85. *The Monastery, 23 Cambridge Road, Hove, E Sussex BN3 1DE* Brighton (0273) 726698

SHARPE, John Edward. b 50. Dur Univ BSc72. St Jo Coll Dur DipTh75. **d** 76 **p** 77. C Woodford Wells *Chelmsf* 76-79; C Ealing St Mary *Lon* 79-83; Min Walsall St Martin *Lich* 83-87; TV Walsall from 87. *St Martin's House, 17 Daffodil Road, Walsall WS5 3DQ* Walsall (0922) 23216

SHARPE, Canon John Leslie. b 33. MInstGA88 Birm Univ DPS71 Open Univ BA75. Kelham Th Coll 54. **d** 58 **p** 59. C Old Charlton *S'wark* 58-63; Papua New Guinea 63-70; P-in-c Southn SS Pet and Paul w All SS *Win* 71-73; TV Southn (City Cen) 73-76; Chapl SW Hants Psychiatric Services from 76; Chapl Knowle Hosp Fareham from 76; Hon Can Portsm Cathl *Portsm* from 86. *The Chaplain's Office, Knowle Hospital, Fareham, Hants PO17 5NA* Wickham (0329) 832271

SHARPE, Canon Kenneth Henry. b 20. Roch Th Coll. **d** 60 **p** 61. Uganda 60-78; Can Nakuru 73-78; Hon Can Nakuru from 78; V Coley *Wakef* 78-89; rtd 89. *54 Bradford Road, Menston, Ilkley, W Yorkshire LS29 6BX* Menston (0943) 77710

SHARPE, Kenneth William. b 40. Univ of Wales (Lamp) BA61. Sarum Th Coll 61. **d** 63 **p** 64. C Hubberston *St D* 63-71; TV Cwmbran *Mon* 71-74; Dioc Children's Adv 72-82; Dioc Youth Chapl 74-82; V Dingestow and Llangovan w Penyclawdd and Tregaer 74-82; V Newport St Mark from 82; Chapl Alltyryn Hosp Gwent from 83. *The Vicarage, 7 Goldtops, Newport, Gwent NP9 4PH* Newport (0633) 263321

SHARPE, Miss Mary. b 31. CQSW71. Dalton Ho Bris 58. **dss** 78 **d** 87. Upton (or Overchurch) *Ches* 78-83; Harlescott *Lich* 83-84; New Brighton All SS *Ches* 85-87;

Par Dn 87-89; rtd 89. *Frondeg, Waunfawr, Caernarfon, Gwynedd*

SHARPE, Mrs Mary Primrose. b 22. Coll of St Matthias Bris CertEd. Gilmore Ho CertRK51 DC51 CMS Tr Coll Chislehurst. **dss** 81 **d** 87. Coley *Wakef* 81-87; Hon Par Dn 87-89; rtd 89. *54 Bradford Road, Menston, Ilkley, W Yorkshire LS29 6BX* Menston (0943) 877710

SHARPE, Richard Gordon. b 48. Birm Univ BA69. St Jo Coll Nottm BA74. **d** 75 **p** 76. C Hinckley H Trin *Leic* 75-78; C Kingston upon Hull H Trin *York* 78-85; Chapl Marston Green Hosp Birm 85-88; Chelmsley Hosp Birm 86-88; TV Chelmsley Wood *Birm* 85-88; P-in-c Dosthill from 88. *The Vicarage, Dosthill, Tamworth, Staffs B77 1LU* Tamworth (0827) 281349

SHARPE, Robert Nelson. b 05. TCD 64. **d** 65 **p** 66. I Sallaghy *Clogh* 67-73; I Clogh w Errigal Portclare 73-80; I Augher 73-80; Preb Clogh Cathl 76-80; rtd 80. *22 Ballyholme Court, Windmill Road, Bangor, Co Down BT20 5QX* Bangor (0247) 454890

SHARPE, Canon Roger. b 35. TCD BA60 MA63. Qu Coll Birm 60. **d** 62 **p** 63. C Stockton H Trin *Dur* 62-64; C Oakdale St Geo *Sarum* 64-68; V Redlynch and Morgan's Vale 68-86; RD Alderbury 82-86; V Warminster St Denys 86-88; R Upton Scudamore 86-88; V Horningsham 86-88; R Warminster St Denys, Upton Scudamore etc from 88; Can and Preb Sarum Cathl from 89; RD Heytesbury from 89; Chmn Dioc Assoc for Deaf from 91. *The Vicarage, Church Street, Warminster, Wilts BA12 8PG* Warminster (0985) 213456

SHARPLES, Canon Alfred Cyril. b 09. Man Univ BA33. Linc Th Coll 33. **d** 35 **p** 36. V Hope St Jas *Man* 51-76; Hon Can Man Cathl 74-76; rtd 76; Perm to Offic *Ches* and *Man* from 77. *30 Greenbank Drive, Bollington, Macclesfield, Cheshire SK10 5LW* 061-207 5073

SHARPLES, David. b 41. Linc Th Coll 71. **d** 73 **p** 74. C Reddish *Man* 73-75; C Prestwich St Mary 76-78; V Ashton St Jas 78-86; V Hope St Jas from 86. *Hope Vicarage, Vicarage Close, Pendleton, Salford M6 8EJ* 061-789 3303

SHARPLES, David. b 58. Lon Univ BD81 AKC81. Coll of Resurr Mirfield. **d** 82 **p** 83. C Prestwich St Mary *Man* 82-87; V Royton St Anne from 87. *St Anne's Vicarage, St Anne's Avenue, Royton, Oldham OL2 5AD* 061-624 2249

SHARPLES, Dr Derek. b 35. SS Paul & Mary Coll Cheltenham CertEd57 Liv Univ DipEd63 Man Univ MEd66 Bath Univ PhD72 Open Univ BA79 FCollP86. W Midl Minl Tr Course 83. **d** 86 **p** 87. NSM Malvern H Trin and St Jas *Worc* 86-90; C St Jo in Bedwardine from 90. *16 Heron Close, Worcester WR2 4BW* Worcester (0905) 429641

SHARPLES, John Charles. b 29. St Jo Coll York TCert48 Lon Univ BSc55. St Deiniol's Hawarden 87. **d** 87 **p** 88. Hon C Wigan St Mich *Liv* 87-89; P-in-c New Springs from 89. *7 Lealholme Avenue, Wigan, Lancs WN2 1EH* Wigan (0942) 43071

SHARPLES, John Stanley. b 11. Lon Univ BA54 MA64. Tyndale Hall Bris 33. **d** 37 **p** 38. C Upper Holloway St Pet *Lon* 37-39; C Dorking St Paul *Guildf* 39-41; Chapl Goldings Tech Sch 41-42; R Man St Phil *Man* 42-44; V Hatherden cum Tangley *Win* 44-52; Canada from 52. *4453 Ontario Street, Beamsville, Ontario, Canada, L0R 1B5* Toronto (416) 563-7949

SHARPLEY, Ven Roger Ernest Dion. b 28. Ch Ch Ox BA52 MA56. St Steph Ho Ox 52. **d** 54 **p** 55. C Southwick St Columba *Dur* 54-60; V Middlesb All SS *York* 60-81; P-in-c Middlesb St Hilda w St Pet 64-72; RD Middlesbrough 70-81; Can and Preb York Minster 74-81; P-in-c Middlesb St Aid 79; V 79-81; V St Andr Holborn *Lon* from 81; Adn Hackney from 81. *St Andrew's Vicarage, 5 St Andrew Street, London EC4A 3AB* 071-353 3544

SHARPUS-JONES, Trevor. b 20. TD66. St And Dioc Tr Course 83. **d** 87 **p** 88. NSM Elie and Earlsferry *St And* from 87; NSM St Andrews St Andr from 87; NSM Pittenweem from 89. *Etta Bank, 40 Leven Road, Lundin Links, Leven, Fife KY8 6AH* Lundin Links (0333) 320510

SHAW, Alan. b 24. Man Univ BSc44 MSc48 PhD51. Ely Th Coll 55. **d** 57 **p** 58. C Orford St Marg *Liv* 57-59; C Bury St Mary *Man* 59-61; Perm to Offic *Liv* 61-71; V Beckermet St Jo *Carl* 71-76; V Lt Leigh and Lower Whitley *Ches* 76-80; V Latchford Ch Ch from 80. *Christchurch Vicarage, Wash Lane, Warrington WA4 1HT* Warrington (0925) 30846

SHAW, Alan Taylor. b 52. Sarum & Wells Th Coll 88. **d** 90 **p** 91. C Beeston *Ripon* from 90. *45 Cardinal Crescent, Leeds LS11 8HQ* Leeds (0532) 774748

SHAW, Canon Alexander Martin. b 44. AKC67. **d** 68 **p** 69. C Glas St Oswald *Glas* 68-70; C Edin Old St Paul *Edin* 70-75; Chapl K Coll Cam 75-77; C St Marylebone All SS *Lon* 77-78; R Dunoon *Arg* 78-81; Succ Ex Cathl *Ex* 81-83; Dioc Miss and Ecum Officer 83-89; TV Cen Ex 83-87; Can Res St E Cathl *St E* from 89. *3 Crown Street, Bury St Edmunds, Suffolk* Bury St Edmunds (0284) 753866

SHAW, Andrew Jonathan. b 50. Leeds Univ CertEd72 Open Univ BA81. Wycliffe Hall Ox 85. **d** 87 **p** 88. C Witton w Brundall and Braydeston *Nor* 87-89; C Postwick 87-89; C Brundall w Braydeston and Postwick 89-90; C Grayswood *Guildf* 90-91; P-in-c from 91; Chapl RN Sch Haslemere from 90. *Church House, Church Close, Grayswood, Haslemere, Surrey GU27 2DB* Haslemere (0428) 56504

SHAW, Ms Anne Lesley. b 50. Linc Th Coll 77. **dss** 80 **d** 87. Camberwell St Luke *S'wark* 80-85; Chapl Asst Lon Hosp (Whitechapel) 85-90; Chapl Lewisham Hosp from 90. *The Chaplain's Office, Lewisham Hospital, London SE13 6LH* 081-690 4311

SHAW, Dr Anne Patricia Leslie. b 39. MRCS LRCP63 MB, BS63 DA68. Qu Coll Birm 79. **dss** 81 **d** 87. Pinner *Lon* 81-84; Rickmansworth *St Alb* 84-87; Hon Par Dn from 87. *37 Sandy Lodge Road, Moor Park, Rickmansworth, Herts WD3 1LP* Northwood (09274) 27663

SHAW, Anthony Keeble. b 36. K Alfred's Coll Win CertEd. SW Minl Tr Course. **d** 81 **p** 82. NSM E Teignmouth *Ex* 81-83; NSM Highweek and Teigngrace 83-87; C Southbourne St Kath *Win* 87-89. *121 Broadway, Bournemouth BH6 4EJ* Bournemouth (0202) 426171

SHAW, Basil Earle. b 06. BNC Ox BA28 DipTh29 MA32. Wells Th Coll 29. **d** 30 **p** 31. V N Frodingham *York* 60-73; rtd 74. *21 Cranbrook Avenue, Hull*

SHAW, Charles Edward. b 10. Man Univ BA33. Egerton Hall Man 33. **d** 35 **p** 36. C Man St Matt w St Jo *Man* 35-38; C Worsley 38; C Moston St Mary 38-43; V Wingates 43-57; V Waterhead from 57. *Holy Trinity Vicarage, Church Street East, Waterhead, Oldham OL4 2JQ* 061-624 4011

SHAW, Colin Clement Gordon. b 39. RMN60 TNC62 DPS72. Linc Th Coll 65. **d** 67 **p** 68. C Tettenhall Regis *Lich* 67-70; C Tile Cross *Birm* 70-72; V Edstaston *Lich* 72-75; V Whixall 72-75; Chapl Stoke Mandeville Hosp and St Jo Hosp 75-90; Manor Ho Hosp and Tindal Gen Hosp Aylesbury 75-90; R Bledlow w Saunderton and Horsenden *Ox* from 90. *The Rectory, Church End, Bledlow, Aylesbury, Bucks HP17 9PD* Princes Risborough (08444) 4762

SHAW, Colin Martin. b 21. Oak Hill Th Coll 68. **d** 69 **p** 70. C Halliwell St Pet *Man* 69-72; V Tonge Fold 72-78; V Gresley *Derby* 78-82; V Gt Marsden *Blackb* 82-87; rtd 87. *Holborn Close, Huntingdon, Cambs PE17 3AJ* Ramsey (0487) 822246

SHAW, Cuthbert Charles. b 08. St Edm Hall Ox BA35 MA46. Westcott Ho Cam 30. **d** 32 **p** 33. R Aveton Gifford *Ex* 61-72; rtd 73; Perm to Offic *Guildf* from 73. *Flat 29, Manormead, Tilford Road, Hindhead, Surrey GU26 6RP* Hindhead (042873) 5722

SHAW, David George. b 40. Lon Univ BD64. Tyndale Hall Bris 58. **d** 65 **p** 66. C Kirkdale St Lawr *Liv* 65-68; C Bebington *Ches* 68-70; V Swadlincote *Derby* 70-75; R Eyam from 75. *The Rectory, Eyam, Sheffield S30 1QH* Hope Valley (0433) 30821

SHAW, David Parlane. b 32. CITC. **d** 69 **p** 70. Bp's C Lower w Upper Langfield *D & R* 69-75; R Chedburgh w Depden and Rede *St E* 75-78; R Chedburgh w Depden, Rede and Hawkedon 79-82; R Desford *Leic* 82-83; R Desford and Peckleton w Tooley 84-91; P-in-c Ramsden Crays w Ramsden Bellhouse *Chelmsf* from 91. *The Rectory, Church Lane, Crays Hill, Billericay, Essex CM11 2UN* Basildon (0268) 521043

SHAW, David Thomas. b 45. Open Univ BA78. W Midl Minl Tr Course 87. **d** 90. C Sheldon *Birm* from 90. *151 Church Road, Sheldon, Birmingham B26 3TT* 021-743 6956

SHAW, Denis. b 26. Westcott Ho Cam. **d** 59 **p** 60. C Bethnal Green St Matt *Lon* 59-63; R Newton Heath St Wilfrid *Man* 63-71; R Clewer St Andr *Ox* from 71. *The Rectory, 14 Parsonage Lane, Windsor, Berks SL4 5EN* Windsor (0753) 65185

SHAW, Denis Alfred Arthur. b 24. Wells Th Coll 64. **d** 65 **p** 66. C Redditch St Steph *Worc* 65-70; R Addingham *Bradf* from 70. *The Rectory, Addingham, Ilkley, W Yorkshire LS29 0QP* Addingham (0943) 830276

SHAW, Canon Denis Walter. b 16. Sarum Th Coll 65. **d** 67 **p** 68. C Bridport *Sarum* 67-70; R Tarrant Rushton, Tarrant Rawston etc 70-76; RD Milton and Blandford

73-81; P-in-c Bere Regis 76-77; Can and Preb Sarum Cathl 77-85; R Bere Regis and Affpuddle w Turnerspuddle 78-85; rtd 85. *29 Martleaves Close, Weymouth, Dorset DT4 9UT* Dorchester (0305) 774738

SHAW, Ernest Ronald. b 16. K Coll Lon BA38. Chich Th Coll 72. **d** 72 **p** 73. Chapl Cov Cathl *Cov* 72-78; Perm to Offic *Sarum* 79-80; C Semley and Sedgehill 80-85; rtd 85. *Fairmead, Church Hill, Stour Row, Shaftesbury, Dorset SP7 0QW* East Stour (074785) 350

SHAW, Mrs Felicity Mary. b 46. UEA BSc67 MSc68 Liv Inst of Educn DipRE87. Nor Ord Course 88. **d** 91. Par Dn Benchill *Man* from 91. *St Luke's House, Brownley Road, Benchill, Manchester M22 4PT* 061-945 7399

SHAW, Frederick Hugh. b 16. CChem MRSC Dur Univ BSc49 MSc66. E Midl Min Tr Course 73. **d** 76 **p** 77. Hon C Wingerworth *Derby* from 76. *1 Frances Drive, Wingerworth, Chesterfield, Derbyshire S42 6SJ* Chesterfield (0246) 78321

SHAW, Gary Robert. b 59. **d** 85 **p** 86. C Dundonald *D & D* 85-87; I Tullaniskin w Clonoe *Arm* from 87. *215 Brackaville Road, Newmills, Dungannon, Co Tyrone BT71 4EJ* Coalisland (08687) 40370

SHAW, Canon Geoffrey Norman. b 26. Jes Coll Ox MA50. Wycliffe Hall Ox 49. **d** 51 **p** 52. Lic to Offic *Sheff* 68-72; Vice-Prin and Lect Oak Hill Th Coll 72-79; Prin Wycliffe Hall Ox 79-88; Hon Can Ch Ch *Ox* 86-88; rtd 88; Lic to Offic *Nor* from 88. *Kingham, The Green, Thorpe Market, Norfolk NR11 8TL* Cromer (0263) 833580

SHAW, Gerald Oliver. b 32. K Coll Lon 56. **d** 60 **p** 61. C Burnley St Cuth *Blackb* 60-62; C Heysham 62-65; C-in-c Oswaldtwistle All SS CD 65-66; V Oswaldtwistle All SS 66-69; Chapl Leavesden Hosp Abbots Langley 69-75; Chapl Broadmoor Hosp Crowthorne 75-88; C Easthampstead *Ox* from 88. *4 Qualitas, Roman Hill, Bracknell, Berks RG12 4QG* Bracknell (0344) 487248

SHAW, Graham. b 44. Worc Coll Ox BA65. Cuddesdon Coll. **d** 69 **p** 70. C Esher *Guildf* 69-73; R Winford *B & W* 73-78; Chapl Ex Coll Ox 78-85; R Farnborough *Roch* from 88. *The Rectory, Farnborough Hill, Orpington, Kent BR6 7EQ* Farnborough (0689) 53471

SHAW, Grahame David. b 44. Lich Th Coll 65. **d** 68 **p** 69. C Grange St Andr *Ches* 68-73; TV E Runcorn w Halton 73-74; TV Thamesmead *S'wark* 74-79; V Newington St Paul from 79; S'wark Adnry Ecum Officer from 90. *The Vicarage, Lorrimore Square, London SE17 3QU* 071-735 2947 or 735 8815

SHAW, Jack Firth. b 11. Dorchester Miss Coll 35. **d** 38 **p** 39. V Mert St Jo *S'wark* 64-76; rtd 77; Perm to Offic *Cant* from 79. *37 The Crescent, Canterbury, Kent* Canterbury (0227) 451963

SHAW, James Alan. b 20. Keble Coll Ox BA42 MA47. Linc Th Coll 42. **d** 44 **p** 45. R Flax Bourton *B & W* 65-80; V Barrow Gurney 77-80; Chapl and Lect St Deiniol's Lib Hawarden 80-81; rtd 81; Perm to Offic *Ban* 82-89; *Mor* from 90. *Ceol na Mara, 25 Dalchalm, Brora, Sutherland KW9 6LP* Brora (0408) 21058

SHAW, John. b 20. K Coll Lon 57. **d** 59 **p** 60. V Burnley St Cuth *Blackb* 63-74; V Goosnargh w Whittingham 74-85; RD Garstang 79-85; rtd 85; Perm to Offic *Newc* from 85. *13 Southlands, Hexham, Northd NE46 2NG* Hexham (0434) 605576

SHAW, John Reginald Derek. b 32. Sarum Th Coll 57. **d** 59 **p** 60. C Thornbury *Bradf* 59-61; C Tong 62-63; C Clifford *York* 63-65; V Bramham from 65. *The Vicarage, Vicarage Lane, Bramham, Wetherby, W Yorkshire LS23 6QG* Boston Spa (0937) 843631

SHAW, John Richard Astley. b 24. St Jo Coll Dur 46. ACT ThL53. **d** 51 **p** 53. R Guernsey St Marguerite de la Foret *Win* 65-90; rtd 90. *St Antony, Clos de Cornus, St Martin's, Guernsey, Channel Islands* Guernsey (0481) 37097

SHAW, Kenneth James. b 36. St Jo Coll Nottm 85 Edin Th Coll 88. **d** 87 **p** 89. NSM Troon *Glas* 87-89; C Glas St Mary 89-90; R Lenzie from 90. *The Rectory, 1A Beech Road, Lenzie, Glasgow G66 4HN* 041-776 4149

SHAW, Michael Howard. b 38. Leeds Univ BSc61. Linc Th Coll 64. **d** 66 **p** 67. C W Hartlepool St Paul *Dur* 66-68; Asst Master Stockbridge Co Sec Sch 68; Totton Coll 69; Gravesend Boys' Gr Sch 70-72; Maidstone Gr Sch from 72; Perm to Offic *Roch* from 82. *2 Bredgar Close, Maidstone, Kent* Maidstone (0622) 673415

SHAW, Neil Graham. b 61. St Jo Coll Nottm LTh89. **d** 91. C Leamington Priors St Paul *Cov* from 91. *49 Wathen Road, Leamington Spa, Warks CV32 5UY* Leamington Spa (0926) 886687

SHAW, Norman. b 33. Cranmer Hall Dur. **d** 82 **p** 83. C Beamish *Dur* 82-84; P-in-c Craghead 84-88; V Cleadon from 88. *The Vicarage, 5 Sunderland Road, Cleadon, Sunderland SR6 7UR* 091-536 7147

SHAW, Peter Haslewood. b 17. Pemb Coll Cam BA39 MA65. Worc Ord Coll 65. **d** 67 **p** 68. V Alderney *Win* 69-78; V Disley *Ches* 78-82; rtd 82; Chapl Athens w Kyfissia, Patras and Corfu *Eur* 82-85; Hon C Las Palmas 84-85; Hon C Breamore *Win* 85-89. *Manor Cottage, Church Road, Greatworth, Banbury, Oxon OX17 2DU* Banbury (0295) 712102

SHAW, Ralph. b 38. Man Univ MEd70. Sarum & Wells Th Coll 78. **d** 80 **p** 81. C Consett *Dur* 80-84; P-in-c Tanfield 84-88; V from 88. *The Vicarage, Tanfield, Stanley, Co Durham DH9 9PX* Stanley (0207) 232750

SHAW, Ralph Michael. b 45. DipAdEd. Lich Th Coll 68. **d** 70 **p** 71. C Dewsbury All SS *Wakef* 70-75; TV Redcar w Kirkleatham *York* 75-76; Dioc Youth Officer *St Alb* 76-91; Chief Exec John Grooms Assn for the Disabled from 91. *c/o John Grooms Association, 10 Gloucester Drive, London N4 2LP* 081-802 7272

SHAW, Richard. b 46. **d** 89 **p** 90. NSM Porchester *S'well* 89-91. *95 Marshall Hill Drive, Nottingham NG3 6HX* Nottingham (0602) 621705

SHAW, Richard Tom. b 42. AKC69. St Aug Coll Cant 69. **d** 70 **p** 71. C Dunston St Nic *Dur* 70-73; C Maidstone All SS w St Phil and H Trin *Cant* 73-75; Chapl RN 75-79; V Barrow-on-Humber *Linc* 79-83; V Linc St Faith and St Martin w St Pet from 83. *165C Carholme Road, Lincoln LN1 1RU* Lincoln (0522) 531477

SHAW, Robert Christopher. b 34. Man Univ BA BD. Union Th Sem (NY) STM. **d** 82 **p** 83. C Sharlston *Wakef* 82-83; C Scissett St Aug 83-85; R Cumberworth w Denby Dale 85-90; P-in-c Denby 85-90; R Bolton w Ireby and Uldale *Carl* from 90. *The Vicarage, Ireby, Carlisle CA5 1EX* Low Ireby (09657) 307

SHAW, Robert William. b 46. Lon Univ BD69. St Aug Coll Cant 69. **d** 70 **p** 71. C Hunslet St Mary and Stourton *Ripon* 70-71; C Hunslet St Mary 71-74; C Hawksworth Wood 74-76; R Stanningley St Thos 76-84; V Potternewton from 84. *St Martin's Vicarage, 2A St Martin's View, Leeds LS7 3LB* Leeds (0532) 624271

SHAW, Ronald Forbes. b 16. FRICS55 RIBA47. S'wark Ord Course 67. **d** 70 **p** 71. C Belmont *S'wark* 70-73; P-in-c Lower Sydenham St Mich 73-83; rtd 83; Hon C Surbiton St Matt *S'wark* 83-88; Hon C Kingswood from 88. *5 Buckland Road, Lower Kingswood, Tadworth, Surrey KT20 7DN* Mogador (0737) 832921

SHAW, Mrs Rosemary Alice. b 44. CertEd65 DipTh75 CQSW78. S'wark Ord Course 87. **d** 89. Par Dn Walworth *S'wark* from 89. *19 Scutari Road, London SE22 0NN* 081-693 6325

SHAW-HAMILTON, Mrs Janet Elizabeth. b 43. W Midl Minl Tr Course 88. **d** 91. NSM Bromsgrove All SS *Worc* from 91. *76 Hanbury Road, Stoke Prior, Bromsgrove, Worcs B60 4DN* Bromsgrove (0527) 79843

SHAYLOR, Denis Freke. Sarum Th Coll 68. **d** 69 **p** 70. C Caversham *Ox* 69-75; Lic to Offic 76-79; Perm to Offic *Win* from 80. *Asante, Lasham, Alton, Hants GU34 5SJ* Herriard (025683) 351

SHEA, Guy Roland John. b 33. Trin Coll Connecticut BA55 Ch Ch Ox BA58 MA62. Coll of Resurr Mirfield 60. **d** 60 **p** 61. C Kennington St Jo *S'wark* 60-63 and 75-77; C N Audley Street St Mark *Lon* 63-67; C Hammersmith St Sav 67-70; P-in-c Gunnersbury St Jas 70-75; Perm to Offic 77-82; Hon C Fulham St Alb from 82. *5C Collier House, 163-169 Brompton Road, London SW3 1PY* 071-584 4036

SHEAD, John Frederick Henry. b 38. ACP74 FCP81. Westcott Ho Cam 72. **d** 74 **p** 75. Hd Master Thaxted Co Primary Sch 70-85; Hon C Thaxted *Chelmsf* 74-85; C Saffron Walden w Wendens Ambo and Littlebury 86-88; P-in-c Wethersfield w Shalford from 88. *The Vicarage, Braintree Road, Wethersfield CM7 4AD* Great Dunmow (0371) 850245

SHEARD, Ernest. b 29. Linc Th Coll 73. **d** 74 **p** 75. Hon C Birstall *Leic* 74-82; Hon C Birstall and Wanlip 82-84; Asst Chapl Loughb Univ and Colls 75-90; Lic to Offic *Leic* from 90. *21 Orchard Road, Birstall, Leicester LE4 4GD* Leicester (0533) 673901

SHEARD, Neil Jeremy. b 58. Chich Th Coll. **d** 84 **p** 85. C Gellygaer *Llan* 84-86; C Caerphilly 86-90; V Treboeth *S & B* from 90. *St Alban's Vicarage, Heol Fach, Treboeth, Swansea SA5 9DE* Swansea (0792) 771332

SHEARER, Very Rev John. b 26. TCD BA48 MA53 BD53. **d** 50 **p** 51. C Magheralin w Dollingstown *D & D* 50-52; C Ballymacarrett St Patr 52-59; I Magheradroll 59-64; I Seagoe 64-85; Adn Dromore 70-85; I Belf St Anne *Conn* from 85; Dean Belf from 85. *The Deanery, 5 Deramore Drive, Belfast BT9 5JQ* Belfast (0232) 660980 or 328332

SHEARER, John Frank. b 35. Ex Univ BSc60. Tyndale Hall Bris 62. **d** 63 **p** 64. C Blackheath St Jo *S'wark* 63-67;

R Nuff *Ox* from 67. *The Rectory, Nuffield, Henley-on-Thames, Oxon RG9 5SN* Nettlebed (0491) 641305

SHEARING, Michael James. b 39. Lanc Univ BA71. Linc Th Coll. **d** 66 **p** 67. Hon C Hartlepool St Paul *Dur* 66-76; Asst Master Dyke Ho Comp Sch Hartlepool 76-87; C Houghton le Spring 87; P-in-c Wheatley Hill from 87. *The Vicarage, Wheatley Hill, Co Durham DH6 3RA* Wellfield (0429) 820496

SHEARLOCK, Very Rev David John. b 32. Birm Univ BA55. Westcott Ho Cam 56. **d** 57 **p** 58. C Guisborough *York* 57-60; C Christchurch *Win* 60-64; V Kingsclere 64-71; V Romsey 71-82; Dioc Dir of Ords 77-82; Hon Can Win Cathl 78-82; Dean Truro from 82; R Truro St Mary from 82; Chapl Cornwall Fire Brigade from 91. *The Deanery, Lemon Street, Truro, Cornwall TR1 2PE* Truro (0872) 72661

SHEARMAN, Michael Alan. b 22. Down Coll Cam BA44 MA48. Coll of Resurr Mirfield 46. **d** 48 **p** 49. V Enfield St Luke *Lon* 58-87; rtd 87; Perm to Offic *Nor* from 87. *18 Thompson Avenue, Holt, Norfolk NR25 6EN* Holt (0263) 713072

SHEARS, Michael George Frederick. b 33. Pemb Coll Cam BA57 MA68. St Steph Ho Ox 57. **d** 59 **p** 60. C Grantham St Wulfram *Linc* 59-68; R Waltham 68-80; R Barnoldby le Beck 74-80; RD Haverstoe 78-80; V Soham *Ely* from 80; RD Fordham from 83. *The Vicarage, Soham, Ely, Cambs CB7 5DU* Ely (0353) 720423

SHEARWOOD, Alexander George Dobbie. b 21. New Coll Ox BA48. Wells Th Coll 49. **d** 50 **p** 51. R Wickenby w Friesthorpe *Linc* 59-81; R Lissington w Holton cum Beckering 60-81; R Snelland w Snarford 63-81; R Wickenby Gp 82; Perm to Offic *Truro* from 82; rtd 86. *Trelowen, 3 Old Road, Boscastle, Cornwall PL35 0AJ* Boscastle (08405) 663

SHEASBY, Adrian. b 29. Open Univ BA89. St Aid Birkenhead 54. **d** 57 **p** 58. C Foleshill St Paul *Cov* 57-60; C Pet St Jo *Pet* 60-65; V Maxey w Northborough from 65. *The Vicarage, Maxey, Peterborough PE6 9EJ* Market Deeping (0778) 343329

SHEDDEN, Mrs Valerie. b 56. Ripon Coll of Educn CertEd77. Cranmer Hall Dur 81. **dss** 84 **d** 87. Tudhoe Grange *Dur* 84-85; Whitworth w Spennymoor 85-87; Par Dn 87-91; Par Dn E Darlington from 91. *12 Vane Terrace, Darlington, Co Durham DL3 7AT* Darlington (0325) 353326

SHEEHY, Jeremy Patrick. b 56. Magd Coll Ox BA78 MA81 New Coll Ox DPhil90. St Steph Ho Ox 78. **d** 81 **p** 82. C Erdington St Barn *Birm* 81-83; C Small Heath St Greg 83-84; Dean Div, Fell and Chapl New Coll Ox 84-90; V Leytonstone St Marg w St Columba *Chelmsf* from 90. *St Margaret's Vicarage, 15 Woodhouse Road, London E11 3NG* 081-519 0813

SHEEKEY, Raymond Arthur. b 23. Chich Th Coll 51. **d** 53 **p** 54. V Brabourne w Smeeth *Cant* 61-79; RD N Lympne 75-78; Chapl Lenham Hosp 79-88; R Lenham w Boughton Malherbe 79-88; rtd 88. *Rosewell Cottage, Leighterton, Tetbury, Glos* Leighterton (0666) 890268

SHEEN, Canon John Harold. b 32. Qu Coll Cam BA54 MA58. Cuddesdon Coll 56. **d** 58 **p** 59. C Stepney St Dunstan and All SS *Lon* 58-62; V Tottenham St Jo 62-68; V Wood Green St Mich 68-78; P-in-c Southgate St Mich 77-78; R Bride *S & M* from 78; Chapl Ramsey Cottage Hosp from 80; V Lezayre St Olave Ramsey from 80; RD Ramsey from 88; Can St German's Cathl from 91. *The Rectory, Kirk Bride, Ramsey, Isle of Man* Kirk Andreas (062488) 351

SHEEN, Canon Victor Alfred. b 17. Tyndale Hall Bris 47. **d** 49 **p** 50. V Clapham St Jas *S'wark* 65-86; RD Clapham and Brixton 75-82 and 85-86; Hon Can S'wark Cathl 80-86; rtd 86; Perm to Offic *Chich* from 86. *10 Porters Way, Polegate, E Sussex BN26 6AP* Polegate (03212) 7487

SHEERAN, Canon Ernest William. b 17. St Aid Birkenhead 47. **d** 50 **p** 51. V Edwalton *S'well* 55-86; RD Bingham S 68-86; Hon Can S'well Minster 72-86; rtd 86; Perm to Offic *S'well* from 86. *Brodick, 20 Taunton Road, Nottingham NG2 6EW* Nottingham (0602) 231895

SHEFFIELD, Michael Julian. b 53. Brentwood Coll of Educn CertEd. Sarum & Wells Th Coll 76. **d** 79 **p** 80. C Locks Heath *Portsm* 79-83; C Waterlooville 83; C Ryde All SS 83-86; P-in-c Ryde H Trin from 86; P-in-c Swanmore St Mich w Havenstreet from 86. *The Vicarage, Wray Street, Ryde, Isle of Wight PO33 3ED* Isle of Wight (0983) 62984

SHEFFIELD, Archdeacon of. See LOWE, Ven Stephen Richard

SHEFFIELD, Bishop of. See LUNN, Rt Rev David Ramsay

SHEFFIELD, Provost of. See GLADWIN, Very Rev John Warren

SHEGOG, Eric Marshall. b 37. Lon Univ DipTh60 City Univ MA88. Lich Th Coll 64. **d** 65 **p** 66. C Benhilton *S'wark* 65-68; Asst Youth Adv 68-70; V Abbey Wood 70-76; Chapl Sunderland Town Cen 76-83; C Bishopwearmouth St Mich w St Hilda *Dur* 76-83; Hd Relig Broadcasting IBA 84-90; Perm to Offic *Lon* 85-90; *St Alb* 85-89; Hon C Harpenden St Nic *St Alb* from 89; Dir Communications for C of E from 90. *c/o Church House, Great Smith Street, London SW1P 3NZ* 071-222 9011

SHEILD, Canon Edward Oscar. b 10. Univ of NZ LLB33 Qu Coll Ox BA36 MA40 BD82. **d** 36 **p** 37. V Chapel Allerton *Ripon* 64-75; rtd 75; Perm to Offic *Carl* from 75; P-in-c Coldstream *Edin* 77-79. *Midtown Cottage, Askham, Penrith, Cumbria CA10 2PF* Hackthorpe (09312) 427

SHELDON, John Gordon. b 22. Trin Coll Cam BA43 MA44. Ridley Hall Cam 43. **d** 45 **p** 46. V Lindfield *Chich* 62-80; P-in-c Cowden *Roch* 80-81; R Cowden w Hammerwood *Chich* 81-87; rtd 87. *Portland Cottage, Thornhill, Stalbridge, Sturminster Newton, Dorset DT10 2SJ* Stalbridge (0963) 62469

SHELDON, Jonathan Mark Robin. b 59. Cam Univ MA83. Ridley Hall Cam 81. **d** 83 **p** 84. C Dulwich St Barn *S'wark* 83-86; C Worle *B & W* 86-88; V Chesterton St Andr *Ely* from 88. *The Vicarage, Church Street, Chesterton, Cambridge CB4 1DT* Cambridge (0223) 354098

SHELLEY, Derrick Sydney David. b 38. Lon Univ LLB60 AKC65. Linc Th Coll. **d** 68 **p** 69. C Weybridge *Guildf* 68-72; Chapl Red Bank Schs 72-77; Lic to Offic *Blackb* from 80. *21 Agnew Street, Lytham St Annes, Lancs FY8 5NJ*

SHELLEY, George. b 18. Qu Coll Birm 56. **d** 57 **p** 58. Miss to Seamen 67-71; R Gt Ringstead *Nor* 71 77; P-in-c Sedgeford w Southmere 71-77; P-in-c Gateshead St Jas *Dur* 77-78; R 78-82; rtd 82; Perm to Offic *Nor* from 82. *18 Burnt Hills, Cromer, Norfolk NR27 9LW* Cromer (0263) 512957

SHELLEY, Robin Arthur. b 34. CEng MIMechE. St Jo Coll Nottm 85. **d** 87 **p** 88. C Countesthorpe w Foston *Leic* 87-90; V Enderby w Lubbesthorpe and Thurlaston from 90. *1 Finch Way, Narborough, Leics LE9 5TP* Leicester (0533) 751564

SHELLOCK, Norman Stanley. b 15. ATCL53 Dur Univ LTh38. St Aug Coll Cant 34. **d** 38 **p** 39. Area Sec (Dios Ely and St E) USPG 59-80; rtd 80; Perm to Offic *Nor* from 80; *St E* from 81. *24 Runnymede Green, Bury St Edmunds, Suffolk IP33 2LH* Bury St Edmunds (0284) 703506

SHELLS, Canon Charles Harry. b 15. St Chad's Coll Dur BA38 MA43. **d** 39 **p** 40. Can Res Bris Cathl *Bris* 71-81; Lic to Offic *B & W* and *Sarum* from 81; rtd 81; Perm to Offic *Bris* from 81. *13 Dod Lane, Glastonbury, Somerset BA6 8BZ* Glastonbury (0458) 32052

SHELTON, Ian Robert. b 52. BEd74 Lon Univ MA79. Ripon Coll Cuddesdon BA81 MA90. **d** 82 **p** 83. C Wath-upon-Dearne w Adwick-upon-Dearne *Sheff* 82-86; TV Grantham *Linc* from 86. *114 Manthorpe Road, Grantham, Lincs NG31 8DL* Grantham (0476) 67047

SHENTON, Brian. b 43. Chich Th Coll 73. **d** 75 **p** 76. C Mill Hill Jo Keble Ch *Lon* 75-78; C New Windsor *Ox* 78-81; TV 81-82; P-in-c Cherbury 82-83; V Calcot 83-89; R Reading St Mary w St Laur from 89. *39 Downshire Square, Reading RG1 6NH* Reading (0734) 51738 or 571057

SHEPHARD, Brian Edward. b 34. Magd Coll Cam BA56 MA60 Ox Univ DipPSA60 CertEd71 HDipRE71. Wycliffe Hall Ox 58. **d** 60 **p** 61. C Wigan St Cath *Liv* 60-62; C Kidderminster St Geo *Worc* 62-65; Lect CA Tr Coll Blackheath 65-70; Lect Hamilton Coll of Educn 70-77; Perm to Offic *Glas* 70-77; Chapl Buchan Sch Castletown 77-88; Lic to Offic *S & M* 77-88; *S'wark* 88-89; Tutor CA Wilson Carlile Coll of Evang 88-89; C Andreas St Jude *S & M* 89-91; C Jurby 89-91; V Lezayre from 91. *The Vicarage, Lezayre, Ramsey, Isle of Man* Ramsey (0624) 812500

SHEPHEARD, Denis Arthur. b 28. Oak Hill Th Coll 56. **d** 59 **p** 60. C Foord St Jo *Cant* 59-64; C Southborough St Pet *Roch* 64-66; C St Marylebone All So w SS Pet and Jo *Lon* 66-72; V Loudwater *Ox* 72-81; CPAS Evang from 81. *14 College Road, Reading, Berks RG6 1QB* Reading (0734) 661268

SHEPHEARD-WALWYN, John. b 16. Or Coll Ox BA38 MA44. Wells Th Coll 38. **d** 40 **p** 42. R Horwood *Ex* 61-78; V Westleigh 61-78; P-in-c Harberton w Harbertonford 78-82; rtd 82; Perm to Offic *Bris* from 82. *12 Luccombe Hill, Bristol BS6 6SN* Bristol (0272) 731261

SHEPHERD, Anthony Michael. b 50. Em Coll Cam BA72 MA76. Westcott Ho Cam 72. **d** 74 **p** 75. C Folkestone St Mary and St Eanswythe *Cant* 74-79; Bp's Dom Chapl *Ripon* 79-87; Dioc Communications Officer 79-87; V High Harrogate St Pet from 87. *St Peter's Vicarage, 13 Beech Grove, Harrogate, N Yorkshire* Harrogate (0423) 871415

SHEPHERD, Christopher Francis Pleydell. b 44. St Steph Ho Ox 68. **d** 69 **p** 70. C Milber *Ex* 69-72; C Ex St Thos 72-74; TV Ilfracombe, Lee and W Down 74-78; TV Ilfracombe, Lee, W Down, Woolacombe and Bittadon 78-80; P-in-c Tregony w St Cuby and Cornelly *Truro* 80-83; R from 83. *The Rectory, Tregony, Truro, Cornwall TR2 5SE* Tregony (087253) 507

SHEPHERD, David. b 42. St Jo Coll Dur BA65 MA68 MLitt76. Edin Th Coll 66. **d** 68 **p** 69. Chapl St Paul's Cathl Dundee *Bre* 68-79; Chapl Dundee Univ 73-79; R Dundee St Mary Magd from 79. *14 Albany Terrace, Dundee DD3 6HR* Dundee (0382) 23510

SHEPHERD, David Mark. b 59. Reading Univ BA81 Nottm Univ BTh86. Linc Th Coll 83. **d** 86 **p** 87. C Wilmslow *Ches* 86-89; C Bromborough from 89. *St Barnabas House, 193 Allport Road, Bromborough, Wirral, Merseyside L62 6BA* 051-334 4181

SHEPHERD, Canon Ernest John Heatley. b 27. TCD BA48 BD53. **d** 50 **p** 51. C Belf St Mary Magd *Conn* 50-54; I Whitehouse from 54; Can Conn Cathl 86-90; Co-ord Aux Min from 87; Treas Conn Cathl 90; Prec Conn Cathl from 90. *283 Shore Road, Newtownabbey, Co Antrim BT37 9SR* Belfast (0232) 851622

SHEPHERD, Frederick John. b 32. Lich Th Coll 54. **d** 57 **p** 58. C Gt Walsingham *Nor* 57-59; C Balham St Jo Bedf Hill *S'wark* 59; C Kennington Park St Agnes 67-68; C Southfields St Barn 68-70; P-in-c Tottenham St Jo *Lon* 70-74; V Enfield SS Pet and Paul 74-83; Bp's Dom Chapl 83-90; Hon Can Fort Worth 89-90; USA from 90; Can Fort Worth from 90. *6300 Ridglea Place, Suite 1100, Fort Worth, Texas 76116, USA* Fort Worth (817) 370-2970

SHEPHERD, Miss Jayne Elizabeth. b 57. Reading Univ BA78. Cranmer Hall Dur 79. **dss** 82 **d** 87. Wombourne *Lich* 82-85; Harlescott 85-87; Par Dn 87-90; Chapl Asst Univ Hosp Nottm from 90. *3 Ash Grove, Stapleford, Nottingham NG9 7GL* Nottingham (0602) 491742

SHEPHERD, Mrs Joan Francis Fleming. b 45. RGN66. **dss** 84 **d** 86. NSM Ellon *Ab* from 84; NSM Cruden from 84. *8 Ythan Court, Ellon, Aberdeenshire AB4 9BL* Ellon (0358) 21894

SHEPHERD, John Donald. b 33. Cranmer Hall Dur BA59 DipTh61. **d** 61 **p** 62. C Dewsbury All SS *Wakef* 61-63; C Chapelthorpe 63-66; V Stainland 66-70; Dioc Youth Chapl *Truro* 70-74; V Newquay 74-84; RD Pydar 81-84; Chapl Borocourt Mental Handicap Hosp from 84; TR Langtree *Ox* from 84. *The Rectory, Checkendon, Reading RG8 0QS* Checkendon (0491) 680252

SHEPHERD, John Michael. b 42. BNC Ox BA63 MA72. Coll of Resurr Mirfield 64. **d** 66 **p** 67. C Clapham H Spirit *S'wark* 66-69; C Kingston All SS 69-72; V Upper Tooting H Trin 73-80; V Wandsworth St Paul 80-90; P-in-c Mitcham SS Pet and Paul from 90. *21 Church Road, Mitcham, Surrey CR4 3BE* 081-648 1566

SHEPHERD, John William. b 20. S'wark Ord Course 67. **d** 70 **p** 71. C Leighton Buzzard *St Alb* 70-77; P-in-c Studham w Whipsnade 77-80; V 80-82; P-in-c Kensworth 82; V Kensworth, Studham and Whipsnade 82-86; rtd 86; Asst Chapl Costa Blanca *Eur* 86-89. *24 Church Road, Studham, Dunstable, Beds LU6 2QA* Whipsnade (0582) 872298

SHEPHERD, Keith Frederick. b 42. E Midl Min Tr Course 86. **d** 89 **p** 90. Hon C Stocking Farm *Leic* from 89. *55 Heacham Drive, Leicester LE4 0LJ* Leicester (0533) 352928

SHEPHERD, Peter James. b 38. Dur Univ BA64. Ridley Hall Cam 64. **d** 66 **p** 67. C Luton Ch Ch *Roch* 66-70; C Belvedere All SS 70-71; C Wisley w Pyrford *Guildf* 71-75; V Thorney Abbey *Ely* 75-85; V Yaxley from 85; RD Yaxley from 88. *The Vicarage, Yaxley, Peterborough PE7 3LH* Peterborough (0733) 240339

SHEPHERD, Peter William. b 48. MBIM DASE Reading Univ BA71 Lon Univ BD80 Brighton Poly MPhil87. Chich Th Coll 77. **d** 80 **p** 81. NSM Eastbourne St Sav and St Pet *Chich* 80-83; Hd Master Wm Temple Sch Preston 83-88; NSM Clitheroe St Mary *Blackb* from 83; Hd Master Canon Slade Sch Bolton from 89. *Homestead Eastham Street, Clitheroe, Lancs BB7 2HY* Clitheroe (0200) 25053

SHEPHERD, Philip Reginald. b 07. Keble Coll Ox BA29 MA36. Cuddesdon Coll 29. **d** 30 **p** 31. R Shepton Beauchamp *B & W* 64-72; rtd 72. *3 Coles Lane, South*

Petherton, Somerset TA13 5AF South Petherton (0460) 40809

SHEPHERD, Timothy Roy. b 34. Selw Coll Cam BA58. Linc Th Coll 62. **d** 64 **p** 65. C Selly Oak St Mary *Birm* 64-67; C Stockland Green 67-72; V Perry Common 72-76; V Holton-le-Clay *Linc* 76-84; V Habrough Gp from 84. *The Vicarage, Killingholme Road, Habrough, S Humberside DN40 3BB* Immingham (0469) 572876

✠**SHEPPARD, Rt Rev David Stuart.** b 29. Trin Hall Cam BA53 MA56. Ridley Hall Cam 53. **d** 55 **p** 56 **c** 69. C Islington St Mary *Lon* 55-58; Chapl & Warden Mayflower Family Cen Canning Town *Chelmsf* 58-69; Suff Bp Woolwich *S'wark* 69-75; Bp Liv from 75. *Bishop's Lodge, Woolton Park, Liverpool L25 6DT*

SHEPPARD, Ian Arthur Lough. b 33. Sarum & Wells Th Coll 71. **d** 74 **p** 75. C Bishop's Cleeve *Glouc* 74-77; Chapl RAF 77-81; V Gosberton *Linc* 81-87; V Leven Valley *Carl* 87-90; Deputation and Gen Appeals Org Children's Soc from 90. *57 St Seymour Grove, Eaglescliffe, Stockton-on-Tees, Cleveland TS16 0LE* Eaglescliffe (0642) 790777

SHEPPARD, Martin. b 37. Hertf Coll Ox BA61 MA65. Chich Th Coll 63. **d** 65 **p** 66. C N Hull St Mich *York* 65-68; C Hove St Jo *Chich* 68-71; V Heathfield St Rich 71-77; V New Shoreham from 77; V Old Shoreham from 77. *The Vicarage, Church Street, Shoreham-by-Sea, W Sussex BN43 5DQ* Shoreham-by-Sea (0273) 452109

SHEPPARD, Stanley Gorton. b 18. St Jo Coll Dur 46. **d** 62 **p** 63. R Cole Orton *Leic* 65-75; V Ashby Folville and Twyford w Thorpe Satchville 75-88; rtd 88; Perm to Offic *Ex* from 89. *1 Peak Coach House, Cotmaton Road, Sidmouth, Devon EX10 8SY* Sidmouth (0395) 516124

SHEPTON, Robert Leonard McIntyre. b 35. Jes Coll Cam BA58 MA61. Oak Hill Th Coll 59. **d** 61 **p** 62. C Weymouth St Jo *Sarum* 61-63; Boys' Ldr Cam Univ Miss Bermondsey 63-66; Warden Ox-Kilburn Club 66-69; Chapl St D Coll Llandudno 69-77; Chief Instructor Carnoch Outdoor Cen 77-80; Chapl Kingham Hill Sch Ox from 80. *Swansea House, Kingham Hill School, Kingham, Oxford OX7 6TH* Kingham (0608) 71479

SHERBORNE, Archdeacon of. *See* WHEATLEY, Ven Paul Charles

SHERBORNE, Area Bishop of. *See* KIRKHAM, Rt Rev John Dudley Galtrey

SHERGOLD, William Frank. b 19. St Chad's Coll Dur BA40 MA47. Coll of Resurr Mirfield 40. **d** 42 **p** 43. V Charlton-by-Dover St Bart *Cant* 69-72; P-in-c Charlton-by-Dover SS Pet and Paul 70-72; R Charlton-in-Dover 72-78; R Tunstall 78-83; rtd 84; TV Poplar 84-87; Hon C from 84. *6 Mountague Place, London E14 0EX* 071-515 5454

SHERLEY-PRICE, Lionel Digby. b 11. SS Coll Cam BA32 MA36. Chich Th Coll 33. **d** 34 **p** 35. V Dawlish *Ex* 69-74; R Manaton 74-78; R N Bovey 74-78; rtd 78; RD Moreton *Ex* 80-83. *7 High Close, Bovey Tracey, Newton Abbot, Devon TQ13 9EX* Bovey Tracey (0626) 833448

SHERLOCK, Charles Patrick. b 51. New Coll Ox BA73 MA76. Ripon Coll Cuddesdon 75. **d** 77 **p** 78. C Ashtead *Guildf* 77-81; Ethiopia 81-82; Chapl Belgrade w Zagreb *Eur* 82-84; USPG (Ethiopia) 84-91; R Dollar *St And* from 91. *St James Rectory, 12 Harviestoun Road, Dollar, Clackmannanshire FK14 7HF* Dollar (0259) 42494

SHERLOCK, Desmond. b 31. K Coll Lon BD60 AKC60. **d** 61 **p** 62. C Mitcham Ascension *S'wark* 61-64; C Reigate St Luke S Park 64-67; V Aldersbrook *Chelmsf* 67-77; RD Redbridge 74-77; V Witham from 77. *The Vicarage, 7 Chipping Dell, Witham, Essex CM8 2JX* Witham (0376) 512056

SHERLOCK, Ewart Templeman. b 03. AKC31. **d** 30 **p** 31. V Dorney *Ox* 60-70; rtd 71. *11 Fairview Road, Taplow, Maidenhead, Berks SL6 0NQ* Burnham (0628) 604226

SHERLOCK, Thomas Alfred. **d** 90 **p** 91. NSM Kilmallock w Kilflynn, Kilfinane, Knockaney etc *L & K* from 90. *Castlequarter, Kildorrey, Co Cork, Irish Republic* Mallow (22) 25280

SHERRATT, Allan Dennis. b 48. Chich Th Coll 78. **d** 79 **p** 80. C Seaford w Sutton *Chich* 79-81; Chapl Eliz Coll Guernsey 81-84; C Guernsey Ste Marie du Castel *Win* 84-85; P-in-c 85-87; C Guernsey St Matt 84-85; P-in-c 85-87; Lic to Offic *Win* 88-89; York 89-90; P-in-c Barmby on the Moor w Fangfoss *York* 90; R Barmby Moor w Allerthorpe, Fangfoss and Yapham from 90. *The Vicarage, Barmby Moor, York YO4 5HF* Pocklington (0759) 305971

SHERSBY, Brian Alfred. b 41. Clifton Th Coll 68. **d** 71 **p** 72. C Stoughton *Guildf* 71-74; C Heref St Pet w St Owen *Heref* 75-79; V Earlham St Mary *Nor* from 79. *St*

Mary's Vicarage, Douglas Haig Road, Norwich NR5 8LD Norwich (0603) 54742

SHERWIN, David Royston. b 56. HNC. St Jo Coll Nottm 84. **d** 89 **p** 90. C Conisbrough *Sheff* from 89. *14 Chestnut Grove, Conisbrough, Doncaster, S Yorkshire DN12 2JE* Rotherham (0709) 863525

SHERWIN, Margaret. b 32. dss 83 **d** 87. Holborn St Alb w Saffron Hill St Pet *Lon* 83-87; Par Dn 87-88; Par Dn Highgate St Mich from 88. *c/o St Michael's Vicarage, 10 The Grove, London N6 6LB* 081-340 7279

SHERWOOD, David James. b 45. St Steph Ho Ox 81. **d** 83 **p** 84. C Westbury-on-Trym H Trin *Bris* 83-85; C Corringham *Chelmsf* 85-87; V Hullbridge from 87. *The Vicarage, 93 Ferry Road, Hullbridge, Essex SS5 6EL* Southend-on-Sea (0702) 232017

SHERWOOD, Denys Charles. b 20. Lon Univ BA49. Oak Hill Th Coll. **d** 51 **p** 52. V Lenton Abbey *S'well* 67-77; V Basford *Lich* 77-85; rtd 85; Perm to Offic *S'well* from 85. *5 Larch Crescent, Eastwood, Nottingham NG16 3RB* Langley Mill (0773) 760922

SHERWOOD, Gordon Frederick. b 29. Sarum & Wells Th Coll 77. **d** 80 **p** 81. Hon C Weeke *Win* 80-82; C Kirk Ella *York* 82-85; P-in-c Burstwick w Thorngumbald 85-87; V 87-90; R Kirby Misperton w Normanby, Edston and Salton from 90. *The Rectory, Normanby, Sinnington, York YO6 6RH* Kirkbymoorside (0751) 31288

SHERWOOD, Ian Walter Lawrence. b 57. TCD BA80 DipTh82. **d** 82 **p** 84. C Dub St Patr Cathl Gp *D & G* 82-83; Chapl Billinge Hosp Wigan 83-86; C Orrell *Liv* 83-86; Chapl Bucharest *Eur* 86-89; Chapl Istanbul w Moda from 89. *c/o British Consulate General, Tepebasi, Bevoglu 80072, Istanbul, Turkey* Istanbul (1) 144-4228

SHERWOOD, Nigel John Wesley. b 58. DipTh. CITC 86. **d** 86 **p** 87. C Kilmore w Ballintemple, Kildallon etc *K, E & A* 86-88; I Tullow w Shillelagh, Aghold and Mullinacuff *C & O* from 88. *The Rectory, Tullow, Co Carlow, Irish Republic* Carlow (503) 51481

SHERWOOD, Suffragan Bishop of. *See* MORGAN, Rt Rev Alan Wyndham

SHEWAN, Alistair Boyd. b 44. Open Univ BA83. Edin Th Coll 63. **d** 67 **p** 68. Prec St Andr Cathl Inverness *Mor* 67-69; C Shepherd's Bush St Steph w St Thos *Lon* 70-72; Hon C Edin St Mich and All SS *Edin* 73-75; Perm to Offic 75-81; Hon C Edin Old St Paul 81-86; NSM Edin St Columba from 87. *3 Castle Wynd North, Edinburgh EH1 2NQ* 031-225 6537

SHEWAN, James William. b 36. Sarum Th Coll 61. **d** 63 **p** 64. C Rainbow Hill St Barn *Worc* 63-64; C Newton Aycliffe *Dur* 64-66; C Harton 66-69; V S Moor 69-72; CF 72-77 and from 81; P-in-c Benwell St Aid *Newc* 77-79; V Longhoughton w Howick 79-88; V Spittal from 88; V Scremerston from 88. *St John's Vicarage, 129 Main Street, Spittal, Berwick-upon-Tweed TD15 1RP* Berwick-upon-Tweed (0289) 307342

SHEWELL, Edward Charles Beaudon. b 12. St Pet Hall Ox BA36 MA46. Ridley Hall Cam 36. **d** 37 **p** 38. V Berry Pomeroy *Ex* 54-77; R Lt Hempston 69-77; rtd 77; Hon C Tetcott w Luffincott *Ex* 77-81; Hon C Clawton 77-81. *3 Dreva Road, Broughton, Biggar, Lanarkshire ML12 6HQ* Broughton (08994) 219

SHIELD, Ian Thomas. b 32. Hertf Coll Ox BA56 MA60 BLitt60. Westcott Ho Cam 59. **d** 61 **p** 62. Tutor Lich Th Coll 64-71; Chapl 67-71; V Dunston w Coppenhall *Lich* 71-79; TV Wolv 79-86; rtd 87; Perm to Offic *Lich* from 87. *13 Duke Street, Penn Fields, Wolverhampton WV3 7DT* Wolverhampton (0902) 337037

SHIELDS, Michael Penton. b 30. Bps' Coll Cheshunt. **d** 64 **p** 65. C Kingsbury St Andr *Lon* 64-67; C Friern Barnet All SS 67-69; V Colindale St Matthias 69-76; Chapl Sevenoaks Hosp from 76; V Sevenoaks St Jo *Roch* from 76; RD Sevenoaks from 84. *The Clergy House, 62 Quakers Hall Lane, Sevenoaks, Kent TN13 3TX* Sevenoaks (0732) 451710

SHIELS, Donald Allan Patterson. b 15. Selw Coll Cam BA38 MA42. Wycliffe Hall Ox 38. **d** 39 **p** 40. V Stoke Gifford *Bris* 62-80; rtd 80; Perm to Offic *Glouc* from 80. *5 Down Hatherley Lane, Gloucester GL2 9PT* Gloucester (0452) 730367

SHIER, John Michael. b 42. St Chad's Coll Dur BA64. **d** 66 **p** 67. C Kenton *Lon* 66-72; C Pimlico St Mary Graham Terrace 72-77; V Finsbury St Clem w St Barn and St Matt from 77; Chapl Moorfields Eye Hosp Lon from 82. *St Clement's Vicarage, King Square, Lever Street, London EC1V 8DA* 071-253 9140

SHILL, Kenneth Leslie. b 49. Leic Univ BA70 Lon Univ BD73 Cam Univ DipTh77. Ridley Hall Cam 75. **d** 77 **p** 78. C Harborne Heath *Birm* 77-83; V Mansf St Jo *S'well* from 83; Bp's Adv on Healing from 89. *The*

Vicarage, St John Street, Mansfield, Notts NG18 1QH Mansfield (0623) 25999

SHILLAKER, Mrs Christine Frances. b 39. Lon Univ DipTh61. Gilmore Ho 74. **dss** 86 **d** 87. Colchester St Leon, St Mary Magd and St Steph *Chelmsf* 86-87; Par Dn Colchester, New Town and The Hythe from 87. *24 New Town Road, Colchester CO1 2EF* Colchester (0206) 570442

SHILLAKER, John. b 34. K Coll Lon BD60 AKC60. **d** 61 **p** 62. C Bush Hill Park St Mark *Lon* 61-65; C Milton *Win* 65-69; C-in-c Moulsham St Luke CD *Chelmsf* 69-78; V Moulsham St Luke 78-85; P-in-c Colchester St Leon, St Mary Magd and St Steph 85-86; R 86-89; TR Colchester, New Town and The Hythe from 89. *The Rectory, 24 New Town Road, Colchester CO1 2EF* Colchester (0206) 570442

SHILLCOCK, Betty. b 33. IDC67. St Mich Ho Ox 65. **d** 88. Par Dn Higher Walton *Blackb* from 88. *38 Kittlingabout Brow, Higher Walton, Preston, Lancs PR5 4DP* Preston (0772) 311460

SHILLING, Ms Audrey Violet. b 26. Dur Univ BA69. CA Tr Coll 51 Cranmer Hall Dur 66. **d** 87. CA from 53; NSM Gillingham H Trin *Roch* from 87. *45 Eastcourt Lane, Gillingham, Kent ME8 6EU* Medway (0634) 33654

SHILLINGFORD, Brian. b 39. Lich Th Coll 65. **d** 68 **p** 69. C Lewisham St Swithun *S'wark* 68-71; C Godstone 71-75; TV Croydon *Cant* 75-81; TV N Creedy *Ex* from 81. *The Rectory, Morchard Bishop, Crediton, Devon EX17 6PJ* Morchard Bishop (03637) 221

SHILSON-THOMAS, Mrs Annabel Margaret. b 60. Jes Coll Ox BA82. Westcott Ho Cam 87. **d** 89. Par Dn Sydenham St Bart *S'wark* from 89. *10 Knighton Park Road, London SE26 5RJ* 081-676 9214

SHILSON-THOMAS, Hugh David. b 64. Ex Coll Ox BA86. Westcott Ho Cam 87. **d** 89 **p** 90. C Sydenham All SS *S'wark* from 89; C Lower Sydenham St Mich from 89. *10 Knighton Park Road, London SE26 5RJ* 081-659 8070

SHILVOCK, Geoffrey. b 47. Univ of Wales (Lamp) BA69. Sarum Th Coll 70. **d** 72 **p** 73. C Kidderminster St Mary *Worc* 72-78; P-in-c Gt Malvern Ch Ch 78-85; V Wolverley and Cookley from 85. *The Vicarage, Wolverley, Kidderminster, Worcs DY11 5XD* Kidderminster (0562) 851133

SHIMWELL, Robert John. b 46. ARCM65. Lon Bible Coll DipTh68 Trin Coll Bris 75. **d** 78 **p** 79. C Richmond H Trin *S'wark* 78-79; C Cullompton *Ex* 79-81; C Kentisbeare w Blackborough 79-81; V S Cave and Ellerker w Broomfleet *York* 81-87; Chapl Lee Abbey 87-88; R Glas St Silas *Glas* from 88. *4 Banavie Road, Glasgow G11 5AN* 041-357 0486

SHINER, Michael Joseph. b 21. Chich Th Coll 51. **d** 53 **p** 54. V Powerstock w W Milton, Witherstone and N Poorton *Sarum* 67-73; V Knutsford St Cross *Ches* 73-75; rtd 86. *1 Clay Lane, Puncknowle, Dorchester, Dorset DT2 9BJ* Burton Bradstock (0308) 897007

SHINN, William Raymond. b 22. Sarum & Wells Th Coll 71. **d** 73 **p** 74. C Letchworth St Paul *St Alb* 73-75; C Dunstable 76-78; TV 78-80; V Luton St Chris Round Green 80-88; rtd 88. *31 Coleridge Close, Hitchin, Herts SG4 0QX* Hitchin (0462) 450899

SHIPLEY, Christopher John. b 44. Leeds Univ BSc65 MSc70 BA72. Coll of Resurr Mirfield 70. **d** 73 **p** 74. C Preston St Jo *Blackb* 73-77; Chapl Lancs (Preston) Poly 75-77; V Blackb St Mich w St Jo 77-81; P-in-c Blackb H Trin 78-81; V Blackb St Mich w St Jo and H Trin 81-82; V Walthamstow St Pet *Chelmsf* 82-85; Gen Sec Mary Feilding Guild Lon 85-86; Org Waltham Forest Coun for Voluntary Service 86-89; Gen Sec Hull 89-91; Dir Grimsby & Cleethorpes from 91; Perm to Offic *York* from 90. *24 Westbourne Avenue, Hull HU5 3HR* Hull (0482) 42563

SHIPLEY, Miss Marjorie. b 17. Gilmore Ho 67. **dss** 72 **d** 87. Acomb St Steph *York* 72-78; rtd 78; Perm to Offic *York* 78-84; NSM Scarborough St Martin from 84. *Flat 25, Normanton Rise, Belvedere Place South, Scarborough YO11 2XD* Scarborough (0723) 353150

SHIPLEY, Stephen Edwin Burnham. b 52. Univ Coll Dur BA74. Westcott Ho Cam 85. **d** 87 **p** 88. C Ipswich St Marg *St E* 87-90; P-in-c Stuntney *Ely* from 90; Min Can, Prec and Sacr Ely Cathl from 90. *Precentor's House, 32 High Street, Ely CB7 4JU* Ely (0353) 662526

SHIPP, Patricia Susan. b 54. Univ of Wales BA76. St Paul's Grahamstown 77 Linc Th Coll 81. **d** 83. C Cyncoed *Mon* 83-87; Par Dn Lawrence Weston *Bris* from 89. *10 Westover Gardens, Bristol BS9 3LE* Bristol (0272) 500370

SHIPSIDES, Brian Kenneth. b 56. Reading Univ BA. Westcott Ho Cam 79. **d** 82 **p** 83. C Bramley *Ripon* 82-85; C Notting Dale St Clem w St Mark and St Jas *Lon* 85-90; Chapl Poly of N Lon from 90. *123 Calabria Road, London N5 1HS* 071-704 9914

SHIPTON, Andrew James. b 60. Leeds Univ BA82. Cranmer Hall Dur 83. **d** 85 **p** 86. C Fishponds St Jo *Bris* 85-88; C Gosforth All SS *Newc* 88-91; V Long Benton St Mary from 91. *St Mary's House, Blackfriars Way, Newcastle upon Tyne NE12 8ST* 091-266 2326

SHIPTON, Miss Linda Anne. b 60. Avery Hill Coll DipHE84. Westcott Ho Cam 84. **dss** 86 **d** 87. Borehamwood *St Alb* 86-87; Par Dn 87-89; Par Dn Sheff St Cuth *Sheff* 89-90; Chapl Asst N Gen Hosp Sheff 89-90; Chapl from 90. *Flat 1, 282 Herries Road, Sheffield S5 7HA*

SHIRE, William Stanley. b 17. TCD BA39 MA43. **d** 40 **p** 41. R Aldwincle w Thorpe Achurch, Pilton, Wadenhoe etc *Pet* 70-82; rtd 82; Lic to Offic *Pet* 82-85; Perm to Offic from 85. *96 Glapthorne Road, Oundle, Peterborough PE8 4PS* Oundle (0832) 272125

SHIREHAMPTON, William John Prankerd. b 10. Qu Coll Cam BA34 MA38. Lon Coll of Div 34. **d** 36 **p** 37. Warden Mon Sch 49-80; Perm to Offic *Heref* from 77; Mon from 80; rtd 80. *Cranford, 17 St Mary Street, Monmouth, Gwent NP5 3DB* Monmouth (0600) 2082

SHIRES, Alan William. b 36. Lon Univ BA60. Oak Hill Th Coll 57. **d** 61 **p** 62. C York St Paul *York* 61-64; C Southgate *Chich* 64-67; V Doncaster St Mary *Sheff* 67-75; Student Counsellor Portsm Poly 75-88; Hd Student Services Portsm Poly from 88. *18 Salisbury Road, Cosham, Portsmouth PO6 2PN* Portsmouth (0705) 843170

SHIRESS, Canon David Henry Faithfull. b 27. St Cath Coll Cam BA49 MA53. Ridley Hall Cam 51. **d** 53 **p** 54. C Southport Ch Ch *Liv* 53-55; C St Helens St Mark 55-58; V Shrewsbury St Julian *Lich* 58-67; V Blackheath Park St Mich *S'wark* from 67; Sub-Dean of Greenwich 81-90; RD Greenwich from 90; Hon Can S'wark Cathl from 89. *St Michael's Vicarage, 2 Pond Road, London SE3 9JL* 081-852 5287

SHIRLEY, Timothy Francis. b 25. Univ Coll Ox BA49 MA49. Qu Coll Birm 49. **d** 51 **p** 52. V Fulham St Etheldreda w St Clem *Lon* 68-90; rtd 90. *70 St Dunstan's Cresent, Worcester WR5 2AQ* Worcester (0905) 353930

SHIRRAS, Ven Edward Scott. b 37. St Andr Univ BSc61. Clifton Th Coll 61. **d** 63 **p** 64. C Surbiton Hill Ch Ch *S'wark* 63-66; C Jesmond Clayton Memorial *Newc* 66-68; Youth Sec CPAS 68-71; Publications Sec 71-74; Asst Gen Sec 74-75; Hon C Wallington H Trin *S'wark* 69-75; V Roxeth Ch Ch *Lon* 75-82; V Roxeth Ch Ch and Harrow St Pet 82-85; AD Harrow 82-85; Adn Northolt from 85. *71 Gayton Road, Harrow, Middx HA1 2LY* 081-863 1530

SHIRRAS, Ms Rachel Joan. b 66. Univ of Wales (Abth) BSc88. St Jo Coll Nottm 88. **d** 91. Par Dn Ockbrook *Derby* from 91. *34 Rutland Avenue, Borrowash, Derbyshire DE7 3JF* Derby (0332) 674252

SHOLL, Preb Ernest Redfern. b 09. AKC33. **d** 33 **p** 34. V Stogursey *B & W* 53-74; Preb Wells Cathl 57-74; R Fiddington 64-74; rtd 74. *Langdale, Kirtlebridge, Lockerbie, Dumfriesshire DG11 3LT* Kirtlebridge (04615) 659

SHONE, John Terence. b 35. Selw Coll Cam BA58 MA64. Linc Th Coll 58. **d** 60 **p** 61. C St Pancras w St Jas and Ch Ch *Lon* 60-62; Chapl Aber Univ *Ab* 62-68; Chapl St Andr Cathl 62-65; V Gt Grimsby St Andr and St Luke *Linc* 68-69; Chapl Stirling Univ *Edin* 69-80; R Bridge of Allan *St And* 69-86; P-in-c Alloa 77-85; Can St Ninian's Cathl Perth 80-89; P-in-c Dollar 81-86; Dean St Andr 82-89; Research and Development Officer 86-89; Dioc Supernumerary 86-89; TV Cullercoats St Geo *Newc* from 89. *St Hilda's Vicarage, Preston Gate, North Shields, Tyne & Wear NE29 9QB* 091-257 6595

SHONE, Raymond. b 21. St Jo Coll Dur BA(Theol)47 MA54 Brighton Poly DCouns81. Linc Th Coll 48. **d** 48 **p** 49. Perm to Offic *Chich* from 66; Sen Lect Eastbourne Coll of Educn 66-76; L Sussex Coll of HE 76-79; Brighton Poly 79-80; Counsellor W Sussex Inst of HE 83-87; rtd 87. *28 Hawthorn Close, Chichester, W Sussex PO19 3DZ* Chichester (0243) 774543

SHONE, Robert Alan. b 16. Qu Coll Cam BA38 MA42. St Steph Ho Ox 39. **d** 39 **p** 40. V Wardleworth St Mary *Man* 63-73; V Wardleworth St Mary w St Jas 73-81; rtd 81; Perm to Offic *Man* from 81. *172 Bar Terrace, Market Street, Whitworth, Rochdale, Lancs OL12 8TB* Rochdale (0706) 344405

SHONE, Ursula Ruth. b 34. Lon Univ DBRS59 Stirling Univ BA75 Open Univ BPhil88. **dss** 81 **d** 86. Bridge of

Allan *St And* 81-85; Lochgelly 85-87; Chapl Cov Cathl *Cov* 87-90; Ind Chapl 87-90; Par Dn Ainsdale *Liv* from 90; Dioc Science Adv from 90. *St John's House, 25 Pinfold Lane, Southport PR8 3QH* Southport (0704) 76098

SHORROCK, John Musgrave. b 29. TCD BA54 MA58. Bps' Coll Cheshunt 54. **d** 56 **p** 57. C Fleetwood *Blackb* 56-59; C Lanc St Mary 59-61; C-in-c Blackpool St Wilfred CD 61-65; V Blackpool St Wilfrid 65-67; Min Can and Sacr Cant Cathl *Cant* 67-70; V Chorley St Geo *Blackb* 71-78; P-in-c Bredgar w Bicknor and Huckinge *Cant* 78-82; P-in-c Frinsted w Wormshill and Milstead 78-82; R Bredgar w Bicknor and Frinsted w Wormshill etc from 82. *The Vicarage, Bredgar, Sittingbourne, Kent ME9 8HA* Wormshill (062784) 387

SHORT, Brian Frederick. b 29. St Jo Coll Nottm 70. **d** 72 **p** 73. C Walton *St E* 72-75; P-in-c Barking w Darmsden and Gt Bricett 75-78; P-in-c Ringshall w Battisford and Lt Finborough 75-78; TV Nor St Pet Parmentergate w St Jo *Nor* 78-88; R Winfarthing w Shelfanger w Burston w Gissing etc 88-90; rtd 90. *31 Nursery Gardens, Blofield, Norwich, Norfolk NR13 4JE* Norwich (0603) 712396

SHORT, Canon John Sinclair. b 33. Oak Hill Th Coll 64. **d** 66 **p** 67. C Islington St Mary *Lon* 66-70; V Becontree St Mary *Chelmsf* 70-76; V New Malden and Coombe *S'wark* 76-90; RD Kingston 79-84; Hon Can S'wark Cathl from 83; P-in-c Peldon w Gt and Lt Wigborough *Chelmsf* from 90. *The Rectory, Church Road, Peldon, Colchester CO5 7PT* Peldon (0206) 35303

SHORT, John Timothy. b 43. Lon Univ DipTh67. Kelham Th Coll 63. **d** 68 **p** 69. C St Marylebone Ch w St Barn *Lon* 68-70; C Southgate Ch 70-72; P-in-c Mosser *Carl* 72-78; Dioc Youth Officer 72-78; R Heyford w Stowe Nine Churches *Pet* 78-87; V Northn St Jas from 87; RD Wootton from 88. *St James's Vicarage, Vicarage Road, Northampton NN5 7AX* Northampton (0604) 51164

SHORT, Kenneth Arthur. b 33. Tyndale Hall Bris 64. **d** 67 **p** 68. C E Twickenham St Steph *Lon* 67-71; C Paddock Wood *Roch* 71-74; SE Area Sec BCMS 74-82; Hon C Sidcup Ch Ch 74-82; V Tollington Park St Mark w St Anne *Lon* 82-86; V Holloway St Mark w Em 86-89; R Alfold and Loxwood *Guildf* from 89. *The Rectory, Loxwood, Billingshurst, W Sussex RH14 0RG* Loxwood (0403) 752320

SHORT, Martin Peter. b 54. Peterho Cam BA77 MA81. Wycliffe Hall Ox 77. **d** 79 **p** 80. C Shipley St Pet *Bradf* 79-82; C Becontree St Mary *Chelmsf* 82-86; V Bolton St Jas w St Chrys *Bradf* from 86. *St James's Vicarage, 1056 Bolton Road, Bradford, W Yorkshire BD2 4LH* Bradford (0274) 637193

SHORT, Canon Michael John. b 38. Univ of Wales (Lamp) BA59. Sarum Th Coll 59. **d** 61 **p** 62. C Swansea St Nic *S & B* 61-64; C Oystermouth 64-69; V Merthyr Vale w Aberfan *Llan* 69-82; RD Merthyr Tydfil 76-82; R Caerphilly from 82; RD Caerphilly from 83; Can Llan Cathl from 89. *The Rectory, St Martin's Road, Caerphilly, M Glam CF8 1EJ* Caerphilly (0222) 882992

SHORT, Neil Robert. b 58. Loughb Univ BSc81 St Jo Coll Dur BA86. Cranmer Hall Dur 83. **d** 86 **p** 87. C Whitfield *Derby* 86-90; C Bradf St Aug Undercliffe *Bradf* from 90. *96 Sydenham Place, Bradford BD3 0LA* Bradford (0274) 630545

SHORT, Terence. b 32. AKC63. **d** 64 **p** 65. P-in-c Sutton in Ashfield St Mich *S'well* 69-75; V Carlton 75-85; R Etwall w Egginton *Derby* 85-91; rtd 91. *19 Monk Street, Tutbury, Staffs*

SHORTEN, Richard Deering. b 08. Qu Coll Cam BA30 MA48. Westcott Ho Cam 30. **d** 32 **p** 33. V Preshute *Sarum* 56-75; Asst Chapl Marlborough Coll Wilts 56-75; rtd 75. *Throg Cottage, Preshute Lane, Marlborough, Wilts SN8 4HQ* Marlborough (0672) 512447

SHORTER, Robert Edward. b 48. Ripon Coll Cuddesdon 89. **d** 91. C Braunton *Ex* from 91. *11 Hazel Avenue, Braunton, Devon EX33 2EZ* Braunton (0271) 814735

SHORTHOUSE, Mervin. b 14. Edin Th Coll. **d** 47 **p** 48. V Cornforth *Dur* 55-75; Chapl Ind Tr Cen Dur 68-74; V Aycliffe 75-79; rtd 79. *23 West Crescent, Darlington, Co Durham DL3 7PS* Darlington (0325) 487433

SHORTHOUSE, Raymond Trevor. b 34. DipAdEd. Ridley Hall Cam 68. **d** 70 **p** 71. C Gt Ilford St Andr *Chelmsf* 70-73; C Ludlow *Heref* 73-75; P-in-c Cressage w Sheinton 76-80; P-in-c Harley w Kenley 76-80; P-in-c Denby *Derby* 80-84; Adult Educn Officer 80-85; RD Heanor 83-84; V Chellaston 84-88; P-in-c Breadsall from 88; Dioc Dir of Studies from 88. *Breadsall Rectory, Derby DE7 6AL* Derby (0332) 831352

SHORTHOUSE, Canon Stephen Arthur. b 20. Trin Coll Cam BA41 MA45. Westcott Ho Cam 41. **d** 43 **p** 44. V

Yardley Wood *Birm* 57-75; V Bartley Green 75-85; Hon Can Birm Cathl 76-85; rtd 85; Perm to Offic *Birm* from 85; *Worc* from 86. *15 Lansdowne Terrace, Malvern, Worcs WR14 2AR* Malvern (0684) 569033

SHORTT, John Buckley. b 04. Linc Coll Ox BA28 MA32. St Aug Coll Cant 26. **d** 29 **p** 30. R River *Cant* 63-74; RD Dover 66-74; rtd 74; Hon C Walmer *Cant* 76-86; Perm to Offic from 86. *8 Herschell Road East, Deal, Kent CT14 7SQ* Deal (0304) 374792

SHORTT, Noel Christopher. b 36. Open Univ BA76 Ulster Univ MA DipContEd DPhil91. Bps' Coll Cheshunt 63. **d** 63 **p** 64. C Belf St Mary *Conn* 63-66; C Agherton 66-68; Chapl RAF 68-69; I Duneane w Ballyscullion *Conn* 69-79; I Belf St Steph w St Luke 79-89; RD M Belf 82-86 and 88-89; I Ballyrashane w Kildollagh from 89. *9 Sandelwood Avenue, Coleraine, Co Londonderry BT52 1JW* Coleraine (0265) 43061

SHOTLANDER, Lionel George. b 27. Cant Univ (NZ) BA49 MA51. **d** 51 **p** 52. New Zealand 60-74; V Curdridge *Portsm* 74-85; R Durley 79-85; V Twyford and Owslebury and Morestead *Win* 85-91; rtd 91. *Cambria, High Street, Shirrell Heath, Southampton SO3 2JN* Wickham (0329) 832353

SHOTTER, Very Rev Edward Frank. b 33. Univ of Wales (Lamp) BA58. St Steph Ho Ox 58. **d** 60 **p** 61. C Plymouth St Pet *Ex* 60-62; Inter-Colleg Sec SCM (Lon) 62-66; Perm to Offic *Lon* 62-69; Dir Lon Medical Gp 63-89; Chapl Lon Univ Medical Students *Lon* 69-89; Dir Inst of Medical Ethics 74-89; Preb St Paul's Cathl *Lon* from 77; Dean Roch from 89. *The Deanery, Rochester, Kent ME1 1TG* Medway (0634) 844023

SHOULER, Simon Frederic. b 54. ARICS77 Pemb Coll Cam MA79. E Midl Min Tr Course 82. **d** 85 **p** 86. NSM Asfordby *Leic* from 85. *Tower Cottage, Wartnaby, Melton Mowbray, Leics LE14 3HU* Melton Mowbray (0664) 822698

SHREEVE, Ven David Herbert. b 34. St Pet Hall Ox BA57 MA61. Ridley Hall Cam 57. **d** 59 **p** 60. C Plymouth St Andr *Ex* 59-64; V Bermondsey St Anne *S'wark* 64-71; V Eccleshill *Bradf* 71-84; RD Calverley 78-84; Hon Can Bradf Cathl 83-84; Adn Bradf from 84. *11 The Rowans, Baildon, Shipley, W Yorkshire BD17 5DB* Bradford (0274) 583735

SHREWSBURY, Preb Michael Buller. b 30. St Jo Coll Dur BA54. Linc Th Coll 54. **d** 56 **p** 57. C Salford St Phil w St Steph *Man* 56-60; Chapl RN 60-63; Chapl HM Pris Pentonville 64-67; Bermuda 67-70; V Dalston H Trin w St Phil *Lon* 70-86; AD Hackney 79-84; Preb St Paul's Cathl from 86; R Stepney St Dunstan and All SS from 86. *Stepney Rectory, Rectory Square, London E1 3NG* 071-791 3545

SHREWSBURY, Suffragan Bishop of. *See* DAVIES, Rt Rev John Dudley

SHRIMPTON, Canon Aner Clive. b 14. Lon Univ BD39. ALCD39. **d** 39 **p** 40. V Ruddington *S'well* 52-84; Hon Can S'well Minster 78-84; rtd 84; Perm to Offic *S'well* from 84. *36 Brookview Drive, Keyworth, Notts NG12 5JN* Plumtree (06077) 2795

SHRIMPTON, George Roderick. b 33. Selw Coll Cam BA56 MA60. Linc Th Coll 56. **d** 58 **p** 59. C Bilston St Leon *Lich* 58-63; C High Wycombe All SS *Ox* 63-67; V Dalton *Sheff* 67-74; V Milborne Port w Goathill *B & W* 74-90; P-in-c Barkston and Hough Gp *Linc* 90; R from 90. *The Parsonage, The Drift, Syston, Grantham, Lincs NG32 2BY* Loveden (0400) 50381

SHRIMPTON, Mrs Sheila Nan. b 32. Qu Mary Coll Lon BA54 LSE CSocStuds55. St Chris Coll Blackheath 57. dss 83 **d** 87. Lic to Offic *B & W* 83-90; NSM Barkston and Hough Gp *Linc* from 90; Asst Local Min Officer from 90. *The Parsonage, The Drift, Syston, Grantham, Lincs NG32 2BY* Loveden (0400) 50381

SHRISUNDER, David Shripat. b 29. Osmania Univ Hyderabad BA52 Serampore Univ BD59 Shivaji Univ Kolhapur MA69. Bp's Coll Calcutta 54. **d** 57 **p** 58. India 57-71, 72-75, 77-79 and 88-90; C Batley All SS *Wakef* 71-72; C Skegness *Linc* 75-77; C Derringham Bank *York* 80-81; TV Grays Thurrock *Chelmsf* 81-85; R Uddingston *Glas* 85-88; R Cambuslang 85-88; P-in-c Sinfin Moor *Derby* from 90. *The Vicarage, 72 Redwood Road, Sinfin Moor, Derby DE2 9LA* Derby (0332) 760016

SHRIVES, Austen Geoffrey. b 28. Lon Univ BD68 MTh77. S'wark Ord Course. **d** 64 **p** 65. C Lower Sydenham St Mich *S'wark* 64-68; Miss to Seamen 68-74; V Epsom St Martin *Guildf* 74-84; V York Town 84-87; R Churchstanton, Buckland St Mary and Otterford *B & W* from 87. *The Rectory, Churchstanton, Taunton, Somerset TA3 7QE* Churchstanton (082360) 228

SHUCKSMITH, John Barry. b 37. FRSA Hull Univ DipTh. Oak Hill Th Coll DipTh68. **d** 68 **p** 69. C Tooting

Graveney St Nic *S'wark* 68-70; S Africa 74-76; P-in-c Liv Ch Ch Norris Green *Liv* 82-86; Chapl RN 86-91; R Broughton *Linc* from 91. *The Rectory, Scawby Road, Broughton, Brigg, S Humberside DN20 0AF*   Brigg (0652) 52506

SHUFFLEBOTHAM, Alastair Vincent. b 32. Nottm Univ CSocSc57. Lich Th Coll 63. **d** 65 **p** 66. C W Kirby St Bridget *Ches* 65-69; V Tranmere St Paul 69-71; V Tranmere St Paul w St Luke 71-78; V Neston from 78. *The Vicarage, Neston, South Wirral L64 9TZ*   051-336 4544

SHUTE, Ronald Archie. b 06. St D Coll Lamp BA32. **d** 32 **p** 33. V Heytesbury w Tytherington and Knook *Sarum* 71-75; rtd 76; Perm to Offic *Chich* from 85. *Aysgarth, Hayes Lane, Slinfold, Horsham, W Sussex RH13 7SQ* Slinfold (0403) 790737

SHUTT, Anthony John. b 57. Brunel Univ BSc79 DipHE89. Trin Coll Bris 87. **d** 89 **p** 90. C Epsom St Martin *Guildf* from 89. *12 Worple Road, Epsom, Surrey KT18 5EE*   Epsom (0372) 720088

SHUTT, Laurence John. b 42. MPS64 MRPharmS88. St Steph Ho Ox 87 Llan Dioc Tr Scheme 80. **d** 84 **p** 85. NSM Whitchurch *Llan* 84-87; C Llanishen and Lisvane 88-90; Chapl RNR from 89; V Middlestown *Wakef* from 90. *The Vicarage, 19 Wood Mount, Overton, Wakefield, W Yorkshire WF4 4SB*   Wakefield (0924) 276159

SHUTT, Rowland James Heath. b 11. St Chad's Coll Dur BA33 PhD36 MA36. **d** 35 **p** 36. Warden Worc Ord Coll 64-69; rtd 77. *7 Greenhill, Bath Road, Worcester WR5 2AT*   Worcester (0905) 355410

SHUTTLEWORTH, Claude Tone. b 16. Solicitor 48 St Cath Coll Cam BA38 MA54. Edin Th Coll 55. **d** 57 **p** 58. R Lamplugh w Ennerdale *Carl* 61-65; rtd 81. *31 Thorntrees Drive, Thornhill, Egremont, Cumbria CA22 2SU*   Egremont (0946) 820014

SIBBALD, Olwyn Eileen. b 57. Linc Th Coll 87. **d** 89. Par Dn Wythenshawe St Martin *Man* from 89. *45 Amberwood Drive, Baguley, Manchester M23 9NZ* 061-998 3220

SIBLEY, Jonathan Paul Eddolls. b 55. Newc Univ BA77. Westcott Ho Cam 78 Ripon Coll Cuddesdon 85. **d** 87 **p** 88. C Waltham Cross *St Alb* 87-90; C Chalfont St Peter *Ox* from 90. *All Saints' Parsonage, Oval Way, Chalfont St Peter, Gerrards Cross, Bucks SL9 8PZ*   Gerrards Cross (0753) 883839

SIBLEY, Peter Linsey. b 40. Selw Coll Cam BA61 MA63 DipHE. Oak Hill Th Coll 79. **d** 81 **p** 82. C Crofton *Portsm* 81-84; TV Cheltenham St Mark *Glouc* from 84. *St Barnabas' Vicarage, 152 Alstone Lane, Cheltenham, Glos GL51 8HL*   Cheltenham (0242) 580568

SIBSON, Edward John. b 39. Brasted Th Coll 61 St Aid Birkenhead 63. **d** 65 **p** 66. C Gt Parndon *Chelmsf* 65-69; C Saffron Walden 69-72; P-in-c Colchester St Leon 72-77; Ind Chapl 72-80; TV Colchester St Leon, St Mary Magd and St Steph 77-80; V Layer-de-la-Haye 80-90; R Chipping Ongar w Shelley from 90. *The Rectory, Shaketons, Ongar, Essex CM5 9AT*   Ongar (0277) 362173

SIBSON, Robert Francis. b 46. Leeds Univ CertEd68. Sarum & Wells Th Coll 78. **d** 80 **p** 81. C Watford St Mich *St Alb* 80-83; TV Digswell and Panshanger 83-90; V Biggleswade from 90. *The Vicarage, Shortmead Street, Biggleswade, Beds SG18 0AT*   Biggleswade (0767) 312243

SICHEL, Stephen Mackenzie. b 59. RGN85 RMN87 UEA BA80. Ripon Coll Cuddesdon 87. **d** 90 **p** 91. C Tettenhall Regis *Lich* from 90. *45 Lower Street, Tettenhall, Wolverhampton WV6 9LR*   Wolverhampton (0902) 755292

SIDAWAY, Geoffrey Harold. b 42. Kelham Th Coll 61. **d** 66 **p** 67. C Beighton *Derby* 66-70; C Chesterfield All SS 70-72; P-in-c Derby St Bart 72-74; V 74-77; V Maidstone St Martin *Cant* 77-86; V Bearsted w Thurnham from 86. *The Vicarage, Church Lane, Bearsted, Maidstone, Kent ME14 4EF*   Maidstone (0622) 37135

SIDDALL, Arthur. b 43. Lanc Univ MA81 DMS90. Lon Coll of Div ALCD67 LTh74. **d** 67 **p** 68. C Formby H Trin *Liv* 67-70; C Childwall All SS 70-72; CMS 72-77; Bangladesh 74-77; V Clitheroe St Paul Low Moor *Blackb* 77-82; V Blackb St Gabr 82-90; Dep Gen Sec Miss to Seamen from 90. *c/o St Michael Paternoster Royal, College Hill, London EC4R 2RL*   071-248 5202 or 248 7442

SIDDLE, Michael Edward. b 33. Dur Univ BA54. St Aid Birkenhead 55. **d** 57 **p** 58. C Fazakerley Em *Liv* 57-59; C Farnworth 59-62; V Swadlincote *Derby* 62-70; Distr Sec (Northd and Durham) BFBS 70-72; Yorkshire 72-82; V Bamber Bridge St Aid *Blackb* 82-87; V Hereford H

Ripon from 87. *St Margaret's Vicarage, Church Lane, Horsforth, Leeds LS18 5LA*   Leeds (0532) 582481

SIDEBOTHAM, Canon Stephen Francis. b 35. Qu Coll Cam BA58 MA80. Linc Th Coll 58. **d** 60 **p** 61. C Bitterne Park *Win* 60-64; Hong Kong 64-83; Dean Hong Kong 76-83; Chapl Gravesend and N Kent Hosp from 83; R Gravesend St Geo *Roch* from 83; RD Gravesend from 91. *St George's Rectory, Gravesend, Kent DA11 0DJ* Gravesend (0474) 534965

SIDEBOTTOM, Andrew John. b 54. FRCO75 FTCL76 LRAM75 Univ of Wales (Abth) BMus76 St Martin's Coll Lanc PGCE78. Sarum & Wells Th Coll 79. **d** 81 **p** 82. C Tenby w Gumfreston *St D* 81-84; C Llanelly 84-86; V Monkton 86-91; V Fairfield *Derby* from 91. *The Vicarage, Fairfield, Buxton, Derbyshire SK17 7EB* Buxton (0298) 23629

SIDEBOTTOM, George. b 16. TCD 43. **d** 49 **p** 50. V Felmersham *St Alb* 62-81; rtd 81; Perm to Offic *St Alb* from 81. *11 Cody Road, Clapham, Bedford*   Bedford (0234) 56189

SIDES, Canon James Robert. b 37. TCD BA66. CITC 68. **d** 67 **p** 68. C Belf St Clem *D & D* 67-70; C Antrim All SS *Conn* 70-73; I Tomregan w Drumlane *K, E & A* 73-80; I Killesher from 80; Preb Kilmore Cathl from 89. *Killesher Rectory, Tully, Florencecourt, Enniskillen, Co Fermanagh BT92 1FN*   Florencecourt (036582) 235

SIGRIST, Richard Martin. b 46. Sarum Th Coll 68. **d** 71 **p** 72. C Yeovil St Mich *B & W* 71-74; Chapl RN 74-84; TV Sidmouth, Woolbrook and Salcombe Regis *Ex* 84-86; TR 86-91; TR Sidmouth, Woolbrook, Salcombe Regis, Sidbury etc from 91; RD Ottery from 90. *The Rectory, Convent Fields, Sidmouth, Devon EX10 8QR* Sidmouth (0395) 513431

SILCOCK, Donald John. b 30. AKC59. **d** 60 **p** 61. C Hackney St Jo *Lon* 60-63; C-in-c Plumstead Wm Temple Ch Abbey Wood CD *S'wark* 63-68; C Felpham w Middleton *Chich* 68-74; R Ightham *Roch* 74-84; R Cliffe at Hoo w Cooling from 84; RD Strood from 85. *St Helen's Rectory, Church Street, Cliffe, Rochester, Kent ME3 7PY*   Medway (0634) 220220

SILK, Ian Geoffrey. b 60. Pemb Coll Cam BA81 MA85. Trin Coll Bris BA89. **d** 89 **p** 90. C Linc St Giles *Linc* from 89. *54 Wolsey Way, Lincoln LN2 4QH*   Lincoln (0522) 536498

SILK, John Arthur. b 52. Selw Coll Cam BA73 MA77 K Coll Lon MTh80. Westcott Ho Cam 75. **d** 77 **p** 78. C Banstead *Guildf* 77-80; C Dorking w Ranmore 80-84; R Ringwould w Kingsdown *Cant* from 84. *The Rectory, Upper Street, Kingsdown, Deal, Kent CT14 8BJ*   Deal (0304) 373951

SILK, Ven Robert David. b 36. Ex Univ BA58. St Steph Ho Ox 58. **d** 59 **p** 60. C Gillingham St Barn *Roch* 59-62; C Lamorbey H Redeemer 63-69; R Swanscombe SS Pet and Paul 69-71; P-in-c Swanscombe All SS 69-71; R Swanscombe 71-75; R Beckenham St Geo 75-80; Adn Leic from 80; TR Leic H Spirit 82-88. *13 Stoneygate Avenue, Leicester LE2 3HE*   Leicester (0533) 704441

SILKSTONE, Harry William James. b 21. St D Coll Lamp BA48. **d** 49 **p** 50. R Debden *Chelmsf* 63-72; V Bocking St Pet 72-78; R Gt Hallingbury 78-86; rtd 86; Perm to Offic *B & W* from 86. *Trevarah, 13 Lye Mead, Winford, Bristol BS18 8AU*   Bristol (0272) 872836

SILKSTONE, Thomas William. b 27. St Edm Hall Ox BA51 MA55 BD68. Wycliffe Hall Ox 51. **d** 53 **p** 54. C Aston SS Pet and Paul *Birm* 54-56; Asst Master Merchant Taylors' Sch Crosby 56-62; Lect K Alfred's Coll *Win* 62-85; Asst Chapl 62-69; Lic to Offic *Win* from 62; Perm to Offic *Truro* from 82. *Trevalyon, Lansallos, Looe, Cornwall*   Polperro (0503) 72110

SILLER, James Robert William. b 44. Pemb Coll Ox BA65 MA70 Qu Coll Cam 69. Westcott Ho Cam 67. **d** 70 **p** 71. C Spring Grove St Mary *Lon* 70-73; C Leeds St Pet *Ripon* 73-77; P-in-c Quarry Hill 73-77; V Gilling and Kirkby Ravensworth 77-82; P-in-c Melsonby 77-82; R Farnley from 82. *The Rectory, 16 Cross Lane, Leeds LS12 5AA*   Leeds (0532) 638064

SILLETT, Mrs Angela Veronica Isabel. See BERNERS-WILSON, Angela Veronica Isabel

SILLEY, Michael John. b 48. Ripon Coll Cuddesdon 82. **d** 84 **p** 85. C Frodingham *Linc* 84-87; V Ingham w Cammeringham w Fillingham from 87; R Aisthorpe w Scampton w Thorpe le Fallows etc from 87. *The Vicarage, Ingham, Lincoln LN1 2YW*   Lincoln (0522) 730519

SILLIS, Eric Keith. b 41. NW Ord Course 75. **d** 78 **p** 79. C Blackpool St Steph *Blackb* 78-82; V Huncoat 82-86; V Blackpool St Wilfrid from 86. *St Wilfrid's Vicarage, 9 Langdale Road, Blackpool FY4 4RT*   Blackpool (0253) 61532

SILLIS, Graham William. b 46. S'wark Ord Course 73. **d** 76 **p** 77. C Palmers Green St Jo *Lon* 76-79; C Dawlish *Ex* 79-81; V Ipswich St Thos *St E* 81-87; V Babbacombe *Ex* from 87. *Babbacombe Vicarage, Cary Park, Torquay, Devon TQ1 3NH* Torquay (0803) 323002

SILLITOE, Pauline Ann. b 42. ACP71 FCP82 CertEd69 Birm Poly DipEd80. Qu Coll Birm 82. **dss** 85 **d** 87. Kingshurst *Birm* 85-86; Castle Bromwich St Clem 86-87; NSM from 87. *St Clement's Vicarage, Lanchester Way, Birmingham B36 9JG* 021-747 4460

SILLITOE, William John. b 37. Lich Th Coll 67. **d** 69 **p** 70. C Ettingshall *Lich* 69-71; C March St Jo *Ely* 72-74; P-in-c Kennett 74-77; V Fordham St Pet 74-77; V Castle Bromwich St Clem *Birm* from 77. *The Vicarage, Lanchester Way, Birmingham B36 9JG* 021-747 4460

SILLS, Peter Michael. b 41. Nottm Univ BA63 LLM68. S'wark Ord Course 78. **d** 81 **p** 82. C W Wimbledon Ch Ch *S'wark* 81-85; P-in-c Barnes H Trin from 85; Wandsworth Adnry Ecum Officer from 90. *162 Castelnau, London SW13 9ET* 081-748 5744

SILVANUS, Brother Superior. See BERRY, Graham Renwick

SILVER, Christopher. b 53. Southn Univ BA77. St Steph Ho Ox 84. **d** 86 **p** 87. C Carnforth *Blackb* 86-89; C Leytonstone H Trin Harrow Green *Chelmsf* from 89. *4 Holloway Road, London E11 4LD* 081-539 7760

SILVERSIDES, Mark. b 51. Lon Univ BD73. St Jo Coll Nottm 74. **d** 76 **p** 77. C Hornchurch St Andr *Chelmsf* 76-80; P-in-c Becontree St Thos 80-85; TR Becontree W 85-86; CPAS Staff from 86. *c/o CPAS, Athena Drive, Tachbrook Park, Leamington Spa, Warks CV34 6NG* Leamington Spa (0926) 334242

SILVERTHORN, Alan. b 37. St Mich Coll Llan 62. **d** 65 **p** 66. C Machen and Rudry *Mon* 65-71; V New Tredegar 71-83; V Llanfrechfa and Llanddewi Fach w Llandegveth from 83. *The Vicarage, Llanfrechfa, Cwmbran, Gwent NP44 8DQ* Cwmbran (0633) 32343

SILVESTER, David. b 59. Qu Mary Coll Lon BSc80 Nottm Univ BCombStuds85. Linc Th Coll 82. **d** 85 **p** 86. C Walthamstow St Mary w St Steph *Chelmsf* 85-90; TV Barking St Marg w St Patr from 90. *The Vicarage, Bastable Avenue, Barking, Essex IG11 0NG* 081-594 1976

SILVESTER, Stephen David. b 59. Chu Coll Cam BA80 MA83 Man Univ PGCE82. St Jo Coll Nottm 88. **d** 91. C Nottm St Jude *S'well* from 91. *19 Kent Road, Nottingham NG3* Nottingham (0602) 620281

SIM, David Hayward. b 29. Qu Coll Birm 57. **d** 59 **p** 60. C Foleshill St Laur *Cov* 59-62; C Kenilworth St Nic 62-64; V Devonport St Aubyn *Ex* 64-69; V Frampton *Linc* 69-74; V Gainsborough St Geo 74-82; V Sturminster Newton and Hinton St Mary *Sarum* 82-89; R Stock and Lydlinch 82-89; Dorchester from 89; Chapl HM Pris Dorchester from 89. *The Parsonage, 10 Treves Road, Dorchester, Dorset DT1 2HD* Dorchester (0305) 69262

SIMCOCK, Canon Michael Pennington. b 27. Qu Coll Cam BA50 MA52. Bps' Coll Cheshunt 50. **d** 52 **p** 53. C Andover w Foxcott *Win* 52-55; C Eastleigh 55-57; Min Tadley St Mary CD 57-67; V Altarnon and Bolventor *Truro* 67-70; V Treleigh 70-87; RD Carnmarth N 75-91; Hon Can Truro Cathl from 82; R Redruth w Lanner 87-88; TR Redruth w Lanner and Treleigh from 88. *The Rectory, 53 Clinton Road, Redruth, Cornwall TR15 2LP* Redruth (0209) 215258

SIMISTER, Charles Arnold. b 19. MM44. Edin Th Coll 49. **d** 52 **p** 53. CF from 63; R Kircudbright *Glas* 63-84; R Gatehouse of Fleet 63-84; rtd 84. *98 High Street, Kirkcudbright DG6 4JQ* Kirkcudbright (0557) 30747

SIMISTER, Thomas Brocklehurst. b 19. Keble Coll Ox BA48 MA53. St Steph Ho Ox 48. **d** 50 **p** 51. V Rushall *Lich* 55-88; rtd 88; Perm to Offic *Nor* from 88. *St Fursey House, Convent of All Hallows, Ditchingham, Bungay NR35 2DZ* Bungay (0986) 892308

SIMMONDS, Clement. b 05. AKC30 Lon Univ BD59. **d** 30 **p** 31. V Heigham St Bart *Nor* 59-74; rtd 74; Hon C Heigham St Barn w St Bart *Nor* from 79. *7 Queen Elizabeth Close, Norwich NR3 1RY* Norwich (0603) 626483

SIMMONDS, David Brian. b 38. Selw Coll Cam BA62 MA66. Ridley Hall Cam. **d** 65 **p** 66. C Newc w Butterton *Lich* 65-69; V Branston from 69. *The Vicarage, Branston, Burton-on-Trent, Staffs DE14 3EX* Burton-on-Trent (0283) 68926

SIMMONDS, Edward Alan. b 32. St Edm Hall Ox MA60. Ripon Coll Cuddesdon 88. **d** 89 **p** 90. NSM Ox St Mich w St Martin and All SS *Ox* from 89. *5 Upland Park Road, Oxford OX2 7RU* Oxford (0865) 512591

SIMMONDS, John. b 24. Sheff Univ BA50. Ridley Hall Cam 50. **d** 52 **p** 53. V W Streatham St Jas *S'wark* 65-73;

V Congresbury *B & W* 73-75; P-in-c Puxton w Hewish St Ann and Wick St Lawrence 73-75; V Congresbury w Puxton and Hewish St Ann 75-84; Warden Home of Divine Healing Crowhurst 84-89; rtd 89. *Beach Villa, 14 The Beach, Clevedon, Avon BS21 7QU* Clevedon (0272) 342295

SIMMONDS, Paul Andrew Howard. b 50. Nottm Univ BSc73 Lon Univ DipTh78. Trin Coll Bris 75. **d** 78 **p** 79. C Leic H Trin w St Jo *Leic* 78-82; CPAS Staff from 82; Perm to Offic *B & W* 83-89; Lic to Offic *Bris* 83-89; Hon C Wolston and Church Lawford *Cov* from 89. *c/o CPAS, Athena Drive, Tachbrook Park, Warwick CV34 6NG* Warwick (0926) 334242

SIMMONDS, Paul Richard. b 38. AKC63. **d** 64 **p** 65. C Newington St Mary *S'wark* 64-67; C Cheam 68-73; P-in-c Stockwell Green St Andr 73-87; V from 87. *St Andrew's Vicarage, Moat Place, London SW9 0TA* 071-274 7531

SIMMONDS, Robert William. b 52. Nottm Univ BTh77 Birm Poly DCG79. Linc Th Coll 72. **d** 80 **p** 81. C Roehampton H Trin *S'wark* 80-83; TV Hemel Hempstead *St Alb* 83-90; V S Woodham Ferrers *Chelmsf* from 90. *The Vicarage, 18 Victoria Road, South Woodham Ferrers, Chelmsford CM3 5LR* Chelmsford (0245) 320201

SIMMONDS, William Hugh Cyril. b 08. Lon Univ DipOAS47. St Jo Hall Highbury. **d** 37 **p** 38. V S Malling *Chich* 67-78; rtd 78; Perm to Offic *Chich* from 82. *79 Grange Close, Horam, Heathfield, E Sussex TN21 0EG* Horam Road (04353) 2743

SIMMONS, Barry Jeremy. b 32. Leeds Univ BA54 MA62. Ridley Hall Cam 61. **d** 63 **p** 64. C Buttershaw St Aid *Bradf* 63-65; Jamaica 65-68; V Earby *Bradf* 68-73; Hong Kong 73-74; Bahrain 75-79; Chapl Luxembourg *Eur* 80-91; V Shoreham *Roch* from 91. *The Vicarage, Shoreham, Sevenoaks, Kent TN14 7SA* Otford (09592) 2363

SIMMONS, Bernard Peter. b 26. CA Tr Coll 48 S'wark Ord Course 86. **d** 88 **p** 88. C Chatham St Wm *Roch* 88-91; rtd 91; P-in-c Underriver *Roch* from 91; P-in-c Seal St Lawr from 91. *St Lawrence Vicarage, Stone Street, Seal, Sevenoaks, Kent TN15 0LQ* Sevenoaks (0732) 61766

SIMMONS, Brian Dudley. b 35. Master Mariner. St Steph Ho Ox 62. **d** 64 **p** 65. C Bournemouth St Pet *Win* 64-67; Miss to Seamen 67-71; Hon C Milton next Gravesend w Denton *Roch* 67-70; Hon C Gravesend St Geo 70-71; V Lamorbey H Trin 71-90; P-in-c Four Elms from 90; R Hever w Mark Beech from 90. *The Rectory, Hever, Edenbridge, Kent TN8 7LH* Edenbridge (0732) 862249

SIMMONS, Christopher John. b 49. Mert Coll Ox MA77. NE Ord Course 88. **d** 90 **p** 91. C Kirkleatham *York* from 90. *44 Ayton Drive, Redcar, Cleveland TS10 4LR* Redcar (0642) 490475

SIMMONS, Eric. b 30. Leeds Univ BA51. Coll of Resurr Mirfield 51. **d** 53 **p** 54. C Chesterton St Luke *Ely* 53-57; Chapl Keele Univ *Lich* 57-61; Lic to Offic *Wakef* 63-65 and from 67; CR from 63; Lic to Offic *Ripon* 65-67; Warden Hostel of the Resurr Leeds 66-67; Superior CR 74-87. *Royal Foundation of St Katharine, 2 Butcher Row, London E14 8DS* 071-790 3540

SIMMONS, Gary David. b 59. Trin Coll Bris BA86. **d** 87 **p** 88. C Ecclesfield *Sheff* 87-90; Min Stapenhill Immanuel CD *Derby* from 90. *Immanuel Vicarage, 150 Hawthorn Crescent, Burton-on-Tent, Staffs DE15 9QW* Burton-on-Trent (0283) 63959

SIMMONS, Godfrey John. b 39. Open Univ BA77. Edin Th Coll 77. **d** 74 **p** 74. Dioc Supernumerary *St And* 74-75 and 80-81; C Strathtay 75-77; C Dunkeld 75-77; C Bridge of Allan 77-80; C Alloa 77-80; Chapl Stirling Univ 79-80; Chapl HM Pris Perth 80-85; Min Crieff *St And* 80-81; R 81-85; Min Muthill 80-81; R 81-85; Min Comrie 80-81; R 81-85; R Stromness *Ab* from 85; R Kirkwall 85-91; Miss to Seamen from 85. *The Rectory, 12 Dundas Crescent, Kirkwall, Isle of Orkney KW15 1JQ* Kirkwall (0856) 2024

SIMMONS, Miss Joan Yvonne. b 14. Gilmore Ho 57. **dss** 61 **d** 87. Adult Educn Officer *Lon* 69-78; rtd 78; Perm to Offic *Chich* from 87. *12 Whittington College, London Road, East Grinstead, W Sussex RH19 2QU* East Grinstead (0342) 312781

SIMMONS, John. b 53. Carl Dioc Tr Course 82. **d** 85 **p** 86. C Wotton St Mary *Glouc* 85-88; P-in-c Amberley from 88. *The Rectory, Amberley, Stroud, Glos GL5 5JG* Amberley (0453) 878515

SIMMONS, John Harold. b 46. FCCA. Sarum & Wells Th Coll 86. **d** 89 **p** 90. NSM The Iwernes, Sutton Waldron and Fontmell Magna *Sarum* from 89. *Fourways, Iwerne Courteney, Blandford Forum, Dorset DT11 8QL* Blandford (0258) 860515

SIMMONS, Canon Maurice Samuel. b 27. St Chad's Coll Dur BA50 DipTh52. **d** 52 **p** 53. C S Shields St Hilda *Dur* 52-58; Youth Chapl 56-60; R Croxdale 58-81; Soc and Ind Adv to Bp Dur 61-70; Gen Sec Soc Resp Gp 70-75; Hon Can Dur Cathl from 71; Sec Dioc Bd for Miss and Unity 75-82; V Norton St Mary from 81; RD Stockton from 85. *Norton Vicarage, Stockton-on-Tees, Cleveland TS20 1EL* Stockton-on-Tees (0642) 558888

SIMMONS, Norman. b 11. Wycliffe Hall Ox 49. **d** 49 **p** 50. V Doncaster St Leon and St Jude *Sheff* 53-74; R Burghwallis w Skelbrooke 74-81; rtd 81. *21 Norseway, Stamford Bridge, York YO4 1DR* Stamford Bridge (0759) 72298

SIMMONS, Raymond Agar. b 35. Linc Th Coll 69. **d** 71 **p** 72. C Hartlepool St Luke *Dur* 71-74; P-in-c Purleigh *Chelmsf* 74-81; Ind Chapl 74-81; P-in-c Cold Norton w Stow Maries 81; Chapl Rampton Hosp Retford from 81. *4 Galen Avenue, Woodbeck, Retford, Notts DN22 0PD* Rampton (077784) 321 or 531

SIMMONS, Richard Andrew Cartwright. b 46. Trin Coll Bris 73. **d** 75 **p** 76. C Worting *Win* 75-80; R Six Pilgrims *B & W* from 80. *The Rectory, North Barrow, Yeovil, Somerset BA22 7LZ* Wheathill (096324) 230

SIMMS, Ernest Desmond Ross. b 25. TCD BA48 MA51 BD51. **d** 51 **p** 52. CF 62-81; R Cheriton w Tichborne and Beauworth *Win* 81-90; RD Alresford 84-90; rtd 90. *11 Buttermere Gardens, Alresford, Hants SO24 9NN* Alresford (0962) 735526

✠**SIMMS, Most Rev George Otto.** b 10. MRIA57 TCD BA32 MA35 BD36 PhD50 DD52 Iona Coll (NY) Hon DD91. **d** 35 **p** 36 **c** 52. C Dub St Bart *D & G* 35-38; Hon CV Ch Ch Cathl Dub 35-52; Chapl Linc Th Coll 38-39; Dean of Residence TCD 39-52; Dean Cork *C, C & R* 52; Bp C, *C & R* 52-56; Abp Dub *D & G* 56-69; Abp Arm 69-80; rtd 80. *62 Cypress Grove Road, Dublin 6W, Irish Republic* Dublin (1) 905594

SIMMS, William Michael. b 41. DMA66 ACIS70 MIPM75 Open Univ BA87. NE Ord Course 84. **d** 87 **p** 88. NSM Croft *Ripon* 87; C 88; NSM Middleton Tyas and Melsonby 87; C 88; C Headingley 88-90; C Richmond w Hudswell from 90; C-in-c Downholme and Marske from 90. *1 Wathcote Place, Richmond, N Yorkshire DL10 7SR* Richmond (0748) 6260

SIMON, Brother. *See* HOLDEN, Jack Crawford

SIMON, David Sidney. b 49. Univ of Wales (Abth) BSc(Econ)70 Hull Univ MA83. NE Ord Course 84. **d** 87 **p** 88. Humberside Poly from 87; NSM Beverley St Mary York from 87. *8 Melrose Park, Beverley, N Humberside HU17 8JL* Hull (0482) 862855

SIMON, Frederick Fairbanks. b 42. Ripon Coll Cuddesdon 75. **d** 77 **p** 78. C Cheddleton *Lich* 77-79; C Woodley *Ox* 79-82; V Spencer's Wood 82-85; P-in-c Steventon w Milton 85-87; Chapl Grenville Coll Bideford from 87; Lic to Offic *Ex* from 88. *Bracken Brae, Belvoir Road, Bideford, Devon EX39 3JR*

SIMON, Oliver. b 45. Dur Univ BA67 Sussex Univ MA68 Ox Univ DipTh71 Man Univ CertRS89. Cuddesdon Coll 69. **d** 71 **p** 72. C Kidlington *Ox* 71-74; C Bracknell 74-78; V Frodsham *Ches* 78-88; R Easthampstead *Ox* from 88. *The Rectory, Easthampstead, Bracknell, Berks RG12 4ER* Bracknell (0344) 425205 or 423253

SIMON, Prof Ulrich Ernst. b 13. K Coll Lon BD38 AKC38 MTh43 DD59. Linc Th Coll 38. **d** 38 **p** 39. C St Helier *S'wark* 38-42; C Upton cum Chalvey *Ox* 42-45; Lect Hebrew and OT K Coll Lon 45-59; FKC from 57; Hon C Bletchingley *S'wark* 50-52; P-in-c Millbrook *St Alb* 52-55; Lic to Offic 55-72; Prof Chr Lit Lon Univ 71-80; Dean K Coll Lon 78-80; Lic to Offic *Lon* from 85. *22 Collingwood Avenue, London N10* 081-883 4852

SIMONS, Miss Christine. b 40. RGN62 RM64 RHV69. St Jo Coll Nottm 82. dss 84 **d** 87. Claygate *Guildf* 84-87; C Camberley St Paul from 87. *70 Inglewood Avenue, Camberley, Surrey GU15 1RS* Camberley (0276) 684702

SIMONS, John Trevor. b 34. Lon Univ BD67. ALCD66. **d** 67 **p** 68. C Becontree St Mary *Chelmsf* 67-71; V Cranham Park 71-78; P-in-c Nailsea H Trin *B & W* 78-83; R from 83; Preb Wells Cathl from 90. *The Rectory, 2 Church Lane, Nailsea, Bristol RS19 2NG* Nailsea (0272) 3227

SIMONS, Mark Anselm. b 38. ARCM62. Oak Hill Th Coll 62. **d** 65 **p** 66. C Nottm St Ann *S'well* 65-68; C N Ferriby *York* 68-75; P-in-c Sherburn 75-78; V Gt and Lt Driffield from 78. *The Vicarage, Driffield, N Humberside YO25 7DU* Driffield (0377) 43394

SIMONS, William Angus. b 18. Keble Coll Ox BA39 MA47. Cuddesdon Coll 40. **d** 41 **p** 42. Chapl Hammersmith Hosp Lon 65-68; St Edm Hosp 68-88;

Northn Gen Hosp 68-72; Lic to Offic *Pet* 68-72 and from 81; P-in-c Northn St Lawr 72-76; C Northn H Sepulchre w St Andr and St Lawr 76-81; Northants Past Coun Service 76-81; rtd 83. *54 Park Avenue North, Northampton NN3 2JE* Northampton (0604) 713767

SIMONSON, Canon Juergen Werner Dietrich. b 24. Lon Univ BD52. ALCD52. **d** 52 **p** 53. V Putney St Marg *S'wark* 69-81; RD Wandsworth 74-81; Hon Can S'wark Cathl 75-90; R Barnes St Mary 81-90; rtd 90. *Elm Cottage, Horseshoe Lane, Ibthorpe, Andover, Hants SP11 0BY* Hurstbourne Tarrant (026476) 381

SIMPER, Canon Allan Frederick. b 32. G&C Coll Cam BA56 MA59. Cuddesdon Coll 56. **d** 58 **p** 59. C Wigan All SS *Liv* 58-61; C Kirkby 61-64; Chapl Dover Coll Kent 64-70; V New Addington *Cant* 70-79; P-in-c Selsdon St Jo w St Fran 79-81; TR 81-84; TR Selsdon St Jo w St Fran *S'wark* 85; V Dover St Mary *Cant* from 85; Miss to Seamen from 85; RD Dover *Cant* from 86; Hon Can Cant Cathl from 90. *The Vicarage, Taswell Street, Dover, Kent CT16 1SE* Dover (0304) 206842

SIMPER, Terence Ernest. b 27. Qu Coll Birm 53. **d** 56 **p** 57. Australia 69-75; P-in-c Bris Lockleaze St Mary Magd w St Fran *Bris* 76-79; P-in-c Brislington St Anne 79-84; P-in-c St Dominic *Truro* 84-87; P-in-c St Mellion w Pillaton 84-87; P-in-c Landulph 84-87; R St Dominic, Landulph and St Mellion w Pillaton 87-90; rtd 90. *21 St Anne's Drive, Oldland Common, Bristol BS15 6RD* Bristol (0272) 322514

SIMPKIN, Mrs Doris Lily. b 30. E Midl Min Tr Course 79. dss 82 **d** 87. Mugginton and Kedleston *Derby* 82-87; Hon Par Dn from 87. *71 Wheeldon Avenue, Derby DF3 1HP* Derby (0332) 43830

SIMPKIN, Paul. b 29. E Midl Min Tr Course. **d** 82 **p** 83. NSM Mugginton and Kedleston *Derby* from 82. *71 Wheeldon Avenue, Derby DE3 1HP* Derby (0332) 43830

SIMPKINS, Frank Charles. b 19. Oak Hill Th Coll 72. **d** 75 **p** 76. C Harrow Weald St Mich *Lon* 75-78; Hon C 81-84; P-in-c Dollis Hill St Paul 78-80; Chapl Northwick Park Hosp Harrow 81-83; Hon C Harrow H Trin St Mich *Lon* from 84. *7 Milne Field, Pinner, Middx HA5 4DP* 081-428 2477

SIMPKINS, Lionel Frank. b 46. UEA BSc68. Lambeth STh77 St Jo Coll Nottm ALCD72 LTh74. **d** 73 **p** 74. C Leic H Apostles *Leic* 73-77; C Bushbury *Lich* 77-80; V Sudbury w Ballingdon and Brundon *St E* from 80; RD Sudbury from 88. *All Saints' Vicarage, Church Street, Sudbury, Suffolk CO10 6BL* Sudbury (0787) 72400

SIMPSON, Alexander. b 31. Oak Hill Th Coll 74. **d** 76 **p** 77. Hon C Lower Homerton St Paul *Lon* 76-81; Hon C Homerton St Barn w St Paul 81-85; TV Hackney Marsh 85-87; V Kensington St Helen w H Trin from 87. *St Helen's Vicarage, St Helen's Gardens, London W10 6LP* 081-969 1520

SIMPSON, Andrew. b 48. Liv Univ BEng69. Sarum Th Coll 83. **d** 86 **p** 87. NSM Canford Magna *Sarum* from 86. *17 Sopwith Crescent, Merley, Wimborne, Dorset BH21 1SH* Wimborne (0202) 883996

SIMPSON, Canon Anthony Cyril. b 30. K Coll Lon BD55 AKC55. **d** 56 **p** 57. C Bishop's Cleeve *Glouc* 56-59; C E Grinstead St Swithun *Chich* 59-62; R E w W Barkwith *Linc* 62-76; R E w W Torrington 63-76; V Hainton w Sixhills 63-76; R S Willingham 63-76; R Barkwith Gp from 76; RD W Wold 78-88; Can and Preb Linc Cathl from 85. *Barkwith Rectory, East Barkwith, Lincoln LN3 5RY* Wragby (0673) 858291

SIMPSON, Athol. b 20. Lich Th Coll 41. **d** 44 **p** 45. V Amble *Newc* 63-90; rtd 90. *63 Briardene Crescent, Gosforth, Newcastle upon Tyne NE3 4RX*

SIMPSON, Canon Brian Shepherd Tinley. b 12. Linc Th Coll 38. **d** 40 **p** 41. R Portnacrois *Arg* 70-80; R Duror 70-80; Can St Jo Cathl Oban 78-80; rtd 80; Hon Can St Jo Cathl Oban *Arg* from 80. *Tigh-na-Crois, Appin, Argyll PA38 4BL* Appin (063173) 297

SIMPSON, Clarence. b 13. Bps' Coll Cheshunt 39. **d** 40 **p** 41. P-in-c Bicknoller *B & W* 66-74; P-in-c Port Isaac *Truro* 74-77; P-in-c Welsh Newton w Llanrothal *Heref* 77-78; C 78-80; rtd 78; Perm to Offic *Glouc* 80-88; Sen Chapl Glouc City Mental Hosp 86-89; Chapl Beauchamp Community 88-90. *12 Handbury Road, Malvern Link, Worcs WR14 1NN* Malvern (0684) 569388

SIMPSON, David John. b 61. Univ Coll Dur BA85 Liv Univ PGCE86. Sarum & Wells Th Coll 89. **d** 91. C Selby Abbey *York* from 91. *57 Woodville Terrace, Selby, N Yorkshire YO8 8AJ* Selby (0757) 705419

SIMPSON, Derek John. b 59. Oak Hill Th Coll BA89. **d** 89 **p** 90. C Alperton *Lon* from 89. *1 Norwood Avenue, Wembley, Middx HA0 1LX* 081-997 0083

SIMPSON, Derrick. b 27. NW Ord Course 72. **d** 75 **p** 76. C Disley *Ches* 75-79; C Stockport St Geo 79-81; R Wistaston 81-90; Chapl Barony Hosp Nantwich 81-89; V Newton in Mottram *Ches* from 90. *St Mary's Vicarage, 39 Bradley Green Road, Hyde, Cheshire SK14 4NA* 061-368 1489

SIMPSON, Edward. b 16. TD67. Leeds Univ BCom38. Bps' Coll Cheshunt 46. **d** 48 **p** 49. R Witcham w Mepal *Ely* 57-70; P-in-c Lockwood *Wakef* 71-73; R 73-80; V Hartshead 80-83; V Armitage Bridge 71-80; rtd 83; Perm to Offic *Chelmsf* from 84. *47 Hunters Way, Saffron Walden, Essex CB11 4DE* Saffron Walden (0799) 24418

SIMPSON, Geoffrey Sedgwick. b 32. Hamilton Coll (NY) BA54 Wisconsin Univ MA Pemb Coll Cam PhD70. Gen Th Sem (NY) STB57. **d** 57 **p** 57. USA 57-77; Chapl Birm Univ *Birm* 77-80; V Shoreham *Roch* 80-90; TR Stigar Team Min *York* from 90. *The Rectory, Barton-le-Street, Malton, N Yorkshire YO17 0PL* Malton (0653) 376

SIMPSON, George William. b 18. Ox NSM Course. **d** 76 **p** 77. NSM Didcot *Ox* 76-87; C Swan 87-89; rtd 89; Perm to Offic *Ex* from 90. *21 Crescent Gardens, Ivybridge, Plymouth PL21 0BS* Plymouth (0752) 894425

SIMPSON, Godfrey Lionel. b 42. Sarum Th Coll 63. **d** 66 **p** 67. C Leintwardine *Heref* 66-70; C Leominster 70-73; P-in-c Whitbourne 73-79; V Barlaston *Lich* from 79; RD Trentham from 85. *The Vicarage, Barlaston, Stoke-on-Trent ST12 9AB* Barlaston (078139) 2452

SIMPSON, Herbert. b 20. Carl Dioc Tr Course. **d** 82 **p** 83. NSM Barrow St Aid *Carl* 82; NSM Barrow St Jo 82-90; rtd 90. *3 Glenridding Drive, Barrow-in-Furness, Cumbria LA14 4PE* Barrow-in-Furness (0229) 23707

SIMPSON, Very Rev John Arthur. b 33. Keble Coll Ox BA56 MA60. Clifton Th Coll 56. **d** 58 **p** 59. C Low Leyton *Chelmsf* 58-59; C Orpington Ch Ch *Roch* 59-62; Tutor Oak Hill Th Coll 62-72; V Ridge *St Alb* 72-79; P-in-c Ridge and Post-Ord Tr 75-81; Hon Can St Alb 77-79; Can Res St Alb 79-81; Adn Cant and Can Res Cant Cathl *Cant* 81-86; Dean Cant from 86. *The Deanery, The Precincts, Canterbury, Kent CT1 2EH* Canterbury (0227) 765983

SIMPSON, Canon John Lawrence. b 33. ARCM60 SS Coll Cam BA55 MA59. Wells Th Coll 63. **d** 65 **p** 66. Chapl Win Cathl *Win* 65-66; C Win St Bart 65-69; Chapl Repton Sch Derby 69-71; Hd of RE Helston Sch 71-78; Lic to Offic *Truro* 71-78; P-in-c Curry Rivel *B & W* 79-80; R Curry Rivel w Fivehead and Swell 80-86; V Tunbridge Wells K Chas *Roch* 86-89; Can Res Bris Cathl *Bris* from 89. *55 Salisbury Road, Bristol BS6 7AS* Bristol (0272) 421452

SIMPSON, John Peter. b 39. ALCD66. **d** 66 **p** 67. C Woodside *Ripon* 66-69; C Burnage St Marg *Man* 69-72; V Rochdale Deeplish St Luke 72-80; R Lamplugh w Ennerdale *Carl* from 80. *The Vicarage, Ennerdale, Cleator, Cumbria CA23 3AG* Lamplugh (0946) 861310

SIMPSON, John Raymond. b 29. Man Univ BA57 Southn Univ CertEd68. Kelham Th Coll 50. **d** 57 **p** 59. V Moulsford *Ox* 68-73; V Hurley 73-75; Perm to Offic *Ex* from 84; rtd 89. *9 Greenbanks Close, Slapton, Kingsbridge, Devon TQ7 2PZ* Kingsbridge (0548) 580887

SIMPSON, John Raymond. b 41. **d** 67 **p** 68. C Scarborough St Martin *York* 67-71; C Grangetown 71-72; Bermuda from 72. *PO Box 62M, Hamilton, Bermuda*

SIMPSON, John Raymond. b 55. Oak Hill Th Coll 88. **d** 90 **p** 91. C Immingham *Linc* from 90. *95 Pilgrim Avenue, Immingham, S Humberside DN40 1DJ* Immingham (0469) 573518

SIMPSON, Mrs June Hall. b 31. LRAM59 Sheff Univ BEd74. E Midl Min Tr Course 83. **dss** 86 **d** 87. Hon Par Dn Carlton-in-Lindrick *S'well* from 87. *57 Arundel Drive, Carlton-in-Lindrick, Worksop, Notts S81 9DL* Worksop (0909) 730665

SIMPSON, Miss Margery Patricia. b 36. SRN57 SCM59. Oak Hill Th Coll BA86. **dss** 86 **d** 87. Rodbourne Cheney *Bris* 86-87; Par Dn 87-90; Par Dn Warmley from 90. *25 Poplar Road, Warmley, Bristol BS15 5JX* Bristol (0272) 609969

SIMPSON, Patrick Verrent. b 26. Fitzw Ho Cam BA49 MA54 Lon Univ PGCE70. Ridley Hall Cam 49. **d** 51 **p** 52. Chapl Prince Rupert Sch Wilhelmshaven 67-71; Chapl Northfleet Girl's Sch 71-81; Hon C Meopham w Nurstead *Roch* 72-81; P-in-c Weare Giffard w Landcross *Ex* 81-82; P-in-c Littleham 81-82; P-in-c Monkleigh 81-82; R Landcross, Littleham, Monkleigh etc 82-86; P-in-c Bovey Tracey SS Pet and Paul 86-91; Chapl Hawkmoor Hosp 86-87; Bovey Tracey Hosp 86-91; rtd 91. *10 Vicarage Close, Burton-in-Kendal, Carnforth, Lancs LA6 1NP* Burton (0524) 782306

SIMPSON, Peter. b 28. Trin Hall Cam BA56 MA60. **d** 57 **p** 58. C Kemp Town St Mark *Chich* 57-60; C Walthamstow St Pet *Chelmsf* 60-64; V Chingford St Anne 64-75; P-in-c Widdington 75; Perm to Offic *Win* 76-79; Chapl Princess Eliz Hosp Guernsey 77-79; R Guernsey St Michel du Valle *Win* from 79. *Vale Rectory, Guernsey, Channel Isles* Guernsey (0481) 44088

SIMPSON, Canon Peter Wynn. b 32. Birm Univ BA53. Ripon Hall Ox 55. **d** 57 **p** 58. C Leamington Priors H Trin *Cov* 57-60; C Croydon *Cant* 60-63; V Foleshill St Laur *Cov* 63-70; V Radford 70-79; RD Cov N 76-79; V Finham from 79; RD Cov S 82-88; Hon Can Cov Cathl from 83. *St Martin's Vicarage, 136 Green Lane South, Coventry CV3 6EA* Coventry (0203) 418330

SIMPSON, Raymond James. b 40. Lon Coll of Div ALCD63 LTh74. **d** 64 **p** 65. C Longton St Jas *Lich* 64-68; C Upper Tooting H Trin *S'wark* 68-71; BFBS Distr Sec E Anglia 71-77; C-in-c Bowthorpe CD *Nor* 78-84; V Bowthorpe from 84. *Church Community House, Bowthorpe Hall Road, Bowthorpe, Norwich NR5 9AA* Norwich (0603) 745698

SIMPSON, Preb Reginald Ernest. b 17. Lon Univ BA38 BD41. ALCD41. **d** 41 **p** 42. V Holloway St Mary w St Jas *Lon* 56-87; P-in-c W Holl St Dav 59-77; Preb St Paul's Cathl 81-87; P-in-c Barnsbury St Dav w St Clem 85-87; rtd 87. *12 Seaford Road, Eastbourne, E Sussex BN22 7JA* Eastbourne (0323) 27470

SIMPSON, Ven Rennie. b 20. LVO74. Lambeth MA70 Kelham Th Coll 39. **d** 45 **p** 46. Prec Westmr Abbey 63-74; P-in-O to HM The Queen 67-74; Sub-Prelate OStJ from 73; Can Res Ches Cathl *Ches* 74-78; Vice-Dean Ches 75-78; Adn Macclesfield 78-85; R Gawsworth 78-85; Chapl to HM The Queen 82-90; rtd 86. *18 Roseberry Green, North Stainley, Ripon, N Yorkshire HG4 3HZ* Ripon (0765) 85286

SIMPSON, Robert. b 21. Leeds Univ BA42. Coll of Resurr Mirfield 42. **d** 44 **p** 45. V Woodhouse St Mark *Ripon* 56-82; R Skipsea w Ulrome and Barmston w Fraisthorpe *York* 82-91; rtd 91. *The Rectory, Barmston, Driffield, N Humberside YO25 8PG* Skipsea (026286) 284

SIMPSON, Robert Charles. b 46. Ridley Hall Cam. **d** 85 **p** 86. C Eastwood *S'well* 85-88; V Yardley St Cypr Hay Mill *Birm* from 88. *The Vicarage, 7 The Fordrough, Birmingham B25 8DL* 021-773 1278

SIMPSON, Robert David. b 61. Fitzw Coll Cam BA83 MA87. Trin Coll Bris DipHE87. **d** 87 **p** 88. C Beckenham Ch Ch *Roch* 87-90; C Heydon w Gt and Lt Chishill *Chelmsf* 90; C Chrishall 90; C Elmdon w Wendon Lofts and Strethall 90; C Heydon, Gt and Lt Chishill, Chrishall etc from 91. *The Vicarage, Bury Lane, Elmdon, Saffron Walden, Essex CB11 4NQ* Royston (0763) 838893

SIMPSON, Robert Theodore. b 34. Linc Coll Ox BA58 MA61 K Coll Lon PhD71 S Africa Univ DTEd81 MEd85. Chich Th Coll 58. **d** 60 **p** 61. C Ellesmere Port *Ches* 60-63; CR 63-66; S Africa 68-88; Chapl Coll of SS Mark and Jo Plymouth 88-90; Chapl Simon of Cyrene Th Inst from 90; Perm to Offic *S'wark* from 91. *Simon of Cyrene Theological College, 2 St Anne's Crescent, London SW18 2LR* 081-874 1353

SIMPSON, Roger Westgarth. b 51. Lon Univ BSc72. St Jo Coll Nottm 77. **d** 79 **p** 80. C St Marylebone All So w SS Pet and Jo *Lon* 79-85; R Edin St Paul and St Geo *Edin* from 85. *St Paul's & St George's Church, 6 Broughton Street, Edinburgh EH1 3RD* 031-556 1335

SIMPSON, Ven Samuel. b 26. TCD BA55 MA69 Div Test56. **d** 56 **p** 57. C Coleraine *Conn* 56-60; I Donagh w Cloncha and Clonmany *D & R* 60-64; I Ballyscullion 64-81; RD Maghera and Kilrea 75-89; Can Derry Cathl from 78; I Errigal w Garvagh from 81; Adn Derry from 89. *St Paul's Rectory, 58 Station Road, Garvagh, Co Londonderry BT51 5LA* Garvagh (02665) 58226

SIMPSON, Thomas Eric. b 31. St Chad's Coll Dur BA55. Ely Th Coll 55. **d** 57 **p** 58. C Jarrow St Paul *Dur* 57-61; C Bishopwearmouth St Mary V w St Pet CD 61-63; V Chopwell from 63; Chapl Norman Riding Hosp Tyne & Wear 79-83; Chapl Shotley Bridge Hosp 83-90. *The Vicarage, Chopwell, Newcastle upon Tyne NE17 7AN* Ebchester (0207) 561248

SIMPSON, William Michael. b 45. Leeds Univ BA66. St Jo Coll Nottm 75. **d** 77 **p** 78. C Desborough *Pet* 77-80; P-in-c Arthingworth w Kelmarsh and Harrington 79-80; Hong Kong 80-85; P-in-c Beetham and Milnthorpe *Carl* from 85. *The Vicarage, Milnthorpe, Cumbria LA7 7QE* Milnthorpe (05395) 62244

SIMPSON, William Thomas. b 10. St Chad's Coll Dur BA35 DipTh36 MA38. **d** 36 **p** 37. R Week St Mary *Truro* 59-81; R Whitstone 62-81; rtd 81. *Waverley, Under*

Road, Gunnislake, Cornwall PL18 9JL Tavistock (0822) 833396

SIMPSON, William Vaughan. b 16. Worc Ord Coll 55. **d** 57 **p** 58. R Willersey w Saintbury *Glouc* 60-73; RD Campden 70-73; P-in-c Cherington 74-76; V Clearwell 76-79; Perm to Offic from 79; rtd 81. *Little Glebe, Cidermill Lane, Chipping Campden, Glos GL55 6HU* Evesham (0386) 840610

SIMS, Christopher Sidney. b 49. Wycliffe Hall Ox 74. **d** 77 **p** 78. C Walmley *Birm* 77-80; V Yardley St Cypr Hay Mill 80-88; V Stanwix *Carl* from 88; RD Carl from 89. *Stanwix Vicarage, Dykes Terrace, Carlisle CA3 9AS* Carlisle (0228) 514600 or 511430

SIMS, David John. b 18. Handsworth Coll Birm 44 St Aug Coll Cant 59. **d** 56 **p** 56. In Meth Ch 47-56; W Indies 47-63; V Haxey *Linc* 63-73; USA 73-83; rtd 83; Perm to Offic *Chich* from 87. *Bungalow 6, Terry's Cross, Brighton Road, Henfield, W Sussex BN5 9SX* Henfield (0273) 493487

SIMS, James Henry. b 35. St Jo Coll Nottm. **d** 89 **p** 91. NSM Ban Abbey *D & D* 89-91; Lic to Offic from 91. *7 Prior's Lea, Holywood, Co Down BT18 9QW* Holywood (02317) 4360

SIMS, Peter George Russell. b 36. Univ of Wales (Swansea) BA57. St Mich Coll Llan 63. **d** 65 **p** 66. C Brecon w Battle *S & B* 65-72; Min Can Brecon Cathl 65-72; V Llanfrynach and Cantref w Llanhamlach from 72. *The Rectory, Llanfrynach, Brecon, Powys LD3 7AJ* Llanfrynach (087486) 667

SIMS, Sidney. b 20. Wycliffe Hall Ox. **d** 64 **p** 65. V Ramsey St Mary's w Ponds Bridge *Ely* 67-70; V Cam St Matt 70-85; Algeria 85-86; rtd 86; Perm to Offic *Nor* from 86. *66 Morston Road, Blakeney, Norfolk NR25 7BE* Cley (0263) 740184

SIMS-WILLIAMS, Michael Vernon Sims. b 09. Trin Hall Cam BA30 MA34. Westcott Ho Cam 32. **d** 33 **p** 35. Teacher St Jo Sch Sittingbourne 60-73; Perm to Offic *Cant* from 73; rtd 75. *Broomfield, Harmans Corner, Borden, Sittingbourne, Kent ME9 8JH* Sittingbourne (0795) 472014

SINCLAIR, Andrew John McTaggart. b 58. Ex Univ BA. Westcott Ho Cam. **d** 84 **p** 85. C Aston cum Aughton *Sheff* 84; C Aston cum Aughton and Ulley 84-87; C Rotherham 87-88; TV Edin Old St Paul *Edin* from 88; Chapl Edin Univ from 89. *Flat 3, 1 Whitehorse Close, 27 Canongate, Edinburgh EH8 8DN* 031-556 7397

SINCLAIR, Arthur Alfred. b 46. **d** 87 **p** 89. Chapl Asst Inverness Hosp from 87; Hon C Inverness St Andr *Mor* from 87; Dioc Chapl from 87. *25 High Street, Fortrose, Ross-shire IV10 8SX* Inverness (0463) 226255

SINCLAIR, Charles Horace. b 19. Keble Coll Ox BA40 MA44. Linc Th Coll 41. **d** 42 **p** 43. Hd Master St Aid Sch Denby Dale 57-64; rtd 84. *Oakstead, 94 Harbour Way, Folkestone, Kent CT20 1NB* Folkestone (0303) 50882

SINCLAIR, Colin. b 30. **d** 84 **p** 85. NSM Ramoan w Ballycastle and Culfeightrin *Conn* from 84. *4 Bushfoot Cottages, Portballintrae, Bushmills, Co Antrim BT57 8RN* Bushmills (02657) 31551

SINCLAIR, Gordon Keith. b 52. MA. Cranmer Hall Dur. **d** 84 **p** 85. C Summerfield *Birm* 84-88; V Aston SS Pet and Paul from 88. *Aston Vicarage, Sycamore Road, Birmingham B6 5UH* 021-327 5856

SINCLAIR, Jane Elizabeth Margaret. b 56. St Hugh's Coll Ox BA78 MA80 Nottm Univ BA82. St Jo Coll Nottm 81. **dss** 83 **d** 87. Herne Hill St Paul *S'wark* 83-86; Chapl and Lect St Jo Coll Nottm from 86. *St John's College, Bramcote, Nottingham NG9 3DS* Nottingham (0602) 251114

✠**SINCLAIR, Rt Rev Maurice Walter.** b 37. Nottm Univ BSc59 Leics Univ PGCE60. Tyndale Hall Bris 62. **d** 64 **p** 65 **c** 90. C Boscombe St Jo *Win* 64-67; SAMS 67-84; Prin Crowther Hall CMS Tr Coll Selly Oak 84-90; Perm to Offic *Birm* 84-90; Bp N Argentina from 90. *Iglesia Anglicana, Casilla 187, CP 4400, Salta, Argentina* Salta (87) 310167

˙**SINCLAIR, Peter.** b 44. Oak Hill Th Coll 86. **d** 88 **p** 89. C Darlington H Trin *Dur* 88-91; C-in-c Bishop Auckland Woodhouse Close CD from 91. *18 Watling Road, Bishop Auckland, Co Durham DL14 6RP* Bishop Auckland (0388) 604086

SINCLAIR, Robert Charles. b 28. Liv Univ LLB49 QUB LLM69 PhD82. Ely Th Coll 58. **d** 60 **p** 61. C Glenavy *Conn* 60-63; Chapl RN 63-67; C Cregagh *D & D* 67-68; Perm to Offic *Conn* from 69. *Juniper Cottage, 11A Glen Road, Glenavy, Crumlin, Co Antrim BT29 4LT* Crumlin (08494) 53126

SINCLAIR, Robert Michael. b 41. Edin Th Coll 63. **d** 66 **p** 67. C Dunfermline *St And* 66-68; C Edin Old St Paul *Edin* 68-72; P-in-c Edin St Dav 72-77; Hon Dioc Supernumerary from 77. *143 Greenbank Road, Edinburgh EH10 5RN* 031-447 5068

SINCLAIR, Thomas. b 04. Edin Th Coll 32. **d** 35 **p** 36. V Mayfair Ch *Lon* 61-69; rtd 69. *Flat 1, 182 Warwick Road, Carlisle*

SINDALL, Mrs Christine Ann. b 42. ALA69. E Anglian Minl Tr Course 84. **d** 87. NSM Sutton *Ely* 87-89; C Cam Ascension from 89. *8 St Catherines, Ely, Cambs CB6 1AP* Ely (0353) 662148

SINFIELD, George Edward. b 16. E Midl Min Tr Course 73. **d** 76 **p** 77. NSM Radcliffe-on-Trent *S'well* 76-79; NSM St Oswald in Lee w Bingfield *Newc* 79-86; rtd 86; Perm to Offic *S'well* from 86; Linc from 89. *62 Station Road, Collingham, Newark, Notts NG23 7RA* Newark (0636) 892766

SINGH, Balwant. b 32. BA60. Saharanpur Th Coll 50. **d** 53 **p** 58. India 53-67 and 71-73; Hon C Handsworth St Jas *Birm* 67-71; Hon C N Hinksey *Ox* 73-80; Lic to Offic 80-81; Hon C S Hinksey from 82. *9 Jersey Road, Rose Hill, Oxford OX4 4RT* Oxford (0865) 717277

SINGH, Vivian Soorat. b 30. Trin Coll Cam MA. Westcott Ho Cam 54. **d** 55 **p** 56. Chapl Framlingham Coll Suffolk 60-72; Chapl Wymondham Coll 72-75; Dep Hd Litcham High Sch 75-88; rtd 88. *Manor Cottage, Wendling Road, Longham, Dereham NR12 2RD* Wendling (036287) 382

SINGLETON, Mrs Editha Mary. b 27. W Midl Minl Tr Course 85. **dss** 84 **d** 87. Lich St Chad *Lich* 84-87; Hon Par Dn 87-90; Hon Par Dn Beaulieu and Exbury and E Boldre *Win* from 90. *The Peregrine, The Lane, Fawley, Southampton SO4 1EY* Southampton (0703) 894364

SINGLETON, Ernest George (Brother Paul). b 15. St Aug Coll Cant 38. **d** 41 **p** 42. Prior St Teilo's Priory Cardiff 61-68; rtd 80. *4 Eyot Lodge, Cross Deep, Twickenham TW1 4QH* 081-892 5496

SINGLETON, Kenneth Miller. b 58. Oak Hill Th Coll DipHE91. **d** 91. C Grove *Ox* from 91. *21 Albermarle Drive, Grove, Wantage, Oxon OX12 0NB*

SINKER, Canon Michael Roy. b 08. Clare Coll Cam BA30 MA34. Cuddesdon Coll 31. **d** 32 **p** 33. R Ipswich St Matt *St E* 67-77; rtd 77. *8 White Horse Way, Westbury, Wilts BA13 3AH* Westbury (0373) 864883

SINNAMON, Canon William Desmond. b 43. TCD BA65. CITC 66. **d** 66 **p** 67. C Seapatrick *D & D* 66-70; C Arm St Mark *Arm* 70-74; VC Arm Cathl 73-74; I Ballinderry 75-80; I Dub St Patr Cathl Gp *D & G* 80-83; Preb Tipperkevin St Patr Cathl Dub 80-83; I Taney w St Nahi *D & G* from 83; RD Taney from 91; Can Ch Ch Cathl Dub from 91. *Taney Rectory, Stoney Road, Dundrum, Dublin 14, Irish Republic* Dublin (1) 984497

SINNICKSON, Charles. b 21. Princeton Univ BA44. Cuddesdon Coll 60. **d** 63 **p** 64. C Staveley St Luke *Lon* 67-72; Hon C S Kensington St Jude 72-81; NSM Upper Chelsea St Simon 81-86; NSM S Kensington St Aug 86-90; rtd 90; Perm to Offic *Lon* from 90. *4 Cranley Mansion, 160 Gloucester Road, London SW7 4QF* 071-373 2767

SINTON, Bernard. b 43. Leic Univ BSc66. Sarum & Wells Th Coll 87. **d** 90 **p** 91. NSM Horsham *Chich* from 90. *Kinsale, 28 Kennedy Road, Horsham, W Sussex RH13 5DA* Horsham (0403) 62991

SINTON, Vera May. b 43. Somerville Coll Ox BA65 MA Bris Univ CertEd66. Trin Coll Bris DipHE81. **dss** 81 **d** 87. Broxbourne w Wormley *St Alb* 81-87; Hon Par Dn 87; Tutor All Nations Chr Coll 81-87; Chapl St Hilda's Coll Ox 87-90; Tutor Wycliffe Hall Ox from 87. *3A Norham Gardens, Oxford OX2 6PS* Oxford (0865) 52397

SIRMAN, Allan George. b 34. Lon Univ BA58. Oak Hill Th Coll 55. **d** 59 **p** 60. C Uphill *B & W* 59-61; C Morden S'wark 61-65; R Chadwell *Chelmsf* 65-75; V Wandsworth All SS *S'wark* from 75. *Wandsworth Vicarage, 11 Rusholme Road, London SW15 3JX* 081-788 7400

SIRR, Very Rev John Maurice Glover. b 42. TCD BA63. CITC 65. **d** 65 **p** 66. C Belf St Mary *Conn* 65-68; C Finaghy 68-69; I Drumcliffe w Lissadell and Munninane K, E & A 69-87; RD S Elphin 75-87; Preb Elphin Cathl 81-87; Dean Limerick and Ardfert *L & K* from 87; I Limerick City from 87. *The Deanery, 7 Kilbane, Castletroy, Co Limerick, Irish Republic* Limerick (61) 338697

SISSON, Trevor. b 54. St Jo Coll Dur 76. **d** 79 **p** 80. C Rainworth *S'well* 79-83; C Worksop Priory 83-85; R Bilborough w Strelley from 85. *St Martin's Rectory, 11 St Agnes Close, Nottingham NG8 4BJ* Nottingham (0602) 291874

SITCH, Keith Frank. b 40. Ex Univ BA63. S'wark Ord Course 72. **d** 75 **p** 76. NSM Romford St Edw *Chelmsf* 75-78; NSM Kidbrooke St Jas *S'wark* from 78.

92 Kidbrooke Park Road, London SE3 0DX 081-856 3843

SIVITER, Cecil Isaac Hill. b 11. Tyndale Hall Bris 36. **d** 41 **p** 42. V Pott Shrigley *Ches* 60-74; V Alsager Ch Ch 74-79; rtd 79; Perm to Offic *Ches* from 79. *193 South Parade, West Kirby, Wirral, Merseyside L48 3HX* 051-625 6676

SIVITER, Hugh Basil. b 21. St Pet Hall Ox MA47. Wycliffe Hall Ox 46. **d** 48 **p** 49. V Knotty Ash St Jo *Liv* 66-84; rtd 85. *2 Heol Bodran, Abergele, Clwyd LL22 7UW* Abergele (0745) 824860

SIZER, Stephen Robert. b 53. Sussex Univ BA DipHE. Trin Coll Bris 80. **d** 83 **p** 84. C St Leonards St Leon *Chich* 83-86; C Guildf St Sav w Stoke-next-Guildf 86-89; R Stoke-next-Guildford from 89. *Stoke Rectory, 2 Joseph's Road, Guildford, Surrey GU1 1DW* Guildford (0483) 32397

SKEET, Edward Kenneth Walter. b 27. Southn Univ BEd70. Chich Th Coll 79. **d** 81 **p** 82. Hon C Denmead *Portsm* 81-85. *76 Whichers Gate Road, Rowland's Castle, Hants PO9 6BB* Rowlands Castle (0705) 412084

SKEET, Hedley Ernest Burt. b 24. Lon Univ DipRE. Sarum & Wells Th Coll. **d** 84 **p** 85. Hon C Frimley *Guildf* from 84. *42 Denton Way, Frimley, Camberley, Surrey GU1 5UQ* Camberley (0276) 27742

SKELDING, Donald Brian. b 23. Trin Coll Cam BA47 MA52. Cuddesdon Coll. **d** 50 **p** 51. V Southport St Paul *Liv* 65-72; R Norton Canes *Lich* 72-81; rtd 84; P-in-c Whiteparish *Sarum* 91; C Alderbury Team from 91. *The Vicarage, Common Road, Whiteparish, Salisbury SP5 5SU* Whiteparish (0794) 884315

SKELDING, Mrs Hazel Betty. b 25. LGSM66 CertEd45. Gilmore Course 80. **dss** 83 **d** 87. Hinstock and Sambrook *Lich* 83-84; Asst Children's Adv RE 86-91; Hon Par Dn Whiteparish *Sarum* 91; Hon Par Dn Alderbury Team from 91. *c/o The Vicarage, Whiteparish, Salisbury, Wilts SP5 2SU* Whiteparish (0794) 884248

SKELTON, Beresford. b 52. St Chad's Coll Dur BA74. Chich Th Coll 74. **d** 76 **p** 77. C Byker St Ant *Newc* 76-80; Chapl Asst Newc Gen Hosp 80-81; C Newc St Jo *Newc* 80-82; Chapl Asst Freeman Hosp Newc 81-82; V Cresswell and Lynemouth *Newc* 82-88; P-in-c Millfield St Mary *Dur* from 88. *St Mary Magdalene's Vicarage, Millfield, Sunderland SR4 6HJ* 091-565 6318

SKELTON, Dennis Michael. b 33. K Coll Lon BSc55. NE Ord Course 76. **d** 79 **p** 80. NSM Pennywell St Thos and Grindon St Oswald CD *Dur* 79-84; V Heatherycleugh from 84; V St John in Weardale from 84; V Westgate from 84. *Heatherycleugh Vicarage, Cowshill, Bishop Auckland, Co Durham DL13 1DA* Bishop Auckland (0388) 537260

SKELTON, Frank Seymour. b 20. DFC and Bar 44 DSO and Bar 45. Trin Hall Cam BA48 MA52. Ridley Hall Cam 48. **d** 50 **p** 51. Dir Lambeth Endowed Charities 69-85; Lic to Offic *S'wark* 69-85; rtd 85. *Flat B, 36 Champion Hill, London SE5 8AP* 071-737 2187

SKELTON, Canon Henry John Nugent. b 13. Linc Th Coll 37. **d** 40 **p** 41. V Holbeach *Linc* 56-73; rtd 78. *Upton Castle, Cosheston, Pembroke Dock, Dyfed SA72 4SE* Pembroke (0646) 682435

✠SKELTON, Rt Rev Kenneth John Fraser. b 18. CBE72. CCC Cam BA40 MA44. Wells Th Coll 40. **d** 41 **p** 42 **c** 62. C Normanton *Derby* 41-43; C Bakewell 43-45; C Bolsover 45-46; PV Wells Cathl *B & W* 46-50; Lect Wells Th Coll 46-50; V Howe Bridge *Man* 50-55; R Walton St Mary *Liv* 55-62; Bp Matabeleland 62-70; Asst Bp Dur 70-75; R Bishopwearmouth St Mich w St Hilda 70-75; RD Wearmouth 70-75; Bp Lich 75-84; rtd 84; Asst Bp Derby from 84; Asst Bp Sheff from 84. *65 Crescent Road, Sheffield S7 1HN* Sheffield (0742) 551260

SKELTON, Melvyn Nicholas. b 38. St Pet Coll Ox BA61 MA65 Selw Coll Cam BA63 MA68. Ridley Hall Cam 62. **d** 64 **p** 65. C St Marychurch *Ex* 64-66; C Bury St Edmunds St Mary *St E* 66-69; Hon C 69-78; Lic to Offic from 78. *22 The Street, Moulton, Newmarket, Suffolk* Newmarket (0638) 750563

SKELTON, Pamela Dora. b 38. Hull Coll of Educn DipEd. Edin Th Coll 80. **dss** 78 **d** 86. Edin St Barn *Edin* 78-86; Dn-in-c 86-90; Dioc Youth Chapl from 82. *112 St Alban's Road, Edinburgh EH9 2PG* 031-667 1280

SKEMP, Canon Stephen Rowland. b 12. Wadh Coll Ox BA34 MA62. Cuddesdon Coll 34. **d** 35 **p** 36. Adn Aegean *Eur* 71-77; Chapl Athens St Paul 74-77; rtd 77; Perm to Offic *Ox* from 83. *Caldicote, Clifton, Deddington, Oxford* Deddington (0869) 38487

SKEOCH, David Windsor. b 37. Ch Ch Ox BA58 MA62. Westcott Ho Cam 73. **d** 74 **p** 75. NSM Pimlico St Mary Graham Terrace *Lon* 74-79; Bp's Dom Chapl *Truro* 79-81; Bp's Dom Chapl *Lon* 81-83; V Pimlico St Gabr

from 83. *St Gabriel's Vicarage, 30 Warwick Square, London SW1V 2AD* 071-834 7520 or 834 2136

SKEPPER, Robert. b 25. **d** 67 **p** 68. C Loughb All SS *Leic* 67-71; R Shelthorpe Gd Shep 71-80; V Loughb Gd Shep 80-82; rtd 90. *c/o 20 The Rise, Thornton Dale, Pickering, N Yorkshire YO18 7TG*

SKETCHLEY, Edward Sydney. b 20. Qu Coll Birm. **d** 49 **p** 50. V Walsgrave on Sowe *Cov* 65-73; V Hound *Win* 73-90; rtd 90. *55 Terminus Terrace, Southampton S01 1FE* Southampton (0703) 233249

SKIDMORE, Mrs Sheila Ivy. b 36. **d** 87. Hon Par Dn Leic Resurr *Leic* 87-91; Par Dn Clarendon Park St Jo w Knighton St Mich from 91. *St Michael and All Angels Vicarage, Scott Street, Leicester* Leicester (0533) 700964

SKILLEN, John Clifford Tainish. b 50. NUU BA72 MA82 QUB DipEd73 TCD BTh89. CITC 86. **d** 89 **p** 90. C Ban Abbey *D & D* from 89. *72 Abbey Park, Bangor, Co Down BT20 4DL* Bangor (0247) 454401

SKILLINGS, Martyn Paul. b 46. St Chad's Coll Dur BA68. Linc Th Coll 68. **d** 70 **p** 71. C Stanley *Liv* 70-72; C Warrington St Elphin 72-75; Ind Chapl 75-76; V Surfleet *Linc* from 88. *The Vicarage, 13 Station Road, Surfleet, Spalding, Lincs PE11 4DA* Surfleet (077585) 230

SKILTON, Christopher John. b 55. Magd Coll Cam BA76 MA80. Wycliffe Hall Ox 77. **d** 80 **p** 81. C Ealing St Mary *Lon* 80-84; C New Boro and Leigh *Sarum* 84-88; TV Gt Baddow *Chelmsf* from 88. *124 Beehive Lane, Great Baddow, Chelmsford CM2 9SH* Chelmsford (0245) 269026

SKILTON, Joseph Laurence. b 41. Univ of Wales (Cardiff) DipTh70 Murdoch Univ Aus BA90. St Mich Coll Llan. **d** 70 **p** 71. C Bicester *Ox* 71-73; C Shrewsbury St Chad *Lich* 73-76; V W Bromwich St Phil 76-80; Australia from 80. *52 Pangbourne Street, Wembley, W Australia 6014* Perth (9) 387-2287 or 387-2487

SKINNER, Basil Garnet. b 23. Ex Univ BSc42 Lon Univ MSc45 BD60 Ball Coll Ox DPhil51 Ex Univ MA73. Chich Th Coll 54. **d** 54 **p** 55. V Brixham *Ex* 69-75; Perm to Offic from 75; rtd 88. *Dell House, 23 Vicarage Hill, Cockington, Torquay TQ2 6HZ* Torquay (0803) 607021

✠SKINNER, Rt Rev Brian Antony. b 39. Reading Univ BSc60. Tyndale Hall Bris 66. **d** 67 **p** 68 **c** 77. C Woking St Pet *Guildf* 67-70; Chile 70-86; Adn Valparaiso 76-77; Suff Bp Valparaiso 77-86; C Chorleywood St Andr *St Alb* from 87. *Dell View, Quickley Lane, Chorleywood, Rickmansworth, Herts WD3 5AF* Chorleywood (0923) 282238

SKINNER, Canon Frederick Arthur. b 08. **d** 35 **p** 36. R Bidborough *Roch* 51-81; Hon Can Roch Cathl 70-81; rtd 81; Perm to Offic *Roch* from 82. *Cornford House, Cornford Lane, Pembury, Kent TN2 4QS* Pembury (089282) 4654

SKINNER, Graeme John. b 57. Southn Univ BSc79. Trin Coll Bris BA. **d** 86 **p** 87. C Bebington *Ches* 86-90; V Ashton on Mersey St Mary from 90. *St Mary's Vicarage, 20 Beeston Road, Sale, Cheshire M33 5AG* 061-973 5118

SKINNER, Mrs Jane Mary. b 59. Leeds Univ BA81. Cranmer Hall Dur 82. **dss** 84 **d** 87. Chatham St Phil and St Jas *Roch* 84-87; Hon Par Dn 87; Hon Par Dn Torver *Carl* from 87; Hon Par Dn Church Coniston from 87. *The Vicarage, Coniston, Cumbria LA21 8DB* Coniston (05394) 41262

SKINNER, John Cedric. b 30. Bris Univ BA55 Lon Univ DipTh57. Tyndale Hall Bris 55. **d** 57 **p** 58. C St Leonard *Ex* 57-62; Sec IVF 62-68; V Guildf St Sav *Guildf* 68-76; R Stoke next Guildf St Jo 74-76; R Guildf St Sav w Stoke-next-Guildf 76-84; R Ex St Leon w H Trin *Ex* from 84. *St Leonard's Rectory, 27 St Leonard's Road, Exeter EX2 4LA* Exeter (0392) 55681

SKINNER, John Richard. b 45. N Ord Course 84. **d** 87 **p** 88. C Allerton *Liv* 87-90; AV Huyton St Mich from 90. *1 The Cross, Stanley Road, Liverpool L36 9XL* 051-449 3800

SKINNER, Leonard Harold. b 36. K Coll Lon BD62 AKC62. **d** 63 **p** 64. C Hackney Wick St Mary of Eton w St Aug *Lon* 63-66; C Palmers Green St Jo 66-70; V Grange Park St Pet 70-80; TV Hanley H Ev *Lich* 80-86; Chapl Sunderland Poly *Dur* from 86. *4 Ashbrooke Mount, Tunstall Road, Sunderland SR2 7SD* 091-522 6872

SKINNER, Maurice Wainwright. b 30. FRSC70 St Jo Coll Ox BA53 MA59. Ox NSM Course. **d** 86 **p** 87. NSM Furze Platt *Ox* from 86. *5 Clarefield Close, Maidenhead, Berks SL6 5DR* Maidenhead (0628) 24875

SKINNER, Michael Thomas. b 39. Open Univ BA88. S'wark Ord Course 73. **d** 78 **p** 79. NSM Orpington St Andr *Roch* 78-82; NSM Orpington All SS from 82.

80 Spur Road, Orpington, Kent BR6 0QN Orpington (0689) 825322

SKINNER, Peter William. b 47. Sarum & Wells Th Coll 85. **d** 87 **p** 88. C Latchford St Jas *Ches* 87-89; C Weymouth St Paul *Sarum* 89. *49E Abbotsbury Road, Weymouth, Dorset* Weymouth (0305) 71000

SKINNER, Raymond Frederick. b 45. St Jo Coll Dur BA67. Cranmer Hall Dur. **d** 70 **p** 71. C High Elswick St Paul *Newc* 70-76; V Newbottle *Dur* 76-87; Ind Chapl 81-87; RD Houghton 84-87; Chapl Oman 87-89; TR Morden *S'wark* from 90; Asst RD Merton from 91. *The Rectory, London Road, Morden, Surrey SM4 5QT* 081-648 3920

SKINNER, Stephen John. b 52. AIA Bris Univ BSc St Jo Coll Dur BA Dur Univ MLitt. Cranmer Hall Dur. **d** 83 **p** 84. C Chatham St Phil and St Jas *Roch* 83-87; P-in-c Torver *Carl* 87-90; P-in-c Church Coniston 87-90; V from 90; R Torver from 90. *The Vicarage, Coniston, Cumbria LA21 8DB* Coniston (05394) 41262

SKIPPER, Joseph Allen. b 17. Selly Oak Coll 45 Lich Th Coll 58. **d** 59 **p** 60. R Bishopstrow and Boreham *Sarum* 64-72; R Fleet *Linc* 72-74; V Sutterton 74-78; P-in-c Wigtoft 77-78; V Sutterton and Wigtoft 78-83; rtd 83; P-in-c Tidworth *Sarum* 83-86; C Tidworth, Ludgershall and Faberstown 86-88. *68 Wellington Court, Weymouth, Dorset DT4 8UE* Weymouth (0305) 777449

SKIPPER, Mrs Joyce Evelyn. b 27. Cam Univ CertEd71. Gilmore Ho 73. **dss** 75 **d** 87. Cranham *Chelmsf* 75-87; Hon Par Dn 87-90; Hon Par Dn Upminster from 90. *53 Tawny Avenue, Upminster, Essex RM14 2EP* Upminster (04022) 25703

SKIPPER, Kenneth Graham. b 34. St Aid Birkenhead 65. **d** 68 **p** 69. C Newland St Aug *York* 68-71; C Newby 71-74; V Dormanstown 74-78; C-in-c Mappleton w Goxhill 78; C-in-c Withernwick 78; V Aldbrough w Cowden Parva 78; V Aldbrough, Mappleton w Goxhill and Withernwick 79-89; R Londesborough from 89; R Burnby from 90; R Nunburnholme and Warter from 90; V Shiptonthorpe w Hayton from 90. *The Rectory, 3 Fairview, Town Street, Shiptonthorpe, York YO4 3PE* Market Weighton (0430) 872513

SKIPPER, Canon Lawrence Rainald. b 17. St Pet Hall Ox BA39 MA43. Wycliffe Hall Ox 39. **d** 41 **p** 41. RD Ches 69-78; R Eccleston and Pulford 72-82; Hon Can Ches Cathl 74-82; rtd 82; Perm to Offic *Ches* from 82. *Stud Farmhouse, Churton, Chester CH3 6LL* Farndon (0829) 270296

SKIPPON, Kevin John. b 54. St Steph Ho Ox 78. **d** 81 **p** 82. C Gt Yarmouth *Nor* 81-84; C Kingstanding St Luke *Birm* 84-86; V Smethwick SS Steph and Mich from 86. *The Vicarage, 94 Regent Street, Smethwick, Warley, W Midlands B66 3BH* 021-558 3583

SKIPWITH, Osmund Humberston. b 06. New Coll Ox BA28 MA33. Cuddesdon Coll 29. **d** 30 **p** 31. C Worle *B & W* 71-74; rtd 74. *16 Kingswood Court, Southcote Road, Reading RG3 2AU* Reading (0734) 571246

SKLIROS, Michael Peter. b 33. Clare Coll Cam BA57 MA62. Ridley Hall Cam 57. **d** 59 **p** 60. C Hornchurch St Andr *Chelmsf* 59-61; Asst Chapl Denstone Coll Uttoxeter 61-65; Chapl RAF 65-77; P-in-c Stowmarket *St E* 77-78; Lic to Offic 78-85; C Gt Finborough w Onehouse and Harleston 85-91; P-in-c from 91. *19 Childer Road, Stowmarket, Suffolk IP14 1PP* Stowmarket (0449) 672844

SKUCE, David. b 56. NUU BSc79 QUB PGCE80 TCD BTh89. CITC 87. **d** 89 **p** 90. C Templemore *D & R* from 89. *4 St Columb's Court, Londonderry BT48 6PT* Londonderry (0504) 267539

SKUSE, Canon Frank Richard. b 18. TCD BA42. Div Test42. **d** 42 **p** 43. I Kilgariffe Union *C, C & R* 68-85; Can Cloyne Cathl 78-85; Preb Cork Cathl 78-85; rtd 85. *Woodbrooke, Gaggin, Bandon, Co Cork, Irish Republic* Bandon (23) 44709

SLACK, Canon Ellis Edward. b 23. Birm Univ BA51 MA53. Qu Coll Birm 51. **d** 53 **p** 53. V N Dulwich St Faith *S'wark* 64-72; V Bethnal Green St Jo w St Simon *Lon* 72-78; V Bethnal Green St Jo w St Bart 78-79; Can Res Portsm Cathl *Portsm* 79-83; V Woodplumpton *Blackb* 83-88; Dir of Post-Ord Tr 83-88; rtd 88. *6 Parkfield, Stillington, York YO6 1JW* Easingwold (0347) 810104

SLACK, Michael. b 53. St Jo Coll Dur BA74. St Steph Ho Ox 74. **d** 76 **p** 77. C Wolv St Steph *Lich* 76-77; NSM Bywell St Pet *Newc* from 89. *1 Croft Cottages, New Ridley Road, Stocksfield, Northd NE43 7LF* Stocksfield (0661) 843027

SLADDEN, Duncan Julius Edward. b 25. K Coll Cam BA50 MA51. Cuddesdon Coll 51. **d** 53 **p** 54. P-in-c Stevenage *St Alb* 65-70; R Johnstone *Glas* 70-76; Prayer

Gp Adv Scottish Chs Renewal 76-81; Sec Scottish Episc Renewal Fellowship 81-84; R E Kilbride 85-90; rtd 90. *17 Bruce Avenue, Dunblane, Perthshire FK15 9JB* Dunblane (0786) 825520

SLADDEN, Canon John Cyril. b 20. Mert Coll Ox BA42 MA46 BD66. Wycliffe Hall Ox 46. **d** 48 **p** 49. V Nether Peover *Ches* 59-86; RD Knutsford 80-85; Hon Can Ches Cathl 80-86; rtd 86. *Rossa, Penmon, Beaumaris, Gwynedd LL58 8SN* Llangoed (024878) 207

SLADDEN, John David. b 49. RN Eng Coll Plymouth BSc74 St Edm Coll Cam MA86. Ridley Hall Cam. **d** 83 **p** 84. C St Bees *Carl* 83-85; Perm to Offic *Lich* 85-87; Miss Co-ord Down to Earth Evangelistic Trust *Lich* 85-87; V Doncaster St Jas *Sheff* from 87. *The Vicarage, 54 Littlemoor Lane, Doncaster, S Yorkshire DN4 0LB* Doncaster (0302) 365544

SLADE, Canon Adrian Barrie. b 47. K Alfred's Coll Win DipEd68. St Jo Coll Nottm BTh73 ALCD72. **d** 73 **p** 74. C Streatham Immanuel w St Anselm *S'wark* 73-76; C Chipping Barnet *St Alb* 76-78; C Chipping Barnet w Arkley 78-80; V Sundon 80-85; Soc Resp Officer *Glouc* from 86; Hon Can Glouc Cathl from 91. *38 Sydenham Villas Road, Cheltenham, Glos GL52 6DZ* Cheltenham (0242) 242672

SLADE, Alfred Laurence. b 12. ACII. Roch Th Coll 67. **d** 69 **p** 70. Hon C Cliftonville *Cant* 69-71; Hon C Westgate St Jas 71-75; Perm to Offic *Sarum* 75-81; *Cant* from 81. *21 McKinlay Court, The Parade, Minnis Bay, Birchington, Kent CT7 9QG* Thanet (0843) 46882

SLADE, Harold Godfrey Rex. **d** 87 **p** 88. NSM Patrick *S & M* from 87; NSM German St Jo from 87; NSM Foxdale from 87. *2 Hamilton Close, Lower Foxdale, Douglas, Isle of Man* St Johns (062471) 431

SLADE, Herbert Edwin William. b 12. Lon Univ BA33. Dorchester Miss Coll 34. **d** 35 **p** 36. C Tuffley *Glouc* 35-39; SSJE from 39; Lic to Offic *Chich* 71-82; rtd 82. *The Anchorhold, Paddockhall Road, Haywards Heath, W Sussex RH16 1HN* Haywards Heath (0444) 52468

SLADE, Canon William Clifford. b 24. St Jo Coll Dur BA47 DipTh49 MA53. **d** 49 **p** 50. R Stokesley *York* 67-71; V Felixkirk w Boltby 71-82; V Kirby Knowle 71-82; Can and Preb York Minster 79-86; C Topcliffe w Dalton and Dishforth 82-86; Abp's Adv for Spiritual Direction 82-86; rtd 86. *Bede House, Beck Lane, South Kilvington, Thirsk, N Yorkshire YO7 3RU* Thirsk (0845) 522915

SLADEN, Philip. b 50. Fitzw Coll Cam BA71 MA75 DipTh. Ripon Hall Ox 72. **d** 75 **p** 76. C Bushey Heath *St Alb* 75-78; Chapl RAF from 78. *c/o MOD, Adastral House, Theobald's Road, London WC1X 8RU* 071-430 7268

SLADER, William Basil. b 16. Sarum Th Coll 55. **d** 57 **p** 58. R Copythorne and Minstead *Win* 60-70; V St Mary Bourne and Woodcott 70-81; rtd 81; Perm to Offic *Win* and *Ely* from 81. *23 Hawthorn Close, Littleport, Ely, Cambs CB6 1NY* Ely (0353) 862366

SLATER, Edward Ian. b 31. E Midl Min Tr Course 81. **d** 84 **p** 85. NSM Cherry Willingham w Greetwell *Linc* 84-86; C Cleethorpes 86-88; TV from 88. *St Francis House, Sandringham Road, Cleethorpes DN35 9HA* Cleethorpes (0472) 691215

SLATER, Gilbert Leonard. b 09. Selw Coll Cam BA31 MA35. Wells Th Coll 31. **d** 32 **p** 34. V Gt and Lt Dalby *Leic* 60-87; rtd 88. *99 Main Street, Asfordby, Melton Mowbray, Leics* Melton Mowbray (0664) 813456

SLATER, James Richard David. b 61. BA83 TCD BTh89. CITC 86. **d** 89 **p** 90. C Clooney w Strathfoyle *D & R* from 89. *102 Knockwellan Park, Londonderry BT47 2JE* Londonderry (0504) 46286

SLATER, John. b 45. K Coll Lon BA67 AKC67 Fitzw Coll Cam BA69 MA73. Westcott Ho Cam 67 Union Th Sem (NY) STM70. **d** 70 **p** 71. C St Marylebone All SS *Lon* 70-77; V Paddington St Sav 77-83; Dir Post-Ord Tr from 82; V St Jo Wood from 83. *St John's House, St John's Wood, London NW8 7NE* 071-722 4378

SLATER, John Albert. b 25. Lon Univ BA52. Oak Hill Th Coll 47. **d** 52 **p** 53. V Bacup St Sav *Man* 61-70; V Blackpool St Thos *Blackb* 70-84; rtd 84; Lic to Offic *Blackb* from 84. *18 Church Road, Thornton Cleveleys, Blackpool FY5 2TZ* Cleveleys (0253) 853330

SLATER, John Allen. b 20. St Aid Birkenhead 60. **d** 62 **p** 63. V Welton w Melton *York* 65-82; P-in-c Burstwick w Thorngumbald 82-84; rtd 85. *103 Burden Road, Beverley, N Humberside HU17 9LN* Hull (0482) 867825

SLATER, John Ralph. b 38. Kent Univ BA90. Linc Th Coll 71. **d** 73 **p** 74. C S Hackney St Mich w Haggerston St Paul *Lon* 73-74; C Leytonstone St Marg w St Columba

Chelmsf 74-77; C Whitstable All SS w St Pet *Cant* 77-80; V Gt Ilford St Alb *Chelmsf* 80-83; V Clipstone *S'well* 83-87; rtd 87. *8 Edgar Close, Whitstable, Kent CT5 2SA* Whitstable (0227) 792154

SLATER, Mark Andrew. b 56. ARCS79 Imp Coll Lon BSc79. Ridley Hall Cam 87. **d** 89 **p** 90. C Northn St Giles *Pet* from 89. *18 The Avenue, Cliftonville, Northampton NN1 5BT* Northampton (0604) 24797

SLATER, Paul John. b 58. CCC Ox MA83 Dur Univ BA83. Cranmer Hall Dur 81. **d** 84 **p** 85. C Keighley St Andr *Bradf* 84-88; Dir Dioc Foundn Course from 88; P-in-c Cullingworth from 88. *The Vicarage, Halifax Road, Cullingworth, Bradford, W Yorkshire BD13 5DE* Cullingworth (0535) 272434

SLATER, Philip David. b 27. K Coll Lon 58. **d** 60 **p** 61. C Havant *Portsm* 60-67; C Leigh Park 68-69; Hants Co RE Adv 69-74; Gosport and Fareham RE Adv 74-82; Hon C Bishops Waltham 76-82; V Bulford, Figheldean and Milston *Sarum* from 82; RD Avon from 85. *The Vicarage, Figheldean, Salisbury SP4 8JL* Stonehenge (0980) 70326

SLATER, Robert Adrian. b 48. St Jo Coll Nottm 76. **d** 79 **p** 80. C Bedworth *Cov* 79-82; TV Billericay and Lt Burstead *Chelmsf* 82-88; V Rounds Green *Birm* from 88. *The Vicarage, Shelsley Avenue, Oldbury, Warley, W Midlands B69 1BG* 021-552 2822

SLATER, Ronald Spencer. b 13. Man Univ BA36. Lich Th Coll 36. **d** 38 **p** 39. V Mabe *Truro* 71-76; rtd 76. *1 Col-Moor Close, Hayle, Cornwall TR27 4PT* Hayle (0736) 754057

SLATER, Thomas Ernest. b 37. Lon Univ BD71. **d** 67 **p** 68. C Bootle Ch Ch *Liv* 67-72; C Stapleford *S'well* 72-75; Supt Tower Hamlets Miss 75-77; Hon C Stepney St Pet w St Benet *Lon* 78-79; Asst Chapl The Lon Hosp (Whitechapel) 79-83; Chapl 83-90; Chapl R Lon Hosp (Whitechapel) from 90. *22 Cephas Street, London E1 4AX* 071-247 5454 or 790 0578

SLATER, Victoria Ruth. b 59. Hertf Coll Ox BA82 MA87 Selw Coll Cam BA89. Westcott Ho Cam 86. **d** 89. Chapl Asst Man R Infirmary from 89. *350 Church Road, Flixton, Manchester M31 3HR* 061-748 3568

SLATER, William Edward. b 51. Bolton Inst of Tech HNC77. Aston Tr Scheme 85 Oak Hill Th Coll 87. **d** 89 **p** 90. C Balderstone *Man* from 89. *2 Buersil Avenue, Balderstone, Rochdale OL16 4TP* Rochdale (0706) 357633

SLATOR, Edward Douglas Humphreys. b 18. TCD BA41 MA47 Hull Univ BPhil75. **d** 43 **p** 44. I Killea *C & O* 60-73; C Taney w St Nahi *D & G* 74-80; P-in-c Rathmolyon w Castlerickard, Rathcore and Agher *M & K* 80-87; rtd 87. *31 St John's, Park Avenue, Dublin 4, Irish Republic*

SLATOR, Canon William Thompson Howard. b 09. TCD BA31 MA34. **d** 33 **p** 34. Preb Elphin Cathl *K, E & A* 66-81; I Kiltoghart 66-81; RD Fenagh 67-81; rtd 81. *Bayside, Haddington Terrace, Dunlaoghaire, Dublin, Irish Republic*

SLAUGHTER, Clive Patrick. b 36. St Paul's Grahamstown DipTh78. **d** 77 **p** 78. S Africa 77-87; R Thorley w Bishop's Stortford H Trin *St Alb* 87-90; R Thorley from 90. *The Rectory, Viceron's Place, Thorley, Bishop's Stortford, Herts CM23 4EL* Bishop's Stortford (0279) 54955

SLAUGHTER, Canon Maurice Basil. b 20. Leeds Univ BA42. Coll of Resurr Mirfield 42. **d** 44 **p** 45. V Skipton Ch Ch *Bradf* 63-78; Hon Can *Bradf* Cathl 67-85; RD Skipton 73-82; P-in-c Bolton Abbey 78-85; P-in-c Rylstone 78-85; P-in-c Arncliffe w Halton Gill 79-82; rtd 85; Perm to Offic *Bradf* and *Wakef* from 85. *Hewitt Gate, Threshfield, Skipton, N Yorkshire BD23 5HB* Grassington (0756) 752158

SLEDGE, Ven Richard Kitson. b 30. Peterho Cam BA52 MA57. Ridley Hall Cam 52. **d** 54 **p** 55. C Compton Gifford *Ex* 54-57; C Ex St Martin, St Steph, St Laur etc 57-63; V Dronfield *Derby* 63-76; TR 76-78; RD Chesterfield 72-78; Adn Huntingdon *Ely* from 78; R Hemingford Abbots 78-89; Hon Can Ely Cathl from 78. *The Rectory, Hemingford Abbots, Huntingdon, Cambs PE18 9AN* St Ives (0480) 69856

SLEE, Canon Colin Bruce. b 45. K Coll Lon BD69 AKC69. St Aug Coll Cant 69. **d** 70 **p** 71. C Nor Heartsease St Fran *Nor* 70-73; C Cam St St Mary w St Mich *Ely* 73-76; Chapl Girton Coll Cam 73-76; Tutor and Chapl K Coll Lon 76-82; Sub-Dean from 82; Can Res St Alb from 82. *The Old Rectory, Sumpter Yard, St Albans, Herts AL1 1BY* St Albans (0727) 54827

SLEE, John Graham. b 51. Brunel Univ BTech73. Oak Hill Th Coll 85. **d** 87 **p** 88. C St Columb Minor and St Colan *Truro* 87-91; R St Mawgan w St Ervan and St

Eval from 91. *The Rectory, St Mawgan, Newquay, Cornwall TR8 4EZ* St Mawgan (0637) 860358

SLEGG, John Edward. b 36. St Pet Coll Ox BA62 MA66. Ridley Hall Cam 62. **d** 64 **p** 65. C Perranzabuloe *Truro* 64-66; CF 66-86; P-in-c Poling *Chich* 86-89; V from 89; P-in-c Lyminster 86-89; V from 89. *The Vicarage, Lyminster, Littlehampton, W Sussex BN17 7QE* Arundel (0903) 882152

SLEIGHT, Gordon Frederick. b 47. AKC69. St Aug Coll Cant 69. **d** 70 **p** 71. C Boston *Linc* 70-74; P-in-c Louth St Mich 74-75; P-in-c Stewton 75; TV Louth 75-81; V Crosby from 81. *St George's Vicarage, 87 Ferry Road, Scunthorpe, S Humberside DN15 8LY* Scunthorpe (0724) 843328

SLIM, David Albert. b 49. CertEd72. Linc Th Coll 88. **d** 90 **p** 91. C Walmley *Birm* from 90. *90 Walmley Ash Road, Sutton Coldfield, W Midlands B76 8JB* 021-351 1245

SLOANE, Isaac Reuben. b 16. TCD BA41 MA60. **d** 42 **p** 43. I Ardstraw w Baronscourt, Badoney Lower etc *D & R* 54-76; I Drumclamph w Lower and Upper Langfield 76-78; rtd 78. *40 Rawdon Place, Moira, Craigavon, Co Armagh* Moira (0846) 611547

SLOGGETT, Donald George. b 49. Trin Coll Bris 81. **d** 83 **p** 84. C Horfield H Trin *Bris* 83-86; C Highworth w Sevenhampton and Inglesham etc 86-88; P-in-c Upavon w Rushall *Sarum* 88-90; R Uphavon w Rushall and Charlton from 90. *The Vicarage, Upavon, Pewsey, Wilts SN9 6AA* Stonehenge (0980) 630248

SLOUGH, Colin Richard. b 40. AKC66. Ripon Hall Ox. **d** 68 **p** 69. Hon C Birm St Luke *Birm* 68-69; Hd of RE Lea-Mason Sch 68-69; P-in-c Portsea St Geo *Portsm* 70-72; Hon Chapl Portsm Cathl 70-72; RE Adv *Ox* 72-75; Lect Cudham Coll 72-75; Dep Hd Master St Luke's Sch Southsea 75-80; P-in-c Sandown Ch Ch *Portsm* 80; V 80-87; P-in-c Lower Sandown St Jo 80; V 80-87; Chapl Birm Poly *Birm* from 87. *156 Skipper Way, Lee-on-the-Solent, Hants PO18 3HS* Lee-on-the-Solent (0705) 551339

SLOW, Leslie John. b 47. Liv Univ BSc68 MSc69. N Ord Course 77. **d** 80 **p** 81. NSM Gt Horton *Bradf* from 80. *25 Grasleigh Way, Bradford, W Yorkshire BD15 9BE* Bradford (0274) 491808

SLUMAN, Richard Geoffrey Davies. b 34. St Jo Coll Ox BA68 MA68. Sarum Th Coll 68. **d** 70 **p** 71. C Gt Yarmouth *Nor* 70-73; V Churchdown *Glouc* 73-82; P-in-c Blockley w Aston Magna 82-83; V Blockley w Aston Magna and Bourton on the Hill from 83. *The Vicarage, Blockley, Moreton-in-Marsh, Glos GL56 9ES* Blockley (0386) 700283

SLY, Christopher John. b 34. Selw Coll Cam BA58 MA62. Wycliffe Hall Ox. **d** 60 **p** 61. C Buckhurst Hill *Chelmsf* 60-64; V Berechurch 64-75; V Southend St Sav Westcliff 75-87; P-in-c Wickham Bishops 87; R 87; RD Witham from 87; R Wickham Bishops w Lt Braxted from 87. *The Rectory, 1 Church Road, Wickham Bishops, Witham, Essex CM8 3LA* Maldon (0621) 891360

SLY, Canon Harold Kenneth. b 15. Kelham Th Coll 34. **d** 38 **p** 39. V Hampton in Arden *Birm* 57-83; rtd 83; Perm to Offic *Worc* from 83; Chapl Convent of the H Name Malvern 83-90. *28 Walstead Road, Fulbrook, Walsall, W Midlands WS5 4LX* Walsall (0922) 21673

SLYFIELD, John David. b 32. Roch Th Coll 66. **d** 68 **p** 69. C St Mary in the Marsh *Cant* 68-71; P-in-c Steeple Claydon *Ox* 71-76; P-in-c Middle w E Claydon 71-76; RD Claydon 73-78; R The Claydons 76-78; V S Westoe *Dur* 78-82; V Tideswell *Derby* from 82; RD Buxton 84-91. *The Vicarage, Tideswell, Buxton, Derbyshire SK17 8LD* Tideswell (0298) 871317

SMAIL, Canon Thomas Allan. b 28. Glas Univ MA49 Edin Univ BD52. **d** 79 **p** 79. Hon C E Twickenham St Steph *Lon* 79; Vice-Prin St Jo Coll Nottm 80-85; TR Sanderstead All SS *S'wark* from 85; Hon Can S'wark Cathl from 91. *The Rectory, 1 Addington Road, South Croydon, Surrey CR2 8RE* 081-657 1366 or 657 0665

SMAILES, Robert Anthony. b 44. Linc Th Coll 79 DipMin88. **d** 81 **p** 82. C Stokesley *York* 81-83; V Lythe 83-85; P-in-c Ugthorpe 83-85; V Lythe w Ugthorpe 85-88; V Saltburn-by-the-Sea from 88. *The Vicarage, Greta Street, Saltburn-by-the-Sea, Cleveland TS12 1LS* Guisborough (0287) 622007

SMALE, Frederick Ronald. b 37. K Coll Lon BD60 AKC60. **d** 61 **p** 62. C Bearsted *Cant* 61-64; C Fishponds St Mary *Bris* 64-69; V Hartlip *Cant* 69-71; P-in-c Stockbury w Bicknor and Huckinge 69-71; V Hartlip w Stockbury 71-75; R River 75-85; V Birchington w Acol and Minnis Bay from 85. *All Saints' Vicarage, 15 Minnis Road, Birchington, Kent CT7 9SE* Thanet (0843) 41117

SMALL, David Binney. b 39. Westcott Ho Cam 63. **d** 65 **p** 66. C Milton *Portsm* 65-69; CF from 69. *c/o MOD (Army), Bagshot Park, Bagshot, Surrey GU19 5PL* Bagshot (0276) 71717

SMALL, Gordon Frederick. b 41. **d** 79 **p** 80. C Belper *Derby* 79-84; NSM Matlock Bath 90-91; C Ripley from 91. *15 Lime Avenue, Ripley, Derbyshire DE5 3HD* Belper (0773) 743799

SMALL, Leonard Norman. b 09. AKC32. **d** 32 **p** 33. V St Ethelburga Bishopgate *Lon* 54-76; rtd 77. *13 Kingston Avenue, Leatherhead, Surrey KT22 7HY* Leatherhead (0372) 372040

SMALLDON, Keith. b 48. Open Univ BA76. Llan St Mich DipTh71. **d** 71 **p** 72. C Cwmbran *Mon* 71-73; C Chepstow 73-75; Dioc Youth Adv *Bradf* 75-79; P-in-c Woolfold *Man* 82-85; Dioc Youth and Community Officer 82-90; P-in-c Thursby *Carl* from 90; Dir of Clergy Tr from 90. *The Vicarage, Church Lane, Thursby, Carlisle CA5 6PF* Dalston (0228) 710303

SMALLEY, Mrs Kathleen. b 23. Linc Th Coll 81. **dss** 84 **d** 87. Leominster *Heref* 84-85; Bridgnorth, Tasley, Astley Abbotts, Oldbury etc 85-87; Hon C from 87. *3 Elizabeth Avenue, Sidney Cottage Drive, Bridgnorth, Shropshire WV16 4PX* Bridgnorth (0746) 766202

SMALLEY, Very Rev Stephen Stewart. b 31. Jes Coll Cam BA55 MA58 PhD79. Eden Th Sem (USA) BD57 Ridley Hall Cam. **d** 58 **p** 59. C Portman Square St Paul *Lon* 58-60; Chapl Peterho Cam 60-63; Dean 62-63; Nigeria 63-69; Lect Th Man Univ 70-77; Prec Cov Cathl *Cov* 77-87; Can Res Cov Cathl 77-87; Vice-Provost Cov Cathl 86-87; Dean Ches from 87. *The Deanery, 7 Abbey Street, Chester CH1 2JF* Chester (0244) 351380

SMALLMAN, Miss Margaret Anne. b 43. Hull Univ BSc64 Bris Univ CertEd65. St Jo Coll Nottm DipTh82. **dss** 83 **d** 87. Bromsgrove St Jo *Worc* 83-87; Par Dn 87-88; Par Dn Stoke Prior, Wychbold and Upton Warren 88-90; TM Tettenhall Wood *Lich* from 91. *21 Tintagel Close, Perton, Wolverhampton WV6 7RG* Wolverhampton (0902) 750232

SMALLWOOD, Canon Graham Marten. b 19. St Pet Hall Ox BA48 MA52. Cuddesdon Coll 48. **d** 50 **p** 51. R Cannock *Lich* 69-76; TR 76-78; RD Rugeley 72-78; P-in-c Hatherton 76-78; Can Res Lich Cathl 78-88; rtd 88. *Brook House, The Cross, Childswickham, Broadway, Worcester WR12 7HJ* Broadway (0386) 853173

SMART, Alfred Ernest. b 14. Leeds Univ BA35 MA42. Coll of Resurr Mirfield 35. **d** 37 **p** 38. V Talbot Village *Sarum* 55-80; rtd 80. *13 Jarman's Field, Orchard Drive, Wye, Ashford, Kent TN25 5AQ* Wye (0233) 812954

SMART, Barry. b 57. Lanc Univ BEd79. St Steph Ho Ox 85. **d** 88 **p** 89. C Wantage *Ox* 88-91; C Abingdon from 91. *The Vicarage, Faringdon Road, Abingdon, Oxon OX14 1BG* Wantage (0235) 520297

SMART, Clifford Edward James. b 28. Kelham Th Coll 48. **d** 53 **p** 54. C Blackb St Pet *Blackb* 53-56; Korea 56-65 and from 66; C Birm St Aid Small Heath *Birm* 65-66. *Anglican Church, 3 Chong-dong, Chung-ku, Seoul 100-120, Republic of Korea* Seoul (2) 794-1846

SMART, Haydn Christopher. b 38. Wells Th Coll 66. **d** 69 **p** 70. C Hillmorton *Cov* 69-72; C Duston *Pet* 72-75; V Woodford Halse 75-79; V Woodford Halse w Eydon 79-82; V Wellingborough All SS from 82; RD Wellingborough from 87. *The Vicarage, 154 Midland Road, Wellingborough, Northants NN8 1NG* Wellingborough (0933) 227101

SMART, Hilary Jean. b 42. SOAS Lon BA63 CSocSc64 DASS67. E Midl Min Tr Course 85. **d** 88. Par Dn Walsall Pleck and Bescot *Lich* from 88. *16 Bescot Drive, Walsall WS2 9DF* Walsall (0922) 613927

SMART, John Francis. b 36. Keble Coll Ox BA59 MA69. Cuddesdon Coll 59. **d** 61 **p** 66. C Cannock *Lich* 61-63; Hon C Gt Wyrley 63-66; C Wednesfield St Thos 66-70; V Brereton 70-85; R E Clevedon and Walton w Weston w Clapton *B & W* from 85. *The Rectory, All Saints' Lane, Clevedon, Avon BS21 6AU* Clevedon (0272) 873257

SMART, Richard Henry. b 22. St Jo Coll Dur 46 Clifton Th Coll 48. **d** 52 **p** 53. C Leeds St Geo *Ripon* 52-54; Kenya 54-56; C New Addington *Cant* 56-59; V Awsworth w Cossall *S'well* 59-63; BFBS Distr Sec E Anglia 63-70; Bp's Ecum Adv *Ely* 70-81; Dioc Missr 70-74; P-in-c Dry Drayton 74-81; Min Bar Hill LEP 74-81; P-in-c Madingley 80-81; V Sandylands *Blackb* from 81. *St John's Vicarage, 2 St John's Avenue, Morecambe, Lancs LA3 1EU* Morecambe (0524) 411299

SMART, Richard Henry. b 23. Lon Univ BA51. Oak Hill Th Coll. **d** 53 **p** 54. V Hanley Road St Sav w St Paul *Lon* 59-71; V Plumstead All SS *S'wark* 71-84; rtd 88.

2 Annington Road, Eastbourne, E Sussex BN22 8NG Eastbourne (0323) 26850

SMART, Canon Sydney. b 15. TCD BA37 MA43. **d** 39 **p** 40. I Belf All SS *Conn* 60-83; Can Belf Cathl 76-83; rtd 83. *43 Norwood Avenue, Belfast BT4 2EF* Belfast (0232) 653932

SMEATON, Archibald John. b 99. Coll of Resurr Mirfield 51. **d** 51 **p** 52. V Barkingside St Laur *Chelmsf* 60-66; rtd 66. *Ramsay Hall, Byron Road, Worthing, W Sussex BN11 3HN* Worthing (0903) 201025

SMEATON, Malcolm John. b 56. BSc(Econ). Coll of Resurr Mirfield 79. **d** 83 **p** 84. C Tynemouth Ch Ch w H Trin *Newc* 83-84; C Long Benton 85-90; V Byker St Martin from 90. *St Martin's Vicarage, 152 Roman Avenue, Newcastle upon Tyne NE6 2RJ* 091-265 5931

SMEATON, Canon William Brian Alexander. b 37. CITC 69. **d** 71 **p** 72. C Belf St Luke *Conn* 71-81; I Tullyaughnish w Kilmacrennan and Killygarvan *D & R* from 81; Dom Chapl to Bp from 87; Can Raphoe Cathl from 88; RD Kilmacrenan E and W from 90; Dioc Radio Officer from 90. *The Rectory, Ramelton, Letterkenny, Co Donegal, Irish Republic* Ramelton (74) 51013

SMEDLEY, Canon Frank. b 17. Kelham Th Coll 35. **d** 40 **p** 41. V Wool, E Burton and Coombe Keynes *Sarum* 71-76; R Wool and E Stoke 76-82; RD Purbeck 76-82; rtd 82. *4 Meadows Drive, Upton, Poole, Dorset BH16 5JG* Lytchett Minster (0202) 622496

SMERDON, Stanley William. b 19. Oak Hill Th Coll 72. **d** 74 **p** 75. C Bournemouth St Paul *Win* 74-81; P-in-c Luccombe *B & W* 81; Perm to Offic from 85; Chapl Sandhill Park Hosp Taunton from 87; rtd 89. *Heather Cottage, The Ball, Minehead, Somerset TA24 5JJ* Minehead (0643) 702933

SMETHURST, David Alan. b 36. Lon Univ BD60 Man Univ MPhil84. Tyndale Hall Bris 57. **d** 61 **p** 62. C Burnage St Marg *Man* 61-64; P-in-c Whalley Range St Marg 64-65; R Haughton St Mary 65-74; R Ulverston St Mary w H Trin *Carl* 74-87; Dean Hong Kong 87; Dir Acorn Chr Healing Trust from 88. *Whitehill Chase, High Street, Bordon, Hants GU35 0AP* Bordon (0420) 472779

SMETHURST, Gordon James. b 33. CEng FIStructE. N Ord Course 79. **d** 82 **p** 83. NSM Halliwell St Marg *Man* 82-87; NSM Bradshaw 87-88; Asst Chapl Bolton R Infirmary from 88; Asst Chapl Bolton Gen Hosp from 88. *91 Albert Road, Bolton BL1 5ED* Bolton (0204) 42561

SMETHURST, Gordon McIntyre. b 40. Man Univ BA62 BD69. **d** 70 **p** 71. C Sandal St Helen *Wakef* 70-72; P-in-c Smawthorpe St Mich 72-75; P-in-c Whitwood 74-75; Asst Master Goole Gr Sch 75-84; Hon C Howden *York* 77-79; Hon C Howden Team 80-84. *35 Beck Road, Everthorpe, Brough, N Humberside HU15 2JH* Howden (0430) 423849

SMETHURST, John Michael Benedict. b 44. St Pet Coll Ox BA66 MA70. St Steph Ho Ox 66. **d** 68 **p** 69. C Gladstone Park St Fran *Lon* 68-71; C St Pancras H Cross w St Jude and St Pet 71-73; C Hendon St Mary 73-76; Chapl S Devon Tech Coll Torbay 76-79; P-in-c N Keyham *Ex* 80; V from 80; RD Plymouth Devonport 83-86. *St Thomas's Presbytery, 90 Royal Navy Avenue, Plymouth PL2 2AJ* Plymouth (0752) 561102

SMETHURST, Leslie Beckett. b 22. CEng. NW Ord Course 72. **d** 75 **p** 76. C Baguley *Man* 75-78; TV Droylsden St Mary 78-81; V Droylsden St Martin 81-86; rtd 87; Perm to Offic *Blackb* from 87. *27 Calf Croft Place, Lytham St Annes, Lancs FY8 4PU* Lytham (0253) 733159

SMILLIE, Linda Barbara. b 46. Oak Hill Th Coll DipHE87. **d** 87. Par Dn Holloway St Mary w St Jas *Lon* 87-88; Par Dn Holloway St Mary Magd 88-90; Ind Chapl from 90. *5 Arvon Road, London N5 1PS* 071-704 7804

SMITH, Alan. b 38. Tyndale Hall Bris 63. **d** 65 **p** 66. C New Milverton *Cov* 65-68; C Cheadle *Ches* 68-71; V Handforth 71-78; Asst Chapl HM Pris Styal 75-78; Chapl HM Pris Wormwood Scrubs 78-79; Chapl HM Borstal Wellingborough 79-83; R Rushden w Newton Bromswold *Pet* from 83. *The Rectory, Rushden, Northants NN10 0HA* Rushden (0933) 312554

SMITH, Alan Gregory Clayton. b 57. Birm Univ BA78 MA79. Wycliffe Hall Ox 79. **d** 81 **p** 82. C Pudsey St Lawr *Bradf* 81-82; C Pudsey St Lawr and St Paul 82-84; Chapl Lee Abbey 84-90; TV Walsall *Lich* from 90; Dioc Missr from 90. *14 Gorway Gardens, Walsall, W Midlands WS1 3BJ* Walsall (0922) 26010

SMITH, Alan Pearce Carlton. b 20. Trin Hall Cam BA40 MA45 LLB46. Westcott Ho Cam 76. **d** 78 **p** 79. Hon C Cherry Hinton St Jo *Ely* 78-82; P-in-c Madingley 82-83; P-in-c Dry Drayton 82-83; P-in-c Swaffham

Bulbeck 84-88; Perm to Offic from 88. *38 Alpha Road, Cambridge CB4 3DG* Cambridge (0223) 358124

SMITH, Alan Thomas. b 35. BA DipEd. Ridley Hall Cam 82. **d** 84 **p** 85. C Bedworth *Cov* 84-89; R Carlton Colville w Mutford and Rushmere *Nor* from 89. *The Rectory, Carlton Colville, Lowestoft, Suffolk NR33 8BB* Lowestoft (0502) 565217

SMITH, Alec John. b 29. AKC53. **d** 54 **p** 55. C Charlton Kings St Mary *Glouc* 54-56; C-in-c Findon Valley CD *Chich* 56-57; V Viney Hill *Glouc* 57-65; V Churchdown St Jo 65-66; V Bishop's Cannings *Sarum* 66-69; CF 69-88; V Douglas St Thos *S & M* from 88. *Church Barn, Church Road, Lonan, Isle of Man* Laxey (0624) 861325

SMITH, Alexander Montgomery. b 36. TCD BA59 MA64 BD65. TCD Div Sch Div Test60. **d** 61 **p** 62. C Knock *D & D* 61-64; C Belf St Thos *Conn* 64-66; Lect St Kath Coll Liv from 66; Sen Lect from 68; Asst Chapl St Kath Coll *Liv* 66-69; Chapl 69-80; Hon C Allerton from 80. *15 Glenathol Road, Liverpool L18 3JS* 051-724 3965

SMITH, Alfred Lawrence. b 23. FCP84 Open Univ BA72 Birm Univ DipEd73. E Midl Min Tr Course 82. **d** 85 **p** 86. NSM Ashover *Derby* 85-86; NSM Ashover and Brackenfield from 86. *Cotton House Farm, Ashover, Chesterfield, Derbyshire S45 0DZ* Chesterfield (0246) 590265

SMITH, Andrew John. b 37. Leeds Univ BA61. Coll of Resurr Mirfield 61. **d** 63 **p** 64. C W Hackney St Barn *Lon* 63-65; Dir and Chapl Northorpe Hall Trust Yorkshire 65-72; Warden Ox Ho Bethnal Green 72-78; Dir and Chapl The Target Trust 78-86; P-in-c Gt Staughton *Ely* 86-88; Norfolk DTI Educn Adv 88-91. *63 Chudleigh Road, Kingsteignton, Newton Abbot, Devon TQ12 3JF* Newton Abbot (0626) 69970

SMITH, Andrew John. b 46. ACGI Lon Univ BScEng67 DIC PhD71 Trin Coll Ox DipTh74 Bath Univ MEd88. Coll of Resurr Mirfield 74. **d** 76 **p** 77. C Swindon New Town *Bris* 76-78; C Southmead 78-79; Perm to Offic from 79. *15 Dyrham Close, Bristol BS9 4TF* Bristol (0272) 428594

SMITH, Andrew John. b 59. Birm Univ BSc80 PhD81. W Midl Minl Tr Course 89. **d** 91. C Lower Mitton *Worc* from 91. *16 Grosvenor Gardens, Church Drive, Stourport-on-Severn, Worcs DY13 9DD* Stourport (0299) 827567

SMITH, Andrew Perry Langton. b 56. Sheff City Poly BSc79 Imp Coll Lon MSc80. Trin Coll Bris 89. **d** 91. C Littleover *Derby* from 91. *4 Merridale Road, Littleover, Derby DE3 7DJ* Derby (0332) 766060

SMITH, Mrs Anita Elisabeth. b 57. Westhill Coll Birm BEd79. Trin Coll Bris DipHE88 ADPS88. **d** 88. Par Dn Bermondsey St Anne *S'wark* from 88. *107 Grange Road, London SE1 3BW* 071-237 5750

SMITH, Anthony Adam Dalziel. b 42. Qu Coll Birm 65. **d** 68 **p** 69. C Peterlee *Dur* 68-71; C Tilehurst St Mich *Ox* 71-76; V Wootton (Boars Hill) 76-88; R Brightwalton w Catmore, Leckhampstead etc from 88. *The Rectory, Chaddleworth, Newbury, Berks RG16 0EW* Chaddleworth (04882) 566

SMITH, Anthony Cyril. b 40. K Coll Lon 65. **d** 69 **p** 70. C Crewkerne *B & W* 69-74; TV Hemel Hempstead *St Alb* 74-76; Asst Chapl K Coll Taunton 76-80; Chapl from 80. *40 South Road, Taunton, Somerset TA1 3DY* Taunton (0823) 275137

SMITH, Anthony Grahame. b 29. ALCD54. **d** 54 **p** 55. C Stratford New Town St Paul *Chelmsf* 54-56; C Woodford Wells 56-58; Canada 58-60; Hon C Gt Ilford St Andr *Chelmsf* 60-62; V Chelmsf St Andr 62-69; R Mistley w Manningtree 69-81; RD Harwich 75-81; R Fordham from 81. *The Rectory, Wood Lane, Fordham Heath, Colchester CO3 5TR* Colchester (0206) 240221

SMITH, Anthony James. b 57. ACA Sheff Univ BA. Ridley Hall Cam 83. **d** 86 **p** 87. C Woking St Pet *Guildf* 86-90; C Reigate St Mary *S'wark* from 90. *63 Chart Lane, Reigate, Surrey RH2 7EA* Reigate (0737) 243085

SMITH, Ven Anthony Michael Percival. b 24. G&C Coll Cam BA48 MA53. Westcott Ho Cam 48. **d** 50 **p** 51. V Yeovil St Jo w Preston Plucknett *B & W* 66-72; RD Merston 68-72; Preb Wells Cathl 70-72; V Addiscombe St Mildred *Cant* 72-79; Adn Maidstone 79-89; Dir of Ords 80-89; Hon Can Cant Cathl 80-89; rtd 89; Perm to Offic *Cant* from 89; Perm to Offic *Chich* 89-91; RD Rye from 91. *The Garden House, Horseshoe Lane, Beckley, E Sussex TN31 6RZ* Beckley (079726) 514

SMITH, Ven Arthur Cyril. b 09. VRD55. Sheff Univ BA34 MA50. St Jo Coll Manitoba 29 Westcott Ho Cam 33. **d** 34 **p** 35. Adn Linc 60-76; Can and Preb Linc Cathl 60-77; R Algarkirk 60-76; rtd 77. *2 Cavendish Court, 14 Blackwater Road, Eastbourne, E Sussex BN21 4JD* Eastbourne (0323) 36204

SMITH, Canon Arthur Eric. b 08. St Edm Hall Ox BA29 MA33. Wycliffe Hall Ox 29. **d** 31 **p** 32. Hon Can Roch Cathl *Roch* 59-74; R Knockholt 65-74; rtd 74; Perm to Offic *Chich* 74-84; from 84. *32 Highfield Road, Chislehurst, Kent BR7 6QZ* Orpington (0689) 26985

SMITH, Austin John Denyer. b 40. Worc Coll Ox BA62. Cuddesdon Coll 64. **d** 66 **p** 67. C Shepherd's Bush St Steph w St Thos *Lon* 66-69; C W Drayton 69-72; Chapl Sussex Univ *Chich* 72-79; V Caddington St Alb from 79. *The Vicarage, Collings Wells Close, Caddington, Luton LU1 4BG* Luton (0582) 31692

SMITH, Mrs Barbara Jean. b 39. Bris Univ BA62. S'wark Ord Course 83. **dss** 86 **d** 87. Chislehurst St Nic *Roch* 86-87; Hon Par Dn 87-90; Hon C Wrecclesham *Guildf* from 90. *Cedar Lodge, 53A Sandrock Hill Road, Wrecclesham, Farnham, Surrey GU10 4RJ* Frensham (025125) 3041

SMITH, Barbara Mary. b 47. Doncaster Coll of Educn TCert68. Cranmer Hall Dur 82. **dss** 85 **d** 87. Beverley St Nic *York* 85-87; Par Dn 87; NSM S'wark H Trin w St Matt *S'wark* 89-90; Ind Chapl Teesside *York* from 91. *12 Fox Howe, Middlesbrough, Cleveland TS8 0RU* Middlesbrough (0642) 597745

SMITH, Canon Barry. b 41. Univ of Wales (Lamp) BA62 Fitzw Ho Cam BA64 MA68. Ridley Hall Cam. **d** 65 **p** 66. C Rhyl w Rhyl St Ann *St As* 65-70; Chapl Scargill Ho N Yorkshire 70-72; C Flint *St As* 72-74; V Broughton 74-86; Dioc Ecum Officer from 82; RD Wrexham 82-86; Cursal Can from 86; R Wrexham from 86. *The Rectory, 7 Westminster Drive, Wrexham, Clwyd LL12 7AT* Wrexham (0978) 263905 or 355808

SMITH, Brian. b 44. Sarum & Wells Th Coll 71. **d** 74 **p** 75. C Pennywell St Thos and Grindon St Oswald CD *Dur* 74-77; Chapl RAF from 77. *c/o MOD, Adastral House, Theobald's Road, London WC1X 8RU* 071-430 7268

SMITH, Ven Brian Arthur. b 43. Edin Univ MA66 Fitzw Coll Cam BA68 MA72 Jes Coll Cam MLitt73. Westcott Ho Cam 66. **d** 72 **p** 73. Tutor and Lib Cuddesdon Coll 72-75; Dir of Studies 75-78; C Cuddesdon *Ox* 76-79; Sen Tutor Ripon Coll Cuddesdon 78-79; P-in-c Halifax St Jo Cragg Vale *Wakef* 79-85; Dir Tr 79-87; Hon Can Wakef Cathl 81-87; Adn Craven *Bradf* from 87. *Brooklands, Bridge End, Long Preston, Skipton, N Yorkshire BD23 4RA* Long Preston (07294) 334

SMITH, Brian Godfrey. b 24. Chich Th Coll 63. **d** 65 **p** 66. C Redcar *York* 68-72; C Kirkleatham 68-72; V Wortley de Leeds *Ripon* 72-76; Chapl Costa del Sol E *Eur* 76-82; Chapl Estoril 82-84; V Worfield *Heref* 84-89; rtd 89. *2 Pineway, Lodge Farm, Bridgnorth, Shropshire* Bridgnorth (0746) 764088

SMITH, Ven Brian John. b 33. Sarum Th Coll 62. **d** 65 **p** 66. C Whitstable All SS *Cant* 65-69; V Woodford w Wilsford *Sarum* 69-74; P-in-c Durnford 74; V Woodford Valley 74-76; V Mere w W Knoyle and Maiden Bradley 76-80; RD Heytesbury 78-80; Can and Preb Sarum Cathl from 80; Adn Wilts from 80; V Bishop's Cannings, All Cannings etc 80-83; Adv Chr Giving 83-90; TV Redhorn from 90. *The Vicarage, 57 The Street, Chirton, Devizes, Wilts SN10 3QS* Devizes (0380) 84271

SMITH, Brian Michael. b 42. Kelham Th Coll 69. **d** 69 **p** 70. C Somers Town St Mary *Lon* 70-74; C Stamford Hill St Jo 74-75; C Stamford Hill St Bart 75-84; P-in-c Edmonton St Pet w St Martin from 84. *The Vicarage, St Peter's Road, London N9 8JP* 081-807 2974

SMITH, Mrs Bridget Mary. b 46. Bp Otter Coll CertEd67 S Dios Minl Tr Scheme 88. **d** 91. C Pet H Spirit Bretton Pet from 91. *98 Benland, Bretton, Peterborough, Cambs PE3 8ED* Peterborough (0733) 269196

SMITH, Canon Charles. b 11. St Jo Coll Dur BA39 MA42. **d** 39 **p** 40. V Heatherycleugh *Dur* 48-83; V St John in Weardale 57-83; V Westgate 57-83; Hon Can Dur Cathl 79-83; rtd 83. *Rutson House, Nunnington, York* Nunnington (04395) 204

SMITH, Charles Frederick. b 18. St Aid Birkenhead 54. **d** 56 **p** 58. R Everleigh *Sarum* 60-74; V Burneside *Carl* 74-79; Perm to Offic *Chich* from 80; rtd 83. *7 Manor Road, Seaford, E Sussex BN25 4NL* Seaford (0323) 890433

SMITH, Charles Henry Neville. b 31. Nottm Univ BA52 MA65. Sarum Th Coll 55. **d** 57 **p** 58. C Thirsk w S Kilvington *York* 57-60; C Linthorpe 60-61; V Danby 61-66; Chapl United Camb Hosps 66-76; Lanc Moor Hosp 76-84; Hon Can Blackb Cathl *Blackb* 81-84; Asst Sec Gen Syn Hosp Chapl Coun 84-88; Hon C Lee St Marg *S'wark* 84-88; Chapl Guy's Hosp Lon from 88. *Guy's Hospital, St Thomas Street, London SE1 9RT* 071-955 4591

SMITH, Charles Rycroft. b 46. Sarum & Wells Th Coll 76. **d** 78 **p** 79. C Heref St Martin *Heref* 78-81; C Southn Maybush St Pet *Win* 81-83; R The Candover Valley from 83; RD Alresford from 90. *The Rectory, Preston Candover, Basingstoke, Hants RG25 2EE*   Preston Candover (025687) 245

SMITH, Charles Septimus. b 23. Bris & Glouc Tr Course. **d** 79 **p** 80. NSM Bris St Agnes and St Simon w St Werburgh *Bris* 79-86; C 86-87; C Bris St Paul's 87-89; rtd 89. *287 Paisley Boulevard West, Mississauga, Ontario, Canada, L5B 2S7*

SMITH, Christine Lydia. See CARTER, Mrs Christine Lydia

SMITH, Christopher Blake Walters. b 63. Univ of Wales (Cardiff) BMus84 BD88. St Mich Coll Llan 85. **d** 88 **p** 89. C Aberdare *Llan* from 88. *9 College Street, Abernant, Aberdare, M Glam CF44 0RN*   Aberdare (0685) 882641

SMITH, Christopher Francis. b 46. K Coll Lon BD68 AKC68. St Aug Coll Cant 69. **d** 70 **p** 71. C Norwood All SS *Cant* 70-72; Asst Chapl Marlborough Coll Wilts 72-76; C Deal St Leon w Sholden *Cant* 77-81; P-in-c Benenden 81-83; V from 83. *The Vicarage, Benenden, Cranbrook, Kent TN17 4DL*   Cranbrook (0580) 240658

SMITH, Christopher John. b 55. Bris Univ BSc76. St Steph Ho Ox 78. **d** 81 **p** 82. C Shirley *Birm* 81-84; C Curdworth w Castle Vale 84-87; V Pet Ch Carpenter *Pet* from 87. *The Vicarage, Chestnut Avenue, Peterborough PE1 4PE*   Peterborough (0733) 67140

SMITH, Canon Christopher Milne. b 44. Selw Coll Cam BA66. Cuddesdon Coll 67. **d** 69 **p** 70. C Liv Our Lady and St Nic *Liv* 69-74; TV Kirkby 74-81; R Walton St Mary 81-91; Can Res Sheff Cathl *Sheff* from 91. *9 Stumperlowe Hall Road, Fulwood, Sheffield S10 3QR*   Sheffield (0742) 304181

SMITH, Clarice Mary. b 25. St Mich Coll Llan 76. dss 77 **d** 80. Llanguicke *S & B* 77-80; C Llwynderw 80-84; C Newton St Pet 84-88; rtd 88. *33 Sherringham Drive, Newton, Swansea SA3 4UG*   Swansea (0792) 367613

SMITH, Clifford. b 31. Lon Univ DipTh60. St Aid Birkenhead 59. **d** 61 **p** 62. C Limehouse St Anne *Lon* 61-63; C Ashtead *Guildf* 63-66; R Bromley All Hallows *Lon* 66-76; V Hillsborough and Wadsley Bridge *Sheff* 76-89; V Stainforth from 89. *The Vicarage, Field Road, Stainforth, Doncaster, S Yorkshire DN7 5AQ*   Doncaster (0302) 841295

SMITH, Clive Leslie. b 50. Leeds Univ BA72 Ch Coll Liv PGCE. Coll of Resurr Mirfield 75. **d** 77 **p** 78. C Goldington *St Alb* 77-81; C Cheshunt 81-84; V Watford St Pet 84-89; Chapl Leavesden Hosp Abbots Langley from 89. *34 Tanner's Hill, Abbots Langley, Watford WD5 0LT*   Watford (0923) 677977

SMITH, Colin Graham. b 59. Hatf Poly BA82 CQSW82. Trin Coll Bris BA88. **d** 88 **p** 89. C Bermondsey St Jas w Ch Ch *S'wark* from 88. *107 Grange Road, London SE1 3BW*   071-237 5750

SMITH, Colin Ian McNaughton. b 28. St Jo Coll Dur BA53. **d** 55 **p** 56. V Weaverthorpe w Helperthorpe and Luttons *York* 57-76; P-in-c Kirby Grindalythe 74-76; RD Buckrose 75-76; V Weaverthorpe w Helperthorpe, Luttons Ambo etc 76-91; rtd 91. *Aynsley House, East Lutton, Malton, N Yorkshire*   West Lutton (09443) 539

SMITH, Colin Richard. b 53. Liv Poly BA80 Liv Univ MTD83. Oak Hill Th Coll 84. **d** 86 **p** 87. C Ormskirk *Liv* 86-89; V Wigan St Cath from 89. *St Catharine's Vicarage, St Catherine Terrace, Wigan, Lancs WN1 3JW*   Wigan (0942) 820668

SMITH, Darren John Anthony. b 62. Nottm Univ BCombStuds84. Linc Th Coll 84. **d** 86 **p** 87. C Leic Ascension *Leic* 86-90; C Curdworth w Castle Vale *Birm* 90; C St Cuth of Lindisfarne, Castle Vale 90-91; C Kingstanding St Luke from 91. *St Luke's House, 49 Caversham Road, Birmingham B44 0LW*   021-324 3281

SMITH, David Earling. b 35. AKC60. **d** 61 **p** 62. R Claxby w Normanby-le-Wold *Linc* 69-74; R Nettleton 69-74; R S Kelsey 69-74; R N Owersby w Thornton le Moor 69-74; R Stainton-le-Vale w Kirmond le Mire 69-74; V Ancaster 74-79; Warden and Chapl St Anne Bedehouses Linc 79-89; C Linc Minster Gp 79-89; rtd 89; Perm to Offic *Linc* from 90. *17 Egerton Road, Lincoln LN2 4PJ*   Lincoln (0522) 510336

SMITH, David Graham. b 08. MBE46. Wadh Coll Ox BA31 MA33. Cuddesdon Coll 31. **d** 32 **p** 33. V Woldingham *S'wark* 59-76; rtd 76; Perm to Offic *B & W* from 86. *St Mary's, Whitegate Road, Minehead, Somerset TA24 5SP*   Minehead (0643) 702036

✠**SMITH, Rt Rev David James.** b 35. AKC58. **d** 59 **p** 60

c 87. C Gosforth All SS *Newc* 59-62; C Newc St Fran 62-64; C Longbenton St Bart 64-68; V Longhirst 68-75; V Monkseaton St Mary 75-82; RD Tynemouth 80-82; Hon Can Newc Cathl 81-87; Adn Lindisfarne 81-87; V Felton 82-83; Suff Bp Maidstone *Cant* from 87; Bp HM Forces from 90. *Bishop's House, Pett Lane, Charing, Ashford, Kent TN27 0DL*   Charing (023371) 2950

SMITH, David John. b 32. Lon Univ BA76 MSc79. Lon Coll of Div 68. **d** 70 **p** 71. C Clerkenwell St Jas and St Jo w St Pet *Lon* 70-73; P-in-c Penge St Paul *Roch* 74-78; V 78-89; RD Beckenham 86-89; Chapl Bromley and Sheppard's Colls from 90; Dioc Clergy Widows and Retirement Officer from 90. *Bromley College, London Road, Bromley, Kent BR1 1PE*   081-460 4712

SMITH, David John. b 42. Oak Hill Th Coll 75. **d** 77 **p** 78. C New Milverton *Cov* 77-81; V Hartshill 81-86; V Attleborough from 86. *Attleborough Vicarage, 5 Fifield Close, Nuneaton, Warks CV11 4TS*   Nuneaton (0203) 382926

SMITH, David John Parker (Brother Victor). b 47. S'wark Ord Course 83. **d** 86. SSF from 71; Hon C Stepney St Dunstan and All SS *Lon* 86-89; Educn Development Officer 86-89; Guardian Hilfield Friary Dorchester from 89; Lic to Offic *Sarum* from 89. *The Friary, Hilfield, Dorchester, Dorset DT2 7BE*   Cerne Abbas (0300) 341345

SMITH, David Leonard. b 37. St Alb Minl Tr Scheme 84. **d** 91. NSM Potton w Sutton and Cockayne Hatley *St Alb* from 91. *11 Judith Gardens, Potton, Beds SG19 2RJ*   Potton (0767) 260583

SMITH, Preb David Lloyd. b 17. TD63. AKC39. **d** 39 **p** 40. R Brierley Hill *Lich* 66-77; RD Himley 68-77; P-in-c Chaddesley Corbett *Worc* 77-83; P-in-c Stone 77-83; rtd 83; Perm to Offic *Lich* from 83. *Jalna, 7 Hyde Lane, Kinver, Stourbridge, Staffs DY7 6AE*   Kinver (0384) 872177

SMITH, David Roland Mark. b 46. ACP78 FRSA87 SSC88 Dur Univ BA68. Edin Th Coll 68. **d** 70 **p** 71. C Southwick St Columba *Dur* 70-74 and 81-82; Asst Chapl Univ of Wales (Cardiff) *Llan* 74-76; Hon C E Bris 76-78; Hon C Filton 78-79; Min Leam Lane CD *Dur* 80-81; V Leam Lane 81; Chapl Sunderland Poly 81-86; Co-ord Chapl Service 81-86; Chapl Birm Univ *Birm* from 86; Perm to Offic *Cov* from 88. *16 The Vale, Edgbaston, Birmingham B15 2RP*   021-455 0287 or 414 7000

SMITH, David Sidney Mark. b 54. Bris Univ BEd76. Ripon Coll Cuddesdon 77. **d** 79 **p** 80. C Wotton-under-Edge w Ozleworth and N Nibley *Glouc* 79-83; TV Malvern Link w Cowleigh *Worc* from 83; Relig Affairs Producer BBC Heref and Worc from 90. *St Peter's House, 49 Yates Hay Road, Malvern, Worcs WR14 1LH*   Malvern (0684) 54041

SMITH, David Stanley. b 41. Ox NSM Course. **d** 84 **p** 85. NSM Burghfield *Ox* 84-86; NSM Stratfield Mortimer 86-88; NSM Mortimer W End w Padworth 86-88; C St Breoke and Egloshayle *Truro* from 88. *3 Broomfield Road, Egloshayle, Wadebridge, Cornwall PL27 6AU*   Wadebridge (0208) 812239

SMITH, David Watson. b 31. Sarum Th Coll 63. **d** 65 **p** 66. C W Wimbledon Ch Ch *S'wark* 65-69; C Cheam 69-74; V Haslington *Ches* 74-83; V Haslington w Crewe Green 83-87; V Daresbury from 87. *The Vicarage, Daresbury, Warrington WA4 4AE*   Moore (0925) 740348

SMITH, David William. b 46. Sarum Th Coll 70. **d** 72 **p** 73. C Stokesley *York* 72-75; C Edin St Mich and All SS *Edin* 75-77; R Galashiels 77-85; R Yarm *York* from 85. *The Rectory, Yarm, Cleveland TS15 9BU*   Middlesbrough (0642) 781115

SMITH, Denis Richard. b 53. St Jo Coll Nottm 83. **d** 85 **p** 86. C Hersham *Guildf* 85-88; C Thatcham *Ox* 88-91; V Shefford *St Alb* from 91. *The Vicarage, 9 The Hollies, Shefford, Beds SG17 5BX*   Hitchin (0462) 811100

SMITH, Dennis Austin. b 50. Lanc Univ BA71 Liv Univ CertEd72. NW Ord Course 74. **d** 77 **p** 78. NSM Gt Crosby St Faith *Liv* 77-83; Hon C from 83; Chapl Merchant Taylors' Sch Crosby from 83. *16 Fir Road, Liverpool L22 4QL*   051-928 5065

SMITH, Dennis Peter. b 35. Qu Coll Birm 83. **d** 85 **p** 86. C Sedgley All SS *Lich* 85-89; C Penkridge w Stretton 89-90; TV Penkridge Team from 90. *The Vicarage, Top Road, Acton Trussell, Stafford ST17 0RQ*   Stafford (0785) 712408

SMITH, Derek Arthur. b 38. Chich Th Coll 63. **d** 66 **p** 67. C Cheadle *Lich* 66-70; C Blakenall Heath 70-72; P-in-c 76-77; TR 77-86; C Knutton 72-76; R Lich St Mary w St Mich from 86; P-in-c Wall from 90. *St Michael's Rectory, St Michael Road, Lichfield, Staffs WS13 6SN*   Lichfield (0543) 262420

SMITH, Derek Arthur Byott. b 26. Hull Univ MA89.

S Dios Minl Tr Scheme 78. **d** 81 **p** 82. NSM Wimborne Minster and Holt *Sarum* 81-83; C Northn St Alb *Pet* 83-85; Ind Chapl *York* 85-89; P-in-c Kingston upon Hull St Mary 88-89; P-in-c Newington w Dairycoates from 89. *1023 Anlaby Road, Hull HU4 7PN* Hull (0482) 52212

SMITH, Derek Arthur Douglas. b 26. Dur Univ BA51. Qu Coll Birm 58. **d** 60 **p** 61. C Evesham *Worc* 60-63; C Bollington St Jo *Ches* 63-68; V Thelwall 68-78; V Whitegate w Lt Budworth from 78. *The New Vicarage, Cinder Hill, Whitegate, Northwich, Cheshire CW8 2AY* Northwich (0606) 882151

SMITH, Derek Graham. b 52. St Cath Coll Cam BA74 MA77. Westcott Ho Cam 74. **d** 76 **p** 77. C Weymouth H Trin *Sarum* 76-79; P-in-c Bradpole 79; TV Bridport 79-84; R Monkton Farleigh, S Wraxall and Winsley from 84. *The Rectory, 6 Millbourn Close, Winsley, Bradford-on-Avon, Wilts BA15 2NN* Limpley Stoke (0225) 722230

SMITH, Donald Edgar. b 56. Oak Hill Th Coll 89. **d** 91. C Holloway St Mark w Em *Lon* from 91. *68 Tollington Park, London N4 3LD* 071-263 5384

SMITH, Ven Donald John. b 26. Clifton Th Coll 50. **d** 53 **p** 54. R Whitton and Thurleston w Akenham *St E* 62-75; Hon Can St E Cathl from 73; R Rickinghall 75-76; P-in-c Redgrave w Botesdale and Wortham 75-76; Adn Suffolk 75-84; R Redgrave cum Botesdale w Rickinghall 76-78; Adn Sudbury 84-91; rtd 91. *St Peter's Cottage, Stretton-on-the-Fosse, Moreton-in-Marsh, Glos GL56 9SE*

✠**SMITH, Rt Rev Donald Westwood.** b 28. Edin Th Coll 54. **d** 54 **p** 55 **c** 90. Asst Dioc Supernumerary *Ab* 54-55; Chapl St Andr Cathl 55-56; Canada 56-57; R Longside *Ab* 57-65; Mauritius 65-85; P-in-c St-Geo-in-the-East St Mary *Lon* 85-86; Madagascar from 86; Bp Toamasina from 90. *BP 531, Toamasina 501, Madagascar*

SMITH, Douglas David Frederick. b 28. Lon Univ BD53. ALCD53. **d** 53 **p** 54. R Higher Openshaw *Man* 69-80; R Church w Chapel Brampton *Pet* 80-81; R Church and Chapel Brampton w Harlestone 81-86; Perm to Offic *Ox* from 86; rtd 89. *27 Green Way, Newton Longville, Milton Keynes MK17 0AP* Milton Keynes (0908) 647257

SMITH, Douglas James. b 29. **d** 57 **p** 58. C Shrewsbury St Mary *Lich* 57-60; C Highgate Rise St Anne Brookfield *Lon* 60-63. *Sir John Cass & Red Coat School, Stepney Way, London E1 0RH* 071-790 6712

SMITH, Edward Leonard Richard. b 27. Lon Univ DipRS77. S'wark Ord Course 74. **d** 77 **p** 78. NSM N Wembley St Cuth *Lon* 77-83; C Broxbourne w Wormley *St Alb* 83-89; R Therfield w Kelshall from 89. *The Rectory, Therfield, Royston, Herts SG8 9QD* Kelshall (076387) 364

SMITH, Miss Elizabeth Jane. b 50. Birm Univ BA72 DCG73. Trin Coll Bris 88. **d** 90. C Lowestoft and Kirkley *Nor* from 90. *5 Magdalen Close, Lowestoft, Suffolk NR32 4TP* Lowestoft (0502) 517841

SMITH, Elvyn Garston. b 09. St Pet Hall Ox BA36 MA40. Wycliffe Hall Ox 36. **d** 37 **p** 38. V Patcham *Chich* 55-75; RD Preston 73-75; rtd 75; Perm to Offic *Chich* from 75. *45 Sheridan Road, Worthing, W Sussex BN14 8EU* Worthing (0903) 208611

SMITH, Eric Alfred Norman. b 25. St D Coll Lamp BA51 LTh53. **d** 53 **p** 54. C Loughb Em *Leic* 53-56; C Leic St Mark 56; Hanson Boys Gr Sch 56-59; Thornton Boys Gr Sch 60-61; Asst Lect Bradf Tech Coll 62-63; Hon C Manningham St Jude *Bradf* 62-63; V 63-65; Tyldesley Sec Sch Blackpool 65-69; J H Whitley Sch Halifax 70-81; C Stocksbridge *Sheff* 81-83; V Deepcar 83-84; R Caister *Nor* from 84. *The Rectory, Caister-on-Sea, Great Yarmouth, Norfolk NR30 5EH* Great Yarmouth (0493) 720287

SMITH, Eric Frederick. b 19. Lon Univ BA40 BD42. ALCD42. **d** 42 **p** 43. R Long Ditton *S'wark* 67-81; V Deal St Geo *Cant* 81-85; RD Sandwich 82-85; rtd 85; Perm to Offic *Cant* 85-88; Chapl Cant Sch of Min from 88. *Beach Cottage, 179 Beach Street, Deal, Kent CT14 6LE* Deal (0304) 367648

SMITH, Ernest John. b 24. ARICS49. Oak Hill Th Coll 59. **d** 61 **p** 62. C Hove Bp Hannington Memorial Ch *Chich* 64-72; V W Hampstead Trin *Lon* 72-89; rtd 90. *11 Oziers, Elsenham, Bishop's Stortford, Herts CM22 6LS* Bishop's Stortford (0279) 816872

SMITH, Esmond Ernest Carrington. b 22. Mert Coll Ox BA43 MA47. Westcott Ho Cam 46. **d** 46 **p** 47. V Aston SS Pet and Paul *Birm* 65-75; RD Aston 71-75; Asst Master Stainitorth Sch Thetford 75-78; Perm to Offic *St E* from 78; rtd 87. *The Saltings, Broad Street, Orford, Suffolk IP12 2NQ* Orford (0394) 405234

SMITH, Eustace. b 20. St Pet Hall Ox BA43 MA46.

Wycliffe Hall Ox 43. **d** 46 **p** 46. V Buckminster w Sewstern *Leic* 59-74; V Buckminster w Sewstern, Sproxton and Coston 74-82; R Algarkirk *Linc* 82-88; V Fosdyke 82-88; rtd 89. *32 Wordsworth Way, Measham, Burton-on-Trent, Staffs DE12 7ER* Measham (0530) 273765

SMITH, Dr Felicity Ann. b 40. Bris Univ MB, ChB63. Qu Coll Birm. **dss** 86 **d** 87. NSM Dioc Bd for Soc Resp *Cov* from 86. *14 Oakwood Grove, Warwick CV34 5TD* Warwick (0926) 492452

SMITH, Francis Armand. b 10. Sarum Th Coll 59. **d** 61 **p** 62. V Upavon w Rushall *Sarum* 63-76; rtd 76; Perm to Offic *S'wark* from 76; *Roch* from 77; *Chich* from 78. *15 High Street, Cowden, Edenbridge, Kent* Cowden (034286) 484

SMITH, Francis Christian Lynford. b 36. Cuddesdon Coll 72. **d** 74 **p** 75. C Catford St Laur *S'wark* 74-79; Mauritius 79-80; C Friern Barnet St Jas *Lon* 80; Chapl Dulwich Coll 81-91. *Address temp unknown*

SMITH, Francis James Prall. b 22. Nor Ord Course 73. **d** 76 **p** 77. NSM Gunthorpe w Bale *Nor* 76-82; NSM Friston *St E* 82-86; NSM Knodishall w Buxlow 82-86; NSM Aldringham w Thorpe, Knodishall w Buxlow etc 86-89; rtd 89; Perm to Offic *St E* from 90. *6 Bluebell Way, Worlingham, Beccles, Suffolk NR34 7BT* Beccles (0502) 711528

SMITH, Frank. b 39. Nottm Univ CertEd65 Open Univ BA76. Paton Congr Coll Nottm 61 Cuddesdon Coll 69. **d** 69 **p** 70. C Davyhulme St Mary *Man* 69-72; V Peak Forest and Wormhill *Derby* 72-78; R W Hallam and Mapperley 78-85; V Henleaze *Bris* from 85. *St Peter's Vicarage, 17 The Drive, Bristol BS9 4LD* Bristol (0272) 620636

SMITH, Frederick Thomas William. b 12. Kelham Th Coll 28. **d** 36 **p** 37. V Whittlebury w Silverstone *Pet* 62-82; rtd 82. *Wellburn House, Ovingham, Prudhoe, Northd NE42 6DE*

SMITH, Geoffrey. b 45. Sarum Th Coll 66. **d** 69 **p** 70. C Hatf *Sheff* 69-71; C Bolton St Pet *Man* 71-75; V Lt Hulton 75-78; Soc Resp Adv *Newc* 78-87; P-in-c Newc St Andr 78-87; Hon Can Newc Cathl 84-87; Public Preacher *Birm* from 87; Dir Cen for Applied Chr Studies 87-91; Team Ldr Birm Drug Prevention Unit from 91. *53 Northfield Road, Birmingham B30 1JD*

SMITH, Canon Geoffrey Cobley. b 30. Bps' Coll Cheshunt 63. **d** 65 **p** 66. C Hockerill *St Alb* 65-68; C Evesham *Worc* 68-72; V Walberswick w Blythburgh *St E* 72-85; RD Halesworth 81-85; R Newmarket St Mary w Exning St Agnes from 85; RD Mildenhall from 86; Hon Can St E Cathl from 87. *The Rectory, 5A Fitzroy Street, Newmarket, Suffolk CB8 0JW* Newmarket (0638) 662448

SMITH, Geoffrey Keith. b 37. Lon Coll of Div 57. **d** 60 **p** 61. C Leek St Luke *Lich* 60-63; C Trentham 63-66; V Lilleshall 66-84; P-in-c Sheriffhales w Woodcote 83-84; V Lilleshall and Sheriffhales 84-87; P-in-c Haughton from 87. *The Rectory, Haughton, Stafford ST18 9HU* Stafford (0785) 780181

SMITH, Geoffrey Raymond. b 49. AKC71. St Aug Coll Cant 71. **d** 72 **p** 73. C Hendon St Alphage *Lon* 72-75; C Notting Hill St Mich and Ch Ch 75-78; P-in-c Isleworth St Fran 78-83; P-in-c Chipping Ongar *Chelmsf* 83-84; R 84-86; R Shelley 84-86; R Chipping Ongar w Shelley 86-89; RD Ongar 88-89; P-in-c Harlow St Mary Magd 89-90; V from 90. *The Vicarage, Harlow, Essex CM17 9ND* Harlow (0279) 422681

SMITH, George Aelbert. b 15. Sarum & Wells Th Coll 77. **d** 80 **p** 81. NSM Milton Abbot w Dunterton *Ex* 80-81; Hon C 80-81; NSM Milton Abbot, Dunterton, Lamerton etc 81-83; Perm to Offic 83-86; NSM Colyton, Southleigh, Offwell, Widworthy etc from 86. *St Mary's, Church Street, Colyton, Devon EX13 6JY* Colyton (0297) 52089

SMITH, George Frederic. b 35. AKC59. **d** 60 **p** 61. C Radford *Cov* 60-64; C Kenilworth St Nic 64-67; V Burton Dassett 67-71; CF 71-74; V Lapley w Wheaton Aston *Lich* 74-80; V Gt Wyrley 80-90; V Shareshill from 90. *The Vicarage, 11 Brookhouse Lane, Featherstone, Wolverhampton WV10 7AW* Wolverhampton (0902) 727579

SMITH, Canon George Robert Henry. b 24. Chich Th Coll 49. **d** 52 **p** 53. C Glouc St Steph *Glouc* 52-56; V Dean Forest St Paul 56-65; P-in-c Clearwell 60-62; V Tuffley 65-82; Hon Can Glouc Cathl from 81; R Leckhampton St Pet from 82. *The Rectory, Leckhampton, Cheltenham, Glos GL51 5XX* Cheltenham (0242) 513647

SMITH, Gerald. b 36. Sarum Th Coll 61. **d** 63 **p** 64. C Menston w Woodhead *Bradf* 63-66; Chapl RAF 66-70; C Hoylake *Ches* 70-72; R Inverurie *Ab* 72-74; R Kemnay

72-74; TV Hucknall Torkard *S'well* 74-75; Falkland Is 75-78; V Luddenden w Luddenden Foot *Wakef* 79-86; V Scopwick Gp *Linc* from 86. *The Vicarage, Scopwick, Lincoln LN4 3NT* Metheringham (0526) 21047

SMITH, Preb Gilbert. b 14. Lon Univ BD64. Lambeth STh57 K Coll Lon 39. **d** 40 **p** 41. V Codsall *Lich* 58-83; RD Penkridge 72-82; Preb Lich Cathl 82-88; rtd 83; P-in-c Blymhill w Weston-under-Lizard *Lich* 83-88. *14 Malthouse Lane, Bradley, Stafford ST18 9DU* Stafford (0785) 780365

SMITH, Godfrey Declan Burfield. b 42. TCD BA64 MA67 PGCE65. Irish Sch of Ecum DipEcum82 Sarum Th Coll. **d** 69 **p** 70. Zambia 70-75; Perm to Offic *D & G* from 81; S Regional Sec (Ireland) CMS from 81; Overseas Sec from 87. *Overseas House, 3 Belgrave Road, Rathmines, Dublin 6, Irish Republic* Dublin (1) 970931 or 280-7452

SMITH, Graeme Richard. b 65. Leeds Univ BA87. Qu Coll Birm 87. **d** 89 **p** 90. C Daventry *Pet* from 90. *48 Trinity Close, Daventry, Northants NN11 4RN* Daventry (0327) 78697

SMITH, Graham Charles Morell. b 47. St Chad's Coll Dur BA74. Westcott Ho Cam 74. **d** 76 **p** 77. C Tooting All SS *S'wark* 76-80; TV Thamesmead 80-87; TR Kidlington w Hampton Poyle *Ox* from 87; RD Ox from 89. *St Mary's Rectory, 19 Mill Street, Kidlington, Oxford OX5 2EE* Kidlington (08675) 2230

SMITH, Graham David Noel. b 37. Oak Hill Th Coll 72. **d** 73 **p** 74. C Southborough St Pet w Ch Ch and St Matt *Roch* 73-76; C Bedworth *Cov* 76-79; C Cov Caludon 79; R Treeton *Sheff* 79-84; V Riddlesden *Bradf* from 84. *The Vicarage, Riddlesden, Keighley, W Yorkshire BD20 5PA* Keighley (0535) 603419

SMITH, Canon Graham Francis. b 27. Leic Univ DSocStuds51 Lon Univ BD57. Wells Th Coll 51. **d** 54 **p** 55. C Howe Bridge *Man* 54-57; C Hatf Hyde St Mary *St Alb* 57-63; V Angell Town St Jo *S'wark* 63-73; V Wandsworth St Anne 73-85; P-in-c Wandsworth St Faith 75-78; RD Wandsworth 81-85; Hon Can S'wark Cathl from 82; Mert Deanery Missr from 85. *30 Gorringe Park Avenue, Mitcham, Surrey CR4 2DG* 081-685 0772

SMITH, Graham John. b 31. SSC. **d** 75 **p** 76. Hon C Devonport St Mark Ford *Ex* 75-81; Hon C Plympton St Maurice 81-90; V Ernesettle from 90. *St Aidan's Vicarage, 122 Rochford Crescent, Plymouth PL5 2QD* Plymouth (0752) 364374

SMITH, Graham John. b 60. BScEng84. Trin Coll Bris BA90. **d** 90 **p** 91. C Herne *Cant* from 90. *7 St Martin's View, Herne, Canterbury, Kent CT6 7AP* Herne Bay (0227) 372470

SMITH, Grahame Clarence. b 32. Lich Th Coll 58. **d** 60 **p** 61. C New Sleaford *Linc* 60-63; R Tydd 63-76; V Barholm w Stowe 76-81; V Tallington 76-81; R Uffington 76-81; P-in-c W Deeping 76-77; R 77-81; R Uffington from 81. *The Rectory, Uffington, Stamford, Lincs PE9 4SN* Stamford (0780) 62430

SMITH, Gregory James. b 52. GGSM73 Lon Univ TCert74 Golds Coll Lon BMus82. Sarum & Wells Th Coll 87. **d** 89 **p** 90. C Welling *S'wark* from 89. *21 Hill View Drive, Welling, Kent DA16 3RS* 081-856 3500

SMITH, Canon Guy Howard. b 33. Man Univ BA54. Coll of Resurr Mirfield 60. **d** 62 **p** 63. C Oswestry H Trin *Lich* 62-66; Malaysia 66-69; V Willenhall St Anne *Lich* 69-79; P-in-c Willenhall St Steph 75-79; Malawi 79-82; Adn Lilongwe Lake Malawi 80-82; V Tettenhall Wood *Lich* 82-89; TR from 89. *Christ Church Rectory, 7 Broxwood Park, Tettenhall Wood, Wolverhampton WV6 8LZ* Wolverhampton (0902) 751116

SMITH, Harold. b 20. Qu Coll Birm 77. **d** 80 **p** 81. NSM Gravelly Hill *Birm* 80-85; NSM Duddeston w Nechells from 85. *3 Dovey Tower, Duddeston Manor Road, Birmingham B7 4LE* 021-359 0568

SMITH, Harold John. b 15. Ridley Hall Cam 49. **d** 51 **p** 51. Chapl CA 63-82; R St Marg Lothbury and St Steph Coleman Street etc *Lon* 73-82; rtd 83. *29 Stream Pit Lane, Sandhurst, Hawkhurst, Kent TN18 5LB* Sandhurst (058085) 463

SMITH, Harvey Jefferson. b 19. AMCT39 FIEE38 FIMechE52 FIPlantE67 ACIArb78. St Alb Minl Tr Scheme 81. **d** 88. Hon C Hemel Hempstead *St Alb* from 88. *43 Garland Close, Hemel Hempstead, Herts HP2 5HU* Hemel Hempstead (0442) 66377

SMITH, Hazel Ferguson Waide (Sister Hazel). b 33. Univ Coll Lon BA55. dss 64 **d** 87. Bedf St Paul *St Alb* 85-87; Par Dn from 87. *St Etheldreda, 4 Conduit Road, Bedford MK40 1EQ* Bedford (0234) 63953

SMITH, Henry Neville. b 25. Chich Th Coll 53. **d** 54 **p** 55. V Ivinghoe w Pitstone *Ox* 63-73; Chapl Qu Anne's Sch Caversham 73-90; rtd 90. *12 Poulner Close, Bognor Regis, W Sussex PO22 8HN* Bognor Regis (0243) 822716

SMITH, Henry Robert. b 41. Lanchester Poly BSc66. Qu Coll Birm 75. **d** 78 **p** 79. Hon C Hillmorton *Cov* 78-81; Lic to Offic *S'well* 81-85; Hon C Radcliffe-on-Trent and Shelford etc 85-89; C Sutton in Ashfield St Mary from 89. *Grosvenor House, Grosvenor Avenue, Sutton-in-Ashfield, Notts NG17 1FG* Mansfield (0623) 552572

SMITH, Howard Alan. b 46. DCouns81 St Jo Coll Dur BA73 DipTh74. **d** 74 **p** 75. C Brighton St Matthias *Chich* 74-77; C Henfield 77-78; C Henfield w Shermanbury and Woodmancote 78-80; R Northiam 80-87; Chapl St Ebba's Hosp Epsom from 87; Chapl Qu Mary's Hosp Carshalton from 87. *The Chaplain's House, Queen Mary's Hospital, Carshalton, Surrey SM5 4NR* 081-643 3300

SMITH, Howard Charles. b 08. St Steph Ho Ox 68. **d** 70 **p** 71. C Kensington St Mary Abbots w St Geo *Lon* 70-71; C Mill Hill Jo Keble Ch 72-77; C Hendon St Alphage 78; rtd 78; Hon C Eastbourne St Sav and St Pet *Chich* 84-87; Perm to Offic from 87. *c/o National Westminster Bank plc, 1 Cavendish Square, London W19 4NU* 071-631 4878

SMITH, Howard Gilbert. b 48. Leeds Univ BA69. St Steph Ho Ox BA71 MA75 Ridley Hall Cam 72. **d** 73 **p** 74. C Wallsend St Luke *Newc* 73-76; C Farnworth and Kearsley *Man* 76-77; P-in-c Farnworth All SS 77-78; TV E Farnworth and Kearsley 78-82; V Belfield from 82. *St Ann's Vicarage, 310 Milnrow Road, Rochdale, Lancs OL16 5BT* Rochdale (0706) 46173

SMITH, Ian. b 62. Hull Univ BA83. Oak Hill Th Coll DipHE87 BA88. **d** 88 **p** 89. C W Hampstead St Luke *Lon* 88-90; C Woking St Pet *Guildf* from 90. *12 Vicarage Road, Kingfield, Woking, Surrey GU22 9BP* Woking (0483) 764134

SMITH, Ian Charles. b 39. Lich Th Coll 65. **d** 68 **p** 69. C Kingshurst *Birm* 68-71; Chapl RAF 72-83; Chapl Winterton Hosp Sedgefield from 83. *Winterton Hospital, Sedgefield, Stockton-on-Tees, Cleveland TS21 3EJ* Sedgefield (0740) 22066 or 20521

SMITH, Canon Ian Walker. b 29. Leeds Univ BA52. Coll of Resurr Mirfield 52. **d** 54 **p** 55. C Moulsecoomb *Chich* 54-61; Chapl K Sch Cant 61-62; C Crawley *Chich* 62-79; TV 79-81; R Clenchwarton *Ely* from 81; RD Lynn Marshland from 84; Hon Can Ely Cathl from 88; Perm to Offic *Nor* from 88. *The Rectory, Clenchwarton, King's Lynn, Norfolk PE34 4DT* King's Lynn (0553) 772089

SMITH, Jack Douglas. b 37. Down Coll Cam BA60 MA64. Westcott Ho Cam 78. **d** 80 **p** 81. C Fincham *Ely* 80-82; P-in-c Barton Bendish w Beachamwell and Shingham 82-83; R 83-90; R Boughton 83-90; V Wereham 83-90; R Silverstone and Abthorpe w Slapton *Pet* from 90. *The Vicarage, High Street, Silverstone, Towcester, Northants NN12 8US* Silverstone (0327) 857996

SMITH, James. b 26. NE Ord Course 76. **d** 79 **p** 80. NSM Seaton Hirst *Newc* 79-82; NSM Cresswell and Lynemouth 82-88; NSM Cambois from 88. *140 Pont Street, Ashington, Northd NE63 0PX* Ashington (0670) 816557

SMITH, James Edward. b 30. Chich Th Coll 57. **d** 58 **p** 59. C Ellesmere Port *Ches* 58-61; C W Bromwich All SS *Lich* 61-63; Chapl RN 63-65; V Walton St Jo *Liv* 65-71; V Anfield St Columba 71-79; V Altcar from 79. *The Vicarage, Lord Sefton Way, Altcar Formby, Liverpool L37 5AG* Formby (07048) 72670

SMITH, James Harold. b 31. Ch Coll Tasmania ThL61. **d** 61 **p** 61. Australia 61-63 and 66-85; Canada 64-65; Chapl St Chris Hospice Sydenham 86-87; Asst Chapl Brook Gen Hosp Lon from 87; Asst Chapl Greenwich Distr Hosp Lon from 87. *The Chaplaincy, Brook Hospital, Shooter's Hill Road, London SE18 4LW* 081-856 5555

SMITH, James Henry. b 32. St Aid Birkenhead. **d** 65 **p** 66. C Wigan St Cath *Liv* 65-68; V Parkfield in Middleton *Man* 68-77; V Bolton Breightmet St Jas from 77. *St James's Vicarage, Roscow Avenue, Bolton BL2 6HU* Bolton (0204) 25640

SMITH, James William. b 47. RGN RMN MRIPIIH. Lambeth STh90 Chich Th Coll 78. **d** 80 **p** 80. C Kenwyn *Truro* 80-82; C Haslemere *Guildf* 82-84; TV Honiton, Gittisham, Combe Raleigh, Monkton etc *Ex* 84-91; Chapl R Marsden Hosp Lon and Surrey from 91; Perm to Offic *S'wark* from 91. *The Chaplain's Office, Royal Marsden Hospital, Sutton, Surrey* 081-642 6011

SMITH, Jeffery Donald Morris. b 23. **d** 53 **p** 54. S Africa 68-73; P-in-c Bintree w Themelthorpe *Nor* 73-76; V Twyford w Guist 73-76; R Twyford w Guist and Bintry w Themelthorpe 76-80; RD Sparham 79-81; R Twyford w Guist w Bintry w Themelthorpe etc 81; TR Hempnall 81-84; R Catfield 84-89; R Ingham w Sutton 84-89; rtd

663

89; Perm to Offic *Nor* from 89. *27 Dale Road, East Dereham, Norfolk NR19 2DD*   Dereham (0362) 697022

SMITH, Jeffry Bradford. b 56. BA82. Ch Div Sch of the Pacific (USA) MDiv85 Ripon Coll Cuddesdon. **d** 86 **p** 87. C Frimley *Guildf* 87-91; R E and W Clandon from 91. *The Rectory, West Clandon, Guildford, Surrey GU4 7RG* Guildford (0483) 222573

SMITH, Mrs Jennifer Pamela. b 63. Girton Coll Cam BA85 MA88. Oak Hill Th Coll BA91. **d** 91. C Rawdon *Bradf* from 91. *69 Leeds Road, Rawdon, Leeds LS19 6NT* Leeds (0532) 508088

SMITH, Jeremy Victor. b 60. Keble Coll Ox BA82. Chich Th Coll 83. **d** 85 **p** 86. C Alton St Lawr *Win* 85-88; C W Hampstead St Jas *Lon* from 88. *2 St James House, Sherriff Road, London NW6 2AP*   071-624 9221

SMITH, Canon John. b 14. Qu Coll Birm 47. **d** 50 **p** 51. R Weston Favell *Pet* 62-72; R Uppingham w Ayston 73-82; P-in-c Wardley w Belton 76-82; Can Pet Cathl 76-82; RD Rutland 77-82; rtd 82; Lic to Offic *Pet* 82-85; Perm to Offic from 85. *149 Braunston Road, Oakham, Leics LE15 6LF*   Oakham (0572) 756745

SMITH, John Alec. b 37. Lon Coll of Div ALCD62 BD63. **d** 63 **p** 64. C Cromer *Nor* 63-66; C Barking St Marg *Chelmsf* 66-69; V Attercliffe *Sheff* 69-75; P-in-c Sheff St Barn 76-78; V Sheff St Barn and St Mary 78-89; Ind Chapl 78-89; RD Ecclesall 80-85; TR Chippenham St Paul w Hardenhuish etc *Bris* from 89. *St Paul's Rectory, 9 Greenway Park, Chippenham, Wilts SN15 1QG* Chippenham (0249) 653839

SMITH, John David Elliott. b 39. Dur Univ BA61. Cranmer Hall Dur 61. **d** 64 **p** 65. C Stratford w Bishopton *Cov* 64-70; P-in-c Tredington 70-76; P-in-c Newbold on Avon 76-81; V 81-89; P-in-c Arlington, Folkington and Wilmington *Chich* from 89. *The Vicarage, The Street, Wilmington, Polegate, E Sussex BN26 5SW*

SMITH, Dr John Denmead. b 44. Ox Univ BA65 MA69 DPhil71. Coll of Resurr Mirfield 72. **d** 75 **p** 76. Asst Chapl Win Coll from 75. *11 Kingsgate Street, Winchester, Hants SO23 9PD*   Winchester (0962) 861820

SMITH, Canon John Douglas. b 20. Roch Th Coll 63. **d** 65 **p** 66. C Hersham *Guildf* 69-72; V Churt 72-80; V Cobham 80-88; RD Leatherhead 83-88; Hon Can Guildf Cathl from 85; rtd 88. *77 Home Park, Oxted, Surrey RH8 0JT*   Oxted (0883) 714861

SMITH, John Eckersley. b 26. **d** 55 **p** 56. C Heywood St Jas *Man* 55-57; C Atherton 57-59; R Gorton All SS 59-65; C Northenden 73-75; V Charlestown 75-82; Perm to Offic from 85. *19 Arthur Street, Swinton, Manchester M27 3HP*   061-793 7707

SMITH, John Edward Allin. b 29. K Coll Lon BA52 Brunel Univ MPhil81. St Aug Coll Cant 49 Ridley Hall Cam 52. **d** 54 **p** 55. C Upper Tooting H Trin *S'wark* 54-57; C Weaste *Man* 57-58; C-in-c Reigate St Phil CD *S'wark* 58-65; V Lewisham St Swithun 65-71; R Wexham *Ox* 71-83; P-in-c Princes Risborough w Ilmer 83-84; R from 84. *The Rectory, Manor Park Avenue, Princes Risborough, Aylesbury, Bucks HP17 9AR*   Princes Risborough (08444) 4784

SMITH, John Ernest. b 52. St Andr Univ MTh77. Wycliffe Hall Ox 78. **d** 79 **p** 80. C Bermondsey St Mary w St Olave, St Jo etc *S'wark* 79-87; P-in-c Whyteleafe from 87. *9 Regents Close, Whyteleafe, Surrey CR3 0AH* 081-660 4015

SMITH, John Graham. b 32. **d** 78 **p** 79. NSM Hordle *Win* from 78. *3 Marryat Road, New Milton, Hants BH25 5LW* New Milton (0425) 615701

SMITH, John Lawrence. b 43. Birm Univ BSc65. Linc Th Coll 67. **d** 70 **p** 71. C Frodingham *Linc* 70-75; TV Gt Grimsby St Mary and St Jas 75-83; V Wolv St Andr *Lich* from 83. *St Andrew's Vicarage, 66 Albert Road, Wolverhampton WV6 0AF*   Wolverhampton (0902) 712935

SMITH, John Leslie. b 44. Trin Coll Cam BA65 MA71. Ripon Coll Cuddesdon 79. **d** 81 **p** 82. C Ollerton *S'well* 81-84; P-in-c Farndon 84-88; P-in-c Thorpe 84-88; P-in-c Langford w Holme from 88; P-in-c Winthorpe from 88; Dioc Chief Insp Ch Schs from 88. *The Rectory, The Spinney, Winthorpe, Newark, Notts NG24 2NT*   Newark (0636) 704985

SMITH, John Macdonald. b 29. Ch Coll Cam BA52 MA56. Wells Th Coll 56. **d** 58 **p** 59. V Kidmore End *Ox* 63-82; rtd 82. *38 Main Road, Norton, Evesham, Worcs WR11 4TL*   Evesham (0386) 870918

SMITH, John Malcolm. b 36. ACIB60. N Ord Course 81. **d** 84 **p** 85. NSM Bury St Pet *Man* from 84. *46 Ajax Drive, Bury, Lancs BL9 8EF*   061-766 8378

SMITH, John Oswald Salkeld. b 32. Oak Hill Th Coll 57. **d** 60 **p** 61. C Peckham St Mary Magd *S'wark* 61-63; C Rodbourne Cheney *Bris* 63-67; V Bradf St Aug

Undercliffe *Bradf* 67-74; P-in-c Hammersmith St Simon *Lon* 74-76; V Chelsea St Jo w St Andr from 76. *St Andrew's Vicarage, 43 Park Walk, London SW10 0AU* 071-352 1675

SMITH, Canon John Reginald. b 15. TCD BA39 MA42. Wycliffe Hall Ox 40. **d** 41 **p** 42. C Heaton Norris Ch Ch *Man* 41-44; C Stretford St Matt 44-47; R Stretford All SS 47-49; V Radcliffe St Thos 49-59; R Sutton *Liv* 59-66; RD Bury *Man* 66-86; R Bury St Mary from 66; Hon Can Man Cathl from 72. *St Mary's Rectory, Bury, Lancs BL9 0JR*   061-764 2452

SMITH, John Roger. b 36. Dur Univ BA59. Tyndale Hall Bris 59. **d** 61 **p** 62. C Chaddesden St Mary *Derby* 61-63; C Gresley 63-66; V Burton Ch Ch *Lich* 66-76; V Doncaster St Mary *Sheff* from 76. *St Mary's Vicarage, 59 St Mary's Road, Doncaster, S Yorkshire DN1 2NR* Doncaster (0302) 342565

SMITH, Canon John Stewart. b 18. St Cath Soc Ox BA42 MA46. Ripon Hall Ox 42. **d** 43 **p** 44. V Shirehampton *Bris* 58-72; V Westbury-on-Trym St Alb 72-83; RD Clifton 73-79; Hon Can Bris Cathl 77-84; rtd 83; Perm to Offic *Bris* from 84. *48A Downs Park West, Bristol BS6 7QL*   Bristol (0272) 629208

SMITH, John Thomas. b 29. Shuttleworth Agric Coll NDA55 Keele Univ DASE72 Wolv Poly MPhil81 PhD87. W Midl Minl Tr Course 87. **d** 91. NSM Drayton in Hales *Lich* from 91. *Red Bank House, Market Drayton, Shropshire TF9 1AY*   Market Drayton (0630) 652302

SMITH, John Thompson. b 30. Wycliffe Hall Ox 64. **d** 66 **p** 67. C Walsall *Lich* 66-69; V Stoke Prior *Worc* 69-75; Asst Gen Sec Red Triangle Club 75-85; Chapl Heath Hosp Tendring from 85; R Tendring and Lt Bentley w Beaumont cum Moze *Chelmsf* 85-89; R Fairstead w Terling and White Notley etc from 89. *The Rectory, New Road, Terling, Chelmsford CM3 2PL*   Chelmsford (0245) 33256

SMITH, John Trevor. b 47. GGSM. Coll of Resurr Mirfield 74. **d** 77 **p** 78. C Loughton St Jo *Chelmsf* 77-80; C Ruislip St Martin *Lon* 80-84; P-in-c Southall Ch Redeemer from 84. *The Clergy House, Allenby Road, Southall, Middx UB1 2HE*   081-578 2711

SMITH, Jonathan Paul. b 60. Univ of Wales (Lamp) BA81. Wycliffe Hall Ox 82. **d** 84 **p** 85. C Baglan *Llan* 84-88; C Gabalfa 88-90; V Llangarten and Llangammarch and Llanfechan etc *S & B* from 90. *The Rectory, Maes Glas, Llangammarch Wells, Powys LD4 4EE*   Llangammarch Wells (05912) 482

SMITH, Jonathan Peter. b 55. K Coll Lon BD77 AKC77 Cam Univ PGCE78. Westcott Ho Cam 79. **d** 80 **p** 81. C Gosforth All SS *Newc* 80-82; C Waltham Abbey *Chelmsf* 82-85; Chapl City Univ *Lon* 85-88; R Harrold and Carlton w Chellington *St Alb* from 88; Chapl Beds Police from 90. *The Rectory, 3 The Moor, Carlton, Bedford MK43 7JR*   Bedford (0234) 720262

SMITH, Julian. b 48. K Coll Lon 70. Linc Th Coll 71. **d** 73 **p** 74. C Taunton Lyngford *B & W* 73-76; TV Wellington and Distr 76-81; R Axbridge w Shipham and Rowberrow from 81; Chapl St Jo Hosp Axbridge from 84. *The Rectory, Cheddar Road, Axbridge, Somerset BS26 2DL*   Axbridge (0934) 732261

SMITH, Keith. b 46. S Dios Minl Tr Scheme. **d** 87 **p** 88. NSM W Worthing St Jo *Chich* from 87. *Sowena, 20 Trent Road, Goring-by-Sea, Worthing, W Sussex BN12 4EL* Worthing (0903) 505850

SMITH, Kenneth Harry. b 21. St Chad's Coll Dur BA49 DipTh50. Linc Th Coll 51. **d** 51 **p** 52. C Nantwich *Ches* 51-52; C Hale 52-54; V Lindal w Marton *Carl* 54-60; V Dacre from 60. *The Vicarage, Stainton, Penrith, Cumbria CA11 0ES*   Penrith (0768) 63179

SMITH, Kenneth Robert. b 48. K Coll Lon BD75 AKC75. St Aug Coll Cant 75. **d** 76 **p** 77. C Birtley *Dur* 76-80; V Lamesley 80-90; R Whitburn from 90. *The Rectory, 51 Front Street, Whitburn, Sunderland SR6 7JD*   091-529 2232

SMITH, Kenneth Victor George. b 37. Lon Univ BD62. ALCD61. **d** 62 **p** 63. Hon C Bromley Common St Aug *Roch* 62-66; Hon C Streatham Immanuel w St Anselm *S'wark* 66-68; Perm to Offic 68-78; Hon C Sanderstead All SS 78-91; Chapl Whitgift Sch and Ho Croydon from 90; Hon C Croydon St Jo from 91. *Bridles Way, Haling Grove, Croydon CR2 6DQ*   081-680 4460

SMITH, Canon Laurence Kenneth Powell. b 17. Lon Coll of Div ALCD41 LTh74. **d** 41 **p** 42. V Iford *Win* 57-72; R Stockbridge and Houghton 72-85; RD Romsey 79-85; Hon Can Win Cathl 82-85; rtd 85; Perm to Offic *Win* from 85. *8 Riverside Gardens, Romsey, Hants SO51 8HN* Romsey (0794) 51862

SMITH, Laurence Sidney. b 37. Sarum & Wells Th Coll

70. **d** 73 **p** 74. C Surbiton St Matt *S'wark* 73-76; C Horley 76-81; V W Ewell *Guildf* 81-90; V W Byfleet from 90. *The Vicarage, 5 Dartnell Avenue, West Byfleet, Weybridge, Surrey KT14 6PJ* Weybridge (0932) 345270

SMITH, Lawrence Paul. b 51. Southn Univ BTh81. Chich Th Coll 76. **d** 79 **p** 80. C Margate St Jo *Cant* 79-84; R Eythorne w Waldershare 84-87; P-in-c Sibertswold w Coldred 85-87; R Eythorne and Elvington w Waldershare etc from 87. *The Rectory, Barfreystone Road, Eythorne, Dover, Kent CT15 4AH* Shepherdswell (0304) 830241

SMITH, Lewis Shand. b 52. Aber Univ MA74 Edin Univ BD78. Edin Th Coll 74. **d** 77 **p** 78. C Wishaw *Glas* 77-79; P-in-c 79-80; C Motherwell 77-79; P-in-c 79-80; R Lerwick *Ab* from 80; R Burravoe from 80; Miss to Seamen from 80. *1 Greenrig, Lerwick, Isle of Shetland ZE1 0AW* Lerwick (0595) 3862

SMITH, Miss Lorna Cassandra. b 43. Open Univ BA76. Cant Sch of Min 82. **dss** 86 **d** 87. Birchington w Acol and Minnis Bay *Cant* 86-87; Par Dn from 87. *9 Sewell Close, Birchington, Kent CT7 0BP* Thanet (0843) 43750

SMITH, Margaret Elizabeth. b 46. Bretton Hall Coll CertEd67. N Ord Course 85. **d** 88. Hon Par Dn Battyeford *Wakef* 88-91; Hon C Mirfield 89-91; Dn-in-c Flockton cum Denby Grange from 91; Chapl HM Pris New Hall from 90. *5 Springfield Park, Mirfield, W Yorkshire WF14 9PD* Mirfield (0924) 498020

SMITH, Mark Gordon Robert Davenport. b 56. St Jo Coll Dur BA77. Ridley Hall Cam 78. **d** 80 **p** 81. C Sheff St Jo *Sheff* 80-83; C Brightside w Wincobank 83-86; V Kimberworth Park from 86. *The Vicarage, 21 Birks Road, Kimberworth Park, Rotherham, S Yorkshire S61 3JX* Rotherham (0709) 552268

SMITH, Mark Graham. b 63. Ex Univ BA86 Qu Coll Cam DipTh89. Westcott Ho Cam 87. **d** 90 **p** 91. C Cottingham *York* from 90. *10 King Tree Avenue, Cottingham, N Humberside HU16 4DS* Hull (0482) 842306

SMITH, Mark Richard Samuel. b 63. UMIST BSc84. Cranmer Hall Dur 86. **d** 89 **p** 90. C Kersal Moor *Man* from 89. *6 Woodward Road, Prestwich, Manchester M25 8TU* 061-773 1109

SMITH, Martin David. b 52. LTCL Hull Univ BA75. Cuddesdon Coll 75. **d** 78 **p** 79. C Brentwood St Thos *Chelmsf* 78-80; C Reading St Giles *Ox* 80-91; R Colkirk w Oxwick w Pattesley, Whissonsett etc *Nor* from 91. *The Rectory, Colkirk, Fakenham, Norfolk NR21 7NU* Fakenham (0328) 863890

SMITH, Martin John. b 59. Qu Coll Birm 86. **d** 89 **p** 90. C Grays Thurrock *Chelmsf* from 89. *48 Parker Road, Grays, Essex RM17 5YN* Grays Thurrock (0375) 379309

SMITH, Martin Lee. b 47. **d** 70 **p** 71. C Digswell *St Alb* 70-71; C Cheshunt 71-73; Perm to Offic *Ox* 74-80; USA from 81. *Emery House, Emery Lane, West Newbury, Massachusetts 01985, USA*

SMITH, Martin William. b 40. JP. K Coll Lon BD63 AKC63. **d** 64 **p** 65. C Ashford St Hilda CD *Lon* 64-67; Malaysia 67-71; V Lakenham St Mark *Nor* 72-85; V N Walsham w Antingham from 85. *28A Yarmouth Road, North Walsham, Norfolk NR28 9AT* North Walsham (0692) 406380

SMITH, Martyn. b 52. CertEd73. Oak Hill Th Coll BA81. **d** 81 **p** 82. C Halliwell St Pet *Man* 81-86; V Cam St Martin *Ely* 86-89; Vineyard Chr Fellowship from 89. *6 Lambeth Close, Horwich, Bolton BL6 6DQ* Horwich (0204) 669529

SMITH, Maurice Jeffrey. b 18. Bps' Coll Cheshunt 56. **d** 56 **p** 57. V Springfield H Trin *Chelmsf* 58-70; Chapl HM Pris Chelmsf 65-70; R Wickham Bishops *Chelmsf* 70-86; RD Witham 76-86; rtd 86; Perm to Offic *Ex* from 88. *88 Valley Way, Exmouth, Devon EX8 4RL* Exmouth (0395) 278524

SMITH, Mervyn Gilbert Morris. b 18. Ripon Hall Ox 56. **d** 58 **p** 59. V Rosherville *Roch* 67-79; R Horsmonden 79-86; Chapl HM Det Cen Blantyre Ho 82-86; rtd 86; Perm to Offic *Portsm* from 86. *9 Golden Ridge, Freshwater, Isle of Wight PO40 9LE* Isle of Wight (0983) 754857

SMITH, Michael. b 54. Matlock Coll of Educn CertEd76 Nottm Univ BEd77 Ridley Hall Cam 87. **d** 89 **p** 90. C Ilkeston St Mary *Derby* from 89. *14 Lower Stanton Road, Ilkeston, Derbyshire DE7 4LN* Ilkeston (0602) 327032

SMITH, Michael Anthony. b 47. Univ of Wales (Abth) MA73. **d** 78 **p** 79. NSM Llandingat w Llanfair and Myddfai 78-82; Chapl Llandovery Coll 81-82; Chapl Pocklington Sch York from 82. *Hosmer Lodge, 35 Percy Road, Pocklington, York YO42 2LZ* Pocklington (0759) 304543

SMITH, Michael David. b 57. BA80. St Steph Ho Ox 81.

d 83 **p** 84. C Beaconsfield *Ox* 83-87; V Wing w Grove from 87. *The Vicarage, 27B Aylesbury Road, Wing, Leighton Buzzard, Beds LU7 0PD* Aylesbury (0296) 688496

SMITH, Michael George. b 33. Univ Coll Ox BA57 MA61 BD65. St Steph Ho Ox 57. **d** 60 **p** 61. C Ex St Thos *Ex* 60-63; C Ox St Mary V *Ox* 63-65; USA 65-70; Chapl Qu Marg Sch Escrick Park 70-74; Chapl Pocklington Sch York 74-82; V Ex St Dav *Ex* 82-91; R Silverton from 91; R Butterleigh from 91. *The Rectory, King Street, Silverton, Exeter EX5 4JG* Exeter (0392) 860350

SMITH, Michael James. b 47. AKC69. St Aug Coll Cant 70. **d** 71 **p** 72. C Corby St Columba *Pet* 71-78; V Collierley *Dur* 78-80; CPAS Evang from 83; V Collierley w Annfield Plain *Dur* 83. *6 Blind Lane, Chester le Street, Co Durham DH3 4AG* 091-388 1977

SMITH, Michael John. b 39. FBIM80 FIIM81. S Dios Minl Tr Scheme 86. **d** 89 **p** 90. NSM Shepton Mallet w Doulting *B & W* from 89. *Whytegates, Barrow Lane, Pilton, Shepton Mallet, Somerset BA4 4BH* Pilton (074989) 481

SMITH, Michael John. b 47. Lon Univ DipTh71. Kelham Th Coll 65. **d** 71 **p** 72. C Cov St Mary *Cov* 71-75; Chapl RN 75-90; CF from 90. *c/o MOD, Bagshot Park, Bagshot, Surrey GU19 5PL* Bagshot (0276) 71717

SMITH, Michael Raymond. b 36. ARCM56 ARCO56 Qu Coll Cam BA59 MA63. Cuddesdon Coll 64. **d** 65 **p** 66. C Redcar *York* 65-70; V Dormanstown 70-73; Prec Worc Cathl *Worc* 73-77; TR Worc St Barn w Ch Ch 77-83; RD Worc E 79-83; V Eskdale, Irton, Muncaster and Waberthwaite *Carl* 83-87; Chapl Uppingham Sch Leics from 87; Lic to Offic *Pet* from 88. *Merion House, 50 High Street West, Uppingham, Leics LE15 9QD* Uppingham (0572) 821468 or 822710

SMITH, Michael Richard Guy. b 55. Man Univ BA77. Ripon Coll Cuddesdon 88. **d** 90 **p** 91. C Wallasey St Hilary *Ches* from 90. *18 Broadway Avenue, Wallasey, Merseyside L45 6TA* 051-638 2612

SMITH, Michael Robin. b 34. ACIB58. Sarum Th Coll. **d** 62 **p** 63. C Perry Hill St Geo *S'wark* 62-65; C Streatham St Leon 65-68; NSM E Brixton St Jude 68-70; Brixton Chr Counselling Min 70-79; Wandsworth Ch Inst from 80. *10 Wiseton Road, London SW17 7EE* 081-672 7374

SMITH, Neil Reginald. b 47. Qu Coll Birm 70. **d** 72 **p** 73. C Horton *Bradf* 72-75; C New Mills *Derby* 76-79; Perm to Offic *Ches* from 79; Lic to Offic *Derby* from 79; Chapl Community of the King of Love Whaley Bridge from 79. *Whaley Hall, Reservoir Road, Whaley Bridge, Stockport, Cheshire SK12 7BL* Whaley Bridge (0663) 32495

SMITH, Nicholas Victor. b 54. St Jo Coll Dur BA76. St Steph Ho Ox 76. **d** 78 **p** 85. C Saltley *Birm* 78-79; C St Marylebone Ch Ch *Lon* 84-87; C Barnsley St Mary *Wakef* 87-90. *16 Maple Road, Sutton Coldfield, W Midlands B72 1JP* 021-355 1744

SMITH, Norman. b 22. Coll of Resurr Mirfield 85. **d** 85 **p** 86. Hon C Greenhill *Sheff* 85-89; rtd 89; Hon C Blackpool St Mary *Blackb* from 89. *21 Cairn Court, Squires Gate Lane, Blackpool FY4 2QQ* Blackpool (0253) 401498

SMITH, Norman George. b 27. K Coll Lon BD52 AKC52. **d** 53 **p** 54. C Pennington *Man* 53-56; C Choriton-cum-Hardy St Clem 56-57; V Heywood St Jas 57-63; R Bedhampton *Portsm* 63-81; V Win St Bart *Win* from 81; RD Win 84-89. *The Vicarage, 1 Abbey Hill Close, Winchester, Hants SO23 7AZ* Winchester (0962) 852032

SMITH, Norman Jordan. b 30. Sarum Th Coll 57. **d** 60 **p** 61. C Dean Forest St Paul *Glouc* 60-61; C Clearwell 60-61; C W Tarring *Chich* 61-65; Australia 65-68; V Chidham *Chich* from 68. *The Vicarage, Chidham, Chichester, W Sussex PO18 8TA* Bosham (0243) 573147

SMITH, Mrs Olwen. b 44. Birm Univ BA66 DPS68. Selly Oak Coll 67. **d** 87. Ind Chapl Black Country Urban Ind Miss *Lich* from 84. *66 Albert Road, Wolverhampton WV6 0AF* Wolverhampton (0902) 712935

SMITH, Paul Aidan. b 59. Birm Univ BA82. Wycliffe Hall Ox 82. **d** 85 **p** 86. C Selly Park St Steph and St Wulstan *Birm* 85-88; C Kensal Rise St Mark and St Martin *Lon* from 88. *26 Ashburnham Road, London NW10 5SD* 081-960 6211

SMITH, Paul Andrew. b 55. St Chad's Coll Dur BA76. Chich Th Coll 78. **d** 80 **p** 81. C Habergham Eaves St Matt *Blackb* 80-83; C Ribbleton 83-86; V Rishton from 86. *The Vicarage, Somerset Road, Rishton, Blackburn BB1 4BP* Great Harwood (0254) 886191

SMITH, Paul Gregory. b 39. Ex Univ BA61. St Steph Ho Ox 61. **d** 63 **p** 64. C Walthamstow St Mich *Chelmsf* 63-66; C Devonport St Mark Ford *Ex* 66-69; C Hemel Hempstead *St Alb* 69-71; TV 71-83; R Bideford *Ex* from

83; Chapl Bideford and Torridge Hosps from 83. *The Rectory, Abbotsham Road, Bideford, Devon EX39 3AB* Bideford (0237) 470228

SMITH, Paul Raymond. b 60. Sheff Univ BA81. Qu Coll Birm 82. d 85 p 86. C Frecheville and Hackenthorpe *Sheff* 85-88; C Rawmarsh w Parkgate 88-89; TV Staveley and Barrow Hill *Derby* from 89. *191 Middlecroft Road, Staveley, Chesterfield S43 3NQ* Chesterfield (0246) 472724

SMITH, Mrs Pauline Frances. b 37. Bris Univ BA58 Lon Univ CertEd59. Sarum & Wells Th Coll 87. d 90. C Cobham *Guildf* from 90. *18 Daymerslea Ridge, Leatherhead, Surrey KT22 8TF* Leatherhead (0372) 376284

SMITH, Peter. d 81 p 83. Hon C Camberwell St Mich w All So w Em *S'wark* from 81. *14 Rignold House, 9 McNeil Road, London SE5 8NU* 071-701 8631

SMITH, Peter. b 36. Keele Univ BA60. Cuddesdon Coll 73. d 75 p 76. C Shrewsbury St Chad *Lich* 75-80; ' Burton St Chad 80-90; P-in-c Berwick w Selmeston and Alciston *Chich* from 90. *The Parsonage, Berwick Polegate, E Sussex BN26 6SR* Alfriston (0323) 870512

SMITH, Peter. b 49. Ex Univ BSc69 PGCE73. Carl Dioc Tr Course. d 82 p 83. NSM Kendal H Trin *Carl* from 82. *10 Castle View, Sedgwick, Kendal, Cumbria LA8 0JL* Sedgwick (05395) 60588

SMITH, Peter Albert. b 26. Keble Coll Ox BA51 MA55. Wells Th Coll 51. d 53 p 54. Bp's Chapl to Students and Lic to Offic *Bradf* 67-73; V Madeley *Lich* 73-77; rtd 81; Lic to Offic *Glouc* from 81. *8 Newport Road, Whitchurch, Shropshire SY13 1QE*

SMITH, Peter Alexander. b 62. UEA BSc83. Westcott Ho Cam 85. d 88 p 89. C Tettenhall Regis *Lich* 88-89; C Cannock from 89. *9 Condor Grove, Heath Hayes, Cannock, Staffs WS12 5YB* Heath Hayes (0543) 270107

SMITH, Peter Anson Stewart. b 16. AKC37. d 39 p 40. V Leavesden All SS *St Alb* 49-73; V Greenhill St Jo *Lon* 73-81; Selection Sec ACCM 75-81; rtd 81; Perm to Offic *Chich* 81-83; P-in-c Brighton St Matthias 83-84; P-in-c Brighton St Pet w Chpl Royal and St Jo 85; P-in-c Brighton St Mich 85-86; P-in-c Moulsecoomb 86-87; TV 88-89; P-in-c Preston 87-88; P-in-c Brighton St Aug and St Sav from 89. *3 West Drive, Brighton BN2 2GD* Brighton (0273) 605042

SMITH, Peter Francis Chasen. b 28. Leeds Univ BA54. Coll of Resurr Mirfield 54. d 56 p 57. C E Dulwich St Clem *S'wark* 56-59; C Sutton St Nic 59-62; C-in-c Wrangbrook w N Elmsall CD *Wakef* 62-68; Chapl St Aid Sch Harrogate 68-85; P-in-c Lower Nidderdale *Ripon* from 85. *The Rectory, Cattal, York YO5 8DX* Boroughbridge (0423) 358662

SMITH, Peter Howard. b 55. St Andr Univ MTh78. Trin Coll Bris 78. d 79 p 80. C Handforth *Ches* 79-82; C Eccleston St Luke *Liv* 82-85; V Leyton St Paul *Chelmsf* 85-91; V Darwen St Barn *Blackb* from 91. *St Barnabas' Vicarage, 68 Park Road, Darwen, Lancs BB3 2LD* Darwen (0254) 72732

SMITH, Peter Howard. b 57. St Jo Coll Dur BSc Selw Coll Cam BA. Ridley Hall Cam 80. d 83 p 84. C Welling *Roch* 83-87; C Hubberston w Herbrandston and Hasguard etc *St D* 87-89; C Hubbertson from 89. *30 Silverstream Drive, Milford Haven, Dyfed SA73 3NL* Milford Haven (0646) 697362

SMITH, Peter James. b 23. K Coll Lon 49. d 53 p 54. Chapl Highcroft Hosp Birm 62-71; C Wolborough w Newton Abbot *Ex* 71-74; C Furze Platt *Ox* 74-78; Travelling Sec Ch Coun for Health and Healing 78-81; P-in-c Bisham *Ox* 82-90; rtd 90. *Church Cottage, Tilford Road, Hindhead, Surrey GU26 6RB* Hindhead (0428) 606782

SMITH, Peter Michael. b 28. Open Univ BA75. K Coll Lon 52. d 56 p 57. C Pokesdown St Jas *Win* 56-59; C Weeke 59-63; V Hutton Roof *Carl* 63-69; V Barrow St Aid 69-72; V Preston Patrick from 72. *St Patrick's Vicarage, Dove Nest Lane, Endmoor, Kendal, Cumbria LA8 0HB* Crooklands (04487) 235

SMITH, Peter William. b 31. Glouc Th Course 74. d 77 p 77. C Coleford w Staunton *Glouc* 77; Hon C 77-87; P-in-c Alderton w Gt Washbourne from 87. *The Rectory, Alderton, Tewkesbury, Glos GL20 8NR* Alderton (024262) 238

SMITH, Philip James. b 32. St Alb Minl Tr Scheme. d 82 p 83. NSM Radlett *St Alb* 82-85; C 85-89; V Codicote from 89. *The Vicarage, 4 Bury Lane, Codicote, Hitchin, Herts SG4 8XT* Stevenage (0438) 820266

SMITH, Philip Lloyd Cyril. b 22. Ch Coll Cam BA47 MA49. Wycliffe Hall Ox 47. d 49 p 50. R Burslem St Jo *Lich* 56-83; P-in-c Burslem St Paul 82-83; R Burslem 83-86; rtd 86; Perm to Offic *Sheff* from

86. *7 Melfort Glen, Sheffield S10 5SU* Sheffield (0742) 304238

SMITH, Canon Philip Morell. b 10. Wadh Coll Ox BA33 MA36. Wells Th Coll 33. d 34 p 35. R Streatham St Leon *S'wark* 64-72; Hon Can S'wark Cathl 68-72; RD Streatham 68-72; R Puttenham and Wanborough *Guildf* 72-78; rtd 78; Perm to Offic *Win* from 78. *43 Windrush Court, Witan Way, Witney, Oxon OX8 6FD* Witney (0993) 779773

SMITH, Philip Sydney Bellman (Brother Luke). b 11. St Cath Soc Ox BA35 DipTh36 MA46. St Steph Ho Ox 35. d 37 p 38. C Storrington *Chich* 39-42; CR from 51; rtd 81. *House of the Resurrection, Mirfield, W Yorkshire WF14 0BN* Mirfield (0924) 494318

SMITH, Raymond Charles William. b 56. K Coll Lon BD78 AKC78. Coll of Resurr Mirfield 79. d 80 p 81. C Iffley *Ox* 80-83; C Wallingford w Crowmarsh Gifford etc 83-86; V Tilehurst St Mary from 86. *St Mary Magdalen's Vicarage, 270 Kentwood Hill, Reading RG3 6DR* Reading (0734) 427234

SMITH, Canon Raymond Douglas. b 31. TCD BA53 MA56 BD56. d 54 p 55. C Belf St Mich *Conn* 54-56; C Ballymacarrett St Patr *D & D* 56-58; CMS Tr Coll Chislehurst 58-60; CMS 60-71; Kenya 60-71; Asst Gen Sec (Hibernian) CMS 71-74; Gen Sec CMS 74-86; CMS Ireland 76-86; Hon Can N Maseno from 78; I Powerscourt w Kilbride and Annacrevy *D & G* from 86. *Powerscourt Rectory, Enniskerry, Bray, Co Wicklow, Irish Republic* Dublin (1) 286-3534

SMITH, Raymond Frederick. b 28. Lon Univ BSc51 Leeds Univ MA65. Oak Hill Th Coll 51. d 53 p 54. V Normanton *Wakef* 66-81; RD Chevet 73-81; R Moreton *Ches* 81-90; rtd 90. *Peniarth Uchaf, Meifod, Powys SY22 6DS* Meifod (093884) 366

SMITH, Raymond Horace David. b 30. FIMLS62. Lon Coll of Div 64. d 67 p 68. C Shoreditch St Leon *Lon* 67-71; Chile 71-80; SAMS 71-73; P-in-c Castle Hedingham *Chelmsf* 80-83; P-in-c Cam St Phil *Ely* 83-86; V 86-91; Chapl Intercon Ch Soc from 91; Ibiza w San Antonio and Santa Eulalia *Eur* from 91. *Apartado 6, 07820 San Antonio Abad, Ibiza, Baleares, Spain* Ibiza (71) 343383

SMITH, Richard. b 47. St D Coll Lamp DipTh75. d 75 p 76. C Aberavon *Llan* 75-78; Ind Chapl 78-81; TV Bournemouth St Pet w St Swithun, St Steph etc *Win* 81-85; Chapl Severalls Hosp Colchester from 85; Chapl Colchester Gen Hosp from 85. *8 Dunncok Way, Longridge Park, Colchester* Colchester (0206) 864733 or 853535

SMITH, Richard Geoffrey. b 46. St Jo Coll Dur BA68 MA69. St Steph Ho Ox BA74 MA78. d 75 p 76. C Brentwood St Thos *Chelmsf* 75-78; C Corringham 78-81; R Shepton Beauchamp w Barrington, Stocklinch etc *B & W* 81-83; TV Redditch, The Ridge *Worc* 85-89; R Teme Valley N from 89. *The Rectory, Lindridge, Tenbury Wells, Worcs WR15 8JQ* Eardiston (058470) 331

SMITH, Richard Harwood. b 34. Sarum Th Coll 57. d 59 p 60. C Kington w Huntington *Heref* 59-62; Br Guiana 62-66; Guyana 66-69; C Broseley w Benthall *Heref* 69-70; Lic to Offic 70-76; USPG Area Sec (Dios Heref and Worc) 70-76; R Wigmore Abbey 76-84; V Eye w Braiseworth and Yaxley *St E* from 84; P-in-c Bedingfield from 84; P-in-c Occold from 84. *The Vicarage, Eye, Suffolk IP23 7AW* Eye (0379) 870277

SMITH, Richard Ian. b 46. Jes Coll Ox BA69 MA80. Ripon Hall Ox 69. d 70 p 71. C Eston *York* 76-79; TV E Ham w Upton Park *Chelmsf* 76-80; R Crook *Dur* 80-86; V Stanley 80-86; V Billingham St Cuth from 86. *St Cuthbert's Vicarage, Billingham, Cleveland TS23 1BW* Stockton-on-Tees (0642) 553236

SMITH, Richard Keith. b 44. Harper Adams Agric Coll NDA69. St Jo Coll Nottm. d 84 p 85. C Wirksworth w Alderwasley, Carsington etc *Derby* 84-87; R Hulland, Atlow, Bradley and Hognaston from 87. *The Vicarage, 16 Eaton Close, Hulland Ward, Derby DE6 3EX* Ashbourne (0335) 70605

SMITH, Richard Michael. b 52. Lon Univ BA74. E Anglian Minl Tr Course 79. d 82 p 83. NSM Cam Ascension *Ely* 82-84; C Rainham *Roch* 84-88; V Southborough St Thos from 88. *The Vicarage, 28 Pennington Road, Southborough, Tunbridge Wells TN4 0SL* Tunbridge Wells (0892) 29624

SMITH, Canon Robert. b 13. Wycliffe Hall Ox 52. d 52 p 53. Home Sec SAMS 61-71; V Pennington *Man* 71-78; rtd 78; NE Area Sec SAMS 79-81; C-in-c Hampstead St Jo Downshire Hill Prop Chpl *Lon* 81-86. *Flat 1, Treetops, Sydney Road, Woodford Green, Essex IG8 0SY* 081-505 2828

SMITH, Robert Harold. b 23. Lon Univ BA49. Oak Hill Th Coll 46. **d** 50 **p** 51. R Upton *Ex* 67-80; P-in-c Fersfield *Nor* 80-81; P-in-c N w S Lopham 80-81; R Bressingham 80-81; R Bressingham w N and S Lopham and Fersfield 81-87; rtd 87; Perm to Offic *Nor* from 87. *22 St Walstan's Road, Taverham, Norwich NR8 6NG*   Norwich (0603) 861285

SMITH, Robert William. b 16. Fitzw Ho Cam BA46 MA51. Ripon Hall Ox. **d** 49 **p** 50. R Hardwick *Ely* 64-73; R Toft w Caldecote 64-72; P-in-c Childerley 64-72; R Toft w Caldecote and Childerley 72-73; rtd 73. *36 Shelford Road, Trumpington, Cambridge CB2 2NA*   Cambridge (0223) 841448

✠**SMITH, Rt Rev Robin Jonathan Norman.** b 36. Worc Coll Ox BA60 MA64. Ridley Hall Cam 60. **d** 62 **p** 63 **c** 90. C Barking St Marg *Chelmsf* 62-67; Chapl Lee Abbey 67-72; V Chesham St Mary *Ox* 72-80; RD Amersham 79-82; TR Gt Chesham 80-90; Hon Can Ch Ch 88-90; Suff Bp Hertf *St Alb* from 90. *Hertford House, Abbey Mill Lane, St Albans AL3 4HE*   St Albans (0727) 866420

SMITH, Rodney Frederic Brittain. b 38. Jes Coll Cam BA61 MA64. St Steph Ho Ox 87. **d** 88 **p** 89. NSM Rainworth *S'well* 88-89; C Basford St Aid 89-91; C Sneinton St Cypr from 91. *41 Cyprus Road, Nottingham NG3 5EB*   Nottingham (0602) 603610

SMITH, Rodney John Boughton. b 19. AKC41. Sarum Th Coll 41. **d** 42 **p** 43. V E Meon *Portsm* 68-84; V Langrish 76-84; rtd 84; Perm to Offic *Ex* from 84. *3 East Orchard, Tipton St John, Sidmouth, Devon EX10 0AN*   Ottery St Mary (040481) 4673

SMITH, Roger Douglas St John. b 12. TD56. Selw Coll Cam BA37 MA41 Jes Coll Ox BA39 MA43 Man Univ BD51. Ripon Hall Ox 37. **d** 39 **p** 40. R Darley w S Darley *Derby* 63-77; rtd 77. *28 Ffordd Penrhwylfa, Prestatyn, Clwyd LL19 8AG*   Prestatyn (0745) 857307

SMITH, Roger Owen. b 50. FRGS Univ of Wales (Abth) BA72 St Chad's Coll Dur CertEd73. S'wark Ord Course 84. **d** 87 **p** 88. NSM Nunhead St Antony w St Silas *S'wark* from 87. *32 Mundania Road, London SE22 0NW*   081-693 4882

SMITH, Roger Stuart. b 41. Chich Th Coll 65. **d** 66 **p** 67. C Garforth *Ripon* 66-70; C Cockley Cley w Gooderstone *Nor* 70-73; C Gt and Lt Cressingham w Threxton 70-73; C Didlington 70-73; C Hilborough w Bodney 70-73; C Oxborough w Foulden and Caldecote 70-73; TV 73-78; V Mendham w Metfield and Withersdale *St E* 78-89; P-in-c Fressingfield w Weybread 86-89; R Fressingfield, Mendham, Metfield, Weybread etc 90-91; RD Hoxne 86-91; R Kelsale-cum-Carlton, Middleton-cum-Fordley etc from 91. *The Rectory, Middleton, Saxmundham, Suffolk IP17 3NR*   Westleton (072873) 421

SMITH, Ronald. b 26. ALCD56. **d** 56 **p** 57. C Gravesend St Jas *Roch* 56-59; C-in-c Istead Rise CD 59-79; V Istead Rise from 79. *The Vicarage, Upper Avenue, Northfleet, Kent DA13 9DA*   Southfleet (047483) 2403

SMITH, Ronald Deric. b 21. Lon Univ BA46. Bps' Coll Cheshunt 59. **d** 61 **p** 62. C W Malling w Offham *Roch* 68-71; V Slade Green 71-78; V Bromley Common St Luke 78-91; rtd 91. *5 Bromley College, London Road, Bromley BR1 1PE*   081-464 0212

SMITH, Ronald George. b 34. St Jo Coll Dur BA56 Bede Coll Dur PGCE73. Cranmer Hall Dur DipTh58. **d** 58 **p** 59. C Shirley *Win* 58-60; C Basingstoke 60-63; R Wolviston *Dur* 63-74; Teacher Hartlepool 74-78; Lic to Offic 74-78; Hd of Relig Studies Loughton Co High Sch 78-80; Perm to Offic *Chelmsf* 78-80; V Harold Hill St Geo 80-86; V Elmstead from 86. *The Vicarage, Church Road, Elmstead, Colchester, Essex CO7 7AW*   Wivenhoe (0206) 822431

SMITH, Ronald James. b 36. Linc Th Coll 73. **d** 75 **p** 76. C Bilborough St Jo *S'well* 75-78; P-in-c Colwick 78-81; R 81-85; P-in-c Netherfield 78-81; V 81-85; C Worksop Priory 85-90; TV Langley and Parkfield *Man* from 90. *316 Windermere Road, Middleton, Manchester M24 4LA*   061-654 8562

SMITH, Ronald William. b 16. ACIS40 FCIS61 Open Univ BA85. Worc Ord Coll 63. **d** 65 **p** 66. V Stretton Grandison w Ashperton, Canon Frome etc *Heref* 71-81; rtd 82; Perm to Offic *Heref* from 82. *17 Knapp Close, Ledbury, Herefordshire HR8 1AW*   Ledbury (0531) 4620

SMITH, Ronald William. b 45. St Jo Coll York CertEd67. Chich Th Coll 70. **d** 73 **p** 74. C Scarborough St Martin *York* 73-76; C Stainton-in-Cleveland 76-80; V Coatham 80-89; V Brookfield from 89. *89 Low Lane, Brookfield, Middlesbrough, Cleveland TS5 8EF*   Middlesbrough (0642) 592136

SMITH, Rowan Quentin. b 43. AKC66. **d** 67 **p** 68. S Africa 67-77 and from 80; C Plumstead All SS *S'wark* 71-72; CR from 80. *Bishopscourt, 16-20 Bishopscourt Drive, Claremont, 7700 South Africa*   Cape Town (21) 797-5476

SMITH, Roy Leonard. b 36. Clifton Th Coll 63. **d** 66 **p** 67. C Clapham St Jas *S'wark* 66-70; C Kennington St Mark 70-74; C-in-c Southall Em CD *Lon* 74-83; V Stonebridge St Mich from 83. *St Michael's Vicarage, Hillside, London NW10 8LB*   081-965 7443

SMITH, Royston. b 55. E Midl Min Tr Course 87. **d** 90. NSM Shirland *Derby* from 90. *40 Birkinstyle Lane, Shirland, Derbyshire DE5 6BS*   Alfreton (0773) 836331

SMITH, Royston Burleigh. b 26. St Deiniol's Hawarden 76. **d** 79 **p** 80. C Prestatyn *St As* 79-83; V Kerry and Llanmerewig 83-90; C Rhyl w Rhyl St Ann 90-91; rtd 91. *18 Garth Clarendon, Kinmel Bay, Rhyl, Clwyd*

SMITH, Canon Stanley. b 10. St D Coll Lamp BA35. **d** 35 **p** 36. C Beamish *Dur* 35-37; Miss to Seamen 37-38 and 49-54; S Africa 38-49; Canada from 54. *Apartment 304, 2710 Lonsdale Avenue, Vancouver, Canada, V7N 3J1*

SMITH, Stephen. b 53. Leeds Poly CQSW78. Sarum & Wells Th Coll 87. **d** 89 **p** 90. C Redcar *York* from 89. *34 Ings Road, Redcar, Cleveland TS10 2DL*   Middlesbrough (0642) 480426

SMITH, Stephen John. b 46. Kelham Th Coll 65. **d** 69 **p** 70. C Warsop *S'well* 69-73; C Heaton Ch Ch *Man* 73-75; V Bolton St Bede 75-78; R Bilborough w Strelley *S'well* 78-84; R E Leake from 84; P-in-c Costock from 84; P-in-c Rempstone from 84; P-in-c Stanford on Soar from 84. *The Rectory, Bateman Road, East Leake, Loughborough, Leics LE12 6LN*   East Leake (0509) 852228

SMITH, Stephen John. b 55. Lon Univ BD80. Trin Coll Bris 77. **d** 81 **p** 82. C Fulham St Matt *Lon* 81-86; C Stoke Gifford *Bris* 86-90; TV from 90. *The Vicarage, Mautravers Close, Bradley Stoke, Bristol BS12 8ED*   Bristol (0272) 312222

SMITH, Stephen John Stanyon. b 49. Sussex Univ BA81 Birm Univ MSocSc83. Westcott Ho Cam 83. **d** 85 **p** 86. C Four Oaks *Birm* 85-89; USA from 89. *Address temp unknown*

SMITH, Steven Barnes. b 60. Cov Poly BA83 Leeds Univ BA86. Coll of Resurr Mirfield 84. **d** 87 **p** 88. C Darlington St Mark w St Paul *Dur* 87-89; C Prescot *Liv* from 89. *St Mary's House, 2A West Street, Prescot, Merseyside L34 1LE*   051-426 0716

SMITH, Steven Gerald Crosland. b 48. Linc Th Coll 82. **d** 84 **p** 85. Chapl St Jo Sch Tiffield Northants 84-87; C Towcester w Easton Neston *Pet* 84-87; P-in-c Kings Heath 87-89; V from 89. *The Vicarage, Church Green, Northampton NN5 7LS*   Northampton (0604) 751778

SMITH, Sydney John. b 21. Univ of Wales (Lamp) BA48. **d** 49 **p** 50. V Scarborough St Luke *York* 59-86; rtd 86. *309 Scalby Road, Scarborough, N Yorkshire YO12 6TF*   Scarborough (0723) 378736

SMITH, Sydney Robert. b 17. St Jo Coll Dur LTh39 BA40 ALCD39. **d** 40 **p** 41. V Fazakerley St Nath *Liv* 64-75; V Westhead 75-82; rtd 82; Perm to Offic *Liv* from 82. *59 Crosshall Brow, Ormskirk, Lancs L40 6JD*   Ormskirk (0695) 75285

SMITH, Terence. b 38. Lon Univ DipTh69. Tyndale Hall Bris 67. **d** 69 **p** 70. C Cheylesmore *Cov* 69-71; C Leamington Priors St Paul 71-74; V Halliwell St Paul *Man* 74-75; Lect Brunel Univ 75-86; R Medstead cum Wield *Win* from 86. *The Rectory, Medstead, Alton, Hants GU34 5LT*   Alton (0420) 62050

SMITH, Terrence Gordon. b 34. TD83. MCSP58 SRN60. St Mich Coll Llan 68. **d** 70 **p** 71. C Gellygaer *Llan* 70-73; CF (TA) from 72; C Aberavon *Llan* 73-75; V Pontlottyn w Fochriw 75-77; V Kenfig Hill 77-84; V Dyffryn from 84. *The Vicarage, Dyffryn, Bryncoch, Neath, W Glam SA10 7AZ*   Skewen (0792) 814237

SMITH, Thomas Robert Selwyn. b 12. Bps' Coll Cheshunt 35. **d** 37 **p** 38. C Workington St Mich *Carl* 37-40; C Wilton Place St Paul *Lon* 40-41; C Cheshunt *St Alb* 41-44; V Dalston *Carl* 44-55; V Box *Bris* from 55. *The Vicarage, Box, Corsham, Wilts SN14 9NR*   Box (0225) 742405

SMITH, Thomas Roger. b 48. Cant Sch of Min 77. **d** 80 **p** 81. NSM Folkestone St Sav *Cant* 80-82; NSM Lyminge w Paddlesworth, Stanford w Postling etc 82-85; Chapl Cant Sch of Min 82-91; R Biddenden and Smarden *Cant* 86-91; P-in-c Totnes and Berry Pomeroy *Ex* from 91. *The Rectory, Crosspark, Bridgetown, Totnes, Devon TQ9 5BQ*   Totnes (0803) 864836

SMITH, Tony. b 23. Roch Th Coll 62. **d** 64 **p** 65. V Hadlow *Roch* 67-78; R Wrotham 78-89; RD Shoreham 80-89; rtd 89. *25 Wye Road, Borough Green, Sevenoaks, Kent TN15 8DX*   Borough Green (0732) 885884

SMITH, Trevor Andrew. b 60. St Jo Coll Dur BA86. Cranmer Hall Dur 83. **d** 87 **p** 88. C Guisborough *York* 87-90; C Northallerton w Kirby Sigston from 90. *8 Friarage Mount, Northallerton, N Yorkshire DL6 1LW* Northallerton (0609) 780975

SMITH, Trevor Bernard. b 33. **d** 64 **p** 65. C Bispham *Blackb* 64-66; C Chesham St Mary *Ox* 66-68; Perm to Offic from 90. *235 Whitecross, Wootton, Abingdon, Berks OX13 6BW*

SMITH, Vernon Hemingway. b 33. St Alb Minl Tr Scheme 83. **d** 86 **p** 87. NSM Leighton Buzzard w Eggington, Hockliffe etc *St Alb* from 86. *41 Orion Way, Leighton Buzzard, Beds LU7 8XJ* Leighton Buzzard (0525) 377391

SMITH, Walter. b 37. Westcott Ho Cam 67. **d** 69 **p** 70. C N Hull St Mich *York* 69-72; C Whitby 72-74; V Newington w Dairycoates 74-77; P-in-c Skipton Bridge 77-78; P-in-c Baldersby 77-78; TV Thirsk 77-88; P-in-c Topcliffe w Dalton and Dishforth 82-87; V Lythe w Ugthorpe from 88. *The Vicarage, Lythe, Whitby, N Yorkshire YO21 3RL* Whitby (0947) 83479

SMITH, Miss Wendy Hamlyn. b 41. ALA70 Open Univ BA85. Ridley Hall Cam 85. **d** 87. C Stroud H Trin *Glouc* 87-90 and from 91; Australia 90-91. *40 Valley View Road, Stroud, Glos GL5 1HP* Stroud (0453) 764447

SMITH, William Carrington. b 16. Selw Coll Cam BA40 MA44. S'wark Ord Course 63. **d** 66 **p** 67. NSM Nunhead St Antony *S'wark* 66-83; rtd 83; Perm to Offic *Roch* from 83. *5 Reed Street, Cliffe, Rochester, Kent ME3 7UN* Medway (0634) 221898

SMITH, William Joseph Thomas. b 20. Chich Th Coll 54. **d** 55 **p** 56. V Boreham *Chelmsf* 65-90; rtd 90. *7 Trelawn, Church Road, Boreham, Chelmsford CM3 3EF* Chelmsford (0245) 466930

SMITH, William Melvyn. b 47. K Coll Lon BD69 AKC69 PGCE70. St Aug Coll Cant 71. **d** 71 **p** 72. C Kingswinford H Trin *Lich* 71-73; Hon C Coseley Ch Ch 73-74; C Wednesbury St Paul Wood Green 75-78; V Coseley St Chad 78-91; RD Himley from 83; TR Wordsley from 91. *The Rectory, 13 Dunsley Drive, Wordsley, Stourbridge, W Midlands DY8 8RA* Kingswinford (0384) 277215

SMITH, Willie Ernest. b 1900. LRCP44 MRCS44 Leeds Univ MA34. St Aid Birkenhead 33. **d** 33 **p** 34. Lic to Offic *Wakef* 46-73; rtd 73. *Ryder Cottage, Main Street, East Keswick, Leeds LS17 9EU* Collingham Bridge (0937) 73483

SMITH-CAMERON, Canon Ivor Gill. b 29. Madras Univ BA50 MA52. Coll of Resurr Mirfield. **d** 54 **p** 55. C Rumboldswyke *Chich* 54-58; Chapl Imp Coll *Lon* 58-72; Dioc Missr *S'wark* from 72; Can Res S'wark Cathl from 72. *100 Prince of Wales Drive, London SW11 4BD* 071-622 3809

SMITHIES, Edwin Henry. b 23. Leeds Univ DBS47. **d** 60 **p** 61. Hd Master Highfields Gr Sch Ossett 62-73; Lic to Offic *Wakef* 68-73; C Beeston *Ripon* 73-79; Perm to Offic 79-81; Lic to Offic 81-83; Hon C Leeds St Pet 83-90; Hon C Leeds City *Ripon* from 90. *8 Noster View, Leeds LS11 8QQ* Leeds (0532) 770154

✠**SMITHSON, Rt Rev Alan.** b 36. Qu Coll Ox BA62 MA68. Qu Coll Birm DipTh64. **d** 64 **p** 65 **c** 90. C Skipton Ch Ch *Bradf* 64-68; C Ox St Mary V w St Cross and St Pet *Ox* 68-72; Chapl Qu Coll Ox 69-72; Chapl Reading Univ *Ox* 72-77; V Bracknell 77-83; TR 83-84; Can Res Carl Cathl *Carl* 84-90; Dir of Tr Inst 84-90; Dioc Dir of Tr 85-90; Suff Bp Jarrow *Dur* from 90. *The Old Vicarage, Hallgarth, Pittington, Co Durham DH6 1AB* 091-372 0225

SMITHSON, Michael John. b 47. FRGS Newc Univ BA68 Lon Univ BD79 Dur Univ PGCE. Trin Coll Bris 76. **d** 79 **p** 80. C S Mimms Ch Ch *Lon* 79-81; Support and Public Relations Sec UCCF 82-84; R Frating w Thorrington *Chelmsf* 84-88; V Portsea St Luke *Portsm* from 88. *St Luke's Vicarage, Greetham Street, Southsea, Hants PO5 4LH* Portsmouth (0705) 826073

SMITS, Eric. b 29. **d** 61 **p** 62. C Thornaby on Tees St Paul *York* 61-66; R Brotton Parva from 66. *The Rectory, Brotton, Saltburn-by-the-Sea, Cleveland TS12 2PJ* Guisborough (0287) 76275

SMOUT, Michael John. b 37. St Pet Coll Ox BA61 MA75 DipTh62 Lon Univ BD64. Lon Coll of Div 62. **d** 64 **p** 65. C Toxteth Park St Philemon w St Silas *Liv* 64-69; C Everton St Sav 69-70; Missr E Everton Gp of Chs 70-74; V Everton St Sav w St Cuth 74-79; R Aughton St Mich from 79; RD Ormskirk 82-89; AD from 89. *The Rectory, 10 Church Lane, Ormskirk, Lancs L39 6SB* Aughton Green (0695) 423204

SMURTHWAITE, William. b 25. Edin Th Coll 54. **d** 57 **p** 58. Miss to Seamen 59-72; Lic to Offic *Linc* 65-72; R Ladybank *St And* 73-90; R Cupar 73-90; rtd 90. *10 Park View, Balmullo, St Andrews KY16 0DN*

SMYTH, Anthony Irwin. b 40. TCD BA63 MA66. Clifton Th Coll 64. **d** 66 **p** 67. C Worthing St Geo *Chich* 66-69; Chile 70-75; C Woodley *Ox* 76-80; V St Leonards St Ethelburga *Chich* from 80. *31 St Saviour's Road, St Leonards-on-Sea, E Sussex TN38 0AS* Hastings (0424) 421488

SMYTH, Francis George. b 20. Ridley Hall Cam 64. **d** 65 **p** 66. C Ormskirk *Liv* 65-70; V Bicton *Lich* 70-90; Chapl HM Pris Shrewsbury 71-90; rtd 90. *The Vicarage, Shrewsbury SY8 6DL* Shrewsbury (0743) 60030

SMYTH, Gordon William. b 47. Open Univ BA. St Jo Coll Nottm 81. **d** 83 **p** 84. C St Keverne *Truro* 83-86; V Landrake w St Erney and Botus Fleming from 86. *The Vicarage, School Road, Landrake, Saltash, Cornwall PL12 5EA* Landrake (0752) 851801

SMYTH, James Desmond. b 12. TCD BA36 MA39. **d** 36 **p** 37. R Wappenham w Abthorpe and Slapton *Pet* 58-77; rtd 77; Perm to Offic *Glouc* from 79. *The Ferns, Vicarage Lane, Frampton on Severn, Gloucester GL2 7EE* Gloucester (0452) 740744

SMYTH, Kenneth James. b 44. TCD BA67 MA72. **d** 68 **p** 69. C Ban Abbey *D & D* 68-71; C Holywood 71-74; I Gilnahirk 74-82; I Newtownards w Movilla Abbey 82-89; I Newtownards from 89. *27 Regent Street, Newtownards, Co Down* Newtownards (0247) 812527

SMYTH, Robert Andrew Laine (Brother Anselm). b 30. Trin Coll Cam BA53 MA59. **d** 79 **p** 80. SSF from 53; Min Prov Eur Province SSF from 79; Lic to Offic *Linc* from 84. *St Francis House, Normanby Road, Scunthorpe, S Humberside DN15 6AR* Scunthorpe (0724) 853899

SMYTH, Trevor Cecil. b 45. Chich Th Coll 66. **d** 69 **p** 70. C Cookridge H Trin *Ripon* 69-73; C Middleton St Mary 73-75; C Felpham w Middleton *Chich* 75-78; P-in-c Wellington Ch Ch *Lich* 78-80; V 80-86; P-in-c W Wittering *Chich* 86; R W Wittering and Birdham w Itchenor from 86. *The Rectory, Cakeham Road, West Wittering, Chichester, W Sussex PO20 8AD* Birdham (0243) 514057

SMYTH, William Ernest. b 23. Sarum & Wells Th Coll 77. **d** 77 **p** 78. C Plympton St Mary *Ex* 77-80; R Beaford, Roborough and St Giles in the Wood 80-83; V Hook *S'wark* 83-87; rtd 87; P-in-c Thrandeston, Stuston and Brome w Oakley *St E* 87-88; Perm to Offic *Nor* 88. *Winsford, The Ridgeway, Ottery St Mary, Devon* Ottery St Mary (040481) 3319

SMYTHE, Angela Mary. b 53. St Jo Coll Nottm 85. **d** 87. Par Dn Forest Town *S'well* 87-90; Dn-in-c Pleasley Hill from 90. *16 Douglas Road, Forest Town, Mansfield, Notts NG19 0LT* Mansfield (0623) 643083

SMYTHE, Harry Reynolds. b 23. Sydney Univ BA45 St Pet Hall Ox BA48 MA51 Ch Ch Ox DPhil51. ACT ThL Moore Th Coll Sydney 43. **d** 51 **p** 53. C Tavistock and Gulworthy *Ex* 51-52; C Ex St Mary Arches 53; Australia 54-70; Dir Angl Cen Rome 70-81; Lib Pusey Ho from 81; Lic to Offic *Ox* from 83. *Pusey House, Oxford OX1 3LZ* Oxford (0865) 278415

SMYTHE, Paul Rodney. b 05. Mert Coll Ox BA28 MA31 BD37. Ripon Hall Ox 34. **d** 35 **p** 36. V Horningsea *Ely* 45-83; rtd 83. *82 High Street, Horningsea, Cambridge CB5 9SH* Cambridge (0223) 860392

SMYTHE, Peter John. b 32. **d** 58 **p** 59. C Maidstone All SS *Cant* 58-62; V Barrow St Jo *Carl* 62-65; V Billesdon w Goadby and Rolleston *Leic* 65-71. *Address temp unknown*

SMYTHE, Ronald Ingoldsby Meade. b 25. Qu Coll Ox BA46 MA48. Ely Th Coll 51. **d** 54 **p** 55. V Hatf Heath *Chelmsf* 62-78; Hon C Writtle 78-81; Hon C Writtle w Highwood 81-85; P-in-c Whatfield w Semer, Nedging and Naughton *St E* 85-89; Dir Ipswich Concern Counselling Cen from 85; Dioc Adv for Counselling 85-89; Dioc Adv for Counselling and Past Care from 89; rtd 90. *94 Wangford Road, Reydon, Southwold, Suffolk IP18 6NY* Southwold (0502) 723413

SNAITH, Bryan Charles. b 33. Univ of Wales BSc55. St Mich Coll Llan 61. **d** 61 **p** 62. C Bargoed w Brithdir *Llan* 61-62; C Llanishen and Lisvane 62-71; Ind Chapl *Dur* 71-76; Ind Chapl *Worc* 76-81; P-in-c Stone 76-81; C Chaddesley Corbett 77-81; Ind Chapl *Chelmsf* from 81; TV Colchester St Leon, St Mary Magd and St Steph 81-86. *2 Colvin Close, Colchester CO3 4BS* Colchester (0206) 767793

SNAPE, Sqn Ldr Bernard Reginald Roy. b 08. OBE56. Sarum Th Coll 69. **d** 69 **p** 70. C W Leigh *Portsm* 69-71; V Arreton 71-75; rtd 75. *23 Shady Bower Close, Salisbury SP1 2RQ* Salisbury (0722) 328645

SNAPE, Harry. b 21. Qu Coll Birm 76. **d** 78 **p** 79. NSM Highters Heath *Birm* 78-82; NSM Stirchley 82-84; TV Corby SS Pet and Andr w Gt and Lt Oakley *Pet* 84-89; rtd 89. *9 Church Vale Road, Bexhill-on-Sea, E Sussex TN40 2ED* Bexhill-on-Sea (0424) 216925

SNASDELL, Antony John. b 39. St Chad's Coll Dur BA63 DipTh65. **d** 65 **p** 66. C Boston *Linc* 65-70; Hon C Worksop Priory *S'well* 71-82; P-in-c Gt Massingham *Nor* 82-84; P-in-c Harpley 82-84; P-in-c Lt Massingham 82-84; R Gt w Lt Massingham and Harpley 84-91; R Thorpe from 91. *The Rectory, 56A Thunder Lane, Norwich NR7 0JW* Norwich (0603) 33578

SNEARY, Michael William. b 38. Brentwood Coll of Educn CertEd71 Open Univ BA79. Ely Th Coll 61. **d** 64 **p** 65. C Loughton St Jo *Chelmsf* 64-67; Youth Chapl 67-70; Hon C Ingrave 70-71; Harold Hill Gr Sch Essex 71-74; Ivybridge Sch 74-76; Coombe Dean Sch Plymouth from 76. *The Lodge, Lower Port View, Saltash, Cornwall PL12 4BY*

SNEATH, Canon Sidney Dennis. b 23. Leeds Univ BA50. Bps' Coll Cheshunt 50. **d** 52 **p** 53. C Nuneaton St Mary *Cov* 52-59; C-in-c Galley Common Stockingford CD 59-68; V Camp Hill w Galley Common from 68; Hon Can Cov Cathl from 80. *The Vicarage, Cedar Road, Nuneaton, Warks CV10 9DL* Chapel End (0203) 392523

SNELGAR, Canon Douglas John. b 17. DSC45. Trin Hall Cam BA48 MA53. Westcott Ho Cam 48. **d** 50 **p** 51. C Fareham SS Pet and Paul *Portsm* 50-53; C Ventnor St Cath 53-57; C Ventnor H Trin 53-57; V Steep from 57; Hon Can Portsm Cathl from 85; P-in-c Froxfield w Privett from 88. *The Vicarage, Steep, Petersfield, Hants GU32 2DB* Petersfield (0730) 64282

✠**SNELGROVE, Rt Rev Donald George.** b 25. TD72. Qu Coll Cam BA48 MA53. Ridley Hall Cam. **d** 50 **p** 51 **c** 81. C Oakwood St Thos *Lon* 50-53; C Hatch End St Anselm 53-56; V Dronfield *Derby* 56-62; CF (TA) 60-73; V Hessle *York* 63-70; RD Hull 67-70 and 81-90; Can and Preb York Minster 69-81; Adn E Riding 70-81; R Cherry Burton 70-78; Suff Bp Hull from 81. *Hullen House, Woodfield Lane, Hessle, N Humberside HU13 0ES* Hull (0482) 649019 or Barton-on-Humber (0652) 34484

SNELL, Brigitte. b 43. BA. E Anglian Minl Tr Course 86. **d** 89. NSM Cam Gt St Mary w St Mich *Ely* from 89. *45 London Road, Cambridge CB2 5QQ* Cambridge (0223) 870542

SNELL, James Osborne. b 13. Selw Coll Cam BA35 MA39. Ely Th Coll 35. **d** 36 **p** 37. R Ramsgate H Trin *Cant* 69-78; rtd 79; Perm to Offic *Cant* from 79. *3 Glebe Close, St Margarets-at-Cliffe, Dover, Kent CT15 6AF* Dover (0304) 852210

SNELL, William Graham Brooking. b 14. Lon Coll of Div 36. **d** 39 **p** 40. R Ashby w Oby, Thurne and Clippesby *Nor* 57-79; rtd 79; Perm to Offic *Nor* from 79. *17 Park Home, Burgh Hall, Fleggburgh, Great Yarmouth NR29 3AF* Fleggburgh (049377) 369776

SNELLGROVE, Frederic Mortimer. b 06. Lon Univ BSc28. Ridley Hall Cam 28. **d** 29 **p** 30. R Bergh Apton w Yelverton *Nor* 60-72; rtd 72; Perm to Offic *Chich* from 74. *64 Rugby Road, Worthing, W Sussex BN11 5NB* Worthing (0903) 505120

SNELLGROVE, Martin Kenneth. b 54. City Univ BSc77 CEng80 MICE84. Aston Tr Scheme 85 Ridley Hall Cam 87. **d** 89 **p** 90. C Four Oaks *Birm* from 89. *12 Clarence Gardens, Sutton Coldfield, W Midlands B74 4AP* 021-308 6279

SNELLING, Brian. b 40. Oak Hill Th Coll DipTh68. **d** 69 **p** 70. C Slough *Ox* 69-72; C Hoole *Ches* 72-76; V Millbrook 76-80; V Homerton St Luke *Lon* 80-90; R Marks Tey w Aldham and Lt Tey *Chelmsf* from 90. *The Rectory, Church Lane, Marks Tey, Colchester CO6 1LW* Colchester (0206) 210396

SNELLING, Stanley Alfred. b 03. Lich Th Coll 54. **d** 55 **p** 56. V Furneux Pelham w Stocking Pelham *St Alb* 62-76; rtd 77; Perm to Offic *St Alb* from 77. *Old School House, Furneux Pelham, Buntingford, Herts SG9 0LH* Brent Pelham (0279) 777418

SNELSON, William Thomas. b 45. Ex Coll Ox BA67 Fitzw Coll Cam BA69 MA75. Westcott Ho Cam 67. **d** 69 **p** 70. C Godalming *Guildf* 69-72; C Leeds St Pet *Ripon* 72-75; V Chapel Allerton 75-81; V Bardsey from 81; Dioc Ecum Officer from 86. *The Vicarage, Wood Acre Lane, Bardsey, Leeds LS17 9DG* Collingham Bridge (0937) 72243

SNOOK, Walter Currie. b 39. Lon Univ DipTh66. Tyndale Hall Bris 64. **d** 67 **p** 68. C Cromer *Nor* 67-70; C Macclesfield St Mich *Ches* 70-74; R Postwick *Nor* 74-87; Chapl Jas Paget Hosp Gorleston from 87. *104 Lackford*

Close, Brundall, Norwich NR13 5NL Norwich (0603) 713949

SNOW, Campbell Martin Spencer. b 35. JP. Roch Th Coll 65. **d** 67 **p** 68. C Dover St Mary *Cant* 67-72; C Birchington w Acol 72-74; V Reculver 74-80; P-in-c New Addington 80-81; V 81-84; V New Addington *S'wark* 85-87; CF (ACF) 84-87; CF (TA) from 87; P-in-c Caterham Valley *S'wark* from 87. *Caterham Valley Vicarage, 51 Crescent Road, Caterham, Surrey CR3 6LH* Caterham (0883) 343188

SNOW, Ven Edward Brian. b 22. CITC. **d** 65 **p** 66. C Cork H Trin w St Paul, St Pet and St Mary *C, C & R* 65-67; C Dun Laoghaire *D & G* 67-72; Hon CV Ch Ch Cathl Dub 69-72; I Rathkeale *L & K* 72-77; I Kilmallock w Kilflynn, Kilfinane, Knockaney etc from 77; Adn Limerick from 81. *The Rectory, Kilmallock, Co Limerick, Irish Republic* Kilmallock (63) 98334

SNOW, Frank. b 31. Lon Univ BD57. **d** 83 **p** 84. Hon C Tweedmouth *Newc* 83-86; Hon C Berwick H Trin 86-89; Hon C Berwick St Mary 86-89; Hon C Berwick H Trin and St Mary 89-90; R Gt Smeaton w Appleton Wiske and Birkby etc *Ripon* from 90. *Great Smeaton Rectory, Northallerton, N Yorkshire DL6 2EP* Great Smeaton (060981) 205

SNOW, Glyn Francis. b 53. Dur Univ BA74 CertEd. St Steph Ho Ox 76. **d** 78 **p** 79. C Pontnewynydd *Mon* 78-82; TV Ebbw Vale 82-91. *25 William Street, Cwmfelinfach, Ynysddu, Newport, Gwent NP1 7GY* Ynysddu (0495) 201354

SNOW, Miss Patricia Margaret. b 21. St Mich Ho Ox 51. **dss** 72 **d** 87. W Ham *Chelmsf* 72-78; Acomb St Steph *York* 78-83; rtd 83. *4 Grove Terrace, Acomb, York YO2 3BP* York (0904) 791270

SNOW, Peter David. b 37. **d** 64 **p** 65. C Kingshurst *Birm* 64-66; USA from 67. *927 36th Avenue, Seattle, Washington 98122, USA*

SNOW, Peter Normington. b 23. St Jo Coll Ox BA48 MA52. Ely Th Coll 48. **d** 50 **p** 51. V Emscote *Cov* 56-89; RD Warw 67-77; rtd 89. *3 Park Lane, Harbury, Leamington Spa, Warks CV33 9HX* Harbury (0926) 612410

SNOW, Richard John. b 57. Bris Univ BSc80. **d** 90 **p** 91. C Preston Plucknett *B & W* from 90. *5 Lime Kiln, Abbey Manor Park, Yeovil, Somerset BA21 3RW* Yeovil (0935) 22553

SNOW, William George Sinclair. b 08. Edin Univ MA31 PhD40. Edin Th Coll 32. **d** 33 **p** 34. V Bognor *Chich* 52-76; rtd 76; Perm to Offic *Chich* from 76. *25 Merton Avenue, Rustington, Littlehampton, W Sussex BN16 2EQ* Rustington (0903) 771610

SNOW, Canon William Harvey. b 13. Univ Coll Dur BA36 LTh36 MA39. Qu Coll Birm 32. **d** 36 **p** 37. R Cromwell *S'well* 61-78; V N and S Muskham 61-78; Hon Can S'well Minster 71-78; P-in-c Caunton 76-78; rtd 78; Perm to Offic *S'well* from 79. *Grange Lodge, Caunton, Newark, Notts NG23 6AB* Caunton (063686) 382

SNOWBALL, Michael Sydney. b 44. Dur Univ BA70 MA72 St Jo Coll Dur DipTh72. **d** 72 **p** 73. C Stockton St Pet *Dur* 72-75; C Dunston St Nic 75-77; C Dunston 77-78; C Darlington St Jo 78-81; V Chilton from 81. *1 New South View, Chilton, Ferryhill, Co Durham DL17 0PS* Bishop Auckland (0388) 720243

SNOWSELL, Raymond Ernest Elijah. b 15. Wycliffe Hall Ox 67. **d** 68 **p** 69. V Oaks (Charnwood Forest) *Leic* 71-79; V Oaks in Charnwood and Copt Oak 79-80; rtd 80; Perm to Offic *B & W* from 81. *Charnwood, Castle Street, Keinton Mandeville, Somerton, Somerset TA11 6DX* Somerton (0458) 223225

SOAR, Arthur Leslie. b 20. ACII. Linc Th Coll 82. **d** 83 **p** 84. NSM Chilham *Cant* 83-86; NSM Crundale w Godmersham 86-90; NSM Elmsted w Hastingleigh 86-90; rtd 90; Perm to Offic *Cant* from 90. *9 Northdowns Close, Old Wives Lees, Canterbury, Kent CT4 8BP* Canterbury (0227) 730205

SOAR, Martin William. b 54. Lon Univ BSc. Wycliffe Hall Ox 86. **d** 88 **p** 89. C Henfynyw w Aberaeron and Llanddewi Aber-arth *St D* from 88. *Hillcrest, Vicarage Hill, Aberaeron, Dyfed SA46 0DY* Aberaeron (0545) 570769

SOBEY, Canon Haydn Norman. b 28. Univ of Wales (Lamp) BA52 Qu Coll Cam BA54 MA56 Univ of W Indies DipEd74. St Mich Coll Llan 54. **d** 55 **p** 56. C Port Talbot St Theodore *Llan* 55-58; Trinidad and Tobago 58-78; Hon Can Trinidad from 71; V Port Talbot St Agnes *Llan* 78-89; R Gellygaer from 89. *The Rectory, Church Road, Gelligaer, Hengoed, M Glam CF8 8FW* Hengoed (0443) 830303

SODOR AND MAN, Bishop of. *See* JONES, Rt Rev Noel Debroy

SOGA, Hector Ian. b 47. **d** 88 **p** 89. NSM Dollar *St And* from 88. *2 Harviestoun Road, Dollar, Clackmannanshire FK14 7HF* Dollar (0259) 43169

SOLOMON, Arthur Creagh. b 33. ACT LTh Ch Coll Hobart. **d** 62 **p** 63. Australia 62-67; C Addiscombe St Mildred *Cant* 67-68; Chapl Pierrepont Sch Frensham 69-72; R Clifton Campville w Chilcote *Lich* from 72; P-in-c Thorpe Constantine from 83. *The Rectory, Clifton Campville, Tamworth, Staffs B79 0AP* Clifton Campville (082786) 257

SOLOMON, Gerald Tankerville Norris. b 12. Lon Univ BA36. Sarum Th Coll 37. **d** 39 **p** 40. R Corsley *Sarum* 63-78; rtd 78. *The Old Forge, Hindon, Salisbury SP3 6DR* Hindon (074789) 255

SOLTAU, Bernard Alick. b 08. Trin Coll Ox BA32 MA50. K Coll Lon 49. **d** 50 **p** 51. V Stubbings *Ox* 53-90; rtd 90. *Stubbings Vicarage, Henley Lane, Maidenhead, Berks SL6 6QW* Maidenhead (0628) 822966

SOMERS-EDGAR, Carl John. b 46. Otago Univ BA69. St Steph Ho Ox 72. **d** 75 **p** 76. C Northwood H Trin *Lon* 75-79; C St Marylebone All SS 79-82; V Liscard St Mary w St Columba *Ches* 82-85; New Zealand from 85. *St Peter's Vicarage, 57 Baker Street, Caversham, Dunedin, New Zealand* Christchurch (3) 455-3961

SOMERS-SMITH, Leslie John. b 17. **d** 61 **p** 63. Australia 61-70; Perm to Offic *Chich* 70-71; C Mon 71-72; Perm to Offic *Win* from 72. *26 Walders Road, Rustington, W Sussex BN16 3PE* Rustington (0903) 770184

SOMERVELL, Katharine Mary. b 30. Edin Univ CSocStuds51. W Midl Minl Tr Course 86. **d** 88. Par Dn Caldmore *Lich* from 88. *56 Glebe Street, Walsall, W Midlands WS1 3NX* Walsall (0922) 22868

SOMERVILLE, John William Kenneth. b 38. St D Coll Lamp 60. **d** 63 **p** 64. C Rhosllanerchrugog *St As* 63-67; C Llangystenyn 67-70; V Gorsedd 70-77; V Gorsedd w Brynford and Ysceifiog from 77. *The Vicarage, Gorsedd, Holywell, Clwyd CH8 8QZ* Holywell (0352) 711675

SOMES, Arthur Marston. b 97. **d** 46 **p** 47. V Gt w Lt Oakley *Pet* 54-67; rtd 67; Perm to Offic *Pet* from 86. *St Christopher's Home, Abington Park Crescent, Northampton NN3 3AL* Northampton (0604) 37125

SONG, James. b 32. Lon Coll of Div 57. **d** 60 **p** 61. C Virginia Water *Guildf* 60-63; C Portman Square St Paul *Lon* 63-66; V Matlock Bath *Derby* 66-76; V Woking St Jo *Guildf* from 76; RD Woking from 87. *St John's Vicarage, St John's Hill Road, Woking, Surrey GU21 1RQ* Woking (0483) 761253

SOOSAINAYAGAM, Xavier. b 50. S'wark Ord Course 89 St Paul's Sem Trichy BTh77 Sri Lanka Nat Sem BPh73. **d** 76 **p** 77. In RC Ch 76-89; C Streatham St Leon *S'wark* from 89. *47 Fernwood Avenue, London SW16 1RD* 081-769 6239

SOPER, Brian Malcolm. b 31. Lon Univ BSc53 Mansf Coll Ox DipTh56. Ripon Hall Ox 63. **d** 63 **p** 64. C Platt *Roch* 63-64; Chapl K Sch Roch 64-72; Chapl Repton Sch Derby 72-75; Chapl Bennett Memorial Sch Tunbridge Wells 75-84; Perm to Offic *Cant* from 70; *Chich* from 87. *The Croft, Point Hill, Rye, E Sussex TN31 7NP* Rye (0797) 222897

SORENSEN, Ms Anna Katrine Elizabeth. b 58. Man Univ BA82. Ripon Coll Cuddesdon 83. **d** 87. Par Dn Ashton H Trin *Man* 87-88; Asst Chapl St Felix Sch Southwold 89-90; Chapl from 90; Hon Par Dn Reydon *St E* from 89. *The Rectory, Moll's Lane, Brampton, Beccles, Suffolk NR34 8DB* Brampton (050279) 859

SORENSEN, Arthur Frank. b 28. S'wark Ord Course 66. **d** 69 **p** 70. C Broadwater Down *Chich* 69-71; P-in-c Shenley *Ox* 72-75; R Loughton and Bradwell 72-73; R Loughton 73-75; P-in-c Thornborough 75-77; P-in-c Beachampton w Thornton and Nash 75-77; R Nash w Thornton, Beachampton and Thornborough 77-83; P-in-c Gt Milton 83-86; P-in-c Lt Milton 83-86; rtd 86. *Shambala, 54 Beaufort Road, Morecambe, Lancs LA4 6UA* Morecambe (0524) 419741

SOULSBY, Michael. b 36. Dur Univ BSc57. Westcott Ho Cam 61. **d** 62 **p** 63. C Selly Oak St Mary *Birm* 62-66; C Kings Norton 66-72; TV K Norton 73-76; TR Sutton *Liv* 76-88; RD Prescot 84-88; P-in-c Orton Longueville *Ely* from 88. *The Rectory, Orton Longueville, Peterborough PE2 0DN* Peterborough (0733) 371071

SOUPER, Patrick Charles. b 28. K Coll Lon BD55 AKC55. **d** 57 **p** 58. Chapl Derby City Hosp 57-62; Chapl Derby Cathl *Derby* 57-62; Asst Chapl Lon Univ *Lon* 62-64; C St Marylebone w H Trin 64-65; Chapl St Paul's Sch Barnes 65-70; Lic to Offic *Win* from 70. *15 Canton Street, Bedford Place, Southampton SO1 2DJ*

SOURBUT, Philip John. b 57. Cam Univ BA MA. Cranmer Hall Dur BA. **d** 85 **p** 86. C Springfield All SS *Chelmsf* 85-88; C Roxeth Ch Ch and Harrow St Pet *Lon* from

88. *69 Southdown Crescent, Harrow, Middx HA2 0RT* 081-422 2340

SOUTH, Gillian. b 51. NE Ord Course 87. **d** 90. C Rothbury *Newc* from 90. *13 Cragside View, Rothbury, Northd NE65 7YU* Rothbury (0669) 21012

SOUTH, Canon Thomas Horsman. b 06. Qu Coll Ox BA31 MA35. Cuddesdon Coll 31. **d** 32 **p** 33. V Latimer w Flaunden *Ox* 62-73; Hon Can Ch Ch 66-73; rtd 73. *Folly Cottage, Deddington, Banbury, Oxon OX15 0ST* Deddington (0869) 38464

SOUTHALL, Colin Edward. b 36. Lich Th Coll 63. **d** 65 **p** 82. C Wylde Green *Birm* 65-67; Perm to Offic *Birm* 68-73; *Pet* 73-81; Hon C Linc St Faith and St Martin w St Pet *Linc* 82-85; Hon C Gt Glen, Stretton Magna and Wistow etc *Leic* from 85. *1 Spinney View, Great Glen, Leicester LE8 0EP*

SOUTHAMPTON, Suffragan Bishop of. See PERRY, Rt Rev John Freeman

SOUTHCOMBE, Hector George. b 07. Clare Coll Cam BA29 MA33. Westcott Ho Cam 67. **d** 69 **p** 70. C Congresbury *B & W* 69-73; V Crimplesham w Stradsett *Ely* 73-80; RD Fincham 76-80; rtd 80; Perm to Offic *B & W* from 80; *Bris* from 88. *264 Wells Road, Knowle, Bristol* Bristol (0272) 715275

SOUTHEARD, Canon Alfred Gordon. b 22. Univ of Wales BA54. Ely Th Coll 49. **d** 51 **p** 52. V Wootton Wawen *Cov* 67-88; RD Alcester 69-79; Hon Can Cov Cathl from 87; rtd 88. *21 Broad Street, Warwick CV34 4LT* Warwick (0926) 499137

SOUTHEND, Archdeacon of. See BAILEY, Ven Jonathan Sansbury

SOUTHERN, Humphrey Ivo John. b 60. Ch Ch Ox BA82 MA86. Ripon Coll Cuddesdon 83. **d** 86 **p** 87. C Rainham *Roch* 86-90; C Walton St Mary *Liv* from 90. *10 Lochinvar Street, Walton, Liverpool L9 1ER* 051-523 6617

SOUTHERN, John Abbott. b 27. Leeds Univ BA47. Coll of Resurr Mirfield. **d** 51 **p** 52. C Leigh St Mary *Man* 51-55; C Gt Grimsby St Jas *Linc* 55-58; V Oldham St Jas *Man* 58-60; V Haigh *Liv* 60-75; R Pemberton St Jo from 75. *The Vicarage, 148 Orrell Road, Orrell, Wigan, Lancs WN5 8HJ* Wigan (0942) 222237

SOUTHERN, Paul Ralph. b 48. Oak Hill Th Coll DipHE. **d** 87 **p** 88. C Chadwell Heath *Chelmsf* 87-91; P-in-c Tolleshunt D'Arcy w Tolleshunt Major from 91. *The Vicarage, Church Street, Tolleshunt D'Arcy, Maldon, Essex CM9 8TS* Maldon (0621) 860521

SOUTHERTON, Peter Clive. b 38. Univ of Wales (Lamp) BA59. Qu Coll Birm DipTh60. **d** 61 **p** 62. C Llandrillo-yn-Rhos *St As* 61-68; Bermuda 68-71; V Esclusham *St As* 72-82; V Prestatyn from 82. *The Vicarage, 109 High Street, Prestatyn, Clwyd LL19 9AR* Prestatyn (0745) 853780

SOUTHEY, George Rubidge. b 34. St Mich Coll Llan 84. **d** 86 **p** 87. C Hessle *York* 86-89; P-in-c Scarborough St Columba from 89. *160 Dean Road, Scarborough, N Yorkshire YO12 7JH* Scarborough (0723) 375070

SOUTHGATE, Geoffrey Trevor Stanley. b 28. AKC56. **d** 57 **p** 58. C Tonge Moor *Man* 57-60; C Lon Docks St Pet w Wapping St Jo *Lon* 60-62; V Upper Clapton St Matt 62-67; V Fleetwood *Blackb* 68-85; R Cov St Jo *Cov* from 85. *St John's Rectory, 9 Davenport Road, Coventry CV5 6QA* Coventry (0203) 673203

SOUTHGATE, Very Rev John Eliot. b 26. St Jo Coll Dur BA53 DipTh55. **d** 55 **p** 56. C Glen Parva and S Wigston *Leic* 55-59; C Lee Gd Shep w St Pet *S'wark* 59-62; V Plumstead St Mark 62-66; R Old Charlton 66-72; Boro Dean of Greenwich 69-72; Hon Can S'wark Cathl 70-72; Can and Preb York Minster *York* 72-84; V Harome 72-77; Adn Cleveland 74-84; Dean York from 84; Chmn Assn of English Cathls from 90. *The Deanery, York YO1 2JD* York (0904) 623608

SOUTHWARD, Canon Douglas Ambrose. b 32. St Jo Coll Nottm LTh74 ALCD57. **d** 57 **p** 58. C Otley *Bradf* 57-61; C Sedbergh 61-63; C Cautley w Dowbiggin 61-63; C Garsdale 61-63; PV Lich Cathl *Lich* 63-65; V Hope *Derby* 65-72; V Crosby Ravensworth *Carl* 72-82; V Bolton 74-82; Sec Dioc Past and Redundant Chs Uses Cttees 78-82; RD Appleby 78-82; Hon Can Carl Cathl from 81; R Asby 81-82; V Hawkshead and Low Wray w Sawrey from 82; P-in-c Windermere St Jo 83-89; RD Windermere 84-89. *The Vicarage, Hawkshead, Ambleside, Cumbria LA22 0PD* Hawkshead (09666) 301

SOUTHWARD, James Fisher. b 57. St Martin's Coll Lanc BEd80. Chich Th Coll 83. **d** 86 **p** 87. C Woodford St Barn *Chelmsf* 86-89; TV Crawley *Chich* from 89. *7 The Parade, Crawley, W Sussex RH10 2DT* Crawley (0293) 520620

SOUTHWARK, Archdeacon of. *See* BARTLES-SMITH, Ven Douglas Leslie
SOUTHWARK, Bishop of. *Vacant*
SOUTHWARK, Provost of. *See* EDWARDS, Very Rev David Lawrence
SOUTHWELL, Peter John Mackenzie. b 43. New Coll Ox BA64 MA68. Wycliffe Hall Ox 66. **d** 67 **p** 68. Lect Sheff Univ 67-70; C Crookes St Thos *Sheff* 67-70; Sen Tutor Wycliffe Hall Ox from 70; Chapl Qu Coll Ox from 82. *Queen's College, Oxford OX1 4AW* Oxford (0865) 279143 or 53829
SOUTHWELL, Ven Roy. b 14. AKC42. **d** 42 **p** 43. V Hendon Ch Ch *Lon* 68-71; Adn Northolt 70-80; rtd 80; Warden Community of All Hallows Ditchingham 83-89; Lic to Offic *Nor* 83-89; Perm to Offic from 89. *397 Sprowton Road, Norwich NR3 4HY* Norwich (0603) 405977
SOUTHWELL-SANDER, Canon Peter George. b 41. G&C Coll Cam BA64 MA67. Westcott Ho Cam 63. **d** 65 **p** 66. C Maidstone All SS w St Phil *Cant* 65-68; C Cam Gt St Mary w St Mich *Ely* 68-71; Chapl Girton Coll Cam 69-73; V Clapham St Paul *S'wark* 73-77; V Mert St Mary 77-84; P-in-c Mert St Jo 77-79; Dir of Min *Chelmsf* from 85; Can Res Chelmsf Cathl from 85. *North House, Church Road, Boreham, Chelmsford CM3 3EJ or, Guy Harlings, 53 New Street, Chelmsford CM1 1NG* Chelmsford (0245) 465946 or 266731
SOUTHWELL, Bishop of. *See* HARRIS, Rt Rev Patrick Burnet
SOUTHWELL, Provost of. *See* LEANING, Very Rev David
SOUTHWOOD, Robert Alfred. b 31. Sarum & Wells Th Coll 72. **d** 74 **p** 75. C Christchurch *Win* 74-76; C Fordingbridge w Ibsley 76-79; P-in-c Ernesettle *Ex* 79-80; V 80-83; R Stoke-in-Teignhead w Combe-in-Teignhead etc from 83. *The Rectory, Stoke-in-Teignhead, Newton Abbot TQ12 4QB* Shaldon (0626) 873493
SOUTTAR, Preb Edward Herbert. b 16. Bps' Coll Cheshunt 38. **d** 46 **p** 47. V Sidmouth St Nic *Ex* 65-73; TR Sidmouth, Woolbrook, Salcombe Regis etc 73-81; Preb Ex Cathl 72-85; rtd 81; Perm to Offic *Ex* from 85. *20 Fosseway Close, Axminster, Devon EX13 5LW* Axminster (0297) 34382
SOWDON, Henry Lewis Malcolm. b 37. TCD BA. Bps' Coll Cheshunt. **d** 64 **p** 65. C Newport w Longford *Lich* 64-66; C Caverswall 66-69; Chapl Clayesmore Sch Blandford 69-72; Hon C Hornsey Ch Ch *Lon* 72-80; Chapl Gordon's Sch Woking 80-86; TV Hodge Hill *Birm* from 86. *1 Ayala Croft, Birmingham B36 8SN* 021-747 9320
SOWERBUTTS, Alan. b 49. Sheff Univ BSc70 PhD73 Qu Coll Cam BA75 MA79. Westcott Ho Cam 74. **d** 76 **p** 77. C Salesbury *Blackb* 76-80; V Lower Darwen St Jas 80-84; V Musbury from 84. *St Thomas's Vicarage, 1 Flaxmoss Close, Helmshore, Rossendale, Lancs BB4 4PX* Rossendale (0706) 213302
SOWERBY, Geoffrey Nigel Rake. b 35. St Aid Birkenhead 56. **d** 60 **p** 61. C Armley St Bart *Ripon* 60-63; Min Can Ripon Cathl 63-65; V Thornthwaite w Thruscross and Darley 65-69; V Leeds All SS 69-73; V Leyburn w Bellerby 73-81; R Edin Old St Paul *Edin* 81-86; V Hawes and Hardraw *Ripon* from 86; Dioc Adv in Deliverance Min from 91. *The Vicarage, Hawes, N Yorkshire DL8 3NP* Wensleydale (0969) 667553
SOWERBY, Mark Crispin Rake. b 63. K Coll Lon BD85 AKC85. Coll of Resurr Mirfield 85. **d** 87 **p** 88. C Knaresborough *Ripon* 87-90; C Darwen St Cuth w Tockholes St Steph *Blackb* from 90. *The Old School House, Rock Lane, Tockholes, Darwen, Lancs BB3 0LX* Darwen (0254) 702676
SOWTER, Dr Colin Victor. b 35. Ball Coll Ox MA59 DPhil60. Oak Hill NSM Course 88. **d** 91. NSM Cranleigh *Guildf* from 91. *Hollycroft, Grantley Avenue, Wonersh Park, Guildford, Surrey GU5 0QN* Guildford (0483) 892094
SOX, Harold David. b 36. N Carolina Univ BA58. NY Th Sem MDiv61. **d** 61 **p** 61. USA 61-74; Hon C Richmond St Mary *S'wark* 74-79; Hon C Richmond St Mary w St Matthias and St Jo 79-82; Hon C Kensington St Mary Abbots w St Geo *Lon* 82-84 and from 89; Perm to Offic 84-89. *72A Campden Hill Court, London W8 7HL* 071-937 9091
SPACKMAN, Ven Peter John. b 37. Southn Univ BSc60. Westcott Ho Cam 65. **d** 66 **p** 67. C Boxmoor St Jo *St Alb* 66-69; C Alnwick St Paul *Newc* 69-72; Jamaica 72-74; Canada from 74; Adn Gaspe from 88. *PO Box 1490, Gaspe, Province of Quebec, Canada G0C 1R0* Gaspe (418) 368-2564

SPAFFORD, Christopher Garnett Howsin. b 24. St Jo Coll Ox BA48 MA54. Wells Th Coll 48. **d** 50 **p** 51. V Shrewsbury St Chad *Lich* 69-76; V Newc St Nic *Newc* 76-89; Provost Ncwc 76-89; rtd 89. *Low Moor, Elm Close, Leominster, Herefordshire HR6 8JX* Leominster (0568) 4395
SPAIGHT, Robert George. b 45. Ridley Hall Cam. **d** 84 **p** 85. C St Columb Minor and St Colan *Truro* 84-87; C Worksop St Jo *S'well* 87-89; V Barlings *Linc* from 89. *The Vicarage, Station Road, Langworth, Lincoln LN3 5BB* Lincoln (0522) 754233
SPALDING, Wilfrid Frank. b 20. Sarum Th Coll. **d** 57 **p** 58. R Hoole *Blackb* 69-85; rtd 85. *5 Park Walk, Fulwood, Preston* Preston (0772) 774663
SPANNER, Douglas Clement. b 16. Lon Univ BSc46 PhD51 DSc72. Local NSM Course. **d** 73 **p** 75. Hon C Ealing St Mary *Lon* 73-78; Hon C Eynsham *Ox* 79-83; Hon C Grove 83-86; Lic to Offic from 86. *Ivy Cottage, Main Street, Grove, Wantage, Oxon OX12 7JY* Wantage (02357) 66845
SPANNER, Handley James. b 51. Lanchester Poly BSc73 BA. Oak Hill Th Coll 82. **d** 85 **p** 86. C Cov H Trin *Cov* 85-89; V Rye Park St Cuth *St Alb* from 89. *St Cuthbert's Vicarage, Ogard Road, Hoddesdon, Herts EN11 0NU* Hoddesdon (0992) 463168
SPARGO, Peter Frederick Duncan. b 21. Kelham Th Coll 47. **d** 51 **p** 52. V N Hylton St Marg Castletown *Dur* 57-84; rtd 84; Perm to Offic *Ches* from 84. *16 Hillside Road, Kelsall, Tarporley, Cheshire CW6 0NT* Kelsall (0829) 52555
SPARHAM, Anthony George. b 41. St Jo Coll Dur BA69 DipTh. Cranmer Hall Dur 66. **d** 71 **p** 72. C Bourne *Linc* 71-74; TV Tong *Bradf* 74-76; V Windhill 76-81; Dir of Educn *St E* 82-85; V Goostrey *Ches* from 85; Dir Lay Tr 85-90; Jt Dir Lay Tr from 90. *The Vicarage, Goostrey, Crewe CW4 8PG* Holmes Chapel (0477) 32109
SPARKES, Colin Anthony. b 37. MIEE Surrey Univ MSc68 Bath Univ MEd83. Ox NSM Course 78. **d** 81 **p** 82. NSM Shrivenham w Watchfield and Bourton *Ox* 81-84; NSM Shellingford from 84. *Cornerstones, High Street, Hinton Waldrist, Faringdon, Oxon SN7 8RN* Longworth (0865) 820769
SPARKES, Donald James Henry. b 33. Oak Hill Th Coll DipTh59. **d** 59 **p** 60. C Southall Green St Jo *Lon* 59-63; P-in-c Pitsmoor *Sheff* 63-70; V 70-73; P-in-c Wicker w Neepsend 70-73; V Pitsmoor w Wicker 73-79; V Pitsmoor w Ellesmere 79-86; V Pitsmoor Ch Ch from 86. *The Vicarage, 257 Pitsmoor Road, Sheffield S3 9AQ* Sheffield (0742) 727756
SPARKES, Richard Graham Brabant. b 21. St Jo Coll Ox BA42 MA47. Westcott Ho Cam 54. **d** 55 **p** 56. V Oulton *Ripon* 69-75; rtd 86. Ty Newydd, Bethel, Llanfyllin, Powys SY22 5HJ* Llanfyllin (069184) 783
SPARKS, Christopher Thomas. b 29. St D Coll Lamp BA53 Lich Th Coll 53. **d** 55 **p** 56. C Macclesfield St Mich *Ches* 55-59; C W Kirby St Bridget 59-61; V Altrincham St Jo 61-68; Lic to Offic *Blackb* 68-79; C Lanc St Mary 79-83; Perm to Offic from 84. *The Hollies, Littlefell Lane, Lancaster LA2 0RG* Lancaster (0524) 67507
SPARKS, Hedley Frederick Davis. b 08. ATCL27 FBA59 BNC Ox BA30 MA34 BD37 DD49 Birm Univ MA47 St Andr Univ Hon DD63. Ripon Hall Ox 30. **d** 33 **p** 34. Oriel Prof Interpr of H Scripture Ox 52-76; R Wytham *Ox* 61-68; Lic to Offic *Cant* from 69; rtd 76. *14 Longport, Canterbury, Kent CT1 1PE* Canterbury (0227) 66265
SPARKS, Herbert Francis. b 23. AKC49. **d** 50 **p** 51. Chapl HM Pris Leyhill 64-69; Lect 69-74; Kirkham 74-76; Liv 76-79; Long Lartin 79-84; rtd 84; Perm to Offic *York* from 84. *21 Chestnut Avenue, Withernsea, N Humberside HU19 2PG* Withernsea (0964) 614183
SPARLING, Arthur Cecil. b 16. TCD BA40 MA44. **d** 41 **p** 42. V Spelsbury and Chadlington *Ox* 51-81; rtd 81; Perm to Offic *Glouc* from 81; *Ox* 81-87. *Parkfield, Mill Lane, Lower Slaughter, Cheltenham, Glos GL54 2HX* Cotswold (0451) 20987
SPARLING, Harold William. b 19. ARCM53 Lon Univ BD40 AKC40. Bps' Coll Cheshunt 40. **d** 41 **p** 43. R Upper Hardres w Stelling *Cant* 60-78; Teacher Ashford Sch Kent 75-80; Perm to Offic *St E* from 81; rtd 84. *89 Langton Green, Eye, Suffolk IP23 7SH* Eye (0379) 870073
SPARROW, Michael Kenneth. St Jo Coll Dur BA74. Coll of Resurr Mirfield 74. **d** 75 **p** 76. C N Hinksey *Ox* 75-78; C Portsea St Mary *Portsm* 78-85; V Midsomer Norton w Clandown *B & W* from 85. *The Vicarage, 83 North Road, Midsomer Norton, Bath BA3 2QH* Midsomer Norton (0761) 412118

SPEAK, Geoffrey Lowrey. b 24. OBE. Cam Univ MA. Ridley Hall Cam 49. **d** 51 **p** 52. Hong Kong 54-85; rtd 91. *Murren, Watery Lane, Donhead St Mary, Shaftesbury, Dorset SP7 9DP* Donhead (0747) 828613

SPEAKMAN, Joseph Frederick. b 26. NW Ord Course 75. **d** 78 **p** 79. NSM Wallasey St Hilary *Ches* 78; C 79-82; V Marthall w Over Peover from 82. *The Vicarage, One Oak, Marthall, Knutsford, Cheshire WA16 7SB* Chelford (0625) 861462

SPEAR, Andrew James Michael. b 60. Dur Univ BA81. Ridley Hall Cam 83. **d** 86 **p** 87. C Haughton le Skerne *Dur* 86-90; C Eastbourne H Trin *Chich* from 90. *33 Hyde Road, Eastbourne, E Sussex BN21 4SX* Eastbourne (0323) 37743

SPEAR, Miss Jennifer Jane. b 53. Westhill Coll Birm BEd76. Trin Coll Bris 82. **dss** 84 **d** 87. Reading St Jo *Ox* 84-87; Par Dn 87-90; Hon Par Dn Devonport St Barn *Ex* 90-91; Hon Par Dn Devonport St Mich 90-91; Par Dn Plymstock from 91. *63 Plymstock Road, Plymstock, Plymouth PL9 7NX*

SPEAR, John Cory. b 33. Open Univ BA87. Ridley Hall Cam 68. **d** 70 **p** 71. C Gerrards Cross *Ox* 70-73; TV Washfield, Stoodleigh, Withleigh etc *Ex* 73-79; R Instow 79-90; V Westleigh 79-90; RD Hartland 82-89; V Pilton w Ashford from 90. *The Vicarage, Northfield Lane, Pilton West, Barnstaple, Devon EX31 1QB* Barnstaple (0271) 45958

SPEAR, Sylvia Grace. b 36. St Chris Coll Blackheath 60. **dss** 76 **d** 87. S Wimbledon H Trin and St Pet *S'wark* 76-80; Lee Gd Shep w St Pet 80-87; Par Dn from 87. *56 Weigall Road, London SE12 8HF* 081-318 2363

SPEARS, Reginald Robert Derek. b 48. Trin Coll Ox BA72 MA75. Cuddesdon Coll 72. **d** 75 **p** 76. C Hampton All SS *Lon* 75-79; C Caversham *Ox* 79-81; C Caversham and Mapledurham 81-84; V Reading St Matt from 84. *St Matthew's Vicarage, 205 Southcote Lane, Reading RG3 3AX* Reading (0734) 573755

SPECK, Peter William. b 42. Univ of Wales BSc64 Birm Univ BA66 DPS67 MA71. Qu Coll Birm 64. **d** 67 **p** 68. C Rhosddu *St As* 67-71; C Wrexham 71-72; Asst Chapl United Sheff Hosps 72-73; Chapl N Gen Hosp Sheff 73-79; Chapl R Free Hosp Lon from 79; Hon Sen Lect Sch of Med from 87. *The Chaplain's Office, Royal Free Hospital, Pond Street, London NW3 2QG* 071-794 0500 or 081-883 3386

SPECK, Raymond George. b 39. Oak Hill Th Coll 64. **d** 67 **p** 68. C Stretford St Bride *Man* 67-70; C Roxeth Ch Ch *Lon* 70-74; V Woodbridge St Jo *St E* 74-85; R Jersey St Ouen w St Geo Win from 85. *The Rectory, St Ouen, Jersey, Channel Islands JE3 2GG* Jersey (0534) 81800

SPEDDING, Geoffrey Osmond. b 46. Hull Univ BA67 Fitzw Coll Cam BA69 MA BD. **d** 70 **p** 71. C Bradf Cathl *Bradf* 70-73; C Sutton St Jas and Wawne *York* 73-76; TV Preston St Jo *Blackb* 76-82; TV Yate New Town *Bris* 82-87; TR Bestwood *S'well* from 87. *The Vicarage, Padstow Road, Bestwood, Nottingham NG5 5GH* Nottingham (0602) 276107

SPEDDING, William Granville. b 39. Lon Univ BD60. Tyndale Hall Bris 57. **d** 62 **p** 63. C Man Albert Memorial Ch *Man* 62-65; Perm to Offic 65-67; Hon C New Bury 67-79; Hon C Bolton St Paul w Em 79-86; Hon C Pennington from 86. *26 Milverton Close, Lostock, Bolton BL6 4RR* Bolton (0204) 41248

SPEEDY, Darrel Craven. b 35. St Chad's Coll Dur BA57. Wells Th Coll 57. **d** 59 **p** 60. C Frodingham *Linc* 59-63; V Heckington w Howell 63-71; V Barton upon Humber 71-79; R Tain *Mor* 79-85; Dioc Sec 82-85; Can St Andr Cathl Inverness 83-85; Syn Clerk 83-85; R Whaley Bridge *Ches* from 85; RD Chadkirk from 88. *St James's Rectory, Taxal Road, Whaley Bridge, Stockport, Cheshire SK12 7DY* Whaley Bridge (0663) 732696

SPEERS, Canon Albert Edward. b 10. Wycliffe Hall Ox. **d** 44 **p** 44. V Barnehurst *Roch* 67-87; Hon Can Roch Cathl from 75; rtd 87. *48 Birch Grove, Hempstead, Gillingham, Kent* Medway (0634) 379464

SPEERS, John Stevenson. b 09. Ripon Hall Ox 41. **d** 43 **p** 43. R Luton Ch Ch *Roch* 50-66; rtd 66. *32 Hengistbury Road, Bournemouth BH6 4DQ* Bournemouth (0202) 417513

SPEERS, Canon Samuel Hall. b 46. TCD BA70 MA75. Cuddesdon Coll 70. **d** 73 **p** 74. C Boreham Wood All SS *St Alb* 73-76; Madagascar 76-88; Hon Can Antananarivo from 85; R S Lafford *Linc* from 88. *The Rectory, Folkingham, Sleaford, Lincs NG34 0SN* Folkingham (05297) 391

SPENCE, Brian Robin. b 39. St Chad's Coll Dur BA61 DipTh63. **d** 63 **p** 64. C Weston *Guildf* 63-67; Lesotho 67-68; C Chobham w Valley End *Guildf* 68-71;

C Gt Yarmouth *Nor* 71-74; V Warnham *Chich* 74-81; V E Grinstead St Mary 81-86; V Crowthorne *Ox* from 86. *The Vicarage, 56 Duke's Ride, Crowthorne, Berks RG11 6NY* Crowthorne (0344) 772413

SPENCE, James Knox. b 30. Worc Coll Ox BA55 MA58. Ridley Hall Cam. **d** 57 **p** 58. C W Hampstead Trin *Lon* 57-60; C Ox St Ebbe w St Pet *Ox* 61-64; Cand Sec CPAS 64-68; V Reading Greyfriars *Ox* 68-78; C St Helen Bishopsgate w St Martin Outwich *Lon* 78-80; C St Helen Bishopsgate w St Andr Undershaft etc 80-82; P-in-c Gt Baddow *Chelmsf* 82-86; V 86-88; TR from 88. *The Vicarage, 12 Church Street, Great Baddow, Chelmsford CM2 7HZ* Chelmsford (0245) 71740

SPENCE, James Timothy. b 35. St Jo Coll Cam BA59 MA63. Wycliffe Hall Ox 59. **d** 61 **p** 62. C Stoke *Cov* 61-64; C Cam H Trin *Ely* 64-67; R Tarrington w Stoke Edith *Heref* 67-72; Dioc Youth Officer 67-72; Lic to Offic *Win* 72-75; R Falstone *Newc* 75-80; TV Bellingham/Otterburn Gp 80-82; Dioc Ecum Adv 82-87; V Dinnington 82-87; V Shap w Swindale *Carl* from 87. *The Vicarage, Shap, Penrith, Cumbria CA10 3LB* Shap (09316) 232

SPENCE, Canon John Edis. b 24. St Edm Hall Ox BA46 MA48. Westcott Ho Cam 47. **d** 48 **p** 49. Chapl RNR from 65; V St Germans *Truro* 65-73; V Tideford 65-73; P-in-c Sheviock 69-70; Perm to Offic 73-76; Dioc Chapl to Bp 76-78; C Newlyn St Newlyn 76-78; Chapl for Maintenance of the Min 78-87; Stewardship Adv 80-87; Hon Can Truro Cathl 84-89; Bp's Dom Chapl 87-89; P-in-c St Allen 87-89; rtd 89; Lic to Offic *Truro* from 89. *2 Halvarras Road, Playing Place, Truro TR3 6HD* Truro (0872) 863699

SPENCE, Philip Arthur. b 39. Lon Univ BD71 Open Univ BA76. Hartley Victoria Coll DipTh67 Westcott Ho Cam 78. **d** 78 **p** 79. In Meth Ch 67-78; C Walthamstow St Pet *Chelmsf* 78-80; Dioc Adv on Evang 80-87; Dep Dir Dept of Miss (Evang Division) 80-85; P-in-c Greensted 80-86; Bp's Adv on Tourism 81-87; Asst Dir of Miss and Unity 85-87; R Greensted-juxta-Ongar w Stanford Rivers 86-87; V Cam St Mark *Ely* from 87; Relig Adv Anglia TV from 91. *St Mark's Vicarage, Barton Road, Cambridge CB3 9JZ* Cambridge (0223) 63339

SPENCE, Very Rev Walter Cyril. b 19. TCD BA40 MA43 BD43. **d** 42 **p** 43. Dean Tuam *T, K & A* 66-81; I Tuam 66-81; Dioc Registrar 66-85; Preb Kilmactalway St Patr Cathl Dub 67-85; I Kilmoremoy w Castleconnor, Easkey, Kilglass etc *T, K & A* 81-85; rtd 85. *Beth Shalom, 1 Gracefield Avenue, Dublin 5, Irish Republic*

SPENCELEY, Malcolm. b 40. St Jo Coll Dur 78. **d** 80 **p** 81. C Redcar *York* 80-85; V Middlesb Ascension from 85. *The Ascension Vicarage, Penrith Road, Middlesbrough, Cleveland TS3 7JR* Middlesbrough (0642) 244857

SPENCER, Preb Christopher John Edward. b 16. AKC41. **d** 41 **p** 42. R Lt Stanmore St Lawr *Lon* 66-82; Preb St Paul's Cathl 79-82; rtd 82; Perm to Offic *St Alb* from 82; Hon C Gt Stanmore *Lon* from 85. *28 Culverlands Close, Stanmore, Middx HA7 3AG* 081-954 8801

SPENCER, David William. b 43. E Anglian Minl Tr Course 80. **d** 81 **p** 82. NSM Wisbech St Aug *Ely* 81-84; C Whittlesey 84-86; R Upwell Ch Ch 86-90; R March St Pet from 90; R March St Mary from 90. *St Peter's Rectory, High Street, March, Cambs PE15 9JR* March (0354) 52297

SPENCER, Geoffrey. b 50. ALCM76 Nottm Univ CertEd78 ACertCM79 Open Univ BA84. Linc Th Coll 85. **d** 87 **p** 88. C Skegness and Winthorpe *Linc* 87-90; V Heckington from 90. *The Vicarage, Heckington, Sleaford, Lincs NG34 9RW* Sleaford (0529) 60302

SPENCER, George. b 56. Cam Univ BA77 MA83. Coll of Resurr Mirfield 80. **d** 83 **p** 84. C Edin Old St Paul *Edin* 83-85; P-in-c Edin St Ninian from 85. *147 Comely Bank Road, Edinburgh EH4 1BH* 031-332 6226

SPENCER, Gilbert Hugh. b 43. Lon Univ BD67. ALCD66. **d** 67 **p** 68. C Bexleyheath Ch Ch *Roch* 67-73; C Bexley St Jo 73-76; P-in-c Bromley St Jo 76-78; V 78-81; R Chatham St Mary w St Jo 81-91; V Minster in Sheppey *Cant* from 91. *The Vicarage, Minster-in-Sheppey, Sheerness, Kent ME12 2HE* Minster (0795) 873185

SPENCER, Gordon Charles Craig. b 13. Oak Hill Th Coll 35. **d** 38 **p** 39. V Bathampton *B & W* 66-81; rtd 81; P-in-c Ditteridge *Bris* 81-86; Perm to Offic from 86; Perm to Offic *B & W* from 86. *26 Elm Grove, Bath BA1 7AZ* Bath (0225) 316570

SPENCER, Graham Lewis. b 48. St Jo Coll Nottm 80. **d** 82 **p** 83. C Leic St Anne *Leic* 82-85; P-in-c Frisby-on-the-Wreake w Kirby Bellars 85-86; TV Melton Gt Framland from 86. *The Vicarage, 2 Carrfields Lane,*

Frisby-on-the-Wreake, Melton Mowbray, Leics LE14 2NT Melton Mowbray (0664) 434878

SPENCER, John Edward. b 36. Bris Univ BA60. Tyndale Hall Bris 57. **d** 61 **p** 62. C St Helens St Mark *Liv* 61-64; Japan 65-70; Area Sec (Dios Leic and Pet) CMS 70-71; Lic to Offic *Leic* 70-71; Warden and Chapl Rikkyo Japanese Sch Rudgwick 71-73; Hd Master Pennthorpe Sch Rudgwick from 73; Lic to Offic *Guildf* 71-73; *Chich* from 73. *Pennthorpe School, Rudgwick, Horsham, W Sussex RH12 3HJ* Rudgwick (040372) 2391

SPENCER, John Leslie. b 09. St Cath Soc Ox BA30 MA34. St Aid Birkenhead 31. **d** 32 **p** 33. V Bramfield and Walpole *St E* 69-74; rtd 74; Perm to Offic *Chich* from 80. *Flat 7, Capel Court, The Burgage, Prestbury, Cheltenham, Glos GL52 3EL* Cheltenham (0242) 577516

SPENCER, Norman Ernest. b 07. FCIS70. **d** 74 **p** 75. NSM Olveston *Bris* 74-82; Perm to Offic from 82. *26 Park Crescent, Bristol BS16 1NZ* Bristol (0272) 568873

SPENCER, Peter Cecil. b 30. Lich Th Coll 58. **d** 61 **p** 62. C Alton St Lawr *Win* 61-63; C Bournemouth St Luke 63-66; C W End 67-70; C Reading St Mary V *Ox* 70-72; C-in-c Reading St Matt CD 72-76; V Reading St Matt 76-78; TV Sidmouth, Woolbrook and Salcombe Regis *Ex* 78-79; TV Sidmouth, Woolbrook and Salcombe Regis 79-86; R Birch w Layer Breton and Layer Marney *Chelmsf* from 86. *The Rectory, Birch, Colchester CO2 0NA* Colchester (0206) 330241

SPENCER, Peter Lane. b 19. St Jo Coll Cam BA40 MA45. Linc Th Coll 41. **d** 43 **p** 45. C Oxhey St Matt *St Alb* 43-46; S Africa from 46. *23 Davdon, 42 Musgrave Road, Durban, 4001 South Africa* Durban (31) 216893

SPENCER, Peter Roy. b 40. CertEd. Sarum & Wells Th Coll 72. **d** 74 **p** 75. C Northn St Alb *Pet* 74-77; TV Cov E *Cov* 77-90; V Erdington St Barn *Birm* from 90. *The Vicarage, 26 Church Road, Erdington, Birmingham B24 9AX* 021-373 0884 or 350 9945

SPENCER, Richard Hugh. b 62. Univ of Wales (Cardiff) LLB84 BD88. St Mich Coll Llan 85. **d** 88 **p** 89. C Barry All SS *Llan* 88-90; Asst Chapl Univ of Wales (Cardiff) from 90. *St Teilo's Vicarage, Flora Street, Cathays, Cardiff CF2 4EP* Cardiff (0222) 232407

SPENCER, Richard William Edward. b 33. W Midl Minl Tr Course 78. **d** 81 **p** 82. NSM The Lickey *Birm* 81-83; Area Sec (Warks and W Midl) Chr Aid from 83; Perm to Offic *Birm* 84-91; Lic from 91; Perm *Cov* from 85. *104 Witherwood Way, Birmingham B29 4AW* 021-472 2041 or 643 2249

SPENCER, Canon Robert. b 27. FRSA. St Aid Birkenhead 48. **d** 51 **p** 52. C Coppenhall St Paul *Ches* 51-53; C Bollington St Jo 53-56; V Lower Tranmere 56-62; V Stockport St Alb Hall Street 62-71; V Crewe All SS and St Paul 71-81; V Over St Chad 81-89; Hon Can Ches Cathl from 89; V Baddiley and Wrenbury w Burleydam from 89. *The Vicarage, Wrenbury, Nantwich, Cheshire CW5 8EY* Crewe (0270) 780398

SPENCER, Roy Primett. b 26. Oak Hill Th Coll 50. **d** 53 **p** 54. V Accrington St Paul *Blackb* 69-78; V Woodplumpton 78-83; Chapl Preston R Hosp 83-91; P-in-c Preston St Luke *Blackb* 83-89; P-in-c Preston St Luke and St Oswald 89-90; rtd 91. *5 Hollywood Avenue, Penwortham, Preston PR1 9AS* Preston (0772) 743783

SPENCER, Stanley. b 11. Clifton Th Coll 32. **d** 36 **p** 37. R Monken Hadley *Lon* 67-77; rtd 77. *27 Chestnut Avenue, Holbeach, Spalding, Lincs PE12 7NE* Holbeach (0406) 22894

SPENCER, Stephen Christopher. b 60. Ball Coll Ox BA82 DPhil90. Edin Th Coll 88. **d** 90 **p** 91. C Harlesden All So *Lon* from 90. *The Hall Flat, 1 Station Road, London NW10 4UJ* 081-961 2750

SPENCER, Stephen Nigel Howard. b 53. Pemb Coll Ox BA75 Jes Coll Cam PGCE76. Trin Coll Bris 80. **d** 82 **p** 83. C Partington and Carrington *Ches* 82-85; C Brunswick *Man* 85-88; Chapl UEA *Nor* from 88. *5 Bridge Farm Lane, Wilberforce Road, Norwich NR5 8NW* Norwich (0603) 57505

SPENCER, Mrs Susan. b 47. E Midl Min Tr Course 87. **d** 90. Par Dn Cotgrave *S'well* from 90. *Church House, 35 East Acres, Cotgrave, Notts NG12 3JP* Nottingham (0602) 893478

SPENCER, Canon William Lowbridge. b 16. Keble Coll Ox BA38 MA46. Wells Th Coll 46. **d** 47 **p** 48. C Swindon New Town *Bris* 50-51; Tanganyika 52-64; Tanzania from 64; Can Masasi from 75; rtd 86. *St Cyprian's College, PO Box 212, Lindi, Tanzania*

SPENCER-THOMAS, Owen Robert. b 40. Lon Univ BSc(Soc)70. Westcott Ho Cam 70. **d** 72 **p** 73. C S Kensington St Luke *Lon* 72-76; Lect Relig Studies S Kensington Inst 74-76; Dir Lon Chs Radio Workshop &

Relig Producer BBC 76-78; Anglia TV from 78; Lic to Offic *Lon* 76-86; Perm *Pet* from 86; *Ely* 85-87; NSM Cam Ascension *Ely* from 87. *52 Windsor Road, Cambridge CB4 3JN* Cambridge (0223) 358446

SPENSER UNDERHILL, Mervyn. b 23. Dur Univ BA49. Chich Th Coll 49. **d** 51 **p** 52. C Northn St Mary *Pet* 51-56; C Pokesdown All SS *Win* 56-61; V Hedge End from 61. *The Vicarage, Vicarage Drive, St John's Road, Hedge End, Southampton SO3 4DF* Botley (0489) 782288

SPERRING, Clive Michael. b 43. Oak Hill Th Coll 71. **d** 75 **p** 76. C Hawkwell *Chelmsf* 75-78; C-in-c Gt Baddow 78-82; New Zealand from 82. *49 Te Arawa Street, Orakei, Auckland 5, New Zealand 1105* Auckland (9) 521-0296

SPICER, David John. b 49. Lon Univ BEd71. Linc Th Coll 76. **d** 78 **p** 79. C Upminster *Chelmsf* 78-80; C Mosborough *Sheff* 80-82; V Frisby-on-the-Wreake w Kirby Bellars *Leic* 82-84; Hon C Gt Ilford St Luke *Chelmsf* 85-88; C Cleethorpes *Linc* 88-90; C-in-c Stamford Ch Ch CD from 90. *Christ Church Parsonage, 14 Queen Street, Stamford, Lincs PE9 1QS* Stamford (0780) 62990

SPICER, David John. b 52. Sussex Univ BA76 Lon Univ MTh78. Westcott Ho Cam 77. **d** 79 **p** 80. C E Dulwich St Jo *S'wark* 79-82; C Richmond St Mary w St Matthias and St Jo 82-87; V Lewisham St Swithun from 87. *St Swithun's Vicarage, 191 Hither Green Lane, London SE13 6QE* 081-852 5088

SPICER, Leigh Edwin. b 56. Sarum & Wells Th Coll 78. **d** 81 **p** 82. C Harborne St Pet *Birm* 81-83; C Bloxwich *Lich* 83-87; Chapl RAF from 87. *c/o MOD, Adastral House, Theobald's Road, London WC1X 8RU* 071-430 7268

SPICER, Nicolas. b 61. Univ of Wales (Lamp) BA84. Coll of Resurr Mirfield 84. **d** 86 **p** 87. C Westbury-on-Trym H Trin *Bris* 86-89; C Willesden Green St Andr and St Fran of Assisi *Lon* from 89. *99 Chambers Lane, London NW10 2RP* 081-459 2670

SPIERS, Ven Graeme Hendry Gordon. b 25. ALCD52. **d** 52 **p** 53. V Aigburth *Liv* 66-80; RD Childwall 75-79; Hon Can Liv Cathl from 77; Adn Liv 79-91; rtd 91. *19 Barkfield Lane, Formby, Merseyside L37 1LY* Formby (07048) 72902

SPIERS, Peter Hendry. b 61. St Jo Coll Dur BA82. Ridley Hall Cam 83. **d** 86 **p** 87. C W Derby St Luke *Liv* 86-90; TV Everton St Pet from 90. *5 Henglers Close, Liverpool L6 1NJ* 051-260 5086

SPIKIN, Simon John Overington. b 48. Linc Th Coll 70. **d** 75 **p** 76. C Sawbridgeworth *St Alb* 75-79; C Odiham w S Warnborough and Long Sutton *Win* 79-81; P-in-c Rushall 81-82; R Dickleburgh w Thelveton w Frenze and Shimpling *Nor* 81-82; R Dickleburgh, Langmere, Shimpling, Thelveton etc from 82. *The Rectory, Dickleburgh, Diss, Norfolk IP21 4NN* Diss (0379) 741313

SPILLER, David Roger. b 44. St Jo Coll Dur BA70 Fitzw Coll Cam BA72 MA76 Nottm Univ DipAdEd80. Ridley Hall Cam 70. **d** 73 **p** 74. C Bradf Cathl *Bradf* 73-77; C Stratford w Bishopton *Cov* 77-80; Chapl Geo Eliot Hosp Nuneaton 80-90; V Chilvers Coton w Astley *Cov* 80-90; RD Nuneaton 84-90; Prin Aston Tr Scheme from 90; Lic to Offic *Birm* from 90. *12 Meadow Rise, Bournville, Birmingham B30 1UZ* 021-472 4247

SPILLER, Edward William. b 32. Cranmer Hall Dur. **d** 82 **p** 83. C Kirkleatham *York* 82-85; R The Thorntons and The Otteringtons from 85. *The Vicarage, Thornton le Moor, Northallerton, N Yorkshire DL7 9DT* Northallerton (0609) 774232

SPILLER, George Dennis. b 30. TD. St Jo Coll Dur BA55 DipTh. **d** 57 **p** 58. C Newc w Butterton *Lich* 57-62; R Armitage 62-65; CF (TA) 63-82; R Church Lawford w Newnham Regis *Cov* 65-73; Lic to Offic 73-81; R Stratford w Bishopton 81-82; TR from 82. *The Rectory, Old Town, Stratford-upon-Avon, Warks CV37 6BG* Stratford-upon-Avon (0789) 293098

SPILMAN, Derrick Geoffrey. b 27. **d** 63 **p** 64. C Dover St Mary *Cant* 63-67; CF 67-71; Canada from 71. *6771 Napier Street, Burnaby, British Columbia, Canada, V9K 1V5*

SPILSBURY, Stephen Ronald Paul. b 39. Nottm Univ BSc69 MPhil72. Linc Th Coll 71. **d** 64 **p** 65. In RC Ch 64-71; C Cricklade w Latton *Bris* 72-75; P-in-c Swindon All SS 76-81; V Lawrence Weston from 81; RD Westbury and Severnside 89-91. *The Vicarage, 335 Long Cross, Bristol BS11 0NN* Avonmouth (0272) 825863

SPINDLER, Jane Diana. b 54. Southn Univ BA75 CertEd76. Wycliffe Hall Ox 87. **d** 89. Par Dn Bishopsworth *Bris* from 89. *30 Brookdale, Headley Park, Bristol BS13 7PZ* Bristol (0272) 645817

SPINK, Canon George Arthur Peter. b 26. Oak Hill Th Coll 54. **d** 56 **p** 57. Chapl Cov Cathl *Cov* 68-70; Can Res Cov Cathl 70-77; Warden The Dorothy Kerin Trust Burrswood 77-81; Prior Omega Order from 80; Lic to Offic *Roch* 80-86; *B & W* from 86; rtd 89. *The Priory, Winford Manor, Winford, Bristol BS18 8DW* Lulsgate (0275) 472262

SPINKS, Bryan Douglas. b 48. FRHistS85 St Chad's Coll Dur BA70 DipTh71 BD79 K Coll Lon MTh72 Dur Univ DD88. **d** 75 **p** 76. C Witham *Chelmsf* 75-78; C Clacton St Jas 78-79; Lic to Offic *Ely* from 80; Chapl Chu Coll Cam from 80; Perm to Offic *St Alb* from 84. *Churchill College, Cambridge CB3 0DS* Cambridge (0223) 336000

SPINKS, Christopher George. b 53. Brighton Poly HND80. Oak Hill Th Coll BA88. **d** 88 **p** 89. C Hove Bp Hannington Memorial Ch *Chich* from 88. *42 Leighton Road, Hove, E Sussex BN3 7AE* Brighton (0273) 724920

SPINKS, John Frederick. b 40. Oak Hill Th Coll 79. **d** 82 **p** 83. NSM Roxbourne St Andr *Lon* 82-89; C Northwood H Trin from 89. *74 Knoll Crescent, Northwood, Middx HA6 1HY* Northwood (09274) 29375

SPINNEY, Giles Martin. b 16. Ch Coll Cam BA39 MA43. Wycliffe Hall Ox 39. **d** 41 **p** 42. R Brixton Deverill *Sarum* 54-72; R Kingston Deverill w Monkton Deverill 55-72; R The Deverills 72-81; rtd 81. *17 Chancery Lane, Warminster, Wilts BA12 9JS* Warminster (0985) 214813

SPITTLE, Ralph Edward. b 23. Qu Coll Birm 75. **d** 77 **p** 78. NSM Cov Caludon *Cov* 77-81; NSM Foleshill St Paul from 82. *227 Tennyson Road, Coventry CV2 5JE* Coventry (0203) 440612

SPITTLE, Robin. b 57. St Jo Coll Nottm 84. **d** 86 **p** 87. C Ipswich St Fran *St E* 86-91; Min Shotley St Mary CD from 91. *6 Sawmill Lane, Nacton, Ipswich IP10 0HS* Ipswich (0473) 659890

SPIVEY, Colin. b 35. ACII61 Ex Univ DSA68. Oak Hill Th Coll 74. **d** 76 **p** 77. C Egham *Guildf* 76-79; C Edgware *Lon* 79-83; R Haworth *Bradf* from 83. *The Rectory, Haworth, Keighley, W Yorkshire BD22 8EN* Haworth (0535) 42169

SPIVEY, Canon Peter. b 19. Edin Th Coll 46. **d** 48 **p** 49. V Meltham *Wakef* 61-85; RD Blackmoorfoot 79-85; Hon Can Wakef Cathl 81-85; rtd 85; Perm to Offic *Wakef* from 85. *3 Follett Avenue, Huddersfield HD4 5LW* Huddersfield (0484) 654674

SPIVEY, Ronald. b 28. ACMA MInstAM. E Midl Min Tr Course 83. **d** 86 **p** 87. NSM Sutton St Mary *Linc* from 86. *5 Lancaster Drive, Long Sutton, Spalding, Lincs PE12 9BD* Holbeach (0406) 362084

SPOKES, David Lawrence. b 57. Nottm Univ BCombStuds85. Linc Th Coll 82. **d** 85 **p** 86. C Rushall *Lich* 85-89; TV Thornaby on Tees *York* from 89. *St Paul's Vicarage, 60 Lanehouse Road, Thornaby, Stockton-on-Tees, Cleveland TS17 8EA* Stockton-on-Tees (0642) 679661

SPOKES, Keith John. b 29. E Anglian Minl Tr Course. **d** 84 **p** 85. NSM Bury St Edmunds St Mary *St E* 84-89; P-in-c Helmingham w Framsden and Pettaugh w Winston from 89. *The Rectory, The Street, Framsden, Stowmarket, Suffolk IP14 6HG* Helmingham (0473) 890858

SPONG, Terence John. b 32. CLJ. Roch Th Coll 63. **d** 66 **p** 67. C Forton *Portsm* 66-68; Rhodesia 68-80; Zimbabwe 80-84; R Christow, Ashton, Trusham and Bridford *Ex* 84-86; Chapl Puerto de la Cruz Tenerife *Eur* from 86; Miss to Seamen from 86. *Apartado 68, Parque Taoro, Puerto de la Cruz, Tenerife, Canary Islands* Tenerife (22) 384038

SPOONER, Anthony Patrick David. b 45. Univ Coll of Rhodesia Univ Coll of Nyasaland BA68 Nottm Univ DipTh72. Linc Th Coll 71. **d** 74 **p** 75. C Glynde, W Firle and Beddingham *Chich* 74-77; Rhodesia 77-80; Zimbabwe 80-86; P-in-c Clacton St Jas *Chelmsf* 86-90; V from 90. *St James's Vicarage, 89 Wash Lane, Clacton-on-Sea, Essex CO15 1DA* Clacton-on-Sea (0225) 422007

SPOOR, Norman Leslie. b 15. BSc PhD DipTh. Ripon Coll Cuddesdon. **d** 83 **p** 83. NSM Steventon w Milton *Ox* 88-90; NSM Abingdon from 90. *4 Ladygrove Paddock, Drayton Road, Abingdon, Oxon OX14 5HT* Abingdon (0235) 528750

SPOTTISWOODE, Anthony Derek. b 25. Solicitor 50 Pemb Coll Cam BA47 MA86. Sarum & Wells Th Coll 85. **d** 86 **p** 87. C Hampstead St Jo *Lon* from 86. *Flat 2, 26 Belsize Lane, London NW3 5AB* 071-435 6756

SPRACKLING, Frederick Phillips. b 16. Bible Churchmen's Coll 37. **d** 40 **p** 41. V Stamford Brook *Lon* 57-81; rtd 81. *Cross Park, Botus Fleming, Saltash, Cornwall PL12 6NH* Saltash (0752) 846174

SPRATLEY, Deryck Edward. b 30. BSc. Oak Hill Th Coll 62. **d** 64 **p** 65. C Ramsgate St Luke *Cant* 64-67; C W Holl St Dav *Lon* 67-73; V Upper Holloway St Pet 73-79; V Upper Holloway St Pet w St Jo 79-82; P-in-c Dagenham *Chelmsf* 82-88; P-in-c Becontree St Geo 84-88; TR Dagenham from 88. *The Vicarage, Church Lane, Dagenham, Essex RM10 9UL* 081-592 1339

SPRATT, Laurence Herbert. b 28. Linc Th Coll 76. **d** 78 **p** 79. C Mexborough *Sheff* 78-80; R Wrentham w Benacre, Covehithe, Frostenden etc *St E* 80-88; P-in-c Inveraray *Arg* 90-91. *Inver, Minard, Inveraray, Argyll PA32 8YB* Minard (0546) 86276

SPRATT, Robert Percival. b 31. MRSH83. Carl Dioc Tr Inst 84. **d** 87 **p** 88. NSM Kendal St Thos *Carl* 87-89; Chapl HM Pris Preston from 89. *The Chaplain's Office, HM Prison, 2 Ribbleton Lane, Preston PR1 5AB* Preston (0772) 57734

SPRAY, Canon Charles Alan Francis Thomas. b 27. ARSM51 Lon Univ BScEng51. Ridley Hall Cam 57. **d** 59 **p** 60. C Chich St Pancras and St Jo *Chich* 59-63; V Shipley 63-69; R Ore 70-85; V Burgess Hill St Andr from 85; Can and Preb Chich Cathl from 88. *St Andrew's Vicarage, 2 Cant's Lane, Burgess Hill, W Sussex RH15 0LG* Burgess Hill (0444) 232023

SPRAY, John William. b 29. Sarum & Wells Th Coll 71. **d** 73 **p** 74. C Clayton *Lich* 73-77; V Hartshill 77-82; P-in-c Aston 82-83; P-in-c Stone St Mich 82-83; P-in-c Stone St Mich w Aston St Sav 83-84; R 84-90; rtd 90. *2 Belvoir Avenue, Trentham, Stoke-on-Trent ST4 8SY* Stoke-on-Trent (0782) 644959

SPRAY, Richard Alan. b 43. **d** 88 **p** 89. NSM Cotgrave S'well from 88. *Church Lodge, Miller Hives Close, Cotgrave, Nottingham* Nottingham (0602) 893562

SPREAD, John Henry Seymour. b 14. MC46. Lon Univ BA37. Chich Th Coll 38. **d** 39 **p** 41. V Sundon w Streatley *St Alb* 53-79; rtd 79; Hon C Gt w Lt Hormead, Anstey, Brent Pelham etc *St Alb* 79-89; Hon C Much Hadham from 89. *Flat 6, Old Red Lion Hotel, Much Hadman, Herts SG10 6DD* Much Hadham (027984) 3140

SPRENT, Michael Francis (Brother Giles). b 34. Ex Coll Ox BA58 MA62. Kelham Th Coll 58. **d** 61 **p** 62. C Plaistow St Andr *Chelmsf* 61-63; SSF from 61; Papua New Guinea 65-69; TV High Stoy *Sarum* 76-77. *La Verna Friary, Hautambu, PO Box 519, Honiara, Solomon Islands*

SPRIGGS, Harold. b 99. Dorchester Miss Coll 29. **d** 31 **p** 32. V Mountfield *Chich* 60-85; V Netherfield 60-85; rtd 85; Perm to Offic *Chich* from 85. *2 Church Cottages, Mountfield, Robertsbridge, E Sussex TN32 5JS* Robertsbridge (0580) 880261

SPRIGGS, John David Robert. b 36. BNC Ox BA58 MA63. S'wark Ord Course 73. **d** 75 **p** 76. Lic to Offic *Ox* from 75. *Bowden Green, Pangbourne College, Pangbourne, Reading RG8 8JL* Pangbourne (0734) 843225

SPRINGATE, Paul Albert Edward. b 48. Oak Hill Th Coll 81. **d** 83 **p** 84. C Pennycross *Ex* 83-87; P-in-c Cossington and Seagrave *Leic* 87-88; TV Sileby, Cossington and Seagrave from 88. *The Vicarage, Main Street, Cossington, Leicester LE7 8UU* Sileby (050981) 3455

SPRINGBETT, John Howard. b 47. Pemb Coll Cam BA70 MA74. Ridley Hall Cam 70. **d** 72 **p** 73. C Ulverston St Mary w H Trin *Carl* 72-76; V Dewsbury Moor *Wakef* 76-84; V Hoddesdon *St Alb* from 84. *The Vicarage, 11 Amwell Street, Hoddesdon, Herts EN11 8TS* Hoddesdon (0992) 462127

SPRINGETT, Robert Wilfred. b 62. Nottm Univ BTh89. Linc Th Coll 86. **d** 89 **p** 90. C Colchester St Jas, All SS, St Nic and St Runwald *Chelmsf* from 89. *Benson House, 13 Roman Road, Colchester CO1 1UR* Colchester (0206) 573038

SPRINGETT, Simon Paul. b 56. Warw Univ LLB78. Wycliffe Hall Ox 78. **d** 81 **p** 82. C Harlow St Mary V *Chelmsf* 81-84; C Gt Clacton 84-86; R Rayne 86-91; Chapl RN from 91. *c/o MOD, Lacon House, Theobald's Road, London WC1X 8RY* 071-430 6847

SPRINGFORD, Patrick Francis Alexander. b 45. Wycliffe Hall Ox 71. **d** 74 **p** 75. C Finchley Ch Ch *Lon* 74-79; CF from 79. *c/o MOD (Army), Bagshot Park, Bagshot, Surrey GU19 5PL* Bagshot (0276) 71717

SPRINGHAM, Desmond John. b 32. Bris Univ BA56. Oak Hill Th Coll 56. **d** 58 **p** 59. C St Alb St Paul *St Alb* 58-61; C Reading St Jo *Ox* 61-66; R Worting *Win* 66-80; V Jersey St Andr from 80. *St Andrew's Vicarage, First Tower, Jersey, Channel Islands* Jersey (0534) 34975

SPRINGTHORPE, David Frederick. b 47. Open Univ BA. AKC72. **d** 73 **p** 74. C Dartford St Alb *Roch* 73-77; C Biggin Hill 77-80; R Ash 80-89; R Ridley 80-89; R Eynsford w Farningham and Lullingstone from 89.

The Rectory, Pollyhaugh, Eynsford, Dartford DA4 0HE
Farningham (0322) 863050

SPROSTON, Bernard Melvin. b 37. St Jo Coll Dur 77.
d 79 **p** 80. C Westlands St Andr *Lich* 79-82; P-in-c Heage
Derby 82-87; V Heath from 87. *The Vicarage, Heath,
Chesterfield, Derbyshire S44 5RX*   Chesterfield (0246)
850339

SPROULE, Gerald Norman. b 26. TCD DBS60. **d** 60
p 61. C Monaghan *Clogh* 60-62; I Cleenish 62-68; I
Magheracross 68-73; Admin Sec (Ireland) BCMS 73-79;
I Belf St Aid *Conn* 79-86; I Magherally w Annaclone
D & D from 86. *46 Kilmacrew Road, Banbridge, Co
Down BT32 4EP* Banbridge (08206) 23655

SPRUYT, John Harry. b 29. St Edm Hall Ox BA56 MA57.
Wycliffe Hall Ox 56. **d** 56 **p** 57. C Southn St Mark *Win*
56-58; C Kidlington *Ox* 58-61; V Lockerley w E Dean
Win 61-68; V Thornton-le-Street w Thornton-le-Moor
etc *York* 68-70; V Milborne St Andrew w Dewlish *Sarum*
71-77; P-in-c Jersey All SS *Win* 77; V 77-85; P-in-c
Jersey St Simon 77-84; V 84-85; Perm to Offic 86-88;
Australia from 88. *4 Ritchies Street, Alonnah, Bruny
Island, Tasmania, Australia 7150* Hobart (2) 931255

SPURGEON, Michael Paul. b 53. MIEx. Linc Th Coll 83.
d 85 **p** 86. C Lillington *Cov* 85-89; C Min Can Ripon
Cathl *Ripon* from 89. *The School House, Sharow, Ripon,
W Yorkshire HG4 5BJ* Ripon (0765) 707017

SPURIN, Richard Mark. b 28. Peterho Cam BA52 MA60.
Wycliffe Hall Ox 54. **d** 55 **p** 56. C Foleshill St Laur *Cov*
55-58; C Atherstone 58-60; CMS 60-61; Kenya 61-73;
C-in-c Ewell St Paul Howell Hill CD *Guildf* 73-82; V
Netherton *Liv* 82-86; V Brandwood *Birm* 86-91; C
Padiham *Blackb* from 91. *5 St John's Road, Padiham,
Burnley, Lancs BB12 7BN*

SPURR, Roger Colin. b 29. Linc Th Coll. **d** 82 **p** 83.
C Street w Walton *B & W* 82-85; R Stogumber w
Nettlecombe and Monksilver from 85. *The Rectory,
Vellow Road, Stogumber, Taunton, Somerset TA4 3TL*
Stogumber (0984) 56221

SPURRELL, John Mark. b 34. FSA87 CCC Ox
BA57 DipTh58 MA61. Linc Th Coll 58. **d** 60 **p** 61. C
Tilbury Docks *Chelmsf* 60-65; C Boston *Linc* 65-76; R
Stow in Lindsey 76-85; P-in-c Willingham 76-85; P-in-c
Coates 76-85; P-in-c Brightwell w Sotwell *Ox* from 85.
The Rectory, Brightwell, Wallingford, Oxon OX10 0RX
Wallingford (0491) 37110

SPURRIER, Richard Patrick Montague. b 25. Bris Univ
BA59. Wycliffe Hall Ox 59. **d** 61 **p** 62. C Weston St Jo
B & W 63-64; rtd 90. *24 Tomlinson Way, Eversley Park,
Sherburn in Elmet, Leeds LS25 6EQ*

SQUAREY, Gerald Stephen Miles. b 36. Lich Th Coll 59.
d 62 **p** 63. C Poplar All SS w St Frideswide *Lon* 62-64;
C Heston 64-67; V Bradf Abbas w Clifton Maybank
Sarum 67-74; P-in-c Corfe Castle 74-79; R 79-84; R
Steeple w Tyneham, Church Knowle and Kimmeridge
79-84; R Corfe Castle, Church Knowle, Kimmeridge etc
84-90; P-in-c Stourpaine, Durweston and Bryanston
90-91; P-in-c Pimperne 90-91; R Pimperne, Stourpaine,
Durweston and Bryanston from 91; RD Milton and
Blandford from 91. *The Vicarage, Shaston Road,
Stourpaine, Blandford Forum, Dorset DT11 8TA*
Blandford (0258) 480580

SQUIRE, Clenyg. b 31. TCert53. Cuddesdon Coll 89. **d** 90
p 91. NSM Hale and Ashley *Ches* from 90. *5 Riddings
Road, Hale, Altrincham, Cheshire WA15 9DS*   061-928
3396

SQUIRE, David George Mitchell. b 31. Worc Coll Ox
BA54 MA58. Qu Coll Birm DipTh66. **d** 67 **p** 68. C
Dursley *Glouc* 67-70; V Cam 71-77; Org Sec (Dios
Birm, Heref, Lich and Worc) CECS 77-88; Perm to
Offic *Heref* from 81; rtd 88. *Ty Gwyn, Dihewyd,
Lampeter, Dyfed SA48 7PP* Lampeter (0570) 470260

SQUIRE, Geoffrey Frank. b 36. Ex & Truro NSM Scheme.
d 83 **p** 84. NSM Barnstaple, Goodleigh and Landkey *Ex*
83-85; NSM Barnstaple from 85. *Little Cross, Northleigh
Hill, Goodleigh, Barnstaple, Devon EX32 7NR*
Barnstaple (0271) 44935

SQUIRE, Humphrey Edward. b 29. St Chad's Coll Dur
BA55. Coll of Resurr Mirfield. **d** 57 **p** 58. C Newbold
and Dunston *Derby* 57-59; C Thorpe *Nor* 59-61; Zanzibar
61-63; C Whittington *Derby* 63-64; R Drayton *Nor*
64-75; Chapl Dover Coll Kent 75-83; TV Wareham
Sarum from 83. *St Martin's Vicarage, Keysworth Drive,
Wareham, Dorset BH20 7DD* Wareham (0929) 552756

SQUIRE, Preb John Brinsmead. b 16. St Edm Hall Ox
BA38 MA43. Linc Th Coll 38. **d** 40 **p** 40. V Taunton St
Andr *B & W* 57-81; Preb Wells Cathl from 77; rtd 81.
*Xanadu, 1 St Mary Street, Nether Stowey, Bridgwater,
Somerset TA5 1LJ* Nether Stowey (0278) 732957

SQUIRES, Malcolm. b 46. St Chad's Coll Dur BA72.
Cuddesdon Coll 72. **d** 74 **p** 75. C Headingley *Ripon*
74-77; C Stanningley St Thos 77-80; V Bradshaw
Wakef 80-85; V Ripponden 85-89; V Barkisland w W
Scammonden 85-89; V Mirfield from 89. *The Vicarage,
Church Lane, Mirfield, W Yorkshire WF14 9HA*
Mirfield (0924) 492188

SSERUNKUMA, Michael Wilberforce. b 54. Trin Coll Bris
DipHE88 BA90 Bp Tucker Coll Mukono 77. **d** 77 **p** 78.
Uganda 77-87; C Gabalfa *Llan* from 90. *27 Pen-y-Bryn
Road, Gabalfa, Cardiff CF4 3LG* Cardiff (0222) 619556

STABLES, Courtley Greenwood. b 13. Keble Coll Ox
BA49 MA54. St Steph Ho Ox 48. **d** 50 **p** 51. Sen Lect
Coll of All SS Tottenham 63-72; Chmn Coun of Ch Schs
Co 68-87; C St Andr Undershaft w St Mary Axe *Lon*
64-72; Hon C Uckfield *Chich* from 72; rtd 78. *Abotslare,
Pound Green, Buxted, E Sussex TN22 4JZ* Buxted
(082581) 2467

STACEY, Dr Helen Norman. Edin Univ MB, ChB45
PhD49. S'wark Ord Course 82. **dss** 83 **d** 87. Notting Hill
St Jo and St Pet *Lon* 83-85; Upper Kennett *Sarum*
85-87; Hon Par Dn from 87. *Greystones House, Green
Street, Avebury, Marlborough, Wilts SN8 1RE* Avebury
(06723) 289

STACEY, John Roderick. b 33. Bris Univ BA54. St D
Coll Lamp LTh56. **d** 56 **p** 57. C Bedwellty *Mon* 56-58; C
Mon 58-62; V New Tredegar 62-66; CF 66-69; TV Ebbw
Vale *Mon* 69-73; CF (TA) from 70; V Mamhilad and
Pontymoile *Mon* 73-77; V Pontnewynydd 77-85; R
Bettws Newydd w Trostrey etc from 85. *The Rectory,
Bettws Newydd, Usk, Gwent NP5 1JN* Nantyderry
(0873) 880258

STACEY, Nicolas David. b 27. St Edm Hall Ox
BA51 MA55. Cuddesdon Coll 52. **d** 53 **p** 54. C Portsea
N End St Mark *Portsm* 53-58; Bp's Dom Chapl *Birm*
58-59; R Woolwich St Mary w H Trin *S'wark* 59-68;
Boro Dean of Greenwich 65-68; Perm to Offic *Ox* 68-71;
Dep Dir Oxfam 68-70; P-in-c Selling *Cant* 76; Perm to
Offic from 79; Six Preacher Cant Cathl from 84. *The
Old Vicarage, Selling, Faversham, Kent ME13 9RD*
Canterbury (0227) 752833

STACEY, Robert George Hugh. b 12. Sarum & Wells Th
Coll 74. **d** 76 **p** 77. NSM Swanage *Sarum* 76-85; rtd 85.
59 Bay Crescent, Swanage, Dorset BH19 1RB Swanage
(0929) 424138

STACEY, Victor George. b 44. NUI BA69 QUB MTh.
CITC 72. **d** 72 **p** 73. C Derriaghy *Conn* 72-76; C Knock
D & D 76-79; I Ballymacarrett St Martin 79-86; I Dub
Santry w Glasnevin *D & G* from 86; Bp's Dom Chapl
from 90; RD Fingal from 90. *The Rectory, Santry,
Dublin 9, Irish Republic* Dublin (1) 428596

STACKPOLE, Robert Aaron. b 59. Williams Coll Mass
BA82 Or Coll Ox MLitt88. St Steph Ho Ox 88. **d** 90
p 91. C Kettering SS Pet and Paul *Pet* from 90. *13 Clifton
Grove, Kettering, Northants NN15 7NB* Kettering
(0536) 84204

STAFF, Mrs Jean. b 44. CertEd64. E Midl Min Tr Course
81. **dss** 84 **d** 87. Old Brumby *Linc* 84-87; C 87-88; C
Gainsborough St Geo from 88. *33 The Pines, Foxby
Lane, Gainsborough, Lincs DN21 1PP* Gainsborough
(0427) 2009

STAFF, Miss Susan. b 59. Leeds Univ BA82. Ridley Hall
Cam 88. **d** 90. Par Dn Mickleover All SS *Derby* from
90. *7 Barnwood Close, Mickleover, Derby DE3 6QY*
Derby (0332) 511340

STAFFORD, David George. b 45. Qu Coll Birm 75. **d** 77
p 78. C Chesterfield St Aug *Derby* 77-80; C Ranmoor
Sheff 80-83; V Bolton-upon-Dearne from 83. *The
Vicarage, 41 Station Road, Bolton-on-Dearne,
Rotherham, S Yorkshire S63 8AA* Rotherham (0709)
893163

STAFFORD, Canon John Ingham Henry. b 31. TCD
BA52 MA56. **d** 53 **p** 55. C Clonallon *D & D* 53-56; C
Belf Malone (St Jo) *Conn* 56-59; Australia 59-64; Min
Can Down Cathl *D & D* 64-68; Hd of S Ch Miss
Ballymacarrett 68-73; I Bright w Killough 73-83; C Ban
Primacy from 83; Can Down Cathl from 90. *4 Glendowan
Way, Gransha Green, Bangor, Co Down BT19 2SP*
Bangor (0247) 456625

STAFFORD, John James. b 31. Linc Th Coll 69. **d** 71 **p** 72.
C Ordsall *S'well* 71-73; V Worksop St Paul 74-78; R
Nuthall 78-85; R Plumtree from 85. *The Rectory,
Plumtree, Church Hill, Nottingham NG12 5ND*
Plumtree (06077) 4245

STAFFORD, Suffragan Bishop of. See SCOTT-JOYNT,
Rt Rev Michael Charles

STAGG, Charles Roy. b 18. G&C Coll Cam BA45 MA47.
Ripon Hall Ox 47. **d** 48 **p** 49. Chapl Dur Sch 48-54; C
The Lickey *Birm* 54-55; Uganda 55-58; Chapl Aldenham

Sch Herts 59-64; Kenya 64-80; Perm to Offic *Glouc* from 81. *Wyck Cottage, Childswickham, Broadway, Worcs WR12 7HF* Broadway (0386) 853229

STAGG, Michael Hubert. b 39. St Chad's Coll Dur 58. **d** 63 **p** 64. C Weston-super-Mare St Sav *B & W* 63-66; P-in-c Fosdyke *Linc* 66-71; R Brompton Regis w Upton and Skilgate *B & W* 71-78; P-in-c Kidderminster St Jo *Worc* 78-80; P-in-c Cannington *B & W* 80-84; R Cannington, Otterhampton, Combwich and Stockland 84-87; Dioc Communications Officer *Nor* from 88; Bp's Chapl from 88. *St Martin-at-Palace Vicarage, Palace Plain, Norwich NR3 1RW* Norwich (0603) 614172

STAINES, Edward Noel. b 26. Trin Coll Ox MA52 MSc85. Chich Th Coll 51 57. **d** 57 **p** 58. V Amberley w N Stoke *Chich* 61-70; V Forest Row 70-75; R Ashurst 70-75; V Bexhill St Aug 75-79; TR Ovingdean w Rottingdean and Woodingdean 79-85; V Rottingdean 85-86; Perm to Offic *Worc* and *Glouc* from 86; Chapl Gtr Lisbon *Eur* 88-90; Chapl Marseille 90; rtd 90. *White House, Harpley Road, Defford, Worcester WR8 9BL* Evesham (0386) 750817

STAINES, Michael John. b 28. Trin Coll Ox BA52 MA56. Wells Th Coll 62. **d** 64 **p** 65. C Southwick *Chich* 64-67; TV Harling Gp *Nor* 67-73; PM S Chilterns Gp *Ox* 74-75; R W Wycombe w Bledlow Ridge, Bradenham and Radnage from 76; RD Wycombe 83-87. *The Rectory, Church Lane, West Wycombe, High Wycombe, Bucks HP14 3AH* High Wycombe (0494) 529988

STALEY, John Colin George. b 44. Hull Univ MA83. Wycliffe Hall Ox 68. **d** 71 **p** 72. C Tinsley *Sheff* 71-73; C Slaithwaite w E Scammonden *Wakef* 73-75; V Wakef St Andr and St Mary 75-80; Warden Scargill Ho N Yorkshire 80-82; P-in-c Macclesfield St Pet *Ches* 82-85; TV Macclesfield Team Par from 85; Dioc Ind Missr from 87. *261 Oxford Road, Macclesfield, Cheshire SK11 8JY* Macclesfield (0625) 423851

STALKER, William John. b 49. Nor Ord Course 89. **d** 91. C Formby H Trin *Liv* from 91. *19 Hampton Road, Formby, Liverpool L37 6EJ* Formby (07048) 76557

STALLARD, Canon Frederick Hugh. b 11. Pemb Coll Cam BA33 MA37. Cuddesdon Coll 33. **d** 34 **p** 35. V Pet All SS *Pet* 46-81; Can Pet Cathl 57-81; rtd 81. *3 Friday Bridge Road, Elm, Wisbech, Cambs* Wisbech (0945) 860812

STALLARD, John Charles. b 34. Selw Coll Cam BA58 MA62. Ripon Hall Ox 62. **d** 64 **p** 65. C Hall Green Ascension *Birm* 64-66; C Sutton Coldfield H Trin 66-68; C-in-c Brandwood CD 68-71; Chapl Dame Allan's Schs Newc 71-74; V Warley Woods *Birm* 75-84; TR Droitwich *Worc* 84-87; P-in-c Dodderhill 84-87; TR Droitwich Spa from 87. *The Rectory, 205 Worcester Road, Droitwich, Worcs WR9 8AS* Droitwich (0905) 773134

STALLEY, Brian Anthony. b 38. Oak Hill Th Coll 60. **d** 63 **p** 64. C Summerstown *S'wark* 63-70; Surrey BFBS Sec 70-73; Manager Action Cen BFBS 73-76; R Branston *Linc* from 76. *The Rectory, Branston, Lincoln LN4 1NN* Lincoln (0522) 791296

STAMFORD, Dean of. *See* IND, Rt Rev William

STAMP, Andrew Nicholas. b 44. Ex Univ BA67. Sarum Th Coll 67. **d** 69 **p** 70. C S Beddington St Mich *S'wark* 69-73; Tutor Sarum & Wells Th Coll 73-76; Chapl RN 76-81; C-in-c W Leigh CD *Portsm* 81-82; V W Leigh 82-87; R Botley from 87. *All Saints' Rectory, Brook Lane, Botley, Southampton SO3 2ER* Botley (0489) 781534

STAMP, Harold William Tremlett. b 08. St Aug Coll Cant 30. **d** 35 **p** 36. R Farway w Northleigh and Southleigh *Ex* 69-72; V Branscombe 72-76; rtd 76; Hon C Nymet Rowland w Coldridge *Ex* 77-81. *9 Clampitt Road, Ipplepen, Newton Abbot, Devon TQ12 5RJ* Ipplepen (0803) 813332

STAMP, Ian Jack. b 47. Aston Tr Scheme 82 N Ord Course 83. **d** 86 **p** 87. C Tonge w Alkrington *Man* 86-89; V Heywood St Marg from 89. *St Margaret's Vicarage, Heys Lane, Heywood, Lancs OL10 3RD* Heywood (0706) 68053

STAMP, Philip Andrew. b 53. Linc Th Coll 86. **d** 88 **p** 89. C Barton w Peel Green *Man* 88-91; R Blackley H Trin from 91. *Holy Trinity Rectory, Goodman Street, Manchester M9 1FE* 061-205 2879

STAMP, Richard Mark. b 36. St Chad's Coll Dur BA60 DipTh62. **d** 62 **p** 63. Australia 62-69 and from 72; C Greenhill St Jo *Lon* 69-72. *69 Sullivan Street, Inglewood, Australia 3517* Inglewood (54) 383055

✠**STANAGE, Rt Rev Thomas Shaun.** b 32. Pemb Coll Ox BA56 MA60 Nashotah Ho Wisconsin Hon DD86. Cuddesdon Coll 56. **d** 58 **p** 59 **c** 78. C Gt Crosby St Faith *Liv* 58-61; Min Orford St Andr CD 61-63; V Orford St Andr 63-70; S Africa from 70; Dean Kimberley 75-78;

Suff Bp Johannesburg from 78; Bp Bloemfontein from 82. *Bishop's House, 16 York Road, Bloemfontein, 9301 South Africa* Bloemfontein (51) 314351

STANBRIDGE, Ven Leslie Cyril. b 20. St Jo Coll Dur BA47 DipTh49 MA54. **d** 49 **p** 50. R Cottingham *York* 64-72; Can and Preb York Minster from 68; Succ Canonicorum from 88; RD Hull 70-72; Adn York 72-88; rtd 88. *1 Deangate, York YO1 2JB* York (0904) 621174

STANBROOK, Harry. b 05. Kelham Th Coll 27. **d** 33 **p** 34. Asst Chapl Chapl Community St Jo Bapt Clewer 63-69; rtd 77. *c/o 20 Bottrells Lane, Chalfont St Giles, Bucks HP8 4EY*

STANCLIFFE, Very Rev David Staffurth. b 42. Trin Coll Ox BA65 MA68. Cuddesdon Coll 65. **d** 67 **p** 68. C Armley St Bart *Ripon* 67-70; Chapl Clifton Coll Bris 70-77; Dir of Ords *Portsm* 77-82; Can Res Portsm Cathl 77-82; Provost Portsm from 82. *Provost's House, Pembroke Road, Portsmouth PO1 2NS* Portsmouth (0705) 824400 or 823300

STANDEN, David Ian. b 57. K Coll Lon BD78 AKC78. St Steph Ho Ox 80. **d** 81 **p** 82. C W Bromwich St Fran *Lich* 81-84; C Sedgley All SS 84-88; V Wolv St Steph from 88. *St Stephen's Vicarage, Hilton Street, Wolverhampton WV10 0LF* Wolverhampton (0902) 454662

STANDEN McDOUGAL, Canon John Anthony Phelps. b 33. AKC58. **d** 59 **p** 60. C Ipswich St Marg *St E* 59-63; C Bury St Edmunds St Mary 63-65; C Wadhurst *Chich* 65-70; C Tidebrook 65-70; R Tollard Royal w Farnham *Sarum* 70-81; P-in-c Gussage St Michael and Gussage All Saints 71-76; R 76-81; RD Milton and Blandford 81-86; R Tollard Royal w Farnham, Gussage St Michael etc 82-86; Can and Preb Sarum Cathl from 86; TR Bride Valley from 86. *The Rectory, Burton Bradstock, Bridport, Dorset DT6 4QS* Burton Bradstock (0308) 359

STANDING, Victor Denis. b 44. FRCO67 Lon Univ BMus66 Ox Univ DipTh77 Clare Coll Cam CertEd68. Ripon Coll Cuddesdon 75. **d** 78 **p** 79. C Wimborne Minster *Sarum* 78-80; TV Wimborne Minster and Holt 80-83; R Ex St Sidwell and St Matt *Ex* from 83; Dep PV Ex Cathl from 83; Chapl R Devon and Ex Hosp from 83; Chapl W England Eye Infirmary Ex from 83. *St Matthew's Vicarage, Spicer Road, Exeter EX1 1TA* Exeter (0392) 71882

STANDISH, Derrick Edgar. b 41. Univ of Wales (Lamp) BA67. Wycliffe Hall Ox 68. **d** 68 **p** 69. C Brynmawr *S & B* 68-69; C Morriston 69-74; V Merthyr Cynog and Dyffryn Honddu 74-76; R Llanwenarth Ultra *Mon* 76-83; V Abersychan and Garndiffaith from 83. *The Vicarage, Abersychan, Pontypool, Gwent NP4 8PL* Talywain (0495) 772213

STANDLEY, Leslie Gordon. b 19. St Chad's Coll Dur BA42 DipTh43 MA45. **d** 43 **p** 44. V Ulceby *Linc* 67-70; V Wootton 67-70; R Croxton 67-70; V Forest Town *S'well* 70-76; V Swineshead *Linc* 76-84; RD Holland W 79-84; rtd 84; Perm to Offic *Linc* from 86. *28 Highfields, Nettleham, Lincoln LN2 2SZ* Lincoln (0522) 754731

STANDLEY, Robert Henry. b 21. Lon Univ BD42. Linc Th Coll 42. **d** 44 **p** 45. V Coleby *Linc* 65-74; V Harmston 65-74; V Skirbeck Quarter 74-86; RD Holland E 80-85; rtd 86; Perm to Offic *Linc* from 86. *23 Burgess Road, Brigg, S Humberside DN20 8DA* Brigg (0652) 52020

STANES, Preb Ian Thomas. b 39. Sheff Univ BSc62 Linacre Coll Ox BA65 MA69. Wycliffe Hall Ox 63. **d** 65 **p** 66. C Leic H Apostles *Leic* 65-69; V Broom Leys 69-76; Warden Marrick Priory *Ripon* 76-82; Officer Miss, Min & Evang (Willesden Episc Area) *Lon* from 82; Continuing Minl Educn Officer from 82; Preb St Paul's Cathl from 89. *48 Whitmore Road, Harrow, Middx HA1 4HD* 081-423 3168

STANESBY, Canon Derek Malcolm. b 31. Leeds Univ BA56 Man Univ MEd75 PhD84. Coll of Resurr Mirfield 56. **d** 58 **p** 59. C Lakenham St Jo *Nor* 58-60; C Welling *S'wark* 60-62; V Bury St Mark *Man* 62-67; R Ladybarn 67-85; Can Windsor from 85; Steward Windsor from 85. *4 The Cloisters, Windsor Castle, Windsor, Berks SL4 1NJ* Windsor (0753) 864142

STANFORD, Ronald John. b 02. Trin Coll Ox BA24 MA28. Ripon Hall Ox 32. **d** 33 **p** 34. V Snape w Friston *St E* 63-73; rtd 73; Perm to Offic *St E* from 73. *Bowling Green, Low Road, Friston, Saxmundham, Suffolk IP17 1PW* Snape (072888) 358

STANIFORD, Mrs Doris Gwendoline. b 43. Gilmore Course. **dss** 80 **d** 87. Hangleton *Chich* 80-82; Durrington 82-87; Par Dn 87-89; Chich Th Coll from 83; Par Dn Crawley from 89. *10 Borrowdale Close, Crawley, W Sussex RH11 8SH* Crawley (0293) 611807

STANLEY, Arthur Patrick. b 32. TCD BA54 MA63. d 55 p 56. C Waterford St Patr *C & O* 55-58; CF 58-74; Dep Asst Chapl Gen 74-83. *Address temp unknown*

STANLEY, Eric William. b 22. TCD BA45 MA58. d 45 p 46. Can Killaloe Cathl *L & K* 65-89; I Nenagh 66-89; Chan Killaloe Cathl 72-79; Adn Killaloe, Kilfenora, Clonfert etc 79-89; Preb Taney St Patr Cathl Dub 81-89; rtd 89. *Cuanbeg, Ballycotton, Midleton, Co Cork, Irish Republic* Midleton (21) 646076

STANLEY, Canon John Alexander. b 31. Tyndale Hall Bris DipTh56. d 56 p 57. C Preston All SS *Blackb* 56-60; C St Helens St Mark *Liv* 60-63; V Everton St Cuth 63-70; P-in-c Everton St Sav 69-70; V Everton St Sav w St Cuth 70-74; V Huyton St Mich from 74; Hon Can Liv Cathl from 87; AD Huyton from 89. *The Vicarage, Huyton, Liverpool L36 7SA* 051-449 3900

STANLEY, Joseph. b 12. Chich Th Coll 37. d 39 p 40. V Swaffham *Nor* 51-60; rtd 77. *Albemarle Rest Home, 50 Kenilworth Road, Leamington Spa CV32 6JW* Leamington Spa (0926) 425629

STANLEY, Robert John. b 27. TCD BA50 MA54. d 50 p 51. C Belf Trin Coll Miss *Conn* 50-52; C Belf St Matt 52-54; I Tamlaghtard w Aghanloo *D & R* 54-60; I Donagheady 60-63; CF 63-79; V Prittlewell St Steph *Chelmsf* from 79. *St Stephen's Vicarage, 213 Manners Way, Southend-on-Sea SS2 6QS* Southend-on-Sea (0702) 341402

STANLEY, Simon Richard. b 44. Wells Th Coll 66. d 69 p 70. C Foleshill St Laur *Cov* 69-71; C Hessle *York* 71-75; P-in-c Flamborough 75-80; R Dunnington from 80. *The Rectory, Dunnington, York YO1 5PW* York (0904) 489349

STANLEY-SMITH, James. b 29. Hatf Coll Dur BA54 DipEd55. S Dios Minl Tr Scheme 81. d 84 p 85. C Bournemouth St Jo w St Mich *Win* 84-87; R Hale w S Charford from 87. *The Rectory, Hale, Fordingbridge, Hants SP6 2AN* Downton (0725) 22307

STANNARD, Brian. b 46. MICE71 MIStructE71. Cranmer Hall Dur 86. d 88 p 89. C Burnage St Marg *Man* 88-91; V Walmersley from 91. *The Vicarage, 14 Springside Road, Bury, Lancs BL9 5JE* 061-797 9273

STANNARD, Ven Colin Percy. b 24. TD66. Selw Coll Cam BA47 MA49. Linc Th Coll 47. d 49 p 50. C St E Cathl *St E* 49-52; C-in-c Nunsthorpe CD *Linc* 52-55; CF (TA) 53-67; V Barrow St Jas *Carl* 55-64; V Upperby St Jo 64-70; R Gosforth 70-75; RD Calder 70-75; P-in-c Natland 75-76; V 76-84; RD Kendal 75-84; Hon Can Carl Cathl 75-84; Adn Carl from 84; Can Res Carl Cathl from 84. *38 Longlands Road, Carlisle CA3 9AE* Carlisle (0228) 27622

STANNARD, Harold Frederick David. b 12. AKC37. d 37 p 38. V W Quantoxhead *B & W* 48-77; rtd 77. *Little Orchard, Bosinver Lane, Polgooth, Cornwall PL26 7BA* St Austell (0726) 68712

STANNARD, Peter Graville. b 59. Univ of Wales (Abth) BSc81 Ox Univ BA85. St Steph Ho Ox 83. d 86 p 87. C Worksop Priory *S'well* 86-89; Ghana from 89. *St Nicholas's Theological College, Cape Coast, Ghana*

STANSBURY, Alan David. b 29. Ridley Hall Cam 59. d 61 p 62. C Kennington St Mark *S'wark* 61-63; S Africa from 63. *PO Box 15, Aliwal North, 5530 South Africa* Aliwal North (551) 2281

STANTON, David John. b 60. FSAScot89 St Andr Univ MTheol82. Ripon Coll Cuddesdon 83. d 85 p 86. C Beckenham St Geo *Roch* 85-88; Asst Chapl Shrewsbury Sch 88-90; Hon C Shrewsbury All SS w St Mich *Lich* 88-90; P-in-c Abbotskerswell *Ex* from 90. *The Vicarage, Church Path, Abbotskerswell, Newton Abbot, Devon TQ12 5NY* Newton Abbot (0626) 334445

STANTON, Gregory John. b 47. Sarum & Wells Th Coll 84. d 86 p 87. C Willenhall H Trin *Lich* 86-89; C Plympton St Mary *Ex* from 89. *9 Horswell Close, Plymptom, Plymouth PL7 3NG* Plymouth (0752) 346485

STANTON, John Maurice. b 18. Univ Coll Ox BA45 MA45. Wycliffe Hall Ox 51. d 52 p 53. Hd Master Blundell's Sch 59-71; Public Preacher *Ex* 71-72; C Ex St Matt *Ex* 72-73; R Chesham Bois *Ox* 73-83; rtd 83; Perm to Offic *Ox* from 83. *37A St Andrew's Road, Oxford OX3 9DL* Oxford (0865) 65206

STANTON, Ronald Geoffrey. b 14. Leeds Univ BA48. Wells Th Coll. d 50 p 51. R Walton D'Eiville *Cov* 61-72; V Finham 72-79; rtd 79; Perm to Offic *Cov* from 79. *8 Margetts Close, Kenilworth, Warks CV8 1EN* Kenilworth (0926) 511036

STANTON, Thomas Hugh (Brother Timothy). b 17. Trin Coll Cam BA38 MA45. Coll of Resurr Mirfield 46. d 47 p 48. CR from 52; S Africa 54-87; rtd 87. *Community of*

the Resurrection, Mirfield, W Yorkshire WF14 0BN Mirfield (0924) 494318

STANTON-HYDE, Mrs Marjorie Elizabeth. b 37. TCert58. Cranmer Hall Dur 86. d 88. Par Dn Elmley Lovett w Hampton Lovett and Elmbridge etc *Worc* from 88; Par Dn Hartlebury from 88; Par Dn Wilden from 88. *Church Rise, Quarry Bank, Hartlebury, Kidderminster, Worcs DY11 7TE* Hartlebury (0299) 251535

STANTON-SARINGER, Maurice Charles. b 49. Bris Univ BSc71 PGCE72 Fitzw Coll Cam BA77 MA81. Ridley Hall Cam 75. d 78 p 79. C Gerrards Cross *Ox* 78-80; C Bletchley 80-83; Lic to Offic 83-91; Chapl Stowe Sch Bucks 83-91; R Sherington w Chicheley, N Crawley, Astwood etc *Ox* from 91. *The Rectory, School Lane, Sherington, Newport Pagnell, Bucks MK16 9NF* Milton Keynes (0908) 610521

STANWAY, Peter David. b 48. K Coll Lon BD71. St Aug Coll Cant 72. d 73 p 74. C Maidstone All SS w St Phil and H Trin *Cant* 73-77; Canada 77-84; C Waterlooville *Portsm* 84-87; R Laughton w Ripe and Chalvington *Chich* 87-90; Chapl Witney Community Hosp from 90. *c/o Armada Cottage, Charlbury, Oxford OX7*

STAPLES, David. b 35. Jes Coll Ox BA59 MA63 BD75. Linc Th Coll 59. d 61 p 62. C Kettering St Andr *Pet* 61-64; C Doncaster St Geo *Sheff* 64-66; Youth Chapl 66-71; V Mexborough 71-83; RD Wath 77-83; Hon Can Sheff Cathl 80-83; V W Haddon w Winwick *Pet* 83-88; RD Brixworth 83-89; V W Haddon w Winwick and Ravensthorpe from 88. *The Vicarage, 4 West End, West Haddon, Northampton NN6 7AY* West Haddon (078887) 207

STAPLES, Canon Edward Eric. b 10. OBE73 CBE77. Chich Th Coll 46. d 48 p 49. Chapl Helsinki w Moscow *Eur* 66-80; Chapl to HM The Queen 73-80; rtd 80; Perm to Offic *Bris* 81-88; *B & W* from 81. *4 Hawthorne Close, Dennedal Tokai, 7945 South Africa* Cape Town (21) 728392

STAPLES, John Wedgwood. b 42. Hertf Coll Ox BA64 MA. Wycliffe Hall Ox 64. d 66 p 67. C Yardley St Edburgha *Birm* 66-69; C Knowle 69-74; R Barcombe *Chich* 74-81; V Old Windsor *Ox* from 81. *The Vicarage, Church Road, Old Windsor, Windsor, Berks SL4 2PQ* Windsor (0753) 865778

STAPLES, Peter. b 35. d 62 p 63. C Fairfield *Derby* 62-63; C Dore 63-66; C Wilne and Draycott w Breaston 66-71; The Netherlands from 72. *c/o The University, Utrecht, The Netherlands*

STAPLES, Peter Brian. b 38. Bps' Coll Cheshunt 66. d 68 p 69. C Birkdale St Jas *Liv* 68-71; C Sevenoaks St Jo *Roch* 71-74; V Treslothan *Truro* 74-80; V Truro St Paul and St Clem from 80. *The Vicarage, 41 Tregolls Road, Truro, Cornwall TR1 1LE* Truro (0872) 72576

STAPLETON, Very Rev Henry Edward Champneys. b 32. FSA74 Pemb Coll Cam BA54 MA58. Ely Th Coll 54. d 56 p 57. C York St Olave w St Giles *York* 56-59; C Pocklington w Yapham-cum-Meltonby, Owsthorpe etc 59-61; R Seaton Ross w Everingham and Bielby and Harswell 61-67; RD Weighton 66-67; R Skelton by York 67-75; V Wroxham w Hoveton *Nor* 75-81; P-in-c Belaugh 76-81; Can Res and Prec Roch Cathl *Roch* 81-88; Dean Carl from 88. *The Deanery, Carlisle CA3 8TZ* Carlisle (0228) 23335

STAPLETON, Canon Kenneth Hargrave. b 11. St Pet Hall Ox BA38 MA42. Wells Th Coll 38. d 39 p 40. V Leeds Halton St Wilfrid *Ripon* 62-78; rtd 78; Perm to Offic *Ripon* from 78; *Wakef* from 90. *29 St Paul's Road, Mirfield, W Yorkshire WF14 8AY* Mirfield (0924) 491746

STAPLETON, Leonard Charles. b 37. Chich Th Coll 75. d 77 p 78. C Crayford *Roch* 77-81; C Lamorbey H Redeemer 81-83; V Belvedere St Aug 83-89; V Beckenham St Jas from 89. *The Vicarage, St James Avenue, Elmers End, Beckenham, Kent BR3 4HF* 081-650 0420

STAPLETON, Robert Michael Vorley. b 25. ALCD51. d 51 p 52. C Plymouth St Andr *Ex* 51-56; Chapl RN 56-60; C Surbiton St Matt *S'wark* 60-64; R Chenies and Lt Chalfont *Ox* 64-87; P-in-c Latimer w Flaunden 86-87; R Chenies and Lt Chalfont, Latimer and Flaunden from 87. *The Rectory, Chenies, Rickmansworth, Herts WD3 6ER* Chorleywood (0923) 284433

STAPLETON, Robert Vauvelle. b 47. Dur Univ BA70. Cranmer Hall Dur DipTh71. d 71 p 72. C Moreton *Ches* 71-73; C Monkwearmouth All SS *Dur* 73-76; C Stranton 76-79; P-in-c Kelloe 79-86; V New Shildon from 86. *All Saints' Vicarage, Shildon, Co Durham DL4 2JT* Bishop Auckland (0388) 772785

STARBUCK, Francis Tony. b 36. Kelham Th Coll 57. d 61 p 62. C Mansf St Mark *S'well* 61-64; C Didcot *Ox* 67-71;

C-in-c California CD 71-75; R Barkham 74-75; V Hagbourne 75-82; V Maidenhead St Luke 82-87; New Zealand from 87. *St John's Vicarage, PO Box 67, Te Puke, New Zealand* Tauranga (75) 737970

STARES, Mrs Beryl. b 33. Sarum Th Coll 83. dss 86 d 87. Crofton *Portsm* 86-87; Hon C from 87. *62 Mancroft Avenue, Hill Head, Fareham, Hants PO14 2DD* Stubbington (0329) 668540

STARES, Brian Maurice William. b 44. St Deiniol's Hawarden 74. d 74 p 75. C Risca *Mon* 74-77; V Newport St Steph and H Trin 77-87; V Fleur-de-Lis from 87. *The Vicarage, Commercial Street, Pengam, Blackwood, Gwent NP2 1TX* Bargoed (0443) 832904

STARK, Preb Edwin George John. b 20. Ex Coll Ox BA48 MA52. Wells Th Coll. d 49 p 50. V Hackney Wick St Mary of Eton w St Aug *Lon* 64-77; P-in-c Falmouth All SS *Truro* 77-80; V Mylor w Flushing 80-83; Preb St Endellion from 81; P-in-c Blisland w St Breward 83-84; R 84-88; rtd 88. *Marnays, Polzeath, Wadebridge, Cornwall PL27 6TN* Trebetherick (0208) 862888

STARK, John Jordan. b 40. Hull Univ BA62 St Chad's Coll Dur DipTh64. d 64 p 65. C Buxton *Derby* 64-67; C Wolborough w Newton Abbot *Ex* 67-74; R Belstone 74-79; P-in-c Plymouth St Gabr 79-80; V from 80. *The Vicarage, 1 Peverell Terrace, Plymouth PL3 4JJ* Plymouth (0752) 663938

STARK, Margaret Alison. b 46. Univ of Wales BA70 BA71. Llan St Mich DPS90. d 90. C Llanishen and Lisvane *Llan* from 90. *Hill View Court, 22B Heol Hir, Llanishen, Cardiff CF4 5AE* Cardiff (0222) 756868

STARK, Michael. b 35. Dur Univ BSc56. Chich Th Coll 58. d 60 p 61. C Middlesb St Paul *York* 60-64; C S Bank 64-66; R Skelton in Cleveland 66-74; P-in-c Upleatham 66-67; R 67-74; Asst Chapl HM Pris Wormwood Scrubs 74-77; Chapl HM Pris Featherstone 77-84; Ex 84-89; Chapl HM Pris Leic from 89. *HM Prison, 116 Welford Road, Leicester LE2 7AJ* Leicester (0533) 546911

STARKEY, Gerald Dennis. b 34. Qu Coll Birm 79. d 82 p 83. C Wilnecote *Lich* 82-86; Min Stoke-upon-Trent 86-90; P-in-c W Bromwich St Pet from 90. *The Vicarage, Oldbury Road, Greets Green, West Bromwich, W Midlands B70 9DP* 021-525 5147

STARKEY, John Douglas. b 23. St Chad's Coll Dur BA47 DipTh48. d 48 p 49. V Freehay *Lich* 66-84; P-in-c Oakamoor w Cotton 78-84; R Dunstall w Rangemore and Tatenhill 84-88; rtd 88; Perm to Offic *Lich* and *Derby* from 88. *34 Park Crescent, Doveridge, Derby DE6 5NE* Uttoxeter (0889) 566384

STARKEY, Simon Mark. b 36. Liv Univ BA78. Clifton Th Coll. d 66 p 67. C Ox St Ebbe w St Pet *Ox* 66-72; Community Chapl CPAS Kirkdale 72-77; TV Toxteth Park St Bede *Liv* 77-78; P-in-c 78-80; V 80-90; RD Toxteth 81-89; Chapl Ches Cath *Ches* from 90. *61 Parkgate Road, Chester CH1 4AQ* Chester (0244) 372003

STARLING, Cyril James. b 18. St D Coll Lamp 63. d 65 p 66. Chapl Basingstoke Distr Hosp 70-73; Australia 74-83; rtd 83. *9 Hillside, Risca, Newport, Gwent NP1 6QD*

STARNES, Peter Henry. b 19. LTCL74 St Jo Coll Cam BA42 MA47 Ch Ch Coll Cant PGCE72. Linc Th Coll 42. d 44 p 45. V Westwell Cant 56-65; R Eastwell w Boughton Aluph 60-65; rtd 84. *Whitebeams, High Halden, Ashford, Kent TN26 3LY* Ashford (0233) 850245

STARR, John Michael. b 50. Southn Univ. Sarum & Wells Th Coll 71. d 74 p 75. C Basingstoke *Win* 74-78; C Southn Maybush St Pet 78-79; C Milton 79-83; V Lupset *Wakef* 83-90; V Kennington St Mark *S'wark* from 90. *St Mark's Vicarage, Kennington Oval, London SE11 5SW* 071-735 1801

STARR, Dr Michael Reginald. b 41. MICE71 Bris Univ BSc63 PhD66. Ox NSM Course 83. d 86 p 87. NSM Gt Faringdon w Lt Coxwell *Ox* from 86. *23 Gloucester Street, Faringdon, Oxon SN7 7JA* Faringdon (0367) 240686

STARR, Michael Richard. b 43. Sarum Th Coll 65. d 68 p 69. C Plymouth St Pet *Ex* 68-72; C Blackpool St Paul *Blackb* 72-74; V Burnley St Cuth 74-79; C Eastbourne St Mary *Chich* 79-84; P-in-c Eastbourne Ch Ch 84-87; V 87-88; R Guernsey Ste Marie du Castel *Win* from 88. *The Rectory, Ste Marie du Castel, Guernsey, Channel Islands* Guernsey (0481) 56793

STARTIN, Geoffrey Neil. b 56. Essex Univ BA81 Ch Ch Ox MSc84 Westmr Coll Ox CertEd85. St Steph Ho Ox 86. d 88 p 89. C Coseley Ch Ch *Lich* 88-90; C Wellingborough All Hallows *Pet* from 90. *2 Troon Crescent, Wellingborough, Northants NN8 3WG* Wellingborough (0933) 679614

STARTIN, Nicola Gail. b 57. K Coll Lon LLB79. St Steph Ho Ox 88. d 90. C Wellingborough All SS *Pet* from 90. *2 Troon Crescent, Wellingborough, Northants NN8 3WG* Wellingborough (0933) 679614

STATHAM, Brian Edward. b 55. K Coll Lon MA AKC76. St Steph Ho Ox 77. d 78 p 79. C Ches H Trin *Ches* 78-81; C Birkenhead Priory 81-82; TV 82-86; V Newton 86-91; SSF from 91. *St Michael's House, Queensbury Road, Newton, Wirral, Merseyside L48 6EP* 051-625 8517

STATHAM, John Francis. b 31. Kelham Th Coll 51. d 56 p 57. C Ilkeston St Mary *Derby* 56-58; C New Mills 58-59; V 69-81; C Newbold and Dunston 59-62; V Ridgeway 62-69; RD Glossop 78-81; R Matlock 81-89; R Killamarsh from 89. *The Rectory, Sheepcote Road, Killamarsh, Sheffield S31 8BN* Sheffield (0742) 482769

STATON, Preb Geoffrey. b 40. Wells Th Coll 64. d 66 p 67. C Wednesfield St Thos *Lich* 66-69; C Cannock 69-72; V Cheddleton 72-82; RD Leek 77-82; V Harlescott 82-90; Preb Lich Cathl from 87; TR Penkridge Team from 90. *The Rectory, Penkridge, Stafford ST19 5DN* Penkridge (0785) 712378

STAUNTON, Richard Steedman. b 25. Wadh Coll Ox BA49 MA50 BSc51. Cuddesdon Coll 63. d 64 p 65. V Tile Hill *Cov* 68-76; V Hillmorton 76-90; rtd 90. *2 Tony-fron, Corris Uchaf, Machynlleth, Powys SY20 9BN* Corris (0654) 761466

STAVELEY, Dennis Frank. b 21. Open Univ BA75. S'wark Ord Course 77. d 80 p 81. C Danbury *Chelmsf* 80-84; P-in-c Lt Hallingbury 84-91; P-in-c Gt Hallingbury 86-91; R Gt Hallingbury and Lt Hallingbury 91; rtd 91. *99 Mumford Road, West Bergholt, Colchester* Colchester (0206) 240965

STAVELEY-WADHAM, Robert Andrew. b 43. Ridley Hall Cam 79. d 81 p 82. C Saffron Walden w Wendens Ambo and Littlebury *Chelmsf* 81-84; P-in-c Austrey *Birm* 84-87; P-in-c Warton 84-87. *Address temp unknown*

STEAD, Andrew Michael. b 63. BA84. Coll of Resurr Mirfield 84. d 87 p 88. C Wellingborough All Hallows *Pet* 87-90; Chapl St Alb Abbey *St Alb* from 90. *The Deanery Barn, Sumpter Yard, St Albans, Herts* St Albans (0727) 54950

STEAD, Canon George Christopher. b 13. FBA80 K Coll Cam BA35 MA38 LittD78 New Coll Ox BA35 Keble Coll Ox MA49. Cuddesdon Coll 38. d 38 p 41. Ely Prof Div Cam Univ 71-80; Can Res Ely Cathl *Ely* 71-80; rtd 80. *13 Station Road, Haddenham, Ely, Cambs* Ely (0353) 740575

STEAD, Leslie Cawthorn. b 11. Oak Hill Th Coll 58. d 59 p 60. V Collier Street *Roch* 62-71; Hon C Ashburnham w Penhurst *Chich* 71-84; rtd 79; Perm to Offic *Chich* from 84. *5 Cornford Court, Cornford Lane, Pembury, Tunbridge Wells TN2 4QS* Pembury (089282) 4635

STEADMAN, Fred. b 11. Univ Coll Ox BA34 MA65. d 65 p 66. V Willaston *Ches* 69-79; P-in-c Capenhurst 71-79; rtd 79; Perm to Offic *Ches* from 79. *24 Glan Aber Park, Chester CH4 8LF* Chester (0244) 682989

STEADMAN, Norman Neil. b 39. QUB BSc61 TCD Div Test63. d 63 p 64. C Newtownards *D & D* 63-65; C Belf Whiterock *Conn* 65-67; Asst Dean of Residences QUB 67-71; Perm to Offic *St Alb* 71-73; Dioc Youth Officer 73-76; P-in-c Hitchin H Sav 76; TV Hitchin 77-84; V Brampton *Carl* from 84. *St Martin's Vicarage, Main Street, Brampton, Cumbria CA8 1SH* Brampton (06977) 2486

STEADMAN-ALLEN, Barbara. b 53. ARCM83 Trent Park Coll of Educn CertEd74 Birm Univ BMus77. Cranmer Hall Dur 88. d 90. C Chessington *Guildf* from 90. *5 Bray Court, North Parade, Chessington, Surrey KT9 1QN* 081-397 3825

STEADMAN-LEWIS, Arthur Edward. b 03. d 39 p 40. V Walton *B & W* 54-76; rtd 76. *11 Beach Court, Beach Road, Weston-super-Mare, Avon BS23 1BD* Weston-super-Mare (0934) 27899

STEADY, Vilda May. b 51. Linc Th Coll 87. d 89. Par Dn Cannock *Lich* from 89. *100 Bond Way, Cannock, Staffs WS12 4SN* Hednesford (05438) 78041

STEAR, Michael Peter Hutchinson. b 47. Wycliffe Hall Ox 71. d 74 p 75. C Streatham Vale H Redeemer *S'wark* 74-77; C Ramsgate St Luke *Cant* 77-82; V Ramsgate St Mark 82-83; Min Jersey St Paul Prop Chpl *Win* from 83. *5 Claremont Avenue, St Saviour, Jersey, Channel Islands* Jersey (0534) 76129

STEARE, Peter Douglas. b 27. S Dios Minl Tr Scheme. d 84 p 85. NSM Upton cum Chalvey *Ox* 84-86; Perm to Offic *Bris* 86-88; Hon C Kington 88-90. *Kensell, Hayes Road, Nailsworth, Glos GL6 0EB* Nailsworth (0453) 833776

STEARN, Peter Reginald. b 38. ARCM. Linc Th Coll 75. d 77 p 78. C St Alb St Pet *St Alb* 77-79; C Bushey 79-82; V Kings Langley from 82. *The Vicarage, The Glebe, Kings Langley, Herts WD4 9HY* Kings Langley (0923) 262939

STEBBING, Michael Langdale (Brother Nicolas). b 46. Univ of Zimbabwe BA68 Univ of S Africa MTh86. Coll of Resurr Mirfield. d 74 p 75. C Borrowdale *Carl* 74-76; Rhodesia 76-79; S Africa 79-86; CR from 80. *House of the Resurrection, Mirfield, W Yorkshire WF14 0BN* Mirfield (0924) 494318

STEDMAN, Michael Sydney. b 34. ARICS58. Clifton Th Coll 62. d 65 p 66. C Lindfield *Chich* 65-68; C Gt Baddow *Chelmsf* 68-73; TV Ashby w Thurton, Claxton and Carleton *Nor* 73-75; P-in-c 75-85; TV Rockland St Mary w Hellington 73-75; P-in-c 75-85; TV Framingham Pigot 73-75; P-in-c 75-85; TV Bramerton w Surlingham 73-75; P-in-c 75-85; TV Bergh Apton w Yelverton 73-75; P-in-c 75-85; RD Loddon 78-85; R Church Stretton *Heref* from 85; RD Condover from 88. *The Rectory, Carding Mill Valley, Church Stretton, Shropshire SY6 6JF* Church Stretton (0694) 722585

STEDMAN, Robert Alfred. b 24. Qu Coll Birm 50. d 52 p 53. V Salehurst *Chich* 61-76; R Newhaven 76-90; rtd 90. *14 Gorham Court, Gorham Way, Telscombe Cliffs, Peacehaven, E Sussex BN10 7BB* Peacehaven (0273) 584254

STEED, Herbert Edward. b 23. St Jo Coll Dur BA51 DipTh52. d 52 p 53. R E Barnet *St Alb* 65-91; rtd 91. *1 Harrier Close, Cranleigh, Surrey GU6 7BS* Cranleigh (0483) 278151

STEEDMAN, Aubrey Wyld. b 11. Dur Univ BA40 MA43. St Aid Birkenhead 34. d 38 p 38. R Beckingham w Fenton *Linc* 49-88; rtd 89. *38 Bullpit Road, Balderton, Newark, Notts NG24 3LY* Newark (0636) 605480

STEEL, David Pitcaithley. b 22. St Andr Univ MA70 Dundee Univ DipEd DipRE71 Jordan Hill Coll Glas HDipRE74 Harley Univ DD82. d 83. NSM Laurencekirk *Bre* from 83; NSM Drumtochty from 84; NSM Fasque 84-91; NSM Drumlithie 84-91. *Churchlands, 29 Arduthie Road, Stonehaven, Kincardineshire AB3 2EH* Stonehaven (0569) 65341

STEEL, Graham Reginald. b 51. Cam Univ MA. Trin Coll Bris 80. d 83 p 84. C Gt Parndon *Chelmsf* 83-86; C Barking St Marg w St Patr 86-89; P-in-c Westcliff St Cedd from 89; Chapl Southend Gen Hosp from 89. *122 Mendip Crescent, Westcliff-on-Sea, Essex SS0 0HN* Southend-on-Sea (0702) 525126

STEEL, Leslie Frederick. Univ of NZ LTh65. St Jo Coll Auckland 57. d 59 p 60. New Zealand 59-91; Chapl Lausanne *Eur* from 91. *Fiet-de-Chapitre 8, CH 1213 Petit Lancy, Lausanne, Switzerland*

STEEL, Norman William. b 53. Sarum & Wells Th Coll 85. d 87 p 88. C S Woodham Ferrers *Chelmsf* from 87. *25 Benbow Drive, South Woodham Ferrers, Essex CM3 5FP* Chelmsford (0245) 325593

STEEL, Richard John. b 57. Dur Univ BA79 Cam Univ MA86. Ridley Hall Cam 81. d 84 p 85. C Hull Newland St Jo *York* 84-87; Relig Broadcasting Officer *Derby* from 88. *19 Elm Avenue, Long Eaton, Nottingham NG10 4LR* Long Eaton (0602) 724811

STEEL, Thomas Molyneux. b 39. Man Univ BA61 Ox Univ DipPSA62. Ripon Hall Ox 61. d 63 p 64. C Newc H Cross *Newc* 63-66; P-in-c Man St Aid *Man* 66-71; R Failsworth St Jo 71-79; P-in-c Farnham Royal *Ox* 79-81; P-in-c Hedgerley 80-81; R Farnham Royal w Hedgerley 81-91; V Prescot *Liv* from 91. *The Vicarage, Prescot, Merseyside L34 1LA* 051-426 6719

STEELE, Charles Edward Ernest. b 24. Cuddesdon Coll 72. d 74 p 75. C Rubery *Birm* 74-77; P-in-c Shaw Hill 77-79; V 79-82; C Curdworth 82-83; C Curdworth w Castle Vale 83-85; rtd 85; Perm to Offic *Birm* from 85. *3 Dominic Drive, Middleton Hall Road, Birmingham B30 1DW* 021-451 3372

STEELE, David Robert. b 29. Peterho Cam BA53 MA57. Oak Hill Th Coll 53. d 56 p 57. C Portman Square St Paul *Lon* 56-59; C Sevenoaks St Nic *Roch* 59-62; Kenya 63-65; Lic to Offic *Lon* 65-83; Chapl Steward's Trust Lon 65-72; Jt Gen Sec Intercon Ch Soc 72-81; Dir 2 Tim 2 Trust from 82; Perm to Offic *Lon & Win* from 83. *Worthy Park Grove, Abbots Worthy, Winchester, Hants SO21 1AN* Winchester (0962) 882082

STEELE, Gerald Robert. b 25. St D Coll Lamp BA49. d 51 p 52. C Glyntaff *Llan* 51-63; V Llangeinor 63-73; R Cadoxton-juxta-Barry from 73; Chapl Barry Community Hosp from 73; Miss to Seamen from 73. *The Rectory, 21 Rectory Road, Cadoxton, Barry, S Glam CF6 6QB* Barry (0446) 733041

STEELE, Gordon John. b 55. Kent Univ BA76 Worc Coll Ox BA82 MA87. Coll of Resurr Mirfield 82. d 84 p 85. C Greenhill St Jo *Lon* 84-88; C Uxbridge St Andr w St Jo 88; C Uxbridge 88; TV from 88. *St Andrew's Vicarage, The Greenway, Uxbridge, Middx UB8 2PJ* Uxbridge (0895) 37853

STEELE, John Thomas Robson. b 02. Qu Coll Ox BA24. d 32 p 33. R Kirkandrews-on-Esk *Carl* 53-70; rtd 70; Lic to Offic *Carl* from 70. *1 The Chestnuts, Cumwhinton, Carlisle CA4 8DY* Wetheral (0228) 61289

STEELE, Keith Atkinson. b 28. CEng MIMechE. Oak Hill Th Coll 80. d 81 p 82. Hon C Westoning w Tingrith *St Alb* 81-87; Hon C Chalgrave 87-88; P-in-c from 88. *Mariner's Lodge, Church Road, Westoning, Bedford MK45 5JW* Flitwick (0525) 714111

STEELE, Terence. b 54. Linc Th Coll 85. d 87 p 88. C New Sleaford *Linc* 87-90; V Cowbit from 90. *The Vicarage, 2 Small Drove, Weston, Spalding, Lincs PE12 6HS* Holbeach (0406) 370152

STEELE-PERKINS, Richard De Courcy. b 36. Clifton Th Coll 61. d 64 p 65. C Stoke Damerel *Ex* 64-65; C Washfield 65-68; P-in-c Wimbledon *S'wark* 68-70; Chapl Lambeth Hosp 70-74; Asst Chapl St Thos Hosp Lon 70-74; P-in-c Tawstock *Ex* 74-75; R 75-81; P-in-c Sticklepath 74-75; R 75-81; V Buckfastleigh w Dean Prior 81-91; TR Camelot Par *B & W* from 91. *The Rectory, Woolston Road, North Cadbury, Yeovil, Somerset BA22 7DS* North Cadbury (0963) 40469

STEER, Frederick Arthur. b 06. Hatf Coll Dur BA38 LTh38. St Boniface Warminster 34. d 38 p 39. V Aldermaston w Wasing *Ox* 69-73; rtd 73; Perm to Offic *Chich* from 73. *3 Holland Avenue, Bexhill-on-Sea, E Sussex TN39 4QD* Cooden (04243) 2835

STEER, Martin Leslie. b 41. Dur Univ BA65. Oak Hill Th Coll 65. d 67 p 68. C Rayleigh *Chelmsf* 67-70; CF 70-76; Past Care, Guidance & Counselling Univ of Wales 76-77; Teacher and Lib Intake High Sch Leeds 77-88; NSM Roundhay St Edm *Ripon* 83-85; NSM Moor Allerton 85-88; Chapl HM Young Offender Inst Portland from 88. *HM Young Offender Institution, Easton, Portland, Dorset DT5 1DL* Portland (0305) 820301

STELL, Peter Donald. b 50. MInstM MBAC MAPCC Leeds Univ 74. Sarum & Wells Th Coll 78. d 81 p 82. C Rothwell w Lofthouse *Ripon* 81-85; TV Brayton *York* 85-87; Chapl Asst Leybourne Grange Hosp W Malling and Kent, Sussex & Pembury Hosps Tunbridge Wells 87-88; C Spalding St Jo w Deeping St Nicholas *Linc* from 88; Chapl S Lincs HA Mental Handicap Unit from 90. *44 West Parade, Spalding, Lincs PE11 1HD* Spalding (0775) 60404

STENHOUSE, William Douglas. b 11. ALCD35. d 36 p 37. V Lamerton w Sydenham Damerel *Ex* 58-76; rtd 76. *Cranmere, Burrator Road, Dousland, Yelverton, Devon PL20 6NE* Yelverton (0822) 852843

STEPHEN, Brother. See BOND, Arthur Edward

STEPHEN, Canon Kenneth George. b 47. Strathclyde Univ BA69 Edin Univ BD72. Edin Th Coll 69. d 72 p 73. C Ayr *Glas* 72-75; R Renfrew 75-80; R Motherwell from 80; R Wishaw from 80; Can St Mary's Cathl from 89. *14 Crawford Street, Motherwell, Lanarkshire ML1 3AD* Motherwell (0698) 62634

STEPHENI, Frederick William. b 28. TD73. FSAScot81 FRSA82 Cranfield Inst of Tech MSc82. Lambeth STh83 Qu Coll Birm 54. d 55 p 56. CF (TA) 60-88; R Cotgrave *S'well* 63-76; V Owthorpe 63-76; Chapl Addenbrooke's Hosp Cam 76-88; Lic to Offic *Ely* from 76; rtd 88. *Thatchers, 13 Tunwells Lane, Great Shelford, Cambridge* Cambridge (0223) 842914

STEPHENS, Canon Archibald John. b 15. Selw Coll Cam BA37 MA44. Wells Th Coll 46. d 47 p 48. Nigeria 70-72; V Ash Vale *Guildf* 72-77; P-in-c Thursley 77-82; rtd 82; Perm to Offic *Guildf* from 85. *Fernhill, 12 Vicarage Lane, Farnham, Surrey GU9 8HN* Farnham (0252) 722514

STEPHENS, Charles Herbert. b 18. Lon Univ BA41 AKC42. d 42 p 43. Asst Master Nottm High Sch 45-78; Perm to Offic *S'well* from 73; rtd 83. *94 Grassington Road, Nottingham NG8 3PE* Nottingham (0602) 291586

STEPHENS, Francis William. b 21. ARCA50. S'wark Ord Course 68. d 70 p 71. C Primrose Hill St Mary w Avenue Road St Paul *Lon* from 70; Ed Ch Pulpit Year Book from 81. *14 St Edmund's Close, London NW8 7QS* 071-722 7931

STEPHENS, Geoffrey Elford. b 19. St Jo Coll Dur BA41 MA58. Ripon Hall Ox 41. d 43 p 44. R Mawdesley *Blackb* 60-86; CF (R of O) 68-74; rtd 86; Perm to Offic *Liv* and *Blackb* from 86. *19 Cambridge Avenue, Southport, Merseyside PR9 9SA* Southport (0704) 212385

STEPHENS, Grosvenor Humphrey Arthur. b 04. Keble Coll Ox BA26 MA31 BLitt31 MLitt80. St Steph Ho Ox 26. **d** 29 **p** 30. V Chislet w Hoath *Cant* 64-71; rtd 71; Perm to Offic *Cant* from 72. *9 Leasingham Gardens, Bexhill-on-Sea, E Sussex TN39 4OZ* Bexhill-on-Sea (0424) 214386

STEPHENS, Harold William Barrow. b 47. Lon Univ BEd. S Dios Minl Tr Scheme 80. **d** 82 **p** 83. NSM Heytesbury and Sutton Veny *Sarum* 82-83; NSM Bishopstrow and Boreham from 83. *14 Prestbury Drive, Warminster, Wilts BA12 9LB* Warminster (0985) 217776

STEPHENS, Horace Alfred Patrick. b 14. MRCVS49. **d** 77 **p** 78. NSM Dingle w Killiney and Kilgobbin *L & K* from 77. *Magharabeg, Castlegregory, Tralee, Co Kerry, Irish Republic* Tralee (66) 39159

STEPHENS, James Charles. b 62. **d** 91. C Kilcolman w Kiltallagh, Killorglin, Knockane etc *L & K* from 91. *Kilderry, Miltown, Co Kerry, Irish Republic* Tralee (66) 67426

STEPHENS, Mrs Jean. b 46. St As Minl Tr Course. **d** 89. NSM Gwernaffield and Llanferres *St As* from 89. *Noddfa, Pen-y-Fron Road, Pantymwyn, Mold, Clwyd CH7 5EF* Mold (0352) 740037

STEPHENS, John James Frederick. b 10. QUB BA34. Lon Coll of Div 34. **d** 37 **p** 38. V Broadheath *Worc* 51-82; rtd 82; Perm to Offic *Worc* from 82. *Jerred Cottage, Church Lane, Lower Broadheath, Worcester* Worcester (0905) 640224

STEPHENS, John Michael. b 29. ARICS52. Lich Th Coll 62. **d** 64 **p** 65. C Birchington w Acol *Cant* 64-70; V Tovil 70-79; V Brabourne w Smeeth from 79; RD N Lympne from 87. *The Rectory, Smeeth, Ashford, Kent TN25 6SA* Sellindge (0303) 812126

STEPHENS, Canon Marcus James Treacher. b 11. Lon Univ BA59. Kelham Th Coll 32. **d** 37 **p** 38. SSM 37-72; S Africa 64-72; Can Bloemfontein Cathl 67-72; Lebanon 73-75; V Battersea St Phil w St Bart *S'wark* 75-78; rtd 76; Chapl Community of the Epiphany Truro 79-81. *Roselyn Cottage, Rose, Truro, Cornwall TR4 9PQ*

STEPHENS, Peter John. b 42. Or Coll Ox BA64 MA67. Clifton Th Coll 63. **d** 68 **p** 68. C Lenton *S'well* 68-71; C Brixton Hill St Sav *S'wark* 71-73; P-in-c 73-82; TV Barnham Broom *Nor* 82-89; V Gorleston St Mary from 89. *The Vicarage, Nuffield Crescent, Gorleston, Great Yarmouth, Norfolk NR31 7LL* Great Yarmouth (0493) 661741

STEPHENS, Preb Peter Stanley. b 33. ALCD59. **d** 59 **p** 60. C Paignton St Paul Preston *Ex* 59-64; V Buckland Monachorum 64-74; RD Tavistock 70-74; V Compton Gifford 74-85; RD Plymouth Sutton 83-86; Preb Ex Cathl from 84; TR Plymouth Em w Efford 85-86; R Thurlestone w S Milton from 86. *The Rectory, Thurlestone, Kingsbridge, Devon TQ7 3NJ* Kingsbridge (0548) 560232

STEPHENS, Richard William. b 37. Dur Univ BSc62 DipTh64. Cranmer Hall Dur 62. **d** 64 **p** 65. C Hensingham *Carl* 64-67; C Norbury *Ches* 67-71; R Elworth and Warmingham 71-79; V Bootle St Matt *Liv* 79-89; P-in-c Litherland St Andr 79-83; P-in-c Failsworth H Trin *Man* from 89. *Holy Trinity Rectory, 103 Oldham Road, Failsworth, Manchester M35 0BH* 061-682 7901

STEPHENS, Ronald John. b 13. Sarum Th Coll 56. **d** 57 **p** 58. V Stanstead Abbots *St Alb* 61-82; rtd 82; Perm to Offic *Nor* from 82. *63 Beechlands Park, Southrepps, Norwich NR11 8NT* Southrepps (0263) 834893

STEPHENS, Simon Edward. b 41. Qu Coll Birm DPS68 PhD80 Bps' Coll Cheshunt 63. **d** 67 **p** 68. C Cov St Mark *Cov* 67-71; C Lillington 71-76; C-in-c Canley CD 76-79; V Canley 79-80; Chapl RN from 80. *c/o MOD, Lacon House, Theobald's Road, London WC1X 8RY* 071-430 6847

STEPHENS, Simon James. b 66. **d** 91. C Caldicot *Mon* from 91. *143 Elan Way, Caldicot, Gwent NP6 4QB* Caldicot (0291) 430586

STEPHENS-HODGE, Lionel Edmund Howard. b 14. Selw Coll Cam BA36 MA40. Ridley Hall Cam 36. **d** 38 **p** 39. R Brindle *Blackb* 64-74; rtd 74; Perm to Offic *Ex* from 79. *4 Fairfield Gardens, King Street, Honiton, Devon EX14 8DW* Honiton (0404) 42420

STEPHENS-WILKINSON, Patricia Ann. b 45. Univ of Wales (Cardiff) BA66 CQSW80 MSc(Econ)91. Bp Burgess Hall Lamp CPS69. **dss** 69 **d** 89. Abth *St D* 69-71; Lic to Offic *Carl* 71-74; Perm to Offic *Mon* 74-89; NSM Machen from 89. *48 St David's Drive, Machen, Newport, Gwent NP1 8RH* Caerphilly (0222) 883769

STEPHENSON, Eric George. b 41. Bede Coll Dur CertEd63. Qu Coll Birm DipTh65. **d** 66 **p** 67. C Wakef St Jo *Wakef* 66-69; C Seaham w Seaham Harbour *Dur*

69-73; C Cockerton 73-75; Lic to Offic 75-85; V E Boldon from 85. *The Vicarage, 2 Ashleigh Villas, East Boldon, Tyne & Wear NE36 0LA* 091-536 2557

STEPHENSON, Ian Clarke. b 24. Lon Univ DipTh69. Tyndale Hall Bris 52. **d** 56 **p** 57. R Biddulph Moor *Lich* 65-70; Hon C Biddulph 70-88; Lic to Offic *Ches* 75; Hon C Burslem *Lich* 85-88; New Zealand from 87; rtd 89. *St John's Vicarage, 165 Union Street, Milton, South Otago, New Zealand* Milton (3) 417-8244

STEPHENSON, John Joseph. b 35. St Jo Coll Dur BA74. Qu Coll Birm 75. **d** 76 **p** 77. C Whitworth w Spennymoor *Dur* 76-79; V Eppleton from 79. *The Vicarage, Church Road, Eppleton, Houghton le Spring, Tyne & Wear DH5 9AJ* 091-526 7412

STEPHENSON, Martin Woodard. b 55. St Cath Coll Cam BA77 MA82. Westcott Ho Cam 78. **d** 81 **p** 82. C Eastleigh *Win* 81-85; C Ferryhill *Dur* 85-87; Asst Dir of Ords 87-89; Chapl St Chad's Coll Dur 87-89; V Clarendon Park St Jo w Knighton St Mich *Leic* from 89. *The Rectory, 9 Springfield Road, Leicester LE2 3BB* Leicester (0533) 706097

STEPHENSON, Michael James. b 29. St Steph Ho Ox 54. **d** 56 **p** 57. V Paddington St Mary Magd *Lon* 64-87; rtd 88. *3 Downing Court, Grenville Street, London WC1N 1LX* 071-833 1392

STEPHENSON, Nicolas William. b 22. Ely Th Coll 60. **d** 62 **p** 63. CR from 68; Hon C Westgate Common *Wakef* 74-75; Lic to Offic 75-87; Asst Chapl HM Pris Wakef 84-87; rtd 87. *5 Dudfleet Lane, Horbury, Wakefield, W Yorkshire WF4 5EX* Wakefield (0924) 270864

STEPHENSON, Robert. b 36. St Chad's Coll Dur BA58 DipTh60. **d** 60 **p** 61. C Whickham *Dur* 60-63; C Gateshead St Mary 63-65; V Low Team 65-67; R Stella 67-74; V Comberton *Ely* from 74. *The Vicarage, Comberton, Cambridge CB3 7ED* Cambridge (0223) 262793

STEPHENSON, Canon Robert Ommanney. b 09. St Cath Coll Cam BA32 MA36. Cuddesdon Coll 32. **d** 33 **p** 34. V Bitterne Park *Win* 47-70; R E Woodhay and Woolton Hill 70-79; RD Whitchurch 72-79; rtd 79; Perm to Offic *B & W* from 79. *Fairlawn, Witcombe Lane, Ash, Martock, Somerset TA12 6AH* Martock (0935) 824330

STEPHENSON, Simon George. b 44. St Jo Coll Dur BA67. Trin Coll Bris 74. **d** 76 **p** 77. C Hildenborough *Roch* 76-82; C Bishopsworth *Bris* 82-85; C-in-c Withywood CD 85-90; TV Wreningham *Nor* from 90. *The Vicarage, 16 The Fields, Tacolneston, Norwich NR16 1DG* Bunwell (095389) 8227

STEPNEY, Area Bishop of. *Vacant*

STERLING, John Haddon. b 40. Pemb Coll Cam BA62 MA66. Cuddesdon Coll 63. **d** 65 **p** 66. S Africa 65-70; Chapl Bris Cathl *Bris* 71-74; Member Dioc Soc & Ind Team 71-74; Ind Chapl *Linc* 74-87; Ind Chapl *Ripon* from 87. *2 Halcyon Hill, Leeds LS7 3PU* Leeds (0532) 693153

STERRY, Christopher. b 54. K Coll Lon BD77 AKC77. St Jo Coll Nottm 79. **d** 80 **p** 81. C Huddersfield St Jo *Wakef* 80-84; V Middlestown 84-89; Chapl N Ord Course from 89; Lic to Offic *Man* from 89. *11 Ackerley Close, Fernhead, Warrington WA2 0DL* Warrington (0925) 851863

STERRY, Timothy John. b 34. Or Coll Ox BA58 MA62 DipTh60. Wycliffe Hall Ox 58. **d** 60 **p** 61. C Cromer *Nor* 60-64; Chapl Oundle Sch Pet 64-72; Chapl Cheam Sch Newbury 72-75; Hd Master Temple Grove Sch E Sussex 75-80; Scripture Union Schs Staffs from 81. *1 The Close, Chart Lane, Reigate, Surrey RH2 7BN* Reigate (0737) 244370

STEVEN, David Bowring. b 38. AKC64. **d** 64 **p** 65. C Grantham St Wulfram *Linc* 64-68; S Africa 68-75; C Bramley *Ripon* 76-77; V Sutton Valence w E Sutton and Chart Sutton *Cant* 77-82; P-in-c Littlebourne 82-86; V Mansf Woodhouse *S'well* from 86. *The Vicarage, 7 Butt Lane, Mansfield Woodhouse, Mansfield, Notts NG19 9JS* Mansfield (0623) 21875

STEVEN, James Gordon. b 08. Birm Univ BA31. ALCD35. **d** 35 **p** 36. R Gt and Lt Bealings w Playford and Culpho *St E* 70-74; rtd 74; Perm to Offic *St E* from 78. *Braemar Retirement Home, 13 Montague Road, Felixstowe, Suffolk IP11 7HF* Felixstowe (0394) 282116

STEVEN, James Henry Stevenson. b 62. CCC Cam MA87 St Jo Coll Dur BA87. Cranmer Hall Dur 84. **d** 87 **p** 88. C Welling *Roch* 87-91; C Bournemouth St Jo w St Mich *Win* from 91. *56 Gordon Road, Branksome, Poole, Dorset BH12 1EB* Poole (0202) 765994

STEVENETTE, John Maclachlan. b 30. St Pet Coll Ox MA60. Ripon Hall Ox 60. **d** 61 **p** 62. C Newhaven *Chich* 61-66; V Lynch w Iping Marsh 66-74; R Birdham w W Itchenor 74-78; R Byfleet *Guildf* 78-86; V Whittlesey

Ely 86-90; TR Whittlesey and Pondersbridge from 91. *The Vicarage, 47 Church Street, Whittlesey, Peterborough PE7 1DB* Peterborough (0733) 203676

STEVENETTE, Simon Melville. b 62. Hull Univ BA83. Wycliffe Hall Ox 84. **d** 87 **p** 88. C Carterton *Ox* 87-90; C Keynsham *B & W* from 90. *9 Chelmer Grove, Keynsham, Bristol BS18 1QA* Bristol (0272) 866390

STEVENS, Alan Robert. b 55. Warw Univ BA77. St Jo Coll Nottm 87. **d** 89 **p** 90. C Ex St Leon w H Trin *Ex* from 89. *27 Barnardo Road, Exeter EX2 4ND* Exeter (0392) 77540

STEVENS, Andrew Graham. b 54. BEd MA. Coll of Resurr Mirfield. **d** 83 **p** 84. C Leigh Park *Portsm* 83-87; TV Brighton Resurr *Chich* from 87. *St Luke's Vicarage, Queen's Park Terrace, Brighton BN2 2YA* Brighton (0273) 603946

STEVENS, Anne Helen. b 61. Warw Univ BA82 Fitzw Coll Cam BA90. Ridley Hall Cam 88. **d** 91. Par Dn E Greenwich Ch Ch w St Andr and St Mich *S'wark* from 91. *37 Chevening Road, London SE10 0LA* 081-858 6936

STEVENS, Arthur Edward Geary. b 14. Lon Coll of Div 34. **d** 37 **p** 38. C Woodside Park St Barn *Lon* 37-40; C W Hampstead St Luke 40-41; C Herne Hill Road St Sav *S'wark* 41-42; V W Hampstead St Cuth *Lon* 42-46; V S'well H Trin *S'well* 46-50; V Sheff St Jo *Sheff* 50-54; V Guernsey H Trin *Win* 54-67; Chapl Castel Hosp Guernsey 60-67; Chapl HM Pris Guernsey 61-67; V Bitterne *Win* 67-72; V Duffield *Derby* from 72. *St Alkmund's Vicarage, Vicarage Lane, Duffield, Derby DE6 4EB* Derby (0332) 841168

STEVENS, Brian Henry. b 28. Oak Hill Th Coll. **d** 69 **p** 70. C Chadwell *Chelmsf* 69-75; V Penge Ch Ch w H Trin *Roch* 75-85; V St Mary Cray and St Paul's Cray from 85. *The Vicarage, Main Road, Orpington, Kent BR5 3EN* Orpington (0689) 827697

STEVENS, Brian Henry. b 45. Open Univ BA80. S Dios Minl Tr Scheme 81. **d** 84 **p** 85. NSM S Malling *Chich* 84-86; C Langney 86-87; TV Wolverton *Ox* 87-88; V Welford w Sibbertoft and Marston Trussell *Pet* 88-91; V Hardingstone and Horton and Piddington from 91. *The Vicarage, 29 Back Lane, Hardingstone, Northants NN4 0BY* Northampton (0604) 760110

STEVENS, Brian Robert. b 49. Qu Mary Coll Lon LLB70 Trin Coll Cam BA LLB72 MA77 LLM84. E Anglian Minl Tr Course 80 Westcott Ho Cam 83. **d** 83 **p** 84. C Diss *Nor* 83-86; V Narborough w Narford 86-87; V Pentney w W Bilney 86-87; Chapl RAF from 87. *c/o MOD, Adastral House, Theobald's Road, London WC1X 8RU* 071-430 7268

STEVENS, Cyril David Richard. b 25. NZ Bd of Th Studies LTh66. **d** 59 **p** 60. New Zealand 59-65 and 67-68; V Playford w Culpho and Tuddenham St Martin *St E* 65-67; R Rendham w Sweffling and Cransford 69-73; RD Saxmundham 72-74; R Rendham w Sweffling from 73. *The Rectory, Sweffling, Saxmundham, Suffolk IP17 2BG* Rendham (072878) 495

STEVENS, David Charles. b 31. Keble Coll Ox BA55 DipTh56 MA59. Wycliffe Hall Ox 55. **d** 57 **p** 58. C Plymouth St Andr *Ex* 57-60; S Rhodesia 61-65; Rhodesia 65-66; Asst Chapl Bryanston Sch Blandford 66-70; Chapl 70-73; P-in-c Shilling Okeford *Sarum* 73-76; Lic to Offic *Chelmsf* 76-86; Chapl Chigwell Sch Essex 76-86; R Tarrant Valley *Sarum* from 86. *The Rectory, Tarrant Hinton, Blandford Forum, Dorset DT11 8JB* Blandford (0258) 89258

STEVENS, David John. b 45. Bris Univ BA67 Lon Univ DipTh69. Clifton Th Coll. **d** 70 **p** 71. C Ex St Leon w H Trin *Ex* 70-75; P-in-c Lt Burstead *Chelmsf* 75-77; TV Billericay and Lt Burstead 77-81; P-in-c Illogan *Truro* 81-83; R from 83. *The Rectory, Illogan, Redruth, Cornwall TR16 4RX* Portreath (0209) 842233

STEVENS, Canon David Johnson (Brother David Stephen). b 13. St Cath Soc Ox BA51 MA55. Wycliffe Hall Ox 49. **d** 52 **p** 53. Ind Chapl *Liv* 57-77; V Warrington St Paul 61-70; Guardian of Franciscan Ho *Liv* 70-77; SSF from 77; Lic to Offic *Newc* from 79; rtd 83. *The Friary, Alnmouth, Alnwick, Northd NE66 3NJ* Alnwick (0665) 830213

STEVENS, David Leonard. b 28. St Edm Hall Ox BA51 MA57. Cuddesdon Coll 60. **d** 62 **p** 63. C Old Brumby *Linc* 62-67; Chapl St Alb Sch Chorley 67-71; V Linc St Faith and St Martin w St Pet *Linc* 72-83; C Wolborough w Newton Abbot *Ex* 83-87; P-in-c from 87. *St Paul's House, 31 Devon Square, Newton Abbot, Devon TQ12 2HH* Newton Abbot (0626) 53119

STEVENS, Douglas George. b 47. Lon Univ BA69. Westcott Ho Cam 69. **d** 72 **p** 73. C Portsea St Geo CD *Portsm* 72-75; C Portsea N End St Mark 75-79; Chapl

NE Lon Poly *Chelmsf* 79-83; C-in-c Orton Goldhay CD *Ely* 83-87; V Elm 87-91; V Coldham 87-91; V Friday Bridge 87-91; R Woodston from 91. *The Rectory, Oundle Road, Woodston, Peterborough PE2 9PJ* Peterborough (0733) 62786

STEVENS, Frank Hayman. b 11. Univ Coll Ox BA32 MA38. Linc Th Coll 64. **d** 65 **p** 66. R Kenn w Kingston Seymour *B & W* 68-74; P-in-c Cossington 74-76; rtd 76. *8 Belfield Court, Poplar Road, Burnham-on-Sea, Somerset TA8 2HD* Burnham-on-Sea (0278) 785732

STEVENS, Frederick Crichton. b 42. K Coll Lon BD78 AKC78. St Steph Ho Ox 78. **d** 79 **p** 80. C Newquay *Truro* 79-81; C St Martin-in-the-Fields *Lon* 81-85; P-in-c Soho St Anne w St Thos and St Pet from 85. *57 Dean Street, London W1V 5HH* 071-437 5006

STEVENS, James Anthony. b 47. Worc Coll Ox MA69. Trin Coll Bris 78. **d** 80 **p** 81. C Heref St Pet w St Owen and St Jas *Heref* 80-84; C Lowestoft and Kirkley *Nor* 84-85; TV 85-89; V Dorridge *Birm* from 89. *The Vicarage, 6 Manor Road, Dorridge, Solihull, W Midlands B93 8DX* Wythall (0564) 772472 or 775652

STEVENS, John David Andrew. b 44. Wycliffe Hall Ox. **d** 68 **p** 69. C Standish *Blackb* 68-71; C Stonehouse *Glouc* 71-76; P-in-c Closworth *B & W* 76-77; P-in-c Barwick 76-77; TV Yeovil 77-80; R Chewton Mendip w Ston Easton, Litton etc from 80. *The Rectory, Chewton Mendip, Bath BA3 4LL* Chewton Mendip (076121) 333

STEVENS, Martin Leonard. b 35. St Jo Coll Dur BA60 MA72. Oak Hill Th Coll 60. **d** 62 **p** 63. C Low Elswick *Newc* 62-65; C S Croydon Em *Cant* 65-69; Hon C 70-74; V Felling *Dur* 74-86. *Address temp unknown*

STEVENS, Michael John. b 37. St Cath Coll Cam BA63. Coll of Resurr Mirfield 63. **d** 65 **p** 66. C Poplar All SS w St Frideswide *Lon* 65-71; Asst Chapl The Lon Hosp (Whitechapel) 71-74; Chapl St Thos Hosp Lon from 75. *2 Walcot Square, London SE11 4TZ* 071-735 7362 or 928 9292

STEVENS, Neville. b 21. Clare Coll Cam BA52 MA54 Or Coll Ox DipTh54. Wycliffe Hall Ox 52. **d** 54 **p** 55. C Bishopsworth *Bris* 54-56; Chapl Leeds Gr Sch 56-84; Perm to Offic *Wakef* from 71; *Ripon* from 85. *6 Hill Top Green, West Ardsley, Tingley, Wakefield, W Yorkshire WF3 1HS* Leeds (0532) 538038

STEVENS, Peter David. b 36. ARICS. Oak Hill Th Coll DipHE81. **d** 81 **p** 82. C Branksome St Clem *Sarum* 81-87; R Moreton and Woodsford w Tincleton from 87. *The Rectory, Moreton, Dorchester, Dorset DT2 8RH* Bindon Abbey (0929) 462466

STEVENS, Philip Terence. b 55. MBIM Man Univ BSc76 Lon Univ BD81 St Jo Coll Dur MA86. Cranmer Hall Dur 81. **d** 83 **p** 84. C Withington St Paul *Man* 83-86; C Middleton 86-88; V Saddleworth from 88. *The Vicarage, Station Road, Uppermill, Oldham OL3 6HQ* Saddleworth (0457) 872412

STEVENS, Canon Ralph. b 11. Selw Coll Cam BA36 MA40. Qu Coll Birm 36. **d** 38 **p** 39. R Colchester Ch Ch w St Mary V *Chelmsf* 65-79; Hon Can Chelmsf Cathl 71-79; rtd 79; Perm to Offic *St E* from 79. *9 York Road, Southwold, Suffolk IP18 6AN* Southwold (0502) 723705

STEVENS, Canon Ralph Samuel Osborn. b 13. Birm Univ BSc34 St Cath Soc Ox BA36 MA41. Ripon Hall Ox 34. **d** 36 **p** 37. V Birm St Paul *Birm* 50-83; Hon Can Birm Cathl 52-83; RD Birm City 58-73; Chapl to HM The Queen 67-83; rtd 83; Perm to Offic *Birm* from 84. *10 Harrison's Green, Birmingham B15 3LH* 021-454 3089

STEVENS, Richard William. b 36. AKC59. **d** 60 **p** 61. C Greenhill St Jo *Lon* 60-63; Chapl RAF 63-79; CF from 79. *c/o MOD (Army), Bagshot Park, Bagshot, Surrey GU19 5PL* Bagshot (0276) 71717

STEVENS, Robin George. b 43. Leic Univ BA65. Cuddesdon Coll 74. **d** 74 **p** 75. C Hemel Hempstead *St Alb* 74-77; Chapl K Coll Sch Wimbledon from 77. *329 Wimbledon Park Road, London SW19 6NS* 081-788 1501

STEVENS, Miss Sylvia Joyce. b 41. Qu Mary Coll Lon BA63 Bris Univ CertEd64 St Jo Coll Dur BA77 DipTh78. Cranmer Hall Dur 75. **dss** 78 **d** 87. Chapl Trent Poly *S'well* from 78. *2 College Drive, Clifton, Nottingham NG11 8NF* Nottingham (0602) 214560

STEVENS, Thomas Walter. b 33. Bps' Coll Cheshunt. **d** 65 **p** 66. C Newc St Matt w St Mary *Newc* 65-69; C Wallsend St Luke 69-70; C Cranford *Lon* 70-87; C Fulwell St Mich and St Geo 87-90; C Teddington SS Pet and Paul and Fulwell 90-91. *The Presbytery, Clonmell Road, Teddington, Middx TW11 0ST*

STEVENS, Ven Timothy John. b 46. Selw Coll Cam BA68 MA72 DipTh. Ripon Coll Cuddesdon 75. **d** 76 **p** 77. C E Ham w Upton Park *Chelmsf* 76-80; TR Canvey Is 80-88; Dep Dir Cathl Cen for Research and Tr 82-84; Bp's Urban Officer 87-91; Hon Can Chelmsf Cathl from 87; Adn W Ham from 91. *86 Aldersbrook Road, London E12 5DH*   081-989 8557

STEVENSEN, Albert. b 24. Wycliffe Hall Ox 61. **d** 62 **p** 63. Chapl HM Pris Brixton 64-70; C Wandsworth All SS *S'wark* 70-71; V Wandsworth St Steph 71-88; rtd 88. *33 Durnsford Avenue, London SW19 8BH*   081-946 3650

STEVENSON, Alastair Rice. b 42. Open Univ BA78. Ripon Coll Cuddesdon 78. **d** 80 **p** 81. C Bexhill St Pet *Chich* 80-82; C Brighton St Matthias 82-84; C Swindon Ch Ch *Bris* 84-87; Bp's Soc and Ind Adv from 87. *15 Sarsen Close, Swindon SN1 4LA*   Swindon (0793) 612385

STEVENSON, Bernard Norman. b 57. Kent Univ BA78 Fitzw Coll Cam BA81 MA86. Ridley Hall Cam. **d** 82 **p** 83. C Mortlake w E Sheen *S'wark* 82-84; C Kensal Rise St Martin *Lon* 84-88; C Headstone St Geo 88-90; V Worfield *Heref* from 90. *The Vicarage, Worfield, Bridgnorth, Shropshire WV15 5JZ*   Worfield (07464) 698

STEVENSON, Brian. b 34. JP66. NW Ord Course 76. **d** 79 **p** 80. C Padiham *Blackb* 79-82; V Clitheroe St Paul Low Moor 82-89; V Blackb St Silas from 89. *St Silas' Vicarage, Preston New Road, Blackburn BB2 6PS*   Blackburn (0254) 671293

STEVENSON, Christopher James. b 43. TCD BA65 MA73 Em Coll Cam BA69 MA73. Westcott Ho Cam 68. **d** 70 **p** 71. C Newc H Cross *Newc* 70-72; C Arm St Mark *Arm* 72-73; C Dub Crumlin *D & G* 73-76; Hon CV Ch Ch Cathl Dub 75-76; C-in-c Appley Bridge All SS CD *Blackb* 76-82; P-in-c Appley Bridge from 82. *The Vicarage, Finch Lane, Appley Bridge, Wigan, Lancs WN6 9DD*   Appley Bridge (02575) 2875

STEVENSON, Derick Neville. b 36. Open Univ BA76. Ridley Hall Cam 79. **d** 80 **p** 81. C Bonchurch *Portsm* 80-84; C-in-c Crookhorn Ch Cen CD 84-87; R Norton Fitzwarren *B & W* from 87. *The Rectory, Rectory Road, Norton Fitzwarren, Taunton, Somerset TA2 6SE*   Taunton (0823) 272570

STEVENSON, Donald Macdonald. b 48. Lon Univ BSc(Econ)70 Leeds Univ MA72 Univ of Wales (Abth) CertEd73 Warw Univ MEd78. Oak Hill Th Coll BA88. **d** 88 **p** 89. C Gt Malvern St Mary *Worc* from 88. *3 Gilbert Road, Malvern, Worcs WR14 3RQ*   Malvern (0684) 892523

STEVENSON, Frank Beaumont. b 39. MInstGA(Lon) Duke Univ(USA) BA61. Episc Th Sch Harvard MDiv64. **d** 64 **p** 64. USA 64-66; Zambia 66-68; Lect Th Ox Univ from 68; Bp's Tr Officer *Ox* 69-70; Chapl Keble Coll Ox 71-72; Chapl Isis Gp Hosps 73-75; Chapl Littlemore Hosp Ox from 75; Officer for Continuing Minl Educn from 90. *The School House, Stanton St John, Oxford OX9 1ET*   Stanton St John (086735) 635

STEVENSON, Frederic Robert. b 14. ARIBA38 FRTPI FRIAS Edin Coll of Art DipArch37 DipTP38 Edin Univ PhD65. **d** 76 **p** 77. Hon C Dunbar *Edin* from 76. *Monk's Orchard, East Linton, East Lothian EH40 3DS*   East Linton (0620) 860218

STEVENSON, Gerald Ernest. b 35. S'wark Ord Course 80. **d** 83 **p** 84. NSM Eltham Park St Luke *S'wark* 83-88; Asst Chapl HM Pris Wormwood Scrubs from 88. *106 Grangehill Road, London SE9 1SE*   081-850 2748

STEVENSON, James Jackson. b 14. TCD BA36 MA44 Div Test38. **d** 39 **p** 40. Prec Clogh Cathl *Clogh* 67-82; I Carrickmacross 73-82; rtd 84. *10 Cairnshill Court, Saintfield Road, Belfast BT8 4TX*   Belfast (0232) 792969

STEVENSON, John. b 39. Glas Univ MA64. St Jo Coll Nottm 87. **d** 87 **p** 88. NSM Eastriggs *Glas* 87-88; NSM Moffat from 88. *Hoppertitty, Beattock, Moffat, Dumfriesshire DG10 9PJ*   Beattock (06833) 337

STEVENSON, John Charles. b 22. St Jo Coll Dur LTh48. Oak Hill Th Coll 45. **d** 49 **p** 50. V Bolton St Bede *Man* 64-75; Asst Chapl HM Pris Wandsworth 75-77; Chapl HM Pris Linc 77-80; R Fiskerton *Linc* 80-87; rtd 87. *15 The Coppice, Redwood Park, Beaufort Road, Morecambe, Lancs LA4 6TY*

STEVENSON, Dr Kenneth William. b 49. FRHistS90 Edin Univ MA70 Southn Univ PhD75 Man Univ DD87. Sarum & Wells Th Coll 70. **d** 73 **p** 74. C Grantham w Manthorpe *Linc* 73-76; C Boston 76-80; Chapl Man Univ 80-86; TV Man Whitworth 80-82; TR 82-86; Lect Man Univ 80-86; R Guildf H Trin w St Mary *Guildf* from 86. *Holy Trinity Rectory, 9 Eastgate Gardens, Guildford, Surrey GU1 4AZ*   Guildford (0483) 575489

STEVENSON, Leslie Thomas Clayton. b 59. TCD BA DipTh MPhil. **d** 83 **p** 84. C Dundela *D & D* 83-87; I Kilmore w Inch from 87. *20 Church Road, Crossgar, Downpatrick, Co Down BT30 9HR*   Crossgar (0396) 830371

STEVENSON, Lorna. b 43. Moray Ho Edin DipEd65. **dss** 85 **d** 86. NSM Dundee St Luke *Bre* from 85. *39 Charleston Drive, Dundee DD2 2HF*   Dundee (0382) 666311

STEVENSON, Michael Richard Nevin. b 52. Univ Coll Lon MA77. CITC DipTh86. **d** 86 **p** 87. C Clooney w Strathfoyle *D & R* 86-89; CF from 89. *c/o MOD (Army), Bagshot Park, Bagshot, Surrey GU19 5PL*   Bagshot (0276) 71717

STEVENSON, Ven Richard Clayton. b 22. TCD BA48 MA56. CITC 48. **d** 48 **p** 49. I Belf St Barn *Conn* 60-70; I Belf St Nic 70-88; Adn Conn 79-88; rtd 88. *42 Malone Heights, Belfast BT9 5PG*   Belfast (0232) 615006

STEVENSON, Robert Brian. b 40. QUB BA61 Qu Coll Cam BA67 MA71 Pemb Coll Ox BA69 BD76 MA76 Birm Univ PhD70. Cuddesdon Coll 69. **d** 70 **p** 71. C Lewisham St Jo Southend *S'wark* 70-73; C Catford (Southend) and Downham 73-74; Lect and Dir Past Studies Chich Th Coll 74-81; Acting Vice-Prin 80-81; V W Malling w Offham *Roch* from 81. *The Vicarage, 138 High Street, West Malling, Maidstone, Kent ME19 6NE*   West Malling (0732) 842245

STEVENSON, Canon Ronald. b 17. Leeds Univ BA38. Coll of Resurr Mirfield 38. **d** 40 **p** 41. C Pontefract All SS *Wakef* 40-44; C-in-c Lundwood CD 44-47; Area Sec Miss to Seamen 47-49; Perm to Offic *Linc, Ches, Man, Blackb, Carl, Leic, Derby, Pet* and Chapl Lanc Moor Hosp 49-65; Chapl N Lancs and S Westmorland Hosps 65-75; Hon Can Blackb Cathl *Blackb* 71-75. *28 Slyne Road, Torrisholme, Morecambe, Lancs*   Morecambe (0524) 410957

STEVENSON, Trevor Donald. b 59. TCD Div Sch BTh. **d** 91. C Magheralin w Dollingstown *D & D* from 91. *1 Victoria Place, Dollingstown, Craigavon, Co Armagh BT66 7LR*   Craigavon (0762) 321515

STEVENTON, June Lesley. b 61. Aston Tr Scheme 86 Sarum & Wells Th Coll BTh91. **d** 91. Par Dn Chatham St Steph *Roch* from 91. *59 Greenway, Chatham, Kent ME5 9UX*   Medway (0634) 861045

STEVINSON, Harold John Hardy. b 34. Selw Coll Cam BA57 MA61. Qu Coll Birm. **d** 59 **p** 60. C Bris St Mary Redcliffe w Temple *Bris* 59-63; C Caversham *Ox* 63-73; Soc Resp Officer *Dur* 74-82; Sec Dioc Bd for Miss and Unity 82-88; P-in-c Croxdale 82-88; P-in-c Leamington Hastings and Birdingbury *Cov* from 88. *The Vicarage, Leamington Hastings, Rugby, Warks CV23 8DY*   Marton (0926) 632455

STEVINSON, Josephine Mary. STh55. Cranmer Hall Dur 86. **dss** 86 **d** 87. Croxdale *Dur* 86-87; Hon Par Dn 87-88; Lic to Offic *Cov* from 88. *The Vicarage, Leamington Hastings, Rugby, Warks CV23 8DY*   Marton (0926) 632455

STEWARD, Mrs Linda Christine. b 46. NE Lon Poly CQSW82. S'wark Ord Course 85. **d** 88. NSM E Ham w Upton Park *Chelmsf* 88-90; Chapl Newham Gen Hosp from 90. *131 Windsor Road, London E7 0RA*   081-552 8877

STEWARDSON, Ian Joseph. b 28. Ex Coll Ox BA52 DipTh54 MA56. Wycliffe Hall Ox 52. **d** 54 **p** 55. C Farnworth *Liv* 54-57; C Mossley Hill St Matt and St Jas 57-60; V New Barnet St Jas *St Alb* 60-72; R Potton w Sutton and Cockayne Hatley 73-82; R Cottered w Broadfield and Throcking from 82. *The Rectory, Cottered, Buntingford, Herts SG9 9QA*   Cottered (076381) 218

STEWART, Canon Alexander Butler. b 25. **d** 58 **p** 59. I Helen's Bay *D & D* 65-72; I Donegal w Killymard, Lough Eske and Laghey *D & R* 72-90; Can Raphoe Cathl 81-90; rtd 90; Lic to Offic *D & D* from 90. *31 Upper Ballygelagh Road, Ardkeen, Newtownards, Co Down BT22 1JH*   Kircubbin (02477) 38601

STEWART, Brian. b 59. **d** 91. C Ballywillan *Conn* from 91. *17 Victoria Street, Portrush, Co Antrim*   Portrush (0265) 824141

STEWART, Charles. b 55. St Jo Coll Cam BA77 CertEd79 MA81. Wycliffe Hall Ox 85. **d** 87 **p** 88. C Bowdon *Ches* 87-90; C Bath Abbey w St Jas *B & W* from 90. *7 Holloway, Calton Gardens, Bath, Avon BA2 4PS*   Bath (0225) 422506

STEWART, Ian Guild. b 43. Edin Th Coll 89. **d** 84 **p** 85. NSM Dundee St Mary Magd *Bre* 84-87; NSM Dundee St Jo 87-90; C from 90; NSM Dundee St Martin 87-90; C from 90. *9 Duff Street, Dundee DD4 7AN*   Dundee (0382) 462486

STEWART, James. b 32. d 69 p 70. C Belf St Donard *D & D* 69-72; C Dundonald 72-74; I Rathmullan w Tyrella 74-80; I Belf St Clem from 80. *80A Sandown Road, Belfast BT5 8GU* Belfast (0232) 657345

STEWART, James Patrick. b 55. Keele Univ BA77 Birm Univ MA78. Ridley Hall Cam 86. d 88 p 89. C Boulton *Derby* from 88. *14 Courtland Drive, Alvaston, Derby DE2 0GJ* Derby (0332) 72198

STEWART, Mrs Janet Margaret. b 41. CertEd62 DipRK70. Cranmer Hall Dur 86. d 87. Hon Par Dn Oulton Broad *Nor* from 87. *St Mark's Vicarage, 212 Bridge Road, Oulton Broad, Lowestoft, Suffolk NR33 9JX* Lowestoft (0502) 572563

STEWART, John. b 09. St Cath Coll Cam BA31 MA35. Cuddesdon Coll 31. d 32 p 33. V Appleton-le-Moors *York* 57-74; V Lastingham 57-74; rtd 74; Chapl Qu Mary's Sch Helmsley 75-85. *Bodney Cottage, Buckingham Square, Helmsley, York YO6 5DZ* Helmsley (0439) 70517

STEWART, John. b 39. Oak Hill Th Coll 75. d 77 p 78. C Accrington Ch Ch *Blackb* 77-79; TV Darwen St Pet w Hoddlesden 79-86; R Coppull St Jo from 86. *St John's Vicarage, Darlington Street, Coppull, Chorley, Lancs PR7 5AB* Coppull (0257) 791258

STEWART, Canon John Roberton. b 29. Sarum Th Coll 63. d 65 p 66. C Gillingham *Sarum* 65-70; R Langton Matravers 70-84; RD Purbeck 82-89; Can and Preb Sarum Cathl 83-90; R Kingston, Langton Matravers and Worth Matravers 84-90; Can Res Sarum Cathl from 90; Treas from 90. *23 The Close, Salisbury SP1 2EH* Salisbury (0722) 322172

STEWART, John Vernon. b 36. BNC Ox BA57 MA66. Coll of Ressur Halki 59. d 61 p 62. R Sibford *Ox* 70-75; R Northolt St Mary *Lon* 75-82; rtd 82. *Rua Jo Arco, Cerdeira 6345, Portugal*

STEWART, John Wesley. b 52. QUB BD76 TCD 76. d 77 p 78. C Lisburn Ch Ch *Conn* 79-85; I Ballybay w Mucknoe and Clontibret *Clogh* 85-90; I Derryvullen S w Garvary from 90. *The Rectory, Tamlaght, Enniskillen, Co Fermanagh* Lisbellaw (0365) 87236

STEWART, Miss Kim Deborah. b 61. Southn Univ LLB82. ASCAT DipApTh86 Trin Coll Bris DipHE88 ADPS89. d 89. Par Dn Bitterne *Win* from 89. *39 Whites Road, Bitterne, Southampton, Hants SO2 7NR* Southampton (0703) 447929

STEWART, Canon Maurice Evan. b 29. TCD BA50 MA53 BD67 QUB PhD75. d 52 p 53. C Belf St Jas *Conn* 52-55; Chapl Bps' Coll Cheshunt 55-58; Hd of Trin Coll Miss Belf 58-61; I Newc *D & D* 61-69; Lect CITC from 69; Vice-Prin CITC from 80; Lect in Div TCD from 72; Chan St Patr Cathl Dub 80-89; Prec St Patr Cathl Dub from 89. *99 Landscape Park, Dublin 14, Irish Republic* Dublin (1) 986989

STEWART, Maxwell Neville Gabriel. b 33. Hertf Coll Ox BA58. Wycliffe Hall Ox DipTh59. d 60 p 61. C Perry Beeches *Birm* 60-62; Chapl Rosenberg Coll St Gallen 62-64; Perm to Offic *Chelmsf* 64-70; Warden Leics Poly from 70; Hon C Leic St Mary *Leic* from 74. *The Warden's Flat, Knighton Lodge, 15 Elms Road, Leicester LE2 3JD* Leicester (0533) 703440

STEWART, Michael. b 65. St Jo Coll Nottm LTh89. d 89 p 90. C Ealing St Paul *Lon* from 89. *23 Littlewood Close, London W13 9XH* 081-567 7834

STEWART, Norman Andrew. b 32. d 58 p 59. C Glas Ch Ch *Glas* 58-59; C Paisley H Trin 59-60; C Glas St Marg 60-62; C Kingsthorpe *Pet* 62-64; Belize from 70. *St Mary's Rectory, PO Box 246, Belize City, Belize*

STEWART, Raymond John. b 55. TCD BA79 MA82. CITC 74 Div Test77. d 79 p 80. C Clooney *D & R* 79-82; I Dunfanaghy 82-87; I Gweedore Union 85-87; Dioc Youth Adv 83-87; I Castledawson from 87; RD Maghera and Kilrea from 89; Ed *D & R* Dioc News from 89. *12 Station Road, Castledawson, Magherafelt, Co Londonderry BT45 8AZ* Castledawson (0648) 68235

STEWART, Canon Robert Stevenson. b 15. TCD BA38. d 39 p 40. I Ballymoney *Conn* 59-82; Can Conn Cathl 78-82; rtd 82. *7 Willan Drive, Portrush, Co Antrim BT56 8PU* Portrush (0265) 824336

STEWART, William Allen. b 43. Trin Coll Cam BA65 MA69. Cranmer Hall Dur DipTh68. d 68 p 69. C Ecclesall *Sheff* 68-72; C Cheltenham St Mary *Glouc* 72-74; V Glouc St Jas 74-80; P-in-c Glouc All SS 78-80; R Upton *Ex* 80-85; V Oulton Broad *Nor* from 85. *St Mark's Vicarage, 212 Bridge Road, Oulton Broad, Lowestoft, Suffolk NR33 9JX* Lowestoft (0502) 572563

STEWART, William James. BA DipTh. d 83 p 84. C Glenageary *D & G* 83-86; Rostrevor Renewal Cen 86-87; I Naas w Kill and Rathmore *M & K* from 87. *St David's*

Rectory, Naas, Co Kildare, Irish Republic Naas (45) 97206

STEWART, William Jones. b 32. Trin Hall Cam BA55 MA59 Cam Univ CertEd56. Edin Th Coll 67. d 69 p 69. Chapl St Ninian's Cathl Perth *St And* 69-71; Bp's Dom Chapl *Ox* 71-75; V Lambourn 75-90; V Lambourn from 90; P-in-c Lambourne Woodlands 83-90; P-in-c Eastbury and E Garston from 83. *Lambourn Vicarage, Newbury, Berks RG16 7PD* Lambourn (0488) 71546

STEWART-DARLING, Dr Fiona Lesley. b 58. Kingston Poly GRSC79 Lon Univ PhD82. Trin Coll Bris BA91. d 91. C Cirencester *Glouc* from 91. *59 North Home Road, Cirencester, Glos GL7 1DS* Cirencester (0285) 654209

STEWART-SMITH, Canon David Cree. b 13. K Coll Cam BA39 MA42. Cuddesdon Coll 40. d 41 p 42. Can Res Roch Cathl *Roch* 69-76; Adn Roch 69-76; Home Sec JMECA 76-78; rtd 78; Perm to Offic *Glouc* from 86. *16 Capel Court, Prestbury, Cheltenham, Glos GL52 3EL* Cheltenham (0242) 510972

STEWART-SYKES, Alistair Charles. b 60. St Andr Univ MA83. Qu Coll Birm. d 89 p 90. C Stevenage St Andr and St Geo *St Alb* from 89. *46 Crossgates, Stevenage, Herts SG1 1LS* Stevenage (0438) 367654

STEWART-SYKES, Teresa Melanie. b 64. Bris Univ BA85. Qu Coll Birm 87. d 89. Par Dn Stevenage St Andr and St Geo *St Alb* from 89. *46 Crossgates, Stevenage, Herts SG1 1LS* Stevenage (0438) 367654

STEYNOR, Victor Albert. b 15. Southn Univ DipEd62. S'wark Ord Course 68. d 71 p 72. C Bognor *Chich* 71-75; P-in-c Kenton and Ashfield w Thorpe *St E* 75-81; P-in-c Aspall 75-81; V Debenham 75-81; V Debenham w Aspall and Kenton 81-82; rtd 82; Perm to Offic *St E* from 82. *74 Elmhurst Drive, Ipswich IP3 0PB* Ipswich (0473) 728922

STIBBE, Dr Mark William Godfrey. b 60. Trin Coll Cam BA83 MA86 Nottm Univ PhD88. St Jo Coll Nottm 83. d 86 p 87. C Stapleford *S'well* 86-90; C Crookes St Thos *Sheff* from 90; Lect Sheff Univ from 90. *79 Glebe Road, Sheffield S10 1FB* Sheffield (0742) 683463

STIBBS, Wilfred James. b 12. Linc Th Coll 67 St Edm Coll Ware 34. d 40 p 41. In RC Ch 40-67; C Hessle 68-70; R Rounton w Welbury *York* 70-72; Master and Chapl Charterhouse Hull 73-76; rtd 77. *51 Back Lane, Sowerby, Thirsk, N Yorkshire YO7 1JT* Thirsk (0845) 23371

STICKLAND, Geoffrey John Brett. b 42. St D Coll Lamp DipTh66. d 66 p 67. C Aberavon H Trin *Llan* 66-69; C Llanrumney *Mon* 69-72; C Tetbury w Beverston *Glouc* 72-75; V Hardwicke 75-82; R Hardwicke, Quedgeley and Elmore w Longney from 82. *The Rectory, Quedgeley, Gloucester GL2 6PN* Gloucester (0452) 720411

STIDOLPH, Robert Anthony. b 54. GRSM ARCM. St Steph Ho Ox 77. d 80 p 80. C Hove All SS *Chich* 80-84; TV Brighton Resurr 84-87; Chapl Cheltenham Coll from 87. *1 Waterfield Close, Cheltenham, Glos GL53 7NL* Cheltenham (0242) 230800

STIEVENARD, Alphonse Etienne Arthur. b 13. Selw Coll Cam BA36 MA40. Lon Coll of Div 36. d 37 p 38. V Jersey Millbrook St Matt *Win* 51-78; rtd 78. *Le Ruisselet, Mont Rossignol, St Ouen, Jersey, Channel Islands* Jersey (0534) 81215

STIFF, Derrick Malcolm. b 40. Lich Th Coll 69. d 72 p 73. C Cov St Geo *Cov* 72-75; R Benhall w Sternfield *St E* 75-79; P-in-c Snape w Friston 75-79; V Cartmel *Carl* 79-87; R Sudbury and Chilton *St E* from 87. *The Rectory, Gainsborough Street, Sudbury, Suffolk CO10 6EU* Sudbury (0787) 72611

STILL, Colin Charles. b 35. Selw Coll Cam BA67 MA71. Cranmer Hall Dur DipTh68 United Th Sem Dayton STM69. d 69 p 70. C Drypool St Columba w St Andr and St Pet *York* 69-72; Abp's Dom Chapl 72-75; Recruitment Sec ACCM 76-80; P-in-c Ockham w Hatchford *Guildf* 76-80; R 80-90; Can Missr and Ecum Officer 80-90. *Flat 9, 16 Lewes Crescent, Brighton BN2 1GB* Brighton (0273) 686014

STILL, Jonathan Trevor Lloyd. b 59. Ex Univ BA81 Qu Coll Cam BA84 MA88. Westcott Ho Cam 82. d 85 p 86. C Weymouth H Trin *Sarum* 85-88; Chapl for Agric *Heref* from 88. *43 Buckfield Road, Leominster, Herefordshire HR6 8SF* Leominster (0568) 5577

STILLINGS, Tom Atkinson. b 33. Llan St Mich DipTh61. d 61 p 62. C Rhosymedre *St As* 61-67; C Minera 67-70; R Llanfynydd 70-74; V Bagillt 74-83; TV Wrexham 83-91; R Trefnant from 91. *The Rectory, Trefnant, Denbigh LL16 5UG* Trefnant (074574) 583

STILLMAN, Roger John. b 47. St Steph Ho Ox 81. d 83 p 84. C St Helier *S'wark* 83-88; P-in-c Falinge *Man* 88;

TV Rochdale from 88. *St Edmund's Vicarage, Clement Royds Street, Rochdale, Lancs OL12 6PL* Rochdale (0706) 46272

STILWELL, Malcolm Thomas. b 54. Coll of Resurr Mirfield 83. **d** 86 **p** 87. C Workington St Mich *Carl* 86-90; P-in-c Flimby from 90. *The Vicarage, Flimby, Maryport, Cumbria CA15 8TJ* Maryport (0900) 812386

STIMPSON, Graham George. b 40. Lon Univ MB BS65 DPM. Cuddesdon Coll 69. **d** 70 **p** 71. NSM Bris St Mary Redcliffe w Temple etc *Bris* from 70. *12 Challoner Court, Bristol BS1 4RG* Bristol (0272) 260802

STINSON, William Gordon. b 29. Lon Univ BSc50. Ely Th Coll 51. **d** 52 **p** 53. C Kingston upon Hull St Alb *York* 52-56; Br Guiana 56-61; V E and W Ravendale w Hatcliffe *Linc* 61-67; R Beelsby 61-67; P-in-c Ashby w Fenby and Brigsley 62-66; R 66-67; V New Cleethorpes 67-76; RD Grimsby and Cleethorpes 73-76; P-in-c Dovercourt *Chelmsf* 76-83; TR Dovercourt and Parkeston from 83; RD Harwich from 87. *The Vicarage, Highfield Avenue, Dovercourt, Harwich, Essex CO12 4DR* Harwich (0255) 2033

STIRK, Peter Francis. b 24. Linc Coll Ox BA49 MA53. Qu Coll Birm 49. **d** 50 **p** 51. P-in-c Kirby-on-the-Moor *Ripon* 68-71; V 71-81; P-in-c Cundall 73-81; V Kirby-on-the-Moor, Cundall w Norton-le-Clay etc 81-90; rtd 90. *Devonshire Cottage, Marton le Moor, Ripon, N Yorkshire HG4 5AT* Harrogate (0423) 322330

STIRLING, Mrs Christina Dorita (Tina). b 48. Lon Univ BEd73. Wycliffe Hall Ox 87. **d** 89. Par Dn Thame w Towersey *Ox* from 89. *29 Chalgrove Road, Thame, Oxon OX9 3TF* Thame (084421) 5217

STIRRUP, Roger. b 34. St Cath Coll Cam BA58 MA62. Linc Th Coll 58. **d** 60 **p** 61. C Selly Oak St Mary *Birm* 60-63; C Battersea St Mary *S'wark* 63-65; Chapl St Andr Univ *St And* 65-68; Chapl Nottm High Sch 68-80; Asst Chapl Rugby Sch Warks 80-85; V Fordingbridge *Win* from 85. *The Vicarage, Fordingbridge, Hants SP6 1BB* Fordingbridge (0425) 53163

STOBART, Judith Audrey. b 43. St Hugh's Coll Ox BA66 MA71 Lon Univ CertEd71 DipEd72. St Alb Minl Tr Scheme 82. **dss** 85 **d** 87. Hatf *St Alb* 85-87; Par Dn Hatf Hyde St Mary 87-91. *23 Park Meadow, Hatfield, Herts AL9 5HA* Hatfield (0707) 264251

STOCK, Canon Kenneth Lawrence. b 28. Leeds Univ BA49 Lon Univ DipEd69. Coll of Resurr Mirfield. **d** 51 **p** 52. C Haggerston St Aug w St Steph *Lon* 51-54; C Bordesley St Alb *Birm* 54-66; V Southwick St Columba *Dur* 66-88; Hon Can Dur Cathl 80-88; P-in-c Spernall, Morton Bagot and Oldberrow *Cov* 88-90; R from 90; P-in-c Coughton 88-90; V from 90. *The Parsonage, Sambourne, Worcs B96 6PA* Astwood Bank (0527) 892372

STOCK, Victor Andrew. b 44. AKC68. **d** 69 **p** 70. C Pinner *Lon* 69-73; Chapl Lon Univ 73-79; R Friern Barnet St Jas 79-86; R St Mary le Bow w St Pancras Soper Lane etc from 86; P-in-c St Mary Aldermary from 87. *The Rector's Lodgings, St Mary le Bow, Cheapside, London EC2V 6AU* 071-248 5139

STOCK, William Nigel. b 50. Dur Univ BA72 Ox Univ DipTh75. Ripon Coll Cuddesdon 76. **d** 76 **p** 77. C Stockton St Pet *Dur* 76-79; Papua New Guinea 79-84; V Shiremoor *Newc* 85-91; TR N Shields from 91. *The Vicarage, 26 Cleveland Road, North Shields, Tyne & Wear NE29 0NG* 091-257 1721

STOCK-HESKETH, Jonathan Philip. b 49. St Chad's Coll Dur BA Cam Univ CertEd Nottm Univ MTh. St Steph Ho Ox. **d** 83 **p** 84. C Leic St Phil *Leic* 83-86; C Loughb Em 86-89. *c/o Theology Department, Nottingham University, Nottingham NG7 2RD* Nottingham (0602) 506101

STOCKBRIDGE, Alan Carmichael. b 33. MBE89. Keble Coll Ox BA55 MA62. Wycliffe Hall Ox 66. **d** 68 **p** 69. CF 68-78 and 82-89; Chapl Reading Sch 78-82; rtd 89. *c/o MOD (Army), Bagshot Park, Bagshot, Surrey GU19 5PL* Bagshot (0276) 71717

STOCKBRIDGE, Nelson William. b 35. Trin Th Coll Auckland 61. **d** 84 **p** 85. New Zealand 85-86; C Shildon w Eldon *Dur* 87; C Norton St Mary 87-88; C Cottingham *York* from 88. *22 Lyndhurst Avenue, Cottingham, N Humberside HU16 4QE* Hull (0482) 845514

STOCKER, David William George. b 37. Bris Univ BA58 CertEd. Qu Coll Birm 59. **d** 60 **p** 61. C Sparkhill St Jo *Birm* 60-64; C Keighley *Bradf* 64-66; V Grenoside *Sheff* 66-83; V Sandbach *Ches* from 83. *The Vicarage, 15 Offley Road, Sandbach, Cheshire CW11 9AY* Crewe (0270) 762379

STOCKLEY, Mrs Alexandra Madeleine Reuss. b 43. Cranmer Hall Dur 80 Carl Dioc Tr Inst. **dss** 84 **d** 87. Upperby St Jo *Carl* 84-87; Par Dn 87-89; Par Dn

Grayrigg 90; Par Dn Old Hutton w New Hutton 90; Dn-in-c Grayrigg, Old Hutton and New Hutton from 90. *The Vicarage, Grayrigg, Kendal, Cumbria LA8 9BU* Grayrigg (053984) 272

STOCKLEY, Michael Ian. b 41. Lon Coll of Div 66. **d** 69 **p** 70. C St Helens St Mark *Liv* 69-74; C Fazakerley Em 74; TV 74-82; V Ince Ch Ch from 82. *The Vicarage, 70 Belle Green Lane, Ince, Wigan, Lancs WN2 2EP* Wigan (0942) 495831

STOCKLEY, Roland. b 23. St Jo Coll Dur BA47 DipTh49. **d** 49 **p** 50. R Pedmore *Worc* 68-88; rtd 88. *64 Hyperion Road, Stourbridge, W Midlands DY7 6SB* Stourbridge (0384) 393463

STOCKPORT, Suffragan Bishop of. See SARGEANT, Rt Rev Frank Pilkington

STOCKS, John Cedric Hawkesworth. b 13. Em Coll Cam BA37 MA40. Westcott Ho Cam 39. **d** 40 **p** 41. V Sheriff Hutton *York* 65-80; rtd 80. *8 Dale Close, Hampsthwaite, Harrogate, N Yorkshire HG3 2EQ* Harrogate (0423) 770834

STOCKTON, Dr Ian George. b 49. Selw Coll Cam BA72 MA76 Hull Univ PhD90. St Jo Coll Nottm CertEd74. **d** 75 **p** 76. C Chell *Lich* 75-78; C Trentham 78-80; R Dalbeattie *Glas* 80-84; P-in-c Scotton w Northorpe *Linc* 84-88; Asst Local Min Officer 84-88; Local Min Officer from 88. *105 Nettleham Road, Lincoln LN2 1RU* Lincoln (0522) 524428 or 542121

STOCKTON, Wilfred. b 32. Roch Th Coll 63. **d** 65 **p** 66. C Shirebrook *Derby* 65-67; C Boulton 67-69; V Ault Hucknall 69-73; R Pinxton 73-83; P-in-c Riddings 83-85; P-in-c Ironville 83-85; V Ladybrook *S'well* from 85. *St Mary's Vicarage, Bancroft Lane, Mansfield, Notts NG18 5LZ* Mansfield (0623) 21709

STOCKWELL, John Nicholas. b 49. Trin Coll Bris 80. **d** 82 **p** 83. C Flixton St Jo *Man* 82-86; V Accrington Ch Ch *Blackb* 86-90; R Chulmleigh Ex from 90; R Chawleigh w Cheldon from 90; R Wembworthy w Eggesford from 90. *The Rectory, Chawleigh, Devon EX18 7HJ* Chulmleigh (0769) 80537

✠**STOCKWOOD, Rt Rev Arthur Mervyn.** b 13. Ch Coll Cam BA35 MA39 Sussex Univ Hon DLitt63. Lambeth DD59 Westcott Ho Cam 35. **d** 36 **p** 37 **c** 59. C Moorfields *Bris* 36-41; V 41-55; Hon Can Bris Cathl 53-55; V Cam Gt St Mary w St Mich *Ely* 55-59; Bp S'wark 59-80; rtd 80; Asst Bp B & W from 81. *15 Sydney Buildings, Bath BA2 6BZ* Bath (0225) 462788

STOKE-ON-TRENT, Archdeacon of. See EDE, Ven Dennis

STOKER, Andrew. b 64. Coll of Ripon & York St Jo BA86. Coll of Resurr Mirfield 87. **d** 90 **p** 91. C Horton *Newc* from 90. *66 Devonworth Place, Cowpen, Blyth, Northd NE24 5AG* Blyth (0670) 361292

STOKER, Mrs Joanna Mary. b 57. Leic Univ BA79 Nottm Univ BCombStuds83. Linc Th Coll 80. **dss** 83 **d** 87. Greenford H Cross *Lon* 83-87; Par Dn 87-89; Par Dn Farnham Royal w Hedgerley *Ox* from 89. *7 Rectory Close, Farnham Royal, Slough SL2 3BG* Farnham Common (0753) 644293

STOKES, Canon Albert Edward. b 21. TCD BA43 MA46 BD46. CITC 43. **d** 46 **p** 47. Lect Ch of Ireland Coll of Educn Dub 49-79; I Powerscourt w Kilbride and Annacrevy *D & G* 56-86; Ch Ch Cathl Dub 70-86; rtd 86. *Cotehele, The Riverwalk, Ashford, Co Wicklow, Irish Republic* Wicklow (404) 40360

STOKES, Andrew John. b 38. G&C Coll Cam BA60 MA64. Ripon Hall Ox 60. **d** 62 **p** 63. C Northn All SS w St Kath *Pet* 62-65; C Endcliffe *Sheff* 65-68; Ind Missr 65-68; Sen Ind Chapl 69-74; P-in-c Bridport *Sarum* 75-79; TR Bridport 79-80; V Holbeach Marsh *Linc* 82-88; Bp's Dom Chapl from 88. *1 Broadway, Lincoln LN2 1SQ* Lincoln (0522) 539531

STOKES, David Lewis. b 49. **d** 75 **p** 76. C Romford St Edw *Chelmsf* 76-78; USA from 78. *61 Broadripple Drive, Princeton, New Jersey 08540-4011, USA*

STOKES, Donald Roy. b 30. K Coll Lon BD79 AKC79. **d** 80 **p** 81. C St-Geo-in-the-East w St Paul *Lon* 80-84; Ind Chapl from 84. *12 The Orchard, London N21 2DH* 081-360 1205

STOKES, George Smithson Garbutt. b 13. Leeds Univ BA35. Coll of Resurr Mirfield 35. **d** 37 **p** 38. V Amport, Grateley and Quarley *Win* 69-74; V Sonning *Ox* 74-85; rtd 85; Perm to Offic *Ox* from 85. *Myrtle Cottage, Sheep Street, Charlbury, Oxon OX7 3RR* Charlbury (0608) 811207

STOKES, Godfrey Julian Fenwick. b 04. SS Coll Cam BA26 MA31. Westcott Ho Cam 29. **d** 30 **p** 31. C Staveley *Derby* 30-34 and 40-42; India 34-40; OSB from 42; Lic to Offic *Ox* from 42; Abbot Nashdom Abbey 84-88; Elmore Abbey from 87. *Elmore Abbey, Church Lane,*

Speen, Newbury, Berks RG13 1SA   Newbury (0635) 33080

STOKES, Leonard Peter Norton. b 21. Jes Coll Cam BA43 MA47. Westcott Ho Cam 44. **d** 45 **p** 46. Chapl Newton Abbot Hosp 59-86; Chapl Forde Park Sch 59-86; R Wolborough w Newton Abbot *Ex* 59-86; rtd 86. *67 Conway Road, Paignton, Devon TQ4 5LH*   Paignton (0803) 529764

STOKES, Miss Mary Patricia. b 39. St Hilda's Coll Ox BA62 MA66. Lanc Univ MA80 Bris Univ CertEd63. E Midl Min Tr Course 78. **d** 87. Par Dn Pheasey *Lich* from 87. *33 Morland Road, Great Barr, Birmingham B43 7JG*   021-360 1723

STOKES, Michael John. b 34. Lich Th Coll 63. **d** 65 **p** 66. C Worplesdon *Guildf* 65-68; Chapl RAF 68-84; Asst Chapl-in-Chief RAF 84-89; QHC from 88; V Chesterton w Middleton Stoney and Wendlebury *Ox* from 89. *Keeper's Cottage, The Tithings, Chesterton, Oxon OX6 8UW*   Bicester (0869) 248744

STOKES, Peter. b 31. Qu Coll Birm 68. **d** 69 **p** 70. C Norton *St Alb* 69-77; V Harlington 77-85; P-in-c Chalgrave 80-85; V Luton St Andr from 85; Asst RD Luton from 89. *St Andrew's Vicarage, Blenheim Crescent, Luton LU3 1HA*   Luton (0582) 32380

STOKES, Richard Spencer. b 29. TCD 66. **d** 68 **p** 69. C Lisburn Ch Ch Cathl *Conn* 68-71; C Dub St Geo and St Thos *D & G* 71-75; C Dub Rathfarnham 75-79; I Blessington w Kilbride, Ballymore Eustace etc from 79; RD Ballymore from 87. *The Rectory, Blessington, Co Wicklow, Irish Republic*   Naas (45) 65178

STOKES, Roger Sidney. b 47. Clare Coll Cam BA68 MA72. Sarum Th Coll 69. **d** 72 **p** 73. C Keighley *Bradf* 72-74; C Bolton St Jas w St Chrys 74-78; V Hightown *Wakef* 78-85; Asst Chapl HM Pris Wakef 85-87; Chapl HM Pris Full Sutton 87-89. *Address temp unknown*

STOKES, Terence Harold. b 46. Man Univ DSPT84 Open Univ BA89. Sarum & Wells Th Coll 71. **d** 73 **p** 74. C Blakenall Heath *Lich* 73-75; C Walsall Wood 75-78; C Northn St Alb *Pet* 78-81; TV Swinton St Pet *Man* 81-85; V Daisy Hill from 85. *The Vicarage, Lower Leigh Road, Daisy Hill, Westhoughton, Bolton BL5 2EH*   Westhoughton (0942) 813155

STOKES, Terence Ronald. b 35. Linc Th Coll. **d** 69 **p** 70. C Bramley *Ripon* 69-72; C Osbournby w Scott Willoughby *Linc* 72-74; C Hykeham 74-77; V Birchwood from 77. *St Luke's Vicarage, Jasmin Road, Lincoln LN6 0YR*   Lincoln (0522) 683507

STOKES, Preb Terence Walter. b 34. Bps' Coll Cheshunt 62. **d** 64 **p** 65. C Wanstead St Mary *Chelmsf* 64-67; C St Alb Abbey *St Alb* 67-70; Asst Dir RE *B & W* 70-75; Youth Chapl 70-75; P-in-c Yeovil 75-77; TV 77-82; R Wellington and Distr from 82; RD Tone from 89; Preb Wells Cathl from 90. *The Rectory, 72 High Street, Wellington, Somerset TA21 8RF*   Wellington (0823) 472248

STOKOE, Rodney James Robert. b 20. Dur Univ BSc46 BA48 DipTh49. Crozer Th Sem Penn ThM67 Atlantic Sch of Th Halifax (NS) Hon DD87. **d** 49 **p** 50. C W Hartlepool St Paul *Dur* 49-53; R Edin Ch Ch *Edin* 53-57; P-in-c Bishopwearmouth St Gabr *Dur* 57-60; Canada from 60; Prof Div K Coll NS 60-71; Prof Past Th Atlantic Sch Th NS 71-85. *403 Prince Street, Ste 206, Truro, Nova Scotia, Canada, B2N 1E6*   Halifax (902) 895-0047

STONE, Albert John. b 44. Loughb Univ BTech67 BSc. Sarum & Wells Th Coll 83. **d** 85 **p** 86. C Plymstock *Ex* 85-88; P-in-c Whitestone from 88; P-in-c Oldridge from 88; P-in-c Holcombe Burnell from 88. *The Rectory, Whitestone, Exeter EX4 2JT*   Longdown (039281) 406

STONE, Andrew Francis. b 43. AKC65. **d** 66 **p** 67. C Walthamstow St Mich *Chelmsf* 66-67; C Ealing St Barn *Lon* 67-70; C E Grinstead St Mary *Chich* 70-74; C-in-c Hydneye CD 74-81; R Denton w S Heighton and Tarring Neville from 81. *The Rectory, 6 Heighton Road, Newhaven, E Sussex BN9 0RB*   Newhaven (0273) 514319

STONE, Christopher John. b 49. Lanc Univ MA88. Lambeth STh84 Linc Th Coll 78. **d** 81 **p** 82. C Bromley St Mark *Roch* 81-84; P-in-c Burgh-by-Sands and Kirkbampton w Kirkandrews etc *Carl* 84; R 84-89; Chapl N Staffs R Infirmary Stoke-on-Trent from 89. *North Staffordshire Royal Infirmary, Princes Road, Stoke-on-Trent ST4 7LN*   Stoke-on-Trent (0782) 49144

STONE, Dr David Adrian. b 56. Or Coll Ox BA78 MA83 BM BCh83. Wycliffe Hall Ox 85. **d** 88 **p** 89. C Holborn St Geo w H Trin and St Bart *Lon* 88-91; C S Kensington St Luke from 91. *St Jude's Vicarage Flat, 20 Collingham Road, London SW5 0LX*   071-373 1693

STONE, Ernest Arthur. b 09. VRD60. AKC34 Open Univ BA81 MPhil91. **d** 34 **p** 35. V Bexhill St Aug *Chich* 54-74; Dioc RE Adv 54-80; rtd 74; Lic to Offic *Chich* 80-86 and from 89; RD Worthing 86-89. *56 Manor Road, Worthing, W Sussex BN11 4SQ*   Worthing (0903) 35120

STONE, Godfrey Owen. b 49. Ex Coll Ox BA71 BA78 MA75 Birm Univ CertEd72. Wycliffe Hall Ox 76. **d** 81 **p** 82. C Rushden w Newton Bromswold *Pet* 81-87; Dir Past Studies Wycliffe Hall Ox from 87. *Wycliffe Hall, 54 Banbury Road, Oxford OX2 6PW*   Oxford (0865) 274207

STONE, Jeffrey Peter. b 34. Nottm Univ TCert72 BEd73. Lich Th Coll 58. **d** 61 **p** 62. C Newark St Mary *S'well* 61-65; C Sutton in Ashfield St Mich 65-69; Robert Smyth Sch Market Harborough 72-89; Perm to Offic *Leic* 88-90; R Waltham on the Wolds, Stonesby, Saxby etc from 90. *The Rectory, Melton Road, Waltham on the Wolds, Melton Mowbray, Leics LE14 4AJ*   Waltham-on-the-Wolds (066478) 774

STONE, John Anthony. b 46. St Chad's Coll Dur BA68 DipTh69. **d** 69 **p** 70. C New Addington *Cant* 69-72; C Tewkesbury w Walton Cardiff *Glouc* 72-76; C-in-c Dedworth CD *Ox* 76-82; V Dedworth 82-86; TV Chipping Barnet w Arkley *St Alb* from 86. *St Stephen's Vicarage, 1 Spring Close, Bells Hill, Barnet, Herts EN5 2UR*   081-449 7758

STONE, John Geoffrey Elliot. b 20. Ch Coll Cam BA41 MA45. Ridley Hall Cam 47. **d** 49 **p** 50. V Southwater *Chich* 59-70; V Thornham w Titchwell *Nor* 70-74; R Copdock w Washbrook and Belstead *St E* 74-77; P-in-c Therfield *St Alb* 77-82; P-in-c Kelshall 77-82; C Littlehampton St Jas *Chich* 82-85; C Littlehampton St Mary 82-85; C Wick 82-85; TV Littlehampton and Wick 86; rtd 86; C Compton, the Mardens, Stoughton and Racton *Chich* from 86. *Forestside Vicarage, Rowlands Castle, Hants PO9 6EE*   Rowlands Castle (0705) 631585

STONE, John Wesley. b 18. TCD BA44. **d** 45 **p** 46. R Woodham Ferrers *Chelmsf* 56-87; rtd 87. *12 Orchid Place, South Woodham Ferrers, Chelmsford, Essex* Chelmsford (0245) 320260

STONE, Michael Graham. b 33. FBCS. S Dios Minl Tr Scheme. **d** 83 **p** 84. NSM Chich St Paul and St Pet *Chich* from 83. *125 Cedar Drive, Chichester, W Sussex PO19 3EL*   Chichester (0243) 784484

STONE, Michael John. b 33. Trin Hall Cam MA56 LLB57. E Anglian Minl Tr Course 78. **d** 80 **p** 81. NSM Whitton and Thurleston w Akenham *St E* 80-84; NSM Westerfield and Tuddenham St Martin w Witnesham from 84. *4 The Granaries, Tuddenham, Ipswich IP6 9BW*   Witnesham (047385) 363

STONE, Nigel John. b 57. Bedf Coll Lon BSc82. St Jo Coll Nottm 82. **d** 85 **p** 86. C Battersea Park St Sav *S'wark* 85-87; C Battersea St Sav and St Geo w St Andr 87-89; P-in-c Brixton St Paul from 89. *St Paul's Vicarage, 73 Baytree Road, London SW2 5RR*   071-274 6907

STONE, Noel Alfred. b 33. St Jo Coll Morpeth 58. **d** 62 **p** 63. Australia 62-74; C The Quinton *Birm* 74-75; Hong Kong 75-78; New Zealand 78-85; P-in-c Witham Gp *Linc* 85; R from 85; RD Beltisloe from 90. *The Rectory, Hill View, High Street, South Witham, Grantham, Lincs NG33 5QW*   Thistleton (057283) 240

STONE, Peter James. b 54. Leic Univ BA75 Qu Coll Cam BA77 MA81. Westcott Ho Cam 76. **d** 78 **p** 79. C Bradford-on-Avon *Sarum* 78-81; R Corsley 81-83; Chapl Dauntsey's Sch Devizes 83-88; V Studley *Sarum* from 89. *The Vicarage, 340 Frome Road, Trowbridge, Wilts BA14 0ED*   Trowbridge (0225) 753162

STONE, Philip William. b 58. Ridley Hall Cam 85. **d** 88 **p** 89. C Hackney Marsh *Lon* from 88. *84 Roding Road, London E5 0DS*   081-533 4034

STONE, Reginald Peter. b 32. Ex Coll Ox BA56 MA61 DipEd57. St Steph Ho Ox 56. **d** 58 **p** 59. C Upper Norwood St Jo *Cant* 58-62; Hon C 62-67; Chapl Abp Tenison's Gr Sch 63-75; Perm to Offic *S'wark* 67-75; Chapl Highgate Sch Lon from 75. *15A Bishopswood Road, London N6 4PB*   081-348 9211 or 340 1524

STONE, Richard Anthony. b 46. Hatf Coll Dur BA68 Nottm Univ DipTh71. Linc Th Coll 70. **d** 73 **p** 74. C Marske in Cleveland *York* 73-78; TV Haxby w Wigginton 78-87; V Osbaldwick w Murton from 87. *The Vicarage, 80 Osbaldwick Lane, York YO1 3AX*   York (0904) 416763

STONE, Rodney Cameron. b 32. Sarum Th Coll 67. **d** 69 **p** 70. C Milton *Portsm* 69-74; CF (TA) from 72; R Rowlands Castle *Portsm* 74-80; V Tividale *Lich* 80-81; C Weeke *Win* 81-88; V Win St Barn from 89. *St Barnabas' Vicarage, Fromond Road, Winchester, Hants SO22 6DY*   Winchester (0962) 882728

STONE, Canon Rodney Milton Robertson. b 25. Ely Th Coll 51. **d** 53 **p** 54. R Gunthorpe w Bale *Nor* 57-70; P-in-c Sharrington 62-70; R Tayport *St And* 70-90; R Newport-on-Tay 70-90; Can St Ninian's Cathl Perth 87-90; rtd 90; Lic to Offic *Newc* from 90. *12 Well Square, Tweedmouth, Berwick-upon-Tweed TD15 2AL* Berwick-upon-Tweed (0289) 307791

STONEBANKS, David Arthur. b 34. Louvain Univ Belgium MA70. Coll of Resurr Mirfield 64. **d** 66 **p** 67. C Burgess Hill St Jo *Chich* 66-68; Chapl City Univ *Lon* 70-73; Chapl Strasbourg w Stuttgart and Heidelberg *Eur* 73-80; Chapl Geneva 80-86; Chapl Zurich w St Gallen and Winterthur 86-89; R Horsted Keynes *Chich* from 89. *The Rectory, Horsted Keynes, Haywards Heath, W Sussex RH17 7ED* Dane Hill (0825) 790317

STONEHOUSE, Joseph Christopher. b 48. Chich Th Coll 68. **d** 71 **p** 72. C Beamish *Dur* 71-76; C Doncaster St Leon and St Jude *Sheff* 76-80; V Copmanthorpe *York* from 80. *The Vicarage, 17 Sutor Close, Copmanthorpe, York YO2 3TX* York (0904) 706280

STONESTREET, George Malcolm. b 38. AKC61. **d** 62 **p** 63. C Leeds St Pet *Ripon* 62-64; C Far Headingley St Chad 64-67; V Askrigg w Stallingbusk 67-82; V Bramley 82-85; TR from 85. *Bramley Vicarage, Hough Lane, Leeds LS13 3NE* Pudsey (0532) 578590

STONEY, Ven Thomas Vesey. b 34. Or Coll Ox BA56 MA60. CITC 58. **d** 58 **p** 59. C Ballywillan *Conn* 58-61; C Carrickfergus 61-66; I Skerry w Rathcavan and Newtowncrommelin from 66; Adn Dalriada from 85. *37 Review Road, Broughshane, Ballymena, Co Antrim BT42 4JL* Broughshane (0266) 861215

STONIER, Peter John. b 53. St Jo Coll Dur BA75. St Steph Ho Ox 76. **d** 79 **p** 80. C Huddersfield St Jo *Wakef* 79-82; C Athersley 82-86; V from 86. *The Vicarage, 27 Laithes Lane, Athersley, Barnsley, S Yorkshire S71 3AF* Barnsley (0226) 245361

STOODLEY, Peter Bindon. b 47. Linc Th Coll 89. **d** 91. C Holbeck *Ripon* from 91. *23 Park View, Leeds LS11 7AY* Leeds (0532) 7775278

STOPFORD, Eric. b 08. Tyndale Hall Bris 31. **d** 34 **p** 35. R Whitmore *Lich* 48-79; rtd 79. *Flat 7, Manor Court, Swan Road, Pewsey, Wilts SN9 5DW* Marlborough (0672) 64028

STOPPARD, Henry. b 16. Worc Ord Coll 60. **d** 61 **p** 62. V Blackwell *Derby* 63-83; rtd 83; Perm to Offic *Bris* from 83. *White Horse Cottage, Church Hill, Olveston, Bristol BS12 3BX* Almondsbury (0454) 615108

STOREY, Mrs Elizabeth Mary. b 37. Cam Univ DipRS80 Man Univ BA84. dss 84 **d** 87. Liv All So Springwood *Liv* 84-87; Par Dn from 87. *27 Mentmore Road, Liverpool L18 4PU* 051-724 2075

STOREY, Gerard Charles Alfred. b 57. GRSC80 Thames Poly BSc80 Lon Univ PhD84. Wycliffe Hall Ox 84. **d** 87 **p** 88. C Broadwater St Mary *Chich* from 87. *28 Loxwood Avenue, Worthing, W Sussex BN14 7QY* Worthing (0903) 38288

STOREY, Michael. b 36. Chich Th Coll 73. **d** 75 **p** 76. C Illingworth *Wakef* 75-78; V Rastrick St Jo 78-87; V Crosland Moor from 87. *The Vicarage, Church Avenue, Crosland Moor, Huddersfield HD4 5DF* Huddersfield (0484) 22381

STOREY, Thomas William. b 08. Clifton Th Coll 52. **d** 52 **p** 53. V Brownhill *Wakef* 64-73; Org Sec (Dios Guildf and S'wark) CECS 64-73; C Beddington *S'wark* 73-79; rtd 80; Hon C S Beddington St Mich *S'wark* from 80. *252 Stafford Road, Wallington, Surrey SM6 8PF* 081-688 9262

STOREY, William Earl Cosbey. b 58. Kent Univ BA. CITC DipTh86. **d** 82 **p** 83. C Drumglass w Moygashel *Arm* 82-86; I Crinken *D & G* from 86. *Crinken Parsonage, Bray, Co Wicklow, Irish Republic* Dublin (1) 282-2048

STOREY, William Leslie Maurice. b 31. Oak Hill Th Coll 67. **d** 69 **p** 70. C Wembley St Jo *Lon* 69-71; C Ealing Dean St Jo 71-75; V W Derby St Luke *Liv* 75-80; V Hunts Cross 80-83; Hon C Brixton St Paul *S'wark* 83-86; P-in-c 87-88; P-in-c Brixton Hill St Sav 83-86; rtd 88. *33A Queens Road, Kingston upon Thames, Surrey* 081-546 3899

STORY, Victor Leonard. b 45. BSc. Ripon Coll Cuddesdon. **d** 81 **p** 82. C Evesham *Worc* 81-85; P-in-c Ilmington w Stretton on Fosse and Ditchford *Cov* 85-90; P-in-c Ilmington w Stretton-on-Fosse etc from 90. *The Rectory, Ilmington, Shipston-on-Stour, Warks CV36 4LB* Ilmington (060882) 210

STOTE-BLANDY, Canon Gordon Blandy. b 12. G&C Coll Cam BA33 MA38. Westcott Ho Cam 33. **d** 35 **p** 36. C Epsom St Martin *Guildf* 35-38; New Zealand from 38;

Hon Can St Paul's Cathl Wellington 65-78. *16 Wren Street, Waikanae, New Zealand* Waikanae (58) 34831

STOTER, David John. b 43. AKC66. **d** 67 **p** 68. C Reading St Giles *Ox* 67-71; C Luton Lewsey St Hugh *St Alb* 71-73; Chapl Westmr Hosp Lon 73-79; Convenor of Chapls Notts Distr HA from 79; Chapl Univ Hosp Nottm from 79; Chapl Nottm Gen Hosp from 79. *The Chaplain's Office, University Hospital, Derby Road, Nottingham* Nottingham (0602) 421421

STOTT, Antony. b 21. Bps' Coll Cheshunt 53. **d** 55 **p** 56. V Bratton *Sarum* 66-74; R Marnhull 74-81; P-in-c Broad Chalke and Bower Chalke 81; P-in-c Ebbesbourne Wake w Fifield Bavant and Alvediston 81; P-in-c Berwick St John 81; V Chalke Valley W 81-87; rtd 87; Perm to Offic *Ex* from 87. *11 Luscombe Close, Ivybridge, Devon PL21 9TT* Plymouth (0752) 896142

STOTT, Christopher John. b 45. Lon Univ BD68. Tyndale Hall Bris. **d** 69 **p** 70. C Croydon Ch Ch Broad Green *Cant* 69-72; Ethiopia 73-76; Area Sec (SW) BCMS 76-78; Tanzania 78-85; R Harwell w Chilton *Ox* from 85; RD Wallingford from 91. *The Rectory, Harwell, Didcot, Oxon OX11 0EW* Abingdon (0235) 835365

STOTT, Eric. b 36. ALCD62. **d** 62 **p** 63. C Penn Fields *Lich* 62-65; C Normanton *Derby* 65-71; R Lower Broughton St Clem w St Matthias *Man* 71-79; V Chadderton Em from 79. *Emmanuel Vicarage, 15 Chestnut Street, Chadderton, Oldham OL9 8HB* 061-681 1310

STOTT, Frederick. b 23. Bris Univ DipFE75 Univ of Wales (Cardiff) CQSW71. Sarum & Wells Th Coll 83. **d** 85 **p** 86. Hon C Sholing *Win* from 85; Perm to Offic *Portsm* from 89. *35 Broadwater Road, Townhill Park, Southampton SO2 2DW* Southampton (0703) 557193

STOTT, Dr John Robert Walmsley. b 21. Trin Coll Cam BA45 MA50. Lambeth DD83 Ridley Hall Cam 44. **d** 45 **p** 46. R St Marylebone All So w SS Pet and Jo *Lon* 50-75; Hon C 75-88; Hon C Langham Place All So from 88; Chapl to HM The Queen 59-91; Extra Chapl from 91; Dir Lon Inst of Contemporary Christianity 82-86; Pres from 86; rtd 91. *92 Weymouth Street, London W1N 3FB* 071-580 1867

STOTT, Wilfrid. b 04. Lon Univ BA26 BD27 Linc Coll Ox BLitt62 DPhil66. Lon Coll of Div 26. **d** 27 **p** 28. Kenya 66-71; rtd 71; P-in-c Croxton and Eltisley *Ely* 71-85. *12 Westfield, Harwell, Didcot, Oxon* Didcot (0235) 832791

STOUT, Trevor. b 24. Qu Coll Birm 77. **d** 77 **p** 77. Hon C Lower Mitton *Worc* 77-85; Hon C Kidderminster St Geo from 85. *9 Ullswater Avenue, Stourport-on-Severn, Worcs DY13 8QP* Stourport (02993) 78073

STOVES, Ernest. b 17. Bps' Coll Cheshunt. **d** 64 **p** 65. V Evenwood *Dur* 68-82; rtd 82. *12 Lady Close, Staindrop, Darlington, Co Durham DL2 3LW* Staindrop (0833) 60369

STOW, John Mark. b 51. Selw Coll Cam BA73 MA77. Linc Th Coll 76. **d** 78 **p** 79. C Harpenden St Jo *St Alb* 78-82; TV Beaminster Area *Sarum* 82-87; P-in-c Hawkchurch 87-90; P-in-c Marshwood Vale 87-88; TR Marshwood Vale Team Min 88-91. *Lower Tytherleigh Farm, Axminster, Devon EX13 7AZ*

STOW, Peter John. b 50. **d** 89 **p** 90. C Forest Gate St Mark *Chelmsf* from 89. *226 Sebert Road, London E7 0NP* 081-534 0426

STOW, Archdeacon of. See WELLS, Ven Roderick John

STOWE, Brian. b 32. Trin Coll Cam BA55 MA59. Ridley Hall Cam. **d** 57 **p** 58. C New Catton St Luke *Nor* 57-59; Chapl R Masonic Sch Bushey 59-70; Chapl Alleyn's Foundn Dulwich 71-75; Hon C Dulwich St Barn *S'wark* 71-75; Chapl Ellerslie Sch Malvern from 75. *31 Park View, Abbey Road, Malvern, Worcs WR14 3HG* Malvern (0684) 568134

STOWE, Nigel James. b 36. Bris Univ BSc57. Clifton Th Coll 59. **d** 61 **p** 62. C Ware Ch Ch *St Alb* 61-64; C Reigate St Mary *S'wark* 64-67; V Islington St Jude Mildmay Park *Lon* 67-75; V Penn Street *Ox* from 75. *The Vicarage, Penn Street, Amersham, Bucks HP7 0PX* High Wycombe (0494) 712194

STOWE, Mrs Rachel Lilian. b 33. Qu Coll Birm 79. dss 83 **d** 87. Dean w Yelden, Melchbourne and Shelton *St Alb* 83-87; Pertenhall w Swineshead 83-87; Bp's Officer for NSM and Asst Dir of Ords from 87. *42 Rodeheath, Luton LU4 9XA* Luton (0582) 584205

STRACHAN, Donald Philip Michael. b 37. St D Coll Lamp 60. **d** 62 **p** 63. C Aber St Mary *Ab* 62-64; P-in-c Aber St Paul 64-66; Chapl St Andr Cathl 65-68; Itinerant Priest *Mor* 68-73; R Coatbridge *Glas* 73-85; Chapl HM Pris Glas (Barlinnie) 84-87; Dioc Supernumerary *Glas* from 85. *50 Monkland View Crescent, Bargeddie, Baillieston, Glasgow G69 7RX* 041-771 4122

STRACHAN, Canon Kenneth Archibald Gibson. b 08. Univ Coll Dur LTh30. **d** 31 **p** 32. Lib Edin Th Coll 70-77; rtd 77; Hon Can St Andr Cathl *Ab* from 78. *11/4 New Orchardfield, Edinburgh EH6 5ET* 031-555 0179

STRAFFORD, Nigel Thomas Bevan. b 53. Univ of Wales (Lamp) BA. Sarum & Wells Th Coll. **d** 82 **p** 84. C Kidderminster St Mary *Worc* 82; C Kidderminster St Mary and All SS etc 82-83; Hon C Stockton St Mark *Dur* 84-86; AP Longwood *Wakef* from 86. *St Mark's Vicarage, 313 Vicarage Road, Huddersfield HD3 4HJ* Huddersfield (0484) 653576

STRAIN, Christopher Malcolm. b 56. MLawSoc Southn Univ LLB73. Wycliffe Hall Ox 83. **d** 86 **p** 87. C Werrington *Pet* 86-89; C Broadwater St Mary *Chich* from 89. *St Stephen's House, 80 Dominion Road, Worthing, W Sussex BN14 8JT* Worthing (0903) 230759

STRANACK, David Arthur Claude. b 43. Chich Th Coll 65. **d** 68 **p** 69. C Forest Gate St Edm *Chelmsf* 68-69; C Colchester St Jas, All SS, St Nic and St Runwald 69-74; V Brentwood St Geo 74-82; V Nayland w Wiston *St E* from 82. *The Vicarage, Bear Street, Nayland, Colchester CO6 4LA* Nayland (0206) 262316

STRANACK, Dr Fay Rosemary. b 30. Lon Univ BSc55 PhD60. Westcott Ho Cam 88. **d** 89. NSM Denmead *Portsm* from 89. *35 Yew Tree Gardens, Denmead, Portsmouth PO7 6LH* Portsmouth (0705) 256785

STRANACK, Richard Nevill. b 40. Leeds Univ BA63. Coll of Resurr Mirfield 63. **d** 65 **p** 66. C Bush Hill Park St Mark *Lon* 65-68; C Brighton St Martin *Chich* 68-72; P-in-c Toftrees w Shereford *Nor* 72-74; V 74-81; P-in-c Pensthorpe 72-74; R 74-81; V Hempton and Pudding Norton 72-81; RD Burnham and Walsingham 78-81; V Par *Truro* from 81; P-in-c St Blazey from 87; Hon Chapl Miss to Seamen from 81. *The Vicarage, 42 Vicarage Road, Tywardreath, Par, Cornwall PL24 2PH* Par (072681) 2775

STRAND, Tyler Alan. b 51. Augustana Coll (USA) BA73. St Steph Ho Ox MDiv78. **d** 77 **p** 78. USA 77-91; Chapl Helsinki w Moscow *Eur* from 91. *Putouskuja 5, B7, 01600 Vantaa 60, Helsinki, Finland* Helsinki (0) 563-4829

STRANEX, Alan. b 37. Oak Hill Th Coll 63. **d** 65 **p** 66. C Stapleford *S'well* 65-68; S Africa from 68. *PO Box 6215, Roggebaai, 8012 South Africa* Cape Town (21) 759162

STRANEX, Douglas. b 07. **d** 40 **p** 41. I Stoneyford *Conn* 53-78; rtd 78. *25 Bannview Heights, Banbridge, Co Down BT32 4LZ* Banbridge (08206) 23967

STRANGE, Alan Michael. b 57. Pemb Coll Ox BA79 MA83. Wycliffe Hall Ox 81. **d** 84 **p** 85. C York St Paul *York* 84-87; Assoc Chapl Brussels Cathl *Eur* from 87; Assoc Chapl Brussels w Charleroi from 87. *29 rue Capitaine Crespel, 1050 Brussels, Belgium* Brussels (2) 646-0827

STRANGE, Bryan. b 26. Sarum & Wells Th Coll 73. **d** 75 **p** 76. C King's Worthy *Win* 75-78; C Wilton *B & W* 78-80; V Kewstoke w Wick St Lawrence 80-89; rtd 89; Perm to Offic *Ex* from 90. *29 Bluebell Avenue, Tiverton, Devon EX16 6SX*

STRANGE, Edward Stanley. b 24. Ab Dioc Tr Course 82 Moray Ord Course 88. **d** 90 **p** 91. Hon C Inverness St Jo *Mor* from 90. *1 Burn Brae Crescent, Westhill, Inverness IV1 2HD* Inverness (0463) 792017

STRANGE, Malcolm. b 58. Sarum & Wells Th Coll 82. **d** 85 **p** 86. C Seaton Hirst *Newc* 85-88; C Ridgeway *Sarum* 88-89; TV from 89. *The Vicarage, Ogbourne St George, Marlborough, Wilts SN8 1SU* Ogbourne St George (067284) 248

STRANGE, Mark Jeremy. b 61. Aber Univ LTh82. Linc Th Coll 87. **d** 89 **p** 90. C Worc St Barn w Ch Ch *Worc* from 89. *22 Salters Close, Worcester WR4 9XT* Worcester (0905) 56903

STRANGE, Canon Peter Robert. b 48. Univ Coll Lon BA69 Ex Coll Ox BA71 MA76. Cuddesdon Coll 71. **d** 72 **p** 73. C Denton *Newc* 72-74; C Newc St Jo 74-79; Chapl for Arts and Recreation 79-90; R Wallsend St Pet 79-86; Can Res Newc Cathl from 86; Angl Adv State Tees TV trom 90. *55 Queen's Terrace, Jesmond, Newcastle upon Tyne NE2 2PL* 091-281 0181

STRANGE, Robert Lewis. b 45. Sarum & Wells Th Coll 72. **d** 74 **p** 75. C Walthamstow St Barn and St Jas Gt *Chelmsf* 74-77; C Wickford 77-80; P-in-c Treverbyn *Truro* 80-83; V 83-86; Asst Stewardship Adv from 82; V Newlyn St Pet from 86; Miss to Seamen from 86. *St Peter's Vicarage, Newlyn, Penzance, Cornwall TR18 5HT* Penzance (0736) 62678

STRANGE, William Anthony. b 53. Qu Coll Cam BA76 MA80 Win Coll CertEd77 Ox Univ DPhil89. Wycliffe Hall Ox. **d** 82 **p** 83. Tutor Wycliffe Hall Ox 82-87; Lic to Offic *Ox* 82-87; C Abth *St D* 87; TV from

87. *The Vicarage, Buarth Road, Aberystwyth, Dyfed SY23 1NB* Aberystwyth (0970) 617015

STRANGEWAYS, Canon David Inderwick. b 12. DSO43 OBE44. Trin Hall Cam BA33 MA36. Wells Th Coll 58. **d** 59 **p** 60. V Bradford-on-Avon Ch Ch *Sarum* 65-73; Chapl Stockholm *Eur* 73-77; Chan Malta Cathl 77-81; rtd 81; Perm to Offic *St E* and *Nor* from 81. *10 Dowes Hill Close, Beccles, Suffolk NR34 9XL* Beccles (0502) 716086

STRANRAER-MULL, Very Rev Gerald Hugh. b 42. AKC69. St Aug Coll Cant 69. **d** 70 **p** 71. C Hexham *Newc* 70-72; C Corbridge w Halton 72; R Cruden *Ab* from 72; R Ellon from 72; Can St Andr Cathl from 81; Dean Ab from 88. *The Rectory, Ellon, Aberdeenshire AB41 9NP* Ellon (0358) 20366

STRAPPS, Robert David. b 28. St Edm Hall Ox BA52 MA56. Wycliffe Hall Ox 52. **d** 54 **p** 55. C Low Leyton *Chelmsf* 54-57; C Ox St Aldate w H Trin *Ox* 57-60; V Sandal St Helen *Wakef* from 60; RD Chevet from 81. *The Vicarage, 313 Barnsley Road, Wakefield, W Yorkshire WF2 6EJ* Wakefield (0924) 255441

STRASZAK, Edmund Norman. b 57. Coll of Resurr Mirfield 88. **d** 90 **p** 91. C Adlington *Blackb* from 90. *17 Broad Oak Close, Adlington, Chorley, Lancs PR6 9RU* Chorley (0257) 482523

STRATFORD, Mrs Anne Barbara. b 38. Southn Univ CertEd58. W Midl Minl Tr Course. **d** 91. Asst Dio Bd of Soc Resp (Family Care) *Lich* from 85; NSM Kinnerley w Melverley and Knockin w Maesbrook from 91. *Pentre Cleddar, Lower Hengoed, Oswestry, Shropshire SY10 7AB* Oswestry (0691) 655469

STRATFORD, Ven Ralph Montgomery. b 30. TCD BA53 MA67. CITC 53. **d** 54 **p** 54. C Dioc Curate *C & O* 54-55; C Waterford Ch Ch 55-56; I Ballisodare w Collooney and Emlaghfad *T, K & A* from 56; RD Straid 61-66 and from 88; Adn Killala and Achonry from 69; Preb Kilmactalway St Patr Cathl Dub from 85. *The Rectory, Ballysodare, Co Sligo, Irish Republic* Sligo (71) 67260

STRATFORD, Terence Stephen. b 45. Chich Th Coll 67. **d** 69 **p** 70. C Old Shoreham *Chich* 69-73; C New Shoreham 69-73; C Uckfield 73-75; C Lt Horsted 73-75; C Isfield 73-75; P-in-c Waldron 76-80; R 80-82; V Blacklands Hastings Ch Ch and St Andr 82-89; P-in-c Ovingdean from 89; Dioc Ecum Officer from 89. *St Wulfran's Rectory, 43 Ainsworth Avenue, Brighton BN2 7BQ* Brighton (0273) 303633

STRATFORD, Timothy Richard. b 61. York Univ BSc82. Wycliffe Hall Ox 83. **d** 86 **p** 87. C Mossley Hill St Matt and St Jas *Liv* 86-89; C St Helens St Helen from 89. *75 King Edward Road, Dentons Green, St Helens, Merseyside WA10 6LE* St Helens (0744) 613122

STRATFORD, William Anthony. b 23. Roch Th Coll 64. **d** 66 **p** 67. C Doncaster St Geo *Sheff* 68-71; V Arksey 71-75; R Armthorpe 75-80; R Harthill 80-82; R Harthill and Thorpe Salvin 82-85; rtd 85; Perm to Offic *Sheff* from 85. *10 Redhall Close, Kirk Sandall, Doncaster, S Yorkshire DN3 1QD* Doncaster (0302) 885289

STRATTA, Antony Charles. b 36. ACIS. S'wark Ord Course 82. **d** 85 **p** 86. C Southborough St Pet w Ch Ch and St Matt *Roch* 85-88; R Gt Mongeham w Ripple and Sutton by Dover *Cant* from 88. *The Rectory, Northbourne Road, Great Mongeham, Deal, Kent CT14 0HB* Deal (0304) 360170

STRATTON, Ven Basil. b 06. Hatf Coll Dur BA29 MA32. **d** 30 **p** 31. Adn Stafford *Lich* 59-74; Can Res and Treas Lich Cathl 60-74; Chapl to HM The Queen 65-76; rtd 74. *Woodlands Cottage, Rook Street, Mere, Warminster, Wilts BA12 6BY* Mere (0747) 235

STRATTON, Geoffrey Frederick. b 25. ARICS52. Oak Hill Th Coll 78. **d** 81 **p** 82. NSM Chipping Barnet w Arkley *St Alb* 81-85; TV 85-90; rtd 90; Perm to Offic *Linc* from 90. *Witsend, 8 Thornton Crescent, Horncastle, Lincs LN9 6JP* Horncastle (0507) 525508

STRATTON, Henry William. b 39. Bris Univ CertEd74 BEd75. Glouc Sch of Min 80. **d** 83 **p** 84. NSM Cainscross w Selsley *Glouc* 83-87; C Odd Rode *Ches* from 87. *53 Heath Avenue, Rode Heath, Stoke-on-Trent ST7 3RY* Alsager (0270) 877762

STRATTON, Ian Herbert Shearing. b 27. St Jo Coll Dur BA52 DipTh53 MA78. **d** 53 **p** 54. P-in-c Chettle *Sarum* 69-72; C Salisbury St Fran 72-80; C Harnham 81-87; rtd 88. *20 Bradley Road, Warminster, Wilts BA12 8BP* Warminster (0985) 212785

STRATTON, John Jefferies. b 27. Bps' Coll Cheshunt 53. **d** 55 **p** 56. C Watford St Mich *St Alb* 55-60; C Stevenage 60-65; R Cottered w Broadfield and Throcking 65-82; RD Buntingford 75-82; V S Mimms St Mary and Potters Bar *Lon* 82-84; V Potters Bar *St Alb* from 85. *The*

Vicarage, 15 The Walk, Potters Bar, Herts EN6 1QN Potters Bar (0707) 44539 or 45080

STRATTON, Canon Leslie Verdun. b 16. Edin Th Coll 36. **d** 39 **p** 40. P-in-c Dundee St Jo *Bre* 50-81; Syn Clerk 71-81; Can St Paul's Cathl Dundee 71-81; Hon Can from 81; rtd 81. *16 Argyle Street, Dundee DD4 7AL* Dundee (0382) 462413

STREATER, David Arthur. b 33. Oak Hill Th Coll 67. **d** 68 **p** 69. C Lindfield *Chich* 68-71; S Africa 71-86; R Kingham w Churchill, Daylesford and Sarsden *Ox* from 86. *The Rectory, Kingham, Oxford OX7 6YT* Kingham (0608) 658230

STREATFEILD, Francis Richard Champion. b 22. Qu Coll Cam BA48 MA59. Cuddesdon Coll 48. **d** 50 **p** 51. India 53-70; V Sacriston *Dur* 70-79; Lic to Offic *Carl* 79-85; Area Sec (Dio Carl) USPG 79-85; C Carl St Aid and Ch Ch *Carl* 85-88; rtd 88; Perm to Offic *Carl* from 88. *Fenton Lane Head, How Mill, Carlisle CA4 9LD* Carlisle (0228) 70470

STREATFEILD-JAMES, Eric Cardew. b 04. OBE45. RN Coll Greenwich RN39. **d** 62 **p** 63. V Hernhill *Cant* 66-75; rtd 75; Perm to Offic *Guildf* from 75. *Arden, Headley Hill Road, Bordon, Hants GU35 8DS* Headley Down (0428) 712248

STREEK, Stanley James. b 11. Man Univ BD42. Wycliffe Hall Ox. **d** 42 **p** 43. V Holmebridge *Wakef* 51-76; rtd 76. *Bridgend, Laurieston, Castle Douglas, Kirkcudbrightshire DG7 2PW* Laurieston (06445) 638

STREET, David Grover. b 24. St Aid Birkenhead 49. **d** 54 **p** 55. Warden Rugby Clubs Notting Hill 68-70; Chapl Milton Abbey Sch Dorset 70; Chapl St Lawr Coll Ramsgate 71; Community Cen Strabane Co Tyrone 73-74; Boys' Welfare Club Hartlepool 74-84; rtd 89. *80 Woodside, Barnard Castle, Co Durham DL12 8AP* Teesdale (0833) 37351

STREET, Peter Ernest. b 17. Oak Hill Th Coll 37. **d** 40 **p** 42. V Cheadle Hulme St Andr *Ches* 68-73; CPAS Evang 74-78; rtd 78; Perm to Offic *Nor* from 78. *49 Eckling Grange, Dereham, Norfolk NR20 3BB* Dereham (0362) 698896

STREET, Peter Jarman. b 29. K Coll Lon BD59 AKC59. **d** 59 **p** 60. C Highters Heath *Birm* 59-60; C Shirley 60-62; Lect Chesh Coll of Educn 62-66; St Pet Coll of Educn Birm 66-70; RE Adv Essex Co Coun from 70; Hon C Gt Dunmow *Chelmsf* 71-85; Sen Insp RE and Humanities from 74; R Gt w Lt Yeldham from 85; RD Belchamp from 90. *The Rectory, Church Road, Great Yeldham, Halstead, Essex CO9 4PT* Great Yeldham (0787) 237358

STREET, Philip. b 47. Lon Univ BPharm68. NW Ord Course 75. **d** 78 **p** 79. C Heaton St Barn *Bradf* 78-81; C Evington *Leic* 82-84; P-in-c Wymondham w Edmondthorpe 84; P-in-c Buckminster w Sewstern, Sproxton and Coston 84; R Wymondham w Edmondthorpe, Buckminster etc 84-88; V Gosberton Clough and Quadring *Linc* from 88; Asst Local Min Officer from 88. *The Vicarage, Gosberton Clough, Spalding, Lincs PE11 4JL* Spalding (0775) 750252

STREETER, Miss Christine Mary. b 50. St Jo Coll Nottm BTh81 LTh81. **dss** 83 **d** 87. Monkwearmouth St Andr *Dur* 83-85; Stranton 85-87; Par Dn 87-90; Par Dn Lastingham w Appleton-le-Moors, Rosedale etc *York* from 90. *16 Rosedale Abbey, Pickering, N Yorkshire YO18 8FA* Lastingham (07515) 7721

STREETER, David James. b 42. Pemb Coll Cam BA64 MA68. Qu Coll Birm 65. **d** 67 **p** 68. C Saffron Walden *Chelmsf* 67-71; C Shrub End 71-73; R Rayne 73-79; V Highams Park All SS 79-82; P-in-c Stradbroke w Horham and Athelington *St E* 82-87; R Stradbroke, Horham, Athelington and Redlingfield from 87; RD Hoxne from 91. *The Rectory, Doctors Lane, Stradbroke, Eye, Suffolk IP21 5HU* Stradbroke (037984) 363

STREETING, Laurence Storey. b 14. VRD65. St Jo Coll Dur BA39 DipTh40 MA42. **d** 40 **p** 41. Chapl RNVR 42-90; R Guernsey St Sampson *Win* 65-71; Windward Is 71-76; Chapl Madeira *Eur* 76-80; Perm to Offic *Win* from 79; rtd 80. *L'Amarrage, La Marette, St Sampson, Guernsey, Channel Islands* Guernsey (0481) 47320

STRETCH, George Peter. b 22. MBE. **d** 70 **p** 71. Malaysia 70-78; V Shireoaks *S'well* 79-85; Perm to Offic *B & W* from 86; rtd 87. *9 The Lerburne, Wedmore, Somerset BS28 4ED* Wedmore (0934) 713244

STRETTON, Reginald John. b 37. MRPharmS63 CBiol70 MIBiol70 Man Univ BSc62 Nottm Univ PhD65. E Midl Min Tr Course 88. **d** 91. NSM Loughb Gd Shep *Leic* from 91. *19 Paddock Close, Quorn, Loughborough, Leics LE12 8BJ* Quorn (0509) 412935

STRETTON, Robert John. b 45. **d** 69 **p** 70. C Hendon St Ignatius *Dur* 69-73; C Middlesb St Thos *York* 73-77;

OSB 77-78; V Brandon *Dur* 78-85; Lic to Offic 85-91; SSM from 85; Tr in Evang Ch in Wales from 91. *18 Woodlands Court, Barry, S Glam CF6 6DR* Barry (0446) 746235

STREVENS, Brian Lloyd. b 49. St Jo Coll Dur BA70. Ripon Hall Ox 70. **d** 73 **p** 74. C Old Trafford St Jo *Man* 73-76; C Bolton St Pet 76-78; Org Sec Southn Coun of Community Service from 78; Perm to Offic *Win* 82-86; NSM Bitterne Park from 86. *186 Hill Lane, Southampton SO1 5DB* Southampton (0703) 333301

STREVENS, Richard Ernest Noel. b 34. Nottm Univ BA60. Linc Th Coll 60. **d** 62 **p** 63. C St Botolph Aldgate w H Trin Minories *Lon* 62-66; C Ealing St Steph Castle Hill 66-68; Hon C St Botolph without Bishopgate 68-76; V Clent *Worc* 76-86; V Pirbright *Guildf* from 86. *The Vicarage, Pirbright, Woking, Surrey GU24 0JE* Brookwood (0483) 473332

STRIBLEY, William Charles Harold. b 29. SW Minl Tr Course. **d** 87 **p** 88. NSM Kenwyn St Geo Truro from 87. *54 Chirgwin Road, Truro, Cornwall TR1 1TT* Truro (0872) 72958

STRICKLAND, Derek. b 26. Bps' Coll Cheshunt 64. **d** 66 **p** 66. C Bray and Braywood *Ox* 66-67; C Hall Green Ascension *Birm* 67-70; V Hamstead St Bernard 70-76; Ind Chapl *St Alb* from 76. *55 Crofts Path, Hemel Hempstead, Herts HP3 8HD* Hemel Hempstead (0442) 254185

STRICKLAND, Mrs Elizabeth Joan Gabrielle. b 61. St Jo Coll Dur BA83. Westcott Ho Cam 87. **d** 90. Par Dn Cayton w Eastfield *York* from 90. *4 Hawson Close, Osgodby, Scarborough, N Yorkshire YO11 3QW* Scarborough (0723) 583282

STRICKLAND, Canon Ernest Armitage. b 24. Ch Coll Cam BA49 MA54. Wycliffe Hall Ox 49. **d** 51 **p** 52. V Southport St Phil *Liv* 64-76; R Broughton *Linc* 76-90; RD Yarborough 81-86; Hon Can Linc Cathl from 85; rtd 90; Perm to Offic *Linc* from 90. *143 Grimsby Road, Waltham, Grimsby, S Humberside DN37 0PU* Grimsby (0472) 821126

STRICKLAND, Canon Paul Lowndes. b 21. Linc Th Coll 46. **d** 49 **p** 50. V Debenham *St E* 61-75; V Lakenheath 75-83; rtd 83. *4 Albany Gardens East, Clacton-on-Sea, Essex CO15 6HW* Clacton-on-Sea (0255) 426303

STRIDE, Clifford Stephen. b 21. Ex & Truro NSM Scheme. **d** 81 **p** 82. NSM Chulmleigh *Ex* 81-83; NSM Hardham *Chich* from 87. *Ambleside, Sandy Lane, Watersfield, Pulborough, W Sussex RH20 1NF* Bury (0798) 831851

STRIDE, Desmond William Adair. b 15. Ch Coll Cam BA37 MA41. Ridley Hall Cam 38. **d** 39 **p** 40. Chapl Heathfield Sch Ascot 67-80; rtd 80; Perm to Offic *Lon* and *Chich* from 90. *5 Oakmede Way, Ringmer, Lewes, E Sussex BN8 5JL* Lewes (0273) 813561

STRIDE, Edgar George. b 23. Tyndale Hall Bris 47. **d** 51 **p** 52. V Becontree St Mary *Chelmsf* 61-70; R Spitalfields Ch Ch w All SS *Lon* 70-89; rtd 89; Perm to Offic *Pet & Linc* from 89. *23 Pembroke Road, Stamford, Lincs PE9 1BS* Stamford (0780) 56325

STRIDE, John David. b 46. Ex Univ BSc68. Oak Hill Th Coll DipHE88. **d** 88 **p** 89. C Ashtead *Guildf* from 88. *1 Oakfield Road, Ashtead, Surrey KT21 2RE* Ashtead (0372) 274578

STRIDE, John Michael. b 48. BA. Oak Hill Th Coll 77. **d** 80 **p** 81. C Edmonton All SS *Lon* 80-82; C Edmonton All SS w St Mich 82-83; C Wembley St Jo 83-85; P-in-c Hockering *Nor* 85-89; R Hockering, Honingham, E and N Tuddenham 89-91; V Tuckswood from 91. *The Vicarage, 22 Little John Road, Norwich NR4 6BH* Norwich (0603) 53739

STRIKE, Maurice Arthur. b 44. FRSA66 NDD66. Sarum & Wells Th Coll 85. **d** 87 **p** 88. C Chippenham St Andr w Tytherton Lucas *Bris* 87-91; R Corfe Castle, Church Knowle, Kimmeridge etc *Sarum* from 91. *The Rectory, Corfe Castle, Wareham, Dorset BH20 5EE* Corfe Castle (0929) 480257

STRINGER, Adrian Nigel. b 60. Univ of Wales (Cardiff) BD82 Lanc Univ PGCE83. Sarum & Wells Th Coll 86. **d** 88 **p** 89. C Barrow St Matt *Carl* from 88. *St Francis's House, Schneider Road, Barrow-in-Furness, Cumbria LA14 5ER* Barrow-in-Furness (0229) 823155

STRINGER, Harold John. b 36. Peterho Cam BA58. Ripon Hall Ox 62. **d** 64 **p** 65. C Hackney St Jo *Lon* 64-68; C Roehampton H Trin *S'wark* 68-71; P-in-c Southn St Mich w H Rood, St Lawr etc *Win* 71-73; TV Southn (City Cen) 73-82; Ind Chapl 77-82; V Notting Hill St Jo *Lon* 82-87; V Notting Hill St Pet 82-87; V Notting Hill St Jo and St Pet from 87. *25 Ladbroke Road, London W11 3PD* 071-727 3439

STRINGER, James Philip. b 05. Lich Th Coll 53. **d** 53 **p** 54. V Horton-in-Ribblesdale *Bradf* 66-72; rtd 72.

17 Castle Road, Whitby, N Yorkshire YO21 3NQ Whitby (0947) 604238

STRINGER, Canon John Roden. b 33. AKC61. **d** 62 **p** 63. C Auckland St Helen *Dur* 62-63; C Hebburn St Cuth 63-67; V Cassop cum Quarrington 67-88; RD Sedgefield 84-88; Hon Can Dur Cathl from 88; V Lumley from 88. *The Vicarage, Great Lumley, Chester le Street, Co Durham DH3 4ER* 091-388 2228

STRINGER, Leonard Gordon. b 14. Westcott Ho Cam 64. **d** 66 **p** 67. C Bath Abbey w St Jas *B & W* 66-80; rtd 80; Perm to Offic *B & W* from 82. *8 Hockley Court, Weston Park West, Bath BA1 4AR* Bath (0225) 318286

STRINGER, Ralph Stuart. b 47. Chich Th Coll 82. **d** 84 **p** 85. C Hadleigh w Layham and Shelley *St E* 84-87; P-in-c Needham Market w Badley 87-89; V from 89. *The Vicarage, Needham Market, Ipswich IP6 8TR* Needham Market (0449) 720316

STROMBERG, Charles Walsham. b 22. St Chad's Coll Dur BA48. Ely Th Coll 48. **d** 49 **p** 50. C-in-c Bishopwearmouth St Mary V w St Pet CD *Dur* 68-73; Chapl Harperbury Hosp Radlett 73-87; rtd 87. *Dulverton Hall, St Martin's Square, Scarborough YO11 2DB* Scarborough (0723) 373082

STRONG, Christopher Patteson. b 43. Ridley Hall Cam. **d** 83 **p** 84. C Dalton-in-Furness *Carl* 83-87; V Wootton *St Alb* from 87. *The Vicarage, Wootton, Bedford MK43 9HF* Bedford (0234) 768391

STRONG, Donald Frederick. b 18. Oak Hill Th Coll 46. **d** 50 **p** 51. R Bedf St Jo *St Alb* 61-75; R Bedf St Jo and St Leon 75-81; rtd 81; Perm to Offic *St Alb* from 81. *Flat 9, Roedean Court, 82B Kimbolton Road, Bedford MK40 2PS* Bedford (0234) 327986

STRONG, George Ian Mossman. b 27. Chich Th Coll 53. **d** 56 **p** 56. RAChD 65-74; V Narborough w Narford *Nor* 74-79; V Pentney w W Bilney 74-79; P-in-c Corsenside *Newc* 79-80; rtd 80. *9 Percy Street, Alnwick, Northd NE66 1AE* Alnwick (0665) 603082

STRONG, Canon George Noel. b 97. St Chad's Coll Dur BA21 DipTh22 MA24. **d** 22 **p** 23. Master St Jo Hosp Lich 64-81; rtd 81. *4 Fecknam Way, Lichfield, Staffs WS13 6BY* Lichfield (0543) 264976

STRONG, Jack. b 16. St Aid Birkenhead 52. **d** 54 **p** 55. V Burgh-by-Sands w Kirkbampton *Carl* 66-83; R Burgh-by-Sands and Kirkbampton w Kirkandrews etc 83; rtd 83; Perm to Offic *Glouc* from 84. *Aballava, 18 Wincel Road, Winchcombe, Cheltenham, Glos GL54 5YE* Cheltenham (0242) 603347

STRONG, Canon John David. b 34. Cuddesdon Coll 59. **d** 61 **p** 62. C Gosforth All SS *Newc* 61-65; Chapl Malvern Coll Worcs 65-71; R Welford w Weston on Avon *Glouc* 72-79; V Nailsworth from 79; RD Tetbury from 83; Hon Can Glouc Cathl from 91. *The Vicarage, Nailsworth, Stroud, Glos GL6 0PJ* Nailsworth (045383) 2181

STRONG, Matthew John. b 60. Lon Univ BA81 Cam Univ BA84 MA89. Ridley Hall Cam 82. **d** 85 **p** 86. C Houghton *Carl* 85-89; C Hirwaun *Llan* from 89. *152 Heol Keir Hardie, Penywaun, Aberdare, M Glam CF44 9AN* Aberdare (0685) 812446

STRONG, Neil. b 34. Bps' Coll Cheshunt 57. **d** 61 **p** 62. C Ludlow *Heref* 69-71; P-in-c Withern *Linc* 71-74; P-in-c N and S Reston w Castle Carlton 71-74; P-in-c Strubby 71-74; P-in-c Gayton le Marsh 71-74; P-in-c Authorpe w Tothill 71-74; P-in-c Swaby w S Thoresby 73-74; C Belleau w Aby and Claythorpe 73-74; R Stanningley St Thos *Ripon* 74-76; P-in-c Bishop Wilton *York* 76-78; P-in-c Full Sutton w Skirpenbeck 76-78; P-in-c Bishop Wilton w Full Sutton 78-80; V Holme-on-Spalding Moor 80-82; V Nunthorpe 82-85; rtd 85. *51 Reeth Road, Linthorpe, Middlesbrough, Cleveland TS5 5JU* Middlesbrough (0642) 821433

STRONG, Rowan Gordon William. b 53. Victoria Univ Wellington BA76. St Jo Coll (NZ) LTh80 Melbourne Coll of Div ThM88. **d** 77 **p** 78. New Zealand 77-83; Australia 83-89; NSM Edin Old St Paul *Edin* from 89. *4 New Street, Edinburgh EH8 8BH* 031-557 3493

STRONG, Preb Stephen Charles. b 16. Em Coll Cam BA38 MA43. Lon Coll of Div 38. **d** 40 **p** 41. V Heref St Pet w St Owen *Heref* 66-79; Preb Heref Cathl 78-85; V Heref St Pet w St Owen and St Jas 79-82; rtd 82; Perm to Offic *Heref* from 83. *27 Westcroft, Leominster, Herefordshire HR6 8HF* Leominster (0568) 5534

STRONG, Capt William (John) Leonard. b 44. CA Tr Coll 64 Chich Th Coll 87. **d** 89 **p** 90. CA from 66; C Mayfield *Chich* from 89. *2 Victoria Cottages, Love Lane, Mayfield, E Sussex TN20 6EN* Mayfield (0435) 873448

STROUD, Ven Ernest Charles Frederick. b 31. St Chad's Coll Dur BA59 DipTh60. **d** 60 **p** 61. C S Kirkby *Wakef* 60-63; C Whitby *York* 63-66; C-in-c Chelmsf All SS CD

Chelmsf 66-69; V Chelmsf All SS 69-75; V Leigh-on-Sea St Marg 75-83; Asst RD Southend 76-79; RD Hadleigh 79-83; Hon Can Chelmsf Cathl 82-83; Adn Colchester from 83. *Archdeacon's House, 63 Powers Hall End, Witham, Essex CM8 1NH* Witham (0376) 513130

STROUD, Robert Owen. b 29. AKC56. **d** 57 **p** 58. C Aylesbury *Ox* 57-60; C Bexhill St Pet *Chich* 60-64; C Gosforth All SS *Newc* 64-66; V High Elswick St Phil 66-72; V Tynemouth Cullercoats St Paul 72-77; R Orlestone w Ruckinge w Warehorne *Cant* 77-81; RD N Lympne 79-81; V Folkestone H Trin w Ch Ch 81-83; TR Folkestone H Trin and St Geo w Ch Ch 83-90; R Folkestone H Trin w Ch Ch from 90; RD Elham from 90. *Holy Trinity Vicarage, 21 Manor Road, Folkestone, Kent CT20 2SA* Folkestone (0303) 53831

STROYAN, John Ronald Angus. b 55. MTh. Qu Coll Birm 81 Bossey Ecum Inst Geneva 82. **d** 83 **p** 84. C Cov E *Cov* 83-87; V Smethwick St Matt w St Chad *Birm* from 87. *1 St Matthew's Road, Smethwick, Warley, W Midlands B66 3TN* 021-558 1653

STRUDWICK, Canon Donald Frank. b 12. Leeds Univ BA33. Coll of Resurr Mirfield 33. **d** 35 **p** 37. V E Dulwich St Clem *S'wark* 49-85; Hon Can S'wark Cathl 73-85; rtd 85; Perm to Offic *Roch* from 85. *8 Mount Avenue, Yalding, Maidstone, Kent ME18 6JG* Maidstone (0622) 814514

STRUDWICK, Canon Vincent Noel Harold. b 32. Nottm Univ BA59 DipEd. Kelham Th Coll 52. **d** 59 **p** 60. Tutor Kelham Th Coll 59-63; Sub-Warden 63-70; C Crawley *Chich* 70-73; Adult Educn Adv 73-77; R Fittleworth 73-77; Planning Officer for Educn Milton Keynes 77-80; Dir of Educn *Ox* 80-89; Hon Can Ch Ch from 82; Continuing Minl Educn Adv 85-89; Dir Dioc Inst for Th Educn from 89; Prin Ox Min Course from 89. *35 Windmill Street, Brill, Aylesbury, Bucks HP18 9TG* Brill (0844) 237748

STRUGNELL, Dr John Richard. b 30. Lon Univ BA52 Leeds Univ MA61 Queensland Univ PhD77. Wells Th Coll 54. **d** 56 **p** 57. C Leeds Halton St Wilfrid *Ripon* 56-59; C Moor Allerton 59-62; Australia from 62. *231 Grandview Road, Pullenvale, Queensland, Australia 4069* Brisbane (7) 374-1776

STRUTT, Susan. b 45. Glouc Sch of Min 87. **d** 90. NSM Eye, Croft w Yarpole and Lucton *Heref* from 90. *Home Farm, Berrington Hall, Leominster, Herefordshire HR6 0DW* Leominster (0568) 5714

STUART, Francis David. b 32. Barrister-at-Law Lon Univ BA54 AKC57. Ridley Hall Cam 62. **d** 64 **p** 65. C Addiscombe St Mildred *Cant* 64-67; Chapl RN 67-71; Lic to Offic *Liv* 76-80; TV Oldham *Man* 84-89; Chapl Oldham and Distr Gen Hosp 84-89; Oldham R Infirmary 86-89; Chapl Oldham R Hosp from 89. *Pine House, Barton Street, Oldham OL1 2NR* 061-626 6804 or 624 0420

STUART, Canon Herbert James. b 26. CB83. TCD BA48 MA55. **d** 49 **p** 50. Chapl RAF 55-73; Asst Chapl-in-Chief RAF 73-80; Chapl-in-Chief RAF 80-83; Can and Preb Linc Cathl *Linc* 81-83; R Cherbury *Ox* 83-87; rtd 87; Perm to Offic *Glouc* & *Ox* from 87. *1 Abbot's Walk, Lechlade, Glos GL7 3DB* Faringdon (0367) 53299

STUART-FOX, Ven Desmond. b 11. Selw Coll Cam BA33 MA37. Bps' Coll Cheshunt 33. **d** 34 **p** 35. C Leic St Pet *Leic* 34-37; C Lich St Mich *Lich* 37-40; Sacr Lich Cathl 37-40; CF (EC) 40-46; V W Bromwich St Andr *Lich* 46-49; Australia from 49. *5/24 Church Street, Goulburn, NSW, Australia 2580* Goulburn (48) 211339

STUART-LEE, Nicholas. b 54. MA. Wycliffe Hall Ox. **d** 83 **p** 84. C Costessey *Nor* 83-85; TV Dewsbury *Wakef* 85-90; R Rowlands Castle *Portsm* from 90. *The Rectory, Manor Lodge Road, Rowlands Castle, Hants PO9 6BA*

STUART-SMITH, David. b 36. St Pet Coll Ox BA61 MA65. Tyndale Hall Bris. **d** 63 **p** 64. C Tooting Graveney St Nic *S'wark* 63-67; C Richmond H Trin 67-70; Lic to Offic 70-74; NSM Canonbury St Steph *Lon* 70-74; Travelling Sec IVF 70-74; Bangladesh 74-79; V Clapham Park St Steph *S'wark* from 79; RD Streatham 83-87. *2 Thornton Road, London SW12 0JU* 081-671 8276

STUART-WHITE, William Robert. b 59. Ox Univ BA. Trin Coll Bris BA. **d** 86 **p** 87. C Upper Armley *Ripon* 86-91; P-in-c Austrey *Birm* from 91. *The Vicarage, Austrey, Atherstone, Warks CV9 3EB* Tamworth (0827) 830572

STUBBINGS, Frank Edward. b 20. Fitzw Coll Cam BA48 MA53. Worc Ord Coll 60. **d** 61 **p** 62. V Catcott *B & W* 64-74; V Burtle 64-74; Chapl St Cath Sch Bramley 74-83; P-in-c Barkestone w Plungar, Redmile and

Stathern *Leic* 83-87; rtd 87; Perm to Offic *B & W* from 88. *35 Main Road, Weston Zoyland, Bridgwater, Somerset TA7 0EB* Weston Zoyland (0278) 691767

STUBBS, Anthony Richard Peter (Brother Aelred). b 23. Ball Coll Ox BA49. Coll of Resurr Mirfield 51. **d** 54 **p** 54. Lic to Offic *Wakef* 54-57 and from 82; CR from 54; Lic to Offic *Llan* 57-59; S Africa 60-77; Lesotho 77-81. *House of the Resurrection, Mirfield, W Yorkshire WF14 0BN* Mirfield (0924) 494318

STUBBS, Ian Kirtley. b 47. Man Univ DipAE90. Kelham Th Coll. **d** 70 **p** 71. C Chandler's Ford *Win* 70-75; C Farnham Royal *Ox* 75-80; Ind Chapl 75-80; Ind Chapl *Man* 81-86; TV Oldham 81-86; TR Langley and Parkfield 86-88; Lic to Offic from 88; Dir Laity Development from 90. *91 Werneth Hall Road, Oldham OL8 4BS* 061-624 4144

STUBBS, John Pattinson. b 27. SS Coll Cam BA48 St Cath Soc Ox BA52 MA67. Wycliffe Hall Ox 50. **d** 53 **p** 54. V Doulting w E and W Cranmore and Downhead *B & W* 64-78; rtd 78. *Ferndale, Hurlingpot Farm, Doulting, Shepton Mallet, Somerset BA4 4PY*

STUBBS, Stanley Peter Handley. b 23. Lon Univ BD52 Lille Univ LesL82. Ely Th Coll 55. **d** 55 **p** 56. C Fletton *Ely* 55-58; Hon Min Can Pet Cathl *Pet* 56-58; C Hounslow Heath St Paul *Lon* 58-63; CF (TA) 59-78; V Northn St Alb *Pet* 63-76; R Brondesbury Ch Ch and St Laur *Lon* from 76. *The Rectory, Chevening Road, London NW6 6DU* 081-969 5961

STUBBS, Trevor Noel. b 48. AKC70. St Aug Coll Cant 73. **d** 74 **p** 75. C Heckmondwike *Wakef* 74-77; Australia 77-80; V Middleton St Cross *Ripon* 80-89; R Wool and E Stoke *Sarum* from 89. *The Vicarage, Wool, Wareham, Dorset BH20 6EB* Bindon Abbey (0929) 462215

STUBENBORD, Jess William. b 48. BA72. Trin Coll Bris 75. **d** 78 **p** 79. C Cromer *Nor* 78-82; C Gorleston St Mary 82-85; P-in-c Saxthorpe and Corpusty 85-89; P-in-c Blickling 86-89; R Saxthorpe w Corpusty, Blickling, Oulton etc from 89. *The Vicarage, Saxthorpe, Norwich NR11 7BJ* Saxthorpe (026387) 228

STUBLEY, Peter Derek. b 28. AKC57 Dur Univ MA79. **d** 58 **p** 59. C Stockton St Chad *Dur* 58-61; V W Hartlepool St Oswald 61-66; Ind Chapl 66-76; Ind Chapl *York* from 76; V Gt Totham *Chelmsf* 83; P-in-c Kingston upon Hull St Mary *York* 83-88. *223 Cottingham Road, Hull HU5 4AU* Hull (0482) 43182

STUCKEY, Frederick Walter. b 04. **d** 77 **p** 77. NSM Wareham *Sarum* 77-84; rtd 84. *16 Shirley Road, Wareham, Dorset BH20 4QE* Wareham (0929) 552766

STUDD, Christopher Sidney. b 25. S'wark Ord Course. **d** 68 **p** 69. C Shenfield *Chelmsf* 68-73; R Stifford 73-83; P-in-c Bowers Gifford w N Benfleet 83-86; R from 83. *The Rectory, Bowers Gifford, Basildon, Essex SS13 2DU* Basildon (0268) 552219

STUDD, John Eric. b 34. Clare Coll Cam BA58 MA62. Coll of Resurr Mirfield 58. **d** 60 **p** 61. C Westmr St Steph w St Jo *Lon* 60-65; Australia 65-69; Hon C Kensington St Mary Abbots w St Geo *Lon* 70-71; P-in-c Monks Risborough *Ox* 72-77; P-in-c Gt and Lt Kimble 72-77; C Aylesbury 78; Chapl to the Deaf 78-82; Chapl Hants, Is of Wight & Channel Is Assn for Deaf 82-91; Perm to Offic *Guildf* and *Portsm* from 82; Chapl to the Deaf *Win* from 91. *Albion Lodge, Halterworth Lane, Romsey, Hants SO51 9AE* Romsey (0794) 512575

STUDDERT, Michael John de Clare. b 39. Trin Coll Cam BA64 MA67. Cuddesdon Coll 64. **d** 66 **p** 67. C Langley All SS and Martyrs *Man* 66-69; C Fleet *Guildf* 69-73; Perm to Offic 73-77; Chapl Eagle Ho Sch Sandhurst 77-88. *Southlands, Churt Road, Hindhead, Surrey GU26 6PS* Hindhead (0428) 604620

STUDDERT, Canon Richard Charles Guy. b 03. Lon Coll of Div 26. **d** 28 **p** 30. I Tullow *C & O* 34-78; Prec Leighlin Cathl 62-78; rtd 78. *Station House, Tullow, Co Carlow, Irish Republic* Carlow (503) 51246

STUDDERT-KENNEDY, Andrew Geoffrey. b 59. Ch Ch Ox BA80 MA86. Ripon Coll Cuddesdon BA88. **d** 89 **p** 90. C Wimbledon *S'wark* from 89. *9 Thorton Road, London SW19 4NE* 081-944 0177

STUDDERT-KENNEDY, Canon Christopher John. b 22. BNC Ox BA49 MA53. Wells Th Coll 49. **d** 51 **p** 52. C Bermondsey St Mary w St Olave and St Jo *S'wark* 51-54; C Clapham H Trin 54-56; V Putney St Marg 56-66; R Godstone from 66; RD Godstone 76-88; Hon Can S'wark Cathl from 80. *The Rectory, Godstone, Surrey RH9 8BJ* Godstone (0883) 742354

STURCH, Richard Lyman. b 36. Ch Ch Ox BA58 MA61 DPhil70. Ely Th Coll. **d** 62 **p** 63. C Hove All SS *Chich* 62-65; C Burgess Hill St Jo 65-66; C Ox St Mich w St Martin and All SS *Ox* 67-68; Tutor Ripon Hall Ox 67-71; Nigeria 71-74; Lect Lon Bible Coll 75-80; Lic to

Offic *Lon* 75-80; TV Wolverton *Ox* 80-86; R Islip w Charlton on Otmoor, Oddington, Noke etc from 86. *The Rectory, 3 The Rise, Islip, Oxford OX5 2TG* Kidlington (08675) 2163

STURDY, John Vivian Mortland. b 33. Ch Ch Ox BA54 MA57 Trin Coll Cam BA58 MA62. Westcott Ho Cam 56. **d** 58 **p** 59. C Hitchin St Mary *St Alb* 58-62; C Ampthill w Millbrook and Steppingley 62-63; Tutor Wells Th Coll 63-65; Lic to Offic *Ely* from 65; Dean G&C Coll Cam from 65. *Gonville and Caius College, Cambridge CB2 1TA* Cambridge (0223) 332400

STURDY, Philip Hugh Francis. b 20. AKC47. **d** 47 **p** 48. Miss to Seamen 62-80; UAE 73-78; V Norton Cuckney S'well 80-84; rtd 85; Perm to Offic *Ches* from 85. *33 The Broadway, Nantwich, Cheshire CW5 6JH* Nantwich (0270) 629531

STURDY, William David Mark. b 28. Ch Coll Cam BA52 MA56. Qu Coll Birm. **d** 55 **p** 56. C Lutterworth w Cotesbach *Leic* 55-59; C Loughb Em 59-61; V Dishley and Thorpe Acre 61-72; R Kegworth 72-82; V Cringleford *Nor* 82-85; R Colney 82-85; R Cringleford w Colney and Bawburgh from 85; RD Humbleyard from 87. *The Vicarage, Cringleford, Norwich NR4 6VE* Norwich (0603) 54424

STURMAN, Robert George. b 50. Nottm Univ BTh79. Linc Th Coll 75. **d** 79 **p** 80. C Cainscross w Selsley *Glouc* 79-83; TV Bottesford w Ashby *Linc* 83-88; V Prescot *Liv* 88-91. *23 Chesterton Park, Cirencester, Glos GL7 1XU* Cirencester (0285) 640140

STURT, Rock Andre Daniel. b 56. Liv Univ BSc79 Lon Univ CertEd80. Oak Hill Th Coll DipTh88 BA88. **d** 88 **p** 89. Chapl St Bede's Sch Cam 88-90; Par Dn Cam St Martin *Ely* 88-90; C from 90. *18 Langham Road, Cambridge CB1 3SE* Cambridge (0223) 214624

STUTZ, Clifford Peter. b 25. **d** 83 **p** 84. NSM Cusop w Clifford, Hardwicke, Bredwardine etc *Heref* from 83. *Burnt House, Middlewood, Clifford, Hereford HR3 5SX* Clifford (04973) 472

STYLER, Geoffrey Marsh. b 15. CCC Ox BA37 MA40 Cam Univ MA44. Union Th Sem (NY) STM39 Cuddesdon Coll 40. **d** 41 **p** 42. Lect Th Cam Univ 53-82; rtd 82. *Middleton Cottage, Sidgwick Avenue, Cambridge CB3 9DA* Cambridge (0223) 358420

STYLER, Jamie Cuming. b 36. Sarum & Wells Th Coll 70. **d** 72 **p** 73. C Whipton *Ex* 72-75; C Paignton St Jo 76-78; V Topsham 78-88; V Plymouth St Simon from 88. *St Simon's Vicarage, 86 Edith Avenue, Plymouth PL4 8TL* Plymouth (0752) 660654

STYLES, Clive William John. b 48. W Midl Minl Tr Course 87. **d** 90 **p** 91. C Burslem *Lich* from 90. *3 Ullswater Avenue, Burslem, Stoke-on-Trent ST6 4JW* Stoke-on-Trent (0782) 827715

STYLES, John Ernest Fredric. b 13. FLCM54 Bris Univ BA34 Ch Ch Ox BA49 MA53. Ely Th Coll 36. **d** 36 **p** 37. Hd Master Edin Cathl Choir Sch 69-73; C Kingston upon Hull H Trin *York* 73-78; rtd 78. *The Dutch Barn, 31 Sands Lane, Barmston, Driffield, N Humberside YO25 8PG* Skipsea (026286) 794

STYLES, Lawrence Edgar. b 19. AM88. Pemb Coll Cam BA48 MA52. Ridley Hall Cam. **d** 50 **p** 51. C Bishop's Stortford St Mich *St Alb* 50-53; V Tyldesley w Shakerley *Man* 53-60; Australia from 60. *25 Carson Street, Kew, Victoria, Australia 3101* Melbourne (3) 861-9749

SUART, Geoffrey Hugh. b 49. Man Univ BSc70 Nottm Univ CertEd71. Oak Hill Th Coll DipHE83. **d** 83 **p** 84. C Ogley Hay *Lich* 83-86; TV Wenlock *Heref* 86-90; TR Kirby Muxloe *Leic* from 90. *The Rectory, 6 Station Road, Kirby Muxloe, Leicester LE9 9EJ* Leicester (0533) 386822

SUCH, Canon Howard Ingram James. b 52. Southn Univ BTh81. Sarum & Wells Th Coll 77. **d** 81 **p** 82. C Cheam S'wark 81-84; Prec Cant Cathl *Cant* 84-91; V Borden from 91; Hon Min Can Cant Cathl from 91. *The Vicarage, Borden, Sittingbourne, Kent ME9 8JS* Sittingbourne (0795) 472986

SUCH, Paul Nigel. b 52. FGA72 BTh84. Chich Th Coll 79. **d** 84 **p** 85. C Handsworth St Andr *Birm* 84-87; C Rugeley *Lich* 87-88; TV from 88. *The Vicarage, 4 Cardigan Avenue, Rugeley, Staffs WS15 1LG* Rugeley (0889) 576401

SUCH, Royston Jeffery. b 46. Solicitor Univ Coll Lon LLB67. Sarum & Wells Th Coll 83. **d** 83 **p** 84. NSM Ringwood *Win* 83-90; R Bishop's Sutton and Ropley and W Tisted from 90. *The Vicarage, Lyeway Lane, Ropley, Alresford, Hants SO24 0DW* Winchester (0962) 772205

SUDBURY, Peter John. b 41. Open Univ BA80. Sarum & Wells Th Coll 78. **d** 79 **p** 80. C Leckhampton SS Phil and Jas w Cheltenham St Jas *Glouc* 79-82; CF (R of O)

from 81; R Siddington w Preston *Glouc* 82-86; P-in-c Rendcomb from 86; Chapl Rendcomb Coll Cirencester from 86; Asst ChStJ from 90. *The Rectory, Rendcomb, Cirencester, Glos GL7 7EZ* North Cerney (028583) 319

SUDBURY, Archdeacon of. *Vacant*

SUDDARDS, John Martin. b 52. Barrister-at-Law 75 Trin Hall Cam BA74 MA77 Birm Univ DipTh89. Qu Coll Birm 86. **d** 89 **p** 90. C Halstead St Andr w H Trin and Greenstead Green *Chelmsf* from 89. *47 Tidings Hill, Halstead, Essex CO9 1BL* Halstead (0787) 475528

SUDWORTH, Frank. b 43. DipHE. Oak Hill Th Coll 76. **d** 78 **p** 79. C Deane *Man* 78-81; C Worksop St Jo *S'well* 82-85; V Wollaton Park 85-90; P-in-c Lenton Abbey 85-86; V 86-90; V Upper Armley *Ripon* from 90. *Christ Church Vicarage, Armley Ridge Road, Leeds LS12 3LE* Leeds (0532) 638788

SUFFERN, Richard William Sefton. b 57. Reading Univ BSc79. Trin Coll Bris DipHE90. **d** 90 **p** 91. C Radipole and Melcombe Regis *Sarum* from 90. *10 Lyndhurst Road, Weymouth, Dorset DT4 7QR* Weymouth (0305) 787368

SUFFOLK, Archdeacon of. *See* ROBINSON, Ven Neil

SUFFRIN, Canon Arthur Charles Emmanuel. b 09. Selw Coll Cam BA30 MA34. Qu Coll Birm 34. **d** 35 **p** 36. V Pirton *St Alb* 68-74; rtd 74. *32 St Michael's Road, Melksham, Wilts SN12 6HN* Melksham (0225) 708041

SUGDEN, Andrew Neville Burn. b 14. ERD54 TD60. St Pet Hall Ox BA37 MA41. Wycliffe Hall Ox 37. **d** 46 **p** 47. V High Harrogate St Pet *Ripon* 67-87; CF (ACF) 68-70; rtd 87. *Crosskeys, 11 Park Chase, Harrogate, N Yorkshire HG1 5AL* Harrogate (0423) 503/58

SUGDEN, Charles Edward. b 59. Magd Coll Cam MA81 PGCE82. Trin Coll Bris DipHE91. **d** 91. C Gidea Park *Chelmsf* from 91. *109 Carlton Road, Romford RM2 5AU* Romford (0708) 741084

SUGDEN, Christopher Michael Neville. b 48. St Pet Coll Ox BA70 MA74 Nottm Univ MPhil74 PhD88. St Jo Coll Nottm 72. **d** 74 **p** 75. C Leeds St Geo *Ripon* 74-77; India 77-83; Lic to Offic *Ox* from 83. *Oxford Centre for Missionary Studies, PO Box 70, Oxford OX2 6HB* Oxford (0865) 56071

SUGDEN, Mrs Kerstin. b 58. Man Univ BSc81 W Midl Coll of Educn PGCE82. Trin Coll Bris BA91. **d** 91. NSM Gidea Park *Chelmsf* from 91. *109 Carlton Road, Romford, Essex RM2 5AU* Romford (0708) 741084

SULLIVAN, Adrian Michael. b 55. Sarum & Wells Th Coll 85. **d** 87 **p** 88. C Louth *Linc* 87-90; P-in-c E and W Keal 90; P-in-c Marden Hill Gp from 90. *The Rectory, West Keal, Spilsby, Lincs PE23 4BJ* Spilsby (0790) 53534

SULLIVAN, Bernard George. b 24. St Jo Coll Dur BA50. **d** 51 **p** 52. C Dudley St Thos *Worc* 51-54; C Braunstone *Leic* 54-55; Chapl RAF 55-58; Chapl Acacam Ho Sch Gosforth 59-63; Chapl St Mary's Hosp Stannington from 62; V Stannington *Newc* from 63. *The Vicarage, Stannington, Morpeth, Northd NE61 6HL* Stannington (067089) 222

SULLIVAN, Julian Charles. b 49. Lon Univ BSc74 CertEd75. Wycliffe Hall Ox 80. **d** 83 **p** 84. C Southall Green St Jo *Lon* 83-87; C Wells St Cuth w Wookey Hole *B & W* 87-90; V Sheff St Barn and St Mary *Sheff* from 90. *St Mary's Vicarage, 42 Charlotte Road, Sheffield S1 4TL* Sheffield (0742) 724987

SULLIVAN, Canon Trevor Arnold. b 40. CITC 69. **d** 70 **p** 71. C Lurgan Ch Ch *D & D* 71-72; C Tralee *L & K* 72-75; Irish Sch of Ecum 75-77; Ind Chapl *D & G* 77-80; I Ematris *Clogh* 80-84; I Aughrim w Ballinasloe etc *L & K* from 84; Can Limerick and Killaloe Cathls from 89. *The Rectory, Aughrim, Ballinasloe, Co Galway, Irish Republic* Ballinasloe (905) 73735

SULLY, Martin John. b 44. AIAS. St Jo Coll Nottm 80. **d** 82 **p** 83. C Lindfield *Chich* 82-86; V Walberton w Binsted from 86. *St Mary's Vicarage, The Street, Walberton, Arundel, W Sussex BN18 0PQ* Yapton (0243) 551488

SUMMERGOOD, Gerard. b 20. Clare Coll Cam BA48 MA53. Cuddesdon Coll 48. **d** 50 **p** 51. C S w N Bersted *Chich* 68-75; V S Patcham 75-87; rtd 87. *1 Arnhem Road, Bognor Regis, W Sussex PO21 5LB* Bognor Regis (0243) 860847

SUMMERS, John Ewart. b 35. MIMechE66. ALCD69. **d** 69 **p** 70. C Fulham St Matt *Lon* 69-72; Chapl RN 72-81; V Devonport St Barn *Ex* from 81. *St Barnabas' Vicarage, 10 De La Hay Avenue, Plymouth PL3 4HU* Plymouth (0752) 666544

SUMMERS, Paul Anthony. b 53. Coll of Resurr Mirfield 77. **d** 80 **p** 81. C Manston *Ripon* 80-83; Prec 83-88; Min Can Ripon Cathl 83-88; Chapl Univ Coll of Ripon & York St Jo 84-88; V Whitkirk *Ripon* from 88. *Whitkirk*

Vicarage, 386 Selby Road, Leeds LS15 0AA Leeds (0532) 645790

SUMMERS, Raymond John. b 41. Univ of Wales TCert63 DPS88 Open Univ BA75. St Mich Coll Llan 77. **d** 77 **p** 78. NSM Mynyddislwyn *Mon* 77-81; NSM Abercarn 81-82; P-in-c 82-89; V from 89. *The Vicarage, Abercarn, Newport, Gwent NP1 5GU* Newbridge (0495) 243919

SUMMERS, Thomas Gresley. b 25. Worc Coll Ox BA53 MA57. Cuddesdon Coll 53. **d** 55 **p** 56. C S Beddington St Mich *S'wark* 55-59; C New Charlton H Trin 59-63; OGS from 61; V Chesterton St Luke *Ely* 63-81; V Brownswood Park *Lon* from 81. *St John's Vicarage, Gloucester Drive, London N4 2LW* 081-800 7875

SUMMERS, Ms Ursula Jeanne. b 35. Birm Univ BA56 Liv Univ CertEd57. Glouc Sch of Min. **dss** 85 **d** 87. Fownhope *Heref* 85-87; Hon C 87; Brockhampton w Fawley 85-87; Hon C 87; C Marden w Amberley and Wisteston from 88. *99 Walkers Green, Marden, Hereford HR1 3EA* Hereford (0432) 880497

SUMNER, Gillian Mansell. b 39. St Anne's Coll Ox BA61 MA65 MLitt76. Wycliffe Hall Ox 83. **dss** 86 **d** 87. Ox St Andr *Ox* 86-87; Hon C 87-91; Tutor Wycliffe Hall Ox 86-89; Vice-Prin Ox Min Course from 89; Prin Ox Adnry Chr Tr Scheme *Ox* from 89; NSM Kirtlington w Bletchingdon, Weston etc from 91. *9 Chalfont Road, Oxford OX2 6TL* Oxford (0865) 58023

SUMNER, John Gordon. b 46. CCC Cam BA68 MA72. Ridley Hall Cam 69. **d** 72 **p** 73. C Liskeard w St Keyne *Truro* 72-75; C Caversham *Ox* 75-81; V Swallowfield from 81; Asst Chapl Reading Univ from 81. *The Vicarage, Swallowfield, Reading RG7 1QY* Reading (0734) 883786

SUNDERLAND, Christopher Allen. b 52. BA75 St Pet Coll Ox MA80 DPhil80 DipTh86. Trin Coll Bris 84. **d** 86 **p** 87. C Stratton St Margaret w S Marston etc *Bris* 86-90; V Barton Hill St Luke w Ch Ch from 90. *St Luke's Vicarage, 60 Barton Hill Road, Bristol BS5 0AW* Bristol (0272) 555947

SUNDERLAND, Preb Geoffrey. b 21. St Edm Hall Ox BA43 MA47 DipTh47. St Steph Ho Ox 46. **d** 48 **p** 49. V Plymstock *Ex* 68-86; RD Plympton 76-81; Preb Ex Cathl from 82; rtd 86; Perm to Offic *B & W* from 86. *Higher Walnut Cottage, Culmstock, Cullompton, Devon EX15 3JU* Hemyock (0823) 680272

SURMAN, Malcolm Colin. b 48. Birm Univ CertEd72 Southn Univ BTh88. Sarum & Wells Th Coll 76. **d** 78 **p** 79. C Basingstoke *Win* 78-81; P-in-c Alton All SS 81-85; V from 85; Chapl Lord Mayor Treloar Hosp Alton from 84. *All Saints' Vicarage, Queen's Road, Alton, Hants GU34 1HU* Alton (0420) 83458

SURREY, Christopher Arthur. b 13. Selw Coll Cam BA35 MA39. Ely Th Coll 35. **d** 36 **p** 37. V Castleton All So *Man* 63-78; rtd 78; Perm to Offic *Blackb* from 78. *34 Black Bull Lane, Fulwood, Preston, Lancs PR2 3PX* Preston (0772) 71679

SURREY, Archdeacon of. *See* WENT, Ven John Stewart

SURTEES, Geoffrey. b 06. St Chad's Coll Dur BA33 DipTh34 MA36. **d** 34 **p** 35. Chapl Community St Laur Belper 57-75; V Bridge Hill *Derby* 75; rtd 75; Perm to Offic *Derby* from 75. *28 Penn Lane, Melbourne, Derby DE6 5NE* Melbourne (0332) 862381

SURTEES, Timothy John de Leybourne. b 31. G&C Coll Cam BA54 MA58. Westcott Ho Cam 54. **d** 56 **p** 57. C Guisborough *York* 56-59; C Grantham St Wulfram *Linc* 59-61; V Cayton w Eastfield *York* 61-72; R Cheam *S'wark* from 72. *Cheam Rectory, Sutton, Surrey SM3 8QD* 081-644 9110

SUSTINS, Nigel. b 46. Lon Univ BEd70. S'wark Ord Course 86. **d** 88 **p** 90. Hon C Mitcham St Mark *S'wark* from 89. *19 Frensham Court, Phipps Bridge Road, Mitcham, Surrey CR4 3PG* 081-685 9603

SUTCH, Christopher David. b 47. AKC69. St Aug Coll Cant 69. **d** 70 **p** 71. C Bris St Andr Hartcliffe *Bris* 70-75; C Swindon Dorcan 75-78; TV 78-79; P-in-c Alveston 79-83; V 83-89; RD Westbury and Severnside 86-89; TR Yate New Town from 89. *The Rectory, Canterbury Close, Yate, Bristol BS17 5TU* Chipping Sodbury (0454) 311483

SUTCH, Canon Christopher Lang. b 21. Or Coll Ox BA47 MA47. Cuddesdon Coll 47. **d** 49 **p** 50. V Hanham *Bris* 58-74; R Brinkworth w Dauntsey 74-86; RD Malmesbury 79-85; Hon Can Bris Cathl 82-86; rtd 86; Hon C E Bris from 86. *42 Henleaze Park Drive, Bristol BS9 4LL* Bristol (0272) 621952

SUTCLIFFE, Allen. b 99. St Aid Birkenhead 30. **d** 32 **p** 33. V Birkenhead St Anne *Ches* 44-74; rtd 75. *96 King John Avenue, Bournemouth BH11 9TG* Bournemouth (0202) 570376

SUTCLIFFE, Crispin Francis Henry. b 48. Keble Coll Ox BA69. Sarum & Wells Th Coll 73. **d** 74 **p** 75. C Truro St Paul *Truro* 74-77; S Africa 77-80; P-in-c Treslothan *Truro* 80-85; V from 85. *The Vicarage, 25 New Road, Troon, Camborne, Cornwall TR14 9ES* Camborne (0209) 714574

SUTCLIFFE, Canon David. b 29. Lon Univ BD57. ALCD56. **d** 57 **p** 58. C Penn *Lich* 57-61; V Ashton St Pet *Man* 61-65; V Eccleshill *Bradf* 65-71; Lic to Offic 71-74; V Manningham St Luke 74-79; V Bolton St Jas w St Chrys 79-85; V Calverley from 85; RD Calverley from 88; Hon Can Bradf Cathl from 89. *The Vicarage, Calverley, Pudsey, W Yorkshire LS28 5NF* Pudsey (0532) 577968

SUTCLIFFE, Geoffrey Alan. b 32. St Jo Coll Dur BA54. Cranmer Hall Dur DipTh57. **d** 58 **p** 59. C Cleveleys *Blackb* 58-61; C Colne St Bart 61-63; V Rochdale Gd Shep *Man* 63-70; V Tottington from 70. *St Anne's Vicarage, Chapel Street, Tottington, Bury, Lancs BL8 4AP* Tottington (0204) 883713

SUTCLIFFE, Howard Guest. b 44. Fitzw Coll Cam BA66 MA70. Birm Univ MA75 Man Univ CertRS88. Westcott Ho Cam 73. **d** 74 **p** 75. C Chorlton-cum-Hardy St Clem *Man* 74-77; Chapl Chetham's Sch of Music Man 77-80; V Oldham St Paul *Man* from 80. *St Paul's Vicarage, 55 Belgrave Road, Oldham OL8 1LU* 061-624 1068

SUTCLIFFE, John Leslie. b 35. Liv Univ BA56. Sarum Th Coll 58. **d** 60 **p** 61. C Lytham St Cuth *Blackb* 60-62; C Altham w Clayton le Moors 62-65; C-in-c Penwortham St Leon CD 65-71; Ind Chapl *Liv* 71-74; V Orford St Andr 74-79; V Burnley St Cuth *Blackb* 79-88; Bp's Adv on UPA *Ripon* from 88; Hon C Leeds Gipton Epiphany from 89. *227 Beech Lane, Leeds LS9 6SW* Leeds (0532) 482153

SUTCLIFFE, Maurice. b 13. St Aug Coll Cant 39. **d** 42 **p** 43. V Barnacre *Blackb* 58-89; rtd 89. *Dean House, Bypass Road, Catterall, Preston PR3 0HL* Garstang (0995) 603643

SUTCLIFFE, Peter John. b 58. BA. Linc Th Coll. **d** 82 **p** 83. C Skipton Ch Ch *Bradf* 82-85; C Tettenhall Regis *Lich* 85-86; TV 86-89; Relig Producer BBC Radio Cov & Warks from 89; TV Warw *Cov* from 89. *1 Cornwall Close, Warwick CV34 5HX* Warwick (0926) 492997

SUTCLIFFE, Canon Thomas Henry. b 07. Qu Coll Cam BA30 MA34. Westcott Ho Cam 30. **d** 31 **p** 32. Org Sec C of E Coun for Deaf 52-74; Hon Can Cant Cathl *Cant* 66-85; rtd 75; Perm to Offic *Ox*, *Cant* & *S'wark* from 85, B & W from 88. *12 Parsonage Court, Bishops Hull, Taunton, Somerset TA1 5HR* Taunton (0823) 332715

SUTCLIFFE, William Norman. b 09. Lich Th Coll 56. **d** 57 **p** 58. V Northmoor Green *B & W* 60-69; V Burrow Bridge 60-69; Perm to Offic *Sarum* 69-72; Lic to Offic 72-89; rtd 74. *The Bungalow, Hollis Hill, Broadwindsor, Beaminster, Dorset DT8 3QS* Broadwindsor (0308) 68476

SUTER, Richard Alan. b 48. Rhodes Univ Grahamstown BA72 St Jo Coll Dur BA74. Cranmer Hall Dur 72. **d** 75 **p** 76. C Darlington H Trin *Dur* 75-77; C Wrexham *St As* 77-82; R Llansantffraid Glan Conway and Eglwysfach 82-87; V Broughton from 87; RD Wrexham from 90. *The Vicarage, Bryn y Gaer Road, Pentre Broughton, Wrexham, Clwyd LL11 6AT* Wrexham (0978) 756210

SUTHERLAND, Alan. b 55. Sarum & Wells Th Coll. **d** 80 **p** 81. C Hessle *York* 80-83; USA from 83. *Box 321, Russellville, Arkansas 72801, USA*

SUTHERLAND, Alistair Campbell. b 31. Lon Univ BSc50 Ex Univ BA77. Wycliffe Hall Ox 77. **d** 78 **p** 79. C Nottm St Jude *S'well* 78-81; R Barton in Fabis from 81; P-in-c Thrumpton 81; V from 81; RD Bingham W from 87. *The Rectory, Church Lane, Barton, Nottingham NG11 0AG* Nottingham (0602) 830252

SUTHERLAND, Donald Frederick Alexander. b 19. S'wark Ord Course. **d** 67 **p** 68. C W Ham *Chelmsf* 67-73; V Leigh-on-Sea St Aid from 73. *St Aidan's Vicarage, Moor Park Gardens, Leigh-on-Sea, Essex SS9 4PY* Southend-on-Sea (0702) 525338

SUTHERLAND, Eric. b 54. AKC76. Sarum & Wells Th Coll 76. **d** 77 **p** 78. C Roehampton H Trin *S'wark* 77-80; C Tattenham Corner and Burgh Heath *Guildf* 80-84; V Guildf All SS from 84; Dep Chapl HM Pris Wandsworth from 91. *HM Prison Wandsworth, PO Box 757, Heathfield Road, London SW18 3HS* 081-874 7292

SUTHERLAND, Mark Robert. b 55. Univ of NZ LLB77 Lon Univ DAC89. Ripon Coll Cuddesdon 82. **d** 85 **p** 86. C Pinner *Lon* 85-88; C Sudbury St Andr from 88; Perm to Offic *S'wark* from 91; Chapl Maudsley Hosp Lon from 91. *30 Priory Close, Wembley, Middx HA0 2SG* 081-904 2315

SUTHERN, William. b 08. St Chad's Coll Dur BA29 DipTh31 MA32. **d** 31 **p** 32. V Hampsthwaite *Ripon* 52-73; rtd 73. *66 Pennywort Grove, Killinghall, Harrogate, N Yorkshire HG3 2XJ* Harrogate (0423) 526588

SUTTERS, Herbert John. b 15. St Jo Coll Ox BA37 MA40. St Steph Ho Ox 37. **d** 39 **p** 40. V Highbridge *B & W* 61-73; V St Margarets on Thames *Lon* 73-80; rtd 80; Perm to Offic *Ox* from 81. *22 Alexandra Road, Oxford OX2 0DB* Oxford (0865) 723549

SUTTLE, Neville Frank. b 38. Reading Univ BSc61 Aber Univ PhD64. **d** 76 **p** 77. NSM Penicuik *Edin* from 76. *44 St James's Gardens, Penicuik, Midlothian EH26 9DU* Penicuik (0968) 73819

SUTTON, Brian Ralph. b 33. Trin Coll Bris DPS81 Sarum & Wells Th Coll. **d** 83 **p** 84. NSM Timsbury *B & W* 83-84; NSM Timsbury and Priston 85-88; V Thorncombe w Winsham and Cricket St Thomas from 89. *The Vicarage, Chard Street, Thorncombe, Chard, Somerset TA20 4NE* Winsham (046030) 479

SUTTON, Charles Edwin. b 53. Bris Univ BEd77 Ox Univ. Ripon Coll Cuddesdon 77. **d** 80 **p** 81. C Stanwix *Carl* 80-84; Warden Marrick Priory *Ripon* 84-88. *7 Beech Close, Baldersby, Thirsk, N Yorkshire YO7 4QB*

SUTTON, Christopher Hope. b 06. St Edm Hall Ox BA31 DipTh32 MA43. Wycliffe Hall Ox 27 and 31. **d** 32 **p** 33. R Aldbury *St Alb* 63-78; rtd 78; Perm to Offic *Chich* from 78. *1 The Twitten, Southwick, Brighton BN42 4DB* Brighton (0273) 593574

SUTTON, Colin Phillip. b 51. Birm Univ BA73. Chich Th Coll 73. **d** 75 **p** 76. C Penarth All SS *Llan* 75-77; C Roath St Marg 77-80; C Caerau w Ely 80-84; V Rhydyfelin from 84. *St Luke's House, 6 Fairfield Lane, Hawthorn, Pontypridd, M Glam CF37 5LN* Pontypridd (0443) 852298

SUTTON, David Robert. b 49. Birm Univ BA69 Ox Univ CertEd72. St Steph Ho Ox 70. **d** 72 **p** 73. C Clitheroe St Mary *Blackb* 72-75; C Fleetwood 75-78; V Calderbrook *Man* 78-88; V Winton from 88. *The Vicarage, Albany Road, Eccles, Manchester M30 8DE* 061-788 8991

SUTTON, Canon Henry. b 16. Tyndale Hall Bris 38. **d** 41 **p** 42. Gen Sec SAMS 59-75; Public Preacher *Chelmsf* 75-78; V Portman Square St Paul *Lon* 78-81; rtd 81. *3 Starling Close, Buckhurst Hill, Essex IG9 5TN* 081-504 0663

SUTTON, James William. b 41. Oak Hill Th Coll 81. **d** 84 **p** 85. NSM Chorleywood St Andr *St Alb* from 84. *Belmount, 7 Hillside Road, Chorleywood, Rickmansworth, Herts WD3 5AP* Chorleywood (0923) 282806

SUTTON, Jeremy John Ernest. b 60. Ridley Hall Cam 83. **d** 86 **p** 87. C Seacombe *Ches* 86-88; C Northwich St Luke and H Trin 88-90; TV Birkenhead Priory from 90. *St Anne's Vicarage, 29 Park Road West, Birkenhead, Merseyside L43 1UR* 051-652 1309

SUTTON, John. b 47. St Jo Coll Dur BA70. Ridley Hall Cam 70. **d** 72 **p** 73. C Denton St Lawr *Man* 72-77; R 77-82; V High Lane *Ches* 82-88; V Sale St Anne from 88. *St Anne's Vicarage, Church Road, Sale, Cheshire M33 3HB* 061-973 4145

SUTTON, John Stephen. b 33. Em Coll Cam BA57 MA61. Wycliffe Hall Ox 57. **d** 59 **p** 60. C Dagenham *Chelmsf* 59-62; C Bishopwearmouth St Gabr *Dur* 62-63; V Over Kellet *Blackb* 63-67; V Darwen St Barn 67-74; V Walthamstow St Jo *Chelmsf* 74-84; V Stebbing w Lindsell from 84. *The Vicarage, High Street, Stebbing, Dunmow, Essex CM6 3SF* Stebbing (037186) 468

SUTTON, John Wesley. b 48. **d** 76 **p** 77. Chile 76-77; Peru 77-85; SAMS from 85; Perm to Offic *Ox* & *St Alb* from 85. *88 Horn Lane, Woodford Green, Essex IG8 9AH* 081-505 7888

✠**SUTTON, Rt Rev Keith Norman.** b 34. Jes Coll Cam BA58 MA62. Ridley Hall Cam. **d** 59 **p** 60. **c** 78. C Plymouth St Andr *Ex* 59-61; Chapl St Jo Coll Cam 62-67; Uganda 68-72; Prin Ridley Hall Cam 73-78; Suff Bp Kingston-upon-Thames *S'wark* 78-84; Bp Lich from 84. *Bishop's House, 22 The Close, Lichfield, Staffs WS13 7LG* Lichfield (0543) 262251

SUTTON, Canon Malcolm David. b 26. Selw Coll Cam BA47 MA52. Ridley Hall Cam 48. **d** 50 **p** 51. C Owlerton *Sheff* 50-52; C Kew *S'wark* 52-54; V Hornchurch St Andr *Chelmsf* 54-56; V Roxeth Ch Ch *Lon* 56-63; R Beccles St Mich *St E* 63-82; TR from 82; RD Beccles 65-73; Hon Can St E Cathl from 72. *The Rectory, 5 Grange Road, Beccles, Suffolk NR34 9NR* Beccles (0502) 712213

SUTTON, Peter. b 20. Ely Th Coll 60. **d** 62 **p** 63. R Hamerton *Ely* 64-77; V Winwick 64-77; V Upton and Copmanford 70-77; V Bradworthy *Ex* 77-90; rtd 90. *The*

Vicarage, Bradworthy, Holsworthy, Devon EX22 7RJ Bradworthy (040924) 200

SUTTON, Peter Allerton. b 59. Ex Univ BA85. Linc Th Coll 85. **d** 87 **p** 88. C Fareham H Trin *Portsm* 87-90; C Alverstoke from 90; Chapl HM Pris Haslar from 90. *1 Newlands Avenue, Gosport, Hants PO12 3QX* Gosport (0705) 522710

SUTTON, Richard Alan. b 39. Reading Univ BSc61. Wycliffe Hall Ox 70. **d** 72 **p** 73. C Galleywood Common *Chelmsf* 72-76; Pakistan 76-79; C Walsall St Martin *Lich* 79-83; V Barton Hill St Luke w Ch Ch *Bris* 83-89; V Sidcup Ch Ch *Roch* from 89. *Christ Church Vicarage, 16 Christ Church Road, Sidcup, Kent DA15 7HE* 081-308 0835

SUTTON, Richard John. b 45. Lon Inst of Educn CertEd68. St Alb Minl Tr Scheme 77 Linc Th Coll 81. **d** 82 **p** 83. C Royston *St Alb* 82-87; C Hatf from 87. *St Michael's House, 31 Homestead Road, Hatfield, Herts AL10 0QJ* Hatfield (0707) 262897

SUTTON, Ronald. b 27. FSCA. NW Ord Course 76. **d** 79 **p** 80. C Helsby and Dunham-on-the-Hill *Ches* 79-81; R Church Lawton from 81; RD Congleton from 91. *The Rectory, Liverpool Road West, Church Lawton, Stoke-on-Trent ST7 3DE* Alsager (0270) 882103

SWABEY, Brian Frank. b 44. BA. Oak Hill Th Coll 79. **d** 82 **p** 83. C Clapham St Jas *S'wark* 82-84; C Wallington H Trin 84-88; Chapl Mt Gould Hosp Plymouth 88-89; V Plymouth St Jude *Ex* from 88. *St Jude's Vicarage, Knighton Road, Plymouth PL4 9BU* Plymouth (0752) 661232

SWABEY, Henry Sandys. b 16. Univ Coll Dur BA37 MA40 BD50. Chich Th Coll 37. **d** 39 **p** 40. V Deeping Fen *Linc* 58-78; R Rippingale 78-82; R Dunsby w Dowsby 78-82; rtd 82; Perm to Offic *Pet* from 82. *29 High Street, Maxey, Peterborough PE6 9EB* Market Deeping (0778) 342800

SWABY, Canon John Edwin. b 11. St Jo Coll Dur BA32 DipTh34 MA35 Leic Univ PhD83. **d** 34 **p** 35. Can and Preb Linc Cathl Linc 69-77; V Barholm w Stowe 71-76; R Uffington 71-76; V Tallington 71-76; rtd 76; Perm to Offic *Pet* from 76. *6 Willoughby Drive, Empingham, Oakham, Leics LE15 8PZ* Empingham (078086) 719

SWABY, Keith Graham. b 48. Southn Univ BA75. St Steph Ho Ox 75. **d** 77 **p** 78. C Lt Stanmore St Lawr *Lon* 77-80; C Hove All SS *Chich* 80-83; C Haywards Heath St Wilfrid 83; TV from 83. *87 New England Road, Haywards Heath, W Sussex RH16 3LE* Haywards Heath (0444) 454417

SWAIN, David Noel. b 36. Wellington Univ (NZ) BA63 MA66. Coll of Resurr Mirfield 65. **d** 67 **p** 68. C Clapham H Trin *S'wark* 67-70; New Zealand 70-75; P-in-c Hermitage *Ox* 75-76; P-in-c Hampstead Norris 75-76; V Hermitage w Hampstead Norreys 76-80; TR Hermitage and Hampstead Norreys, Cold Ash etc 80-82; R Bingham *S'well* from 82. *The Rectory, Bingham, Nottingham NG13 8DR* Bingham (0949) 837335

SWAIN, John Edgar. b 44. **d** 69 **p** 70. C E Dereham w Hoe *Nor* 69-73; V Haugh *Linc* 73-74; R S Ormsby w Ketsby, Calceby and Driby 73-74; R Harrington w Brinkhill 73-74; R Oxcombe 73-74; R Ruckland w Farforth and Maidenwell 73-74; R Somersby w Bag Enderby 73-74; R Tetford and Salmonby 73-74; R Belchford 73-74; V W Ashby 73-74; C Attleborough *Nor* 74-78; Canada 78-90; P-in-c Kirton w Falkenham *St E* from 90; Chapl Suffolk Constabulary from 90. *The Rectory, Kirton, Ipswich IP10 0PT* Kirton (03948) 226

SWAIN, Canon John Roger. b 30. Fitzw Ho Cam BA55 MA59. Bps' Coll Cheshunt 55. **d** 57 **p** 58. C Headingley *Ripon* 57-60; C Moor Allerton 60-65; V Wyther Ven Bede 65-75; V Horsforth 75-86; P-in-c Roundhay St Edm 86-88; V from 88; RD Allerton from 89; Hon Can Ripon Cathl from 89. *St Edmund's Vicarage, 5A North Park Avenue, Leeds LS8 1DN* Leeds (0532) 662550

SWAIN, Peter John. b 44. NCA63. Sarum & Wells Th Coll 86. **d** 88 **p** 89. C Beaminster Area *Sarum* from 88. *25A Clay Lane, Beaminster, Dorset DT8 3BX* Beaminster (0308) 863156

SWAIN, Raymond Thomas. b 60. Oak Hill Th Coll BA89. **d** 89 **p** 90. C New Clee *Linc* from 89. *73 Carr Lane, Cleethorpes, S Humberside DN35 7SA* Grimsby (0472) 356416

SWAIN, Ronald Charles Herbert. b 08. Dur Univ LTh32 BA42 MA50. St Aug Coll Cant 29. **d** 32 **p** 33. V Shipley *Chich* 70-74; rtd 74; Perm to Offic *St E* from 74. *81 Westley Road, Bury St Edmunds, Suffolk IP33 3RU* Bury St Edmunds (0284) 761655

SWAIN, Sharon Juanita. b 46. Sussex Univ BA75 CertEd76. Glouc Sch of Min 84 Qu Coll Birm.

dss 84 **d** 87. Upton St Leonards *Glouc* 84-87; C 87-88; Children's Officer *Worc* from 88. *35 Lobelia Close, Worcester WR5 2RR* Worcester (0905) 359666

SWAIN, William Allan. b 38. Kelham Th Coll 63. **d** 68 **p** 69. C Welwyn Garden City *St Alb* 68-72; C Romsey *Win* 72-74; C Weeke 74-78; V Bournemouth H Epiphany 78-91; P-in-c Moordown from 91. *St John's Vicarage, 2 Vicarage Road, Moordown, Bournemouth, Dorset BH9 2SA* Bournemouth (0202) 546400

SWAINE, John Arthur. b 45. St Steph Ho Ox 68. **d** 71 **p** 72. C Kilburn St Aug *Lon* 71-74; C Lavender Hill Ascension *S'wark* 74-77; C Deptford St Paul 77-78; Hon C 78-80; Warden St Mark's Youth & Community Cen Deptford 78-80; V Leic St Chad *Leic* 80-86; V Leytonstone H Trin Harrow Green *Chelmsf* from 86. *Holy Trinity Clergy House, 4 Holloway Road, Leytonstone, London E11 4LD* 081-539 7760

SWAINSON, Norman. b 38. Salford Univ MSc75. St Jo Coll Nottm 77. **d** 79 **p** 80. C Levenshulme St Pet *Man* 79-84; R Jarrow Grange *Dur* from 84. *Christ Church Rectory, Clayton Street, Jarrow, Tyne & Wear NE32 3JR* 091-489 4682

SWALES, David James. b 58. Warw Univ BA. Cranmer Hall Dur. **d** 84 **p** 85. C Eccleshill *Bradf* 84-88; C Prenton *Ches* from 88. *83 Bramwell Avenue, Birkenhead, Merseyside L43 0RQ* 051-608 4692

SWALES, Peter. b 52. ACIB78. Ridley Hall Cam 85. **d** 87 **p** 88. C Allestree *Derby* 87-91; P-in-c Horsley from 91. *The Vicarage, Horsley, Derby DE2 5BR* Derby (0332) 880284

SWALES, Shaun Redmayne Staveley. b 60. Keble Coll Ox BA82 MA87. Coll of Resurr Mirfield 85. **d** 87 **p** 88. C Preston St Matt *Blackb* 87-89; C Penistone and Thurlstone *Wakef* from 89. *38 Park Avenue, Penistone, Sheffield S30 6DN* Barnsley (0226) 763768

SWALLOW, Mrs Alice Gillian. b 51. Birm Univ BA72 CertEd73. NE Ord Course 82. dss 84 **d** 87. Morpeth *Newc* 84-86; Uttoxeter w Bramshall *Lich* 86-87; Par Dn 87-88; Par Dn Rocester 88; Chapl to the Deaf *Man* 88-90; Par Dn Goodshaw and Crawshawbooth from 88. *St John's Vicarage, 508 Burnley Road, Rossendale, Lancs BB4 8LZ* Rossendale (0706) 212340

SWALLOW, Arnold Birkett. b 04. SS Coll Cam BA27 MA30. Westcott Ho Cam 37. **d** 38 **p** 39. R Fulbourn *Ely* 57-76; rtd 76. *40 Pierce Lane, Fulbourn, Cambs* Cambridge (0223) 880358

SWALLOW, John Allen George. b 28. St Jo Coll Dur BA53 DipTh54. **d** 54 **p** 55. C Billericay St Mary *Chelmsf* 54-57; C Bishop's Stortford St Mich *St Alb* 57-59; V Roxwell *Chelmsf* 59-64; V S Weald 64-81; R W w E Mersea from 81. *The Rectory, 69 Kingsland Road, West Mersea, Colchester CO5 8QZ* West Mersea (0206) 382303

SWALLOW, John Brian. b 36. **d** 84 **p** 85. C Cleveleys *Blackb* 84-87; V Blackpool St Mich from 87. *St Michael's Vicarage, Calvert Place, Blackpool FY3 7RU* Blackpool (0253) 397755

SWALLOW, Robert Andrew. b 52. Leeds Univ BA73 Sheff Univ PGCE74 Keele Univ MA76. Linc Th Coll 76. **d** 78 **p** 79. C Gt Wyrley *Lich* 78-81; C Blakenall Heath 81-83; TV 83-90; TV Fareham H Trin *Portsm* from 90. *21 Miller Drive, Fareham, Hants PO16 7LZ* Fareham (0329) 281518

SWAN, Owen. b 28. ACP71. Edin Th Coll 56. **d** 59 **p** 60. C Lewisham St Jo Southend *S'wark* 59-64; CF (TA) from 60; V Richmond St Luke *S'wark* 64-82; C-in-c Darlington St Hilda and St Columba CD *Dur* 82-84; R Feltwell *Ely* 84-87; R Holywell w Needingworth from 87. *The Rectory, Holywell, St Ives, Huntingdon, Cambs PE17 3TQ* St Ives (0480) 494287

SWAN, Philip Douglas. b 56. Wye Coll Lon BSc78 Qu Coll Cam MA81 CertEd81 Nottm Univ DipTh87. St Jo Coll Nottm 86. **d** 88 **p** 89. C Birm St Martin w Bordesley St Andr *Birm* from 88. *90 Durley Dean Road, Birmingham B29 6RX* 021-471 3027

SWAN, Preb Ronald Frederick. b 35. St Cath Coll Cam BA59 MA. Coll of Resurr Mirfield. **d** 61 **p** 62. C Staveley *Derby* 61-66; Chapl Lon Univ *Lon* 66-72; C St Martin-in-the-Fields 72-77; V Ealing St Barn 77-88; V Ealing St Steph Castle Hill 81-88; AD Ealing E 84-87; V Harrow St Mary from 88; AD Harrow from 89; Preb St Paul's Cathl from 91. *St Mary's Vicarage, Church Hill, Harrow, Middx HA1 3HL* 081-422 2652

SWAN, Thomas Hugh Winfield. b 26. New Coll Ox MA62. Ridley Hall Cam 63. **d** 65 **p** 66. C Yaxley *Ely* 65-68; P-in-c Sawtry 69; R 69-79; P-in-c Fordham St Mary 79-82; V 82-87; P-in-c Hilgay 79-82; R 82-87; P-in-c Southery 79-82; R 82-87. *6 Brookside Grove, Littleport, Ely, Cambs CB6 1JN* Ely (0353) 860080

SWANBOROUGH, Alan William. b 38. Southn Univ BEd75. Sarum & Wells Th Coll 77. **d** 80 **p** 81. NSM Ventnor H Trin *Portsm* 80-85; NSM Ventnor St Cath 80-85; Chapl Upper Chine Sch Shanklin from 85; NSM Shanklin St Blasius *Portsm* from 91. *The Dell, 10 Church Road, Shanklin, Isle of Wight PO37 6NU* Isle of Wight (0983) 864034

SWANBOROUGH, Robert Charles. b 28. Sarum & Wells Th Coll 75. **d** 77 **p** 78. C Woodley *Ox* 77-78; C Bray and Braywood 79-80; V Gt Coxwell w Buscot, Coleshill & Eaton Hastings from 80. *The Vicarage, Great Coxwell, Faringdon, Oxon SN7 7NG* Faringdon (0367) 240665

SWANN, Antony Keith. b 34. Lon Univ DipTh60. St Aid Birkenhead 58. **d** 61 **p** 62. C Bilston St Leon *Lich* 61-66; Sierra Leone 66-70; V W Bromwich St Phil *Lich* 70-75; Nigeria 76-78; R Church Lench w Rous Lench and Abbots Morton *Worc* 78-88; Chapl HM Pris Coldingley 88-91; Chapl HM Pris Leyhill from 91. *HM Prison Leyhill, Wotton-under-Edge, Glos GL12 8HL* Falfield (0454) 260681

SWANN, Canon Edgar John. b 42. TCD BA66 MA70 BD77. CITC 68. **d** 68 **p** 69. C Crumlin *Conn* 68-70; C Howth *D & G* 70-73; I Greystones from 73; Can Ch Ch Cathl Dub from 90. *The Rectory, Greystones, Co Wicklow, Irish Republic* Dublin (1) 287-4077

SWANN, Frederick David. b 38. **d** 69 **p** 70. C Lurgan Ch Ch *D & D* 69-77; I Ardmore w Craigavon 77-79; I Comber 79-85; I Drumglass w Moygashel *Arm* from 85. *The Rectory, 24 Circular Road, Dungannon, Co Tyrone* Dungannon (08687) 22614

SWANN, Paul David James. b 59. Ch Ch Ox BA81 MA88. St Jo Coll Nottm DTS89 DPS90. **d** 90 **p** 91. C Old Hill H Trin *Worc* from 90. *15 Highland Road, Cradley Heath, Warley, W Midlands B64 5NB* Dudley (0384) 67103

SWANN, Robert Edgar. b 50. Salford Univ BSc72 Leeds Univ DipTh79. Coll of Resurr Mirfield 77. **d** 80 **p** 81. C Southport H Trin *Liv* 80-84; R Rufford *Blackb* from 84. *St Mary's Vicarage, 17 Church Road, Rufford, Lancs L40 1TA* Rufford (0704) 821261

SWANNELL, George Alfred Roderick. b 20. St Edm Hall Ox BA44 MA51. Ridley Hall Cam 47. **d** 49 **p** 50. V Hildenborough *Roch* 68-80; Lic to Offic from 80; Chapl Kent and Sussex Hosp Tunbridge Wells 80-86; rtd 85; Chapl Sevenoaks Hosp from 86. *68 Mount Ephraim, Tunbridge Wells, Kent TN4 8BG* Tunbridge Wells (0892) 29674

SWANSEA AND BRECON, Bishop of. See BRIDGES, Rt Rev Dewi Morris

SWARBRIGG, David Cecil. b 42. TCD BA64 MA67. **d** 65 **p** 66. C Lisburn Ch Ch *Conn* 65-67; C Thames Ditton *Guildf* 72-76; Chapl Hampton Sch Middx from 76. *The Chaplain's Office, Hampton School, Hampton, Middx TW12 3HD* 081-979 5526

SWART-RUSSELL, Dr Phoebe. b 58. Cape Town Univ BA79 MA82 DPhil88. Ox NSM Course 89. **d** 90. C Riverside *Ox* from 90. *3 Leigh Park, Datchet, Slough, Berks SL3 9JP* Slough (0753) 40395

SWEATMAN, John. b 44. Open Univ BA89. Oak Hill Th Coll 68. **d** 71 **p** 72. C Rayleigh *Chelmsf* 71-73; C Seaford w Sutton *Chich* 73-77; Chapl RN 77-82; CF 82-85; V Hellingly and Upper Dicker *Chich* 85-90. *6 Middleham Close, Ringmer, Lewes, E Sussex BN8 5EN* Ringmer (0273) 814057

SWEED, John William. b 35. Bernard Gilpin Soc Dur 58 Clifton Th Coll 59. **d** 62 **p** 63. C Shrewsbury St Julian *Lich* 62-64; C Sheff St Jo *Sheff* 64-70; V Doncaster St Jas 70-79; V Hatf from 79; RD Snaith and Hatf from 84. *The Vicarage, Hatfield, Doncaster, S Yorkshire DN7 6RS* Doncaster (0302) 840280

SWEENEY, Robert Maxwell. b 38. Ch Ch Ox BA63 MA66 Birm Univ MA78. Cuddesdon Coll 63. **d** 65 **p** 66. C Prestbury *Glouc* 65-68; C Handsworth St Andr *Birm* 68-70; Asst Chapl Lancing Coll Sussex 70-73; Perm to Offic *Chich* 70-73; V Wotton St Mary *Glouc* 74-79; V Ox St Thos w St Frideswide and Binsey *Ox* from 79; Chapl Magd Coll Ox 82-88. *19 Botley Road, Oxford OX2 0BL* Oxford (0865) 251403

SWEET, Canon John Philip McMurdo. b 27. New Coll Ox BA49 MA52. Westcott Ho Cam 53 Yale Div Sch 54. **d** 55 **p** 56. C Mansf St Mark *S'well* 55-58; Chapl Selw Coll Cam 58-83; Lic to Offic *Ely* from 58; Wiccamical Preb Chich Cathl *Chich* from 62; Asst Lect Div Cam Univ 60-63; Lect from 64; Dean of Chapl Selw Coll Cam from 83. *Selwyn College, Cambridge CB3 9DQ* Cambridge (0223) 335846

SWEET, Reginald Charles. b 36. Open Univ BA74. Ripon Hall Ox 61. **d** 62 **p** 63. C Styvechale *Cov* 62-65; Chapl RN 65-69 and from 74; R Riddlesworth w Gasthorpe and Knettishall *Nor* 69-74; R Brettenham w Rushford 69-74;

c/o MOD, Lacon House, Theobald's Road, London WC1X 8RY 071-430 6847

SWEET, Vaughan Carroll. b 46. Aston Univ BSc69 MSc70. Linc Th Coll 89. **d** 91. C Uttoxeter w Bramshall *Lich* from 91. *5 Beech Close, Uttoxeter, Staffs ST14 7PY* Uttoxeter (0889) 567677

SWEET-ESCOTT, Richard Mark. b 28. Hertf Coll Ox BA51 MA53. Westcott Ho Cam 56. **d** 58 **p** 59. C Leeds St Pet *Ripon* 58-62; C Littlehampton St Mary *Chich* 62-65; C Seaford w Sutton 65-72; P-in-c Burpham 72-75; V Easebourne 75-79; V Crawley Down All SS from 79. *The Vicarage, Vicarage Road, Crawley Down, Crawley, W Sussex RH10 4JJ* Copthorne (0342) 713246

SWEETMAN, Denis Harold. b 22. Roch Th Coll 61. **d** 63 **p** 64. C Riverhead *Roch* 63-70; C Dunton Green 67-70; Chapl Sevenoaks Hosp 70-72; R Eynsford w Lullingstone *Roch* 71-73; R Eynsford w Farningham and Lullingstone 73-89; rtd 89; Perm to Offic *Newc* from 89. *31 Gloster Park, Amble, Morpeth, Northd NE65 0JQ* Alnwick (0665) 711863

SWENARTON, Canon John Creighton. b 19. TCD BA41 MA45. **d** 42 **p** 43. I Donaghadee *D & D* 60-84; rtd 84. *3 Slievenamaddy Avenue, Newcastle, Co Down BT33 0DT* Newcastle (03967) 24387

SWENSSON, Sister Gerd Inger. b 51. Lon Univ MPhil Uppsala Univ 70. **dss** 74 **d** 87. In Ch of Sweden 74-75; Notting Hill *Lon* 75-77; CSA from 75; Abbey Ho Malmesbury Wilts 77-79; R Foundn of St Cath 79-81; Notting Hill All SS w St Columb *Lon* 81-84; Kensington St Mary Abbots w St Geo 85-89. *St Andrew's House, 2 Tavistock Road, London W11 1BA* 071-229 2662

SWIDENBANK, Stephen. b 37. Lich Th Coll 58. **d** 61 **p** 62. V Kells *Carl* 67-76; V Staveley w Kentmere 76-85; rtd 85; Perm to Offic *Carl* from 86. *Flat 1, Engadine, New Road, Windermere, Cumbria LA23 2LA* Windermere (09662) 6507

SWIFT, Christopher James. b 65. Hull Univ BA86. Westcott Ho Cam 89. **d** 91. C Longton *Blackb* from 91. *66 Franklands, Longton, Preston PR4 5WD* Preston (0772) 615473

SWIFT, Christopher John. b 54. Linc Coll Ox BA76 MA Selw Coll Cam BA80. Westcott Ho Cam 79. **d** 81 **p** 82. C Portsea N End St Mark *Portsm* 81-84; C Alverstoke 84-87; V Whitton SS Phil and Jas *Lon* from 87. *The Vicarage, 205 Kneller Road, Twickenham, Middx TW2 7DY* 081-894 1932

SWIFT, Francis Bernard. b 06. Dur Univ LTh32. Lich Th Coll 28. **d** 31 **p** 32. V Ireby w Uldale *Carl* 58-72; rtd 72; Lic to Offic *Carl* 72-77; Perm to Offic from 77. *5 Westhaven, Thursby, Carlisle CA5 6PH* Dalston (0228) 710099

SWIFT, James Theodore. b 11. Ripon Hall Ox 67. **d** 68 **p** 69. C Highfield *Ox* 68-72; P-in-c Lyford w Charney 72-78; P-in-c Denchworth 72-78; R Cherbury 78-81; rtd 81; Perm to Offic *Ox* from 81. *5 Cedar Road, Faringdon, Oxon SN7 8AY* Faringdon (0367) 21158

SWIFT, John Russell. b 07. K Coll Lon. **d** 33 **p** 34. V Healey *Man* 57-81; rtd 81; Perm to Offic *Man* from 81. *3 Thornton Old Road, Royton, Oldham* 061-624 2428

SWIFT, Ms Pamela Joan. b 47. Liv Univ BSc68. NE Ord Course 85. **d** 88. Par Dn Bermondsey St Jas w Ch Ch *S'wark* 88-91; Par Dn Middleton St Cross *Ripon* from 91. *87 Helston Walk, Middleton, Leeds LS10 4NW* Leeds (0532) 771034

SWIFT, Richard Barrie. b 33. Selw Coll Cam BA58 MA64. Ripon Hall Ox. **d** 60 **p** 61. C Stepney St Dunstan and All SS *Lon* 60-64; C Sidmouth St Nic *Ex* 64-72; P-in-c W Hyde St Thos *St Alb* 72-77; V Mill End 72-77; V Mill End and Heronsgate w W Hyde 77-82; V Axminster *Ex* 82-83; P-in-c Chardstock 82-83; P-in-c Combe Pyne w Rousdon 82-83; TR Axminster, Chardstock, Combe Pyne and Rousdon from 83. *The Vicarage, Axminster, Devon EX13 5AQ* Axminster (0297) 32264

SWIFT, Selwyn. b 41. Trin Coll Bris 73. **d** 76 **p** 77. C Melksham *Sarum* 76-79; TV 79-81; TV Whitton 81-84; V Derry Hill 84-89; R Bunwell, Carleton Rode, Tibenham, Gt Moulton etc *Nor* from 89. *The Rectory, Carleton Rode, Norwich NR16 1RN* Bunwell (095389) 218

SWIFT, Stanley. b 47. ACIS71 Nottm Univ DipTh73 Open Univ BA86. Linc Th Coll 71. **d** 74 **p** 75. C Heaton St Barn *Bradf* 74-77; C Bexhill St Pet *Chich* 77-81; R Crowland *Linc* 81-86; RD Elloe W 82-86; R Upminster *Chelmsf* from 86. *The Rectory, Gridiron Place, Upminster, Essex RM14 2BE* Upminster (04022) 20174

SWINBANK, Peter. b 19. Linc Coll Ox BA41 MA47. Ridley Hall Cam. **d** 43 **p** 44. V W Hampstead Trin *Lon* 56-72; R Hinton w Dinnington *B & W* 72-78; V Stebbing w Lindsell *Chelmsf* 78-84; rtd 84; Perm to Offic *Ely* from 85. *27 Doggett Road, Cherry Hinton, Cambridge CB1 4LF* Cambridge (0223) 210029

SWINBURNE, Harold Noel. b 27. Univ Coll Lon BA49 St Chad's Coll Dur DipTh. **d** 53 **p** 54. C Cockerton *Dur* 53-57; C Wisbech St Aug *Ely* 57-59; V Chilton Moor *Dur* 59-71; Lect Relig Studies New Coll Dur from 71; Lic to Offic *Dur* 71-85; V Bishopwearmouth St Nic from 85. *St Nicholas' Vicarage, Queen Alexandra Road, Sunderland SR3 1XQ* 091-522 6444

SWINDELL, Anthony Charles. b 50. Selw Coll Cam BA73 MA77 Leeds Univ MPhil77. Ripon Hall Ox 73. **d** 75 **p** 76. C Hessle *York* 75-78; Adult Educn Adv E Sussex 78-80; P-in-c Litlington w W Dean *Chich* 78-80; Chapl York Univ *York* 80-81; TV Heslington 80-81; R Harlaxton *Linc* from 81; RD Grantham 85-90. *The Rectory, Harlaxton, Grantham, Lincs NG32 1HD* Grantham (0476) 75019

SWINDELL, Brian. b 35. St Jo Coll Nottm 86. **d** 88 **p** 89. C Wombwell *Sheff* from 88. *62 Dove Road, Wombwell, Barnsley, S Yorkshire S73 0TE* Barnsley (0226) 754976

SWINDELL, Richard Carl. b 45. FCollP87 Didsbury Coll Man CertEd67 Open Univ BA73 Leeds Univ MEd86. N Ord Course 79 Qu Coll Birm. **d** 82 **p** 83. Hd Teacher Moorside Jun Sch from 86; NSM Halifax St Aug *Wakef* from 82. *38 The Gardens, Heath Road, Halifax, W Yorkshire HX1 2PL* Halifax (0422) 361972

SWINDELLS, Philip John. b 34. St Edm Hall Ox BA56 MA60. Ely Th Coll 56. **d** 58 **p** 59. C Upton cum Chalvey *Ox* 58-62; C Bishops Hull St Jo *B & W* 62-66; C Stevenage St Geo *St Alb* 66-71; V Stevenage All SS Pin Green 71-78; R Clophill from 78; P-in-c Upper w Lower Gravenhurst from 83. *The Rectory, Great Lane, Clophill, Bedford MK45 4BQ* Silsoe (0525) 60792

SWINDELLS, Stephen Seel Sherwood. b 17. Mert Coll Ox BA38 MA43. Wycliffe Hall Ox 38. **d** 40 **p** 41. R Whitfield *Newc* 65-75; V Ninebanks and Carrshield 66-75; P-in-c Bolam 75-79; P-in-c Whalton 77-79; R Bolam w Whalton 79-82; rtd 82. *36 Fountain Head Bank, Seaton Sluice, Whitley Bay, Tyne & Wear NE26 4HU* 091-237 3598

SWINDLEHURST, Canon Michael Robert Carol. b 29. Worc Coll Ox BA52 MA56. Cuddesdon Coll 61. **d** 63 **p** 64. C Havant *Portsm* 63-66; C Hellesdon *Nor* 66-69; V Brightlingsea *Chelmsf* from 69; Miss to Seamen from 69; RD St Osyth *Chelmsf* from 84; Hon Can Chelmsf Cathl from 89. *The Vicarage, Richard Avenue, Brightlingsea, Colchester CO7 0LP* Brightlingsea (0206) 302407

SWINDLEY, Canon Geoffrey. b 25. St Mich Coll Llan 59. **d** 61 **p** 62. C Flint *St As* 61-68; V Buttington and Pool Quay 68-77; R Welshpool w Castle Caereinion from 77; RD Pool from 77; Hon Can St As Cathl from 83. *The Vicarage, Church Street, Welshpool, Powys SY21 7DP* Welshpool (0938) 3164

SWINDON, Archdeacon of. See CLARK, Ven Kenneth James

SWINGLER, Preb Jack Howell. b 19. St Jo Coll Cam BA41 MA47. Ridley Hall Cam 46. **d** 48 **p** 49. V Henstridge *B & W* 53-79; RD Merston 74-84; P-in-c Charlton Horethorne w Stowell 78-79; Preb Wells Cathl from 79; R Henstridge and Charlton Horethorne w Stowell 79-85; rtd 85. *St Andrew's, March Lane, Galhampton, Yeovil, Somerset BA22 7AN* North Cadbury (0963) 40842

SWINGLER, Canon Leslie Ronald. b 12. Lich Th Coll 35. **d** 38 **p** 39. Sec Ox Dioc Coun of Educn 62-78; Dioc Youth and Community Officer *Ox* 74-77; rtd 77; Perm to Offic *Nor* from 77. *54 Folly Road, Wymondham, Norfolk NR18 0QR* Wymondham (0953) 604763

SWINGLER, Phillip Frank. b 45. Keble Coll Ox BA67 MA71 DipEd68 Cam Univ PGCE69. Westcott Ho Cam 68. **d** 70 **p** 71. C Aldenham *St Alb* 70-72; Aldenham Sch Herts 70-72; Eton Coll Windsor 72-75; Lic to Offic *Ox* 72-75; Pet 75-90; Chapl Oundle Sch Pet 75-89; V Luton St Sav *St Alb* from 90. *St Saviour's Vicarage, St Saviour's Crescent, Luton LU1 5HG* Luton (0582) 30445

SWINHOE, Terence Leslie. b 49. Man Univ BA71 PGCE72. N Ord Course. **d** 84 **p** 85. C Harborne St Pet *Birm* 84-87; V Warley *Wakef* from 87. *The Vicarage, 466 Burnley Road, Warley, Halifax, W Yorkshire HX2 7LW* Halifax (0422) 363623

SWINN, Gerald Robert. b 40. Leeds Univ BSc60 Lon Univ BD70. Oak Hill Th Coll 63. **d** 66 **p** 67. C Weston-super-Mare Ch Ch *B & W* 66-69; C Harefield *Lon* 70-72; Lic to Offic *Sarum* from 72. *16 Heddington Drive, Blandford Forum, Dorset DT11 7TP* Blandford (0258) 51637

SWINNERTON, Edward. b 26. St Aid Birkenhead 62. **d** 64 **p** 65. C Prescot *Liv* 64-67; C S Shore H Trin *Blackb*

67-69; V Hambleton 69-88; P-in-c Out Rawcliffe 84-88; V Hambleton w Out Rawcliffe 88-89; V Barnacre w Calder Vale from 89. *The Vicarage, Barnacre, Garstang, Lancs PR3 1GL* Garstang (0995) 602117

SWINNERTON, Ernest George Francis. b 33. Clare Coll Cam BA54 MA57. Linc Th Coll 56. **d** 58 **p** 59. C Kirkholt *Man* 58-61; C Swindon Ch Ch *Bris* 61-67; C-in-c Walcot St Andr CD 67-75; P-in-c Chilton Foliat *Sarum* 76; TV Whitton 76-85; V Bolton St Matt w St Barn *Man* from 85. *St Matthew's Vicarage, Stowell Street, Bolton BL1 3RQ* Bolton (0204) 22810

SWINNEY, Fergus William. b 37. **d** 69 **p** 70. C Benwell St Jas *Newc* 69-72; C Willington 72-75; V Longhirst 75-80. *Address temp unknown*

SWINNEY, Thomas. b 14. Kelham Th Coll 32. **d** 38 **p** 39. V Witton le Wear *Dur* 59-79; V Fir Tree 77-79; rtd 79. *6 Wesley Grove, Bishop Auckland, Co Durham DL14 7TG* Bishop Auckland (0388) 603739

SWINTON, Garry Dunlop. b 59. SS Mark & Jo Coll Plymouth BA81 CertEd82. Ripon Coll Cuddesdon 85. **d** 88 **p** 89. C Surbiton St Andr and St Mark *S'wark* from 88. *Flat B, St Andrew's Hall, Balaclava Road, Surbiton, Surrey KT6 5PN* 081-399 6518

SWITHINBANK, Kim Stafford. b 53. SS Coll Cam BA77 MA80. Cranmer Hall Dur 78. **d** 80 **p** 81. C Heigham H Trin *Nor* 80-83; Chapl Monkton Combe Sch Bath 83-85; C St Marylebone All So w SS Pet and Jo *Lon* 85-88; C Langham Place All So 88-89; R Stamford St Geo w St Paul *Linc* from 90. *St George's Rectory, Stamford, Lincs PE9 2BN* Stamford (0780) 63351

SWITZERLAND, Archdeacon of. See HAWKER, Ven Peter John

SWYER, David Martin. b 64. **d** 91. C Killay *S & B* from 91. *The Parsonage, 79 Ashgrove, Killay, Swansea SA2 7QZ* Swansea (0792) 206631

SWYER (nee HARRIS), Mrs Rebecca Jane. b 67. **d** 91. C Sketty *S & B* from 91. *The Parsonage, 79 Ashgrove, Killay, Swansea SA2 7QZ* Swansea (0792) 206631

SWYNNERTON, Brian Thomas. b 31. JP77. FRGS62 LCP62 Ox Univ Inst of Educn 56 NY Univ BA74 PhD75. Lich Th Coll 67. **d** 69 **p** 70. C Swynnerton *Lich* 69-71; CF (TAVR) 70-80; C Eccleshall *Lich* 71-74; C Croxton w Broughton 74-80; Chapl and Lect Stafford Coll 80-84; Chapl Naples w Sorrento, Capri and Bari *Eur* 84-85; Perm to Offic *Lich & Wakef* from 85; Chapl Rishworth Sch Ripponden 85-88; Chapl Acton Reynald Sch Shrewsbury from 88. *Acton Reynald School, Shrewsbury SY4 4DX* Clive (093928) 365

SYER, Canon George Vivian. b 11. AKC39. ACT ThL56. **d** 39 **p** 42. R Chagford *Ex* 71-76; rtd 76; Perm to Offic *Ex* from 76. *48 Newtown, Milborne Port, Sherborne, Dorset DT9 5BJ* Milborne Port (0963) 250375

SYKES, Albert. b 08. Man Egerton Hall 33. **d** 35 **p** 36. V Pelynt *Truro* 67-73; R Lanreath 67-73; rtd 73; Hon C St Austell *Truro* from 78. *32 Biscovey Road, Par, Cornwall PL24 2HW* Par (072681) 4139

SYKES, Arthur. b 14. Lon Univ BA34. St Deiniol's Hawarden 77. **d** 77 **p** 78. Hon C Birkenhead Priory *Ches* 77-83; rtd 83; Perm to Offic *Ches* from 83. *15 Village Close, Wallasey, Merseyside L45 3PB* 051-630 1796

SYKES, Colin George. b 30. K Coll Cam BA52 MA56 Lon Univ BD61 MTh65. **d** 61 **p** 62. C Bournemouth St Pet *Win* 61-64; C Llan w Capel Llanilterne *Llan* 64-66; Lib and Lect St Mich Coll Llan 66-70; Chapl Bradfield Coll Berks 70-75; R Bodiam *Chich* 75-81; R Ewhurst 75-81; Chapl SS Mary and Anne's Sch Abbots Bromley 81-82; V Hove St Phil *Chich* 82-87; V Abergavenny St Mary w Llanwenarth Citra *Mon* from 88. *St Mary's Vicarage, Priory Meadow, Abergavenny, Gwent NP7 5PR* Abergavenny (0873) 3168

SYKES, Frederick Drummond. b 11. CCC Cam BA33 MA37. Ely Th Coll 33. **d** 34 **p** 35. V Hepworth *Wakef* 71-76; rtd 76; Perm to Offic *Wakef* from 85. *4 West Lodge Crescent, Huddersfield HD2 2EH* Halifax (0422) 372223

SYKES, Ian. b 44. Lon Univ DipTh Leic Univ DipEd. Bris Bapt Coll 64 Ripon Coll Cuddesdon 84. **d** 85 **p** 86. In Bapt Ch 64-84; C Headington *Ox* 85-88; TV Bourne Valley *Sarum* from 88. *The Rectory, High Street, Porton, Salisbury SP4 0LH* Idmiston (0980) 610305

SYKES, James Clement. b 42. Keble Coll Ox BA64 MA71. Westcott Ho Cam 65. **d** 67 **p** 68. C Bishop's Stortford St Mich *St Alb* 67-71; Chapl St Jo Sch Leatherhead 71-73; Bermuda 74-79; V Northaw *St Alb* 79-87; Chapl St Marg Sch Bushey from 87. *The Chaplain's House, St Margaret's School, Bushey, Herts WD2 1DT* 081-950 4616

SYKES, Miss Jean. b 45. Leeds Univ BA66 Bris Univ CertEd67. Ripon Coll Cuddesdon 86. **d** 88. C N

Huddersfield *Wakef* from 88. *60 Tanfield Road, Huddersfield HD1 5HD* Huddersfield (0484) 422645

SYKES, Jeremy Jonathan Nicholas. b 61. Wycliffe Hall Ox. **d** 89 **p** 90. C Knowle *Birm* from 89. *St Anne's Cottage, 1713 High Street, Knowle, Solihull, W Midlands B93 0LN* Knowle (0564) 775672

SYKES, John. b 39. Man Univ BA62. Ripon Hall Ox 61. **d** 63 **p** 64. C Heywood St Luke *Man* 63-67; Chapl Bolton Colls of FE 67-71; C Bolton H Trin *Man* 67-71; R Reddish 71-78; V Saddleworth 78-87; TR Oldham from 87. *The Vicarage, 15 Grotton Hollow, Oldham OL4 4LN* 061-678 6767 or 624 4866

SYKES, John Trevor. b 35. Lich Th Coll 60. **d** 62 **p** 63. C Lillington *Cov* 62-65; C Cov St Marg 65-68; P-in-c Bubbenhall 68-77; V Ryton on Dunsmore 68-77; V Ryton on Dunsmore w Bubbenhall from 77. *The Vicarage, Ryton on Dunsmore, Coventry CV8 3ET* Coventry (0203) 303570

✠SYKES, Rt Rev Stephen Whitefield. b 39. St Jo Coll Cam BA61 MA65. Ripon Hall Ox 61. **d** 64 **p** 65 **c** 90. Fell and Dean St Jo Coll Cam 64-74; Asst Lect Div Cam Univ 64-68; Lect 68-74; Can Res Dur Cathl *Dur* 74-85; Van Mildert Prof Div Dur Univ 74-85; Regius Prof Div Cam Univ 85-90; Hon Can Ely Cathl *Ely* 85-90; Bp Ely from 90. *Bishop's House, Ely, Cambs CB7 4DW* Ely (0353) 662749

SYKES, William George David. b 39. Ball Coll Ox BA63 MA68. Wycliffe Hall Ox 63. **d** 65 **p** 66. Chapl Bradf Cathl *Bradf* 65-69; Chapl Univ Coll Lon 69-78; Chapl Univ Coll Ox from 78. *University College, Oxford OX1 4BH* Oxford (0865) 276663

SYLVIA, Keith Lawrence Wilfred. b 63. Chich Th Coll 85. **d** 88 **p** 89. C Newbold and Dunston *Derby* 88-91; C Heston *Lon* from 91. *24 Hogarth Gardens, Hounslow, Middlesex TW5 0QS*

SYMES, Collin. b 20. Birm Univ BA47 MA48. Bps' Coll Cheshunt 56. **d** 58 **p** 59. Hon C Rusthall *Roch* 68-85; Chapl W Kent Coll of FE 68-73; Chapl Chapl RN Sch Haslemere 81-84; rtd 84; Chapl St Elphin's Sch Matlock 85-86. *3 Eden Walk, Tunbridge Wells, Kent TN1 1TT* Tunbridge Wells (0892) 32283

SYMES, Percy Peter. b 24. Leeds Univ BA50. Coll of Resurr Mirfield 50. **d** 52 **p** 53. V Reading St Luke *Ox* 61-81; V Drayton St Pet (Berks) 81-89; rtd 89. *107 Abingdon Road, Standlake, Witney, Oxon OX8 7QN*

SYMES-THOMPSON, Hugh Kynard. b 54. Peterho Cam BA76 MA81 St Jo Coll Dur DipTh79. **d** 79 **p** 80. C Summerfield *Birm* 79-82; C Harlow New Town w Lt Parndon *Chelmsf* 82-83; Australia 84-89; TV Dagenham *Chelmsf* from 89. *St George's Vicarage, 86 Rogers Road, Dagenham, Essex RM10 8JX* 081-593 2760

SYMINGTON, Canon Alexander Aitken. b 02. Hertf Coll Ox BA26 MA29. **d** 29 **p** 30. R Pertenhall w Swineshead *St Alb* 57-71; rtd 71. *Ramsay Hall, Byron Road, Worthing, W Sussex BN11 3HW* Worthing (0903) 36880

SYMINGTON, Ms Patricia Ann. *See* TURNER, Ms Patricia Ann

SYMMONS, Roderic Paul. b 56. Chu Coll Cam MA77. Oak Hill Th Coll BA83. **d** 83 **p** 84. C Ox St Aldate w St Matt *Ox* 83-88; USA 89-90; R Ardingly *Chich* from 90. *The Rectory, Church Lane, Ardingly, Haywards Heath, W Sussex RH17 6UR* Ardingly (0444) 892332

SYMON, Canon John Francis Walker. b 26. Edin Univ MA50. Edin Th Coll 50. **d** 52 **p** 53. C Edin St Cuth *Edin* 52-56; CF 56-59; R Forfar *St And* 59-68; R Dunblane 68-85; Can St Ninian's Cathl Perth from 74; Chapl Trin Coll Glenalmond from 85. *Roberts, Back Avenue, Glenalmond, Perth PH1 3RY* Glenalmond (073888) 268

SYMON, Canon Roger Hugh Crispin. b 34. St Jo Coll Cam BA59. Coll of Resurr Mirfield 59. **d** 61 **p** 62. C Westmr St Steph w St Jo *Lon* 61-66; P-in-c Hascombe *Guildf* 66-68; Chapl Surrey Univ 66-74; V Paddington Ch Ch *Lon* 74-78; V Paddington St Jas 78-79; USPG 80-87; Abp Cant's Acting Sec for Angl Communion Affairs from 87. *28 Hillcrest Road, London W3 9RZ or, Lambeth Palace, London SE1 7JU* 071-928 8282

SYMONDS, Edward George. b 03. Launde Abbey 58. **d** 59 **p** 60. V Leic All SS *Leic* 64-74; rtd 74. *19 Victoria Square, Penarth, S Glamorgan CF6 2EJ* Penarth (0222) 705546

SYMONDS, James Henry. b 31. Ripon Hall Ox 67. **d** 69 **p** 70. C Southn (City Cen) *Win* 69-71; CF 71-78 and from 79; P-in-c Arrington *Ely* 78-79; V 79; P-in-c Orwell 78-79; R 79; P-in-c Wimpole 78-79; R 79; P-in-c Croydon w Clopton 78-79; R 79. *c/o MOD (Army), Bagshot Park, Bagshot, Surrey GU19 5PL* Bagshot (0276) 71717

SYMONDS, Canon Robert Pinder. b 10. CCC Cam BA32 MA37. Linc Th Coll 32. **d** 34 **p** 35. OGS from 44;

V Leic St Mary *Leic* 56-74; Sub-Warden St Deiniol's Lib Hawarden 74-78; rtd 75; Chapl Trin Hosp Retford 78-87; Perm to Offic *Chich* from 87. *67 Church Lane, Beeding, Steyning, W Sussex BN44 3HP* Steyning (0903) 813999

SYMONS, Fernley Rundle. b 39. Peterho Cam BA61 MA71. St Steph Ho Ox 61. **d** 64 **p** 65. C Chesterton St Geo *Ely* 64-67; C Henleaze *Bris* 67-72; V Shirehampton from 72. *St Mary's Vicarage, 8 Priory Gardens, Shirehampton, Bristol BS11 0BZ* Bristol (0272) 822737

SYMONS, James Edward. b 28. AKC57. **d** 58 **p** 59. C Benwell St Jas *Newc* 58-62; C Alnwick St Mich 62-65; C Prudhoe 65-67; V Mickley from 67. *The Vicarage, Mickley, Stocksfield, Northd NE43 7LS* Stocksfield (0661) 843342

SYMONS, Peter Henry. b 25. AKC51. **d** 52 **p** 53. V Woolacombe *Ex* 61-75; V Kingsteignton 75-89; rtd 89. *13 Harbour Court, Penzance, Cornwall*

SYMONS, Stewart Burlace. b 31. Keble Coll Ox BA55 MA59. Clifton Th Coll 55. **d** 57 **p** 58. C Hornsey Rise St Mary *Lon* 57-60; C Gateshead St Geo *Dur* 60-61; C Patcham *Chich* 61-64; R Stretford St Bride *Man* 64-71; V Waterloo St Jo *Liv* 71-83; R Ardrossan *Glas* from 83; C-in-c Irvine St Andr LEP from 83; Miss to Seamen from 83. *31 Milgarholm Avenue, Irvine, Ayrshire KA12 0EL* Irvine (0294) 78341

SYMS, Richard Arthur. b 43. Ch Coll Cam BA66 MA71. Wycliffe Hall Ox 66. **d** 68 **p** 69. C New Eltham All SS *S'wark* 68-72; Chapl to Arts and Recreation *Dur* 72-73; C Hitchin St Mary *St Alb* 73-76; TV Hitchin 77-78; Perm to Offic from 78. *94 Pondcroft Road, Knebworth, Herts SG3 6DE* Stevenage (0438) 811933

SYNNOTT, Alan Patrick Sutherland. b 59. **d** 85 **p** 86. C Lisburn Ch Ch *Conn* 85-88; CF from 88. *c/o MOD (Army), Bagshot Park, Bagshot, Surrey GU19 5PL* Bagshot (0276) 71717

SYNNOTT, Canon Patrick Joseph. b 18. **d** 52 **p** 54. I Magheralin *D & D* 63-74; RD Shankill 70-74; I Belf St Donard 74-89; Can Down Cathl 80-89; Chan Down Cathl 87-89; rtd 89; Lic to Offic *D & D* from 90. *7 Norwood Drive, Belfast BT4 2EA* Belfast (0232) 652365

T

TABERN, James. b 23. St Aid Birkenhead 57. **d** 59 **p** 60. V Litherland St Paul Hatton Hill *Liv* 61-72; V Gillingham St Mark *Roch* 72-79; V Lindow *Ches* 79-85; rtd 85; Perm to Offic *Liv* from 86. *12 Dickinson Road, Formby, Merseyside L37 4BX* Formby (07048) 31131

TABERNACLE, Peter Aufrere. b 22. S'wark Ord Course 72. **d** 74 **p** 75. NSM Enfield St Geo *Lon* 75-80; C Corby Epiphany w St Jo *Pet* 80-83; V Wellingborough St Mark 83-88; P-in-c Wilby 83-88; rtd 88; Perm to Offic *Pet* from 88. *15 Archfield Court, Oxford Street, Wellingborough, Northants NN8 4HH* Wellingborough (0933) 228570

TABOR, John Tranham. b 30. Ball Coll Ox BA56 MA58. Ridley Hall Cam 55. **d** 58 **p** 59. C Lindfield *Chich* 58-62; Tutor Ridley Hall Cam 62-63; Chapl 63-68; Warden Scargill Ho N Yorkshire 68-75; V Berkhamsted St Mary *St Alb* from 75. *The Rectory, 80 High Street, Northchurch, Berkhamsted, Herts HP4 3QW* Berkhamsted (0442) 865312

TABOR, Leonard Frank. b 15. St Steph Ho Ox 47. **d** 50 **p** 51. V Margate All SS *Cant* 66-86; rtd 86; Perm to Offic *Cant* from 86. *Appleshaw, 18B Whitehall Gardens, Canterbury, Kent CT2 8BD* Canterbury (0227) 464342

TABRAHAM, Canon Albert John. b 14. Birm Univ DipTh71. Coll of Resurr Mirfield 55. **d** 56 **p** 57. V Stockland Green *Birm* 59-70; RD Aston 68-70; V Acocks Green 70-80; RD Yardley 74-77; Hon Can Birm Cathl 78-80; rtd 80; Hon C Duns *Edin* from 80. *10 Gourlays Wynd, Duns, Berwickshire TD11 3AZ* Duns (0361) 82483

TADMAN, John Christopher. b 33. Lon Coll of Div 54. **d** 58 **p** 59. C Blackheath St Jo *S'wark* 58-61; C Surbiton Hill Ch Ch 61-64; R Cratfield w Heveningham and Ubbeston *St E* 65-70; R Kelsale w Carlton 70-74; R Ashurst *Roch* 74-76; V Fordcombe 74-77; P-in-c Penshurst 76-77; R Penshurst and Fordcombe 77-85; V Felsted *Chelmsf* from 85. *The Vicarage, Felsted, Dunmow, Essex CM6 3DQ* Great Dunmow (0371) 820242

TADMAN-ROBINS, Christopher Rodney. b 47. JP82. LRAM ARCM GNSM68 Lon Univ CertEd Westmr Coll Ox BA. Ox NSM Course 86. **d** 89 **p** 90. Hon C Burford w Fulbrook and Taynton *Ox* from 89. *Rest Harrow, Meadow Lane, Fulbrook, Oxford OX8 4BS* Burford (099382) 3551

TAGGART, Geoffrey Marmaduke. b 11. Man Univ 52. Qu Coll Birm 54. **d** 56 **p** 57. V Oldham St Steph and All Martyrs *Man* 59-71; V Denshaw 71-76; rtd 76; Perm to Offic *Liv* from 79. *4 Pilling Lane, Lydiate, Liverpool L31 4HF* 051-526 0456

TAGGART, Canon Justin Paul. b 11. Linc Th Coll 32. **d** 34 **p** 35. V Woodhall Spa and Kirkstead *Linc* 52-76; R Langton w Woodhall 52-76; Can and Preb Linc Cathl 68-76; rtd 76. *Reedsbeck, Droghadfayle Road, Port Erin, Isle of Man* Port Erin (0624) 834204

TAGGART, William Joseph. b 54. **d** 85 **p** 86. C Belf St Mich *Conn* 85-90; Chmn Dioc Youth Coun from 90; I Belf St Kath from 90. *St Katharine's Rectory, 24 Lansdowne Road, Belfast BT15 4DB* Belfast (0232) 777647

TAILBY, Mark Kevan. b 36. K Coll Lon 60. **d** 64 **p** 65. C Newbold on Avon *Cov* 64-67; C Stratford w Bishopton 67-70; CF 70-76; P-in-c S Shoebury *Chelmsf* 76-79; P-in-c Stambridge 79-89; Chapl Rochford Gen Hosp 79-89; TV Dovercourt and Parkeston *Chelmsf* from 89. *41 Seafield Road, Dovercourt, Harwich, Essex CO12 4EH* Harwich (0255) 551471

TAILBY, Peter Alan. b 49. Chich Th Coll 83. **d** 85 **p** 86. C Stocking Farm *Leic* 85-88; C Knighton St Mary Magd 88-90; P-in-c Thurnby Lodge from 90. *Christ Church Vicarage, 73 Nursery Road, Leicester LE5 2HQ* Leicester (0533) 413848

TAIT, Henry Alexander. b 29. DipEd DipTh. St Chad's Coll Dur 65. **d** 66 **p** 67. C Hexham *Newc* 66-69; R Elmsett w Aldham *St E* 69-75; Dir of Educn 69-74; P-in-c Kersey w Lindsey 74-75; R Sandiacre *Derby* 75-81; V E Dereham *Nor* 81-88; P-in-c Scarning 81-88; R E Dereham and Scarning 89-90; RD Hingham and Mitford 86-90; V Gilling and Kirkby Ravensworth *Ripon* from 90; Asst RD Richmond from 91. *The Vicarage, Gilling West, Richmond, N Yorkshire DL10 5JG* Richmond (0748) 4466

TAIT, James Laurence Jamieson. b 47. St Jo Coll Dur 78. **d** 80 **p** 81. C Heyside *Man* 80-81; C Westhoughton 81-84; R Aldingham and Dendron and Rampside *Carl* 84-88; V Flookburgh from 88. *The Vicarage, Flookburgh, Grange-over-Sands, Cumbria LA11 7JY* Flookburgh (044853) 245

TAIT, Philip (Leslie). b 52. Ex Univ BA73 Hull Univ PGCE74. NE Ord Course 87. **d** 90. NSM Osbaldwick w Murton *York* from 90; Chapl Burnholme Sch York from 90. *Dunneoc, 6 Givendale Grove, Osbaldwick, York* York (0904) 412790

TAIT, Thomas William. b 07. St Cath Soc Ox BA30 MA33. Clifton Th Coll 40 Edin Th Coll 42. **d** 43 **p** 44. R Church Lawton *Ches* 64-67; rtd 72. *43 Hanover Gardens, Cuckoofield Lane, Mulbarton, Norwich NR14 8DA* Mulbarton (0508) 70598

TALBOT, Alan John. b 23. BNC Ox BA49 MA55. Coll of Resurr Mirfield 49. **d** 51 **p** 52. V Stepney St Aug w St Phil *Lon* 69-78; V Twickenham All Hallows 78-86; rtd 88. *46 Brandon Street, London SE17 1NL*

TALBOT, Allan Peter Surman. b 09. Worc Coll Ox BA30 MA69. St Andr Coll Pampisford 46. **d** 46 **p** 47. V Midgham w Brimpton *Ox* 62-75; rtd 75; Perm to Offic *St E* from 79. *8 Canberra, Stonehouse, Glos GL10 2PR* Stonehouse (0453) 825632

TALBOT, Derek Michael. b 55. St Jo Coll Dur BSc77 Nottm Univ DipTh85. St Jo Coll Nottm 84. **d** 87 **p** 88. C Rushden w Newton Bromswold *Pet* 87-90; C Barton Seagrave w Warkton from 90. *9 Churchill Way, Kettering, Northants NN15 5DP* Kettering (0536) 512828

TALBOT, George Brian. b 37. Qu Coll Birm 78. **d** 80 **p** 81. C Heref St Martin *Heref* 80-83; R Bishop's Frome w Castle Frome and Fromes Hill 83-90; P-in-c Acton Beauchamp and Evesbatch w Stanford Bishop 83-90; R Burstow *S'wark* from 90. *The Rectory, Church Road, Burstow, Horley, Surrey RH6 9RG* Smallfield (034284) 2224

TALBOT, John Frederick Gordon. b 12. Chich Th Coll 47. **d** 50 **p** 51. R Wednesbury St Jo *Lich* 57-73; R W Felton 73-87; rtd 87. *8 Rose Hill Close, Whittington, Shropshire SY11 4DY* Oswestry (0691) 657962

TALBOT, John Herbert Boyle. b 30. TCD BA51 MA57. CITC 52. **d** 53 **p** 54. C Dub St Pet *D & G* 53-57; Chan Vicar St Patrick's Cathl Dub 56-61; C Dub Zion Ch 57-61; Chapl Asst St Thos Hosp Lon 61-64; Min Can and Sacr Cant Cathl *Cant* 64-67; R Brasted *Roch* 67-84;

R Ightham from 84; P-in-c Shipbourne from 87; RD Shoreham from 89. *The Rectory, Tonbridge Road, Ightham, Sevenoaks, Kent TN15 9BG* Borough Green (0732) 884176

TALBOT, Dr John Michael. b 23. FRSM FRCPath68 Lon Univ MD52. S'wark Ord Course 75. **d** 78 **p** 79. NSM S Croydon Em *Cant* 78-81; Perm to Offic *Nor* 82-85; NSM Hethersett w Canteloff w Lt and Gt Melton from 85. *3 White Gates Close, Hethersett, Norwich NR9 3JG* Norwich (0603) 811709

TALBOT, Mrs June Phyllis. b 46. Ripon Coll of Educn CertEd67. NE Ord Course 88. **d** 91. NSM Cleadon *Dur* from 91. *66 Wheatall Drive, Whitburn, Sunderland, Tyne & Wear SR6 7HQ* 091-529 2265

TALBOT, Mrs Marian. b 25. Qu Coll Birm 76. dss 78 **d** 87. Droitwich *Worc* 78-87; Chapl Droitwich Hosps 83-88; Par Dn Droitwich Spa 87-88; Asst Chapl Alexandra Hosp Redditch from 88. *Talbot House, Foredraught Lane, Tibberton, Droitwich, Worcs WR9 7NH* Spetchley (090565) 404

TALBOT, Very Rev Maurice John. b 12. TCD BA35 MA43. **d** 35 **p** 36. Dean Limerick *L & K* 54-71; Preb St Patr Cathl Dub 59-73; C Kilmallock *L & K* 71-73; Lic to Offic 75-80; I Drumcliffe 80-84; Bp's C Banagher *M & K* 85-86; rtd 86. *Woodbrook, Lower Main Street, Abbeyleix, Co Laois, Irish Republic* Abbeyleix (502) 31721

TALBOT, Richard Allen. b 06. MC40. St D Coll Lamp BA32 BD45. **d** 32 **p** 33. R Hunsingore w Cowthorpe *Ripon* 65-74; rtd 74. *25 Boroughbridge Road, Knaresborough, N Yorkshire HG5 0LY* Harrogate (0423) 863164

TALBOT, Stephen Richard. b 52. BSc. Trin Coll Bris DipHE. **d** 84 **p** 85. C Tonbridge SS Pet and Paul *Roch* 84-89; P-in-c Hemingford Grey *Ely* from 89; P-in-c Hemingford Abbots from 89. *The Vicarage, Braggs Lane, Hemingford Grey, Huntingdon PE18 9BW* St Ives (0480) 67305

TALBOT-PONSONBY, Preb Andrew. b 44. Leeds Univ DipTh66. Coll of Resurr Mirfield 66. **d** 68 **p** 70. C Radlett *St Alb* 68-70; C Salisbury St Martin *Sarum* 70-73; P-in-c Acton Burnell w Pitchford *Heref* 73-80; P-in-c Frodesley 73-80; P-in-c Cound 73-80; Asst Youth Officer 73-80; P-in-c Bockleton w Leysters 80-81; V from 81; P-in-c Kimbolton w Middleton-on-the-Hill 80-81; V Kimbolton w Hamnish and Middleton-on-the-Hill from 81; Preb Heref Cathl from 87. *The Vicarage, Kimbolton, Leominster, Herefordshire HR6 0HQ* Leominster (0568) 612024

TALBOT-PONSONBY, Mrs Jill. b 50. Sarum & Wells Th Coll 89. **d** 91. C Leominster *Heref* from 91. *Kimbolton Vicarage, Leominster, Herefordshire HR6 0HQ* Leominster (0568) 612024

TALBOTT, Brian Hugh. b 34. RD78. St Pet Hall Ox BA57 MA64. Westcott Ho Cam. **d** 59 **p** 60. C Newc H Cross *Newc* 59-61; C Newc St Jo 61-64; Chapl RNR 63-77; Sen Chapl RNR from 77; Chapl RN from 91; Chapl Barnard Castle Sch 64-71; Hon C Bishop's Stortford St Mich *St Alb* from 71; Chapl Bishop's Stortford Coll Herts from 71. *c/o Bishop's Stortford College, Bishop's Stortford, Herts CM23 2QZ* Bishop's Stortford (0279) 657911

TALBOTT, Simon John. b 57. Pontifical Univ Maynooth BD81. **d** 81 **p** 82. In RC Ch 81-87; C Headingley *Ripon* 88-91; V Gt and Lt Ouseburn w Marton-cum-Grafton from 91. *The Vicarage, Great Ouseburn, York YO5 9RQ* Boroughbridge (0423) 330928

TALENT, Canon Jack. b 23. AKC49. **d** 50 **p** 51. C Grantham St Wulfram *Linc* 50-59; R Corsley *Sarum* 59-62; S Africa from 62; Hon Can Kimberley and Kuruman from 81. *27 Armenia Crescent, Plattekloof Glen, Goodwoodt, 7460 South Africa* Cape Town (21) 559-1431

TALLANT, John. b 45. Edin Th Coll 86. **d** 88 **p** 89. C Cayton w Eastfield *York* 88-90; C N Hull St Mich 90-91; V Scarborough St Sav w All SS from 91. *St Saviour's Vicarage, 1 Manor Road, Scarborough, N Yorkshire YO12 7RZ* Scarborough (0723) 360648

TAMBLING, Peter Francis. b 20. St Pet Hall Ox BA47. Westcott Ho Cam. **d** 49 **p** 50. R Zeals and Stourton *Sarum* 64-73; P-in-c Bourton w Silton 71-73; R Upper Stour 73-74; R Glenfield *Leic* 74-85; RD Sparkenhoe III 76-81; rtd 85; Perm to Offic *B & W* from 86. *20 Balsam Fields, Wincanton, Somerset BA9 9HF* Wincanton (0963) 34237

TAMPLIN, Peter Harry. b 44. Sarum & Wells Th Coll 71. **d** 73 **p** 74. C Digswell *St Alb* 73-76; C Chesterton St Luke *Ely* 76-82; V Chesterton St Geo from 82. *St*

George's Vicarage, 8 Chesterfield Road, Cambridge CB4 1LN Cambridge (0223) 423374

TAMS, Gordon Thomas Carl. b 37. LLCM76 Leeds Univ BMus60 Reading Univ CertEd61 Newc Univ MLitt84. Edin Dioc NSM Course 83. **d** 90. NSM Kelso *Edin* from 90. *Old Joiners Cottage, Eckford, Kelso, Roxburghshire TD5 8LG* Crailing (08355) 323

TAMS, Paul William. b 56. Huddersfield Poly CertEd77. E Anglian Minl Tr Course 87. **d** 90 **p** 91. NSM Mildenhall *St E* from 90. *28 Raven Close, Mildenhall, Bury St Edmunds IP28 7LF* Mildenhall (0638) 715475

TANBURN, John Walter. b 30. Jes Coll Cam BA53 MA57. Clifton Th Coll 54. **d** 56 **p** 57. C Orpington Ch Ch *Roch* 56-59; C-in-c St Paul's Cray St Barn CD 59-64; V St Paul's Cray St Barn 64-67; Chapl Stowe Sch Bucks 67-72; Chapl Wymondham Coll 72-82; R Morley *Nor* 72-82. *Address temp unknown*

TANCRED-LAWSON, Christopher. b 24. Trin Coll Cam BA49 MA65. Chich Th Coll 63. **d** 65 **p** 66. C Uckfield *Chich* 65-70; R Wrington *B & W* 70-73; R Wrington w Butcombe 73-79; Perm to Offic *Chich* from 80; Hon C Battersea St Luke *S'wark* from 83; rtd 89. *Flat 3, Minterne House, Dorchester, Dorset DT2 7AX* Cerne Abbas (0300) 341328

TANKARD, Reginald Douglas Alan. b 37. Sarum Th Coll 60. **d** 62 **p** 63. C Howden *York* 62-65; C Heckmondwike *Wakef* 65-67; CF 67-70; C Thornbury *Bradf* 82-88; P-in-c Rockcliffe and Blackford *Carl* 88-90; V from 90. *The Vicarage, Rockcliffe, Carlisle CA6 4AA* Rockcliffe (022874) 209

TANN, Canon David John. b 31. K Coll Lon BD57 AKC57. **d** 58 **p** 59. C Wandsworth St Anne *S'wark* 58-60; C Sholing *Win* 60-64; Asst Chapl Lon Univ *Lon* 64-65; C Fulham All SS 65-68; Hon C 72-82; Lic to Offic 68-72; Teacher Godolphin and Latymer Sch Hammersmith 68-73; Ealing Boys Gr Sch 69-73; Hd of RE Green Sch Isleworth 73-82; V Dudley St Jas *Worc* from 82; Chapl Burton Rd Hosp Dudley from 83; Hon Can Worc Cathl *Worc* from 90. *St James's Vicarage, The Parade, Dudley, W Midlands DY1 3JA* Dudley (0384) 253570

TANNER, Preb Alan John. b 25. Linc Coll Ox BA52 MA65. Coll of Resurr Mirfield 52. **d** 54 **p** 55. C Hendon St Mary *Lon* 54-58; V S Harrow St Paul 58-60; Dir Coun for Chr Stewardship 60-65; Dir Lay Tr 65-71; Sec Coun for Miss and Unity 65-80; V St Nic Cole Abbey 66-78; Preacher of the Charterhouse from 73; Sec Gtr Lon Chs' Coun 76-83; P-in-c St Ethelburga Bishopsgate *Lon* 78-85; R St Botolph without Bishopgate from 78; P-in-c All Hallows Lon Wall from 80; Bp's Ecum Officer from 81; AD The City from 90; Preb St Paul's Cathl from 71. *St Botolph's Vestry, Bishopsgate, London EC2M 3TL* 071-588 3388 or 588 1053

TANNER, Frank Hubert. b 38. St Aid Birkenhead. **d** 66 **p** 67. C Ipswich St Marg *St E* 66-69; C Mansf St Pet *S'well* 69-72; V Huthwaite 72-79; Chapl to the Deaf from 79; Hon Can S'well Minster from 90. *28 Alexandra Avenue, Mansfield, Notts NG18 5AB* Mansfield (0623) 23847

TANNER, Frederick James. b 24. **d** 64 **p** 65. Uganda 64-69; Hd Master Summerhill Jun Mixed Sch Bris from 69; Perm to Offic *Bris* from 69; Hon C Chew Magna w Dundry *B & W* 81-86; Perm to Offic from 86. *The Byre, Eastfields, Charlton, Horethorne, Sherborne, Dorset DT9 4PB* Corton Denham (096322) 641

TANNER, Canon Laurence Ernest. b 17. St Cath Coll Cam BA39 MA43. St Mich Coll Llan. **d** 40 **p** 41. V Shamley Green *Guildf* 64-71; RD Cranleigh 68-71; Can Res Guildf Cathl 71-82; Sub-Dean 72-82; Dir of Ords 71-82; rtd 82; Perm to Offic *St E* from 82. *Homestead Cottage, South Green, Southwold, Suffolk IP18 6EU* Southwold (0502) 722602

TANNER, Mark Stuart. b 59. Nottm Univ BA81. Sarum & Wells Th Coll. **d** 85 **p** 86. C Radcliffe-on-Trent *S'well* 85, C Radcliffe-on-Trent and Shelford etc 85-88; C Bestwood 88-89; TV from 89. *45 Pine Hill Close, Nottingham NG5 9DA* Nottingham (0602) 277229

TANNER, Martin Philip. b 54. Univ Coll Lon BSc(Econ)75. Ridley Hall Cam 79. **d** 82 **p** 83. C Bitterne *Win* 82-85; C Weeke 85-88; V Long Buckby w Watford *Pet* from 88. *The Vicarage, 10 Hall Drive, Long Buckby, Northampton NN6 7QU* Long Buckby (0327) 842909

TANSILL, Canon Derek Ernest Edward. b 36. Univ of Wales (Lamp) BA61. Ripon Hall Ox 61. **d** 63 **p** 64. C Chelsea St Luke *Lon* 63-67; C-in-c Saltdean CD *Chich* 67-69; V Saltdean 69-73; V Billingshurst 73-82; RD Horsham 77-82 and from 85; Can and Preb Chich Cathl from 81; R Bexhill St Pet 82-85; RD Battle and Bexhill 84-86; V Horsham 85-86; TR from 86. *The Vicarage,*

The Causeway, Horsham, W Sussex RH12 1HE Horsham (0403) 53762

TAPLIN, John. b 35. St Alb Minl Tr Scheme 78. **d** 81 **p** 82. NSM Knebworth *St Alb* 81-88; C Braughing, Lt Hadham, Albury, Furneux Pelham etc 88; R Lt Hadham w Albury from 88. *The Vicarage, Parsonage Lane, Albury, Ware, Herts SG11 2HU* Albury (027974) 361

TAPPER, John A'Court. b 42. FCA64. Sarum & Wells Th Coll 89. **d** 91. C Ashford *Cant* from 91. *19 The Weald, Ashford, Kent TN24 8RA* Ashford (0233) 629819

TARGETT, Kenneth. b 28. Qu Coll Birm 54. **d** 57 **p** 58. C Mansf Woodhouse *S'well* 57-59; C Skipton Ch Ch *Bradf* 59-62; V Bradf St Jo 62-65; Perm to Offic from 65; Australia 82-87; V Old Leake w Wrangle *Linc* from 87. *The Vicarage, Old Leake, Boston, Lincs PE22 9NS* Boston (0205) 870130

TARLETON, Denis Reginald. b 12. TCD BA35 MA45. CITC 36. **d** 36 **p** 37. I Devenish w Boho *Clogh* 59-63; rtd 63; Perm to Offic *D & D* from 67. *33 Drumkeen Court, Belfast BT8 4TU* Belfast (0232) 691003

TARLETON, Peter. b 46. TCD BA72 Div Test73 HDipEd77 MA80. **d** 73 **p** 74. C Cork St Luke w St Ann C, *C & R* 73-75; C Dub Drumcondra *D & G* 75-78; I Limerick City *L & K* 78-82; I Drumgoon w Dernakesh, Ashfield etc *K, E & A* 82-85; Chapl HM Young Offender Inst Hindley 85-89; Chapl HM Pris Lindholme from 89. *HM Prison, Bawtry Road, Hatfield Woodhouse, Doncaster, S Yorkshire DN7 6DG* Doncaster (0302) 846600

TARLING, Paul. b 53. Oak Hill Th Coll BA. **d** 85 **p** 86. C Old Hill H Trin *Worc* 85-89; V Walford w Bishopswood *Heref* 89-90; P-in-c Goodrich w Welsh Bicknor and Marstow 89-90; R Walford and Saint John, w Bishopswood etc from 90. *The Vicarage, Walford, Ross-on-Wye, Herefordshire* Ross-on-Wye (0989) 62703

TARPER, Ann Jennifer. b 47. SRN71 BCombStuds82. Linc Th Coll 79. dss 83 **d** 87. Stamford All SS w St Jo *Linc* 82-85; Witham *Chelmsf* 85-87; Par Dn 87-90; Min and Educn Adv to Newmarch Gp Min *Heref* from 90. *St Mary's Vicarage, Almeley, Hereford HR3 6LB* Eardisley (0544) 68497

TARR, James Robert. b 39. Bps' Coll Cheshunt 64. **d** 67 **p** 68. C Wortley de Leeds *Ripon* 67-69; C Hunslet St Mary and Stourton St Andr 70-73; V Moorends *Sheff* 73-77; V Cross Stone *Wakef* 77-83; V Chilworth w N Baddesley *Win* 83-90; V Andover St Mich from 90. *St Michael's Vicarage, 13 The Avenue, Andover, Hants SP10 3EW* Andover (0264) 352553

TARRANT, Ian Denis. b 57. Cam Univ BA MA Nottm Univ DipTh. St Jo Coll Nottm 81. **d** 84 **p** 85. C Ealing St Mary *Lon* 84-87; CMS from 88; Zaire from 88. *c/o Postles Lodge, 52 Orchard Way, Knebworth, Herts*

TARRANT, John Michael. b 38. St Jo Coll Cam BA59 MA63 Ball Coll Ox BA62. Ripon Hall Ox 60. **d** 62 **p** 63. C Chelsea All SS *Lon* 62-65; Chapl St Pet Coll Saltley 66-70; Br Honduras 70-73; Belize 73-75; V Forest Row *Chich* 75-87. *Address temp unknown*

TARRANT, Paul John. b 57. BA. Chich Th Coll. **d** 82 **p** 83. C Southgate Ch Ch *Lon* 82-85; C Hornsey St Mary w St Geo 85-90; USA from 90. *St Thomas's Rectory, 115 High Street, Taunton, Massachusetts 02780, USA*

TARRIS, Canon Geoffrey John. b 27. Em Coll Cam BA50 MA55. Westcott Ho Cam 51. **d** 53 **p** 54. C Abbots Langley *St Alb* 53-55; Prec St E Cathl *St E* 55-59; V Bungay H Trin w St Mary 59-72; RD S Elmham 65-72; V Ipswich St Mary le Tower 72-78; Hon Can St E Cathl 74-82; V Ipswich St Mary le Tower w St Lawr and St Steph 78-82; Can Res St E Cathl from 82; Dioc Dir of Lay Min and Warden of Readers 82-87; Dioc Dir of Ords from 87. *1 Abbey Precincts, Bury St Edmunds, Suffolk IP33 1RS* Bury St Edmunds (0284) 761982

TARRY, Gordon Malcolm. b 54. Leeds Univ BSc75. Lon Bible Coll BA83 Ridley Hall Cam. **d** 85 **p** 86. C Gt Ilford St Andr *Chelmsf* 85-89; C Rainham from 89. *8A Frederick Road, Rainham, Essex RM13 8NT* Rainham (04027) 54458

TASH, Stephen Ronald. b 56. Warw Univ BEd79. W Midl Minl Tr Course 88. **d** 91. C Studley *Cov* from 91. *Plot 1, Westmead Avenue, Studley, Warks* Studley (052785) 7688

TASKER, Canon Harry Beverley. b 41. BA76. Wycliffe Hall Ox 64. **d** 67 **p** 68. C Withington St Paul *Man* 67-71; C Bingley All SS *Bradf* 71-72; Chapl RAF 72-76; R Publow w Pensford, Compton Dando and Chelwood *B & W* 76-84; V Long Ashton from 84; Hon Can Bris Cathl *Bris* from 86; RD Portishead *B & W* from 86. *The Vicarage, 7 Church Lane, Long Ashton, Bristol BS18 9LU* Long Ashton (0272) 393109

TASSELL, Douglas Rene. b 15. St Edm Hall Ox BA37 MA52. Wycliffe Hall Ox 37. **d** 39 **p** 40. R Delamere *Ches* 69-74; RD Middlewich 69-74; P-in-c Welland *Worc* 75-79; Chapl St Jas Sch Malvern 77-81; AP Hanley Castle, Hanley Swan & Welland 79; rtd 80; Lic to Offic *Worc* 80-85; Perm to Offic from 85. *12 Gardens Walk, Upton-upon-Severn, Worcester WR8 0LL* Upton-upon-Severn (06846) 2205

TASSELL, Canon Dudley Arnold. b 16. K Coll Lon BD49 AKC49. **d** 49 **p** 50. R Rotherhithe St Mary w All SS *S'wark* 63-77; RD Bermondsey 69-76; Hon Can S'wark Cathl 72-76; V Spring Park *Cant* 76-84; RD Croydon Addington 81-84; V Spring Park All SS *S'wark* 85-86; RD Croydon Addington 85; rtd 86; Perm to Offic *Guildf* from 86. *80 Sandy Lane, Woking, Surrey GU22 8BH* Woking (0483) 766154

TATE, Harold Richard. b 24. St Jo Coll Dur BA50. **d** 51 **p** 52. R Blackley St Pet *Man* 60-79; V Alsager Ch Ch *Ches* 79-89; rtd 89. *57 Neville Road, Gargrave, Skipton, N Yorkshire BD23 3RE* Skipton (0756) 748315

TATE, Henry Charles Osmond. b 13. K Coll Lon 64. **d** 65 **p** 66. R Winfrith Newburgh w Chaldon Herring *Sarum* 68-78; V Chardstock 78; V Chardstock *Ex* 78-82; rtd 82. *St Andrews, 31 High Street Close, Wool, Wareham, Dorset BH20 6BW* Wareham (0929) 462890

TATE, John Robert. b 38. Dur Univ BA61 MA71. Cranmer Hall Dur DipTh69. **d** 70 **p** 71. C Bare *Blackb* 70-73; V Over Darwen St Jas 73-81; V Caton w Littledale from 81. *The Vicarage, Brookhouse Road, Brookhouse, Lancaster LA2 9NX* Caton (0524) 770300

TATE, Robert John Ward. b 24. St Jo Coll Morpeth ThL48. **d** 49 **p** 50. Australia from 49; Chapl RN 53-79; QHC 76-79. *58 Sky Point Road, Carey Bay, NSW, Australia 2283* Maitland (49) 592921

TATNALL, Alec James. b 09. Codrington Coll Barbados 51. **d** 52 **p** 53. USA 69-71; I Belf St Mary *Conn* 71-75; C Hale *Guildf* 75-79; rtd 79; Perm to Offic *Ex* from 79. *15 Ashdown Close, Ashdown Road, Reigate, Surrey RH2 7QS* Reigate (0737) 224964

TATTERSALL, Canon George Neville. b 10. Em Coll Cam BA32 MA36. Ridley Hall Cam 32. **d** 33 **p** 34. V Batley All SS *Wakef* 50-85; Hon Can Wakef Cathl 68-85; rtd 85; Perm to Offic *Wakef* from 85; *Ely* from 86. *22 Beach Road, Grafham, Huntingdon, Cambs PE18 0BA* Huntingdon (0480) 811013

TATTERSALL, James. b 31. Sheff Univ BSc53 DipEd54. Linc Th Coll 81. **d** 82 **p** 83. C Boston *Linc* 82-84; C Tyldesley w Shakerley *Man* 84-85; TV Sutton *Liv* from 89. *80 Waterdale Crescent, St Helens, Merseyside WA9 3PD* Marshalls Cross (0744) 815158

TATTON-BROWN, Simon Charles. b 48. Qu Coll Cam BA70 MA78 Man Univ CQSW72. Coll of Resurr Mirfield 78. **d** 79 **p** 80. C Ashton St Mich *Man* 79-82; P-in-c Prestwich St Gabr 82-87; V 87-88; Bp's Dom Chapl 82-88; TR Westhoughton from 88. *St Bartholomew's Rectory, Market Street, Westhoughton, Bolton BL5 3AZ* Westhoughton (0942) 813280

TATTUM, Ian Stuart. b 58. N Lon Poly BA79 Lanc Univ DipRS86 Fitzw Coll Cam BA89. Westcott Ho Cam 87. **d** 90 **p** 91. C Beaconsfield *Ox* from 90. *North Flat, Old Rectory, Beaconsfield, Bucks HP9 2JW* Beaconsfield (0494) 674506

TAUNTON, Archdeacon of. *See* OLYOTT, Ven Leonard Eric

TAUNTON, Suffragan Bishop of. *See* McCULLOCH, Rt Rev Nigel Simeon

TAVERNOR, James Edward. b 23. Lich Th Coll 41 St D Coll Lamp BA49. **d** 50 **p** 51. C Buxton *Derby* 67-69; Perm to Offic *Derby* 70-75; Heref 75-83; St D from 83; rtd 88. *Trenova, Aberarth, Aberaeron, Dyfed SA46 0LT* Aberaeron (0545) 570930

TAVERNOR, William Noel. b 16. Lich Th Coll 37. **d** 40 **p** 41. V Canon Pyon w Kings Pyon and Birley *Heref* 65-88; rtd 88. *Vine Cottage, Kingsland, Leominster, Hereford* Kingsland (056881) 8817

TAVINOR, Michael Edward. b 53. ARCO77 Univ Coll Dur BA75 Em Coll Cam CertEd76 K Coll Lon MMus77 AKC77 Ox Univ BA81 MA86. Ripon Coll Cuddesdon 79. **d** 82 **p** 83. C Ealing St Pet Mt Park *Lon* 82-85; Prec Ely Cathl *Ely* 85-90; Min Can and Sacr 85-90; P-in-c Stuntney 87-90; V Tewkesbury w Walton Cardiff *Glouc* from 90. *The Abbey House, Tewkesbury, Glos GL20 5SR* Tewkesbury (0684) 293333

TAWN, Andrew. b 61. Trin Coll Cam BA83 Ox Univ BA88. Ripon Coll Cuddesdon 86. **d** 89 **p** 90. C Dovecot *Liv* from 89. *8B Grant Road, Liverpool L14 0LQ* 051-489 2163

TAYLER, Michael Frederick. b 20. Fitzw Ho Cam BA50 MA55. Linc Th Coll. **d** 52 **p** 53. C Testwood *Win*

69-70; R Chawton and Farringdon 70-85; RD Alton 74-79; rtd 86. *c/o White, Brooks & Gilman, 19 St Peter's Street, Winchester, Hants SO23 8BU*

TAYLOR, Alan Cecil. b 34. Keble Coll Ox BA57 MA63. Cuddesdon Coll 58. **d** 60 **p** 61. C Blackpool St Steph *Blackb* 60-63; C Chorley St Laur 63-65; V Burnley St Mark from 65. *St Mark's Vicarage, 9 Rossendale Road, Burnley, Lancs BB11 5DQ* Burnley (0282) 28178

TAYLOR, Alan Clive. b 48. Southn Univ BTh79. Sarum Th Coll 69. **d** 74 **p** 75. C Watford St Pet *St Alb* 74-78; C Broxbourne w Wormley 78-83; Chapl to the Deaf 83-91; V Shefford 83-91; R Portishead *B & W* from 91. *The Rectory, Church Road South, Portishead, Bristol BS20 9PU* Portishead (0272) 842284

TAYLOR, Alan Gerald. b 33. Roch Th Coll 61 St Aid Birkenhead 61. **d** 63 **p** 64. C W Bridgford *S'well* 63-66; C E w W Barkwith *Linc* 66-69; V E Stockwith 69-76; V Morton 69-76; Countryside Officer 69-88; R Ulceby w Fordington 76-88; R Willoughby w Sloothby w Claxby 76-88; R Woolpit w Drinkstone *St E* from 88; Rural Min Adv from 88. *The Rectory, Woolpit, Bury St Edmunds, Suffolk IP30 9QP* Elmswell (0359) 42244

TAYLOR, Alan Leonard. b 43. Chich Th Coll 67. **d** 69 **p** 70. C Walton St Mary *Liv* 69-73; C Toxteth St Marg 73-75; V Stanley 75-83; V Leeds St Aid *Ripon* from 84. *The Vicarage, Elford Place, Leeds LS8 5QD* Leeds (0532) 486992

TAYLOR, Alfred Harry Bryant. b 17. St Deiniol's Hawarden 77. **d** 79 **p** 80. Hon C Woodchurch *Ches* 79-85; C 85-87; Hon C from 87. *111 New Hey Road, Birkenhead, Merseyside L49 7NE* 051-677 4933

TAYLOR, Andrew David. b 58. Toronto Univ 82 Ox Univ BA81 MA86. Westcott Ho Cam 85. **d** 87 **p** 89. C Leckhampton SS Phil and Jas w Cheltenham St Jas *Glouc* 87-91; C Cheltenham St Pet from 91. *25 Great Norwood Street, Cheltenham, Glos GL50 2AW* Cheltenham (0242) 583515

TAYLOR, Arthur Alfred. b 32. MA. Ox NSM Course. **d** 83 **p** 84. NSM Monks Risborough *Ox* from 83. *9 Place Farm Way, Monks Risborough, Aylesbury, Bucks HP17 9JJ* Princes Risborough (08444) 7197

TAYLOR, Arthur Harry. b 17. **d** 48 **p** 49. C Kilburn St Aug *Lon* 50-55; rtd 82. *Buckfast Abbey, Buckfastleigh, Devon TQ11 0EE* Buckfastleigh (0364) 43301

TAYLOR, Arthur John. b 17. Lon Univ BD39 BA52. ALCD39. **d** 40 **p** 41. Asst Master K Sch Ely 56-80; Perm to Offic *Ely* 56-85; rtd 80; Perm to Offic *Mon* from 86. *44 Homeforge House, Goldwire Lane, Monmouth, Gwent NP5 3HA* Monmouth (0600) 6269

TAYLOR, Arthur Robert. b 26. ACIS59. Oak Hill Th Coll 67. **d** 68 **p** 69. C Wilmington *Roch* 68-71; C Polegate *Chich* 71-73; R Chesterton w Haddon *Ely* 73-80; P-in-c Alwalton 73-75; R 75-80; R Sawtry 80-91; rtd 91. *10 Faraday Ride, Tonbridge, Kent TN10 4RL* Tonbridge (0732) 358694

TAYLOR, Bernard Richmond Hartley. b 30. Leeds Univ Reading Univ MEd. S Dios Minl Tr Scheme 82. **d** 85 **p** 86. NSM Englefield Green *Guildf* 85-90; NSM Lyddington w Stoke Dry and Seaton *Pet* from 90. *4 Windmill Way, Lyddington, Oakham, Leics LE15 9LY* Uppingham (0572) 822717

TAYLOR, Brian. b 29. FSA83 FRHistS84 Keble Coll Ox BA52 MA56. Linc Th Coll 54. **d** 57 **p** 58. C Spalding St Jo *Linc* 57-60; PC 60-61; Sarawak 62-68; V Leic St Gabr *Leic* 69-75; R Guildf St Nic *Guildf* from 75. *The Rectory, The Flower Walk, Guildford, Surrey GU2 5EP* Guildford (0483) 504895

TAYLOR, Brian. b 38. MBIM Bris Univ BA60 Liv Univ BA70 Southn Univ MA90. Ridley Hall Cam 60. **d** 66 **p** 66. Nigeria 66-72; Perm to Offic *Derby* 74-78; Chapl Chapl Newbury Coll from 76; P-in-c Shaw cum Donnington *Ox* 89-90; R from 90. *The Rectory, Well Meadow, Shaw, Newbury, Berks* Newbury (0635) 40450

TAYLOR, Brian. b 42. St Deiniol's Hawarden 78. **d** 80 **p** 81. C Mold *St As* 80-84; V Bagillt from 84. *The Vicarage, Bagillt, Clwyd CH6 6BZ* Flint (03526) 2732

TAYLOR, Brian Valentine. b 34. St Deiniol's Hawarden 69. **d** 71 **p** 72. C Workington St Mich *Carl* 71-72; C Carl St Aid and Ch Ch 73-74; Chapl Rotterdam Miss to Seamen *Eur* 74-75; Asst Chapl Madrid 75-76; Chapl Marseille w St Raphael Aix-en-Provence etc 77-78; Chapl Alassio w Genoa and Rapallo 78-81; C Higher Broughton *Man* 82-83; P-in-c Cheetwood St Alb 83-84; Lic to Offic 84-85; rtd 85; Perm to Offic *Man* from 85. *5 Kimberley Street, Higher Broughton, Salford M7 0AF* 061-792 2442

TAYLOR, Charles Derek. b 36. Trin Hall Cam BA59 MA62. Ripon Hall Ox 59. **d** 61 **p** 62. C Nottm All SS *S'well* 61-64; C Binley *Cov* 64-67; C Stoke 67-70; R

Purley *Ox* 70-74; V Milton *B & W* from 74; RD Locking 86-87 and from 90. *Milton Vicarage, 461 Locking Road, Weston-super-Mare, Avon BS22 8QW* Weston-super-Mare (0934) 625651

TAYLOR, Charles William. b 53. Selw Coll Cam BA74 MA78. Cuddesdon Coll 74. d 76 p 77. C Wolv *Lich* 76-79; Chapl Westmr Abbey 79-84; V Stanmore *Win* 84-90; R N Stoneham from 90. *The Rectory, 62 Glen Eyre Road, Bassett, Southampton SO2 3NL* Southampton (0703) 768123

TAYLOR, Preb Clive Cavanagh. b 28. MBE91. Cranmer Hall Dur 61. d 63 p 64. C Wembley St Jo *Lon* 63-66; C Edmonton All SS 66-69; V Tottenham St Jo 69-76; RD E Haringey 73-76; Chapl Metrop Police Coll Hendon from 76; Sen Chapl Metrop Police from 78; Dir of Ords 76-85; V Temple Fortune St Barn from 76; Preb St Paul's Cathl from 78; AD W Barnet 79-85. *St Barnabas's Vicarage, 7 Oakfields Road, London NW11 0JA* 081-458 7828

TAYLOR, Dennis James. b 31. ACIS62. Ripon Hall Ox 63. d 68 p 69. C Baswich (or Berkswich) *Lich* 68-77; P-in-c Hastings H Trin *Chich* 77-81; V 81-86; R Catsfield and Crowhurst from 86. *The Rectory, Church Lane, Catsfield, Battle, E Sussex TN33 9DR* Ninfield (0424) 892319

TAYLOR, Very Rev Derek John. b 31. Univ of Wales (Lamp) BA52 Fitzw Ho Cam BA54 MA58 Ex Univ CertEd70. St Mich Coll Llan 55. d 55 p 56. C Newport St Paul *Mon* 55-59; CF (TA) 57-59 and 62-64; CF 59-62; V Bettws *Mon* 62-64; V Exminster *Ex* 64-70; Chapl Prince Rupert Sch Wilhelmshaven 71-75; Chapl R Russell Sch Croydon 75-79; P-in-c Croydon St Andr *Cant* 79-81; V 81-84; Chapl St Andr Sch Croydon 79-84; Chapl Bromsgrove Sch Worcs 84-89; Provost St Chris Cathl Bahrain from 90; Hon Chapl Miss to Seamen from 90. *St Christopher's Cathedral, PO Box 36, Manama, Bahrain* Bahrain (973) 253866

TAYLOR, Edward Frank. b 23. Lon Univ BSc44. Chich Th Coll 50. d 52 p 53. V Hangleton *Chich* 63-73; V Wivelsfield 73-88; rtd 88; Perm to Offic *Bradf* from 88. *4 Clarendon Street, Haworth, Keighley, W Yorkshire BD22 8PT* Haworth (0535) 642493

TAYLOR, Canon Edwin Norman. b 24. Trin Coll Ox BA50 MA50. Ripon Hall Ox 49. d 51 p 52. V Radcliffe St Thos *Man* 59-71; RD Heaton 71-88; R Heaton Moor 71-89; Hon Can Man Cathl 75-89; rtd 89. *79 Mauldeth Road, Stockport, Cheshire SK4 3NB* 061-442 0780

TAYLOR, Eric Hargreaves. b 21. Oak Hill Th Coll 47. d 51 p 52. V Camerton H Trin W Seaton *Carl* 62-71; V Ramsgate St Luke Ch Ch *Cant* 71-85; Chapl Ramsgate Gen Hosp 71-85; rtd 85; Perm to Offic Cant 85-90; Blackb from 89. *27 Pilling Lane, Preesall, Blackpool, Lancs FY6 0EX* Knott End (0253) 811046

TAYLOR, Eric William. b 17. St Jo Coll Dur BA40 DipTh41 MA43. d 41 p 42. V Wingate Grange *Dur* 63-83; rtd 83. *2 The Cottage, West Row, Greatham, Hartlepool, Cleveland TS25 2HW* Hartlepool (0429) 870150

TAYLOR, Francis Oswald. b 10. Chich Th Coll 37. d 40 p 41. P-in-c Flimwell *Chich* 67-78; rtd 78. *12 St Richard's House, Pevensey Road, St Leonards-on-Sea, E Sussex* Hastings (0424) 440537

TAYLOR, Frank. b 02. Kelham Th Coll 22. d 28 p 29. V Lambourn *Ox* 61-70; rtd 70; Perm to Offic *Ox* from 74. *18 Bertie Road, Cumnor, Oxford OX2 9PS* Oxford (0865) 863239

TAYLOR, Frank Hampton. b 49. St Jo Coll Nottm 80. d 82 p 83. C Hoole *Ches* 82-85; C Timperley 85-89; V Birkenhead Ch Ch from 89. *Christ Church Vicarage, 7 Palm Grove, Birkenhead, Merseyside L43 1TE* 051-652 5647 or 652 3990

TAYLOR, Frank Leslie. b 05. St Jo Coll Ox BA27 DipTh28 MA30. Wycliffe Hall Ox 27. d 29 p 30. R E Hoathly *Chich* 62-72; rtd 72. *Manormead Nursing Home, Tilford Road, Hindhead, Surrey GU26 6RA* Hindhead (0428) 604780

TAYLOR, Garry Kenneth. b 53. Edin Univ BMus75 Southn Univ BTh81. Sarum & Wells Th Coll 76. d 79 p 80. C Southsea H Spirit *Portsm* 79-82; C Croydon *Cant* 82-84; C Croydon St Jo *S'wark* 85-86; VC S'well Minster *S'well* 86-90; V Portsea St Alb *Portsm* from 90. *St Alban's Vicarage, Copnor Road, Portsmouth PO3 5AL* Portsmouth (0705) 662626

TAYLOR, George Davidson. b 27. St Aid Birkenhead 60. d 62 p 63. V Shuttleworth *Man* 65-71; V Litherland St Phil *Liv* 71-85; rtd 85. *34 Beckwith Crescent, Harrogate, N Yorkshire HG2 0BQ* Harrogate (0423) 560023

TAYLOR, George James Trueman. b 36. Ripon Hall Ox 66. d 69 p 70. C Wavertree H Trin *Liv* 69-73; V Newton-le-Willows 73-79; V Stoneycroft All SS 79-83; V Haigh from 83. *The Vicarage, Copperas Lane, Haigh, Wigan, Lancs WN2 1PA* Wigan (0942) 831255

TAYLOR, Godfrey Alan. b 36. Oak Hill Th Coll DipTh60. d 61 p 62. C Herne Bay Ch Ch *Cant* 61-64; C Tunbridge Wells St Jas *Roch* 64-68; V Guernsey H Trin *Win* 68-81; V Boscombe St Jo from 81. *St John's Vicarage, 17 Browning Avenue, Bournemouth BH5 1NR* Bournemouth (0202) 396667

TAYLOR, Gordon. b 46. AKC68. St Aug Coll Cant 69. d 70 p 71. C Rotherham *Sheff* 70-74; P-in-c Brightside St Thos 74-79; P-in-c Brightside St Marg 77-79; V Brightside St Thos and St Marg 79-82; R Kirk Sandall and Edenthorpe from 82. *The Rectory, 31 Doncaster Road, Kirk Sandall, Doncaster, S Yorkshire DN3 1HP* Doncaster (0302) 882861

TAYLOR, Gordon Clifford. b 15. VRD56 and Bars 66. FSA Ch Coll Cam BA37 MA41. Ripon Hall Ox 37. d 38 p 39. C Ealing St Steph Castle Hill *Lon* 38-40; Chapl RNVR 40-58; Asst Master Eton Coll 46-49; R St Giles-in-the-Fields *Lon* from 49; RD Finsbury and Holborn 54-67; Chapl RNR 58-70. *St Giles's Rectory, 15A Gower Street, London WC1E 6HG* 071-636 4646

TAYLOR, Henry. b 46. St Cath Coll Ox BA69 MA73. Liturg Inst Trier DipLit Cuddesdon Coll 70. d 73 p 74. C Tettenhall Regis *Lich* 73-76; C Walsall 76-80; V Witton le Wear and Firtree *Dur* from 80. *Fir Tree Vicarage, Hargill Hill, Howden-le-Wear, Crook, Co Durham DL15 8HL* Bishop Auckland (0388) 764938

TAYLOR, Canon Herbert Cyril. b 06. Em Coll Cam BA29 MA34. Ridley Hall Cam 29. d 31 p 32. V Orpington Ch Ch *Roch* 42-73; Hon Can Roch Cathl 64-73; rtd 73. *Room 3, Abbeyfield, 7 Dry Hill Park Crescent, Tonbridge, Kent TN10 3BJ* Tonbridge (0732) 359340

✠**TAYLOR, Rt Rev Humphrey Vincent.** b 38. Pemb Coll Cam BA61 MA66 Lon Univ MA70. Coll of Resurr Mirfield 61. d 63 p 64 c 91. C N Hammersmith St Kath *Lon* 63-64; C Notting Hill St Mark 64-66; USPG 67-71; Malawi 67-71; Chapl Bp Grosseteste Coll Linc 72-74; Sec Chapls in HE Gen Syn Bd of Educn 75-80; Sec Miss Progr USPG 80-84; Sec USPG 84-91; Hon Can Bris Cathl *Bris* from 86; Lic to Offic *S'wark* 89-91; Suff Bp Selby *York* from 91. *8 Bankside Close, Upper Poppleton, York YO2 6LH* York (0904) 795342

TAYLOR, James McMurray. b 16. TCD BA38 MA. d 39 p 40. I Castle Archdale and Killadeas *Clogh* 57-80; rtd 80. *42 Main Street, Lisbellaw, Co Fermanagh BT94 5ER* Lisbellaw (0365) 87259

TAYLOR, Jan William Karel. b 59. QUB BD82 MSocSc89 TCD DipTh84. d 84 p 85. C Belf St Simon w St Phil *Conn* 84-87; I Belf St Paul from 87. *The Parsonage, 50 Sunningdale Park, Belfast BT14 6RW* Belfast (0232) 715413

TAYLOR, Canon John Ambrose. b 19. K Coll Lon 45. Coll of Resurr Mirfield 49. d 50 p 51. V Ches St Oswald w Lt St Jo *Ches* 63-72; TV Ches 72-74; Hon Can Gib Cathl *Eur* from 74; V Withyham St Jo *Chich* 74-88; RD Rotherfield 77-87; P-in-c Withyham St Mich 87; rtd 88. *11 Park View, Buxted, Uckfield, E Sussex TN22 4LS* Uckfield (0825) 813475

TAYLOR, John Andrew. b 53. Linc Th Coll 86. d 88 p 89. C Stanley *Liv* from 88. *The Vicarage Flat, 8 Derwent Square, Liverpool L13 6QT* 051-228 5252

TAYLOR, John Andrew Wemyss. b 27. RCS LDS51 PhD62. Sarum & Wells Th Coll 70. d 72 p 73. C Ashburton w Buckland-in-the-Moor *Ex* 72-76; P-in-c E Portlemouth 76-79; P-in-c S Pool w Chivelstone 76-79; R E Portlemouth, S Pool and Chivelstone 79-81; Miss to Seamen from 81; V Salcombe *Ex* 81-88; RD Woodleigh 83-88; Perm to Offic from 88. *Waverley, Grand View Road, Hope Cove, Kingsbridge, Devon TQ7 3HF* Kingsbridge (0548) 561332

✠**TAYLOR, Rt Rev John Bernard.** b 29. Ch Coll Cam BA50 MA54 Jes Coll Cam 52 Hebrew Univ Jerusalem 54. Ridley Hall Cam 55. d 56 p 57 c 80. C Morden *S'wark* 56-59; V Henham *Chelmsf* 59-64; V Elsenham 59-64; Sen Tutor Oak Hill Th Coll 64-65; Vice-Prin 65-72; V Woodford Wells 72-75; Dioc Dir of Ords 72-80; Adn W Ham 75-80; Bp St Alb from 80. *Abbey Gate House, 4 Abbey Mill Lane, St Albans, Herts AL3 4HD* St Albans (0727) 53305

TAYLOR, John Charles Browne. b 23. CEng58 MIEE58. Oak Hill Th Coll 81. d 82 p 83. NSM Havering-atte-Bower *Chelmsf* 82-85; NSM Collier Row St Jas and Havering-atte-Bower 86-89; rtd 89; Lic to Offic *Chelmsf* from 89. *Giffords, North Road, Havering-atte-Bower, Romford RM4 1PX* Romford (0708) 742072

TAYLOR, John Denys. b 20. Leeds Univ BA49. Coll of Resurr Mirfield. **d** 51 **p** 52. C Leeds St Marg *Ripon* 51-54; India 54-59; C Gt Grimsby St Jas *Linc* 59-66; New Zealand from 66. *155 Queen Street, Northcote, Auckland 9, New Zealand* Auckland (9) 480-5968

TAYLOR, Canon John Frederick. b 20. St Chad's Coll Dur 39. Ely Th Coll 59. **d** 61 **p** 62. V Middlesb St Cuth *York* 64-71; V Skipsea w Ulrome 71-79; P-in-c Barmston w Fraisthorpe 77-79; Can and Preb York Minster from 79; R Skipsea w Ulrome and Barmston w Fraisthorpe 79-82; V Hemingbrough 82-85; rtd 85. *19 Willow Garth, Eastrington, Goole, N Humberside DN14 7QP* Howden (0430) 410647

TAYLOR, Canon John Michael. b 30. St Aid Birkenhead 56. **d** 59 **p** 60. C Chorley St Jas *Blackb* 59-62; C Broughton 62-64; Chapl St Boniface Coll Warminster 64-68; V Altham w Clayton le Moors *Blackb* 68-76; RD Accrington 71-76; Can Res Blackb Cathl from 76. *22 Billinge Avenue, Blackburn BB2 6SD* Blackburn (0254) 61152

✠**TAYLOR, Rt Rev John Mitchell.** b 32. Aber Univ MA54. Edin Th Coll 54. **d** 56 **p** 57 **c** 91. C Aber St Marg *Ab* 56-58; R Glas H Cross *Glas* 58-64; R Glas St Ninian 64-73; R Dumfries 73-91; Chapl Dumfries and Galloway R Infirmary 73-91; Can St Mary's Cathl *Glas* 79-91; Bp Glas from 91. *Bishop's House, 48 Drymen Road, Bearsden, Glasgow G61 2RH* 041-943 0612

TAYLOR, John Ralph. b 48. St Jo Coll Nottm BTh74. **d** 74 **p** 75. C Clitheroe St Jas *Blackb* 74-77; C Kidsgrove *Lich* 77-79; C Hawkwell *Chelmsf* 79-82; V Linc St Geo Swallowbeck *Linc* from 82. *St George's Vicarage, Eastbrook Road, Lincoln LN6 7EW* Lincoln (0522) 683394

TAYLOR, Canon John Rowland. b 29. OBE74. St Mich Coll Llan 57. **d** 58 **p** 59. C Caerau St Cynfelin *Llan* 58-59; C Aberdare 59-61; Miss to Seamen 61-88; Tanganyika 61-64; Tanzania 64-73; Adn Dar-es-Salaam 65-73; V Gen Dar-es-Salaam 67-73; Thailand 73-84; Chapl Rotterdam w Schiedam *Eur* 84-88; V Warnham Chich from 88. *The Vicarage, Warnham, Horsham, W Sussex RH12 3QW* Horsham (0403) 65041

✠**TAYLOR, Rt Rev John Vernon.** b 14. Trin Coll Cam BA36 St Cath Soc *Ox* BA38 MA41. Wycliffe Coll Toronto Hon DD64 Wycliffe Hall Ox 36. **d** 38 **p** 39 **c** 75. C St Marylebone All So w SS Pet and Jo *Lon* 38-40; C St Helens St Helen *Liv* 40-43; CMS 43-63; Gen Sec CMS 63-74; Bp Win 75-85; rtd 85; Perm to Offic *Ox* from 86. *Camleigh, 65 Aston Street, Oxford OX4 1EW* Oxford (0865) 248502

TAYLOR, Joseph Robin Christopher. b 34. St Aid Birkenhead 58. **d** 61 **p** 62. C Aldershot St Mich *Guildf* 61-64; C Fleet 64-68; R Manaton *Ex* 69-74; R N Bovey 69-74; V Dawlish 74-87; P-in-c Christow, Ashton, Trusham and Bridford 87-88; R from 88. *The Rectory, Christow, Exeter EX6 7PE* Christow (0647) 52845

TAYLOR, Justin Wray Lindsay. b 39. Moray Ord Course 77. **d** 84 **p** 87. Hon C Nairn *Mor* 84-87; Hon C Inverness St Andr from 87. *68 High Street, Ardersier, Inverness IV1 2QF* Ardersier (0667) 62509

TAYLOR, Kenneth Charles. b 24. St Deiniol's Hawarden 76. **d** 76 **p** 77. C Wilmslow *Ches* 76-79; V Willaston from 79; Chapl Clatterbridge Hosp Wirral from 86. *The Vicarage, Willaston, South Wirral* 051-327 4737

TAYLOR, Kenneth Gordon. b 30. Selw Coll Cam BA54 MA58. Chich Th Coll 54. **d** 56 **p** 57. C S Lynn *Nor* 56-60; C Holbeck St Matt *Ripon* 60-62; C Moor Allerton 62-71; R Northwold *Ely* 71-81; P-in-c Harlton 81-87; R 87-89; P-in-c Haslingfield 81-87; V 87-89; P-in-c Thornage w Brinton w Hunworth and Stody *Nor* from 89; P-in-c Briningham from 89; P-in-c Melton Constable w Swanton Novers from 89. *The Rectory, Brinton, Melton Constable, Norfolk NR24 2QF* Melton Constable (0263) 860295

TAYLOR, Canon Marcus Beresford. b 13. TCD BA35 MA43. CITC 36. **d** 36 **p** 37. I Stillorgan *D & G* 47-78; Can Ch Ch Cathl Dub 71-86; I Stillorgan w Blackrock 78-86; rtd 86. *78 Beech Trees, Galloping Green Lane, Stillorgan, Dublin, Irish Republic* Dublin (1) 288-4196

TAYLOR, Marcus Iles. b 16. Ely Th Coll 48. **d** 49 **p** 50. V Cookham Dean *Ox* 56-71; rtd 81. *Kimbers, Budnick, Perranporth, Cornwall* Truro (0872) 572143

TAYLOR, Mrs Marian Alexandra. b 62. Newc Univ BA85. Qu Coll Birm 89. **d** 91. C Earls Barton *Pet* from 91. *The Methodist Manse, 96A Kingsway, Wellingborough, Northants NN8 2PD* Wellingborough (0933) 222357

TAYLOR, Mark Frederick. b 62. N Ireland Poly BA84. TCD DipTh87. **d** 87 **p** 88. C Ballymacarrett St

Patr *D & D* 87-90; C Dundela from 90; Hon Chapl Miss to Seamen from 90. *2A Sydenham Avenue, Belfast BT4 2DR* Belfast (0232) 655969

TAYLOR, Michael Alan. b 47. Bris Univ CertEd70 Lon Univ BD85. Trin Coll Bris 72. **d** 76 **p** 77. C Chilwell *S'well* 76-79; Chapl RAF 79-87; New Zealand from 87. *1 Merton Place, Bryndwr, Christchurch 5, New Zealand* Christchurch (3) 352-4788

TAYLOR, Michael Allan. b 50. Nottm Univ BTh80. St Jo Coll Nottm 76. **d** 80 **p** 81. C Bowling St Jo *Bradf* 80-82; C Otley 82-85; P-in-c Low Moor St Mark from 85. *St Mark's Vicarage, Low Moor, Bradford, W Yorkshire BD12 0UA* Bradford (0274) 677754

TAYLOR, Michael Barry. b 38. Bps' Coll Cheshunt 63. **d** 65 **p** 66. C Leeds St Cypr Harehills *Ripon* 65-68; C Stanningley St Thos 68-70; V Hunslet Moor St Pet and St Cuth 70-78; V Starbeck from 78. *The Vicarage, High Street, Harrogate, N Yorkshire HG2 7LW* Harrogate (0423) 883036 or 889856

TAYLOR, Michael Frank Chatterton. b 30. St Aid Birkenhead 59. **d** 61 **p** 62. C Knighton St Jo *Leic* 61-65; V Briningham *Nor* 65-86; R Melton Constable w Swanton Novers 65-86; P-in-c Thornage w Brinton w Hunworth and Stody 85-86; R Lyng w Sparham 86-90; R Elsing w Bylaugh 86-90; R Lyng, Sparham, Elsing and Bylaugh from 90. *The Rectory, Lyng, Norwich NR9 5RA* Norwich (0603) 872381

TAYLOR, Michael John. b 63. Lanc Univ BA85. Linc Th Coll 86. **d** 88 **p** 89. C Carl St Aid and Ch Ch *Carl* 88-91; C Loughton St Jo *Chelmsf* from 91. *St Francis House, 68 Grosvenor Drive, Loughton, Essex IG10 2LG* 081-508 0690

TAYLOR, Michael Joseph. b 49. Gregorian Univ Rome STB72 PhL74 Birm Univ MA81. English Coll Rome 67. **d** 72 **p** 73. In RC Ch 72-83; Hon C Newport Pagnell w Lathbury *Ox* 83-86; TV Langley Marish 86-90; Vice Prin E Midl Min Tr Course *S'well* from 90. *52 Parkside Gardens, Wollaton, Nottingham NG8 2PQ* Nottingham (0602) 283111

TAYLOR, Michael Laurence. b 43. ARCM68 Ch Coll Cam BA66 MA70 CertEd72 MPhil88. Cuddesdon Coll 66. **d** 68 **p** 69. C Westbury-on-Trym H Trin *Bris* 68-72; Asst Chapl Wellington Coll Berks 72-76; C St Helier *S'wark* 76-78; TV Bedminster *Bris* 78-82; P-in-c Chippenham St Andr w Tytherton Lucas 82-88; V 88-89; Dioc Ecum Officer *B & W* 89-90; P-in-c Rodney Stoke w Draycott 89-90. *21 Bath Road, Wells, Somerset BA5 2DJ* Wells (0749) 670348

TAYLOR, Michael Stewart. St Mich Coll Llan BTh. **d** 91. C Llangunnor and Cwmffrwd *St D* from 91. *6 Awel Tywi, Penymorfa, Llangynnwr, Carmarthen, Dyfed SA31 2NL* Carmarthen (0267) 234606

TAYLOR, Neil Hamish. b 48. Open Univ BA87. Linc Th Coll 72. **d** 75 **p** 76. C Rotherham *Sheff* 75-78; C Doncaster St Geo 78-82; P-in-c Knaresdale 82-87; V Alston cum Garrigill w Nenthead and Kirkhaugh *Newc* 82-87; TR Alston Team 87-88; V Maidstone St Paul *Cant* from 88. *St Paul's Vicarage, 130 Boxley Road, Maidstone, Kent ME14 2AH* Maidstone (0622) 691926

TAYLOR, Neville Patrick. b 40. Trin Coll Bris DipTh82. **d** 82 **p** 83. C Old Trafford St Jo *Man* 82-84; C Hurst 84-87; R Levenshulme St Mark from 87. *St Mark's Rectory, 331 Mount Road, Levenshulme, Manchester M19 3HW* 061-224 9551

TAYLOR, Nicholas James. b 46. St Chad's Coll Dur BA67 DipTh68. **d** 69 **p** 70. C Beamish *Dur* 69-74; C Styvechale *Cov* 74-77; P-in-c Wilmcote w Billesley 77-79; P-in-c Aston Cantlow 77-79; V Aston Cantlow and Wilmcote w Billesley 79-87; V Cov St Fran N Radford from 87. *St Francis's Vicarage, Treherne Road, Coventry CV6 3DY* Coventry (0203) 595178

TAYLOR, Nigel Thomas Wentworth. b 60. Bris Univ BA82 Ox Univ BA86. Wycliffe Hall Ox 84. **d** 87 **p** 88. C Ches Square St Mich w St Phil *Lon* from 87. *2 Elizabeth Street, London SW1W 9RB* 071-824 8873

TAYLOR, Norman. b 26. CCC Cam BA49 MA52. Cuddesdon Coll 49. **d** 51 **p** 52. R Lt Wilbraham *Ely* 55-71; Chapl St Faith's Sch Cam from 71; Lic to Offic *Ely* from 72; rtd 91. *57 De Freville Avenue, Cambridge CB4 1HW* Cambridge (0223) 321201

TAYLOR, Norman Adrian. b 48. St D Coll Lamp DipTh73. **d** 73 **p** 74. C Fleur-de-Lis *Mon* 73-75; C W Drayton *Lon* 75-79; C-in-c Hayes St Edm CD 79-85; V Hayes St Edm 85-87; V Pilton w Ashford *Ex* 87-89; V Sidley Chich from 89. *All Saints' Vicarage, Bexhill-on-Sea, E Sussex TN39 5HA* Bexhill-on-Sea (0424) 221071

TAYLOR, Norman Wyatt. b 23. Wells Th Coll 58. **d** 60 **p** 61. V Bishop's Cannings *Sarum* 69-77; V Bishop's Cannings, All Cannings etc 77-80; V W Moors 80-87;

rtd 88; Perm to Offic *Ex* from 89. *3 Kits Close, Chudleigh, Newton Abbot, Devon TQ13 0LG*   Newton Abbot (0626) 852733

TAYLOR, Paul Frank David. b 60. ARICS87 Leic Poly BSc84. Trin Coll Bris BA91. **d** 91. C Edin St Thos *Edin* from 91. *81 Glasgow Road, Corstorphine, Edinburgh EH12 8LJ*   031-334 4434

TAYLOR, Paul Latham. b 11. **d** 49 **p** 50. Chapl Milford Chest Hosp 70-72; Warden Coll of St Barn Lingfield 72-77; rtd 77; Perm to Offic *Win* from 83. *22 Halton Close, Bransgore, Christchurch, Dorset BH23 8HZ*   Bransgore (0425) 72137

TAYLOR, Paul Stanley. b 53. Ox Univ BEd. Westcott Ho Cam. **d** 84 **p** 85. C Bush Hill Park St Steph *Lon* 84-88; Asst Dir Post Ord Tr Edmonton Episc Area from 87; V Southgate St Andr from 88. *St Andrew's Vicarage, 184 Chase Side, London N14 5HN*   081-886 7523

TAYLOR, Peter David. b 38. FCA. N Ord Course 77. **d** 80 **p** 81. C Penwortham St Mary *Blackb* 80-84; V Farington from 84. *St Paul's Vicarage, 150 Croston Road, Farington, Preston, Lancs PR5 3PR*   Preston (0772) 38999

TAYLOR, Peter David. b 47. Liv Univ BEd74 Man Univ MEd78 Lanc Univ MA88. N Ord Course 78. **d** 81 **p** 82. C Formby H Trin *Liv* 81-84; V Stoneycroft All SS from 84. *All Saints' Vicarage, West Oakhill Park, Liverpool L13 4BW*   051-228 3581

TAYLOR, Peter Flint. b 44. Qu Coll Cam BA65 MA69. Lon Coll of Div BD70. **d** 70 **p** 71. C Highbury New Park St Aug *Lon* 70-73; C Plymouth St Andr w St Paul and St Geo *Ex* 73-77; V Ironville *Derby* 77-83; P-in-c Riddings 82-83; R Rayleigh *Chelmsf* from 83; Chapl HM Young Offender Inst Bullwood Hall 85-90; RD Rochford *Chelmsf* from 89. *The Rectory, Hockley Road, Rayleigh, Essex SS6 8BA*   Rayleigh (0268) 742151

TAYLOR, Peter John. b 40. Oak Hill Th Coll 62. **d** 65 **p** 66. C St Paul's Cray St Barn *Roch* 65-69; C Woking St Jo *Guildf* 69-77; R Necton w Holme Hale *Nor* from 77; RD Breckland from 86. *The Rectory, Necton, Swaffham, Norfolk PE37 8HT*   Swaffham (0760) 22021

TAYLOR, Peter John. b 46. Trin Coll Bris 71. **d** 73 **p** 74. C Walshaw Ch Ch *Man* 73-75; C Rodbourne Cheney *Bris* 75-78; Asst Chapl HM Pris Pentonville 78-79; Chapl HM Borstal Roch 79-84; HM Pris Highpoint 84-90; Asst Chapl Gen of Pris from 90. *c/o Home Office, Calthorpe House, Hagley Road, Birmingham B16 8QR*   021-455 9855

TAYLOR, Peter John. b 60. Edin Th Coll 83. **d** 87 **p** 88. C Edin SS Phil and Jas *Edin* 87-90; USA from 90. *St Paul's Episcopal Church, 1221 Wass Street, Tustin, California 92680, USA*   Tustin (714) 573-0755

TAYLOR, Peter Joseph. b 41. Bps' Coll Cheshunt 66. **d** 68 **p** 69. C Wollaton *S'well* 68-71; C Cockington *Ex* 71-74; V Broadhembury 74-79; V Broadhembury w Payhembury 79-81; V Gt Staughton *Ely* 81-86; Chapl HM Young Offender Inst Gaynes Hall from 81; R Offord D'Arcy w Offord Cluny *Ely* from 86; V Gt Paxton from 86. *The Rectory, Offord D'Arcy, Huntingdon, Cambs PE18 9RH*   Huntingdon (0480) 810588

TAYLOR, Philip George. b 49. Bp Otter Coll BEd78 St Jo Coll Nottm 86. **d** 88 **p** 89. C Margate H Trin *Cant* 88-91; TV Whitstable from 91. *St Alphege House, 11 Kimberley Grove, Seasalter, Whitstable, Kent CT5 4AY*   Whitstable (0227) 276795

TAYLOR, Ralph Urmson. b 28. Tulsa Univ MA72 Man Coll of Educn DipEd74. Kelham Th Coll BD56. **d** 56 **p** 57. C Redcar *York* 56-60; C Bridlington Quay H Trin 60-62; C Sewerby w Marton 60-62; USA 62-65; Chapl Holland Hall Sch from 65. *230 Garforth, Chadderton, Oldham*

TAYLOR, Raymond. b 34. Lon Coll of Div 62. **d** 65 **p** 66. C Pennington *Man* 65-70; P-in-c Wombridge *Lich* 70-80; R S Normanton *Derby* 80-88; RD Alfreton 86-88; V Youlgreave, Middleton, Stanton-in-Peak etc from 88. *The Vicarage, Youlgreave, Bakewell, Derbys DE4 1WL*   Bakewell (0629) 636285

TAYLOR, Raymond Montgomery. b 43. Oak Hill Th Coll 77. **d** 80 **p** 81. Hon C Cricklewood St Pet *Lon* 80-85; Hon C Golders Green 85-87; V New Southgate St Paul from 87. *St Paul's Vicarage, 11 Woodland Road, London N11 1PN*   081-361 1946

TAYLOR, Richard. b 46. Reading Univ BA68. Sarum & Wells Th Coll 70. **d** 73 **p** 74. C Swindon Ch Ch *Bris* 73-76; P-in-c Charlton w Brokenborough and Hankerton 76-79; P-in-c Croydon St Matt *Cant* 79-81; V 81-84; V Croydon St Matt *S'wark* from 85. *The Vicarage, 7 Brownlow Road, Croydon CR0 5JT*   081-688 5055

TAYLOR, Richard David. b 44. Worc Coll Ox BA67 MA70. Coll of Resurr Mirfield 67. **d** 69 **p** 70. C

Barrow St Geo w St Luke *Carl* 69-73; C Gosforth All SS *Newc* 73-80; TR Newc Epiphany 80-83; V Tynemouth Priory from 83. *Holy Saviour Vicarage, 1 Crossway, North Shields, Tyne & Wear NE30 2LB*   091-257 1636

TAYLOR, Preb Richard John. b 21. Kelham Th Coll 38. **d** 45 **p** 46. R Edgmond *Lich* 68-77; V Streetly 77-87; Preb Lich Cathl 78-87; rtd 87; Perm to Offic *Lich* from 87. *15 Covey Close, Lichfield, Staffs WS13 6BS*   Lichfield (0543) 268558

TAYLOR, Richard John. b 46. Ripon Coll Cuddesdon 85. **d** 85 **p** 86. C Moseley St Mary *Birm* 85-87; V Kingsbury 87-91; TR Hodge Hill from 91. *The Rectory, Hodge Hill Common, Birmingham B36 8AG*   021-747 2094 or 747 9262

TAYLOR, Roger. b 21. Birkb Coll Lon BA50 Leeds Univ MA59. Oak Hill Th Coll 47. **d** 51 **p** 52. V Felixstowe SS Pet and Paul *St E* 68-81; P-in-c Gt and Lt Thurlow w Lt Bradley 81-82; TV Haverhill w Withersfield, the Wrattings etc 82-84; R Hopton, Market Weston, Barningham etc 84-86; rtd 86; Perm to Offic *St E* from 87. *Chapel House, Lindsey, Ipswich, Suffolk IP7 6QA*   Boxford (0787) 211120

TAYLOR, Canon Roland Haydn. b 29. St Chad's Coll Dur BA53 DipTh55. **d** 55 **p** 56. C N Gosforth *Newc* 55-58; C Barnsley St Mary *Wakef* 58-61; V Brotherton 61-68; V Purston cum S Featherstone 68-76; RD Pontefract from 74; R Badsworth from 76; Hon Can Wakef Cathl from 81. *The Rectory, Main Street, Badsworth, Pontefract, W Yorkshire WF9 1AF*   Pontefract (0977) 643642

TAYLOR, Canon Rowland Wilfred. b 09. AKC34. **d** 34 **p** 35. V Tunbridge Wells St Barn *Roch* 62-74; RD Tunbridge Wells 73-74; rtd 74; Perm to Offic *Chich* from 74. *College of St Barnabas, Blackberry Lane, Lingfield, Surrey RH7 6NT*   Dormans Park (034287) 352

TAYLOR, Roy William. b 37. Ch Coll Cam BA61 MA65. Clifton Th Coll 61. **d** 63 **p** 64. C Blackb Sav *Blackb* 63-66; C Hensingham *Carl* 66-68; Taiwan 71-79; TV Bushbury *Lich* 79-85; OMF from 85; Perm to Offic *Lich* from 85. *81 Newbridge Crescent, Tettenhall, Wolverhampton WV6 0LH*   Wolverhampton (0902) 754474

TAYLOR, Stella Isabelle. b 31. S Dios Minl Tr Scheme 86. **d** 89. NSM Haworth *Bradf* from 89. *Home Cottage, 4 Clarendon Street, Haworth, Keighley, W Yorkshire BD22 8PT*   Haworth (0535) 642493

TAYLOR, Stephen Gordon. b 35. Bris Univ BA60. Ridley Hall Cam 60. **d** 62 **p** 63. C Gt Baddow *Chelmsf* 62-65; C Portsdown *Portsm* 65-69; P-in-c Elvedon *Ex* 69-70; R 70-75; P-in-c Eriswell 69-70; R 70-75; P-in-c Icklingham 69-70; R 70-75; Chapl St Felix Sch Southwold 75-77; R Lt Shelford w Newton *Ely* from 77. *The Rectory, Manor Road, Little Shelford, Cambridge CB2 5HF*   Cambridge (0223) 843710

TAYLOR, Stephen James. b 48. Chich Th Coll 70. **d** 73 **p** 74. C Tottenham St Paul *Lon* 73-76; St Vincent 78-85; Grenada 85-88; C-in-c Hammersmith SS Mich and Geo White City Estate CD *Lon* from 88. *The Parsonage, 1 Commonwealth Avenue, London W12 7QR*   081-743 7100

TAYLOR, Stephen Ronald. b 55. Cranmer Hall Dur 80. **d** 83 **p** 84. C Ches le Street *Dur* 83-87; V Newbottle from 87. *The Vicarage, Newbottle, Houghton le Spring, Tyne & Wear DH4 4EP*   091-584 3244

TAYLOR, Stewart. b 51. St Jo Coll Dur 74. **d** 77 **p** 78. C Norwood *S'wark* 77-81; C Surbiton Hill Ch Ch from 81. *181 Elgar Avenue, Surbiton, Surrey KT5 9JX*   081-399 1503

TAYLOR, Stuart Bryan. b 40. St Chad's Coll Dur BA64 DipTh66. **d** 66 **p** 67. C Portsea N End St Mark *Portsm* 66-70; C Epsom St Martin *Guildf* 70-76; Perm to Offic *Bris* from 76; Chapl Clifton Coll Bris 76-88; Dir Bloxham Project from 88. *62 Providence Lane, Long Ashton, Bristol BS18 9DN*   Bristol (0272) 393625

TAYLOR, Mrs Susan Mary. b 48. Univ of Wales (Swansea) BA69 Univ of Wales (Lamp) LTh72. St D Coll Lamp 70. **dss** 72 **d** 87. Chepstow *Mon* 72-73; Mynyddislwyn 73-75; Perm to Offic *Lon* 75-79; Hayes St Edm 79-87; NSM Pilton w Ashford *Ex* 87-89; NSM Sidley *Chich* from 89. *All Saints' Vicarage, Sidley, Bexhill-on-Sea, E Sussex TN39 5HA*   Bexhill-on-Sea (0424) 221071

TAYLOR, Thomas. b 33. Sarum & Wells Th Coll 77. **d** 80 **p** 81. NSM Heatherlands St Jo *Sarum* 80-82; TV Kinson 82-88; TV Shaston from 88. *The Vicarage, Motcombe, Shaftesbury, Dorset SP7 9NX*   Shaftesbury (0747) 2168

TAYLOR, Thomas. b 42. Dur Univ BA64. Linc Th Coll 64. **d** 66 **p** 67. C Clitheroe St Mary *Blackb* 66-69; C Skerton St Luke 69-71; C-in-c Penwortham St Leon CD

71-72; V Penwortham St Leon 72-78; R Poulton-le-Sands 78-81; P-in-c Morecambe St Lawr 78-81; R Poulton-le-Sands w Morecambe St Laur 81-85; Chapl Ld Wandsworth Coll Long Sutton from 85. *Lord Wandsworth College, Long Sutton, Basingstoke, Hants* Basingstoke (0256) 862206

TAYLOR, Thomas Fish. b 13. Glas Univ MA46. Kelham Th Coll 30. **d** 36 **p** 37. P-in-c Rattery *Ex* 69-79; rtd 79; Perm to Offic *Ex* from 79. *Digby House, 40 Avenue Road, Wimborne, Dorset* Wimborne (0202) 841596

TAYLOR, Thomas Ronald Bennett. b 23. TCD BA46 MA54. **d** 47 **p** 48. I Tynan w Middletown *Arm* 68-85; rtd 85. *34 Kernan Park, Portadown, Co Armagh BT63 5QY* Portadown (0762) 337230

TAYLOR, William Austin. b 36. Linc Th Coll 65. **d** 67 **p** 68. C Tyldesley w Shakerley *Man* 67-71; R Cheetham St Mark 71-79; V Peel 79-90; AD Farnworth 83-90; V Pelton *Dur* from 90. *The Vicarage, Church Road, Pelton, Chester le Street, Co Durham DH2 1XB* 091-370 2204

TAYLOR, William David. b 60. Southn Univ BTh90. Sarum & Wells Th Coll 87. **d** 90 **p** 91. C Washington *Dur* from 90. *101 Barmston Way, Washington, Tyne & Wear NE38 8DE* 091-415 1487

TAYLOR, William Henry. b 56. FRAS MA MTh MPhil86. Westcott Ho Cam. **d** 83 **p** 84. C Maidstone All SS and St Phil w Tovil *Cant* 83-86; Abp's Adv on Orthodox Affairs 86-88; C St Marylebone All SS *Lon* 86-88; Chapl Guy's Hosp Lon 88; CMS from 88; Jordan from 88. *Church of the Redeemer, PO Box 598, Amman, Jordan*

TAYLOR, William Richard de Carteret Martin. b 33. CCC Cam MA57. Westcott Ho Cam 58. **d** 59 **p** 60. C Eastney *Portsm* 59-63; Chapl RN 63-67 and 70-87; V Childe Okeford *Sarum* 67-70; V Manston w Hamoon 67-70; QHC from 83; TR Tisbury *Sarum* 87-89; Chapl Hatf Poly *St Alb* from 89. *Hatfield Polytechnic, College Lane, Hatfield AL10 9AB* Hatfield (0707) 279000

TAYLOR, William Walter Joseph. b 11. Lon Coll of Div ALCD42 LTh74. **d** 41 **p** 42. R Fulmer *Ox* 64-74; rtd 74. *8 Manormead, Tilford Road, Hindhead, Surrey GU26 6RA* Hindhead (0428) 606924

TEAGE, Alan Dixon. b 17. Ripon Hall Ox 59. **d** 61 **p** 62. V Blackawton *Ex* 63-76; V Blackawton and Stoke Fleming 76-83; RD Woodleigh 80-83; rtd 83; Perm to Offic *Ex* from 83. *Honeysuckle Cottage, Stoke Fleming, Dartmouth, Devon TQ6 0PZ* Stoke Fleming (0803) 770354

TEAGUE, Dr Gaythorne Derrick. b 24. MRCGP53 Bris Univ MB, ChB49 DPH. **d** 74 **p** 75. NSM Bris St Andr Hartcliffe *Bris* 74-86; Perm to Offic *B & W* 79-86; NSM Blagdon w Compton Martin and Ubley from 86. *Innisfree, Bell Square, Blagdon, Bristol BS18 6UB* Blagdon (0761) 62671

TEAGUE, Robert Hayden. b 15. Univ of Wales (Ban). Dorchester Miss Coll 36 St Deiniol's Hawarden. **d** 63 **p** 64. V Llangernyw, Gwytherin and Llanddewi *St As* 66-77; V Meliden and Gwaenysgor 77-83; rtd 83. *4 Ffordd Tanrallt, Melidan, Prestatyn, Clwyd LL19 8PR* Prestatyn (0745) 857419

TEAL, Andrew Robert. b 64. Birm Univ BA85. Ripon Coll Cuddesdon 86. **d** 88 **p** 89. C Wednesbury St Paul Wood Green *Lich* from 88. *St Luke's House, 49 Oldbury Street, Wednesbury, W Midlands WS10 0QJ* 021-556 0443

TEALE, Adrian. b 53. Univ of Wales (Abth) BA74 CertEd77 MA80 Univ of Wales (Cardiff) MTh89. Wycliffe Hall Ox 78. **d** 80 **p** 81. C Bettws St Dav *St D* 80-84; V Brynaman w Cwmllynfell from 84. *The Vicarage, 23 Llandeilo Road, Brynaman, Dyfed SA18 1BA* Amman Valley (0269) 822275

TEALE, Ernest Burdett. b 20. Keble Coll Ox BA42 MA46. Westcott Ho Cam 42. **d** 43 **p** 45. P-in-c Radbourne *Derby* 69-70; Adv for Primary and Middle Schs *Lon* 70-85; rtd 85; Lic to Offic *Lon* from 85. *103 Sandringham Gardens, London N12 0PA* 081-445 2037

TEARE, Robert John Hugh. b 39. Bris Univ BSc62 Leeds Univ DipTh69. Coll of Resurr Mirfield 67. **d** 70 **p** 71. C Fareham SS Pet and Paul *Portsm* 70-73; Chapl K Alfred Coll *Win* 73-78; V Pokesdown St Jas 78-82; P-in-c Win H Trin 82; P-in-c Win St Jo cum Winnall 82; R Winnall from 82; RD Win from 89. *The Rectory, 22 St John's Street, Winchester, Hants SO23 8HF* Winchester (0962) 63891

TEARNAN, John Herman Janson. b 37. Bris Univ BSc59. Kelham Th Coll 62. **d** 66 **p** 67. C Kettering SS Pet and Paul *Pet* 66-71; Lic to Offic 71-85; Perm to Offic *St Alb* from 82; *Pet* from 85; Sub-Chapl HM Young Offender Inst Wellingborough from 89; Chapl HM Young Offender Inst Glen Parva from 90. *HM Young Offender Institute, Glen Parva, Tigers Road, Wigston, Leicester LE8 2TN* Leicester (0533) 772022

TEASDALE, Keith. b 56. Cranmer Hall Dur 86. **d** 88 **p** 89. C Crook *Dur* from 88. *Cherry Tree House, Park Avenue, Crook, Co Durham DL15 9HX* Bishop Auckland (0388) 762451

TEBBOTH, Alfred Thomas Henderson. b 09. Qu Coll Birm 51. **d** 52 **p** 53. R Kelshall *St Alb* 69-76; R Therfield 69-76; rtd 77. *5 Wheatfield Crescent, Royston, Herts SG8 7EN* Royston (0763) 242276

TEBBOTH, John Arthur. b 17. PhD. **d** 60 **p** 61. V Crofton St Paul *Roch* 67-79; RD Orpington 76-79; C Speldhurst w Groombridge and Ashurst 79-82; rtd 82; Perm to Offic *Ex* from 82. *21 Venborough Close, Seaton, Devon EX12 2EY* Seaton (0297) 21074

TEBBS, Richard Henry. b 52. Southn Univ BTh. Sarum & Wells Th Coll 75. **d** 78 **p** 79. C Cinderhill *S'well* 78-82; C Nor St Pet Mancroft *Nor* 82; C Nor St Pet Mancroft w St Jo Maddermarket 82-85; TV Bridport *Sarum* from 85. *The Vicarage, Higher Street, Bradpole, Bridport, Dorset DT6 3JA* Bridport (0308) 56635

TEBBUTT, Simon Albert. b 27. Qu Coll Birm 88. **d** 89 **p** 90. NSM Northn St Matt *Pet* from 89. *Home Close, Moulton Lane, Boughton, Northampton NN2 8RF* Northampton (0604) 843240

TEDMAN, Alfred. b 33. AKC59. **d** 60 **p** 61. C Newington St Mary *S'wark* 60-64; C Milton *Portsm* 64-68; R Bonchurch from 68; RD E Wight 78-83; P-in-c Whitwell 79-82; P-in-c St Lawrence 82-84; V Wroxall from 84. *The Rectory, Bonchurch, Ventnor, Isle of Wight PO38 1NU* Isle of Wight (0983) 852357

TEE, John. b 59. **d** 82 **p** 83. C Walworth *S'wark* 82-85; Chapl RAF 85-89; CF from 89. *c/o MOD, Army, Bagshot Park, Bagshot, Surrey GU19 5PL* Bagshot (0276) 71717

TEESDALE, Ian Bruce. b 60. Lanc Univ BA83. Linc Th Coll 83. **d** 86 **p** 87. C Wigan All SS *Liv* 86-90; TV Liv Our Lady and St Nic w St Anne from 90. *14 Priory Park, Riverside Drive, Liverpool L17 5AX* 051-727 2804

TEGGIN, John. b 26. **d** 83 **p** 84. NSM Dub Sandford w Milltown *D & G* from 84; Leprosy Miss from 86. *5 St James's Terrace, Clonskeagh Road, Dublin 6, Irish Republic* Dublin (1) 269-8804

TELFER, Canon Frank Somerville. b 30. Trin Hall Cam BA53 MA58. Ely Th Coll 53. **d** 55 **p** 56. C Liv Our Lady and St Nic *Liv* 55-58; Chapl Down Coll Cam 58-62; Bp's Chapl *Nor* 62-65; Chapl Kent Univ *Cant* 65-73; Can Res Guildf Cathl *Guildf* from 73. *2 Cathedral Close, Guildford, Surrey GU2 5TL* Guildford (0483) 60329

TELFORD, Alan. b 46. St Jo Coll Nottm. **d** 83 **p** 84. C Normanton *Derby* 83-86; TV N Wingfield, Pilsley and Tupton 86-90; TV N Wingfield, Clay Cross and Pilsley from 90. *The Vicarage, Ankerbold Road, Tupton, Chesterfield, Derbyshire S42 6BX* Chesterfield (0246) 864524

TELFORD, Cyril Harry. b 22. S Dios Minl Tr Scheme. **d** 54 **p** 55. C Gt Crosby St Faith *Liv* 54-57; C Liv Our Lady and St Nic 57-60; V Lt Lever *Man* from 60. *The Vicarage, Market Street, Little Lever, Bolton BL3 1HH* Farnworth (0204) 73574

TELFORD, Canon Edward Cecil. b 17. Selw Coll Cam BA47 MA52. Linc Th Coll 47. **d** 49 **p** 50. R Langdon Hills *Chelmsf* 59-70; R Shenfield 70-85; Hon Can Chelmsf Cathl 75-85; RD Brentwood 76-84; rtd 85; Perm to Offic *Ely* from 86. *13 Harlestones Road, Cottenham, Cambridge CB4 4TR* Cottenham (0954) 51184

TELFORD, John Edward. b 16. TCD BA40 MA46. CITC 40. **d** 41 **p** 42. I Dub Irishtown *D & G* 44-60; rtd 60. *12 Woodbine Avenue, Blackrock, Co Dublin, Irish Republic* Dublin (1) 269-1187

TELLINI, Canon Dr Gianfranco. b 36. Franciscan Sem Trent 57. **d** 61 **p** 61. In RC Ch 61-66; C Mill Hill Jo Keble Ch *Lon* 66; C Roxbourne St Andr 66-67; Lect Sarum Th Coll 67-69; Sen Tutor 69-74; Vice-Prin Edin Th Coll 74-82; Lect Th Edin Univ from 74; R Pittenweem *St And* 82-85; R Elie and Earlsferry 82-85; R Dunblane from 85; Can St Ninian's Cathl Perth from 90. *The Rectory, Smithy Loan, Dunblane, Perthshire FK15 0HQ* Dunblane (0786) 824225

TEMPERLEY, Robert Noble. b 29. JP. ACP52 St Jo Coll York CertEd50 Dur Univ DAES62. NE Ord Course 85. **d** 88 **p** 88. NSM Ryhope *Dur* from 88. *18 Withernsea Grove, Ryhope, Sunderland SR2 0BU* 091-521 1813

TEMPLE, Donald Hubert. b 08. **d** 41 **p** 42. Uganda 68-72; Kenya 72-75; rtd 76; Perm to Offic *Ex* 77-82; *S'wark* from 82. *7 Arkendale, Whittington College, Felbridge, East Grinstead, W Sussex RH19 2QU* East Grinstead (0342) 314165

✛**TEMPLE, Rt Rev Frederick Stephen.** b 16. Ball Coll Ox BA39 MA45 Trin Hall Cam BA47 MA52. Westcott Ho Cam 45. **d** 47 **p** 48 **c** 73. C Arnold *S'well* 47-49; C Newark w Coddington 49-51; R Birch St Agnes *Man* 51-53; Dean Hong Kong 53-59; Abp's Sen Chapl *Cant* 59-61; V Portsea St Mary *Portsm* 61-70; Hon Can Portsm Cathl 65-69; Adn Swindon *Bris* 70-73; Hon Can Bris Cathl 70-83; Suff Bp Malmesbury 73-83; rtd 83; Asst Bp Bris from 83; Asst Bp Sarum from 83. *7 The Barton, Wood Street, Wootton Bassett, Swindon SN4 7BG* Swindon (0793) 851227

TEMPLE, Ven George Frederick. b 33. Wells Th Coll 66. **d** 68 **p** 69. C Gt Bookham *Guildf* 68-70; C Penzance St Mary *Truro* 70-72; V St Just in Penwith 72-74; V Sancreed 72-74; V St Gluvias 74-81; Hon Can Truro Cathl from 81; Adn Bodmin 81-89; V Saltash St Nich and St Faith 82-85; Dioc Dir of Ords 85-89; rtd 89. *50 Athelstan Park, Bodmin, Cornwall PL31 1DT* Bodmin (0208) 77568

TEMPLEMAN, Peter Morton. b 49. Ch Ch Ox BA71 MA75 BTh75. Wycliffe Hall Ox 73. **d** 76 **p** 77. C Cheltenham St Mary, St Matt, St Paul and H Trin *Glouc* 76-79; Chapl St Jo Coll Cam 79-84; P-in-c Finchley St Paul Long Lane *Lon* 84-85; P-in-c Finchley St Luke 84-85; V Finchley St Paul and St Luke from 85. *St Paul's Vicarage, 50 Long Lane, London N3 2PU* 081-346 8729

TEMPLETON (nee McCUTCHEON), Irene. b 41. QUB BEd. Dalton Ho Bris 65. **d** 89 **p** 90. Lic to Offic *Conn* 89; Hon Par Dn Kilmakee 89-90; C from 90. *15 Cairnshill Avenue, Belfast BT8 4NR* Belfast (0232) 701686

TEMPLETON, Canon John Herbert. b 97. TCD BA25 MA36 BD36 BLitt43 PhD46 MLitt61. **d** 25 **p** 26. I Dunseverick *Conn* 64-78; Chan Conn Cathl 65-73; rtd 73. *2 Chichester Court, Antrim Road, Belfast BT15 5DS* Belfast (0232) 771806

TENNANT, Charles Roger. b 19. Open Univ PhD75. Linc Th Coll 49. **d** 51 **p** 52. V Bitteswell *Leic* 62-88; P-in-c Misterton w Walcote 80-88; rtd 88. *Middle House, Station Road, Ullesthorpe, Lutterworth, Leics LE17 5BS* Hinckley (0455) 209703

TENNANT, Cyril Edwin George. b 37. Keble Coll Ox BA59 MA63 Lon Univ BD61. Clifton Th Coll 59. **d** 62 **p** 63. C Stapleford *S'well* 62-65; C Felixstowe SS Pet and Paul *St E* 65-69; V Gipsy Hill Ch Ch *S'wark* 69-84; V Lee St Mildred 84-90; V Ilfracombe SS Phil and Jas w W Down *Ex* from 90. *St James's Vicarage, Kingsley Avenue, Ilfracombe, Devon EX34 8ET* Ilfracombe (0271) 863519

TENNANT, Osmond Roy. b 21. Worc Ord Coll 62. **d** 63 **p** 64. V Escot *Ex* 67-89; R Talaton 67-89; P-in-c Clyst Hydon and Clyst St Lawrence 74-87; rtd 89; Perm to Offic *Ex* from 89. *Rockleigh, 29 West Clyst, Exeter EX1 3TL* Exeter (0392) 65515

TENNICK, Edward. b 10. St Aid Birkenhead 38. **d** 40 **p** 41. V Southborough St Thos *Roch* 62-75; rtd 75; Perm to Offic *Chich* from 87. *Flat 3, 7 Chatsworth Gardens, Eastbourne, E Sussex BN20 7JP* Eastbourne (0323) 648490

TER BLANCHE, Harold Daniel. b 35. St Paul's Grahamstown LTh85. **d** 63 **p** 64. S Africa 63-82; Miss to Seamen 82-84; Chapl Grimsby Distr Gen Hosp from 84. *Grimsby District General Hospital, Scartho Road, Grimsby, S Humberside DN33 2PY* Grimsby (0472) 74111

TERESA, Sister. See WHITE, Teresa Joan

TERRANOVA, Jonathan Rossano. b 62. Sheff Poly BA85. Oak Hill Th Coll BA88. **d** 88 **p** 89. C Carl St Jo *Carl* 88-91; C Stoughton *Guildf* from 91. *12 Grange Close, Guildford, Surrey GU2 6QJ* Guildford (0483) 573154

TERRELL, Richard Charles Patridge. b 43. Wells Th Coll 69. **d** 71 **p** 72. C Shepton Mallet *B & W* 71-76; P-in-c Drayton 76-78; P-in-c Muchelney 76-78; TV Langport Area Chs 78-82; P-in-c Tatworth 82-89; V from 89. *The Vicarage, Tatworth, Chard, Somerset TA20 2PD* South Chard (0460) 20404

TERRETT, Mervyn Douglas. b 43. AKC65. **d** 66 **p** 67. C Pet St Mary *Pet* 66-69; C Sawbridgeworth *St Alb* 69-74; V Stevenage H Trin 74-85; Perm to Offic from 86. *131 Walkern Road, Stevenage, Herts* Stevenage (0438) 720152

TERRY, Christopher Laurence. b 51. FCA80. St Alb Minl Tr Scheme. **d** 83 **p** 84. Hon C Dunstable *St Alb* 83-89; C Abbots Langley from 89. *40 Kindersley Way, Abbots Langley, Watford WD5 0DQ* Kings Langley (0923) 265729

TERRY, Ian Andrew. b 53. Dur Univ BA74 St Jo Coll York PGCE75. Coll of Resurr Mirfield 78. **d** 80 **p** 81. C Beaconsfield *Ox* 80-83; C N Lynn w St Marg and St Nic *Nor* 83-84; Chapl Eliz Coll Guernsey 84-89; Chapl St Jo

Sch Leatherhead from 89. *The Chaplain's House, 5 Linden Pit Path, Leatherhead, Surrey KT22 7JD* Leatherhead (0372) 376424

TERRY, John Arthur. b 32. S'wark Ord Course. **d** 66 **p** 67. C Plumstead All SS *S'wark* 66-69; C Peckham St Mary Magd 69-72; V Streatham Vale H Redeemer 72-80; R Sternfield w Benhall and Snape *St E* 80-84; V Stevenage St Mary Shephall *St Alb* 84-86; V Stevenage St Mary Sheppall w Aston 86-90; V Cople w Willington from 90; Chapl Shuttleworth Agric Coll from 90. *The Vicarage, Cople, Bedford MK44 3TT* Bedford (0234) 838431

TERRY, Stephen John. b 49. K Coll Lon BD72 AKC74. **d** 75 **p** 76. C Tokyngton St Mich *Lon* 75-78; C Hampstead St Steph w All Hallows 78-81; V Whetstone St Jo 81-89; TR Aldrington *Chich* from 89; OStJ from 89. *The Rectory, 77 New Church Road, Hove, E Sussex BN3 4BB* Brighton (0273) 737915

TESTA, Luigi Richard Frederick. b 30. Nottm Univ CTPS85. **d** 85 **p** 86. NSM Castle Donington and Lockington cum Hemington *Leic* from 85. *40 Hillside, Castle Donington, Derby DE7 2NH* Derby (0332) 810823

TESTER, Clarence Albert. b 20. Qu Coll Birm 47. **d** 50 **p** 51. Chapl Ham Green Hosp Bris 55-70; V Halberton *Ex* 70-85; rtd 85; Perm to Offic *B & W* from 86. *Brays Batch, Chewton Mendip, Bath BA3 4LH* Chewton Mendip (076121) 218

TESTER, Canon Francis Edward. b 24. Leeds Univ BA46. Coll of Resurr Mirfield 45. **d** 47 **p** 48. V Hockerill *St Alb* 64-71; Chapl Highwood and St Faith's Hosps Brentwood 71-89; V Brentwood St Thos *Chelmsf* 71-89; RD Brentwood 84-89; Hon Can Chelmsf Cathl 87-89; rtd 89; Perm to Offic Nor and Chelmsf from 89. *Wythe, Burnt Street, Wells-next-the-Sea, Norfolk NR23 1HW* Fakenham (0328) 711306

TETLEY, Brian. b 38. FCA BA. Cranmer Hall Dur 80. **d** 83 **p** 84. C Chipping Sodbury and Old Sodbury *Glouc* 83-86; Chapl and Succ Roch Cath *Roch* 86-89; R Gravesend H Family w Ifield from 89. *The Rectory, 2 Wilberforce Way, Gravesend, Kent DA12 5DQ* Gravesend (0474) 363038

TETLEY, Canon Joy Dawn. b 46. dss 77 **d** 87. Bentley *Sheff* 77-79; Buttershaw St Aid *Bradf* 79-80; Dur Cathl *Dur* 80-83; Lect Trin Coll Bris 83-86; Chipping Sodbury and Old Sodbury *Glouc* 83-86; Roch Cathl *Roch* 87-89; Assoc Dir of Post Ord Tr 87-88; Dir Post Ord Tr from 88; Hon Can Roch Cathl from 90. *The Rectory, 2 Wilberforce Way, Gravesend, Kent DA12 5DQ* Gravesend (0474) 363038

TETLEY, Matthew David. b 61. Bucks Coll of Educn BSc83. Sarum & Wells Th Coll BTh89. **d** 87 **p** 88. C Kirkby *Liv* 87-90; AV Hindley St Pet from 90. *67 Cashmore Drive, Hindley, Wigan, Lancs WN2 3JJ* Wigan (0942) 57030

TETLOW, John. b 46. St Steph Ho Ox 73. **d** 76 **p** 77. C Stanwell *Lon* 76-77; C Hanworth All SS 77-80; C Somers Town St Mary 80-83; TV Wickford and Runwell *Chelmsf* 83-90; P-in-c Walthamstow St Mich from 90. *St Michael's Vicarage, Palmerston Road, London E17 6PQ* 081-520 6328

TETLOW, Richard Jeremy. b 42. Trin Coll Cam MA66 Golds Coll Lon CQSW74. Qu Coll Birm 81. **d** 83 **p** 84. C Birm St Martin *Birm* 83-85; C Birm St Martin w Bordesley St Andr 85-88; V Birm St Jo Ladywood from 89. *St John's Vicarage, Darnley Road, Birmingham B16 8TF* 021-454 0973

TEWKESBURY, Alec. b 13. Dur Univ LTh38. ALCD36. **d** 36 **p** 37. V Loxwood *Chich* 70-78; rtd 78; Perm to Offic *Chich* from 78. *1 Stonefield Close, Crawley, W Sussex RH10 6AU* Crawley (0293) 534420

TEWKESBURY, Noel. b 44. Hull Univ BA67. Wycliffe Hall Ox 70. **d** 72 **p** 73. C Bishops Waltham *Portsm* 72-76; C Havant 76-77; C Filey *York* 77-79; V Monk Fryston 79-84; V Hambleton 79-84; TV Bolventor *Truro* 84-86; TR from 86. *5 Hendra Tor View, Five Lanes, Launceston, Cornwall PL15 7RG* Pipers Pool (0566) 86579

TEWKESBURY, Suffragan Bishop of. See WALSH, Rt Rev Geoffrey David Jeremy

THACKER, Charles Kent. b 09. K Coll Cam BA31 MA35. Ely Th Coll 31. **d** 32 **p** 34. Chapl Victoria Coll Jersey 63-74; C Jersey St Clem *Win* 73-74; rtd 74. *Sea Court, Bel Royal, Jersey, Channel Islands* Jersey (0534) 20019

THACKER, Ian David. b 59. DCR DRI. Oak Hill Th Coll BA91. **d** 91. C Illogan *Truro* from 91. *46 Bosmoor Park, Illogan, Redruth, Cornwall TR15 3JN* Redruth (0209) 219268

THACKER, Jonathan William. b 53. Lon Univ BA74 Nottm Univ DipTh78. Linc Th Coll 76. **d** 79 **p** 80.

C Bromyard *Heref* 79-82; C Penkridge w Stretton *Lich* 82-87; V Brothertoft Gp *Linc* from 87. *The Vicarage, Main Road, Brothertoft, Boston, Lincs PE20 3SW* Langrick (020573) 267

THACKER, Kenneth Ray. b 31. Open Univ BA73. Tyndale Hall Bris 56. **d** 59 **p** 60. C Penn Fields *Lich* 59-61; C Tipton St Martin 62-64; V Moxley 64-71; R Leigh from 71. *The Rectory, Leigh, Stoke-on-Trent ST10 4PT* Field (0889) 502237

THACKER, Roger Ailwyn Mackintosh. b 46. CCC Cam BA68 MA73. Westcott Ho Cam 68. **d** 70 **p** 71. C St Jo Wood *Lon* 70-74; P-in-c Hammersmith St Paul 74-79; V from 79. *21 Lower Mall, Hammersmith Road, London W6* 071-603 4303 or 748 3855

THACKRAY, John Adrian. b 55. ACIB81 Southn Univ BSc76. Coll of Resurr Mirfield 81. **d** 84 **p** 85. C Loughton St Jo *Chelmsf* 84-87; Chapl Bancroft's Sch Woodford Green from 87. *Bancroft's School, Woodford Green, Essex IG8 0RF* 081-505 1486 or 505 4821

THACKRAY, Peter Michael. b 29. Coll of Resurr Mirfield BA52. **d** 54 **p** 55. C St Mary-at-Lambeth *S'wark* 54-57; C Primrose Hill St Mary w Avenue Road St Paul *Lon* 57-59; C-in-c S Kenton Annunciation CD 59-61; Chapl Pierrepont Sch Frensham 61-67; Chapl Windsor Girls' Sch, Hamm 67-73; CF 73-78; Lic to Offic *Eur* 78-84; Hon C Sellindge w Monks Horton and Stowting *Cant* 84-86; Hon C Lympne w W Hythe 84-86; Hon C Sellindge w Monks Horton and Stowting etc from 86. *The Friars' School, Great Chart, Ashford, Kent TN23 3DJ* Ashford (0233) 620493

THACKRAY, William Harry. b 44. Leeds Univ CcrtEd66. Chich Th Coll 70. **d** 73 **p** 74. C Sheff St Cuth *Sheff* 73-76; C Stocksbridge 76-78; P-in-c Newark St Leon *S'well* 79-80; TV Newark w Hawton, Cotham and Shelton 80-82; VC S'well Minster 82-85; V Bawtry w Austerfield 85; P-in-c Misson 85; V Bawtry w Austerfield and Misson from 86; RD Bawtry from 90. *The Vicarage, Martin Lane, Bawtry, Doncaster, S Yorkshire DN10 6NJ* Doncaster (0302) 710298

THADDEUS, Brother. *See* BURGOYNE-JOHNSON, Philip Simon

THAKE, Terence. b 41. ALCD65. **d** 66 **p** 67. C Gt Faringdon w Lt Coxwell *Ox* 66-70; C Aldridge *Lich* 70-73; V Werrington 73-82; Chapl HM Det Cen Werrington Ho 73-82; TR Chell *Lich* from 82; Chapl Westcliffe Hosp from 82; RD Stoke N from 91. *The Rectory, 203 St Michael's Road, Stoke-on-Trent ST6 6JT* Stoke-on-Trent (0782) 838708

THAME, Miss Margaret Eve. b 31. SRN54 SCM55. Glouc Sch of Min 85. **d** 88. NSM Pittville *Glouc* from 88. *13 Brighton Road, Cheltenham, Glos GL52 6BA* Cheltenham (0242) 41228

THATCHER, Barbara Mary. b 25. **d** 90. NSM Helensburgh *Glas* from 90. *228 West Princes Street, Helensburgh, Dunbartonshire G84 8HA* Helensburgh (0436) 72003

THATCHER, Rodney David. b 38. Sarum & Wells Th Coll 83. **d** 86 **p** 87. NSM Wilton *B & W* 86-89; C Bridgwater St Mary, Chilton Trinity and Durleigh 89-91; P-in-c Charlton Musgrove, Cucklington and Stoke Trister from 91. *The Rectory, Charlton Musgrove, Wincanton, Somerset BA9 8HN* Wincanton (0963) 33233

THATCHER, Stephen Bert. b 58. St Jo Coll Nottm LTh87. **d** 87 **p** 88. C Bargoed and Deri w Brithdir *Llan* 87-89; C Llanishen and Lisvane 89-91; V Llanwnda, Goodwick, w Manorowen and Llanstinan *St D* from 91. *The Vicarage, Goodwick, Dyfed* Fishguard (0348) 873251

THAWLEY, Very Rev David Laurie. b 24. St Edm Hall Ox BA47 MA49. Cuddesdon Coll 49. **d** 51 **p** 52. C Bitterne Park *Win* 51-56; C-in-c Andover St Mich CD 56-60; Australia from 60; Can Res Brisbane 64-72; Dean Wangaratta 72-89. *Lavender Cottage, 2 Bond Street, North Caulfield, Victoria, Australia 3161* Melbourne (3) 571-0513

THAYER, Michael David. b 52. Sarum & Wells Th Coll 77. **d** 80 **p** 81. C Minehead *B & W* 80-85; Chapl RN 85-89; TV Lowestoft and Kirkley *Nor* from 89. *St Peter's Rectory, Kirkley, Lowestoft, Suffolk NR33 0ED* Lowestoft (0502) 65391

THEAKSTON, Ms Sally Margaret. b 62. UEA BSc84 Ox Univ BA89. Ripon Coll Cuddesdon 86. **d** 89. C Hackney *Lon* from 89. *21B Blurton Road, London E5 0NL* 081-986 5668

THELWALL, George de Crespigny. b 05. ACT ThL38 St Jo Coll Morpeth 37. **d** 38 **p** 39. R Brushford *B & W* 65-75; rtd 75. *Flat 1, Harbour Court Esplanade, Minehead, Somerset TA24 5BG* Minehead (0643) 2295

THELWALL, Canon Robert Champion de Crespigny. St Paul's Grahamstown. **d** 48 **p** 48. S Rhodesia 48-65; Rhodesia 65-73; Zimbabwe 81-83; Perm to Offic *Derby*

from 83. *28 Greenfield Crescent, Mickleover, Derby DE3 5RF* Derby (0332) 516997

THELWELL, John Berry. b 49. Univ of Wales (Ban) BD72. Qu Coll Birm 73. **d** 73 **p** 74. C Minera *St As* 73-80; Dioc Youth Chapl 78-86; V Gwernaffield and Llanferres from 80; Chapl to Clwyd Fire Service from 88; RD Mold from 91. *The Vicarage, Cilcain Road, Gwernaffield, Mold, Clwyd CH7 5DQ* Mold (0352) 740205

THEOBALD, Graham Fitzroy. b 43. ALCD63. **d** 67 **p** 68. C Crookham *Guildf* 67-71; C York Town 71-74; V Wrecclesham 74-83; R Frimley 83-85; Perm to Offic *Ox* from 90. *4 Tawfield, Bracknell, Berks RG12 4YU* Bracknell (0344) 483921

THEOBALD, Henry Charles. b 32. Lon Univ DBS. S'wark Ord Course 60. **d** 63 **p** 64. C Battersea St Phil *S'wark* 63-65; C Caterham 65-68; C Reigate St Luke S Park 68-73; Chapl S Lon Hosp for Women & St Jas Hosp Balham 73-83; Chapl St Mary's Gen Hosp Portsm from 83. *141 Warren Avenue, Southsea, Hants PO4 8PP* Portsmouth (0705) 817443 or 822331

THEOBALD, John Walter. b 33. St Aid Birkenhead. **d** 65 **p** 66. C Hindley All SS *Liv* 65-68; C Beverley Minster *York* 68-71; R Loftus 71-86; P-in-c Carlin How w Skinningrove 73-86; Asst Chapl HM Pris Leeds 86-89; Chapl HM Pris Rudgate from 89; Chapl HM Pris Thorp Arch from 89. *HM Prison Thorpe Arch, Wetherby, W Yorkshire LS23 7KY* Boston Spa (0937) 844241

THEODOSIUS, Hugh John. b 32. Trin Coll Cam BA56 MA60. Cuddesdon Coll 56. **d** 58 **p** 59. C Milton *Win* 58-62; C Romsey 62-64; C Southn Maybush St Pet 64-70; V Malden St Jo *S'wark* 70-81; V Billingborough *Linc* from 81; V Horbling from 81; V Sempringham w Pointon and Birthorpe from 81; RD Aveland and Ness w Stamford from 87. *The Vicarage, Billingborough, Sleaford, Lincs NG34 0QA* Sleaford (0529) 240750

THEODOSIUS, Richard Francis. b 35. Fitzw Coll Cam BA59. Lich Th Coll 69. **d** 71 **p** 72. C Bloxwich *Lich* 71-73; Chapl Blue Coat Comp Sch Walsall 71-73; Lic to Offic *S'well* from 73; Chapl Ranby Ho Sch Retford from 73. *Downlea, 51 Town Street, Lound, Retford, Notts DN22 8RT* Retford (0777) 818744

THETFORD, Suffragan Bishop of. *See* DUDLEY-SMITH, Rt Rev Timothy

THEWLIS, Andrew James. b 64. Man Univ BSc86. Cranmer Hall Dur 87. **d** 90 **p** 91. C Walshaw Ch Ch *Man* from 90. *2 Acresbrook Walk, Tottinston, Bury, Lancs BL8 3JR* Bolton (0204) 887109

THEWLIS, Dr John Charles. b 49. Van Mildert Coll Dur BA70 PhD75. N Ord Course 78. **d** 81 **p** 82. NSM Hull Sculcoates St Mary *York* 81-83; C Spring Park *Cant* 83-84; C Spring Park All SS *S'wark* 85-86; V Eltham Park St Luke from 86. *St Luke's Vicarage, 107 Westmount Road, London SE9 1XX* 081-850 3030

THICKE, James Balliston. b 43. Sarum & Wells Th Coll 74. **d** 77 **p** 78. C Wareham *Sarum* 77-80; Dioc Youth Adv *Dur* 83-87; C Portishead *B & W* 87-90; V Westf from 90. *Westfield Vicarage, Midsomer Norton, Bath BA3 4BJ* Midsomer Norton (0761) 412101

THIEME, Paul Henri. b 22. Ecclesiastical Sem Vent Cathl Holland. **d** 50 **p** 50. V Kingston upon Hull St Sav and St Mark *York* 63-73; V Middlesb St Aid 73-79; rtd 87. *Haagweg 174, 2282 A J Rijswijk ZH, The Netherlands* Rijswijk (70) 390-9296

✠**THIRD, Rt Rev Richard Henry McPhail.** b 27. Em Coll Cam BA50 MA55 Kent Univ Hon DCL90. Linc Th Coll 50. **d** 52 **p** 53 **c** 76. C Mottingham St Andr *S'wark* 52-55; C Sanderstead All SS 55-59; V Sheerness H Trin w St Paul *Cant* 59-67; V Orpington All SS *Roch* 67-76; RD Orpington 73-76; Hon Can Roch Cathl 74-76; Suff Bp Maidstone from 76-80; Suff Bp Dover from 80. *Upway, 52 St Martin's Hill, Canterbury, Kent CT1 1PR* Canterbury (0227) 459382 or 464537

THISELTON, Anthony Charles. b 37. Novi Testamenti Societas 75 Lon Univ BD59 K Coll Lon MTh64 Sheff Univ PhD77. Oak Hill Th Coll 58. **d** 60 **p** 61. C Sydenham H Trin *S'wark* 60-63; Tutor Tyndale Hall Bris 63-67; Sen Tutor 67-70; Lect Bibl Studies Sheff Univ 70-79; Sen Lect 79-85; Prof Calvin Coll Grand Rapids 82-83; Special Lect Th Nottm Univ 86-88; Prin St Jo Coll Nottm 86-88; Prin St Jo Coll w Cranmer Hall Dur from 88. *St John's College, University of Durham, Durham DH1 3RJ* 091-374 3561

THISTLETHWAITE, Dr Nicholas John. b 51. Selw Coll Cam BA73 MA77 PhD80 Ox Univ BA78 MA83 Ripon Coll Cuddesdon BA78. **d** 79 **p** 80. C Newc St Gabr *Newc* 79-82; Lic to Offic *Ely* 82-90; Chapl G&C Coll Cam 82-90; V Trumpington *Ely* from 90. *The Vicarage,*

Trumpington, Cambridge CB2 2LH Cambridge (0223) 841262

THISTLEWOOD, Michael John. b 31. Ch Coll Cam BA53 MA57. Linc Th Coll 54. **d** 56 **p** 57. V Newland St Aug *York* 67-72; Asst Master Bemrose Sch Derby 72-80; V Derby St Andr w St Osmund *Derby* 80-82; Lic to Offic *Ox* from 84; rtd 88; Perm to Offic *Carl* from 88. *9 Lightburn Road, Ulverston, Cumbria LA12 0AU* Ulverston (0229) 54687

THOM, Alastair George. b 60. ACA86 G&C Coll Cam BA81 MA84. Ridley Hall Cam 88. **d** 91. C Lindfield *Chich* from 91. *32 Noah's Ark Lane, Lindfield, Haywards Heath, W Sussex RH16 2LT* Lindfield (0444) 482989

THOM, James. b 31. St Chad's Coll Dur BA53 DipTh57. **d** 57 **p** 58. C Middlesb St Thos *York* 57-60; C Hornsea and Goxhill 60-62; C S Bank 62-63; V Copmanthorpe 63-75; V Coxwold 75-77; RD Easingwold 77-82; V Coxwold and Husthwaite 77-87; Abp's Adv for Spiritual Direction from 86; P-in-c Topcliffe from 87. *St Columba's Vicarage, Topcliffe, Thirsk, N Yorkshire YO7 3RU* Thirsk (0845) 577939

THOM, Thomas Kennedy Dalziel. b 29. Pemb Coll Cam BA53 MA57. St Steph Ho Ox 60. **d** 61 **p** 62. C Colchester St Jas, All SS, St Nic and St Runwald *Chelmsf* 61-65; USPG 65-70; Ghana 65-70; V Colchester St Jas 71; Chapl Essex Univ *Chelmsf* 73-80; Sec Chapls in HE Gen Syn Bd of Educn 81-87; Partnership Sec and Dep Gen Sec USPG from 87. *c/o USPG, Partnership House, 157 Waterloo Road, London SE1 8XA* 071-928 8681

THOMAS, Adrian Leighton. b 37. St D Coll Lamp BA62 DipTh. **d** 63 **p** 64. C Port Talbot St Theodore *Llan* 63-70; V Troedrhiwgarth 70-73; C Sandhurst *Ox* 73-77; V Streatley 77-84; P-in-c Moulsford 81-84; V Streatley w Moulsford 84-90; P-in-c Sutton Courtenay w Appleford from 90. *The Vicarage, Tullis Close, Sutton Courtenay, Abingdon, Oxon OX14 4BD* Abingdon (0235) 848297

THOMAS, Alan. b 42. Univ of Wales (Cardiff) BA65. St Mich Coll Llan 65. **d** 67 **p** 68. C Fairwater *Llan* 67-69; C Llanishen and Lisvane 69-73; V Troedyrhiw w Merthyr Vale 73-77; Chapl S Pemb Hosp from 77; V Pemb Dock *St D* from 77; RD Castlemartin from 83; P-in-c Cosheston w Nash and Upton from 85; Can St D Cathl from 89. *The Vicarage, Church Street, Pembroke Dock, Dyfed SA72 6AR* Pembroke (0646) 682943

THOMAS, Alan William Charles. b 19. Liv Univ BA41. St Aid Birkenhead 42. **d** 43 **p** 44. V Wolv St Jude *Lich* 67-87; rtd 87; Perm to Offic Lich 87-89; Ex from 89. *Gable Cottage, Radway, Sidmouth, Devon EX10 8TW* Sidmouth (0395) 513302

THOMAS, Albert. b 19. St Aid Birkenhead 57. **d** 59 **p** 60. V Parr Mt *Liv* 64-72; V Toxteth Park Ch Ch 72-84; rtd 84; Perm to Offic *Liv* from 84. *181 South Mossley Hill Road, Liverpool L19 9BB*

THOMAS, Albert Kenneth. b 18. St D Coll Lamp BA40 St Mich Coll Llan 40. **d** 42 **p** 43. R Charlton Musgrove *B & W* 67-80; R Charlton Musgrove, Cucklington and Stoke Trister 80-83; rtd 83; Perm to Offic *B & W* 84-86. *Chelwood, 32 Shreen Way, Gillingham, Dorset SP8 4EL* Gillingham (0747) 822093

THOMAS, Aled Huw. b 59. Univ of Wales (Abth) BD81 DPS83. St Mich Coll Llan 84. **d** 85 **p** 86. C Llandilo Fawr and Taliaris *St D* 85-86; P-in-c Llangrannog and Llandysiliogogo 86-88; Chapl RAF from 88. *c/o MOD, Adastral House, Theobald's Road, London WC1X 8RU* 071-730 7350

THOMAS, Alfred James Randolph. b 48. St D Coll Lamp DipTh71. **d** 71 **p** 72. C Kidwelly and Llandefaelog *St D* 71-74; C Carmarthen St Dav 74-76; TV Abth 76-81; V Bettws St Dav from 81; RD Dyffryn Aman from 90. *The Vicarage, College Street, Ammanford, Dyfed SA18 3AB* Ammanford (0269) 592084

THOMAS, Andrew Herbert Redding. b 41. Lon Coll of Div 66. **d** 69 **p** 70. C Cromer *Nor* 69-72; Holiday Chapl 72-76; R Grimston w Congham 76-83; R Roydon All SS 76-83; C-in-c Ewell St Paul Howell Hill CD *Guildf* 83-89; V Howell Hill from 89. *St Paul's Vicarage, Northey Avenue, Cheam, Surrey SM2 7HS* 081-643 3838

THOMAS, Arthur George. b 19. Univ of Wales (Swansea) BA40. St Mich Coll Llan 40. **d** 42 **p** 43. R Llanganten w Llanafan Fawr, Maesmynis etc *S & B* 69-79; R Llanganten, Llanafan Fawr, Llangammarch etc 79-84; rtd 84. *37 Gwernyfed Avenue, Three Cocks, Brecon, Powys LD3 0RT* Glasbury (04974) 451

THOMAS, Arthur Norman. b 17. St Aid Birkenhead 54. **d** 56 **p** 57. R Seacroft *Ripon* 65-70; TR 70-76; R Thornton Watlass w Thornton Steward and E Witton 76-86; rtd 86. *Christmas Cottage, Emmerdale Garth, Kirkby*

Malzeard, Ripon, N Yorkshire HG4 3SH Kirkby Malzeard (076583) 8884

THOMAS, Canon Arthur Roy. b 25. St Steph Ho Ox 55. **d** 58 **p** 59. C St Mary Aldermary *Lon* 66-72; Regional Officer SPCK 67-72; V Canning Town St Cedd *Chelmsf* 72-80; P-in-c Victoria Docks Ascension 78-79; P-in-c Runwell 80-81; P-in-c Wickford 80-81; TR Wickford and Runwell 81-85; V Gosfield 85-91; RD Halstead and Coggeshall 87-91; Hon Can Chelmsf Cathl 90-91; rtd 91; Perm to Offic *St E* from 91. *1 Beech Cottage, Stoke by Nayland, Colchester CO6 4QH* Colchester (0206) 262110

THOMAS, Austin George. b 23. Open Univ BA75. Wells Th Coll 65. **d** 67 **p** 68. C Brislington St Luke *Bris* 67-73; P-in-c Bris St Geo 73-74; P-in-c Bris St Leon Redfield 74-75; TV E Bris 75-80; R Lyddington w Wanborough 80-88; rtd 88; Perm to Offic *Bris* from 88. *11 College Road, Fishponds, Bristol BS16 2HN* Bristol (0272) 583511

THOMAS, Canon Barry Wilfred. b 41. Univ of Wales (Cardiff) BD75. St Mich Coll Llan 72. **d** 75 **p** 76. C Porthmadog *Ban* 75-78; V Llanegryn and Llanfihangel-y-Pennant w Talyllyn 78-82; Sec Dioc Coun for Miss and Unity from 81; R Llanbeblig w Caernarfon and Betws Garmon etc from 82; Can Ban Cathl from 89. *The Rectory, 4 Ffordd Menai, Caernarfon, Gwynedd LL55 1LF* Caernarfon (0286) 3750

THOMAS, Benjamin Lewis. b 10. **d** 56 **p** 57. V Kineton *Cov* 63-70; V Combroke w Compton Verney 63-70; V Cutcombe w Luxborough *B & W* 70-75; rtd 75; Perm to Offic Ex 75-78; Truro from 78. *4 St Martin's Close, Tregurthen Road, Camborne, Cornwall TR14 7DY* Camborne (0209) 714446

THOMAS, Bryan. b 36. Univ of Wales (Abth) BA59. St Deiniol's Hawarden 68. **d** 70 **p** 71. C Llangynwyd w Maesteg *Llan* 70-72; V Cwmllynfell *St D* 72-76; V Gorslas 76-82; R Yarnbury *Sarum* from 82. *The Rectory, Steeple Langford, Salisbury SP3 4NH* Salisbury (0722) 790337

THOMAS, Ven Charles Edward. b 27. Univ of Wales (Lamp) BA51. Coll of Resurr Mirfield 51. **d** 53 **p** 54. C Ilminster w Whitelackington *B & W* 53-56; Chapl St Mich Coll Tenbury 56-57; C St Alb St Steph *St Alb* 57-58; V Boreham Wood St Mich 58-66; R Monksilver w Brompton Ralph and Nettlecombe *B & W* 66-74; P-in-c Nettlecombe 68-69; R S Petherton w the Seavingtons 74-83; RD Crewkerne 77-83; Adn Wells, Can Res and Preb Wells Cathl from 83. *6 The Liberty, Wells, Somerset BA5 2SU* Wells (0749) 72224

THOMAS, Charles Moray Stewart Reid. b 53. BNC Ox BA74 MA79. Wycliffe Hall Ox 75. **d** 78 **p** 79. C Bradf Cathl *Bradf* 78-81; C Barnsbury St Andr and H Trin w All SS *Lon* 81-90; TV Barnsbury from 90. *10 Thornhill Square, London N1 1BQ* 071-609 5525

THOMAS, Cheeramattathu John. b 25. Travancore Univ BA46 BT49 Serampore Coll BD55. United Th Coll Bangalore Andover Newton Th Coll MA66. **d** 55 **p** 57. C Eastham *Ches* 66-74; V Gt Sutton 75-83; USA from 83; rtd 91. *2706 Burke Road, Pasadena, Texas 77502, USA* Pasadena (713) 947-7548

THOMAS, Colin Norman. b 41. Open Univ BA78. Trin Coll Bris 72. **d** 74 **p** 75. C Handforth *Ches* 74-77; C Bucknall and Bagnall *Lich* 77-80; TV 80-86; V Ogley Hay from 86. *St James's Vicarage, 37 New Road, Brownhills, Walsall WS8 6AT* Brownhills (0543) 372187

THOMAS, Canon Cyril. b 15. Univ of Wales BA38 Ex Coll Ox BA40 MA45. **d** 41 **p** 42. V Llandingat w Myddfai *St D* 58-82; Can St D Cathl 72-82; rtd 82. *33 Glanaber, Burry Port, Dyfed* Burry Port (05546) 4819

THOMAS, David. b 42. Keble Coll Ox BA64 BA(Theol)66 MA67. St Steph Ho Ox 64. **d** 67 **p** 68. C Hawarden *St As* 67-69; Lect St Mich Coll Llan 69-70; Chapl 70-75; Sec Ch in Wales Liturg Commn 70-75; Vice-Prin St Steph Ho Ox 75-79; Prin 82-87; V Chepstow *Mon* 79-82; Lic to Offic *Ox* 82-87; V Newton St Pet *S & B* from 87. *The Vicarage, Mary Twill Lane, Newton, Swansea SA3 4RB* Swansea (0792) 368348

THOMAS, David Brian. b 45. MIEEE. St D Dioc Tr Course 82. **d** 85 **p** 86. NSM Llandyssul *St D* 85-87; NSM Lamp Pont Steffan w Silian from 88. *Rock House, Bridge Street, Llandysul, Dyfed SA44 4BA* Lampeter (0570) 422706

THOMAS, David Edward. b 60. Univ of Wales (Lamp) BA83 LTh85. Llan St Mich DPS86. **d** 86 **p** 87. C Killay *S & B* 86-89; P-in-c Newbridge-on-Wye and Llanfihangel Brynpabuan 89-90; V 90-91; V Brecon St David w Llanspyddid and Llanilltyd from 91. *St David's Vicarage, Llanfaes, Brecon, Powys LD3 8DR* Brecon (0874) 622707

THOMAS, Canon David Geoffrey. b 24. AKC48. **d** 49 **p** 50. Miss to Seamen 52-53 and 68-81; V Milford Haven *St D* 68-89; Can St D Cathl from 77; Treas from 85; rtd 89. *49 Pill Lane, Milford Haven, Dyfed* Milford Haven (0646) 695792

THOMAS, David Geoffrey. b 37. Univ of Wales (Cardiff) BA58. Launde Abbey 70. Qu Coll Birm 71. **d** 71 **p** 72. Hon C Fenny Drayton *Leic* 71-75; Chapl Community of the H Family Baldslow Chich 75-77; Perm to Offic *Chich* 77-79; P-in-c Mill End and Heronsgate w W Hyde *St Alb* 79-81; Perm to Offic 82-91; Sen Lect Watford Coll 82-91; R Walgrave w Hannington and Wold and Scaldwell *Pet* from 91. *The Rectory, Walgrave, Northampton NN6 9QB* Northampton (0604) 781377

THOMAS, Canon David Glynne. b 41. Dur Univ BSc63. Westcott Ho Cam 64. **d** 67 **p** 68. C St Jo Wood *Lon* 67-70; Min Can St Alb 70-72; Chapl Wadh Coll Ox 72-75; C Ox St Mary V w St Cross and St Pet *Ox* 72-75; Bp's Dom Chapl 75-78; P-in-c Burnham 78-82; TR Burnham w Dropmore, Hitcham and Taplow 82-83; Australia 83-87; Can Res Worc Cathl *Worc* from 87. *Chanson, Battenhall Road, Worcester WR5 2BJ* Worcester (0905) 350223

THOMAS, David Godfrey. b 50. St Chad's Coll Dur BA71 Fitzw Coll Cam BA74 MA78. Westcott Ho Cam 72. **d** 75 **p** 76. C Kirkby *Liv* 75-78; TV Cov E *Cov* 78-88; TR Canvey Is *Chelmsf* from 88. *The Rectory, 210 Long Road, Canvey Island, Essex SS8 0JR* Canvey Island (0268) 511098

THOMAS, David John. b 34. Univ of Wales (Swansea) St D Coll Lamp. St D Dioc Tr Course 85. **d** 88 **p** 89. NSM Cwmaman *St D* from 88. *9 New School Road, Garnant, Ammanford, Dyfed SA18 1LL* Amman Valley (0269) 823936

THOMAS, David Noel. b 08. Univ of Wales BA30. St Mich Coll Llan 31. **d** 32 **p** 33. V Harwich *Chelmsf* 61-74; rtd 74. *24 Mays Avenue, Balsham, Cambridge CB1 6ER* Cambridge (0223) 893047

THOMAS, Dr David Richard. b 48. BNC Ox BA71 MA74 Fitzw Coll Cam BA75 MA80 Lanc Univ PhD83. Ridley Hall Cam 73 Qu Coll Birm 79. **d** 80 **p** 81. C Anfield St Columba *Liv* 80-83; C Liv Our Lady and St Nic w St Anne 83-85; Chapl CCC Cam 85-90; V Witton *Blackb* from 90; Bp's Adv on Inter-Faith Relns from 90. *St Mark's Vicarage, Buncer Lane, Blackburn BB2 6SY* Blackburn (0254) 676615

THOMAS, David Ronald Holt. b 28. Lich Th Coll 55. **d** 58 **p** 59. C Uttoxeter w Bramshall *Lich* 58-61; C Hednesford 61-66; R Armitage from 66; RD Rugeley from 88. *The Rectory, Hood Lane, Armitage, Rugeley, Staffs WS15 4AG* Armitage (0543) 490278

THOMAS, David Thomas. b 44. St Cath Coll Cam BA66 MA70 St Jo Coll Dur DipTh68. **d** 71 **p** 72. C Chorlton-cum-Hardy St Clem *Man* 71-74; Chapl Salford Tech Coll 74-79; P-in-c Pendleton St Thos *Man* 75-77; V 77-80; TR Gleadless *Sheff* 80-90; RD Attercliffe 86-90; V Benchill *Man* from 90. *St Luke's Vicarage, Brownley Road, Benchill, Manchester M22 4PT* 061-998 2071

THOMAS, Canon David William. b 17. Univ of Wales BA63 MA67. St D Coll Lamp BA38 St Mich Coll Llan 39. **d** 41 **p** 43. V Pontyberem *St D* 67-76; V Llanilar w Rhostie and Llangwyryfon etc 76-83; Hon Can St D Cathl from 88; rtd 83. *138 Stryd Margoed, Rhydaman, Dyfed SA18 2NN* Ammanford (0269) 594986

THOMAS, David William Wallace. b 51. St Chad's Coll Dur BA72. St Mich Coll Llan 72. **d** 75 **p** 76. C Bargoed and Deri w Brithdir *Llan* 75-79; Hon C 79-81; V Nantymoel w Wyndham 81-84; Chapl RN from 84. *c/o MOD, Lacon House, Theobald's Road, London WC1X 8RY* 071-430 6847

THOMAS, David Wynford. b 48. Univ of Wales (Abth) LLB70. Qu Coll Birm 76. **d** 79 **p** 80. C Swansea St Mary w H Trin and St Mark *S & B* 79-83; P-in-c Swansea St Mark 83-89; Lic to Assist RD 90. *74 Terrace Road, Swansea SA1 6HU*

THOMAS, Canon Dillwyn Morgan. b 26. Univ of Wales (Lamp) BA50. Qu Coll Birm 50. **d** 52 **p** 53. V Bargoed w Brithdir *Llan* 68-74; V Bargoed and Deri w Brithdir 74-75; V Penarth All SS 75-88; Can Llan Cathl from 86; rtd 88. *11 Baroness Place, Penarth, S Glam CF61UL* Penarth (0222) 704090

THOMAS, Canon Donald George. b 22. DFC44. Qu Coll Cam BA47 MA52. Ridley Hall Cam 47. **d** 49 **p** 50. V Runcorn All SS *Ches* 61-88; RD Frodsham 82-88; Hon Can Ches Cathl from 84; rtd 88. *11 Parc Capel, Lixwm, Holywell, Clwyd CH8 8NA* Holywell (0352) 780163

THOMAS, Edward Bernard Meredith. b 21. Leeds Univ BA44 Queensland Univ BEd68 BD72. Coll of Resurr Mirfield 47. **d** 49 **p** 50. C St Mary-at-Lambeth *S'wark*

49-54; C Portsea N End St Mark *Portsm* 54-56; V Portsea All SS 56-64; Australia from 64. *33 Highfield Street, Durack, Queensland, Australia 4077* Brisbane (7) 372-3517

THOMAS, Canon Edward Maldwyn. b 12. Univ of Wales BA34. St Mich Coll Llan 37. **d** 38 **p** 39. V Duddeston *Birm* 51-83; Hon Can Birm Cathl 72-83; rtd 83; Perm to Offic *Birm* from 83. *3 Birchtree Grove, Solihull, W Midlands B91 1HD* 021-705 3706

THOMAS, Edward Walter Dennis. b 32. St Mich Coll Llan 61. **d** 63 **p** 64. C Lougher *S & B* 63-69; V Ystradfellte 69-74; V Dukinfield St Mark and St Luke *Ches* from 74; Chapl Gtr Man Police from 77; OCF from 88. *St Mark's Vicarage, Dukinfield, Cheshire SK16 4PR* 061-330 2783

THOMAS, Miss Eileen Anne Harwood. b 35. Univ of Wales (Swansea) BA59 Kent Univ MA80. Cant Sch of Min 80. **dss** 83 **d** 87. Mill Hill Jo Keble Ch *Lon* 83-86; The Lydiards *Bris* 86-87; Par Dn from 87. *63 Beverley, Toothill, Swindon SN5 8BL* Swindon (0793) 496421

THOMAS, Eirwyn Wheldon. b 35. St Mich Coll Llan 58. **d** 61 **p** 62. C Glanadda *Ban* 61-67; R Llantrisant and Llandeusant 67-75; V Nevin w Pistyll w Tudweiliog w Llandudwen etc from 75. *The Vicarage, Nefyn, Pwllheli, Gwynedd LL53 6BS* Nefyn (0758) 720481

THOMAS (nee REEVES), Mrs Elizabeth Anne. b 45. Sheff Univ BA67 PGCE75. SW Minl Tr Course 87. **d** 90. Par Dn Stoke Damerel *Ex* from 90. *5 Waterloo Street, Plymouth PL1 5RW* Plymouth (0752) 565723

THOMAS, Elwyn Bernard. b 45. Univ of Wales (Swansea) BSc68. Llan St Mich BD71. **d** 71 **p** 72. C Aberdare St Fagan *Llan* 71-74; C Merthyr Dytan 74-76; R Dowlais 76-86; V Llangynwyd w Maesteg from 86. *The Vicarage, 33 Brynmawr Place, Maesteg, Bridgend, M Glam CF34 9PB* Maesteg (0656) 733194

THOMAS, Erwin Arthur. b 09. Boston Univ BA42. Nashotah Ho BD46. **d** 45 **p** 45. SSJE from 42; Lic to Offic *Ox* 56-79; rtd 79; Lic to Offic *Lon* from 79. *St John's Home, St Mary's Road, Oxford OX4 1QE* Oxford (0865) 247725

✠**THOMAS, Rt Rev Eryl Stephen.** b 10. St Jo Coll Ox BA32 MA38. Wells Th Coll 32. **d** 33 **p** 34 **c** 68. C Colwyn Bay *St As* 33-38; C Hawarden 38-43; V Risca *Mon* 43-48; Warden St Mich Coll Llan 48-54; Dean Llan 54-68; Bp Mon 68-71; Bp Llan 71-75; rtd 75; Asst Bp *S & B* from 88. *17 Orchard Close, Gilwern, Abergavenny, Gwent NP7 0EN* Gilwern (0873) 831050

THOMAS, Euros Lloyd. b 53. Bris Poly LLB75. Llan St Mich DipTh79. **d** 79 **p** 80. C Llanelly *St D* 79-84; R Cilgerran w Bridell and Llantwyd from 84. *The Rectory, Cilgerran, Cardigan, Dyfed SA43 2RZ* Cardigan (0239) 614500

THOMAS, Evan Tudor. b 11. St Mich Coll Llan 49. **d** 51 **p** 53. R Pontfaen, Morfil, Llanychllwydog, Puncheston etc *St D* 59-78; rtd 78; Perm to Offic *Cant* from 78. *17 Western Avenue, Ashford, Kent TN23 1LY* Ashford (0233) 628811

THOMAS, Frank Lowth. b 22. Lon Coll of Div 64. **d** 66 **p** 67. C Bickenhill w Elmdon *Birm* 68-71; R Carlton Colville *Nor* 71-81; R Smallburgh w Dilham w Honing and Crostwight 81-85; rtd 85; Perm to Offic *Nor* from 86. *7 Mill Close, Salhouse, Norwich NR13 6QB* Norwich (0603) 720376

THOMAS, Frederick Eric. b 16. Bps' Coll Cheshunt 57. **d** 59 **p** 60. C Alverstoke *Portsm* 72-79; Chapl HM Youth Cust Cen Hewell Grange 79-83; C Tardebigge *Worc* 79-81; TV Redditch, The Ridge 81-83; rtd 83; Perm to Offic *Ox* from 84. *9 Orchard Way, Chinnor, Oxford OX9 4UD* Kingston Blount (0844) 51261

THOMAS, Geler Harries. b 28. St D Coll Lamp BA55. **d** 57 **p** 58. C Llanelly Ch Ch *St D* 57-62; V Llandyssilio and Egremont 62-69; V Llanedy 69-79; V Llangennech and Hendy 79-88; V Llanegwad w Llanfynydd from 88; RD Llangadog and Llandeilo 89-90. *Llanegwad Vicarage, Heol Alltyferin, Nantgaredig, Carmarthen, Dyfed SA32 7NE* Nantgaredig (0267) 290516

THOMAS, Geoffrey Brynmor. b 34. K Coll Lon BA56 AKC56. Ridley Hall Cam 58. **d** 60 **p** 61. C Harlow New Town w Lt Parndon *Chelmsf* 60-65; V Leyton All SS 65-74; V Halifax All So *Wakef* 74-82; R The Winterbournes and Compton Valence *Sarum* 82-89; TV Cheltenham St Mark *Glouc* from 89. *St Aidan's Vicarage, 21 Brooklyn Road, Cheltenham, Glos GL51 8DT* Cheltenham (0242) 514179

THOMAS, Geoffrey Charles. b 30. St Jo Coll Nottm LTh ALCD64. **d** 64 **p** 65. C York St Paul *York* 64-67; C Cheltenham Ch Ch *Glouc* 67-70; V Whitgift w Adlingfleet *Sheff* 70-74; P-in-c Eastoft 72-74; V Mortomley 74-88; R Middleton Cheney w Chacombe *Pet* from 88. *The Rectory, 3 High Street, Middleton*

Cheney, Banbury, Oxon OX17 2PB   Banbury (0295) 710254

THOMAS, Geoffrey Heale. b 29. St Mich Coll Llan 58. **d** 60 **p** 61. C Llansamlet *S & B* 60-63; Nigeria 63-67; V Swansea St Nic *S & B* 67-80; CF (TA) 72; V Oystermouth *S & B* from 80. *The Vicarage, 9 Western Close, Mumbles, Swansea SA3 4HF*   Swansea (0792) 369971 or 361684

THOMAS, George. b 46. Leeds Univ BEd69. St Jo Coll Dur 75 Cranmer Hall Dur DipTh77. **d** 78 **p** 79. C Highfield *Liv* 78-83; V Chorley St Jas *Blackb* from 83. *St James's Vicarage, St James's Place, Chorley, Lancs PR6 0NA*   Chorley (02572) 63153

THOMAS, Glyn. b 36. Lon Univ BPharm61. St Deiniol's Hawarden 80. **d** 82 **p** 83. C Rhyl w Rhyl St Ann *St As* 83-85; R Llanycil w Bala and Frongoch and Llangower etc from 85. *The Rectory, Heol-y-Castell, Bala, Gwynedd LL23 7YA*   Bala (0678) 521047

THOMAS, Gwilym Ivor. b 20. St D Coll Lamp BA41. **d** 43 **p** 44. V Llansantffraed *St D* 62-70; V Llansantffraed and Llanbadarn Trefeglwys 70-80; V Llansantffraed and Llanbadarn Trefeglwys etc 80-85; RD Glyn Aeron 78-85; rtd 85. *Stanley House, 9 Hill Street, New Quay, Dyfed SA45 9QD*   New Quay (0545) 560167

THOMAS, Gwyn Aubrey. b 12. St D Coll Lamp BA35. **d** 35 **p** 36. R S Perrott w Mosterton and Chedington *Sarum* 66-79; rtd 79. *Flat 7, Miller House, Merchants Road, Bristol*   Bristol (0272) 734665

THOMAS, Gwynfor. b 13. St D Coll Lamp BA40. **d** 46 **p** 47. V Wookey *B & W* 69-74; V Wookey w Henton 74-78; rtd 78; Lic to Offic *B & W* from 79. *10 Fairfield, Somerton, Somerset TA11 7PE*   Somerton (0458) 72549

THOMAS, Harold Heath. b 08. Man Univ BA32 AKC47. Linc Th Coll 47. **d** 47 **p** 48. V Low Marple *Ches* 53-75; rtd 75; Perm to Offic from 75; Ches from 76. *102 Hollins Lane, Marple Bridge, Stockport, Cheshire SK6 5DA*   061-449 8176

THOMAS, Herbert John. b 13. AKC42. **d** 42 **p** 43. R Bridgwater St Jo w Chedzoy *B & W* 62-73; R Compton Martin w Ubley 73-79; rtd 79; Perm to Offic *B & W* from 79. *25 Delmore Road, Frome, Somerset BA11 4EG*   Frome (0373) 63762

THOMAS, Howard Donald Lewis. b 19. Chich Th Coll 46. **d** 49 **p** 50. R Hanborough *Ox* 67-84; rtd 84; Chapl Soc of All SS Sisters of the Poor 84-87; Perm to Offic *Ox* from 84. *7 Marlborough Crescent, Long Hanborough, Oxford OX7 2JP*   Freeland (0993) 881805

THOMAS, Hugh. b 14. St D Coll Lamp BA36. **d** 37 **p** 38. R Clocaenog and Gyffylliog *St As* 55-79; rtd 79. *2 Hafan Deg, Clawdd Newydd, Ruthin, Clwyd LL15 2ND*   Clawdd Newydd (08245) 716

THOMAS, Hugh. b 25. St D Coll Lamp BA50. **d** 51 **p** 52. V Llanfynydd *St D* 63-74; V Pontyates 74-80; V Pontyates and Llangyndeyrn 80-90; rtd 91. *90 Priory Street, Kidwelly, Dyfed SA17 4TY*   Kidwelly (0554) 890114

THOMAS, Hugh Meredith. b 39. Univ of Wales (Lamp) BA61. St Mich Coll Llan 61. **d** 63 **p** 64. C Llandeilo Fawr and Llandefeisant *St D* 63-70; V Gwynfe and Llanddeusant 70-74; V Llanpumsaint 74-80; V Llanpumsaint w Llanllawddog 80-85; R Newport w Cilgwyn and Dinas w Llanllawer from 85. *The Rectory, Long Street, Newport, Dyfed SA42 0TY*   Newport (0239) 820380

THOMAS, Canon Huw Glyn. b 42. Univ of Wales (Lamp) BA62 Linacre Coll Ox BA65 MA69. Wycliffe Hall Ox 62. **d** 65 **p** 66. C Oystermouth *S & B* 65-68; Asst Chapl Solihull Sch Warks 68-69; Chapl Solihull Sch W Midl 69-73; Selection Sec ACCM 73-78; C Loughton St Jo *Chelmsf* 74-77; V Bury St Jo *Man* 78-83; Dir of Ords 82-87; V Bury St Jo w St Mark 83-86; Can Res and Treas Liv Cathl *Liv* from 87. *2 Cathedral Close, Liverpool L1 7BR*   051-708 0932

THOMAS, Ian Melville. b 50. Jes Coll Ox BA71 MA75. St Steph Ho Ox 71. **d** 73 **p** 74. PV St D Cathl *St D* 73-77; Chapl RAF from 77. *c/o MOD, Adastral House, Theobald's Road, London WC1X 8RU*   071-430 7268

THOMAS, Idris. b 48. St D Coll Lamp DipTh71. **d** 71 **p** 72. C Llanbeblig w Caernarfon and Betws Garmon etc *Ban* 71-75; P-in-c Llanaelhaiarn 75-77; R Llanaelhaearn w Clynnog Fawr from 77. *The Rectory, Trefor, Caernarfon, Gwynedd LL54 5HN*   Clynnogfawr (028686) 547

THOMAS, Ven Ilar Roy Luther. b 30. St D Coll Lamp BA51. St Mich Coll Llan 51. **d** 53 **p** 54. C Oystermouth *S & B* 53-56; C Gorseinon 56-59; R Llanbadarn Fawr and Llandegley 59-60; R Llanbadarn Fawr, Llandegley and Llanfihangel 60-66; CF (ACF) 62-90; Children's Adv *S & B* 63-77; RD Knighton 66-79; V Knighton and Norton 66-79; Can Brecon Cathl from 75; V Sketty 79-89; Treas 87-88; Chan 88-90; Adn Gower from 90.

104 West Cross Lane, West Cross, Swansea SA3 5NQ   Swansea (0792) 402464 or 404043

THOMAS, Iris. b 18. Univ of Wales (Abth) BA39 DipEd40. **d** 80. Hon C Tylorstown *Llan* 80-84; Hon C Ferndale w Maerdy 84-85; rtd 85; Perm to Offic *Llan* from 86. *18 Richard Street, Maerdy, Ferndale, M Glam CF43 4AU*   Ferndale (0443) 755235

THOMAS, James Morris. b 02. **d** 37 **p** 38. R Tintern Parva w Chapel Hill *Mon* 57-73; rtd 73; Perm to Offic Mon from 73; Heref 74-90. *c/o 23 Dundee Court, Duncraig, Australia 6023*

THOMAS, John Albert. b 13. **d** 51 **p** 52. R Kirton *S'well* 65-74; V Walesby 65-74; V Sutton cum Lound 74-78; rtd 78; Perm to Offic *S'well* from 78. *2 Trinity Hospital, Retford, Notts DN22 7BD*   Retford (0777) 707333

THOMAS, John Arun. b 47. Bombay Univ BA69 MA72 Nottm Univ CertEd80. Oak Hill Th Coll 84. **d** 88 **p** 89. C Liv Ch Ch Norris Green *Liv* 88-89; C Wavertree St Mary from 89. *24 Orford Street, Wavertree, Liverpool L15 8HX*   051-733 7116

THOMAS, John Bryn. b 37. Lich Th Coll 63. **d** 66 **p** 67. C Stoke upon Trent *Lich* 66-71; R Wotton *Guildf* 71-79; P-in-c Holmbury St Mary 78-79; R Wotton and Holmbury St Mary 79-86; C Easthampstead *Ox* 86-88; TV Chambersbury (Hemel Hempstead) *St Alb* from 88. *The Vicarage, Peascroft Road, Hemel Hempstead, Herts HP3 8EP*   Hemel Hempstead (0442) 43934

THOMAS, Canon John Degwel. b 11. Univ of Wales BSc33. St Steph Ho Ox 34. **d** 36 **p** 37. V Chesterton St Geo *Ely* 51-74; R Rampton 74-81; Press and Communications Officer 74-86; Hon Can Ely Cathl 77-81; rtd 81. *17 King Street, Over, Cambridge CB4 5PS* Swavesey (0954) 31198

THOMAS, Canon John Elwern. b 14. Univ of Wales BA35. Coll of Resurr Mirfield 35. **d** 37 **p** 38. Can Cursal Ban Cathl 68-70; Warden Ruthin w Llanrhydd *St As* 70-79; Can Cursal St As Cathl 77-79; rtd 79. *Fron Deg, Ffordd Goch, Llandyrnog, Denbigh, Clwyd LL16 4LE* Llandyrnog (08244) 445

THOMAS, John Herbert Samuel. b 34. Pemb Coll Cam BA57 MA64. St Mich Coll Llan 57. **d** 58 **p** 59. C Port Talbot St Theodore *Llan* 58-60; C Llantwit Major and St Donat's 60-67; P-in-c Barry All SS 67-74; V Dinas w Penygraig 74-85; V Pontypridd St Cath 85-90; V Pontypridd St Cath w St Matt from 90; RD Pontypridd from 90. *St Catherine's Vicarage, Gelliwastad Grove, Pontypridd, M Glam CF37 2BS*   Pontypridd (0443) 402021

✠**THOMAS, Rt Rev John James Absalom.** b 08. Univ of Wales BA29 Keble Coll Ox BA36 MA36. Lambeth DD58. **d** 31 **p** 32 **c** 58. C Llanguicke *S & B* 31-34; C Sketty 34-36; Bp's Messenger 36-40; Lect Th Univ Coll Ban 40-44; I Swansea *S & B* 45-58; RD 52-54; Hon Can Brecon Cathl 46-53; Can and Prec 53-54; Adn Gower 54-58; Bp *S & B* 58-76; rtd 76. *Woodbine Cottage, St Mary's Street, Tenby, Dyfed*   Tenby (0834) 2013

THOMAS, Canon John Keble Holliday. b 09. St D Coll Lamp BA31. **d** 32 **p** 33. R Ripple *Worc* 52-78; Hon Can Worc Cathl 75-78; rtd 78; Perm to Offic *Worc* from 78. *Brook House, Wyre Piddle, Pershore, Worcs*   Pershore (0386) 553635

THOMAS, Dr John Thurston. b 28. CChem FRSC65 Univ of Wales (Swansea) BSc48 DipEd49 Leeds Univ PhD58. Glouc Sch of Min 88. **d** 90. NSM S Cerney w Cerney Wick and Down Ampney *Glouc* from 90. *Samantha, Silver Street, South Cerney, Cirencester, Glos GL7 5TP* Cirencester (0285) 860382

THOMAS, Joseph Neville. b 33. Univ of Wales (Lamp) BA57. St Mich Coll Llan. **d** 59 **p** 60. C Porthmadog *Ban* 59-62; C Cardiff St Jo *Llan* 62-65; CF 65-88; R Sherfield-on-Loddon and Stratfield Saye etc *Win* from 88. *The Rectory, Breach Lane, Sherfield-on-Loddon, Basingstoke, Hants RG27 0EU*   Basingstoke (0256) 882209

THOMAS, Judith Ann Bower. b 37. Lon Bible Coll DipTh60. Trin Coll Bris 77. **dss** 78 **d** 87. Portsea St Geo CD *Portsm* 78-80; Ch Sister Princess Marg Hosp Swindon 80-81; CMS Personnel Dept from 82. *c/o CMS, Partnership House, 157 Waterloo Road, London SE1 8UU*   071-928 8681

THOMAS, June Marion. b 31. Univ of Wales BA53 DipEd54. NE Ord Course 83. **dss** 86 **d** 87. Stockton St Pet *Dur* 86-87; Hon Par Dn 87-89; Hon Par Dn Stockton St Mark from 89. *50 Brisbane Grove, Stockton-on-Tees, Cleveland TS18 5BP*   Stockton-on-Tees (0642) 582408

THOMAS, Leslie Richard. b 45. Lon Coll of Div 65. **d** 69 **p** 70. C Knotty Ash St Jo *Liv* 69-72; C Sutton 72-74; TV 74-77; V Banks 77-82; V Gt Crosby All SS from

82. *All Saints' Vicarage, 17 Moor Coppice, Crosby, Liverpool L23 2XJ* 051-924 6436

THOMAS, Lewis Llewellyn. b 21. Univ of Wales (Lamp) BA41 Selw Coll Cam BA44 MA48. Westcott Ho Cam 44. d 45 p 46. V Bilston St Mary *Lich* 55-75; Perm to Offic 75-80 and 82-89; Hon C Wolv St Jo 80-82; rtd 86; Perm to Offic *Glouc* from 86. *Flat 14, Capel Court, The Burgage, Prestbury, Cheltenham, Glos GL52 3EL* Cheltenham (0242) 576384

THOMAS, Ms Margaret. b 41. Bris Univ BSc63 Leeds Univ CertEd64 Ex Univ ADC70. Cranmer Hall Dur 81. dss 83 d 87. Maghull *Liv* 83-86; Asst Chapl Liv Univ from 86; St Luke in the City 86-87; Par Dn 87; Chapl St Helen's and Knowsley HA from 89; Chapl Whiston Hosp from 89. *Chapel House, Whiston Hospital, Prescot, Merseyside L35 5DR* 051-430 1657

THOMAS, Mark Wilson. b 51. Dur Univ BA72 Hull Univ MA89. Ripon Coll Cuddesdon 76. d 78 p 79. C Chapelthorpe *Wakef* 78-81; C Seaford w Sutton *Chich* 81-84; V Gomersal *Wakef* from 84. *The Vicarage, 404 Spen Lane, Gomersal, Cleckheaton, W Yorkshire BD19 4LS* Cleckheaton (0274) 872131

THOMAS, Sister Mary Josephine. b 30. Ripon Dioc Tr Coll TCert50 Carl Dioc Tr Course 88. d 90. NSM Hawes Side *Blackb* from 90. *112 St Andrew's Road North, St Annes-on-Sea, Lancs FY8 2JQ* St Annes (0253) 728016

THOMAS, Melvyn. b 04. St D Coll Lamp BA32. d 33 p 34. V Llangadog *St D* 60-74; rtd 74. *4 Ger-y-Llan, Carmarthen, Dyfed SA31 1LY* Carmarthen (0267) 233412

THOMAS, Michael Longdon Sanby. b 34. Trin Hall Cam BA55 MA60. Wells Th Coll 56. d 58 p 59. C Sandal St Helen *Wakef* 58-60; Chapl Portsm Cathl *Portsm* 60-64; V Shedfield 64-69; V Portchester from 69. *The Vicarage, 164 Castle Street, Portchester, Fareham, Hants PO16 9QH* Cosham (0705) 376289

THOMAS, Michael Paul. b 29. d 52 p 53. V Ardeley *St Alb* 67-86; rtd 86; Perm to Offic *Nor* from 87. *Mead House, 7 Eagle Close, Erpingham, Norwich NR11 7AW* Cromer (0263) 768432

THOMAS, Preb Owen. b 17. Selw Coll Cam BA40 MA58. St Mich Coll Llan 40. d 41 p 42. R Welshpool w Castle Caereinion *St As* 65-77; RD Pool 76-77; Preb St As Cathl 77-87; Adn Montgomery 77-87; V Berriew and Manafon 80-87; rtd 87. *Oaklands, Fron, Montgomery, Powys SY15 6RZ* Berriew (0686) 640675

THOMAS, Owen James. b 17. Univ of Wales BA38. Tyndale Hall Bris 38. d 40 p 41. Chapl and Lect Lon Bible Coll 62-76; Hon C Northwood Em *Lon* 70-76; V Canonbury St Steph 76-85; rtd 85; Perm to Offic *Chich* from 85. *22 Woodland Way, Fairlight, Hastings, E Sussex TN35 4AU* Hastings (0424) 813613

THOMAS, Ms Pamela Sibyl. b 38. Ripon Coll Cuddesdon 88. d 90. C Preston w Sutton Poyntz and Osmington w Poxwell *Sarum* 90; Par Dn from 91. *7 Wyke Oliver Close, Preston, Weymouth, Dorset DT3 6DR* Preston (0305) 835018

THOMAS, Mrs Patricia Margaret. b 44. Hockerill Coll Cam TCert65. Sarum & Wells Th Coll 79. dss 82 d 87. Verwood *Sarum* 82-87; Hon Par Dn 87-88; Chapl Asst Friern Hosp Lon 88-90; Par Dn Upton cum Chalvey *Ox* from 90. *11 Cooper Way, Windsor Meadows, Slough SL1 9JA* Slough (0753) 38714

THOMAS, Patrick Hungerford Bryan. b 52. St Cath Coll Cam BA73 MA77 Leeds Univ BA78 Univ of Wales PhD82. Coll of Resurr Mirfield 76. d 79 p 80. C Abth *St D* 79-81; C Carmarthen St Pet 81-82; R Llangeitho and Blaenpennal w Bettws Leiki etc 82-84; Warden of Ords 83-86; R Brechfa w Abergorlech etc from 84. *The Rectory, Brechfa, Carmarthen, Dyfed SA32 7RA* Brechfa (0267) 202389

THOMAS, Paul Robert. b 42. N Ord Course. d 82 p 83. C Hull Newland St Jo *York* 82-84; P-in-c Rowley 84-87; Soc Resp Officer Hull 84-87; R Rowley w Skidby 87-88; TR Barking St Marg w St Patr *Chelmsf* from 88. *The Rectory, 166 Longbridge Road, Barking, Essex IG11 7NR* 081-594 2932

THOMAS, Paul Wyndham. b 55. Or Coll Ox BA76 BTh78 MA80. Wycliffe Hall Ox 77. d 79 p 80. C Llangynwyd w Maesteg *Llan* 79-85; TV Langport Area Chs *B & W* 85-90; P-in-c Thorp Arch w Walton *York* from 90; Clergy Tr Officer from 90. *The Vicarage, Church Causeway, Thorp Arch, Wetherby, W Yorkshire LS23 7AE* Boston Spa (0937) 842430

THOMAS, Peter George Hartley. b 38. AKC63. d 64 p 65. C Leigh Park St Fran CD *Portsm* 64-69; V Cosham 69-77; R Hayes *Roch* from 77. *The Rectory, Hayes Street, Bromley BR2 7LH* 081-462 1373

THOMAS, Peter James. b 53. Lon Univ BSc75. Trin Coll Bris 77. d 80 p 81. C Hucclecote *Glouc* 80-84; C Loughb Em *Leic* 84-85; TV Parr *Liv* from 85. *459 Fleet Lane, St Helens, Merseyside WA9 2NQ* St Helens (0744) 21213

THOMAS, Peter Rhys. b 37. MInstPkg MIPM. TCD BA59 MA72. d 72 p 73. C Cong *T, K & A* 73-75; I 75-77; C Bingley All SS *Bradf* 77-79; V Shelf 79-81; Producer Relig Broadcasting Viking Radio 81-84; P-in-c Croxton *Linc* 81-82; P-in-c Ulceby 81-82; P-in-c Wootton 81-82; P-in-c Ulceby Gp 82; V Ulceby Gp 82-84; R E and W Tilbury and Linford *Chelmsf* 84-89; I Celbridge w Straffan and Newcastle-Lyons *D & G* from 89. *The Rectory, Maynooth Road, Celbridge, Co Kildare, Irish Republic* Dublin (1) 628-8231

THOMAS, Peter Wilson. b 58. BD AKC. Ripon Coll Cuddesdon. d 82 p 83. C Stockton St Pet *Dur* 82-85; TV Solihull *Birm* 85-90; V Rednal from 90. *St Stephen's Vicarage, Edgewood Road, Rednal, Birmingham B45 8SG* 021-453 3347

THOMAS, Philip Edward. b 13. Lon Univ BA35 AKC36. d 36 p 37. Hd Master Friern Barnet Gr Sch 54-60; rtd 78. *29 Clay Hall Drive, Spalding, Lincs PE11 1ST* Spalding (0775) 760147

THOMAS, Philip Harold Emlyn. b 41. Cant Univ (NZ) BA64 MA77 Dur Univ PhD82. Melbourne Coll of Div BD68. d 68 p 69. Australia 68-71; New Zealand 71-77; Fell and Chapl Univ Coll Dur 77-83; V Heighington *Dur* from 84. *The Vicarage, Heighington, Co Durham DL5 6PP* Aycliffe (0325) 312134

THOMAS, Philip Mansell. b 59. Hatf Coll Dur BA81. Chich Th Coll. d 86 p 87. C Wythenshawe St Martin *Man* 86-89; C Bedf Leigh from 89. *30 Carisbrooke Road, Leigh, Lancs WN7 2XA* Leigh (0942) 607893

THOMAS, Philip Sewell. b 09. Linc Coll Ox BA32 MA38. Ely Th Coll 32. d 33 p 34. C Odiham w S Warnborough *Win* 33-36; C Midsomer Norton *B & W* 36-42; PV Wells Cathl 42-46; C Easton 42-46; C Eastover 46-49; V Barton St David w Kingweston from 49. *The Vicarage, Barton St David, Somerton, Somerset TA11 6BN* Baltonsborough (0458) 257

THOMAS, Ralph Pilling. b 23. Univ of Wales (Lamp) BA49. Wycliffe Hall Ox 49. d 51 p 52. Chapl HM Pris Leeds 69-74; R Kirklington w Burneston and Wath *Ripon* 74-88; RD Wensley 85-88; rtd 88. *20 The Maltings, Staithe Road, Bungay, Suffolk NR35 1EJ* Bungay (0986) 895118

THOMAS, Richard. b 45. St D Coll Lamp 68. d 71 p 72. C Llanelly St Paul *St D* 71-74; Chapl RN 74-90; V St Ishmael's w Llansaint and Ferryside *St D* from 90. *Vicarage, Ferryside, Dyfed SA17* Ferryside (026785) 288

THOMAS, Richard Frederick. b 24. Qu Coll Cam BA45 MA49. Ridley Hall Cam 47. d 49 p 50. Jerusalem 67-73; Ho Master Bp Luffa Sch Chich 74-80; Lic to Offic *Chich* 75-77; Hon C Chich St Pancras and St Jo 78-80; R N Mundham w Hunston and Merston 80-89; rtd 89. *16 Brent Cross, Emsworth, Hants PO10 7JA* Emsworth (0243) 378974

THOMAS, Richard Paul. b 50. MIPR. Wycliffe Hall Ox 74. d 76 p 77. C Abingdon w Shippon *Ox* 76-80; R Win All SS w Chilcomb and Chesil *Win* 80-88; Dioc Communications Officer 83-89; Dioc Communications Officer *Ox* from 89. *18 Eason Drive, Abingdon, Oxon* Abingdon (0235) 553360

THOMAS, Robert Stanley. b 31. Lon Univ BD65 Man Univ MEd78. Sarum Th Coll 66. d 67 p 68. C Maltby *Sheff* 67-70; Lic to Offic St Alb 70-72; Man 72-79; St As 80-82; Dioc RE Adv *St As* from 82; V Glyndyfrdwy and Llansantffraid Glyn Dyfrdwy from 82; RD Edeyrnion from 88. *The Vicarage, Glyndyfrdwy, Corwen, Clwyd LL21 9HG* Glyndwr (049083) 201

THOMAS, Robin. b 57. Coll of Art Lon NDD50. St Steph Ho Ox 89. d 89 p 90. NSM Clifton All SS w St Jo *Bris* from 89. *Garden Flat, 8 Ashgrove Road, Bristol BS6 6LY* Bristol (0272) 730729

THOMAS, Roger James. b 37. Bris Univ BA59. Wells Th Coll 59. d 61 p 62. C Henbury *Bris* 61-64; C Stapleton 64-69; P-in-c Hardenhuish 69-71; R 71-75; P-in-c Kington 69-71; V 71-75; V Bris St Andr Hartcliffe 75-81; RD Bedminster 79-81; P-in-c Frenchay 81-86; P-in-c Winterbourne Down 81-86; R Frenchay and Winterbourne Down from 86. *The Rectory, Frenchay, Bristol BS16 1NB* Bristol (0272) 567616

THOMAS, Ronald Stuart. b 13. Univ of Wales BA35. St Mich Coll Llan 35. d 36 p 37. R Aberdaron and Bodferin w Rhiw w Llanfaelrhys *Ban* 72-78; rtd 78. *Sarn-y-Plas, Rhiw, Pwllheli, Gwynedd* Rhiw (075888) 279

THOMAS, Russen William. b 30. Univ of Wales (Lamp) BA55. St Mich Coll Llan 55. d 57 p 58. C Newport St

Jo Bapt *Mon* 57-59; C Pemb Dock *St D* 59-62; R St Florence and Redberth 62-69; V Newport St Julian *Mon* 69-79; V Stratton *Truro* 79-88; RD Stratton 83-88; V Lanteglos by Fowey from 88; Miss to Seamen from 88. *The Vicarage, Battery Lane, Polruan, Fowey, Cornwall PL23 1PR* Polruan (0726) 870213

THOMAS, Preb Stephen Blayney. b 35. St D Coll Lamp BA62. Bp Burgess Hall Lamp DipTh63. **d** 63 **p** 64. C Ledbury *Heref* 63-67; C Bridgnorth w Tasley 67-68; C Clun w Chapel Lawn, Bettws-y-Crwyn and Newc 68-73; C Clungunford w Clunbury and Clunton, Bedstone etc 68-73; V Worfield 73-84; RD Bridgnorth 81-83; R Kingsland from 84; P-in-c Aymestrey and Leinthall Earles w Wigmore etc from 84; P-in-c Eardisland from 84; Preb Heref Cathl from 85. *Kingsland Rectory, Leominster, Herefordshire HR6 9QW* Kingsland (056881) 255

THOMAS, Stuart Grahame. b 54. Pemb Coll Cam BA77 MA81. Ridley Hall Cam 85. **d** 87 **p** 88. C Guildf H Trin w St Mary *Guildf* 87-91; V Churt from 91. *The Vicarage, Old Kiln Lane, Churt, Farnham, Surrey GU10 2HX* Headley Down (0428) 713368

THOMAS, Sydney Robert. b 44. Univ of Wales (Swansea) BA65 MA83. St D Coll Lamp LTh67. **d** 67 **p** 68. C Llanelly *St D* 67-77; V Pontyberem from 77. *The Vicarage, 56 Llannon Road, Pontyberem, Llanelli, Dyfed SA15 5LY* Pontyberem (0269) 870345

THOMAS, Telford Ifano. b 17. Univ of Wales BA38. St D Coll Lamp 38. **d** 40 **p** 41. V Llangennech and Hendy *St D* 61-79; V Llansteffan and Llan-y-bri etc 79-82; rtd 82. *Flat 33, Ty Rhys, The Parade, Carmarthen, Dyfed SA31 1LY*

THOMAS, Theodore Eilir. b 36. Univ of Wales (Lamp) BA58. Sarum Th Coll 58. **d** 60 **p** 61. C Fenton *Lich* 60-63; C Stourport All SS and St Mich CD *Worc* 63-67; V Worc H Trin 67-74; P-in-c Dudley St Fran 74-79; V 79-83; R Plympton St Maurice *Ex* from 83. *St Maurice's Rectory, 31 Wain Park, Plympton, Plymouth PL7 3HX* Plymouth (0752) 346114

THOMAS, Thomas Alan. b 37. K Coll Lon BD60 AKC60. St Boniface Warminster 60. **d** 61 **p** 62. C Washington *Dur* 61-65; C Bishopwearmouth St Mary w St Pet CD 65-70; V Ruishton w Thornfalcon *B & W* 70-82; R Hutton from 82. *The Rectory, Church Lane, Hutton, Weston-super-Mare, Avon BS24 9SL* Bleadon (0934) 812366

THOMAS, Thomas Hugh. b 25. Open Univ BA77. St D Coll Lamp 59. **d** 60 **p** 61. C Cwmaman *St D* 60-63; V Martletwy and Lawrenny w Minwear 63-78; V Martletwy w Lawrenny and Minwear and Yerbeston 78-79; R Narberth w Mounton w Robeston Wathen and Crinow from 79; RD Narberth from 82. *The Rectory, Adams Drive, Narberth, Dyfed SA67 7AE* Narberth (0834) 860370

THOMAS, Thomas John. b 15. St D Coll Lamp BA37 St Mich Coll Llan 37. **d** 38 **p** 39. V St Benet Paul's Wharf *Lon* 64-82; C-in-c Paddington St Dav Welsh Ch 64-82; Perm to Offic S'wark from 74; Chapl R Hosp and Home Putney from 74; rtd 82. *5 Amberley Drive, Twyford, Reading RG10 9BX* Twyford (0734) 345018

THOMAS, Thomas John Samuel. b 21. St D Coll Lamp BA48. **d** 49 **p** 50. Chapl RAF 52-77; QHC 73-85; V Horsham *Chich* 77-85; rtd 85; Perm to Offic *St D* from 85. *1 Glynhir Road, Llandybie, Ammanford, Dyfed SA18 2TA* Llandybie (0269) 850726

THOMAS, Canon Thomas Vernon. b 21. St D Coll Lamp BA42 Selw Coll Cam BA(Theol)44 MA48. St Mich Coll Llan 44. **d** 45 **p** 46. V Beeston *Ripon* 55-77; Hon Can Ripon Cathl from 75; R Spofforth w Kirk Deighton 77-89; rtd 89. *The Lodge, Main Street, East Keswick, Leeds LS17 9DB* Collingham Bridge (0937) 73033

THOMAS, Trevor Wilson. b 17. Adelaide Univ BA39. St Barn Coll Adelaide 40 ACT ThL41. **d** 41 **p** 42. V Littlehampton St Jas *Chich* 65-76; R W Blatchington 76-82; rtd 82; Hon C Westbourne *Chich* 82-86; Hon C Stansted 82-86; Perm to Offic from 86. *16 All Saints' Lane, Bexhill-on-Sea, E Sussex TN39 5HA* Bexhill-on-Sea (0424) 217936

THOMAS, Tristan Emmanuel Douglas. b 38. Mysore Univ BA60. Bp's Coll Calcutta DipTh65. **d** 65 **p** 66. India 65-70; Miss to Seamen 70-72; Chapl Rotterdam w Schiedam etc *Eur* 70-71; C Gt Clacton *Chelmsf* 72-74; Chapl Hamburg w Kiel *Eur* 74-85; V Halliwell St Marg *Man* from 85. *The Vicarage, 1 Somerset Road, Bolton BL1 4NE* Bolton (0204) 40850

THOMAS, Vernon Douglas Ronald. b 13. Univ of Wales BSc35. K Coll Lon 36. **d** 37 **p** 38. V Bournemouth St Fran *Win* 70-78; rtd 78. *14 Melrose Street, Leederville, Perth, W Australia 6007*

THOMAS, Victor George Frederick Woolcott. b 02. Lich Th Coll 59. **d** 60 **p** 61. V Colden *Win* 63-70; rtd 70; Perm to Offic *Ex* from 71. *St Andrew's House, Marsh Green, Exeter EX5 2EX* Whimple (0404) 822116

THOMAS, Wallis Huw Wallis. b 06. Univ of Wales BA27. St Mich Coll Llan 30. **d** 31 **p** 32. R Llanelltyd *Ban* 66-76; rtd 76. *The Vicarage, Llanelltyd, Dolgellau, Gwynedd LL40 2SU* Dolgellau (0341) 422517

THOMAS, William Alwyn. b 11. St D Coll Lamp BA33 St Mich Coll Llan 33. **d** 34 **p** 35. R Weyhill cum Penton Newsey *Win* 66-78; rtd 78. *The Brow, Ferryside, Dyfed SA17 5RS* Ferryside (026785) 369

THOMAS, William Brynmor. b 11. St D Coll Lamp BA33 BD41 Wycliffe Hall Ox 34. **d** 35 **p** 36. V Belper *Derby* 53-76; rtd 76. *42 Eastfield Avenue, Haxby, York YO3 8EY* York (0904) 760110

THOMAS, William George. b 29. JP. FRSA Birm Univ BA50 CertEd51. E Anglian Minl Tr Course 82. **d** 85 **p** 86. NSM Brampton *Ely* 85-87; NSM Bluntisham w Earith 87-89; P-in-c Foxton from 89. *The Vicarage, 7 West Hill Road, Foxton, Cambridge CB2 6SZ* Cambridge (0223) 870375

THOMAS, William John. b 11. St D Coll Lamp BA48. **d** 49 **p** 50. V Formby St Pet *Liv* 53-76; rtd 76. *Bro Gain, 49 Pen-y-Cefn Road, Caerwys, Mold, Clwyd CH7 5BH* Mold (0352) 720811

THOMAS, William John Charles. b 17. St D Coll Lamp BA50. **d** 51 **p** 52. Chapl Springfield Hosp Lon 64-82; rtd 82; Perm to Offic S'wark from 82. *101 Heybridge Avenue, London SW16 3DS*

THOMAS, Ven William Jordison. b 27. K Coll Cam BA50 MA55. Cuddesdon Coll 51. **d** 53 **p** 54. C Byker St Ant *Newc* 53-56; C Berwick H Trin 56-59; V Alwinton w Holystone and Alnham 59-70; V Alston cum Garrigill w Nenthead and Kirkhaugh 70-80; P-in-c Lambley w Knaresdale 72-80; RD Bamburgh and Glendale 81-83; TR Glendale Gp 80-83; Adn Northd and Can Res Newc Cathl from 83. *80 Moorside North, Newcastle upon Tyne NE4 9DU* 091-273 8245

THOMAS, Canon William Kenneth. b 19. Mert Coll Ox BA40 MA44. Westcott Ho Cam 40. **d** 42 **p** 43. V Minety w Oaksey *Bris* 71-82; P-in-c 82-84; RD Malmesbury 73-79; Hon Can Bris Cathl 77-84; P-in-c Crudwell w Ashley 82-84; rtd 84; Perm to Offic *Bris* from 84. *27 Hamilton Road, Bristol BS3 4EN* Bristol (0272) 632198

THOMAS, William Phillip. b 43. Lich Th Coll 68. **d** 70 **p** 71. C Llanilid w Pencoed *Llan* 70-74; C Pontypridd St Cath 74-76; V Tonyrefail 76-84; Youth Chapl 78-80; RD Rhondda 81-84; R Neath w Llantwit from 84. *The Rectory, London Road, Neath, W Glam SA11 1LE* Neath (0639) 644612

THOMAS, William Rhys Ithel Phillips. b 16. St Jo Coll Dur BA38 DipTh41 MA42. **d** 41 **p** 42. Lic to Offic *St E* 68-78; Chapl Asst Addenbrooke's Hosp Cam 78-81; rtd 81; Perm to Offic *Ely* from 85. *19 Brooklyn Court, Cherry Hinton Road, Cambridge CB1 4HF* Cambridge (0223) 246348

THOMAS, William Ronald. b 13. St D Coll Lamp BA34. **d** 38 **p** 39. C Hamstead St Paul *Birm* 38-40; C Fleur-de-Lis *Mon* 40-49; R Llandogo w Whitebrook 49-73; RD Chepstow 63-78; R Llandogo and Tintern 73-83; Lic to Offic from 83. *Wye Meadow View, Llandogo, Monmouth, Gwent NP5 4TE* Dean (0594) 530254

THOMAS ANTHONY, Brother. See DE HOOP, Thomas Anthony

THOMPSON, Alfred. b 13. Linc Th Coll 55. **d** 55 **p** 56. V Harwood *Man* 60-72; V Stubbins 72-78; rtd 78; Perm to Offic *Man* from 79. *66 Old Lane, Shevington, Wigan, Lancs WN6 8AS* Wigan (0942) 426024

THOMPSON, Anthony Edward. b 38. Bris Univ BA61. Ridley Hall Cam 61. **d** 63 **p** 64. C Peckham St Mary Magd *S'wark* 63-66; Paraguay 67-72; C Otley *Bradf* 72-75; TV Woughton *Ox* 75-82; P-in-c Lower Nutfield *S'wark* from 82. *136 Mid Street, South Nutfield, Redhill RH1 5RP* Nutfield Ridge (0737) 822211

THOMPSON, Ven Arthur Hugh. b 08. TCD BA37 MA56. **d** 37 **p** 38. I Boyle Union *K, E & A* 52-78; Adn Elphin and Ardagh 66-78; rtd 78. *Rivermead, Maguiresbridge, Co Fermanagh BT94 4RG* Lisnaskea (03657) 21767

THOMPSON, Athol James Patrick. b 34. St Paul's Grahamstown 72. **d** 74 **p** 75. S Africa 74-83; P-in-c Dewsbury St Matt and St Jo *Wakef* 84; TV Dewsbury from 84; Chapl Staincliffe & Dewsbury Gen Hosps Wakef 84-90; Chapl Dewsbury Distr Hosp from 90. *St Matthew's Vicarage, Quarry Road, Dewsbury, W Yorkshire WF13 2RZ* Dewsbury (0924) 450598

THOMPSON, Barry (Brother Aidan). b 33. St Jo Coll Lusaka. **d** 69 **p** 70. SSF from 59; Zambia 69-76; Miss to

Seamen from 76; Tanzania 76-81; Korea 81-82; Australia 83-85; Chapl Vlissingen (Flushing) Miss to Seamen *Eur* from 85. *Amstelstraat 53, 4388 RK Oost-Souburg, The Netherlands* Vlissingen (1184) 78788

THOMPSON, Canon Barry Pearce. b 40. St Andr Univ BSc63 Ball Coll Ox PhD66 Hull Univ MA82. NW Ord Course 76. **d** 79 **p** 80. C Cottingham *York* 79-82; V Swine 82-83; Lect Th Hull Univ 83-88; Ind Chapl *York* 83-85; Abp's Adv on Ind Issues 85-88; Can Res Chelmsf Cathl *Chelmsf* from 88. *2 Harlings Grove, Waterloo Lane, Chelmsford CM1 1YQ* Chelmsford (0245) 355041

THOMPSON, Beverley Francis. b 40. Bps' Coll Cheshunt 61. **d** 64 **p** 65. C St Ives Truro 64-67; Guyana 67-69; C Madron w Morvah *Truro* 69-72; R Mawgan w St Martin-in-Meneage 73-78; P-in-c Landulph 78-84; P-in-c St Dominic 78-84; P-in-c Crantock 84-89; P-in-c Newlyn St Newlyn 84-89; V Mullion from 89; Miss to Seamen from 89. *The Vicarage, Nancmellyon Road, Mullion, Helston, Cornwall TR12 7DH* Mullion (0326) 240325

THOMPSON, Brian. b 34. BSc. St Jo Coll Nottm. **d** 84 **p** 85. C Bletchley *Ox* 84-87; V Sneyd Green *Lich* from 87. *St Andrew's Vicarage, 42 Granville Avenue, Sneyd Green, Stoke-on-Trent ST1 6BH* Stoke-on-Trent (0782) 215139

THOMPSON, David Arthur. b 37. Clifton Th Coll. **d** 69 **p** 70. C Finchley Ch Ch *Lon* 69-72; C Barking St Marg w St Patr *Chelmsf* 72-75; TV 75-81; V Toxteth Park St Clem *Liv* 81-91; TR Parr from 91. *The Rectory, Delta Road, Parr, St Helens WA9 2DZ* St Helens (0744) 23726

THOMPSON, David Frank. b 44. Hull Univ BA65 MA69. St Steph Ho Ox 73. **d** 75 **p** 76. C Sidmouth, Woolbrook and Salcombe Regis *Ex* 75-78; C Lamorbey H Redeemer *Roch* 78-80; Chapl R Masonic Sch for Girls Rickmansworth from 81. *Rickmansworth Masonic School, Rickmansworth, Herts* Rickmansworth (0923) 773168

THOMPSON, David John. b 17. Selw Coll Cam BA48 MA52. Ridley Hall Cam 48. **d** 50 **p** 51. V Wallington H Trin *S'wark* 62-74; R Hambledon *Guildf* 74-84; rtd 84; Perm to Offic *Chich* from 85. *1 Pond Willow, North Trade Road, Battle, E Sussex TN33 0HU* Battle (04246) 3000

THOMPSON, Denise. b 50. Chich Th Coll 88. **d** 90. Par Dn Eighton Banks *Dur* from 90. *5 Springfield Avenue, Eighton Banks, Gateshead, Tyne and Wear NE9 7HL* 091-491 0638

THOMPSON, Canon Donald Frazer. b 20. St Cath Coll Cam BA46 MA49. Coll of Resurr Mirfield 46. **d** 48 **p** 49. V Leeds St Aid *Ripon* 62-73; RD Allerton 70-73; R Adel 73-87; Hon Can Ripon Cathl 75-87; RD Headingley 85-87; rtd 87. *2 Brooklands, Main Street, East Keswick, Leeds LS17 9DD* Wetherby (0937) 72704

THOMPSON, Edward Ronald Charles. b 25. AKC51. **d** 52 **p** 53. C Hinckley St Mary *Leic* 52-54; Jerusalem 54-55; Chapl St Boniface Coll Warminster 56-59; R Hawkchurch w Fishpond *Sarum* 59-63; V Camberwell St Mich w All So w Em *S'wark* 63-67; P-in-c St-Mary-le-Strand w St Clem Danes *Lon* 67-74; R from 74. *3 Woodsyre, London SE26 6SS* 081-670 8289

THOMPSON, Eric John. b 41. Chich Th Coll 83. **d** 85 **p** 86. C Newbold and Dunston *Derby* 85-88; P-in-c Taddington and Chelmorton 88-90; P-in-c Earl Sterndale and Monyash 88-90; V Taddington, Chelmorton and Flagg, and Monyash from 90. *The Vicarage, Monyash, Bakewell, Derbyshire DE4 1JH* Bakewell (0629) 812234

THOMPSON, Frank. b 08. Liv Univ BA36. St Aid Birkenhead 36. **d** 36 **p** 37. R Helmdon w Stuchbury and Radstone *Pet* 68-73; rtd 73. *Ashton House, Minster Precincts, Peterborough PE1 1XX* Peterborough (0733) 53792

THOMPSON, Frederick Robert. b 15. Dur Univ LTh40. St Aug Coll Cant 37. **d** 40 **p** 41. V Tutbury *Lich* 64-80; rtd 80. *1 Panorama Road, Sandbanks, Poole, Dorset BH13 7RA* Canford Cliffs (0202) 700735

✠**THOMPSON, Rt Rev Geoffrey Hewlett.** b 29. Trin Hall Cam BA52 MA56. Cuddesdon Coll 52. **d** 54 **p** 55 **c** 74. C Northn St Matt *Pet* 54-59; V Wisbech St Aug *Ely* 59-66; V Folkestone St Sav *Cant* 66-74; Suff Bp Willesden *Lon* 74-79; Area Bp Willesden 79-85; Bp Ex from 85. *The Palace, Exeter EX1 1HY* Exeter (0392) 72362

THOMPSON, George Harry Packwood. b 22. Qu Coll Ox BA48 MA48 BTh49. Qu Coll Birm 50. **d** 51 **p** 52. V Combe *Ox* 64-85; Perm to Offic from 85; rtd 87. *12 Briar Thicket, Woodstock, Oxford OX7 1NT* Woodstock (0993) 811915

THOMPSON, Gerald George. b 17. TCD BA40. CITC 40. **d** 41 **p** 42. Sec N Ireland ICM from 49; Lic to Offic

D & D 51-78; rtd 78. *40 Loopland Park, Belfast BT6 9DY* Belfast (0232) 732047

THOMPSON, Gordon George. b 37. Brasted Place Coll 64. Edin Th Coll 66. **d** 68 **p** 69. C Ches St Jo *Ches* 68-71; C Hackney *Lon* 72-76; P-in-c Craghead *Dur* 76-77; V 77-79; Warden Pemb Coll Miss Walworth *S'wark* 79-82; TV Walworth 79-82; V Mitcham St Olave from 82. *St Olave's Vicarage, 22 Church Walk, London SW16 5JH* 081-764 2048

THOMPSON, Preb Gordon Henry Moorhouse. b 41. K Coll Lon 63. St Boniface Warminster 66. **d** 67 **p** 68. C Leominster *Heref* 67-70; C Burford II w Greete and Hope Bagot 70-74; TV 74-89; C Burford III w Lt Heref 70-74; TV 74-89; C Tenbury 70-74; TV 74-89; TV Burford I 74-89; RD Ludlow 83-89; Preb Heref Cathl from 85; rtd 89. *The Poplars, Bitterley, Ludlow, Shropshire SY8 3HQ* Ludlow (0584) 891093

THOMPSON, Harold Anthony. b 41. N Ord Course 84. **d** 87 **p** 88. C Leeds Belle Is St Jo and St Barn *Ripon* 87-90; V Leeds St Cypr Harehills from 90. *St Cyprian's Vicarage, 43A Coldcotes Avenue, Leeds LS9 6ND* Leeds (0532) 493746

THOMPSON, Ian Charles. b 58. Wycliffe Hall Ox 80. **d** 83 **p** 84. C Knutsford St Jo and Toft *Ches* 83-86; C Birkenhead Ch Ch 86-88; V Balderstone *Man* from 88. *The Sett, Badger Lane, Craiglands, Rochdale, Lancs OL16 4RD* Rochdale (0706) 49886

THOMPSON, James. b 30. MNACH90 DipHyp84 Nottm Univ DipEd65 DipTh65. Paton Congr Coll Nottm 61 Wycliffe Hall Ox 66. **d** 66 **p** 67. C Woodlands *Sheff* 66-69; R Firbeck w Letwell 69-71; V Milnsbridge *Wakef* 71-80; Lic to Offic 80-84; Dioc Chapl Aber Hosps 84-89; Dioc Supernumerary *Ab* 84-89; R Buckie from 89; R Portsoy from 89. *All Saints' Rectory, Cluny Square, Buckie, Banffshire AB5 1HA* Buckie (0542) 32312

THOMPSON, James. b 37. Coll of Resurr Mirfield 64. **d** 67 **p** 68. C Shieldfield Ch Ch *Newc* 67-69; C Hendon *Dur* 69-74; V Gateshead St Chad Bensham 74-85; R Easington 85-90; Chapl Thorpe Hosp Easington from 85; V Cassop cum Quarrington *Dur* from 90. *The Vicarage, Bowburn, Co Durham DH6 5DL*

✠**THOMPSON, Rt Rev James Lawton.** b 36. ACA59 FCA70 Em Coll Cam BA64 MA71 Hon DLitt89. Cuddesdon Coll 64. **d** 66 **p** 67 **c** 78. C E Ham St Geo *Chelmsf* 66-68; Chapl Cuddesdon Coll 68-71; Lic to Offic *S'wark* 71-72; TR Thamesmead 72-78; Suff Bp Stepney *Lon* 78-79; Area Bp Stepney 79-91; Bp B & W from 91. *The Palace, Wells, Somerset BA5 2PD* Wells (0749) 72341

THOMPSON, John David. b 40. Lon Univ BD65 Ch Ch Ox DPhil69. St Steph Ho Ox 65. **d** 67 **p** 68. C Solihull *Birm* 67-71; C Biddestone w Slaughterford *Bris* 71-73; Lect Wells Th Coll 71-72; C Yatton Keynell *Bris* 71-73; C Castle Combe 71-73; V Braughing *St Alb* 74-77; R Digswell 77-82; TR Digswell and Panshanger from 82. *The Rectory, 354 Knightsfield, Welwyn Garden City, Herts AL8 7NG* Welwyn Garden (0707) 326677

THOMPSON, John Michael. b 47. Nottm Univ BTh77 Cam Univ BA84 Hull Univ CLRHist90. Linc Th Coll 73. **d** 77 **p** 78. C Old Brumby *Linc* 77-80; C Grantham 80-81; TV 81-84; V Holton-le-Clay from 84. *The Vicarage, Church Walk, Holton-le-Clay, Grimsby, S Humberside DN36 5AN* Grimsby (0472) 824082

THOMPSON, John Miller. b 26. St Deiniol's Hawarden. **d** 63 **p** 64. C Hawarden *St As* 63-66; C Connah's Quay 66-67; V Askern *Sheff* 67-72; P-in-c Moss 69-72; Ind Chapl 72-85; P-in-c Brightside St Marg 72-77; P-in-c Sheff St Silas 77-88; Chapl Weston Park Hosp Sheff from 85; C Ranmoor *Sheff* from 88; Chapl to Homes for the Aged from 88. *2 Knab Close, Sheffield S7 2ER* Sheffield (0742) 586790

THOMPSON, John Turrell. b 57. Sheff Univ BA(Econ)79 Southn Univ BTh88. Sarum & Wells Th Coll 83. **d** 86 **p** 87. C Tavistock and Gulworthy *Ex* 86-90; TV Pinhoe and Broadclyst from 90. *The Vicarage, Broadclyst, Exeter EX5 3EW* Exeter (0392) 61280

THOMPSON, John Wilfred. b 44. CA Tr Coll 66. St Deiniol's Hawarden 84. **d** 85 **p** 86. C Rhyl w Rhyl St Ann *St As* 85-87; R Fritwell w Souldern and Ardley w Fewcott *Ox* from 87. *The Vicarage, 44 Forge Place, Fritwell, Bicester, Oxon OX6 9QQ* Fritwell (0869) 346739

THOMPSON (nee LILLIE), Mrs Judith Virginia. b 44. LMH Ox BA66 Univ of E Africa DipEd67 Essex Univ MA73. Gilmore Course 77. **dss** 82 **d** 87. Asst Chapl Bris Univ *Bris* 76-80; Lawrence Weston 82-85; E Bris 85-87; Hon Par Dn from 87; Chapl HM Rem Cen Pucklechurch 87-91; Chapl Southmead Hosp Bris from 91. *St Aidan's*

Vicarage, 2 Jockey Lane, Bristol BS5 8NZ   Bristol (0272) 677812

THOMPSON, Kenneth. b 31. St Deiniol's Hawarden. **d** 87 **p** 88. Hon Par Dn Upton (or Overchurch) *Ches* 87-90; NSM Tranmere St Cath from 90. *33 Meadway, Upton, Wirral, Merseyside L49 6JQ*   051-677 6433

THOMPSON, Kevin. b 55. Sheff Univ BEd77. Oak Hill Th Coll DipHE89. **d** 89 **p** 90. C Brinsworth w Catcliffe *Sheff* from 89. *18 St George's Drive, Brinsworth, Rotherham, S Yorkshire S60 5NG*   Rotherham (0709) 361677

THOMPSON, Canon Leslie. b 09. Univ Coll Dur LTh36. St Aid Birkenhead 38. **d** 38 **p** 39. R Middleton-in-Teesdale *Dur* 51-81; RD Barnard Castle 72-80; Hon Can Dur Cathl 74-84; rtd 81. *Sunnymead, Alston Road, Middleton-in-Teesdale, Barnard Castle, Co Durham DL12 0UU*   Teesdale (0833) 40625

THOMPSON, Mark William. b 52. St Jo Coll Nottm 77. **d** 81 **p** 82. C Barnsbury St Andr and H Trin w All SS *Lon* 81-84; C Addiscombe St Mary *Cant* 84; C Addiscombe St Mary *S'wark* 85-87; V Thorpe Edge *Bradf* from 87. *The Vicarage, Northwood Crescent, Bradford, W Yorkshire BD10 9HX*   Bradford (0274) 613246

THOMPSON, Michael. b 49. NE Ord Course 83. **d** 86 **p** 87. C Ashington *Newc* 86-88; C Ponteland 88-91; TV Newc Epiphany from 91. *7 Fawdon Lane, Newcastle upon Tyne NE3 2RR*   091-285 5403

THOMPSON, Michael James. b 55. St Andr Univ MTh78. St Mich Coll Llan 78. **d** 79 **p** 80. C Aberavon *Llan* 79-81; C Kensington St Mary Abbots w St Geo *Lon* 81-85; Chapl Westmr Abbey 85-88; P-in-c R Westmr St Marg 86-87; Sacr Westmr Abbey 86-88; R Lowick w Sudborough and Slipton *Pet* 88-91; P-in-c Islip 88-91; P-in-c Ryhall w Essendine from 91. *The Vicarage, Ryhall, Stamford, Lincs PE9 4HR*

THOMPSON, Canon Michael Reginald. b 34. Roch Th Coll 66. **d** 68 **p** 69. C Aldrington *Chich* 68-70; Dioc Youth Chapl 70-78; R Litlington w W Dean 70-77; RD Seaford 75-77; RD Lewes and Seaford from 77; P-in-c Bishopstone 77; V Seaford w Sutton from 78; Can and Preb Chich Cathl from 85. *The Vicarage, Sutton Road, Seaford, E Sussex BN25 1SS*   Seaford (0323) 893508

THOMPSON, Nathanael (Brother Nathanael). b 29. St Deiniol's Hawarden 76. **d** 78 **p** 79. SSF from 62; C Llanbeblig w Caernarfon *Ban* 78-80; C Swansea St Gabr *S & B* 84-87; C Swansea St Mary w H Trin 87. *The Monastery, Shrawley, Worcester WR6 6TQ*   Great Witley (0299) 896345

THOMPSON, Neil Hamilton. b 48. SS Hild & Bede Coll Dur BEd72 Leic Univ MA75. S'wark Ord Course 77. **d** 80 **p** 81. C Mert St Mary *S'wark* 80-82; C Dulwich St Barn 82-84; V Shooters Hill Ch Ch 84-87; V S Dulwich St Steph from 87. *St Stephen's Vicarage, College Road, London SE21 7HN*   081-693 3797

THOMPSON, Patrick Arthur. b 36. Dur Univ BA59. Qu Coll Birm DipTh61. **d** 61 **p** 62. C W Wickham St Fran *Cant* 61-65; C Portchester *Portsm* 65-68; C Birchington w Acol *Cant* 68-71; V S Norwood St Mark 71-77; P-in-c Norbury St Oswald 77-81; V Norbury St Oswald *S'wark* from 81. *220 Norbury Avenue, Thornton Heath, Surrey CR7 8AJ*   081-764 2853

THOMPSON, Paul. b 58. Ox Univ BA. Ripon Coll Cuddesdon 80. **d** 83 **p** 84. Chapl Fazakerley Hosp 83-86; C Kirkby *Liv* 83-86; TV Chapl Kirkby Coll of FE 86-89; CF from 89. *c/o MOD (Army), Bagshot Park, Bagshot, Surrey GU19 5PL*   Bagshot (0276) 71717

THOMPSON, Paul. b 65. TCD BA87. CITC 87. **d** 89 **p** 90. C Orangefield w Moneyreagh *D & D* from 89. *412 Castlereagh Road, Belfast BT5 6BH*   Belfast (0232) 794824

THOMPSON, Paul Noble. b 54. Univ of Wales (Cardiff) BMus77. Coll of Resurr Mirfield DipTh79. **d** 80 **p** 81. C Bargoed and Deri w Brithdir *Llan* 80-83; C Whitchurch 83-84; V Porth w Trealaw 84-89; V Llanharan w Peterston-s-Montem from 89. *The Vicarage, Brynna Road, Llanharan, Pontyclun, M Glam CF7 9QE*   Newtown Llantwit (0443) 226307

THOMPSON, Mrs Pauline. b 44. E Midl Min Tr Course 81. **dss** 84 **d** 87. Derby St Aug *Derby* 84-87; Par Dn 87-88; Par Dn Boulton 88-90; Par Dn Allestree from 91. *26 Coronation Avenue, Alvaston, Derby DE2 0LQ*   Derby (0332) 752902

THOMPSON, Peter Homer. b 17. Chich Th Coll 39. **d** 41 **p** 42. V Ruislip St Mary *Lon* 59-81; V Mullion *Truro* 81-87; rtd 87. *Glen Cairn, La Flounder Fields, Mullion, Helston, Cornwall TR12 7EJ*   Mullion (0326) 240613

THOMPSON, Dr Peter Ross. b 26. St Jo Coll Cam BA47 MB50 BChir50. Tyndale Hall Bris. **d** 60 **p** 61. C New Malden and Coombe *S'wark* 60-61; Burma 61-66; R Slaugham *Chich* 66-72; V Polegate from 72. *St John's*

Vicarage, 1 Church Road, Polegate, E Sussex BN26 5BX   Polegate (03212) 3259

THOMPSON, Randolph. b 25. Lich Th Coll 63. **d** 65 **p** 66. P-in-c Cornholme *Wakef* 69-71; V 71-72; Chapl Barnsley Hall & Lea Hosps Bromsgrove 72-84; V Hanley Castle, Hanley Swan and Welland *Worc* 84-89; rtd 89. *37 Hampton Fields, Oswestry, Shropshire SY11 1TL*   Oswestry (0691) 658484

THOMPSON, Raymond Craigmile. b 42. **d** 84 **p** 85. C Clooney *D & R* 84-86; I Urney w Sion Mills from 86. *112 Melmount Road, Sion Mills, Strabane, Co Tyrone BT82 9EX*   Sion Mills (06626) 58020

THOMPSON, Richard Brian. b 60. Sheff Poly BSc83. Ripon Coll Cuddesdon 86. **d** 89 **p** 90. C Thorpe Bay *Chelmsf* from 89. *62 Bunters Avenue, Shoeburyness, Essex SS3 9NF*   Southend-on-Sea (0702) 295376

THOMPSON, Robert. b 36. AKC61. **d** 62 **p** 63. C Cockerton *Dur* 62-65; C Dur St Marg 65-70; V Wallsend St Jo *Newc* 70-78; V Norham and Duddo from 78. *The Vicarage, Norham, Berwick-upon-Tweed TD15 2LF*   Berwick-upon-Tweed (0289) 382325

THOMPSON, Ronald. b 08. DFC43. Linc Th Coll. **d** 60 **p** 61. R Saham Toney *Nor* 65-78; rtd 78; Perm to Offic *Nor* from 79. *4 Oval Avenue, Norwich NR5 0DP*   Norwich (0603) 744139

THOMPSON, Ross Edwards. b 42. Otago Univ BA63 TDip64. Coll of Resurr Mirfield 66. **d** 68 **p** 69. C Fareham SS Pet and Paul *Portsm* 68-71; C W Hackney St Barn *Lon* 71-72; C Northolt St Mary 72-75; P-in-c Wells St Thos w Horrington *B & W* 75-80; V 80-81; TR Cowley St Jas *Ox* 81-87; Gen Sec Ch Union 87-89; V Petts Wood *Roch* from 89. *The Vicarage, Willett Way, Petts Wood, Orpington, Kent BR5 1QE*   Orpington (0689) 829971

THOMPSON, Dr Ross Keith Arnold. b 53. Sussex Univ BA75 Bris Univ PhD82. Coll of Resurr Mirfield 80. **d** 82 **p** 83. C Knowle *Bris* 82-85; TV E Bris from 85. *St Aidan's Vicarage, 2 Jockey Lane, Bristol BS5 8NZ*   Bristol (0272) 677812

THOMPSON, Ruth Jean. b 47. St Alb Minl Tr Scheme 85. **d** 90. Par Dn Stonebridge St Mich *Lon* from 90. *3 Alric Avenue, London NW10*   081-459 0788

THOMPSON, Thomas. b 25. NE Ord Course. **d** 85 **p** 86. NSM Ford *Newc* 85-86; NSM Tweedmouth from 86. *35 Magdalene Drive, Berwick-upon-Tweed TD15 1PX*   Berwick-upon-Tweed (0289) 305725

THOMPSON, Thomas Oliver. b 27. TCD 61. **d** 63 **p** 64. C Lisburn Ch Ch *Conn* 63-68; Chapl to Ch of Ireland Miss to Deaf and Dumb 68-76; I Glenavy w Tunny and Crumlin from 77. *Glenavy Vicarage, Crumlin, Co Antrim BT29 4LG*   Crumlin (08494) 22361

THOMPSON, Canon Timothy. b 34. Fitzw Ho Cam BA59 MA64. Cuddesdon Coll 59. **d** 61 **p** 62. C Noel Park St Mark *Lon* 61-64; C Shrub End *Chelmsf* 64-67; New Zealand 67-70; R Tolleshunt Knights w Tiptree *Chelmsf* 70-81; R Colchester St Jas, All SS, St Nic and St Runwald 81-88; RD Colchester 84-88; Hon Can Chelmsf Cathl 85-88; Vice-Provost Chelmsf from 88; Can Res Chelmsf Cathl from 88. *115 Rainsford Road, Chelmsford, Essex CM1 2PH*   Chelmsford (0245) 267773

THOMPSON, Timothy Charles. b 51. Lon Univ BSc73 AKC. Westcott Ho Cam 75. **d** 78 **p** 79. C Ipswich St Mary at Stoke w St Pet & St Mary Quay *St E* 78-81; Ind Chapl *Nor* 81-88; C Lowestoft and Kirkley 81-83; TV 83-88; V Coney Hill *Glouc* from 88. *St Oswald's Vicarage, Coney Hill, Gloucester GL4 7LX*   Gloucester (0452) 23618

THOMPSON, Timothy William. b 48. Bris Univ CertEd70 Open Univ BA78. E Midl Min Tr Course. **d** 88 **p** 89. C Scartho *Linc* from 88. *25 Waltham Road, Grimsby DN33 2LY*   Grimsby (0472) 70373

THOMPSON, Tom Malcolm. b 38. Dur Univ BA60. Bps' Coll Cheshunt 60. **d** 62 **p** 63. C Standish *Blackb* 62-65; C Lanc St Mary 65-67; V Chorley All SS 67-72; V Barrowford 72-78; RD Pendle 75-78; R Northfield *Birm* 78-82; RD Kings Norton 79-82; V Longton *Blackb* from 82; RD Leyland from 89. *Longton Vicarage, Birchwood Avenue, Hutton, Preston PR4 5EE*   Longton (0772) 612179

THOMPSON, William George. b 32. Leeds Univ BA54. Coll of Resurr Mirfield 54. **d** 56 **p** 57. C Southport St Luke *Liv* 56-60; R Man St Aid *Man* 60-64; V Bradshaw 64-83; Perm to Offic *Liv* from 83. *178 High Street, Skelmersdale, Lancs WN8 8AF*   Skelmersdale (0695) 22054

THOMPSON-McCAUSLAND, Marcus Perronet. b 31. Trin Coll Cam BA54 MA60. Coll of Resurr Mirfield 57. **d** 59 **p** 60. C Perry Barr *Birm* 59-65; V Rubery 65-72; R Cradley *Heref* 72-82; P-in-c Storridge 72-82; P-in-c Mathon 72-82; P-in-c Castle Frome 72-82; Hon C Camberwell St Giles *S'wark* 82-88; Hon C Lydbury N

Heref 88-89; Hon C Lydbury N w Hopesay and Edgton from 89. *3 Round Oak, Hopesay, Craven Arms, Shropshire SY7 8HQ* Lydbury North (05888) 369

THOMPSTONE, John Deaville. b 39. BNC Ox BA63 MA67. Ridley Hall Cam 63. **d** 65 **p** 66. C Hoole *Ches* 65-68; C Fulwood *Sheff* 68-71; V Skirbeck H Trin *Linc* 71-77; V Shipley St Pet *Bradf* from 77; RD Airedale 82-88. *The Vicarage, 2 Glenhurst Road, Shipley, W Yorkshire BD18 4DZ* Bradford (0274) 584488 or 583381

THOMSON, Alexander Keith. b 38. Cranmer Hall Dur BA63. **d** 64 **p** 65. C Middleton *Man* 64-68; Chapl Rannoch Sch Perthshire 68-72; P-in-c Kinloch Rannoch *St And* 68-72; Asst Chapl Oundle Sch Pet from 72; Lic to Offic *Pet* from 73; Chapl Laxton Sch Oundle from 88. *34 Kings Road, Oundle, Peterborough PE8 4AY* Oundle (0832) 273416

THOMSON, Preb Clarke Edward Leighton. b 19. TD65. Pemb Coll Ox BA41 MA45. Wycliffe Hall Ox 44. **d** 45 **p** 46. C Penge Lane H Trin *Roch* 45-47; Egypt 47-50; C Chelsea All SS *Lon* 50-51; V from 51; CF (TA) 52-69; Preb St Paul's Cathl *Lon* from 86. *4 Old Church Street, London SW3 5DQ* 071-352 5627

THOMSON, Colin Hugh. b 21. **d** 91. C Galway w Kilcummin *T, K & A* from 91. *Luimnagh West, Corrandulla, Co Galway, Irish Republic* Galway (91) 91482

THOMSON, Cyril Raby. b 12. Serampore Coll BD60 Lon Univ DipTh64. Tyndale Hall Bris 32. **d** 36 **p** 37. V S'wark H Trin *S'wark* 67-73; C Southall Green St Jo *Lon* 73-76; C-in-c Wimbledon Em Ridgway Prop Chpl *S'wark* 76-81; rtd 81; Perm to Offic *S'wark* from 85. *2 Coppice Close, London SW20 9AS* 081-540 7748

THOMSON, Dr David. b 52. Keble Coll Ox MA78 DPhil78 Selw Coll Cam BA80 MA84. Westcott Ho Cam 78. **d** 81 **p** 82. C Maltby *Sheff* 81-84; Sec Par and People from 84; TV Banbury *Ox* from 84. *St Paul's House, Prescott Avenue, Banbury, Oxon OX16 0LR* Banbury (0295) 264003

THOMSON, George Miller McMillan. b 33. Edin Th Coll 59. **d** 62 **p** 63. C Edin Old St Paul *Edin* 62-64; USA 64-68; C Brookfield St Mary *Lon* 68-72; V Noel Park St Mark 72-81; RD E Haringey 77-81; Chapl Newark Hosp 81-87; TR Newark w Hawton, Cotham and Shelton *S'well* 81-87; R Glas St Bride *Glas* from 87. *St Bride's Rectory, 25 Queensborough Gardens, Glasgow G12 9QP* 041-334 1401

THOMSON, John Bromilow. b 59. York Univ BA81 Ox Univ BA84. Wycliffe Hall Ox 82. **d** 85 **p** 86. C Ecclesall *Sheff* 85-89; S Africa from 89. *St Paul's College, PO Box 77, Grahamstown, 6140 South Africa* Grahamstown (461) 23332

THOMSON, Julian Harley. b 43. AKC70. St Aug Coll Cant 70. **d** 71 **p** 72. C Wellingborough All Hallows *Pet* 71-74; Min Can, Prec and Sacr Ely Cathl *Ely* 74-80; P-in-c Stuntney 76-80; V Arrington 80-91; R Croydon w Clopton 80-91; R Orwell 80-91; R Wimpole 80-91; V Linton from 91; R Bartlow from 91; P-in-c Castle Camps from 91. *The Vicarage, Church Lane, Linton, Cambridge CB1 6JX* Cambridge (0223) 891291

THOMSON, Oliver Miles. b 38. Magd Coll Cam BA61 MA65. Wycliffe Hall Ox 61. **d** 63 **p** 64. C St Marylebone All So w SS Pet and Jo *Lon* 63-67; C Fulwood *Sheff* 67-70; R Wick w Doynton *Bris* 70-74; V Harold Wood *Chelmsf* 74-87; R Sevenoaks St Nic *Roch* from 87. *The Rectory, Rectory Lane, Sevenoaks, Kent TN13 1JA* Sevenoaks (0732) 740340

THOMSON, Peter Malcolm. b 44. Trin Coll Bris 75. **d** 78 **p** 79. C Tonbridge St Steph *Roch* 78-82; R Cobham w Luddesdowne and Dode 82-90; V Wythall *Birm* from 90. *St Mary's Vicarage, 27 Lea Green Lane, Wythall, Birmingham B47 6HE* Wythall (0564) 823381

THOMSON, Canon Richard Irving. b 32. Oak Hill Th Coll 57. **d** 60 **p** 61. C Kingston upon Hull H Trin *York* 60-63; C S Croydon Em *Cant* 63-66; V Shoreditch St Leon *Lon* 66-73; Chapl Vevey w Chateau d'Oex and Villars *Eur* 73-78; V Reigate St Mary *S'wark* from 78; Hon Can S'wark Cathl from 90. *St Mary's Vicarage, 76 Church Street, Reigate, Surrey RH2 0SP* Reigate (0737) 242973

THOMSON, Richard William Byars. b 60. Birm Univ BA86. Ripon Coll Cuddesdon 86. **d** 88 **p** 89. C Moulsecoomb *Chich* 88-90; P-in-c Kirriemuir *St And* from 90. *St Mary's Rectory, 128 Glengate, Kirriemuir, Angus DD8 4JG* Kirriemuir (0575) 72730

THOMSON, Robert Douglass. b 37. Dur Univ BEd75. Cranmer Hall Dur 76. **d** 79 **p** 80. NSM Shincliffe *Dur* from 79. *11 Hill Meadows, High Shincliffe, Durham DH1 2PE* 091-386 3358

THOMSON, Canon Ronald. b 24. Leeds Univ BA49. Coll of Resurr Mirfield 49. **d** 51 **p** 52. V Shiregreen St Hilda *Sheff* 57-73; RD Ecclesfield 72-73; V Worsbrough 73-88; RD Tankersley 75-85; Hon Can Sheff Cathl 77-88; rtd 88. *34 Kingwell Road, Worsbrough, Barnsley, S Yorkshire S70 4HF* Barnsley (0226) 203553

THOMSON, Ronald Arthur. b 29. G&C Coll Cam BA53 MA57. Ripon Hall Ox. **d** 57 **p** 58. C Sanderstead All SS *S'wark* 57-60; C Kidbrooke St Jas 60-62; Chapl RAF 62-68; C Amersham *Ox* 68; R Watton at Stone *St Alb* from 68. *The Rectory, Watton at Stone, Hertford SG14 3RD* Ware (0920) 830262

THOMSON, Russell. b 39. AKC62. **d** 63 **p** 64. C Hackney *Lon* 63-66; C Plumstead Wm Temple Ch Abbey Wood CD *S'wark* 66-69; TV Strood *Roch* 69-75; V Gillingham St Mary 75-89; V Roch from 89. *The Vicarage, Delce Road, Rochester, Kent ME1 2EH* Medway (0634) 845122

THOMSON, Preb Sidney Seward Chartres. b 01. OBE. **d** 54 **p** 55. V Worfield *Heref* 56-72; Preb Heref Cathl 70-72; rtd 72; Perm to Offic *Heref* from 72. *8C Cliff Road, Bridgnorth, Shropshire WV16 4EY* Bridgnorth (0746) 761368

THOMSON, Mrs Winifred Mary. b 35. St Mary's Coll Dur BA57 MA58 Lon Univ 86. Qu Coll Birm 79. **dss** 82 **d** 87. Leic H Spirit *Leic* 82-86; Oadby 86-87; Par Dn from 87. *140 Knighton Church Road, Leicester LE2 3JJ* Leicester (0533) 705863

THOMSON-GLOVER, Canon William Hugh. b 28. Trin Hall Cam BA52 MA56. Cuddesdon Coll 52. **d** 54 **p** 55. C Stepney St Dunstan and All SS *Lon* 54-58; C Tiverton St Andr *Ex* 58-60; P-in-c 60-63; Chapl Clifton Coll Bris 63-69; V Bris Lockleaze St Mary Magd w St Fran *Bris* 70-76; P-in-c Sherston Magna w Easton Grey 76-81; P-in-c Luckington w Alderton 76-81; V Sherston Magna, Easton Grey, Luckington etc from 81; P-in-c Foxley w Bremilham 84-86; RD Malmesbury from 88; Hon Can Bris Cathl from 91. *The Vicarage, Sherston, Malmesbury, Wilts SN16 0NP* Malmesbury (0666) 840209

THORBURN, Austin Noel. b 13. Trin Coll Cam BA36 MA40. Bps' Coll Cheshunt 36. **d** 38 **p** 39. C Langley Marish *Ox* 71-76; TV 76-79; rtd 79; Perm to Offic Carl from 79; Ox from 88. *28 Blacklands Road, Benson, Wallingford, Oxon OX10 6NW* Wallingford (0491) 32365

THORBURN, Guy Douglas Anderson. b 50. Ridley Hall Cam. **d** 83 **p** 84. C Putney St Marg *S'wark* 83-87; R Moresby *Carl* from 87. *The Rectory, Low Moresby, Whitehaven, Cumbria CA28 6RR* Whitehaven (0946) 3970

THORBURN, Peter Hugh. b 17. Worc Coll Ox BA41 MA43. Wells Th Coll 46. **d** 47 **p** 48. V Chipping Sodbury and Old Sodbury *Glouc* 68-72; Chapl Withington Univ Hosp Man 72-82; rtd 82; Perm to Offic B & W from 83; Bris from 85; Warden Servants of Ch the King from 89. *12 Drake Road, Wells, Somerset BA5 3JX* Wells (0749) 72919

THORBURN, Simon Godfrey. b 51. Newc Univ BSc73 Fitzw Coll Cam BA77 MA81. Westcott Ho Cam 75. **d** 78 **p** 79. C Stafford St Mary and St Chad *Lich* 78-79; C Stafford 79-82; C Tettenhall Regis 82-83; TV 83-90; Soc Resp Officer *S'wark* from 90. *104 Queens Road, London SW19 8LS* 081-543 8874

THORLEY-PAICE, Alan. b 26. AKC53. **d** 55 **p** 56. C Eton w Boveney *Ox* 63-74; P-in-c Hawridge w Cholesbury 74-83; P-in-c Lee 74-83; V 83-86; P-in-c Aston Clinton St Leon 79-83; R Hawridge w Cholesbury and St Leonard 83-86; rtd 86. *Glaston, Kingstone, Hereford HR2 9ES* Golden Valley (0981) 250195

THORMAN, Canon Peter. b 10. SS Coll Cam BA32 MA36. Cuddesdon Coll 32. **d** 33 **p** 34. C Headingley *Ripon* 33-37; Ox Miss Calcutta from 37; Can Calcutta from 59; Superior Brotherhood of the Epiphany (Ox Miss) 55-84. *Oxford Mission, Barisha, Calcutta 700 008, India*

THORN, Peter. b 50. BEd79. Ridley Hall Cam 82. **d** 84 **p** 85. C Aughton Ch Ch *Liv* 84-87; C Skelmersdale St Paul 87-90; Dioc Children's Officer from 90; P-in-c Croft w Southworth from 90. *Croft Rectory, 76 New Lane, Croft, Warrington WA3 7JL* Culcheth (092576) 2294

THORN, Robert Anthony D'Venning. b 54. AKC76. Chich Th Coll 75. **d** 77 **p** 78. C Bodmin *Truro* 77-80; TV N Hill w Altarnon, Bolventor and Lewannick 80-83; V Feock 83-90; Dioc Ecum Officer 83-90; Broadcasting Officer *Linc* from 90. *4 Grange Close, Canwick, Lincoln LN4 2RH* Lincoln (0522) 528266

THORNBURGH, Richard Hugh Perceval. b 52. Sarum & Wells Th Coll. **d** 84 **p** 85. C Broadstone *Sarum* 84-87; TV Beaminster Area from 87. *The Vicarage, Orchard*

Mead, Broadwindsor, Beaminster, Dorset DT8 3RA Broadwindsor (0308) 68805

THORNE, Anita Dawn. b 46. Trin Coll Bris 84. **dss** 86 **d** 87. Chapl Bris Poly *Bris* 86-88; Par Dn Olveston from 88. *The Vicarage, The Street, Olveston, Bristol BS12 3DA* Almondsbury (0454) 612296

THORNE, Clifford Graham. b 16. St Jo Coll Cam BA38 MA50. Westcott Ho Cam 78. **d** 78 **p** 79. Hon C Ponteland *Newc* from 78. *Dissington Old Hall, Dalton, Newcastle upon Tyne NE18 0BN* Ponteland (0661) 25258

THORNE, Mrs Marie Elizabeth. b 47. E Midl Min Tr Course 83. **dss** 86 **d** 87. Cleethorpes *Linc* 86-87; C 87-90; C Brigg from 90. *5 Winston Way, Brigg, S Humberside DN20 8UA* Brigg (0652) 55609

THORNE, Canon Ralph Frederick. b 14. ALCD36 St Jo Coll Dur LTh36 BA37. **d** 37 **p** 38. R Heaton Reddish *Man* 62-80; Hon Can Man Cathl 74-80; rtd 80; Perm to Offic *Man* from 80. *9 Greenfield Road, Atherton, Manchester M29 9LW* Atherton (0942) 873894

THORNETT, Frederick Charles. b 34. Harris Coll CQSW68. Local NSM Course. **d** 85 **p** 86. NSM Skegness and Winthorpe *Linc* 85-90; C New Sleaford from 90. *24 North Parade, Sleaford, Lincs NG34 8AN* Sleaford (0529) 303754

THORNEWILL, Canon Mark Lyon. b 25. ALCD56. **d** 56 **p** 58. R Lifton *Ex* 62-66; R Kelly w Bradstone 62-66; USA from 66; Hon Can Louisville Cathl from 70; rtd 90. *173 Sears Avenue, Suite 270, Louisville, Kentucky 40207, USA*

THORNEYCROFT, Mrs Pippa Hazel Jeanetta. b 44. Ex Univ BA65. Qu Coll Birm 85 W Midl Minl Tr Course. **d** 88. NSM Badger *Lich* from 90; NSM Beckbury from 90; NSM Ryton from 90; NSM Kemberton, Sutton Maddock and Stockton from 90. *Kemberton Hall, Shifnal, Shropshire TF11 9LH* Telford (0952) 580588

THORNHILL, Raymond. b 16. St Chad's Coll Dur BA38 MA41. **d** 40 **p** 41. Lic to Offic *Dur* 40-80; rtd 80. *6 Mayorswell Close, Durham DH1 1JU* 091-386 4856

THORNLEY, Arthur Richard. b 15. Selw Coll Cam BA38. Westcott Ho Cam 38. **d** 39 **p** 40. Chapl Lon Ho 70-75; PV Truro Cathl *Truro* 75-80; Chapl Truro Cathl Sch 75-80; rtd 80; Hon PV Truro Cathl *Truro* from 80. *Flat 5, Rydal Mount, St John's Road, Eastbourne, E Sussex BN20 7JA* Eastbourne (0323) 647686

THORNLEY, David Howe. b 43. Wycliffe Hall Ox 77. **d** 79 **p** 80. C Burgess Hill St Andr *Chich* 79-83; P-in-c Amberley w N Stoke 83-84; P-in-c Parham and Wiggonholt w Greatham 83-84; V Amberley w N Stoke and Parham, Wiggonholt etc from 84. *The Vicarage, Amberley, Arundel, W Sussex BN18 9ND* Bury (0798) 831500

THORNLEY, Geoffrey Pearson. b 23. Pemb Coll Cam BA47 MA52. Cuddesdon Coll. **d** 50 **p** 51. Chapl RN 53-73; Bp's Dom Chapl *Linc* 73-75; P-in-c Riseholme 73-78; P-in-c Scothern w Sudbrooke 77-78; V Dunholme 75-85; Hon PV Linc Cathl 75-85; rtd 85; Chapl Allnutt's Hosp Goring Heath from 85. *The Chaplaincy, Goring Heath, Reading RG8 7RR* Checkendon (0491) 680261

THORNLEY, Nicholas Andrew. b 56. St Jo Coll Nottm BTh81. **d** 81 **p** 84. C Frodingham *Linc* 81-84; P-in-c Belton All SS 84-85; V 85-90; V Horncastle w Low Toynton from 90. *9 Langton Drive, Horncastle, Lincs LN9 5AJ* Horncastle (06582) 3537

THORNTON, Canon Cecil. b 26. Lon Univ BD PhD. Tyndale Hall Bris 47. **d** 50 **p** 51. I Fahan Lower and Upper *D & R* 65-88; RD Innishowen 67-88; Can Raphoe Cathl 79-88; rtd 88. *Cluain-Fois, 38 Ballywillan Road, Portrush, Co Antrim BT56 8JN* Portrush (0265) 824270

THORNTON, David John Dennis. b 32. Kelham Th Coll 52. **d** 56 **p** 57. C New Eltham All SS *S'wark* 56-58; C Stockwell Green St Andr 58-62; V Tollesbury *Chelmsf* 62-74; P-in-c Salcot Virley 72-74; V Kelvedon from 74. *The Vicarage, Church Street, Kelvedon, Colchester CO5 9AL* Kelvedon (0376) 70373

THORNTON, John. b 26. St Edm Hall Ox BA53 MA57. Westcott Ho Cam 53. **d** 55 **p** 56. R Gt Witcombe *Glouc* 63-91; Chapl HM Pris Glouc 82-91; rtd 91. *24 Spencer Close, Hucclecote, Gloucester GL3 3EA* Gloucester (0452) 619775

THORNTON, Canon Kenneth. b 27. Open Univ BA77. ALCD55. **d** 55 **p** 56. C Fazakerley Em *Liv* 55-61; V Widnes St Paul 61-69; V Childwall All SS 69-82; RD Childwall 79-82; V Ormskirk from 82; Hon Can Liv Cathl from 87. *The Vicarage, Ormskirk, Lancs L39 3AJ* Ormskirk (0695) 572143

THORNTON, Peter Stuart. b 36. St Pet Hall Ox BA59 MA67. Cuddesdon Coll 59. **d** 61 **p** 62. C Coatham *York* 61-64; C Scarborough St Martin 64-67; R Seaton

Ross w Everingham and Bielby and Harswell 67-81; RD Weighton 75-85; P-in-c Thornton w Allerthorpe 80-81; R Seaton Ross Gp of Par 81-85; V York St Lawr w St Nic from 85. *St Lawrence's Vicarage, 11 Newland Park Close, York YO1 3HW* York (0904) 411916

THORNTON, Ronald Edward William. b 14. TCD BA36 HDipEd37 BD39. **d** 39 **p** 40. I Antrim All SS *Conn* 68-80; Can Conn Cathl 76-80; rtd 80; Hon C Bride *S & M* 80-88; Hon C Lezayre St Olave Ramsey 80-88. *Flat 2, Oban House, Ballure Road, Ramsey, Isle of Man* Ramsey (0624) 814976

THORNTON, Stanley John. b 23. Ely Th Coll. **d** 58 **p** 59. Ind Chapl HM Dockyard Devonport 68-76; V Devonport St Aubyn *Ex* 69-76; V Illingworth *Wakef* 76-81; R Clayton W w High Hoyland 81-83; rtd 83; Perm to Offic *Wakef* from 83. *13 Green Lane North, Timperley, Altrincham, Cheshire WA15 7NQ* 061-980 7916

THORNTON, Timothy Charles Gordon. b 35. Ch Ch Ox BA58 MA61. Linc Th Coll 60. **d** 62 **p** 63. C Kirkholt CD *Man* 62-64; Tutor Linc Th Coll 64-68; Chapl 66-68; Fiji 69-73; Chapl Brasted Place Coll Westerham 73-74; Can Missr *Guildf* 74-79; P-in-c Hascombe 74-79; V Chobham w Valley End 79-84; V Spelsbury and Chadlington *Ox* 84-87; V Chadlington and Spelsbury, Ascott under Wychwood from 87. *The Vicarage, Church Road, Chadlington, Oxford OX7 3LY* Chadlington (060876) 572

THORNTON, Timothy Martin. b 57. Southn Univ BA78. St Steph Ho Ox 78. **d** 80 **p** 81. C Todmorden *Wakef* 80-82; P-in-c Walsden 82-85; Lect Univ of Wales (Cardiff) 85-87; Asst Chapl Univ of Wales (Cardiff) *Llan* 85-86; Sen Chapl 86-87; Bp's Chapl *Wakef* from 87-91; Dir of Ords from 88-91. Bp's Dom Chapl *Lon* from 91. *4 Midhurst Avenue, London N10 3EN* 081-444 3552

THOROGOOD, John Martin. b 45. Birm Univ BA68 PGCE69. Ox NSM Course 82. **d** 85 **p** 86. NSM Sunningdale *Ox* 85-90; Chapl St Geo Sch Ascot 88-90; TV Camelot Par *B & W* from 90. *The Rectory, Holton, Wincanton, Somerset BA9 8AN* Wincanton (0963) 32163

THOROLD, Henry Croyland. b 21. Cuddesdon Coll 42. **d** 44 **p** 45. Chapl Summer Fields Sch Ox 68-75; Lic to Offic *Ox* 69-81; rtd 81. *Marston Hall, Grantham, Lincs* Loveden (0400) 50225

THOROLD, John Robert Hayford. b 16. K Coll Cam BA43 MA45. Cuddesdon Coll 42. **d** 42 **p** 43. V Mitcham SS Pet and Paul *S'wark* 52-86; OGS from 53; rtd 87; Perm to Offic *Blackb* from 87. *St Deiniol's Library, Hawarden, Deeside, Clwyd CH5 3DF* Hawarden (0244) 531256

THOROLD, John Stephen. b 35. Bps' Coll Cheshunt 61. **d** 63 **p** 64. C Cleethorpes *Linc* 63-70; V Cherry Willingham w Greetwell 70-77; P-in-c Firsby w Gt Steeping 77-79; R 79-86; R Aswardby w Sausthorpe 77-86; R Halton Holgate 77-86; R Langton w Sutterby 77-86; V Spilsby w Hundleby 77-86; R Lt Steeping 79-86; R Raithby 79-86; V New Sleaford from 86; RD Lafford from 87. *The Vicarage, Sleaford, Lincs NG34 7SH* Sleaford (0529) 302177

THOROLD, Trevor Neil. b 63. Hull Univ BA87. Ripon Coll Cuddesdon 87. **d** 89 **p** 90. C W Bromwich St Andr w Ch Ch *Lich* from 89. *23 Rowley View, West Bromwich, W Midlands B70 8QR* 021-553 3538

THORP, Adrian. b 55. Clare Coll Cam BA77 MA80 Lon Univ BD80. Trin Coll Bris 77. **d** 80 **p** 81. C Kendal St Thos *Carl* 80-83; C Handforth *Ches* 83-86; V Siddal *Wakef* from 86. *St Mark's Vicarage, 15 Whitegate Road, Siddal, Halifax, W Yorkshire HX3 9AD* Halifax (0422) 69538

THORP, Mrs Helen Mary. b 54. Bris Univ BA75 MA77 DipHE. Trin Coll Bris 78. **d** 87. NSM Siddal *Wakef* from 87. *St Mark's Vicarage, 15 Whitegate Road, Siddal, Halifax, W Yorkshire HX3 9AD* Halifax (0422) 369538

THORP, Norman Arthur. b 29. DMA63. Tyndale Hall Bris 63. **d** 65 **p** 66. C Southsea St Jude *Portsm* 65-68; C Braintree *Chelmsf* 68-73; P-in-c Tolleshunt D'Arcy w Tolleshunt Major 73-75; V 75-83; R N Buckm *Ox* from 83; RD Buckm from 90. *The Rectory, Maids Moreton, Buckingham MK18 1QD* Buckingham (0280) 813246

THORP, Robert Penfold. b 29. Chich Th Coll 54. **d** 57 **p** 58. C-in-c Goodrington CD *Ex* 64-84; V Goodrington 84-88; rtd 88; Perm to Offic *Ex* from 88. *St Hugh of Lincoln, 43 Belmont Road, Torquay, Devon TQ1 1ND* Torquay (0803) 326906

THORP, Roderick Cheyne. b 44. Ch Ch Ox BA65 MA69. Ridley Hall Cam 66. **d** 69 **p** 70. C Reading Greyfriars *Ox* 69-73; C Kingston upon Hull St Martin *York* 73-76; C Heworth 76-79; C-in-c N Bletchley CD *Ox* 79-86; TV Washfield, Stoodleigh, Withleigh etc *Ex* from 86. *The*

Vicarage, 3 Court Gardens, Stoodleigh, Tiverton, Devon EX16 9PL Oakford (03985) 373

THORP, Thomas Malcolm. b 49. AKC. St Aug Coll Cant 71. **d** 72 **p** 73. C Derby St Bart *Derby* 72-76; C Newport Pagnell *Ox* 76-79; C Newport Pagnell w Lathbury 79; Dioc Youth and Community Officer 79-82; TV Schorne from 82. *The Vicarage, White Horse Lane, Whitchurch, Aylesbury, Bucks HP22 4JZ* Aylesbury (0296) 641768

THORPE, Christopher David Charles. b 60. Cov Poly BA83. Ripon Coll Cuddesdon 85. **d** 88 **p** 89. C Norton *St Alb* from 88. *63 Kimberley, Letchworth, Herts SG6 4RB* Letchworth (0462) 672256

THORPE, Donald Henry. b 34. St Aid Birkenhead 57. **d** 60 **p** 61. C Mexborough *Sheff* 60-64; C Doncaster St Leon and St Jude 64-67; V Doncaster Intake 67-74; V Millhouses H Trin 74-85; Prec Leic Cathl *Leic* 85-89; TR Melton Gt Framland from 89. *The Rectory, 67 Dalby Road, Melton Mowbray, Leics LE13 0BQ* Melton Mowbray (0664) 62417

THORPE, Canon Harry Fletcher Cyprian. b 12. Kelham Th Coll 30. **d** 36 **p** 37. S Africa 36-73; R Ecton *Pet* 73-78; rtd 78; Perm to Offic *Portsm* from 81. *9 Borough Hill, Petersfield, Hants GU32 3LQ* Petersfield (0730) 61413

THORPE, John Wellburn. b 31. Lich Th Coll 55. **d** 58 **p** 59. C Heref St Martin *Heref* 58-61; C Dudley St Fran *Worc* 61-65; R Gt w Lt Witley 65-70; C Tuffley *Glouc* 70-72; P-in-c Blaisdon w Flaxley 73-76; P-in-c Westbury-on-Severn w Flaxley and Blaisdon 76-77; V 77-84; P-in-c Walton on Trent w Croxall etc *Derby* from 84. *The Rectory, Walton-on-Trent, Burton-on-Trent, Staffs DE12 8NA* Barton under Needwood (0283) 712442

THORPE, Kerry Michael. b 51. Lon Univ BD78. Oak Hill Th Coll DipTh76. **d** 78 **p** 79. C Upton (or Overchurch) *Ches* 78-81; C Ches le Street *Dur* 81-84; V Fatfield from 84. *49 Larchwood, Harraton, Washington, Tyne & Wear NE38 9BT* 091-416 3134

THORPE, Michael William. b 42. Lich Th Coll 67. **d** 70 **p** 71. C Walthamstow St Mich *Chelmsf* 70-71; C Plaistow St Andr 71; P-in-c Plaistow St Mary 72-74; TV Gt Grimsby St Mary and St Jas *Linc* 74-78; Chapl Grimsby Distr Hosps 78-83; Roxbourne, Northwick Park and Harrow Hosps 83-87; Chapl St Geo Hosp Linc from 87; Chapl Linc Co Hosp from 87. *The Chaplain's Office, County Hospital, Greetwell Road, Lincoln* Lincoln (0522) 512512

THORPE, Trevor Cecil. b 21. Em Coll Cam BA47 MA52. Ridley Hall Cam 48. **d** 50 **p** 51. C Farnborough *Guildf* 50-53; C W Ham All SS *Chelmsf* 53-57; V N Weald Bassett from 57. *The Vicarage, Vicarage Lane, North Weald, Essex CM16 6AL* North Weald (037882) 2246

THRALL, Margaret Eleanor. b 28. Girton Coll Cam BA50 MA54 PhD60. **d** 82. Asst Chapl Univ of Wales (Ban) *Ban* 82-88; Lect Th Univ of Wales (Ban) from 83. *25 Y Rhos, Bangor, Gwynedd LL57 2LT* Bangor (0248) 364957

THREADGILL, Alan Roy. b 31. St Alb Minl Tr Scheme 77. **d** 80 **p** 81. NSM Bedf St Andr *St Alb* 80-83; Chapl RAD 83-86; C Melton Gt Framland *Leic* 86-89; R Wymondham w Edmondthorpe, Buckminster etc from 89. *The Rectory, Sycamore Lane, Wymondham, Melton Mowbray, Leics LE14 2AZ* Wymondham (057284) 238

THROSSELL, John Julian. b 30. Nottm Univ BSc53 Syracuse Univ PhD56. Oak Hill Th Coll 72. **d** 75 **p** 76. NSM Wheathampstead *St Alb* 75-82; V Codicote 82-88; rtd 91. *20 Dakings Drift, Halesworth, Suffolk IP19 8TQ* Halesworth (0986) 874602

THROWER, Clive Alan. b 41. CEng90 Sheff Univ BSc62. E Midl Min Tr Course 76. **d** 79 **p** 80. C Derby Cathl *Derby* 79-86; C Spondon 86-91; Soc Resp Officer 86-91; Faith in the City Link Officer 88-91; P-in-c Ashford w Sheldon from 91; Dioc Rural Officer from 91. *The Vicarage, Ashford in the Water, Bakewell, Derbyshire DE4 1QN* Bakewell (0629) 812298

THROWER, George. b 06. St Paul's Coll Burgh 26. **d** 30 **p** 31. V Spratton *Pet* 68-71; rtd 71; Perm to Offic *Chich* from 78. *Dover Court, 12 St Leonard's Gardens, Hove, E Sussex BN3 4QB* Brighton (0273) 414353

THROWER, Philip Edward. b 41. Kelham Th Coll 61. **d** 66 **p** 67. C Hayes St Mary *Lon* 66-69; C Yeovil *B & W* 69-71; C Shirley St Jo *Cant* 71-77; P-in-c S Norwood St Mark 77-81; V 81-84; V S Norwood St Mark *S'wark* from 85. *St Mark's Vicarage, 101 Albert Road, London SE25 4JE* 081-656 9462

THRUSH, Alfred William Cyril. b 09. St Aid Birkenhead 43. **d** 45 **p** 46. V Grays Thurrock *Chelmsf* 59-79; rtd 80. *20 St George's Avenue, Grays, Essex* Grays Thurrock (0375) 383189

THUBRON, Thomas William. b 33. Edin Th Coll 62. **d** 65 **p** 66. C Gateshead St Mary *Dur* 65-66; C Shildon 66-67;

E Pakistan 68-71; Bangladesh 71-80; V Wheatley Hill *Dur* 80-87; V Dur St Giles from 87. *St Giles's Vicarage, Durham DH1 1QH* 091-386 4241

THURBURN-HUELIN, David Richard. b 47. St Chad's Coll Dur BA69. Westcott Ho Cam 69. **d** 71 **p** 72. C Poplar *Lon* 71-76; Chapl Liddon Ho Lon 76-80; R Harrold and Carlton w Chellington *St Alb* 81-88; V Goldington from 88. *St Mary's Vicarage, Church Lane, Goldington, Bedford MK41 0EX* Bedford (0234) 355024

THURGOOD, John William Voce. b 96. Roch Th Coll. **d** 60 **p** 60. V Wellingore w Temple Bruer *Linc* 62-71; rtd 71. *College of St Barnabas, Blackberry Lane, Lingfield, Surrey RH7 6NJ* Dormans Park (034287) 260

THURMER, Canon John Alfred. b 25. Or Coll Ox BA50 MA55. Linc Th Coll 50. **d** 52 **p** 53. Chapl Ex Univ *Ex* 64-73; Lect 64-85; Can Res and Chan Ex Cathl 73-91; rtd 91. *38 Velwell Road, Exeter EX4 4LD* Exeter (0392) 72277

THURNELL, David Christopher. b 37. Open Univ BA83. Sarum & Wells Th Coll 88. **d** 90. NSM Chippenham St Pet *Bris* from 90. *81 Westcroft, Chippenham, Wilts SN14 0LZ* Chippenham (0249) 654828

THURSFIELD, John Anthony. b 21. Magd Coll Ox BA47 MA51. Cuddesdon Coll 47. **d** 49 **p** 50. V Basing *Win* 60-72; Chapl Bonn w Cologne *Eur* 72-75; R E Clandon *Guildf* 75-79; R W Clandon 75-79; V Reydon *St E* 79-83; Perm to Offic *Heref* from 84; rtd 86. *Little Homend, The Homend, Ledbury, Herefordshire HR8 1AR* Ledbury (0531) 2935

THURSFIELD, John Richard. b 22. ALAM64. Roch Th Coll 60. **d** 62 **p** 63. C Battersea St Luke *S'wark* 69-71; C Wandsworth St Mich 71-72; Chapl St Ebba's Hosp Epsom 72-86; Qu Mary's Carshalton & Henderson Sutton 73-86; rtd 87. *PO Box 184, Worthing, W Sussex BN11 2ED*

THURSFIELD, Preb Raymond John. b 14. St Aid Birkenhead 43. **d** 45 **p** 46. Preb Heref Cathl *Heref* 65-80; R Ross 67-79; P-in-c Watermillock *Carl* 79-80; rtd 80; Perm to Offic *Heref* from 81; *Glouc* from 85; P-in-c France Lynch *Glouc* 84-85. *Flat 2, The Willows, Lansdown Road, Gloucester GL1 3LA* Gloucester (0452) 380198

THURSTON, Colin Benedict. b 47. Chich Th Coll 88. **d** 90 **p** 91. C Up Hatherley *Glouc* from 90. *St James's House, Reddings Road, The Reddings, Cheltenham, Glos GL51 6PA* Gloucester (0452) 856980

THURSTON, Ian Charles. b 54. St Hild Coll Dur CertEd78. S Dios Minl Tr Scheme 87 Sarum & Wells Th Coll 89. **d** 89 **p** 90. Bahrain 89-90; C All Hallows by the Tower etc *Lon* from 91. *14 Codling Close, London E1 9UX* 071-709 0609

THURSTON-SMITH, Trevor. b 59. Chich Th Coll 83. **d** 86 **p** 87. C Rawmarsh w Parkgate *Sheff* 86-87; C Horninglow *Lich* 87-91. *103 Carlton Road, Littleover, Derby DE3 6HE* Derby (0332) 770270

TIBBO, George Kenneth. b 29. Reading Univ BA50 MA54. Coll of Resurr Mirfield 55. **d** 57 **p** 58. C W Hartlepool St Aid *Dur* 57-61; V Darlington St Mark 61-74; V Darlington St Mark w St Paul 74-75; R Crook 75-80; V Stanley 76-80; V Oldham St Chad Limeside *Man* 80-87; V Hipswell *Ripon* from 87; OCF from 90. *The Vicarage, Piper Hill, Catterick Garrison, N Yorkshire DL9 4PN* Richmond (0748) 833320

TIBBOTT, Joseph Edwards. b 14. K Coll Lon. **d** 55 **p** 56. V Stockwell St Mich *S'wark* 59-71; V Llanguicke *S & B* 76-77; R Llangammarch w Garth, Llanlleonfel etc 77-80; rtd 80. *Pellingbridge Farm House, Scaynes Hill, Haywards Heath, W Sussex* Scaynes Hill (044486) 409

TIBBS, Canon Howard Abraham Llewellyn Thomas. b 13. Univ of Wales BA39. Coll of Resurr Mirfield 39. **d** 41 **p** 42. V Northn H Sepulchre w St Andr *Pet* 66-76; RD Northn 70-79; Can Pet Cathl 75-85; V Northn H Sepulchre w St Andr and St Lawr 76-85; rtd 85; Perm to Offic *Pet* from 85. *30 Fairway, Northampton NN2 7JZ* Northampton (0604) 716863

TIBBS, Canon John Andrew. b 29. AKC53. **d** 54 **p** 55. V Sompting *Chich* 69-73; R Ifield 73-78; TR 78-83; V Elstow *St Alb* 83-89; rtd 90; Chapl Bedf Gen Hosp from 90; Hon Can St Alb from 91. *15 Alexandra Road, Bedford MK40 1JA* Bedford (0234) 59579

TICEHURST, David. b 29. K Coll Lon 50. **d** 55 **p** 56. Hd Master Hawley Place Camberley 67-76; P-in-c Bury and Houghton *Chich* 76-81; V 81-89; P-in-c Bignor *Bognor* 78; P-in-c Barlavington 78; rtd 89. *34 Outerwyke Road, Felpham, Bognor Regis, W Sussex PO22 8HX* Bognor Regis (0243) 863985

TICKLE, Robert Peter. b 51. St Chad's Coll Dur BA74. St Steph Ho Ox 74. **d** 76 **p** 77. C Kingston upon Hull St

Alb *York* 76-80; C Leic St Chad *Leic* 80-81; Chapl Tewkesbury Abbey Choir Sch 81-82; Chapl Bradfield Coll Berks 82-86; Hon C Perivale *Lon* 86-89; Chapl St Cath Sch Bramley 89-91; Chapl Denstone Coll Uttoxeter from 91. *Denstone College, Uttoxeter, Staffs ST14 5HN* Uttoxeter (0889) 590372

TICKNER, Colin de Fraine. b 37. Chich Th Coll. **d** 66 **p** 67. C Huddersfield SS Pet and Paul *Wakef* 66-68; C Dorking w Ranmore *Guildf* 68-74; V Shottermill 74-91; RD Godalming 89-91; R Ockley w Okewood and Forest Green from 91. *The Rectory, Ockley, Dorking, Surrey RH5 5SY* Dorking (0306) 711550

TICKNER, David Arthur. b 44. MBE89. AKC67. **d** 69 **p** 70. C Thornhill Lees *Wakef* 69-71; C Billingham St Aid *Dur* 71-74; TV 74-78; CF from 78. *c/o MOD (Army), Bagshot Park, Bagshot, Surrey GU19 5PL* Bagshot (0276) 71717

TICKNER, Geoffrey John. b 55. BD. St Mich Coll Llan. **d** 82 **p** 83. C Bourne *Guildf* 82-85; C Grayswood 85-90; V New Haw from 90. *The Vicarage, 149 Woodham Lane, New Haw, Weybridge, Surrey KT15 3NJ* Byfleet (0932) 343187

TICQUET, Cyril Edward. b 11. DipTh. Ripon Hall Ox 63. **d** 64 **p** 65. V Castle Bromwich St Clem *Birm* 68-76; rtd 76; Hon C Stokenham w Sherford *Ex* from 77. *Bay Trees, Slapton, Kingsbridge, Devon TQ7 2PN* Kingsbridge (0548) 580564

TIDMARSH, Canon Peter Edwin. b 29. Keble Coll Ox BA52 MA56 DipEd. St Steph Ho Ox 52. **d** 54 **p** 55. C Stepney St Dunstan and All SS *Lon* 54-58; C Streatham St Pet *S'wark* 58-62; Chapl Shiplake Coll Henley 62-64; Hd Master All SS Choir Sch 64-68; C St Marylebone All SS *Lon* 64-68; V Cubert *Truro* from 68; Dir of Educn 69-85; Hon Can Truro Cathl from 73. *The Vicarage, St Cubert, Newquay, Cornwall TR8 5HA* Crantock (0637) 830301

TIDMARSH, Philip Reginald Wilton. b 14. G&C Coll Cam BA36 MA40. Ridley Hall Cam 46. **d** 48 **p** 49. V Odiham w S Warnborough *Win* 66-76; P-in-c Abbotts Ann 76-79; Perm to Offic *Heref* from 79; rtd 86. *The Gravel Pit Bungalow, Broadheath, Presteigne, Powys* Presteigne (0544) 267275

TIDY, John Hylton. b 48. AKC72. St Aug Coll Cant 73. **d** 73 **p** 74. C Newton Aycliffe *Dur* 73-78; V Auckland St Pet 78-84; V Burley in Wharfedale *Bradf* from 84. *The Vicarage, Burley-in-Wharfedale, Ilkley, W Yorkshire LS29 7DR* Burley-in-Wharfedale (0943) 863216

TIERNAN, Paul Wilson. b 54. Man Univ BA76. Coll of Resurr Mirfield 77. **d** 79 **p** 80. C Lewisham St Mary *S'wark* 79-83; V Sydenham St Phil from 83. *St Philip's Vicarage, 122 Wells Park Road, London SE26 6AS* 081-699 4930

TIGWELL, Brian Arthur. b 36. S'wark Ord Course 74. **d** 77 **p** 78. C Purley St Mark Woodcote *S'wark* 77-80; TV Upper Kennett *Sarum* 80-85; V Devizes St Pet from 85; Wilts Adnry Ecum Officer from 88. *The Vicarage, Bath Road, Devizes, Wilts SN10 2AP* Devizes (0380) 722621

TILL, Ven Michael Stanley. b 35. Linc Coll Ox BA60 MA67. Westcott Ho Cam. **d** 64 **p** 65. C St Jo Wood *Lon* 64-67; Chapl K Coll Cam 67-70; Dean K Coll Cam 70-81; AD Hammersmith *Lon* 81-86; V Fulham All SS 81-86; Adn Cant and Can Res Cant Cathl *Cant* from 86. *29 The Precincts, Canterbury, Kent CT1 2EP* Canterbury (0227) 463036

TILLER, Charles Edgar Gregory. b 61. St Mich Coll Llan BD. **d** 89 **p** 90. C Ex St Thos and Em *Ex* from 89. *3 Ferndale Road, Exeter EX14 1DF* Exeter (0392) 39501

TILLER, Edgar Henry. b 22. ACP71 Open Univ BA78. Wells Th Coll 57. **d** 59 **p** 60. V Stoke Lane *B & W* 62-67; V Leigh upon Mendip 62-67; Perm to Offic *Ex* from 67; rtd 91. *3 Byron Close, Pilton, Barnstaple, Devon EX31 1QH* Barnstaple (0271) 72483

TILLER, Canon John. b 38. Ch Ch Ox BA60 MA64 Bris Univ MLitt72. Tyndale Hall Bris 60. **d** 62 **p** 63. C Bedf St Cuth *St Alb* 62-65; C Widcombe *B & W* 65-67; Tutor Tyndale Hall Bris 67-71; Chapl 67-71; Lect Trin Coll Bris 71-73; P-in-c Bedf Ch Ch *St Alb* 73-78; Chief Sec ACCM 78-84; Hon Can St Alb 79-84; Can Res and Chan Heref Cathl *Heref* from 84. *The Canon's House, 3 St John Street, Hereford HR1 2NB* Hereford (0432) 265659

TILLETT, Leslie Selwyn. b 54. Peterho Cam BA75 MA79 Leeds Univ BA80. Coll of Resurr Mirfield 78. **d** 81 **p** 82. C W Dulwich All SS and Em *S'wark* 81-85; R Purleigh, Cold Norton and Stow Maries *Chelmsf* from 85. *The Rectory, Purleigh, Chelmsford CM3 6QH* Maldon (0621) 828743

TILLEY, David Robert. b 38. Kelham Th Coll 58. **d** 63 **p** 64. C Bournemouth St Fran *Win* 63-67; C Moulsecoomb *Chich* 67-70; C Ifield 70-75; C Warw St Mary *Cov* 76; TV 76; TV Warw 76-85; P-in-c Alderminster 85-89; P-in-c Halford 85-89; Dioc Min Tr Adv from 85; P-in-c Alderminster and Halford from 90; Minl Educn Adv from 90. *The Vicarage, Alderminster, Stratford-upon-Avon, Warks CV37 8PE* Alderminster (0789) 450208

TILLEY, Derise Ralph. b 21. Sarum Th Coll 55. **d** 57 **p** 58. V Millbrook *Truro* 64-80; P-in-c Antony w St Jo 76-80; R St John w Millbrook 80-90; rtd 90. *25 York Road, Torpoint, Cornwall PL11 2LG* Plymouth (0752) 815450

TILLEY, James Stephen. b 55. Nottm Univ BTh84. St Jo Coll Nottm. **d** 84 **p** 85. C Nottm St Jude *S'well* 84-88; C Ches le Street *Dur* from 88. *16 Park Road North, Chester le Street, Co Durham DH3 3SD* 091-388 9633

TILLEY, Peter Robert. b 41. Bris Univ BA62. Sarum & Wells Th Coll 77. **d** 79 **p** 80. C Wandsworth St Paul *S'wark* 79-82; V Mitcham St Mark from 82; RD Merton from 89. *St Mark's Vicarage, Locks Lane, Mitcham, Surrey CR4 2JX* 081-648 2397

TILLIER, Dr Jane Yvonne. b 59. New Hall Cam BA81 PhD85. Ripon Coll Cuddesdon BA(Theol)90. **d** 91. Par Dn Sheff Broomhall St Mark *Sheff* from 91. *46 Newbould Lane, Sheffield S10 2PL* Sheffield (0742) 686740

TILLMAN, Miss Mary Elizabeth. b 43. S Dios Minl Tr Scheme 86. **d** 89. NSM Bridgemary *Portsm* from 89. *391 Fareham Road, Gosport, Hants PO13 0AD* Fareham (0329) 232589

TILLYARD, James Donald. b 16. St D Coll Lamp BA38 Ripon Hall Ox 38. **d** 39 **p** 40. CF 42-71; V Uffington w Woolstone and Baulking *Ox* 71-81; rtd 81; Perm to Offic *Ox* 82-87. *Wingleting, Chapel Lane, Uffington, Faringdon, Oxon SN7 7RY* Uffington (036782) 513

TILLYER, Desmond Benjamin. b 40. Ch Coll Cam BA63 MA67. Coll of Resurr Mirfield 64. **d** 66 **p** 67. C Hanworth All SS *Lon* 66-70; Chapl Liddon Ho Lon 70-74; V Pimlico St Pet w Westmr Ch Ch *Lon* from 74; AD Westmr St Marg from 85. *24 Chester Square, London SW1W 9HS* 071-730 4354

TILNEY, Harold Arthur Rhodes. b 04. OBE45. **d** 52 **p** 53. R Southrepps *Nor* 59-69; rtd 69; Perm to Offic *Nor* from 70. *The Old Victoria House, Burnham Market, King's Lynn, Norfolk* Fakenham (0328) 738437

TILSON, Alan Ernest. b 46. TCD. **d** 70 **p** 71. C Londonderry Ch Ch *D & R* 70-73; I Inver w Mountcharles, Killaghtee and Killybegs 73-79; I Leckpatrick w Dunnalong 79-89; Bermuda from 89. *Holy Trinity Rectory, PO Box CR 186, Hamilton Parish, CRBX, Bermuda* Bermuda (1809) 293-1710

TILSTON, Derek Reginald. b 27. NW Ord Course. **d** 73 **p** 74. NSM Bury St Mark *Man* 73-77; NSM Holcombe 77-82; NSM Bury St Jo 82-83; NSM Bury St Jo w St Mark 83-84; C Bramley *Ripon* 85-87; TV 87-90; R Tendring and Lt Bentley w Beaumont cum Moze *Chelmsf* from 90. *The Rectory, Tendering, Clacton-on-Sea, Essex CO16 0BW* Clacton-on-Sea (0225) 830586

TILTMAN, Alan Michael. b 48. Selw Coll Cam BA70 MA74. Cuddesdon Coll 71. **d** 73 **p** 74. C Chesterton Gd Shep *Ely* 73-77; C Preston St Jo *Blackb* 77-79; Chapl Lancs (Preston) Poly 77-79; TV Man Whitworth *Man* 79-86; Chapl Man Univ (UMIST) 79-86; V Urmston from 86. *St Clement's Vicarage, Manor Avenue, Urmston, Manchester M31 1HH* 061-748 3972

TIMBERLAKE, Neil Christopher. b 26. Kelham Th Coll 47. **d** 51 **p** 52. Australia 68-70; C Leyland St Ambrose *Blackb* 70-72; C Bilborough w Strelley *S'well* 72-74; V Langold 74-86; rtd 86. *7 Thirlmere Avenue, Colne, Lancs BB8 7DD* Colne (0282) 863879

TIMBRELL, Keith Stewart. b 48. Edin Th Coll 72. **d** 74 **p** 75. C Chorley St Pet *Blackb* 74-77; C Altham w Clayton le Moors 77-79; Chapl Whittingham Hosp Preston from 79. *The Chaplain's Office, Whittingham Hospital, Goosnargh, Preston, Lancs PR3 2JH* Preston (0772) 865531

TIMBRELL, Maxwell Keith. b 28. St Jo Coll Morpeth ThL51. **d** 51 **p** 52. Australia 51-58 and 64-82; C Hanworth All SS *Lon* 59-63; P-in-c Kildale *York* 83-85; V Ingleby Greenhow w Bilsdale Priory 83-85; V Ingleby Greenhow w Bilsdale Priory, Kildale etc from 85. *The Vicarage, Ingleby Greenhow, Middlesbrough, Cleveland TS9 6LL* Great Ayton (0642) 723947

TIMINS, John Francis Holmer. b 03. Clare Coll Cam MA29. Ely Th Coll 33. **d** 34 **p** 35. R Horringer cum Ickworth *St E* 59-65; Lic to Offic 67-75; rtd 68. *Tudor*

Lodge, 6 St Michael's Road, Worthing, W Sussex BN11 4SD Worthing (0903) 206326

TIMMS, Ven George Boorne. b 10. St Edm Hall Ox BA33 MA45. Coll of Resurr Mirfield 33. d 35 p 36. Dir of Ords Lon 64-81; V St Andr Holborn 65-81; Adn Hackney 71-81; Perm to Offic Cant from 78; rtd 81. Cleve Lodge, Minster-in-Thanet, Ramsgate, Kent CT12 4BA Thanet (0843) 821777

TIMMS, Robert Newell. b 13. Dur Univ LTh36. Dorchester Miss Coll 33. d 36 p 37. R Watton at Stone St Alb 64-68; rtd 69; Perm to Offic Glouc 76-84; Worc from 85. 76 Red Hall Road, Gornall Wood, Dudley, W Midlands DY3 2NL Dudley (0384) 241383

TIMOTHY, Brother. See STANTON, Thomas Hugh

TIMPERLEY, Patrick. b 65. St D Coll Lamp BA86. St Jo Coll Dur 86. d 88 p 89. C Pemb St Mary and St Mich St D 88-91; C Higher Bebington Ches from 91. 3 Beech Road, Bebington, Wirral, Merseyside L63 8PE 051-645 9074

TINDALL, Edward Frederick. b 08. St Andr Coll Pampisford 44. d 45 p 46. V Arkengarthdale Ripon 66-75; rtd 75. 2 Mallard Road, Scotton, Catterick Garrison, N Yorkshire DL9 3NP Richmond (0748) 832345

TINDALL, Canon Frederick Cryer. b 1900. Lon Univ AKC22 BD23. Ely Th Coll 23. d 24 p 25. Prin Sarum Th Coll 50-65; Can and Preb Sarum Cathl Sarum 50-81; rtd 70. 16 The Close, Salisbury SP1 2EB Salisbury (0722) 22373

TINGAY, Kevin Gilbert Xavier. b 43. Sussex Univ BA79. Chich Th Coll 79. d 80 p 81. C W Tarring Chich 80-83; TV Worth 83-90; R Bradf w Oake, Hillfarrance and Heathfield B & W from 90. The Rectory, Bradford on Tone, Taunton, Somerset TA4 1HG Bradford-on-Tone (0823) 461423

TINGLE, Michael Barton. b 31. Bps' Coll Cheshunt 65. d 67 p 68. C Totteridge St Alb 67-70; C Hitchin St Mary 70-73; V Gt Gaddesden 73-78; V Belmont Lon 78-86; V Burford w Fulbrook and Taynton Ox from 86. The Vicarage, Burford, Oxford OX8 4SE Burford (099382) 2275

TINKER, Preb Eric Franklin. b 20. OBE89. Ex Coll Ox BA42 MA46 Lon Univ Hon DD89. Linc Th Coll 42. d 44 p 45. Preb St Paul's Cathl Lon from 69; Sen Chapl Lon Univs and Polys 69-90; Dir of Educn (Dios Lon and S'wark) 72-80; Gen Sec Lon Dioc Bd of Educn 80-82; rtd 90. 35 Theberton Street, London N1 0QY 071-359 4750

TINKER, Melvin. b 55. Hull Univ BSc Ox Univ MA. Wycliffe Hall Ox 80. d 83 p 84. C Wetherby Ripon 83-85; Chapl Keele Univ Lich 85-90; V Cheadle All Hallows Ches from 90. All Hallows' Vicarage, 222 Councillor Lane, Cheadle, Chesire SK8 2JG 061-428 9071

TINKER, Michael Jonathan Russell. b 50. York Univ BA72. Qu Coll Birm DipTh74. d 75 p 76. C Castle Vale Birm 75-78; Bp's Dom Chapl 78-80; R Stretford All SS Man 80-88; V Stalybridge from 88. The Vicarage, 2 Tintagel Court, Astley Road, Stalybridge, Cheshire SK15 1RA 061-338 2368

TINKLER, Ian Henry. b 32. Selw Coll Cam BA57 MA61. Westcott Ho Cam. d 60 p 61. C Gosforth All SS Newc 60-65; Asst Chapl Brussels Eur 65-68; R S Ferriby Linc 68-85; V Horkstow 68-85; R Saxby All Saints 72-85; V Humberston from 85. The Vicarage, Tetney Road, Humberston, Grimsby, S Humberside DN36 4JF Grimsby (0472) 813158

TINNISWOOD, Robin Jeffries. b 41. K Coll Lon BSc64 Bris Univ DipTh69. Wells Th Coll 67. d 70 p 71. C Yeovil St Mich B & W 70-72; C Gt Marlow Ox 72-74; C Christow, Ashton, Trusham and Bridford Ex 74-77; P-in-c Ex St Paul 77; TV Heavitree w Ex St Paul 78-79; TV Ifield Chich 79-85. Address temp unknown

TINSLEY, Bernard Murray. b 26. Nottm Univ BA51 Birm Univ DPS. Westcott Ho Cam 51. d 53 p 54. R Alverdiscott w Huntshaw Ex 61-78; R Newton Tracey 61-78; R Beaford and Roborough 67-78; V St Giles in the Wood 67-78; V Yarnscombe 67-78; R Newton Tracey, Alverdiscott, Huntshaw etc 78-88; RD Torrington 81-86; rtd 88; Perm to Offic Ex from 88. The Grange, Grange Road, Bideford, Devon EX39 4AS Bideford (0237) 471414

TINSLEY, Derek. b 31. ALCM65. NW Ord Course 73. d 76 p 77. C Gt Crosby St Faith Liv 76-80; V Wigan St Anne 80-85; V Colton w Satterthwaite and Rusland Carl from 85. The Vicarage, Colton, Ulverston, Cumbria LA12 8HF Greenodd (022986) 361

TINSLEY, Preb Derek Michael. b 35. Lon Coll of Div ALCD66 LTh. d 66 p 67. C Rainhill Liv 66-68; C Chalfont St Peter Ox 68-74; R N Buckm 74-82; RD Buckm 78-82; P-in-c Alstonfield Lich 82-84; P-in-c

Butterton 82-84; P-in-c Warslow and Elkstones 82-84; P-in-c Wetton 82-84; RD Alstonfield from 82; V Alstonfield, Butterton, Warslow w Elkstone etc from 85; Preb Lich Cathl from 91. The Vicarage, Alstonefield, Ashbourne, Derbyshire DE6 2FX Alstonefield (033527) 216

✠TINSLEY, Rt Rev Ernest John. b 19. St Jo Coll Dur BA40 BA42 MA43 BD45. Westcott Ho Cam 43. d 42 p 43 c 76. C Dur St Mary le Bow w St Mary the Less Dur 42-44; C S Westoe 44-46; Lect Th Hull Univ 46-54; C Newland St Jo York 47-48; C Kingston upon Hull St Alb 48-55; Sen Lect Hull Univ 54-61; Lic to Offic Ripon 62-66; Prof Th Leeds Univ 62-76; Hon Can Ripon Cathl Ripon 66-76; Bp Bris 76-85; rtd 85; Perm to Offic Ox from 85. 100 Acre End Street, Eynsham, Oxford OX8 1PD Oxford (0865) 880822

TINSLEY, Canon John. b 17. AKC49. d 49 p 50. V Wandsworth St Paul S'wark 56-70; RD Wandsworth 69-70; V Redhill St Jo 70-80; RD Reigate 76-80; Hon Can S'wark Cathl 80-81; P-in-c Othery B & W 80; P-in-c Middlezoy 80; P-in-c Moorlinch w Stawell and Sutton Mallet 80; V Middlezoy and Othery and Moorlinch 81-85; rtd 85. Cedar House, 1 Quantock Rise, Kingston St Mary, Taunton, Somerset TA2 8HJ Taunton (0823) 451317

TIPLADY, Dr Peter. b 42. MRCGP72 FFPHM86 Dur Univ MB, BS65. Carl Dioc Tr Course 86. d 89 p 90. NSM Wetheral w Warw Carl from 89. The Arches, The Green, Wetheral, Carlisle CA4 8ET Wetheral (0228) 61611 or 41996

TIPP, James Edward. b 45. Oak Hill Th Coll 73. d 75 p 76. C St Mary Cray and St Paul's Cray Roch 75-78; C Southborough St Pet w Ch Ch and St Matt 78-82; R Snodland All SS w Ch Ch from 82. The Vicarage, St Katherine's Lane, Snodland, Kent ME6 5JB Snodland (0634) 240232

TIPPER, David Allen. b 21. Tyndale Hall Bris 54. d 56 p 57. V Balderstone Man 65-79; P-in-c Linton w Upton Bishop and Aston Ingham Heref 79; R 80-87; rtd 87. 4 Monkscroft Drive, Belmont, Hereford HR2 7XB Hereford (0432) 357801

TIPPER, Michael William. b 38. Hull Univ BSc59 MSc61. Em Coll Saskatoon 72. d 73 p 74. Canada 73-77 and 79-80 and 83-88; R Amcotts Linc 77-79; V Aycliffe Dur 80-83; V Kneesall w Laxton and Wellow S'well from 88. The Vicarage, 19 Baulk Lane, Kneesall, Newark, Notts NG22 0AA Mansfield (0623) 835820

TIPPING, John Henry. b 27. St Mich Coll Llan 63. d 65 p 66. C Clydach S & B 65-68; C Oystermouth 68-70; R Llangynllo and Bleddfa 70-79; V Cwmddauddwr w St Harmon's and Llanwrthwl 79-80; R Ashton Gifford Sarum from 80. The Rectory, Green Lane, Codford, Warminster, Wilts BA12 0NY Warminster (0985) 50320

TIPPING, John Woodman. b 42. AKC65. d 66 p 67. C Croydon St Sav Cant 66-70; C Plaistow St Mary Roch 70-72; V Brockley Hill St Sav S'wark 72-83; P-in-c Sittingbourne St Mary Cant 83-86; V from 86. St Mary's Vicarage, 88 Albany Road, Sittingbourne, Kent ME10 1EL Sittingbourne (0795) 472535

TIRRELL, Canon Leslie Burditt. b 07. Lon Univ BSc27. Sarum Th Coll 28. d 30 p 31. Dir of RE (Dios Lon and S'wark) 49-71; Hon Can S'wark Cathl S'wark 51-71; rtd 72; Perm to Offic Guildf from 82. Fairwinds, Park Corner Drive, East Horsley, Leatherhead, Surrey KT24 6SF East Horsley (04865) 3376

TITCOMBE, Peter Charles. b 57. Llan St Mich DipTh83. d 83 p 84. C Pontnewynydd Mon 83-85; C Bassaleg 85-86; C Cwmbran 87; TV from 87. The Vicarage, 87 Bryn Eglwys, Croesyceiliog, Cwmbran, Gwent NP44 2LF Cwmbran (0633) 33425

TITFORD, Richard Kimber. b 45. UEA BA67. Ripon Coll Cuddesdon 78. d 80 p 80. C Middleton Man 80-83; P-in-c Edwardstone w Groton and Lt Waldingfield St E 83-90; R from 90. The Vicarage, Edwardstone, Colchester CO6 5PG Boxford (0787) 210026

TITLEY, David Joseph. b 47. Ex Univ BSc Surrey Univ PhD. Wycliffe Hall Ox. d 82 p 83. C Stowmarket St E 82-85; C Bloxwich Lich 85-90; TV from 90. 9 Sanstone Road, Bloxwich, Walsall WS3 3SJ Bloxwich (0922) 479160

TITLEY, Robert John. b 56. Ch Coll Cam BA78 MA82. Westcott Ho Cam DipTh83. d 85 p 86. C Lower Sydenham St Mich S'wark 85-88; C Sydenham All SS 85-88; Chapl Whitelands Coll of HE from 88. Whitelands College, London SW15 3SN 081-788 8268

TITTERINGTON, Canon John Milne. b 23. St Cath Soc Ox BA49 MA53. Linc Th Coll 49. d 51 p 52. V Langley All SS and Martyrs Man 68-72; RD Rossendale 72-80; R Newchurch St Nic 72-73; R Newchurch 73-80; Hon

Can Man Cathl 77-80; Papua New Guinea from 80; rtd 90. *St John's Cathedral, PO Box 6, Port Moresby, Papua New Guinea*

TITTERINGTON, Mark. b 24. St Aid Birkenhead 66. **d** 67 **p** 67. C Chorley St Laur *Blackb* 67-71; C Blackpool St Steph 71-75; V Woodplumpton 75-78; V Preston St Matt 78-85; P-in-c Over Wyresdale 85-88; rtd 88. *5 New Links Avenue, Ingol, Preston, Lancs PR2 7EX* Preston (0772) 725524

TITTLEY, Donald Frank. b 22. ACP70 LCP74. NE Ord Course 78. **d** 80 **p** 81. NSM Tynemouth Cullercoats St Paul *Newc* from 80. *22 Selwyn Avenue, Whitley Bay, Tyne & Wear NE25 9DH* 091-252 6655

TIZZARD, Canon David John. b 40. LRAM. Sarum Th Coll 65. **d** 68 **p** 69. C Foley Park *Worc* 68-70; Hon C Gravesend St Geo *Roch* 70-73; Miss to Seamen 70-72; PV Truro Cathl *Truro* 73-75; TV Bemerton *Sarum* 75-79; Soc Resp Adv 79-85; Chapl to the Deaf 79-85; Can and Preb Sarum Cathl 84-85; R S Hill w Callington *Truro* 85-87; P-in-c Linkinhorne 86-87; Relig Affairs Producer BBC Radio Solent from 87; V Portswood St Denys *Win* from 87. *34 Whitworth Road, Southampton SO2 4GF* Southampton (0703) 227160

TIZZARD, Dudley Frank. b 19. Roch Th Coll 63. **d** 65 **p** 66. C Cant St Martin w St Paul *Cant* 68-71; Chapl HM Pris Cant 68-71; V Petham w Waltham *Cant* 71-75; C Sevenoaks St Jo *Roch* 75-78; rtd 84; Lic to Offic *Cant* from 84. *61 Robins Avenue, Lenham, Maidstone, Kent ME17 2HP* Maidstone (0622) 850110

TIZZARD, Peter Francis. b 53. Oak Hill Th Coll DipHE88. **d** 90 **p** 91. C Letchworth St Paul w Willian *St Alb* from 90. *89 Howard Drive, Letchworth, Herts SG6 2BX* Letchworth (0462) 673888

TOAN, Robert Charles. b 50. Oak Hill Th Coll. **d** 84 **p** 85. C Upton (or Overchurch) *Ches* 84-87; V Rock Ferry from 87. *The Vicarage, St Peter's Road, Birkenhead, Merseyside L42 1PY* 051-645 1622

TOBIAS, Edwin John Rupert. b 16. TCD BA40 MA59. **d** 40 **p** 41. RD Loughscudy and Mullingar *M & K* 68-82; I Killucan 77-82; rtd 82. *Sue Ryder House, Chalet 7, Ballyroan, Co Laois, Irish Republic* Portlaoise (502) 31071

TOBIAS, William Trevor. b 10. St Steph Ho Ox 62. **d** 63 **p** 64. P-in-c Hanwell St Mark *Lon* 69-80; rtd 80; Perm to Offic *Lon* from 81. *58 Claremont Road, London W13 0DG* 081-997 6023

TOBIN, Richard Francis. b 44. CertEd. Chich Th Coll 76. **d** 78 **p** 79. C W Leigh CD *Portsm* 78-79; C Halstead St Andr *Chelmsf* 79; C Halstead St Andr w H Trin 79; C Halstead St Andr w H Trin and Greenstead Green 79-87; Youth Chapl 82-87; V S Shields St Simon *Dur* from 87. *St Simon's Vicarage, Wenlock Road, South Shields, Tyne & Wear NE34 9AL* 091-455 3164

TODD, Alastair. b 20. CMG71. CCC Ox BA45 Lon Univ DipTh65. Sarum & Wells Th Coll 71. **d** 73 **p** 74. C Willingdon *Chich* 73-77; P-in-c Brighton St Aug 77-78; V Brighton St Aug and St Sav 78-86; rtd 86; Perm to Offic *Chich* from 86. *59 Park Avenue, Eastbourne, E Sussex BN21 2XH* Eastbourne (0323) 505843

TODD, Andrew John. b 61. Keble Coll Ox. Univ Coll Dur BA84. Coll of Resurr Mirfield 85. **d** 87 **p** 88. C Thorpe *Nor* from 87. *14 Acacia Road, Thorpe St Andrew, Norwich NR7 0PP* Norwich (0603) 35228

TODD, Clive. b 57. Linc Th Coll 89. **d** 91. C Consett *Dur* from 91. *Church House, 1C Aynsley Terrace, Consett, Co Durham DH8 5LX* Consett (0207) 508420

TODD, Edward Peter. b 44. Cranmer Hall Dur 86. **d** 88 **p** 89. C Hindley All SS *Liv* 88-91; P-in-c Wigan St Steph from 91. *St Stephen's Vicarage, Wigan, Lancs WN2 1BL* Wigan (0942) 42579

TODD, George Robert. b 21. Sarum & Wells Th Coll 74. **d** 76 **p** 77. Hon C Wellington and Distr *B & W* from 76. *15 John Grinter Way, Wellington, Somerset TA21 9AR* Wellington (0823) 662828

TODD, John Lindsay. b 22. Univ of Wales (Ban) BA49. St Mich Coll Llan 49. **d** 51 **p** 52. C Chirk *St As* 51-53; C Llanrhos 53-58; R Guilsfield from 58. *The Vicarage, Guilsfield, Welshpool, Powys SY21 9NF* Welshpool (0938) 3879

TODD, Joy Gertrude. b 28. Local NSM Course. **d** 90. NSM Guildf H Trin w St Mary *Guildf* from 90. *165 Stoke Road, Guildford, Surrey GU1 1EY* Guildford (0483) 67500

TODD, Leslie Alwill. b 15. St Aid Birkenhead 46. **d** 48 **p** 49. Bahamas 70-73; C Clerkenwell H Redeemer w St Phil *Lon* 73-74; Chapl Nat Hosp for Nervous Diseases Lon 74-80; rtd 80; P-in-c Ipswich St Mary at the Elms *St E* 80-85; Perm to Offic *Man* 86-88; Wakef from

88. *3 Park Avenue, Denby Dale Road, Wakefield, W Yorkshire WF2 8DS* Wakefield (0924) 382461

TODD, Canon Norman Henry. b 19. PhC Lon Univ BPharm42 Fitzw Ho Cam BA50 MA55 Nottm Univ PhD78. Westcott Ho Cam 50. **d** 52 **p** 53. R Elston w Elston Chapelry *S'well* 71-76; R E Stoke w Syerston 72-76; V Sibthorpe 72-76; Bp's Adv on Tr 76-83; C Averham w Kelham 76-80; V Rolleston w Morton 80-83; P-in-c Upton 80-83; Hon Can S'well Minster from 82; V Rolleston w Fiskerton, Morton and Upton 83-88; rtd 88; Abp's Adv Induction & Continuing Minl Educn of Bps from 88. *70 Park Road, Nottingham NG7 1JG* Nottingham (0602) 418345

TODD, Rupert Granville. b 31. ALCD61. **d** 61 **p** 62. I Lissan *Arm* 66-69; rtd 69; Dioc Curate *Arm* 70-83. *13 Cranfield Court, Portstewart, Co Londonderry* Portstewart (026583) 2725

TODD, William Colquhoun Duncan. b 26. AKC53 St Boniface Warminster 53. **d** 54 **p** 55. C Westmr St Steph w St Jo *Lon* 54-59; C-in-c Leigh Park CD *Portsm* 59-69; V Leigh Park 69-72; Win Coll Missr 60-72; Angl Adv Southern TV 62-72; Thames TV from 72; R Hatf *St Alb* from 72. *The Rectory, 1 Fore Street, Hatfield, Herts AL9 5AN* Hatfield (0707) 262072

TODD, William Moorhouse. b 26. Lich Th Coll 54. **d** 57 **p** 58. C W Derby St Mary *Liv* 57-61; V Liv St Chris Norris Green from 61. *St Christopher's Vicarage, Lorenzo Drive, Norris Green, Liverpool L11 1BQ* 051-226 1637

TOFTS, Jack. b 31. Roch Th Coll 66. **d** 68 **p** 69. C Richmond *Ripon* 68-71; C Croydon *Cant* 71-74; P-in-c Welney *Ely* 74-78; P-in-c Upwell Ch Ch 74-79; V Gorefield from 78; R Newton from 78; R Tydd St Giles from 78. *The Rectory, Newton, Wisbech, Cambs PE13 5EX* Wisbech (0945) 870205

TOLL, Brian Arthur. b 35. Ely Th Coll 62 Linc Th Coll 64. **d** 65 **p** 66. C Cleethorpes *Linc* 65-68; C Hadleigh w Layham and Shelley *St E* 69-72; R Claydon and Barham 72-86; P-in-c Capel w Lt Wenham from 86; P-in-c Holton St Mary w Gt Wenham from 87; Bp's Adv on Deliverance and Exorcism from 89. *The Rectory, Days Road, Capel St Mary, Ipswich IP9 2LE* Great Wenham (0473) 310236

TOLLER, Elizabeth Margery. b 53. Leeds Univ BA75. Ripon Coll Cuddesdon 84. **d** 87. Perm to Offic *Nor* from 87. *The Rectory, Rectory Road, Cottishall, Norwich NR12 7HL* Norwich (0603) 737255

TOLLER, Heinz Dieter. b 52. Bonn Univ DipTh77. NE Ord Course 86. **d** 87 **p** 88. C Leeds Gipton Epiphany *Ripon* 87-90; R Coltishall w Gt Hautbois and Horstead *Nor* from 90. *The Rectory, Coltishall, Norwich NR12 7HL* Norwich (0603) 737255

TOLLEY, Canon George. b 25. FRSC CBIM Lon Univ BSc45 MSc48 PhD52 Sheff Univ Hon DSc83. Linc Th Coll 65. **d** 67 **p** 68. C Sheff Sharrow *Sheff* 67-90; Hon Can Sheff Cathl from 76. *74 Furniss Avenue, Sheffield S17 3QP* Sheffield (0742) 360538

TOLWORTHY, Colin. b 37. Chich Th Coll 64. **d** 67 **p** 68. C Hulme St Phil *Man* 67-70; C Lawton Moor 70-71; C Hangleton *Chich* 72-76; V Eastbourne St Phil 76-87; V Hastings H Trin from 87. *Holy Trinity Vicarage, 72 Priory Avenue, Hastings, E Sussex TN34 1UG* Hastings (0424) 441766

TOMBLING, Canon Arthur John. b 32. St Jo Coll Cam BA54 MA58. Ridley Hall Cam 55. **d** 57 **p** 58. C Rushden Pet 57-59; Asst Chapl Repton Sch Derby 59-61; C Reigate St Mary *S'wark* 61-64; V Battersea Park St Sav 64-87; P-in-c Battersea St Geo w St Andr 74-87; RD Battersea 85-90; V Battersea St Sav and St Geo w St Andr from 87; P-in-c Battersea Park All SS from 89; Hon Can S'wark Cathl from 89. *St Saviour's Vicarage, 7 Alexandra Avenue, London SW11 4DZ* 071-622 4526

TOMKINS, Clive Anthony. b 47. Cant Sch of Min 85. **d** 88 **p** 89. C Eastry and Northbourne w Tilmanstone etc *Cant* from 88. *The Rectory, The Street, Northbourne, Deal, Kent CT14 0LG* Deal (0304) 374967

✠TOMKINS, Rt Rev Oliver Stratford. b 08. Ch Coll Cam BA32 MA35 Edin Univ Hon DD53. Westcott Ho Cam 32. **d** 35 **p** 36 **c** 59. C Prittlewell St Mary *Chelmsf* 35-39; Lic to Offic *Lon* 39-40; V Millhouses H Trin *Sheff* 40-45; Assoc Gen Sec & Sec Cttee on Faith & Order WCC 45-52; Warden Linc Th Coll 53-58; Can and Preb Linc Cathl *Linc* 53-58; Bp Bris 75-79; rtd 75; Asst Bp Worc 76-91. *23 St Paul's Road West, Dorking, Surrey RH4 2HT* Dorking (0306) 885536

TOMKINSON, Raymond David. b 47. RGN MSSCh. E Anglian Minl Tr Course 86. **d** 89 **p** 90. NSM Chesterton St Geo *Ely* 89-91; C Sawston from 91; C Babraham from

91. *23 Teversham Way, Sawston, Cambridge CB2 4DF* Cambridge (0223) 832955

TOMLIN, Graham Stuart. b 58. Linc Coll Ox MA80. Wycliffe Hall Ox BA85. **d** 86 **p** 87. C Ex St Leon w H Trin *Ex* 86-89; Tutor Wycliffe Hall Ox from 89; Chapl Jes Coll Ox from 89. *Jesus College, Oxford OX1 3DW* Oxford (0865) 279757

TOMLIN, Henry Alfred. b 14. Worc Ord Coll 62. **d** 64 **p** 65. V Smallthorne *Lich* 68-79; rtd 79; Perm to Offic *Man* from 80. *13 Billinge Avenue, Blackburn* Blackburn (0254) 580515

TOMLIN, Keith Michael. b 53. Imp Coll Lon BSc75. Ridley Hall Cam 77. **d** 80 **p** 81. C Heywood St Jas *Man* 80-83; C Rochdale 83-84; TV 84-85; Chapl Rochdale Tech Coll 83-85; R Benington w Leverton *Linc* from 85. *The Rectory, Benington, Boston, Lincs PE22 0BT* Boston (0205) 760962

TOMLINE, Stephen Harrald. b 35. Dur Univ BA57. Cranmer Hall Dur DipTh61. **d** 61 **p** 62. C Blackley St Pet *Man* 61-66; V Audenshaw St Steph 66-90; V Newhey from 90. *St Thomas's Vicarage, Newhey, Rochdale, Lancs OL16 3QS* Shaw (0706) 845159

TOMLINSON, Arthur John Faulkner. b 20. Clare Coll Cam BA41 MA45. Ridley Hall Cam 46. **d** 48 **p** 49. R Sarratt *St Alb* 62-85; rtd 85; Perm to Offic *Nor* from 85. *The Retreat, The Heath, Buxton, Norwich NR10 5JA* Buxton (060546) 470

TOMLINSON, Barry William. b 47. Reading Univ DipTh. Clifton Th Coll 72. **d** 72 **p** 73. C Pennington *Man* 72-76; SAMS 76-80; Chile 77-80; C-in-c Gorleston St Mary CD *Nor* 80; Chapl Jas Paget Hosp Gorleston 81-87; V Gorleston St Mary *Nor* 80-88; P-in-c Gt w Lt Plumstead 88-89; R Gt w Lt Plumstead and Witton from 89. *The Rectory, 9 Lawn Crescent, Thorpe End, Norwich NR13 5BP* Norwich (0603) 34778

TOMLINSON, Eric Joseph. b 45. Qu Coll Birm 70. **d** 73 **p** 74. C Cheadle *Lich* 73-76; C Sedgley All SS 77-79; V Ettingshall from 79. *The Vicarage, Ettingshall, Wolverhampton WV4 6QH* Sedgley (09073) 4616

TOMLINSON, Frederick William. b 58. Glas Univ MA80 Edin Univ BD83. Edin Th Coll 80. **d** 83 **p** 84. C Cumbernauld *Glas* 83-86; C Glas St Mary 86-88; R Edin St Hilda *Edin* from 88; R Edin St Fillan from 88. *8 Buckstone Drive, Edinburgh EH10 6PD* 031-445 2942

TOMLINSON, Canon Geoffrey. b 15. Linc Coll Ox BA37 MA47. Westcott Ho Cam 37. **d** 39 **p** 40. V Lanc St Mary *Blackb* 66-81; Hon Can Blackb Cathl from 67; RD Lanc 71-82; V Overton 81-86; rtd 86; Perm to Offic *Bradf* from 86; *Blackb* from 87. *3 Kirk Beck Close, Brookhouse, Lancaster LA2 9JN* Caton (0524) 770051

TOMLINSON, Ian James. b 50. K Coll Lon AKC72 MA90. St Aug Coll Cant 72. **d** 73 **p** 74. C Thirsk w S Kilvington and Carlton Miniott etc *York* 73-76; C Harrogate St Wilfrid *Ripon* 76-79; R Appleshaw, Kimpton, Thruxton and Fyfield *Win* from 79. *The Rectory, Ragged Appleshaw, Andover, Hants SP11 9HX* Weyhill (0264) 772414

TOMLINSON, Mrs Jean Mary. b 32. K Coll Lon CertRK53 BEd75. S Dios Minl Tr Scheme 84. **d** 87. Hon Par Dn Spring Park All SS *S'wark* from 87; Bp's Exam Chapl from 88. *32 Maresfield, Chepstow Road, Croydon, Surrey CR0 5UA* 081-680 8790

TOMLINSON, John Coombes. b 34. Nottm Univ DipEd76. Lich Th Coll 60. **d** 62 **p** 63. C Cheadle *Lich* 62-66; Warden Lich Dioc Tr Cen 66-73; C Alstonfield 66-68; P-in-c Ilam w Blore Ray and Okeover 68-73; Dioc Youth Tr Officer 68-73; Bp's Youth Chapl *Derby* 73-84; Dep Dir of Educn 78-79; Dir of Educn 79-84; TR Buxton w Burbage and King Sterndale from 84; Dioc Adv Past Care and Counselling from 85; RD Buxton from 91. *The Rectory, Lismore Park, Buxton, Derbyshire SK17 9AU* Buxton (0298) 22151

TOMLINSON, Peter Robert Willis. b 19. CertEd49. Linc Th Coll 53. **d** 55 **p** 56. V Barrow Gurney *B & W* 70-77; Asst Chapl and Lect Coll of St Matthias Bris 70-77; TV Langport Area Chs 78-80; R Flax Bourton 80-84; V Barrow Gurney 80-84; rtd 84. *Flat 2, Vernon Lodge, 87 Hampton Park, Bristol BS6 6LQ* Bristol (0272) 466011

TOMLINSON, Robert Herbert. b 12. Lon Univ BD38. ALCD38. **d** 38 **p** 39. V Docking *Nor* 62-78; V Fring 66-78; R Stanhoe w Barwick 71-78; P-in-c 78-85; rtd 78; Perm to Offic *Nor* from 85. *The Chantry, Stanhoe, King's Lynn, Norfolk PE31 8PT* Docking (04858) 456

TOMLINSON, Miss Thelma Marcelle. b 20. K Coll Lon 46. **dss** 67. Liv Cathl *Liv* 69-81; Liv Univ 69-75; Dioc Lay Min Adv 75-81; rtd 81; Hon C Worle *B & W* from 81. *Cranbrook, 16 Greenwood Road, Worle,*

Weston-super-Mare, Avon BS22 0EX Weston-super-Mare (0934) 515112

TOMLINSON, Vincent Bellini. b 11. Bps' Coll Cheshunt 66. **d** 67 **p** 68. C Ipswich H Trin *St E* 70-73; R Westerfield w Tuddenham St Martin 73-77; rtd 77. *11 Edward Terrace, Sun Lane, Alresford, Hants SO24 9LY* Alresford (0962) 734449

TOMPKINS, David John. b 32. Oak Hill Th Coll 55. **d** 58 **p** 59. C Northn St Giles *Pet* 58-61; C Heatherlands St Jo *Sarum* 61-63; V Selby St Jas *York* 63-73; V Wistow 63-73; V Retford *S'well* 73-87; P-in-c Clarborough w Hayton 84-87; V Kidsgrove *Lich* 87-90; V Tockwith and Bilton w Bickerton *York* from 90. *The Vicarage, Westfield Road, Tockwith, York YO5 8PY* Boroughbridge (0423) 358338

TOMPKINS, Francis Alfred Howard. b 26. St Jo Coll Dur BA50 DipTh52. **d** 52 **p** 53. V Donington *Linc* 65-79; RD Holland W 69-78; V Silloth *Carl* 79-91; rtd 91; Perm to Offic *Linc* from 91. *22 Silver Street, Branston, Lincoln LN4 1LR* Lincoln (0522) 791689

TOMPKINS, Canon James Charles Harrison. b 20. Peterho Cam BA41 MA45. Westcott Ho Cam 45. **d** 47 **p** 48. C Rugby St Andr *Cov* 47-51; Chapl Eton Coll Windsor 51-55; R Handsworth St Mary *Birm* from 55; Lect Qu Coll Birm from 57; Hon Can Birm Cathl *Birm* from 76; RD Handsworth 77-83. *The Rectory, 288 Hamstead Road, Birmingham B20 2RB* 021-554 3407

TOMPKINS, Michael John Gordon. b 35. JP76. Man Univ BSc58 MPS59. N Ord Course 82. **d** 85 **p** 86. C Abington *Pet* 85-87; TV Daventry from 87; P-in-c Braunston from 87. *The Rectory, High Street, Braunston, Daventry, Northants NN11 7HS* Rugby (0788) 890235

TOMSETT, James. b 08. S'wark Ord Course 61. **d** 64 **p** 65. V Compton Bishop *B & W* 70-79; V Compton Bishop w Loxton and Christon 79-80; rtd 80; Perm to Offic *B & W* from 81. *9 St Andrew's Road, Cheddar, Somerset BS27 3NE* Cheddar (0934) 742694

TONBRIDGE, Archdeacon of. See MASON, Ven Richard John

TONBRIDGE, Suffragan Bishop of. See BARTLEET, Rt Rev David Henry

TONES, Kevin Edward. b 64. Hertf Coll Ox BA85. Ridley Hall Cam 88. **d** 91. C Warmsworth *Sheff* from 91. *The White Church House, 23 Wrightson Avenue, Warmsworth, Doncaster, S Yorkshire* Doncaster (0302) 311086

TONG, Canon Peter Laurence. b 29. Lon Univ BA50. Oak Hill Th Coll 52. **d** 54 **p** 55. C Everton St Chrys *Liv* 54-56; P-in-c Liv St Sav 56-59; V Blackb Sav *Blackb* 59-65; Chapl Blackb R Infirmary 63-65; V Islington St Andr w St Thos and St Matthias *Lon* 65-75; V Welling *Roch* 75-82; R Bedworth *Cov* from 82; Hon Can Cov Cathl from 88; Hon Can Chile from 89. *The Vicarage, 1 Linden Lea, Bedworth, Nuneaton, Warks CV12 8ES* Coventry (0203) 310219

TONGE, Brian. b 36. Dur Univ BA58. Ely Th Coll 59. **d** 61 **p** 62. C Fleetwood *Blackb* 61-65; Chapl Ranby Ho Sch Retford 65-69; Hon C Burnley St Andr w St Marg *Blackb* from 69. *230 Barden Lane, Burnley, Lancs BB10 1TD* Burnley (0282) 23185

TONGE, David Theophilus. b 30. Wells Th Coll 68. **d** 70 **p** 71. C Kidderminster St Mary *Worc* 70-76; P-in-c Finstall 76-82; V from 82; Chapl to HM The Queen from 85. *The Vicarage, Finstall, Bromsgrove, Worcs B60 2EA* Bromsgrove (0527) 72459

TONGE, Lister. b 51. AKC74. St Aug Coll Cant 74. **d** 75 **p** 76. C Liv Our Lady and St Nic w St Anne *Liv* 75-78; S Africa 78-83; CR 79-91; Lic to Offic *Wakef* 83-91; Perm to Offic *Man* from 89; Perm to Offic *Ches* from 91. *c/o 47 Moreton Street, Chadderton, Oldham OL9 0LT* 061-620 8847

TONGUE, Denis Harold. b 15. Em Coll Cam BA37 MA41. Tyndale Hall Bris 37. **d** 38 **p** 39. Lect NT Tyndale Hall Bris 46-72; Trin Coll Bris 72-77; rtd 80. *Eaglehurst, Bassetts Gardens, Exmouth, Devon EX8 4EE* Exmouth (0395) 264695

TONGUE, Paul. b 41. St Chad's Coll Dur BA63 DipTh64. **d** 64 **p** 65. C Dudley St Edm *Worc* 64-69; C Sedgley All SS *Lich* 69-70; V Amblecote *Worc* from 70. *The Vicarage, 4 The Holloway, Amblecote, Stourbridge, W Midlands DY8 4DL* Stourbridge (0384) 394057

TONKIN, Canon Richard John. b 28. Lon Coll of Div ALCD59 BD60. **d** 60 **p** 61. C Leic Martyrs *Leic* 60-63; C Keynsham *B & W* 63-66; V Hinckley H Trin *Leic* 66-74; RD Sparkenhoe II 71-74; R Oadby 74-84; Hon Can Leic Cathl from 83; V Leic H Apostles from 84. *Holy Apostles' Vicarage, 281 Fosse Road South, Leicester LE3 1AE* Leicester (0533) 824336

TONKINSON, David Boyes. b 47. K Coll Lon BD71 AKC71. St Aug Coll Cant 71. **d** 72 **p** 73. C Surbiton St Andr *S'wark* 72-74; C Selsdon St Jo w St Fran *Cant* 75-81; V Croydon St Aug 81-84; V Croydon St Aug *S'wark* 85-89; Ind Chapl *Ox* from 89; Easthampstead from 89. *1 Ardingly, Mill Park, Bracknell, Berks RG12 4XR* Bracknell (0344) 423131

TOOBY, Anthony Albert. b 58. Sarum & Wells Th Coll 89. **d** 91. C Warsop *S'well* from 91. *Churchside Cottage, Church Road, Warsop, Mansfield, Notts NG20 0DP* Mansfield (0623) 847687

TOOBY, Derrick David Johnson. b 35. Lich Th Coll 66. **d** 68 **p** 69. C Stratford w Bishopton *Cov* 68-69; C Leamington Priors H Trin 69-71; V E Green from 71. *St Andrew's Vicarage, Church Lane, Coventry CV5 7BX* Coventry (0203) 466215

TOOGOOD, Noel Hare. b 32. Birm Univ BSc54. Wells Th Coll 59. **d** 61 **p** 62. C Rotherham *Sheff* 61-65; C Darlington St Jo *Dur* 65-70; V Burnopfield 70-81; P-in-c Roche *Truro* 81-84; P-in-c Withiel 81-84; R Roche and Withiel 84-91; RD St Austell 88-91; V Madron from 91. *The Vicarage, Madron, Penzance, Cornwall TR20 8SW* Penzance (0736) 3116

TOOGOOD, Robert Charles. b 45. AKC70. St Aug Coll Cant 70. **d** 71 **p** 72. C Shepperton *Lon* 71-74; C Kirk Ella *York* 74-76; P-in-c Levisham w Lockton 76-81; P-in-c Ebberston w Allerston 76-81; R Kempsey and Severn Stoke w Croome d'Abitot *Worc* from 81. *The Vicarage, Old Road South, Kempsey, Worcester WR5 3NJ* Worcester (0905) 820202

TOOKE, Mrs Sheila. b 44. E Anglian Minl Tr Course 88. **d** 91. NSM March St Wendreda *Ely* from 91. *79 Creek Road, March, Cambs PE15 8RE* March (0354) 54575

TOOKEY, Preb Christopher Tom. b 41. AKC67. **d** 68 **p** 69. C Stockton St Pet *Dur* 68-71; C Burnham *B & W* 71-77; R Clutton w Cameley 77-81; V Wells St Thos w Horrington from 81; RD Shepton Mallet from 86; Preb Wells Cathl from 90. *St Thomas's Vicarage, St Thomas's Street, Wells, Somerset BA5 2UZ* Wells (0749) 72193

TOOLEY, Geoffrey Arnold. b 27. Lon Coll of Div 55. **d** 58 **p** 59. C Chalk *Roch* 58-60; C Meopham 60-62; P-in-c Snodland and Paddlesworth 62-68; P-in-c Burham 68-76; C Riverhead w Dunton Green 76-79; C S w N Bersted *Chich* 79-83; C-in-c N Bersted CD from 83. *330 Chichester Road, North Bersted, Bognor Regis, W Sussex PO21 5AU* Bognor Regis (0243) 823800

TOOLEY, Norman Oliver. b 27. Roch Th Coll. **d** 65 **p** 66. C Gravesend St Mary *Roch* 65-68; C Ormskirk *Liv* 68-73; Chapl Merseyside Cen for the Deaf 73-78; C Bootle Ch Ch 78-80; C W Ham *Chelmsf* 80-86; Chapl RAD from 86. *42 Richford Road, London E15 3PQ* 081-534 4538

TOOMBS, Alan Trevor. b 33. Man Univ BA54. Ripon Hall Ox 54. **d** 56 **p** 57. C Hope St Jas *Man* 56-61; R Moston St Mary 61-74; V Weaste 74-81; R Newchurch 81-85; R Newchurch from 85. *The Rectory, 539 Newchurch Road, Newchurch, Rossendale, Lancs BB4 9HH* Rossendale (0706) 215098

TOON, Norman. b 22. Launde Abbey 75. **d** 76 **p** 77. C Shepshed *Leic* 76-80; P-in-c Kimcote w Walton w Bruntingthorpe 80-82; rtd 82. *1 Primethorpe Walk, Broughton Astley, Leicester LE9 6RJ* Hinckley (0455) 284675

TOON, Dr Peter. b 39. K Coll Lon BD65 MTh67 Liv Univ MA72. Ch Ch Ox DPhil77 DD. Lambeth STh65 NW Ord Course 72. **d** 73 **p** 74. C Skelmersdale St Paul *Liv* 73-74; Lib Latimer Ho Ox 74-76; C Ox St Ebbe w St Pet *Ox* 74-76; Hon Lect St Giles-in-the-Fields *Lon* 76-82; Tutor Oak Hill Th Coll 76-82; Dir of Post-Ord Tr *St E* 82-87; P-in-c Boxford 82-88; V Staindrop *Dur* 88-91; USA from 91. *Nashotah Episcopal Seminary, Nashotah, Wisconsin 53058, USA*

TOONE, Canon Lawrence Raymond. b 32. Open Univ BA79. Roch Th Coll 60 St Aid Birkenhead 61. **d** 63 **p** 64. C Birch St Agnes *Man* 63-66; C Didsbury Ch Ch 66-69; V Oldham St Paul 69-79; V Greenfield from 79; AD Oldham from 80; Hon Can Man Cathl from 82. *St Mary's Vicarage, 1 Park Lane, Greenfield, Oldham OL3 7DX* Saddleworth (0457) 872346

TOOP, Alan Neil. b 49. St Alb Minl Tr Scheme 79 Linc Th Coll 82. **d** 83 **p** 84. C Kempston Transfiguration *St Alb* 83-87; C Ludlow *Heref* from 87. *St Giles's Vicarage, Sheet Road, Ludlow, Shropshire SY8 1LR* Ludlow (0584) 875912

TOOP, William John. b 07. Lon Univ BSc27 K Coll Cam BA38 MA42. **d** 41 **p** 42. R Torwood St Mark *Ex* 52-79; P-in-c Torquay H Trin 74-79; R Torwood St Mark w H Trin 79; rtd 79. *Green Pastures, 4 Seaton Close, Torquay TQ1 3UH* Torquay (0803) 323696

TOOTH, Nigel David. b 47. Sarum & Wells Th Coll 71. **d** 74 **p** 75. C S Beddington St Mich *S'wark* 74-77; C Whitchurch *Bris* 77-83; TV Bedminster 83-87; Chapl Dorchester Hosps from 87; Chapl Herrison Hosp Dorchester from 87. *20 Herrison Cottages, Herrison Hospital, Dorchester, Dorset DT4 9RL* Dorchester (0305) 260271

TOOVEY, Preb Kenneth Frank. b 26. K Coll Lon BD51 AKC51. **d** 52 **p** 53. C Munster Square St Mary Magd *Lon* 52-60; V Upper Teddington SS Pet and Paul 60-70; V Ruislip St Martin 70-81; RD Hillingdon 75-81; V Greenhill St Jo from 81; Preb St Paul's Cathl from 83. *St John's Vicarage, 11 Flambard Road, Harrow, Middx HA1 2NB* 081-907 7956 or 863 3690

TOOZE, Margaret Elizabeth. b 27. St Mich Ho Ox 54. **dss** 83 **d** 89. Miss Bible Churchmen's Soc (Kenya) 61-88; Par Dn Bath Walcot *B & W* from 89. *38 The Paragon, Bath BA1 5LY* Bath (0225) 465642

TOPHAM, Paul Raby. b 31. MIL66 Columbia Pacific Univ MA81. Cen Sch of Religion LTh80. **d** 85 **p** 86. Chapl St Paul's Prep Sch Barnes 85-91; Chapl Toulouse w Biarritz, Cahors and Pau *Eur* from 91. *1 rue Pasteur, 31700 Cornebarrieu, France* France (33) 61 85 17 67

TOPLEY, John Ernest Wilmot. b 21. Keble Coll Ox BA48 Ox Univ MA80. Ely Th Coll. **d** 49 **p** 50. Chapl Middlewood & Wharncliffe Hosps Sheff 66-72; V Broadwoodwidger *Ex* 72-73; R Stowford 72-73; rtd 79. *10 South Lea Avenue, Hoyland, Barnsley, S Yorkshire* Barnsley (0226) 745128

TOPPING, Kenneth Bryan Baldwin. b 27. Bps' Coll Cheshunt 58. **d** 59 **p** 60. C Fleetwood *Blackb* 59-63; V Ringley *Man* 63-70; V Cleator Moor w Cleator *Carl* from 70. *The Vicarage, Trumpet Road, Cleator, Cumbria CA23 3EF* Cleator Moor (0946) 810510

TOPPING, Norman. b 32. NW Ord Course 73. **d** 76 **p** 77. NSM Prenton *Ches* 76-79; C E Runcorn w Halton 79-80; C Halton 80; P-in-c Newton Flowery Field 80-81; V 81-86; V Bredbury St Mark from 86. *St Mark's Vicarage, George Lane, Bredbury, Stockport, Cheshire SK6 1AT* 061-406 6552

TORDOFF, Donald William. b 45. Nottm Univ BA69. Qu Coll Birm 69. **d** 71 **p** 72. C High Harrogate Ch Ch *Ripon* 71-75; C Moor Allerton 75-80; V Bilton from 80. *Bilton Vicarage, Harrogate, N Yorkshire HG1 3DT* Harrogate (0423) 565129

TORDOFF (nee PARKER), Mrs Margaret Grace. b 40. SRN65 SCM67. Cranmer Hall Dur 81. **dss** 83 **d** 87. Bilton *Ripon* 83-87; C from 87. *St John's Vicarage, Elm Tree Avenue, Harrogate, N Yorkshire HG1 3DT* Harrogate (0423) 565129

TORRENS, Robert Harrington. b 33. Trin Coll Cam BA56 MA61. Ridley Hall Cam 56. **d** 58 **p** 59. C Bromley SS Pet and Paul *Roch* 58-60; C Aylesbury *Ox* 60-63; V Eaton Socon *St Alb* 63-73; Lic to Offic 73-75; V Pittville *Glouc* 75-84; Chapl Frenchay Hosp Bris from 84; Chapl Manor Park Hosp Bris from 84. *21 Church Road, Winterborne Down, Bristol BS17 1BX* Winterbourne (0454) 775445

TORRINGTON, Norman Russell. b 17. Kelham Th Coll 37. **d** 43 **p** 44. TR Rugeley *Lich* 61-72; RD Hodnet 72-82; V Cheswardine 72-78; V Hales 73-78; R Hodnet w Weston under Redcastle 78-84; rtd 84; Perm to Offic *Lich* from 84. *24 Longford Road, Newport, Shropshire TF10 7PU* Newport (0952) 814827

TORRY, Alan Kendall. b 33. Ex & Truro NSM Scheme. **d** 77 **p** 79. NSM Truro St Paul *Truro* 77-80; TV Probus, Ladock and Grampound w Creed 80-84; P-in-c Gulval 84-88; V from 88; P-in-c Marazion 85-88; V from 88. *The Vicarage, Gulval, Penzance, Cornwall TR18 3BG* Penzance (0736) 62699

TORRY, Malcolm Norman Alfred. b 55. St Jo Coll Cam BA76 MA80 Lon Univ BD78 K Coll Lon MTh79 PhD90. Cranmer Hall Dur 79. **d** 80 **p** 81. C S'wark H Trin w St Matt *S'wark* 80-83; C S'wark Ch Ch 83-88; Ind Chapl 83-88; V Hatcham St Cath from 88. *St Catherine's Vicarage, 102 Pepys Road, London SE14 5SG* 071-639 1050

TOSTEVIN, Alan Edwin John. b 41. BA. Trin Coll Bris 83. **d** 86 **p** 87. C Hildenborough *Roch* 86-89; TV Ipsley *Worc* from 89. *29 Sheldon Road, Redditch, Worcs B98 7QS* Redditch (0527) 501092

TOSTEVIN, Ronald Edwin. b 26. Selw Coll Cam BA51 MA56. Ely Th Coll 51. **d** 53 **p** 54. C Lower Broughton Ascension *Man* 53-55; Bp's Dom Chapl *Ely* 55-57; V Coppenhall St Paul *Ches* 57-71; R Woodchurch 71-85; RD Birkenhead 74-85; Hon Can Ches Cathl 78-85; R Somerton w Compton Dundon, the Charltons etc *B & W* from 85. *The Vicarage, Vicarage Lane, Somerton, Somerset TA11 7NQ* Somerton (0458) 72216

TOTNES, Archdeacon of. *See* TREMLETT, Ven Anthony Frank

TOTTEN, Andrew James. b 64. QUB BA87 TCD BTh90. CITC. **d** 90 **p** 91. C Newtownards *D & D* from 90. *10 Londonderry Road, Newtownards, Co Down BT23 3AY* Newtownards (0247) 814750

TOTTY, Canon Lawrence Harold. b 07. Tyndale Hall Bris 46. **d** 46 **p** 47. R Kingswood *Glouc* 65-72; rtd 72; Perm to Offic *Glouc* from 72. *10 Kingscote Close, Cheltenham, Glos GL51 6JU* Cheltenham (0242) 522809

TOUW, Dennis Frank Pieter. b 49. Chich Th Coll 77. **d** 80 **p** 81. C Pinner *Lon* 80-83; C Willesden Green St Andr and St Fran of Assisi 83-88; V Enfield SS Pet and Paul from 88. *The Vicarage, 177 Ordnance Road, Enfield, Middx EN3 6AB* Lea Valley (0992) 719770

TOVAR, Miss Gillian Elaine. b 48. Sussex Univ CertEd69. Trin Coll Bris BA86. dss 86 **d** 87. Tonbridge SS Pet and Paul *Roch* 86-87; Par Dn from 87. *2 Larch Crescent, Tonbridge, Kent TN10 3NN* Tonbridge (0732) 361204

TOVEY, Phillip Noel. b 56. Societas Liturgica MSLS Lon Univ BA77 Nottm Univ MPhil88. Lon Bible Coll BA83 St Jo Coll Nottm 85. **d** 87 **p** 88. C Beaconsfield *Ox* 87-90; C Banbury from 90; SSF from 90. *10 Hardwick Park, Banbury, Oxford OX16 7YD* Banbury (0295) 275449

TOVEY, Ronald. b 27. AKC51. **d** 52 **p** 53. C Glossop *Derby* 52-55; C Chorlton upon Medlock *Man* 55-57; C Hulme St Phil 55-57; C Hulme St Jo 55-57; C Hulme H Trin 55-57; Malawi 57-69; Lesotho 69-85; Adn S Lesotho 77-85; R Reddish *Man* from 85. *The Rectory, Bedford Street, Stockport, Cheshire SK5 6DJ* 061-432 3033

TOWARD, Stanley. b 25. Cranmer Hall Dur 65. **d** 66 **p** 67. C S Westoe *Dur* 66-69; V Swalwell 69-74; R Ryton 74-86; R Ryton w Hedgefield from 86. *The Rectory, Barmoor House, Main Road, Ryton, Tyne & Wear NE40 3AJ* 091-413 4592

TOWELL, Alan. b 37. Sarum & Wells Th Coll 86 W Midl Minl Tr Course 87. **d** 89 **p** 90. C Boultham *Linc* from 89. *46 Moorland Avenue, Lincoln LN6 7RD* Lincoln (0522) 680683

TOWELL, Geoffrey Leonard. b 37. K Coll Lon BA59. Linc Th Coll 59. **d** 61 **p** 62. C Ashbourne w Mapleton *Derby* 61-65; C Claxby w Normanby-le-Wold *Linc* 65-67; V Alkborough w Whitton 67-80; R W Halton 68-80; P-in-c Winteringham 75-80; V Alkborough 81-85; Dioc Ecum Officer from 85. *Antares, Church Street, Hemswell, Gainsborough, Lincs DN21 5UN* Hemswell (042773) 608

TOWELL, Canon John William. b 16. St Jo Coll Dur BA38 DipTh39 MA41. **d** 39 **p** 40. Can Res Bradf Cathl *Bradf* 67-77; rtd 77; Perm to Offic *Bradf* from 77. *4 Ashfield Avenue, Shipley, W Yorkshire BD18 3AL* Bradford (0274) 583905

TOWERS, Canon David Francis. b 32. G&C Coll Cam BA56 MA60. Clifton Th Coll 56. **d** 58 **p** 59. C Gresley *Derby* 58-63; V Brixton St Paul *S'wark* 63-75; V Chatteris *Ely* 75-87; RD March 82-87; Hon Can Ely Cathl from 85; R Burnley St Pet *Blackb* from 87. *The Rectory, 42 Pasturegate, Burnley, Lancs BB11 4DE* Burnley (0282) 39490

TOWERS, John Keble. b 19. Keble Coll Ox BA41 MA57. Edin Th Coll 41. **d** 43 **p** 44. V Bradf St Oswald Chapel Green *Bradf* 71-78; P-in-c Holme Cultram St Mary *Carl* 78-80; V 80-85; rtd 85. *Glengarth, Beattock, Moffat, Dumfriesshire DG10 9QX* Beattock (06833) 351

TOWERS, John William. b 60. **d** 85 **p** 86. C Pimlico St Gabr *Lon* 85-88; C S Kensington St Steph from 88. *Flat 1, 66 Cornwall Gardens, London SW7 4BD* 071-937 0318

TOWERS, Patrick Leo. b 43. AKC68 Hull Univ CertEd69. **d** 74 **p** 75. Japan 74-81; TV Bourne Valley *Sarum* 81-83; Dioc Youth Officer 81-83; Chapl Oundle Sch *Pet* 83-86; I Rathkeale w Askeaton and Kilcornan *L & K* 86-89; RD Limerick 88-89; I Nenagh from 89. *St Mary's Rectory, Nenagh, Co Tipperary, Irish Republic* Nenagh (67) 32598

TOWERS, Terence John. b 33. AKC60. **d** 61 **p** 62. C Bishopwearmouth Gd Shep *Dur* 61-65; V Runham *Nor* 65-67; R Stokesby w Herringby 65-67; V Ushaw Moor *Dur* from 67. *The Vicarage, Ushaw Moor, Durham DH7 7PB* 091-373 0298

TOWLER, David George. b 42. Cranmer Hall Dur 73. **d** 76 **p** 77. C Newbarns w Hawcoat *Carl* 76-80; V Huyton St Geo *Liv* from 80. *St George's Vicarage, St George's Road, Huyton, Liverpool L36 8BE* 051-489 1997

TOWLER, John Frederick. b 42. Bps' Coll Cheshunt 63. **d** 66 **p** 67. C Lowestoft St Marg *Nor* 66-71; R Horstead 71-77; Prec Worc Cathl *Worc* 77-81; Min Can Worc Cathl 78-81. *Address temp unknown*

TOWLSON, Arthur Stanley. b 20. St Jo Coll Dur LTh48 BA49 ALCD48. **d** 50 **p** 51. R Blithfield *Lich* 57-70; R Colton 57-70; R Longton St Jas 70-71; Lic to Offic 71-78; P-in-c Checkley 78-84; P-in-c Croxden 78-84; rtd 85; Perm to Offic *Lich* from 85. *4 The Close, Lichfield, Staffs WS13 7LD* Lichfield (0543) 258608

TOWLSON, George Eric. b 40. N Ord Course 81. **d** 83 **p** 84. NSM Wakef St Andr and St Mary *Wakef* 83-86; NSM Ox St Mich w St Martin and All SS *Ox* 84-86; Perm to Offic from 86; NSM Hoar Cross w Newchurch *Lich* from 87. *58 Church Lane, Barton under Needwood, Burton-on-Trent, Staffs DE13 8HX*

TOWNDROW, Ven Frank Noel. b 11. K Coll Cam BA34 MA38. Coll of Resurr Mirfield 35. **d** 37 **p** 38. Can Res Pet Cathl *Pet* 66-77; Adn Oakham 67-77; Chapl to HM The Queen 75-81; rtd 77; Perm to Offic *Pet* from 77. *17 Croake Hill, Swinstead, Grantham, Lincs NG33 4PE* Corby Glen (047684) 478

TOWNE, David William. b 34. St Jo Coll Dur BA58. Cranmer Hall Dur DipTh60. **d** 60 **p** 61. C Bromley St Jo *Roch* 60-63; Lect Watford St Mary *St Alb* 63-66; V Prestonville St Luke *Chich* 66-73; R Slaugham 73-79; V Wilmington *Roch* 79-85; V Otford from 85. *The Vicarage, The Green, Otford, Sevenoaks, Kent TN14 5PD* Otford (09592) 3185

TOWNEND, John Philip. b 52. Sarum & Wells Th Coll 89. **d** 91. C Sherborne w Castleton and Lillington *Sarum* from 91. *Askwith House, 1 Quarr Drive, Sherborne, Dorset DT9 4HZ* Sherborne (0935) 814277

TOWNEND, Noel Alexander Fortescue. b 06. Selw Coll Cam BA28 MA32. Cuddesdon Coll 29. **d** 30 **p** 32. V Port Isaac *Truro* 68-73; rtd 73; Hon C N Petherton w Northmoor Green *B & W* from 73. *Rose Cottage, Clare Street, North Petherton, Bridgwater, Somerset TA6 6RG* North Petherton (0278) 662135

TOWNER, Paul. b 51. Bris Univ BSc72 BTh81. Oak Hill Th Coll 78. **d** 81 **p** 82. C Aspley *S'well* 81-84; R Gt Hanwood *Heref* from 84. *The Rectory, Hanwood, Shrewsbury SY5 8LJ* Shrewsbury (0743) 860074

TOWNLEY, Peter Kenneth. b 55. Sheff Univ BA78 Man Univ DSPT87. Ridley Hall Cam 78. **d** 80 **p** 81. C Ashton Ch Ch *Man* 80-83; C-in-c Holts CD 83-88; R Stretford All SS from 88. *The Rectory, 233 Barton Road, Stretford, Manchester M32 9RB* 061-865 1350

TOWNLEY, Very Rev Robert Keith. b 44. St Jo Coll Auckland LTh67. **d** 67 **p** 68. New Zealand 67-70; C Lisburn Ch Ch *Conn* 71-74; C Portman Square St Paul *Lon* 75-80; Chan Cork Cathl *C, C & R* from 82; Dean Ross from 82; I Ross Union from 82. *The Deanery, Roscarbery, Co Cork, Irish Republic* Bandon (23) 48166

TOWNLEY, Roger. b 46. Man Univ BSc York Univ MSc. St Deiniol's Hawarden 82. **d** 84 **p** 85. C Longton *Blackb* 84-88; V Penwortham St Leon from 88. *St Leonard's Vicarage, Marshall's Brow, Penwortham, Preston, Lancs PR1 9HY* Preston (0772) 742367

TOWNROE, Canon Edward John. b 20. St Jo Coll Ox BA42 MA48. Linc Th Coll 42. **d** 43 **p** 44. Warden St Boniface Coll Warminster 56-69; Can and Preb Sarum Cathl *Sarum* from 69; rtd 85. *St Boniface Lodge, Church Street, Warminster, Wilts BA12 8PG* Warminster (0985) 212355

TOWNROE, Canon Michael Dakeyne. b 15. Linc Th Coll 35. **d** 38 **p** 39. R Bexhill St Pet *Chich* 59-82; RD Battle and Bexhill 64-77; Can and Preb Chich Cathl from 69; rtd 82. *Robin's Mount, 1 Portsdown Way, Willingdon, Eastbourne, E Sussex BN20 9LL* Eastbourne (0323) 503669

TOWNSEND, Dr Anne Jennifer. b 38. Lon Univ MB, BS60 MRCS60 LRCP60. S'wark Ord Course 88. **d** 91. NSM Wandsworth St Paul *S'wark* from 91; Chapl Asst St Geo Hosp Tooting from 91. *16 Roebuck Court, Rodney Road, New Malden, Surrey KT3 5BJ* 081-942 7425

TOWNSEND, Christopher Robin. b 47. St Jo Coll Nottm LTh74. **d** 74 **p** 75. C Gt Horton *Bradf* 74-77; C Heaton St Barn 77-78; C Wollaton *S'well* 78-80; V Slaithwaite w E Scammonden *Wakef* from 80. *The Vicarage, Station Road, Slaithwaite, Huddersfield HD7 5AW* Huddersfield (0484) 842748

TOWNSEND, Dr Derek William. b 52. Fitzw Coll Cam BA74 Man Univ PhD89. St Jo Coll Nottm DTS91. **d** 91. C Hazlemere *Ox* from 91. *101 Rose Avenue, Hazlemere, High Wycombe, Bucks HP15 7UP* Penn (049481) 5561

TOWNSEND, Canon John Clifford. b 24. St Edm Hall Ox BA48 MA49. Wells Th Coll. **d** 50 **p** 51. Chapl RNR 58-75; V Branksome St Aldhelm *Sarum* 60-70; R Melksham 70-73; TR 73-80; Can and Preb Sarum Cathl from 72; RD Bradf 73-80; P-in-c Harnham 80-81; V 81-90; RD Salisbury 80-85; rtd 90. *19 Wyke Oliver Close,*

Preston, Weymouth, Dorset DT3 6DR Weymouth (0305) 833641

TOWNSEND, John Elliott. b 39. ALCD63. d 64 p 65. C Harold Wood *Chelmsf* 64-68; C Walton *St E* 68-72; V Kensal Rise St Martin *Lon* 72-83; V Hornsey Ch Ch from 83. *Christ Church Vicarage, 32 Crescent Road, London N8 8AX* 081-340 1566

TOWNSEND, John Errington. b 20. St Aug Coll Cant 64. d 65 p 66. R Droxford *Portsm* 69-74; Soc Work Org Sec 74-78; Perm to Offic from 82; rtd 85. *Greytiles, Frogmore, East Meon, Petersfield, Hants GU32 1QQ* East Meon (073087) 374

TOWNSEND, Peter. b 35. AKC63. d 64 p 65. C Norbury St Oswald *Cant* 64-67; C New Romney w Hope 67-69; C Westborough *Guildf* 69-74; P-in-c Wicken *Pet* 74-87; R Paulerspury 74-84; P-in-c Whittlebury w Silverstone 82-84; V Whittlebury w Paulerspury 84-87; V Greetham and Thistleton w Stretton and Clipsham from 87. *The Vicarage, Greetham, Oakham, Leics LE15 7NF* Oakham (0572) 812015

TOWNSEND, Peter. b 37. Open Univ BA87. Wells Th Coll 67. d 69 p 70. C Desborough *Pet* 69-72; C Bramley *Ripon* 72-75; C-in-c Newton Hall LEP *Dur* 75-80; P-in-c Newton Hall 80-81; V Hartlepool St Luke from 81. *St Luke's Vicarage, 5 Tunstall Avenue, Hartlepool TS26 8NF* Hartlepool (0429) 272893

TOWNSEND, Philip Roger. b 51. Sheff Univ BA78. Trin Coll Bris 78. d 80 p 81. C W Streatham St Jas *S'wark* 80-85; C Ardsley *Sheff* 85-88; V Crookes St Tim from 88. *St Timothy's Vicarage, 152 Slinn Street, Sheffield S10 1NZ* Sheffield (0742) 661745

TOWNSHEND, Charles Hume. b 41. St Pet Coll Ox BA64 MA69. Westcott Ho Cam 64. d 66 p 67. C Warlingham w Chelsham and Farleigh *S'wark* 66-75; R Old Cleeve, Leighland and Treborough *B & W* 75-85; R Bishops Lydeard w Bagborough and Cothelstone from 85. *The Rectory, Bishops Lydeard, Taunton, Somerset TA4 3AT* Bishops Lydeard (0823) 432414

TOWNSHEND, David William. b 57. Lon Univ PGCE80 Ox Univ MA85. Cranmer Hall Dur 81. d 84 p 85. C Barking St Marg w St Patr *Chelmsf* 84-87; Canada from 87. *The Rectory, Newboro, Ontario, Canada, K0G 1P0* Kingston (613) 272-2664

TOWNSHEND, Edward George Hume. b 43. Pemb Coll Cam BA66 MA70. Westcott Ho Cam 68. d 70 p 71. C Helleston *Nor* 70-74; Ind Chapl 74-81; TV Lowestoft St Marg 74-79; TV Lowestoft and Kirkley 79-81; V Stafford St Jo *Lich* 81-85; P-in-c Tixall w Ingestre 81-85; V Stafford St Jo and Tixall w Ingestre 85-87; R Lich St Chad from 87. *St Chad's Rectory, The Windings, Lichfield, Staffs WS13 7EX* Lichfield (0543) 262254

TOWNSON, Eric James. b 34. St Aid Birkenhead 60. d 62 p 63. C Heysham *Blackb* 62-65; C Preston St Jo 65-69; Rwanda 69-74; C Burley *Ripon* 74-85; V 85-87; P-in-c Kelbrook *Bradf* from 87; Dioc Adv in Evang from 87. *The Vicarage, Kelbrook, Colne, Lancs BB8 6TQ* Earby (0282) 842984

TOWSE, Anthony Norman Beresford. b 21. Linc Coll Ox BA48 MA72. Westcott Ho Cam 48. d 50 p 51. V Appledore *Cant* 64-72; V Appledore w Stone in Oxney and Ebony 72-75; V Appledore w Stone in Oxney and Ebony etc 75-82; RD S Lympne 81-90; V Appledore w Brookland, Fairfield, Brenzett etc 82-90; rtd 90. *3 Oaks Road, Tenterden, Kent TN30 6RD* Tenterden (05806) 6402

TOY, Elizabeth Margaret. b 37. NDAD59 CQSW77. Oak Hill NSM Course 85. d 88. NSM Hildenborough *Roch* from 88. *2 Francis Cottages, London Road, Hildenborough, Tonbridge, Kent TN11 8NQ* Hildenborough (0732) 833886

TOY, Canon John. b 30. Hatf Coll Dur BA53 MA62 Leeds Univ PhD82. Wells Th Coll 53. d 55 p 56. C Newington St Paul *S'wark* 55-58; S Sec SCM 58-60; Chapl Ely Th Coll 60-64; Chapl Gothenburg w Halmstad and Jonkoping *Eur* 65-69; Asst Chapl St Jo Coll York 69-72; Sen Lect 72-79; Prin Lect 79-83; Can Res and Chan York Minster *York* from 83. *10 Precentor's Court, York YO1 2EJ* York (0904) 620877

TOZER, Frank William. b 21. Wells Th Coll 61. d 63 p 64. C Crawley *Chich* 65-73; V Heathfield 73-87; rtd 87. *30 Orchid Close, Eastbourne, E Sussex BN23 8DE* Eastbourne (0323) 768270

TOZER, Reginald Ernest. b 25. St Aid Birkenhead 57. d 59 p 60. C Plaistow St Andr *Chelmsf* 59-62; P-in-c Clayton *Lich* 62-69; V E Ham w Upton Park *Chelmsf* 69-75; V Hatf Peverel w Ulting from 75. *The Vicarage, Hatfield Peverel, Chelmsford CM3 2DS* Chelmsford (0245) 380958

TRACEY, Thomas Patrick. b 14. Sarum Th Coll 54. d 56 p 57. R Rotherfield Peppard *Ox* 71-75; P-in-c Stadhampton w Chislehampton 75-77; P-in-c Warborough 75-77; TV Dorchester 78-81; rtd 81; Perm to Offic *Ox* from 85. *14 Myrtle Close, Long Hanborough, Oxford OX7 2DE* Freeland (0993) 882412

TRAFFORD, Mrs Joyce. b 35. N Ord Course 84. d 87. Par Dn Chapelthorpe *Wakef* from 87. *1 Gillion Crescent, Durkar, Wakefield, W Yorkshire WF4 6PP* Wakefield (0924) 252033

TRAFFORD, Peter. b 39. Chich Th Coll. d 83 p 84. C Bath Bathwick *B & W* 83-86; Chapl RN 86-90; P-in-c Donnington *Chich* from 90. *65 Stockbridge Road, Donnington, Chichester, W Sussex PO20 2QE* Chichester (0243) 776395

TRANTER, Paul Trevor William. b 10. Qu Coll Cam BA32. Clifton Th Coll 34. d 34 p 35. V Bere Regis *Sarum* 61-76; rtd 76. *The Knapp, North Gorley, Fordingbridge, Hants SP6 2PL* Fordingbridge (0425) 652709

TRAPNELL, Stephen Hallam. b 30. G&C Coll Cam BA53 MA57. Ridley Hall Cam 53. Virginia Th Sem BD56 MDiv70. d 56 p 57. C Upper Tulse Hill St Matthias *S'wark* 56-59; C Reigate St Mary 59-61; V Richmond Ch Ch 61-72; P-in-c Sydenham H Trin 72-80; R Worting *Win* from 80. *The Rectory, Glebe Lane, Basingstoke, Hants RG23 8QA* Basingstoke (0256) 22095

✠**TRAPP, Rt Rev Eric Joseph.** b 10. Leeds Univ BA32. Trin Coll Toronto Hon DD67 Coll of Resurr Mirfield 32. d 34 p 35 c 47. C Mitcham St Olave *S'wark* 34-37; Basutoland 37-40 and 43-47; S Africa 40-43; Can Bloemfontein Cathl 44-47; Bp Zululand 47-57; Bp Swaziland 47-57; Sec USPG 57-70; Bp Bermuda 70-75; rtd 75; Asst Bp St Alb 76-80. *Flat 15, Manormead, Tilford Road, Hindhead, Surrey GU26 6RA* Hindhead (0428) 607301

TRASLER, Graham Charles George. b 44. Ch Ch Ox BA65 MA69. Cuddesdon Coll 66. d 68 p 69. C Gateshead St Mary *Dur* 68-71; P-in-c Monkwearmouth St Pet 71-79; P-in-c Bentley *Guildf* 79; R Binsted w Ovington and Itchen Stoke from 84. *The Rectory, 37 Jacklyns Lane, New Alresford SO24 9LF* Alresford (0962) 732105

TRAVERS, Colin James. b 49. St Pet Coll Ox BA70 MA74. Ridley Hall Cam 70. d 72 p 73. C Hornchurch St Andr *Chelmsf* 72-75; Youth Chapl 75-77; C Aldersbrook 75-77; V Barkingside St Laur 77-82; V Waltham Abbey 82-88; V S Weald from 88. *The Vicarage, Wigley Bush Lane, South Weald, Brentwood, Essex CM14 5QP* Brentwood (0277) 212054

TRAVERS, John William. b 48. Open Univ BA84 Hull Univ MA86. Linc Th Coll 75. d 78 p 79. C Headingley *Ripon* 78-81; TV Louth *Linc* 81-89; P-in-c Shingay Gp of Par *Ely* 89; V from 90. *The Vicarage, Church Street, Guilden Morden, Royston, Herts SG8 0JP*

TRAVERSE, Ernest. b 28. Oak Hill Th Coll 73. d 75 p 76. C Roby *Liv* 75-76; C Rainhill 76-78; V Wigan St Barn Marsh Green 78-80; TV Bemerton *Sarum* 80-83; C Hednesford *Lich* 83-86; rtd 86; Perm to Offic *Liv* from 86. *20 Ashgrove Crescent, Billinge, Wigan, Lancs WN5 7NH* Billinge (0744) 894257

TRAVIS, Robert Leonard. b 15. Sarum Th Coll 55. d 56 p 57. V Sevenoaks Weald *Roch* 61-66; rtd 66. *Shelly Beach, RD1 Helensville, N Island, New Zealand*

TREADGOLD, Very Rev John David. b 31. LVO90. Nottm Univ BA58. Wells Th Coll 58. d 59 p 60. VC S'well Minster *S'well* 59-64; CF (TA) 62-67 and 74-78; R Wollaton *S'well* 64-74; V Darlington St Cuth w St Hilda *Dur* 74-81; Chapl in the Gt Park 81-89; Can Windsor 81-89; Chapl to HM The Queen 81-89; Dean Chich from 89. *The Deanery, Chichester, W Sussex PO19 1PX* Chichester (0243) 783286

TREADWELL, Albert Frederick. K Coll Lon. St Boniface Warminster 55. d 57 p 58. V Barnes St Mich *S'wark* 65-85; rtd 85; Hon C Wexham *Ox* 87; Perm to Offic S'wark from 85; Lon & Ox from 87. *11 Misbourne Court, High Street, Langley, Slough SL3 8LG* Slough (0753) 581672

TREANOR, Canon Desmond Victor. b 28. St Jo Coll Dur BA53 DipTh54 MA59. d 54 p 55. C Oakwood St Thos *Lon* 54-57; C Sudbury St Andr 57-59; V Lansdown *B & W* 59-66; V Derby St Werburgh *Derby* 66-68; V Leic St Anne *Leic* 68-75; V Humberstone 75-86; Hon Can Leic Cathl from 78; P-in-c Leic St Eliz Nether Hall 81-86; RD Christianity (Leic) N 82-86; R Gt Bowden w Welham, Glooston and Cranoe from 86; RD Gartree I (Harborough) from 88. *The Rectory, Dingley Road, Great Bowden, Market Harborough, Leics LE16 7ET* Market Harborough (0858) 462032

TREANOR, Terence Gerald. b 29. St Jo Coll Ox BA52 MA56. Wycliffe Hall Ox 52. **d** 54 **p** 55. C Hornsey Ch Ch *Lon* 54-57; C Cam H Trin *Ely* 57-60; V Doncaster St Mary *Sheff* 60-66; Chapl Oakham Sch Leics from 66; Lic to Offic *Pet* from 66. *35 Glebe Way, Oakham, Leics LE15 6LX* Oakham (0572) 757495

TREASURE, Andrew Stephen. b 51. Or Coll Ox BA73 MA77. St Jo Coll Nottm BA76. **d** 77 **p** 78. C Beverley Minster *York* 77-81; C Cam H Trin *Ely* 81-84; C Cam H Trin w St Andr Gt 84-85; V Eccleshill *Bradf* from 85. *The Vicarage, Fagley Lane, Eccleshill, Bradford, W Yorkshire BD2 3NS* Bradford (0274) 636403

TREASURE, Canon Herbert John. b 16. Keble Coll Ox BA37 MA41. Cuddesdon Coll 38. **d** 39 **p** 40. R Puddletown w Athelhampton and Burleston *Sarum* 69-75; P-in-c Barford St Martin 76-79; P-in-c Dinton 76-79; P-in-c Baverstock 76-79; R Barford St Martin, Dinton, Baverstock etc 79-82; Can and Preb Sarum Cathl 76-82; rtd 82. *Avening, Oddford Vale, Tisbury, Salisbury SP3 6NJ* Tisbury (0747) 870944

TREASURE, Mrs Joy Elvira. b 23. St Anne's Coll Ox MA50 CertEd. S Dios Minl Tr Scheme 80. **dss** 82 **d** 87. Tisbury *Sarum* 82-87; Hon Par Dn from 87. *Avening, Oddford Vale, Tisbury, Salisbury SP3 6NJ* Tisbury (0747) 870944

TREASURE, Ronald Charles. b 24. Or Coll Ox BA48 MA52. Cuddesdon Coll. **d** 50 **p** 51. V New Malton *York* 62-89; RD Malton 63-75; rtd 89. *Castle Walls, Castlegate, Kirkbymoorside, York YO6 6BW* Kirkbymoorside (0751) 32916

TREBLE, Harry. b 06. Lon Univ BD55 BA61. AKC32. **d** 32 **p** 33. V Barkingside St Cedd *Chelmsf* 61-83; rtd 83. *8 Fairlight Avenue, Woodford Green, Essex IG8 9JP*

TREDENNICK, Ms Angela Nicolette (Nicky). b 38. SRN62 SCM64 HVCert67. S'wark Ord Course 87. **d** 90. NSM Charlwood *S'wark* from 90. *Mill View, The Street, Charlwood, Horley, Surrey RH6 0DF* Horley (0293) 862406

TREDENNICK, John Edwin Foster. b 06. ALCD33 St Jo Coll Dur LTh33 BA35. **d** 36 **p** 37. V Lambeth St Andr w St Thos *S'wark* 56-75; rtd 76. *Roselle, Kenwyn Road, Truro, Cornwall TR1 3SH* Truro (0872) 72246

TREEBY, Stephen Frank. b 46. Man Univ LLB67 Nottm Univ DipTh69. Cuddesdon Coll 69. **d** 71 **p** 72. C Ashbourne w Mapleton *Derby* 71-74; C Boulton 74-76; Chapl Trowbridge Coll *Sarum* 76-79; TV Melksham 79-87; V Dilton Marsh from 87. *The Vicarage, Dilton Marsh, Westbury, Wilts BA13 4BU* Westbury (0373) 822560

TREEN, Anthony Robert. b 37. Chich Th Coll 72. **d** 74 **p** 75. C Haywards Heath St Rich *Chich* 74-77; Ind Chapl 77-80; V Burgess Hill St Jo 80-85; P-in-c Walpole St Andrew *Ely* 85-86; P-in-c Walpole St Peter 85-86; R Walpole St Peter w St Andr from 86. *The Rectory, Walpole St Peter, Wisbech, Cambs PE14 7NX* Wisbech (0945) 780252

TREEN, Preb Robert Hayes Mortlock. b 19. New Coll Ox BA46 MA46. Westcott Ho Cam 45. **d** 47 **p** 48. R Bath St Sav *B & W* 61-76; Preb Wells Cathl from 74; V Bishops Hull 76-84; RD Taunton S 77-81; RD Taunton 81-84; rtd 84. *13 The Leat, Bishops Lydeard, Taunton, Somerset TA4 3NY* Bishops Lydeard (0823) 433437

TREETOPS, Ms Jacqueline. b 47. NE Ord Course 83. **dss** 86 **d** 87. Low Harrogate St Mary *Ripon* 86-87; C Roundhay St Edm from 87. *43 Lincombe Bank, Leeds LS8 1QG* Leeds (0532) 667223

TREFUSIS, Charles Rodolph. b 61. Hull Univ BA83. Wycliffe Hall Ox 85. **d** 90 **p** 91. C Blackheath St Jo *S'wark* from 90. *15C St John's Park, London SE3 7TD* 081-858 1442

TREHERNE, Alan Thomas Evans. b 30. Univ of Wales (Lamp) BA53. Wycliffe Hall Ox. **d** 55 **p** 56. C Heref St Pet w St Owen *Heref* 55-57; India 57-72; C-in-c Netherley Ch Ch CD *Liv* 72-74; R Gateacre 74-75; TR from 75; RD Farnworth 81-89. *St Stephen's Rectory, Belle Vale Road, Liverpool L25 2PQ* 051-487 9338

TRELEAVEN, Robert Samuel. b 38. S'wark Ord Course. **d** 82 **p** 83. NSM Caterham *S'wark* from 82. *3 Dunedin Drive, Caterham, Surrey CR3 6BA* Caterham (0883) 47766

TRELLIS, Oswald Fitz-Burnell. b 35. Chich Th Coll 73. **d** 74 **p** 75. C Chelmsf All SS *Chelmsf* 74-78; C-in-c N Springfield CD 79-85; V Heybridge w Langford from 85. *The Vicarage, 1A Crescent Road, Heybridge, Maldon, Essex CM9 7SJ* Maldon (0621) 856938

TREMBATH, Martyn Anthony. b 65. Leeds Univ BA86. Ripon Coll Cuddesdon. **d** 90 **p** 91. C Bodmin w Lanhydrock and Lanivet *Truro* from 90. *23 Tanwood*

View, Bodmin, Cornwall PL31 2PN Bodmin (0208) 72961

TREMLETT, Andrew. b 64. Pemb Coll Cam BA86 Qu Coll Ox BA88. Wycliffe Hall Ox 86. **d** 89 **p** 90. C Torquay St Matthias, St Mark and H Trin *Ex* from 89. *St Martin, 9 Lower Warberry Road, Torquay TQ1 1QP* Torquay (0803) 212872

TREMLETT, Ven Anthony Frank. b 37. Ex & Truro NSM Scheme 78. **d** 81 **p** 82. C Southway *Ex* 81-82; P-in-c 82-84; V 84-88; RD Plymouth Moorside 86-88; Adn Totnes from 88. *38 Huxhams Cross, Dartington, Totnes, Devon TQ9 6NT* Staverton (080426) 263

✠**TREMLETT, Rt Rev Anthony Paul.** b 14. K Coll Cam BA36 MA46. Cuddesdon Coll 37. **d** 38 **p** 39 **c** 64. C Northolt Park St Barn *Lon* 38-41; CF (EC) 41-46; Trinidad and Tobago 46-50; Chapl Trin Hall Cam 50-58; V Westmr St Steph w St Jo *Lon* 58-64; Suff Bp Dover *Cant* 64-80; rtd 80; Asst Bp Glouc from 80. *Doctors Commons, The Square, Northleach, Cheltenham, Glos GL54 3EH* Cotswold (0451) 60426

TRENCHARD, Hubert John. b 26. S Dios Minl Tr Scheme. **d** 83 **p** 84. NSM Sturminster Marshall *Sarum* 83-87; NSM Blandford Forum and Langton Long etc 87-88; NSM Blandford Forum and Langton Long from 88. *20 Chapel Gardens, Blandford Forum, Dorset DT11 7UY* Blandford (0258) 459576

TRENCHARD, Hugh. b 50. Llan St Mich BD75. **d** 75 **p** 76. C Caerleon *Mon* 75-80; Dioc Chapl GFS 78-86; Asst Chapl Mon Sch 80-84; R Llanarth w Clytha, Llansantffraed and Bryngwyn *Mon* 80-84; TV Cyncoed from 84. *62 Hollybush Road, Cyncoed, Cardiff CF2 6TA* Cardiff (0222) 755306

TRENCHARD, Paul Charles Herbert Anstiss. b 53. Liv Univ LLB76. St Steph Ho Ox 77. **d** 80 **p** 81. C Torquay St Martin Barton *Ex* 80-84; R Ashprington, Cornworthy and Dittisham from 84. *The Rectory, Prior View, Cornworthy, Totnes, Devon TQ9 7HN* Harbertonford (080423) 384

TRENDALL, Peter John. b 43. Oak Hill Th Coll 66. **d** 69 **p** 70. C Beckenham Ch Ch *Roch* 69-73; C Bedworth *Cov* 73-76; V Hornsey Rise St Mary *Lon* 76-82; P-in-c Upper Holloway St Steph 80-82; V Hornsey Rise St Mary w St Steph 82-84; V Walthamstow St Mary w St Steph *Chelmsf* 84-85; TR from 85. *St Mary's Rectory, 117 Church Hill, London E17 3BD* 081-520 4281

TRENDER, Lawrence. b 37. Bps' Coll Cheshunt 64. **d** 66 **p** 67. C Petersham *S'wark* 66-71; C Malden St Jo 71-73; R Thornham Magna w Thornham Parva *St E* 73-81; P-in-c Mellis 73-81; P-in-c Gislingham 73-81; R Thornhams Magna and Parva, Gislingham and Mellis 81-87; RD Hartismere 85-87. *2 Settles House, Kerrison, Thorndon, Eye, Suffolk IP23 7JQ* Occold (037971) 768

TRENEER, Cyril George Howard. b 14. Leeds Univ BA36. Coll of Resurr Mirfield 36. **d** 38 **p** 39. V Plymouth St Gabr *Ex* 60-79; rtd 79. *2 Headborough Road, Ashburton, Newton Abbot, Devon TQ13 7QP* Ashburton (0364) 52159

TRENGOVE, Harry Christopher. b 04. Coll of Resurr Mirfield 55. **d** 56 **p** 58. V Shalford *Chelmsf* 64-66; Perm to Offic 66-70; rtd 67; Perm to Offic *Ox* 70-72; Llan 72-76; *Pet* 80-81; *Chich* 82-88. *Balmoral Rest Home, 18 Helena Road, Southsea, Hants PO4 9RH* Portsmouth (0705) 829884

TRETHEWEY, Frederick Martyn. b 49. Lon Univ BA70 DipTh77. Lambeth STh79 Oak Hill Th Coll 75. **d** 78 **p** 79. C Tollington Park St Mark w St Anne *Lon* 78-82; C Whitehall Park St Andr Hornsey Lane 82-87; TV Hornsey Rise Whitehall Park Team 87-88; V Brockmoor *Lich* from 88. *5 Leys Road, Brockmoor, Brierley Hill, W Midlands DY5 3UR* Brierley Hill (0384) 263327

TREVELYAN, James William Irvine. b 37. Selw Coll Cam BA64 MA67. Cuddesdon Coll 62. **d** 65 **p** 66. C Heston *Lon* 65-68; C Folkestone St Sav *Cant* 68-72; R Lenham w Boughton Malherbe 72-78; P-in-c Honiton, Gittisham and Combe Raleigh *Ex* 78-79; R Honiton, Gittisham, Combe Raleigh and Monkton 79-83; TR Honiton, Gittisham, Combe Raleigh, Monkton etc from 83; P-in-c Farway w Northleigh and Southleigh 84-86. *The Rectory, Exeter Road, Honiton, Devon EX14 8AN* Honiton (0404) 42925

TREVOR, Canon Charles Frederic. b 27. Sarum Th Coll 54. **d** 56 **p** 57. C Sutton in Ashfield St Mich *S'well* 56-58; C Birstall *Leic* 58-61; V Prestwold w Hoton 61-66; V Thornton in Lonsdale w Burton in Lonsdale *Bradf* 66-74; V Kirkby Malham 74-85; P-in-c Coniston Cold 81-85; Hon Can Bradf Cathl from 85; V Sutton from 85; RD S Craven from 86. *The Vicarage, Sutton-in-Craven,*

Keighley, W Yorkshire BD20 7JS Cross Hills (0535) 633372

TREVOR-MORGAN, Canon Basil Henry. b 27. Univ of Wales (Lamp) BA51. Wells Th Coll 51. **d** 53 **p** 54. C Chepstow *Mon* 53-56; C Halesowen *Worc* 56-59; CF (TA) from 59; V Stourbridge St Thos *Worc* 59-76; Chapl Christchurch Hosp from 76; V Christchurch *Win* from 76; Hon Can Win Cathl from 84. *The Priory Vicarage, Quay Road, Christchurch, Dorset BH23 1BU* Christchurch (0202) 483102

TREW, Alen Robert. b 30. Llan St Mich BD77. **d** 77 **p** 78. C Abergavenny St Mary w Llanwenarth Citra *Mon* 77-79; Hon C Broughty Ferry *Bre* from 81. *4 Bridge Lane, Broughty Ferry, Dundee DD5 2SZ* Dundee (0382) 736218

TREW, Robin Nicholas. b 52. UWIST BSc74. St Jo Coll Nottm 87. **d** 89 **p** 90. C Cov H Trin *Cov* from 89. *85 Stoney Road, Coventry CV3 6HH* Coventry (0203) 504141

TREWEEKS, Mrs Angela Elizabeth. b 35. Gilmore Ho 57. **dss** 59 **d** 87. Chapl St Nic Hosp Newc from 87; Hon C Newc St Geo *Newc* 87-90. *10 Beatty Avenue, Jesmond, Newcastle upon Tyne NE2 3QP* 091-285 2090

TRIBE, Arthur Wilfrid Newton. b 03. Trin Coll Ox BA25 MA31. Ridley Hall Cam 25. **d** 27 **p** 28. R High Ongar w Norton Mandeville *Chelmsf* 61-76; rtd 76. *19 Longfields, Ongar, Essex CM5 9BZ* Ongar (0277) 364211

TRICKETT, Judith. b 50. St Jo Coll Nottm 89. **d** 91. Par Dn Kimberworth *Sheff* from 91. *32 Hill View Road, Kimberworth, Rotherham, S Yorkshire S61 2AJ* Rotherham (0709) 559010

TRICKETT, Stanley Mervyn Wood. b 27. Lich Th Coll 64. **d** 66 **p** 67. C Kington w Huntington *Heref* 66-70; P-in-c Old Radnor 70-81; P-in-c Knill 70-81; V Shrewton *Sarum* from 81; P-in-c Winterbourne Stoke from 81; RD Wylye and Wilton 85-89. *The Vicarage, Chapel Lane, Shrewton, Salisbury SP3 4BX* Shrewton (0980) 620580

TRICKEY, Frederick Marc. b 35. Dur Univ BA62. Cranmer Hall Dur DipTh64. **d** 64 **p** 65. C Alton St Lawr *Win* 64-68; V Win St Jo cum Winnall 68-77; R Guernsey St Martin from 77. *The Rectory, Grande rue St Martins, Guernsey, Channel Islands* Guernsey (0481) 38303

TRICKEY, Jolyon. b 57. Barrister-at-Law 80. Jes Coll Cam BA79 MA83. Trin Coll Bris BA90. **d** 90 **p** 91. C Chesham Bois *Ox* from 90. *67A Woodley Hill, Chesham, Bucks HP5 1SP* Chesham (0494) 774868

TRICKLEBANK, Steven. b 56. Nottm Univ BTh88. Linc Th Coll 85. **d** 88 **p** 89. C Ditton St Mich *Liv* 88-91; C Wigan All SS from 91. *The Glebe House, The Hall, Wigan WN1 1HN* Wigan (0942) 43793

TRIGG, Jeremy Michael. b 51. Open Univ BA88. Ripon Coll Cuddesdon 80. **d** 81 **p** 82. C Roundhay St Edm *Ripon* 81-84; C Harrogate St Wilfrid and St Luke 84-87; TV Pocklington Team *York* 87-90; R Rowley w Skidby from 90. *The Rectory, Southwold, Little Weighton, Hull HU20 3UQ* Hull (0482) 843317

TRIGG, John Alfred. b 29. Keble Coll Ox BA64 MA64. Ripon Hall Ox 64. **d** 65 **p** 66. C Dursley *Glouc* 65-67; C Glouc St Geo 67-68; C Swan *Ox* 68-72; P-in-c Stokenchurch and Cadmore End 72-76; V Stokenchurch and Ibstone from 76. *The Vicarage, Wycombe Road, Stokenchurch, High Wycombe, Bucks HP14 3RG* Radnage (024026) 3384

TRIGG, Jonathan David. b 49. Ex Coll Ox BA71 MA75. Cranmer Hall Dur BA82. **d** 83 **p** 84. C Enfield St Andr *Lon* 83-87; V Oakwood St Thos from 87. *St Thomas's Vicarage, 2 Sheringham Avenue, London N14 4UE* 081-360 1749

TRILL, Barry. b 42. Chich Th Coll 65. **d** 68 **p** 69. C W Hackney St Barn *Lon* 68-73; TV Is of Dogs Ch Ch and St Jo w St Luke 73-79; P-in-c Hastings All So *Chich* 78-79; V from 79. *All Souls' Vicarage, 16 Berlin Road, Hastings, E Sussex TN35 5JD* Hastings (0424) 421441

TRILL, Victor Alfred Mansfield. b 21. St Deiniol's Hawarden. **d** 81 **p** 82. Hon C Prestbury *Ches* 81-83; Hon C Church Hulme 83-85; V Marbury 85-90; rtd 90. *5 Maisterson Court, Nantwich, Cheshire CW5 5TZ* Nantwich (0270) 628948

✠**TRILLO, Rt Rev Albert John.** b 15. K Coll Lon BD38 AKC38 MTh44. **d** 38 **p** 39 **c** 63. C Fulham Ch Ch *Lon* 38-41; P-in-c Cricklewood St Mich 41-45; NE Sch Sec SCM 45-50; Lic to Offic Ripon 50-55; St Alb 55-63; R Friern Barnet St Jas 50-55; Lect K Coll Lon 50-55; Prin Bps' Coll Cheshunt 55-63; Hon Can St Alb 58-63; Can Res St Alb 63-65; Suff Bp Bedf 63-68; Suff Bp Hertf 68-71; Bp Chelmsf 71-85; rtd 85; Perm to Offic *St E* from 85. *Copperfield, Back Road, Wenhaston,*

Halesworth, Suffolk IP19 9DY Blythburgh (050270) 505

TRIMBLE, John Alexander. b 33. Lon Univ BD65. Edin Th Coll 55. **d** 58 **p** 59. C Glas St Mary *Glas* 58-60; C Edin St Jo *Edin* 60-65; R Baillieston *Glas* 65-69; R Falkirk *Edin* 69-86; R Troon *Glas* from 86. *70 Bentinck Drive, Troon, Ayrshire KA10 6HZ* Troon (0292) 313731

TRIMBLE, Thomas Henry. b 36. TCD DipTh82 BTh90. CITC 79. **d** 82 **p** 83. C Seapatrick *D & D* 82-85; I Magheracross *Clogh* 85-90; Bp's Appeal Sec 89-90; I Donegal w Killymard, Lough Eske and Laghey *D & R* from 90. *The Rectory, Ballyshannon Road, Donegal, Co Donegal, Irish Republic* Donegal (73) 21075

TRIMBY, George Henry. b 44. DipTh. Trin Coll Bris 84. **d** 86 **p** 87. C Newtown w Llanllwchaiarn w Aberhafesp *St As* 86-88; P-in-c Llanfair D C, Derwen, Llanelidan and Efenechtyd 88-90; V from 90. *The Vicarage, Llanfair Dyffryn Clwyd, Ruthin, Clwyd LL15 2SA* Ruthin (08242) 4551

TRINDER, John Derek. b 28. Glouc Th Course 74. **d** 77 **p** 78. C Forest of Dean Ch Ch w English Bicknor *Glouc* 77; Hon C 77-79; Hon C Chepstow *Mon* 79-81; C Newport St Paul 81-82; V Dingestow and Llangovan w Penyclawdd and Tregaer 82-87; V Kirton in Holland *Linc* from 87. *The Vicarage, Willington Road, Kirton, Boston, Lincs PE20 1EH* Boston (0205) 722380

TRIPLOW, Keith John. b 44. Selw Coll Cam BA66 MA70. Chich Th Coll 70. **d** 72 **p** 73. C Ipswich All Hallows *St E* 72-76; C Dartford H Trin *Roch* 76-78; V Fyfield w Tubney and Kingston Bagpuize *Ox* from 78. *The Vicarage, Fyfield, Abingdon, Oxon OX13 5LR* Frilford Heath (0865) 390803

TRIPPASS, Canon William Arthur. b 08. Birm Univ BA30. Wells Th Coll 30. **d** 31 **p** 32. V Bidford-on-Avon *Cov* 68-73; rtd 73; C Alveston *Cov* 73-81. *19 Grange Road, Bidford-on-Avon, Alcester, Warks B50 4BY* Bidford-on-Avon (0789) 778957

TRISTRAM, Catherine Elizabeth. b 31. Somerville Coll Ox BA53 MA57. **dss** 83 **d** 87. Holy Is *Newc* 84-87; Hon C from 87. *Marygate House, Holy Island, Berwick-upon-Tweed TD15 2SD* Berwick-upon-Tweed (0289) 89246

TRISTRAM, Geoffrey Robert. b 53. K Coll Lon BA76 Pemb Coll Cam BA78 MA80. Westcott Ho Cam 77. **d** 79 **p** 80. C Weymouth H Trin *Sarum* 79-82; C Gt Berkhamsted *St Alb* 83-85; OSB from 85; Lic to Offic *Pet* from 86; Asst Chapl Oundle Sch *Pet* from 86; Sen Chapl from 88. *3 Cottesmore, West Street, Oundle, Peterborough PE8 4EN* Oundle (0832) 73187

TRISTRAM, Michael Anthony. b 50. Solicitor 76 Ch Coll Cam BA72 MA76. Ripon Coll Cuddesdon 79. **d** 82 **p** 83. C Stanmore *Win* 82-85; R Abbotts Ann and Upper and Goodworth Clatford from 85. *The Rectory, Upper Clatford, Andover, Hants SP11 7QP* Andover (0264) 352906

TRIVASSE, Keith Malcolm. b 59. Man Univ BA81 CertEd82 MPhil90 Birm Univ DipTh86. Qu Coll Birm 84. **d** 86 **p** 87. C Prestwich St Marg *Man* 86-88; C Orford St Marg *Liv* 88-90; TV Sunderland *Dur* 90-91; P-in-c N Hylton St Marg Castletown from 91. *St Margaret's Presbytery, Hylton Castle Road, Sunderland SR5 3ED* 091-548 4491

TRNKA, Oldrich. b 15. Inst of Th Olomouc 32. **d** 37 **p** 38. V Penton Street St Silas w All SS *Lon* 66-68; rtd 68. *2 Carlton Court, Bosanquet Close, Cowley, Middx UB8 3PF* Uxbridge (0895) 54390

TRODDEN, Canon Hugh. b 20. St Chad's Coll Dur BA48 DipTh50. **d** 50 **p** 51. V Bury St Edmunds All SS *St E* 63-85; Hon Can St E Cathl 79-85; rtd 85; Perm to Offic *Chelmsf* from 85; *Ely* and *St E* from 86. *11 St Stephen's Place, Westfield Road, Cambridge CB3 0JE* Cambridge (0223) 328083

TRODDEN, Michael John. b 54. K Coll Lon BD77 AKC77 CertEd. Wycliffe Hall Ox 79. **d** 80 **p** 81. C Woodford St Mary w St Phil and St Jas *Chelmsf* 80-87; V Aldborough Hatch from 87. *The Vicarage, St Peter's Close, Oaks Lane, Ilford, Essex IG2 7QN* 081-599 0524

TROLLOPE, David Harvey. b 41. BSc63. Lon Coll of Div 66. **d** 68 **p** 69. C Bermondsey St Jas w Ch Ch *S'wark* 68-71; Uganda 71-77; Kenya 77-82; V Gt Crosby St Luke *Liv* from 82. *St Luke's Vicarage, 71 Liverpool Road, Crosby, Liverpool L23 5SE* 051-924 1737

TROOP, John Richard. b 37. Ely Th Coll 61. **d** 64 **p** 65. C Linc St Andr *Linc* 64-66; C Linc St Swithin 64-66; C Gt Grimsby St Andr and St Luke 66-70; V Wrangle 70-78; V S Moor *Dur* 78-85; Chapl Dur and Northd ATC from 82; V Darlington St Hilda and St Columba from 85. *239 Parkside, Darlington, Co Durham DL1 5TG* Darlington (0325) 486712

TROSS, Canon Julian Chamings. b 14. AKC35. Bps' Coll Cheshunt 37. **d** 37 **p** 38. R Datchworth *St Alb* 55-77; Hon Can St Alb 72-79; P-in-c Tewin 76-77; R Datchworth w Tewin 77-79; rtd 79; Perm to Offic *St Alb* from 79. *63 Colestrete, Stevenage, Herts SG1 1RE* Stevenage (0438) 354150

TROTMAN, Anthony Edward Fiennes. b 11. Ex Coll Ox BA33 MA56. Wycliffe Hall Ox 46. **d** 48 **p** 49. R Chilmark *Sarum* 59-76; rtd 76. *17 Estcourt Road, Salisbury SP1 3AP* Salisbury (0722) 324857

TROTT, Stephen John. b 57. FRSA86 Hull Univ BA79 Fitzw Coll Cam BA83 MA87. Westcott Ho Cam 81. **d** 84 **p** 85. C Hessle *York* 84-87; C Kingston upon Hull St Alb 87-88; R Pitsford w Boughton *Pet* from 88; Sec Continuing Minl Educn from 88. *The Rectory, Humfrey Lane, Boughton, Northampton NN2 8RQ* Northampton (0604) 821387

TROTTER, Donald McIntoch. b 35. S Dios Minl Tr Scheme. **d** 83 **p** 84. C Middlesb All SS *York* 83-86; V N Ormesby from 86. *The Vicarage, James Street, North Ormesby, Middlesbrough, Cleveland TS3 6LD* Middlesbrough (0642) 225272

TROTTER, Harold Barrington. b 33. Sarum Th Coll 64. **d** 66 **p** 67. C Salisbury St Fran *Sarum* 66-69; Dioc Youth Officer 69-72; R Holt St Jas, Hinton Parva, Horton and Chalbury 69-73; R Frenchay *Bris* 73-81; V Henbury from 81. *St Mary's Vicarage, Station Road, Bristol BS10 7QQ* Bristol (0272) 500536

TROTTER, Torrens James. b 31. St Jo Coll Dur BA54. Westcott Ho Cam 54. **d** 56 **p** 57. TV Billingham St Aid *Dur* 68-70 and 70-77; Community Chapl Gateshead 77-84; TV Gateshead 77-84; R Birm St Geo *Birm* 84-88; rtd 89. *37 St Paul's Court, St Paul's Street, Stockton-on-Tees, Cleveland TS19 0AB* Stockton-on-Tees (0642) 671133

TROUNSON, Ronald Charles. b 26. Em Coll Cam BA48 MA52. Ripon Hall Ox 54. **d** 56 **p** 57. C Plymouth St Gabr *Ex* 56-58; Chapl Denstone Coll Uttoxeter 58-76; Bursar 76-78; Prin St Chad's Coll Dur 78-88; R Easton on the Hill, Collyweston w Duddington etc *Pet* from 89. *The Rectory, Easton On The Hill, Stamford, Lincs PE9 3LS* Stamford (0780) 2616

TRUBRIDGE, George Ernest Samuel. b 11. ALCD35. **d** 35 **p** 36. R Broughton *Linc* 52-76; rtd 76. *27 Clarendon Road, Broadstone, Dorset BH18 9HT* Broadstone (0202) 695808

TRUBY, David Charles. b 57. BA79 Nottm Univ DipTh80. Linc Th Coll 79. **d** 82 **p** 83. C Stanley *Liv* 82-85; C Hindley St Pet 85-90; R Brimington *Derby* from 90. *The Rectory, Brimington, Chesterfield, Derbyshire S43 1JG* Chesterfield (0246) 73103

TRUDGILL, Harry Keith. b 25. Leeds Univ DipEd49 LCP54 Lon Univ BD61. St Deiniol's Hawarden 76. **d** 76 **p** 76. C Glas St Marg *Glas* 76-78; R Lenzie 78-86; Perm to Offic *Bradf* from 86. *Darrowby, 33 Cowpasture Road, Ilkley, W Yorkshire LS29 8SY* Ilkley (0943) 603175

TRUEMAN, Reginald. b 24. K Coll Cam BA47 MA49 Man Univ BD54. St Jo Coll Winnipeg Hon DD58 Ely Th Coll 49 Union Th Sem (NY) STM50. **d** 50 **p** 51. C Bolton St Pet *Man* 50-53; Hong Kong 53-61; Lect K Coll Lon 63-74; Lect N Co Coll of Educn from 75. *17 Burnt Ash Cottages, Sheep Marsh, Petersfield, Hants GU32 2BB* Petersfield (0730) 61341

TRUMAN, John Malcolm. b 33. Cuddesdon Coll 61. **d** 63 **p** 64. C Billingham St Aid *Dur* 63-65; C Alnwick St Mich *Newc* 65-68; R Ford 68-75; V Fenham St Jas and St Basil 75-84; Chapl HM Young Offender Inst Castington from 84; V Chevington *Newc* 84-87; Lic to Offic from 87. *1 Churchill Way, Acklington, Morpeth, Northd NE65 9DB* 091-760 942

TRUMPER, Roger David. b 52. Ex Univ BSc74 K Coll Lon MSc75 Ox Univ BA80 MA85. Wycliffe Hall Ox 78. **d** 81 **p** 82. C Tunbridge Wells St Jo *Roch* 81-84; C Slough *Ox* 84-87; TV Shenley and Loughton 87-88; TV Watling Valley from 88. *2 Symington Court, Shenley Lodge, Milton Keynes MK5 7AN* Milton Keynes (0908) 675943

TRUNDLE, Herbert Edward. b 11. Lich Th Coll 33. **d** 36 **p** 37. V Cheam Common St Phil *S'wark* 52-76; rtd 76. *Westlands, Mappowder, Sturminster Newton, Dorset DT10 2EH* Sturminster Newton (0258) 817694

TRURO, Bishop of. See BALL, Rt Rev Michael Thomas

TRURO, Dean of. See SHEARLOCK, Very Rev David John

TRUSS, Charles Richard. b 42. Reading Univ BA63 K Coll Lon MPhil79 Linacre Coll Ox BA66 MA69. Wycliffe Hall Ox 64. **d** 66 **p** 67. C Leic H Apostles *Leic* 66-69; C Hampstead St Jo *Lon* 69-72; V Belsize Park 72-79; V Wood Green St Mich 79-82; TR Wood Green St Mich w Bounds Green St Gabr etc 82-85; R Shepperton from

85. *The Rectory, Church Square, Shepperton, Middx TW17 9JY* Walton-on-Thames (0932) 220511

TRUSTRAM, David Geoffrey. b 49. Pemb Coll Ox BA71 MA76 Qu Coll Cam BA73 MA77. Westcott Ho Cam 74. **d** 75 **p** 76. C Surbiton St Mark *S'wark* 75-77; C Surbiton St Andr and St Mark 77-78; C Richmond St Mary 78-79; C Richmond St Mary w St Matthias and St Jo 79-82; P-in-c Eastry *Cant* 82-88; Chapl Eastry Hosp 82-90; R Eastry and Northbourne w Tilmanstone etc *Cant* 88-90; V Tenterden St Mildred w Smallhythe from 90. *The Vicarage, Church Road, Tenterden, Kent TN30 6AT* Tenterden (05806) 3118

TSIPOURAS, John George. b 38. Trin Coll Bris 76. **d** 78 **p** 79. C Cheadle Hulme St Andr *Ches* 78-82; V Hurdsfield from 82. *197A Hurdsfield Road, Macclesfield, Cheshire SK10 2PY* Macclesfield (0625) 24587

TUAM, Archdeacon of. See GRANT, Very Rev William James

TUAM, Dean of. See GRANT, Very Rev William James

TUAM, KILLALA AND ACHONRY, Bishop of. See NEILL, Rt Rev John Robert Winder

TUAM, Provost of. See FORREST, Very Rev Leslie David Arthur

TUBBS, Brian Ralph. b 44. AKC66. **d** 67 **p** 68. C Ex St Thos *Ex* 67-72; TV Sidmouth, Woolbrook and Salcombe Regis 72-77; R Ex St Jas from 77; RD Christianity from 89. *St James's Rectory, 4 Rosebank Crescent, Exeter EX4 6EJ* Exeter (0392) 55871

TUBBS, Canon Christopher Norman. b 25. G&C Coll Cam BA51 MA54. Wycliffe Hall Ox. **d** 52 **p** 53. C Neston *Ches* 52-55; C Nor St Pet Mancroft *Nor* 55-59; V Scalby *York* 59-68; V Scalby w Ravenscar and Staintondale from 68; RD Scarborough 76-82; Can and Preb York Minster from 85. *The Vicarage, Scalby, Scarborough, N Yorkshire YO13 0PS* Scarborough (0723) 362740

TUBBS, Peter Alfred. b 22. G&C Coll Cam BA48 MA53. Linc Th Coll 55. **d** 57 **p** 58. V Cardington *St Alb* 69-85; RD Elstow 77-82; C Sandy 85-89; rtd 89; Perm to Offic *St Alb* from 89. *1 Foster Grove, Sandy, Beds SG19 1HP* Sandy (0767) 682803

TUCK, Andrew Kenneth. b 42. Kelham Th Coll 63. **d** 68 **p** 69. C Poplar *Lon* 68-74; TV 74-76; V Walsgrave on Sowe *Cov* 76-90; R Farnham *Guildf* from 90. *The Rectory, Farnham, Surrey GU9 7PW* Farnham (0252) 716119

TUCK, David John. b 36. St Cath Coll Cam BA61 MA65. Cuddesdon Coll 61. **d** 63 **p** 64. C Kelling w Salthouse *Nor* 63-69; C Holt 63-69; Zambia 69-73; V Sprowston *Nor* 73-84; R Beeston St Andr 73-84; RD Nor N 81-84; V Pinner *Lon* from 84. *The Vicarage, 2 Church Lane, Pinner, Middx HA5 3AA* 081-866 3869

TUCK, Nigel Graham. b 57. Chich Th Coll 82. **d** 85 **p** 86. C Port Talbot St Theodore *Llan* 85-87; C Llantrisant 87-90; TV Duston Team *Pet* from 90. *St Francis House, Eastfield Road, Duston, Northampton* Northampton (0604) 753679

TUCK, Ralph Thomas. b 42. Worc Coll Ox BA64 Bris Univ CertEd66 Leeds Univ DipFE81. N Ord Course 87. **d** 90 **p** 91. NSM S Crosland *Wakef* from 90; NSM Helme from 90. *5 Nields Road, Slaithwaite, W Yorkshire HD7 5HT* Huddersfield (0484) 843583

TUCK, Ronald James. b 47. S'wark Ord Course 75. **d** 78 **p** 79. C Upper Holloway St Pet *Lon* 78-79; C Upper Holloway St Pet w St Jo 79-81; P-in-c Scottow *Nor* 81-88; P-in-c Swanton Abbott w Skeyton 81-88; R Bradwell from 88. *The Rectory, Church Walk, Bradwell, Great Yarmouth, Norfolk NR31 8QQ* Great Yarmouth (0493) 663219

TUCKER, Anthony Ian. b 50. CYCW78. CA Tr Coll 73 S'wark Ord Course 81. **d** 85 **p** 86. NSM E Ham w Upton Park *Chelmsf* 85-86; NSM S'well Minster *S'well* 86-90; C Rolleston w Fiskerton, Morton and Upton from 90. *The Vicarage, 29 Marlock Close, Fiskerton, Southwell, Notts NG25 0UB* Newark (0636) 830331

✛**TUCKER, Rt Rev Cyril James.** b 11. CBE75. St Cath Coll Cam BA33 MA37. Ridley Hall Cam 33. **d** 35 **p** 36 **c** 63. C Dalston St Mark and Highgate Sch Miss Lon 35-37; C Cam St Barn *Ely* 37-38; Youth Sec BFBS 38-39; Chapl RAFVR 39-46; Warden Mon Sch 46-49; Chapl Ox Pastorate 49-57; Cam 57-63; Chapl Wadh Coll Ox 51-57; V Cam H Trin *Ely* 57-63; Bp in Argentina and E S America 63-75; Bp Falkland Is 63-76; rtd 76; Perm to Offic *Ely* from 77. *202 Gilbert Road, Cambridge CB4 3PB* Cambridge (0223) 358345

TUCKER, Desmond Robert. b 29. Bris Sch of Min 83. **d** 86 **p** 87. C Bris St Mich *Bris* 86-88; P-in-c from 88. *94 Fremantle House, Dove Street, Bristol BS2 8LH* Bristol (0272) 246803

TUCKER, Douglas Greening. b 17. Lon Univ DipTh53. St Aid Birkenhead 49. **d** 52 **p** 53. V Elsham *Linc* 62-85; V Worlaby 62-85; V Bonby 73-85; rtd 85. *Balintore, Main Street, Bowsden, Northd TD15 2TW*   Berwick-upon-Tweed (0289) 88630

TUCKER, Canon Ernest Henry. b 09. Sarum Th Coll 34. **d** 37 **p** 38. V Stroud H Trin *Glouc* 59-76; Hon Can Glouc Cathl 74-78; rtd 76; RD Bisley *Glouc* 76-78; Perm to Offic from 78. *Bidstone, Hampton Green, Box, Stroud, Glos GL6 9AD*   Brimscombe (0453) 882798

TUCKER, Harold George. b 21. St Aug Coll Cant 48 Sarum Th Coll 50. **d** 51 **p** 52. R Bratton Fleming *Ex* 64-73; P-in-c Goodleigh 67-73; P-in-c Stoke Rivers 67-73; P-in-c Parracombe 69-73; P-in-c Martinhoe 69-73; R Whimple 73-86; rtd 86. *Lansdowne, The Crescent, Widemouth Bay, Bude, Cornwall EX23 0AE*   Bude (0288) 361396

TUCKER, Ian Malcolm. b 46. HND69. S Dios Minl Tr Scheme 86. **d** 89 **p** 90. NSM Pill w Easton in Gordano and Portbury *B & W* from 89. *4 Priory Road, Portbury, Bristol BS20 9TH*   Pill (0275) 373769

TUCKER, John Yorke Raffles. b 24. Magd Coll Cam BA49 MA56. Westcott Ho Cam 49. **d** 51 **p** 52. V Belmont *Lon* 67-78; V Sunbury 78-89; rtd 89; Perm to Offic *Ex* from 89. *Brook House, Millhayes, Stockland, Devon EX14 9DB*   Stockland (040488) 376

TUCKER, Maurice Grahame. b 12. FPhS73 Bris Univ BA34 DipEd35 MA37. Coll of Resurr Mirfield 37. **d** 39 **p** 40. C Henbury *Bris* 63-74; P-in-c Brentry 63-74; P-in-c Greenbank 74-75; C Eastville St Thos w St Anne 75-79; Hon C 79-84; rtd 79; Hon C Eastville St Anne w St Mark and St Thos *Bris* from 84. *Abbeyfields House, 5 Hughenden Road, Bristol BS8 2TT*   Bristol (0272) 734041

TUCKER, Michael. b 33. MA. **d** 84 **p** 85. NSM Sawston *Ely* 84-87; C Ely 87-90; P-in-c Barton Bendish w Beachamwell and Shingham from 90. *The Rectory, Barton Bendish, Kings Lynn, Norfolk PE33 9DP*   Fincham (03664) 363

TUCKER, Michael Owen. BSc PhD. **d** 84 **p** 85. NSM Uley w Owlpen and Nympsfield *Glouc* from 84. *East Cottage, 3 The Green, Uley, Dursley, Glos GL11 5SN*   Dursley (0453) 860492

TUCKER, Richard Parish. b 51. Cam Univ BA72 MA76 Lon Univ BD83. Wycliffe Hall Ox 80. **d** 83 **p** 84. C Wellington w Eyton *Lich* 83-84; C Walsall 84-88; TV Dronfield *Derby* 88-90; TV Dronfield w Holmesfield from 90. *11 Rothay Close, Dronfield, Woodhouse, Sheffield S18 5PR*   Dronfield (0246) 416893

TUCKER, Stephen Reid. b 51. New Coll Ox MA76 DipTh76. Ripon Coll Cuddesdon 75. **d** 77 **p** 78. C Hove All SS *Chich* 77-80; Lect Chich Th Coll 80-86; V Portsea St Alb *Portsm* 86-90; Chapl and Dean of Div New Coll Ox from 90; Lic to Offic *Ox* from 90. *New College, Oxford OX1 3BN*   Oxford (0865) 279541

TUCKETT, Christopher Mark. b 48. Qu Coll Cam MA71 Lanc Univ PhD79. Westcott Ho Cam 71. **d** 75 **p** 76. C Lanc St Mary *Blackb* 75-77; Chapl and Fell Qu Coll Cam 77-79; Lect NT Man Univ 79-89; Sen Lect from 89; Prof Bibl Studies from 91. *Kidd Road Farm, Moorfield, Glossop, Derbyshire SK13 9PN*   Glossop (0457) 860150

TUCKEY, John William Townsend. b 19. TCD BA41 MA. **d** 43 **p** 44. V Milton *B & W* 65-74; P-in-c E Brent 74-75; R E Brent w Lympsham 75-81; rtd 84; Perm to Offic *B & W* from 85. *10 Hill Head Close, Glastonbury, Somerset BA6 8AL*   Glastonbury (0458) 33728

TUCKWELL, Christopher Howard Joseph. b 45. Chich Th Coll 70. **d** 73 **p** 74. C Upper Clapton St Matt *Lon* 73-76; St Vincent 76-85; C Shepherd's Bush St Steph w St Thos *Lon* 85-86; V Tottenham St Mary from 86. *St Mary's Vicarage, Lansdowne Road, London N17 9XE*   081-808 6644

TUCKWELL, Paul. b 12. Magd Coll Ox BA35 MA38. Westcott Ho Cam 36. **d** 38 **p** 39. R Appleton *Ox* 66-79; rtd 79; Perm to Offic *Glouc* from 79. *18 Canonbury Street, Berkeley, Glos GL13 9BG*   Dursley (0453) 810120

TUDBALL, Arthur James. b 28. AKC54. **d** 54 **p** 55. Malaya 57-63; Malaysia 63-79; Singapore from 79; rtd 89. *Orchard Point, PO Box 160, Singapore 9123*   Singapore (65) 259-4298

TUDGE, Paul Quartus. b 55. Leeds Univ BEd78. Cranmer Hall Dur 84. **d** 87 **p** 88. C Roundhay St Edm *Ripon* 87-90; C Leeds St Pet 90; C Leeds City 91; V Woodside from 91. *St James's Vicarage, 1 Scotland Close, Horsforth, Leeds LS18 5SG*   Horsforth (0532) 582433

TUDGEY, Stephen John. b 51. St Jo Coll Nottm BTh81 LTh. **d** 81 **p** 82. C Grays Thurrock *Chelmsf* 81-83; C Grays SS Pet and Paul, S Stifford and W Thurrock 83-84; C Grays Thurrock 84; C Madeley *Heref* 84-87; R Chilcompton w Downside and Stratton on the Fosse *B & W* from 87. *The Rectory, The Street, Chilcompton, Bath BA3 4HN*   Stratton-on-the-Fosse (0761) 232219

TUDOR, David Charles Frederick. b 42. Sarum & Wells Th Coll 70. **d** 73 **p** 74. C Plymouth St Pet *Ex* 73-75; C Reddish *Man* 75-78; P-in-c Hamer 78-80; V Goldenhill *Lich* 80-87; V Meir 87-91; Chapl Asst Nottm City Hosp from 91. *79 Henrietta Street, Bulwell, Nottingham*   Nottingham (0602) 794767

TUDOR, David St Clair. b 55. K Coll Lon BD77 AKC77. Ripon Coll Cuddesdon 77. **d** 78 **p** 79. C Plumstead St Nic *S'wark* 78-80; C Redhill St Matt 80-83; C-in-c Reigate St Phil CD 83-87; Asst Sec Gen Syn Bd for Miss and Unity from 87. *Flat 3, 68 Venner Road, London SE26*   081-676 9582

TUDOR, Malcolm George Henry Booth. b 36. Nottm Univ BA71. Linc Th Coll 72. **d** 60 **p** 61. In RC Ch 60-71; C Cinderhill *S'well* 72-74; P-in-c Broxtowe 74-78; P-in-c E Drayton w Stokeham 78-86; R E Markham and Askham 78-86; P-in-c Headon w Upton 78-86; V Llandinam w Trefeglwys w Penstrowed *Ban* from 86. *The Vicarage, Llandinam, Powys SY17 5BS*   Caersws (068684) 341

TUFFEL, Kennedy Joseph. b 20. Worc Ord Coll 64. **d** 66 **p** 67. C Goring-by-Sea *Chich* 68-72 and 81-89; NSM from 89; V Barnham 72-78; Hon C W Worthing St Jo 78-81; rtd 89. *10 Brook Barn Way, Goring-by-Sea, Worthing, W Sussex BN12 4DW*   Worthing (0903) 49657

TUFFIELD, Canon Basil Thomas. b 23. Fitzw Ho Cam BA49 MA54. Wells Th Coll 50. **d** 52 **p** 53. V Carshalton Beeches *S'wark* 65-79; P-in-c Crosscanonby *Carl* 79-82; V 82-90; P-in-c Allonby w W Newton 81-82; V Allonby 82-90; RD Solway 84-90; Hon Can Carl Cathl from 87; rtd 90. *Hafod y Cwm, Nannerch, Mold, Clwyd CH7 5RP*   Mold (0352) 741234

TUFNELL, Edward Nicholas Pember. b 45. Chu Coll Cam MA68. St Jo Coll Nottm BA73. **d** 73 **p** 74. C Ealing St Mary *Lon* 73-76; BCMS 76-88; Tanzania 76-88; P-in-c Lt Thurrock St Jo *Chelmsf* 89-91; V from 91; Chapl Thurrock Hosp from 89. *St John's Vicarage, Victoria Avenue, Grays, Essex RM16 2RP*   Grays Thurrock (0375) 372101

TUFT, Patrick Anthony. b 31. Selw Coll Cam BA56 MA60. Edin Th Coll 56. **d** 58 **p** 59. C Keighley *Bradf* 58-63; PV Chich Cathl *Chich* 63-68; Min Can St Paul's Cathl *Lon* 68-74; Hon Min Can from 74; V Chiswick St Nic w St Mary from 74; PV Westmr Abbey 74-79; AD Hounslow *Lon* from 87; P-in-c Chiswick St Paul Grove Park 88-90. *Chiswick Vicarage, The Mall, London W4 2PJ*   081-995 4717

TUFTON, Canon Colin Charles Guy. b 24. Or Coll Ox BA48 MA53. Ely Th Coll 49. **d** 51 **p** 52. V Maidstone All SS w St Phil and H Trin *Cant* 67-74; RD Sutton 67-74; Hon Can Cant Cathl 68-89; Tutor St Aug Coll Cant 74-76; Master Eastbridge Hosp Cant 76-89; R Cant St Pet w St Alphege and St Marg etc *Cant* 76-89; rtd 89; Perm to Offic *Chich* from 89. *3 Manor Road North, Seaford, E Sussex BN25 3RA*   Seaford (0323) 893452

TULL, Preb Christopher Stuart. b 36. Hertf Coll Ox BA60 MA64. Oak Hill Th Coll 60. **d** 62 **p** 63. C Stoodleigh *Ex* 62-71; C Washfield 62-71; TV Washfield, Stoodleigh, Withleigh etc 71-74; RD Tiverton 74-75; R Bishops Nympton w Rose Ash 75-77; V Mariansleigh 75-77; TR Bishopsnympton, Rose Ash, Mariansleigh etc from 77; RD S Molton 80-87; Preb Ex Cathl from 84. *The Rectory, Bishops Nympton, South Molton, Devon EX36 4NY*   Bishops Nympton (07697) 427

TULLOCH, Richard James Anthony. b 52. Wadh Coll Ox BA74 Selw Coll Cam BA79. Ridley Hall Cam 76. **d** 79 **p** 80. C Morden *S'wark* 79-83; C Jesmond Clayton Memorial *Newc* from 83. *56 Holly Avenue, Jesmond, Newcastle upon Tyne NE2 2QA*   091-281 9046

TULLOCH, Walter Harold. b 16. AIMLS53 MRSH62. St Deiniol's Hawarden 79. **d** 79 **p** 80. NSM Maghull *Liv* 79-86; Hon C from 88; rtd 86; Perm to Offic *Liv* 86-88. *8 Tailor's Lane, Maghull, Liverpool L31 3HD*   051-526 1936

TULLY, David John. b 56. St Jo Coll Dur BA77 Nottm Univ PGCE78. Ridley Hall Cam 81. **d** 84 **p** 85. C Gosforth St Nic *Newc* 84-86; C Newburn 86-90; TV Whorlton from 90. *St John's Vicarage, Whorlton, Newcastle upon Tyne NE5 1NN*   091-286 9648

TULLY, Ross. b 22. Clare Coll Cam BA44 MA48. Ridley Hall Cam 47. **d** 49 **p** 50. Pakistan 53-73; Chapl St Bernard's Hosp Southall 74-80; C Eastbourne H Trin *Chich* 80-86; rtd 87. *40 Thornton Court, Girton, Cambridge CB3 0NS*   Cambridge (0223) 276223

TUNBRIDGE, John Stephen. b 31. Keble Coll Ox BA54 MA59. Ely Th Coll 54. **d** 56 **p** 57. C Upper

Norwood All SS w St Marg *Cant* 56-57; C Ramsgate St Geo 57-60; P-in-c 76-84; C Folkestone St Mary and St Eanswythe 60-62; R Gt Chart 62-67; V Womenswold 67-76; C-in-c Aylesham CD 67-76; R Harbledown from 84. *The Rectory, Summerhill, Harbledown, Canterbury CT2 8NW* Canterbury (0227) 464117

TUNNICLIFFE, Martin Wyndham. b 31. Keele Univ BA56. Qu Coll Birm 59. **d** 60 **p** 61. C Castle Bromwich SS Mary and Marg *Birm* 60-65; V Shard End 65-73; R Over Whitacre w Shustoke 73-78; V Tanworth from 78; RD Solihull from 89. *The Vicarage, Tanworth-in-Arden, Solihull, W Midlands B94 5EB* Tanworth-in-Arden (05644) 2565

TUNSTALL, Barry Anthony. b 29. Sarum Th Coll 53. **d** 55 **p** 56. C Croxley Green All SS *St Alb* 55-58; C Apsley End 58-63; V N Mymms 63-81; P-in-c Kirkby Overblow *Ripon* 81; R Kirkby Overblow from 81. *The Rectory, Kirkby Overblow, Harrogate, N Yorkshire HG3 1HD* Harrogate (0423) 872314

TUPPER, Michael Heathfield. b 20. St Edm Hall Ox BA41 MA46. Ridley Hall Cam 41. **d** 43 **p** 44. C Win Ch Ch *Win* 43-45; Chapl Monkton Combe Sch Bath 45-48; Asst Chapl Shrewsbury Sch 48-59 and 60-79; Kenya 59-60; Hon C Bayston Hill *Lich* from 80. *9 Eric Lock Road, Bayston Hill, Shrewsbury SY3 0HQ* Shrewsbury (0743) 722674

TURNBULL, Brian Robert. b 43. Chich Th Coll 71. **d** 74 **p** 75. C Norbury St Phil *Cant* 74-76; C Folkestone St Sav 76-77; Hon C Tong *Lich* 83-88; C Jarrow *Dur* 88-89; TV from 89. *St John the Baptist House, Iona Road, Jarrow, Tyne & Wear NE32 4HX* 091-489 2043

TURNBULL, Charles Philip. b 13. Ely Th Coll 37. **d** 38 **p** 39. V Hornsey St Pet *Lon* 64-76; Chapl Laleham Abbey 76-79; rtd 79; Perm to Offic *Chich* from 79. *3 Clarence Drive, East Preston, Littlehampton, W Sussex BN16 1EH* Littlehampton (0903) 774043

TURNBULL, Canon Colin. b 22. St Chad's Coll Dur BA46 DipTh48. **d** 48 **p** 49. V Monkseaton St Mary *Newc* 68-75; RD Tynemouth 70-75; V Embleton w Rennington and Rock 75-87; Hon Can Newc Cathl from 79; RD Alnwick 81-86; rtd 87. *38 Eastfield Avenue, Whitley Bay, Tyne & Wear NE25 8LU* 091-251 5806

TURNBULL, David Charles. b 44. Leeds Univ BA65. Chich Th Coll 67. **d** 69 **p** 70. C Jarrow St Paul *Dur* 69-74; V Carlinghow *Wakef* 74-83; V Penistone 83-86; TR Penistone and Thurlstone from 86; RD Barnsley from 88. *The Vicarage, Shrewbury Road, Penistone, Sheffield S30 6DY* Barnsley (0226) 763241

TURNBULL, Canon Eric Samuel. b 17. Clare Coll Cam BA48 MA52. Cuddesdon Coll. **d** 48 **p** 49. Can Res Worc Cathl *Worc* 71-82; rtd 82; Perm to Offic *Nor* from 83. *Mill Leet, High Street, Cley, Holt, Norfolk NR25 1BB* Cley (0263) 740772

TURNBULL, George William Warwick. b 47. CQSW75 Lon Univ DipEd68 DipDA68 Leeds Poly BEd84. N Ord Course 85. **d** 88. Chapl Asst Leeds Gen Infirmary 88-91. *11 North Parade, Leeds LS16 5AY* Leeds (0532) 752382

TURNBULL, James. b 19. St Aug Coll Cant 57. **d** 58 **p** 59. R Twineham *Chich* 61-75; P-in-c Kingston Buci 75-80; Perm to Offic *B & W* from 80; rtd 84. *34 Hood Close, Glastonbury, Somerset BA6 8ES* Glastonbury (0458) 33796

TURNBULL, James Awty. b 28. Solicitor. Cranmer Hall Dur 89. **d** 89 **p** 90. NSM Bolton Abbey *Bradf* from 89. *Deerstones Cottage, Deerstones, Skipton, N Yorkshire BD23 6JB*

TURNBULL, Canon John Smith Gardiner. b 13. Kelham Th Coll 30. **d** 36 **p** 37. V Auckland St Helen *Dur* 53-78; Hon Can Dur Cathl 58-78; rtd 79. *32 The Ridgeway, Mount Park Drive, Lanchester, Durham DH7 0PT* Lanchester (0207) 520541

✠**TURNBULL, Rt Rev Michael.** b 35. Keble Coll Ox BA58 MA62. Cranmer Hall Dur DipTh60. **d** 60 **p** 61 **c** 88. C Middleton *Man* 60-61; C Luton w E Hyde *St Alb* 61-65; Dir of Ords *York* 65-69; Abp's Dom Chapl 65-69; Chapl York Univ 69-76; V Heslington 69-76; Chief Sec CA 76-84; Can Res Roch Cathl *Roch* 84-88; Adn Roch 84-88; Bp Roch from 88. *Bishopscourt, Rochester, Kent ME1 1TS* Medway (0634) 842721

TURNBULL, Peter Frederick. b 64. SS Mark & Jo Coll Plymouth BA85. Sarum & Wells Th Coll 89. **d** 91. C Upper Norwood All SS *S'wark* from 91. *51 Chevening Road, London SE19 3TD* 081-768 0269

TURNBULL, Stephen. b 40. Nottm Univ BTh74. Linc Th Coll 70. **d** 74 **p** 75. C Kirkstall *Ripon* 74-76; C Fairfield *Derby* 76-79; TV Seacroft *Ripon* 79-84; Lic to Offic *Derby* from 84; Chapl Derbyshire Children's Hosp from 84; Chapl Derby City Hosp from 84. *City Hospital, Uttoxeter Road, Derby DE3 3NE* Derby (0332) 40131

TURNBULL, William George. b 25. Lich Th Coll 63. **d** 65 **p** 66. C Portishead *B & W* 69-73; C Holsworthy w Cookbury *Ex* 73-76; P-in-c Bridgerule 76-79; P-in-c Pyworthy w Pancraswyke 77-79; P-in-c Pyworthy, Pancrasweek and Bridgerule 79-80; R 80-81; V Otterton and Colaton Raleigh 81-90; rtd 90; Chapl Convent Companions Jes Gd Shep W Ogwell from 90. *10 Croft Road, East Ogwell, Newton Abbot, Devon TQ12 6BD* Newton Abbot (0626) 62770

TURNER, Alan James. b 40. Oak Hill Th Coll BA81. **d** 81 **p** 82. C Bradley *Wakef* 81-84; C Sandal St Helen 84-86; P-in-c Sileby *Leic* 86-88; TR Sileby, Cossington and Seagrave from 88. *The Rectory, 11 Mountsorrel Lane, Sileby, Loughborough, Leics LE12 7NE* Sileby (050981) 2493

TURNER, Albert Edward. b 41. Glouc Sch of Min 83. **d** 89 **p** 90. C Woodford St Mary w St Phil and St Jas *Chelmsf* from 89. *33 Elmhurst Drive, London E18 1BP* 081-989 3958

TURNER, Andrew John. b 52. St Jo Coll Nottm LTh. **d** 83 **p** 84. C Framlingham w Saxtead *St E* 83-86; P-in-c Badingham w Bruisyard and Cransford 86-88; P-in-c Dennington 86-88; R Badingham w Bruisyard, Cransford and Dennington 88-91; Chapl RAF from 91. *c/o MOD, Adastral House, Theobald's Road, London WC1X 8RU* 071-430 7268

TURNER, Mrs Ann Elizabeth Hamer. b 38. Ex Univ BA59 CertEd60. Trin Coll Bris 84. **dss** 86 **d** 87. Bath St Luke *B & W* 86-87; Hon C 87-91; Chapl Dorothy Ho Foundn 89-91; C Bath Twerton-on-Avon from 91. *24 Edgeworth Road, Bath BA2 2LY* Bath (0225) 424234

TURNER, Anthony John. b 49. **d** 91. C Coity w Nolton *Llan* from 91. *100 Fairfield Road, Bridgend, M Glam CF31 3DS* Bridgend (0656) 652948

TURNER, Ven Antony Hubert Michael. b 30. FCA63 Lon Univ DipTh56. Tyndale Hall Bris 54. **d** 56 **p** 57. C Nottm St Ann *S'well* 56-58; C Cheadle Ches 58-62; V Macclesfield Ch Ch 62-68; Lic to Offic *S'wark* 68-74; Home Sec BCMS 68-74; V Southsea St Jude *Portsm* 74-86; P-in-c Portsea St Luke 75-80; RD Portsm 79-84; Hon Can Portsm Cathl 85-86; Adn Is of Wight from 86. *3 Beech Grove, Ryde, Isle of Wight PO33 3AN* Isle of Wight (0983) 65522

TURNER, Benjamin John. b 45. Bolton Inst of Tech CEng MICE. N Ord Course 82. **d** 85 **p** 86. C Worsley *Man* 85-88; V Elton St Steph from 88. *St Stephen's Vicarage, 44 Peers Street, Elton, Bury BL9 2QF* 061-764 1775

TURNER, Mrs Beryl Rose. b 31. Nottm Univ CertEd75 BEd76. **dss** 84 **d** 87. Mortomley *Sheff* 84-86; Whitgift w Adlingfleet and Eastoft 86; The Marshland 86-87; Par Dn Goole from 87. *49 Colonel's Walk, Goole, N Humberside DN14 6HJ* Goole (0405) 69193

TURNER, Carl Francis. b 60. St Chad's Coll Dur BA81. St Steph Ho Ox 83. **d** 85 **p** 86. C Leigh-on-Sea St Marg *Chelmsf* 85-88; C Brentwood St Thos 88-90; TV Plaistow from 90. *St Martin's Vicarage, 34 St Martin's Avenue, London E6 3DX* 081-470 3262

TURNER, Charles Maurice Joseph. b 13. **d** 79 **p** 80. Hon C Brislington St Luke *Bris* 79-83; Hon C Bris Ch Ch w St Ewen and All SS 83-84; Hon C Bris St Steph w St Nic and St Leon 83-84; Hon C City of Bris from 84. *31 Eagle Road, Bristol BS4 3LQ* Bristol (0272) 776329

TURNER, Christopher James Shepherd. b 48. Ch Ch Ox BA70 MA74. Wycliffe Hall Ox 71. **d** 74 **p** 75. C Rusholme *Man* 74-78; C Chadderton Ch Ch 78-80; V 80-89; V Selly Park St Steph and St Wulstan *Birm* from 89. *St Stephen's Vicarage, 20 Elmdon Road, Birmingham B29 7LF* 021-472 0050

TURNER, Colin Peter John. b 42. Clifton Th Coll 63. **d** 66 **p** 67. C Kinson *Sarum* 66-68; C York St Paul *York* 68-72; Org Sec (SE Area) CPAS 73-78; TV Weymouth St Jo *Sarum* 78-87; TV Radipole and Melcombe Regis 78-87; R Radstock w Writhlington *B & W* from 90; R Kilmersdon w Babington from 90. *The Rectory, 1 Bristol Road, Radstock, Bath BA3 3EF* Radstock (0761) 33182

TURNER, David. b 40. St Andr Univ BSc63. Ridley Hall Cam 63. **d** 65 **p** 66. C Bootle St Matt *Liv* 65-68; C Wigan St Barn Marsh Green 68-73; V Huyton St Geo 73-79; V Meltham Mills *Wakef* 79-89; V Wilshaw 79-89; P-in-c Helme 81-85; P-in-c Meltham 85-89; V 89; V Gawber from 89. *The Vicarage, Church Street, Gawber, Barnsley, S Yorkshire S75 2RL* Barnsley (0226) 207140

TURNER, David Stanley. b 35. Lon Univ CertRK69 Westmr Coll Ox BA84. W Midl Minl Tr Course 86. **d** 87 **p** 88. NSM Worc St Mich *Worc* 87-90; C Walsall Wood *Lich* from 90. *Church House, 25 Green Lane, Shelfield, Walsall WS4 1RN* Walsall (0922) 682604

TURNER, Derek John. b 54. Univ of Wales (Ban) BSc81 PhD86. St Jo Coll Nottm. **d** 87 **p** 88. C Pelsall *Lich* from

87. *21 Dovedale Avenue, Pelsall, Walsall WS3 4HG* Pelsall (0922) 682196

TURNER, Donald. b 29. S'wark Ord Course. **d** 71 **p** 72. C Hounslow St Steph *Lon* 71-76; Hon C Isleworth St Jo 76-78; C Brighton St Pet w Chpl Royal *Chich* 78-80; C Brighton St Pet w Chpl Royal and St Jo 80-85; P-in-c St Leonards SS Pet and Paul 85-87; V 87-91; rtd 91. *22 High Beech Close, St Leonards-on-Sea, E Sussex TN37 7TT* Hastings (0424) 854687

TURNER, Douglas John. b 15. Ely Th Coll 45. **d** 47 **p** 48. V Ventnor H Trin *Portsm* 66-72; V Ventnor St Cath 66-72; V Ryde All SS 72-81; rtd 81; Perm to Offic *Chich* from 81. *102 Wallace Avenue, Worthing, W Sussex BN11 5QA* Worthing (0903) 46973

TURNER, Canon Edward Robert. b 37. Em Coll Cam BA62 BTh66 MA67. Westcott Ho Cam 64. **d** 66 **p** 67. C Salford St Phil w St Steph *Man* 66-69; Chapl Tonbridge Sch Kent 69-81; Adv for In-Service Tr *Roch* 81-89; Dir of Educn from 81; Can Res Roch Cathl from 81; Vice-Dean Roch Cathl from 88. *1 King's Orchard, The Precinct, Rochester, Kent ME1 1TG* Medway (0634) 42756 or 830333

TURNER, Canon Eric Gurney Hammond. b 11. St Edm Hall Ox BA40 MA44. Cuddesdon Coll 40. **d** 41 **p** 42. R Colchester St Jas, All SS, St Nic and St Runwald *Chelmsf* 69-81; Hon Can Chelmsf Cathl 74-81; RD Colchester 75-81; rtd 81. *D'Arcy Cottage, South Street, Tolleshunt D'Arcy, Maldon, Essex CM9 8TR* Maldon (0621) 860232

TURNER, Canon Francis Edwin. b 29. Sarum Th Coll 54. **d** 57 **p** 58. C Cheriton Street *Cant* 57-61; C Willesborough w Hinxhill 61-64; P-in-c Betteshanger w Ham 64-65; R Northbourne w Betteshanger and Ham 64-70; R Northbourne, Tilmanstone w Betteshanger and Ham 70-74; V Sittingbourne St Mich from 74; RD Sittingbourne 78-84; Hon Can Cant Cathl from 84. *St Michael's Vicarage, Valenciennes Road, Sittingbourne, Kent ME10 1EN* Sittingbourne (0795) 472874

TURNER, Frederick Charles Jesse. b 07. St Boniface Warminster 31. **d** 36 **p** 37. V Hooe *Chich* 65-74; R Ninfield 65-74; rtd 74. *1 Birchwood Road, Malvern, Worcs WR14 1LD* Leigh Sinton (0886) 32453

TURNER, Canon Frederick Glynne. b 30. Univ of Wales (Lamp) BA52. St Mich Coll Llan 52. **d** 54 **p** 55. C Aberaman *Llan* 54-60; C Oystermouth *S & B* 60-64; V Abercynon *Llan* 64-71; V Ton Pentre 71-73; V Ystradyfodwg 73-77; R Caerphilly 77-82; V Whitchurch from 82; Can Llan Cathl from 84. *The Vicarage, 6 Penlline Road, Whitchurch, Cardiff CF4 2AD* Cardiff (0222) 626072

TURNER, Geoffrey. b 46. **d** 87 **p** 88. C Lougher *S & B* 87-89; C Swansea St Pet 89-90; V New Radnor and Llanfihangel Nantmelan etc from 90. *The Rectory, New Radnor, Presteigne, Powys LD8 2SS* New Radnor (054421) 258

TURNER, Geoffrey Edwin. b 45. Aston Univ BSc68 Newc Univ MSc69 PhD72. Cranmer Hall Dur BA74 DipTh75. **d** 75 **p** 76. C Wood End *Cov* 75-79; V Huyton Quarry *Liv* 79-86; Press and Communications Officer *Ely* from 86; P-in-c Gt w Lt Abington from 86; P-in-c Hildersham from 86. *The Vicarage, Church Lane, Little Abington, Cambridge CB1 6BQ* Cambridge (0223) 891350

TURNER, Canon Geoffrey Martin. b 34. Oak Hill Th Coll 60. **d** 63 **p** 64. C Tonbridge St Steph *Roch* 63-66; C Heatherlands St Jo *Sarum* 66-69; V Derby St Pet *Derby* 69-73; V Chadderton Ch Ch *Man* 73-79; R Bebington *Ches* from 79; Hon Can Ches Cathl from 89; RD Wirral N from 89. *The Rectory, Bebington, Cheshire L63 3EX* 051-645 6478

TURNER, Geoffrey Raymond. b 28. Sarum & Wells Th Coll 71. **d** 73 **p** 74. C Pokesdown All SS *Win* 73-76; R N Waltham and Steventon, Ashe and Deane from 76; CF(TA) from 77. *The Rectory, North Waltham, Basingstoke, Hants RG25 2BQ* Dummer (0256) 379256

TURNER, Canon Gerald Garth. b 38. Univ of Wales (Lamp) BA61 St Edm Hall Ox BA63 MA67. St Steph Ho Ox 63. **d** 65 **p** 66. C Drayton in Hales *Lich* 65-68; Chapl Prebendal Sch Chich 68-70; PV Chich Cathl *Chich* 68-70; C Forest Row 70-72; V Hope *Derby* 72-78; Prec Man Cathl *Man* 78-86; Can Res 78-86; R Tattenhall and Handley *Ches* from 86. *The Rectory, Tattenhall, Chester CH3 9QE* Tattenhall (0829) 70328

TURNER, Graham Colin. b 55. Bradf Univ BTech. Oak Hill Th Coll BA81. **d** 81 **p** 82. C Upper Armley *Ripon* 81-86; V Bordesley Green *Birm* from 86. *The Vicarage, 405 Belcher's Lane, Bordesley Green, Birmingham B9 5SY* 021-772 0418

TURNER, Mrs Heather Winifred. b 43. SRN65. Cant Sch of Min 89. **d** 90. Par Dn Orpington All SS *Roch* from

90. *62 Bark Hart Road, Orpington, Kent BR6 0QD* Orpington (0689) 821733

TURNER, Canon Prof Henry Ernest William. b 07. St Jo Coll Ox BA39 MA33 Linc Coll Ox BD40 DD55. Wycliffe Hall Ox 31. **d** 31 **p** 32. Can Res Dur Cathl *Dur* 51-73; Prof Div Dur Univ 58-74; rtd 74; Perm to Offic *Carl* from 77. *Realands, Eskdale Green, Holmrook, Cumbria CA19 1TW* Eskdale (09403) 321

TURNER, Henry John Mansfield. b 24. Magd Coll Cam BA45 MA48 Man Univ PhD85. Westcott Ho Cam 48. **d** 50 **p** 51. C Crosby *Linc* 50-52; C Chorlton upon Medlock *Man* 52-55; Inter-Colleg Sec SCM (Man) 52-55; C Leigh St Mary *Man* 55-57; V Rochdale Gd Shep 57-62; India 63-67; V Becontree St Geo *Chelmsf* 67-71; R Weeley 71-79; Chapl St Deiniol's Lib Hawarden 79-80; Sub-Warden 80-86; Perm to Offic *St As & Chelmsf* from 86; Hon C St Botolph without Bishopgate *Lon* from 87; Lic to Offic from 87. *25 Fourth Avenue, Frinton-on-Sea, Essex CO13 9DU* Frinton-on-Sea (0255) 677554

TURNER, Miss Jessica Mary. b 60. SS Coll Cam BA81 PGCE82. Trin Coll Bris 88. **d** 91. Par Dn Preston Em *Blackb* from 91. *144 Inkerman Street, Preston, Lancs PR2 2BN* Preston (0772) 720296

TURNER, Miss Jessie Irene. b 06. Qu Mary Coll Lon BSc29 DipEd30. **dss** 60 **d** 87. Coleford w Staunton *Glouc* 60-69; Chingford St Edm *Chelmsf* 69-87; Hon Par Dn from 87. *57 Normanshire Drive, London E4 9HE* 081-524 4108

TURNER, John Arthur. b 05. St Jo Coll Dur BA37 DipTh38 MA40. **d** 38 **p** 39. V Chasetown *Lich* 56-76; rtd 76. *103 Leomansley View, Lichfield, Staffs WS13 8AP* Lichfield (0543) 268597

TURNER, John David Maurice. b 22. Keble Coll Ox BA45 MA48. Ripon Hall Ox 69. **d** 70 **p** 71. C Crowthorne *Ox* 70-73; V Cropredy w Gt Bourton 73-79; V Cropredy w Gt Bourton and Wardington 80-83; Perm to Offic *Ox* and *Pet* from 83; rtd 87. *Appletree Cottage, The Close, Greatworth, Banbury, Oxon OX17 2EB* Banbury (0295) 711326

TURNER, John Edward. b 19. S Dios Minl Tr Scheme. **d** 82 **p** 83. NSM Radipole and Melcombe Regis *Sarum* from 82. *95 Weymouth Bay Avenue, Weymouth, Dorset DT3 5AD* Weymouth (0305) 771024

TURNER, John Gilbert. b 06. Cranmer Hall Dur. **d** 66 **p** 67. C Tithby w Cropwell Butler *S'well* 71-77; C Colston Bassett 71-77; C Cropwell Bishop 71-77; C Langar 71-77; C Granby w Elton 71-77; rtd 77; Perm to Offic *S'well* from 79. *Landyke, Iythby Road, Cropwell Butler, Nottingham* Nottingham (0602) 333166

TURNER, John Girvan. b 54. Glas Univ MA Dur Univ BA. **d** 82 **p** 83. C Kippax *Ripon* 82-85; C Kippax w Allerton Bywater 85; Chapl Glas and Strathclyde Univs from 86. *212 Wilton Street, Glasgow G20 6DE* 041-946 1145

TURNER, John William. b 43. Sheff Univ BSc73. Wycliffe Hall Ox 86. **d** 88 **p** 89. C Clayton *Bradf* from 88. *4 Crestville Close, Clayton, Bradford, W Yorkshire BD14 6DZ* Bradford (0274) 816547

TURNER, Keith Howard. b 50. Southn Univ BA71. Wycliffe Hall Ox 72. **d** 75 **p** 76. C Enfield Ch Ch Trent Park *Lon* 75-79; C Chilwell *S'well* 79-83; P-in-c Linby w Papplewick 83-90; R from 90. *The Rectory, Main Street, Linby, Nottingham NG15 8AE* Nottingham (0602) 632346

TURNER, Lawrence John. b 43. Kelham Th Coll 65. **d** 70 **p** 71. C Lower Gornal *Lich* 70-73; C Wednesbury St Paul Wood Green 73-74; C Porthill 75-77; C Wilton *York* 77-80; P-in-c 80-82; R Jersey St Martin *Win* from 82; Chmn Jersey Miss to Seamen from 82. *St Martin's Rectory, Jersey, Channel Islands JE3 6HW* Jersey (0534) 54294

TURNER, Leslie. b 29. NE Lon Poly BSc87. St Aid Birkenhead 51. **d** 54 **p** 55. C Darwen St Cuth *Blackb* 54-56; C Haslingden w Grane and Stonefold 56-59; V Oswaldtwistle St Paul 59-65; Chapl Belmont and Henderson Hosps Sutton 65-71; St Ebba's Hosp Epsom 65-71; Qu Mary's Carshalton 67-71; Lic to Offic *Pet* 71; Chapl Princess Marina & St Crispin's Hosps 71-87; Chapl Northn Gen Hosp, Manfield Hosp Northn and St Edm Hosp Northn from 87. *The Chaplain's Office, General Hospital, Northampton NN1 5BD* Northampton (0604) 34700

TURNER, Mark Richard Haythornthwaite. b 41. TCD MA67 Linc Coll Ox BA68. Wycliffe Hall Ox 65. **d** 68 **p** 69. C Birtley *Newc* 68-71; C Cam Gt St Mary w St Mich *Ely* 71-74; Chapl Loughb Univ *Leic* 74-79; P-in-c Keele *Lich* 80-85; Chapl Keele Univ 80-85; P-in-c

Ashley from 85. *The Rectory, Ashley, Market Drayton, Shropshire TF9 4LQ* Ashley (063087) 2210

TURNER, Martin John. b 34. Trin Hall Cam BA55 MA59. Cuddesdon Coll 58. **d** 60 **p** 61. C Rugby St Andr *Cov* 60-65; C Cov Cathl 65-68; USA 68-70; V Rushmere *St E* 70-82; V Monkwearmouth St Pet *Dur* 82-90; V Bathford *B & W* from 90. *Bathford Vicarage, Ostlings Lane, Bath BA1 7RW* Bath (0225) 858325

TURNER, Maureen. b 55. Leeds Univ BA78. St Jo Coll Nottm 84. **d** 87. Par Dn Darlaston St Lawr *Lich* from 87. *21 Dovedale Avenue, Pelsall, Walsall WS3 4HG* Pelsall (0922) 682196

TURNER, Maurice William. b 27. Sarum Th Coll 53. **d** 56 **p** 57. C Thornhill *Wakef* 56-60; V Gawber 60-71; V Alverthorpe 71-74; V Oxon and Shelton *Lich* 74-81; P-in-c Battlefield w Albrighton 81-82; V Leaton 81-82; V Leaton and Albrighton w Battlefield from 82. *The Vicarage, Baschurch Road, Bomere Heath, Shrewsbury SY4 3PN* Bomere Heath (0939) 290259

TURNER, Michael Andrew. b 34. K Coll Cam BA59 MA62. Cuddesdon Coll 59. **d** 61 **p** 62. C Luton St Andr *St Alb* 61-64; V 70-77; C Northolt St Mary *Lon* 64-70; Lic to Offic *St Alb* from 78; Lic to Offic *Lon* from 85; Dep Hd and Chapl Greycoat Hosp Sch from 85. *35 Culverhouse Road, Luton LU3 1PY* Luton (0582) 391835

TURNER, Michael John Royce. b 43. St Jo Coll Dur BA65. Chich Th Coll 65. **d** 67 **p** 68. C Hodge Hill *Birm* 67-71; C Eling, Testwood and Marchwood *Win* 71-72; TV 72-77; R Kirkwall *Ab* 77-85; R Laurencekirk *Bre* from 85; R Drumtochty from 85; R Fasque from 85; R Drumlithie from 85. *Beattie Lodge, Laurencekirk, Kincardineshire AB3 1HJ* Laurencekirk (05617) 380

TURNER, Nicholas Anthony. b 51. Clare Coll Cam BA73 MA77 Keble Coll Ox BTh77 MA81. Ripon Coll Cuddesdon 78. **d** 78 **p** 79. C Stretford St Matt *Man* 78-80; Tutor St Steph Ho Ox 80-84; V Leeds Richmond Hill *Ripon* from 84. *All Saints' Vicarage, Pontefract Lane, Leeds LS9 9AE* Leeds (0532) 480971

TURNER, Noel Macdonald Muncaster. b 08. Ch Coll Cam BA31. Ely Th Coll 32. **d** 32 **p** 33. R Gonalston *S'well* 41-73; R Epperstone 41-73; Chapl HM Youth Cust Cen Lowdham Grange 45-73; P-in-c Oxton *S'well* 67-73; rtd 73; Perm to Offic *Chich* and *Portsm* from 73. *27 West Close, Fernhurst, Haslemere, Surrey* Haslemere (0428) 53542

TURNER (nee SYMINGTON), Ms Patricia Ann. b 46. SRN68 RMN71 SCM72 Cam Univ DipRS82. St Steph Ho Ox 82. **dss** 84 **d** 87. Buttershaw St Aid *Bradf* 84-87; TM Manningham from 87. *All Saints' Vicarage, 7 Pontefract Lane, Leeds LS9 9AE* Leeds (0532) 480971

TURNER, Peter Carpenter. b 39. Oak Hill Th Coll 63. **d** 66 **p** 67. C Chadwell *Chelmsf* 66-69; C Braintree 69-73; R Fyfield 73-87; P-in-c Moreton 77-87; C-in-c Bobbingworth 82-87; P-in-c Willingale w Shellow and Berners Roding 84-87; P-in-c E Ham St Geo from 87. *The Vicarage, Buxton Road, London E6 3NB* 081-472 2111

TURNER, Peter Robin. b 42. Open Univ BA79. AKC65. **d** 66 **p** 67. C Crediton *Ex* 66-69; Chapl RAF 70-88; Asst Chapl-in-Chief RAF from 88. *c/o MOD, Adastral House, Theobald's Road, London WC1X 8RU* 071-430 7268

TURNER, Philip William. b 25. CM65. Worc Coll Ox BA50 MA62. Chich Th Coll 49. **d** 51 **p** 52. Relig Broadcasting Org BBC Midl Region 66-71; Asst Master Brian Mill Sch Droitwich 71-73; Chapl Eton Coll Windsor 73-75; Chapl Malvern Coll Worcs 75-84; Chapl St Jas & Abbey Schs Malvern 84-86; rtd 90. *181 West Malvern Road, Malvern, Worcs WR14 4AY* Malvern (0684) 563852

TURNER, Canon Robert Edgar. b 20. TCD BA42 MA51. Linc Th Coll 44. **d** 45 **p** 46. I Belf St Geo *Conn* 58-90; Can Belf Cathl 71-76; Preb Clonmethan St Patr Cathl Dub 76-90; Dioc Registrar *Conn* from 82; rtd 90. *19 Cricklewood Park, Belfast BT9 5GU* Belfast (0232) 663214

TURNER, Robin Edward. b 35. Selw Coll Cam BA57 MA63. Qu Coll Birm DipTh63. **d** 63 **p** 64. C Aveley *Chelmsf* 63-67; C Upminster 67-71; R Goldhanger w Lt Totham 71-80; R Lt Baddow from 80. *The Rectory, Colam Lane, Little Baddow, Chelmsford CM3 4SY* Danbury (024541) 3488

TURNER, Roger Dyke. b 39. Trin Coll Bris 79. **d** 81 **p** 82. C Clevedon St Andr *B & W* 81-82; C Clevedon St Andr and Ch Ch 83-85; R Freshford, Limpley Stoke and Hinton Charterhouse 85-88; V Kenilworth St Jo *Cov* from 88; RD Kenilworth from 90. *St John's Vicarage, Clarke's Avenue, Kenilworth, Warks CV8 1HX* Kenilworth (0926) 53203

TURNER, St John Alwin. b 31. Dur Univ BA57 MA61. Cranmer Hall Dur DipTh58. **d** 59 **p** 60. C W Hartlepool St Paul *Dur* 59-62; C S Shore H Trin *Blackb* 62-65; V Huncoat 65-67; Org Sec (Dios Ripon and York) CMS 67-72; V Harrogate St Mark *Ripon* from 72. *The Vicarage, 13 Wheatlands Road, Harrogate, N Yorkshire HG2 8BB* Harrogate (0423) 504959

TURNER, Walter. b 21. Lich Th Coll 51. **d** 53 **p** 54. V Frizington *Carl* 65-70; V Underbarrow w Helsington and Crook 70-77; V Allithwaite 77-79; TV Kirkby Lonsdale 79-82; TV Penrith w Newton Reigny and Plumpton Wall 82-86; rtd 86; Perm to Offic *Carl* from 86. *69 Lansdowne Crescent, Carlisle CA3 9ES* Carlisle (0228) 401177

TURNER, Canon Walter John. b 29. Bris Univ BA53. Clifton Th Coll 49. **d** 54 **p** 55. C W Bromwich All SS *Lich* 54-58; C-in-c Oxley 58-60; V 60-65; V Wednesfield St Thos 65-74; RD Shifnal 75-83; V Boningale 75-83; V Shifnal 75-83; Preb Lich Cathl 80-83; Can Res and Prec Lich Cathl from 83. *23 The Close, Lichfield, Staffs WS13 7LD* Lichfield (0543) 263337

TURNER, William Edward. b 41. Keble Coll Ox BA63 MA73. Linc Th Coll 76. **d** 78 **p** 79. C Lich St Chad *Lich* 78-80; Chapl Trent Poly *S'well* 80-89; Chapl Lancs (Preston) Poly *Blackb* from 89. *10 Queens Road, Fulwood, Preston PR2 3EA* Preston (0772) 717791

TURNHAM, Derek Lynn. b 52. Kelham Th Coll 71. **d** 75 **p** 76. C Worc St Martin w St Pet *Worc* 75-78; C Maidstone All SS w St Phil and H Trin *Cant* 78-81; C Maidstone All SS and St Phil w Tovil 81; V New Rossington *Sheff* 81-90; TR Thornaby on Tees *York* from 90. *Thornaby Rectory, Trenchard Avenue, Thornaby, Stockton-on-Tees, Cleveland TS17 0EF* Stockton-on-Tees (0642) 761655

TURNOCK, Geoffrey. MSOSc Leeds Univ BSc61 PhD64. E Midl Min Tr Course 84. **d** 87 **p** 88. NSM Oadby *Leic* from 87. *51 Brambling Way, Oadby, Leicester LE2 5PB* Leicester (0533) 714115

TURP, Paul Robert. b 48. Oak Hill Th Coll BA79. **d** 79 **p** 80. C Southall Green St Jo *Lon* 79-83; V Shoreditch St Leon w St Mich 83-88; TR Shoreditch St Leon and Hoxton St Jo from 88. *The Vicarage, 36 Hoxton Square, London N1 6NN* 071-739 2063

TURPIN, John Richard. b 41. St D Coll Lamp BA63 Magd Coll Cam BA65 MA70. Cuddesdon Coll 65. **d** 66 **p** 67. C Tadley St Pet *Win* 66-71; V Southn Thornhill St Chris 71-85; V Ringwood from 85. *The Vicarage, 65 Southampton Road, Ringwood, Hants BH24 1HE* Ringwood (0425) 473219

TURRALL, Albert Thomas George. b 19. Linc Th Coll 64. **d** 66 **p** 67. R Astley *Worc* 69-74; V Montford w Shrawardine *Lich* 74-77; R Montford w Shrawardine and Fitz 77-84; rtd 84; Perm to Offic *Heref* from 86; *Lich* from 87. *15 Whippley Close, Shrewsbury SY2 6SN* Shrewsbury (0743) 249831

TURRELL, Stephen John. b 35. S'wark Ord Course. **d** 83 **p** 84. NSM W Wickham St Jo *Cant* 83-84; NSM Addington S'wark from 85. *60 Courtfield Rise, West Wickham, Kent BR4 9EH* 081-462 6515

TURTLE, Malcolm. b 28. ACP66 FCollP88 CertEd51. Qu Coll Birm 77. **d** 80 **p** 81. NSM Worfield *Heref* 80-83; Dioc Schs Officer from 83; P-in-c Stoke Lacy, Moreton Jeffries w Much Cowarne etc 83-88; R from 88. *The Rectory, Stoke Lacy, Bromyard, Hereford HR7 4HH* Munderfield (0885) 490257

TURTON, Arthur Bickerstaffe. b 19. Oak Hill Th Coll 46. **d** 48 **p** 49. V Southborough St Pet w Ch Ch and St Matt *Roch* 68-76; V Histon *Ely* 76-82; rtd 84; Perm to Offic *Chich* from 82; Ely from 88. *20 St Peter's Drive, Chatteris, Cambs PE16 6BY* Chatteris (03543) 5551

TURTON, Douglas Walter. b 38. Kent Univ BA77 Surrey Univ MSc90. Oak Hill Th Coll 77. **d** 78 **p** 79. C Cant St Mary Bredin *Cant* 78-80; P-in-c Thornton Heath St Paul 80-81; V 81-84; V Thornton Heath St Paul *S'wark* 85-91; R Eastling w Ospringe and Stalisfield w Otterden *Cant* from 91. *The Rectory, Newnham Lane, Eastling, Faversham, Kent ME13 0AS* Eastling (079589) 487

TURTON, Neil Christopher. b 45. Wycliffe Hall Ox 77. **d** 79 **p** 80. C Guildf Ch Ch *Guildf* 79-83; C Godalming 83-86; V Wyke from 86. *Wyke Vicarage, Guildford Road, Normandy, Guildford, Surrey GU3 2DA* Guildford (0483) 811332

TURTON, Paul Edward. b 26. St Pet Hall Ox BA50 MA55. Qu Coll Birm 50. **d** 52 **p** 53. Perm to Offic *S'wark* 68-70; Dir of Educn *Nor* 70-75; Dep Dir Nat Soc Cen Camberwell 75-77; Dir Nat Soc RE Cen Kensington 78-84; C Eastbourne St Mary *Chich* 84-86; rtd 86; Perm to Offic *Chich* from 87. *32 Churchill Close, Eastbourne, E Sussex BN20 8AJ* Eastbourne (0323) 638089

TURVEY, Raymond Hilton. b 16. St Cath Coll Cam BA38 MA42. Ridley Hall Cam 38. **d** 40 **p** 41. V Leeds St Geo *Ripon* 58-72; V Onslow Square St Paul *Lon* 72-78; V Brompton H Trin 76-78; V Brompton H Trin w Onslow Square St Paul 78-80; rtd 80; Perm to Offic *Ox* from 83. *3 Peacock Road, Oxford OX3 0DQ* Oxford (0865) 246898

✠**TUSTIN, Rt Rev David.** b 35. Magd Coll Cam BA57 MA61. Cuddesdon Coll 58. **d** 60 **p** 61 **c** 79. C Stafford St Mary *Lich* 60-63; C St Dunstan in the West *Lon* 63-67; Asst Gen Sec C of E Coun on Foreign Relns 63-67; V Wednesbury St Paul Wood Green *Lich* 67-71; V Tettenhall Regis 71-79; RD Trysull 76-79; Suff Bp Grimsby *Linc* from 79; Can and Preb Linc Cathl from 79. *Bishop's House, Church Lane, Irby-upon-Humber, Grimsby, S Humberside DN37 7JR* Grimsby (0472) 371715

TUTE, James Stanley. b 11. Bps' Coll Cheshunt 30. **d** 34 **p** 35. V Stamford Hill St Bart *Lon* 56-80; rtd 81; Perm to Offic *Sarum* from 81. *24 Oakwood Drive, Iwerne Minster, Blandford Forum, Dorset DT11 8QT* Fontmell Magna (0747) 811761

TUTE, John Armytage. b 13. Lich Th Coll 37. **d** 40 **p** 41. R Hawkridge w Withypool *B & W* 66-80; rtd 80; Perm to Offic *Sarum* from 81. *24 Oakwood Drive, Iwerne Minster, Blandford Forum, Dorset DT11 8QT* Fontmell Magna (0747) 811761

TUTTON, Canon John Knight. b 30. Man Univ BSc51. Ripon Hall Ox 53. **d** 55 **p** 56. C Tonge w Alkrington *Man* 55-57; C Bushbury *Lich* 57-59; R Blackley St Andr *Man* 59-67; R Denton Ch Ch from 67; Hon Can Man Cathl from 90. *Christ Church Rectory, 1 Windmill Lane, Denton, Manchester M34 3RN* 061-336 2126

TWADDELL, Canon William Reginald. b 33. TCD 61. **d** 62 **p** 63. C Belf Whiterock *Conn* 62-65; I Loughgilly w Clare *Arm* 65-71; I Milltown 71-84; I Portadown St Mark from 84; RD Kilmore from 86; Preb Arm Cathl from 88. *The Rectory, Brownstown Road, Portadown, Co Armagh BT62 3QA* Portadown (0762) 332368

TWEDDLE, David William Joseph. b 28. ATCL56 Dur Univ BSc50. Wycliffe Hall Ox 54. **d** 56 **p** 57. C Darlington H Trin *Dur* 56-60; P-in-c Prestonpans *Edin* 60-63; PV Linc Cathl *Linc* 63-65; C Pet St Jo *Pet* 65-71; Hon Min Can Pet Cathl from 68; V Southwick w Glapthorn 71-83; P-in-c Benefield 80-83; R Benefield and Southwick w Glapthorn from 83; RD Oundle 84-89. *The Vicarage, Southwick, Peterborough PE8 5BL* Oundle (0832) 74026

TWEED, Andrew. b 48. Univ of Wales (Cardiff) BA69. St Deiniol's Hawarden. **d** 81 **p** 84. NSM Llandrindod w Cefnllys *S & B* 81-87; NSM Llandrindod w Cefnllys and Disserth from 87. *Gwenallt, Wellington Road, Llandrindod Wells, Powys LD1 5NB* Llandrindod Wells (0597) 823671

TWEEDIE-SMITH, Ian David. b 60. Newc Univ BA83. Wycliffe Hall Ox 83. **d** 85 **p** 86. C Hatcham St Jas *S'wark* 85-89; C Bury St Edmunds St Mary *St E* from 89. *St Mary's House, 18 Vinery Road, Bury St Edmunds IP33 2JR* Bury St Edmunds (0284) 705035

TWENTYMAN, Trevor Lawrence Holme. b 35. Chich Th Coll 67. **d** 70 **p** 71. C N Holmwood *Guildf* 70; C Sheff Parson Cross St Cecilia *Sheff* 71; C S Kensington St Aug *Lon* 76-83; Colombia from 89. *c/o Sotwell Manor, Wallingford, Oxon*

TWIDELL, William James. b 30. St Mich Coll Llan 58. **d** 60 **p** 61. C Tonge w Alkrington *Man* 60-63; C High Wycombe All SS *Ox* 63-65; P-in-c Elkesley w Bothamsall S'well 65-66; V Bury St Thos *Man* 66-72; V Daisy Hill 72-84; R Flixton St Mich from 84; AD Stretford from 88. *The Rectory, 348 Church Road, Flixton, Urmston, Manchester M31 3HR* 061-748 2884

TWISLETON, Dr John Fiennes. b 48. St Jo Coll Ox MA73 DPhil73. Coll of Resurr Mirfield DipTh75. **d** 76 **p** 77. C New Bentley *Sheff* 76-79; P-in-c Moorends 79-80; V 80-86; USPG 86-90; Coll of the Ascension Selly Oak 86-87; Guyana 87-90; V Holbrooks *Cov* from 90. *St Luke's Vicarage, Rotherham Road, Coventry CV6 4FE* Coventry (0203) 688604

TWISLETON, Peter. b 50. Linc Th Coll. **d** 84 **p** 85. C Bodmin w Lanhydrock and Lanivet *Truro* 84-87; C Par 87-90; R St Breoke and Egloshayle from 90. *The Rectory, 31 Trevanion Road, Wadebridge, Cornwall PL27 7NZ* Wadebridge (0208) 812501

TWISLETON-WYKEHAM-FIENNES, Very Rev the Hon Oliver William. b 26. New Coll Ox BA54 MA55. Cuddesdon Coll 52. **d** 54 **p** 55. Can and Preb Linc Cathl *Linc* from 69; Dean Linc 69-89; rtd 89; Perm to Offic *Pet* from 89. *Home Farm House, Colsterworth, Grantham, Lincs NG33 5NE* Grantham (0476) 860811

TWISS, Dorothy Elizabeth. Gilmore Ho 68 Linc Th Coll 70. **dss** 71 **d** 87. Portsea St Mary *Portsm* 71-75; Chapl Asst RAF 78-91; TM Pewsey Team Min *Sarum* from 91. *The Vicarage, Cross Roads, Easton Royal, Pewsey, Wilts SN9 5LS* Marlborough (0672) 810970

TWITTY, Rosamond Jane. b 54. Univ of Wales (Ban) BSc75 CertEd76. Trin Coll Bris BA89. **d** 90. C Lt Thurrock St Jo *Chelmsf* from 90. *141 Southend Road, Grays, Essex RM17 5NP* Grays Thurrock (0375) 377249

TWOHIG, Dr Brian Robert. b 48. La Trobe Univ Victoria BA77 PhD86. St Mich Th Coll Crafers 70. **d** 72 **p** 73. Australia 72-78 and 80-82; C Leatherhead *Guildf* 78-80; TV New Windsor *Ox* from 82. *Church Lodge, St Alban's Street, Windsor, Berks SL4 1PF* Windsor (0753) 865157

TWOMEY, Jeremiah Thomas Paul. b 46. CITC 87. **d** 87 **p** 88. C Derryloran *Arm* 87-90; I Brackaville w Donaghendry and Ballyclog from 90. *27 Ferguy Heights, Cookstown, Co Tyrone BT80 8EE* Cookstown (06487) 64852

TWYCROSS, Christopher John. **d** 64 **p** 65. P-in-c Shenley *St Alb* from 90; Chapl Shenley Hosp Radlett Herts from 90. *The Rectory, 63 London Road, Shenley, Radlett, Herts WD7 9BW* Radlett (0923) 855383

TWYCROSS, Stephen Jervis. b 33. Nottm Univ BEd73 Leic Univ MA85. Lambeth STh88 Kalk Bay Bible Inst S Africa 56 Wycliffe Hall Ox 58. **d** 60 **p** 61. C Hinckley H Trin *Leic* 60-64; V Barlestone 64-71; NSM Dio Leic 71-87; P-in-c Stokesay *Heref* 87-91; P-in-c Sibdon Carwood w Halford 87-91; Chapl Utrecht w Amersfoort, Harderwijk & Zwolle *Eur* from 91. *van Hogendorpstraat 26, 3581 KE Utrecht, The Netherlands* Utrecht (30) 513424

TWYFORD, Canon Arthur Russell. b 36. ALCD60. **d** 60 **p** 61. C Speke All SS *Liv* 60-64; Asst Dioc Youth Officer *Ox* 64-70; R Maids Moreton w Foxcote 64-72; P-in-c Lillingstone Dayrell w Lillingstone Lovell 70-72; V Desborough *Pet* 72-88; P-in-c Braybrook 73-77; P-in-c Brampton Ash w Dingley 73-77; R Brampton Ash w Dingley and Braybrooke 77-88; RD Kettering 79-87; Can Pet Cathl from 81; R Stanwick w Hargrave from 88. *The Rectory, Stanwick, Wellingborough, Northants NN9 6PP* Wellingborough (0933) 622317

TWYMAN, George Charles William. b 12. ISO. ARICS36 FRICS73. S'wark Ord Course 71. **d** 72 **p** 73. C Wandsworth All SS *S'wark* 72-75; P-in-c Kings Nympton Ex 75-79 and 81-83; C S Molton, Nymet St George, High Bray etc 79-83; P-in-c Romansleigh 81-83; rtd 83; Perm to Offic *Chich* 84-91. *15 Oak House, Alasdair Place, Claydon, Suffolk IP6 0ET* Ipswich (0473) 832233

TYDEMAN, Canon Richard. b 16. St Jo Coll Ox BA39 MA43. Ripon Hall Ox 38. **d** 39 **p** 40. R St Sepulchre w Ch Ch Greyfriars etc *Lon* 63-81; Dep Min Can St Paul's Cathl 63-81; Preacher Lincoln's Inn 72-81; rtd 81; Perm to Offic *St E* from 82. *10 Colneis Road, Felixstowe, Suffolk IP11 9HP* Felixstowe (0394) 283214

TYE, Eric John. b 37. St Alb Minl Tr Scheme. **d** 81 **p** 82. NSM Rushden w Newton Bromswold *Pet* from 81. *24 Lodge Road, Rushden, Northants NN10 9HA* Rushden (0933) 53274

TYE, John Raymond. b 31. Lambeth STh64 Linc Th Coll 66. **d** 68 **p** 69. C Crewe St Mich *Ches* 68-71; C Wednesfield St Thos *Lich* 71-76; P-in-c Petton w Cockshutt 76-79; P-in-c Hordley 79; P-in-c Weston Lullingfield 79; R Petton w Cockshutt and Weston Lullingfield etc 79-81; V Hadley 81-84; R Ightfield w Calverhall 84-89; V Ash 84-89; R Calton, Cauldon, Grindon and Waterfall from 89. *The Vicarage, Waterfall Lane, Waterhouses, Stoke-on-Trent ST10 3HT* Waterhouses (0538) 308506

TYE, Leslie Bernard. b 14. AKC40. **d** 40 **p** 41. V Ambergate *Derby* 69-79; rtd 79; Perm to Offic *Derby* from 79. *31 Cromwell Drive, Swanwick, Derby DE5 3TS* Leabrooks (0773) 602895

TYERS, Canon Gerald Seymour. b 22. St Pet Hall Ox BA46 MA49. Linc Th Coll 47. **d** 49 **p** 50. C Perry Street *Roch* 49-52; C Gillingham St Aug 52-53; V 60-67; V Orpington St Andr 53-60; V Erith Ch Ch 67-82; Chapl Erith and Distr Hosp 67-82; RD Erith 79-82; R Foots Cray *Roch* from 82; Hon Can Roch Cathl from 82. *The Rectory, Rectory Lane, Sidcup, Kent DA14 5BP* 081-300 7096

TYERS, Canon John Haydn. b 31. Lon Univ BSc51. Ridley Hall Cam 53. **d** 55 **p** 56. C Nuneaton St Nic *Cov* 55-58; C Rugby St Andr 58-62; V Cov St Anne 62-71; V Keresley and Coundon 71-78; V Atherstone 78-85; P-in-c Pleshey *Chelmsf* 85-91; Warden Pleshey Retreat Ho 85-91; Hon Can Chelmsf Cathl *Chelmsf* from 86; P-in-c Ash *Lich* from 91; P-in-c Ightfield w Calverhall from 91. *The Rectory, Ightfield, Whitchurch, Shropshire SY13 4NU* Calverhall (094876) 639

TYERS, Philip Nicolas. b 56. Nottm Univ BTh84. St Jo Coll Nottm 80. **d** 84 **p** 85. C Rugby St Matt *Cov* 84-88; TV Cov E from 88. *St Barnabas's Vicarage, 55 St Paul's Road, Coventry CV6 5DE* Coventry (0203) 688264

TYLDESLEY, Douglas Wilfred. b 31. CCC Cam BA54 MA58. Oak Hill Th Coll 54. **d** 56 **p** 57. C Skellingthorpe *Linc* 56-58; C Doddington 57-58; C Beckenham St Jo *Roch* 58-61; V Walthamstow St Luke *Chelmsf* 61-66; V Prestwold w Hoton *Leic* 66-72; R Sapcote 72-83; R Sapcote and Sharnford w Wigston Parva from 83. *The Rectory, 4 Sharnford Road, Sapcote, Leicester LE9 6JN* Sapcote (045527) 2215

TYLER, Alan William. b 60. Univ of Wales (Ban) DipTh84. Ridley Hall Cam 84. **d** 86 **p** 87. C Bedwellty *Mon* 86-89; C St Mellons and Michaelston-y-Fedw from 89. *The Rectory, Michaelston-y-Fedw, Cardiff CF3 9XS* Cardiff (0222) 680414

TYLER, Andrew. b 57. Univ of Wales (Lamp) BA79 Warw Univ MA80 Man Univ BD86. Coll of Resurr Mirfield 83. **d** 87 **p** 88. C Glen Parva and S Wigston *Leic* 87-90; C Didcot All SS *Ox* from 90. *All Saints' Curate's House, 114 Oxford Crescent, Didcot, Oxon OX11 7EA* Didcot (0235) 819470

TYLER, Mrs Frances Elizabeth. b 55. Linc Th Coll 81. **dss** 84 **d** 87. Hampton All SS *Lon* 84-87; Par Dn Brentford 87-91; NSM Walsgrave on Sowe *Cov* from 91. *The Vicarage, 4 Farber Road, Coventry CV2 2BG* Coventry (0203) 615152

TYLER, Preb Frank Cecil. b 08. AKC32. **d** 32 **p** 33. V Hillingdon St Jo *Lon* 49-77; Preb St Paul's Cathl 61-77; rtd 77. *The Vicarage, 4 Faber Road, Coventry CV2 2BG* Coventry (0203) 615152

TYLER, Mrs Gaynor. b 46. Univ of Wales (Abth) BA68. S'wark Ord Course 87. **d** 90. NSM Reigate St Luke S Park S'wark from 90. *2 Sheep Walk Cottage, The Clears, Reigate, Surrey RH2 9JQ* Reigate (0737) 247160

TYLER, John Arthur Preston. b 19. Em Coll Cam BA42 MA46. Wycliffe Hall Ox 42. **d** 44 **p** 45. R Ickham w Wickhambreaux and Stodmarsh *Cant* 65-85; rtd 85; Perm to Offic *Ox* 86-89; *Cant* from 89. *Church Orchard, Church Lane, Kingston, Canterbury, Kent CT4 6HY* Canterbury (0227) 830193

TYLER, John Thorne. b 46. Selw Coll Cam BA68 MA72. Sarum Th Coll 70. **d** 72 **p** 73. C Frome St Jo *B & W* 72-74; Chapl Huish Coll Taunton from 74; Hon C Stoke St Gregory w Burrowbridge and Lyng *B & W* from 77. *1 Borough Post, North Curry, Taunton, Somerset TA3 6NB* North Curry (0823) 490206

TYLER, Ven Leonard George. b 20. Liv Univ BA41 Ch Coll Cam BA46 MA50. Westcott Ho Cam. **d** 43 **p** 44. Prin Wm Temple Coll 66-73; R Easthampstead *Ox* 73-85; rtd 85; Perm to Offic *Ox* from 85. *11 Ashton Place, Kintbury, Newbury, Berks RG15 0XS* Kintbury (0488) 58510

TYLER, Malcolm. b 56. Kent Univ BSc77 Cam Univ BA84. Ridley Hall Cam 82. **d** 85 **p** 86. C Twickenham St Mary *Lon* 85-88; C Acton St Mary 88-91; V Walsgrave on Sowe *Cov* from 91. *The Vicarage, 4 Farber Road, Coventry CV2 2BG* Coventry (0203) 615152

TYLER, Paul Graham Edward. b 58. Cranmer Hall Dur. **d** 83 **p** 84. C Stranton *Dur* 83-86; C Collierley w Annfield Plain 86-89; V Esh from 89; V Hamsteels from 89. *The Vicarage, Church Street, Langley Park, Durham DH6 9TZ* 091-373 1344

TYLER, Samuel John. b 32. Lon Univ BD57. Oak Hill Th Coll 57. **d** 58 **p** 59. C W Ham All SS *Chelmsf* 58-61; V Berechurch 61-64; R Aythorpe w High and Leaden Roding 64-72; Perm to Offic 73-74; P-in-c Gt Ilford St Jo 74-76; V from 76. *St John's Vicarage, 2 Regent Gardens, Ilford, Essex IG3 8UL* 081-590 5884

TYLER (nee WAITE), Mrs Sheila Margaret. b 25. SRN47 Lon Univ DipTh73. Trin Coll Bris. **dss** 79 **d** 87. Easton H Trin w St Gabr and St Lawr *Bris* 79-80; Westbury-on-Trym St Alb 81-85; rtd 85; Hon Par Dn Henleaze *Bris* from 87; Chapl Stoke Park and Purdown Hosps Stapleton 88-90. *7 Remenham Drive, Henleaze, Bristol BS9 4HY* Bristol (0272) 628394

TYLER, William Stanley. b 12. Ripon Hall Ox 54. **d** 55 **p** 56. R Woodleigh and Loddiswell *Ex* 68-76; rtd 76. *5 Chatfield Crescent, Willingdon, Eastbourne, E Sussex BN22 0EZ* Eastbourne (0323) 501401

TYLER-WHITTLE, Michael Sidney. b 27. FRSL71 FLS77 Peterho Cam BA49 MA51. Wells Th Coll 53. **d** 55 **p** 56. C Wymondham *Nor* 55-58; Hon Chapl Bp Nor 57-59; PC Old Buckenham 58-69; Chapl UEA 65-67; Lic to Offic Nor 69-80; Eur 69-72; Chapl Amalfi Coast Eur 72-80; P-in-c Forton *Lich* 80-83; P-in-c Norbury 80-83; R Mereworth w W Peckham *Roch* 83-85; R Penshurst

and Fordcombe from 85. *Penshurst Rectory, Tonbridge, Kent TN11 8BN* Penshurst (0892) 870316

TYMMS, Canon Wilfrid Widdas. b 18. Ch Coll Cam BA40 MA44. Linc Th Coll 40. **d** 41 **p** 42. R Middleton St Geo *Dur* 70-78; Can Res Dur Cathl 78-83; rtd 83. *9A Low Road, Gainford, Darlington, Co Durham DL2 3DW* Darlington (0325) 730086

TYNDALE-BISCOE, John Annesley. b 08. Cam Univ BA33 MA61. Westcott Ho Cam 34. **d** 34 **p** 35. R Gilston w Eastwick *St Alb* 60-76; rtd 76; Perm to Offic *Chelmsf* from 76. *33 Hadleigh Road, Frinton-on-Sea, Essex CO13 9HQ* Frinton-on-Sea (0255) 671520

TYNDALE-BISCOE, William Francis. b 04. Trin Coll Ox BA25 MA29. Westcott Ho Cam 27. **d** 28 **p** 29. SSF from 37; Cen Africa 62-74; Australia 74-77 and from 86; Melanesia 77-86; rtd 86. *Hermitage of St Bernadine, Stroud, NSW, Australia 2425*

TYNDALL, Mrs Elizabeth Mary. b 30. St Andr Univ MA51 DipEd52 DPS82. Qu Coll Birm 81. **dss** 83 **d** 87. Rugby St Andr *Cov* 83-87; Par Dn Feltham *Lon* from 87. *39A St Dunstan's Road, Feltham, Middx 081-751 4075*

TYNDALL, Jeremy Hamilton. b 55. St Jo Coll Nottm BTh81 LTh81. **d** 81 **p** 82. C Oakwood St Thos *Lon* 81-84; C Upper Holloway St Pet w St Jo 84-87; TV Halewood *Liv* from 87. *The Rectory, 3 Rectory Drive, Halewood, Liverpool L26 6LJ* 051-487 5610

TYNDALL, Simon James. b 54. Lon Univ BSc(Econ)77 PGCE82. St Jo Coll Nottm 88. **d** 90 **p** 91. C Yeovil w Kingston Pitney *B & W* from 90. *67 Preston Grove, Yeovil BA20 2BJ* Yeovil (0935) 25452

TYNDALL, Canon Timothy Gardner. b 25. Jes Coll Cam BA50. Wells Th Coll 50. **d** 51 **p** 52. V Sherwood *S'well* 60-75; P-in-c Bishopwearmouth St Mich w St Hilda *Dur* 75-85; RD Wearmouth 75-85; Hon Can Dur Cathl from 83; Chief Sec ACCM 85-90; rtd 90; Perm to Offic *Lon* from 90. *27 Beverley Road, London W4 2LP* 081-994 4516

TYNEY, James Derrick. b 33. TCD. **d** 62 **p** 63. C Ballynafeigh St Jude *D & D* 62-64; C Ban St Comgall 64-69; I Clonallon w Warrenpoint 69-75; I Groomsport from 75; RD Ban from 91. *32 Bangor Road, Bangor, Co Down BT19 2JF* Bangor (0247) 464476

TYRER, Ms Jayne Linda. b 59. Golds Coll Lon BA81 CertEd82. Sarum & Wells Th Coll 85. **d** 87. C Rochdale *Man* 87-88; Par Dn Heywood St Luke w All So 88-91; Hon Par Dn Burneside *Carl* from 91. *All Souls' Vicarage, 173 Rochdale Road East, Heywood, Lancs OL10 1QU* Heywood (0706) 624005

TYRRELL, Canon Charles Robert. b 51. SRN73 Open Univ BA80. Oak Hill Th Coll 74. **d** 77 **p** 78. C Halewood *Liv* 77-80; C St Helens St Helen 80-83; V Banks 83-88; New Zealand from 88; Can Wellington from 88. *9 Williamson Way, Karori, Wellington, New Zealand* Wellington (4) 763511

TYRRELL, Frank Englefield. b 20. DSC44 VRD. Qu Coll Birm 70. **d** 72 **p** 73. C S Gillingham *Roch* 72-76; Chapl N Staffs R Infirmary Stoke-on-Trent 76-78; Chapl Stoke-on-Trent City Hosp 76-78; rtd 86. *Daneway, 2 Minfford, Tyn-y-Gongl, Gwynedd* Tyn-y-Gongl (0248) 853104

TYRRELL, John Patrick Hammond. b 42. Cranmer Hall Dur 62. **d** 65 **p** 66. C Edin St Jo *Edin* 65-68; Chapl RN 68-72; Hong Kong 72-74 and 79-82; R Westborough *Guildf* 74-78; C Yateley *Win* 82-83; C-in-c Darby Green CD 83-88; V Darby Green from 88. *St Barnabas House, Green Lane, Blackwater, Camberley, Surrey GU17 0NU* Yateley (0252) 877817

TYRRELL, Stephen Jonathan. b 39. Sheff Univ BA62. Clifton Th Coll. **d** 65 **p** 66. C Rodbourne Cheney *Bris* 65-68; C Lillington *Cov* 68-72; P-in-c Bishop's Itchington 73-78; V 78-86; V Kingston upon Hull St Nic *York* from 86. *St Nicholas's Vicarage, 898 Hessle High Road, Hull HU4 6SA* Hull (0482) 507944

TYSOE, James Raymond. b 19. Qu Coll Birm 70. **d** 75 **p** 76. NSM Cov E *Cov* 75-85; NSM Cov Cathl from 85. *Primrose Cottage, Norton Lindsey, Warwick CV35 8JN* Claverdon (092684) 2522

TYSON, John Wood Worsley. b 22. ACII50. Ripon Hall Ox 54. **d** 56 **p** 57. V Sneinton St Steph w St Alb *S'well* 59-87; rtd 87. *5 St Peter's Court, 398 Woodborough Road, Nottingham NG3 4JF* Nottingham (0602) 856177

TYSON, Peter. b 47. Reading Univ BSc70 MSc75. Trin Coll Bris 87. **d** 89 **p** 90. C Walsall *Lich* from 89. *164 Birmingham Road, Walsall WS1 2NJ* Walsall (0922) 645445

TYSON, Canon William Edward Porter. b 25. St Cath Coll Cam BA49 MA52. Ridley Hall Cam 49. **d** 51 **p** 52. V Over Tabley *Ches* 62-70; V High Legh 62-70; CF (TA) 64-91; V Church Hulme *Ches* 70-91; Chapl Cranage Hall

Hosp 70-91; Hon Can Ches Cathl *Ches* from 82; RD Congleton 85-90; rtd 91. *Cairngorm, Kirkhead Road, Allithwaite, Grange-over-Sands, Cumbria LA11 7DD* Grange-over-Sands (05395) 35291

TYTE, Ven Keith Arthur Edwin. b 31. St D Coll Lamp BA55. **d** 57 **p** 58. C Mynyddislwyn *Mon* 57-61; C Llanfrechfa All SS 61-64; V Bettws 64-71; V Griffithstown 71-77; RD Pontypool 74-77; Can St Woolos Cathl from 77; V Malpas 77-87; Adn Mon from 86; R Llanmartin from 87. *The Rectory, Llanmartin, Newport, Gwent NP6 2EB* Llanwern (0633) 412661

✠TYTLER, Rt Rev Donald Alexander. b 25. Ch Coll Cam BA47 MA52. Ridley Hall Cam 47. **d** 49 **p** 50 **c** 82. C Yardley St Edburgha *Birm* 49-52; SCM Sec Birm Univ 52-55; Prec Birm Cathl 55-57; Dir RE 57-63; V Londonderry 63-72; RD Warley 63-72; Hon Can Birm Cathl 71-72; Can Res Birm Cathl 72-77; Adn Aston and Can Res Birm Cathl 77-82; Suff Bp Middleton *Man* from 82. *The Hollies, Manchester Road, Rochdale, Lancs OL11 3QY* Rochdale (0706) 358550

TYZACK, Canon Leonard George. b 37. BA DipTh. Chich Th Coll. **d** 63 **p** 64. C Folkestone St Mary and St Eanswythe *Cant* 63-67; Abp's Dom Chapl 67-69; C-in-c Buckland Valley CD 69-72; R Buckland in Dover w Buckland Valley from 72; RD Dover 81-86; Hon Can Cant Cathl from 83; Dir of Ords *Eur* from 86. *St Andrew's Rectory, London Road, Dover, Kent CT17 0TF* Dover (0304) 201324

U

UCHIDA, Job Minoru. b 28. St Paul's Univ Tokyo BA51. **d** 54 **p** 55. Japan 54-56 and 59-86; SSM 56-59; Chapl to Japanese in England from 89. *St Martin's Cottage, Hale Gardens, London W3 9SQ* 081-993 4227

UDALL, Dr Geoffrey Sturt. b 17. Cam Univ MA MB BChir. Ripon Coll Cuddesdon 82. **d** 82 **p** 83. NSM Reading St Matt *Ox* 82-86; Asst RD Reading from 85; NSM Whitley Ch Ch from 86. *Trunkwell Fields, Beech Hill, Reading RG7 2AT* Reading (0734) 883252

UDY, John Francis. b 24. E Midl Min Tr Course 78. **d** 81 **p** 82. NSM Kirton in Holland *Linc* from 81; NSM Sutterton w Fosdyke and Algarkirk from 89. *26 Grosvenor Road, Frampton, Boston, Lincs PE20 1DB* Boston (0205) 722043

UFFINDELL, David Wilfred George. b 37. Qu Coll Birm 72. **d** 75 **p** 76. NSM Harlescott *Lich* from 75. *13 Kenley Avenue, Heath Farm, Shrewsbury SY1 3HA* Shrewsbury (0743) 52029

UFFINDELL, Harold David. b 61. Down Coll Cam MA87. Wycliffe Hall Ox BA86 MA91 Oak Hill Th Coll 86. **d** 87 **p** 88. C Kingston Hill St Paul *S'wark* 87-91; C Surbiton St Matt from 91. *127 Hamilton Avenue, Surbiton, Surrey KT6 7QA* 081-397 4294

UNDERDOWN, Steven. b 61. Hull Univ BSc75 CertEd76. **d** 88. CSWG from 82; Lic to Offic *Chich* from 88. *The Monastery, Crawley Down, Crawley, W Sussex RH10 4LH* Copthorne (0342) 712074

UNDERHILL, Edward Mark Thomas. b 24. Univ Coll Dur BA50. St Aid Birkenhead 50. **d** 52 **p** 53. C Meopham *Roch* 52-54; Kenya 55-57; PC Gateshead St Geo *Dur* 57-68; V Gateshead St Geo from 68. *St George's Vicarage, 327 Durham Road, Gateshead, Tyne & Wear NE9 5AJ* 091-487 5587

UNDERHILL, Very Rev Michael Leeke. b 10. CBE. Qu Coll Ox BA34 MA38. Westcott Ho Cam 34. **d** 35 **p** 36. C Millom H Trin *Carl* 35-38; New Zealand from 38; Dean Christchurch 66-81. *95 Church Street, Rangiora, New Zealand* Rangiora (502) 313-5261

UNDERHILL, Stanley Robert. b 27. Cant Sch of Min. **d** 82 **p** 83. C New Addington *Cant* 82-84; C Cannock *Lich* 84-86; TV 86-88; R Dymchurch w Burmarsh and Newchurch *Cant* from 88. *The New Rectory, 135 High Street, Dymchurch, Romney Marsh, Kent TN29 0LD* Dymchurch (0303) 872150

UNDERWOOD, Brian. b 35. Dur Univ BA57 Keble Coll Ox PGCE76 Dur Univ MA72. Clifton Th Coll 57. **d** 59 **p** 60. C Blackpool Ch Ch *Blackb* 59-61; C New Malden and Coombe *S'wark* 61-64; Travel Sec Pathfinders 64-68; Chapl Chantilly *Eur* 68-69; Home Sec CCCS 69-71; P-in-c Gatten St Paul *Portsm* 71-72; Chapl Lyon w Grenoble and Aix-les-Bains *Eur* 72-75; Lic to Offic *Derby* 76-80; *Blackb* 80-85; Asst Chapl Trent Coll Nottm 76-80; Chapl Qu Eliz Gr Sch *Blackb* 80-85; R Bentham

St Jo *Bradf* from 85. *The Rectory, Bentham, Lancaster LA2 7DD* Bentham (05242) 61422

UNDERWOOD, Charles Brian. b 23. Leeds Univ BA48 CertEd. Coll of Resurr Mirfield 48. **d** 50 **p** 51. Dioc Youth Chapl *Bradf* 63-72; R Carleton-in-Craven 63-76; V Twyning *Glouc* 76-88; RD Tewkesbury 81-88; rtd 88. *9 Ellendene Drive, Pamington, Tewkesbury, Glos GL20 8LU* Bredon (0684) 72504

UNDERWOOD, David Richard. b 47. AKC St Osyth Coll of Educn CertEd. St Aug Coll Cant. **d** 70. NSM Chevington w Hargrave and Whepstead w Brockley *St E* from 82. *8 Barn Field, Chevington, Bury St Edmunds, Suffolk* Bury St Edmunds (0284) 850610

UNDERWOOD, Jack Maurice. b 13. Leeds Univ BA36 Lon Univ BD41. Coll of Resurr Mirfield 36. **d** 38 **p** 39. Prin Stroud Court Ox 60-71; Perm to Offic *Eur* 73-78; rtd 78. *Willow Lea, Hatford, Faringdon, Oxon* Stanford in the Vale (0367) 710364

UNDERWOOD, Canon James Derrick. b 09. Trin Hall Cam BA33 MA39. Linc Th Coll 34. **d** 35 **p** 36. Hon Can S'wark Cathl *S'wark* 61-71; R Oxted 65-71; RD Godstone 66-71; rtd 71. *27 Gresham Road, Oxted, Surrey RH8 0BU* Oxted (0883) 715302

UNDERWOOD, Luke William. b 21. SW Minl Tr Course. **d** 85 **p** 86. NSM Duloe w Herodsfoot *Truro* 85-87; P-in-c 87-89; rtd 89. *Harewold, Tredinnick, Duloe, Liskeard, Cornwall PL14 4PJ* Looe (05036) 3541

UNGOED-THOMAS, Peter. Pemb Coll Ox BA51 MA67. St Mich Coll Llan. **d** 60 **p** 61. C Llangeinor *Llan* 60-64; I Dub Donnybrook *D & G* 64-67; RAChD 67-70; Chapl Leigh C of E Schs 70-74; C Leigh St Mary *Man* 70-74; Lect Warley Coll 74-86; Perm to Offic *Birm & St D* from 75; Lect Sandwell Coll of F&HE from 86. *93 Heol Felin-Foel, Llanelli, Dyfed SA15 3JQ*

UNSWORTH, Thomas Foster. b 28. Lon Univ BA56. Lich Th Coll 60. **d** 62 **p** 63. V Leyburn *Ripon* 68-73; V Bellerby 68-73; Chapl Whittingham Hosp Preston 73-79; V Freckleton *Blackb* 79-83; V S Yardley St Mich *Birm* 83-86; V Sutton w Carlton and Normanton upon Trent etc *S'well* 86-90; rtd 90; Chapl St Raphael *Eur* from 90. *Oakdell Lodge, 16 Page Heath Lane, Bickley, Kent BR1 2DS*

UNWIN, Christopher Michael Fairclough. b 31. Dur Univ BA57. Linc Th Coll 65. **d** 67 **p** 68. C S Shields St Hilda w St Thos *Dur* 67-73; R Tatsfield *S'wark* 73-81; RE Adv to Ch Secondary Schs 73-81; V Newc St Gabr *Newc* from 81. *St Gabriel's Vicarage, 9 Holderness Road, Heaton, Newcastle upon Tyne NE6 5RH* 091-276 3957

UNWIN, Christopher Philip. b 17. TD63. Magd Coll Cam BA39 MA63. Qu Coll Birm 39. **d** 40 **p** 41. Adn Northd and Can Res Newc Cathl *Newc* 63-82; rtd 82. *60 Sandringham Avenue, Benton, Newcastle upon Tyne NE12 8JX* 091-270 0418

UNWIN, Ven Kenneth. b 26. St Edm Hall Ox BA48 MA52. Ely Th Coll 49. **d** 51 **p** 52. C Leeds All SS *Ripon* 51-55; C Dur St Marg *Dur* 55-59; V Dodworth *Wakef* 59-69; V Royston 69-73; V Wakef St Jo 73-82; Hon Can Wakef Cathl 80-82; RD Wakef 80-81; Adn Pontefract from 82. *19A Tithe Barn Street, Horbury, Wakefield, W Yorkshire WF4 6JL* Wakefield (0924) 263777

UNWIN, Percival Alexander. b 04. St Jo Coll Dur BA28 DipTh29 MA33. **d** 29 **p** 30. V Canford Magna *Sarum* 61-71; rtd 71; Perm to Offic *Win* from 81. *58 Canon Street, Winchester, Hants SO23 9JW* Winchester (0962) 65481

UNWIN, Reginald Christopher. b 02. TD78. St Jo Coll Dur BA24 DipTh25 MA29. **d** 25 **p** 26. R Ousby w Melmerby *Carl* 65-68; rtd 68; P-in-c Bishopwearmouth St Gabr *Dur* 69; Perm to Offic from 69. *The Close, 13 Sea View Park, Whitburn, Tyne & Wear SR6 7JS* 091-529 3492

UPCOTT, Derek Jarvis. b 26. CEng FIMechE FBIM. S'wark Ord Course 81. **d** 84 **p** 85. NSM Gt Chesham *Ox* from 84; Perm to Offic *St Alb* from 90. *Bluff Cottage, Blackthorne Lane, Ballinger, Great Missenden, Bucks HP16 9LN* The Lee (024020) 505

UPHILL, Keith Ivan. b 35. Keble Coll Ox BA70 MA74. Wycliffe Hall Ox 67. **d** 70 **p** 71. C Maghull *Liv* 70-73; V Wroxall *Portsm* 73-77; TV Fareham H Trin 77-82; C Havant 82-84; P-in-c Mert St Jo *S'wark* 84-85; V from 85. *St John's Vicarage, High Path, London SW19 2JY* 081-542 3283

UPRICHARD, Horace Launcelot. b 17. TCD BA42 MA47. **d** 42 **p** 43. I Drumbeg *D & D* 53-82; rtd 82. *3 Fairview Drive, Upper Malone, Belfast BT9 5ND* Belfast (0232) 616380

UPRICHARD, Jervis. b 17. **d** 42 **p** 43. V Edgeside *Man* 60-66; rtd 82; Perm to Offic *Man* from 82. *14 Chestnut Drive, Rawtenstall, Lancs* Rossendale (0706) 211502

UPTON, Anthony Arthur. b 30. Wells Th Coll 61. d 63 p 64. C Milton *Portsm* 63-67; Chapl RN 67-83; V Foleshill St Laur *Cov* from 83. *St Laurence's Vicarage, 142 Old Church Road, Coventry CV6 7ED* Coventry (0203) 688271

UPTON, Clement Maurice. b 49. Linc Th Coll 88. d 90 p 91. C Northn St Alb *Pet* from 90. *12 Oulton Rise, Northampton NN3 1EW* Northampton (0604) 492965

UPTON, Donald George Stanley. b 16. Peterho Cam BA38 MA44. Westcott Ho Cam 39. d 40 p 41. Lic to Offic St Alb from 69; Chapl St Alb High Sch for Girls 69-73; Ch Hosp Sch Hertf 73-80; rtd 81. *The Pump House, Braughing, Ware, Herts SG11 2QS*

UPTON, Julie. b 61. Ripon Coll Cuddesdon 87. d 88. C Kirkstall *Ripon* 88-91; Par Dn E Greenwich Ch Ch w St Andr and St Mich *S'wark* from 91. *52 Earlswood Street, London SE10 9ES* 081-853 5950

UPTON, Kenneth Roy. b 19. K Coll Cam BA40 MA48. Oak Hill Th Coll 46. d 48 p 49. V Derby St Chad *Derby* 65-86; rtd 86; Perm to Offic *Derby* from 86. *31 Stone Hill Road, Derby DE3 6TJ* Derby (0332) 43765

UPTON, Michael Gawthorne. b 29. AKC53. d 54 p 55. C Middleton *Man* 54-57; C Plymouth St Andr *Ex* 57-59; Dep Dir of Educn *Cant* 59-63; Hon C Riverhead *Roch* 63-70; Youth Chapl 63-70; Lic to Offic *Ex* from 70; Chr Aid Area Sec (Devon and Cornwall) from 70; Chr Aid SW Region Co-ord 73-89. *Otter Dell, Harpford, Sidmouth, Devon EX10 0NH* Colaton Raleigh (0395) 68448

UPTON, Robert de Courcy Everard. b 26. Lon Univ DipTh57. St Aid Birkenhead. d 57 p 58. P-in-c Tilstock *Lich* 69-83; C Penn 83-85; C Harlescott 85-87; Perm to Offic from 87; rtd 88. *Riverside, Wollerton, Market Drayton, Shropshire TF9 3NB* Hodnet (063084) 495

URCH, Harold Henry. b 08. Roch Th Coll 59. d 60 p 61. R Sticklepath *Ex* 63-73; rtd 74. *Fosbrooke House, 8 Clifton Drive, Lytham, Lancs FY8 5RQ* Lytham (0253) 737291

UREN, Malcolm Lawrence. b 37. AKC63. d 64 p 65. C Cant St Martin w St Paul *Cant* 64-67; C Falmouth K Chas *Truro* 67-71; V St Blazey 71-79; P-in-c Tuckingmill 79-83; V 83-89; V Launceston St Steph w St Thos from 89. *8 St Cuthbert Close, Launceston, Cornwall* Launceston (0566) 2679

URQUHART, Colin. b 40. AKC62. d 63 p 64. C Cheshunt *St Alb* 63-67; C Norton 67-70; V Luton Lewsey St Hugh 70-76; Perm to Offic *Guildf* 76-78; Lic to Offic *Chich* from 78. *Kingdom Faith Ministries, 26 Redkiln Way, Horsham RH13 5QH* Horsham (0403) 210432

URQUHART, David Andrew. b 52. BA77. Wycliffe Hall Ox 82. d 84 p 85. C Kingston upon Hull St Nic *York* 84-87; TV Drypool from 87. *St Andrew's House, 2 Harcourt Drive, Hull HU9 2AR* Hull (0482) 23840

URQUHART, Edmund Ross. b 39. Univ Coll Ox BA62 DipTh63 MA68. St Steph Ho Ox 62. d 64 p 65. C Milton *Win* 64-69; C Norton *Derby* 69-73; V Bakewell from 73. *The Vicarage, Bakewell, Derbyshire DE4 1FD* Bakewell (0629) 812256

URSELL, Philip Elliott. b 42. Univ of Wales BA66 Ox Univ MA82. St Steph Ho Ox 66. d 68 p 69. C Newton Nottage *Llan* 68-71; Asst Chapl Univ of Wales (Cardiff) 71-77; Chapl Poly of Wales 74-77; Lic to Offic *Llan* from 77; Chapl Em Coll Cam 77-82; Prin Pusey Ho Ox from 82; Lic to Offic *Ox* from 82. *Pusey House, Oxford OX1 3LZ* Oxford (0865) 278415

URWIN, John Hope. b 09. Lich Th Coll 29. d 32 p 33. V Trysull *Lich* 60-74; rtd 74. *77 Fountain Fold, Gnosall, Stafford ST20 0DR* Stafford (0785) 822601

URWIN, Lindsay Goodall. b 55. Ripon Coll Cuddesdon 77. d 80 p 81. C Walworth *S'wark* 80-83; V N Dulwich St Faith 83-88; Dioc Missr *Chich* from 88. *1 New Dorset Street, Brighton BN1 3LL* Brighton (0273) 202497

URWIN, Preb Roger Talbot. b 22. Ex Coll Ox BA43 MA47. Sarum Th Coll 48. d 50 p 50. CF (R of O) 56-77; R Littleham w Exmouth *Ex* 66-72; TR 72-87; R Aylesbeare 69-73; P-in-c Withycombe Raleigh 72-74; Preb Ex Cathl 82-87; rtd 87. *Bishop's Lodge, Kelly Park, St Mabyn, Bodmin, Cornwall* St Mabyn (020884) 606

USHER, George. b 30. Univ of Wales (Swansea) BSc51. St Deiniol's Hawarden 73. d 75 p 76. NSM Clun w Chapel Lawn *Heref* 75-78; NSM Clun w Chapel Lawn, Bettws-y-Crwyn and Newc 79-80; C Shrewsbury St Giles *Lich* 80-83; C Shrewsbury St Giles w Sutton and Atcham 83-84; R Credenhill w Brinsop, Mansel Lacey, Yazor etc *Heref* from 84. *St Mary's Rectory, Credenhill, Hereford HR4 7DL* Hereford (0432) 760687

USHER, Robin Reginald. b 50. AKC74. St Aug Coll Cant 75. d 76 p 77. C Hulme Ascension *Man* 76-80; P-in-c

Newall Green 80-85; C Atherton 85-87; TV 87-90; V Leigh St Jo from 90. *The Vicarage, Gordon Street, Leigh, Lancs WN7 1RT* Leigh (0942) 672868

UTLEY, Canon Edward Jacob. b 24. AKC52. d 53 p 54. C Bexhill St Pet *Chich* 56-60; Chapl Asst Bexhill Hosp 56-60; Chapl Dudley Road Hosp Birm from 60; RD Birm City 75-82; Hon Can Birm Cathl 80-89; rtd 89; Perm to Offic *Birm* from 89. *St Raphael, 50 Wheatsheaf Road, Birmingham B16 0RY* 021-454 2666

UTTLEY, Mrs Valerie Gail. b 43. Man Univ BA64. N Ord Course 80. dss 83 d 87. Otley *Bradf* 83-87; Hon Par Dn 87-89; Par Dn Calverley from 89. *11 St Richard's Road, Otley, W Yorkshire LS21 2AL* Otley (0943) 463722

V

VAIL, David William. b 30. Dur Univ BA56 Sheff Univ DipEd71. Oak Hill Th Coll 56. d 58 p 59. C Toxteth Park St Bede *Liv* 58-61; Kenya 61-77; Chapl Versailles *Eur* 77-82; Gen Sec Rwanda Miss 82-88; V Virginia Water *Guildf* from 88. *Christ Church Vicarage, Virginia Water, Surrey GU25 4LD* Wentworth (0344) 842374

VAIZEY, Martin John. b 37. AKC64. d 65 p 66. C Bishopwearmouth Gd Shep *Dur* 65-69; C Darlington H Trin 69-72; V Easington Colliery 72-80; C-in-c Bishopwearmouth St Mary V w St Pet CD 80-85; V Sunderland Springwell w Thorney Close 85-88; R Witton Gilbert from 88. *The Rectory, Witton Gilbert, Durham DH7 6ST* 091-371 0376

VALE, David Phipps. b 37. Lon Univ BSc64. St Steph Ho Ox 64. d 66 p 67. C Chiswick St Nic w St Mary *Lon* 66-70; Trinidad and Tobago 70-72; Ind Chapl *Wakef* 72-73; V Huddersfield St Andr 72-73; Asst Chapl St Olave and St Sav Sch Orpington 73-75; Perm to Offic *St E* 76-78; Hon C Ipswich St Clem w H Trin 78-80; TV Wolstanton *Lich* 80-89; V Ramsbottom St Jo and St Paul *Man* from 89. *St Paul's Vicarage, Maple Grove, Ramsbottom, Bury, Lancs BL0 0AN* Ramsbottom (0706) 821036

VALE, Thomas Stanley George. b 52. Chich Th Coll 85. d 87 p 88. C Leic St Phil *Leic* 87-90; C Knighton St Mary Magd from 90. *41 Cairnsford Road, West Knighton, Leicester LE2 6GC* Leicester (0533) 886097

VALENTINE, Derek William. b 24. S'wark Ord Course 65. d 68 p 69. NSM Battersea St Luke *S'wark* 68-77; NSM Fenstanton *Ely* 77-88; Perm to Offic *Bradf* from 88. *4 Woodland Drive, Skipton, N Yorkshire BD23 1QU* Skipton (0756) 69399

VALENTINE, Hugh William James. b 56. Bradf Univ BA83 CQSW. S'wark Ord Course 86. d 89 p 90. NSM Stoke Newington Common St Mich *Lon* from 89. *4 Leigh House, 1 Halcrow Street, London E1 2HF* 071-377 7500

VALENTINE, Jeremy Wilfred. b 38. NW Ord Course 76. d 79 p 80. C Cundall *Ripon* 79-82; TV Huntington *York* 82-87; V Sand Hutton from 87. *The Vicarage, Sand Hutton, York YO4 1LB* Flaxton Moor (090486) 443

VALENTINE, Robin James. b 41. Lich Th Coll 63. d 66 p 67. C Ipswich All Hallows *St E* 66-69; C Staveley *Derby* 69-73; P-in-c Pleasley 74-81; C Mackworth St Fran from 81. *St Francis House, Collingham Gardens, Mackworth Estate, Derby DE3 4FQ* Derby (0332) 383288

VALLINS, Christopher. b 43. Lich Th Coll 63. d 66 p 67. C Cuddington *Guildf* 66-70; C Aldershot St Mich 70-73; V W Ewell 73-81; R Worplesdon 81-89; Chapl Merrist Wood Coll of Agric 81-89; RD Guildf 86-89; Chapl Epsom Distr Hosp from 89. *The Chaplain's Office, Epsom District Hospital, Dorking Road, Epsom, Surrey KT18 7EG* Epsom (0372) 726100

VAMPLEW, Peter Gordon. Jes Coll Cam BA57 MA61. Ridley Hall Cam 57. d 59 p 60. C Tooting Graveney St Nic *S'wark* 59-65; C Poole *Sarum* 70-76. *Address temp unknown*

VAN CARRAPIETT, Timothy Michael James. b 39. Chich Th Coll 60. d 63 p 64. C Sugley *Newc* 63-65; C Newc St Fran 65-69; P-in-c Wrangbrook w N Elmsall CD *Wakef* 69-74; P-in-c Flushing *Truro* 74-75; P-in-c Mylor w Flushing 75-76; P-in-c St Day 76-82; R Aldrington *Chich* 82-87; V Bexhill St Barn from 87. *The Vicarage, Cantelupe Road, Bexhill-on-Sea, E Sussex TN40 1JG* Bexhill-on-Sea (0424) 212036

VAN CULIN, Canon Samuel. b 30. Princeton Univ AB52. Virginia Th Sem DB55 Hon DD. d 55 p 56. USA 55-83; Hon Can Cant Cathl *Cant* from 83; Sec Gen ACC from

83. *c/o ACC, Partnership House, 157 Waterloo Road, London SE1 8UT* 071-620 1110

VAN DE KASTEELE, Peter John. b 39. Magd Coll Cam BA61 MA65. Clifton Th Coll 61. **d** 63 **p** 64. C Eastbourne H Trin *Chich* 63-66; C N Pickenham w S Pickenham etc *Nor* 66-70; R Mursley w Swanbourne and Lt Horwood *Ox* 70-80; Perm to Offic *Glouc* 83-88; Admin Sec Clinical Th Assn from 83; Gen Dir from 88; Hon C Westcote w Icomb and Bledington from 88. *St Mary's House, Church Westcote, Oxford OX7 6SF* Shipton-under-Wychwood (0993) 830209

van de WEYER, Robert William Bates. b 50. Lanc Univ BA76. S'wark Ord Course 78. **d** 81 **p** 82. Warden Lt Gidding Community from 77; Hon C Gt w Lt Gidding and Steeple Gidding *Ely* 81-83; P-in-c from 83; P-in-c Winwick from 83; P-in-c Hamerton from 83; P-in-c Upton and Copmanford from 83. *Castle House, Leighton, Bromswold, Huntingdon, Cambs PE18 0SJ* Huntingdon (0480) 890333

VAN DEN BERG, Jan Jacob. b 56. Sarum & Wells Th Coll 86. **d** 88 **p** 89. C Glouc St Aldate *Glouc* 88-91; C Ollerton w Boughton *S'well* from 91. *The Glebe House, Church Road, Boughton, Newark, Notts NG22 9RJ* Mansfield (0623) 835665

VAN DER LINDE, Herbert John. b 43. Rhodes Univ Grahamstown BA66. Coll of Resurr Mirfield. **d** 68 **p** 69. C Kingston St Luke *S'wark* 68-75; C Chipping Campden w Ebrington *Glouc* 75-78; V Cheltenham St Pet 78-84; V Bussage from 84. *St Michael's Vicarage, Bussage, Stroud, Glos GL6 8BB* Brimscombe (0453) 883556

VAN DER PUMP, Charles Lyndon. b 25. ARCM. S'wark Ord Course 86. **d** 88 **p** 89. NSM Primrose Hill St Mary w Avenue Road St Paul *Lon* from 88. *48 Canfield Gardens, London NW6 3EB* 071-624 4517

VAN DER VALK, Jesse. b 59. Nottm Univ BTh84 PGCE85 Birm Univ MPhil88. St Jo Coll Nottm 81. **d** 88 **p** 89. C Droitwich Spa *Worc* from 88. *61 Drovers Way, Droitwich, Worcs WR9 9DA* Droitwich (0905) 772841

VAN GORDER, Lloyd Franklin. b 11. **d** 73 **p** 74. V Hartley Wintney and Elvetham *Win* 74-76; Perm to Offic *Chich* 76-78; *Portsm* from 79. *Hoxall Cottage, Hoxall Lane, Mottistone, Newport, Isle of Wight PO33 4EE* Isle of Wight (0983) 740235

VANDERSTOCK, Alan. b 31. **d** 59 **p** 60. C Kersal Moor *Man* 59-63. *14 Annsworthy Crescent, Grange Road, London SE25*

VANE, Walter Brian. b 21. Liv Univ BSc46 MA50. Coll of Resurr Mirfield 51. **d** 53 **p** 54. Hon C Heaton Norris Ch Ch *Man* 66-70; Lic to Offic Man & Ches 71-84; Chapl Costa del Sol W *Eur* 84-88; rtd 88. *6 The Mead, Cirencester, Glos GL7 2BB* Cirencester (0285) 653235

VANN, Ms Cherry Elizabeth. b 58. ARCM78 GRSM80. Westcott Ho Cam 86. **d** 89. Par Dn Flixton St Mich *Man* from 89. *350 Church Road, Flixton, Urmston, Manchester M31 3HR* 061-748 3568

VANN, Paul. b 41. St D Coll Lamp DipTh65. **d** 65 **p** 66. C Griffithstown *Mon* 65-67; C Llanfrechfa All SS 67-71; Dioc Youth Chapl 69-74; Chapl St Woolos Cathl 71-72; P-in-c Llanrumney 72-76; V from 76; Asst Chapl HM Pris Cardiff 75-78; RD Bassaleg *Mon* from 90. *The Vicarage, Countisbury Avenue, Cardiff CF3 9RN* Cardiff (0222) 792761

VANNOZZI, Peter. b 62. Lon Univ BA83 Ox Univ BA86. Ripon Coll Cuddesdon 84. **d** 87 **p** 88. C Kenton *Lon* 87-90; C Fleet *Guildf* from 90. *91 Kings Road, Fleet, Aldershot, Hants GU13 9AR* Fleet (0252) 614147

VANSTON, Ven William Francis Harley. b 24. TCD BA48 MA52. **d** 48 **p** 49. I Arklow w Inch *D & G* 67-73; I Arklow w Inch and Kilbride 73-89; RD Rathdrum 77-89; Adn Glendalough 83-89; rtd 89. *11 Seabank Court, Sandycove, Dun Laoghaire, Co Dublin, Irish Republic* Dublin (1) 280-4575

VANSTONE, Walford David Frederick. b 38. Open Univ BA81. AKC69. **d** 70 **p** 71. C Feltham *Lon* 70-75; TV E Runcorn w Halton *Ches* 75-80; V Grange St Andr 80-82; V Hampton All SS *Lon* from 82. *All Saints' Vicarage, 40 The Avenue, Hampton, Middx TW12 3RS* 081-979 2102

VANSTONE, Canon William Hubert. b 23. Ball Coll Ox BA48 St Jo Coll Cam BA50. Lambeth DLitt88 Westcott Ho Cam 48 Union Th Sem (NY) STM50. **d** 50 **p** 51. V Kirkholt *Man* 64-76; Hon Can Man Cathl 68-76; V Hattersley *Ches* 77-78; Can Res Ches Cathl 78-90; Six Preacher Cant Cathl *Cant* from 83; rtd 91. *6 Hodges Close, Tetbury, Glos* Tetbury (0666) 502689

VARAH, Preb Edward Chad. b 11. OBE69 RPC68 ASGM72 LDA74. Keble Coll Ox BA33 MA46 Leic Univ Hon LLD79. Linc Th Coll 34. **d** 35 **p** 36. C Linc St Giles *Linc* 35-38; C Putney St Mary *S'wark* 38-40; C

Barrow St Jo *Carl* 40-42; V Blackb H Trin *Blackb* 42-49; V Battersea St Paul *S'wark* 49-53; P-in-c St Steph Walbrook and St Swithun etc *Lon* 53-54; R from 54; Founder The Samaritans 53; Dir 53-74; Preb St Paul's Cathl *Lon* from 75. *St Stephen's Vestry, 39 Walbrook, London EC4N 8BP* 071-283 4444 or 626 8242

VARAH, Paul Hugh. b 46. St Deiniol's Hawarden 83. **d** 85 **p** 86. C Prestatyn *St As* 85-87; P-in-c Hawarden 87-88; TV 88-89; V Esclusham from 89. *The Vicarage, Vicarage Hill, Rhostyllen, Wrexham, Clwyd LL14 4AR* Wrexham (0978) 354438

VARGAS, Eric Arthur Dudley. b 27. BD. S Dios Minl Tr Scheme 81. **d** 83 **p** 84. C Farncombe *Guildf* 83-86; R Ockley w Okewood and Forest Green 86-90; V Kirdford *Chich* from 90. *The Vicarage, Kirdford, Billingshurst, W Sussex RH14 0LU* Kirdford (040377) 605

VARGESON, Peter Andrew. b 53. Wycliffe Hall Ox 85. **d** 87 **p** 88. C Yateley *Win* from 87. *18 Hall Farm Crescent, Yateley, Camberley, Surrey GU17 7HT* Yateley (0252) 876416

VARLEY, Robert. b 36. St Jo Coll Cam BA57 MA64. NW Ord Course 71. **d** 74 **p** 75. C Wallasey St Hilary *Ches* 74-77; V Rock Ferry 77-81; Perm to Offic *Man* 82-83; Hon C E Farnworth and Kearsley 83-86; Hon C Walkden Moor 86-87; C 87-89; V Lt Hulton 89-90. *66 Normanby Road, Worsley, Manchester M28 5TS* 061-790 8420

VARNEY, Donald James. b 35. Chich Th Coll 84. **d** 86. Hon C Liss *Portsm* from 86. *12 Birch Close, Liss, Petersfield, Hants GU33 7HS* Liss (0730) 893945

VARNEY, Peter David. b 38. Dur Univ BA61 MA64 Birm Univ DipTh63. Qu Coll Birm 61. **d** 64 **p** 65. C Newington St Paul *S'wark* 64-66; C Camberwell St Mich w All So w Em 66-67; Malaysia 67-68; Hon C Croxley Green All SS *St Alb* 69; Perm to Offic *Roch* 69-72 and 74-84; Asst Chapl Chapl Community St Jo Bapt Clewer 72-73; Asst Sec Chrs Abroad 74-79; Dir Bloxham Project 84-86; Perm to Offic *Cant* 84-85; S'wark 85-86; Nor from 89; P-in-c Thornage w Brinton w Hunworth and Stody *Nor* 87; P-in-c Briningham 87; P-in-c Melton Constable w Swanton Novers 87; Chapl Yare and Norvic Clinics and St Andr Hosp Nor from 90. *8 High Green, Norwich NR1 4AP* Norwich (0603) 34855

VARNEY, Stephen Clive. b 59. Qu Mary Coll Lon BSc80 Sussex Univ MSc82 Southn Univ BTh88. Sarum & Wells Th Coll 83. **d** 86 **p** 87. C Riverhead w Dunton Green *Roch* 86-91; V Bostall Heath from 91. *St Andrew's Parsonage, 276 Brampton Road, Bexleyheath, Kent DA7 5SF* 081-303 9332

VARNEY, Wilfred Davies. b 10. Sarum & Wells Th Coll 71. **d** 71 **p** 72. C Glouc St Paul *Glouc* 71-74; V Lydbrook 74-77; rtd 77; Hon C Felpham w Middleton *Chich* 77-80; Hon C Overbury w Alstone, Teddington and Lt Washbourne *Worc* 80-82; P-in-c Nor St Andr *Nor* 87-91; Perm to Offic 82-87 and from 91. *12 Westwood House, 75 Edinburgh Road, Norwich NR2 3RL* Norwich (0603) 627021

VARNEY, William James Granville. b 22. St D Coll Lamp 62. **d** 65 **p** 66. C Burry Port and Pwll *St D* 65-68; V Strata Florida 68-71; V Llandyfriog, Llanfair Trelygen, Troedyraur etc 72-78; R Aber-porth w Tre-main and Blaen-porth 78-87; P-in-c Penbryn and Betws Ifan w Bryngwyn from 88. *Am-Nawr, 19 Fordd y Bedol, Aberporth, Cardigan, Dyfed SA43 2ET* Aberporth (0239) 810217

VARNHAM, Gerald Stanley. b 29. Sarum & Wells Th Coll 74. **d** 77 **p** 78. Hon C Portchester *Portsm* from 77. *15 Southampton Road, Fareham, Hants PO16 7DZ* Fareham (0329) 234182

VARTY, John Eric. b 44. Tyndale Hall Bris 68. **d** 71 **p** 72. C Barrow St Mark *Carl* 71-74; C Cheadle *Ches* 74-82; V Cheadle All Hallows 82-89; V Alsager Ch Ch from 89. *Christ Church Vicarage, 43 Church Road, Alsager, Stoke-on-Trent ST7 2HS* Alsager (0270) 873727

VARTY, Robert. b 46. LRAM. Sarum & Wells Th Coll 84. **d** 86 **p** 87. C Plympton St Mary *Ex* 86-89; TV Northam w Westward Ho and Appledore from 89. *The Vicarage, Meeting Street, Appledore, Bideford, Devon EX39 1RJ* Bideford (0237) 470469

VASEY, Arthur Stuart. b 37. Qu Coll Birm 68. **d** 71 **p** 72. C Shelf *Bradf* 71-73; Australia 74-76; Chapl St Jo Hosp Linc 76-79; P-in-c Tanfield *Dur* 79-84; C Birtley 84-85; C Middlesb St Thos *York* 85-86. *Address temp unknown*

VASEY, David. b 26. St Aid Birkenhead 56. **d** 58 **p** 59. V Leeds St Cypr Harehills *Ripon* 68-78; V Scarborough St Columba *York* 78-87; rtd 87. *45 Newlands Park Grove, Scarborough, N Yorkshire YO12 6PU* Scarborough (0723) 352122

VASEY, Michael Richard. b 46. Ball Coll Ox BA68 MA71. Wycliffe Hall Ox 68. **d** 71 **p** 72. C Tonbridge SS Pet and Paul *Roch* 71-75; Lic to Offic *Dur* from 75; Tutor St Jo Coll Dur from 75. *St John's College, Durham DH1 3RJ* 091-374 3584 or 384 0593

VASS, Robert James Templeton. b 28. Lon Coll of Div 62. **d** 64 **p** 68. C Horsell *Guildf* 64-65; Kenya from 72. *PO Box 11860, Nairobi, Kenya*

VAUGHAN, Andrew Christopher James. b 61. Linc Th Coll BA. **d** 84 **p** 85. C Caerleon *Mon* 84-86; C Magor w Redwick and Undy 86-88; Ind Chapl from 89. *16 Steynton Path, Fairwater, Cwmbran, Gwent NP44 4QJ* Cwmbran (0633) 362414

✠**VAUGHAN, Rt Rev Benjamin Noel Young.** b 17. Univ of Wales (Lamp) BA40 St Edm Hall Ox BA(Theol)42 MA46. Westcott Ho Cam 42. **d** 43 **p** 44 **c** 61. C Llan-non *St D* 43-45; C Carmarthen St Dav 45-48; Barbados 48-52; Lect St D Coll Lamp 52-55; Trinidad and Tobago 55-61; Dean Port of Spain 55-61; Jamaica 61-67; Suff Bp Mandeville 61-67; Adn S Middx 61-64; Bp Br Honduras 67-71; Dean Ban 71-76; Asst Bp Ban 71-76; Bp S & B 76-87; Pres Coun of Ch for Wales 79-82; rtd 87. *4 Caswell Drive, Newton, Swansea* Swansea (0792) 360646

VAUGHAN, Brian John. b 38. Lich Th Coll 65. **d** 68 **p** 69. C Fisherton Anger *Sarum* 68-70; C Wareham w Arne 70-73; Australia from 73. *The Rectory, PO Box 33, Murray Street, Pinjarra, W Australia 6208* Pinjarra (95) 311248

VAUGHAN, Charles Jeremy Marshall. b 52. Man Univ BSc75 LTh. St Jo Coll Nottm 83. **d** 85 **p** 86. C Epsom Common Ch Ch *Guildf* 85-88; C Woking Ch Ch from 88. *4 Orchard Drive, Woking, Surrey GU21 4BN* Woking (0483) 771551

VAUGHAN, Idris Samuel. b 46. Sarum Th Coll 70. **d** 72 **p** 73. C Workington St Jo *Carl* 72-76; C Foley Park *Worc* 76-79; P-in-c Hayton St Mary *Carl* 79; V 79-85; Chapl Asst Univ Hosp Nottm 85-90; Chapl Asst Nottm Gen Hosp 85-90; Chapl Stafford Distr Gen Hosp from 90. *The Chaplain's Office, Stafford District General Hospital, Weston Road, Stafford ST16 3RS* Stafford (0785) 57731

VAUGHAN, Jeffrey Charles. b 45. S'wark Ord Course 85. **d** 88 **p** 89. NSM Tottenham St Paul *Lon* from 88. *11 Trulock Road, London N17 0PH* 081-801 1551

VAUGHAN, John. b 30. Sarum Th Coll 53. **d** 56 **p** 57. C Wigan St Andr *Liv* 56-59; Australia 59-64; P-in-c Riddings *Derby* 64-71; R Hasland 71-80; V Temple Normanton 71-80; TV Dronfield 80-86; V Bradwell from 86. *The Vicarage, Bradwell, Sheffield S30 2HJ* Hope Valley (0433) 20485

VAUGHAN, Canon Dr Patrick Handley. b 38. TCD BA60 BD65 Selw Coll Cam BA62 MA66 Nottm Univ PhD88. Ridley Hall Cam 61. **d** 63 **p** 64. Min Can Bradf Cathl *Bradf* 63-66; Uganda 67-73; P-in-c Slingsby *York* 74-77; Tutor NW Ord Course 74-77; P-in-c Hovingham *York* 74-77; Prin E Midl Min Tr Course *S'well* 77-90; Hon Can Leic Cathl *Leic* 87-90. *232 Psalter Lane, Sheffield S11 8QT* Sheffield (0742) 666579

✠**VAUGHAN, Rt Rev Peter St George.** b 30. Selw Coll Cam BA55 MA59 BNC Ox MA63. Ridley Hall Cam. **d** 57 **p** 58 **c** 89. C Birm St Martin *Birm* 57-63; Chapl to Ox Pastorate 63-67; Asst Chapl BNC Ox 63-67; Ceylon 67-72; New Zealand 72-75; Lic to Offic *Birm* 75-83; Prin Crowther Hall CMS Tr Coll Selly Oak 75-83; Adn Westmorland and Furness *Carl* 83-89; Hon Can Carl Cathl 83-89; Area Bp Ramsbury *Sarum* from 89; Can and Preb Sarum Cathl from 89. *Bishop's House, High Street, Urchfont, Devizes, Wilts SN10 4QH* Devizes (0380) 84373

VAUGHAN, Richard John. b 09. MC45. St Edm Hall Ox BA34 DipTh35 MA38. Wycliffe Hall Ox 34. **d** 35 **p** 36. V Headstone St Geo *Lon* 55-81; rtd 81; Perm to Offic *Lon* from 83. *3 Brookshill Avenue, Harrow Weald, Middx HA3 6RZ* 081-954 7855

VAUGHAN, Roger Maxwell. b 39. AKC62. **d** 63 **p** 64. C W Bromwich All SS *Lich* 63-65; C Wolv 65-70; V Tunstall Ch Ch 70-79; V Tunstall 79; V Abbots Bromley 79-86; P-in-c Blithfield 85-86; V Abbots Bromley w Blithfield from 86. *The Vicarage, Abbots Bromley, Rugeley, Staffs WS15 3BP* Burton-on-Trent (0283) 840242

VAUGHAN, Ronald Alfred. b 38. S'wark Ord Course 78. **d** 81 **p** 82. NSM Stepney St Pet w St Benet *Lon* 81-86; NSM St Jo on Bethnal Green from 87. *14 Cephas Street, London E1 4AX* 071-791 1205

VAUGHAN, Trevor. b 41. Linc Th Coll 66. **d** 69 **p** 70. C Wyken *Cov* 69-72; C Stratford w Bishopton 72-73; P-in-c Monks Kirby w Withybrook and Copston Magna 73-75; P-in-c Wolvey, Burton Hastings and Stretton Baskerville 73-77; P-in-c Withybrook w Copston Magna 73-77; V Heyhouses *Blackb* 77-80; V Chorley St Geo 80-83; R Bolton by Bowland w Grindleton *Bradf* 83-89; V Settle from 89. *The Vicarage, Townhead Way, Settle, N Yorkshire BD24 9JB* Settle (07292) 2288

VAUGHAN-JONES, Canon Frederick Edward Cecil. b 19. Selw Coll Cam BA40 MA44. Cuddesdon Coll 40. **d** 42 **p** 43. C Leigh-on-Sea St Marg *Chelmsf* 42-46; S Africa 46-62 and from 65; R Gt w Lt Gransden *Ely* 63-65; Can Grahamstown 70-73; Adn Johannesburg 82-86. *PO Box 282, Port Edward, 4295 South Africa* Port Edward (3930) 32553

VAUGHAN-JONES, Canon Geraint James. b 29. JP77. St D Coll Lamp 50 St Deiniol's Hawarden 68. **d** 70 **p** 71. C Llanaber w Caerdeon *Ban* 70-73; TV Dolgelly w Llanfachreth and Brithdir etc 73-76; R Mallwyd w Cemaes and Llanymawddwy from 76; RD Cyfeiliog and Mawddwy from 85; Can Ban Cathl from 86; Prec Ban Cathl from 89. *The Rectory, Mallwyd, Machynlleth, Powys SY20 9HJ* Dinas Mawddwy (06504) 217

VAUGHAN-JONES, Canon John Paschal. b 18. Keble Coll Ox BA39 MA43. St Steph Ho Ox 39. **d** 41 **p** 42. R Chipping Ongar *Chelmsf* 49-83; R Shelley 49-83; RD Ongar 72-82; Hon Can Chelmsf Cathl 78-83; rtd 83. *Ryecroft, Old Harwich Road, Little Bentley, Colchester, Essex CO7 8SX* Colchester (0206) 250238

VAUGHAN-WILSON, Jane Elizabeth. b 61. Magd Coll Ox MA87. Cranmer Hall Dur. **d** 89. Par Dn Ormesby *York* from 89. *9 Lobelia Close, Ormesby, Middlesbrough, Cleveland* Middlesbrough (0642) 315850

VEAR, Frank Henry. b 12. K Coll Lon 67. **d** 68 **p** 69. C N Stoneham *Win* 68-75; V Southbourne St Chris 75-86; rtd 86; Perm to Offic *Win* from 86. *St Boniface, 3 Glenroyd Gardens, Bournemouth BH6 3JN* Bournemouth (0202) 427021

VEAZEY, Harry Christopher Hurford. b 11. Westcott Ho Cam 33. **d** 35 **p** 36. V Doddington w Wychling *Cant* 57-80; V Newnham 57-80; RD Ospringe 78-80; rtd 80; Perm to Offic *Cant* from 80. *Five Oaks, Pluckley Road, Charing, Ashford, Kent* Charing (023371) 2300

VEITCH, Thomas. b 12. Glas Univ MA37. **d** 40 **p** 41. R Edin St Paul and St Geo *Edin* 56-84; rtd 85. *17 Falcon Road West, Edinburgh EH10 4AD* 031-447 3207

VELLACOTT, John Patrick Millner. b 29. Ox NSM Course 86. **d** 89 **p** 90. NSM Cholsey *Ox* from 89. *Old Blackalls, Cholsey, Wallingford, Oxon OX10 9HD* Cholsey (0491) 651394 or 652281

VENABLES, Arthur Peter. b 20. Vancouver Sch of Th LTh47. **d** 49 **p** 50. V Kensington St Phil Earl's Court *Lon* 69-74; P-in-c Uxbridge Moor 74-82; rtd 82; Perm to Offic *Lon* from 82. *4 Wharf Court, Iver Lane, Cowley, Middx UB8 2JD* Uxbridge (0895) 71442

VENABLES, Dudley James. b 17. Cant Sch of Min 77. **d** 80 **p** 81. NSM Ramsgate H Trin *Cant* 80-82; Chapl Asst St Aug Hosp Cant from 83; NSM Wye w Brook from 83. *48 Abbots Walk, Wye, Ashford, Kent* Wye (0233) 813000

VENABLES, Gregory James. b 49. Lon Univ CertEd74. **d** 84 **p** 84. SAMS 77-90; Paraguay 78-90; C Rainham *Chelmsf* from 90. *34 Warwick Road, Rainham, Essex RM13 9XU* Rainham (04027) 55810

VENABLES, Margaret Joy. b 37. CertEd57 ADB. S Dios Minl Tr Scheme 86. **d** 89. NSM Wilton *B & W* from 89. *11 Henley Road, Taunton, Somerset TA1 5BN* Taunton (0823) 335023

VENABLES, Philip Richard Meredith. b 58. Magd Coll Ox BA79 CertEd80. Wycliffe Hall Ox 85. **d** 88 **p** 89. C Gillingham St Mark *Roch* from 88. *The Garden House, Vicarage Road, Gillingham, Kent ME7 5JA* Medway (0634) 53687

VENESS, David Roger. b 48. Brunel Univ BTech70. St Jo Coll Nottm 73. **d** 75 **p** 76. C Selly Hill St Steph *Birm* 75-80; V Colney Heath St Mark *St Alb* from 80; RD Hatf from 88. *St Mark's Vicarage, Colney Heath, St Albans, Herts AL4 0NQ* Bowmansgreen (0727) 22040

VENNER, Canon Stephen Squires. b 44. Birm Univ BA65 Linacre Coll Ox BA67 MA71 Lon Univ PGCE72. St Steph Ho Ox 65. **d** 68 **p** 69. C Streatham St Pet *S'wark* 68-71; C Streatham Hill St Marg 71-72; C Balham Hill Ascension 72-74; Bp's Chapl to Overseas Students 74-76; V Clapham St Pet 74-76; P-in-c Studley *Sarum* 76; V 76-82; V Weymouth H Trin from 82; RD Weymouth from 88; Can and Preb Sarum Cathl from 89. *Holy Trinity Vicarage, 7 Glebe Close, Weymouth, Dorset DT4 9LR* Weymouth (0305) 760354

VENNING, Nigel Christopher. b 50. K Coll Lon BD75 AKC75. St Aug Coll Cant 75. **d** 76 **p** 77. C Minehead *B & W* 76-80; C Fawley *Win* 80-83; P-in-c

Combe St Nicholas w Wambrook *B & W* 83-89; P-in-c Whitestaunton 83-89; R Staplegrove from 89. *The Rectory, Rectory Drive, Staplegrove, Taunton, Somerset TA2 6AP* Taunton (0823) 272787

VENTON, Bertram Ernest. b 1900. K Coll Lon. **d** 50 **p** 51. V Molland *Ex* 59-68; rtd 68; Lic to Offic *Ex* from 68. *33 Ocean View Road, Bude, Cornwall EX23 8NL*

VENUS, John Charles. b 29. AKC53. **d** 54 **p** 55. C Havant *Portsm* 54-59; S Africa 60-65; Chapl RN 66-70 and 78-83; Chapl Trin Coll Glenalmond 70-78; R Abinger cum Coldharbour *Guildf* from 83. *The Rectory, Abinger Common, Dorking, Surrey RH5 6HZ* Dorking (0306) 730746

VERE HODGE, Preb Francis. b 19. MC43. Worc Coll Ox BA46 MA46. Cuddesdon Coll 46. **d** 48 **p** 49. V Moorlinch w Stawell and Sutton Mallet *B & W* 65-79; R Greinton 68-79; RD Glastonbury 75-79; Preb Wells Cathl 79-85; P-in-c Lydeard St Lawrence w Combe Florey and Tolland 79-84; rtd 84; Perm to Offic *B & W* from 84. *Rose Cottage, Ham Street, Baltonsborough, Glastonbury, Somerset BA6 8PN* Baltonsborough (0458) 50032

VERITY, Cecil Beaumont. b 01. Trin Coll Cam BA22 MA26. Ridley Hall Cam 24. **d** 25 **p** 26. V Barton Stacey w Bullington *Win* 58-69; rtd 69; Perm to Offic *Cant* from 81. *9 Conyngham Lane, Bridge, Canterbury, Kent CT4 5JX* Canterbury (0227) 830940

✠**VERNEY, Rt Rev Stephen Edmund.** b 19. MBE45. Ball Coll Ox BA48 MA48. **d** 50 **p** 51 **c** 77. C Gedling *S'well* 50-52; C-in-c Clifton CD 52-57; V Clifton St Fran 57-58; Dioc Missr *Cov* 58-64; V Leamington Hastings 58-64; Can Res Cov Cathl 64-70; Can Windsor 70-77; Suff Bp Repton *Derby* 77-85; Hon Can Derby Cathl 77-85; Dioc Dir of Post-Ord Tr 83-85; rtd 86; Perm to Offic *Ox* from 86. *Charity School House, Church Road, Blewbury, Didcot, Oxon OX11 9PY*

VERNON, Bryan Graham. b 50. Qu Coll Cam BA72 MA76. Qu Coll Birm DipTh74. **d** 75 **p** 76. C Newc St Gabr *Newc* 75-79; Chapl Newc Univ 79-91; Chmn Newc Mental Health Trust from 91; C Benwell Team from 91. *34 Queens Road, Newcastle upon Tyne NE2 2PQ* 091-281 3861

VERNON, Charles Harold. b 09. AKC38. Westcott Ho Cam 38. **d** 39 **p** 40. V Bishopstone *Chich* 70-76; RD Seaford 72-75; rtd 76; Perm to Offic *Chich* from 76. *Marecottes, Mount Pleasant, Waldron, Heathfield, E Sussex TN21 0QU* Horam Road (04353) 2096

VERNON, John Christie. b 40. Lon Univ BSc62. Linc Th Coll 63. **d** 65 **p** 66. C Barnard Castle *Dur* 65-69; CF from 69. *c/o MOD (Army), Bagshot Park, Bagshot, Surrey GU19 5PL* Bagshot (0276) 71717

VERNON, Michael Helm. b 33. G&C Coll Cam BA56 MA61. Clifton Th Coll 56. **d** 58 **p** 59. C Higher Openshaw *Man* 58-61; Argentina 61-69; C Leeds St Geo *Ripon* 69-70; V Skellingthorpe *Linc* 70-76; R Doddington 72-76; TR Marfleet *York* 76-82; V Hull Newland St Jo from 82. *St John's Vicarage, Clough Road, Newland, Hull HU6 7PA* Hull (0482) 43658

VERNON, Reginald Joseph. b 08. Lon Coll of Div 49. **d** 51 **p** 52. V Steeple Claydon *Ox* 59-71; rtd 71. *Bethany, 46 Blenheim Place, Aylesbury, Bucks HP21 8AQ* Aylesbury (0296) 84516

VERNON, Robert Leslie. b 47. Sarum & Wells Th Coll 73. **d** 76 **p** 77. C Hartlepool St Luke *Dur* 76-79; C Birm St Geo *Birm* 79-82; V Bordesley Green 82-86; Dioc Youth Officer *Carl* 86-89; P-in-c Holme 86-89; Dioc Youth Adv *Newc* from 89. *9 Winsford Avenue, North Shields, Tyne & Wear NE29 9EE* 091-258 1183

VERNON, William Bradney. b 05. St Jo Coll Ox BA28 MA32. Wells Th Coll 28. **d** 29 **p** 30. R Winterslow *Sarum* 65-70; rtd 70. *9 Brooke Court, Parkleys, Ham, Richmond, Surrey TW10 5LX* 081-546 8495

VERRELLS, Canon Herbert Stuart. b 1900. Hatf Coll Dur BA25. **d** 25 **p** 26. R Ringsfield w Redisham *St E* 33-70; Hon Can St E Cathl 59-70; rtd 70; Lic to Offic *St E* from 70. *9 Marsh Lane, Worlingham, Beccles, Suffolk* Beccles (0502) 712094

VESSEY, Andrew John. b 45. Bp Otter Coll CertEd67 Sarum & Wells Th Coll 84. **d** 86 **p** 87. C Framlingham w Saxtead *St E* 86-89; V Catshill and Dodford *Worc* from 89. *The Vicarage, 403 Stourbridge Road, Catshill, Bromsgrove, Worcs* Bromsgrove (0527) 579619

VESSEY, Peter Allan Beaumont. b 36. Lon Coll of Div ALCD65 LTh74. **d** 64 **p** 65. C Rayleigh *Chelmsf* 64-67; C Cam H Trin *Ely* 67-71; V Kingston upon Hull Southcoates St Aid *York* 71-80; V Swannick and Pentrich *Derby* from 80. *The Vicarage, Broadway, Swanwick, Derby DE55 1DQ* Leabrooks (0773) 602684

VETTERS, Shirley Jacqueline Margaret. b 34. S'wark Ord Course 85. **d** 88. NSM E Ham w Upton Park *Chelmsf*

from 88. *Flat 1, St Bartholomew's Court, St Bartholomew's Road, London E6 3AG* 081-470 3411

VEVAR, Canon John Harvard. b 14. Univ of Wales BA36. St Mich Coll Llan 37. **d** 38 **p** 40. R Meyllteyrn w Botwnnog and Llandygwnnin etc *Ban* 51-84; Can Ban Cathl 78-84; rtd 84; Perm to Offic *Ban* from 84. *Gwynant, Tudweiliog, Gwynedd LL53 8AJ* Tudweiliog (075887) 270

VEVERS, Eric. b 22. Oak Hill Th Coll 54. **d** 56 **p** 57. V Ealing St Mary *Lon* 68-78; V Sidmouth All SS *Ex* 78-88; rtd 88. *16 Clayton Drive, Guildford, Surrey GU2 6TZ* Guildford (0483) 506269

VEVERS, Geoffrey Martin. b 51. Oak Hill Th Coll. **d** 82 **p** 83. C Wealdstone H Trin *Lon* 82-84; C Harrow H Trin St Mich 84-88; V Wandsworth St Steph *S'wark* from 88. *St Stephen's Vicarage, 2A Oakhill Road, London SW15 2QU* 081-874 5610

VEYSEY, John Norris. b 14. **d** 47 **p** 48. Chapl to the Deaf *B & W* 50-79; rtd 79; Perm to Offic *B & W* from 80. *8 Richmond Place, Lansdown, Bath BA1 5PZ* Bath (0225) 313965

VIBERT, Simon David Newman. b 63. Oak Hill Th Coll BA89. **d** 89 **p** 90. C Houghton *Carl* from 89. *224 Kingstown Road, Carlisle CA3 0DE* Carlisle (0228) 34711

VICARS, David. b 22. Leeds Univ BA48. Coll of Resurr Mirfield 48. **d** 50 **p** 51. Area Sec (Llan, Mon, St D and S & B) USPG 67-77; R Coychurch w Llangan and St Mary Hill *Llan* 77-90; rtd 90. *43 Brynrhedyn, Pencoed, Bridgend, M Glam CF35 6TL* Bridgend (0656) 860920

VICARY, Canon Douglas Reginald. b 16. Trin Coll Ox BA38 BSc39 DipTh40 MA42. Wycliffe Hall Ox 39. **d** 40 **p** 41. Hd Master K Sch Roch 57-75; Hon Can Roch Cathl *Roch* 57-75; Can Res and Prec Wells Cathl *B & W* 75-88; Chapl to HM The Queen 77-87; rtd 88. *8 Tor Street, Wells, Somerset BA5 2US* Wells (0749) 679137

VICK, Samuel Kenneth Lloyd. b 31. Univ of Wales (Lamp) BA53. Linc Th Coll. **d** 55 **p** 56. C Shotton *St As* 55-56; C Wrexham 56-61; C Knowle H Nativity *Bris* 61-67; V Mirfield Eastthorpe St Paul *Wakef* 67-78; V Altofts from 78. *The Vicarage, Altofts, Normanton, W Yorkshire WF6 2QG* Wakefield (0924) 892299

VICKERMAN, John. b 42. Chich Th Coll 69. **d** 72 **p** 73. C Horbury *Wakef* 72-76; C Elland 76-78; V Glasshoughton 78-89; V Bruntcliffe from 89. *St Andrew's Vicarage, 4 Lewisham Street, Morley, Leeds LS27 0LA* Morley (0532) 523783

VICKERS, Allan Frederick. b 24. St Jo Coll Dur BA50 DipTh52. **d** 52 **p** 53. Chapl RAF 57-77; Asst Chapl HM Pris Wandsworth 78-79; Chapl HM Pris Ford 79-87; rtd 87. *23 Ashurst Close, Bognor Regis, W Sussex PO21 5UJ*

VICKERS, Dennis William George. b 30. RIBA72. Glouc Th Course 83. **d** 86 **p** 87. NSM Bucknell w Buckton, Llanfair Waterdine and Stowe *Heref* 88-91; NSM Bucknell w Chapel Lawn, Llanfair Waterdine etc from 91. *The Shear, Reeves Lane, Stanage, Knighton, Powys LD7 1NA* Bucknell (05474) 577

VICKERS, Mrs Mary Janet. b 57. St Jo Coll Nottm BTh85. dss 85 **d** 87. Worc City St Paul and Old St Martin etc *Worc* 85-87; Par Dn 87-89; World Miss Officer from 89. *186 Birmingham Road, Kidderminster, Worcs DY10 2SJ* Kidderminster (0562) 820275

✠**VICKERS, Rt Rev Michael Edwin.** b 29. Worc Coll Ox BA56 MA56. Dur Univ DipTh59. **d** 59 **p** 60 **c** 88. C Bexleyheath Ch Ch *Roch* 59-62; Chapl Lee Abbey 62-67; V Hull Newland St Jo *York* 67-81; AD W Hull Deanery 72-81; Can and Preb York Minster 81-88; Adn E Riding 81-88; Area Bp Colchester *Chelmsf* from 88. *1 Fitzwalter Road, Colchester CO3 3SS* Colchester (0206) 576648

VICKERS, Peter. b 56. St Jo Coll Nottm LTh85. **d** 85 **p** 86. C Worc St Barn w Ch Ch *Worc* 85-88; TV Kidderminster St Mary and All SS etc 88-90; TV Kidderminster St Mary and All SS w Trimpley etc from 90; Ind Chapl from 88. *186 Birmingham Road, Kidderminster, Worcs DY10 2SJ* Kidderminster (0562) 746332

VICKERS, Randolph. b 36. MCIM65. St Alb Minl Tr Scheme 77. **d** 80 **p** 82. NSM Hitchin *St Alb* 80-87; NSM Luton Lewsey St Hugh 87-89; NSM Shotley *Newc* from 89. *Beggar's Roost, 26 Painshawfield Road, Stocksfield, Northd NE43 7PF* Stocksfield (0661) 842364

VICKERY, Charles William Bryan. b 38. Lich Th Coll 63. **d** 65 **p** 66. C Hove St Barn *Chich* 65-73; Chapl Hostel of God Clapham 73-76; P-in-c Kingston St Luke *S'wark* 76-82; V from 82. *The Vicarage, 4 Burton Road, Kingston upon Thames, Surrey KT2 5TE* 081-546 4064

VICKERY, Jonathan Laurie. b 58. Bretton Hall Coll CertEd79 Leeds Univ BEd80. Wycliffe Hall Ox 81. **d** 84 p 85. C Gorseinon *S & B* 84-86; P-in-c Whitton and Pilleth and Cascob etc 86-87; V from 87. *The Rectory, Whitton, Knighton, Powys LD7 1NP*   Whitton (05476) 231

VICKERY, Robin Francis. b 48. K Coll Lon BD73 AKC73. d 74 p 75. C Clapham St Jo *S'wark* 74-77; C Clapham Ch Ch and St Jo 75-77; C Reigate St Luke S Park 77-79; Hon C Clapham H Spirit 80-87; Hon C Clapham Team Min from 87. *Norfolk House, 13 Chelsham Road, London SW4 6NR*   071-622 4792

VICKERY, Trevor Hopkin. b 17. Univ of Wales BA39. St Mich Coll Llan 39. d 40 p 41. C Ban St Jas *Ban* 40-43; Lic to Offic Ban 43-47; Cant 48-51; Chapl RN 43-47; C Heacham *Nor* 47-48; Chapl Cranbrook Sch Kent 48-51; R Staplehurst *Cant* from 51; Chapl HM Det Cen Blantyre Ho 54-80. *The Rectory, Staplehurst, Kent TN12 0DH*   Staplehurst (0580) 891258

VICTOR, Brother. See SMITH, David John Parker

VIDAL-HALL, Roderic Mark. b 37. Sheff Univ BSc60 Birm Univ DPS70. Lich Th Coll 62. d 64 p 65. C Ilkeston St Mary *Derby* 64-67; C Nether and Over Seale 67-70; V Chellaston 70-84; C Marchington w Marchington Woodlands *Lich* from 84; C Kingstone w Gratwich from 85. *13 Moisty Lane, Marchington, Uttoxeter, Staffs ST14 8JY*   Burton-on-Trent (0283) 820030

VIGAR, Gilbert Leonard. b 12. Lon Univ BD46 BA50 MA52 Nottm Univ MPhil72. Kelham Th Coll 32. d 38 p 39. Prin Lect Bp Grosseteste Coll Linc 61-77; Lic to Offic *Linc* 61-77; rtd 77; Hon C Win H Trin *Win* 79-85; Hon C Eastbourne St Sav and St Pet *Chich* from 85. *5 Chatsworth Gardens, Eastbourne, E Sussex BN20 7JP*   Eastbourne (0323) 644121

VIGARS, Anthony Roy. b 54. St Jo Coll Dur BA75. Trin Coll Bris 77. d 78 p 79. C Barking St Marg w St Patr *Chelmsf* 78-81; C Littleover *Derby* 81-84; C-in-c Stapenhill Immanuel CD 84-90; V Meltham *Wakef* from 90. *The Vicarage, 150 Huddersfield Road, Meltham, Huddersfield HD7 3AL*   Huddersfield (0484) 850050

VIGEON, Owen George. b 28. Peterho Cam BA52 MA57. Ely Th Coll 52. d 54 p 55. C Barrow St Luke *Carl* 54-58; Chapl St Jo Coll York 58-61; V Burnley St Steph *Blackb* 61-69; V Bilsborrow 69-73; Asst Dir RE 69-73; V St Annes 74-85; RD Fylde 80-85; R Halton w Aughton from 85. *The Rectory, Halton, Lancaster LA2 6PU*   Halton-on-Lune (0524) 811370

VIGERS, Neil Simon. b 62. K Coll Lon BD84 MTh87. Linc Th Coll 88. d 90 p 91. C Chelsea St Luke and St Ch *Lon* from 90. *30 St Luke's Street, London SW3 3RP*   071-352 6433

VIGOR, Miss Margaret Ann. b 45. Leeds Univ CertEd66. Ripon Coll Cuddesdon 85. d 87. Chapl Asst All SS Convent Ox 87-89; Par Dn Basildon, St Martin of Tours w Nevendon *Chelmsf* 89-91; Iona Community from 91. *Bishop's House, Isle of Iona, Argyll PA76 6SJ*   Iona (06817) 306

VILE, Canon Donald Arthur. b 15. Down Coll Cam BA37 MA41. Cuddesdon Coll 37. d 38 p 39. Hon Can S'wark Cathl *S'wark* 64-80; V Caterham Valley 68-80; rtd 80; Perm to Offic *Chich* from 80. *1 Loxwood Close, Bexhill-on-Sea, E Sussex TN39 4LX*   Cooden (04243) 4760

VILLER, Allan George Frederick. b 38. E Anglian Minl Tr Course 78. d 81 p 82. NSM Ely 81-85; V Emneth from 85. *The Vicarage, Church Road, Emneth, Wisbech, Cambs PE14 8AF*   Wisbech (0945) 583089

VILLIERS, Preb Tony. b 35. Lich Th Coll 59. d 62 p 63. C Shifnal *Lich* 62-65; C Wednesbury St Paul Wood Green 65-67; R Llanymynech from 67; V Morton from 72; RD Oswestry 82-87; Preb Lich Cathl from 89. *Llanymynech Rectory, Pant, Oswestry, Shropshire SY10 9RA*   Oswestry (0691) 830446

VINCE, Mrs Barbara Mary Tudor. b 29. St Alb Minl Tr Scheme 79. dss 82 d 87. Northwood H Trin *Lon* 82-86; Belmont 86-87; Par Dn 87-89; rtd 90; Perm to Offic *Lon* from 90. *22 St Mary's Avenue, Northwood, Middx HA6 3AZ*   Northwood (09274) 25730

VINCE, David Eric. b 59. Birm Univ BA Nottm Univ BCombStuds Lon Univ PGCE. Linc Th Coll. d 85 p 86. C Gt Malvern St Mary *Worc* 85-87; C All Hallows by the Tower etc Lon 88-89; AP St Giles Cripplegate w St Bart Moor Lane etc from 89. *Waverley, 4 Chandos Square, Broadstairs, Kent CT10 1QW*

VINCE, Edwin George. b 13. Leeds Univ BA36. Coll of Resurr Mirfield 36. d 39 p 40. C Glouc St Aldate *Glouc* 66-73; Chapl Convent Companions Jes Gd Shep W Ogwell 74-77; rtd 77. *The Grey House, Church Street, Chiseldon, Swindon, Wiltshire SN4 0NJ*   Swindon (0793) 740240

VINCE, Raymond Michael. b 45. Lon Univ BD69 Bris Univ MA72 K Coll Lon MTh80 LSE MSc83. Tyndale Hall Bris 66. d 71 p 72. C Southsea St Jude *Portsm* 71-75; Hon C Islington St Mary *Lon* 75-83; Chapl Poly of N Lon 75-83; USA from 83. *373 Pierremont, Shreveport, Louisiana 71106, USA*

VINCENT, Preb Alfred James. b 30. Bris Univ BA54 Lon Univ BD56. Tyndale Hall Bris 50. d 54 p 55. C Shrewsbury St Julian *Lich* 54-56; C Camborne *Truro* 56-59; V Kenwyn 59-68; Lic to Offic *St Alb* 68; Lect Qu Coll Birm 68-70; Lic to Offic *Birm* 68-70; V Bordesley St Oswald 70-76; V S Shields St Hilda w St Thos *Dur* 76-84; Miss to Seamen from 84; V Bude Haven *Truro* 84-89; R Bude Haven and Marhamchurch from 89; RD Stratton from 88; Preb St Endellion from 90. *The Rectory, 8 Falcon Terrace, Bude, Cornwall EX23 8LJ*   Bude (0288) 352318

VINCENT, Brother. See GIRLING, Francis Richard

VINCENT, Bruce Matthews. b 24. Univ of Wales (Swansea) DipYW50 Open Univ BA76 Surrey Univ MPhil83. d 88 p 88. Hon C Sidcup St Jo *Roch* from 88. *497 Footscray Road, London SE9 3UH*   081-850 5450

VINCENT, Christopher Robin. b 30. Sarum Th Coll 57. d 60 p 61. C Frome St Jo *B & W* 60-64; V Puxton w Hewish St Ann and Wick St Lawrence 64-70; V Buckland Dinham w Elm 70-71; V Buckland Dinham w Elm, Orchardleigh etc 71-77; P-in-c Frome H Trin 77-90; Chapl St Adhelm's Hosp Frome 77-88; RD Frome *B & W* 85-89; V Kewstoke w Wick St Lawrence from 90. *The Vicarage, 35 Kewstoke Road, Kewstoke, Weston-super-Mare, Avon BS22 9YE*   Weston-super-Mare (0934) 416162

VINCENT, David Cyril. b 37. Selw Coll Cam BA60 MA64. Coll of Resurr Mirfield 60. d 62 p 63. C Cheetwood St Alb *Man* 62-65; C Lawton Moor 65-67; V Wandsworth Common St Mary *S'wark* 67-84; RD Tooting 75-80; R Stoke D'Abernon *Guildf* from 84. *The Rectory, Blundell Lane, Stoke D'Abernon, Cobham, Surrey KT11 2SE*   Cobham (0932) 62502

VINCENT, George William Walter. b 13. ALCD40. d 40 p 41. R Alderton w Ramsholt and Bawdsey *St E* 55-86; rtd 86; Perm to Offic *St E* from 86. *The Rectory, Alderton, Woodbridge, Suffolk*   Shottisham (0394) 411306

VINCENT, Henry William Gordon. b 16. Leeds Univ BA42. Coll of Resurr Mirfield 42. d 44 p 45. V Whitton St Aug *Lon* 64-81; rtd 81. *20 West Mills Road, Dorchester, Dorset DT1 1SR*   Dorchester (0305) 263933

VINCENT, John Leonard. b 61. Univ of Wales (Lamp) BA83 Southn Univ BTh87. Chich Th Coll 84. d 87 p 88. C Hampton All SS *Lon* 87-90; C Shepperton from 90. *Flat 2, The Rectory, Church Square, Shepperton, Middx TW17 9JY*   Walton-on-Thames (0932) 241846

VINCENT, Michael Francis. b 48. CertEd70 Open Univ BA83. Sarum & Wells Th Coll 85. d 87 p 88. C Nuneaton St Mary *Cov* 87-90; C Stockingford 90-91; P-in-c from 91. *The Vicarage, Church Road, Stockingford, Nuneaton, Warks CV10 8LG*   Nuneaton (0203) 383024

VINCENT, Canon Noel Thomas. b 36. Fitzw Ho Cam BA60 MA64. Ridley Hall Cam 61. d 63 p 64. C Fenham St Jas and St Basil *Newc* 63-67; C Prudhoe 67-70; V Holbrooke *Derby* 70-74; P-in-c Lt Eaton 73-74; P-in-c Osmaston w Edlaston 74-78; Dioc Info Officer 74-78; Hon C Osmaston w Edlaston 78-85; Sen Producer Relig Progr BBC Man from 82; Hon C Brailsford w Shirley and Osmaston w Edlaston *Derby* 85-86; Hon Can Derby Cathl from 85; Perm to Offic *Ches* from 86. *St Elizabeth's House, Ashley, Altrincham, Cheshire WA14 3QE*   061-928 0063

VINCENT, Roy David. b 37. Univ of Wales (Swansea) DipYW. Chich Th Coll 81. d 83 p 84. C Atherton *Man* 83-86; V E Crompton from 86. *East Crompton Vicarage, Salts Street, Shaw, Oldham OL2 7TE*   Shaw (0706) 847454

VINCENT, Canon William Alfred Leslie. b 11. Bris Univ BA33 St Edm Hall Ox BLitt44 DPhil68. d 39 p 40. Chapl R Wanstead Sch 39-41; C S Woodford H Trin CD *Chelmsf* 39-41; Lic to Offic *Mon* from 42; Chapl Ch Ch Ox 45-51; Chapl Dioc Tr Coll Ches 51-64; Lic to Offic *Ches* from 52; *Bris* from 74; Can Res Bris Cathl 74-77. *80 College Road, Fishponds, Bristol*

VINCER, Michael. b 41. Sarum & Wells Th Coll 77. d 80 p 81. Hon C Littleham w Exmouth *Ex* from 80; Miss to Seamen from 80; Area Sec (Dios Ex and Truro) USPG from 86. *5 Albion Hill, Exmouth, Devon EX8 1JS*   Exmouth (0395) 273630

VINE, John. b 24. Keble Coll Ox BA45 MA50. St Steph Ho Ox 45. d 48 p 49. C Hackney Wick St Mary of Eton w St Aug *Lon* 48-50; C Holborn St Alb w Saffron Hill

St Pet 50-53; Chapl Ely Th Coll 53-56; Vice-Prin Ely Th Coll 56-60; Hon C St Leonards Ch Ch *Chich* 60-62; Chapl Lich Th Coll 62-67; R Wrington *B & W* 67-69; V Earl's Court St Cuth w St Matthias *Lon* from 69. *St Cuthbert's Clergy House, 50 Philbeach Gardens, London SW5 9EB*   071-370 3263

VINE, Michael Charles. b 51. Worc Coll Ox BA73 MA80. Cuddesdon Coll 73. **d** 76 **p** 77. C Wallsend St Luke *Newc* 76-79; C Denton 79-81; V Sugley 81-91; V Shiremoor from 91. *St Mark's Vicarage, Brenkley Avenue, Shiremoor, Newcastle upon Tyne NE27 0PP*   091-253 3291

VINE, Michael Derek. b 35. Ch Ch Ox BA58 MA63. Ely Th Coll 58. **d** 60 **p** 61. C Syston *Leic* 60-63; C S Ascot *Ox* 63-66; Chapl RN 66-70; Perm to Offic *Portsm* 71-74; Lon from 74. *The Hall School, Crossfield Road, London NW3 4NU*   071-222 1700

VINE, Neville Peter. b 54. K Coll Lon BD80 AKC80. Linc Th Coll 80. **d** 81 **p** 82. C Peterlee *Dur* 81-86; Chapl Peterlee Coll 84-86; V Auckland St Pet *Dur* 86-89; Perm to Offic 89-91; R Easington from 91. *The Rectory, 5 Tudor Grange, Easington, Peterlee, Co Durham SR8 3DF*   091-527 0287

VINER, John Eckstein. b 11. MICE37 Lon Univ BSc31. ALCD48. **d** 48 **p** 49. V Bris St Paul w St Barn *Bris* 61-76; rtd 76; Perm to Offic *Bris* from 76. *75 Malmesbury Road, Chippenham, Wilts SN15 1PU*   Chippenham (0249) 653656

VINER, Canon Leonard Edwin. b 20. Univ Coll Dur LTh41 BA43. St Aug Coll Cant 38. **d** 43 **p** 44. Malawi 64-71; R Honing w Crostwight *Nor* 71-75; P-in-c E Ruston 71-73; V 73-75; P-in-c Witton w Ridlington 71-73; V 73-75; C Corby Epiphany w St Jo *Pet* 75-79; V Brigstock w Stanion 79-86; rtd 86; Asst Chapl Lisbon *Eur* 86-87; Chapl Tangier 87-89. *8 Clive Close, Kettering, Northants NN15 5BQ*   Kettering (0536) 519734

VINEY, Arthur William. b 32. BEd. S Dios Minl Tr Scheme. **d** 82 **p** 83. NSM Clayton w Keymer *Chich* 82-86; NSM Streat w Westmeston from 86. *The Rectory, Streat, Hassocks, W Sussex BN6 8RX*   Plumpton (0273) 890607

VINEY, Peter. b 43. Ox NSM Course. **d** 76 **p** 77. NSM High Wycombe *Ox* from 76. *5 Avery Avenue, Downley, High Wycombe, Bucks HP13 5UE*   High Wycombe (0494) 436065

VIPERS, Christopher James. b 63. Man Univ BA84. St Steph Ho Ox 87. **d** 89 **p** 90. C Wood Green St Mich w Bounds Green St Gabr etc *Lon* from 89. *20 Cornwall Avenue, London N22 4DA*   081-888 8120

VIPOND, Canon John. b 17. Lon Univ BD48. ALCD48. **d** 48 **p** 49. V Pudsey St Lawr and St Paul *Bradf* 56-73; V St Austell *Truro* 73-83; rtd 83. *Wisteria, 15 Coffeelake Meadow, Lostwithiel, Cornwall PL22 0LT*   Bodmin (0208) 873141

VIRGO, Canon Leslie Gordon. b 25. Linc Th Coll 56. **d** 58 **p** 59. C Hatcham Park All SS *S'wark* 58-61; C Selsdon St Jo *Cant* 61-65; Chapl Warlingham Park Hosp Croydon 65-73; Dioc Adv on Past Care and Counselling from 74; R Chelsfield *Roch* from 74; Hon Can Roch Cathl from 83. *The Rectory, Skibbs Lane, Orpington, Kent BR6 7RH*   Orpington (0689) 25749

VIRTUE, Thomas James. b 32. QUB BA56 TCD 58 Liv Univ DipRS80. **d** 58 **p** 59. C Belf St Mich *Conn* 58-61; C Belf St Bart 61-63; I Tempo *Clogh* 63-66; P-in-c Glynn w Raloo and Templecorran *Conn* 66-70; TV Ellesmere Port *Ches* 70-74; TV Ches Team 74-83; V Gt Sutton from 83. *St John's Vicarage, 1 Church Lane, Great Sutton, South Wirral L66 4RE*   051-339 9916

VITTLE, Cyril Wilfred. b 13. **d** 55 **p** 56. V Brislington St Cuth *Bris* 69-76; C Thornbury *Glouc* 76-79; rtd 79; Perm to Offic *Glouc* from 80. *39 Hyde Avenue, Thornbury, Avon BS12 1HZ*   Thornbury (0454) 415614

VIVIAN, Adrian John. b 42. K Coll Lon BD65 AKC66. **d** 66 **p** 67. C Bromley St Andr *Roch* 66-69; C Egg Buckland *Ex* 69-73; Perm to Offic *Ex* 83-84; P-in-c Newton Ferrers w Revelstoke 84-87. *The Parsonage Farm, Parsonage Road, Newton Ferrers, Plymouth PL8 1AT*

VIVIAN, Thomas Keith. b 27. St Jo Coll Cam BA48 MA52. St Deiniol's Hawarden 76. **d** 80 **p** 81. Hd Master Lucton Sch Leominster 62-85; Lic to Offic *Heref* 80-85; P-in-c Chew Stoke w Nempnett Thrubwell *B & W* 85-88; R from 88; P-in-c Norton Malreward 85-88; R from 88. *The Rectory, Chew Stoke, Bristol BS18 8TU*   Chew Magna (0272) 332554

VOAKE, Andrew James Frederick. b 28. Dur Univ BA55. Oak Hill Th Coll 51. **d** 55 **p** 56. Chapl Millfield Sch Somerset 63-71; R Bp Latimer Memorial Ch *Birm* 71-73; R Birm Bishop Latimer w All SS 73-80; V Crondall and Ewshot *Guildf* 80-90; rtd 90. *Garthowen, Street Road,*

Glastonbury, Somerset BA6 9EG   Glastonbury (0458) 31557

VOCKINS, Michael David. b 44. Univ of Wales (Abth) BSc69. Glouc Sch of Min 85. **d** 88 **p** 89. NSM Cradley w Mathon and Storridge *Heref* from 88; Perm to Offic *Worc* from 88. *Birchwood Lodge, Birchwood, Storridge, Malvern, Worcs WR13 5EZ*   Suckley (0886) 884366

✠**VOCKLER, Rt Rev John Charles (Brother John-Charles).** b 24. Queensland Univ BA53. ACT ThL48 ThD61 Gen Th Sem (NY) STB54 STM56 STD61 St Jo Coll Morpeth 48. **d** 48 **p** 48 **c** 59. Australia 48-53, 56-62 and 75-81; USA 54-56 and from 81; Bp Coadjutor Adelaide 59-62; Adn Eyre Peninsula 59-62; Bp Polynesia 62-68; SSF from 69; Perm to Offic *Sarum* 69-72; Asst Bp Worc 71-72; Perm to Offic *Lon* 72-75; Asst Bp Chelmsf 72-73; Asst Bp S'wark 73-75; Hon Can S'wark Cathl 75; rtd 90; Asst Bp Quincy from 90; Superior Franciscan Order Divine Compassion from 90. *The Friar's Lodgings, PO Box 281, Monmouth, Illinois 61462-0281, USA*

VODEN, Capt Raymond William Lang. b 35. CQSW74. SW Minl Tr Course 85. **d** 88 **p** 89. CA from 60; NSM Bideford *Ex* from 88. *The Retreat, 28 Westcombe, Bideford, Devon EX39 3JQ*   Bideford (0237) 475693 or 479220

VOGEL, Charles Edward. b 06. Trin Coll Ox BA28 MA31. Cuddesdon Coll 64. **d** 65 **p** 65. C-in-c Childrey *Ox* 69-75; P-in-c Sparsholt w Kingston Lisle 73-75; rtd 75. *Flat 12, Ellesborough Manor, Butlers Cross, Aylesbury, Bucks HP17 0XF*   Aylesbury (0296) 696125

VOGT, Charles William Derek. b 36. Portsm Poly DipSocWork76 Sheff Sch of Counselling & Psychology CertAnPsych85. E Midl Min Tr Course 83. **d** 86 **p** 87. NSM Ilkeston H Trin *Derby* 86-87; C Derby St Anne and St Jo 87-90; TV Staveley and Barrow Hill from 90. *St Francis Vicarage, Cedar Street, Hollingwood, Chesterfield S43 2LE*   Chesterfield (0246) 472175

VOGT, Robert Anthony. b 25. Jes Coll Cam BA50 MA54. S'wark Ord Course 60. **d** 63 **p** 64. C Kidbrooke St Jas *S'wark* 67-72; V Wood End *Cov* 72-80; RD Cov E 77-80; R Kidbrooke St Jas *S'wark* 80-85; TR 85-90; rtd 90. *16 Tristan Square, London SE3 9UB*   081-297 2361

VOKES, Prof Frederick Ercolo. b 10. FTCD74 St Jo Coll Cam BA33 MA46 BD53 TCD MA67. Westcott Ho Cam 33. **d** 34 **p** 35. Prof of Div TCD 57-80; rtd 80. *97 Westbourne Road, Lancaster LA1 5JY*   Lancaster (0524) 69428

VOKES-DUDGEON, Preb Thomas Pierre. b 09. Univ of NZ BA32 St Jo Coll Auckland 29. **d** 32 **p** 33. V St Marychurch *Ex* 51-75; Preb Ex Cathl 72-75; rtd 75; Perm to Offic *Ex* from 75. *Flat No 3, Petroc House, Falkland Road, Torquay TQ2 5JP*   Torquay (0803) 293968

VON BENZON, Charles Nicholas. b 54. Solicitor. Kent Univ BA. S'wark Ord Course 82. **d** 85 **p** 86. NSM Bromley SS Pet and Paul *Roch* 85-87; Ed Newsletter among Ministers at Work from 89. *Kirkholme, Tilsmore Road, Heathfield, E Sussex TN21 0XT*   Heathfield (04352) 2013

VON MALAISE, Nicolas Christoph Axel. b 62. Univ Coll Ox BA84. Ripon Coll Cuddesdon BA86. **d** 87 **p** 88. C Oxhey St Matt *St Alb* 87-90; C Northfield *Birm* from 90. *10 Pine View, Birmingham B31 2RD*   021-277 9179

VONBERG, Canon Michael. b 27. Lon Univ BA51. Wells Th Coll 58. **d** 59 **p** 60. C Bournemouth St Andr *Win* 59-61; C Milton 61-64; V Camberwell St Geo *S'wark* 64-74; V Kenley from 75; RD Croydon S from 85; Hon Can S'wark Cathl from 89. *The Vicarage, 3 Valley Road, Kenley, Surrey CR8 5DJ*   081-660 3263

VOOGHT, Canon Michael George Peter. b 38. St Pet Hall Ox BA61 MA65. Chich Th Coll 61. **d** 63 **p** 64. C E Dulwich St Jo *S'wark* 63-66; C Prestbury *Glouc* 66-72; R Minchinhampton 72-85; RD Stonehouse 79-85; V Thornbury from 85; Hon Can Glouc Cathl from 86. *The Vicarage, Castle Street, Thornbury, Bristol BS12 1HQ*   Thornbury (0454) 413209

VORLEY, Kenneth Arthur. b 27. Sarum Th Coll 65. **d** 67 **p** 68. C Ashbourne w Mapleton and Clifton *Derby* 67-71; R W Hallam and Mapperley 71-77; V Hemingford Grey *Ely* 78-88; rtd 88. *The Old Manor, Little Braithwaite, Keswick, Cumbria CA12 5SR*   Braithwaite (07687) 82535

VOSS, Mrs Philomena Ann. **d** 90. NSM Nazeing *Chelmsf* from 90. *21 Queen's Road, Hertford SG13 8AZ*   Hertford (0992) 554676

VOUSDEN, Alan Thomas. b 48. K Coll Lon BSc69. Qu Coll Birm DipTh71. **d** 72 **p** 73. C Orpington All SS *Roch* 72-76; C Belvedere All SS 76-80; R Cuxton and Halling 80-86; V Bromley St Mark from 86. *St Mark's Vicarage, 51 Hayes Road, Bromley, Kent BR2 9AE*   081-460 6220

VOUT, Victor Alan. b 25. Lon Univ BA53 Hull Univ BA56. Ripon Hall Ox 63. **d** 65 **p** 66. C Norton Woodseats St Paul *Sheff* 65-70; V Clifton St Jas from 70. *10 Clifton Crescent North, Rotherham, S Yorkshire S65 2AS* Rotherham (0709) 363082

VOWLES, Miss Patricia. b 50. S'wark Ord Course 84. **d** 87. NSM Nunhead St Antony w St Silas *S'wark* from 87. *USPG Network 21 Promoter, 157 Waterloo Road, London SE1 8XA* 071-928 8681

VOWLES, Canon Peter John Henry. b 25. Magd Coll Ox BA50 MA55. Westcott Ho Cam 50. **d** 52 **p** 53. V 64-72; R Cottingham *York* 72-83; R Man St Ann *Man* 83-91; Hon Can Man Cathl from 83; rtd 91. *10 Redshaw Close, Fallowfield, Manchester M14 6JB* 061-257 2065

VYSE, Canon Jack Walter Miller. b 15. CCC Cam BA37 MA41. Westcott Ho Cam 38. **d** 39 **p** 40. V St Mary Abchurch *Lon* 61-70; Vice-Prin S'wark Ord Course 66-70; P-in-c Alby w Thwaite *Nor* 70-81; V Aylsham 70-88; Chapl St Mich Hosp Aylsham 70-88; RD Ingworth *Nor* 74-88; Hon Can Nor Cathl 81-88; rtd 88; Perm to Offic *Linc* 88-89; RD Louthesk from 89. *The Old Post Office, Ludford Magna, Lincs LN3 6AD* Burgh-on-Bain (0507) 313740

VYVYAN, John Philip. b 28. New Coll Ox BA51 MA59. Cuddesdon Coll 57. **d** 59 **p** 60. C Notting Hill St Mark *Lon* 59-61; USPG (Sarawak & Borneo) 61-64; V Adderbury w Milton *Ox* from 64. *The Vicarage, 13 Dog Close, Adderbury, Banbury, Oxon OX17 3EF* Banbury (0295) 810309

W

WADDINGTON, Very Rev John Albert Henry. b 10. MBE TD. **d** 33 **p** 34. Provost St E 58-76; rtd 76; Perm to Offic *St E* from 76. *67 Churchgate Street, Bury St Edmunds, Suffolk IP33 1RH* Bury St Edmunds (0284) 754494

WADDINGTON, Very Rev Robert Murray. b 27. Selw Coll Cam BA51 MA55. Ely Th Coll 51. **d** 53 **p** 54. C Bethnal Green St Jo w St Simon *Lon* 53-56; Australia 56-59 and 61-71; C Chesterton St Luke *Ely* 59-61; OGS from 60; Can Res Carl Cathl *Carl* 72-77; Bp's Adv for Educn 72-77; Hon Can Carl Cathl 77-84; Gen Sec Gen Syn Bd of Educn 77-84; Gen Sec Nat Soc 77-84; Dean Man from 84. *Deanery, 44 Shrewsbury Road, Prestwich, Manchester M25 8GQ* 061-773 2959 or 834 7503

WADDINGTON-FEATHER, John Joseph. b 33. FRSA89 Leeds Univ BA54. St Deiniol's Hawarden 75. **d** 77 **p** 78. Hon C Longden and Annscroft w Pulverbatch *Heref* from 77; Sub-Chapl HM Pris Shrewsbury from 77; Chapl Prestfelde Sch Shrewsbury from 86. *Fair View, Old Coppice, Lyth Bank, Shrewsbury SY3 0BW* Bayston Hill (074372) 2177

WADDLE, William. b 31. Linc Th Coll 64. **d** 66 **p** 67. C Tynemouth Priory *Newc* 66-69; C Longbenton St Bart 69-75; V Denton 75-81; V Beadnell 81; V Beadnell w Ellingham from 81; RD Bamburgh and Glendale from 83. *The Vicarage, Beadnell, Chathill, Northd NE67 5BR* Seahouses (0665) 720223

WADDLETON, Edwin Henry. b 12. Clifton Th Coll 37. **d** 39 **p** 40. R Chippenham St Paul w Langley Burrell *Bris* 65-77; rtd 77; Perm to Offic *Bris* from 77. *66 Sadler's Mead, Chippenham, Wilts SN15 3PL* Chippenham (0249) 653721

WADDY, Richard Patteson Stacy. b 04. Ball Coll Ox BA26 MA30. Cuddesdon Coll 26. **d** 27 **p** 28. Chapl Qu Anne's Sch Caversham 67-72; rtd 72. *Manormead, Tilford Road, Hindhead, Surrey GU26 6RA* Hindhead (0428) 604780

WADE, Andrew James Bentinck. b 54. Sheff Univ BA76. Sarum & Wells Th Coll 83. **d** 85 **p** 86. C Redhill St Jo *S'wark* 85-88; C Norbury St Steph and Thornton Heath 88-90. *Address temp unknown*

WADE, Andrew John. b 50. Trin Coll Bris. **d** 86 **p** 87. C St Keverne *Truro* 86-89; TV Probus, Ladock and Grampound w Creed from 89. *74 Trencreek Close, St Erme, Truro, Cornwall TR4 9RA* Truro (0872) 40835

WADE, Anthony Austen. b 14. Leeds Univ BA36 MA38. Coll of Resurr Mirfield 36. **d** 38 **p** 39. V Sudbury St Andr *Lon* 68-79; rtd 79; Perm to Offic *Bris* from 80. *28 Claremont Road, Bristol BS7 8DH* Bristol (0272) 243966

WADE, Canon John Martin. b 22. Wells Th Coll. **d** 54 **p** 55. V Nayland w Wiston *St E* 60-74; Chapl Jane Walker Hosp Nayland 62-74; V Shrivenham w Watchfield and

Bourton *Ox* 74-88; RD Vale of White Horse 83-87; Hon Can Ch Ch from 86; rtd 88; Perm to Offic *Ox* from 88; Glouc from 90. *Cranham, 13 Besbury Park, Minchinhampton, Stroud, Glos GL6 9EN* Stroud (0453) 885449

WADE, Very Rev Kenneth Ernest. b 14. K Coll Lon 37. Coll of Resurr Mirfield 40. **d** 41 **p** 42. R Bocking St Mary *Chelmsf* 64-89; Dean Bocking 64-89; rtd 89. *120 School Road, Copford, Essex CO6 1BX* Colchester (0206) 212498

WADE, Robert Edward. b 56. Trin Coll Bris. **d** 85. C Monkwearmouth St Andr *Dur* 85-87. *21 Dale Terrace, Fulwell, Sunderland*

WADE, Walter. b 29. Oak Hill Th Coll 64. **d** 66 **p** 67. C Denton Holme *Carl* 66-69; V Jesmond H Trin *Newc* 69-78; R Moresby *Carl* 78-87; P-in-c Langdale from 87. *The Vicarage, Chapel Stile, Ambleside, Cumbria LA22 9JG* Langdale (09667) 267

WADE-STUBBS, Edward Pomery Flood. b 17. St Jo Coll Dur LTh39 BA40. Tyndale Hall Bris 36. **d** 40 **p** 41. V Norton Bavant *Sarum* 63-66; R Sutton Veny 63-66; rtd 69; Perm to Offic *Sarum* from 90. *6 Blair Court, 18 Blair Avenue, Poole, Dorset BH14 0DA* Parkstone (0202) 715519

WADGE, Alan. b 46. Grey Coll Dur BA68 MA72 St Chad's Coll Dur DipTh69. **d** 70 **p** 71. C Cockerton *Dur* 70-74; C Whitworth w Spennymoor 74-75; P-in-c Shipton Moyne w Westonbirt and Lasborough *Glouc* 75-80; Chapl Westonbirt Sch 75-80; V Dean Forest H Trin *Glouc* 80-83; Chapl Gresham's Sch Holt 83-91; R Ridgeway *Ox* from 91. *The Rectory, Letcombe Regis, Wantage, Oxon OX12 9LD* Wantage (02357) 3805

WADSWORTH, Andrew James. b 56. St Jo Coll Dur BA79 Cam Univ CertEd80. Sarum & Wells Th Coll 84 Chich Th Coll 86. **d** 87 **p** 88. NSM Forest Row *Chich* 87-89; NSM E Grinstead St Swithun 87-89; C Shrewsbury St Chad w St Mary *Lich* 89-91; TV Honiton, Gittisham, Combe Raleigh, Monkton etc *Ex* from 91. *The Vicarage, Awliscombe, Honiton, Devon EX14 0PJ* Honiton (0404) 42983

WADSWORTH, Jean. b 44. Cranmer Hall Dur BA71 St Jo Coll Dur. **d** 87. Par Dn Thamesmead *S'wark* from 87. *6 Sorrel Close, Waterfield Gardens, London SE28 8ER* 081-310 9351 or 310 6814

WADSWORTH, Michael Philip. b 43. Qu Coll Ox BA65 MA68 DPhil75 Cam Univ PhD78. Ripon Hall Ox 67. **d** 70 **p** 71. C Sutton St Mich *York* 70-73; Lect Sussex Univ 73-78; Fell 78-81; Hon C Hove St Jo *Chich* 75-78; Chapl SS Coll Cam 78-81; Dir Th Studies 79-81; CF (TA) from 80; C Ditton St Mich *Liv* 81; TV 82-84; Dioc Lay Tr Officer 83-89; V Orford St Marg 84-89; V Haddenham *Ely* from 89; V Wilburton from 89. *The Vicarage, Haddenham, Ely, Cambs CB6 3TB* Ely (0353) 740309

WADSWORTH, Norman Charles. b 26. Bps' Coll Cheshunt 62. **d** 64 **p** 65. C Leighton Buzzard *St Alb* 64-69; P-in-c Wing *Ox* 69-73; P-in-c Grove St Mic 69-73; P-in-c Wingrave 69-74; V Wing w Grove 73-79; R Didcot All SS from 79. *The Rectory, 140 Lydalls Road, Didcot, Oxon OX11 7EA* Didcot (0235) 813244

WADSWORTH, Peter Richard. b 52. Qu Coll Ox BA73 MA77. Cuddesdon Coll 74 English Coll Rome 76. **d** 77 **p** 78. C High Wycombe *Ox* 77-81; C Farnham Royal 81; C Farnham Royal w Hedgerley 81-84; Dioc Ecum Officer *Portsm* 84-90; V E Meon from 84; V Langrish from 84. *The Vicarage, East Meon, Petersfield, Hants GU32 1NL* East Meon (073087) 221

WADSWORTH, Roy. b 37. NE Ord Course. **d** 89 **p** 90. NSM Alne *York* from 89. *Rosery, Tollerton, York YO6 2DX* Tollerton (03473) 212

WAGGETT, Geoffrey James. b 49. Sarum & Wells Th Coll 83. **d** 85 **p** 86. C Newton Nottage *Llan* 85-88; TV Glyncorrwg w Afan Vale and Cymmer Afan 88-89; R from 89. *The Vicarage, Church Street, Glyncorrwg, Port Talbot, W Glam SA13 3BW* Cymmer (0639) 851301

WAGHORN, Geoffrey Brian. b 28. St Aid Birkenhead 62. **d** 64 **p** 65. C Gillingham H Trin *Roch* 64-66; C St Mary Cray and St Paul's Cray 66-68; C Lavington w Ingoldsby *Linc* 68-70; V Messingham 70-77; R Fishtoft 77-85; R Durley *Portsm* from 85; V Curdridge from 85. *The Vicarage, Curdridge, Southampton SO3 2DR* Botley (04892) 2795

WAGHORNE, Frederick Charles. b 07. St Jo Coll Dur BA32 MA35 DipTh35. **d** 33 **p** 34. V Bearsted *Cant* 63-73; rtd 73; Perm to Offic *Cant* from 73. *Townfield, Burleigh Road, Charing, Ashford, Kent* Charing (023371) 3130

WAGNER, Canon Peter Frederick. b 30. Lon Univ BSc56. Westcott Ho Cam. **d** 60 **p** 61. C Longbridge *Birm* 60-64; V Nechells 64-70; Rhodesia 70-80; Zimbabwe from 80;

Dean Gweru 84-87. *PO Box 75, Kwekwe, Zimbabwe* Kwekwe (55) 2535

WAGSTAFF, Alan Robert Joseph. b 21. Lon Univ DipTh69. S'wark Ord Course 67. **d** 70 **p** 71. C St Paul's Cray St Barn *Roch* 70-76; V Southborough St Pet w Ch Ch and St Matt 76-86; RD Tunbridge Wells 83-86; rtd 86; Perm to Offic Chich & Roch from 86. *27A The Green, St Leonards-on-Sea, E Sussex TN38 0SX* Hastings (0424) 425895

WAGSTAFF, Andrew Robert. b 56. K Coll Lon BD79 AKC79. Coll of Resurr Mirfield 81. **d** 83 **p** 84. C Newark w Hawton, Cotham and Shelton *S'well* 83-86; C Dub St Bart w Ch Ch Leeson Park *D & G* 86-89; V Nottm St Geo w St Jo *S'well* from 89. *St George's Vicarage, Strome Close, Nottingham NG2 1HD* Nottingham (0602) 864881

WAGSTAFF, Ven Christopher John Harold. b 36. St D Coll Lamp BA62 DipTh63. **d** 63 **p** 64. C Queensbury All SS *Lon* 63-68; V Tokyngton St Mich 68-73; V Coleford w Staunton *Glouc* 73-83; RD Forest S 76-82; Adn Glouc from 83. *Christ Church Vicarage, 6 Spa Villas, Gloucester GL1 1LB* Gloucester (0452) 28500

WAGSTAFF, Miss Joan. b 33. Gilmore Ho. **dss** 75 **d** 87. Ellesmere Port *Ches* 86-87; Par Dn from 87. *16 Westminster Road, Ellesmere Port, South Wirral L65 2EG* 051-355 9011

WAGSTAFF, Michael. b 59. R Holloway Coll Lon BA81. Coll of Resurr Mirfield 86. **d** 89 **p** 90. C Worksop Priory *S'well* from 89. *268 Kilton Road, Worksop, Notts S80 2DZ* Worksop (0909) 485642

WAGSTAFF, Robert Hugh. b 22. Pemb Coll Ox BA43 MA47. Wycliffe Hall Ox 47. **d** 49 **p** 50. V Ince St Mary *Liv* 58-75; V Glazebury 75-87; rtd 87. *22 Greenfield Avenue, Parbold, Wigan, Lancs WN8 7DH* Parbold (0257) 463467

WAGSTAFF, Robert William. b 36. Edin Th Coll 61. **d** 63 **p** 64. C Harringay St Paul *Lon* 63-64; C Mill Hill Jo Keble Ch 64-69; Perm to Offic *S'wark* 76-81; Lic to Offic *Worc* from 81. *The Red House, Quarry Bank, Hartlebury, Kidderminster, Worcs* Hartlebury (0299) 250883

WAGSTAFFE, Eric Herbert. b 25. St Aid Birkenhead 55. **d** 57 **p** 58. V Pendlebury St Jo *Man* 69-84; V Hoghton *Blackb* 84-91; rtd 91. *3 Chelwood Close, Springfield Heights, Bolton BL1 7LN* Bolton (0204) 596048

WAIN, Frank. b 13. Leeds Univ BA35. Coll of Resurr Mirfield 35. **d** 37 **p** 38. R Kinwarton w Gt Alne and Haselor *Cov* 55-83; rtd 83; Perm to Offic *Cov* from 83. *21 Queensway, Bidford-on-Avon, Alcester, Warks B50 4BA* Bidford-on-Avon (0789) 778586

WAINAINA, Francis Samson Kamoko. b 51. BA84 Dur Univ MA89. Oak Hill Th Coll 81. **d** 84 **p** 85. Kenya 84-88; C Upton (or Overchurch) *Ches* from 89. *65 Devonshire Road, Upton, Wirral, Merseyside*

✠**WAINE, Rt Rev John.** b 30. Man Univ BA51. Ridley Hall Cam 53. **d** 55 **p** 56 **c** 75. C W Derby St Mary *Liv* 55-58; C Sutton 58-60; V Ditton St Mich 60-64; V Southport H Trin 64-69; V Kirkby 69-71; TR 71-75; Suff Bp Stafford *Lich* 75-78; Preb Lich Cathl 75-78; Bp St E 78-86; Bp Chelmsf from 86; Clerk of the Closet to HM The Queen from 89. *Bishopscourt, Margaretting, Ingatestone, Essex CM4 0HD* Ingatestone (0277) 352001

WAINE, Stephen John. b 59. BA. Westcott Ho Cam 81. **d** 84 **p** 85. C Wolv *Lich* 84-88; Min Can and Succ St Paul's Cathl *Lon* from 88. *8A Amen Court, London EC4M 7BU* 071-248 6115

WAINWRIGHT, Barrington Herbert. b 08. St Cath Coll Cam BA31 MA35. Wycliffe Hall Ox 31. **d** 33 **p** 34. V St Marylebone St Mark Hamilton Terrace *Lon* 65-79; rtd 79. *98 Bargates, Leominster, Herefordshire HR6 8QT* Leominster (0568) 4657

WAINWRIGHT, David Bernard Pictor. b 25. St Jo Coll Dur BA50 MA53. Chich Th Coll 50. **d** 51 **p** 52. Sen Soc Worker Bd for Soc Resp Man 69-73; V Scouthead *Man* 69-72; Asst Sec Gen Syn Bd for Soc Resp 74-78; Dep Sec 78-79; P-in-c Charlton on Otmoor and Oddington *Ox* 79-85; Soc Resp Officer 79-88; RD Bicester and Islip 82-85; Sec Ox Dioc Bd for Soc Resp 85-88; rtd 88. *4 Eleanor Road, Harrogate, N Yorkshire HG2 7AJ* Harrogate (0423) 881081

WAINWRIGHT, Frank Alan. b 18. Leeds Univ BA39. Coll of Resurr Mirfield 39. **d** 41 **p** 42. V Woodham *Guildf* 64-72; rtd 83. *Roydon, Pendoggett, St Kew, Bodmin, Cornwall PL30 3HH* Port Isaac (020888) 528

WAINWRIGHT, John Pounsberry. b 42. St Steph Ho Ox 64. **d** 66 **p** 67. C Palmers Green St Jo *Lon* 66-70; C Primrose Hill St Mary w Avenue Road St Paul 70-71; P-in-c St Jo Wood All SS 71-73; V Hendon All SS

Childs Hill from 73. *All Saints' Vicarage, Church Walk, London NW2 2JT* 071-435 3182

WAINWRIGHT, Joseph Allan. b 21. K Coll Lon BD50 AKC50. Columbia Pacific Univ PhD82 Sussex Univ DPhil85. **d** 50 **p** 51. Lect Moray Ho Coll of Educn Edin 66-78; Perm to Offic *Chich* from 79; rtd 86. *Beggar's Roost, Lewes, E Sussex BN7 1LX* Lewes (0273) 477453

WAINWRIGHT, Kevin Frank. b 46. Linc Th Coll 73. **d** 75 **p** 76. C Stand *Man* 75-78; C Radcliffe St Thos and St Jo 78-80; V Kearsley Moor from 80. *St Stephen's Vicarage, Blair Street, Kearsley, Bolton BL4 8QP* Farnworth (0204) 72535

WAINWRIGHT, Maurice Sidney. b 30. Lon Univ BSc54. Bps' Coll Cheshunt 54. **d** 56 **p** 57. C Twickenham St Mary *Lon* 56-59; C Caversham *Ox* 59-61; Lic to Offic *Chelmsf* from 61. *60 Eastwood Road, London E18* 081-989 1529

WAINWRIGHT, Miss Pauline Barbara. b 40. St Deiniol's Hawarden 83. **dss** 84 **d** 87. New Ferry *Ches* 84-87; Par Dn 87-90; Par Dn Hallwood from 90. *284 The Glen, Palace Fields, Runcorn WA7 2TF* Runcorn (0928) 715688

WAINWRIGHT, Peter Anthony. b 45. **d** 75 **p** 76. C Ashtead *Guildf* 76-79; V Woking St Paul 79-84. *Address temp unknown*

WAINWRIGHT, Raymond Laycock. b 25. Lon Univ BD60. Ho of Resurr Mirfield 55. **d** 56 **p** 57. V Gawthorpe and Chickenley Heath *Wakef* 60-74; V New Mill 74-89; V Thurstonland 74-89; TV Upper Holme Valley 89-91; rtd 91. *7 Greenlaws Close, Holmfirth, Huddersfield HD7 2GB* Huddersfield (0484) 683779

WAIT, Alan Clifford. b 33. St Cath Soc Ox BA58 MA70. Coll of Resurr Mirfield. **d** 60 **p** 61. C Old Charlton *S'wark* 60-67; C Caterham 67-72; V N Dulwich St Faith 72-83; RD Dulwich 78-83; V Purley St Barn from 83. *St Barnabas's Vicarage, 84 Higher Drive, Purley, Surrey CR8 2HJ* 081-660 3251

WAITE, Harry. b 21. Linc Th Coll. **d** 55 **p** 56. Youth Chapl Pet 69-88; rtd 88; Perm to Offic *Linc* from 90. *37 Tor O'Moor Road, Woodhall Spa, Lincs LN10 6TD* Woodhall Spa (0526) 53387

WAITE, John Langton. b 10. Solicitor 34. ACP37 Man Univ 30. Wycliffe Hall Ox 37. **d** 39 **p** 40. V Woking St Jo *Guildf* 58-76; rtd 76; Perm to Offic *Portsm* from 82. *11 The Crescent, Alverstoke, Gosport, Hants PO12 2DN* Gosport (0705) 521458

WAITE, Julian Henry. b 47. Brasted Th Coll 68 Ridley Hall Cam 70. **d** 72 **p** 73. C Wollaton *S'well* 72-76; C Herne Bay Ch Ch *Cant* 76-79; P-in-c Mersham 79-87; P-in-c Sevington 79-87; R Mersham w Hinxhill 87; V Marden from 87; Chapl HM Pris Blantyre Ho from 90. *The Vicarage, Marden, Tonbridge, Kent TN12 9DR* Maidstone (0622) 831379

WAITE, Sheila Margaret. See TYLER, Mrs Sheila Margaret

WAKE, Colin Walter. b 50. Or Coll Ox BA72 MA. Cuddesdon Coll 74. **d** 75 **p** 76. C Sandhurst *Ox* 75-78; C Faversham *Cant* 79-80; TV High Wycombe *Ox* 80-89; R Weston Favell *Pet* from 89. *The Rectory, Churchway, Weston Favell, Northampton NN3 3BX* Northampton (0604) 784679

WAKE, Hugh. b 16. St Aug Coll Cant. **d** 62 **p** 63. R Stanningfield w Bradfield Combust *St E* 67-74; V Gt Finborough w Onehouse and Harleston 75-84; rtd 84; Perm to Offic *St E* from 84. *1 Burroughs Piece Road, Sudbury, Suffolk CO10 6PR* Sudbury (0787) 76760

WAKEFIELD, Allan. b 31. Qu Coll Birm 72. **d** 74 **p** 75. C Kingsthorpe w Northn St Dav *Pet* 74-77; TV Clifton *S'well* 77-81; V Bilborough St Jo 81-85; R Bere Ferrers *Ex* 85-91; R Mevagissey and St Ewe *Truro* from 91. *The Vicarage, 58 Church Steet, Mevagissey, St Austell, Cornwall PL26 6SR* Mevagissey (0726) 842488

WAKEFIELD, Andrew Desmond. b 55. K Coll Lon BD77 AKC77. Coll of Resurr Mirfield 77. **d** 78 **p** 79. C Mitcham Ascension *S'wark* 78-81; C Putney St Mary 81-86; TV Wimbledon 86-91; Ind Chapl from 90; P-in-c S Wimbledon St Andr from 91; Dioc Urban Missr from 91. *St Andrew's Vicarage, 47 Wilton Grove, London SW19 3QU* 081-542 1794

WAKEFIELD, David Geoffrey. b 43. AMIC90. S'wark Ord Course 84. **d** 87 **p** 88. C Addiscombe St Mildred *S'wark* 87-89; C Reigate St Luke S Park from 89. *St Peter's House, Lynn Walk, Reigate, Surrey RH2 7NZ* Reigate (0737) 245560

WAKEFIELD, Gavin Tracy. b 57. Van Mildert Coll Dur BSc Sheff Univ CertEd Nottm Univ DipTh. St Jo Coll Nottm 83. **d** 86 **p** 87. C Anston *Sheff* 86-89; C Aston cum Aughton and Ulley 89-91; TV Billericay and

Lt Burstead *Chelmsf* from 91. *10 Chestwood Close, Billericay, Essex CM12 0PB* Billericay (0277) 652659

WAKEFIELD, Canon Kenneth Eyles. b 25. St Jo Coll Dur BA50 DipTh51 MA56. **d** 51 **p** 52. Chapl Bartlet Hosp Felixstowe 59-89; V Walton *St E* 59-88; Hon Chapl Miss to Seamen 64-88; RD Colneys *St E* 73-86; Hon Can St E Cathl 75-88; rtd 89. *14 Fleetwood Road, Felixstowe, Suffolk IP11 7EQ* Felixstowe (0394) 672113

WAKEFIELD, Peter. b 48. Nottm Univ BTh72 DipAdEd85. St Jo Coll Nottm 68 ALCD72. **d** 72 **p** 73. C Hinckley H Trin *Leic* 72-75; C Kirby Muxloe 75-78; V Barlestone 78-85; TV Padgate *Liv* 85-88; V Quinton w Marston Sicca *Glouc* from 91. *The Vicarage, Lower Quinton, Stratford-upon-Avon, Warks CV37 8SG* Stratford-upon-Avon (0789) 720707

WAKEFIELD, Bishop of. *Vacant*

WAKEFIELD, Provost of. *See* ALLEN, Very Rev John Edward

WAKEFORD, Victor David. b 16. Ex Coll Ox BA37 MA41. Ripon Hall Ox 41. **d** 46 **p** 47. Chapl K Sch Glouc 58-71; Perm to Offic *Chich* from 71; rtd 81. *Flat 5, Grantley Court, London Road, Tunbridge Wells, Kent TN1 1BX*

WAKELIN, Alan Frank. b 32. Univ of Wales (Lamp) BA58. Coll of Resurr Mirfield 58. **d** 60 **p** 61. C Northn St Matt *Pet* 60-63; C Pet All SS 63-65; C Spalding *Linc* 65-68; R Skirbeck St Nic from 68. *The Rectory, Skirbeck, Boston, Lincs PE21 0DJ* Boston (0205) 63216

WAKELING, Bruce. b 50. Lon Univ BA74. Westcott Ho Cam 74. **d** 77 **p** 78. C Weymouth H Trin *Sarum* 77-82; TV Oakdale St Geo 82-89; R Clopton w Otley, Swilland and Ashbocking *St E* from 89. *The Rectory, Clopton, Woodbridge, Suffolk IP13 6SE* Grundisburgh (047335) 765

WAKELING, Hugh Michael. b 42. CEng MIMechE82 Cape Town Univ BSc63. Wycliffe Hall Ox 71. **d** 74 **p** 75. C Kennington St Mark *S'wark* 74-78; C Surbiton Hill Ch Ch 78-80; Hon C Richmond H Trin and Ch Ch 80-84; Hon C California *Ox* 85-89; Hon C Arborfield w Barkham from 89. *Pine Lodge, 52 Pine Drive, Wokingham, Berks RG11 3LE* Eversley (0734) 734078

✠**WAKELING, Rt Rev John Denis.** b 18. MC45. St Cath Coll Cam BA40 MA44 Nottm Univ Hon DD84. Ridley Hall Cam 46. **d** 47 **p** 48 **c** 70. C Barwell w Potters Marston and Stapleton *Leic* 47-50; Chapl Clare Coll Cam 50-52; Lic to Offic *Ely* 50-52; V Plymouth Em *Ex* 52-59; Preb Ex Cathl 57-59; V Barking St Marg *Chelmsf* 59-65; P-in-c Barking St Patr 60-65; Adn W Ham 65-70; Bp S'well 70-85; rtd 85. *The Maples, The Avenue, Porton, Salisbury, Wilts SP4 0NT* Idmiston (0980) 610666

WAKELING, Stanley George. b 11. St Cath Coll Cam BA35 MA39. Wycliffe Hall Ox 35. **d** 37 **p** 38. V Tulse Hill H Trin *S'wark* 69-73; V Lower Nutfield 73-76; rtd 76; Hon C Nether Stowey w Over Stowey *B & W* 77-80; Perm to Offic from 86. *3 Suffolk Crescent, Taunton, Somerset TA1 4JL* Taunton (0823) 271007

WAKELY, Marcus. b 40. Solicitor 62 FRSA88. E Midl Min Tr Course 84. **d** 87 **p** 88. NSM Carrington *S'well* 87-91; C Worksop Priory from 91. *148 Edwards Lane, Nottingham NG5 3HZ* Nottingham (0602) 203299

WAKELY, Roger. b 42. St Paul's Cheltenham CertEd. S'wark Ord Course 67. **d** 70 **p** 71. C Ealing St Mary *Lon* 70-76; Chapl Bp Wand's Sch Sunbury-on-Thames 76-82; R Gaulby *Leic* 82-87; V Galleywood Common *Chelmsf* from 87; Warden of Ords from 89. *Galleywood Vicarage, 450 Beehive Lane, Chelmsford CM2 8RN* Chelmsford (0245) 353922

WAKEMAN, Mrs Hilary Margaret. b 38. E Anglian Minl Tr Course. **dss** 85 **d** 87. Heigham St Thos *Nor* 85-87; C 87-90; C Nor St Mary Magd w St Jas 90-91; Dn-in-c Norwich-over-the-Water Colegate St Geo 90-91; TM Nor Over-the-Water from 91. *32 Grosvenor Road, Norwich NR2 2PZ* Norwich (0603) 666455

WAKER, Anthony Francis. b 30. St Chad's Coll Dur BA56 DipTh57. **d** 57 **p** 58. C Stokenchurch *Ox* 57-60; C Summertown 60-65; R Iron Acton *Bris* from 65. *The Rectory, High Street, Iron Acton, Bristol BS17 1UQ* Rangeworthy (045422) 412

WAKERELL, Richard Hinton. b 55. Qu Coll Birm. **d** 84 **p** 85. C Gillingham St Mary *Roch* 84-87; C Kingswinford St Mary *Lich* from 87. *28 Foundry Road, Kingswinford, W Midlands DY6 9BD* Kingswinford (0384) 273961

WALDEN, John Edward Frank. b 38. FInstSMM. Oak Hill Th Coll 67. **d** 69 **p** 70. C Rainham *Chelmsf* 69-73; P-in-c Bris H Cross Inns Court *Bris* 73-78; Conf and Publicity Sec SAMS 78-81; Hon C Southborough St Pet w Ch Ch and St Matt *Roch* 78-81; Exec Sec Spanish and Portuguese Ch Aid Soc 80-81; Hon C Tonbridge St Steph 81-84; R Earsham w Alburgh and Denton *Nor*

84-89. *c/o Michael Hall & Co, Garsett House, Norwich* Norwich (0603) 617772

WALDEN, Samuel. b 15. Richmond Th Coll 45. **d** 57 **p** 58. USA 57-71; R Blackley H Trin *Man* 71-74; Chapl Prestwich Hosp Man 74-80; rtd 80. *5 Castlegate, New Brook Street, Ilkley, W Yorkshire LS29 8DF* Ilkley (0943) 601860

WALDRON, Geoffrey Robert. b 15. Selw Coll Cam BA37 MA41. Ely Th Coll 37. **d** 38 **p** 39. R Barwick *B & W* 63-76; R Closworth 63-76; P-in-c Charlton Adam w Charlton Mackrell 76-78; R Charlton Adam w Charlton Mackrell and Kingsdon 78-80; rtd 80; Perm to Offic *B & W* from 81. *Roseland, Castle Street, Keinton Mandeville, Somerton, Somerset TA11 6DX* Charlton Mackrell (045822) 3224

WALDRON, Laurence Charles. b 22. Bps' Coll Cheshunt 58. **d** 59 **p** 60. V Lea Hall *Birm* 66-77; V Wiggenhall St Mary Magd *Ely* 77-87; V Wiggenhall St Germans and Islington 77-87; rtd 87. *16 Heath Gardens, Stone, Staffs ST15 0AW* Stone (0785) 818237

WALES, David Neville. b 55. Rhodes Univ Grahamstown BA78. Coll of Resurr Mirfield 80. **d** 82 **p** 83. Zimbabwe 82-88; C Linslade *Ox* 89-91; P-in-c Weston Turville from 91. *The Rectory, Church Walk, Weston Turville, Aylesbury, Bucks HP22 5SH* Aylesbury (0296) 613212

WALES, Archbishop of. *Vacant*

WALFORD, David. b 45. S'wark Ord Course 75. **d** 78 **p** 79. NSM Hackbridge and N Beddington *S'wark* 78-83; C Fawley *Win* 83-87; C-in-c Boyatt Wood CD 87-90; V Boyatt Wood from 90. *St Peter's Church House, 53 Sovereign Way, Boyatt Wood, Eastleigh SO5 4SA* Eastleigh (0703) 642188

WALFORD, David John. b 47. St Luke's Coll Ex CertEd68 AKC71. St Aug Coll Cant. **d** 72 **p** 73. C Oxton *Ches* 72-77; C Neston 77-80; Youth Chapl 80-81; V Backford 80-81; C Woodchurch 81; Chapl Fulbourn Hosp and Ida Darw Hosp Cam 82-83; Chapl N Man Gen Hosp 83-86; Distr Chapl in Mental Health Ex HA and Chapl Ex Hosp Gp from 86. *Dean Clarke House, Southernhay East, Exeter EX1 1PQ* Exeter (0392) 411222

WALFORD, David Sanderson. b 23. BEM49. Chich Th Coll 78. **d** 79 **p** 80. Hon C Chich St Pet *Chich* 79-81; C Chich St Paul and St Pet 81-83; P-in-c Wisbech St Aug *Ely* 83-86; rtd 88. *Sibford, Church Hill, Marnhull, Sturminster Newton, Dorset DT10 1PU* Marnhull (0258) 820201

WALFORD, Dr Frank Roy. b 35. Birm Univ MB, ChB58. Qu Coll Birm 78. **d** 80 **p** 81. Hon C Walsall Pleck and Bescot *Lich* 80-85; Chr Healing Cen Bordon 85-88; Dep Medical Dir St Wilfrid's Hospice Chich from 88; Perm to Offic *Chich* from 88. *15 Grove Road, Chichester, W Sussex PO19 2AR* Chichester (0243) 533947

WALFORD, Robin Peter. b 46. Qu Coll Birm 75. **d** 78 **p** 79. C Radcliffe-on-Trent *S'well* 78-81; TV Newark w Hawton, Cotham and Shelton 81-84; P-in-c Forest Town from 84. *The Vicarage, Old Mill Lane, Forest Town, Mansfield, Notts NG19 0EP* Mansfield (0623) 21120

WALKER, Alan Robert Glaister. b 52. K Coll Cam BA76 MA79 New Coll Ox BA76 MA84 Cen Lon Poly LLB91. St Steph Ho Ox 82. **d** 84 **p** 85. C St Jo Wood *Lon* 84-86; Chapl Poly of Cen Lon from 87. *4A Luxborough Street, London W1M 3LG* 071-911 5050

WALKER, Albert William John. b 14. Linc Th Coll 43. **d** 45 **p** 46. V Kingston St Luke *S'wark* 67-74; V Mickleton *Glouc* 74-79; rtd 79; Chapl Convent of St Mary at the Cross Edgware from 79; Lic to Offic *Lon* from 79; Perm to Offic *Carl* from 87. *Shepherd's Fold, 4 Fairview Cottages, Ambleside, Cumbria LA22 9EE* Ambleside (05394) 32418

WALKER, Allen Ross. b 46. Chich Th Coll 86. **d** 88. C Cosham *Portsm* from 88. *39 Magdala Road, Cosham, Portsmouth PO6 2QG* Cosham (0705) 325121

WALKER, Andrew Stephen. b 58. St Chad's Coll Dur BA80. St Steph Ho Ox 83. **d** 85 **p** 86. C Fareham SS Pet and Paul *Portsm* 85-87; C St Jo Wood *Lon* from 87. *3 Cochrane Street, London NW8 7PA* 071-722 4766

WALKER, Anthony Charles St John. b 55. Trin Coll Ox MA80. Wycliffe Hall Ox 78. **d** 81 **p** 82. C Bradf Cathl *Bradf* 81-84; C Nottm St Ann w Em *S'well* 84-88; V Retford from 88. *St Saviour's Vicarage, 31 Richmond Road, Retford, Notts DN22 6SJ* Retford (0777) 703800

WALKER, Canon Arthur Keith. b 33. Dur Univ BSc57 Fitzw Ho Cam BA60 MA64 Leeds Univ PhD68. Lich Th Coll 62. **d** 63 **p** 64. C Slaithwaite w E Scammonden *Wakef* 63-66; Lect Wells Th Coll 66-71; V N Wootton *B & W* 66-71; Can Res and Prec Chich Cathl *Chich* 71-80; TV Basingstoke *Win* 81-87; Can Res Win Cathl from 87. *5 The Close, Winchester, Hants SO23 9LS* Winchester (0962) 864923

WALKER, Barry Donovan. b 28. Linc Coll Ox BA52 MA56. Linc Th Coll 52. **d** 54 **p** 55. V Kensal Rise St Martin *Lon* 61-71; V Palmers Green St Jo 71-83; R Takeley w Lt Canfield *Chelmsf* 83-88; rtd 88. *17 The Maltings, Dunmow, Essex CM6 1BY* Great Dunmow (0371) 874778

WALKER, Brian Cecil. b 28. FCA62. Cranmer Hall Dur 68. **d** 70 **p** 71. C Heworth w Peasholme St Cuth *York* 70-73; C Attenborough w Chilwell *S'well* 73-75; C Chilwell 75-78; R Trowell 78-89; rtd 89. *1 Kendal Close, Bromsgrove, Worcs B60 2HW* Bromsgrove (0527) 579382

WALKER, Charles Edward Cornwall. b 18. Selw Coll Cam BA39 MA43. Cuddesdon Coll 40. **d** 41 **p** 42. C Gillingham *Sarum* 41-46; C Evesham *Worc* 46-48; V Gt Amwell *St Alb* 48-81; P-in-c Stanstead St Marg 74-81; V Gt Amwell w St Marg from 81. *The Vicarage, St John's Lane, Great Amwell, Ware, Herts SG12 9SR* Ware (0920) 870139

WALKER, Christopher James Anthony. b 43. Sarum & Wells Th Coll 85. **d** 87 **p** 88. Hon C Durrington *Sarum* 87-89; CF from 87. *c/o MOD (Army), Bagshot Park, Bagshot, Surrey GU19 5PL* Bagshot (0276) 71717

WALKER, Christopher John. b 52. ALA74. Chich Th Coll 75. **d** 78 **p** 79. C Reading All SS *Ox* 78-82; C Stony Stratford 82-84; C Wokingham All SS 84-90; V Headington St Mary from 90. *St Mary's Vicarage, Bayswater Road, Oxford OX3 9EY* Oxford (0865) 61886

WALKER, Christopher John Deville. b 42. St Jo Coll Dur BA69. Westcott Ho Cam 69. **d** 71 **p** 72. C Portsea St Mary *Portsm* 71-75; C Saffron Walden w Wendens Ambo and Littlebury *Chelmsf* 75-77; C St Martin-in-the-Fields *Lon* 77-80; V Riverhead w Dunton Green *Roch* 80-89; V Chatham St Steph from 89. *St Stephen's Vicarage, 181 Maidstone Road, Chatham, Kent ME4 6JG* Medway (0634) 49791

WALKER, David. b 48. Linc Th Coll 71. **d** 74 **p** 75. C Arnold *S'well* 74-77; C Crosby *Linc* 77-79; V Scrooby *S'well* 79-86; V Sutton in Ashfield St Mary from 86; P-in-c Sutton in Ashfield St Mich from 89. *The Vicarage, Church Avenue, Sutton-in-Ashfield, Notts NG17 2EB* Mansfield (0623) 554509

WALKER, David Andrew. b 52. St Andr Univ MTh75 MA. Linc Th Coll 79. **d** 81 **p** 82. C Hessle *York* 81-84; C N Hull St Mich 84-86; V from 86. *St Michael's Vicarage, 214 Orchard Park Road, Hull HU6 9BX* Hull (0482) 803375

WALKER, Canon David Grant. b 23. FSA60 FRHistS62 Bris Univ BA49 Ball Coll Ox DPhil54. **d** 62 **p** 62. Hon C Swansea St Mary w H Trin *S & B* 62-86; Chapl and Lect Univ of Wales (Swansea) 62; Sen Lect 63-82; Dir of Post-Ord Tr from 65; Can Brecon Cathl from 72; Prec 79-90; Chan from 90; Chapl Univ of Wales (Swansea) 75-76; Dir of In-Service Tr from 77; P-in-c Caereithin 86-87. *52 Eaton Crescent, Swansea SA1 4QN* Swansea (0792) 472624

WALKER, David Ian. b 41. DipCM. Bernard Gilpin Soc Dur 64 Bps' Coll Cheshunt 65. **d** 68 **p** 69. C Todmorden *Wakef* 68-72; V Rastrick St Jo 72-77; V Crosland Moor 77-86; V Kirton in Lindsey *Linc* from 86; R Grayingham from 86; R Manton from 88; OCF from 88. *28 Southcliffe Road, Kirton-in-Lindsey, Gainsborough, Lincs DN21 4NR* Kirton Lindsey (0652) 648009

WALKER, David John. b 47. St Jo Coll Nottm 88. **d** 90 **p** 91. C Strood St Fran *Roch* from 90. *81 Laburnham Road, Strood, Rochester ME2 2LB* Medway (0634) 720339

WALKER, David Stuart. b 57. Cam Univ MA. Qu Coll Birm DipTh. **d** 83 **p** 84. C Handsworth *Sheff* 83-86; TV Maltby from 86; Ind Chapl from 86. *The Vicarage, 5 Haids Road, Maltby, Rotherham, S Yorkshire S66 8BH* Rotherham (0709) 814951

WALKER, Dennis Richard. b 25. Bp Gray Coll Cape Town LTh57. **d** 57 **p** 58. S Africa 57-73; V Catterick *Ripon* 73-78; V Manston 78-86; rtd 86. *Micklegarth, Cliff Road, Sewerby, Bridlington, N Humberside YO15 1EW* Bridlington (0262) 678417

WALKER, Derek Fred. b 46. Trin Coll Bris 71. **d** 74 **p** 75. C St Paul's Cray St Barn *Roch* 74-78; C Rushden w Newton Bromswold *Pet* 78-80; R Kirkby Thore w Temple Sowerby and w Newbiggin *Carl* 80-83; V Coppull *Blackb* 83-87; V New Ferry *Ches* from 87. *St Mark's Vicarage, New Chester Road, New Ferry, Wirral, Merseyside L62 1DG* 051-645 2638

WALKER, Douglas. b 36. Lich Th Coll 61. **d** 63 **p** 64. C Bris St Ambrose Whitehall *Bris* 63-68; P-in-c Easton

All Hallows 68-71; V Penhill 71-79; P-in-c Crundale w Godmersham *Cant* 79-83; P-in-c Elmsted w Hastingleigh 79-83; V Sheerness H Trin w St Paul from 83. *The Vicarage, 241 High Street, Sheerness, Kent ME12 1UR* Sheerness (0795) 662589

WALKER, Duncan Andrew. b 59. **d** 90 **p** 91. C Gorseinon *S & B* from 90. *138 Frampton Road, Gorseinon, Swansea SA4 2YG* Swansea (0792) 895191

WALKER, Canon Edward William Murray (Brother Dominic). b 48. AKC73. **d** 72 **p** 72. CGA 67-83; C Wandsworth St Faith *S'wark* 72-73; Bp's Dom Chapl 73-76; R Newington St Mary 76-85; RD S'wark and Newington 80-85; OGS from 83; Superior from 90; RD Brighton *Chich* from 85; V Brighton St Pet w Chpl Royal and St Jo 85-86; P-in-c Brighton St Nic 85-86; Can and Preb Chich Cathl from 85; TR Brighton St Pet and St Nic w Chpl Royal from 86. *Brighton Vicarage, 87 London Road, Brighton BN1 4JF* Brighton (0273) 682960

WALKER, Eric Henry. b 15. Lon Univ BD54. AKC39. **d** 39 **p** 40. V Rotherhithe St Kath w St Barn *S'wark* 56-81; RD Bermondsey 78-81; rtd 81. *10 Barton Road, Ely, Cambs CB7 4DE* Ely (0353) 665927

WALKER, Ernest Alwyn. b 18. Clifton Th Coll 54. **d** 56 **p** 57. V Kingston upon Hull St Barn *York* 59-70; V Shiptonthorpe w Hayton 70-77; V Daubhill *Man* 77-84; rtd 84; Perm to Offic *Bradf* from 84. *1 Hillside View, Pudsey, W Yorkshire LS28 9DH* Leeds (0532) 578468

WALKER, Gavin Russell. b 43. FCA78. Coll of Resurr Mirfield 76. **d** 78 **p** 79. C Wakef St Jo *Wakef* 78-81; C Northallerton w Kirby Sigston *York* 81-83; V Whorlton w Carlton and Faceby 83-85; Chapl Pontefract Gen Infirmary 85-89; P-in-c Brotherton *Wakef* 85-89; V Earlsheaton from 89. *St Peter's Vicarage, 256 Wakefield Road, Dewsbury, W Yorkshire WF12 8AH* Dewsbury (0924) 461490

WALKER, Geoffrey Frederick. b 23. Oak Hill Th Coll 57. **d** 59 **p** 60. C Clayton *Bradf* 59-62; V Clapham 62-66; R Necton w Holme Hale *Nor* 66-71; P-in-c Mundham w Seething 71-74; V 74-83; P-in-c Thwaite 71-75; R 75-83; V Trowse from 83; V Arminghall from 83; R Caistor w Markshall from 83; RD Loddon from 90. *The Vicarage, Trowse, Norwich NR14 8TN* Norwich (0603) 21732

WALKER, Canon George Percival John. b 13. Dur Univ LTh38. St Boniface Warminster 35. **d** 38 **p** 39. St Kitts-Nevis 52-78; Hon Can Antigua 55-78; Adn St Kitts 64-78; rtd 78. *St Peter's Cottage, Monkey Hill, St Kitts, West Indies* St Kitts (809) 461-4091

WALKER, Gerald Roger. b 41. K Coll Lon BD67 AKC67. **d** 68 **p** 69. C High Elswick St Phil *Newc* 68-70; C Goring-by-Sea *Chich* 70-75; R Selsey 75-81; V Hove St Andr Old Ch from 81. *The Vicarage, 17 Vallance Gardens, Hove, E Sussex BN3 2DB* Brighton (0273) 734859

WALKER, Canon Graham. b 35. Ex Coll Ox BA58 BTh60 MA62 Leeds Univ MPhil80. Sarum Th Coll 60. **d** 61 **p** 62. C Guiseley *Bradf* 61-64; C Ingrow cum Hainworth 64-68; Lic to Offic 68-80; V Hellifield from 80; RD Bowland from 86; Hon Can Bradf Cathl from 89. *The Vicarage, Hellifield, Skipton, N Yorkshire BD23 4HY* Hellifield (07295) 243

WALKER, Canon Harvey William. b 26. Edin Univ MA52. St Steph Ho Ox 58. **d** 60 **p** 61. C Newc St Matt w St Mary *Newc* 60-64; V from 64; Hon Can Newc Cathl from 80. *St Matthew's Vicarage, 10 Winchester Terrace, Newcastle upon Tyne NE4 6EH* 091-232 2866

WALKER, Helen Margaret. b 58. RGN80 DON80 Lon Univ DN83. Cranmer Hall Dur 86. **d** 89. C Newark-upon-Trent *S'well* from 89. *35 Kingsnorth Close, Newark, Notts NG24 1PS* Newark (0636) 605849

WALKER, Ian Richard Stevenson. b 51. Univ of Wales (Lamp) BA73. Qu Coll Birm DipTh75. **d** 76 **p** 77. C Stainton-in-Cleveland *York* 76-79; C Fulford 79-81; C Kidderminster St Mary *Worc* 81-82; TV Kidderminster St Mary and All SS etc 82-86; R Keyingham w Ottringham, Halsham and Sunk Is *York* from 86. *The Rectory, Keyingham, Hull HU12 9RX* Withernsea (0964) 622171

WALKER, Jack. b 21. Kelham Th Coll 37. **d** 45 **p** 46. C Tynemouth Ch Ch *Newc* 45-49; C Wallsend St Luke 49-51; C Linthorpe *York* 51-55; V Newbald from 55; V Sancton from 55. *The Vicarage, North Newbald, York YO4 3SY* Market Weighton (0430) 827284

WALKER, John. b 49. Sheff Univ BSc74. Qu Coll Birm DipTh77. **d** 79 **p** 79. C Loughb Em *Leic* 78-81; C Nottm All SS *S'well* 81-84; V Radford St Pet from 84. *St Peter's Vicarage, Hartley Road, Old Radford, Nottingham NG7 3DW* Nottingham (0602) 784450

WALKER, John. b 51. Aber Univ MA74. Edin Th Coll BD78. **d** 78 **p** 79. C Broughty Ferry *Bre* 78-81; P-in-c

Dundee St Jo 81-85; Ind Chapl 83-88; R Dundee St Luke from 85. *The Rectory, 4 St Luke's Road, Dundee DD3 0LD* Dundee (0382) 825165

WALKER, John Anthony Patrick. b 58. Trin Coll Bris BA86. **d** 86 **p** 87. C Canford Magna *Sarum* 86-90; TV Glyncorrwg w Afan Vale and Cymmer Afan *Llan* from 90. *The Vicarage, 17 School Road, Cymmer, Port Talbot, W Glam SA13 3EG* Cymmer (0639) 851058

WALKER, John Cameron. b 31. St Andr Univ MA52. Edin Th Coll 63. **d** 65 **p** 66. C Edin H Cross *Edin* 65-67; C Perth St Jo *St And* 67-70; Chapl Angl Students Glas 70-74; Youth Chapl Warks Educn Cttee 75-77; Officer Gen Syn Bd of Educn 78-82; C W Hendon St Jo *Lon* 79-82; PV Westmr Abbey 82-84; Chapl Ghent w Ypres *Eur* from 84; Miss to Seamen from 84. *Blankenbergestraat 39, 9000 Gent, Belgium* Ghent (91) 223659

WALKER, John David. b 44. St Jo Coll Dur BA76 DipTh77. **d** 77 **p** 78. C Heworth *York* 77-81; P-in-c Barmby on the Moor w Fangfoss 81-83; P-in-c Allerthorpe 81-83; TV Pocklington Team 84-89; P-in-c Hovingham 89; TV Street Team Min from 89. *The Rectory, Amotherby, Malton, N Yorkshire YO17 0TN* Malton (0653) 093503

WALKER, John Frank. b 53. Leeds Univ BEd76. NW Ord Course 78. **d** 81 **p** 82. NSM Whitkirk *Ripon* 81-82; C 82-85; V Sutton Courtenay w Appleford *Ox* 85-90; Dioc Children's Adv *S'wark* from 90. *48 Union Street, London SE1 1TD or, 139 Perry Vale, London SE23 2JB* 071-407 7911 or 081-291 5245

WALKER, John Frederick. b 21. St Jo Coll Dur BA47 DipTh49 MA51. **d** 49 **p** 50. V Halifax All So *Wakef* 59-74; V Hampsthwaite *Ripon* 74-86; P-in-c Killinghall 76-86; rtd 86. *36 Rockwood Drive, Skipton, N Yorkshire* Skipton (0756) 799835

WALKER, John Howard. b 47. Clifton Th Coll 69. **d** 72 **p** 73. C Upton (or Overchurch) *Ches* 72-76; Asst Chapl Liv Univ *Liv* 76-80; V Everton St Chrys 80-82; C Parr Mt 83-86; Area Sec (NE and E Midl) SAMS 86-89; Paraguay from 89. *Iglesia Anglicana Paraguaya, Casilla 1124, Asuncion, Paraguay*

WALKER, John Hugh. b 34. K Coll Lon BD57 AKC57 Lon Univ MTh75 MA85. **d** 58 **p** 59. C Southend St Alb *Chelmsf* 58-61; V Gt Ilford St Alb 61-67; Perm to Offic 67-68; Hon C Forest Gate St Edm 68-74; Perm to Offic *Cant* 75-82 and from 87; R Dymchurch w Burmarsh and Newchurch 82-87. *Aberfeldy, Covet Lane, Kingston, Canterbury, Kent CT4 6HU* Canterbury (0227) 830818

WALKER, John Michael. b 32. Qu Coll Birm. **d** 57 **p** 58. C Ruddington *S'well* 57-60; C Horsham *Chich* 60-64; C Sullington 64-70; C Storrington 64-70; V Peasmarsh 70-73; V Washington 73-77; R Ashington w Buncton, Wiston and Washington from 77. *The Rectory, Ashington, Pulborough, W Sussex RH20 3BH* Ashington (0903) 892304

WALKER, John Percival. b 45. CITC 68. **d** 71 **p** 72. C Belf St Clem *D & D* 71-74; C Magheraculmoney *Clogh* 74-78; C Lisburn St Paul *Conn* 78-81; I Belf St Ninian 81-88; I Belf St Mary 88-89; I Belf St Mary w H Redeemer from 89. *558 Crumlin Road, Belfast BT14 7GL* Belfast (0232) 391120

WALKER, John Thomas. b 14. RD70. Univ of Wales BA37. Linc Th Coll 38. **d** 39 **p** 40. Chapl RNR 58-70; V Brislington St Anne *Bris* 69-78; P-in-c Bishopstone w Hinton Parva 78-84; rtd 84; Perm to Offic *Bris* from 84. *16 The Wyncies, Bishopstone, Swindon, Wilts SN6 8PJ* Swindon (0793) 790183

WALKER, John Wolfe. b 15. LRAM38 Trin Coll Cam BA37 MA47. Cuddesdon Coll 46. **d** 47 **p** 48. V Pilton *B & W* 57-72; V Pilton w N Wootton 72-80; RD Shepton Mallet 75-79; rtd 80; Perm to Offic *B & W* from 81. *58 Compton Road, Shepton Mallet, Somerset BA4 5QT* Shepton Mallet (0749) 344190

WALKER, Keith. b 48. Linc Th Coll 82. **d** 84 **p** 85. C Whickham *Dur* 84-87; C Trimdon Station 87; P-in-c 87-89; V 89-90; R Penshaw from 90. *All Saints' Rectory, Penshaw, Houghton le Spring, Tyne & Wear DH4 7ER* 091-584 2631

WALKER, Kenneth Saxon Watkinson. b 21. Jes Coll Cam BA47 MA50. Westcott Ho Cam 67. **d** 68 **p** 69. Hon C W Kirby St Bridget *Ches* 68-70; Lic to Offic *Ches* 70-78; *Arg* 77-82; Hon C Ashbury, Compton Beauchamp and Longcot w Fernham *Ox* from 84. *Church Cottage, Compton Beauchamp, Swindon SN6 8NN* Ashbury (079371) 334

WALKER, Mrs Lesley Ann. b 53. S Dios Minl Tr Scheme 85. **d** 88. Par Dn Oakdale St Geo *Sarum* from 88. *328 Wimborne Road, Poole, Dorset BH15 3EG* Poole (0202) 673296

WALKER, Mrs Margaret Joy. b 44. Avery Hill Coll DipHE80. CA Tr Coll 80. **dss** 86 **d** 87. Scargill Ho N Yorkshire 86-87; Hon Par Dn Monkwearmouth St Andr *Dur* 87; Hon Par Dn Ches le Street from 87. *The Rectory, Lindisfarne Avenue, Chester le Street, Co Durham DH3 3PT* 091-388 4027

WALKER, Martin Frank. b 39. St Jo Coll Nottm 71. **d** 73 **p** 74. C Penn *Lich* 73-78; V Bentley 78-82; V Kinver 82-88; R Kinver and Enville 88-91; V Harlescott from 91. *Harlescott Vicarage, Meadow Farm Drive, Shrewsbury SY1 4NG* Shrewsbury (0743) 62883

WALKER, Martin John. b 52. Linc Coll Ox BA73 PGCE74 Chateau de Bossey Geneva DipEcum78. Cranmer Hall Dur BA78. **d** 79 **p** 80. C Harlow New Town w Lt Parndon *Chelmsf* 79-81; C Dorchester *Ox* 81-83; Chapl Bath Coll of FE 83-89; TV Southn (City Cen) *Win* from 89. *2 Arthur Road, Southampton SO1 5DY* Southampton (0703) 230128

WALKER, Canon Michael John. b 32. BNC Ox BA55 MA59. Clifton Th Coll 55. **d** 57 **p** 58. C Patcham *Chich* 57-61; V Stapleford *S'well* 61-66; R Saxmundham *St E* 66-71; V New Beckenham St Paul *Roch* 71-78; V Bury St Edmunds St Mary *St E* from 78; Hon Can St E Cathl from 86. *The Vicarage, St Mary's Square, Bury St Edmunds, Suffolk IP33 2AJ* Bury St Edmunds (0284) 754680

WALKER, Michael John. b 39. Univ of Wales (Lamp) BA61. St Aid Birkenhead 61. **d** 63 **p** 64. C Clifton *York* 63-66; C Marfleet 66-69; V Salterhebble St Jude *Wakef* 69-83; RD Llangollen from 83. *The Vicarage, Abbey Road, Llangollen, Clwyd LL20 8SN* Llangollen (0978) 860231

WALKER, Michael Sykes. b 10. TD. Trin Hall Cam BA33 MA40. Wycliffe Hall Ox. **d** 49 **p** 50. R Escrick *York* 61-75; rtd 75; Hon C Ryther *York* 75-80. *2 Rawcliffe Grove, Clifton Lane, York YO3 6NR* York (0904) 636453

WALKER, Nigel Maynard. b 39. ALCD66. **d** 67 **p** 68. C Southsea St Jude *Portsm* 67-70; S Africa 70-76; C Abingdon w Shippon *Ox* 76-80; V Upton (or Overchurch) *Ches* from 80. *The Vicarage, Upton, Wirral, Merseyside L49 6JZ* 051-677 4810 or 677 1186

WALKER, Mrs Pamela Sarah. b 52. Somerville Coll Ox BA73 MA77 St Jo Coll Dur BA78. Cranmer Hall Dur 76. **dss** 79 **d** 87. Harlow New Town w Lt Parndon *Chelmsf* 79-81; Dorchester *Sarum* 82-83; Bath St Bart *B & W* 85-87; Hon C 87-88; Par Dn Warmley *Bris* 88-89; Par Dn Bitton 88-89; Par Dn Southn (City Cen) *Win* from 89. *2 Arthur Road, Southampton SO1 5DY* Southampton (0703) 39001

WALKER, Paul Gary. b 59. Lon Univ BD. St Jo Coll Nottm 82. **d** 84 **p** 85. C Bowling St Steph *Bradf* 84-87; C Tong 87-90; P-in-c Oakenshaw cum Woodlands from 90. *589 Bradford Road, Oakenshaw, Bradford BD12 7FS* Bradford (0274) 676410

WALKER, Paul Laurence. b 63. St Chad's Coll Dur BA84. Chich Th Coll BTh90. **d** 88 **p** 89. C Shildon w Eldon *Dur* 88-91; C Barnard Castle w Whorlton from 91. *The Glebe House, Newgate Street, Barnard Castle, Co Durham DL12 8NW* Teesdale (0833) 690435

WALKER, Peter Anthony. b 57. Pemb Coll Cam BA79 MA83 St Jo Coll Dur BA86. Cranmer Hall Dur 84. **d** 87 **p** 88. C Chesham Bois *Ox* 87-90; Chapl Bradf Cathl *Bradf* from 90. *Cathedral Cottage, Stott Hill, Bradford BD1 4ET* Bradford (0274) 728955

WALKER, Peter Anthony Ashley. b 46. Chich Th Coll 67. **d** 70 **p** 71. C Stamford Hill St Thos *Lon* 70-74; C Bethnal Green St Matt 74-77; V Hackney Wick St Mary of Eton w St Aug 77-84; Warden Rydal Hall *Carl* from 84; P-in-c Rydal from 84. *Rydal Hall, Ambleside, Cumbria LA22 9LX* Ambleside (05394) 32050

WALKER, Peter Jeffrey. b 46. Kelham Th Coll 65. **d** 70 **p** 71. C Middlesb All SS *York* 70-75 and 77-78; SSF 75-77; C-in-c Wrangbrook w N Elmsall CD *Wakef* 78-82; V Athersley 82-86; Perm to Offic *Blackb* 86-87; *Dur* from 87; V Hartlepool H Trin *Dur* from 89. *Holy Trinity Vicarage, Davison Drive, Hartlepool, Cleveland TS24 9BX* Hartlepool (0429) 267618

✠**WALKER, Rt Rev Peter Knight.** b 19. Qu Coll Ox BA47 MA47 Cam Univ Hon DD78. Westcott Ho Cam 53. **d** 54 **p** 55 **c** 72. Asst Master Merchant Taylors' Sch Lon 50-56; C Hemel Hempstead St Mary *St Alb* 56-58; Fell Dean and Lect Th CCC 58-62; Asst Tutor 59-62; Prin Westcott Ho Cam 62-72; Hon Can Ely Cathl *Ely* 66-72; Suff Bp Dorchester *Ox* 72-77; Can Res Ch Ch 72-77; Bp Ely 77-89; rtd 89; Asst Bp Ox from 89. *Anchorage House, The Lanes, Bampton, Oxford OX8 2LA* Bampton Castle (0993) 850943

WALKER, Peter Sidney Caleb. b 50. DipMin80. St Mich Th Coll Crafers 76. **d** 80 **p** 81. Australia 80-88; R Swallow *Linc* from 88. *The Rectory, Beelsby Road, Swallow, Lincoln LN7 6DG* Swallow (047289) 560

WALKER, Peter Stanley. b 56. SRN RMN Nottm Univ BCombStuds. Linc Th Coll 80. **d** 83 **p** 84. C Woodford St Barn *Chelmsf* 83-86; C Brentwood St Thos 86-88; V Colchester St Barn from 88. *The Vicarage, 13 Abbots Road, Colchester CO2 8BE* Colchester (0206) 47817

WALKER, Peter William Leyland. b 61. CCC Cam BA82 MA86 PhD87. Wycliffe Hall Ox 87. **d** 89 **p** 90. C Tonbridge SS Pet and Paul *Roch* from 89. *14 Salisbury Road, Tonbridge, Kent TN10 4PB* Tonbridge (0732) 355200

WALKER, Philip Geoffrey. b 47. St Jo Coll Dur BA70 Or Coll Ox BA72 MA76. Ripon Hall Ox 70. **d** 74 **p** 75. C Sheff St Geo *Sheff* 74-77; C Cam Gt St Mary w St Mich *Ely* 77-81; V Monkwearmouth St Andr *Dur* 81-87; R Ches le Street from 87; RD Ches le Street from 89. *The Rectory, Lindisfarne Avenue, Chester le Street, Co Durham DH3 3PT* 091-388 4027

WALKER, Philip Kingsley. b 47. Ox Univ BA70 Univ of Wales DPS90. St Mich Coll Llan. **d** 90 **p** 91. C Newport Maindee St Jo Ev *Mon* from 90. *16 Kensington Place, Maindee, Newport, Gwent NP9 8GL* Newport (0633) 281053

WALKER, Raymond. b 28. Carl Dioc Tr Inst 83. **d** 86 **p** 87. NSM Gt Salkeld w Lazonby *Carl* 86-91; C Greystoke, Matterdale, Mungrisdale & W'millock from 91. *Matterdale Vicarage, Penrith, Cumbria CA11 0LD* Glenridding (07684) 82301

WALKER, Richard Mainprize. b 43. Keele Univ BA DipEd. Wycliffe Hall Ox 84. **d** 86 **p** 87. C Guildf Ch Ch *Guildf* 86-90; V Bradley St Martin *Lich* from 90. *St Martin's Vicarage, King Street, Bradley, Bilston, W Midlands WV14 8PQ* Bilston (0902) 493109

WALKER, Robert Edward Lea. b 23. Qu Coll Ox MA49. Wycliffe Hall Ox 49. **d** 51 **p** 52. V Wroxton w Balscott *Ox* 61-80; P-in-c Shenington and Alkerton w Shutford 79-80; R Wroxton w Balscote, Shenington, Alkerton etc 80-85; R Wroxton w Balscote and Shenington w Alkerton 85-88; rtd 88. *11 Tanners Court, Charlbury, Oxford OX7 3RP* Charlbury (0608) 810461

WALKER, Mrs Ruth Elizabeth. b 58. St Jo Coll Dur BA79 Cam Univ CertEd81. St Jo Coll Nottm 86. **d** 88. Par Dn Princes Risborough w Ilmer *Ox* 88-90; Chapl Bradf Cathl *Bradf* from 90. *Cathedral Cottage, Bradford BD1 4ET* Bradford (0274) 728955

WALKER, Stanley Frederick. b 48. St Jo Coll Nottm. **d** 84 **p** 85. C Ellesmere Port *Ches* 84-89; V Seacombe from 89. *The Vicarage, 5 Brougham Road, Wallasey, Merseyside L44 6PN* 051-638 3677

WALKER, Canon Stephen. b 09. St Jo Coll Dur BA30 DipTh31 MA33. **d** 32 **p** 33. V Beverley St Mary *York* 58-77; RD Beverley 63-73; Can and Preb York Minster 64-77; rtd 77. *Dulverton Hall, St Martin's Square, Scarborough, N Yorkshire YO11 2DQ* Scarborough (0723) 373082

WALKER, Stephen Michael Maynard. b 62. St Jo Coll Dur BA84. Trin Coll Bris 86. **d** 88 **p** 89. C Eastwood *S'well* from 88. *2 Church Walk, Eastwood, Nottingham NG16 3BG* Langley Mill (0773) 710280

WALKER, Stephen Patrick. b 62. York Univ BSc83 PGCE84. St Jo Coll Nottm DipTh89 DPS90. **d** 90 **p** 91. C Hull Newland St Jo *York* from 90. *75 Desmond Avenue, Hull HU6 7JX* Hull (0482) 43789

WALKER, Mrs Susan Joy. b 52. Univ of Wales (Lamp) BA73 Hull Univ MA91. Qu Coll Birm 75. **dss** 83 **d** 87. Kidderminster St Mary and All SS etc *Worc* 83-86; Keyingham w Ottringham, Halsham and Sunk Is *York* 86-87; Hon Par Dn from 87; Chapl Hull Coll of FE from 89. *The Rectory, Keyingham, Hull HU12 9RX* Withernsea (0964) 622171

WALKER, Thomas. b 18. St Aid Birkenhead 58. **d** 60 **p** 61. V Wrightington *Blackb* 69-87; rtd 87. *6 Cranford Close, Eastham, South Wirral L62 9DH* 051-327 1380

WALKER, Ven Thomas Overington. b 33. Keble Coll Ox BA58 MA61. Oak Hill Th Coll 58. **d** 60 **p** 61. C Woking St Paul *Guildf* 60-62; C St Leonards St Leon *Chich* 62-64; Travelling Sec IVF 64-67; Succ Birm Cathl *Birm* 67-70; V Harborne Heath 70-91; Hon Can Birm Cathl 80-91; P-in-c Edgbaston St Germain 83-91; RD Edgbaston 89-91; Adn Nottm *S'well* from 91. *16 Woodthorpe Avenue, Woodthorpe, Nottingham NG5 4FD* Nottingham (0602) 267349

WALKER, Trevor John. b 51. Southn Univ BTh80. Sarum & Wells Th Coll 75. **d** 78 **p** 79. C Standish *Blackb* 78-81; P-in-c N Somercotes *Linc* 81-82; P-in-c S Somercotes 81-82; V Somercotes 82-85; R Binbrook Gp from 85. *The Rectory, Binbrook, Lincoln LN3 6BJ* Binbrook (047283) 227

WALKER, Victor John. b 05. TCD BA36 MA49. **d** 38 **p** 39. V Toxteth Park St Andr Aigburth Road *Liv* 51-71; rtd 71. *12 Menlove Court, Menlove Avenue, Liverpool L18 2EF* 051-724 3876

WALKER, Canon Walter Stanley. b 21. AKC42. Cuddesdon Coll 42. **d** 44 **p** 45. R Bromborough *Ches* 66-77; R Wallasey St Hilary 77-86; RD Wallasey 77-86; Hon Can Ches Cathl 80-86; rtd 86; Perm to Offic *Ches* from 86. *39 Lyndhurst Road, Wallasey, Merseyside L45 6XB* 051-630 4237

WALKER, William. b 10. **d** 51 **p** 52. Chapl, Lect and Tutor Stanford Hall Loughb 52-70; V Daybrook *S'well* 70-80; rtd 80; Perm to Offic *S'well* from 80. *278 Rutland Road, West Bridgford, Nottingham* Nottingham (0602) 869353

WALKER, Canon William George Leslie. b 10. TCD BA39 MA42. **d** 39 **p** 40. I Knockbreda *D & D* 59-78; Can Down Cathl 70-78; rtd 78. *160 Ballylesson Road, Belfast BT8 8JU* Drumbo (023126) 578

WALKEY, Malcolm Gregory Taylor. b 44. Lon Univ DipTh68. Kelham Th Coll 63. **d** 68 **p** 69. C Oadby *Leic* 68-72; TV Corby SS Pet and Andr w Gt and Lt Oakley *Pet* 72-79; R Ashton w Hartwell 79-86; TR Halesworth w Linstead, Chediston, Holton etc *St E* from 86. *The Vicarage, Banfield Road, Wenhaston, Suffolk IP19 9EA* Halesworth (09867) 2602

WALL, Charles William. b 20. Kelham Th Coll 39. **d** 44 **p** 45. P-in-c Sidlow Bridge *S'wark* 71-76; R Feltwell *Ely* 76-78; rtd 78; Perm to Offic *Chich* from 80. *56 Barrack Road, Bexhill-on-Sea, E Sussex TN40 2AZ* Bexhill-on-Sea (0424) 219711

WALL, Colin Edward. b 35. Open Univ BA76. K Coll Lon 55. **d** 59 **p** 60. C Tynemouth Ch Ch *Newc* 59-62; C Cowley St Jas *Ox* 62-65; V Syston *Leic* 65-82; RD Goscote II 75-82; TV Langley and Parkfield *Man* 82-86; V Claremont H Angels 86-89; P-in-c Lake *Portsm* from 89. *46 Sandown Road, Lake, Isle of Wight PO36 9JT* Isle of Wight (0983) 405666

WALL, David Oliver. b 39. TD JP. OStJ. Bps' Coll Cheshunt 62. **d** 65 **p** 66. C Lt Ilford St Mich *Chelmsf* 65-68; CF 68-73; R Sudbourne w Orford *St E* 73-76; R Orford w Sudbourne and Chillesford w Butley 76-79; P-in-c Iken 76-79; P-in-c Ipswich St Bart 77-79; R Drinkstone 79-82; R Rattlesden 79-82; R Chedburgh w Depden, Rede and Hawkedon from 82. *The Rectory, Rede, Bury St Edmunds, Suffolk IP29 4BE* Hawkedon (028489) 342

✠**WALL, Rt Rev Eric St Quintin.** b 15. BNC Ox BA37 MA46. Wells Th Coll 37. **d** 38 **p** 39 **c** 72. C Boston *Linc* 38-41; Chapl RAFVR 41-45; V Sherston Magna w Easton Grey *Bris* 44-53; RD Malmesbury 51-53; V Cricklade w Latton 53-60; Bp's Chapl 60-66; Dioc Adv in Chr Stewardship 60-66; Hon Can Bris Cathl 60-72; V Westbury-on-Trym St Alb 66-72; RD Clifton 67-72; Suff Bp Huntingdon *Ely* 72-80; Can Res Ely Cathl 72-80; rtd 80; Perm to Offic *Nor* from 80; *St E* from 81; *Ely* from 86. *7 Peregrine Close, Diss, Norfolk IP22 3PG* Diss (0379) 644331

WALL, James Leach. b 19. Leeds Univ BA40. **d** 64 **p** 65. C Prenton *Ches* 66-71; C Auckland St Andr and St Anne *Dur* 71-74; V Hart w Elwick Hall 74-80; rtd 81. *191 Park Road, Hartlepool, Cleveland TS26 9LP* Hartlepool (0429) 275105

WALL, John Caswallen. b 60. York Univ BA83 MA85 Ox Univ BA89. St Steph Ho Ox 86. **d** 89 **p** 90. C Ifield *Chich* from 89. *86 Warren Drive, Ifield, Crawley, W Sussex RH11 0DL* Crawley (0293) 22337

WALL, Martyn Philip Lucas. b 17. Hertf Coll Ox BA38 MA43. Wells Th Coll 69. **d** 71 **p** 72. C Highworth w Sevenhampton and Inglesham etc *Bris* 71-74; R Wick w Doynton 74-85; rtd 85. *9 Woburn Close, Trowbridge, Wilts BA14 9TJ* Trowbridge (0225) 754323

WALL, Nicholas John. b 46. Brasted Th Coll 69 Trin Coll Bris 71. **d** 73 **p** 74. C Morden *S'wark* 73-78; V Dunkeswell and Dunkeswell Abbey *Ex* 78-83; V Sheldon 78-83; P-in-c Luppitt 81-83; V Dunkeswell, Sheldon and Luppitt from 83. *The Rectory, Dunkeswell, Honiton, Devon EX14 0RE* Luppitt (040489) 1243

WALL, Mrs Pauline Ann. b 39. Bris Sch of Min 87. **dss** 85 **d** 87. Bris Ch the Servant Stockwood *Bris* 85-87; Hon Par Dn from 87. *41 Ladman Road, Stockwood, Bristol BS14 8QD* Bristol (0272) 833083

WALL, Philip John. b 12. St Chad's Coll Dur BA34 DipTh35 MA37. **d** 35 **p** 36. R Norwood St Mary *Lon* 69-81; rtd 81; Perm to Offic Lon from 82; Ox from 89. *9 Hervines Court, Amersham, Bucks HP6 5HH* Amersham (0494) 728124

WALL, Robert William. b 52. Ex Coll Ox MA Ex Univ BPhil77. Trin Coll Bris 80. **d** 83 **p** 84. C Blackb Sav *Blackb* 83-86; C Edgware *Lon* 86-89; C Barnsbury 89-90; TV from 90. *43 Matilda Street, London N1 0LA* 071-278 5208

WALLACE, Alastair Robert. b 50. St Cath Coll Cam BA71 MA75 Lon Univ BD75. Trin Coll Bris 72. **d** 75 **p** 76. C Ex St Leon w H Trin *Ex* 75-79; Chapl Ridley Hall Cam 79-80; R Bath St Mich w St Paul *B & W* from 83; RD Bath from 90. *71 Priory Close, Combe Down, Bath BA2 5AP* Bath (0225) 835490

WALLACE, Mrs Brenda Claire. b 52. Linc Th Coll 73. S'wark Ord Course 78. **dss** 80 **d** 87. Sutton at Hone *Roch* 80-83; Borstal 83-87; Hon Par Dn 87-89; HM Pris Cookham Wood 83-89; Asst Chapl 87-89; Hon Par Dn Stansted Mountfitchet *Chelmsf* from 89. *The Vicarage, 5 St John's Road, Stansted, Essex CM24 8JP* Bishop's Stortford (0279) 812203

WALLACE, Derek George. b 33. Glas Univ MA55. Edin Th Coll 55. **d** 57 **p** 58. C Falkirk *Edin* 57-60; C Ayr *Glas* 60-62; Chapl Netherton Tr Sch Morpeth 62-67; V Oldham St Jo *Man* 67-70; R Burravoe *Ab* 70-78; R Lerwick 70-78; R Port Glas from 78; Miss to Seamen from 78. *The Rectory, Bardrainney Avenue, Port Glasgow, Renfrewshire PA14 6HB* Port Glasgow (0475) 707444

WALLACE, Edgar Walker. b 17. St D Coll Lamp BA40. **d** 42 **p** 43. Ind Chapl *Chelmsf* 65-84; rtd 84. *18 Gotts Park Road, Southgate, Crawley, W Sussex RH11 8AX* Crawley (0293) 22713

WALLACE, Godfrey Everingham. b 32. Tyndale Hall Bris BA57. **d** 58 **p** 59. C Broadwater St Mary *Chich* 58-61; V Shipton Bellinger w S Tidworth *Win* 61-70; V Bournemouth St Paul 70-84; V Throop from 84. *St Paul's Vicarage, Chesildene Avenue, Bournemouth BH8 0AZ* Bournemouth (0202) 531064

WALLACE, Hugo. b 31. **d** 56 **p** 57. C Hornchurch St Andr *Chelmsf* 56-58; Uganda 58-60; C Bermondsey St Mary w St Olave and St Jo *S'wark* 61; S Africa from 61. *Shalom, 7 Ixia Avenue, Kommetjie Cape, 7976 South Africa* Cape Town (21) 831466

WALLACE, Mrs Julie Michele. b 58. Cam Univ DipRS82 Lon Univ DipSC88. CA Tr Coll 77. **d** 88. Chapl Middx Poly *Lon* from 86; Voc Adv CA from 90. *Church Army Headquarters, Independents Road, London SE3 9LG* 081-318 1226

WALLACE, Miss Marjorie Emily. b 17. FIPM Birm Univ BA38. Linc Th Coll 77. **dss** 79 **d** 87. Hammersmith St Paul *Lon* 79-87; Hon Par Dn from 87; rtd 84. *1 Mall Villas, Mall Road, London W6* 081-748 5604 or 081-748 7479

WALLACE, Canon Martin William. b 48. K Coll Lon BD70 AKC70. St Aug Coll Cant 70. **d** 71 **p** 72. C Attercliffe *Sheff* 71-74; C New Malden and Coombe *S'wark* 74-77; V Forest Gate St Mark *Chelmsf* from 77; RD Newham 82-91; P-in-c Forest Gate Em w Upton Cross 85-89; Hon Can Chelmsf Cathl from 89. *St Mark's Vicarage, Tylney Road, Forest Gate, London E7 0LS* 081-555 2988

WALLACE, Raymond Sherwood. b 28. Selw Coll Dunedin (NZ). St J 52 **p** 54. V Stroud Green H Trin *Lon* 67-79; V Penwerris *Truro* 79-84; R Wymington w Podington *St Alb* 84-87; rtd 87; Perm to Offic *St Alb* from 87. *141 Dunsmore Road, Luton LU1 5JX* Luton (0582) 455882

WALLACE, Richard Colin. b 39. Mert Coll Ox BA61 MA64. St Chad's Coll Dur 69. **d** 71 **p** 72. Tutor St Chad's Coll Dur 71-72; P-in-c Kimblesworth *Dur* 72-74; Chapl Bradf Univ *Bradf* 74-79; C Bingley All SS 79-80; TV 80-89; V Earby from 89. *The Vicarage, Earby, Colne, Lancs BB8 6JL* Earby (0282) 842291

WALLACE, Richard John. b 56. Coll of Resurr Mirfield. **d** 82 **p** 83. C Catford St Laur *S'wark* 82-85; C Bellingham St Dunstan 85-87; V from 87. *St Dunstan's Vicarage, 32 Bellingham Green, London SE6 3JB* 081-698 3291

WALLACE, Richard Samuel. b 17. TCD BA39 MA53. **d** 41 **p** 42. V Teddington St Mark *Lon* 60-83; rtd 83; Perm to Offic *Ex* from 83. *St Christopher, 17 Hartley Road, Exmouth, Devon EX8 2SG* Exmouth (0395) 279595

WALLACE, Robert. b 52. Sussex Univ BSc73 Nottm Univ DipTh75. Linc Th Coll 73. **d** 76 **p** 77. C Plaistow St Mary *Roch* 76-79; C Dartford H Trin 79-83; Chapl The Foord Almshouses 83-89; V Borstal *Roch* 83-89; Chapl HM Pris Cookham Wood 83-89; V Stansted Mountfitchet *Chelmsf* from 89; P-in-c Farnham from 89. *The Vicarage, 5 St John's Road, Stansted, Essex CM24 8JP* Bishop's Stortford (0279) 812203

WALLACE-HADRILL, David Sutherland. b 20. CCC Ox BA41 MA45 Man Univ BD44 DD60. **d** 43 **p** 44. V Eston

---

York 55-62; Lic to Offic *St Alb* from 62; rtd 85. *1 The Almshouse, High Street, Elstree, Borehamwood, Herts WD6 3EY* 081-207 2919

WALLBANK, Preb Newell Eddius. b 14. Qu Coll Cam BA34 MusB34 MA40 TCD MusD36 Lon Univ BA40 PhD56. Ripon Hall Ox 35. **d** 37 **p** 38. R Smithfield St Bart Gt *Lon* 45-79; Preb St Paul's Cathl 64-79; Select Preacher Ox Univ 68; rtd 79; Perm to Offic *Lon* from 80. *Meldrum, Boveney Road, Dorney, Windsor, Berks SL4 6QD* Burnham (0628) 602399

WALLER, Arthur Henry Naunton. b 06. Selw Coll Cam BA30 MA34. Wycliffe Hall Ox. **d** 31 **p** 32. R Frostenden w S Cove *St E* 45-74; rtd 74. *Mill Field Mill Road, Waldringfield, Woodbridge, Suffolk* Waldringfield (047336) 291

WALLER, David Arthur. b 61. Leeds Univ BA83. Chich Th Coll 89. **d** 91. C Aldwick *Chich* from 91. *59 Westminster Drive, Aldwick, Bognor Regis, W Sussex PO21 3RE* Bognor Regis (0243) 830124

WALLER, David James. b 58. Whitelands Coll Lon BA85. Ripon Coll Cuddesdon 85. **d** 88 **p** 89. C Tettenhall Regis *Lich* from 88. *38 Barnhurst Lane, Wolverhampton WV8 1XB* Wolverhampton (0902) 756249

WALLER, Derek James Keith. b 54. Em Coll Cam BA75 PGCE76. Trin Coll Bris 88. **d** 91. C Church Stretton *Heref* from 91. *3 Alison Road, Church Stretton, Shropshire SY6 6DQ*

WALLER, Miss Elizabeth Jean. b 58. Keswick Hall Coll BEd BTh. Linc Th Coll 84. **d** 87. Par Dn Mile End Old Town H Trin *Lon* 87-90; Manna Chr Cen from 90. *177 Coughton Lane, Greenford, Middx UB6 9AD*

WALLER, Canon Gordon Hamilton. b 18. AKC49. **d** 49 **p** 50. V Biscot *St Alb* 62-71; R Meppershall 71-86; R Upper Stondon 71-86; Hon Can St Alb 82-86; R Campton 82-86; rtd 86; Perm to Offic *St Alb* from 86. *102 High Street, Meppershall, Shefford, Beds SG17 5LZ* Hitchin (0462) 816368

WALLER, John. b 60. Man Univ BA84. St Jo Coll Nottm 85. **d** 87 **p** 88. C Chorlton-cum-Hardy St Clem *Man* 87-90; R Openshaw from 90. *St Barnabas's Rectory, South Street, Openshaw, Manchester M11 2EW* 061-231 4365

WALLER, John Pretyman. b 41. Sarum Th Coll 68. **d** 71 **p** 72. C Ipswich St Jo *St E* 71-74; R Waldringfield w Hemley 74-78; P-in-c Newbourn 74-78; R Waldringfield w Hemley and Newbourn from 78. *The Rectory, Waldringfield, Woodbridge, Suffolk* Waldringfield (047336) 247

✠**WALLER, Rt Rev John Stevens.** b 24. Peterho Cam BA48 MA53. Wells Th Coll 48. **d** 50 **p** 51 **c** 79. C Hillingdon St Jo *Lon* 50-52; C Twerton *B & W* 52-55; C-in-c Weston-super-Mare St Andr Bournville CD 55-59; V Weston-super-Mare St Andr Bournville 59-60; R Yarlington 60-63; Youth Chapl 60-63; Tr Officer C of E Youth Coun 63-67; V Frindsbury w Upnor *Roch* 67-72; P-in-c Strood St Fran 67-72; P-in-c Strood St Mary 67-72; P-in-c Strood St Nic 67-72; RD Strood 67-73; TR Strood 72-73; R Harpenden St Nic 73-79; Hon Can Lich Cathl *Lich* 79-87; Suff Bp Stafford 79-87; Asst Bp B & W from 87; P-in-c Long Sutton w Long Load 87-88; TV Langport Area Chs 88-89; rtd 89. *Grey Cottage, The Green, Beaminster, Dorset DT8 3SD* Beaminster (0308) 862284

WALLER, John Watson. b 35. Qu Mary Coll Lon BSc57 St Cath Soc Ox DipTh60. Wycliffe Hall Ox 59. **d** 61 **p** 62. C Pudsey St Lawr *Bradf* 61-65; V 74-82; V Mortomley *Sheff* 65-74; V Pudsey St Lawr and St Paul *Bradf* 82-88; Hon Can Bradf Cathl 84-88; RD Calverley 84-88; V Kingston upon Hull H Trin *York* from 88. *Holy Trinity Vicarage, 66 Pearson Park, Hull HU5 2TQ* Hull (0482) 42292

WALLER, Orlando Alfred. b 12. St Aid Birkenhead 39. **d** 41 **p** 42. V Bearpark *Dur* 71-76; rtd 77. *22 Thornley Close, Broom Park, Durham DH7 7NN*

WALLER, Philip Thomas. b 56. Ex Coll Ox BA78 MA88. St Jo Coll Dur BA87. **d** 88 **p** 89. C Enfield St Andr *Lon* 88-91; C Belper *Derby* from 91. *St Mark's House, Openwoodgate, Belper, Derbyshire DE5 0FD* Belper (0773) 825727

WALLER, Canon Trevor. b 04. Selw Coll Cam BA27 MA31. Ridley Hall Cam 27. **d** 29 **p** 30. R Waldringfield w Hemley *St E* 48-74; R Newbourn 50-74; Hon Can St E Cathl 65-74; rtd 74; Perm to Offic *St E* 74-90. *Whitehall Cottage, Waldringfield, Woodbridge, Suffolk* Waldringfield (047336) 348

WALLING, Mrs Caroline. b 47. **d** 86. Par Dn Greenwich St Alfege w St Pet and St Paul *S'wark* 89; Saudi Arabia 89; Par Dn Mottingham St Andr *S'wark* 90; Par

Dn Battersea St Mary from 91. *83 Whitgift House, 61 Westbridge Road, London SW11 3TJ* 071-924 4858

WALLIS, Ian George. b 57. Sheff Univ BA79 St Edm Ho Cam MLitt87. Ridley Hall Cam 88. **d** 90 **p** 91. C Armthorpe *Sheff* from 90. *55 Fernbank Drive, Armthorpe, Doncaster, S Yorkshire DN3 2HB* Doncaster (0302) 832815

WALLIS, Canon John. b 13. Pemb Coll Ox BA36 MA40. Wells Th Coll 36. **d** 37 **p** 38. RD Birstall *Wakef* 59-79; Hon Can Wakef Cathl 65-79; V Hartshead 69-79; rtd 79; Perm to Offic *Wakef* from 79. *Dulverton Hall, St Martin's Square, Scarborough YO11 2DB* Scarborough (0723) 373082

WALLIS, John Anthony. b 36. St Pet Coll Ox BA60 MA64. Clifton Th Coll 60. **d** 62 **p** 63. C Blackpool St Mark *Blackb* 62-65; C Leeds St Geo *Ripon* 65-69; Korea 69-74; Nat Sec (Scotland) OMF 75-78; Home Dir OMF 78-89; Hon C Sevenoaks St Nic *Roch* 82-89; Chapl The Hague *Eur* from 89. *Riouwstraat 2, 2585 HA, The Hague, The Netherlands* The Hague (70) 355-5359

WALLIS, Canon John Charles. b 12. DSC44. Hatf Coll Dur BA38 LTh38 MA51. St Boniface Warminster 34. **d** 39 **p** 40. R Wareham w Arne *Sarum* 61-76; RD Purbeck 66-73; Can and Preb Sarum Cathl 66-79; rtd 79; C Wimborne Minster and Holt *Sarum* 81; C Witchampton and Hinton Parva, Long Crichel etc 82-90. *50 West Borough, Wimborne, Dorset BH21 1NQ* Wimborne (0202) 883756

WALLIS, Paul Justin. b 65. St Jo Coll Nottm BTh90. **d** 90. C Somers Town St Mary *Lon* from 90. *2A Camden Terrace, London NW1 9BP* 071-267 8704

WALLIS, Raymond Christopher. b 38. Moor Park Coll Farnham 61. Sarum Th Coll 63. **d** 66 **p** 67. C Allerton *Bradf* 66-68; C Langley Marish *Ox* 68-69; C Caister *Nor* 69-73; P-in-c E w W Bradenham 73-80; R Outwell *Ely* 80-84; R Upwell St Pet 80-84; V Bishopstone *Chich* from 84. *The Vicarage, Bishopstone Road, Bishopstone-Seaford, E Sussex BN25 2UD* Seaford (0323) 892972

WALLIS, Roderick Vaughan. b 37. Leic Univ BA79 Warw Univ MA80 Leeds Univ CertEd82 E Lon Poly DCouns90. Lich Th Coll 64. **d** 66 **p** 67. C Cookham *Ox* 66-70; C Daventry *Pet* 70-72; TV Northn Em 72-76; Hon C 81-89; Hon C Northn St Matt 76-81; Perm to Offic from 89. *28 Lingswood Park, Northampton NN3 4TA* Northampton (0604) 401578

WALLIS, Roland Seabon. b 17. MBE44. Lon Univ BSc38 Ex Univ BSc57. St Aug Coll Cant 75. **d** 77 **p** 78. Hon C Whitstable All SS w St Pet *Cant* 77-84; Hon C Whitstable 84-87; Perm to Offic from 87. *22 Mickleburgh Avenue, Herne Bay, Kent CT6 6HA* Canterbury (0227) 372263

WALLIS, Canon Michael Peter. b 38. Cape Town Univ BA57 Lon Univ DipTh61. Wells Th Coll 59. **d** 61 **p** 62. C Morecambe St Barn *Blackb* 61-64; C Birm St Paul *Birm* 64-66; Ind Chapl 64-74; V Temple Balsall 66-74; Chapl Wroxall Abbey Sch 72-74; V Kings Heath *Birm* 74-76; Hon C Small Heath St Greg 76-78; Chapl Oakham Sch *Leics* 78-83; P-in-c Leic St Sav *Leic* 83-85; P-in-c Knossington and Cold Overton 85-87; P-in-c Owston and Withcote 85-87; V Tilton w Lowesby 85-87; P-in-c 87; V Whatborough Gp of Par 87-90; Bp's Adv Relns with People of Other Faiths from 89; Hon Can Leic Cathl from 89; V Leic St Mary from 90. *The Vicarage, 15 Castle Street, Leicester LE1 5WN* Leicester (0533) 628727

WALLS, Canon Raymond William. b 10. AKC35. **d** 35 **p** 36. R Ufford *St E* 59-77; Hon Can St E Cathl 65-77; rtd 77. *Flat 14, Bromley College, London Road, Bromley BR1 1PE* 081-464 7906

WALLS, Simon Conor. b 67. Dur Univ BA89 TCD MPhil90. **d** 91. C Castleknock and Mulhuddart w Clonsilla *D & G* from 91. *42 Oakview Avenue, Clonsilla, Dublin 15, Irish Republic* Dublin (1) 217672

WALMISLEY, Andrew John. b 55. Ex Univ BA75. Ridley Hall Cam 76. **d** 78 **p** 79. C W Brompton St Mary w St Pet *Lon* 78-81; USA from 81. *Trinity School, 101 West 91st Street, New York, New York 10024, USA*

WALMSLEY, Alexander David. b 07. **d** 34 **p** 35. R Whitchurch St Mary *Ox* 64-74; rtd 74; Perm to Offic *Glouc* from 74. *1 College Yard, Gloucester GL1 2PL* Gloucester (0452) 412040

WALMSLEY, Derek. b 57. Oak Hill Th Coll DipHE91. **d** 91. C Bletchley *Ox* from 91. *65 Bushy Close, Bletchley, Milton Keynes MK3 6PX* Milton Keynes (0908) 379853

WALMSLEY, George Bernard. b 07. Leeds Univ BA29. Coll of Resurr Mirfield 25. **d** 31 **p** 32. V Meerbrook *Lich* 59-72; P-in-c Quarnford 65-72; rtd 72. *46 Parker Street, Leek, Staffs ST13 6LB* Leek (0538) 373927

WALMSLEY, John William. b 37. Hull Univ BA71 MA73 PhD81. Wycliffe Hall Ox 71. **d** 72 **p** 73. C Clifton *York*

72-74; C Acomb St Steph 74-76; P-in-c Newton upon Ouse 76-81; P-in-c Shipton w Overton 76-81; V York St Thos w St Maurice 81-89; V Barkingside St Laur *Chelmsf* from 89. *St Laurence's Vicarage, Donnington Avenue, Ilford, Essex IG6 1AJ* 081-554 2003

WALMSLEY-McLEOD, Paul Albert. b 56. St Cuth Soc Dur BA82 Cam Univ CertEd83. Westcott Ho Cam 85. **d** 87 **p** 88. C Gt Bookham *Guildf* 87-90; Asst Chapl St Chris Hospice Sydenham from 90. *5 Lawrence Court, 77 Lawrie Park Road, London SE26 6ED* 081-676 9994

WALNE, John Clifford. b 29. Wycliffe Hall Ox. **d** 87 **p** 88. NSM Hedsor and Bourne End *Ox* 87-88; Hon C Lezayre St Olave Ramsey *S & M* from 88; Hon C Bride from 88. *St Olave's Vicarage, Ramsey, Isle of Man* Ramsey (0624) 812104

WALROND-SKINNER, Susan Mary. b 42. Bris Univ BA63 CertEd68 Univ of Wales DASS70. Bris Minl Tr Scheme 82 Ripon Coll Cuddesdon. **dss** 84 **d** 87. Assoc Dir of Ords *Bris* 84-86; Continuing Minl Educn Officer from 87. *St Stephen's Vicarage, Wigton Crescent, Bristol BS10 6RU* Bristol (0272) 590610

WALSER, Ven David. b 23. St Edm Hall Ox BA48 DipTh49 MA53. St Steph Ho Ox 48. **d** 50 **p** 51. C Horfield St Greg *Bris* 50-54; Vice-Prin St Steph Ho Ox 54-60; Asst Chapl Ex Coll Ox 56-57; Asst Chapl Mert Coll Ox 57-60; Min Can Ely Cathl *Ely* 61-70; Chapl K Sch Ely 61-71; V Linton *Ely* 71-81; R Bartlow 73-81; RD Linton 76-81; Adn Ely from 81; R Cam St Botolph 81-89; Hon Can Ely Cathl from 81. *St Botolph's Rectory, Cambridge CB3 9HE* Cambridge (0223) 350684

WALSER, Emil Jonathan. b 16. St Jo Coll Dur LTh38 BA39 MA43. Oak Hill Th Coll 35. **d** 39 **p** 40. V Baslow *Derby* 65-82; RD Bakewell and Eyam 78-81; rtd 82. *2 Almond Grove, Filey, N Yorkshire YO14 9EH* Scarborough (0723) 515582

WALSH, Bertram William Nicholas. b 21. TCD BA44. CITC 46. **d** 46 **p** 47. Chapl St Columba's Coll Dub 60-87; rtd 87. *130 Grange Road, Rathfarnham, Dublin 14, Irish Republic* Dublin (1) 931229

✠**WALSH, Rt Rev Geoffrey David Jeremy.** b 29. Pemb Coll Cam BA53 MA58. Linc Th Coll 53. **d** 55 **p** 56 **c** 86. C Southgate Ch Ch *Lon* 55-58; SCM Sec Cam 58-61; C Cam Gt St Mary w St Mich *Ely* 58-61; V Moorfields *Bris* 61-66; R Marlborough *Sarum* 66-76; Can and Preb Sarum Cathl 73-76; R Elmsett w Aldham *St E* 76-80; Adn Ipswich 76-86; Suff Bp Tewkesbury *Glouc* from 86. *Green Acre, 166 Hempstead Lane, Gloucester GL2 6LG* Gloucester (0452) 21824

WALSH, Geoffrey Malcolm. b 46. Sarum & Wells Th Coll. **d** 84 **p** 85. C Wellington and Distr *B & W* 84-87; TV Axminster, Chardstock, Combe Pyne and Rousdon *Ex* 87-90; Chapl RN from 90. *c/o MOD, Lacon House, Theobald's Road, London WC1X 8RY* 071-430 6847

WALSH, John Alan. b 37. Chich Th Coll 63. **d** 66 **p** 67. C Wigan St Anne *Liv* 66-69; C Newport w Longford *Lich* 69-73; V Dunstall 73-83; V Rangemore 73-83; P-in-c Tatenhill 77-83; R Dunstall w Rangemore and Tatenhill 83; V Hartshill from 83. *Holy Trinity Vicarage, Hartshill, Stoke-on-Trent ST4 7NJ* Newcastle-under-Lyme (0782) 616965

WALSH, Julia Christine (Sister Julian). b 20. K Coll Lon DipTh49. Gilmore Ho 46. **dss** 56 **d** 87. CSA from 53. *St Andrew's House, 2 Tavistock Road, London W11 1BA* 071-229 2662

WALSH, Preb Lionel Ernest. b 10. Hatf Coll Dur BA31. Bps' Coll Cheshunt 31. **d** 33 **p** 34. Preb Wells Cathl *B & W* from 63; R Ditcheat 65-75; rtd 75. *Abbey Close, Ditcheat, Shepton Mallet, Somerset BA4 6RB* Ditcheat (074986) 314

WALSH, Peter. b 64. Liv Univ BA86 Nottm Univ BTh90. Linc Th Coll 87. **d** 90 **p** 91. C Cantley *Sheff* from 90. *40 Cantley Manor Avenue, Cantley, Doncaster, S Yorkshire DN4 6TN* Doncaster (0302) 531520

WALSH, Thomas Laurence. b 11. BNC Ox BA38 MA38. Ripon Hall Ox 38. **d** 39 **p** 40. V Staveley in Cartmel *Carl* 60-76; rtd 76; Perm to Offic *Carl* from 77. *Tarn Potts, Newby Bridge, Ulverston, Cumbria LA12 8AW* Newby Bridge (05395) 31808

WALSH, Canon William Arthur. b 12. St Jo Coll Dur BA34 MA41 DipTh41. **d** 35 **p** 36. V Dartford Ch Ch *Roch* 44-77; Hon Can Roch Cathl 71-77; rtd 77. *33 Correnden Road, Tonbridge, Kent*

WALSHE, Canon Brian. b 28. AKC49. St Boniface Warminster. **d** 54 **p** 55. R Langley Marish *Ox* 68-76; Chapl Manfield Hosp Northn 76-88; V Northn St Alb *Pet* 76-88; Dir Mountbatten Community Trust from 76; Chief Exec Lon Youth Trust from 87; rtd 88; Perm to Offic *Pet* from 88. *9/10 Warrior Court, 16 Warrior Way, St Leonards-on-Sea, E Sussex*

WALT, Trevor. RMN74 RNT79. Ox NSM Course 83. **d** 86 **p** 87. NSM Crowthorne *Ox* from 86; Chapl Asst Broadmoor Hosp Crowthorne 86-89; Chapl from 89. *Redwoods, Kentigern Drive, Crowthorne, Berks RG11 7HJ* Crowthorne (0344) 773999

WALTER, Canon Arthur Reginald. b 13. Keble Coll Ox BA34 MA38. St Mich Coll Llan 35. **d** 36 **p** 37. R Swanton Morley w Worthing *Nor* 60-78; Hon Can Nor Cathl 75-78; rtd 78; Chapl Madeira *Eur* 80-90; Perm to Offic *Nor* from 90. *4 Southern Reach, Mulbarton, Norfolk NR14 8BU* Mulbarton (0508) 78107

WALTER, Donald Alex. b 34. Ripon Hall Ox 57. **d** 60 **p** 61. C Ealing St Steph Castle Hill *Lon* 60-63; Jamaica 63-80; V Twickenham Common H Trin *Lon* from 81. *Holy Trinity Vicarage, 1 Vicarage Road, Twickenham TW2 5TS* 081-898 1168

WALTER, Giles Robert. b 54. Cam Univ MA76. Cranmer Hall Dur 78. **d** 82 **p** 83. C Finchley Ch Ch *Lon* 82-86; C Cam H Sepulchre w All SS *Ely* from 86. *9 Victoria Street, Cambridge CB1 1JP* Cambridge (0223) 359314

WALTER, Ian Edward. b 47. Edin Univ MA69 Keble Coll Ox BA71 MA78. Cuddesdon Coll 71. **d** 73 **p** 74. C Greenock *Glas* 73-76; C Glas St Mary 76-79; Chapl Angl Students Glas 76-79; R Paisley St Barn 79-84; P-in-c Bolton St Phil *Man* 84-86; V 86-91; Bp's Ecum Adv from 89; V Elton All SS from 91. *All Saints' Vicarage, 90 Tottington Road, Bury, Lancs BL8 1LR* 061-764 1431

WALTER, Michael. b 36. AKC62. **d** 63 **p** 64. C Middlesb St Jo the Ev *York* 63-65, C Sherborne *Win* 65-68; C Bournemouth St Fran 68-69; Prec Newc Cathl *Newc* 69-71; C Dur St Marg *Dur* 72-74; P-in-c Deaf Hill cum Langdale 74-77; V Newington w Dairycoates *York* 77-88; Perm to Offic from 88. *2 Davenport Avenue, Hessle, N Humberside HU13 0RP* Hull (0482) 645740

WALTER, Noel. b 41. St D Coll Lamp DipTh66. **d** 66 **p** 67. C Mitcham Ascension *S'wark* 66-71; C Caterham 71-74; V Welling 74-82; C Warlingham w Chelsham and Farleigh 82-88; Chapl R Earlswood Hosp Redhill from 88; Chapl Redhill Gen Hosp from 88; Chapl E Surrey Hosp Redhill from 88. *11 Ringwood Avenue, Redhill, Surrey RH1 2DY* Redhill (0737) 765043

WALTER, Peter John. b 44. CEng MIGasE. Chich Th Coll 80. **d** 82 **p** 83. C Leominster *Heref* 82-85; P-in-c Brimfield 85-90; P-in-c Orleton 85-90; R Orleton w Brimfield from 91. *The Vicarage, Orleton, Ludlow, Shropshire SY8 4HW* Yarpole (056885) 258

WALTER, Robin. b 37. Univ Coll Dur BA63 MA90 Linacre Coll Ox BA65 MA69. St Steph Ho Ox 63. **d** 66 **p** 68. C Peckham St Jo *S'wark* 66-69; Chapl Lon Univ *Lon* 69-70; C Dur St Marg *Dur* 70-74; R Burnmoor 74-79; Asst Master Barnard Castle Sch from 79; Lic to Offic 79-82; Hon C Whorlton 82-88; NSM Barnard Castle Deanery from 88. *4 Montalbo Road, Barnard Castle, Co Durham DL12 8BP* Teesdale (0833) 31741

WALTERS, Andrew Farrar. b 42. ACP67. **d** 81 **p** 82. Warden St Mich Coll Tenbury 77-85; Chapl Ex Cathl Sch 85-87; Hd Master Homefield Sch Sutton from 87; Perm to Offic *S'wark* from 87. *32 Tate Road, Sutton, Surrey SM1 2TD* 081-642 0965

WALTERS, Christopher John Linley. b 24. St Pet Hall Ox BA47 MA49. Linc Th Coll 48. **d** 50 **p** 51. V Newc St Paul *Lich* 61-70; V Pattingham 70-85; P-in-c Patshull 77-85; V Pattingham w Patshull 85-89; rtd 89. *Old School House, 19 Cardington, Church Stretton, Shropshire SY6 7JZ* Longville (06943) 528

WALTERS, David Michael Trenham. b 46. Open Univ BA86. St D Coll Lamp DipTh69. **d** 69 **p** 70. C Killay *S & B* 69-72; CF 72-89 and from 91; Chapl Eagle Ho Prep Sch Crowthorne from 89. *30 Duke's Wood, Crowthorne, Berks RG11 6NF* Crowthorne (0344) 780120

WALTERS, Canon David Miles Ivor. b 12. Qu Coll Cam BA34 MA38. Wells Th Coll 34. **d** 35 **p** 36. V Rottingdean *Chich* 55-74; Chapl Butlin's Ocean Hotel 55-72; Can and Preb Chich Cathl 72-80; TR Ovingdean w Rottingdean and Woodingdean 74-78; rtd 78; Perm to Offic *Chich* from 80. *8 Elmstead Gardens, West Wittering, Chichester, W Sussex PO20 8NG* Birdham (0243) 513644

WALTERS, David Trevor. b 37. Ex Coll Ox BA58 MA62. St Steph Ho Ox 62. **d** 64 **p** 65. C Cardiff St Mary *Llan* 64-69; V Brecon w Battle *S & B* 69-73; Min Can Brecon Cathl 69-73; V Llanddew and Talachddu 73-78; V Cefncoed and Capel Nantddu 78-80; V Cefn Coed and Capel Nantddu w Vaynor etc 80-87; V Talgarth and Llanelieu from 87. *The Vicarage, 10 Bronant, Talgarth, Brecon, Powys LD3 0HF* Talgarth (0874) 711249

WALTERS, Canon Douglas Lewis. b 20. Univ of Wales BA41. St Mich Coll Llan 41. **d** 43 **p** 44. V Kidwelly *St D* 58-80; RD Cydweli 77-85; Can St D Cathl 78-86; V Kidwelly and Llandefaelog 80-86; rtd 86. *83 Ashburnham Road, Burry Port, Dyfed SA16 0TW* Burry Port (05546) 4139

WALTERS, Preb Egerton Edward Farrar. b 04. Qu Coll Cam BA25 MA29. Cuddesdon Coll 27. **d** 27 **p** 28. V Shrewsbury St Mary *Lich* 56-68; rtd 68. *Tyrgroes, Cwmcamlais, Brecon, Powys* Sennybridge (087482) 530

WALTERS, Francis Raymond. b 24. Ball Coll Ox BA49 MA54. Wycliffe Hall Ox 51. **d** 53 **p** 54. C Boulton *Derby* 53-56; Lect Qu Coll Birm 56-64; Succ Birm Cathl *Birm* 56-58; C Harborne St Pet 58-64; V Leic St Nic *Leic* 64-74; Chapl Leic Univ 64-74; R Appleby 74-77; Dir of Educn 77-89; Hon Can Leic Cathl 77-89; P-in-c Swithland from 77. *The Rectory, 165 Main Street, Swithland, Loughborough, Leics LE12 8QT* Woodhouse Eaves (0509) 890357

WALTERS, Ian Robert. b 51. ACA75 FCA81. Local NSM Course 80. **d** 85 **p** 86. NSM Ingoldsby *Linc* from 85. *Dairy Farmhouse, Westby, Grantham, Lincs NG33 4EA* Ingoldsby (047685) 542

WALTERS, John Eurof Thomas. b 20. St D Coll Lamp BA46. **d** 47 **p** 48. V Burntwood *Lich* 56-81; P-in-c Edingale 81-89; P-in-c Harlaston 81-89; rtd 89. *Harlaston Rectory, Tamworth, Staffs* Harlaston (082785) 646

WALTERS, John Morgan. b 09. **d** 34 **p** 35. V High Wych *St Alb* 52-74; rtd 74; Perm to Offic *St E* from 75. *5 Cannonfields, Bury St Edmunds, Suffolk IP33 1JX* Bury St Edmunds (0284) 61010

WALTERS, John Philip Hewitt. b 50. Coll of Resurr Mirfield 72. **d** 73 **p** 74. C Llanguicke *S & B* 73-76; Min Can Brecon Cathl 76-79; C Brecon w Battle 76-79; V Merthyr Cynog and Dyffryn Honddu etc 79-83; V Llandilo Talybont from 83. *The Vicarage, 28 Bolgoed Road, Pontardulais, Swansea SA4 1JE* Pontardulais (0792) 882468

WALTERS, Leslie Ernest Ward. b 27. Wadh Coll Ox BA51 MA55. Ridley Hall Cam 55. **d** 57 **p** 58. C Heref St Pet w St Owen *Heref* 57-59; C Morden *S'wark* 59-61; V Felbridge 61-68; V Streatham Immanuel w St Anselm 68-81; V Cotmanhay *Derby* from 81; Chapl Ilkeston Gen Hosp 81-88; Chapl Ilkeston Community Hosp from 88. *Cotmanhay Vicarage, Ilkeston, Derbyshire DE7 8QL* Ilkeston (0602) 325670

WALTERS, Michael William. b 39. Dur Univ BSc61. Clifton Th Coll 61. **d** 63 **p** 64. C Aldershot H Trin *Guildf* 63-66; C Upper Armley *Ripon* 66-69; Area Sec (NE) CPAS 69-75; V Hyde St Geo *Ches* 75-82; V Knutsford St Jo and Toft from 82. *The Vicarage, 11 Gough's Lane, Knutsford, Cheshire WA16 8QL* Knutsford (0565) 632834

WALTERS, Nicholas Humphrey. b 45. K Coll Lon BD67 AKC67. **d** 68 **p** 69. C Weston *Guildf* 68-71; Chapl and Lect NE Surrey Coll of Tech Ewell 71-77; Hon C Ewell 71-77; Warden Moor Park Coll Farnham 77-80; Tutor Surrey Univ *Guildf* from 80; Dir of Studies Guildf Inst from 82. *9 Valley View, Godalming, Surrey* Godalming (04868) 5106

WALTERS, Peter. b 27. Leeds Univ BSc48 Univ of Wales (Abth) MSc52. Ripon Coll Cuddesdon 78. **d** 79 **p** 80. C Kingswood *Bris* 79-82; R Stanton St Quintin, Hullavington, Grittleton etc 82-88; rtd 88. *Rose Cottage, Duntisbourne Abbots, Cirencester, Glos GL7 7JN* Cirencester (0285) 82777

WALTERS, Peter Shane. b 54. SS Paul & Mary Coll Cheltenham DipRS83 Univ of Wales (Cardiff) BD87. St Mich Coll Llan 84. **d** 87 **p** 88. C Newport St Julian *Mon* 87-90; Asst Admin of Shrine of Our Lady of Walsingham from 91; Lic to Offic *Nor* from 91. *The College, Walsingham, Norfolk NR22 6EF* Fakenham (0328) 820266

WALTERS, Very Rev Rhys Derrick Chamberlain. b 32. LSE BSc55. Ripon Hall Ox. **d** 57 **p** 58. C Manselton *S & B* 57-58; C Swansea St Mary and H Trin 58-62; Chapl Univ of Wales (Swansea) 58-62; V Totley *Sheff* 62-67; V Boulton *Derby* 67-74; Dioc Missr *Sarum* 74-83; P-in-c Burcombe 74-79; Can and Preb Sarum Cathl 77-79; Can Res and Treas Sarum Cathl 79-83; Dean Liv from 83. *The Deanery, 1 Cathedral Close, Liverpool L1 7BR* 051-708 0924

WALTERS, Mrs Sheila Ann Beatrice. b 37. Bris Univ DipEd58. E Midl Min Tr Course 85. **d** 89. NSM Ashby-de-la-Zouch St Helen w Coleorton *Leic* from 89. *115 Loughborough Road, Coleorton, Leicester LE6 4HH* Coalville (0530) 32267

WALTERS, Thomas. b 24. St Deiniol's Hawarden. **d** 79 **p** 80. Hon C Bardsley *Man* 79-89; rtd 90. *49 Fir Tree Avenue, Oldham, Lancs OL8 2QS*   061-652 4108

WALTERS, Thomas Hubert. b 16. Univ of Wales BA39. St Mich Coll Llan 39. **d** 40 **p** 41. V Blacklands Hastings Ch Ch and St Andr *Chich* 70-81; rtd 81; Perm to Offic *Chich* from 81. *125 Ashford Road, Hastings, E Sussex TN34 2HY*   Hastings (0424) 442653

WALTON, Brian. b 53. Sarum & Wells Th Coll 83. **d** 85 **p** 86. C Silksworth *Dur* 85-86; C Bishopwearmouth St Mich w St Hilda 86-88; Chapl RN from 88. *c/o MOD, Lacon House, Theobald's Road, London WC1X 8RY*   071-430 6847

WALTON, Ven Geoffrey Elmer. b 34. Dur Univ BA59. Qu Coll Birm DipTh61. **d** 61 **p** 62. C Warsop *S'well* 61-65; Dioc Youth Chapl 65-69; V Norwell 65-69; Recruitment Sec ACCM 69-75; V Weymouth H Trin *Sarum* 75-82; RD Weymouth 79-82; Can and Preb Sarum Cathl from 81; Adn Dorset from 82; P-in-c Witchampton and Hinton Parva, Long Crichel etc from 82. *The Vicarage, Witchampton, Wimborne, Dorset BH21 5AP*   Witchampton (0258) 840422

WALTON, John Sidney. b 99. Linc Th Coll 22. **d** 24 **p** 25. V Hatherden cum Tangley *Win* 53-60; rtd 64. *31 River Way, Christchurch, Dorset BH23 2QQ*   Christchurch (0202) 484448

WALTON, John Victor. b 45. Lon Univ BSc67. Linc Th Coll 79. **d** 81 **p** 82. C Stevenage St Mary Shephall *St Alb* 81-85; TV Bourne Valley *Sarum* from 85. *The Vicarage, Winterbourne Earls, Salisbury SP4 6HA*   Idmiston (0980) 611350

WALTON, Philip William. b 28. Dur Univ BScAgr52. Tyndale Hall Bris 54. **d** 56 **p** 58. C Clerkenwell St Jas and St Jo w St Pet *Lon* 56-57; C St Alb St Paul *St Alb* 57-59; C Haydock St Mark *Liv* 58-60; V Wiggenhall St Mary Magd *Ely* 60-66; Sec CCCS 66-69; Chapl Maisons-Lafitte w Versailles and Caen *Eur* 69-74; V Worthing Ch Ch *Chich* 74-85; R Wigmore Abbey *Heref* from 85. *The Rectory, Leintwardine, Craven Arms, Shropshire SY7 0LL*   Leintwardine (05473) 235

WALTON, Reginald Arthur. b 40. St Jo Coll Nottm 80. **d** 81 **p** 82. C Woodthorpe *S'well* 81-84; P-in-c Nottm St Andr 84-85; V 85-91; R Moreton *Ches* from 91. *The Rectory, Dawpool Drive, Moreton, South Wirral L46 0PH*   051-677 3540

WALTON, Stephen John. b 55. Birm Univ BSc76 Fitzw Coll Cam BA79 MA82. Ridley Hall Cam 77. **d** 83 **p** 84. C Bebington *Ches* 83-86; Voc and Min Adv CPAS from 86; Lic to Offic *St Alb* from 86. *c/o CPAS, Athena Drive, Tachbrook Park, Warwick CV34 6NG*   Warwick (0926) 334242

WALTON, Wilfred James. b 14. St Jo Coll Dur BA39 MA51. **d** 39 **p** 40. Lic to Offic *Sheff* from 68; rtd 79; Perm to Offic *Derby* from 79. *25 Main Avenue, Totley, Sheffield S17 4FH*   Sheffield (0742) 367183

WANDSWORTH, Archdeacon of. *See* GERRARD, Ven David Keith Robin

WANJIE, Lukas Macharia. b 50. Fitzw Coll Cam BA79 MA83. St Paul's Coll Limuru 72 Ridley Hall Cam 76. **d** 75 **p** 76. Kenya 75-76 and 80-91; Prin Trin Bib Coll Nairobi 85-91; C Mill End and Heronsgate w W Hyde *St Alb* 79; C St Alb St Steph from 91. *12 Tavistock Avenue, St Albans, Herts AL1 2NH*   St Albans (0727) 50215

WANSEY, John. b 07. Selw Coll Cam BA30 MA34. Westcott Ho Cam 31. **d** 31 **p** 32. V W Lavington *Chich* 61-78; rtd 78; Perm to Offic *Chich* from 78. *Manormead Residential Home, Tilford Road, Hindhead, Surrey GU26 6RA*   Hindhead (0428) 604780

WANSEY, Joseph Christopher. b 10. Selw Coll Cam BA32 MA36. Westcott Ho Cam 33. **d** 34 **p** 35. V Roydon *Chelmsf* 64-75; rtd 75; Lic to Offic *Ely* from 81; Perm to Offic *Cov* from 85. *6 Margetts Close, Kenilworth, Warks CV8 1EN*   Kenilworth (0926) 54762

WANSEY, Canon Paul Raymond. b 06. MC44. Selw Coll Cam BA28 MA32. Westcott Ho Cam. **d** 29 **p** 30. R Woodbridge St Mary *St E* 68-74; rtd 74; Perm to Offic *St E* from 75. *3 Warren Hill Road, Woodbridge, Suffolk IP12 4DT*   Woodbridge (03943) 7807

WANSTALL, Miss Noelle Margaret. b 53. Wolfs Coll Cam BEd76. Sarum & Wells Th Coll 84. dss 86 **d** 87. Hythe *Cant* 86-87; Par Dn 87-89; Par Dn Reculver and Herne Bay St Bart from 89. *St Bartholomew's House, 25 Dence Park, Herne Bay, Kent CT6 6BQ*   Herne Bay (0227) 360948

WARBURTON, Andrew James. b 44. Oak Hill Th Coll 64. **d** 69 **p** 70. C New Milverton *Cov* 69-72; C Fulham St Matt *Lon* 72-76; C Chesham St Mary *Ox* 76-80; TV Gt Chesham from 80. *14A Manor Way, Chesham, Bucks HP5 3BG*   Chesham (0494) 784372

WARBURTON, John Bryce. b 33. St Aid Birkenhead 64. **d** 66 **p** 67. C Padiham *Blackb* 66-69; C Burnley St Pet 69-70; V Tideswell *Derby* 70-81; V Bollington St Jo *Ches* 81-91; V Capesthorne w Siddington and Marton from 91. *The Vicarage, School Lane, Marton, Macclesfield, Cheshire SK11 9HD*   Marton Heath (0260) 224447

WARBURTON, Piers Eliot de Dutton. b 30. Cranmer Hall Dur BA65. **d** 65 **p** 66. C Grassendale *Liv* 65-68; Bermuda 68-71; R Sherborne *Win* 71-76; V Yateley 76-82; R Guernsey St Andr 82-89; V Hartley Wintney, Elvetham, Winchfield etc from 89. *The Vicarage, Hartley Wintney, Basingstoke, Hants RG27 8DZ*   Hartley Wintney (025126) 2670

WARBURTON, Canon Robert Tinsley. b 23. MBE66 TD69. Jes Coll Cam BA47 MA52. Oak Hill Th Coll 47. **d** 47 **p** 48. C Ipswich St Marg *St E* 47-50; R Dallinghoo and Pettistree 50-54; P-in-c Playford w Culpho and Tuddenham St Martin 52-54; V Attenborough w Bramcote *S'well* 54-67; CF (TA) from 55; RD Beeston *S'well* 60-67; Chapl Mansf Gen Hosp from 67; RD Mansf *S'well* from 67; V Mansf St Pet from 67; P-in-c Teversal 68-72; Hon Can S'well Minster from 72. *The Vicarage, Lindhurst Lane, Mansfield, Notts NG18 4JE*   Mansfield (0623) 21600

WARBURTON, Walter George. b 16. Bede Coll Dur BA40 DipTh42 MA43. **d** 41 **p** 42. V Gt Marsden *Blackb* 60-81; rtd 81; Lic to Offic *Blackb* from 81. *145 Halifax Road, Nelson, Lancs BB9 0EL*   Nelson (0282) 697589

WARCHUS, Michael Edward George. b 37. Lon Univ DipTh67. Roch Th Coll 65. **d** 68 **p** 69. C Buckhurst Hill *Chelmsf* 68-71; C Stainton-in-Cleveland *York* 71-76; V Carlton and Drax 76-86; V Acomb St Steph from 86. *32 Carr Lane, Acomb, York YO2 5HX*   York (0904) 798106

WARD, Alan William. b 56. Trin Coll Bris 80. **d** 81 **p** 82. C New Ferry *Ches* 81-86; Dioc Youth Officer 86-91; C Charlesworth and Dinting Vale *Derby* from 91. *7 Burwell Close, Glossop, Derbyshire SK13 9PG*   Glossop (0457) 856831

WARD, Albert George. b 27. K Coll Lon BD54 AKC54. **d** 55 **p** 56. TR Usworth *Dur* 69-78; V S Shields St Simon 78-86; C Darlington St Cuth 86-88; rtd 88. *25 West Crescent, Darlington, Co Durham DL3 7PS*   Darlington (0325) 351572

WARD, Allan Edward Neville. b 11. Kelham Th Coll 29. **d** 35 **p** 36. V Shalfleet *Portsm* 67-73; V Thorley 67-73; R Chale 73-80; R Niton 77-80; rtd 80; Perm to Offic *Portsm* from 80. *2 Fairy Hill, Seaview Lane, Seaview, Isle of Wight PO34 5DG*   Isle of Wight (0983) 612474

WARD, Anthony. b 55. Wycliffe Hall Ox 78. **d** 80 **p** 81. Zimbabwe 80-85; S Africa 85-90; C Leic H Trin w St Jo *Leic* from 90. *83 Regent Road, Leicester LE1 6YG*   Leicester (0533) 553808

WARD, Anthony Peter. b 46. Bris Univ BSc67 Ox Univ DipEd68. St Jo Coll Nottm. **d** 82 **p** 83. C Hellesdon *Nor* 82-85; P-in-c Nor St Aug w St Mary 85-91; P-in-c Norwich-over-the-Water Colegate St Geo 85-90; Norfolk Churches' Radio Officer from 85; TV Nor Over-the-Water from 91. *St Paul's Vicarage, 1 Mill Lane, Norwich NR3 4LD*   Norwich (0603) 622240

WARD, Ven Arthur Frederick. b 12. Armstrong Coll Dur BA33. Ridley Hall Cam 33. **d** 35 **p** 36. Preb Ex Cathl *Ex* from 70; Adn Ex and Can Res Ex Cathl 70-81; Prec 72-81; rtd 81. *Melrose, Christow, Exeter EX6 7LY*   Christow (0647) 52498

WARD, Arthur John. b 32. Lon Univ BD57. St Aid Birkenhead 57. **d** 57 **p** 58. C Ecclesfield *Sheff* 57-60; C Fulwood 60-63; Tutor St Aid Birkenhead 63-66; R Denton St Lawr *Man* 66-74; CMS 74-82; TV Wolv *Lich* 82-90; V Edgbaston SS Mary and Ambrose *Birm* from 90. *St Ambrose Vicarage, 15 Raglan Road, Birmingham B5 7RA*   021-440 2196

WARD, Calvin. b 34. Univ of Wales BA57 DipEd60 Fitzw Ho Cam BA63 MA67. Westcott Ho Cam 61. **d** 64 **p** 65. C Handsworth St Mich *Birm* 64-66; C Shaw Hill 66-69; V Windhill *Bradf* 69-76; V Esholt 76-81; V Oakworth 81-91; V Allerton from 91. *The Vicarage, Leytop Lane, Allerton, Bradford, W Yorkshire BD15 7LT*   Bradford (0274) 41948

WARD, Canon Charles Leslie. b 16. Lich Th Coll 36. **d** 39 **p** 40. V Minehead *B & W* 67-76; V Kewstoke w Wick St Lawrence 76-81; Can Treas Wells Cathl 78-84; rtd 84; NSM Hardwicke, Quedgeley and Elmore w Longney *Glouc* from 90. *23 Clover Drive, Hardwicke, Glos GL2 6TG*   Gloucester (0452) 720015

WARD, Christopher John William. b 36. Qu Coll Birm 68. d 69 p 70. C Wednesbury St Bart *Lich* 69-73; CF from 73. *c/o MOD (Army), Bagshot Park, Bagshot, Surrey GU19 5PL* Bagshot (0276) 71717

WARD, David. b 40. St Jo Coll Nottm 83. d 85 p 86. C Aspley *S'well* 85-89; V from 89. *St Margaret's Vicarage, 319 Aspley Lane, Nottingham NG8 5GA* Nottingham (0602) 292920

WARD, David Conisbee. b 33. St Jo Coll Cam BA54 MA59. S'wark Ord Course 77. d 80 p 81. NSM Surbiton St Matt *S'wark* 80-83; C Streatham Immanuel w St Anselm 83-84; P-in-c 84-87; V Hook from 87. *The Vicarage, 278 Hook Road, Chessington, Surrey KT9 1PF* 081-397 3521

WARD, David Robert. b 51. Oak Hill Th Coll 74. d 77 p 78. C Kirkheaton *Wakef* 77-81; V Earlsheaton 81-88; V Bradley from 88. *The Vicarage, 87 Bradley Road, Huddersfield HD2 1RA* Huddersfield (0484) 427838

WARD, David Towle Greenfield. b 22. Ch Coll Cam BA47 MA49. Linc Th Coll 47. d 49 p 50. V Potter Heigham *Nor* 64-77; V Repps 64-77; R Ditchingham w Pirnough 77-87; R Broome 77-87; R Hedenham 77-87; rtd 87; Perm to Offic *Nor* from 87. *Manor Cottage, 58 Mount Street, Diss, Norfolk IP22 3QQ* Diss (0379) 651328

WARD, Ven Edwin James Greenfield. b 19. LVO63. Ch Coll Cam BA46 MA48. Ridley Hall Cam 46. d 48 p 49. Chapl to HM The Queen 55-90; R W Stafford w Frome Billet *Sarum* 67-84; Can and Preb Sarum Cathl 67-84; Adn Sherborne 67-84; rtd 85. *Manor Cottage, Poxwell, Dorchester, Dorset DT2 8ND* Warmwell (0305) 852062

WARD, Ms Frances Elizabeth Fearn. b 59. St Andr Univ MTh83 Jes Coll Cam DipTh89. Westcott Ho Cam 87. d 89. Par Dn Westhoughton *Man* from 89. *1 Furze Avenue, Westhoughton, Bolton BL5 2NW* Wigan (0942) 818030

WARD, Frank Neal. b 16. E Anglian Minl Tr Course 78. d 80 p 81. NSM Weybourne w Upper Sheringham *Nor* 80-84; NSM Kelling w Salthouse 80-84; NSM Briningham from 84. *The Street, Sharrington, Melton Constable, Norfolk NR24 2AB* Melton Constable (0263) 860337

WARD, Geoffrey. b 35. Cranmer Hall Dur 77. d 79 p 80. C Garforth *Ripon* 79-81; V Holmfield *Wakef* 81-85; TV Thornaby on Tees *York* from 85. *The Vicarage, 80 Acklam Road, Thornaby, Stockton-on-Tees, Cleveland TS17 7HD* Stockton-on-Tees (0642) 607210

WARD, Geoffrey Edward. b 30. Linc Th Coll 62. d 64 p 65. C Oundle *Pet* 64-68; C Weston Favell 68-70; TV 70-72; R Cottingham w E Carlton from 72. *The Rectory, Cottingham, Market Harborough, Leics LE16 8GX* Rockingham (0536) 771277

WARD, George Henry. b 08. Sheff Univ BA29 MA30 DipEd30. Ridley Hall Cam 36. d 37 p 38. V Worsbrough *Sheff* 67-73; rtd 73. *Fosbrooke House, 8 Clifton Drive, Lytham, Lancs FY8 5RE* Lytham (0253) 735904

WARD, Graham John. b 55. Fitzw Coll Cam BA80 Selw Coll Cam MA83. Westcott Ho Cam 87. d 90 p 91. C Bris St Mary Redcliffe w Temple etc *Bris* from 90. *2 Colston Parade, Bristol BS1 6RA* Bristol (0272) 260587

WARD, Ian Stanley. b 62. K Coll Lon BD83. Cranmer Hall Dur 84. d 86 p 87. C Moreton *Ches* 86-89; Chapl RAF from 89. *c/o MOD, Adastral House, Theobald's Road, London WC1X 8RU* 071-430 7268

WARD, Jack. b 08. Tyndale Hall Bris. d 57 p 58. V Mow Cop *Lich* 61-79; rtd 79. *9 Wentworth Drive, Rookery, Stoke-on-Trent ST7 4SU* Stoke-on-Trent (0782) 773316

WARD, John Frederick. b 55. St Mich Coll Llan 81. d 84 p 85. C Pemb Dock *St D* 84-86; PV Llan Cathl *Llan* 86-89; R St Bride's Minor w Bettws from 89. *St Bride's Rectory, Sarn, Bridgend, M Glam CF32 9RH* Bridgend (0656) 720274

WARD, John Raymond. b 31. St Jo Coll Dur BA54 DipTh56. d 56 p 57. C Leeds St Pet *Ripon* 56-60; C Seacroft 60-63; V Kirkstall 63-75; V Bramhope from 75. *The Vicarage, 26 Leeds Road, Bramhope, Leeds LS16 9BQ* Leeds (0532) 842543

WARD, Prof John Stephen Keith. b 38. Univ of Wales (Cardiff) BA 62 Linacre Coll Ox BLitt68 Trin Hall Cam MA72. Westcott Ho Cam 72. d 72 p 73. Hon C Hampstead St Jo *Lon* 72-75; Fell and Dean Trin Hall Cam 75-82; Prof Moral and Soc Th K Coll Lon 82-85; Prof Hist and Philosophy of Religion from 85. *King's College, Strand, London WC2R 2LS* 071-274 6222

WARD, John Stewart. b 43. St Jo Coll Dur BA66. Ripon Coll Cuddesdon 77. d 79 p 80. C High Harrogate Ch Ch *Ripon* 79-82; V Ireland Wood 82-86; Chapl Wells Cathl Sch 86-88; V Menston w Woodhead *Bradf* from 88. *The Vicarage, 12 Fairfax Gardens, Menston, Ilkley, W Yorkshire LS29 6ET* Menston (0943) 72818

WARD, Keith Raymond. b 37. Dur Univ BSc60. Chich Th Coll 63. d 65 p 66. C Wallsend St Luke *Newc* 65-68; C Wooler 68-74; V Dinnington 74-81; V Bedlington from 81. *The Vicarage, 21 Church Lane, Bedlington, Northd NE22 5EL* Bedlington (0670) 829220

WARD, Kenneth Arthur. b 22. St D Coll Lamp BA50 Chich Th Coll 50. d 52 p 53. R Daventry *Pet* 58-72; RD Daventry 68-76; R Daventry w Norton 73-79; R Daventry 79-82; V Pattishall w Cold Higham 82-88; rtd 88; Perm to Offic *Pet* from 89. *43 Inlands Rise, Daventry, Northants NN11 4DQ*

WARD, Dr Kevin. b 47. Edin Univ MA69 Trin Coll Cam PhD76. d 78 p 79. CMS from 75; Uganda 76-90; Qu Coll Birm from 91; Perm to Offic *Birm* from 91. *Queen's College, Somerset Road, Birmingham B15 2QH* 021-454 5748

WARD, Canon Leslie Alan James. b 38. AKC61. d 62 p 63. C Earlham St Anne *Nor* 62-65; C Gt Yarmouth 65-70; R Belton 70-83; R Burgh Castle 71-83; Chapl Norfolk and Nor Hosp from 83; Chapl N Norwich and Colman Hosp from 83; Hon Can Nor Cathl *Nor* from 86. *24 Carnoustie, Sunningdale, Norwich NR4 6AY* Norwich (0603) 58245 or 628377

WARD, Lionel Owen. b 37. Univ of Wales (Cardiff) BA58 Univ of Wales (Swansea) DipEd59 MA65 Lon Univ PhD70. St Mich Coll Llan 83. d 85 p 86. NSM Swansea St Mary w H Trin *S & B* 85-89; P-in-c Swansea St Matt w Greenhill from 89. *96 Glanbrydan Avenue, Uplands, Swansea SA2 0JH* Swansea (0792) 208081

WARD, Louis Arthur. b 13. Ripon Hall Ox 72. d 73 p 74. C Corsham *Bris* 73-77; Bp's Chapl for the Arts from 76; V Bitton 78-80; rtd 80; Perm to Offic *Bris* from 80; *Glouc* from 86. *10 Orchard Close, Lower Paddock, Stoke Bishop, Bristol BS9 1AS* Bristol (0272) 628332

WARD, Mrs Marjorie. b 38. Univ of Wales (Abth) BA59 DipEd60. N Ord Course 83. dss 86 d 87. Keighley St Andr *Bradf* 86-87; Hon Par Dn 87-88; Hon Par Dn Oakworth 88-90; C Allerton from 91. *St Peter's Vicarage, Leytop Lane, Allerton, Bradford BD15 7LT* Bradford (0274) 541948

WARD, Michael Anthony. b 42. Sarum Th Coll 67. d 70 p 71. C Bridport *Sarum* 70-74; TV Swanborough 74-77; P-in-c Chute w Chute Forest 77-79; P-in-c Shalbourne w Ham 77-79; TR Wexcombe 79-86; V Southbroom from 86. *Southbroom Vicarage, London Road, Devizes, Wilts SN10 1LT* Devizes (0380) 723891

WARD, Michael Reginald. b 31. BNC Ox BA54 MA58. Tyndale Hall Bris 54. d 56 p 57. C Ealing St Mary *Lon* 56-59; C Morden *S'wark* 59-61; Area Sec (Midl and E Anglia) CCCS 61-66; V Chelsea St Jo *Lon* 66-73; P-in-c Chelsea St Andr 72-73; V Chelsea St Jo w St Andr 73-76; P-in-c Hawkesbury *Glouc* 76-80; P-in-c Alderley w Hillesley 79-80; P-in-c Bibury w Winson and Barnsley 80-85; V Barkby and Queniborough *Leic* 85-90; R Gunthorpe w Bale w Field Dalling, Saxlingham and Sharrington *Nor* from 90. *The Rectory, Bale, Fakenham, Norfolk NR21 0QJ* Fakenham (0328) 878292

WARD, Patricia. b 43. d 91. NSM Swansea St Mary w H Trin *S & B* from 91. *96 Glanbrydan Avenue, Uplands, Swansea SA2 0JH* Swansea (0792) 208081

WARD, Peter Garnet. b 28. GRSM51 LRAM. Ridley Hall Cam 59. d 61 p 62. C Maghull *Liv* 61-64; Kenya 64-73; Master St Leon Mayfield Sch Sussex 73-83; Perm to Offic *Chich* 74-75; P-in-c Coleman's Hatch 75-77; Lic to Offic 77-83; P-in-c Herstmonceux 83-84; P-in-c Wartling 83-84; R Herstmonceux and Wartling from 84. *The Rectory, Herstmonceux, Hailsham, E Sussex BN27 4NY* Herstmonceux (0323) 833124

WARD, Philip Paul Ben. b 35. Toronto Univ BA61. ALCD66. d 66 p 67. C Chenies and Lt Chalfont *Ox* 66-68; C Ardsley *Sheff* 68-70; C Finham *Cov* 70-73; V Terrington St Clement *Ely* 73-81; Canada from 81. *369 Main Street, Saint John, New Brunswick, Canada, E2K 1J1*

WARD, Philip Percival Ford. b 33. City Univ BSc61. Wells Th Coll 67. d 69 p 70. C Clifton All SS *Bris* 69-72; P-in-c Bedminster Down 72-76; V 76-77; P-in-c Fishponds All SS 77-80; V Fishponds St Jo 77-83; V Walney Is *Carl* 83-90; V Hambleton w Out Rawcliffe *Blackb* from 90. *The Vicarage, Church Lane, Hambleton, Blackpool FY6 9BZ* Blackpool (0253) 700231

WARD, Richard. b 09. St Aug Coll Cant 63. d 64 p 65. V Hoar Cross *Lich* 69-78; P-in-c Newborough w Ch Ch on Needwood 76-78; rtd 78. *Rose Cott, Abbots Bromley Road, Hoar Cross, Burton-on-Trent, Staffs DE13 8RA* Hoar Cross (028375) 215

WARD, Robert. b 60. Em Coll Cam BA81 MA85. Chich Th Coll. **d** 86 **p** 87. C Horfield H Trin *Bris* 86-90; C Stantonbury and Willen *Ox* 90; TV from 90. *The Vicarage, Bradwell Road, Bradville, Milton Keynes MK13 7AX* Milton Keynes (0908) 314224

WARD, Robert Arthur Philip. b 53. Lon Univ BD82 Open Univ BA88. Qu Coll Birm 77. **d** 79 **p** 80. C Balsall Heath St Paul *Birm* 79-82; Chapl RAF from 82. *c/o MOD, Adastral House, Theobald's Road, London WC1X 8RU* 071-430 7268

WARD, Robert Charles Irwin. b 48. Leic Univ LLB70. St Jo Coll Dur 78. **d** 80 **p** 81. C Byker St Mich w St Lawr *Newc* 80-85; Perm to Offic from 86. *1 Hawthorn Villas, The Green, Wallsend, Tyne & Wear NE28 7NT* 091-234 3969

WARD, Robin. b 66. Magd Coll Ox BA87 MA91. St Steph Ho Ox 88. **d** 91. C Romford St Andr *Chelmsf* from 91. *24 Eastbury Road, Romford, Essex RM7 9AL* Romford (0708) 734047

WARD, Stanley. b 34. NE Ord Course. **d** 84 **p** 85. NSM Jarrow *Dur* 84-90; P-in-c Thornley from 90. *The Vicarage, 10 Church Walk, Thornley, Durham DH6 3EN* Hartlepool (0429) 820363

WARD, Stanley Gordon. b 21. Qu Coll Cam BA43 MA47. E Midl Min Tr Course 76. **d** 79 **p** 80. NSM Wollaton *S'well* 79-83; NSM Plympton St Mary *Ex* 84-88; Perm to Offic from 88. *60 Wain Park, Plympton, Plymouth PL7 3HX* Plymouth (0752) 344042

WARD, Timothy William. b 49. Open Univ BA74. St Deiniol's Hawarden 78. **d** 79 **p** 80. Hon C Handsworth St Mary *Birm* from 79. *3 Dale Close, Birmingham B43 6AS* 021-358 1880

WARD, William. b 13. Wycliffe Hall Ox 63. **d** 64 **p** 65. V Stillington w Marton and Farlington *York* 68-73; V Langtoft w Foxholes, Butterwick and Cottam 73-78; rtd 78. *14 Park Close, Easingwold, York YO6 3BR* Easingwold (0347) 23009

WARD, William Edward. b 48. FSAScot71. AKC71. **d** 72 **p** 73. C Heref St Martin *Heref* 72-77; C Blakenall Heath *Lich* 77-78; TV 78-82; V Astley, Clive, Grinshill and Hadnall from 82. *The Vicarage, Hadnall, Shrewsbury SY4 4AQ* Hadnall (09397) 241

WARD, William Francis. b 35. Ely Th Coll 61 Coll of Resurr Mirfield 64. **d** 64 **p** 65. C Byker St Ant *Newc* 64-67; C Glas St Marg *Glas* 67-69; R Glas Ascension 69-74; Chapl RNR 72-74; Chapl RN 74-78; P-in-c Auchmithie *Bre* 79-90; R Arbroath from 78; Hon Chapl Miss to Seamen from 78. *The Rectory, 2 Springfield Terrace, Arbroath DD11 1EL* Arbroath (0241) 73392

WARD-ANDREWS, Canon Lewes. b 12. Kelham Th Coll 29. **d** 36 **p** 37. SSM from 36; P-in-c Nottm St Geo w St Jo *S'well* 60-82; Hon Can S'well Minster 66-82; rtd 82; Perm to Offic *Blackb* 82-90. *Woodlands Nursing Home, Sleights, Whitby, N Yorkshire YO21 1RY* Whitby (0947) 810449

WARD-BODDINGTON, Canon Douglas. b 20. S'wark Ord Course 69. **d** 72 **p** 73. C S'wark Ch Ch *S'wark* 72-77; Admin S Lon Ind Miss 72-77; Chapl Algarve *Eur* 77-80 and 83-89; V-Gen to Bp Eur 80-83; Can Gib Cathl from 80; rtd 89; Chapl Porto (or Oporto) *Eur* from 89. *Rua do Campo Alegre 640-5 D, 4100 Porto, Portugal* Oporto (2) 691006

WARD-DAVIES, Thomas John. b 09. Lon Univ BSc35 St Cath Soc Ox MA42. Cuddesdon Coll 40. **d** 41 **p** 42. V Wall *Lich* 56-78; V Stonnall 56-78; rtd 78. *c/o Moseley, Chapman & Skemp, 18 Bore Street, Lichfield, Staffs WS13 6LW* Lichfield (0543) 414100

WARDALE, Dr Harold William. b 40. BSc PhD. Wycliffe Hall Ox 83. **d** 85 **p** 86. C Bedminster St Mich *Bris* 85-89; C Bishopston 89; TV from 89. *89 King's Drive, Bristol BS7 8JQ* Bristol (0272) 243424

WARDALE, Robert Christopher. b 46. Newc Univ BA69. Coll of Resurr Mirfield 77. **d** 79 **p** 80. C Cockerton *Dur* 79-84; P-in-c Hedworth 84-87; V from 87. *St Nicholas Vicarage, Hedworth Lane, Boldon Colliery, Tyne & Wear NE35 9JA* 091-536 7552

WARDEN, John Michael. b 41. Univ Coll Lon BA63 Trin Coll Ox BA65 MA. NE Ord Course 80. **d** 82 **p** 83. NSM Osmotherley w E Harlsey and Ingleby Arncliffe *York* 82-86; V Kirkdale from 86. *Kirkdale Vicarage, Nawton, York YO6 5ST* Helmsley (0439) 71206

WARDEN, Richard James. b 57. BA MTh. Wycliffe Hall Ox 81. **d** 83 **p** 84. C Fulham St Mary N End *Lon* 83-85; CF 85-89; Chapl Wycombe Abbey Sch High Wycombe from 89. *Wycombe Abbey School, High Wycombe, Bucks* High Wycombe (0494) 20381

WARDLE, Edward Christian. b 13. **d** 62 **p** 63. C Farnley *Ripon* 62-64; C Wortley de Leeds 64-66; R Llanwyddelan w Manafon *St As* 66-79; P-in-c Stottesdon *Heref* 79-82;

Perm to Offic *Ripon* from 82. *The Gables Nursing Home, Swinnow Road, Pudsey, Leeds* Pudsey (0532) 570123

WARDLE, John Alexander. b 30. TD73. Lon Univ BA59 Man Univ MA81. Oak Hill Th Coll 53. **d** 57 **p** 58. C Blackpool St Mark *Blackb* 57-60; C Tunbridge Wells St Jo *Roch* 60-62; V Maidstone St Luke *Cant* 62-69; CF (TA) 62-73; V Hartford *Ches* 69-79; R Barton Seagrave w Warkton *Pet* from 79. *The Rectory, Barton Seagrave, Kettering, Northants NN15 6SR* Kettering (0536) 513629

WARDLE, John Argyle. b 47. ARCM67 St Jo Coll Dur BA71 CertEd73. Cranmer Hall Dur DipTh72. **d** 73 **p** 74. C Mansf St Pet *S'well* 73-77; Chapl St Felix Sch Southwold 77-87; TV Haverhill w Withersfield, the Wrattings etc *St E* 87-90; VC S'well Minster *S'well* from 90. *3 Vicars' Court, Southwell, Notts NG25 0HP* Southwell (0636) 813767

WARDLE-HARPUR, Canon Charles Noel. b 03. St Edm Hall Ox BA25 MA29. Wycliffe Hall Ox 26. **d** 26 **p** 27. TR Stockton *Dur* 58-71; Hon Can Dur Cathl 59-71; RD Stockton 59-71; rtd 71. *19 Elm Crescent, The Paddocks, Charlbury, Oxford OX7 3PZ* Charlbury (0608) 810600

WARDLE-HARPUR, Canon James. b 31. St Jo Coll Dur BA55. Wells Th Coll 55. **d** 56 **p** 57. C Sheff Parson Cross St Cecilia *Sheff* 56-59; C Maltby 59-61; V Doncaster St Jude 61-64; Pakistan 64-68; R Man Victoria Park *Man* 68-75; V Foxton w Gumley and Laughton *Leic* 75-79; V Foxton w Gumley and Laughton and Lubenham 79-82; TR Leic Resurr 82-88; Hon Can Leic Cathl from 88; V Burrough Hill Pars from 88. *The Rectory, High Street, Somerby, Melton Mowbray, Leics LE14 2PZ* Somerby (066477) 318

WARDROBE, Bevan. b 26. Hatf Coll Dur BA53. Cuddesdon Coll 53. **d** 54 **p** 55. Hd Master York Minster Song Sch 67-85; VC York Minster *York* 67-85; Chapl Rome *Eur* 85-91; rtd 91; Chapl San Remo *Eur* from 91. *Corso Matuzia 1, 18038 San Remo (Imperia), Italy* San Remo (184) 667575

WARDROP, David John. b 34. ALCD59. **d** 59 **p** 60. C Harrow Weald All SS *Lon* 59-62; Chapl RNR from 61; V Ernesettle *Ex* 62-64; V Broadclyst 64-67; Dioc Miss and Ecum Officer 64-67; Asst Gen Sec Ind Chr Fellowship 67-76; P-in-c Pertenhall w Swineshead *St Alb* 76-80; R Wymington w Podington 80-83; R Cavendish *St E* 83-89; P-in-c Clare w Poslingford 86-89; P-in-c Stoke by Clare w Wixoe 86-89; R Clare w Poslingford, Cavendish etc 89-91; RD Clare 87-91; Chapl Bordeaux w Monteton, Tocane, Limeuil etc *Eur* from 91. *4 rue de Larmont Village, 33310 Larmont, France* France (33) 56 06 37 17

WARE, Austin Neville. b 14. St D Coll Lamp BA37 St Mich Coll Llan 37. **d** 39 **p** 41. V Knapton *York* 58-75; R W and E Heslerton w Knapton 75-79; rtd 79. *Craigsmoor, Lon Crescent, Trearddur Bay, Holyhead, Gwynedd LL65 2BQ* Trearddur Bay (0407) 860106

WARE, John Franklin Jones. b 07. Univ of Wales BA30 Keble Coll Ox BA33 MA36. **d** 32 **p** 33. V Hove St Phil *Chich* 65-79; rtd 79; Perm to Offic *B & W* from 80. *10 Evelyn Terrace, Bath BA1 6EX* Bath (0225) 311003

WARE, Canon John Lawrence. b 37. Nottm Univ BA59. Ridley Hall Cam 62. **d** 62 **p** 63. C Attercliffe *Sheff* 62-66; C Ranmoor 66-68; R Liddington *Bris* 68-74; Soc and Ind Adv 74-79; P-in-c City of Bris 74-79; Hon Can Bris Cathl from 76; V Kingswood 79-88; RD Bitton 85-87; P-in-c Blunsdon from 88; P-in-c Broad Blunsdon from 88; RD Cricklade from 88. *The Rectory, Burytown Lane, Broad Blunsdon, Swindon, Wilts SN2 4DQ* Swindon (0793) 729592

WARE, Stephen John. b 55. Univ of Wales (Lamp) BA76. Ripon Coll Cuddesdon 77. **d** 79 **p** 80. C Lighthorne *Cov* 79-82; Chapl RAF from 82. *c/o MOD, Adastral House, Theobald's Road, London WC1X 8RU* 071-430 7268

WAREHAM, Mrs Caroline. b 32. Lightfoot Ho Dur 55. **dss** 80 **d** 87. Stanwell *Lon* 80-87; Par Dn 87-88; C Epsom St Barn *Guildf* from 88. *St Barnabas House, 63 Temple Road, Epsom, Surrey KT19 8EY* Epsom (03727) 45473

WAREHAM, Sheila. b 36. CertEd56. N Ord Course 85. **d** 88. NSM Lostock Hall *Blackb* 88-90; NSM Allithwaite Carl from 90. *Lyng Nook, Church Road, Allithwaite, Cumbria LA11 7RD* Cartmel (05395) 35237

WARING, Graham George Albert. b 37. ACII. Portsm Dioc Tr Course 86. **d** 87. Chapl Asst Qu Alexandra's Hosp Portsm from 87. *5 Pennant Hills, Bedhampton, Havant, Hants PO9 3JZ* Havant (0705) 450898

WARING, Jeffery Edwin. b 53. Trin Coll Bris 80. **d** 83 **p** 84. C Harpurhey Ch Ch *Man* 83-86; TV Eccles from 86. *St Andrew's Vicarage, 11 Abbey Grove, Eccles, Manchester M30 9QN* 061-707 1742

WARING, John Valentine. b 29. St Deiniol's Hawarden 65. **d** 67 **p** 68. C Bistre *St As* 67-71; C Blackpool St Thos *Blackb* 71-72; R Levenshulme St Pet *Man* 72-87; R Caerwys and Bodfari *St As* from 87. *The Rectory, Caerwys, Mold, Clwyd CH7 5AQ* Caerwys (0352) 720223

WARING, Roger. b 32. ACP66 CertEd56 Open Univ BA74. SW Minl Tr Course 83. **d** 86 **p** 87. NSM Ex St Sidwell and St Matt *Ex* 86-90; NSM Tavistock and Gulworthy from 90. *St Eustace, 32 Plym Crescent, Tavistock, Devon PL19 9HX* Tavistock (0822) 615501

WARING, Ruth. b 44. Keele Univ CertEd65. SW Minl Tr Course 86. **d** 90. Par Dn Tavistock and Gulworthy *Ex* from 90. *St Eustace, 32 Plym Crescent, Tavistock, Devon PL19 9HX* Tavistock (0822) 615501

WARING, Mrs Sheila May. b 29. SS Paul & Mary Coll Cheltenham CertEd49. Oak Hill Th Coll 85. **dss** 86 **d** 87. Eastwood *Chelmsf* 86-87; NSM from 87; Chapl Rochford Hosp from 87. *42 Manchester Drive, Leigh-on-Sea, Essex SS9 3HR* Southend-on-Sea (0702) 711046

WARING, Wilfrid Harold. b 11. TD46. Jes Coll Cam BA33 MA37. Ripon Hall Ox 33. **d** 34 **p** 35. V Saddleworth *Man* 67-77; rtd 77. *Trinity Close, 8A Kirkby Road, Ripon, N Yorkshire HG4 2ET* Ripon (0765) 605880

✠**WARKE, Rt Rev Robert Alexander.** b 30. TCD BA52 BD60 DipEcon. Union Th Sem (NY) 60. **d** 53 **p** 54 **c** 88. C Newtownards *D & D* 53-56; C Dub St Cath w St Victor *D & G* 56-58; C Dub Rathfarnham 58-64; Min Can St Patr Cathl Dub 59-64; I Dunlavin w Ballymore Eustace and Hollywood *D & G* 64-67; I Dub Drumcondra w N Strand 67-71; I Dub St Barn 67-71; I Dub Zion Ch 71-88; RD Taney 77-80; Adn Dub 80-88; Bp C, C & R from 88. *The Palace, Bishop Street, Cork, Irish Republic* Cork (21) 271214

WARLAND, Preb Cyril John. b 21. St Cath Soc Ox BA43 MA56. Cuddesdon Coll. **d** 44 **p** 45. R Marytavy *Ex* 56-88; RD Tavistock 77-88; P-in-c Walkhampton 80-83; Preb Ex Cathl 82-88; R Peter Tavy 82-88; rtd 88; Lic to Offic *Ex* from 88. *2 Rowantree Road, Newton Abbot, Devon TQ1 4LL* Newton Abbot (0626) 55369

WARLAND, Peter William. b 35. K Coll Lon 56. **d** 60 **p** 61. C Pemberton St Jo *Liv* 60-64; C Warrington St Elphin 64-66; V Farnworth All SS *Man* 66-71; Chapl RN from 71; Chapl to HM The Queen from 88. *c/o MOD, Lacon House, Theobald's Road, London WC1X 8RY* 071-430 6847

WARMAN, Canon Cyril Aidan Oswald. b 08. Pemb Coll Ox BA30 MA35. Ridley Hall Cam 30. **d** 31 **p** 32. Hon Can Wakef Cathl *Wakef* 62-74; V Kellington w Whitley 66-74; rtd 74; Perm to Offic *York* from 74. *34 St Oswald Road, Bridlington, N Humberside YO15 5SD* Bridlington (0262) 673436

WARMAN, John Richard. b 37. Pemb Coll Ox BA61 MA. Ridley Hall Cam 61. **d** 63 **p** 64. C Huyton St Mich *Liv* 63-67; Asst Chapl Liv Univ 67-68; Chapl 68-74; P-in-c Holbrooke *Derby* 74-80; P-in-c Lt Eaton 74-80; R Sawley from 80; RD Ilkeston from 82. *The Rectory, Tamworth Road, Long Eaton, Nottingham NG10 3AB* Long Eaton (0602) 734900

WARMAN, Miss Marion Alice. b 20. Newnham Coll Cam BA43 MA50. S'wark Ord Course 76. **dss** 79 **d** 87. Spring Grove St Mary *Lon* 79-87; Hon Par Dn from 87; Chapl Asst W Middx Hosp Isleworth from 80. *43 Thornbury Road, Isleworth, Middx TW7 4LE* 081-560 5905

WARNER, Alan Winston. b 51. Lon Univ BSc73 Leeds Univ DipTh75. Coll of Resurr Mirfield 73. **d** 76 **p** 77. C Willenhall St Anne *Lich* 76-78; C Baswich (or Berkswich) 78-81; V Wednesfield St Greg 81-87; Chapl Frimley Park Hosp from 87. *14 The Cloisters, Frimley, Camberley, Surrey GU16 5JR* Camberley (0276) 64685 or 692777

WARNER, Andrew Compton. b 35. Fitzw Ho Cam BA58 MA62. Westcott Ho Cam 59. **d** 60 **p** 61. C Addlestone *Guildf* 60-64; C-in-c Ash Vale CD 64-71; V Hinchley Wood 71-80; R Gt Bookham from 80; RD Leatherhead from 88. *The Rectory, 2A Fife Way, Leatherhead, Surrey KT23 3PH* Bookham (0372) 452405

WARNER, Clifford Chorley. b 38. Hull Univ MA88. E Midl Min Tr Course 76. **d** 79 **p** 80. NSM Swanwick and Pentrich *Derby* from 79; NSM Allestree from 88. *17 Amber Heights, Ripley, Derby DE5 3SP* Ripley (0773) 745089

WARNER, David. b 40. AKC63. **d** 64 **p** 65. C Castleford All SS *Wakef* 64-68; Warden Hollowford Tr and Conf Cen Sheff 68-72; R Wombwell *Sheff* 72-83; V Wortley 83-84; V Wortley w Thurgoland from 84; RD Tankersley from 88. *The Vicarage, Park Avenue, Wortley, Sheffield S30 7DR* Sheffield (0742) 882238

WARNER, David Leonard John. b 24. Kelham Th Coll 47. **d** 51 **p** 52. V Bournemouth H Epiphany *Win* 68-78; V Whitchurch w Tufton and Litchfield 78-89; RD Whitchurch 79-89; rtd 89. *9 Sparkford Close, Winchester, Hants SO22 4NH* Winchester (0962) 867343

WARNER, Dennis Vernon. b 46. Lon Univ BA68 K Coll Lon BD71. **d** 72 **p** 73. C W Bromwich All SS *Lich* 72-75; C Uttoxeter w Bramshall 75-79; Lic to Offic from 79. *17 Shrewsbury Road, Stretton, Burton-on-Trent, Staffs DE13 0JF* Burton-on-Trent (0283) 48058

WARNER, Canon George Francis. b 36. Trin Coll Ox BA60 MA64 Qu Coll Cam BA63. Westcott Ho Cam 61. **d** 63 **p** 64. C Birm St Geo *Birm* 63-66; C Maidstone All SS w St Phil and H Trin *Cant* 66-69; Chapl Wellington Coll Berks 69-78; TR Cov Caludon *Cov* from 78; Hon Can Cov Cathl from 85; RD Cov E from 89. *Stoke Rectory, Walsgrave Road, Coventry CV2 4BG* Coventry (0203) 635731

WARNER, James Morley. b 32. S'wark Ord Course 66. **d** 69 **p** 70. C S Mymms K Chas *Lon* 69-72; C Bush Hill Park St Steph 72-75; V W Hendon St Jo from 75. *St John's Vicarage, Vicarage Road, London NW4 3PX* 081-202 8606

WARNER, John Philip. b 59. Keble Coll Ox BA80 MA85. St Steph Ho Ox. **d** 83 **p** 84. C Brighton Resurr *Chich* 83-87; C Paddington St Mary *Lon* 87-90; V Teddington St Mark and Hampton Wick St Jo from 90. *The Vicarage, St Mark's Road, Teddington, Middx TW11 9DE* 081-977 4067

WARNER, Martin Clive. b 58. St Chad's Coll Dur BA80 MA85. St Steph Ho Ox. **d** 84 **p** 85. C Plymouth St Pet *Ex* 84-88; TV Leic Resurr *Leic* from 88. *St Matthew's House, Kamloops Crescent, Leicester LE1 2HX* Leicester (0533) 623038

WARNER, Michael John William. b 41. Sarum Th Coll 68. **d** 71 **p** 72. C Plympton St Mary *Ex* 71-75; V St Goran w St Mich Caerhays *Truro* 75-78; V Bishops Tawton *Ex* 78-79; V Newport 78-79; Perm to Offic *Truro* 79-83; V St Stythians w Perranarworthal and Gwennap from 83. *The Vicarage, Old Vicarage Close, Stithians, Truro, Cornwall TR3 7DZ* Stithians (0209) 860123

WARNER, Nigel Bruce. b 51. ALCM67 St Jo Coll Cam BA72 DipTh73 MA76. Wycliffe Hall Ox 75. **d** 77 **p** 78. C Luton St Mary *St Alb* 77-80; Prec Dur Cathl *Dur* 80-84; R St Jo Lee *Newc* from 84. *St John Lee Rectory, Hexham, Northd NE46 4PE* Hexham (0434) 602220

WARNER, Canon Robert William. b 32. TCD BA54 MA65 BD65. TCD Div Sch Div Test56. **d** 56 **p** 57. C Wythenshawe St Martin CD *Man* 56-60; R Hulme St Steph w St Mark 60-66; R Droylsden St Mary 66-76; R Stand from 76; AD Radcliffe and Prestwich from 85; Hon Can Man Cathl from 87. *Stand Rectory, Church Lane, Whitefield, Manchester M25 7NF* 061-766 2619

WARNER, Canon Samuel John. b 10. TCD BA34 MA50. **d** 34 **p** 35. I Laghey *D & R* 64-79; Can Raphoe Cathl 72-79; rtd 79. *Coolkelure, Laghey, Donegal, Irish Republic*

WARNER, Dr Thomas Edward. b 06. TCD BA28 BD32 MA39 MLitt60 Lon Univ BD49 PhD54. **d** 30 **p** 30. C Rathkeale w Nantenan *L & K* 30-33; India 33-34; I Corbally *L & K* 34-36; Chapl Pannal Ash Coll 36-37; C Gt and Lt Driffield *York* 37-40; Chapl RAF 41-61; Chapl Wycliffe Coll Stonehouse Glos 61-75. *West End, Pearcroft Road, Stonehouse, Glos GL10 2JY* Stonehouse (0453) 822065

WARNES, Brian Leslie Stephen. b 40. Natal Univ BSocSc76. Kelham Th Coll 59. **d** 67 **p** 68. C Tonge Moor *Man* 67-71; S Africa 71-87; V Blean *Cant* from 87. *The Vicarage, 24 Tyler Hill Road, Blean, Canterbury, Kent CT2 9HT* Canterbury (0227) 471261

WARNES, Frank William. b 18. Bps' Coll Cheshunt 61. **d** 62 **p** 63. V Roxton w Gt Barford *St Alb* 68-74; V Gulval *Truro* 74-83; rtd 83. *1 Sylverton Place, Heamoor, Penzance, Cornwall TR18 3EP* Penzance (0736) 68408

WARNES, Miss Marjorie. b 32. Leeds Inst of Educn CertEd53. St Jo Coll Nottm 85. **d** 87. C Leamington Priors St Mary *Cov* from 87. *78 Lewis Road, Radford Semele, Leamington Spa CV31 1UQ* Leamington Spa (0926) 420811

WARNES, Warren Hugh. b 23. St Barn Coll Adelaide ThL49. **d** 50 **p** 50. V Kings Heath *Pet* 64-71; V Rockingham w Caldecote 71-73; V Gretton w Rockingham and Caldecote 73-83; V Marston St Lawrence w Warkworth and Thenford 83-89; rtd 89; Perm to Offic *Pet* from 89. *17 Thorpe Road, Earls Barton, Northampton NN6 0PJ* Northampton (0604) 812935

WARR, Timothy Gerald. b 59. Trin Coll Bris BA86. d 88
p 89. C Yateley *Win* from 88. *37 Walnut Close, Yateley,
Camberley, Surrey GU17 7DA* Yateley (0252) 875798

WARREN, Very Rev Alan Christopher. b 32. CCC Cam
BA56 MA60. Ridley Hall Cam 56. d 57 p 58. C
Cliftonville *Cant* 57-59; C Plymouth St Andr *Ex* 59-62;
Chapl Kelly Coll Tavistock 62-64; V Leic H Apostles
Leic 64-72; Hon Can Cov Cathl *Cov* 72-78; Dioc Missr
72-78; Provost Leic from 78. *The Provost's House, 1 St
Martin's East, Leicester LE1 5FX* Leicester (0533)
25294 or 25295

WARREN, Canon Christopher Bruce. TCD BA58 MA61.
d 62 p 63. C Waterford H Trin *C & O* 62-64; I Askeaton
w Shanagolden and Loghill *L & K* 64-66; I Kilcolman
66-73; I Dub St Werburgh *D & G* 73-74; I Kilrossanty
C & O 74-80; I Fenagh w Myshall, Aghade and Ardoyne
80-86; Preb Ossory Cathl 85-88; I Castlecomer w
Colliery Ch, Mothel and Bilbo 86-88; Finland from 88.
*Virkamiehenkatu 15, 35880 Mantta or, Vaasa University,
PL 297, 65101 Vaasa, Finland* Mantta (34) 428607 or
Vaasa-vasa (61) 248120

WARREN, Clifford Frederick. b 32. Univ of Wales (Lamp)
BA53. St Mich Coll Llan 54. d 56 p 57. C Whitchurch
Llan 56-68; Lic to Offic 68-70; C Llanedeyrn *Mon* 70-76;
R Machen from 76. *The Rectory, Machen, Newport,
Gwent NP1 8SA* Machen (0633) 440321

WARREN, David. b 39. S'wark Ord Course. d 87 p 88.
NSM Mottingham St Andr *S'wark* from 87. *26 Longcroft,
London SE9 3BQ* 081-851 4824

WARREN, Desmond Benjamin Moore. b 22. TCD
BA44 MA49. Bps' Coll Cheshunt 46. d 48 p 49. R Sandy
St Alb 63-78; P-in-c Gt Munden 78-79; P-in-c Westmill
78-79; R Westmill w Gt Munden 79-84; rtd 84; Lic to
Offic (Lismore) *C & O* 84-90; Lic to Offic *C, C & R* from
91. *Dysert, Ardmore, Youghal, Co Cork, Irish Republic*
Youghal (24) 94110

WARREN, Eric Anthony. b 28. MBE. Ex & Truro NSM
Scheme. d 83 p 84. NSM Chudleigh *Ex* from 83. *Lower
Radway House, Bishopsteignton, Teignmouth, Devon
TQ14 9SS* Teignmouth (0626) 770217

WARREN, Ernest Bruce. b 24. K Coll Lon BD54 AKC54.
d 54 p 55. V Lostwithiel *Truro* 67-77; V Perranzabuloe
77-89; rtd 89. *22 Coombe Road, Saltash, Cornwall
PL12 4ER* Saltash (0752) 844058

WARREN, Canon Frederick Noel. b 30. TCD BA52 MA58
BD66 QUB PhD72. d 53 p 54. C Belf St Matt *Conn*
53-56; C Belf St Geo 56-59; I Castlewellan *D & D* 59-65;
I Clonallon w Warrenpoint 65-69; I Newc 69-87; Can
Belf Cathl 73-76; Preb Wicklow St Patr Cathl Dub 76-88;
I Dunfanaghy, Raymunterdoney and Tullaghbegley
D & R from 87; Preb Swords St Patr Cathl Dub from
89. *The Rectory, Dunfanaghy, Letterkenny, Co Donegal,
Irish Republic* Letterkenny (74) 36187

WARREN, Geoffrey Richard. b 44. Middx Poly MA91.
Bps' Coll Cheshunt 66 Qu Coll Birm 68. d 69 p 70. C
Waltham Cross *St Alb* 69-73; C Radlett 73-78; C Tring
78-80; TV Tring from 80. *The Vicarage, Aldbury, Tring,
Herts HP23 5RS* Aldbury Common (044285) 244

WARREN, Preb Henry Fiennes. b 21. Keble Coll Ox
BA42 MA47. Cuddesdon Coll 42. d 48 p 49. R Exford
B & W 53-75; RD Wiveliscombe 65-73; Preb Wells Cathl
from 73; R W Monkton 75-86; rtd 86. *6 Brookside,
Broadway, Ilminster, Somerset TA19 9RT* Ilminster
(0460) 57922

WARREN, Malcolm Clive. b 46. St D Coll Lamp DipTh74.
d 74 p 75. C Newport St Andr *Mon* 74-78; C Risca
78-79; V St Hilary Greenway 79-84; TV Grantham *Linc*
84-90; Ind Chapl 87-90; Ind Chapl *Worc* from 90.
9 Tansley Hill Road, Dudley, West Midlands DY2 7ER
Dudley (0384) 258112

WARREN, Martin John. b 59. Ch Coll Cam BA81 MA85
LTh DPS. St Jo Coll Nottm 83. d 86 p 87. C Littleover
Derby 86-90; C Hermitage and Hampstead Norreys,
Cold Ash etc *Ox* from 90. *The Rectory, Yattendon,
Newbury, Berks RG16 0UR* Hermitage (0635) 201213

WARREN, Michael John. b 40. d 64 p 65. C Withington
St Chris *Man* 64-67; C Worsley 67-69; C Witney *Ox*
69-72; V S Hinksey 72-80; Canada from 80. *14 Wild Hay
Drive, Devon, Alberta, Canada, T0C 1EO*

WARREN, Michael Meade King. b 18. Lich Th Coll 38.
d 42 p 43. S Africa 69-72; R Witham Friary w Marston
Bigot *B & W* 72-83; rtd 83. *10 North Crescent, Garlieston,
Newton Stewart, Wigtownshire DG8 8BA* Garlieston
(09886) 620

WARREN, Ven Norman Leonard. b 34. CCC Cam
BA58 MA62. Ridley Hall Cam 58. d 60 p 61. C Bedworth
Cov 60-63; V Leamington Priors St Paul 63-77; R
Morden *S'wark* 77-88; TR 88-89; RD Merton 86-89;
Adn Roch from 89; Can Res Roch Cathl from 89.

The Archdeaconry, Rochester, Kent ME1 1SX Medway
(0634) 842527

WARREN, Canon Paul Kenneth. b 41. Selw Coll Cam
BA63 MA67. Cuddesdon Coll 64. d 67 p 68. C Lanc St
Mary *Blackb* 67-70; Chapl Lanc Univ 70-78; V Langho
Billington 78-83; Bp's Dom Chapl 83-88; Chapl Whalley
Abbey 83-88; R Standish from 88; Hon Can Blackb
Cathl from 91. *The Rectory, 13 Rectory Lane, Standish,
Wigan, Lancs WN6 0XA* Standish (0257) 421396

WARREN, Peter. b 40. FCA64. Oak Hill Th Coll 77. d 79
p 80. C Newc w Butterton *Lich* 79-82; TV Sutton St Jas
and Wawne *York* 82-87; V Ledsham w Fairburn from
87. *The Vicarage, 11 Main Street, Ledston, Castleford,
W Yorkshire WF10 2AA* Castleford (0977) 556946

WARREN, Peter John. b 55. CertEd76 BA86. Trin Coll
Bris 83. d 86 p 87. C W Streatham St Jas *S'wark* 86-91;
P-in-c Edin Clermiston Em *Edin* from 91. *127 Clermiston
Road, Edinburgh EH12 6UR* 031-316 4706

WARREN, Robert. b 54. TCD BA78 MA81. CITC 76.
d 78 p 79. C Limerick City *L & K* 78-81; Dioc Youth
Adv (Limerick) 79-86; I Adare w Kilpeacon and
Croom 81-88; Bp's Dom Chapl from 81; Dioc Registrar
(Limerick etc) from 81; Dioc Registrar (Killaloe etc)
from 86; I Tralee w Ballymacelligott, Kilnaughtin etc
from 88; RD Tralee from 89. *St John's Rectory, Ashe
Street, Tralee, Co Kerry, Irish Republic* Tralee (66)
22245

WARREN, Robert Geoffrey. b 51. DipHE. Trin Coll Bris
79. d 82 p 83. C Felixstowe SS Pet and Paul *St E* 82-86;
V Gazeley w Dalham, Moulton and Kentford 86-90;
P-in-c Ipswich St Clem w St Luke and H Trin from 90.
42 Clapgate Lane, Ipswich, Suffolk IP3 0RD Ipswich
(0473) 723467

WARREN, Robert Irving. b 38. Univ of BC BA58 Ox
Univ MA(Theol)73. Angl Th Coll (BC) LTh61. d 61
p 63. Canada 61-89; R Northfield *Birm* from 89. *The
Rectory, Rectory Road, Birmingham B31 2NA* 021-477
3111 or 475 1518

WARREN, Canon Robert Peter Resker. b 39. Jes Coll
Cam BA63 MA. ALCD65. d 65 p 66. C Rusholme *Man*
65-68; C Bushbury *Lich* 68-71; V Crookes St Thos *Sheff*
71-90; TR from 90; RD Hallam 78-83; Hon Can Sheff
Cathl from 82. *The Vicarage, 18A Hallam Gate Road,
Sheffield S10 5BT* Sheffield (0742) 671090

WARREN, William Frederick. b 55. Sarum & Wells Th
Coll 83. d 86 p 87. C E Greenwich Ch Ch w St Andr
and St Mich *S'wark* 86-91; C Richmond St Mary w St
Matthias and St Jo from 91. *22A Cambrian Road,
Richmond, Surrey TW10 6JQ* 081-948 7217

WARRICK, Mark. b 54. Aston Univ BSc76 Nottm Univ
BCombStuds83. Linc Th Coll 80. d 83 p 84. C Cirencester
Linc 83-87; C Cirencester *Glouc* 87-91; V Over *Ely*
from 91. *The Vicarage, Over, Cambridge CB4 5NH*
Swavesey (0954) 30329

WARRILLOW, Brian Ellis. b 39. Linc Th Coll 81. d 83
p 84. C Tunstall Ch Ch *Lich* 83; C Tunstall 83-85; C
Shrewsbury H Cross 86-87; P-in-c Whixall 88; P-in-c
Tilstock 88; V Tilstock and Whixall from 89. *The
Vicarage, Tilstock, Whitchurch, Shropshire SY13 3JL*
Whixall (094872) 552

WARRILOW, Christine. b 42. Lanc Univ BA86. N Ord
Course 86. d 89. C Netherton *Liv* from 89. *57 Park Lane
West, Bootle, Merseyside L30 3SX* 051-521 5977

WARRINER, Leonard. b 15. Ox NSM Course. d 79 p 80.
NSM Chalfont St Peter *Ox* from 79. *Briar Rose, Winkers
Lane, Chalfont St Peter, Gerrards Cross, Bucks SL9 0AJ*
Gerrards Cross (0753) 884443

WARRINGTON, Clement Egbert. b 05. Dur Univ LTh35.
Lon Coll of Div 31. d 34 p 35. V Spotland *Man* 47-82;
rtd 82; Perm to Offic *Man* 88. *390 Fencepiece Road,
Chigwell, Essex*

WARRINGTON, Gwynfa Lewis Jones. b 44. St D Coll
Lamp 64. d 67 p 68. C Gorseinon *S & B* 67-70; C Pemb
Dock *St D* 70-74; V Rosemarket and Freystrop 74-78; R
Llangwm and Freystrop 78-79; V Ystradfellte *S & B*
79-84; V Abercynon *Llan* 84-87; V Beguildy and Heyope
S & B from 87. *The Vicarage, Beguildy, Knighton, Powys
LD7 1YE* Beguildy (05477) 252

WARRINGTON, William Leslie. b 03. Chich Th Coll 26.
d 28 p 29. V Salt *Lich* 52-68; rtd 69. *Sunny Corner,
223 Weston Road, Stafford ST16 3RZ* Stafford (0785)
42184

WARRINGTON, Archdeacon of. *See* WOODHOUSE,
Ven Charles David Stewart

WARRINGTON, Suffragan Bishop of. *See* HENSHALL,
Rt Rev Michael

WARWICK, Gordon Melvin. b 31. N Ord Course 79. d 80
p 81. NSM Darrington w Wentbridge *Wakef* 80-87; TV
Almondbury w Farnley Tyas from 87. *The Vicarage,*

125A Hall Cross Road, Huddersfield HD5 8LD Huddersfield (0484) 547239

WARWICK, Canon John Michael. b 37. Fitzw Ho Cam BA58 MA62. Ely Th Coll 58. **d** 60 **p** 61. C Towcester w Easton Neston *Pet* 60-63; C Leighton Buzzard *St Alb* 63-64; C Boston *Linc* 64-66; P-in-c Sutterton 66-72; V 72-74; V Sutton St Mary 74-84; V Bourne from 84; Chapl Bourne Hosps Lincs from 84; Hon Can Linc Cathl from 89. *The Vicarage, Bourne, Lincs PE10 9LX* Bourne (0778) 422412

WARWICK, Archdeacon of. See PAGET-WILKES, Ven Michael Jocelyn James

WARWICK, Suffragan Bishop of. See HANDFORD, Rt Rev George Clive

WASH, John. **d** 81 **p** 83. Hon C Newington St Mary S'wark from 81. *15 Canterbury Place, London SE17 3AD* 071-582 9280

WASHINGTON, Patrick Leonard. b 44. Nottm Univ BSc66. St Steph Ho Ox 65. **d** 68 **p** 69. C Fleet *Guildf* 68-71; C Farnham 71-74; TV Staveley and Barrow Hill *Derby* 74-83; V Norbury St Phil *Cant* 83-84; V Norbury St Phil *S'wark* from 85; RD Croydon N from 90. *St Philip's Vicarage, 66 Pollards Hill North, London SW16 4NY* 081-764 1812

WASSALL, Keith Leonard. b 45. Bede Coll Dur TCert67. Chich Th Coll 68. **d** 71 **p** 72. C Upper Gornal *Lich* 71-74; C Codsall 74-75; C Shelton 75-76; TV Hanley All SS 76-79; Bermuda 79-81; V Rickerscote *Lich* from 81. *St Peter's Vicarage, 106 Rickerscote Road, Stafford ST17 4HB* Stafford (0785) 52878

WASTELL, Canon Eric Morse. b 33. St Mich Coll Llan DipTh62. **d** 62 **p** 63. C Oystermouth *S & B* 62-65; Antigua 65-74; Hon Can Antigua 71-74; V Swansea St Gabr *S & B* from 74; RD Clyne from 88; Can Brecon Cathl from 90. *St Gabriel's Vicarage, Bryn Road, Brynmill, Swansea SA2 0AP* Swansea (0792) 464011

WASTIE, David Vernon. b 37. BA84. Chich Th Coll 79. **d** 81 **p** 82. C Bitterne Park *Win* 81-83; TV Chambersbury (Hemel Hempstead) *St Alb* 83-87; V Jersey St Luke *Win* from 87; P-in-c Jersey St Jas from 87. *The Vicarage, St James Street, St Helier, Jersey, Channel Islands* Jersey (0534) 34433

WATCHORN, Brian. b 39. Em Coll Cam BA61 MA65 Ex Coll Ox BA62. Ripon Hall Ox 61. **d** 63 **p** 64. C Bolton St Pet *Man* 63-66; Chapl G&C Coll Cam 66-74; V Chesterton St Geo *Ely* 75-82; Fell Dean and Chapl Pemb Coll Cam from 82; Lic to Offic *Ely* from 82. *Pembroke College, Cambridge CB2 1RF* Cambridge (0223) 338100

WATERER, Anthony Tatham. b 14. ARCA38. Cuddesdon Coll 45. **d** 47 **p** 48. V Staveley w Copgrove *Ripon* 53-72; R Rawreth w Rettendon *Chelmsf* 73-82; rtd 82; Perm to Offic *Chich* from 83. *9 Stafford Way, Keymer, Hassocks, W Sussex BN6 8QG* Hassocks (07918) 4341

WATERFORD, Dean of. See NEILL, Very Rev William Benjamin Alan

WATERHOUSE, Eric Thomas Benjamin. b 24. Lon Univ DipTh60. Qu Coll Birm 50. **d** 51 **p** 52. C Wolv St Pet *Lich* 51-56; C Lower Gornal 56-57; V Walsall St Mark 57-60; R Kington w Dormston *Worc* 60-64; R Worc St Clem 64-77; P-in-c Abberton, Naunton Beauchamp and Bishampton etc 77-50; R from 80. *The Rectory, Bishampton, Pershore, Worcs WR10 2LT* Bishampton (038682) 648

WATERHOUSE, Peter. b 46. Leeds Univ DipTh68. Linc Th Coll 68. **d** 70 **p** 71. C Conset Dur 70-73; C Heworth St Mary 73-76; V Stockton St Chad 76-83; V Lanchester from 83; RD Lanchester from 90. *The Vicarage, 1 Lee Hill Court, Lanchester, Durham DH7 0QE* Lanchester (0207) 521170

WATERMAN, Albert Thomas. b 33. Roch Th Coll 61. **d** 64 **p** 65. C Dartford St Alb *Roch* 64-67; V from 79; V Ilkeston St Jo *Derby* 67-75; V Mackworth St Fran 75-79; RD Dartford *Roch* from 84. *St Alban's Vicarage, 51 Watling Street, Dartford DA1 1RW* Dartford (0322) 224052

WATERMAN, Mrs Jacqueline Mahalah. b 45. ALCM71. Cant Sch of Min 82. dss 85 **d** 87. Wavertree H Trin *Liv* 85-87; Par Dn 87-90; Par Dn Anfield St Columba from 90. *110 Ince Avenue, Liverpool L4 7UY* 051-263 4523

WATERS, Arthur Brian. b 34. St Deiniol's Hawarden 71. **d** 73 **p** 74. C Bedwellty *Mon* 73-76; P-in-c Newport All SS 76-81; V Mynyddislwyn 81-91; C-in-c Maesglas Newport CD from 91. *15 St Bride's Crescent, Maesglas, Newport, Gwent NP9 3AS* Newport (0633) 815738

WATERS, Charles Eric. b 34. Hatf Coll Dur LTh37 BA38. St Aug Coll Cant 34. **d** 38 **p** 39. R Bromham *Sarum* 62-79; V Chittoe 73-79; rtd 79. *3 St Mary's Court, Silver Street, Bridgwater, Somerset TA6 3EG* Bridgwater (0278) 453675

WATERS, Miss Jill Christine. b 43. CertEd64. Cranmer Hall Dur 82. dss 82 **d** 87. New Milverton *Cov* 82-86; Draycott-le-Moors w Forsbrook *Lich* 86-87; Par Dn from 87. *366 Uttoxeter Road, Blythe Bridge, Stoke-on-Trent ST11 9LY* Blythe Bridge (0782) 392707

WATERS, John Michael. b 30. Qu Coll Cam BA53 MA58. Ridley Hall Cam 53. **d** 55 **p** 56. C Southport Ch Ch *Liv* 55-57; C Farnworth 57-62; V Blackb H Trin *Blackb* 63-70; Sec Birm Coun Chr Chs 70-77; Chapl Birm Cathl *Birm* 70-74; Dioc Ecum Officer 74-77; V Hednesford *Lich* from 77; RD Rugeley 78-88. *The Vicarage, Church Hill, Hednesford, Cannock, Staffs WS12 5BD* Hednesford (0543) 422635

WATERS, Mark. b 51. Sarum & Wells Th Coll. **d** 82 **p** 83. C Clifton All SS w St Jo *Bris* 82-85; P-in-c Brislington St Anne 85-91; Dioc Soc Resp Officer *Sheff* from 91. *9 The Copse, Bramley, Rotherham, S Yorkshire S66 0TB* Rotherham (0709) 701740

WATERS, Nicholas Marshall Stephenson. b 35. Selw Coll Cam BA59 MA63. Wells Th Coll 59. **d** 61 **p** 62. C Eastbourne St Mary *Chich* 61-64; Asst Chapl Ardingly Coll Haywards Heath from 64. *6 Standgrove, Ardingly, Haywards Heath, W Sussex RH17 6SF* Ardingly (0444) 256

WATERS, Stephen. b 49. Chich Th Coll 83. **d** 85 **p** 86. C Baildon *Bradf* 85-87; C Altrincham St Geo *Ches* 87-89; TV Ellesmere Port from 89. *The Vicarage, Vale Road, Ellesmere Port, South Wirral L65 9AY* 051-355 2516

WATERS, William Paul. b 52. Aston Tr Scheme 84 Chich Th Coll 86. **d** 88 **p** 89. C Tottenham St Paul *Lon* 88-91; C Stroud Green H Trin from 91. *30 Tregaron Avenue, London N8*

WATERSON, Harold. b 03. Tyndale Hall Bris 42. **d** 42 **p** 44. V Upper Holloway St Pet *Lon* 58-72; rtd 73. *9 Ashurst Road, Maidstone, Kent ME14 5PZ* Maidstone (0622) 750788

WATERSON, John Hayden Lionel. b 13. K Coll Cam BA35 MA39. Cuddesdon Coll 35. **d** 36 **p** 37. R Stoke D'Abernon *Guildf* 49-83; rtd 83. *Duck End, The Street, Corpusty, Norwich NR11 6QP* Saxthorpe (026387) 703

WATERSON, Raymond Arthur. b 25. Wells Th Coll 69. **d** 70 **p** 71. C Wotton St Mary *Glouc* 70-74; C Cirencester 74-79; P-in-c Falfield w Rockhampton 79-90; P-in-c Oldbury-on-Severn 85-90; rtd 90. *91 Brampton Way, Portishead, Bristol BS20 9YT* Bristol (0272) 845134

WATERSTONE, Canon Albert Thomas. b 23. TCD BA45 BD67. CITC 46. **d** 46 **p** 47. I Tullamore w Lynally and Rahan *M & K* 64-73; I Tullamore w Durrow, Newtownfertullagh, Rahan etc 73-90; Can Meath 81-90; rtd 90. *Lynally House, Mocklagh, Bluebalt, Co Offaly, Irish Republic* Tullamore (506) 21367

WATERSTREET, Canon John Donald. b 34. Trin Hall Cam BA58 MA62. Lich Th Coll 58. **d** 60 **p** 61. C Blackheath *Birm* 60-64; C Aston SS Pet and Paul 64-67; R Sheldon 67-77; RD Coleshill 75-77; V Selly Oak St Mary 77-89; RD Edgbaston 84-89; Hon Can Birm Cathl from 86; R The Whitacres and Shustoke from 89. *The Rectory, Dog Lane, Coleshill, Birmingham B46 2DU* Furnace End (0675) 81252

WATHEN, Sydney Gordon. Open Univ BA. E Midl Min Tr Course. **d** 86 **p** 87. NSM W Hallam and Mapperley *Derby* from 86. *40 Station Road, West Hallam, Derby DE7 6GW* Ilkeston (0602) 329255

WATHERSTON, Peter David. b 42. FCA76 Lon Univ BSc69. Ridley Hall Cam 75. **d** 77 **p** 78. C Barnsbury St Andr *Lon* 77-78; C Barnsbury St Andr w H Trin 79-80; C Barnsbury St Andr and H Trin w All SS 81; Chapl Mayflower Family Cen Canning Town *Chelmsf* from 81. *Mayflower Family Centre, Vincent Street, London E16 1LZ* 071-476 1171

WATKIN, David William. b 42. FCA70. Qu Coll Birm 84. **d** 86 **p** 87. C Tunstall *Lich* 86-89; Camberwell Deanery Missr S'wark from 89. *36 Finsen Road, London SE5 9AX* 071-274 4652

WATKIN, Stephen Roy. b 23. DFC. BSc. Worc Ord Coll 66. **d** 68 **p** 69. C Sutton St Geo *Ches* 68-73; V Aston by Sutton 73-76; P-in-c Eaton and Hulme Walfield 76-77; V 77-80; P-in-c Ipstones *Lich* 80-83; P-in-c Onecote cum Bradnop 80-83; V Ipstones w Berkhamsytch and Onecote w Bradnop 83-87; rtd 87. *2 Hawthorne Close, Upper Tean, Stoke-on-Trent ST10 4NL* Tean (0538) 723475

WATKINS, Alfred Felix Maceroni. b 20. Glouc Th Course 70. **d** 72 **p** 73. C Yate *Glouc* 72-75; V Dean Forest St Paul 75-90; rtd 90. *Leylines, 26 Southbank Road, Hereford HR1 2TJ* Hereford (0432) 341014

WATKINS, Anthony John. b 42. St D Coll Lamp BA64 St Steph Ho Ox 64. **d** 66 **p** 67. C E Dulwich St Jo *S'wark*

66-71; C Tewkesbury w Walton Cardiff *Glouc* 71-75; Prec 75-81; Chapl Choral Ches Cathl *Ches* 75-81; V Brixworth w Holcot *Pet* from 81. *The Vicarage, Brixworth, Northampton NN6 9DF* Northampton (0604) 880286

WATKINS, Christopher. b 43. Sarum & Wells Th Coll 88. **d** 90 **p** 91. C Abergavenny St Mary w Llanwenarth Citra *Mon* from 90. *12A Park Court, Abergavenny, Gwent NP7 5SR* Abergavenny (0873) 2407

WATKINS, David James Hier. b 39. Trin Coll Carmarthen CertEd60 Univ of Wales DipEd67 BEd76. **d** 90 **p** 91. NSM Oystermouth *S & B* from 90. *10 Lambswell Close, Langland, Swansea SA3 4HJ* Swansea (0792) 369742

WATKINS, Gordon Derek. b 29. **d** 53 **p** 54. Australia 53-61; C Harrogate St Wilfrid *Ripon* 61-63; V Upton Park *Chelmsf* 63-67; V Gt and Lt Bentley 67-73; R Gt Canfield 73-78; Dioc Past Sec *Lon* 78-84; Sec Dioc Adv Cttee from 84; PV Westmr Abbey 84-89; P-in-c St Martin Ludgate *Lon* 84-89; P-in-o to HM The Queen from 84. *21 The Drummonds, Epping, Essex CM16 4PJ* 071-821 9386

WATKINS, Mrs Gwyneth. Univ of Wales (Swansea) BA MEd. St Mich Coll Llan. **d** 91. NSM Llanbadarn Fawr w Capel Bangor *St D* from 91. *Minafon, Capel Bangor, Aberystwyth, Dyfed SY23 3LU* Capel Bangor (097084) 325

WATKINS, Herbert Ernest. b 22. Clifton Th Coll 39 Oak Hill Th Coll 43. **d** 46 **p** 47. V Rodbourne Cheney *Bris* 58-73; V Bilton St Helen *York* 73-77; V Tockwith 73-77; V Hurdsfield *Ches* 77-82; V Pott Shrigley 82-87; rtd 87; Perm to Offic *Cov* 87-88; Chapl to the Deaf *Bradf* from 88. *41 Hawkcliffe View, Silsden, Keighley, W Yorkshire BD20 0BS* Steeton (0535) 656284

WATKINS, Miss Lorna Ann Frances Charles. b 59. Trin Coll Carmarthen BEd82. St Steph Ho Ox 82. **d** 84. C Tenby and Gumfreston *St D* 84-89; C Pemb Dock 89-91; Dn-in-c Cosheston w Nash and Upton from 91. *St Michael's House, The Garth, Cosheston, Pembroke Dock, Dyfed SA72 4UD* Pembroke (0646) 682477

WATKINS, Michael Morris. b 32. MRCS LRCP. St Jo Coll Nottm 77. **d** 81 **p** 81. C Hornchurch St Andr *Chelmsf* 81-84; P-in-c Snitterfield w Bearley *Cov* 84-90; V from 90. *The Vicarage, Snitterfield, Stratford-upon-Avon CV37 0LN* Stratford-upon-Avon (0789) 731263

WATKINS, Peter. b 51. Oak Hill Th Coll BA. **d** 82 **p** 83. C Whitnash *Cov* 82-86; V Wolston and Church Lawford from 86. *The Vicarage, Brook Street, Wolston, Coventry CV8 3HD* Coventry (0203) 542722

WATKINS, Peter Gordon. b 34. St Pet Coll Ox BA57 MA61. Wycliffe Hall Ox 58. **d** 59 **p** 60. C Wolv St Geo *Lich* 59-60; C Burton St Chad 60-61; C Westmr St Jas *Lon* 61-63; USA 63-65; V Ealing Common St Matt *Lon* from 67. *St Matthew's Vicarage, 7 North Common Road, London W5 2QA* 081-567 3820

WATKINS, Robert Henry. b 30. New Coll Ox BA54 MA60. Westcott Ho Cam 59. **d** 60 **p** 61. V Delaval *Newc* 67-80; V Lanercost w Kirkcambeck and Walton *Carl* 80-90; rtd 90. *Lowpark, Loweswater, Cockermouth, Cumbria CA13 0RU* Lorton (090085) 242

WATKINS, Walter. b 27. St Deiniol's Hawarden 80. **d** 81 **p** 82. C Lache cum Saltney *Ches* 81-84; P-in-c Over Tabley and High Legh from 84. *The Vicarage, The Avenue, High Legh, Knutsford, Cheshire WA16 6ND* Lymm (092575) 3612

WATKINS, William Hywel. b 36. Univ of Wales (Lamp) BA58. Wycliffe Hall Ox 58. **d** 61 **p** 62. C Llanelly *St D* 61-68; V Llwynhendy 68-78; V Slebech and Uzmaston w Boulston from 78; RD Daugleddau from 87. *The Vicarage, Uzmaston, Haverfordwest, Dyfed SA62 4AE* Haverfordwest (0437) 762325

WATKINS-JONES, Arthur Basil. b 24. Sarum Th Coll 67. **d** 69 **p** 70. C Broadstone *Sarum* 69-73; P-in-c Winterbourne Stickland and Turnworth etc 73-76; R 76-78; P-in-c Lilliput 78-82; V 82-89; rtd 89. *Oak Cottage, 31 Danecourt Road, Poole, Dorset BH14 0PG* Parkstone (0202) 746074

WATKINS-WRIGHT, Richard Kenneth David. b 39. Westcott Ho Cam 66. **d** 70 **p** 71. C Bilton *Cov* 70-74; Asst Chapl St Geo Hosp Gp Lon 74-75; Chapl Oakwood Hosp Maidstone 76-78; R Gt w Lt Gransden *Ely* from 78. *The Vicarage, Webb's Meadow, Great Gransden, Sandy, Beds SG19 3BL* Great Gransden (07677) 227

WATLING, Arthur Edward. b 28. St Chad's Coll Dur BA57. Linc Th Coll 57. **d** 59 **p** 60. C Middlesb St Cuth *York* 59-61; C Whitby 61-64; V Eastwood *Sheff* 64-88; R Easington w Skeffling, Kilnsea and Holmpton *York* from 88. *The Rectory, Hull Road, Easington, Hull HU12 0TE* Withernsea (0964) 650203

WATLING, Charles Arthur. b 10. **d** 40 **p** 41. Chapl Leeds Gen Infirmary 57-62; rtd 75; Perm to Offic *Carl* from 77. *Westlands, Town Head, Dean, Workington, Cumbria CA14 4TJ* Lamplugh (0946) 861610

WATLING, His Honour Judge David Brian. b 35. QC79. Barrister-at-Law (Middle Temple) 57. K Coll Lon LLB56 LLM90. E Anglian Minl Tr Course 84. **d** 87 **p** 88. Hon C Lavenham *St E* 87-90; Hon C Nayland w Wiston from 90. *The Mead House, Stoke-by-Nayland, Suffolk CO6 4QE* Nayland (0206) 263494

WATLING, Sister Rosemary Dawn. b 32. Newnham Coll Cam BA70 MA73. Gilmore Course 70. **dss** 85 **d** 87. CSA 79-90; Paddington St Mary *Lon* 85-86; E Bris 86-87; Hon Par Dn 87; Par Dn Clifton H Trin, St Andr and St Pet from 87. *St Leonard's Vicarage, Parkfield Avenue, St George, Bristol BS5 8DP* Bristol (0272) 556286

WATSON, Canon Alan. b 34. Lon Univ LLB58. Linc Th Coll 58. **d** 60 **p** 61. C Spring Park *Cant* 60-63; C Sheerness H Trin w St Paul 63-68; R Allington 68-73; P-in-c Maidstone St Pet 73; R Allington and Maidstone St Pet from 73; Hon Can Cant Cathl from 85; RD Sutton from 86. *The Rectory, 35 Poplar Grove, Allington, Maidstone, Kent ME16 0DE* Maidstone (0622) 58704

WATSON, Alan. b 41. AKC64. St Boniface Warminster. **d** 65 **p** 66. C Hendon *Dur* 65-68; C Sheff Parson Cross St Cecilia *Sheff* 68-70; C Harton Colliery *Dur* 70-72; TV 72-74; R Gorton Our Lady and St Thos *Man* 74-82; R Swinton St Pet 82-87; TR Swinton and Pendlebury 87-89; R Rawmarsh w Parkgate *Sheff* from 89. *The Rectory, High Street, Rawmarsh, Rotherham, S Yorkshire S62 6NE* Rotherham (0709) 527160

WATSON, Alan William Martin. b 03. OBE46. Keble Coll Ox BA23. Sarum Th Coll 29. **d** 31 **p** 32. R Spexhall w Wissett *St E* 58-69; rtd 69; Lic to Offic *St E* from 69. *Martin Cottage, Bridge Road, Levington, Ipswich IP10 0NA* Nacton (0473) 659288

WATSON, Albert Victor. b 44. Ridley Hall Cam 85. **d** 87 **p** 88. C Hornchurch St Andr *Chelmsf* from 87. *85 Kenilworth Gardens, Hornchurch, Essex RM12 4SG* Hornchurch (04024) 42275

WATSON, Andrew John. b 61. CCC Cam BA82 MA90. Ridley Hall Cam 84. **d** 87 **p** 88. C Ipsley *Worc* 87-91; C Notting Hill St Jo and St Pet *Lon* from 91. *48 Ladbroke Road, London W11 3NW* 071-229 7275

WATSON, Basil Alderson. b 16. OBE65. Selw Coll Cam BA38 MA44. Westcott Ho Cam 39. **d** 40 **p** 41. Chapl RN 46-70; V St Lawr Jewry *Lon* 70-86; RD The City 76-79; rtd 86. *19 Straightsmouth, London SE10 9LB* 081-853 0643

WATSON, Canon Cecil Henry Barrett. b 14. Jes Coll Ox BA35 MA39. Bps' Coll Cheshunt 35. **d** 37 **p** 38. RD Gedling *S'well* 58-85; R Gedling 58-85; Hon Can S'well Minster 61-85; rtd 85; Perm to Offic *S'well* from 85. *65 Lambley Lane, Burton Joyce, Nottingham NG14 5BL* Burton Joyce (060231) 2490

WATSON, Derek Richard. b 38. Selw Coll Cam BA61 MA65. Cuddesdon Coll 62. **d** 64 **p** 65. C New Eltham All SS *S'wark* 64-66; Chapl Ch Coll Cam 66-70; Bp's Dom Chapl *S'wark* 70-73; V Surbiton St Mark 73-77; V Surbiton St Andr and St Mark 77-78; Can Res and Treas S'wark Cathl 78-82; Dioc Dir of Ords 78-82; P-in-c Chelsea St Luke *Lon* 82-85; R 85-87; P-in-c Chelsea Ch Ch 86-87; R Chelsea St Luke and Ch Ch from 87. *St Luke's Rectory, 29 Burnsall Street, London SW3 3SR* 071-352 6331 or 351 7365

WATSON, Preb Donald Wace. b 17. Qu Coll Cam BA39 MA43. Lich Th Coll 39. **d** 41 **p** 42. V Kinver *Lich* 55-82; Preb Lich Cathl 78-82; rtd 82. *Criddon Cottage, Upton Cressett, Bridgnorth, Shropshire WV16 6UJ* Middleton Scriven (07464535) 661

WATSON, Douglas John Muirhead. b 29. Keble Coll Ox BA52 MA56 DipEd. Ely Th Coll 58. **d** 60 **p** 61. C Charlton-by-Dover SS Pet and Paul *Cant* 60-62; C St Peter-in-Thanet 62-66; V W Wickham St Fran 66-72; V Headcorn from 72. *The Vicarage, 64 Oak Lane, Headcorn, Ashford, Kent TN27 9TB* Headcorn (0622) 890342

WATSON, Edward John. b 48. Chu Coll Cam BA70 MA74. Chich Th Coll 79. **d** 81 **p** 82. C Liv Our Lady and St Nic w St Anne *Liv* 81-84; C Clayton w Keymer *Chich* 84-87; V Frizington and Arlecdon *Carl* from 87. *The Vicarage, Arlecdon, Frizington, Cumbria CA26 3UB* Lamplugh (0946) 861353

WATSON, Canon Edward Vincent Cornelius. b 14. TCD BA39 MA61. **d** 40 **p** 40. I Dub Rathmines *D & G* 61-84; Can Ch Ch Cathl Dub 80-84; rtd 84. *The Mews, Tyrrellstown House, Mulhuddart, Co Dublin, Irish Republic* Dublin (1) 211186

WATSON, Elsada Beatrice. W Midl Minl Tr Course. **d** 89. NSM Birm St Pet *Birm* 89-90; NSM Lozells St Paul and St Silas from 90. *206 Albert Road, Aston, Birmingham B6 5NL* 021-328 7225

WATSON, Geoffrey. b 48. Liv Univ BEd71. Linc Th Coll 81. **d** 83 **p** 84. C Hartlepool St Luke *Dur* 83-87; P-in-c Shadforth from 87; Soc Resp Officer from 87; Dioc Rural Development Adv from 90. *The Rectory, 1 Rectory View, Shadforth, Durham DH6 1LF* 091-372 0223

WATSON, George. b 11. New Coll Ox BA32 MA43. St Steph Ho Ox 32. **d** 34 **p** 35. V Southend St Alb *Chelmsf* 65-76; rtd 76. *46 Penlands Vale, Steyning, W Sussex BN44 3PL* Steyning (0903) 814865

WATSON, Graeme Campbell Hubert. b 35. Ch Ch Ox BA58 MA61. Coll of Resurr Mirfield 59. **d** 61 **p** 62. C Edin St Mary *Edin* 61-63; C Carrington *S'well* 63-67; Tanzania 67-77; P-in-c Kingston St Mary w Broomfield *B & W* 77-80; V 80-81; R Kingston St Mary w Broomfield etc from 81. *The Vicarage, Kingston St Mary, Taunton, Somerset TA2 8HW* Kingston St Mary (0823) 451257

WATSON, Hartley Roger. b 40. K Coll Lon. **d** 64 **p** 65. C Noel Park St Mark *Lon* 64-67; C Munster Square St Mary Magd 67-68; C Stamford Hill St Jo 68-70; Chapl RAF 70-76; R St Breoke *Truro* 76-84; P-in-c Egloshayle 82-84; R Wittering w Thornhaugh and Wansford *Pet* from 84. *The Rectory, Wittering, Peterborough PE8 6AQ* Stamford (0780) 782428

WATSON, Henry Stanley. b 36. **d** 72 **p** 74. Hon C Bethnal Green St Jas Less *Lon* 72-83; Hon C Old Ford St Paul w St Steph and St Mark 83-88; Hon C Bethnal Green St Jas Less from 89. *6 Medhurst Close, London E3 5DE* 081-981 6977

WATSON, Ian Leslie Stewart. b 50. Wycliffe Hall Ox 79. **d** 81 **p** 82. C Plymouth St Andr w St Paul and St Geo *Ex* 81-85; TV Ipsley *Worc* 85-90; V Woodley *Ox* from 90. *The Vicarage, 36 Church Road, Reading RG5 4GJ* Reading (0734) 692316

WATSON, Canon Jeffrey John Seagrief. b 39. Em Coll Cam BA61 MA65. Clifton Th Coll 62. **d** 65 **p** 66. C Beckenham Ch Ch *Roch* 65-69; C Southsea St Jude *Portsm* 69-71; V Win Ch Ch *Win* 71-81; V Bitterne from 81; RD Southn from 83; Hon Can Win Cathl from 91. *The Vicarage, 2 Bursledon Road, Bitterne, Southampton SO2 7LW* Southampton (0703) 446488

WATSON, John. b 16. Oak Hill Th Coll 76. **d** 78 **p** 79. Hon C Lexden *Chelmsf* 78-81; Perm to Offic *Ches* 81-85; Hon C Alsager St Mary from 85. *9 Woolaston Drive, Alsager, Stoke-on-Trent* Alsager (0270) 874565

WATSON, John Davidson. b 25. Kelham Th Coll. **d** 58 **p** 59. C Brixham *Ex* 61-70; V Treverbyn *Truro* 70-73; V S Shields St Jude *Dur* 73-78; V Rekendyke 78-84; V Coleford w Holcombe *B & W* 84-91; rtd 91. *La Ribouilliere, 53510 Chatillon sur Colmont, France*

WATSON, John Derrick. b 35. K Coll Lon 56. Edin Th Coll 60. **d** 61 **p** 62. C Fulham St Etheldreda *Lon* 61-64; P-in-c Stevenage H Trin *St Alb* 64-71; V 71-74; V Leagrave 74-84; RD Luton 80-82; V Eaton Socon from 84. *St Mary's Vicarage, 34 Drake Road, Eaton Socon, Huntingdon, Cambs PE19 3HS* Huntingdon (0480) 212219

WATSON, Preb John Francis Wentworth. b 28. St Jo Coll Nottm LTh59. **d** 59 **p** 60. C Egham *Guildf* 59-62; C-in-c Ewell St Paul Howell Hill CD 62-66; R Ashtead 66-72; V Plymouth St Andr w St Paul and St Geo *Ex* from 72; Angl Adv TV South West from 83; Preb Ex Cathl from 84. *St Andrew's Vicarage, 13 Bainbridge Avenue, Plymouth PL3 5QZ* Plymouth (0752) 772139 or 661414

WATSON, John Lionel. b 39. G&C Coll Cam BA61 MA65. Ridley Hall Cam 62. **d** 64 **p** 65. C Toxteth Park St Philemon w St Silas *Liv* 64-69; C Morden *S'wark* 69-73; C Cam St Phil *Ely* 73-74; Chapl Elstree Sch Woolhampton 74-77; R Woolhampton w Midgham *Ox* 77-81; R Woolhampton w Midgham and Beenham Valance from 81. *The Rectory, New Road Hill, Midgham, Reading RG7 5RY* Woolhampton (0734) 712264

WATSON, Canon John Robertson Thomas. b 27. CITC 68. **d** 70 **p** 71. C Belf St Steph *Conn* 71-73; Bp's C Swanlinbar w Templeport *K, E & A* 73-82; I Arvagh w Carrigallen, Gowna and Columbkille from 82; Preb Kilmore Cathl from 88. *The Rectory, Arva, Cavan, Irish Republic* Cavan (49) 35233

WATSON, Jonathan Ramsay George. b 38. Or Coll Ox BA61 MA65 DipEd62. Ridley Hall Cam 88. **d** 90 **p** 91. C Locks Heath *Portsm* from 90. *11 Laurel Road, Locks Heath, Southampton SO3 6QG* Locks Heath (0489) 572699

WATSON, Kenneth Roy. b 27. CEng68 MIMechE68. E Midl Min Tr Course 83. **d** 86 **p** 87. NSM Ashby-de-la-Zouch St Helen w Coleorton *Leic* 86-90; R Breedon

cum Isley Walton and Worthington from 90. *The Rectory, Melbourne Lane, Breedon-on-the-Hill, Derby DE7 1AT* Melbourne (0332) 864056

WATSON, Laurence Leslie. b 31. Keble Coll Ox BA55 MA59. Ely Th Coll. **d** 57 **p** 58. C Solihull *Birm* 57-60; C Digswell *St Alb* 60-62; V Smethwick St Steph *Birm* 62-67; V Billesley Common from 67. *Holy Cross Vicarage, 29 Beauchamp Road, Birmingham B13 0NS* 021-444 1737

WATSON, Leonard Alexander David. b 37. Man Univ BSc59. Coll of Resurr Mirfield 62. **d** 64 **p** 65. C Rawmarsh w Parkgate *Sheff* 64-68; S Africa 69-74; TV E Runcorn w Halton *Ches* 74-79; TV Sanderstead All SS *S'wark* 79-86; TR Selsdon St Jo w St Fran from 86; RD Croydon Addington from 90. *The Rectory, Upper Selsdon Road, Selsdon, South Croydon, Surrey CR2 8DD* 081-657 2343

WATSON, Paul Frederick. b 44. MRCVS69 RVC(Lon) BSc66 BVetMed69 Sydney Univ PhD73. Oak Hill NSM Course 86. **d** 88 **p** 89. Hon C Muswell Hill St Jas w St Matt *Lon* from 88. *43 Grasmere Road, London N10 2DH* 081-444 7158

WATSON, Paul William. b 55. Huddersfield Poly BA. St Jo Coll Nottm. **d** 86 **p** 87. C Meltham Mills *Wakef* 86-89; C Meltham 89-90; TV Borehamwood *St Alb* from 90. *The Vicarage, 142 Brook Road, Borehamwood, Herts WD6 5EQ* 081-953 2362

WATSON, Philip. b 60. RGN83. Qu Coll Birm 86. **d** 89 **p** 90. C Ordsall *S'well* from 89. *Croft Cottage, Church Lane, Retford, Notts DN22 7TU* Retford (0777) 700733

✠**WATSON, Rt Rev Richard Charles Challinor.** b 23. New Coll Ox BA48 MA48. Westcott Ho Cam 50. **d** 51 **p** 52 **c** 70. C Stratford St Jo *Chelmsf* 51-53; Tutor and Chapl Wycliffe Hall Ox 54-57; Chapl to Ox Pastorate 57-61; Chapl Wadh Coll Ox 57-62; V Hornchurch St Andr *Chelmsf* 62-70; Hon Can Blackb Cathl *Blackb* 70-88; R Burnley St Pet 70-77; Suff Bp Burnley 70-87; Asst Bp Ox from 87; rtd 88. *6 Church Road, Thame, Oxon OX9 3AJ* Thame (084421) 3853

WATSON, Richard Rydill. b 47. Sarum & Wells Th Coll 74. **d** 77 **p** 78. C Cayton w Eastfield *York* 77-80; C Howden Team Min 80-82; P-in-c Burton Pidsea and Humbleton w Elsternwick 82-83; V Dormanstown 83-87; V Cotehill and Cumwhinton *Carl* 87-89; Chapl Harrogate Distr Hosp from 89. *10 Manor Road, Knaresborough, N Yorkshire HG5 0BN* Harrogate (0423) 864816

WATSON, Robert Bewley. b 34. Bris Univ BA59. Clifton Th Coll 56. **d** 61 **p** 62. C Bebington *Ches* 61-65; C Woking St Jo *Guildf* 65-68; V Knaphill from 68. *Trinity House, Trinity Road, Knaphill, Woking, Surrey GU21 2SY* Brookwood (04867) 3489

WATSON, Robert Bruce Scoular Jameson. Dur Univ LTh32 Keble Coll Ox BA43 MA47. Lich Th Coll 29. **d** 31 **p** 32. V Bayford *St Alb* 56-75; rtd 75; Perm to Offic *Lon* and *St Alb* from 75. *83 Overstone Road, Harpenden, Herts AL5 5PL* Harpenden (0582) 761651

WATSON, Robert Leslie. b 01. Wells Th Coll 24. **d** 25 **p** 26. R Withycombe *B & W* 64-68; rtd 68; Perm to Offic *Glouc* 68-74; *B & W* from 74. *24 Golf Links Road, Burnham-on-Sea, Somerset TA8 2PW* Burnham (0628) 785520

WATSON, Ronald Marwood. b 25. Roch Th Coll 68. **d** 70 **p** 71. C Horsforth *Ripon* 70-71; C Leeds All SS 71-73; C Baildon *Bradf* 73-75; R Salford Stowell Memorial *Man* 75-77; C Tonge Moor 77-83; P-in-c Crawshawbooth 83-84; C Goodshaw and Crawshawbooth 84-88; rtd 88; Perm to Offic *S'wark* from 91. *179 Grangehill Road, London SE9 1SR* 081-859 3906

WATSON, Mrs Sheila Anne. b 53. St Andr Univ MA75 MPhil80. Edin Th Coll 78. **dss** 79 **d** 87. Bridge of Allan *St And* 79-80; Alloa 79-80; Monkseaton St Mary *Newc* 80-84; Adult Educn Officer *Lon* 84-87; Hon Par Dn Chelsea St Luke and Ch Ch from 87. *29 Burnsall Street, London SW3 3SR* 071-352 6331 or 351 7365

WATSON, Miss Stephanie Abigail. b 61. Heriot-Watt Univ BA84 St Jo Coll Dur CCSk90. Cranmer Hall Dur 86. **d** 90. C Bishop's Castle w Mainstone *Heref* from 90. *7 Lavender Bank, Bishops Castle, Shropshire SY9 5BD* Bishops Castle (0588) 638024

WATSON, Terence David. b 38. Jes Coll Ox BA61 MA67. Chich Th Coll 73. **d** 74 **p** 75. C Sidley *Chich* 74-78; C Woodham *Guildf* 78-86; C Willesborough w Hinxhill *Cant* 86-87; C Willesborough from 87. *19 Gladstone Road, Willesborough, Ashford, Kent TN24 0BY* Ashford (0233) 639985

WATSON, Thomas Anthony. b 23. Chich Th Coll 50. **d** 52 **p** 53. V Honicknowle *Ex* 65-72; R Butterleigh 72-90; R Silverton 72-90; rtd 90; Chapl Palermo w Taormina *Eur*

from 90. *Via Manin 2, 90139 Palermo, Sicily, Italy*
Palermo (91) 581787

WATSON, Thomas Heys. b 16. Clifton Th Coll 36. **d** 40 **p** 41. V Whittle-le-Woods *Blackb* 61-75; R Hesketh w Becconsall 75-80; rtd 81; Lic to Offic *Blackb* from 81. *78 Sandy Lane, Leyland, Preston PR5 1EE* Leyland (0772) 431821

WATSON, Timothy Patrick. b 38. ALCD66. **d** 66 **p** 67. C Northwood Em *Lon* 66-70; TV High Wycombe *Ox* 70-76; Gen Sec Intercon Ch Soc 76-82; R Bath Weston All SS w N Stoke *B & W* from 82. *The Vicarage, Weston, Bath BA1 4BU* Bath (0225) 421159

WATSON, Miss Violet Hazel. b 29. SRN52 SCM54 RSCN59. Linc Th Coll 83. **dss** 85 **d** 87. Hammersmith SS Mich and Geo White City Estate CD *Lon* 85-86; Sunbury 86; Fulham St Dionis Parson's Green 86-87; Par Dn 87; Perm to Offic *St Alb* 88-90. *4 Hayes Terrace, Crown Lane, Shorne, Gravesend, Kent DA12 3DZ* Shorne (047482) 3579

WATSON, William. b 36. Ripon Hall Ox 64. **d** 66 **p** 67. C Leamington Priors H Trin *Cov* 66-69; V Salford Priors 69-74; V Malin Bridge *Sheff* 74-79; Chapl Shrewsbury R Hosps 79-89; Chapl R Hallamshire Hosp Sheff from 89. *396 Stannington Road, Sheffield S6 5QQ* Sheffield (0742) 324005 or 766222

WATSON, William Lysander Rowan. b 26. TCD BA47 MA50 Clare Coll Cam MA52 St Pet Hall Ox MA57. **d** 49 **p** 50. Chapl St Pet Hall Ox 57-91; Fell and Tutor St Pet Hall Ox 59-91; Lect Th Ox Univ 60-91; Sen Tutor 77-81; Vice Master St Pet Coll Ox 83-85; rtd 91. *65 Chalfont Road, Oxford OX1 2DL* Oxford (0865) 278903

WATSON-PEGMAN, John Basil. b 24. **d** 58 **p** 59. Miss to Seamen 68-87; E Regional Dir 74-87; Lic to Offic Chelmsf 69-74; Linc 74-87; R Skelsmergh w Selside and Longsleddale *Carl* 87-90; rtd 90. *Little Owl Cottage, Brook Lane, Thornton Dale, Pickering, N Yorkshire YO18 7RZ* Pickering (0751) 76238

WATSON WILLIAMS, Richard Hamilton Patrick. b 31. SS Coll Cam BA57 MA62. St Aug Coll Cant. **d** 59 **p** 60. C Dorking St Paul *Guildf* 59-63; C Portsea St Mary *Portsm* 63-66; V Culgaith *Carl* 66-71; V Kirkland 66-71; V Wigton 72-79; Warden Dioc Conf Ho Crawshawbooth *Man* 79-82; P-in-c Crawshawbooth 79-82; Master Lady Kath Leveson Hosp from 82; P-in-c Temple Balsall *Birm* 82-84; V from 84. *The Master's House, Knowle, Solihull, W Midlands B93 0AL* Knowle (0564) 772415

WATT, Very Rev Alfred Ian. b 34. Edin Th Coll 57. **d** 60 **p** 61. Chapl St Paul's Cathl Dundee *Bre* 60-63; Prec 63-66; P-in-c Dundee H Cross 64-66; R Arbroath 66-69; R Perth St Ninian *St And* 69-82; Provost St Ninian's Cathl Perth 69-82; Can St Ninian's Cathl Perth from 82; R Kinross from 82; Dean St Andr from 89. *St Paul's Rectory, 55 Muirs, Kinross KY13 7AU* Kinross (0577) 62271

WATT, William Montgomery. b 09. Edin Univ MA30 PhD44 Ball Coll Ox BA32 MA36 BLitt36 Aber Univ Hon DD66. Cuddesdon Coll 38. **d** 39 **p** 40. C W Brompton St Mary *Lon* 39-41; C Edin Old St Paul *Edin* 41-43; Hon C 46-60; Jerusalem 43-46; Hon C Edin St Columba *Edin* 60-67; Hon C Dalkeith from 80; Hon C Lasswade from 80. *The Neuk, Bridgend, Dalkeith, Midlothian EH22 1JT* 031-663 3197

WATT-WYNESS, Gordon. b 25. Cranmer Hall Dur 70 St Jo Coll Dur 70. **d** 72 **p** 73. C Scarborough St Mary w Ch Ch, St Paul and St Thos *York* 72-76; R Rossington *Sheff* 76-90; rtd 90. *29 Church Street, Filey, N Yorkshire YO14 9ED* Scarborough (0723) 516608

WATTERSON, Mrs Susan Mary. b 87. NSM Rushen *S & M* from 87; Dioc Youth Officer from 88. *46 Ballahane Close, Port Erin, Isle of Man* Port Erin (0624) 832835

WATTERSON, William Howard. b 16. Dur Univ LTh39 BA47 MA58. St Aid Birkenhead 36. **d** 39 **p** 40. Hd of RE Waterloo Gr Sch 53-72; Lic to Offic *Liv* 70-81; Hd of RE Aylesbury High Sch Bucks 72-77; Perm to Offic *Ox* 72-77; rtd 81; Perm to Offic *Liv* from 81. *10 Dinorwic Road, Southport, Merseyside PR8 4DL* Southport (0704) 65682

WATTHEY, Arthur Edward. b 20. St Cath Coll Cam BA45 MA48. St Aug Coll Cant 73. **d** 73 **p** 74. NSM Glen Magna w Stretton Magna *Leic* 73-76; NSM Carlton Curlieu, Illston on the Hill etc 76-81; Perm to Offic *Leic* from 81; *Pet* from 85; Bp's Insp of Par Registers & Records from 90. *2 The Chase, Great Glen, Leicester LE8 0EQ* Great Glen (053759) 2603

WATTON, Robert Newman Kingsley. b 45. Qu Coll Birm 72. **d** 74 **p** 75. C Madron w Morvah *Truro* 74-78; Dioc Adv in RE 78-81; P-in-c Lostwithiel 78-83; P-in-c Lanhydrock 81-83; P-in-c Lanivet 81-82; V Launceston

83-91; RD Trigg Major 89-91; R Kingston, Langton Matravers and Worth Matravers *Sarum* from 91. *The Rectory, Langton Matravers, Swanage, Dorset BH19 3HB* Swanage (0929) 422559

WATTS, Anthony George. b 46. K Coll Lon BD69 AKC69 Lon Univ CertEd70. Sarum & Wells Th Coll 82. **d** 84 **p** 85. C Wimborne Minster and Holt *Sarum* 84-87; Chapl Croft Ho Sch Shillingstone from 87; P-in-c Shilling Okeford *Sarum* from 87. *The Rectory, Shillingstone, Blandford, Dorset DT11 0SL* Child Okeford (0258) 860261

WATTS, Anthony John. b 30. AKC59. **d** 60 **p** 61. C Whitburn *Dur* 60-63; C Croxdale 63-65; V Warrington St Pet *Liv* 65-70; V Peel *Man* 70-78; P-in-c Bury St Mark 78-81; V Davyhulme Ch Ch from 81. *Christ Church Vicarage, 14 Welbeck Avenue, Urmston, Manchester M31 1GJ* 061-748 2018

WATTS, Canon Arthur James. b 08. Hatf Coll Dur BA30 MA47. **d** 32 **p** 33. R Harpsden w Bolney *Ox* 51-77; Hon Can Ch Ch 59-77; rtd 77. *Juniper Cottage, Harpsden, Henley-on-Thames, Oxon RG9 4HL* Henley-on-Thames (0491) 5343

WATTS, Charles George. b 08. ALCD37. **d** 37 **p** 38. R Limehouse *Lon* 71-75; rtd 75. *Crwys Villa, Irfon Terrace, Llanwrtyd Wells, Powys* Llanwrtyd Wells (05913) 463

WATTS, David Henry. b 27. Ex Coll Ox BA50 MA55. Wells Th Coll 57. **d** 53 **p** 54. Educn Officer Essex Educn Cttee 62-70; HMI of Schs 70-87; Hon C Wetherby *Ripon* 83-87; P-in-c Healaugh w Wighill, Bilbrough and Askham Richard *York* 87-89; Chapl HM Pris Askham Grange from 87; rtd 89. *3 Westwood Way, Boston Spa, Wetherby, W Yorkshire LS23 6DX* Boston Spa (0937) 845005

WATTS, Dr Fraser Norman. b 46. FBPsS80 CPsychol89 Magd Coll Ox BA68 MA74 Lon Univ MSc70 PhD75 Magd Coll Cam DipTh90. Westcott Ho Cam 88. **d** 90 **p** 91. NSM Harston w Hauxton *Ely* from 90. *81 Church Road, Hauxton, Cambridge CB2 5HS* Cambridge (0223) 871810

WATTS, Geoffrey Frederick. b 46. Chich Th Coll 70. **d** 73 **p** 74. C Torquay St Martin Barton *Ex* 73-76; C Ex St Jas 76-79; TV Littleham w Exmouth 79-84; R Ogwell and Denbury from 84. *The Rectory, St Bartholomew Way, Ogwell, Newton Abbot, Devon TQ12 6YW* Newton Abbot (0626) 54330

WATTS, George Reginald. b 15. Or Coll Ox BA37 MA43. **d** 57 **p** 58. Hd Master Gonvena Ho Sch and C of St Minver 57-71; R St Mellion w Pillaton *Truro* 71-83; rtd 83. *The Fish Cellars, Port Quin, Port Isaac, Cornwall PL29 3SU* Port Isaac (020888) 774

WATTS, Gordon Sidney Stewart. b 40. CITC 63. **d** 66 **p** 67. C Belf St Steph *Conn* 66-69; CF from 69. *c/o MOD (Army), Bagshot Park, Bagshot, Surrey GU19 5PL* Bagshot (0276) 71717

WATTS, Canon Horace Gordon. b 20. TCD BA42 MA52. **d** 43 **p** 44. I Fanlobbus Union *C, C & R* 56-76; Preb Cork Cathl 67-88; Treas Cloyne Cathl 68-88; I Douglas w Frankfield 76-86; I Douglas Union w Frankfield 86-88; rtd 88. *St Anton, 29 Carrigcourt, Carrigaline, Co Cork, Irish Republic* Cork (21) 373406

WATTS, Ian Charles. b 63. Hull Univ BA85. Linc Th Coll 86. **d** 88 **p** 89. C W Kirby St Bridget *Ches* from 88. *13 Caldy Road, West Kirby, Wirral, Merseyside L48 2HE* 051-625 2731

WATTS, Ian Harold. b 15. St Pet Coll Ox BA39 MA47. Wycliffe Hall Ox. **d** 65 **p** 66. Chapl Uppingham Sch Leics 68-73; Hon C Mirfield *Wakef* 73-79; Chapl Cannes *Eur* 80-87; rtd 87. *67 Arden Street, Marchmont, Edinburgh EH9 1BT* 031-447 6760

WATTS, John Harry. b 24. St Aid Birkenhead 57. **d** 59 **p** 60. V S Wingfield *Derby* 65-86; C-in-c Wessington CD 77-86; V S Wingfield and Wessington 86-89; rtd 89. *57 Abbotts Road, Alfreton, Derby DE5 7HD* Alfreton (0773) 521063

WATTS, John Robert. b 39. Leeds Univ BSc60 MSc63 DipEd63. Oak Hill Th Coll 88. **d** 90 **p** 91. C Partington and Carrington *Ches* from 90. *18 Langdale Road, Partington, Urmston, Manchester M31 4NE* 061-775 7666

WATTS, John Stanley. b 28. LCP62 Birm Univ DipEd65 MEd72 Nottm Univ MPhil83. Qu Coll Birm 83. **d** 86 **p** 87. Hon C Dudley St Fran *Worc* 86-91; Hon C Sedgley St Mary *Lich* from 91. *5 Warren Drive, Sedgley, Dudley, W Midlands DY3 3RQ* Sedgley (0902) 661265

WATTS, Kenneth Francis. b 17. St Fran Coll Brisbane ACT ThL39. **d** 40 **p** 41. V Cheriton All So w Newington *Cant* 64-80; New Zealand from 80; rtd 82. *Shechinah, Okau Road, RD 27, Whangamomona, Taranaki, New Zealand* Whangamomona (6) 762-5585

WATTS, Mary Kathleen. b 31. Lon Univ DipRS73 BA(Theol)86. Gilmore Ho 73. **dss** 75 **d** 87. C Streatham Immanuel w St Anselm *S'wark* 87-88; C Lower Streatham St Andr 87-88; C Streatham Immanuel and St Andr 90-91; rtd 91; Perm to Offic *S'wark* from 91. *25 Hilldown Road, London SW16 3DZ* 081-764 6165

WATTS, Michael. b 24. NE Ord Course. **d** 82 **p** 83. NSM Stockton St Pet *Dur* from 82. *59 Richmond Road, Stockton-on-Tees, Cleveland TS18 4DT* Stockton-on-Tees (0642) 675602

WATTS, Michael. b 32. St Cath Soc Ox BA57 MA61. St Steph Ho Ox 57. **d** 58 **p** 59. C Ox St Mich *Ox* 58-60; Chapl New Coll Ox 60-72; Chapl Ch Ch *Ox* 60-81; C Ox St Mary Magd 63-73; Prec Ch Ch 64-81; R Sulhamstead Abbots and Bannister w Ufton Nervet from 81; PV Westmr Abbey from 82. *The Rectory, Ufton Nervet, Reading RG7 4DH* Burghfield Common (073529) 2328

WATTS, Paul George. b 43. Nottm Univ MA67. Wells Th Coll 67. **d** 69 **p** 70. C Sherwood *S'well* 69-74; Chapl Trent Poly 74-80; V Nottm All SS 80-84; Lic to Offic from 84. *16 Grosvenor Avenue, Mapperley Park, Nottingham NG5 3DX* Nottingham (0602) 609964

WATTS, Canon Peter Alan Witney. b 37. Dur Univ BA59 Birm Univ MSocSc83. Qu Coll Birm DipTh61. **d** 61 **p** 62. C Hamstead St Paul *Birm* 61-65; C Ward End 65-66; V Burney Lane 66-73; V Sutton Coldfield St Chad from 73; Hon Can Birm Cathl from 89. *The Vicarage, 41 Hollyfield Road, Sutton Coldfield, W Midlands B75 7SN* 021-329 2995

WATTS, Peter Francis. b 48. Univ of Wales (Cardiff) DipTh71. Llan St Mich 67. **d** 71 **p** 72. C Swansea St Mary and H Trin *S & B* 71-74; C Newton Nottage *Llan* 74-77; V Hirwaun 77-80; P-in-c Menheniot *Truro* 80-81; V 81-84; P-in-c Falmouth All SS 84-89; V from 89; Co-Chmn Cornwall Miss to Seamen from 90. *All Saints' Vicarage, 72 Dracaena Avenue, Falmouth, Cornwall TR11 2EN* Falmouth (0326) 314141

WATTS, Raymond Ivor. b 31. DIM. Local NSM Course. **d** 85 **p** 86. NSM Scotter w E Ferry *Linc* from 85. *5 St Peter's Road, Scotter, Gainsborough, Lincs DN21 3SG* Scunthorpe (0724) 762691

WATTS, Miss Rebecca Harriet. b 61. St Cath Coll Cam BA83 MA. Wycliffe Hall Ox 87. **d** 90. C Goldsworth Park *Guildf* from 90. *1 Hamble Walk, Goldsworth Park, Woking, Surrey GU21 3LG* Woking (0483) 730442

WATTS, Roger Edward. b 39. S'wark Ord Course 85. **d** 88 **p** 89. C Belmont *S'wark* from 88. *65 Downs Road, Sutton, Surrey SM2 5NR* 081-642 9775

WATTS, Roger Mansfield. b 41. CEng76 MIEE76 Univ of Wales (Cardiff) BSc63 Southn Univ. Chich Th Coll 89. **d** 91. C Chippenham St Andr w Tytherton Lucas *Bris* from 91. *18 Downham Mead, Chippenham, Wilts SN15 3LN* Chippenham (0249) 653932

WATTS, Ronald. b 21. St D Coll Lamp BA47. **d** 48 **p** 49. R Kilkhampton *Truro* 58-72; P-in-c Morwenstow 63-72; R Kilkhampton w Morwenstow 72-86; rtd 86. *St Peter's, Stibb, Kilkhampton, Bude, Cornwall EX23 9HW* Bude (0288) 354080

WATTS, Wilfred Richard James. b 11. St Mich Coll Llan 64. **d** 66 **p** 66. V Viney Hill *Glouc* 69-82; rtd 82; Perm to Offic *Glouc* from 82. *5 Lambert Drive, Shurdington, Cheltenham, Glos GL51 5SP* Cheltenham (0242) 862377

WATTS, William George Duncan. b 12. Kelham Th Coll 32. **d** 38 **p** 39. R Benefield *Pet* 70-80; rtd 80; Lic to Offic *Pet* 80-85; Perm from 85; Perm *Ely* 80-85. *5 Lime Avenue, Oundle, Peterborough PE8 4PJ* Oundle (0832) 72643

WATTS, William Henry Norbury. b 51. CertEd. St Jo Coll Nottm 87. **d** 89 **p** 90. C S Molton w Nymet St George, High Bray etc *Ex* from 89. *2 North Road, South Molton, Devon EX36 3AZ* South Molton (07695) 3919

WATTS-JONES, William Vyvyan Francis Kynaston. b 22. Em Coll Cam BΛ43 MΛ47 CertEd72. Ridley Hall Cam 47. **d** 49 **p** 50. V Bilton *Ripon* 60-70; Asst Master St Pet Colleg Ch Sch Wolv 72-74; R Brampton St Thos *Derby* 74-84; rtd 84; Perm to Offic *Derby* from 84. *91 Abbeydale Park Rise, Sheffield S17 3PE* Sheffield (0742) 366733

WAUD, John David. b 31. N Ord Course 82. **d** 85 **p** 86. C Cayton w Eastfield *York* 85-88; R Brandesburton from 88. *The New Rectory, Main Street, Brandesburton, Driffield, N Humberside YO25 8RG* Hornsea (0964) 542015

WAUDBY, Miss Christine. b 45. TCert66. Trin Coll Bris DipHE. **d** 90. C Weston-super-Mare Ch Ch *B & W* from 90. *44 Brendon Avenue, Weston-super-Mare, Avon BS23 2TF* Weston-super-Mare (0934) 641639

WAUGH, Mrs Jane Leitch. b 38. DMusEd60 CertEd61 Toronto Univ MDiv83. Trin Coll Toronto 80. **d** 84. Canada 84-87; Par Dn Dunnington *York* 88-90. *Moonrakers, Rectory Corner, Brandsby, York YO6 4RJ* Brandsby (03475) 637

WAUGH, Canon Nigel John William. b 56. TCD BA78 MA81. CITC 76. **d** 79 **p** 80. C Ballymena *Conn* 79-82; C Ballyholme *D & D* 82-84; I Bunclody w Kildavin *C & O* 84-86; I Bunclody w Kildavin and Clonegal from 86; RD New Ross from 86; Preb Ferns Cathl from 88; Treas from 91; Radio Officer (Cashel) 90-91; Dioc Info Officer (Ferns) from 91. *The Rectory, Bunclody, Enniscorthy, Co Wexford, Irish Republic* Enniscorthy (54) 77652

WAXHAM, Derek Frank. b 33. Oak Hill Th Coll 76. **d** 79 **p** 80. Hon C Old Ford St Paul w St Steph *Lon* 79-82; Hon C Old Ford St Paul w St Steph and St Mark from 82. *39 Hewlett Road, London E3 5NA* 081-980 1748

WAY, Albert James. b 27. St D Coll Lamp BA61 DipTh63. **d** 63 **p** 64. C Neath w Llantwit *Llan* 63-68; C Watford St Jo *St Alb* 68; R Clayhidon *Ex* 68-76; V Llanbadog and Llanllowell *Mon* 76-83; V Llanhilleth from 83. *The Rectory, Aberbeeg, Abertillery, Gwent NP3 2DA* Abertillery (0495) 214236

WAY, Andrew Lindsay. b 43. Linc Th Coll 76. **d** 78 **p** 79. C Shenfield *Chelmsf* 78-82; C Waltham *Linc* 82-84; V New Waltham 84-89; R Duxford *Ely* from 89; V Hinxton from 89; V Ickleton from 89. *The Rectory, St John's Street, Duxford, Cambridge CB2 4RA* Cambridge (0223) 832137

WAY, Anthony Hilton. b 21. ARIBA. Chich Th Coll 57. **d** 59 **p** 60. C Chich St Paul and St Bart *Chich* 59-61; C Hangleton 61-63; V Horam 63-70; V Ditchling 70-77; Asst Dioc Sec 77-83; Chapl Dioc Ch Ho 79-83; V Linchmere from 83. *The Vicarage, Linchmere, Haslemere, Surrey GU27 3NF* Liphook (0428) 723197

WAY, Mrs Barbara Elizabeth. b 47. Open Univ BA82 Hull Univ PGCE86. Linc Th Coll 76. **dss** 78 **d** 87. Shenfield *Chelmsf* 78-82; Adult Educn Adv *Linc* 82-85; Dioc Lay Min Adv 84; New Waltham 82-87; Hon Par Dn 87-89; Tetney 86-87; Dn-in-c 87-89; Hon Par Dn Duxford *Ely* from 89; Hon Par Dn Ickleton from 89; Hon Par Dn Hinxton from 89; Dir of Past Studies 91; Dir of Past Studies E Anglian Min Tr Course from 91. *The Rectory, 13 St John's Road, Duxford, Cambridge CB2 4RA* Cambridge (0223) 832137

WAY, Colin George. b 31. St Cath Coll Cam BA55 MA59 Lon Inst of Educn PGCE58. E Anglian Minl Tr Course. **d** 84 **p** 85. NSM Hempnall *Nor* 84-87; C Gaywood, Bawsey and Mintlyn 87-90; R Acle w Fishley and N Burlingham from 90. *The Rectory, Acle, Norwich NR13 3BU* Great Yarmouth (0493) 750393

WAY, David Victor. b 54. Pemb Coll Ox MA DPhil. Cranmer Hall Dur BA Cuddesdon Coll 83. **d** 85 **p** 86. C Chenies and Lt Chalfont *Ox* 85-87; C Chenies and Lt Chalfont, Latimer and Flaunden 87-88; Tutor and Dir of Studies Sarum & Wells Th Coll from 88. *66 The Close, Salisbury, Wilts SP1 2EL* Salisbury (0722) 320519

WAY, Lawrence William. b 32. St Mich Coll Llan 77. **d** 79 **p** 80. C Merthyr Dyfan *Llan* 79-82; V Abercynon 82-84; TV Cwmbran *Mon* 84-86; V Caerwent w Dinham and Llanfair Discoed etc 86-90; V Llanfrechfa Upper from 90. *The Vicarage, Church Road, Pontnewydd, Cwmbran, Gwent NP44 1AT* Cwmbran (0633) 32300

WAY, Michael David. b 57. K Coll Lon BD78 AKC78. St Steph Ho Ox 79. **d** 80 **p** 83. C Bideford *Ex* 80-81; Hon C Wembley Park St Aug *Lon* 81-84; C Kilburn St Aug w St Jo 84-89; V Earlsfield St Jo *S'wark* from 89. *St John's Vicarage, 40 Atheldene Road, London SW18 3BW* 081-874 2837

WAY, Winfrid Hilary. b 07. Lich Th Coll 29. **d** 32 **p** 34. R Stow on the Wold *Glouc* 67-83; rtd 83; Perm to Offic *Heref* 83-88. *The Cottage, Old Gore, Ross-on-Wye, Hereford HR9 7QT* Ross-on-Wye (0989) 85456

WAYNE, Kenneth Hammond. b 31. Bps' Coll Cheshunt 58. **d** 61 **p** 62. C Eyres Monsell CD *Leic* 61-62; C Loughb Em 62-65; C-in-c Staunton Harold 65-73; R Breedon w Isley Walton 65-73; V Leic St Phil 73-85; V Ault Hucknall *Derby* from 85. *59 The Hill, Glapwell, Chesterfield, Derbyshire S44 5LX* Chesterfield (0246) 850371

WAYTE, Alleyn Robert. b 33. Trin Coll Ox BA56 MA60. Westcott Ho Cam 60. **d** 61 **p** 62. C Cannock *Lich* 61-66; P-in-c Dawley 66-75; V Stretton w Claymills from 75. *The Vicarage, Church Road, Stretton, Burton-on-Trent, Staffs DE13 0HD* Burton-on-Trent (0283) 65141

WAYTE, Christopher John. b 28. Lon Univ BSc54. Wells Th Coll 54. **d** 56 **p** 57. C Maidstone St Martin *Cant* 56-60; C W Wickham St Jo 60-61; C Birchington w Acol

61-64; C-in-c Buckland Valley CD 64-68; R Biddenden 68-80; P-in-c Boughton Monchelsea 80-85; V St Margarets-at-Cliffe w Westcliffe etc from 85. *The Vicarage, Sea Street, St Margarets-at-Cliffe, Dover, Kent CT15 6AB* Dover (0304) 852179

WEALE, Colin Alexander. b 26. Univ of Wales (Lamp) BA49 Lon Univ DipRS77 Open Univ MPhil87. Lambeth STh81 Sarum Th Coll 49. **d** 51 **p** 52. C Swansea St Mary and H Trin *S & B* 51-55; Min Can Brecon Cathl 55-59; C Brecon w Battle 55-59; V Llanbister and Llanbadarn Fynydd w Llananno 59-61; R Bengeo H Trin *St Alb* 61-69; R Bengeo from 69. *The Rectory, Byde Street, Hertford SG14 3BS* Hertford (0992) 584537

WEARMOUTH, Alan Wilfred. b 54. St Paul's Cheltenham CertEd75 Bris Univ BEd76. Glouc Sch of Min 85. **d** 88 **p** 89. Hon C Coleford w Staunton *Glouc* from 88. *22 Forest Patch, Christchurch, Coleford, Glos GL16 8RB* Dean (0594) 32660

WEARMOUTH, Paul Frederick. b 37. Wells Th Coll 60. **d** 62 **p** 63. Ho Master Castleview Sch Sunderland 68-84; rtd 84; Perm to Offic *Dur* from 84. *9 Withernsea Grove, Ryhope, Sunderland, Tyne and Wear SR2 0BU* 091-521 0127

WEARN, William Frederick. b 51. S Dios Minl Tr Scheme. **d** 85 **p** 86. NSM Hythe *Win* from 85. *117 Cedar Road, Hythe, Southampton SO4 6QA* Southampton (0703) 849390

WEATHERBY, Peter John James. b 58. Keble Coll Ox BA80 MA91. St Steph Ho Ox 81. **d** 83 **p** 84. C Latchford St Jas *Ches* 83-85; C Calcot *Ox* 85-88; Asst Chapl HM Pris Reading 85-88; TV Cowley St Jas *Ox* from 88. *The Vicarage, 85 Temple Road, Oxford OX4 2EX* Oxford (0865) 778333

WEATHERHEAD, Very Rev Thomas Leslie. b 13. Hatf Coll Dur BA37 LTh37. St Aug Coll Cant 32. **d** 37 **p** 38. Dean and V-Gen Nassau 65-72; R Felmingham *Nor* 72-79; R Colby w Banningham and Tuttington 74-79; R Suffield 74-79; RD Tunstead 76-79; rtd 79. *St Nicholas's Lodge, 25 Bishopton Lane, Ripon, N Yorkshire HG4 2QN* Ripon (0765) 600413

WEATHERLEY, Miss Mary Kathleen. b 36. SRN57 SCM59 MTD72. SW Minl Tr Course 78. **dss** 82 **d** 87. Littleham w Exmouth *Ex* 82-84; Heavitree w Ex St Paul 85-87; Hon Par Dn 87-88; Chapl Asst R Devon and Ex Hosp from 85; Lic to Offic *Ex* from 88. *Flat 5, 36 Douglas Avenue, Exmouth, Devon EX8 2HB* Exmouth (0395) 265528

WEAVER, Prof Arthur Kenneth. b 17. MRAeS Trin Coll Cam MA. Wycliffe Hall Ox 81 Ox NSM Course 81. **d** 81 **p** 82. NSM Ashbury, Compton Beauchamp and Longcot w Fernham *Ox* from 81. *White Lodge, Longcot, Faringdon, Oxon SN7 7SS* Swindon (0793) 782364

WEAVER, Brian John. b 34. Oak Hill Th Coll 82. **d** 84 **p** 85. C Nailsea H Trin *B & W* 84-88; R Nettlebed w Bix and Highmore *Ox* from 88. *The Rectory, Nettlebed, Henley-on-Thames, Oxon RG9 5DD* Nettlebed (0491) 641575

WEAVER, David Anthony. b 43. Hatf Coll Dur BSc65. Lich Th Coll 68. **d** 71 **p** 72. C Walsall Wood *Lich* 71-75; C Much Wenlock w Bourton *Heref* 75-76; Canada 76-79 and 82; V Mow Cop *Lich* 79-82; P-in-c Burntwood from 82; Chapl St Matt Hosp Burntwood from 83. *The Vicarage, Church Road, Burntwood, Walsall WS7 9EA* Burntwood (0543) 675014

WEAVER, George Edward. b 1900. **d** 53 **p** 54. R Drayton Bassett *Lich* 64-71; P-in-c Canwell CD 64-71; rtd 71. *26 Priory Road, Stourbridge, W Midlands DY8 2HG* Stourbridge (0384) 6888

WEAVER, Ven John. b 28. Ex Coll Ox BA51 MA55. St Steph Ho Ox 52. **d** 55 **p** 56. C Ex St Dav *Ex* 55-58; S Africa from 58; Adn Midl from 84. *PO Box 21, Himeville, 4585 South Africa* Himeville (33722) 13

WEAVER, Michael Howard. b 39. Chich Th Coll 63. **d** 66 **p** 67. C Kidderminster St Jo *Worc* 66-69; Br Honduras 69-71; TV Droitwich *Worc* 71-76; V Arundel w Tortington and S Stoke *Chich* from 76; Sub-Chapl HM Pris Ford from 77; P-in-c Clymping 84-87; RD Arundel and Bognor from 88. *The Vicarage, 26 Maltravers Street, Arundel, W Sussex BN18 9BU* Arundel (0903) 882573

WEAVER, Raymond Alexander. Bris Univ BA. Sarum Th Coll. **d** 86 **p** 87. NSM Weymouth H Trin *Sarum* from 86. *1 Fairclose, Weymouth, Dorset DT4 0DF* Weymouth (0305) 783681

WEAVER, Canon Thomas James. b 04. **d** 53 **p** 54. V Liv Ch Ch Kensington *Liv* 60-74; RD Toxteth 72-77; P-in-c Edge Hill St Cypr 74-75; V Toxteth St Cypr w Ch Ch 75-77; rtd 77. *24 Wirral View, Connah's Quay, Deeside, Clwyd CH5 4TE* Deeside (0244) 818564

WEAVER, William. b 40. Man Univ BA63 BD65. **d** 74 **p** 75. Lect Leeds Univ from 74; Hon C Clifford *York* 82-86. *Stepping Stones, 2 Nidd View, Cattal, York YO5 8DZ* Harrogate (0423) 358512

WEBB, Canon Albert. b 22. AKC49. **d** 50 **p** 51. V Evesham *Worc* 66-87; RD Evesham 73-79; Hon Can Worc Cathl from 75; rtd 87. *2 Dolphin Close, Worcester WR2 6BG* Worcester (0905) 422230

WEBB, Andrew David. b 60. St Chad's Coll Dur BA81. Coll of Resurr Mirfield 82. **d** 84 **p** 85. C Hemsworth *Wakef* 84-87; C Leytonstone H Trin Harrow Green *Chelmsf* 87-89; OSB 89-90; C Willesden Green St Andr and St Fran of Assisi *Lon* from 90. *150 Ellesmere Road, London NW10 1JT* 081-452 4118

WEBB, Anthony John. b 24. Sarum & Wells Th Coll 79. **d** 81 **p** 82. C Yeovil *B & W* 81-84; P-in-c Cossington 84-87; P-in-c Woolavington 84-87; P-in-c Bawdrip 87; V Woolavington w Cossington and Bawdrip 87-91; rtd 91. *4 Brue Crescent, Burnham-on-Sea, Somerset TA8 1LR* Burnham-on-Sea (0278) 787483

WEBB, Arthur Robert. b 33. FRSA LCP67 Lanc Univ MA82. Wells Th Coll 69. **d** 70 **p** 70. C W Drayton *Lon* 70-72; Hd Master St Jas Cathl Sch Bury St Edmunds 72-86; Min Can St E Cathl *St E* 72-87; Succ St E Cathl 81-87; P-in-c Seend and Bulkington *Sarum* 87-88; V from 88. *The Vicarage, Seend, Melksham, Wilts SN12 6LR* Devizes (0380) 828615

WEBB, Cyril George. b 19. Roch Th Coll 64. **d** 66 **p** 67. C Bournemouth St Andr *Win* 66-71; V Micheldever 71-72; V Micheldever and E Stratton, Woodmancote etc 72-79; V Bubwith w Ellerton and Aughton *York* 79-83; I Tomregan w Drumlane *K, E & A* 83-86; rtd 86. *62 Columbia Avenue, Whitstable, Kent CT5 4EH* Whitstable (0227) 264687

WEBB, David Basil. b 30. Ch Coll Cam BA54 MA58. Ripon Hall Ox 54. **d** 55 **p** 56. C Wimbledon *S'wark* 55-57; Chapl Em Coll Cam 57-60; V Langley Mill *Derby* 60-64; R Farnborough *Roch* 64-73; R Dunstable *St Alb* 73-78; TR 78-84; RD Dunstable 81-84; TR Bemerton *Sarum* 84-90; V Haslingden w Grane and Stonefold *Blackb* from 90. *St James's Vicarage, Church Lane, Haslingden, Rossendale, Lancs BB4 5QZ* Rossendale (0706) 215533

WEBB, David William. b 30. MRINA Kent Univ DipTh84. Cant Sch of Min 86. **d** 89 **p** 90. NSM Sittingbourne St Mary *Cant* from 89; NSM Iwade from 89. *5 Windermere Grove, Sittingbourne, Kent ME10 1UU* Sittingbourne (0795) 424502

WEBB, Mrs Gillian Anne. b 49. Whitelands Coll Lon CertEd71. St Alb Minl Tr Scheme 83. **dss** 86 **d** 87. Kempston Transfiguration *St Alb* 86-87; Hon Par Dn from 87. *2 Hillson Close, Marston Moreteyne, Bedford MK43 0QN* Bedford (0234) 767256

WEBB, Gregory John. b 55. Man Univ LLB77. Oak Hill Th Coll 89. **d** 91. C Bury St Edmunds St Geo *St E* from 91. *165 Tollgate Lane, Bury St Edmunds, Suffolk IP32 6DF* Bury St Edmunds (0284) 768970

WEBB, Harold William. b 37. Dur Univ BA59. St Steph Ho Ox 59. **d** 61 **p** 62. C Plumstead St Nic *S'wark* 61-65; S Africa 65-70; Sacr Wakef Cathl *Wakef* 71-72; P-in-c Lane End *Ox* 72-76; V Lane End w Cadmore End 76-84; Chapl to the Deaf *Guildf* from 84. *1 Lindfield Gardens, London Road, Guildford, Surrey GU1 1TP* Guildford (0483) 573228

WEBB, John Christopher Richard. b 38. ACA63 FCA73. Wycliffe Hall Ox 64. **d** 67 **p** 68. C Hendon St Paul Mill Hill *Lon* 67-71; CF from 71. *c/o MOD (Army), Bagshot Park, Bagshot, Surrey GU19 5PL* Bagshot (0276) 71717

WEBB, Marjorie Valentine (Sister Elizabeth). b 31. Bedf Coll Lon. **d** 88. CSF from 55; Rev Mother 71-86; Lic to Bp Heref 86-90; Perm to Offic *Lon* 88-90; Lic to Offic *Lich* 90-91. *Compton Durville Manor House, South Petherton, Somerset TA13 5ES*

WEBB, Michael David. b 59. K Coll Lon BD82 PGCE83. Ripon Coll Cuddesdon 88. **d** 90 **p** 91. C Broughton Astley *Leic* from 90. *1 Aland Gardens, Broughton Astley, Leicester LE9 6NE* Sutton Elms (0455) 283081

WEBB, Michael John. b 49. Linc Coll Ox BA70 MA74. Linc Th Coll 70. **d** 72 **p** 73. C Tring *St Alb* 72-75; C Chipping Barnet 75-78; C Chipping Barnet w Arkley 78-82; TV Cullercoats St Geo *Newc* 82-89; V Newc H Cross from 89. *Holy Cross Vicarage, 16 Whittington Grove, Newcastle upon Tyne NE5 2QP* 091-274 4476

WEBB, Nicholas David Jon. b 38. Dur Univ BA61. Coll of Resurr Mirfield 61. **d** 63 **p** 64. C Royston *Wakef* 63-66; Prec Wakef Cathl 66-70; R Thornhill from 70; V Lower Whitley from 73. *The Rectory, 51 Frank Lane, Dewsbury, W Yorkshire WF12 0JW* Dewsbury (0924) 465064

WEBB, Pauline (Nikola). b 49. W Midl Minl Tr Course. **d** 87. C Walsgrave on Sowe *Cov* 87-91; TM Grantham *Linc* from 91; Ind Chapl from 91. *St John's Vicarage, 4 Station Road, Grantham, Lincs NG31 6JY* Grantham (0476) 592432

WEBB, Peter Henry. b 55. Nottm Univ BA77. St Steph Ho Ox 77. **d** 79 **p** 80. C Lancing w Coombes *Chich* 79-82; C Hydneye CD 82-84; C-in-c 84-86; Chapl Sunderland Distr Hosps from 86. *The Chaplain's Office, Sunderland District General Hospital, Kayll Road, Sunderland SR4 7TP* 091-565 6256

WEBB, Richard Frederick. b 42. Cant Sch of Min. **d** 84 **p** 85. C Ipswich St Clem w H Trin *St E* 84-87; R Rougham and Beyton w Hessett 87-91; R Rougham, Beyton w Hessett and Rushbrooke from 91. *The Rectory, Rougham, Bury St Edmunds, Suffolk IP30 9JJ* Beyton (0359) 70250

WEBB, Richard Lacey. b 09. ALCD30. **d** 32 **p** 33. V Lakenham St Alb *Nor* 66-77; rtd 77; Hon C Nor St Andr *Nor* 83-86; Perm to Offic from 86. *32 Ipswich Road, Eaton Rise, Norwich NR4 6QR* Norwich (0603) 51348

WEBB, Rowland James. b 33. Roch Th Coll 64. **d** 67 **p** 68. C Tavistock and Gulworthy *Ex* 67-70; Chapl RN 70-86; R Mundford w Lynford *Nor* 86-90; V Burnham *Chelmsf* from 90. *The Vicarage, 2A Church Road, Burnham-on-Crouch, Essex CM0 8DA* Maldon (0621) 782071

WEBB, William John. b 43. Cuddesdon Coll 68. **d** 71 **p** 72. C Weston Favell *Pet* 71-73; C Newport w Longford *Lich* 74-77; C Baswich (or Berkswich) 77-79; P-in-c Stonnall 79-83; P-in-c Wall 79-83; V Fauls from 83; V Prees from 83. *The Vicarage, Prees, Whitchurch, Shropshire SY13 2EE* Whitchurch (0948) 840243

WEBBER, David Price. b 39. Chich Th Coll 90. **d** 91. NSM Shoreham Beach *Chich* from 91. *69 Grinstead Lane, Lancing, W Sussex BN15 9DT* Lancing (0903) 753950

WEBBER, Eric Michael. b 16. AKC43 ATh(SA)55 Lon Univ BD54 Univ of Tasmania MEd77 MHums85. **d** 43 **p** 44. C Clapham H Spirit *S'wark* 43-47; C Wimbledon 47-50; S Africa 50-58; Australia from 58; Sen Lect Relig Studies Tasmanian Coll Adv Educn 71-81. *1 Hean Street, Hobart, Tasmania, Australia 7004* Hobart (2) 236413

WEBBER, Harry Gill. b 09. AKC41. **d** 41 **p** 42. Chapl St Jo Hosp Linc 69-74; rtd 74; Perm to Offic *Linc* from 77. *124 Highgate, Cleethorpes, S Humberside DN35 8NU* Cleethorpes (0472) 693794

WEBBER, Canon Lionel Frank. b 35. Kelham Th Coll Llan St Mich. **d** 60 **p** 61. C Bolton Sav *Man* 60-63; C Aberavon *Llan* 63-65; R Salford Stowell Memorial *Man* 65-69; V Aberavon H Trin *Llan* 69-74; TV Stantonbury *Ox* 74-76; TR Basildon St Martin w H Cross and Laindon *Chelmsf* 76-79; P-in-c Nevendon 77-79; RD Basildon 79-89; TR Basildon, St Martin of Tours w Nevendon from 79; Hon Can Chelmsf Cathl from 84. *The Rectory, Pagel Mead, Basildon, Essex SS14 1DX* Basildon (0268) 22455

WEBBER, Michael Champneys Wilfred. b 48. Man Univ BA71 MA(Theol)78. Cuddesdon Coll 73. **d** 75 **p** 76. C Caterham *S'wark* 75-79; P-in-c Kidbrooke St Jas 79-84; TV 84-85; V Earls Barton *Pet* from 87. *The Vicarage, 7 High Street, Earls Barton, Northampton NN6 0JG* Northampton (0604) 810447

WEBBER, Peter Cecil. b 21. Lon Coll of Div ALCD55 LTh. **d** 55 **p** 56. V Foord St Jo *Cant* 67-86; RD Elham 80-83; rtd 86; Perm to Offic *Chich* from 86. *15 Goodwin Close, Hailsham, E Sussex BN27 3DE* Hailsham (0323) 848668

WEBBER, Raymond John. b 40. Lon Univ DipTh65. Linc Th Coll 84. **d** 85 **p** 86. C Helston *Truro* 85; C Helston and Wendron 85-90; TV from 90. *The Vicarage, Wendron, Helston, Cornwall TR13 0EA* Helston (0326) 572169

WEBER, Douglas John Craig. b 20. Ex Coll Ox BA46 MA46. Sarum Th Coll. **d** 49 **p** 50. V Hook w Warsash *Portsm* 55-88; rtd 88; Perm to Offic *Portsm* from 88. *1 Trevose Way, Titchfield, Fareham, Hants PO14 4NG* Locks Heath (0489) 583065

WEBLEY, Robin Bowen. b 32. Univ of Wales (Cardiff) DPS. St Mich Coll Llan 87. **d** 89 **p** 90. C St D Cathl *St D* 89-91; Min Can St D Cathl 89-91; R Castlemartin w Warren and Angle etc from 91. *The Rectory, Angle, Pembroke, Dyfed SA71 5AN* Angle (0646) 641368

WEBSTER, Very Rev Alan Brunskill. b 18. KCVO88. Qu Coll Ox BA39 MA43 BD54. Lon Univ Hon DD. Westcott Ho Cam 41. **d** 42 **p** 43. Warden Linc Th Coll 59-70; Can and Preb Linc Cathl *Linc* 64-70; Dean Nor 70-78; Dean St Paul's *Lon* 78-87; rtd 88. *20 Beechbank, Norwich NR2 2AL* Norwich (0603) 55833

WEBSTER, David Edward. b 39. K Coll Lon 60 Edin Th Coll 62. **d** 64 **p** 65. C Maghull *Liv* 64-69; R Wavertree St Mary 69-76; TV Greystoke, Matterdale and Mungrisdale *Carl* 76-81; R Lowton St Luke *Liv* 81-88; Chapl Nat Agric Cen from 88; R Stoneleigh w Ashow and Baginton *Cov* from 88. *The Rectory, Church Lane, Stoneleigh, Coventry CV8 3DN* Coventry (0203) 415506

WEBSTER, David Robert. b 32. Selw Coll Cam BA56 MA60. Linc Th Coll 56. **d** 58 **p** 59. C Billingham St Cuth *Dur* 58-61; C Doncaster St Geo *Sheff* 61-64; Chapl Doncaster R Infirmary 61-64; V Lumley *Dur* 64-76; V Belmont from 76. *The Vicarage, Broomside Lane, Durham DH1 2QW* 091-386 1545

WEBSTER, Dennis Eric. b 39. Fitzw Ho Cam BA60 MA64 Linacre Coll Ox MA70 Lon Univ CertEd61. Wycliffe Hall Ox 62. **d** 65 **p** 66. C Herne Bay Ch Ch *Cant* 65-68; C Tulse Hill H Trin *S'wark* 68-69; Kenya 70-75; Chapl Pierrepont Sch Frensham from 75. *Sylvan Cottage, Longdown Road, Lower Bourne, Farnham, Surrey GU10 3JL* Farnham (0252) 713919

WEBSTER, Derek Herbert. b 34. FRSA82 Hull Univ BA55 Lon Univ BD55 Leic Univ MEd68 PhD73. Lambeth STh67 Linc Th Coll 76. **d** 76 **p** 77. Lect Hull Univ from 72; Hon C Cleethorpes *Linc* from 76. *60 Queen's Parade, Cleethorpes, S Humberside DN35 0DG* Cleethorpes (0472) 693786

WEBSTER, Geoffrey William. b 36. St Alb Minl Tr Scheme 77. **d** 80 **p** 81. NSM Harlington *St Alb* 80-82; C Belmont *Dur* 82-86; R Gateshead Fell from 86. *The Rectory, 45 Shotley Gardens, Low Fell, Gateshead, Tyne & Wear NE9 5DP* 091-487 3537

WEBSTER, Glyn Hamilton. b 51. SRN73. St Jo Coll Dur 74. **d** 77 **p** 78. C Huntington *York* 77-81; Sen Chapl York Distr Hosp from 80; V York St Luke from 81. *St Luke's Vicarage, 79 Burton Stone Lane, York YO3 6BZ* York (0904) 54232

WEBSTER, James George William. b 46. Qu Coll Birm 81. **d** 83 **p** 84. C Pennsett *Lich* 83-85; C Cannock 85-88; TV from 88. *St Aidan's Vicarage, Albert Street, West Chadsmoor, Cannock, Staffs WS11 2JD* Cannock (0543) 505674

WEBSTER, Prof John Bainbridge. b 55. Clare Coll Cam MA81 PhD82. **d** 83 **p** 84. Chapl and Dep Sen Tutor St Jo Coll Dur 83-86; Hon C Bearpark *Dur* 83-86; Canada from 86; Assoc Prof Systematic Th Wycliffe Coll Tor Univ from 86. *Wycliffe College, 5 Hoskin Avenue, Toronto, Ontario, Canada, M5S 1H7* Toronto (416) 979-2870

WEBSTER, John Maurice. b 34. Sarum & Wells Th Coll 73. **d** 76 **p** 77. Hon C Hythe *Win* from 76. *Avery Lodge, Long Lane, Marchwood, Southampton SO4 4WR* Southampton (0703) 862388

WEBSTER, Martin Duncan. b 52. Nottm Univ BSc74 DipTh76. Linc Th Coll 75. **d** 78 **p** 79. C Thundersley *Chelmsf* 78-81; C Canvey Is 81-82; TV 82-86; V Nazeing from 86; RD Harlow from 88. *The Vicarage, Betts Lane, Nazeing, Waltham Abbey, Essex EN9 2DB* Nazeing (099289) 3167

WEBSTER, Martyn Richard. b 54. St Chad's Coll Dur BA76. St Steph Ho Ox 76. **d** 78 **p** 79. C Worc St Martin w St Pet *Worc* 78-81; C Swindon New Town *Bris* 81-84; V Walham Green St Jo w St Jas *Lon* from 84. *The Vicarage, 40 Racton Road, London SW6 1LP* 071-385 3676

WEBSTER, Patricia Eileen. b 34. St Gabr Coll Lon TCert54. Gilmore Ho 56. **d** 87. Par Dn Belmont *Dur* from 87. *The Vicarage, Broomside Lane, Durham DH1 2QW* 091-386 1545

WEBSTER, Peter. b 26. FASI. Cranmer Hall Dur 68. **d** 70 **p** 71. C Tickhill w Stainton *Sheff* 70-72; C Conisbrough 72-73; V Walkley 73-77; V Rawcliffe 77-84; V Barrow-on-Humber *Linc* 84; P-in-c Goxhill 84; V Barrow and Goxhill from 84. *The Vicarage, Thornton Street, Barrow-on-Humber, S Humberside DN19 7DG* Barrow-on-Humber (0469) 30357

WEBSTER, Sarah Vernoy (Sally). b 38. Univ of Georgia BSc61. S'wark Ord Course 87. **d** 90. NSM Primrose Hill St Mary w Avenue Road St Paul *Lon* from 90. *15 Elsworthy Rise, London NW3 3QY* 071-722 5756

WEBSTER, Mrs Sheila Mary. b 22. Bedf Coll Lon CSocStuds43. Gilmore Ho 69. **dss** 81 **d** 87. Patcham *Chich* 77-83; Hove All SS 84-87; Hon Par Dn 87-90; rtd 90. *108 Surrenden Road, Brighton BN1 6WB* Brighton (0273) 561222

WEBSTER-SMITH, Preb Alfred William. b 10. St Chad's Coll Dur BA32 DipTh33 MA35. **d** 33 **p** 34. R Pontesbury I and II *Heref* 66-76; Preb Heref Cathl 73-81; Perm to Offic 76-80; rtd 76; Perm to Offic *S'wark* from 80.

6 Frederick Gardens, Cheam, Surrey SM1 2HX 081-641
0226

WEDDERBURN, John Alroy. b 07. St Aid Birkenhead
46. **d** 47 **p** 48. V Hornby w Claughton *Blackb* 54-82; rtd
72. *Flat 3, Manormead, Tilford Road, Hindhead, Surrey
GU26 6RA* Hindhead (0428) 605428

WEDDERSPOON, Very Rev Alexander Gillan. b 31. Jes
Coll Ox BA54 MA61 Lon Univ BD62. Cuddesdon Coll.
d 61 **p** 62. C Kingston All SS *S'wark* 61-63; Lect RE
Lon Univ 63-66; Educn Adv C of E Sch Coun 66-70;
Can Res Win Cathl *Win* 70-87; Vice-Dean 80-87;
Treas 80-85; Dean Guildf from 87. *1 Cathedral Close,
Guildford, Surrey GU2 5TL* Guildford (0483) 60328 or
65287

WEDGBURY, John William. b 53. RMCS BSc78. St Jo
Coll Nottm 84. **d** 87 **p** 88. C Foord St Jo *Cant* 87-91; V
Mangotsfield *Bris* from 91. *The Vicarage, Rodway Hill,
Mangotsfield, Bristol BS17 3JA* Bristol (0272) 560510

WEDGWOOD, Preb Charles Mervyn. b 16. Selw Coll
Cam BA38 MA46. Wycliffe Hall Ox 38. **d** 40 **p** 41. Preb
Wells Cathl *B & W* from 63; V Combe Down w Monkton
Combe 73-81; RD Bath 76-81; V Combe Down w
Monkton Combe and S Stoke 81; rtd 81; Perm to Offic
Ex from 86. *10 Earlswood Drive, Plymouth PL6 8SF*
Plymouth (0752) 793425

WEDGWOOD, George Peter. b 26. St Jo Coll Dur
BA51 DipTh52 MA56. **d** 52 **p** 53. Prin Lect St Kath Coll
69-83; Lic to Offic *Bradf* 83-86; Hd of Div Liv Coll of
HE 84-86; P-in-c Kirkoswald, Renwick and Ainstable
Carl 86-88; rtd 88; Perm to Offic *Carl* from 88.
Brunt House, Kirkoswald, Penrith, Cumbria CA10 1EX
Lazonby (076883) 791

WEDGWOOD, Keith. b 20. Hertf Coll Ox BA42 MA46.
Wycliffe Hall Ox 42. **d** 43 **p** 44. Canada 68-72; P-in-c
Osmington w Poxwell *Sarum* 72-77; TV The Iwernes
and Sutton Waldron 77-78; P-in-c 78-81; V The
Iwernes, Sutton Waldron and Fontmell Magna 81-85;
rtd 85. *18 Walton Road, Bournemouth BH10 4BJ*
Bournemouth (0202) 532116

WEDGWOOD, Peter John. b 20. Worc Ord Coll. **d** 66
p 67. C Claines St Jo *Worc* 66-90; Chapl Alice Ottley
Sch Upper Tything from 73; rtd 90. *28 Cornmeadow
Lane, Worcester WR3 7NY* Worcester (0905) 53730

WEDGWOOD GREENHOW, Stephen John Francis. b 57.
Man Univ BA82. Edin Th Coll MTh84. **d** 84 **p** 85. C
Wythenshawe Wm Temple Ch *Man* 84-87; USA from 87.
*1802 Avondale Avenue, Sacramento, California 95825,
USA*

WEEDEN, Simon Andrew. b 55. York Univ BA79.
Wycliffe Hall Ox 88. **d** 90 **p** 91. C Gt Chesham *Ox* from
90. *31 Chapman's Crescent, Chesham, Bucks HP5 2QT*
Chesham (0494) 786686

WEEDING, Paul Stephen. b 62. Leic Poly BSc. Ripon
Coll Cuddesdon. **d** 90 **p** 91. C Llanishen and Lisvane
Llan from 90. *25 Mountbatten Close, Cardiff CF2 5QG*
Cardiff (0222) 757190

✠**WEEKES, Rt Rev Ambrose Walter Marcus.** b 19. CB70.
AKC41 Linc Th Coll 41. **d** 42 **p** 43 **c** 77. C New Brompton
St Luke *Roch* 42-44; Chapl RNVR 44-46; Chapl RN
46-69; Chapl of the Fleet and Adn for the RN 69-72;
QHC from 69; Can Gib Cathl *Eur* 71-73; Chapl Tangier
72-73; Dean Gib 73-77; Aux Bp Eur 77-80 and from 89;
Suff Bp Eur 80-86; Dean Brussels 81-86; rtd 86; Asst
Bp Roch 86-88; Chapl Montreux w Gstaad *Eur* from 89.
92 Ave de Chillon, 1820 Territet, Montreux, Switzerland
Montreux (21) 963-4354

WEEKES, Very Rev Cecil William. b 31. CITC. **d** 78 **p** 79.
NSM Glenageary *D & G* 78-80; Bp's V Kilkenny Cathl
C & O 80-83; I Carlow w Urglin and Staplestown 83-90;
Preb Leighlin Cathl from 88; Preb Ossory Cathl from
88; I Lismore w Cappoquin, Kilwatermoy, Dungarvan
etc from 90; Dean Lismore from 90; Chan Cashel Cathl
from 90; Prec Waterford Cathl from 90. *The Deanery,
The Mall, Lismore, Co Waterford, Irish Republic*
Lismore (58) 54137

WEEKES, David John. b 34. Magd Coll Cam BA59 MA68
Lon Univ CertEd68 Aber Univ MTh79. Clifton Th Coll
62. **d** 64 **p** 65. C Cheadle *Ches* 64-68; Uganda 69-73;
Perm to Offic *St And* 73-74; Chapl Fettes Coll Edin
from 74; Lic to Offic *Edin* from 74. *Arniston House,
Fettes College, Edinburgh EH4 1QU* 031-332 6301

WEEKS, John Huguenin. b 28. TCD BA53 MA61. Sarum
Th Coll 61. **d** 63 **p** 64. C Hillingdon St Jo *Lon* 63-69; V
Brentford St Faith 69-74; V Yiewsley 74-84; AD
Hillingdon 81-85; R Hanwell St Mary 84-91; P-in-c
Hanwell St Chris 87-91; R Hanwell St Mary w St Chris
from 91. *The Rectory, 91 Church Road, London W7
3BP* 081-567 6185

WEETMAN, John Charles. b 66. Qu Coll Ox BA87. Trin
Coll Bris BA91. **d** 91. C Hull Newland St Jo *York* from
91. *St Faith's House, Dunswell Lane, Hull HU6 0AS*
Hull (0482) 854526

WEIGALL, Anthony Fitzroy. b 12. Ch Ch Ox BA34 MA38.
Westcott Ho Cam 34. **d** 36 **p** 37. R Barming *Roch* 56-77;
rtd 78. *College of St Barnabas, Blackberry Lane,
Lingfield, Surrey RH7 6NJ* Dormans Park (034287) 260

WEIL, Canon Ernest James. b 13. Sarum Th Coll 50. **d** 53
p 53. V Bawtry w Austerfield *S'well* 68-74; V Misson
68-74; RD Bawtry 68-74; Hon Can S'well Minster 73-78;
R Epperstone 74-78; P-in-c Oxton 74-78; R Gonalston
75-78; rtd 78; Perm to Offic *S'well* from 79. *48 Springfield
Road, Southwell, Notts NG25 0BT* Southwell (0636)
814325

WEIR, Graham Francis. b 52. GSM LASI. Nor Ord
Course 88. **d** 91. NSM High Crompton *Man* from 91.
*49 Cliff Hill Road, Crompton, Shaw, Oldham, Lancs
OL2 8DE* Shaw (0706) 846319

WEIR, John Michael Vavasour. b 48. K Coll Lon
BD72 AKC72. **d** 73 **p** 74. C Hatf Hyde St Mary *St Alb*
73-76; C Watford St Mich 76-79; Asst Chapl Oslo St
Edm *Eur* 80-81; V Bethnal Green St Pet w St Thos *Lon*
from 81; Chapl Qu Eliz Hosp for Children Lon from 81.
St Peter's Vicarage, St Peter's Close, London E2 7AE
071-739 2717

WEIR, John William Moon. b 36. St Luke's Coll Ex
CertEd69 Ex Univ BEd76. SW Minl Tr Course 82. **d** 85
p 86. NSM Meavy, Sheepstor and Walkhampton *Ex*
85-87; NSM Yelverton, Meavy, Sheepstor and
Walkhampton from 87; Hd Master Princetown Primary
Sch from 87; Sub-Chapl HM Pris Dartmoor from 87.
Goblin's Green, Dousland, Yelverton, Devon PL20 6ND
Yelverton (0822) 852671

WEIR, William Daniel Niall. b 57. BA. Ripon Coll
Cuddesdon. **d** 83 **p** 84. C Chelsea St Luke *Lon* 83-87;
PV Westmr Abbey from 85; C Poplar *Lon* 87-88; TV
from 88. *St Michael's Vicarage, St Leonard's Road,
London E14 6PW* 071-987 1795

WELANDER, Canon David Charles St Vincent. b 25.
FSA. Lon Coll of Div BD47 ALCD47. **d** 48 **p** 49. V
Cheltenham Ch Ch *Glouc* 63-75; RD Cheltenham 73-75;
Can Res Glouc Cathl 75-91; rtd 91. *Willow Cottage,
1 Sandpits Lane, Sherston Magna, Malmesbury, Wilts
SN16 0NN* Malmesbury (0666) 840180

WELBOURN, David Anthony. b 41. K Coll Lon
BD63 AKC63 DMS. **d** 64 **p** 65. C Stockton St Chad *Dur*
64-67; C S Westoe 69-74; Ind Chapl 69-80; Ind Chapl
Nor 80-90; Industry and Commerce Officer *Guildf*
from 90. *81 Collingwood Crescent, Guildford, Surrey
GU1 2NU* Guildford (0483) 570600

WELBY, Peter Edlin Brown. b 34. Open Univ BA75. St
Jo Coll Dur 75. **d** 77 **p** 78. C Auckland St Andr and St
Anne *Dur* 77-79; C S Westoe 79-81; V Tudhoe from
81. *19 York Villas, Tudhoe Village, Spennymoor, Co
Durham DL16 6LP* Spennymoor (0388) 818418

WELBY, Richard Alexander Lyon. b 58. St Jo Coll Nottm
BTh81 LTh Ridley Hall Cam 83. **d** 84 **p** 85. C Stoke
Bishop *Bris* 84-88; V Bowling St Steph *Bradf* from
88. *St Stephen's Vicarage, 48 Newton Street, Bradford,
W Yorkshire BD5 7BH* Bradford (0274) 720784

WELCH, Miss Alice. b 41. Trin Coll Bris 77. dss 85 **d** 87.
Chesterfield H Trin *Derby* 85-87; Par Dn 87-89; Chapl
to the Deaf from 89; Dn-in-c Rowsley from 89.
The Vicarage, Rowsley, Matlock, Derbyshire DE4 2EA
Matlock (0629) 733296

WELCH, Derek. b 27. Keble Coll Ox BA51 MA57. Coll
of Resurr Mirfield 51. **d** 53 **p** 54. C Middlesb St Jo the
Ev *York* 53-58; C Oswaldtwistle Immanuel *Blackb* 58-59;
V Accrington St Andr 59-65; V Salesbury 66-72; V
Heyhouses on Sea from 73. *The Vicarage, Church Road,
St Annes, Lytham St Annes, Lancs FY8 3BB* St Annes
(0253) 722725

WELCH, Francis Hughan. b 16. Lon Univ BD67. S'wark
Ord Course 67. **d** 70 **p** 71. C St Alb St Steph *St Alb*
71-75; P-in-c 75-80; Perm to Offic *Lon* from 80; Chapl
St Alb City Hosp 80-90; rtd 81; Perm to Offic *St Alb*
80-81 and from 90; Hon C St Alb St Pet 81-89; Hon C
St Alb St Mich 89-90. *Bryntelor, Sanau, Llandysul,
Dyfed SA44 6QN* Aberporth (0239) 654573

WELCH, Frederick George. b 23. St Cath Coll Cam
BA44 MA48 Lon Univ BD59. St Aug Coll Cant 63.
d 74 **p** 75. Kenya 74-87; rtd 87; Asst Chapl Tenerife *Eur*
87-88; Hon C Tamworth *Lich* 88-89; Hon C Hordle
Win from 89. *Church Cottage, Sway Road, Tiptoe,
Lymington, Hants SO41 6FR* New Milton (0425)
616670

WELCH, Gordon Joseph. b 47. Man Univ BSc68 PhD72.
N Ord Course 84. **d** 87 **p** 88. NSM Upton Ascension

Ches from 87. *6 St James Avenue, Chester CH2 1NA* Chester (0244) 382196

WELCH, Canon Grant Keith. b 40. AKC63. **d** 64 **p** 65. C Nottm St Mary *S'well* 64-68; V Cinderhill 68-73; Master St Jo Hosp Weston Favell 73-88; R Weston Favell *Pet* 73-88; Can Pet Cathl 83-88; P-in-c Gt Houghton 84-85; V Wymondham *Nor* 88; C Loughton St Jo *Chelmsf* from 89. *St Gabriel's House, Grosvenor Drive, Loughton, Essex IG10 2LG* 081-508 5790

WELCH, Harold Gerald. b 16. St Cath Soc Ox BA48 MA53. Wycliffe Hall Ox 48. **d** 50 **p** 51. V Austrey *Birm* 66-83; V Warton 66-83; rtd 83; Perm to Offic *Birm* and *Linc* from 88. *2 Clifford Close, Tamworth, Staffs B77 2DD* Tamworth (0827) 53678

WELCH, Ivor Thomas Ronald. b 29. Dur Univ BA53 DipEd54. Trin Coll Bris 79. **d** 81 **p** 81. C Desborough *Pet* 81-84; P-in-c Burlingham St Edmund w Lingwood *Nor* 84-88; P-in-c Buckenham w Hassingham and Strumpshaw 86-88; R Burlingham St Edmund w Lingwood, Strumpshaw etc from 88. *The Rectory, Barn Close, Lingwood, Norwich NR13 4TS* Norwich (0603) 713880

WELCH, John Harry. b 52. Oak Hill Th Coll 85. **d** 87 **p** 88. C Parr *Liv* 87-90; V W Derby St Luke from 90. *St Luke's Vicarage, Princess Drive, West Derby, Liverpool L14 8XG* 051-228 6025

WELCH, Michael Robin. b 33. MBE81. St Chad's Coll Dur BSc55. Wells Th Coll 57. **d** 59 **p** 60. C St Shields St Hilda *Dur* 59-63; CF (R of O) 61-88; Warden and Tr Officer Dioc Youth Cen *Newc* 63-68; Soc and Ind Adv *Portsm* from 68; V Portsea All SS 72-85; V Swanmore St Barn from 85; RD Bishops Waltham from 88. *The Vicarage, Swanmore, Southampton SO3 2PA* Bishops Waltham (0489) 892105

WELCH, Paul Baxter. b 47. Lanc Univ BEd74 MA75. St Alb Minl Tr Scheme 80. **d** 83 **p** 84. NSM Heath and Reach St Alb 83-84; Bp's Sch Adv *Win* 84-89; P-in-c Clungunford w Clunbury and Clunton, Bedstone etc *Heref* from 89. *Clungunford Rectory, Craven Arms, Shropshire SY7 0PN* Little Brampton (05887) 342

WELCH, Stephan John. b 50. Hull Univ BA74. Qu Coll Birm DipTh76. **d** 77 **p** 78. C Waltham Cross *St Alb* 77-80; P-in-c Reculver *Cant* 80-86; P-in-c Herne Bay St Bart 82-86; V Reculver and Herne Bay St Bart from 86. *The Vicarage, 29 Burlington Drive, Herne Bay, Kent CT6 6PG* Canterbury (0227) 375154

✠**WELCH, Rt Rev William Neville.** b 06. Keble Coll Ox BA27 MA32. Wycliffe Hall Ox 27. **d** 29 **p** 30 **c** 68. C Kidderminster *Worc* 29-32; C St Alb St Mich *St Alb* 32-34; Miss to Seamen 34-39; V Grays Thurrock *Chelmsf* 39-43; V Gt Ilford St Clem 43-53; RD Barking 46-53; Hon Can Chelmsf Cathl 51-53; V Gt Burstead 53-56; Adn Southend 53-72; Suff Bp Bradwell 68-73; rtd 73; Perm to Offic *Nor* from 73. *112 Earlham Road, Norwich NR2 3HE* Norwich (0603) 618192

WELCHMAN, Richard Neville de Beaufort. b 11. St Pet Hall Ox BA33 DipTh34 MA37. Wycliffe Hall Ox 33. **d** 34 **p** 35. V Pinhoe *Ex* 62-76; rtd 77. *Flat 5, Culver House, Longdown, Exeter EX6 7BD* Exeter (0392) 81392

WELDON, William Ernest. b 41. TCD BA62 MA66. **d** 64 **p** 65. C Belf Trin Coll Miss *Conn* 64-67; C Carnmoney 67-71; Chapl RN from 71. *c/o MOD, Lacon House, Theobald's Road, London WC1X 8RY* 071-430 6847

WELFORD, Alan Traviss. b 14. St Jo Coll Cam BA35 MA39 ScD64. **d** 37 **p** 38. Australia 68-79; rtd 79; Perm to Offic *Win* 87-90. *187A High Street, Aldeburgh, Suffolk IP15 5AL* Felixstowe (0394) 278536

WELHAM, Clive Richard. b 54. **d** 80 **p** 81. C Bellingham St Dunstan *S'wark* 80-84; Chapl Golds Coll Lon from 84. *20 Shardeloes Road, London SE14 6NZ* 081-691 3064 or 692 0211

WELLER, John Beresford. b 15. Lon Univ BD52. Tyndale Hall Bris 39. **d** 42 **p** 43. V Harlow St Mary V *Chelmsf* 60-77; RD Harlow 73-80; V Hatf Broad Oak 77-80; rtd 80; Hon C Duffield *Derby* from 81. *8 Chudleigh Road, Duffield, Derby DE6 4DU* Derby (0332) 842271

WELLER, Canon John Christopher. b 25. St Pet Hall Ox BA49 MA52 Nottm Univ BD57. Qu Coll Birm 50. **d** 51 **p** 52. Zambia 64-71; V W Heath *Birm* 71-81; Warden and Chapl Resthaven Home Stroud 81-84; P-in-c Duddeston 84-85; Zimbabwe 85-90; Can Harare 87-90; rtd 90. *42 Mallard Close, Acocks Green, Birmingham B27 6BN* 021-706 7535

WELLER, Richard Morton. b 33. Selw Coll Cam BA57 MA61. Wells Th Coll 61. **d** 63 **p** 64. C Stockingford *Cov* 63-66; C Pontefract St Giles *Wakef* 66-68; C-in-c Stockton St Jas CD *Dur* 68-74; V E Ardsley *Wakef* 74-83; V Heckmondwike 83-91; V Birstall from 91. *The*

Vicarage, Kings Drive, Birstall, Batley, W Yorkshire WF17 9JJ Batley (0924) 473715

WELLER, Ronald Howden. b 18. Wycliffe Hall Ox. **d** 60 **p** 61. V Broxbourne *St Alb* 63-70; Singapore 70-74; New Zealand from 74; rtd 83. *Address temp unknown*

WELLER, William John France. b 12. MBE58. Ridley Hall Cam 60. **d** 61 **p** 62. C-in-c Hartley Wespall w Stratfield Turgis *Win* 65-74; RD Odiham 69-74; P-in-c Southwick w Boarhunt *Portsm* 75-77; rtd 77; Perm to Offic *Ex* from 77. *10 Kingsley Terrace, Portreath, Redruth, Cornwall TR16 4LX*

WELLING, Anthony Wyndham. b 29. Ely Th Coll 55. **d** 58 **p** 83. C Coppenhall St Paul *Ches* 58-60; Lic to Offic *Ox* 82; Hon C Cookham from 83. *Broadway Barn, High Street, Ripley, Woking, Surrey GU23 6AQ* Guildford (0483) 225384

WELLINGTON, James Frederick. b 51. Leic Univ LLB72 Fitzw Coll Cam BA76. Ridley Hall Cam 74. **d** 77 **p** 78. C Mill Hill Jo Keble Ch *Lon* 77-80; C Wood Green St Mich 80-82; C Wood Green St Mich w Bounds Green St Gabr etc 82-83; V Stocking Farm *Leic* 83-90; V Gt Glen, Stretton Magna and Wistow etc from 90; Warden of Readers from 91. *St Cuthbert's Vicarage, Great Glen, Leicester LE8 0FE* Great Glen (053759) 2238

WELLS, Andrew Stuart. b 48. St Jo Coll Dur BA71. Cranmer Hall Dur DipTh73. **d** 74 **p** 75. C Walmsley *Man* 74-77; C Failsworth H Family 77-79; R Openshaw 79-90; V Hindsford from 90. *St Anne's Vicarage, Powys Street, Atherton, Manchester M29 9AR* Atherton (0942) 883902

WELLS, Anthony Martin Giffard. b 42. St Jo Coll Nottm 72. **d** 74 **p** 75. C Orpington Ch Ch *Roch* 74-78; P-in-c Odell *St Alb* 78-82; R 82-86; P-in-c Pavenham 78-82; V 82-86; RD Sharnbrook 81-86; R Angmering *Chich* from 86. *The Rectory, Angmering, Littlehampton, W Sussex BN16 4JU* Rustington (0903) 4979

WELLS, Antony Ernest. b 36. Oak Hill Th Coll 58. **d** 61 **p** 62. C Bethnal Green St Jas Less *Lon* 61-64; SAMS 64-69; Paraguay 64-69; V Kirkdale St Athanasius *Liv* 69-73; SAMS 73-75; Argentina 73-75; V Warfield *Ox* 75-81; V Fairfield *Liv* 81-83; C Rainhill 83-85; TV Cheltenham St Mark *Glouc* 85-89; P-in-c Forest of Dean Ch Ch w English Bicknor from 89. *Christ Church Vicarage, Ross Road, Coleford, Glos GL16 7NS* Dean (0594) 32334

WELLS, Bryan Arthur. b 47. Golds Coll Lon BMus72 DipEd83 MA85. Coll of Resurr Mirfield 77. **d** 79 **p** 82. C Leigh-on-Sea St Marg *Chelmsf* 79-80; Hon C Limpsfield and Titsey *S'wark* 81-85; C Weymouth St Paul *Sarum* 86-89; TV Selsdon St Jo w St Fran *S'wark* from 89. *St Francis's Vicarage, Tedder Road, Selsdon, Croydon CR2 8AH* 081-657 7864

WELLS, Miss Cecilia Isabel. b 24. Bedf Coll Lon BA45. St Mich Ho Ox 56. **dss** 62 **d** 87. Ches le Street *Dur* 74-84; rtd 84; NSM Nantwich *Ches* from 84. *20 Hawthorn Avenue, Nantwich, Cheshire CW5 6HZ* Nantwich (0270) 627258

WELLS, Canon Charles. b 07. Ch Coll Cam BA28 MA32. Westcott Ho Cam 28. **d** 30 **p** 31. V Win St Bart *Win* 55-73; Hon Can Win Cathl 70-73; rtd 73; Perm to Offic *Win* from 73; *Portsm* from 83. *7 Park Court, Park Road, Winchester, Hants SO23 7BE* Winchester (0962) 69015

WELLS, Charles Francis. b 39. Oak Hill Th Coll DipHE. **d** 85 **p** 86. C Southend St Sav Westcliff *Chelmsf* 85-89; P-in-c E and W Horndon w Lt Warley from 89. *The Rectory, Thorndon Avenue, Brentwood, Essex CM13 3TR* Brentwood (0277) 811223

WELLS, Christopher Paul. b 49. St Mich Coll Llan DipTh77. **d** 77 **p** 78. C Flint *St As* 77-80; CF from 80. *c/o MOD (Army), Bagshot Park, Bagshot, Surrey GU19 5PL* Bagshot (0276) 71717

WELLS, Colin Durant. b 20. Lon Univ BSc43. St Deiniol's Hawarden 76. **d** 78 **p** 80. C Llanidan w Llanddaniel-fab w Llanedwen *Ban* 78; Perm to Offic *Ches* 80-84; *Ban* from 84. *Cae Coch, Brynsiencyn, Llanfairpwllgwyngyll, Gwynedd LL61 6SZ* Brynsiencyn (0248) 430308

WELLS, David Henry Nugent. b 20. St Chad's Coll Dur BA42 MA46 DipTh47. **d** 47 **p** 48. V Alrewas *Lich* 64-73; V Wychnor 64-73; R Upton Magna 73-81; V Withington 73-81; P-in-c Uffington 81; R Uffington, Upton Magna and Withington 81-85; rtd 85; Perm to Offic *Lich* from 85. *13 Belvidere Avenue, Shrewsbury SY2 5PF* Shrewsbury (0743) 65822

WELLS, Canon Edward Arthur. b 23. SRN. Oak Hill Th Coll. **d** 57 **p** 58. R Sproughton w Burstall *St E* 62-74; V Ipswich St Nic 74-80; Hon Can St E Cathl from 80; Chapl Ipswich Hosp 80-90; rtd 88. *74 Christchurch Street, Ipswich, Suffolk IP4 2DH* Ipswich (0473) 254046

WELLS, George Reginald. b 11. K Coll Cam BA33. Cuddesdon Coll 33. **d** 34 **p** 35. V Hagbourne *Ox* 61-74; P-in-c Gt Coxwell 74-80; P-in-c Buscot 74-80; P-in-c Coleshill 74-80; P-in-c Eaton Hastings 74-80; P-in-c Gt Coxwell w Buscot, Coleshill & Eaton Hastings 80; rtd 80. *8 Greystone Avenue, Dumfries DG1 1PE* Dumfries (0387) 68294

WELLS, Jeremy Stephen. b 47. Nottm Univ BA69 Univ of Wales DPS87. Chich Th Coll 72. **d** 73 **p** 74. C S Yardley St Mich *Birm* 73-76; C St Marychurch *Ex* 76-78; P-in-c Bridgwater H Trin *B & W* 78-82; P-in-c Brent Knoll 82-84; P-in-c E Brent w Lympsham 82-84; R Brent Knoll, E Brent and Lympsham from 84. *The Rectory, Church Road, East Brent, Highbridge, Somerset TA9 4HZ* Brent Knoll (0278) 760271

WELLS, John. b 11. Kelham Th Coll 29. **d** 34 **p** 35. Chapl N Staffs R Infirmary Stoke-on-Trent 62-76; Stoke-on-Trent City Hosp 62-76; rtd 76; Perm to Offic *S'well* from 76. *4 Upton Fields, Southwell, Notts NG25 0QA* Southwell (0636) 812310

WELLS, John Michael. b 35. Mert Coll Ox BA58 MA61. Westcott Ho Cam 60. **d** 62 **p** 63. C Hornchurch St Andr *Chelmsf* 62-64; C Barking St Marg 64-66; C Wanstead H Trin Hermon Hill 66-69; V Elm Park St Nic Hornchurch 69-76; R Wakes Colne w Chappel 76-79; Project Officer Cathl Cen for Research and Tr 79-81; Area Sec (Dios Chelmsf and Ely) CMS 81-88; E Cen Co-ord from 85; Area Sec (Dios Chelmsf and St E) from 88; Perm to Offic *St E* from 88. *Arlington, Links Drive, Chelmsford CM2 9AW* Chelmsford (0245) 355090

WELLS, Ven John Rowse David. b 27. Kelham Th Coll 53. **d** 57 **p** 58. SSM from 57; Lic to Offic *S'well* 57-59; Australia 59-65; Basutoland 65-66; Lesotho from 66; Can SS Mary and Jas Cathl Maseru from 77; Adn Cen Lesotho from 85. *PO Box 1579, Maseru, Lesotho 100* Lesotho (266) 315979

WELLS, Mark Wynne-Eyton. b 20. Peterho Cam BA48 MA54. Westcott Ho Cam 48. **d** 50 **p** 51. V Stoke by Nayland w Leavenheath *St E* 62-88; RD Hadleigh 71-76 and 85-86; rtd 88; Perm to Offic *Nor* from 88. *Red House, The Street, Great Snoring, Fakenham, Norfolk NR21 0AH* Fakenham (0328) 820641

WELLS, Nicholas Anthony. b 60. Cranmer Hall Dur 88. **d** 91. C Accrington St Jo w Huncoat *Blackb* from 91. *167 Manor Street, Accrington, Lancs BB5 6DZ* Accrington (0254) 301297

WELLS, Norman Charles. b 18. Keble Coll Ox BA40 MA44. St Steph Ho Ox 40. **d** 42 **p** 43. V St Margarets on Thames *Lon* 62-73; V Highbridge *B & W* 73-84; RD Burnham 76-82; rtd 84; Perm to Offic *B & W* from 85. *40 Mount Road, Nether Stowey, Bridgwater, Somerset TA5 1LU* Nether Stowey (0278) 732609

WELLS, Oswald Bertie. b 18. Linc Th Coll. **d** 48 **p** 49. C Loughton St Jo *Chelmsf* 81-84; Hon C from 84; rtd 84. *2 Baldwins Hill, Loughton, Essex IG10 1SD* 081-508 4602

WELLS, Peter Robert. b 59. Wilson Carlile Coll 78 Sarum & Wells Th Coll 87. **d** 89 **p** 90. CA from 81; C Mortlake w E Sheen *S'wark* from 89. *5 Vernon Road, London SW14 8NH* 081-876 9696

WELLS, Philip Anthony. b 57. BA MPhil. Coll of Resurr Mirfield. **d** 84 **p** 85. C Wylde Green *Birm* 84-87; Chapl and Succ Birm Cathl 87-91; Bp's Dom Chapl from 91. *East Wing, Bishop's Croft, Old Church Road, Birmingham B17 0BE* 021-427 1163 or 427 2295

WELLS, Richard John. b 46. Llan St Mich DipTh70 Cuddesdon Coll 70. **d** 71 **p** 72. C Kingston upon Hull St Alb *York* 71-75; C Addlestone *Guildf* 75-80; V Weston 80-88; V Milford from 88. *The Vicarage, Milford, Godalming, Surrey GU8 5BX* Godalming (04868) 4710

WELLS, Robert Crosby. b 28. St Jo Coll Dur BA52. **d** 54 **p** 55. C S Shore H Trin *Blackb* 54-59; C-in-c Lea CD 59-69; V Ribby w Wrea from 69. *The Vicarage, 10 Ribby Road, Wrea Green, Preston PR4 2NA* Kirkham (0772) 683587

WELLS, Ven Roderick John. b 36. Dur Univ BA63 Hull Univ MA85. Cuddesdon Coll 63. **d** 65 **p** 66. C Lambeth St Mary the Less *S'wark* 65-68; P-in-c 68-71; R Skegness *Linc* 71-77; P-in-c Winthorpe 77; R Skegness and Winthorpe 77-78; TR Gt and Lt Coates w Bradley 78-89; RD Grimsby and Cleethorpes 83-89; Hon Can Linc Cathl from 86; Adn Stow from 89; V Hackthorn w Cold Hanworth from 89; P-in-c N w S Carlton from 89. *The Vicarage, Hackthorn, Lincoln LN2 3PF* Welton (0673) 60382

WELLS, Ronald Charles. b 20. AKC50. **d** 51 **p** 52. C Prittlewell St Mary *Chelmsf* 51-56; C-in-c Leigh-on-Sea St Aid CD 56; V Leigh-on-Sea St Aid 56-65; R

Springfield All SS 65-80; Chapl Southend Gen Hosp from 80; V Prittlewell St Pet *Chelmsf* 80-90; P-in-c from 91. *28 Eastbourne Grove, Westcliff-on-Sea, Essex SS0 0QF* Southend-on-Sea (0702) 49545

WELLS, Samuel Martin. b 65. Mert Coll Ox BA87. Edin Th Coll 88. **d** 91. C Wallsend St Luke *Newc* from 91. *St Luke's Church House, Hugh Street, Wallsend, Tyne and Wear NE25 8SY* 091-251 7587

WELLS, Stephen Glossop. b 22. CCC Ox BA48 MA48. Westcott Ho Cam 48. **d** 50 **p** 51. R Saltford *B & W* 56-80; P-in-c Corston w Newton St Loe 76-80; RD Chew Magna 80-85; R Saltford w Corston and Newton St Loe 80-87; Preb Wells Cathl 84-90; TV Wellington and Distr 87-90; rtd 90. *57 Meadow Road, Berkhamsted, Herts HP4 1JL* Berkhamsted (0442) 870981

WELLS, Canon William Alan John. St Fran Coll Brisbane ThL51. **d** 52 **p** 53. Australia 52-57; Chapl Southport Sch 57-61; Chapl St Hilda's Sch Whitby 62-63; Chapl OHP 62-63; Br Honduras 64-68; Bahamas 68-70; C Penton Street St Silas w All SS *Lon* 71; Grenada 72-73; St Vincent 73-75; Belize 74-79; Can Belize Cathl from 77; Asst Chapl HM Pris Liv 79-82; Chapl HM Pris Rudgate and HM Rem Cen Thorp Arch 82-87; V Middlesb St Thos *York* from 87. *1A Cherwell Terrace, Brambles Farm, Middlesbrough, Cleveland TS3 9DQ* Middlesbrough (0642) 244908

WELLS, Canon William David Sandford. b 41. JP. Or Coll Ox BA64 MA66. Ridley Hall Cam 63. **d** 65 **p** 66. C Gt Malvern St Mary *Worc* 65-70; V Crowle 70-84; P-in-c Himbleton w Huddington 78-84; V E Bowbrook 84-89; Hon Can Worc Cathl from 84; RD Droitwich from 84; R Bowbrook S from 89. *The Vicarage, Crowle, Worcester WR7 4AT* Upton Snodsbury (090560) 617

WELLS, Archdeacon of. *See* THOMAS, Ven Charles Edward

WELLS, Dean of. *See* LEWIS, Very Rev Richard

WELSBY, Canon Paul Antony. b 20. Univ Coll Dur BA42 MA45 Sheff Univ PhD58. Linc Th Coll 42. **d** 44 **p** 45. Can Res Roch Cathl *Roch* 66-88; Dir Post Ord Tr 66-88; Chapl to HM The Queen 80-90; rtd 88; Bp's Dom Chapl *Roch* 88-90. *20 Knights Ridge, Pembury, Tunbridge Wells, Kent TN2 4HP* Pembury (089282) 3053

WELSH, Angus Alexander. b 30. Trin Coll Cam BA54 MA59 St Jo Coll Dur DipTh56. **d** 56 **p** 57. C Jesmond Clayton Memorial *Newc* 56-60; C Fenham St Jas and St Basil 60-62; V Bacup St Jo *Man* 62-68; Tristan da Cunha 68-71; St Vincent 72-78; R Heysham *Blackb* 78-88; V Blackb St Steph from 88. *St Stephen's Vicarage, 285 Whalley Old Road, Blackburn BB1 5RS* Blackburn (0254) 55546

WELSH, Jennifer Ann. b 48. Univ Coll Lon BA. **d** 81. NSM Newport St Matt *Mon* 81-85; NSM Risca from 85. *470 Caerleon Road, Newport, Gwent NP9 7LW* Newport (0633) 258287

WELSH, Jennifer Lee. b 59. Calgary Univ BSc81. Cam Episc Div Sch (USA) MDiv87. **d** 87 **p** 88. Canada 87-89; Sub-Chapl HM Pris Linc from 89. *46 Yarborough Crescent, Lincoln LN1 3LU* Lincoln (0522) 512650

WELSH, Miss Mary Elizabeth. b 22. St Hilda's Coll Ox BA44 MA48 Lon Univ DipEd45 BD50. Lambeth STh64. dss 68 **d** 87. Ex St Mark *Ex* 70-82; Lic to Offic 82-85; Yatton Moor *B & W* 85-87; Perm to Offic from 87. *26 Rectory Way, Yatton, Bristol BS19 4JF* Yatton (0934) 833329

WELSH, Maxwell Wilfred. b 29. Bp's Coll Calcutta 55. **d** 58 **p** 59. India 58-72; C Cannock *Lich* 73-76; C Wednesfield 76-79; V Milton 79-86; V Croxton w Broughton and Adbaston from 86. *Broughton Vicarage, Wetwood, Stafford ST21 6NR* Wetwood (063082) 231

WELSH, Philip Peter. b 48. Keble Coll Ox BA69 MA73 Selw Coll Cam BA72 MA76. Westcott Ho Cam 71. **d** 73 **p** 74. C W Dulwich All SS and Em *S'wark* 73-76; C Surbiton St Andr 76-77; C Surbiton St Andr and St Mark 77-79; India 79-81; V Malden St Jo *S'wark* 81-87; Min Officer *Linc* from 87. *46 Yarborough Crescent, Lincoln LN1 3LU* Lincoln (0522) 512650

WELSH, Robert Leslie. b 32. Sheff Univ BA54 St Jo Coll Dur DipTh58. **d** 58 **p** 59. C S Westoe *Dur* 58-62; C Darlington St Cuth 62-66; CF (TA) 64-67; V E Rainton *Dur* 66-85; R W Rainton 66-85; R Wolsingham and Thornley from 85. *The Rectory, 14 Rectory Lane, Wolsingham, Bishop Auckland, Co Durham DL13 3AJ* Bishop Auckland (0388) 527340

WELTON, Peter Abercrombie. b 62. Ball Coll Ox BA84. Qu Coll Birm 84. **d** 86 **p** 87. C Walthamstow St Pet *Chelmsf* 86-89; CP from 89. *2 Boreham Avenue, London E16 3AG* 071-476 0267

WEMYSS, Gary. b 52. St Jo Coll Dur 79. **d** 80 **p** 81. C Blackb St Jas *Blackb* 80-83; C Padiham 83-86; V Stalmine 86-90; P-in-c Egton-cum-Newland and Lowick *Carl* from 90. *The Vicarage, Penny Bridge, Ulverston, Cumbria LA12 7RQ* Ulverston (0229) 861285

WENHAM, David. b 45. MA PhD. Ridley Hall Cam. **d** 84 **p** 85. Lic to Offic *Ox* from 84; Tutor Wycliffe Hall Ox from 84. *Wycliffe Hall, Banbury Road, Oxford OX2 6PW* Oxford (0865) 274208

WENHAM, John William. b 13. Pemb Coll Cam BA35 MA39 Lon Univ BD43. **d** 38 **p** 39. Warden Latimer Ho Ox 70-73; Lic to Offic *Ox* 70-73; C Cottisford 73-75; C Hardwick w Tusmore 73-75; rtd 78. *55 Bainton Road, Oxford OX2 7AG* Oxford (0865) 58820

WENHAM, Michael Timothy. b 49. Pemb Coll Cam MA75. Wycliffe Hall Ox DipTh85. **d** 86 **p** 87. C Norbury *Ches* 86-89; V Stanford in the Vale w Goosey and Hatford *Ox* from 89. *The Vicarage, Stanford in the Vale, Faringdon, Oxon SN7 8HU* Stanford in the Vale (0367) 710267

WENSLEY, Mrs Beryl Kathleen. b 29. CertRK55. Selly Oak Coll 53. **dss** 76 **d** 87. Raynes Park St Sav *S'wark* 76-83; Chapl Asst St Geo Hosp Gp Lon 83-89; rtd 89; Chapl Win HA and Chapl R Hants Co Hosp Win from 89. *Flat 6, Normans, Norman Road, Winchester SO23 9BX* Winchester (0962) 863992

WENT, Ven John Stewart. b 44. CCC Cam BA66 MA70. Oak Hill Th Coll 67. **d** 69 **p** 70. C Northwood Em *Lon* 69-75; V Margate H Trin *Cant* 75-83; Vice-Prin Wycliffe Hall Ox 83-89; Adn Surrey *Guildf* from 89; Chmn Dioc Coun for Unity and Miss from 90. *Tarawera, 71 Boundstone Road, Rowledge, Farnham, Surrey GU10 4AT* Frensham (025125) 3987

WENZEL, Peggy Sylvia. STh. Gilmore Ho. **d** 88. Perm to Offic *Sarum* from 88. *Church Cottage, Church Street, Pewsey, Wilts SN9 5DL* Marlborough (0672) 63834

WERNER, David Robert Edmund. b 33. Clifton Th Coll 61. **d** 63 **p** 64. C Holywell *St As* 63-68; C Llanrhos 68-70; R Tedburn St Mary *Ex* from 71; RD Kenn 80-83. *The Rectory, Tedburn St Mary, Exeter EX6 6EN* Tedburn St Mary (06476) 253

WERNER, Donald Kilgour. b 39. Univ of Wales BA61 Linacre Coll Ox BA64 MA67. Wycliffe Hall Ox 61. **d** 64 **p** 65. C Wrexham *St As* 64-69; Chapl Brasted Place Coll Westerham 69-73; Chapl Bris Univ *Bris* 73-76; Hon C Clifton St Paul 73-76; Chapl Keele Univ *Lich* 77-79; P-in-c Keele 77-79; C York St Mich-le-Belfrey *York* 79-83; Dir of Evang 79-83; R Holborn St Geo w H Trin and St Bart *Lon* from 83. *13 Doughty Street, London WC1N 2PL* 071-831 0588

WERRELL, Ralph Sidney. b 29. Tyndale Hall Bris 54. **d** 56 **p** 57. C Penn Fields *Lich* 56-60; C Champion Hill St Sav *S'wark* 60-61; R Danby Wiske w Yafforth *Ripon* 61-65; P-in-c Hutton Bonville *York* 61-65; R Combs *St E* 65-75; V Bootle Ch Ch *Liv* 75-80; R Scole w Billingford and Thorpe Parva *Nor* 80; P-in-c Brockdish w Thorpe Abbots 80; R Scole, Brockdish, Billingford, Thorpe Abbots etc 80-83; R Southam w Stockton *Cov* 83-89; R Southam from 89. *The Rectory, Park Lane, Southam, Leamington Spa, Warks CV33 0JA* Southam (092681) 2413

WERWATH, Wolfgang Albert Richard Kurt. b 22. Ripon Hall Ox 54. **d** 56 **p** 57. V Whitfield *Derby* 67-75; V Bretby w Newton Solney 75-88; rtd 88; Perm to Offic *Derby* from 88. *28 D'Ayncourt Walk, Farnsfield, Newark, Notts NG22 8DP* Mansfield (0623) 882635

WESLEY, Charles Boyd. b 43. Westcott Ho Cam 76. **d** 79 **p** 80. C Haverhill *St E* 79-82; C Cayton w Eastfield *York* 82-83; TV Usworth *Dur* 84-88; V Stockton St Mark from 88. *The Vicarage, 76 Fairfield Road, Stockton-on-Tees, Cleveland TS19 7BP* Stockton-on-Tees (0642) 588904

WESSON, Basil. b 24. **d** 83 **p** 84. NSM Belper Ch Ch and Milford *Derby* from 83. *Wescot, Belper Lane End, Belper, Derby DE5 2DL* Belper (0773) 7566

WESSON, Canon John Graham. b 38. St Pet Coll Ox BA62 DipTh63 MA68. Clifton Th Coll 63. **d** 65 **p** 66. C Southport Ch Ch w St Andr *Liv* 65-68; C Ox St Ebbe w St Pet *Ox* 68-71; Chapl Poly of Cen Lon 71-76; C-in-c Edin St Thos *Edin* 76-82; Dir Past Studies Trin Coll Bris 82-86; R Birm St Martin w Bordesley St Andr *Birm* from 86; RD Birm City from 88; Hon Can Birm Cathl from 91. *The Rectory, 37 Barlows Road, Birmingham B15 2PN* 021-454 0119

WEST, Andrew Victor. b 59. Wycliffe Hall Ox 87. **d** 90. C Leyland St Andr *Blackb* from 90. *3 Beech Avenue, Leyland, Preston PR5 2AL* Leyland (0772) 622446

WEST, Arthur. b 20. Linc Th Coll 59. **d** 60 **p** 61. V Nether w Upper Poppleton *York* 68-85; RD Ainsty 77-85; rtd 85. *8 River View, Linton-on-Ouse, York* Linton-on-Ouse (03474) 463

WEST, Bryan Edward. b 39. Avery Hill Coll CertEd69 BEd80 Kent Univ MA86. Cant Sch of Min 85. **d** 88 **p** 89. NSM Gravesend H Family w Ifield *Roch* from 88. *66 South Hill Road, Gravesend, Kent DA12 1JZ* Gravesend (0474) 332974

WEST, Clive. QUB BD75. CITC. **d** 64 **p** 65. C Lisburn Ch Ch Cathl *Conn* 64-68; Asst Master Lisnagarvey Sec Sch Lisburn 68-70; C Belf All SS 70-75; I from 84; I Mullabrack w Kilcluney *Arm* 76-84. *25 Rugby Road, Belfast BT7 1PT* Belfast (0232) 323327

WEST, David Marshall. b 48. St Jo Coll Dur BA70. Qu Coll Birm DipTh72. **d** 73 **p** 74. C Wylde Green *Birm* 73-76; C Wokingham St Paul *Ox* 76-79; V Hurst 79-88; V Maidenhead St Luke from 88. *St Luke's Vicarage, 26 Norfolk Road, Maidenhead, Berks SL6 7AX* Maidenhead (0628) 22733

WEST, Derek Elvin. b 47. Hull Univ BA69. Westcott Ho Cam 71. **d** 73 **p** 74. C Walthamstow St Pet *Chelmsf* 73-77; C Chingford SS Pet and Paul 77-80; TV W Slough *Ox* 80-88; Slough Community Chapl from 88. *16 Buckland Avenue, Slough, Berks SL3 7PH* Slough (0753) 24293

WEST, Eric Edward. b 32. Leeds Univ BA60. Bps' Coll Cheshunt 63. **d** 64 **p** 65. C Biscot *St Alb* 64-71; V from 71. *The Vicarage, 161 Bishopscote Road, Luton LU3 1PD* Luton (0582) 573421

✠WEST, Rt Rev Francis Horner. b 09. Magd Coll Cam BA31 MA35. Ridley Hall Cam 31. **d** 33 **p** 34 **c** 62. C Burmantofts St Steph and St Agnes *Ripon* 33-36; C Cam H Trin *Ely* 36; Chapl and Tutor Ridley Hall Cam 36-38; V Starbeck *Ripon* 38-42; CF (R of O) 39-46; V Upton *S'well* 46-51; Adn Newark 47-62; V E Retford 51-54; RD Retford 51-53; R Dinder *B & W* 62-71; Preb Wells Cathl 62-77; Suff Bp Taunton 62-77; rtd 77. *11 Castle Street, Aldbourne, Marlborough, Wilts SN8 2DA* Marlborough (0672) 40630

WEST, George Edward. b 08. Roch Th Coll 62. **d** 63 **p** 64. V Barrow-on-Trent w Twyford and Swarkestone *Derby* 66-74; rtd 74. *Fosbrooke House, 8 Clifton Drive, Lytham, Lancs FY8 5RE* Lytham (0253) 738812

WEST, Gerald Eric. b 18. ACII48. St Deiniol's Hawarden. **d** 80 **p** 81. Hon C Bramhall *Ches* 80-82; C 82-87; rtd 87; Perm to Offic *Ches* from 87. *255 Bramhall Moor Lane, Hazel Grove, Stockport, Cheshire SK7 5JL* 061-439 3029

WEST, Harold Reginald. b 15. Dur Univ BA43 MA46. Coll of Resurr Mirfield 43. **d** 45 **p** 46. V Newc St Luke *Newc* 61-82; rtd 82. *42 Linden Road, Gosforth, Newcastle upon Tyne NE3 4HB* 091-284 4291

WEST, Henry Cyrano. b 28. K Coll Lon. **d** 51 **p** 52. V Sculcoates *York* 63-71; P-in-c Kingston upon Hull St Jude w St Steph 67-71; Lic to Offic *Cov* 71-75; *Man* 75-87; Hon C Hulme Ascension *Man* from 87; rtd 91. *6 King's Drive, Middleton, Manchester M24 4PB* 061-643 4410

WEST, James. b 15. Lon Univ BA39 BD44. Sarum Th Coll 39. **d** 40 **p** 41. V Pilton w Ashford *Ex* 56-81; rtd 81. *10 Park Place, Wadebridge, Cornwall PL27 7EA* Wadebridge (020881) 3945

WEST, Canon Michael Brian. b 39. Bris Univ BSc60. Linc Th Coll 64. **d** 66 **p** 67. C Hatf *St Alb* 66-69; Ind Chapl 69-81; Hon Can St Alb 78-81; Sen Ind Chapl *Sheff* from 81; Hon Can Sheff Cathl from 81. *21 Endcliffe Rise Road, Sheffield S11 8RU* Sheffield (0742) 661921

WEST, Michael Frederick. b 50. Trin Coll Ox BA72 MA76. Westcott Ho Cam 72. **d** 74 **p** 75. C Wolv *Lich* 74-78; C Wolv 78; C Hanley H Ev 78-79; TV 79-82; Dioc Youth Officer *St E* 83-88; V Ipswich St Thos from 88. *St Thomas's Vicarage, 102 Cromer Road, Ipswich IP1 5EP* Ipswich (0473) 41215

WEST, Michael John. b 33. ARSM54 CEng60 FIMM68 FEng89 Imp Coll Lon BScEng54. S'wark Ord Course 85. **d** 88 **p** 89. Hon C Caterham *S'wark* from 88. *1 Church Road, Kenley, Surrey CR8 5DW* 081-668 1548

WEST, Michael Oakley. b 31. Wells Th Coll 62. **d** 63 **p** 64. C Swindon Ch Ch *Bris* 63-66; Libya 66-68; R Lydiard Millicent w Lydiard Tregoz *Bris* 68-75; V Breage w Germoe *Truro* 75-82; CMS 82-91; Israel 82-91; Chapl Shiplake Coll Henley from 91. *Chiltern Cottage, Chalkhouse Green, Reading RG4 9AH*

WEST, Miss Penelope Anne Margaret. b 44. City of Birm Coll CertEd68. Glouc Sch of Min 74 Ridley Hall Cam 85. **dss** 86 **d** 87. Portishead *B & W* 86-87; C from 87. *7 Channel View Road, Portishead, Bristol BS20 9LZ* Portishead (0272) 847417

WEST, Philip William. b 48. Magd Coll Ox BA70 MA78. St Jo Coll Nottm BA74 DPS75. **d** 75 **p** 76. C Rushden w

Newton Bromswold *Pet* 75-79; C Pitsmoor w Ellesmere *Sheff* 79-83; V Attercliffe 83-89; Ind Chapl 85-90; P-in-c Darnall H Trin 86-89; V Stannington from 89. *The Vicarage, 334 Oldfield Road, Stannington, Sheffield S6 6EA* Sheffield (0742) 345586 or 324490

WEST, Reginald George. b 14. ACA39 FCA57. Worc Ord Coll 66. **d** 68 **p** 69. C Oundle *Pet* 68-73; V Weedon Lois w Plumpton and Moreton Pinkney 73-79; rtd 79. *57 Greenacres Way, Newport, Shropshire TF10 7PH* Newport (0952) 812645

WEST, Reginald Roy. b 28. St Deiniol's Hawarden 74. **d** 74 **p** 75. C Abergavenny St Mary w Llanwenarth Citra *Mon* 74-77; V Tredegar St Jas from 77. *St James's Vicarage, Poplar Road, Tredegar, Gwent NP2 4LH* Tredegar (0495) 252510

WEST, Richard Wilfrid Anthony. b 20. Magd Coll Cam BA41 MA45. Wells Th Coll 41. **d** 43 **p** 44. V Brockham Green *S'wark* 50-86; P-in-c Betchworth 81-86; rtd 86. *2 Abbotts Walk, Cerne Abbas, Dorchester, Dorset DT2 7JN* Cerne Abbas (0300) 341567

WEST, Canon Ronald Cameron. b 06. AKC33. **d** 33 **p** 34. V Freeland *Ox* 55-80; RD Woodstock 76-80; Hon Can Ch Ch 79-80; rtd 80; Perm to Offic *Truro* from 80. *Flat 22, Chynance, Alexandra Road, Penzance, Cornwall TR18 4LY* Penzance (0736) 66612

WEST, Stephen Peter. b 52. Liv Univ CertEd74. Oak Hill Th Coll 87. **d** 89 **p** 90. C Gateacre *Liv* from 89. *20 Wellgreen Road, Liverpool L25 1QP* 051-487 4653

WEST, Thomas. b 13. Worc Ord Coll 63. **d** 64 **p** 65. V Marton *Linc* 68-75; V Leake 75-80; rtd 80. *6 Ravendale, Barton-on-Humber, S Humberside DN18 6AR* Barton-on-Humber (0652) 34529

WEST, Thomas Roderic. b 55. DipTh BTh90. TCD Div Sch. **d** 86 **p** 87. C Dromore Cathl *D & D* 86-89; I Carrowdore w Millisle from 89. *The Rectory, 40 Woburn Road, Millisle, Newtownards, Co Down BT22 2HY* Millisle (0247) 861226

WEST, Timothy Ralph. b 53. Bath Univ BSc75. Ridley Hall Cam 82. **d** 85 **p** 86. C Mildenhall *St E* 85-88; TV Melbury *Sarum* from 88. *The Vicarage, Summer Lane, Evershot, Dorchester, Dorset DT2 0JP* Evershot (093583) 238

WEST CUMBERLAND, Archdeacon of. See PACKER, Ven John Richard

WEST HAM, Archdeacon of. See STEVENS, Ven Timothy John

WEST-LINDELL, Stein Eric. b 54. BA. Linc Th Coll 82. **d** 84 **p** 85. C Allington and Maidstone St Pet *Cant* 84-87; R Orlestone w Snave and Ruckinge w Warehorne from 87. *The Rectory, Cock Lane, Ham Street, Ashford, Kent TN26 2HU* Ham Street (023373) 2274

WESTALL, Robert Cyril. b 07. St Chad's Coll Dur BA28. **d** 30 **p** 31. R Dodbrooke *Ex* 66-76; rtd 76. *Pynes House, Cheriton Fitzpaine, Crediton, Devon EX17 4JA* Cheriton Fitzpaine (03636) 505

WESTBROOK, Canon Colin David. b 36. Or Coll Ox BA59. St Steph Ho Ox DipTh60 MA63. **d** 61 **p** 62. C Roath St Martin *Llan* 61-66; C Roath St Marg 66-74; V Llantarnam *Mon* 74-79; V Newport St Jo Bapt from 79; Hon Can St Woolos Cathl 88-91; Can from 91; Warden of Ords from 91. *St John's Vicarage, Oakfield Road, Newport, Gwent NP9 4LP* Newport (0633) 265581

WESTBROOK, Mrs Ethel Patricia Ivy. b 42. Bris Univ CertEd63. Cant Sch of Min 82. **dss** 84 **d** 87. Fawkham and Hartley *Roch* 84-85; Asst Dir of Educn 84-86; Cliffe at Hoo w Cooling 85-86; Corby SS Pet and Andr w Gt and Lt Oakley *Pet* 86-87; Par Dn 87-90; Par Dn Roch from 90. *47 Roebuck Road, Rochester, Kent ME1 1UE* Medway (0634) 826821

WESTBROOK, Richard Henry. b 09. **d** 67 **p** 68. R Carlton Curlieu and Illston on the Hill etc *Leic* 70-76; R Carlton Curlieu, Illston on the Hill etc 76-81; rtd 81; Perm to Offic *Roch* from 90. *47 Roebuck Road, Rochester, Kent ME1 1UE* Medway (0634) 826821

WESTCOTT, Cuthbert Philip Brooke. b 09. Magd Coll Ox BA32 MA36. Westcott Ho Cam 36. **d** 36 **p** 37. Chapl Palermo w Taormina *Eur* 75-77; rtd 77; Chapl St Jean-de-Luz w Pau and Biarritz *Eur* 77-80; Perm to Offic *Birm* 81-86; *Linc* and *Pet* from 87. *Karnak House, Second Drift, Wothorpe, Stamford, Lincs PE9 3JH* Stamford (0780) 56174

WESTCOTT, Donald Ralph. b 27. Bris Univ BA51. Ridley Hall Cam 51. **d** 53 **p** 54. V Benchill *Man* 63-70; R Islip *Ox* 70-86; R Noke 70-86; P-in-c Woodeaton 70-86; R Roydon St Remigius *Nor* 86-90; rtd 90. *54 Arosa Drive, Malvern, Worcs WR14 3QF* Malvern (0684) 568653

WESTERN, Canon Robert Geoffrey. b 37. Man Univ BSc60. Qu Coll Birm DipTh62. **d** 62 **p** 63. C Sedbergh *Bradf* 62-65; PV Linc Cathl *Linc* 65-73; Hd Master Linc

Cathl Sch from 74; Can and Preb Linc Cathl *Linc* from 74. *Headmaster's House, 8 Eastgate, Lincoln LN2 1QG* Lincoln (0522) 28489 or 23769

WESTLAKE, Michael Paul. b 34. Ex Coll Ox BA56 MA64. Wells Th Coll 59. **d** 61 **p** 62. C Southmead *Bris* 61-67; V Eastville St Thos 67-74; V Eastville St Thos w St Anne 74-83; P-in-c Easton St Mark 79-83; V Marshfield w Cold Ashton and Tormarton etc from 83. *The Vicarage, Church Lane, Marshfield, Chippenham, Wilts SN14 8NT* Bath (0225) 891850

WESTLAKE, Peter Alan Grant. b 19. CMG72 MC43. FRAS. CCC Ox MA48 Univ of Wales (Ban) BD81 MSc81. **d** 81 **p** 82. Hon C Llandegfan w Llandysilio *Ban* from 81. *53 Church Street, Beaumaris, Gwynedd LL58 8AB* Beaumaris (0248) 810114

WESTLAND, Richard Theodore. b 27. Local NSM Course. **d** 87 **p** 88. NSM Freiston w Butterwick *Linc* from 87. *17 Homers Lane, Freiston, Boston, Lincs PE22 0PB* Boston (0205) 760572

WESTLEY, Stuart. b 24. Em Coll Cam BA48 MA52 Man Univ DASE84. Wells Th Coll 49. **d** 50 **p** 51. Lic to Offic *Blackb* 51-70; Asst Chapl Denstone Coll Uttoxeter 70-73; Chapl Ermysted's Gr Sch Skipton 73-85; Hon C Blackpool St Mich *Blackb* 75-77; Perm to Offic *Bradf* 77-78; Lic to Offic 78-85; C Padiham *Blackb* 85-89; rtd 89. *Ad Viam, Side Gate Lane, Lothersdale, Keighley, W Yorkshire BD20 8EU* Keighley (0535) 635646

WESTMACOTT, Preb Ian Field. b 19. Wells Th Coll 60. **d** 60 **p** 61. V Long Ashton *B & W* 63-84; RD Portishead 72-82; Preb Wells Cathl 77-84; rtd 84; Perm to Offic Bris from 84; B & W from 85. *8A York Place, Bristol B58 1AH* Bristol (0272) 736057

WESTMINSTER, Archdeacon of. See HARVEY, Ven Anthony Ernest

WESTMINSTER, Dean of. See MAYNE, Very Rev Michael Clement Otway

WESTMORLAND AND FURNESS, Archdeacon of. See PEAT, Ven Lawrence Joseph

WESTMUCKETT, John Spencer. b 30. Lon Univ BA54. Oak Hill Th Coll. **d** 55 **p** 56. C Sydenham H Trin *S'wark* 55-57; CF 57-83; P-in-c Brightling w Dallington *Chich* 83-85; R Brightling, Dallington, Mountfield & Netherfield 85-87. *Address temp unknown*

WESTNEY, Michael Edward William. b 29. Lich Th Coll 64. **d** 65 **p** 66. C Hughenden *Ox* 65-68; C Banbury 68-71; TV Trunch *Nor* 71-78; V Reading St Matt *Ox* 78-83; TV W Slough 83-88; TR from 88. *St Andrew's House, Washington Drive, Cippenham, Slough SL1 5RE* Burnham (0628) 661994

WESTON, Christopher James. b 20. G&C Coll Cam BA46 MA49. Ridley Hall Cam 47. **d** 49 **p** 50. V Clifton St Jas *Sheff* 63-70; P-in-c Stevenage St Nic *St Alb* 70-71; V 71-87; rtd 87. *15 Coltsfoot Close, Cherry Hinton, Cambridge CB1 4YH* Cambridge (0223) 242604

WESTON, David Wilfrid Valentine. b 37. **d** 67 **p** 68. OSB 60-84; Lic to Offic *Ox* 67-84; Prior Nashdom Abbey 71-74; Abbot 74-84; C Chorley St Pet *Blackb* 84-85; V Pilling 85-89; Bp's Dom Chapl *Carl* from 89. *The Chaplain's House, Rose Castle, Dalston, Carlisle CA5 7BZ*

WESTON, Ven Frank Valentine. b 35. Qu Coll Ox BA60 MA64. Lich Th Coll 60. **d** 61 **p** 62. C Atherton *Man* 61-65; Chapl USPG Coll of the Ascension Selly Oak 65-69; Prin 69-76; Prin Edin Th Coll 76-82; Can St Mary's Cathl *Edin* 76-82; Adn Ox and Can Res Ch Ch *Ox* from 82. *Archdeacon's Lodging, Christ Church, Oxford OX1 1DP* Oxford (0865) 276185

WESTON, Frederick Victor Henry. b 41. Qu Coll Cam BA63 MA67. St D Coll Lamp LTh65. **d** 65 **p** 66. C Grangetown *Llan* 65-67; C Cwmmer w Abercregan CD 67-69; C Haverhill *St E* 69-74; R Gt and Lt Whelnetham 74-79; Perm to Offic from 84. *154 Southgate Street, Bury St Edmunds, Suffolk*

WESTON, Harold John. b 24. Worc Ord Coll 65. **d** 67 **p** 68. C Northn St Mich *Pet* 67-71; C Pet St Jo 71-74; R Peakirk w Glinton 75-89; rtd 89. *8 Delph Court, Delph Street, Whittlesey, Peterborough PE7 1QQ* Peterborough (0733) 205516

WESTON, Ivan John. b 45. MBE88. Chich Th Coll 71. **d** 74 **p** 75. C Harlow St Mary Magd *Chelmsf* 74-77; Chapl RAF from 77. *c/o MOD, Adastral House, Theobald's Road, London WC1X 8RU* 071-430 7268

WESTON, John Oglivy. b 30. St Pet Coll Ox BA66 MA70. Linc Th Coll 71. **d** 71 **p** 72. Lect Trent Poly 66-82; Hon C Long Clawson and Hose *Leic* 71-82; Hon C Bingham *S'well* 82-85; Lic to Offic from 85. *10 Morkinshire Lane, Cotgrave, Notts NG12 3HJ* Nottingham (0602) 893336

WESTON, Mrs Judith. b 36. MSR56 Open Univ BA75. St Jo Coll Nottm 84. **dss** 85 **d** 87. Huddersfield H Trin

Wakef 85-87; Par Dn from 87. *8 Newlands Road, Huddersfield HD5 0QT* Huddersfield (0484) 421490

WESTON, Canon Keith Aitken Astley. b 26. Trin Hall Cam BA51 MA55. Ridley Hall Cam 51. **d** 53 **p** 54. C Weston-super-Mare Ch Ch *B & W* 53-56; C Cheltenham St Mark *Glouc* 56-59; V Clevedon Ch Ch *B & W* 59-64; R Ox St Ebbe w H Trin and St Pet *Ox* 64-85; RD Ox 71-76; Hon Can Ch 81-85; Dir of Post-Ord Tr *Nor* 85-90; Dioc Dir of Ords from 85; P-in-c Nor St Steph from 85; Hon Brigade Chapl to Norfolk Co Fire Service from 90. *12 The Crescent, Norwich NR2 1SA* Norwich (0603) 623045

WESTON, Neil. b 51. Jes Coll Ox BA73 MA78. Ridley Hall Cam 74. **d** 76 **p** 77. C Ealing St Mary *Lon* 76-80; P-in-c Pertenhall w Swineshead *St Alb* 80-89; P-in-c Dean w Yelden, Melchbourne and Shelton 80-89; R The Stodden Churches 89-91; R Newhaven *Chich* from 91. *The Rectory, 36 Second Avenue, Newhaven, E Sussex BN9 9HN* Newhaven (0273) 5251

WESTON, Paul David Astley. b 57. Trin Hall Cam BA80 MA83. Wycliffe Hall Ox 83. **d** 85 **p** 86. C New Malden and Coombe *S'wark* 85-89; Lect Oak Hill Th Coll from 89. *Oak Hill College, Southgate, London N14 4PS* 081-449 0467

WESTON, Ralph Edward Norman. b 30. Worc Ord Coll 67. **d** 69 **p** 70. C Harborne St Pet *Birm* 69-71; CF 71-75; Chapl Oswestry Sch 75-85; Chapl Rotherham Distr HA from 85; CF (ACF) from 87. *Rotherham District Hospital, Moorgate Road, Rotherham, S Yorkshire S60 2UD* Rotherham (0709) 820000

WESTON, Stephen. b 48. St Steph Ho Ox 74. **d** 77 **p** 78. C Wigston Magna *Leic* 77-82; C Corringham *Chelmsf* 82-84; V Southtown *Nor* 84-89; R Catfield from 90. *The Rectory, Catfield, Great Yarmouth, Norfolk NR29 5DB* Stalham (0692) 82290

WESTON, Stephen John Astley. b 55. Aston Univ BSc77. Ridley Hall Cam 78. **d** 81 **p** 82. C Gt Chesham *Ox* 81-85; C Southport Ch Ch *Liv* 85-87; P-in-c Gayhurst w Ravenstone, Stoke Goldington etc *Ox* 87-91; R from 91. *The Rectory, Stoke Goldington, Newport Pagnell, Bucks MK16 8LL* Stoke Goldington (090855) 221

WESTON, Mrs Virginia Anne. b 58. UEA BSc79. Wycliffe Hall Ox 84. **d** 87. Par Dn New Malden and Coombe *S'wark* 87-89; Lic to Offic *Lon* from 89. *Oak Hill College, Southgate, London N14 4PS* 081-441 0315

WESTROPP, Canon Ralph Michael Lanyon. b 07. New Coll Ox BA29 MA42. Westcott Ho Cam 42. **d** 43 **p** 44. V Natland *Carl* 70-75; Hon Can Carl Cathl 72-75; rtd 75; Perm to Offic *Carl* from 77. *Inglewood House, Kirkby Lonsdale, Carnforth, Lancs LA6 2DH* Kirkby Lonsdale (05242) 71409

WESTRUP, Wilfrid Allan. b 08. Ch Coll Cam BA30 MA34. Westcott Ho Cam 30. **d** 32 **p** 33. Chapl Cranbrook Sch Kent 52-64; rtd 73. *Sharon, Hartley Hill, Cranbrook, Kent TN17 3QD* Cranbrook (0580) 712595

WESTWELL, Ven George Leslie Cedric. b 31. Lich Th Coll. **d** 61 **p** 63. C Rothwell *Ripon* 61-63; C Armley St Bart 63-66; C Maidstone St Martin *Cant* 65-68; V 72-77; R Otham 68-72; V Bethersden w High Halden 77-79; R Lichborough w Maidford and Farthingstone *Pet* 79-80; Perm to Offic *Chich* 80-83; Chapl Florence w Siena and Assisi *Eur* from 83; Adn Italy from 85. *16/18 via Maggio, 50125 Florence, Italy* Florence (55) 294764

WESTWOOD, John Richard. b 55. Clare Coll Cam BA77 MA81. Ripon Coll Cuddesdon 77. **d** 79 **p** 80. C Oakham w Hambleton and Egleton *Pet* 79-81; C Oakham, Hambleton, Egleton, Braunston and Brooke 81-83; V Gt w Lt Harrowden and Orlingbury 83-90; V Wellingborough St Andr from 90. *The Vicarage, Berrymoor Road, Wellingborough, Northants NN8 2HU* Wellingborough (0933) 222692

WESTWOOD, Peter. b 38. Open Univ BA76. AKC64. **d** 65 **p** 66. C Acomb St Steph *York* 65-68; Chapl HM Youth Cust Cen Onley 69-73; Chapl HM Pris *Leic* 73-77; Maidstone 77-81; Dur 81-87; Chapl HM Pris Brixton from 87. *The Chaplain's Office, HM Prison, Jebb Avenue, London SW2 5XF* 081-674 9811

✠**WESTWOOD, Rt Rev William John.** b 25. Em Coll Cam BA50 MA55. Westcott Ho Cam 50. **d** 52 **p** 53 **c** 75. C Kingston upon Hull H Trin *York* 52-57; R Lowestoft St Marg *Nor* 57-65; RD Lothingland 59-65; V Nor St Pet Mancroft 65-75; RD Nor 66-71; Hon Can Nor Cathl 68-75; Suff Bp Edmonton *Lon* 75-79; Area Bp Edmonton 79-84; Bp Pet from 84. *The Palace, Peterborough PE1 1YA* Peterborough (0733) 62492

WETHERALL, Canon Cecil Edward. b 29. St Jo Coll Dur 49. **d** 56 **p** 57. C Ipswich St Aug *St E* 56-59; R Hitcham 59-79; P-in-c Brettenham 61-63; P-in-c Kettlebaston from 71; R Hitcham w Lt Finborough from 79; Hon Can St E

Cathl from 83; P-in-c Preston from 85. *The Rectory, Hitcham, Ipswich IP7 7NF* Bildeston (0449) 740350

WETHERALL, Nicholas Guy. b 52. Lon Univ BMus73 Ox Univ CertEd75. Chich Th Coll 82. **d** 84 **p** 85. C Cleobury Mortimer w Hopton Wafers *Heref* 84-87; TV Leominster from 87. *118 Buckfield Road, Leominster, Hereford HR6 8SQ* Leominster (0568) 2124

WETHERELL, Philip Anthony. b 45. Leic Univ MPhil87. AKC72. **d** 73 **p** 74. C Walthamstow St Sav *Chelmsf* 73-75; Chapl Bp Namibia & Tutor Namibia Int Peace Cen 75-76; C Knighton St Mary Magd *Leic* 76-80; TV Southn (City Cen) *Win* 80-84; Personnel Officer USPG from 84. Miss Personnel Sec USPG from 88; *c/o USPG, Partnership House, 157 Waterloo Road, London SE1 8XA* 071-928 8681

WETZ, Peter Joseph Patrick. b 37. **d** 62 **p** 62. C Hatf Hyde St Mary *St Alb* 85; C Stevenage St Pet Broadwater 85-87; V Irlam *Man* from 87. *The Vicarage, Vicarage Road, Irlam, Manchester M30 6WA* 061-775 2461

WEYMAN, John Derek Henry. b 31. Wells Th Coll 69. **d** 70 **p** 71. C Headley All SS *Guildf* 70-76; V Westcott from 76; RD Dorking 84-89. *The Vicarage, Westcott, Dorking, Surrey RH4 3QB* Dorking (0306) 885309

WEYMAN, Richard Darrell George. b 46. Lon Univ BA Bris Univ PhD. Sarum & Wells Th Coll. **d** 84 **p** 85. C Sherborne w Castleton and Lillington *Sarum* 84-88; V Malden St Jo *S'wark* from 88. *329 Malden Road, New Malden, Surrey KT3 6AL* 081-942 3297

WEYMONT, Gillian. b 41. SRN67. Trin Coll Bris 88. **d** 90. C Wincanton *B & W* from 90. *10 Elm Drive, Wincanton, Somerset BA9 9EZ* Wincanton (0963) 31246

WEYMONT, Martin Eric. b 48. St Jo Coll Dur BA69 MA74 CertEd73 Lon Univ PhD88. Westcott Ho Cam 71. **d** 73 **p** 74. C Blackheath *Birm* 73-76; Hon C Willesden St Matt *Lon* 76-77; Hon C Belmont 76-79; P-in-c W Twyford 79-85; P-in-c Cricklewood St Mich 85-88; Chapl St Pet Colleg Sch Wolv 88-91; Hon C Wolv *Lich* 88-91. *St Peter's Flat, 4 Exchange Street, Wolverhampton WV1 1TS* Wolverhampton (0902) 28491

WHALE, Desmond Victor. b 35. Bris Sch of Min 81. **d** 84 **p** 85. Lic to Offic *Bris* 84-88; C Parr *Liv* 88-91; R Winfarthing w Shelfanger w Burston w Gissing etc *Nor* from 91. *The Rectory, Winfarthing, Diss, Norfolk IP22 2EA* Diss (0379) 642543

WHALE, Canon Jeffery Walter George. b 33. Lon Univ BSc60. Cuddesdon Coll 60. **d** 62 **p** 63. C Rugby St Andr *Cov* 62-68; C-in-c Britwell St Geo CD *Ox* 68-77; P-in-c Datchet 77-78; TR Riverside 78-88; RD Burnham 83-87; Hon Can Ch Ch from 85; TR New Windsor from 88. *The Rectory, Park Street, Windsor, Berks SL4 1LU* Windsor (0753) 864572

WHALE, Dr Peter Richard. b 49. Down Coll Cam BA74 MA78 Auckland Univ BSc71 MA72 Otago Univ BD78 Ex Univ PhD89. St Jo Coll Auckland 75. **d** 77 **p** 78. New Zealand 77-85; TV Saltash *Truro* 85-90; Jt Dir SW Min Tr Course Truro 86-90; Preb St Endellion 89-90; Prin W Midl Minl Tr Course from 90. *7 Somerset Road, Birmingham B15 2QB* 021-455 7579

WHALER, Herbert Riggall. b 13. St Andr Pampisford 47. **d** 49 **p** 50. R Bucknall w Tupholme *Linc* 52-82; R Horsington w Stixwould 52-82; R Kirkby-on-Bain 61-82; V Martin w Thornton 61-82; R Roughton w Haltham 61-82; R Scrivelsby w Dalderby 66-82; P-in-c Thimbleby 80-82; rtd 82. *Stocks Hill Lodge, Stixwould, Lincoln LN3 5HP*

WHALES, Jeremy Michael. b 31. Bris Univ MA82. Lambeth STh72 Wycliffe Hall Ox 59. **d** 61 **p** 62. C W Wimbledon Ch Ch *S'wark* 61-64; Lect St Paul's Coll Cheltenham 64-67; Asst Chapl and Sen Lect 67-74; Chapl 74-78; Assoc Chapl & Sen Lect Coll of St Mary & St Paul 78-84; V Cheltenham St Luke and St Jo *Glouc* from 85. *St Luke's Vicarage, College Road, Cheltenham, Glos GL53 7HX* Cheltenham (0242) 513940

WHALEY, Stephen John. b 57. York Univ BA79. Cranmer Hall Dur BA85 **d** 86 **p** 87. C Selby Abbey *York* 86-90; V Derringham Bank from 90. *110 Calvert Road, Hull HU5 5DH* Hull (0482) 52175

WHALLEY, Anthony Allen. b 41. Linc Th Coll 77. **d** 79 **p** 80. C Upton cum Chalvey *Ox* 79-83; R Newton Longville w Stoke Hammond and Whaddon from 83. *The Rectory, Drayton Road, Newton Longville, Milton Keynes MK17 0BH* Milton Keynes (0908) 377847

WHALLEY, George Peter. b 40. **d** 86 **p** 86. NSM Ellon *Ab* from 86; NSM Cruden from 86. *128 Braehead Drive, Cruden Bay, Aberdeenshire AB4 7NW* Cruden Bay (0779) 812511

WHALLEY, Michael Thomas. b 30. AKC55. **d** 56 **p** 57. C Nottm All SS *S'well* 56-58; C Clifton St Fran 58-60; C

Mansf St Pet 60; V N Wilford St Faith 60-66; Asst Chapl HM Pris Man 66-67; Chapl HM Youth Cust Cen Dover 67-69; Lic to Offic *Linc* 70-75; Chapl HM Pris Aylesbury 75-79; C Aylesbury *Ox* 79-83; P-in-c Bierton w Hulcott 83-89; TV Aylesbury w Bierton and Hulcott from 89. *The Vicarage, St James's Way, Bierton, Aylesbury HP22 5ED* Aylesbury (0296) 23920

WHARTON, Christopher Joseph. b 33. Keble Coll Ox BA57 MA61. **d** 79 **p** 80. NSM Harpenden St Nic *St Alb* from 79. *97 Overstone Road, Harpenden, Herts AL5 5PL* Harpenden (0582) 761164

WHARTON, Canon John Martin. b 44. Van Mildert Coll Dur BA69 Linacre Coll Ox BTh71 MA76. Ripon Hall Ox 69. **d** 72 **p** 73. C Birm St Pet *Birm* 72-75; C Croydon *Cant* 76-77; Dir Past Studies Ripon Coll Cuddesdon 77-83; C Cuddesdon *Ox* 79-83; Sec to Bd of Min and Tr *Bradf* from 83; Dir Post-Ord Tr from 84; Hon Can Bradf Cathl from 84. *6 Woodvale Crescent, Bingley, W Yorkshire BD16 4AL* Bradford (0274) 565789

WHARTON, Thomas Anthony. b 21. Bps' Coll Cheshunt 49. **d** 52 **p** 53. V Chipping Norton *Ox* 65-86; Chapl Bern *Eur* 86-89; rtd 89. *4 Bowling Green Crescent, Cirencester, Glos GL7 2HA* Cirencester (0285) 659043

WHATLEY, Preb Henry Lawson. b 16. Worc Coll Ox BA38. Wells Th Coll 38. **d** 39 **p** 40. R Colwall *Heref* 63-82; Preb Heref Cathl 76-82; rtd 82; Perm to Offic *Heref* from 84. *2 The Priory, Worcester Road, Ledbury, Herefordshire HR8 1PL* Ledbury (0531) 4795

WHATMORE, Terence James Brian. b 38. St Mich Coll Llan 64. **d** 66 **p** 67. C Sevenoaks St Jo *Roch* 66-70; C Newport St Julian *Mon* 70-72; V Bordesley St Benedict *Birm* 72-81; Chapl Florence w Siena and Assisi *Eur* 81-83; V Hove St Thos *Chich* 83-89; V Tipton St Jo *Lich* from 89. *St John's Vicarage, Upper Church Lane, Tipton, W Midlands DY4 9ND* 021-557 1793

WHATMOUGH, Michael Anthony. b 50. ARCO71 Ex Univ BA72. Edin Th Coll BD81. **d** 81 **p** 82. C Edin St Hilda *Edin* 81-84; C Edin St Fillan 81-84; C Salisbury St Thos and St Edm *Sarum* 84-86; R from 86; RD Salisbury from 90. *The Rectory, St Thomas's Square, Salisbury SP1 1BA* Salisbury (0722) 322537

WHATSON, Mark Edwin Chadwick. b 57. CEng83 MIMechE83 Southn Univ BSc79. N Ord Course 86. **d** 88 **p** 91. NSM Church Hulme *Ches* from 88. *Credo, 1 Gleneagles Drive, Holmes Chapel, Crewe CW4 7JA* Holmes Chapel (0477) 33117

WHAWELL, Arthur Michael. b 38. Sarum & Wells Th Coll 74. **d** 76 **p** 77. C Cottingham *York* 76-79; P-in-c Bessingby 79-84; P-in-c Carnaby 79-84; V Birchencliffe *Wakef* 84-87; Chapl St Bart Hosp Lon from 87; V St Bart Less *Lon* from 87. *The Vicar's Office, St Bartholomew's Hospital, London EC1A 7BE* 071-601 8888

WHEALE, Alan Leon. b 43. HNC65 AKC69. St Aug Coll Cant 69 DipMin89. **d** 70 **p** 71. C Tamworth *Lich* 70-73; C Cheddleton 73-75; V Garretts Green *Birm* 75-78; V Perry Beeches 78-83; V Winshill *Derby* 83-84; Deputation Appeals Org (E Midl) CECS 84-86; C Arnold *S'well* 86-88; V Daybrook from 88. *St Paul's Vicarage, 241 Oxclose Lane, Nottingham NG5 6FB* Nottingham (0602) 262686

WHEALE, Canon Gerald Arnold. b 32. St Jo Coll Dur BA56 Man Univ MEd74 PhD79. Ridley Hall Cam 56. **d** 58 **p** 59. C Tonge w Alkrington *Man* 58-60; Nigeria 60-62; R Moss Side St Jas *Man* 62-73; R Moss Side St Jas w St Clem from 73; AD Hulme from 82; Hon Can Man Cathl from 84. *The Rectory, 68 Dudley Road, Whalley Range, Manchester M16 8DE* 061-226 1684 or 226 4211

WHEAT, Charles Donald Edmund. b 37. Nottm Univ BA70 Sheff Univ MA76. Kelham Th Coll 58. **d** 62 **p** 63. C Sheff Arbourthorne *Sheff* 62-67; Lic to Offic *S'well* 67-69; SSM from 69; Chapl St Martin's Coll Lanc 70-73; Prior SSM Priory Sheff 73-75; Lic to Offic *Sheff* from 73; C Ranmoor 75-77; Asst Chapl Sheff Univ 75-77; Chapl 77-80; Prov SSM in England from 81; Dir 82-89; Lic to Offic *Blackb* 81-88; V Middlesb All SS *York* from 88. *All Saints' Vicarage, Grange Road, Middlesbrough, Cleveland TS1 2LR* Middlesbrough (0642) 245035

WHEATLEY, Canon Arthur. b 31. Edin Th Coll 68. **d** 70 **p** 70. C Dundee St Salvador *Bre* 70-71; C Dundee St Martin 70-71; P-in-c Dundee St Ninian 71-76; R Lossiemouth *Mor* 76-80; R Elgin 76-80; Can St Andr Cathl Inverness 78-80 and from 83; Provost St Andr Cathl Inverness 80-83; R Inverness St Andr 80-83; P-in-c Grantown-on-Spey from 83; P-in-c Rothiemurchus from 83. *The Rectory, Grant Road, Grantown-on-Spey, Morayshire PH26 3ER* Grantown-on-Spey (0479) 2866

WHEATLEY, Gordon Howard. b 29. Trin Coll Cam MA52. Lon Bible Coll DipTh58. **d** 90. C Cockley Cley w Gooderstone *Nor* from 90; C Didlington from 90; C Gt and Lt Cressingham w Threxton from 90; C Hilborough w Bodney from 90; C Oxborough w Foulden and Caldecote from 90. *The White House, Great Cressingham, Thetford, Norfolk IP25 6NL* Great Cressingham (07606) 304

WHEATLEY, James. b 40. Linc Th Coll 66. **d** 68 **p** 69. C Morpeth *Newc* 68-72; C Cowgate 72-74; C Tynemouth Cullercoats St Paul 74-76; V Newsham 76-84; R Bothal 84-89; C Newc St Geo 89-91; C Mexborough *Sheff* from 91. *The Vicarage, Church Street, Mexborough, S Yorkshire S64 0ER* Mexborough (0709) 582321

WHEATLEY, John. b 14. **d** 77 **p** 78. NSM Cambois *Newc* 77-87; rtd 87; Perm to Offic *Newc* from 87. *20 Cypress Gardens, Blyth, Northd NE24 2LP* Blyth (0670) 353353

WHEATLEY, Canon Maurice Samuel. b 13. AKC36. Chich Th Coll 36. **d** 37 **p** 38. SPG Area Sec (Dios Derby, Leics & S'well) 50-54; Youth & Educn Sec 54-60; Cand Sec 60-64; Appt & Tr Sec 64-72; Bermuda 72-80; Hon Can N Queensland from 62; rtd 80. *30 Barnes Close, Sturminster Newton, Dorset DT10 1BN* Sturminster Newton (0258) 73066

WHEATLEY, Ven Paul Charles. b 38. Dur Univ BA61. Linc Th Coll 61. **d** 63 **p** 64. C Bishopston *Bris* 63-68; Youth Chapl 68-73; V Swindon St Paul 73-77; TR Swindon Dorcan 77-79; R Ross *Heref* 79-81; P-in-c Brampton Abbotts 79-81; RD Ross and Archenfield 79-91; TR Ross w Brampton Abbotts, Bridstow and Peterstow 81-91; Preb Heref Cathl 87-91; Adn Sherborne *Sarum* from 91; P-in-c W Stafford w Frome Billet from 91. *The Rectory, West Stafford, Dorchester, Dorset DT2 8AB* Dorchester (0305) 264637

WHEATLEY, Peter William. b 47. Qu Coll Ox BA69 MA73 Pemb Coll Cam BA71 MA75. Ripon Hall Ox 72. **d** 73 **p** 74. C Fulham All SS *Lon* 73-78; V St Pancras H Cross w St Jude and St Pet 78-82; P-in-c Hampstead All SS 82-90; P-in-c Kilburn St Mary 82-90; V W Hampstead St Jas from 82; Dir Post-Ord Tr from 85; AD N Camden (Hampstead) from 88; P-in-c Kilburn St Mary w All So from 90. *St Mary's Vicarage, 134A Abbey Road, London NW6 4SN* 071-624 5434

WHEATLEY PRICE, Canon John. b 31. Em Coll Cam BA54 MA58. Ridley Hall Cam 54. **d** 56 **p** 57. C Drypool St Andr and St Pet *York* 56-59; CMS 59-76; Uganda 61-74; Adn Soroti 72-74; Kenya 74-76; Adn N Maseno 74-76; V Clevedon St Andr *B & W* 76-82; V Clevedon St Andr and Ch Ch 83-87; Hon Can Soroti from 78; Chapl Amsterdam *Eur* from 87. *Christ Church, Groenburgwal 42, 1011 HW Amsterdam, The Netherlands* Amsterdam (20) 624-8877

WHEATON, Christopher. b 49. St Jo Coll Nottm BTh80 LTh80. **d** 80 **p** 81. C Hatcham St Jas *S'wark* 80-83; C Warlingham w Chelsham and Farleigh 83-87; V Carshalton Beeches from 87. *The Vicarage, 38 Beeches Avenue, Carshalton, Surrey SM5 3LW* 081-647 6056

WHEATON, Canon David Harry. b 30. St Jo Coll Ox BA53 MA56 Lon Univ BD55. Oak Hill Th Coll 58. **d** 59 **p** 60. Tutor Oak Hill Th Coll 59-62; Prin 71-86; C Enfield Ch Ch Trent Park *Lon* 59-62; R Ludgershall *Ox* 62-66; V Onslow Square St Paul *Lon* 66-71; Chapl Brompton Hosp 69-71; Hon Can St Alb from 76; V Ware Ch Ch from 86; RD Hertf from 88; Chapl to HM The Queen from 90. *The Vicarage, 15 Hanbury Close, Ware, Herts SG12 7BZ* Ware (0920) 463165

WHEATON, Canon Ralph Ernest. b 32. St Jo Coll Dur BA54. Cranmer Hall Dur DipTh58. **d** 58 **p** 59. C Evington *Leic* 58-63; V Bardon Hill 63-71; V Whitwick St Jo the B 71-81; RD Akeley S (Coalville) 79-81; V Blyth *S'well* from 81; P-in-c Scofton w Osberton 83-86; V from 86; RD Worksop from 83; Hon Can S'well Minster from 86; P-in-c Langold from 86. *The Vicarage, Blyth, Worksop, Notts S81 8EQ* Blyth (0909) 591229

WHEBLE, Eric Clement. b 23. S'wark Ord Course 68. **d** 71 **p** 72. C Croydon H Trin *Cant* 71-78; Hon C Croydon St Sav 78-80; Hon C Norbury St Oswald 80-81; TV Selsdon St Jo w St Fran 81-84; TV Selsdon St Jo w St Fran *S'wark* 85-88; rtd 88. *20 Michael's Way, Fair Oak, Eastleigh, Hants S05 7NT* Southampton (0703) 693239

WHEELDON, John Graham. b 32. Sarum & Wells Th Coll 86. **d** 87 **p** 88. C Winchcombe, Gretton, Sudeley Manor etc *Glouc* 87-90; R Huntley and Longhope from 90. *The Rectory, 56 Byford Road, Huntley, Glos GL19 3EL* Gloucester (0452) 830800

✠**WHEELDON, Rt Rev Philip William.** b 13. OBE46. Down Coll Cam BA35 MA42. Westcott Ho Cam 35. **d** 37 **p** 38 **c** 54. C Farnham *Guildf* 37-40; CF (EC) 39-46; Abp's Dom Chapl *York* 46-49; Gen Sec CACTM 49-54; Preb Wells Cathl *B & W* 52-54; Suff Bp Whitby *York*

54-61; S Africa 61-65 and 68-76; Bp Kimberley and Kuruman 61-65 and 68-76; Asst Bp Worc 66-68; rtd 76; Asst Bp Wakef 77-85. *11 Toothill Avenue, Brighouse, W Yorkshire HD6 3SA*   Brighouse (0484) 715414

WHEELDON, Thomas Frederick Ronald. b 10. St Chad's Coll Dur 43. **d** 45 **p** 46. R Redmarshall *Dur* 52-75; R Elton 54-75; rtd 75. *7 Lilac Close, Carlton, Stockton-on-Tees, Cleveland TS21 1DS*   Sedgefield (0740) 30643

WHEELDON, William Dennis. b 25. Leeds Univ BA51. Coll of Resurr Mirfield 52. **d** 54 **p** 56. CR 55-76; Prin Coll of Resurr Mirfield 66-75; P-in-c Neuw Whittington *Derby* 83-87; P-in-c Belper Ch Ch and Milford 87-90; rtd 90. *10 Brooklyn, Threshfield, Skipton, N Yorkshire BD23 5ER*   Grassington (0756) 753187

WHEELER, Alban Massy. b 19. Dur Univ 40. Bps' Coll Cheshunt 40. **d** 43 **p** 44. Perm to Offic Glouc 68-81; Ex 81-84; rtd 84. *Dunster House, St Martin's Avenue, Shanklin, Isle of Wight PO37 6HB*   Isle of Wight (0983) 614379

WHEELER, Alexander Quintin Henry (Alastair). b 51. Lon Univ BA73 Nottm Univ DipTh75. St Jo Coll Nottm 74. **d** 77 **p** 78. C Kenilworth St Jo *Cov* 77-80; C Madeley *Heref* 80-83; P-in-c Draycott-le-Moors *Lich* 83-84; P-in-c Forsbrook 83-84; R Draycott-le-Moors w Forsbrook 84-91; V Nailsea Ch Ch *B & W* from 91. *The Vicarage, Christ Church Close, Nailsea, Bristol BS19 2DL*   Nailsea (0272) 855789

WHEELER, Andrew Charles. b 48. CCC Cam MA69 Makerere Univ Kampala MA72 Leeds Univ CertEd72. Trin Coll Bris BA88. **d** 88 **p** 88. CMS from 76; C Whitton *Sarum* 88-89; Egypt 89-90; Sudan from 90. *PO Box 87, Zamalek, Cairo, Egypt*

WHEELER, Anthony William. b 28. **d** 76 **p** 77. NSM Shirehampton *Bris* from 76; Chmn Avonmouth Miss to Seamen from 76. *76 Kingsweston Avenue, Bristol BS11 0AL*   Avonmouth (0272) 822261

WHEELER, David Ian. b 49. Southn Univ BSc70 PhD78. N Ord Course 87. **d** 90 **p** 91. C Blackpool St Jo *Blackb* from 90. *52 Leeds Road, Blackpool FY1 4HJ*   Blackpool (0253) 24036

WHEELER, David James. b 49. S Dios Minl Tr Scheme 87. **d** 90 **p** 91. C Hythe *Cant* from 90. *2 Palmarsh Avenue, Hythe, Kent CT21 6NT*   Hythe (0303) 261699

WHEELER, Desmond Reginald Sessel. b 18. Rhodes Univ Grahamstown BA49. St Paul's Grahamstown LTh51. **d** 50 **p** 51. V Sutton on Plym *Ex* 63-70; V Bishopsteignton 71-85; rtd 85; Perm to Offic *Ex* from 85. *30 Odlehill Grove, Abbotskerswell, Newton Abbot, Devon TQ12 5NJ*   Newton Abbot (0626) 51162

WHEELER, Sister Eileen Violet. b 28. TCert48 Newnham Coll Cam MA52. Chich Th Coll 85. **dss** 86 **d** 87. Bexhill St Pet *Chich* 86-87; Hon Par Dn 87-90; Par Dn from 90. *14 Barrack Road, Bexhill-on-Sea, E Sussex TN40 2AT*   Bexhill-on-Sea (0424) 215115

WHEELER, Frank George Michael. b 10. Reading Univ BA33. Linc Th Coll 68. **d** 69 **p** 70. C Nottm St Pet and St Jas *S'well* 69-81; rtd 81; Perm to Offic *S'well* from 81. *52 Milton Court, Nottingham NG5 7JB*   Nottingham (0602) 263123

WHEELER, Graham John. b 39. Llan St Mich DipTh66 BD78. **d** 66 **p** 67. C Roath St Martin *Llan* 66-71; C Cadoxton-juxta-Barry 71-75; Perm to Offic 75-79; C Highcliffe w Hinton Admiral *Win* 79-83; C Milton 83-90; P-in-c Bournemouth St Ambrose from 90. *St Ambrose Vicarage, 72 West Cliff Road, Bournemouth BH4 8BE*   Bournemouth (0202) 764957

WHEELER, Henry Gilbert Reginald. b 07. **d** 66 **p** 69. C Wear St Luke *Ex* 66-81; rtd 81. *23 Lucas Avenue, Exeter EX4 6LZ*   Exeter (0392) 73827

WHEELER, James Albert. b 49. Sarum & Wells Th Coll 74. **d** 76 **p** 77. C Orpington All SS *Roch* 76-79; C Roch 79-81; C Bexley St Jo 81-84; V Penge Lane H Trin from 84. *Holy Trinity Vicarage, 64 Lennard Road, London SE20 7LX*   081-778 7258

WHEELER, John David. b 31. Selw Coll Cam BA54 MA58. Ely Th Coll 54. **d** 56 **p** 57. C Old Charlton *S'wark* 56-60; C Northolt St Mary *Lon* 61-63; V Bush Hill Park St Mark 64-71; V Ealing St Pet Mt Park 71-74; V Truro St Paul *Truro* 74-79; V Truro St Paul and St Clem 79-80; P-in-c Hammersmith St Sav *Lon* 80-83; V Cobbold Road St Sav w St Mary from 83. *St Saviour's Vicarage, Cobbold Road, London W12 9LQ*   081-743 4769

WHEELER, Julian Aldous. b 48. Nottm Univ BTh74. Kelham Th Coll 70. **d** 75 **p** 76. C Bideford *Ex* 75-79; Lic to Offic 79-86; Hon C Parkham, Alwington, Buckland Brewer etc from 86. *Forge Cottage, Pump Lane, Abbotsham, Bideford, Devon EX39 5AY*   Bideford (0237) 473948

WHEELER, Mrs Madeleine. b 42. Gilmore Course 76. **dss** 78 **d** 87. Ruislip Manor St Paul *Lon* 78-87; Par Dn from 87; Chapl for Women's Min (Willesden Episc Area) from 86. *68 College Drive, Ruislip, Middx HA4 8SB*   Ruislip (0895) 633697

WHEELER, Nicholas Gordon Timothy. b 59. BCombStuds84. Linc Th Coll. **d** 84 **p** 85. C Hendon St Alphage *Lon* 84-87; C Wood Green St Mich w Bounds Green St Gabr etc 87-89; TV from 89. *27 Collings Close, London N22 4RL*   081-881 9836

WHEELER, Nicholas Paul. b 60. Ox Univ BA86 MA91. Wycliffe Hall Ox 83. **d** 87 **p** 88. C Wood Green St Mich w Bounds Green St Gabr etc *Lon* from 87. *218 Bracknell Close, London N22 5TA*   081-889 9475

WHEELER, Richard Anthony. b 23. St Chad's Coll Dur BA46 MA48 DipTh48. **d** 48 **p** 49. R Dorchester H Trin w Frome Whitfield *Sarum* 64-73; TV Dorchester 73-87; rtd 87. *25 Victoria Road, Dorchester, Dorset DT1 1SB*   Dorchester (0305) 262803

WHEELER, Richard Roy. b 44. K Coll Lon BD72. St Aug Coll Cant. **d** 74 **p** 74. C Brixton St Matt *S'wark* 74-78; Dir St Matt Meeting Place Brixton 78-79; Sec BCC Community Work Resource Unit 79-82; TV Southn (City Cen) *Win* 83-88; TR from 88. *St Michael's Vicarage, 55 Bugle Street, Southampton SO1 0AG*   Southampton (0703) 224242

WHEELER, William Thomas Pope. b 1900. Chich Th Coll 40. **d** 42 **p** 42. V Mountsorrel St Pet *Leic* 65-67; rtd 67; Lic to Offic Liv 68-69; Pet & Ely 69-72; Perm to Offic *Pet* from 72; Lic *Leic* 72-74; *S'wark* 74-79. *Abbeyfield, 146 London Road, Gloucester GL2 0RS*   Gloucester (0452) 505450

WHEELOCK, Canon John Richard. b 18. TCD BA41 MA51. CITC 42. **d** 42 **p** 43. I Annagh Union K, E & A 56-83; Preb Kilmore Cathl 72-83; rtd 83. *c/o Mrs J Elliott, Tomkin Road, Belturbet, Co Cavan, Irish Republic*

WHEELWRIGHT, Michael Harvey. b 39. Bps' Coll Cheshunt 64. **d** 67 **p** 68. C Glen Parva and S Wigston *Leic* 67-70; C Evington 70-74; V Leic St Eliz Nether Hall 74-79; Chapl Prudhoe Hosp Northd from 79. *61 Dene Road, Wylam, Northd NE41 8HB*   Prudhoe (0661) 32501 or 852508

WHELAN, Canon John Bernard. b 17. Dur Univ LTh41. Oak Hill Th Coll 38. **d** 47 **p** 48. C Bury St Mary *Man* 68-71; Asst Chapl Crumpsall Hosp Man 71-73; Chapl N Man Gen Hosp 73-82; rtd 82; Chapl Gran Canary Las Palmas *Eur* 82-84; Asst Chapl Valletta w Sliema from 84; Can Malta Cathl from 87. *Bishop's House, Rudolphe Street, Sliema, Malta*   Malta (356) 330575

WHELAN, Miss Patricia Jean. b 33. ACA55 FCA82. Dalton Ho Bris 58. **dss** 64 **d** 87. Stapleford *S'well* 62-69; Aylesbury *Ox* 69-75; Bushbury *Lich* 75-77; Patchway *Bris* 77-81; Trin Coll Bris 81-82; W Swindon LEP 82-86; High Wycombe *Ox* 86-87; Par Dn 87-91; Par Dn Ox St Ebbe w H Trin and St Pet from 91. *32 Dale Close, Oxford OX1 1TU*   Oxford (0865) 727447

WHELAN, Peter Warwick Armstrong. b 34. Southn Univ BTh80 Open Univ BA80. Sarum Th Coll 69. **d** 71 **p** 72. C Salisbury St Mark *Sarum* 71-73; C Solihull *Birm* 73-77; TR Shirley 77-86; Chapl Whittington Hosp Lon from 86; Chapl R N and Hornsey Cen Hosps Lon from 86. *51 Tytherton Road, London N19 4PZ*   071-272 5309 or 272 3070

WHELAN, Raymond Keith. b 40. Cant Sch of Min 85. **d** 88 **p** 91. C Eastbourne St Andr *Chich* from 88. *35 Martello Road, Eastbourne, E Sussex BN22 7SS*   Eastbourne (0323) 39395

WHERRY, Anthony Michael. b 44. Nottm Univ BA65 Univ Coll Lon DAA66. W Midl Minl Tr Course 88. **d** 91. NSM Worc City St Paul and Old St Martin etc *Worc* from 91. *2 Redfern Avenue, Red Hill, Worcester WR5 1PU*   Worcester (0905) 358532

WHETTEM, John Curtiss. b 27. Peterho Cam BA50 MA55. Wycliffe Hall Ox 50. **d** 52 **p** 53. C Clifton Ch Ch *Bris* 52-55; C Wandsworth All SS *S'wark* 55-58; V Soundwell *Bris* 58-63; Youth Chapl 63-68; Chapl Bris Cathl 64-68; R N Mundham w Hunston *Chich* 68-80; P-in-c Oving w Merston 75-80; TR Swanborough *Sarum* from 80; RD Pewsey 84-89. *The Rectory, Manningford Bruce, Pewsey, Wilts SN9 6JW*   Stonehenge (0980) 630308

WHETTER, Michael Arnold. b 30. Bris Univ BA51. Wells Th Coll 53. **d** 55 **p** 56. C Dursley *Glouc* 55-58; C Coppenhall *Ches* 58-61; R Ches H Trin 61-71; V Stockport St Alb Hall Street from 72; Chapl Cherry Tree Hosp Stockport from 72; Chapl Offerton Hosp Stockport from 72. *St Alban's Vicarage, Offerton Lane, Stockport, Cheshire SK2 5AG*   061-480 3773

WHETTINGSTEEL, Raymond Edward. b 44. S Dios Minl Tr Scheme 79. **d** 82 **p** 83. NSM Sholing *Win* 82-84; C Southn Maybush St Pet 84-89; V Hatherden w Tangley, Weyhill and Penton Mewsey from 89. *The Rectory, Penton Mewsey, Andover, Hants SP11 0RD* Weyhill (0264) 773554

WHETTON, Nicholas John. b 56. St Jo Coll Nottm 83. **d** 86 **p** 87. C Hatf *Sheff* 86-90; V Cornholme *Wakef* from 90. *30 Cross Lee Road, Todmorden, Lancs OL14 8EH* Todmorden (0706) 813604

WHIFFEN, Canon William Timothy. b 25. SS Coll Cam BA50 MA54. Linc Th Coll. **d** 52 **p** 53. C Wigan St Mich *Liv* 52-56; India 57-69; V Clay Cross *Derby* 69-74; Sec (Overseas Division) USPG 74-79; TR Woughton *Ox* 79-85; P-in-c Seer Green and Jordans from 85; Hon Can Ch Ch from 91. *The Vicarage, 43 Long Grove, Seer Green, Beaconsfield, Bucks HP9 2YN* Beaconsfield (04946) 5013

WHILD, Canon James Edward. b 24. Bris Univ BA52. Tyndale Hall Bris 48. **d** 53 **p** 54. Australia from 56; Hon Can Sydney 73-77; Can from 77; rtd 89. *53 Darling Point Road, Darling Point, NSW, Australia 2027* Sydney (2) 363-3657

✠**WHINNEY, Rt Rev Michael Humphrey Dickens.** b 30. Pemb Coll Cam BA55 MA59. Gen Th Sem (NY) STM90 Ridley Hall Cam 55. **d** 57 **p** 58 **c** 82. C Rainham *Chelmsf* 57-60; Hd Cam Univ Miss Bermondsey 60-67; Chapl 67-73; V Bermondsey St Jas w Ch Ch *S'wark* 67-73; Adn S'wark 73-82; Suff Bp Aston *Birm* 82-85; Bp S'well 85-88; Asst Bp Birm from 88. *3 Moor Green Lane, Moseley, Birmingham B13 8NE or, Diocesan Office, Birmingham B17 0BQ* 021-449 2856 or 428 2228

WHINTON, William Francis Ivan. b 35. N Ord Course 77. **d** 80 **p** 81. NSM Stockport St Mary *Ches* 80-82; NSM Disley 82-87; V Birtles from 87; Dioc Officer for Disabled from 89. *The Vicarage, Birtles, Macclesfield, Cheshire SK10 4RX* Chelford (0625) 861238

WHIPP, Anthony Douglas. b 46. Leeds Univ BSc68. Ripon Coll Cuddesdon 84. **d** 86 **p** 87. C Dalston *Carl* 86-89; V Holme Cultram St Mary from 89; V Holme Cultram St Cuth from 89. *The Vicarage, Abbey Town, Carlisle CA5 4SP* Abbeytown (09656) 246

WHIPP, Dr Margaret Jane. b 55. MRCP82 FRCR86 LMH Ox BA76 Sheff Univ MB, ChB79. N Ord Course 87. **d** 90. NSM Wickersley *Sheff* from 90. *7 Scholey Road, Wickersley, Rotherham, S Yorkshire S66 0HU* Rotherham (0709) 548661

WHITAKER, David Arthur Edward. b 27. New Coll Ox BA50 MA55. Wells Th Coll 51. **d** 53 **p** 54. C W Bridgford *S'well* 53-56; CF 56-58; V Clifton St Fran *S'well* 58-63; Basutoland 63-66; Lesotho 66-69; R Buckerell *Ex* 69-76; R Feniton 69-76; P-in-c Tiverton St Pet 76-79; R from 79. *St Peter's Rectory, Park Hill, Tiverton, Devon EX16 6RW* Tiverton (0884) 254079

WHITAKER, Michael Benjamin. b 60. Nottm Univ BA83. Sarum & Wells Th Coll 85. **d** 87 **p** 88. C Gt Grimsby St Mary and St Jas *Linc* from 87. *56 Cartergate, Grimsby, S Humberside DN31 1RT* Grimsby (0472) 356385

WHITBY, Suffragan Bishop of. *See* BATES, Rt Rev Gordon

WHITCOMBE, Michael George Stanley. b 34. Keble Coll Ox BA58 MA62. Wycliffe Hall Ox DipTh59. **d** 60 **p** 61. C Nuneaton St Nic *Cov* 60-63; Malaysia 63-67; V Warw St Paul *Cov* 67-68; Hong Kong 68-72; V Lightcliffe *Wakef* 72-79; R Largs *Glas* 79-81; P-in-c Ipswich St Fran *St E* 81-82; TR from 82. *St Francis's Rectory, 190 Hawthorn Drive, Ipswich IP2 0QQ* Ipswich (0473) 684983

WHITCOMBE, Stanley Edward Cuthbert. b 07. K Coll Lon 42. **d** 42 **p** 42. R Bourton w Frankton *Cov* 65-72; rtd 72; Perm to Offic Wakef 73-79 and from 81; Glas 79-81. *10 Cricketers Close, Ackworth, Pontefract, W Yorkshire WF7 7PW* Hemsworth (0977) 616477

WHITCROFT, Graham Frederick. b 42. Oak Hill Th Coll 64. **d** 66 **p** 67. C Attercliffe *Sheff* 69-72; V Kimberworth Park 72-85; V Lepton *Wakef* from 85. *The Vicarage, 138 Wakefield Road, Lepton, Huddersfield HD8 0EJ* Huddersfield (0484) 602172

WHITE, Alan. b 18. Man Univ BSc39 MSc40 St Cath Soc Ox BA42 MA46 Leeds Univ MEd52. Ripon Hall Ox 40. **d** 42 **p** 43. Lic to Offic *Worc* from 56; Chapl Bromsgrove Sch *Worcs* 72-83; rtd 83. *25 Leadbetter Drive, Bromsgrove, Worcs B61 7JG* Bromsgrove (0527) 77955

WHITE, Alan. b 43. Ex Univ BA65. Chich Th Coll 65. **d** 68 **p** 69. C Upper Clapton St Matt *Lon* 68-72; C Southgate Ch Ch 72-76; P-in-c Friern Barnet St Pet le Poer 76-79; V 79-85; TR Ex St Thos and Em *Ex* from

85. *St Thomas's Vicarage, 57 Cowick Street, Exeter EX4 1HR* Exeter (0392) 55219

WHITE, Mrs Alison Mary. b 56. St Aid Coll Dur BA78. Cranmer Hall Dur 83. **d** 86. NSM Ches le Street *Dur* 86-89; Hon Par Dn Birtley from 89; Adv in Local Miss from 89. *6 Ruskin Road, Birtley, Co Durham DH3 1AD*

WHITE, Andrew Paul Bartholomew. b 64. MIOT85 ABIST85 St Thos Hosp Lon DipSurg84 DA84 CertMBiol84. Ridley Hall Cam 86. **d** 90. C Battersea Rise St Mark *S'wark* from 90. *24 Parma Crescent, London SW11 1LT* 071-223 9341

WHITE, Basil Rowntree. b 14. Lon Univ BA36. St Deiniol's Hawarden. **d** 62 **p** 63. Hon C Stoke-upon-Trent *Lich* 62-75; Hd Master St Pet High Sch Stoke-on-Trent 62-75; Perm to Offic *Ripon* 75-80; P-in-c Fornham St Martin w Timworth *St E* 80-83; rtd 84; Hon C Bishop's Stortford St Mich *St Alb* from 87. *Cowell House, 24 Apton Road, Bishop's Stortford, Herts CM23 3SN* Bishop's Stortford (0279) 654414

WHITE, Charles William Langston. b 13. Lon Coll of Div 52. **d** 54 **p** 55. R St Leonards St Leon *Chich* 68-76; Jerusalem 76-78; rtd 78. *Shalom, Church Knowle, Wareham, Dorset BH20 5NQ* Wareham (0929) 480728

WHITE, Canon Christopher Norman Hessler. b 32. TD76. St Cath Coll Cam BA56 MA60. Cuddesdon Coll 57. **d** 59 **p** 60. C Solihull *Birm* 59-62; C Leeds St Aid *Ripon* 62-65; CF (TA) 64-85; V Aysgarth *Ripon* 65-74; R Richmond 74-76; P-in-c Hudswell w Downholme and Marske 75-76; R Richmond w Hudswell from 76; RD Richmond 75-80; Hon Can Ripon Cathl from 89. *The Rectory, Richmond, N Yorkshire DL10 7AQ* Richmond (0748) 923398

WHITE, Clement. b 25. AKC50. **d** 51 **p** 52. V Monkseaton St Pet *Newc* 69-89; rtd 89. *18 Beach Road, Tynemouth, Tyne & Wear NE30 2NS* 091-258 7505

WHITE, Colin Davidson. b 44. St And Dioc Tr Course 85. **d** 88 **p** 89. NSM Glenrothes *St And* 88-91. *23 Ivanhoe Drive, Glenrothes, Fife KY6 2NB* Glenrothes (0592) 759386

WHITE, Crispin Michael. b 42. Bps' Coll Cheshunt 62. **d** 65 **p** 66. C S Harrow St Paul *Lon* 65-67; C Mill Hill St Mich 67-68; Canada 68-71; Toc H Padre (W Region) 71-75; (E Midl Region) 75-82; Ind Chapl *Portsm* from 82. *11 Burnham Wood, Fareham, Hants PO16 7UD* Fareham (0329) 239390

WHITE, David Christopher. b 51. Lon Univ LLB73. St Jo Coll Nottm 86. **d** 88 **p** 89. C Bulwell St Mary *S'well* from 88. *123 Squires Avenue, Nottingham NG6 8GL* Nottingham (0602) 761130

WHITE, David John. b 26. Leeds Univ BA53. Coll of Resurr Mirfield 53. **d** 55 **p** 56. C Brighton St Pet *Chich* 55-58; C Wednesbury St Jas *Lich* 58-60; C Bishops Hull St Jo *B & W* 60-61; R Morton *Derby* 61-62; In RC Ch 62-73; Perm to Offic *Nor* from 73; Lect Whitelands Coll Lon 72-75; R Tregony w St Cuby and Cornelly *Truro* 75-79; R Castle Bromwich SS Mary and Marg *Birm* 79-83; V Plymouth St Simon *Ex* 83-88; R Lapford, Nymet Rowland and Coldridge from 88. *The Rectory, Lapford, Crediton, Devon EX17 6PX* Lapford (0363) 83321

WHITE, David Martin. b 50. St Jo Coll Dur BA72. Cranmer Hall Dur DipTh73. **d** 74 **p** 75. C Ripley *Derby* 74-78; C Normanton 78-80; C-in-c Sinfin 78-80; P-in-c 80; V 80-88; P-in-c Belper from 88. *St Peter's Vicarage, Chesterfield Road, Belper, Derby DE5 1FD* Belper (0773) 2148

WHITE, David Paul. b 58. Oak Hill Th Coll. **d** 84 **p** 85. C Toxteth Park St Clem *Liv* 84-87; C Woodford Wells *Chelmsf* 87-89; C Woodside Park St Barn *Lon* 89-90; TV Canford Magna *Sarum* from 90. *The Vicarage, 359 Sopwith Crescent, Wimborne, Dorset BH21 1XQ* Wimborne (0202) 886320

WHITE, Derek. b 35. **d** 84 **p** 85. Hon C St Marylebone St Cypr *Lon* 84-87; C from 87; Bp's Chapl for the Homeless from 87. *80 Coleraine Road, London SE3 7BE or, 17 Homer Row, London W1H 1HU* 081-858 3622 or 071-723 3501

WHITE, Derek James. Birm Univ BA56. Chich Th Coll 56. **d** 58 **p** 59. C Stanmer w Falmer and Moulsecoomb *Chich* 58-61; Asst Chapl Ardingly Coll Haywards Heath 61-63; Chapl 63-72; C Glynde, W Firle and Beddingham *Chich* 72-73; R Bramber w Botolphs 73-87; R Beeding and Bramber w Botolphs from 87. *The Rectory, Church Lane, Beeding, Steyning, W Sussex BN44 3HP* Steyning (0903) 815474

WHITE, Douglas Richard Leon. b 49. Linc Th Coll. **d** 83 **p** 84. C Warsop *S'well* 83-88; R Kirkby in Ashfield St Thos from 88. *109 Diamond Avenue, Kirkby-in-Ashfield, Nottingham NG17 7LX* Mansfield (0623) 755131

WHITE, Dudley William. b 33. Univ of Wales (Ban) BSc53. St Mich Coll Llan BD69. **d** 59 **p** 60. C Sketty *S & B* 59-66; R New Radnor and Llanfihangel Nantmelan 66-70; V Penyfai w Tondu *Llan* 70-77; V Swansea St Jude *S & B* from 77. *St Jude's Vicarage, Hillside Crescent, Swansea SA2 0RD* Swansea (0792) 473154

WHITE, Egbert Douglas. b 06. Keble Coll Ox BA28 MA32. Wycliffe Hall Ox 28. **d** 34 **p** 35. C Weston-super-Mare St Paul *B & W* 34-36; P-in-c Locking 40-42; C Kewstoke 44-49; V Mudford 49-87; R Chilton Cantelo w Ashington 67-87; R Chilton Cantelo, Ashington, Mudford, Rimpton etc from 87. *The Vicarage, Mudford, Yeovil, Somerset BA21 5TJ* Marston Magna (0935) 850381

WHITE, Francis. b 49. Univ of Wales (Cardiff) BSc(Econ)70 DSocStuds71. St Jo Coll Nottm DipTh78. **d** 80 **p** 81. C Dur St Nic *Dur* 80-84; C Ches le Street 84-87; Chapl Dur and Ches le Street Hosps 87-89; C Birtley *Dur* from 89. *The Vicarage, 6 Ruskin Road, Birtley, Chester le Street, Co Durham DH3 1AD* 091-410 2115

WHITE, Frederick Stanley. b 28. Lon Univ DHRK66. S'wark Ord Course 62. **d** 67 **p** 68. C Eastham *Ches* 67-72; Asst Chapl Miss to Seamen 72-75; OCF from 75; V Andreas St Jude *S & M* from 75; V Jurby from 75; R Andreas from 79; RD Ramsey 78-88. *The Rectory, Village Road, Andreas, Ramsey, Isle of Man* Ramsey (0624) 880419

WHITE, Frederick William Hartland. b 22. MBE62. Kelham Th Coll 39. **d** 45 **p** 46. CF 50-70; Asst Chapl Gen 70-74; QHC from 73; V Harrow St Mary *Lon* 74-87; rtd 87. *Whitesfield House, 5 Seend Cleeve, Melksham, Wilts SN12 6PS*

WHITE, Gavin Donald. b 27. Toronto Univ BA49 Lon Univ PhD70. Trin Coll Toronto BD61 Gen Th Sem (NY) STM68 St Steph Ho Ox 51. **d** 53 **p** 54. Canada 53-58; Zanzibar 59-62; Kenya 62-66; C Hampstead St Steph *Lon* 68-70; Lect Glas Univ from 71; Lic to Offic *Glas* 71-83; Hon C Glas St Marg from 83. *99 Mossgiel Road, Glasgow G43 2BY* 041-632 3151

WHITE, Geoffrey Brian. b 54. Jes Coll Ox BA76 MA80. St Steph Ho Ox 76. **d** 79 **p** 80. C Huddersfield St Pet *Wakef* 79-82; C Flixton St Mich *Man* 82-84; TV Westhoughton 84-91; V Stevenage St Mary Sheppall w Aston *St Alb* from 91. *St Mary's Vicarage, 148 Hydean Way, Sheppall, Stevenage, Herts SG2 9YA* Stevenage (0438) 351963

WHITE, Preb Geoffrey Gordon. b 28. Selw Coll Cam BA50 MA54. Cuddesdon Coll 51. **d** 53 **p** 54. C Bradford-on-Avon *Sarum* 53-56; C Kennington St Jo *S'wark* 56-61; V Leeds St Wilfrid *Ripon* 61-63; Chapl K Coll Hosp *Lon* 63-66; V Aldwick *Chich* 66-76; V Brighton Gd Shep Preston from 76; Preb Chich Cathl from 90. *The Good Shepherd Vicarage, 272 Dyke Road, Brighton BN1 5AE* Brighton (0273) 552737

WHITE, Gordon Benjamin James. b 13. Worc Ord Coll 60. **d** 62 **p** 63. V Leonard Stanley *Glouc* 65-83; RD Stonehouse 67-79; rtd 83. *The Old Vicarage, Honeyhill, Wootton Bassett, Swindon SN4 7DY* Swindon (0793) 851363

WHITE, Harold Kent. b 05. St Cath Soc Ox BA27 MA37. St Steph Ho Ox 28. **d** 28 **p** 29. V St Mary Aldermary *Lon* 62-75; rtd 75; Chapl Venice w Trieste *Eur* 75-76. *3 Pickwick Road, London SE21 7JN* 071-274 1006

WHITE, Howard Christopher Graham. b 43. Leeds Univ BA65. Coll of Resurr Mirfield 67. **d** 67 **p** 68. C Friern Barnet St Jas *Lon* 67-71; P-in-c Uxbridge Moor 71-73; Asst Chapl RADD 73-77; Hon C Corringham *Chelmsf* 73-77; Team Ldr St Sav Cen for the Deaf Acton 77-84; Perm to Offic *Guildf* from 86. *Drake Cottage, Hook Hill Lane, Woking, Surrey GU22 0PS*

WHITE, Ian Terence. b 56. CertEd. Ripon Coll Cuddesdon 83. **d** 86 **p** 87. C Maidstone St Martin *Cant* 86-89; C Earley St Pet *Ox* 89-91; TV Schorne from 91. *The Rectory, Quainton, Aylesbury, Bucks HP22 4AP* Aylesbury (0296) 75237

WHITE, Janice. b 49. Trin Coll Bris IDC76. **d** 91. C Claygate *Guildf* from 91. *The Church Hall Flat, Church Road, Claygate, Esher, Surrey KT10 0JP* Esher (0372) 464894

WHITE, Jeremy Spencer. b 54. St Luke's Coll Ex BEd78. Wycliffe Hall Ox 81. **d** 84 **p** 85. C S Molton w Nymet St George, High Bray etc *Ex* 84-87; TV from 87. *The Vicarage, Chittlehampton, Umberleigh, Devon EX37 9QL* Chittlehamholt (07694) 654

WHITE, Canon John Austin. b 42. Hull Univ BA64. Coll of Resurr Mirfield 64. **d** 66 **p** 67. C Leeds St Aid *Ripon* 66-69; Asst Chapl Leeds Univ 69-73; Chapl N Ord Course 73-82; Can and Prec Windsor from 82. *8 The*

Cloisters, Windsor Castle, Windsor, Berks SL4 1NJ Windsor (0753) 860409

WHITE, John Bernard Valentine. b 07. TCD BA30 MA36. **d** 30 **p** 31. Dioc Curate (Cork) *C, C & R* 58-65; Miss to Seamen 58-65; rtd 70. *Raintree, Fort View, Ardbrack, Kinsale, Co Cork, Irish Republic*

WHITE, John Christopher. b 62. Keble Coll Ox BA84. Wycliffe Hall Ox 86. **d** 89 **p** 90. C Southway *Ex* from 89. *160 Bampfylde Way, Plymouth PL6 6ST* Plymouth (0752) 702050

WHITE, John Cooper. b 58. LTCL K Alfred's Coll Win BEd82. St Steph Ho Ox 86. **d** 89 **p** 90. C Christchurch *Win* from 89. *105B Stour Road, Christchurch, Dorset BH23 1JN* Christchurch (0202) 486644

WHITE, John Emlyn. b 34. St Aid Birkenhead 59. **d** 62 **p** 63. C Cricklade w Latton *Bris* 62-63; C Kingswood 63-66; C Ashton-on-Ribble St Andr *Blackb* 66-69; V Heyhouses 69-71; Chapl Roundway Hosp Devizes 71-77; Chapl R Variety Children's Hosp 77-89; Chapl K Coll and Belgrave Hosps Lon 77-89; Regional Community Relns Co-ord from 89. *26 Harbour Street, Whitstable, Kent CT5 1AH* Whitstable (0227) 265572

WHITE, John Francis. b 47. Qu Coll Cam BA69 MA73. Cuddesdon Coll 72. **d** 72 **p** 73. Sacr Wakef Cathl *Wakef* 72-73; Prec 73-76; V Thurlstone 76-82; P-in-c Hoyland Swaine 81-82; V Chapelthorpe from 82. *The Vicarage, Church Lane, Chapelthorpe, Wakefield, W Yorkshire WF4 3JB* Wakefield (0924) 255360

WHITE, John Malcolm. b 54. Aston Univ BSc77. Trin Coll Bris BA87. **d** 87 **p** 88. C Harborne Heath *Birm* from 87. *58 Station Road, Harborne, Birmingham B17 9LX* 021-426 6228

WHITE, John McKelvey. b 57. QUB BA. TCD DipTh82. **d** 82 **p** 83. C Clooney *D & R* 82-84; C Belf H Trin *Conn* 84-86; I Kilcronaghan w Draperstown and Sixtowns *D & R* from 86. *The Rectory, 10 Rectory Road, Tobermore, Magherafelt, Co Londonderry BT45 5QP* Draperstown (0648) 28823

WHITE, John Neville. b 41. Edin Univ MA63. Cranmer Hall Dur DipTh65. **d** 65 **p** 66. C Sedgefield *Dur* 65-68; C Stoke *Cov* 68-72; V Wrose *Bradf* 72-90; V Farsley from 90. *The Vicarage, 9 St John's Avenue, Farsley, Pudsey, W Yorkshire LS28 5DJ* Pudsey (0532) 574009

WHITE, Jonathan Roger. b 36. Lon Univ BSc61. Cuddesdon Coll 63. **d** 65 **p** 66. C Swinton St Pet *Man* 65-67; C Prestwich St Mary 67-70; R Salford Stowell Memorial 70-74; TV Swan *Ox* 74-78; P-in-c Monks Risborough 78-84; P-in-c Gt and Lt Kimble 78-84; P-in-c Prestwood 84-87; P-in-c Gt w Lt Hampden 85-87; P-in-c Prestwood and Gt Hampden from 87; RD Wendover from 89. *The Vicarage, Prestwood, Great Missenden, Bucks HP16 0HJ* Great Missenden (02406) 2130

WHITE, Canon Joseph George. b 19. Liv Univ DPA50 Leeds Univ CertEd57. St Deiniol's Hawarden 61. **d** 61 **p** 62. V Rainow w Saltersford *Ches* 65-72; P-in-c Macclesfield Forest w Wildboarclough 66-72; TV Ches 72-75; Dir of Educn 74-88; Hon Can Ches Cathl from 79; P-in-c Capenhurst 79-87; rtd 88. *17 Endsleigh Close, Chester CH2 1LX* Chester (0244) 382376

WHITE, Julian Edward Llewellyn. b 53. St D Coll Lamp BA79 Chich Th Coll 79. **d** 79 **p** 80. C Newport St Mark *Mon* 79-83; TV Llanmartin 83-86; R Llandogo and Tintern from 86. *The Rectory, Llandogo, Monmouth, Gwent NP5 4TW* Dean (0594) 530887

WHITE, Keith. b 54. Liv Poly BA78 Lon Univ BD82. Wycliffe Hall Ox 78. **d** 81 **p** 82. C Edin St Thos *Edin* 81-84; C Fulwood Sheff 84-87; R Heigham H Trin *Nor* from 87. *The Rectory, Essex Street, Norwich NR2 2BL* Norwich (0603) 621120

WHITE, Keith Robert. b 48. St Jo Coll Nottm. **d** 84 **p** 85. C Erith St Paul *Roch* 84-88; Chapl Salisbury Coll of Tech *Sarum* 88. *22 Chapel Hill, Dartford, Kent DA1 4BY* Dartford (0322) 523779

WHITE, Kenneth Charles. b 15. TD. FCIS FHSM. St Deiniol's Hawarden 76. **d** 77 **p** 78. Hon C Upton Ascension *Ches* 77-79; R Warburton 79-82; rtd 82; Perm to Offic *Ches* from 82; Chapl Asst Countess of Ches Hosp from 84. *9 Barons Court, Liverpool Road, Chester CH2 1BE* Chester (0244) 383194

WHITE, Kenneth Charles. b 26. Tyndale Hall Bris 48. **d** 54 **p** 56. V Leyton Ch Ch *Chelmsf* 66-81; V Totland Bay *Portsm* 81-91; rtd 91. *30 Pendwyallt Road, Whitchurch, Cardiff CF4 7EG* Cardiff (0222) 611529

WHITE, Malcolm Robert. b 46. Man Univ BSc68. St Jo Coll Dur 74. **d** 77 **p** 78. C Linthorpe *York* 77-81; C Sutton St Jas and Wawne 81-83; V Upper Holloway St Pet w St Jo *Lon* from 83. *St Peter's Vicarage, 2 Anatola Road, London N19 5HN* 071-263 6915

WHITE, Marilyn. d 88. NSM Westbury-on-Severn w Flaxley and Blaisdon *Glouc* from 88. *Beacon View, Northwood Green, Westbury-on-Severn, Glos* Westbury-on-Severn (045276) 419

WHITE, Maureen Barbara. b 42. Bris Univ BA63. Oak Hill NSM Course 87. d 89. NSM Wallington H Trin *S'wark* from 89. *20 Woodcote Avenue, Wallington, Surrey SM6 0QY* 081-647 1639

WHITE, Nicolas John. b 54. BEd. Wycliffe Hall Ox. d 83 p 84. C Islington St Mary *Lon* 83-87; Chapl Univ Coll Lon 87-89. *3 Carleton Villas, Leighton Grove, London NW5 2TU* 071-482 2133

WHITE, Noel Louis. b 11. TCD BA45 MA58. CITC 46. d 46 p 47. I Belf St Silas *Conn* 62-74; Asst Gen Sec CMS Ireland 74-81; Lic to Offic *D & D* 75-82; rtd 82; Hon C Newtownards *D & D* from 82. *90 Hamilton Road, Bangor, Co Down* Bangor (0247) 450121

WHITE, Peter Francis. b 27. St Edm Hall Ox BA51 MA55. Ridley Hall Cam 51. d 53 p 54. CF 62-78; R Barming *Roch* 78-89; rtd 89. *Wilmington, 10 Fauchons Lane, Bearsted, Maidstone, Kent ME14 4AH* Maidstone (0622) 30278

WHITE, Canon Peter John. b 23. Hertf Coll Ox BA45 MA49. Wycliffe Hall Ox 45. d 47 p 48. V Chipping Campden *Glouc* 69-75; P-in-c Ebrington 69-75; RD Campden 73-88; V Chipping Campden w Ebrington 75-88; Hon Can Glouc Cathl from 86; rtd 88. *14 Mannington Way, West Moors, Wimborne, Dorset BH22 0JE* Wimborne (0202) 872254

WHITE, Peter John. b 26. St Aid Birkenhead 57. d 60 p 61. C Toxteth Park St Gabr *Liv* 60-62; C Huyton St Mich 62-63; V Thornham w Gravel Hole *Man* 63-68; C Keighley *Bradf* 68-71; C Newington w Dairycoates *York* 71-75; C Frodingham *Linc* 75-80; R Mareham-le-Fen and Revesby 80-86; V Wrawby from 86; V Melton Ross w New Barnetby from 86. *The Vicarage, Wrawby, Brigg, S Humberside DN20 8RR* Brigg (0652) 57605

WHITE, Philip William. b 53. Bede Hall Dur CertEd75. St Jo Coll Nottm DipCM91. d 91. C Clifton *York* from 91. *59 The Garlands, Clifton, York YO3 6NZ* York (0904) 645937

WHITE, Canon Phillip George. b 33. Univ of Wales (Lamp) BA54. St Mich Coll Llan 54. d 56 p 57. C Tongwynlais *Llan* 56-58; C Mountain Ash 58-60; C Aberavon 60-62; Area Sec (Middx) CMS 62-64; V Treherbert *Llan* 64-76; P-in-c Treorchy 75-76; V Treherbert w Treorchy 76-77; V Pyle w Kenfig from 77; RD Margam from 86; Can Llan Cathl from 91. *The Vicarage, Pyle, Bridgend, M Glam CF33 6PG* Bridgend (0656) 740500

WHITE, Mrs Priscilla Audrey. b 62. St Hugh's Coll Ox BA84. Wycliffe Hall Ox 87. d 89. Par Dn Southway *Ex* from 89. *160 Bampfylde Way, Plymouth PL6 6ST* Plymouth (0752) 702050

WHITE, Canon Richard. b 18. Sarum Th Coll 46. d 49 p 50. V Marske in Cleveland *York* 59-85; Can and Preb York Minster 78-86; rtd 85. *68 West Dyke Road, Redcar, Cleveland TS10 1HL* Redcar (0642) 479784

WHITE, Richard Alfred. b 49. DipSocWork CQSW. St Jo Coll Nottm. d 90 p 91. C Leic St Phil *Leic* from 90. *22 Trueway Road, Leicester LE5 5UP* Leicester (0533) 738528

WHITE, Richard Allen. b 25. Open Univ BA78 Southn Univ MPhil88. Sarum & Wells Th Coll 78. d 81 p 82. NSM Bursledon *Win* 81-85; C W End 85-90; C Fareham SS Pet and Paul *Portsm* from 90. *Manor Cottage, Church Path, Osborn Road, Fareham, Hants PO16 7DT* Fareham (0329) 280226

WHITE, Robert Bruce. b 42. Sarum & Wells Th Coll 71. d 73 p 74. C Woodford St Barn *Chelmsf* 73-75; Youth Chapl 75-79; C-in-c Sutton 75-78; P-in-c 78-79; C-in-c Shopland 75-78; P-in-c 78-79; TR Southend St Jo w St Mark, All SS w St Fran etc 79-82; P-in-c Southend St Alb 80-82; TR Southend 82-89; P-in-c Brentwood St Thos from 89. *The Vicarage, 91 Queen's Road, Brentwood, Essex CM14 4EY* Brentwood (0277) 225700

WHITE, Robert Charles. b 61. Mansf Coll Ox BA83. St Steph Ho Ox 83. d 85 p 86. C Forton *Portsm* 85-88; C Portsea N End St Mark from 88. *St Francis's House, 186 Northern Parade, Portsmouth PO2 9LU* Portsmouth (0705) 662467

WHITE, Canon Robin Edward Bantry. b 47. TCD BA70 BD79. CITC 72. d 72 p 73. C Dub Zion Ch *D & G* 72-76; Min Can St Patr Cathl Dub 76-79; C Taney Ch Ch *D & G* 76-79; I Abbeystrewry Union C, C & R 79-89; RD Mid W Cork 87-89; I Douglas Union w Frankfield from 89; Preb Ross Cathl from 89; Preb Cork Cathl

from 89; RD Cork City from 89. *The Rectory, Carrigaline Road, Douglas, Cork, Irish Republic* Cork (21) 891539

WHITE, Roderick Harry. b 55. Trin Coll Bris BA86. d 86 p 87. C Northn St Giles *Pet* 86-89; C Godley cum Newton Green *Ches* from 89. *The Vicarage, 43 Sheffield Road, Hyde, Cheshire SK14 2JR* 061-368 2159

WHITE, Roger Charles. b 37. St Alb Minl Tr Scheme 77. d 80 p 81. NSM Wilshamstead and Houghton Conquest *St Alb* from 80. *31 Mendip Crescent, Putnoe, Bedford MK41 9ER* Bedford (0234) 266172

WHITE, Roger David. b 37. Llan St Mich DipTh66. d 66 p 67. C Mountain Ash *Llan* 66-71; C Port Talbot St Theodore 71-74; V Caerhun w Llangelynnin *Ban* 74-85; R Llanbedrog w Llannor w Llanfihangel etc 85-88; V Llangeinor *Llan* 88-90; V Spittal w Treffgarne and Ambleston w St Dogwells *St D* from 90. *The Vicarage, West Gate, Spittal, Haverfordwest, Dyfed SA26 5QP* Treffgarne (043787) 505

✠**WHITE, Rt Rev Roger John.** b 41. Kelham Th Coll. d 66 p 67 c 84. C Manston *Ripon* 66-69; USA from 69; Bp Milwaukee from 85. *804 East Juneau Avenue, Milwaukee, Wisconsin 53202, USA*

WHITE, Ronald Henry. b 36. Bris Univ BSc58 Ox Univ DipEd59 Lon Univ DipTh64. SW Minl Tr Course 82. d 85 p 86. C Ivybridge *Ex* 85-87; C Ivybridge w Harford 87-88; V Blackawton and Stoke Fleming from 88. *The Vicarage, Stoke Flemming, Dartmouth, Devon TQ6 0QB* Stoke Fleming (0803) 770361

WHITE, Canon Roy Sidney. b 34. Sarum Th Coll 62. d 65 p 66. C Selsdon St Jo *Cant* 65-68; C Ranmoor *Sheff* 68-72; V Croydon St Andr *Cant* 72-78; Dir Abp Coggan Tr Cen 78-85; Hon Can S'wark Cathl *S'wark* from 85; Dir of Chr Stewardship from 85. *70 Pollards Hill North, London SW16 4NY* 081-679 4908

WHITE, Simon Inigo Dexter. b 58. York Univ BA80 Nottm Univ PGCE81. St Jo Coll Nottm 87. d 90 p 91. C Chadkirk *Ches* from 90. *29 Urwick Road, Romiley, Stockport, Cheshire SK6 3JS* 061-494 0547

WHITE, Stephen Ross. b 58. Hull Univ BA Ox Univ BA. Ripon Coll Cuddesdon 82. d 85 p 86. C Redcar *York* 85-88; P-in-c Gweedore (Bunbeg), Carrickfin and Templecrone *D & R* from 88; Dom Chapl to Bp from 91. *The Rectory, Bunbeg, Letterkenny, Co Donegal, Irish Republic* Bunbeg (75) 31043

WHITE, Teresa Joan (Sister Teresa). b 36. Wellesley Coll (USA) BA58. Harvard Univ STB61 Lon Univ CertEd74 Hon DD86. dss 75 d 87. CSA from 72. *St Andrew's House, 2 Tavistock Road, London W11 1BA* 071-229 2662

WHITE, Thomas Arthur. b 11. Univ of Wales (Swansea) BA38. St Mich Coll Llan 39. d 39 p 40. V Bris St Jude w St Matthias *Bris* 50-80; CF (TA) 64-80; rtd 80; Perm to Offic *Bris* from 80. *63 George Street South, Salisbury SP2 7BQ* Salisbury (0722) 22096

WHITE, Trevor John. b 37. St Pet Coll Ox BA61 MA65. Wycliffe Hall Ox. d 63 p 64. C Walsall *Lich* 63-67; V Greasbrough *Sheff* 67-73; Chapl Nat Nautical Sch Portishead 73-82; Chapl Bris Cathl Sch from 82; Perm to Offic *B & W* from 82. *4 Gardner Road, Portishead, Bristol BS20 9ER* Bristol (0272) 847855

WHITE, Vernon Philip. b 53. Clare Coll Cam BA75 MA79 Or Coll Ox MLitt80. Wycliffe Hall Ox DipTh76. d 77 p 78. Tutor Wycliffe Hall Ox 77-83; Chapl and Lect Ex Univ 83-87; R Wotton and Holmbury St Mary *Guildf* from 87; Dir of Ords from 87. *The Rectory, Holmbury St Mary, Dorking, Surrey RH5 6NL* Dorking (0306) 730285

WHITE, William John. b 54. BSc. Wycliffe Hall Ox. d 84 p 85. C Bowdon *Ches* 84-87; C Chadkirk 87-90; R Wistaston from 90. *The Rectory, 44 Church Lane, Wistaston, Crewe CW2 8HA* Crewe (0270) 67119

WHITE-THOMSON, Very Rev Ian Hugh. b 04. BNC Ox BA27 MA37 Kent Univ Hon DCL71. Cuddesdon Coll 28. d 29 p 30. Dean Cant 63-76; rtd 76; Perm to Offic *Cant* from 76. *Camphill, Harville Road, Wye, Ashford, Kent TN25 5EY* Wye (0233) 812210

WHITEFIELD, Keith Russell. b 60. Edin Th Coll. d 91. Haddington *Edin* from 91; C Dunbar from 91. *17 Victoria Street, Dunbar, East Lothian EH42 1HP* Dunbar (0368) 62278

WHITEHEAD, Barry. b 30. Or Coll Ox BA53 MA62. St Steph Ho Ox 53. d 55 p 56. C Edge Hill St Dunstan *Liv* 55-58; C Upholland 58-61; Ind Chapl 61-90; CF (TA) 64-78; V Aspull *Liv* from 77. *St Elizabeth's Vicarage, Bolton Road, Aspull, Wigan, Lancs WN2 1PR* Wigan (0942) 831236

WHITEHEAD, Brian. b 36. DipTh SRN. S'wark Ord Course 74. d 75 p 77. C Croydon St Aug *Cant* 75-78; C St Marychurch *Ex* 78-80; V Devonport St Mark Ford

80-87; V Castle Donington and Lockington cum Hemington *Leic* from 87; RD Scarborough from 91. *The Vicarage, 6 Delven Lane, Castle Donington, Derby DE7 2LJ* Derby (0332) 810364

WHITEHEAD, Christopher Martin Field. b 36. ALCD62. d 62 p 63. C Higher Openshaw *Man* 62-63; C Halliwell St Pet 64-66; V Owlerton *Sheff* 66-75; V Hunmanby w Muston *York* from 75. *The Vicarage, Hunmanby, Filey, N Yorkshire YO14 0NT* Scarborough (0723) 890294

WHITEHEAD, Denys Gordon. b 22. Pemb Coll Ox BA50 MA55. Linc Th Coll 49. d 52 p 53. Zambia from 60; Adn S Zambia 80-89; rtd 89. *29 Airport Road, PO Box 60648, Livingstone, Zambia* Livingstone (3) 323565

WHITEHEAD, Canon Derek. b 27. St Jo Coll Cam BA50 MA55 Lon Univ BD60 Lanc Univ PhD73. Wells Th Coll 55. d 56 p 57. C Lower Broughton Ascension *Man* 56-59; Chapl Highgate Sch Lon 63-65; Lect Div Preston Poly 65-79; Dir of Educn *Chich* from 79; Can and Preb Chich Cathl from 82. *The Rectory, Maresfield, Uckfield, E Sussex TN22 2HB* Uckfield (0825) 763817

WHITEHEAD, Frederick Keith. b 35. K Coll Lon BD58 AKC58. St Boniface Warminster 58. d 59 p 60. C S Shore H Trin *Blackb* 59-63; C Whitfield *Derby* 63-66; Lic to Offic from 66. *Steepways, 3 Simmondley New Road, Glossop, Derbyshire SK13 9LP* Glossop (0457) 852717

WHITEHEAD, Gordon James. b 42. Clifton Th Coll 66. d 73 p 74. Chile 73-87; C Coleraine *Conn* from 87. *19 Adelaide Avenue, Coleraine, Co Londonderry BT52 1LT* Coleraine (0265) 43474

WHITEHEAD, John Stanley. b 38. Jes Coll Cam BA63 MA67 MPhil. Westcott Ho Cam 63. d 64 p 65. C Batley All SS *Wakef* 64-67; C Mitcham St Mark *S'wark* 67-70; C Frindsbury w Upnor *Roch* 70-72; TV Strood 72-75; R Halstead 75-82; V Betley *Lich* 82-85; Asst Chapl Keele Univ from 82; V Betley and Keele from 85. *The Vicarage, Betley, Crewe CW3 9AX* Crewe (0270) 820245

WHITEHEAD, Matthew Alexander. b 44. Leeds Univ BA65 St Chad's Coll Dur DipEd66 Birm Univ MA75. Qu Coll Birm DipTh68. d 69 p 70. C Bingley All SS *Bradf* 69-72; C Keele *Lich* 72-74; Asst Chapl Keele Univ 72-74; Bp's Dom Chapl *Dur* 74-80; V Escomb 74-80; V Witton Park 74-80; V Birtley 80-89; RD Ches le Street 84-89; V Stockton St Pet from 89. *The Vicarage, 77 Yarm Road, Stockton-on-Tees, Cleveland TS18 3PJ* Stockton-on-Tees (0642) 676625

WHITEHEAD, Canon Michael Hutton. b 33. St Chad's Coll Dur 54. d 58 p 59. C Southwick St Columba *Dur* 58-64; V Hendon St Ignatius 64-70; P-in-c Sunderland 67-80; V Hendon 70-80; V Hendon and Sunderland 80-87; Hon Can Dur Cathl from 84; V Hartlepool St Aid from 87; RD Hartlepool from 91. *The Vicarage, St Aidan's Street, Hartlepool, Cleveland TS25 1SN* Hartlepool (0429) 273539

WHITEHEAD, Nicholas James. b 53. AIB. Ridley Hall Cam 86. d 88 p 89. C Bourne *Guildf* from 88. *Heavitree, 5 Dene Lane, Lower Bourne, Farnham, Surrey GU10 3PN* Farnham (0252) 725879

WHITEHEAD, Philip. b 34. Kelham Th Coll 55. d 59 p 60. C Sugley *Newc* 59-62; C Alnwick St Paul 62-63; C Newc St Gabr 63-66; C Gosforth All SS 66-67; V Kenton Ascension 67-75; V Spittal 75-88; P-in-c Scremerston 81-88; V Cresswell and Lynemouth from 88. *The Vicarage, 33 Till Grove, Ellington, Morpeth, Northd NE61 5ER* Morpeth (0670) 860242

WHITEHEAD, Robin Lawson. b 53. Bris Univ BA76. St Steph Ho Ox 77. d 80 p 81. C Cheshunt *St Alb* 80-83; C E Grinstead St Swithun *Chich* 83-85; V Friern Barnet St Pet le Poer *Lon* from 85. *St Peter's Vicarage, 163 Colney Hatch Lane, London N10 1HA* 081-883 1526

WHITEHEAD, Roger Milton. b 25. Pemb Coll Ox BA50 MA54. Ely Th Coll 50. d 52 p 53. V Oakfield St Jo *Portsm* 64-72; V Albrighton *Lich* 72-80; R Euston w Barnham and Fakenham *St E* 80-85; R Euston w Barnham, Elvedon and Fakenham Magna 85-89; rtd 89. *Groveways, Spur Road, Barnham Broom, Norwich NR9 4BY* Barnham Broom (060545) 779

WHITEHORN, Arthur Basil. b 24. W Midl Minl Tr Course. d 84 p 85. Asst Chapl Bromsgrove & Redditch Health Auth 84-89; NSM Bromsgrove St Jo *Worc* from 84. *15 Perry Lane, Bromsgrove, Worcs B61 7JL* Bromsgrove (0527) 74857

WHITEHORN, Jean Margaret. b 28. Lon Univ DipSocSc49 Cam Univ TCert70 Lon Univ DipRS85. S'wark Ord Course 87. d 89. NSM Orsett *Chelmsf* 89-90; NSM Orsett

and Bulphan from 90. *46 Monkshaven, Stanford-le-Hope, Essex SS17 7EF* Stanford-le-Hope (0375) 676074

WHITEHOUSE, Robert Edward. b 64. d 91. C Sheff Norwood St Leon *Sheff* from 91. *29 Piper Road, Sheffield S5 7HZ* Sheffield (0742) 426875

WHITEHOUSE, Susan Clara. b 48. R Holloway Coll Lon BA70. Westcott Ho Cam 87. d 89. Par Dn Farnley *Ripon* from 89. *4 Kirkdale Grove, Farnley, Leeds LS12 6AU* Leeds (0532) 633909

WHITELAM, Canon John. b 20. Kelham Th Coll 36. d 43 p 44. V Kennington Park St Agnes *S'wark* 54-86; Hon Can S'wark Cathl 83-86; rtd 86. *9 Cloister Walk, Monkgate, York YO3 7HZ* York (0904) 631591

WHITELEY, Alan. b 42. ACII. Lich Th Coll 68. d 71 p 72. C Wales *Sheff* 71-75; TV Frecheville and Hackenthorpe 75-79; V Malin Bridge from 79. *St Polycarp's Vicarage, 33 Wisewood Lane, Sheffield S6 4WA* Sheffield (0742) 343450

WHITELEY, Donal Royston. b 27. Qu Coll Birm 54. d 57 p 58. C Handsworth St Mary *Birm* 57-60; C Kingswinford St Mary *Lich* 60-63; R Norton Canes 63-71; V Wetley Rocks from 71. *St John's Vicarage, Wetley Rocks, Stoke-on-Trent ST9 0AP* Wetley Rocks (0782) 550251

WHITELEY, Robert. b 36. d 67 p 68. C Maidstone All SS w St Phil and H Trin *Cant* 67-70; Asst Chapl K Sch Roch 70-71; Chapl 71-82. *c/o Mrs L E Walton, 10 Greenway, Wilmslow, Cheshire* Wilmslow (0625) 524019

WHITELEY, Canon Robert Louis. b 28. Leeds Univ BA48. Coll of Resurr Mirfield. d 52 p 53. C Hollinwood *Man* 52-55; Br Honduras 56-61; V Illingworth *Wakef* 61-68; V Westgate Common 68-75; Can Res Wakef Cathl 75-80; Hon Can from 80; V Almondbury 80-82; RD Almondbury from 81; TR Almondbury w Farnley Tyas from 82. *The Vicarage, 2 Westgate, Almondbury, Huddersfield HD5 8XE* Huddersfield (0484) 21753

WHITEMAN, Canon Cedric Henry. b 28. Lich Th Coll 59. d 61 p 62. C Abington *Pet* 61-64; V Kettering St Andr 64-79; RD Kettering 73-79; Can Pet Cathl 77-79; V Rotherham *Sheff* 79-87; RD Rotherham 79-86; Hon Can Sheff Cathl from 85; Bp's Dom Chapl from 86; V Wentworth from 87. *The Vicarage, Wentworth, Rotherham, S Yorkshire S62 7TW* Barnsley (0226) 742274

WHITEMAN, Christopher Henry Raymond. b 51. Portsm Poly BA73 Worc Coll of Educn PGCE74. St Jo Coll Nottm DipTh90. d 90 p 91. C Rockland St Mary w Hellington, Bramerton etc *Nor* from 90. *Lowen Lodge, The Green, Surlingham, Norwich NR14 7HE* Surlingham (05088) 497

WHITEMAN, Ven Rodney David Carter. b 40. Ely Th Coll 61. d 64 p 65. C Kings Heath *Birm* 64-70; V Rednal 70-79; V Erdington St Barn 79-89; RD Aston 81-86 and 88-89; Hon Can Birm Cathl 85-89; Adn Bodmin *Truro* from 89; P-in-c Cardynham from 89; P-in-c Helland from 89; Hon Can Truro Cathl from 89. *The Rectory, Cardinham, Bodmin, Cornwall PL30 4BL* Cardinham (020882) 614

WHITESIDE, Canon Peter George. b 30. St Cath Coll Cam BA55. Cuddesdon Coll MA59. d 57 p 58. C Westmr St Steph w St Jo *Lon* 57-61; Chapl Clifton Coll Bris 61-70; Hd Linc Cathl Sch 70-73; Australia from 74. *16 Hearn Street, Dromana, Victoria, Australia 3936* Dromana (59) 872156

WHITFIELD, Canon Benjamin Owen. b 17. Saskatchewan Univ BA43. Em Coll Saskatoon LTh43 BD53. d 43 p 44. V Clee *Linc* 62-70; Can and Preb Linc Cathl from 70; V Gainsborough All SS 70-81; RD Corringham 72-78; V Morton 76-81; V Melton Ross w New Barnetby 81-85; V Wrawby 81-85; rtd 85. *6 The Copse, Bigby High Road, Brigg, S Humberside DN20 9HY* Brigg (0652) 52695

WHITFIELD, Charles. b 25. St Pet Hall Ox BA49 MA53. Ridley Hall Cam 49. d 51 p 52. V Egg Buckland *Ex* 68-90; rtd 90. *23 Chapel Meadow, Buckland Monachorum, Yelverton, Devon PL20 7LR*

WHITFIELD, George Joshua Newbold. b 09. Lon Univ AKC30 MA35. Bps' Coll Cheshunt. d 62 p 63. Hon C Hampton St Mary *Lon* 62-74; Gen Sec Gen Syn Bd of Educn 69-74; rtd 74; Lic to Offic *Ex* from 78. *Bede Lodge, 31A Rolle Road, Exmouth, Devon EX8 2AW* Exmouth (0395) 274162

WHITFIELD, George Oakley. b 17. St Jo Coll Dur 43. d 45 p 46. R Hemingby *Linc* 50-81; V Baumber w Gt Sturton 51-81; R Hatton w Sotby 60-81; R Hemingby 81-82; rtd 83. *High Acres, Sotby, Lincoln LN3 5LH*

WHITFIELD, Miss Joy Verity. b 46. SRN67 SCM71 MTD80. Trin Coll Bris BA88. d 88. C Littleover *Derby* from 88. *8 Thornhill Road, Littleover, Derby DE3 6FZ* Derby (0332) 763263

WHITFIELD, Kenneth. b 18. Lich Th Coll 54. **d** 56 **p** 57. V Leeds St Marg *Ripon* 64-73; Chapl Community of St Pet Horbury 73-84; rtd 83; Perm to Offic *Nor* from 84. *47 Charles Road, Holt, Norfolk NR25 6DA* Holt (0263) 712004

WHITFIELD, Trevor. b 48. Lon Univ BSc71. Ridley Hall Cam BA78. **d** 79 **p** 80. C Battersea St Pet and St Paul *S'wark* 79-82; Chapl Stockholm w Uppsala *Eur* 82-83; C-in-c Roundshaw CD *S'wark* 83-89; Asst Chapl R Victoria Infirmary Newc from 89. *41 Hampstead Road, Newcastle upon Tyne NE4 8AD* 091-272 3907

WHITING, Antony Gerald Stroud. b 26. CITC 81. **d** 86 **p** 87. NSM Clonmel Union *C, C & R* 86-87; Cork St Fin Barre's Union 87-88; Lic to Offic from 88. *Edgwater, Midleton, Co Cork, Irish Republic* Cork (21) 631876

WHITING, Arthur. K Coll Lon 54. **d** 55 **p** 56. V Southn St Jude *Win* 58-78; Chapl Southn Gen Hosp 59-73; rtd 78; Perm to Offic *Win* and *Sarum* from 78. *10 Paget Close, Colehill, Wimborne, Dorset BH21 2SW* Wimborne (0202) 884948

WHITING, Graham James. b 58. Bris Univ BSc81. Chich Th Coll 83. **d** 86 **p** 88. C Portslade St Nic and St Andr *Chich* 86-87; C W Tarring 87-91; C Seaford w Sutton from 91. *51 Chyngton Gardens, Seaford, E Sussex BN25 3RS* Seaford (0323) 893876

WHITING, Joseph Alfred. b 41. Oak Hill Th Coll 82. **d** 85 **p** 86. Hon C Sidcup St Andr *Roch* 85-88; C Southborough St Pet w Ch Ch and St Matt from 88. *72 Power Mill Lane, Tunbridge Wells, Kent TN4 9EJ* Tunbridge Wells (0892) 29098

WHITING, Leslie John. b 27. St Deiniol's Hawarden 59. **d** 61 **p** 62. C E Dulwich St Clem *S'wark* 61-64; C Parkstone St Pet w Branksea *Sarum* 64-69; C Lt Coates *Linc* 69-70; C Willesden St Matt *Lon* 70-74; V from 74. *St Matthew's Vicarage, St Mary's Road, London NW10 4AU* 081-965 3748

WHITLEY, Charles Francis. TCD BA42 MA45 BD45 PhD49 Ox Univ MA66 MLitt82. **d** 43 **p** 44. C Dundalk *Arm* 43-45; C Dub Zion Ch *D & G* 45-49; Lect OT Dur Univ 49-52; Tutor St Jo Coll Dur 49-52; V Bolton St Barn *Man* 52-53; Lect Hebrew and OT Univ of Wales (Ban) 53-67; Sen Lect 67-84; Prof Bibl Studies from 84. *Elmbank, Llandegfan, Menai Bridge, Gwynedd*

WHITLEY, Eric Keir. b 47. Salford Univ BSc68. Trin Coll Bris 77. **d** 79 **p** 80. C Nottm St Ann w Em *S'well* 79-83; V Donisthorpe and Moira w Stretton-en-le-Field *Leic* from 83. *St John's Vicarage, Donisthorpe, Burton-on-Trent, Staffs DE12 7PX* Measham (0530) 71456

WHITLEY, John Duncan Rooke. b 29. Trin Coll Cam BA51 MA55. Coll of Resurr Mirfield 52. **d** 54 **p** 55. C Ashington *Newc* 54-59; C Chiswick St Nic w St Mary *Lon* 59-61; V Ware St Mary *St Alb* 61-71; Can Missr St Mary's Cathl Edin 71-74; Dioc Educn Officer 71-74; Lic to Offic from 74. *19 Primrose Bank Road, Edinburgh EH5 3JQ* 031-552 2085

WHITLEY, John William. b 46. TCD BA68. Cranmer Hall Dur BA71. **d** 71 **p** 72. C Belf St Mary Magd *Conn* 71-73; C Toxteth St Philemon w St Gabr *Liv* 73-78; P-in-c Toxteth Park St Cleopas 78-88; TV Toxteth St Philemon w St Gabr and St Cleopas from 89. *St Cleopas Vicarage, Beresford Road, Liverpool L8 4SG* 051-727 0633

WHITLOCK, James Frederick. b 44. Ch Coll Cam BA75 MA78. Westcott Ho Cam 73. **d** 76 **p** 77. C Newquay *Truro* 76-79; P-in-c St Mawgan w St Ervan and St Eval 79-81; R 81; Bp's Dom Chapl 82-85; Dioc Dir of Ords 82-85; V Leagrave *St Alb* 85-89; TR Probus, Ladock and Grampound w Creed *Truro* from 89. *The Sanctuary, Wagg Lane, Probus, Truro, Cornwall TR2 4JX* St Austell (0726) 882746

WHITLOW, Brian William. b 14. St Edm Hall Ox BA36 DipTh37 Bp's Univ Lennoxville MEd52 BD59 DD67. Westcott Ho Cam 37. **d** 38 **p** 39. C Leeds St Aid *Ripon* 38-41; Chapl RAFVR 41-46; Canada from 46; Dean Ch Ch Cathl Victoria 55-80. *1347 Craigdarroch Road, Victoria, British Columbia, Canada, V8S 2A6* Victoria (604) 592-6109

WHITMORE, Mrs Dorothy Mary. b 28. Sheff Univ BA49 DipEd50. Gilmore Course 79. **dss** 81 **d** 87. Marston Green *Birm* 81-87; Hon Par Dn from 87. *116 Elmdon Lane, Birmingham B37 7EG* 021-779 2695

WHITMORE, Edward James. b 36. Lon Univ BD66. Tyndale Hall Bris. **d** 68 **p** 69. Tanzania 68-76; Lic to Offic *Blackb* from 77. *74 Greencroft, Penwortham, Preston PR1 9LB* Preston (0772) 746522

WHITMORE, Jane Frances. b 30. dss 79 **d** 87. Elloughton and Brough w Brantingham *York* 79-83; Foley Park *Worc* 83-87; C Frimley *Guildf* from 87. *20 Winterbourne*

Walk, Frimley, Camberley, Surrey GU16 5YB Camberley (0276) 837425

WHITMORE, Stephen Andrew. b 53. Sheff Univ BSc74. St Jo Coll Nottm DTS89. **d** 91. C Newbury *Ox* from 91. *10 Braunfels Walk, Newbury, Berks RG14 5NQ* Newbury (0635) 47018

WHITNALL, Robert Edward (Brother Dominic). b 14. Magd Coll Ox BA37. Cuddesdon Coll 37. **d** 38 **p** 39. S Africa 47-66; CR from 47; Hon C Battyeford *Wakef* from 68; rtd 84. *House of the Resurrection, Mirfield, W Yorkshire WF14 0BN* Mirfield (0924) 494318

WHITTA, Rex Alfred Rought. b 28. Leeds Inst of Educn CertEd52 Open Univ BA88 Lon Univ CertTESOL89. Qu Coll Birm DipTh63. **d** 63 **p** 64. V Elloughton and Brough w Brantingham *York* 68-74; TR Redcar w Kirkleatham 74-78; V Redcar 78-84; V Bassenthwaite, Isel and Setmurthy *Carl* 84-86; P-in-c Cloughton *York* 86-88; P-in-c Hackness w Harwood Dale 86-88; rtd 89. *14 Candler Street, Scarborough, N Yorkshire YO12 7DF* Scarborough (0723) 375740

WHITTAKER, Arthur. b 30. Oak Hill Th Coll. **d** 60 **p** 61. C Bispham *Blackb* 60-64; V Edge Hill St Cypr *Liv* 64-73; Area Sec (Dios Ban, St A, Ches and S & M) CMS 73-74; C Maghull *Liv* 74; V Bilsborrow *Blackb* from 74. *The Vicarage, Church Lane, Bilsborrow, Preston PR3 0RL* Brock (0995) 40269

WHITTAKER, Arthur George. b 14. MRIPHH38 LTCL57 Man Univ 48. **d** 60 **p** 61. V Hadfield *Derby* 63-72; V Coldham *Ely* 72-81; V Friday Bridge 72-81; rtd 81; Perm to Offic *Glouc* from 81. *27 Mosley Crescent, Cashes Green, Stroud, Glos GL5 4LT* Stroud (0453) 763622

WHITTAKER, Brian Lawrence. b 39. Clifton Th Coll 63. **d** 66 **p** 67. C Whitton and Thurleston w Akenham *St E* 66-69; C Normanton *Wakef* 69-74; P-in-c Castle Hall *Ches* 74-77; P-in-c Dukinfield Ch Ch 74-77; P-in-c Stalybridge H Trin and Ch Ch 74-77; V 77-83; TR Bucknall and Bagnall *Lich* from 83. *The Rectory, Werrington Road, Bucknall, Stoke-on-Trent ST2 9AQ* Stoke-on-Trent (0782) 214455

WHITTAKER, Bryan. b 58. Southn Univ BTh82. Chich Th Coll 82. **d** 84 **p** 85. C Whitleigh *Ex* 84-88; C Corringham *Chelmsf* from 88. *St John's House, Corringham, Essex SS17 7LF* Stanford-le-Hope (0375) 675463

WHITTAKER, Garry. b 59. St Jo Coll Nottm DipCM91. **d** 91. C Denton Ch Ch *Man* from 91. *65 Hulme Road, Denton, Manchester M34 2WX* 061-336 3455

WHITTAKER, George Brian. b 13. Lon Univ BD36. ALCD36. **d** 36 **p** 37. R Roche *Truro* 62-72; R Withiel 63-72; V Lelant 72-78; rtd 78. *4 Lelant Meadows, Lelant, St Ives, Cornwall TR26 3JS* Hayle (0736) 756234

WHITTAKER, Ivan Harrison. b '08. Westcott Ho Cam 44. **d** 46 **p** 47. Chapl St Mich Sch Otford 65-73; rtd 73; Perm to Offic *Chich* from 73. *1 Manor Close, North Lancing, W Sussex BN15 0QY* Lancing (0903) 752387

WHITTAKER, James Rawstron. b 14. Worc Coll Ox BA38 MA46. Wells Th Coll 38. **d** 40 **p** 41. V Almeley *Heref* 70-80; P-in-c Kinnersley w Norton Canon 74-80; rtd 81; Perm to Offic *Heref* from 82. *Eign Gate House, 142 Eign Street, Hereford HR4 0AP* Hereford (0432) 268961

WHITTAKER, Jeremy Paul. b 59. Ox Univ MA. Ripon Coll Cuddesdon 82. **d** 84 **p** 85. C Crowthorne *Ox* 84-87; C Westborough *Guildf* 87-88; TV from 88. *St Clare's Vicarage, Cabell Road, Guildford, Surrey GU2 6JW* Guildford (0483) 503348

WHITTAKER, Canon John. b 20. Ch Coll Cam BA47 MA49. Ridley Hall Cam 46. **d** 48 **p** 49. V New Bury *Man* 66-75; Hon Can Man Cathl 71-87; R Middleton 75-87; rtd 87. *5 Farnborough Road, Bolton BL1 7HJ* Bolton (0204) 595499

WHITTAKER, John. b 27. Oak Hill Th Coll 53. **d** 55 **p** 56. V Skelmersdale St Paul *Liv* 67-77; V Gt Faringdon w Lt Coxwell *Ox* 77-83; RD Vale of White Horse 80-83; rtd 83; Perm to Offic *Ox* 83-88; C Broughton Poggs w Filkins, Broadwell etc from 88. *26 The Pines, Faringdon, Oxon SN7 8AU* Faringdon (0367) 241009

WHITTAKER, Peter Harold. b 39. AKC62. **d** 63 **p** 64. C Walton St Mary *Liv* 63-67; C Ross *Heref* 67-70; R Bridgnorth St Mary 70-78; P-in-c Oldbury 70-78; TR Bridgnorth, Tasley, Astley Abbotts and Oldbury 78-81; RD Bridgnorth 78-81; Preb Heref Cathl 80-81; P-in-c Billington *St Alb* 81; P-in-c Eggington 81; P-in-c Hockliffe 81; V Leighton Buzzard 81; V Leighton Buzzard w Eggington, Hockliffe etc from 81; RD Dunstable 84-85. *The Vicarage, Pulford Road, Leighton Buzzard, Beds LU7 7AB* Leighton Buzzard (0525) 373217

WHITTAKER, Robert Andrew. b 49. DipEd Open Univ BA75 Nottm Univ MA83. Linc Th Coll 85. **d** 87 **p** 88. C

Mansf Woodhouse *S'well* 87-90; V Norwell w Ossington, Cromwell and Caunton from 90. *The Vicarage, Norwell, Newark, Notts NG23 6JT* Caunton (063686) 329

WHITTAKER, Canon William Joseph. b 04. TCD BA33 MA48. Div Sch TCD 35. **d** 36 **p** 37. I Knock *D & D* 50-76; Preb St Patr Cathl Dub 74-76; rtd 76. *23 Barton Drive, Rathfarnham, Dublin 14, Irish Republic* Dublin (1) 931308

WHITTAM, Canon Kenneth Michael. b 26. Ball Coll Ox BA50 MA54. Cuddesdon Coll 50. **d** 52 **p** 53. Chapl Highgate Sch Lon 66-75; V Shotwick *Ches* 75-89; Can Res Ches Cathl and Dioc Missr 75-85; Hon Can Ches Cathl from 85; Clergy Study Officer 85-91; rtd 91. *22 Warwick Close, Little Neston, South Wirral L64 0SR*

WHITTINGHAM, Peter. b 58. Sheff Univ BA79. St Jo Coll Nottm 88. **d** 90 **p** 91. C Northowram *Wakef* from 90. *34 Stephen Close, Northowram, Halifax, W Yorkshire HX3 7BY* Halifax (0422) 206808

WHITTINGHAM, Ronald Norman. b 43. Linc Coll Ox BA65 MA68. Coll of Resurr Mirfield 65. **d** 67 **p** 68. C Horninglow *Lich* 67-69; C Drayton in Hales 69-70; C Uttoxeter w Bramshall 71-75; P-in-c Burton St Paul 75-80; V Shareshill 80-83; V Silverdale and Knutton Heath 83-89; P-in-c Alsagers Bank 83-89; V Silverdale and Alsagers Bank from 89. *St John's Vicarage, High Street, Alsagers Bank, Stoke-on-Trent ST7 8BQ* Stoke-on-Trent (0782) 723312

WHITTINGTON, David John. b 45. Qu Coll Ox BA67 MA71. Coll of Resurr Mirfield 69. **d** 71 **p** 72. Chapl St Woolos Cathl *Mon* 71-72; C Ox St Mary V w St Cross and St Pet *Ox* 72-76; Chapl Qu Coll Ox 72-76; V Stockton *Dur* from 77. *The Victoria Flat, Bishop Auckland, Co Durham DL14 7NP* Bishop Auckland (0388) 661740

WHITTLE, Alan. b 29. K Coll Lon BD52 AKC52. **d** 53 **p** 54. C Combe Down *B & W* 53-55; C Bath Twerton-on-Avon 55-57; Australia 57-66; R Aston Rowant w Crowell *Ox* 66-68; Lic to Offic *S'wark* 69-72; V Mitcham Ch Ch from 72. *Christ Church Vicarage, Christchurch Road, London SW19 2NY* 081-542 5125

WHITTLE, Fred. b 17. Keble Coll Ox BA40 MA44. Cuddesdon Coll 40. **d** 41 **p** 42. R Gt w Lt Addington *Pet* 71-82; rtd 82; Lic to Offic *Pet* 82-85; Perm to Offic from 85. *6 Coleman Street, Raunds, Wellingborough, Northants NN9 6NJ* Wellingborough (0933) 624989

WHITTLE, Ian Christopher. b 60. Univ Coll Dur BA81 Fitzw Coll Cam BA87. Ridley Hall Cam. **d** 88 **p** 89. C S Petherton w the Seavingtons *B & W* from 88. *8 Summer Shard, South Petherton, Somerset TA13 5DW* South Petherton (0460) 41143

WHITTLE, John William. b 46. Qu Mary Coll Lon BA68. Sarum & Wells Th Coll 84. **d** 86 **p** 87. C Blandford Forum and Langton Long etc *Sarum* 86-88. *Leslie House, The Tabernacle, Blandford Forum, Dorset* Blandford (0258) 51943

WHITTLE, Robin Jeffrey. b 51. Bris Univ BA72 Leic Univ CQSW75. Sarum & Wells Th Coll 85. **d** 87 **p** 88. C Henbury *Bris* 87-91; V Capel *Guildf* from 91. *The Vicarage, Capel, Dorking, Surrey RH5 5LN* Dorking (0306) 711260

WHITTOCK, Michael Graham. b 47. Hull Univ BA69 Fitzw Ho Cam BA71 MA76. Westcott Ho Cam 69 Union Th Sem Richmond 71. **d** 72 **p** 73. C Kirkby *Liv* 72-76; C Prescot 76-79; R Methley w Mickletown *Ripon* from 79; RD Whitkirk from 88. *The Rectory, Church Side, Methley, Leeds LS26 9BJ* Castleford (0977) 515278

WHITTOME, Donald Marshall. b 26. S Dios Minl Tr Scheme. **d** 84 **p** 85. NSM Henfield w Shermanbury and Woodmancote *Chich* from 84. *Field House, Furners Lane, Henfield, W Sussex BN5 9HS* Henfield (0273) 492231

WHITTON, Norman. b 17. Edin Th Coll 65. **d** 67 **p** 68. V Brough w Stainmore *Carl* 70-76; C P-in-c Harraby 76-80; rtd 80; Perm to Offic *Carl* from 83. *Hartley Fold Cottage, Hartley, Kirkby Stephen, Cumbria CA17 4JH* Kirkby Stephen (07683) 71047

WHITTY, Gordon William. b 35. W Midl Minl Tr Course. **d** 82 **p** 83. NSM Willenhall St Giles *Lich* 82-84; NSM Coseley Ch Ch 84-85; C 85-87; TV Hanley H Ev from 87. *45 Parkway, Hanley, Stoke-on-Trent ST1 3BB* Stoke-on-Trent (0782) 266066

WHITTY, Harold George. b 41. TCD BA64 MA67. CITC Div Test65. **d** 65 **p** 66. C Willowfield *D & D* 65-68; C Lisburn Ch Ch *Conn* 68-71; Bp's Dom Chapl 70-71; Asst Dir Exhibitions CMJ from 71; C Enfield Ch Ch Trent Park *Lon* 72-75; TV Washfield, Stoodleigh, Withleigh etc *Ex* 75-83; TR from 83; RD Tiverton 82-84.

The Rectory, Withleigh, Tiverton, Devon EX16 8JG Tiverton (0884) 254004

WHITWELL, John Peter. b 36. Qu Coll Birm 62. **d** 65 **p** 66. C Stepney St Dunstan and All SS *Lon* 65-68; C Chingford SS Pet and Paul *Chelmsf* 68-71; V Walthamstow St Sav 71-78; P-in-c Lt Ilford St Mich 78-88; R from 88; RD Newham from 91. *The Rectory, Church Road, London E12 6HA* 081-478 2182

WHITWELL, Martin Corbett. b 32. Pemb Coll Ox BA55 MA59. Clifton Th Coll 55. **d** 57 **p** 58. Chapl Sandbach Co Secondary Sch 68-74; C Chipping Campden *Glouc* 70-71; Perm to Offic *Chich* 74-75; *Bris* 75-76; C Tranmere St Cath *Ches* 76-80; V Lt Leigh and Lower Whitley 80-90; rtd 90. *11 Hollies Drive, Bayston Hill, Shrewsbury, Shropshire* Bayston Hill (0743) 874241

WHITWORTH, Alan. b 24. ACP66 Nottm Univ BEd66 MEd. St Deiniol's Hawarden 80. **d** 80 **p** 81. NSM Capesthorne w Siddington and Marton *Ches* 80-81; P-in-c 83-85; P-in-c Eaton and Hulme Walfield 81-85; V 85-87; R Burnsall *Bradf* 87-89; P-in-c Rylstone 87-89; R Burnsall w Rylstone 89-91; rtd 91. *4 Twemlow Parade, Morecambe, Lancs LA3 1PD* Morecambe (0524) 850174

WHITWORTH, Benjamin Charles Battams. b 49. CCC Ox BA71 MA85. Linc Th Coll 83. **d** 85 **p** 86. C Swanborough *Sarum* 85-88; C Sherborne w Castleton and Lillington 88-91; V Milborne Port w Goathill *B & W* from 91. *The Vicarage, Bathwell Lane, Milborne Port, Sherborne, Dorset DT9 5AN* Milborne Port (0963) 250248

WHITWORTH, Duncan. b 47. K Coll Lon BD69 AKC69. **d** 70 **p** 71. C Tonge Moor *Man* 70-73; C Upper Norwood St Jo *Cant* 73-78; Asst Chapl Madrid *Eur* 78-82; Chapl Br Emb Ankara 82-83; V Douglas St Matt *S & M* from 84; RD Douglas from 91. *St Matthew's Vicarage, Alexander Drive, Douglas, Isle of Man* Douglas (0624) 676310

WHITWORTH, Eric Watkinson. b 06. Univ Coll Dur 25. Lich Th Coll 28. **d** 30 **p** 32. R Drayton St Leon *Ox* 68-74; V Stadhampton w Chislehampton 68-74; rtd 74. *5 Waldron Court, Longbridge Deverill, Warminster, Wilts BA12 7DJ* Warminster (0985) 218574

WHITWORTH, Patrick John. b 51. Ch Ch Ox BA72 MA76 St Jo Coll Dur DipTh75 MA78. **d** 76 **p** 77. C York St Mich-le-Belfrey *York* 76-79; C Brompton H Trin w Onslow Square St Paul *Lon* 79-84; V Gipsy Hill Ch Ch *S'wark* from 84. *Christ Church Vicarage, 1 Highland Road, London SE19 1DP* 081-670 0385

WHITWORTH-HARRISON, Bernard. b 05. St Cath Coll Ox BA36 MA38. St Chad's Coll Dur 28 K Coll Lon 28. **d** 34 **p** 36. R Langham *Chelmsf* 62-75; rtd 75. *19 Trinity Close, Balsham, Cambridge CB1 6DW* Cambridge (0223) 893921

WHYBORN, Robert. b 42. Loughb Coll of Educn CSD69. N Ord Course 87. **d** 90 **p** 91. NSM Milnrow *Man* from 90. *5 Delamere Avenue, Shaw, Oldham OL2 8HN* Shaw (0706) 843644

WHYBRAY, Prof Roger Norman. b 23. Keble Coll Ox BA44 MA48 DPhil62 BD81 DD81. Linc Th Coll 44. **d** 46 **p** 47. Lect Th Hull Univ 65-71; Reader 71-78; Prof Hebrew and OT 78-82; rtd 88. *45 Hills Lane, Ely, Cambs CB6 1AY* Ely (0353) 663897

WHYE, Canon Alexander George. b 01. Keble Coll Ox BA23 MA27. St Aug Coll Cant 23. **d** 25 **p** 26. V S Hinksey *Ox* 59-72; Hon Can Ch 62-79; rtd 72. *St Luke's Nursing Home, Latimer Road, Oxford OX3 7PG* Oxford (0865) 750220

WHYMAN, Oliver. b 27. ALCM52 LCP57. S'wark Ord Course 60. **d** 63 **p** 64. C Streatham Ch Ch *S'wark* 63-68; Lic to Offic 68-87; NSM Sutton New Town St Barn from 87. *37 Jubilee Court, London Road, Thornton Heath, Surrey CR7 6JL* 081-684 5320

WHYTE, Alastair John. b 61. Coll of Ripon & York St Jo BA83. Sarum & Wells Th Coll 83. **d** 85 **p** 86. C Chorley St Geo *Blackb* 85-88; C Poulton-le-Fylde 88-91; V Wesham from 91; Chapl Wesham Park Hosp Blackb from 91. *The Vicarage, Mowbreck Lane, Wesham, Preston PR4 3HA* Kirkham (0772) 682206

WHYTE, Duncan Macmillan. b 25. St Jo Coll Dur BA50 St Cath Soc Ox BA51 MA57. Wycliffe Hall Ox. **d** 51 **p** 53. C Garston *Liv* 51-56; C St Leonards St Leon *Chich* 56-59; V Southsea St Simon *Portsm* 59-66; Gen Sec Lon City Miss from 66; Hon C Blackheath St Jo *S'wark* from 66. *192 Charlton Road, London SE7 7DW* 081-856 7306 or 071-407 7585

WHYTE, Henry Lewis. b 38. Lon Coll of Div ALCD70 LTh74. **d** 70 **p** 71. C Crawley *Chich* 70-74; V Bermondsey St Jas w Ch Ch *S'wark* 74-82; V Kingston Hill St Paul from 82. *The Vicarage, 33 Queen's Road, Kingston upon Thames, Surrey KT2 7SF* 081-549 8597

WHYTE, Canon Herbert Blayney. b 21. TCD BA43 MA53. d 44 p 45. CV Ch Ch Cathl Dub *D & G* 68-91; I Dub Crumlin 68-91; Can Ch Ch Cathl Dub 80-86; Chan 86-91; rtd 91. *238 Redford Park, Greystones, Co Wicklow, Irish Republic* Dublin (1) 287-7264

WHYTE, Malcolm Dorrance. b 29. Man Univ BA50 BD53. Wycliffe Hall Ox 57. d 57 p 58. C Roch St Pet w St Marg *Roch* 57-60; V Ravenhead *Liv* 60-67; V Southport Em from 67; RD N Meols 78-89; AD from 89. *Emmanuel Vicarage, 12 Allerton Road, Southport, Merseyside PR9 9NJ* Southport (0704) 32743

WHYTE, Canon Robert Angus. b 12. Wycliffe Hall Ox. d 43 p 44. C Gravesend St Jas *Roch* 43-47; C Hove Bp Hannington Memorial Ch *Chich* 47-54; V Tunbridge Wells St Luke *Roch* from 54; Hon Can Roch Cathl from 78. *158 Upper Grosvenor Road, Tunbridge Wells, Kent TN1 2EQ* Tunbridge Wells (0892) 21374

WHYTE, Robert Euan. b 44. St Pet Coll Ox BA67. Cuddesdon Coll 67. d 69 p 70. C Blackheath Ascension *S'wark* 69-73; NSM Lewisham St Swithun 73-76; NSM Heston *Lon* 76-77; NSM Rusthall *Roch* 77-87; C 87-88; V from 88; RD Tunbridge Wells from 91. *The Vicarage, Bretland Road, Rusthall, Tunbridge Wells, Kent TN4 8PB* Tunbridge Wells (0892) 21357

WHYTE, Thomas Arthur. b 15. Man Univ BA48. Wycliffe Hall Ox 56. d 56 p 57. V Hunts Cross *Liv* 59-71; V Roby 71-83; rtd 83; Perm to Offic *Ches* 83-90; *Liv* from 83; NSM Aston by Sutton *Ches* from 90. *11 Acres Crescent, Westbrook Park, Kingsley, Warrington WA6 3DZ* Kingsley (0928) 88194

WIBBERLEY, Anthony Norman. b 36. K Coll Lon BSc58 AKC58. Sarum & Wells Th Coll 76. d 79 p 80. Hon C Tavistock and Gulworthy *Ex* 79-86; R Hoby cum Rotherby w Brooksby, Ragdale & Thru'ton *Leic* 86-90; V Ingol *Blackb* from 90. *St Margaret's Vicarage, 299 Tag Lane, Ingol, Preston, Lancs PR2 3XA* Preston (0772) 727208

WIBROE, Andrew Peter. b 56. K Coll Lon BD83 AKC83. Ripon Coll Cuddesdon 83. d 86 p 87. C Purley St Mark Woodcote *S'wark* 86-89; C Boyne Hill *Ox* 89-90. *15 Pinnocks Avenue, Gravesend, Kent DA11 7QD*

WICK, Patricia Anne. b 54. Lon Bible Coll BA80 Oak Hill Th Coll DipHE86. dss 86 d 87. Halliwell St Luke *Man* 86-87; Par Dn 87-91; Par Dn Drypool *York* from 91. *3 Caledonia Park, Victoria Dock, Hull HU9 1TE* Hull (0482) 589786

WICKENS, John Philip. b 33. Open Univ BA76. K Coll Lon 57. d 61 p 62. C Hatcham Park All SS *S'wark* 61-64; USA 64-66; Tutor Richmond Fellowship Coll from 66; Hon C Sutton Ch Ch *S'wark* 68-83; Hon C Benhilton from 83. *8 Orchard Road, Sutton, Surrey SM1 2QA* 081-642 8071

✠**WICKHAM, Rt Rev Edward Ralph.** b 11. Lon Univ BD37 Salford Univ Hon DLitt73. St Steph Ho Ox 38. d 38 p 39 c 59. C Shieldfield Ch Ch *Newc* 38-41; Chapl Ordnance Factory Swynnerton 41-44; P-in-c Swynnerton *Lich* 43-44; Ind Chapl *Sheff* 44-59; Can Res Sheff Cathl 51-59; Suff Bp Middleton *Man* 59-82; rtd 82; Asst Bp Man from 82. *12 Westminster Road, Ellesmere Park, Eccles, Manchester M30 9HF* 061-789 3144

WICKHAM, Lionel Ralph. b 32. LRAM St Cath Coll Cam BA57 MA61 PhD. Westcott Ho Cam 57. d 59 p 60. C Boston *Linc* 59-61; Tutor Cuddesdon Coll 61-63; V Cross Stone *Wakef* 63-67; Lect Th Southn Univ 67-78; Sen Lect 78-81; V Honley 81-87; Lect Cam Univ from 87; NSM W Wratting *Ely* from 89. *Divinity Faculty, Divinity School, Trinity Street, Cambridge*

WICKHAM, Nicholas John. b 27. Trin Coll Cam BA51 MA56. Coll of Resurr Mirfield 54 Ox NSM Course 85. d 87 p 88. NSM Banbury *Ox* from 87. *19 Britannia Wharf, Britannia Road, Banbury, Oxon OX16 8DS* Banbury (0295) 256537

WICKHAM, Canon Norman George. b 25. Kelham Th Coll 42. d 51 p 52. TP Edin St Jo *Edin* 69-79; Can and Vice-Provost St Mary's Cathl Edin 74-79; R Edin Ch Ch 79-88; Can St Mary's Cathl from 86; rtd 88. *Linton Mill, Mill Wynd, East Linton, East Lothian EH40 3AE* East Linton (0620) 860142

WICKHAM, Robert George. b 05. Hertf Coll Ox BA27 MA31. Wycliffe Hall Ox 27. d 29 p 30. Chapl Marlboro' Coll Wilts 37-84; Chapl Twyford Sch Win 37-63; Hd Master Twyford Sch Win 37-63; Perm to Offic *Win* from 84; rtd 85. *Primrose Cottage, Exton, Southampton SO3 1NW* Southampton (0703) 877390

WICKINGS, Luke Iden. b 59. Sheff Poly BA81. Oak Hill Th Coll BA90. d 90 p 91. C Fulham St Mary N End *Lon* from 90. *72 Edith Road, London W14* 071-603 5909

WICKS, Christopher Blair. b 59. BA. Oak Hill Th Coll 85. d 88 p 89. C Edmonton All SS w St Mich *Lon* from 88. *60 Tillotson Road, London N9 9AH* 081-803 1590

WICKSTEAD, Gavin John. b 46. St Chad's Coll Dur BA67. Linc Th Coll 82. d 84 p 85. C Louth *Linc* 84-87; P-in-c E Markham and Askham *S'well* 87-89; P-in-c Headon w Upton 87-89; P-in-c Grove 87-89; R E Markham w Askham, Headon w Upton and Grove from 90. *The Rectory, Lincoln Road, East Markham, Newark, Notts NG22 0SH* Tuxford (0777) 871731

WIDDAS, Preb John Anderson. b 38. Kelham Th Coll 58. d 63 p 64. C Willenhall H Trin *Lich* 63-66; C Tamworth 66-69; V from 86; V Chesterton 69-74; R Lich St Chad 74-86; RD Lich 77-86; Preb Lich Cathl from 80; P-in-c Gentleshaw 80-82; P-in-c Farewell 80-82. *The Vicarage, Hospital Street, Tamworth, Staffs B79 7EE* Tamworth (0827) 62446

WIDDECOMBE, Canon Malcolm Murray. b 37. Tyndale Hall Bris 57. d 62 p 63. C Bris H Trin *Bris* 62-65; C Barton Hill St Luke w Ch Ch 65-67; P-in-c Bris St Phil and St Jacob w Em 67-74; V from 74; RD Bris City 79-85; Hon Can Bris Cathl from 86. *The Vicarage, 7 King's Drive, Bristol BS7 8JW* Bristol (0272) 43169

WIDDESS, Peter Henry. b 53. Jes Coll Cam BA74. Ripon Coll Cuddesdon 75. d 77 p 78. C Darlington St Cuth *Dur* 77-79; C Ancoats *Man* 79-82; Asst Chapl Wiesbaden *Eur* 82. *Address temp unknown*

WIDDICOMBE, Alexander Charles Ernest. b 11. Jes Coll Cam BA32 MA36. Wells Th Coll 33. d 34 p 35. R Chedburgh w Depden and Rede *St E* 66-71; S Africa from 72; rtd 79. *PO Box 20, Saldanha, 7395 South Africa* Vredenburg (2281) 42662

WIDDICOMBE, Peter John. b 52. Univ of Manitoba BA74 St Cath Coll Ox MPhil77 St Cross Coll Ox DPhil90. Wycliffe Coll Toronto MDiv81. d 81 p 82. C Canada 81-84; C Ox St Andr *Ox* 84-86; Acting Chapl Trin Coll Ox 88; Acting Chapl Linc Coll Ox 89; P-in-c Penn from 90. *The Vicarage, Paul's Hill, Penn, High Wycombe, Bucks HP10 8NZ* Penn (049481) 3254

WIDDOWS, David Charles Roland. b 52. Hertf Coll Ox BA75 MA79. St Jo Coll Nottm BA77. d 79 p 80. C Blackley St Andr *Man* 79-83; P-in-c Rochdale Deeplish St Luke 83-84; V from 84. *St Luke's Vicarage, 70 Deeplish Road, Rochdale, Lancs OL11 1PQ* Rochdale (0706) 354628

WIDDOWS, Edward John. b 45. Lon Coll of Div 66. d 70 p 71. C Formby St Pet *Liv* 70-72; C Uckfield *Chich* 72-73; C Isfield 72-73; C Lt Horsted 72-73; C Babbacombe *Ex* 73-76; V Sithney *Truro* 76-78; RD Kerrier 77-78; V Bude Haven 78-84; P-in-c Laneast w St Clether and Tresmere 84-85; P-in-c N Hill w Altarnon, Bolventor and Lewannick 84-85; P-in-c Boyton w N Tamerton 84-85; P-in-c N Petherwin 84-85; R Collingham w S Scarle and Besthorpe and Girton *S'well* from 85. *The Rectory, 1 Vicarage Close, Collingham, Newark, Notts NG23 7PQ* Newark (0636) 892317

WIDDOWS, John Christopher (Kit). b 46. Trin Coll Cam BA69 MA72. Cuddesdon Coll 69. d 71 p 72. C Herrington *Dur* 71-76; Chapl Nat Exhibition Cen 76-80; TV Chelmsley Wood *Birm* 76-80; V Halifax St Hilda *Wakef* from 80. *St Hilda's Vicarage, Gibraltar Road, Halifax, W Yorkshire HX1 4HE* Halifax (0422) 354448

WIDDOWSON, Robert William. b 47. Linc Th Coll 83. d 85 p 86. C Syston *Leic* 85-88; R Husbands Bosworth w Mowsley and Knaptoft etc from 88. *The Rectory, Husbands Bosworth, Lutterworth, Leics LE17 6LY* Market Harborough (0858) 880351

WIERSUM, Timothy Peter. b 55. MA. Cranmer Hall Dur. d 83 p 84. C Boldmere *Birm* 83-86; C Ashton St Mich *Man* 86-88; CMS from 89; Guinea from 90. *Cathedrale Toussaint, BP 1187, Conakry, Guinea*

WIFFEN, Richard Austin. b 58. St Pet Coll Ox BA80. Trin Coll Bris BA90. d 90 p 91. C Bowdon *Ches* from 90. *Stamford Cottage, Stamford Road, Bowdon, Altrincham, Cheshire WA14 2TR* 061-928 4084

WIGAN, Bernard John. b 18. St Edm Hall Ox BA40 MA44. Cuddesdon Coll 40. d 42 p 43. V Mark Beech *Roch* 59-65; rtd 65; Hon Can Roch Cathl *Roch* 68-84; Hon C Brighton St Paul *Chich* from 89. *119 Western Road, Hurstpierpoint, W Sussex BN6 9SY*

WIGFIELD, Thomas Henry Paul. b 26. Edin Th Coll 46. d 49 p 50. Asst Dir Chr TV Cen 63-79; Perm to Offic *Lon* from 63; Perm to Offic *St Alb* from 66; Hd of Services Foundn for Chr Communication 79-84; Chs' Liaison Officer 84-91; rtd 91. *16 Fishers Field, Buckingham, Bucks MK18 1SF* Buckingham (0280) 817893

WIGGEN, Richard Martin. b 42. Open Univ BA78 Hull Univ MA86. Qu Coll Birm 64. d 67 p 68. C Penistone w

Midhope *Wakef* 67-70; C Leeds St Pet *Ripon* 70-73; Asst Youth Chapl *Glouc* 73-76; Youth Officer *Liv* 76-80; V Kirkstall *Ripon* 80-90; V Meanwood from 90. *Meanwood Vicarage, 9 Parkside Green, Leeds LS6 4NY* Leeds (0532) 757885

WIGGINS, **Karl Patrick.** b 38. FRICS64 Lon Univ BD72. Trin Coll Bris 71. **d** 72 **p** 73. C Hildenborough *Roch* 72-76; Hon C Reading St Barn *Ox* 76-78; Lic to Offic 78-83; NSM Reading St Jo from 83. *93 Crescent Road, Reading RG1 5SC* Reading (0734) 663832

WIGGINTON, **Canon Peter Walpole.** b 20. Dur Univ LTh44. Edin Th Coll 40. **d** 43 **p** 44. R W Keal *Linc* 56-83; R E Keal 57-83; RD Bolingbroke 66-88; Can and Preb Linc Cathl from 77; R E and W Keal 83-88; R Bolingbroke 83-88; R Toynton All Saints w Toynton St Peter 83-88; rtd 88; Chapl Trin Hosp Retford from 88. *The Rectory Farm, Rectory Road, Retford, Notts DN22 7AY* Retford (0777) 860352

WIGGS, **Robert James.** b 50. Pemb Coll Cam BA72 MA CertEd. Qu Coll Birm 78. **d** 80 **p** 81. C Stratford St Jo and Ch Ch w Forest Gate St Jas *Chelmsf* 80-83; C E Ham w Upton Park 83-86; TV 86-91; TR Grays Thurrock from 91. *The Rectory, 10 High View Avenue, Grays, Essex RM17 6RU* Grays Thurrock (0375) 373215

WIGHT, **Dennis Marley.** b 53. Southn Univ BTh87. Sarum & Wells Th Coll 82. **d** 85 **p** 86. C Gillingham *Sarum* 85-87; Appeals Org CECS from 87; Perm to Offic *Birm* from 89; V Coseley Ch Ch *Lich* from 90. *The Vicarage, Church Road, Coseley, Bilston, W Midlands WV14 8YB* Bilston (0902) 353551

WIGHT, **Mrs Sian Hilary.** b 54. CertEd75 Birm Univ BEd76 Southn Univ BTh87. Sarum & Wells Th Coll 82. **dss** 85 **d** 87. Ex St Sidwell and St Matt *Ex* 85-87; Par Dn 87-88; Perm to Offic *Lich* from 89; Hon Par Dn Coseley Ch Ch from 90. *Christchurch Vicarage, Church Road, Coseley, Bilston, Wolverhampton WV14 8YB* Wolverhampton (0902) 353551

WIGHTMAN, **Very Rev William David.** b 39. Birm Univ BA61. Wells Th Coll 61. **d** 63 **p** 64. C Rotherham *Sheff* 63-67; C Castle Church *Lich* 67-70; V Buttershaw St Aid *Bradf* 70-76; V Cullingworth 76-83; R Peterhead *Ab* 83-91; R Strichen 90-91; R Old Deer 90-91; R Longside 90-91; Provost St Andr Cathl from 91; R Aber St Andr from 91; P-in-c Aber St Ninian from 91. *15 Morningfield Road, Aberdeen AB2 4AP* Aberdeen (0224) 314765

WIGLEY, **Brian Arthur.** b 31. Qu Coll Birm. **d** 82 **p** 83. C Houghton le Spring *Dur* 82-85; C Louth *Linc* 85-86; TV 86-89; Chapl Dudley Road Hosp Birm from 89. *Dudley Road Hospital, Birmingham B18* 021-554 3801

WIGLEY, **Canon Harry Maxwell.** b 38. Oak Hill Th Coll 61. **d** 64 **p** 65. C Upton (or Overchurch) *Ches* 64-67; C Gateacre *Liv* 67-69; C Chadderton Ch Ch *Man* 67; V Gt Horton *Bradf* 69-88; Hon Can Bradf Cathl from 85; V Pudsey St Lawr and St Paul from 88. *The Vicarage, Vicarage Drive, Pudsey, W Yorkshire LS28 7RL* Pudsey (0532) 577843

WIGLEY, **Ms Jennifer.** b 53. Bris Univ BA74 Birm Univ MA75 Ox Univ CertEd76. Qu Coll Birm 86. **d** 87. C Llangollen w Trevor and Llantysilio *St As* 87-89; C Swansea St Jas *S & B* from 89. *12 Worcester Drive, Langland, Swansea, W Glam SA3 4HL* Swansea (0792) 366712

WIGNALL, **Paul Graham.** b 49. **d** 74 **p** 75. C Chesterton Gd Shep *Ely* 74-76; Min Can Dur Cathl *Dur* 76-79; Tutor Ripon Coll Cuddesdon 80-84; P-in-c Chinnor w Emmington and Sydenham etc *Ox* 81-84; C Shepherd's Bush St Steph w St Thos *Lon* 84. *Address temp unknown*

WIGRAM, **Andrew Oswald.** b 39. Lon Univ BD64. Bps' Coll Cheshunt 61. **d** 64 **p** 65. C Marton-in-Cleveland *York* 64-69; Kenya 69-82; V Westcliff St Mich *Chelmsf* from 82; RD Southend-on-Sea from 89. *St Michael's Vicarage, 5 Mount Avenue, Westcliff-on-Sea, Essex SS0 8PS* Southend-on-Sea (0702) 78462

WIGRAM, **Canon Sir Clifford Woolmore, Bt.** b 11. Trin Coll Cam BA32 MA36. Ely Th Coll 33. **d** 34 **p** 35. V Marston w Warkworth *Pet* 45-75; V Marston St Lawrence w Warkworth and Thenford 75-83; Can Pet Cathl 73-83; rtd 83; Perm to Offic *B & W* from 84. *2 Mold Cottages, Marston St Lawrence, Banbury, Oxon OX17 2DB* Banbury (0295) 711779

WIGRAM, **Miss Ruth Margaret.** b 41. CertEd63. Cranmer Hall Dur 83. **dss** 84 **d** 87. Shipley St Paul and Frizinghall *Bradf* 84-87; Par Dn 87-90; Asst Dioc Dir of Ords from 90; C Skipton H Trin from 90. *7 Princes Drive, Skipton, N Yorkshire BD23 1HN* Skipton (0756) 701063

WIGSTON, **Kenneth Edmund.** b 28. Lich Th Coll 55. **d** 58 **p** 59. C Sheff Sharrow *Sheff* 58-61; C Kidlington *Ox* 61-68; R Airdrie *Glas* 68-78; R Gartcosh 68-78; R Glas

St Oswald 78-85; R Onich *Arg* from 85; R Glencoe from 85; R Ballachulish from 85. *The Rectory, Glencoe, Argyll PA39 4HP* Ballachulish (08552) 335

WIKELEY, **John Roger Ian.** b 41. AKC64. **d** 65 **p** 66. C Southport H Trin *Liv* 65-69; C Padgate Ch Ch 69-71; TV Padgate 71-73; R 73-74; TR 74-85; TR W Derby St Mary from 85; AD W Derby from 89. *The Rectory, West Derby, Liverpool L12 5EA* 051-256 6600

WILBOURNE, **David Jeffrey.** b 55. Jes Coll Cam BA78 MA82. Westcott Ho Cam 79. **d** 81 **p** 82. C Stainton-in-Cleveland *York* 81-85; Chapl Asst Hemlington Hosp 81-85; R Monk Fryston and S Milford 85-91; Abp's Dom Chapl from 91; Dir of Ords from 91. *Brew House Cottage or, Bishopthorpe Palace, Bishopthorpe, York YO2 1QU* York (0904) 706822 or 707021

WILBOURNE, **Geoffrey Owen.** b 29. Lich Th Coll 60. **d** 62 **p** 63. V Ellerton Priory w Aughton and E Cottingwith *York* 65-70; TV Scalby w Ravenscar and Staintondale 70-73; V Kingston upon Hull St Nic 73-76; V Keyingham 76-85; V Hemingbrough 85-91; rtd 91. *4 Eastleigh Court, Hasland, Chesterfield, Derbyshire*

WILBRAHAM, **David.** b 59. Oak Hill Th Coll BA88. **d** 88 **p** 89. C Ince Ch Ch *Liv* 88-91; C St Helens St Helen from 91. *45B Cowley Hill Lane, St Helens, Merseyside WA10 2AR* St Helens (0744) 453681

WILBY, **Mrs Jean.** b 38. Open Univ BA82. Wycliffe Hall Ox 83. **dss** 85 **d** 87. Maidenhead St Andr and St Mary Magd *Ox* 85-87; C 87; TM Hermitage and Hampstead Norreys, Cold Ash etc from 87. *The Vicarage, Cold Ash Hill, Cold Ash, Newbury, Berks RG16 9PT* Newbury (0635) 64395

WILBY, **Timothy David.** b 59. Univ Coll Dur BA80 MA87. Ripon Coll Cuddesdon 81. **d** 83 **p** 84. C Standish *Blackb* 83-86; CF 86-89; V Chorley All SS *Blackb* from 89. *All Saints' Vicarage, Moor Road, Chorley, Lancs PR7 2LR* Chorley (02572) 65665

WILBY, **Wendy Ann.** b 49. ARCM69 LRAM72 St Hugh's Coll Ox BA71. NE Ord Course. **d** 90. Par Dn Barwick in Elmet *Ripon* from 90. *Rosemead, St John's Avenue, Thorner, Leeds LS14 3BZ* Leeds (0532) 892013

WILCOCK, **Christopher John.** b 45. TCD BA68 MA72. CITC 75. **d** 77 **p** 78. C Holywood *D & D* 77-82; C Dub St Ann's Gp *D & G* 82-83; I Inishmacsaint *Clogh* 83-89; Dioc Info Officer 86-89; Bp's C Stoneyford *Conn* from 89; Chapl R Victoria Hosp Belf from 89. *The Rectory, Stoneyford, Lisburn, Co Antrim BT28 3SP* Stoneyford (084664) 300

WILCOCK, **Michael Jarvis.** b 32. Dur Univ BA54. Tyndale Hall Bris 60. **d** 62 **p** 63. C Southport Ch Ch *Liv* 62-65; C St Marylebone All So w SS Pet and Jo *Lon* 65-69; V Maidstone St Faith *Cant* 69-77; Dir Past Studies Trin Coll Bris 77-82; V Dur St Nic *Dur* from 82. *St Nicholas' Vicarage, Kepier Rise, Durham DH1 1JP* 091-384 6066

WILCOCK, **Paul Trevor.** b 59. Bris Univ BA. Trin Coll Bris 83. **d** 87 **p** 88. C Kirkheaton *Wakef* 87-90; Chapl Huddersfield Poly from 90. *85 New North Road, Huddersfield* Huddersfield (0484) 530655

WILCOCKSON, **Stephen Anthony.** b 51. Nottm Univ BA73 Ox Univ BA75 MA81. Wycliffe Hall Ox 73. **d** 76 **p** 77. C Pudsey St Lawr *Bradf* 76-78; C Wandsworth All SS *S'wark* 78-81; V Rock Ferry *Ches* 81-86; V Lache cum Saltney from 86. *St Mark's Vicarage, 5 Cliveden Road, Chester CH4 8DR* Chester (0244) 671702

WILCOX, **Anthony Gordon.** b 41. Lon Coll of Div LTh67 ALCD67. **d** 67 **p** 68. C Cheltenham Ch Ch *Glouc* 67-72; C Beccles St Mich *St E* 72-74; TV 74-81; V Ipswich All SS from 81. *All Saints' Vicarage, 264 Norwich Road, Ipswich IP1 4BT* Ipswich (0473) 252975

WILCOX, **Brian Howard.** b 46. Westcott Ho Cam 71. **d** 73 **p** 74. C Kettering SS Pet and Paul *Pet* 73-78; V Eye 78-82; R Clipston w Naseby and Haselbech w Kelmarsh 82-90; V Hornsea w Atwick from 90. *The Vicarage, 9 Newbeggin, Hornsea, N Humberside HU18 1AB* Hornsea (0964) 532531

WILCOX, **Colin John.** b 43. St Mich Coll Llan 84. **d** 86 **p** 87. C Newport St Andr *Mon* 86-88; C Llanmartin 88-90; TV from 90. *The Vicarage, Station Road, Llanwern, Newport, Gwent NP6 2DW* Llanwern (0633) 413457

WILCOX, **David.** b 35. Roch Th Coll 66. **d** 68 **p** 69. C Newington St Mary *S'wark* 68-73; C Mottingham St Andr 73-77; P-in-c Shooters Hill 77-84; R Kirtlington w Bletchingdon, Weston etc *Ox* from 84. *The Rectory, Troy Lane, Kirtlington, Oxford OX5 3HA* Bletchingdon (0869) 50224

✠WILCOX, **Rt Rev David Peter.** b 30. St Jo Coll Ox BA52 MA56. Linc Th Coll 52. **d** 54 **p** 55 **c** 86. C St Helier *S'wark* 54-56; C Ox St Mary V *Ox* 56-59; Tutor Linc Th Coll 59-60; Chapl 60-61; Sub-Warden 61-63; India 64-70; R Gt w Lt Gransden *Ely* 70-72; Can Res Derby Cathl

Derby 72-77; Warden E Midl Min Tr Course 73-77; Prin Ripon Coll Cuddesdon 77-85; V Cuddesdon *Ox* 77-85; Suff Bp Dorking *Guildf* from 86. *13 Pilgrims Way, Guildford, Surrey GU4 8AD* Guildford (0483) 570829

WILCOX, Graham James. b 43. Qu Coll Ox BA64 MA75. Ridley Hall Cam 64. **d** 66 **p** 67. C Edgbaston St Aug *Birm* 66-69; C Sheldon 69-72; Asst Chapl Wrekin Coll Shropshire 72-74; C Asterby w Goulceby *Linc* 74-77; P-in-c 77; R 77-81; R Benniworth w Market Stainton and Ranby 77-81; R Donington on Bain 77-81; R Stenigot 77-81; R Gayton le Wold w Biscathorpe 77-81; V Scamblesby w Cawkwell 77-81; R Asterby Gp 81-88; V Sutton le Marsh 88-90; R Sutton, Huttoft and Anderby from 90. *The Vicarage, Huttoft Road, Mablethorpe, Lincs LN12 2RU* Mablethorpe (0521) 441169

WILCOX, Haydon Howard. b 56. Sarum & Wells Th Coll. **d** 82 **p** 83. C Fishponds St Jo *Bris* 82-85; TV Hucknall Torkard *S'well* 85-91; R Bilsthorpe from 91; R Eakring from 91; V Maplebeck from 91; P-in-c Winkburn from 91. *The Rectory, Church Hill, Bilsthorpe, Newark, Notts NG22 8RU* Mansfield (0623) 870256

WILCOX, Hugh Edwin. b 37. St Edm Hall Ox BA62 MA66. St Steph Ho Ox 62. **d** 64 **p** 65. C Colchester St Jas, All SS, St Nic and St Runwald *Chelmsf* 64-66; Hon C Clifton St Paul *Bris* 66-68; SCM 66-68; Sec Internat Dept BCC 68-76; Asst Gen Sec 74-76; V Ware St Mary *St Alb* from 76. *The Vicarage, 31 Thunder Court, Milton Road, Ware, Herts SG12 0PT* Ware (0920) 464817

WILCOX, Jeffry Reed. b 40. K Coll Lon AKC65 BA78. **d** 66 **p** 67. C Ryhope *Dur* 66-69; C Cockerton 69-71; P-in-c Pallion 71-82; R Streatham St Leon *S'wark* from 82. *The Rectory, 1 Becmead Avenue, London SW16 1UH* 081-769 4366 or 769 1216

WILCOX, Joe. b 21. ACT LTh62 Lich Th Coll. **d** 62 **p** 63. V Leek St Luke *Lich* 67-75; P-in-c Ellington *Ely* 75-80; P-in-c Spaldwick w Barham and Woolley 75-80; P-in-c Easton 75-80; P-in-c Grafham 75-80; R Holywell w Needingworth 80-86; rtd 86; Perm to Offic *Ely* from 87. *16 Silver Birch Avenue, St Ives, Huntingdon, Cambs PE17 4TS* St Ives (0480) 496846

WILCOX, John Bower. b 28. AKC55. **d** 58 **p** 59. C Orford St Marg *Liv* 58-60; C W Derby St Mary 60-63; R Aisthorpe w W Thorpe and Scampton *Linc* 63-74; R Brattleby 64-74; Ind Chapl *York* 74-89; P-in-c Middlesb St Cuth from 89; Urban Development Officer from 89. *95 Southwell Road, Middlesbrough, Cleveland TS5 6NG* Middlesbrough (0642) 620838

WILCOX, Peter Jonathan. b 61. St Jo Coll Dur BA84 BA86. Ridley Hall Cam 84. **d** 87 **p** 88. C Preston on Tees *Dur* 87-90. *19 Hart-Synnot House, Leckford Road, Oxford OX2 6JL* Oxford (0865) 511762

WILCOX, Raymond Trevor. b 22. St D Coll Lamp BA47. **d** 48 **p** 49. V Bentley *Lich* 50-78; P-in-c Blithfield 78-84; P-in-c Colton 78-84; V Llanddewi Rhydderch w Llangattock-juxta-Usk etc *Mon* 84-87; rtd 87. *8 Orchard Close, Uttoxeter, Staffs ST14 7QZ* Uttoxeter (0889) 566308

WILD, Edwin Arnold. b 13. Peterho Cam BA35 MA44. Wells Th Coll 36. **d** 37 **p** 38. R Barton-le-Cley w Higham Gobion *St Alb* 62-69; V Ash w Westmarsh *Cant* 70-77; rtd 77; Perm to Offic Chich from 77; Cant from 78. *Lapwings, 12 The Suttons, Camber, Rye, E Sussex TN31 7SA* Rye (0797) 497

WILD, Very Rev John Herbert Severn. b 04. DD. **d** 29 **p** 30. Dean Dur 51-73; rtd 73; Lic to Offic *B & W* from 73. *Deacon's Farm House, Rapps, Ilminster, Somerset TA19 9LG* Ilminster (0460) 53398

WILD, Robert David Fergusson. b 10. MC45 MBE46 TD50. Ex Coll Ox BA33 MA36. Westcott Ho Cam 34. **d** 35 **p** 36. C Eastleigh *Win* 35-36; Bp's Dom Chapl 36-37; Lic to Offic 37; Chapl Eton Coll Windsor 37-69; CF (TA) 39-50; Select Preacher Cam Univ 52; P-in-c Staplegrove *B & W* 70-71; P-in-c Bicknoller 73-74; Perm to Offic from 74. *Yard End, Carters Lane, Crowcombe, Taunton, Somerset TA4 4AA* Crowcombe (09848) 640

WILD, Roger Bedingham Barratt. b 40. ALCD64. **d** 65 **p** 66. C Shipley St Pet *Bradf* 65-68; C Pudsey St Lawr 68-71; P-in-c Rawthorpe *Wakef* 71-73; V 73-78; V Ripon H Trin *Ripon* from 78; RD Ripon from 86. *Holy Trinity Vicarage, College Road, Ripon, N Yorkshire HG4 2AE* Ripon (0765) 5865

WILD, Roger Longson. b 13. K Coll Lon 55. **d** 57 **p** 58. V Kingston Hill St Paul *S'wark* 63-74; R Easton and Martyr Worthy *Win* 74-82; rtd 82; Perm to Offic *Win* from 83. *Escallonia, Cottagers Lane, Hordle, Lymington, Hants SO41 0FE* New Milton (0425) 613501

WILDE, David Wilson. b 37. Lon Coll of Div ALCD61 BD62. **d** 62 **p** 63. C Kirkheaton *Wakef* 62-66; C

Attenborough w Chilwell *S'well* 66-72; P-in-c Bestwood Park 72-83; R Kimberley from 83. *The Rectory, Kimberley, Nottingham NG16 2LL* Nottingham (0602) 383565

WILDEY, Ian Edward. b 51. St Chad's Coll Dur BA72. Coll of Resurr Mirfield 72. **d** 74 **p** 75. C Westgate Common *Wakef* 74-77; C Barnsley St Mary 77-81; V Ravensthorpe from 81. *St Saviour's Vicarage, Ravensthorpe, Dewsbury, W Yorkshire WF13 3LA* Dewsbury (0924) 465959

WILDING, David. b 43. K Coll Lon BD67 AKC67. **d** 68 **p** 69. C Thornhill *Wakef* 68-70; C Halifax St Jo Bapt 70-72; V Scholes 72-79; V Lightcliffe from 79. *The Vicarage, Wakefield Road, Lightcliffe, Halifax, W Yorkshire HX3 8TH* Halifax (0422) 202424

WILDING, Joseph. b 14. Edin Th Coll 50. **d** 52 **p** 53. R Alexandria *Glas* 56-80; P-in-c 80-84; rtd 84. *Ash House Farm, Ulnes Walton, Preston PR5 3LU*

WILDING, Michael Paul. b 57. Chich Th Coll 82. **d** 85 **p** 86. C Treboeth *S & B* 85-87; C Llanguicke 87-88; V Devynock w Rhydybriw and Llandilo'r-fan from 88. *The Vicarage, Sennybridge, Brecon, Powys LD3 8TB* Sennybridge (0874) 828927

WILDRIDGE, Peter. b 24. Univ of Wales (Lamp) BA51. St D Coll Lamp BA51. **d** 52 **p** 53. V Islington St Pet *Lon* 60-80; rtd 89. *66 Queensborough Terrace, London W2 3SH* 071-221 0022

WILDS, Anthony Ronald. b 43. Dur Univ BA64. Bps' Coll Cheshunt 64. **d** 66 **p** 67. C Newport Pagnell *Ox* 66-72; Zambia 72-75; V Chandler's Ford *Win* 75-85; V Andover w Foxcott from 85; RD Andover from 89. *St Mary's Vicarage, Church Close, Andover, Hants SP10 1DP* Andover (0264) 352729

WILES, David James. b 50. Univ Coll Lon BSc72 K Coll Lon CertEd73. St Jo Coll Nottm 85. **d** 88 **p** 89. C Clapham Park St Steph *S'wark* from 88. *153 Hydethorpe Road, London SW12 0JG* 081-673 6066

WILES, Canon Prof Maurice Frank. b 23. FBA Ch Coll Cam BA47 MA52 DD. Ridley Hall Cam 48. **d** 50 **p** 51. Prof Chr Doctrine K Coll Lon 67-70; Can Res Ch Ch *Ox* from 70; Regius Prof Div Ox Univ from 70; rtd 91. *11 Baytree Close, Oxford OX4 4DT* Oxford (0865) 777091

WILES, Canon Eric. b 22. Dur Univ BA51. St Steph Ho Ox 50. **d** 53 **p** 54. C Shrewsbury All SS *Lich* 53-55; C Leeds St Aid *Ripon* 55-58; C Cowley St Jo *Ox* 58-63; V Toxteth Park St Marg *Liv* 63-71; V Orford St Marg 71-83; Hon Can Liv Cathl 76-83; R Shepton Beauchamp w Barrington, Stocklinch etc *B & W* from 83; RD Ilminster from 87. *The Rectory, Church Street, Shepton Beauchamp, Ilminster, Somerset TA19 0LQ* South Petherton (0460) 40338

WILKES, Canon Keith Reid. b 30. Pemb Coll Cam BA53 MA55 Bris Univ MA71. Linc Th Coll 53. **d** 55 **p** 56. C Welwyn Garden City *St Alb* 55-59; Chapl St Fran Hall Birm Univ 59-64; SCM Sec Birm Univ 59-64; Chapl St Matthias's Coll Bris 64-70; Dir of Educn *Bris* 70-80; Chapl Bris Cathl 70-74; R Bris Ch Ch w St Ewen 70-74; R Bris St Ewen and All SS 74-80; Hon Can Bris Cathl 74-80; Provost Woodard Schs (Midl Division) from 80; Perm to Offic *S'well* and *Derby* from 80; Lic to Offic *Lich* from 80. *The Mount, St John's Hill, Ellesmere, Shropshire SY12 0EY* Ellesmere (0691) 622466

WILKES, Robert Anthony. b 48. Trin Coll Ox BA70 MA73. Wycliffe Hall Ox 71. **d** 74 **p** 75. C Netherton *Liv* 74-77; V 77-81; Bp's Dom Chapl 81-85; CMS from 85; Pakistan 85-86; Regional Sec Middle East and Pakistan from 87; Perm to Offic *S'wark* 87-90; *Ox* from 90. *28 Lonsdale Road, Oxford OX2 7EW* Oxford (0865) 59362

WILKES, Thomas Clement Broadbery. b 14. Lon Univ BA37. Chich Th Coll 37. **d** 38 **p** 39. R Stambridge *Chelmsf* 69-79; rtd 79. *31 Radford Court, Billericay, Essex*

WILKIE, Alan James. b 17. Chich Th Coll 39. **d** 42 **p** 43. V Lindale *Carl* 69-71; P-in-c Field Broughton 71; V Lindale w Field Broughton 71-85; rtd 85; Perm to Offic *Carl* from 85. *Fernlea, Beckermet, Cumbria CA21 2YF* Beckermet (094684) 284

WILKIN, Kenneth. b 54. S'wark Ord Course 86 Wilson Carlile Coll. **d** 88 **p** 89. C Wolv *Lich* from 88. *3 Westland Gardens, Wolverhampton WV3 9NU* Wolverhampton (0902) 23739

WILKIN, Paul John. b 56. Linc Th Coll 88. **d** 90 **p** 91. C Leavesden All SS *St Alb* from 90. *24 Kimpton Place, Garston, Watford, Herts WD2 6RD* Garston (0923) 670318

WILKIN, Rose Josephine. *See* HUDSON-WILKIN, Rose Josephine

WILKINS, Peter. b 11. St Jo Coll Ox BA33 MA37. St Steph Ho Ox 55. **d** 56 **p** 57. V Cassington *Ox* 58-79; rtd 79; Lic to Offic *Heref* from 79. *Kilmer House, Kings Pyon, Hereford HR4 8PS* Canon Pyon (043271) 589

WILKINS, Ralph Herbert. b 29. Lon Univ BD61. St Aug Coll Cant 72. **d** 73 **p** 74. C Epsom Common Ch Ch *Guildf* 73-76; C Haslemere 77-79; P-in-c Market Lavington and Easterton *Sarum* 79-82; V 82-90; P-in-c Puddletown and Tolpuddle from 90. *The Vicarage, The Square, Puddletown, Dorchester, Dorset DT2 8SL* Puddletown (0305) 848216

WILKINS, Miss Susan Stafford. b 47. Dur Univ BA. Sarum Th Coll. **dss** 82 **d** 87. Redlynch and Morgan's Vale *Sarum* 82-88; Hon Par Dn 87-88; Hon Par Dn Bemerton 88-90; Par Dn Hilperton w Whaddon and Staverton etc from 90. *10 Hayes Close, Wyke Farm Estate, Trowbridge, Wilts BA14 7ND* Trowbridge (0225) 766330

WILKINS, Vernon Gregory. b 53. Trin Coll Cam MA74 Ox Univ BA88. Wycliffe Hall Ox 86. **d** 89 **p** 90. C Boscombe St Jo *Win* 89-91; C Bursledon from 91. *15 Old Bridge Close, Bursledon, Southampton SO3 8AX* Bursledon (042121) 6980

WILKINSON, Canon Alan Bassindale. b 31. St Cath Coll Cam BA54 MA58 PhD59. Coll of Resurr Mirfield 57. **d** 59 **p** 60. C Kilburn St Aug w St Jo *Lon* 59-61; Chapl St Cath Coll Cam 61-67; V Barrow Gurney *B & W* 67-70; Asst Chapl St Matthias's Coll Bris 67-70; Prin Chich Th Coll 70-74; Can and Preb Chich Cathl *Chich* 70-74; Warden Verulam Ho 74-75; Dir of Aux Min Tr *St Alb* 74-75; Sen Lect Crewe & Alsager Coll 75-78; Dioc Dir of Tr *Ripon* 78-84; Hon Can Ripon Cathl from 84; P-in-c Thornthwaite w Thruscross and Darley 84-88; Hon C Portsm Cathl *Portsm* from 88. *Hope Cottage, 27 Great Southsea Street, Portsmouth PO5 3BY* Portsmouth (0705) 825788

WILKINSON, David Andrew. b 62. Edge Hill Coll of HE BA83. Oak Hill Th Coll BA85. **d** 88 **p** 89. C Upton (or Overchurch) *Ches* 88-91; C Fulham St Matt *Lon* from 91. *2A Clancarty Road, London SW6 3AB* 071-736 4421

WILKINSON, David Edward Paul. b 36. Univ of Wales (Swansea) BSc57. St Mich Coll Llan 57. **d** 59 **p** 60. C Brecon w Battle *S & B* 59-60; Min Can Brecon Cathl 60-66; R Llanelwedd w Llanfaredd, Cwmbach Llechryd etc 66-72; V Tycoch 72-74; Asst Master Churchmead Sch Datchet 75-82; Perm to Offic *Ox* 80-82; TV Seacroft *Ripon* from 82. *St Paul's Vicarage, 58 Whinmoor Crescent, Leeds LS14 1EW* Leeds (0532) 655649

WILKINSON, David James. b 45. St D Coll Lamp 65 Wycliffe Hall Ox 68. **d** 69 **p** 70. C Swansea St Thos and Kilvey *S & B* 69-73; C Clydach 73-76; R Llanbadarn Fawr, Llandegley and Llanfihangel R'n 76-81; V Swansea St Nic 81-88; V Killay from 88. *The Vicarage, 30 Goetre Fach Road, Killay, Swansea SA2 7SG* Swansea (0792) 204233

WILKINSON, Canon David Reginald. b 16. St Edm Hall Ox BA38 MA48. Wells Th Coll 38. **d** 39 **p** 40. V Swansea St Barn *S & B* 69-82; Can Brecon Cathl 76-82; rtd 82. *12 Pantgwyn, Sketty Park Road, Sketty, Swansea SA2 9BA* Swansea (0792) 297901

WILKINSON, Edward. b 55. Cranmer Hall Dur 86. **d** 88 **p** 89. C Bishopwearmouth St Nic *Dur* from 88. *3 Highside Drive, Sunderland SR3 1UW* 091-522 7035

WILKINSON, Edward Arthur Hewson. b 20. CITC. **d** 84 **p** 85. NSM Dub Irishtown w Donnybrook *D & G* 84-85; NSM Dub St Geo and St Thos 85-90; NSM Dub Zion Ch from 90. *Ferndale, 62 Beaumont Avenue, Churchtown, Dublin 14, Irish Republic* Dublin (1) 983769

WILKINSON, Edwin. b 29. Oak Hill Th Coll 53. **d** 56 **p** 57. C Blackb Ch Ch *Blackb* 56-58; C Cheltenham St Mark *Glouc* 58-61; V Tiverton St Geo *Ex* 61-66; V Rye Harbour *Chich* 66-73; V Camber and E Guldeford 73-79; V Westf 79-87; V Bexhill St Steph from 87. *67 Woodsgate Park, Bexhill-on-Sea, E Sussex TN39 4DL* Bexhill-on-Sea (0424) 211186

WILKINSON, Guy Alexander. b 48. Magd Coll Cam BA69. Ripon Coll Cuddesdon 85. **d** 87 **p** 88. C Cov Caludon *Cov* 87-90; P-in-c Ockham w Hatchford *Guildf* from 90; Bp's Dom Chapl from 90. *The Rectory, Ockham Lane, Ockham, Woking, Surrey GU23 6NP* Guildford (0483) 225358

WILKINSON, Canon James Noel Batthews. b 30. LRAM66 TCD BA53 MA65 BD65. CITC 55. **d** 55 **p** 56. C Dundonald *D & D* 55-57; C Lurgan Ch Ch 57-62; R Harrington *Carl* 62-66; C Antrim All SS *Conn* 66-70; I

Belf Ardoyne 70-79; Min Can Belf Cathl 72-88; RD M Belf *Conn* 78-79; I Derryvolgie from 79; Can Belf Cathl from 88. *53 Kennedy Drive, Belsize Road, Lisburn, Co Antrim BT27 4JA* Lisburn (0846) 663707

WILKINSON, John Andrew. b 59. Pemb Coll Ox BA83 MA87 St Jo Coll Dur BA86. Cranmer Hall Dur 84. **d** 87 **p** 88. C Broadheath *Ches* 87-91; TV Worthing Ch the King *Chich* from 91. *5 Christchurch Road, Worthing, W Sussex BN11 1JH* Worthing (0903) 202433

WILKINSON, John David. b 36. AKC59. **d** 60 **p** 61. C Wythenshawe Wm Temple Ch CD *Man* 60-63; C Morley St Pet w Churwell *Wakef* 63-65; V Roberttown 65-75; V Battyeford 75-88; V Airedale w Fryston from 88. *The Vicarage, The Mount, Airedale, Castleford, W Yorkshire WF10 3JL* Castleford (0977) 553157

WILKINSON, John Donald. b 29. **d** 56. C Stepney St Dunstan and All SS *Lon* 56-59; Tutor Ely Th Coll 60; Jerusalem 61-75 and from 79; Can Jerusalem 73-75; P-in-c S Kensington H Trin w All SS *Lon* 75-78; Lic to Offic 79. *British School of Archaeology, PO Box 19283, Jerusalem, Israel*

WILKINSON, John Lawrence. b 43. Ch Coll Cam BA65 MA69. Qu Coll Birm DipTh68 Gen Th Sem (NY) STB69. **d** 69 **p** 70. C Braunstone *Leic* 69-71; C Hodge Hill *Birm* 71-74; P-in-c Aston St Jas 75-84; Tutor Qu Coll Birm from 85; Hon C Birm St Geo *Birm* from 86. *The Queen's College, Somerset Road, Birmingham B15 2QH* 021-455 8177 or 359 3440

WILKINSON, John Stoddart. b 47. Univ of Wales (Cardiff) CQSW83. St D Coll Lamp DipTh70. **d** 70 **p** 71. C Kells *Carl* 70-72; C Barrow St Geo w St Luke 72-74; Perm to Offic *Mon* 74-89; Sub-Chapl HM Young Offender Inst Hewell Grange from 89; HM Rem Cen Brockhill from 89. *HM Young Offender Institute, Hewell Grange, Redditch, Worcs B97 6QQ* Redditch (0527) 550843

WILKINSON, Jonathan Charles. b 61. Leeds Univ BA83. Wycliffe Hall Ox 85. **d** 87 **p** 88. C Plymouth St Andr w St Paul and St Geo *Ex* 87-90; C Oulton Broad *Nor* from 90. *3 Windward Way, Oulton Broad, Lowestoft, Suffolk NR33 9HF* Lowestoft (0502) 582083

WILKINSON, Joseph Henry. b 09. K Coll Lon. **d** 44 **p** 45. Chapl Kingham Hill Sch Ox 49-77; rtd 77. *Two Ways, Churchill, Oxford OX7 6ND* Kingham (0608) 658583

WILKINSON, Keith Howard. b 48. Hull Univ BA70 Em Coll Cam MA74. Westcott Ho Cam 74. **d** 76 **p** 77. C Pet St Jude *Pet* 76-79; Chapl Eton Coll Windsor 79-84; Perm to Offic *Pet* from 82; Chapl Malvern Coll Worcs 84-89; Hd Master Berkhamsted Sch Herts from 89. *Wilson House, Castle Street, Berkhamsted, Herts HP4 2BE* Berkhamsted (0442) 863236

WILKINSON, Ven Kenneth Samuel. b 31. TCD BA60 MA69. CITC 60. **d** 60 **p** 61. C Dub St Michan w St Paul *D & G* 60-63; Min Can St Patr Cathl Dub 62-67; C Dub Ch Ch Leeson Park *D & G* 63-67; I Killegney *C & O* 67-70; I Enniscorthy w Clone, Clonmore, Monart etc from 70; Preb Ferns Cathl 83-88; Adn Ferns from 88. *The Rectory, Enniscorthy, Co Wexford, Irish Republic* Enniscorthy (54) 33249

WILKINSON, Canon Lewis. b 14. HND(IMechE)36. Ripon Hall Ox 60. **d** 61 **p** 62. Malaysia 68-75; C Lindley *Wakef* 75-78; C Almondbury 78-81; rtd 81; Hon Can Kuala Lumpur from 89. *12 Carey Park, Truro, Cornwall TR1 2LD*

WILKINSON, Michael Alan. b 27. Selw Coll Cam BA51. Westcott Ho Cam 52. **d** 53 **p** 54. C Swindon Ch Ch *Bris* 53-57; C Knowle St Barn 57-59; C Eltham St Jo *S'wark* 59-65; C Sydenham St Bart 65-77; Perm to Offic *Ex* 77-84; P-in-c Yealmpton from 84; P-in-c Brixton from 87. *The Vicarage, Yealmpton, Plymouth, Devon PL8 2JX* Plymouth (0752) 880229

WILKINSON, Norman Ellis. b 10. Peterho Cam BA31 MA35. Sarum Th Coll 32. **d** 33 **p** 34. V Broadhempston and Woodland *Ex* 59-75; rtd 75. *Manor Farmhouse, Walditch, Bridport, Dorset* Bridport (0308) 56025

WILKINSON, Paul. b 51. Sarum & Wells Th Coll 75. **d** 78 **p** 79. C Allerton *Bradf* 78-80; C Baildon 80-83; V Hengoed w Gobowen *Lich* 83-90; V Potterne w Worton and Marston *Sarum* from 90. *The Vicarage, 4 Rookes Lane, Potterne, Devizes, Wilts SN10 5NF* Devizes (0380) 723189

WILKINSON, Paul Martin. b 56. Brunel Univ BSc. Wycliffe Hall Ox 83. **d** 86 **p** 87. C Hinckley H Trin *Leic* 86-90; V Newbold on Avon *Cov* from 90. *The Vicarage, Main Street, Newbold, Rugby, Warks CV21 1HH* Rugby (0788) 543055

WILKINSON, Peter Francis. b 20. Cuddesdon Coll 63. **d** 65 **p** 66. C Chobham w Valley End *Guildf* 65-78; V Yalding *Roch* 68-72; V Yalding w Collier Street 72-87; rtd

87. *Chartfield, Flimwell, Wadhurst, E Sussex TN5 7PA* Flimwell (058087) 372

WILKINSON, Peter Howarth. b 32. St Pet Hall Ox BA54 MA58. Ridley Hall Cam 56. **d** 58 **p** 59. V Nettlebed *Ox* 62-68; rtd 68; Hon C Cheadle *Ches* 69-82. *10 Norbreck Avenue, Cheadle, Cheshire* 061-428 7699

WILKINSON, Canon Raymond Stewart. b 19. AKC42. Bps' Coll Cheshunt 42. **d** 43 **p** 44. R Woodchurch *Ches* 61-71; R Solihull *Birm* 71-79; TR 79-87; Hon Can Birm Cathl 76-87; Chapl to HM The Queen 83-87; rtd 87; Perm to Offic *Cov* from 87. *42 Coten End, Warwick CV34 4NP* Warwick (0926) 493510

WILKINSON, Robert Ian. b 43. MIMunE73 MICE84 CEng73. Oak Hill NSM Course. **d** 88 **p** 89. NSM Hawkwell *Chelmsf* 88-89; NSM Thundersley 89-91; C New Thundersley from 91. *18 Hornbeams, Benfleet, Essex SS7 4NP* South Benfleet (0268) 751759

WILKINSON, Canon Robert Matthew. b 21. TCD BA46. CITC 47. **d** 47 **p** 48. I Derryloran *Arm* 55-73; Can Arm Cathl 67-73; I Ballymore 73-87; Treas Arm Cathl 73-75; Chan 75-83; Prec 83-87; rtd 87. *60 Coleraine Road, Portrush, Co Antrim BT56 8HN* Portrush (0265) 822758

WILKINSON, Roger. b 46. Lon Univ BA68 AKC68 AKC72. St Aug Coll Cant 72. **d** 73 **p** 74. C Lt Stanmore St Lawr *Lon* 73-76; Asst Chapl St Geo Hosp Gp Lon 76-78; Chapl Hounslow and Spelthorne HA 78-88; TV Langley and Parkfield *Man* 88-89; C Shelf *Bradf* 89-90; C Buttershaw St Aid 90; Chapl Ipswich Hosp from 90. *Heath Road, Ipswich, Suffolk IP4 5PD or, 74 Newbury Road, Ipswich, Suffolk IP4 5EY* Ipswich (0473) 704101 or 719702

WILKINSON, Roy Geoffrey. b 42. Sarum Th Coll 67. **d** 70 **p** 71. C Belsize Park *Lon* 70-73; C Heston 73-75; C Hythe *Cant* 75-79; P-in-c Croydon Woodside 79-81; V 81-84; V Croydon Woodside *S'wark* 85-86. *Sundown, Church Lane, Winthorpe, Skegness PE25 1EG* Skegness (0754) 66727

WILKINSON, Simon Evelyn. b 49. Nottm Univ BA74. Cuddesdon Coll 74. **d** 76 **p** 77. C Cheam *S'wark* 76-78; P-in-c Warlingham w Chelsham and Farleigh 78-83; Radley Coll Abingdon 83-89; R Bishops Waltham *Portsm* from 89; R Upham from 89. *The Rectory, Bishops Waltham, Southampton SO3 1EE* Bishops Waltham (0489) 892618

WILKINSON, Walter Edward Robert. b 38. St Andr Univ MA60. Lon Coll of Div BD63 ALCD63. **d** 63 **p** 64. C High Wycombe *Ox* 63-70; PV, Succ and Sacr Roch Cathl *Roch* 70-73; P-in-c Asby w Ormside *Carl* 73-80; R Cherry Burton from 80; RD Beverley from 88. *The Rectory, Cherry Burton, Beverley, N Humberside HU17 7RF* Hornsea (0964) 550293

WILKINSON, Canon Wilfred Badger. b 21. K Coll Lon BD50 AKC50. **d** 50 **p** 51. R Clifton w Glapton *S'well* 65-71; TR Clifton 71-86; Hon Can S'well Minster 83-86; rtd 86; Perm to Offic *S'well* from 86. *13 Farthingate Close, Southwell, Notts NG25 0HU* Southwell (0636) 814047

WILKS, Basil Worsley. b 18. Ripon Hall Ox 61. **d** 62 **p** 63. C Leatherhead *Guildf* 62-64; Lic to Offic *Ox* 64-66; Chapl Shiplake Coll Henley 64-81; Perm to Offic *Ox* from 66. *5 New Cottages, Fawley, Henley-on-Thames, Oxon* Henley-on-Thames (0491) 573574

WILKS, Eric Percival. b 32. **d** 68 **p** 69. C Fladbury w Throckmorton, Wyre Piddle and Moor *Worc* 68-70; Perm to Offic from 70. *4 Catherine Cottages, Torton, Hartlebury, Kidderminster, Worcs DY10 4EL* Hartlebury (0299) 251580

WILKS, Ernest Howard. b 26. Oak Hill Th Coll 64. **d** 66 **p** 67. C Slough *Ox* 66-69; R Gressenhall w Longham and Bittering Parva *Nor* 69-77; Area Sec (Dios St E & I and Nor) CMS 77-83; P-in-c Deopham w Hackford *Nor* 83-84; P-in-c Morley 83-84; P-in-c Wicklewood and Crownthorpe 83-84; R Morley w Deopham, Hackford, Wicklewood etc 84-87; CMS from 89; Nigeria from 89. *Bishopscourt, Egbu, PO Box 31, Owerri, Nigeria*

WILKS, Leslie Ronald. b 10. Oak Hill Th Coll 67. **d** 68 **p** 69. C Hanley Road St Sav w St Paul *Lon* 68-72; R Easton w Letheringham *St E* 72-79; rtd 79; P-in-c Polstead *St E* 79-88. *21 Windmill Fields, Coggeshall, Colchester CO6 1PJ* Coggeshall (0376) 562816

WILLANS, Jonathan Michael Arthur. b 60. QUB BD DipTh. **d** 85 **p** 86. C Larne and Inver *Conn* 85-88; R Hawick *Edin* from 88. *2 Trystside, Hawick, Roxburghshire TD9 0DX* Hawick (0450) 72043

WILLARD, John Fordham. b 38. K Coll Lon BD62 AKC62. **d** 63 **p** 64. C Balham Hill Ascension *S'wark* 63-67; C Leigh Park *Portsm* 67-73; C-in-c Leigh Park St Clare CD 73-75; R Bishops Waltham 75-87; P-in-c Upham 78-79; R 79-87; V Dalston H Trin w St

Phil *Lon* from 87; P-in-c Haggerston All SS from 90. *Holy Trinity Vicarage, 89 Forest Road, London E8 3BL* 071-254 5062

WILLCOCK, Albert. b 13. St D Coll Lamp BA41. **d** 41 **p** 42. V Long Clawson and Hose *Leic* 61-74; R Stonton Wyville w Glooston, Slawston and Cranoe 74-78; rtd 78; Perm to Offic Linc & Leic from 78. *19 Teesdale Road, Grantham, Lincs NG31 8ES* Grantham (0476) 73774

WILLCOCK, Donald Thomas. b 07. Chich Th Coll 52. **d** 54 **p** 55. V Gt Totham *Chelmsf* 58-81; rtd 81. *7 Hawkes Road, Coggeshall, Colchester CO6 1QP* Coggeshall (0376) 561803

WILLCOCK, Richard William. b 39. Hertf Coll Ox BA62 MA66. Ripon Hall Ox 62. **d** 64 **p** 65. C Ashton St Mich *Man* 64-68; Bp's Dom Chapl 68-72; V Charlestown 72-73; V Charlestown 73-75; Chapl Casterton Sch Cumbria 75-80; V Bamford *Man* from 80. *St Michael's Vicarage, Bury and Rochdale Old Road, Heywood, Lancs OL10 4AT* Heywood (0706) 69610

WILLCOX, Frederick John. b 29. Kelham Th Coll 49. **d** 54 **p** 55. C Tranmere St Paul *Ches* 54-56; Lic to Offic *S'well* 57-61; S Africa 62-70; P-in-c Derby St Andr w St Osmund *Derby* 70-74; V 74-80; V Netherton St Andr *Worc* from 80. *The Vicarage, Highbridge Road, Netherton, Dudley, W Midlands DY2 0HT* Dudley (0384) 253118

WILLCOX, Ralph Arthur. b 32. Westhill Coll Birm CertYS59 Cranfield Inst of Tech MSc80. St Alb Minl Tr Scheme 86. **d** 89 **p** 90. NSM Aspley Guise w Husborne Crawley and Ridgmont *St Alb* from 89. *5 Church Road, Woburn Sands, Milton Keynes MK17 8TE* Milton Keynes (0908) 582510

WILLCOX, Dr Richard John Michael. b 39. Birm Univ BSc62 PhD67. Qu Coll Birm 78. **d** 80 **p** 81. C Boldmere *Birm* 80-85; V Edgbaston SS Mary and Ambrose 83-89; V Evercreech w Chesterblade and Milton Clevedon *B & W* from 89; Dioc Development Rep from 90. *The Vicarage, Church Lane, Evercreech, Shepton Mallet, Somerset BA4 6HU* Evercreech (0749) 830322

WILLCOX, Sydney Harold. b 36. Univ of Wales (Lamp) BA58. St Mich Coll Llan. **d** 60 **p** 61. C Pwllheli *Ban* 60-62; C Llandegfan w Beaumaris and Llanfaes 62-65; R Llanenddwyn 65-70; R Dolgellau, Llanfachreth, Brithdir etc 70-76; TR Ridgeway *Sarum* 76-86; RD Marlborough 81-86; TR Cockermouth w Embleton and Wythop *Carl* from 86; RD Derwent from 89. *The Rectory, Lorton Road, Cockermouth, Cumbria CA13 9DU* Cockermouth (0900) 823269

WILLENBROCK, Dr Philip Charles. b 42. Ox Univ MA BM BCh. Ex & Truro NSM Scheme. **d** 82 **p** 83. NSM Treslothan *Truro* 82-87; NSM Redruth w Lanner and Treleigh 87-89; Perm to Offic Sarum 89-90; Chelmsf from 90. *18 The Dale, Wivenhoe, Colchester CO7 9NL* Colchester (0206) 823812

WILLESDEN, Area Bishop of. *Vacant*

WILLETT, Canon Allen Gardiner. b 20. Bris Univ BA51 Lon Univ BD54. Clifton Th Coll 47. **d** 54 **p** 55. V Galleywood Common *Chelmsf* 68-87; RD Chelmsf 81-86; Hon Can Chelmsf Cathl 85-87; rtd 87; Perm to Offic *Pet* from 87; Linc & Ely from 90. *4 Abbotts Grove, Werrington, Peterborough PE4 5BT* Peterborough (0733) 77532

WILLETT, Frank Edwin. b 45. Lon Univ DipTh68. Kelham Th Coll 64. **d** 68 **p** 69. C Oswestry H Trin *Lich* 68-71; C Bilston St Leon 71-74; USPG Coll of the Ascension Selly Oak 74-75; USPG 74-80; Zambia 75-80; V Curbar and Stoney Middleton *Derby* 80-88; Area Sec (Dios Derby and Leic) USPG 88-91; V Chesterfield St Aug *Derby* from 91. *St Augustine's Vicarage, 1 Whitecotes Lane, Chesterfield, Derbys S40 3HJ* Chesterfield (0246) 273942

WILLETT, Canon Geoffrey Thomas. b 38. Dur Univ BA59 MA82. Cranmer Hall Dur DipTh61. **d** 62 **p** 63. C Widnes St Paul *Liv* 62-65; C Harborne Heath *Birm* 65-68; V Wakef St Andr and St Mary *Wakef* 68-75; V Hinckley H Trin *Leic* 75-89; TR 89; RD Sparkenhoe II 84-87; RD Sparkenhoe W (Hinkley & Bosworth) 87-89; Hon Can Leic Cathl from 87; P-in-c Markfield 89-90; R from 90. *The Rectory, The Nook, Markfield, Leicester LE6 0WE* Markfield (0530) 242844

WILLETT, John Ivon. b 40. Ch Ch Ox BA63 MA65. Chich Th Coll 61. **d** 63 **p** 64. C Leic St Andr *Leic* 63-66; C Bordesley St Alb *Birm* 66-72; Min Can, Prec and Sacr Pet Cathl *Pet* 72-82; R Uppingham w Ayston and Wardley w Belton from 82. *The Rectory, Uppingham, Oakham, Leics LE15 9TJ* Uppingham (0572) 823381

WILLETT, Stephen John. b 54. Ridley Hall Cam 88. **d** 90 **p** 91. C Chapeltown *Sheff* from 90. *9 Maple Place, Chapeltown, Sheffield S30 3NF* Sheffield (0742) 461860
WILLETTS, Alfred. b 15. **d** 62 **p** 63. R Man St Phil w St Mark *Man* 67-75; R Man Apostles 75-84; rtd 85; Perm to Offic Man & Ches from 85. *22 Larne Drive, Broughton, Chester CH4 0QF* Chester (0244) 533485
WILLEY, David Geoffrey. b 53. Imp Coll Lon BSc74 BA86. Oak Hill Th Coll 83. **d** 86 **p** 87. C Cromer *Nor* 86-90; R High Halstow w All Hallows and Hoo St Mary *Roch* from 90. *2 Cooling Road, High Halstow, Rochester, Kent ME3 8SA* Medway (0634) 250637
WILLIAMS, Aled Jones. b 56. Univ of Wales (Ban) BA77 Univ of Wales (Cardiff) DipTh79. St Mich Coll Llan 77. **d** 79 **p** 80. C Conwy w Gyffin *Ban* 79-82; R Llanrug 82-86; R Machynlleth and Llanwrin 86-87; Member L'Arche Community from 88. *42 Kelso Road, Liverpool L6 3AQ* 051-260 9724
WILLIAMS, Aled Wyn. b 47. Univ of Wales (Abth) BA69. St Mich Coll Llan 69. **d** 71 **p** 72. C Llanelly *St D* 71-73; P-in-c Capel Colman w Llanfihangel Penbedw etc 73-74; V 74-81; V Llanddewi Brefi w Llanbadarn Odwyn 81-84; V Llanddewibrefi w Llanbadarn Odwyn and Cellan etc from 84. *The Vicarage, Llanddewi Brefi, Tregaron, Dyfed SY25 6PE* Tregaron (0974) 298937
WILLIAMS, Alexander Ernest. b 14. Fitzw Ho Cam BA35 MA46 Regent's Park Coll Ox 35. Coll of Resurr Mirfield 79. **d** 79 **p** 80. Hon C Carshalton Beeches *S'wark* 79-87; rtd 87. *88 Grosvenor Avenue, Carshalton, Surrey SM5 3EP* 081-647 8446
WILLIAMS, Alfred Donald. b 26. St Aid Birkenhead 57. **d** 59 **p** 60. V Ladybrook *S'well* 62-70; P-in-c Newark Ch Ch 70-71; R Gotham 72-88; P-in-c W Leake w Kingston-on-Soar etc 72-81; rtd 88; Perm to Offic *Bradf* from 88. *20 Grassington Road, Skipton, N Yorkshire BD23 1LL* Skipton (0756) 794496
WILLIAMS, Alfred George. b 21. St D Coll Lamp BA42. **d** 46 **p** 47. V Rock Ferry *Ches* 64-77; V Lache cum Saltney 77-86; rtd 86; Perm to Offic *Ches* from 86. *7 Lache Park Avenue, Chester CH4 8HR* Chester (0244) 678768
WILLIAMS, Allen Philpin. b 10. St D Coll Lamp BA32 St Mich Coll Llan. **d** 34 **p** 35. V Manordeilo and Taliaris *St D* 70-78; rtd 78. *7 Diana Road, Llandeilo, Dyfed SA19 6RR* Llandeilo (0558) 822376
WILLIAMS, Andrew Gibson. b 31. Edin Univ MA57. Edin Th Coll 56. **d** 59 **p** 60. C Todmorden *Wakef* 59-61; C Clitheroe St Mary *Blackb* 61-63; V Burnley St Jas 63-65; CF (TA) 64-65; CF 65-71; R Winterslow *Sarum* 71-84; P-in-c Condover *Heref* 84-88; P-in-c Acton Burnell w Pitchford 84-88; P-in-c Frodesley 84-88; R Condover w Frodesley, Acton Burnell etc 88-90; R Whimple, Talaton and Clyst St Lawr *Ex* from 90. *The Rectory, Grove Road, Whimple, Exeter EX5 2TP* Whimple (0404) 822521
WILLIAMS, Andrew Joseph. b 55. St Jo Coll Nottm BTh81. **d** 81 **p** 82. C Hollington St Leon *Chich* 81-84; C Sutton Coldfield H Trin *Birm* 84-87; Perm to Offic from 87. *10 Midland Drive, Sutton Coldfield, W Midlands B72 1TV* 021-355 3352
WILLIAMS, Mrs Anthea Elizabeth. b 50. Trevelyan Coll Dur BA71. Linc Th Coll 72. **dss** 79 **d** 87. St Marylebone Ch Ch *Lon* 79-84; Maidstone St Martin *Cant* 84-87; Par Dn 87-91; Par Dn Rolvenden 91; Dn-in-c from 91. *The Vicarage, Rolvenden, Cranbrook, Kent TN17 4ND* Cranbrook (0580) 241235
WILLIAMS, Dr Anthony David. b 38. MRCGP68 LRCP62 MRCS62 DRCOG65 FPACert65. S Dios Minl Tr Scheme 87. **d** 90 **p** 91. Hon C Jersey St Pet *Win* from 90. *Beau Vallon, Mont de la Rosiere, St Saviour, Jersey, Channel Islands JE2 7HF* Jersey (0534) 63859
WILLIAMS, Anthony Francis. b 21. Trin Coll Ox BA49 MA53. Coll of Resurr Mirfield 49. **d** 51 **p** 52. V Lindridge *Worc* 67-77; P-in-c Bluntisham w Earith *Ely* 77-79; R 79-88; rtd 88. *21 Kings Hedges, St Ives, Huntingdon, Cambs PE17 6XU* St Ives (0480) 67686
WILLIAMS, Canon Anthony Riley. b 36. Univ of Wales BA60. Chich Th Coll 57. **d** 59 **p** 60. C Llandinorwic *Ban* 59-61; C Llandegfan w Beaumaris and Llanfaes 61-64; R Ludchurch and Templeton *St D* 64-72; V Lamphey w Hodgeston 72-83; RD Castlemartin 75-83; V Llanelly from 83; Can *St D* Cathl from 86; Chapl Bryntirion Hosp Llanelli from 90. *The Vicarage, 11 Old Road, Llanelli, Dyfed SA15 3HW* Llanelli (0554) 772072
WILLIAMS, Arfon. b 58. Univ of Wales (Abth) BD83. Wycliffe Hall Ox 83. **d** 84 **p** 85. C Carmarthen St Dav *St D* 84-86; C Abth 86-87; TV 87-88; V Glanogwen *Ban* from 88. *Glanogwen Vicarage, Bethesda, Bangor, Gwynedd LL57 3PP* Bethesda (0248) 600294

WILLIAMS, Preb Arthur Edwin. b 33. Leeds Univ BA57. Coll of Resurr Mirfield 57. **d** 59 **p** 60. C Wednesfield St Thos *Lich* 59-62; C Codsall 62-65; V from 83; V Coseley St Chad 65-73; R Kingswinford H Trin 73-81; TR Wordsley 81-83; RD Himley 77-83; Preb Lich Cathl from 82; RD Penkridge from 89. *The Vicarage, Church Road, Codsall, Wolverhampton WV8 1EH* Codsall (09074) 2168
WILLIAMS, Canon Arthur James Daniel. b 24. Univ of Wales (Lamp) BA49. St Mich Coll Llan 49. **d** 51 **p** 52. V Llantwit Fadre *Llan* 66-89; RD Pontypridd 84-88; Can Llan Cathl 86-89; rtd 89. *Typica, Efail Isaf, Church Village, Pontypridd, M Glam*
WILLIAMS, Barrie. b 33. Em Coll Cam BA54 MA58 Bris Univ MLitt71. Lambeth STh75 Ripon Hall Ox 62. **d** 63 **p** 64. C Penwortham St Mary *Blackb* 63-65; Hon C Salisbury St Martin *Sarum* 65-77; Chapl St Edw King & Martyr Cam *Ely* 77-84; Asst Chapl Trin Hall Cam 77-84; R Ashley w Weston by Welland and Sutton Bassett *Pet* 84-85; Asst Chapl St Hilda's Sch Whitby from 85. *Flat 5, Crinkle Court, 9 Chubb Hill, Whitby, N Yorkshire* Whitby (0947) 600766
WILLIAMS, Benjamin Clive. b 24. Lon Univ BD59. Westcott Ho Cam 59. **d** 61 **p** 62. R Denton w S Heighton and Tarring Neville *Chich* 66-74; Dioc Stewardship Adv 74-81; P-in-c Clapham w Patching 76-81; V Ticehurst and Flimwell 81-89; rtd 89. *14 Lindfield Avenue, Seaford, E Sussex BN25 4DY* Seaford (0323) 491019
WILLIAMS, Brian. b 48. W Midl Minl Tr Course. **d** 83 **p** 84. NSM Lich St Chad *Lich* from 83. *82 Walsall Road, Lichfield, Staffs WS13 8AF* Lichfield (0543) 253120
WILLIAMS, Brian Luke. b 54. AKC75. St Steph Ho Ox 76. **d** 77 **p** 78. C Kettering St Mary *Pet* 77-80; C Walsall St Gabr Fullbrook *Lich* 80-83; P-in-c Sneyd 83-85; V from 85. *Sneyd Vicarage, Hamil Road, Stoke-on-Trent ST6 1AP* Stoke-on-Trent (0782) 825841
WILLIAMS, Brian Thomas. b 48. GSM69. Linc Th Coll 89. **d** 91. C Liss *Portsm* from 91. *13 Woodbourne Close, Liss, Hants GU33 7BA* Liss (0730) 892764
WILLIAMS, Ms Carol Jean. b 45. FIPM89. Ox NSM Course 86. **d** 89. NSM High Wycombe *Ox* from 89. *3 Pimms Close, High Wycombe, Bucks HP13 7EG* Penn (049481) 4571
WILLIAMS, Cecil Augustus Baldwin. b 09. TCD BA31 MA39. CITC 32. **d** 32 **p** 33. I Crinken *D & G* 71-81; rtd 81. *3 St John's Close, Portstewart, Co Londonderry BT55 7HJ* Portstewart (026583) 4249
WILLIAMS, Dr Cecil Peter. b 41. TCD BA63 MA67 Lon Univ BD67 PhD86 Bris Univ MLitt77. Clifton Th Coll 64. **d** 67 **p** 68. C Maghull *Liv* 67-70; Lic to Offic *Bris* 70-91; Tutor Clifton Th Coll 70-72; Tutor Trin Coll Bris 72-91; Lib 73-81; Course Ldr 81-85; Vice-Prin 85-91; V Ecclesall *Sheff* from 91. *Ecclesall Vicarage, Ringinglow Road, Sheffield S11 7PQ* Sheffield (0742) 360084
WILLIAMS, Charles Henry. b 11. Dorchester Miss Coll 38. **d** 40 **p** 41. V Kirk Hammerton *Ripon* 69-7?; V Nun Monkton 69-74; rtd 74. *34 Larkfield Drive, Harrogate, N Yorkshire HG2 0BX* Harrogate (0423) 507164
WILLIAMS, Canon Clifford Rex. b 06. **d** 43 **p** 44. V Herne Hill St Paul *S'wark* 66-78; Hon C S'wark Cathl 77-78; rtd 78; Perm to Offic *Chich* from 78. *Blue Horizon, 13 Marine Parade, Seaford, E Sussex BN25 2PL* Seaford (0323) 895699
WILLIAMS, Clifford Smith. b 48. Univ of Wales (Ban) BD79. St Deiniol's Hawarden 79. **d** 80 **p** 81. C Llanbeblig w Caernarfon and Betws Garmon etc *Ban* 80-82; R Llanfair Mathafarneithaf w Llanbedrgoch from 82. *The Rectory, Bay View Road, Benllech, Tyn-y-Gongl, Gwynedd* Tyn-y-Gongl (0248) 852348
WILLIAMS, Clive Gregory. b 45. Trin Coll Bris 83. **d** 85 **p** 86. C Bedhampton *Portsm* 85-88; V Highley *Heref* from 88. *The Vicarage, Church Street, Highley, Bridgnorth, Shropshire WV16 6NA* Highley (0746) 861612
WILLIAMS, Colin Henry. b 52. Pemb Coll Ox BA73 MA78. St Steph Ho Ox BA80. **d** 81 **p** 82. C Liv St Paul Stoneycroft *Liv* 81-84; TV Walton St Mary 84-89; Chapl Walton Hosp Liv 86-89; Bp's Dom Chapl *Blackb* from 89; Chapl Whalley Abbey from 89. *Whalley Lodge, Whalley Abbey, Whalley, Blackburn BB6 9SS* Blackburn (0254) 824679
WILLIAMS, Creswell. b 13. Univ of Wales BA36. St D Coll Lamp 37. **d** 38 **p** 39. V Eglwysfach and Llangynfelin *St D* 67-78; rtd 78; Lic to Offic *Ban* from 78. *4 Londonderry Terrace, Machynlleth, Powys SY20 8BG* Machynlleth (0654) 2349
WILLIAMS, Cyril. b 06. Univ of Wales BA34. St Mich Coll Llan 34. **d** 35 **p** 36. R Denbigh *St As* 61-77; rtd 77. *Bryniog, 13 Nant y Patrick, St Asaph, Clwyd LL17 0BN* Trefnant (074574) 264

WILLIAMS, David. b 11. Univ of Wales BA57. St Mich Coll Llan 51. **d** 53 **p** 54. V Llandygwydd and Cenarth w Cilrhedyn *St D* 71-77; rtd 77. *Trem Hudol, Ynyslas, Borth, Dyfed SY24 5LA* Borth (0970) 871241

WILLIAMS, David. b 19. **d** 66 **p** 67. Hon C Dean Forest St Paul *Glouc* 66-78; Hon C Coleford w Staunton 78-83; Perm to Offic from 83. *The Nook, Parkend Road, Bream, Lydney, Glos GL15 6JZ* Dean (0594) 562240

WILLIAMS, David. b 33. Ch Coll Cam BA56 MA60 Cranfield Inst of Tech MSc72. Sarum & Wells Th Coll 71. **d** 73 **p** 74. C Ex St Jas *Ex* 73-75; Lic to Offic 75-84; Teacher St Wilfrid Sch Ex 75-76; Teacher Hele's Sch Ex 76-84; TV Thorverton, Cadbury, Upton Pyne etc from 84. *The Vicarage, Newton St Cyres, Exeter EX5 5BN* Exeter (0392) 851230

WILLIAMS, David. b 43. ACA65 K Coll Lon AKC69 BD70. St Aug Coll Cant 69. **d** 70 **p** 71. C Walkden Moor *Man* 70-72; C Deane 72-75; V Horwich St Cath 75-81; Hon C Chorley All SS *Blackb* 84-86; P-in-c Weeton 86-87; V Singleton w Weeton from 86. *St Michael's Vicarage, Church Road, Weeton, Preston PR4 3WD* Weeton (039136) 249

WILLIAMS, David. b 49. BTh DTechM. **d** 88 **p** 89. C Lurgan etc w Ballymachugh, Kildrumferton etc *K, E & A* 88-91; I Kinsale Union *C, C & R* from 91. *The Rectory, Kinsale, Co Cork, Irish Republic* Cork (21) 772220

WILLIAMS, David Albert. b 15. St D Coll Lamp BA35 St Mich Coll Llan 36. **d** 38 **p** 39. Lic to Offic *Heref* 69-80; rtd 80; Perm to Offic *St D* from 81. *London House, Llanwrda, Dyfed SA19 8AA*

WILLIAMS, David Gareth. b 58. Lon Univ BD81. Ripon Coll Cuddesdon 82. **d** 84 **p** 85. C Chandler's Ford *Win* 84-88; C Alton St Lawr 88-90; R Crawley and Littleton and Sparsholt w Lainston from 90. *The Rectory, Church Lane, Littleton, Winchester, Hants SO22 6QY* Winchester (0962) 881898

WILLIAMS, Canon David Gerald Powell. b 35. St Mich Coll Llan DipTh62. **d** 62 **p** 63. C Canton St Jo *Llan* 62-64; Field Tr Officer Ch in Wales Prov Youth Coun 63-70; Prov Youth Chapl 65-70; V Treharris *Llan* 70-75; R Flemingston w Gileston and St Hilary 75-78; Warden of Ords 77-80; Dir Past Studies and Chapl St Mich Coll Llan 78-80; Sub-Warden 79-80; Dir Ch in Wales Publications and Communications 80-85; Prov Dir of Educn Ch in Wales 80-85; Hon Can Llan Cathl *Llan* from 84; Dir of Miss Ch in Wales 85-87; V Pendoyln and Welsh St Donats *Llan* from 87. *The Vicarage, Pendoylan, Cowbridge, S Glam CF7 7UJ* Peterston-super-Ely (0446) 760210

WILLIAMS, David Gordon. b 43. Selw Coll Cam BA65 MA69. Oak Hill Th Coll 66. **d** 68 **p** 69. C Maidstone St Luke *Cant* 68-71; C Rugby St Matt *Cov* 71-73; P-in-c Budbrooke 73-74; V 74-81; V Lenton *S'well* 81-87; TR Cheltenham St Mark *Glouc* from 87. *St Mark's Rectory, Fairmount Road, Cheltenham, Glos GL51 7AQ* Cheltenham (0242) 580036

WILLIAMS, David Grant. b 61. Bris Univ BSocSc83. Wycliffe Hall Ox 86. **d** 89 **p** 90. C Ecclesall *Sheff* from 89. *11 Mylor Road, Sheffield S11 7PF* Sheffield (0742) 662313

WILLIAMS, David Griffith. b 35. Univ of Wales (Lamp) BA57. St Mich Coll Llan 57. **d** 59 **p** 60. C Kidwelly *St D* 59-63; C Haverfordwest St Mary 63-64; V Rosemarket and Freystrop 64-73; R Begelly w Kilgetty 73-84; R Begelly w Ludchurch and Crunwere from 84. *The Rectory, Begelly, Kilgetty, Dyfed SA68 0YG* Saundersfoot (0834) 812348

WILLIAMS, David Henry. b 33. Trin Coll Cam BA56 MA60 PhD77. St D Coll Lamp 67. **d** 69 **p** 70. C Mon 69-70; Chapl St Woolos Cathl 70-71; P-in-c Six Bells 71-76; Libya 76-79; P-in-c Crumlin *Mon* 79-80; R Llanddewi Skirrid w Llanvetherine etc 80-83; Perm to Offic 83-87; Guest Master Caldey Abbey 83-87; V Buttington and Pool Quay *St As* from 87. *The Vicarage, Buttington, Welshpools, Powys SY21 8HD* Welshpool (0938) 553351

WILLIAMS, Canon David Humphrey. b 23. Em Coll Cam BA49 MA54. St Steph Ho Ox 49. **d** 51 **p** 52. RD Bulwell *S'well* 70-88; P-in-c Bestwood Park 71-78; R Hucknall Torkard 63-71; TR 71-88; Hon Can S'well Minster from 75; rtd 88. *12 Wollaton Paddocks, Trowell Road, Nottingham NG8 2ED* Nottingham (0602) 280639

WILLIAMS, David James. b 42. Chich Th Coll 67. **d** 70 **p** 71. C Charlton-by-Dover St Bart *Cant* 70-74; C Dorking w Ranmore *Guildf* 74-77; C Guildf H Trin w St Mary 77-78; P-in-c E Molesey St Paul 78-88; V Burpham from 88. *5 Orchard Road, Burpham, Guildford, Surrey GU4 7JH* Guildford (0483) 68494

WILLIAMS, David John. b 30. Open Univ BA79. St D Coll Lamp 64. **d** 66 **p** 67. C Mold *St As* 66-69; C Llanrhos 69-71; R Llangynhafal and Llanbedr Duffryn Clwyd 71-86; P-in-c Llanynys w Llanychan from 77; RD Dyffryn Clwyd from 86; R Ruthin w Llanrhydd from 86. *The Cloisters, Ruthin, Clwyd LL15 1BL* Ruthin (08242) 2068

WILLIAMS, David John. b 38. AKC62. **d** 63 **p** 64. C Benchill *Man* 63-66; C Heywood St Jas 66-69; V Leesfield 69-73; Chapl TS Arethusa 73-74; TV Southend St Jo w St Mark, All SS w St Fran etc *Chelmsf* 74-80; V Horndon on the Hill from 80; RD Thurrock from 83. *The Vicarage, Orsett Road, Horndon-on-the-Hill, Stanford-le-Hope SS17 8NS* Stanford-le-Hope (0375) 673806

WILLIAMS, David John. b 43. Wadh Coll Ox BA64. St Jo Coll Nottm 73. **d** 75 **p** 76. C Newc w Butterton *Lich* 75-79; P-in-c Oulton 79-89; P-in-c Stone Ch Ch 84-89; V Stone Ch Ch and Oulton from 89. *Christ Church Vicarage, Bromfield Court, Stone, Staffs ST15 8DA* Stone (0785) 812669

WILLIAMS, David Leslie. b 35. ALCD63. **d** 63 **p** 64. C Bexleyheath Ch Ch *Roch* 63-64; C Gt Faringdon w Lt Coxwell *Ox* 64-66; CMS from 67; Uganda 67-73; C Shortlands *Roch* 73-74; Fiji 74-76; V Bromley H Trin *Roch* 77-86; RD Cobham from 86; R Meopham w Nurstead from 86. *The Rectory, Shipley Hills Road, Meopham, Gravesend, Kent DA13 0AD* Meopham (0474) 813106

WILLIAMS, David Michael Rochfort. b 40. Hull Univ DipTh81. St Mich Coll Llan DipTh65. **d** 65 **p** 66. C Pemb Dock *St D* 65-68; Miss to Seamen 68-71; Ind Chapl *St D* 68-71; P-in-c Walwyn's Castle w Robeston W 68-70; R 70-71; Ind Chapl *Mon* 71-74; V Blaenavon w Capel Newydd 74-77; Ind Chapl *St As* 77-88; V Whitford 81-87; V Ruabon from 87. *The Vicarage, Park Street, Ruabon, Wrexham, Clwyd LL14 6LF* Ruabon (0978) 810176

WILLIAMS, David Norman. b 54. Lanc Univ BSc Leeds Univ BA. Coll of Resurr Mirfield. **d** 84 **p** 85. C Ireland Wood *Ripon* 84-87; C Beeston from 87. *St David's House, Waincliffe Drive, Leeds LS11 8ET* Leeds (0532) 702829

WILLIAMS, David Roger. b 49. St D Coll Lamp DipTh73. **d** 73 **p** 74. C Llansamlet *S & B* 73-76; C Oystermouth 76-79; V Aberedw w Llandilo Graban and Llanbadarn etc 79-81; V Brynmawr 81-89; V Newport St Julian *Mon* from 89. *St Julian's Vicarage, 41 St Julian's Avenue, Newport, Gwent NP9 7JT* Newport (0633) 258046

WILLIAMS, David Terence. b 32. Univ of Wales (Lamp) BA57. St Steph Ho Ox 57. **d** 59 **p** 60. C Oystermouth *S & B* 59-61; Hon C Pentonville St Silas w All SS and St Jas *Lon* 73-83. *12 Legion Close, London N1* 071-609 5651

WILLIAMS, Derek. b 27. Man Univ BSc49. St Deiniol's Hawarden 76. **d** 78 **p** 79. NSM Abergele *St As* from 78. *48 Eldon Drive, Abergele, Clwyd LL22 7DA* Abergele (0745) 833479

WILLIAMS, Derek Lawrence. b 45. Lon Univ DipTh68. Tyndale Hall Bris 65. **d** 69 **p** 70. C Cant St Mary Bredin *Cant* 69-71; Gen Sec Inter-Coll Chr Fellowship 71-75; Lic to Offic *St Alb* 78-84; *Bris* from 85. *39 Greenway Lane, Chippenham, Wilts SN15 1AE* Chippenham (0249) 658652

WILLIAMS, Diana Mary. b 36. Leeds Univ BSc57 CertEd58. Oak Hill Th Coll 86. **d** 87. NSM S Mymms K Chas *St Alb* from 87. *The Vicarage, 40 Dugdale Hill Lane, Potters Bar, Herts EN6 2DW* Potters Bar (0707) 54219

WILLIAMS, Ms Diane Patricia. b 53. Dur Univ CertEd74 Liv Univ DipRE83 Lanc Univ MA84. Cranmer Hall Dur 84. **dss** 86 **d** 87. Clubmoor *Liv* 86-87; Par Dn 87-90; Par Dn Everton St Geo from 90; Dioc Lay Tr Officer from 90. *2 Stanfield Avenue, Liverpool L5 4TA* 051-264 8835

WILLIAMS, Ven Edward Bryan. b 36. Univ of Wales (Lamp) BA58. St Mich Coll Llan 58. **d** 60 **p** 61. C Rhyl w Rhyl St Ann *St As* 60-68; Dioc Youth Chapl 66-78; V Dyserth and Trelawnyd and Cwm 68-77; R Denbigh 77-82; Can St As Cathl 81-87; R Denbigh and Nantglyn 82-87; Adn Wrexham from 87; V Bwlchgwyn from 87. *The Vicarage, 8 Whiteoaks, Bwlchgwyn, Wrexham, Clwyd LL11 5UB* Wrexham (0978) 752627

WILLIAMS, Edward Ffoulkes. b 34. ALA65. Chich Th Coll 71. **d** 73 **p** 74. C Kidderminster St Geo *Worc* 73-78; TV Worc St Barn w Ch Ch 78-82; V Exhall w Wixford *Cov* from 82; V Temple Grafton w Binton from 82. *The Vicarage, Temple Grafton, Alcester, Warks B49 6PA* Bidford-on-Avon (0789) 772314

WILLIAMS, Edward Heaton. b 18. St Aid Birkenhead 56. d 58 p 59. R Wistaston *Ches* 66-81; V Burton 81-85; rtd 85; Perm to Offic Pet & Ox from 85. *4 Bowmens Lea, Aynho, Banbury, Oxon OX17 3AG* Croughton (0869) 810533

WILLIAMS, Prof Edward Sydney. b 23. FRCP FRCR K Coll Lon BSc PhD MB, BS MD AKC. Sarum & Wells Th Coll 84. d 87 p 88. NSM Bramley and Grafham *Guildf* from 87; Hon AP Shamley Green from 89. *Bisney Cottage, Shamley Green, Guildford, Surrey GU5 0TB* Guildford (0483) 892591

WILLIAMS, Elfed Owain. b 24. Newc Univ DipAdEd74. St Deiniol's Hawarden 79. d 81 p 82. Hon C Whorlton *Newc* 81-82; Hon C Elham w Denton and Wootton *Cant* 82-86; R Barham w Bishopsbourne and Kingston 86-91; rtd 91. *Chusan, 31 Ryecroft Way, Wooler, Northd NE71 6DY* Wooler (0668) 81253

WILLIAMS, Eric Rees. b 30. Roch Th Coll 60 St Deiniol's Hawarden 71. d 72 p 73. C Llanelly *St D* 72-75; P-in-c Tregaron 75-76; V 76-82; RD Lamp and Ultra Aeron 82-87; V Tregaron w Ystrad Meurig and Strata Florida 82-87; V St Dogmael's w Moylgrove and Monington from 87. *The Vicarage, St Dogmaels, Cardigan, Dyfed SA43 3DX* Cardigan (0239) 612030

WILLIAMS, Evelyn Joyce. b 37. Cant Sch of Min 86. d 89. NSM Sittingbourne H Trin w Bobbing *Cant* from 89. *32 Rock Road, Sittingbourne, Kent ME10 1JF* Sittingbourne (0795) 470372

WILLIAMS, Frederick Errol. b 41. MBIM80. Sarum & Wells Th Coll 86. d 88 p 89. C Milton *Win* 88-91; P-in-c Chilbolton cum Wherwell from 91. *The Rectory, Chilbolton, Stockbridge, Hants SO20 6BA* Chilbolton (0264) 860258

WILLIAMS, Frederick John. b 11. Oak Hill Th Coll 71. d 74 p 75. NSM Bexley St Mary *Roch* 74-76; C Shirwell w Loxhore *Ex* 76-77; NSM Heanton Punchardon 77-79; NSM S Molton, Nymet St George, High Bray etc 79-84; rtd 84; Perm to Offic *Ex* from 84. *Dawn Glow, Deans Park, South Molton, Devon EX36 3DY* South Molton (07695) 3491

WILLIAMS, Frederick Vivian. b 08. St Andr Pampisford 47. d 48 p 49. V Croydon St Martin *Cant* 60-73; rtd 73. *1 St Augustine's Close, Cooden Drive, Bexhill-on-Sea, E Sussex TN39 3AZ* Bexhill-on-Sea (0424) 221370

WILLIAMS, Fredric Barry. b 41. Man Univ BSc62 CertEd63 Man Poly DMEd87. N Ord Course 79. d 82 p 83. NSM Darwen St Cuth *Blackb* 82-85; NSM Darwen St Cuth w Tockholes St Steph 85-88; V Rillington w Scampston, Wintringham etc *York* from 88; RD Buckrose from 90. *The Vicarage, 2 High Street, Rillington, Malton, N Yorkshire YO17 8LA* Rillington (09442) 8891

WILLIAMS, Gareth Wynn. b 67. d 91. C Mold *St As* from 91. *2 Harrowby Road, Mold, Clwyd CH7 1DN* Mold (0352) 753624

WILLIAMS, Gavin John. b 61. Barrister-at-Law 85. Down Coll Cam BA84. Wycliffe Hall Ox BA88. d 89 p 90. C Muswell Hill St Jas w St Matt *Lon* from 89. *67 St James's Lane, London N10 3QY* 081-883 7417

WILLIAMS, Canon Geoffrey Ainsworth. b 16. Univ Coll Dur BA38 MA41. d 39 p 40. Can Res and Chan Blackb Cathl *Blackb* 65-90; Warden of Readers 69-90; Warden Whalley Abbey from 77; rtd 90. *22 Buncer Lane, Blackburn, Lancs BB2 6SE* Blackburn (0254) 56706

WILLIAMS, Geoffrey Thomas. b 35. Ox NSM Course 77. d 80 p 81. NSM Earley St Bart *Ox* 80-82; NSM Reading St Luke 82-85; C Wembley Park St Aug *Lon* 85-86; C-in-c S Kenton Annunciation CD 86-90; V Streatham Hill St Marg *S'wark* from 90. *St Margaret's Vicarage, 165 Barcombe Avenue, London SW2 3BH* 081-674 7348

WILLIAMS, George Harold. b 20. Lon Univ BSc49. d 67 p 68. C Bishopsworth *Bris* 67-70; V Weston-super-Mare Ch Ch *B & W* 70-85; rtd 85; Perm to Offic *B & W* from 86. *15 Elmhurst Road, Hutton, Weston-super-Mare, Avon BS24 9RJ* Weston-super-Mare (0934) 813342

WILLIAMS, George Maxwell Frazer. b 42. TCD BA65 MA69. Cuddesdon Coll 65. d 67 p 68. C Bolton St Jas w St Chrys *Bradf* 67-70; C Lich St Chad *Lich* 70-73; V Shawbury 73-79; P-in-c Moreton Corbet 73-79; V Willenhall H Trin 79-86; TR 86-88; V Penn from 88. *St Bartholemew's Vicarage, 68 Church Hill, Penn, Wolverhampton WV4 5JD* Wolverhampton (0902) 341399

WILLIAMS, George Melvin (Kim). b 24. Worc Ord Coll 64. d 66 p 67. C Holdenhurst *Win* 66-70; V Yateley 70-75; V St Leonards and St Ives 75-90; rtd 90. *Amen Cottage, 23 Edifred Road, Muscliffe, Bournemouth BH9 3PB* Bournemouth (0202) 521763

WILLIAMS, Canon Giles Peter. b 54. Lon Univ BA77 MA78. Trin Coll Bris 80. d 82 p 83. C Reading Greyfriars *Ox* 82-85; Rwanda Miss 85-90; Mid-Africa Min (CMS) from 90; Can Kigali Cathl Rwanda from 90. *Eglise Episcopale au Rwanda, BP 61, Kigali, Rwanda* Rwanda (250) 76504

WILLIAMS, Glyn. b 54. K Coll Lon BD77 AKC77. Ripon Coll Cuddesdon 77. d 78 p 79. C Coppenhall *Ches* 78-81; C Northn St Alb *Pet* 81-82; TV Birkenhead Priory *Ches* 82-85; Chapl RAF 85-90; Dep Chapl HM Pris Wandsworth 90-91; Chapl HM Pris Elmley from 91. *HM Prison Elmley, Eastchurch, Sheerness, Kent*

WILLIAMS, Glyn Alun. b 17. St D Coll Lamp BA40. d 41 p 42. V Pencarreg and Llanycrwys *St D* 71-73; rtd 73. *11 Tirwaun, Pwll, Llanelli, Dyfed SA15 4AY* Llanelli (0554) 759850

WILLIAMS, Graham Ivor. b 23. Jes Coll Ox BA48 MA48. Cuddesdon Coll 48. d 49 p 50. C Swansea St Mary and H Trin *S & B* 49-53; C Edgbaston St Bart *Birm* 53-55; R Nutfield *S'wark* from 55. *The Rectory, Blechingley Road, Nutfield, Redhill RH1 4HN* Nutfield Ridge (0737) 822286

WILLIAMS, Graham John. b 49. Univ of Wales (Ban) DipTh71. St Steph Ho Ox 71. d 72 p 73. C Cardiff St Jo *Llan* 72-76; C Middlesb Ascension *York* 76-78; V Dormanstown 78-83; V Hockley *Chelmsf* 83-90; V Newc Ch Ch w St Ann *Newc* from 90. *The Vicarage, 11 Gibson Street, Newcastle upon Tyne NE1 6PY* 091-232 0516

WILLIAMS, Graham Parry. b 46. Bp Burgess Hall Lamp 67 St D Coll Lamp DipTh70. d 70 p 71. C Ebbw Vale *Mon* 70-73; C Trevethin 73-74; V Nantyglo 74-76; Chapl RN 76-85; R Northlew w Ashbury *Ex* 85-87; R Bratton Clovelly w Germansweek 85-87; TV Pontypool *Mon* 88-90; C Skegness and Winthorpe *Linc* 90-91; V Sutton Bridge from 91. *The Vicarage, 79 Bridge Road, Sutton Bridge, Spalding, Lincs PE12 9SD* Holbeach (0406) 350288

WILLIAMS, Gwilym Elfed. b 33. Univ of Wales (Lamp) BA53. St Mich Coll Llan 53. d 56 p 57. C Llandudno *Ban* 56-59; C Aberdare *Llan* 59-63; C Penarth All SS 63-65; R Eglwysilan 65-70; V Mountain Ash 70-81; V Llanblethian w Cowbridge and Llandough etc from 81; P-in-c St Hilary 87-91. *The Vicarage, Broadway, Llanblethian, Cowbridge, S Glam CF7 7EY* Cowbridge (0446) 772302

WILLIAMS, Canon Gwilym Kenneth. b 12. Univ of Wales BA34. St Mich Coll Llan 34. d 35 p 36. RD Llanbadarn Fawr *St D* 71-80; Can St D Cathl 75-80; V Borth and Eglwysfach w Llangynfelin 79-80; rtd 80. *2 Clos-y-Drindod, Buarth Road, Aberystwyth, Dyfed* Aberystwyth (0970) 615756

WILLIAMS, Ven Harold Edgar. b 17. Univ of Wales (Lamp) BA39. AKC42. d 42 p 43. Dir of Ords *S & B* 55-79; V Brynmawr 67-76; Can Brecon Cathl 72-83; Sec Prov Selection Bd for Ords 73-76; V Newton St Pet 76-87; Chan Brecon Cathl 79-83; Adn Gower 83-87; rtd 87. *10 Budehaven Terrace, Mumbles, Swansea SA3 5PY* Swansea (0792) 404728

WILLIAMS, Harry Abbott. b 19. Trin Coll Cam BA41 MA45. Cuddesdon Coll 41. d 43 p 44. Fell and Lect Trin Coll Cam 51-69; Dean of Chpl and Tutor 58-69; CR from 72; Lic to Offic *Wakef* from 80; rtd 89. *House of the Resurrection, Mirfield, W Yorkshire WF14 0BN* Mirfield (0924) 493272

WILLIAMS, Mrs Heather Marilyn. b 42. Oak Hill Th Coll 82. dss 85 d 87. Taunton Lyngford *B & W* 85-87; Hon C 87-89; C Worle from 89. *6 Gannet Road, Worle, Weston-super-Mare, Avon BS22 8UR* Weston-super-Mare (0934) 521765

WILLIAMS, Helena Maria Alija. b 43. d 88. NSM Roath St Marg *Llan* 88-91. *25 Hampton Court Road, Penylan, Cardiff CF3 7DH* Cardiff (0222) 492934

WILLIAMS, Henry Gordon. b 33. JP83. St Aid Birkenhead 57. d 60 p 61. C Radcliffe St Mary *Man* 60-63; Australia from 63; OStJ from 78. *PO Box 259, Northampton, W Australia 6535* Northampton (99) 341259

WILLIAMS, Ven Henry Leslie. b 19. Univ of Wales (Lamp) BA41. St Mich Coll Llan 41. d 43 p 44. V Barnston *Ches* 53-84; RD Wirral N 67-75; Hon Can Ches Cathl 72-75; Adn Ches 75-88; rtd 88. *1 Bartholomew Way, Westminster Park, Chester CH4 7RJ* Chester (0244) 675296

WILLIAMS, Herbert Brian. b 18. BNC Ox BA39 MA48. Linc Th Coll 80. d 81 p 82. NSM Asterby Gp *Linc* from 81; rtd 88. *Mill House, Goulceby, Louth, Lincs LN11 9UB* Stenigot (050784) 684

WILLIAMS, Canon Howard. b 08. Univ of Wales BA29 MA32 St Jo Coll Cam MLitt45. St Steph Ho Ox 30. d 31 p 32. Chapl Llanelli Gen Hosp 57-75; V Llanelly

St D 57-75; Can St D Cathl 60-75; Treas 73-75; rtd 75. *Cwm Eithin, 53 Maeshendre, Waunfawr, Aberystwyth, Dyfed SY23 3PS* Aberystwyth (0970) 615311

WILLIAMS, Howard Graham (Brother Anthony). b 04. **d** 52 **p** 53. OSB from 48; Perm to Offic *Ox* from 52. *Elmore Abbey, Church Lane, Speen, Newbury, Berks RG13 1SA* Newbury (0635) 33080

WILLIAMS, Howell Mark. b 56. Univ of Wales (Cardiff) BD87. St Mich Coll Llan 84. **d** 87 **p** 88. C Swansea St Thos and Kilvey *S & B* 87-89; TV Abth *St D* from 89. *St Anne's Vicarage, Penparcau, Aberystwyth, Dyfed SY23 1RZ* Aberystwyth (0970) 617819

WILLIAMS, Canon Hugh. b 27. MRIPHH ACP48. AKC53. **d** 54 **p** 55. C Kirkby *Liv* 54-57; C Blackpool St Jo *Blackb* 57-58; V Foulridge 58-65; V Over Darwen H Trin 65-74; P-in-c Hoddlesden 65-74; P-in-c Over Darwen St Jo 68-74; P-in-c Darwen St Geo 69-74; TR Darwen St Pet w Hoddlesden 74-77; RD Darwen 75-77; R Burnley St Pet 77-85; RD Burnley 78-85; Hon Can Blackb Cathl from 78; V Bolton le Sands from 85. *The Vicarage, Bolton le Sands, Carnforth, Lancs LA5 8DS* Hest Bank (0524) 822335

WILLIAMS, Hugh Llewelyn. b 09. St D Coll Lamp BA32. **d** 32 **p** 33. V Alsager Ch Ch *Ches* 63-73; rtd 74; Perm to Offic *Ches* from 74. *Winterbourne, 1 Laureston Avenue, Crewe CW1 1HU*

WILLIAMS, Hugh Martin. b 45. AKC73. St Aug Coll Cant 73. **d** 74 **p** 75. C Heston *Lon* 74-78; Chapl City Univ 78-84; PV Westmr Abbey 82-84; V Newquay *Truro* from 84. *The Vicarage, 8 Pentire Road, Newquay, Cornwall TR7 1NX* Newquay (0637) 872724

WILLIAMS, Hugh Wynford. b 16. Selw Coll Cam BA40 MA44. St D Coll Lamp BA38 St Mich Coll Llan 40. **d** 41 **p** 42. Perm to Offic *Pet* 51-74; Chapl Oundle Sch Pet 54-74; R Tichmarsh *Pet* 74-88; P-in-c Clapton 77-88; rtd 88. *28 Church Street, Tichmarsh, Kettering, Northants NN14 3DB* Thrapston (08012) 4529

WILLIAMS, Ian Geoffrey. b 50. Lon Univ BD71 AKC71 CertEd. St Jo Coll Nottm 72. **d** 74 **p** 75. C Harborne Heath *Birm* 74-76; C Hazlemere *Ox* 77-84; V Littleover *Derby* 84-90. *The Minstead Community, The Old Vicarage, Church Lane, Horsley Woodhouse, Derby DE7 6BB* Derby (0332) 780598

WILLIAMS, Ian Kenneth. b 44. MMS83 MBIM87. E Midl Min Tr Course 84. **d** 87 **p** 88. NSM Corby Glen *Linc* from 87. *6 Market Place, Corby Glen, Grantham, Lincs NG33 4NH* Corby Glen (047684) 595

WILLIAMS, Ian Withers. b 43. Linc Th Coll 68. **d** 69 **p** 70. C Burney Lane *Birm* 69-72; C Cleobury Mortimer w Hopton Wafers *Heref* 72-75; P-in-c Coreley w Doddington 75-79; V Knowbury 75-79; V Lich Ch Ch *Lich* from 79. *Christ Church Vicarage, Lichfield, Staffs WS13 8AL* Lichfield (0543) 264431

WILLIAMS, Ieuan Merchant. b 13. St D Coll Lamp BA36. **d** 39 **p** 40. R Brightwell Baldwin *Ox* 71-80; R Cuxham w Easington 72-80; P-in-c Britwell Salome 76-80; P-in-c Ewelme 76-80; rtd 80; Perm to Offic *Ox* from 80. *4 The Cloisters, Ewelme, Oxford* Oxford (0865) 38897

WILLIAMS, Ifan. b 24. St D Coll Lamp 54. **d** 56 **p** 57. Area Sec (Merioneth) USPG 63-89; V Festiniog w Blaenau Festiniog *Ban* 67-89; RD Ardudwy 80-89; rtd 89. *Cil y Coed, 6 Penrallt, Llanystumdwy, Criccieth, Gwynedd* Criccieth (0766) 522978

WILLIAMS, Jack. b 26. Univ of Wales (Ban) BSc50. St Mich Coll Llan 50. **d** 52 **p** 53. Hd Master Rishworth Sch Ripponden 68-86; V Halifax St Jo Cragg Vale *Wakef* 86-89; rtd 89. *36 Tros-yr-Afon, Llangoed, Beaumaris, Gwynedd* Llangoed (024878) 839

WILLIAMS, James Einon. b 18. St Mary's Univ (NS) BEd63. St D Coll Lamp BA39. **d** 46 **p** 47. Chapl RCN 52-70; V Mydroilyn and Llanarth w Llanina *St D* 73-80; rtd 80. *244 Hartland Avenue, Victoria, British Columbia, Canada, U8X 4M6*

WILLIAMS, James Nicholas Owen. b 39. MBE. CEng DipTh. S'wark Ord Course. **d** 82 **p** 83. C Petersfield w Sheet *Portsm* 82-86; TV Droitwich *Worc* 86-87; TV Droitwich Spa 87-88; R Church Lench w Rous Lench and Abbots Morton from 88. *The Rectory, Church Lench, Evesham, Worcs WR11 4UB* Evesham (0386) 870345

WILLIAMS, Preb John. b 31. AKC56. **d** 57 **p** 58. C Cockerton *Dur* 57-60; C Camberwell St Geo *S'wark* 60-62; C Stockton St Chad *Dur* 62-65; V 65-68; R Longnewton 68-75; Soc Resp Officer 68-83; Hon Can Dur Cathl 80-83; Bp's Officer for Min *Lich* from 83; Preb Lich Cathl from 83. *200E Upper St John Street, Lichfield, Staffs WS14 9EF* Lichfield (0543) 253480

WILLIAMS, John Anthony. b 53. G&C Coll Cam BA75 MA79 St Jo Coll Dur BA83 PhD86. Cranmer Hall

Dur 81. **d** 86 **p** 87. C Beverley Minster *York* 86-89; C Cloughton 89-90; P-in-c from 90; Clergy Tr Officer E Riding from 89. *The Vicarage, Mill Lane, Cloughton, Scarborough, N Yorkshire YO13 0AB* Scarborough (0723) 870270

WILLIAMS, John Barrie. b 38. Lon Univ DSocStuds68 Univ of Wales (Cardiff) MSc77 DipEd80. St Mich Coll Llan 89. **d** 87 **p** 88. NSM Newc *Llan* 87-89; C Port Talbot St Theodore 89. *Shorncliffe, 11 Priory Oak, Bridgend, M Glam CF31 2HY* Bridgend (0656) 660369

WILLIAMS, John Beattie. b 42. Univ of Wales BA66. Cuddesdon Coll 67. **d** 69 **p** 69. C St Helier *S'wark* 69-70; C Yeovil H Trin *B & W* 70-76; P-in-c Ebbesbourne Wake w Fifield Bavant and Alvediston *Sarum* 76-78; Chapl to the Deaf 76-78; Chapl to the Deaf *B & W* 78-83; TV Fareham H Trin *Portsm* from 83. *St Columba Vicarage, Hillson Drive, Fareham, Hants PO15 6PF* Titchfield (0329) 43705

WILLIAMS, Ven John Charles. b 12. Univ Coll Ox 34 St D Coll Lamp BA34. Qu Coll Birm 36. **d** 37 **p** 38. R Halesowen *Worc* 59-70; Hon Can Worc Cathl 65-75; Adn Dudley 68-75; V Dodderhill 70-75; Adn Worc and Can Res Worc Cathl 75-80; Dir of Ords 75-79; rtd 80; Lic to Offic *Worc* from 80; Perm to Offic *Cov* from 80; Asst Chapl HM Pris Long Lartin 82-87. *The Old Vicarage, Church Lane, Norton, Evesham, Worcs WR11 4TL* Evesham (0386) 870213

WILLIAMS, John David Anthony. b 55. St Steph Ho Ox 85. **d** 87 **p** 88. C Paignton St Jo *Ex* 87-90; C Heavitree w Ex St Paul from 90. *St Lawrence Vicarage, Lower Hill Barton Road, Exeter EX1 3EH* Exeter (0392) 66302

WILLIAMS, John Edward. b 31. Univ of Wales (Abth) DipTh55. St Deiniol's Hawarden 76. **d** 76 **p** 77. C Llansamlet *S & B* 76-78; V Aberffraw and Llangwyfan w Llangadwaladr *Ban* 78-83; rtd 83. *17 Pontwillim Estate, Brecon, Powys*

WILLIAMS, John Elwyn Askew. b 09. St Jo Coll Cam BA32 MA36. Ridley Hall Cam 32. **d** 34 **p** 35. V Whitchurch w Creslow *Ox* 61-81; R Hardwick St Mary 76-81; R Quainton 76-81; R Schorne 76-81; rtd 81; Perm to Offic *Ox* from 81. *15 Manor Park, Maids Moreton, Buckingham MK18 1OY* Buckingham (0280) 814101

WILLIAMS, John Francis Meyler. b 34. St Jo Coll Cam BA56 MA60. Sarum & Wells Th Coll 79. **d** 81 **p** 82. C Hadleigh w Layham and Shelley *St E* 81-84; P-in-c Parham w Hacheston 84-87; P-in-c Campsey Ashe and Marlesford 84-87; R Campsea Ashe w Marlesford, Parham and Hacheston from 87. *The Rectory, Marlesford, Woodbridge, Suffolk IP13 0AT* Wickham Market (0728) 746747

WILLIAMS, Canon John Francis Oliver. b 15. TCD BA40 MA43. **d** 40 **p** 41. I Dalkey St Patr *D & G* 73-82; Can Ch Ch Cathl Dub 81-82; rtd 82. *Wayside, Church Road, Greystones, Co Wicklow, Irish Republic* Dublin (1) 287-4953

WILLIAMS, John Frederick Arthur. b 26. Lon Univ BSc50 Southn Univ PhD53. Ridley Hall Cam 63. **d** 65 **p** 66. C Cam H Sepulchre w All SS *Ely* 65-66; P-in-c Cam St Mark 66-67; V Portswood Ch Ch *Win* 67-90; AV from 90. *6 Royston Close, Southampton SO2 1TB* Southampton (0703) 595015

WILLIAMS, John Gilbert. b 36. St Aid Birkenhead 64. **d** 67 **p** 68. C Bollington St Jo *Ches* 67-69; C Oxton 69-72; P-in-c Acton Beauchamp and Evesbatch 72-76; P-in-c Castle Frome *Heref* 72-76; P-in-c Bishop's Frome 72-76; R Kingsland 76-83; P-in-c Eardisland 77-83; P-in-c Aymestry and Leinthall Earles 82-83; R Cradley w Mathon and Storridge from 83. *The Rectory, Cradley, Malvern, Worcs WR13 5LQ* Ridgway Cross (0886) 880438

WILLIAMS, John Glyn. b 18. Lon Univ BA47. St Mich Coll Llan 46. **d** 49 **p** 50. Org Sec (S Wales) CECS 59-83; P-in-c Llanharry *Llan* from 83; rtd 83. *St Caron's, 40 Parkfields Road, Bridgend, M Glam CF31 4BJ* Bridgend (0656) 654110

WILLIAMS, John Gordon. b 06. Lon Univ BA27. Ridley Hall Cam 30. **d** 32 **p** 33. Chapl and Educn Officer SPCK 57-72; rtd 72. *2 Sunnybank Place, Borrage Lane, Ripon, N Yorkshire HG4 2PZ* Ripon (0765) 3352

WILLIAMS, Canon John Heard. b 35. Bris Univ BA58. Clifton Th Coll 59. **d** 59 **p** 60. C Tunbridge Wells Ch Ch *Roch* 59-65; V Forest Gate St Sav *Chelmsf* 65-75; P-in-c W Ham St Matt 72-75; TR Forest Gate St Sav w W Ham St Matt from 75; Hon Can Chelmsf Cathl from 82. *St Saviour's Rectory, Sidney Road, London E7 0EF* 081-534 6109

WILLIAMS, John Herbert. b 19. LVO89. St D Coll Lamp BA41 Sarum & Wells Th Coll 41. **d** 43 **p** 44. Chapl HM Pris Birm 57-64; Wormwood Scrubs 64-71; SE Regional

Chapl 71-74; Dep Chapl Gen of Pris 74-83; P-in-O to HM The Queen 79-83; Chapl RVO 83-89; Chapl to Qu Chpl of the Savoy 83-89; Chapl to HM The Queen 87-89; rtd 89. *75 Monks Drive, London W3 0ED* 081-992 5206

WILLIAMS, John James. b 08. Qu Coll Cam BA31 MA35. Ely Th Coll 31. **d** 32 **p** 33. R Wokingham St Paul *Ox* 62-73; P-in-c N w S Moreton 73-77; rtd 77; Perm to Offic *Ox* from 77. *Iona, Coopers Lane, Wantage, Oxon OX12 8HQ* Wantage (02357) 67904

WILLIAMS, Canon John James. b 20. TD61. Linc Coll Ox BA42 MA46. St Mich Coll Llan 42. **d** 44 **p** 45. V Powyke *Worc* 64-85; Hon Can Worc Cathl 77-85; rtd 85; Perm to Offic *Worc* from 85. *9 St Nicholas's Road, Peopleton, Pershore, Worcs WR10 2EN* Worcester (0905) 840032

WILLIAMS, John Mark Gruffydd. MA MSc DPhil. **d** 89 **p** 90. NSM Girton *Ely* 89-91; Perm to Offic *Ban* from 91. *Department of Psychology, University of Wales (Bangor), Gwynedd LL57 2DG*

WILLIAMS, John Michael. b 44. MBASW Univ of Wales (Cardiff) CQSW74. St Deiniol's Hawarden 80. **d** 83 **p** 84. NSM Llanrhos *St As* from 83. *35 Marston Road, Rhos on Sea, Colwyn Bay, Clwyd LL28 4SG* Colwyn Bay (0492) 44153

WILLIAMS, John Peter Philip. b 49. Univ of Wales (Ban) DipTh70 Open Univ BA84. Chich Th Coll 71. **d** 72 **p** 73. C Abergele *St As* 72-77; R Henllan and Llannefydd 77-82; R Henllan and Llannefydd and Bylchau from 82. *The Rectory, Henllan, Denbigh, Clwyd LL16 5BB* Denbigh (074571) 2628

WILLIAMS, John Richard. b 48. Rhodes Univ Grahamstown BA68 K Coll Lon BD72 AKC72. **d** 73 **p** 74. S Africa 73-76; C Addington *Cant* 77-80; C Minster in Sheppey 80-86; R Temple Ewell w Lydden 86-90; V Hound *Win* from 90. *The Vicarage, Grange Road, Netley Abbey, Southampton S03 5FF* Southampton (0703) 452209

WILLIAMS, John Roger. b 31. Bris Univ BA55 Lon Univ BD57. Tyndale Hall Bris 57. **d** 57 **p** 58. C Islington H Trin Cloudesley Square *Lon* 57-60; Travelling Sec IVF 60-64; V Selly Hill St Steph *Birm* 64-74; P-in-c Chilwell *S'well* 74-75; V 75-90; Dioc Tourism Chapl from 90; P-in-c Perlethorpe from 90; P-in-c Norton Cuckney from 90. *The Chaplain's House, Perlethorpe, Newark, Notts NG22 9EF* Mansfield (0623) 822106

WILLIAMS, Canon John Roger. b 37. Lich Th Coll 60. **d** 63 **p** 64. C Wem *Lich* 63-66; C Wolv St Pet 66-69; R Pudleston w Hatf *Heref* 69-74; P-in-c Stoke Prior and Ford w Humber 69-74; P-in-c Docklow 69-74; V Fenton *Lich* 74-81; P-in-c Honington w Idlicote *Cov* 81; P-in-c Shipston-on-Stour w Tidmington 81; R Shipston-on-Stour w Honington and Idlicote from 81; RD Shipston 83-90; Hon Can Cov Cathl from 90. *Shipston Rectory, 8 Glen Close, Shipston-on-Stour CV36 4ED* Shipston-on-Stour (0608) 62661

WILLIAMS, John Strettle. b 44. DipEd73 BA84. N Ord Course 77. **d** 80 **p** 81. NSM Liv St Paul Stoneycroft *Liv* 80-83; Chapl Cen Liv Coll of FE from 80; Hon C Liv Our Lady and St Nic w St Anne 83-90; Chapl RNR 84-90; Chapl City Coll of FE Liv from 85; Chapl to High Sheriff of Merseyside from 90. *28 Brook Street, Whiston, Prescot, Merseyside L35 5AP* 051-426 9598

WILLIAMS, John Trefor. b 23. Worc Ord Coll 65. **d** 67 **p** 68. C Paignton St Jo *Ex* 67-72; V Winkleigh 72-80; P-in-c Ashreigney 73-79; R 79-80; P-in-c Brushford 75-79; V 79-80; R Broadwoodkelly 79-80; P-in-c Berrynarbor 80-81; P-in-c Combe Martin 80-81; R Combe Martin and Berrynarbor from 81. *The Rectory, Combe Martin, Ilfracombe, Devon EX34 0NS* Combe Martin (027188) 3203

WILLIAMS, Jonathan Simon. b 60. Univ of Wales (Cardiff) BSc81. Coll of Resurr Mirfield 83. **d** 86 **p** 87. C Gellygaer *Llan* 86-89; C Cwmbran *Mon* 89-90; TV from 90. *The Vicarage, Llantarnam, Cwmbran, Gwent NP44 3BW* Cwmbran (0633) 33532

WILLIAMS, Miss Joy Margaret. b 30. Lon Univ BD69. Linc Th Coll 82. **dss** 83 **d** 87. Pershore w Pinvin, Wick and Birlingham *Worc* 83-87; Par Dn 87-88; Par Dn Dudley St Jo 88-90; rtd 90. *Pixie Cottage, 40 Ridge Street, Pershore, Worcs WR10 1AT* Pershore (0386) 556867

WILLIAMS, Julian Thomas. b 65. Clare Coll Cam BA87. Wycliffe Hall Ox BA(Theol)90. **d** 91. Min Can St D Cathl *St D* from 91. *Pembroke Cottage, Glasfryn Lane, St David's, Haverfordwest, Dyfed SA62 6ST* St Davids (0437) 720252

WILLIAMS, Keith. b 37. St Jo Coll Nottm 83. **d** 85 **p** 86. C Holbeck *Ripon* 85-88; R Swillington from 88. *The*

Rectory, Wakefield Road, Swillington, Leeds LS26 8DS Leeds (0532) 860172

WILLIAMS, Keith Douglas. b 41. E Midl Min Tr Course 86. **d** 89 **p** 90. Hon C Netherfield w Colwick *S'well* from 89. *15 Mile End Road, Nottingham NG4 2DW* Nottingham (0602) 614850

WILLIAMS, Keith Graham. b 38. ARICS62 Reading Univ MSc70 St Jo Coll Dur DipTh77. **d** 77 **p** 78. C Almondbury *Wakef* 77-81; C Chapelthorpe 81-82; V Ryhill 82-88; V E Ardsley from 88. *The Vicarage, Church Lane, East Ardsley, Wakefield, W Yorkshire WF3 2LJ* Wakefield (0924) 822184

WILLIAMS, Kelvin George John. b 36. ALCD62. **d** 62 **p** 63. C Bath Abbey w St Jas *B & W* 62-65; CF (TA) 64-65 and 70-79; Chapl R Nat Hosp for Rheumatic Diseases Bath 64-65; CF 65-68; C Clevedon St Andr *B & W* 68-70; V Ston Easton w Farrington Gurney 70-74; P-in-c Bradf 74-75; R Bradf w Oake, Hillfarrance and Heathfield 75-76; NSM Puriton and Pawlett 89-91; NSM Bridgwater Deanery from 91. *48 Main Road, West Huntspill, Highbridge, Somerset TA9 3DW* Burnham-on-Sea (0278) 786136

WILLIAMS, Kenneth Hooper. b 30. St D Coll Lamp BA49 LTh51. **d** 53 **p** 54. C Pemb Dock *St D* 53-56; C Burry Port and Pwll 56-58; CF 58-83; R Hope *St As* from 83. *The Rectory, Hawarden Road, Hope, Wrexham, Clwyd LL12 9NH* Caergwrle (0978) 762127

WILLIAMS, Ven Leslie Arthur. b 09. Down Coll Cam BA40 MA45. Clifton Th Coll 34. **d** 34 **p** 35. Hon Can Bris Cathl *Bris* 58-79; Adn Bris 67-79; rtd 79. *St Monica's Rest Home, Cote Lane, Bristol BS9 3UN* Bristol (0272) 621703

WILLIAMS, Llewelyn Owen. b 09. St Pet Hall Ox 28. Clifton Th Coll 35. **d** 38 **p** 39. R Bawdrip *B & W* 67-68; rtd 74. *Coombe Lodge Flat, Wotton-under-Edge, Glos GL12 7NB* Dursley (0453) 843165

WILLIAMS, Lloyd. b 43. Oak Hill Th Coll 71. **d** 74 **p** 75. C Laisterdyke *Bradf* 74-77; C Hoole Ches 77-80; V Rawthorpe *Wakef* 80-84; HM Pris Leeds 84-85; Chapl HM Pris Cardiff 85-88; Chapl HM Pris Aldington from 88; R Aldington w Bonnington and Bilsington *Cant* from 88. *The Rectory, Aldington, Ashford, Kent TN25 7ES* Ashford (0233) 720898

WILLIAMS, Mrs Louise Margaret. b 66. Lanc Univ BA87. St Jo Coll Nottm DPS91. **d** 91. Par Dn W Ham *Chelmsf* from 91. *181 Balaam Street, London E13 8AA* 081-470 2531

WILLIAMS, Malcolm Kendra. b 34. Oak Hill NSM Course. **d** 85 **p** 86. NSM Margate H Trin *Cant* 85-87; P-in-c Austrey *Birm* 87-90; V Wonersh *Guildf* from 90. *The Vicarage, Wonersh, Guildford, Surrey GU5 0PF* Guildford (0483) 893131

WILLIAMS, Mark Naylor. b 28. CCC Cam BA52 MA56 CertEd. Ripon Hall Ox 58. **d** 59 **p** 60. C Dorchester *Ox* 59-65; R Gt and Lt Braxted *Chelmsf* 65-70; R E Kilbride *Glas* 70-74; R Norton *Sheff* 74-89; R Lt w Gt Ellingham w Rockland *Nor* from 89. *The Rectory, Great Ellingham, Attleborough, Norfolk NR17 1LD* Attleborough (0953) 453200

WILLIAMS, Martin Inffeld. b 37. SS Coll Cam BA62. Chich Th Coll 62. **d** 64 **p** 65. C Greenford H Cross *Lon* 64-70; Tutor Chich Th Coll 70-75; Vice-Prin 75-77; V Roath St German *Llan* from 77. *St German's Clergy House, Metal Street, Roath, Cardiff CF2 1LA* Cardiff (0222) 494488

WILLIAMS, Maxwell Holman Bentley. b 24. Reading Univ BA50. Cuddesdon Coll 56. **d** 58 **p** 59. R Bemerton *Sarum* 67-75; rtd 89. *70 Doncaster Road, Weymouth, Dorset DT4 9JH* Weymouth (0305) 779081

WILLIAMS, Mervyn Rees. b 28. Univ of Wales (Swansea) BA49 Lon Univ PGCE54. St Deiniol's Hawarden 68. **d** 72 **p** 73. NSM Llangollen w Trevor and Llantysilio *St As* from 72. *12 Wern Road, Llangollen, Clwyd LL20 8DU* Llangollen (0978) 860369

WILLIAMS, Michael John. b 31. St Edm Hall Ox BA53 MA57. Wells Th Coll 53. **d** 55 **p** 56. C Thatcham *Ox* 66-70; Perm to Offic *Ex* 70-81; C Rainhill *Liv* 81-86; Chapl Whiston Hosp 83-86; rtd 86; Perm to Offic *Ex* from 86. *1 Bramble Lane, Crediton, Devon EX17 1DA* Crediton (03632) 4005

WILLIAMS, Michael John. b 48. Ox NSM Course. **d** 84 **p** 85. NSM Prestwood *Ox* 84-87; NSM Terriers from 87. *87 Amersham Road, High Wycombe, Bucks HP13 5AA* High Wycombe (0494) 29257

WILLIAMS, Michael Joseph. b 42. Cranmer Hall Dur BA68. **d** 70 **p** 71. C Toxteth Park St Philemon *Liv* 70-75; TV Toxteth St Philemon w St Gabr 75-78; Dir Past Studies St Jo Coll Dur 78-89; Prin N Ord Course from

89. *75 Framingham Road, Brooklands, Sale, Cheshire M33 3RH* 061-962 7513

WILLIAMS, Michael Robert John. b 41. Cranmer Hall Dur 67. **d** 70 **p** 71. C Middleton *Man* 70-73; C-in-c Blackley White Moss St Mark CD 73-79; R Blackley White Moss St Mark 79-86; R Gorton Em from 86. *Emmanuel Rectory, 35 Blackwin Street, Manchester M12 5LS* 061-223 3510

WILLIAMS, Monrelle Theophilus. b 54. Univ of W Indies BA79 TCD MPhil84. **d** 78 **p** 79. C Ferryhill *Dur* from 88. *15 Osbourne Terrace, Ferryhill, Co Durham DL17 8AS* Ferryhill (0740) 55447

WILLIAMS, Norman Ernest. b 23. IEng FIEEE AMIEE Cardiff Coll of Tech HNC. Llan Dioc Tr Scheme 78. **d** 82 **p** 83. NSM Llanblethian w Cowbridge and Llandough etc *Llan* from 82. *The Poplars, Cowbridge, S Glam CF7 7BD* Cowbridge (0446) 772107

WILLIAMS, Norman Henry. b 17. Bris Univ BA43. Qu Coll Birm 77. **d** 77 **p** 78. NSM Cov Cathl *Cov* from 77. *63 Daventry Road, Coventry CV3 5DH* Coventry (0203) 502448

WILLIAMS, Norman Leigh. b 26. Open Univ BA86 Trin Coll Carmarthen 83. **d** 85 **p** 86. NSM Lougher *S & B* from 85; NSM Adnry Gower from 87. *Gorwydd Villa, 13 The Woodlands, Gowerton, Swansea SA4 3DP* Gowerton (0792) 874853

WILLIAMS, Ogwen Lloyd. b 20. Univ of Wales (Ban) BA42. St Mich Coll Llan 42. **d** 44 **p** 45. V Bistre *St As* 65-80; V Llansantffraid GC and Llanarmon DC and Pontfadog 80-85; rtd 85; Perm to Offic *St D* from 85. *Gwendraeth, 3 Heol y Gof, Newcastle Emlyn, Dyfed SA38 9HW* Newcastle Emlyn (0239) 710295

WILLIAMS, Owen David. b 38. S'wark Ord Course 72. **d** 75 **p** 76. NSM Tatsfield *S'wark* 75-80; C Maidstone All SS w St Phil and H Trin *Cant* 80-81; C Maidstone All SS and St Phil w Tovil 81-82; V St Nicholas at Wade w Sarre and Chislet w Hoath from 82. *The Vicarage, The Length, St Nicholas-at-Wade, Birchington, Kent CT7 0PW* Thanet (0843) 47200

WILLIAMS, Paul Andrew. b 62. Oak Hill Th Coll BA91. **d** 91. C Ware Ch Ch *St Alb* from 91. *10 Cromwell Road, Ware, Herts SG12 7JZ* Ware (0920) 467918

WILLIAMS, Paul Rhys. b 58. St Andr Univ MTh82. Westcott Ho Cam 83. **d** 86 **p** 87. Asst Chapl Selw Coll Cam 86-87; C Chatham St Steph *Roch* 87-90; V Gillingham St Aug from 90. *St Augustine's Vicarage, Rock Avenue, Gillingham, Kent ME7 5PW* Medway (0634) 50288

WILLIAMS, Peris Llewelyn. b 39. Univ of Wales (Lamp) BA59. Qu Coll Birm 59. **d** 62 **p** 63. C Upton (or Overchurch) *Ches* 62-65; C Davenham 65-68; C Grange St Andr 68-73; TV E Runcorn w Halton 73-74; V Backford 74-80; Youth Chapl 74-80; V Witton 80-86; V Hoylake from 86. *The Vicarage, Stanley Road, Hoylake, Wirral, Merseyside L47 1HW* 051-632 3897

WILLIAMS, Peter David. b 32. **d** 64 **p** 65. C Southport St Phil *Liv* 64-68; Kenya from 68; CMS from 76. *Lutheran Theological College, Makumira, PO Box 55, USA River, Tanzania*

WILLIAMS, Peter Hurrell. b 34. Keble Coll Ox BA58 MA61. Tyndale Hall Bris 62. **d** 64 **p** 65. C Sparkbrook Ch Ch *Birm* 64-67; C Rushden St Pet 67-70; P-in-c Clapham Park All SS *S'wark* 70-78; R Stanford-le-Hope w Mucking *Chelmsf* from 78. *The Rectory, The Green, Stanford-le-Hope, Essex SS17 0EP* Stanford-le-Hope (0375) 672271

WILLIAMS, Peter John. b 55. Southn Univ BTh80 Univ of Wales (Swansea) DSocStuds90. Chich Th Coll 76. **d** 80 **p** 81. C Chepstow *Mon* 80-84; C Morriston *S & B* 84-85; V Glantawe 85-88; R Reynoldston w Penrice and Llangennith from 88; Dioc Soc Resp Officer from 88. *The Vicarage, Llangennith, Swansea SA3 1HU* Swansea (0792) 386391

WILLIAMS, Peter Rodney. b 22. Chich Th Coll 60. **d** 62 **p** 63. P-in-c Wivelsfield *Chich* 65-72; V Eastbourne St Jo 72-87; rtd 87. *7 The Paragon, Wannock Lane, Willingdon, Eastbourne, E Sussex BN20 9SH* Polegate (03212) 7570

WILLIAMS, Philip Allan. b 48. Bris Univ BSc69 CertEd74. Trin Coll Bris 86. **d** 88 **p** 89. C Heref St Pet w St Owen and St Jas *Heref* from 88. *23 St James Road, Hereford HR1 2QS* Hereford (0432) 354197

WILLIAMS, Philip Andrew. b 64. Sheff Univ BA86. St Jo Coll Dur 88. **d** 90 **p** 91. C Hillsborough and Wadsley Bridge *Sheff* from 90. *10 Welney Place, Sheffield S6 1JX* Sheffield (0742) 313876

WILLIAMS, Philip James. b 52. St Chad's Coll Dur BA73. Coll of Resurr Mirfield 74. **d** 76 **p** 77. C Stoke upon Trent *Lich* 76-80; TV 80; Chapl N Staffs Poly 80-84;

TV Stoke-upon-Trent 80-84; R Shrewsbury St Giles w Sutton and Atcham from 84. *St Giles's Rectory, 127 Abbey Foregate, Shrewsbury SY2 6LY* Shrewsbury (0743) 56426

WILLIAMS, Ray. b 23. Birm City Tech Coll DipMechEng41 Lon Univ DipEd46. St Aid Birkenhead 56. **d** 58 **p** 59. C Sparkhill St Jo *Birm* 58-60; Area Sec (Dios St Alb and Chelmsf) CMS 60-65; V Shenstone *Lich* 65-73; New Zealand from 73. *178 St Vincent Street, Nelson, New Zealand* Nelson (54) 69078

WILLIAMS, Raymond Howel. b 27. St Jo Coll Cam BA49 MA51 Ball Coll Ox BLitt63. St Jo Coll Nottm 72 NW Ord Course 73. **d** 73 **p** 74. C Derby St Pet *Derby* 73-76; C Enfield Ch Ch Trent Park *Lon* 75-81; V S Mymms K Chas *St Alb* from 81. *The Vicarage, 40 Dugdale Hill Lane, Potters Bar, Herts EN6 2DW* Potters Bar (0707) 54219

WILLIAMS, Richard Dennis. b 57. LTCL79. Coll of Resurr Mirfield 79. **d** 82 **p** 83. C Roath St Marg *Llan* 82-85; C Penarth w Lavernock 85-88; V Abertillery *Mon* from 88. *The Vicarage, Church Street, Abertillery, Gwent NP3 1DA* Abertillery (0495) 212246

WILLIAMS, Richard Elwyn. b 57. Hull Univ BA79. Coll of Resurr Mirfield 79. **d** 81 **p** 82. C Altrincham St Geo *Ches* 81-84; C Stockport St Thos 84-85; C Stockport St Thos w St Pet 86; R Withington St Crispin *Man* from 86. *St Crispin's Rectory, 2 Hart Road, Manchester M14 7LE* 061-224 3452

WILLIAMS, Canon Richard Glyndwr. b 18. St D Coll Lamp BA39 BD50. **d** 41 **p** 42. Warden Ch Hostel Ban 62-70; Chapl Univ of Wales (Ban) Ban 62-70; Dir of Ords 62-70 and 84-86; Prec Ban Cathl 68-88; Can from 68; R Llanbeblig w Caernarfon 70-71; R Llanbeblig w Caernarfon and Betws Garmon etc 71-81; V Llandysilio and Llandegfan 81-88; RD Tindaethwy 82-88; rtd 88. *Borth, 9 Cae Cil Melyn, Penrhos, Bangor, Gwynedd* Bangor (0248) 362883

WILLIAMS, Canon Richard Henry Lowe. b 31. Liv Univ BA52. K Coll (NS) BD64 Ridley Hall Cam 54. **d** 56 **p** 57. C Drypool St Andr and St Pet *York* 56-59; Canada 59-64; V Kirkdale St Athanasius *Liv* 64-68; R Much Woolton 68-79; R Croft w Southworth 79-89; Dioc Communications Officer from 79; Hon Can Liv Cathl from 88; R Wavertree St Mary from 89. *St Mary's Rectory, 1 South Drive, Wavertree, Liverpool L15 8JJ* 051-734 3103

WILLIAMS, Richard Huw. b 63. Bradf and Ilkley Coll BA85. St Jo Coll Nottm LTh88 DPS89. **d** 89 **p** 90. C Forest Gate St Edm *Chelmsf* 89-90; C Plaistow from 90. *181 Balaam Street, London E13* 081-470 2531

WILLIAMS, Richard Pierce. b 09. Univ of Wales BSc31. St Mich Coll Llan 32. **d** 35 **p** 36. V Bettws-yn-Rhos *St As* 62-73; rtd 73. *42 Penrhyn Isaf Road, Penrhyn Bay, Llandudno, Gwynedd LL30 3LT* Llandudno (0492) 48834

WILLIAMS, Robert. b 07. **d** 70 **p** 71. Hon C Glanadda *Ban* 70-77; rtd 77; Perm to Offic *Ban* from 77. *38 Belmont Avenue, Bangor, Gwynedd LL57 2HT* Bangor (0248) 364683

WILLIAMS, Canon Robert. b 20. OBE90. Univ of Wales (Ban) BA43. St Mich Coll Llan 43. **d** 45 **p** 46. R Llangwnnadl w Penllech and Bryncroes *Ban* 55-90; RD LLyn 76-90; Hon Can Ban Cathl 84-90; R Aberdaron and Bodferin w Rhiw w Llanfaelrhys 89-90; rtd 90. *Hendre Bach, Aberdaron, Pwllheli, Gwynedd* Aberdaron (075886) 624

WILLIAMS, Robert David. b 05. St D Coll Lamp BA32. **d** 33 **p** 34. V Llandysilio (or Menai Bridge) *Ban* 62-75; rtd 75. *31 Parc Henblas, Llanfairfechan, Gwynedd LL33 0RW* Llanfairfechan (0248) 680102

WILLIAMS, Canon Robert Edward. b 17. St Mich Coll Llan 45. **d** 47 **p** 48. V Llanwnda w Llanfaglan *Ban* 55-87; Hon Can Ban Cathl 86-87; rtd 87. *Bodfryn, 49 Llyn Beuno, Bontnewydd, Caernarfon, Gwynedd LL49 2UH* Caernarfon (0286) 3877

WILLIAMS, Robert Edward. b 42. Ex Univ BA63. Lich Th Coll. **d** 65 **p** 66. C Wednesbury St Paul Wood Green *Lich* 65-67; C Whitchurch 67-69; P-in-c Whixall 69-72; P-in-c Edstaston 69-72; CF 72-91; R Cheriton w Tichborne and Beauworth *Win* from 91. *The Rectory, Cheriton, Alresford, Hants SO24 0QH* Bramdean (0962) 771226

WILLIAMS, Robert Edward. b 50. Univ of Wales (Ban) DipTh71. St Mich Coll Llan BD74 CertEd79. **d** 74 **p** 75. C Flint Llan 74-77; Asst Chapl Sandbach Sch Cheshire 79-80; Chapl and Hd of RE 80-88; Perm to Offic *Ches* from 86; *St As* from 87; CF from 88. *c/o MOD (Army), Bagshot Park, Bagshot, Surrey GU19 5PL* Bagshot (0276) 71717

WILLIAMS, Robert Ellis Greenleaf. b 12. St D Coll Lamp BA34 Lich Th Coll 34. **d** 36 **p** 37. V Rochdale St Aid *Man* 66-75; TV Weston-super-Mare Cen Par *B & W* 75-78; P-in-c Castleton All So *Man* 78-80; rtd 80; Perm to Offic *Man* from 81. *18 Barrowdale Drive, Meadway Estate, Rochdale, Lancs OL11 3JZ* Rochdale (0706) 356582

WILLIAMS, Robert George Dibdin. b 20. St Mich Coll Llan 56. **d** 58 **p** 59. V Cilcain and Nannerch *St As* 68-75; V Gwersyllt 75-85; rtd 85. *30 Ffordd y Gaer, Bradley, Wrexham, Clwyd LL11 4BW* Wrexham (0978) 754007

WILLIAMS, Robert Gwynne. b 15. St D Coll Lamp BA38. **d** 41 **p** 42. R Goodrich w Welsh Bicknor and Marstow *Heref* 51-81; rtd 81. *The Arch Bungalow, Goodrich, Ross-on-Wye, Herefordshire*

WILLIAMS, Robert Jeffrey Hopkin. b 62. ALAM Univ of Wales (Abth) BA84. Chich Th Coll BTh90. **d** 90 **p** 91. C Eastbourne St Mary *Chich* from 90. *20 Motcombe Road, Eastbourne, E Sussex BN21 1QT* Eastbourne (0323) 29667

WILLIAMS, Robert John. b 51. Cartrefle Coll of Educn CertEd73 Univ of Wales (Ban) BEd. St Mich Coll Llan BD76. **d** 76 **p** 77. C Swansea St Mary and H Trin *S & B* 76-78; Chapl Univ of Wales (Swansea) 78-84; Children's Adv 81-88; Asst Dir of Educn 81-88; Bp's Chapl for Th Educn 83-88; R Reynoldston w Penrice and Llangennith 84-88; R Denbigh and Nantglyn *St As* from 88. *The Rectory, St David's Lane, Denbigh, Clwyd LL16 3EP* Denbigh (0745) 712970

WILLIAMS, Robert Wilfred Callard. b 16. St D Coll Lamp BA37 Chich Th Coll 37. **d** 39 **p** 40. V Manorbier *St D* 63-83; rtd 83. *17 The Green, Lydstep, Tenby, Dyfed* Manorbier (0834) 871247

WILLIAMS, Roger Anthony. b 54. Univ of Wales (Lamp) BA76. Bp Burgess Hall Lamp 72 Qu Coll Birm 76. **d** 78 **p** 79. C Llanelly *St D* 78-82; V Monkton 82-86; Chapl to the Deaf *B & W* 86-90; Chapl to the Deaf *Ox* from 90. *Hagbourne Vicarage, East Hagbourne, Didcot, Oxon OX11 9LR* Didcot (0235) 815047

WILLIAMS, Roger Arthur. b 15. St Pet Hall Ox BA37 MA45. Wycliffe Hall Ox 37. **d** 38 **p** 39. R Hartley *Roch* 58-76; Chapl Bromley Coll Kent 76-80; rtd 80; Perm to Offic *Ex* from 85. *13 Great Close, Culmstock, Cullompton, Devon EX15 3HQ* Cullompton (0884) 840842

WILLIAMS, Roger Stewart. b 54. Qu Coll Cam BA75 MA79. Wycliffe Hall Ox BA78 MA82. **d** 79 **p** 80. C Hamstead St Paul *Birm* 79-82; C Barking St Marg w St Patr *Chelmsf* 82-85; V Mildmay Grove St Jude and St Paul *Lon* from 85. *The Vicarage, 71 Marquess Road, London N1 2PT* 071-226 5924

WILLIAMS, Ronald Hywel. b 35. St D Coll Lamp BA62. **d** 63 **p** 64. C Machynlleth and Llanwrin *Ban* 63-66; C Llanaber 66-69; C Hawarden *St As* 69-73; R Llansantffraid Glan Conway and Eglwysfach 73-77; V Rhosllanerchrugog 77-88; R Cilcen and Nannerch and Rhydymwyn from 88. *The Rectory, 9 Pen-y-Coed, Nannerch, Mold, Clwyd CH7 5RS* Mold (0352) 741376

WILLIAMS, Canon Rowan Douglas. b 50. FBA90 Ch Coll Cam BA71 MA75 Wadh Coll Ox DPhil75 DD85. Coll of Resurr Mirfield 75. **d** 77 **p** 78. Tutor Westcott Ho Cam 77-80; Hon C Chesterton St Geo *Ely* 80-83; Lect Div Cam Univ 80-86; Dean Clare Coll Cam 84-86; Can Th *Leic* Cathl *Leic* from 81; Can Res Ch Ch *Ox* from 86; Lady Marg Prof of Div Ox Univ from 86. *Christ Church, Oxford OX1 1DP* Oxford (0865) 276247

WILLIAMS, Canon Roy. b 28. Lon Univ DipTh60. Ely Th Coll 58. **d** 60 **p** 61. C Daybrook *S'well* 60-63; V Bilborough St Jo 63-73; V Arnold from 73; Hon Can S'well Minster from 85. *St Mary's Vicarage, Church Lane, Nottingham NG5 8HJ* Nottingham (0602) 262946

WILLIAMS, Royce. b 35. Leeds Univ BA56 Lanc Univ MA82. St Steph Ho Ox 58. **d** 60 **p** 61. C Ardwick St Benedict *Man* 60-62; C Bedf Leigh 62-64; V Blackb St Pet *Blackb* 64-68; Perm to Offic 70-78; Chapl W R Tuson Coll Preston 75-78; C Burnley St Cath 78-81; P-in-c Burnley St Alb w St Paul 78-81; V Burnley St Cath w St Alb and St Paul from 81. *St Catherine's Vicarage, 156 Todmorden Road, Burnley, Lancs BB11 3ER* Burnley (0282) 23351

WILLIAMS, Shamus Frank Charles. b 57. St Cath Coll Cam BA79 MA83. Ripon Coll Cuddesdon 81. **d** 84 **p** 85. C Swanage and Studland *Sarum* 84-87; C St Alb St Pet *St Alb* 87-90; TV Saffron Walden w Wendens Ambo and Littlebury *Chelmsf* from 90. *The Vicarage, Church Walk, Littlebury, Saffron Walden, Essex CB11 4TT* Saffron Walden (0799) 21004

WILLIAMS, Preb Sidney Austen. b 12. CVO79. St Cath Coll Cam BA36 MA56. Westcott Ho Cam 36. **d** 37 **p** 38.

V St Martin-in-the-Fields *Lon* 56-84; Chapl to HM The Queen from 61; Extra Chapl from 82; Preb St Paul's Cathl *Lon* 73-84; rtd 84. *37 Tulsemere Road, London SE27 9EH* 081-670 7945

WILLIAMS, Stephen Geoffrey. b 54. St Jo Coll Nottm BTh79 LTh79. **d** 79 **p** 80. C Skelmersdale St Paul *Liv* 79-81; C Burley *Ripon* 81-86. *24 Coronation Drive, Penketh, Warrington WA5 2DD* Penketh (092572) 3599

WILLIAMS, Stephen Grant. b 51. K Coll Lon BD73 AKC73. **d** 75 **p** 76. C Paddington Ch Ch *Lon* 75-78; C Paddington St Jas 78-80; Chapl LSE 80-91; Sen Chapl Lon Univs and Polys from 91. *15 Ormonde Mansions, 106 Southampton Row, London WC1B 4BP* 071-242 2574

WILLIAMS, Ven Stephen Heath. b 51. LTh DipRE DipMin. **d** 74 **p** 75. Australia 74-76 and from 78; Adn Wagga Wagga from 89; C Leigh Park *Portsm* 76-78. *The Rectory, Church Street, Wagga Wagga, NSW, Australia 2650* Wagga Wagga (69) 212323

WILLIAMS, Stephen James. b 52. Lon Univ BSc73. Ridley Hall Cam 73. **d** 78 **p** 79. C Waltham Abbey *Chelmsf* 78-82; C Bedf St Paul *St Alb* 82-86; P-in-c Chalgrave 86-88; V Harlington from 86. *The Vicarage, Church Road, Harlington, Dunstable, Beds LU5 6LE* Toddington (05255) 2413

WILLIAMS, Stephen Stuart. b 60. Magd Coll Ox BA82 Dur Univ BA88. Cranmer Hall Dur 86. **d** 89 **p** 90. C W Derby Gd Shep *Liv* from 89. *345 Utting Avenue East, Liverpool L11 1DF* 051-256 0510

WILLIAMS, Terence. b 36. Univ of Wales (Abth) BSc57 Univ of Wales (Cardiff) MA67 Aston Univ PhD71. Glouc Sch of Min 78. **d** 81 **p** 81. NSM Deerhurst, Apperley w Forthampton and Chaceley *Glouc* 81-87; NSM Tarrington w Stoke Edith, Aylton, Pixley etc *Heref* 87-88; P-in-c Upper and Lower Slaughter w Eyford and Naunton *Glouc* from 88. *The Rectory, Lower Slaughter, Cheltenham, Glos GL54 2HY* Cotswold (0451) 20401

WILLIAMS, Terence John. b 36. Univ of Wales BSc62. St Deiniol's Hawarden 85. **d** 86 **p** 87. C Llangyfelach *S & B* 86-88; C Morriston 88-89; V Llanwrtyd w Llanddulas in Tir Abad etc 89-91; V Llanedy w Tycroes and Saron *St D* from 91. *The Vicarage, 37 Hendre Road, Tycroes, Ammanford, Dyfed SA18 3LA* Ammanford (0269) 592384

WILLIAMS, Thomas Bruce. b 41. **d** 76 **p** 77. C Liskeard w St Keyne and St Pinnock *Truro* 76-79; Australia from 79. *Milpo, Bandiana, Victoria, Australia 3694*

WILLIAMS, Canon Thomas Gerald. b 14. Ex Coll Ox BA35 MA39. Chich Th Coll 35. **d** 37 **p** 38. R Willesborough w Hinxhill *Cant* 62-80; Hon Can Cant Cathl 73-81; rtd 80; Perm to Offic *Cant* from 81. *2 Heathfield Court, Heathfield Road, Ashford, Kent TN24 8QD* Ashford (0233) 639328

WILLIAMS, Timothy John. b 54. **d** 89 **p** 90. NSM Llansamlet *S & B* from 89. *6 Lucas Road, Glais, Swansea SA7 9EU* Swansea (0792) 843807

WILLIAMS, Timothy John. b 64. Kent Univ BA86. St Mich Coll Llan BD89. **d** 89 **p** 90. C Killay *S & B* 89-91; C Llwynderw from 91. *23 Mayals Avenue, Blackpill, Swansea SA3 5DE* Swansea (0792) 401703

WILLIAMS, Tom David. b 19. St D Coll Lamp BA41 St Mich Coll Llan 41. **d** 43 **p** 45. V Llanidloes w Llangurig *Ban* 60-75; RD Arwystli 73-75; R Criccieth w Treflys 75-82; V Llanfihangel Ysceifog and Llanffinan etc 82-84; rtd 84; Perm to Offic *Ban* from 84. *Trefri Fach, Llangaffo, Gaerwen, Gwynedd LL60 6LT* Newborough (024879) 687

WILLIAMS, Trevor Russell. b 48. TCD BA71. St Jo Coll Nottm BA73. **d** 74 **p** 75. C Maidenhead St Andr and St Mary Magd *Ox* 74-77; Asst Chapl QUB 78-80; Relig Broadcasting Producer BBC 81-88; Lic to Offic *Conn* 81-88; I Newc *D & D* from 88. *St John's Rectory, 1 King Street, Newcastle, Co Down BT33 0HD* Newcastle (03967) 22439

WILLIAMS, Trevor Stanley Morlais. b 38. Jes Coll Ox BA63 Univ of E Africa MA67. Westcott Ho Cam BA67. **d** 67 **p** 68. C Clifton St Paul *Bris* 67-70; Asst Chapl Bris Univ 67-70; Chapl and Fell Trin Coll Ox from 70. *Trinity College, Oxford OX1 3BH* Oxford (0865) 279886

WILLIAMS, Vincent Handley. b 24. LRAM LLCM ARCM CertEd. St Deiniol's Hawarden 76. **d** 78 **p** 79. Hon C Barrow *Ches* 78-81; C Dodleston 81-83; V Lostock Gralam 83-90; rtd 90. *2 Springfield Close, Higher Kinnerton, Chester CH4 9BU* Chester (0244) 660983

WILLIAMS, Walter Haydn. b 31. Univ of Wales (Lamp) BA53 Selw Coll Cam BA55 MA60. St Mich Coll Llan 55. **d** 56 **p** 57. C Denbigh *St As* 56-58; VC St As Cathl 58-61; C St As 58-61; R Llanfyllin and Bwlchycibau 61-68; V Northop 68-73; V Mold 73-86; Can St As Cathl

77-82; Prec 81-82; Preb and Chan 82-86; RD Mold 79-86; R Overton and Erbistock and Penley from 86; Chmn Ch of Wales Liturg Cttee from 86. *The Rectory, 4 Sundorne, Overton, Wrexham, Clwyd LL13 0ED* Wrexham (0978) 73229

WILLIAMS, William Arwyn. b 15. Univ of Wales (Abth) BA37. Clifton Th Coll 38. **d** 40 **p** 41. CF 48-72; Chapl to HM The Queen from 69; Chapl Salisbury Hosps 72-80; rtd 80; Perm to Offic Bris from 84; B & W from 85. *The Coach House, Entry Hill Drive, Bath BA2 5NJ* Bath (0225) 312658

WILLIAMS, William David Brynmor. b 48. Univ of Wales (Swansea) DipTh71 Open Univ BA89. St D Coll Lamp 71. **d** 72 **p** 73. C Killay *S & B* 72-74; C Wokingham All SS *Ox* 74-75; CF 75-77; C Spilsby w Hundleby *Linc* 83-87; R Meppershall w Campton and Stondon *St Alb* 87-90; V Hemsby *Nor* from 90. *The Vicarage, Hemsby, Great Yarmouth, Norfolk NR29 4EU* Great Yarmouth (0493) 730308

WILLIAMS, Canon William David Conwyl. b 09. MBE OBE. BA. **d** 32 **p** 33. R Devizes St Jo w St Mary *Sarum* 60-77; RD Devizes 60-77; Can and Preb Sarum Cathl from 74; rtd 77; Master St Nic Hosp Salisbury 77-86. *11A St Nicholas Road, Salisbury SP1 2SN* Salisbury (0722) 330536

WILLIAMS, William John. b 23. Fitzw Ho Cam BA50 MA55. Wycliffe Hall Ox. **d** 54 **p** 55. V Cholsey *Ox* 69-73; rtd 88. *8 Heol-y-Deryn Du, Llangewydd Court, Bridgend, M Glam CF31 4UD* Bridgend (0656) 69259

WILLIAMS-HUNTER, Ian Roy. b 44. Trin Coll Bris 71. **d** 73 **p** 74. C Redhill H Trin *S'wark* 73-75; C Deane *Man* 76-80; R Hartshorne *Derby* from 80. *The Rectory, 74 Woodville Road, Hartshorne, Burton-on-Trent, Staffs DE11 7ET* Burton-on-Trent (0283) 217866

WILLIAMSON, Alfred Michael. b 28. Kelham Th Coll 53. **d** 58 **p** 59. C Nottm St Geo w St Jo *S'well* 58-64; V Kenwyn St Geo *Truro* 64-73; V St Agnes 73-87; Australia from 87. *The Rectory, 64 John Street, Beverley, W Australia 6304* Perth (9) 461112

WILLIAMSON, Andrew John. b 39. MRPharmS. St Alb Minl Tr Scheme 82. **d** 85 **p** 86. NSM Oxhey All SS *St Alb* 85-88; NSM Bricket Wood from 88. *148 Penrose Avenue, Watford WD1 5AH* 081-421 0623

WILLIAMSON, Anthony William. b 33. OBE77. Trin Coll Ox BA56 MA60. Cuddesdon Coll 56. **d** 60 **p** 61. Hon C Cowley St Jas *Ox* 60-79; TV 79-89; Dir of Educn (Schs) from 89. *9 The Goggs, Watlington, Oxford OX9 5JX* Watlington (049161) 2143

WILLIAMSON, David Barry. b 56. St Jo Coll Nottm. **d** 83 **p** 84. C N Mymms *St Alb* 83-86; C Burley *Ripon* from 86. *33 Stanmore Crescent, Leeds LS4 2RY* Leeds (0532) 781920

WILLIAMSON, Edward McDonald. b 42. CITC 67. **d** 69 **p** 70. CF 70-73; C Penzance St Mary w St Paul *Truro* 73-76; V Mullion 76-81; rtd 81. *Hazelmere, The Commons, Mullion, Helston, Cornwall TR12 7HZ* Mullion (0326) 240865

WILLIAMSON, Canon Frank. b 98. Toronto Univ BA25 BD30. **d** 31 **p** 32. Hon Can Man Cathl *Man* 51-70; V Eccles St Mary 56-70; rtd 70. *5 Birchfield Drive, Boothstown, Worsley, Manchester M28 4ND* 061-790 6453

WILLIAMSON, Gavin Leslie. b 59. FRSA Hull Univ BA82 TCD DipTh85. **d** 85 **p** 86. C Stillorgan w Blackrock *D & G* 85-87; Min Can St Patr Cathl Dub from 86; Warden Guild of Lay Readers from 86; I Dunboyne w Kilcock, Maynooth, Moyglare etc *M & K* from 87; Treas St Patr Cathl Dub from 90. *The Rectory, Lismahon, Batterstown, Co Meath, Irish Republic* Dublin (1) 250020

WILLIAMSON, Ivan Alister. TCD BTh. **d** 90 **p** 91. C Lisburn St Paul *Conn* from 90. *12 Belvoir Crescent, Lisburn, Co Antrim BT28 1UA* Lisburn (0846) 664189

WILLIAMSON, John. b 33. Bede Coll Dur. NE Ord Course 81. **d** 84 **p** 85. NSM Beamish *Dur* 84-85; C Sedgefield 85-88; P-in-c Trimdon 88-89; V from 89. *The Vicarage, Trimdon, Trimdon Station, Co Durham TS29 6LX* Wellfield (0429) 880430

WILLIAMSON, John Brian Peter. b 30. CEng FIMechE FIEE FInstP FWeldI Selw Coll Cam PhD55. W Midl Minl Tr Course. **d** 84 **p** 87. NSM Malvern H Trin and St Jas *Worc* from 84. *Monkfield House, Malvern, Worcs WR13 5BB* Worcester (0905) 830522

WILLIAMSON, John Mark. b 43. FCP87 Birm Univ BA65 Univ of Wales (Cardiff) MEd75 MA82. St D Coll Lamp LTh67. **d** 67 **p** 68. C Shepton Mallet *B & W* 67-70; Hon C Dinder 70-71; Chapl Clifton Coll Bris 71-75; Lect All SS Bris 75-78; Chapl Bris Cathl *Bris* 77-78; Perm to

Offic *Pet* 78-84; *B & W* from 84. *6 Upper Lansdown Mews, Bath BA1 5HG* Bath (0225) 429938

WILLIAMSON, Michael John. b 39. ALCD63. **d** 64 **p** 65. C Pennington *Man* 64-67; C Higher Openshaw 67-69; P-in-c Man St Jerome w Ardwick St Silas 69-72; C-in-c Holts CD 72-77; R Droylsden St Mary from 77. *The Rectory, Dunkirk Street, Droylsden, Manchester M35 7FB* 061-370 1569

WILLIAMSON, Paul Stewart. b 48. K Coll Lon BD71 AKC71. **d** 72 **p** 73. C Deptford St Paul *S'wark* 72-75; Hon C Kennington St Jo 76-77; C Hoxton H Trin w St Mary *Lon* 78-83; C St Marylebone All SS 83-84; C Willesden St Mary 84-85; Perm to Offic 86-89; C Hanworth St Geo from 89. *7 Blakewood Close, Hanworth, Middx TW13 7NL* 081-844 0475

WILLIAMSON, Peter Barry Martin. b 21. Wycliffe Hall Ox 61. **d** 62 **p** 63. V Bentley Common *Chelmsf* 68-77; Lt Thurrock St Jo 77-86; rtd 86; Perm to Offic *St E* from 86. *Corner Cottage, The Street, Kelsale, Saxmundham, Suffolk IP17 2PB* Saxmundham (0728) 602963

WILLIAMSON, Ralph James. b 62. LSE BSc(Econ)84. Ripon Coll Cuddesdon BA89. **d** 90 **p** 91. C Southgate St Andr *Lon* from 90. *10 The Woodlands, London N14* 081-368 3276

WILLIAMSON, Reginald. b 13. Roch Th Coll 66. **d** 67 **p** 68. R Soulby w Crosby Garrett *Carl* 70-72; R Warcop, Musgrave, Soulby and Crosby Garrett 74-78; rtd 78; Perm to Offic *Liv* from 78. *Flat 2, 75A Virginia Street, Southport, Merseyside PR8 6SP* Southport (0704) 41527

WILLIAMSON, Robert John. b 55. K Coll Lon BA77. Coll of Resurr Mirfield 78. **d** 79 **p** 80. C Kirkby *Liv* 79-82; C Warrington St Elphin 82-84; P-in-c Burneside *Carl* 84-90; V Walney Is from 90. *The Vicarage, Promenade, Walney, Barrow-in-Furness, Cumbria LA14 3QU* Barrow-in-Furness (0229) 471268

✠**WILLIAMSON, Rt Rev Robert Kerr.** b 32. Oak Hill Th Coll 61. **d** 63 **p** 64 **c** 84. C Crowborough *Chich* 63-66; V Hyson Green *S'well* 66-72; V Nottm St Ann w Em 72-76; V Bramcote 76-79; Adn Nottm 78-84; Bp Bradf from 84. *Bishopscroft, Ashwell Road, Heaton, Bradford, W Yorkshire BD9 4AU* Bradford (0274) 545414

WILLIAMSON, Thomas George. b 33. AKC57. **d** 58 **p** 59. C Winshill *Derby* 58-61; C Hykeham *Linc* 61-64; V Brauncewell w Dunsby 64-78; R S w N Leasingham 64-78; RD Lafford 78-87; V Cranwell 78-80; R Leasingham 78-80; V Billinghay 80-87; V Gosberton from 87. *The Vicarage, Wargate Way, Gosberton, Spalding, Lincs PE11 4NH* Spalding (0775) 840694

WILLIE, Andrew Robert. b 43. Bris Univ BA65 Fitzw Coll Cam BA73 MA77. Ridley Hall Cam 71. **d** 74 **p** 75. Chapl St Woolos Cathl *Mon* 74-79; Chapl St Woolos Hosp Newport 75-79; V Newbridge *Mon* 79-85; V Mathern and Mounton w St Pierre from 85; Post-Ord Tr Officer from 85; Warden of Readers from 91. *St Tewdric's Vicarage, Mathern, Chepstow, Gwent NP6 6JA* Chepstow (0291) 622317

WILLIMENT, Paul. b 47. **d** 73 **p** 74. C Guiseley *Bradf* 73-76; C Northn St Mary *Pet* 76-79; Malaysia from 80. *Box 347, Kuching, Sarawak, Malaysia*

WILLIS, Andrew Lyn. b 48. Univ of Wales (Lamp) BA73. **d** 74 **p** 75. C Swansea St Mary w H Trin and St Mark *S & B* 74-81; V Glasbury and Llowes 81-83; Chapl RAF from 83. *c/o MOD, Adastral House, Theobald's Road, London WC1X 8RU* 071-430 7268

WILLIS, Anthony David. b 40. Sarum & Wells Th Coll 87. **d** 89 **p** 90. C Ivybridge w Harford *Ex* from 89. *12 Buddle Close, Ivybridge, Devon PL21 0JU* Plymouth (0752) 690797

WILLIS, Anthony John. b 38. Univ of Wales (Lamp) BA62. Qu Coll Birm DipTh74. **d** 64 **p** 65. C Kidderminster St Jo *Worc* 64-68; C Dunstable *St Alb* 68-72; V Rubery *Birm* 72-80; R Salwarpe and Hindlip w Martin Hussingtree *Worc* from 80; Agric Chapl from 85. *The Rectory, Salwarpe, Droitwich, Worcs WR9 0AH* Droitwich (0905) 778757

WILLIS, Christopher Charles Billopp. b 32. Bps' Coll Cheshunt 57. **d** 59 **p** 60. C Golders Green St Alb *Lon* 59-61; C N Harrow St Alb 61-64; V Shaw and Whitley *Sarum* 64-69; Ind Chapl *Ex* 69-77; C Swimbridge 70-77; Chapl W Buckland Sch Barnstaple from 77. *Lower Upcott, Chittlehampton, Umberleigh, Devon EX37 9RX* Chittlehamholt (07694) 289

WILLIS, Donald. b 09. Oak Hill Th Coll 56. **d** 57 **p** 58. C Farnborough *Roch* 70-74; rtd 74; Hon C Green Street Green *Roch* 74-77. *Flat 20, Bromley College, London Road, Bromley, Kent BR1 1PE* 081-460 7128

WILLIS, Geoffrey Stephen Murrell. b 58. Sussex Univ BA80. Wycliffe Hall Ox 83. **d** 86 **p** 87. C Ashtead *Guildf*

86-89; Chapl Lee Abbey from 89. *Lee Abbey, Lynton, Devon EX35 6JJ* Lynton (0598) 52621

WILLIS, Preb George Arnold. b 16. Liv Univ BVSc46. Ely Th Coll 52. **d** 53 **p** 53. R Ex St Martin, St Steph, St Laur etc *Ex* 64-74; Preb Ex Cathl 73-81; TV Cen Ex 74-78; TR 78-81; rtd 81; Perm to Offic *Ox* from 90. *11 Knox Green, Binfield, Bracknell, Berks RG12 5NZ* Bracknell (0344) 428522

WILLIS, Joyce Muriel. b 42. CQSW73 Open Univ BA86. E Anglian Minl Tr Course 86. **d** 89. NSM Hadleigh w Layham and Shelley *St E* from 89. *26 Ramsey Road, Hadleigh, Ipswich* Hadleigh (0473) 823165

WILLIS, Peter Ambrose Duncan. b 34. Kelham Th Coll 55 Lich Th Coll 58. **d** 59 **p** 60. C Sevenoaks St Jo *Roch* 59-63; Trinidad and Tobago 63-68; P-in-c Diptford *Ex* 68-69; R 69-85; P-in-c N Huish 68-69; R 69-85; R Diptford, N Huish, Harberton and Harbertonford from 85. *The Rectory, Diptford, Totnes, Devon TQ9 7NY* Gara Bridge (054882) 392

WILLIS, Canon Robert Andrew. b 47. Warw Univ BA68 Worc Coll Ox DipTh71. Cuddesdon Coll 70. **d** 72 **p** 73. C Shrewsbury St Chad *Lich* 72-75; VC Sarum Cathl *Sarum* 75-78; TR Tisbury 78-87; Chapl Cranborne Chase Sch Wilts from 78; RD Chalke *Sarum* 82-87; V Sherborne w Castleton and Lillington from 87; Can and Preb Sarum Cathl from 88; RD Sherborne from 91. *The Vicarage, Sherborne, Dorset DT9 3LQ* Sherborne (0935) 812452

WILLIS, Stephen Anthony. b 65. Univ of Wales BA86. Chich Th Coll 87. **d** 90 **p** 91. C Bethnal Green St Matt w St Jas the Gt *Lon* from 90. *The Rectory Flat, Hereford Street, London E2 6EX* 071-729 0878

WILLIS, Thomas Charles. b 30. Bps' Coll Cheshunt 55. **d** 58 **p** 59. C Anlaby Common St Mark *York* 58-61; C Middlesb St Martin 61-63; V Kingston upon Hull St Paul w Sculcoates Ch Ch 63-69; P-in-c Sculcoates St Silas 67-69; V Sculcoates St Paul w Ch Ch and St Silas 69-80; V Bridlington H Trin and Sewerby w Marton from 80. *The Vicarage, Sewerby, Cloverley Road, Bridlington, N Humberside YO16 5TX* Bridlington (0262) 675725

WILLMER, Derek Franklin. b 37. Wells Th Coll 67. **d** 69 **p** 70. C Cheadle Hulme All SS *Ches* 69-72; C Ches 72-75; TV Ches Team from 75; Chapl to the Deaf from 75; Chapl Ches R Infirmary from 83. *Christ Church Vicarage, 5 Gloucester Street, Chester CH1 3HR* Chester (0244) 380625

WILLMINGTON, Canon John Henry William. b 14. AKC37. St Steph Ho Ox 35. **d** 37 **p** 38. V Selsdon St Jo w St Fran *Cant* 63-79; Hon Can Cant Cathl 74-79; rtd 79; Perm to Offic Cant from 79; S'wark from 82. *22 Barrow Green Road, Oxted, Surrey RH8 0NL* Oxted (0883) 715669

WILLMINGTON, John Martin Vanderlure. b 45. St D Coll Lamp BA69. St Steph Ho Ox 69. **d** 71 **p** 72. C Upper Teddington SS Pet and Paul *Lon* 71-75; C Kensington St Mary Abbots w St Geo 75-83; R Perivale 83-91; V Acton Green from 91. *St Peter's Vicarage, 206 St Alban's Avenue, London W4 5JU* 081-994 5735

WILLMONT, Anthony Vernon. b 35. Lich Th Coll 62. **d** 63 **p** 64. C Yardley St Edburgha *Birm* 63-65; C Smethwick H Trin w St Alb 65-68; V Ropley w W Tisted *Win* 68-77; V Ipswich St Aug *St E* 77-84; R King's Worthy *Win* 84-90; R Headbourne Worthy 84-90; R Lapworth *Birm* from 90; R Baddesley Clinton from 90. *The Rectory, Church Lane, Lapworth, Solihull, W Midlands B94 5NX* Lapworth (05643) 2098

WILLMOT, Philip Boulton. b 15. St Pet Hall Ox BA36 MA41. Westcott Ho Cam 38. **d** 38 **p** 39. Chapl Win Coll 50-77; Lic to Offic *Win* 60-84; Chapl St Jo and St Mary Magd Hosps Win 79-80; rtd 80; Perm to Offic *Win* from 84. *34 Hatherley Road, Winchester, Hants SO22 6RT* Winchester (0962) 852360

WILLMOTT, Oliver Leonard. b 10. Lon Univ DipTh41. Kelham Th Coll 31. **d** 38 **p** 39. V Loders *Sarum* 47-82; R Askerswell 52-82; rtd 82. *Bell Cottage, West Milton, Bridport, Dorset DT6 3SW* Bridport (0308) 24291

WILLMOTT, Robert Owen Noel. b 41. Lich Th Coll 65. **d** 68 **p** 69. C Perry Hill St Geo *S'wark* 68-71; C Denham *Ox* 71-76; P-in-c Tingewick w Water Stratford 76-77; P-in-c Radclive 76-77; R Tingewick w Water Stratford, Radclive etc 77-89; R Wingrave w Rowsham, Aston Abbotts and Cublington from 89. *The Rectory, Leighton Road, Wingrave, Aylesbury, Bucks HP22 4PA* Aylesbury (0296) 681623

WILLMOTT, Trevor. b 50. St Pet Coll Ox BA71 MA74. Westcott Ho Cam DipTh73. **d** 74 **p** 75. C Norton *St Alb* 74-77; Asst Chapl Chapl Oslo w Bergen, Trondheim and Stavanger *Eur* 78-79; Chapl Naples w Sorrento,

Capri and Bari 79-83; Warden Ecton Ho 83-89; R Ecton *Pet* 83-89; Dir of Post-Ord Tr from 86; Dir of Ords from 86; Can Res, Prec and Sacr Pet Cathl from 89. *The Precentor's Lodging, Minster Precincts, Peterborough PE1 1XX* Peterborough (0733) 343389

WILLOUGHBY, Canon Bernard Digby. b 96. Bps' Coll Cheshunt 39. **d** 42 **p** 43. I Cong *T, K & A* 50-73; I Ballinrobe w Kilcommon and Ballyovie 50-73; rtd 73. *Maneys, Salruck, Renvyle, Co Galway, Irish Republic* Lettergesh (95) 43404

WILLOUGHBY, Ven David Albert. b 31. St Jo Coll Dur BA53 DipTh57. **d** 57 **p** 58. C Shipley St Pet *Bradf* 57-61; C Barnoldswick w Bracewell 61-62; R Moston St Chad *Man* 62-72; V Marown *S & M* 72-80; Dioc Stewardship Adv from 76; V Douglas St Geo and St Barn from 80; RD Douglas 80-82; Adn Man from 82. *St George's Vicarage, 16 Devonshire Road, Douglas, Isle of Man* Douglas (0624) 675430

WILLOUGHBY, Francis Edward John. b 38. St Jo Coll Nottm. **d** 83 **p** 84. C Tonbridge SS Pet and Paul *Roch* 83-87; V Sutton at Hone from 87. *The Vicarage, Main Road, Sutton at Hone, Dartford DA4 9HQ* Farningham (0322) 862253

WILLOUGHBY, Ven George Charles. b 20. TCD BA43 MA46. CITC 44. **d** 44 **p** 45. I Clooney *D & R* 59-85; Dioc Dir of Ords 62-72; Adn Derry 79-85; rtd 85. *21 Tyler Avenue, Limavady, Co Londonderry BT49 0DT* Limavady (05047) 65382

✠**WILLOUGHBY, Rt Rev Noel Vincent.** b 26. TCD BA48 MA52. **d** 50 **p** 51 **c** 80. C Drumglass *Arm* 50-53; C Dub St Cath *D & G* 53-55; C Bray Ch Ch 55-59; I Delgany 59-69; I Glenageary 69-80; Treas St Patr Cathl Dub 77-80; Adn Dub *D & G* 78-80; Bp C & O from 80. *The Palace, Kilkenny, Irish Republic* Kilkenny (56) 21560

WILLOUGHBY, Paul Moore. b 60. DipTh BA. **d** 86 **p** 87. C Dub St Patr Cathl Gp *D & G* 86-90; C Glenageary from 90. *10 Silchester Park, Glengeary, Co Dublin, Irish Republic* Dublin (1) 280-7543

WILLOWS, Michael John. b 35. Sarum & Wells Th Coll 70. **d** 72 **p** 73. C Pershore w Wick *Worc* 72-75; P-in-c Astley 75-81; Ind Chapl from 75; P-in-c Hallow 81-85; V 85-88; V Wollaston from 88. *The Vicarage, 46 Vicarage Road, Wollaston, Stourbridge, W Midlands DY8 4NP* Stourbridge (0384) 395674

WILLOX, Peter. b 63. Sunderland Poly BSc85. St Jo Coll Dur 86. **d** 89 **p** 90. C Bradley *Wakef* from 89. *14 Bradley Quarry Close, Huddersfield HD2 1XQ* Huddersfield (0484) 430859

WILLS, David Ernest. b 37. St Jo Coll Cam BA58 MA62. Ridley Hall Cam 58. **d** 60 **p** 61. C Kenilworth St Jo *Cov* 60-63; C Northwood Em *Lon* 63-66; V Huyton St Geo *Liv* 66-73; V Littleover *Derby* 73-84; V Mossley Hill St Matt and St Jas *Liv* from 84. *The Vicarage, Rose Lane, Mossley Hill, Liverpool L18 8DB* 051-724 2650

WILLS, David Stuart Ralph. b 36. Chich Th Coll 64. **d** 66 **p** 67. C Bodmin *Truro* 66-70; V Bude Haven 70-78; TV Banbury *Ox* 78-83; Accredited Counsellor from 81; V Launceston St Steph w St Thos *Truro* 83-88; P-in-c Kenwyn St Geo from 88. *St George's Vicarage, St George's Road, Truro TR1 3NW* Truro (0872) 72630

WILLS, Herbert Ashton Peter. b 24. St Edm Hall Ox BA46 MA50. Qu Coll Birm 60. **d** 60 **p** 61. C Stocksbridge *Sheff* 60-63; Chapl Repton Sch *Derby* 64-69; Chapl St Matthias's Coll Bris 69-78; Asst Chapl Sheff Univ *Sheff* 78-80; Chapl 80-84; R Flax Bourton *B & W* from 84; V Barrow Gurney from 84. *The Rectory, Main Road, Flax Bourton, Bristol BS19 3QJ* Flax Bourton (027583) 2582

WILLS, Ian Leslie. b 49. Wycliffe Hall Ox 77. **d** 80 **p** 81. C Henbury *Bris* 80; C Gtr Corsham 80-83; C Whitchurch 83-86; Chapl HM Rem Cen Pucklechurch from 86; P-in-c Pucklechurch and Abson w Dyrham *Bris* 86-87; V Pucklechurch and Abson from 87. *The Vicarage, Westerleigh Road, Pucklechurch, Bristol BS17 3RD* Abson (027582) 2260

WILLS, John Trevethan. b 21. **d** 50 **p** 51. C Cockermouth All SS w Ch Ch *Carl* 50-54; Chapl Maryhull Hosp 54-59; Torryburn Sch 60-61. *Address temp unknown*

WILLS, Canon Kenneth Charles Austen. b 21. Cuddesdon Coll 68. **d** 70 **p** 71. C Petersfield w Sheet *Portsm* 70-73; R W Meon and Warnford from 73; RD Petersfield 85-90; Hon Can Portsm Cathl from 89. *The Rectory, West Meon, Petersfield, Hants GU32 1LR* West Meon (0730) 829226

WILLS, Morley. b 35. Ex & Truro NSM Scheme. **d** 80 **p** 81. NSM St Enoder *Truro* 80-82; NSM Kenwyn St Geo 82-85; NSM Truro St Paul and St Clem 85-88; NSM Crantock from 89. *The Vicarage, Crantock, Newquay, Cornwall TR8 5RE* Crantock (0637) 830294

WILLSON, Andrew William. b 64. Or Coll Ox BA85 Nottm Univ BTh90. Linc Th Coll 87. **d** 90 **p** 91. C Northn St Mary *Pet* from 90. *54 Bowden Road, Northampton NN5 5LT* Northampton (0604) 759841

WILLSON, Stephen Geoffrey. b 63. Nottm Univ BTh90. St Jo Coll Nottm. **d** 90 **p** 91. C Newport St Andr *Mon* from 90. *23 Nash Grove, Lliswerry, Newport, Gwent NP9 0NL* Newport (0633) 271118

WILLSON, Stuart Leslie. b 61. Nottm Univ BA83. Sarum & Wells Th Coll 83. **d** 84 **p** 85. C Llandrindod w Cefnllys *S & B* 84-85; Asst Chapl Angl Students Univ of Wales (Swansea) 85-88; C Llwynderw 85-88; Chapl Gatwick Airport *Chich* from 88. *18 Aldingbourne Close, Ifield, Crawley, W Sussex RH11 0QJ* Crawley (0293) 541139 or 503857

WILMAN, Arthur Garth. b 37. E Anglian Minl Tr Course 84. **d** 87 **p** 88. NSM Swavesey *Ely* 87-90; NSM Fen Drayton w Conington 87-90; NSM Hardwick from 90; NSM Toft w Caldecote and Childerley from 90. *37 Prentice Close, Longstanton, Cambridge CB4 5DY* Crafts Hill (0954) 781400

WILMAN, Mrs Dorothy Ann Jane. b 38. Reading Univ BSc60 Lon Univ DipTh67. Westcott Ho Cam 89. **d** 90. NSM Toft w Caldecote and Childerley *Ely* from 90. *37 Prentice Close, Longstanton, Cambridge CB4 5DY* Crafts Hill (0954) 781400

WILMAN, Leslie Alan. b 37. Selw Coll Cam BA61 MA65. Ridley Hall Cam 61. **d** 63 **p** 64. C Skipton H Trin *Bradf* 63-67; C Guiseley 67-69; V Morton St Luke 69-79; R Swanton Morley w Worthing *Nor* 79-82; P-in-c E Bilney w Beetley 79-82; P-in-c Hoe 80-82; R Swanton Morley w Worthing, E Bilney, Beetley etc 82-89; R Swanton Morley w Beetley w E Bilney and Hoe from 89; RD Brisley and Elmham from 87. *The Rectory, Beetley, Dereham, Norfolk NR20 4AB* Dereham (0362) 860328

WILMER, John Watts. b 26. Lich Th Coll 56. **d** 58 **p** 59. C Wolv Ch Ch *Lich* 58-60; C Fenton 60-63; V Dresden 63-76; TV Sutton St Jas and Wawne *York* 76-80; R Bishop Wilton w Full Sutton 80; P-in-c Kirby Underdale w Bugthorpe 80; R Bishop Wilton w Full Sutton, Kirby Underdale etc 80-87; V York St Hilda from 87. *St Hilda's Vicarage, Tang Hall Lane, York* York (0904) 413150

WILMOT, David Mark Baty. b 60. Liv Univ BA82. Sarum & Wells Th Coll 84. **d** 87 **p** 88. C Penrith w Newton Reigny and Plumpton Wall *Carl* 87-91; C St Alb St Pet *St Alb* from 91. *4 The Willows, St Albans, Herts AL1 1UL* St Albans (0727) 865087

WILMOT, Jonathan Anthony de Burgh. b 48. St Jo Coll Nottm LTh73 BTh74. **d** 74 **p** 75. C Cam St Martin *Ely* 74-77; Chapl Chantilly *Eur* 77-83; Asst Chapl Chapl Paris St Mich 80-82; Chapl Versailles 82-87; V Blackheath St Jo *S'wark* from 88. *146 Langton Way, London SE3 7JS* 081-293 0023

WILMOT, Stuart Leslie. b 42. Oak Hill Th Coll 64. **d** 68 **p** 69. C Spitalfields Ch Ch w All SS *Lon* 68-71; C Islington St Mary 71-74; P-in-c Brixton St Paul *S'wark* 75-81; R Mursley w Swanbourne and Lt Horwood *Ox* from 81. *The Rectory, Mursley, Milton Keynes MK17 0RT* Mursley (029672) 369

WILMUT, Ronald William. b 09. Ripon Hall Ox. **d** 61 **p** 62. V Birchfield *Birm* 63-78; rtd 78; Perm to Offic Birm from 80; Cov from 85. *2 St Alphege Close, Church Hill Road, Solihull, W Midlands B91 3RQ* 021-704 3708

WILSON, Dr Alan Thomas Lawrence. b 55. St Jo Coll Cam BA77 MA81 Ball Coll Ox DPhil89. Wycliffe Hall Ox 77. **d** 79 **p** 80. Hon C Eynsham *Ox* 79-81; C 81-82; C Caversham and Mapledurham 82-89; V Caversham St Jo from 89. *St John's Vicarage, 9 South View Avenue, Caversham, Reading RG4 0AB* Reading (0734) 471814

WILSON, Canon Alfred Michael Sykes. b 32. Jes Coll Cam BA56 MA61. Ridley Hall Cam 56. **d** 58 **p** 59. C Fulwood *Sheff* 58-63; V Gt Horton *Bradf* 63-69; R Rushden w Newton Bromswold *Pet* 69-76; RD Higham 75-83; P-in-c Rushden St Pet 75-77; R Rushden w Newton Bromswold 77-83; Can Pet Cathl from 77; R Preston and Ridlington w Wing and Pilton from 83; RD Rutland from 85. *The Rectory, Preston, Oakham, Leics LE15 9NN* Manton (057285) 287

WILSON, Canon Allen. b 22. TCD BA44 BD50. **d** 45 **p** 46. C Dub St Michan w St Paul *D & G* 46-51; C Dub St Mary 51-56; I Gt Connell *M & K* 56-64; I Carnalway w Kilcullen 60-64; I Dub Santry w Glasnevin *D & G* 64-73; I Dub Rathfarnham from 73; Preb Rathmichael St Patr Cathl Dub from 86. *Rathfarnham Rectory, Terenure, Dublin 6W, Irish Republic* Dublin (1) 905543

WILSON, Andrew Alan. b 47. Nottm Univ BA68. St Steph Ho Ox 68. **d** 71 **p** 72. C Streatham St Paul *S'wark* 71-75;

TV Catford (Southend) and Downham 75-80; V Malden St Jas 80-89; Chapl Croydon Community Mental Health Unit from 89; Chapl Warlingham Park Hosp Croydon from 89. *7 Leas Road, Warlingham, Surrey CR6 9LN* Upper Warlingham (0883) 627463

WILSON, Andrew Kenneth. b 62. CertJourn. Oak Hill Th Coll BA91. **d** 91. C Springfield H Trin *Chelmsf* from 91. *15 Shelley Road, Chelmsford, Essex CM2 6ER* Chelmsford (0245) 351813

WILSON, Arthur. b 20. Worc Ord Coll 62. **d** 64 **p** 65. V Altofts *Wakef* 71-78; V Staincross 78-84; rtd 84. *Flat 1, Hastings House, South Milford, Leeds LS25 5LL* South Milford (0977) 684591

WILSON, Arthur Guy Ross. b 28. St Aid Birkenhead 58. **d** 59 **p** 60. C Bexley St Mary *Roch* 59-63; C Gravesend St Geo 63-66; C Belvedere All SS 66-70; V Brighton St Matthias *Chich* 70-77; V Bradf St Clem *Bradf* 77-84; Lic to Offic 84-87; C Baildon 87-88; V Skirwith, Ousby and Melmerby w Kirkland *Carl* from 88. *The Vicarage, Skirwith, Penrith, Cumbria CA10 1RQ* Culgaith (076888) 663

WILSON, Arthur Neville. b 43. ACGI Lon Univ BScEng65 Linacre Coll Ox BA70 MA74. St Steph Ho Ox 68. **d** 71 **p** 72. C Whitton St Aug *Lon* 71-73; C Chiswick St Nic w St Mary 73-76; C Littlehampton St Jas *Chich* 76-81; C Littlehampton St Mary 76-81; C Wick 76-81; V Whitworth *Man* 81-88; V Shaw from 88. *The Vicarage, 13 Church Road, Shaw, Oldham OL2 7AT* Shaw (0706) 847369

WILSON, Barry Richard. b 46. W Midl Minl Tr Course 88. **d** 91. NSM Leek and Meerbrook *Lich* from 91. *7 Brackendale, Leek, Staffs ST13 8PD* Leek (0538) 385512

WILSON, Bernard Martin. b 40. St Jo Coll Cam BA63 MA68. Ripon Hall Ox 72. **d** 73 **p** 74. C Bilton *Cov* 73-77; Dioc Development Officer *Birm* 78-83; Soc Resp Officer *Derby* 83-90; V Darley Abbey 83-90; Chapl Derbyshire R Infirmary 88-90; Educn Unit Dir Tearcraft from 91. *c/o Tear Fund, 100 Church Road, Teddington, Middx TW11 8QE* 081-977 9144

WILSON, Bertram Arthur Cuthbert David. b 11. Lon Univ BA35 AKC37. **d** 37 **p** 38. R Colchester St Mary Magd *Chelmsf* 71-76; rtd 76; Perm to Offic *St Alb* from 77. *39 Mayfield Court, Sandy, Beds* Sandy (0767) 82019

WILSON, Brian Arthur. b 37. Portsm Dioc Tr Course 84 Chich Th Coll. **d** 85. NSM S w N Hayling *Portsm* 85-88; Chapl Asst RN from 88. *c/o MOD, Lacon House, Theobald's Road, London WC1X 8RY* 071-430 6847

WILSON, Cecil Henry. b 40. CITC 67. **d** 69 **p** 70. C Lurgan St Jo *D & D* 69-72; Min Can Dromore Cathl 72-75; Youth Sec CMS Ireland 75-80; N Regional Sec 80-87; Gen Sec CMS Ireland from 87. *20 Knockbreda Road, Belfast BT6 0JA* Belfast (0232) 644011

WILSON, Canon Cecil Moffat. b 26. TCD BA51. **d** 52 **p** 53. C Urney *K, E & A* 52-54; I Templeharry *L & K* 56-59; I Cloughjordan 59-64; I Mountmellick *M & K* 64-76; Can Kildare Cathl 72-75; Adn Kildare 75-76; I Raheny w Coolock *D & G* from 76; Preb Dunlavin St Patr Cathl Dub from 88. *403 Howth Road, Dublin 5, Irish Republic* Dublin (1) 313929

WILSON, Charles Michael. b 39. Magd Coll Ox BA63 MA66. NE Ord Course 76. **d** 79 **p** 80. NSM Darlington St Jas *Dur* from 79. *29 Prescott Street, Darlington, Co Durham DL1 2ND* Darlington (0325) 460442

WILSON, Charles Roy. b 30. Brasted Place Coll 56. St Aid Birkenhead 57. **d** 59 **p** 60. C Kirkdale St Paul N Shore *Liv* 59-62; C St Helens St Mark 62-66; V Wolv St Matt *Lich* 66-74; V Ripley *Derby* 74-88; V Willington from 88; V Findern from 88. *The Vicarage, The Castle Way, Willington, Derby DE6 6BU* Burton-on-Trent (0283) 702203

WILSON, Christopher Harry. b 59. Man Univ MusB80. Wycliffe Hall Ox 88. **d** 91. C S Lafford *Linc* from 91. *The Vicarage, 1 The Drove, Osbournby, Sleaford, Lincs NG34 0DH*

WILSON, Mrs Claire Frances. b 43. Hull Univ BA65. SW Minl Tr Course 85. **d** 87. Par Dn Belsize Park *Lon* from 87. *26 Frognal Lane, London NW3 7DT* 071-794 9408

WILSON, Colin Myles. b 40. St Aid Birkenhead 64. **d** 66 **p** 67. C Frodsham *Ches* 66-68; C Heald Green St Cath 68-70; C Kirkby *Liv* 70-73; CF from 73. *c/o MOD (Army), Bagshot Park, Bagshot, Surrey GU19 5PL* Bagshot (0276) 71717

WILSON, David Brian. b 47. QUB BA68. CITC 71. **d** 71 **p** 72. C Ballyholme *D & D* 71-74; C Guildf Ch Ch *Guildf* 74-78; I Arvagh w Carrigallen, Gowna and Columbkille *K, E & A* 78-81; I Clogherney w Seskinore and

Drumnakilly *Arm* from 81. *96 Church Road, Beragh, Omagh, Co Tyrone* Beragh (06627) 72219

WILSON, David Gordon. b 40. Man Univ BSc61 Clare Coll Cam BA63 MA68. Ridley Hall Cam 63. **d** 65 **p** 66. C Clapham Common St Barn *S'wark* 65-69; C Onslow Square St Paul *Lon* 69-73; V Leic H Apostles *Leic* 73-84; V Spring Grove St Mary *Lon* from 84. *St Mary's Vicarage, Osterley Road, Isleworth, Middx TW7 4PW* 081-560 3555

WILSON, David Mark. b 53. Lon Univ BSc75. Wycliffe Hall Ox BA77 MA82. **d** 78 **p** 79. C Romford Gd Shep Collier Row *Chelmsf* 78-81; C Cheadle Hulme St Andr *Ches* 81-85; V Huntington from 85. *St Luke's Vicarage, 14 Celandine Close, Huntington, Chester CH3 6DT* Chester (0244) 347345

WILSON, David Merritt. b 26. S'wark Ord Course 61. **d** 64 **p** 65. C Brixton St Paul *S'wark* 64-69; Perm to Offic from 69. *18 Calais Street, London SE5 9LP* 071-274 5707

WILSON, Derrick. b 33. Oak Hill Th Coll 69. **d** 71 **p** 72. C Lurgan (Shankill) *D & D* 71-74; C Willowfield 74-75; I 83-88; I Knocknamuckley 75-83; I Tullylish from 88. *The Rectory, 100 Banbridge Road, Gilford, Craigavon, Co Armagh BT63 6DL* Gilford (0762) 831298

WILSON, Mrs Dorothy Jean. b 35. St Mary's Coll Dur BA57 DipEd58 Newc Poly LLB78. NE Ord Course 86. **d** 88. NSM Dur St Giles *Dur* from 88; Perm to Offic *Newc* from 88. *86 Gilesgate, Durham DH1 1HY* 091-386 5016

WILSON, Edward Thomas. b 48. Southn Univ BTh82. Chich Th Coll 78. **d** 82 **p** 83. C Cardiff St Jo *Llan* 82-86; V Aberavon H Trin from 86. *Holy Trinity Vicarage, Fairway, Port Talbot, W Glam SA12 7HG* Port Talbot (0639) 884409

WILSON, Erik. b 51. Lanc Univ BA72. Trin Coll Bris 83. **d** 85 **p** 86. C Linthorpe *York* 85-89; V Hull St Martin w Transfiguration from 89. *St Martin's Vicarage, 942 Anlaby Road, Hull HU4 6AH* Hull (0482) 52995

WILSON, Francis. b 34. ACP67. Cuddesdon Coll 71. **d** 73 **p** 74. C Newc St Fran *Newc* 73-79; V Wallsend St Jo from 79. *St John's Vicarage, Station Road, Wallsend, Tyne & Wear NE28 8DT* 091-262 3944

WILSON, Frank Cecil. b 03. **d** 65 **p** 66. V N Clifton *S'well* 68-75; P-in-c S Scarle w Besthorpe w Girton w Spatford 68-75; rtd 75; Perm to Offic *S'well* from 75. *Colanroy, Church Lane, Collingham, Newark, Notts* Newark (0636) 892625

WILSON, Frederick John. b 25. Lon Univ BScEng45. Oak Hill Th Coll 68. **d** 70 **p** 71. C Wandsworth All SS *S'wark* 70-75; P-in-c Garsdon w Lea and Cleverton *Bris* 75-84; P-in-c Charlton w Brokenborough and Hankerton 80-84; Chapl Barn Fellowship Whatcombe Ho 84-87; C Corby Epiphany w St Jo *Pet* from 87. *17 Blake Road, Corby, Northants NN18 9LL* Corby (0536) 201213

WILSON, Canon Harold. b 29. St Jo Coll Ox BA53 MA57. Ridley Hall Cam 57. **d** 59 **p** 60. C Leamington Priors St Mary *Cov* 59-61; C Walsgrave on Sowe 61-64; V Potters Green 64-67; Chapl Barcelona *Eur* 67-73; V Bursledon *Win* 73-83; RD Eastleigh 75-83; V Yateley from 83; RD Odiham 85-88; Hon Can Win Cathl from 87. *The Vicarage, 99 Reading Road, Yateley, Camberley, Surrey GU17 7LR* Yateley (0252) 873133

WILSON, Harold Marcus. b 32. St Jo Coll Dur BA55 DipTh57. **d** 57 **p** 58. C Adlington *Blackb* 57-60; Miss to Seamen 60-81; Iraq 60-63; Japan 63-67; P-in-c Crowfield w Stonham Aspal and Mickfield *St E* from 81. *The Rectory, Stonham Aspal, Stowmarket, Suffolk IP14 6AQ* Stowmarket (0449) 711409

WILSON, Ian Andrew. b 57. Nottm Univ BTh89. Linc Th Coll 86. **d** 89 **p** 90. C Whitton and Thurleston w Akenham *St E* from 89. *530 Norwich Road, Ipswich IP1 6JR* Ipswich (0473) 463676

WILSON, James Andrew Christopher. b 48. Ex & Truro NSM Scheme. **d** 82 **p** 83. NSM Plymouth Crownhill Ascension *Ex* 82-83; NSM Yelverton 83-85; C Plymstock 85-87; R Lifton from 87; R Kelly w Bradstone from 87; V Broadwoodwidger from 87. *The Rectory, Lifton, Devon PL16 0BJ* Lifton (0566) 84291

WILSON, James Charles. b 58. TCD MA DipTh85. **d** 85 **p** 86. C Ban Abbey *D & D* 85-87; C Dub Rathfarnham *D & G* 87-91; I Ardtrea w Desertcreat *Arm* from 91. *Tullyhogue Rectory, 50 Lower Grange Road, Cookstown, Co Tyrone BT80 8SL* Cookstown (06487) 61163

WILSON, James Kenneth. b 47. **d** 88 **p** 89. C Holyhead w Rhoscolyn w Llanfair-yn-Neubwll *Ban* 88-91; Chapl RAF from 91. *c/o MOD, Adastral House, Theobald's Road, London WC1X 8RU* 071-430 7268

WILSON, James Lewis. b 39. TCD BA62 HDipEd63 MA65 BD71. CITC 74. **d** 74 **p** 75. C Enniskillen *Clogh*

74-76; C Belf St Matt *Conn* 76-79; I Killeshandra w Killegar *K, E & A* 79-81; I Derrylane 79-81; I Loughgilly w Clare *Arm* from 81. *124 Gosford Road, Loughgilly, Armagh BT60 2DE* Glenanne (086157) 265

WILSON, James Robert. b 36. CITC. **d** 66 **p** 67. C Ballywillan *Conn* 67-73; I Drummaul 73-79; I Drummaul w Duneane and Ballyscullion from 79. *The Vicarage, 1A Glenkeen, Randalstown, Antrim BT41 3JX* Randalstown (08494) 72561

WILSON, Miss Jane Jennifer. b 43. Ch Ch Coll Cant TCert65 Open Univ BA84. Wycliffe Hall Ox 89. **d** 91. Par Dn Northwood Em *Lon* from 91. *27 Foxfield Close, Northwood, Middx HA6 3NU* Northwood (09274) 25390

WILSON, John Anthony. b 34. Linc Th Coll. **d** 83 **p** 84. C Nunthorpe *York* 83-85; V Whorlton w Carlton and Faceby from 85. *Whorlton Vicarage, Swainby, Northallerton, N Yorkshire DL6 3EA* Stokesley (0642) 700321

WILSON, Canon John Christopher Heathcote. b 13. Qu Coll Ox BA39 MA41. Cuddesdon Coll 40. **d** 41 **p** 42. V Kirk Ella *York* 59-88; AD W Hull Deanery 72-79; Can and Preb York Minster from 79; rtd 88. *14 Tremayne Avenue, Brough, N Humberside HU15 1BL* Hull (0482) 668481

WILSON, John Clifford. b 32. AKC56. **d** 57 **p** 58. C Bordesley St Andr *Birm* 57-59; C Kings Norton 59-61; Somalia and Aden 61-63; V Lydbrook *Glouc* 64-67; TV Bow w Bromley St Leon *Lon* 69-73; P-in-c Stepney St Pet w St Benet 73-80; P-in-c Long Marton w Dufton and w Milburn *Carl* 80-81; R 81-87; V Annesley Our Lady and All SS *S'well* from 87. *The Vicarage, Annesley Cutting, Annesley, Nottingham NG15 0AJ* Mansfield (0623) 759666

WILSON, John Frederick. b 33. Qu Coll Birm 58. **d** 61 **p** 62. C Jarrow St Paul *Dur* 61-65; C Monkwearmouth All SS 65-68; Br Honduras 68-71; V Scunthorpe Resurr *Linc* 71-90; Chapl Divine Healing Miss Crowhurst 90-91; V Terrington St Clement *Ely* from 91. *The Vicarage, 27 Sutton Road, Terrington St Clement, King's Lynn, Norfolk PE34 4RQ* King's Lynn (0553) 828430

WILSON, Canon John Hamilton. b 29. St Chad's Coll Dur BA53. Sarum Th Coll 53. **d** 55 **p** 56. C W End *Win* 55-59; C Fishponds St Mary *Bris* 59-64; V Bedminster St Fran 64-73; RD Bedminster 68-73; R Horfield H Trin from 73; Hon Can Bris Cathl from 77. *The Rectory, Wellington Hill, Bristol BS7 8ST* Bristol (0272) 46185

WILSON, Canon John Hewitt. b 24. CB77. TCD BA46 Div Test47 MA61. **d** 47 **p** 48. C Dub St Geo *D & G* 47-50; Chapl RAF 50-73; Chapl-in-Chief RAF 73-80; QHC 73-80; Can and Preb Linc Cathl *Linc* 74-80; R The Heyfords w Rousham and Somerton *Ox* from 81. *Glencree, Philcote Street, Deddington, Banbury, Oxford OX15 0TB* Deddington (0869) 38903

WILSON, John Lake. b 34. Linc Th Coll 74. **d** 76 **p** 77. C N Lynn w St Marg and St Nic *Nor* 76-80; V Narborough w Narford 80-85; V Pentney w W Bilney 80-85; V Lakenham St Mark from 85. *The Vicarage, 2 Conesford Drive, Bracondale, Norwich NR1 2BB* Norwich (0603) 22579

WILSON, Dr John Michael. b 16. MRCP48 Lon Univ MB, BS42 MD48. **d** 53 **p** 56. Birm Univ Research Fell 67-71; Lect 71-78; Sen 78-81; rtd 81. *4 Eastern Road, Birmingham B29 7JP* 021-472 1051

WILSON, John Stafford. b 21. Bible Churchmen's Coll 49. **d** 51 **p** 52. V Packington w Normanton-le-Heath *Leic* 68-72; V Worthing St Geo *Chich* 72-84; P-in-c Ashby w Fenby and Brigsley *Linc* 84; P-in-c Beelsby 84; P-in-c E and W Ravendale w Hatcliffe 84; R Ravendale Gp 84-87; rtd 88. *88 Bruce Avenue, Worthing, W Sussex BN11 5LA* Worthing (0903) 45844

WILSON, Canon John Walter. b 25. St Jo Coll Dur BA67 Hatf Coll Dur MSc74. Cranmer Hall Dur. **d** 67 **p** 68. C Auckland St Helen *Dur* 67-69; V S Hetton 69-75; Lect Sunderland Poly 75-82; V Ormesby w Scratby *Nor* from 82; RD Flegg from 89; Hon Can Nor Cathl from 91. *The Vicarage, Ormesby, Great Yarmouth, Norfolk NR29 3PZ* Great Yarmouth (0493) 730234

WILSON, Joseph William Sidney. b 23. St Aid Birkenhead 62. **d** 64 **p** 65. C Birkdale St Jo *Liv* 68-71; V Eppleton *Dur* 71-78; V Riccall *York* 78-84; V Freckleton *Blackb* 84-87; rtd 87. *27 Sandy Lane, Wallasey, Merseyside L45 3JY* 051-639 9083

WILSON, Keith. b 38. UEA BA87 MA90. Chich Th Coll 60. **d** 63 **p** 64. C W Bromwich St Fran *Lich* 63-66; C Kirkley *Nor* 66-70; R Swainsthorpe w Newton Flotman 70-75; R Acle 75-89; R Fishley 77-89; RD Blofield 79-87; P-in-c Burlingham St Andr w St Pet 85-89; R Acle w Fishley and N Burlingham 89; TV Thetford from 89;

Ind Chapl from 89; Dioc Rep for Abp's Commn on UPA from 91. *44 Monksgate, Thetford, Norfolk IP24 1BY* Thetford (0842) 766074

WILSON, Kenneth. b 59. ARICS84 Selw Coll Cam MA82 DipRS88. S'wark Ord Course 86. **d** 89 **p** 90. C Walthamstow St Pet *Chelmsf* from 89. *1 Beech Court, Bisterne Avenue, London E17 3QX* 081-521 3333

WILSON, Canon Leslie Rule. b 09. Univ Coll Dur 27. Edin Th Coll 29. **d** 33 **p** 34. Dean Geraldton Cathl Aus 62-66; Hon Can from 65; V Holmside *Dur* 69-74; rtd 74; Perm to Offic *Dur* from 74. *11 Norwich Close, Great Lumley, Chester le Street, Co Durham DH3 4QL* 091-389 2366

WILSON, Malcolm Richard Milburn. b 30. Edin Th Coll 57. **d** 59 **p** 60. C Dumbarton *Glas* 59-61; India 62-63; C Dunfermline *St And* 63-65; R Newport-on-Tay 65-70; R Tayport 65-70; R Baillieston *Glas* 70-74; R Milngavie 74-84; R Bearsden 74-84; R Dalbeattie 84-88; R Gourock from 88. *The Rectory, 86 Albert Road, Gourock, Renfrewshire PA19 1NN* Gourock (0475) 31828

WILSON, Marjorie Jayne. b 59. Hull Univ BA80 K Alfred's Coll Win PGCE81. St Jo Coll Dur 85. **dss** 86 **d** 87. Ormesby *York* 86-87; Par Dn 87-89; Chapl Asst Newc Gen Hosp 89-91; Chapl from 91. *Newcastle General Hospital, Westgate Road, Newcastle upon Tyne NE4 6BE* 091-273 8811

WILSON, Mark Anthony John. b 56. TCD BA80. CITC 75. **d** 80 **p** 81. C Dub Rathfarnham *D & G* 80-83; Bp's C Dub Finglas 83-85; I Celbridge w Straffan and Newcastle-Lyons 85-88; CF from 88. *c/o MOD (Army), Bagshot Park, Bagshot, Surrey GU19 5PL* Bagshot (0276) 71717

WILSON, Mark John Crichton. b 46. Clare Coll Cam BA67 MA70. Ridley Hall Cam 67. **d** 69 **p** 70. C Luton w E Hyde *St Alb* 69-72; C Ashtead *Guildf* 72-77; Chapl Epsom Coll Surrey 77-81; V Epsom Common Ch Ch *Guildf* from 81; RD Epsom from 87. *Christ Church Vicarage, Epsom, Surrey KT19 8NE* Epsom (0372) 720302

WILSON, Mrs Mavis Kirby. b 42. Cam Univ CertEd71 Ex Univ BA64. S Dios Minl Tr Scheme 82. **dss** 84 **d** 87. Chessington *Guildf* 84-85; Epsom St Martin 85-86; Epsom Common Ch Ch 86-87; C 87-90; Dioc Adv in Miss and Evang from 90. *Christ Church Vicarage, Epsom, Surrey KT19 8NE* Epsom (0372) 720302

WILSON, Mervyn Raynold Alwyn. b 33. Qu Coll Cam BA57 MA61. Ripon Hall Ox 57. **d** 59 **p** 60. C Rubery *Birm* 59-62; C Kings Norton 62-63; V Hamstead St Bernard 63-69; R Bermondsey St Mary w St Olave, St Jo etc *S'wark* 69-78; R Bulwick, Blatherwycke w Harringworth and Laxton *Pet* from 78. *The Rectory, Bulwick, Corby, Northants NN17 3DY* Bulwick (078085) 249

WILSON, Very Rev Mervyn Robert. b 22. Bris Univ BA51 Lon Univ BD58. Tyndale Hall Bris 52. **d** 52 **p** 53. C Ballymacarrett St Patr *D & D* 52-56; C Donaghcloney 56-59; C Newtownards 59-61; I Ballyphilip w Ardquin 61-70; I Newry St Patr from 70; RD Newry and Mourne 77-83; RD Kilbroney 77-83; Preb Dromore Cathl 83-85; Can St Anne's Cathl *Conn* 85-89; Dean Dromore *D & D* from 90. *1 Arthur Street, Newry, Co Down BT34 1HR* Newry (0693) 62227

WILSON, Michael. b 13. Trin Coll Cam BA35 MA39. Westcott Ho Cam 37. **d** 38 **p** 39. C Bournemouth St Clem w St Mary *Win* 68-73; V Appleshaw 73-78; rtd 78. *The Friary, 19 St Cross Road, Winchester, Hants SO23 9JA* Winchester (0962) 860171

WILSON, Canon Michael. b 44. Liv Univ BA66 Fitzw Coll Cam BA68 MA73. Westcott Ho Cam. **d** 69 **p** 70. C Worksop Priory *S'well* 69-71; C St Martyn St Mary *Worc* 71-75; V Leic St Anne *Leic* 75-85; TR Leic Ascension 85-88; Hon Can Leic Cathl 85-88; Can Res and Treas from 88. *7 St Martins East, Leicester LE1 5FX* Leicester (0533) 530580

WILSON, Neil. b 61. Newc Univ BA83. Ripon Coll Cuddesdon 85. **d** 88 **p** 89. C Wallsend St Luke *Newc* 88-91; C Monkseaton St Pet from 91. *30 Paignton Avenue, Whitley Bay, Tyne & Wear NE25 8SY* 091-262 3631

WILSON, Paul Edward. b 43. Ridley Hall Cam 81. **d** 83 **p** 84. C Brighstone and Brooke w Mottistone *Portsm* 83-86; C Shorwell w Kingston 83-86; TV Tring *St Alb* 86-90; P-in-c Renhold from 90; Chapl HM Pris Bedf from 90. *The Vicarage, 46 Church End, Renhold, Bedford MK41 0LU* Bedford (0234) 771317

WILSON, Paul Hugh. b 26. Glouc Sch of Min 80. **d** 83 **p** 84. NSM Much Birch w Lt Birch, Much Dewchurch etc *Heref* 83-86; C from 86. *Covertside, Lyston Lane, Wormelow, Hereford HR2 8EW* Golden Valley (0981) 540598

WILSON, Paul Thomas Wardley. b 43. AKC67. St Aug Coll Cant. **d** 70 **p** 71. C Tokyngton St Mich *Lon* 70-74; Soc Community Worker *Roch* 74-81; Perm to Offic from 81; Lic to Offic *Cant* from 83; Sen Adv Coun for Soc Resp from 83; Chief Exec Carr Gomm Soc from 88. *Carr Gomm Society, Telegraph Hill Centre, Kitto Road, London SE14 5TY* 071-277 5050

WILSON, Peter James. b 65. Natal Univ BA85 Cape Town Univ HDipEd86 BA87. **d** 89 **p** 89. S Africa 89-91; C Newton Aycliffe *Dur* from 91; OGS from 91. *99 Winterburn Place, Newton Aycliffe, Co Durham DL5 7ET* Aycliffe (0325) 321533

WILSON, Peter John. b 43. CertEd76 BEd84. Linc Th Coll. **d** 71 **p** 72. C Stretford St Matt *Man* 71-73; C Rugby St Andr *Cov* 73-76; TV from 86; Hon C Bilton 76-79; Asst Dir of Educn *Blackb* 79-81; P-in-c Accrington St Paul 79-81. *St Michael's House, 43 Bow Fell, Rugby CV21 1JF* Rugby (0788) 73696

WILSON, Peter Sheppard. b 39. TCD BA61. CITC 62. **d** 62 **p** 63. C Killowen *D & R* 62-68; C Portadown St Columba *Arm* 68-70; I Convoy w Monellan and Donaghmore *D & R* 70-78; P-in-c Castletown *S & M* 78; V 78-83; R Kilmacolm *Glas* 83-84; R Bridge of Weir 83-84; I Camus-juxta-Bann *D & R* from 85; Dom Chapl to Bp from 90. *19 Dunderg Road, Macosquin, Coleraine, Co Londonderry BT51 4PN* Coleraine (0265) 43918

WILSON, Quentin Harcourt. b 45. FTCL75 K Coll Lon AKC68 BD76. St Aug Coll Cant 69. **d** 70 **p** 71. C Is of Dogs Ch Ch and St Jo w St Luke *Lon* 70-72; C Muswell Hill St Jas 72-77; Succ and Sacr Ex Cathl *Ex* 77-81; Min Can Windsor 81-84; V Langho Billington *Blackb* from 84; Chapl Brockhall Hosp Blackb from 85; RD Whalley *Blackb* from 89. *St Leonard's Vicarage, Whalley Road, Billington, Blackburn BB6 9NA* Whalley (0254) 822246

WILSON, Richard Rennison. b 38. TCD MA. **d** 65 **p** 66. C Derryloran *Arm* 65-68; USA 68-69; C Stormont *D & D* 69-70; I Rathdowney *C & O* 70-77; RD Baltinglass 77-87; I Baltinglass w Ballynure etc 77-87; Preb Leighlin Cathl 85-87; I Dundalk w Heynestown *Arm* from 87; Miss to Seamen from 87. *The Rectory, Haggardstown, Dundalk, Co Louth, Irish Republic* Dundalk (42) 21402

WILSON, Robert Brian. b 29. AKC55. **d** 56 **p** 57. V Hunslet Moor St Pet and St Cuth *Ripon* 63-70; V Bilton 70-80; V Gt and Lt Ouseburn w Marton-cum-Grafton 80-90; rtd 90. *56 Church Avenue, Harrogate, N Yorkshire* Harrogate (0423) 504398

WILSON, Robert Malcolm. b 35. St Andr Univ MA59. ALCD62. **d** 62 **p** 63. C Wallington H Trin *S'wark* 62-66; C Dur St Nic *Dur* 66-70; V Colchester St Pet *Chelmsf* from 70. *The Vicarage, Balkerne Close, Colchester CO1 1NZ* Colchester (0206) 572641

WILSON, Robert Michael. b 33. Linc Th Coll 73. **d** 75 **p** 76. C Knottingley *Wakef* 75-78; P-in-c Cleckheaton St Luke 78-84; Ind Chapl from 78; P-in-c Cleckheaton St Luke and Whitechapel 84; V 84-86; V Batley All SS from 86; RD Dewsbury from 90. *The Vicarage, Churchfield Street, Batley, W Yorkshire WF17 5DL* Batley (0924) 473049

WILSON, Robert Stoker. b 39. Dur Univ BSc62. Oak Hill Th Coll 62. **d** 64 **p** 65. C High Elswick St Paul *Newc* 64-68; C Kirkheaton 68-70; Youth Chapl *Liv* 70-73; P-in-c S Shields St Steph *Dur* 73-78; R 78-83; Youth Chapl 73-77; P-in-c S Shields St Aid 81-83; V Greenside from 83. *The Vicarage, Greenside, Ryton, Tyne & Wear NE40 4AA* 091-413 8281

✠**WILSON, Rt Rev Roger Plumpton.** b 05. KCVO74. Keble Coll Ox BA28 MA34. Lambeth DD49 Westcott Ho Cam 35. **d** 35 **p** 36 **c** 49. C Prince's Park St Paul *Liv* 35-38; C Westmr St Jo 38-39; V S Shore H Trin *Blackb* 39-44; V Radcliffe-on-Trent *S'well* 44-49; Adn Nottm 44-49; V Shelford 46-49; Bp Wakef 49-58; Bp Chich 58-74; Clerk of the Closet to HM The Queen 63-74; rtd 74; Asst Bp B & W from 74. *Kingsett, Wrington, Bristol BS18 7NH* Wrington (0934) 862464

WILSON, Canon Ronald. b 11. St Aid Birkenhead. **d** 51 **p** 52. V Pinchbeck *Linc* 63-78; Can and Preb Linc Cathl 72-78; rtd 78. *14 Windermere Gardens, Linslade, Leighton Buzzard, Beds LU7 7QP* Leighton Buzzard (0525) 379676

WILSON, Canon Spencer William. b 08. AKC35. **d** 35 **p** 36. V Haydock St Jas *Liv* 42-82; Hon Can Liv Cathl 71-82; rtd 82; Perm to Offic *Chich* from 83. *College of St Barnabas, Blackberry Lane, Lingfield, Surrey RH7 6NJ* Dormans Park (034287) 260

WILSON, Stanley. b 24. TCD BA45 MA50. **d** 46 **p** 47. C Belf St Bart *Conn* 46-50; C Finaghy 50-54; C Seapatrick *D & D* 54-55; I Ballymascanlan *Arm* 55-60; I Woodschapel 60-63; Ind Chapl *Glouc* 63-65; P-in-c Worc St Paul *Worc* 65-67; Chapl Worc Hosps 67-77; V The

Guitings, Cutsdean and Farmcote *Glouc* from 77, *The Vicarage, Temple Guiting, Cheltenham, Glos GL54 5RP* Guiting Power (0451) 850268

WILSON, Stephen Charles. b 51. Newc Univ BA73 Cam Univ MA82. Westcott Ho Cam BA78. **d** 79 **p** 80. C Fulham All SS *Lon* 79-82; C W Hampstead St Jas 82-85; P-in-c Alexandra Park St Sav from 85. *St Saviour's Vicarage, 268 Alexandra Park Road, London N22 4BG* 081-888 5683

WILSON, Stuart Michael. b 47. Surrey Univ BSc71. St Steph Ho Ox BA73 MA78. **d** 74 **p** 75. C Tottenham St Paul *Lon* 74-78; C-in-c S Kenton Annunciation CD 78-82; V Hoxton H Trin w St Mary from 82. *Holy Trinity Vicarage, 3 Bletchley Street, London N1 7QG* 071-253 4796

WILSON, Thomas Irven. b 30. TCD BA51 MA58. **d** 53 **p** 54. Chapl RAF 56-85; QHC from 80; rtd 85. *Rathclaren House, Kilbrittain, Co Cork, Irish Republic*

WILSON, Canon Thomas Roderick. b 26. St Pet Hall Ox BA50 MA55. Sarum Th Coll 50. **d** 52 **p** 53. V Habergham Eaves H Trin *Blackb* 58-78; RD Burnley 70-78; Hon Can Blackb Cathl from 75; V Bare 78-81; P-in-c Accrington St Jas 81-82; P-in-c Accrington St Paul 81-82; V Accrington St Jas w St Paul 82-89; rtd 89. *33 Nook Terrace, Cherry Tree, Blackburn BB2 4SW* Blackburn (0254) 209390

WILSON, Timothy Charles. b 62. Oak Hill Th Coll BA90. **d** 90 **p** 91. C Highley *Heref* from 90. *43 Yew Tree Grove, Highley, Bridgnorth, Shropshire WV16 6DG* Highley (0746) 861218

WILSON, Timothy John. b 58. St Pet Coll Ox MA80. Trin Coll Bris 81. **d** 83 **p** 84. C Gt Horton *Bradf* 83-86; C Handforth *Ches* 86-90; V Salterhebble All SS *Wakef* from 90. *All Saints' Vicarage, Greenroyd Avenue, Halifax, W Yorkshire HX3 0LP* Halifax (0422) 365805

WILSON, Victor Isaac. b 23. St Deiniol's Hawarden 69. **d** 71 **p** 72. C Davenham *Ches* 71-75; V Latchford Ch Ch 75-80; V Stalybridge St Paul 80-88; rtd 88. *Bod Awen, Top y Rhos, Treuddyn, Mold, Clwyd CH7 4NE* Pontybodkin (0352) 770060

WILSON, Walter. b 33. **d** 60 **p** 61. C Sheff St Swithun *Sheff* 60-64; Ind Chapl 64-66; C Attercliffe 66-69; R Swallow w Cabourn *Linc* 69-72; Dioc Youth Officer *Heref* 72-77; Chapl Ipswich Sch from 77. *37 Henley Road, Ipswich* Ipswich (0473) 55561

WILSON, William Adam. b 53. Sheff Univ BA74 St Jo Coll Dur BA84. Cranmer Hall Dur 82. **d** 85 **p** 86. C S Croydon Em *S'wark* 85-89; C Wandsworth All SS from 89. *56 Lebanon Gardens, London SW18 1RH* 081-874 3438

WILSON, William Bell. b 04. AKC28. **d** 27 **p** 28. V Cov St Geo *Cov* 39-71; rtd 71. *2 St James's Close, Kissing Tree Lane, Alveston, Stratford-upon-Avon, Warks* Stratford-upon-Avon (0789) 267987

WILSON, William Gerard. b 42. St Chad's Coll Dur BA65 DipTh67. **d** 67 **p** 68. C Hollinwood *Man* 67-71; V Oldham St Jas 71-79; R Birch w Fallowfield from 79. *197 Old Hall Lane, Manchester M14 6HJ* 061-224 1310

✠**WILSON, Rt Rev William Gilbert.** b 18. TCD BA36 MA44 BD44 PhD49. CITC 40. **d** 41 **p** 42 **c** 81. C Belf St Mary Magd *Conn* 41-44; C Ban St Comgall *D & D* 44-47; I Armoy w Loughguile *Conn* 47-76; Can Conn Cathl 64-76; I Lisburn Ch Ch 76-81; Dean Conn 76-81; Bp K, E & A from 81. *The See House, Kilmore, Cavan, Irish Republic* Cavan (49) 31336

WILSON, William Hubert. b 08. Clare Coll Cam BA31 MA34. Westcott Ho Cam 31. **d** 32 **p** 33. R Church Stretton *Heref* 64-72; Israel 72-76; rtd 76. *Anchorage Cottage, Denhead, St Andrews, Fife KY16 8PB* Strathkinness (033485) 589

WILSON, William John. b 25. CEng MIEE. S Dios Minl Tr Scheme 79 **d** 82 **p** 83. NSM Weeke *Win* 82-88; NSM Win St Barn from 89. *23 Buriton Road, Winchester, Hants SO22 6JE* Winchester (0962) 881904

WILTON, Albert Edward. b 10. St Paul's Grahamstown 69. **d** 67 **p** 68. S Africa 69-77; rtd 77; Perm to Offic *St E* 77-86. *College of St Barnabas, Blackberry Lane, Lingfield, Surrey RH7 6NJ* Dormans Park (034287) 609

WILTON, Gary Ian. b 60. Bath Univ BSc83. Wycliffe Hall Ox 85. **d** 88 **p** 89. C Clevedon St Andr and Ch Ch *B & W* from 88. *23 Turner Way, Clevedon, Avon BS21 7YN* Bristol (0272) 872134

WILTON, Glenn Warner Paul. b 33. Miami Univ BSc55 Washington Univ MSocWork76. Ch Div Sch of the Pacific (USA) 77. **d** 65 **p** 66. In RC Ch 65-72; USA 77-81; Chapl Pastures Hosp Derby 82-88; Chapl St Aug Hosp Cant from 89. *The Chaplaincy, St Augustine's Hospital, Chartham, Canterbury, Kent CT4 7LL* Canterbury (0227) 738382

WILTON, Harry Owens. b 22. St Aid Birkenhead 43. **d** 46 **p** 47. C Edge Hill St Cypr *Liv* 46-49; C Kingston upon Hull H Trin *York* 49-51; Area Sec (NW England) CCCS 51-53; V Southport All So *Liv* 53-56. *Crantock, 34 Prenton Lane, Prenton, Wirral, Merseyside L42 8LB* 051-608 4540

WILTSE, Joseph August Jean Paul. b 41. **d** 66 **p** 67. C Airedale w Fryston *Wakef* 66-70; Canada from 70. *6983 Richmond Street, Powell River, British Columbia, Canada, V8A 1H7*

WILTSHIRE, Albert. b 19. Qu Coll Birm 49. **d** 51 **p** 52. V Woodhorn w Newbiggin *Newc* 63-71; V Chatton w Chillingham 71-75; Chapl OHP 75-77; P-in-c Felton *Newc* 77-80; V Cornhill w Carham 80-85; V Branxton 80-85; rtd 85. *The Levers, Yeavering, Wooler, Northd NE71 6HG* Milfield (06686) 427

WILTSHIRE, John Herbert Arthur. b 27. S'wark Ord Course 63. **d** 66 **p** 67. C Lee Gd Shep w St Pet *S'wark* 66-69; Min W Dulwich Em CD 69-79; R Coulsdon St Jo from 79. *The Rectory, Coulsdon, Surrey CR5 1ED* Downland (07375) 52152

WILTSHIRE, Robert Michael. b 50. W Midl Minl Tr Course. **d** 89 **p** 90. NSM Droitwich Spa *Worc* from 89. *29 Arkle Road, Droitwich, Worcs WR9 7RJ* Worcester (0905) 771988

WILTSHIRE, Archdeacon of. See SMITH, Ven Brian John

✠**WIMBUSH, Rt Rev Richard Knyvet.** b 09. Or Coll Ox BA32 MA35. Cuddesdon Coll 32. **d** 34 **p** 35 **c** 63. Chapl Cuddesdon Coll 34-37; C Pocklington w Yapham-cum-Meltonby, Owsthorpe etc *York* 37-39; C Harrogate St Wilfrid *Ripon* 39-42; R Melsonby 42-48; Hon Can St Mary's Cathl *Edin* 48-63; Prin Edin Th Coll 48-63; Bp Arg 63-77; Primus 74-77; Asst Bp York from 77; P-in-c Etton w Dalton Holme 77-83; rtd 83. *5 Tower Place, York YO1 1RZ* York (0904) 641971

WIMBUSH, Timothy. b 44. JP. St Steph Ho Ox. **d** 68 **p** 69. C Hobs Moat *Birm* 68-71; C W Wycombe *Ox* 71-76; R Epwell w Sibford, Swalcliffe and Tadmarton from 76; RD Deddington from 86. *The Rectory, Sibford Gower, Banbury, Oxon OX15 5RW* Swalcliffe (029578) 555

WIMSETT, Paul. b 58. Univ of Wales (Abth) BSc(Econ)79 Hull Univ MA86. St Jo Coll Nottm DipTh83. **d** 85 **p** 86. C Nuneaton St Nic *Cov* 85-89; C Loughb Em *Leic* from 89. *46 Forest Road, Loughborough, Leics LE11 3NP* Loughborough (0509) 261581

WIMSHURST, Michael Alexander. b 33. St Jo Coll Ox BA58. Westcott Ho Cam 59. **d** 60 **p** 61. C Lewisham St Mary *S'wark* 60-65; India 66-70; V Battersea St Pet *S'wark* 71-73; V Battersea St Pet and St Paul from 73. *St Peter's Vicarage, Plough Road, London SW11 2DE* 071-228 8027

WINBOLT LEWIS, Martin John. b 46. Fitzw Coll Cam BA69 MA72. St Jo Coll Nottm LTh75. **d** 75 **p** 76. C Highbury Ch Ch *Lon* 75-78; C Nottm St Nic *S'well* 79-82; R Carlton Colville *Nor* 82-83; R Carlton Colville w Mutford and Rushmere 83-88; V Burley *Ripon* from 88. *The Vicarage, 271 Burley Road, Leeds LS4 2EL* Leeds (0532) 785872

WINCH, Victor Edward. b 17. AIB41 Selw Coll Cam BA47 MA52. Ridley Hall Cam. **d** 48 **p** 49. V Kirdford *Chich* 69-82; rtd 82; Perm to Offic *Heref* from 83. *16 Whitehouse Drive, Kingstone, Hereford HR2 9ER* Golden Valley (0981) 250796

WINCHESTER, Gordon Law. b 50. LTCL LRAM ARCM. Trin Coll Bris. **d** 82 **p** 83. C Cheadle *Ches* 82-84; Asst Chapl Amsterdam *Eur* 84-88; C Hove Bp Hannington Memorial Ch *Chich* from 88. *43 Hogarth Road, Hove, E Sussex BN3 5RH* Brighton (0273) 725642

WINCHESTER, Paul. b 44. St Pet Coll Ox BA66 MA70. Ridley Hall Cam 67. **d** 69 **p** 70. C Wednesfield Heath *Lich* 69-72; Perm to Offic *Sarum* 73-84; R Tushingham and Whitewell *Ches* from 84. *The Vicarage, Tushingham, Whitchurch, Shropshire SY13 4QS* Hampton Heath (094485) 328

WINCHESTER, Paul Marc. b 53. Univ of Wales (Lamp) BA80 DipTh. St Mich Coll Llan 82. **d** 84 **p** 85. C Bedwellty *Mon* 84-86; C Chepstow 86-89; V Cwmcarn from 89. *The Vicarage, Park Street, Cwmcarn, Gwent NP1 7EL* Cwm (0495) 270479

WINCHESTER, Archdeacon of. See CLARKSON, Ven Alan Geoffrey

WINCHESTER, Bishop of. See JAMES, Rt Rev Colin Clement Walter

WINCHESTER, Dean of. See BEESON, Very Rev Trevor Randall

WINDEBANK, Clive Leonard. b 41. New Coll Ox BA62 MA85. Ox NSM Course 75. **d** 78 **p** 79. Kuwait

78-83; NSM Brompton H Trin w Onslow Square St Paul *Lon* 83-84; NSM Basildon w Aldworth and Ashampstead *Ox* from 85. *The Coombe House, The Coombe, Streatley, Reading* Goring-on-Thames (0491) 872174

WINDER, John William. b 15. SS Coll Cam BA37 MA41. Ridley Hall Cam 37. **d** 39 **p** 40. R Bolton by Bowland *Bradf* 66-81; rtd 81; Perm to Offic *Bradf* from 81. *2 Croft Rise, Menston, Ilkley, W Yorkshire LS29 6LU* Menston (0943) 872084

WINDLE, Christopher Rodney. b 45. Univ of Wales (Lamp) BA66. Qu Coll Birm DipTh68. **d** 70 **p** 71. C Lache cum Saltney *Ches* 70-73; C Stockton Heath 73-76; P-in-c Bredbury St Barn 76-83; V from 83. *St Barnabas's Vicarage, Osborne Street, Stockport, Cheshire SK6 2DA* 061-494 1191

WINDMILL, Roy Stanley. b 17. Sarum Th Coll. **d** 54 **p** 55. C-in-c Kineton *Cov* 70-75; C-in-c Combroke w Compton Verney 70-75; C Wraxall *B & W* 76-78; P-in-c Holton 78-82; rtd 82. *The Garden Flat, 38B Berrow Road, Burnham-on-Sea, Somerset TA8 2EX* Burnham-on-Sea (0278) 782715

WINDRIDGE, Peter William Roland. b 23. ACGI MIMechE BScEng. Sarum & Wells Th Coll 82. **d** 84 **p** 85. Hon C Shirley St Jo *Cant* 84; Hon C Shirley St Jo *S'wark* 85-86; Hon C New Addington from 86. *3 Devonshire Way, Croydon CR0 8BU* 081-776 0952

WINDROSS, Andrew. b 49. Univ of Wales (Ban) BA71. Cuddesdon Coll 71. **d** 74 **p** 75. C Wakef St Jo *Wakef* 74-78; C Bromley All Hallows *Lon* 78-83; V De Beauvoir Town St Pet from 83; AD Hackney from 89. *St Peter's Vicarage, 86 De Beauvoir Road, London N1 5AT* 071-254 5670

WINDSLOW, Miss Kathryn Alison. b 62. Southn Univ BTh83. Linc Th Coll 84. **dss** 86 **d** 87. Littlehampton and Wick *Chich* 86-87; Par Dn 87-89; Dn-in-c Scotton w Northorpe *Linc* from 89; Asst Local Min Officer from 89. *The Rectory, Scotton, Gainsborough, Lincs DN21 3QP* Scunthorpe (0724) 764020

WINDSOR, Dean of. *See* MITCHELL, Very Rev Patrick Reynolds

WINFIELD, Ms Flora Jane Louise. b 64. Univ of Wales (Lamp) BA85. Ripon Coll Cuddesdon 87. **d** 89. Par Dn Stantonbury and Willen *Ox* from 89. *41 Yarrow Place, Conniburrow, Milton Keynes MK14 7AY* Milton Keynes (0908) 666866

WINFIELD, June Mary. b 29. Gilmore Ho 57. **dss** 66 **d** 87. Bracknell *Ox* 68-74; Dean of Women's Min 74-80; St Marylebone w H Trin *Lon* 80-82; Ind Chapl 82-89; rtd 89. *3 Clementine Close, London W13 9UB* 081-840 5696

WINGATE, Andrew David Carlile. b 44. Worc Coll Ox BA66 MPhil68 MA71. Linc Th Coll 70. **d** 72 **p** 73. C Halesowen *Worc* 72-75; India 76-82; Prin W Midl Minl Tr Course 82-90; Prin Coll of Ascension Selly Oak from 90. *12 Shenley Fields Road, Selly Oak, Birmingham B29 5AQ* 021-472 1667

WINGATE, Canon David Hugh. b 22. Qu Coll Cam BA48 MA53. Qu Coll Birm 47. **d** 49 **p** 50. Chapl United Leeds Hosp 66-71; Chapl Garlands Cumberland and Westmoreland Hosps 71-86; V Cotehill and Cumwhinton *Carl* 72-86; Hon Can Carl Cathl 85-86; rtd 87; Perm to Offic *Carl* from 87. *26 Beechwood Avenue, Carlisle CA3 9BW* Carlisle (0228) 38061

WINGFIELD, Eric John. b 16. Queensland Univ BA51. ACT ThL43 St Fran Coll Brisbane. **d** 44 **p** 44. R Wadingham w Snitterby *Linc* 59-77; V Cowbit 77-78; P-in-c Moulton St Jas 77-78; P-in-c Weston 78; V Cowbit 78-81; rtd 81. *1A Fallowfield, Luton LU3 1UL* Luton (0582) 592208

WINGFIELD-DIGBY, Andrew Richard. b 50. Keble Coll Ox BA72. Wycliffe Hall Ox 74. **d** 77 **p** 78. C Cockfosters Ch Ch CD *Lon* 77-80; C Enfield Ch Ch Trent Park 80-84; Hon C Ox St Aldate w St Matt *Ox* from 84; Dir Chrs in Sport from 84. *Christians in Sport, PO Box 93, Oxford OX2 7YP* Oxford (0865) 311211

WINGFIELD DIGBY, Very Rev Richard Shuttleworth. b 11. Ch Coll Cam BA35 MA39. Westcott Ho Cam 35. **d** 36 **p** 37. Dean Pet 66-80; rtd 80; Perm to Offic *B & W* from 81. *Byways, Higher Holton, Wincanton, Somerset BA9 8AP* Wincanton (0963) 32137

WINGFIELD-DIGBY, Ven Stephen Basil. b 10. MBE. Ox Univ MA. Wycliffe Hall Ox. **d** 36 **p** 37. Can Res Sarum Cathl *Sarum* 68-79; Adn Sarum 68-79; rtd 79. *The Old Rectory, Nunton, Salisbury* Salisbury (0722) 327479

WINKS, Paul David. b 45. Ex Univ BA67. Cuddesdon Coll 68. **d** 70 **p** 71. C Rickerscote *Lich* 70-73; Chapl RAF 73-75; C Yate *Bris* 76-77; TV Yate New Town 77-83; P-in-c Leigh upon Mendip w Stoke St Michael *B & W*

83-84; V from 84. *The Vicarage, Leigh Street, Leigh upon Mendip, Bath BA3 5QP* Mells (0373) 812559

WINLO, Ronald. b 14. Open Univ BA74. AKC41. **d** 41 **p** 42. V Kirkby Malzeard w Dallow Gill *Ripon* 66-81; rtd 81. *146 Whitcliffe Lane, Ripon, N Yorkshire HG4 2LD* Ripon (0765) 2854

WINN, Mrs Jean Elizabeth. b 58. Man Univ BSc80. Wycliffe Hall Ox 85. **d** 88. C W Derby St Luke *Liv* 88-89. *345 Utting Avenue East, Liverpool L11 1DS* 051-256 0510

WINN, Paul William James. b 44. Liv Univ BSc66. E Midl Min Tr Course 86. **d** 89 **p** 90. NSM Spalding St Paul *Linc* from 89. *10 Holland Road, Spalding, Lincs PE11 1UL* Spalding (0775) 722802

WINN, Peter Anthony. b 60. Worc Coll Ox BA82 MA86. Wycliffe Hall Ox 83. **d** 86 **p** 87. C W Derby Gd Shep *Liv* 86-89; V Seaforth from 89. *St Thomas's Vicarage, Elm Road, Liverpool L21 1BH* 051-928 1889

WINNARD, Jack. b 30. Oak Hill Th Coll 79. **d** 81 **p** 82. C Skelmersdale St Paul *Liv* 81-84; C Goose Green 84-85; V Wigan St Barn Marsh Green from 85. *St Barnabas' Vicarage, Lancaster Road, Wigan, Lancs WN5 0PT* Wigan (0942) 222092

WINNINGTON-INGRAM, David Robert. b 59. Hertf Coll Ox BA82 MA85 K Coll Cam BA89. Westcott Ho Cam 87. **d** 90 **p** 91. C Bishop's Cleeve *Glouc* from 90. *2A Orchard Road, Bishops Cleeve, Cheltenham, Glos GL52 4LX* Bishops Cleeve (024267) 5431

WINSOR, Anthony Geoffrey. b 56. Univ of Wales (Abth) BSc76 BTh87. Linc Th Coll 84. **d** 87 **p** 88. C Cobbold Rd St Sav w St Mary *Lon* 87-88; Barnardo's CANDL Project 88-89. *Saxon Court, 502 Avebury Boulevard, Central Milton Keynes, Milton Keynes MK9 3HF* Milton Keynes (0908) 692692

✠**WINSTANLEY, Rt Rev Alan Leslie.** b 49. Nottm Univ BTh72. St Jo Coll Nottm 68 ALCD72. **d** 72 **p** 73 **c** 88. C Livesey *Blackb* 72-75; C Gt Sankey *Liv* 75-76; P-in-c Penketh 76-77; V 78-81; SAMS from 81; Bp Bolivia and Peru from 88. *Apartado 18-1032, Miraflores, Lima 18, Peru* Lima (14) 453878

WINSTANLEY, Canon Cyril Henry. b 04. Liv Univ BA26 MA30. Ridley Hall Cam 30. **d** 32 **p** 33. V Liv Ch Ch Norris Green *Liv* 41-72; Hon Can Liv Cathl 66-72; rtd 72; Perm to Offic *Liv* from 83. *49 Menlove Gardens West, Liverpool L18 2ET* 051-722 9177

WINSTANLEY, John Graham. b 47. K Coll Lon 67. **d** 71 **p** 72. C Wandsworth St Paul *S'wark* 71-74; Chapl Salford Univ *Man* 75-79; R Kersal Moor 79-87. *Address temp unknown*

WINSTON, Jeremy Hugh. b 54. Univ of Wales BEd76. St Steph Ho Ox BA78. **d** 79 **p** 80. C Bassaleg *Mon* 79-83; Dioc Children's Adv from 79; V Itton and St Arvans w Penterry and Kilgwrrwg etc from 83. *The Vicarage, St Arvans, Chepstow, Gwent NP6 6EU* Chepstow (0291) 622064

WINSTONE, Canon Peter John. b 30. Jes Coll Ox BA52 MA56. Ridley Hall Cam 53. **d** 55 **p** 56. C Bitterne *Win* 55-58; C Keighley *Bradf* 58-60; V Fairweather Green 60-67; V Clapham 67-84; R Leathley w Farnley, Fewston and Blubberhouses from 84; Hon Can Bradf Cathl from 89. *The Rectory, Leathley, Otley, W Yorkshire LS21 2LF* Arthington (0532) 843692

WINTER, Anthony Cathcart. b 28. FCA. Ridley Hall Cam 54. **d** 56 **p** 57. C Childwall St Dav *Liv* 56-58; C Hackney St Jo *Lon* 58-63; V Newmarket All SS *St E* 63-74; Lic to Offic 74-81; Perm to Offic *Lon* 78-81; Hon C St Andr-by-the-Wardrobe w St Ann, Blackfriars 81-86; Hon C Smithfield St Bart Gt from 86. *239 Crescent House, London EC1Y 0SL* 071-250 0741

WINTER, David Brian. b 29. K Coll Lon BA53 CertEd54. Oak Hill NSM Course. **d** 87 **p** 88. Hon C Finchley St Paul and St Luke *Lon* 87-89; Hd Relig Broadcasting BBC from 87; Bp's Officer for Evang *Ox* from 89; P-in-c Ducklington from 89. *The Rectory, 6 Standlake Road, Ducklington, Witney, Oxon OX8 7XG* Witney (0993) 776625

WINTER, Canon Dennis Graham St Leger. b 33. K Coll Lon BSc54 AKC54. Tyndale Hall Bris BD62. **d** 61 **p** 62. C Pennycross *Ex* 61-64; C Maidstone St Faith *Cant* 64-66; V Paddock Wood *Roch* from 66; RD Tonbridge from 89; Hon Can Roch Cathl from 90. *The Vicarage, Maidstone Road, Paddock Wood, Tonbridge, Kent TN12 6DZ* Paddock Wood (089283) 3917

WINTER, Ernest Philip. b 18. Bris Univ BA49 St Cath Coll Ox BLitt54 MA56. Worc Ord Coll 57. **d** 58 **p** 59. V Reddal Hill St Luke *Worc* 61-79; P-in-c Upper Arley 79-86; P-in-c Wribbenhall 81-83; rtd 86; Perm to Offic *Worc* from 86; *Heref* from 87. *4 Summit Road, Clows*

Top, Kidderminster, Worcs DY14 9HN Clows Top (029922) 342

WINTER, Henry David. b 24. Sarum Th Coll 51. **d** 53 **p** 54. C Hope St Jas *Man* 53-55; C Heywood St Luke 55-58; R Hulme St Mich 58-63; Chapl Essex Co Hosp Colchester 63-85; V Colchester St Paul *Chelmsf* from 63. *The Vicarage, 141 North Station Road, Colchester CO1 1UX* Colchester (0206) 578383

WINTER, Jonathan Gay. b 37. **d** 65 **p** 66. C W Dulwich All SS and Em *S'wark* 65-69; Asst Master Kidbrooke Sch 69-77; Norwood Sch from 77; Hon C Dulwich St Barn from 90. *160 Turney Road, London SE21 7JJ* 071-274 3060

WINTER, Norman Gladwyn. b 50. Ch Ch Ox BA72 MA76. Wycliffe Hall Ox 72. **d** 76 **p** 77. C Huyton St Mich *Liv* 76-80; C-in-c Skelmersdale Ecum Cen 80-82; V Skelmersdale Ch at Cen 82-87; Producer BBC Relig Broadcasting Unit Man from 87. *43 Falstone Close, Birchwood, Warrington WA3 6SU* Padgate (0925) 831953

WINTER, Raymond McMahon. b 23. FSA73 Selw Coll Cam BA52 MA60. Wycliffe Hall Ox 59. **d** 61 **p** 62. P-in-c Horstead w Frettenham w Stanninghall *Nor* 64-71; Youth Chapl 64-71; Warden Dioc Conf Ho 64-71; Chapl Loretto Sch Musselburgh 71-74; P-in-c Latchingdon w Mundon and N Fambridge *Chelmsf* 74-75; P-in-c Brettenham w Rushford *Nor* 75-83; P-in-c Riddlesworth w Gasthorpe and Knettishall 76-83; P-in-c Garboldisham w Blo' Norton 77-83; Chapl Bedgebury Sch Kent 83-91; Hon C Kilndown *Cant* 83-87; Hon C Goudhurst w Kilndown 87-91; Warden St Barn Coll Lingfield 88-91; rtd 91. *The Lodge, College of St Barnabas, Blackberry Lane, Lingfield, Surrey RH7 6NJ* Dormans Park (034287) 366

WINTER, Stephen Christopher. b 55. Southn Univ BA76. Trin Coll Bris 85. **d** 88 **p** 89. C Birm St Luke *Birm* from 88. *63 Princess Road, Birmingham B5 7PZ* 021-440 6794

WINTER, Thomas Andrew. b 24. Wadh Coll Ox BA51 MA63. Ely Th Coll 51. **d** 53 **p** 54. S Africa 56-83; R Woodston *Ely* 83-90; rtd 90. *6 The Close, Shoreham-by-Sea, W Sussex BN4 5AH* Shoreham-by-Sea (0273) 452606

WINTERBOTHAM, Canon Anthony James Marshall. b 27. Magd Coll Cam BA51 MA55. Wells Th Coll 55. **d** 57 **p** 58. C Portsea St Mary *Portsm* 57-63; Asst Chapl Wellington Coll Berks 63-67; Hon Chapl Portsm Cathl *Portsm* from 67; Chapl Portsm Gr Sch from 67; Hon Can Portsm Cathl *Portsm* from 90. *4 Poynings Place, St Nicholas Street, Portsmouth PO1 2PB* Portsmouth (0705) 825068

WINTERBOTTOM, Ian Edmund. b 42. St Andr Univ MA66 Nottm Univ DipTh68. Linc Th Coll 66. **d** 68 **p** 69. C Blackb St Steph *Blackb* 68-71; C Wingerworth *Derby* 71-73; P-in-c Brimington 73-77; R 77-89; RD Bolsover and Staveley from 86; R Pleasley from 89. *The Rectory, 57 Newboundmill Lane, Pleasley, Notts NG19 7PT* Sheffield (0742) 482769

WINTERBOURNE, George. b 20. S'wark Ord Course 64. **d** 67 **p** 68. C Cove St Jo *Guildf* 67-71; Perm to Offic 72; Hon C Aldershot St Mich 73-78; Perm to Offic *B & W* 79-80. *Address temp unknown*

WINTERBURN, Derek Neil. b 60. Bris Univ BSc82 Ox Univ BA85. Wycliffe Hall Ox 83. **d** 86 **p** 87. C Mildmay Grove St Jude and St Paul *Lon* 86-89; C Hackney Marsh 89-91; TV from 91. *The Vicarage, Overbury Street, London E5 0AJ* 081-986 5076

WINTERBURN, Ieuan Thomas. b 16. Univ of Wales BA37 Univ of S Africa BA48 Witwatersrand Univ MA52. K Coll Lon 37. **d** 39 **p** 40. S Africa 70-72; Rhodesia 72-80; Zimbabwe 80-81; V Borth and Eglwysfach w Llangynfelin *St D* 81-85; rtd 85. *209 Willsborough Mansions, Seaview Street, Durban, 4000 South Africa*

WINTERBURN, Maurice. b 14. Oak Hill Th Coll 61. **d** 62 **p** 63. V Stambermill *Worc* 68-79; P-in-c The Lye 74-79; rtd 79; Perm to Offic *Worc* from 79. *36 Whittingham Road, Halesowen, W Midlands B63 3TF* 021-550 0434

WINTERSGILL, Allan Vernon. b 19. St Jo Coll Dur BA49. Ely Th Coll 49. **d** 50 **p** 51. V Pet St Barn *Pet* 57-70; V Northn St Jas 70-81; V Staverton w Helidon and Catesby 81-89; rtd 89; Perm to Offic *Pet* from 89. *20 Church Lane, Nether Heyford, Northampton NN7 3LQ*

WINTLE, Anthony Robert. b 44. K Coll Lon 64. St Mich Coll Llan DipTh68. **d** 68 **p** 69. C Llan N *Llan* 68-70; C Baglan 70-75; V Treharris 75-86; V Treharris w Bedlinog 86-90; R St Fagans w Michaelston-s-Ely from 90. *The*

Rectory, Greenwood Lane, St Fagans, Cardiff CF5 6EL Cardiff (0222) 565869

WINTLE, Graham. b 52. Bris Univ BSc73. Oak Hill Th Coll BA86. **d** 86 **p** 87. C Southgate *Chich* 86-89; C New Malden and Coombe *S'wark* from 89. *12 Rosebery Avenue, New Malden, Surrey KT3 4JS* 081-942 2523

WINTLE, Canon Ruth Elizabeth. b 31. Westf Coll Lon BA53 St Hugh's Coll Ox BA67 MA74. St Mich Ho Ox 63. **dss** 72 **d** 87. Tutor St Jo Coll Dur 72-74; Selection Sec ACCM 74-83; St Jo in Bedwardine *Worc* 83-87; C from 87; Dir of Ords from 84; Hon Can Worc Cathl from 87. *72 Henwick Road, Worcester WR2 5NT* Worcester (0905) 422841

WINTON, Alan Peter. b 58. Sheff Univ BA83 PhD87. Linc Th Coll CMM91. **d** 91. C Southgate Ch Ch *Lon* from 91. *62 Oakfield Road, London N14 6LX* 081-886 3346

WINTON, Mrs Philippa. b 56. Nottm Univ BA78. Trin Coll Bris DipHE82. **dss** 83 **d** 87. Sheff St Jo *Sheff* 83-86; Chapl Asst R Hallamshire Hosp Sheff 87; Hon Par Dn Sheff St Silas *Sheff* 87-90; Hon Par Dn Linc St Faith and St Martin w St Pet *Linc* from 90. *15 Albert Crescent, Lincoln LN1 1LX* Lincoln (0522) 539831

WINTON, Stanley Wootton. b 30. Sarum & Wells Th Coll 70. **d** 72 **p** 73. C Birkenhead St Jas w St Bede *Ches* 72-75; V 75-79; TR Ellesmere Port 79-88; Chapl Ellesmere Port and Manor Hosps from 79; R Delamere *Ches* from 88. *The Rectory, Delamere, Northwich, Cheshire CW8 2HS* Sandiway (0606) 882184

WINWARD, Stuart James. b 36. Open Univ BA85. Lich Th Coll 65. **d** 68 **p** 69. C Lytham St Cuth *Blackb* 68-71; C Padiham 71-73; V Musbury 73-84; R Old Trafford St Hilda *Man* 84-89; V Davyhulme St Mary from 89. *St Mary's Vicarage, Vicarage Road, Davyhulme, Manchester M31 3TP* 061-748 2210

WIPPELL, David Stanley. b 46. Queensland Univ BSc67. Westcott Ho Cam BA77 MA. **d** 78 **p** 79. C Wolvercote w Summertown *Ox* 78; Hon C from 78; Asst Chapl St Edw Sch Ox from 78; Chapl St Hugh's Coll Ox from 80. *Segar's House, St Edward's School, Oxford OX2 7NN* Oxford (0865) 58239

WISBECH, Archdeacon of. *See* FLEMING, Ven David

WISE, David Reginald. b 46. Glas Univ BSc65 QUB PhD74. Edin Th Coll 72. **d** 74 **p** 75. Chapl St Andr Cathl *Ab* 74-75; C Ayr *Glas* 75-78; R Airdrie 78-81; P-in-c Gartcosh 78-81; P-in-c Leic St Nic *Leic* 81-82; Chapl Leic Univ 81-89; TV Leic H Spirit 82-89; Chapl St Hilda's Priory and Sch Whitby from 89. *56 Ruswarp Lane, Whitby, N Yorkshire YO21 1ND* Whitby (0947) 603619

WISE, Geoffrey John. b 23. Qu Coll Birm 61. **d** 63 **p** 64. S Rhodesia 63-65; Rhodesia 65-76; P-in-c Cottesmore *Pet* 76; R 76-79; P-in-c Ashwell w Burley 76; R Cottesmore and Barrow w Ashwell and Burley 79-89; rtd 89. *14 Butterslade Grove, Ynysforgan, Swansea SA6 6QU* Swansea (0792) 774734

WISE, Ms Pamela Margaret. b 51. CertEd73 BA79. Ripon Coll Cuddesdon 89. **d** 91. Par Dn Tokyngton St Mich *Lon* from 91. *120 Wyld Way, Wembley, Middx HA9 6PU* 081-903 8625

WISE, Very Rev Randolph George. b 25. VRD64. MBIM Qu Coll Ox BA49 MA55. Linc Th Coll 49. **d** 51 **p** 52. C Walworth Lady Marg w St Mary *S'wark* 51-53; V 55-60; C Stocksbridge *Sheff* 53-55; V 60-66; Ind Chapl *Lon* 66-76; V St Botolph without Aldersgate 72-76; TR Notting Hill 76-81; Dean Pet from 81. *The Deanery, Peterborough PE1 1XS* Peterborough (0733) 62780

WISEMAN, David John. b 51. Lon Univ BD80 Birm Univ DipIslam87. Cranmer Hall Dur 77. **d** 80 **p** 81. C Bilston *Lich* 80-84; P-in-c W Bromwich St Phil 84-86; V 86-89; P-in-c Cheetham St Mark *Man* from 89; Dioc Community Relns Officer from 89. *6 Cheltenham Crescent, Higher Broughton, Salford M7 0FE* 061-792 7161

WISEMAN, John. b 56. Sarum & Wells Th Coll 80. **d** 83 **p** 84. C Swinton St Pet *Man* 83-87; C Swinton and Pendlebury 87-88; TV Atherton from 88. *6 Mickleton, Sandringham Gardens, Atherton, Manchester M29 9HT* Atherton (0942) 892379

WISHART, Michael Leslie. b 45. St Mich Coll Llan DipTh73. **d** 73 **p** 74. C Llangyfelach *S & B* 73-76; Chapl RN 77-80 and from 85; Chapl RNR 80-85; V Beguildy and Heyope *S & B* 80-84; V Gowerton 84-85. *c/o MOD, Lacon House, Theobald's Road, London WC1X 8RY* 071-430 6847

WISKEN, Canon Brian Leonard. b 34. Dur Univ BA58. Linc Th Coll 58. **d** 60 **p** 61. C Lobley Hill *Dur* 60-63; C Ipswich All Hallows *St E* 63-65; P-in-c Scunthorpe All SS *Linc* 65-69; V 69-71; Dioc Stewardship Adv 70-75; R Panton w Wragby 71-75; V Langton by Wragby 71-75;

R Cleethorpes 75-77; TR Cleethorpes 77-89; Hon Can Linc Cathl from 88; V Linc St Nic w St Jo Newport from 89. *St Nicholas Vicarage, 103 Newport, Lincoln LN1 3EE* Lincoln (0522) 525653

WISKEN, Robert Daniel. b 30. ACT. **d** 60 **p** 60. Australia 60-63 and from 86; V Winton *Man* 63-65; R Luddington w Hemington and Thurning *Pet* 65-69; P-in-c Clopton *St E* 66-69; V Ipswich All SS 69-73; V Sompting *Chich* 74-78; Org Sec (SW England) CECS 78-80; R Edmundbyers w Muggleswick *Dur* 80-83; R Wexham *Ox* 83-86. *The Rectory, Geeveston, Tasmania, Australia 7116* Geeveston (02) 971440

WISKER, George Richard. b 35. S'wark Ord Course 69. **d** 72 **p** 73. C Croydon Ch Ch Broad Green *Cant* 72-76; C Barking St Erkenwald *Chelmsf* 76-77; P-in-c 77-82; V from 82. *St Erkenwald's Vicarage, Levett Road, Barking, Essex IG11 9JZ* 081-594 2271

WITCHELL, David William. b 47. St Jo Coll Nottm BTh75 LTh75. **d** 75 **p** 76. C Northn St Mary *Pet* 75-78; C Oakham w Hambleton and Egleton 78-81; C Oakham, Hambleton, Egleton, Braunston and Brooke 81-82; V Weedon Bec w Everdon 82-90; V Wellingborough St Barn from 90. *St Barnabas's Vicarage, Wellingborough, Northants NN8 3HB* Wellingborough (0933) 226337

WITCOMB, Canon Cyril Albert. b 14. Mert Coll Ox BA38 MA43. Westcott Ho Cam 39. **d** 40 **p** 41. Can and Preb Sarum Cathl *Sarum* 65-81; V Calne and Blackland 70-76; V Woodford Valley 76-81; rtd 81. *6 Park Lane, Salisbury SP1 3NP* Salisbury (0722) 331982

WITCOMBE, John Julian. b 59. Cam Univ MA84. St Jo Coll Nottm BA83 DPS84. **d** 84 **p** 85. C Birtley *Dur* 84-87; C Chilwell S'well 87-91; V Lodge Moor St Luke *Sheff* from 91. *St Luke's House, 18 Blackbrook Road, Sheffield S10 4LP* Sheffield (0742) 305271

WITCOMBE, Mrs Maureen Dorothy. b 56. CertEd77 Nottm Univ BTh83. St Jo Coll Nottm 80. **dss** 84 **d** 87. Birtley *Dur* 84-85; Hon Par Dn Chilwell S'well 87-91; Par Dn Lodge Moor St Luke *Sheff* from 91. *St Luke's Vicarage, 18 Blackbrook Road, Sheffield S10 4LP* Sheffield (0742) 305271

WITCOMBE, Michael David. b 53. Univ of Wales (Lamp) BA76. Qu Coll Birm 76. **d** 78 **p** 79. C Neath w Llantwit *Llan* 78-80; C Whitchurch 80-83; V Newc from 83; P-in-c Ewenny 84-86. *The Vicarage, 1 Walters Road, Bridgend, M Glam CF31 4HE* Bridgend (0656) 55999

WITCOMBE, Simon Christopher. b 61. Dundee Univ MA83 PGCE84 Dur Univ BA(Theol)90. St Jo Coll Dur 88. **d** 91. C Earlham St Anne *Nor* from 91. *8 Corie Road, Earlham, Norwich NR4 7JB* Norwich (0603) 54509

WITHERIDGE, John Stephen. b 53. Kent Univ BA76 Ch Coll Cam BA78 MA82. Ridley Hall Cam 78. **d** 79 **p** 80. C Luton St Mary *St Alb* 79-82; Asst Chapl Marlborough Coll Wilts 82-84; Abp's Chapl *Cant* 84-87; Conduct Eton Coll Windsor from 87. *Eton College, Windsor, Berks SL4 6DW* Windsor (0753) 865411

WITHERS, Mrs Christine Mary. b 37. ALA60. Qu Coll Birm DipRS81. **dss** 81 **d** 87. Chorleywood Ch Ch *St Alb* 81-86; Darley Abbey 86-87; C from 87. *Bent Farm, Farley, Matlock, Derbyshire DE4 5LT* Matlock (0629) 582792

WITHERS, John Geoffrey. b 39. St Jo Coll Dur BA61 Birm Univ CertEd63 Reading Univ DipEdG70 CQSW72. SW Minl Tr Course 84. **d** 87 **p** 88. NSM Drewsteignton *Ex* from 87. *St Levan, Chagford, Newton Abbot, Devon TQ13 8DD* Chagford (0647) 432340

WITHERS, Michael. b 41. TCD BA66 Edin Univ BD70 QUB MTh83. Union Th Sem (NY) STM71. **d** 71 **p** 73. C Seagoe *D & D* 71-77; C Seapatrick 77-80; I Belf St Chris 80-89; I Movilla from 89. *27 Old Movilla Road, Newtownards, Co Down BT23 3HH* Newtownards (0247) 810787

WITHERS GREEN, Timothy. b 30. K Coll Lon 51. **d** 55 **p** 56. C Greenhill St Jo *Lon* 55-58; C St Helier S'wark 58-61; V Belmont 61-79; CF (TA) 71-79; R Hexham *Newc* 79-84; R Weldon w Deene *Pet* from 84. *The Rectory, 13 School Lane, Weldon, Corby, Northants* Corby (0536) 3671

WITHEY, Michael John. b 45. Open Univ BA80. Oak Hill Th Coll 71. **d** 74 **p** 75. C St Alb St Paul *St Alb* 74-76; C Luton St Mary 77; C Luton St Fran 77-80; V Woodside w E Hyde 80-87; CF (TA) 83-87; Dioc Stewardship Adv *Ox* 87-89; Chapl HM Young Offender Inst Onley 89-91; V Hengoed w Gobowen *Lich* from 91; Chapl Robert Jones and Agnes Hunt Orthopaedic Hosp from 91. *The Vicarage, Old Chirk Road, Gobowen, Oswestry, Shropshire SY11 3LL* Oswestry (0691) 661226

WITHINGTON, George Kenneth. b 37. Birm Univ BA59. Wells Th Coll 59. **d** 61 **p** 62. C Hartcliffe St Andr CD *Bris* 61-65; V Swindon St Jo 65-73; V Cricklade w Latton from 73. *The Vicarage, Cricklade, Swindon, Wilts SN6 6DA* Swindon (0793) 750300

WITHINGTON, Harold. b 04. St Andr Whittlesford. **d** 42 **p** 43. R Ebchester *Dur* 61-70; rtd 70. *1 Front Street, Ebchester, Consett, Co Durham DH8 0PJ* Ebchester (0207) 560997

WITHINGTON, Canon Keith. b 32. Univ of Wales (Lamp) BA55. Qu Coll Birm 55. **d** 57 **p** 58. C Bournville *Birm* 57-61; V from 61; RD Moseley 81-91; Hon Can Birm Cathl from 83. *The Vicarage, 61 Linden Road, Birmingham B30 1JT* 021-472 1209 or 472 7215

WITHNELL, Roderick David. b 55. Leic Univ CTPS89. E Midl Min Tr Course 86 Ridley Hall Cam 89. **d** 90 **p** 91. C Shenfield *Chelmsf* from 90. *53 Friars Avenue, Shenfield, Brentwood, Essex CM15 8HU* Brentwood (0277) 201487

WITHY, John Daniel Forster. b 38. Bible Tr Inst Glas CertRK61 ALCD64. **d** 64 **p** 65. C Belf St Aid *Conn* 64-68; Dir Chr Conf Cen Sion Mills from 68. *Zion House, 120 Melmont Road, Strabane, Co Tyrone BT82 9ET* Sion Mills (06626) 58672

WITT, Bryan Douglas. b 52. Llan St Mich BD84. **d** 84 **p** 85. C Bettws St Dav *St D* 84-87; V Llanllwni from 87. *The Vicarage, Llanllwni, Maesycrugiau, Pencader, Dyfed SA39 3DG* Maesycrugiau (055935) 450

WITTEY, William Francis George. b 05. AKC31. **d** 31 **p** 32. V Torpenhow *Carl* 63-72; rtd 72; Perm to Offic Carl from 72. *14 High Croft Drive, Allithwaite, Grange-over-Sands, Cumbria LA11 7QL* Grange-over-Sands (04484) 3979

WITTON-DAVIES, Ven Carlyle. b 13. Univ of Wales BA34 Ex Coll Ox BA37 MA40. Cuddesdon Coll 36. **d** 37 **p** 38. Adn Ox and Can Res Ch Ch Ox 56-82; rtd 82; Perm to Offic *Ox* from 82. *Hill Rise, 199 Divinity Road, Oxford OX4 1LS* Oxford (0865) 247301

WITTS, Cyril Charles. b 14. Sarum Th Coll 47. **d** 49 **p** 50. V Enfield Chase St Mary *Lon* 67-78; rtd 78; Perm to Offic *Win* from 81. *18 Southlea Avenue, Bournemouth BH6 3AB* Bournemouth (0202) 431633

WITTS, Donald Roger. b 47. Cranmer Hall Dur 86. **d** 88 **p** 89. C Leyland St Ambrose *Blackb* 88-90; C Staines St Mary and St Pet *Lon* from 90. *Peterhouse, St Peter's Close, Staines, Middx TW18 2ED* Staines (0784) 450861

WITTS, Graham Robert. b 53. Newc Univ BEd. Linc Th Coll 79. **d** 82 **p** 83. C Horncastle w Low Toynton *Linc* 82-85; TV Gt Grimsby St Mary and St Jas 85-89; TR Yelverton, Meavy, Sheepstor and Walkhampton *Ex* from 89. *The Rectory, Yelverton, Devon PL20 6AE* Yelverton (0822) 832362

WITTWER, Kurt Ian. b 60. Trin Coll Ox BA82 MA87. Linc Th Coll 82. **d** 84 **p** 85. C Kennington *Cant* 84-87; C Whitstable 87-90; TV from 90. *St Andrew's Church House, Saddleton Road, Whitstable, Kent CT5 4JH* Whitstable (0227) 263152

WIXON, Jack. b 44. Lich Th Coll 68. **d** 71 **p** 72. C Adlington *Blackb* 71-74; C St Annes 74-76; V Chorley St Jas 76-82; V Preston Em from 82. *Emmanuel Vicarage, 2 Cornthwaite Road, Preston, Lancs PR2 3DA* Preston (0772) 717136

WOADDEN, Christopher Martyn. b 56. St Jo Coll Nottm LTh. **d** 87 **p** 88. C Mickleover All SS *Derby* 87-90; C Wirksworth w Alderwasley, Carsington etc from 90. *41 Yokecliffe Crescent, Wirksworth, Derbyshire DE4 4ER* Wirksworth (0629) 822337

WODEHOUSE, Armine Boyle. b 24. Oak Hill Th Coll 84. **d** 86 **p** 86. NSM Gt Parndon *Chelmsf* from 86. *Great Hyde Hall, Sawbridgeworth, Herts CM21 9JA* Bishop's Stortford (0279) 723953

WODEHOUSE, Lady Carol Lylie. b 51. St Hugh's Coll Ox BA73 CertEd74 MA77. Ripon Coll Cuddesdon 87. **d** 89. NSM Hambleden Valley *Ox* from 89. *Derry House, Northend, Henley-on-Thames, Oxon RG9 6LQ* Turville Heath (049163) 293

WODEMAN, Cyril Peter Guy. b 28. ARCO54 LRAM58 ARCM58 Qu Coll Cam BA50 MA55. Cranmer Hall Dur 72. **d** 73 **p** 74. C Penwortham St Mary *Blackb* 73-77; V Burnley St Steph 77-85; V Hornby w Claughton from 85. *The Vicarage, Main Street, Hornby, Lancaster LA2 8JY* Hornby (05242) 21238

WOLFE, Dr Kenneth Wesley. b 19. QUB MB42. Linc Th Coll 52. **d** 57 **p** 61. C Rugby St Matt *Cov* 76-80; Hon C Northn St Alb *Pet* 80-84; rtd 84; Perm to Offic *Pet* from 84. *40 Greenfield Avenue, Northampton NN3 2AF* Northampton (0604) 406369

WOLFE, Canon Michael Matheson. b 29. Pemb Coll Ox BA49 MA53. Cuddesdon Coll 51. **d** 53 **p** 54. C Moorfields *Bris* 53-57; P-in-c Fochabers *Mor* 57-58; Sub-Warden Aberlour Orphanage 58-59; V Southport St Paul *Liv*

59-65; V Upholland 65-73; TR 73-82; RD Ormskirk 78-82; Hon Can Liv Cathl 78-82; Merseyside Ecum Officer from 82; Can Res Liv Cathl from 82; AD Toxteth and Wavertree from 89. *23 Hunters Lane, Liverpool L15 8HL*   051-733 1541

WOLFENDEN, Peter Graham. b 40. St Pet Coll Ox BA63 MA66. Linc Th Coll 62. **d** 64 **p** 65. C Adlington *Blackb* 64-66; Asst Master Barton Peveril Gr Sch 66-69; Chapl Bp Wordsworth Sch Salisbury 69-72; Hon C Ponteland *Newc* from 72; Hd Master Coates Middle Sch Ponteland from 78. *16 Fern Avenue, Jesmond, Newcastle upon Tyne NE2 2QT*   091-281 9346

WOLFF, Curt Heinz. b 20. St Paul's Grahamstown LTh65. **d** 64 **p** 65. S Africa 64-86; Hon C Allendale w Whitfield *Newc* from 86. *2 The Villas, Whitfield, Hexham, Northd NE47 8HA*   Haltwhistle (0434) 345314

WOLLASTON, Canon Barbara Kathleen. b 30. LSE BSc(Soc)64. Gilmore Ho 51. **d** 87. Dir Past Studies Qu Coll Birm 80-89; Dioc Dir of Ords *S'wark* from 89. *29 Cornwall Road, Sutton, Surrey SM2 6DU*   081-642 6554

WOLLEY, John. BSc. **d** 85 **p** 86. Hon C Croydon St Aug *S'wark* 85-89; Perm to Offic *Linc* from 89. *7 Royal Oak Court, Upgate, Louth, Lincs*   Louth (0507) 601614

WOLLEY, Richard. b 33. Ox Univ MA. S Dios Minl Tr Scheme 82. **d** 85 **p** 86. NSM Brighton Resurr *Chich* 85-88; C 88-89; C Brighton St Geo w St Anne and St Mark from 89. *28 Henley Road, Brighton BN2 5NA*   Brighton (0273) 607876

WOLSTENCROFT, Canon Alan. b 37. Cuddesdon Coll. **d** 69 **p** 70. C Halliwell St Thos *Man* 69-71; C Stand 71-73; V Wythenshawe St Martin 73-80; AD Withington 78-91; Chapl Wythenshawe Hosp Man 80-89; V Baguley *Man* 80-91; Hon Can Man Cathl from 86; V Bolton St Pet from 91. *St Peter's Vicarage, Churchgate, Bolton BL1 1PS*   Bolton (0204) 33847

WOLSTENHULME, Arthur James. b 20. Leeds Univ BA42. Coll of Resurr Mirfield 42. **d** 44 **p** 46. R Kingsthorpe *Pet* 66-73; TR Kingsthorpe w Northn St Dav 73-86; rtd 86; Perm to Offic *Pet* from 86. *2 Springbanks Way, Northampton NN4 0QA*   Northampton (0604) 766405

WOLVERHAMPTON, Suffragan Bishop of. See MAYFIELD, Rt Rev Christopher John

WOMERSLEY, Walter John. b 28. AKC52. **d** 53 **p** 54. C Linc St Pet-at-Gowts *Linc* 53-59; S Rhodesia 59-65; Rhodesia 65-70; S Africa 70-87; C E and W Keal *Linc* 87-90; Chapl St Jas Choir Sch Grimsby from 90. *St James's School, 22 Bargate, Grimsby, S Humberside DN34 4SY*

WONNACOTT, Charles Edward. b 14. Wycliffe Hall Ox 62. **d** 63 **p** 64. C Sidley *Chich* 70-73; P-in-c Peasmarsh 73-76; R Beckley and Peasmarsh 76-81; rtd 81; Perm to Offic *Win* from 81. *The Grove, 3 Cedar Avenue, St Leonards, Ringwood, Hants BH24 2QF*   Ferndown (0202) 895457

WOOD, Ann Rene. b 49. St Deiniol's Hawarden 87. **d** 90. Par Dn Bamber Bridge St Aid *Blackb* from 90. *17 Station Road, Bamber Bridge, Preston, Lancs PR5 6QR*   Preston (0772) 312663

WOOD, Anthony James. b 38. Kelham Th Coll 58. **d** 63 **p** 64. C Shrewsbury St Almund *Lich* 63; C Harlescott 63-66; C Porthill 66-70; P-in-c Priorslee 70-76; Chapl Telford Town Cen 73-74; V Barton under Needwood from 76. *The Vicarage, Barton under Needwood, Burton-on-Trent DE13 8HU*   Barton under Needwood (0283) 712359

WOOD, Ven Arnold. b 18. Clifton Th Coll 66. **d** 65 **p** 66. V Mt Pellon *Wakef* 67-73; R Lanreath *Truro* 73-81; V Pelynt 73-81; RD W Wivelshire 76-81; Lib Truro Cathl 81-88; Can Res Truro Cathl 81-88; Adn Cornwall 81-88; Warden Community of the Epiphany Truro from 85; rtd 88. *Cobblers, Quethiock, Liskeard, Cornwall PL14 3SQ*   Liskeard (0579) 44788

WOOD, Barry. b 56. CQSW81 CYCW81 Open Univ BA87. St Steph Ho Ox 87. **d** 89 **p** 90. C Tranmere St Paul w St Luke *Ches* from 89. *St Paul's House, 48 Hesketh Avenue, Birkenhead, Merseyside L42 6RS*   051-644 7414

WOOD, Miss Beryl Jean. b 54. Linc Th Coll 85. **d** 87. C Gaywood, Bawsey and Mintlyn *Nor* from 87. *Church Bungalow, Gayton Road, King's Lynn, Norfolk PE30 4DZ*   King's Lynn (0553) 766552

WOOD, Canon Brian Frederick. b 31. Leeds Univ BA52. Coll of Resurr Mirfield 55. **d** 57 **p** 58. C Wigan St Anne *Liv* 57-60; C Elland *Wakef* 60-63; V Carlinghow 63-73; V Drighlington from 73; RD Birstall from 83; Hon Can Wakef Cathl from 89. *The Vicarage, Drighlington, Bradford, W Yorkshire BD11 1LS*   Leeds (0532) 852402

WOOD, Charles Laver. b 14. Wells Th Coll 66. **d** 68 **p** 69. C Stoke *Cov* 68-71; V Ramsey w Lt Oakley *Chelmsf* 71-85; P-in-c Wrabness w Wix 82-85; V Ramsey w Lt Oakley and Wrabness 85-88; RD Harwich 81-87; rtd 88. *9 Richards Way, Salisbury, Wilts SP2 8NT*

WOOD, Christoper William. b 44. Rhodes Univ Grahamstown BA66 Univ of S Africa BTh82. St Bede's Coll Umtata 79. **d** 80 **p** 82. S Africa 80-87; C Houghton Regis *St Alb* from 87. *The New Clergy House, Lowry Drive, Houghton Regis, Dunstable, Beds LU5 5SJ*   Dunstable (0582) 863292

WOOD, Colin Arthur. b 41. CEng MICE68 MIStructE68. S'wark Ord Course 86. **d** 89 **p** 90. C Tadworth *S'wark* from 89. *22 Station Approach Road, Tadworth, Surrey KT20 5AD*   Tadworth (0737) 812006

WOOD, Canon David Abell. b 25. Qu Coll Cam BA50 MA54. Wells Th Coll 50. **d** 50 **p** 51. C Bodmin *Truro* 50-52; Ind Chapl *Lich* 52-55; P-in-c Wolv St Geo 55-56; Warden St Geo Ho Wolv 56-67; V Wolv St Geo 56-67; Perm to Offic *Heref* 67-70; Warden Communicare Ho *Newc* 70-88; V Mitford from 88; Chapl Northgate Mental Handicap Unit Morpeth from 88; Hon Can Newc Cathl *Newc* from 88. *The Vicarage, Mitford, Morpeth, Northd NE61 3PZ*   Morpeth (0670) 512527

WOOD, David Arthur. b 30. Man Univ BA51 DSA55. Lich Th Coll 59. **d** 61 **p** 62. C Ashton Ch Ch *Man* 61-64; C Elton All SS 64-68; Dioc Youth Adv *Newc* 68-72; R Cramlington 72-73; TR 73-83; V Walham 83-86; TV Egremont and Haile *Carl* from 86. *1 Bridge End Park, Egremont, Cumbria CA22 2RE*   Egremont (0946) 822051

WOOD, David Christopher. b 52. Oak Hill Th Coll DipHE91. **d** 91. C Kendal St Thos *Carl* from 91. *6 Caroline Street, Kendal, Cumbria LA9 4SH*   Kendal (0539) 728482

WOOD, David Michael. b 39. Chich Th Coll. **d** 82 **p** 83. C Epping St Jo *Chelmsf* 82-85; C Totton *Win* 85-88; V Southway *Ex* from 88. *The Vicarage, 70 Inchkeith Road, Plymouth PL6 6EJ*   Plymouth (0752) 771938

WOOD, Dennis William. b 28. Qu Mary Coll Lon BSc53 Glas Univ PhD57. NE Ord Course 82. **d** 85 **p** 85. NSM Stanhope *Dur* 85-86; NSM Stanhope w Frosterley from 86; NSM Eastgate w Rookhope from 86. *The Vicarage, Frosterley, Bishop Auckland, Co Durham DL13 2QT*   Weardale (03885) 527320

WOOD, Edward Berryman. b 33. Ely Th Coll 54. **d** 57 **p** 58. C Aldershot St Mich *Guildf* 57-60; C Worplesdon 60-62; V Littleport St Matt *Ely* 62-64; V Balham St Jo Bedf Hill *S'wark* 64-71; V New Eltham All SS 71-84; RD Eltham (Sub-deanery) 79-82; P-in-c Woldingham from 84. *The Rectory, Woldingham, Caterham, Surrey CR3 7DB*   Caterham (0883) 652192

WOOD, Edward Francis. b 28. Chich Th Coll 56. **d** 58 **p** 59. C Newc St Fran *Newc* 58-62; C High Elswick St Phil 62-64; C Delaval 64-67; C-in-c Shiremoor CD 67-68; Dioc Broadcasting Adv 68-78; V Shiremoor 68-78; C Newc St Geo 78-82; C Newc Epiphany from 82. *52 Albemarle Avenue, Jesmond, Newcastle upon Tyne NE2 3NQ*   091-284 5338

WOOD, Eric Basil. b 25. St Edm Hall Ox BA50 MA50. Cuddesdon Coll 50. **d** 51 **p** 52. P-in-c Drayton St Pet (Berks) *Ox* 68-72; V 72-81; P-in-c Buckland 81-84; V 84-88; P-in-c Littleworth 81-84; V 84-88; P-in-c Pusey 81-84; R 84-88; Master Hugh Sexey's Hosp Bruton from 88; rtd 89. *The Master's House, Hugh Sexey's Hospital, Bruton, Somerset BA10 0AS*   Bruton (0749) 813369

WOOD, Eric Stanley. b 16. AKC40. **d** 40 **p** 41. R Lowton St Luke *Liv* 64-81; rtd 81. *12 Cranham Avenue, Lowton, Warrington WA3 2PQ*   Leigh (0942) 674045

WOOD, Ernest Charles Anthony. b 06. RMA 25. Wycliffe Hall Ox 52. **d** 53 **p** 54. R Nurstead w Ifield *Roch* 55-78; rtd 78. *14 Maryland Drive, Barming, Maidstone, Kent ME16 9EW*   Maidstone (0622) 27120

WOOD, Francis Gilbert. b 10. Bp Wilson Coll 31. **d** 34 **p** 35. R Ditchingham w Pirnough *Nor* 69-76; R Hedenham 71-76; R Broome 75-76; rtd 76. *3 Bligh Close, Framingham Earl, Norwich NR14 7SF*   Framingham Earl (05086) 3929

WOOD, Frederick Leonard. b 19. BEM59. Worc Ord Coll. **d** 64 **p** 65. V Charles w St Matthias Plymouth *Ex* 68-81; rtd 82; Perm to Offic *B & W* from 85. *The Brambles, 3 Windrush Heights, Hartsleap Road, Camberley, Surrey GU17 8ET*

WOOD, Geoffrey. b 33. Tyndale Hall Bris 56. **d** 61 **p** 62. C Tranmere St Cath *Ches* 61-64; C Newburn *Newc* 64-68; R Gt Smeaton w Appleton upon Wiske *Ripon* 69-79; P-in-c Cowton w Birkby 73-79; P-in-c Danby Wiske w Yafforth and Hutton Bonville 76-79; R Gt Smeaton w Appleton Wiske and Birkby etc 79-89; P-in-c

Bishop Monkton and Burton Leonard 89. *9 Gordon's Bank, Eggleston, Barnard Castle, Co Durham*

WOOD, Geoffrey James. b 47. Nor Ord Course 88. **d** 91. C Stainton-in-Cleveland *York* from 91. *116 Cedarwood Glade, Stainton, Middlesbrough, Cleveland TS8 9DL* Middlesbrough (0642) 597615

WOOD, George Albert. b 22. St Paul's Grahamstown. **d** 54 **p** 55. S Africa 63-77; Area Sec (Dio Chich) USPG from 78; TV Littlehampton and Wick *Chich* 86-88; rtd 88. *3 Orchard Gardens, Rustington, Littlehampton, W Sussex BN16 3HS* Rustington (0903) 787746

WOOD, George John Edmund. b 09. ACP50. Roch Th Coll 69. **d** 70 **p** 71. C Thornton Heath St Jude *Cant* 70-72; C W Wickham St Mary 72-76; rtd 76; Perm to Offic *Chich* from 76. *91 Cross Road, Southwick, Brighton BN4 4HH* Brighton (0273) 591755

WOOD, George Robert. b 26. Em Coll Cam BA52. Oak Hill Th Coll 52. **d** 53 **p** 54. R Watermillock *Carl* 61-74; V Holme Eden 74-76; Chapl Lindley Lodge N Yorkshire 76-78; C Kingston upon Hull H Trin *York* 78-80; V Chipping *Blackb* 80-81; P-in-c Whitewell 80-81; V Chipping and Whitewell 82-83; R Bunwell w Carleton Rode and Tibenham *Nor* 83-88; P-in-c Wray w Tatham Fells *Blackb* 88-89; rtd 89. *5 Rimington Way, Penrith, Cumbria CA11 8TG* Penrith (0768) 890177

WOOD, Gordon Cooper. b 20. St Pet Hall Ox BA43 MA46. Wycliffe Hall Ox. **d** 44 **p** 45. V Roundhay St Jo *Ripon* 65-90; rtd 90. *Flat 55, Moorland Drive, Moortown, Leeds LS17 6JP*

WOOD, Lt-Col Gordon Edward. b 12. Ely Th Coll 63. **d** 64 **p** 65. R Houghton *Ely* 66-74; R Wyton 66-74; V Billingborough *Linc* 74-80; V Horbling 75-80; V Sempringham w Pointon and Birthorpe 75-80; rtd 80; C Broughton *Ely* 81-91. *4 Kings Hedges, St Ives, Huntingdon, Cambs PE17 4XR* St Ives (0480) 61806

WOOD, Harold George. b 08. Lon Univ BD34. Lon Coll of Div 31. **d** 34 **p** 35. V Bitton *Bris* 70-74; rtd 74; Hon C Sutton New Town St Barn *S'wark* 75-83; Perm to Offic from 83. *1 Blenkarne Road, London SW11 6HZ* 071-228 9071

WOOD, Jack Barrington. b 24. St Aug Coll Cant 56. **d** 57 **p** 58. V Bradpole *Sarum* 65-74; rtd 89. *37 Princess Road, Bridport, Dorset DT6 5AZ*

WOOD, Miss Jane. b 38. Wye Coll Lon BSc59. St Jo Coll Nottm LTh89. **d** 89. NSM Newtown w Llanllwchaiarn w Aberhafesp *St As* from 89. *The Rectory Close, Old Kerry Road, Newtown, Powys SY22 6RN* Newtown (0686) 622309

WOOD, John. b 37. **d** 77 **p** 79. NSM Dunbar *Edin* from 77; NSM Haddington from 77. *7 Herdmanflatt, Haddington, East Lothian EH41 3LN* Haddington (062082) 2838

WOOD, John Anthony Scriven. b 48. Leeds Univ BSc70. St Jo Coll Nottm 76. **d** 79 **p** 80. C Colwich *Lich* 79-82; C W Bridgford *S'well* 82-90; R Gamston and Bridgford from 90. *59 Burleigh Road, Nottingham NG2 6FQ* Nottingham (0602) 235070

WOOD, John Arthur. b 23. Roch Th Coll 68. **d** 70 **p** 71. C Wetherby *Ripon* 70-71; P-in-c Sheff Arbourthorne *Sheff* 71-75; TV Sheff Manor 75-81; R Rodney Stoke w Draycott *B & W* 81-88; rtd 88. *36 Vicarage Crescent, Grenoside, Sheffield S30 3RE* Sheffield (0742) 460272

WOOD, John Maurice. b 58. Qu Coll Cam BA80 MA83. Wycliffe Hall Ox BA87. **d** 87 **p** 88. C Northwood Em *Lon* 87-91; C Muswell Hill St Jas w St Matt from 91. *8 St James's Lane, London N10 3DB* 081-883 0636

WOOD, John Samuel. b 47. Lanchester Poly BSc69 Sheff Univ DipEd. Westcott Ho Cam 72. **d** 81 **p** 82. NSM Haverhill *St E* 81-83; C Haverhill w Withersfield, the Wrattings etc 83; C Whitton and Thurleston w Akenham 83-86; P-in-c Walsham le Willows 86-88; P-in-c Finningham w Westhorpe 86-88; R Walsham le Willows and Finningham w Westhorpe from 88; Min Can St E Cathl from 89. *The Priory, Walsham-le-Willows, Bury St Edmunds, Suffolk IP33 1RS* Walsham-le-Willows (0359) 259310

WOOD, Keith. b 49. St Steph Ho Ox 76. **d** 78 **p** 79. C Bognor *Chich* 78-81; C Hangleton 81-83; R W Blatchington 83-87; V W Worthing St Jo from 87. *St John's Vicarage, 15 Reigate Road, Worthing, W Sussex BN11 5NF* Worthing (0903) 47340

WOOD, Keith Ernest. b 33. Qu Coll Ox BA55 BCL56 DipTh57 MA70. Wycliffe Hall Ox 56. **d** 58 **p** 59. C Barking St Marg *Chelmsf* 58-61; Min Basildon St Andr ED 61-70; V Brampton Bierlow *Sheff* 70-82; R Grasmere *Carl* from 82; RD Windermere from 89. *The Rectory, Grasmere, Ambleside, Cumbria LA22 9SW* Grasmere (05394) 35326

WOOD, Laurence Henry. b 27. Kelham Th Coll 47. **d** 52 **p** 53. C Ravensthorpe *Wakef* 52-55; C Almondbury 55-58; V Linthwaite 58-64; R Bonsall *Derby* 64-70; V Cromford 64-70; V Longwood *Wakef* 70-76; V Liversedge from 76. *Christ Church Vicarage, Knowler Hill, Liversedge, W Yorkshire WF15 6LJ* Heckmondwike (0924) 402414

WOOD, Mrs Lorna. b 43. E Anglian Minl Tr Course 85. **d** 88. Hon C Sprowston *Nor* 88-90; Hon C Sprowston w Beeston from 90. *39 Inman Road, Norwich NR7 8JT* Norwich (0603) 408710

✠**WOOD, Rt Rev Maurice Arthur Ponsonby.** b 16. DSC44. Qu Coll Cam BA38 MA42. Ridley Hall Cam 40. **d** 40 **p** 41 **c** 71. C Portman Square St Paul *Lon* 40-43; Chapl RNVR 43-46; R Ox St Ebbe *Ox* 47-52; V Islington St Mary *Lon* 52-61; RD Islington 52-61; Prin Oak Hill Th Coll 61-71; Preb St Paul's Cathl *Lon* 69-71; Bp Nor 71-85; Chapl RNR from 71; rtd 85; Asst Bp Lon from 85; Hon C Theale and Englefield *Ox* from 88; Asst Bp Ox from 89. *St Mark's House, Englefield, Reading RG7 5EN* Reading (0734) 302227

WOOD, Michael Frank. b 55. Nottm Univ BCombStuds. Linc Th Coll. **d** 84 **p** 85. C Marton *Blackb* 84-88; TV Ribbleton from 88. *The Ascension House, 450 Watling Street Road, Preston, Lancs PR2 6TU* Preston (0772) 700568

WOOD, Nicholas Martin. b 51. AKC74. **d** 75 **p** 76. C E Ham w Upton Park *Chelmsf* 75-78; C Leyton St Luke 78-81; V Rush Green 81-91; Chapl Barking Tech Coll 81-91; TR Elland *Wakef* from 91. *Elland Rectory, 50 Victoria Road, Elland, W Yorkshire HX5 0QA* Elland (0422) 72133

WOOD, Nowell Wakeley. b 07. FRICS46. Ripon Hall Ox 63. **d** 64 **p** 65. R Halstead *Roch* 67-75; rtd 75; Perm to Offic *Chich* from 80. *3 Broadwater Down, Tunbridge Wells, Kent TN2 5NJ* Tunbridge Wells (0892) 25089

WOOD, Peter Palmer. b 36. Nottm Univ BA58. Bps' Coll Cheshunt 58. **d** 60 **p** 61. C Aldrington *Chich* 60-64; C Brighton St Matthias 64-67; C Lewes St Anne 67-70; C The Quinton *Birm* 70-72; V Kirkby Wharfe *York* 72-85; V Riccall from 85. *The Vicarage, Church Street, Riccall, York YO4 6PN* Selby (0757) 248326

WOOD, Peter Thomas. b 31. Clifton Th Coll 57. **d** 60 **p** 61. C Woodford Wells *Chelmsf* 60-63; SAMS 63-72; Chile 63-72; V Clevedon Ch Ch *B & W* 72-82; Chapl St Brandon's Sch Clevedon 72-82; Chapl Heref Gen Hosp from 82; V Heref St Pet w St Owen and St Jas *Heref* from 82; Chapl to Police from 86; RD Heref City from 90. *St James's Vicarage, 102 Green Street, Hereford HR1 2QW* Hereford (0432) 273676

WOOD, Philip Hervey. b 42. Sarum & Wells Th Coll 73. **d** 74 **p** 75. C Cov H Trin *Cov* 74-75; C Finham 75-77; C Wandsworth Common St Mary *S'wark* 78-81; R Bodiam *Chich* 81-87; R Ewhurst 81-87; Asst Chapl HM Pris Wandsworth 88-89. *Address temp unknown*

WOOD, Philip James. b 48. Bris Univ BSc69. Oak Hill Th Coll 71. **d** 74 **p** 75. C Islington St Mary *Lon* 74-77; C Stapenhill w Cauldwell *Derby* 77-80; V Walthamstow St Luke *Chelmsf* from 80; RD Waltham Forest from 89. *St Luke's Vicarage, Greenleaf Road, London E17 6QQ* 081-520 2885

WOOD, Raymond John Lee. b 28. ACII55 ACIArb. Linc Th Coll 66. **d** 68 **p** 69. C Beaconsfield *Ox* 68-72; CF 70-72; V Wath-upon-Dearne w Adwick-upon-Dearne *Sheff* 72-77; R St Tudy w Michaelstow *Truro* 77-86; P-in-c St Mabyn 82-86; R St Tudy w St Mabyn and Michaelstow from 86; Chapl Bodmin Fire Brigade from 91. *The Rectory, St Tudy, Bodmin, Cornwall PL30 3NH* Bodmin (0208) 850374

WOOD, Reginald John. b 16. Worc Ord Coll 61. **d** 63 **p** 64. V The Seavingtons w Lopen *B & W* 68-80; rtd 81; Perm to Offic *Ex* from 82. *Downside, Station Road, Budleigh Salterton, Devon EX9 6RW* Budleigh Salterton (03954) 2389

✠**WOOD, Rt Rev Richard James.** b 20. Wells Th Coll 51. **d** 52 **p** 53 **c** 73. C Calne *Sarum* 52-55; S Africa 55-73; Namibia 73-77; Suff Bp Damaraland 73-77; Asst Bp Damaraland 77; V Kingston upon Hull St Mary *York* 77-79; Chapl Hull Coll of HE 77-79; Tanzania 79-85; rtd 85; Asst Bp York 79 and from 85. *90 Park Lane, Cottingham, N Humberside HU16 5RX* Hull (0482) 843928

WOOD, Richard Olivier Ronald. b 19. TCD BA42 MA51. **d** 43 **p** 44. CF 47-74; V Kemble w Poole Keynes *Glouc* 74-77; V Kemble, Poole Keynes, Somerford Keynes etc 77-81; rtd 81. *73 Newbarn Lane, Prestbury, Cheltenham, Glos GL52 3LB* Cheltenham (0242) 57752

WOOD, Roger Graham. b 49. K Coll Lon BD. Chich Th Coll 74. **d** 76 **p** 77. C Skipton H Trin *Bradf* 76-79; Dioc

Youth Chapl 79-87; V Queensbury from 87. *7 Russell Hall Lane, Queensbury, Bradford, W Yorkshire BD13 2AJ* Bradford (0274) 880573

WOOD, Roger William. b 43. Leeds Univ BA65 MA67 Fitzw Coll Cam BA69 MA75. Westcott Ho Cam 67. d 70 p 71. C Bishop's Stortford St Mich *St Alb* 70-74; C Sundon w Streatley 75-79; V Streatley from 80. *17 Sundon Road, Streatley, Luton* Luton (0582) 882780

WOOD, Ron. b 49. Sarum & Wells Th Coll 79. d 81 p 82. C Weston-super-Mare Cen Par *B & W* 81-84; C Forest of Dean Ch Ch w English Bicknor *Glouc* 84-88; R Handley w Gussage St Andrew and Pentridge *Sarum* from 88. *The Vicarage, 60 High Street, Sixpenny Handley, Salisbury SP5 5ND* Handley (0725) 52608

WOOD, Stanley Charles. b 26. Glouc Th Course. d 83 p 84. NSM Lower Cam w Coaley *Glouc* 83-87; P-in-c Shipton Moyne w Westonbirt and Lasborough from 87. *The Rectory, Shipton Moyne, Tetbury, Glos GL8 8PW* Westonbirt (066688) 244

✠**WOOD, Rt Rev Stanley Mark.** b 19. Univ of Wales BA40. Coll of Resurr Mirfield 40. d 42 p 43 c 71. C Cardiff St Mary *Llan* 42-45; S Africa 45-55; S Rhodesia 55-65; Rhodesia 65-77; Can Mashonaland 61-65; Dean Salisbury 65-71; Bp Matabeleland 71-77; Asst Bp Heref 77-81; Preb Heref Cathl 77-87; Suff Bp Ludlow 81-87; Adn Ludlow 82-83; rtd 87. *Glen Cottage, The Norton, Tenby, Dyfed SA70 8AG* Tenby (0834) 3463

WOOD, Sylvia Marian. b 40. Gilmore Ho 77. dss 80 d 87. Tolleshunt Knights w Tiptree *Chelmsf* 80-83; Leigh-on-Sea St Jas 83-86; Canvey Is 86-87; Par Dn from 87; Miss to Seamen from 87; Warden of Ords *Chelmsf* from 89. *17 The Ridings, Canvey Island, Essex SS8 9QZ* Canvey Island (0268) 682586

WOOD, Thomas Henry. Glassboro Coll (USA) BEcon84. St D Coll Lamp 57. d 60 p 61. C Pontnewynydd *Mon* 60-62; C Middlesb All SS *York* 64-69; C Fleetwood *Blackb* 69-73; V Ferndale *Llan* 73-77; C Sheff Parson Cross St Cecilia *Sheff* from 88. *St Cecilia's Priory, Chaucer Close, Sheffield S5 9QE* Sheffield (0742) 321084

WOOD, Canon Thomas Patrick Scarborough. b 19. TCD BA41 BD54. d 42 p 43. C Portarlington w Ballykean and Cloneyhurke *M & K* 42-44; C Dub St Geo *D & G* 44-46; I Rathaspick w Russagh and Streete *K, E & A* 46-56; P-in-c Ballysumaghan 46-49; I Calry from 56; RD S Elphin 67-75; Preb Elphin Cathl 67-83; Preb Mulhuddart St Patr Cathl Dub from 83. *Calry Rectory, The Mall, Sligo, Irish Republic* Sligo (71) 42656

✠**WOOD, Rt Rev Dr Wilfred Denniston.** b 36. Lambeth DipHT62 Gen Th Sem (NY) Hon DD86 Codrington Coll Barbados 57. d 61 p 62 c 85. C Hammersmith St Steph *Lon* 62-63; C Shepherd's Bush St Steph w St Thos 63-74; Bp's Chapl for Community Relns 67-74; V Catford St Laur *S'wark* 74-82; Hon Can S'wark Cathl 77-82; RD E Lewisham 77-82; Boro Dean of S'wark 82-85; Adn S'wark 82-85; Suff Bp Croydon 85-91; Area Bp Croydon from 91. *53 Stanhope Road, Croydon CR0 5NS* 081-686 1822

WOOD, William. b 03. St Jo Coll Morpeth 28 ACT ThL31. d 31 p 32. OGS from 28; Chapl and Trustee Lon Healing Miss 68-71; rtd 71; Perm to Offic *Ox & S'wark* from 83. *32 The Maltings, Kennet Road, Newbury, Berks RG14 5HZ* Newbury (0635) 523447

WOOD, William Alfred. b 16. FCIS63. Qu Coll Birm 73. d 74 p 75. NSM Sutton Coldfield H Trin *Birm* from 74. *1 Vaughton Drive, Sutton Coldfield, W Midlands B75 6AQ* 021-378 4061

WOOD, William George. b 31. Oak Hill Th Coll 61. d 63 p 64. C Woking St Jo *Guildf* 63-69; V Camberwell All SS *S'wark* 69-88; R Horne from 88; P-in-c Outwood from 88. *The Rectory, Church Road, Horne, Horley, Surrey RH6 9LA* Smallfield (034284) 2054

WOODALL, Hugh Gregory. b 11. Keble Coll Ox BA33 MA37. Cuddesdon Coll 33. d 34 p 35. V Boston Spa *York* 55-80; RD Tadcaster 72-78; rtd 80. *Kirklea, Gracious Street, Huby, York YO6 1HR* York (0904) 810705

WOODALL, Reginald Homer. b 38. Univ of Wales DipTh59. St Mich Coll Llan 59. d 61 p 62. C Newtown w Llanllwchaiarn w Aberhafesp *St As* 61-65; C Rhosddu 65-66; C Hawarden 66-70; CF 70-74; C Thornton Heath St Jude *Cant* 74-77; TV Cannock *Lich* 77-79; TV Basildon St Martin w H Cross and Laindon etc *Chelmsf* 79-84; P-in-c Canning Town St Cedd from 84. *St Cedd's Vicarage, 301 Newham Way, London E16 4ED* 071-474 3711

WOODBRIDGE, Trevor Geoffrey. b 31. Lon Univ BSc52. ALCD57. d 58 p 59. C Bitterne *Win* 58-61; C Ilkeston St Mary *Derby* 61-65; Area Sec (Dios Ex and Truro)

CMS 65-81; SW Regional Sec 70-81; TV Clyst St George, Aylesbeare, Clyst Honiton etc *Ex* 82-84; V Aylesbeare, Rockbeare, Farringdon etc from 85. *The Vicarage, Rockbeare, Exeter EX5 2EG* Whimple (0404) 822569

WOODBURN, William John. b 19. St Aug Coll Cant 61. d 62 p 63. V Bridgwater H Trin *B & W* 70-78; C Midsomer Norton 78-82; rtd 83; Perm to Offic *B & W & Bris* from 83. *32 Canterbury Close, Weston-super-Mare, Avon BS22 0TS* Weston-super-Mare (0934) 514490

WOODCOCK, Nicholas Ethelbert. b 46. FRSA90. Cant Sch of Min 80. d 90 p 91. Chief Exec and Co Sec Keston Coll Kent from 89; NSM Clerkenwell H Redeemer w St Phil *Lon* from 90. *The Clergy House, 24 Exmouth Market, London EC1R 4QE* 071-837 1861

WOODD, Basil John. b 07. Jes Coll Cam BA31 MA35. Westcott Ho Cam 31. d 32 p 33. R Gt Gonerby *Linc* 59-68; rtd 68. *College of St Barnabas, Blackberry Lane, Lingfield, Surrey RH7 6NJ* Dormans Park (034287) 260

WOODERSON, Marguerite Ann. b 44. RGN SCM. Qu Coll Birm 86. d 89. Par Dn Stoneydelph St Martin CD *Lich* 89-90; Par Dn Glascote and Stonydelph from 90. *The Vicarage, 158A High Street, Chasetown, Walsall WS7 8XG* Burntwood (0543) 686276

WOODERSON, Preb Michael George. b 39. Southn Univ BA61. Lon Coll of Div BD69. d 69 p 70. C Morden *S'wark* 69-73; C Aldridge *Lich* 73-81; V Chasetown from 81; RD Lich from 86; Preb Lich Cathl from 89. *The Vicarage, 158A High Street, Chasetown, Walsall WS7 8XG* Burntwood (0543) 686276

WOODERSON, Timothy George Arthur. b 39. St Chad's Coll Dur BA61 DipTh63. d 63 p 64. C S w N Hayling *Portsm* 63-66; Papua New Guinea 66-70; C Rowner *Portsm* 71-77; R Bermondsey St Mary w St Olave, St Jo etc *S'wark* 78-89; V Redhill St Jo from 89. *St John's Vicarage, Church Road, Redhill RH1 6QA* Redhill (0737) 766562

WOODFIELD, Robert Ronald. b 13. Ch Coll Cam BA35 MA49. Ridley Hall Cam 35. d 37 p 38. R Shaw cum Donnington *Ox* 53-71; R Leadenham *Linc* 71-78; R Welbourn 73-78; rtd 78. *Laurenti, Rolls Bridge, Gillingham, Dorset SP8 4BB* Gillingham (0747) 822522

WOODFORD, Frank. b 14. d 53 p 54. V Billinghay *Linc* 68-79; rtd 79. *13 Flintham Close, Metheringham, Lincoln LN4 3EW* Metheringham (0526) 21288

WOODGATE, Douglas Digby. b 09. Bris Univ BA32. Wells Th Coll 33. d 34 p 35. V Elkesley w Bothamsall *S'well* 45-80; rtd 80; Perm to Offic *S'well* from 80. *4 Elm Tree Court, Potter Street, Worksop, Notts* Worksop (0909) 484740

WOODGATE, Michael James. b 35. Dur Univ BA60. St Steph Ho Ox 60. d 62 p 63. C Streatham St Pet *S'wark* 62-69; V 69-84; RD Streatham 78-84; R St Magnus the Martyr w St Marg New Fish Street *Lon* from 84; P-in-c St Clem Eastcheap w St Martin Orgar from 89. *St Magnus' Vestry House, Lower Thames Street, London EC3R 6DN* 071-626 4481

WOODGER, John McRae. b 36. Tyndale Hall Bris 60. d 63 p 64. C Heref St Pet w St Owen *Heref* 63-66; C Macclesfield St Mich *Ches* 66-69; V Llangarron w Llangrove *Heref* 69-74; P-in-c Garway 70-74; R Church Stretton 74-84; Preb Heref Cathl 82-84; V Watford *St Alb* from 84. *20 Devereux Drive, Watford WD1 3DE* Watford (0923) 54005 or 225189

WOODGER, John Page. b 30. Master Mariner 56 Lon Univ DipTh58. St Aid Birkenhead 56. d 59 p 60. C Kimberworth *Sheff* 59-62; Chapl HM Borstal Pollington 62-70; C Goole *Sheff* 62-63; V Balne 63-70; C Halesowen *Worc* 70-74; V Cookley 74-81; TV Droitwich 81-85; TV Bedminster *Bris* from 85. *St Dunstan's Vicarage, 66 Bedminster Down Road, Bristol BS13 7AA* Bristol (0272) 635977

WOODGER, Richard William. b 50. Sarum & Wells Th Coll 76. d 79 p 80. C Chessington *Guildf* 79-82; C Frimley 82-85; C Frimley Green 82-85; V N Holmwood 85-90; TR Headley All SS from 90. *The Rectory, 8 Elderberry Road, Lindford, Bordon, Hants GU35 0YE* Bordon (0420) 478135

WOODHALL, Michael Leslie. b 36. d 74 p 75. C S Shields St Hilda w St Thos *Dur* 74-76; C Barnard Castle 76-78; C-in-c Bishopwearmouth St Mary V w St Pet CD 78-80; V Leeds St Cypr Harehills *Ripon* 80-83. *Address temp unknown*

WOODHALL, Peter. b 32. Edin Th Coll 57. d 60 p 61. C Carl St Barn *Carl* 60-63; Hon Chapl Estoril St Paul *Eur* 63-65; Chapl RN 66-82; TR Scilly Is *Truro* 82-90; V Mithian w Mt Hawke from 90. *The Vicarage, Mount Hawke, Truro, Cornwall TR4 8DE* Porthtowan (0209) 890926

WOODHAM, Richard Medley Swift. b 43. Master Mariner 70 DipTh. S'wark Ord Course 71. **d** 73 **p** 74. C Gravesend St Aid *Roch* 73-75; C Chessington *Guildf* 75-78; Warden Dioc Conf Ho Horstead *Nor* 78-87; R Horstead 78-87; Youth Chapl from 78; V Nor St Mary Magd w St Jas 87-91; TR Nor Over-the-Water from 91. *The Vicarage, Crome Road, Norwich NR3 4RQ* Norwich (0603) 618612

WOODHAMS, Ven Brian Watson. b 11. St Jo Coll Dur BA36. Oak Hill Th Coll 32. **d** 36 **p** 37. Adn Newark *S'well* 65-80; R Staunton w Flawborough 71-80; R Kilvington 71-80; rtd 80; Hon C Kilvington *S'well* 80-90; Hon C Staunton w Flawborough 80-90. *2 Lunn Lane, Collingham, Newark, Notts NG23 7LP* Newark (0636) 892207

WOODHAMS, Mrs Sophie Harriet. b 27. Cranmer Hall Dur 66. dss 80 **d** 87. Raveningham *Nor* 80-81; Henleaze *Bris* 81-87; rtd 87. *31 Hanover Close, Shaftgate Avenue, Shepton Mallet, Somerset BA4 5YQ* Shepton Mallet (0749) 344124

WOODHEAD, Alan Howard. b 37. Open Univ BA73. St Aid Birkenhead 62. **d** 65 **p** 66. C Kirkstall *Ripon* 65-68; C Marfleet *York* 68-71; V Barmby on the Moor w Fangfoss 71-80; Chapl R Russell Sch Croydon from 81. *Old Ballard's Cottage, Hollingsworth Road, Croydon CR0 5RP* 081-651 2756 or 657 4433

WOODHEAD, Christopher Godfrey. b 26. Pemb Coll Cam BA50 MA55. Ely Th Coll 50. **d** 52 **p** 53. C Barnsley St Edw *Wakef* 52-54; C Mill Hill St Mich *Lon* 54-58; C Sandridge *St Alb* 58-66; R Earl Stonham *St E* 66-72; V Hoo St Werburgh *Roch* 72-88; C Cheam *S'wark* from 88. *49 Brocks Drive, North Cheam, Surrey SM3 9UW* 081-641 1516

WOODHEAD, Miss Helen Mary. b 35. Bedf Coll Lon BA57. Westcott Ho Cam 86. **d** 87. Par Dn Daventry *Pet* 87-90; C Godalming *Guildf* from 90; Asst Dioc Dir of Ords from 90. *St Mark's House, 29 Franklyn Road, Godalming, Surrey GU7 2LD* Guildford (0483) 424710

WOODHEAD, Canon Henry Hamilton. b 22. TCD BA45. **d** 47 **p** 48. I Killowen *D & R* 65-91; Can Derry Cathl 81-91; rtd 91. Miss to Seamen from 91. *7 Woodland Park, Coleraine, Co Londonderry BT52 1JG* Coleraine (0265) 51382

WOODHEAD, Michael. b 51. St Jo Coll Nottm 88. **d** 90 **p** 91. C Stannington *Sheff* from 90. *50 Goodison Crescent, Stannington, Sheffield S6 5HU* Sheffield (0742) 342136

WOODHEAD, Mrs Sandra Buchanan. b 42. Man Poly BA82 Man Univ BD85. St Deiniol's Hawarden. dss 86 **d** 87. High Lane *Ches* 86-87; Hon Par Dn 87-90; Par Dn Brinnington w Portwood from 90. *Woodbank, Light Alders Lane, Disley, Stockport, Cheshire SK12 2LW* Disley (0663) 765708

WOODHEAD-KEITH-DIXON, James Addison. b 25. St Aid Birkenhead 44. **d** 48 **p** 49. C Upperby St Jo *Carl* 48-50; C Dalton-in-Furness 50-52; V Blawith w Lowick 52-59; V Lorton 59-80; Chapl Puerto de la Cruz Tenerife *Eur* 80-82; TV Bellingham/Otterburn Gp *Newc* 82-83; TR from 83. *The Rectory, Falstone, Hexham, Northd NE48 1AE* Hexham (0434) 40213

WOODHOUSE, Miss Alison Ruth. b 43. Bedf Coll of Educn CertEd64 Lon Univ DipTh70. Dalton Ho Bris 68. dss 79 **d** 87. Bayston Hill *Lich* 79-81; W Derby St Luke *Liv* 81-86; Burscough Bridge 86-87; Par Dn from 87. *32 Manor Avenue, Burscough, Ormskirk, Lancs L40 7TT* Burscough (0704) 894731

WOODHOUSE, Ven Andrew Henry. b 23. DSC45. Qu Coll Ox BA48 MA49. Linc Th Coll 48. **d** 50 **p** 51. V W Drayton 56-70; RD Hillingdon 67-70; Adn Ludlow *Heref* 70-82; R Wistanstow 70-82; P-in-c Acton Scott 70-73; Can Res Heref Cathl 82-91; Treas 82-85; Adn Heref 82-91; rtd 91. *Orchard Cottage, Bracken Close, Woking, Surrey GU22 7HD* Woking (0483) 760671

WOODHOUSE, Andrew Laurence. b 40. NW Ord Course. **d** 82 **p** 83. NSM Bedale *Ripon* from 82. *86 South End, Bedale, N Yorkshire DL8 2DS* Bedale (0677) 23573

WOODHOUSE, Ven Charles David Stewart. b 34. Kelham Th Coll 55. **d** 59 **p** 60. C Leeds Halton St Wilfrid *Ripon* 59-63; Youth Chapl *Liv* 63-66; Bermuda 66-69; Asst Gen Sec CEMS 69-70; Gen Sec 70-76; Bp's Dom Chapl *Ex* 76-81; R Ideford, Luton and Ashcombe 76-81; V Hindley St Pet *Liv* from 81; Adn Warrington from 81; Hon Can Liv Cathl from 83. *St Peter's Vicarage, Wigan Road, Hindley, Wigan, Lancs WN2 3DF* Wigan (0942) 55505

WOODHOUSE, Canon David. b 36. FRSA FCollP Selw Coll Cam BA60 MA64. St Steph Ho Ox 60. **d** 62 **p** 63. C Boston *Linc* 62-64; C Pimlico St Gabr *Lon* 64-66; Chapl Woodbridge Sch Suffolk 66-73; V Heap Bridge *Man* 73-75; Can Res Wakef Cathl *Wakef* 76-85; Dir of Educn 76-85; Hon Can Liv Cathl *Liv* from 85; Dir of Educn from 85. *5 Cathedral Close, Liverpool L1 7BR* 051-708 0942

WOODHOUSE, David Edwin. b 45. Lon Univ BSc68. Cuddesdon Coll 68. **d** 71 **p** 72. C E Dulwich St Jo *S'wark* 71-74; Lic to Offic S'wark 74-77; Perm Bris 77-79; Lic from 79. *St Augustine's Vicarage, Morris Street, Swindon SN2 2HT* Swindon (0793) 22741

WOODHOUSE, David Maurice. b 40. Lon Univ BA62. Clifton Th Coll 63. **d** 65 **p** 66. C Wellington w Eyton *Lich* 65-69; C Meole Brace 69-71; V Colwich 71-82; P-in-c Gt Haywood 78-82; R Clitheroe St Jas *Blackb* 82-88; Ellel Grange Chr Healing Cen 88-91; V The Lye and Stambermill *Worc* from 91. *The Vicarage, High Street, Lye, Stourbridge, W Midlands DY9 8LF* Lye (0384) 823142

WOODHOUSE, Hugh Frederic. b 12. TCD BA34 BD37 DD52. **d** 37 **p** 38. Regius Prof Div TCD 63-82; rtd 82. *4591 West 16th Avenue, Vancouver, British Columbia, Canada, V6R 3E8* Vancouver (604) 224-4812

WOODHOUSE, James. b 29. Lon Univ BA52. Lich Th Coll. **d** 61 **p** 62. C Whitby *York* 61-64; C Pocklington w Yapham-cum-Meltonby, Owsthorpe etc 64-66; P-in-c Roos w Tunstall 66-69; R 69-72; C Garton w Grimston and Hilston 66-69; V 69-72; V Nunthorpe 72-82; V Pocklington w Yapham-cum-Meltonby, Owsthorpe etc 82-83; P-in-c Millington w Gt Givendale 82-83; TR Pocklington Team 84-89; RD Pocklington 84-86; RD S Wold 86-90; V Coatham from 89. *9 Blenheim Terrace, Redcar, Cleveland TS10 1QP* Redcar (0642) 482870

WOODHOUSE, Canon Keith Ian. b 33. K Coll Lon 54. **d** 58 **p** 59. C Stockton St Chad CD *Dur* 58-61; C Man St Aid *Man* 61-64; V Peterlee *Dur* from 64; RD Easington from 72; Hon Can Dur Cathl from 79. *The Vicarage, Manor Way, Peterlee, Co Durham SR8 5QW* 091-586 2630

WOODHOUSE, Patrick Henry Forbes. b 47. Ch Ch Ox BA69 MA81. St Jo Coll Nottm 69 Lon Coll of Div ALCD71 LTh71. **d** 72 **p** 73. C Birm St Martin *Birm* 72-74; C Whitchurch *Bris* 75-76; C Harpenden St Nic *St Alb* 76-80; Tanzania 80-81; Soc Resp Officer *Carl* 81-85; P-in-c Dean 81-85; Dir Soc Resp *Win* 85-90; V Chippenham St Andr w Tytherton Lucas *Bris* from 90. *The Vicarage, St Mary Street, Chippenham, Wilts SN15 7JW* Chippenham (0249) 656834

WOODHOUSE, Ven Samuel Mostyn Forbes. b 12. Ch Ch Ox BA34 MA42. Wells Th Coll 35. **d** 36 **p** 37. Adn Lon and Can Res St Paul's Cathl *Lon* 67-78; rtd 78. *Under Copse Cottage, Redhill, Wrington, Bristol BS18 7SH* Wrington (0934) 862711

WOODHOUSE, William Henry. b 12. SS Coll Cam BA36 MA40. Chich Th Coll 36. **d** 38 **p** 39. R Yate *Bris* 61-74; P-in-c Wapley w Codrington and Dodington 67-71; R N Cerney w Bagendon *Glouc* 74-82; RD Cirencester 77-82; rtd 82; Perm to Offic *Glouc* from 82. *2 Burford Road, Cirencester, Glos GL7 1AF* Cirencester (0285) 658938

WOODING JONES, Andrew David. b 61. Oak Hill Th Coll BA91. **d** 91. C Welling *Roch* from 91. *52 Clifton Road, Welling, Kent DA16 1QD* 081-304 4179

WOODLAND, Robert Alan. b 29. Bps' Coll Cheshunt 59. **d** 61 **p** 62. V Oxhey All SS *St Alb* 66-76; V Hainault *Chelmsf* 76-81; R Bicknoller w Crowcombe and Sampford Brett *B & W* 81-89; rtd 90. *13 Paganel Close, Minehead, Somerset TA24 5HD* Minehead (0643) 704598

WOODLEY, David James. b 38. K Coll Lon BD61 AKC61. **d** 62 **p** 63. C Lancing St Jas *Chich* 62-64; C St Alb St Pet *St Alb* 64-67; Malaysia 67-70; Lic to Offic *Linc* 71-72; V Westoning w Tingrith *St Alb* 72-77; Asst Chapl HM Pris Wormwood Scrubs 77-78; Chapl HM Pris Cardiff 78-84; Chapl HM Rem Cen Risley from 84. *HM Remand Centre, Warrington Road, Risley, Warrington WA3 6BP* Warrington (0925) 763871

WOODLEY, Canon John Francis Chapman. b 33. Univ of Wales (Lamp) BA58. Edin Th Coll 58. **d** 60 **p** 61. C Edin St Mich and All SS *Edin* 60-65; Chapl St Andr Cathl *Ab* 65-67; Prec 67-71; R Glas St Oswald *Glas* 71-77; P-in-c Cumbernauld from 77; Can St Mary's Cathl from 82; CSG from 82. *Holy Name House, Fleming Road, Cumbernauld, Glasgow G67 1LJ* Cumbernauld (0236) 721599

WOODLEY, Ven Ronald John. b 25. Bps' Coll Cheshunt 50. **d** 53 **p** 54. V Middlesb Ascension *York* 66-71; R Stokesley 71-85; RD Stokesley 77-85; Can and Preb York Minster from 82; Adn Cleveland 85-91; rtd 91. *52 South Parade, Northallerton, N Yorkshire DL7 8SL* Northallerton (0609) 778818

WOODLIFFE, Leslie Jestyn Lewis. b 35. St Mich Coll Llan 76. d 78 p 79. C Henfynyw w Aberaeron and Llanddewi Aber-arth *St D* 78-80; V Llangeler from 80. *The Vicarage, Saron, Llandysul, Dyfed SA44 5EX* Velindre (0559) 370449

WOODMAN, Brian Baldwin. b 35. Leeds Univ BA57 PhD73. N Ord Course 84. d 87 p 88. C Guiseley w Esholt *Bradf* 87-90; TV Bingley All SS from 90. *Winston Grange, Otley Road, Eldwick, Bingley BD16 3EQ* Bradford (0274) 568266

WOODMAN, Oliver Nigel. b 47. FIPM MIPM73 HNC73. Sarum Th Coll 67. d 70 p 82. C Stepney St Dunstan and All SS *Lon* 70-71; NSM Ovingdean w Rottingdean and Woodingdean *Chich* 81-87; NSM Eastbourne St Sav and St Pet from 88. *56 Upper Kings Drive, Eastbourne, E Sussex BN20 9AS* Eastbourne (0323) 507208

WOODMAN, Canon Peter Wilfred. b 36. Univ of Wales (Lamp) BA58. Wycliffe Hall Ox 58. d 60 p 61. C New Tredegar *Mon* 60-61; C Newport St Paul 61-64; C Llanfrechfa All SS 64-66; Abp of Wales's Messenger 66-67; V Llantillio Pertholey w Bettws Chpl etc *Mon* 67-74; V Bassaleg 74-90; Can St Woolos Cathl from 84; V Caerwent w Dinham and Llanfair Discoed etc from 90. *The Vicarage, Vicarage Gardens, Caerwent, Newport, Gwent NP6 4BF* Caldicot (0291) 424984

WOODMANSEY, Michael Balfour. b 55. Leic Univ BSc. Ridley Hall Cam. d 83 p 84. C St Paul's Cray St Barn *Roch* 83-89; C S Shoebury *Chelmsf* from 89. *56 Wakering Road, Shoebury, Essex SS3 9SY* Southend-on-Sea (0702) 292078

WOODROFFE, Ian Gordon. b 46. Edin Th Coll 69. d 72 p 73. C Soham *Ely* 72-75; P-in-c Swaffham Bulbeck 75-80; Youth Chapl 75-80; V Cam St Jas 80-87; Chapl Mayday Hosp Thornton Heath from 87. *Mayday Hospital, 137 Downs Road, Coulsdon, Surrey CR5 1AD* 081-684 6999

WOODROW, Canon Norman Wilson. b 21. TCD BA44 MA50. CITC 46. d 46 p 47. C Newc *D & D* 46-50; C Leytonstone St Jo *Chelmsf* 50-54; R Pitsea 54-63; C Newtownards *D & D* 63-64; I Saintfield from 64; RD Killinchy from 79; Can Belf Cathl from 85. *11 Lisburn Road, Saintfield, Ballynahinch, Co Down BT24 7AL* Saintfield (0238) 510286

WOODRUFF, Barry Mark Edmund. b 59. St Chad's Coll Dur BA80. Coll of Resurr Mirfield 82. d 84 p 85. C Leeds Halton St Wilfrid *Ripon* 84-88; C Primrose St Gabr *Lon* 88-89; Prec St E Cathl *St E* 89-91; Min Can St E Cathl 89-91; V Grange Park St Pet *Lon* from 91; Chapl Highlands Hosp Lon from 91. *St Peter's Vicarage, Langham Gardens, London N21 1DJ* 081-360 2294

WOODS, Alan Geoffrey. b 42. ACCA65 FCCA80. Sarum Th Coll 67. d 70 p 71. C Bedminster St Fran *Bris* 70-73; Youth Chapl 73-76; Warden Legge House Res Youth Cen 73-76; P-in-c Neston 76-79; TV Gtr Corsham 79-81; P-in-c Charminster *Sarum* 81-83; V Charminster and Stinsford 83-90; RD Dorchester 85-90; P-in-c Calne and Blackland 90; V from 90; RD Calne from 90. *The Vicarage, Vicarage Close, Calne, Wilts SN11 8DD* Calne (0249) 812340

WOODS, Albert. b 12. St Paul's Coll Burgh St Chad's Coll Regina LTh47. d 41 p 42. V Upper w Nether Swell *Glouc* 71-78; rtd 78; Perm to Offic *Liv* 85-91. *4 Priors Court, Tolsey Quay, Tewkesbury, Glos GL20 5US* Tewkesbury (0684) 274228

WOODS, Allan Campbell. b 32. MIEH59. Ox NSM Course 85. d 89 p 90. NSM W Wycombe w Bledlow Ridge, Bradenham and Radnage *Ox* from 89. *4 Pitcher's Cottages, Bennett End, Radnage, Bucks HP14 4EF* High Wycombe (0494) 482083

WOODS, Charles William. b 31. Lich Th Coll 55. d 58 p 59. C Hednesford *Lich* 58-62; V Wilnecote 62-67; V Basford 67-76; V Chasetown 76-81; P-in-c Donington 81-83; R from 83; P-in-c Boningale 83; V from 83; RD Shifnal 84-89. *Donington Rectory, Albrighton, Wolverhampton WV7 3EP* Albrighton (0902) 372279

WOODS, Christopher Guy Alistair. b 35. Dur Univ BA60. Clifton Th Coll 60. d 62 p 63. C Rainham *Chelmsf* 62-65; C Edin St Thos *Edin* 65-69; Sec Spanish and Portuguese Ch Aid Soc 69-79; C Willesborough w Hinxhill *Cant* 75-80; P-in-c Murston w Bapchild and Tonge 80-87; R 87-90; R Gt Horkesley *Chelmsf* from 90; RD Dedham and Tey from 91. *The Rectory, Ivy Lodge Road, Great Horkesley, Colchester CO6 4EN* Colchester (0206) 271242

WOODS, Christopher Samuel. b 43. Cant Univ (NZ) BA. Qu Coll Birm 75. d 76 p 77. C Childwall All SS *Liv* 76-79; V Parr Mt from 79. *The Vicarage, Traverse Street, St Helens, Merseyside WA9 1BW* St Helens (0744) 22778

WOODS, David Arthur. b 28. Bris Univ BA52. Tyndale Hall Bris 48. d 53 p 54. C Camborne *Truro* 53-56; C Bromley Ch Ch *Roch* 56-58; V Tewkesbury H Trin *Glouc* 58-66; V Stapleford *S'well* 66-70; Miss to Seamen from 70; V Fowey *Truro* from 70; RD St Austell 80-88. *The Vicarage, Fowey, Cornwall PL23 1BU* Fowey (0726) 833535

WOODS, David Benjamin. b 42. Linc Th Coll 88. d 90 p 91. C Louth *Linc* from 90. *15 Grosvenor Crescent, Louth, Lincs LN11 0BD* Louth (0507) 603635

WOODS, David Winston. b 39. K Coll Lon BD62 AKC62. d 63 p 64. C Barrow St Luke *Carl* 63-65; C Workington St Jo 65-67; V Appleby *Linc* 67-71; V Scunthorpe St Jo 71-76; R Mablethorpe w Stain 76-78; P-in-c Trusthorpe 76-78; R Mablethorpe w Trusthorpe 78-87; RD Calcewaithe and Candleshoe 87; V Urswick *Carl* from 87; V Bardsea from 87. *The Vicarage, Great Urswick, Ulverston, Cumbria LA12 0TA* Ulverston (0229) 56254

WOODS, Edward Christopher John. b 44. NUI BA67. CITC 66. d 67 p 68. C Drumglass *Arm* 67-70; C Belf St Mark *Conn* 70-73; I Kilcolman *L & K* 73-78; RD Killarney 75-78; I Portarlington w Cloneyhurke and Lea *M & K* 78-84; Chan Kildare Cathl 81-84; I Killiney (Ballybrack) *D & G* from 85; RD Killiney from 90. *The Rectory, 21 Killiney Avenue, Killiney, Co Dublin, Irish Republic* Dublin (1) 285-6180

WOODS, Eric John. b 51. Magd Coll Ox BA72 MA77 Trin Coll Cam BA77 MA83. Westcott Ho Cam 75. d 78 p 79. C Bris St Mary Redcliffe w Temple etc *Bris* 78-81; Hon C Clifton St Paul 81-83; Asst Chapl Bris Univ 81-83; R Wroughton from 83; RD Wroughton from 88. *The Vicarage, Wroughton, Swindon SN4 9JS* Swindon (0793) 812301

✠WOODS, Most Rev Sir Frank. b 07. KBE72. Trin Coll Cam BA30 MA33 Monash Univ Aus LLD73. Lambeth DD57 Westcott Ho Cam 30. d 31 p 32 c 52. C Portsea St Mary *Portsm* 31-33; Chapl Trin Coll Cam 33-36; Vice-Prin Wells Th Coll 36-45; CF (R of O) 39-45; I Huddersfield *Wakef* 45-52; RD 45-52; Hon Can Wakef Cathl 47-52; Chapl to HM The King 51-52; Chapl to HM The Queen from 52; Suff Bp Middleton *Man* 52-57; Can Res Man Cathl 52-57; Australia from 57; Abp Melbourne 57-77; Primate of Australia 71-77; rtd 77. *18 Victoria Road, Camberwell, Victoria, Australia 3124* Melbourne (3) 882-9945

WOODS, Frederick James. b 45. Southn Univ BA66 MPhil74 Fitzw Coll Cam BA76 MA79. Ridley Hall Cam 74. d 77 p 78. C Stratford w Bishopton *Cov* 77-81; V Warminster Ch Ch *Sarum* from 81. *The Vicarage, 13 Avon Road, Warminster, Wilts BA12 9PR* Warminster (0985) 212219

WOODS, Geoffrey Edward. b 49. Tyndale Hall Bris BD70. d 73 p 74. C Gipsy Hill Ch Ch *S'wark* 73-76; C Uphill *B & W* 76-79; R Swainswick w Langridge 79-84. *22 Watergates, Colerne, Chippenham, Wilts SN14 8DR* Box (0225) 743675

WOODS, Howard Charles. b 04. Trin Coll Ox BA26 MA30. Westcott Ho Cam 32. d 33 p 34. R Stratton Audley w Godington *Ox* 64-71; rtd 71. *Manormead, Tilford Road, Hindhead, Surrey GU26 6RA*

WOODS, Canon John Mawhinney. b 19. Edin Th Coll 55. d 58 p 59. R Walpole St Peter *Ely* 60-75; R Inverness St Andr *Mor* 75-80; Provost St Andr Cathl Inverness 75-80; Hon Can from 80; V The Suttons w Tydd *Linc* 80-85; rtd 85; Perm to Offic *Nor* from 85. *1 Purfleet Place, King's Lynn, Norfolk PE30 1JH* King's Lynn (0553) 775599

WOODS, John William Ashburnham. b 22. Reading Univ BSc50. NW Ord Course 73 St Jo Coll Lusaka 69. d 71 p 74. Zambia 71-72; C Goole *Sheff* 73-75; P-in-c Firbeck w Letwell 75-76; R 76-82; P-in-c Woodsetts 75-76; V 76-82; Bp's Rural Adv from 80; R Barnburgh w Melton on the Hill from 82; RD Wath from 86. *The Rectory, Barnburgh, Doncaster, S Yorkshire DN5 7ET* Rotherham (0709) 892598

WOODS, Joseph Richard Vernon. b 31. Solicitor 57. Cuddesdon Coll 58. d 60 p 61. C Newc St Gabr *Newc* 60-63; Trinidad and Tobago 63-67; Chapl Long Grove Hosp Epsom 67-76; P-in-c Ewell St Fran *Guildf* 76-79; V 79-87; V Englefield Green from 87. *The Vicarage, 21 Willow Walk, Englefield Green, Egham, Surrey TW20 0DQ* Egham (0784) 432553

WOODS, Michael Spencer. b 44. K Coll Lon BD66 AKC66 Hull Univ DipMin88. d 67 p 68. C Sprowston *Nor* 67-70; Malaysia 70-74; TV Hempnall *Nor* 74-79; TV Halesworth w Linstead and Chediston *St E* 79-80; TV Halesworth w Linstead, Chediston, Holton etc 80-85; TR Braunstone *Leic* from 85; RD Sparkenhoe E from 89. *The Rectory,*

Braunstone, Leicester LE3 3AL   Leicester (0533) 893377

WOODS, Canon Norman Harman. b 35. K Coll Lon BD62 AKC62. **d** 63 **p** 64. C Poplar All SS w St Frideswide *Lon* 63-68; C-in-c W Leigh CD *Portsm* 68-76; V Hythe *Cant* from 76; RD Elham 83-89; Hon Can Cant Cathl from 90. *St Leonard's Vicarage, Oak Walk, Hythe, Kent CT21 5DN* Hythe (0303) 266217

WOODS, Richard Thomas Evelyn Brownrigg. b 51. St Steph Ho Ox 83. **d** 85 **p** 86. C Southgate Ch Ch *Lon* 85-88; C Northn All SS w St Kath *Pet* 88-89; V Maybridge *Chich* from 89. *56 The Boulevard, Worthing, W Sussex BN13 1LA* Worthing (0903) 49463

✠**WOODS, Rt Rev Robert Wylmer.** b 14. KCMG89 KCVO71. Trin Coll Cam BA37 MA40. Westcott Ho Cam 37. **d** 38 **p** 39 **c** 71. C St Edm the King w St Nic Acons etc *Lon* 38-39; C Hoddesdon *St Alb* 39-42; CF (EC) 42-46; V Glen Parva and S Wigston *Leic* 46-51; Adn Singapore 51-58; R Tankersley *Sheff* 58-62; Adn Sheff 58-62; Dean of Windsor and Dom Chapl to HM the Queen 62-71; Bp Worc 71-81; rtd 81; Asst Bp Glouc from 81. *Torsend House, Tirley, Gloucester GL19 4EU* Tirley (045278) 327

WOODS, Ven Samuel Edward. b 10. Trin Coll Cam BA34 MA37. Westcott Ho Cam 35. **d** 36 **p** 37. New Zealand 36-46 and from 55; V Southport H Trin *Liv* 46-50; R Hatf *St Alb* 50-55; Adn Rangiora and Westland 55-59 and 63-68; Adn Sumner 59-63; Timaru 68-71; Akaroa and Asburton 73-74. *19B Sumnervale Drive, Sumner, Christchurch 8, New Zealand* Christchurch (3) 266521

WOODS, Theodore Frank Spreull. b 37. Trin Coll Cam 58. Wells Th Coll 60. **d** 62 **p** 63. C Stocking Farm CD *Leic* 62-67; Papua New Guinea 67-77; V Knighton St Jo *Leic* 77-80; Australia from 80. *257 Bennetts Road, Norman Park, Queensland, Australia 4170* Brisbane (7) 354-3422

WOODS, Timothy James. b 52. BA MSc. Qu Coll Birm. **d** 83 **p** 84. C Brierley Hill *Lich* 83-86; C Stoneydelph St Martin CD 86-88; Chr Aid Area Sec (SE Lon) from 88. *Inter-Church House, 35-41 Lower Marsh, London SE1 7RL* 071-620 4444

WOODS, Mrs Valerie Irene. b 44. Trin Coll Bris DipHE84. **dss** 84 **d** 87. Coleford w Staunton *Glouc* 84-87; C 87-88; TM Bedminster *Bris* from 88. *St Paul's Vicarage, 2 Southville Road, Bristol BS3 1DG* Bristol (0272) 663189

WOODSFORD, Andrew Norman. b 43. Nottm Univ BA65. Ridley Hall Cam 65. **d** 67 **p** 68. C Radcliffe-on-Trent *S'well* 67-70; P-in-c Ladybrook 70-73; P-in-c Barton in Fabis 73-81; P-in-c Thrumpton 73-81; Chapl Bramcote Sch Gamston 81-88; R Gamston w Eaton and W Drayton *S'well* 81-88; Warden of Readers from 88. *The Rectory, Gamston, Retford, Notts DN22 0QB* Gamston (077783) 706

WOODSIDE, David. b 60. St Jo Coll Dur BA81. Cranmer Hall Dur 87. **d** 90 **p** 91. C Stoke Newington St Mary *Lon* from 90. *The Rectory Flat, Church Street, London N16 9ES* 071-249 6138

WOODWARD, Anthony John. b 50. Salford Univ BSc78. St Jo Coll Nottm DipTh79. **d** 81 **p** 82. C Deane *Man* 81-84; CF 84-87; R Norris Bank *Man* 87-90; rtd 90. *6 Barrisdale Close, Ladybridge, Bolton BL3 4TR* Bolton (0204) 654863

WOODWARD, Arthur Robert Harry. b 28. **d** 76 **p** 77. Rhodesia 76-80; Zimbabwe 80-87; Adn E Harare 82-87; R Wymington w Podington *St Alb* from 87; RD Sharnbrook from 89. *The Rectory, Manor Lane, Wymington, Rushden, Northants NN10 9LL* Rushden (0933) 57800

WOODWARD, Geoffrey Wallace. b 23. St Jo Coll Cam BA47 MA50. Westcott Ho Cam 47. **d** 49 **p** 50. V Nunthorpe *York* 65-72; V Scarborough St Martin 72-79; V Goathland 79-88; rtd 88; Chapl E Netherlands (Nijmegen and Twente) *Eur* from 89. *Yemscroft, 2 Grange Drive, Cottingham HU16 5RE* Hull (0482) 841423

WOODWARD, Canon Horace James. b 22. AKC49. **d** 50 **p** 51. V Redhill St Matt *S'wark* 67-74; R Warlingham w Chelsham and Farleigh 74-84; Hon Can S'wark Cathl 79-84; RD Caterham 83-84; V Glynde, W Firle and Beddingham *Chich* 84-90; rtd 90. *15 Grove Road, Seaford, E Sussex BN25 1TP* Seaford (0323) 891075

WOODWARD, James Welford. b 61. K Coll Lon BD82 AKC82. Birm Univ MPhil91. Westcott Ho Cam 84 Lambeth STh85. **d** 85 **p** 86. C Consett *Dur* 85-87; Bp's Dom Chapl *St E* 87-90; Chapl Qu Eliz Hosp Birm from 90. Dist Chaplaincy Co-ord S Birm HA from 90. *142 Dawlish Road, Selly Oak, Birmingham B29 7AR or,*

Queen Elizabeth Medical Centre, Edgbaston, Birmingham B15 2TH 021-472 3932 or 472 1311

WOODWARD, Canon John Clive. b 35. Univ of Wales (Lamp) BA56. St Jo Coll Dur 56. **d** 58 **p** 59. C Risca *Mon* 58-63; C Chepstow 63-66; V Ynysddu 66-74; V Christ Church 74-84; Can St Woolos Cathl from 82; R Cyncoed from 84. *The Rectory, 256 Cyncoed Road, Cardiff CF2 6RU* Cardiff (0222) 752138

WOODWARD, Maurice George. b 29. Selw Coll Cam BA56 MA58. Wells Th Coll 56. **d** 58 **p** 59. C Gedling *S'well* 58-61; Succ Leic Cathl *Leic* 61-64; Chapl Leic R Infirmary 62-64; CF (R of O) from 63; V Barrow upon Soar *Leic* 64-77; Hon Chapl Leic Cathl 64-77; V Clare w Poslingford *St E* 77-85; P-in-c Stoke by Clare w Wixoe 84-85; R How Caple w Sollarshope, Sellack etc *Heref* from 85. *The Rectory, Kings Caple, Hereford HR1 4TX* Hereford (0432) 840485

WOODWARD, Canon Peter Cavell. b 36. St Cath Coll Cam BA58 MA62. Bps' Coll Cheshunt 58. **d** 60 **p** 61. C Chingford St Anne *Chelmsf* 60-63; Madagascar 63-75; V Weedon Bec *Pet* 75-76; P-in-c Everdon 75-76; V Weedon Bec w Everdon 76-81; RD Daventry 79-81; Can Pet Cathl from 81; V Brackley St Pet w St Jas from 81; RD Brackley 82-88. *The Vicarage, Old Town, Brackley, Northants NN13 5BZ* Brackley (0280) 702767

WOODWARD, Reginald Charles Huphnill. b 19. FRGS Lon Univ BA41 DipEd. Wells Th Coll 41. **d** 43 **p** 44. Lic to Offic *Linc* from 53; Teacher K Sch Grantham 53-74; Hd Master K Lower Sch Grantham 74-79; rtd 79. *104 Harrowby Road, Grantham, Lincs NG31 9DS* Grantham (0476) 71912

WOODWARD, Richard Tharby. b 39. Man Univ BA60. Chich Th Coll 60. **d** 62 **p** 63. C Mansf St Mark *S'well* 62-65; Chapl Liddon Ho Lon 65-69; C-in-c Beaconsfield St Mich CD *Ox* 69-76; TV Beaconsfield from 76. *St Michael's Parsonage, St Michael's Green, Beaconsfield, Bucks HP9 2BN* Beaconsfield (0494) 673464

WOODWARD, Roger David. b 38. W Midl Minl Tr Course 87. **d** 90. C Castle Bromwich SS Mary and Marg *Birm* from 90. *4 Wasperton Close, Castle Bromwich, Birmingham B36 9DZ* 021-747 7467

WOODWARD-COURT, John Blunden. b 13. Ripon Hall Ox 52. **d** 53 **p** 54. P-in-c Snitterfield w Bearley *Cov* 55-74; P-in-c Barton-on-the-Heath 74-83; R Barcheston 76-83; R Cherington w Stourton 76-83; V Wolford w Burmington 76-83; rtd 83; Perm to Offic *Cov* from 83; Glouc from 83; Ox from 84. *2 Orchard Close, Lower Brailes, Banbury, Oxon OX15 5AH* Brailes (060885) 411

WOODWARDS, Canon David George. b 36. K Coll Lon BD62 MTh73. Oak Hill Th Coll 62. **d** 64 **p** 65. C Heworth H Trin *York* 64-66; Nigeria 67-71; V Edwardstone w Groton *St E* 72-82; RD Sudbury 81-88; R Glemsford 82-88; P-in-c Stanstead w Shimplingthorne and Alpheton 85-86; P-in-c Hartest w Boxted 85-86; P-in-c Lawshall 85-86; P-in-c Hartest w Boxted, Somerton and Stanstead 86-88; Hon Can St E Cathl from 87; R Thorndon w Rishangles, Stoke Ash, Thwaite etc from 88; RD Hartismere from 88. *The Rectory, Standwell Green, Thorndon, Eye, Suffolk IP23 7JL* Occold (037971) 603

WOODWORTH, Very Rev Gerald Mark David. b 39. TCD BA62 MA69. CITC 64. **d** 64 **p** 65. C Dub Zion Ch *D & G* 64-67; Min Can St Patr Cathl Dub 65-67; Dioc Registrar and Lib (Ossory) *C & O* 67-70; VC Kilkenny Cathl 67-70; C Kilkenny St Canice Cathl 67-70; I Bandon Union *C, C & R* 70-84; RD Mid W Cork 79-84; Preb Tymothan St Patr Cathl Dub 82-84; I Cashel w Magorban, Tipperary, Clonbeg etc *C & O* from 84; Dean Cashel, Chan Waterford Cathl and Chan Lismore Cathl from 84; Adn Cashel 84-86; Adn Cashel, Waterford and Lismore from 86. *The Deanery, Cashel, Co Tipperary, Irish Republic* Tipperary (62) 61232

WOOKEY, Stephen Mark. b 54. Em Coll Cam BA76 MA80. Wycliffe Hall Ox 77. **d** 80 **p** 81. C Enfield Ch Ch Trent Park *Lon* 80-84; Chapl Paris St Mich *Eur* 84-87; C Langham Place All So *Lon* from 87. *12 Duke's Mews, London W1M 5RB* 071-486 0006

WOOLCOCK, John. b 47. DipRK70 Open Univ BA82 BA86. Wm Temple Coll Rugby 69 Sarum & Wells Th Coll 70. **d** 72 **p** 73. C Kells *Carl* 72-76; C Barrow St Matt 76-78; R Distington 78-86; V Staveley w Kentmere from 86; Soc Resp Officer from 89. *The Vicarage, Kentmere Road, Staveley, Kendal, Cumbria LA8 9PA* Staveley (0539) 821267

WOOLDRIDGE, Derek Robert. b 33. Nottm Univ BA57. Oak Hill Th Coll. **d** 59 **p** 60. C Chesterfield H Trin *Derby* 59-63; C Heworth w Peasholme St Cuth *York* 63-70; R York St Paul from 70. *St Paul's Rectory, 100 Acomb Road, York YO2 4ER* York (0904) 792304

WOOLDRIDGE, John Bellamy. b 27. Tyndale Hall Bris 54. **d** 56 **p** 57. C Norbury *Ches* 56-58; C Bramcote *S'well* 58-60; R Eccleston *Ches* 60-66; Area Sec (NW) CPAS 66-68; P-in-c Knutsford St Jo *Ches* 68-71; V Knutsford St Jo and Toft 71-79; V Gt Clacton *Chelmsf* 79-82; V Disley *Ches* 82-88; Min Buxton Trin Prop Chpl *Derby* from '88. *Trinity Parsonage, Hardwick Square East, Buxton, Derbyshire SK17 6PT* Buxton (0298) 23461

WOOLF, William John. b 05. **d** 53 **p** 54. V N Somercotes *Linc* 58-73; R S Somercotes 59-73; rtd 73. *Beech Grove Hall Nursing Home, Manby, Louth, Lincs*

WOOLFENDEN, Dennis George. b 12. Leeds Univ BSc35. Cranmer Hall Dur 66. **d** 68 **p** 69. C Barking St Marg *Chelmsf* 68-72; R Wakes Colne w Chappel 72-76; V Elm Park St Nic Hornchurch 76-80; rtd 80; Perm to Offic *Chich* from 80; *Portsm* from 90. *2 Tollhouse Close, Chichester, W Sussex PO19 1SE* Chichester (0243) 528593

WOOLFENDEN, Thomas. b 11. Ely Th Coll 45. **d** 47 **p** 48. V Geddington w Newton le Willows *Pet* 63-73; V Geddington w Weekley 73-88; rtd 88; Perm to Offic *Pet* from 88. *135 Headlands, Kettering, Northants NN15 6AE* Kettering (0536) 517728

WOOLHOUSE, Kenneth. b 38. BNC Ox BA61 MA65. Cuddesdon Coll 61. **d** 64 **p** 65. C Old Brumby *Linc* 64-67; Chapl Cov Cathl *Cov* 68-74; C-in-c Hammersmith SS Mich and Geo White City Estate CD *Lon* 75-81; Dir Past Studies Chich Th Coll from 81; P-in-c Birdham w W Itchenor *Chich* 81-86; Chapl W Sussex Inst of HE from 86. *Bishop Otter College, College Lane, Chichester PO19 4PE* Chichester (0243) 787911

WOOLHOUSE, Miss Linda June. b 49. ACP76 CertEd70. W Midl Minl Tr Course 85. **d** 88. Hon Par Dn Old Swinford Stourbridge *Worc* from 88. *10 Rectory Gardens, Old Swinford, Stourbridge, W Midlands DY8 2HB* Stourbridge (0384) 376587

WOOLLARD, Ms Bridget Marianne. b 56. K Coll Cam BA77 MA80 Sheff Univ CertEd78 St Jo Coll Dur BA81 Birm Univ MPhil87. **dss** 82 **d** 87. Battersea St Pet and St Paul *S'wark* 82-84; Chapl Southn Univ *Win* 84-89; Tutor Past Th from 89; Dir Past Studies Qu Coll Birm from 89. *9 East Pathway, Harborne, Birmingham B17 9DN* 021-427 1411 or 454 1765

WOOLLARD, David John. b 39. Leic Univ BSc62. Trin Coll Bris DipHE88. **d** 88 **p** 89. C Clifton *York* 88-91; C York St Luke from 91. *91 Burton Stone Lane, York YO3 6BZ* York (0904) 655653

WOOLLASTON, Brian. b 53. CertEd76 DipTh83. St Paul's Grahamstown 81. **d** 83 **p** 84. C Kington w Huntington, Old Radnor, Kinnerton etc *Heref* 88-89; C Tupsley from 89. *2 Litley Close, Tupsley, Hereford HR1 1TN* Hereford (0432) 50805

WOOLLCOMBE, Mrs Juliet. b 38. St Mary's Coll Dur BA60 DipEd61. Gilmore Course 74. **dss** 77 **d** 87. St Marylebone Ch Ch *Lon* 77-80; Dean of Women's Min (Lon Area) 87-89; Dn-in-c Upton Snodsbury and Broughton Hackett etc *Worc* from 89. *4 Flax Piece, Upton Snodsbury, Worcester WR7 4PA* Upton Snodsbury (090560) 886

✠**WOOLLCOMBE, Rt Rev Kenneth John.** b 24. St Jo Coll Ox BA49 MA53 S Sewanee Univ STD63 Trin Coll Hartford (USA) Hon DD75. Westcott Ho Cam 49. **d** 51 **p** 52 **c** 71. C Gt Grimsby St Jas *Linc* 51-53; Fell Chapl and Lect St Jo Coll Ox 53-60; Tutor St Jo Coll Ox 56-60; USA 60-63; Prof Dogmatic Th Gen Th Sem NY 60-63; Prin Edin Th Coll 63-71; Can St Mary's Cathl *Edin* 63-71; Bp Ox 71-78; Asst Bp Lon 78-81; Can Res and Prec St Paul's Cathl 81-89; rtd 89; Asst Bp Worc from 89. *4 Flax Piece, Upton Snodsbury, Worcester WR7 4PA* Upton Snodsbury (090560) 886

WOOLLEY, Canon Christopher Andrew Lempriere. b 15. Ch Ch Ox BA37 MA70. Ely Th Coll 37. **d** 39 **p** 40. Tanganyika 46-64; Tanzania 64-70; Adn Njombe 64-70; P-in-c Hanwell *Ox* 70-84; V Horley w Hornton 70-84; rtd 84; Perm to Offic *B & W* from 86. *Springfield, Street Road, Glastonbury, Somerset BA6 9EG* Glastonbury (0458) 35175

WOOLLEY, Cyril George. b 22. **d** 70 **p** 71. SSJE from 60; Lic to Offic *Lon* 70-76; Perm from 90; Lic *Ox* 76-80; *Leic* from 80; Perm *Cant* 88-90; Chapl Bede Ho Staplehurst 88-90. *St Edward's House, 22 Great College Street, London SW1P 3QA* 071-222 9234

WOOLLEY, Francis Bertram Hopkinson. b 43. Sarum & Wells Th Coll 75. **d** 78 **p** 79. C Halesowen *Worc* 78-81; TV Droitwich 81-86; TV Cam Ascension *Ely* from 86. *2 Stretten Avenue, Cambridge CB4 3EP* Cambridge (0223) 315320

WOOLLEY, John Alexander. b 28. St Deiniol's Hawarden 61. **d** 63 **p** 64. C Garston *Liv* 63-65; C Gt Crosby St Luke 65-71; R Croft w Southworth 71-75; Chapl Cherry Knowle & Ryhope Hosps Sunderland 75-83; Chapl Cell Barnes Hosp St Alb from 83; Chapl Hill End Hosp St Alb from 83. *4 Nelsons Avenue, St Albans, Herts AL1 3UD* St Albans (0727) 53149

WOOLLEY, William Burrell. b 17. Kelham Th Coll 34. **d** 40 **p** 41. V Burton St Paul *Lich* 59-75; P-in-c Church Eaton 75-78; P-in-c Bradeley St Mary and All SS 75-80; P-in-c Moreton 76-78; R Moreton and Church Eaton 78-82; rtd 82. *72 Waverley Lane, Burton-on-Trent, Staffs DE14 2HG* Burton-on-Trent (0283) 36594

WOOLMER, John Shirley Thursby. b 42. Wadh Coll Ox BA63 MA69. St Jo Coll Nottm 70. **d** 71 **p** 72. Asst Chapl Win Coll 72-75; C Ox St Aldate w H Trin *Ox* 75-82; C Ox St Aldate w St Matt 82; R Shepton Mallet w Doulting *B & W* from 82. *The Rectory, Peter Street, Shepton Mallet, Somerset BA4 5BL* Shepton Mallet (0749) 2163

WOOLSTENHOLMES, Cyril Esmond. b 16. Bede Coll Dur BA37 DipTh38 MA41. **d** 39 **p** 40. R Shadforth *Dur* 67-82; rtd 82. *12 Wearside Drive, The Sands, Durham DH1 1LE* 091-384 3763

WOOLVEN, Ronald. b 36. Oak Hill Th Coll 60. **d** 63 **p** 64. C Romford Gd Shep Collier Row *Chelmsf* 63-68; C Widford 68-73; P-in-c Barling w Lt Wakering 73-84; V from 84. *154 Little Wakering Road, Great Wakering, Southend-on-Sea SS3 0JN* Southend-on-Sea (0702) 219200

WOOLVERIDGE, Gordon Hubert. b 27. Barrister-at-Law 52 CCC Cam BA51 MA55. S Dios Minl Tr Scheme 81. **d** 84 **p** 85. NSM St Edm the King w St Nic Acons etc *Lon* 84-85; NSM Chich St Paul and St Pet *Chich* 85-88; P-in-c Greatham w Empshott *Portsm* from 88; P-in-c Hawkley w Priors Dean from 88. *The Vicarage, Hawkley, Liss, Hants GU33 6NF* Hawkley (073084) 459

WOOLWICH, Area Bishop of. See HALL, Rt Rev Albert Peter

WOOSTER, Patrick Charles Francis. b 38. Qu Coll Birm 63. **d** 65 **p** 66. C Chippenham St Andr w Tytherton Lucas *Bris* 65-70; C Cockington *Ex* 70-72; V Stone w Woodford *Glouc* 72-73; P-in-c Hill 72-73; V Stone w Woodford and Hill from 73. *The Vicarage, Stone, Berkeley, Glos GL13 9LB* Falfield (0454) 260277

WORBOYS, Charles William. b 19. Oak Hill Th Coll 61. **d** 62 **p** 63. V W Thurrock *Chelmsf* 65-71; V Shalford 71-75; Warden Holbeck & Bethel Trust 75-88; rtd 84; Perm to Offic *Nor* from 91. *Flaxley, Holme-next-the-Sea, Norfolk PE36 6LQ* Holme (048525) 216

WORCESTER, Archdeacon of. See BENTLEY, Ven Frank William Henry

WORCESTER, Bishop of. See GOODRICH, Rt Rev Philip Harold Ernest

WORCESTER, Dean of. See JEFFERY, Very Rev Robert Martin Colquhoun

WORDSWORTH, Jeremy Nathaniel. b 30. Clare Coll Cam BA54 MA58. Ridley Hall Cam 54. **d** 56 **p** 57. C Gt Baddow *Chelmsf* 56-59; Chapl Felsted Sch Essex 59-63; Chapl Sherborne Sch Dorset 63-71; PV and Succ S'wark Cathl *S'wark* 71-73; P-in-c Stone *Worc* 73-77; V Malvern St Andr 77-82; V Combe Down w Monkton Combe and S Stoke *B & W* from 82. *The Vicarage, 141 Bradford Road, Combe Down, Bath BA2 5BS* Combe Down (0225) 833152

WORDSWORTH, Paul. b 42. Birm Univ BA64 Hull Univ DipMin89. Wells Th Coll 64. **d** 66 **p** 67. C Anlaby St Pet *York* 66-71; C Marfleet 71-72; TV 72-77; V Sowerby 77-90; P-in-c Sessay 77-90; V York St Thos w St Maurice from 90; Dioc Community Miss Project Ldr from 90. *St Thomas's Vicarage, 157 Haxby Road, York YO3 7JL* York (0904) 652228

WORGAN, Maurice William. b 40. Ely Th Coll 62 Sarum Th Coll 64. **d** 65 **p** 66. C Cranbrook *Cant* 65-69; C Maidstone St Martin 69-72; P-in-c Stanford w Postling and Radegund 72-73; R Lyminge w Paddlesworth 72-73; R Lyminge w Paddlesworth, Stanford w Postling etc 73-88; V Cant St Dunstan w H Cross from 88. *St Dunstan's Vicarage, 5 Harkness Drive, Canterbury, Kent CT2 7RW* Canterbury (0227) 463654

WORKMAN, David Andrew. b 22. MICS49 AMBIM78 FBIM80. Arm Aux Min Course 87. **d** 90 **p** 91. C Dundalk w Heynestown *Arm* from 90. *Dunbeag, Togher, Drogheda, Co Louth, Irish Republic* Drogheda (41) 52171

WORKMAN, John Lewis. b 26. St Deiniol's Hawarden 82. **d** 83 **p** 84. C Brecon St Mary and Battle w Llanddew *S & B* 83-86; Min Can Brecon Cathl 83-86; P-in-c Cwmbwrla 86-87; V from 87. *St Luke's Vicarage, 8 Vicarage Lane, Cwmdu, Swansea SA5 8EU* Swansea (0792) 586300

WORLEY, William. b 37. TD89. Cranmer Hall Dur 69. **d** 72 **p** 73. C Consett *Dur* 72-76; V Seaton Carew from 76; CF (TA) from 77. *The Vicarage, 11 Ruswarp Grove, Seaton Carew, Hartlepool, Cleveland TS25 2BA* Hartlepool (0429) 262463

WORMALD, Louis Percival. b 03. Leeds Univ BSc23. **d** 43 **p** 44. V Assington *St E* 59-68; rtd 68. *55 Blenheim Road, Clacton-on-Sea, Essex CO15 1DN* Clacton-on-Sea (0225) 35106

WORMALD, Roy Henry. b 42. Chich Th Coll 64. **d** 67 **p** 68. C Walthamstow St Mich *Chelmsf* 67-69; C Cov St Thos *Cov* 69-72; C Cov St Jo 69-72; C Wood Green St Mich *Lon* 72-77; P-in-c Hanwell St Mellitus 77-80; P-in-c Hanwell St Mellitus w St Mark 80-81; V from 81. *St Mellitus Vicarage, Church Road, London W7 3BA* 081-567 6535

WORN, Nigel John. b 56. Sarum & Wells Th Coll. **d** 84 **p** 85. C Walworth St Jo *S'wark* 84-88; Succ S'wark Cathl from 88. *St Paul's Vicarage, Kipling Street, London SE1 3RU* 071-407 8290

WORRALL, Frederick Rowland. **d** 86 **p** 87. NSM Chellaston *Derby* from 86. *37 St Peter's Road, Chellaston, Derby DE7 1UU* Derby (0332) 701890

WORRALL, Miss Suzanne. b 63. Trin Coll Bris BA86. **d** 87. Par Dn Kingston upon Hull St Nic *York* 87-91; Par Dn Kingston upon Hull Southcoates St Aid from 91. *76 Southcoates Avenue, Hull HU9 3HD* Hull (0482) 783233

WORSDALL, John Robin. b 33. Dur Univ BA57. Linc Th Coll 62. **d** 63 **p** 64. C Manthorpe w Londonthorpe *Linc* 63-66; C Folkingham w Laughton 66-68; V New Bolingbroke w Carrington 68-74; P-in-c S Somercotes 74-80; V N Somercotes 74-80; P-in-c Stickney 80-82; P-in-c E Ville and Mid Ville 80-82; P-in-c Stickford 80-82; V Stickney Gp from 82. *The Rectory, Horbling Lane, Stickney, Boston, Lincs PE22 8DQ* Boston (0205) 480049

WORSDELL, William Charles. b 35. AKC59. **d** 60 **p** 61. C Glouc St Aldate *Glouc* 60-66; V Devonport St Barn *Ex* 66-72; R Uplyme 72-77; R Withington and Compton Abdale w Haselton *Glouc* 77-87; V Badgeworth w Shurdington from 87. *The Vicarage, Shurdington, Cheltenham, Glos GL51 5TQ* Cheltenham (0242) 862241

WORSFOLD, Ms Caroline Jayne. b 61. St Steph Ho Ox. **d** 88. Chapl Asst Leic R Infirmary 88-90; C Sunderland Pennywell St Thos *Dur* 90-91; Chapl Cherry Knowle Hosp Sunderland from 91; Sunderland HA Chapl from 91. *St Thomas's Vicarage, Parkhurst Road, Sunderland SR4 9DB* 091-534 2100

WORSFOLD, John. b 24. Keble Coll Ox BA50 MA50. Cuddesdon Coll 50. **d** 51 **p** 52. C Shirley St Geo *Cant* 63-80; C Croydon H Sav 80-84; C Croydon H Sav *S'wark* 85-89; rtd 90. *26 Links Road, West Wickham, Kent BR4 0QW* 081-777 7463

WORSLEY, Ms Christine Anne. b 52. Hull Univ BA73 Bris Univ CertEd74. W Midl Minl Tr Course 82. **dss** 84 **d** 87. Smethwick St Mary *Birm* 84-87; Par Dn 87; Par Dn Smethwick H Trin w St Alb 87-89; Par Dn Cov Caludon *Cov* from 89. *Wyken Vicarage, Wyken Croft, Coventry CV2 3AD* Coventry (0203) 602332

WORSLEY, James Duncan. b 14. Dur Univ LTh40. Tyndale Hall Bris 37. **d** 40 **p** 41. V Ullenhall cum Aspley *Cov* 61-72; V Wappenbury w Weston under Wetherley 72-79; V Hunningham 72-79; Chapl Weston-under-Wetherley Hosp 72-79; rtd 79. *24 Banneson Road, Nether Stowey, Bridgwater, Somerset TA5 1NW* Nether Stowey (0278) 732169

WORSLEY, Richard John. b 52. Qu Coll Cam BA74 MA78. Qu Coll Birm DipTh79. **d** 80 **p** 81. C Styvechale *Cov* 80-84; V Smethwick H Trin w St Alb *Birm* 84-89; TV Cov Caludon *Cov* from 89. *Wyken Vicarage, Wyken Croft, Coventry CV2 3AD* Coventry (0203) 602332

WORSLEY, Ronald Freeman. b 23. St Deiniol's Hawarden 59. **d** 61 **p** 62. C Chorley *Ches* 61-64; C Timperley 64-68; R Waverton 68-75; V Congleton St Steph 75-82; V Eastham from 82. *The Vicarage, Ferry Road, Eastham, Wirral, Merseyside L62 0AJ* 051-327 2182

WORSTEAD, Eric Henry. b 14. Lon Univ BD44 BA46 MTh54. **d** 64 **p** 64. Hon C Southborough St Thos *Roch* 67-72; Dep Prin Whitelands Coll Lon 67-72; P-in-c High Hurstwood *Chich* 72-78; rtd 78. *Flat 2, Waterside, Crowborough Hill, Crowborough, E Sussex TN6 2RS* Crowborough (0892) 664330

WORT, Ernest Winstone. b 13. S'wark Ord Course 66. **d** 68 **p** 69. C Aldwick *Chich* 68-72; Hon C from 79; V Mendham w Metfield and Withersdale *St E* 72-77; C Haverhill 77-79; rtd 79. *5 St John's Close, Bognor Regis, W Sussex PO21 5RX* Bognor Regis (0243) 823156

WORTH, Douglas Albert Victor. b 09. St Cath Coll Cam BA32 MA47. Wells Th Coll 32. **d** 33 **p** 34. Prin Lect Coll of SS Mark and Jo Chelsea 67-71; Perm to Offic *Glouc* from 71; rtd 74. *Rose Cottage, Chalford Hill, Stroud, Glos GL6 8QH* Brimscombe (0453) 882572

WORTH, Frederick Stuart. b 30. Oak Hill Th Coll 60. **d** 62 **p** 63. C Okehampton w Inwardleigh *Ex* 62-68; V Dunkeswell and Dunkeswell Abbey 68-78; P-in-c Luppitt 69-72; P-in-c Upottery 72-76; V Sheldon 73-78; RD Honiton 77-84 and 86-90; R Uplyme 78-86; R Uplyme w Axmouth from 86. *The Rectory, Rhode Lane, Uplyme, Lyme Regis, Dorset DT7 3TX* Lyme Regis (0297) 43256

WORTHEN, Peter Frederick. b 38. Oak Hill Th Coll 71. **d** 71 **p** 72. C Tonbridge SS Pet and Paul *Roch* 71-75; P-in-c High Halstow w Hoo St Mary 75-76; R High Halstow w All Hallows and Hoo St Mary 76-83; V Welling from 83. *St John's Vicarage, Danson Lane, Welling, Kent DA16 2BQ* 081-303 1107

WORTHINGTON, George. b 35. AKC60. **d** 61 **p** 62. C Stockton St Pet *Dur* 61-65; C Poulton-le-Fylde *Blackb* 65-67; V Trawden 67-76; P-in-c Gressingham 76-78; P-in-c Arkholme 76-78; P-in-c Whittington 77-78; V Whittington w Arkholme and Gressingham 78-91; V Warton St Paul from 91. *The Vicarage, Church Road, Warton, Preston PR4 1BD* Freckleton (0772) 632227

WORTHINGTON, John Clare. b 17. St Jo Coll Cam BA39 MA46. Westcott Ho Cam 39 and 46. **d** 48 **p** 49. V Ellingham and Harbridge and Ibsley *Win* 65-85; RD Christchurch 79-82; rtd 85; Perm to Offic *Win* from 85. *Moorland Cottage, Godshill, Fordingbridge, Hants SP6 2LG* Fordingbridge (0425) 654448

WORTLEY, Prof John Trevor. b 34. FRHistS Dur Univ BA57 MA60 DD86 Lon Univ PhD69. Edin Th Coll 57. **d** 59 **p** 60. C Huddersfield St Jo *Wakef* 59-64; Canada from 64; Prof Hist Manitoba Univ from 69. *298 Yale Avenue, Winnipeg, Canada, R3M 0M1 or, Manitoba University, Winnipeg, Canada, R3T 2N2* Winnipeg (204) 284-7554 or 474-9830

WORTON, David Reginald (Brother Paschal). b 56. St Steph Ho Ox 88. **d** 90 **p** 90. SSF from 77. *St Francis House, 68 Laurel Road, Liverpool L7 0LW* 051-263 8581

WORTON, Norman. b 10. ALCD38. **d** 38 **p** 39. V Hove St Phil *Chich* 59-65; Australia from 65; rtd 75. *7A Esther Road, Balmoral Beach, Mosman, NSW, Australia 2088* Sydney (2) 969-5587

WORWOOD, Canon Frank Edward. b 11. ALCD34. **d** 34 **p** 35. RD Bingham W *S'well* 61-81; R W Bridgford 61-81; Hon Can S'well Minster 72-81; rtd 81; Perm to Offic *S'well* from 81. *1 Eastwood Road, Radcliffe-on-Trent, Nottingham NG12 2FZ* Radcliffe-on-Trent (0602) 335647

WOSTENHOLM, Dr David Kenneth. b 56. Edin Univ BSc77 MB, ChB80 Southn Univ BTh88. Chich Th Coll 82. **d** 85 **p** 86. C Leytonstone St Marg w St Columba *Chelmsf* 85-90; V Brighton Annunciation *Chich* from 90. *Annunciation Vicarage, 89 Washington Street, Brighton BN2 2SR* Brighton (0273) 681341

WOTHERSPOON, David Colin. b 36. Portsm Coll of Tech CEng65 MIMechE65. St Jo Coll Dur 76. **d** 78 **p** 79. C Blackb St Gabr *Blackb* 78-81; V Witton 81-90; Chapl Bern w Neuchatel *Eur* from 90. *St Ursula, Jubilaumsplatz 2, 3005 Bern, Switzerland* Berne (31) 430343

WOTTON, David Ashley. b 44. Chich Th Coll 71. **d** 74 **p** 75. C Allington and Maidstone St Pet *Cant* 74-77; C Ham St Andr *S'wark* 78-79; Chapl HM Rem Cen Latchmere Ho 78-79; C Tattenham Corner and Burgh Heath *Guildf* 85-88; P-in-c E Molesey St Mary from 88. *The Vicarage, St Mary's Road, East Molesey, Surrey KT8 0ST* 081-979 1441

WOULDHAM, Ralph Douglas Astley. b 19. Leeds Univ BA48. Coll of Resurr Mirfield 48. **d** 50 **p** 51. V Cleadon *Dur* 69-79; V Lowick and Kyloe w Ancroft *Newc* 79-84; rtd 84. *55 Northumberland Road, Tweedmouth, Berwick-upon-Tweed TD15 2AS* Berwick-upon-Tweed (0289) 308240

WRAGG, John Gordon. b 17. Sheff Univ BA39. ALCD41. **d** 41 **p** 42. V Spittal *Newc* 62-75; R Wark 75-82; V Birtley 77-82; rtd 82. *21 The Croft, Filey, N Yorkshire YO14 9LT* Scarborough (0723) 514824

WRAGG, Peter Robert. b 46. Lon Univ BSc68. Sarum & Wells Th Coll 71. **d** 74 **p** 75. C Feltham *Lon* 74-79; TV Hackney 79-85; P-in-c Isleworth St Mary from 85. *St Mary's Vicarage, 11 Paget Lane, Isleworth, Middx TW7 6ED* 081-560 6166

WRAIGHT, John Radford. b 38. St Chad's Coll Dur BA62 DipTh64. **d** 64 **p** 65. C Shildon *Dur* 64-67; C Newton Aycliffe 67-70; C Darlington St Jo 70-75; P-in-c Livingston LEP *Edin* 75-80; TV Carl H Trin and St Barn *Carl* 80-85; P-in-c Lindale w Field Broughton from 85. *The Vicarage, School Hill, Lindale, Grange-over-Sands, Cumbria LA11 6LD* Grange-over-Sands (05395) 34717

WRANGHAM HARDY, Canon John Francis. b 11. MBE57 TD50. Leeds Univ BA32 Indiana Univ Hon DLitt87. Wells Th Coll 34. **d** 35 **p** 36. OStJ 38-60; Asst ChStJ 60-77; Sub ChStJ 77-85; ChStJ from 85; QHC 62-64 and from 67; R Green's Norton w Bradden *Pet* 67-84; RD Towcester 70-82; rtd 84; Lic to Offic *Pet* 84-85; Perm to Offic from 85. *5 High Street North, Tiffield, Towcester, Northants NN12 8AD* Towcester (0327) 53104

WRAPSON, Donald. b 36. St Aid Birkenhead 61. **d** 65 **p** 66. C Bacup St Sav *Man* 65-69; C Wolv St Matt *Lich* 69-72; C Normanton *Derby* 72-78; V Dordon *Birm* 78-82; Chapl Birm Accident Hosp from 82; Chapl Selly Oak Hosp Birm from 82. *37 Walkers Heath Road, Birmingham B38 0AB* 021-458 2995 or 472 5313

WRATTEN, Martyn Stephen. b 34. AKC58 St Boniface Warminster 58. **d** 59 **p** 60. C Wandsworth Common St Mary *S'wark* 59-62; C Putney St Mary 62-65; C Pembury *Roch* 65-70; R Stone 70-76; Chapl Joyce Green Hosp Dartford 70-73; Stone Ho Hosp Kent 73-76; Hillcrest Hosp and Netherne Hosp Coulsdon 76-87; Hon C Netherne St Luke CD *S'wark* 76-87; V Gt Doddington *Pet* 87-88; V Gt Doddington and Wilby from 88. *The Vicarage, Great Doddington, Wellingborough, Northants NN9 7TH* Wellingborough (0933) 78181

WRAW, John Michael. b 59. Linc Coll Ox BA81 Fitzw Ho Cam BA84. Ridley Hall Cam 82. **d** 85 **p** 86. C Bromyard *Heref* 85-88; TV Sheff Manor *Sheff* from 88. *St Paul's Vicarage, East Bank Road, Sheffield S2 2AD* Sheffield (0742) 398533

WRAY, Christopher. b 48. Hull Univ BA70 New Coll Ox DipTh73. Cuddesdon Coll 70. **d** 73 **p** 74. C Brighouse *Wakef* 73-76; C Almondbury 76-78; C Tong *Bradf* 78-80; V Ingleton w Chapel le Dale 80-86; R Brompton Regis w Upton and Skilgate *B & W* 86-91; P-in-c Yoxford *St E* from 91. *The Vicarage, Yoxford, Saxmundham, Suffolk IP17 3EP* Yoxford (072877) 712

WRAY, Christopher Brownlow. b 46. Oak Hill Th Coll 86. **d** 88 **p** 89. C Quidenham *Nor* from 88. *Church House, 78 Quidenham Road, Kenninghall, Norwich NR16 2EF* Quidenham (095387) 637

WRAY, Karl. b 51. St And Coll Greystoke 72 Ian Ramsey Coll 74 Coll of Resurr Mirfield 75. **d** 78 **p** 79. C Salford St Phil w St Steph *Man* 78-83; CF 83-86 and from 89; V Sculcoates St Paul w Ch Ch and St Silas *York* 86-89. *c/o MOD (Army), Bagshot Park, Bagshot, Surrey GU19 5PL* Bagshot (0276) 71117

WRAY, Kenneth Martin. b 43. Linc Th Coll 72. **d** 75 **p** 76. C Shipley St Paul *Bradf* 75-79; V Edlington *Sheff* 79-85; V Nether Hoyland St Pet from 85. *The Vicarage, 104 Hawshaw Lane, Hoyland, Barnsley, S Yorkshire S74 0HH* Barnsley (0226) 749231

WRAY, Martin John. b 51. St Steph Ho Ox 86. **d** 88 **p** 89. C E Boldon *Dur* 88-90; C Seaham w Seaham Harbour from 90. *234 The Avenue, Seaham, Co Durham* 091-581 6664

WRAY, Michael. b 49. RGN87 Univ of Wales (Cardiff) BSc(Econ)77. Ripon Coll Cuddesdon 80. **d** 82 **p** 83. C Blackpool St Steph *Blackb* 82-83; C Torrisholme 83-84. *7 Honeysuckle Grove, Oxford OX4 5UL*

WRAYFORD, Geoffrey John. b 38. Ex Coll Ox BA61 MA65. Linc Th Coll 61. **d** 63 **p** 64. C Cirencester *Glouc* 63-69; Chapl Chelmsf Cathl *Chelmsf* 69-74; V 70-74; V Canvey Is 74-76; TR 76-80; P-in-c Woodlands *B & W* 80-88; V from 89; P-in-c Frome St Jo 80-88; P-in-c Frome Ch Ch 80-85; P-in-c Frome St Mary 85-88; V Frome St Jo and St Mary from 89. *The Vicarage, Vicarage Street, Frome, Somerset BA11 1PU* Frome (0373) 62325

WREN, Christopher John. b 54. Dur Univ BEd76 MA85. St Steph Ho Ox 77. **d** 79 **p** 80. C Stockton St Pet *Dur* 79-82; C Newton Aycliffe 82-85; V Gateshead St Chad Bensham 85-91; TR Bensham from 91. *St Chad's Vicarage, Dunsmuir Grove, Gateshead, Tyne & Wear NE8 4QL* 091-477 1964

WREN, Douglas Peter. b 59. Lanc Univ BA82. Trin Coll Bris BA88. **d** 88 **p** 89. C Nantwich *Ches* 88-91; C Chatham St Phil and St Jas *Roch* from 91. *3A Kit Hill Avenue, Chatham, Kent ME5 9ET* Medway (0634) 864348

WREN, John Aubrey. b 46. St Chad's Coll Dur BA69. Cuddesdon Coll 72. **d** 74 **p** 75. C Fenny Stratford and

Water Eaton *Ox* 74-77; TV Brighton Resurr *Chich* 77-84; V Eastbourne St Andr from 84. *St Andrew's Vicarage, 425 Seaside, Eastbourne, E Sussex BN22 7RT* Eastbourne (0323) 23739

WREN, Mrs Kathleen Ann. b 50. St Steph Ho Ox 83. dss 85 **d** 87. Gateshead St Cuth w St Paul *Dur* 85-86; Gateshead St Chad Bensham 86-87; Par Dn 87-91; Adv for Women's Min from 90; Par Dn Bensham from 91. *St Chad's Vicarage, Dunsmuir Grove, Gateshead, Tyne & Wear NE8 4QL* 091-477 1964

WREN, Richard. b 35. S Dios Minl Tr Scheme. **d** 90 **p** 91. NSM Tisbury *Sarum* from 90. *Gaston House, Tisbury, Salisbury SP3 6LG* Tisbury (0747) 870674

WRENBURY, Rev and Rt Hon Lord (John Burton Buckley). b 27. Solicitor 52 K Coll Cam BA48 MA48. S'wark Ord Course 87. **d** 90 **p** 91. NSM Brightling, Dallington, Mountfield & Netherfield *Chich* from 90. *Oldcastle, Dallington, Heathfield, E Sussex TN21 9JP* Rushlake Green (0435) 830400

WRENN, Peter Henry. b 34. Lon Univ BA56. Qu Coll Birm 58. **d** 60 **p** 61. C Dronfield *Derby* 60-64; C Hessle *York* 64-65; V Loscoe *Derby* 65-70; Asst Chapl Solihull Sch W Midl 71-77; Chapl from 77. *63 Shakespeare Drive, Shirley, Solihull, W Midlands B90 2AN* 021-744 3941 or 705 4409

WREXHAM, Archdeacon of. See WILLIAMS, Ven Edward Bryan

WRIGHT, Alan James. b 38. Chich Th Coll 63. **d** 66 **p** 67. C Edge Hill St Dunstan *Liv* 66-69; Swaziland 69-71; P-in-c Seaforth *Liv* 71-76; V Taunton All SS *B & W* from 76. *All Saints' Vicarage, Outer Circle, Taunton, Somerset TA1 2DE* Taunton (0823) 331545

WRIGHT, Alfred John. b 22. Wycliffe Hall Ox 66. **d** 66 **p** 67. C Newbury St Jo *Ox* 66-71; V E Challow 71-91; Chapl Community of St Mary V Wantage 75-89; rtd 91. *3 Latton Close, Southmoor, Abingdon, Oxon* Longworth (0865) 820625

WRIGHT, Andrew David Gibson. b 58. St Andr Univ MTheol81. Ridley Hall Cam. **d** 83 **p** 84. C W Derby Gd Shep *Liv* 83-86; C Carl H Trin and St Barn *Carl* 86-88; V Wigan St Jas w St Thos *Liv* from 88. *St James's Vicarage, Worsley Mesnes, Wigan, Lancs WN3 5HL* Wigan (0942) 43896

WRIGHT, Anthony John. b 47. ACA70 FCA77. Ripon Coll Cuddesdon 86. **d** 88 **p** 89. C Kidderminster St Mary and All SS etc *Worc* 88-90; C Kidderminster St Mary and All SS w Trimpley etc from 90. *44 Broadwaters Drive, Kidderminster, Worcs DY10 2RY* Kidderminster (0562) 68533

WRIGHT, Anthony Robert. b 49. Lanchester Poly BA70. St Steph Ho Ox 70. **d** 73 **p** 74. C Amersham on the Hill *Ox* 73-76; C Reading St Giles 76-78; P-in-c Prestwood 78-84; P-in-c Wantage 84-87; V from 87; RD Wantage from 84; P-in-c w E Hanney 88-91. *The Vicarage, Wantage, Oxon OX12 8AQ* Wantage (02357) 2214

WRIGHT, Antony John. b 31. St Pet Coll Saltley CertEd53. Chan Sch Truro 76. **d** 79 **p** 80. NSM St Breoke *Truro* 79-84; TV Probus, Ladock and Grampound w Creed 84-89; V Perranzabuloe from 89. *The Vicarage, Perranporth, Cornwall TR6 0DD* Truro (0872) 573375

WRIGHT, Canon Aubrey Kenneth William. b 21. K Coll Lon BD43 AKC43 BA44. Linc Th Coll 43. **d** 44 **p** 45. R W Wickham St Jo *Cant* 63-72; RD Croydon Cen 66-72; RD E Charing 72-81; Hon Can Cant Cathl 72-86; V Ashford 72-81; R Barham w Bishopsbourne and Kingston 81-86; rtd 86. *Stable End, The Street, Newchurch, Romney Marsh, Kent TN29 0DZ* Dymchurch (0303) 874286

WRIGHT, Canon Barry Owen. b 38. S'wark Ord Course 66. **d** 69 **p** 70. C Plumstead Ascension *S'wark* 69-74; Hon C Welling 74-89; Hon Can S'wark Cathl 79-89; Chapl W Midl Police *Birm* from 89. *256 Portland Road, Birmingham B17 8LR* 021-429 7784

WRIGHT, Miss Caroline Peggy. b 34. RMN75. Gilmore Ho 57. dss 59 **d** 88. Badsey *Worc* 62-66; Wickhamford 62-66; Wolverley 66-67; Warden St Mary's Abbey Leiston 67-74; Perm to Offic *St E* 74-88; Par Dn Bungay H Trin w St Mary from 88. *4 Kerrison Road, Bungay, Suffolk NR35 1RZ* Bungay (0986) 2023

WRIGHT, Charles Frederick Peter. b 16. Qu Coll Ox BA39 MA42. Westcott Ho Cam 40. **d** 41 **p** 42. Lic to Offic *Linc* 69-81; rtd 81. *The Hermitage, Snelland, Lincoln LN3 5AA* Wickenby (06735) 325

WRIGHT, Christopher Joseph Herbert. b 47. St Cath Coll Cam BA69 MA73 PhD77. Ridley Hall Cam 75. **d** 77 **p** 78. C Tonbridge SS Pet and Paul *Roch* 77-81; Perm to Offic *St Alb* from 82; India 83-88; Tutor and Dir Studies All Nations Chr Coll Ware from 88. *All Nations Christian*

College, Easneye, Ware, Herts SG12 8LX Ware (0920) 61243

WRIGHT, Christopher Nigel. b 39. Kelham Th Coll 60. **d** 65 **p** 66. C Latchford Ch Ch *Ches* 69-72; C Gt Budworth 72-75; C Wigan St Andr *Liv* 75-76; V New Springs 77-82; C Dovecot 82-85; C Rainford 85-89; rtd 89. *105 Ilfracombe Road, Sutton Leach, St Helens, Merseyside WA9 4NN* Marshalls Cross (0744) 821199

WRIGHT, Canon Clifford Nelson. b 35. K Coll Lon BD59 AKC59. **d** 60 **p** 61. C Stevenage *St Alb* 60-67; V Camberwell St Luke *S'wark* 67-81; RD Camberwell 75-80; Hon Can S'wark Cathl 79-80; TR Basingstoke *Win* from 81; RD Basingstoke from 84; Hon Can Win Cathl from 89. *The Rectory, Church Street, Basingstoke, Hants RG21 1QT* Basingstoke (0256) 26654

WRIGHT, Colin Trevor. b 33. **d** 61 **p** 62. Canada 61-72 and from 77; V Birchwood *Linc* 72-77. *518-24th Street East, Prince Albert, Saskatchewan, Canada, S6V 1S2*

WRIGHT, David Evan Cross. b 35. K Coll Lon BD64 AKC64. **d** 65 **p** 66. C Morpeth *Newc* 65-69; C Benwell St Jas 69-70; C Bushey *St Alb* 70-74; V High Wych 74-77; R High Wych and Gilston w Eastwick 77-80; V St Alb St Mary Marshalswick 80-89; P-in-c Sandridge 87-89; R Lenham w Boughton Malherbe *Cant* from 89. *The Vicarage, Old Ashford Road, Lenham, Maidstone, Kent ME17 2PX* Maidstone (0622) 858245

WRIGHT, David Hanson. b 14. Hertf Coll Ox BA36 MA46. **d** 61 **p** 62. C Westhoughton *Man* 62-67; C Bolton St Matt w St Barn 67-77; Hon C New Bury 77-79; Hon C Bolton St Phil 79-84; Perm to Offic from 84. *8 Moorside Avenue, Bolton BL1 6BE* Bolton (0204) 40121

WRIGHT, David Henry. b 23. Keble Coll Ox BA49. St Steph Ho Ox 52. **d** 54 **p** 55. C Penton Street St Silas w All SS *Lon* 54-57; V Barnsbury St Clem 57-66; V Wandsworth St Anne *S'wark* 66-73; R Dunkeld *St And* from 73; P-in-c Stanley 73-75; R Strathtay from 75. *St Mary's Rectory, St Mary's Road, Birnam, Dunkeld PH8 0BJ* Dunkeld (03502) 329

WRIGHT, Derek Anthony. b 35. ACP66 Lon Univ CertEd57. Cranmer Hall Dur 80. **d** 81 **p** 82. C Auckland St Andr and St Anne *Dur* 81-83; V Cornforth 83-87; P-in-c Thornley 87-88; R Gt and Lt Glemham, Blaxhall etc *St E* 88-90; V Evenwood *Dur* from 90. *The Vicarage, Brookside, Evenwood, Bishop Auckland, Co Durham DL14 9RA* Bishop Auckland (0388) 834671

WRIGHT, Edward Maurice. b 54. **d** 88. C Maidstone St Luke *Cant* from 88. *75 Snowden Avenue, Maidstone, Kent ME14 5NT* Maidstone (0622) 55774

WRIGHT, Edward Michael. b 37. St Cath Soc Ox BA61 MA65. Cuddesdon Coll DipTh63. **d** 64 **p** 65. C Willesden St Andr *Lon* 64-68; Bahamas 68-71; V Lewisham St Steph and St Mark *S'wark* 72-80; V Ox St Barn and St Paul *Ox* from 80. *St Barnabas' Vicarage, St Barnabas' Street, Oxford OX2 6BG* Oxford (0865) 57530

WRIGHT, Ven Evan Gilbert. b 03. Liv Univ MA49. St D Coll Lamp BA31 BD42. **d** 31 **p** 32. Adn Ban 62-73; rtd 73. *20 Penrhos Road, Bangor, Gwynedd* Bangor (0248) 352105

WRIGHT, Frank Albert. b 51. Sarum & Wells Th Coll 80. **d** 83 **p** 84. C Buckm *Ox* 83-86; C Newport Pagnell w Lathbury and Moulsoe 86-89; TV W Slough from 89. *298 Stoke Poges Lane, Slough SL1 3LL* Slough (0753) 539062

WRIGHT, Canon Frank Sidney. b 22. St Pet Hall Ox BA45 MA47. Westcott Ho Cam 47. **d** 49 **p** 50. Can Res Man Cathl *Man* 66-74; Sub-Dean 72-74; Min Can Man Cathl 74-83; Tutor Man Univ 74-83; rtd 83; Perm to Offic *Carl* from 83; *Ches* from 87. *Windyridge, Aaronstown Lonning, Brampton, Cumbria CA8 1QR* Brampton (06977) 2752

WRIGHT, Frederick John. b 15. AKC42. **d** 42 **p** 43. R Romsley *Worc* 67-80; rtd 80. *Rosevear, 3 Dury Lane, Colne, Huntingdon, Cambs PE17 3NB* Ramsey (0487) 840518

WRIGHT, Frederick John. b 21. Glouc Th Course 67. **d** 70 **p** 71. C Glouc Ch Ch *Glouc* 70-73; C Wotton-under-Edge 73-75; C Wotton-under-Edge w Ozleworth 75-76; R Woolstone w Gotherington and Oxenton 76-89; P-in-c Kemerton 80-89; R Woolstone w Gotherington and Oxenton etc 90; rtd 90. *6 Stevans Close, Farmscroft, Longford, Gloucester GL2 9AN* Gloucester (0452) 330672

WRIGHT, George Frederick. b 12. Kelham Th Coll 30. **d** 36 **p** 37. R E Markham and Askham *S'well* 62-77; P-in-c Headon w Upton 76-77; rtd 77; Perm to Offic *S'well* from 77. *Rutland House, Low Street, Collingham, Newark, Notts NG23 7NL* Newark (0636) 892876

WRIGHT, Gerald Grattan. b 32. Delaware State Coll BSc72. Ripon Hall Ox 73. **d** 76 **p** 77. Hon C Wolvercote w Summertown *Ox* 76-87; C Ox St Mich w St Martin and All SS 87-88; NSM Wolvercote w Summertown from 88. *28 Davenant Road, Oxford OX2 8BX* Oxford (0865) 52617

WRIGHT, Graham. b 50. Oak Hill Th Coll 73. **d** 76 **p** 77. C Northn St Giles *Pet* 76-79; C Man Resurr *Man* 79-82; V Barkingside St Laur *Chelmsf* 82-88; Chapl K Geo V Hosp Ilford 82-88; P-in-c Yoxford *St E* 88-90; Chapl Suffolk Constabulary 88-90. *8-10 Dixons Fold, North Walsham Road, Old Catton, Norwich NR6 7QD* Norwich (0603) 459960

WRIGHT, Graham Ewen. b 44. Lon Univ DipRS. S'wark Ord Course 86. **d** 89 **p** 90. NSM Aveley and Purfleet *Chelmsf* from 89. *2 Palmers, Corringham, Stanford-le-Hope, Essex SS17 7JA* Stanford-le-Hope (0375) 671747

WRIGHT, Horace Edward. b 12. AKC36. **d** 36 **p** 37. V Brailes *Cov* 65-78; RD Shipston 68-78; R Sutton under Brailes 76-78; rtd 78; Perm to Offic *St E* from 78. *19 Debenham Road, Debenham, Stowmarket, Suffolk IP14 6PY* Debenham (0728) 860530

WRIGHT, Hugh Edward. b 57. BNC Ox BA79 MA87 Ex Univ CertEd81. Sarum & Wells Th Coll 85. **d** 87 **p** 88. C Hobs Moat *Birm* 87-90; C W Drayton *Lon* from 90. *31 Swan Road, West Drayton, Middx UB7 7JY* West Drayton (0895) 422475

WRIGHT, Miss Jacqueline Anne. b 39. Dalton Ho Bris 67. dss 76 **d** 87. BCMS 71-88; Uganda 71-77; N Area Sec BCMS 78-88; Pudsey St Lawr and St Paul *Bradf* 82-87; Hon Par Dn 87-88; Par Dn Kingston upon Hull H Trin *York* from 88. *43 Trinity Court, Fish Street, Hull HU1 2NB* Hull (0482) 23120

WRIGHT, John Alastair. b 30. FRSA72. Cranmer Hall Dur 62. **d** 64 **p** 65. Miss to Seamen 67-72; V Darlington St Luke *Dur* 72-78; Community Chapl Darlington 78-89; rtd 89. *8 Trinity Road, Darlington, Co Durham DL3 7AS* Darlington (0325) 462714

WRIGHT, John Douglas. b 42. Birm Univ BSc64 CertEd66. St Steph Ho Ox 69. **d** 69 **p** 70. C Swanley St Mary *Roch* 69-74; C Stockwell Green St Andr *S'wark* 74-79; V Leigh St Jo *Man* 79-82; P-in-c Whitehawk *Chich* from 82. *St Cuthman's Vicarage, 1 St Cuthman's Close, Whitehawk, Brighton BN2 5LJ* Brighton (0273) 699424

WRIGHT, John Gordon. b 27. Birm Univ MA51. St D Coll Lamp BA50. **d** 52 **p** 53. Chapl St Olave and St Sav Sch Orpington 68-86; Hon C Crayford *Roch* 68-76; Lic to Offic 76-86; R Whimple *Ex* 87-88; R Whimple, Talaton and Clyst St Lawr 89-90; rtd 90; Perm to Offic *Lich* and *Heref* from 90. *Danesford, High Street, Albrighton, Wolverhampton WV7 3LA* Albrighton (0902) 373709

WRIGHT, John Harold. b 36. ATCL Dur Univ BA58 ACertCM. Ely Th Coll 58. **d** 61 **p** 62. C Boston *Linc* 61-64; C Willesborough w Hinxhill *Cant* 64-68; V Westwell 68-75; R Eastwell w Boughton Aluph 68-75; V Rolvenden 75-84; R Cheriton from 84. *St Martin's Rectory, Horn Street, Folkestone, Kent CT20 3JJ* Folkestone (0303) 238509

WRIGHT, Canon John Richard Martin. b 12. St Jo Coll Dur BA34 MA37 DipTh35. **d** 35 **p** 36. R Barrow *St E* 53-76; V Denham St Mary 53-76; R Edmundbyers w Muggleswick *Dur* 76-80; rtd 80; Perm to Offic *St E* from 80. *26 Out Risbygate, Bury St Edmunds, Suffolk IP33 3RJ* Bury St Edmunds (0284) 703848

WRIGHT, Canon Joseph James. b 16. Lon Univ BD39 AKC39. Ely Th Coll 39. **d** 39 **p** 40. V Forest Gate Em w Upton Cross *Chelmsf* 62-84; Hon Can Chelmsf Cathl 82-84; rtd 84. *87 Burnham Road, Southminster, Essex CM0 7ES* Maldon (0621) 773640

WRIGHT, Canon Kenneth William. b 13. Coll of Resurr Mirfield 37. **d** 39 **p** 40. Hon Can Ch Ch *Ox* 70-79; TR Fenny Stratford and Water Eaton 74-79; rtd 80; Perm to Offic *S'well* from 80. *St Martin's, Station Road, Collingham, Newark, Notts NG23 7RA* Newark (0636) 892800

WRIGHT, Canon Kenyon Edward. b 32. Glas Univ MA53 Fitzw Coll Cam BA55 Serampore Coll MTh61. Wesley Ho Cam 53. **d** 57 **p** 57. India 57-72; Dir of Internat Min Cov Cathl 72-81; Lic to Offic *Cov* 72-74; Can Res Cov Cathl 74-81; Gen Sec Scottish Chs Coun 81-90; Dir Scottish Chs Ho Dunblane 81-90; Hon C Knightswood H Cross Miss *Glas* from 91. *c/o The Rectory, 64 Cowdenhill Road, Glasgow G13 2HE* 041-954 6078

WRIGHT, Leonard John. b 24. Sarum & Wells Th Coll 77. **d** 80 **p** 81. Hon C Gillingham *Sarum* 80-90; rtd 90. *37 Saxon Mead Close, Peacemarsh, Gillingham, Dorset SP8 4HG* Gillingham (0747) 823261

WRIGHT, Leslie Frank. b 08. Coll of Resurr Mirfield 71. **d** 71 **p** 72. Hon C Northn St Alb *Pet* 71-78; Lic to Offic *Lich* 78-81; Perm to Offic *Ex* from 81. *65 Pellew Way, Teignmouth, Devon TQ14 9LU* Teignmouth (0626) 776032

WRIGHT, Leslie Vandernoll. b 24. Trin Hall Cam MA50. Ridley Hall Cam 49. **d** 51 **p** 52. Chapl Vevey *Eur* 68-73; Hd St Geo Sch Clarens 73-89; rtd 89; Chapl Lugano *Eur* from 89. *Residenza Falcieu E/1, 6914 Ciona di Carona, Switzerland* Lugano (91) 685573

WRIGHT, Mrs Louisa Mary. b 33. S'wark Ord Course. **d** 87. NSM Streatham Hill St Marg *S'wark* from 87. *19 Hillside Road, London SW2 3HL* 081-671 8037

WRIGHT, Martin Neave. b 37. AKC61 Leic Univ DSRS67. St Boniface Warminster. **d** 62 **p** 63. C Corby St Columba *Pet* 62-65; Ind Chapl 65-71; Nigeria 71-75; P-in-c Honiley *Cov* 75-84; P-in-c Wroxall 75-84; Ind Chapl 75-84; Soc Resp Officer from 84. *The New Rectory, Baginton, Coventry CV8 3AR* Coventry (0203) 302508 or 227597

WRIGHT, Canon Michael. b 30. St Chad's Coll Dur BA55 DipTh56. **d** 56 **p** 57. C New Cleethorpes *Linc* 56-59; C Skegness 59-62; V Louth St Mich 62-73; R Stewton 62-73; R Warmsworth *Sheff* 73-86; Warden Dioc Readers' Assn 81-86; Hon Can Sheff Cathl from 82; V Wath-upon-Dearne w Adwick-upon-Dearne from 86. *The Vicarage, Church Street, Wath-upon-Dearne, Rotherham, S Yorkshire S63 7RD* Rotherham (0709) 872299

WRIGHT, Michael Christopher. b 44. Leeds Univ BA65 CertEd67 MSc75. Wells Th Coll 65. **d** 67 **p** 68. C Dormanstown *York* 67-69; Perm to Offic *Linc* from 69; *Sheff* from 71; Hd Master Eastmoor High Sch Wakef 84-87; Lic to Offic *Wakef* from 84; Hd Master Carleton High Sch Pontefract from 87. *Orchard End, Finkle Street, Hensall, Goole, N Humberside DN14 0QY* Whitley Bridge (0977) 661900

WRIGHT, Michael John. b 38. DipTM. Chich Th Coll 59. **d** 62 **p** 63. C Yate *Glouc* 62-65; C Kirby Moorside w Gillamoor *York* 65-68; V 68-72; V Bransdale cum Farndale 68-72; V Kirkbymoorside w Gillamoor, Farndale & Bransdale 72-73; Dioc Communications Officer 72-74; V Ormesby 74-80; P-in-c Middlesb St Cuth 81-88; Perm to Offic 88-90; NSM W Acklam from 91. *25 Thornfield Road, Middlesbrough, Cleveland TS5 5DD* Middlesbrough (0642) 816247

WRIGHT, Michael Mat. b 32. St Edm Hall Ox BA55 MA59. Wells Th Coll. **d** 57 **p** 58. CF 62-87; rtd 87. *c/o MOD (Army), Bagshot Park, Bagshot, Surrey GU19 5PL* Bagshot (0276) 71717

WRIGHT, Nicholas Mark. b 59. Loughb Univ BSc80. Qu Coll Birm 82. **d** 85 **p** 86. C Coney Hill *Glouc* 85-89; C Rotherham *Sheff* from 89. *3 Reneville Road, Rotherham, S Yorkshire S60 2AR* Rotherham (0709) 364729

WRIGHT, Nicholas Thomas. b 48. Ex Coll Ox BA71 MA75 DPhil81. Wycliffe Hall Ox BA(Theol)73. **d** 75 **p** 76. Fell Mert Coll Ox 75-78; Asst Chapl 76-78; Chapl and Fell Down Coll Cam 78-81; Canada 81-86; Asst Prof NT Studies McGill Univ Montreal 81-86; Chapl and Fell Worc Coll Ox and Univ Lect Th from 86. *Worcester College, Oxford OX1 2HB* Oxford (0865) 278359

WRIGHT, Paul. b 54. K Coll Lon BD78 AKC78 Heythrop Coll Lon MTh90. Ripon Coll Cuddesdon 78. **d** 79 **p** 80. C Beckenham St Geo *Roch* 79-83; Chapl Ch Sch Richmond 83-85; C Richmond St Mary w St Matthias and St Jo *S'wark* 83-85; V Gillingham St Aug *Roch* 85-90; R Crayford from 90. *1 Claremont Crescent, Crayford, Dartford, Kent DA1 4RJ* Crayford (0322) 522078

WRIGHT, Peter. b 35. Hull Univ MA. AKC61 St Boniface Warminster. **d** 62 **p** 63. C Goole *Sheff* 62-67; V Norton Woodseats St Chad 67-80; R Aston cum Aughton 80-84; P-in-c Ulley 80-84; R Aston cum Aughton and Ulley from 84; RD Laughton from 85. *The Rectory, 91 Worksop Road, Aston, Sheffield S31 0EB* Sheffield (0742) 872272

WRIGHT, Peter Gordon. b 27. St Aid Birkenhead 55. **d** 57 **p** 58. C Mansf Woodhouse *S'well* 57-61; V Coddington w Barnby in the Willows from 61. *All Saints' Vicarage, Coddington, Newark, Notts NG24 2QF* Newark (0636) 703084

WRIGHT, Peter Reginald. b 34. Dur Univ BA60. Linc Th Coll 60. **d** 62 **p** 63. C Lt Ilford St Mich *Chelmsf* 62-65; C Billingham St Aid *Dur* 65-68; TV 68-71; TR 71-76; Chapl Portsm Poly *Portsm* 76-87; Sec Chapls in HE Gen Syn Bd of Educn from 88. *c/o Church House, Great Smith Street, London SW1P 3NZ* 071-222 9011

WRIGHT, Peter Westrope. b 24. Kelham Th Coll 43. **d** 48 **p** 49. R E Blatchington *Chich* 59-73; P-in-c Lewes St Mich 73-75; TV Lewes All SS, St Anne, St Mich and St

Thos 75-84; TR 84-87; rtd 89. *41 Victoria Street, Brighton BN1 3FQ* Brighton (0273) 730969

WRIGHT, Philip. b 32. G&C Coll Cam BA53 MA57. Wells Th Coll 56. **d** 57 **p** 58. C Barnard Castle *Dur* 57-60; C Heworth St Mary 60-64; V Tow Law 64-70; V Tanfield 70-78; V Gateshead Ch Ch from 78. *Christ Church Vicarage, Bewick Road, Gateshead, Tyne & Wear NE8 4DR* 091-477 1840

WRIGHT, Phillip. b 35. Kelham Th Coll 57 St Aid Birkenhead 59. **d** 61 **p** 62. C Goldthorpe *Sheff* 61-65; V Doncaster St Jude 65-71; V Kettering All SS *Pet* 71-82; V S Kirkby *Wakef* from 82. *The Vicarage, Bull Lane, South Kirkby, Pontefract, W Yorkshire WF9 3QD* Pontefract (0977) 642795

WRIGHT, Robert Charles. b 31. Roch Th Coll 65. **d** 67 **p** 68. C Manston *Ripon* 67-70; C Moor Allerton 70-74; P-in-c Terrington St John *Ely* 74-79; P-in-c Walpole St Andrew 74-75; P-in-c Tilney All Saints w Tilney St Lawrence 79; V Terrington St John from 80; V Tilney St Lawrence from 80; V Tilney All Saints from 80. *The Vicarage, Church Road, Terrington St John, Wisbech, Cambs PE14 7SA* Wisbech (0945) 880259

WRIGHT, Canon Robert Doogan. b 24. TCD BA46. **d** 47 **p** 48. C Belf St Mark *Conn* 64-70; I Carrickfergus 70-82; Can Conn Cathl 79-86; I Killead w Gartree 82-86; Chan Conn Cathl 83-86; rtd 86. *123 Station Road, Greenisland, Carrickfergus, Co Antrim* Belfast (0232) 862779

✠**WRIGHT, Rt Rev Royston Clifford.** b 22. Univ of Wales BA42. St Steph Ho Ox 43. **d** 45 **p** 46 **c** 86. C Bedwas *Mon* 45-47; C Newport St Jo Bapt 47-49; C Walton St Jo *Liv* 49-51; Chapl RNVR 50-51; Chapl RN 51-68; V Blaenavon w Capel Newydd *Mon* 68-74; RD Pontypool 73-74; Can St Woolos Cathl 74-77; R Ebbw Vale 74-77; Adn Newport 77-86; Adn Mon 77-86; Bp Mon from 86. *Bishopstow, Stow Hill, Newport, Gwent NP9 4EA* Newport (0633) 263510

WRIGHT, Samuel John. b 18. St D Coll Lamp BA50. **d** 52 **p** 53. V Birkenhead St Pet w St Matt *Ches* 58-74; V Marbury 75-84; RD Malpas 84; rtd 85; Perm to Offic *Lich & St As* from 85. *Bodwen, Llansantffraid, Powys SY22 6AQ* Llansantffraid (0691) 828896

WRIGHT, Simon Christopher. b 44. AKC67. **d** 68 **p** 69. C Bitterne Park *Win* 68-72; C Kirkby 72-74; V Wigan St Anne *Liv* 74-79; Abp's Dom Chapl *York* 79-84; Dir of Ords 79-84; V W Acklam from 84; RD Middlesbrough from 87. *The Vicarage, Church Lane, West Acklam, Middlesbrough, Cleveland TS5 7EB* Middlesbrough (0642) 817150

WRIGHT, Stephen Irwin. b 58. Ex Coll Ox BA80 MA84 Selw Coll Cam BA85 MA90. Ridley Hall Cam 83. **d** 86 **p** 87. C Newbarns w Hawcoat *Carl* 86-90; C Burton and Holme from 90. *The Vicarage, Holme, Carnforth, Lancs LA6 1PZ* Burton (0524) 781372

WRIGHT, Stephen Mark. b 60. Keele Univ BA83. Trin Coll Bris 86. **d** 89 **p** 90. C Thorne *Sheff* from 89. *154 Grampian Way, Thorne, Doncaster, S Yorkshire DN8 5YW* Thorne (0405) 815415

WRIGHT, Thomas Stephen. b 31. Fitzw Ho Cam BA54 MA58. Bps' Coll Cheshunt 56. **d** 57 **p** 58. C Bishop's Stortford St Mich *St Alb* 57-61; C St E Cathl *St E* 61-64; R Hartest w Boxted 64-82; Chapl RAF 64-71; RD Sudbury *St E* 70-81; P-in-c Somerton 71-82; P-in-c Stansfield from 82; Min Can St E Cathl from 82. *Cornerstones, Bury Road, Stradishall, Newmarket, Suffolk* Haverhill (0440) 820580

WRIGHT, Timothy. b 63. NUU BSc85. Cranmer Hall Dur 86. **d** 89 **p** 90. C Bramcote *S'well* from 89. *50 Bankfield Drive, Nottingham NG9 3EG* Nottingham (0602) 221502

WRIGHT, Timothy John. b 41. K Coll Lon BD63 AKC63. **d** 64 **p** 65. C Highfield *Ox* 64-68; Asst Chapl Worksop Coll Notts 68-71; Chapl Malvern Coll Worcs 71-77; Ho Master and Asst Chapl 77-87; Hd Master Jn Lyon Sch Harrow from 87. *Capers Mead, Whitmore Road, Harrow, Middx HA1 4AA* 081-864 9964

WRIGHT, Mrs Vyvienne Mary. b 35. S Dios Minl Tr Scheme 80. dss 83 **d** 87. Martock w Ash *B & W* 83-87; Hon C from 87. *29 North Street, Martock, Somerset TA12 6DH* Martock (0935) 823292

WRIGHT, William Easton. b 20. Linc Th Coll 52. **d** 53 **p** 54. R Offwell w Widworthy *Ex* 69-72; P-in-c Cotleigh 69-72; R Offwell, Widworthy, Cotleigh, Farway etc 72-85; rtd 85; Perm to Offic *Ex* from 85. *17 North Street, Ottery St Mary, Devon EX11 1DR* Ottery St Mary (0404) 813744

WRIGHT, William Henry Laurence. b 11. Em Coll Cam BA35 MA45. **d** 37 **p** 38. R Campbeltown *Arg* 71-79; rtd 79. *6 Moray Place, Edinburgh EH3 6DS* 031-255 1348

WRIGHT, Canon William Hutchinson. b 27. St Jo Coll Dur BA50 DipTh52. **d** 55 **p** 56. C Kimberworth *Sheff* 55-59; Ind Chapl *Dur* from 59; Hon Can Dur Cathl from 72. *109 Bishopton Road, Stockton-on-Tees, Cleveland TS18 4PL* Stockton-on-Tees (0642) 678817

WRIGHT, William Samuel. b 59. TCD DipTh87 BTh89. **d** 87 **p** 88. C Belf St Aid *Conn* 87-91; Sec Dioc Bd of Miss 90-91; I Cleenish w Mullaghdun *Clogh* from 91. *Cleenish Rectory, Bellanaleck, Enniskillen, Co Fermanagh BT92 2BP* Florencecourt (036582) 259

WRIGHTSON, Bernard. b 25. Linc Th Coll. **d** 83 **p** 84. Hon C Alford w Rigsby *Linc* 83-86; Perm to Offic 86-89; NSM Mablethorpe w Trusthorpe from 89. *Pipits Acre, Church Lane, Mablethorpe, Lincs LN12 2NU* Mablethorpe (0521) 72394

WRIGLEY, Canon Philip Arthur. b 07. St Jo Coll Dur LTh33 BA34. St Aid Birkenhead 29. **d** 34 **p** 35. R Stoke Bliss w Kyre Wyard *Worc* 69-72; rtd 72; Hon C Worc City St Paul and Old St Martin etc *Worc* 72-76; Hon C Middleton *Man* 76-80; Perm to Offic *Heref* from 80. *1 Highwell Avenue, Bromyard, Herefordshire HR7 4EL* Bromyard (0885) 483725

WRIGLEY, William Vickers. b 10. K Coll Cam BA32 MA36. Wells Th Coll 32. **d** 33 **p** 35. V Hutton Buscel *York* 57-70; V Old Malton 70-75; rtd 76; Hon C Rillington w Scampston, Wintringham etc *York* 76-83; RD Buckrose 77-80. *Beech House, Low Moorgate, Rillington, Malton, N Yorkshire YO17 8JW* Rillington (09442) 513

WRISDALE, Jean May. b 40. Local NSM Course. **d** 90. NSM Fotherby *Linc* from 90. *The Meadows, Livesey Road, Ludborough, S Humberside DN36 5SG* Grimsby (0472) 840474

WRIST-KNUDSEN, Svend (Michael). b 61. Cranfield Inst of Tech DipTh87. St Jo Coll Dur BA(Theol)91. **d** 91. C Newton Aycliffe *Dur* from 91. *St Clare's Rectory, St Cuthbert's Way, Newton Aycliffe, Co Durham DL5 5NT* Darlington (0325) 313613

WYATT, Colin. b 27. Ex Coll Ox BA54 MA55 Lon Univ BD62. Tyndale Hall Bris 60. **d** 63 **p** 64. C Radipole *Sarum* 63-66; C Southborough St Pet *Roch* 66-67; V Tetsworth *Ox* 67-72; Lect Bible Tr Inst Glas 72-74; R Hurworth *Dur* 74-79; P-in-c Dinsdale w Sockburn 74-76; R 76-79; R Sadberge 79-84; P Bacton w Wyverstone and Cotton *St E* from 84. *The Rectory, Church Road, Bacton, Stowmarket, Suffolk IP14 4LJ* Bacton (0449) 781245

WYATT, Canon David Stanley Chadwick. b 36. Fitzw Ho Cam BA59 MA71. Ely Th Coll 59. **d** 61 **p** 62. C Rochdale *Man* 61-63; Bp's Dom Chapl 63-68; R Salford St Paul w Ch Ch from 68; Hon Can Man Cathl from 82. *St Paul's Church House, Broadwalk, Salford M6 5AN* 061-736 8868

WYATT, Norman Dick. b 01. St Aid Birkenhead 35. **d** 36 **p** 37. R Dalbeattie *Glas* 64-70; rtd 70. *24 Gordon Crescent, Newton Mearns, Glasgow G77 6HZ* 041-639 4201

WYATT, Peter John. b 38. Kelham Th Coll 58. **d** 64 **p** 65. C N Stoneham *Win* 64-68; C Brixham *Ex* 68-69; Dominica 69-75; Zambia 76-78; P-in-c Ettington *Cov* 78-79; V Butlers Marston and the Pillertons w Ettington 79-86; V Codnor and Loscoe *Derby* 86-91; Chapl to the Deaf from 91. *10 Kirkstead Close, Oakwood, Derby DE2 2HN*

WYATT, Richard Norman. b 21. LVCM. **d** 84 **p** 85. C Puttenham and Wanborough *Guildf* 84-90; rtd 91. *1 High Meadow, Cocking, Midhurst, W Sussex GU29 0EZ* Midhurst (0730) 816269

WYATT, Royston Dennis. b 36. FRICS67. Sarum & Wells Th Coll 74. **d** 77 **p** 78. NSM Canford Magna *Sarum* 77-82; V Abbotsbury, Portesham and Langton Herring 82-88; Dioc Missr *Linc* from 88. *Spinneyfields, Main Street, Honington, Grantham, Lincs NG32 2PG* Loveden (0400) 50123

WYBREW, Canon Hugh Malcolm. b 34. Qu Coll Ox BA58 MA. Linc Th Coll 59. **d** 60 **p** 61. C E Dulwich St Jo *S'wark* 60-64; Tutor St Steph Ho Ox 65-71; Chapl Bucharest *Eur* 71-73; V Pinner *Lon* 73-83; Sec Fellowship of SS Alb and Sergius 84-86; Dean Jerusalem 86-89; V Ox St Mary Magd *Ox* from 89; Hon Can Gib Cathl *Eur* from 89. *15 Beaumont Street, Oxford OX1 2NA* Oxford (0865) 247836

WYER, Keith George. b 45. K Coll Lon BD71 AKC71. St Aug Coll Cant 71. **d** 72 **p** 73. C Moseley St Mary *Birm* 72-76; Chapl RNR 73-77 and from 80; C Walsall *Lich* 76-77; C Walsall St Martin 77-79; Chapl Colston's Sch Bris 79-86; Chapl Kelly Coll Tavistock from 86. *The Lodge, Kelly College, Tavistock, Devon PL19 0HJ* Tavistock (0822) 612841

WYLAM, John. b 43. AKC66. **d** 67 **p** 68. C Derby St Bart *Derby* 67-70; SSF 70-73; C Seaton Hirst *Newc* 74-77; V Byker St Silas 77-83; V Alwinton w Holystone and Alnham from 83. *The Vicarage, Alwinton, Morpeth, Northd NE65 7BE* Rothbury (0669) 50203

WYLD, Kevin Andrew. b 58. St Cath Coll Ox BA79 MA85 Univ Coll Dur MSc83 Edin Univ BD85. Edin Th Coll 82. **d** 85 **p** 86. C Winlaton *Dur* 85-87; C Houghton le Spring 87-90; V Medomsley from 90. *The Vicarage, Manor Road, Medomsley, Consett, Co Durham DH8 6QW* Ebchester (0207) 560289

WYLD, Peter Houldsworth. b 20. Magd Coll Ox BA53 MA53. Cuddesdon Coll 53. **d** 55 **p** 56. USPG 66-74; Gen Ed 71-74; Dir C of E Enquiry Cen 74-78; C Hatf *St Alb* 78-79; R Appleton *Ox* 79-89; P-in-c Besselsleigh w Dry Sandford 85-89; rtd 89. *2 Jubilee Terrace, Oxford OX1 4LN* Oxford (0865) 792506

WYLIE, Clive George. b 64. QUB BSc TCD BTh MITD. CITC. **d** 90 **p** 91. C Drumglass w Moygashel *Arm* from 90. *Kinore, 84 Killyman Road, Dungannon, Co Tyrone BT71 6DQ* Dungannon (08687) 27131

WYLIE-SMITH, Ms Megan Judith. b 52. BD74. S'wark Ord Course 88. **d** 91. Par Dn Greenstead juxta Colchester *Chelmsf* from 91. *6 Patmore Road, Colchester CO4 3PN* Colchester (0206) 871658

WYMAN, Arthur Howard. b 23. Kelham Th Coll 46. **d** 50 **p** 51. P-in-c Uxbridge Moor *Lon* 58-71; V Harrow St Pet 71-80; R Belton and Osgathorpe *Leic* 80-88; rtd 88. *40 Pantain Road, Loughborough, Leics LE11 3NA* Loughborough (0509) 214975

WYNBURNE, John Paterson Barry. b 48. St Jo Coll Dur BA70. Wycliffe Coll Toronto MDiv72 Ridley Hall Cam 72. **d** 73 **p** 74. C Gt Stanmore *Lon* 73-76; Chapl Bucharest w Sofia *Eur* 76-77; C Dorking w Ranmore *Guildf* 77-80; V Send 80-88; V York Town from 88. *The Vicarage, 286 London Road, Camberley, Surrey GU15 3JP* Camberley (0276) 23602

WYNBURNE, Victor Barry. b 06. MBE. **d** 33 **p** 34. R Ickenham *Lon* 68-77; rtd 77; Perm to Offic *Chich* from 87. *5A Pelham Road, Lindfield, Haywards Heath, W Sussex RH16 2EW* Lindfield (0444) 482008

WYNES, Michael John. b 33. AKC57. **d** 58 **p** 59. C Gt Berkhamsted *St Alb* 58-62; C Silverhill St Matt *Chich* 62-65; C Wilton *B & W* 65-68; R Berkley w Rodden 68-77; V Priddy 77-86; V Westbury sub Mendip w Easton 77-86; C Milton from 86. *475 Locking Road, Weston-super-Mare, Avon BS22 8QW* Weston-super-Mare (0934) 419294

WYNGARD, Canon Ernest Clive. b 30. Leeds Univ BA52. Coll of Resurr Mirfield 52. **d** 54 **p** 55. C Bishopwearmouth St Mich *Dur* 54-59; C Winlaton 59-61; V Castleside 61-67; V Beamish 67-80; RD Lanchester 74-80; V Dur St Giles 80-87; Hon Can Dur Cathl from 83; Master Greatham Hosp from 87; V Greatham *Dur* from 87. *Greatham Hall, Greatham, Hartlepool, Cleveland TS25 2HS* Hartlepool (0429) 871148

WYNN-EVANS, Canon James Naylor. b 34. Magd Coll Ox BA55 MA59. Linc Th Coll 57. **d** 59 **p** 60. C Goole *Sheff* 59-62; C Hatf 62-63; Chapl HM Borstal Hatf 62-67; C-in-c Dunscroft CD *Sheff* 63-67; Bp's Dom Chapl *Edin* 67-75; C Edin St Columba 67-69; R Edin St Marg 69-85; P-in-c Edin SS Phil and Jas 76-85; P-in-c Edin St Dav from 85; Can St Mary's Cathl from 86. *1 Gayfield Place, Edinburgh EH7 4AB* 031-556 1566

WYNNE, Alan John. b 46. St Luke's Coll Ex CertEd71. St Steph Ho Ox BA71 MA75. **d** 71 **p** 72. C Watford St Pet *St Alb* 71-74; Chapl Liddon Ho Lon 74-75; Chapl Abp Tenison Gr Sch Kennington 75-86; Hon C St Marylebone Annunciation Bryanston Street *Lon* 81-86; V Hoxton St Anne w St Columba from 86. *St Anne's Vicarage, 37 Hemsworth Street, London N1 5LF* 071-729 1243

WYNNE, Canon Edward. b 15. St D Coll Lamp BA37. **d** 39 **p** 40. V Blackb St Gabr *Blackb* 53-81; RD Blackb 70-79; Hon Can Blackb Cathl 77-81; rtd 81; Lic to Offic *Blackb* from 82. *18 St Peter's Close, Blackburn BB1 9HH* Blackburn (0254) 48546

WYNNE, Frederick John Gordon. b 44. Chu Coll Cam BA66 MA70. CITC DipTh84. **d** 84 **p** 85. C Dub St Patr Cathl Gp *D & G* 84-86; C Romsey *Win* 86-89; R Broughton, Bossington, Houghton and Mottisfont from 89. *The Rectory, Broughton, Stockbridge, Hants SO20 8AB* Romsey (0794) 301287

WYNNE, Preb Geoffrey. b 41. K Coll Lon BD64 AKC64 Lon Univ BSc(Soc)75 Heythrop Coll Lon MTh86. **d** 66 **p** 67. C Wolv St Pet *Lich* 66-70; Chapl Wolv Poly from 70; Sen Chapl from 79; Dir of Ords 76-83; Preb Lich Cathl from 83. *The Principal's House, 1 Compton Park,*

Wolverhampton WV3 9DU Wolverhampton (0902) 712051

WYNNE, James Arthur Hill. b 13. BSP45. **d** 47 **p** 48. V Coundon *Dur* 67-82; rtd 82; Perm to Offic *Dur* and *Newc* from 82. *44 Hermiston, Monkseaton, Whitley Bay, Tyne & Wear NE25 9AN* 091-253 0302

WYNNE, Canon Richard William Maurice. b 19. TCD BA44 MA68. TCD Div Sch Div Test44. **d** 44 **p** 45. I Monkstown St Mary *D & G* 58-78; Founder Member Irish Samaritans 59; Member from 59; Preb Dunlavin St Patr Cathl Dub 76-87; I Dub St Ann w St Mark and St Steph *D & G* 78-87; Chmn. Nat Sec and Deputation Sec Miss to Seamen from 83; rtd 87. *17 Brookville Park, Stradbrook, Blackrock, Co Dublin, Irish Republic* Dublin (1) 289-2315

WYNNE, Canon Ronald Charles. b 16. Selw Coll Cam BA38 MA42 Cape Town Univ MA79. Bp's Coll Calcutta 41. **d** 42 **p** 43. Botswana 68-82; rtd 82; Perm to Offic *Glouc* from 83. *19 Ricardo Road, Minchinhampton, Stroud, Glos GL6 9BY* Brimscombe (0453) 883372

WYNNE, Trefor. b 35. St Mich Coll Llan 72. **d** 74 **p** 75. C Llangynwyd w Maesteg *Llan* 74-77; V Trealaw 77-83; R Llanbeulan w Llanfaelog and Talyllyn *Ban* from 83. *The Rectory, Rhosneigr, Gwynedd LL64 5JX* Rhosneigr (0407) 810412

WYNNE-GREEN, Roy Rowland. b 36. Chich Th Coll 67. **d** 70 **p** 71. C Fleetwood *Blackb* 70-73; C Cen Torquay *Ex* 73-75; Chapl SW Hosp & Chapl Asst St Thos Hosp Lon 75-85; Chapl R Surrey and Distr Hosp Guildf from 85. *14 Broadacres, Guildford, Surrey GU3 3AZ* Guildford (0483) 571122

WYNNE-JONES, Dyfed. b 56. St Mich Coll Llan DipTh79. **d** 79 **p** 80. C Porthmadog *Ban* 79-82; R Llangelynnin w Rhoslefain 82-86; Dioc Youth Officer 82-88; V Llanllechid 86-88; Chapl RAF from 88. *c/o MOD, Adastral House, Theobald's Road, London WC1X 8RU* 071-430 7268

WYNNE-JONES, Nicholas Winder. b 45. Jes Coll Ox BA67 MA72. Oak Hill Th Coll 69. **d** 72 **p** 73. C St Marylebone All So w SS Pet and Jo Lon 72-75; Chapl Stowe Sch Bucks 75-83; V Gt Clacton *Chelmsf* from 83. *St John's Vicarage, Valley Road, Great Clacton, Clacton-on-Sea CO15 4AR* Clacton-on-Sea (0225) 423435

WYNNE-OWEN, Canon David. b 99. **d** 22 **p** 23. SSF from 47; Min 58-63; Min Gen 63-70; Can and Preb Sarum Cathl *Sarum* 66-70; rtd 70. *Glasshampton Monastery, Shrawley, Worcester WR6 6TG* Great Witley (0299) 896345

WYSS, Joan. b 30. **d** 88. NSM Woodhorn w Newbiggin *Newc* 88-90; rtd 90. *11 Sandridge, Newbiggin-by-the-Sea, Northd NE64 6DX* Ashington (0670) 813356

Y

YABBACOME, David Wallace. b 55. Bp Otter Coll BEd Linc Th Coll DipTh. **d** 83 **p** 84. C Egham Hythe *Guildf* 83-86; C Cen Telford *Lich* 86-87; TV from 87. *Holy Trinity Vicarage, Stirchley Lane, Dawley, Telford TF4 3SZ* Telford (0952) 595915

YABSLEY, Mrs Janet. b 42. St Alb Minl Tr Scheme 81. dss 84 **d** 87. Luton St Andr *St Alb* 84-87; Hon C Luton St Aug Limbury from 87. *11 Dale Road, Dunstable, Beds LU5 4PY* Dunstable (0582) 661480

YACOMENI, Peter Frederick. b 34. Worc Coll Ox BA58 MA61. Wycliffe Hall Ox 58. **d** 60 **p** 61. C New Malden and Coombe *S'wark* 60-64; C Bethnal Green St Jas Less Lon 64-68; V Barton Hill St Luke w Ch Ch *Bris* 68-75; V Bishopsworth 75-86; RD Bedminster 84-86; P-in-c Wick w Doynton 86-87; V Wick w Doynton and Dyrham from 87. *The Vicarage, 78A High Street, Wick, Bristol BS15 5QH* Abson (027582) 3281

YALLOP, John. b 47. BA79. Oak Hill Th Coll 79. **d** 79 **p** 80. C Brinsworth w Catcliffe *Sheff* 79-81; C Heeley 81-83; C Pitsmoor Ch Ch 83-86; V Ellesmere St Pet 86-88; C Worksop St Jo *S'well* from 90. *17 Westminster Close, Worksop, Notts S81 0PN* Worksop (0909) 472397

YANDELL, Canon Owen James. b 20. Trin Hall Cam BA42 MA46. Wycliffe Hall Ox 42. **d** 44 **p** 45. C Farlington *Portsm* 44-47; C Bath Abbey w St Jas *B & W* 47-50; V Langley St Mich *Birm* 50-57; V Stoneycroft All SS *Liv* 57-67; V Birkdale St Jo 67-73; Dir of Educn 73-85; R Sefton from 73; Hon Can Liv Cathl from 76. *The Rectory, Glebe End, Liverpool L29 6YB* 051-531 7021

YARKER, Canon Francis Bospidnick. b 12. Lon Univ BD38. ALCD38. **d** 38 **p** 39. V St Laurence in Thanet *Cant* 66-77; Hon Can Cant Cathl 76-79; rtd 77; Perm to Offic *Chich* from 77; Cant from 79. *5 Seaview Terrace, Rye, E Sussex TN31 7JZ* Rye (0797) 223744

YARNOLD, Canon Grenville Dennis. b 09. DPhil. **d** 42 **p** 43. V Llanwddyn and Llanfihangel and Llwydiarth *St As* 62-73; RD Llanfyllin 69-73; Can Res St As Cathl 74-77; rtd 78. *13 Ffordd Siarl, St Asaph, Clwyd LL17 0PT* St Asaph (0745) 582024

YATES, Andrew Martin. b 55. St Chad's Coll Dur BA77. Linc Th Coll 78. **d** 80 **p** 81. C Brightside St Thos and St Marg *Sheff* 80-83; TV Haverhill w Withersfield, the Wrattings etc *St E* 84-90; Ind Chapl 84-90; R Aylesham w Adisham *Cant* from 90. *St Peter's Vicarage, Dorman Avenue North, Aylesham, Canterbury CT3 3BL Nonington* (0304) 840266

YATES, Anthony Hugh. b 39. Univ of Wales BA62. Wycliffe Hall Ox 62. **d** 65 **p** 66. C Withington St Crispin *Man* 65-68; C Sheff Parson Cross St Cecilia *Sheff* 68-73; V Middlesb St Thos *York* 73-82; V Fenton *Lich* from 82. *The Clergy House, 65 Glebedale Road, Fenton, Stoke-on-Trent ST4 3AQ* Stoke-on-Trent (0782) 412417

YATES, Dr Arthur Stanley. b 11. Lon Univ BD43 BA45 Leeds Univ PhD49. Ripon Hall Ox. **d** 61 **p** 62. Sen Lect Coll of SS Jo and Mark Plymouth 63-77; Lic to Offic *Ex* from 74; rtd 77; Ex Univ *Ex* from 77. *The Homestead, Thornhill Road, Plymouth PL3 5NA* Plymouth (0752) 663774

YATES, David. b 56. Oak Hill Th Coll DipHE90. **d** 90 **p** 91. C Parkham, Alwington, Buckland Brewer etc *Ex* from 90. *5 Manor Court, Parkham, Bideford, Devon EX39 5PG* Horns Cross (0237) 451800

YATES, David Herbert. b 10. **d** 70 **p** 73. Rhodesia 70-80; rtd 80; C Verwood *Sarum* 80-85; Perm to Offic from 85. *67 Joys Road, Three Legged Cross, Wimborne, Dorset BH21 6SJ* Wimborne (0202) 824499

YATES, James Ainsworth. b 21. Bps' Coll Cheshunt 56. **d** 58 **p** 59. V Shillington *St Alb* 60-79; V Upper Gravenhurst 62-72; R Lower Gravenhurst 62-72; RD Shefford 69-79; V Upper w Lower Gravenhurst 72-79; V Sandon and Wallington w Rushden 79; R Sandon, Wallington and Rushden w Clothall 79-87; rtd 87. *97 Grove Road, Hitchin, Herts SG5 1SQ* Hitchin (0462) 434959

YATES, Miss Joanna Mary. b 49. St Anne's Coll Ox BA71 MA74 K Coll Lon PGCE72. S'wark Ord Course 89. **d** 91. NSM Regents Park St Mark *Lon* from 91. *68 Eton Rise, Eton College Road, London NW3 2DA* 071-586 6825

✠**YATES, Rt Rev John.** b 25. Jes Coll Cam BA49 MA52. Linc Th Coll 49. **d** 51 **p** 52 **c** 72. C Southgate Ch Ch *Lon* 51-54; Lic to Offic *Linc* 54-59; Tutor Linc Th Coll 54-59; Chapl 56-59; V Bottesford *Linc* 59-65; Lic to Offic *Lich* 66-72; Prin Lich Th Coll 66-72; Preb Lich Cathl *Lich* 72; Suff Bp Whitby *York* 72-75; Bp Glouc from 75. *Bishopscourt, Pitt Street, Gloucester GL1 2BQ* Gloucester (0452) 24598

YATES, Canon John Dennis. b 28. Wells Th Coll. **d** 57 **p** 58. C Elton All SS *Man* 57-60; C Cannock *Lich* 60-62; R Moston St Jo *Man* 62-73; V Bury St Pet 73-76; R Ipswich St Mary at Stoke w St Pet & St Mary Quay *St E* 76-80; TR from 80; P-in-c Wherstead from 77; Hon Can St E Cathl from 87. *The Rectory, 74 Ancaster Road, Ipswich IP2 9AJ* Ipswich (0473) 601895

YATES, Keith Leonard. b 36. K Coll Lon BD AKC61 Nottm Univ MPhil79. Wells Th Coll. **d** 69 **p** 70. C Luton Ch Ch *St Alb* 69-73; Hon C Luton St Andr 73-76; R Grimoldby w Manby *Linc* 76-80; P-in-c Yarburgh 76-78; R 78-80; P-in-c Alvingham w N and S Cockerington 76-78; V 78-80; P-in-c Gt w Lt Carlton 77-78; R 78-80; Lect Sarum & Wells Th Coll 80-87; R Upper Chelsea H Trin w St Jude *Lon* from 87. *Upper Chelsea Rectory, 97A Cadogan Lane, London SW1X 9DU* 071-235 3383

YATES, Kenneth. b 44. Leeds Univ CQSW80. Kelham Th Coll 65. **d** 70 **p** 71. C Leeds City *Ripon* 70-74; C Worksop Priory *S'well* 74-75; Hon C Bawtry w Austerfield 75-78; Hon C Cantley *Sheff* 80-83; Hon C Doncaster St Jude 83-86; Hon C Ashford St Matt *Lon* 86-88; TV Brighton Resurr *Chich* from 88. *St Alban's Vicarage, 10 Natal Road, Brighton BN2 4BN* Brighton (0273) 602357

YATES, Michael Anthony. b 48. Oak Hill Th Coll. **d** 82 **p** 83. C Hebburn St Jo *Dur* 82-85; C Sheldon *Birm* 85-87; V Lea Hall from 87. *St Richard's Vicarage, Hallmoor Road, Birmingham B33 9QY* 021-783 2319

YATES, Michael John Whitworth. b 39. Selw Coll Cam BA62. Oak Hill Th Coll 62. **d** 64 **p** 65. C New Catton St Luke *Nor* 64-68; C Lowestoft St Jo 68-74; Perm to Offic

Bradf from 75. *5 Belle Hill, Giggleswick, Settle, N Yorkshire BD24 0BA* Settle (07292) 2690

YATES, Michael Peter. b 47. Leeds Univ BA69 MA70 MPhil85. Coll of Resurr Mirfield 69. **d** 71 **p** 72. C Crewe St Andr *Ches* 71-76; V Wheelock 76-79; Chapl Rainhill Hosp *Liv* 79-89; Chapl Barnsley Distr Gen Hosp from 89. *The Chaplain's Office, Barnsley Hospital, Gawber Road, Barnsley, S Yorkshire S75 2EP* Barnsley (0226) 730000

YATES, Dr Paul David. b 47. Sussex Univ BA73 DPhil80. Sarum & Wells Th Coll 88. **d** 91. NSM Lewes All SS, St Anne, St Mich and St Thos *Chich* from 91. *17 St Swithun's Terrace, Lewes, E Sussex BN7 1UJ* Brighton (0273) 473463

YATES, Peter Francis. b 47. Sheff Univ BA69 Nottm Univ DipTh71. Kelham Th Coll 69. **d** 74 **p** 75. C Mexborough *Sheff* 74-78; C Sevenoaks St Jo *Roch* 78-81; CSWG from 81. *The Monastery, Crawley Down, Crawley, W Sussex RH10 4LH* Copthorne (0342) 712074

YATES, Raymond Paul. b 55. Oak Hill Th Coll BA88. **d** 88 **p** 89. C Bootle St Mary w St Paul *Liv* 88-91; C Drypool *York* from 91. *383 Southcoates Lane, Hull HU9 3UN*

YATES, Dr Roger Alan. b 47. MRCP77 Trin Coll Cam BA68 MB71 BChir71 MA72 Bris Univ PhD75. N Ord Course 84. **d** 87 **p** 88. NSM Wilmslow *Ches* from 87. *3 Racecourse Park, Wilmslow, Cheshire SK9 5LU* Wilmslow (0625) 520246

YATES, Mrs Sian. b 57. Univ of Wales (Ban). Linc Th Coll 78. **d** 80. C Risca *Mon* 80-83; Chapl Ch Hosp Horsham 83-85; TM Haverhill w Withersfield, the Wrattings etc *St E* 85-90; Dioc Youth Chapl *Cant* from 90. *Diocesan House, 1 Lady Wootton's Green, Canterbury, Kent CT1 1TL* Canterbury (0227) 459401

YATES, Canon Timothy Edward. b 35. Magd Coll Cam BA59 MA62 Uppsala Univ DTh78. Ridley Hall Cam 58. **d** 60 **p** 61. C Tonbridge SS Pet and Paul *Roch* 60-63; Tutor St Jo Coll Dur 63-71; Warden Cranmer Hall Dur 71-79; P-in-c Darley w S Darley *Derby* 79-82; R Darley 82-90; Dioc Dir of Ords from 85; Hon Can Derby Cathl from 89. *Great Longstone Vicarage, Bakewell, Derbyshire DE4 1TB* Great Longstone (062987) 257

YATES, Warwick John. b 52. Univ of Wales (Lamp) BA78. Wycliffe Hall Ox 87. **d** 89 **p** 90. C Hoddesdon *St Alb* from 89. *St Catherine's House, Paul's Lane, Hoddesdon, Herts EN11 8TR* Hoddesdon (0992) 443724

YATES, William Herbert. b 35. Man Univ BA59. Chich Th Coll 60. **d** 61 **p** 62. C Blackpool St Steph *Blackb* 61-65; C Wednesbury St Jo *Lich* 65-69; V Porthill 69-78; R Norton in the Moors 78-84; R Church Aston from 84. *St Andrew's Rectory, Church Aston, Newport, Shropshire TF10 9JG* Newport (0952) 810942

YATES-ROUND, Joseph Laurence John. b 25. S'wark Ord Course 75. **d** 76 **p** 77. NSM Tonbridge SS Pet and Paul *Roch* 76-83; Chapl Palma and Balearic Is w Ibiza etc *Eur* 83-90; rtd 90. *5 Willowtree Grove, Road Heath, Alsager, Stoke-on-Trent ST7 3TE* Alsager (0270) 883425

YAXLEY, Canon Robert William. b 05. ARIC27 Birm Univ BSc25. Ripon Hall Ox 29. **d** 31 **p** 32. V Moseley St Anne *Birm* 51-75; Hon Can Birm Cathl 65-76; rtd 76; Perm to Offic *Birm* from 79. *Flat 24, 20 Moor Green Lane, Birmingham B13 8ND* 021-449 8647

YEANDLE-HIGNELL, Dr John Wilfred. b 05. St Cath Soc Ox BA46 MA46. K Coll Lon. **d** 30 **p** 31. V Binsey *Ox* 42-50; R Wytham 42-50; rtd 75. *Underdown Farm, Yarcombe, Honiton, Devon EX14 9BJ* Honiton (0404) 86329

YEATS, Charles. b 56. Ball Coll Ox BA85 MA90 K Coll Lon MTh90. Wycliffe Hall Ox 85. **d** 87 **p** 88. C Islington St Mary *Lon* 87-90; Research Fell Whitefield Inst Ox from 90. *2 Mere Road, Wolvercote, Oxford OX2 8AN* Oxford (0865) 510037

YEATS, Peter Derek. b 62. Leeds Univ BA84. Cranmer Hall Dur 85. **d** 87 **p** 88. C Tynemouth Cullercoats St Paul *Newc* 87-90; USPG from 90. *c/o USPG, Partnership House, 157 Waterloo Road, London SE1 8XA* 071-928 8681

YEEND, Walter Archibald John. b 12. AKC40. **d** 40 **p** 41. C W Molesey *Guildf* 40-42; V from 45; C Westmr St Matt *Lon* 43-45. *The Vicarage, 518 Walton Road, West Molesey, Surrey* 081-979 2805

YENDALL, John Edward Thomas. b 52. St Jo Coll Dur BA88. Cranmer Hall Dur. **d** 88 **p** 89. C Ban 88-90; C Meylllteyrn w Botwnnog and Llandygwnnin etc from 90. *Bron Philip Farm, Botwnnog, Pwllheli, Gwynedd LL53 8PY* Botwnnog (075883) 359

YEO, Lester John. b 55. Ex Coll Ox BA77 MA81. Coll of Resurr Mirfield 78. **d** 80 **p** 81. C Plymstock *Ex* 80-83; C Northam w Westward Ho and Appledore 83-85; TV 85-89; P-in-c Devonport St Mark Ford from 89. *1 Home Park, Plymouth PL2 1BQ* Plymouth (0752) 560828

YEO, Richard Ellery. b 25. Ex Coll Ox MA49 DipEd49. Cant Sch of Min 86. **d** 89 **p** 90. NSM Broadstairs *Cant* from 89. *Skaigh, 1A Stanley Road, Broadstairs, Kent CT10 1DA* Thanet (0843) 61523

YEOMAN, David. b 44. Univ of Wales DipTh69. St Mich Coll Llan 66. **d** 70 **p** 71. C Cardiff St Jo *Llan* 70-72; C Caerphilly 72-76; V Ystrad Rhondda w Ynyscynon 76-81; V Mountain Ash from 81. *The Vicarage, Duffryn Road, Mountain Ash, M Glam CF45 4DA* Mountain Ash (0443) 473700

YEOMAN, Douglas. b 35. ACII63. **d** 77 **p** 78. NSM Edin St Martin *Edin* from 77; NSM Edin St Luke 79-91. *6 Craiglockhart Crescent, Edinburgh EH14 1EY* 031-443 5449

YEOMAN, Miss Ruth Jane. b 60. Sheff Univ BSc82 MSc85 Dur Univ PGCE83. Ripon Coll Cuddesdon BA90. **d** 91. C Coleshill *Birm* from 91. *30 Temple Way, Coleshill, Warks B46 1HN* Coleshill (0675) 464297

YEOMANS, Ernest Harold. b 07. K Coll (NS) STh44 St Paul's Coll Burgh. **d** 39 **p** 39. V Newfoundpool *Leic* 61-75; rtd 75; Lic to Offic *Leic* 75-81; Perm to Offic from 81. *7 The Courtyard, Bancks Street, Minehead, Somerset TA24 5NJ* Minehead (0643) 704746

YEOMANS, Robert John. b 44. AKC66. **d** 67 **p** 68. C Pontesbury I and II *Heref* 67-70; Asst Youth Officer *St Alb* 70-72; Project Officer (Dio St Alb) Gen Syn Bd of Educn 73-77; V Is of Dogs Ch Ch and St Jo w St Luke *Lon* 77-87; V Waterloo St Jo w St Andr *S'wark* from 87. *St John's Vicarage, Secker Street, London SE1 8UF* 071-928 4470 or 633 9819

YEOMANS, Thomas Henry. b 14. **d** 60 **p** 61. V Helme *Wakef* 62-71; V Wincle and Wildboarclough *Ches* 73-79; rtd 79; Perm to Offic *Ches* from 80. *14 Dean Close, Sandbach, Cheshire* Crewe (0270) 765638

YERBURGH, Canon David Savile. b 34. Magd Coll Cam BA57 MA61. Wells Th Coll 57. **d** 59 **p** 60. C Cirencester *Glouc* 59-63; C Bitterne Park *Win* 63-67; V Churchdown St Jo *Glouc* 67-74; RD Glouc N 73-74; V Charlton Kings St Mary 74-85; R Minchinhampton from 85; Hon Can Glouc Cathl from 86. *The Rectory, Butt Street, Minchinhampton, Stroud, Glos GL6 9JP* Brimscombe (0453) 882289

YERBURGH, Peter Charles. b 31. Magd Coll Cam BA53 MA57. Wells Th Coll 53. **d** 55 **p** 56. Chapl Wells Cathl Sch 58-71; Chapl Durlston Court Sch Barton on Sea 71-91; rtd 91. *2 Mill Race Close, Mill Road, Salisbury SP2 7RX* Salisbury (0722) 327796

YEULETT, George Eric. b 04. Qu Coll Cam BA27 MA30. Bps' Coll Cheshunt 27. **d** 28 **p** 29. V W Acton St Martin *Lon* 53-71; rtd 71; Perm to Offic *Chich* from 76. *2 Poole Farm Court, South Road, Hailsham, E Sussex BN27 3NU* Hailsham (0323) 842452

YEWDALL, Mrs Mary Doreen. b 23. Nottm Univ DipEd71 BTh85. E Midl Min Tr Course 76. **dss** 79 **d** 87. Kirkby in Ashfield St Thos *S'well* 79-81; Daybrook 81-87; Par Dn 87-89; rtd 89; Hon Par Dn Bilsthorpe *S'well* 89-91; Hon Par Dn Eakring 89-91; Hon Par Dn Winkburn 89-91; Hon Par Dn Maplebeck 89-91. *2A The Avenue, Norton, Malton, N Yorkshire YO17 9EF* Malton (0653) 697773

YIN, Canon Roy Henry Bowyer. b 10. K Coll Cam BA32 MA36. Cuddesdon Coll 32. **d** 33 **p** 34. Singapore from 64; rtd 75; Hon Can Singapore from 80. *114-A Newton Court, Newton Road, Singapore 1130* Singapore (65) 252-5108

YORK, Canon Humphrey Bowmar. b 28. St Chad's Coll Dur BA54. **d** 55 **p** 56. C Beamish *Dur* 55-57; C Tettenhall Regis *Lich* 57-62; P-in-c Lansallos w Pelynt *Truro* 62-63; R Lanreath 62-67; V Pelynt 63-67; P-in-c Lanlivery 67-74; P-in-c Luxulyan 67-74; P-in-c Lanlivery w Luxulyan 74-83; RD Bodmin 76-82; R Antony w Sheviock from 83; Hon Can Truro Cathl from 90. *The Rectory, Sheviock, Torpoint, Cornwall PL11 3EH* St Germans (0503) 30477

YORK, Archbishop of. See HABGOOD, Most Rev and Rt Hon John Stapylton

YORK, Archdeacon of. See AUSTIN, Ven George Bernard

YORK, Dean of. See SOUTHGATE, Very Rev John Eliot

YORKE, Edward Frederick. b 06. G&C Coll Cam BA28 MA32. Tyndale Hall Bris 28. **d** 31 **p** 32. R Denver *Ely* 66-70; rtd 71; Hon C Portman Square St Paul *Lon* 84-88; Hon C Langham Place All So 88-90. *Flat 28, Grace Darling House, Vallis Close, Poole, Dorset BH15 1XZ* Poole (0202) 681739

YORKE, John Andrew. b 47. Cranmer Hall Dur 70. **d** 73 **p** 74. C Spitalfields Ch Ch w All SS *Lon* 73-78; Canada from 78. *St Matthew's Anglican Church, PO Box 65, Fort McPherson, NWT, Canada, X0E 0J0* Fort McPherson (403) 952-2375

YORKE, Canon Leslie Henry. b 09. Dur Univ LTh34. St Aug Coll Cant 33. **d** 33 **p** 34. V Christchurch *Win* 62-76; rtd 76; Perm to Offic *Chich* 76-88 and from 89; P-in-c Aldrington 88-89. *5 Burlington Court, George V Avenue, Worthing, W Sussex BN11 5RG* Worthing (0903) 48549

YORKE, Canon Michael Leslie. b 39. Magd Coll Cam BA62 MA66. Cuddesdon Coll 62. **d** 64 **p** 65. C Croydon *Cant* 64-68; Succ Chelmsf Cathl *Chelmsf* 68-69; Prec and Chapl 69-73; Dep Dir Cathl Cen for Research and Tr 72-74; P-in-c Ashdon w Hadstock 74-76; R 76-78; Can Res Chelmsf Cathl 78-88; Vice-Provost 84-88; P-in-c N Lynn w St Marg and St Nic *Nor* from 88; Chmn Dioc Adv Bd for Min from 90. *St Margaret's Vicarage, St Margaret's Place, King's Lynn PE30 5DL* King's Lynn (0553) 772858

YORKSTONE, Peter. b 48. Loughb Univ BTech72. Oak Hill Th Coll 79. **d** 81 **p** 82. C Blackpool St Thos *Blackb* 81-85; V Copp from 85. *St Anne's Vicarage, Copp Lane, Great Eccleston, Preston PR3 0ZN* Great Eccleston (0995) 70231

YOUELL, Canon George. b 10. Keele Univ MA69. St Steph Ho Ox 33. **d** 33 **p** 34. Adn Stoke *Lich* 56-70; Can Res Ely Cathl *Ely* 70-81; Vice-Dean 73-81; rtd 81; Perm to Offic *St E* from 82; *Ely* from 85. *Stranton Cottage, Wattisfield Road, Walsham-le-Willows, Bury St Edmunds IP31 3BD* Walsham-le-Willows (0359) 8888

YOUENS, Ven John Ross. b 14. CB70 OBE59 MC45. Kelham Th Coll 31. **d** 39 **p** 40. Chapl Gen 66-74; Chapl to HM The Queen 69-85; rtd 74. *Osbourne House, East Cowes, Isle of Wight PO32 6JY*

YOULD, Guy Martin. b 37. FSAScot Keble Coll Ox BA61 DipTh62 MA65 BD68 Hull Univ PhD80. Lambeth STh75 St Steph Ho Ox 61. **d** 63 **p** 64. C Middlesb St Jo the Ev *York* 63-65; Chapl Magd Coll Ox 65-68; C Cowley St Jo *Ox* 65-68; Lic to Offic 68-71 and from 87; Asst Chapl Radley Coll Abingdon 68-71; C W Kirby St Bridget *Ches* 71-74; Chapl Loretto Sch Musselburgh 74; V Liscard St Mary w St Columba *Ches* 74-78; Australia 78-80; C Doncaster St Leon and St Jude *Sheff* 80-81; V Brodsworth w Hooton Pagnell, Frickley etc 81-87; Chapl St Mary's Sch Wantage from 87. *Alma House, 35 Newbury Street, Wantage, Oxford OX12 8BZ* Wantage (02357) 3617 or 3571

YOULE, Peter William. b 36. S'wark Ord Course. **d** 89 **p** 90. NSM Gt Totham *Chelmsf* from 89. *3 Seagers Hall Road, Great Totham, Maldon, Essex CM9 8PB* Maldon (0621) 892314

YOULL, Cyril Thomas. b 26. Qu Coll Birm DipTh74. **d** 74 **p** 75. C Leamington Priors H Trin *Cov* 75-76; C Lillington 76-77; Canada from 78. *Christ Church Rectory, PO Box 33, Bridgenorth, Ontario, Canada, K0L 1H0* Bridgenorth (705) 292-7104

YOUNG, Andrew John. b 50. St Jo Coll Dur BA73. Westcott Ho Cam 73. **d** 75 **p** 89. C Nailsworth *Glouc* 75-76; NSM Yeovil w Kingston Pitney *B & W* from 89. *17 Stone Lane, Yeovil, Somerset BA21 4NN* Yeovil (0935) 76394

YOUNG, Aubrey William. b 38. **d** 91. NSM Tallaght *D & G* from 91. *27 Flower Grove, Dun Laoghaire, Irish Republic* Dublin (1) 285-5069

YOUNG, Brian Thomas. b 42. Linc Th Coll 67. **d** 70 **p** 71. C Monkseaton St Mary *Newc* 70-73; C Berwick H Trin 73-77; P-in-c Gt Broughton *Carl* 77-80; P-in-c Gt Broughton and Broughton Moor 80; V 80-83; V Chorley *Ches* 83-90; V Alderley Edge from 90. *The Vicarage, Church Lane, Alderley Edge, Cheshire SK9 7UZ* Alderley Edge (0625) 583249

YOUNG, Canon Charles John. b 24. Qu Coll Birm 52. **d** 55 **p** 56. C Dudley St Thos *Worc* 55-58; C Beeston S'well 58-61; V Lady Bay 61-66; R Kirkby in Ashfield 66-75; V Balderton from 75; RD Newark 82-90; Hon Can S'well Minster from 84. *The Vicarage, Main Street, Balderton, Newark, Notts NG24 3NN* Newark (0636) 704811

YOUNG, Clive. b 48. St Jo Coll Dur BA70. Ridley Hall Cam 70. **d** 72 **p** 73. C Neasden cum Kingsbury St Cath *Lon* 72-75; C Hammersmith St Paul 75-79; P-in-c Old Ford St Paul w St Steph 79-82; V Old Ford St Paul w St Steph and St Mark from 82; AD Tower Hamlets from 88. *Old Ford Vicarage, St Stephen's Road, London E3 5JL* 081-980 9020

YOUNG, Colin James. b 60. TCD BA DipTh85. **d** 85 **p** 86. C Templemore *D & R* 85-88; C Malahide w Balgriffin *D & G* 88-91; C Limerick City *L & K* from 91.

14 Springfield Drive, Dooradoyle, Limerick, Irish Republic Limerick (61) 302038

YOUNG, Daniel George Harding. b 52. New Coll Ox BA73 MA83. Cranmer Hall Dur 77. **d** 80 **p** 81. C Bushbury *Lich* 80-83; Chapl Dean Close Sch Cheltenham from 83. *15 Harrington Drive, Up Hatherley, Cheltenham, Glos* Cheltenham (0242) 528922 or 519275

YOUNG, David. b 37. Open Univ PhD89. Lambeth STh79 Ely Th Coll 61 Linc Th Coll 64. **d** 67 **p** 68. C Crofton *Wakef* 67-68; C Heckmondwike 68-71; V Stainland 71-76; R Patrington w Winestead *York* 76-80; Chapl St Jo Hosp Linc 80-90; Chapl N Lincs Mental Health Unit from 90; Chapl Witham Court ESMI Unit from 90. *Westview, Aisthorpe, Lincoln LN1 2SG* Lincoln (0522) 730912

YOUNG, David Charles. b 44. Or Coll Ox BA66 MA70. S'wark Ord Course 74. **d** 77 **p** 78. C Harborne St Pet *Birm* 77-81; P-in-c Edgbaston St Germain 81-83; P-in-c Birm St Paul 83-85; Perm to Offic *St Alb* from 85. *18 Tamar Walk, Leighton Buzzard, Beds LU7 8DD* Leighton Buzzard (0525) 382881

YOUNG, David John. b 43. Nottm Univ BA64 MPhil89. Lambeth STh87 Coll of Resurr Mirfield 64. **d** 66 **p** 67. C Warsop *S'well* 66-68; C Harworth 68-71; P-in-c Hackenthorpe Ch Ch *Derby* 71-73; TV Frecheville and Hackenthorpe 73-75; V Chaddesden St Phil 75-83; R Narborough and Huncote *Leic* 83-89; RD Guthlaxton I (Blaby) 87-90; Chapl Leic Univ from 90. *23 Victoria Park Road, Leicester LE2 1XE* Leicester (0533) 522007

✠**YOUNG, Rt Rev David Nigel de Lorentz.** b 31. Ball Coll Ox BA54 MA58. Wycliffe Hall Ox 57. **d** 59 **p** 60 **c** 77. C Allerton *Liv* 59-62; C St Marylebone St Mark Hamilton Terrace *Lon* 62-63; CMS 63-67; Perm to Offic *Ches & Man* 67-70; Lect Man Univ 67-70; V Burwell *Ely* 70-75; Hon Can Ely Cathl 75-77; Adn Huntingdon 75-77; V Gt w Lt Gidding and Steeple Gidding 75-77; R Hemingford Abbots 77; Bp Ripon from 77. *Bishop Mount, Ripon, N Yorkshire HG4 5DP* Ripon (0765) 2045

YOUNG, Derek John. b 42. St D Coll Lamp DipTh73. **d** 73 **p** 74. C Griffithstown *Mon* 73-76; C Ebbw Vale 76-77; V Penmaen 77-81; V Penmaen and Crumlin 81-87; Chapl Oakdale Hosp Gwent from 83; V New Tredegar *Mon* from 87. *The Vicarage, Gorse Terrace, New Tredegar, Gwent NP2 6NR* Bargoed (0443) 821087

YOUNG, Desmond Terence. b 17. TCD BA40. **d** 41 **p** 42. P-in-c Thomastown *C & O* 62-74; I Inistioge w the Rower 62-74; RD Kells 65-74; C Roundhay St Edm *Ripon* 74-77; V Leeds Gipton Epiphany 77-83; rtd 83; Perm to Offic *Guildf* from 83. *St Edwards, Barton Road, Bramley, Guildford, Surrey GU5 0HZ* Guildford (0483) 893711

YOUNG, Frederick Charles. b 32. TCD BA56 MA59 MLitt63 DTh68. **d** 58 **p** 59. C Dub Donnybrook *D & G* 58-63; C Taney Ch Ch 63-66; I Bray 66-70; I Dalkey St Patr 70-73; C Upper Norwood All SS w St Marg *Cant* 81-84; Warden Coll of Preachers from 84; P-in-c Morton w Hacconby *Linc* 84-90; V from 90. *The Vicarage, Morton, Bourne, Lincs PE10 0NR* Morton (0778) 570660

YOUNG, Canon Geoffrey Maxwell. b 12. Ch Coll Cam BA34 MA38. Westcott Ho Cam 34. **d** 35 **p** 36. V W Malling w Offham *Roch* 67-81; Hon Can Roch Cathl 73-81; rtd 81; Perm to Offic *Roch* 82-84; Hon PV Roch Cathl from 84. *4 Albany Road, Rochester, Kent ME1 3ET* Medway (0634) 844608

YOUNG, George William. b 31. Lon Coll of Div ALCD55 LTh74. **d** 56 **p** 57. C Everton Em *Liv* 56-58; C Halliwell St Pet *Man* 58-61; V Newburn *Newc* 61-67; P-in-c Tylers Green *Ox* 67-69; V 69-80; Lic to Offic 80-84; Area Sec (W England) SAMS 80-84; Hon C Purley Ch Ch *S'wark* 84-87; V Beckenham St Jo *Roch* from 87. *St John's Vicarage, 249 Eden Park Avenue, Beckenham, Kent BR3 3JN* 081-650 3515

YOUNG, Henry Lawrence. b 19. TCD MA46. **d** 47 **p** 48. R Gt and Lt Casterton w Pickworth and Tickencote *Pet* 64-70; rtd 70; Hon C Perth St Jo *St And* from 70. *6 Pullar Terrace, Hillyland, Perth PH1 2QF* Perth (0738) 36797

YOUNG, Iain Clavering. b 56. Newc Poly BA79. Coll of Resurr Mirfield 80. **d** 83 **p** 84. C Wallsend St Luke *Newc* 83-86; C Horton 86-87; V from 87. *St Benedict's Vicarage, Brierley Road, Cowpen, Blyth, Northd NE24 5AU* Blyth (0670) 367035

YOUNG, Jeremy Michael. b 54. Ch Coll Cam BA76 MA80. Coll of Resurr Mirfield 78. **d** 80 **p** 81. C Whitworth w Spennymoor *Dur* 80-83; C Boxmoor St Jo *St Alb* 83-86; V Croxley Green St Oswald from 86. *The Vicarage, 159 Baldwins Lane, Croxley Green, Rickmansworth, Herts WD3 3LL* Watford (0923) 32386

YOUNG, John David. b 37. DLC60 Lon Univ BD65 Sussex Univ MA77. Clifton Th Coll 62. **d** 65 **p** 66. C Plymouth St Jude *Ex* 65-68; Hd of RE Northgate Sch Ipswich 68-71; Lic to Offic *St E* 68-71; Chapl and Sen Lect Bp Otter Coll Chich 71-81; Chapl and Sen Lect W Sussex Inst of HE 77-81; Chapl and Sen Lect Coll of Ripon & York St Jo 81-87; C York St Paul *York* 87-88; Dioc Ev from 88. *73 Middlethorpe Grove, York YO2 2JX* York (0904) 704195

YOUNG, John Kenneth. Edin Th Coll 62. **d** 64 **p** 65. C Gosforth All SS *Newc* 64-67; C Newc St Gabr 67-69; R Bowers Gifford *Chelmsf* 69-72; R Bowers Gifford w N Benfleet 72-75; P-in-c Kirkwhelpington *Newc* 75-79; P-in-c Kirkheaton 75-79; P-in-c Cambo 77-79; P-in-c Kirkharle 77-79; V Kirkwhelpington, Kirkharle, Kirkheaton and Cambo 79-82; V Gosforth St Nic from 82. *The Vicarage, 17 Rectory Road, Gosforth, Newcastle upon Tyne NE3 1XR* 091-285 1326

YOUNG, John Strang Walker. b 55. Magd Coll Ox MA80. St Steph Ho Ox 77. **d** 80 **p** 81. C N Lynn w St Marg and St Nic *Nor* 80-82; C St Marylebone All SS *Lon* 82-86; V Crewe St Andr *Ches* from 86. *St Andrew's Vicarage, 303 Nantwich Road, Crewe CW2 6PF* Crewe (0270) 69000

YOUNG, Canon Jonathan Frederick. b 25. Univ of Wales (Lamp) BA51 Birm Univ MA81. St Mich Coll Llan 51. **d** 53 **p** 54. Lic to Offic *Ox* 59-74; SSJE 62-71; Bp's Chapl for Community Relns *Birm* 71-74; Chapl Coun for Soc Resp 74-85; Hon Can Birm Cathl 84-85; USA from 85; rtd 90. *193 Salem Street, Boston, Massachusetts 02113, USA*

YOUNG, Jonathan Priestland. b 44. AKC68. **d** 69 **p** 70. C Clapham H Trin *S'wark* 69-73; C Mitcham St Mark 73-74; V Godmanchester *Ely* 74-82; P-in-c Cam St Giles w St Pet 82; P-in-c Chesterton St Luke 82; TR Cam Ascension from 82. *Ascension Rectory, Cambridge CB4 3PS* Cambridge (0223) 61919

YOUNG, Miss Katharine Jane. b 65. Westmr Coll Ox BA87. Sarum & Wells Th Coll 89. **d** 91. Par Dn Basingstoke *Win* from 91. *17 Deep Lane, Basingstoke, Hants RG21 1RY* Basingstoke (0256) 466694

YOUNG, Kathleen Margaret. QUB BD BTh. **d** 88 **p** 90. C Carrickfergus *Conn* from 88. *3 The Avenue, Carrickfergus, Co Antrim BT38 8LT* Carrickfergus (09603) 67758

YOUNG, Malcolm Ryswinn. b 36. Ch Coll Cam BA60 MA64. Lon Coll of Div ALCD63 LTh74 St Jo Coll Nottm. **d** 63 **p** 64. C Egham *Guildf* 63-67; Lic to Offic 67-71; Asst Chapl K Sch Roch 71-88; C Patcham Chich from 88. *66 Eldred Avenue, Brighton BN1 5EG* Brighton (0273) 503926

YOUNG, Martin Edward. b 20. Or Coll Ox BA41 MA45. Cuddesdon Coll 41. **d** 43 **p** 44. R Wootton w Quinton *Pet* 64-72; R Wootton w Quinton and Preston Deanery 72-78; V Welford w Sibbertoft 78-82; V Welford w Sibbertoft and Marston Trussell 82-88; rtd 88. *29 St Andrew's Road, Headington, Oxford OX3 9DL* Oxford (0865) 64022

YOUNG, Margaret Dorothy. *See* COOLING, Mrs Margaret Dorothy

YOUNG, Canon Noel. b 26. St Aid Birkenhead 53. **d** 56 **p** 57. C Garston *Liv* 56-59; C Oldham St Paul *Man* 59-61; R Goldhanger w Lt Totham *Chelmsf* 61-65; C-in-c Leigh-on-Sea St Aid CD 65-69; V Leigh-on-Sea St Aid 69-72; I Kilnasoolagh *L & K* 73-78; I Tullow w Shillelagh, Aghold and Mullinacuff *C & O* 79-88; Preb Leighlin Cathl 83-88; Preb Ossory Cathl 83-88; Treas (Ossory and Leighlin Cathls) 85-88; I Templemore w Thurles, Kilfithmone, Holycross etc from 88. *The Rectory, Roscrea Road, Templemore, Co Tipperary, Irish Republic* Templemore (504) 31175

YOUNG, Norman Keith. b 35. E Anglian Minl Tr Course. **d** 87 **p** 88. C Burwell *Ely* from 87. *St Mary's Vicarage, Swaffham Prior, Cambridge CB5 0JT* Newmarket (0638) 741409

YOUNG, Paul Goodwin. b 07. Em Coll Cam BA30 MA38. Coll of Resurr Mirfield 30. **d** 32 **p** 33. R Redmarley D'Abitot *Worc* 59-74; rtd 74; Perm to Offic *Ex* from 74. *8 Shepherds Meadow, Beaford, Winkleigh, Devon EX19 8NF* Beaford (08053) 351

YOUNG, Peter John. b 26. Pemb Coll Cam BA49. Ridley Hall Cam 49. **d** 51 **p** 52. C Cheadle *Ches* 51-54; Malaya 54-63; Malaysia from 63. *247 Jalan 5/48, 46000 Petaling Jaya, Selangor, Malaysia* Kuala Lumpur (3) 792-9269

YOUNG, Canon Raymond Grant. b 11. MBE81. **d** 43 **p** 44. Chapl to Deaf (Dios Win and Portsm) 70-81; Hon Can Win Cathl *Win* 77-81; rtd 81; Perm to Offic *Win* from 81. *66 Chalvington Road, Eastleigh, Hants SO5 3DT* Chandler's Ford (0703) 261519

YOUNG, Roger Edward. b 40. Dur Univ BSc62. Cuddesdon Coll 64. **d** 66 **p** 67. C Eglwysilan *Llan* 66-68; C Llanishen and Lisvane 68-74; C-in-c Rhydyfelin CD 74-78; TV Ystradyfodwg 78-81; V 81-88; Chapl Tyntyla, Llwynypia and Porth and Distr Hosps from 81; Dir of Tr for the NSM from 86; R Peterston-super-Ely w St Brides-super-Ely *Llan* from 88. *The Rectory, Peterston-super-Ely, Cardiff CF5 6LH* Peterston-super-Ely (0446) 760297

YOUNG, Canon Stanley. b 14. St Jo Coll Dur BA36. Ely Th Coll 36. **d** 37 **p** 38. C Camberwell St Luke *S'wark* 37-40; Min Can Carl Cathl *Carl* 40-45; Warden St Anne's Ch Ho Soho 45-48; C Pimlico St Mary Graham Terrace *Lon* 48-50; Warden Pemb Coll Miss Walworth *S'wark* 50-53; V Aldermaston w Wasing *Ox* 53-69; RD Bradfield 63-68; V Long Crendon 70-80; P-in-c Chearsley w Nether Winchendon 77-80; V Long Crendon w Chearsley and Nether Winchendon from 80; Hon Can Ch Ch from 81. *The Vicarage, Long Crendon, Aylesbury, Bucks HP18 9AL* Long Crendon (0844) 208363

YOUNG, Stephen. b 33. St Edm Hall Ox MA61. St Jo Coll Nottm 75 ALCD77. **d** 77 **p** 78. C Crofton *Portsm* 77-81; C Rainham *Chelmsf* 81-87; V Ramsgate Ch Ch *Cant* from 87. *23 Pegwell Road, Ramsgate, Kent CT11 0JB* Thanet (0843) 589848

YOUNG, Stephen Edward. b 52. K Coll Lon BD73 AKC73 Ch Ch Coll Cant CertEd74. **d** 75 **p** 76. C Walton St Mary *Liv* 75-79; C St Marylebone All SS *Lon* 83; C Pimlico St Gabr 83-85; Chapl Whitelands Coll of HE *S'wark* 85-88; Chapl St Paul's Sch Barnes from 88; Dep P-in-O to HM The Queen from 91. *St Paul's School, Lonsdale Road, London SW13 9JT* 081-748 9162

YOUNG, Walter Howlett. b 08. Clifton Th Coll 32. **d** 34 **p** 35. R Chelwood *B & W* 67-73; rtd 73. *West Moorlands, 8 Watery Lane, Nailsea, Bristol BS19 2AX* Nailsea (0272) 852944

YOUNG, William Maurice. b 32. St Jo Coll Nottm 80. **d** 81 **p** 82. C Harlescott *Lich* 81-84; V Hadley from 84. *The Vicarage, 19 Manor Road, Hadley, Telford, Shropshire TF1 4PN* Telford (0952) 254251

YOUNGER, Jeremy Andrew. b 46. Nottm Univ BA68 Bris Univ MA71. Wells Th Coll 68. **d** 70 **p** 71. C Basingstoke *Win* 70-74; C Harpenden St Nic *St Alb* 74-76; Dir Communications & Chapl Sarum & Wells Th Coll 77-81; V Clifton All SS w St Jo *Bris* 81-84; Relig Affairs Producer BBC Radio Nottm *S'well* 84-86; C Bow w Bromley St Leon *Lon* 86-88; Projects and Min Manager St Jas Piccadilly from 89; Hon C St Marylebone All SS from 89. *8 Margaret Street, London WC1N 8JQ* 071-636 0451

YOUNGMAN, Donald Arthur. b 10. AKC37. **d** 37 **p** 38. P-in-c Rampton *Ely* 69-74; rtd 74. *4 Church Close, Hunstanton, Norfolk PE36 6BE* Hunstanton (0485) 533322

YOUNGMAN, Frank Arthur. b 05. Magd Coll Cam BA27 MA31. Westcott Ho Cam 35. **d** 35 **p** 36. R Studland *Sarum* 66-72; rtd 72. *Brook Cottage, Wass, York YO6 4BH* Coxwold (03476) 472

YOUNGSON, David Thoms. b 38. Cuddesdon Coll 71. **d** 73 **p** 74. C Norton St Mary *Dur* 73-76; C Hartlepool St Paul 76-79; P-in-c Stockton St Jo CD 79-84; V Stockton St Jo 84-86; V Owton Manor 86-90; rtd 90. *36 Stokesley Road, Seaton Carew, Hartlepool TS25 1EE*

YULE, John David. b 49. G&C Coll Cam BA70 MA74 PhD76. Westcott Ho Cam 79. **d** 81 **p** 82. C Cherry Hinton St Andr *Ely* 81-84; C Almondbury w Farnley Tyas *Wakef* 84-87; V Swavesey *Ely* from 87; V Fen Drayton w Conington from 87. *The Vicarage, Honey Hill, Fen Drayton, Cambridge CB4 5SF* Swavesey (0954) 31903

YULE, Robert White. b 49. FCMA81. St Jo Coll Nottm LTh88. **d** 88 **p** 89. C Wilford *S'well* 88-91; TV Bestwood from 91. *Emmanuel Vicarage, 10 Church View Close, Arnold, Nottingham NG5 9QP* Nottingham (0602) 208879

Z

ZACHAU, Eric. b 31. AKC57. **d** 58 **p** 59. C Bishopwearmouth St Mich *Dur* 58-62; C Ryhope 62-63; V Beadnell *Newc* 63-69; V Carsdon 69-81; V Bamburgh and Lucker from 81. *The Vicarage, 7 The Wynding, Bamburgh, Northd NE69 7DB* Bamburgh (06684) 295

ZAIR, Richard George. b 52. Newc Univ BSc74. Trin Coll Bris 75 St Jo Coll Dur 79. **d** 80 **p** 81. C Bishopsworth *Bris* 80-83; C New Malden and Coombe *S'wark* 83-91; Dir of Evang CPAS from 91. *64 Kingsway, Leamington Spa, Warwick CV31 3LE*   Leamington Spa (0926) 424634

ZASS-OGILVIE, Ian David. b 38. ARICS72 FRICS80. AKC65. **d** 66 **p** 67. C Washington *Dur* 66-70; Bp's Soc and Ind Adv for N Dur 70-73; Lic to Offic *Newc* 73-75; V Tynemouth St Jo 75-78; Hon C St Marylebone St Mary *Lon* 78-81; V Bromley St Jo *Roch* 81-84; R Keith *Mor* 84-88; R Huntly 84-88; R Aberchirder 84-88; R Edin St Pet *Edin* from 88. *3 Brights Crescent, Edinburgh EH9 2DB*   031-667 6224

ZEAL, Stanley Allan. b 33. Leeds Univ BA55. Coll of Resurr Mirfield. **d** 57 **p** 58. C Perry Hill St Geo *S'wark* 57-61; C Cobham *Guildf* 61-64; V Ash Vale 64-69; R Ash 64-69; Chapl Northfield Hosp Aldershot from 69; V Aldershot St Mich *Guildf* from 69. *St Michael's Vicarage, 120 Church Lane East, Aldershot, Hants GU11 3SS*   Aldershot (0252) 20108

ZIETSMAN, Sheila. **d** 90. C Geashill w Killeigh and Ballycommon *M & K* 90-91; C Mullingar, Portnashangan, Moyliscar, Kilbixy etc from 91; Chapl Wilson's Hosp Sch Multyfarnham from 91. *Wilson's Hospital School, Multyfarnham, Mullingar, Westmeath, Irish Republic*   Mullingar (44) 71115

ZWALF, Willem Anthony Louis. b 46. AKC68. **d** 71 **p** 72. C Fulham St Etheldreda w St Clem *Lon* 71-74; Chapl City Univ 74-78; V Coalbrookdale *Heref* 78; P-in-c Ironbridge 78; P-in-c Lt Wenlock 78; R Coalbrookdale, Iron-Bridge and Lt Wenlock 78-90; V Wisbech SS Pet and Paul *Ely* from 90. *The Vicarage, Love Lane, Wisbech, Cambs PE13 1HP*   Wisbech (0945) 583559

DEACONESSES

The biographies of women deacons and assistant curates are to be found in the preceding section.

ANDERSON, Mary. b 15. St Mary's Ho Dur 38. **dss** 43. Warden S'wark Dioc Ho 66-70; Clapham H Trin *S'wark* 70-75; rtd 75. *1 Barrett Crescent, Wokingham, Berks RG11 1UR* Wokingham (0734) 783676

ATHERFOLD, Mrs Evelyne Sara. b 43. **dss** 85. Fishlake w Sykehouse, Kirk Bramwith, Fenwick etc *Sheff* 87-90; Adult Educn Officer 89-90. *Padley House, Hawkeshouse Green, Moss, Doncaster, S Yorkshire* Doncaster (0302) 700452

BALL, Marjorie. b 98. Gilmore Ho. **dss** 31. Gt Grimsby St Mary and St Jas *Linc* 57-63; rtd 63. *Manormead Nursing Home, Tilford Road, Hindhead, Surrey GU26 6RA* Hindhead (042873) 4780

BANYARD, Sheila Kathryn. b 53. Univ of Wales (Ban) BA75 K Coll Lon MA83. Cranmer Hall Dur 76. **dss** 82. Sunbury *Lon* 82-85; Asst Chapl Ch Hosp Horsham 85-90; Chapl Malvern Girls' Coll *Worcs* from 90. *11 Wilton Road, Great Malvern, Worcs WR14 3RG* Malvern (0684) 892418

BENNETT, Doreen. b 29. St Mich Ho Ox 60. **dss** 79. Moreton *Ches* 79-80; Dewsbury Moor *Wakef* 80-86; W Germany 86-90; Germany from 90; rtd 89. *6B Fairlawn Road, Lytham, Lancs FY8 5PT* Lytham (0253) 795217

BLACKBURN, Mary Paterson. b 16. St Chris Coll Blackheath 45 Wm Temple Coll Rugby 59. **dss** 76. Sawston *Ely* 74-78; rtd 78. *30 Maple Avenue, Sawston, Cambridge CB2 4TB* Cambridge (0223) 833843

BRIERLY, Margaret Ann. b 32. Dalton Ho Bris 54. **dss** 85. Wreningham *Nor* 85-86; Tetsworth, Adwell w S Weston, Lewknor etc *Ox* from 86. *The Rectory, 46 High Street, Tetsworth, Oxford OX9 7AS* Tetsworth (084428) 267

BULLOCK, Florence Mabel (Prudence). b 90. St Chris Coll Blackheath 29 St Andr Ho Portsm 22. **dss** 25. Adv RE Newc 47-60; rtd 60; Lic to Offic *Bris* 60-70. *The Close, Vicarage Road, Staines, Middx TW18 4YG* Staines (0784) 452094

BUTLER, Ann. b 41. St Mich Ho Ox 67 Dalton Ho Bris IDC69. **dss** 82. Bucknall and Bagnall *Lich* 82-87; Leyton St Mary w St Edw *Chelmsf* from 89. *14 Vicarage Road, London E10 5EA* 081-558 4200

BYATT, Margaret Nelly. b 18. Bedf Coll Lon BA40. Lon Bible Coll DipTh50 Gilmore Ho 59. **dss** 62. Lee Gd Shep w St Pet *S'wark* 66-78; rtd 78. *41 Woodlands, Overton, Basingstoke, Hants RG25 3HW* Basingstoke (0256) 770347

BYWORTH, Mrs Ruth Angela. b 49. Cranmer Hall Dur BA82. **dss** 83. Kirkby *Liv* 83-89; Aintree St Pet from 89. *The Vicarage, 51A Rainford Road, St Helens, Merseyside WA10 6BZ* St Helens (0744) 22067

CARTER, Crystal Dawn. b 49. **dss** 82. Hengrove *Bris* 82-86; Dagenham *Chelmsf* 86-88. *c/o St Peter & St Paul Parish Office, Church Lane, Dagenham, Essex RM10 9UL*

CECILIA MARY, Sister. *See* GILL, Mary Louise

COLEBROOK, Vera Gwendoline. b 06. Greyladies Coll Gilmore Ho 45. **dss** 49. Lewisham St Steph *S'wark* 61-67; rtd 67. *Flat 57, Charles Clore Court, 139 Appleford Road, Reading RG3 3NT* Reading (0734) 583960

COOK, Gwendoline. b 14. Greyladies Coll 50 St Andr Ho Ox 51. **dss** 56. Dss Ho Hindhead 69-74; rtd 74; Perm to Offic *S'wark* from 74. *2 Lancaster Avenue, London SW19 5DE* 081-947 1096

COOPER, Janet Pamela. b 46. Glos Coll of Educn TCert67 Ox Poly CertEdD79. Trin Coll Bris DipHE83. **dss** 83. Patchway *Bris* 83-88. *Bethel, Kington Mead Farm, Kington Road, Thornbury, Bristol BS12 1PQ* Thornbury (0454) 414230

COPE, Melia Lambrianos. b 53. Cape Town Univ BSW73. W Midl Minl Tr Course 83. **dss** 86. W Bromwich All SS *Lich* from 86. *7 Hopkins Drive, West Bromwich, W Midlands B71 3RR* 021-588 3744

CUZNER, Amabel Elizabeth Callow. b 17. Gilmore Ho 63. **dss** 72. Catshill *Worc* 72-82; rtd 82; Perm to Offic *Worc* from 82. *12 Blake Road, Catshill, Bromsgrove, Worcs B61 0LZ* Bromsgrove (0527) 35063

DAVIDSON, Helen Beatrice. b 98. Greyladies Coll 40. **dss** 45. Norbury St Steph *Cant* 48-50; rtd 50; Perm to Offic *Chich* 50-70. *The Close, Vicarage Road, Staines, Middx TW18 4YG* Staines (0784) 452094

DEE, Mary. b 21. **dss** 55. Cumnor *Ox* 76-81; rtd 81. *Flat 4, 45 Oxford Avenue, Bournemouth BH6 5HT* Bournemouth (0202) 424240

DENCE, Barbara Irene (Sister Verity). b 20. **dss** 52. CSA from 48. *St Andrew's House, 2 Tavistock Road, London W11 1BA* 071-229 2662

DIMENT, Grace Joan. b 22. DipTh50. Wm Temple Coll Rugby 47 Gilmore Ho 48 Lambeth STh51. **dss** 76. Tavistock and Gulworthy *Ex* 76-77; Nor Cathl *Nor* 77-85; rtd 85. *53 The Close, Norwich NR1 4EG* Norwich (0603) 622136

DRIVER, Janet Mary. b 43. **dss** 80. CMS from 85; Sri Lanka from 86. *368/1 Bauddhaloka Mawatha, Colombo 7, Sri Lanka*

DUCKERING, Alice Muriel. b 07. Gilmore Ho 43. **dss** 46. USPG 45-70; Kegworth *Leic* 71-77; rtd 77. *The Close, Vicarage Road, Staines, Middx TW18 4YG* Staines (0784) 452094

ELKINGTON, Mrs Audrey Anne. b 57. St Cath Coll Ox BA80 UEA PhD83 Nottm Univ DipTh86. St Jo Coll Nottm 85 E Anglian Minl Tr Course 86. **dss** 88. Monkseaton St Mary *Newc* 88-91; Ponteland from 91. *12 Shannon Court, Newcastle upon Tyne NE3 2XF* 091-286 4050

ENTWISTLE, Phyllis. b 18. Gilmore Ho 49. **dss** 54. Northallerton w Kirby Sigston *York* 70-78; rtd 78. *15 Kent Road, Harrogate, N Yorkshire HG1 2LH* Harrogate (0423) 560564

ESSAM, Susan Catherine. b 46. **dss** 84. CMS from 83; Nigeria from 83. *c/o Bishopscourt, PO Box 6283, Jos, Nigeria*

EVANS, Mrs Diana. b 59. Somerville Coll Ox BA81 MA85. St Steph Ho Ox 81. **dss** 84. Sherborne w Castleton and Lillington *Sarum* 84-88. *The Rectory, 17 Panmure Place, Montrose DD10 8ER* Montrose (0674) 72212

EVENDEN, Joyce Nellie. b 15. Ranyard Tr Ho 46. **dss** 63. Wembley St Jo *Lon* 67-72; Warden Dss Ho Staines 72-76; rtd 76. *27 Dowe House, The Glebe, London SE3 9TU* 081-318 2158

FINDER, Miss Patricia Constance. b 30. Dalton Ho Bris 63. **dss** 79. rtd 90. *8 Brighton Road, Ilkley, W Yorkshire LS29 8PS* Ilkley (0943) 607023

FISH, Margaret. b 18. St Mich Ho Ox 49. **dss** 77. rtd 78; Perm to Offic *Nor* 78-89. *35 Ashwell Court, Norwich NR5 9BS* Norwich (0603) 746123

FROST, Constance Mary. b 09. Gilmore Ho 34. **dss** 37. Bilston *Lich* 49-73; rtd 73. *17 Church Way, Worthing, W Sussex BN13 1HD*

GILES, Susan. b 58. BSc. **dss** 83. Balsall Heath St Paul *Birm* 83-85; Asst Chapl Southmead Hosp Bris 86-90. *13 Beverley Road, Bristol BS7 0JL* Bristol (0272) 513854

GILL, Mary Louise (Sister Cecilia Mary). b 1900. Lon Coll of Div. **dss** 30. CSA from 40; Sister-in-charge Graden St Andr Finchley 60-70; Abbey Ho Malmesbury 70-76; rtd 76. *St Andrew's House, 2 Tavistock Road, London W11 1BA* 071-229 2662

GOUGH, Mrs Janet Ainley. b 46. SRN RSCN SCM Lon Univ CertRK73. Trin Coll Bris 70. **dss** 76. Leic H Apostles *Leic* 73-80; USA 80-81; Perm to Offic *Leic* from 81. *410 Hinckley Road, Leicester LE3 0WA* Leicester (0533) 854284

GREAVES, Dorothea Mary. b 16. St Denys Warminster 39. **dss** 62. Willesden St Andr *Lon* 63-76; rtd 76. *5 Norfolk House, Ellenslea Road, St Leonards-on-Sea, E Sussex TN37 6HZ* Hastings (0424) 432965

GRIERSON, Miss Janet. b 13. Westf Coll Lon BA34. Lambeth STh37 MA82 Greyladies Coll 34 K Coll Lon 34. **dss** 48. Prin Lect RE Summerfield Coll Kidderminster 63-75; rtd 75. *Flat 8, Parkview, Abbey Road, Malvern, Worcs WR14 3HG* Malvern (0684) 569341

GRIFFIN, Joan Angela. b 35. Qu Coll Birm 82. **dss** 85. Moseley St Mary *Birm* from 85. *389 Wake Green Road, Birmingham B13 0BH* 021-777 8772

HAMBLY, Miss Winifred Kathleen. b 18. Lambeth DipTh55 Gilmore Ho 54. **dss** 55. Cricklewood St Pet *Lon* 55-78; Eastbourne St Mich *Chich* from 78. *4 Tutts Barn Court, Tutts Barn Lane, Eastbourne, E Sussex BN22 8XP* Eastbourne (0323) 640735

HAMILTON, Miss Pamela Moorhead. b 43. SRN64 SCM66. Trin Coll Bris DipTh75. **dss** 77. Derby St Pet and Ch Ch w H Trin *Derby* 77-84; Bedworth *Cov* from 85. *10 William Street, Bedworth, Nuneaton, Warks CV12 9DS*   Nuneaton (0203) 491608

HARRIS, Audrey Margaret. b 39. Dalton Ho Bris 68. **dss** 82. Collier Row St Jas *Chelmsf* 82-85; Woking St Mary *Guildf* from 85. *46 Hawthorn Road, Woking, Surrey GU22 0BA*   Woking (0483) 64056

HARRISON, Mrs Ann. b 55. Ex Univ BSc77. Linc Th Coll DipHE81. **dss** 82. Acomb H Redeemer *York* 82-83; Lic to Offic *Wakef* from 83. *The Rectory, 8 Viking Road, Stamford Bridge, York YO4 1BR*   Stamford Bridge (0759) 71353

HEDLEY, Elsie. b 16. Lon Univ DipTh51. St Chris Coll Blackheath 46. **dss** 58. St D Cathl *St D* 65-74; Bradford-on-Avon *Sarum* 74-75; rtd 75. *13A Connaught Road, Sidmouth, Devon EX10 8TT*   Sidmouth (0395) 516963

HEWITT, Joyce Evelyn. b 30. SRN51 SCM55. St Mich Ho Ox IDC61. **dss** 67. Spitalfields Ch Ch w All SS *Lon* 67-70; CMJ 71-73; Canonbury St Steph *Lon* 73-75; Chorleywood RNIB Coll for Blind Girls 75-80; rtd 90. *38 Ashridge Court, Station Road, Newbury, Berks RG14 7LL*   Newbury (0635) 47829

HIDER, Miss Margaret Joyce Barbara. b 25. St Mich Ho Ox 52. **dss** 72. Bris H Cross Inns Court *Bris* 77-84; Uphill *B & W* 84-89; rtd 89; Perm to Offic *B & W* from 89. *Bethany, 8 Uphill Way, Weston-super-Mare, Avon BS23 4TH*   Weston-super-Mare (0934) 414191

HINDE, Miss Mavis Mary. b 29. Lightfoot Ho Dur. **dss** 65. Hitchin St Mary *St Alb* 65-68; Ensbury *Sarum* 69-70; Portsea St Alb *Portsm* 70-76; Houghton Regis *St Alb* 77-85; Eaton Socon from 85. *53 Shakespeare Road, Eaton Socon, St Neots, Huntingdon, Cambs PE19 3HG*   Huntingdon (0480) 214980

HOAD, Anne Elizabeth. b 42. Bris Univ BA63. **dss** 69. Asst Chapl Imp Coll *Lon* 69-74; S'wark Lay Tr Scheme 74-77; Brixton St Matt *S'wark* 77-80; Charlton St Luke w H Trin 80-88; Project Worker Community of Women and Men from 88. *17 Foyle Road, London SE3 7RQ*   081-858 5522

HOWARD, Jean Elizabeth. b 37. Man Univ BA59 Univ of Wales (Cardiff) TDip61 Lon Univ DipTh BD86. St Mich Ho Ox 61. **dss** 82. Tottenham St Ann *Lon* 82-84; Dagenham *Chelmsf* 88-90; Perm to Offic from 90. *4 Lavenham House, Brettenham Road, Walthamstow, London E17 5AS*

HURFORD, Alma Janie. b 07. St Andr Ho Portsm 40 Gilmore Ho 41. **dss** 42. Jamaica 57-74; rtd 74. *Amy Muschett Home, Duncans PO, Trelawny, Jamaica* Jamaica (1809) 954-2424

JACKSON, Margaret Elizabeth. b 47. MIPM89 Lon Univ BSc68 DipRS83. S'wark Ord Course. **dss** 83. Surbiton Hill Ch Ch *S'wark* 83-84; Saffron Walden w Wendens Ambo and Littlebury *Chelmsf* 84-87; Dulwich St Barn *S'wark* from 87. *4 Ferrings, College Road, London SE21 7LU*   081-299 1872

JAMES, Grace. b 18. **dss** 72. Chatham St Wm *Roch* 70-78; rtd 79. *46 Oastview, Rainham, Kent ME8 8JQ*   Medway (0634) 360276

JENKS, Miss Patricia Anne. b 37. MCSP59. Dalton Ho Bris 62. **dss** 80. W Holl St Luke *Lon* 80-85; Camborne *Truro* from 85. *6 St Meriadoc Road, Camborne, Cornwall TR14 7HL*   Camborne (0209) 713160

KELLY, Miss Philippa. b 14. St Chris Coll Blackheath 37. **dss** 61. Jamaica 69-71; Kidderminster St Mary *Worc* 72-75; rtd 75. *15 Lax Lane, Bewdley, Worcs DY12 2DY* Bewdley (0299) 400313

LEACH, Edith. b 22. St Mich Ho Ox 51. **dss** 81. Halliwell St Luke *Man* 77-83; rtd 82. *13 London Road, Blackpool FY3 8DL*   Blackpool (0253) 34616

McCLATCHEY, Mrs Diana. b 20. LMH Ox MA44 DPhil49 Lon Univ DBRS69. **dss** 71. Adv for Women's Min *Dur* 70-74; Adv Lay Min *Worc* 74-80; Wilden 80-85; rtd 85. *10 Bellars Lane, Malvern, Worcs WR14 2DN*   Malvern (0684) 560336

MACCORMACK, Mrs June Elizabeth. b 45. Local NSM Course 82. **dss** 86. Bieldside *Ab* from 86. *5 Overton Park, Dyce, Aberdeen AB2 0FT*   Aberdeen (0224) 722691

MASKREY, Mrs Susan Elizabeth. b 43. IDC CertRK. Cranmer Hall Dur St Jo Coll Dur 67. **dss** 76. Littleover *Derby* 76-77; Billingham St Aid *Dur* from 88. *1 Lanchester Avenue, Billingham, Cleveland TS23 2TD* Stockton-on-Tees (0642) 562566

MAYBURY, Doreen Lorna. b 33. RGN54 SCM56. Edin Th Coll 76. **dss** 81. Jedburgh *Edin* 81-84; Duns 84-91; Warden Whitchester Conf Cen 84-91; Whitchester Chr Guest Ho and Retreat Cen 91; Hawick *Edin* from 91. *Whitchester Christian Centre, Borthaugh, Hawick, Roxburghshire TD9 7LN*   Hawick (0450) 77477

MOORE, Sister Hildegard. b 03. St Andr Ho Ox CWWCh38. **dss** 41. CSA from 41; Perm to Offic *Lon*

from 41. *St Andrew's House, 2 Tavistock Road, London W11 1BA*   071-229 2662

MOORHOUSE, Olga Marian. b 28. Dalton Ho Bris. **dss** 63. Fazakerley Em *Liv* 68-70; Huyton St Geo 70-76; Blurton *Lich* 76-88; rtd 88. *37 Rosalind Grove, Wednesfield, Wolverhampton WV11 3RZ*   Willenhall (0902) 630128

MORGAN, Beryl. b 19. Dalton Ho Bris 47. **dss** 77. Princess Marg Hosp Swindon 69-79; rtd 79. *Ty Clyd, Llanfihangel, Nant-Bran, Brecon, Powys LD3 9NA*   Sennybridge (087482) 500

MOURANT, Julia Caroline. b 58. Sheff Univ BA79. St Jo Coll Nottm DPS84. **dss** 84. Cropwell Bishop w Colston Bassett, Granby etc *S'well* 84-86; Marple All SS *Ches* 86-89; Harlow St Mary V *Chelmsf* from 89. *The Vicarage, 5 The Staffords, Harlow, Essex CH17 0JR*   Harlow (0279) 450633

MULLER, Louise Irmgard. b 12. **dss** 64. Prestonville St Luke *Chich* 65-72; rtd 73. *24 Clifton Road, Worthing, W Sussex BN11 4DP*   Worthing (0903) 206541

NELSON, Olive Margaret. b 21. **dss** 52. Auckland St Andr and St Anne *Dur* 76; Heanor *Derby* 76-78; Littleover 78-82; rtd 82; Blagreaves St Andr CD *Derby* 82. *Address temp unknown*

OBEE, Monica May. b 37. **dss** 82. Radford *Cov* from 82. *53 Cheveral Avenue, Coventry CV6 3ED*   Coventry (0203) 594350

OLD, Constance Nellie. b 11. St Cath Coll Lon 37 St Mich Ho Ox 38. **dss** 40. Pakistan 47-71; Gt Ilford St Andr *Chelmsf* 72-86; rtd 86. *230 Wanstead Park Road, Ilford, Essex IG1 3TT*   081-554 2781

OLIVER, Miss Kathleen Joyce. b 44. Man Univ BA65. N Ord Course 80. **dss** 83. Littleborough *Man* 83-87; Perm to Offic from 88. *Littleborough Church Centre, Todmorden Road, Littleborough, Lancs OL15 9EA* Littleborough (0706) 74074

OLPHIN, Miss Maureen Rose. b 30. Lon Univ BSc Sheff Univ DipEd Man Univ DipTh. **dss** 84. Sheff St Barn and St Mary *Sheff* 84-90; rtd 90. *41A Queen Street, Mosborough, Sheffield S19 5BP*   Sheffield (0742) 473009

PALMER, Kathleen. b 09. Gilmore Ho 43. **dss** 65. Chapl Asst S Ockendon Hosp 65-70; S Ockendon *Chelmsf* 65-70; rtd 70; Lee St Marg *S'wark* 70-80; Lewisham St Mary 70-80. *The Close, Vicarage Road, Staines, Middx TW18 4YG*   Staines (0784) 452094

PATRICK, Ruby Olivia. b 16. Gilmore Ho 69. **dss** 72. E Ham w Upton Park *Chelmsf* 72-74; Becontree St Eliz 74-75; Trinidad and Tobago 75-82; rtd 82. *41A New River Crescent, London N13 5RD*   081-882 5146

PIERSON, Mrs Valerie Susan. b 44. CertEd65. Trin Coll Bris 76. **dss** 79. Fulham St Matt *Lon* from 79. *48 Peterborough Road, London SW6 3EB*   071-731 6544

PLATT, Marjorie. b 18. Qu Coll Birm 76. **dss** 78. Hinckley St Mary *Leic* from 78. *The Vicarage, St Mary's Road, Hinckley, Leics LE10 1EQ*   Hinckley (0455) 637691

POLLARD, Shirley Ann. b 27. Wm Temple Coll Rugby 67 Cranmer Hall Dur 69. **dss** 84. Cramlington *Newc* 78-85; rtd 85. *62 Bath Road, Banbury, Oxon OX16 0TR* Banbury (0295) 252414

RAIKES, Miss Gwynneth Marian Napier. b 51. Somerville Coll Ox MA72 Lon Univ BD81. Trin Coll Bris 79. **dss** 81. Asst Chapl Bris Poly *Bris* 81-86; Beckenham Ch Ch *Roch* from 86. *25 Rectory Road, Beckenham, Kent BR3 1HL*   081-650 8025

RAINEY, Miss Irene May. b 14. SRN36 SCM38. Gilmore Ho 69. **dss** 72. Filton *Bris* 70-74; Crowthorne *Ox* 74-79; rtd 79. *12 Stevens Close, Cottenham, Cambridge CB4 4TT*   Cottenham (0954) 51634

RANSLEY, Frances Mary. b 12. St Andr Ho Portsm 52. **dss** 61. Linc St Jo *Linc* 69-72; rtd 72; Lic to Offic *Portsm* from 72. *The Home of Comfort, 17 Victoria Grove, Southsea, Hants PO5 1NF*   Portsmouth (0705) 820920

ROBINSON, Philippa. b 09. R Holloway Coll Lon BA31 Nottm Univ CTPS76. **dss** 75. Branksome St Aldhelm *Sarum* 76-83; Lic to Offic from 83; Tutor Bp's Cert 84-86. *132 Parkstone Avenue, Poole, Dorset BH14 9LS*   Poole (0202) 748415

SAMPSON, Miss Hazel. b 35. Lightfoot Ho Dur 58. **dss** 64. Fenton *Lich* 64-67; Gt Wyrley 67-69; Chapl Asst Manor Hosp Walsall 69-76; Lich St Mary w St Mich from 76. *12 Green Court, Birmingham Road, Lichfield WS13 6UU*   Lichfield (0543) 255888

SCHMIEGELOW, Miss Patricia Kate Lunn. b 37. St Mich Ho Ox 63. **dss** 86. The Hague *Eur* from 86. *Franken Slag 161, 2582 HK den Haag, The Netherlands*   The Hague (70) 555729

SHUKMAN, Mrs Ann Margaret. b 31. Girton Coll Cam BA53 MA58 LMH Ox DPhil74. Qu Coll Birm. **dss** 84. Steeple Aston w N Aston and Tackley *Ox* from 84. *Old*

School House, Tackley, Oxford OX5 3AH   Tackley
(086983) 761

SILL, Grace Mary. b 11. St Chris Coll Blackheath 53. **dss**
62. Southmead Hosp Bris 63-77; rtd 77. *10 Tyndale
Court, Chertsey Road, Bristol BS6 6NF*   Bristol (0272)
732903

SIMPSON, Mrs Elizabeth Ann. b 59. Lon Bible Coll
BA80 Trin Coll Bris 84. **dss** 86. Thornbury *Glouc* 86-87;
Beckenham Ch Ch *Roch* 87-90; Heydon, Gt and Lt
Chishill, Chrishall etc *Chelmsf* from 90. *The Vicarage,
Bury Lane, Elmdon, Saffron Walden, Essex CB11 4NQ*
Royston (0763) 838893

SMEDBERG, Dr Daphne. b 17. MRCPsych MB, ChB
DPM. S'wark Ord Course 73. **dss** 76. Chipstead *S'wark*
from 76. *76 Woodplace Lane, Coulsdon, Surrey CR5 1NF*
Downland (0737) 554440

SNOW, Marjorie Eveline. b 07. St Chris Coll Blackheath
30. **dss** 45. Jamaica 57-72; rtd 72. *The Close, Vicarage
Road, Staines, Middx TW18 4YC*   Staines (0784) 452094

SPROSON, Doreen. b 31. St Mich Ho Ox IDC58. **dss** 70.
Wandsworth St Mich *S'wark* 68-71; Women's Sec CMS
71-74; Goole *Sheff* 74-76; Kirby Muxloe *Leic* 76-77;
Perm to Offic *S'wark* from 85; rtd 91. *Flat 2, 629 Upper
Richmond Road West, Richmond, Surrey TW10 5DU*
081-876 4281

STOWE, Ann Jessica Margaret. b 41. St Mich Ho Ox. **dss**
87. Watford *St Alb* 87-88; Spitalfields Ch Ch w All SS
Lon 88-89; rtd 89. *31 Burham Road, London E4*
081-529 9618

SYMES, Miss Annabel. b 41. AIMLS68. S Dios Minl Tr
Scheme 79. **dss** 85. Barford St Martin, Dinton,
Baverstock etc *Sarum* from 89; Chapl Asst Salisbury
Hosps from 85. *7 Shaftesbury Road, Barford St Martin,
Salisbury*   Salisbury (0722) 744110

TAYLOR, Miss Jean. b 37. St Andr Coll Pampisford 62.
dss 68. CSA from 62; E Crompton *Man* from 79.
1A Crossley Street, Shaw, Oldham, Lancs OL2 8EN
Shaw (0706) 844061

TAYLOR, Muriel. b 28. CA Tr Coll 48. **dss** 76. Gateshead
Fell *Dur* 76-86; Gateshead Harlow Green 86-88; rtd 88.

*18 Beechwood Avenue, Low Fell, Gateshead, Tyne &
Wear NE9 6PP*   091-487 6902

THUMWOOD, Janet Elizabeth. b 30. STh60 DipRE61.
Trin Coll Toronto 58. **dss** 62. CSF 66-77; rtd 90.
66 Headley Grove, Tadworth, Surrey KT20 5JF   Tadworth (0737) 371076

TURNER, Miss Rosie (Poppy). b 22. St Mich Ho Ox 56.
dss 61. Wealdstone H Trin *Lon* 62-70; CMJ 71-72; CMS
73-74; Dss Ho Hindhead 74-76; Sutton Ch Ch *S'wark*
77-80; rtd 80. *Bungalow 16, Huggens' College, College
Road, Northfleet, Kent DA11 9DL*   Gravesend (0474)
357722

van DONGEN, Wilhelmina Gerardina. b 26. St Chris Coll
Blackheath 51. **dss** 76. Hon Asst Rotterdam *Eur* from
84. *Frederik Hendrikstraat 13, 3143 LB Maassluis, The
Netherlands*   Maassluis (1899) 11102

VERITY, Sister. *See* DENCE, Barbara Irene

WAKELING, Joan. b 44. Hockerill Coll Cam CertEd65
Lon Univ DipTh79. S'wark Ord Course 76. **dss** 79.
Surbiton Hill Ch Ch *S'wark* 79-80; Richmond H Trin
and Ch Ch 80-84; California *Ox* 84-89; Arborfield w
Barkham from 89. *52 Pine Drive, Wokingham, Berks
RG11 3LE*   Eversley (0734) 734078

WARR, Sister Dorothy Lilian Patricia. b 14. Selly Oak
Coll 38. **dss** 53. CSA from 53; S'wark St Sav w All
Hallows *S'wark* 59-65; rtd 75. *St Andrew's House,
2 Tavistock Road, London W11 1BA*   071-229 2662

WEBB, Sybil Janet. b 20. SRN42 SCM43. Gilmore Course
69. **dss** 77. Worthing St Geo *Chich* 77-80; rtd 80. *42 Ham
Road, Worthing, W Sussex BN11 2QX*   Worthing (0903)
202997

WRIGHT, Edith Mary. b 22. St Hugh's Coll Ox
MA46 DipEd46. Gilmore Ho STh58. **dss** 61. St
Marylebone St Mary *Lon* 58-71; Lect Linc Th Coll
71-73; Oatlands *Guildf* 73-76; Roehampton H Trin
S'wark 76-82; rtd 82. *39A Radnor Road, Harrow, Middx
HA1 1SA*   081-863 7320

WRIGHT, Gloria Mary. b 40. **dss** 83. Smethwick St Matt
w St Chad *Birm* 83-84; Tottenham H Trin *Lon* 84-86.
*3 Barelees Cottages, Cornhill-on-Tweed, Northd TD12
4SF*   Crookham (089082) 327

CHURCH HOUSE PUBLISHING

The Imprint of the General Synod of the Church of England
Publishing key titles for the Church's life and worship

REPORTS COMMISSIONED BY GENERAL SYNOD
Recent publications have included:
Good News in Our Times on the Gospel and modern culture
Christian Initiation: A Policy for the Church of England
From Power to Partnership on Britain, the Commonwealth and the Anglican
Communion
All God's Children? (co-published with The National Society) on children and
evangelism
For 1992: *The Report of the Archbishops' Commission on Church Music* (co-published
with Hodder)

LITURGICAL REPORTS AND APPROVED EDITIONS
of which the latest is *The Promise of His Glory.*
New editions of *Patterns for Worship* are due to appear in 1992.

CHRISTIAN EDUCATION AND NURTURE
Co-publications with The National Society
Recent titles:
How Faith Grows an appraisal of Faith Development research
The RE Teacher's Christmas Carol

CHURCH CARE AND MAINTENANCE
Published for the Council for the Care of Churches
Recent titles:
Church Plate a popular illustrated history
The Repair and Maintenance of Glass in Churches
Coming in 1992: *Open All Hours: A Church Cleaner's Guide* by Graham Jeffrey

WORLDWIDE ANGLICAN CONCERNS
Publications for the Anglican Consultative Council
The Reports of ARCIC II (co-published with the Catholic Truth Society)
The Anglican Cycle of Prayer 1993 edition available September 1992

THE CHURCH OF ENGLAND YEAR BOOK
The natural complement to *Crockford*, published each year in February.

All titles carrying the CHP imprint are available through your local bookseller. If
you are not already on our mailing list, write for a complete catalogue to:

CHURCH HOUSE PUBLISHING
Great Smith Street, London SW1P 3NZ

CHURCH HOUSE BOOKSHOP

THE COMPREHENSIVE SERVICE

Church House Bookshop has a distinctive name in the world of religious bookselling:

* Covering the whole spectrum of theology and church practice with an ecumenical dimension

* Having a wide range of books on worship and devotion, biography, Bible study, as well as Bibles and service books, children's books, religious poetry and fiction

* Stocking all official reports of the Church of England's General Synod

* Being sole supplier of the approved *Parish Accounts Book* and material on *Covenants* and *Tax Recovery*

* Supplying the series of leaflets *Explaining the Church of England*, now fifteen titles in all, covering such subjects as Marriage, Christening, Funerals, General Synod, Becoming a Priest (send for an order form giving details of discounts for parishes)

* Selling recorded music on cassette and compact disc, greetings cards and wrapping paper

* Operating a *Standing Order* service for items such as General Synod Agenda, Papers and Report of Proceedings, The Church of England Year Book, Anglican Cycle of Prayer and Church Measures (full details on application)

* Providing books for *Book Agents* who run church bookstalls

* Sending books all over the world from the *Mail Order Department.*

For mail orders please ring 071-222 9011 Ext. 201/202. preferably quoting your Visa/Access account number

For bookshop enquiries ring through direct on 071-222 5520

CHURCH HOUSE BOOKSHOP
Great Smith Street, London SW1P 3BN

INDEX OF ENGLISH BENEFICES
AND CHURCHES

An index of benefices, conventional districts, local ecumenical projects, and proprietary chapels (shown in bold type), together with entries for churches and other licensed places of worship listed on the Parish Index of the Central Board of Finance. Where the church name is the same as the benefice (or the first place name in the benefice), the church entry is omitted. Church dedications are indicated in brackets.

The benefice entries give the full legal name, together with the diocese, a reference number to the deanery (listed on page   ), the patron(s), and the names and appointments of clergy serving there. The following are the main abbreviations used; for others see the full list of abbreviations:—

C	Curate	P	Patron
C-in-c	Curate-in-charge	P-in-c	Priest-in-charge
Dn-in-c	Deacon-in charge	Par Dn	Parish Deacon
Dss	Deaconess	R	Rector
Hon C	Honorary Curate	TM	Team Minister
Hon Par Dn	Honorary Parish Deacon	TR	Team Rector
Min	Minister	TV	Team Vicar
NSM	Non-stipendiary Minister	V	Vicar

Listed below are the elements in place names which are not normally treated as substantive in the index:—

CENTRAL	HIGHER	MUCH	OVER
EAST	LITTLE	NETHER	SOUTH
GREAT	LOW	NEW	THE
GREATER	LOWER	NORTH	UPPER
HIGH	MIDDLE	OLD	WEST

Thus, WEST WIMBLEDON (Christ Church) appears as **WIMBLEDON, WEST (Christ Church)** and CENTRAL TELFORD as **TELFORD, CENTRAL**. The only exception occurs where the second element of the place name is a common noun – thus NEW LANE remains as **NEW LANE**, and WEST TOWN as **WEST TOWN**.

AB KETTLEBY Group, The (St James) *Leic 3*
  P *V Rothley, K J M Madocks Wright Esq, and MMCET (jt)* R *Vacant* Melton Mowbray (0664) 822153
ABBAS and Templecombe w Horsington *B & W 2* P *Bp and Ch Trust Fund (jt)* R A J ROSE
ABBERLEY (St Mary) (St Michael) *Worc 12* P *Bp*
  R H R BEVAN
ABBERTON (St Andrew) w Langenhoe *Chelmsf 19*
  P *Ld Chan and Bp (alt)* R R J HANDSCOMBE
ABBERTON (St Edburga), Naunton Beauchamp and Bishampton w Throckmorton *Worc 4* P *Ld Chan and Bp (alt)* R E T B WATERHOUSE
ABBESS RODING (St Edmund), Beauchamp Roding and White Roding *Chelmsf 21* P *Viscount Gough (1 turn) and Bp (2 turns)* R E W C EXELL
ABBEY CHAPEL (St Mary) Annesley Our Lady and All SS *S'well*
ABBEY HEY (St George) *Man 1* P *Bp* R B HOLT
ABBEY HULTON (St John) Bucknall and Bagnall *Lich*
ABBEY WOOD (St Michael and All Angels) *S'wark 1*
  P *Bp* V M W NEALE
ABBEY WOOD (William Temple) Thamesmead *S'wark*
ABBEYDALE (St John the Evangelist) *Sheff 2* P *Lady Judith Roberts, Mrs C Longworth, P Hayward Esq and J Roebuck Esq (jt)* V G G MacINTOSH
ABBEYDALE (St Peter) Sheff Abbeydale St Pet *Sheff*
ABBEYDORE (St Mary) Ewyas Harold w Dulas, Kenderchurch etc *Heref*
ABBOTS BICKINGTON (St James) and Bulkworthy *Ex 9*
  P *Bp* V *Vacant*
ABBOTS BROMLEY (St Nicholas) w Blithfield *Lich 4*
  P *Bp and D&C (jt)* V R M VAUGHAN
ABBOTS LANGLEY (St Lawrence) *St Alb 13* P *Bp*
  V B K ANDREWS, C C L TERRY
ABBOTS LEIGH (Holy Trinity) w Leigh Woods *Bris 5*
  P *Bp* V P W ROWE
ABBOTS MORTON (St Peter) Church Lench w Rous Lench and Abbots Morton *Worc*
ABBOTS RIPTON (St Andrew) w Wood Walton *Ely 9*
  P *Lord de Ramsey (2 turns), D&C (1 turn)*
  P-in-c B J HYDER-SMITH
ABBOTSBURY (St Mary) Highweek and Teigngrace *Ex*
ABBOTSBURY (St Nicholas), Portesham and Langton Herring *Sarum 5* P *Hon Charlotte Morrison and P R FitzGerald Esq (jt), and Bp (alt)* V P T SEAL
ABBOTSHAM (St Helen) Parkham, Alwington, Buckland Brewer etc *Ex*
ABBOTSKERSWELL (Blessed Virgin Mary) *Ex 11*
  P *Ld Chan* **P-in-c** D J STANTON
ABBOTSLEY (St Margaret) *Ely 12* P *Ball Coll Ox*
  V W J PATTERSON

ABBOTSWOOD (St Nicholas Family Centre) Yate New Town *Bris*
ABBOTTS ANN (St Mary) and Upper Clatford and Goodworth Clatford *Win 3* P *T P de Paravicini Esq and Bp (jt)* R M A TRISTRAM, NSM N J JUDD
ABDON (St Margaret) *Heref 12* P *Bp* R I E GIBBS
ABENHALL (St Michael) w Mitcheldean *Glouc 3* P *DBP*
  R K R KING
ABERFORD (St Ricarius) w Saxton *York 1* P *Abp and Or Coll Ox (jt)* V B W HARRIS
ABINGDON (Christ Church) (St Helen) (St Michael and All Angels) (St Nicholas) *Ox 10* P *Patr Bd*
  TR D MANSHIP, TV G N MAUGHAN, M LOVERING,
  C D J BRYAN, B SMART, A G DOIG,
  Par Dn J M LOVERING,
  NSM M C SAMS, G W COX, A MITRA, N L SPOOR
ABINGER (St James) cum Coldharbour *Guildf 7*
  P *Ch Patr Trust and J P M H Evelyn Esq (alt)*
  R J C VENUS
ABINGTON (St Peter and St Paul) *Pet 4* P *Bp*
  R F E PICKARD, C R C PARRISH
ABINGTON, GREAT (St Mary the Virgin) w Little Abington *Ely 4* P *MMCET* **P-in-c** G E TURNER
ABINGTON, LITTLE (St Mary) Gt w Lt Abington *Ely*
ABINGTON PIGOTTS (St Michael and All Angels) Shingay Gp of Par *Ely*
ABNEY (Mission Room) Bradwell *Derby*
ABRAM (St John) *Liv 14* P *R Wigan* V J JORDAN
ABRIDGE (Holy Trinity) Lambourne w Abridge and Stapleford Abbotts *Chelmsf*
ABSON (St James the Great) Pucklechurch and Abson *Bris*
ABTHORPE (St John the Baptist) Silverstone and Abthorpe w Slapton *Pet*
ACASTER MALBIS (Holy Trinity) *York 1*
  P *R A G Raimes Esq* V P RATHBONE
ACASTER SELBY (St John) Appleton Roebuck w Acaster Selby *York*
ACCRINGTON (Christ Church) *Blackb 1* P *Trustees*
  V K LOGAN
ACCRINGTON (St James) (St Paul) (St Andrew) (St Peter) *Blackb 1* P *DBP* **TR** F R COOKE
ACCRINGTON (St John the Evangelist) w Huncoat (St Augustine) *Blackb 1* P *Bp and V Accrington St Jas w St Paul (jt)* V D E CROOK,
  C E A SAVILLE, N A WELLS
ACCRINGTON (St Mary Magdalen) Milnshaw *Blackb 1*
  P *V Accrington St Jas* **P-in-c** A I DALTON
ACKLAM (St John the Baptist) Burythorpe, Acklam and Leavening w Westow *York*
ACKLAM, WEST (St Mary) *York 19* P *Trustees*
  V S C WRIGHT, NSM M J WRIGHT
ACKLETON (Mission Room) Worfield *Heref*

ACKLINGTON (St John the Divine)   Warkworth and
Acklington *Newc*
ACKWORTH (All Saints) (St Cuthbert) *Wakef 11*
P *Duchy of Lanc*   R P MOORHOUSE
ACLE (St Edmund) w Fishley and North Burlingham *Nor 1*
P *Bp and Ch Soc Trust (jt)*   R C G WAY
ACOCKS GREEN (St Mary) *Birm 10*   P *Trustees*
V R H POSTILL,   C J G RICHARDS
ACOL (St Mildred)   Birchington w Acol and Minnis Bay
Cant
ACOMB (Holy Redeemer) *York 8*   P *The Crown*
V J BEECH
ACOMB (St Stephen) *York 8*   P *J H Murray Esq and
J B Deby Esq (jt)*   V M E G WARCHUS,
Par Dn P A BROOKFIELD
ACOMB MOOR (James the Deacon) *York 8*   P *Abp*
V J W HORTON
ACRISE (St Martin)   Hawkinge w Acrise and Swingfield
Cant
ACTON (All Saints) w Great Waldingfield *St E 12*   P *Bp*
P-in-c L R PIZZEY
ACTON (St Mary) *Lon 22*   P *Bp*   R R JONES,
C D E NENO
ACTON (St Mary) and Worleston *Ches 15*
P *R C Roundell Esq and Bp (alt)*   V M J RYLANDS,
Par Dn A C RYLANDS
ACTON, EAST (St Dunstan w St Thomas) *Lon 22*   P *Bp*
V W J MORGAN,   C P J KNIGHT
ACTON, NORTH (St Gabriel) *Lon 22*   P *Bp*
V E J ALCOCK
ACTON, SOUTH (All Saints)   Acton Green *Lon*
ACTON, WEST (St Martin) *Lon 22*   P *Bp*
P-in-c N P HENDERSON,   NSM R K ROWLAND
ACTON BEAUCHAMP (St Giles) and Evesbatch w
Stanford Bishop *Heref 2*   P *Bp and MMCET (alt)*
R *Vacant*
ACTON BURNELL (St Mary)   Condover w Frodesley,
Acton Burnell etc *Heref*
ACTON GREEN (St Alban) (St Peter) *Lon 22*   P *Bp*
V J M V WILLMINGTON,   C A H G JONES
ACTON ROUND (St Mary) *Heref 9*   P *DBP*
Hon C H J PATTERSON
ACTON SCOTT (St Margaret) *Heref 11*   P *DBP*
P-in-c R S PAYNE
ACTON TRUSSELL (St James)   Penkridge Team *Lich*
ACTON TURVILLE (St Mary)   Badminton w Lt
Badminton, Acton Turville etc *Glouc*
ADBASTON (St Michael and All Angels)   Croxton w
Broughton and Adbaston *Lich*
ADDERBURY (St Mary) w Milton *Ox 5*   P *New Coll Ox*
V J P VYVYAN
ADDERLEY (St Peter) *Lich 24*   P *Lt-Col Sir John
Corbet, Bt*   R P A LEONARD-JOHNSON
ADDINGHAM (St Michael), Edenhall, Langwathby and
Culgaith *Carl 4*   P *D&C*   V R A MOATT,
Hon C T G DOWNS,   NSM A R BEAUMONT
ADDINGHAM (St Peter) *Bradf 4*   P *J R Thompson-
Ashby Esq*   R D A A SHAW,   Hon C J E LLOYD
ADDINGTON (St Margaret)   Birling, Addington,
Ryarsh and Trottiscliffe *Roch*
ADDINGTON (St Mary)   Winslow w Gt Horwood and
Addington *Ox*
ADDINGTON (St Mary) *S'wark 19*   P *Abp*
V C J MORGAN-JONES,   C W A BUCK,
NSM S J TURRELL
ADDINGTON, GREAT (All Saints) w Little Addington *Pet
10*   P *Bp*   NSM P R NEEDLE
ADDINGTON, LITTLE (St Mary the Virgin)   Gt w Lt
Addington *Pet*
ADDINGTON, NEW (St Edward) *S'wark 19*   P *Bp*
V R SCREECH,   Par Dn A O NICOLL,
Hon C P W R WINDRIDGE
ADDISCOMBE (St Mary Magdalene) *S'wark 20*
P *Trustees*   V M R McKINNEY,   C M C DEARNLEY
ADDISCOMBE (St Mildred) *S'wark 20*   P *Bp*
V G D S GALILEE
ADDLESTONE (St Augustine) (St Paul) *Guildf 11*   P *Bp*
V W M POWELL,   C A R ARNOLD
ADDLETHORPE (St Nicholas)   Ingoldmells w
Addlethorpe *Linc*
ADEL (St John the Baptist) *Ripon 7*
P *Brig R G Lewthwaite, D R Lewthwaite Esq, and
J V Lewthwaite Esq (jt)*   R G C DARVILL,   C J P RAFFAY
DEYFIELD (St Barnabas)   Hemel Hempstead *St Alb*
´DISHAM (Holy Innocents)   Aylesham w Adisham
´ant
ˏESTROP (St Mary Magdalene)   Broadwell,
ˏnlode, Oddington and Adlestrop *Glouc*
NGFLEET (All Saints)   The Marshland *Sheff*

ADLINGTON (St John's Mission Church)   Prestbury
Ches
ADLINGTON (St Paul) *Blackb 4*   P *Bp*
V D F C MORGAN,   C E N STRASZAK
ADSTOCK (St Cecilia)   Lenborough *Ox*
ADSTONE (All Saints)   Blakesley w Adstone and
Maidford etc *Pet*
ADSWOOD (St Gabriel's Mission Church)   Stockport St
Geo *Ches*
ADVENT (St Adwena)   Lanteglos by Camelford w
Advent *Truro*
ADWELL (St Mary)   Tetsworth, Adwell w S Weston,
Lewknor etc *Ox*
ADWICK-LE-STREET (St Laurence) *Sheff 8*
P *J C M Fullerton Esq*   R R J BUCKLEY
ADWICK-UPON-DEARNE (St John the Baptist)
Wath-upon-Dearne w Adwick-upon-Dearne *Sheff*
AFFPUDDLE (St Lawrence)   Bere Regis and Affpuddle
w Turnerspuddle *Sarum*
AIGBURTH (St Anne) *Liv 4*   P *Trustees*   V J C ANDERS,
C N J PATTERSON
AIKTON (St Andrew) *Carl 3*   P *Earl of Lonsdale*
R I F BLACK
AINDERBY STEEPLE (St Helen) w Yafforth and Kirby
Wiske w Maunby *Ripon 4*   P *Bp and Duke of
Northd (jt)*   R J E COLSTON
AINSDALE (St John) *Liv 9*   P *R Walton, Bp, and
Adn (jt)*   V A RENSHAW,   Par Dn U R SHONE
AINSTABLE (St Michael and All Angels)   Kirkoswald,
Renwick and Ainstable *Carl*
AINSWORTH (Christ Church) *Man 14*   P *Bp*   V *Vacant*
Bolton (0204) 22662
AINTREE (St Giles) *Liv 7*   P *Bp*   V D K KING
AINTREE (St Peter) *Liv 7*   P *R Sefton*   Dss R A BYWORTH
AIREDALE (Holy Cross) w Fryston *Wakef 11*   P *Bp*
V J D WILKINSON
AIRMYN (St David)   Hook w Airmyn *Sheff*
AISHOLT (All Saints) *B & W 15*   P *MMCET*   V *Vacant*
AISLABY (St Margaret) and Ruswarp *York 23*   P *Abp*
P-in-c D W PROUT
AISTHORPE (St Peter) w Scampton w Thorpe le Fallows w
Brattleby *Linc 3*   P *DBP and J M Wright Esq (jt)*
R M J SILLEY
ALBERBURY (St Michael and All Angels) w Cardeston
Heref 13   P *Bp and Sir Michael Leighton, Bt (alt)*
V H J EDWARDS
ALBOURNE (St Bartholomew) w Sayers Common and
Twineham *Chich 9*   P *Bp (2 turns), Ex Coll Ox (1 turn)*
R D F PIKE
ALBRIGHTON (St John the Baptist)   Leaton and
Albrighton w Battlefield *Lich*
ALBRIGHTON (St Mary Magdalene) *Lich 26*
P *Haberdashers' Co and Ch Hosp Horsham (alt)*
V R B BALKWILL
ALBURGH (All Saints)   Earsham w Alburgh and
Denton *Nor*
ALBURY (St Mary)   Lt Hadham w Albury *St Alb*
ALBURY (St Peter and St Paul) (St Martha) *Guildf 2*
P *Marquess of Linlithgow and R G H Smith Esq (jt)*
R D H GUMMER,   NSM J V M GORDON CLARK
ALBURY Tiddington (St Helen)   Holton and
Waterperry w Albury and Waterstock *Ox*
ALBY (St Ethelbert)   Erpingham w Calthorpe, Ingworth,
Aldborough etc *Nor*
ALCESTER (St Nicholas) and Arrow w Oversley and
Weethley *Cov 7*   P *Marquess of Hertf*
P-in-c D C CAPRON
ALCISTON (not known)   Berwick w Selmeston and
Alciston *Chich*
ALCOMBE (St Michael the Archangel) *B & W 17*   P *Bp*
V A F MILLS
ALCONBURY (St Peter and St Paul) w Alconbury Weston
Ely 9   P *D&C Westmr*   V J A COOMBE
ALDBOROUGH (St Andrew) w Boroughbridge and
Roecliffe *Ripon 3*   P *D&C York and Bp (alt)*
V R T COOPER
ALDBOROUGH (St Mary)   Erpingham w Calthorpe,
Ingworth, Aldborough etc *Nor*
ALDBOROUGH HATCH (St Peter) *Chelmsf 7*
P *The Crown*   V M J TRODDEN
ALDBOURNE (St Michael)   Whitton *Sarum*
ALDBROUGH (St Bartholomew) and Mappleton w Goxhill
and Withernwick *York 12*   P *Ld Chan, Abp, and Adn
E Riding (by turn)*   NSM S FOSTER
ALDBROUGH (St Paul)   Forcett and Aldbrough and
Melsonby *Ripon*
ALDBURY (St John the Baptist)   Tring *St Alb*
ALDEBURGH (St Peter and St Paul) w Hazlewood *St E 19*
P *Mrs A C V Wentworth*   V W D HUTCHINSON

ALDEBY (St Mary)　Raveningham *Nor*

ALDENHAM (St John the Baptist) *St Alb 1*　**P** *Lord Aldenham*　**V** *Vacant*　Radlett (0923) 855905

ALDERBROOK (St Richard)　Crowborough *Chich*

ALDERBURY (St Mary the Virgin)　Alderbury Team *Sarum*

ALDERBURY Team, The (St Mary the Virgin) *Sarum 11*　**P** *Patr Bd*　**TR** G ROWSTON,　**TV** P R BOSHER, **C** D B SKELDING,　**NSM** G F H MITCHELL, **Hon Par Dn** H B SKELDING, C HUNT

ALDERCAR (St John)　Langley Mill *Derby*

ALDERFORD (St John the Baptist) w Attlebridge and Swannington *Nor 8*　**P** *Bp and D&C (alt)* **R** A J HAWES

ALDERHOLT (St James) *Sarum 10*　**P** *DBP* **V** P J MARTIN

ALDERLEY (St Kenelm)　Kingswood w Alderley and Hillesley *Glouc*

ALDERLEY (St Mary) *Ches 12*　**P** *Trustees* **R** P ROBERTS

ALDERLEY EDGE (St Philip) *Ches 12*　**P** *Trustees* **V** B T YOUNG

ALDERMASTON (St Mary the Virgin) w Wasing and Brimpton *Ox 12*　**P** *Bp, DBP, Sir William Mount, Bt, and Worc Coll Ox (jt)*　**V** R B MILLER

ALDERMINSTER (St Mary and Holy Cross) and Halford *Cov 9*　**P** *Bp and SMF (jt)*　**P-in-c** D R TILLEY

ALDERNEY (St Anne) *Win 14*　**P** *The Crown* **V** S C INGHAM

ALDERSBROOK (St Gabriel) *Chelmsf 7*　**P** *R Wanstead* **V** D C L MAY

ALDERSHOT (Holy Trinity) *Guildf 1*　**P** *CPAS* **V** R F PARKER

ALDERSHOT (St Augustine) *Guildf 1*　**P** *Bp* **V** K M HODGES

ALDERSHOT (St Michael) (Ascension) *Guildf 1*　**P** *Bp* **V** S A ZEAL, C R MARTIN

ALDERSLEY (Christ the King)　Tettenhall Regis *Lich*

ALDERTON (St Andrew) w Ramsholt and Bawdsey *St E 7* **P** *Sir Anthony Quilter (1 turn), F G A Beckett Esq (2 turns), and Bp (1 turn)*　**P-in-c** J K COTTON, **Hon C** M H INMAN

ALDERTON (St Giles)　Sherston Magna, Easton Grey, Luckington etc *Bris*

ALDERTON (St Margaret)　Stoke Bruerne w Grafton Regis and Alderton *Pet*

ALDERTON (St Margaret of Antioch) w Great Washbourne *Glouc 17*　**P** *Bp (2 turns), DBP (1 turn)* **P-in-c** P W SMITH

ALDERWASLEY (All Saints)　Wirksworth w Alderwasley, Carsington etc *Derby*

ALDFIELD (St Lawrence)　Fountains Gp *Ripon*

ALDFORD (St John the Baptist) and Bruera *Ches 5* **P** *Duke of Westmr and D&C (alt)*　**R** C A BARTON

ALDHAM (St Margaret and St Catherine)　Marks Tey w Aldham and Lt Tey *Chelmsf*

ALDHAM (St Mary)　Elmsett w Aldham *St E*

ALDINGBOURNE (St Mary the Virgin), Barnham and Eastergate *Chich 1*　**P** *Bp and D&C (jt)* **NSM** D J FARNHAM

ALDINGHAM (St Cuthbert) and Dendron and Rampside *Carl 8*　**P** *The Crown and V Dalton-in-Furness (alt)* **R** P HUMPLEBY

ALDINGTON (St Martin) w Bonnington and Bilsington *Cant 12*　**P** *Abp*　**R** L WILLIAMS

ALDRIDGE (St Mary the Virgin) (St Thomas) *Lich 7* **P** *MMCET*　**R** N J H REEVES,　C G R DAVIES

ALDRIDGE (St Thomas) Conventional District *Lich 7* **Min** D J BUTTERFIELD

ALDRINGHAM (St Andrew) w Thorpe, Knodishall w Buxlow and Friston *St E 19*　**P** *Mrs A C V Wentworth, Ch Patr Trust, and Ch Soc Trust (by turn)*　**R** I J MANN

ALDRINGTON (St Leonard) *Chich 4*　**P** *Bp* **TR** S J TERRY,　**TV** C R BREEDS, J W RICHARDSON

ALDSWORTH (St Bartholomew)　Sherborne, Windrush, the Barringtons etc *Glouc*

ALDWARK (St Stephen)　Alne *York*

ALDWICK (St Richard) *Chich 1*　**P** *Bp*　**V** L C J NAGEL, **C** D A WALLER,　**Hon C** E W WORT

ALDWINCLE (St Peter) w Thorpe Achurch and Pilton w Wadenhoe and Stoke Doyle *Pet 12*　**P** *Soc Merchant Venturers Bris (2 turns), G C Capron Esq (1 turn), and Wadenhoe Trust (1 turn)*　**R** J A ROBERTS

ALDWORTH (St Mary the Virgin)　Basildon w Aldworth and Ashampstead *Ox*

ALEXANDRA PARK (St Andrew) *Lon 20*　**P** *Bp* **V** A F PYBUS

ALEXANDRA PARK (St Saviour) *Lon 20*　**P** *Bp* **P-in-c** S C WILSON

ALFINGTON (St James and St Anne)　Ottery St Mary, Alfington, W Hill, Tipton etc *Ex*

ALFOLD (St Nicholas) and Loxwood *Guildf 2*　**P** *Bp and CPAS (jt)*　**R** K A SHORT

ALFORD (All Saints)　Six Pilgrims *B & W*

ALFORD (St Wilfrid) w Rigsby *Linc 8*　**P** *Bp* **V** G I GEORGE-JONES

ALFRETON (St Martin) *Derby 1*　**P** *Bp*　**V** C W SEEDS

ALFRICK (St Mary Magdalene) and Lulsley and Suckley and Leigh and Bransford *Worc 3*　**P** *Prime Min and Bp (alt)*　**R** J W HERBERT,　**NSM** J C GUISE

ALFRISTON (St Andrew) w Lullington, Litlington and West Dean *Chich 18*　**P** *Ld Chan (3 turns), R A Brown Esq (1 turn), and Duke of Devonshire (1 turn)*　**R** J DAVEY

ALGARKIRK (St Peter and St Paul)　Sutterton w Fosdyke and Algarkirk *Linc*

ALHAMPTON (Mission Church)　Ditcheat w E Pennard and Pylle *B & W*

ALKBOROUGH (St John the Baptist) *Linc 4*　**P** *Em Coll Cam and Bp (alt)*　**V** G P GUNNING

ALKERTON (St Michael and All Angels)　Horley w Hornton and Hanwell, Shenington etc *Ox*

ALKHAM (St Anthony) w Capel le Ferne and Hougham *Cant 4*　**P** *Abp*　**V** C HENDEY

ALKMONTON (St John), Cubley, Marston, Montgomery and Yeaveley *Derby 14*　**P** *Bp (3 turns), V Shirley (1 turn)*　**P-in-c** R HILL

ALL CANNINGS (All Saints)　Bishop's Cannings, All Cannings etc *Sarum*

ALL STRETTON (St Michael and All Angels)　Church Stretton *Heref*

ALLENDALE (St Cuthbert) w Whitfield *Newc 4* **P** *Viscount Allendale and J C Blackett-Ord Esq (alt)* **R** A M ROFF,　**Hon C** C H WOLFF

ALLENS CROSS (St Bartholomew) *Birm 4*　**P** *Bp* **V** E W FOSKETT

ALLENS GREEN (Mission Church)　High Wych and Gilston w Eastwick *St Alb*

ALLEN'S ROUGH (Worship Centre)　Willenhall H Trin *Lich*

ALLENSMORE (St Andrew)　Kingstone w Clehonger, Eaton Bishop etc *Heref*

ALLENTON (St Edmund) and Shelton Lock *Derby 15* **P** *Bp*　**V** A LUKE

ALLER (St Andrew)　Langport Area Chs *B & W*

ALLERSTON (St John)　Brompton-by-Sawdon w Snainton, Ebberston etc *York*

ALLERTHORPE (St Botolph)　Barmby Moor w Allerthorpe, Fangfoss and Yapham *York*

ALLERTON (All Hallows) *Liv 4*　**P** *J Bibby Esq* **V** R J LEE,　C C DOWDLE,　**Hon C** A M SMITH

ALLERTON (not known)　Mark w Allerton *B & W*

ALLERTON (St Peter) (St Francis of Assisi) *Bradf 1* **P** *Bp*　**V** C WARD,　C M WARD

ALLERTON BYWATER (St Mary)　Kippax w Allerton Bywater *Ripon*

ALLESLEY (All Saints) *Cov 2*　**P** *J R W Thomson-Bree Esq*　**R** J T H BRITTON,　**C** J BURROWS

ALLESLEY PARK (St Christopher) and Whoberley *Cov 3* **P** *Bp*　**V** F J CURTIS

ALLESTREE (St Edmund) *Derby 11*　**P** *Bp* **V** A T REDMAN,　**C** I ALDERSLEY, **Par Dn** P THOMPSON,　**NSM** C C WARNER

ALLESTREE (St Nicholas) *Derby 11*　**P** *Bp* **V** G K G GRIFFITH,　**NSM** J L H RICE

ALLEXTON (St Peter)　Hallaton w Horninghold, Allexton, Tugby etc *Leic*

ALLHALLOWS (All Saints) *Carl 7*　**P** *Bp*　**V** *Vacant*

ALLINGTON (St John the Baptist)　Bourne Valley *Sarum*

ALLINGTON (St Nicholas) and Maidstone St Peter *Cant 15* **P** *Abp*　**R** A WATSON

ALLINGTON (St Swithin)　Bridport *Sarum*

ALLINGTON, EAST (St Andrew), Slapton and Strete *Ex 14*　**P** *Bp*　**R** A DURANT

ALLINGTON, WEST (Holy Trinity) w East Allington and Sedgebrook *Linc 19*　**P** *Ld Chan*　**R** J M ASHLEY, **NSM** S J HADLEY

ALLITHWAITE (St Mary) *Carl 10*　**P** *Bp* **V** H C KNIGHT,　**NSM** S WAREHAM

ALLONBY (Christ Church) *Carl 7*　**P** *D&C and V Bromfield w Waverton (jt)*　**V** J LEONARDI

ALMELEY (St Mary)　Lyonshall w Titley, Almeley and Kinnersley *Heref*

ALMER (St Mary)　Red Post *Sarum*

ALMONDBURY (St Michael and St Helen) (St Mary) (All Hallows) w Farnley Tyas *Wakef 1*　**P** *DBP* **TR** R L WHITELEY,　**TV** G M WARWICK, D MATHERS

ALMONDSBURY (St Mary the Virgin) *Bris 8*   **P** *Bp*
  V B G CARNE
ALNE (St Mary) *York 5*   **P** *CPAS and MMCET (alt)*
  V W R HENDERSON, **NSM** R WADSWORTH
ALNE, GREAT (St Mary Magdalene)   Kinwarton w Gt
  Alne and Haselor *Cov*
ALNHAM (St Michael and All Angels)   Alwinton w
  Holystone and Alnham *Newc*
ALNMOUTH (St John the Baptist)   Lesbury w
  Alnmouth *Newc*
ALNWICK (St Michael and St Paul) *Newc 9*   **P** *Duke of*
  Northd   **V** C P ANDREWS, **C** R C MILLS
ALPERTON (St James) *Lon 21*   **P** *CPAS*   **V** J B ROOT,
  C D J SIMPSON
ALPHAMSTONE (not known) w Lamarsh and Pebmarsh
  Chelmsf 17   **P** *Earl of Verulam and Ld Chan (alt)*
  R M T MORGAN
ALPHETON (St Peter and St Paul)   Lawshall w
  Shimplingthorne and Alpheton *St E*
ALPHINGTON (St Michael and All Angels) *Ex 3*   **P** *DBP*
  R L M BATE
ALRESFORD (St Andrew) *Chelmsf 26*   **P** *Bp*
  R G R COBB
ALRESFORD, NEW (St John the Baptist) w Ovington and
  Itchen Stoke *Win 1*   **P** *Bp*   **R** G C G TRASLER
ALRESFORD, OLD (St Mary) and Bighton *Win 1*   **P** *Bp*
  R M CAMPLING
ALREWAS (All Saints) *Lich 1*   **P** *Bp*   **V** S J MORRIS
ALSAGER (Christ Church) *Ches 11*   **P** *Bp*   **V** J E VARTY
ALSAGER (St Mary Magdalene) (St Patrick's Mission
  Church) *Ches 11*   **P** *Bp*   **V** M LINDSAY-PARKINSON,
  Hon C J WATSON
ALSAGERS BANK (St John)   Silverdale and Alsagers
  Bank *Lich*
ALSOP EN LE DALE (St Michael and All Angels)
  Parwich w Alsop en le Dale *Derby*
ALSTON Team, The (St Augustine) *Newc 4*   **P** *Bp*
  TR L T ATHERTON
ALSTONE (St Margaret)   Overbury w Teddington,
  Alstone etc *Worc*
ALSTONFIELD (St Peter), Butterton, Warslow w Elkstone
  and Wetton *Lich 11*   **P** *H F Harpur-Crewe Esq, Bp,*
  and V Mayfield (jt)   **V** D M TINSLEY
ALSWEAR (not known)   Bishopsnympton, Rose Ash,
  Mariansleigh etc *Ex*
ALTARNON (St Nonna)   Bolventor *Truro*
ALTCAR (St Michael and All Angels) *Liv 5*   **P** *Bp*
  V J E SMITH
ALTHAM (St James) w Clayton le Moors *Blackb 1*
  P *DBP and Trustees (alt)*   **V** P H DEARDEN,
  C C J NELSON
ALTHORNE (St Andrew)   Creeksea w Althorne,
  Latchingdon and N Fambridge *Chelmsf*
ALTHORPE (St Oswald)   N Axholme Gp *Linc*
ALTOFTS (St Mary Magdalene) *Wakef 9*   **P** *Meynall*
  Ingram Trustees   **V** S K L VICK
ALTON (All Saints) *Win 2*   **P** *Bp*   **V** M C SURMAN
ALTON (St Lawrence) *Win 2*   **P** *D&C*
  V R W S L GUSSMAN, **C** G R ANTHONY-ROBERTS
ALTON (St Peter) w Bradley-le-Moors and Oakamoor w
  Cotton *Lich 12*   **P** *Earl of Shrewsbury and Talbot,*
  DBP, and R Cheadle (jt)   **V** C BROWN
ALTON BARNES (St Mary the Virgin)   Swanborough
  Sarum
ALTON COMMON (Mission Room)   Alton w Bradley-
  le-Moors and Oakamoor w Cotton *Lich*
ALTON PANCRAS (St Pancras)   Piddletrenthide w
  Plush, Alton Pancras etc *Sarum*
ALTRINCHAM (St George) *Ches 10*   **P** *V Bowdon*
  V B R McCONNELL, **C** A D LYON
ALTRINCHAM (St John the Evangelist) *Ches 10*   **P** *Bp*
  V D P BROCKBANK
ALVANLEY (St John the Evangelist) *Ches 3*   **P** *Bp*
  V M J FENTON
ALVASTON (St Michael and All Angels) *Derby 15*
  P *PCC*   **P-in-c** C F MEEHAN
ALVECHURCH (St Lawrence) *Worc 7*   **P** *Bp*   **R** *Vacant*
  021-445 1087
ALVEDISTON (St Mary)   Chalke Valley W *Sarum*
ALVELEY (St Mary the Virgin) and Quatt *Heref 9*
  P *J W H Thompson Esq and Lady Labouchere (jt)*
  R M J BENNETT, **NSM** C R ROE, W R PRYCE
ALVERDISCOTT (All Saints)   Newton Tracey,
  Alverdiscott, Huntshaw etc *Ex*
ALVERSTOKE (St Faith) (St Francis) (St Mary) *Portsm 3*
  P *Bp*   **R** N CHATFIELD, **C** A G DAVIS, P A SUTTON
ALVERSTONE (Church Hall)   Brading w Yaverland
  Portsm

ALVERTHORPE (St Paul) *Wakef 12*   **P** *Bp*
  V S P KELLY, **C** R C GEDDES
ALVESCOT (St Peter) w Black Bourton, Shilton, Holwell
  and Westwell *Ox 8*   **P** *Mrs P Allen (1 turn), Ch Ch Ox*
  (2 turns), J Heyworth Esq (1 turn), and O N Colvile Esq
  (1 turn)   **R** R H LLOYD, **NSM** F M RIGBY
ALVESTON (St Helen) *Bris 8*   **P** *D&C*   **V** D J POLE
ALVESTON (St James) *Cov 8*   **P** *R Hampton Lucy w*
  Charlecote and Loxley   **V** R A NOISE
ALVINGHAM (St Adelwold)   Mid Marsh Gp *Linc*
ALVINGTON (St Andrew)   Woolaston w Alvington
  Glouc
ALVINGTON, WEST (All Saints)   Malborough w S
  Huish, W Alvington and Churchstow *Ex*
ALWALTON (St Andrew) and Chesterton *Ely 13*
  P *Sir Stephen Hastings*   **R** *Vacant*
ALWINGTON (St Andrew)   Parkham, Alwington,
  Buckland Brewer etc *Ex*
ALWINTON (St Michael and All Angels) w Holystone and
  Alnham *Newc 9*   **P** *Ld Chan and Duke of Northd (alt)*
  V J WYLAM
ALWOODLEY (St Barnabas)   Moor Allerton *Ripon*
AMBER HILL (St John the Baptist)   Brothertoft Gp
  Linc
AMBERGATE (St Anne) *Derby 11*   **P** *Exors*
  M A T Johnson Esq   **P-in-c** D J T RYMER
AMBERLEY (Holy Trinity) *Glouc 8*   **P** *DBP*
  P-in-c J SIMMONS
AMBERLEY (no dedication)   Marden w Amberley and
  Wisteston *Heref*
AMBERLEY (St Michael) w North Stoke and Parham,
  Wiggonholt and Greatham *Chich 12*   **P** *Bp and Parham*
  Estate Trustees (jt)   **V** D H THORNLEY
AMBLE (St Cuthbert) *Newc 9*   **P** *Bp*
  V J A MACNAUGHTON
AMBLECOTE (Holy Trinity) *Worc 11*   **P** *Bp*
  V P TONGUE, **C** A K LANE
AMBLESIDE (St Mary) w Brathay *Carl 10*   **P** *DBP*
  V L G HIGDON
AMBROSDEN (St Mary the Virgin) w Merton and
  Piddington *Ox 2*   **P** *Trustees F A W Page-Turner Esq,*
  Ex Coll Ox, and DBF (jt)   **V** *Vacant*   Charlton-on-
  Otmoor (086733) 212
AMCOTTS (St Mark)   N Axholme Gp *Linc*
AMERSHAM (St Mary the Virgin) *Ox 20*   **P** *Capt*
  F Tyrwhitt Drake   **R** A M PRIDDIS, **C** J R BAKER,
  NSM B M BLACKSHAW
AMERSHAM ON THE HILL (St Michael and All Angels)
  Ox 20   **P** *Bp*   **V** G B GRIFFITHS
AMESBURY (St Mary and St Melor) *Sarum 12*   **P** *D&C*
  Windsor   **V** P R LEWIS, **NSM** S C DAVIS
AMINGTON (St Editha) *Birm 12*   **P** *Bp*   **V** *Vacant*
  Tamworth (0827) 62573
AMOTHERBY (St Helen)   Street Team Min *York*
AMPFIELD (St Mark)   Hursley and Ampfield *Win*
AMPLEFORTH (St Hilda) and Oswaldkirk and Gilling
  East *York 18*   **P** *Abp and Trin Coll Cam (jt)*
  R D E NEWTON
AMPNEYS (St Mary) (St Peter) (Holy Rood) w Driffield
  and Poulton, The *Glouc 13*   **P** *Bp and Col Sir Piers*
  Bengough (jt)   **R** P G C JEFFRIES
AMPORT (St Mary), Grateley, Monxton and Quarley
  Win 3   **P** *D&C Chich, T P de Paravicini Esq,*
  Mrs E D Collie, Bp, and R Foundn of St Kath (jt)
  V R S BENNETT
AMPTHILL (St Andrew) w Millbrook and Steppingley
  St Alb 15   **P** *Ld Chan*   **R** R L HODSON,
  Par Dn V J ROCKALL
AMPTON (St Peter)   Ingham w Ampton and Gt and Lt
  Livermere *St E*
AMWELL, GREAT (St John the Baptist) w St Margaret's
  St Alb 8   **P** *Bp and Haileybury & Imp Service Coll (jt)*
  V C E C WALKER
AMWELL, LITTLE (Holy Trinity) *St Alb 8*   **P** *Ch Patr*
  Trust   **V** J V BUDD
ANCASTER (St Martin)   Ancaster Wilsford Gp *Linc*
ANCASTER WILSFORD Group, The *Linc 23*   **P** *Bp*
  (2 turns), DBP (1 turn), and Mrs G V Hoare (1 turn)
  R I R CARDINAL, **NSM** J E COULTHURST, I D McGRATH
ANCHORSHOLME (All Saints) *Blackb 9*   **P** *Bp,*
  V Bispham, and Ch Soc Trust (jt)   **V** P R NUNN
ANCOATS (All Souls)   Man Gd Shep *Man*
ANCROFT (St Anne)   Lowick and Kyloe w Ancroft
  Newc
ANDERBY (St Andrew)   Sutton, Huttoft and Anderby
  Linc
ANDOVER (St Mary the Virgin) (St Thomas) w Foxcott
  Win 3   **P** *St Mary's Coll Win*   **V** A R WILDS,
  C P BRADFORD, J C COWBURN

ANDOVER (St Michael and All Angels) *Win 3*   **P** *Bp*
  V J R TARR
ANDREAS (St Andrew) *S & M 4*   **P** *The Crown*
  R F S WHITE
ANDREAS (St Jude Chapelry) *S & M 4*   **P** *R Andreas*
  V F S WHITE
ANERLEY Christ Church *Roch 12*   **P** *CPAS*
  V R J GROVES
ANFIELD (St Columba) *Liv 7*   **P** *Bp*   **V** P B CAVANAGH,
Par Dn J M WATERMAN,   **NSM** K L MILLER
ANFIELD (St Margaret) *Liv 3*   **P** *Bp*   **V** J H DAVIES
ANGELL TOWN (St John the Evangelist) *S'wark 9*   **P** *Bp*
  V M S ARMITAGE,   **NSM** D J DERRICK
ANGERSLEIGH (St Michael)   Trull w Angersleigh
B & W
ANGMERING (St Margaret) *Chich 1*
  P *J F P Somerset Esq*   **R** A M G WELLS
ANLABY (St Peter) *York 15*   **P** *Trustees*
  V T R J DICKENS
ANLABY COMMON (St Mark) Hull *York 15*   **P** *Abp*
  V R EVELEIGH
ANMER (St Mary)   Dersingham w Anmer and
Shernborne *Nor*
ANNESLEY (Our Lady and All Saints) *S'well 4*   **P** *Major
R P Chaworth-Musters*   **V** J C WILSON
ANNFIELD PLAIN (St Aidan)   Collierley w Annfield
Plain *Dur*
ANNSCROFT (Christ Church)   Longden and Annscroft
w Pulverbatch *Heref*
ANSFORD (St Andrew)   Castle Cary w Ansford *B & W*
ANSLEY (St Lawrence) *Cov 5*   **P** *Ch Patr Trust*
  V J R JASPER
ANSLOW (Holy Trinity) *Lich 20*   **P** *MMCET*
  V M D BIRT
ANSTEY (St George)   Hormead, Wyddial, Anstey,
Brent Pelham etc *St Alb*
ANSTEY (St Mary) *Leic 12*   **P** *R Thurcaston*   **R** J E HALL
ANSTEY, EAST (St Michael)   Bishopsnympton, Rose
Ash, Mariansleigh etc *Ex*
ANSTEY, WEST (St Petrock)   as above
ANSTON (St James) *Sheff 5*   **P** *Bp*   **V** W E HOWE,
C M R BURKE
ANSTY (St James)   Bulkington w Shilton and Ansty *Cov*
ANSTY (St James)   Tisbury *Sarum*
ANSTY (St John)   Cuckfield *Chich*
ANTINGHAM (St Mary)   Trunch *Nor*
ANTONY (St James the Great) w Sheviock *Truro 11*
  P *Bp and Col Sir John Carew-Pole, Bt (alt)*
  R H B YORK
ANTROBUS (St Mark)   Gt Budworth and Antrobus
Ches
ANWICK (St Edith)   Kirkby Laythorpe *Linc*
APETHORPE (St Leonard)   King's Cliffe w Apethorpe
Pet
APLEY (St Andrew)   Bardney *Linc*
APPERLEY (Holy Trinity)   Deerhurst, Apperley w
Forthampton and Chaceley *Glouc*
APPLEBY (St Bartholomew)   Winterton Gp *Linc*
APPLEBY (St Lawrence) *Carl 1*   **P** *D&C and Bp (jt)*
  V P E P NORTON
**APPLEBY MAGNA (St Michael and All Angels) and
Swepstone w Snarestone** *Leic 9*   **P** *DBP and
MMCET (jt)*   **R** N D GREENWOOD
APPLEDORE (St Mary)   Northam w Westward Ho and
Appledore *Ex*
**APPLEDORE (St Peter and St Paul) w Brookland and
Fairfield and Brenzett w Snargate and Kenardington**
Cant 13   **P** *Abp*   **V** L J HAMMOND
APPLEDRAM (St Mary the Virgin) *Chich 3*   **P** *D&C*
  V *Vacant*
APPLEFORD (St Peter and St Paul)   Sutton Courtenay
w Appleford *Ox*
**APPLESHAW (St Peter) and Kimpton and Thruxton and
Fyfield** *Win 3*   **P** *Bp, D&C, and M H Routh Esq (jt)*
  R I J TOMLINSON
APPLETHWAITE (St Mary) *Carl 10*   **P** *Bp*
  V W E BARKER
APPLETON (All Saints)   Street Team Min *York*
APPLETON (St Lawrence) *Ox 10*   **P** *Magd Coll Ox*
  P-in-c R G PENMAN
APPLETON (St Mary Magdalene)   Stockton Heath *Ches*
APPLETON-LE-MOORS (Christ Church)   Lastingham
w Appleton-le-Moors, Rosedale etc *York*
APPLETON ROEBUCK (All Saints) w Acaster Selby
York 1   **P** *Abp*   **P-in-c** J M RODEN
APPLETON THORN (St Cross)   Stretton and Appleton
Thorn *Ches*
APPLETON WISKE (St Mary)   Gt Smeaton w Appleton
Wiske and Birkby etc *Ripon*

APPLETREEWICK (St John the Baptist)   Burnsall w
Rylstone *Bradf*
APPLEY BRIDGE (All Saints) *Blackb 4*   **P** *Bp*
P-in-c C J STEVENSON
APULDRAM (St Mary the Virgin)   Appledram *Chich*
ARBORFIELD (St Bartholomew) w Barkham *Ox 16*
  P *DBP*   **Hon C** H M WAKELING, **Dss** J WAKELING
ARBORY (St Columba) *S & M 1*   **P** *The Crown*
  V G B CLAYTON
ARBOURTHORNE (St Paul)   Sheff Manor *Sheff*
ARDELEY (St Lawrence) *St Alb 5*   **P** *D&C St Paul's*
P-in-c E J POOLE,   **NSM** B KNIGHT
ARDINGLY (St Peter) *Chich 6*   **P** *MMCET*
  R R P SYMMONS
ARDINGTON (Holy Trinity)   Wantage Downs *Ox*
ARDLEIGH (St Mary the Virgin) *Chelmsf 20*   **P** *Ld Chan*
  V R A DONCASTER
ARDLEY (St Mary)   Fritwell w Souldern and Ardley w
Fewcott *Ox*
ARDSLEY (Christ Church) *Sheff 12*   **P** *R Darfield*
  V R G R EVANS,   **C** S DONALD
ARDSLEY, EAST (St Gabriel) (St Michael) *Wakef 12*
  P *E C S J G Brudenell Esq*   **V** K G WILLIAMS
ARDSLEY, WEST *Wakef 10*   **P** *E C S J G Brudenell Esq*
  V T R KING
ARDWICK (St Benedict) *Man 1*   **P** *Keble Coll Ox*
  R D LOWE
ARDWICK (St Jerome and St Silas)   Man Gd Shep *Man*
ARELEY KINGS (St Bartholomew) *Worc 12*   **P** *R Martley*
  R G E COOKE
ARKENDALE (St Bartholomew)   Farnham w Scotton,
Staveley, Copgrove etc *Ripon*
ARKENGARTHDALE (St Mary)   Swaledale *Ripon*
ARKESDEN (St Mary the Virgin)   Clavering w Langley
and Arkesden *Chelmsf*
ARKHOLME (St John the Baptist)   Whittington w
Arkholme and Gressingham *Blackb*
ARKLEY (St Peter)   Chipping Barnet w Arkley *St Alb*
ARKSEY (All Saints) *Sheff 8*   **P** *DBP*   **V** C J A HICKLING
ARLECDON (St Michael)   Frizington and Arlecdon *Carl*
ARLESEY (St Andrew) (St Peter) w Astwick *St Alb 22*
  P *DBP*   **V** T MAINES
ARLEY (St Michael and All Angels) (St Wilfred) *Cov 5*
  P *A C D Ransom Esq and N W H Sylvester Esq (jt)*
  R *Vacant*   Fillongley (0676) 40378
ARLEY, UPPER (St Peter)   Kidderminster St Mary and
All SS w Trimpley etc *Worc*
ARLINGHAM (St Mary the Virgin)   Frampton on
Severn, Arlingham, Saul etc *Glouc*
ARLINGTON (St James)   Shirwell, Loxhore,
Kentisbury, Arlington, etc *Ex*
ARLINGTON (St Pancras), Folkington and Wilmington
Chich 18   **P** *Bp Lon, Mrs M P Gwynne-Longland, and
Duke of Devonshire (by turn)*   **P-in-c** J D E SMITH
ARMATHWAITE (Christ and St Mary)   Hesket-in-the-
Forest and Armathwaite *Carl*
ARMINGHALL (St Mary) *Nor 14*   **P** *D&C*
  V G F WALKER
ARMITAGE (Holy Trinity) *Lich 4*   **P** *Bp*
  R D R H THOMAS
ARMITAGE (St John the Baptist)   Armitage *Lich*
ARMITAGE BRIDGE (St Paul)   Newsome and
Armitage Bridge *Wakef*
ARMLEY (St Bartholomew) w New Wortley (St Mary)
Ripon 6   **P** *Bp, DBP, and Hyndman Trustees (jt)*
  V R G N PLANT,   **C** D C BRANFORD
ARMLEY, UPPER (Christ Church) *Ripon 6*   **P** *Ch Patr
Trust*   **V** F SUDWORTH,   **C** T P PARKER, M JARVIS
ARMLEY HEIGHTS (Church of the Ascension)   Upper
Armley *Ripon*
ARMTHORPE (St Leonard and St Mary) *Sheff 9*   **P** *Bp*
  R D J DRYE,   **C** I G WALLIS
ARNCLIFFE (St Oswald)   Kettlewell w Conistone,
Hubberholme etc *Bradf*
ARNE (St Nicholas)   Wareham *Sarum*
ARNESBY (St Peter) w Shearsby and Bruntingthorpe
Leic 10   **P** *Bp*   **R** M H HARDY
ARNOLD (St Mary) *S'well 11*   **P** *Bp*   **V** R WILLIAMS,
  C J A BANKS, D HOLLIS
ARNSIDE (St James) *Carl 9*   **P** *Bp*   **V** *Vacant*   Arnside
(0524) 761319
ARRETON (St George) *Portsm 7*   **P** *Bp*   **V** *Vacant*
ARRINGTON (St Nicholas) *Ely 8*   **P** *Bp and DBP (alt)*
  V *Vacant*
ARROW (Holy Trinity)   Alcester and Arrow w Oversley
and Weethley *Cov*
ARTHINGTON (St Peter)   Pool w Arthington *Ripon*
**ARTHINGWORTH (St Andrew) and Harrington w
Oxendon and East Farndon** *Pet 2*   **P** *St Jo Coll Ox*

(2 turns), E G Nugee Esq (2 turns), and Bp (1 turn)
R T H ROPER
ARTHURET (St Michael and All Angels) *Carl 2*
  P *Sir Charles Graham, Bt* J L HIGGINS
ARUNDEL (St Nicholas) w Tortington and South Stoke
  Chich 1   **P** *Bp (2 turns), Duke of Norfolk (1 turn)*
  V M H WEAVER, **Hon C** M C LEAL
ASBY (St Peter) *Carl 1*   **P** *Bp*   **R** J W HAYWOOD
ASCOT, NORTH (St Mary and St John)   Ascot Heath
  Ox
ASCOT, SOUTH (All Souls) *Ox 11*   **P** *Bp*   **V** D S JONES
ASCOT HEATH (All Saints) *Ox 11*   **P** *Bp*
  R P le S V NASH-WILLIAMS, **C** K G O'DONNELL
ASCOTT UNDER WYCHWOOD (Holy Trinity)
  Chadlington and Spelsbury, Ascott under Wychwood
  Ox
ASFORDBY (All Saints) *Leic 3*   **P** *DBP*
  R H J EDWARDS, **NSM** S F SHOULER
ASGARBY (St Andrew)   Kirkby Laythorpe *Linc*
ASH (Christ Church) *Lich 29*   **P** *R Whitchurch*
  P-in-c J H TYERS
ASH (Holy Trinity)   Martock w Ash *B & W*
ASH (St Nicholas) w Westmarsh *Cant 1*   **P** *Abp*
  V C C BARLOW
ASH (St Peter) *Guildf 1*   **P** *Win Coll*   **R** H F JACKSON
ASH (St Peter and St Paul) *Roch 1*   **P** *J R A B Scott Esq*
  R L W G KEVIS
ASH (Thomas Chapel)   Sampford Peverell, Uplowman,
  Holcombe Rogus etc *Ex*
ASH PRIORS (Holy Trinity)   Lydeard St Lawrence w
  Brompton Ralph etc *B & W*
ASH VALE (St Mary) *Guildf 1*   **P** *Bp*   **V** P C BAKER
ASHAMPSTEAD (St Clement)   Basildon w Aldworth
  and Ashampstead *Ox*
ASHBOCKING (All Saints)   Clopton w Otley, Swilland
  and Ashbocking *St E*
ASHBOURNE (St John the Baptist) *Derby 8*   **P** *Wright*
  Trustees   **V** D H SANSUM
ASHBOURNE (St Oswald) w Mapleton *Derby 8*   **P** *Bp*
  V D H SANSUM
ASHBRITTLE (St John the Baptist)   Wellington and
  Distr *B & W*
ASHBURNHAM (St Peter) w Penhurst *Chich 14*
  P *Ashburnham Chr Trust*   **P-in-c** K L BARHAM,
  Hon C J D BICKERSTETH
ASHBURTON (St Andrew) w Buckland in the Moor and
  Bickington *Ex 11*   **P** *D&C*   **V** P J GREGSON
ASHBURY (St Mary the Virgin), Compton Beauchamp and
  Longcot w Fernham *Ox 17*   **P** *Ld Chan*   **V** B P R PEGG,
  Hon C K S W WALKER, **NSM** A K WEAVER
ASHBY (St Catherine)   Bottesford w Ashby *Linc*
ASHBY (St Mary)   Somerleyton w Ashby, Fritton and
  Herringfleet *Nor*
ASHBY (St Mary)   Thurton *Nor*
ASHBY (St Paul)   Bottesford w Ashby *Linc*
ASHBY, WEST (All Saints)   Hemingby *Linc*
ASHBY-BY-PARTNEY (St Helen)   Partney *Linc*
ASHBY-CUM-FENBY (St Peter)   Ravendale Gp *Linc*
ASHBY DE LA LAUNDE (St Hibald)   Digby *Linc*
ASHBY-DE-LA-ZOUCH (Holy Trinity) *Leic 9*   **P** *Bp*
  V L A DUTTON
ASHBY-DE-LA-ZOUCH (St Helen) w Coleorton *Leic 9*
  P *D A G Shields Esq*   **V** C P DOBBIN, **C** J N KING,
  NSM S A B WALTERS
ASHBY FOLVILLE (St Mary)   S Croxton Gp *Leic*
ASHBY MAGNA (St Mary)   Willoughby Waterleys,
  Peatling Magna etc *Leic*
ASHBY PARVA (St Peter)   Leire w Ashby Parva and
  Dunton Bassett *Leic*
ASHBY PUERORUM (St Andrew)   Fulletby w
  Greetham and Ashby Puerorum *Linc*
ASHBY ST LEDGERS (Blessed Virgin Mary and
  St Leodegarius)   Welton w Ashby St Ledgers *Pet*
ASHCHURCH (St Nicholas) *Glouc 9*   **P** *K Storey Esq*
  R K R CORLESS, **C** D G S BATTERSBY
ASHCOMBE (St Nectan)   Teignmouth, Ideford w
  Luton, Ashcombe etc *Ex*
ASHCOTT (All Saints)   Shapwick w Ashcott and Burtle
  B & W
ASHDON (All Saints) w Hadstock *Chelmsf 25*
  P *E H Vestey Esq and Ld Chan (alt)*   **R** J D SAVILLE
ASHE (Holy Trinity and St Andrew)   N Waltham and
  Steventon, Ashe and Deane *Win*
ASHEN (St Augustine)   Ridgewell w Ashen, Birdbrook
  and Sturmer *Chelmsf*
ASHENDON (St Mary)   Ludgershall w Wotton
  Underwood and Ashendon *Ox*
ASHFIELD, GREAT (All Saints)   Badwell Ash w Gt
  Ashfield, Stowlangtoft etc *St E*

ASHFIELD CUM THORPE (St Mary)   Earl Soham w
  Cretingham and Ashfield cum Thorpe *St E*
ASHFORD (Holy Trinity) w Sheldon *Derby 2*
  P *V Bakewell*   **P-in-c** C A THROWER
ASHFORD (St Hilda) *Lon 13*   **P** *Bp*   **V** S J BLOOD
ASHFORD (St Mary the Virgin) *Cant 10*   **P** *Abp*
  V J W EVERETT, **C** J C TAPPER
ASHFORD (St Matthew) *Lon 13*   **P** *Ld Chan*
  V R E HORTON
ASHFORD (St Peter)   Pilton w Ashford *Ex*
ASHFORD, SOUTH (Christ Church) (St Francis of Assisi)
  Cant 10   **P** *Abp*   **V** R G E GAZZARD, **C** B P SHARP
ASHFORD BOWDLER (St Andrew)   Ashford
  Carbonell w Ashford Bowdler *Heref*
ASHFORD CARBONELL (St Mary) w Ashford Bowdler
  Heref 12   **P** *Bp Birm*   **P-in-c** J F BAULCH
ASHFORD COMMON (St Benedict)   Upper Sunbury St
  Sav *Lon*
ASHFORD HILL (St Paul) w Headley *Win 6*
  P *V Kingsclere*   **V** *Vacant*   Headley (0635) 268217
ASHILL (St Nicholas) w Saham Toney *Nor 18*   **P** *Bp and*
  New Coll Ox (alt)   **P-in-c** M J DOWN
ASHILL (St Stephen)   Uffculme *Ex*
ASHILL (The Blessed Virgin Mary)   Donyatt w Horton,
  Broadway and Ashill *B & W*
ASHINGDON (St Andrew) w South Fambridge *Chelmsf 14*
  P *CCC Cam*   **R** S HANKEY
ASHINGTON (Holy Sepulchre) *Newc 11*   **P** *Bp*
  V P O BENNISON
ASHINGTON (St Matthew)   Canford Magna *Sarum*
ASHINGTON (St Peter and St Paul) w Buncton, Wiston
  and Washington *Chich 12*   **P** *Bp and J Goring Esq (alt)*
  R J M WALKER
ASHINGTON (St Vincint)   Chilton Cantelo, Ashington,
  Mudford, Rimpton etc *B & W*
ASHLEWORTH (St Bartholomew)   Hasfield w Tirley
  and Ashleworth *Glouc*
ASHLEY (St Elizabeth)   Hale and Ashley *Ches*
ASHLEY (St James the Greater), Crudwell, Hankerton,
  Long Newnton and Oaksey *Bris 12*   **P** *Trustees*
  R *Vacant*   Crudwell (06667) 226
ASHLEY (St John the Baptist) *Lich 13*   **P** *Meynell*
  Ch Trustees   **P-in-c** M R H TURNER
ASHLEY (St Mary the Virgin) w Weston by Welland and
  Sutton Bassett *Pet 9*   **P** *Bp and DBP (alt)*   **R** *Vacant*
  Medbourne Green (085883) 827
ASHLEY (St Mary) w Silverley *Ely 4*   **P** *Bp and*
  DBP (alt)   **R** A F HOMER
ASHLEY (St Peter and St Paul)   Somborne w Ashley
  Win
ASHLEY GREEN (St John the Evangelist) *Ox 20*
  P *R A S Dorrien-Smith Esq*   **V** *Vacant*   Berkhamsted
  (0442) 863764
ASHMANHAUGH (St Swithin)   Horning w Beeston St
  Laurence and Ashmanhaugh *Nor*
ASHMANSWORTH (St James)   Highclere and
  Ashmansworth w Crux Easton *Win*
ASHMORE (St Nicholas)   Tollard Royal w Farnham,
  Gussage St Michael etc *Sarum*
ASHMORE PARK (St Alban)   Wednesfield *Lich*
ASHOVER (All Saints) and Brackenfield *Derby 5*
  P *Rev J Nodder and DBF (jt)*   **R** T B JOHNSON,
  NSM A L SMITH
ASHOW (The Assumption of Our Lady)   Stoneleigh w
  Ashow and Baginton *Cov*
ASHPERTON (St Bartholomew)   Bosbury w Wellington
  Heath etc *Heref*
ASHPRINGTON (St David), Cornworthy and Dittisham
  Ex 13   **P** *Bp*   **P** P C H A TRENCHARD
ASHREIGNEY (St James) *Ex 16*   **P** *DBP*   **R** P NIXSON
ASHTEAD (St George) (St Giles) *Guildf 10*   **P** *Bp*
  R C C HUGHES, **C** J D STRIDE, M P MELLUISH
ASHTON (Annunciation)   Breage w Germoe *Truro*
ASHTON (Chapel)   Oundle *Pet*
ASHTON (St John the Baptist)   Christow, Ashton,
  Trusham and Bridford *Ex*
ASHTON (St Michael and All Angels)   Roade and
  Ashton w Hartwell *Pet*
ASHTON, WEST (St John)   Trowbridge St Thos and W
  Ashton *Sarum*
ASHTON GATE (St Francis)   Bedminster *Bris*
ASHTON GIFFORD *Sarum 16*   **P** *DBP, Ld Chan, and*
  Pemb Coll Ox (by turn)   **R** J H TIPPING
ASHTON HAYES (St John the Evangelist) *Ches 2*
  P *Keble Coll Ox*   **V** W B FAULL
ASHTON-IN-MAKERFIELD (Holy Trinity) *Liv 15*   **P** *Bp*
  R D R ABBOTT

ASHTON-IN-MAKERFIELD (St Thomas) *Liv 15*
 P *R Ashton-in-Makerfield H Trin* **V** D W PERCIVAL,
 C D J HOOTON

ASHTON KEYNES (Holy Cross), Leigh and Minety *Bris 12*
 P *Bp* **V** P S HUGHES

ASHTON ON MERSEY (St Mary Magdalene) *Ches 10*
 P *Trustees* **V** G J SKINNER, **C** A CLARK,
 Par Dn T M BINLEY

ASHTON-ON-RIBBLE (St Andrew) *Blackb 14*
 P *Trustees* **V** J R POWELL

ASHTON-ON-RIBBLE (St Michael and All Angels)
 Blackb 14 **P** *Bp* **P-in-c** W G GRIMES,
 Par Dn B PARKINSON

ASHTON UNDER HILL (St Barbara) Overbury w
 Teddington, Alstone etc *Worc*

ASHTON-UNDER-LYNE (Christ Church) *Man 17* **P** *Bp*
 V S CARTWRIGHT, **Par Dn** J HEIL

ASHTON-UNDER-LYNE (Holy Trinity) *Man 17*
 P *Trustees* **V** C A E LAWRENCE

ASHTON-UNDER-LYNE (St James) (Queen Victoria
 Memorial Church) *Man 17* **P** *Bp and*
 Lord Deramore (jt) **V** *Vacant* 061-330 2771

ASHTON-UNDER-LYNE (St Michael and All Angels)
 (St Gabriel) *Man 17* **P** *Lord Deramore*
 C K F McGARAHAN

ASHTON-UNDER-LYNE (St Peter) *Man 17* **P** *R Ashton-*
 under-Lyne St Mich **P-in-c** A BROWN

ASHTON UPON MERSEY (St Martin) *Ches 10* **P** *SMF*
 R P M FREEMAN

ASHURST (St James) *Chich 12* **P** *MMCET*
 R P J BURCH

ASHURST (St Martin of Tours) Speldhurst w
 Groombridge and Ashurst *Roch*

ASHURST WOOD (St Dunstan) Forest Row *Chich*

ASHWATER (St Peter ad Vincula), Halwill, Beaworthy,
 Clawton and Tetcott w Luffincott *Ex 9* **P** *Ld Chan*
 (1 turn), Major L J Melhuish, Lt-Col Sir John
 Molesworth-St Aubyn, Bt and Bp (jt) ((2 turns)
 R L BROOKHOUSE

ASHWELL (St Mary) Cottesmore and Barrow w
 Ashwell and Burley *Pet*

ASHWELL (St Mary the Virgin) *St Alb 5* **P** *Bp*
 R P J M BRIGHT

ASHWELLTHORPE (All Saints) Wreningham *Nor*

ASHWICK (St James) w Oakhill and Binegar *B & W 9*
 P *Bp* **R** J CLOWES

ASHWICKEN (All Saints) Gayton Gp of Par *Nor*

ASHWORTH (St James) Norden w Ashworth *Man*

ASKAM (St Peter) Ireleth w Askam *Carl*

ASKERN (St Peter) *Sheff 8* **P** *Bp* **V** P H NOBLE

ASKERSWELL (St Michael), Loders and Powerstock
 Sarum 3 **P** *Ld Chan, Lady Laskey, Bp, and D&C*
 (by turn) **R** E G A W PAGE-TURNER

ASKHAM (Church Centre) Ireleth w Askam *Carl*

ASKHAM (St Nicholas) E Markham w Askham,
 Headon w Upton and Grove *S'well*

ASKHAM (St Peter) Lowther and Askham *Carl*

ASKHAM BRYAN (St Nicholas) *York 1* **P** *Trustees of*
 Rev G Nussey **V** *Vacant*

ASKHAM RICHARD (St Mary) Healaugh w Wighill,
 Bilbrough and Askham Richard *York*

ASKRIGG (St Oswald) w Stallingbusk *Ripon 4*
 P *V Aysgarth* **V** C W MALPASS

ASLACKBY (St James) Rippingale Gp *Linc*

ASLACTON (St Michael) Bunwell, Carleton Rode,
 Tibenham, Gt Moulton etc *Nor*

ASLOCKTON (St Thomas) Whatton w Aslockton,
 Hawksworth, Scarrington etc *S'well*

ASPALL (St Mary of Grace) Debenham w Aspall and
 Kenton *St E*

ASPATRIA (St Kentigern) w Hayton *Carl 7* **P** *Bp*
 V G G DOUGLAS

ASPENDEN (St Mary) and Layston w Buntingford *St Alb 5*
 P *CPAS and MMCET (alt)* **R** N J RICHARDS

ASPLEY (St Margaret) *S'well 14* **P** *Trustees*
 V D WARD, **C** I A HILTON

ASPLEY GUISE (St Botolph) w Husborne Crawley and
 Ridgmont *St Alb 15* **P** *Ld Chan (1 turn), Trustees Bedf*
 Estates (1 turn), and Bp (2 turns) **NSM** R A WILLCOX

ASPULL (St Elizabeth) *Liv 14* **P** *R Wigan*
 V B WHITEHEAD

ASSINGTON (St Edmund) w Newton Green and Little
 Cornard *St E 12* **P** *DBP (1 turn), Peterho Cam*
 (1 turn), and Bp (2 turns) **R** A R GEORGE

ASTBURY (St Mary) and Smallwood *Ches 11*
 P *Sir Richard Baker Wilbraham, Bt* **R** P A CAMPBELL

ASTERBY Group, The *Linc 11* **P** *Bp, DBP,*
 J N Heneage Esq, F Smith Esq, and Mrs J Fox (jt)
 R D F COOMBES, **NSM** H B WILLIAMS

ASTHALL (St Nicholas) and Swinbrook w Widford *Ox 8*
 P *Bp and Capt D Mackinnon (alt)* **V** J T M HINE

ASTLEY (St Mary the Virgin) Chilvers Coton w Astley
 Cov

ASTLEY (St Mary), Clive, Grinshill and Hadnall *Lich 29*
 P *D R B Thompson Esq* **V** W E WARD

ASTLEY (St Peter) Shrawley and Witley w Astley *Worc*

ASTLEY (St Stephen) *Man 13* **P** *V Leigh St Mary*
 C R W LAWRANCE

ASTLEY ABBOTTS (St Calixtus) Bridgnorth, Tasley,
 Astley Abbotts, Oldbury etc *Heref*

ASTLEY BRIDGE (St Paul) *Man 16* **P** *The Crown*
 V T P CHALLIS, **NSM** B E HAWORTH

ASTON cum Aughton (All Saints) and Ulley *Sheff 5* **P** *Bp*
 R P WRIGHT, **C** P J HOPPER

ASTON (St Giles) Wigmore Abbey *Heref*

ASTON (St Mary) Woore and Norton in Hales *Lich*

ASTON (St Mary) Stevenage St Mary Sheppall w Aston
 St Alb

ASTON (St Saviour) Stone St Mich w Aston St Sav *Lich*

ASTON, LITTLE (St Peter) *Lich 2* **P** *Trustees*
 V R J OLIVER

ASTON, NORTH (St Mary the Virgin) Steeple Aston w
 N Aston and Tackley *Ox*

ASTON ABBOTS (St James the Great) Wingrave w
 Rowsham, Aston Abbotts and Cublington *Ox*

ASTON BOTTERELL (St Michael and All Angels)
 Ditton Priors w Neenton, Burwarton etc *Heref*

ASTON BY SUTTON (St Peter) *Ches 3* **P** *B H Talbot Esq*
 NSM T A WHYTE

ASTON CANTLOW (St John the Baptist) and Wilmcote w
 Billesley *Cov 7* **P** *SMF* **V** T J HENDERSON

ASTON CLINTON (St Michael and All Angels) w Buckland
 and Drayton Beauchamp *Ox 22* **P** *Exors Major*
 S W Jenney, Jes Coll Ox, and Bp (by turn)
 R A W BENNETT, **NSM** I CORNISH

ASTON EYRE (not known) Morville w Aston Eyre
 Heref

ASTON FLAMVILLE (St Peter) Burbage w Aston
 Flamville *Leic*

ASTON INGHAM (St John the Baptist) Linton w
 Upton Bishop and Aston Ingham *Heref*

ASTON JUXTA BIRMINGHAM (St James) *Birm 6*
 P *V Aston* **V** D H HORN

ASTON JUXTA BIRMINGHAM (St Peter and St Paul)
 Birm 6 **P** *Patr Bd* **V** G K SINCLAIR, **C** C A GILBERT,
 Hon C C M GILBERT

ASTON LE WALLS (St Leonard) Chipping Warden w
 Edgcote and Aston le Walls *Pet*

ASTON-ON-TRENT (All Saints) and Weston-on-Trent
 Derby 15 **P** *Winterbottom Trustees and Bp (alt)*
 R B H MUNRO

ASTON ROWANT (St Peter and St Paul) Chinnor w
 Emmington and Sydenham etc *Ox*

ASTON SANDFORD (St Michael and All Angels)
 Haddenham w Cuddington, Kingsey etc *Ox*

ASTON SOMERVILLE (St Mary) Childswyckham w
 Aston Somerville, Buckland etc *Glouc*

ASTON-SUB-EDGE (St Andrew) Willersey, Saintbury,
 Weston-sub-Edge etc *Glouc*

ASTON TIRROLD (St Michael) S w N Moreton, Aston
 Tirrold and Aston Upthorpe *Ox*

ASTON UPTHORPE (All Saints) as above

ASTWICK (St Guthlac) Arlesey w Astwick *St Alb*

ASTWOOD (St Peter) Sherington w Chicheley, N
 Crawley, Astwood etc *Ox*

ASTWOOD BANK (St Matthias and St George) *Worc 7*
 P *DBP* **P-in-c** K A BOYCE

ASWARBY (St Denys) S Lafford *Linc*

ASWARDBY (St Helen) w Sausthorpe *Linc 7* **P** *DBP*
 R G ROBSON

ATCHAM (St Eata) Shrewsbury St Giles w Sutton and
 Atcham *Lich*

ATHELINGTON (St Peter) Stradbroke, Horham,
 Athelington and Redlingfield *St E*

ATHERINGTON (St Mary) and High Bickington *Ex 16*
 P *DBP and D&C (alt)* **R** V GILLETT

ATHERSLEY (St Helen) *Wakef 7* **P** *Bp* **V** P J STONIER,
 C P HARROP

ATHERSTONE (St Mary) *Cov 5* **P** *V Mancetter*
 V P I HARRIS

ATHERSTONE ON STOUR (St Mary) Ilmington w
 Stretton-on-Fosse etc *Cov*

ATHERTON (St John the Baptist) (St George) (St Philip)
 Man 13 **P** *Bp* **TR** W BALDWIN, **TV** J WISEMAN

ATLOW (St Philip and St James) Hulland, Atlow,
 Bradley and Hognaston *Derby*

ATTENBOROUGH (St Mary the Virgin) *S'well 7*
  P *CPAS*   **V** B DAWSON, **Assoc Min** A M M PARKER,
  Hon C D J DAVIES
ATTERCLIFFE (St Alban)   Darnall-cum-Attercliffe
  Sheff
**ATTLEBOROUGH (Assumption of the Blessed Virgin
  Mary) w Besthorpe** *Nor 17*   **P** *CR and
  Mrs S P J Scully (jt)*   **R** J A AVES
ATTLEBOROUGH (Holy Trinity) *Cov 5* **P** *V Nuneaton*
  V D J SMITH, **NSM** J REID
ATTLEBRIDGE (St Andrew)   Alderford w Attlebridge
  and Swannington *Nor*
ATWICK (St Lawrence)   Hornsea w Atwick *York*
**ATWORTH (St Michael and All Angels) w Shaw and
  Whitley** *Sarum 17* **P** *D&C Bris and R Melksham (alt)*
  V G E GRIFFITHS
AUBOURN (St Peter) w Haddington *Linc 18*
  P *Capt H N Nevile*   **V** D T OSBORN
AUCKLAND (St Andrew) (St Anne) *Dur 10*   **P** *Bp*
  V J MARSHALL, **C** G LIDDLE
AUCKLAND (St Helen) *Dur 10* **P** *Bp* **V** J BLAKESLEY
AUCKLAND (St Peter) *Dur 10* **P** *The Crown* **V** P K LEE
AUCKLEY (St Saviour)   Finningley w Auckley *S'well*
AUDENSHAW (St Hilda) *Man 17* **P** *Bp*
  V J H KERSHAW
AUDENSHAW (St Stephen) *Man 17* **P** *Bp* **V** P R DIXON
AUDLEM (St James the Great) *Ches 15* **P** *Bp*
  V D ROSTRON
AUDLEY (St James the Great) *Lich 15* **P** *Ch Soc Trust*
  V P T W DAVIES
AUGHTON (All Saints)   Bubwith w Skipwith *York*
AUGHTON (Christ Church) *Liv 11* **P** *R Aughton St Mich*
  V E BRAMHALL, **C** F R CAIN
AUGHTON (St Michael) *Liv 11* **P** *Bp* **R** M J SMOUT,
  C S E DRAPER
AUGHTON (St Saviour)   Halton w Aughton *Blackb*
AUKBOROUGH (St John the Baptist)   Alkborough
  Linc
AULT HUCKNALL (St John the Baptist) *Derby 3*
  P *Duke of Devonshire* **V** K H WAYNE
AUNSBY (St Thomas of Canterbury)   S Lafford *Linc*
AUST (not known)   Olveston *Bris*
AUSTERFIELD (St Helen)   Bawtry w Austerfield and
  Misson *S'well*
AUSTREY (St Nicholas) *Birm 12* **P** *Ld Chan*
  P-in-c W R STUART-WHITE
AUSTWICK (Epiphany)   Clapham-with-Keasden and
  Austwick *Bradf*
AVEBURY (St James)   Upper Kennett *Sarum*
AVELEY (St Michael) and Purfleet *Chelmsf 16* **P** *Bp*
  V C J NORRIS, **NSM** G E WRIGHT
AVENING (Holy Cross) w Cherington *Glouc 16*
  P *Mrs D C Fetherston-Godley (1 turn), D&C (2 turns)*
  P-in-c J W HOLDER, **NSM** C CARTER
AVERHAM (St Michael and All Angels) w Kelham
  S'well 3 **P** *DBP* **R** R B FEARN
AVETON GIFFORD (St Andrew) *Ex 14* **P** *Bp*
  R J S COLE
AVINGTON (St Mary)   Itchen Abbas cum Avington *Win*
**AVON DASSETT (St Peter and St Clare) w Farnborough
  and Fenny Compton** *Cov 8* **P** *G V L Holbech and Mrs
  A D Seyfried (jt), CCC Ox, and Bp (alt)* **R** D P PYM
AVONMOUTH (St Andrew) *Bris 8* **P** *Bp* **V** C F PENN
AWBRIDGE (All Saints) w Sherfield English *Win 11*
  P *Bp and CPAS (jt)* **R** A R CROAD
AWLISCOMBE (St Michael and All Angels)   Honiton,
  Gittisham, Combe Raleigh, Monkton etc *Ex*
AWRE (St Andrew)   Newnham w Awre and Blakeney
  Glouc
AWSWORTH (St Peter) w Cossall *S'well 7* **P** *Bp*
  V J A PARFITT
**AXBRIDGE (St John the Baptist) w Shipham and
  Rowberrow** *B & W 1* **P** *Bp and D&C (alt)* **R** J SMITH
AXFORD (St Michael)   Whitton *Sarum*
**AXMINSTER (St Mary the Virgin), Chardstock, Combe
  Pyne and Rousdon** *Ex 5* **P** *Bp* **TR** R B SWIFT,
  C A J ASHWELL, **Par Dn** D M BROWN
AXMOUTH (St Michael)   Uplyme w Axmouth *Ex*
AYCLIFFE (Church Centre)   Dover St Mary *Cant*
AYCLIFFE (St Andrew) *Dur 14* **P** *D&C* **V** P D DAVEY
AYLBURTON (St Mary)   Lydney w Aylburton *Glouc*
AYLBURTON COMMON (Mission Church)   as above
**AYLESBEARE (Blessed Virgin Mary), Rockbeare,
  Farringdon, Clyst Honiton and Sowton** *Ex 1* **P** *Bp and
  D&C (jt)* **V** T G WOODBRIDGE, **NSM** P RYDEN
AYLESBURY (St Mary the Virgin) w Bierton and Hulcott
  Ox 21 **P** *Bp and Patr Bd (jt)* **TR** T J HIGGINS,
  TV M T WHALLEY, L E PEPPER, S M B ROWE,
  Par Dn C E ROWE

AYLESBY (St Lawrence)   Keelby w Riby and Aylesby
  Linc
AYLESFORD (St Peter and St Paul) *Roch 7* **P** *D&C*
  V P E FRANCIS
AYLESHAM (St Peter) w Adisham *Cant 1* **P** *Abp*
  R A M YATES
AYLESTONE (St Andrew) w St James *Leic 2* **P** *Bp*
  R J HICKLING, **C** P ENNION, D H LEIGH
AYLMERTON (St John the Baptist) w Runton *Nor 7*
  P *Bp* **R** P H ATKINS
AYLSHAM (St Mary)   Burgh *Nor*
AYLSHAM (St Michael) *Nor 3* **P** *D&C Cant*
  V R D BRANSON, **NSM** N J A PUMPHREY
AYLTON (not known)   Tarrington w Stoke Edith,
  Aylton, Pixley etc *Heref*
**AYMESTREY (St John the Baptist and St Alkmund) and
  Leinthall Earles w Wigmore and Leinthall Starkes**
  Heref 7 **P** *Ld Chan and Bp (alt)* **P-in-c** S B THOMAS,
  Priest (w Past Care) E J BRYANT, **NSM** G N PRIDAY
AYNHO (St Michael) and Croughton w Evenley *Pet 1*
  P *Bp, Ms E A J Cartwright-Hignett, and Magd Coll Ox
  (by turn)* **R** G J GREEN
AYOT ST LAWRENCE (St Lawrence)   Kimpton w
  Ayot St Lawrence *St Alb*
AYOT ST PETER (St Peter)   Welwyn w Ayot St Peter
  St Alb
AYSGARTH (St Andrew) and Bolton cum Redmire
  Ripon 4 **P** *Trin Coll Cam and R Wensley (alt)*
  V M E BROWN, **Hon C** J H RICHARDSON
AYSTON (St Mary the Virgin)   Uppingham w Ayston
  and Wardley w Belton *Pet*
AYTHORPE (St Mary) w High and Leaden Roding
  Chelmsf 21 **P** *Ld Chan and Ch Soc Trust and Bp
  (by turn)* **P-in-c** C H OVERTON
AYTON, EAST (St John the Baptist)   Seamer w E Ayton
  York
**AYTON, GREAT (All Saints) (Christ Church) w Easby and
  Newton in Cleveland** *York 22* **P** *Abp* **V** P A W JONES
BABBACOMBE (All Saints) *Ex 10* **P** *V St Marychurch*
  V G W SILLIS
BABCARY (Holy Cross)   Six Pilgrims *B & W*
BABINGTON (St Margaret)   Kilmersdon w Babington
  B & W
BABRAHAM (St Peter) *Ely 7* **P** *H R T Adeane Esq*
  P-in-c R L POWELL, **C** R D TOMKINSON
BABWORTH (All Saints) w Sutton-cum-Lound *S'well 5*
  P *Bp and Major Sir James Whitaker, Bt (jt)*
  R G E HOLLOWAY
BACKFORD (St Oswald) and Capenhurst *Ches 9* **P** *Bp*
  R D E HARDWICK
BACKWELL (St Andrew) *B & W 14* **P** *DBP*
  R P J BLAKE
BACKWORTH (St John)   Earsdon and Backworth *Newc*
BACONSTHORPE (St Mary)   Barningham w Matlaske
  w Baconsthorpe etc *Nor*
**BACTON (St Andrew) w Edingthorpe w Witton and
  Ridlington** *Nor 9* **P** *Duchy of Lanc (1 turn), Bp and
  Earl of Kimberley (1 turn)* **P-in-c** J M S PICKERING
BACTON (St Faith)   Ewyas Harold w Dulas,
  Kenderchurch etc *Heref*
BACTON (St Mary the Virgin) w Wyverstone and Cotton
  St E 6 **P** *MMCET, Ld Chan, and J C S Priston Esq
  (by turn)* **R** C WYATT
BACUP (Christ Church) *Man 15* **P** *Trustees* **V** *Vacant*
  Bacup (0706) 878293
BACUP (St John the Evangelist) *Man 15* **P** *Wm Hulme
  Trustees* **V** M HOLT
BACUP (St Saviour) *Man 15* **P** *Ch Soc Trust*
  V D H KINGHAM
BADBY (St Mary) w Newnham *Pet 3* **P** *Bp*
  V S P ADAMS
BADDESLEY, NORTH (All Saints' Mission Church)
  Chilworth w N Baddesley *Win*
BADDESLEY, NORTH (St John the Baptist)   Valley
  Park *Win*
BADDESLEY, SOUTH (St Mary)   Boldre w S
  Baddesley *Win*
BADDESLEY CLINTON (St Michael) *Birm 13*
  P *T W Ferrers-Walker Esq* **R** A V WILLMONT
BADDESLEY ENSOR (St Nicholas) w Grendon *Birm 12*
  P *Bp, V Polesworth, and PCC (jt)* **V** J CHAPMAN
BADDILEY (St Michael) and Wrenbury w Burleydam
  Ches 15 **P** *V Acton and Bp (alt)* **V** R SPENCER
**BADDOW, GREAT (Meadgate Church Centre) (St Mary
  the Virgin) (St Paul)** *Chelmsf 11* **P** *Patr Bd*
  TR J K SPENCE, **TV** P C NICHOLSON, C J SKILTON,
  C R C MATTHEWS, **Hon Par Dn** M J COTTEE
BADDOW, LITTLE (St Mary the Virgin) *Chelmsf 11*
  P *Bp* **R** R E TURNER

BADGER (St Giles) *Lich 26* **P** *Ld Chan*
NSM P H J THORNEYCROFT
BADGEWORTH (Holy Trinity) w Shurdington *Glouc 11*
P *Bp* **V** W C WORSDELL
BADGWORTH (St Congar) Crook Peak *B & W*
BADINGHAM (St John the Baptist) w Bruisyard,
Cransford and Dennington *St E 18* **P** *R C Rous Esq*
(1 turn), DBP *(2 turns)* **R** *Vacant* Badingham
(072875) 784
BADLESMERE (St Leonard) Selling w Throwley,
Sheldwich w Badlesmere etc *Cant*
BADMINTON (St Michael and All Angels) w Little
Badminton, Acton Turville and Hawkesbury *Glouc 7*
P *Duke of Beaufort* **V** T T GIBSON
BADMINTON, LITTLE (St Michael and All Angels)
Badminton w Lt Badminton, Acton Turville etc *Glouc*
BADSEY (St James) w Aldington and Wickhamford *Worc 1*
P *Ch Ch Ox* **V** P D MITCHELL
BADSHOT LEA (St George) Conventional District *Guildf 3*
P-in-c P W C HOLT
BADSWORTH (St Mary the Virgin) *Wakef 11* **P** *DBP*
R R H TAYLOR, **C** J M GRIFFITHS
BADWELL ASH (St Mary) w Great Ashfield, Stowlangtoft,
Langham and Hunston *St E 9* **P** *Bp (2 turns),* DBP
(1 turn) **R** G L PATTISON
BAG ENDERBY (St Margaret) S Ormsby Gp *Linc*
BAGBOROUGH (St Pancras) Bishops Lydeard w
Bagborough and Cothelstone *B & W*
BAGBY (St Mary) Thirkleby w Kilburn and Bagby *York*
BAGENDON (St Margaret) N Cerney w Bagendon
Glouc
BAGINTON (St John the Baptist) Stoneleigh w Ashow
and Baginton *Cov*
BAGNALL (St Chad) Bucknall and Bagnall *Lich*
BAGSHOT (Good Shepherd) Wexcombe *Sarum*
BAGSHOT (St Anne) *Guildf 6* **P** *Ld Chan* **V** D HOLT
BAGULEY Brooklands (St John the Divine) *Man 8* **P** *Bp*
and A W Hargreaves Esq (jt) **V** J C FINDON,
C C E MANSLEY, **NSM** A W HARGREAVES
BAGWORTH (The Holy Rood) Thornton, Bagworth
and Stanton *Leic*
BAILDON (St John the Evangelist) (St Hugh Mission
Church) (St James) *Bradf 1* **P** *Major M W V*
Hammond-Maude **V** D A CARPENTER,
C M H CANNON, R HOWARD
BAINTON (St Andrew) w North Dalton, Middleton-on-the-
Wolds and Kilnwick *York 11* **P** *Abp, St Jo Coll Ox,*
and Exors M P Winter (jt) **R** H L ARTLEY
BAINTON (St Mary) Barnack w Ufford and Bainton *Pet*
BAKEWELL (All Saints) *Derby 2* **P** *D&C Lich*
V E R URQUHART, **NSM** L E ELLSWORTH
BALBY (St John the Evangelist) *Sheff 10* **P** *Bp*
V J F COOKE
BALCOMBE (St Mary) *Chich 6* **P** *Rev P B Secretan*
R N G PRINT
BALDERSBY (St James) w Dalton, Dishforth and Skipton
on Swale *York 20* **P** *Abp and Viscount Downe (jt)*
V D F BAKER
BALDERSTONE (St Leonard) *Blackb 2* **P** *V Blackb*
V D E ASHFORTH
BALDERSTONE (St Mary) *Man 19* **P** *Trustees*
V I C THOMPSON, **C** W E SLATER
BALDERTON (St Giles) *S'well 3* **P** *Ld Chan*
V C J YOUNG
BALDHU (St Michael) Highertown and Baldhu *Truro*
BALDOCK (St Mary the Virgin) w Bygrave *St Alb 12*
P *Marquess of Salisbury and Bp (alt)* **R** J D ATKINSON,
C T E JESSIMAN
BALDWIN (St Luke) Marown *S & M*
BALE (All Saints) Gunthorpe w Bale w Field Dalling,
Saxlingham etc *Nor*
BALHAM (St Mary and St John the Divine) *S'wark 16*
P *Rp and Keble Coll Ox (jt)* **V** T J N HULL,
Par Dn P J ROSE-CASEMORE, **Hon C** W A PENNEY
BALHAM HILL (Ascension) *S'wark 16* **P** *Bp*
V M P N JEWITT
BALKWELL (St Peter) *Newc 8* **P** *Bp* **V** O BLOXHAM
BALLAM (St Matthew) Ribby w Wrea *Blackb*
BALLAUGH (St Mary) (St Mary Old Church) *S & M 3*
P *The Crown* **V** J D GELLING
BALLIDON (All Saints) Bradbourne and Brassington
Derby
BALLINGER (St Mary Mission Hall) Gt Missenden w
Ballinger and Lt Hampden *Ox*
BALLINGHAM (St Dubricius) Lt Dewchurch,
Aconbury w Ballingham and Bolstone *Heref*
BALSALL COMMON (St Peter) *Birm 13* **P** *Bp*
V J N HACKETT

BALSALL HEATH (St Barnabas) Sparkbrook St
Agatha w Balsall Heath St Barn *Birm*
BALSALL HEATH (St Paul) *Birm 8* **P** *Bp*
Par Dn A G BUCKNALL
BALSCOTE (St Mary Magdalene) Broughton w N
Newington and Shutford etc *Ox*
BALSHAM (Holy Trinity) *Ely 4* **P** *Charterhouse*
R W N C GIRARD
BALTERLEY (All Saints' Memorial Church)
Barthomley *Ches*
BALTONSBOROUGH (St Dunstan) w Butleigh and West
Bradley *B & W 5* **P** *Bp* **V** B H ADAMS
BAMBER BRIDGE (St Aidan) *Blackb 6* **P** *Bp*
V J F HARPER, **Par Dn** A R WOOD
BAMBER BRIDGE (St Saviour) *Blackb 6* **P** *V Blackb*
V W T BARNES
BAMBURGH (St Aidan) and Lucker *Newc 10* **P** *Lord*
Armstrong (2 turns), Newc Dioc Soc (1 turn)
V E ZACHAU
BAMFORD (St John the Baptist) *Derby 2*
P *A C H Barnes Esq* **R** N P GOWER
BAMFORD (St Michael) *Man 19* **P** *Bp*
V R W WILLCOCK
BAMFURLONG (Good Shepherd) Abram *Liv*
BAMPTON (Holy Trinity) (St James) (St Mary) w Clanfield
Ox 8 **P** *Bp,* DBP, *St Jo Coll Ox, D&C Ex, and*
B Babington-Smith Esq (jt) **V** A C G SCOTT
BAMPTON (St Michael and All Angels), Morebath,
Clayhanger and Petton *Ex 8* **P** *DBP and D&C (jt)*
V J G M SCOTT
BAMPTON (St Patrick) w Mardale *Carl 1* **P** *Earl of*
Lonsdale **P-in-c** C P EDMONDSON, **NSM** W E SANDERS
BAMPTON ASTON (St James) Bampton w Clanfield
Ox
BAMPTON LEW (Holy Trinity) as above
BAMPTON PROPER (St Mary) as above
BANBURY (St Mary) *Ox 5* **P** *Bp*
TV D THOMSON, A J MILTON, S W CURRIE,
C P N TOVEY, **Par Dn** J V DURELL,
NSM S R FAIRBAIRN, N J WICKHAM, V BALL
BANHAM (St Mary) Quidenham *Nor*
BANKFOOT (St Matthew) *Bradf 2* **P** *Bp* **V** J R POOLE
BANKS (St Stephen in the Banks) *Liv 9* **P** *R N Meols*
P-in-c B J GERRARD
BANNINGHAM (St Botolph) Colby w Banningham and
Tuttington *Nor*
BANSTEAD (All Saints) *Guildf 9* **P** *Bp* **V** T S NEW,
C S HARDAKER
BANWELL (St Andrew) *B & W 12* **P** *D&C Bris*
V C A R MOORSOM
BAPCHILD (St Lawrence) Murston w Bapchild and
Tonge *Cant*
BAR HILL (not known) Local Ecumenical Project *Ely 5*
P-in-c J W S NEWCOME, **C** J C LAWRENCE
BARBON (St Bartholomew) Kirkby Lonsdale *Carl*
BARBOURNE (St Stephen) *Worc 6* **P** *Bp* **V** G L YALL
BARBROOK (St Bartholomew) Lynton, Brendon,
Countisbury, Lynmouth etc *Ex*
BARBY (St Mary) w Kilsby *Pet 3* **P** *Bp* **R** *Vacant*
Rugby (0788) 890252
BARCHESTON (St Martin) *Cov 9* **P** *Bp* **R** D C BROWN
BARCOMBE (St Bartholomew) (St Fancis) (St Mary the
Virgin) *Chich 18* **P** *Ld Chan* **R** T FLETCHER
BARDFIELD (St Peter and St Paul) Gt w Lt Saling
Chelmsf
BARDFIELD, GREAT (St Mary the Virgin) and Little
Bardfield *Chelmsf 21* **P** *Ch Union Trust* **V** *Vacant*
Great Dunmow (0371) 810267
BARDFIELD, LITTLE (St Katherine) Gt and Lt
Bardfield *Chelmsf*
BARDNEY (St Laurence) *Linc 11* **P** *DBP (1 turn), Bp*
(2 turns), and St Jo Coll Cam (1 turn) **R** S GREEN,
Hon C J A GREEN
BARDON HILL (St Peter) Coalville and Bardon Hill
Leic
BARDSEA (Holy Trinity) *Carl 8* **P** *DBP* **V** D W WOODS
BARDSEY (All Hallows) *Ripon 1* **P** *G L Fox Esq*
V W T SNELSON
BARDSLEY (Holy Trinity) *Man 17* **P** *Wm Hulme*
Trustees **V** L S IRELAND, **Hon Par Dn** L A IRELAND
BARDWELL (St Peter and St Paul) Ixworth and
Bardwell *St E*
BARE (St Christopher) *Blackb 12* **P** *Bp*
V D J GREENMAN
BARFORD (St Botolph) Barnham Broom *Nor*
BARFORD (St John) Deddington w Barford, Clifton
and Hempton *Ox*
BARFORD (St Michael) as above

BARFORD (St Peter) w Wasperton and Sherbourne *Cov 8* **P** *Major J M Mills, R Hampton Lucy, and Lady Jeryl Smith-Ryland (jt)* **R** G BENFIELD

BARFORD, GREAT (All Saints) Roxton w Gt Barford *St Alb*

BARFORD ST MARTIN (St Martin), Dinton, Baverstock and Burcombe *Sarum 13* **P** *All So Coll Ox, A K I Mackenzie-Charrington Esq, Bp, and St Jo Hosp Wilton (jt)* **R** J LEEMING, **Dss** A SYMES

BARFREYSTONE (St Nicholas) Eythorne and Elvington w Waldershare etc *Cant*

BARHAM (St Giles) Spaldwick w Barham and Woolley *Ely*

BARHAM (St John the Baptist) w Bishopsbourne and Kingston *Cant 1* **P** *Abp* **R** *Vacant* Canterbury (0227) 831340

BARHAM (St Mary) Claydon and Barham *St E*

BARHOLME (St Martin) Uffington *Linc*

BARKBY (St Mary) and Queniborough *Leic 6* **P** *Peache Trustees and A J Peacock Pochin Esq (jt)* **V** *Vacant* Leicester (0533) 695539

BARKESTONE (St Peter and St Paul) w Plungar, Redmile and Stathern *Leic 3* **P** *The Crown and Peterho Cam (alt)* **R** E W RUPP

BARKHAM (St James) Arborfield w Barkham *Ox*

BARKING (St Erkenwald) *Chelmsf 1* **P** *Bp* **V** G R WISKER

BARKING (St Margaret) (St Patrick) *Chelmsf 1* **P** *Patr Bd* **TR** P R THOMAS, **TV** D SILVESTER, A R HURLE, **C** D A EATON, **NSM** J G FROUD

BARKING (St Mary) Ringshall w Battisford, Barking w Darmsden etc *St E*

BARKINGSIDE (Holy Trinity) *Chelmsf 7* **P** *V Ilford* **V** C REEVES

BARKINGSIDE (St Cedd) *Chelmsf 7* **P** *Bp* **P-in-c** R C MATTHEWS, **C** M J KETLEY

BARKINGSIDE (St Francis of Assisi) *Chelmsf 7* **P** *Bp* **V** R H S EASTOE

BARKINGSIDE (St George) *Chelmsf 7* **P** *Bp* **V** J V FISHER

BARKINGSIDE (St Laurence) *Chelmsf 7* **P** *Bp* **V** J W WALMSLEY

BARKISLAND (Christ Church) w West Scammonden *Wakef 4* **P** *V Halifax* **V** C W DIXON, **C** H N LAWRANCE

BARKSTON (St Nicholas) and Hough Group, The *Linc 23* **P** *Capt Sir Anthony Thorold, Bt, Rev J R H and H C Thorold, Lord Brownlow, and Sir Lyonel Tollemache, Bt (by turn)* **R** G R SHRIMPTON, **NSM** S N SHRIMPTON

BARKSTON ASH (Holy Trinity) Sherburn in Elmet *York*

BARKWAY (St Mary Magdalene), Reed and Buckland w Barley *St Alb 5* **P** *The Crown and DBP (alt)* **R** C C KEVILL-DAVIES

BARKWITH Group, The *Linc 5* **P** *D&C, J N Heneage Esq, K Coll Lon, and DBP (by turn)* **R** A C SIMPSON

BARKWITH, EAST (St Mary) Barkwith Gp *Linc*

BARLASTON (St John the Baptist) *Lich 19* **P** *Countess of Sutherland* **V** G L SIMPSON

BARLAVINGTON (St Mary), Burton w Coates and Sutton w Bignor *Chich 11* **P** *Lord Egremont and Miss J B Courtauld (jt)* **R** R G JOHNSON

BARLBOROUGH (St James) *Derby 3* **P** *S R Sitwell Esq* **R** H J DOBBIN

BARLBY (All Saints) *York 4* **P** *V Hemingbrough* **V** R L BROWN

BARLESTONE (St Giles) *Leic 13* **P** *Bp* **P-in-c** L R CARPENTER

BARLEY (St Margaret of Antioch) Barkway, Reed and Buckland w Barley *St Alb*

BARLING (All Saints) w Little Wakering *Chelmsf 14* **P** *D&C St Paul's and Bp (alt)* **V** R WOOLVEN

BARLING MAGNA (All Saints) Barling w Lt Wakering *Chelmsf*

BARLINGS (St Edward) *Linc 3* **P** *DBP (2 turns), Earl of Scarborough (1 turn)* **V** R G SPAIGHT

BARLOW (not known) Brayton *York*

BARLOW (St Lawrence) *Derby 5* **P** *R Stavely* **P-in-c** H B HOSKIN

BARLOW, GREAT (St Lawrence) Barlow *Derby*

BARLOW MOOR (Emmanuel) Didsbury St Jas and Em *Man*

BARMBY MARSH (St Helen) Howden Team Min *York*

BARMBY MOOR (St Catherine) w Allerthorpe, Fangfoss and Yapham *York 7* **P** *Abp* **R** A D SHERRATT

BARMING (St Margaret of Antioch) w West Barming *Roch 7* **P** *Ld Chan* **R** A DAUNTON-FEAR

BARMING HEATH (St Andrew) *Cant 15* **P** *Abp* **V** B REED

BARMSTON (All Saints) Skipsea w Ulrome and Barmston w Fraisthorpe *York*

BARNACK (St John the Baptist) w Ufford and Bainton *Pet 8* **P** *Bp and St Jo Coll Cam (alt)* **R** G AUSTEN

BARNACRE (All Saints) w Calder Vale *Blackb 10* **P** *Bp and Mrs V O Shepherd-Cross (alt)* **V** E SWINNERTON

BARNARD CASTLE (St Mary) w Whorlton *Dur 11* **P** *Trin Coll Cam* **V** P W LIND-JACKSON, **C** P L WALKER

BARNARDISTON (All Saints) Hundon w Barnardiston *St E*

BARNBURGH (St Peter) w Melton on the Hill *Sheff 12* **P** *Ld Chan (2 turns), Bp (1 turn)* **R** J W A WOODS, **Hon Par Dn** P RUSSELL

BARNBY (St John the Baptist) Worlingham w Barnby and N Cove *St E*

BARNBY, EAST (Mission Chapel) Lythe w Ugthorpe *York*

BARNBY DUN (St Peter and St Paul) *Sheff 9* **P** *Bp* **V** T W HARRIS

BARNBY IN THE WILLOWS (All Saints) Coddington w Barnby in the Willows *S'well*

BARNEHURST (St Martin) *Roch 14* **P** *Bp* **V** J C BLAKE

BARNES (Holy Trinity) *S'wark 15* **P** *R Barnes St Mary* **P-in-c** P M SILLS

BARNES (St Mary) *S'wark 15* **P** *D&C St Paul's* **P-in-c** R AMES-LEWIS, **NSM** R CHAPMAN

BARNES (St Michael and All Angels) *S'wark 15* **P** *D&C St Paul's* **P-in-c** R B RUDDOCK

BARNET (Christ Church) S Mimms Ch Ch *Lon*

BARNET (St Stephen) Chipping Barnet w Arkley *St Alb*

BARNET, EAST (St Mary the Virgin) *St Alb 2* **P** *The Crown* **R** *Vacant* 081-368 3840

BARNET, NEW (St James) *St Alb 2* **P** *Ch Patr Trust* **V** M G H LACKEY, **C** D G ALEXANDER

BARNET VALE (St Mark) *St Alb 2* **P** *Bp* **V** C J GAY

BARNETBY LE WOLD Group, The (St Barnabas) *Linc 6* **P** *Bp (2 turns), DBP (1 turn), and D&C (1 turn)* **V** S R KENYON

BARNEY (St Mary), Fulmodeston w Croxton, Hindringham and Thursford *Nor 22* **P** *CCC Cam, Lord Hastings, and D&C (by turn)* **R** K W FARMER

BARNHAM (St Gregory) Euston w Barnham, Elvedon and Fakenham Magna *St E*

BARNHAM (St Mary) Aldingbourne, Barnham and Eastergate *Chich*

BARNHAM BROOM (St Peter and St Paul) *Nor 12* **P** *Patr Bd* **TR** D R RYE, **TM** P M HOPKINS

BARNINGHAM (St Andrew) Hopton, Market Weston, Barningham etc *St E*

BARNINGHAM (St Mary the Virgin) w Matlaske w Baconsthorpe w Plumstead w Hempstead *Nor 22* **P** *Duchy of Lanc (1 turn), Sir Charles Mott-Radclyffe, CPAS and D&C (jt) (1 turn)* **R** D C CANDLER

BARNINGHAM (St Michael and All Angels) w Hutton Magna and Wycliffe *Ripon 2* **P** *Bp and V Gilling and Kirkby Ravensworth (jt)* **R** W A CLAYTON

BARNINGHAM, LITTLE (St Andrew) Wickmere w Lt Barningham, Itteringham etc *Nor*

BARNINGHAM WINTER (St Mary the Virgin) Barningham w Matlaske w Baconsthorpe etc *Nor*

BARNOLDBY LE BECK (St Helen) *Linc 10* **P** *Ld Chan* **R** W J A NUNNERLEY

BARNOLDSWICK (Holy Trinity) (St Mary le Gill) w Bracewell *Bradf 7* **P** *Bp* **V** J R LANCASTER

BARNSBURY (St Andrew) *Lon 6* **P** *Patr Bd* **TR** A E HARVEY, **TV** C M S R THOMAS, R W WALL

BARNSLEY Old Town (St Paul) Barnsley St Mary *Wakef*

BARNSLEY (St Edward the Confessor) *Wakef 7* **P** *Bp* **V** G H HALL

BARNSLEY (St George's Parish Church Centre) *Wakef 7* **P** *Bp* **V** P J MUNBY

BARNSLEY (St Mary) Bibury w Winson and Barnsley *Glouc*

BARNSLEY (St Mary) *Wakef 7* **P** *Bp* **R** P MILLS, **C** G R CALVERT, M DAVIES

BARNSLEY (St Peter and St John the Baptist) *Wakef 7* **P** *Bp* **V** J E G ASHMAN

BARNSTAPLE (St Peter and St Mary Magdalene) (Holy Trinity) w Goodleigh, Landkey and Sticklepath *Ex 15* **P** *DBP* **TV** M J PEARSON, D J PHIPPS, G CHAVE-COX, **C** H G POLLOCK, **NSM** G F SQUIRE, **Hon Par Dn** P D PILDITCH

BARNSTON (Christ Church) *Ches 8*   **P** *Bp*
  V K I HOBBS, **C** P H GEDDES
BARNSTON (St Mary the Virgin) and Little Dunmow
  Chelmsf 21   **P** *CPAS*   **R** A R JACK
BARNSTONE (St Mary Mission Room)   Cropwell
  Bishop w Colston Bassett, Granby etc *S'well*
BARNT GREEN (St Andrew)   Cofton Hackett w Barnt
  Green *Birm*
BARNTON (Christ Church) *Ches 4*   **P** *Bp*
  V D R BUCKLEY
BARNWELL (All Saints) (St Andrew) w Tichmarsh,
  Thurning and Clapton *Pet 12*   **P** *Soc of Merchant*
  Venturers, MMCET, Em Coll Cam, and DBP (by turn)
  R *Vacant*   Oundle (0832) 72374
BARNWOOD (St Lawrence) *Glouc 5*   **P** *D&C*
  P-in-c P MINALL
BARR, GREAT (St Margaret) *Lich 7*   **P** *Exors*
  Mrs V C A Norbury   **V** J S REANEY
BARRINGTON (All Saints) *Ely 8*   **P** *Trin Coll Cam*
  V M W BAKER
BARRINGTON (Blessed Virgin Mary)   Shepton
  Beauchamp w Barrington, Stocklinch etc *B & W*
BARRINGTON, GREAT (St Mary)   Sherborne,
  Windrush, the Barringtons etc *Glouc*
BARRINGTON, LITTLE (St Peter)   as above
BARROW (All Saints) w Denham St Mary and Higham
  Green *St E 13*   **P** *Bp, St Jo Coll Cam, and*
  D W Barclay Esq (by turn)   **R** J B DAVIS
BARROW and Goxhill *Linc 6*   **P** *Ld Chan*
  V P WEBSTER
BARROW (St Bartholomew) *Ches 2*   **P** *D Okell Esq*
  R J H A HAYES
BARROW (St Giles)   Linley w Willey and Barrow *Heref*
BARROW, NORTH (St Nicholas)   Six Pilgrims *B & W*
BARROW, SOUTH (St Peter)   as above
BARROW GURNEY (Blessed Virgin Mary and St Edward
  King and Martyr) *B & W 14*   **P** *Major M A Gibbs*
  V H A P WILLS
BARROW HILL (St Andrew)   Staveley and Barrow Hill
  Derby
BARROW-IN-FURNESS (St Aidan) *Carl 8*   **P** *Bp*
  V D LE BERRY
BARROW-IN-FURNESS (St George) (St Luke) *Carl 8*
  P *Bp*   **TR** C GILLHESPEY
BARROW-IN-FURNESS (St James) *Carl 8*   **P** *DBP*
  V N J P HAYTON
BARROW-IN-FURNESS (St John the Evangelist) *Carl 8*
  P *DBP*   **V** A N BOYD
BARROW-IN-FURNESS (St Mark) *Carl 10*   **P** *Bp*
  V P G DAY, **C** K KITCHIN
BARROW-IN-FURNESS (St Mary the Virgin)   Walney
  Is *Carl*
BARROW-IN-FURNESS (St Matthew) *Carl 8*   **P** *Bp*
  V C G JOHNSON, **C** A N STRINGER,
  Hon C D H MARSTON
BARROW-ON-HUMBER (Holy Trinity)   Barrow and
  Goxhill *Linc*
BARROW-ON-TRENT (St Wilfrid) w Twyford and
  Swarkestone *Derby 15*   **P** *Repton Sch and H F Harpur-*
  Crewe Esq (jt)   **V** H T LINDLEY
BARROW UPON SOAR (Holy Trinity) w Walton le Wolds
  Leic 7   **P** *St Jo Coll Cam and DBP (jt)*
  R S J MITCHELL
BARROWBY (All Saints) *Linc 19*   **P** *Duke of Devonshire*
  R C W CALCOTT-JAMES
BARROWDEN (St Peter) and Wakerley w South
  Luffenham *Pet 8*   **P** *Burghley Ho Preservation Trust*
  and Ball Coll Ox (alt)   **R** B SCOTT
BARROWFORD (St Thomas) *Blackb 7*   **P** *DBF*
  V B MORGAN
BARSHAM (Holy Trinity)   Ringsfield w Redisham,
  Barsham, Shipmeadow etc *St E*
BARSHAM, EAST (All Saints) w North Barsham (All
  Saints) and West Barsham (Assumption of the Blessed
  Virgin Mary) *Nor 20*   **P** *Capt J D A Keith*
  P-in-c B R ROBERTS
BARSTON (St Swithin) *Birm 13*   **P** *MMCET*
  P-in-c A V GOLTON
BARTESTREE (St James)   Lugwardine w Bartestree
  and Weston Beggard *Heref*
BARTHOMLEY (St Bertoline) *Ches 11*   **P** *Lord O'Neill*
  R O J HORROCKS
BARTLEY (Mission Church)   Copythorne and Minstead
  Win
BARTLEY GREEN (St Michael and All Angels) *Birm 2*
  P *Bp*   **V** N E BALL, **C** E PITTS
BARTLOW (St Mary) *Ely 4*   **P** *Brig A N Breitmeyer*
  R J H THOMSON

BARTON (St Cuthbert w St Mary) and Manfield w Cleasby
  Ripon 2   **P** *Bp, D&C, and V Forcett and Stanwick w*
  Aldbrough (jt)   **V** *Vacant*   Darlington (0325) 377274
BARTON (St Lawrence) *Blackb 10*   **P** *DBP*
  V J H RANDELL
BARTON (St Mark's Chapel) w Peel Green (St Michael and
  All Angels) (St Catherine) *Man 2*   **P** *Bp and TR Eccles*
  V A PARK
BARTON (St Martin)   Torquay St Martin Barton *Ex*
BARTON (St Michael), Pooley Bridge and Martindale
  Carl 4   **P** *Bp and Earl of Lonsdale (jt)*   **V** N S DIXON
BARTON (St Paul) *Portsm 8*   **P** *R Whippingham*
  P-in-c C G LANE
BARTON (St Peter) *Ely 1*   **P** *Ld Chan*   **V** H D SEARLE
BARTON, GREAT (Holy Innocents) *St E 13*
  P *Sir Michael Bunbury, Bt*   **V** A BEARDSMORE
BARTON BENDISH (St Andrew) w Beachamwell and
  Shingham *Ely 16*   **P** *Bp and DBP (alt)*
  P-in-c M TUCKER
BARTON HARTSHORN (St James)   Swan *Ox*
BARTON HILL (St Luke w Christ Church) *Bris 4*
  P *V Bris St Phil (2 turns) and CPAS (1 turn)*
  V C A SUNDERLAND
BARTON IN FABIS (St George) *S'well 10*   **P** *Ld Chan*
  R A C SUTHERLAND
BARTON-LE-CLEY (St Nicholas) w Higham Gobion and
  Hexton *St Alb 15*   **P** *The Crown (3 turns),*
  Mrs F A A Cooper (1 turn)   **R** I H G GRAHAM-ORLEBAR
BARTON-LE-STREET (St Michael)   Street Team Min
  York
BARTON MILLS (St Mary)   Mildenhall *St E*
BARTON-ON-THE-HEATH (St Lawrence)   Long
  Compton, Whichford and Barton-on-the-Heath *Cov*
BARTON SEAGRAVE (St Botolph) w Warkton *Pet 11*
  P *Ch Soc Trust (2 turns), Duke of Buccleugh (1 turn)*
  R J A WARDLE, **C** D M TALBOT, D COURT,
  Hon C G MORGAN, **NSM** H EASTWOOD
BARTON ST DAVID (St David) w Kingweston *B & W 3*
  P *Bp and Mrs E J Burden (alt)*   **V** P S THOMAS
BARTON STACEY (All Saints) and Bullington and
  Hurstbourne Priors and Longparish *Win 6*   **P** *Bp,*
  D&C, and J Woodcock Esq (jt)   **V** D J COTTRILL
BARTON TURF (St Michael)   Neatishead, Barton Turf
  and Irstead *Nor*
BARTON UNDER NEEDWOOD (St James) *Lich 20*
  P *Bp*   **V** A J WOOD
BARTON UPON HUMBER (St Mary) *Linc 6*   **P** *Bp*
  V E J P HEPWORTH, **C** I S PARTRIDGE
BARTON UPON IRWELL (St Catherine)   Barton w
  Peel Green *Man*
BARWELL (St Mary) w Potters Marston and Stapleton
  Leic 13   **P** *R J W Titley Esq*   **R** G T RIMMINGTON
BARWICK (St Mary Magdalene) *B & W 8*
  P *Ms Y L Bennett and Ms R S Mullen (jt)*   **R** *Vacant*
  Yeovil (0935) 20661
BARWICK IN ELMET (All Saints) *Ripon 8*   **P** *Duchy of*
  Lanc   **R** T G MUNRO, **Par Dn** W A WILBY
BASCHURCH (All Saints) and Weston Lullingfield w
  Hordley *Lich 23*   **P** *Ch Patr Trust and Bp (jt)*
  R D R D JONES
BASEGREEN (St Peter)   Gleadless *Sheff*
BASFORD (St Aidan) *S'well 13*   **P** *Bp*   **V** W H JARVIS
BASFORD (St Leodegarius) w Hyson Green *S'well 13*
  P *Bp and CPAS (jt)*   **V** G E JONES,
  C R J St C HARLOW-TRIGG, M T PHILLIPS, P DENISON
BASFORD (St Mark) *Lich 15*   **P** *Bp*   **V** F POWELL
BASFORD, NEW (St Augustine)   Basford w Hyson
  Green *S'well*
BASHLEY (St John)   Milton *Win*
BASILDON (St Andrew) (Holy Cross) *Chelmsf 9*   **P** *Bp*
  P-in-c H A MATTY, **C** R HANKEY
BASILDON (St Stephen) w Aldworth and Ashampstead
  Ox 12   **P** *St Jo Coll Cam, Simeon's Trustees, and DBF*
  (by turn)   **V** D G MEARA, **NSM** C L WINDEBANK
BASILDON, (St Martin of Tours) w Nevendon (St Peter)
  Chelmsf 9   **P** *Bp*   **TR** L F WEBBER, **TV** H A MATTY
BASING (St Mary) *Win 4*   **P** *Magd Coll Ox*
  V A D PICTON
BASINGSTOKE (All Saints) (St Michael) *Win 4*
  P *Patr Bd*   **TR** C N WRIGHT,
  TV P FURBER, P M GILKS, C J BANNISTER,
  Par Dn K J YOUNG, **NSM** E A GEORGE
BASINGSTOKE Brighton Hill (Christ the King)
  Basingstoke *Win*
BASINGSTOKE Popley (Bethlehem Chapel)   as above
BASINGSTOKE South Ham (St Peter)   as above
BASLOW (St Anne) *Derby 2*   **P** *Duke of Devonshire*
  V M F LEIGH

BASSENTHWAITE (St Bega) (St John), Isel and Setmurthy *Carl 6*   **P** *Bp, D&C, and Exors Mrs M Austen-Leigh (by turn)*   **V** J H HARKER

BASSINGBOURN (St Peter and St Paul) *Ely 8*   **P** *D&C Westmr*   **V** J F AITCHISON

BASSINGHAM (St Michael and All Angels) *Linc 18*   **P** *CCC Ox*   **R** D T OSBORN,   **NSM** J T ROOKE

BASSINGTHORPE (St Thomas a Becket) Ingoldsby *Linc*

BASTON (St John the Baptist) Langtoft Gp *Linc*

BASWICH (Holy Trinity) *Lich 16*   **P** *Bp*   **V** J POTTS, **C** G E T BENNETT,   **Par Dn** P CORBETT

BATCOMBE (St Mary) Yetminster w Ryme Intrinseca and High Stoy *Sarum*

BATCOMBE (The Blessed Virgin Mary) Bruton and Distr *B & W*

BATH Abbey (St Peter and St Paul) w St James *B & W 10*   **P** *Simeon's Trustees*   **R** R G ASKEW,   **C** C STEWART

BATH Bathwick (St John the Baptist) (Blessed Virgin Mary) *B & W 10*   **P** *Bp*   **NSM** J B DOUGLAS

BATH (Christ Church) Proprietary Chapel *B & W 11*   **P** *R Walcot*   **Hon C** M C R BRAYBROOKE

BATH (Holy Trinity) *B & W 10*   **P** *SMF*   **R** *Vacant* Bath (0225) 422311

BATH Odd Down (St Philip and St James) w Combe Hay *B & W 10*   **P** *Simeon's Trustees*   **V** A BAIN, **NSM** T D H CATCHPOOL

BATH (St Barnabas) w Englishcombe *B & W 10*   **P** *Bp*   **V** T R BONIWELL

BATH (St Bartholomew) *B & W 10*   **P** *Simeon's Trustees*   **V** I R LEWIS

BATH (St Luke) *B & W 10*   **P** *Simeon's Trustees*   **V** D F PERRYMAN,   **C** S C COUPLAND

BATH St Mary Magdalene Holloway (Extra-parochial Chapelry) *B & W 11*   **P** *Bath Municipal Charities for Ld Chan*   **Min** G S MOWAT

BATH St Michael (Group Ministry with Bath Abbey) *B & W 11*   **P** *Bath Municipal Charities for Ld Chan* *Vacant*

BATH (St Michael) w St Paul *B & W 10*   **P** *Exors Rev W G M C Colburn, and Rev D B Bubbers, Canon A R Henderson and CPAS (jt)*   **R** A R WALLACE

BATH (St Saviour) *B & W 10*   **P** *Ch Patr Trust*   **R** *Vacant* Bath (0225) 311637

BATH (St Stephen) Charlcombe w Bath St Steph *B & W*

BATH Twerton-on-Avon (Ascension) (St Michael) *B & W 10*   **P** *Patr Bd*   **TR** R G CLARKE, **TV** M F BAYNHAM,   **C** M S PERSSON, A E H TURNER

BATH Walcot (St Andrew) (St Swithin) *B & W 10*   **P** *Simeon's Trustees*   **R** G M DODDS, **Par Dn** M E TOOZE,   **NSM** N J L PEARCE

BATH Weston (All Saints) w North Stoke *B & W 10*   **P** *Ld Chan*   **R** T P WATSON,   **C** A N PERRY,

BATH Weston (St John the Evangelist) (Emmanuel) w Kelston *B & W 10*   **P** *Ld Chan*   **R** *Vacant* Bath (0225) 27206

BATH Widcombe (St Matthew) (St Thomas a Becket) *B & W 10*   **P** *Simeon's Trustees*   **V** R A RUSSELL, **NSM** G M GARDNER

BATHAMPTON (St Nicholas) *B & W 10*   **P** *D&C Bris*   **P-in-c** O J D BAYLEY

BATHEALTON (St Bartholomew) Wellington and Distr *B & W*

BATHEASTON (St John the Baptist) (St Catherine) *B & W 10*   **P** *Ch Ch Ox*   **V** J W B PERRY

BATHFORD (St Swithun) *B & W 10*   **P** *D&C Bris*   **V** M J TURNER

BATLEY (All Saints) *Wakef 10*   **P** *E C S J G Brudenell Esq and Trustees D Stubley Esq (jt)*   **V** R M WILSON

BATLEY (St Thomas) *Wakef 10*   **P** *V Batley*   **V** L C DEW

BATLEY CARR (Holy Trinity) Dewsbury *Wakef*

BATSFORD (St Mary) Moreton-in-Marsh w Batsford, Todenham etc *Glouc*

BATTERSEA (Christ Church and St Stephen) *S'wark 13*   **P** *Bp and V Battersea St Mary (alt)*   **V** P CLARK, **C** G N OWEN

BATTERSEA (St Luke) *S'wark 13*   **P** *Bp*   **P-in-c** J A RUSSELL,   **C** D FROST, **Hon C** C TANCRED-LAWSON, J A BAKER

BATTERSEA (St Peter) (St Paul) *S'wark 13*   **P** *V Battersea St Mary*   **V** M A WIMSHURST, **Par Dn** C E LATHAM

BATTERSEA (St Philip w St Bartholomew) *S'wark 13*   **P** *Bp*   **V** I R FORSTER

BATTERSEA (St Saviour) (St George w St Andrew) *S'wark 13*   **P** *CPAS and Ch Patr Soc (jt)*   **V** A J TOMBLING,   **Par Dn** A BAKER

BATTERSEA Wandsworth Common (St Michael) *S'wark 13*   **P** *V Battersea St Mary*   **P-in-c** A C HORTON

BATTERSEA PARK (All Saints) *S'wark 13*   **P** *Bp*   **P-in-c** A J TOMBLING

BATTERSEA RISE (St Mark) *S'wark 13*   **P** *V Battersea St Mary*   **P-in-c** P J S PERKIN,   **C** A P B WHITE

BATTERSEA ST MARY (St Mary) *S'wark 13*   **P** *Earl Spencer*   **V** J M CLARKE,   **C** I M HUBBARD, **Par Dn** C WALLING

BATTISFORD (St Mary) Ringshall w Battisford, Barking w Darmsden etc *St E*

BATTLE (Church of the Ascension) (St Mary the Virgin) *Chich 14*   **P** *The Crown*   **V** W A V CUMMINGS

BATTLE HILL (Good Shepherd) Willington Team *Newc*

BATTLESDEN (St Peter and All Saints) Woburn w Eversholt, Milton Bryan, Battlesden etc *St Alb*

BATTYEFORD (Christ the King) *Wakef 10*   **P** *V Mirfield*   **V** D B FOSS,   **Hon C** R E WHITNALL

BAUGHURST (St Stephen) and Ramsdell and Wolverton w Ewhurst and Hannington *Win 4*   **P** *Ld Chan, Duke of Wellington, and Bp (by turn)*   **R** J E FRANKS

BAULKING (St Nicholas) Uffington w Woolstone and Baulking *Ox*

BAUMBER (St Swithin) Hemingby *Linc*

BAUNTON (St Mary Magdalene) Stratton w Baunton *Glouc*

BAVERSTOCK (St Editha) Barford St Martin, Dinton, Baverstock etc *Sarum*

BAWBURGH (St Mary and St Walstan) Cringleford w Colney and Bawburgh *Nor*

BAWDESWELL (All Saints) w Foxley *Nor 8*   **P** *Bp*   **P-in-c** G L HUMPHRIES

BAWDRIP (St Michael and All Angels) Woolavington w Cossington and Bawdrip *B & W*

BAWDSEY (St Mary) Alderton w Ramsholt and Bawdsey *St E*

BAWTRY (St Nicholas) w Austerfield and Misson *S'well 1*   **P** *Bp*   **V** W H THACKRAY,   **Hon C** P E SARGAN

BAXENDEN (St John the Baptist) *Blackb 1*   **P** *Bp*   **V** M C IRELAND

BAXTERGATE (St Ninian) Whitby *York*

BAXTERLEY (not known) w Hurley and Wood End and Merevale w Bentley *Birm 12*   **P** *Ld Chan (1 turn), Bp and Sir William Dugdale, Bt (1 turn)*   **R** *Vacant* Tamworth (0827) 874252

BAYDON (St Nicholas) Whitton *Sarum*

BAYFORD (Mission Room) Charlton Musgrove, Cucklington and Stoke Trister *B & W*

BAYFORD (St Mary) Lt Berkhamsted and Bayford, Essendon etc *St Alb*

BAYLHAM (St Peter) Gt and Lt Blakenham w Baylham and Nettlestead *St E*

BAYSTON HILL (Christ Church) *Lich 27*   **P** *V Shrewsbury H Trin w St Julian*   **V** G C GRIFFITHS, **Hon C** M H TUPPER

BAYSWATER (St Matthew) *Lon 2*   **P** *Dame Jewell Magnus-Allcroft*   **V** G M EVANS, **Hon Par Dn** P D PERKINS

BAYTON (St Bartholomew) Mamble w Bayton, Rock w Heightington etc *Worc*

BEACHAMPTON (Assumption of the Blessed Virgin Mary) Nash w Thornton, Beachampton and Thornborough *Ox*

BEACHAMWELL (St Mary) Barton Bendish w Beachamwell and Shingham *Ely*

BEACHLEY (St John the Evangelist) Tidenham w Beachley and Lancaut *Glouc*

BEACONSFIELD (St Mary and All Saints) (St Michael and All Angels) *Ox 20*   **P** *Patr Bd*   **TR** M M FITZWILLIAMS, **TV** P W LOCKYER, R T WOODWARD,   **C** I S TATTUM, **NSM** W T EVANS, R A JOHNSON, G R ANDERSON

BEADLAM (St Hilda) Kirkdale *York*

BEADNELL (St Ebba) w Ellingham *Newc 10*   **P** *D&C Dur and V Bamburgh (jt)*   **V** W WADDLE

BEAFORD (All Saints), Roborough and St Giles in the Wood *Ex 20*   **P** *Bp, Ld Chan, and MMCET (by turn)*   **P-in-c** T C OAKLEY

BEALINGS, GREAT and LITTLE (St Mary) w Playford and Culpho *St E 7*   **P** *Lord Cranworth (1 turn), Bp (3 turns)*   **R** *Vacant* Ipswich (0473) 623884

BEALINGS, LITTLE (All Saints) Gt and Lt Bealings w Playford and Culpho *St E*

BEAMINSTER AREA (St Mary of the Annunciation) *Sarum 1*   **P** *Patr Bd*   **TR** T M F BILES, **TV** J LILLEY, R H P THORNBURGH,   **C** P J SWAIN, **NSM** L F A HOLLAND

BEAMISH (St Andrew) Stanley *Dur*

BEARD (St James the Less) New Mills *Derby*

BEARLEY (St Mary the Virgin) Snitterfield w Bearley *Cov*

BEARPARK (St Edmund) *Dur 2* P *D&C* V C R MASON

BEARSTED (Holy Cross) w Thurnham *Cant 15* P *Abp*
V G H SIDAWAY, C S J BETTS

BEARWOOD (St Catherine) *Ox 16* P *Bp*
R H D ETCHES

BEARWOOD (St Mary the Virgin) *Birm 5*
P *V Smethwick* V H G JAMES

BEAUCHAMP RODING (St Botolph) Abbess Roding, Beauchamp Roding and White Roding *Chelmsf*

BEAUDESERT (St Nicholas) and Henley-in-Arden w Ullenhall *Cov 7* P *MMCET, Bp, and High Bailiff of Henley-in-Arden (jt)* P-in-c J F GANJAVI

BEAULIEU (Blessed Virgin and Holy Child) and Exbury and East Boldre w Beaulieu (jt) *Win 10* P *Bp and Lord Montagu of Beaulieu (jt)* V D T P ABERNETHY,
Hon Par Dn E M SINGLETON

BEAUMONT CUM MOZE (St Leonard and St Mary) Tendring and Lt Bentley w Beaumont cum Moze *Chelmsf*

BEAUMONT LEYS (Christ the King) *Leic 2* P *Bp*
V D V OSBORNE

BEAUWORTH (St James) Cheriton w Tichborne and Beauworth *Win*

BEAUXFIELD (St Peter) Whitfield w Guston *Cant*

BEAWORTHY (St Alban) Ashwater, Halwill, Beaworthy, Clawton etc *Ex*

BEBINGTON (St Andrew) *Ches 8* P *Ch Soc Trust*
R G M TURNER, C P S McVEAGH, R I McLAREN,
NSM E P BICKERSTETH

BEBINGTON, HIGHER (Christ Church) *Ches 8*
P *C J C Saunders-Griffiths Esq* V R K FAULKNER,
C P TIMPERLEY, Hon C R RAWLINSON

BECCLES (St Michael the Archangel) (St Luke's Church Centre) *St E 14* P *Patr Bd* TR M D SUTTON,
TV G H CLOTHIER

BECCONSALL (All Saints) Hesketh w Becconsall *Blackb*

BECK ROW (St John) Mildenhall *St E*

BECKBURY (St Milburga) *Lich 26* P *Ld Chan*
P-in-c D F CHANTREY, NSM P H J THORNEYCROFT

BECKENHAM (Christ Church) *Roch 12* P *Ch Trust Fund Trust* V A P BAKER, C R E SEED,
Hon C J T ANSCOMBE,
NSM M D COOKE, Dss G M N RAIKES

BECKENHAM (Holy Trinity) Penge Lane H Trin *Roch*

BECKENHAM (St Barnabas) *Roch 12* P *Keble Coll Ox*
V *Vacant* 081-650 3332

BECKENHAM (St George) *Roch 12* P *Bp*
R D G E CARPENTER, C W T MARSTON

BECKENHAM (St James) Elmers End *Roch 12* P *Bp*
V L C STAPLETON

BECKENHAM (St John the Baptist) Eden Park *Roch 12*
P *Ch Trust Fund Trust, Bp and Adn Bromley (jt)*
V G W YOUNG, Par Dn P J AVANN

BECKENHAM (St Michael and All Angels) w St Augustine *Roch 12* P *SMF and Bp (jt)* V R S FAYERS

BECKENHAM, NEW (St Paul) *Roch 12* P *Bp*
V J FROST

BECKERMET (St Bridget) (St Bridget Old Church) (St John) w Ponsonby *Carl 5* P *Bp, Adn W Cumberland, P Stanley Esq, and PCCs of Beckermet St Jo and St Bridget (jt)* V P EVANS

BECKFORD (St John the Baptist) Overbury w Teddington, Alstone etc *Worc*

BECKHAM, WEST (St Helen and All Saints) Weybourne Gp *Nor*

BECKINGHAM (All Saints) Brant Broughton and Beckingham *Linc*

BECKINGHAM (All Saints) w Walkeringham *S'well 1*
P *Bp and Ld Chan (alt)* V *Vacant* Saundby (042784) 266

BECKINGTON (St George) w Standerwick, Berkley, Rodden, Lullington and Orchardleigh *B & W 4* P *Bp (3 turns), Ch Soc Trust (1 turn), and Exors of A Duckworth (1 turn)* R H B B BAKER

BECKLEY (All Saints) and Peasmarsh *Chich 20* P *Univ Coll Ox and SS Coll Cam (alt)* R C F HOPKINS

BECKLEY (Assumption of the Blessed Virgin Mary) *Ox 1*
P *W A Cooke Esq* V A G A de VERE

BECKTON, EAST (Christian Centre) E Ham w Upton Park *Chelmsf*

BECKWITHSHAW (St Michael and All Angels) Pannal w Beckwithshaw *Ripon*

BECONTREE (St Elizabeth) *Chelmsf 1* P *Bp*
P-in-c R LOVE

BECONTREE (St George) Dagenham *Chelmsf*

BECONTREE (St Mary) *Chelmsf 1* P *CPAS*
V R HERBERT, C J E PERRYMAN, Par Dn A NEWTON

BECONTREE West (St Cedd) (St Peter) (St Thomas) *Chelmsf 1* P *DBP* TR D N BAXTER,
TV J R CARR, R J COWEN

BECONTREE SOUTH (St Alban) (St John the Divine) *Chelmsf 1* P *Peache Trust* TR D S AINGE,
TV J A V FLORANCE

BEDALE (St Gregory) *Ripon 4* P *Sir Henry Beresford-Peirce, Bt* R M D EMMEL, C R W GROSSE,
NSM H K DEWIS, A L WOODHOUSE

BEDDINGHAM (St Andrew) Glynde, W Firle and Beddingham *Chich*

BEDDINGTON (St Francis' Church Hall) S Beddington St Mich *S'wark*

BEDDINGTON (St Mary) *S'wark 25* P *K Bond Esq*
R D A RICHARDSON

BEDDINGTON, SOUTH (St Michael and All Angels) *S'wark 25* P *Bp* V J M DEAN, C T W STOREY

BEDFIELD (St Nicholas) Worlingworth, Southolt, Tannington, Bedfield etc *St E*

BEDFONT, EAST (St Mary the Virgin) *Lon 11*
P *Ld Chan* V P G HUTTON, C N G KELLEY

BEDFORD (All Saints) *St Alb 16* P *Bp* V N J ELDER,
Par Dn M A McLEAN

BEDFORD (Christ Church) *St Alb 16* P *Bp*
V D R HARRIS, C R M McCONNELL

BEDFORD (St Andrew) *St Alb 16* P *Ld Chan*
V J A L HULBERT, C M W PERCY, Par Dn E M PERCY

BEDFORD (St John the Baptist) (St Leonard) *St Alb 16*
P *MMCET* M J PARKER, Hon C C MOSS

BEDFORD (St Martin) *St Alb 16* P *Bp* V *Vacant*
Bedford (0234) 357862

BEDFORD (St Michael and All Angels) *St Alb 16* P *Bp*
V J R FOWLER

BEDFORD (St Paul) *St Alb 16* P *Bp*
V C P COLLINGWOOD,
Par Dn J A BLUNDEN, H F W SMITH, NSM M H BULL,
Hon Par Dn M ARTHINGTON, J CROSSLAND

BEDFORD (St Peter de Merton) w St Cuthbert *St Alb 16*
P *Ld Chan* R J SCHILD, NSM B V I GREENISH

BEDFORD LEIGH (St Thomas) (All Saints Mission) *Man 13* P *V Leigh St Mary* V R J ALDERSON,
C P M THOMAS

BEDFORD PARK (St Michael and All Angels) *Lon 11*
P *Bp* V P A BUTLER, Hon C G IBALL

BEDGROVE (Holy Spirit) *Ox 21* P *DBP*
C S J D FOSTER, NSM N M DICK

BEDHAMPTON (St Nicholas's Mission Church) (St Thomas) *Portsm 4* P *Bp* R I G COOMBER,
C W A McCOUBREY

BEDINGFIELD (St Mary) *St E 16* P *MMCET*
P-in-c R H SMITH

BEDINGHAM (St Andrew) Hempnall *Nor*

BEDLINGTON (St Cuthbert) *Newc 1* P *D&C Dur*
V K R WARD

BEDMINSTER (St Aldhelm) (St Dunstan) (St Paul) *Bris 1*
P *Bp* TV J P WOODGER, TM J I WOODS,
NSM J F HOUSE, R DURBIN, R A LANE

BEDMINSTER (St Michael and All Angels) *Bris 1* P *Bp*
V T J BAILLIE, C D B HARREX

BEDMINSTER DOWN (St Oswald) *Bris 1* P *Bp*
V C M PILGRIM

BEDMONT (Ascension) Abbots Langley *St Alb*

BEDNALL (All Saints) Penkridge Team *Lich*

BEDSTONE (St Mary) Clungunford w Clunbury and Clunton, Bedstone etc *Heref*

BEDWORTH (All Saints) *Cov 5* P *MMCET*
R P L TONG, C P J NORTON, Dss P M HAMILTON

BEDWYN, GREAT (St Mary), Little Bedwyn and Savernake Forest *Sarum 21* P *Bp* V T SALISBURY

BEDWYN, LITTLE (St Michael) Gt and Lt Bedwyn and Savernake Forest *Sarum*

BEECH (St Peter) Alton St Lawr *Win*

BEECH, HIGH (Holy Innocents) Waltham H Cross *Chelmsf*

BEECH HILL (St Mary the Virgin), Grazeley and Spencers Wood *Ox 15* P *Bp* V *Vacant* Reading (0734) 883215

BEECHDALE ESTATE (St Chad) Blakenall Heath *Lich*

BEECHINGSTOKE (St Stephen) Swanborough *Sarum*

BEEDING (St Peter) and Bramber w Botolphs *Chich 12*
P *Bp* R D J WHITE

BEEDING, LOWER (Holy Trinity) (St John the Evangelist) *Chich 8* P *Bp* V J F FORD

BEEDON (St Nicholas) and Peasemore w West Ilsley and Farnborough *Ox 14* P *Bp* P-in-c P M RENOUF

BEEFORD (St Leonard) w Frodingham and Foston
York 12 **P** *Abp and Ch Soc Trust (jt)*
R J N CHARTERS
BEELEY (St Anne) and Edensor *Derby 2* **P** *Duke of*
Devonshire **P-in-c** R A BEDDOES
BEELSBY (St Andrew) Ravendale Gp *Linc*
BEENHAM VALENCE (St Mary) Woolhampton w
Midgham and Beenham Valance *Ox*
BEER (St Michael) and Branscombe *Ex 5* **P** *Lord Clinton*
and D&C (jt) **V** N H FREATHY
BEER HACKETT (St Michael) Bradf Abbas and
Thornford w Beer Hackett *Sarum*
BEERCROCOMBE (St James) Hatch Beauchamp w
Beercrocombe, Curry Mallet etc *B & W*
BEESANDS (St Andrew) Stokenham w Sherford *Ex*
BEESBY (St Andrew) Saleby w Beesby *Linc*
BEESTON (St Andrew) Sprowston w Beeston *Nor*
BEESTON (St John the Baptist) *S'well 7* **P** *Duke of*
Devonshire **V** S A LOWE, **C** M EVANS,
Par Dn J E LAMB
BEESTON (St Laurence) Horning w Beeston St
Laurence and Ashmanhaugh *Nor*
BEESTON (St Mary the Virgin) *Ripon 6* **P** *V Leeds St Pet*
V J M OLIVER, **C** D N WILLIAMS, A T SHAW,
Par Dn A C JENKINS
BEESTON HILL (Holy Spirit) *Ripon 6* **P** *V Leeds St Pet*
P-in-c J P GUTTERIDGE
BEESTON NEXT MILEHAM (St Mary the Virgin)
Litcham, Kempston, Lexham, Mileham, Beeston etc
Nor
BEESTON REGIS (All Saints) *Nor 7* **P** *Duchy of Lanc*
R S H GILBERT
BEESTON RYLANDS (St Mary) Beeston *S'well*
BEETHAM (St Michael and All Angels) and Milnthorpe
Carl 9 **P** *Bp and V Heversham (jt)*
P-in-c W M SIMPSON
BEETLEY (St Mary) Swanton Morley w Beetley w E
Bilney and Hoe *Nor*
BEGBROKE (St Michael) Yarnton w Begbroke and
Shipton on Cherwell *Ox*
BEIGHTON (All Saints) Freethorpe w Wickhampton,
Halvergate etc *Nor*
BEIGHTON (St Mary the Virgin) *Sheff 1* **P** *Bp*
Par Dn S K PROCTOR
BEKESBOURNE (St Peter) Patrixbourne w Bridge and
Bekesbourne *Cant*
BELAUGH (St Peter) Wroxham w Hoveton and
Belaugh *Nor*
BELBROUGHTON (Holy Trinity) w Fairfield and Clent
Worc 11 **P** *Ld Chan and St Jo Coll Ox (alt)*
R J GLOVER, **NSM** T F BARLOW
BELCHALWELL (St Aldheim) Okeford Fitzpaine,
Ibberton, Belchalwell etc *Sarum*
BELCHAMP OTTEN (St Ethelbert and All Saints) w
Belchamp Walter and Bulmer *Chelmsf 17*
P *M Raymond Esq (1 turn), DBP (2 turns)*
R R T HOWARD
BELCHAMP ST PAUL (St Paul and St Andrew)
Chelmsf 17 **P** *D&C Windsor* **P-in-c** H A HARKER
BELCHAMP WALTER (St Mary the Virgin) Belchamp
Otten w Belchamp Walter and Bulmer *Chelmsf*
BELCHFORD (St Peter and St Paul) *Linc 11* **P** *Ld Chan*
R *Vacant*
BELFIELD (St Ann) *Man 19* **P** *Bp* **V** H G SMITH
BELFORD (St Mary) *Newc 10* **P** *Bp* **V** P HEYWOOD
BELGRAVE (St Gabriel) Leic Resurr *Leic*
BELGRAVE (St Michael and All Angels) as above
BELGRAVE (St Paul) Wilnecote *Lich*
BELGRAVE (St Peter) *Leic 1* **P** *Bp* **V** E K L QUINE
BELHUS PARK (All Saints) *Chelmsf 16* **P** *Bp*
V *Vacant* South Ockendon (0708) 853246
BELLE GREEN (Mission) Ince Ch Ch *Liv*
BELLEAU (St John the Baptist) Withern *Linc*
BELLERBY (St John) Leyburn w Bellerby *Ripon*
BELLFIELD (St Mark) Sutton St Jas and Wawne *York*
BELLINGDON (St John the Evangelist) Gt Chesham
Ox
BELLINGHAM (St Cuthbert) Bellingham/Otterburn
Gp *Newc*
BELLINGHAM (St Dunstan) *S'wark 3* **P** *Bp*
V R J WALLACE, **J** A McKNIGHT, **Hon C** R B CRANE
BELLINGHAM/OTTERBURN Group, The *Newc 2*
P *Patr Bd* **TR** J A WOODHEAD-KEITH-DIXON,
TV B A McKAY, T R HARPER
BELMONT (St Anselm) *Lon 23* **P** *Bp* **V** P J EDGE,
C I M McINTOSH
BELMONT (St John) *S'wark 25* **P** *R Cheam*
V E J S PLAXTON, **C** R E WATTS, **NSM** G F PEGG

BELMONT (St Mary Magdalene) *Dur 2* **P** *The Crown*
V D R WEBSTER, **Par Dn** P E WEBSTER
BELMONT (St Peter) *Man 16* **P** *V Bolton-le-Moors*
St Pet **P-in-c** B P HUMPHRIES
BELPER (Christ Church) (St Faith's Mission Church) and
Milford *Derby 11* **P** *Bp* **P-in-c** M J KIRKHAM,
NSM B WESSON
BELPER (St Peter) *Derby 11* **P** *V Duffield*
P-in-c D M WHITE, **C** J P GREENWOOD, P T WALLER
BELSIZE PARK (St Peter) *Lon 16* **P** *D&C Westmr*
V D E BARNES, **Par Dn** C F WILSON
BELSTEAD (St Mary the Virgin) Copdock w
Washbrook and Belstead *St E*
BELSTONE (St Mary) S Tawton and Belstone *Ex*
BELTINGHAM (St Cuthbert) w Henshaw *Newc 4*
P *V Haltwhistle* **V** J E LINTON
BELTON (All Saints) and Burgh Castle *Nor 2* **P** *Bp and*
Ld Chan (alt) **R** J J QUINN
BELTON (St John the Baptist) Hathern, Long Whatton
and Diseworth w Belton etc *Leic*
BELTON (St Peter) Uppingham w Ayston and Wardley
w Belton *Pet*
BELTON (St Peter and St Paul) Barkston and Hough
Gp *Linc*
BELTON IN THE ISLE OF AXHOLME (All Saints) *Linc 1*
P *Bp* **V** A D O'BRIEN
BELVEDERE (All Saints) *Roch 14* **P** *DBP*
V G LAMBERT
BELVEDERE (St Augustine) *Roch 14* **P** *Bp*
V R L FEATHERSTONE
BEMBRIDGE (Holy Trinity) (St Luke's Mission Church)
Portsm 7 **P** *V Brading* **V** A P MENNISS
BEMERTON (St Andrew) (St John the Evangelist)
(St Michael and All Angels) *Sarum 15* **P** *Prime Min*
(2 turns) and Bp (1 turn) **Hon Par Dn** P D NEWTON
BEMPTON (St Michael) *York 10* **P** *DBP*
V B le G PETFIELD
BEN RHYDDING (St John the Evangelist) *Bradf 4*
P *V Ilkey* **V** M A SAVAGE
BENCHILL (St Luke) *Man 8* **P** *Bp* **V** D T THOMAS,
Par Dn F M SHAW
BENEFIELD (St Mary the Virgin) and Southwick w
Glapthorn *Pet 12* **P** *Mrs G S Watts-Russell and*
G C Capron Esq (alt) **R** D W J TWEDDLE
BENENDEN (St George and St Margaret) *Cant 11* **P** *Abp*
V C F SMITH
BENFIELDSIDE (St Cuthbert) *Dur 8* **P** *Bp*
V D E BREED, **C** J R DOBSON
BENFLEET, NORTH (All Saints) Bowers Gifford w N
Benfleet *Chelmsf*
BENFLEET, SOUTH (St Mary the Virgin) *Chelmsf 12*
P *D&C Westmr* **V** M E GALLOWAY
BENGEO (Holy Trinity) (St Leonard) and Christ Church
St Alb 8 **P** *R M A Smith Esq* **R** C A WEALE
BENGEWORTH (St Peter) *Worc 1* **P** *Bp* **V** L L BURN,
NSM F L MIDDLEMISS
BENHALL (St Mary) Sternfield w Benhall and Snape
St E
BENHILTON (All Saints) *S'wark 25* **P** *Bp*
V M A JOADES, **Hon C** J P WICKENS
BENINGTON (All Saints) w Leverton *Linc 20* **P** *Ld Chan*
R K M TOMLIN
BENINGTON (St Peter) w Walkern *St Alb 12* **P** *Trustees*
Ripon Coll Ox and K Coll Cam (alt) **R** P M HICKLEY
BENNIWORTH (St Julian) Asterby Gp *Linc*
BENSHAM (St Chad) *Dur 4* **P** *Bp* **TR** C J WREN,
TV T L JAMIESON, **Par Dn** K A WREN, M JAMIESON
BENSINGTON (St Helen) Benson *Ox*
BENSON (St Helen) *Ox 1* **P** *Ch Ch Ox* **V** A E BARTON
BENTHALL (St Bartholomew) Broseley w Benthall
Heref
BENTHAM (St John the Baptist) *Bradf 6* **P** *Bp*
R B UNDERWOOD
BENTHAM (St Margaret) *Bradf 6* **P** *Bp*
V N J A KINSELLA
BENTILEE (St Stephen) Bucknall and Bagnall *Lich*
BENTLEY (Emmanuel) *Lich 10* **P** *Bp and Personal Reps*
Sir Alfred Owen (jt) **V** J S BARNES
BENTLEY (St Mary) and Binsted *Win 2* **P** *Adn Surrey*
and D&C (jt) **R** W A ROGERS
BENTLEY (St Mary) w Tattingstone *St E 5* **P** *Bp and*
DBP (alt) **P-in-c** R R J LAPWOOD
BENTLEY (St Peter) *Sheff 8* **P** *Bp* **V** G J KEATING
BENTLEY (St Peter) Rowley w Skidby *York*
BENTLEY, GREAT (St Mary the Virgin) *Chelmsf 26*
P *Bp* **V** J G JARMAN
BENTLEY, LITTLE (St Mary) Tendring and Lt Bentley
w Beaumont cum Moze *Chelmsf*
BENTLEY, LOWER (St Mary) Tardebigge *Worc*

BENTLEY, NEW (St Philip and St James) *Sheff 8* **P** *Bp*
V M C F KING
BENTLEY COMMON (St Paul) *Chelmsf 10* **P** *Bp*
P-in-c C CHARLTON, **NSM** N K OTAGIRI
BENTLEY HEATH (St James) Dorridge *Birm*
BENTWORTH (St Mary) and Shalden and Lasham *Win 2*
P J L Jervoise Esq **R** J O MANN
**BENWELL Team, The (St James) (St John) (Venerable
Bede)** *Newc 7* **P** *Bp* **TV** A P RUGG,
C A S ADAMSON, B G VERNON
BEOLEY (St Leonard) (St Andrew's Church Centre)
Worc 7 **P** *Patr Bd* **V** D ROGERS, **Par Dn** C E HOUGH
BEPTON (St Mary) Cocking, Bepton, and W Lavington
Chich
BERDEN (St Nicholas) Manuden w Berden *Chelmsf*
BERE ALSTON (Holy Trinity) Bere Ferrers *Ex*
BERE FERRERS (St Andrew) *Ex 25* **P** *DBP* **R** *Vacant*
Tavistock (0822) 840229
**BERE REGIS (St John the Baptist) and Affpuddle w
Turnerspuddle** *Sarum 7* **P** *Ball Coll Ox (2 turns),
Bp (1 turn)* **R** J BURKE
BERECHURCH (St Margaret w St Michael) *Chelmsf 19*
P *Bp* **V** C J A HARVEY
BERGH APTON (St Peter and St Paul) Thurton *Nor*
BERGHOLT, EAST (St Mary the Virgin) *St E 5* **P** *Em
Coll Cam* **R** J P DRUCE
BERGHOLT, WEST (St Mary the Virgin) *Chelmsf 20*
P *Bp* **R** W C FREWIN
BERINSFIELD (St Mary and St Berin) Dorchester *Ox*
**BERKELEY (St Mary the Virgin) w Wick, Breadstone and
Newport** *Glouc 2* **P** *R J G Berkeley Esq and Sir Hugo
Huntington-Whiteley (jt)* **V** E T PETTENGELL
BERKHAMSTED (St Mary) *St Alb 3* **P** *Bp*
V J T TABOR
BERKHAMSTED, GREAT (All Saints) (St Peter) *St Alb 3*
P *Bp* **R** H R DAVIS, **C** M T C BAYNES,
NSM J MACPHERSON
**BERKHAMSTED, LITTLE (St Andrew) and Bayford,
Essendon and Ponsbourne** *St Alb 8* **P** *Marquess of
Salisbury (2 turns), CPAS (1 turn), and Bp (1 turn)*
P-in-c J H B COTTON, **C** J N PRICE,
Hon Par Dn M E COTTON
BERKHAMSYTCH (St Mary and St John) Ipstones w
Berkhamsytch and Onecote w Bradnop *Lich*
BERKLEY (The Blessed Virgin Mary) Beckington w
Standerwick, Berkley, Rodden etc *B & W*
BERKSWELL (St John the Baptist) *Cov 4* **P** *Trustees
Col C J H Wheatley* **R** *Vacant* Berkswell (0676)
33605
BERKSWICH (Holy Trinity) Baswich *Lich*
BERMONDSEY (St Anne) *S'wark 5* **P** *F W Smith Esq*
Par Dn A E SMITH
BERMONDSEY (St Crispin w Christ Church) *S'wark 5*
P *Hyndman Trustees* **V** P GRAY
**BERMONDSEY St Hugh Charterhouse Mission
Conventional District** *S'wark 5* **Min** D J FUDGER
BERMONDSEY (St James w Christ Church) *S'wark 5*
P *The Crown, Bp, and R Bermondsey St Mary (by turn)*
C C G SMITH, **Hon C** R W MAYO, **NSM** I J DAVOLL
**BERMONDSEY (St Mary Magdalen w St Olave, St John
and St Luke)** *S'wark 5* **P** *Ch Patr Soc (2 turns),
Ld Chan (1 turn), and Bp (1 turn)*
P-in-c J A BRADSHAW, **NSM** T C COCKERTON
BERMONDSEY, SOUTH (St Augustine) *S'wark 5* **P** *Bp*
V P E H GOLDING
BERMONDSEY, SOUTH (St Bartholomew) *S'wark 5*
P *Bp* **P-in-c** T HOPPERTON
BERRICK SALOME (St Helen) Chalgrove w Berrick
Salome *Ox*
BERRINGTON (All Saints) and Betton Strange *Heref 11*
P *DBP* **R** *Vacant* Cross Houses (074375) 214
BERROW (Blessed Virgin Mary) and Breane *B & W 1*
P *Adn Wells* **R** W St J KEMM
**BERROW (St Faith) w Pendock, Eldersfield, Hollybush
and Birtsmorton** *Worc 5* **P** *Bp, D&C, and Sir Berwick
Lechmere, Bt (jt)* **R** J R PARKINSON
BERRY POMEROY (St Mary) Totnes and Berry
Pomeroy *Ex*
BERRYNARBOR (St Peter) Combe Martin and
Berrynarbor *Ex*
BERSTED, NORTH (Holy Cross) Conventional District
Chich 1 **C-in-c** G A TOOLEY
BERSTED, NORTH (St Peter) see below
BERSTED, SOUTH (St Mary Magdalene) w North Bersted
Chich 1 **P** *Abp* **V** H G PRUEN
BERWICK (Holy Trinity) (St Mary) *Newc 12* **P** *Bp
(2 turns), D&C (1 turn)* **V** M H BURDEN
BERWICK (St John) Chalke Valley W *Sarum*

**BERWICK (St Michael and All Angels) w Selmeston and
Alciston** *Chich 18* **P** *Miss I M Newson and Miss
R Fitzherbert (1 turn), D&C (1 turn)* **P-in-c** P SMITH
BERWICK PARK (The Good Shepherd) Wood Green
St Mich w Bounds Green St Gabr etc *Lon*
BERWICK ST JAMES (St James) Stapleford w Berwick
St James *Sarum*
BESFORD (St Peter's Chapelry) Defford w Besford
Worc
BESSACARR, WEST (St Francis of Assisi) *Sheff 9* **P** *Bp*
V J DRAYCOTT
BESSELSLEIGH (St Lawrence) w Dry Sandford *Ox 10*
P *Ox Ch Trust* **R** *Vacant* Frilford Heath (0865)
390403
BESSINGBY (St Magnus) (St Mark) *York 10* **P** *Reps
George Wright Esq* **V** T J DAVIDSON
BESSINGHAM (St Mary) Roughton and Felbrigg,
Metton, Sustead etc *Nor*
BESTHORPE (All Saints) Attleborough w Besthorpe
Nor
BESTHORPE (Holy Trinity) Collingham w S Scarle and
Besthorpe and Girton *S'well*
**BESTWOOD (St Luke's Church Hall) (St Mark)
(St Matthew on the Hill)** *S'well 13* **P** *Patr Bd*
TR G O SPEDDING, **TM** S J GRIFFITHS,
TV M STANNER, R W YULE, **Par Dn** J HENDERSON
BESTWOOD/RISE PARK Local Ecumenical Project
S'well 10 **Min** S J GRIFFITHS
BESTWOOD PARK (Emmanuel) Bestwood *S'well*
BESWICK (St Margaret) Hutton Cranswick w Skerne,
Watton and Beswick *York*
BETCHWORTH (St Michael and All Angels) *S'wark 24*
P *D&C Windsor* **P-in-c** J B GOULD
BETHERSDEN (St Margaret) w High Halden *Cant 11*
P *Abp* **V** B C GURD
BETHESDA (Shared Church) Hallwood *Ches*
BETHNAL GREEN (St Barnabas) *Lon 7* **P** *D&C Cant*
P-in-c F M ROLLINSON
BETHNAL GREEN (St James the Less) *Lon 7* **P** *CPAS*
P-in-c B S CASTLE, **Hon C** W C HARRAP, H S WATSON
BETHNAL GREEN (St Matthew w St James the Great)
Lon 7 **P** *Bp* **R** C J C BEDFORD, **C** S A WILLIS,
Hon C J L OLDLAND
BETHNAL GREEN (St Peter) (St Thomas) *Lon 7*
P *City Corp* **V** J M V WEIR
BETLEY (St Margaret) and Keele *Lich 15*
P *T G H Howard-Sneyd Esq and DBP (jt)*
V J S WHITEHEAD
BETTESHANGER (St Mary the Virgin) Eastry and
Northbourne w Tilmanstone etc *Cant*
BETTISCOMBE (St Stephen) Marshwood Vale Team
Min *Sarum*
BETTON STRANGE (St Margaret) Berrington and
Betton Strange *Heref*
BETTWS-Y-CRWYN (St Mary) Clun w Bettws-y-Crwyn
and Newc *Heref*
BEVENDEAN (Holy Nativity) Moulsecoomb *Chich*
BEVERLEY (St Mary) *York 9* **P** *Abp* **V** D W HOSKIN,
Hon C H A HALL, **NSM** D S SIMON,
Hon Par Dn K HAILSTONE
BEVERLEY (St Nicholas) *York 9* **P** *Abp* **V** R R DIXON,
Par Dn S RICHARDSON
BEVERLEY MINSTER (St John and St Martin) *York 9*
P *Simeon's Trustees* **C** W E J MASH, P MARR
BEVERSTON (St Mary the Virgin) Tetbury w
Beverston *Glouc*
BEWBUSH (Community Centre) Ifield *Chich*
**BEWCASTLE (St Cuthbert), Stapleton and Kirklinton w
Hethersgill** *Carl 2* **P** *Bp, D&C, and DBP (jt)*
R J R REPATH
BEWDLEY (St Anne) Ribbesford w Bewdley and
Dowles *Worc*
BEWERLEY GRANGE (Chapel) Upper Nidderdale
Ripon
BEWHOLME (St John the Baptist) Sigglesthorne and
Rise w Nunkeeling and Bewholme *York*
BEWICK, OLD (Holy Trinity) Glendale Gp *Newc*
BEXHILL (All Saints) Sidley *Chich*
BEXHILL (St Andrew) Conventional District *Chich 14*
NSM G G DANIELS
BEXHILL (St Augustine) *Chich 14* **P** *Bp* **V** D RANKIN
BEXHILL (St Barnabas) *Chich 14* **P** *Bp*
V T M J VAN CARRAPIETT
BEXHILL (St Mark) *Chich 14* **P** *Bp* **R** S P GAMESTER
BEXHILL (St Peter) (St Michael) (Good Shepherd)
Chich 14 **P** *Bp* **TR** J W COTTON, **TV** R L HAWKES,
Par Dn E V WHEELER, **Hon Par Dn** E A HAWKES
BEXHILL (St Stephen) *Chich 14* **P** *Bp* **V** E WILKINSON

BEXLEY (St John the Evangelist) *Roch 16*   **P** *The Crown* **Hon C** A F DALLING
BEXLEY (St Mary the Virgin) *Roch 16*   **P** *Bp* **V** D L KNIGHT,   **Hon Par Dn** G ATFIELD
BEXLEYHEATH (Christ Church) *Roch 14*   **P** *Bp* **V** M G GRIBBLE,   **Hon Par Dn** S M DATSON
BEXLEYHEATH (St Peter) *Roch 14*   **P** *Bp* **V** M H CLUMGAIR,   **C** J P HARTLEY,   **NSM** J DAY
BEXWELL (St Mary)   Downham Market w Bexwell *Ely*
BEYTON (All Saints)   Rougham, Beyton w Hessett and Rushbrooke *St E*
BIBURY (St Mary) w Winson and Barnsley *Glouc 13*   **P** *Bp and W H Wykeham-Musgrave Esq (alt)* **V** F B BRUCE
BICESTER (St Edburg) w Bucknell, Caversfield and Launton *Ox 2*   **P** *Patr Bd* **TR** J S BAGGLEY,   **TV** J D NIXON,   **C** J M GOODALL
BICKENHILL (St Peter) *Birm 13*   **P** *Birm Dioc Trustees* **P-in-c** A J EYLES
BICKER (St Swithin) and Wigtoft *Linc 21*   **P** *Bp and D&C (alt)* **V** N A G BURNET
BICKERSHAW (St James and St Elizabeth) *Liv 14*   **P** *Bp* **V** J JORDAN
BICKERSTAFFE Four Lane Ends (not known) Bickerstaffe *Liv*
BICKERSTAFFE (Holy Trinity) *Liv 11*   **P** *Lord Derby* **V** *Vacant*   Skelmersdale (0695) 22304
BICKERTON (Holy Trinity) w Bickley *Ches 5*   **P** *DBP, Marquess of Cholmondeley, Adn, and Bp (jt)* **V** J M R G REES
BICKINGTON (St Andrew)   Fremington *Ex*
BICKINGTON (St Mary the Virgin)   Ashburton w Buckland in the Moor and Bickington *Ex*
BICKINGTON, HIGH (St Mary)   Atherington and High Bickington *Ex*
BICKLEIGH (Plymouth) (St Mary the Virgin) *Ex 21*   **P** *Patr Bd*   **TR** K FELTHAM,   **TV** R J CARLTON
BICKLEIGH (St Mary)   Washfield, Stoodleigh, Withleigh etc *Ex*
BICKLEIGH DOWN (School)   Bickleigh (Plymouth) *Ex*
BICKLEY (St George) *Roch 13*   **P** *SMF* **V** D A S HERBERT,   **NSM** C M HALL
BICKLEY (St Wenefrede)   Bickerton w Bickley *Ches*
BICKNACRE (St Andrew)   Woodham Ferrers and Bicknacre *Chelmsf*
BICKNOLLER (St George) w Crowcombe and Sampford Brett *B & W 19*   **P** *Bp and V Stogumber (jt)* **R** M D BOLE
BICKNOR (St James)   Bredgar w Bicknor and Frinsted w Wormshill etc *Cant*
BICTON (Holy Trinity), Montford w Shrawardine and Fitz *Lich 27*   **P** *Earl of Powis, Sir Offley Wakeman, Bt, and C J Wingfield Esq (jt)* **R** K J F MACLEAN
BICTON (St Mary)   E Budleigh and Bicton *Ex*
BIDBOROUGH (St Lawrence) *Roch 10*   **P** *Mabledon Trust* **R** M R HODGE
BIDDENDEN (All Saints) and Smarden *Cant 11*   **P** *Abp* **R** P A NAYLOR,   **C** M R S RANDOLPH
BIDDENHAM (St James) *St Alb 16*   **P** *Bp* **V** J M SCHOFIELD
BIDDESTONE (St Nicholas) w Slaughterford *Bris 9*   **P** *Win Coll*   **P-in-c** J N A BRADBURY,   **NSM** J E B MARSH
BIDDICK HALL ESTATE (St Martin)   S Shields All SS *Dur*
BIDDISHAM (St John the Baptist)   Crook Peak *B & W*
BIDDLESDEN (St Margaret)   Westbury w Turweston, Shalstone and Biddlesden *Ox*
BIDDULPH (St Lawrence) *Lich 14*   **P** *MMCET* **V** R E CARTER,   **C** D J DITCH
BIDDULPH MOOR (Christ Church) *Lich 14*   **P** *MMCET* **R** J McGUIRE
BIDEFORD (St Mary) (St Peter East the Water) *Ex 17*   **P** *DBP*   **R** P G SMITH,   **NSM** R W L VODEN
BIDFORD-ON-AVON (St Laurence) *Cov 7*   **P** *Bp* **V** W A RICHARDS
BIDSTON (St Oswald) *Ches 1*   **P** *Bp*   **V** P M KIRBY,   **C** J E M NEWMAN
BIELBY (St Giles)   Seaton Ross Gp of Par *York*
BIERLEY (St John the Evangelist) *Bradf 2*   **P** *DBP* **V** I R LANE
BIERLEY, EAST (St Luke)   Birkenshaw w Hunsworth *Wakef*
BIERTON (St James the Great)   Aylesbury w Bierton and Hulcott *Ox*
BIGBURY (St Lawrence), Ringmore and Kingston *Ex 14*   **P** *MMCET and Canon N M Ramm (alt)* **R** A DROWLEY
BIGBY (All Saints)   Barnetby le Wold Gp *Linc*

BIGGIN (St Thomas)   Hartington, Biggin and Earl Sterndale *Derby*
BIGGIN HILL (St Mark) *Roch 13*   **P** *Bp* **V** E H HESELWOOD,   **C** A J DOBSON
BIGGLESWADE (St Andrew) *St Alb 17*   **P** *Bp* **V** R F SIBSON
BIGHTON (All Saints)   Old Alresford and Bighton *Win*
BIGNOR (Holy Cross)   Barlavington, Burton w Coates, Sutton and Bignor *Chich*
BIGRIGG (St John)   Egremont and Haile *Carl*
BILBOROUGH (St John the Baptist) *S'well 14*   **P** *Bp* **V** A S G HART,   **C** E P BAILEY
BILBOROUGH (St Martin) w Strelley *S'well 14*   **P** *SMF* **R** T SISSON
BILBROOK (Holy Cross)   Codsall *Lich*
BILBROUGH (St James)   Healaugh w Wighill, Bilbrough and Askham Richard *York*
BILDESTON (St Mary Magdalene) w Wattisham *St E 3*   **P** *Abp, Bp, and CPAS (by turn)*   **P-in-c** R J DEDMAN
BILHAM *Sheff 12*   **P** *Bp, Major W Warde-Aldam, W G A Warde-Norbury Esq, and Mrs S Grant-Dalton (jt)* **V** J K MOORE
BILLERICAY (St Mary Magdalen) (Christ Church) and Little Burstead *Chelmsf 9*   **P** *Bp*   **TR** P D ASHTON,   **TV** N HAWKINS, G T WAKEFIELD,   **P** R HYSON,   **Hon Par Dn** M L ASHTON
BILLESDON (St John the Baptist) and Skeffington *Leic 4*   **P** *Bp* **V** *Vacant*   Billesdon (053755) 284
BILLESLEY COMMON (Holy Cross) *Birm 8*   **P** *Bp* **V** L L WATSON
BILLING, GREAT (St Andrew) w Little Billing *Pet 4*   **P** *BNC Ox and Bp (alt)*   **R** K P ASHBY
BILLING, LITTLE (All Saints)   Gt w Lt Billing *Pet*
BILLINGBOROUGH (St Andrew) *Linc 13*   **P** *The Crown* **V** H J THEODOSIUS
BILLINGE (St Aidan) *Liv 15*   **P** *R Wigan*   **V** D LYON,   **C** A K GOODE
BILLINGFORD (St Leonard)   Scole, Brockdish, Billingford, Thorpe Abbots etc *Nor*
BILLINGFORD (St Peter)   N Elmham w Billingford and Worthing *Nor*
BILLINGHAM (St Aidan) (St Luke) *Dur 16*   **P** *Patr Bd*   **TR** C O HURFORD,   **TV** G V MILLER, D R HANSON,   **Dss** S E MASKREY
BILLINGHAM (St Cuthbert) *Dur 16*   **P** *D&C* **V** R I SMITH
BILLINGHAM (St Mary Magdalene)   Wolviston *Dur*
BILLINGHAY (St Michael) *Linc 22*   **P** *Sir Stephen Hastings*   **V** L F B CUMINGS
BILLINGSHURST (St Mary the Virgin) *Chich 8*   **P** *Bp* **V** J E LLOYD-JAMES
BILLINGSLEY (St Mary) w Sidbury, Middleton Scriven, Chetton, Glazeley, Deuxhill and Chelmarsh *Heref 9*   **P** *Bp and Woodward Schools (jt)*   **R** P R J LAMB
BILLINGTON (St Michael and All Angels)   Leighton Buzzard w Eggington, Hockliffe etc *St Alb*
BILLOCKBY (All Saints)   Rollesby w Burgh w Billockby w Ashby w Oby etc *Nor*
BILLY MILL (St Aidan)   Cullercoats St Geo *Newc*
BILNEY, EAST (St Mary)   Swanton Morley w Beetley w E Bilney and Hoe *Nor*
BILNEY, WEST (St Cecilia)   Pentney w W Bilney *Nor*
BILSBORROW (St Hilda) *Blackb 10*   **P** *V St Michael's-on-Wyre*   **V** A WHITTAKER
BILSBY (Holy Trinity) w Farlesthorpe *Linc 8*   **P** *Bp* **V** G I GEORGE-JONES
BILSDALE MIDCABLE (St John)   Upper Ryedale *York*
BILSDALE PRIORY (St Hilda)   Ingleby Greenhow w Bilsdale Priory, Kildale etc *York*
BILSINGTON (St Peter and St Paul)   Aldington w Bonnington and Bilsington *Cant*
BILSON (Mission Church)   Cinderford St Steph w Littledean *Glouc*
BILSTHORPE (St Margaret) *S'well 15*   **P** *DBP* **R** H H WILCOX
BILSTON (St Leonard) (St Chad) (St Mary the Virgin) *Lich 10*   **P** *Patr Bd*   **TR** P J CHAPMAN,   **TV** G E MORRIS,   **Par Dn** C L GILBERT,   **NSM** C CHAPMAN
BILTON (St John the Evangelist) *Ripon 1*   **P** *Bp* **V** D W TORDOFF,   **C** M G TORDOFF (nee PARKER),   **NSM** K A FITZSIMONS
BILTON (St Mark) *Cov 6*   **P** *N M Assheton Esq* **R** G R CORNWALL-JONES,   **C** R W DEIMEL,   **NSM** A J HOBSON
BILTON, NEW (St Oswald) *Cov 6*   **P** *Dioc Trustees* **V** J T RANDALL

BILTON-IN-AINSTY (St Helen) Tockwith and Bilton w Bickerton *York*

BILTON IN HOLDERNESS (St Peter) *York 13* **P** *Abp*
V R J E MAJOR

BINBROOK Group, The (St Mary) *Linc 10* **P** *Ld Chan DBP and M M Sleight Esq (alt)* **R** T J WALKER

BINCOMBE (Holy Trinity) w Broadwey, Upwey and Buckland Ripers *Sarum 5* **P** *G&C Coll Cam (2 turns), Miss M B F Frampton (1 turn), and Bp (1 turn)*
R A S B FREER

BINEGAR (Holy Trinity) Ashwick w Oakhill and Binegar *B & W*

BINFIELD (All Saints) (St Mark) *Ox 11* **P** *Ld Chan*
R O R M BLATCHLY

BINGFIELD (St Mary) St Oswald in Lee w Bingfield *Newc*

BINGHAM (St Mary and All Saints) *S'well 8* **P** *The Crown* **R** D N SWAIN, **Par Dn** D CHAPMAN, **Hon C** J B DAVIS

BINGLEY (All Saints) *Bradf 1* **P** *Bp* **TR** M W BULL, **TV** B B WOODMAN

BINGLEY (Holy Trinity) *Bradf 1* **P** *Bp* **V** J COOPER

BINHAM (St Mary) Stiffkey and Cockthorpe w Morston, Langham etc *Nor*

BINLEY (St Bartholomew) *Cov 1* **P** *Bp*
P-in-c D J HOWARD, **C** T D BUCKLEY, S F SEWELL

BINLEY WOODS Local Ecumenical Project *Cov 1*
Min T D BUCKLEY

BINSEY (St Margaret) Ox St Thos w St Frideswide and Binsey *Ox*

BINSTEAD (Holy Cross) *Portsm 7* **P** *Bp*
P-in-c S M CHALONER, **NSM** T I CARD

BINSTED (Holy Cross) Bentley and Binsted *Win*

BINSTED (St Mary) Walberton w Binsted *Chich*

BINTON (St Peter) Temple Grafton w Binton *Cov*

BINTREE (St Swithin) Twyford w Guist w Bintry w Themelthorpe etc *Nor*

BIRCH (St Agnes) *Man 3* **P** *Bp* **R** J M MacGILLIVRAY

BIRCH (St James) w Fallowfield *Man 4* **P** *Bp*
R W G WILSON, **C** D M IND

BIRCH (St Mary) Rhodes *Man*

BIRCH w Layer Breton and Layer Marney *Chelmsf 22* **P** *Col J G Round, N S Charrington Esq, and Bp (jt)*
R P C SPENCER

BIRCH-IN-RUSHOLME (St James) Birch w Fallowfield *Man*

BIRCHAM, GREAT (St Mary the Virgin) Docking w The Birchams and Stanhoe w Barwick *Nor*

BIRCHAM NEWTON (All Saints) as above

BIRCHANGER (St Mary the Virgin) *Chelmsf 24* **P** *New Coll Ox* **R** T G EVANS-PUGHE

BIRCHENCLIFFE (St Philip the Apostle) *Wakef 5*
P *V Lindley* **V** D N CALVIN-THOMAS

BIRCHES HEAD (St Matthew) Hanley H Ev *Lich*

BIRCHFIELD (Holy Trinity) *Birm 3* **P** *Bp*
V R W HUNT, **C** J E I HAWKINS

BIRCHILLS, THE (St Andrew) Walsall St Andr *Lich*

BIRCHIN COPPICE (St Peter) Kidderminster St Jo and H Innocents *Worc*

BIRCHINGTON (All Saints) w Acol and Minnis Bay *Cant 9* **P** *Abp* **V** F R SMALE, **Par Dn** L C SMITH

BIRCHMOOR (St John) Polesworth *Birm*

BIRCHOVER (St Michael) Youlgreave, Middleton, Stanton-in-Peak etc *Derby*

BIRCHWOOD (Mission Church) Churchstanton, Buckland St Mary and Otterford *B & W*

BIRCHWOOD (St Luke) *Linc 15* **P** *Bp* **V** T R STOKES

BIRCHWOOD (Transfiguration) Padgate *Liv*

BIRCLE (St John the Baptist) *Man 10* **P** *R Middleton St Leon* **V** M H MAXWELL

BIRDBROOK (St Augustine) Ridgewell w Ashen, Birdbrook and Sturmer *Chelmsf*

BIRDHAM (St James) W Wittering and Birdham w Itchenor *Chich*

BIRDINGBURY (St Leonards) Leamington Hastings and Birdingbury *Cov*

BIRDLIP (St Mary in Hamlet) Brimpsfield, Cranham, Elkstone and Syde *Glouc*

BIRDSALL (St Mary) w Langton *York 2*
P *Lord Middleton and Ld Chan (alt)*
Hon C B A BROWNBRIDGE

BIRKBY (St Peter) Gt Smeaton w Appleton Wiske and Birkby etc *Ripon*

BIRKDALE Carr Lane (St Mary) Birkdale St Jo *Liv*

BIRKDALE (St James) *Liv 9* **P** *Trustees* **V** *Vacant* Southport (0704) 66255

BIRKDALE (St John) *Liv 9* **P** *Trustees*
V J W C HARDING, **C** P W DAWKIN

BIRKDALE (St Peter) *Liv 9* **P** *Trustees* **V** *Vacant* Southport (0704) 68448

BIRKENHEAD (Christ Church) *Ches 1* **P** *Bp*
V F H TAYLOR, **C** A J MAUNDER

BIRKENHEAD (St James) w St Bede *Ches 1* **P** *Trustees*
C S T PENDLEBURY, G J COUSINS

BIRKENHEAD (St Winifred) Welsh Church *Ches 1*
C-in-c D T P EVANS

BIRKENHEAD PRIORY (St Peter w St Matthew) (St Mary) *Ches 1* **P** *Bp, Simeon's Trustees, and Ch Patr Trust (jt)* **TR** R J GILLINGS, **TV** J J E SUTTON

BIRKENHEAD (St Paul) w Hunsworth *Wakef 8*
P *V Birstall* **V** M J CASTERTON

BIRKIN (St Mary) Haddlesey w Hambleton and Birkin *York*

BIRLEY (St Peter) Canon Pyon w Kings Pyon and Birley *Heref*

BIRLING (All Saints), Addington, Ryarsh and Trottiscliffe *Roch 7* **P** *Bp* **R** G C M MILES

BIRLING, LOWER (Christ Church) Snodland All SS w Ch Ch *Roch*

BIRLINGHAM (St James the Great) Pershore w Pinvin, Wick and Birlingham *Worc*

BIRMINGHAM (Bishop Latimer w All Saints) *Birm 1*
P *St Martin's Trustees* **R** R F BASHFORD

BIRMINGHAM (St Aidan) Small Heath *Birm 8*
P *Trustees* **V** J F P MORRISON-WELLS

BIRMINGHAM (St George) *Birm 1* **P** *St Martin's Trustees* **R** R A KENWAY, **Hon C** J L WILKINSON

BIRMINGHAM (St John the Evangelist) Ladywood *Birm 1*
P *R Birm St Martin w Bordesley* **V** R J TETLOW

BIRMINGHAM (St Luke) *Birm 1* **P** *Trustees*
C S C WINTER

BIRMINGHAM (St Martin) w Bordesley St Andrew *Birm 1*
P *St Martin's Trustees* **R** J G WESSON,
C A D J COE, N H BENSON, P D SWAN,
NSM J S LAWRENCE, **Hon Par Dn** H C BENSON

BIRMINGHAM (St Paul) *Birm 1* **P** *St Martin's Trustees*
V D L CLARINGBULL

BIRMINGHAM (St Peter) *Birm 1* **P** *Bp* **V** C F MORTON

BIRSTALL (St James the Greater) and Wanlip *Leic 6*
P *Bp and C A Palmer-Tomkinson Esq (jt)*
V C A BRADSHAW, **C** M J PEERS

BIRSTALL (St Peter) *Wakef 8* **P** *Bp* **V** R M WELLER

BIRSTWITH (St James) *Ripon 1* **P** *Exors Col B C Greenwood* **P-in-c** P GARNER

BIRTLES (St Catherine) *Ches 13* **P** *Bp*
V W F I WHINTON

BIRTLEY (St Giles) Chollerton w Birtley and Thockrington *Newc*

BIRTLEY (St John the Evangelist) *Dur 1* **P** *R Chester-le-Street* **V** F WHITE, **Hon Par Dn** A M WHITE

BIRTSMORTON (St Peter and St Paul) Berrow w Pendock, Eldersfield, Hollybush etc *Worc*

BIRWOOD (Mission church) Churcham w Bulley and Minsterworth *Glouc*

BISBROOKE (St John the Baptist) Morcott w Glaston and Bisbrooke *Pet*

BISCATHORPE (St Helen) Asterby Gp *Linc*

BISCOT (Holy Trinity) *St Alb 20* **P** *Bp* **V** E E WEST

BISHAM (All Saints) *Ox 13* **P** *Mrs D M P Thoresby*
P-in-c N J MOLONY

BISHAMPTON (St James) Abberton, Naunton Beauchamp and Bishampton etc *Worc*

BISHOP AUCKLAND Woodhouse Close Area of Ecumenical Experiment (Conventional District) *Dur 10*
C-in-c P SINCLAIR

BISHOP BURTON (All Saints) w Walkington *York 9*
P *Abp and DBP (alt)* **R** R P BURTON

BISHOP CAUNDLE (not known) The Caundles w Folke and Holwell *Sarum*

BISHOP MIDDLEHAM (St Michael) *Dur 14* **P** *Ld Chan*
V R P PEARSON

BISHOP MONKTON (St John the Baptist) and Burton Leonard *Ripon 3* **P** *D&C* **P** P HULETT

BISHOP NORTON (St Peter), Waddingham and Snitterby *Linc 6* **P** *Bp and The Crown (alt)* **R** *Vacant* Bishop Norton (067381) 796

BISHOP SUTTON (Holy Trinity) and Stanton Drew and Stowey *B & W 11* **P** *Bp and Adn Bath (alt)*
V J HIGGINS

BISHOP THORNTON (St John the Evangelist) Markington w S Stainley and Bishop Thornton *Ripon*

BISHOP WILTON (St Edith) w Full Sutton, Kirby Underdale and Bugthorpe *York 7* **P** *Abp, D&C, and Earl of Halifax (jt) (3 turns), Ld Chan (1 turn)*
R *Vacant* Bishop Wilton (07596) 230

BISHOPDALE (Mission Room) Aysgarth and Bolton cum Redmire *Ripon*

BISHOP'S CANNINGS (St Mary the Virgin), All Cannings and Etchilhampton *Sarum 19* **P** *DBP* **V** F M HENLY

BISHOP'S CASTLE (St John the Baptist) w Mainstone *Heref 10* **P** *Earl of Powis and Ld Chan (alt)* **C** S A WATSON

BISHOP'S CLEEVE (St Michael and All Angels) *Glouc 9* **P** *DBP* **R** J H MEAD, **C** D R WINNINGTON-INGRAM, **Hon C** G E PARSONS

BISHOP'S FROME (St Mary the Virgin) w Castle Frome and Fromes Hill *Heref 2* **P** *Bp* **R** *Vacant* Munderfield (0885) 490204

BISHOP'S HATFIELD (St Etheldreda) Hatf *St Alb*

BISHOP'S HULL (St John the Evangelist) Taunton St Jo *B & W*

BISHOPS HULL (St Peter and St Paul) *B & W 20* **P** *Adn Taunton* **V** C M S RANDALL

BISHOP'S ITCHINGTON (St Michael) *Cov 10* **P** *Bp* **P-in-c** R D CLUCAS

BISHOP'S LAVINGTON (All Saints) W Lavington and the Cheverells *Sarum*

BISHOPS LYDEARD (Blessed Virgin Mary) w Bagborough and Cothelstone *B & W 20* **P** *D&C Wells (3 turns), Ms P M G Mitford (1 turn)* **R** C H TOWNSHEND

BISHOPS NORTON (St John the Evangelist) Twigworth, Down Hatherley, Norton, The Leigh etc *Glouc*

BISHOP'S STORTFORD (Holy Trinity) *St Alb 4* **P** *Bp* **R** J R HAYNES

BISHOP'S STORTFORD (St Michael) *St Alb 4* **P** *Bp* **V** J H RICHARDSON, **Hon C** B H TALBOTT, B R WHITE, **NSM** D C HINGE

BISHOP'S SUTTON (St Nicholas) and Ropley and West Tisted *Win 1* **P** *Peache Trustees* **R** R J SUCH

BISHOP'S TACHBROOK (St Chad) *Cov 10* **P** *Bp* **V** W R LARGE

BISHOPS TAWTON (St John the Baptist) Newport, Bishops Tawton and Tawstock *Ex*

BISHOPS WALTHAM (St Peter) *Portsm 1* **P** *Bp* **R** S E WILKINSON, **C** W C DAY, **Hon C** H G PRIDEAUX

BISHOP'S WOOD (St Mary) Hartlebury *Worc*

BISHOPSBOURNE (St Mary) Barham w Bishopsbourne and Kingston *Cant*

BISHOPSNYMPTON (St Mary the Virgin), Rose Ash, Mariansleigh, Molland, Knowstone, East Anstey and West Anstey *Ex 19* **P** *DBP* **TR** C S TULL, **TV** B P CHAVE

BISHOPSTEIGNTON (St John the Evangelist) Teignmouth, Ideford w Luton, Ashcombe etc *Ex*

BISHOPSTOKE (St Mary) (St Paul) *Win 9* **P** *Bp* **R** G H ROSE, **Hon C** N JACKSON

BISHOPSTON (Church of the Good Shepherd) (St Michael and All Angels) *Bris 6* **P** *Patr Bd* **TR** W G CHALLIS, **TV** H W WARDALE

BISHOPSTONE (St Andrew) *Chich 18* **P** *Bp Lon* **V** R C WALLIS

BISHOPSTONE (St John the Baptist) Chalke Valley E *Sarum*

BISHOPSTONE (St Lawrence) *Heref 4* **P** *Major D J C Davenport* **R** *Vacant*

BISHOPSTROW (St Aldhelm) and Boreham *Sarum 14* **P** *DBP* **R** A B ELKINS, **NSM** H W B STEPHENS

BISHOPSWOOD (All Saints) Walford and Saint John, w Bishopswood etc *Heref*

BISHOPSWOOD (St John the Evangelist) *Lich 3* **P** *V Brewood* **V** T H GREEN

BISHOPSWORTH (St Peter) *Bris 1* **P** *Bp* **V** P G HUZZEY, **Par Dn** J D SPINDLER, **NSM** P J BEVAN, **Hon Par Dn** W J BISHOP

BISHOPTHORPE (St Andrew) *York 1* **P** *Abp* **V** P RATHBONE

BISHOPTON (St Peter) w Great Stainton *Dur 16* **P** *Ld Chan* **V** P S ATKINSON

BISHOPWEARMOUTH (Christ Church) *Dur 9* **P** *Bp* **V** R I DAVISON

BISHOPWEARMOUTH (Good Shepherd) *Dur 9* **P** *Bp* **V** G ROBERTS

BISHOPWEARMOUTH Millfield (St Mary) Millfield St Mary *Dur*

BISHOPWEARMOUTH (St Gabriel) *Dur 9* **P** *V Sunderland* **C** C JAY

BISHOPWEARMOUTH (St Mark) Millfield St Mark *Dur*

BISHOPWEARMOUTH (St Michael) Sunderland *Dur*

BISHOPWEARMOUTH (St Nicholas) *Dur 9* **P** *Bp* **V** H N SWINBURNE, **C** E WILKINSON

BISLEY (All Saints), Oakridge, Miserden and Edgeworth *Glouc 1* **P** *Major M T N H Wills, Ld Chan, and Bp (by turn)* **V** E S PYECROFT

BISLEY (St John the Baptist) and West End (Holy Trinity) *Guildf 6* **P** *Bp* **R** C EDMONDS, **C** T COLEMAN, **NSM** D ROBINSON, D H ROBINSON

BISPHAM (All Hallows) *Blackb 9* **P** *Ch Soc Trust* **R** D J N MADDOCK, **C** J P MILTON-THOMPSON

BISTERNE (St Paul) Ringwood *Win*

BITCHFIELD (St Mary Magdalene) Ingoldsby *Linc*

BITTADON (St Peter) Ilfracombe, Lee, Woolacombe, Bittadon etc *Ex*

BITTERING PARVA (St Peter and St Paul) Gressenhall w Longham w Wendling etc *Nor*

BITTERLEY (St Mary) w Middleton, Stoke St Milborough w The Heath and Hopton Cangeford, Clee St Margaret and Cold Weston *Heref 12* **P** *Bp, DBP, Walcott Trustees, and Miss M F Rouse-Boughton (jt)* **R** A G SEABROOK

BITTERNE (Holy Saviour) *Win 12* **P** *Bp* **V** J J S WATSON, **C** A L McPHERSON, **Par Dn** K D STEWART

BITTERNE PARK (All Hallows) (Ascension) *Win 12* **P** *Bp* **Par Dn** R A CORNE, **NSM** B L STREVENS

BITTESWELL (St Mary) *Leic 11* **P** *Haberdashers' Co* **P-in-c** J BACKHOUSE

BITTON (St Mary) *Bris 2* **P** *Bp* **P-in-c** D G MITCHELL

BIX (St James) Nettlebed w Bix and Highmore *Ox*

BLABY (All Saints) *Leic 10* **P** *Bp* **V** M D PETITT

BLACK BOURTON (St Mary the Virgin) Alvescot w Black Bourton, Shilton, Holwell etc *Ox*

BLACK NOTLEY (St Peter and St Paul) *Chelmsf 18* **P** *St Jo Coll Cam* **R** A G MORRISON

BLACK TORRINGTON (St Mary), Bradford w Cookbury, Thornbury and Highampton *Ex 9* **P** *DBP* **R** *Vacant* Black Torrington (040923) 279

BLACKAWTON (St Michael) and Stoke Fleming *Ex 14* **P** *Bp and DBP (jt)* **V** R H WHITE

BLACKBIRD LEYS (Holy Family) *Ox 4* **P** *Bp* **V** J A RAMSAY

BLACKBOROUGH (All Saints) Kentisbeare w Blackborough *Ex*

BLACKBURN (Christ Church w St Matthew) *Blackb 2* **P** *Bp* **V** J G RILEY, **Hon Par Dn** L A RILEY

BLACKBURN (Church of the Redeemer) *Blackb 2* **P** *Bp* **C** N J HAY

BLACKBURN (Saviour) *Blackb 2* **P** *CPAS* **V** A K ROYLE

BLACKBURN (St Aidan) *Blackb 5* **P** *Bp* **V** J S McDONALD

BLACKBURN (St Barnabas) *Blackb 2* **P** *Bp* **V** H H DANIEL

BLACKBURN (St Bartholomew) Ewood *Blackb*

BLACKBURN (St Gabriel) *Blackb 2* **P** *Bp* **V** J CORBYN, **C** D L HEAP

BLACKBURN (St James) *Blackb 2* **P** *Bp* **V** R BRAITHWAITE

BLACKBURN (St Luke) w St Philip *Blackb 2* **P** *Bp* **V** P S GRIERSON

BLACKBURN (St Michael and All Angels) (Holy Trinity Worship Centre) w St John the Evangelist *Blackb 2* **P** *V Blackb* **V** S EDWARDS, **C** G LEWIS

BLACKBURN (St Silas) *Blackb 2* **P** *Trustees* **V** B STEVENSON

BLACKBURN (St Stephen) *Blackb 2* **P** *Trustees* **V** A A WELSH

BLACKBURN St Thomas (St Jude) *Blackb 2* **P** *Bp and Trustees (alt)* **V** P R HAPGOOD-STRICKLAND

BLACKDOWN (Holy Trinity) Beaminster Area *Sarum*

BLACKFEN (Good Shepherd) Lamorbey H Redeemer *Roch*

BLACKFORD (Holy Trinity) Wedmore w Theale and Blackford *B & W*

BLACKFORD (St John the Baptist) Rockcliffe and Blackford *Carl*

BLACKFORD (St Michael) Camelot Par *B & W*

BLACKFORDBY (St Margaret) *Leic 9* **P** *Bp* **V** M J PENNY

BLACKHALL (St Andrew) *Dur 3* **P** *Bp* **V** W E L BROAD

BLACKHAM (All Saints) Withyham St Mich *Chich*

BLACKHEATH (All Saints) *S'wark 3* **P** *V Lewisham St Mary* **V** H K BURGIN

BLACKHEATH (Ascension) *S'wark 3* **P** *V Lewisham St Mary* **P-in-c** P C KNAPPER, **Hon C** E R NEWNHAM, **NSM** J M PRESTON

BLACKHEATH (St John the Evangelist) *S'wark 1* **P** *CPAS* **V** J A de B WILMOT, **C** C R TREFUSIS, **Hon C** D M WHYTE, **NSM** A M BESWETHERICK

BLACKHEATH (St Martin) and Chilworth *Guildf 2* **P** *Bp* **V** E GIBBONS

BLACKHEATH (St Paul) *Birm 5* **P** *Bp* **V** D H GARNER, **Par Dn** G C FRANCIS

BLACKHEATH PARK (St Michael and All Angels) *S'wark 1* **P** *Bp* **V** D H F SHIRESS, **C** D N LEAVER, **NSM** A SCOTT

BLACKHILL (St Aidan) *Dur 8* **P** *Bp* **V** G HEPPLE

BLACKLAND (St Peter) Calne and Blackland *Sarum*

BLACKLANDS Hastings (Christchurch and St Andrew) *Chich 17* **P** *Ch Patr Trust* **V** P J LE SUEUR

BLACKLEY (Holy Trinity) *Man 5* **P** *Bp* **R** P A STAMP

BLACKLEY (St Andrew) *Man 5* **P** *Bp* **R** D J ERRIDGE, **C** T M MALONEY

BLACKLEY (St Paul) *Man 5* **P** *Bp* **R** R MORRIS

BLACKLEY (St Peter) *Man 5* **P** *D&C* **R** L St J R AITKEN

BLACKLEY White Moss (St Mark) *Man 5* **P** *D&C* **R** R LEATHERBARROW

BLACKMOOR (St Matthew) *Portsm 5* **P** *Earl of Selborne* **V** R J INKPEN

BLACKMORE (St Laurence) and Stondon Massey *Chelmsf 6* **P** *Bp* **V** M G SELLIX

BLACKPOOL (Christ Church w All Saints) (St Andrew) *Blackb 9* **P** *Bp and Trustees (jt)* **V** P GASCOIGNE

BLACKPOOL (Holy Cross) South Shore *Blackb 9* **P** *Bp* **V** *Vacant* Blackpool (0253) 41263

BLACKPOOL (St John the Evangelist) *Blackb 9* **P** *Trustees* **V** R IMPEY, **C** D I WHEELER

BLACKPOOL (St Mark) *Blackb 9* **P** *CPAS* **V** D G MANNING, **Par Dn** D M HANKEY

BLACKPOOL (St Mary) South Shore *Blackb 9* **P** *Bp* **V** G F GILCHRIST, **Hon C** N SMITH

BLACKPOOL (St Michael and All Angels) *Blackb 9* **P** *Bp* **V** J B SWALLOW, **C** L LAYCOCK

BLACKPOOL (St Paul) *Blackb 9* **P** *Trustees* **V** C J ENTWISTLE, **Par Dn** P I IMPEY

BLACKPOOL (St Stephen on the Cliffs) *Blackb 9* **P** *Trustees* **V** A D AINSLEY, **C** I G PAGE

BLACKPOOL (St Thomas) *Blackb 9* **P** *CPAS* **V** J E DENNETT

BLACKPOOL (St Wilfrid) Mereside *Blackb 9* **P** *Bp* **V** E K SILLIS

BLACKROD (St Catherine) (Scot Lane School) *Man 11* **P** *V Bolton-le-Moors St Pet* **V** R C COOPER

BLACKTOFT (Holy Trinity) Howden Team Min *York*

BLACKWATER (St Barnabas) Arreton *Portsm*

BLACKWELL (All Saints) Darlington St Cuth *Dur*

BLACKWELL (St Catherine) The Lickey *Birm*

BLACKWELL (St Werburgh) *Derby 1* **P** *Bp* **V** A P de BERRY

BLADON (St Martin) w Woodstock *Ox 9* **P** *Duke of Marlborough* **P-in-c** J D BECKWITH

BLAGDON (St Andrew) w Compton Martin and Ubley *B & W 11* **P** *Bp and Sir John Wills, Bt (jt)* **R** C A HADLEY, **C** H A MATTHEWS, **NSM** G D TEAGUE

BLAGREAVES (St Andrew) *Derby 10* **P** *Bp, Churchwardens, and CPAS (jt)* **V** K W HORLESTON

BLAISDON (St Michael and All Angels) Westbury-on-Severn w Flaxley and Blaisdon *Glouc*

BLAKEDOWN (St James) Churchill-in-Halfshire w Blakedown and Broome *Worc*

BLAKEMERE (St Leonard) Madley w Tyberton, Preston-on-Wye and Blakemere *Heref*

BLAKENALL HEATH (Christ Church) *Lich 7* **P** *Patr Bd* **TR** D P LINGWOOD, **C** J BALL

BLAKENEY (All Saints) Newnham w Awre and Blakeney *Glouc*

BLAKENEY (St Nicholas w St Mary and St Thomas) w Cley, Wiveton, Glandford and Letheringsett *Nor 22* **P** *Bp and Keble Coll Ox (jt)* **R** N R MARTIN, **C** B N CARLING, **NSM** R H ROE

BLAKENHALL (St Luke) Wolv St Luke *Lich*

BLAKENHAM, GREAT (St Mary) and Little Blakenham w Baylham and Nettlestead *St E 1* **P** *Bp and MMCET (jt)* **P-in-c** G E NOBLE

BLAKENHAM, LITTLE (St Mary) Gt and Lt Blakenham w Baylham and Nettlestead *St E*

BLAKESLEY (St Mary) w Adstone and Maidford and Farthingstone *Pet 5* **P** *Sons of Clergy Corp, Bp, Hertf Coll Ox, and Capt R Grant-Renwick (by turn)* **R** *Vacant* Blakesley (0327) 860507

BLANCHLAND (St Mary's Abbey) w Hunstanworth and Edmundbyers and Muggleswick *Newc 3* **P** *D E Scott-Harden, Lord Crewe's Trustees and D&C (alt)* **R** J E DURNFORD

BLANDFORD FORUM (St Peter and St Paul) and Langton Long *Sarum 7* **P** *Bp* **R** R A BABINGTON, **C** A G MARLEY, **NSM** H J TRENCHARD, **Hon Par Dn** M C MILES

BLANDFORD ST MARY (St Mary) Spetisbury w Charlton Marshall and Blandford St Mary *Sarum*

BLANKNEY (St Oswald) Metheringham w Blankney *Linc*

BLASTON (St Giles) Six Saints circa Holt *Leic*

BLATCHINGTON, EAST (St John the Evangelist) (St Peter) *Chich 19* **P** *Bp* **R** R S CRITTALL

BLATCHINGTON, WEST (St Peter) *Chich 4* **P** *Bp* **R** M S PORTEOUS

BLAXHALL (St Peter) Gt and Lt Glemham, Blaxhall etc *St E*

BLEADON (St Peter and St Paul) *B & W 12* **P** *Guild of All So* **R** D T PARKINSON

BLEAN (St Cosmus and St Damian) *Cant 3* **P** *Eastbridge Hosp* **V** B L S WARNES

BLEASBY (St Mary) Thurgarton w Hoveringham and Bleasby etc *S'well*

BLEASDALE (St Eadmor) Whitechapel w Admarsh-in-Bleasdale *Blackb*

BLEATARN (Chapel of Ease) Brough w Stainmore, Musgrave and Warcop *Carl*

BLEDINGTON (St Leonard) Westcote w Icomb and Bledington *Glouc*

BLEDLOW (Holy Trinity) w Saunderton and Horsenden *Ox 21* **P** *Lord Carrington* **R** C C G SHAW

BLEDLOW RIDGE (St Paul) W Wycombe w Bledlow Ridge, Bradenham and Radnage *Ox*

BLENDON (St James) Bexley St Jo *Roch*

BLENDON (St James the Great) *Roch 16* **P** *The Crown* **V** M G KICHENSIDE

BLENDWORTH (Holy Trinity) w Chalton w Idsworth *Portsm 4* **P** *Bp* **R** E M PINSENT

BLETCHINGDON (St Giles) Kirtlington w Bletchingdon, Weston etc *Ox*

BLETCHINGLEY (St Andrew) (St Mary) *S'wark 23* **P** *Em Coll Cam* **R** J B M FREDERICK, **NSM** P H BRADSHAW

BLETCHLEY (St Mary) *Ox 25* **P** *DBP* **R** I J PUSEY, **C** J E HOLBROOK, D WALMSLEY, **Par Dn** A MACKENZIE

BLETSOE (St Mary) Riseley w Bletsoe *St Alb*

BLEWBURY (St Michael and All Angels), Hagbourne and Upton *Ox 18* **P** *Bp* **R** E G CLEMENTS, **C** B W BARRETT

BLICKLING (St Andrew) Saxthorpe w Corpusty, Blickling, Oulton etc *Nor*

BLIDWORTH (St Mary) *S'well 2* **P** *Ld Chan* **V** R BEARDALL

BLIDWORTH, NEW (St Andrew) Blidworth *S'well*

BLINDLEY HEATH (St John the Evangelist) *S'wark 23* **P** *R Godstone* **P-in-c** H G C CLARKE

BLISLAND (St Protus and St Hyacinth) w St Breward *Truro 10* **P** *SMF and D&C (alt)* **R** F E HARRIS, **C** J F KIRBY

BLISWORTH (St John the Baptist) *Pet 5* **P** *MMCET* **R** H BUNKER

BLITHFIELD (St Leonard) Abbots Bromley w Blithfield *Lich*

BLO' NORTON (St Andrew) Garboldisham w Blo' Norton, Riddlesworth etc *Nor*

BLOCKLEY (St Peter and St Paul) w Aston Magna and Bourton on the Hill *Glouc 10* **P** *Lord Dulverton and DBP (jt)* **V** R G D SLUMAN

BLOFIELD (St Andrew) w Hemblington *Nor 1* **P** *G&C Coll Cam* **R** A G BAKER

BLOOMSBURY (St George) w Woburn Square (Christ Church) *Lon 17* **P** *Ld Chan* **P-in-c** M DAY

BLORE RAY (St Bartholomew) Ilam w Blore Ray and Okeover *Lich*

BLOXHAM (Our Lady of Bloxham) w Milcombe and South Newington *Ox 5* **P** *Ex Coll Ox and Eton Coll (jt)* **V** E F CONDRY

BLOXHOLME (St Mary) Digby *Linc*

BLOXWICH (All Saints) (Holy Ascension) *Lich 7* **P** *Patr Bd* **TR** S C RAWLING, **TV** D E CLAYDEN, D J TITLEY

BLOXWORTH (St Andrew) Red Post *Sarum*

BLUBBERHOUSES (St Andrew) Leathley w Farnley, Fewston and Blubberhouses *Bradf*

BLUCHER (St Cuthbert) Newburn *Newc*

BLUE BELL HILL (St Alban) Chatham St Steph *Roch*

BLUNDELLSANDS (St Michael) *Liv 5* **P** *Trustees* **V** P C N CONDER, **Hon C** R E DENNIS

BLUNDELLSANDS (St Nicholas) *Liv 5* **P** *Trustees* **V** R D BAKER

BLUNDESTON (St Mary the Virgin) w Flixton and Lound *Nor 15* **P** *SMF* **R** J S HUNT

BLUNHAM (St Edmund and St James) w Tempsford and Little Barford *St Alb 17* **P** *Ball Coll Ox and The Crown (alt)* **R** P W RICKETTS

BLUNSDON (St Andrew) *Bris 10*   P *Bp*   P-in-c J L WARE
BLUNTISHAM (St Mary) cum Earith w Colne and
   Woodhurst *Ely 11*   P *Ch Ch Ox*   P-in-c C BACKHOUSE
BLURTON (St Bartholomew) (St Alban) *Lich 19*   P *Bp*
   V C R BOOTH,   C C M CASE
BLYBOROUGH (St Alkmund)   Corringham *Linc*
BLYFORD (All Saints)   Halesworth w Linstead,
   Chediston, Holton etc *St E*
BLYMHILL (St Mary) w Weston-under-Lizard *Lich 3*
   P *Earl of Bradf*   P-in-c R F DABORN,
   Hon C R C W DAMPIER
BLYTH (St Cuthbert) *Newc 1*   P *Bp*   V J G O'CONNOR
BLYTH (St Mary) *Newc 1*   P *Bp*   V M NELSON,
   C N J HENSHALL
BLYTH (St Mary and St Martin) *S'well 6*   P *Trin Coll*
   Cam   V R E WHEATON
BLYTHBURGH (Holy Trinity)   Walberswick w
   Blythburgh *St E*
BLYTON (St Martin) w Pilham *Linc 2*   P *Ld Chan*
   V M W PAGE-CHESTNEY
BOARHUNT (St Nicholas)   Southwick w Boarhunt
   Portsm
BOARSTALL (St James)   Brill, Boarstall, Chilton and
   Dorton *Ox*
BOBBING (St Bartholomew)   Sittingbourne H Trin w
   Bobbing *Cant*
BOBBINGTON (Holy Cross)   Wombourne w Trysull
   and Bobbington *Lich*
BOBBINGWORTH (St Germain)   Fyfield and Moreton
   w Bobbingworth *Chelmsf*
BOCKING (St Mary) *Chelmsf 18*   P *Abp*   R A M HAIG
BOCKING (St Peter) *Chelmsf 18*   P *Abp*   V M C S BEVER
BOCKLETON (St Michael) w Leysters *Heref 7*   P *Bp*
   V A TALBOT-PONSONBY
BOCONNOC (not known)   Lostwithiel, St Winnow w St
   Nectan's Chpl etc *Truro*
BODDINGTON (St John the Baptist)   Byfield w
   Boddington *Pet*
BODDINGTON (St Mary Magdalene)   Staverton w
   Boddington and Tredington etc *Glouc*
BODENHAM (St Michael and All Angels) w Hope-under-
   Dinmore, Felton and Preston Wynne *Heref 4*   P *Bp*
   R D C MILLER
BODHAM (All Saints)   Weybourne Gp *Nor*
BODIAM (St Giles) *Chich 20*   P *All So Coll Ox*
   R M D MUMFORD
BODICOTE (St John the Baptist) *Ox 5*   P *New Coll Ox*
   V C J BUTLAND
BODINNICK (St John)   Lanteglos by Fowey *Truro*
BODLE STREET GREEN (St John the Evangelist)
   Warbleton and Bodle Street Green *Chich*
BODMIN (St Leonard) (St Petroc) w Lanhydrock and
   Lanivet *Truro 10*   P *DBP*   TR K ROGERS,
   TV S R F DRAKELEY,   C M A TREMBATH,
   NSM F B J COOMBES, J MARSHALL
BODNEY (St Mary)   Hilborough w Bodney *Nor*
BOGNOR (St Wilfrid) *Chich 1*   P *Abp*   V J H NICHOLL
BOLAM (St Andrew)   Heighington *Dur*
BOLAM (St Andrew) w Whalton and Hartburn w Meldon
   Newc 11   P *Ld Chan (2 turns), J I K Walker Esq*
   (1 turn), and D&C Dur (1 turn)   R W A GOFTON
BOLAS MAGNA (St John the Baptist)   Tibberton w
   Bolas Magna and Waters Upton *Lich*
BOLDMERE (St Michael) *Birm 9*   P *Birm Dioc Trustees*
   V J D PIGOTT,   C D J R FLEET
BOLDON (St Nicholas) *Dur 7*   P *Bp*   R T A MIDDLETON
BOLDON, EAST (St George) *Dur 7*   P *Bp*
   V E G STEPHENSON
BOLDRE (St John) w South Baddesley *Win 10*   P *Bp and*
   Lord Teynham (jt)   V J RICHARDS
BOLDRE, EAST (St Paul)   Beaulieu and Exbury and E
   Boldre *Win*
BOLDRON (Mission Room)   Startforth w Bowes *Ripon*
BOLE (St Martin)   N Wheatley, W Burton, Bole,
   Saundby, Sturton etc *S'well*
BOLINGBROKE (St Peter and St Paul)   Marden Hill Gp
   Linc
BOLINGBROKE, NEW (St Peter)   Sibsey w Frithville
   Linc
BOLLINGHAM (St Silas)   Eardisley w Bollingham,
   Willersley, Brilley etc *Heref*
BOLLINGTON (Holy Trinity)   Rostherne w Bollington
   Ches
BOLLINGTON (St John the Baptist) *Ches 13*
   P *V Prestbury*   C J E DRAYTON
BOLLINGTON CROSS (St Oswald)   Bollington St Jo
   Ches
BOLNEY (St Mary Magdalene) *Chich 6*   P *K Coll Lon*
   V A R HARCUS

BOLNHURST (St Dunstan)   Keysoe w Bolnhurst and Lt
   Staughton *St Alb*
BOLSOVER (St Mary and St Laurence) *Derby 3*   P *Bp*
   V J EASTON
BOLSTERSTONE (St Mary) *Sheff 7*   P *R R Rimington-*
   Wilson Esq   V K J BARNARD,   Hon C P B MIALL
BOLTBY (Holy Trinity)   Felixkirk w Boltby *York*
BOLTON (All Saints) *Carl 1*   P V *Morland w Thrimby etc*
   V J W HAYWOOD
BOLTON (All Saints) w Ireby and Uldale *Carl 6*   P *Earl*
   of Lonsdale, D&C, and Qu Coll Ox (by turn)
   R R C SHAW
BOLTON Breightmet (St James) *Man 16*   P *The Crown*
   V J H SMITH
BOLTON Chapel (unknown)   Whittingham and
   Edlingham w Bolton Chapel *Newc*
BOLTON (St James w St Chrysostom) *Bradf 3*   P *Bp*
   V M P SHORT,   C A B KNAPP
BOLTON (St John the Evangelist) Top o' th' Moss *Man 16*
   P *The Crown*   V H CALLAGHAN
BOLTON (St Thomas) *Man 9*   P *Trustees*
   V D ROTTLEY,   C W S BRISON
BOLTON ABBEY (St Mary and St Cuthbert) *Bradf 7*
   P *Duke of Devonshire*   R R G HIRST,
   NSM J A TURNBULL
BOLTON BY BOWLAND (St Peter and St Paul) w
   Grindleton *Bradf 5*   P *Bp and V Hurst Green and*
   Mitton (jt)   R C GREENWELL
BOLTON LE MOORS (St Bede) *Man 11*   P *Bp*
   V K B ASHWORTH
BOLTON LE MOORS (St Matthew w St Barnabas) *Man 9*
   P *Bp*   V E G F SWINNERTON
BOLTON LE MOORS (St Paul) (Emmanuel) *Man 9*
   P *Patr Bd*   TR R C CRASTON,   TV R J N COOK,
   Par Dn B H FULLALOVE
BOLTON LE MOORS (St Peter) (Holy Trinity) *Man 9*
   P *Bp*   V A WOLSTENCROFT,   C J E PAXTON,
   Lect R W LAWRANCE
BOLTON LE MOORS (St Philip) *Man 9*   P *Bp and*
   Hulme Trustees (alt)   V M W J HILLS
BOLTON LE MOORS (St Simon and St Jude) *Man 9*
   P *Trustees*   V F G DOWNING
BOLTON LE SANDS (Holy Trinity) *Blackb 15*   P *Bp*
   V H WILLIAMS
BOLTON ON SWALE (St Mary)   Easby w Brompton on
   Swale and Bolton on Swale *Ripon*
BOLTON PERCY (All Saints) *York 1*   P *Abp*
   P-in-c F A R MINAY
BOLTON-UPON-DEARNE (St Andrew the Apostle)
   Sheff 12   P *Meynall Ch Trust*   V D G STAFFORD
BOLVENTOR (Holy Trinity) *Truro 9*   P *Ld Chan, Duchy*
   of Cornwall, and Patr Bd (by turn)
   TR N TEWKESBURY,   TV W J F COX
BOMERE HEATH (Mission Room)   Leaton and
   Albrighton w Battlefield *Lich*
BONBY (St Andrew) *Linc 6*   P *DBP*   V S W ANDREW
BONCHURCH (St Boniface) (St Boniface Old Church)
   Portsm 7   P *Ch Patr Trust*   R A TEDMAN
BONDLEIGH (St James the Apostle)   N Tawton,
   Bondleigh, Sampford Courtenay etc *Ex*
BONINGALE (St Chad) *Lich 26*   P *MMCET*
   V C W WOODS
BONNINGTON (St Rumwold)   Aldington w Bonnington
   and Bilsington *Cant*
BONSALL (St James the Apostle) *Derby 7*   P *Bp*
   R *Vacant* Wirksworth (062982) 2124
BOOKER (St Birinus' Mission Church)   High Wycombe
   Ox
BOOKHAM, GREAT (St Nicholas) *Guildf 10*   P *Bp*
   R A C WARNER,   C O R PAGE,   NSM T E MORALEE
BOOKHAM, LITTLE (not known)   Effingham w Lt
   Bookham *Guildf*
BOOSBECK (St Aidan) w Moorsholm *York 17*   P *Abp*
   V D R SAMWAYS
BOOTHBY GRAFFOE (St Andrew)   Graffoe *Linc*
BOOTHBY PAGNELL (St Andrew)   Ingoldsby *Linc*
BOOTHSTOWN (St Andrew's Church Institute)
   Worsley *Man*
BOOTLE (Christ Church) *Liv 1*   P *Bp*
   P-in-c D C JOHNSTON,   NSM C R SANDS
BOOTLE (St Leonard) *Liv 1*   P *Simeon's Trustees*
   V C D BENGE
BOOTLE (St Mary w St Paul) *Liv 1*   P *Bp and*
   Trustees (jt)   V A HETHERINGTON
BOOTLE (St Matthew) *Liv 1*   P *Bp*   P-in-c C H JONES
BOOTLE (St Michael and All Angels), Corney, Whicham
   and Whitbeck *Carl 5*   P *Earl of Lonsdale*
   R M C RIDYARD
BORASTON (not known)   Burford I *Heref*

BORDEN (St Peter and St Paul) *Cant 14*   **P** *SMF*
   V H I J SUCH
BORDESLEY (St Alban and St Patrick) *Birm 7*   **P** *Keble Coll Ox*   **V** M H BRYANT,   **Hon C** D P BAZEN,
   NSM S KERSHAW
BORDESLEY (St Benedict) *Birm 10*   **P** *Keble Coll Ox*
   V S J PIMLOTT,   **Hon C** W ROMANES
BORDESLEY (St Oswald) *Birm 7*   **P** *Bp and Trustees (alt)*
   P-in-c J F P MORRISON-WELLS
BORDESLEY GREEN (St Paul) *Birm 10*   **P** *The Crown*
   V G C TURNER
BORDON (St Mark)   Headley All SS *Guildf*
BOREHAM (St Andrew) *Chelmsf 11*   **P** *Bp*
   P-in-c D W A KING
BOREHAM (St John the Evangelist)   Bishopstrow and Boreham *Sarum*
BOREHAMWOOD (All Saints) (Holy Cross) (St Michael and All Angels) *St Alb 1*   **P** *Patr Bd*   **TR** S PURVIS,
   TV P W WATSON, A F BUNDOCK,   **C** N R HARTLEY,
   Par Dn M E PARTRIDGE
BORLEY (not known)   Pentlow, Foxearth, Liston and Borley *Chelmsf*
BOROUGH GREEN (Good Shepherd) *Roch 9*   **P** *Bp*
   V A J POWELL
BOROUGHBRIDGE (St James)   Aldborough w Boroughbridge and Roecliffe *Ripon*
BORROWASH (St Stephen's Chapel)   Ockbrook *Derby*
BORROWDALE (St Andrew) *Carl 6*   **P** *V Crosthwaite*
   P-in-c P K BARBER
BORSTAL (St Matthew) *Roch 5*   **P** *V Rochester St Marg*
   V J KING
BORWICK (St Mary)   Warton St Oswald w Yealand Conyers *Blackb*
BOSBURY (Holy Trinity) w Wellington Heath, Stretton Grandison, Ashperton and Canon Frome *Heref 6*   **P** *Bp and D&C (jt)*   **V** J R HAWKINS
BOSCASTLE w Davidstow *Truro 10*   **P** *Duchy of Cornwall (1 turn) and DBP (2 turns)*   **TR** J M AYLING,
   Hon C S W DORAN
BOSCOMBE (St Andrew)   Bourne Valley *Sarum*
BOSCOMBE (St Andrew) *Win 7*   **P** *Bp*   **V** D HASLAM
BOSCOMBE (St John) *Win 7*   **P** *Peache Trustees*
   V G A TAYLOR
BOSHAM (Holy Trinity) *Chich 13*   **P** *Bp*   **V** T J INMAN
BOSLEY (St Mary the Virgin) and North Rode (St Michael) w Wincle (St Michael) and Wildboarclough (St Saviour) *Ches 13*   **P** *Bp, V Prestbury, and Earl of Derby (jt)*
   V P BARRATT
BOSSALL (St Botolph)   Sand Hutton *York*
BOSSINGTON (St James)   Broughton, Bossington, Houghton and Mottisfont *Win*
BOSTALL HEATH (St Andrew) *Roch 14*   **P** *DBP*
   V S C VARNEY
BOSTON (St Botolph) (St Christopher) *Linc 20*   **P** *Bp*
   V P E FLUCK,   **C** H HALL, R J MORRISON, N S D GIBSON
BOSTON SPA (St Mary) *York 1*   **P** *Ch Ch Ox*
   V R M C SEED,   **C** M L KAVANAGH,   **Par Dn** S MORTON
BOTCHERBY (St Andrew)   Carl St Aid and Ch Ch *Carl*
BOTESDALE (St Botolph)   Redgrave cum Botesdale w Rickinghall *St E*
BOTHAL (St Andrew) *Newc 11*   **P** *Bp*   **P-in-c** W S DEETH
BOTHAMSALL (Our Lady and St Peter)   Elkesley w Bothamsall *S'well*
BOTHENHAMPTON (Holy Trinity)   Bridport *Sarum*
BOTLEY (All Saints) *Portsm 1*   **P** *Bp*   **R** A N STAMP,
   Par Dn J K FRENCH
BOTLEY (St Peter and St Paul)   N Hinksey and Wytham *Ox*
BOTLEYS and Lyne (Holy Trinity) *Guildf 11*   **P** *Bp*
   P-in-c A B OLSEN
BOTOLPHS (St Botolph)   Beeding and Bramber w Botolphs *Chich*
BOTTESFORD (St Mary the Virgin) and Muston *Leic 3*
   P *Duke of Rutland*   **R** K A DYKE
BOTTESFORD (St Peter) w Ashby *Linc 4*   **P** *Patr Bd*
   TR M J BOUGHTON,   **TV** J C BAKER, I ROBINSON,
   C T H ATKINSON, P A McCULLOCK,   **NSM** M L MILLSON
BOTTISHAM (Holy Trinity) and Lode with Longmeadow
   Ely 6   **P** *Trin Coll Cam and Bp (jt)*   **V** P A FROSTICK
BOTUS FLEMING (St Mary)   Landrake w St Erney and Botus Fleming *Truro*
BOUGHTON (All Saints) *Ely 16*   **P** *Bp*   **R** *Vacant*
BOUGHTON (St John the Baptist)   Pitsford w Boughton *Pet*
BOUGHTON (St Matthew)   Ollerton w Boughton *S'well*
BOUGHTON ALUPH (All Saints)   Westwell, Hothfield, Eastwell and Boughton Aluph *Cant*
BOUGHTON ALUPH (St Christopher)   as above

BOUGHTON MALHERBE (St Nicholas)   Lenham w Boughton Malherbe *Cant*
BOUGHTON MONCHELSEA (St Augustine) (St Peter)
   Cant 15   **P** *Abp*   **V** R G DAVIS
BOUGHTON UNDER BLEAN (St Barnabas) (St Peter and St Paul) w Dunkirk and Hernhill *Cant 6*   **P** *Abp*
   V J W R MOWLL
BOULGE (St Michael) w Burgh and Grundisburgh *St E 7*
   P *Bp and DBP (jt)*   **R** N DAVIS
BOULMER (St Andrew)   Longhoughton w Howick *Newc*
BOULTHAM (Holy Cross) (St Helen) (St Mary Magdalene) (St Matthew) *Linc 15*   **P** *DBP*   **R** J D BROWN,
   C E HORNER, A TOWELL
BOULTON (St Mary the Virgin) *Derby 15*   **P** *Bp*
   P-in-c R J HARRIS,   **C** J P STEWART
BOUNDSTONE (Mission Church)   Wrecclesham *Guildf*
BOURN (St Helena and St Mary) and Kingston w Caxton and Longstowe *Ely 1*   **P** *Bp, Ch Coll Cam, D&C Windsor, and Selw Coll Cam (jt)*   **R** H BOURNE
BOURNE (St Peter and St Paul) *Linc 13*   **P** *DBP*
   V J M WARWICK,   **C** J COOK
BOURNE (St Thomas on the Bourne) *Guildf 3*   **P** *Adn Surrey*   **V** P W DYSON,
   C N J WHITEHEAD, P R FLEMING,   **NSM** J D A ADAMS
BOURNE, LOWER (St Martin)   Bourne *Guildf*
BOURNE END (St John)   Sunnyside w Bourne End *St Alb*
BOURNE END (St Mark)   Hedsor and Bourne End *Ox*
BOURNE STREET (St Mary)   Pimlico St Mary Graham Terrace *Lon*
BOURNE VALLEY *Sarum 11*   **P** *Patr Bd*
   TR S P BURTWELL,   **TV** J V WALTON, I SYKES
BOURNEMOUTH (Christ Church)   Westbourne Ch Ch *CD Win*
BOURNEMOUTH (Holy Epiphany) *Win 7*   **P** *Bp*
   P-in-c R S COSSINS,   **Hon C** D G KINGSLAND
BOURNEMOUTH Queen's Park (St Barnabas)   Holdenhurst *Win*
BOURNEMOUTH (St Alban) *Win 7*   **P** *Bp*
   V A H BAILEY
BOURNEMOUTH (St Ambrose) *Win 7*   **P** *Bp*
   P-in-c G J WHEELER
BOURNEMOUTH (St Andrew) Bennett Road *Win 7*
   P *Trustees*   **V** A R ROAKE
BOURNEMOUTH (St Augustine) *Win 7*   **P** *Bp*
   V *Vacant*   Bournemouth (0202) 26861
BOURNEMOUTH (St Clement) *Win 7*   **P** *DBP*
   V W A ARIES
BOURNEMOUTH (St Francis) *Win 7*   **P** *CR*
   V P G BERRETT
BOURNEMOUTH (St John) (St Michael and All Angels)
   Win 7   **P** *Bp and Exors R Ives Esq (jt)*
   P-in-c K J RANDALL,   **C** J H S STEVEN,
   NSM P V J LLOYD
BOURNEMOUTH (St Luke) *Win 7*   **P** *Bp*   **V** *Vacant*
   Bournemouth (0202) 516653
BOURNEMOUTH (St Mary) *Win 7*   **P** *DBP*
   P-in-c D DUNN
BOURNEMOUTH (St Peter) (St Swithun) (St Stephen) and Holy Trinity *Win 7*   **P** *Patr Bd*   **TR** D H R JONES,
   TV A J LANE, P HASTROP,   **NSM** P V J LLOYD
BOURNVILLE (St Andrew)   Weston-super-Mare St Andr Bournville *B & W*
BOURNVILLE (St Francis of Assisi) *Birm 8*   **P** *Bp*
   V K WITHINGTON,   **NSM** H A A YKROYD
BOURTON (Holy Trinity)   Wenlock *Heref*
BOURTON (St George)   Upper Stour *Sarum*
BOURTON (St James)   Shrivenham w Watchfield and Bourton *Ox*
BOURTON (St Peter) w Frankton and Stretton on Dunsmore w Princethorpe *Cov 6*   **P** *Bp (2 turns), Simeon's Trustees (1 turn), and Mrs J H Shaw-Fox (1 turn)*   **R** G W BROUGH
BOURTON, GREAT (All Saints)   Cropredy w Gt Bourton and Wardington *Ox*
BOURTON ON THE HILL (St Lawrence)   Blockley w Aston Magna and Bourton on the Hill *Glouc*
BOURTON-ON-THE-WATER (St Lawrence) w Clapton
   Glouc 15   **P** *Wadh Coll Ox*   **R** *Vacant*   Cotswold (0451) 20386
BOVEY, NORTH (St John the Baptist)   Moretonhampstead, N Bovey and Manaton *Ex*
BOVEY TRACEY (St John the Evangelist) w Chudleigh Knighton and Heathfield *Ex 11*   **P** *DBP and Guild of All So (jt)*   **V** J A PEASE
BOVEY TRACEY (St Peter and St Paul and St Thomas of Canterbury) *Ex 11*   **P** *The Crown*   **V** *Vacant*   Bovey Tracey (0626) 833813

BOVINGDON (St Lawrence) *St Alb 3*　**P**　*Ch Soc Trust*　**Hon C**　R H METCALFE
BOW (Holy Trinity) (All Hallows) *Lon 7*　**P**　*Patr Bd*　**TR**　J M PEET,　**TM**　M F SCHLEGER,　**NSM**　A M BELL
BOW (St Bartholomew) w Broad Nymet *Ex 2*　**P**　*DBP*　**R**　B H GALES
BOW (St Mary) w Bromley (St Leonard) *Lon 7*　**P**　*Bp*　**R**　G W GARNER
BOW BRICKHILL (All Saints) Gt Brickhill w Bow Brickhill and Lt Brickhill *Ox*
BOW COMMON (St Paul) (St Luke) *Lon 7*　**P**　*Bp*　**V**　R G KIRKBY
BOWBROOK NORTH: Feckenham and Hanbury and Stock and Bradley *Worc 8*　**P**　*Bp*　**R**　F J GILBERT
BOWBROOK SOUTH: Crowle w Bredicot and Hadzor w Oddingley and Tibberton and Himbleton and Huddington *Worc 8*　**P**　*Bp, D&C, R J G Berkeley Esq, and J F Bennett Esq (jt)*　**R**　W D S WELLS,　**C**　C D BULL
BOWBURN (Christ the King) Cassop cum Quarrington *Dur*
BOWDEN, GREAT (St Peter and St Paul) w Welham, Glooston and Cranoe *Leic 4*　**P**　*Bp and E Brudenell Esq*　**R**　D V TREANOR
BOWDEN HILL (St Anne) Lacock w Bowden Hill *Bris*
BOWDON (St Luke) (St Mary the Virgin) *Ches 10*　**P**　*Bp*　**V**　A B MARTIN,　**C**　R A WIFFEN
BOWERCHALKE (Holy Trinity) Chalke Valley W *Sarum*
BOWERS GIFFORD (St John) (St Margaret) w North Benfleet *Chelmsf 9*　**P**　*Em Coll Cam and Brig R H C Bryhers (alt)*　**R**　C S STUDD
BOWES (St Giles) Startforth w Bowes *Ripon*
BOWES PARK (St Michael-at-Bowes) Wood Green St Mich w Bounds Green St Gabr etc *Lon*
BOWLEE (St Thomas) Rhodes *Man*
BOWLING (St John) *Bradf 2*　**P**　*V Bradford*　**V**　H K ASTIN
BOWLING (St Stephen) *Bradf 2*　**P**　*CPAS*　**V**　R A L WELBY
BOWNESS (St Michael) *Carl 3*　**P**　*Earl of Lonsdale*　**R**　R BRIGHT
BOWTHORPE (St Michael) *Nor 5*　**P**　*Bp and CPAS (jt)*　**V**　R J SIMPSON
BOX (St Barnabas) Minchinhampton *Glouc*
BOX (St Thomas a Becket) *Bris 9*　**P**　*Bp*　**V**　T R S SMITH
BOX HILL (St Andrew) Headley w Box Hill *Guildf*
BOXFORD (St Andrew) Welford w Wickham and Gt Shefford, Boxford etc *Ox*
BOXFORD (St Mary) *St E 12*　**P**　*The Crown*　**P-in-c**　E C HAMLYN
BOXGROVE (St Mary and St Blaise) *Chich 3*　**P**　*Earl of March and Kinrara*　**Hon Par Dn**　B R RUNDLE
BOXLEY (St Mary the Virgin and All Saints) w Detling *Cant 15*　**P**　*Abp*　**V**　M M BRADSHAW,　**C**　J A C MANTLE
BOXMOOR (St John the Evangelist) (St Francis of Assisi) *St Alb 3*　**P**　*Bp*　**V**　A J S FREEMAN,　**C**　I R DOWSE
BOXTED (Holy Trinity) Glem Valley United Benefice *St E*
BOXTED (St Peter) w Langham *Chelmsf 20*　**P**　*Bp and Duchy of Lanc (alt)*　**R**　D LANCASHIRE
BOXWELL (St Mary the Virgin), Leighterton, Didmarton, Oldbury-on-the-Hill and Sopworth *Glouc 16*　**P**　*Duke of Beaufort and J F B Hutley Esq (alt)*　**R**　N C J MULHOLLAND,　**Hon C**　D G EMERSON
BOXWORTH (St Peter) *Ely 1*　**P**　*G E P Thornhill Esq*　**R**　H A MOSEDALE
BOYATT WOOD (St Peter) *Win 9*　**P**　*Bp*　**V**　D WALFORD
BOYLESTONE (St John the Baptist) Ch Broughton w Barton Blount, Boylestone etc *Derby*
BOYNE HILL (All Saints) *Ox 13*　**P**　*Bp*　**V**　N J BROWN
BOYNTON (St Andrew) Rudston w Boynton and Kilham *York*
BOYTHORPE (St Francis) Chesterfield St Aug *Derby*
BOYTON (Holy Name) Bolventor *Truro*
BOYTON (St Andrew) w Capel St Andrew and Hollesley *St E 7*　**P**　*Mary Warner Charity and DBP (alt)*　**R**　J M GATES
BOYTON (St Mary the Virgin) Ashton Gifford *Sarum*
BOZEAT (St Mary) w Easton Maudit *Pet 6*　**P**　*Bp and Marquess of Northn (alt)*　**V**　P H BLIGH
BRABOURNE (St Mary the Blessed Virgin) w Smeeth *Cant 12*　**P**　*Abp*　**V**　J M STEPHENS
BRACEBOROUGH (St Margaret) Langtoft Gp *Linc*
BRACEBRIDGE (All Saints) *Linc 15*　**P**　*Mrs B M Ellison-Lendrum*　**V**　A J KERSWILL
BRACEBRIDGE HEATH (St John the Evangelist) *Linc 15*　**P**　*Bp*　**V**　I W MACKIE
BRACEBY (St Margaret) Sapperton w Braceby *Linc*

BRACEWELL (St Michael) Barnoldswick w Bracewell *Bradf*
BRACKENFIELD (Holy Trinity) Ashover and Brackenfield *Derby*
BRACKLEY (St Peter w St James) *Pet 1*　**P**　*Bp*　**V**　P C WOODWARD,　**Par Dn**　R E H BATES
BRACKNELL (Holy Trinity) *Ox 11*　**P**　*Bp*　**TR**　C G CLARKE,　**TV**　P E BANNISTER, J M ALLEN,　**C**　J HOWARD,　**Par Dn**　C H REDGRAVE
BRACON ASH (St Nicholas) Wreningham *Nor*
BRADBOURNE (All Saints) and Brassington *Derby 7*　**P**　*Duke of Devonshire and Bp (alt)*　**TV**　M J HANCOCK
BRADDAN (St Brendan) *S & M 2*　**P**　*Bp*　**V**　H ALDRIDGE
BRADDEN (St Michael and All Angels) Greens Norton w Bradden and Lichborough *Pet*
BRADLEY (St Mary and All Saints) *Lich 16*　**P**　*Bp*　**V**　*Vacant*
BRADENHAM (St Botolph) W Wycombe w Bledlow Ridge, Bradenham and Radnage *Ox*
BRADENHAM, EAST (St Mary) Shipdham w E and W Bradenham *Nor*
BRADENHAM, WEST (St Andrew) as above
BRADENSTOKE (St Mary) Lyneham w Bradenstoke *Sarum*
BRADFIELD (St Andrew) and Stanford Dingley *Ox 12*　**P**　*Ch Soc Trust*　**R**　N A BARKER
BRADFIELD (St Clare) Cockfield w Bradfield St Clare, Felsham etc *St E*
BRADFIELD (St George) Gt and Lt Whelnetham w Bradfield St George *St E*
BRADFIELD (St Giles) Trunch *Nor*
BRADFIELD (St Laurence) Mistley w Manningtree and Bradfield *Chelmsf*
BRADFIELD (St Nicholas) *Sheff 7*　**P**　*V Ecclesfield*　**R**　P J DENNIS
BRADFIELD COMBUST (All Saints) Hawstead and Nowton w Stanningfield etc *St E*
BRADFORD (All Saints) Black Torrington, Bradf w Cookbury etc *Ex*
BRADFORD (St Augustine) Undercliffe *Bradf 3*　**P**　*V Bradford*　**V**　R P GAMBLE,　**C**　N R SHORT
BRADFORD (St Clement) *Bradf 3*　**P**　*Bp (2 turns) and Trustees (1 turn)*　**P-in-c**　S NAYLOR
BRADFORD (St Columba w St Andrew) *Bradf 2*　**P**　*Bp*　**V**　C I JUDD
BRADFORD (St Giles) w Oake, Hillfarrance and Heathfield *B & W 21*　**P**　*Bp and M V Spurway Esq (jt)*　**R**　K G X TINGAY
BRADFORD (St Oswald) Chapel Green *Bradf 2*　**P**　*Bp*　**V**　*Vacant*　Bradford (0274) 574830
BRADFORD (St Wilfrid) Lidget Green *Bradf 2*　**P**　*Bp*　**V**　P M BILTON,　**NSM**　L F CRAWLEY
BRADFORD, WEST (St Catherine) Waddington *Bradf*
BRADFORD ABBAS (St Mary the Virgin) and Thornford w Beer Hackett *Sarum 4*　**P**　*Major K S D Wingfield Digby and Win Coll (alt)*　**R**　D A K GREENE
BRADFORD-ON-AVON (Christ Church) *Sarum 17*　**P**　*V Bradf H Trin*　**V**　D R R SEYMOUR,　**NSM**　B F CHAPMAN
BRADFORD-ON-AVON (Holy Trinity) *Sarum 17*　**P**　*D&C*　**V**　W A MATTHEWS,　**C**　D R A BRETT
BRADFORD ON TONE (St Giles) Bradf w Oake, Hillfarrance and Heathfield *B & W*
BRADFORD PEVERELL (Church of the Assumption), Stratton, Frampton and Sydling St Nicholas *Sarum 2*　**P**　*Win Coll and Bp (alt)*　**R**　K J SCOTT
BRADING (St Mary the Virgin) w Yaverland *Portsm 7*　**P**　*Hon Mrs I S T Monck and Trin Coll Cam (jt)*　**R**　D L LONGENECKER
BRADLEY (All Saints) Hulland, Atlow, Bradley and Hognaston *Derby*
BRADLEY (All Saints) The Candover Valley *Win*
BRADLEY (St George) Gt and Lt Coates w Bradley *Linc*
BRADLEY (St John the Baptist) Bowbrook N *Worc*
BRADLEY (St Martin) *Lich 10*　**P**　*Baldwin Pugh Trustees*　**V**　R M WALKER
BRADLEY (St Mary) Cononley w Bradley *Bradf*
BRADLEY (St Thomas) *Wakef 5*　**P**　*Bp*　**V**　D R WARD,　**C**　P WILLOX
BRADLEY, GREAT (St Mary the Virgin) Haverhill w Withersfield, the Wrattings etc *St E*
BRADLEY, LITTLE (All Saints) as above
BRADLEY, NORTH (St Nicholas) Southwick and Heywood *Sarum 17*　**P**　*Win Coll*　**P-in-c**　P M POTTER
BRADLEY, WEST (not known) Baltonsborough w Butleigh and W Bradley *B & W*
BRADLEY-LE-MOORS (St Leonard) Alton w Bradley-le-Moors and Oakamoor w Cotton *Lich*

BRADMORE (Mission Room)　Bunny w Bradmore
S'well
BRADNINCH (St Disen) and Clyst Hydon *Ex 4*　**P** *D&C
and D&C Windsor (jt)*　**R** *E J ILLING*
BRADNOP (Mission Church)　Ipstones w Berkhamsytch
and Onecote w Bradnop *Lich*
BRADOC (Blessed Virgin Mary)　Liskeard, St Keyne, St
Pinnock, Morval etc *Truro*
BRADPOLE (Holy Trinity)　Bridport *Sarum*
BRADSHAW (St John the Evangelist) *Wakef 4*　**P** *Bp*
V *C HAYNES*
BRADSHAW (St Maxentius) *Man 16*　**P** *V Bolton-le-
Moors St Pet*　**V** *D M DUNN*
BRADSTONE (St Nonna)　Kelly w Bradstone *Ex*
BRADWELL (St Barnabas) *Derby 2*　**P** *D&C Lich*
V *J VAUGHAN*
BRADWELL (St Barnabas)　Wolstanton *Lich*
BRADWELL (St Laurence and Methodist United)
Stantonbury and Willen *Ox*
BRADWELL (St Nicholas) *Nor 2*　**P** *Bp*　**R** *R J TUCK*
BRADWELL, NEW (St James)　Stantonbury and Willen
Ox
BRADWELL AND PATTISWICK (Holy Trinity)
Stisted w Bradwell and Pattiswick *Chelmsf*
BRADWELL ON SEA (St Thomas) *Chelmsf 13*　**P** *Bp*
P-in-c *G A CATCHPOLE*
BRADWORTHY (St John the Baptist) *Ex 9*　**P** *The Crown*
V *Vacant* Bradworthy (040924) 200
**BRAFFERTON (St Peter) w Pilmoor, Myton on Swale and
Thormanby** *York 5*　**P** *Abp and Sir Anthony
Milnes Coates (jt)*　**R** *J D HARRIS-DOUGLAS*
BRAFIELD ON THE GREEN (St Laurence)　Gt and Lt
Houghton w Brafield on the Green *Pet*
BRAILES (St George) *Cov 9*　**P** *Provost and Chapter*
V *N J MORGAN*,　**NSM** *J W ROLFE*
**BRAILSFORD (All Saints) w Shirley and Osmaston w
Edlaston** *Derby 8*　**P** *Bp, Earl Ferrers, and Sir Peter
Walker-Okeover, Bt (by turn)*　**R** *M F H HULBERT*
BRAINTREE (St Michael) (St Paul) *Chelmsf 18*
P *Ch Trust Fund Trust*　**V** *B DAVIES*,
C *D N KELLY, S R LLOYD*
BRAISHFIELD (All Saints)　Michelmersh, Timsbury,
Farley Chamberlayne etc *Win*
BRAITHWAITE (St Herbert)　Thornthwaite cum
Braithwaite and Newlands *Carl*
BRAITHWELL (St James) w Bramley *Sheff 10*
P *Sir Stephen Hastings*　**V** *Vacant* Rotherham (0709)
812665
BRAMBER (St Nicholas)　Beeding and Bramber w
Botolphs *Chich*
BRAMBLETON (not known)　Bourne *Guildf*
BRAMCOTE (St Michael and All Angels) *S'well 7*
P *CPAS*,　**V** *J G HUMPHREYS*,　**C** *T WRIGHT*,
NSM *D EDINBOROUGH*
BRAMDEAN (St Simon and St Jude)　Hinton Ampner w
Bramdean and Kilmeston *Win*
BRAMDEAN COMMON (Church in the Wood)　as
above
BRAMERTON (St Peter)　Rockland St Mary w
Hellington, Bramerton etc *Nor*
BRAMFIELD (St Andrew)　Thorington w Wenhaston
and Bramfield *St E*
BRAMFIELD (St Andrew) w Stapleford and Waterford
St Alb 8　**P** *R M A Smith Esq and Grocers' Co (alt)*
R *G D BOOKER*
BRAMFORD (St Mary the Virgin) *St E 4*　**P** *D&C Cant*
V *Vacant* Ipswich (0473) 41105
BRAMHALL (St Michael and All Angels) (Hall Chapel)
Ches 17　**P** *Trustees*　**V** *R H HACK*,　**C** *J T OWEN*
BRAMHAM (All Saints) *York 1*　**P** *G Lane Fox Esq*
V *J R D SHAW*
BRAMHOPE (St Giles) *Ripon 7*　**P** *Trustees*　**V** *J R WARD*
BRAMLEY (Holy Trinity) and Grafham *Guildf 2*
P *Ld Chan*　**V** *M F H GODWIN*,　**NSM** *E S WILLIAMS*
BRAMLEY (St Francis) and Ravenfield *Sheff 6*　**P** *Bp*
C *A T COATES*
BRAMLEY (St James) *Win 4*　**P** *Qu Coll Ox*　**V** *Vacant*
Basingstoke (0256) 881373
BRAMLEY (St Peter) *Ripon 6*　**P** *DBP*
TR *G M STONESTREET*,　**TV** *J E PALIN*,　**TM** *G R LURIE*
BRAMPFORD SPEKE (St Peter)　Thorverton,
Cadbury, Upton Pyne etc *Ex*
BRAMPTON (St Mark) *Derby 5*　**P** *Bp*　**V** *W M FELL*
BRAMPTON (St Martin) *Carl 2*　**P** *Mrs J M Matthews and
Mrs S Dean (jt)*　**V** *N N STEADMAN*
BRAMPTON (St Mary Magdalene) *Ely 9*　**P** *Bp*
R *W M DEBNEY*,　**Par Dn** *D M OSBORN*
BRAMPTON (St Peter)　Buxton w Oxnead, Lammas and
Brampton *Nor*

BRAMPTON (St Peter)　Hundred River Gp of Par *St E*
BRAMPTON (St Thomas the Martyr) *Derby 5*　**P** *Bp*
R *C J C FRITH*,　**C** *B J H PORTER, J N JEE*
BRAMPTON, OLD (Cutthorpe Institute)　Old
Brampton and Loundsley Green *Derby*
**BRAMPTON, OLD (St Peter and St Paul) and Loundsley
Green** *Derby 5*　**P** *Bp*　**TR** *P J BOWLES*
BRAMPTON ABBOTTS (St Michael)　Ross w
Brampton Abbotts, Bridstow and Peterstow *Heref*
BRAMPTON ASH (St Mary) w Dingley and Braybrooke
Pet 11　**P** *Earl Spencer (2 turns), DBP (1 turn)*
R *R J CHAPMAN*
BRAMPTON BIERLOW (Christ Church) *Sheff 12*
P *V Wath-upon-Dearne*　**V** *C W M BALDOCK*
BRAMPTON BRYAN (St Barnabas)　Wigmore Abbey
Heref
BRAMSHALL (St Laurence)　Uttoxeter w Bramshall
Lich
BRAMSHAW (St Peter) and Landford w Plaitford
Sarum 11　**P** *Bp and D&C (alt)*　**R** *D P CLACEY*
BRAMSHILL (Mission Church)　Eversley *Win*
BRAMSHOTT (St Mary the Virgin) *Portsm 5*　**P** *Qu Coll
Ox*　**R** *R A EWBANK*,　**C** *J EVANS*
**BRANCASTER (St Mary the Virgin) w Burnham Deepdale
and Titchwell** *Nor 21*　**P** *Bp and H S N Simms-
Adams Esq (alt)*　**R** *L H CAMPBELL*
BRANCEPETH (St Brandon) *Dur 2*　**P** *Bp*
P-in-c *A H NUGENT*
BRANCEPETH, NEW (St Catherine)　Brandon *Dur*
BRANDESBURTON (St Mary) *York 12*　**P** *St Jo Coll
Cam*　**R** *J D WAUD*
BRANDESTON (All Saints) w Kettleburgh *St E 18*
P *Capt J L Round-Turner (2 turns), C Austin Esq
(1 turn)*　**P-in-c** *R J DIXON*
BRANDLESHOLME (St Francis House Chapel)　Elton
All SS *Man*
BRANDON (Chapel)　Barkston and Hough Gp *Linc*
BRANDON (St John the Evangelist) *Dur 2*
P *R Brancepeth*　**P-in-c** *D B GODSELL*,　**C** *P BROWN*
BRANDON (St Peter) and Santon Downham *St E 11*
P *Ld Chan (1 turn), M F Carter Esq (2 turns), and Bp
(1 turn)*　**R** *Vacant* Thetford (0842) 811221
BRANDON PARVA (All Saints)　Barnham Broom *Nor*
BRANDSBY (All Saints)　Crayke w Brandsby and
Yearsley *York*
BRANDWOOD (St Bede) *Birm 4*　**P** *Bp*　**V** *Vacant*
021-444 4631
BRANKSEA ISLAND (St Mary)　Parkstone St Pet w
Branksea and St Osmund *Sarum*
BRANKSOME (St Aldhelm) (St Francis) *Sarum 8*　**P** *Bp*
V *Vacant* Poole (0202) 764420
BRANKSOME (St Clement) (St Barnabas) *Sarum 8*
P *MMCET*　**V** *M G BOULTER*
BRANKSOME PARK (All Saints) *Sarum 8*　**P** *MMCET*
V *M S LOWE*
BRANSCOMBE (St Winifred)　Beer and Branscombe
Ex
BRANSDALE (St Nicholas)　Kirkbymoorside w
Gillamoor, Farndale & Bransdale *York*
BRANSFORD (St John the Baptist)　Alfrick, Lulsley,
Suckley, Leigh and Bransford *Worc*
BRANSGORE (St Mary the Virgin) *Win 8*
P *P W J Jesson Esq*　**V** *P C ELKINS*
BRANSHOLME (St John)　Sutton St Jas and Wawne
York
BRANSTON (All Saints) *Linc 18*　**P** *Stowe Sch*
R *B A STALLEY*
BRANSTON (St Saviour) *Lich 20*　**P** *Simeon's Trustees*
V *D B SIMMONDS*
BRANSTON BY BELVOIR (St Guthlac)　Croxton
Kerrial, Knipton, Harston, Branston etc *Leic*
BRANT BROUGHTON (St Helen) and Beckingham
Linc 23　**P** *Bp, Exors Sir Richard Sutton, Bt, and
Rev J R H and H C Thorold Esq (by turn)*　**R** *R CLARK*
BRANT ROAD (Church Centre)　Bracebridge *Linc*
BRANTHAM (St Michael and All Angels) w Stutton *St E 5*
P *Bp and Em Coll Cam (alt)*　**R** *A S JONES*
BRANTINGHAM (All Saints)　Elloughton and Brough
w Brantingham *York*
BRANXTON (St Paul) *Newc 12*　**P** *D&C Dur*
P-in-c *R BLEWETT*
BRASSINGTON (St James)　Bradbourne and
Brassington *Derby*
BRASTED (St Martin) *Roch 8*　**P** *Abp*　**R** *A B CURRY*
BRATHAY (Holy Trinity)　Ambleside w Brathay *Carl*
BRATOFT (St Peter and St Paul) w Irby-in-the-Marsh
Linc 8　**P** *Bp*　**R** *Vacant*
BRATTLEBY (St Cuthbert)　Aisthorpe w Scampton w
Thorpe le Fallows etc *Linc*

BRATTON (St James the Great) (Oratory) *Sarum 14*
  P *V Westbury* **V** J P R SAUNT
BRATTON CLOVELLY (St Mary the Virgin) w
  Germansweek *Ex 12* **P** *Bp* **R** J REASON
BRATTON FLEMING (St Peter) Shirwell, Loxhore,
  Kentisbury, Arlington, etc *Ex*
BRATTON ST MAUR (St Nicholas) Bruton and Distr
  B & W
BRAUGHING (St Mary the Virgin) w Furneux Pelham and
  Stocking Pelham *St Alb 4* **P** *Bp and Lord*
  Hamilton (alt) **R** R H NOKES
  P-in-c M J G TOMPKINS
BRAUNSTON (All Saints) *Pet 3* **P** *Jes Coll Ox*
  P-in-c M J G TOMPKINS
BRAUNSTON (All Saints) Oakham, Hambleton,
  Egleton, Braunston and Brooke *Pet*
BRAUNSTONE (St Peter) (St Crispin) *Leic 12* **P** *Bp*
  TR M S WOODS, **TV** D F MILLS, A R ARCHER
BRAUNTON (St Brannock) *Ex 15* **P** *Bp* **V** R P REEVE,
  C R E SHORTER, **Hon C** G MORGAN
BRAXTED, GREAT (All Saints) Tolleshunt Knights w
  Tiptree and Gt Braxted *Chelmsf*
BRAXTED, LITTLE (St Nicholas) Wickham Bishops w
  Lt Braxted *Chelmsf*
BRAY (St Michael) and Braywood *Ox 13* **P** *Bp*
  V G D REPATH, **Par Dn** J F RAMSBOTTOM
BRAY, HIGH (All Saints) S Molton w Nymet St
  George, High Bray etc *Ex*
BRAYBROOKE (All Saints) Brampton Ash w Dingley
  and Braybrooke *Pet*
BRAYDESTON (St Michael) Brundall w Braydeston
  and Postwick *Nor*
BRAYTON (St Wilfrid) *York 6* **P** *Abp*
  TR D H REYNOLDS, **TV** D G RICHARDSON,
  C P E GRIGSBY, **NSM** K MANNERS
BREADSALL (All Saints) *Derby 13* **P** *H F Harpur-*
  Crewe Esq and Miss A I M Harpur-Crewe (jt)
  P-in-c R T SHORTHOUSE, **NSM** B A LEESON
BREADSTONE (St Michael and All Angels) Berkeley
  w Wick, Breadstone and Newport *Glouc*
BREAGE (St Breaca) w Germoe *Truro 4* **P** *The Crown*
  V J E COX
BREAM (St James) *Glouc 4* **P** *Bp* **NSM** G M PEMBERY
BREAMORE (St Mary) *Win 8* **P** *Sir Westrow Hulse, Bt*
  V *Vacant*
BREAN (St Bridget) Berrow and Breane *B & W*
BREARTON (St John the Baptist) Knaresborough
  Ripon
BREASTON (St Michael) Wilne and Draycott w
  Breaston *Derby*
BRECKLES (St Margaret) Caston w Griston, Merton,
  Thompson etc *Nor*
BREDBURY (St Barnabas) *Ches 16* **P** *V Bredbury*
  St Mark **V** C R WINDLE
BREDBURY (St Mark) *Ches 16* **P** *Bp* **V** N TOPPING
BREDE (St George) w Udimore *Chich 20* **P** *Bp and*
  Mrs M E Crook (alt) **R** R W COTTON
BREDENBURY (St Andrew) w Grendon Bishop and
  Wacton, Edwyn Ralph, Collington, Thornbury,
  Pencombe and Marston Stannett and Little Cowarne
  Heref 2 **P** *DBP, V Bromyard, and*
  Lt-Col H H Barneby (jt) **R** C S HARPER
BREDFIELD (St Andrew) Ufford w Bredfield and
  Hasketon *St E*
BREDGAR (St John the Baptist) w Bicknor and Frinsted w
  Wormshill and Milstead *Cant 14* **P** *Abp,*
  R L Pemberton Esq, M Nightingale Esq, and
  Mrs McCandish (jt) **R** J M SHORROCK
BREDHURST (St Peter) S Gillingham *Roch*
BREDICOT (St James the Less) Bowbrook S *Worc*
BREDON (St Giles) w Bredon's Norton *Worc 4* **P** *Bp*
  R C J RIDOUT
BREDON'S NORTON (not known) Bredon w Bredon's
  Norton *Worc*
BREDWARDINE (St Andrew) Cusop w Clifford,
  Hardwicke, Bredwardine etc *Heref*
BREDY, LITTLE (St Michael and All Angels) Bride
  Valley *Sarum*
BREEDON-ON-THE-HILL (St Mary and St Hardulph)
  cum Isley Walton and Worthington *Leic 9*
  P *D A G Shields Esq and Ch Coll Cam (alt)*
  R K R WATSON
BREIGHTMET Top o' th' Moss (St John the Evangelist)
  Bolton St Jo *Man*
BREINTON (St Michael) (Mission Hall) *Heref 4* **P** *Bp*
  P-in-c B IRONS
BREMHILL (St Martin) w Foxham and Hilmarton
  Sarum 18 **P** *Prime Min* **V** G H JONES,
  NSM J W SCOTT

BRENCHLEY (All Saints) *Roch 11* **P** *D&C Cant*
  V J F BOYCE
BRENDON (St Brendon) Lynton, Brendon,
  Countisbury, Lynmouth etc *Ex*
BRENT, EAST (The Blessed Virgin Mary) Brent Knoll,
  E Brent and Lympsham *B & W*
BRENT, SOUTH (St Petroc) *Ex 13* **P** *Bp*
  P-in-c J H HARPER
BRENT ELEIGH (St Mary) Monks Eleigh w
  Chelsworth and Brent Eleigh etc *St E*
BRENT KNOLL (St Michael) and East Brent and
  Lympsham *B & W 1* **P** *Adn Wells (1 turn), Bp (2 turns)*
  R J S WELLS
BRENT PELHAM (St Mary the Virgin) Hormead,
  Wyddial, Anstey, Brent Pelham etc *St Alb*
BRENTFORD (St Paul w St Lawrence and St George) (St
  Faith) *Lon 11* **P** *Bp* **TR** M J BRIDGER,
  Par Dn M J BULMAN, **Hon C** J S BOWDEN
BRENTOR (Christ Church) Lydford, Brent Tor,
  Bridestowe and Sourton *Ex*
BRENTOR (St Michael) as above
BRENTRY (St Mark) Henbury *Bris*
BRENTS (St John the Evangelist) and Davington w Oare
  and Luddenham, The *Cant 6* **P** *Abp and Ld Chan (alt)*
  V P J E GELDARD
BRENTWOOD (St George the Martyr) *Chelmsf 10*
  P *DBP* **P-in-c** G F JENKINS
BRENTWOOD (St Thomas) *Chelmsf 10* **P** *DBP*
  P-in-c R B WHITE, **C** M HUME
BRENZETT (St Eanswith) Appledore w Brookland,
  Fairfield, Brenzett etc *Cant*
BRERETON (St Michael) *Lich 4* **P** *R Rugeley*
  V P A HARDWICKE
BRERETON (St Oswald) w Swettenham *Ches 11* **P** *DBP*
  and MMCET (jt) **R** J M INNES
BRESSINGHAM (St John the Baptist) w North and South
  Lopham and Fersfield *Nor 16* **P** *R D A Woode Esq,*
  MMCET, and St Jo Coll Cam (by turn) **R** D M HUNTER
BRETBY (St Wystan) w Newton Solney *Derby 16* **P** *Bp*
  and DBP (alt) **NSM** G GOODALL
BRETFORTON (St Leonard) Offenham and Bretforton
  Worc
BRETHERTON (St John the Baptist) *Blackb 4*
  P *R Croston* **R** R S LADDS
BRETTENHAM (St Andrew) Garboldisham w Blo'
  Norton, Riddlesworth etc *Nor*
BRETTENHAM (St Mary) Rattlesden w Thorpe
  Morieux and Brettenham *St E*
BRETTON PARK (St Bartholomew) Woolley *Wakef*
BREWHAM, SOUTH (St John the Baptist) Bruton and
  Distr *B & W*
BREWOOD (St Mary and St Chad) *Lich 3* **P** *Bp*
  V T H GREEN, **NSM** E J EDMUNDS
BRICETT, GREAT (St Mary and St Lawrence)
  Ringshall w Battisford, Barking w Darmsden etc *St E*
BRICKENDON (Holy Cross and St Alban) Lt
  Berkhamsted and Bayford, Essendon etc *St Alb*
BRICKET WOOD (St Luke) *St Alb 1* **P** *CPAS*
  NSM A J WILLIAMSON
BRICKHILL, GREAT (St Mary) w Bow Brickhill and
  Little Brickhill *Ox 26* **P** *Sir Philip Duncombe, Bt, Bp,*
  and St Edw Sch Ox (by turn) **R** H R M HARRIES
BRICKHILL, LITTLE (St Mary Magdalene) Gt
  Brickhill w Bow Brickhill and Lt Brickhill *Ox*
BRICKHILL, NORTH (St Mark) and Putnoe *St Alb 16*
  P *Bp* **V** C ROYDEN
BRICKLEHAMPTON (St Michael) Elmley Castle w
  Bricklehampton and Combertons *Worc*
BRIDE (St Bridget of Kildare) *S & M 4* **P** *The Crown*
  R J H SHEEN, **Hon C** J C WALNE
BRIDE VALLEY *Sarum 3* **P** *Patr Bd*
  TR J A P STANDEN McDOUGAL, **TV** A M B SALMON
BRIDEKIRK (St Bridget) *Carl 6* **P** *Trustees*
  V C H COWPER
BRIDESTOWE (St Bridget) Lydford, Brent Tor,
  Bridestowe and Sourton *Ex*
BRIDFORD (St Thomas a Becket) Christow, Ashton,
  Trusham and Bridford *Ex*
BRIDGE (St Peter) Patrixbourne w Bridge and
  Bekesbourne *Cant*
BRIDGE SOLLARS (St Andrew) Kenchester and
  Bridge Sollers *Heref*
BRIDGEMARY (St Matthew) *Portsm 3* **P** *Bp*
  V J R H RAILTON, **NSM** M E TILLMAN
BRIDGERULE (St Bridget) Pyworthy, Pancrasweek
  and Bridgerule *Ex*
BRIDGETOWN (St John the Evangelist) Totnes and
  Berry Pomeroy *Ex*

BRIDGFORD, EAST (St Peter) and Kneeton *S'well 8*
  P *Magd Coll Ox (2 turns), C G Neale Esq (1 turn)*
  R A HAYDOCK
BRIDGFORD, WEST (St Giles) (St Luke) *S'well 10*
  P *Waddington Trustees* **R** P N HUMPHREYS,
  NSM G CLEAVER, **Hon Par Dn** J M GORICK
BRIDGHAM (St Mary) E w W Harling and Bridgham w
  Roudham *Nor*
BRIDGNORTH (St Mary Magdalene) (St Leonard)
  (St James), Tasley, Astley Abbotts, Oldbury and
  Quatford *Heref 9* **P** *DBP (3 turns) and Ld Chan*
  (1 turn) **TR** J F BUTTERWORTH, **TV** M J KNEEN,
  C C H DEE, **Hon C** W A D BAKER, K SMALLEY
BRIDGWATER (Holy Trinity) *B & W 15* **P** *Bp*
  V J P HART
BRIDGWATER (St Francis of Assisi) *B & W 15* **P** *Bp*
  V D ARNOTT
BRIDGWATER (St John the Baptist) *B & W 15* **P** *Bp*
  V I G PIDOUX
BRIDGWATER (St Mary) and Chilton Trinity and
  Durleigh *B & W 15* **P** *Ld Chan* **V** R E J PACKER
BRIDLINGTON (Emmanuel) *York 10* **P** *Trustees*
  V M EXLEY
BRIDLINGTON (Holy Trinity) and Sewerby w Marton
  York 10 **P** *Abp* **V** T C WILLIS
BRIDLINGTON (St Mary's Priory Church) *York 10*
  P *Simeon's Trustees* **R** J C MEEK, **C** A MAUCHAN
BRIDLINGTON QUAY (Christ Church) *York 10*
  P *R Bridlington Priory* **V** J G COUPER
BRIDPORT (St Mary) *Sarum 3* **P** *Patr Bd (2 turns) and*
  Ld Chan (1 turn) **TR** J W GANN,
  TV R H TEBBS, R W SHAMBROOK, **Par Dn** J E CURTIS
BRIDSTOW (St Bridget) Ross w Brampton Abbotts,
  Bridstow and Peterstow *Heref*
BRIERCLIFFE (St James) *Blackb 3* **P** *Hulme Trustees*
  V P H HALLAM, **C** J D HODGKINSON
BRIERFIELD (St Luke the Evangelist) *Blackb 7* **P** *Bp*
  V S P BALLARD
BRIERLEY (St Paul) Felkirk w Brierley *Wakef*
BRIERLEY HILL (St Michael) (St Paul) *Lich 1*
  P *R Wordsley* **R** C S MINCHIN
BRIGG (St John the Evangelist) *Linc 6* **P** *Bp*
  V G A NEALE, **C** M E THORNE
BRIGHAM (St Bridget) *Carl 6* **P** *Earl of Lonsdale*
  V C GODDARD
BRIGHOUSE (St Chad) (St Martin) *Wakef 2* **P** *Bp*
  TR J R FLACK, **TV** D C BROOKES, **C** M G RAWSON
BRIGHSTONE (St Mary the Virgin) and Brooke w
  Mottistone *Portsm 8* **P** *Bp (2 turns), D&C St Paul's*
  (1 turn) **R** *Vacant* Isle of Wight (0983) 740267
BRIGHTLING (St Thomas of Canterbury) Dallington,
  Mountfield and Netherfield *Chich 15* **P** *Bp, Adn Lewes*
  and Hastings, Mrs R Hope Grissell, P S Wilmot-
  Sitwell Esq, and N S Cobbold Esq (jt) **R** D D FRICKER,
  NSM Lord WRENBURY
BRIGHTLINGSEA (All Saints) (St James) *Chelmsf 26*
  P *Ld Chan* **V** M R C SWINDLEHURST
BRIGHTON (Annunciation) *Chich 2* **P** *Wagner Trustees*
  V D K WOSTENHOLM
BRIGHTON (Good Shepherd) Preston *Chich 2* **P** *Bp*
  V G G WHITE, **Par Dn** M A LEPPARD
BRIGHTON (Resurrection) (St Luke) (St Martin w
  St Wilfrid) *Chich 2* **P** *Patr Bd* **TR** B L BRANDIE,
  TV A G STEVENS, K YATES, **C** R BIGGERSTAFF,
  NSM A D OTTERWELL
BRIGHTON (St Augustine and St Saviour) *Chich 2* **P** *Bp*
  P-in-c P A S SMITH
BRIGHTON (St Bartholomew) *Chich 2* **P** *Wagner*
  Trustees **V** J M HOLDROYD
BRIGHTON (St George w St Anne and St Mark) *Chich 2*
  P *Bp and V Brighton (jt)* **V** B J LOVATT, **C** R WOLLEY
BRIGHTON (St John) Preston *Chich*
BRIGHTON (St Mary the Virgin) Kemp Town St Mary
  Chich
BRIGHTON (St Matthias) *Chich 2* **P** *V Preston*
  V A D MACDONALD, **C** P A BOSTOCK
BRIGHTON (St Michael and All Angels) *Chich 2*
  P *V Brighton* **V** F G JACKSON, **NSM** D G HEWETSON
BRIGHTON (St Paul) *Chich 2* **P** *Wagner Trustees*
  P-in-c G R O'LOUGHLIN, **Hon C** J N BALDRY, B J WIGAN
BRIGHTON (St Peter) (St Nicholas) (Chapel Royal)
  Chich 2 **P** *Bp* **TR** E W M WALKER,
  TV W R D CAPSTICK, D F MOODY, **C** A C LEE
BRIGHTON, NEW (All Saints) *Ches 7* **P** *DBP*
  V E R ROYDEN
BRIGHTON, NEW (Emmanuel) *Ches 7* **P** *Bp*
  V R W DENT
BRIGHTON, NEW (St James) *Ches 7* **P** *Bp*
  V A J JEYNES

BRIGHTSIDE (St Thomas and St Margaret) w Wincobank
  Sheff 3 **P** *The Crown and Sheff Ch Burgesses (alt)*
  Dn-in-c S HOPE
BRIGHTWALTON (All Saints) w Catmore,
  Leckhampstead, Chaddleworth and Fawley *Ox 14*
  P *Bp, P L Wroughton Esq, and D&C Westmr (jt)*
  R A A D SMITH
BRIGHTWELL (St Agatha) w Sotwell *Ox 18* **P** *Bp*
  P-in-c J M SPURRELL
BRIGHTWELL (St John the Baptist) Martlesham w
  Brightwell *St E*
BRIGHTWELL BALDWIN (St Bartholomew)
  Ewelme, Brightwell Baldwin, Cuxham w Easington *Ox*
BRIGNALL (St Mary) Rokeby w Brignall *Ripon*
BRIGSLEY (St Helen) Ravendale Gp *Linc*
BRIGSTOCK (St Andrew) w Stanion *Pet 9* **P** *Bp*
  V R D HOWE
BRILL (All Saints), Boarstall, Chilton and Dorton *Ox 21*
  P *Sir John Aubrey-Fletcher, Bt and Earl Temple of*
  Stowe (jt) **V** P R BUGG
BRILLEY (St Mary) Eardisley w Bollingham,
  Willersley, Brilley etc *Heref*
BRIMFIELD (St Michael) Orleton w Brimfield *Heref*
BRIMINGTON (St Michael) *Derby 3* **P** *V Chesterfield*
  R D C TRUBY
BRIMPSFIELD (St Michael), Cranham, Elkstone and Syde
  Glouc 1 **P** *Bp, Wg Comdr H T Price, Mrs N Owen,*
  and DBP (jt) **R** P NEWING
BRIMPTON (St Peter) Aldermaston w Wasing and
  Brimpton *Ox*
BRIMSCOMBE (Holy Trinity) *Glouc 8* **P** *Simeon's*
  Trustees **P-in-c** D N GREEN
BRINDLE (St James) *Blackb 4* **P** *Trustees*
  P-in-c J W FINCH
BRINGHURST (St Nicholas) Six Saints circa Holt *Leic*
BRINGTON (All Saints) w Molesworth and Old Weston
  Ely 10 **P** *Bp* **R** G L NORTH
BRINGTON (St Mary w St John) w Whilton and Norton
  Pet 3 **P** *DBP and Earl Spencer (alt)* **R** N V KNIBBS
BRININGHAM (St Maurice) *Nor 22* **P** *J S Howlett Esq*
  P-in-c K G TAYLOR, **NSM** F N WARD
BRINKBURN (not known) Longframlington w
  Brinkburn *Newc*
BRINKHILL (St Philip) S Ormsby Gp *Linc*
BRINKLEY (St Mary), Burrough Green and Carlton *Ely 4*
  P *St Jo Coll Cam, Mrs B O Killander, and*
  E H Vestey Esq (by turn) **P-in-c** N E H HOLMES
BRINKLOW (St John the Baptist) *Cov 6* **P** *Ld Chan*
  R P S RUSSELL, **NSM** D J BAYFORD
BRINKWORTH (St Michael and All Angels) w Dauntsey
  Bris 12 **P** *Bp* **R** D ORMSTON
BRINNINGTON (St Luke) w Portwood St Paul *Ches 18*
  P *Bp* **V** A OWENS, **Par Dn** S B WOODHEAD
BRINSCALL (St Luke) Withnell *Blackb*
BRINSLEY (St James the Great) w Underwood *S'well 4*
  P *Bp* **V** D L HARPER
BRINSOP (St George) Credenhill w Brinsop, Mansel
  Lacey, Yazor etc *Heref*
BRINSWORTH (St Andrew) w Catcliffe (St Mary) *Sheff 6*
  P *Bp* **C** K THOMPSON
BRINTON (St Andrew) Thornage w Brinton w
  Hunworth and Stody *Nor*
BRISLEY (St Bartholomew) Colkirk w Oxwick w
  Pattesley, Whissonsett etc *Nor*
BRISLINGTON (St Anne) *Bris 3* **P** *Bp* **V** *Vacant*
  Bristol (0272) 776667
BRISLINGTON (St Christopher) *Bris 3* **P** *Simeon's*
  Trustees **Dn-in-c** C R EDWARDS
BRISLINGTON (St Cuthbert) *Bris 3* **P** *Bp*
  P-in-c G R M FISON
BRISLINGTON (St Luke) *Bris 3* **P** *Bp*
  NSM C A G LEGGATE
BRISTOL (Christ the Servant) Stockwood *Bris 3* **P** *Bp*
  V J N HARRISON, **C** R J C NEWTON,
  Hon Par Dn P A WALL
BRISTOL (Holy Cross) Inns Court *Bris 3* **P** *Bris Ch*
  Trustees **V** J F JENKINS
BRISTOL Lockleaze (St Mary Magdalene w St Francis)
  Bris 6 **P** *Bp* **V** P H DENYER
BRISTOL Redfield (St Leonard) E Bris *Bris*
BRISTOL (St Andrew) Hartcliffe *Bris 1* **P** *Bp*
  V J M FRANCIS, **Par Dn** A I FESSEY
BRISTOL (St Andrew w St Bartholomew) *Bris 6* **P** *Bp*
  P-in-c A C HORNE
BRISTOL (St Mary the Virgin) Redcliffe w Temple and
  Bedminster St John the Baptist *Bris 1* **P** *Bp*
  V D FRAYNE, **C** G J WARD, **Par Dn** P J HAYWARD,
  NSM G G STIMPSON, C R PIPE-WOLFERSTAN,
  Hon Par Dn C HERBERT

BRISTOL (St Matthew) (St Nathanael w St Katharine) *Bris 6* **P** *Bp and CPAS (jt)* **V** R V BRAZIER, **NSM** E D DELVE
BRISTOL (St Michael the Archangel on the Mount Without) *Bris 4* **P** *Trustees* **P-in-c** D R TUCKER
BRISTOL St Paul's (St Agnes) *Bris 4* **P** *Ld Chan and Patr Bd (alt)* **TR** P G BARNETT, **TV** J B BISHOP, **NSM** P BARTLE-JENKINS
BRISTOL (St Philip and St Jacob w Emmanuel) *Bris 4* **P** *Trustees* **V** M M WIDDECOMBE
BRISTOL, The City of (Christ Church w St George) (St James w St Peter) (St Stephen w St James and St John the Baptist) *Bris 4* **P** *Ld Chan (1 turn)*, *Trustees (2 turns)* **R** E A MORRIS, **Hon C** C M J TURNER, C W GONIN
BRISTOL, EAST (St Aidan) (St Ambrose) (St George) (St Matthew) (St Leonard) *Bris 2* **P** *Patr Bd* **TR** R D JAMES, **TV** R K A THOMPSON, B W JONES, **Hon C** C L SUTCH, J M HALL, N G BAILEY, **Hon Par Dn** J V THOMPSON (nee LILLIE)
BRISTON (All Saints) Burgh Parva w Briston *Nor*
BRITFORD (St Peter) *Sarum 11* **P** *D&C* **P-in-c** R P HOLLINGSHURST
BRITWELL (St George) W Slough *Ox*
BRITWELL SALOME (St Nicholas) Swyncombe w Britwell Salome *Ox*
BRIXHAM (St Mary) w Churston Ferrers and Kingswear *Ex 10* **P** *The Crown* **TR** I D CAMPBELL, **TV** D R MILTON
BRIXHAM, LOWER (All Saints) Brixham w Churston Ferrers and Kingswear *Ex*
BRIXTON (St Mary) *Ex 21* **P** *D&C Windsor* **P-in-c** M A WILKINSON
BRIXTON St Matthew *S'wark 9* **P** *Abp* **V** C B OXENFORTH, **Par Dn** M DURRAN
BRIXTON (St Paul) *S'wark 9* **P** *Ch Soc Trust* **P-in-c** N J STONE
BRIXTON, EAST (St Jude) *S'wark 9* **P** *Ch Soc Trust* **V** D PETERSON
BRIXTON, NORTH (Christ Church) Brixton Rd Ch Ch *S'wark*
BRIXTON DEVERILL (St Michael) The Deverills *Sarum*
BRIXTON HILL (St Saviour) *S'wark 9* **P** *Ch Soc Trust* **P-in-c** C R B BIRD, **Par Dn** S F COUGHTREY, **Hon C** J MARSHALL
BRIXTON ROAD (Christ Church) *S'wark 10* **P** *CPAS* **V** N P GODFREY, **Hon C** H J N FULLERTON, M S KEEN, V A ROBERTS
BRIXWORTH (All Saints) w Holcot *Pet 2* **P** *Bp* **V** A J WATKINS
BRIZE NORTON (St Britius) Minster Lovell and Brize Norton *Ox*
BROAD BLUNSDON (St Leonard) *Bris 10* **P** *Bp* **P-in-c** J L WARE
BROAD CAMPDEN (St Michael and All Angels) Chipping Campden w Ebrington *Glouc*
BROAD HINTON (St Peter ad Vincula) Upper Kennett *Sarum*
BROAD LANE (Licensed Room) Wybunbury w Doddington *Ches*
BROAD OAK (St George) Heathfield *Chich*
BROAD TOWN (Christ Church), Clyffe Pypard and Tockenham *Sarum 18* **P** *DBP and Ld Chan (alt)* **R** A G CAPES
BROADBOTTOM (St Mary Magdalene) Mottram in Longdendale w Woodhead *Ches*
BROADBRIDGE HEATH (St John) Horsham *Chich*
BROADCHALKE (All Saints) Chalke Valley W *Sarum*
BROADCLYST (St John the Baptist) Pinhoe and Broadclyst *Ex*
BROADFIELD (Christ the Lord) Southgate *Chich*
BROADHEATH (Christ Church), Crown East and Rushwick *Worc 3* **P** *Bp and D&C (jt)* **V** M NOTT
BROADHEATH (St Alban) *Ches 10* **P** *Bp* **V** J BEANEY, **C** T S McCABE, **NSM** E C COMBE
BROADHEMBURY (St Andrew the Apostle and Martyr), Payhembury and Plymtree *Ex 7* **P** *W Drewe Esq*, *Ex Coll Ox, and Or Coll Ox (by turn)* **R** A M ROBERTS
BROADHEMPSTON (St Peter and St Paul), Woodland, Staverton w Landscove and Littlehempston *Ex 13* **P** *Prime Min (1 turn)*, *D&C and Bp (1 turn)* **R** J CRUSE
BROADMAYNE (St Martin), West Knighton, Owermoigne and Warmwell *Sarum 2* **P** *Major G A M Cree (1 turn)*, *MMCET (2 turns)*, *and Sir Robert Williams, Bt (1 turn)* **R** R B GREGORY
BROADOAK (St Paul) Symondsbury and Chideock *Sarum*

BROADSTAIRS (Holy Trinity) *Cant 9* **P** *V St Peter-in-Thanet* **R** E J POWE, **NSM** R E YEO
BROADSTONE (not known) Diddlebury w Munslow, Holdgate and Tugford *Heref*
BROADSTONE (St John the Baptist) *Sarum 8* **P** *Bp* **V** S J T BUFFREY, **C** P J W MURPHY
BROADWAS (St Mary Magdalene) Martley and Wichenford, Knightwick etc *Worc*
BROADWATER (St Mary) (St Stephen) *Chich 5* **P** *MMCET* **R** P J DOMINY, **C** C M STRAIN, G C A STOREY, **Par Dn** M J HANSEN, **NSM** J E M HULETT, **Hon Par Dn** E T HARDING
BROADWATER DOWN (St Mark) Tunbridge Wells St Mark *Roch*
BROADWATERS (St Oswald) Kidderminster St Mary and All SS w Trimpley etc *Worc*
BROADWAY (St Aldhem and St Eadburga) Donyatt w Horton, Broadway and Ashill *B & W*
BROADWAY (St Eadburgha) (St Michael and All Angels) *Worc 1* **P** *Peache Trustees* **V** J W HAMPTON
BROADWELL (St Paul), Evenlode, Oddington and Adlestrop *Glouc 15* **P** *Bp, Ch Soc Trust, Lord Leigh, and DBP (jt)* **P-in-c** R N MANN
BROADWELL (St Peter and St Paul) Broughton Poggs w Filkins, Broadwell etc *Ox*
BROADWELL (Good Shepherd) Coleford w Staunton *Glouc*
BROADWEY (St Nicholas) Bincombe w Broadwey, Upwey and Buckland Ripers *Sarum*
BROADWINDSOR (St John the Baptist) Beaminster Area *Sarum*
BROADWOODKELLY (All Saints) *Ex 16* **P** *DBP* **R** P NIXSON
BROADWOODWIDGER (St Nicholas) *Ex 25* **P** *Bp* **V** J A C WILSON
BROCKDISH (St Peter and St Paul) Scole, Brockdish, Billingford, Thorpe Abbots etc *Nor*
BROCKENHURST (St Nicholas) (St Saviour) *Win 10* **P** *Trustees of E Mourant Esq* **V** D P BREWSTER, **Hon C** R DROWN
BROCKHALL (St Peter and St Paul) Flore w Dodford and Brockhall *Pet*
BROCKHAM GREEN (Christ Church) *S'wark 24* **P** *Hon J L Hamilton* **V** *Vacant*
BROCKHAMPTON (All Saints) w Fawley *Heref 4* **P** *D&C* **P-in-c** R H GARNETT
BROCKHAMPTON (Chapel) Bromyard *Heref*
BROCKHOLES (St George) Honley *Wakef*
BROCKLESBY (All Saints) Gt Limber w Brocklesby *Linc*
BROCKLEY (St Andrew) Chevington w Hargrave and Whepstead w Brockley *St E*
BROCKLEY HILL (St Saviour) *S'wark 4* **P** *V Forest Hill Ch Ch* **V** I FOWLE
BROCKMOOR (St John) *Lich 1* **P** *Prime Min* **V** F M TRETHEWEY
BROCKWORTH (St George) *Glouc 6* **P** *DBP* **V** P H NAYLOR
BROCTON (All Saints) Baswich (or Berkswich) *Lich*
BRODSWORTH (St Michael and All Angels) Bilham *Sheff*
BROKENBOROUGH (St John the Baptist) Malmesbury w Westport and Brokenborough *Bris*
BROKERS WOOD (All Saints) Dilton Marsh *Sarum*
BROMBOROUGH (St Barnabas) *Ches 9* **P** *D&C* **R** N P CHRISTENSEN, **C** D M SHEPHERD
BROME (St Mary) N Hartismere *St E*
BROMESWELL (St Edmund) Eyke w Bromeswell, Rendlesham, Tunstall etc *St E*
BROMFIELD (St Mary the Virgin) Culmington w Onibury, Bromfield etc *Heref*
BROMFIELD (St Mungo) w Waverton *Carl 3* **P** *Bp* **V** *Vacant* Aspatria (06973) 20261
BROMFORD FIRS (not Known) Hodge Hill *Birm*
BROMHAM (St Nicholas), Chittoe and Sandy Lane *Sarum 18* **P** *DBP and S Spicer Esq (jt)* **R** R G BROWN
BROMHAM (St Owen) w Oakley and Stagsden *St Alb 19* **P** *Bp* **V** D V DRAPER, **C** L R McDONALD
BROMLEY (All Hallows) Bow H Trin and All Hallows *Lon*
BROMLEY (Christ Church) *Roch 13* **P** *CPAS* **V** M C LAWSON, **C** C M GREEN, **Hon C** N E BAINES
BROMLEY (Holy Trinity Mission Church) Pensnett *Lich*
BROMLEY (St Andrew) *Roch 13* **P** *Bp* **V** H A ATHERTON
BROMLEY (St John the Evangelist) *Roch 13* **P** *Bp* **V** C D ELLIOTT

BROMLEY (St Mark) *Roch 13* P *V Bromley SS Pet & Paul* V A T VOUSDEN, C D G BACON
BROMLEY (St Peter and St Paul) *Roch 13* P *Bp* V M P BEEK, C R M JOHNSON
BROMLEY, GREAT (St George) The Bromleys *Chelmsf*
BROMLEY COMMON (Holy Trinity) *Roch 13* P *The Crown* V H P C BROADBENT
BROMLEY COMMON (St Augustine) *Roch 13* P *Bp* V B J ASH, C R B JACKSON
BROMLEY COMMON (St Luke) *Roch 13* P *Bp* Par Dn H HESELWOOD
BROMLEY CROSS (St Andrew's Mission Church) Walmsley *Man*
BROMLEYS, The *Chelmsf 23* P *CR and Wadh Coll Ox (alt)* R P M DAVIS
BROMPTON (Holy Trinity) w Onslow Square (St Paul) *Lon 8* P *Bp and MMCET (jt)* V J A K MILLAR, C N G P GUMBEL, T A GILLUM, N K LEE
BROMPTON (St Thomas) w Deighton *York 20* P *D&C Dur* V *Vacant* Northallerton (0609) 2436
BROMPTON, NEW (St Luke) *Roch 3* P *Bp* P-in-c D A GIBBONS
BROMPTON, WEST (St Mary) (St Peter) *Lon 8* P *Bp* V S G H BARTLETT
BROMPTON-BY-SAWDON (All Saints) w Snainton, Ebberston and Allerston *York 21* P *Abp* V C C FORSTER
BROMPTON ON SWALE (St Paul) Easby w Brompton on Swale and Bolton on Swale *Ripon*
BROMPTON RALPH (The Blessed Virgin Mary) Lydeard St Lawrence w Brompton Ralph etc *B & W*
BROMPTON REGIS (Blessed Virgin Mary) w Upton and Skilgate *B & W 17* P *Bp, Em Coll Cam, and Keble Coll Ox (jt)* R *Vacant* Brompton Regis (03987) 239
BROMSBERROW (St Mary the Virgin) Redmarley D'Abitot, Bromesberrow w Pauntley etc *Glouc*
BROMSGROVE (All Saints) *Worc 7* P *V Bromsgrove St Jo* V J E COOK, NSM J E SHAW-HAMILTON
BROMSGROVE (St John the Baptist) *Worc 7* P *D&C* V F J MUSHEN, Par Dn J E BAYLISS, NSM A B WHITEHORN
BROMWICH, WEST (All Saints) *Lich 9* P *Bp* V M MORETON, C J M E COOPER, Par Dn F D DIXON, Dss M L COPE
BROMWICH, WEST (Good Shepherd w St John) *Lich 9* P *Bp* V D J BELCHER
BROMWICH, WEST (Holy Trinity) *Lich 9* P *Peache Trustees* V G St C CAMPBELL
BROMWICH, WEST (St Andrew) (Christ Church) *Lich 9* P *Bp and V W Bromwich All SS (jt)* V A J G COOPER, C T N THOROLD
BROMWICH, WEST (St Francis of Assisi) *Lich 9* P *Bp* V A J JONES, C R J S GRIGSON
BROMWICH, WEST St James Hill Top *Lich 9* P *Bp* V M C RUTTER, Par Dn S R EMTAGE
BROMWICH, WEST (St Mary Magdalene) Conventional District *Lich 9* Min P J COPE
BROMWICH, WEST (St Paul) Golds Hill *Lich 9* P *V Tipton St Martin* P-in-c M C RUTTER, Par Dn S R EMTAGE
BROMWICH, WEST (St Peter) *Lich 9* P *Bp* P-in-c G D STARKEY
BROMWICH, WEST (St Philip) *Lich 9* P *Bp* V R C DESON
BROMYARD (St Peter) *Heref 2* P *Bp* V D W GOULD, C S W DEANE, NSM D H GOOD
BROMYARD DOWNS (Mission Church) Bromyard *Heref*
BRONDESBURY (Christ Church) (St Laurence) *Lon 21* P *Ld Chan* R S P H STUBBS
BRONDESBURY (St Anne) w Kilburn (Holy Trinity) *Lon 21* P *Bp and Ch Patr Soc (alt)* V G C BEAUCHAMP, NSM D NEW
BROOK (St Mary) Wye w Brook *Cant*
BROOKE (St Mary the Virgin) Brighstone and Brooke w Mottistone *Portsm*
BROOKE (St Peter) Oakham, Hambleton, Egleton, Braunston and Brooke *Pet*
BROOKE (St Peter), Kirstead, Mundham w Seething and Thwaite *Nor 11* P *G&C Coll Cam, Gt Hosp and Countess Ferrers, and Ld Chan (by turn)* R P E HALLS
BROOKE STREET (St Alban) Holborn St Alb w Saffron Hill St Pet *Lon*
BROOKEND (Mission Room) Sharpness w Purton and Brookend *Glouc*
BROOKFIELD (St Margaret) *York 22* P *Abp* V R W SMITH

BROOKFIELD (St Mary) *Lon 17* P *Bp* V C G POPE, C H S PENNINGTON
BROOKHURST (St Peter's Chapel) Eastham *Ches*
BROOKING (St Barnabas) Dartington *Ex*
BROOKLAND (St Augustine) Appledore w Brookland, Fairfield, Brenzett etc *Cant*
BROOKLANDS Baguley *Man*
BROOKMANS PARK (St Michael) N Mymms *St Alb*
BROOKSBY (St Michael and All Angels) Hoby cum Rotherby w Brooksby, Ragdale & Thru'ton *Leic*
BROOKSIDE (Pastoral Centre) Cen Telford *Lich*
BROOKTHORPE (St Swithun) The Edge, Pitchcombe, Harescombe and Brookthorpe *Glouc*
BROOKWOOD (St Saviour) Woking St Jo *Guildf*
BROOM (St Matthew) Bidford-on-Avon *Cov*
BROOM LEYS (St David) *Leic 8* P *Bp* V J B BARNES
BROOM VALLEY (St Barnabas) Rotherham *Sheff*
BROOME (St Michael) Ditchingham, Hedenham and Broome *Nor*
BROOME (St Peter) Churchill-in-Halfshire w Blakedown and Broome *Worc*
BROOMFIELD (St Margaret) Hollingbourne and Hucking w Leeds and Broomfield *Cant*
BROOMFIELD (St Mary and All Saints) Kingston St Mary w Broomfield etc *B & W*
BROOMFIELD (St Mary w St Leonard) *Chelmsf 11* P *Bp* P-in-c A W D RITSON
BROOMFLEET (St Mary) S Cave and Ellerker w Broomfleet *York*
BROSELEY (All Saints) w Benthall *Heref 14* P *Lord Forester* R W W LUCAS, NSM B J HARRISON
BROTHERTOFT Group, The (Christ Church) (St Gilbert of Sempringham) *Linc 21* P *Bp (2 turns), V Algarkirk (1 turn)* V J W THACKER, NSM D J CLARKE
BROTHERTON (St Edward the Confessor) *Wakef 11* P *D&C York* Dn--in-c M BAMFORD
BROTTON PARVA (St Margaret) *York 17* P *Abp* R E SMITS
BROUGH (All Saints) Elloughton and Brough w Brantingham *York*
BROUGH (St Michael) w Stainmore, Musgrave and Warcop *Carl 1* P *Bp (2 turns) and Lord Hothfield (1 turn)* R K S CAMPBELL
BROUGHAM (St Wilfrid Chapel) Clifton, Brougham and Cliburn *Carl*
BROUGHTON (All Saints) *Ely 11* P *Bp* P-in-c D J EVANS
BROUGHTON (All Saints), Marton and Thornton *Bradf 7* P *Ch Ch Ox and Exors of Dame Harriet Nelson (jt)* R *Vacant* Earby (0282) 842332
BROUGHTON (St Andrew) w Loddington and Cransley and Thorpe Malsor *Pet 11* P *Ld Chan (1 turn), Bp (2 turns), and Keble Coll Ox (1 turn)* R C HILTON
BROUGHTON (St John the Baptist) *Blackb 14* P *Trustees* V S J FINCH, NSM E AMBROSE
BROUGHTON (St John the Evangelist) *Man 6* P *Bp* P-in-c E W DIMOND, C J APPLEGATE
BROUGHTON (St Mary) *Lich 29* P *D R B Thompson Esq* V C P COLLIS SMITH
BROUGHTON (St Mary) *Linc 6* P *MMCET* R J B SHUCKSMITH
BROUGHTON (St Mary Magdalene) (Holy Innocents) and Duddon *Carl 8* P *V Millom, Lt-Col D A S Pennefather, and Ch Patr Trust (by turn)* V P F BARNES
BROUGHTON (St Mary the Virgin) w North Newington and Shutford, Wroxton w Balscote and Drayton *Ox 5* P *Lord Saye and Sele, New Coll Ox, and Bp (by turn)* R W I MEADS
BROUGHTON (St Mary) w Bossington and Houghton and Mottisfont *Win 11* P *Ld Chan (1 turn), E J M Dent Esq and Ms M Dent, A Humbert Esq and Miss R A Humbert (jt) (2 turns)* R F J G WYNNE
BROUGHTON (St Peter) Croxton w Broughton and Adbaston *Lich*
BROUGHTON, GREAT (Christ Church) and Broughton Moor *Carl 7* P *Bp* V E J M HOGAN
BROUGHTON, HIGHER (St James) *Man 6* P *Bp* R E W DIMOND, C J APPLEGATE, NSM S HORROCKS
BROUGHTON, LOWER (Ascension) *Man 6* P *Trustees* R P H MILLER, NSM W N PRICE
BROUGHTON, LOWER (St Clement w St Matthias) *Man 6* P *Trustees and CPAS (alt)* C J APPLEGATE
BROUGHTON, NETHER (St Mary the Virgin) Old Dalby and Nether Broughton *Leic*
BROUGHTON, UPPER (St Luke) Hickling w Kinoulton and Broughton Sulney *S'well*
BROUGHTON ASTLEY (St Mary) *Leic 10* P *Woodard Schs* R P BURROWS, C M D WEBB

BROUGHTON GIFFORD (St Mary the Virgin), Great Chalfield and Holt St Katharine *Sarum 17* **P** *D&C Bris (3 turns)*, *Ld Chan (2 turns)*, *and R C Floyd Esq (1 turn)* **R** P F B FISKE
BROUGHTON HACKETT (St Leonard) Upton Snodsbury and Broughton Hackett etc *Worc*
BROUGHTON IN FURNESS (St Mary Magdalene) Broughton and Duddon *Carl*
BROUGHTON MILLS (Holy Innocents) as above
BROUGHTON MOOR (St Columba) Gt Broughton and Broughton Moor *Carl*
BROUGHTON POGGS (St Peter) w Filkins, Broadwell w Kelmscot, Kencot, Langford and Little Faringdon *Ox 8* **P** *Bp, Ch Soc Trust, and F R Goodenough Esq (jt)* **V** W L GLAZEBROOK,
    C J WHITTAKER, D T CASSON, J J CRESSWELL
BROWN CANDOVER (St Peter) The Candover Valley *Win*
BROWN EDGE (St Anne) *Lich 14* **P** *Bp*
    V D J FAIRWEATHER
BROWNHILL (St Saviour) *Wakef 10* **P** *V Batley*
    V R ADAIR
BROWNSWOOD PARK (St John the Evangelist) *Lon 5* **P** *City Corp* **V** T G SUMMERS
BROXBOURNE (St Augustine) w Wormley *St Alb 6* **P** *Bp and Peache Trustees (jt)* **R** R A POTTER,
    C J R JAMES, J F MILBURN
BROXTED (St Mary the Virgin) w Chickney and Tilty and Great and Little Easton *Chelmsf 21* **P** *Mrs F Spurrier (2 turns)*, *DBP (1 turn)*, *and MMCET (1 turn)*
    R J M FILBY
BROXTOWE (St Martha) *S'well 14* **P** *Bp*
    V J S M HARDING,   **C** D B NEVILLE
BRUERA (St Mary) Aldford and Bruera *Ches*
BRUISYARD (St Peter) Badingham w Bruisyard, Cransford and Dennington *St E*
BRUMBY, OLD (St Hugh) *Linc 4* **P** *Bp*
    TR A G D HAYDAY, **TV** P M MULLINS, **C** D C PEACOCK
BRUNDALL (St Lawrence) w Braydeston and Postwick *Nor 1* **P** *Bp and MMCET (jt)* **R** R M BAKER,
    C M T BAILEY
BRUNDISH (St Lawrence) Wilby w Brundish *St E*
BRUNSTEAD (St Peter) Stalham and E Ruston w Brunstead *Nor*
BRUNSWICK (Christ Church) *Man 4* **P** *Ch Soc Trust*
    R M L GOODER
BRUNSWICK (St Cuthbert) Ch the King in the Dio of Newc *Newc*
BRUNTCLIFFE (St Andrew) *Wakef 8* **P** *V Batley and V St Peter Morley (alt)* **V** J VICKERMAN
BRUNTINGTHORPE (St Mary) Arnesby w Shearsby and Bruntingthorpe *Leic*
BRUNTON PARK (St Aidan) Ch the King in the Dio of Newc *Newc*
BRUSHFORD (St Mary the Virgin) *Ex 16* **P** *D&C*
    V P NIXSON
BRUSHFORD (St Nicholas) Dulverton and Brushford *B & W*
BRUTON (Blessed Virgin Mary) and District *B & W 2* **P** *Patr Bd* **TR** D J RICHARDS, **TV** A F NICHOLLS,
    Hon C D C BARKER
BRYANSTON SQUARE (St Mary) w St Marylebone (St Mark) *Lon 4* **P** *The Crown* **R** D EVANS,
    Hon Par Dn V D MAKIN
BRYHER (All Saints) Scilly Is *Truro*
BRYMPTON (St Andrew) *B & W 7* **P** *C E B Clive-Ponsby-Fane Esq* **R** *Vacant*
BRYN (St Chad) Clun w Bettws-y-Crwyn and Newc *Heref*
BRYN (St Peter) *Liv 15* **P** *Bp* **V** P MORRIS
BUBBENHALL (St Giles) Ryton on Dunsmore w Bubbenhall *Cov*
BUBWITH (All Saints) w Skipwith *York 4* **P** *Abp and D&C, and Ld Chan (alt)* **V** G E JOHNSON
BUCKDEN (St Mary) *Ely 12* **P** *Bp* **P-in-c** J S FRANCIS
BUCKENHAM, NEW (St Martin) Quidenham *Nor*
BUCKENHAM, OLD (All Saints) as above
BUCKERELL (St Mary and St Giles) Feniton, Buckerell and Escot *Ex*
BUCKFAST SANCTUARY (not known) Buckfastleigh w Dean Prior *Ex*
BUCKFASTLEIGH (Holy Trinity) (St Luke's Mission) w Dean Prior *Ex 13* **P** *D&C (2 turns)*, *DBP (1 turn)*
    NSM J N CIRWIN
BUCKHORN WESTON (St John the Baptist) Gillingham *Sarum*
BUCKHURST HILL (St Elisabeth) (St John the Baptist) (St Stephen) *Chelmsf 2* **P** *Bp* **TV** T J GLOW,
    P-in-c K P HALLETT, **C** G F KIMBER, **NSM** G M KIMBER

BUCKINGHAM (St Peter and St Paul) *Ox 22* **P** *Bp*
    V J W BELL, **Par Dn** P HARDY, **NSM** R M BUNDOCK
BUCKINGHAM, NORTH *Ox 22* **P** *Ch Soc Trust, Mrs J M Williams, and D J Robarts Esq (by turn)*
    R N A THORP
BUCKLAND (All Saints) Aston Clinton w Buckland and Drayton Beauchamp *Ox*
BUCKLAND (St Mary the Virgin) *Ox 17* **P** *DBP, Bp and Or Coll Ox (by turn)* **V** C R RUDD
BUCKLAND (St Mary the Virgin) *S'wark 24* **P** *All So Coll Ox* **P-in-c** J B GOULD
BUCKLAND (St Michael) Childswyckham w Aston Somerville, Buckland etc *Glouc*
BUCKLAND, EAST (St Michael) S Molton w Nymet St George, High Bray etc *Ex*
BUCKLAND, WEST (St Peter) Swimbridge and W Buckland *Ex*
BUCKLAND, WEST (Blessed Virgin Mary) Wellington and Distr *B & W*
BUCKLAND BREWER (St Mary and St Benedict) Parkham, Alwington, Buckland Brewer etc *Ex*
BUCKLAND DINHAM (St Michael and All Angels) Mells w Buckland Dinham, Elm, Whatley etc *B & W*
BUCKLAND FILLEIGH (St Mary and Holy Trinity) Shebbear, Buckland Filleigh, Sheepwash etc *Ex*
BUCKLAND IN DOVER (St Andrew) w Buckland Valley (St Nicholas) *Cant 4* **P** *Abp* **R** L G TYZACK,
    C G G GILL
BUCKLAND IN THE MOOR (St Peter) Ashburton w Buckland in the Moor and Bickington *Ex*
BUCKLAND MONACHORUM (St Andrew) *Ex 25* **P** *Bp*
    V G M COTTER, **NSM** R M PRESTON
BUCKLAND NEWTON (Holy Rood) Dungeon Hill *Sarum*
BUCKLAND RIPERS (St Nicholas) Bincombe w Broadwey, Upwey and Buckland Ripers *Sarum*
BUCKLAND ST MARY (Blessed Virgin Mary) Churchstanton, Buckland St Mary and Otterford *B & W*
BUCKLAND TOUT SAINTS (St Peter) Charleton w Buckland Tout Saints etc *Ex*
BUCKLAND VALLEY (St Nicholas) Buckland in Dover w Buckland Valley *Cant*
BUCKLEBURY (St Mary) w Marlston *Ox 14* **P** *C J Pratt Esq* **V** A D R HOLMES
BUCKLEBURY, UPPER (All Saints) Bucklebury w Marlston *Ox*
BUCKLERS HARD (St Mary) Beaulieu and Exbury and E Boldre *Win*
BUCKLESHAM (St Mary) Nacton and Levington w Bucklesham and Foxhall *St E*
BUCKMINSTER (St John the Baptist) Wymondham w Edmondthorpe, Buckminster etc *Leic*
BUCKNALL (St Margaret) w Tupholme *Linc 11* **P** *Bp*
    P-in-c R I McMASTER
BUCKNALL (St Mary the Virgin) and Bagnall *Lich 18* **P** *Patr Bd* **TR** B L WHITTAKER,
    TV N M LADD, B J NASH, B H G BRADLEY,
    Par Dn A de C LADD
BUCKNELL (St Mary) w Chapel Lawn, Llanfair Waterdine and Stowe *Heref 10* **P** *Earl of Powis, Grocers' Co, and J Coltman Rogers Esq (jt)*
    V D R P HAYES, **NSM** D W G VICKERS
BUCKNELL (St Peter) Bicester w Bucknell, Caversfield and Launton *Ox*
BUCKS MILLS (St Anne) Woolfardisworthy and Buck Mills *Ex*
BUCKWORTH (All Saints) *Ely 9* **P** *Bp* **R** J A COOMBE
BUDBROOKE (St Michael) *Cov 4* **P** *MMCET*
    V T J JOHNSON
BUDE HAVEN (St Michael and All Angels) and Marhamchurch *Truro 8* **P** *Bp and PCC (jt)*
    R A J VINCENT, **Hon C** A G B PARSONS,
    NSM D G ADAMS
BUDLEIGH, EAST (All Saints) and Bicton *Ex 1* **P** *Lord Clinton* **V** D O'L MARKHAM
BUDLEIGH SALTERTON (St Peter) *Ex 1* **P** *Lord Clinton* **NSM** M M CAMERON
BUDOCK (St Budock) *Truro 3* **P** *Bp* **V** J T R HAM
BUDWORTH, GREAT (St Mary and All Saints) and Antrobus *Ches 4* **P** *Ch Ch Ox* **V** G D MILLS
BUDWORTH, LITTLE (St Peter) Whitegate w Lt Budworth *Ches*
BUGBROOKE (St Michael and All Angels) *Pet 3* **P** *Exors E W Harrison Esq* **R** T R PARTRIDGE
BUGLAWTON (St John the Evangelist) *Ches 11* **P** *R Astbury* **V** J K MOWLL
BUGTHORPE (St Andrew) Bishop Wilton w Full Sutton, Kirby Underdale etc *York*

BUILDWAS (Holy Trinity) and Leighton w Eaton
Constantine and Wroxeter *Lich 30*　**P** *Bp*, *Lord
Barnard*, *and MMCET (jt)*　**R** T W B FOX
BULCOTE (Holy Trinity)　Burton Joyce w Bulcote
S'well
BULFORD (St Leonard), Figheldean and Milston *Sarum 12*
P *Bp (1 turn)*, *MOD (2 turns)*　**V** P D SLATER
BULKELEY (All Saints)　Bickerton w Bickley *Ches*
BULKINGTON (Christ Church)　Seend and Bulkington
Sarum
BULKINGTON (St James) w Shilton and Ansty *Cov 5*
P *Ld Chan*　**V** K ROBINSON
BULKWORTHY (St Michael)　Abbots Bickington and
Bulkworthy *Ex*
BULLEY (St Michael and All Angels)　Churcham w
Bulley and Minsterworth *Glouc*
BULLINGHOPE, UPPER (St Peter) and Lower w Grafton
Heref 3　**P** *Bp*　**V** T P JONES,　**TV** R NORTH
BULLINGTON (St Michael and All Angels)　Barton
Stacey and Bullington etc *Win*
BULMER (St Andrew)　Belchamp Otten w Belchamp
Walter and Bulmer *Chelmsf*
BULMER (St Martin) w Dalby, Terrington and Welburn
York 3　**P** *Abp and Hon S B G Howard (jt)*
R E T CHAPMAN
BULPHAN (St Mary the Virgin)　Orsett and Bulphan
Chelmsf
BULWELL (St John the Divine) *S'well 13*　**P** *Bp*
V J P FEWKES
BULWELL (St Mary the Virgin and All Souls) *S'well 13*
P *Bp*　**R** W S BEASLEY,　**C** D C WHITE,
Par Dn C M BROWNE
BULWICK (St Nicholas) and Blatherwycke w
Harringworth and Laxton *Pet 8*　**P** *G T G Conant Esq
(3 turns)*, *F & A George Ltd (1 turn)*　**R** M R A WILSON
BUNBURY (St Boniface) *Ches 5*　**P** *Haberdashers' Co*
V *Vacant*　Bunbury (0829) 260283
BUNCTON (All Saints)　Ashington w Buncton, Wiston
and Washington *Chich*
BUNGAY (Holy Trinity) w St Mary *St E 14*　**P** *DBP*
V S C MORRIS,　**C** G L CARTER,　**Par Dn** C P WRIGHT
BUNNY (St Mary the Virgin) w Bradmore *S'well 9*
P *Lady Shrigley-Ball*　**V** C E JONES
BUNWELL (St Michael and All Angels), Carleton Rode,
Tibenham, Great Moulton and Aslacton *Nor 11*　**P** *Bp
and DBP (alt)*　**R** S SWIFT
BURBAGE (All Saints)　Wexcombe *Sarum*
BURBAGE (Christ Church)　Buxton w Burbage and
King Sterndale *Derby*
BURBAGE (St Catherine) w Aston Flamville *Leic 13*
P *Ball Coll Ox*　**R** F D JENNINGS,　**C** A E MUMFORD
BURCOMBE (St John the Baptist)　Barford St Martin,
Dinton, Baverstock etc *Sarum*
BURES (St Mary the Virgin) *St E 12*　**P** *DBP*
V C D G PATTERSON
BURFORD 1st Portion *Heref 12*　**P** *DBP*, *Bp Birm*, *Bp*,
and Lady More (jt)　**R** D S DORMOR
BURFORD 2nd Portion (St Mary) w Greete and Hope
Bagot *Heref 12*　**P** *DBP*　**TV** G P HOWELL
BURFORD 3rd Portion (St Mary) w Little Hereford
Heref 12　**P** *DBP and Bp Birm (jt)*　**TV** G P HOWELL
BURFORD (St John the Baptist)　Fulbrook and Taynton
Ox 8　**P** *Bp*　**V** M B TINGLE,　**Par Dn** M E FRAMPTON,
Hon C C R TADMAN-ROBINS
BURGATE (St Mary)　N Hartismere *St E*
BURGESS HILL (St Andrew) *Chich 9*　**P** *Bp*
V C A FTSPRAY
BURGESS HILL (St John the Evangelist) (St Edward)
Chich 9　**P** *R Clayton w Keymer*　**V** R A JUPP,
C T G BUXTON
BURGH (St Botolph)　Boulge w Burgh and
Grundisburgh *St E*
BURGH (St Margaret and St Mary)　Rollesby w Burgh w
Billockby w Ashby w Oby etc *Nor*
BURGH (St Peter)　Raveningham *Nor*
BURGH-BY-SANDS (St Michael) and Kirkbampton w
Kirkandrews on Eden, Beaumont and Grinsdale *Carl 3*
P *DBP and Earl of Lonsdale (jt)*　**R** D R KING
BURGH CASTLE (St Peter and St Paul)　Belton and
Burgh Castle *Nor*
BURGH HEATH (St Mary the Virgin)　Tattenham
Corner w Burgh Heath *Guildf*
BURGH LE MARSH (St Peter and St Paul) *Linc 8*　**P** *Bp*
V B K NEWTON
BURGH NEXT AYLSHAM (St Mary the Virgin) *Nor 2*
P *J M Roberts Esq*　**R** *Vacant*
BURGH-ON-BAIN (St Helen)　Asterby Gp *Linc*
BURGH PARVA (St Mary) w Briston *Nor 22*　**P** *Bp*
R H J BLACKER

BURGHCLERE (Ascension) (All Saints) w Newtown and
Ecchinswell w Sydmonton *Win 6*　**P** *Earl of Carnarvon*
R M W GARNER
BURGHFIELD (St Mary the Virgin) *Ox 12*　**P** *Earl of
Shrewsbury*　**R** A B GRUNDY
BURGHILL (St Mary the Virgin) *Heref 4*　**P** *DBP*
P-in-c M A KELK
BURGHWALLIS (St Helen) w Skelbrooke *Sheff 8*
P *Mrs E H I Donovan-Anne (2 turns)*, *Bp (1 turn)*
P-in-c A D LENNON
BURHAM (Methodist Church) and Wouldham *Roch 5*
P *Bp and Ld Chan (alt)*　**R** W S AITKEN
BURITON (St Mary the Virgin) *Portsm 5*　**P** *Bp*
R C LOWSON
BURLESCOMBE (St Mary)　Sampford Peverell,
Uplowman, Holcombe Rogus etc *Ex*
BURLEY (St Matthias) *Ripon 7*　**P** *G M Bedford Esq*,
J C Yeadon Esq, *E Beety Esq*, *Mrs M E Dunham*, *and
Mrs L M Rawse (jt)*　**V** M J WINBOLT LEWIS,
C D B WILLIAMSON
BURLEY IN WHARFEDALE (St Mary the Virgin) *Bradf 4*
P *Bp*　**V** J H TIDY,　**Par Dn** E M McLEAN
BURLEY VILLE (St John the Baptist) *Win 8*
P *V Ringwood*　**V** A G CLARKSON,
Par Dn M A BARTON
BURLEYDAM (St Mary and St Michael)　Baddiley and
Wrenbury w Burleydam *Ches*
BURLINGHAM (St Andrew)　Acle w Fishley and N
Burlingham *Nor*
BURLINGHAM (St Edmund) w Lingwood, Strumpshaw w
Hassingham and Buckenham *Nor 1*　**P** *Ch Soc Trust*,
MMCET, *and Bp (jt)*　**R** I T R WELCH
BURLTON (St Anne)　Loppington w Newtown *Lich*
BURMANTOFTS (St Stephen and St Agnes) *Ripon 5*
P *Ch Trust Fund Trust*　**V** J C BURCH
BURMARSH (All Saints)　Dymchurch w Burmarsh and
Newchurch *Cant*
BURMINGTON (St Nicholas and St Barnabas)　Wolford
w Burmington *Cov*
BURNAGE (St Margaret) *Man 3*　**P** *Bp*　**R** A PUGMIRE,
C I BROWN
BURNAGE (St Nicholas) *Man 8*　**P** *Trustees*
R T S R CHOW,　**Hon Par Dn** A C ASHCROFT
BURNBY (St Giles) *York 7*　**P** *Trustees*　**R** K G SKIPPER
BURNESIDE (St Oswald) *Carl 9*　**P** *J A Cropper Esq*,
Mrs B Snowdon and Mrs E Bingham (jt)　**V** N L DAVIES,
Hon Par Dn J L TYRER
BURNESTON (St Lambert)　Kirklington w Burneston
and Wath and Pickhill *Ripon*
BURNETT (St Michael)　Keynsham *B & W*
BURNEY LANE (Christ Church) *Birm 10*　**P** *Bp*
V P H LAWRENCE
BURNHAM (St Andrew) *B & W 1*　**P** *D&C*　**V** R C DEAN
BURNHAM (St Mary the Virgin) *Chelmsf 13*
P *N D Beckett Esq and Walsingham Coll Trust (jt)*
V R J WEBB
BURNHAM (St Peter) w Dropmore, Hitcham and Taplow
Ox 23　**P** *Patr Bd*　**TR** S N D BROWN,
TV A C DIBDEN,　P D DERBYSHIRE,　**Par Dn** S HAYTER
BURNHAM DEEPDALE (St Mary)　Brancaster w
Burnham Deepdale and Titchwell *Nor*
BURNHAM NORTON (St Margaret)　Burnham Gp of
Par *Nor*
BURNHAM-ON-CROUCH (St Mary the Virgin)
Burnham *Chelmsf*
BURNHAM-ON-SEA (St Andrew)　as above
BURNHAM OVERY (St Clement)　Burnham Gp of Par
Nor
BURNHAM THORPE (All Saints)　as above
BURNHAM ULPH (All Saints)　as above
BURNHAM WESTGATE (St Mary), Burnham Norton,
Burnham Overy, Burnham Thorpe, and Burnham
Sutton w Ulph (The Burnham Group of Parishes) *Nor 20*
P *Ch Coll Cam (1 turn)*, *Ld Chan (2 turns)*, *and DBP
(1 turn)*　**R** A D PARSONS
BURNLEY Habergham Eaves (St Matthew the Apostle)
(Holy Trinity) *Blackb 3*　**P** *R Burnley*
V R McCULLOUGH,　**C** S M AIKEN
BURNLEY (St Andrew) w St Margaret *Blackb 3*
P *R Burnley*　**V** B ROBINSON,　**Hon C** B TONGE
BURNLEY (St Catherine) (St Alban and St Paul) *Blackb 3*
P *R Burnley*　**V** R WILLIAMS,　**C** A C HUTCHINSON,
NSM H DICKINSON
BURNLEY (St Cuthbert) *Blackb 3*　**P** *R Burnley*
V H LEE
BURNLEY (St James) *Blackb 3*　**P** *The Crown*
V J K RUSSON
BURNLEY (St Mark) *Blackb 3*　**P** *Bp*　**V** A C TAYLOR
BURNLEY (St Peter) *Blackb 3*　**P** *Bp*　**R** D F TOWERS

BURNLEY (St Stephen) *Blackb 3*   **P**   *R Burnley*
  V   H PUGH
BURNLEY, WEST (All Saints w St John the Baptist)
Blackb 3   **P**   *Bp and V Burnley St Pet (jt)*
  V   J HODGSON,   **C**   L ADAM,   M J HAMPSON
BURNMOOR (St Barnabas) *Dur 6*   **P**   *Lord Lambton*
  R   M G BISHOP
BURNOPFIELD (St James) *Dur 8*   **P**   *Bp*
  V   P D SADDINGTON
BURNSALL (St Wilfrid) w Rylstone *Bradf 7*   **P**   *Exors*
Earl of Craven and CPAS (jt)   **R**   *Vacant Burnsall*
(075672) 238
BURNT YATES (St Andrew) *Ripley Ripon*
BURNTWOOD (Christ Church) *Lich 2*   **P**   *D&C*
  P-in-c   D A WEAVER,   **C**   D C BLISS
BURPHAM (St Luke) Guildford *Guildf 5*   **P**   *Bp*
  V   D J WILLIAMS
BURPHAM (St Mary the Virgin) *Chich 1*   **P**   *D&C*
  P-in-c   E R GILLIES
BURRADON (Good Shepherd) *Weetslade Newc*
BURRILL (Mission Church) *Bedale Ripon*
BURRINGTON (Holy Trinity) *Ex 16*   **P**   *DBP*
  V   V GILLETT
BURRINGTON (Holy Trinity) and Churchill *B & W 12*
  P   *D&C Bris and Burrington PCC (jt)*   **V**   J C ABDY
BURRINGTON (St George) *Wigmore Abbey Heref*
BURROUGH GREEN (St Augustine of Canterbury)
Brinkley, Burrough Green and Carlton Ely
BURROUGH HILL PARISHES, The: Burrough on the
Hill, Great Dalby, Little Dalby, Pickwell and Somerby
Leic 3   **P**   *Bp, DBP, and F R D Burdett Fisher Esq (jt)*
  V   J WARDLE-HARPUR
BURROUGH ON THE HILL (St Mary the Virgin)
see above
BURROWBRIDGE (St Michael) *Stoke St Gregory w*
Burrowbridge and Lyng B & W
BURRSVILLE (St Mark) *Gt Clacton Chelmsf*
BURSCOUGH BRIDGE (St John) (St Andrew)
(St Cyprian) *Liv 11*   **P**   *V Ormskirk*   **V**   B ROBINSON,
Par Dn   A R WOODHOUSE
BURSDON MOOR (St Martin) *Hartland and*
Welcombe Ex
BURSEA (Chapel) *Holme-on-Spalding Moor York*
BURSLEDON Pilands Wood (St Paul) *Bursledon Win*
BURSLEDON (St Leonard) *Win 9*   **P**   *Bp*
  V   J D ALDERMAN,   **C**   V G WILKINS
BURSLEM (St John the Baptist) (St Paul) *Lich 17*   **P**   *Bp*
and MMCET (jt)   **R**   C R JOHNSON,   **C**   C W J STYLES
BURSLEM (St Werburgh) *Lich 17*   **P**   *Bp*   **V**   D J MELLOR
BURSTALL (St Mary the Virgin) *Sproughton w Burstall*
St E
BURSTEAD, GREAT (St Mary Magdalene) *Chelmsf 9*
  P   *Bp*   **V**   P D ELVY
BURSTEAD, LITTLE (St Mary) *Billericay and Lt*
Burstead Chelmsf
BURSTOCK (St Andrew) *Beaminster Area Sarum*
BURSTON (St Mary) *Winfarthing w Shelfanger w*
Burston w Gissing etc Nor
BURSTON (St Rufin) *Salt and Sandon w Burston Lich*
BURSTOW (St Bartholomew) *S'wark 24*   **P**   *Ld Chan*
  R   G B TALBOT,   **Hon C**   K W RAMSAY
BURSTWICK (All Saints) w Thorngumbald *York 13*
  P   *Abp*   **V**   F W R LA TOUCHE
BURTLE (St Philip and St James) *Shapwick w Ashcott*
and Burtle B & W
BURTON (All Saints) w Christ Church *Lich 20*   **P**   *CPAS*
and Ch Soc Trust (jt)   **V**   J G BLACKETT
BURTON (St James) and Holme *Carl 9*   **P**   *Simeon's*
Trustees   **V**   J J C NODDER,   **C**   S I WRIGHT
BURTON (St Luke) and Sopley *Win 8*   **P**   *Bp and D&C*
Cant (alt)   **V**   A SESSFORD
BURTON (St Nicholas) and Shotwick *Ches 9*   **P**   *D&C*
(1 turn) and St Jo Hosp Lichf (2 turns)   **V**   H J ALDRIDGE
BURTON w COATES (St Agatha) *Barlavington,*
Burton w Coates, Sutton and Bignor Chich
BURTON AGNES (St Martin) w Harpham and Lowthorpe
w Ruston Parva *York 11*   **P**   *Ld Chan (2 turns),*
C T Legard Esq (1 turn)   **R**   D S HAWKINS
BURTON BRADSTOCK (St Mary) *Bride Valley Sarum*
BURTON BY LINCOLN (St Vincent) *Linc 2*   **P**   *Lord*
Monson   **P-in-c**   E R COOK
BURTON COGGLES (St Thomas a Becket) *Ingoldsby*
Linc
BURTON DASSETT (All Saints) *Cov 8*   **P**   *Bp*
  V   P T FRANCIS
BURTON FLEMING (St Cuthbert) w Fordon, Grindale
and Wold Newton *York 10*   **P**   *Abp and MMCET (jt)*
  P-in-c   J R BROADHURST

BURTON GREEN (Chapel of Ease) *Kenilworth St Nic*
Cov
BURTON HASTINGS (St Botolph) *Wolvey w Burton*
Hastings, Copston Magna etc Cov
BURTON IN LONSDALE (All Saints) *Thornton in*
Lonsdale w Burton in Lonsdale Bradf
BURTON JOYCE (St Helen) w Bulcote *S'well 11*
  P   *MMCET*   **V**   A GRAHAM
BURTON LATIMER (St Mary the Virgin) *Pet 11*   **P**   *Bp*
  R   *Vacant Burton Latimer (0536) 722098*
BURTON LAZARS (St James) *Melton Gt Framland*
Leic
BURTON LEONARD (St Leonard) *Bishop Monkton*
and Burton Leonard Ripon
BURTON-ON-TRENT (All Saints) *Burton All SS w Ch*
Ch Lich
BURTON-ON-TRENT (St Aidan) *Shobnall Lich*
BURTON-ON-TRENT (St Chad) *Lich 20*   **P**   *Bp*
  V   *Vacant Burton-on-Trent (0283) 64044*
BURTON-ON-TRENT (St Modwen) (St Paul) *Lich 20*
  P   *Bp and Lord Burton (jt)*   **V**   D M MORRIS,
  Res Min   D E H MOLE,   **Hon Par Dn**   V R MORRIS
BURTON OVERY (St Andrew) *Gaulby Leic*
BURTON PEDWARDINE (St Andrew and the Blessed
Virgin Mary and St Nicholas) *Heckington Linc*
BURTON PIDSEA (St Peter) and Humbleton w
Elsternwick *York 13*   **P**   *Ld Chan and D&C (alt)*
  V   *Vacant Withernsea (0964) 670896*
BURTON UPON STATHER (St Andrew) *Flixborough*
w Burton upon Stather Linc
BURTONWOOD (St Michael) *Liv 16*   **P**   *R Warrington*
  V   R S NAYLOR,   **Hon C**   F H BOARDMAN
BURWARDSLEY (St John) *Harthill and Burwardsley*
Ches
BURWASH (St Bartholomew) *Chich 14*   **P**   *BNC Ox*
  R   R P B DURRANT
BURWASH WEALD (St Philip) *Chich 15*   **P**   *Bp*
  P-in-c   M J L AUSTIN
BURWELL (St Andrew) (St Mary) *Ely 3*   **P**   *DBP*
  V   I R SECRETT,   **C**   N K YOUNG
BURY (Christ the King) (Holy Trinity) *Man 10*   **P**   *Patr Bd*
  TR   J K McCOLLOUGH,   **TV**   J ARCUS
BURY (Holy Cross) *Ely 11*   **P**   *Bp*   **P-in-c**   S O LEEKE
BURY (St John the Evangelist) and Houghton *Chich 11*
  P   *Pemb Coll Ox*   **P-in-c**   B A CRADDOCK
BURY (St John w St Mark) *Man 10*   **P**   *R Bury St Mary*
  V   J B KELLY
BURY (St Mary the Virgin) *Man 10*   **P**   *Earl of Derby*
  R   J R SMITH
BURY (St Paul) *Man 10*   **P**   *Trustees*   **V**   A BORSLEY
BURY (St Peter) *Man 10*   **P**   *R Bury St Mary*
  V   G G ROXBY,   **C**   D A AKKER,   **NSM**   J M SMITH
BURY, NEW (St James) *Man 12*   **P**   *Bp*   **TR**   P T KERR,
  TV   P J BARNETT,   **Par Dn**   J KERR
BURY ST EDMUNDS (All Saints) *St E 13*   **P**   *Bp*
  V   D S HILL
BURY ST EDMUNDS (St George) *St E 13*   **P**   *Bp*
  V   D W HERRICK,   **C**   G J WEBB
BURY ST EDMUNDS (St John the Evangelist) *St E 13*
  P   *Bp*   **V**   S PETTITT
BURY ST EDMUNDS (St Mary) (St Peter's District
Church) *St E 13*   **P**   *Hyndman Trustees*
  V   M J WALKER,   **C**   I D TWEEDIE-SMITH
BURYTHORPE (All Saints), Acklam and Leavening w
Westow *York 2*   **P**   *Abp*   **P-in-c**   G B NEWTON,
  C   T J ROBINSON
BUSBRIDGE (St John the Baptist) *Guildf 4*   **P**   *DBP*
  R   P J PARTINGTON,   **C**   J C MILLS
BUSCOT (St Mary) *Gt Coxwell w Buscot, Coleshill &*
Eaton Hastings Ox
BUSH END (St John the Evangelist) *Hatf Broad Oak*
and Bush End Chelmsf
BUSH HILL PARK (St Mark) *Lon 18*   **P**   *Bp*
  V   D G BROOKER
BUSH HILL PARK (St Stephen) *Lon 18*   **P**   *V Edmonton*
All SS   **V**   R J ANNIS
BUSHBURY (St Mary) *Lich 10*   **P**   *Patr Bd*
  TR   R A HINTON,   **TV**   N R HOGG,   P I DENNISON,
  C   K A L DENNIS,   M R CLEVELAND
BUSHEY (Holy Trinity) (St James) (St Paul) *St Alb 1*
  P   *Bp*   **R**   P B MORGAN,   **C**   R A FLETCHER,
  Par Dn   V E RAYMER,   **NSM**   R J ROBY
BUSHEY HEATH (St Peter) *St Alb 1*   **P**   *Bp*   **V**   W R LOW,
  NSM   J R BELITHER
BUSHLEY (St Peter) *Longdon, Castlemorton, Bushley,*
Queenhill etc Worc
BUSSAGE (St Michael and All Angels) *Glouc 1*   **P**   *Bp*
  V   H J VAN DER LINDE

BUTCOMBE (St Michael and All Angels) Wrington w
Butcombe *B & W*
BUTLEIGH (St Leonard) Baltonsborough w Butleigh
and W Bradley *B & W*
**BUTLERS MARSTON (St Peter and St Paul) and the
Pillertons w Ettington** *Cov 9* **P** *Ch Ch Ox (1 turn), Bp,
Major & Mrs J E Shirley, and Miss M L P Shirley (jt)
(1 turn), and Mr & Mrs G Howell (1 turn)* **V** D CHING
BUTLEY (St John the Baptist) Orford w Sudbourne,
Chillesford, Butley and Iken *St E*
BUTTERCRAMBE (St John the Evangelist) Sand
Hutton *York*
BUTTERLEIGH (St Matthew) *Ex 4* **P** *Bp* **R** M G SMITH
BUTTERMERE (St James) Lorton and Loweswater w
Buttermere *Carl*
BUTTERMERE (St James the Great) Wexcombe
Sarum
BUTTERSHAW (St Aidan) (Horton Bank Top) *Bradf 2*
P *Bp* **P-in-c** D PEEL
BUTTERSHAW (St Paul) *Bradf 2* **P** *Bp* **V** M COWGILL
BUTTERTON (St Bartholomew) Alstonfield,
Butterton, Warslow w Elkstone etc *Lich*
BUTTERTON (St Thomas) Newc w Butterton *Lich*
BUTTERWICK (Mission Chapel) Street Team Min
York
BUTTERWICK (St Andrew) Freiston w Butterwick
Linc
BUTTERWICK (St Nicholas) Langtoft w Foxholes,
Butterwick, Cottam etc *York*
BUTTERWICK, EAST (St Andrew) Messingham *Linc*
BUTTERWICK, WEST (St Mary) *Linc 1* **P** *V Owston*
V A J RHODES
BUTTSBURY (St Mary) Ingatestone w Buttsbury
Chelmsf
BUXHALL (St Mary) w Shelland *St E 6* **P** *Bp*
P-in-c C N KENDALL
**BUXTED (St Margaret the Queen) (St Mary) and Hadlow
Down** *Chich 21* **P** *Abp, Bp, and Wagner Trustees (jt)*
R *Vacant* Buxted (082581) 3103
BUXTON (St Andrew) w Oxnead, Lammas and Brampton
Nor 3 **P** *Bp* **R** G R DRAKE
**BUXTON (St Anne) (St John the Baptist) (St Mary the
Virgin) w Burbage and King Sterndale** *Derby 4*
P *Patr Bd* **TR** J C TOMLINSON,
TV M J LEWIS, L N CHILDS, **Par Dn** E D PACKHAM
BUXTON (Trinity Chapel) Proprietary Chapel *Derby 4*
Min J B WOOLDRIDGE
BUXWORTH (St James) Chinley w Buxworth *Derby*
BYERS GREEN (St Peter) *Dur 10* **P** *Bp*
P-in-c A L BELL
BYFIELD (Holy Cross) w Boddington *Pet 1* **P** *Em Coll
Cam, CCC Ox, and Bp (by turn)* **R** J N JOHNSON
BYFLEET (St Mary) *Guildf 12* **P** *Ld Chan*
R J V M KIRKBY, **C** D J ADAMS
BYFLEET, WEST (St John) *Guildf 12* **P** *Bp*
V L S SMITH
BYFORD (St John the Baptist) Letton w Staunton,
Byford, Mansel Gamage etc *Heref*
BYGRAVE (St Margaret of Antioch) Baldock w
Bygrave *St Alb*
BYKER (St Anthony) *Newc 6* **P** *Bp* **V** D C MUMFORD
BYKER (St Mark) *Newc 6* **P** *Ch Trust Fund Trust*
P-in-c K MOULDER
BYKER (St Martin) Newcastle upon Tyne *Newc 6* **P** *Bp*
V M J SMEATON
BYKER (St Michael w St Lawrence) *Newc 6* **P** *Bp*
V A P DAVIES
BYKER (St Silas) *Newc 6* **P** *Bp* **P-in-c** I G FALCONER
BYLAND, OLD (All Saints) Upper Ryedale *York*
BYLAUGH (St Mary) Lyng, Sparham, Elsing and
Bylaugh *Nor*
BYLEY CUM LEES (St John the Evangelist)
Middlewich w Byley *Ches*
BYRNESS (St Francis) Bellingham/Otterburn Gp *Newc*
BYTHAM, LITTLE (St Medardus) *Linc 14* **P** *Bp and
D&C (alt)* **R** *Vacant*
BYTHORN (St Lawrence) Keyston and Bythorn *Ely*
BYTON (St Mary) Pembridge w Moorcourt, Shobdon,
Staunton etc *Heref*
BYWELL (St Peter) *Newc 3* **P** *Adn Northd*
V T EMMETT, **NSM** M SLACK
BYWORTH (St Francis) Farnham *Guildf*
CABOURN (St Nicholas) Swallow *Linc*
CADBURY (St Michael and All Angels) Thorverton,
Cadbury, Upton Pyne etc *Ex*
CADBURY, NORTH (St Michael the Archangel)
Camelot Par *B & W*
CADBURY, SOUTH (St Thomas a Becket) as above

CADDINGTON (All Saints) *St Alb 20* **P** *D&C St Paul's*
V A J D SMITH
CADEBY (All Saints) Market Bosworth, Cadeby w
Sutton Cheney etc *Leic*
CADELEIGH (St Bartholomew) Washfield, Stoodleigh,
Withleigh etc *Ex*
CADGWITH (St Mary) St Ruan w St Grade and
Landewednack *Truro*
CADISHEAD (St Mary the Virgin) *Man 2* **P** *Bp*
V D RIDLEY, **Par Dn** L RIDLEY
CADMORE END (St Mary le Moor) Lane End w
Cadmore End *Ox*
CADNEY (All Saints) *Linc 6* **P** *Bp* **V** R J G PARKER
CADOGAN SQUARE (St Simon Zelotes) Upper
Chelsea St Simon *Lon*
CAERHAYS (St Michael) St Goran w St Mich Caerhays
Truro
CAGE GREEN (Church Hall) Tonbridge SS Pet and
Paul *Roch*
CAINSCROSS (St Matthew) w Selsley *Glouc 8* **P** *Bp and
Sir Charles Marling, Bt (alt)* **V** G G C MINORS,
C M J CAIN
**CAISTER NEXT YARMOUTH (Holy Trinity) (St
Edmund)** *Nor 2* **P** *SMF* **R** E A N SMITH
CAISTOR (St Edmund) w Markshall *Nor 14*
P *Mrs D Pott* **R** G F WALKER
CAISTOR (St Peter and St Paul) w Clixby *Linc 5* **P** *Bp*
V D J DAVIS
CALBOURNE (All Saints) w Newtown *Portsm 8* **P** *Bp*
V J F R RYALL
CALCOT (St Birinus) *Ox 15* **P** *Magd Coll Ox*
V A D BARNES, **C** H A N PLATTS
**CALDBECK (St Mungo) (Fellside), Castle Sowerby and
Sebergham** *Carl 3* **P** *Bp and D&C (alt)* **R** C G REID
CALDECOTE (All Saints) *St Alb 17* **P** *Grocers' Co*
V *Vacant* Biggleswade (0767) 315578
CALDECOTE (St John the Evangelist) Gretton w
Rockingham and Caldecote *Pet*
CALDECOTE (St Michael and All Angels) Toft w
Caldecote and Childerley *Ely*
CALDECOTE (St Theobald and St Chad) Weddington
and Caldecote *Cov*
CALDER GROVE (St John the Divine) Chapelthorpe
Wakef
CALDER VALE (Mission) Barnacre w Calder Vale
Blackb
CALDER VALE (St John the Evangelist) as above
CALDERBROOK (St James the Great) *Man 19* **P** *Bp*
P-in-c C D DOUGLAS
CALDMORE (St Michael and All Angels) *Lich 7* **P** *Bp*
P-in-c N A MPUNZI, **Par Dn** K M SOMERVELL
CALDWELL (Chapel) Forcett and Aldbrough and
Melsonby *Ripon*
CALDWELL (St Giles) Stapenhill w Cauldwell *Derby*
CALDY (Church of the Resurrection and All Saints)
W Kirby St Bridget *Ches*
CALEDONIAN ROAD (All Saints Hall) Barnsbury
Lon
CALIFORNIA (St Mary and St John) *Ox 16* **P** *DBP*
V K G HUMPHREYS
CALLINGTON (St Mary) S Hill w Callington *Truro*
CALLOW (St Mary) Dewsall w Callow *Heref*
CALLOW END (St James) Powyke w Guarlford *Worc*
CALMORE (St Anne) Totton *Win*
CALNE (Holy Trinity) (St Mary the Virgin) and Blackland
Sarum 18 **P** *Bp* **V** A G WOODS, **C** R P LODGE
CALOW (St Peter) and Sutton cum Duckmanton *Derby 3*
P *Bp and V Chesterfield (jt)* **R** N V JOHNSON
CALSHOT (St George) Fawley *Win*
CALSTOCK (St Andrew) *Truro 11* **P** *Duchy of Cornwall*
R G W RUMING
CALSTONE WELLINGTON (St Mary the Virgin)
Oldbury *Sarum*
CALTHORPE (Our Lady w St Margaret) Erpingham w
Calthorpe, Ingworth, Aldborough etc *Nor*
CALTHWAITE (All Saints) Hesket-in-the-Forest and
Armathwaite *Carl*
**CALTON (St Mary the Virgin), Cauldon, Grindon and
Waterfall** *Lich 11* **P** *Bp* **R** J R TYE
CALVELEY CHURCH (not known) Bunbury *Ches*
CALVERHALL or CORRA (Holy Trinity) Ightfield w
Calverhall *Lich*
CALVERLEIGH (St Mary the Virgin) Washfield,
Stoodleigh, Withleigh etc *Ex*
CALVERLEY (St Wilfrid) *Bradf 3* **P** *Bp*
V D SUTCLIFFE, **Par Dn** V G UTTLEY,
NSM D B MUMFORD
CALVERTON (All Saints) *Ox 25* **P** *DBP*
R C H J CAVELL-NORTHAM

CALVERTON (St Wilfrid) *S'well 15*   **P** *Bp*
  V R CATCHPOLE

CAM (St George) w Stinchcombe *Glouc 2*   **P** *Bp*
  V C M MALKINSON

CAM, LOWER (St Bartholomew) w Coaley *Glouc 2*
  P *Bp*   **V** I A ROBB

CAMBER (St Thomas)   Rye *Chich*

CAMBERLEY (St Martin)   York Town *Guildf*

CAMBERLEY (St Michael)   as above

CAMBERLEY (St Paul) (St Mary) *Guildf 6*   **P** *Bp*
  TR R S CROSSLEY,   **TV** A R HOWE,   J H G CARTER,
  C C SIMONS

CAMBERLEY HEATHERSIDE (Community Centre)
  Camberley St Paul *Guildf*

CAMBERWELL (All Saints) Blenheim Grove *S'wark 6*
  P *Ch Trust Fund Trust*   **V** 071-639 3052

CAMBERWELL (Christ Church) *S'wark 6*   **P** *Trustees*
  V H R BALFOUR

CAMBERWELL (St George) *S'wark 6*   **P** *Bp and*
  Trin Coll Cam (jt)   **V** S J ROBERTS,   **C** C D HARRISON,
  Hon C J E PAWSEY

CAMBERWELL (St Giles) (St Matthew) *S'wark 6*   **P** *Bp*
  V R W G BOMFORD,   **C** R DANIELL, A C BECK,
  Hon C S D HAINES

CAMBERWELL (St Luke) *S'wark 6*   **P** *Bp*
  V A P DAVEY,   **Par Dn** H H NESBITT

CAMBERWELL (St Matthew)   Herne Hill *S'wark*

CAMBERWELL (St Michael and All Angels w All Souls w
  Emmanuel) *S'wark 8*   **P** *DBP*   **P-in-c** M A HART,
  Hon C B H MOAKES, P SMITH

CAMBERWELL (St Philip) and St Mark *S'wark 5*   **P** *The*
  Crown   **V** J D JELLEY

CAMBO (Holy Trinity)   Kirkwhelpington, Kirkharle,
  Kirkheaton and Cambo *Newc*

CAMBOIS (St Peter) (St Andrew's Mission Church)
  Newc 1   **P** *D&C*   **NSM** J SMITH

CAMBORNE (St Martin and St Meriadoc) *Truro 2*
  P *Ch Soc Trust*   **R** N J POCOCK,
  Hon C G E BOTTOMLEY, **Dss** P A JENKS

CAMBRIDGE Ascension (St Giles) (St Luke the Evangelist)
  (St Augustine of Canterbury) (All Souls Chapel) *Ely 2*
  P *Bp*   **TR** J P YOUNG,   **TV** F B H WOOLLEY,
  C C A SINDALL,   **NSM** O R SPENCER-THOMAS

CAMBRIDGE (Holy Sepulchre) w All Saints *Ely 2*
  P *PCC*   **V** M H ASHTON,   **C** G R WALTER

CAMBRIDGE (Holy Trinity) w St Andrew the Great *Ely 2*
  P *D&C and Peache Trustees (jt)*   **V** D HUMPHRIES,
  C A L HARGRAVE,   **Par Dn** P M HOYLE,
  Hon C G G AKURU

CAMBRIDGE (St Andrew the Less) (Christ Church) *Ely 2*
  P *Ch Trust Fund Trust*   **V** M L DIAMOND

CAMBRIDGE (St Barnabas) *Ely 2*   **P** *V Cam St Paul*
  C M S BECKETT,   **Hon Par Dn** J E KEILLER

CAMBRIDGE (St Benedict) *Ely 2*   **P** *CCC Cam*
  V T A DE HOOP

CAMBRIDGE (St Botolph) *Ely 2*   **P** *Qu Coll Cam*
  NSM W HORBURY

CAMBRIDGE (St Clement) *Ely 2*   **P** *Jes Coll Cam*
  V *Vacant*

CAMBRIDGE St Edward Proprietary Chapel *Ely 2 Vacant*

CAMBRIDGE (St James) *Ely 2*   **P** *Bp*   **V** H W DAWES

CAMBRIDGE (St John the Evangelist)   Cherry Hinton
  St Jo *Ely*

CAMBRIDGE (St Mark) *Ely 2*   **P** *DBP*   **V** P A SPENCE

CAMBRIDGE (St Martin) (St Thomas) *Ely 2*   **P** *V Cam*
  St Paul   **V** S D ARMSTRONG,   **C** R A D STURT

CAMBRIDGE (St Mary the Great) w St Michael *Ely 2*
  P *Trin Coll Cam*   **V** D J CONNER,
  C M J A BARR, D L GOSLING, **Hon C** A S HOPKINSON,
  NSM B SNELL

CAMBRIDGE (St Mary the Less) *Ely 2*   **P** *Peterho Cam*
  V J OWEN,   **Hon C** A K BERGQUIST,
  NSM N J HANCOCK

CAMBRIDGE (St Matthew) *Ely 2*   **P** *V Cam St Andr the*
  Less   **P-in-c** E P J FOSTER

CAMBRIDGE (St Paul) *Ely 2*   **P** *Ch Trust Fund Trust*
  V M R W FARRER

CAMBRIDGE (St Philip) (St Stephen) *Ely 2*   **P** *Ch Trust*
  Fund Trust   **V** *Vacant*   Cambridge (0223) 247652

CAMDEN SQUARE (St Paul) *Lon 17*   **P** *D&C St Paul's*
  V P DYSON

CAMDEN TOWN (St Michael) (All Saints and St Thomas)
  Lon 17   **P** *D&C St Paul's*   **V** A R B PAGE

CAMEL, WEST (All Saints)   Queen Camel w W Camel,
  Corton Denham etc *B & W*

CAMELFORD (St Julitta)   Lanteglos by Camelford w
  Advent *Truro*

CAMELFORD (St Thomas of Canterbury)   as above

CAMELOT Parishes, The *B & W 3*   **P** *Patr Bd*
  TR R D C STEELE-PERKINS,   **TV** J M THOROGOOD

CAMELSDALE (St Paul) *Chich 10*   **P** *The Crown*
  V G BOTTOMLEY

CAMERTON (St Peter) w Dunkerton, Foxcote and
  Shoscombe *B & W 13*   **P** *Bp*   **R** D E COOPER

CAMERTON (St Peter), Seaton and West Seaton *Carl 7*
  P *D&C and Ch Trust Fund Trust (jt)*   **V** J D KELLY

CAMMERINGHAM (St Michael)   Ingham w
  Cammeringham w Fillingham *Linc*

CAMP HILL (St Mary and St John) w Galley Common
  Cov 5   **P** *Bp*   **V** S D SNEATH

CAMPBELL ROOMS (not known)   Parr Mt *Liv*

CAMPSALL (St Mary Magdalene) *Sheff 8*   **P** *Bp*
  V T B CLARK

CAMPSEA ASHE (St John the Baptist) w Marlesford,
  Parham and Hacheston *St E 18*   **P** *Prime Min, Ch Soc*
  Trust, and J S Schreiber Esq (by turn)
  R J F M WILLIAMS

CAMPTON (All Saints)   Meppershall w Campton and
  Stondon *St Alb*

CANDLESBY (St Benedict)   Partney *Linc*

CANDOVER VALLEY, THE *Win 1*   **P** *D&C and Lord*
  Ashburton (jt)   **R** C R SMITH

CANEWDON (St Nicholas) w Paglesham *Chelmsf 14*
  P *D&C Westmr and Hyndman Trustees (alt)*
  V N J KELLY

CANFIELD, GREAT (St Mary) *Chelmsf 21*
  P *A C Sainthill Esq*   **P-in-c** A L POULTON

CANFIELD, LITTLE (All Saints)   Takeley w Lt
  Canfield *Chelmsf*

CANFORD CLIFFS (Transfiguration) and Sandbanks
  Sarum 8   **P** *Bp*   **V** R A HOWE

CANFORD HEATH (St Paul)   Oakdale St Geo *Sarum*

CANFORD MAGNA (Bearwood) (Lantern) *Sarum 10*
  P *Patr Bd*   **TR** P F SERTIN,   **TV** A D EDWARDS,
  D P WHITE,   **NSM** A SIMPSON,
  J W KNOTT

CANLEY (St Stephen) *Cov 3*   **P** *Bp*   **V** *Vacant*
  Coventry (0203) 469016

CANNING TOWN (St Cedd) *Chelmsf 5*   **P** *Bp*
  P-in-c R H WOODALL

CANNING TOWN (St Matthias) *Chelmsf 5*   **P** *Bp*
  P-in-c R I BRIGGS

CANNINGTON (Blessed Virgin Mary), Otterhampton,
  Combwich and Stockland *B & W 15*   **P** *Bp*
  R P MARTIN

CANNOCK (St Luke) *Lich 4*   **P** *Patr Bd*
  TV R J DREWETT, P M DOWN, J G W WEBSTER,
  C D COLE, P A SMITH, D K BEEDON,
  Par Dn V M STEADY

CANON FROME (St James)   Bosbury w Wellington
  Heath etc *Heref*

CANON PYON (St Lawrence) w Kings Pyon and Birley
  Heref 7   **P** *Bp and D&C (alt)*   **V** C M BURKE

CANONBURY (St Stephen) *Lon 6*   **P** *V Islington St Mary*
  V D P LITTLE

CANTERBURY (All Saints) *Cant 3*   **P** *Abp*
  V B J COOPER

CANTERBURY (St Dunstan w Holy Cross) *Cant 3*   **P** *Abp*
  V M W WORGAN

CANTERBURY (St Martin) (St Paul) *Cant 3*   **P** *Abp*
  R P T MACKENZIE

CANTERBURY (St Mary Bredin) *Cant 3*   **P** *Simeon's*
  Trustees   **V** J M GLEDHILL,   **C** M P M BOOKER

CANTERBURY (St Peter) (St Mildred) w St Alphege and
  St Margaret w St Mary de Castro *Cant 3*   **P** *The Crown*
  R D M H HAYES

CANTERBURY (St Stephen)   Hackington *Cant*

CANTLEY (St Margaret)   Reedham w Cantley w
  Limpenhoe and Southwood *Nor*

CANTLEY (St Wilfrid) *Sheff 9*   **P** *Guild of All So*
  V D N GIBBS,   **C** T A PARKINSON, P WALSH

CANTLEY, NEW (St Hugh of Lincoln) *Sheff 9*   **P** *Guild*
  of All So   **V** C J FLETCHER

CANTRIL FARM (St Jude) *Liv 2*   **P** *Bp and*
  R W Derby (jt)   **V** T R EVANS,   **C** R GRIFFITH-JONES

CANVEY ISLAND (St Anne) (St Katherine's Worship
  Centre) (St Nicholas) *Chelmsf 12*   **P** *Bp and Patr Bd (jt)*
  TR D G THOMAS,   **TV** C A G JENKIN,   **C** M D MOORE,
  Par Dn S M WOOD,   **NSM** J E MOORE

CANWELL (St Mary, St Giles and All Saints) *Lich 5*
  P *Bp*   **V** H J BAKER

CANWICK (All Saints)   Washingborough w Heighington
  and Canwick *Linc*

CAPEL (St John the Baptist) *Guildf 7*   **P** *Ld Chan*
  V R J WHITTLE

CAPEL (St Mary) w Little Wenham *St E 5*   **P** *SMF*
  P-in-c B A TOLL

CAPEL LE FERNE (St Radigund)   Alkham w Capel le
Ferne and Hougham *Cant*
CAPENHURST (Holy Trinity)   Backford and
Capenhurst *Ches*
CAPESTHORNE (Holy Trinity) w Siddington and Marton
Ches 13   **P** *Exors Lt-Col Sir Walter Bromley-Davenport*
V J B WARBURTON
CAR COLSTON (St Mary) w Screveton *S'well 8*
P *H S Blagg Esq*   **R** J PULMAN
CARBIS BAY (St Anta and All Saints) w Lelant (St Uny)
Truro 5   **P** *Bp*   **V** M H FISHER
CARBROOKE (St Peter and St Paul)   Watton w
Carbrooke and Ovington *Nor*
CARBURTON (St Giles)   Worksop Priory *S'well*
CARDESTON (St Michael)   Alberbury w Cardeston
Heref
CARDINGTON (St James) *Heref 11*   **P** *Rt Hon*
Sir Frederick Corfield   **V** M BROMFIELD
CARDINGTON (St Mary) *St Alb 19*
P *S C Whitbread Esq*   **R** J K DIXON,   **Hon C** L R MOORE
CARDYNHAM (St Mewbud) *Truro 10*   **P** *DBP and*
Personal Reps R M Coode Esq (jt)
P-in-c R D C WHITEMAN,   **NSM** J L BRENDON-COOK
CAREBY (St Stephen) w Holywell and Aunby *Linc 14*
P *D&C and Bp (jt)*   **R** *Vacant*
CARHAM (St Cuthbert)   Cornhill w Carham *Newc*
CARHAMPTON (St John the Baptist)   Dunster,
Carhampton and Withycombe w Rodhuish *B & W*
CARHARRACK (St Piran's Mission Church)   St Day
Truro
CARISBROOKE (St John the Baptist)   Newport St Jo
Portsm
CARISBROOKE (St Mary the Virgin) *Portsm 8*
P *Qu Coll Ox*   **V** M S COOPER
CARISBROOKE St Nicholas in the Castle *Portsm 8*
P *Qu Coll Ox*   **V** M S COOPER
CARLBY (St Stephen)   Thurlby w Carlby *Linc*
CARLECOATES (St Anne)   Penistone and Thurlstone
Wakef
CARLETON (St Mary) and Lothersdale *Bradf 7*   **P** *Ch Ch*
Ox   **R** S G HOARE
CARLETON (St Michael) *Wakef 11*   **P** *V Pontefract*
V F L BROOKS,   **Par Dn** S V BROOKS
CARLETON (St Peter)   Rockland St Mary w Hellington,
Bramerton etc *Nor*
CARLETON, EAST (St Mary)   Swardeston w E
Carleton, Intwood, Keswick etc *Nor*
CARLETON IN CRAVEN   Carleton and Lothersdale
Bradf
CARLETON RODE (All Saints)   Bunwell, Carleton
Rode, Tibenham, Gt Moulton etc *Nor*
CARLIN HOW (St Helen)   Loftus and Carlin How w
Skinningrove *York*
CARLINGHOW (St John the Evangelist) *Wakef 10*
P *V Brownhill and V Batley (alt)*   **V** M C McCREADIE
CARLISLE Belah (St Mark)   Stanwix *Carl*
CARLISLE Harraby (St Elizabeth)   Harraby *Carl*
CARLISLE (Holy Trinity) (St Barnabas) *Carl 3*
P *Patr Bd*   **TR** M D J BARROW,   **Par Dn** M J MURRAY
CARLISLE (St Aidan) and Christ Church *Carl 3*   **P** *Bp*
V N M E CLAPP
CARLISLE (St Cuthbert) *Carl 3*   **P** *D&C*
V D T I JENKINS
CARLISLE (St Herbert) w St Stephen *Carl 3*   **P** *Bp*
C H GRAINGER
CARLISLE (St James)   Denton Holme *Carl*
CARLISLE (St John the Evangelist) *Carl 3*   **P** *CPAS*
V P J BYE,   **C** J R BAXENDALE
CARLISLE (St Luke) Morton *Carl 3*   **P** *Bp*
V R P H FRANK,   **NSM** A J MARSHALL
CARLISLE Stanwix (St Michael)   Stanwix *Carl*
CARLISLE Upperby (St John the Baptist)   Upperby St
Jo *Carl*
CARLTON (St Aidan)   Helmsley *York*
CARLTON (St Andrew)   Nailstone and Carlton w
Shackerstone *Leic*
CARLTON (St Bartholomew)   Guiseley w Esholt *Bradf*
CARLTON (St Botolph)   Whorlton w Carlton and
Faceby *York*
CARLTON (St John the Baptist) *S'well 11*   **P** *Bp*
V A M LUCKCUCK
CARLTON (St John the Evangelist) *Wakef 7*   **P** *DBP*
P-in-c J L HUDSON
CARLTON (St Mary)   Harrold and Carlton w
Chellington *St Alb*
CARLTON (St Peter)   Brinkley, Burrough Green and
Carlton *Ely*
CARLTON (St Peter)   Kelsale-cum-Carlton, Middleton-
cum-Fordley etc *St E*

CARLTON, EAST (St Peter)   Cottingham w E Carlton
Pet
CARLTON, GREAT (St John the Baptist)   Mid Marsh
Gp *Linc*
CARLTON, NORTH (St Luke) w South Carlton *Linc 3*
P *Lord Monson*   **P-in-c** R J WELLS
CARLTON, SOUTH (St John the Baptist)   N w S
Carlton *Linc*
CARLTON BY SNAITH (St Mary) and Drax *York 6*
P *Abp and Ch Trust Fund Trust (jt)*   **V** J H DAVIS
CARLTON COLVILLE (St Peter) w Mutford and
Rushmere *Nor 15*   **P** *Bp, G&C Coll Cam, and Simeon's*
Trustees (jt)   **R** A T SMITH
CARLTON CURLIEU (St Mary the Virgin)   Gaulby
Leic
CARLTON FOREHOE (St Mary)   Barnham Broom *Nor*
CARLTON HUSTHWAITE (St Mary)   Coxwold and
Husthwaite *York*
CARLTON-IN-LINDRICK (St John the Evangelist)
S'well 6   **P** *Ld Chan*   **R** J C A LAMBERT,
Hon Par Dn J H SIMPSON
CARLTON-IN-THE-WILLOWS (St Paul) *S'well 11*
P *MMCET*   **R** W W HARRISON
CARLTON-LE-MOORLAND (St Mary) w Stapleford
Linc 18   **P** *Lord Middleton*   **V** D T OSBORN
CARLTON MINIOTT (St Lawrence)   Thirsk *York*
CARLTON-ON-TRENT (St Mary)   Sutton w Carlton
and Normanton upon Trent etc *S'well*
CARLTON SCROOP (St Nicholas)   Caythorpe *Linc*
CARNABY (St John the Baptist) *York 10*   **P** *Abp*
V T J DAVIDSON
CARNFORTH (Christ Church) *Blackb 15*   **P** *Bp*
V R P PRICE,   **C** J M HALL
CARR CLOUGH (St Andrew)   Kersal Moor *Man*
CARR MILL (St David) *Liv 10*   **P** *V St Helens St Mark*
and Bp (jt)   **V** G N ROBERTS
CARRINGTON (St John the Evangelist) *S'well 13*   **P** *Bp*
V A BURNHAM,   **C** J HEMSTOCK,   **Par Dn** P HEMSTOCK,
NSM D C GILL
CARRINGTON (St Paul)   Sibsey w Frithville *Linc*
CARSHALTON (All Saints) *S'wark 25*   **P** *Bp*
R L C EDWARDS,   **Hon C** L A BREWSTER,   **NSM** J Z RAY
CARSHALTON BEECHES (Good Shepherd) *S'wark 25*
P *Bp*   **V** C WHEATON
CARSINGTON (St Margaret)   Wirksworth w
Alderwasley, Carsington etc *Derby*
CARTERTON (St John the Evangelist) *Ox 8*   **P** *Ch Ch Ox*
V R J HUMPHREYS,   **Par Dn** M P CARNEY
CARTMEL (St Mary and St Michael) *Carl 10*
P *R H Cavendish Esq*   **V** C L V ATKINSON
CARTMEL FELL (St Anthony) *Carl 9*   **P** *Bp*
V K PARTINGTON
CASSINGTON (St Peter)   Eynsham and Cassington *Ox*
CASSOP cum Quarrington *Dur 14*   **P** *Bp*
V J THOMPSON,   **Par Dn** P E MARTIN
CASTERTON (Holy Trinity)   Kirkby Lonsdale *Carl*
CASTERTON, GREAT (St Peter and St Paul) and Little
Castertonw Pickworth and Tickencote *Pet 8*
P *Burghley Ho Preservation Trust (2 turns), Lord*
Chesham (1 turn), and Bp (1 turn)   **R** J BUTLER
CASTERTON, LITTLE (All Saints)   Gt and Lt
Casterton w Pickworth and Tickencote *Pet*
CASTLE ACRE (St James) w Newton, Rougham and
Southacre *Nor 19*   **P** *Viscount Coke, T F North Esq, Bp*
and H Birkbeck Esq (jt) (by turn)   **R** D W PRICE
CASTLE ASHBY (St Mary Magdalene)   Yardley
Hastings, Denton and Grendon etc *Pet*
CASTLE BOLTON (St Oswald)   Aysgarth and Bolton
cum Redmire *Ripon*
CASTLE BROMWICH (St Clement of Alexandria) *Birm 11*
P *Bp*   **V** W J SILLITOE,   **C** C HODGSON,
Hon C M W MORECROFT,   **NSM** P A SILLITOE
CASTLE BROMWICH (St Mary and St Margaret) *Birm 11*
P *Earl of Bradf*   **R** C J BOYLE,   **C** R D WOODWARD
CASTLE BYTHAM (St James) *Linc 14*   **P** *Bp and D&C*
(alt)   **V** *Vacant*   Castle Bytham (078081) 308
CASTLE CAMPS (All Saints) *Ely 4*   **P** *Charterhouse*
P-in-c J H THOMSON,   **NSM** M W B O'LOUGHLIN
CASTLE CARROCK (St Peter) w Cumrew and Croglin
Carl 2   **P** *D&C*   **R** K P O'DONOHUE
CASTLE CARY (All Saints) w Ansford *B & W 3*   **P** *Bp*
V P W M REVELL,   **C** R H AXFORD
CASTLE CHURCH (St Mary) *Lich 16*   **P** *Bp*
V J T H PYE
CASTLE COMBE (St Andrew) *Bris 9*   **P** *Bp*
P-in-c J N A BRADBURY,   **NSM** J E B MARSH
CASTLE DONINGTON (St Edward the King and Martyr)
and Lockington cum Hemington *Leic 7*   **P** *Lady Gretton*

and C H C Coaker Esq (jt)   **V**   B WHITEHEAD,
NSM L R F TESTA
CASTLE EATON (St Mary the Virgin)   Meysey
Hampton w Marston Meysey and Castle Eaton *Glouc*
CASTLE EDEN (St James) w Monkhesleden *Dur 3*   **P**   *Bp*
R   G G DEWHURST
CASTLE FROME (St Michael)   Bishop's Frome w
Castle Frome and Fromes Hill *Heref*
CASTLE HEDINGHAM (St Nicholas) *Chelmsf 22*
P   *Hon T R Lindsay*   **V**   *Vacant*   Halstead (0787) 60274
CASTLE HILL (St Philip)   Hindley All SS *Liv*
CASTLE RISING (St Lawrence) *Nor 21*
P   *G Howard Esq*   **P-in-c**   G R HALL
CASTLE SOWERBY (St Kentigern)   Caldbeck, Castle
Sowerby and Sebergham *Carl*
CASTLE TOWN (St Thomas and St Andrew) *Lich 16*
P   *Hyndman Trustees*   **V**   A L HUGHES
CASTLE VALE (St Cuthbert of Lindisfarne) *Birm 9*
P   *Bp*   **R**   J L SALTER
CASTLE VIEW ESTATE (St Francis)   Langley Marish
Ox
CASTLECROFT (The Good Shepherd)   Tettenhall
Wood *Lich*
CASTLEFORD (All Saints) *Wakef 11*   **P**   *Duchy of Lanc*
R   E GEE,   **NSM**   G DRAKE
CASTLEFORD (St Michael and All Angels)
Smawthorpe St Mich *Wakef*
CASTLEMORTON (St Gregory)   Longdon,
Castlemorton, Bushley, Queenhill etc *Worc*
CASTLESIDE (St John the Evangelist) *Dur 8*   **P**   *Bp*
V   R L FERGUSON
CASTLETHORPE (St Simon and St Jude)   Hanslope w
Castlethorpe *Ox*
CASTLETON (St Edmund)   Hope and Castleton *Derby*
CASTLETON (St Mary Magdalene)   Sherborne w
Castleton and Lillington *Sarum*
CASTLETON (St Michael and St George)   Danby *York*
CASTLETON MOOR (St Martin) *Man 19*   **P**   *Bp*
V   I McVEETY
CASTLETHORPE (St Margaret)   N Hylton St Marg
Castletown *Dur*
CASTLETOWN (St Mary) *S & M 1*   **P**   *Bp*   **V**   W N KELLY
**CASTON (St Cross) w Griston, Merton, Thompson, Stow
Bedon and Breckles** *Nor 18*   **P**   *Bp and Lord
Walsingham (alt)*   **R**   J H RICHARDSON
CASTOR (St Kyneburgha) w Sutton and Upton *Pet 13*
P   *Bp (2 turns) and Mrs V S V Gunnery (1 turn)*
R   J A HARPER
CATCLIFFE (St Mary)   Brinsworth w Catcliffe *Sheff*
CATCOTT (St Peter)   W Poldens *B & W*
CATERHAM (St Mary the Virgin) (St Laurence) (St Paul)
S'wark 18   **P**   *Bp*   **P-in-c**   C J L BOSWELL,   **C**   T W PAGE,
Par Dn V M HAMER,   **Hon C**   E M HILL, M J WEST,
NSM   R S TRELEAVEN
CATERHAM VALLEY (St John the Evangelist) *S'wark 18*
P   *Bp*   **P-in-c**   C M S SNOW
CATESBY (St Mary)   Staverton w Helidon and Catesby
Pet
CATFIELD (All Saints) *Nor 10*   **P**   *Bp*   **R**   S WESTON
CATFORD (Southend) and Downham *S'wark 3*   **P**   *Bp*
TR   J D FRYAR,
TV   N A W DAVIS, K P ROBINSON, P H ALLEN
CATFORD (St Andrew) *S'wark 3*   **P**   *Bp*   **V**   R B JORDAN
CATFORD (St Laurence) *S'wark 3*   **P**   *Bp*
V   C F PICKSTONE,   **C**   J A McKNIGHT
CATHERINGTON (All Saints) and Clanfield *Portsm 4*
P   *Bp*   **V**   C BEARDSLEY,   **Hon C**   D R DIVALL
CATHERSTON LEWESTON (St Mary)   Charmouth
and Catherston Leweston *Sarum*
CATON (St Paul) w Littledale *Blackb 12*   **P**   *V Lanc*
V   J R TATE
CATSFIELD (St Laurence) and Crowhurst *Chich 14*
P   *Bp and J P Papillon (alt)*   **R**   D J TAYLOR
CATSHILL (Christ Church) and Dodford *Worc 7*   **P**   *Bp
and V Bromsgrove St Jo (alt)*   **V**   A J VESSEY,
Par Dn W J RIOCH
CATTERICK (St Anne) *Ripon 2*   **P**   *Bp*   **V**   W R HOGG
CATTHORPE (St Thomas)   Swinford w Catthorpe,
Shawell and Stanford *Leic*
CATTISTOCK (St Peter and St Paul)   Melbury *Sarum*
CATTON (All Saints)   Stamford Bridge Gp of Par *York*
CATTON (St Margaret) *Nor 4*   **P**   *D&C*
V   A D RAYMENT
CATTON (St Nicholas and the Blessed Virgin Mary)
Walton on Trent w Croxall etc *Derby*
CATTON, NEW (Christ Church) *Nor 4*   **P**   *R Colegate
St Geo*   **V**   J F McGINLEY
CATTON, NEW (St Luke) *Nor 4*   **P**   *CPAS*
V   D A G G DOLMAN

CATWICK (St Michael)   Leven w Catwick *York*
CATWORTH, GREAT   Catworth Magna *Ely*
CATWORTH MAGNA (St Leonard) *Ely 10*   **P**   *BNC Ox*
P-in-c   J HINDLEY,   **NSM**   B A BEARCROFT
CAULDON (St Mary and St Laurence)   Calton,
Cauldon, Grindon and Waterfall *Lich*
CAUNDLE MARSH (St Peter and St Paul)   The
Caundles w Folke and Holwell *Sarum*
CAUNDLES w Folke and Holwell, The *Sarum 4*   **P**   *Major
K S D Wingfield Digby, Bp, and D&C (jt)*
R   J D HILLIER
CAUNTON (St Andrew)   Norwell w Ossington,
Cromwell and Caunton *S'well*
CAUSEWAY HEAD (St Paul)   Silloth *Carl*
CAUTLEY (St Mark)   Sedbergh, Cautley and Garsdale
Bradf
CAVENDISH (St Mary)   Clare w Poslingford, Cavendish
etc *St E*
CAVENHAM (St Andrew)   Mildenhall *St E*
CAVERSFIELD (St Laurence)   Bicester w Bucknell,
Caversfield and Launton *Ox*
CAVERSHAM (St Andrew) *Ox 15*   **P**   *Bp*
R   W B CARPENTER
CAVERSHAM (St John the Baptist) *Ox 15*   **P**   *Bp*
V   A T L WILSON
CAVERSHAM (St Peter) (Park Church) and Mapledurham
Ox 15   **P**   *Eton Coll (1 turn) and Ch Ch Ox (3 turns)*
R   R J KINGSBURY,   **C**   P J ABREY, C ALLSOPP
CAVERSHAM HEIGHTS (St Andrew)   Caversham St
Andr *Ox*
CAVERSHAM PARK Local Ecumenical Project *Ox 15*
Min   P J ABREY
CAVERSWALL (St Peter) *Lich 12*   **P**   *Mrs D E Parker-
Jervis*   **V**   N JEFFERYES,   **Par Dn**   R M POLLIT,
NSM   J A JEFFERYES
CAWOOD (All Saints) *York 6*   **P** *Abp*   **P-in-c**   R E MESSER
CAWSAND (St Andrew's Mission Church)   Maker w
Rame *Truro*
**CAWSTON (St Agnes) w Haveringland, Booton and
Brandiston** *Nor 3*   **P**   *Pemb Coll Cam (3 turns), DBP
(1 turn)*   **R**   M C KING
CAWTHORNE (All Saints) *Wakef 7*   **P**   *S W Fraser Esq*
V   R T G SHARP
CAWTHORPE, LITTLE (St Helen)   Legbourne *Linc*
CAXTON (St Andrew)   Bourn and Kingston w Caxton
and Longstowe *Ely*
CAYNHAM (St Mary) *Heref 12*   **P**   *Bp*
P-in-c   J F BAULCH
CAYTHORPE (St Aidan)   Lowdham *S'well*
CAYTHORPE (St Vincent) *Linc 23*   **P**   *Bp, J F Fane Esq,
and S J Packe-Drury-Lowe Esq (by turn)*
R   H C MIDDLETON
CAYTON (St John the Baptist) w Eastfield *York 16*
P *Abp*   **v**   M D B LONG,   **Par Dn**   E J G STRICKLAND
CENTRAL: *see under substantive place names*
**CERNE ABBAS (St Mary) w Godmanstone and Minterne
Magna** *Sarum 2*   **P**   *Adn Sherborne (1 turn),
D H C Batten Esq (1 turn), Lord Digby (2 turns), and
G E H Gallia Esq (1 turn)*   **P-in-c**   D JACKSON
CERNEY, NORTH (All Saints) w Bagendon *Glouc 12*
P   *Jes Coll Ox and Univ Coll Ox (alt)*
P-in-c   H A S COCKS,   **NSM**   D H S LEESON
**CERNEY, SOUTH (All Hallows) w Cerney Wick and Down
Ampney** *Glouc 13*   **P**   *Bp and Ch Ch Ox (alt)*
V   J R CALVERT,   **NSM**   J T THOMAS
CERNEY WICK (Holy Trinity)   S Cerney w Cerney
Wick and Down Ampney *Glouc*
CHACELEY (St John the Baptist)   Deerhurst, Apperley
w Forthampton and Chaceley *Glouc*
CHACEWATER (St Paul) *Truro 6*   **P**   *V Kenwyn*
P-in-c   K HILL
CHACOMBE (St Peter and St Paul)   Middleton Cheney
w Chacombe *Pet*
CHADDERTON (Christ Church) (St Saviour) *Man 18*
P   *Trustees*   **V** D P BANTING,   **C**   C L ALBIN
CHADDERTON (Emmanuel) (St George) *Man 18*
P   *Trustees*   **V**   E STOTT
CHADDERTON (St Luke) *Man 18*   **P**   *Bp*
V   G G MARSHALL
CHADDERTON (St Mark) *Man 18*   **P**   *The Crown*
V   A COOKE
CHADDERTON (St Matthew) *Man 18*   **P**   *The Crown*
V   R W BAILEY
CHADDESDEN (St Mary) *Derby 9*   **P**   *MMCET*
V   I F R JARVIS,   **C**   D J HORSFALL,   **Par Dn**   M A BEXON
CHADDESDEN (St Philip) *Derby 9*   **P**   *Bp*   **C**   S J DOBSON
CHADDESLEY CORBETT (St Cassian) and Stone
Worc 10   **P**   *Ld Chan*   **V**   J A COX

CHADDLEWORTH (St Andrew) Brightwalton w Catmore, Leckhampstead etc *Ox*
CHADKIRK (St Chad) *Ches 16* **P** *R Stockport St Mary*
   V T D BARLOW, **C** S I D WHITE
CHADLINGTON (St Nicholas) and Spelsbury, Ascott under Wychwood *Ox 3* **P** *Bp and Ch Ch Ox (alt)*
   V T C G THORNTON
CHADSMOOR (St Aidan) Cannock *Lich*
CHADSMOOR (St Chad) as above
CHADWELL (Emmanuel) (St Mary) *Chelmsf 16*
   P *Ch Soc Trust* **R** S BAILEY,
   C A J PUGSLEY, B J ROBSON
CHADWELL HEATH (St Chad) *Chelmsf 1*
   P *Vs Dagenham and Ilford (alt)* **V** J A A FLETCHER,
   C E W COCKETT, **NSM** M JOYCE
CHAFFCOMBE (St Michael and All Angels) Chard, Furnham w Chaffcombe, Knowle St Giles etc *B & W*
CHAGFORD (St Michael) w Gidleigh and Throwleigh *Ex 12* **P** *Lady Anne Hayter-Hames, Guild of All So., and Bp (jt)* **R** P L BAYCOCK
CHAILEY (St Peter) *Chich 21* **P** *Major Gen Philip Tillard* **R** E MATTHIAS
CHALBURY (All Saints) Horton and Chalbury *Sarum*
CHALDON (St Peter and St Paul) *S'wark 18* **P** *Bp*
   P-in-c C J L BOSWELL
CHALDON HERRING (St Nicholas) The Lulworths, Winfrith Newburgh and Chaldon *Sarum*
CHALE (St Andrew) *Portsm 7* **P** *Keble Coll Ox*
   P-in-c J W RUSSELL, **NSM** C A B MARKE
CHALFIELD, GREAT (All Saints) Broughton Gifford, Gt Chalfield and Holt *Sarum*
CHALFONT, LITTLE (St George) Chenies and Lt Chalfont, Latimer and Flaunden *Ox*
CHALFONT ST GILES *Ox 20* **P** *Bp* **R** P W POOLE
CHALFONT ST PETER (St Peter) *Ox 20* **P** *St Jo Coll Ox*
   R D M MURRAY, **C** J P E SIBLEY, W P L GAMMON,
   NSM L WARRINER
CHALFORD (Christ Church) *Glouc 1* **P** *Adn Glouc*
   V *Vacant* Brimscombe (0453) 883375
CHALGRAVE (All Saints) *St Alb 18* **P** *DBP*
   P-in-c K A STEELE
CHALGROVE (St Mary) w Berrick Salome *Ox 1*
   P *Ch Ch Ox* **V** I G H COHEN, **Par Dn** J D PORTER
CHALK (St Mary) *Roch 4* **P** *R Milton* **V** J R FRY
CHALKE VALLEY West *Sarum 13* **P** *Bp, DBP, and K Coll Cam (by turn)* **V** R W HOWARD,
   C T A M SANKEY, **Hon C** E R BROADBENT
CHALKE VALLEY EAST *Sarum 13* **P** *D&C, CCC Ox, and Bp (by turn)* **R** P BYRON-DAVIES
CHALLACOMBE (Holy Trinity) Shirwell, Loxhore, Kentisbury, Arlington, etc *Ex*
CHALLOCK (St Cosmas and St Damian) w Molash *Cant 2*
   P *Abp* **P-in-c** C R DUNCAN
CHALLOW, EAST (St Nicholas) *Ox 19* **P** *Bp*
   P-in-c A HOGG
CHALLOW, WEST (St Laurence) Ridgeway *Ox*
CHALTON (St Michael and All Angels) Blendworth w Chalton w Idsworth *Portsm*
CHALVEY (St Peter) Upton cum Chalvey *Ox*
CHALVINGTON (St Bartholomew) Laughton w Ripe and Chalvington *Chich*
CHAMBERSBURY (Hemel Hempstead) (Holy Trinity) (St Mary) (St Benedict) *St Alb 3* **P** *DBP*
   TR M R ABBOTT, **TV** A S ALLEN, J B THOMAS,
   Hon C D A BUTLER
CHANDLER'S FORD (St Boniface) Valley Park *Win*
CHANDLER'S FORD (St Martin) *Win 9* **P** *Bp*
   V A G HARBIDGE, **C** P D BAIRD, D S BENNETT
CHANTRY (Holy Trinity) Mells w Buckland Dinham, Elm, Whatley etc *B & W*
CHAPEL ALLERTON (St Matthew) *Ripon 5* **P** *V Leeds St Pet* **V** M A CROSS, **NSM** A P BERRY
CHAPEL CHORLTON (St Laurence), Maer and Whitmore *Lich 13* **P** *Bp and R G D Cavenagh-Mainwaring Esq (jt)* **R** J D D PORTER
CHAPEL-EN-LE-FRITH (St Thomas a Becket) *Derby 4*
   P *PCC* **V** N R BRALESFORD
CHAPEL HILL (Holy Trinity) Brothertoft Gp *Linc*
CHAPEL HOUSE (Holy Nativity) Whorlton *Newc*
CHAPEL LAWN (St Mary) Bucknell w Chapel Lawn, Llanfair Waterdine etc *Heref*
CHAPEL LE DALE (St Leonard) Ingleton w Chapel le Dale *Bradf*
CHAPEL PLAISTER (not known) Box *Bris*
CHAPEL ST LEONARDS (St Leonard) w Hogsthorpe *Linc 8* **P** *R Willoughby* **V** A E R EMERSON
CHAPELTHORPE (St James) *Wakef 9* **V** *V Sandal*
   V J F WHITE, **Par Dn** J TRAFFORD

CHAPELTOWN (St John the Baptist) *Sheff 7* **P** *Bp*
   V P J CRAIG-WILD, **C** S J WILLETT,
   Par Dn D E CRAIG-WILD
CHAPMANSLADE (St Philip and St James) Corsley *Sarum*
CHAPPEL (St Barnabas) Gt Tey and Wakes Colne w Chappel *Chelmsf*
CHARBOROUGH (St Mary) Red Post *Sarum*
CHARD (Blessed Virgin Mary) *B & W 16* **P** *Bp*
   V M S KIVETT
CHARD Furnham (Good Shepherd) w Chaffcombe, Knowle St Giles and Cricket Malherbie *B & W 16*
   P *Rs Shepton Beauchamp etc and Bishops Lydeard etc (jt)* **P-in-c** D M FLETCHER
CHARDSTOCK (All Saints) Axminster, Chardstock, Combe Pyne and Rousdon *Ex*
CHARDSTOCK (St Andrew) as above
CHARFIELD (St John) *Glouc 7* **P** *R W Neeld Esq*
   R K G GRANT
CHARFORD (St Andrew) Bromsgrove St Jo *Worc*
CHARING (St Peter and St Paul) w Charing Heath (Holy Trinity) and Little Chart *Cant 10* **P** *Abp and D&C (jt)*
   V B CHALMERS
CHARLBURY (St Mary the Virgin) w Shorthampton *Ox 3*
   P *St Jo Coll Ox* **V** M J CHADWICK
CHARLCOMBE (Blessed Virgin Mary) w Bath (St Stephen) *B & W 10* **P** *DBP and Simeon's Trustees (jt)* **R** R OSBORNE
CHARLECOTE (St Leonard) Hampton Lucy w Charlecote and Loxley *Cov*
CHARLES (St John the Baptist) S Molton w Nymet St George, High Bray etc *Ex*
CHARLES w St Matthias, Plymouth *Ex 24* **P** *Ch Patr Trust* **P-in-c** R H V PAYNE, **C** M J BURTON
CHARLESTOWN (St George) Pendleton St Thos w Charlestown *Man*
CHARLESTOWN (St Paul) *Truro 1* **P** *The Crown*
   V D R APPS, **C** M G BARTLETT, **Hon C** A D J JAGO,
   NSM D C B PECKETT
CHARLESTOWN (St Thomas the Apostle) *Wakef 4*
   P *V Halifax* **V** L GREENWOOD
CHARLESWORTH (St John the Evangelist) and Dinting Vale *Derby 6* **P** *The Crown (2 turns), Bp (1 turn)*
   V G G MOATE, **C** A W WARD, **NSM** W ILLINGWORTH
CHARLETON (St Mary) w Buckland Tout Saints, East Portlemouth, South Pool and Chivelstone *Ex 14*
   P *Ld Chan (2 turns), E Roberts, S Tyler and N Tyler Esqs (1 turn), Bp (1 turn), and DBP (1 turn)*
   R P HANCOCK
CHARLTON (Holy Trinity) Wantage *Ox*
CHARLTON (St John) Cropthorne w Charlton *Worc*
CHARLTON (St John the Baptist) Garsdon, Lea and Cleverton and Charlton *Bris*
CHARLTON (St John the Baptist) The Donheads *Sarum*
CHARLTON (St Luke w Holy Trinity) (St Richard) *S'wark 1* **P** *Viscount Gough* **R** A M CROWE,
   Par Dn B M C BROGGIO
CHARLTON (St Peter) Uphavon w Rushall and Charlton *Sarum*
CHARLTON (St Thomas the Apostle) Andover w Foxcott *Win*
CHARLTON, SOUTH (St James) Glendale Gp *Newc*
CHARLTON ABBOTS (St Martin) Sevenhampton w Charlton Abbotts and Hawling etc *Glouc*
CHARLTON ADAM (St Peter and St Paul) Somerton w Compton Dundon, the Charltons etc *B & W*
CHARLTON ALL SAINTS (All Saints) *Sarum 11*
   P *V Downton* **P-in-c** R P HOLLINGSHURST
CHARLTON HORETHORNE (St Peter and St Paul) Henstridge and Charlton Horethorne w Stowell *B & W*
CHARLTON-IN-DOVER (St Peter and St Paul) *Cant 4*
   P *Keble Coll Ox* **R** N D L DE KEYSER,
   NSM L R CRUTTENDEN
CHARLTON KINGS (Holy Apostles) *Glouc 14*
   P *R Cheltenham* **V** E M DUTHIE
CHARLTON KINGS (St Mary) *Glouc 11* **P** *Bp*
   V G T BRYANT, **C** N S McGREGOR, **NSM** R E ROBERTS
CHARLTON MACKRELL (Blessed Virgin Mary) Somerton w Compton Dundon, the Charltons etc *B & W*
CHARLTON MARSHALL (St Mary the Virgin) Spetisbury w Charlton Marshall and Blandford St Mary *Sarum*
CHARLTON MUSGROVE (St John) (St Stephen), Cucklington and Stoke Trister *B & W 2* **P** *Bp*
   P-in-c R D THATCHER
CHARLTON ON OTMOOR (St Mary) Islip w Charlton on Otmoor, Oddington, Noke etc *Ox*
CHARLWOOD (St Nicholas) *S'wark 24* **P** *DBP*
   Hon C R C GAUNT, **NSM** A N TREDENNICK

CHARMINSTER (St Mary the Virgin) and Stinsford *Sarum 2* **P** *Hon Charlotte Morrison and P R FitzGerald (jt), and Bp (alt)* **P-in-c** G M BOULT, **NSM** F W BELCHER

CHARMOUTH (St Andrew) and Catherston Leweston *Sarum 3* **P** *MMCET* **R** *Vacant* Charmouth (0297) 60409

CHARNEY BASSETT (St Peter) Cherbury *Ox*

CHARNOCK RICHARD (Christ Church) *Blackb 4* **P** *DBF* **V** B G MOORE

CHARSFIELD w Debach (St Peter), Monewden, Hoo, Dallinghoo and Letheringham *St E 18* **P** *MMCET and CPAS (1 turn), Ld Chan (1 turn), and Ch Patr Trust (1 turn)* **V** G R ADDINGTON HALL

CHART, GREAT (St Mary) *Cant 10* **P** *Abp* **R** A J DAVIS

CHART, LITTLE (St Mary) Charing w Charing Heath and Lt Chart *Cant*

CHART SUTTON (St Michael) Sutton Valence w E Sutton and Chart Sutton *Cant*

CHARTERHOUSE-ON-MENDIP (St Hugh) Blagdon w Compton Martin and Ubley *B & W*

CHARTHAM (St Mary) *Cant 2* **P** *Abp* **R** M E KIDD

CHARWELTON (Holy Trinity) w Fawsley and Preston Capes *Pet 3* **P** *Bp* **R** S P ADAMS, **P-in-c** A C FRYER

CHASE TERRACE St John District Church *Lich 2* **Min** C T ROOME

CHASETOWN (St Anne) (St John) *Lich 2* **P** *V Burntwood* **V** M G WOODERSON

CHASETOWN (St John) Chase Terrace St Jo Distr Ch *Lich*

CHASTLETON (St Mary the Virgin) Lt Compton w Chastleton, Cornwell etc *Ox*

CHATBURN (Christ Church) *Blackb 8* **P** *DBF* **V** W DRAIN

CHATHAM (St Mary and St John the Divine) *Roch 5* **P** *D&C* **Hon C** J L M LE MARCHAND

CHATHAM (St Paul w All Saints) *Roch 5* **P** *Bp* **V** R K BILLINGS

CHATHAM (St Philip and St James) *Roch 5* **P** *Ch Soc Trust* **V** K A GARDINER, **C** D P WREN

CHATHAM (St Stephen) *Roch 5* **P** *Bp* **V** C J D WALKER, **Par Dn** J L STEVENTON, **Hon C** O MATON

CHATHAM (St William) (St David) *Roch 5* **P** *Bp* **V** P E LONGBOTTOM, **C** P J MILLS

CHATTERIS (St Peter and St Paul) *Ely 18* **P** *G&C Coll Cam* **V** C J MYHILL

CHATTISHAM (All Saints and St Margaret) Hintlesham w Chattisham *St E*

CHATTON (Holy Cross) Glendale Gp *Newc*

CHAULDEN (St Stephen) Hemel Hempstead *St Alb*

CHAVEY DOWN (St Martin) Winkfield and Cranbourne *Ox*

CHAWLEIGH (St James) w Cheldon *Ex 16* **P** *Bp* **R** J N STOCKWELL

CHAWTON (St Nicholas) and Farringdon *Win 2* **P** *Bp* **R** G A HODGE

CHEADLE (All Hallows) (St Philip's Mission Church) *Ches 17* **P** *R Cheadle* **V** M TINKER, **C** S J SCOTT

CHEADLE (St Cuthbert) (St Mary) *Ches 17* **P** *Ch Soc Trust* **R** D S ALLISTER, **C** P S DANIEL, N C HALL, **NSM** S POOLE, R J COEKIN

CHEADLE (St Giles) w Freehay *Lich 12* **P** *DBP* **R** *Vacant* Cheadle (0538) 753337

CHEADLE HEATH (St Augustine) *Ches 18* **P** *Bp* **V** J B ELLIS

CHEADLE HULME (All Saints) *Ches 17* **P** *Bp* **V** S A FOSTER, **C** C M KEMP

CHEADLE HULME (St Andrew) (Emmanuel) *Ches 17* **P** *R Cheadle* **V** C P COOK, **C** G J RENISON, T Q FORRYAN, **NSM** R P MOSS

CHEAM (St Dunstan) (St Alban the Martyr) *S'wark 25* **P** *St Jo Coll Ox* **R** T J de L SURTEES, **C** C G WOODHEAD, F T LYNN

CHEAM, NORTH (St Oswald) Cheam *S'wark*

CHEAM COMMON (St Philip) *S'wark 25* **P** *R Cheam* **V** M R GOODLAD, **C** R J FARMAN, **Par Dn** B M SCALES, **Hon C** H R NAUNTON

CHEARSLEY (St Nicholas) Long Crendon w Chearsley and Nether Winchendon *Ox*

CHEBSEY (All Saints) *Lich 13* **P** *D&C* **P-in-c** G G HODSON

CHECKENDON (St Peter and St Paul) Langtree *Ox*

CHECKLEY (Mission Room) Woolhope *Heref*

CHECKLEY (St Mary and All Saints) *Lich 21* **P** *Mrs M Philips* **P-in-c** A G SADLER, **C** A O L HODGSON

CHEDBURGH (All Saints) w Depden, Rede and Hawkedon *St E 8* **P** *Bp (1 turn), Ld Chan (4 turns)* **R** D O WALL

CHEDDAR (St Andrew) *B & W 1* **P** *D&C* **V** V L DALEY

CHEDDINGTON (St Giles) w Mentmore and Marsworth *Ox 26* **P** *Bp and Earl of Rosebery (jt)* **R** R A HALE

CHEDDLETON (St Edward the Confessor) *Lich 14* **P** *Bp* **V** E A FARLEY, **C** D W KESTERTON

CHEDDON FITZPAINE (The Blessed Virgin Mary) Kingston St Mary w Broomfield etc *B & W*

CHEDGRAVE (All Saints) w Hardley and Langley *Nor 14* **P** *Gt Hosp (1 turn), Sir Christopher Beauchamp, Bt (2 turns)* **R** D A J MacPHERSON

CHEDISTON (St Mary) Halesworth w Linstead, Chediston, Holton etc *St E*

CHEDWORTH (St Andrew), Yanworth and Stowell, Coln Rogers and Coln St Denys *Glouc 14* **P** *Ld Chan (2 turns), Qu Coll Ox (1 turn)* **V** P J DRAYCOTT

CHEDZOY (The Blessed Virgin Mary) Weston Zoyland w Chedzoy *B & W*

CHEETHAM (St John the Evangelist) *Man 5* **P** *Bp* **R** J PRESTON

CHEETHAM St Luke and Lower Crumpsall (St Thomas) *Man 5* **P** *Bp and CPAS (jt)* **R** H W MAYOR

CHEETHAM (St Mark) Barton w Peel Green *Man*

CHEETHAM (St Mark) (Hamilton Memorial Hall) *Man 5* **P** *D&C* **P-in-c** D J WISEMAN

CHEETWOOD (St Alban) *Man 6* **P** *D&C* **P-in-c** M J G MELROSE, P H MILLER

CHELBOROUGH, EAST (St James) Melbury *Sarum*

CHELBOROUGH, WEST (St Andrew) as above

CHELDON (St Mary) Chawleigh w Cheldon *Ex*

CHELFORD (St John the Evangelist) w Lower Withington *Ches 12* **P** *J M Dixon Esq* **V** J FELLIS

CHELL (St Michael) *Lich 17* **P** *Patr Bd* **TR** T THAKE, **TV** S R J FRENCH, **C** N J ROOMS

CHELL HEATH (Saviour) Chell *Lich*

CHELLASTON (St Peter) *Derby 15* **P** *Bp* **V** R J ANDREWS, **NSM** F R WORRALL

CHELMARSH (St Peter) Billingsley w Sidbury, Middleton Scriven etc *Heref*

CHELMONDISTON (St Andrew) w Harkstead and Shotley w Erwarton *St E 5* **P** *Ld Chan (1 turn), Bp (3 turns)* **R** R D NEWTON

CHELMORTON AND FLAGG (St John the Baptist) Taddington, Chelmorton and Flagg, and Monyash *Derby*

CHELMSFORD (All Saints) (St Michael's Church Centre) *Chelmsf 11* **P** *Bp* **V** M J ATKINSON

CHELMSFORD (Ascension) *Chelmsf 11* **P** *Bp* **P-in-c** I L MORRIS

CHELMSFORD (St Andrew) *Chelmsf 11* **P** *Bp* **P-in-c** J E HANSEN

CHELMSLEY WOOD (St Andrew) *Birm 11* **P** *Bp* **TR** D R CARRIVICK, **TM** G BLOOMFIELD

CHELMSLEY WOOD (St Augustine) Conventional District *Birm 11* **C-in-c** S A JONES

CHELSEA (All Saints) (Old Church) *Lon 8* **P** *R Chelsea St Luke and Earl Cadogan (jt)* **V** C E L THOMSON, **Hon C** J H L CROSS

CHELSEA (St John w St Andrew) *Lon 8* **P** *CPAS and Lon Coll of Div (jt)* **V** J O S SMITH

CHELSEA (St Luke) (Christ Church) *Lon 8* **P** *Earl Cadogan* **R** D R WATSON, **C** S H H ACLAND, N S VIGERS, **Hon C** D G BUSTON, **Hon Par Dn** S A WATSON

CHELSEA (St Saviour) Upper Chelsea St Sav *Lon*

CHELSEA, UPPER (Holy Trinity) (St Jude) *Lon 8* **P** *Earl Cadogan* **R** K L YATES

CHELSEA, UPPER (St Saviour) *Lon 8* **P** *R Upper Chelsea Holy Trin w St Jude* **V** F H ANDERSON

CHELSEA, UPPER (St Simon Zelotes) *Lon 8* **P** *Hyndman Trustees* **P-in-c** J J G JAMES

CHELSFIELD (St Martin of Tours) *Roch 15* **P** *All So Coll Ox* **R** L G VIRGO, **Hon C** R S BODY

CHELSHAM (St Christopher) Warlingham w Chelsham and Farleigh *S'wark*

CHELSHAM (St Leonard) as above

CHELSTON (St Peter) Cockington *Ex*

CHELSWORTH (All Saints) Monks Eleigh w Chelsworth and Brent Eleigh etc *St E*

CHELTENHAM (Christ Church) *Glouc 11* **P** *Simeon's Trustees* **C** R E INGLESBY

CHELTENHAM (Emmanuel) *Glouc 11* **P** *Bp* **P-in-c** I E BURBERY

CHELTENHAM (St Luke and St John) *Glouc 11* **P** *R Cheltenham and Simeon's Trustees (alt)* **V** J M WHALES, **C** G E HISCOCK

CHELTENHAM (St Mark) (St Silas) (St Barnabas) (St Aidan) (Emmanuel) *Glouc 11* **P** *Patr Bd*

TR D G WILLIAMS, **TV** S F KIMBER, G B THOMAS, P L SIBLEY, **C** R J FACER, **NSM** N A D SCOTLAND, H J DAVIES
CHELTENHAM (St Mary) (St Matthew) (St Paul) (Holy Trinity) *Glouc 11* **P** *Patr Bd* **TR** G W HART, **TV** P HARRIS, F COLLARD, **C** D I GIBSON, **NSM** L A FITZ
CHELTENHAM (St Michael) *Glouc 11* **P** *Bp* **P-in-c** D I LAWRENCE, **NSM** G L EDWARDS
CHELTENHAM (St Peter) *Glouc 11* **P** *DBP* **V** W F J EVERITT, **C** A D TAYLOR
CHELTENHAM (St Stephen) *Glouc 11* **P** *Bp* **P-in-c** J H HEIDT
CHELVESTON (St John the Baptist) Higham Ferrers w Chelveston *Pet*
CHELVEY (St Bridget) Cleeve w Chelvey and Brockley *B & W*
CHELWOOD (St Leonard) Publow w Pensford, Compton Dando and Chelwood *B & W*
CHELWOOD GATE (not known) Danehill *Chich*
CHENIES (St Michael) and Little Chalfont, Latimer and Flaunden *Ox 23* **P** *Bedf Estates Trustees and Lord Chesham (jt)* **R** R M V STAPLETON, **C** S A FRANKLIN, J G HARFORD
CHEQUERBENT (St Thomas) Westhoughton *Man*
CHEQUERFIELD (St Mary) Pontefract St Giles *Wakef*
CHERBURY *Ox 17* **P** *Bp, Jes Coll Ox, and Worc Coll Ox (jt)* **R** D J HOWSON
CHERHILL (St James the Great) Oldbury *Sarum*
CHERINGTON (St John the Baptist) w Stourton *Cov 9* **P** *Bp* **R** D C BROWN
CHERINGTON (St Nicholas) Avening w Cherington *Glouc*
CHERITON (All Souls) w Newington *Cant 5* **P** *Abp* **V** G H GREEN
CHERITON (St Martin) *Cant 5* **P** *Abp* **R** J H WRIGHT
CHERITON (St Michael and All Angels) w Tichborne and Beauworth *Win 1* **P** *The Crown* **R** R E WILLIAMS
CHERITON, NORTH (St John the Baptist) Camelot Par *B & W*
CHERITON BISHOP (St Mary) *Ex 6* **P** *Bp* **P-in-c** N CLARKE
CHERITON FITZPAINE (St Matthew) N Creedy *Ex*
CHERRY BURTON (St Michael) *York 9* **P** *R H Burton Esq* **R** W E R WILKINSON
CHERRY HINTON (St Andrew) *Ely 2* **P** *Peterho Cam* **V** C D BOULTON, **C** P K REED, M N HAWORTH, **Hon C** W G PRENTICE
CHERRY HINTON (St John the Evangelist) *Ely 2* **P** *Bp* **V** B N JONES, **Par Dn** E A HUBBARD
CHERRY WILLINGHAM (St Peter and St Paul) w Greetwell *Linc 3* **P** *D&C* **V** K J SAUNDERS
CHERTSEY (St Peter w All Saints) *Guildf 11* **P** *Haberdashers' Co* **V** D L H HEAD, **C** P C AVES, K A ELFORD
CHESELBORNE (St Martin) Milton Abbas, Hilton w Cheselbourne etc *Sarum*
CHESHAM, GREAT (Christ Church) (Emmanuel) (St Mary the Virgin) *Ox 20* **P** *Patr Bd* **TR** R J SALISBURY, **TV** J A HAWKINS, A J WARBURTON, **C** S A WEEDEN, **Par Dn** M M HALL, **NSM** A DAVIS, A W MEEK, D J UPCOTT, J O EDIS
CHESHAM BOIS (St Leonard) *Ox 20* **P** *Peache Trustees* **R** M A HILL, **C** J TRICKEY, **NSM** A P HOPWOOD
CHESHUNT (St Mary the Virgin) *St Alb 6* **P** *Marquess of Salisbury* **V** T D L LLOYD, **C** A R GOOD, F J MERCURIO
CHESSINGTON (St Mary the Virgin) *Guildf 9* **P** *Mert Coll Ox* **V** C M SAVAGE, **C** B STEADMAN-ALLEN
CHESTER (Holy Trinity without the Walls) *Ches 2* **P** *Bp* **R** D A BOYD, **C** I A DAVENPORT
CHESTER (St Mary on the Hill) *Ches 2* **P** *Duke of Westmr* **R** C W J SAMUELS, **Hon C** J R CARHART
CHESTER (St Paul) *Ches 2* **P** *R Ches* **V** N W PYATT
CHESTER Team, The (Christ Church) (St Barnabas) (St John the Baptist) (St Peter) (St Thomas of Canterbury) *Ches 2* **P** *DBP* **TR** R S LUNT, **TV** C M POTTER, D F WILLMER
CHESTER LE STREET (St Mary and St Cuthbert) *Dur 1* **P** *St Jo Coll Dur* **P** P G WALKER, **C** J S TILLEY, N P DENHAM, **Par Dn** E A BLACK, **Hon Par Dn** M J WALKER
CHESTER SQUARE (St Michael) (St Philip) *Lon 3* **P** *Duke of Westmr* **V** D C L PRIOR, **C** N T W TAYLOR, W J H CROSSLEY
CHESTERBLADE (Blessed Virgin Mary) Evercreech w Chesterblade and Milton Clevedon *B & W*
CHESTERFIELD (Christ Church) *Derby 5* **P** *R Chesterfield H Trin* **V** V C MOSS

CHESTERFIELD (Holy Trinity) *Derby 5* **P** *CPAS* **R** A J ASHTON
CHESTERFIELD (St Augustine) *Derby 5* **P** *Bp* **V** F E WILLETT
CHESTERFIELD (St Mary and All Saints) *Derby 5* **P** *Bp* **V** M W JARRETT, **C** N L CUTTS, **NSM** D KING
CHESTERFORD, GREAT (All Saints) w Little Chesterford *Chelmsf 25* **P** *Bp* **V** A KEMP
CHESTERFORD, LITTLE (St Mary the Virgin) Gt w Lt Chesterford *Chelmsf*
CHESTERTON (Good Shepherd) *Ely 2* **P** *Bp* **V** P S G CAMERON
CHESTERTON (Holy Trinity) (St Chad) *Lich 15* **P** *Prime Min* **V** V T OXFORD
CHESTERTON (St Andrew) *Ely 2* **P** *Trin Coll Cam* **V** J M R SHELDON, **C** L DAZELEY, **Par Dn** L L RANDALL
CHESTERTON (St George) *Ely 2* **P** *Bp* **V** P H TAMPLIN
CHESTERTON (St Giles) *Cov 8* **P** *Lady Willoughby de Broke* **P-in-c** E J A BRAZIER
CHESTERTON (St Lawrence) Cirencester *Glouc*
CHESTERTON (St Michael) Alwalton and Chesterton *Ely*
CHESTERTON w Middleton Stoney and Wendlebury *Ox 2* **P** *New Coll Ox, Ch Ch Ox, and Bp (by turn)* **V** M J STOKES
CHESTERTON, GREAT (St Mary) Chesterton w Middleton Stoney and Wendlebury *Ox*
CHESWARDINE (St Swithun) *Lich 24* **P** *Adn Salop* **V** A D KEAY
CHETNOLE (St Peter) Yetminster w Ryme Intrinseca and High Stoy *Sarum*
CHETTISHAM (St Michael and All Angels) *Ely 14* **P** *D&C* **V** A BARTLE, **Hon Par Dn** M A GUITE
CHETTLE (St Mary) Tollard Royal w Farnham, Gussage St Michael etc *Sarum*
CHETTON (St Giles) Billingsley w Sidbury, Middleton Scriven etc *Heref*
CHETWODE (St Mary and St Nicholas) Swan *Ox*
CHETWYND (St Michael and All Angels) Newport w Longford and Chetwynd *Lich*
CHEVELEY (St Mary) *Ely 4* **P** *DBP and Mrs D A Bowlby (alt)* **R** A F HOMER
CHEVENING (St Botolph) *Roch 8* **P** *Abp* **R** M G HEWETT
CHEVERELL, GREAT (St Peter) W Lavington and the Cheverells *Sarum*
CHEVERELL, LITTLE (St Peter) as above
CHEVINGTON (All Saints) w Hargrave and Whepstead w Brockley *St E 13* **P** *DBP (1 turn), Guild of All So (2 turns), and Bp (2 turns)* **R** J W MOTT, **NSM** D R UNDERWOOD, **Hon Par Dn** L S McCORMACK
CHEVINGTON (St John the Divine) *Newc 9* **P** *Bp* **V** T D DAWSON
CHEVITHORNE (St Thomas) Washfield, Stoodleigh, Withleigh etc *Ex*
CHEW MAGNA (St Andrew) w Dundry *B & W 11* **P** *Mrs D H F Luxmoore-Ball* **V** J D HEWITT
CHEW STOKE (St Andrew) w Nempnett Thrubwell *B & W 11* **P** *Bp and SMF (jt)* **R** T K VIVIAN
CHEWTON (Mission Church) Keynsham *B & W*
CHEWTON MENDIP (St Mary Magdalene) w Ston Easton, Litton and Emborough *B & W 9* **P** *Earl Waldegrave (2 turns), Bp (1 turn)* **R** J D A STEVENS
CHEYLESMORE (Christ Church) *Cov 3* **P** *Ch Trust Fund Trust* **V** A F MUNDEN
CHICHELEY (St Laurence) Sherington w Chicheley, N Crawley, Astwood etc *Ox*
CHICHESTER (St Pancras and St John) *Chich 3* **P** *Simeon's Trustees (2 turns), St Jo Chpl Trustees (1 turn)* **R** R B M GRIFFITHS
CHICHESTER (St Paul) and St Peter the Great *Chich 3* **P** *D&C* **V** K W CATCHPOLE, **J** M W SEDGWICK, **NSM** M G STONE, **Hon Par Dn** P KING
CHICHESTER (St Wilfred) Parklands St Wilfrid CD *Chich*
CHICKERELL (St Mary) w Fleet *Sarum 5* **P** *Bp* **R** O J NEWNHAM
CHICKLADE (All Saints) Tisbury *Sarum*
CHIDDINGFOLD (St Mary) *Guildf 4* **P** *Ld Chan* **R** *Vacant* Wormley (0428) 682008
CHIDDINGLY (not known) w East Hoathly *Chich 21* **P** *Bp* **R** P H AMOS
CHIDDINGSTONE (St Mary) w Chiddingstone Causeway *Roch 10* **P** *Abp and Bp (jt)* **R** J R LEE, **NSM** E J LORIMER
CHIDDINGSTONE CAUSEWAY (St Luke) Chiddingstone w Chiddingstone Causeway *Roch*

CHIDEOCK (St Giles)   Symondsbury and Chideock
Sarum
CHIDHAM (St Mary) *Chich 13*   **P**   *Bp*   **V** N J SMITH
**CHIEVELEY (St Mary the Virgin) w Winterbourne and
Oare** *Ox 14*   **P** *Adn Berks*   **V** C T SCOTT-DEMPSTER
CHIGNAL SMEALEY (St Nicholas)   The Chignals w
Mashbury *Chelmsf*
CHIGNALS w Mashbury, The *Chelmsf 11*   **P** *CPAS*
(2 turns), Bp (1 turn)   **R** *Vacant*
CHIGWELL (St Mary) (St Winifred) *Chelmsf 2*   **P** *Bp*
TR H R DIBBENS,   **TV** A J BISHOP
CHIGWELL ROW (All Saints) *Chelmsf 2*   **P** *The Crown*
R V C BROWN
CHILBOLTON (St Mary) cum Wherwell *Win 3*   **P** *Bp
and Marquess of Camden (alt)*   **P-in-c** F E WILLIAMS
CHILCOMB (St Andrew)   Win All SS w Chilcomb and
Chesil *Win*
CHILCOMBE (not known)   Bride Valley *Sarum*
**CHILCOMPTON (St John the Baptist) w Downside and
Stratton on the Fosse** *B & W 13*   **P** *Bp, MMCET, and
V Midsomer Norton (jt)*   **R** S J TUDGEY
CHILCOTE (St Matthew's Chapel)   Clifton Campville w
Chilcote *Lich*
**CHILDE OKEFORD (St Nicholas), Manston, Hammoon
and Hanford** *Sarum 6*   **P** *DBP*   **P-in-c** D N BOX
CHILDERDITCH (All Saints and St Faith)   Gt Warley w
Childerditch and Ingrave *Chelmsf*
CHILDREY (St Mary the Virgin)   Ridgeway *Ox*
CHILDS ERCALL (St Michael and All Angels) *Lich 24*
P *Lt-Col Sir John Corbet, Bt*   **V** D W RENSHAW
**CHILDSWYCKHAM (St Mary the Virgin) w Aston
Somerville, Buckland and Snowshill** *Glouc 17*   **P** *Bp*
R A M LEE
CHILDWALL (All Saints) *Liv 4*   **P** *Bp*
V C J ROOKWOOD
CHILDWALL (St David) *Liv 4*   **P** *Bp*   **V** S W C GOUGH
CHILDWALL VALLEY (St Mark)   Gateacre *Liv*
CHILDWICK (St Mary)   St Alb St Mich *St Alb*
CHILFROME (Holy Trinity)   Melbury *Sarum*
CHILHAM (St Mary) *Cant 2*   **P** *Viscount Massereene and
Ferrard*   **V** C R DUNCAN
CHILLENDEN (All Saints)   Nonington w Wymynswold
and Goodnestone etc *Cant*
CHILLESFORD (St Peter)   Orford w Sudbourne,
Chillesford, Butley and Iken *St E*
CHILLINGHAM (St Peter)   Glendale Gp *Newc*
CHILLINGTON (St James)   Dowlishwake w Kingstone,
Chillington etc *B & W*
CHILMARK (St Margaret of Antioch)   Tisbury *Sarum*
CHILTHORNE DOMER (Blessed Virgin Mary)
Tintinhull w Chilthorne Domer, Yeovil Marsh etc
B & W
CHILTINGTON, EAST (not known)   Plumpton *Chich*
CHILTINGTON, WEST (St Mary) *Chich 12*   **P** *Bp*
R J L REEVES
CHILTON (All Saints)   Harwell w Chilton *Ox*
CHILTON (St Aidan) *Dur 14*   **P** *Bp*   **V** M S SNOWBALL
CHILTON (St Mary)   Brill, Boarstall, Chilton and
Dorton *Ox*
**CHILTON CANTELO (St James) w Ashington, Mudford,
Rimpton and Marston Magna** *B & W 8*   **P** *DBP and
D&C (1 turn), D&C Bris (1 turn), and Bp Lon (1 turn)*
R E D WHITE
CHILTON FOLIAT (St Mary)   Whitton *Sarum*
CHILTON MOOR (St Andrew) *Dur 6*   **P** *Bp*
V G HARRIS
CHILTON POLDEN (St Edward)   W Poldens *B & W*
CHILTON TRINITY (Holy Trinity)   Bridgwater St
Mary, Chilton Trinity and Durleigh *B & W*
CHILVERS COTON (All Saints) w Astley *Cov 5*
P *Viscount Daventry*   **V** J D PHILPOTT,
C S F HARDWICK
CHILWELL (Christ Church) *S'well 7*   **P** *CPAS*
V D M MOORE,   **C** A J HULME
CHILWORTH (St Denys) w North Baddesley *Win 11*
P *Mrs P M A T Chamberlayne-Macdonald*
V A W DOUGHTY
CHILWORTH (St Thomas)   Blackheath and Chilworth
Guildf
CHINEHAM (Christ Church) *Win 4*   **P** *Bp*   **V** P J LAW
CHINESE CONGREGATION   St Martin-in-the-Fields
Lon
CHINGFORD (All Saints) (St Peter and St Paul) *Chelmsf 8*
P *Bp*   **R** R W MARRIOTT,   **C** D J DALAIS
CHINGFORD (St Anne) *Chelmsf 8*   **P** *Bp*
V J A L HARRISSON,   **Hon C** P G ROLPH
CHINGFORD (St Edmund) *Chelmsf 8*   **P** *Bp*
V E C FORD,   **Hon Par Dn** J I TURNER

CHINLEY (St Mary) w Buxworth *Derby 6*   **P** *Bp*
V L E GILCHRIST
CHINNOCK, EAST (Blessed Virgin Mary)
W Coker w Hardington Mandeville, E Chinnock etc
B & W
CHINNOCK, MIDDLE (St Margaret)   Norton sub
Hamdon, W Chinnock, Chiselborough etc *B & W*
CHINNOCK, WEST (Blessed Virgin Mary)   as above
**CHINNOR (St Andrew) w Emmington and Sydenham and
Aston Rowant w Crowell** *Ox 1*   **P** *Bp, DBP, and Peache
Trustees (jt)*   **R** R A CARTMILL,   **C** T R HEWSON
CHIPPENHAM (St Andrew) w Tytherton Lucas *Bris 9*
P *Ch Ch Ox*   **V** P H F WOODHOUSE,   **C** R M WATTS
CHIPPENHAM (St Margaret) *Ely 3*   **P** *Mrs A Crawley*
P-in-c D J KIGHTLEY
**CHIPPENHAM (St Paul) w Hardenhuish and Langley
Burrell** *Bris 9*   **P** *Patr Bd*   **TR** J A SMITH
CHIPPENHAM (St Peter) *Bris 9*   **P** *Bp*   **V** J G BRAY,
NSM B H BOLLEN, D C THURNELL
CHIPPERFIELD (St Paul) *St Alb 10*   **P** *Trustees*
V A J G ELLERY,   **Hon Par Dn** A M BUTLER
CHIPPING (St Bartholomew) and Whitewell (St Michael)
Blackb 8   **P** *Bp and Hulme Trustees (jt)*
V H F K CHEALL
CHIPPING BARNET (St John the Baptist) w Arkley
St Alb 2   **P** *The Crown*   **TR** A G K ESDAILE,
TV J A STONE, M S CHERRY,   **C** M J AINSWORTH
CHIPPING CAMPDEN (St James) w Ebrington *Glouc 10*
P *Peache Trustees (1 turn), Earl of Harrowby (2 turns)*
V P J MILLAM
CHIPPING NORTON (St Mary the Virgin) *Ox 3*
P *D&C Glouc*   **V** T J CURTIS
CHIPPING ONGAR (St Martin) w Shelley *Chelmsf 6*
P *Guild of All So and Keble Coll Ox*   **R** E J SIBSON
**CHIPPING SODBURY (St John the Baptist) and Old
Sodbury** *Glouc 7*   **P** *D&C Worc*   **V** N R E JACOBS,
C E P A GREEN
**CHIPPING WARDEN (St Peter and St Paul) w Edgcote
and Aston le Walls** *Pet 1*   **P** *Bp, Mrs D A Bowlby, and
R Courage Esq (by turn)*   **R** S E CRAWLEY
**CHIPSTABLE (All Saints) w Huish Champflower and
Clatworthy** *B & W 21*   **P** *Bp (2 turns), Major T F
Trollope-Bellew (1 turn)*   **R** J P BIRD
CHIPSTEAD (Good Shepherd)   Chevening *Roch*
CHIPSTEAD (St Margaret of Antioch) *S'wark 24*   **P** *Abp*
R J M P GOODDEN,   **Dss** D SMEDBERG
CHIRBURY (St Michael) *Heref 13*   **P** *Sir David
Wakeman, Bt, and Bp (alt)*   **V** P D HARRATT
CHIRTON (St John the Baptist)   Redhorn *Sarum*
CHISELBOROUGH (St Peter and St Paul)   Norton sub
Hamdon, W Chinnock, Chiselborough etc *B & W*
CHISHILL, GREAT (St Swithun)   Heydon, Gt and Lt
Chishill, Chrishall etc *Chelmsf*
CHISHILL, LITTLE (St Nicholas)   as above
CHISLEDON (Holy Cross)   Ridgeway *Sarum*
CHISLEHURST (Annunciation) *Roch 13*   **P** *Keble Coll*
V W B BEER
CHISLEHURST (Christ Church) *Roch 13*   **P** *CPAS*
V R W COTTON
CHISLEHURST (St Nicholas) *Roch 13*   **P** *Bp*
R J C ALLEN,   **NSM** J B HURN
CHISLET (St Mary the Virgin)   St Nicholas at Wade w
Sarre and Chislet w Hoath *Cant*
CHISWICK (St Michael) *Lon 11*   **P** *V St Martin-in-the-
Fields*   **V** M F BARNEY
CHISWICK (St Nicholas w St Mary Magdalene) *Lon 11*
P *D&C St Paul's*   **V** P A TUFT,   **C** C J FULLER,
Hon C J W CHARLES,   **NSM** D W RANDALL
CHISWICK (St Paul) Grove Park *Lon 11*   **P** *V Chiswick*
V M C RILEY
CHITHURST (St Mary)   Rogate w Terwick and Trotton
w Chithurst *Chich*
CHITTERNE (All Saints and St Mary)   Tilshead,
Orcheston and Chitterne *Sarum*
CHITTERNE (St Mary Chancel)   as above
CHITTLEHAMHOLT (St John)   S Molton w Nymet St
George, High Bray etc *Ex*
CHITTLEHAMPTON (St Hieritha)   as above
CHITTS HILL (St Cuthbert) *Lon 19*   **P** *CPAS*
V S P CORBETT
CHIVELSTONE (St Sylvester)   Charleton w Buckland
Tout Saints etc *Ex*
CHOBHAM (St Lawrence) w Valley End *Guildf 6*   **P** *Bp
and Brig R W Acworth (alt)*   **V** A J H SALMON
CHOLDERTON (St Nicholas)   Bourne Valley *Sarum*
CHOLESBURY (St Lawrence)   Hawridge w Cholesbury
and St Leonard *Ox*

CHOLLERTON w Birtley and Thockrington *Newc 2*
 P *Mrs P I Enderby (2 turns)*, *Newc Dioc Soc (1 turn)*
 R *Vacant* Hexham (0434) 681721
CHOLSEY (St Mary) *Ox 18* **P** *Ld Chan* **V** J R HALL,
 NSM J P M VELLACOTT
CHOPPARDS (Mission Room) Upper Holme Valley
 Wakef
CHOPPINGTON (St Paul the Apostle) *Newc 1* **P** *D&C*
 V R G FORD
CHOPWELL (St John the Evangelist) *Dur 5* **P** *Bp*
 V T E SIMPSON
CHORLEY (All Saints) *Blackb 4* **P** *Bp* **V** T D WILBY
CHORLEY (St George) *Blackb 4* **P** *R Chorley*
 V K BARRETT, **C** A H McMICHAEL
CHORLEY (St James) *Blackb 4* **P** *R Chorley*
 V G THOMAS
CHORLEY (St Laurence) *Blackb 4* **P** *Bp* **R** E V JONES
CHORLEY (St Peter) *Blackb 4* **P** *R Chorley*
 V J D BURNS
CHORLEY (St Philip) Alderley Edge *Ches*
CHORLEYWOOD (Christ Church) *St Alb 10* **P** *CPAS*
 Par Dn A P DOUGLAS
CHORLEYWOOD (St Andrew) *St Alb 10* **P** *Bp*
 V G E D PYTCHES, **C** B J KISSELL, B A SKINNER,
 Par Dn M O KNIGHT,
 NSM J G ROBERTS, J W SUTTON, R W MAYNARD
CHORLTON-CUM-HARDY (St Clement) (St Barnabas)
 Man 4 **P** *D&C* **R** R J GILPIN, **C** G C BURROWS
CHORLTON-CUM-HARDY (St Werburgh) *Man 4* **P** *Bp*
 R A R M SEAMAN
CHRISHALL (Holy Trinity) Heydon, Gt and Lt
 Chishill, Chrishall etc *Chelmsf*
CHRIST THE KING in the Diocese of Newcastle *Newc 5*
 P *Patr Bd* **TR** P KENNEY,
 TV P G H HISCOCK, R FINDLAYSON
CHRISTCHURCH (Holy Trinity) *Win 8* **P** *Bp*
 V B H TREVOR-MORGAN,
 C G A HARRIS, J C WHITE, M J CLAYTON, P A MacCARTY
CHRISTCHURCH Stourvale (St George) Christchurch
 Win
CHRISTIAN MALFORD (All Saints) w Sutton Benger and
 Tytherton Kellaways *Bris 9* **P** *D&C Sarum (2 turns)*,
 Bp (2 turns), and R W Neeld Esq (1 turn)
 R Lord MILVERTON
CHRISTLETON (St James) *Ches 2* **P** *Exors*
 Major H C L Garnett **R** D C GARNETT
CHRISTON (Blessed Virgin Mary) Crook Peak *B & W*
CHRISTOW (St James), Ashton, Trusham and Bridford
 Ex 6 **P** *SMF, MMCET, Viscount Exmouth, Bp, and*
 E A Beard Esq (jt) **R** J R C TAYLOR,
CHUDLEIGH (St Mary and St Martin) *Ex 11*
 P *MMCET* **V** C T PIDSLEY, **NSM** E A WARREN
CHUDLEIGH KNIGHTON (St Paul) Bovey Tracey St
 John, Chudleigh Knighton etc *Ex*
CHULMLEIGH (St Mary Magdalene) *Ex 16* **P** *MMCET*
 R J N STOCKWELL
CHURCH ASTON (St Andrew) *Lich 22* **P** *R Edgmond*
 R W H YATES
CHURCH BRAMPTON (St Botolph) w Chapel Brampton
 and Harleston, East Haddon and Holdenby *Pet 2*
 P *Earl Spencer, Bp, The Crown, and CCC Ox (by turn)*
 R J B DOTY
CHURCH BROUGHTON (St Michael and All Angels) w
 Barton Blount, Boylestone, Sutton on the Hill and
 Trusley *Derby 14* **P** *Exors R H R Buckston, Worc Coll*
 Ox, Mrs F H Coke-Steel (2 turns each), Miss C M Auden
 and J W Pratt Esq (1 turn each) **R** A J F SHARP
CHURCH CONISTON (St Andrew) *Carl 8* **P** *Peache*
 Trustees **V** S J SKINNER, **Hon Par Dn** J M SKINNER
CHURCH EATON (St Editha) Moreton and Church
 Eaton *Lich*
CHURCH HONEYBOURNE (St Ecgwyn) Pebworth w
 Dorsington and Honeybourne *Glouc*
CHURCH HULME (St Luke) *Ches 11* **P** *V Sandbach*
 V J EARDLEY, **NSM** M E C WHATSON
CHURCH KIRK (St James) *Blackb 1* **P** *Hulme Trustees*
 R N A ASHTON
CHURCH KNOWLE (St Peter) Corfe Castle, Church
 Knowle, Kimmeridge etc *Sarum*
CHURCH LANGTON (St Peter) w Tur Langton, Thorpe
 Langton and Stonton Wyville *Leic 4* **P** *Bp and*
 E Brudenell Esq (jt) **P-in-c** E Z MBALI
CHURCH LAWFORD (St Peter) Wolston and Church
 Lawford *Cov*
CHURCH LAWTON (All Saints) *Ches 11*
 P *J A Lawton Esq* **R** R SUTTON
CHURCH LENCH (All Saints) w Rous Lench and Abbots
 Morton *Worc 1* **P** *Bp* **R** J N O WILLIAMS

CHURCH MINSHULL (St Bartholomew) *Ches 15* **P** *Bp*
 P-in-c G D GEDDES
CHURCH OAKLEY (St Leonard) and Wootton (St
 Lawrence) *Win 4* **P** *Qu Coll Ox and D&C (alt)*
 R C L ATKINS
CHURCH PREEN (St John the Baptist) Wenlock *Heref*
CHURCH STRETTON (St Laurence) *Heref 11* **P** *Ch Patr*
 Trust **R** M S STEDMAN, **C** D J K WALLER, T F PRICE,
 NSM D E JANES
CHURCHAM (St Andrew) w Bulley and Minsterworth
 Glouc 3 **P** *Bp and D&C (alt)* **V** G P JENKINS
CHURCHDOWN (St Andrew) (St Bartholomew) *Glouc 6*
 P *D&C* **V** M W NORTHALL
CHURCHDOWN (St John the Evangelist) *Glouc 6* **P** *Bp*
 V E F GILES, **C** S MOTH
CHURCHILL (All Saints) Kingham w Churchill,
 Daylesford and Sarsden *Ox*
CHURCHILL (St James) Churchill-in-Halfshire w
 Blakedown and Broome *Worc*
CHURCHILL (St John the Baptist) Burrington and
 Churchill *B & W*
CHURCHILL (St Michael) Peopleton and White Ladies
 Aston etc *Worc*
CHURCHILL-IN-HALFSHIRE w Blakedown and Broome
 Worc 11 **P** *Viscount Cobham and H A C Bourne Esq*
 (alt) **R** N J DAVIS
CHURCHOVER (Holy Trinity) w Willey *Cov 6* **P** *Bp*
 P-in-c P S BALLANTINE, **C** A S REED
CHURCHSTANTON (St Peter and St Paul), Buckland
 St Mary and Otterford *B & W 20* **P** *DBP and*
 Mrs M E Mcdonald (jt) **R** A G SHRIVES
CHURCHSTOKE (St Nicholas) w Hyssington and Sarn
 Heref 10 **P** *The Crown (1 turn), Earl of Powis (2 turns)*
 V W T BRYAN, **NSM** I R BALL, G LLOYD
CHURCHSTOW (St Mary) Malborough w S Huish, W
 Alvington and Churchstow *Ex*
CHURSTON FERRERS (St Mary the Vigin) Brixham w
 Churston Ferrers and Kingswear *Ex*
CHURT (St John the Evangelist) *Guildf 3* **P** *Adn Surrey*
 V S G THOMAS
CHURWELL (All Saints) Morley St Pet w Churwell
 Wakef
CHUTE (St Nicholas) Wexcombe *Sarum*
CHYNGTON (St Luke) Seaford w Sutton *Chich*
CINDERFORD (St John the Evangelist) *Glouc 4*
 P *The Crown* **V** J K MARTIN
CINDERFORD (St Stephen) w Littledean *Glouc 4*
 P *Ch Patr Trust* **V** G C BOWYER, **NSM** B J DAVIES
CINDERHILL (Christ Church) *S'well 14* **P** *Bp*
 V C H KNOWLES, **Par Dn** M J O'CONNELL
CINNAMON BROW (Resurrection) Padgate *Liv*
CIPPENHAM (St Andrew) W Slough *Ox*
CIRENCESTER (St John the Baptist) *Glouc 12* **P** *Bp*
 V H S RINGROSE, **C** J E BECK, F L STEWART-DARLING,
 NSM P G W PRIDGEON, S G ENSON
CLACTON, GREAT (St John the Baptist) *Chelmsf 26*
 P *Ch Patr Trust* **V** N W WYNNE-JONES, **C** J J CLARK
CLACTON, LITTLE (St James) Weeley and Lt Clacton
 Chelmsf
CLACTON-ON-SEA (St Christopher) (St James)
 Chelmsf 26 **P** *Bp* **V** A P D SPOONER,
 C V R DUNSTAN-MEADOWS, **NSM** I A O LEE
CLACTON-ON-SEA (St Paul) *Chelmsf 26* **P** *Ch Patr*
 Trust **V** A F RICHARDS, **Hon C** D W HART
CLAINES (St John the Baptist) *Worc 6* **P** *Bp*
 V W D OWEN
CLANDON, EAST (St Thomas of Canterbury) and West
 Clandon *Guildf 5* **P** *Earl of Onslow and Bp (alt)*
 R J B SMITH
CLANDON, WEST (St Peter and St Paul) E and W
 Clandon *Guildf*
CLANFIELD (St James) Catherington and Clanfield
 Portsm
CLANFIELD (St Stephen) Bampton w Clanfield *Ox*
CLANNABOROUGH (St Petrock) N Creedy *Ex*
CLAPHAM (St James) *S'wark 9* **P** *CPAS* **V** C E GALE,
 Par Dn H EDWARDS
CLAPHAM (St Mary the Virgin) Findon w Clapham and
 Patching *Chich*
CLAPHAM (St Thomas of Canterbury) *St Alb 19*
 P *MMCET* **V** M K M SCOTT
CLAPHAM Team Ministry, The (Christ Church and
 St John) (Holy Spirit) (Holy Trinity) (St John the
 Evangelist) (St Paul) (St Peter) *S'wark 9* **P** *Patr Bd*
 TR J HACKETT,
 TV D N HEAD, S EDWARDS, D J HOUGHTON,
 TM H M CUNLIFFE, **C** J P HAWES,
 Hon C R F VICKERY, **NSM** S MOSS

CLAPHAM COMMON (St Barnabas) *S'wark 13*
  P *Ch Trust Fund Trust* **P-in-c** D PAGE
CLAPHAM PARK (All Saints) *S'wark 9* **P** *CPAS and*
  R Clapham (jt) **V** M J BREEN
CLAPHAM PARK (St Stephen) *S'wark 10* **P** *Trustees*
  V D STUART-SMITH, **C** D J WILES
CLAPHAM-WITH-KEASDEN (St James) and Austwick
  Bradf 6 **P** *Bp* **V** J DALBY
CLAPTON (St James) Bourton-on-the-Water w Clapton
  Glouc
CLAPTON (St Peter) Barnwell w Tichmarsh, Thurning
  and Clapton *Pet*
CLAPTON, UPPER (St Matthew) *Lon 5* **P** *D&C Cant*
  V L W S PHILLIPS
CLAPTON IN GORDANO (St Michael) E Clevedon
  and Walton w Weston w Clapton *B & W*
CLARBOROUGH (St John the Baptist) w Hayton *S'well 5*
  P *Bp* **P-in-c** D A MINSHULL
CLARE (St Peter and St Paul) w Poslingford, Cavendish,
  Stoke by Clare w Wixoe *St E 8* **P** *Duchy of Lanc,*
  DBP, Jes Coll Cam, and Lord Loch (by turn)
  TV D BROAD, **C** A K GAIR
CLAREMONT (Holy Angels) *Man 6* **P** *Bp*
  V A BUTLER, **Par Dn** P BUTLER
CLARENDON PARK (St John the Baptist) w Knighton
  (St Michael and All Angels) *Leic 2* **P** *Bp*
  V M W STEPHENSON, **Par Dn** S I SKIDMORE,
  Hon C A J BALLARD
CLATFORD, UPPER (All Saints) Abbotts Ann and
  Upper and Goodworth Clatford *Win*
CLATWORTHY (St Mary Magdalene) Chipstable w
  Huish Champflower and Clatworthy *B & W*
CLAUGHTON (St Chad) Hornby w Claughton *Blackb*
CLAUGHTON VILLAGE (St Bede) Birkenhead St Jas
  w St Bede *Ches*
CLAVERDON (St Michael and All Angels) w Preston Bagot
  Cov 7 **P** *Bp* **P-in-c** C P C HUNT
CLAVERHAM (St Barnabas) Cleeve w Chelvey and
  Brockley *B & W*
CLAVERING (St Mary and St Clement) w Langley and
  Arkesden *Chelmsf 24* **P** *Ch Hosp and Keble Coll Ox*
  (alt) **V** D S McGUFFIE
CLAVERLEY (All Saints) (Heathton Mission) w Tuckhill
  Heref 9 **P** *Bp and Miss L Amphlett (jt)* **V** R SHARP
CLAVERTON (Blessed Virgin Mary) (St Hugh) *B & W 10*
  P *Personal Reps of the late R L D Skrine Esq*
  R D W HARVEY
CLAVERTON DOWN (St Hugh) Claverton *B & W*
CLAWTON (St Leonard) Ashwater, Halwill,
  Beaworthy, Clawton etc *Ex*
CLAXBY (St Mary) Walesby *Linc*
CLAXTON (St Andrew) Rockland St Mary w
  Hellington, Bramerton etc *Nor*
CLAY CROSS (St Bartholomew N Wingfield, Clay Cross
  and Pilsley *Derby*
CLAY HILL (St John the Baptist) (St Luke) *Lon 18*
  P *V Enfield St Andr and Bp (jt)* **V** J H NODDINGS
CLAYBROOKE (St Peter) cum Wibtoft and Frolesworth
  Leic 11 **P** *The Crown and Adn Loughb (by turn)*
  R S A HADDELSEY
CLAYDON and Barham *St E 1* **P** *Mrs M Rusinow and*
  G K Drury Esq (alt) **R** *Vacant* Ipswich (0473) 830362
CLAYDON (St James the Great) w Mollington *Ox 5*
  P *Bp* **P-in-c** R J CHARD
CLAYDONS, The (St Mary) (All Saints) *Ox 24*
  P *Sir Ralph Verney, Bt* **R** W J A RANKIN
CLAYGATE (Holy Trinity) *Guildf 8* **P** *Ch Patr Trust*
  C J WHITE
CLAYHANGER (St Peter) Bampton, Morebath,
  Clayhanger and Petton *Ex*
CLAYHIDON (St Andrew) Hemyock w Culm Davy and
  Clayhidon *Ex*
CLAYPOLE (St Peter) *Linc 23* **P** *DBP* **R** G MUNN
CLAYTON (St James the Great) *Lich 15* **P** *Bp*
  V R K LEGG, **Par Dn** P M JELF
CLAYTON (St John the Baptist) *Bradf 2* **P** *V Bradf*
  V J A N B HOWELL, **C** J W TURNER
CLAYTON (St John the Baptist) w Keymer *Chich 9*
  P *BNC Ox* **R** R L CLARKE, **C** J P COOPER
CLAYTON BROOK (Community Church) Whittle-le-
  Woods *Blackb*
CLAYTON LE MOORS (All Saints) Altham w Clayton
  le Moors *Blackb*
CLAYTON LE MOORS (St James) as above
CLAYTON WEST w HIGH HOYLAND (All Saints)
  High Hoyland, Scissett and Clayton W *Wakef*
CLAYWORTH (St Peter) Everton and Mattersey w
  Clayworth *S'well*

CLEADON (All Saints) *Dur 7* **P** *R Whitburn*
  V N SHAW, **NSM** J P TALBOT
CLEADON PARK (St Mark and St Cuthbert) *Dur 7*
  P *Bp* **V** J MAUGHAN
CLEARWELL (St Peter) Newland and Redbrook w
  Clearwell *Glouc*
CLEASBY (St Peter) Barton and Manfield w Cleasby
  Ripon
CLEATOR MOOR (St John the Evangelist) w Cleator
  (St Leonard) *Carl 5* **P** *Earl of Lonsdale and Bp (alt)*
  V K B B TOPPING
CLECKHEATON (St John the Evangelist) *Wakef 8*
  P *V Birstall* **V** M G INMAN
CLECKHEATON (St Luke) (Whitechapel) *Wakef 8* **P** *Bp*
  and Sir Martin Wilson (jt) **V** I M GASKELL,
  NSM M GASKELL
CLEDFORD (Mission Room) Middlewich w Byley *Ches*
CLEE, NEW (St John the Evangelist) (St Stephen) *Linc 9*
  P *Bp* **V** J WELLIS, **C** R T SWAIN
CLEE, OLD (Holy Trinity and St Mary the Virgin) *Linc 9*
  P *Bp* **V** R S R PATSTON
CLEE ST MARGARET (St Margaret) Bitterley w
  Middleton, Stoke St Milborough etc *Heref*
CLEETHORPE (Christ Church) Clee *Linc*
CLEETHORPES (St Aidan) (St Francis) (St Peter) *Linc 9*
  P *Bp* **TR** T H ROBINSON,
  TV J C HETHERINGTON, E I SLATER,
  Hon C D H WEBSTER
CLEETON (St Mary) Stottesdon w Farlow, Cleeton and
  Silvington *Heref*
CLEEVE (Holy Trinity) w Chelvey and Brockley *B & W 14*
  P *Bp and V Yatton (jt)* **V** D M JONES
CLEEVE, OLD (St Andrew), Leighland and Treborough
  B & W 17 **P** *Selw Coll Cam (2 turns), Personal Reps*
  G R Wolseley Esq (1 turn) **R** H E ALLEN
CLEEVE HILL (St Peter) Bishop's Cleeve *Glouc*
CLEEVE PRIOR (St Andrew) and The Littletons *Worc 1*
  P *D&C and Ch Ch Ox (alt)* **V** D R EVANS
CLEHONGER (All Saints) Kingstone w Clehonger,
  Eaton Bishop etc *Heref*
CLENCHWARTON (St Margaret) *Ely 17* **P** *Bp*
  R I W SMITH
CLENT (St Leonard) Belbroughton w Fairfield and
  Clent *Worc*
CLEOBURY MORTIMER (St Mary the Virgin) w Hopton
  Wafers *Heref 12* **P** *Keble Coll Ox and Mrs*
  R C Woodward (jt) **R** R A HORSFIELD,
  C A E DICKSON, **NSM** B H GADD
CLEOBURY NORTH (St Peter and St Paul) Ditton
  Priors w Neenton, Burwarton etc *Heref*
CLERKENWELL (Holy Redeemer) (St Philip) *Lon 6*
  P *Trustees* **P-in-c** B A BOUCHER,
  NSM N E WOODCOCK
CLERKENWELL (St James and St John) (St Peter) *Lon 6*
  P *Ch Patr Trust and PCC (jt)* **P-in-c** T C COLLETT-
  WHITE
CLEVEDON (St Andrew) (Christ Church) (St Peter)
  B & W 14 **P** *Simeon's Trustees (1 turn), Ld Chan*
  (2 turns) **V** M G W HAYES, **C** G I WILTON, R H M LEGG
CLEVEDON (St John the Evangelist) *B & W 14* **P** *SMF*
  V R D HARRIS, **C** D J MERCERON
CLEVEDON, EAST (All Saints) and Walton w Weston w
  Clapton in Gordano *B & W 14* **P** *Bp and SMF (jt)*
  R J F SMART, **C** M E RICHARDS
CLEVELEYS (St Andrew) *Blackb 13* **P** *Trustees*
  V D E REEVES, **C** J P ATACK
CLEWER (St Andrew) *Ox 13* **P** *Eton Coll* **R** D SHAW
CLEWER (St Stephen) *Ox 13* **P** *SMF* **V** *Vacant*
  Windsor (0753) 863955
CLEY (St Margaret) Blakeney w Cley, Wiveton,
  Glandford etc *Nor*
CLIBURN (St Cuthbert) Clifton, Brougham and Cliburn
  Carl
CLIDDESDEN (St Lawrence) and Ellisfield and Farleigh
  Wallop and Dummer *Win 4* **P** *Earl of Portsm and*
  DBP (jt) **R** T F KIME
CLIFFE (St Andrew) Hemingbrough *York*
CLIFFE, NORTH (St John) N Cave w Cliffe *York*
CLIFFE AT HOO (St Helen) w Cooling *Roch 6* **P** *D&C*
  R D J SILCOCK
CLIFFE VALE (St Stephen) Hartshill *Lich*
CLIFFORD (St Luke) *York 1* **P** *G Lane-Fox Esq*
  P-in-c R M C SEED
CLIFFORD (St Mary the Virgin) Cusop w Clifford,
  Hardwicke, Bredwardine etc *Heref*
CLIFFORD CHAMBERS (St Helen) Welford w
  Weston and Clifford Chambers *Glouc*
CLIFFORDS MESNE (St Peter) Newent and Gorsley w
  Cliffords Mesne *Glouc*

CLIFFSEND (St Mary the Virgin) St Laurence in Thanet *Cant*

CLIFTON (All Saints) *St Alb 22* P *Bp* R P J PAVEY

CLIFTON (All Saints w St John) *Bris 5* P *Bp*
V P G COBB, C M R FREEMAN, NSM R THOMAS

CLIFTON (Christ Church w Emmanuel) *Bris 5*
P *Simeon's Trustees* V P M BERG, C R A HIGGINS,
Par Dn G C MILLS

CLIFTON (Holy Trinity) *Derby 8* P *Lt-Col
J R G Stanton, T W Clowes Esq, and V Ashbourne w
Mapleton (by turn)* V J R J READ

CLIFTON (Holy Trinity, St Andrew the Less and St Peter)
Bris 5 P *Simeon's Trustees* V J J R COLLINGWOOD,
Par Dn R D WATLING

CLIFTON (Mission Church) Conisbrough *Sheff*

CLIFTON (St Anne) *Man 2* P *Bp* V W J GASH

CLIFTON (St Cuthbert), Brougham and Cliburn *Carl 4*
P *Earl of Lonsdale and Lord Hothfield (alt)*
R P H HOCKEY

CLIFTON (St Francis) (St Mary the Virgin) *S'well 10*
P *DBP* TR A HEATON, TV C C LEVY, C F ANDREWS,
C S BROCKLEHURST, Hon Par Dn P A EDWARDS

CLIFTON (St James) *Sheff 6* P *Bp* V V A VOUT

CLIFTON (St John) *Wakef 2* P *Bp* V J A RICHARDSON

CLIFTON (St Luke) *Carl 4* P R *Workington*
V P M BADEN, NSM J V HINE

CLIFTON (St Paul) *Bris 5* P *Bp* P-in-c J S F HADLEY,
C A C BRYER

CLIFTON (St Philip and St James) *York 8* P *Trustees*
V R G FLETCHER, C P W WHITE, Par Dn S E MUTCH,
NSM N E ECKERSLEY

CLIFTON, NEW (Holy Trinity) Clifton *S'well*

CLIFTON, NORTH (St George) Harby w Thorney and
N and S Clifton *S'well*

CLIFTON CAMPVILLE (St Andrew) w Chilcote *Lich 5*
P *Brig W J Reed* R A C SOLOMON

CLIFTON GREEN (St Thomas) *Man 2* P *Bp*
V K J MASSEY

CLIFTON HAMPDEN (St Michael and All Angels)
Dorchester *Ox*

CLIFTON-ON-TEME (St Kenelm), Lower Sapey and the
Shelsleys *Worc 3* P *Bp and A F Evans Esq (jt)*
R P C OWEN

CLIFTON REYNES (St Mary the Virgin) Lavendon w
Cold Brayfield, Clifton Reynes etc *Ox*

CLIFTON UPON DUNSMORE (St Mary) and Newton
Cov 6 P *H A F W Boughton Leigh Esq*
P-in-c P S BALLANTINE, C A S REED

CLIFTONVILLE (St Paul) *Cant 9* P *Ch Patr Trust*
V D A LUGG

CLIPPESBY (St Peter) Rollesby w Burgh w Billockby w
Ashby w Oby etc *Nor*

CLIPSHAM (St Mary) Greetham and Thistleton w
Stretton and Clipsham *Pet*

CLIPSTON (All Saints) w Naseby and Haselbech w
Kelmarsh *Pet 2* P *Ch Coll Cam, DBP, M F Harris
Esq, and Miss C V Lancaster (by turn)* R D W FAULKS

CLIPSTONE (All Saints) *S'well 2* P *Bp* V C S FULLER

CLITHEROE (St James) *Blackb 8* P *Trustees*
R H L CLARK

CLITHEROE (St Mary Magdalene) *Blackb 8*
P *J R Peel Esq* V J A D ROBERTS, C P HARTLEY,
NSM P W SHEPHERD

CLITHEROE (St Paul) Low Moor *Blackb 8* P *Bp*
V R NICHOLSON

CLIVE (All Saints) Astley, Clive, Grinshill and Hadnall
Lich

CLIVE VALE (All Souls) Hastings All So *Chich*

CLODOCK (St Clydog) and Longtown w Craswall,
Llanveynoe, St Margaret's, Michaelchurch Escley and
Newton *Heref 1* P *DBP (2 turns), MMCET (1 turn)*
V F E RODGERS, NSM G G DAVIES

CLOFORD (St Mary) Nunney and Witham Friary,
Marston Bigot etc *B & W*

CLOPHILL (St Mary the Virgin) *St Alb 22* P *Ball Coll
Ox* R P J SWINDELLS

CLOPTON (St Mary) w Otley, Swilland and Ashbocking
St E 7 P *Ld Chan and Bp (alt)* R B WAKELING

CLOSWORTH (All Saints) E Coker w Sutton Bingham
and Closworth *B & W*

CLOTHALL (St Mary Virgin) Sandon, Wallington and
Rushden w Clothall *St Alb*

CLOUGHTON (St Mary) *York 16* P *V Scalby*
P-in-c J A WILLIAMS

CLOVELLY (All Saints) (St Peter) *Ex 17*
P *Hon Mrs Asquith's Trustees* R D A BATES

CLOWNE (St John the Baptist) *Derby 3* P *Ld Chan*
R L R R HARRIS

CLOWS TOP (Mission Room) Mamble w Bayton, Rock
w Heightington etc *Worc*

CLUBMOOR (St Andrew) *Liv 8* P *Bp* V R J G PANTER

CLUMBER PARK (St Mary the Virgin) Worksop
Priory *S'well*

CLUN (St George) w Bettws-y-Crwyn and Newcastle
Heref 10 P *Earl of Powis* Hon AP J E M ROBERTS

CLUNBURY (St Swithin) Clungunford w Clunbury and
Clunton, Bedstone etc *Heref*

CLUNGUNFORD (St Cuthbert) w Clunbury and Clunton,
Bedstone and Hopton Castle *Heref 10* P *Earl of Powis,
Mrs S B Rocke, M S C Brown Esq, and
Sir Hugh Ripley, Bt (jt)* P-in-c P B WELCH

CLUNTON (St Mary) Clungunford w Clunbury and
Clunton, Bedstone etc *Heref*

CLUTTON (St Augustine of Hippo) w Cameley *B & W 11*
P *Earl of Warw (2 turns), and Exors J P Hippisley
(1 turn)* R A V SAUNDERS

CLYFFE PYPARD (St Peter) Broad Town, Cliffe
Pypard and Tockenham *Sarum*

CLYMPING (St Mary the Virgin) and Yapton w Ford
Chich 1 P *Bp (2 turns), Ld Chan (1 turn)*
V D S FARRANT, NSM A R BRANT

CLYST HONITON (St Michael and All Angels)
Aylesbeare, Rockbeare, Farringdon etc *Ex*

CLYST HYDON (St Andrew) Bradninch and Clyst
Hydon *Ex*

CLYST ST GEORGE (St George) Clyst St Mary, Clyst
St George etc *Ex*

CLYST ST LAWRENCE (St Lawrence) Whimple,
Talaton and Clyst St Lawr *Ex*

CLYST ST MARY (St Mary), Clyst (St George) and
Woodbury Salterton *Ex 1* P *Lord Wraxall, D&C, and
S Radcliffe (jt)* R G L ROWE

COALBROOKDALE (Holy Trinity), Iron-Bridge and
Little Wenlock *Heref 14* P *Bp, Lord Forester,
Vs Madeley and Much Wenlock (jt)* R *Vacant*
Ironbridge (095245) 3309

COALEY (St Bartholomew) Lower Cam w Coaley
Glouc

COALPIT HEATH (St Saviour) *Bris 7* P *Bp*
V B RAVEN

COALVILLE (Christ Church) and Bardon Hill *Leic 8*
P *Simeon's Trust and R Hugglescote (jt)* V S M LEE

COATES (Holy Trinity) *Ely 18* P *Ld Chan*
R A BENNETT

COATES (St Edith) *Linc 2* P *Bp*
P-in-c G S RICHARDSON

COATES (St Matthew), Rodmarton and Sapperton w
Frampton Mansell *Glouc 12* P *Bp, Lord Bathurst, and
Guild of All So (jt)* R R A BOWDEN,
NSM J M FRANCIS

COATES, GREAT (St Nicholas) Gt and Lt Coates w
Bradley *Linc*

COATES, GREAT and LITTLE (Bishop Edward King
Church) (St Michael) w Bradley *Linc 9* P *Patr Bd*
TR A V DOUGLAS, TV P T DAVIS, R PROSSER,
Par Dn P A GOLDSMITH

COATES, NORTH (St Nicholas) Tetney, Marshchapel
and N Coates *Linc*

COATHAM (Christ Church) *York 17* P *Trustees*
V J WOODHOUSE

COATHAM, EAST (Christ Church) Coatham *York*

COBBOLD ROAD (St Saviour) (St Mary) *Lon 9* P *Bp*
V J D WHEELER

COBERLEY (St Giles) w Cowley *Glouc 12* P *Ld Chan
and H W G Elwes Esq (alt)* R S I PULFORD

COBHAM Sole Street (St Mary's Church Room)
Cobham w Luddesdowne and Dode *Roch*

COBHAM (St Andrew) (St John the Divine) *Guildf 10*
P *D C H Combe Esq* V B L PREECE, C P F SMITH

COBHAM (St Mary Magdalene) w Luddesdowne and Dode
Roch 1 P *Earl of Darnley and CPAS (alt)*
P-in-c M P P HOWARD

COBRIDGE (Christ Church) Hanley H Ev *Lich*

COCKAYNE HATLEY (St John the Baptist) Potton w
Sutton and Cockayne Hatley *St Alb*

COCKERHAM (St Michael) w Winmarleigh St Luke and
Glasson Christ Church *Blackb 12* P *Bp (2 turns),
Trustees (1 turn)* V R N HAMBLIN

COCKERINGTON, SOUTH (St Leonard) Mid Marsh
Gp *Linc*

COCKERMOUTH (All Saints) (Christ Church) w
Embleton and Wythop *Carl 6* P *Patr Bd*
TR S H WILLCOX, TV N D PERKINSON,
NSM J M CHAMBERLIN

COCKERNHOE (St Hugh) Luton St Fran *St Alb*

COCKERTON (St Mary) *Dur 12* P *Bp* V M P KENT,
C N A CHAMBERLAIN

COCKFIELD (St Mary) *Dur 11* **P** *Bp* **R** *Vacant*
Bishop Auckland (0388) 718447
COCKFIELD (St Peter) w Bradfield St Clare, Felsham
and Gedding *St E 10* **P** *St Jo Coll Cam (3 turns), R*
(2 turns), and *Lt-Col J G Aldous (1 turn)*
R B H MANNING, **Hon C** M M FORD
COCKING (not known), Bepton and West Lavington
Chich 10 **P** *Ld Chan, Bp and Cowdray Trust (alt)*
R *Vacant* Midhurst (07308) 3281
COCKINGTON (St George and St Mary) (St Matthew)
Ex 10 **P** *Bp* **V** A K F MACEY **C** P J NORMAN
COCKLEY CLEY (All Saints) w Gooderstone w
P *Bp* **P-in-c** C W T HALCRAFT, C W W BAILEY
COCKSHUTT (St Simon and St Jude) Petton w
Cockshutt, Welshampton and Leeal etc (*w*)
COCKWARD (Church) with Chapel-en-le-Frith *Derby*
CODDENHAM (not known) w Gosbeck and Hemingstone w
Henley *St E 7* **P** *Pemb Coll Cam (2 turns),*
J Suarez (1 turn) **R** D CUTTS
CODDINGTON (All Saints) Colwall w Upper Colwall
and Coddington *Heref*
CODDINGTON (All Saints) w Barnby in the Willows
S'well 3 **P** *Bp* **V** R G WRIGHT
CODDINGTON (St Mary) Farndon and Coddington
Ches
CODFORD (St Mary) Ashton Gifford *Sarum*
CODFORD (St Peter) as above
CODICOTE (St Giles) *St Alb 7* **P** *Abp* **V** P I SMITH
CODNOR (St Thomas) and Loscoe *Derby 13* **P** *The Crown*
V *Vacant* Ripley (0773) 742516
CODSALL (St Nicholas) *Lich 2* **P** *R and Lady*
Wrottesley (jt) **V** A F WILLIAMS, **C** J C GOLDBATCH
CODSALL WOOD (St Peter) Codsall *Lich*
COFFLE HALL (Community Church) Woughton etc *Ox*
COFFINSWELL (St Bartholomew) Kingskerswell w
Coffinswell *Ex*
COFTON (St Mary) Kenton, Mamhead, Powderham,
Cofton and Starcross *Ex*
COFTON HACKETT (St Michael) w Barnt Green *Birm 4*
P *Bp* **V** J GREY, **C** M E REAVIL
COGENHOE (St Peter) *Pet 7* **P** *DBP* **R** D W JOHNSON
COGGES (St Mary) *Ox 8* **P** *Trustees* **V** J DUSSEK
COGGESHALL (St Peter ad Vincula) w Markshall
Chelmsf 22 **P** *Bp (2 turns), DBP (1 turn)*
V D A M DILLON, **NSM** R M ATKINSON
COGGESHALL (St Peter) (St Nicholas) Coggeshall w
Markshall *Chelmsf*
CONKLEY (St Michael and All Angels) w South
Dingham and Closworth *B & W 8* **P** *DBC Ex*
V R J HUNT
COKER, WEST (St Martin of Tours) w Hardington
Mandeville, East Chinnock and Pendomer *B & W 8*
P *DBF and Sx Chs Trust, DBP (alt)*
V D M OSMOND
COLATON RALEIGH (St John the Baptist) Ottery and
and Colaton Raleigh *Ex*
COLBURN (St Cuthbert) Hipswell *Ripon*
COLBURY (Christ Church) *Win 10* **P** *Mrs A V Hudson-*
Davies **V** *Vacant* Ashurst (0703) 292132
COLBY (Belle Abbey Church) Arbory *S & M*
COLBY (St Giles) w Banningham and Tuttington *Nor 9*
P *Bp (3 turns), P H C Barber Esq (1 turn)* **R** *Vacant*
COLCHESTER (Christ Church w St Mary at the Walls)
Chelmsf 19 **P** *Bp* **R** C J HASLAM-JONES
COLCHESTER (St Anne) *Chelmsf 19* **P** *Bp*
V T W HODDER
COLCHESTER (St Barnabas) Old Heath *Chelmsf 19*
P *Bp* **V** P S WALKER
COLCHESTER (St Botolph w Holy Trinity and St Giles)
Chelmsf 19 **P** *Bp* **V** P G EVANS,
Hon Par Dn P B J GREGORY
COLCHESTER (St James) w All Saints and St Nicholas
and St Runwald *Chelmsf 19* **P** *Bp* **R** M J FOX,
C R W SPRINGETT, **Hon C** P S LANSLEY
COLCHESTER (St John the Evangelist) *Chelmsf 19*
P *Adn Colchester* **V** B W NICHOLSON,
Par Dn M CORSTORPHINE
COLCHESTER (St Mary Magdalen) Colchester, New
Town and The Hythe *Chelmsf*
COLCHESTER (St Michael) Myland *Chelmsf 19*
P *Ball Coll Ox* **R** J F BLORE
COLCHESTER (St Paul) *Chelmsf 19* **P** *Bp*
V H D WINTER
COLCHESTER (St Peter) *Chelmsf 19* **P** *Simeon's*
Trustees **V** R M WILSON
COLCHESTER (St Stephen) Colchester, New Town
and The Hythe *Chelmsf*
COLCHESTER, New Town and The Hythe (St Stephen,
St Mary Magdalen and St Leonard) *Chelmsf 19*

P Ball Coll Ox (2 turns)
TW WILLAKER, Pe
COLD ASH (St Mark) He
Norreys, Cold Ash etc *Ox*
COLD ASHBY (St Denys)
and Cold Ashby *Pet*
COLD ASHTON (Holy Trinity)
Acton and Dormarton etc *Bris*
COLD ASTON (St Andrew) w
Glouc 14 **P** *Ld Chan (2 turns)*
P-in-c J P BROWN, **C** J W S F
NSM D W HITCHIN
COLD BRAYFIELD (St Mary)
Brayfield, Clifton Reynes etc *Ox*
COLD HIGHAM (St Luke) Pattishall
with Dayton w Tiffield *Pet*
COLD KIRBY (St Michael) Upper Rye
COLD NORTON (St Stephen) Purleigh
and Stow Maries *Chelmsf*
COLD OVERTON (St John the Baptist)
Vp of Par *Leic*
COLD SALPERTON (All Saints) Dowdeswell w
Andoversford w the Shiptons etc *Glouc*
COLDEAN (St Mary Magdalene) Moulsecoomb
COLDEN (Holy Trinity) *Win 9* **P** *V Thwaites*
V W EVANS
COLDHAM (St Etheldreda) *Ely 19* **P** *Bp*
V G L BARRETT
COLD HARBOUR (Christ Church) Abinger *cum*
Coldharbour *Guildf*
COLDHURST (Holy Trinity) Oldham *Man*
COLD INMERED (St Pancras) Lythorne and Fishbourn w
Waldershare etc *Cant*
COLDRIDGE (St Matthew) Lapford, Nymet Rowland
and Coldridge *Ex*
COLDWALTHAM (St Giles) *Chich 12* **P** *DBC*
V G A GENT
COLEBROOKE (St Andrew) *Ex 1* **P** *D & C*
V W GALES
COLEBY (All Saints) *Linc 18* **P** *Or Coll Ox* **V** R C BELL
COLEFORD (Holy Trinity) w Holcombe *B & W 13* **P** *Bp*
and J Somersett (jt) **V** *Vacant* Mells (0373) 812300
COLEFORD (St John the Evangelist) w Staunton *Glouc 4*
P *R* **V** P W SEMPLE, **C** P E PINKERTON,
Hon C A W WEARMOUTH
COLEHILL (St Michael and All Angels) *Sarum 10*
P *Wimborne Minster Sch* **P-in-c** J W GOODALL
COLEMAN'S HATCH (Holy Trinity) Hartfield w
Coleman's Hatch *Chich*
COLEORTON (St Mary the Virgin) Ashby-de-la-Zouch
St Helen w Coleorton *Leic*
COLERNE (St John the Baptist) w North Wraxall *Bris 9*
P *New Coll Ox and Or Coll Ox (alt)*
P-in-c R C CLIFTON
COLESBOURNE (St James) *Glouc 12*
P *H W G Elwes Esq* **P-in-c** S I PULFORD
COLESHILL (All Saints) Amersham *Ox*
COLESHILL (All Saints) Gt Coxwell w Buscot,
Coleshill & Eaton Hastings *Ox*
COLESHILL (St Peter and St Paul) *Birm 11*
P *K S D Wingfield Digby Esq* **V** R G BOLLARD,
C R J YEOMAN, **NSM** L LEWIS
COLEY Norwood Green (St George) Coley *Wakef*
COLEY (St John the Baptist) *Wakef 2* **P** *V Halifax*
V A M EARNSHAW
COLGATE (St Saviour) *Chich 8* **P** *Mrs E C Calvert*
P-in-c P H ADDENBROOKE
COLINDALE (St Matthias) *Lon 15* **P** *Bp*
V S MOSELING
COLKIRK (St Mary) w Oxwick w Pattesley, Whissonsett,
Horningtoft and Brisley *Nor 19* **P** *DBP, Ch Coll Cam,*
and C S P D Lane Esq (jt) **R** M D SMITH
COLLATON (St Mary the Virgin) Stoke Gabriel and
Collaton St Mary *Ex*
COLLIER ROW (St James) and Havering-atte-Bower
Chelmsf 4 **P** *CPAS and Bp (jt)* **V** C G THERRELL,
C D R W ROBBINS, **Par Dn** B S RAWLINGS
COLLIER STREET (St Margaret) Yalding w Collier
Street *Roch*
COLLIERLEY (St Thomas) w Annfield Plain *Dur 8* **P** *Bp*
and The Crown (alt) **V** G H LAWES
COLLIERS END (St Mary) High Cross *St Alb*
COLLINGBOURNE DUCIS (St Andrew) Wexcombe
Sarum
COLLINGBOURNE KINGSTON (St Mary) as above
COLLINGHAM (All Saints) (St John the Baptist) w South
Scarle and Besthorpe and Girton *S'well 3* **P** *Ld Chan*
and D & C Pet (alt) **R** E J WIDDOWS

CLIFFSEND (St Mary the Virgin)   St Laurence in Thanet *Cant*
CLIFTON (All Saints) *St Alb 22*   P *Bp*   R P J PAVEY
CLIFTON (All Saints w St John) *Bris 5*   P *Bp*
V P G COBB,   C M R FREEMAN,   NSM R THOMAS
CLIFTON (Christ Church w Emmanuel) *Bris 5*
P *Simeon's Trustees*   V P M BERG,   C R A HIGGINS,
Par Dn G C MILLS
CLIFTON (Holy Trinity) *Derby 8*   P *Lt-Col
J R G Stanton, T W Clowes Esq, and V Ashbourne w
Mapleton (by turn)*   V J R J READ
CLIFTON (Holy Trinity, St Andrew the Less and St Peter)
Bris 5   P *Simeon's Trustees*   V J J R COLLINGWOOD,
Par Dn R D WATLING
CLIFTON (Mission Church)   Conisbrough *Sheff*
CLIFTON (St Anne) *Man 2*   P *Bp*   V W J GASH
CLIFTON (St Cuthbert), Brougham and Cliburn *Carl 4*
P *Earl of Lonsdale and Lord Hothfield (alt)*
R P H HOCKEY
CLIFTON (St Francis) (St Mary the Virgin) *S'well 10*
P *DBP*   TR A HEATON,   TV C C LEVY, C F ANDREWS,
C S BROCKLEHURST,   Hon Par Dn P A EDWARDS
CLIFTON (St James) *Sheff 6*   P *Bp*   V V A VOUT
CLIFTON (St John) *Wakef 2*   P *Bp*   V J A RICHARDSON
CLIFTON (St Luke) *Carl 4*   R *Workington*
V P M BADEN,   NSM J V HINE
CLIFTON (St Paul) *Bris 5*   P *Bp*   P-in-c J S F HADLEY,
C A C BRYER
CLIFTON (St Philip and St James) *York 8*   P *Trustees*
V R G FLETCHER,   C P W WHITE,   Par Dn S E MUTCH,
NSM N E ECKERSLEY
CLIFTON, NEW (Holy Trinity)   Clifton *S'well*
CLIFTON, NORTH (St George)   Harby w Thorney and
N and S Clifton *S'well*
CLIFTON CAMPVILLE (St Andrew) w Chilcote *Lich 5*
P *Brig W J Reed*   R A C SOLOMON
CLIFTON GREEN (St Thomas) *Man 2*   P *Bp*
V K J MASSEY
CLIFTON HAMPDEN (St Michael and All Angels)
Dorchester *Ox*
CLIFTON-ON-TEME (St Kenelm), Lower Sapey and the
Shelsleys *Worc 3*   P *Bp and A F Evans Esq (jt)*
R P C OWEN
CLIFTON REYNES (St Mary the Virgin)   Lavendon w
Cold Brayfield, Clifton Reynes etc *Ox*
CLIFTON UPON DUNSMORE (St Mary) and Newton
Cov 6   P *H A F W Boughton Leigh Esq*
P-in-c P S BALLANTINE,   C A S REED
CLIFTONVILLE (St Paul) *Cant 9*   P *Ch Patr Trust*
V D A LUGG
CLIPPESBY (St Peter)   Rollesby w Burgh w Billockby w
Ashby w Oby etc *Nor*
CLIPSHAM (St Mary)   Greetham and Thistleton w
Stretton and Clipsham *Pet*
CLIPSTON (All Saints) w Naseby and Haselbech w
Kelmarsh *Pet 2*   P *Ch Coll Cam, DBP, M F Harris
Esq, and Miss C V Lancaster (by turn)*   R D W FAULKS
CLIPSTONE (All Saints) *S'well 2*   P *Bp*   V C S FULLER
CLITHEROE (St James) *Blackb 8*   P *Trustees*
R H L CLARK
CLITHEROE (St Mary Magdalene) *Blackb 8*
P *J R Peel Esq*   V J A D ROBERTS,   C P HARTLEY,
NSM P W SHEPHERD
CLITHEROE (St Paul) Low Moor *Blackb 8*   P *Bp*
V R NICHOLSON
CLIVE (All Saints)   Astley, Clive, Grinshill and Hadnall
Lich
CLIVE VALE (All Souls)   Hastings All So *Chich*
CLODOCK (St Clydog) and Longtown w Craswall,
Llanveynoe, St Margaret's, Michaelchurch Escley and
Newton *Heref 1*   P *DBP (2 turns), MMCET (1 turn)*
V F E RODGERS,   NSM G G DAVIES
CLOFORD (St Mary)   Nunney and Witham Friary,
Marston Bigot etc *B & W*
CLOPHILL (St Mary the Virgin) *St Alb 22*   P *Ball Coll
Ox*   R P J SWINDELLS
CLOPTON (St Mary) w Otley, Swilland and Ashbocking
St E 7   P *Ld Chan and Bp (alt)*   R B WAKELING
CLOSWORTH (All Saints)   E Coker w Sutton Bingham
and Closworth *B & W*
CLOTHALL (St Mary Virgin)   Sandon, Wallington and
Rushden w Clothall *St Alb*
CLOUGHTON (St Mary) *York 16*   P *V Scalby*
P-in-c J A WILLIAMS
CLOVELLY (All Saints) (St Peter) *Ex 17*
P *Hon Mrs Asquith's Trustees*   R D A BATES
CLOWNE (St John the Baptist) *Derby 3*   P *Ld Chan*
R L R R HARRIS

CLOWS TOP (Mission Room)   Mamble w Bayton, Rock
w Heightington etc *Worc*
CLUBMOOR (St Andrew) *Liv 8*   P *Bp*   V R J G PANTER
CLUMBER PARK (St Mary the Virgin)   Worksop
Priory *S'well*
CLUN (St George) w Bettws-y-Crwyn and Newcastle
Heref 10   P *Earl of Powis*   Hon AP J E M ROBERTS
CLUNBURY (St Swithin)   Clungunford w Clunbury and
Clunton, Bedstone etc *Heref*
CLUNGUNFORD (St Cuthbert) w Clunbury and Clunton,
Bedstone and Hopton Castle *Heref 10*   P *Earl of Powis,
Mrs S B Rocke, M S C Brown Esq, and
Sir Hugh Ripley, Bt (jt)*   P-in-c P B WELCH
CLUNTON (St Mary)   Clungunford w Clunbury and
Clunton, Bedstone etc *Heref*
CLUTTON (St Augustine of Hippo) w Cameley *B & W 11*
P *Earl of Warw (2 turns), and Exors J P Hippisley
(1 turn)*   R A V SAUNDERS
CLYFFE PYPARD (St Peter)   Broad Town, Clyffe
Pypard and Tockenham *Sarum*
CLYMPING (St Mary the Virgin) and Yapton w Ford
Chich 1   P *Bp (2 turns), Ld Chan (1 turn)*
V D S FARRANT,   NSM A R BRANT
CLYST HONITON (St Michael and All Angels)
Aylesbeare, Rockbeare, Farringdon etc *Ex*
CLYST HYDON (St Andrew)   Bradninch and Clyst
Hydon *Ex*
CLYST ST GEORGE (St George)   Clyst St Mary, Clyst
St George etc *Ex*
CLYST ST LAWRENCE (St Lawrence)   Whimple,
Talaton and Clyst St Lawr *Ex*
CLYST ST MARY (St Mary), Clyst (St George) and
Woodbury Salterton *Ex 1*   P *Lord Wraxall, D&C, and
S Radcliffe (jt)*   R G L ROWE
COALBROOKDALE (Holy Trinity), Iron-Bridge and
Little Wenlock *Heref 14*   P *Bp, Lord Forester,
Vs Madeley and Much Wenlock (jt)*   R *Vacant*
Ironbridge (095245) 3309
COALEY (St Bartholomew)   Lower Cam w Coaley
Glouc
COALPIT HEATH (St Saviour) *Bris 7*   P *Bp*
V B RAVEN
COALVILLE (Christ Church) and Bardon Hill *Leic 8*
P *Simeon's Trust and R Hugglescote (jt)*   V S M LEE
COATES (Holy Trinity) *Ely 18*   P *Ld Chan*
R A BENNETT
COATES (St Edith) *Linc 2*   P *Bp*
P-in-c G S RICHARDSON
COATES (St Matthew), Rodmarton and Sapperton w
Frampton Mansell *Glouc 12*   P *Bp, Lord Bathurst, and
Guild of All So (jt)*   R R A BOWDEN,
NSM J M FRANCIS
COATES, GREAT (St Nicholas)   Gt and Lt Coates w
Bradley *Linc*
COATES, GREAT and LITTLE (Bishop Edward King
Church) (St Michael) w Bradley *Linc 9*   P *Patr Bd*
TR A V DOUGLAS,   TV P T DAVIS, R PROSSER,
Par Dn P A GOLDSMITH
COATES, NORTH (St Nicholas)   Tetney, Marshchapel
and N Coates *Linc*
COATHAM (Christ Church) *York 17*   P *Trustees*
V J WOODHOUSE
COATHAM, EAST (Christ Church)   Coatham *York*
COBBOLD ROAD (St Saviour) (St Mary) *Lon 9*   P *Bp*
V J D WHEELER
COBERLEY (St Giles) w Cowley *Glouc 12*   P *Ld Chan
and H W G Elwes Esq (alt)*   R S I PULFORD
COBHAM Sole Street (St Mary's Church Room)
Cobham w Luddesdowne and Dode *Roch*
COBHAM (St Andrew) (St John the Divine) *Guildf 10*
P *D C H Combe Esq*   V B L PREECE,   C P F SMITH
COBHAM (St Mary Magdalene) w Luddesdowne and Dode
Roch 1   P *Earl of Darnley and CPAS (alt)*
P-in-c M P P HOWARD
COBRIDGE (Christ Church)   Hanley H Ev *Lich*
COCKAYNE HATLEY (St John the Baptist)   Potton w
Sutton and Cockayne Hatley *St Alb*
COCKERHAM (St Michael) w Winmarleigh St Luke and
Glasson Christ Church *Blackb 12*   P *Bp (2 turns),
Trustees (1 turn)*   V R N HAMBLIN
COCKERINGTON, SOUTH (St Leonard)   Mid Marsh
Gp *Linc*
COCKERMOUTH (All Saints) (Christ Church) w
Embleton and Wythop *Carl 6*   P *Patr Bd*
TR S H WILLCOX,   TV N D PERKINSON,
NSM J M CHAMBERLIN
COCKERNHOE (St Hugh)   Luton St Fran *St Alb*
COCKERTON (St Mary) *Dur 12*   P *Bp*   V M P KENT,
C N A CHAMBERLAIN

COCKFIELD (St Mary) *Dur 11* **P** *Bp* **R** *Vacant*
Bishop Auckland (0388) 718447
COCKFIELD (St Peter) w Bradfield St Clare, Felsham and Gedding *St E 10* **P** *St Jo Coll Cam (3 turns), Bp (2 turns), and Lt-Col J G Aldous (1 turn)*
R B H MANNING, **Hon C** H M FORD
COCKING (not known), Bepton and West Lavington *Chich 10* **P** *Ld Chan, Bp and Cowdray Trust (alt)*
R *Vacant* Midhurst (073081) 3281
COCKINGTON (St George and St Mary) (St Matthew) *Ex 10* **P** *Bp* **V** A K F MACEY, **C** P J NORMAN
COCKLEY CLEY (All Saints) w Gooderstone *Nor 18* **P** *Bp* **P-in-c** C W T CHALCRAFT, **C** G H WHEATLEY
COCKSHUTT (St Simon and St Jude) Petton w Cockshutt, Welshampton and Lyneal etc *Lich*
COCKYARD (Church Hall) Chapel-en-le-Frith *Derby*
CODDENHAM (St Mary) w Gosbeck and Hemingstone w Henley *St E 1* **P** *Pemb Coll Cam (2 turns), Lord de Saumarez (1 turn)* **R** D CUTTS
CODDINGTON (All Saints) Colwall w Upper Colwall and Coddington *Heref*
CODDINGTON (All Saints) w Barnby in the Willows *S'well 3* **P** *Bp* **V** P G WRIGHT
CODDINGTON (St Mary) Farndon and Coddington *Ches*
CODFORD (St Mary) Ashton Gifford *Sarum*
CODFORD (St Peter) as above
CODICOTE (St Giles) *St Alb 7* **P** *Abp* **V** P J SMITH
CODNOR (St James) and Loscoe *Derby 12* **P** *The Crown* **V** *Vacant* Ripley (0773) 742516
CODSALL (St Nicholas) *Lich 3* **P** *Bp and Lady Wrottesley (jt)* **V** A E WILLIAMS, **C** J C GREATBATCH
CODSALL WOOD (St Peter) Codsall *Lich*
COFFEEHALL (Community Church) Woughton *Ox*
COFFINSWELL (St Bartholomew) Kingskerswell w Coffinswell *Ex*
COFTON (St Mary) Kenton, Mamhead, Powderham, Cofton and Starcross *Ex*
COFTON HACKETT (St Michael) w Barnt Green *Birm 4* **P** *Bp* **V** I A VEYARD, **C** M E REAVIL
COGENHOE (St Peter) *Pet 7* **P** *DBP* **R** D W JOHNSON
COGGES (St Mary) *Ox 8* **P** *Trustees* **V** S L BESSENT
COGGESHALL (St Peter ad Vincula) w Markshall *Chelmsf 22* **P** *Bp (2 turns), SMF (1 turn)* **V** D A M BEETON, **NSM** F J JACKSON
COGGESHALL, LITTLE (St Nicholas) Coggeshall w Markshall *Chelmsf*
COKER, EAST (St Michael and All Angels) w Sutton Bingham and Closworth *B & W 8* **P** *D&C Ex* **V** D J HUNT
COKER, WEST (St Martin of Tours) w Hardington Mandeville, East Chinnock and Pendomer *B & W 8* **P** *MMCET and Ox Chs Trust, DBP (alt)* **R** D M OSMOND
COLATON RALEIGH (St John the Baptist) Otterton and Colaton Raleigh *Ex*
COLBURN (St Cuthbert) Hipswell *Ripon*
COLBURY (Christ Church) *Win 10* **P** *Mrs A V Hudson-Davies* **V** *Vacant* Ashurst (0703) 292132
COLBY (Belle Abbey Church) Arbory *S & M*
COLBY (St Giles) w Banningham and Tuttington *Nor 9* **P** *Bp (2 turns), P H C Barber Esq (1 turn)* **R** *Vacant*
COLCHESTER (Christ Church w St Mary at the Walls) *Chelmsf 19* **P** *Bp* **R** C J HASLAM-JONES
COLCHESTER (St Anne) *Chelmsf 19* **P** *Bp* **V** T V HODDER
COLCHESTER (St Barnabas) Old Heath *Chelmsf 19* **P** *Bp* **V** P S WALKER
COLCHESTER (St Botolph w Holy Trinity and St Giles) *Chelmsf 19* **P** *Bp* **V** P G EVANS, **Hon Par Dn** P B J GREGORY
COLCHESTER (St James) w All Saints and St Nicholas and St Runwald *Chelmsf 19* **P** *Bp* **R** M J FOX, **C** R W SPRINGETT, **Hon C** P S LANSLEY
COLCHESTER (St John the Evangelist) *Chelmsf 19* **P** *Adn Colchester* **V** B W NICHOLSON, **Par Dn** M CORSTORPHINE
COLCHESTER (St Mary Magdalen) Colchester, New Town and The Hythe *Chelmsf*
COLCHESTER (St Michael) Myland *Chelmsf 19* **P** *Ball Coll Ox* **R** J F BLORE
COLCHESTER (St Paul) *Chelmsf 19* **P** *Bp* **V** H D WINTER
COLCHESTER (St Peter) *Chelmsf 19* **P** *Simeon's Trustees* **V** R M WILSON
COLCHESTER (St Stephen) Colchester, New Town and The Hythe *Chelmsf*
COLCHESTER, New Town and The Hythe (St Stephen, St Mary Magdalen and St Leonard) *Chelmsf 19*

P *Ball Coll Ox (2 turns), Ld Chan (1 turn)*
TR J SHILLAKER, **Par Dn** C F SHILLAKER
COLD ASH (St Mark) Hermitage and Hampstead Norreys, Cold Ash etc *Ox*
COLD ASHBY (St Denys) Guilsborough w Hollowell and Cold Ashby *Pet*
COLD ASHTON (Holy Trinity) Marshfield w Cold Ashton and Tormarton etc *Bris*
COLD ASTON (St Andrew) w Notgrove and Turkdean *Glouc 14* **P** *Ld Chan (2 turns), Bp (1 turn)*
P-in-c J P BROWN, **C** J W S FIELDGATE, **NSM** D W HUTCHIN
COLD BRAYFIELD (St Mary) Lavendon w Cold Brayfield, Clifton Reynes etc *Ox*
COLD HIGHAM (St Luke) Pattishall w Cold Higham and Gayton w Tiffield *Pet*
COLD KIRBY (St Michael) Upper Ryedale *York*
COLD NORTON (St Stephen) Purleigh, Cold Norton and Stow Maries *Chelmsf*
COLD OVERTON (St John the Baptist) Whatborough Gp of Par *Leic*
COLD SALPERTON (All Saints) Dowdeswell and Andoversford w the Shiptons etc *Glouc*
COLDEAN (St Mary Magdalene) Moulsecoomb *Chich*
COLDEN (Holy Trinity) *Win 9* **P** *V Twyford* **V** J R EVANS
COLDHAM (St Etheldreda) *Ely 19* **P** *Bp* **V** J E BARRETT
COLDHARBOUR (Christ Church) Abinger cum Coldharbour *Guildf*
COLDHURST (Holy Trinity) Oldham *Man*
COLDRED (St Pancras) Eythorne and Elvington w Waldershare etc *Cant*
COLDRIDGE (St Matthew) Lapford, Nymet Rowland and Coldridge *Ex*
COLDWALTHAM (St Giles) *Chich 12* **P** *D&C* **V** R V HODGSON
COLEBROOKE (St Andrew) *Ex 2* **P** *D&C* **V** B H GALES
COLEBY (All Saints) *Linc 18* **P** *Or Coll Ox* **V** R C BELL
COLEFORD (Holy Trinity) w Holcombe *B & W 13* **P** *Bp and V Kilmersdon (jt)* **V** *Vacant* Mells (0373) 812300
COLEFORD (St John the Evangelist) w Staunton *Glouc 4* **P** *Bp* **V** P W SEMPLE, **C** P E PINKERTON, **Hon C** A W WEARMOUTH
COLEHILL (St Michael and All Angels) *Sarum 10* **P** *Wimborne Minster Sch* **P-in-c** J W GOODALL
COLEMAN'S HATCH (Holy Trinity) Hartfield w Coleman's Hatch *Chich*
COLEORTON (St Mary the Virgin) Ashby-de-la-Zouch St Helen w Coleorton *Leic*
COLERNE (St John the Baptist) w North Wraxall *Bris 9* **P** *New Coll Ox and Or Coll Ox (alt)*
P-in-c R G CLIFTON
COLESBOURNE (St James) *Glouc 12* **P** *H W G Elwes Esq* **P-in-c** S I PULFORD
COLESHILL (All Saints) Amersham *Ox*
COLESHILL (All Saints) Gt Coxwell w Buscot, Coleshill & Eaton Hastings *Ox*
COLESHILL (St Peter and St Paul) *Birm 11* **P** *K S D Wingfield Digby Esq* **V** R G BOLLARD, **C** R J YEOMAN, **NSM** L LEWIS
COLEY Norwood Green (St George) Coley *Wakef*
COLEY (St John the Baptist) *Wakef 2* **P** *V Halifax* **V** A M EARNSHAW
COLGATE (St Saviour) *Chich 8* **P** *Mrs E C Calvert* **P-in-c** P H ADDENBROOKE
COLINDALE (St Matthias) *Lon 15* **P** *Bp* **V** S MOSELING
COLKIRK (St Mary) w Oxwick w Pattesley, Whissonsett, Horningtoft and Brisley *Nor 19* **P** *DBP, Ch Coll Cam, and C S P D Lane Esq (jt)* **R** M D SMITH
COLLATON (St Mary the Virgin) Stoke Gabriel and Collaton St Mary *Ex*
COLLIER ROW (St James) and Havering-atte-Bower *Chelmsf 4* **P** *CPAS and Bp (jt)* **V** C G T HERBERT, **C** D R W ROBBINS, **Par Dn** B S RAWLINGS
COLLIER STREET (St Margaret) Yalding w Collier Street *Roch*
COLLIERLEY (St Thomas) w Annfield Plain *Dur 8* **P** *Bp and The Crown (alt)* **V** G H LAWES
COLLIERS END (St Mary) High Cross *St Alb*
COLLINGBOURNE DUCIS (St Andrew) Wexcombe *Sarum*
COLLINGBOURNE KINGSTON (St Mary) as above
COLLINGHAM (All Saints) w South Scarle and Besthorpe and Girton *S'well 3* **P** *Ld Chan and D&C Pet (alt)* **R** E J WIDDOWS

COLLINGHAM (St Oswald) w Harewood *Ripon 1*
P *Earl of Harewood and G H H Wheler Esq (jt)*
V J M HECKINGBOTTOM
COLLINGTON (St Mary) Bredenbury w Grendon
Bishop and Wacton etc *Heref*
COLLINGTREE (St Columba) w Courteenhall and Milton
Malsor *Pet 7* **P** *Major Sir Hereward Wake, G Phipps-*
Walker, and Hyndman Trustees (by turn)
R R J ORMSTON
COLLYHURST (Saviour) *Man 5* **P** *Bp and Trustees (jt)*
R D W BAILEY, **C** A I SALMON
COLLYWESTON (St Andrew) Easton on the Hill,
Collyweston w Duddington etc *Pet*
COLMWORTH (St Denys) Wilden w Colmworth and
Ravensden *St Alb*
COLN ROGERS (St Andrew) Chedworth, Yanworth
and Stowell, Coln Rogers etc *Glouc*
COLN ST ALDWYN (St John the Baptist), Hatherop,
Quenington, Eastleach and Southrop *Glouc 13* **P** *Earl*
St Aldwyn, D&C, Wadh Coll Ox, and DBP (jt)
V D L COWMEADOW
COLN ST DENYS (St James the Great) Chedworth,
Yanworth and Stowell, Coln Rogers etc *Glouc*
COLNBROOK (St Thomas) Riverside *Ox*
COLNE (Christ Church) *Blackb 7* **P** *DBF*
V J C PRIESTLEY
COLNE (Holy Trinity) *Blackb 7* **P** *Bp* **V** G S INGRAM,
NSM K ALLEN
COLNE (St Bartholomew) *Blackb 7* **P** *DBF* **R** *Vacant*
Colne (0282) 863479
COLNE (St Helen) Bluntisham cum Earith w Colne and
Woodhurst *Ely*
COLNE ENGAINE (St Andrew) *Chelmsf 22* **P** *Ch Hosp*
P-in-c J E F JASPER
COLNEY (St Andrew) Cringleford w Colney and
Bawburgh *Nor*
COLNEY (St Peter) *St Alb 1* **P** *Bp* **V** M T BEER,
Hon C J M BEER, **NSM** R W HEINZE
COLNEY HEATH (St Mark) *St Alb 7* **P** *Trustees*
V D R VENESS, **Hon C** A D T GORTON,
NSM B R McMAHON
COLSTERWORTH Group, The (St John the Baptist)
Linc 14 **P** *Bp (2 turns), Mrs R S McCorquodale and*
Rev J R H and H C Thorold (jt) (1 turn) **R** *Vacant*
Grantham (0476) 860080
COLSTON BASSETT (St John the Divine) Cropwell
Bishop w Colston Bassett, Granby etc *S'well*
COLTISHALL (St John the Baptist) w Great Hautbois and
Horstead *Nor 3* **P** *D&C and K Coll Cam (jt)*
R H D TOLLER, **NSM** N H KHAMBATTA
COLTON (Holy Trinity) w Satterthwaite and Rusland
Carl 10 **P** *V Hawkshead etc and Landowners (jt)*
V D TINSLEY
COLTON (St Andrew) Easton w Colton and
Marlingford *Nor*
COLTON (St Mary the Virgin) *Lich 4* **P** *Bp* **R** *Vacant*
Rugeley (08894) 3623
COLTON (St Paul) Bolton Percy *York*
COLWALL (St Crispin's Chapel) (St James the Great) w
Upper Cold Coddington *Heref 6* **P** *Bp*
R C N H ATTWOOD, **C** I St J FISHER
COLWALL, UPPER (Good Shepherd) Colwall w
Upper Colwall and Coddington *Heref*
COLWICH (St Michael and All Angels) w Great Haywood
Lich 4 **P** *Bp and Trustees (jt)* **V** K C JONES
COLWICK (St John the Baptist) Netherfield w Colwick
S'well
COLYFORD (St Michael) Colyton, Southleigh, Offwell,
Widworthy etc *Ex*
COLYTON (St Andrew), Southleigh, Offwell, Widworthy,
Farway, Northleigh and Musbury *Ex 5* **P** *Patr Bd*
TR D A GUNN-JOHNSON, **TV** N T SCHOFIELD,
NSM A RICHMOND, G A SMITH
COMBE (St Lawrence) Stonesfield w Combe *Ox*
COMBE (St Swithin) W Woodhay w Enborne,
Hampstead Marshall etc *Ox*
COMBE DOWN (Holy Trinity) (St Andrew) w Monkton
Combe and South Stoke *B & W 10* **P** *R Bath, Ox Chs*
Trust, and Comdr H R Salmer (jt)
V J N WORDSWORTH, **C** N S ATKINS
COMBE FLOREY (St Peter and St Paul) Lydeard St
Lawrence w Brompton Ralph etc *B & W*
COMBE HAY (not known) Bath Odd Down w Combe
Hay *B & W*
COMBE-IN-TEIGNHEAD (All Saints) Stoke-in-
Teignhead w Combe-in-Teignhead etc *Ex*
COMBE MARTIN (St Peter) and Berrynarbor *Ex 18*
P *Bp* **R** J T WILLIAMS, **Hon C** R O H EPPINGSTONE

COMBE PYNE (St Mary the Virgin) Axminster,
Chardstock, Combe Pyne and Rousdon *Ex*
COMBE RALEIGH (St Nicholas) Honiton, Gittisham,
Combe Raleigh, Monkton etc *Ex*
COMBE ST NICHOLAS (St Nicholas) w Wambrook
B & W 16 **P** *Bp and T V D Eames Esq (jt)*
P-in-c P REGAN
COMBERFORD (St Mary and St George) Wigginton
Lich
COMBERTON (St Mary) *Ely 1* **P** *Jes Coll Cam*
V R STEPHENSON, **NSM** M J REISS
COMBERTON, GREAT (St Michael) Elmley Castle w
Bricklehampton and Combertons *Worc*
COMBERTON, LITTLE (St Peter) as above
COMBROKE (St Mary and St Margaret) w Compton
Verney *Cov 8* **P** *Bp* **V** R MIGHALL
COMBS (St Mary) *St E 6* **P** *Bp* **R** *Vacant*
Stowmarket (0449) 612076
COMBWICH (St Peter) Cannington, Otterhampton,
Combwich and Stockland *B & W*
COMER GARDENS (St David) Worc St Clem *Worc*
COMMONDALE (St Peter) Danby *York*
COMPSTALL (St Paul) Werneth *Ches*
COMPTON (All Saints) and Otterbourne *Win 13* **P** *Bp*
and Mrs P M A T Chamberlayne-Macdonald (jt)
R P L S BARRETT
COMPTON (St Mary) Farnham *Guildf*
COMPTON (St Mary and St Nicholas) w East Ilsley *Ox 14*
P *Bp* **V** J B LEWIS
COMPTON (St Mary), the Mardens, Stoughton and
Racton *Chich 13* **P** *Bp Lon (1 turn), Bp (2 turns)*
V J L W ROBINSON, **C** J G E STONE
COMPTON (St Nicholas) w Shackleford and Peper Harow
Guildf 4 **P** *Bp and Major J R More-Molyneux (jt)*
R J M FELLOWS
COMPTON, LITTLE (St Denys) w Chastleton, Cornwell,
Little Rollright and Salford *Ox 3* **P** *Ch Ch Ox, DBP,*
and Bp (by turn) **P-in-c** G P EVANS,
NSM S U LAMBERT
COMPTON, NETHER (St Nicholas) Queen Thorne
Sarum
COMPTON, OVER (St Michael) as above
COMPTON ABBAS (St Mary the Virgin) Shaston
Sarum
COMPTON ABDALE (St Oswald) Withington and
Compton Abdale w Haselton *Glouc*
COMPTON BASSETT (St Swithin) Oldbury *Sarum*
COMPTON BEAUCHAMP (St Swithun) Ashbury,
Compton Beauchamp and Longcot w Fernham *Ox*
COMPTON BISHOP (St Andrew) Crook Peak *B & W*
COMPTON CHAMBERLAYNE (St Michael) Fovant,
Sutton Mandeville and Teffont Evias etc *Sarum*
COMPTON DANDO (Blessed Virgin Mary) Publow w
Pensford, Compton Dando and Chelwood *B & W*
COMPTON DUNDON (St Andrew) Somerton w
Compton Dundon, the Charltons etc *B & W*
COMPTON GREENFIELD (All Saints) Pilning w
Compton Greenfield *Bris*
COMPTON MARTIN (St Michael) Blagdon w Compton
Martin and Ubley *B & W*
COMPTON PAUNCEFOOT (Blessed Virgin Mary)
Camelot Par *B & W*
COMPTON VALENCE (St Thomas a Beckett) The
Winterbournes and Compton Valence *Sarum*
CONCHAN (St Peter) Onchan *S & M*
CONDICOTE (St Nicholas) Longborough, Sezincote,
Condicote and the Swells *Glouc*
CONDOVER (St Andrew and St Mary) w Frodesley, Acton
Burnell and Pitchford *Heref 11* **P** *Bp, Rev*
E W Serjeantson, and Mrs C R Colthurst (jt) **R** *Vacant*
Bayston Hill (074372) 2251
CONEY HILL (St Oswald) *Glouc 5* **P** *The Crown*
V T C THOMPSON, **C** M SHARLAND, P A BRIGHTMAN
CONEY WESTON (St Mary) Hopton, Market Weston,
Barningham etc *St E*
CONEYSTHORPE (Chapel) Street Team Min *York*
CONGERSTONE (St Mary the Virgin) Market
Bosworth, Cadeby w Sutton Cheney etc *Leic*
CONGHAM (St Andrew) Grimston, Congham and
Roydon *Nor*
CONGLETON (St James) *Ches 11* **P** *Bp* **V** A COOK
CONGLETON (St Peter) *Ches 1* **P** *Simeon's Trustees*
V R P SCOONES
CONGLETON (St Stephen) *Ches 11* **P** *Bp*
V R McGREEVY
CONGRESBURY (St Andrew) w Puxton and Hewish
St Ann *B & W 12* **P** *MMCET* **V** R H SALMON

CONINGSBY (St Michael and All Angels) w Tattershall
Linc 11   **P** *DBP and Baroness Willoughby de Eresby*
(alt)   **R** B PARSONS
CONINGTON (St Mary)   Fen Drayton w Conington *Ely*
CONISBROUGH (St Peter) *Sheff 10*   **P** *Bp*
V I S CHISHOLM,   **C** D R SHERWIN, G A FISHER
CONISCLIFFE (St Edwin) *Dur 12*   **P** *Bp*   **P-in-c** P CRICK
CONISHOLME (St Peter)   Somercotes and Grainthorpe
w Conisholme *Linc*
CONISTON (St Andrew)   Church Coniston *Carl*
CONISTON COLD (St Peter)   Kirkby-in-Malhamdale w
Coniston Cold *Bradf*
CONISTONE (St Mary)   Kettlewell w Conistone,
Hubberholme etc *Bradf*
CONONLEY (St John the Evangelist) w Bradley *Bradf 8*
P *Bp*   **V** C R PENFOLD,   **Hon C** S I PENFOLD
CONSETT (Christ Church) *Dur 8*   **P** *Bp*   **V** J HOGARTH,
C C TODD,   **Par Dn** B DAVISON
CONSTABLE LEE (St Paul) *Man 15*   **P** *CPAS*
V P HEYWOOD
CONSTANTINE (St Constantine) *Truro 4*   **P** *D&C*
V V A D HOLYER
COOKBURY (St John the Baptist and the Seven
Maccabees)   Black Torrington, Bradf w Cookbury etc
Ex
COOKHAM (Holy Trinity) *Ox 13*   **P** *Mrs Rogers*
V D D J ROSSDALE,   **Hon C** A W WELLING
COOKHAM DEAN (St John the Baptist) *Ox 13*
P *V Cookham*   **V** J F W V COPPING
COOKHILL (St Paul)   Inkberrow w Cookhill and
Kington w Dormston *Worc*
COOKLEY (St Michael and All Angels)   Cratfield w
Heveningham and Ubbeston etc *St E*
COOKLEY (St Peter)   Wolverley and Cookley *Worc*
COOKRIDGE (Holy Trinity) *Ripon 7*   **P** *R Adel*
V C ISBISTER
COOMBE (Christ Church)   New Malden and Coombe
S'wark
COOMBE BISSET (St Michael and All Angels)   Chalke
Valley E *Sarum*
COOMBES (not known)   Lancing w Coombes *Chich*
COOMBS WOOD (St Ambrose)   Blackheath *Birm*
COOPERSALE (St Alban) *Chelmsf 2*   **P** *Bp*
V R J HARDING
COPDOCK (St Peter) w Washbrook and Belstead *St E 5*
P *DBP*   **R** *Vacant*
COPFORD (St Michael and All Angels) w Easthorpe
Chelmsf 22   **P** *Ld Chan and Duchy of Lanc (alt)*
R L J MIDDLETON
COPGROVE (St Michael)   Farnham w Scotton,
Staveley, Copgrove etc *Ripon*
COPLE (All Saints) w Willington *St Alb 17*   **P** *Bp and*
D&C Ox (alt)   **V** J A TERRY
COPLEY (St Stephen) *Wakef 4*   **P** *V Halifax*   **V** *Vacant*
Halifax (0422) 52964
COPMANTHORPE (St Giles) *York 1*   **P** *R Micklegate*
H Trin   **V** J C STONEHOUSE
COPP (St Anne) *Blackb 10*   **P** *V St Michael's-on-Wyre*
V P YORKSTONE
COPPENHALL (All Saints and St Paul)   Crewe All SS
and St Paul *Ches*
COPPENHALL (St Laurence)   Penkridge Team *Lich*
COPPENHALL (St Michael) *Ches 15*   **P** *Bp*
R J MACKEY,   **C** D M OVERTON
COPPULL (not known) *Blackb 4*   **P** *R Standish*
V J HUDSON
COPPULL (St John the Divine) *Blackb 4*   **P** *R Standish*
R J STEWART
COPSTON MAGNA (St John the Baptist)   Wolvey w
Burton Hastings, Copston Magna etc *Cov*
COPT OAK (St Peter)   Oaks in Charnwood and Copt
Oak *Leic*
COPTHORNE (St John the Evangelist) *Chich 7*   **P** *Bp*
V *Vacant*   Copthorne (0342) 712063
COPYTHORNE (St Mary) and Minstead *Win 10*
P *Bp Liv and J P Green Esq (jt)*   **R** M E DELANY,
NSM T J SELWOOD
CORBRIDGE w Halton (St Andrew) and Newton Hall
Newc 3   **P** *D&C Carl*   **V** L CONSTANTINE,
NSM H H HUNTER
CORBY (Epiphany) (St John the Baptist) *Pet 9*
P *E Brudenell Esq*   **R** P M BROAD,   **C** F J WILSON
CORBY (St Columba and the Northern Saints) *Pet 9*
P *Bp*   **C** R A HATHWAY
CORBY (St Peter and St Andrew) (Kingswood Church) w
Great and Little Oakley *Pet 9*   **P** *Bp, Boughton Estates,*
and H W G de Capell Brooke (jt)   **TR** M A CRAGGS,
TV M D GLENN,   **C** A A ERDAL

CORBY GLEN (St John the Evangelist) *Linc 14*
P *Ld Chan (2 turns), Sir Simon Benton Jones, Bt (1 turn)*
NSM I K WILLIAMS
CORELEY (St Peter) w Doddington *Heref 12*   **P** *DBP and*
Mrs R C Woodward (jt)   **P-in-c** J V ROBERTS
CORFE (St Nicholas)   Pitminster w Corfe *B & W*
CORFE CASTLE (St Edward the Martyr), Church
Knowle, Kimmeridge Steeple w Tyneham *Sarum 9*
P *Major M J A Bond and Major J C Mansel (jt)*
R M A STRIKE,   **NSM** D J ROBERTS
CORFE MULLEN (St Hubert) *Sarum 10*   **P** *Bp*
R M R LAMBERT
CORHAMPTON (not known)   Meonstoke w
Corhampton cum Exton *Portsm*
CORLEY (not known)   Fillongley and Corley *Cov*
CORNARD, GREAT (St Andrew) *St E 12*   **P** *Bp*
V *Vacant*   Sudbury (0787) 73579
CORNARD, LITTLE (All Saints)   Assington w Newton
Green and Lt Cornard *St E*
CORNELLY (St Cornelius)   Tregony w St Cuby and
Cornelly *Truro*
CORNEY (St John the Baptist)   Bootle, Corney,
Whicham and Whitbeck *Carl*
CORNFORTH (Holy Trinity) *Dur 14*   **P** *Bp*
P-in-c A C RUSSELL
CORNHILL (St Helen) w Carham *Newc 12*   **P** *D&C Dur*
(2 turns), Exors W J Straker-Smith (1 turn)
P-in-c R BLEWETT
CORNHOLME (St Michael and All Angels) *Wakef 3*
P *DBP*   **V** N J WHETTON
CORNISH HALL END (St John the Evangelist)
Finchingfield and Cornish Hall End *Chelmsf*
CORNWELL (St Peter)   Lt Compton w Chastleton,
Cornwell etc *Ox*
CORNWOOD (St Michael and All Angels) *Ex 21*   **P** *Bp*
V E J PERRY
CORNWORTHY (St Peter)   Ashprington, Cornworthy
and Dittisham *Ex*
CORONATION SQUARE (St Aidan)   Cheltenham St
Mark *Glouc*
CORRINGHAM (St John the Evangelist) (St Mary the
Virgin) *Chelmsf 16*   **P** *SMF*   **R** D H PRIOR,
C B WHITTAKER
CORRINGHAM (St Lawrence) *Linc 2*   **P** *Bp*   **R** *Vacant*
Corringham (042783) 652
CORSCOMBE (St Mary the Virgin)   Melbury *Sarum*
CORSE (St Margaret)   Hartpury w Corse and Staunton
Glouc
CORSENSIDE (All Saints)   Bellingham/Otterburn Gp
Newc
CORSENSIDE (St Cuthbert)   as above
CORSHAM (St Bartholomew)   Gtr Corsham *Bris*
CORSHAM, GREATER (St Bartholomew) *Bris 9*
P *Patr Bd*   **TR** M H DREWETT,   **TV** V W BEYNON,
C G A B KING-SMITH,   **NSM** L F FLOWERDAY
CORSLEY (St Mary) *Sarum 14*   **P** *DBP*   **R** D G J CADDY
CORSLEY (St Mary the Virgin)   Corsley *Sarum*
CORSTON (All Saints)   Saltford w Corston and Newton
St Loe *B & W*
CORSTON (All Saints)   Gt Somerford, Lt Somerford,
Seagry, Corston etc *Bris*
CORTON (St Bartholomew)   Hopton w Corton *Nor*
CORTON (St Bartholomew)   Abbotsbury, Portesham
and Langton Herring *Sarum*
CORTON DENHAM (St Andrew)   Queen Camel w W
Camel, Corton Denham etc *B & W*
CORYTON (St Andrew)   Marystowe, Coryton,
Stowford, Lewtrenchard etc *Ex*
COSBY (St Michael and All Angels) *Leic 10*   **P** *Bp*
V S B HEYGATE
COSELEY (Christ Church) (St Cuthbert) *Lich 1*   **P** *Bp*
V D M WIGHT,   **C** L FOSTER,   **Hon Par Dn** S H WIGHT
COSELEY (St Chad) *Lich 1*   **P** *Bp*   **V** *Vacant*   021-526
2240
COSGROVE (St Peter and St Paul)   Potterspury,
Furtho, Yardley Gobion and Cosgrove *Pet*
COSHAM (St Philip) *Portsm 6*   **P** *Bp*   **V** T E LOUDEN,
C A R WALKER
COSSALL (St Catherine)   Awsworth w Cossall *S'well*
COSSINGTON (All Saints)   Sileby, Cossington and
Seagrave *Leic*
COSSINGTON (Blessed Virgin Mary)   Woolavington w
Cossington and Bawdrip *B & W*
COSTESSEY (St Edmund) *Nor 4*   **P** *Gt Hosp Nor*
V C J COLLISON,   **C** A KNIGHT
COSTESSEY, NEW (St Helen)   Costessey *Nor*
COSTOCK (St Giles) *S'well 8*   **P** *Bp*   **P-in-c** S J SMITH
COSTON (St Andrew)   Wymondham w Edmondthorpe,
Buckminster etc *Leic*

COTEBROOKE (St John and Holy Cross)   Tarporley *Ches*

COTEHELE HOUSE (Chapel)   Calstock *Truro*

COTEHILL (St John the Evangelist) and Cumwhinton *Carl 2*   P *The Crown*   P-in-c J G PEART

COTES HEATH (St James)   Standon and Cotes Heath *Lich*

COTESBACH (St Mary)   Lutterworth w Cotesbach *Leic*

COTGRAVE (All Saints) *S'well 8*   P *DBP*   R G B BARRODALE,   Par Dn S SPENCER,   NSM R A SPRAY

COTHAM (St Saviour w St Mary) *Bris 5*   P *Bp*   V G N BOUNDY,   NSM G CALWAY

COTHELSTONE (St Thomas of Canterbury)   Bishops Lydeard w Bagborough and Cothelstone *B & W*

COTHERIDGE (St Leonard)   Martley and Wichenford, Knightwick etc *Worc*

COTHERSTONE (St Cuthbert)   Romaldkirk w Laithkirk *Ripon*

COTLEIGH (St Michael and All Angels) *Ex 5*   P *PCC*   P-in-c P D GOTELEE

COTMANHAY (Christ Church) *Derby 13*   P *Bp*   V L E W WALTERS,   C R G LAWRENCE

COTON (St Peter) *Ely 1*   P *St Cath Coll Cam*   R H D SEARLE

COTON IN THE ELMS (St Mary)   Walton on Trent w Croxall etc *Derby*

COTTAM (Holy Trinity)   Rampton w Laneham, Treswell, Cottam and Stokeham *S'well*

COTTENHAM (All Saints) *Ely 5*   P *Bp*   R C A BARBER

COTTERED (St John the Baptist) w Broadfield and Throcking *St Alb 5*   P *Bp*   R I J STEWARDSON

COTTERIDGE (St Agnes) *Birm 4*   P *R Kings Norton*   V M W BLOOD,   NSM R R COLLINS

COTTERSTOCK (St Andrew)   Warmington, Tansor, Cotterstock and Fotheringhay *Pet*

COTTESBROOKE (All Saints) w Great Creaton and Thornby *Pet 2*   P *Bp (2 turns), Macdonald-Buchanan Trustees (1 turn)*   P-in-c W G GIBBS

COTTESMORE (St Nicholas) and Barrow w Ashwell and Burley *Pet 14*   P *E R Hanbury Esq, Viscount Downe, and DBP (by turn)*   R M H W ROGERS

COTTIMORE (St John)   Walton-on-Thames *Guildf*

COTTINGHAM (St Mary) *York 15*   P *Abp*   R T G GRIGG,   C M G SMITH, N W STOCKBRIDGE

COTTINGHAM (St Mary Magdalene) w East Carlton *Pet 9*   P *BNC Ox and Sir Geoffrey Palmer (alt)*   R G E WARD

COTTINGLEY (St Michael and All Angels) *Bradf 1*   P *Bp*   V R S ANDERSON

COTTINGWITH, EAST (St Mary)   Elvington w Sutton on Derwent and E Cottingwith *York*

COTTISFORD (St Mary the Virgin)   Finmere w Mixbury, Cottisford, Hardwick etc *Ox*

COTTON (St Andrew)   Bacton w Wyverstone and Cotton *St E*

COTTON (St John the Baptist)   Alton w Bradley-le-Moors and Oakamoor w Cotton *Lich*

COTTON MILL (St Julian)   St Alb St Steph *St Alb*

COUGHTON (St Peter) *Cov 7*   P *Bp*   V K L STOCK

COULSDON (St Andrew) *S'wark 21*   P *Bp*   V C J E LUNN,   Par Dn H A EVE,   Hon C K V McKIE

COULSDON (St John) *S'wark 21*   P *Abp*   R J H A WILTSHIRE,   C N D BIDEN

COULSTON, EAST (St Thomas of Canterbury)   Edington and Imber, Erlestoke and E Coulston *Sarum*

COUND (St Peter) *Heref 11*   P *Bp*   R *Vacant*

COUNDON (St James) *Dur 10*   P *Bp*   V H HUTCHINSON

COUNTESS WEAR (St Luke)   Wear St Luke *Ex*

COUNTESS WEAR (St Luke's Hall)   as above

COUNTESTHORPE (St Andrew) w Foston *Leic 10*   P *DBP and Bp (alt)*   V B DAVIS,   Hon C J C DUDLEY,   NSM M D GILLESPIE

COUNTISBURY (St John the Evangelist)   Lynton, Brendon, Countisbury, Lynmouth etc *Ex*

COURTEENHALL (St Peter and St Paul)   Collingtree w Courteenhall and Milton Malsor *Pet*

COVE (St John the Baptist) (St Christopher) *Guildf 1*   P *Bp*   TR A J BUTCHER,   TV J M ADAMS

COVEHITHE (St Andrew)   Wrentham w Benacre, Covehithe, Frostenden etc *St E*

COVEN (St Paul) *Lich 3*   P *V Brewood*   V *Vacant* Standeford (0902) 790230

COVEN HEATH (Mission Church)   Bushbury *Lich*

COVENEY (St Peter ad Vincula) *Ely 14*   P *Bp*   R R J MACKLIN

COVENHAM (Annunciation of the Blessed Virgin Mary)   Fotherby *Linc*

COVENT GARDEN (St Paul) *Lon 3*   P *Bp*   R D ELLIOTT

COVENTRY Caludon *Cov 1*   P *Bp and Ld Chan (alt)*   TR G F WARNER,   TV R J WORSLEY,   TM (Dn-in-c) G E B LLOYD,   TV C A LAMB,   C N D ADAMS, D W ROSAMOND,   Par Dn C A WORSLEY,   NSM C ADAMS

COVENTRY Holbrooks (St Luke)   Holbrooks *Cov*

COVENTRY (Holy Trinity) *Cov 2*   P *Ld Chan*   V G G DOW,   C A D BRADLEY, R N TREW

COVENTRY (St Francis of Assisi) North Radford *Cov 2*   P *Bp*   V N J TAYLOR,   C A M CLARK

COVENTRY (St George) *Cov 2*   P *Bp*   V M D S GREIG

COVENTRY (St John the Baptist) *Cov 2*   P *Trustees*   R G T S SOUTHGATE,   C B REGAN

COVENTRY (St Mary Magdalen) *Cov 3*   P *Bp*   V A E DARBY,   C P C CANNING

COVENTRY EAST (St Anne and All Saints) (St Barnabas) (St Margaret) (St Peter) *Cov 1*   P *Patr Bd*   TR W G HARRIS-EVANS,   TV N A J BLACKWELL, P G EDWARDS, P N TYERS, J F BLACKMAN,   Par Dn S EDWARDS,   NSM P N ASPINALL

COVERACK (St Peter)   St Keverne *Truro*

COVERDALE (St Botolph)   Middleham w Coverdale and E Witton *Ripon*

COVINGHAM (St Paul)   Swindon Dorcan *Bris*

COVINGTON (All Saints) *Ely 10*   P *Sir Stephen Hastings*   P-in-c J HINDLEY,   NSM B A BEARCROFT

COWARNE, LITTLE (not known)   Bredenbury w Grendon Bishop and Wacton etc *Heref*

COWARNE, MUCH (St Mary the Virgin)   Stoke Lacy, Moreton Jeffries w Much Cowarne etc *Heref*

COWBIT (St Mary) *Linc 17*   P *Ld Chan, DBP, and V Moulton (by turn)*   V T STEELE

COWCLIFFE (St Hilda)   N Huddersfield *Wakef*

COWDEN (St Mary Magdalene) w Hammerwood *Chich 7*   P *Ch Soc Trust*   R A CALDWELL

COWES (St Faith) *Portsm 8*   P *Bp*   V R W PIKE

COWES (St Mary the Virgin) *Portsm 8*   P *V Carisbrooke*   C C B BURLAND

COWES, EAST (St James)   Whippingham w E Cowes *Portsm*

COWES, WEST (Holy Trinity) *Portsm 8*   P *Trustees*   V *Vacant*

COWESBY (St Michael) *York 20*   P *Abp*   P-in-c P R A R HOARE

COWFOLD (St Peter) *Chich 9*   P *Bp Lon*   V B BRENTON

COWGATE (St Peter) *Newc 7*   P *Bp*   V G A PRICE

COWGILL (St John the Evangelist)   Dent w Cowgill *Bradf*

COWICK (Holy Trinity)   Gt Snaith *Sheff*

COWLAM (St Mary)   Sledmere and Cowlam w Fridaythorpe, Fimer etc *York*

COWLEIGH (St Peter)   Malvern Link w Cowleigh *Worc*

COWLEY (St James) (St Francis) (St Luke) *Ox 4*   P *Patr Bd*   TR K F HAYDON,   TV P J J WEATHERBY,   C S J GRIGG

COWLEY (St John) (St Alban) (St Bartholomew) (St Mary and St John) *Ox 4*   P *St Steph Ho Ox*   V M E FLATMAN,   C M J HALSALL,   NSM W CHAND

COWLEY (St Laurence) *Lon 24*   P *Bp*   P-in-c R CHRISTIAN

COWLEY (St Mary)   Coberley w Cowley *Glouc*

COWLEY CHAPEL (St Antony)   Thorverton, Cadbury, Upton Pyne etc *Ex*

COWLING (Holy Trinity) *Bradf 8*   P *Bp*   V R D CARTER

COWLINGE (St Margaret)   Lydgate w Ousden and Cowlinge *St E*

COWPEN (St Benedict)   Horton *Newc*

COWPLAIN (St Wilfrid) *Portsm 4*   P *Bp*   V P HANCOCK,   C T St J HAWKINS

COWTONS, The (All Saints) (St Luke's Pastoral Centre) *Ripon 2*   P *V Gilling (1 turn), DBP (2 turns)*   P-in-c G F DEAR

COX GREEN (Good Shepherd) *Ox 13*   P *Bp*   V D J CAWTE

COXFORD Group, The: East and West Rudham, Houghton-next-Harpley, Syderstone w Barmer, Tattersett and Tatterford *Nor 20*   P *Marquess Townshend, Most Rev G D Hand, Bp, Mrs R E Russell, Marquess of Cholmondeley, and DBP (by turn)*   R V M SCOTT

COXHEATH (Chapel) w East Farleigh, Hunton and Linton *Roch 7*   P *Abp, Ld Chan and Lord Cornwallis (by turn)*   R R J CASTLE,   NSM H C H BIRD, G R ELLMORE

COXHOE (St Mary) *Dur 14*   P *Bp*   V I S PELTON

COXLEY (Christ Church), Henton and Wookey *B & W 9*   P *Bp*   V R R B PLOWMAN

COXWELL, GREAT (St Giles) w Buscot, Coleshill and Eaton Hastings *Ox 17* **P** *Bp and Lord Faringdon (jt)* **V** R C SWANBOROUGH

COXWELL, LITTLE (St Mary)   Gt Faringdon w Lt Coxwell *Ox*

COXWOLD (St Michael) and Husthwaite *York 5* **P** *Abp* **V** D F JOHNSON

CRABBS CROSS (St Peter)   Redditch, The Ridge *Worc*

CRADLEY (St James) w Mathon and Storridge *Heref 6* **P** *Bp and D&C Westmr (jt)* **R** J G WILLIAMS, **NSM** M D VOCKINS

CRADLEY (St Peter) (St Katherine's Mission Church) *Worc 9* **P** *R Halesowen* **V** D J BLACKBURN

CRADLEY HEATH (St Luke)   Reddal Hill St Luke *Worc*

CRAGHEAD (St Thomas)   Stanley *Dur*

CRAKEHALL (St Gregory) *Ripon 4* **P** *Sir Henry Beresford-Peirse, Bt* **V** R J PEARSON

CRAMBE (St Michael)   Whitwell w Crambe, Flaxton, Foston etc *York*

CRAMLINGTON (St Nicholas) *Newc 1* **P** *Bp* **TR** M N F HAIG, **TV** A PATTISON, M F LAYBOURNE, **TM** V C NICHOLSON

CRAMPMOOR (St Swithun)   Romsey *Win*

CRANBORNE (St Mary and St Bartholomew) w Boveridge, Edmondsham, Wimborne St Giles and Woodlands *Sarum 10* **P** *Marquess of Salisbury, Earl of Shaftesbury, and Mrs C M Medlycott (jt)* **R** B R DIXON

CRANBOURNE (St Peter)   Winkfield and Cranbourne *Ox*

CRANBROOK (St Dunstan) *Cant 11* **P** *Abp* **V** M L COOPER, **NSM** J P MOY

CRANFIELD (St Peter and St Paul) and Hulcote w Salford *St Alb 19* **P** *MMCET* **R** D H HUNT

CRANFORD (Holy Angels) (St Dunstan) *Lon 11* **P** *R J G Berkeley Esq and Sir Hugo Huntingdon-Whiteley (jt)* **R** M A M ST JOHN-CHANNELL

CRANFORD (St Andrew) (St John the Baptist) w Grafton Underwood and Twywell *Pet 11* **P** *Boughton Estates, DBP, and Sir John Robinson (by turn)* **R** D H P FOOT

CRANHAM (All Saints) *Chelmsf 4* **P** *St Jo Coll Ox* **P-in-c** R P BROPHY

CRANHAM (St James the Great)   Brimpsfield, Cranham, Elkstone and Syde *Glouc*

CRANHAM PARK Moor Lane (not known)   Cranham Park *Chelmsf*

CRANHAM PARK (St Luke) *Chelmsf 4* **P** *Bp* **V** C St G CLEVERLY, **C** R G SAUNDERS, J A K GUEST

CRANLEIGH (St Nicolas) *Guildf 2* **P** *Bp* **R** N P NICHOLSON, **C** A W H ASHDOWN, **NSM** C V SOWTER

CRANMORE (Christ the King)   Shirley *Birm*

CRANMORE, WEST (St Bartholomew)   Shepton Mallet w Doulting *B & W*

CRANOE (St Michael)   Gt Bowden w Welham, Glooston and Cranoe *Leic*

CRANSFORD (St Peter)   Badingham w Bruisyard, Cransford and Dennington *St E*

CRANSLEY (St Andrew)   Broughton w Loddington and Cransley etc *Pet*

CRANTOCK (St Carantoc) *Truro 7* **P** *SMF* **NSM** M WILLS

CRANWELL (St Andrew) *Linc 22* **P** *DBP* **V** F RODGERS

CRANWICH (St Mary) *Nor 18* **P** *CPAS* **P-in-c** R O DAVIES

CRANWORTH (St Mary the Virgin)   Reymerston w Cranworth, Letton, Southburgh etc *Nor*

CRASSWALL (St Mary)   Clodock and Longtown w Craswall, Llanveynoe etc *Heref*

CRASTER (Mission Church)   Embleton w Rennington and Rock *Newc*

CRATFIELD (St Mary) w Heveningham and Ubbeston w Huntingfield and Cookley *St E 15* **P** *Hon Mrs S Peel and Simeon's Trustees (alt)* **P-in-c** L M HIPKINS

CRATHORNE (All Saints) *York 22* **P** *Baron Crathorne, Hon David Dugdale, and J Southern Esq (jt)* **P-in-c** P KITCHING

CRAWCROOK (Church of the Holy Spirit)   Greenside *Dur*

CRAWFORD (District Church)   Upholland *Liv*

CRAWLEY (St John the Baptist) *Chich 7* **P** *Bp* **TR** M A J GOODE, **TV** M F H GRAY, R C MARSH, B L HACKSHALL, J F SOUTHWARD, **Par Dn** D G STANIFORD, **Hon C** I W NATHANIEL, I D F MOSS

CRAWLEY (St Mary) and Littleton and Sparsholt w Lainston *Win 13* **P** *Ld Chan and DBP (alt)* **R** D G WILLIAMS

CRAWLEY, NORTH (St Firmin)   Sherington w Chicheley, N Crawley, Astwood etc *Ox*

CRAWLEY DOWN (All Saints) *Chich 7* **P** *R Worth* **V** R M SWEET-ESCOTT

CRAWSHAWBOOTH (St John)   Goodshaw and Crawshawbooth *Man*

CRAY (St Mary and St Paulinus)   St Mary Cray and St Paul's Cray *Roch*

CRAY, NORTH (St James) w Ruxley *Roch 16* **P** *Bp* **R** P H ROLTON

CRAYFORD (St Paulinus) *Roch 14* **P** *Bp* **R** P WRIGHT, **C** C D DENCH

CRAYKE (St Cuthbert) w Brandsby and Yearsley *York 5* **P** *The Crown and Abp (alt)* **P-in-c** W H BATES

CRAZIES HILL (Mission Room)   Wargrave *Ox*

CREACOMBE (St Michael and All Angels)   Witheridge, Thelbridge, Creacombe, Meshaw etc *Ex*

CREAKE, NORTH (St Mary) AND SOUTH (St Mary) w Waterden *Nor 20* **P** *Bp, Viscount Coke, Earl Spencer, and Guild of All So (jt)* **R** B R ROBERTS

CREATON, GREAT (St Michael and All Angels)   Cottesbrooke w Gt Creaton and Thornby *Pet*

CREDENHILL (St Mary) w Brinsop, Mansel Lacey, Yazor and Wormesley *Heref 4* **P** *Major D J Davenport (2 turns), Bp (1 turn), and R Ecroyd Esq(1 turn)* **R** G USHER

CREDITON (Holy Cross) (St Lawrence) and Shobrooke *Ex 2* **P** *12 Govs of Crediton Ch* **R** A E GEERING, **C** V C ARMSTRONG-MacDONNELL

CREECH ST MICHAEL (St Michael) *B & W 20* **P** *MMCET* **V** *Vacant*   Henlade (0823) 442237

CREED (St Crida)   Probus, Ladock and Grampound w Creed *Truro*

CREEDY, NORTH: Cheriton Fitzpaine, Woolfardisworthy East, Kennerleigh, Washford Pyne, Puddington, Poughill, Stockleigh English, Morchard Bishop, Stockleigh Pomeroy, Down St Mary and Clannaborough *Ex 2* **P** *Ld Chan (1 turn), DBP (3 turns)* **TR** J L DAVIDSON, **TV** S A R BEVERIDGE, B SHILLINGFORD

CREEKMOOR (Christ Church)   Oakdale St Geo *Sarum*

CREEKSEA (All Saints) w Althorne and Latchingdon w North Fambridge *Chelmsf 13* **P** *Bp, Abp and Ld Chan (by turn)* **V** M L LANGAN, **NSM** D I GORDON, K I DUNSTAN

CREETING (St Peter)   Creeting St Mary, Creeting St Peter etc *St E*

CREETING ST MARY (St Mary), Creeting St Peter and Earl Stonham w Stonham Parva *St E 1* **P** *DBP (2 turns), Pemb Coll Cam (1 turn)* **R** A PYKE

CREETON (St Peter) *Linc 14* **P** *Baroness Willoughby de Eresby (1 turn), Ld Chan (2 turns)* **V** *Vacant*

CREGNEISH (St Peter)   Rushen *S & M*

CRESSAGE (Christ Church)   Wenlock *Heref*

CRESSBROOK (St John the Evangelist)   Tideswell *Derby*

CRESSING (All Saints) *Chelmsf 18* **P** *Bp* **P-in-c** M JENNINGS

CRESSINGHAM, GREAT (St Michael) and Little, w Threxton *Nor 18* **P** *Bp and Sec of State for Defence* **P-in-c** C W T CHALCRAFT, **C** G H WHEATLEY

CRESSINGHAM, LITTLE (St Andrew)   Gt and Lt Cressingham w Threxton *Nor*

CRESSWELL (St Bartholomew) and Lynemouth *Newc 11* **P** *Bp* **V** P WHITEHEAD

CRESWELL (St Mary Magdalene)   Elmton *Derby*

CRETINGHAM (St Peter)   Earl Soham w Cretingham and Ashfield cum Thorpe *St E*

CREWE (All Saints and St Paul) *Ches 15* **P** *Bp* **V** C ALSBURY

CREWE (Christ Church) (St Peter) *Ches 15* **P** *Bp* **V** W C W FOSS

CREWE (St Andrew) *Ches 15* **P** *Bp* **V** J S W YOUNG, **C** D T PEEBLES

CREWE (St Barnabas) *Ches 15* **P** *Bp* **V** R D POWELL

CREWE (St John the Baptist) *Ches 15* **P** *Bp* **V** *Vacant* Crewe (0270) 68835

CREWE GREEN (St Michael and All Angels)   Haslington w Crewe Green *Ches*

CREWKERNE (St Bartholomew) w Wayford *B & W 16* **P** *Ld Chan* **R** P B CURTIS

CREWTON (St Peter)   Boulton *Derby*

CRICH (St Mary) *Derby 1* **P** *Ch Trust Fund Trust* **V** J M C COLBOURN

CRICK (St Margaret) and Yelvertoft w Clay Coton and Lilbourne *Pet 2* **P** *MMCET and St Jo Coll Ox (jt)* **R** R M BARLOW

CRICKET MALHERBIE (St Mary Magdalene)   Chard, Furnham w Chaffcombe, Knowle St Giles etc *B & W*

CRICKET ST THOMAS (St Thomas) Thorncombe w Winsham and Cricket St Thomas *B & W*

CRICKLADE (St Sampson) w Latton *Bris 10* **P** *D&C, Bp, and Hon P N Eliot (by turn)* **V** G K WITHINGTON, **NSM** A EVANS

CRICKLEWOOD (St Gabriel) Willesden Green St Gabr *Lon*

CRICKLEWOOD (St Michael) *Lon 21* **P** *Bp* **P-in-c** D F LAMBERT

CRICKLEWOOD (St Peter) *Lon 21* **P** *Bp* **P-in-c** K MITCHELL

CRIFTINS (St Matthew) *Lich 23* **P** *Bp* **V** A W MOSELEY

CRIMPLESHAM (St Mary) w Stradsett *Ely 16* **P** *Bp* **V** P F KEELING

CRINGLEFORD (St Peter) w Colney and Bawburgh *Nor 13* **P** *Gt Hosp Nor, Exors E H Barclay and D&C (alt)* **R** W D M STURDY

CROCKENHILL (All Souls) *Roch 2* **P** *Bp* **V** S C HEMMING CLARK

CROCKERNWELL (Holy Trinity) Cheriton Bishop *Ex*

CROCKHAM HILL (Holy Trinity) *Roch 10* **P** *J St A Warde Esq* **V** *Vacant* Edenbridge (0732) 866515

CROFT (All Saints) The Wainfleets and Croft *Linc*

CROFT (Christ Church) w Southworth *Liv 16* **P** *Bp* **P-in-c** P THORN

CROFT (St Michael and All Angels) Eye, Croft w Yarpole and Lucton *Heref*

CROFT (St Michael and All Angels) and Stoney Stanton *Leic 13* **P** *Bp and A I Steel Esq (jt)* **NSM** V T GOODMAN

CROFT (St Peter) Middleton Tyas w Croft and Eryholme *Ripon*

CROFTON (All Saints) *Wakef 9* **P** *Duchy of Lanc* **R** B McCLELLAN

CROFTON (Holy Rood) (St Edmund) *Portsm 2* **P** *Bp* **V** J M MAYBURY, **Hon C** B STARES

CROFTON (St Paul) *Roch 15* **P** *V Orpington* **V** C J REED

CROFTON PARK (St Hilda) w St Cyprian *S'wark 4* **P** *V Lewisham St Mary* **P-in-c** G L PRESTON

CROGLIN (St John the Baptist) Castle Carrock w Cumrew and Croglin *Carl*

CROMER (St Peter and St Paul) *Nor 7* **P** *CPAS* **V** D F HAYDEN, **C** R J K BAKER, **Hon C** J A RIVERS

CROMFORD (St Mary) *Derby 7* **P** *DBP* **V** *Vacant*

CROMHALL (St Andrew) w Tortworth and Tytherington *Glouc 7* **P** *Earl of Ducie, Or Coll Ox, and MMCET (jt)* **R** C G LEE

CROMPTON, EAST (St James) *Man 18* **P** *Bp* **V** R D VINCENT, **C** D K BARNES, **Dss** J TAYLOR

CROMPTON, HIGH (St Mary) *Man 18* **P** *Bp* **V** H S EDWARDS, **NSM** G F WEIR

CROMPTON FOLD (St Saviour) E Crompton *Man*

CROMWELL (St Giles) Norwell w Ossington, Cromwell and Caunton *S'well*

CRONDALL (All Saints) and Ewshot *Guildf 3* **P** *Bp* **V** P M RICH

CROOK (St Catherine) *Carl 9* **P** *CPAS* **V** R A MACHIN

CROOK (St Catherine) *Dur 15* **P** *R Brancepeth* **R** A FEATHERSTONE, **C** K TEASDALE

CROOK PEAK *B & W 1* **P** *Ld Chan, Bp, Bp Lon, and R M Dod Esq (by turn)* **R** D T M SERVICE

CROOKES (St Thomas) *Sheff 4* **P** *Patr Bd* **TR** R P R WARREN, **TV** D J FRANK, K J DAVIES, **C** M W G STIBBE

CROOKES (St Timothy) *Sheff 4* **P** *Sheff Ch Burgesses* **V** P R TOWNSEND

CROOKHAM (Christ Church) *Guildf 1* **P** *V Crondall and Ewshot* **V** F J M EVANS, **C** P S J GARLAND

CROOKHORN (Good Shepherd) *Portsm 4* **P** *Simeon's Trustees* **P** D CONNOLLY

CROPREDY (St Mary the Virgin) w Great Bourton and Wardington *Ox 5* **P** *Bp* **V** P G ATKINSON

CROPTHORNE (St Michael) w Charlton *Worc 4* **P** *D&C (2 turns), Bp (1 turn)* **P-in-c** C J R ARMSTRONG

CROPTON (St Gregory) Lastingham w Appleton-le-Moors, Rosedale etc *York*

CROPWELL BISHOP (St Giles) w Colston Bassett, Granby w Elton, Langar cum Barnstone and Tythby w Cropwell Butler *S'well 8* **P** *CPAS and Bp, and Ld Chan (alt)* **V** C B PERKINS, **C** M P D KENNARD, **NSM** J A CONLEY

CROSBY (St George) (St Michael) *Linc 4* **P** *Sir Reginald Sheffield, Bt* **V** G F SLEIGHT, **Par Dn** J E ANDERSON

CROSBY, GREAT (All Saints) *Liv 5* **P** *R Sefton, Bp, V St Luke, and CPAS (jt)* **V** L R THOMAS

CROSBY, GREAT (St Faith) *Liv 1* **P** *St Chad's Coll Dur* **V** R CAPPER, **C** N P ANDERSON, V J ENEVER, **Hon C** D A SMITH, **NSM** G GILFORD

CROSBY, GREAT (St Luke) *Liv 5* **P** *R Sefton* **V** D H TROLLOPE, **NSM** W J PIERCE

CROSBY GARRETT (St Andrew) Kirkby Stephen w Mallerstang etc *Carl*

CROSBY-ON-EDEN (St John the Evangelist) Irthington, Crosby-on-Eden and Scaleby *Carl*

CROSBY RAVENSWORTH (St Lawrence) *Carl 1* **P** *DBP* **V** J W HAYWOOD

CROSCOMBE (Blessed Virgin Mary) Pilton w Croscombe, N Wootton and Dinder *B & W*

CROSLAND, SOUTH (Holy Trinity) *Wakef 1* **P** *R Almondbury* **V** M C RUSSELL, **NSM** R T TUCK

CROSLAND MOOR (St Barnabas) *Wakef 5* **P** *Bp* **V** M STOREY, **NSM** D A KIRBY

CROSS GREEN (St Hilda) Leeds Richmond Hill *Ripon*

CROSS GREEN (St Saviour) as above

CROSS HEATH (St Michael and All Angels) *Lich 15* **P** *Bp* **V** A J DAVIES

CROSS IN HAND (St Bartholomew) Waldron *Chich*

CROSS ROADS cum Lees (St James) *Bradf 8* **P** *Bp* **V** *Vacant* Haworth (0535) 42210

CROSS STONE (St Paul) *Wakef 3* **P** *V Halifax* **P-in-c** P N CALVERT

CROSSCANONBY (St John the Evangelist) *Carl 7* **P** *D&C* **V** J LEONARDI

CROSSCRAKE (St Thomas) *Carl 9* **P** *V Heversham* **V** D HAMPSON

CROSSENS (St John) *Liv 9* **P** *Trustees* **V** R S J CHARLES

CROSSFLATTS (St Aidan) Bingley All SS *Bradf*

CROSSPOOL (St Columba) *Sheff 4* **P** *Bp* **V** E G CLARKSON

CROSTHWAITE (St Kentigern) Keswick *Carl 6* **P** *Bp* **V** R T HUGHES

CROSTHWAITE (St Mary) Kendal *Carl 9* **P** *DBP* **V** K PARTINGTON

CROSTON (St Michael and All Angels) *Blackb 4* **P** *Exors of Canon R G Rawstorne* **R** R J BRUNSWICK

CROSTWICK (St Peter) Spixworth w Crostwick *Nor*

CROSTWIGHT (All Saints) Smallburgh w Dilham w Honing and Crostwight *Nor*

CROUCH END HILL (Christ Church) Hornsey Ch Ch *Lon*

CROUGHTON (All Saints) Aynho and Croughton w Evenley *Pet*

CROWAN (St Crewenna) w Godolphin *Truro 4* **P** *Bp and D L C Roberts Esq (alt)* **V** R F LAW

CROWBOROUGH (All Saints) *Chich 19* **P** *Ld Chan* **V** A C J CORNES, **C** M J OVEY, **NSM** J A HOBBS

CROWCOMBE (Holy Ghost) Bicknoller w Crowcombe and Sampford Brett *B & W*

CROWELL (Nativity of the Blessed Virgin Mary) Chinnor w Emmington and Sydenham etc *Ox*

CROWFIELD (All Saints) w Stonham Aspal and Mickfield *St E 1* **P** *DBP, Bp, and Lord de Saumarez (alt)* **P-in-c** H M WILSON

CROWHURST (St George) Catsfield and Crowhurst *Chich*

CROWHURST (St George) Lingfield and Crowhurst *S'wark*

CROWLAND (St Mary and St Bartholomew and St Guthlac) *Linc 17* **P** *Earl of Normanton* **R** J A CRUST

CROWLE (St John the Baptist) Bowbrook S *Worc*

CROWLE (St Oswald) *Linc 1* **P** *Bp* **V** D SCHOFIELD, **Hon C** D E CORNELIUS

CROWMARSH GIFFORD (St Mary Magdalene) Wallingford w Crowmarsh Gifford etc *Ox*

CROWN EAST AND RUSHWICK (St Thomas) Broadheath, Crown E and Rushwick *Worc*

CROWNHILL (Ascension) Plymouth Crownhill Ascension *Ex*

CROWTHORNE (St John the Baptist) *Ox 16* **P** *Bp* **V** B R SPENCE, **NSM** T WALT

CROWTON (Christ Church) Norley and Crowton *Ches*

CROXALL-CUM-OAKLEY (St John the Baptist) Walton on Trent w Croxall etc *Derby*

CROXBY (All Saints) Swallow *Linc*

CROXDALE (St Bartholomew) *Dur 2* **P** *D&C* **P-in-c** J R SCORER

CROXDEN (St Giles) *Lich 21* **P** *Bp* **V** *Vacant* Rocester (0889) 590424

CROXLEY GREEN (All Saints) *St Alb 10* **P** *V Rickmansworth* **V** L G-H LEE

CROXLEY GREEN (St Oswald) *St Alb 10* **P** *Bp* **V** J M YOUNG

CROXTETH (St Paul) *Liv 8* **P** *R W Derby and Bp (jt)*
V I G BROOKS
CROXTON (All Saints) Thetford *Nor*
CROXTON Group, The SOUTH (St John the Baptist)
Leic 3 **P** *DBP, Ch Soc Trust, and MMCET (jt)*
R D L PRISTON
CROXTON (St James) and Eltisley *Ely 1* **P** *Bp*
R T J MARKS
CROXTON (St John the Evangelist) *Linc 6* **P** *Ld Chan*
R S PHILLIPS
CROXTON (St Paul) w Broughton and Adbaston *Lich 13*
P *Bp and J Hall Esq* **V** M W WELSH
CROXTON KERRIAL (St Botolph and St John the
Baptist), Knipton, Harston, Branston by Belvoir, Saltby
and Sproxton *Leic 3* **P** *Duke of Rutland and Sir Lyonel*
Tollemache, Bt (jt) **R** A E H CLAYTON
CROYDE (St Mary Magdalene) Georgeham *Ex*
CROYDON (All Saints) w Clopton *Ely 8* **P** *Bp and DBP*
(alt) **R** *Vacant* Cambridge (0223) 208008
CROYDON (Christ Church) Broad Green *S'wark 20*
P *Simeon's Trustees* **V** C D FORD, **C** P A HOLMES,
NSM R SCHRAM
CROYDON (Holy Saviour) *S'wark 22* **P** *Bp*
V R N HARLEY, **C** P S DAVIES
CROYDON (St Andrew) *S'wark 20* **P** *Trustees*
V P D HENDRY
CROYDON (St Augustine) *S'wark 20* **P** *Bp*
V G S DERRIMAN, **Hon C** S G HILL
CROYDON (St John the Baptist) *S'wark 20* **P** *Abp*
V C A CHILL, **TV** P G ENSOR,
C M J BULL, T F CRITCHLOW,
Hon C S J F GEDGE, K V G SMITH
CROYDON (St Martin) *S'wark 20* **P** *Bp*
P-in-c C J ROSEWEIR
CROYDON (St Matthew) *S'wark 20* **P** *V Croydon*
V R TAYLOR
CROYDON (St Michael and All Angels w St James)
S'wark 20 **P** *Trustees* **V** N GODWIN
CROYDON (St Peter) *S'wark 20* **P** *V Croydon*
V F E RUSBY
CROYDON Woodside (St Luke) *S'wark 22* **P** *Bp*
V P EVANS, **C** A B COKER
CROYDON, SOUTH (Emmanuel) *S'wark 21* **P** *Ch Trust*
Fund Trust **V** J S JONES, **C** S J OBERST,
NSM D J RICHARDSON, S J H GOATCHER
CROYDON, SOUTH (St Augustine) Croydon St Aug
S'wark
CROYLAND (St Mary and St Bartholomew and St
Guthlac) Crowland *Linc*
CRUDWELL (All Saints) Ashley, Crudwell,
Hankerton, Long Newnton etc *Bris*
CRUMPSALL (St Matthew w St Mary) *Man 5* **P** *Bp*
R C LAYCOCK
CRUNDALE (St Mary the Blessed Virgin) w Godmersham
Cant 2 **P** *Abp* **NSM** R I MARTIN
CRUWYS MORCHARD (Holy Cross) Washfield,
Stoodleigh, Withleigh etc *Ex*
CRUX EASTON (St Michael and All Angels) Highclere
and Ashmansworth w Crux Easton *Win*
CUBBINGTON (St Mary) *Cov 11* **P** *Bp* **V** K LINDOP
CUBERT (St Cubert) *Truro 7* **P** *DBP* **V** P E TIDMARSH
CUBLEY (St Andrew) Alkmonton, Cubley, Marston,
Montgomery etc *Derby*
CUBLINGTON (St Nicholas) Wingrave w Rowsham,
Aston Abbotts and Cublington *Ox*
CUCKFIELD (Holy Trinity) *Chich 6* **P** *Bp*
V E H A HAYDEN, **NSM** J-H D BOWDEN
CUCKLINGTON (St Lawrence) Charlton Musgrove,
Cucklington and Stoke Trister *B & W*
CUDDESDON (All Saints) *Ox 1* **P** *Bp* **V** J H GARTON
CUDDINGTON (St Mary) *Guildf 9* **P** *Bp*
V C H CHEESEMAN
CUDDINGTON (St Nicholas) Haddenham w
Cuddington, Kingsey etc *Ox*
CUDHAM (St Peter and St Paul) and Downe *Roch 15*
P *Ch Soc Trust and Bp (jt)* **V** T R HATWELL
CUDWORTH (St John) *Wakef 7* **P** *Bp* **V** D GLOVER,
C B W PIERCE
CUDWORTH (St Michael) Dowlishwake w Kingstone,
Chillington etc *B & W*
CUFFLEY (St Andrew) Northaw *St Alb*
CULBONE (St Beuno) Oare w Culbone *B & W*
CULFORD (St Mary), West Stow and Wordwell w
Flempton, Hengrave and Lackford *St E 13* **P** *Bp*
(2 turns), R W Gough Esq (1 turn) **R** R W CLIFTON
CULGAITH (All Saints) Addingham, Edenhall,
Langwathby and Culgaith *Carl*
CULHAM (St Paul) Dorchester *Ox*

CULLERCOATS (St George) *Newc 8* **P** *Patr Bd*
TR G F REVETT, **TV** J T SHONE, R A BAILY,
C M D CATLING, **Hon C** R A MACEY
CULLINGWORTH (St John the Evangelist) *Bradf 8*
P *Bp* **P-in-c** P J SLATER
CULLOMPTON (St Andrew) (Langford Chapel) *Ex 4*
P *CPAS* **V** D A SAUNDERS, **C** J G PERKIN
CULM DAVY (St Mary Chapel) Hemyock w Culm
Davy and Clayhidon *Ex*
CULMINGTON (All Saints) w Onibury, Bromfield and
Stanton Lacy *Heref 12* **P** *Lady Magnus-Allcroft*
(1 turn), Earl of Plymouth (2 turns) **R** K J M EWEN,
NSM E H M PERKS
CULMSTOCK (All Saints) *Ex 4* **P** *D&C*
V M HANCOCK
CULPHO (St Botolph) Gt and Lt Bealings w Playford
and Culpho *St E*
CULWORTH (St Mary the Virgin) w Sulgrave and Thorpe
Mandeville *Pet 1* **P** *Ch Patr Trust (1 turn),*
T M Sergison-Brooke Esq (1 turn), DBP (2 turns), and
D L P Humfrey Esq (1 turn) **R** S E CRAWLEY
CUMBERWORTH (St Helen) Sutton, Huttoft and
Anderby *Linc*
CUMBERWORTH (St Nicholas) w Denby Dale *Wakef 6*
P *Bp* **P-in-c** D J CLARKSON
CUMDIVOCK (St John) Dalston *Carl*
CUMMERSDALE (St James) Denton Holme *Carl*
CUMNOR (St Michael) *Ox 10* **P** *St Pet Coll Ox*
V N D DURAND, **Par Dn** A BEECH, **NSM** C H HOLMES
CUMREW (St Mary the Virgin) Castle Carrock w
Cumrew and Croglin *Carl*
CUMWHINTON (St John's Hall) Cotehill and
Cumwhinton *Carl*
CUMWHITTON (St Mary the Virgin) *Carl 2* **P** *D&C*
V K P O'DONOHUE
CUNDALL (St Mary and All Saints) Kirby-on-the-
Moor, Cundall w Norton-le-Clay etc *Ripon*
CURBAR (All Saints) and Stoney Middleton *Derby 2*
P *V Baslow and V Hathersage (alt)* **V** *Vacant* Hope
Valley (0433) 30387
CURBRIDGE (St Barnabas) Sarisbury *Portsm*
CURBRIDGE (St John the Baptist) Witney *Ox*
CURDRIDGE (St Peter) *Portsm 1* **P** *D&C Win*
V G B WAGHORN
CURDWORTH (St Nicholas and St Peter ad Vincula) (St
George) *Birm 9* **P** *Bp and Lord Norton (jt)*
R M GARLAND, **NSM** C HOARE
CURRY, NORTH (St Peter and St Paul) *B & W 20*
P *D&C* **V** B SHACKLETON
CURRY MALLET (All Saints) Hatch Beauchamp w
Beercrocombe, Curry Mallet etc *B & W*
CURRY RIVEL (St Andrew) w Fivehead and Swell
B & W 18 **P** *D&C Bris (1 turn), P G H Speke Esq*
(2 turns) **R** P C LAMBERT
CURY (St Corentine) and Gunwalloe w St Mawgan-in-
Meneage *Truro 4* **P** *Bp* **R** P R LONG
CUSOP (St Mary) w Clifford, Hardwicke, Bredwardine,
Brobury and Moccas *Heref 1* **P** *CPAS, MMCET,*
R T G Chester Master Esq, and Slade Penoyre Esq (jt)
R P W M BYLLAM-BARNES, **NSM** C P STUTZ
CUTCOMBE (St John the Evangelist) Exton and
Winsford and Cutcombe w Luxborough *B & W*
CUTSDEAN (St James) The Guitings, Cutsdean and
Farmcote *Glouc*
CUXHAM (Holy Rood) Ewelme, Brightwell Baldwin,
Cuxham w Easington *Ox*
CUXTON (St Michael and All Angels) and Halling *Roch 6*
P *Bp and D&C (jt)* **R** R I KNIGHT
CUXWOLD (St Nicholas) Swallow *Linc*
CWM HEAD (St Michael) Wistanstow *Heref*
DACRE (Holy Trinity) w Hartwith and Darley w
Thornthwaite *Ripon 3* **P** *Bp, D&C, V Masham and*
Healey, and Mrs K A Dunbar (jt) **Par Dn** M J DUXBURY
DACRE (St Andrew) *Carl 4* **P** *Trustees* **V** K H SMITH
DADLINGTON (St James) Stoke Golding w Dadlington
Leic
DAGENHAM (St Luke) (St Peter and St Paul) *Chelmsf 1*
P *Patr Bd* **TR** D E SPRATLEY, **TV** H K SYMES-
THOMPSON, **C** R HURLEY
DAGENHAM (St Martin) *Chelmsf 1* **P** *Bp*
V G W J NUNN
DAGLINGWORTH (Holy Rood) w the Duntisbournes and
Winstone *Glouc 12* **P** *Ld Chan, DBP, and CCC Ox*
(by turn) **R** E HISCOX
DAGNALL (All Saints) Kensworth, Studham and
Whipsnade *St Alb*
DAISY HILL (St James) *Man 11* **P** *Bp* **V** T H STOKES
DALBURY (All Saints) Longford, Long Lane, Dalbury
and Radbourne *Derby*

DALBY (St James)   Patrick *S & M*
DALBY (St Lawrence and Blessed Edward King)
   Partney *Linc*
DALBY (St Peter)   Bulmer w Dalby, Terrington and
   Welburn *York*
DALBY, GREAT (St Swithun)   Burrough Hill Pars *Leic*
DALBY, LITTLE (St James)   as above
DALBY, OLD (St John the Baptist) and Nether Broughton
   Leic 3   **P** *Bp*   **P-in-c** K MORLEY
DALE ABBEY (All Saints)   Stanton-by-Dale w Dale
   Abbey *Derby*
DALE HEAD (St James)   Long Preston w Tosside *Bradf*
DALHAM (St Mary)   Gazeley w Dalham, Moulton and
   Kentford *St E*
DALLAM (St Mark) *Liv 12*   **P** *R Warrington and Bp (jt)*
   V P J MARSHALL
DALLINGHOO (St Mary)   Charsfield w Debach,
   Monewden, Hoo etc *St E*
DALLINGTON (St Giles)   Brightling, Dallington,
   Mountfield & Netherfield *Chich*
DALLINGTON (St Mary) *Pet 7*   **P** *Earl Spencer*
   V A E PANTON
DALLOWGILL (St Peter)   Fountains Gp *Ripon*
DALSTON (Holy Trinity) (St Philip) *Lon 5*   **P** *Bp*
   V J F WILLARD
DALSTON (St Mark w St Bartholomew) *Lon 5*   **P** *Ch Patr*
   Trust   **V** D H PATEMAN
DALSTON (St Michael) *Carl 3*   **P** *Bp*   **V** W KELLY,
   C I M RUMSEY
DALTON (Holy Trinity)   Newburn *Newc*
DALTON (Holy Trinity) *Sheff 6*   **P** *Bp*   **V** J R CORBYN
DALTON (St James)   Gilling and Kirkby Ravensworth
   Ripon
DALTON (St John the Evangelist)   Baldersby w Dalton,
   Dishforth etc *York*
DALTON (St Michael and All Angels) *Liv 11*   **P** *Bp*
   V T C BARTON
DALTON, NORTH (All Saints)   Bainton w N Dalton,
   Middleton-on-the-Wolds etc *York*
DALTON, SOUTH   Dalton le Dale *Dur*
DALTON HOLME (St Mary)   Etton w Dalton Holme
   York
DALTON-IN-FURNESS (St Mary) *Carl 8*   **P** *Bp*
   C M R EAST
DALTON LE DALE (Holy Trinity) (St Andrew) *Dur 3*
   P *D&C*   **V** E B PATEMAN,   **NSM** L HOOD
DALWOOD (St Peter)   Stockland w Dalwood *Ex*
DAMERHAM (St George)   W Downland *Sarum*
DANBURY (St John the Baptist) *Chelmsf 11*   **P** *Lord*
   Fitzwalter   **R** B J LLOYD,   **C** N A J BELCHER
DANBY (St Hilda) *York 23*   **P** *Viscount Downe*
   V T M RHODES
DANBY WISKE (not known)   Gt Smeaton w Appleton
   Wiske and Birkby etc *Ripon*
DANEHILL (All Saints) *Chich 21*   **P** *Ch Soc Trust*
   P-in-c P L PICKETT
DANESMOOR (St Barnabas)   N Wingfield, Clay Cross
   and Pilsley *Derby*
DARBY END (St Peter) *Worc 9*   **P** *Bp*   **V** N LAMBERT
DARBY GREEN (St Barnabas) *Win 5*   **P** *Bp*
   V J P H TYRRELL
DARENTH (St Margaret) *Roch 2*   **P** *D&C*   **V** R J FORD
DARESBURY (All Saints) *Ches 4*   **P** *D G Greenhall Esq*
   V D W SMITH
DARFIELD (All Saints) *Sheff 12*   **P** *MMCET*
   R M D BROWN,   **C** S P HACKING
DARLASTON (All Saints) *Lich 8*   **P** *Simeon's Trustees*
   P-in-c C S BUTLER
DARLASTON (St Lawrence) *Lich 8*   **P** *Bp and Simeon's*
   Trustees (jt)   **R** G W LLOYD,   **Par Dn** M TURNER
DARLEY (Christ Church)   Dacre w Hartwith and Darley
   w Thornthwaite *Ripon*
DARLEY (St Helen) *Derby 7*   **P** *Bp*   **R** R E QUARTON,
   C C M WITHERS
DARLEY, SOUTH (St Mary the Virgin), Elton and
   Winster *Derby 7*   **P** *Bp and DBF (jt)*   **R** K E SERVANTE
DARLEY ABBEY (St Matthew) *Derby 9*   **P** *DBP*
   V *Vacant*   Derby (0332) 553192
DARLINGSCOTT (St George)   Tredington and
   Darlingscott w Newbold on Stour *Cov*
DARLINGTON (Holy Trinity) (Salutation Church) *Dur 12*
   P *Adn Dur*   **Par Dn** A V MACKEITH
DARLINGTON (St Cuthbert) *Dur 12*   **P** *Lord Barnard*
   V L G READY,   **C** J P JENNINGS,   **Par Dn** J E CHAPMAN
DARLINGTON (St Hilda and St Columba) *Dur 12*   **P** *Bp*
   V J R TROOP
DARLINGTON (St James) *Dur 12*   **P** *The Crown*
   V I L GRIEVES,   **NSM** C M WILSON

DARLINGTON (St Mark) w St Paul *Dur 12*   **P** *Bp and*
   St Jo Coll Dur   **V** J R PILKINGTON
DARLINGTON (St Matthew and St Luke) *Dur 12*   **P** *Bp*
   V J R RICE-OXLEY,   **C** S G RADLEY
DARLINGTON, EAST (St John) (St Herbert) *Dur 12*
   P *The Crown*   **TR** J CLASPER,   **TV** T F BARNFATHER,
   Par Dn V SHEDDEN
DARLTON (St Giles)   Dunham-on-Trent w Darlton,
   Ragnall etc *S'well*
DARNALL (Church of Christ)   Darnall-cum-Attercliffe
   Sheff
DARNALL-CUM-ATTERCLIFFE *Sheff 1*   **P** *Patr Bd*
   TR J H MARTIN,   **TV** M L FUDGER
DARRINGTON (St Luke and All Saints) w Wentbridge
   Wakef 11   **P** *Bp*   **V** R I J MATTHEWS
DARSHAM (All Saints) *St E 19*   **P** *Exors Earl of*
   Stradbroke   **V** R J GINN
DARTFORD (Christ Church) *Roch 2*   **P** *V Dartford*
   H Trin   **V** D B KITLEY,   **C** M A MALCOLM,
   NSM C CROOK
DARTFORD (Holy Trinity) *Roch 2*   **P** *Bp*
   V P H D'ALOCK,   **C** P J LOW
DARTFORD (St Alban) *Roch 2*   **P** *V Dartford H Trin*
   V A T WATERMAN
DARTFORD (St Edmund the King and Martyr) *Roch 2*
   P *Bp*   **V** R P CALLAGHAN
DARTINGTON (St Mary) (Old St Mary's Church Tower)
   Ex 13   **P** *Bp*   **R** *Vacant*   Totnes (0803) 863206
DARTMOUTH (St Petrox) (St Saviour) *Ex 13*   **P** *DBP*
   and Sir John Seale, Bt (jt)   **V** I J BUTLER,
   Hon C P A RILEY
DARTON (All Saints) *Wakef 7*   **P** *Bp*   **V** S McCARRAHER
DARWEN (St Barnabas) *Blackb 5*   **P** *Bp*   **V** P H SMITH
DARWEN (St Cuthbert) w Tockholes St Stephen *Blackb 5*
   P *Bp*   **V** J COOPER,   **C** M C R SOWERBY
DARWEN (St Peter) w Hoddlesden St Paul *Blackb 5*
   P *V Blackburn and DBP (jt)*   **TV** R FARNWORTH,
   C G SENIOR
DARWEN, LOWER (St James) *Blackb 5*   **P** *V Blackb*
   V R P CARTMELL,   **NSM** A HADWIN
DARWEN, OVER (St James) *Blackb 5*   **P** *V Blackb*
   V J FARADAY
DASSETT MAGNA (All Saints)   Burton Dassett *Cov*
DATCHET (St Mary the Virgin)   Riverside *Ox*
DATCHWORTH (All Saints) w Tewin *St Alb 10*   **P** *Bp*
   and Jes Coll Cam (alt)   **R** P R BETTS
DAUBHILL (St George the Martyr) *Man 9*   **P** *Trustees*
   V S J ABRAM
DAUNTSEY (St James Great)   Brinkworth w Dauntsey
   Bris
DAVENHAM (St Wilfrid) *Ches 6*   **P** *Bp*   **R** C J REES
DAVENTRY (Holy Cross) *Pet 3*   **P** *Patr Bd*
   R G J JOHNSON,
   TV M J G TOMPKINS,   J W HARGREAVES,   **C** G R SMITH
DAVIDSTOW (St David)   Boscastle w Davidstow *Truro*
DAVINGTON (St Mary Magdalene)   The Brents and
   Davington w Oare and Luddenham *Cant*
DAVYHULME (Christ Church) *Man 7*   **P** *Bp*
   V A J WATTS,   **Hon C** J C HOOGERWERF
DAVYHULME (St Mary) *Man 7*   **P** *Bp*   **V** S J WINWARD
DAWDON (St Hild and St Helen) *Dur 3*   **P** *Bp*
   V J C G POLLOCK
DAWLEY (Holy Trinity)   Cen Telford *Lich*
DAWLEY (St Jerome) *Lon 24*   **P** *Hyndman Trustees*
   V N A MANNING
DAWLISH (St Gregory) *Ex 6*   **P** *D&C*   **V** W D SLARK,
   C T W BRIGHTON
DAWLISH WARREN (Church Hall)   Kenton,
   Mamhead, Powderham, Cofton and Starcross *Ex*
DAYBROOK (St Paul) *S'well 13*   **P** *Bp*   **V** A L WHEALE
DAYLESFORD (St Peter)   Kingham w Churchill,
   Daylesford and Sarsden *Ox*
DE BEAUVOIR TOWN (St Peter) *Lon 5*   **P** *Bp*
   V A WINDROSS,   **Par Dn** S F REDGRAVE
DEAL (St Andrew) *Cant 8*   **P** *Abp*   **R** J D KING
DEAL (St George the Martyr) *Cant 8*   **P** *Abp*
   V G W LINGS
DEAL (St Leonard) (St Richard) and Sholden (St Nicholas)
   Cant 8   **P** *Abp*   **R** R A V MARCHAND,   **C** R G A RIEM,
   NSM G F MACK
DEAN (All Hallows)   The Stodden Churches *St Alb*
DEAN (St Oswald) *Carl 6*   **P** *A R Sherwen Esq and*
   R Workington (jt)   **R** P M BADEN,   **NSM** J V HINE
DEAN, EAST (All Saints) *Chich 13*   **P** *Bp*
   V P M JENKINS
DEAN, EAST (St Simon and St Jude) w Friston and
   Jevington *Chich 16*   **P** *Duke of Devonshire (1 turn)*,
   D&C (2 turns)   **R** A H H HARBOTTLE

DEAN, EAST (St Winifred)   Lockerley and E Dean w E and W Tytherley *Win*

DEAN, WEST (All Saints)   Alfriston w Lullington, Litlington and W Dean *Chich*

DEAN, WEST (St Andrew) *Chich 13*   P *D&C*   V *Vacant*

DEAN, WEST (St Mary)   Alderbury Team *Sarum*

DEAN COURT (St Andrew)   Cumnor *Ox*

DEAN FOREST (Holy Trinity) *Glouc 4*   P *The Crown*   V A N JAMES

DEAN FOREST (St Paul) *Glouc 4*   P *Bp*   V I L DAVIES, NSM G W J BATTEN

DEAN PRIOR (St George the Martyr)   Buckfastleigh w Dean Prior *Ex*

DEANE (All Saints)   N Waltham and Steventon, Ashe and Deane *Win*

DEANE (St Mary the Virgin) *Man 11*   P *Patr Bd* TR R B JACKSON,   TV A R HAZLEHURST, C M W SAUNDERS

DEANSHANGER (Holy Trinity)   Passenham *Pet*

DEARHAM (St Mungo) *Carl 7*   P *Bp*   V M P BRION

DEARNLEY (St Andrew) *Man 19*   P *Bp*   V D FINNEY

DEBDEN (St Mary the Virgin) and Wimbish w Thunderley *Chelmsf 25*   P *Bp*   R R W REED

DEBENHAM (St Mary Magdalene) w Aspall and Kenton *St E 18*   P *Lord Henniker (2 turns), Bp (1 turn)* V H G PEARSON,   C R W JACK

DEDDINGTON (St Peter and St Paul) Barford, Clifton and Hempton *Ox 5*   P *D&C Windsor and Bp (jt)* V K G REEVES

DEDHAM (St Mary the Virgin) *Chelmsf 20*   P *Duchy of Lanc and Lectureship Trustees (alt)*   V N S BEDFORD

DEDWORTH (All Saints) *Ox 13*   P *Bp*   V P D ATKINSON

DEEPCAR (St John the Evangelist) *Sheff 7*   P *Bp* V R W PALMER

DEEPING (St Nicholas)   Spalding St Jo w Deeping St Nicholas *Linc*

DEEPING, WEST (St Andrew)   Uffington *Linc*

DEEPING ST JAMES (St James) *Linc 13*   P *Burghley Ho Preservation Trust*   V S R HAWORTH

DEERHURST (St Mary) and Apperley w Forthampton and Chaceley *Glouc 9*   P *Bp, Exors G J Yorke, and V Longdon (jt)*   P-in-c J E FORRYAN

DEFFORD (St James) w Besford *Worc 4*   P *D&C Westmr* V R H HOWES

DEIGHTON (All Saints)   Brompton w Deighton *York*

DELABOLE (St John the Evangelist)   St Teath *Truro*

DELAMERE (St Peter) *Ches 6*   P *The Crown* R S W WINTON

DELAVAL (Our Lady) *Newc 1*   P *Lord Hastings* V M F FENWICK

DEMBLEBY (St Lucia)   S Lafford *Linc*

DENABY, OLD (Mission Church)   Mexborough *Sheff*

DENABY MAIN (All Saints) *Sheff 8*   P *Bp* V R C DAVIES

DENBURY (St Mary the Virgin)   Ogwell and Denbury *Ex*

DENBY (St John the Evangelist) *Wakef 6*   P *V Penistone* V *Vacant*

DENBY (St Mary the Virgin) *Derby 12*   P *Exors Capt P J B Drury-Lowe*   P-in-c D J PHYPERS

DENBY DALE (Holy Trinity)   Cumberworth w Denby Dale *Wakef*

DENCHWORTH (St James) *Ox 19*   P *Worc Coll Ox* P-in-c A HOGG

DENDRON (St Matthew)   Aldingham and Dendron and Rampside *Carl*

DENESIDE (All Saints)   Seaham w Seaham Harbour *Dur*

DENFORD (Holy Trinity) w Ringstead *Pet 10* P *L Stopford-Sackville Esq*   V F COLEMAN

DENGIE (St James) w Asheldham *Chelmsf 13* P *D&C St Paul's and Bp*   P-in-c I M FINN

DENHAM (St John the Baptist)   Hoxne w Denham, Syleham and Wingfield *St E*

DENHAM (St Mark) (St Mary the Virgin) *Ox 20* P *L J Way Esq*   R J A HIRST,   C F R A MASON

DENHAM (St Mary)   Barrow w Denham St Mary and Higham Green *St E*

DENHAM, NEW (St Francis)   Denham *Ox*

DENHOLME GATE (St Paul) *Bradf 8*   P *Bp* P-in-c C B HOLLIS

DENMEAD (All Saints) *Portsm 4*   P *Ld Chan* V J R HERKLOTS,   NSM F R STRANACK

DENNINGTON (St Mary)   Badingham w Bruisyard, Cransford and Dennington *St E*

DENSHAW (Christ Church) *Man 18*   P *Bp* V S C L CLAYTON

DENSTON (St Nicholas)   Wickhambrook w Stradishall and Denston *St E*

DENSTONE (All Saints) w Ellastone and Stanton *Lich 21* P *Bp and Col Sir Walter Bromley-Davenport (jt)* V *Vacant*   Rocester (0889) 590263

DENT (St Andrew) w Cowgill *Bradf 6*   P *Bp and Sidesmen of Dent (alt)*   V A E ORMISTON

DENTON (Christ Church) *Man 17*   P *Bp*   R J K TUTTON, C J HANNA,   G WHITTAKER

DENTON Dane Bank (St George)   Denton Ch Ch *Man*

DENTON (Holy Spirit) *Newc 7*   P *Bp*   V B BENISON, C G EVANS

DENTON (St Andrew)   Harlaxton *Linc*

DENTON (St Helen)   Weston w Denton *Bradf*

DENTON (St Lawrence) *Man 17*   P *Earl of Wilton* R R CASSIDY,   C M A S GOODMAN

DENTON (St Leonard) w South Heighton and Tarring Neville *Chich 18*   P *MMCET and Bp (alt)* R A F STONE

DENTON (St Margaret)   Yardley Hastings, Denton and Grendon etc *Pet*

DENTON (St Mary)   Earsham w Alburgh and Denton *Nor*

DENTON (St Mary) and Ingleton *Dur 12*   P *V Staindrop (2 turns), V Gainford (1 turn)*   P-in-c J W BOOCOCK

DENTON (St Mary Magdalene)   Elham w Denton and Wootton *Cant*

DENTON, NETHER (St Cuthbert)   Farlam and Nether Denton *Carl*

DENTON HOLME (St James) *Carl 3*   P *Trustees* V J D RUSHTON,   C D K PHILLIPS

DENVER (St Mary) *Ely 16*   P *G&C Coll Cam* R R JEFFREE

DENVILLE (Christchurch Centre)   Havant *Portsm*

DEOPHAM (St Andrew)   Morley w Deopham, Hackford, Wicklewood etc *Nor*

DEPDEN (St Mary the Virgin)   Chedburgh w Depden, Rede and Hawkedon *St E*

DEPTFORD Brockley (St Peter) *S'wark 2*   P *Bp* V T J L HARPER

DEPTFORD Edward Street (St Mark)   Deptford St Paul *S'wark*

DEPTFORD (St John) (Holy Trinity) *S'wark 2*   P *Peache Trustees and Ch Trust Fund Trust (jt)*   V T OLDROYD

DEPTFORD (St Nicholas) (St Luke) *S'wark 2* P *MMCET, Peache Trustees, and CPAS (jt)* V W G CORNECK,   C T G JACQUET

DEPTFORD (St Paul) (St Mark) *S'wark 2*   P *Bp* R D J DIAMOND,   C M J D ANDERSON

DERBY (St Alkmund and St Werburgh) *Derby 9* P *Simeon's Trustees*   Par A CORRIE,   C R C SAMME

DERBY (St Andrew w St Osmund) *Derby 10*   P *Bp* V D C MACDONALD,   Par Dn N K PRITCHARD

DERBY (St Anne) (St John the Evangelist) *Derby 9*   P *Bp* V C M G BRINKWORTH

DERBY (St Augustine) *Derby 10*   P *V Derby St Chad* P-in-c M W S PARSONS,   C G I KOVOOR, Par Dn S R PITE

DERBY (St Barnabas) *Derby 9*   P *Bp*   V G D KENDREW

DERBY (St Bartholomew) *Derby 10*   P *Bp* V A G MESSOM

DERBY (St Chad) Mill Hill *Derby 10*   P *CPAS* P-in-c D N GOUGH

DERBY (St James the Great) *Derby 10*   P *Bp* P-in-c M R FUTERS

DERBY (St Luke) *Derby 9*   P *Bp*   C J H FLINT, NSM C R OXLEY

DERBY (St Mark) *Derby 9*   P *Bp*   P-in-c B A NORTH, NSM B A KEELING

DERBY (St Paul) *Derby 9*   P *Bp*   V J F LEE

DERBY (St Peter and Christ Church w Holy Trinity) *Derby 10*   P *CPAS*   P-in-c V J PRICE

DERBY (St Thomas the Apostle) *Derby 10*   P *Bp* V M N W EDWARDS

DERBY, WEST (Good Shepherd) *Liv 8*   P *Bp and R W Derby (jt)*   C S S WILLIAMS

DERBY, WEST (St James) *Liv 8*   P *Trustees* V P W PLUNKETT

DERBY, WEST St John *Liv 8*   P *Trustees* V F SAMPSON,   C I R SHACKLETON

DERBY, WEST (St Luke) *Liv 2*   P *Bp*   V J H WELCH, C S ELLIS

DERBY, WEST (St Mary) *Liv 8*   P *Bp* TR J R I WIKELEY,   TV T M LATHAM,   C J BOARDMAN, Par Dn J E BOWEN

DERBYHAVEN (Chapel)   Malew *S & M*

DEREHAM, EAST (St Nicholas) and Scarning *Nor 12* P *Ld Chan*   R D W A RIDER

DEREHAM, WEST (St Andrew) *Ely 16*   P *Bp* V R JEFFREE

DERRINGHAM BANK (Ascension) *York 15* **P** *Abp*
V S J WHALEY, **Par Dn** J BRAY
DERRINGTON (St Matthew) Seighford, Derrington
and Cresswell *Lich*
DERRY HILL (Christ Church) *Sarum 18* **P** *V Calne and
Blackland* **V** J R CARDWELL
DERSINGHAM (St Nicholas) w Anmer and Shernborne
Nor 21 **P** *Ld Chan* **R** T P JARDINE
DESBOROUGH (St Giles) *Pet 11* **P** *Bp*
V R J CHAPMAN, **C** C M SCARGILL
DESFORD (St Martin) and Peckleton w Tooley *Leic 12*
P *Ld Chan* **R** *Vacant* Desford (04557) 2276
DETHICK (St John the Baptist) Tansley, Dethick, Lea
and Holloway *Derby*
DETLING (St Martin) Boxley w Detling *Cant*
DEVERILLS, The *Sarum 14* **P** *DBP (3 turns),* Bp
(1 turn) **R** P R L MORGAN
DEVIZES (St John) (St Mary) *Sarum 19* **P** *Ld Chan*
R C BRYANT, **Hon Par Dn** L M CATER
DEVIZES (St Peter) *Sarum 19* **P** *Bp* **V** B A TIGWELL
DEVONPORT (St Aubyn) *Ex 22* **P** *The Crown and
R Stoke Damerel (alt)* **P-in-c** G D CRYER,
Hon Par Dn J GODFREY
DEVONPORT (St Barnabas) *Ex 22* **P** *R Stoke Damerel*
V J E SUMMERS
DEVONPORT (St Bartholomew) *Ex 22* **P** *Bp*
V A R LEIGH
DEVONPORT (St Boniface) (St Philip) *Ex 22* **P** *Bp*
TR J D A HUTCHINGS, **TV** N R C PEARKES
DEVONPORT (St Mark) Ford *Ex 22* **P** *Trustees*
P-in-c L J YEO
DEVONPORT (St Michael) Stoke *Ex 22* **P** *R Stoke
Damerel* **P-in-c** R J HILL
DEVONPORT ST BUDEAUX *Ex 22* **P** *V Plymouth
St Andr w St Paul and St Geo* **V** M D D JONES,
C P R EVANS, **Hon Par Dn** L S C FRY
DEVORAN (St John the Evangelist and St Petroc) *Truro 6*
P *Bp* **V** M C PALMER, **NSM** R RADCLIFFE
**DEWCHURCH, LITTLE (St David) and Aconbury w
Ballingham and Bolstone** *Heref 4* **P** *D&C and Bp (alt)*
V T P JONES, **TV** R NORTH
DEWCHURCH, MUCH (St David) Much Birch w Lt
Birch, Much Dewchurch etc *Heref*
DEWLISH (All Saints) Milborne St Andrew w Dewlish
Sarum
DEWSALL (St Michael) w Callow *Heref 3* **P** *D&C*
R T P JONES, **TV** R NORTH
**DEWSBURY (All Saints) (St Mark) (St Matthew and
St John)** *Wakef 10* **P** *Bp, Adn Pontefract, RD
Dewsbury, and Lay Chmn Dewsbury Deanery Syn (jt)*
TR J A HAWLEY, **TV** R JONES, A J P THOMPSON
DEWSBURY MOOR (St John the Evangelist)
Dewsbury *Wakef*
DHOON (Christ Church) Maughold *S & M*
DIBDEN (All Saints) *Win 10* **P** *MMCET* **R** C R MILES
DIBDEN PURLIEU (St Andrew) Dibden *Win*
DICKER, UPPER (Holy Trinity) Hellingly and Upper
Dicker *Chich*
**DICKLEBURGH (All Saints) w Langmere and Shimpling,
Thelveton w Frenze, Rushall** *Nor 16* **P** *Ld Chan, Bp,
Trin Coll Cam, MMCET, and Lady Mann (by turn)*
R S J O SPIKIN, **NSM** B J SASADA
DIDBROOK (St George) Toddington, Stanton,
Didbrook w Hailes etc *Glouc*
DIDCOT (All Saints) *Ox 18* **P** *BNC Ox*
R N C WADSWORTH, **C** A TYLER
DIDCOT (St Peter) *Ox 18* **P** *Bp* **V** I N RANDALL,
C C J PATCHING
DIDDINGTON (St Laurence) *Ely 12*
P *G E P Thornhill Esq* **V** P G LEWIS
**DIDDLEBURY (St Peter) w Munslow, Holdgate and
Tugford** *Heref 12* **P** *Bp (3 turns), D&C (1 turn)*
R I E GIBBS
DIDLINGTON (St Michael) *Nor 18* **P** *CPAS*
P-in-c C W T CHALCRAFT, **C** G H WHEATLEY
DIDMARTON (St Michael and All Angels) Boxwell,
Leighterton, Didmarton, Oldbury etc *Glouc*
DIDSBURY (Christ Church) Barlow Moor Road *Man 8*
P *Trustees* **R** C J S JONES
DIDSBURY (St James) (Emmanuel) *Man 8* **P** *Patr Bd*
TR D M HUGHES, **TV** J K MILLS, **C** G F JOYCE
DIGBY (St Thomas of Canterbury) *Linc 22* **P** *DBP and
Mrs H E Gillatt (alt)* **V** C R M POYNTING
DIGMOOR (Christ the Servant) Upholland *Liv*
**DIGSWELL (St John the Evangelist) (Christ the King) and
Panshanger** *St Alb 7* **P** *Patr Bd* **TR** J D THOMPSON,
TM J E FORDHAM, **TV** R COPPING, **C** T W GLADWIN,
NSM J M B POTIPHER

DILHAM (St Nicholas) Smallburgh w Dilham w Honing
and Crostwight *Nor*
DILHORNE (All Saints) *Lich 12* **P** *D&C*
P-in-c N JEFFERYES
DILSTON (St Mary Magdalene) Corbridge w Halton
and Newton Hall *Newc*
DILTON or LEIGH (Holy Saviour) Westbury *Sarum*
DILTON MARSH (Holy Trinity) *Sarum 14* **P** *Bp*
V S F TREEBY
DILWYN AND STRETFORD (St Mary the Virgin)
Leominster *Heref*
DINDER (St Michael and All Angels) Pilton w
Croscombe, N Wootton and Dinder *B & W*
DINEDOR (St Andrew) Holme Lacy w Dinedor *Heref*
DINGLEY (All Saints) Brampton Ash w Dingley and
Braybrooke *Pet*
DINNINGTON (St Leonard) *Sheff 5* **P** *J C Athorpe Esq*
R S P BAILEY, **C** R A FITZHARRIS
DINNINGTON (St Matthew) Ch the King in the Dio of
Newc *Newc*
DINNINGTON (St Nicholas) Merriott w Hinton,
Dinnington and Lopen *B & W*
DINSDALE (St John the Baptist) w Sockburn *Dur 12*
P *D&C and Sherburn Hosp (alt)* **R** R R A GRAHAM
DINTING VALE (Holy Trinity) Charlesworth and
Dinting Vale *Derby*
DINTON (St Mary) Barford St Martin, Dinton,
Baverstock etc *Sarum*
DINTON (St Peter and St Paul) Stone w Dinton and
Hartwell *Ox*
**DIPTFORD (St Mary the Virgin), North Huish, Harberton
and Harbertonford** *Ex 13* **P** *D R Buchanan-Allen Esq,
D&C, and Bp (jt)* **R** P A D WILLIS,
Hon C J T GEORGE, R H CHITTENDEN, M F FURLONGER
DIPTON (St John the Evangelist) *Dur 8* **P** *Bp* **V** *Vacant*
Dipton (0207) 570226
DISCOED (St Michael) Presteigne w Discoed, Kinsham
and Lingen *Heref*
DISEWORTH (St Michael and All Angels) Hathern,
Long Whatton and Diseworth w Belton etc *Leic*
DISHFORTH (Christ Church) Baldersby w Dalton,
Dishforth etc *York*
DISHLEY (All Saints) and Thorpe Acre *Leic 7* **P** *Bp*
C I D FARLEY
DISLEY (St Mary the Virgin) *Ches 16* **P** *Lord Newton*
V S J COX
DISS Heywood (St James the Great) see below
DISS (St Mary) *Nor 16* **P** *Bp* **R** G C JAMES,
NSM B J SASADA
DISTINGTON (Holy Spirit) *Carl 7* **P** *Earl of Lonsdale*
R C P ARNESEN
**DITCHEAT (St Mary Magdalene) w East Pennard and
Pylle** *B & W 9* **P** *Bp and Canon D S Salter (jt)*
R G O FARRAN, **Hon Par Dn** A KEMP
DITCHINGHAM (St Mary), Hedenham and Broome
Nor 11 **P** *Countess Ferrers and Bp (jt)* **R** R C HOLMES
DITCHLING (St Margaret) *Chich 9* **P** *Bp*
V K C JEFFERY
DITTERIDGE (St Christopher) *Bris 9* **P** *Bp*
NSM J AYERS
DITTISHAM (St George) Ashprington, Cornworthy
and Dittisham *Ex*
DITTON (St Michael) *Liv 13* **P** *Patr Bd* **TR** D R LESLIE,
TV J N MANSFIELD, R S BRIDSON, **C** S HOWARD
DITTON (St Peter ad Vincula) *Roch 7* **P** *Ch Trust Fund
Trust* **R** R A GRINSTED, **C** K D MENTZEL
**DITTON PRIORS (St John the Baptist) w Neenton,
Burwarton, Cleobury North, Aston Botterell, Wheathill
and Loughton** *Heref 9* **P** *Bp, Viscount Boyne, and
Princess Josephine zu Loewenstein (jt)*
R M A J HARDING
DIXON GREEN (St Thomas) *Man 12* **P** *Bp* **V** *Vacant*
Farnworth (0204) 72455
DIXTON (St Peter) *Heref 8* **P** *DBP* **V** R E D W PHILLIPS
DOBCROSS (Holy Trinity) w Scouthead (St Paul) *Man 18*
P *Bp* **V** C W M BARLOW
DOBWALLS (St Peter) Liskeard, St Keyne, St Pinnock,
Morval etc *Truro*
DOCCOMBE (Chapel) Moretonhampstead, N Bovey
and Manaton *Ex*
DOCK (Mission Church) Immingham *Linc*
DOCKENFIELD (Church of the Good Shepherd)
Frensham *Guildf*
**DOCKING (St Mary) w The Birchams and Stanhoe w
Barwick** *Nor 21* **P** *The Crown, R S C Ralli Esq, Bp,
and Col J H R Orlebar (by turn)* **R** N A LLEWELLYN
DOCKLOW (St Bartholomew) Leominster *Heref*
DODBROOKE (St Thomas à Beckett) Kingsbridge and
Dodbrooke *Ex*

DODDERHILL (St Augustine)   Droitwich Spa *Worc*
DODDINGHURST (All Saints) and Mountnessing
Chelmsf 10   **P** *Bp*   **R** J T HOWDEN
DODDINGTON (All Saints)   Quantoxhead *B & W*
DODDINGTON (St John)   Wybunbury w Doddington *Ches*
DODDINGTON (St John the Baptist)   Coreley w Doddington *Heref*
DODDINGTON (St John the Baptist), Newnham and Wychling *Cant 6*   **P** *Abp, Adn, and Exors Sir John Croft, Bt (jt)*   **V** D K INNES
DODDINGTON (St Mary and St Michael)   Glendale Gp *Newc*
DODDINGTON (St Mary) w Benwick *Ely 18*   **P** *Lady Glover-Hurlimann and Bp (alt)*   **P-in-c** K G PRATT
DODDINGTON (St Peter)   Skellingthorpe w Doddington *Linc*
DODDINGTON, GREAT (St Nicholas) and Wilby *Pet 6*   **P** *Exors Lt-Col H C M Stockdale and Ld Chan (alt)*   **V** M S WRATTEN
DODDISCOMBSLEIGH (St Michael)   Dunsford and Doddiscombsleigh *Ex*
DODFORD (Holy Trinity and St Mary)   Catshill and Dodford *Worc*
DODFORD (St Mary the Virgin)   Flore w Dodford and Brockhall *Pet*
DODLESTON (St Mary) *Ches 2*   **P** *D&C*   **NSM** N BALL
DODWORTH (St John the Baptist) *Wakef 7*   **P** *V Silkstone*   **V** H P JONES
DOGMERSFIELD (All Saints)   Hartley Wintney, Elvetham, Winchfield etc *Win*
DOLPHINHOLME (St Mark) w Quernmore St Peter *Blackb 12*   **P** *Bp and V Lanc (alt)*   **V** L J HAKES
DOLTON (St Edmund) *Ex 20*   **P** *Ch Soc Trust*   **R** *Vacant* Dolton (08054) 264
DONCASTER (Christ Church) *Sheff 9*   **P** *SMF* **P-in-c** D N GIBBS,   **C** J HARRIS
DONCASTER Intake (All Saints) *Sheff 9*   **P** *Bp* **V** B G FRETWELL,   **Hon C** J S B CROSSLEY
DONCASTER (St George) (St Edmund's Church Centre) *Sheff 9*   **P** *Bp*   **V** H J J BIRD
DONCASTER (St James) *Sheff 10*   **P** *Bp* **V** J D SLADDEN,   **Par Dn** M E GREEN
DONCASTER (St Jude) *Sheff 10*   **P** *Hyndman Trustees* **V** *Vacant*   Doncaster (0302) 852057
DONCASTER (St Leonard and St Jude) *Sheff 8*   **P** *The Crown*   **V** N J PAY,   **C** J W MATHER
DONCASTER (St Mary) *Sheff 9*   **P** *Hyndman Trustees* **V** J R SMITH
DONHEAD ST ANDREW (St Andrew)   see below
DONHEAD ST MARY (St Mary the Virgin)   see below
DONHEADS, The *Sarum 13*   **P** *DBP and New Coll Ox (alt)*   **P-in-c** T C CURRY
DONINGTON (St Cuthbert) *Lich 26*   **P** *MMCET* **R** C W WOODS
DONINGTON (St Mary and the Holy Rood) *Linc 21* **P** *Simeon's Trustees*   **V** J P PATRICK
DONINGTON-ON-BAIN (St Andrew)   Asterby Gp *Linc*
DONISTHORPE (St John) and Moira w Stretton-en-le-Field *Leic 9*   **P** *Ch Soc Trust (1 turn), and Bp (3 turns)* **V** E K WHITLEY,   **Hon C** W POPEJOY
DONNINGTON (St George) *Chich 3*   **P** *Bp* **P-in-c** P TRAFFORD
DONNINGTON WOOD (St Matthew) *Lich 28*   **P** *Bp* **V** H J PASCOE
DONYATT (Blessed Virgin Mary) w Horton, Broadway and Ashill *B & W 18*   **P** *Bp and W P Palmer Esq (jt)* **R** J F SERTIN
DONYLAND, EAST (St Lawrence)   Fingringhoe w E Donyland *Chelmsf*
DORCHESTER (St George) (St Mary the Virgin) (St Peter, Holy Trinity and All Saints) *Sarum 2*   **P** *Patr Bd (3 turns), Ld Chan (1 turn)*   **TV** D J LETCHER, D C W FAYLE, **NSM** I M G SCOTT,   D H SIM
DORCHESTER (St Peter and St Paul) *Ox 1*   **P** *Patr Bd* **TR** J Y CROWE,   **TV** A R MOORE, P L DEWEY, D J COCKERELL, **Par Dn** S M COLE-KING,   **NSM** R M GODFREY, M J GIBB
DORDON (St Leonard) *Birm 12*   **P** *V Polesworth* **V** J D POTTER
DORE (Christ Church) *Sheff 2*   **P** *Sir Stephen Hastings* **V** J FROGGATT
DORKING (St Martin) w Ranmore *Guildf 7*   **P** *Bp* **V** M J FARRANT,   **C** D J SAYER
DORKING (St Paul) *Guildf 7*   **P** *Ch Patr Trust* **V** A S W CULLIS,   **C** G P READ

DORMANSLAND (St John) *S'wark 23*   **P** *Bp* **V** B F MOBBS
DORMANSTOWN (All Saints) *York 17*   **P** *Abp* **V** J E D CAVE
DORMINGTON (St Peter)   Hampton Bishop and Mordiford w Dormington *Heref*
DORMSTON (St Nicholas)   Inkberrow w Cookhill and Kington w Dormston *Worc*
DORNEY (St James the Less)   Riverside *Ox*
DORRIDGE (St Philip) *Birm 13*   **P** *Bp*   **V** J A STEVENS, **C** P A REYNOLDS
DORRINGTON (St Edward) *Heref 11*   **P** *Lady More* **P-in-c** J D M FALL
DORRINGTON (St James)   Digby *Linc*
DORSINGTON (St Peter)   Pebworth w Dorsington and Honeybourne *Glouc*
DORSTONE (St Faith)   Peterchurch w Vowchurch, Turnastone and Dorstone *Heref*
DORTON (St John the Baptist)   Brill, Boarstall, Chilton and Dorton *Ox*
DOSTHILL (St Paul) *Birm 12*   **P** *Bp*   **P-in-c** R G SHARPE
DOTTERY (St Saviour)   Askerswell, Loders and Powerstock *Sarum*
DOUGLAS (Christ Church) *Blackb 4*   **P** *Bp* **V** B E HARDING
DOUGLAS (St George) and St Barnabas w (All Saints) *S & M 2*   **P** *Bp*   **V** D A WILLOUGHBY,   **C** M ROBERTS, **Hon C** J P HEBDEN
DOUGLAS (St Matthew the Apostle) *S & M 2*   **P** *Bp* **V** D WHITWORTH,   **Hon C** J W R C SARKIES
DOUGLAS (St Ninian) *S & M 2*   **P** *CPAS*   **V** *Vacant* Douglas (0624) 676310
DOUGLAS (St Thomas the Apostle) *S & M 2*   **P** *Bp* **V** A J SMITH
DOUGLAS-IN-PARBOLD (Christ Church)   Douglas *Blackb*
DOULTING (St Aldhelm)   Shepton Mallet w Doulting *B & W*
DOVE HOLES (St Paul)   Wormhill, Peak Forest w Peak Dale and Dove Holes *Derby*
DOVECOT (Holy Spirit) *Liv 2*   **P** *Bp*   **V** P D D BRADLEY, **C** A TAWN
DOVER Buckland Valley (St Nicholas)   Buckland in Dover w Buckland Valley *Cant*
DOVER (St Martin) *Cant 4*   **P** *CPAS*   **V** B J DUCKETT, **NSM** J H COLEMAN
DOVER (St Mary the Virgin) *Cant 4*   **P** *Abp, Ld Warden of Cinque Ports, and Ld-Lt of Kent (jt)*   **V** A F SIMPER
DOVER (St Peter and St Paul)   Charlton-in-Dover *Cant*
DOVERCOURT (All Saints) and Parkeston *Chelmsf 23* **P** *Bp*   **TR** W G STINSON, **TV** R M C PAXON, M K TAILBY,   **NSM** O BERGER
DOVERDALE (St Mary)   Ombersley w Doverdale *Worc*
DOVERIDGE (St Cuthbert) *Derby 14*   **P** *Duke of Devonshire*   **P-in-c** D MILNER,   **NSM** P R JONES
DOVERSGREEN (St Peter)   Reigate St Luke S Park *S'wark*
DOWDESWELL (St Michael) and Andoversford w the Shiptons and Cold Salperton *Glouc 14* **P** *Mrs L E Evans, MMCET, and Bp (jt)*   **NSM** J ELLIS
DOWLAND (not known)   Iddesleigh w Dowland *Ex*
DOWLES Button Oak (St Andrew)   Ribbesford w Bewdley and Dowles *Worc*
DOWLISHWAKE (St Andrew) w Kingstone, Chillington and Cudworth *B & W 16*   **P** *Bp, D&C, and P G H Speke Esq (by turn)*   **R** D J RACTLIFFE
DOWN, East (St John the Baptist)   Shirwell, Loxhore, Kentisbury, Arlington, etc *Ex*
DOWN AMPNEY (All Saints)   S Cerney w Cerney Wick and Down Ampney *Glouc*
DOWN HATHERLEY (St Mary and Corpus Christi)   Twigworth, Down Hatherley, Norton, The Leigh etc *Glouc*
DOWN ST MARY (St Mary the Virgin)   N Creedy *Ex*
DOWNDERRY (St Nicholas)   St Germans *Truro*
DOWNE (St Mary Magdalene)   Cudham and Downe *Roch*
DOWNEND (Christ Church) (Church Centre) *Bris 7* **P** *Peache Trustees*   **V** A O JOYCE, **C** C W BOWLER,   G G HOWARD,   **NSM** P J ROBERTS
DOWNHAM (St Barnabas)   Catford (Southend) and Downham *S'wark*
DOWNHAM (St Leonard) *Blackb 8*   **P** *Lord Clitheroe* **V** *Vacant*   Clitheroe (0200) 41379
DOWNHAM (St Leonard) *Ely 14*   **P** *Bp*   **R** R J MACKLIN
DOWNHAM (St Luke)   Catford (Southend) and Downham *S'wark*
DOWNHAM (St Margaret) w South Hanningfield *Chelmsf 11*   **P** *Bp*   **R** D J ATKINS

DOWNHAM, NORTH (St Mark)   Catford (Southend) and Downham *S'wark*

DOWNHAM MARKET (St Edmund) w Bexwell *Ely 16* **P** *Bp*   **R** P F KEELING,   **Par Dn** A M MITCHAM

DOWNHEAD (All Saints)   Leigh upon Mendip w Stoke St Michael *B & W*

DOWNHOLME (St Michael and All Angels) and Marske *Ripon 2* **P** *Bp*   **C-in-c** W M SIMMS

DOWNLEY (St James the Great)   High Wycombe *Ox*

DOWNS BARN and NEAT HILL (Community Church) Stantonbury and Willen *Ox*

DOWNSBY (St Andrew)   Rippingale Gp *Linc*

DOWNSIDE (St Michael's Chapel)   Ockham w Hatchford *Guildf*

DOWNSWAY (All Souls Worship Centre)   Southwick *Chich*

DOWNTON (St Giles)   Wigmore Abbey *Heref*

DOWNTON (St Lawrence) *Sarum 11* **P** *Win Coll*   **V** M C GALLAGHER

DOYNTON (Holy Trinity)   Wick w Doynton and Dyrham *Bris*

DRAKES BROUGHTON (St Barnabas)   Stoulton w Drake's Broughton and Pirton etc *Worc*

DRAUGHTON (St Augustine)   Skipton H Trin *Bradf*

DRAUGHTON (St Catherine)   Maidwell w Draughton, Lamport w Faxton *Pet*

DRAX (St Peter and St Paul)   Carlton and Drax *York*

DRAYCOT CERNE (St James) *Bris 9* **P** *Bp*   **P-in-c** J C POARCH,   **NSM** G H BOLT

DRAYCOTT (St Mary)   Wilne and Draycott w Breaston *Derby*

DRAYCOTT (St Peter)   Rodney Stoke w Draycott *B & W*

DRAYCOTT IN THE CLAY (St Augustine)   Hanbury w Newborough *Lich*

DRAYCOTT-LE-MOORS (St Margaret) w Forsbrook *Lich 12* **P** *Bp*   **Par Dn** J C WATERS

DRAYTON (Church of the Resurrection)   Farlington *Portsm*

DRAYTON (Iron Mission Room)   Chaddesley Corbett and Stone *Worc*

DRAYTON (St Catherine)   Langport Area Chs *B & W*

DRAYTON (St Leonard and St Catherine)   Dorchester *Ox*

DRAYTON (St Margaret) w Felthorpe *Nor 4* **P** *Bp*   **R** R G ROBINSON

DRAYTON (St Peter)   Broughton w N Newington and Shutford etc *Ox*

DRAYTON (St Peter) Berks *Ox 10* **P** *Bp*   **P-in-c** J M LOVELAND

DRAYTON, EAST (St Peter)   Dunham-on-Trent w Darlton, Ragnall etc *S'well*

DRAYTON, LITTLE (Christ Church) *Lich 24* **P** *V Drayton in Hales*   **V** J O DAVIES

DRAYTON, WEST (St Martin) *Lon 24* **P** *Bp*   **V** T SAMUEL,   **C** H E WRIGHT

DRAYTON, WEST (St Paul)   Gamston w Eaton and W Drayton *S'well*

DRAYTON BASSETT (St Peter) *Lich 5* **P** *Bp*   **R** H J BAKER,   **Res Min** J R BALL

DRAYTON-BEAUCHAMP (St Mary the Virgin)   Aston Clinton w Buckland and Drayton Beauchamp *Ox*

DRAYTON IN HALES (St Mary) *Lich 24* **P** *Lt-Col Sir John Corbet, Bt*   **V** P A LEONARD-JOHNSON, **NSM** J T SMITH

DRAYTON PARSLOW (Holy Trinity)   Stewkley w Soulbury and Drayton Parslow *Ox*

DRESDEN (Resurrection) *Lich 18* **P** *V Blurton*   **V** H F HARPER

DREWSTEIGNTON (Holy Trinity) *Ex 12* **P** *Exors B Drewe*   **R** C J L NAPIER,   **NSM** J G WITHERS

DRIFFIELD (St Mary)   The Ampneys w Driffield and Poulton *Glouc*

DRIFFIELD, GREAT (All Saints) and LITTLE (St Peter) *York 11* **P** *Abp*   **V** M A SIMONS

DRIGG (St Peter)   Seascale and Drigg *Carl*

DRIGHLINGTON (St Paul) *Wakef 8* **P** *Bp*   **V** B F WOOD

DRIMPTON (St Mary)   Beaminster Area *Sarum*

DRINGHOUSES (St Edward the Confessor) *York 8* **P** *Abp*   **V** A M GIRLING,   **Par Dn** S E FLETCHER

DRINKSTONE (All Saints)   Woolpit w Drinkstone *St E*

DROITWICH SPA (St Andrew w St Mary de Witton) (St Nicholas) (St Peter) (St Richard) *Worc 8* **P** *Bp*   **TR** J C STALLARD,   **TM** P A HARVEY,   **C** J VAN DER VALK,   **Hon C** S W GODFREY,   **NSM** D F GUTTERIDGE, R M WILTSHIRE

DRONFIELD (St John the Baptist) w Holmesfield *Derby 5* **P** *Ld Chan*   **R** D G PALMER,   **TV** R P TUCKER, P R SANDFORD, D GARLICK

DROPMORE (St Anne)   Burnham w Dropmore, Hitcham and Taplow *Ox*

DROXFORD (St Mary and All Saints) *Portsm 1* **P** *Bp*   **R** D E HENLEY,   **NSM** J R BARNETT

DROYLSDEN (St Andrew) *Man 17* **P** *Bp*   **R** P L SCOTT

DROYLSDEN (St Martin) *Man 17* **P** *Bp*   **V** R LIVINGSTON

DROYLSDEN (St Mary) (St John) *Man 17* **P** *Bp*   **R** M J WILLIAMSON,   **Par Dn** E HOPE

DRY DODDINGTON (St James)   Claypole *Linc*

DRY DRAYTON (St Peter and St Paul) *Ely 5* **P** *MMCET*   **P-in-c** D L GOSLING

DRY SANDFORD (St Helen)   Besselsleigh w Dry Sandford *Ox*

DRYBROOK (Holy Trinity)   Dean Forest H Trin *Glouc*

DRYPOOL (St Columba) (St John) *York 15* **P** *Patr Bd*   **TR** P R W HARRISON,   **TV** D A URQUHART,   **C** R P YATES, D J CHRISTIE,   **Par Dn** P A WICK

DUCKLINGTON (St Bartholomew) *Ox 8* **P** *DBP*   **P-in-c** D B WINTER

DUCKMANTON (St Peter and St Paul)   Calow and Sutton cum Duckmanton *Derby*

DUDDENHOE END (The Hamlet Church)   Heydon, Gt and Lt Chishill, Chrishall etc *Chelmsf*

DUDDESTON (St Matthew) w Nechells St Clement *Birm 1* **P** *Trustees*   **V** J H LANGSTAFF,   **Par Dn** I M BROTHERSTON,   **NSM** H SMITH

DUDDINGTON (St Mary)   Easton on the Hill, Collyweston w Duddington etc *Pet*

DUDDO (All Saints)   Norham and Duddo *Newc*

DUDDON (St Peter)   Tarvin *Ches*

DUDLESTON (St Mary the Virgin) *Lich 23* **P** *V Ellesmere*   **V** A W MOSELEY

DUDLEY Eve Hill (St James the Great) *Worc 9* **P** *V Dudley*   **V** D J TANN

DUDLEY Holly Hall (St Augustine) *Worc 9* **P** *V Dudley*   **V** J L SAMUEL,   **C** M J ROGERS

DUDLEY Kate's Hill (St John) *Worc 9* **P** *V Dudley*   **V** J W KNIGHTS

DUDLEY (St Andrew)   Netherton St Andr *Worc*

DUDLEY (St Barnabas) *Worc 9* **P** *Bp*   **V** P G GREEN

DUDLEY (St Edmund King and Martyr) *Worc 9* **P** *V Dudley*   **V** M C BRAIN,   **Hon C** A REED

DUDLEY (St Francis) *Worc 9* **P** *Bp*   **V** R G JONES,   **C** S M MILLER

DUDLEY (St Paul)   Weetslade *Newc*

DUDLEY (St Thomas and St Luke) *Worc 9* **P** *Bp*   **V** M J GOSS

DUDLEY WOOD (St John) *Worc 9* **P** *V Netherton*   **V** S G F OWENS

DUFFIELD (St Alkmund) *Derby 11* **P** *Ch Soc Trust*   **V** A E G STEVENS,   **Hon C** J B WELLER

DUFTON (St Cuthbert)   Long Marton w Dufton and w Milburn *Carl*

DUKINFIELD (St John) (St Alban Mission Church) *Ches 14* **P** *R Stockport St Mary*   **V** B HEWITT

DUKINFIELD (St Mark) (St Luke) *Ches 14* **P** *Bp*   **V** E W D THOMAS

DULAS (St Michael)   Ewyas Harold w Dulas, Kenderchurch etc *Heref*

DULCOTE (All Saints)   Wells St Cuth w Wookey Hole *B & W*

DULLINGHAM (St Mary) *Ely 4* **P** *P B Taylor Esq*   **P-in-c** G I ARNOLD

DULOE (St Cuby) w Herodsfoot *Truro 12* **P** *Ball Coll Ox*   **NSM** B P BARNES

DULVERTON (All Saints) and Brushford *B & W 17* **P** *D&C and E A M H M Herbert Esq (jt)*   **R** R M AIRD

DULWICH (St Barnabas) *S'wark 7* **P** *Bp*   **V** R M CATTLEY,   **C** C R BAKER,   **Hon C** A R DAWSON, J G WINTER,   **NSM** B JOHNSON, J BROTHWOOD, **Dss** M E JACKSON

DULWICH (St Clement) St Peter *S'wark 7* **P** *Bp*   **V** P J E MACAN

DULWICH, EAST (St John) *S'wark 7* **P** *Ripon Coll Cuddesdon*   **V** J B NAYLOR,   **Par Dn** H M BAKER,   **NSM** B E C PATE

DULWICH, NORTH (St Faith) *S'wark 7* **P** *Bp*   **V** S M BURDETT,   **C** D P LLOYD

DULWICH, SOUTH (St Stephen) *S'wark 7* **P** *Dulwich Coll*   **V** N H THOMPSON,   **NSM** J F ANDREWS

DULWICH, WEST (All Saints) and Emmanuel *S'wark 12* **P** *Bp*   **V** P ADAMS

DULWICH, WEST (Emmanuel) Conventional District *S'wark 7*   **C-in-c** C H KEY

DUMBLETON (St Peter) w Wormington *Glouc 17* **P** *DBP, Viscount Monsell, and Hon S K L Evetts (by turn)*   **R** P L C RICHARDS

DUMMER (All Saints) Cliddesden, Ellisfield, Farleigh Wallop etc *Win*

DUNCHIDEOCK (St Michael and All Angels) and Shillingford (St George) w Ide *Ex 6* **P** *D&C and Mrs J M Michelmore (alt)* **R** J W G GODECK

DUNCHURCH (St Peter) *Cov 6* **P** *Bp*
V R P C ELVERSON, **NSM** J W T ROGERS

DUNCTON (Holy Trinity) *Chich 11* **P** *Lord Egremont*
R G A EVANS

DUNDRY (St Michael) Chew Magna w Dundry *B & W*

DUNGEON HILL *Sarum 4* **P** *DBP, Col J L Yeatman, Mrs C B Ireland-Smith, and N G Halsey Esq (jt)*
R D HOPLEY

DUNHAM, GREAT (St Andrew) and LITTLE (St Margaret), w Great and Little Fransham and Sporle *Nor 19* **P** *Hertf Coll Ox, Ch Soc Trust, Magd Coll Cam, and DBP (by turn)* **R** B R A COLE

DUNHAM MASSEY (St Margaret) (All Saints) *Ches 10*
P *J G Turnbull Esq* **V** *Vacant* 061-928 1609

DUNHAM MASSEY (St Mark) *Ches 10*
P *J G Tunrbull Esq* **V** E G SEDDON

DUNHAM-ON-THE-HILL (St Luke) Helsby and Dunham-on-the-Hill *Ches*

DUNHAM-ON-TRENT (St Oswald) w Darlton, Ragnall, Fledborough and East Drayton *S'well 5* **P** *Bp (2 turns), D&C York (1 turn)* **Dn-in-c** J CALVERT

DUNHOLME (St Chad) *Linc 3* **P** *Bp and DBP (alt)*
V D SAUNDERS

DUNKERTON (All Saints) Camerton w Dunkerton, Foxcote and Shoscombe *B & W*

DUNKESWELL (Holy Trinity) (St Nicholas), Sheldon and Luppitt *Ex 5* **P** *MMCET and Bp (jt)* **V** N J WALL

DUNMOW, GREAT (St Mary the Virgin) *Chelmsf 21*
P *Ld Chan* **P-in-c** K G HOLLOWAY

DUNMOW, LITTLE (not known) Barnston and Lt Dunmow *Chelmsf*

DUNNINGTON (not known) Salford Priors *Cov*

DUNNINGTON (St Nicholas) Beeford w Frodingham and Foston *York*

DUNNINGTON (St Nicholas) *York 4* **P** *Abp*
R S R STANLEY, **Par Dn** C J COPLAND

DUNS TEW (St Mary Magdalen) Westcote Barton w Steeple Barton, Duns Tew etc *Ox*

DUNSBY (All Saints) Rippingale Gp *Linc*

DUNSCROFT (Christ Church) *Sheff 11* **P** *Bp*
V S J RAINE

DUNSDEN (All Saints) Shiplake w Dunsden *Ox*

DUNSFOLD (St Mary and All Saints) *Guildf 2*
P *Ld Chan* **R** B J PARADISE

DUNSFORD (St Mary) and Doddiscombsleigh *Ex 6*
P *Exors Lt-Col F E A Fulford (2 turns), J F N Buckingham Esq (1 turn)* **P-in-c** N CLARKE

DUNSFORTH (St Mary) Aldborough w Boroughbridge and Roecliffe *Ripon*

DUNSLAND (Mission Church) Ashwater, Halwill, Beaworthy, Clawton etc *Ex*

DUNSLEY (Mission Room) Aislaby and Ruswarp *York*

DUNSMORE (Chapel of the Ressurection) Ellesborough, The Kimbles and Stoke Mandeville *Ox*

DUNSOP BRIDGE (St George) Slaidburn *Bradf*

DUNSTABLE (St Augustine of Canterbury) (St Fremund the Martyr) (St Peter) *St Alb 18* **P** *Bp* **TR** D C SELF, **TV** G D GRAHAM, P V HUGHES, **Hon Par Dn** E J HUGHES

DUNSTALL (St Mary) w Rangemore and Tatenhill *Lich 20* **P** *Lord Burton, Sir Rupert Hardy, Bt, and Bp (jt)* **R** R F ROESCHLAUB

DUNSTAN (St Leonard) Penkridge Team *Lich*

DUNSTAN (St Peter) Nocton w Dunston and Potterhanworth *Linc*

DUNSTER (St George), Carhampton and Withycombe w Rodhuish *B & W 17* **P** *Bp* **R** R E F DORE

DUNSTON (Church House) Newbold and Dunston *Derby*

DUNSTON (St Nicholas) w (Christ Church) *Dur 5* **P** *Bp*
V D H FROST

DUNSTON (St Remigius) Stoke H Cross w Dunston *Nor*

DUNSWELL (St Faith's Mission Church) Hull Newland St Jo *York*

DUNTERTON (All Saints) Milton Abbot, Dunterton, Lamerton etc *Ex*

DUNTISBOURNE ABBOTS (St Peter) Daglingworth w the Duntisbournes and Winstone *Glouc*

DUNTISBOURNE ROUS (St Michael and All Angels) as above

DUNTON (St Martin) Schorne *Ox*

DUNTON (St Mary Magdalene) w Wrestlingworth and Eyeworth *St Alb 17* **P** *Ld Chan and DBP (alt)*
R G M BRISCOE

DUNTON BASSETT (All Saints) Leire w Ashby Parva and Dunton Bassett *Leic*

DUNWICH (St James) Westleton w Dunwich *St E*

DURHAM (St Cuthbert) *Dur 2* **P** *D&C*
V J N GREAVES, **NSM** B MIDDLEBROOK

DURHAM (St Giles) *Dur 2* **P** *D&C* **V** T W THUBRON, **NSM** D J WILSON

DURHAM (St Margaret of Antioch) *Dur 2* **P** *D&C*
R I D HOSKINS, **Hon C** S D CONWAY

DURHAM (St Nicholas) *Dur 2* **P** *CPAS*
V M J WILCOCK, **C** J PAYNE

DURHAM (St Oswald King and Martyr) *Dur 2* **P** *D&C*
V B J H de la MARE

DURLEIGH (not known) Bridgwater St Mary, Chilton Trinity and Durleigh *B & W*

DURLEY (Holy Cross) *Portsm 1* **P** *Ld Chan*
R G B WAGHORN

DURNFORD (St Andrew) Woodford Valley *Sarum*

DURRINGTON (All Saints) *Sarum 12* **P** *D&C Win*
R K J PIPER

DURRINGTON (St Symphorian) *Chich 5* **P** *Bp*
V R N AITON, **C** R A BROMFIELD

DURSLEY (St James the Great) *Glouc 2* **P** *Bp*
R J B HUNNISETT

DURSTON (St John the Baptist) N Newton w St Michaelchurch, Thurloxton etc *B & W*

DURWESTON (St Nicholas) Pimperne, Stourpaine, Durweston and Bryanston *Sarum*

DUSTON Team, The (St Francis) (St Luke) *Pet 7* **P** *Bp*
TR P GARLICK, **TV** N G TUCK

DUSTON, NEW (Mission Church) see above

DUTTON (Licensed Room) Lt Leigh and Lower Whitley *Ches*

DUXFORD (St Peter) w St John *Ely 7* **P** *Bp*
R A L WAY, **Hon Par Dn** B E WAY

DYMCHURCH (St Peter and St Paul) w Burmarsh and Newchurch *Cant 13* **P** *Abp* **R** S R UNDERHILL

DYMOCK (St Mary the Virgin) w Donnington and Kempley *Glouc 3* **P** *Pemb Coll Ox, Bp, and R D Marcon Esq (by turn)* **P-in-c** R J LEGG

DYRHAM (St Peter) Wick w Doynton and Dyrham *Bris*

EAGLE (All Saints) Swinderby *Linc*

EAKRING (St Andrew) *S'well 15* **P** *DBP*
R H H WILCOX

EALING (All Saints) *Lon 22* **P** *Bp*
P-in-c N P HENDERSON, **C** A P GODSALL

EALING (Ascension) Hanger Hill Ascension and W Twyford St Mary *Lon*

EALING (Christ the Saviour) *Lon 22* **P** *Bp*
V A F DAVIS, **C** G F OLIVER, **NSM** D E BIRT

EALING (St Barnabas) *Lon 22* **P** *Bp*
V G A REDDINGTON

EALING (St Mary) *Lon 22* **P** *Bp* **V** D R HOLT, **C** J H E ROSKELLY

EALING (St Paul) *Lon 22* **P** *Bp* **P-in-c** M V HAWKEN, **C** M STEWART

EALING (St Peter) Mount Park *Lon 22* **P** *Bp*
NSM J H ROBINSON

EALING (St Stephen) Castle Hill *Lon 22*
P *D&C St Paul's* **V** D C RUNCORN, **C** T S EVANS

EALING, WEST (St John) St James *Lon 22* **P** *Bp*
V S F DAKIN, **C** J O HEREWARD

EALING COMMON (St Matthew) *Lon 22* **P** *Bp*
V P G WATKINS

EARBY (All Saints) *Bradf 7* **P** *Bp* **V** R C WALLACE, **NSM** G L HALL

EARDISLAND (St Mary the Virgin) *Heref 7* **P** *Bp Birm*
P-in-c S B THOMAS, **NSM** G N PRINGLE

EARDISLEY (St Mary Magdalene) w Bollingham, Willersley, Brilley, Michaelchurch, Whitney and Winforton *Heref 5* **P** *Bp, Mrs C E Hope, and Exors Mrs A M Dew (jt)* **R** K NEWBON

EARL SHILTON (St Simon and St Jude) w Elmesthorpe *Leic 13* **P** *Bp* **V** G GITTINGS

EARL SOHAM (St Mary) w Cretingham and Ashfield cum Thorpe *St E 18* **P** *Lord Henniker, Ld Chan, and Wadh Coll Ox (by turn)* **P-in-c** D A S BOYES

EARL STERNDALE (St Michael and All Angels) Hartington, Biggin and Earl Sterndale *Derby*

EARL STONHAM (St Mary) Creeting St Mary, Creeting St Peter etc *St E*

EARLESTOWN (St John the Baptist) *Liv 16*
P *R Wargrave* **V** M BUCKLEY

EARLEY (St Nicolas) *Ox 15* **P** *DBP* **C** P J GRIFFIN, **Hon C** W P COOPER

EARLEY (St Peter) *Ox 15* **P** *DBP* **V** P L BATSON,
C D H JENKINS, **Par Dn** A R NIXON, **NSM** C G BASS
**EARLEY, LOWER Trinity Church Local Ecumenical
Project** *Ox 15* **Min** N A B DAVIES
EARLHAM (St Anne) *Nor 5* **P** *Bp* **V** P R OLIVER,
C S C WITCOMBE
EARLHAM (St Elizabeth) *Nor 5* **P** *Bp* **R** *Vacant*
EARLHAM (St Mary) *Nor 5* **P** *Bp* **V** B A SHERSBY
EARLS BARTON (All Saints) *Pet 6* **P** *DBP*
V M C W WEBBER, **C** M A TAYLOR
EARLS COLNE (St Andrew) and White Colne *Chelmsf 22*
P *DBP* **P-in-c** J E F JASPER
EARL'S COURT (St Cuthbert) (St Matthias) *Lon 12*
P *Trustees* **V** J VINE, **NSM** W J A KIRKPATRICK
EARLS CROOME (St Nicholas) Ripple, Earls Croome
w Hill Croome and Strensham *Worc*
EARLSDON (St Barbara) *Cov 3* **P** *Bp* **V** T C BROOKE,
NSM M M RITCHIE
EARLSFIELD (St Andrew) *S'wark 17* **P** *Bp*
V E C PROBERT, **Par Dn** A MILLS
EARLSFIELD (St John the Divine) *S'wark 17* **P** *Bp*
V M D WAY
EARLSHEATON (St Peter) *Wakef 10* **P** *R Dewsbury*
V G R WALKER
EARLY (St Bartholomew) Reading St Luke w St Bart
Ox
EARNLEY (not known) and East Wittering *Chich 3* **P** *Bp*
(2 turns), Bp Lon (1 turn) **R** P I CARMICHAEL
EARNSHAW BRIDGE (St John) Leyland St Andr
Blackb
EARSDON (St Alban) and Backworth *Newc 8* **P** *Bp*
V R K BRYANT
EARSHAM (All Saints) w Alburgh and Denton *Nor 16*
P *Abp, J M Meade Esq, and St Jo Coll Cam (by turn)*
R J S READ
EARSWICK, NEW (St Andrew) Huntington *York*
EARTHAM (St Margaret) Slindon, Eartham and
Madehurst *Chich*
EASBY (Chapel) Gt Ayton w Easby and Newton in
Cleveland *York*
**EASBY (St Agatha) w Brompton on Swale and Bolton on
Swale** *Ripon 2* **P** *Bp* **V** A GLEDHILL
EASEBOURNE (St Mary) *Chich 10* **P** *Cowdray Trust*
V M C JUDGE
EASINGTON (All Saints) w Liverton *York 17* **P** *Ld Chan*
R E J HOSKIN
**EASINGTON (All Saints) w Skeffling, Kilnsea and
Holmpton** *York 13* **P** *Ld Chan* **R** A E WATLING
EASINGTON (St Hugh) Banbury *Ox*
EASINGTON (St Mary) *Dur 3* **P** *Bp* **R** N P VINE
EASINGTON (St Peter) Ewelme, Brightwell Baldwin,
Cuxham w Easington *Ox*
EASINGTON COLLIERY (Ascension) *Dur 3* **P** *Bp*
V R McLEAN-REID
**EASINGWOLD (St John the Baptist and All Saints) w
Raskelfe** *York 5* **P** *Abp* **V** D M PORTER
EAST: *see also under substantive place names*
EAST FERRY (St Mary the Virgin) Scotter w E Ferry
Linc
EAST LANE (St Mary) W Horsley *Guildf*
EAST ORCHARD (St Thomas) Shaston *Sarum*
EASTBOURNE (All Saints) *Chich 16* **P** *Trustees*
V G T RIDEOUT, **Hon C** P S PLUNKETT,
NSM C A BOYCE
EASTBOURNE (All Souls) *Chich 16* **P** *Ch Soc Trust and
J H Cordle Esq (jt)* **V** R H G MASON
EASTBOURNE (Christ Church) *Chich 16*
P *V Eastbourne* **V** P A S FORDHAM
EASTBOURNE (Holy Trinity) *Chich 16* **P** *V Eastbourne*
V K H BLYTH, **C** A J M SPEAR, **NSM** K C CLARK
EASTBOURNE (St Andrew) *Chich 16* **P** *Bp*
V J A WREN, **C** R K WHELAN
EASTBOURNE (St Elizabeth) *Chich 16* **P** *Bp*
V B H KING
EASTBOURNE (St John) Meads *Chich 16* **P** *Trustees*
V A McCABE, **NSM** B H JEFFORD
EASTBOURNE (St Mary) *Chich 16* **P** *Bp*
V N S READE, **C** R J H WILLIAMS, J R LEES
EASTBOURNE (St Michael and All Angels) Ocklynge
Chich 16 **P** *V Eastbourne*
V J C T HARRINGTON, **Dss** W K HAMBLY
EASTBOURNE (St Philip) *Chich 16* **P** *Bp* **V** R C COLES
EASTBOURNE (St Richard of Chichester) Langney
Chich
EASTBOURNE (St Saviour and St Peter) *Chich 16*
P *Keble Coll Ox* **Hon C** G L VIGAR,
NSM O N WOODMAN, J HAY
EASTBURY (St James the Great) and East Garston *Ox 14*
P *Bp and Ch Ch Ox (alt)* **P-in-c** W J STEWART

EASTCHURCH (All Saints) w Leysdown and Harty
Cant 14 **P** *Abp and Keble Coll Ox (jt)*
R L C MEPSTED
EASTCOMBE (St Augustine) Bussage *Glouc*
EASTCOTE (St Lawrence) *Lon 24* **P** *Bp*
V D COLEMAN, **C** J S FOULDS
**EASTER, HIGH (St Mary the Virgin) and Good Easter w
Margaret Roding** *Chelmsf 21* **P** *Bp Lon, Trustees
R K Shepherd, and D&C St Paul's (by turn)*
R G F BARTLAM
EASTERGATE (St George) Aldingbourne, Barnham
and Eastergate *Chich*
EASTERN GREEN (St Andrew) *Cov 3* **P** *R Allesley*
V D D J TOOBY
EASTERTON (St Barnabas) Market Lavington and
Easterton *Sarum*
EASTFIELD (Holy Nativity) Cayton w Eastfield *York*
EASTGATE (All Saints) w Rookhope *Dur 15* **P** *Bp and
Ld Chan (alt)* **V** C N LOVELL, **NSM** D W WOOD
**EASTHAM (St Mary the Blessed Virgin) (St Peter's
Chapel) (Chapel of the Holy Spirit)** *Ches 9* **P** *D&C*
V R F WORSLEY, **NSM** D J BURLEIGH
EASTHAM (St Peter and St Paul) Teme Valley S *Worc*
EASTHAMPSTEAD (St Michael and St Mary Magdalene)
Ox 11 **P** *Ch Ch Ox* **R** O SIMON, D B TONKINSON,
C G O SHAW, **Par Dn** M G CLARKE
EASTHOPE (St Peter) Wenlock *Heref*
EASTHORPE (St Mary the Virgin) Copford w
Easthorpe *Chelmsf*
EASTINGTON (St Michael and All Angels) and Frocester
Glouc 8 **P** *Lady Cooper and DBP (alt)*
R N E L BAKER
EASTLEACH (St Andrew) Coln St Aldwyn, Hatherop,
Quenington etc *Glouc*
EASTLEIGH (All Saints) *Win 9* **P** *Bp* **V** B N HARLEY,
C B R G FLENLEY
EASTLEIGH Nightingale Avenue (St Francis) Eastleigh
Win
**EASTLING (St Mary) w Ospringe and Stalisfield w
Otterden** *Cant 6* **P** *The Crown* **R** D W TURTON
EASTMOORS (St Mary Magdalene) Helmsley *York*
EASTNEY (St Margaret) *Portsm 6* **P** *Bp* **V** P H KELLY,
NSM A DEAN
EASTNOR (St John the Baptist) Ledbury w Eastnor
Heref
EASTOFT (St Bartholomew) The Marshland *Sheff*
EASTON (All Hallows) *Bris 4* **P** *R Bris St Steph*
V D CHAMBERLAIN
EASTON (All Saints) Wickham Market w Pettistree and
Easton *St E*
**EASTON (Holy Trinity w St Gabriel and St Lawrence and
St Jude)** *Bris 4* **P** *Trustees* **V** W R DONALDSON,
Par Dn H J CHADWICK
EASTON (St Mary) and Martyr Worthy *Win 1*
P *Ld Chan* **P-in-c** A F KNIGHT
EASTON (St Paul) Westbury sub Mendip w Easton
B & W
EASTON (St Peter) *Ely 10* **P** *Bp* **P-in-c** A T SCHOFIELD
EASTON (St Peter) w Colton and Marlingford *Nor 12*
P *Ld Chan, E C Evans-Lombe Esq, and Adn Norfolk
(by turn)* **P-in-c** M S ALLEN
EASTON, GREAT (St Andrew) Six Saints circa Holt
Leic
EASTON, GREAT (St John and St Giles) Broxted w
Chickney and Tilty etc *Chelmsf*
EASTON, LITTLE (not known) as above
EASTON GREY (not known) Sherston Magna, Easton
Grey, Luckington etc *Bris*
EASTON IN GORDANO (St George) Pill w Easton in
Gordano and Portbury *B & W*
EASTON MAUDIT (St Peter and St Paul) Bozeat w
Easton Maudit *Pet*
EASTON NESTON (St Mary) Towcester w Easton
Neston *Pet*
**EASTON ON THE HILL (All Saints) and Collyweston w
Duddington and Tixover** *Pet 8* **P** *Ld Chan, Bp, and
Burghley Ho Preservation Trust (by turn)*
R R C TROUNSON
EASTON ROYAL (Holy Trinity) Pewsey Team Min
Sarum
EASTRINGTON (St Michael) Howden Team Min *York*
EASTROP (St Mary) *Win 4* **P** *CPAS* **R** C L HAWKINS,
NSM D B ROWE, R P BOWSKILL
**EASTRY (St Mary Blessed Virgin) and Northbourne w
Tilmanstone and Betteshanger w Ham** *Cant 8* **P** *Abp
and Lord Northbourne (jt)* **C** C A TOMKINS
EASTVILLE (St Anne w St Mark and St Thomas) *Bris 4*
P *Bp* **V** D L CAWLEY, **C** G S COLE,
Hon C M G TUCKER

EASTVILLE (St Paul)   Stickney Gp *Linc*

EASTWELL (St Michael)   Scalford w Goadby Marwood and Wycombe etc *Leic*

EASTWICK (St Botolph)   High Wych and Gilston w Eastwick *St Alb*

EASTWOOD (St David) *Chelmsf 12*   **P** *Bp*   **V** F A OSWIN

EASTWOOD (St Laurence and All Saints) *Chelmsf 12*   **P** *Ld Chan*   **NSM** S M WARING

EASTWOOD (St Mary) *S'well 4*   **P** *J N Plumptre Esq*   **R** T D ATKINS,   **C** S M M WALKER

EASTWOOD (St Stephen) *Sheff 6*   **P** *Bp*   **V** *Vacant*   Rotherham (0709) 377615

EATON (All Saints)   Gamston w Eaton and W Drayton *S'well*

EATON (Christ Church) and Hulme Walfield *Ches 11*   **P** *Bp and R Astbury (alt)*   **V** R B ROBERTS

EATON (Christ Church) (St Andrew) *Nor 5*   **P** *D&C*   **V** R J HANMER,   **C** S W HEWITT, N J H GARRARD

EATON (St Denys)   Scalford w Goadby Marwood and Wycombe etc *Leic*

EATON (St Thomas)   Tarporley *Ches*

EATON, LITTLE (St Paul)   Holbrook and Lt Eaton *Derby*

EATON BISHOP (St Michael and All Angels)   Kingstone w Clehonger, Eaton Bishop etc *Heref*

EATON BRAY (St Mary the Virgin) w Edlesborough *St Alb 18*   **P** *DBP*   **V** B P MOORE

EATON HASTINGS (St Michael and All Angels)   Gt Coxwell w Buscot, Coleshill & Eaton Hastings *Ox*

EATON SOCON (St Mary) *St Alb 17*   **P** *E W Harper Esq*   **V** J D WATSON, **Dss** M M HINDE

EATON SQUARE (St Peter)   Pimlico St Pet w Westmr Ch Ch *Lon*

EATON-UNDER-HEYWOOD (St Edith)   Hope Bowdler w Eaton-under-Heywood *Heref*

EBBERSTON (St Mary)   Brompton-by-Sawdon w Snainton, Ebberston etc *York*

EBBESBOURNE WAKE (St John the Baptist)   Chalke Valley W *Sarum*

EBCHESTER (St Ebba) *Dur 8*   **P** *Bp*   **R** R D BUTT

EBERNOE (Holy Trinity)   N Chapel w Ebernoe *Chich*

EBONY (St Mary the Virgin)   Wittersham w Stone-in-Oxney and Ebony *Cant*

EBREY WOOD (Mission Chapel)   Uffington, Upton Magna and Withington *Lich*

EBRINGTON (St Eadburgha)   Chipping Campden w Ebrington *Glouc*

ECCHINSWELL (St Lawrence)   Burghclere w Newtown and Ecchinswell w Sydmonton *Win*

ECCLES (St Mary the Virgin)   Quidenham *Nor*

ECCLES (St Mary the Virgin) (St Andrew) *Man 2*   **P** *Ld Chan and Patr Bd (alt)*   **TR** M ARUNDEL, **TV** J E WARING

ECCLESALL (St Gabriel)   Greystones *Sheff*

ECCLESALL BIERLOW (All Saints) *Sheff 2*   **P** *Provost Sheff*   **V** C P WILLIAMS, **C** C GUILLOTEAU, D G WILLIAMS

ECCLESFIELD (St Mary the Virgin) *Sheff 3*   **P** *DBF*   **V** J O FORRESTER

ECCLESFIELD (St Paul)   Sheff St Paul Wordsworth Avenue *Sheff*

ECCLESHALL (Holy Trinity) *Lich 13*   **P** *Bp*   **V** J S COOKE

ECCLESHILL (St Luke) *Bradf 3*   **P** *V Bradf*   **V** A S TREASURE,   **C** J T BIRBECK

ECCLESTON (Christ Church) *Liv 10*   **P** *F Webster Esq, Lord Blanch, Canon J A Lawton, Rev D G Mellors, and Bp (jt)*   **V** S G RICHARDS, **NSM** D G MELLORS, F NAYLOR

ECCLESTON (St Luke) *Liv 10*   **P** *Trustees*   **V** *Vacant*   St Helens (0744) 22456

ECCLESTON (St Mary the Virgin) *Blackb 4*   **P** *DBP*   **R** P G ASPDEN

ECCLESTON (St Mary the Virgin) and Pulford *Ches 2*   **P** *Duke of Westmr*   **R** F H LINN

ECCLESTON (St Thomas) *Liv 10*   **P** *Bp*   **P-in-c** S P ATTWATER

ECCLESTON, GREAT   Copp *Blackb*

ECCLESTON PARK (St James) *Liv 10*   **P** *Bp*   **P-in-c** A OVEREND

ECKINGTON (Holy Trinity) *Worc 4*   **P** *D&C Westmr*   **V** R H HOWES

ECKINGTON (St Peter and St Paul) w Handley and Ridgeway *Derby 3*   **P** *The Crown and Patr Bd (alt)*   **TR** N R HARVEY

ECKINGTON, UPPER (St Luke)   Eckington w Handley and Ridgeway *Derby*

ECTON (St Mary Magdalene) *Pet 6*   **P** *The Crown*   **R** P E NAYLOR

EDALE (Holy and Undivided Trinity) *Derby 2*   **P** *Rep Landowners*   **P-in-c** A J G MURRAY-LESLIE

EDBURTON (St Andrew)   Poynings w Edburton, Newtimber and Pyecombe *Chich*

EDENBRIDGE (St Peter and St Paul) *Roch 10*   **P** *Bp*   **V** S A J MITCHELL,   **C** R JONES

EDENFIELD (not known) and Stubbins *Man 10*   **P** *Bp*   **V** G N HIGHAM

EDENHALL (St Cuthbert)   Addingham, Edenhall, Langwathby and Culgaith *Carl*

EDENHAM (St Michael) w Witham-on-the-Hill *Linc 13*   **P** *Bp and Baroness Willoughby de Eresby (alt)*   **V** A T HAWES

EDENSOR (St Paul) *Lich 18*   **P** *Prime Min*   **V** C CRUMPTON

EDENSOR (St Peter)   Beeley and Edensor *Derby*

EDGBASTON (St Augustine) *Birm 2*   **P** *Bp*   **V** R F PRICE

EDGBASTON (St Bartholomew) *Birm 2*   **P** *Sir Euan Anstruther-Gough-Calthorpe, Bt*   **V** E D COOMBES

EDGBASTON (St George w St Michael) (St Michael's Hall) *Birm 2*   **P** *Sir Euan Anstruther-Gough-Calthorpe, Bt*   **V** R W GRIMLEY

EDGBASTON (St Germain) *Birm 2*   **P** *Trustees*   **P-in-c** A P NORRIS

EDGBASTON (St Mary and St Ambrose) *Birm 2*   **P** *Bp and Sir Euan Anstruther-Gough-Calthorpe, Bt (jt)*   **V** A J WARD

EDGCOTE (St James)   Chipping Warden w Edgcote and Aston le Walls *Pet*

EDGCOTT (St Michael)   Swan *Ox*

EDGE, THE (St John the Baptist), Pitchcombe, Harescombe and Brookthorpe *Glouc 1*   **P** *Bp and D&C (jt)*   **R** P B MYATT

EDGE HILL (St Dunstan) Earle Road *Liv 6*   **P** *Trustees*   **V** R F JONES

EDGE HILL (St Mary) *Liv 3*   **P** *Bp*   **V** A GODSON

EDGEFIELD (School Room)   Worsley *Man*

EDGEFIELD (St Peter and St Paul)   Wickmere w Lt Barningham, Itteringham etc *Nor*

EDGESIDE (St Anne) *Man 15*   **P** *Trustees*   **V** *Vacant*   Rossendale (0706) 215090

EDGEWORTH (St Mary)   Bisley, Oakridge, Miserden and Edgeworth *Glouc*

EDGMOND (St Peter) w Kynnersley and Preston Wealdmoors *Lich 22*   **P** *Bp, Adn Salop, Chan Lich, MMCET, and Preston Trust Homes Trustees (jt)*   **R** *Vacant*   Newport (0952) 820217

EDGTON (St Michael the Archangel)   Lydbury N w Hopesay and Edgton *Heref*

EDGWARE Burnt Oak (St Alphege)   Hendon St Alphage *Lon*

EDGWARE (St Andrew) (St Margaret) (St Peter) *Lon 15*   **P** *MMCET*   **C** S R DINSMORE, J A FAIRBAIRN

EDINGALE (Holy Trinity) *Lich 5*   **P** *Bp*   **V** *Vacant*

EDINGLEY (St Giles) w Halam *S'well 15*   **P** *Bp*   **V** *Vacant*

EDINGTHORPE (All Saints)   Bacton w Edingthorpe w Witton and Ridlington *Nor*

EDINGTON (St George)   W Poldens *B & W*

EDINGTON (St Mary, St Katharine and All Saints) and Imber, Erlestoke and East Coulston *Sarum 19*   **P** *Bp*   **R** N C HEAVISIDES

EDITH WESTON (St Mary) w North Luffenham and Lyndon w Manton *Pet 14*   **P** *Baroness Willoughby de Eresby, Sir John Conant, and Em Coll Cam (by turn)*   **R** R J M BLACKALL

EDITHMEAD (Mission)   Burnham *B & W*

EDLASTON (St James)   Brailsford w Shirley and Osmaston w Edlaston *Derby*

EDLINGHAM (St John the Baptist w Bolton Chapel)   Whittingham and Edlingham w Bolton Chapel *Newc*

EDLINGTON (St Helen)   Hemingby *Linc*

EDLINGTON (St John the Baptist) *Sheff 10*   **P** *Bp*   **V** J T ARCHER

EDMONDSHAM (St Nicholas)   Cranborne w Boveridge, Edmondsham etc *Sarum*

EDMONDTHORPE (St Michael and All Angels)   Wymondham w Edmondthorpe, Buckminster etc *Leic*

EDMONTON (All Saints) (St Michael) *Lon 18*   **P** *D&C St Paul's*   **V** B W OAKLEY,   **C** C B WICKS

EDMONTON (St Aldhelm) *Lon 18*   **P** *V Edmonton All SS*   **V** *Vacant*   081-807 5336

EDMONTON (St Alphege) *Lon 18*   **P** *Bp*   **P-in-c** C W COPPEN

EDMONTON (St Mary w St John) (St Mary's Centre) *Lon 18*   **P** *D&C St Paul's*   **V** D W GOUGH, **Hon C** J S ALDIS,   R H JORDAN

EDMONTON (St Peter w St Martin) *Lon 18*   **P** *Bp*   **P-in-c** B M SMITH

EDMUNDBYERS (St Edmund) Blanchland w
Hunstanworth and Edmundbyers etc *Newc*
EDSTASTON (St Mary the Virgin) *Lich 29* **P** *R Wem*
P-in-c P J RICHMOND
EDSTON (St Michael) Kirby Misperton w Normanby,
Edston and Salton *York*
EDVIN LOACH (St Mary) w Tedstone Delamere, Tedstone
Wafer, Upper Sapey, Wolferlow and Whitbourne *Heref 2*
P *Bp, BNC Ox, Sir Francis Winnington, Bt, and*
D P Barneby (jt) **R** R J COLBY
EDWALTON (Holy Rood) *S'well 9* **P** *Major R P*
Chaworth-Musters **V** D C BIGNELL
EDWARDSTONE (St Mary the Virgin) w Groton and Little
Waldingfield *St E 12* **P** *DBP (2 turns) and Hon*
Thomas Lindsay (1 turn) **R** R K TITFORD
EDWINSTOWE (St Mary) w Carburton *S'well 6* **P** *Earl*
Manvers' Trustees **V** J FORD
EDWYN RALPH (St Michael) Bredenbury w Grendon
Bishop and Wacton etc *Heref*
EFFINGHAM (St Lawrence) w Little Bookham *Guildf 10*
P *Keble Coll Ox* **V** A P HODGETTS
EFFORD (St Paul) Plymouth Em w Efford *Ex*
EGDEAN (St Bartholomew) *Chich 11* **P** *Bp* **R** *Vacant*
EGERTON (St James) w Pluckley *Cant 10* **P** *Abp*
R M J HIGGS
EGG BUCKLAND (St Edward) *Ex 23* **P** *Ld Chan*
V *Vacant* Plymouth (0752) 701399
EGGESFORD (All Saints) Wembworthy w Eggesford
Ex
EGGINTON (St Michael) Leighton Buzzard w
Eggington, Hockliffe etc *St Alb*
EGGINTON (St Wilfrid) Etwall w Egginton *Derby*
EGGLESCLIFFE (St John the Baptist) *Dur 16* **P** *Bp*
R R V CHADWICK
EGGLESTON (Holy Trinity) *Dur 11* **P** *The Crown*
V G LINDEN
EGHAM (St John the Baptist) *Guildf 11* **P** *Ch Soc Trust*
V A J MAGOWAN, **C** M E BROWN
EGHAM HYTHE (St Paul) *Guildf 11* **P** *Bp* **V** M S KING
EGLETON (St Edmund) Oakham, Hambleton,
Egleton, Braunston and Brooke *Pet*
EGLINGHAM (St Maurice) Glendale Gp *Newc*
EGLOSHAYLE (St Petroc) St Breoke and Egloshayle
Truro
EGLOSKERRY (St Petrock and St Keri) Bolventor
Truro
EGMANTON (Our Lady of Egmanton) *S'well 3* **P** *SMF*
V I CLARK
EGREMONT (St John) *Ches 7* **P** *Bp* **V** B E LEE,
NSM T JORDAN
EGREMONT (St Mary and St Michael) and Haile *Carl 5*
P *Patr Bd* **TR** P E MANN, **TV** D A WOOD,
Par Dn C E FARRER
EGTON (St Hilda) w Grosmont *York 23* **P** *Abp*
V P A BURKITT
EGTON-CUM-NEWLAND (St Mary the Virgin) and
Lowick *Carl 8* **P** *Trustees* **P-in-c** G WEMYSS
EIGHT ASH GREEN (All Saints) Fordham *Chelmsf*
EIGHTON BANKS (St Thomas) *Dur 4* **P** *Bp*
V A W HODGSON, **Par Dn** D THOMPSON
ELBERTON (St John the Evangelist) Littleton on
Severn w Elberton *Bris*
ELBURTON (St Matthew) *Ex 24* **P** *CPAS*
V K H S COOMBE
ELDENE (not known) Swindon Dorcan *Bris*
ELDERSFIELD (St John the Baptist) Berrow w
Pendock, Eldersfield, Hollybush etc *Worc*
ELDON (St Mark) Shildon w Eldon *Dur*
ELDWICK (St Lawrence) Bingley All SS *Bradf*
ELFORD (St Peter) *Lich 5* **P** *Bp* **P-in-c** B L COX
ELHAM (St Mary the Virgin) w Denton and Wootton
Cant 5 **P** *Abp and Mert Coll Ox (jt)* **V** T PITT,
Hon C R J C LLOYD, **NSM** M J LEVERTON,
Hon Par Dn P V LLOYD
ELING (St Mary) Totton *Win*
ELKESLEY (St Giles) w Bothamsall *S'well 5* **P** *SMF*
V *Vacant* Gamston (077783) 293
ELKINGTON, SOUTH (All Saints) Louth *Linc*
ELKSTONE (St John the Baptist) Alstonfield,
Butterton, Warslow w Elkstone etc *Lich*
ELKSTONE (St John the Evangelist) Brimpsfield,
Cranham, Elkstone and Syde *Glouc*
ELLACOMBE (Christ Church) Torquay St Jo and
Ellacombe *Ex*
ELLAND (All Saints) (St Mary the Virgin) *Wakef 2* **P** *Bp,*
Adn Halifax, and V Halifax (jt) **TR** N M WOOD,
TV S COOPER, **NSM** B S COCKCROFT
ELLASTONE (St Peter) Denstone w Ellastone and
Stanton *Lich*

ELLEL (St John the Evangelist) *Blackb 12*
P *V Cockerham* **V** W GUY
ELLENBROOK (St Mary's Chapel) Worsley *Man*
ELLENHALL (St Mary) w Ranton *Lich 13* **P** *Trustees*
Earl of Lichfield **V** *Vacant*
ELLERBURNE (St Hilda) Thornton Dale and
Ellerburne w Wilton *York*
ELLERBY (St James) Swine *York*
ELLERKER (not known) S Cave and Ellerker w
Broomfleet *York*
ELLESBOROUGH (St Peter and St Paul), The Kimbles
and Stoke Mandeville *Ox 28* **P** *Chequers Trustees,*
Hon I Hope-Morley, and D&C Linc (by turn)
R S F B HEYWOOD, **NSM** D J FREEMAN, H W HESLOP
ELLESMERE (St Mary) and Welsh Frankton *Lich 23*
P *Bp* **V** C R CORNWELL, **NSM** A C NETHERWOOD
ELLESMERE (St Peter) *Sheff 3* **P** *Bp* **V** W F MASON
ELLESMERE PORT (Christ Church) *Ches 9* **P** *Bp*
TV D H McINTOSH, D R HERBERT, S WATERS,
Par Dn J WAGSTAFF
ELLINGHAM (St Mary) Gillingham w Geldeston,
Stockton, Ellingham etc *Nor*
ELLINGHAM (St Mary and All Saints) and Harbridge and
Ibsley *Win 8* **P** *Earl of Normanton* **V** J T BEECH
ELLINGHAM (St Maurice) Beadnell w Ellingham *Newc*
ELLINGHAM, LITTLE (St Peter) w GREAT (St James) w
Rockland (All Saints) and (St Andrew and St Peter)
Nor 17 **P** *Bp and CCC Cam (alt)* **R** M N WILLIAMS
ELLINGTON (All Saints) *Ely 10* **P** *Peterho Cam*
P-in-c A T SCHOFIELD
ELLISFIELD (St Martin) Cliddesden, Ellisfield,
Farleigh Wallop etc *Win*
ELLISTOWN (St Christopher) Hugglescote w
Donington, Ellistown and Snibston *Leic*
ELLOUGHTON (St Mary) and Brough w Brantingham
York 14 **P** *Abp and D&C Dur (jt)* **V** B HERITAGE,
Par Dn J V CARR
ELM (All Saints) *Ely 19* **P** *Bp* **V** J E BARRETT
ELM (St Mary Magdalene) Mells w Buckland Dinham,
Elm, Whatley etc *B & W*
ELM PARK (St Nicholas) Hornchurch *Chelmsf 4* **P** *Bp*
V D S MILLER, **C** M S McCREADY
ELMBRIDGE (St Mary) Elmley Lovett w Hampton
Lovett and Elmbridge etc *Worc*
ELMDON (St Nicholas) Heydon, Gt and Lt Chishill,
Chrishall etc *Chelmsf*
ELMDON (St Nicholas) (St Stephen's Church Centre) (St
Nicholas's Hall) *Birm 13* **P** *Ch Trust Fund Trust*
R A S GRAESSER
ELMDON HEATH (St Francis of Assisi) Solihull *Birm*
ELMESTHORPE (St Mary) Earl Shilton w Elmesthorpe
Leic
ELMHAM, NORTH (St Mary) w Billingford and Worthing
Nor 19 **P** *Bp (1 turn), Viscount Coke (2 turns), and*
G & C Coll Cam (1 turn) **R** *Vacant* Elmham
(036281) 244
ELMHAM, SOUTH (St Cross) Flixton w Homersfield
and S Elmham *St E*
ELMHAM, SOUTH (St James) Rumburgh w S Elmham
w the Ilketshalls *St E*
ELMHAM, SOUTH (St Margaret) Flixton w
Homersfield and S Elmham *St E*
ELMHAM, SOUTH (St Michael and All Angels)
Rumburgh w S Elmham w the Ilketshalls *St E*
ELMHAM, SOUTH (St Peter) Flixton w Homersfield
and S Elmham *St E*
ELMHURST (Mission Room) Lich St Chad *Lich*
ELMLEY CASTLE (St Mary) w Bricklehampton and the
Combertons *Worc 4* **P** *Bp* **R** S K CLARK
ELMLEY LOVETT (St Michael) w Hampton Lovett and
Elmbridge w Rushdock *Worc 8* **P** *Bp and Ch Coll Cam*
(alt) **P-in-c** C R LEVEY, **Par Dn** M E STANTON-HYDE
ELMORE (St John the Baptist) Hardwicke, Quedgeley
and Elmore w Longney *Glouc*
ELMSALL, NORTH (St Margaret) Badsworth *Wakef*
ELMSALL, SOUTH (St Mary the Virgin) *Wakef 11* **P** *Bp*
V G MOFFAT, **C** N CLEWS
ELMSETT (St Peter) w Aldham *St E 3* **P** *Bp and*
MMCET (alt) **P-in-c** W J SANDS
ELMSTEAD (St Anne and St Laurence) *Chelmsf 23* **P** *Jes*
Coll Cam **V** R G SMITH
ELMSTED (St James the Great) w Hastingleigh *Cant 2*
P *Abp* **V** *Vacant* Elmsted (023375) 414
ELMSTONE (not known) Wingham w Elmstone and
Preston w Stourmouth *Cant*
ELMSTONE HARDWICKE (St Mary Magdalene)
Swindon w Uckington and Elmstone Hardwicke *Glouc*
ELMSWELL (St John) *St E 10* **P** *MMCET*
R J A C PERROTT

ELMTON (St Peter) *Derby 3*   **P** *Bp*   **V** B M CROWTHER-
ALWYN
ELSDON (St Cuthbert)   Bellingham/Otterburn Gp *Newc*
ELSECAR (Holy Trinity) *Sheff 7*   **P** *Sir Stephen Hastings*
V *Vacant*   Barnsley (0226) 742149
ELSENHAM (St Mary the Virgin)   Henham and
Elsenham w Ugley *Chelmsf*
ELSFIELD (St Thomas of Canterbury) *Ox 1*   **P** *Ch Ch Ox*
V A G A de VERE
ELSHAM (All Saints) *Linc 6*   **P** *Bp*   **V** S W ANDREW
ELSING (St Mary)   Lyng, Sparham, Elsing and Bylaugh
Nor
ELSON (St Thomas) *Portsm 3*   **V** K W JACKSON,
Hon C F H RAZEY
ELSTEAD (St James) *Guildf 4*   **P** *Adn Surrey*
R J T McDOWALL,   **NSM** J J F FOSTER
ELSTED (St Paul)   Stedham w Iping, Elsted and
Treyford-cum-Didling *Chich*
ELSTERNWICK (St Laurence)   Burton Pidsea and
Humbleton w Elsternwick *York*
ELSTON (All Saints) w Elston Chapelry *S'well 3*
P J C S Darwin Esq   **R** G A FIRTH
ELSTOW (St Mary and St Helena) *St Alb 19*
P S C Whitbread Esq   **V** R W HUBAND,   **NSM** J POOLE
ELSTREE (St Nicholas) *St Alb 1*   **P** *Ld Chan*
R W J ELLIOTT
ELSWICK, HIGH (St Paul) *Newc 7*   **P** *Trustees*
V B E SEAMAN
ELSWICK, HIGH (St Philip)   Newc St Phil and St Aug
Newc
ELSWICK, LOW (St Stephen) *Newc 7*   **P** *Ch Soc Trust*
V G R CURRY
ELSWORTH (Holy Trinity) w Knapwell *Ely 1*   **P** *Bp*
(4 turns), The Crown (1 turn)   **R** H A MOSEDALE
ELTHAM (Holy Trinity) *S'wark 1*   **P** *Bp*   **V** *Vacant*
081-850 1246
ELTHAM (St Barnabas) *S'wark 1*   **P** *Bp*   **V** J E NEAL
ELTHAM (St John the Baptist) *S'wark 1*   **P** *DBP*
V P V L JOHNSTONE
ELTHAM (St Saviour) *S'wark 1*   **P** *Bp*   **V** *Vacant*
081-850 6829
ELTHAM, NEW (All Saints) *S'wark 1*   **P** *Bp*
V C PULLIN
ELTHAM PARK (St Luke) *S'wark 1*   **P** *Bp*
V J C THEWLIS,   **Hon Par Dn** M J MABBS
ELTISLEY (St Pandionia and St John the Baptist)
Croxton and Eltisley *Ely*
ELTON (All Saints)   S Darley, Elton and Winster *Derby*
ELTON (All Saints) *Ely 13*   **P** *Sir Peter Proby*
R P O POOLEY
ELTON (All Saints) *Man 10*   **P** *R Bury St Mary*
V I E WALTER,   **C** D O FORSHAW,
Hon C P J BEDDINGTON
ELTON (St John)   Longnewton w Elton *Dur*
ELTON (St Mary the Virgin)   Wigmore Abbey *Heref*
ELTON (St Michael and All Angels)   Cropwell Bishop w
Colston Bassett, Granby etc *S'well*
ELTON (St Stephen) *Man 10*   **P** *V Elton All SS*
V B J TURNER
ELVASTON (St Bartholomew) and Shardlow *Derby 15*
P *Earl of Harrington and DBP (alt)*
P-in-c P E HARDING
ELVEDEN (St Andrew and St Patrick)   Euston w
Barnham, Elvedon and Fakenham Magna *St E*
**ELVINGTON (Holy Trinity) w Sutton on Derwent and East
Cottingwith** *York 4*   **P** J Darlington Esq   **R** J R PAYNE
ELWICK HALL (St Peter)   Hart w Elwick Hall *Dur*
ELWORTH (St Peter) and Warmingham *Ches 11*
P V Sandbach, Q H Crewe Esq and J C Crewe Esq (alt)
R C D JEFFERSON
ELY (Holy Trinity w St Mary) (St Peter) *Ely 14*   **P** *D&C*
V A BARTLE,   **Par Dn** A M GUITE,
Hon Par Dn M A GUITE
EMBERTON (All Saints)   Olney w Emberton *Ox*
EMBLETON (Holy Trinity) w Rennington and Rock
Newc 9   **P** *Mert Coll Ox*   **V** P ELLIOTT
EMBLETON (St Cuthbert)   Cockermouth w Embleton
and Wythop *Carl*
EMBROOK (Community of St Nicholas)   Wokingham St
Paul *Ox*
EMBSAY (St Mary the Virgin) w Eastby *Bradf 7*
P R Skipton H Trin   **P-in-c** R P MARSHALL
EMERY DOWN (Christ Church)   Lyndhurst and Emery
Down *Win*
EMLEY (St Michael the Archangel) *Wakef 6*   **P** *Lord
Savile*   **P-in-c** J A A LODGE
EMMER GREEN (St Barnabas) *Ox 15*   **P** *Bp*
R N J HARDCASTLE

EMMINGTON (St Nicholas)   Chinnor w Emmington and
Sydenham etc *Ox*
EMNETH (St Edmund) *Ely 19*   **P** *Bp*   **V** A G F VILLER
EMPINGHAM (St Peter) and Exton w Horn w Whitwell
Pet 14   **P** *Bp and Earl of Gainsborough (alt)*
R N C ROM
EMPSHOTT (Holy Rood)   Greatham w Empshott
Portsm
EMSCOTE (All Saints) *Cov 11*   **P** *Earl of Warw*
V A PLURY,   **C** A G R BRISTOW
EMSWORTH (St James)   Warblington and Emsworth
Portsm
ENBORNE (St Michael and All Angels)   W Woodhay w
Enborne, Hampstead Marshall etc *Ox*
ENDCLIFFE (St Augustine) *Sheff 2*   **P** *Ch Burgesses*
V A G RICHARDS
**ENDERBY (St John the Baptist) w Lubbesthorpe and
Thurlaston** *Leic 10*   **P** *Bp and F B Drummond Esq*
V R A SHELLEY,   **Hon C** T J R KING
ENDON (St Luke) w Stanley *Lich 14*
P R Leek and Meerbrook   **V** E OSMAN
ENFIELD (Christ Church) Trent Park *Lon 18*
P Ch Trust Fund Trust   **V** P A E REES,
C R M COOMBS, A G PURSER,   **NSM** S J NORTHAM
ENFIELD (St Andrew) *Lon 18*   **P** *Trin Coll Cam*
V P B MORGAN,   **C** J R LIBBY,   **NSM** R H DUNN,
Hon Par Dn O R COPE
ENFIELD (St George) *Lon 18*   **P** *Bp*   **V** A C J ROGERS
ENFIELD (St James) (St Barnabas) *Lon 18*   **P** *V Enfield*
V J M BOWERS,   **C** J F REDVERS HARRIS,
Par Dn J D MITCHELL
ENFIELD (St Michael and All Angels) *Lon 18*
P V Enfield   **V** Vacant   081-363 2483
ENFIELD (St Peter and St Paul) *Lon 18*   **P** *Bp*
V D F P TOUW
ENFIELD CHASE (St Mary Magdalene) *Lon 18*   **P** *Bp*
V J A SAMPFORD,   **C** J W SEWELL
ENFORD (All Saints)   Netheravon w Fittleton and
Enford *Sarum*
ENGLEFIELD (St Mark)   Theale and Englefield *Ox*
ENGLEFIELD GREEN (St Jude) *Guildf 11*   **P** *Bp*
V J R V WOODS
ENGLISH BICKNOR (St Mary)   Forest of Dean Ch Ch
w English Bicknor *Glouc*
ENGLISHCOMBE (St Peter)   Bath St Barn w
Englishcombe *B & W*
ENHAM ALAMEIN (St George)   Smannell w Enham
Alamein *Win*
ENMORE (St Michael)   Spaxton w Goathurst, Enmore
and Charlynch *B & W*
ENMORE GREEN (St John the Evangelist)   Shaston
Sarum
ENNERDALE (St Mary)   Lamplugh w Ennerdale *Carl*
ENSBURY PARK (St Thomas) *Sarum 8*   **P** *Bp*
V E FARROW
ENSTONE (St Kenelm) and Heythrop *Ox 3*   **P** *Bp*
V N D J CARNE
ENVILLE (St Mary the Virgin)   Kinver and Enville *Lich*
EPPERSTONE (Holy Cross) *S'well 11*   **P** *Bp, Ld Chan,
and Comdr M B P Francklin (by turn)*   **R** M J BROCK
EPPING (St John the Baptist) *Chelmsf 2*   **P** *DBP*
V A J ABBEY,   **C** A J FORAN
EPPING UPLAND (All Saints) *Chelmsf 2*   **P** *Bp*
P-in-c C F J BARD,   **NSM** J H B DODD
EPPLETON (All Saints) *Dur 6*   **P** *The Crown*
V J J STEPHENSON
EPSOM (St Barnabas) *Guildf 9*   **P** *Bp*   **V** M C PRESTON,
C C WAREHAM
EPSOM (St Martin) (St Stephen on the Downs) *Guildf 9*
P *Bp*   **V** P J LLOYD,   **C** A J SHUTT,
Hon C M D RANKEN
EPSOM COMMON (Christ Church) *Guildf 9*   **P** *Bp*
V M J C WILSON,   **C** C J COCKSWORTH
EPWELL (St Anne) w Sibford, Swalcliffe and Tadmarton
Ox 5   **P** *Worc Coll Ox (1 turn), New Coll Ox (2 turns)*
R T W IMBUSH,   **NSM** S T B FORBES ADAM
EPWORTH (St Andrew) and Wroot *Linc 1*   **P** *Prime Min
(2 turns), Ld Chan (1 turn)*   **R** A MAKEL
**ERCALL MAGNA (St Michael and All Angels) (St Mary
Mission Church)** *Lich 30*   **P** *Lord Barnard*
V K D MINTY
ERDINGTON (St Barnabas) *Birm 6*   **P** *Trustees*
V P R SPENCER,   **C** A T BULLOCK
ERDINGTON (St Chad) *Birm 6*   **P** *Bp*   **V** A R BROOKS
ERIDGE GREEN (Holy Trinity)   Frant w Eridge *Chich*
ERISWELL (St Laurence and St Peter)   Mildenhall *St E*
ERITH (Christ Church) *Roch 14*   **P** *Bp*   **V** J A PEAL,
Par Dn I F DURNDELL

ERITH Northumberland Heath (St Paul) *Roch 14*
  P *CPAS* V JR BALCH, C E BUTT
ERITH (St John the Baptist) *Roch 14* P *Bp*
  P-in-c J A PEAL
ERLESTOKE (Holy Saviour) Edington and Imber,
  Erlestoke and E Coulston *Sarum*
ERMINGTON (St Peter and St Paul) *Ex 21* P *The Crown
  and Bp (alt)* P-in-c P R LEVERTON
ERNESETTLE (St Aidan) *Ex 22* P *Bp* V GJ SMITH
ERPINGHAM (St Mary) w Calthorpe, Ingworth,
  Aldborough, Thurgarton and Alby w Thwaite *Nor 3*
  P *Bp, Lord Walpole, Gt Hosp Nor, Mrs S M Lilly, and
  DBP (by turn)* R B G MIDDLETON
ERWARTON (St Mary the Virgin) Chelmondiston w
  Harkstead and Shotley w Erwarton *St E*
ERYHOLME (St Mary) Middleton Tyas w Croft and
  Eryholme *Ripon*
ESCOMB (St John) *Dur 10* P *Bp* V N M J-W BEDDOW
ESCOT (St Philip and St James) Feniton, Buckerell and
  Escot *Ex*
ESCRICK (St Helen) and Stillingfleet w Naburn *York 4*
  P *Abp, D&C, and N C Forbes Adam Esq (jt)*
  R G D HARRIS
ESH (St Michael) *Dur 8* P *The Crown* V P G E TYLER,
  Par Dn G M POCOCK
ESHER (Christ Church) (St George) *Guildf 8* P *Wadh
  Coll Ox* R C M SCOTT, C J BROWN
ESHOLT (St Paul) Guiseley w Esholt *Bradf*
ESKDALE (St Catherine) (St Bega's Mission), Irton,
  Muncaster and Waberthwaite *Carl 5* P *Bp, Adn
  W Cumberland, Mrs W P Gordon-Duff-Pennington, and
  P Stanley Esq (jt)* V P G ASHBY, NSM I M HALL
ESKDALESIDE (St John) w Ugglebarnby and Sneaton
  York 23 P *Abp* N N JONES
ESSENDINE (St Mary the Virgin) Ryhall w Essendine
  Pet
ESSENDON (St Mary the Virgin) Lt Berkhamsted and
  Bayford, Essendon etc *St Alb*
ESSINGTON (St John the Evangelist) *Lich 10* P *Bp,
  R Bushbury, R Wednesfield, and Simeon's Trustees (jt)*
  V B PRENTICE
ESTON (Christ Church) w Normanby *York 19* P *Abp*
  TR A G C LEIGHTON, TV L N CAVAN, J W R HATTAN
ESTOVER (Christ Church) *Ex 23* P *Bp* V *Vacant*
  Plymouth (0752) 703713
ETAL (St Mary the Virgin) Ford *Newc*
ETCHILHAMPTON (St Andrew) Bishop's Cannings,
  All Cannings etc *Sarum*
ETCHING HILL (The Holy Spirit) Rugeley *Lich*
ETCHINGHAM (Assumption and St Nicholas) *Chich 15*
  P *Bp* R F W BUTLER
ETHERLEY (St Cuthbert) *Dur 10* P *Bp* R D G F HINGE
ETON (St John the Evangelist) Riverside *Ox*
ETON WICK (St John the Baptist) as above
ETTINGSHALL (Holy Trinity) *Lich 10* P *Bp*
  V E J TOMLINSON
ETTINGTON (Holy Trinity and St Thomas of
  Canterbury) Butlers Marston and the Pillertons w
  Ettington *Cov*
ETTON (St Mary) w Dalton Holme *York 9* P *Lord
  Hotham* P-in-c H E HUTCHINSON
ETTON (St Stephen) w Helpston *Pet 13* P *Sir Stephen
  Hastings* R W C H SEAL
ETWALL (St Helen) w Egginton *Derby 14* P *Bp,
  Sir H J M Every, Major J W Chandos-Pole, and DBP
  (by turn)* R *Vacant* Etwall (028373) 2349
EUSTON (St Genevieve) w Barnham, Elvedon and
  Fakenham Magna *St E 9* P *Duke of Grafton (2 turns),
  and Earl of Iveagh (1 turn)* Par Dn E S FOGDEN
EUXTON (not known) *Blackb 4* P *Bp* V D RAITT
EVEDON (St Mary) Kirkby Laythorpe *Linc*
EVENLEY (St George) Aynho and Croughton w
  Evenley *Pet*
EVENLODE (St Edward King and Martyr) Broadwell,
  Evenlode, Oddington and Adlestrop *Glouc*
EVENWOOD (St Paul) *Dur 11* P *Bp* V D A WRIGHT
EVERCREECH (St Peter) w Chesterblade and Milton
  Clevedon *B & W 2* P *DBP* V R J M WILLCOX
EVERDON (St Mary) Weedon Bec w Everdon *Pet*
EVERINGHAM (St Everilda) Seaton Ross Gp of Par
  York
EVERSDEN, GREAT (St Mary) w Little Eversden *Ely 1*
  P *Qu Coll Cam (2 turns), Ld Chan (1 turn)* R *Vacant*
EVERSDEN, LITTLE (St Helen) Gt w Lt Eversden *Ely*
EVERSHOLT (St John the Baptist) Woburn w
  Eversholt, Milton Bryan, Battlesden etc *St Alb*
EVERSHOT (St Osmund) Melbury *Sarum*
EVERSLEY (St Mary) *Win 5* P *DBP* R G D FULLER

EVERTON (Holy Trinity) and Mattersey w Clayworth
  S'well 1 P *Ld Chan (2 turns), Bp (2 turns)*
  R G A MUMFORD
EVERTON (St George) *Liv 3* P *Bp* V GJ BUTLAND,
  Par Dn D P WILLIAMS
EVERTON (St John Chrysostom) (Emmanuel) *Liv 3*
  P *Adn, CPAS, and PCC (jt)* V P H JORDAN
EVERTON (St Mary) Milford *Win*
EVERTON (St Mary) w Tetworth *Ely 12* P *Clare Coll
  Cam* V W J PATTERSON
EVERTON (St Peter) *Liv 3* P *Patr Bd* TR H CORBETT,
  TV P H SPIERS
EVESBATCH (St Andrew) Acton Beauchamp and
  Evesbatch w Stanford Bishop *Heref*
EVESHAM (All Saints w St Lawrence) *Worc 1* P *Bp*
  V R N ARMITAGE
EVINGTON (St Denys) *Leic 1* P *Bp* V C FINCH,
  Par Dn P J GRAY, NSM D JELLEY
EVINGTON (St Stephen) Twigworth, Down Hatherley,
  Norton, The Leigh etc *Glouc*
EVINGTON, NORTH (St Stephen) *Leic 1* P *Bp*
  P-in-c I St C RICHARDS, NSM W C BURLEIGH
EWELL (St Francis of Assisi) Ruxley Lane *Guildf 9* P *Bp*
  V D J CLEEVES
EWELL (St Mary the Virgin) *Guildf 9* P *Bp*
  V W R HANFORD
EWELL, WEST (All Saints) *Guildf 9* P *Bp* V A J HURD
EWELME (St Mary the Virgin), Brightwell Baldwin,
  Cuxham w Easington *Ox 1* P *F D Wright Esq and Mert
  Coll Ox, Prime Min (alt)* R P S K RENSHAW
EWERBY (St Andrew) Kirkby Laythorpe *Linc*
EWHURST (St James the Great) *Chich 20* P *K Coll Cam*
  R M D MUMFORD
EWHURST (St Peter and St Paul) *Guildf 2* P *Ld Chan*
  R D ACKROYD
EWOOD (St Bartholomew) *Blackb 5* P *Bp*
  V R W JORDAN, Par Dn E A JORDAN
EWSHOT (St Mary the Virgin) Crondall and Ewshot
  Guildf
EWYAS HAROLD (St Michael and All Angels) w Dulas,
  Kenderchurch, Abbeydore, Bacton, Kentchurch,
  Llangua, Rowlestone, Llancillo, Walterstone, Kilpeck, St
  Devereux and Wormbridge *Heref 1* P *Patr Bd*
  TR M M EDGE, C S B BELL
EXBOURNE (St Mary the Virgin) Hatherleigh, Meeth,
  Exbourne and Jacobstowe *Ex*
EXBURY (St Katherine) Beaulieu and Exbury and E
  Boldre *Win*
EXE, WEST (St Paul) *Ex 8* P *Peache Trustees*
  P-in-c D E CAVAGHAN
EXE VALLEY Washfield, Stoodleigh, Withleigh etc *Ex*
EXETER (St David) (St Michael and All Angels) *Ex 3*
  P *D&C* NSM P A LEE
EXETER (St James) *Ex 3* P *D&C* R B R TUBBS,
  C J D H CLEMENTS
EXETER (St Leonard w Holy Trinity) *Ex 3* P *CPAS*
  R J C SKINNER, C A R STEVENS
EXETER (St Mark) *Ex 3* P *Bp* V J J LAVERACK
EXETER (St Mary Steps) *Ex 3* P *SMF*
  P-in-c M J MORETON
EXETER (St Paul) Heavitree w Ex St Paul *Ex*
EXETER (St Sidwell) (St Matthew) *Ex 3* P *D&C*
  R V D STANDING, Par Dn J E HOWES
EXETER (St Thomas the Apostle) (Emmanuel) (St Andrew)
  (St Philip) *Ex 3* P *Bp* TR A WHITE,
  TV R A BOWYER, C C E G TILLER
EXETER, CENTRAL (St Martin) (St Mary Arches)
  (St Olave) (St Pancras) (St Petrock) (St Stephen) *Ex 3*
  P *Patr Bd* TR M R SELMAN, Hon C M J HATT,
  NSM P M BEACHAM
EXFORD (St Mary Magdalene), Exmoor, Hawkridge and
  Withypool *B & W 17* P *Bp (1 turn), Peterho Cam
  (2 turns)* R J A ATKIN
EXHALL (St Giles) *Cov 5* P *Bp* V M POWELL,
  C M E JACKSON
EXHALL (St Giles) w Wixford *Cov 7* V E F WILLIAMS
EXMINSTER (St Martin) and Kenn *Ex 6*
  P *Mrs M P L Bate and 12 Govs of Crediton Ch (jt)*
  R J H GOOD
EXMOOR (St Luke) Exford, Exmoor, Hawkridge and
  Withypool *B & W*
EXMOUTH (All Saints) Withycombe Raleigh *Ex*
EXMOUTH (Holy Trinity) Littleham w Exmouth *Ex*
EXMOUTH (St Andrew) as above
EXMOUTH (St Saviour) as above
EXNING (St Agnes) Newmarket St Mary w Exning St
  Agnes *St E*
EXNING (St Martin) (St Philip) w Landwade *St E 11*
  P *D&C Cant* V C T CATTON, C V J BROOKS

EXTON (St Andrew)   Woodbury *Ex*

EXTON (St Peter and St Paul)   Empingham and Exton w Horn w Whitwell *Pet*

EXTON (St Peter and St Paul)   Meonstoke w Corhampton cum Exton *Portsm*

EXTON (St Peter) and Winsford and Cutcombe w Luxborough *B & W 17*   **P** *Ld Chan (2 turns), Em Coll Cam (1 turn), and Rev H F and M M K Warren (1 turn)*   **R** C J BUDDEN

EXWICK (St Andrew) *Ex 3*   **P** *Lord Wraxall*   **V** J FAIRWEATHER

EYAM (St Lawrence) *Derby 2*   **P** *Earl Temple*   **R** D G SHAW

EYDON (St Nicholas)   Woodford Halse w Eydon *Pet*

EYE (St Matthew) *Pet 13*   **P** *Bp*   **V** S CHOLROYD

EYE (St Peter and St Paul) w Braiseworth and Yaxley *St E 16*   **P** *SMF*   **V** R H SMITH

EYE (St Peter and St Paul), Croft w Yarpole and Lucton *Heref 7*   **P** *Exors Mrs E Parr (2 turns), Ld Chan (2 turns), Lucton Sch (1 turn)*   **P-in-c** F T RUMBALL, NSM S STRUTT

EYEWORTH (All Saints)   Dunton w Wrestlingworth and Eyeworth *St Alb*

EYKE (All Saints) w Bromeswell, Rendlesham, Tunstall and Wantisden *St E 7*   **P** *Bp, Mrs R M L Darling, J H Kemball Esq, and MMCET (jt)*   **P-in-c** J K COTTON, **C** A H MOORE

EYNESBURY (St Mary) *Ely 12*   **P** *Bp*   **R** T J McCABE

EYNSFORD (St Martin) w Farningham and Lullingstone *Roch 9*   **P** *D&C*   **R** D F SPRINGTHORPE

EYNSHAM (St Leonard) and Cassington *Ox 9*   **P** *Wycliffe Hall Ox and Ch Ch Ox (alt)*   **NSM** C A W SANDERS

EYPE (St Peter)   Symondsbury and Chideock *Sarum*

EYRES MONSELL (St Hugh) *Leic 2*   **P** *Bp*   **V** K J HOOPER,   **C** W E P DAVAGE

EYTHORNE (St Peter and St Paul) and Elvington w Waldershare and Barfreystone w Sherdswell and Coldred *Cant 4*   **P** *Abp, St Jo Coll Ox, and Earl of Guilford (jt)*   **R** L P SMITH,   **NSM** M G HINTON,   R G ROGERS

EYTON (All Saints)   Leominster *Heref*

EYTON (St Catherine)   Wellington, All SS w Eyton *Lich*

FACCOMBE (St Barnabas)   Hurstbourne Tarrant, Faccombe, Vernham Dean etc *Win*

FACEBY (St Mary Magdalene)   Whorlton w Carlton and Faceby *York*

FACIT (St John the Evangelist) (St Michael the Archangel) *Man 19*   **P** *Bp*   **V** A J HOWELL

FAILAND (St Bartholomew)   Wraxall *B & W*

FAILSWORTH (Holy Family) *Man 18*   **P** *Bp*   **R** *Vacant* 061-681 3644

FAILSWORTH (Holy Trinity) *Man 18*   **P** *The Crown*   **P-in-c** R W STEPHENS

FAILSWORTH (St John) (St John the Evangelist) *Man 18*   **P** *Bp*   **R** J D QUANCE

FAIR OAK (St Thomas) *Win 9*   **P** *Bp*   **V** K M BELL

FAIRBURN (St James)   Ledsham w Fairburn *York*

FAIRFIELD (St John the Divine) *Liv 3*   **P** *MMCET*   **V** D J ROWLAND

FAIRFIELD (St Mark)   Belbroughton w Fairfield and Clent *Worc*

FAIRFIELD (St Matthew) *Linc 9*   **P** *Bp*   **V** D P ROWETT

FAIRFIELD (St Peter) *Derby 4*   **P** *Ch Govs*   **V** A J SIDEBOTTOM

FAIRFIELD (St Thomas a Becket)   Appledore w Brookland, Fairfield, Brenzett etc *Cant*

FAIRFORD (St Mary the Virgin) *Glouc 13*   **P** *D&C*   **V** D M BELL-RICHARDS

FAIRHAVEN (St Paul) *Blackb 11*   **P** *J C Hilton Esq*   **V** J R HASLAM

FAIRLIGHT *Chich 20*   **P** *MMCET*   **V** L C CROWE

FAIRSEAT (Holy Innocents)   Stansted w Fairseat and Vigo *Roch*

FAIRSTEAD (St Mary) w Terling and White Notley w Faulkbourne *Chelmsf 27*   **P** *Bp, Exors Lord Rayleigh, and C W O Parker Esq (by turn)*   **R** J T SMITH

FAIRWARP (Christ Church) *Chich 21*   **P** *Bp*   **V** I GIBSON

FAIRWEATHER GREEN (St Saviour) *Bradf 1*   **P** *Bp*   **V** P AINSWORTH

FAKENHAM (St Peter and St Paul) w Alethorpe *Nor 20*   **P** *Trin Coll Cam*   **R** A J BELL,   **C** L E FLETCHER

FAKENHAM MAGNA (St Peter)   Euston w Barnham, Elvedon and Fakenham Magna *St E*

FALCONWOOD (Bishop Ridley Church) *Roch 14*   **P** *Bp*   **V** R J IRETON

FALDINGWORTH (All Saints)   Wickenby Gp *Linc*

FALFIELD (St George) w Rockhampton *Glouc 7*   **P** *Adn Glouc, V Thornbury, J Leigh Esq, and Bp (by turn)*   **P-in-c** R W MARTIN

FALINGE (St Edmund)   Rochdale *Man*

FALKENHAM (St Ethelbert)   Kirton w Falkenham *St E*

FALMER (St Laurence)   Stanmer w Falmer *Chich*

FALMOUTH (All Saints) *Truro 3*   **P** *Bp*   **V** P F WATTS

FALMOUTH (King Charles the Martyr) *Truro 3*   **P** *Bp*   **R** R G GILBERT

FALSTONE (St Peter)   Bellingham/Otterburn Gp *Newc*

FAMBRIDGE, NORTH (Holy Trinity)   Creeksea w Althorne, Latchingdon and N Fambridge *Chelmsf*

FAMBRIDGE, SOUTH (All Saints)   Ashingdon w S Fambridge *Chelmsf*

FANGFOSS (St Martin)   Barmby Moor w Allerthorpe, Fangfoss and Yapham *York*

FAR FOREST (Holy Trinity)   Mamble w Bayton, Rock w Heightington etc *Worc*

FAR HEADINGLEY St Chad (St Oswald) *Ripon 7*   **P** *Lord Grimthorpe*   **V** B M OVEREND,   **C** J P CLARKE, R BROWN

FARCET (St Mary)   Stanground and Farcet *Ely*

FAREHAM (Holy Trinity) (St Columba) *Portsm 2*   **P** *Bp*   **TR** R W H KINGSTON,   **TV** J B WILLIAMS, R A SWALLOW,   **Hon C** A P BURR,   **NSM** E T JONES, D M JACKSON

FAREHAM (St John the Evangelist) *Portsm 2*   **P** *CPAS*   **V** H CHANT,   **C** V ROSS

FAREHAM (St Peter and St Paul) *Portsm 2*   **P** *Bp*   **V** L F CHADD,   **C** R A WHITE

FAREWELL (St Bartholomew) *Lich 2*   **P** *MMCET*   **V** W E HASSALL

FARFORTH (St Peter)   S Ormsby Gp *Linc*

FARINGDON, GREAT (All Saints) w Little Coxwell *Ox 17*   **P** *Simeon's Trustees*   **V** A J BAILEY,   **NSM** M R STARR

FARINGDON, LITTLE (not known)   Broughton Poggs w Filkins, Broadwell etc *Ox*

FARINGTON (St Paul) *Blackb 6*   **P** *V Penwortham*   **V** P D TAYLOR

FARLAM (St Thomas a Becket) and Nether Denton *Carl 2*   **P** *Bp*   **P-in-c** C T MATTHEWS

FARLEIGH (St Mary)   Warlingham w Chelsham and Farleigh *S'wark*

FARLEIGH, EAST (not known)   Coxheath w E Farleigh, Hunton and Linton *Roch*

FARLEIGH, WEST (All Saints)   Wateringbury w Teston and W Farleigh *Roch*

FARLEIGH HUNGERFORD (St Leonard)   Rode Major *B & W*

FARLEIGH WALLOP (St Andrew)   Cliddesden, Ellisfield, Farleigh Wallop etc *Win*

FARLESTHORPE (St Andrew)   Bilsby w Farlesthorpe *Linc*

FARLEY (All Saints)   Alderbury Team *Sarum*

FARLEY CHAMBERLAYNE (St John)   Michelmersh, Timsbury, Farley Chamberlayne etc *Win*

FARLEY GREEN (St Michael)   Albury w St Martha *Guildf*

FARLEY HILL (St John the Baptist) *St Alb 20*   **P** *Bp*   **V** N P MORRELL

FARLEY HILL (St John the Evangelist)   Swallowfield *Ox*

FARLINGTON (St Andrew) *Portsm 6*   **P** *Mrs V M Brooks and Dr R A L Leatherdale (jt)*   **R** J R PINDER

FARLINGTON (St Leonard)   Sheriff Hutton and Farlington *York*

FARLOW (St Giles)   Stottesdon w Farlow, Cleeton and Silvington *Heref*

FARMBOROUGH (All Saints) and Marksbury and Stanton Prior *B & W 10*   **P** *MMCET (3 turns), Duchy of Cornwall (1 turn), and DBF (1 turn)*   **R** A KENNEDY

FARMCOTE (St Faith)   The Guitings, Cutsdean and Farmcote *Glouc*

FARMINGTON (St Peter)   Northleach w Hampnett and Farmington *Glouc*

FARMOOR (St Mary)   Cumnor *Ox*

FARNBOROUGH (All Saints)   Beedon and Peasemore w W Ilsley and Farnborough *Ox*

FARNBOROUGH (St Botolph)   Avon Dassett w Farnborough and Fenny Compton *Cov*

FARNBOROUGH (St Giles) (St Nicholas) *Roch 15*   **P** *Em Coll Cam*   **R** G SHAW,   **C** A D KIRKWOOD

FARNBOROUGH (St Peter) *Guildf 1*   **P** *CPAS*   **R** A C P BODDINGTON,   **C** A L FLOWERDAY, J R M COOK, E HUGHES

FARNBOROUGH, SOUTH (St Mark) *Guildf 1*   **P** *Bp*   **V** I C HEDGES

FARNCOMBE (St John the Evangelist) *Guildf 4*   **P** *Bp*   **R** D W HEDGES,   **C** D A CAMERON

FARNDALE (St Mary)   Kirkbymoorside w Gillamoor, Farndale & Bransdale *York*

FARNDON (St Chad) and Coddington *Ches 5*   **P** *Duke of Westmr and D&C (jt)*   **V** R R BARRETT

FARNDON (St Peter) w Thorpe, Hawton and Cotham
S'well 3   **P** Ld Chan   **R** J B QUARRELL
FARNDON, EAST (St John the Baptist)   Arthingworth,
Harrington w Oxendon and E Farndon Pet
FARNHAM (St Andrew) Guildf 3   **P** Bp   **R** A K TUCK,
C A N BERRY, S E FORD
FARNHAM (St Laurence)   Tollard Royal w Farnham,
Gussage St Michael etc Sarum
FARNHAM (St Mary)   Gt and Lt Glemham, Blaxhall etc
St E
FARNHAM (St Mary the Virgin) Chelmsf 24
P Lt-Col W D Gosling   **P-in-c** R WALLACE
FARNHAM (St Oswald) w Scotton and Staveley and
Copgrove and Arkendale Ripon 1   **P** Bp, DBP,
R Knaresborough, MMCET, and Major Sir Arthur
Collins (jt)   **R** P L DUNBAR
FARNHAM COMMON (St John the Evangelist)
Farnham Royal w Hedgerley Ox
FARNHAM ROYAL (St Mary the Virgin) w Hedgerley
Ox 23   **P** Bp and Eton Coll (jt)   **Par Dn** J M STOKER
FARNHAM ROYAL SOUTH (St Michael)   W Slough
Ox
FARNINGHAM (St Peter and St Paul)   Eynsford w
Farningham and Lullingstone Roch
FARNLEY (All Saints)   Leathley w Farnley, Fewston
and Blubberhouses Bradf
FARNLEY (St Michael) Ripon 6   **P** Bp   **R** J R W SILLER,
Par Dn S C WHITEHOUSE
FARNLEY, NEW (St James)   Farnley Ripon
FARNLEY TYAS (St Lucias)   Almondbury w Farnley
Tyas Wakef
FARNSFIELD (St Michael) S'well 15   **P** Bp
V D J BARTLETT, **NSM** F CLARKE
FARNWORTH (All Saints)   E Farnworth and Kearsley
Man
FARNWORTH (St George)   New Bury Man
FARNWORTH (St John)   E Farnworth and Kearsley
Man
FARNWORTH (St Luke) (Bold Mission) (Cronton Mission)
Liv 13   **P** V Prescot St Mary   **V** M C FREEMAN,
Par Dn J MITSON
FARNWORTH (St Peter)   E Farnworth and Kearsley
Man
FARNWORTH, EAST (All Saints) (St John) (St Peter) and
Kearsley Man 12   **P** Bp (2 turns), Ld Chan (1 turn)
TR D T N PARRY.   **TV** C A BRACEGIRDLE
FARRINGDON (All Saints)   Chawton and Farringdon
Win
FARRINGDON (St Petrock and St Barnabas)
Aylesbeare, Rockbeare, Farringdon etc Ex
FARRINGTON GURNEY (St John the Baptist) B & W 13
P Bp   **V** J E INGHAM
FARSLEY (St John the Evangelist) Bradf 3
P V Calverley   **V** J N WHITE.   **Par Dn** B LOFTHOUSE
FARTHINGHOE (St Michael and All Angels) w Hinton-in-
the-Hedges w Steane Pet 1   **P** Ld Chan and Bp (alt)
R M BERRY
FARTHINGSTONE (St Mary the Virgin)   Blakesley w
Adstone and Maidford etc Pet
FARWAY (St Michael and All Angels)   Colyton,
Southleigh, Offwell, Widworthy etc Ex
FATFIELD (St George) Dur 1   **P** Lord Lambton
V K M THORPE, **C** A J FARISH
FAULKBOURNE (St Germanus)   Fairstead w Terling
and White Notley etc Chelmsf
FAULS (Holy Emmanuel) Lich 29   **P** V Prees
V W J WEBB
FAVERSHAM (St Mary of Charity) Cant 6   **P** D&C
V G R D MANLEY, **C** A M DURKIN.
Par Dn J K BUTTERWORTH
FAWDON (St Mary the Virgin)   Newc Epiphany Newc
FAWKENHURST Cant 12   **P** DBP   **R** Vacant
FAWKHAM (St Mary) and Hartley Roch 1   **P** Bp and
D&C (jt)   **R** G B McCORMACK, **Hon C** K C BLACKBURN
FAWLEY (All Saints) Win 10   **P** Bp   **R** G J PHILBRICK,
Par Dn P MANHOOD
FAWLEY (St Mary)   Brightwalton w Catmore,
Leckhampstead etc Ox
FAWLEY (St Mary the Virgin)   Hambleden Valley Ox
FAWSLEY (St Mary the Virgin)   Charwelton w Fawsley
and Preston Capes Pet
FAZAKERLEY (Emmanuel) (St Paul) Liv 7   **P** Patr Bd
TR D H HARRISON, **TV** I D ELLIOTT, J E DUFFIELD
FAZAKERLEY Sparrow Hall (St George)   Fazakerley
Em Liv
FAZAKERLEY (St Nathanael) Liv 7   **P** Bp
P-in-c G AMOS
FAZELEY (St Paul) (St Barnabas) Lich 5   **P** Bp
V H J BAKER, **C** D G ANDERSON, J R BALL

FEATHERSTONE (All Saints) Wakef 11   **P** Ch Ch Ox
V Vacant   Pontefract (0977) 792280
FEATHERSTONE (School chapel)   Haltwhistle and
Greenhead Newc
FECKENHAM (St John the Baptist)   Bowbrook N Worc
FEERING (All Saints) Chelmsf 22   **P** Bp   **V** A R MOODY
FELBRIDGE (St John) S'wark 23   **P** DBP   **V** S G BOWEN
FELBRIGG (St Margaret)   Roughton and Felbrigg,
Metton, Sustead etc Nor
FELIXKIRK (St Felix) w Boltby York 20   **P** Abp
P-in-c P R A R HOARE
FELIXSTOWE (St John the Baptist) (St Edmund) St E 2
P Bp   **V** K FRANCIS, **C** J R GLAISTER
FELIXSTOWE (St Peter and St Paul) (St Andrew)
(St Nicholas) St E 2   **P** Ch Trust Fund Trust
V H L BOREHAM, **C** A F HOGARTH
FELKIRK (St Peter) w Brierley Wakef 7   **P** Bp
V A N DAWKINS
FELLING (Christ Church) Dur 4   **P** CPAS   **V** M HOUGH
FELLISCLIFFE (Mission Church)   Hampsthwaite Ripon
FELMERSHAM (St Mary) St Alb 21   **P** Bp
P-in-c D E CLAYPOLE WHITE
FELMINGHAM (St Andrew) Nor 9   **P** Bp   **R** Vacant
North Walsham (0692) 402382
FELPHAM (St Mary the Virgin) w Middleton Chich 1
P D&C   **R** J A HESLOP
FELSHAM (St Peter)   Cockfield w Bradfield St Clare,
Felsham etc St E
FELSTED (Holy Cross) Chelmsf 18   **P** CPAS
V J C TADMAN
FELTHAM (Christ Church) (St Dunstan) Lon 11   **P** Bp
V D J CHAPMAN.   **Par Dn** E M TYNDALL,
NSM M J COLLETT
FELTHORPE (St Margaret)   Drayton w Felthorpe Nor
FELTON (St Katharine and the Noble Army of Martyrs)
Winford w Felton Common Hill B & W
FELTON (St Michael and All Angels) Newc 9   **P** Bp
V A A CLEMENTS
FELTON (St Michael the Archangel)   Bodenham w
Hope-under-Dinmore, Felton etc Heref
FELTON, WEST (St Michael) Lich 25   **P** Bp
R A M BRANNAGAN
FELTWELL (St Mary) w St Nicholas Ely 15   **P** Bp
R J H RICHARDS
FEN DITTON (Holy Cross) (St Mary Magdalene) (St Mary
the Virgin) Ely 6   **P** Bp   **R** L A MARSH
FEN DRAYTON (St Mary the Virgin) w Conington Ely 5
P The Crown and Ch Coll Cam (alt)   **V** J D YULE
FENCE-IN-PENDLE (St Anne) and Newchurch-in-Pendle
(St Mary) Blackb 7   **P** Ld Chan   **V** T N HOWARD
FENCOTE (St Andrew)   Kirkby Fleetham w Langton on
Swale and Scruton Ripon
FENHAM (St James and St Basil) Newc 7   **P** Bp
V V G ASHWIN
FENISCLIFFE (St Francis) Blackb 5   **P** Bp   **V** P D LAW-
JONES
FENISCOWLES (Immanuel) Blackb 5   **P** V Blackb
V J R CREE
FENITON (St Andrew), Buckerell and Escot Ex 7
P DBP, D&C and J-M Kennaway Esq (jt)
R W H C KINGSTON
FENNY BENTLEY (St Edmund King and Martyr),
Kniveton, Thorpe and Tissington Derby 8   **P** Bp and
Sir John FitzHerbert, Bt (jt)   **R** A P BETTS
FENNY DRAYTON (St Michael and All Angels)
Higham-on-the-Hill w Fenny Drayton and Witherley
Leic
FENNY STRATFORD (St Martin) Ox 25   **P** Bp
V S L HUCKLE
FENSTANTON (St Peter and St Paul) Ely 9   **P** Bp
V N E GREEN
FENTON (All Saints)   Brant Broughton and Beckingham
Linc
FENTON (Christ Church) Lich 18   **P** R Stoke-on-Trent
V A H YATES
FENWICK and MOSS (St John)   Fishlake w Sykehouse,
Kirk Bramwith, Fenwick etc Sheff
FEOCK (St Feock) Truro 6   **P** Bp   **P-in-c** D J P HEWLETT
FERHAM PARK (St Paul)   Masbrough Sheff
FERNDOWN (St Mary)   Hampreston Sarum
FERNHAM (St John the Evangelist)   Ashbury, Compton
Beauchamp and Longcot w Fernham Ox
FERNHURST (St Margaret) Chich 10   **P** Cowdray Trust
V Vacant   Haslemere (0428) 52229
FERNILEE (Holy Trinity)   Whaley Bridge Ches
FERRIBY, NORTH (All Saints) York 15   **P** Patr Bd
TR C J ASTILL, **TV** R H O HILL
FERRIBY, SOUTH (St Nicholas) Linc 6   **P** Bp
R A J DRAPER

FERRING (St Andrew) *Chich 5*   **P** *D&C*
   V R D T PATERSON
FERRYBRIDGE (St Andrew) *Wakef 11*   **P** *D&C York*
   V G HOLLAND
FERRYHILL (St Luke) (St Mary and St Martha) *Dur 14*
   P *D&C*   **V** K LUMSDON,
   C R E MASSHEDAR, M T WILLIAMS
FERRYHILL STATION (St Oswald) Chilton *Dur*
FERSFIELD (St Andrew) Bressingham w N and S
   Lopham and Fersfield *Nor*
FETCHAM (St Mary) *Guildf 10*   **P** *Bp*   **R** D J BAKER
FEWSTON (St Michael and St Lawrence) Leathley w
   Farnley, Fewston and Blubberhouses *Bradf*
FIDDINGTON (St Martin) Stogursey w Fiddington
   B & W
FIELD BROUGHTON (St Peter) Lindale w Field
   Broughton *Carl*
FIELD DALLING (St Andrew) Gunthorpe w Bale w
   Field Dalling, Saxlingham etc *Nor*
FIFEHEAD MAGDALEN (St Mary Magdalene)
   Gillingham *Sarum*
FIFEHEAD NEVILLE (All Saints) Hazelbury Bryan w
   Stoke Wake etc *Sarum*
FIFIELD (St John the Baptist) Shipton-under-
   Wychwood w Milton-under-Wychwood *Ox*
FIFIELD BAVANT (St Martin) Chalke Valley W *Sarum*
FIGHELDEAN (St Michael and All Angels) Bulford,
   Figheldean and Milston *Sarum*
FILBY (All Saints) w Thrigby w Mautby, w Stokesby w
   Herringby w Runham *Nor 2*   **P** *Bp, Adn Nor,*
   1 F M Lucas Esq, R T Daniel Esq, and
   Mrs Z K Cognetti (jt)   **R** M HALL
FILEY (St John) (St Oswald) *York 16*   **P** *DBF*
   V C W HUMPHRIES,   **Par Dn** E BUTTERWORTH
FILKINS (St Peter) Broughton Poggs w Filkins,
   Broadwell etc *Ox*
FILLEIGH (St Paul) S Molton w Nymet St George,
   High Bray etc *Ex*
FILLINGHAM (St Andrew) Ingham w Cammeringham
   w Fillingham *Linc*
FILLONGLEY (St Mary and All Saints) and Corley *Cov 5*
   P *Bp and Ch Soc Trust (jt)*   **V** J F LAW
FILTON (St Peter) *Bris 6*   **P** *Bp*   **R** B R ARMAN,
   Par Dn E F CULLY,   **NSM** G C HART
FIMBER (St Mary) Sledmere and Cowlam w
   Fridaythorpe, Fimer etc *York*
FINBOROUGH, GREAT (St Andrew) w Onehouse and
   Harleston *St E 6*   **P** *Bp*   **P-in-c** M P SKLIROS
FINBOROUGH, LITTLE (St Mary) Hitcham w Lt
   Finborough *St E*
FINCHAM (St Martin) *Ely 16*   **P** *Bp*   **R** J D A LINN
FINCHAMPSTEAD (St James) *Ox 16*   **P** *DBP*
   R D T CROSSLEY
FINCHFIELD (St Thomas) Tettenhall Wood *Lich*
FINCHINGFIELD (St John the Baptist) and Cornish Hall
   End *Chelmsf 18*   **P** *Mrs E M Bishop*   **P-in-c** A D JONES
FINCHLEY (Christ Church) *Lon 14*   **P** *Ch Patr Trust*
   V P N L PYTCHES
FINCHLEY (Holy Trinity) *Lon 16*   **P** *Bp*   **V** L B HILL
FINCHLEY (St Mary) *Lon 14*   **P** *Bp*   **R** D J BARNETT,
   C J D HANNAH
FINCHLEY (St Paul) (St Luke) *Lon 14*   **P** *Simeon*
   Trustees and Ch Patr Trust (jt)   **V** P M TEMPLEMAN,
   C N H GREEN
FINCHLEY, EAST (All Saints) *Lon 14*   **P** *Bp*
   V D B PAUL
FINDERN (All Saints) *Derby 16*   **P** *Bp*   **V** C R WILSON
FINDON (St John the Baptist) w Clapham and Patching
   Chich 5   **P** *Abp, Bp, and J E P Somerset Esq (jt)*
   V Z E ALLEN
FINDON VALLEY (All Saints) *Chich 5*   **P** *Bp*
   V Q M RONCHETTI
FINEDON (St Mary the Virgin) *Pet 10*   **P** *Bp*
   V J P BEAUMONT
FINGEST (St Bartholomew) Hambleden Valley *Ox*
FINGHALL (St Andrew) Spennithorne w Finghall and
   Hauxwell *Ripon*
FINGRINGHOE (St Andrew) w East Donyland *Chelmsf 19*
   P *Bp*   **R** R J HANDSCOMBE,   **C** P M ARNOLD
FINHAM (St Martin in the Fields) *Cov 3*   **P** *Bp*
   V P W SIMPSON
FINMERE (St Michael) w Mixbury, Cottisford, Hardwick
   w Tusmore and Newton Purcell w Shelswell *Ox 2*   **P** *Bp,*
   J F Vallings, and Baroness von Maltzahn (jt)
   R R B JENNISON
FINNINGHAM (St Bartholomew) Walsham le Willows
   and Finningham w Westhorpe *St E*
FINNINGLEY (Holy Trinity and St Oswald) w Auckley
   S'well 1   **P** *DBP*   **R** J D J GOODMAN

FINSBURY (St Clement) (St Barnabas) (St Matthew) *Lon 5*
   P *D&C St Paul's*   **V** J M SHIER
FINSBURY PARK (St Thomas) *Lon 5*   **P** *Abp*
   V S R COLES
FINSTALL (St Godwald) *Worc 7*   **P** *V Stoke Prior*
   V D T TONGE
FINSTHWAITE (St Peter) Leven Valley *Carl*
FIR VALE (St Cuthbert) Sheff St Cuth *Sheff*
FIRBANK (St John the Evangelist), Howgill and Killington
   Bradf 6   **P** *Ld Chan and V Sedbergh (alt)*
   V R A C GREENLAND,   **Hon C** A W FELL
FIRBECK (St Martin) w Letwell *Sheff 5*   **P** *Bp*
   R H LIDDLE
FIRLE, WEST (St Peter) Glynde, W Firle and
   Beddingham *Chich*
FIRSBY (St Andrew) w Great Steeping *Linc 7*
   P *Mrs J M Fox-Robinson*   **R** G ROBSON
FIRTREE (St Mary the Virgin) Witton le Wear and
   Firtree *Dur*
FISH HALL (Mission Church) Tonbridge SS Pet and
   Paul *Roch*
FISHBOURNE, NEW (St Peter and St Mary) *Chich 3*
   P *Ld Chan*   **R** M A COLLIS
FISHBURN (St Catherine) Sedgefield *Dur*
FISHERMEAD (Trinity Church) Woughton *Ox*
FISHERTON ANGER (St Paul) *Sarum 15*   **P** *Ch Patr*
   Trust   **R** M T CHRISTIAN-EDWARDS,
   NSM M G HUXTABLE
FISHLAKE (St Cuthbert) w Sykehouse, Kirk Bramwith,
   Fenwick and Moss *Sheff 11*   **P** *Duchy of Lanc (1 turn),*
   D&C Dur (2 turns), and Bp (1 turn)   **R** J M OSGERBY
FISHLEY (St Mary) Acle w Fishley and N Burlingham
   Nor
FISHPOND (St John the Baptist) Marshwood Vale
   Team Min *Sarum*
FISHPONDS (All Saints) *Bris 7*   **P** *Bp*   **V** R J BURBRIDGE
FISHPONDS (St John) *Bris 7*   **P** *Bp*   **V** S JARRATT,
   Par Dn J E NORMAN
FISHPONDS (St Mary) *Bris 7*   **P** *Bp*   **V** B L CURNEW,
   NSM K R G MILES
FISHTOFT (St Guthlac) *Linc 20*   **P** *DBP*   **R** J B PAVEY
FISKERTON (St Clement) w Reepham *Linc 3*   **P** *D&C*
   and Mercers' Co (jt)   **R** M K ROBERTS
FITTLETON (All Saints) Netheravon w Fittleton and
   Enford *Sarum*
FITTLEWORTH (St Mary the Virgin) Stopham and
   Fittleworth *Chich*
FITTON HILL (St Cuthbert) Bardsley *Man*
FITZ (St Peter and St Paul) Bicton, Montford w
   Shrawardine and Fitz *Lich*
FITZHEAD (St James) Milverton w Halse and Fitzhead
   B & W
FITZWILLIAM (St Maurice) Kinsley w Wragby *Wakef*
FIVE ASHES (Church of the Good Shepherd) Mayfield
   Chich
FIVE OAK GREEN (St Luke) Tudeley w Capel *Roch*
FIVEHEAD (St Martin) Curry Rivel w Fivehead and
   Swell *B & W*
FIXBY (St Francis) N Huddersfield *Wakef*
FLACKWELL HEATH (Christ Church) Lt Marlow *Ox*
FLADBURY (St John the Baptist), Wyre Piddle and Moor
   Worc 4   **P** *Bp*   **R** J O C CHAMPION
FLAGG (School Mission Room) Taddington,
   Chelmorton and Flagg, and Monyash *Derby*
FLAMBOROUGH (St Oswald) *York 10*   **P** *Abp*
   V B le G PETFIELD
FLAMSTEAD (St Leonard) *St Alb 14*   **P** *Univ Coll Ox*
   V D C KING,   **C** D J KERR,   **Hon C** G H KING
FLAUNDEN (St Mary Magdalene) Chenies and Lt
   Chalfont, Latimer and Flaunden *Ox*
FLAWBOROUGH (St Peter) Staunton w Flawborough
   S'well
FLAX BOURTON (St Michael and All Angels) *B & W 14*
   P *Lord Wraxall*   **R** H A P WILLS
FLAXLEY (St Mary the Virgin) Westbury-on-Severn w
   Flaxley and Blaisdon *Glouc*
FLAXTON (St Lawrence) Whitwell w Crambe, Flaxton,
   Foston etc *York*
FLECKNEY (St Nicholas) and Kilby *Leic 5*   **P** *Bp and*
   Hon Ann Brooks (jt)   **V** B R GLOVER
FLECKNOE (St Mark) Grandborough w Willoughby
   and Flecknoe *Cov*
FLEET (All Saints) (St Philip and St James) *Guildf 1*
   P *Bp*   **V** C H JOBSON,   **C** P VANNOZZI, J A BIRDSEYE,
   Hon C W J SELLERS,   **NSM** P P MOYSE
FLEET (Holy Trinity) Chickerell w Fleet *Sarum*
FLEET (St Mary Magdalene) w Gedney *Linc 16*
   P *The Crown and DBP (alt)*   **R** D F BRATLEY

FLEETWOOD (St David) *Blackb 13* **P** *Bp and Meynell Trustees (jt)* **V** J B A COPE
FLEETWOOD (St Nicholas) *Blackb 13* **P** *Bp and Meynell Trustees (jt)* **V** R W BUSSELL
FLEETWOOD (St Peter) *Blackb 13* **P** *Meynell Trustees* **V** J CAYTON
FLEMPTON (St Catherine of Alexandria) Culford, W Stow and Wordwell w Flempton etc *St E*
FLETCHAMSTEAD (St James) *Cov 3* **P** *Bp* **V** P G GUINNESS, **C** J C RAINER
FLETCHING (St Mary and St Andrew) *Chich 21* **P** *Abp* **V** J F ELSON
FLETTON (St Margaret) *Ely 13* **P** *Sir Stephen Hastings* **P-in-c** D J BOXALL
FLIMBY (St Nicholas) *Carl 7* **P** *Bp* **P-in-c** M T STILWELL
FLIMWELL (St Augustine of Canterbury) Ticehurst and Flimwell *Chich*
FLINTHAM (St Augustine of Canterbury) *S'well 8* **P** *M T Hildyard Esq* **V** J PULMAN
FLITCHAM (St Mary the Virgin) *Nor 21* **P** *The Crown* **P-in-c** G R HALL
FLITTON (St John the Baptist) Silsoe, Pulloxhill and Flitton *St Alb*
FLITWICK (St Andrew) (St Peter and St Paul) *St Alb 15* **P** *DBP* **V** M F J BRADLEY, **Par Dn** M J BETTIS
FLIXBOROUGH (All Saints) w Burton upon Stather *Linc 4* **P** *Sir Reginald Sheffield, Bt* **V** P B HEARN
FLIXTON (St John) *Man 7* **P** *Bp* **V** J A DEY
FLIXTON (St Mary) w Homersfield, South Elmham (St Margaret), South Elmham (St Peter) and South Elmham (St Cross) *St E 14* **P** *Bp* **P-in-c** S C MORRIS, **NSM** A B DINES
FLIXTON (St Michael) *Man 7* **P** *Bp* **R** W J TWIDELL, **Par Dn** C E VANN, **NSM** N R LITHERLAND
FLOCKTON (St James the Great) cum Denby Grange *Wakef 6* **P** *R Carter's Trustees* **Dn-in-c** M E SMITH
FLOOKBURGH (St John the Baptist) *Carl 10* **P** *R H Cavendish Esq* **V** J L J TAIT, **NSM** A BUTLER
FLORDON (St Michael) Tasburgh w Tharston, Forncett and Flordon *Nor*
FLORE (All Saints) w Dodford and Brockhall *Pet 3* **P** *Bp and Ch Ch Ox (alt)* **V** J W LATHAM
FLOWTON (St Mary) Somersham w Flowton and Offton w Willisham *St E*
FLUSHING (St Peter) Mylor w Flushing *Truro*
FLYFORD FLAVELL (St Peter) Upton Snodsbury and Broughton Hackett etc *Worc*
FOBBING (St Michael) *Chelmsf 16* **P** *The Crown* **P-in-c** G W DAVIES
FOLESHILL (St Laurence) *Cov 2* **P** *Ld Chan* **V** A A UPTON
FOLESHILL (St Paul) *Cov 2* **P** *Ld Chan* **V** A J CANNING, **NSM** R E SPITTLE
FOLEY PARK (Holy Innocents) Kidderminster St Jo and H Innocents *Worc*
FOLKE (St Lawrence) The Caundles w Folke and Holwell *Sarum*
FOLKESTONE Foord (St John the Baptist) Foord St Jo *Cant*
FOLKESTONE (Holy Trinity w Christ Church) *Cant 5* **P** *Abp* **R** R O STROUD
FOLKESTONE (St Augustine) (St Mary and St Eanswythe) *Cant 5* **P** *Abp* **V** J W DILNOT, **C** C J LAXON
FOLKESTONE (St George) *Cant 5* **P** *Abp* **R** W J ADAMSON
FOLKESTONE (St Peter) *Cant 5* **P** *Trustees* **V** M A HOUGHTON
FOLKESTONE (St Saviour) *Cant 5* **P** *Abp* **V** G J BUTLER
FOLKESWORTH (St Helen) Stilton w Denton and Caldecote etc *Ely*
FOLKINGHAM (St Andrew) S Lafford *Linc*
FOLKINGTON (St Peter ad Vincula) Arlington, Folkington and Wilmington *Chich*
FOLKTON (St John) Willerby w Ganton and Folkton *York*
FOLLIFOOT (St Joseph and St James) Spofforth w Kirk Deighton *Ripon*
FONTHILL BISHOP (All Saints) Tisbury *Sarum*
FONTHILL GIFFORD (Holy Trinity) as above
FONTMELL MAGNA (St Andrew) The Iwernes, Sutton Waldron and Fontmell Magna *Sarum*
FOOLOW (St Hugh) Eyam *Derby*
FOORD (St John the Baptist) *Cant 5* **P** *CPAS* **V** H W J HARLAND, **C** R D KING
FOOTS CRAY (All Saints) *Roch 16* **P** *Ld Chan* **R** G STYERS

FORCETT (St Cuthbert) and Aldbrough and Melsonby *Ripon 2* **P** *DBP and Univ Coll Ox (alt)* **R** M D GRAY
FORD (St Andrew) Clymping and Yapton w Ford *Chich*
FORD (St John) Colerne w N Wraxall *Bris*
FORD (St John of Jerusalem) Leominster *Heref*
FORD (St Michael) *Heref 13* **P** *Bp* **V** H J EDWARDS
FORD (St Michael and All Angels) *Newc 12* **P** *Lord Joicey* **P-in-c** W P HEWITT
FORD END (St John the Evangelist) Gt Waltham w Ford End *Chelmsf*
FORDCOMBE (St Peter) Penshurst and Fordcombe *Roch*
FORDHAM (All Saints) *Chelmsf 20* **P** *Reform Ch Trust (2 turns), Ball Coll Ox (2 turns)* **R** A G SMITH
FORDHAM (St Peter and St Mary Magdalene) *Ely 3* **P** *Jes Coll Cam* **V** A F NICHOLAS
FORDHOUSES (St James) Bushbury *Lich*
FORDINGBRIDGE (St Mary) *Win 8* **P** *K Coll Cam* **V** R STIRRUP
FORDON (St James) Burton Fleming w Fordon, Grindale etc *York*
FORDWICH (St Mary the Virgin) Sturry w Fordwich and Westbere w Hersden *Cant*
FOREMARK (St Saviour) *Derby 16* **P** *Major F R D Burdett Fisher (1 turn), H F Harpur-Crewe Esq (2 turns)* **V** J R P BARKER
FOREST (St Stephen) Rainow w Saltersford and Forest *Ches*
FOREST GATE (All Saints) *Chelmsf 5* **P** *Bp* **V** *Vacant* 081-472 0592
FOREST GATE (Emmanuel w St Peter) Upton Cross *Chelmsf 5* **P** *Bp* **V** T G REILLY, **C** J M GLASSPOOL, **Hon Par Dn** A R EASTER
FOREST GATE (St Edmund w St Michael and All Angels) *Chelmsf 5* **P** *Bp* **V** C C DALLISTON
FOREST GATE (St James) Stratford St Jo and Ch Ch w Forest Gate St Jas *Chelmsf*
FOREST GATE (St Mark) *Chelmsf 5* **P** *Ch Patr Trust* **V** M W WALLACE, **C** P J STOW
FOREST GATE (St Saviour) w West Ham (St Matthew) *Chelmsf 5* **P** *Patr Bd* **TR** J H WILLIAMS, **C** R J GARNETT
FOREST GREEN (Holy Trinity) Ockley w Okewood and Forest Green *Guildf*
FOREST HILL (Christ Church) *S'wark 4* **P** *Earl of Dartmouth* **P-in-c** J M P CALDICOTT, **C** N J CALVER, **NSM** T G BURMAN
FOREST HILL (St Augustine) Honor Oak Park *S'wark 4* **P** *Bp* **V** M J R COUNSELL
FOREST HILL (St Nicholas) Wheatley w Forest Hill and Stanton St John *Ox*
FOREST HILL (St Paul) *S'wark 4* **P** *Bp and V Forest Hill Ch Ch (alt)* **P-in-c** J M P CALDICOTT
FOREST-IN-TEESDALE (St Mary the Virgin) Middleton-in-Teesdale w Forest and Frith *Dur*
FOREST OF DEAN (Christ Church) w English Bicknor *Glouc 4* **P** *The Crown (3 turns), SMF (1 turn)* **P-in-c** A E WELLS
FOREST ROW (Holy Trinity) *Chich 7* **P** *V E Grinstead* **V** J S HASTWELL, **NSM** A W B LEACH
FOREST TOWN (St Alban) *S'well 2* **P** *Bp* **P-in-c** R P WALFORD
FORESTSIDE (Christ Church) Stansted *Chich*
FORMBY (Holy Trinity) *Liv 5* **P** *Trustees* **V** C A QUINE, **C** M J CARTLEDGE, W J STALKER
FORMBY (St Luke) *Liv 5* **P** *Bp* **V** T A MOON
FORMBY (St Peter) *Liv 5* **P** *R Walton* **V** M C BOYLING, **NSM** K L MILLER, J D ENGEL
FORNCETT (St Peter) Tasburgh w Tharston, Forncett and Flordon *Nor*
FORNCETT END (St Edmund) as above
FORNHAM (All Saints) (St Martin) w Timworth *St E 13* **P** *Bp* **R** C G G EVERETT
FORRABURY (St Symphorian) Boscastle w Davidstow *Truro*
FORSBROOK (St Peter) Draycott-le-Moors w Forsbrook *Lich*
FORTHAMPTON (St Mary) Deerhurst, Apperley w Forthampton and Chaceley *Glouc*
FORTON (All Saints) *Lich 13* **P** *D&C* **P-in-c** R T HIBBERT
FORTON (St John the Evangelist) *Portsm 3* **P** *DBP* **P-in-c** H O ALBY, **C** R W F BEAKEN, **NSM** D KING
FORTY HILL (Jesus Church) *Lon 18* **P** *V Enfield* **V** *Vacant* 081-363 1935
FOSDYKE (All Saints) Sutterton w Fosdyke and Algarkirk *Linc*
FOSTON (All Saints) Whitwell w Crambe, Flaxton, Foston etc *York*

FOSTON (St Bartholomew) Countesthorpe w Foston *Leic*

FOSTON (St Peter) Long Bennington w Foston *Linc*

FOSTON-ON-THE-WOLDS (St Andrew) Beeford w Frodingham and Foston *York*

FOTHERBY (St Mary) *Linc 12* **P** *Ld Chan (1 turn)*, *DBP, MMCET and M M Sleight Esq (1 turn)*, *and Bp (1 turn)* **R** D N LAMBERT, **NSM** A HUNDLEBY, J M WRISDALE

FOTHERINGHAY (St Mary and All Saints) Warmington, Tansor, Cotterstock and Fotheringhay *Pet*

FOULDEN (All Saints) Oxborough w Foulden and Caldecote *Nor*

FOULNESS (St Mary the Virgin) Gt Wakering w Foulness *Chelmsf*

FOULRIDGE (St Michael and All Angels) *Blackb 7* **P** *Bp* **V** W NUTTALL

FOULSHAM (Holy Innocents) Hindolveston and Guestwick *Nor 8* **P** *Lord Hastings, Mrs M E E Bulwer-Long and D&C (alt)* **R** B T FAULKNER

FOUNTAINS Group, The *Ripon 3* **P** *D&C* **R** A E ATKINSON

FOUR ELMS (St Paul) *Roch 10* **P** *Bp* **P-in-c** B D SIMMONS

FOUR MARKS (Good Shepherd) *Win 2* **P** *Bp* **V** C M NOYCE

FOUR OAKS (All Saints) *Birm 9* **P** *Bp* **V** D E McCORMACK, **C** M K SNELLGROVE

FOURSTONES (St Aidan) Warden w Newbrough *Newc*

FOVANT (St George), Sutton Mandeville and Teffont Evias w Teffont Magna and Compton Chamberlayne *Sarum 13* **P** *Reformation Ch Trust, Bp, and Ch Soc Trust (jt)* **R** J C EADE

FOWEY (St Fimbarrus) *Truro 1* **P** *Ch Soc Trust* **V** D A WOODS

FOWLMERE (St Mary) *Ely 8* **P** *Bp* **P-in-c** J B MYNORS

FOWNHOPE (St Mary) (Ferry Lane Chapel) *Heref 4* **P** *D&C* **P-in-c** R H GARNETT

FOXCOTE (St James the Less) Camerton w Dunkerton, Foxcote and Shoscombe *B & W*

FOXDALE (St Paul) *S & M 3* **P** *The Crown and Bp (alt)* **V** B H PARTINGTON, **NSM** H G R SLADE

FOXEARTH (St Peter and St Paul) Pentlow, Foxearth, Liston and Borley *Chelmsf*

FOXHAM (St John the Baptist) Bremhill w Foxham and Hilmarton *Sarum*

FOXHILL (Chapel) Frodsham *Ches*

FOXHOLE (St Boniface) Paignton St Jo *Ex*

FOXHOLES (St Mary) Langtoft w Foxholes, Butterwick, Cottam etc *York*

FOXLEY (Not Known) Sherston Magna, Easton Grey, Luckington etc *Bris*

FOXLEY (St Thomas) Bawdeswell w Foxley *Nor*

FOXT (St Mark the Evangelist) w Whiston *Lich 12* **P** *Personal Reps Major R J Beech and Mrs C I Townley (alt)* **V** J B HARROP

FOXTON (St Andrew) w Gumley and Laughton and Lubenham *Leic 4* **P** *Bp, A M Finn Esq, and D&C Linc (by turn)* **V** J J W EDMONDSON

FOXTON (St Laurence) *Ely 8* **P** *Bp* **P-in-c** W G THOMAS

FOY (St Mary) How Caple w Sollarshope, Sellack etc *Heref*

FRADLEY (St Stephen) Alrewas *Lich*

FRADSWELL (St James the Less), Gayton, Milwich and Weston on Trent *Lich 16* **P** *Bp, Personal Reps Earl of Harrowby, Hertf Coll Ox and T J A Dive Esq (jt)* **V** *Vacant* Weston (0889) 270490

FRAISTHORPE (St Edmund) Skipsea w Ulrome and Barmston w Fraisthorpe *York*

FRAMFIELD (St Thomas a Becket) *Chich 21* **P** *Mrs E R Wix* **V** G T DAINTREE

FRAMILODE (St Peter) Frampton on Severn, Arlingham, Saul etc *Glouc*

FRAMINGHAM EARL (St Andrew) *Nor 14* **P** J D Alston Esq **R** R B HEMS

FRAMINGHAM PIGOT (St Andrew) Thurton *Nor*

FRAMLINGHAM (St Michael) w Saxtead *St E 18* **P** *Pemb Coll Cam* **R** D J PITCHER, **C** N D G DEAR

FRAMPTON (St Mary) Bradf Peverell, Stratton, Frampton etc *Sarum*

FRAMPTON (St Mary) (St Michael) *Linc 21* **P** *Trustees* **V** N RUSSELL

FRAMPTON COTTERELL (St Peter) *Bris 7* **P** *SMF* **P-in-c** J M CLUTTERBUCK

FRAMPTON MANSELL (St Luke) Coates, Rodmarton and Sapperton etc *Glouc*

FRAMPTON ON SEVERN (St Mary), Arlingham, Saul, Fretherne and Framilode *Glouc 8* **P** *DBP, V Standish*

---

w Haresfield etc, Brig Sir Jeffrey Darell, Bt, and Bp (jt) **V** P CHEESMAN

FRAMSDEN (St Mary) Helmingham w Framsden and Pettaugh w Winston *St E*

FRAMWELLGATE MOOR (St Aidan) Dur St Cuth *Dur*

FRANCE LYNCH (St John the Baptist) *Glouc 1* **P** *DBP* **P-in-c** P R KESLAKE, **Hon C** W R P MORRIS

FRANCHE (St Barnabas) Kidderminster St Mary and All SS w Trimpley etc *Worc*

FRANKBY (St John the Divine) w Greasby St Nicholas *Ches 8* **P** *D&C* **V** K PLEE, **C** J A PATRICK

FRANKLEY (St Leonard) *Birm 4* **P** *Bp* **R** M T DENNY

FRANKTON (St Nicholas) Bourton w Frankton and Stretton on Dunsmore etc *Cov*

FRANSHAM, GREAT (All Saints) Gt and Lt Dunham w Gt and Lt Fransham and Sporle *Nor*

FRANSHAM, LITTLE (St Mary) as above

FRANT (St Alban) w Eridge *Chich 19* **P** *Bp and Marquess of Abergavenny (jt)* **R** C H ATHERSTONE

FRATING (St Mary Magdalene) w Thorrington *Chelmsf 26* **P** *St Jo Coll Cam* **P-in-c** J G JARMAN

FREASLEY (St Mary) Dordon *Birm*

FRECHEVILLE (St Cyprian) *Sheff 2* **P** *Bp* **R** M J GILLINGHAM

FRECKENHAM (St Andrew) Mildenhall *St E*

FRECKLETON (Holy Trinity) *Blackb 11* **P** *Bp* **V** S F BRIAN

FREEBY (St Mary) Melton Gt Framland *Leic*

FREEHAY (St Chad) Cheadle w Freehay *Lich*

FREELAND (St Mary the Virgin) Hanborough and Freeland *Ox*

FREEMANTLE (Christ Church) *Win 12* **P** *Bp* **R** R G DISS

FREETHORPE (All Saints) w Wickhampton, Halvergate, Tunstall, Beighton and Moulton *Nor 1* **P** *Bp, Ch Soc Trust, and K M Mills Esq (jt)* **R** R F GIBSON

FREISTON (St James) w Butterwick *Linc 20* **P** *Bp* **V** B R GRELLIER, **NSM** L HALL, R T WESTLAND

FREMINGTON (St Peter) *Ex 15* **P** *MMCET* **V** R G HOVIL, **C** A C BING

FRENCHAY (St John the Baptist) and Winterbourne Down *Bris 7* **P** *St Jo Coll Ox and SMF (jt)* **R** R J THOMAS, **Hon C** C F MOSLEY

FRENSHAM (St Mary the Virgin) *Guildf 3* **P** *Ld Chan* **V** M W H KIRBY, **NSM** J C NEWELL PRICE

FRESHFORD (St Peter) w Limpley Stoke and Hinton Charterhouse *B & W 10* **P** *Simeon's Trustees and V Norton St Phil (jt)* **R** D J CLARK

FRESHWATER (All Saints) (St Agnes) *Portsm 8* **P** *St Jo Coll Cam* **R** B W E BANKS

FRESSINGFIELD (St Peter and St Paul), Menham, Metfield, Weybread and Withersdale *St E 17* **P** *Bp, Em Coll Cam, Ch Soc Trust, and SMF (jt)* **R** *Vacant* Fressingfield (037986) 488

FRESTON (St Peter) Holbrook w Freston and Woolverstone *St E*

FRETHERNE (St Mary the Virgin) Frampton on Severn, Arlingham, Saul etc *Glouc*

FRETTENHAM (St Swithin) w Stanninghall *Nor 4* **P** *Ch Soc Trust* **R** *Vacant*

FRIAR PARK (St Francis of Assisi) W Bromwich St Fran *Lich*

FRIARMERE (St Thomas) *Man 18* **P** *Bp* **V** D J COX

FRICKLEY (All Saints) Bilham *Sheff*

FRIDAY BRIDGE (St Mark) *Ely 19* **P** *Bp* **V** J E BARRETT

FRIDAYTHORPE (St Mary) Sledmere and Cowlam w Fridaythorpe, Fimer etc *York*

FRIERN BARNET (All Saints) *Lon 14* **P** *Bp* **V** A V BENJAMIN

FRIERN BARNET (St James the Great) (St John the Evangelist) *Lon 14* **P** *D&C St Paul's* **C** P A ROBERTS

FRIERN BARNET (St Peter le Poer) *Lon 14* **P** *D&C St Paul's* **V** R L WHITEHEAD

FRIESTHORPE (St Peter) Wickenby Gp *Linc*

FRIETH (St John the Baptist) Hambleden Valley *Ox*

FRIEZELAND (Christ Church) Friezland *Man*

FRIEZLAND (Christ Church) *Man 18* **P** *Bp* **V** D W HIRST

FRILSHAM (St Frideswide) Hermitage and Hampstead Norreys, Cold Ash etc *Ox*

FRIMLEY (St Francis) (St Peter) *Guildf 6* **P** *R Ash* **R** B J COLEMAN, **C** J F WHITMORE, **Hon C** H E B SKEET

FRIMLEY GREEN (St Andrew) *Guildf 6* **P** *Bp* **V** B K BESSANT

FRINDSBURY (All Saints) w Upnor (St Phillip and St James) *Roch 6* **P** *Bp* **V** *Vacant* Medway (0634) 77580

FRING (All Saints) Snettisham w Ingoldisthorpe and Fring *Nor*
FRINGFORD (St Michael) Stratton Audley and Godington, Fringford etc *Ox*
FRINSTED (St Dunstan) Bredgar w Bicknor and Frinsted w Wormshill etc *Cant*
FRINTON (St Mary Magdalene) *Chelmsf 26* **P** *CPAS* **R** R H ELPHICK, **C** D W BARTLETT
FRISBY ON THE WREAKE (St Thomas of Canterbury) Melton Gt Framland *Leic*
FRISKNEY (All Saints) *Linc 8* **P** *Bp* **V** *Vacant* Friskney (075484) 530
FRISTON (St Mary Magdalene) Aldringham w Thorpe, Knodishall w Buxlow etc *St E*
FRISTON (St Mary the Virgin) E Dean w Friston and Jevington *Chich*
FRITCHLEY (Mission Room) Crich *Derby*
FRITHELSTOCK (St Mary and St Gregory) Gt and Lt Torrington and Frithelstock *Ex*
FRITHVILLE (St Peter) Sibsey w Frithville *Linc*
FRITTENDEN (St Mary) Sissinghurst w Frittenden *Cant*
FRITTON (St Catherine) Hempnall *Nor*
FRITTON (St Edmund) Somerleyton w Ashby, Fritton and Herringfleet *Nor*
FRITWELL (St Olave) w Souldern and Ardley w Fewcott *Ox 2* **P** *DBP, St Jo Coll Cam, and Wadh Coll Ox (by turn)* **R** J W THOMPSON
FRIZINGHALL (St Margaret) Shipley St Paul and Frizinghall *Bradf*
FRIZINGTON (St Paul) and Arlecdon *Carl 5* **P** *Bp* **V** E J WATSON
FROCESTER (St Andrew) Eastington and Frocester *Glouc*
FRODESLEY (St Mark) Condover w Frodesley, Acton Burnell etc *Heref*
FRODINGHAM (St Lawrence) *Linc 4* **P** *Lord St Oswald* **V** M P COONEY, **C** C R KENNEDY, **NSM** M DUNFORD
FRODINGHAM, NORTH (St Elgin) Beeford w Frodingham and Foston *York*
FRODSHAM (St Lawrence) *Ches 3* **P** *Ch Ch Ox* **V** E LOWE
FROGMORE (Holy Trinity) *St Alb 1* **P** *CPAS* **V** G R BARTER, **Hon C** J W MOSS
FROLESWORTH (St Nicholas) Claybrooke cum Wibtoft and Frolesworth *Leic*
FROME (Christ Church) *B & W 4* **P** *Bp* **V** C E ROLFE
FROME (Holy Trinity) *B & W 4* **P** *Bp* **V** G D COOPER
FROME (St John the Baptist) (Blessed Virgin Mary) *B & W 4* **P** *Bp and DBP (jt)* **V** G J WRAYFORD, **C** P N LITTLEWOOD
FROME ST QUINTON (St Mary) Melbury *Sarum*
FROME VAUCHURCH (St Mary) as above
FROMES HILL (St Matthew) Bishop's Frome w Castle Frome and Fromes Hill *Heref*
FROSTENDEN (All Saints) Wrentham w Benacre, Covehithe, Frostenden etc *St E*
FROSTERLEY (St Michael and All Angels) Stanhope w Frosterley *Dur*
FROXFIELD (All Saints) Whitton *Sarum*
FROXFIELD (St Peter) (St Peter on the Green) w Privett *Portsm 5* **P** *Magd Coll Cam* **P-in-c** D J SNELGAR
FROYLE (Assumption of the Blessed Virgin Mary) and Holybourne *Win 2* **P** *Guild of All So and D&C (jt)* **V** C R ARDAGH-WALTER, **Hon C** R M ROYLE
FRYERNING (St Mary the Virgin) w Margaretting *Chelmsf 10* **P** *Wadh Coll Ox* **P-in-c** P E COULTON, **C** C J N MARTIN
FRYSTON (St Peter) Airedale w Fryston *Wakef*
FUGGLESTONE (St Peter) Wilton w Netherhampton and Fugglestone *Sarum*
FULBECK (St Nicholas) Caythorpe *Linc*
FULBOURN (St Vigor w All Saints) *Ely 6* **P** *St Jo Coll Cam* **R** B E KERLEY, **C** N A BRICE
FULBROOK (St James the Great) Burford w Fulbrook and Taynton *Ox*
FULFORD (St Oswald) *York 8* **P** *Abp* **V** R A HALL, **NSM** H A HARTLEY
FULFORD-IN-STONE (St Nicholas) w Hilderstone *Lich 19* **P** *D&C* **V** P D BROOKS
FULHAM (All Saints) *Lon 9* **P** *Bp* **V** K N BOWLER
FULHAM (Christ Church) *Lon 9* **P** *CPAS* **V** C H MAY
FULHAM (St Alban) *Lon 9* **P** *Bp* **V** G PALMER, **Hon C** G R J SHEA
FULHAM (St Andrew) Fulham Fields *Lon 9* **P** *Bp* **V** D R PAGET, **NSM** D F EASTON
FULHAM (St Augustine) *Lon 9* **P** *City Corp* **V** *Vacant* 071-385 5760
FULHAM (St Dionis) Parson's Green *Lon 9* **P** *Bp* **P-in-c** A S ATKINS, **Hon Par Dn** P E BATES

FULHAM (St Etheldreda) (St Clement) *Lon 9* **P** *Bp* **V** J F H HENLEY
FULHAM (St Mary) North End *Lon 9* **P** *Ch Soc Trust* **V** R W CURL, **C** L J WICKINGS
FULHAM (St Matthew) *Lon 9* **P** *Ch Patr Trust* **V** G Q D PIPER, **C** D A WILKINSON, **Dss** V S PIERSON
FULHAM (St Peter) *Lon 9* **P** *Bp* **V** R P HARRISON
FULKING (Good Shepherd) Poynings w Edburton, Newtimber and Pyecombe *Chich*
FULL SUTTON (St Mary) Bishop Wilton w Full Sutton, Kirby Underdale etc *York*
FULLBROOK (St Gabriel) Walsall St Gabr Fullbrook *Lich*
FULLETBY (St Andrew) w Greetham and Ashby Puerorum *Linc 11* **P** *D&C (2 turns), Keble Coll Ox (1 turn)* **R** *Vacant* Winceby (065888) 671
FULMER (St James) Gerrards Cross and Fulmer *Ox*
FULMODESTON (Christ Church) Barney, Fulmodeston w Croxton, Hindringham etc *Nor*
FULSHAW (St Anne) Wilmslow *Ches*
FULSTOW (St Laurence) Fotherby *Linc*
FULWELL (St Michael and St George) Teddington SS Pet and Paul and Fulwell *Lon*
FULWOOD (Christ Church) *Blackb 14* **P** *V Lanc* **V** E J BURNS
FULWOOD (Christ Church) *Sheff 4* **P** *Rev A R Henderson, Rev A C P Boddington, P L Harden Esq, and CPAS (jt)* **V** P H HACKING, **C** G J McGRATH
FULWOOD Lodge Moor (St Luke) Lodge Moor St Luke *Sheff*
FUNDENHALL (St Nicholas) Wreningham *Nor*
FUNTINGTON (St Mary) and Sennicotts *Chich 13* **P** *Bp* **V** D A JOHNSON
FUNTLEY (St Francis) Fareham SS Pet and Paul *Portsm*
FURNACE GREEN (St Andrew) Southgate *Chich*
FURNESS VALE (St John) Disley *Ches*
FURNEUX PELHAM (St Mary the Virgin) Braughing w Furneux Pelham and Stocking Pelham *St Alb*
FURNHAM (Good Shepherd) Chard, Furnham w Chaffcombe, Knowle St Giles etc *B & W*
FURTHO (St Bartholomew) Potterspury, Furtho, Yardley Gobion and Cosgrove *Pet*
FURZE PLATT (St Peter) *Ox 13* **P** *Bp* **V** J E R POLLARD, **NSM** D FOOTE, M W SKINNER
FURZEBANK (Worship Centre) Willenhall H Trin *Lich*
FURZTON (not known) Watling Valley *Ox*
FYFIELD (St Nicholas) Upper Kennett *Sarum*
FYFIELD (St Nicholas) Appleshaw, Kimpton, Thruxton and Fyfield *Win*
FYFIELD (St Nicholas) and Moreton w Bobbingworth *Chelmsf 6* **P** *MMCET* **R** R MORGAN, **NSM** R H R DARK
FYFIELD (St Nicholas) w Tubney and Kingston Bagpuize *Ox 10* **P** *St Jo Coll Ox* **V** K J TRIPLOW
FYLINGDALES (St Stephen) and Hawsker cum Stainsacre *York 23* **P** *Abp* **V** A J MILLS
GADDESBY (St Luke) S Croxton Gp *Leic*
GADDESDEN, GREAT (St John the Baptist) *St Alb 3* **P** *N G Halsey Esq* **P-in-c** N ROSKROW, **Hon Par Dn** P M ROSKROW
GADDESDEN, LITTLE (St Peter and St Paul) *St Alb 3* **P** *Bp* **P-in-c** B G SAUNDERS
GADEBRIDGE (St Peter) Hemel Hempstead *St Alb*
GAINFORD (St Mary) *Dur 11* **P** *Trin Coll Cam* **V** T J D OLLIER
GAINSBOROUGH (All Saints) *Linc 2* **P** *Bp* **V** P W DADD, **C** M T HURLEY, **NSM** M R M LYONS
GAINSBOROUGH (St George) *Linc 2* **P** *Bp* **C** J STAFF
GAINSBOROUGH (St John the Divine) *Linc 2* **P** *Bp* **V** B M DODDS
GALLEY COMMON (St Peter) Camp Hill w Galley Common *Cov*
GALLEYWOOD (Junior School Worship Centre) Galleywood Common *Chelmsf*
GALLEYWOOD COMMON (St Michael and All Angels) *Chelmsf 11* **P** *CPAS* **V** R WAKELY, **C** R T BASHFORD, **NSM** J M ALLWRIGHT
GALMINGTON (St Michael) Wilton *B & W*
GALMPTON (Chapel of The Good Shepherd) Brixham w Churston Ferrers and Kingswear *Ex*
GAMBLESBY (St John) Addingham, Edenhall, Langwathby and Culgaith *Carl*
GAMESLEY (Bp Geoffrey Allen Church and County Centre) Charlesworth and Dinting Vale *Derby*
GAMLINGAY (St Mary the Virgin) w Hatley (St George) and East Hatley *Ely 12* **P** *Bp and Down Coll Cam (jt)* **R** E A NOBES
GAMLINGAY HEATH (St Sylvester) Gamlingay w Hatley St Geo and E Hatley *Ely*

GAMSTON and Bridgford S'well 5   P   DPB
  R J A S WOOD,   NSM B E F CLANCEY
GAMSTON (St Peter) w Eaton and West Drayton S'well 5
  P D&C York and Bp (alt)   R Vacant Gamston
  (077783) 706
GANAREW (St Swithin)   Llangarron w Llangrove,
  Whitchurch and Ganarew Heref
GANTON (St Nicholas)   Willerby w Ganton and Folkton
  York
**GARBOLDISHAM (St John the Baptist) w Blo' Norton,
Riddlesworth, Brettenham and Rushford** Nor 17
  P DBP, Sir John Musker, Mrs C Noel, and
  C P B Goldson Esq (by turn)   R R E FARTHING
GARFORD (St Luke)   Marcham w Garford Ox
GARFORTH (St Mary the Virgin) Ripon 8   P DBP
  R F A CHAPPELL,   NSM J CAWTHORNE
GARGRAVE (St Andrew) Bradf 5   P Bp   V K C GRAIN
GARRETTS GREEN (St Thomas) Birm 11   P Bp
  V A E ASH
GARRIGILL (St John)   Alston Team Newc
GARSDALE (St John the Baptist)   Sedbergh, Cautley
  and Garsdale Bradf
GARSDON (All Saints), Lea and Cleverton and Charlton
  Bris 12   P Ch Soc Trust and Bp (jt)   R Vacant
  Malmesbury (0666) 823861
GARSINGTON (St Mary) and Horspath Ox 1   P DBP
  and Trin Coll Ox (jt)   R C J BUTLER
GARSTANG (St Helen) Churchtown Blackb 10
  P A R Pedder Esq   V D J LEYLAND
GARSTANG (St Thomas the Apostle) Blackb 10
  P V Churchtown St Helen   V R G GREENALL
GARSTON (St Michael) Liv 4   P Trustees
  V W N LETHEREN,   Par Dn V E HUGHES
GARSTON, EAST (All Saints)   Eastbury and E Garston
  Ox
GARSWOOD (St Andrew)   Ashton-in-Makerfield
  H Trin Liv
GARTHORPE (St Mary)   Wymondham w
  Edmondthorpe, Buckminster etc Leic
GARTHORPE (St Mary)   N Axholme Gp Linc
GARTON IN HOLDERNESS (St Michael)   Roos and
  Garton in Holderness w Tunstall etc York
**GARTON-ON-THE-WOLDS (St Michael and All
Angels)**   Wetwang and Garton-on-the-Wolds w
  Kirkburn York
GARVESTON (St Margaret)   Barnham Broom Nor
GARWAY (St Michael)   St Weonards w Orcop, Garway,
  Tretire etc Heref
GASTARD (St John the Baptist)   Gtr Corsham Bris
GATCOMBE (St Olave) Portsm 8   P Qu Coll Ox
  P-in-c J W RUSSELL,   NSM M K NICHOLAS, C A B MARKE
GATE BURTON (St Helen) Linc 2   P Exors Lt-Col
  J E W G Sandars   R J S CROFT
GATE HELMSLEY (St Mary)   Sand Hutton York
GATEACRE (St Stephen) Liv 4   P Bp
  TR A T E TREHERNE,   TV N K LEIPER, A W ROBINSON,
  C J T CLEGG, S P WEST,   NSM W O BALMER
GATEFORTH (St Mary's Mission Room)   Haddlesey w
  Hambleton and Birkin York
GATELEY (St Helen)   Gt and Lt Ryburgh w Gateley
  and Testerton Nor
GATESHEAD (Christ Church) Dur 4   P Bp
  V P WRIGHT
GATESHEAD Harlow Green (St Ninian) Dur 4   P Bp
  V B MOSS
GATESHEAD Lobley Hill (All Saints)   Lobley Hill Dur
GATESHEAD (St Chad)   Bensham Dur
**GATESHEAD (St Edmund's Chapel w Holy Trinity)
(Venerable Bede)** Dur 4   P Bp and The Crown (alt)
  TR K HUXLEY,   TM R A NIXON,   TV J D F INKPIN
GATESHEAD (St George) Dur 4   P Trustees
  V E M T UNDERHILL
GATESHEAD (St Helen) Dur 4   P Bp   V B M HARRISON
GATESHEAD FELL (St John) Dur 4   P Bp
  R G W WEBSTER
GATLEY (St James) Ches 17   P R Stockport St Thos
  V R E READ
GATTEN (St Paul) Portsm 7   P Ch Patr Trust
  V P G ALLEN
GATTON (St Andrew)   Merstham and Gatton S'wark
GAULBY (St Peter) Leic 5   P MMCET, Ch Soc Trust,
  and Sir Geoffrey Palmer, Bt (jt)   R A F B CHEESMAN
GAUTBY (All Saints)   Bardney Linc
GAWBER (St Thomas) Wakef 7   P V Darton
  V D TURNER
GAWCOTT (Holy Trinity)   Lenborough Ox
GAWSWORTH (St James) Ches 13
  P T R R Richards Esq   R K V POVEY

GAWTHORPE (St Mary) and Chickenley Heath Wakef 10
  P Bp   V S MITCHELL
GAYDON (St Giles) w Chadshunt Cov 8   P Bp
  V P T FRANCIS
**GAYHURST (St Peter) w Ravenstone, Stoke Goldington
and Weston Underwood** Ox 27   P Bp and Lord
  Hesketh (jt)   R S J A WESTON
**GAYTON Group of Parishes, The: Gayton (St Nicholas),
Gayton Thorpe w East Walton, Westacre, Ashwicken w
Leziate and Bawsey (Eastern)** Nor 23   P Bp and Capt
  H Birkbeck (alt)   R Vacant Gayton (055386) 227
GAYTON (St Mary)   Pattishall w Cold Higham and
  Gayton w Tiffield Pet
GAYTON (St Peter)   Fradswell, Gayton, Milwich and
  Weston Lich
GAYTON LE WOLD (St Peter)   Asterby Gp Linc
GAYTON THORPE (St Mary)   Gayton Gp of Par Nor
GAYWOOD (St Faith), Bawsey and Mintlyn Nor 23
  P Bp   C B J WOOD, M E ELLSON
GAZELEY (All Saints) w Dalham, Moulton and Kentford
  St E 11   P Bp (2 turns), Personal Reps Major the Hon
  J P Philipps (1 turn), and Ch Coll Cam (1 turn)
  V B R W HAYES
GEDDING (St Mary the Virgin)   Cockfield w Bradfield
  St Clare, Felsham etc St E
GEDDINGTON (St Mary Magdalene) w Weekley Pet 11
  P Boughton Estates   V R B DORRINGTON
GEDLING (All Hallows) S'well 11   P DBP   R D DAVIES,
  Hon C F ANDREWS
GEDNEY (St Mary Magdalene)   Fleet w Gedney Linc
GEDNEY DROVE END (Christ Church)   Lutton w
  Gedney Drove End, Dawsmere Linc
GEDNEY HILL (Holy Trinity) (St Polycarp) Linc 16
  P Bp   V Vacant
GEE CROSS (Holy Trinity) (St Philip's Mission Room)
  Ches 14   P V Werneth   V G D OSGOOD,
  C P N BROMILEY
GELDESTON (St Michael)   Gillingham w Geldeston,
  Stockton, Ellingham etc Nor
GENTLESHAW (Christ Church) Lich 2   P MMCET
  V W E HASSALL
GEORGEHAM (St George) Ex 15   P MMCET
  R D W T RUDMAN
GERMAN (St German) S & M 3   P Bp   V B H KELLY
GERMAN (St John the Baptist) S & M 3   P Bp
  V B H PARTINGTON,   Hon C P C H MATTHEWS,
  NSM H G R SLADE
GERMANSWEEK (St German)   Bratton Clovelly w
  Germansweek Ex
GERMOE (St Germoe)   Breage w Germoe Truro
GERRANS (St Saviour) w St Anthony in Roseland Truro 6
  P Bp   R M L H BOYNS
GERRARDS CROSS (St James) and Fulmer Ox 20   P Bp
  and Simeon's Trustees (jt)   R N A RUSSELL,
  C P I MOUNSTEPHEN
GESTINGTHORPE (St Mary)   Gt and Lt Maplestead w
  Gestingthorpe Chelmsf
**GIDDING, GREAT (St Michael) w LITTLE (St John) and
Steeple Gidding** Ely 10   P Sir Stephen Hastings and Bp
  (alt)   P-in-c R W B van de WEYER,   NSM I D GIBSON
GIDEA PARK (St Michael) Chelmsf 4   P Bp
  V E R PILKINGTON,   C C E SUGDEN,   NSM K SUGDEN
GIDLEIGH (Holy Trinity)   Chagford w Gidleigh and
  Throwleigh Ex
GIGGETTY LANE (The Venerable Bede)   Wombourne
  w Trysull and Bobbington Lich
**GIGGLESWICK (St Alkelda) and Rathmell w
Wigglesworth** Bradf 5   P Bp and Ch Trust Fund
  Trust (jt)   V G D RHODES
GILCRUX (St Mary)   Plumbland and Gilcrux Carl
GILDERSOME (St Peter) Wakef 8   P V Batley
  V D R D MARTINEAU
GILLAMOOR (St Aidan)   Kirkbymoorside w
  Gillamoor, Farndale & Bransdale York
GILLING (St Agatha) and Kirkby Ravensworth Ripon 2
  P Bp and Mrs M W Ringrose-Wharton (jt)   V H A TAIT
GILLING EAST (Holy Cross)   Ampleforth and
  Oswaldkirk and Gilling E York
GILLINGHAM (Holy Trinity) Roch 3   P Bp
  NSM A V SHILLING
GILLINGHAM (St Augustine) Roch 3   P Bp
  V P R WILLIAMS
GILLINGHAM (St Barnabas) Roch 3   P Bp
  V D F PRESTON
GILLINGHAM (St Mark) Roch 3   P Hyndman Trustees
  V C O BUCHANAN,   C P R M VENABLES
GILLINGHAM (St Mary Magdalene) Roch 3   P DBP
  V O P HARVEY,   Par Dn M D PALMER

GILLINGHAM (St Mary the Virgin) *Sarum 6* P *Bp*
TR J McNEISH, TV P BIRT, W T RIDDING,
NSM J R HEDGES
GILLINGHAM (St Mary) w Geldeston w Stockton w
Ellingham St Mary and Kirby Cane *Nor 14* P *Ld Chan
(1 turn), Bp, MMCET and Ch Trust Fund Trust (1 turn)*
R R H BLANKLEY, Hon C D E PENNY,
NSM R D HARVEY
GILLINGHAM, SOUTH (St Matthew) *Roch 3* P *Patr Bd*
TR S H DUNN, TV G E HOVENDEN, A C OEHRING
GILLOW HEATH (Mission Room) Biddulph *Lich*
GILMORTON (All Saints) w Peatling Parva and Kimcote
cum Walton *Leic 11* P *Bp and Guild All So (jt)*
R *Vacant* Lutterworth (04555) 2119
GILSLAND (St Mary Magdalene) *Carl 2* P *Bp*
P-in-c C T MATTHEWS
GILSTEAD (St Wilfrid) Bingley H Trin *Bradf*
GILSTON (St Mary) High Wych and Gilston w Eastwick
St Alb
GIMINGHAM (All Saints) Trunch *Nor*
GIPPING (Chapel of St Nicholas) Old Newton w
Stowupland *St E*
GIPSY HILL (Christ Church) *S'wark 12* P *CPAS*
V P J WHITWORTH, C R C PAGET
GIRLINGTON (St Philip) *Bradf 1* P *Simeon's Trustees*
V A D GREENHILL
GIRTON (St Andrew) *Ely 5* P *Ld Chan*
R R G J MACKINTOSH, NSM R M NANCARROW
GIRTON (St Cecilia) Collingham w S Scarle and
Besthorpe and Girton *S'well*
GISBURN (St Mary the Virgin) *Bradf 5* P *Bp*
P-in-c J B LUMBY
GISLEHAM (Holy Trinity) Kessingland w Gisleham
Nor
GISLINGHAM (St Mary) Thornhams Magna and Parva,
Gislingham and Mellis *St E*
GISSING (St Mary the Virgin) Winfarthing w Shelfanger
w Burston w Gissing etc *Nor*
GITTISHAM (St Michael) Honiton, Gittisham, Combe
Raleigh, Monkton etc *Ex*
GIVENDALE, GREAT (St Ethelberga) Pocklington
and Owsthorpe and Kilnwick Percy etc *York*
GLAISDALE (St Thomas) *York 23* P *Abp*
V D M BUIKE
GLANDFORD (St Martin) Blakeney w Cley, Wiveton,
Glandford etc *Nor*
GLANTON (St Peter) Whittingham and Edlingham w
Bolton Chapel *Newc*
GLAPTHORN (St Leonard) Benefield and Southwick w
Glapthorn *Pet*
GLAPWELL (St Andrew) Ault Hucknall *Derby*
GLASCOTE (St George) and Stonydelph *Lich 5*
P *Patr Bd* TR K M JUKES, TV C E BERESFORD,
Par Dn M A WOODERSON, S A CHAPMAN
GLASSHOUGHTON (St Paul) *Wakef 11* P *Bp*
V G DRIVER
GLASSON (Christ Church) Cockerham w Winmarleigh
and Glasson *Blackb*
GLASTON (St Andrew) Morcott w Glaston and
Bisbrooke *Pet*
GLASTONBURY (St John the Baptist) (St Benedict) w
Meare, West Pennard and Godney *B & W 5* P *Bp*
V P J RILEY, C S LOW, E M CROSS,
Hon C W M MARSHALL
GLATTON (St Nicholas) *Ely 13* P *Bp* R G J SHARPE
GLAZEBURY (All Saints) Newchurch and Glazebury
Liv
GLAZELEY (St Bartholomew) Billingsley w Sidbury,
Middleton Scriven etc *Heref*
GLEADLESS (Christ Church) *Sheff 1* P *DBP*
TR C J W HEDLEY, TV R F ATKINS, Par Dn D ATKINS,
NSM S D HOLDAWAY
GLEADLESS VALLEY (Holy Cross) *Sheff 1* P *DBP*
TR D J GOSS, Par Dn B PARKER
GLEMHAM, GREAT (All Saints) and LITTLE (St
Andrew), Blaxhall, Stratford St Andrew and Farnham
St E 19 P *Earl of Guilford, Mr C J V Hope Johnstone,
Mr P M Cobbold (1 turn), and DBP (1 turn)* R *Vacant*
Saxmundham (0728) 603180
GLEMSFORD (St Mary the Virgin), Hartest w Boxted,
Somerton and Stanstead (Glem Valley United Benefice)
St E 12 P *Bp, Prime Min, and Ch Soc Trust (by turn)*
P-in-c A S MASON
GLEN AULDYN (Mission Church) Lezayre *S & M*
GLEN PARVA and South Wigston *Leic 5* P *Bp*
V G RICHERBY, C M R EAREY, NSM P G HOLMES
GLENDALE Group, The *Newc 10* P *Patr Bd (4 turns),
Ld Chan (1 turn)* TR R B S BURSTON,

TV A J HUGHES, P J BRYARS, R K KENNEDY,
NSM T R ROCHESTER
GLENFIELD (St Peter) *Leic 12* P *Bp*
R A L LATTIMORE, C A J BURGESS
GLENHOLT (St Anne) Bickleigh (Plymouth) *Ex*
GLENTHAM (St Peter) Owmby and Normanby w
Glentham *Linc*
GLENTWORTH (St Michael) *Linc 2* P *Earl of
Scarbrough* V N BRUNNING
GLINTON (St Benedict) Peakirk w Glinton *Pet*
GLODWICK (St Mark w Christ Church) *Man 18* P *Bp*
V M A NARUSAWA
GLOOSTON (St John the Baptist) Gt Bowden w
Welham, Glooston and Cranoe *Leic*
GLOSSOP (All Saints) *Derby 6* P *Patr Bd* V P H HEATH
GLOUCESTER (St Aldate) Finlay Road *Glouc 5* P *Bp*
V D C SAWYER
GLOUCESTER (St Barnabas) Tuffley *Glouc*
GLOUCESTER (St Catharine) *Glouc 5* P *Bp*
V R J LLEWELYN
GLOUCESTER (St George) w Whaddon *Glouc 5* P *Bp*
V B A McQUILLEN, C S B MORRIS, NSM F A EVANS
GLOUCESTER (St James and All Saints) *Glouc 5* P *Bp*
V M W BUTLER, C T E MASON
GLOUCESTER St Luke the Less *Glouc 5* P *Bp*
V D G HUMPHRIES
GLOUCESTER (St Mark) *Glouc 5* P *Bp*
P-in-c A M LYNETT
GLOUCESTER (St Mary de Crypt) (St John the Baptist)
(Christ Church) *Glouc 5* P *Bp and Ld Chan (alt)*
R D A BRAZINGTON
GLOUCESTER (St Mary de Lode and St Nicholas) *Glouc 5*
P *Bp and D&C (alt)* V S J RIGGS,
Hon C M J P BINGHAM
GLOUCESTER (St Michael) Tuffley *Glouc*
GLOUCESTER (St Oswald) Coney Hill *Glouc*
GLOUCESTER (St Paul) *Glouc 5* P *Bp* V R C KEY
GLOUCESTER (St Stephen) Glouc St Steph *Glouc*
GLOUCESTER DOCKS Mariners' Church Extra-
Parochial District *Glouc 5* P *Ch Soc Trust*
Chapl T B GRETTON
GLOUCESTER ROAD (St Stephen) S Kensington St
Steph *Lon*
GLUSBURN (All Saints) Sutton *Bradf*
GLYMPTON (St Mary) Wootton w Glympton and
Kiddington *Ox*
GLYNDE (St Mary), West Firle and Beddingham *Chich 18*
P *Bp and D&C Windsor (alt)* V P A LYNN
GNOSALL (St Lawrence) *Lich 13* P *Bp* V M J POPE
GOADBY (St John the Baptist) Billesdon and
Skeffington *Leic*
GOADBY MARWOOD (St Denys) Scalford w Goadby
Marwood and Wycombe etc *Leic*
GOATHILL (St Peter) Milborne Port w Goathill *B & W*
GOATHLAND (St Mary) *York 23* P *Abp*
P-in-c E NEWLYN
GOATHURST (St Edward the King and Martyr)
Spaxton w Goathurst, Enmore and Charlynch *B & W*
GOBOWEN (All Saints) Hengoed w Gobowen *Lich*
GOBOWEN ROAD (Mission Room) Oswestry H Trin
Lich
GODALMING (St Peter and St Paul) *Guildf 4* P *Bp*
V M C BROWN, C H M WOODHEAD
GODINGTON (Holy Trinity) Stratton Audley and
Godington, Fringford etc *Ox*
GODLEY cum Newton Green (St John the Baptist) *Ches 14*
P *R Cheadle* P-in-c J H DARCH, C R H WHITE
GODMANCHESTER (St Mary) *Ely 9* P *D&C Westmr*
V D H G CLARK, C N R T FOLLETT
GODMANSTONE (Holy Trinity) Cerne Abbas w
Godmanstone and Minterne Magna *Sarum*
GODMERSHAM (St Lawrence the Martyr) Crundale w
Godmersham *Cant*
GODNEY (Holy Trinity) Glastonbury w Meare, W
Pennard and Godney *B & W*
GODOLPHIN (St John the Baptist) Crowan w
Godolphin *Truro*
GODSHILL (All Saints) (St Alban) *Portsm 7* P *Guild of
All So* V T P J HEWITT
GODSHILL (St Giles) Fordingbridge *Win*
GODSTONE (St Nicholas) *S'wark 23* P *C K G Hoare Esq*
R C J STUDDERT-KENNEDY
GOFF'S OAK (St James) *St Alb 6* P *V Cheshunt*
V J W BRIDSTRUP
GOLBORNE (St Thomas) *Liv 16* P *Bp* R H CUNLIFFE
GOLCAR (St John the Evangelist) *Wakef 5*
P *V Huddersfield* V R M F CROMPTON
GOLDEN GREEN (Mission) Hadlow *Roch*

GOLDEN VALLEY (St Matthias)   Riddings and Ironville *Derby*

GOLDENHILL (St John the Evangelist) *Lich 17*   P *Bp*   V J C G SELVINI

GOLDERS GREEN (St Alban the Martyr and St Michael) *Lon 15*   P *Bp*   V P G BAKER

GOLDHANGER (St Peter) w Little Totham *Chelmsf 13*   P *Ld Chan*   R D J ALLAN

GOLDINGTON (St Mary the Virgin) *St Alb 16*   P *Bp*   V D R THURBURN-HUELIN, C N C LAW, Par Dn J M COLLINS, NSM D G PRESTON

GOLDSBOROUGH (St Mary)   Knaresborough *Ripon*

GOLDSWORTH PARK (St Andrew) *Guildf 12*   P *Bp*   V A W A KNOWLES, C R H WATTS

GOLDTHORPE (St John the Evangelist and St Mary Magdalene) w Hickleton *Sheff 12*   P *CR (2 turns), Earl of Halifax (1 turn)*   V A J DELVES

GOMERSAL (St Mary) *Wakef 8*   P *Bp*   V M W THOMAS, C P A CRABB

GONALSTON (St Laurence) *S'well 11*   P *Comdr M B P Francklin, Bp, and Ld Chan (by turn)*   R M J BROCK

GONERBY, GREAT (St Sebastian) *Linc 19*   P *R Grantham*   R P HOPKINS

GOOD EASTER (St Andrew)   High and Gd Easter w Margaret Roding *Chelmsf*

GOODERSTONE (St George)   Cockley Cley w Gooderstone *Nor*

GOODLEIGH (St Gregory)   Barnstaple *Ex*

GOODMANHAM (All Saints) *York 7*   P *Abp*   R Vacant

GOODMAYES (All Saints) *Chelmsf 7*   P *Hyndman Trustees*   V C R KEATING, C T C JONES, NSM M OKELLO

GOODMAYES (St Paul) *Chelmsf 7*   P *Bp*   V D J BAKER

GOODNESTONE (Holy Cross)   Nonington w Wymynswold and Goodnestone etc *Cant*

GOODRICH (St Giles)   Walford and Saint John, w Bishopswood etc *Heref*

GOODRINGTON (St George) *Ex 10*   P *Bp*   V B D PROTHERO

GOODSHAW (St Mary and All Saints) and Crawshawbooth *Man 15*   P *Bp and Wm Hulme Trustees (jt)*   V R E MALLINSON, Par Dn A G SWALLOW

GOODWORTH CLATFORD (St Peter)   Abbotts Ann and Upper and Goodworth Clatford *Win*

GOOLE (St John the Evangelist) (St Mary) (Mariners' Club and Chapel) *Sheff 11*   P *Bp*   V T E LEACH, Par Dn B R TURNER

GOOSE GREEN (St Paul) *Liv 15*   P *Bp*   V J J HARTLEY

GOOSEY (All Saints)   Stanford in the Vale w Goosey and Hatford *Ox*

GOOSNARGH (St Mary) w Whittingham *Blackb 10*   P *Bp*   V R A ANDREW

GOOSTREY (St Luke) *Ches 11*   P *V Sandbach*   V A G SPARHAM

GORAN HAVEN (St Just)   St Goran w St Mich Caerhays *Truro*

GOREFIELD (St Paul) *Ely 19*   P *Bp*   V J TOFTS

GORING (St Thomas of Canterbury) w South Stoke *Ox 6*   P *Ch Ch Ox*   V P E NIXON, Hon C B W BARRETT

GORING-BY-SEA (St Mary) (St Laurence) *Chich 4*   P *Bp*   V F J FOX-WILSON, NSM K J TUFFEL

GORLESTON (St Andrew) *Nor 2*   P *Ch Trust Fund Trust*   V C C COOPER, C T H BERRY, NSM A FROGGATT, A T CADMORE

GORLESTON (St Mary Magdalene) *Nor 2*   P *Bp and Ch Trust Fund Trust (jt)*   V P J STEPHENS

GORNAL, LOWER (St James the Great) *Lich 1*   P *Bp*   V P E HUTCHINSON

GORNAL, UPPER (St Peter) *Lich 1*   P *V Sedgley All SS*   V M K BATE

GORSLEY (Christ Church)   Newent and Gorsley w Cliffords Mesne *Glouc*

GORTON (Emmanuel) *Man 1*   P *Bp*   R M R J WILLIAMS

GORTON (Our Lady and St Thomas) *Man 1*   P *Trustees*   R R G J HERRON

GORTON (St James) *Man 1*   P *D&C*   R Vacant 061-223 0708

GORTON (St Philip) *Man 1*   P *The Crown*   R F J T BRUMWELL

GOSBECK (St Mary)   Coddenham w Gosbeck and Hemingstone w Henley *St E*

GOSBERTON (St Peter and St Paul) *Linc 17*   P *D&C*   V T G WILLIAMSON

GOSBERTON CLOUGH (St Gilbert and St Hugh) and Quadring *Linc 17*   P *Bp*   V P STREET

GOSCOTE, EAST (St Hilda) w Ratcliffe on the Wreake and Rearsby *Leic 6*   P *Adn and Bp (jt)*   V Vacant Leicester (0533) 605938

GOSFIELD (St Katherine) *Chelmsf 22*   P *Mrs G M Lowe and Mrs M A Wilson*   V Vacant Colchester (0206) 262110

GOSFORTH (All Saints) *Newc 5*   P *Bp*   V R B HILL, C M J HILLS

GOSFORTH (St Hugh)   Newc Epiphany *Newc*

GOSFORTH (St Mary) w Nether Wasdale and Wasdale Head *Carl 5*   P *Bp, Earl of Lonsdale, V St Bees, and PCCs (jt)*   R D C BICKERSTETH

GOSFORTH (St Nicholas) *Newc 5*   P *Bp*   V J K YOUNG

GOSFORTH, NORTH (St Columba)   Ch the King in the Dio of Newc *Newc*

GOSFORTH VALLEY (St Andrew)   Dronfield w Holmesfield *Derby*

GOSPEL END (St Barnabas)   Sedgley All SS *Lich*

GOSPEL LANE (St Michael) *Birm 13*   P *Bp*   V R K JOHNSON

GOSPORT (Christ Church) *Portsm 3*   P *Bp*   V D G JAMES, C B M HAMMOND, NSM R A FORSE

GOSPORT (Holy Trinity) *Portsm 3*   P *DBP*   V J R CAPPER

GOSSOPS GREEN (St Alban)   Ifield *Chich*

GOTHAM (St Lawrence) *S'well 10*   P *Bp*   P-in-c D C GORICK, NSM J H MOORE

GOUDHURST (St Mary the Virgin) w Kilndown *Cant 11*   P *Abp and Prime Min (alt)*   V R C CAMPBELL-SMITH

GOULCEBY (All Saints)   Asterby Gp *Linc*

GOXHILL (All Saints)   Barrow and Goxhill *Linc*

GOXHILL (St Giles)   Aldbrough, Mappleton w Goxhill and Withernwick *York*

GRADE (St Grada and the Holy Cross)   St Ruan w St Grade and Landewednack *Truro*

GRAFFHAM (St Giles) w Woolavington *Chich 11*   P *Bp*   P-in-c K F HYDE-DUNN

GRAFFOE *Linc 18*   P *J C M Fullerton Esq, Ch Coll Cam, D&C, and Viscountess Chaplin (by turn)*   V M K LITTLER

GRAFHAM (All Saints) *Ely 10*   P *Bp*   P-in-c A T SCHOFIELD

GRAFHAM (St Andrew)   Bramley and Grafham *Guildf*

GRAFTON, EAST (St Nicholas)   Wexcombe *Sarum*

GRAFTON FLYFORD (St John the Baptist)   Upton Snodsbury and Broughton Hackett etc *Worc*

GRAFTON REGIS (St Mary)   Stoke Bruerne w Grafton Regis and Alderton *Pet*

GRAFTON UNDERWOOD (St James the Apostle)   Cranford w Grafton Underwood and Twywell *Pet*

GRAHAME PARK (St Augustine) Conventional District *Lon 15*   C-in-c J S FAIRHEAD

GRAIN (St James) w Stoke *Roch 6*   P *DBP*   V A E NORRIS

GRAINSBY (St Nicholas) *Linc 10*   P *Personal Reps of C L E Haigh*   R R K EMM

GRAINTHORPE (St Clement)   Somercotes and Grainthorpe w Conisholme *Linc*

GRAMPOUND (St Nun)   Probus, Ladock and Grampound w Creed *Truro*

GRAMPOUND ROAD Mission Church   as above

GRANBOROUGH (St John the Baptist)   Schorne *Ox*

GRANBY (All Saints)   Cropwell Bishop w Colston Bassett, Granby etc *S'well*

GRANDBOROUGH (St Peter) w Willoughby and Flecknoe *Cov 6*   P *Bp*   P-in-c A J HOBSON

GRANGE (Holy Trinity)   Borrowdale *Carl*

GRANGE (St Andrew) *Ches 3*   P *Bp*   V D R FELIX

GRANGE FELL (not known)   Grange-over-Sands *Carl*

GRANGE MOOR (St Bartholomew)   Kirkheaton *Wakef*

GRANGE-OVER-SANDS (St Paul) *Carl 10*   P *Bp*   V A GIBSON

GRANGE PARK (St Peter) *Lon 18*   P *Bp*   V B M E WOODRUFF

GRANGE VILLA (St Columba)   W Pelton *Dur*

GRANGETOWN (St Aidan) *Dur 9*   P *V Ryhope*   V C COLLINS

GRANGETOWN (St Hilda of Whitby) *York 19*   P *Abp*   V C P HORTON, C R G S DEADMAN

GRANSDEN, GREAT (St Bartholomew) w LITTLE (St Peter and St Paul) *Ely 12*   P *Clare Coll Cam*   R R K D WATKINS-WRIGHT

GRANTCHESTER (St Andrew and St Mary) *Ely 7*   P *CCC Cam*   V J S BEER

GRANTHAM (St Anne) (St Wulfram) (Ascension) (Epiphany) *Linc 19*   P *Bp*   TR R P REISS, TV P J MANDER, I R SHELTON, G A PLUMB, C P CRAVEN, TM P N WEBB, C J A KIRBY, NSM J T FARLEY, V A CORY, F H LONG

GRANVILLES WOOTTON (St Mary the Virgin)   Dungeon Hill *Sarum*

GRAPPENHALL (St Wilfrid) *Ches 4* **P** *P G Greenall Esq*
Hon C S BECKETT, **NSM** M JONES
GRASBY (All Saints) *Linc 5* **P** *Lord Tennyson*
P-in-c D SAUNDERS
GRASMERE (St Oswald) *Carl 10* **P** *Qu Coll Ox*
R K E WOOD
GRASSENDALE (St Mary) *Liv 4* **P** *Trustees*
V G D BUCKLAND
GRATELEY (St Leonard) Amport, Grateley, Monxton
and Quarley *Win*
GRATWICH (St Mary the Virgin) Kingstone w
Gratwich *Lich*
GRAVELEY (St Botolph) w Papworth St Agnes w Yelling
and Toseland *Ely 1* **P** *Jes Coll Cam,*
T J H Sperling Esq, and Ld Chan (by turn)
R T J MARKS
GRAVELEY (St Mary) Gt and Lt Wymondley w
Graveley and Chivesfield *St Alb*
GRAVELLY HILL (All Saints) *Birm 6* **P** *Bp*
V D E NEWSOME
GRAVENEY (All Saints) Preston next Faversham,
Goodnestone and Graveney *Cant*
GRAVENHURST, UPPER (St Giles) w Lower Gravenhurst
St Alb 22 **P** *Bp* **P-in-c** P J SWINDELLS
GRAVESEND (Holy Family) w Ifield *Roch 4* **P** *Bp and*
Lt-Col F B Edmeades (jt) **R** B TETLEY,
Par Dn J P LITTLEWOOD, **NSM** B E WEST
GRAVESEND (St Aidan) *Roch 4* **P** *Bp* **V** B PEARSON
GRAVESEND (St George) *Roch 4* **P** *Bp*
R S F SIDEBOTHAM, **C** R J BRALEY, P J DAVIES
GRAVESEND (St Mary) *Roch 4* **P** *R Gravesend*
V C W KITCHENER
GRAYINGHAM (St Radegunda) *Linc 6* **P** *Bp*
R D I WALKER
GRAYRIGG (St John the Evangelist), Old Hutton and New
Hutton *Carl 9* **P** *V Kendal* **Dn-in-c** A M R STOCKLEY
GRAYS THURROCK (St Peter and St Paul) *Chelmsf 16*
P *DBP* **TR** R J WIGGS, **TV** P E PIMENTEL,
C M J SMITH, **Par Dn** M IVIN
GRAYSHOTT (St Luke) *Guildf 3* **P** *Bp* **V** W J MEYER
GRAYSWOOD (All Saints) *Guildf 4* **P** *Bp*
P-in-c A J SHAW
GRAYTHWAITE (Mission Room) Hawkshead and
Low Wray w Sawrey *Carl*
GRAZELEY (Holy Trinity) Beech Hill, Grazeley and
Spencers Wood *Ox*
GREASBROUGH (St Mary) *Sheff 6* **P** *Sir Stephen*
Hastings **V** P J ANDERSON, **C** K J E HALE
GREASBY (St Nicholas) Frankby w Greasby *Ches*
GREASLEY (St Mary) *S'well 4* **P** *Bp* **V** T A JOYCE,
C M R PEATMAN
GREAT: *see also under substantive place names*
GREAT CAMBRIDGE ROAD (St John the Baptist and
St James) *Lon 19* **P** *D&C St Paul's* **V** P B LYONS
GREAT GLEN (St Cuthbert), Stretton Magna and Wistow
cum Newton Harcourt *Leic 5* **P** *Bp and Hon Ann*
Brooks (jt) **V** J F WELLINGTON, **Hon C** C E SOUTHALL
GREAT MOOR (St Saviour) Stockport St Sav *Ches*
GREATER: *see under substantive place names*
GREATFORD (St Thomas à Becket) Uffington *Linc*
GREATHAM (not known) Amberley w N Stoke and
Parham, Wiggonholt etc *Chich*
GREATHAM (St John the Baptist) *Dur 13* **P** *Greatham*
Hosp **V** E C WYNGARD
GREATHAM (St John the Baptist) w Empshott *Portsm 5*
P *Bp and Personal Reps Mrs F E Luttrell-West (alt)*
P-in-c G H WOOLVERIDGE
GREATSTONE (St Peter) Lydd *Cant*
GREATWORTH (St Peter) and Marston St Lawrence w
Warkorth and Thenford *Pet 1* **P** *Bp (2 turns),* DBP
(1 turn) **R** *Vacant* Banbury (0295) 711696
GREAVE FOLD (Holy Innocents) Chadkirk *Ches*
GREEN HAMMERTON (St Thomas) Whixley w Green
Hammerton *Ripon*
GREEN HAWORTH (St Clement) Accrington *Blackb*
GREEN HEATH (St Saviour) Hednesford *Lich*
GREEN STREET GREEN (St Mary) *Roch 15* **P** *Bp*
V P MILLER, **C** A M LEIGH, **NSM** R S LEIGH
GREEN VALE (Holy Trinity) Stockton Green Vale H
Trin CD *Dur*
GREENFIELD (St Mary) *Man 18* **P** *Bp* **V** L R TOONE,
C F J JONES
GREENFIELDS (United Church) Shrewsbury All SS w
St Mich *Lich*
GREENFORD (Holy Cross) (St Edward the Confessor)
Lon 22 **P** *K Coll Cam* **R** N RICHARDSON,
Par Dn S J ROGERS
GREENFORD, NORTH (All Hallows) *Lon 22* **P** *Bp*
NSM R W BUCKLEY

GREENGATES (St John the Evangelist) *Bradf 3* **P** *D&C*
V T COLLIN
GREENHAM (St Mary the Virgin) *Ox 14* **P** *Bp*
V R E F CANHAM
GREENHAM (St Peter) Wellington and Distr *B & W*
GREENHEAD (St Cuthbert) Haltwhistle and
Greenhead *Newc*
GREENHILL (St John the Baptist) *Lon 23* **P** *Bp, Adn,*
and V Harrow St Mary (jt) **V** K F TOOVEY,
C K A ROBUS
GREENHILL (St Peter) *Sheff 2* **P** *Bp* **V** R C PANNELL,
C K A MITCHELL
GREENHITHE (St Mary) *Roch 2* **P** *Ch Soc Trust and*
Canon T L Livermore (jt) **R** R D BARRON
GREENHOW HILL (St Mary) Upper Nidderdale *Ripon*
GREENLANDS (St Anne) *Blackb 9* **P** *Bp and*
V Blackpool St Stephen (jt) **V** S L JONES
GREENLANDS (St John the Evangelist) Ipsley *Worc*
GREENS NORTON (St Bartholomew) w Bradden and
Lichborough *Pet 5* **P** *J E Grant-Ives Esq (1 turn),* The
Crown *(3 turns), and Melanesian Miss Trust (1 turn)*
R J D V EVANS
GREENSIDE (St John) *Dur 5* **P** *R Ryton w Hedgefield*
V R S WILSON
GREENSTEAD (St Andrew) (St Edmund's Church Hall)
(St Matthew) *Chelmsf 19* **P** *Ld Chan*
P-in-c B L BIRCHMORE, **C** I L MORT,
Par Dn M J WYLIE-SMITH
GREENSTEAD GREEN (St James Apostle) Halstead
St Andr w H Trin and Greenstead Green *Chelmsf*
GREENSTED-JUXTA-ONGAR (St Andrew) w Stanford
Rivers *Chelmsf 6* **P** *Bp Lon and Duchy of Lanc (alt)*
R T A GARDINER
GREENWICH (St Alfege w St Peter and St Paul) *S'wark 1*
P *The Crown* **V** G S HARCOURT,
C G A BERRIMAN, I SALONIA, **NSM** K N SHACKELL
GREENWICH, EAST (Christ Church) (St Andrew and
St Michael) *S'wark 1* **P** *V Greenwich St Alphege*
V I H OWERS, **C** T W HURCOMBE,
Par Dn J UPTON, A H STEVENS
GREET (St Bede) Sparkhill w Greet and Sparkbrook
Birm
GREETE (St James) Burford II w Greete and Hope
Bagot *Heref*
GREETHAM (All Saints) Fulletby w Greetham and
Ashby Puerorum *Linc*
GREETHAM (St Mary the Virgin) and Thistleton w
Stretton and Clipsham *Pet 14* **P** *Bp and Sir David*
Davenport-Handley (alt) **V** P TOWNSEND
GREETLAND (St Thomas) and West Vale *Wakef 2*
P *V Halifax* **V** D J HUMPHRIES
GREETWELL (All Saints) Cherry Willingham w
Greetwell *Linc*
GREINTON (St Michael and All Angels) *B & W 5* **P** *Bp*
R D C EVANS
GRENDON (All Saints) Baddesley Ensor w Grendon
Birm
GRENDON (St Mary) Yardley Hastings, Denton and
Grendon etc *Pet*
GRENDON BISHOP (St John the Baptist) Bredenbury
w Grendon Bishop and Wacton etc *Heref*
GRENDON UNDERWOOD (St Leonard) Swan *Ox*
GRENOSIDE (St Mark) *Sheff 3* **P** *Bp and*
V Ecclesfield (jt) **V** R W JACKSON, **C** P DOBSON
GRESHAM (All Saints) *Nor 7* **P** *Guild of All So*
P-in-c D F HAYDEN
GRESLEY (St George and St Mary) *Derby 16*
P *Simeon's Trustees* **V** D A HESLOP, **Par Dn** A LOVE
GRESSENHALL (Assumption of the Blessed Virgin Mary)
w Longham w Wendling and Bittering Parva *Nor 19*
P *Ld Chan (1 turn), J E T H Dodson Esq (2 turns)*
R J E BELHAM
GRESSINGHAM (St John the Evangelist) Whittington
w Arkholme and Gressingham *Blackb*
GRETTON (Christ Church) Winchcombe, Gretton,
Sudeley Manor etc *Glouc*
GRETTON (St James the Great) w Rockingham and
Caldecote *Pet 9* **P** *Bp (2 turns), Comdr L M M*
Saunders-Watson (1 turn) **V** G H RICHMOND
GREWELTHORPE (St James) Fountains Gp *Ripon*
GREYSTEAD (St Luke) Bellingham/Otterburn Gp
Newc
GREYSTOKE (St Andrew), Matterdale, Mungrisdale and
Watermillock *Carl 4* **P** *DBP* **TR** D C ELLIS,
C R WALKER
GREYSTONES (St Gabriel) Ecclesall *Sheff*
GREYSTONES (St Gabriel) *Sheff 2* **P** *Provost Sheff*
V P W BECKLEY

GREYWELL (St Mary)   Newnham w Nately Scures w Mapledurwell etc *Win*

GRIMEHILLS (St Mary Mission Church)   Darwen St Barn *Blackb*

GRIMETHORPE (St Luke) *Wakef 7*   **P** *Bp* **V** A S MACPHERSON

GRIMLEY (St Bartholomew) w Holt *Worc 3*   **P** *Bp* **P-in-c** C P COPELAND

GRIMOLDBY (St Edith)   Mid Marsh Gp *Linc*

GRIMSARGH (St Michael) *Blackb 14*   **P** *R Preston* **V** A J HASLAM

GRIMSBURY (St Leonard)   Banbury *Ox*

GRIMSBY (All Saints) *Linc 9*   **P** *Bp*   **P-in-c** M D LILES

GRIMSBY (St Augustine of Hippo) *Linc 9*   **P** *TR Gt Grimsby SS Mary and Jas*   **V** M C KING

GRIMSBY, GREAT (St Andrew w St Luke) *Linc 9*   **P** *Bp* **Dn-in-c** M M E ISAM

GRIMSBY, GREAT (St Mary and St James) (St Hugh) (St Mark) (St Martin) *Linc 9*   **P** *Bp*   **TR** M O HUNTER, **TV** G A CURTIS, P R DOWN,   **C** M B WHITAKER, **Hon C** M D LILES, E MARSHALL

GRIMSBY, LITTLE (St Edith)   Fotherby *Linc*

GRIMSTEAD, EAST (Holy Trinity)   Alderbury Team *Sarum*

GRIMSTEAD, WEST (St John)   as above

GRIMSTON (St Botolph), Congham and Roydon *Nor 23*   **P** *Qu Coll Cam, Bp, and G Howard Esq (jt)* **R** W A HOWARD,   **NSM** S E HEWER

GRIMSTON (St John the Baptist)   Ab Kettleby Gp *Leic*

GRIMSTON, NORTH (St Nicholas)   Settrington w N Grimston and Wharram *York*

GRINDALE (St Nicholas)   Burton Fleming w Fordon, Grindale etc *York*

GRINDLEFORD (St Helen)   Eyam *Derby*

GRINDLETON (St Ambrose)   Bolton by Bowland w Grindleton *Bradf*

GRINDON (All Saints)   Calton, Cauldon, Grindon and Waterfall *Lich*

GRINDON (St James) and Stillington *Dur 16*   **P** *Bp* **V** M GOODALL

GRINDON (St Oswald)   Sunderland Pennywell St Thos *Dur*

GRINGLEY-ON-THE-HILL (St Peter and St Paul) *S'well 1*   **P** *Bp*   **V** I R BAKER

GRINSDALE (St Kentigern)   Burgh-by-Sands and Kirkbampton w Kirkandrews etc *Carl*

GRINSHILL (All Saints)   Astley, Clive, Grinshill and Hadnall *Lich*

GRINSTEAD, EAST (St Mary the Virgin) *Chich 7*   **P** *Bp* **V** G BOND

GRINSTEAD, EAST (St Swithun) *Chich 7*   **P** *Bp* **V** J R BROWN,   **C** E J POLLARD, R P M ARRANDALE, **NSM** I M EDYE

GRINSTEAD, WEST (St George) *Chich 8*   **P** *Bp* **R** W E M HARRIS

GRINTON (St Andrew)   Swaledale *Ripon*

GRISTHORPE (St Thomas)   Filey *York*

GRISTON (St Peter and St Paul)   Caston w Griston, Merton, Thompson etc *Nor*

GRITTLETON (St Mary the Virgin)   Stanton St Quintin, Hullavington, Grittleton etc *Bris*

GRIZEBECK (The Good Shepherd)   Kirkby Ireleth *Carl*

GROBY (St Philip and St James)   Ratby w Groby *Leic*

GROOMBRIDGE (St John the Evangelist)   Speldhurst w Groombridge and Ashurst *Roch*

GROOMBRIDGE, NEW (St Thomas) *Chich 19*   **P** *R Withyham*   **V** C M HENLEY

GROSMONT (St Matthew)   Egton w Grosmont *York*

GROSVENOR CHAPEL (no dedication) (Chapel of Ease in the parish of Hanover Square St George w St Mark) *Lon 3*   **C-in-c** A W MARKS

GROTON (St Bartholomew)   Edwardstone w Groton and Lt Waldingfield *St E*

GROVE (St Helen)   E Markham w Askham, Headon w Upton and Grove *S'well*

GROVE (St John the Baptist) *Ox 19*   **P** *D&C Windsor* **V** R J FRENCH,   **C** K M SINGLETON

GROVEHILL (Resurrection)   Hemel Hempstead *St Alb*

GRUNDISBURGH (St Mary the Virgin)   Boulge w Burgh and Grundisburgh *St E*

GUARLFORD (St Mary)   Newland, Guarlford and Madresfield *Worc*

GUERNSEY (Holy Trinity) *Win 14*   **P** *Trustees* **V** P C DELIGHT

GUERNSEY L'Islet (St Mary)   Guernsey St Sampson *Win*

GUERNSEY (St Andrew de la Pommeraye) *Win 14*   **P** *The Crown*   **R** J A GUILLE

GUERNSEY (St John the Evangelist) *Win 14*   **P** *Trustees* **V** P HENRY

GUERNSEY (St Marguerite de la Foret) *Win 14*   **P** *The Crown*   **R** W A CANHAM

GUERNSEY (St Martin) *Win 14*   **P** *The Crown* **R** F M TRICKEY

GUERNSEY (St Matthew) *Win 14*   **P** *R St Marie du Castel* **V** N GRIFFITHS

GUERNSEY (St Michel du Valle) *Win 14*   **P** *The Crown* **R** P SIMPSON

GUERNSEY (St Peter Port) *Win 14*   **P** *The Crown* **R** J R FENWICK,   **NSM** G J BARRETT

GUERNSEY (St Philippe de Torteval) *Win 14*   **P** *The Crown*   **R** A F RIDLEY

GUERNSEY (St Pierre du Bois) *Win 14*   **P** *The Crown* **R** A F RIDLEY

GUERNSEY (St Sampson) *Win 14*   **P** *The Crown* **R** J E IRONSIDE

GUERNSEY (St Saviour) (Chapel of St Apolline) *Win 14*   **P** *The Crown*   **R** L G CRASKE

GUERNSEY (St Stephen) *Win 14*   **P** *R St Peter Port* **V** M C MILLARD,   **Hon C** H S RIDGE

GUERNSEY (Ste Marie du Castel) *Win 14*   **P** *The Crown* **R** M R STARR

GUESTLING (St Lawrence) and Pett *Chich 20*   **P** *Bp and DBP (alt)*   **R** N J C GREENFIELD

GUESTWICK (St Peter)   Foulsham w Hindolveston and Guestwick *Nor*

GUILDEN MORDEN (St Mary)   Shingay Gp of Par *Ely*

GUILDEN SUTTON (St John the Baptist)   Plemstall w Guilden Sutton *Ches*

GUILDFORD (All Saints) *Guildf 5*   **P** *Bp*   **V** *Vacant* Guildford (0483) 572006

GUILDFORD (Christ Church) *Guildf 5*   **P** *Simeon's Trustees*   **NSM** D H BEVIS

GUILDFORD (Holy Spirit)   Burpham *Guildf*

GUILDFORD (Holy Trinity) (St Mary) (St Michael) *Guildf 5*   **P** *Bp*   **R** K W STEVENSON,   **C** S A BAKER, **NSM** J K MOORE, J G TODD

GUILDFORD (St Clare)   Westborough *Guildf*

GUILDFORD (St Francis)   as above

GUILDFORD (St Luke)   Burpham *Guildf*

GUILDFORD (St Nicolas) *Guildf 5*   **P** *Bp*   **R** B TAYLOR

GUILDFORD (St Peter)   Stoke Hill *Guildf*

GUILDFORD (St Saviour) *Guildf 5*   **P** *Simeon's Trustees* **R** D J BRACEWELL

GUILSBOROUGH (St Ethelreda) w Hollowell and Cold Ashby *Pet 2*   **P** *Mrs G S Collier (2 turns) and Bp (1 turn)*   **V** W G GIBBS

GUISBOROUGH (St Nicholas) *York 17*   **P** *Abp* **R** P L BISHOP,   **C** N A BAILEY

GUISELEY (St Oswald King and Martyr) w Esholt *Bradf 4*   **P** *Patr Bd*   **TR** G L SANDERS,   **C** R MARSH

GUIST (St Andrew)   Twyford w Guist w Bintry w Themelthorpe etc *Nor*

GUITING POWER (St Michael)   The Guitings, Cutsdean and Farmcote *Glouc*

GUITINGS, Cutsdean and Farmcote, The *Glouc 17*   **P** *E R Cochrane Esq and Ch Ch Ox (alt)*   **V** S WILSON

GULDEFORD, EAST (St Mary)   Rye *Chich*

GULVAL (St Gulval) *Truro 5*   **P** *Ld Chan*   **V** A K TORRY

GULWORTHY (St Paul)   Tavistock and Gulworthy *Ex*

GUMLEY (St Helen)   Foxton w Gumley and Laughton and Lubenham *Leic*

GUNBY (St Nicholas)   Witham Gp *Linc*

GUNBY (St Peter)   Welton-le-Marsh w Gunby *Linc*

GUNHOUSE (otherwise Gunness) (St Barnabas) w Burringham *Linc 4*   **P** *Bp Lon*   **R** *Vacant* Scunthorpe (0724) 783550

GUNN CHAPEL (Holy Name)   Swimbridge and W Buckland *Ex*

GUNNESS (St Barnabas)   Gunhouse w Burringham *Linc*

GUNNISLAKE (St Anne)   Calstock *Truro*

GUNTHORPE (St John the Baptist)   Lowdham *S'well*

GUNTHORPE (St Mary) w Bale w Field Dalling, Saxlingham and Sharrington *Nor 22*   **P** *Keble Coll Ox, MMCET, Bp, and DBP (by turn)*   **R** M R WARD

GUNTON St Peter (St Benedict) *Nor 15*   **P** *CPAS* **R** R J CLARKE

GUNWALLOE (St Winwalloe)   Cury and Gunwalloe w Mawgan *Truro*

GUSSAGE (St Andrew)   Handley w Gussage St Andrew and Pentridge *Sarum*

GUSSAGE ALL SAINTS (All Saints)   Tollard Royal w Farnham, Gussage St Michael etc *Sarum*

GUSSAGE ST MICHAEL (St Michael)   as above

GUSTARD WOOD (St Peter)   Wheathampstead *St Alb*

GUSTON (St Martin of Tours)   Whitfield w Guston *Cant*

GUYHIRN (St Mary Magdalene) w Ring's End *Ely 19*
  P *Bp*   **V** R J SEAMAN
GWEEK (Mission Church) Constantine *Truro*
GWENNAP (St Weneppa) St Stythians w
  Perranarworthal and Gwennap *Truro*
GWINEAR (St Winnear) Phillack w Gwithian and
  Gwinear *Truro*
GWITHIAN (St Gwithian) as above
HABBERLEY (St Mary) *Heref 13*   **P** *Bp*   **R** *Vacant*
HABERGHAM EAVES (St Matthew the Apostle)
  Burnley (Habergham Eaves) St Matt w H Trin *Blackb*
HABROUGH Group, The (St Margaret) *Linc 10*   **P** *DBP*
  V T R SHEPHERD
HABTON, GREAT (St Chad) Kirby Misperton w
  Normanby, Edston and Salton *York*
HACCOMBE (St Blaise) Stoke-in-Teignhead w Combe-
  in-Teignhead etc *Ex*
HACCONBY (St Andrew) Morton w Hacconby *Linc*
HACHESTON (St Andrew) Campsea Ashe w
  Marlesford, Parham and Hacheston *St E*
HACKBRIDGE and North Beddington (All Saints)
  S'wark 25   **P** *Bp*   **V** W M MULLENGER
HACKENTHORPE (Christ Church) *Sheff 2*   **P** *Bp*
  V C L NORWOOD
HACKFORD (St Mary the Virgin) Morley w Deopham,
  Hackford, Wicklewood etc *Nor*
HACKINGTON (St Stephen) *Cant 3*   **P** *Adn Cant*
  R M J CHANDLER
HACKNESS (St Peter) w Harwood Dale *York 16*   **P** *Lord*
  Derwent   **V** *Vacant*
HACKNEY Mount Pleasant Lane (St Matthew) Upper
  Clapton St Matt *Lon*
HACKNEY (St James) (St John) *Lon 5*   **P** *Patr Bd*
  TR W R HURDMAN,   **TV** N R J FUNNELL,
  C S M THEAKSTON, H D J RAYMENT-PICKARD,
  Par Dn C F A B J LE VAY
HACKNEY (St Thomas) Stamford Hill St Thos *Lon*
HACKNEY, OVER (St Philip and St James) Darley
  Derby
HACKNEY, SOUTH (St John) (Christ Church) *Lon 5*
  P *Lord Amherst*   **R** E H JONES,
  Par Dn P A FARQUHAR
HACKNEY, SOUTH (St Michael and All Angels) London
  Fields w Haggerston (St Paul) *Lon 5*   **P** *R S Hackney*
  St Jo w Ch Ch   **V** C J BRICE
HACKNEY, WEST St Barnabas (St Paul) *Lon 5*   **P** *Bp*
  R F A PRESTON
HACKNEY MARSH (All Souls) *Lon 5*   **P** *Patr Bd*
  TV D N WINTERBURN,   **C** P W STONE,   **NSM** B N MANN
HACKNEY WICK (St Mary of Eton) (St Augustine) *Lon 5*
  P *Eton Coll*   **V** D G ROSS
HACKTHORN (St Michael and All Angels) w Cold
  Hanworth *Linc 3*   **P** *Mrs B K Eley*   **V** R J WELLS
HADDENHAM (Holy Trinity) *Ely 14*   **P** *Adn Ely*
  V M P WADSWORTH
HADDENHAM (St Mary the Virgin) w Cuddington,
  Kingsey and Aston Sandford *Ox 20*   **P** *D&C Roch*
  V D W A GREGG,   **Hon C** P McEACHRAN
HADDLESEY (St John the Baptist) Haddlesey w
  Hambleton and Birkin *York*
HADDISCOE (St Mary) Raveningham *Nor*
HADDLESEY w Hambleton and Birkin *York 6*   **P** *Abp*
  and Simeon's Trustees (jt)   **R** A G GREENHOUGH
HADDON (St Mary) Stilton w Denton and Caldecote
  etc *Ely*
HADDON, EAST (St Mary the Virgin) Church
  Brampton, Chapel Brampton, Harleston etc *Pet*
HADDON, OVER (St Anne) Bakewell *Derby*
HADDON, WEST (All Saints) w Winwick and
  Ravensthorpe *Pet 2*   **P** *DBP*   **V** D STAPLES
HADFIELD (St Andrew) *Derby 6*   **P** *Bp*   **V** A BUCKLEY
HADHAM, LITTLE (St Cecilia) w Albury *St Alb 4*
  P *Bp Lon*   **R** J TAPLIN
HADHAM, MUCH (St Andrew) *St Alb 4*   **P** *Bp Lon*
  R M A McADAM,   **Hon C** J H S SPREAD
HADLEIGH (St Barnabas) *Chelmsf 12*   **P** *Bp*
  V J G AMBROSE
HADLEIGH (St James the Less) *Chelmsf 12*
  P *Dr P W M Copeman*   **R** A J MORLEY
HADLEIGH (St Mary) w Layham and Shelley *St E 2*
  P *Abp and St Jo Coll Cam (alt)*   **R** G W ARRAND,
  C S H COWLEY, T P B BREENE,
  NSM J M WILLIS, J H DOSSOR
HADLEY (Holy Trinity) *Lich 28*   **P** *Bp, Adn Salop,*
  V Wrockwardine, R Kynnersley, and V Wellington w
  Eyton (jt)   **V** W M YOUNG
HADLEY WOOD (St Paul) Enfield Ch Ch Trent Park
  Lon

HADLOW (St Mary) *Roch 10*   **P** *Exors Miss I N King*
  V G LANE,   **Hon Par Dn** L M LANE
HADLOW DOWN (St Mark) Buxted and Hadlow
  Down *Chich*
HADNALL (St Mary Magdalene) Astley, Clive,
  Grinshill and Hadnall *Lich*
HADSTOCK (St Botolph) Ashdon w Hadstock *Chelmsf*
HADZOR w Oddingley (St James) Bowbrook S *Worc*
HAGBOURNE (St Andrew) Blewbury, Hagbourne and
  Upton *Ox*
HAGGERSTON (All Saints) *Lon 5*   **P** *Ld Chan*
  P-in-c J F WILLARD,   **C** R J S PEARSON
HAGGERSTON (St Chad) *Lon 5*   **P** *The Crown*
  V D H T LEE
HAGLEY (St John the Baptist) *Worc 11*   **P** *Viscount*
  Cobham   **R** A W BROOKSBANK,   **NSM** H G PLATT
HAGLEY, WEST (St Saviour) Hagley *Worc*
HAGNABY (St Andrew) Marden Hill Gp *Linc*
HAGWORTHINGHAM (Holy Trinity) as above
HAIGH (St David) *Liv 14*   **P** *R Wigan*   **V** G J T TAYLOR
HAIL WESTON (St Nicholas) *Ely 12*   **P** *Mert Coll Ox*
  R W N BROOK
HAILE (not known) Egremont and Haile *Carl*
HAILES (Chapel) Toddington, Stanton, Didbrook w
  Hailes etc *Glouc*
HAILEY (St John the Evangelist) Witney *Ox*
HAILSHAM (St Mary) *Chich 16*   **P** *Ch Soc Trust*
  V R G H PORTHOUSE,   **C** T R N JONES, A W EVERETT
HAINAULT (St Paul) *Chelmsf 7*   **P** *Bp*
  V M W LEARMOUTH
HAINFORD (All Saints) Hevingham w Hainford and
  Stratton Strawless *Nor*
HAINTON (St Mary) Barkwith Gp *Linc*
HALA (St Paul's Centre) Scotforth *Blackb*
HALAM (St Michael) Edingley w Halam *S'well*
HALBERTON (St Andrew) Sampford Peverell,
  Uplowman, Holcombe Rogus etc *Ex*
HALDEN, HIGH (St Mary the Virgin) Bethersden w
  High Halden *Cant*
HALDENS (Christ the King) Digswell and Panshanger
  St Alb
HALE (St David) Timperley *Ches*
HALE (St John the Evangelist) *Guildf 3*   **P** *Bp*
  C R JACKSON, J A PATERSON
HALE (St Mary) *Liv 13*   **P** *Trustees*   **V** N J EDWARDS
HALE (St Mary) w South Charford *Win 8*
  P *P N Hickman Esq*   **R** J STANLEY-SMITH
HALE (St Peter) and Ashley *Ches 10*   **P** *V Bowdon*
  V D ASHWORTH,   **Par Dn** D C P MOORE,
  NSM C SQUIRE
HALE, GREAT (St John the Baptist) Helpringham w
  Hale *Linc*
HALE, UPPER (St Mark) Hale *Guildf*
HALEBANK (St Mary Mission) as above
HALES (St Mary) *Lich 24*   **P** *R N C Hall Esq*
  V A D KEAY
HALESOWEN (St John the Baptist) *Worc 9*   **P** *Patr Bd*
  TR J K KIMBER,
  TV S R BUCKLEY, B A L CAMP, G S JOHNSTON,
  C D G MOSS,   **Hon C** C A KENT
HALESWORTH (St Mary) w Linstead, Chediston, Holton
  St Peter, Blyford, Spexhall, Wissett and Walpole *St E 15*
  P *Ld Chan and DBP (alt)*   **TR** M G T WALKEY,
  TV J M KINCHIN-SMITH, P B ALLAN
HALEWOOD (St Nicholas) (St Mary) *Liv 4*   **P** *Bp*
  TR J M BURGESS,   **TV** J H TYNDALL,
  NSM C CRITCHLEY
HALFORD (Our Blessed Lady) Alderminster and
  Halford *Cov*
HALFORD (St Thomas) Sibdon Carwood w Halford
  Heref
HALFWAY (St Peter) Minster in Sheppey *Cant*
HALIFAX Haley Hill (All Souls) *Wakef 4*   **P** *Simeon's*
  Trustees   **P-in-c** A P BOWSHER
HALIFAX (St Anne in the Grove) *Wakef 2*   **P** *V Halifax*
  V M J HALL
HALIFAX (St Augustine) *Wakef 4*   **P** *Trustees*
  V J H G BUNKER,   **NSM** R C SWINDELL
HALIFAX (St Hilda) *Wakef 4*   **P** *Bp*   **V** J C WIDDOWS
HALIFAX (St James and St Mary) (St John the Baptist)
  Wakef 4   **P** *The Crown*   **TR** R S GIBSON,
  TV M R BRUNDLE
HALIFAX (St John the Baptist in the Wilderness) *Wakef 3*
  P *V Halifax*   **V** *Vacant*   Halifax (0422) 882572
HALIFAX (St Jude) *Wakef 4*   **P** *Trustees*
  V D R G LOCKYER
HALL GREEN (Ascension) *Birm 13*   **P** *Bp, V Yardley,*
  and Vice-Chmn of PCC (jt)   **V** J G RUSSELL,
  Par Dn K M RICKETTS

HALL GREEN (St Peter) *Birm 8*   **P** *Bp*
  V R BROOKSTEIN, **C** K M ROBERTS
HALL STREET (St Andrew)   Stockport St Mary *Ches*
HALLAM, WEST (St Wilfred) and Mapperley *Derby 13*
  P *Bp* **R** E C LYONS, **Hon C** S KRZEMINSKI,
  NSM S G WATHEN
**HALLATON (St Michael and All Angels) w Horninghold
  and Allexton, Tugby and East Norton and Slawston**
  Leic 4   **P** *Bp, DBP, and E Brudenell Esq (jt)*
  R J ADAMS
HALLING (St John the Baptist)   Cuxton and Halling
  Roch
**HALLINGBURY, GREAT (St Giles) (St Andrew) and
  LITTLE (St Mary the Virgin)** *Chelmsf 3*   **P** *Bp and
  Govs Charterhouse (jt)*   **R** *Vacant*   Bishop's Stortford
  (0279) 723341
HALLIWELL (St Luke) *Man 9*   **P** *MMCET*
  V S T REID, **Hon C** E M CULBERTSON
HALLIWELL (St Margaret) *Man 9*   **P** *Trustees*
  V T E D THOMAS
HALLIWELL (St Paul) *Man 9*   **P** *Ch Soc Trust*
  V J HURST
**HALLIWELL (St Peter) (Barrow Bridge Mission)
  (St Andrew's Mission Church)** *Man 9*   **P** *Trustees*
  V R F OLDFIELD,
  C G HARPER, P J RAWLINGS, J A MINNS
HALLIWELL (St Thomas)   Bolton St Thos *Man*
HALLOUGHTON (St James)   Thurgarton w
  Hoveringham and Bleasby etc *S'well*
HALLOW (St Philip and St James) *Worc 3*   **P** *Bp*
  V J A DALE, **Hon Par Dn** J W BAINBRIDGE
HALLWOOD (St Mark) *Ches 3*   **P** *DBP*
  V M R GRAYSHON, **Par Dn** P B WAINWRIGHT
HALSALL (St Cuthbert) *Liv 11*   **P** *Brig D H Blundell-
  Hollinshead-Blundell*   **R** *Vacant*   Halsall (0704)
  840321
HALSE (Mission Church)   Brackley St Pet w St Jas *Pet*
HALSE (St James)   Milverton w Halse and Fitzhead
  B & W
HALSETOWN (St John's in the Fields) *Truro 5*   **P** *D&C*
  NSM J DIBB SMITH
HALSHAM (All Saints)   Keyingham w Ottringham,
  Halsham and Sunk Is *York*
**HALSTEAD (St Andrew) w Holy Trinity and Greenstead
  Green** *Chelmsf 22*   **P** *Bp*   **V** B E ROSE,
  C J M SUDDARDS, **Hon C** H HEATH
HALSTEAD (St Margaret)   Knockholt w Halstead *Roch*
HALSTOCK (St Mary)   Melbury *Sarum*
**HALSTOW, HIGH (St Margaret) (All Hallows) and Hoo
  (St Mary)** *Roch 6*   **P** *MMCET and Ch Soc Trust (jt)*
  R D G WILLEY
HALSTOW, LOWER (St Margaret)   Upchurch w Lower
  Halstow *Cant*
HALTER DEVIL (Mission Room)   Mugginton and
  Kedleston *Derby*
HALTON (St Andrew)   Corbridge w Halton and Newton
  Hall *Newc*
HALTON (St Mary) *Ches 3*   **P** *Bp*   **V** R J SAMUELS,
  Par Dn A E SAMUELS
HALTON (St Michael and All Angels) *Ox 28*   **P** *DBF*
  P-in-c A F MEYNELL
HALTON (St Oswald and St Cuthbert and King Alfwald)
  Corbridge w Halton and Newton Hall *Newc*
HALTON (St Wilfred) w Aughton *Blackb 15*   **P** *Exors of
  R T Sanderson Esq*   **R** O G VIGEON
HALTON, EAST (St Peter)   Habrough Gp *Linc*
HALTON, WEST (St Etheldreda)   Alkborough *Linc*
HALTON HOLGATE (St Andrew) *Linc 7*   **P** *Bp*
  R G ROBSON
HALTON QUAY (St Indract's Chapel)   St Dominic,
  Landulph and St Mellion w Pillaton *Truro*
HALTON WEST (Mission Church)   Hellifield *Bradf*
HALTWHISTLE (Holy Cross) and Greenhead *Newc 4*
  P *Bp*   **V** R B COOK
HALVERGATE (St Peter and St Paul)   Freethorpe w
  Wickhampton, Halvergate etc *Nor*
HALWELL (St Leonard) w Moreleigh *Ex 13*   **P** *Bp*
  (1 turn) and D&C (2 turns)   **V** R J LAW
HALWILL (St Peter and St James)   Ashwater, Halwill,
  Beaworthy, Clawton etc *Ex*
HAM (All Saints)   Wexcombe *Sarum*
HAM (St Andrew) *S'wark 14*   **P** *K Coll Cam*
  V D R MOORE, **Hon C** D S MARKWELL
HAM (St Barnabas Mission Church)   Combe St Nicholas
  w Wambrook *B & W*
HAM (St James the Less)   Plymouth St Jas Ham *Ex*
HAM (St Richard) *S'wark 15*   **P** *Bp*   **V** W G M LEWIS
**HAM, EAST (St Bartholomew) (St Mary Magdalene) w
  Upton Park St Alban** *Chelmsf 5*   **P** *Patr Bd*

  TR F R BENTLEY, **TV** D JONES, C L OWENS,
  C F B CAPIE, **NSM** S J M VETTERS
HAM, EAST (St George w St Ethelbert) *Chelmsf 5*   **P** *Bp*
  P-in-c P C TURNER
HAM, EAST (St Paul) *Chelmsf 5*   **P** *Ch Patr Trust*
  V M J LOWLES
HAM, HIGH (St Andrew)   Langport Area Chs *B & W*
HAM, LOW (Chapel)   as above
HAM, WEST (All Saints) *Chelmsf 5*   **P** *The Crown*
  P-in-c U E E J SCHARF, **C** J H SETTIMBA,
  Par Dn L M WILLIAMS
HAM, WEST (St Matthew)   Forest Gate St Sav w W
  Ham St Matt *Chelmsf*
HAMBLE LE RICE (St Andrew) *Win 9*   **P** *St Mary's Coll
  Win*   **V** K P BIDGOOD, **NSM** A R BEVIS
HAMBLEDEN VALLEY (St Mary the Virgin) *Ox 29*
  P *Bp, Viscount Hambleden, and Miss M Mackenzie (jt)*
  R P B BIBBY, **C** P R NICOLSON, **NSM** C L WODEHOUSE
HAMBLEDON (St Peter) *Guildf 4*   **P** *MMCET*
  P-in-c C J BLISSARD-BARNES
HAMBLEDON (St Peter and St Paul) *Portsm 1*
  P *Ld Chan*   **V** A V SEARLE-BARNES
**HAMBLETON (Blessed Virgin Mary) w Out Rawcliffe
  (St John)** *Blackb 10*   **P** *V Kirkham and V St Michaels-
  on-Wyre (jt)*   **V** P P F WARD
HAMBLETON (St Andrew)   Oakham, Hambleton,
  Egleton, Braunston and Brooke *Pet*
HAMBLETON (St Mary)   Haddlesey w Hambleton and
  Birkin *York*
HAMBRIDGE (St James the Less)   Ilton w Hambridge,
  Earnshill, Isle Brewers etc *B & W*
HAMER (All Saints) *Man 19*   **P** *Bp*   **V** B L CORDINGLEY
HAMERINGHAM (All Saints) w Scrafield and Winceby
  Linc 11   **P** *DBP*   **R** *Vacant*
HAMERTON (All Saints) *Ely 10*   **P** *G R Petherick Esq*
  P-in-c R W B van de WEYER, **NSM** I D GIBSON
HAMMER (St Michael)   Linchmere *Chich*
HAMMERFIELD (St Francis of Assisi)   Boxmoor St Jo
  St Alb
HAMMERSMITH (Holy Innocents) *Lon 9*   **P** *Bp*
  P-in-c M W GRANT, **NSM** G MORGAN
HAMMERSMITH (St John the Evangelist) *Lon 9*   **P**
  V Hammersmith St Paul   **P-in-c** M P ANDREW,
  NSM A H MEAD
HAMMERSMITH (St Luke) *Lon 9*   **P** *Bp*
  P-in-c S J A FARRER
HAMMERSMITH (St Matthew) *Lon 9*   **P** *Trustees*
  V G H CHIPLIN
**HAMMERSMITH (St Michael and St George) White City
  Estate Conventional District** *Lon 9*   **C-in-c** S J TAYLOR
HAMMERSMITH (St Paul) *Lon 9*   **P** *Bp*
  V R A M THACKER, **Hon Par Dn** M E WALLACE
HAMMERSMITH (St Peter) *Lon 9*   **P** *Bp*
  V G W F LANG
HAMMERSMITH (St Simon) *Lon 9*   **P** *Simeon's Trustees*
  V T J MARSHALL
HAMMERSMITH, NORTH (St Katherine) *Lon 9*   **P** *Bp*
  V J G ELLIS
HAMMERWICH (St John the Baptist) *Lich 2*   **P**
  Hammerwich Ch Lands Trustees   **V** J A FIELDING-FOX
HAMMERWOOD (St Stephen)   Cowden w
  Hammerwood *Chich*
HAMMOON (St Paul)   Childe Okeford, Manston,
  Hammoon and Hanford *Sarum*
HAMNISH (St Dubricius and All Saints)   Kimbolton w
  Hamnish and Middleton-on-the-Hill *Heref*
HAMPDEN, GREAT (St Mary Magdalene)   Prestwood
  and Gt Hampden *Ox*
HAMPDEN, LITTLE (not known)   Gt Missenden w
  Ballinger and Lt Hampden *Ox*
HAMPDEN PARK (St Mary-in-the-Park) *Chich 16*   **P** *Bp*
  V D G NEWMAN, **NSM** D J M CAFFYN
HAMPNETT (St George)   Northleach w Hampnett and
  Farmington *Glouc*
HAMPNETT, WEST (St Peter) *Chich 3*   **P** *Bp*   **V** *Vacant*
  Chichester (0243) 782704
HAMPRESTON (All Saints) *Sarum 10*   **P** *Patr Bd*
  TR R G L LUTHER, **TV** G D PRICE, **C** P W GIBBS,
  Hon Par Dn M A BARBER
HAMPSTEAD Belsize Park (St Peter)   Belsize Park *Lon*
HAMPSTEAD (Christ Church) *Lon 16*   **P** *Trustees*
  V C J F SCOTT
**HAMPSTEAD Downshire Hill (St John) Proprietary
  Chapel** *Lon 16*   **Min** D R CROAD
HAMPSTEAD (Emmanuel) West End *Lon 16*   **P** *Trustees*
  P-in-c P J GALLOWAY
HAMPSTEAD (St John) *Lon 16*   **P** *DBP*
  V P J W BUCKLER, **C** A D SPOTTISWOODE, M R COBB

HAMPSTEAD (St Stephen w All Hallows) *Lon 16* **P** *DBP and D&C Cant (jt)* **V** D N C HOULDING
HAMPSTEAD, SOUTH (St Saviour) *Lon 16*
　P *V Hampstead St Jo* **V** *Vacant* 071-722 4621
HAMPSTEAD, WEST (Holy Trinity) *Lon 16*
　P *MMCET* **V** M NOLAN
HAMPSTEAD, WEST (St Cuthbert) *Lon 16* **P** *Ch Trust Fund Trust* **P-in-c** C O MASON
HAMPSTEAD, WEST (St James) *Lon 16* **P** *Trustees*
　V P W WHEATLEY,
　C N H ASBRIDGE, J V SMITH, M R POOLE, S B ROBERTS
HAMPSTEAD, WEST (St Luke) *Lon 16* **P** *CPAS*
　V B J MORRISON
HAMPSTEAD GARDEN SUBURB (St Jude on the Hill)
　Lon 15 **P** *Bp* **V** J J BUNTING
HAMPSTEAD NORREYS (St Mary) Hermitage and Hampstead Norreys, Cold Ash etc *Ox*
HAMPSTHWAITE (St Thomas a Becket) *Ripon 1*
　P *Sir Cecil Aykroyd, Bt* **P-in-c** A G HUDSON
HAMPTON (All Saints) *Lon 10* **P** *Ld Chan*
　V W D F VANSTONE
HAMPTON (St Andrew) Herne Bay Ch Ch *Cant*
HAMPTON (St Andrew) *Worc 1* **P** *Ch Ch Ox*
　V R E MEYER, **C** R A BLOCK
HAMPTON (St Mary the Virgin) *Lon 10* **P** *The Crown*
　V J A ROGERS, **Par Dn** K M PLATT,
　Hon C G CLARKSON
HAMPTON BISHOP (St Andrew) and Mordiford w Dormington *Heref 4* **P** *Bp, A T Foley Esq, and Major R J Hereford (by turn)* **P-in-c** J D REESE
HAMPTON GAY (St Giles) Kirtlington w Bletchingdon, Weston etc *Ox*
HAMPTON HILL (St James) *Lon 10*
　P *V Hampton St Mary* **V** B LEATHARD
HAMPTON IN ARDEN (St Mary and St Bartholomew)
　Birm 13 **P** *Guild of All So* **V** A T W REYNOLDS
HAMPTON LOVETT (St Mary and All Saints) Elmley Lovett w Hampton Lovett and Elmbridge etc *Worc*
HAMPTON LUCY (St Peter ad Vincula) w Charlecote and Loxley *Cov 8* **P** *Sir Edmund Fairfax-Lucy, Bt (3 turns), Col A M H Gregory-Hood (1 turn)*
　R J H CORKE
HAMPTON POYLE (St Mary the Virgin) Kidlington w Hampton Poyle *Ox*
HAMPTON WICK (St John the Baptist) Teddington St Mark and Hampton Wick St Jo *Lon*
HAMSEY (St Peter) *Chich 18* **P** *Bp* **P-in-c** D BASTIDE
HAMSTALL RIDWARE (St Michael and All Angels) The Ridwares and Kings Bromley *Lich*
HAMSTEAD (St Bernard) *Birm 3* **P** *Bp*
　V J R BARNETT, **C** I COUTTS
HAMSTEAD (St Paul) *Birm 3* **P** *Bp* **V** J W MASDING,
　C G H P PETRICHER, **NSM** A BALL
HAMSTEAD MARSHALL (St Mary) W Woodhay w Enborne, Hampstead Marshall etc *Ox*
HAMSTEELS (St John the Baptist) *Dur 8* **P** *The Crown*
　V P G E TYLER
HAMSTERLEY (St James) (Mission Room) *Dur 10* **P** *Bp*
　V R D LEAMING
HAMWORTHY (St Gabriel) (St Michael) *Sarum 8*
　P *MMCET* **P-in-c** R J FORBES, **C** D J LLOYD,
　Par Dn J W POOLE
HANBOROUGH (St Peter and St Paul) and Freeland *Ox 9*
　P *St Jo Coll Ox* **R** C A RANDALL
HANBURY (St Mary the Virgin) Bowbrook N *Worc*
HANBURY (St Werburgh) w Newborough *Lich 20*
　P *DBP* **V** D C FELIX
HANCHURCH (Chapel of Ease) Trentham *Lich*
HANDCROSS (All Saints) Slaugham *Chich*
HANDFORTH (St Chad) *Ches 17* **P** *R Cheadle*
　V S P ISHERWOOD, **C** C A PELL
HANDLEY (All Saints) Tattenhall and Handley *Ches*
HANDLEY (St John the Baptist) Eckington w Handley and Ridgeway *Derby*
HANDLEY (St Mark) N Wingfield, Clay Cross and Pilsley *Derby*
HANDLEY (St Mary) w Gussage St Andrew and Pentridge
　Sarum 7 **P** *D&C Windsor and Earl of Shaftesbury (alt)*
　R R WOOD
HANDSACRE (St Luke) Armitage *Lich*
HANDSWORTH (St Andrew) *Birm 3* **P** *Bp*
　V D J COLLYER, **C** J AUSTEN
HANDSWORTH (St James) *Birm 3* **P** *Bp*
　V R J MORRIS, **C** J V MARCH
HANDSWORTH (St Mary) *Sheff 1* **P** *DBP* **R** B E LENG
HANDSWORTH (St Mary) (Epiphany) *Birm 3* **P** *Bp*
　R J C H TOMPKINS, **Hon C** T W WARD
HANDSWORTH (St Michael) (St Peter) *Birm 3* **P** *Bp*
　V D HARE, **NSM** D R FOUNTAIN

HANDSWORTH Woodhouse (St James) *Sheff 1* **P** *Bp*
　V B R CRANWELL, **Hon C** P E LAWRIE,
　NSM P S BAGSHAW
HANFORD (St Matthias) *Lich 19* **P** *Bp* **V** *Vacant*
　Stoke-on-Trent (0782) 657848
HANGER HILL (Ascension) and West Twyford (St Mary)
　Lon 22 **P** *Bp and DBP (jt)* **V** F J BERNARDI,
　C R BURGESS, **Hon C** J HOCKRIDGE
HANGING HEATON (St Paul) *Wakef 10* **P** *R Dewsbury*
　V S G D PARKINSON
HANGLETON (St Helen) (St Richard) *Chich 4* **P** *Bp*
　V J B A JOYCE, **C** T A MARTIN
HANHAM (Christ Church) (St George) *Bris 2* **P** *Bp*
　V J W FURST, **NSM** J A PLUMMER
HANKERTON (Holy Cross) Ashley, Crudwell, Hankerton, Long Newnton etc *Bris*
HANLEY (All Saints) Stoke-upon-Trent *Lich*
HANLEY Holy Evangelists (St Luke) *Lich 17* **P** *Bp*
　TR R P OWEN, **TV** A R OSBORNE, G W WHITTY,
　NSM C LOWNDES
HANLEY (St Chad) Hanley H Ev *Lich*
HANLEY CASTLE (St Mary), Hanley Swan and Welland
　Worc 5 **P** *Ld Chan and Sir Berwick Lechmere, Bt (alt)*
　V P E FAINT
HANLEY CHILD (St Michael and All Angels) Teme Valley S *Worc*
HANLEY ROAD (St Saviour) (St Paul) *Lon 6* **P** *CPAS*
　P-in-c J O HUTCHINSON
HANLEY SWAN (St Gabriel) Hanley Castle, Hanley Swan and Welland *Worc*
HANLEY WILLIAM (All Saints) Teme Valley S *Worc*
HANNAH (St Andrew) cum Hagnaby w Markby *Linc 8*
　P *Bp and Mrs E Smyth (alt)* **R** G I GEORGE-JONES
HANNEY, WEST (St James the Great) w East Hanney
　Ox 19 **P** *Bp* **P-in-c** A HOGG
HANNINGFIELD, EAST (All Saints) *Chelmsf 11*
　P *CPAS* **P-in-c** G H G PLASTOW
HANNINGFIELD, WEST (St Mary and St Edward)
　Chelmsf 11 **P** *DBP* **P-in-c** D J ATKINS,
　NSM B G HALL
HANNINGTON (All Saints) Baughurst, Ramsdell, Wolverton w Ewhurst etc *Win*
HANNINGTON (St John the Baptist) Highworth w Sevenhampton and Inglesham etc *Bris*
HANNINGTON (St Peter and St Paul) Walgrave w Hannington and Wold and Scaldwell *Pet*
HANOVER SQUARE (St George) (St Mark) *Lon 3* **P** *Bp*
　R W M ATKINS
HANSLOPE (St James the Great) w Castlethorpe *Ox 27*
　P *Bp* **V** C M G BEAKE
HANWELL (St Mary) (St Christopher) *Lon 22* **P** *Bp*
　R J H WEEKS, **Par Dn** J R LUCAS
HANWELL (St Mellitus w St Mark) *Lon 22* **P** *Bp*
　V R H WORMALD
HANWELL (St Peter) Horley w Hornton and Hanwell, Shenington etc *Ox*
HANWELL (St Thomas) *Lon 22* **P** *The Crown*
　V P A ANDREWS
HANWOOD, GREAT (St Thomas) *Heref 13* **P** *Lt-Col H de Grey-Warter* **R** P TOWNER
HANWORTH (All Saints) *Lon 11* **P** *Bp*
　V J A FLETCHER
HANWORTH (St Bartholomew) Roughton and Felbrigg, Metton, Sustead etc *Nor*
HANWORTH (St George) *Lon 11* **P** *Lee Abbey Trust*
　P-in-c J A FLETCHER, **C** P S WILLIAMSON
HANWORTH (St Richard of Chichester) *Lon 11* **P** *Bp*
　V A JACKSON
HAPPISBURGH (St Mary the Virgin) w Walcot, Hempstead, Lessingham and Eccles *Nor 10* **P** *Bp (3 turns), E Coll Cam (2 turns), K C Evans-Lombe Esq and Bp (1 turn)* **R** *Vacant* Walcott (0692) 313
HAPTON (St Margaret) Padiham *Blackb*
HAPTON (St Margaret) Wreningham *Nor*
HARBERTON (St Andrew) Diptford, N Huish, Harberton and Harbertonford *Ex*
HARBERTONFORD (St Peter) as above
HARBLEDOWN (St Michael and All Angels) *Cant 3*
　P *Abp* **R** J S TUNBRIDGE
HARBORNE (St Faith and St Laurence) *Birm 2* **P** *Bp*
　V I M MICHAEL, **NSM** T R BOTT
HARBORNE (St Peter) *Birm 2* **P** *Bp* **V** C J EVANS,
　Par Dn J K D FULLJAMES
HARBORNE HEATH (St John the Baptist) *Birm 2*
　P *Ch Soc Trust* **C** J M WHITE, P D HARDINGHAM
HARBOROUGH MAGNA (All Saints) *Cov 6* **P** *A H F W Boughton-Leigh Esq* **R** P S RUSSELL,
　NSM D J BAYFORD

HARBRIDGE (All Saints)   Ellingham and Harbridge and Ibsley *Win*

HARBURY (All Saints) and Ladbroke *Cov 10*   **P**   *Bp*   **R**   A S BROWE

HARBY (All Saints) w Thorney and North and South Clifton *S'well 3*   **P**   *Ld Chan and Bp (alt)*   **R**   M W BRIGGS

HARBY (St Mary the Virgin), Long Clawson and Hose *Leic 3*   **P**   *Duke of Rutland, Bp, and DBP (alt)*   **R**   S BAILEY

HARDEN (St Saviour) and Wilsden *Bradf 8*   **P**   *Bp, Adn, V Bradf, and R Bingley Esq (jt)*   **V**   J C PEET

HARDENHUISH (St Nicholas)   Chippenham St Paul w Hardenhuish etc *Bris*

HARDHAM (St Botolph) *Chich 12*   **P**   *Col Sir Brian Barttelot, Bt*   **NSM**   C S STRIDE

HARDINGHAM (St George)   Barnham Broom *Nor*

HARDINGSTONE (St Edmund) and Horton and Piddington *Pet 7*   **P**   *Bp*   **V**   B H STEVENS

HARDINGTON MANDEVILLE (Blessed Virgin Mary)   W Coker w Hardington Mandeville, E Chinnock etc *B & W*

HARDLEY (St Margaret)   Chedgrave w Hardley and Langley *Nor*

HARDMEAD (St Mary)   Sherington w Chicheley, N Crawley, Astwood etc *Ox*

HARDRAW (St Mary and St John)   Hawes and Hardraw *Ripon*

HARDRES, LOWER (St Mary)   Petham and Waltham w Lower Hardres etc *Cant*

HARDRES, UPPER (St Peter and St Paul)   as above

HARDSTOFT (St Peter)   Ault Hucknall *Derby*

HARDWICK (St James)   Stockton St Jas *Dur*

HARDWICK (St Leonard)   Mears Ashby and Hardwick and Sywell etc *Pet*

HARDWICK (St Margaret)   Hempnall *Nor*

HARDWICK (St Mary) *Ely 1*   **P**   *Bp*   **R**   A R McKEARNEY, **NSM**   A G WILMAN

HARDWICK, EAST (St Stephen) *Wakef 11*   **P**   *Cawood Trustees*   **V**   F L BROOKS, **Par Dn**   S V BROOKS

HARDWICK-CUM-TUSMORE (St Mary)   Finmere w Mixbury, Cottisford, Hardwick etc *Ox*

HARDWICKE (Holy Trinity)   Cusop w Clifford, Hardwicke, Bredwardine etc *Heref*

HARDWICKE (St Mary the Virgin)   Schorne *Ox*

HARDWICKE (St Nicholas), Quedgeley and Elmore w Longney *Glouc 8*   **P**   *Adn Glouc and Sir John Guise (1 turn), Bp (2 turns), and Ld Chan (1 turn)*   **R**   G J B STICKLAND, **C**   B HUMPHREY, **NSM**   C L WARD

HAREBY (St Peter and St Paul)   Marden Hill Gp *Linc*

HAREFIELD (St Mary the Virgin) *Lon 24*   **P**   *Viscount Daventry*   **V**   D G A CONNOR, **C**   J D CORNISH

HARESCOMBE (St John the Baptist)   The Edge, Pitchcombe, Harescombe and Brookthorpe *Glouc*

HARESFIELD (St Peter)   Standish w Haresfield and Moreton Valence etc *Glouc*

HAREWOOD (Methodist Chapel)   Collingham w Harewood *Ripon*

HARFORD (St Petroc)   Ivybridge w Harford *Ex*

HARGRAVE (All Saints)   Stanwick w Hargrave *Pet*

HARGRAVE (St Edmund)   Chevington w Hargrave and Whepstead w Brockley *St E*

HARGRAVE (St Peter) *Ches 5*   **P**   *Bp*   **R**   K HARRIS

HARKSTEAD (St Mary)   Chelmondiston w Harkstead and Shotley w Erwarton *St E*

HARLASTON (St Matthew) *Lich 5*   **P**   *Bp*   **R**   *Vacant*

HARLAXTON (St Mary and St Peter) *Linc 19*   **P**   *Bp, Sir Richard Welby, Bt, D&C, and DBP (jt)*   **R**   A C SWINDELL

HARLESCOTT (Holy Spirit) *Lich 27*   **P**   *Bp*   **V**   M F WALKER, **C**   A J BURTON, **NSM**   D W G UFFINDELL

HARLESDEN (All Souls) *Lon 21*   **P**   *The Crown*   **V**   M D MOORHEAD, **C**   S C SPENCER

HARLESDEN (St Mark)   Kensal Rise St Mark and St Martin *Lon*

HARLESTON (St Augustine)   Gt Finborough w Onehouse and Harleston *St E*

HARLESTON (St John the Baptist)   Redenhall, Harleston, Wortwell and Needham *Nor*

HARLESTONE (St Andrew)   Church Brampton, Chapel Brampton, Harleston etc *Pet*

HARLEY (St Mary)   Wenlock *Heref*

HARLING, EAST (St Peter and St Paul) w West Haling and Bridgham w Roudham *Nor 17*   **P**   *Ld Chan, DBP, Sir R G C Nugent, Bt, and Mrs Juliet Barry and C D F Musker Esq (by turn)*   **R**   H R ELLIOT

HARLINGTON (Christ Church)   Waltham Avenue Conventional District *Lon 24*   **C-in-c**   R N McCANN

HARLINGTON (St Mary the Virgin) *St Alb 18*   **P**   *Bp*   **V**   S J WILLIAMS

HARLINGTON (St Peter and St Paul) *Lon 24*   **P**   *Bp*   **R**   D R JENKINS

HARLOW (St Mary Magdalene) *Chelmsf 3*   **P**   *V Harlow*   **V**   G R SMITH, **Hon C**   G R NEAVE

HARLOW (St Mary the Virgin) *Chelmsf 3*   **P**   *Simeon's Trustees and Bp (alt)*   **V**   S P E MOURANT, **C**   J G BLAKELEY, **Dss**   J C MOURANT

HARLOW GREEN (St Ninian)   Gateshead Harlow Green *Dur*

HARLOW HILL (All Saints)   Low Harrogate St Mary *Ripon*

HARLOW NEW TOWN (St Paul) w St Mary Little Parndon *Chelmsf 3*   **P**   *Patr Bd*   **R**   G OGILVIE, **C**   A R B HIGGS, T B JONES, **Par Dn**   I E CRAWFORD

HARLSEY, EAST (St Oswald)   Osmotherley w E Harlsey and Ingleby Arncliffe *York*

HARLTON (Assumption of the Blessed Virgin Mary) *Ely 7*   **P**   *Jes Coll Cam*   **R**   J P GILDING

HARMANSWATER (St Paul)   Bracknell *Ox*

HARMER HILL (St Andrew)   Myddle *Lich*

HARMONDSWORTH (St Mary) *Lon 24*   **P**   *DBP*   **Par Dn**   S J FERNANDO

HARMSTON (All Saints) *Linc 18*   **P**   *DBP*   **V**   R C BELL

HARNHAM (St George) (All Saints) *Sarum 15*   **P**   *Bp (1 turn), V Britford (2 turns)*   **P-in-c**   D P SCRACE, **Par Dn**   D JONES, **Hon Par Dn**   S V COLLINS

HARNHILL (St Michael and All Angels)   The Ampneys w Driffield and Poulton *Glouc*

HAROLD HILL (St George) *Chelmsf 4*   **P**   *Bp*   **V**   S R JONES, **C**   R KANERIA, **Par Dn**   R MORTON

HAROLD HILL (St Paul) *Chelmsf 4*   **P**   *Bp*   **V**   C S CARTER

HAROLD WOOD (St Peter) *Chelmsf 4*   **P**   *New Coll Ox*   **V**   W P BENN, **C**   D F P RUTHERFORD, G M REAKES-WILLIAMS

HAROME (St Saviour) w Stonegrave, Nunnington and Pockley *York 18*   **P**   *Lady Clarissa Collin, Abp, Adn Cleveland and V Helmsley, The Crown, and Abp (by turn)*   **R**   J M MATHER

HARPENDEN (St John the Baptist) *St Alb 14*   **P**   *DBP*   **V**   G A J MARTIN, **C**   D C MYLNE, **NSM**   D PRICE

HARPENDEN (St Nicholas) (All Saints) *St Alb 14*   **P**   *Ld Chan*   **R**   N COLLINGS, **C**   R ENYARD, R PLUCK, J M CHILDS, **Hon C**   E M SHEGOG, **NSM**   C J WHARTON

HARPFORD (St Gregory the Great)   Newton Poppleford w Harpford *Ex*

HARPHAM (St John of Beverley)   Burton Agnes w Harpham and Lowthorpe etc *York*

HARPLEY (St Lawrence)   Gt w Lt Massingham and Harpley *Nor*

HARPOLE (All Saints) *Pet 3*   **P**   *Sir Stephen Hastings*   **R**   M S D LEAFE

HARPSDEN (St Margaret) w Bolney *Ox 6*   **P**   *All So Coll Ox*   **P-in-c**   D T W SALT

HARPSWELL (St Chad)   Hemswell w Harpswell *Linc*

HARPTREE, EAST (St Laurence) w West Harptree and Hinton Blewett *B & W 11*   **P**   *Duchy of Cornwall*   **R**   R G HARVEY

HARPTREE, WEST (Blessed Virgin Mary)   E w W Harptree and Hinton Blewett *B & W*

HARPUR HILL (St James)   Buxton w Burbage and King Sterndale *Derby*

HARPURHEY cum Moston (Christ Church) *Man 5*   **P**   *Bp, Dean, K Greenwood Esq, Mrs M V Johnson, and V Morley Esq (jt)*   **R**   T R HINDLEY

HARPURHEY (St Stephen) *Man 5*   **P**   *Bp*   **R**   T R HINDLEY, **C**   P E HOLDEN

HARRABY (St Elisabeth) *Carl 3*   **P**   *Bp*   **V**   *Vacant* Carlisle (0228) 26440

HARRIETSHAM (St John the Baptist) w Ulcombe *Cant 15*   **P**   *The Crown*   **R**   *Vacant* Maidstone (0622) 859466

HARRINGAY (St Paul) *Lon 19*   **P**   *Bp*   **V**   J F SEELEY

HARRINGTON (St Mary) *Carl 7*   **P**   *Exors E S C Curwen*   **R**   E REDHEAD

HARRINGTON (St Mary)   S Ormsby Gp *Linc*

HARRINGTON (St Peter and St Paul)   Arthingworth, Harrington w Oxendon and E Farndon *Pet*

HARRINGWORTH (St John the Baptist)   Bulwick, Blatherwycke w Harringworth and Laxton *Pet*

HARROGATE (St Mark) *Ripon 1*   **P**   *Peache Trustees*   **V**   St J A TURNER

HARROGATE (St Wilfrid and St Luke) *Ripon 1*   **P**   *Bp*   **V**   B R PEARSON, **C**   J B BLACKMAN, J F DICKINSON, **NSM**   G P CORNISH

HARROGATE, HIGH (Christ Church) *Ripon 1*   **P**   *Bp*   **V**   R T W McDERMID, **C**   C J ENGELSEN

HARROGATE, HIGH (St Peter) *Ripon 1* **P** *Ch Patr Trust* **V** A M SHEPHERD, **Par Dn** L C PEARSON
HARROGATE, LOW (St Mary) *Ripon 4* **P** *Peache Trustees* **V** A BODY
HARROLD (St Peter and All Saints) and Carlton w Chellington *St Alb 21* **P** *Bp* **R** J P SMITH
HARROW (Church of the Holy Spirit) Kenton *Lon*
HARROW (Holy Trinity and St Michael and All Angels) *Lon 23* **P** P A BROADBENT, **C** A R LEIGHTON, W B HERD, **Par Dn** A R SALISBURY, **Hon C** F C SIMPKINS
HARROW, NORTH (St Alban) *Lon 23* **P** *Bp* **V** P HEMINGWAY, **C** S D MANSFIELD, **Hon C** D S ARDEN
HARROW, SOUTH (St Paul) *Lon 23* **P** *R St Bride Fleet Street* **P-in-c** B C COLLINS
HARROW GREEN (Church of Holy Trinity and St Augustine of Hippo) Leytonstone H Trin Harrow Green *Chelmsf*
HARROW ON THE HILL (St Mary) *Lon 23* **P** *Bp, Adn, and Hd Master Harrow Sch (jt)* **V** R F SWAN
HARROW WEALD (All Saints) *Lon 23* **P** *Bp, Adn, V Harrow St Mary, and R Bushey (jt)* **V** F D JAKEMAN, **Par Dn** S LEIGHTON
HARROWBARROW (All Saints) Calstock *Truro*
HARROWDEN, GREAT (All Saints) w LITTLE (St Mary the Virgin) and Orlingbury *Pet 6* **P** *Sir Stephen Hastings and Bp (alt)* **V** J E COOPER
HARSTON (All Saints) w Hauxton *Ely 7* **P** *Bp (2 turns), D&C (1 turn)* **V** M T ALLEN, **NSM** F N WATTS
HARSTON (St Michael and All Angels) Croxton Kerrial, Knipton, Harston, Branston etc *Leic*
HARSWELL (St Peter) Seaton Ross Gp of Par *York*
HART (St Mary Magdalene) w Elwick Hall *Dur 13* **P** *Bp and DBP (alt)* **V** J E LUND
HART COMMON (not known) Westhoughton *Man*
HARTBURN (All Saints) Stockton St Pet *Dur*
HARTBURN (St Andrew) Bolam w Whalton and Hartburn w Meldon *Newc*
HARTCLIFFE (St Andrew) Bris St Andr Hartcliffe *Bris*
HARTEST (All Saints) Glem Valley United Benefice *St E*
HARTFIELD (St Mary) w Coleman's Hatch *Chich 19* **P** *Earl de la Warr* **R** P T CRAIG
HARTFORD (All Saints) Huntingdon *Ely*
HARTFORD (All Souls) Hartley Wintney, Elvetham, Winchfield etc *Win*
HARTFORD (St John the Baptist) *Ches 6* **P** *Mrs I H Wilson, Mrs R H Emmet, and Mrs J M Wearne (jt)* **V** P D GARDNER, **C** M A PICKLES
HARTHILL (All Hallows) and Thorpe Salvin *Sheff 5* **P** *Bp* **R** K E JONES
HARTHILL (All Saints) and Burwardsley *Ches 5* **P** *Bp and G R Barbour Esq (jt)* **P-in-c** J R D HUGHES
HARTING (St Mary and St Gabriel) *Chich 10* **P** *Bp* **R** D R C GIBBONS
HARTINGTON (St Giles), Biggin and Earl Sterndale *Derby 4* **P** *Duke of Devonshire* **V** D V GIBLING
HARTISMERE, NORTH *St E 16* **P** *MMCET, K Coll Cam, Bp, and DBP (jt)* **R** C M IDLE
HARTLAND (St Nectan) and Welcombe *Ex 17* **P** *Bp* **V** L M COULSON
HARTLEBURY (St James) *Worc 12* **P** *Bp* **P-in-c** C R LEVEY, **Par Dn** M E STANTON-HYDE
HARTLEPOOL (Holy Trinity) (St Barnabas) *Dur 13* **P** *Bp* **V** P J WALKER, **C** D HAWTHORN
HARTLEPOOL (St Aidan) (St Columba) *Dur 13* **P** *Bp* **V** M H WHITEHEAD, **C** P A BAKER, M G T GOBBETT
HARTLEPOOL (St Hilda) *Dur 13* **P** *Bp* **R** S P FLETCHER, **Par Dn** J L COOK
HARTLEPOOL (St Luke) *Dur 13* **P** *Bp* **V** P TOWNSEND, **C** A MILNE
HARTLEPOOL (St Oswald) *Dur 13* **P** *Bp* **V** C W JACKSON, **C** D HUTTON
HARTLEPOOL (St Paul) *Dur 13* **P** *Bp* **V** B McKENZIE, **C** T M BARON
HARTLEY (All Saints) Fawkham and Hartley *Roch*
HARTLEY, NEW (St Michael and All Angels) Delaval *Newc*
HARTLEY BROOK (Mission Hall) Becontree St Mary *Chelmsf*
HARTLEY MAUDITT (St Leonard) E and W Worldham, Hartley Mauditt w Kingsley etc *Win*
HARTLEY WESPALL (St Mary) Sherfield-on-Loddon and Stratfield Saye etc *Win*
HARTLEY WINTNEY (St John the Evangelist), Elvetham, Winchfield and Dogmersfield *Win 5* **P** *Bp and Sir Euan Anstruther-Gough-Calthorpe, Bt (jt)* **V** P E de D WARBURTON, **C** R DODGSON

HARTLIP (St Michael and All Angels) Newington w Hartlip and Stockbury *Cant*
HARTOFT (Mission Room) Lastingham w Appleton-le-Moors, Rosedale etc *York*
HARTON (All Saints) S Shields All SS *Dur*
HARTON (St Lawrence) Horsley Hill S Shields *Dur*
HARTON (St Peter) *Dur 7* **P** *D&C* **V** A M BARTLETT
HARTPLAIN *Portsm 4* **P** *DBP* **V** D M POWER, **Hon C** J POWER
HARTPOOL (St Mark) Hartlepool H Trin *Dur*
HARTPURY (St Mary the Virgin) w Corse and Staunton *Glouc 6* **P** *Bp (2 turns), DBP (1 turn)* **P-in-c** J G EVANS
HARTSHEAD (St Peter) and Hightown *Wakef 8* **P** *R Dewsbury* **V** *Vacant* Cleckheaton (0274) 873786
HARTSHILL (Holy Trinity) *Cov 5* **P** *V Mancetter* **V** J A DAVIES, **NSM** P DODDS
HARTSHILL (Holy Trinity) *Lich 18* **P** *Bp* **V** J A WALSH
HARTSHORNE (St Peter) *Derby 16* **P** *MMCET* **R** I R WILLIAMS-HUNTER
HARTWELL (St John the Baptist) Roade and Ashton w Hartwell *Pet*
HARTWITH (St Jude) Dacre w Hartwith and Darley w Thornthwaite *Ripon*
HARTY (St Thomas Apostle) Eastchurch w Leysdown and Harty *Cant*
HARVINGTON (St James), Norton and Lenchwick *Worc 1* **P** *D&C* **R** B J FREETH
HARWELL (St Matthew) w Chilton *Ox 18* **P** *DBP and CPAS (jt)* **R** C J STOTT, **Par Dn** J M IMPEY
HARWICH (St Nicholas) *Chelmsf 23* **P** *Bp* **V** *Vacant* Harwich (0255) 2817
HARWOOD (Christ Church) *Man 16* **P** *DBP* **V** D J BRIERLEY, **C** E G MANN, **Hon C** D A HILES
HARWOOD, GREAT (St Bartholomew) *Blackb 8* **P** *V Blackb* **V** K P ARKELL
HARWOOD, GREAT (St John) *Blackb 8* **P** *Trustees* **V** *Vacant* Great Harwood (0254) 886309
HARWOOD DALE (St Margaret) Hackness w Harwood Dale *York*
HARWORTH (All Saints) *S'well 1* **P** *Sir James Whitaker, Bt* **V** J A BRITTON
HASBURY (St Margaret) Halesowen *Worc*
HASCOMBE (St Peter) *Guildf 4* **P** *SMF* **R** R C D MACKENNA
HASELBECH (St Michael) Clipston w Naseby and Haselbech w Kelmarsh *Pet*
HASELBURY PLUCKNETT (St Michael and All Angels), Misterton and North Perrott *B & W 16* **P** *Ld Chan (2 turns), Bp (2 turns), and H W F Hoskyns Esq (1 turn)* **V** R D MARTIN
HASELEY (St Mary) Hatton w Haseley, Rowington w Lowsonford etc *Cov*
HASELEY, GREAT (St Peter) Gt w Lt Milton and Gt Haseley *Ox*
HASELOR (St Mary and All Saints) Kinwarton w Gt Alne and Haselor *Cov*
HASELTON (St Andrew) Withington and Compton Abdale w Haselton *Glouc*
HASFIELD (St Mary) w Tirley and Ashleworth *Glouc 6* **P** *W G F Meath-Baker Esq, Ld Chan, and Bp (by turn)* **R** *Vacant* Tirley (045278) 360
HASKETON (St Andrew) Ufford w Bredfield and Hasketon *St E*
HASLAND (St Paul) *Derby 5* **P** *V Chesterfield* **R** H R O ANDERSON
HASLEMERE (St Bartholomew) (St Christopher) *Guildf 4* **P** *Ld Chan* **R** R N MORTON
HASLINGDEN (St James the Great) w Grane (St Stephen) and Stonefold (St John) *Blackb 1* **P** *Bp and Hulme Trustees (jt)* **V** D B WEBB
HASLINGFIELD (All Saints) *Ely 7* **P** *DBP* **V** J P GILDING
HASLINGTON (St Matthew) w Crewe Green St Michael *Ches 15* **P** *Bp* **V** M R M RAMSAY
HASSALL GREEN (St Philip) Wheelock *Ches*
HASSINGHAM (St Mary) Burlingham St Edmund w Lingwood, Strumpshaw etc *Nor*
HASTINGLEIGH (St Mary the Virgin) Elmsted w Hastingleigh *Cant*
HASTINGS (All Souls) Clive Vale *Chich 17* **P** *R Upper St Leon* **V** B TRILL
HASTINGS (Christ Church and St Andrew) Blacklands Hastings Ch Ch and St Andr *Chich*
HASTINGS (Emmanuel and St Mary in the Castle) *Chich 17* **P** *MMCET and Hyndman Trustees (alt)* **V** J T HENDERSON
HASTINGS (Holy Trinity) *Chich 17* **P** *Bp* **V** C TOLWORTHY

HASTINGS (St Clement) (All Saints) *Chich 17*   **P** *Bp*
  R *Vacant*   Hastings (0424) 422023
HASWELL (St Paul)   S Hetton w Haswell *Dur*
HATCH, WEST (St Andrew)   Hatch Beauchamp w
  Beercrocombe, Curry Mallet etc *B & W*
HATCH BEAUCHAMP (St John the Baptist) w
  Beercrocombe, Curry Mallet and West Hatch *B & W 20*
  P *Duchy of Cornwall (1 turn), Ch Trust Fund Trust*
  (2 turns), and D&C (1 turn)   **R** *R H M JAY*
HATCH END (St Anselm) *Lon 23*   **P** *Bp*   **V** *C PEARCE*
HATCHAM (St Catherine) *S'wark 2*   **P** *Haberdashers' Co*
  V *M N A TORRY*,   **Hon C** *D H HAINES, R M G MORRELL*
HATCHAM (St James) (St George) (St Michael) *S'wark 2*
  P *Ch Patr Soc*   **C** *D A CRAWFORD*,
  Par Dn *J A CARROLL*
HATCHAM PARK (All Saints) *S'wark 2*   **P** *Hyndman*
  Trustees (2 turns), Haberdashers' Co (1 turn)
  V *O J BEAMENT*
HATCLIFFE (St Mary)   Ravendale Gp *Linc*
HATFIELD (St Etheldreda) (St John) (St Michael and All
  Angels) (St Luke) *St Alb 7*   **P** *Marquess of Salisbury*
  R *W C D TODD*,
  C *R J SUTTON, A J PROUD, M FREDRIKSEN*
HATFIELD (St Lawrence) *Sheff 11*   **P** *Bp*   **V** *J W SWEED*,
  C *I A DAVIS*
HATFIELD (St Leonard)   Leominster *Heref*
HATFIELD BROAD OAK (St Mary the Virgin) and Bush
  End *Chelmsf 3*   **P** *Bp*   **P-in-c** *D P HODGSON*
HATFIELD HEATH (Holy Trinity) and Sheering
  Chelmsf 3   **P** *V Hatfield Broad Oak*   **R** *T J POTTER*
HATFIELD HYDE (St Mary Magdalene) *St Alb 7*
  P *Marquess of Salisbury*   **V** *S M BANNISTER*,
  C *K PASSANT*
HATFIELD PEVEREL (St Andrew) w Ulting *Chelmsf 27*
  P *Bp*   **V** *R E TOZER*
HATFIELD REGIS   Hatf Broad Oak and Bush End
  Chelmsf
HATHERDEN (Christ Church) w Tangley and Weyhill and
  Penton Mewsey *Win 3*   **P** *Bp and Qu Coll Ox (jt)*
  V *R E WHETTINGSTEEL*
HATHERLEIGH (St John the Baptist) Meeth, Exbourne
  and Jacobstowe *Ex 12*   **P** *CPAS, Lord Clinton, DBP,*
  and Keble Coll Ox (jt)   **R** *N H P McKINNEL*
HATHERN (St Peter and St Paul), Long Whatton and
  Diseworth w Belton and Osgathorpe *Leic 7*   **P** *Ld Chan,*
  Haberdashers' Co, and Bp (by turn)   **P** *S SAMUEL*,
  Par Dn *S M CHANTRY*,   **Hon C** *E B DAVIES*
HATHEROP (St Nicholas)   Coln St Aldwyn, Hatherop,
  Quenington etc *Glouc*
HATHERSAGE (St Michael and All Angels) *Derby 2*
  P *Duke of Devonshire*   **V** *J W ALLUM*
HATHERTON (St Saviour) *Lich 3*   **P** *A R W Littleton Esq*
  V *Vacant*
HATLEY ST GEORGE (St George)   Gamlingay w
  Hatley St Geo and E Hatley *Ely*
HATTERS LANE (St Andrew)   High Wycombe *Ox*
HATTERSLEY (St Barnabas) *Ches 14*   **P** *Bp*
  V *J E W BOWERS*,   **C** *M J COMER*
HATTON (All Saints Mission Church)   Marston on Dove
  w Scropton *Derby*
HATTON (Chapel of Ease)   E Bedfont *Lon*
HATTON (Holy Trinity) w Haseley, Rowington w
  Lowsonford and Honiley and Wroxall *Cov 4*   **P** *Bp*
  R *B A RITCHIE*,   **NSM** *M M RITCHIE*
HATTON (St Stephen)   Hemingby *Linc*
HAUGH (St Leonard)   S Ormsby Gp *Linc*
HAUGHLEY (St Mary the Virgin) w Wetherden *St E 6*
  P *Ld Chan and Bp (alt)*   **P-in-c** *D P BURRELL*
HAUGHTON (Mission Room)   Bunbury *Ches*
HAUGHTON (St Anne) *Man 17*   **P** *DBP*   **R** *P SAMUELS*
HAUGHTON (St Chad)   W Felton *Lich*
HAUGHTON (St Giles) *Lich 16*   **P** *Mrs M N Nutt*
  P-in-c *G K SMITH*
HAUGHTON (St Mary the Virgin) *Man 17*   **P** *Bp*
  R *M J DOWLAND*,   **C** *A R BROCKBANK*
HAUGHTON LE SKERNE (St Andrew) *Dur 12*   **P** *Bp*
  R *C C MARNHAM*,   **C** *T D MULLINS, C H PATTERSON*
HAUTBOIS, GREAT (Holy Trinity)   Coltishall w Gt
  Hautbois and Horstead *Nor*
HAUXTON (St Edmund)   Harston w Hauxton *Ely*
HAUXWELL (St Oswald)   Spennithorne w Finghall and
  Hauxwell *Ripon*
HAVANT (St Faith) *Portsm 4*   **P** *Bp*   **R** *D F BROWN*
HAVEN STREET (St Peter)   Swanmore St Mich w
  Havenstreet *Portsm*
HAVERHILL (St Mary the Virgin) w Withersfield, the
  Wrattings, the Thurlows and the Bradleys *St E 8*
  P *Patr Bd*   **TR** *E J BETTS*
HAVERIGG (St Luke)   Millom *Carl*

HAVERING-ATTE-BOWER (St John)   Collier Row St
  Jas and Havering-atte-Bower *Chelmsf*
HAVERINGLAND (St Peter)   Cawston w
  Haveringland, Booton and Brandiston *Nor*
HAVERSHAM (St Mary) w Little Linford, Tyringham w
  Filgrave *Ox 27*   **P** *CPAS*   **R** *D LUNN*
HAVERSTOCK HILL (Holy Trinity) w Kentish Town
  (St Barnabas) *Lon 17*   **P** *D&C St Paul's*   **V** *I M SCOTT*
HAVERTHWAITE (St Anne)   Leven Valley *Carl*
HAWES (St Margaret) and Hardraw *Ripon 4*   **P** *Bp,*
  V Aysgarth and Bolton cum Redmire, Mrs R Metcalfe,
  and W H Willan Esq (jt)   **V** *G N R SOWERBY*
HAWES SIDE (St Christopher) *Blackb 9*   **P** *Bp*
  V *R G RAINFORD*,   **NSM** *M J THOMAS*
HAWKCHURCH (St John the Baptist)   Marshwood
  Vale Team Min *Sarum*
HAWKEDON (St Mary)   Chedburgh w Depden, Rede
  and Hawkedon *St E*
HAWKESBURY (St Mary)   Badminton w Lt
  Badminton, Acton Turville etc *Glouc*
HAWKHURST (St Lawrence) *Cant 11*   **P** *Ch Ch Ox*
  V *J RECORD*
HAWKINGE (St Luke) w Acrise and Swingfield *Cant 5*
  P *Abp*   **R** *Vacant*   Hawkinge (030389) 2369
HAWKLEY (St Peter and St Paul) w Priors Dean
  Portsm 5   **P** *Bp*   **P-in-c** *G H WOOLVERIDGE*
HAWKRIDGE (St Giles)   Exford, Exmoor, Hawkridge
  and Withypool *B & W*
HAWKSHAW LANE (St Mary) *Man 10*
  P *F Whowell Esq*   **V** *E A RUEHORN*
HAWKSHEAD (St Michael and All Angels) and Low Wray
  w Sawrey *Carl 10*   **P** *Bp*   **V** *D A SOUTHWARD*
HAWKSWOOD   Hailsham *Chich*
HAWKSWORTH (St Mary and All Saints)   Whatton w
  Aslockton, Hawksworth, Scarrington etc *S'well*
HAWKSWORTH WOOD (St Mary) *Ripon 7*   **P** *Patrons*
  Leeds St Pet   **V** *C M MORRIS*,   **C** *J MURPHY*
HAWKWELL (Emmanuel) (St Mary the Virgin)
  Chelmsf 14   **P** *CPAS*   **R** *A R HIGTON*,
  NSM *A C EDMUNDS*
HAWKWOOD (St Francis)   Chingford SS Pet and Paul
  Chelmsf
HAWLEY (Holy Trinity) *Guildf 1*   **P** *Keble Coll Ox*
  V *I M HANCOCK*,   **C** *I G BOOTH*
HAWLEY, SOUTH (All Saints)   Hawley H Trin *Guildf*
HAWLING (St Edward)   Sevenhampton w Charlton
  Abbotts and Hawling etc *Glouc*
HAWNBY (All Saints)   Upper Ryedale *York*
HAWORTH (St Michael and All Angels) *Bradf 8*
  P *V Bradf and Haworth Ch Lands Trust (jt)*
  R *C SPIVEY*,   **NSM** *S I TAYLOR*
HAWRIDGE (St Mary) w Cholesbury and St Leonard
  Ox 28   **P** *Bp, Chapel Trust, and Neale's Charity (jt)*
  R *G A de BURGH-THOMAS*,   **NSM** *P R BINNS*
HAWSKER (All Saints)   Fylingdales and Hawsker cum
  Stainsacre *York*
HAWSTEAD (All Saints) and Nowton w Stanningfield and
  Bradfield Combust *St E 13*   **P** *Mrs J Oakes (2 turns), Bp*
  (3 turns)   **R** *Vacant*   Sicklesmere (028486) 529
HAWTHORN (St Michael and All Angels) *Dur 3*
  P *I Pemberton Esq*   **R** *E B PATEMAN*,   **NSM** *L HOOD*
HAWTON (All Saints)   Farndon w Thorpe, Hawton and
  Cotham *S'well*
HAXBY (St Mary) w Wigginton *York 8*   **P** *Abp and*
  Ld Chan (alt)   **TR** *M W ESCRITT*,   **TV** *A A HORSMAN*
HAXEY (St Nicholas) *Linc 1*   **P** *Ld Chan*   **V** *Vacant*
  Haxey (0427) 752351
HAY MILL (St Cyprian)   Yardley St Cypr Hay Mill
  Birm
HAYDOCK (St James) *Liv 16*   **P** *R Ashton-in-Makerfield*
  V *P E NENER*
HAYDOCK (St Mark) *Liv 10*   **P** *MMCET*   **V** *P POTTER*
HAYDON BRIDGE (St Cuthbert) *Newc 4*   **P** *Bp*
  V *K FLETCHER*
HAYDON WICK (St John)   Rodbourne Cheney *Bris*
HAYES (St Anselm) *Lon 24*   **P** *Bp*   **V** *R P ANDREW*,
  NSM *J R MOTHERSOLE*
HAYES (St Edmund of Canterbury) *Lon 24*   **P** *Bp*
  V *P J BALL*
HAYES (St Mary) *Lon 24*   **P** *Keble Coll Ox*
  R *R C JENNINGS*
HAYES (St Mary the Virgin) *Roch 13*   **P** *D&C*
  R *P G H THOMAS*,   **Par Dn** *F L MATTHEWS*
HAYES (St Nicholas) Raynton Drive Conventional District
  Lon 24   **C-in-c** *L V GIDDENS*
HAYFIELD (St Matthew) *Derby 6*   **P** *Resident*
  Freeholders   **V** *R W HIGGINBOTTOM*
HAYLE (St Elwyn) *Truro 5*   **P** *D&C*
  V *C L MACDONNELL*

HAYLING, SOUTH (St Mary) (St Andrew) w North Hayling *Portsm 4* **P** *DBP* **V** P S G ROYLE, **C** M R ATKINSON, B M C MORRIS

HAYNES (St Mary) (Mission Room) *St Alb 22* **P-in-c** K LORAINE

HAYTON (St James) Aspatria w Hayton *Carl*

HAYTON (St Martin) Shiptonthorpe w Hayton *York*

HAYTON (St Mary Magdalene) *Carl 2* **P** *D&C* **P-in-c** A S PYE

HAYTON (St Peter) Clarborough w Hayton *S'well*

HAYWARDS HEATH (St Richard) *Chich 6* **P** *Bp* **NSM** M A EGGERT

HAYWARDS HEATH (St Wilfrid) (Church of the Ascension) (Church of the Good Shepherd) (Church of the Presentation) *Chich 6* **P** *Bp* **TR** I J BRACKLEY, **TV** S GUISE, K G SWABY, A T CUNNINGTON, **NSM** D J HOLLIS

HAYWOOD, GREAT (St Stephen) Colwich w Gt Haywood *Lich*

HAZELBURY BRYAN (St Mary and St James) w Stoke Wake, Fifehead Neville and Mappowder *Sarum 6* **P** *Duchess of Northd and Duke of Buccleuch (5 turns), Personal Reps F N Kent Esq (1 turn), and Bp (2 turns)* **P-in-c** D M PINE

HAZELWELL (St Mary Magdalen) *Birm 8* **P** *Bp* **V** A C PRIESTLEY

HAZELWOOD (St John the Evangelist) *Derby 11* **P** *Bp* **V** N DAUGHTRY

HAZLEMERE (Holy Trinity) *Ox 29* **P** *Peache Trustees* **V** C COLLIER, **C** P C ROBERTS, D W TOWNSEND

HEACHAM (St Mary) and Sedgeford *Nor 21* **P** *Bp and D&C (jt)* **P** P W L RATCLIFFE, **C** P DUNTHORNE

HEADBOURNE WORTHY (St Swithun) *Win 13* **P** *Univ Coll Ox and Exors Lord Northbrook (alt)* **R** *Vacant*

HEADCORN (St Peter and St Paul) *Cant 15* **P** *Abp* **V** D J M WATSON

HEADINGLEY (St Chad) Far Headingley St Chad *Ripon*

HEADINGLEY (St Michael and All Angels) *Ripon 7* **P** *V Leeds St Pet* **C** J M LEAK, **Par Dn** K D JACKSON

HEADINGLEY (St Oswald) Far Headingley St Chad *Ripon*

HEADINGTON (St Andrew) *Ox 4* **P** *Keble Coll Ox* **V** W M BREWIN, **C** J P KENNINGTON

HEADINGTON (St Mary) *Ox 4* **P** *Bp* **V** C J WALKER

HEADINGTON QUARRY (Holy Trinity) *Ox 4* **P** *Bp* **P-in-c** C HEWETSON

HEADLESS CROSS (St Luke) Redditch, The Ridge *Worc*

HEADLEY (All Saints) *Guildf 3* **P** *Patr Bd* **TR** R W WOODGER, **TV** S GOODWIN, **C** B NICOLE, **NSM** S E GOODWIN

HEADLEY (St Mary the Virgin) w Box Hill (St Andrew) *Guildf 9* **P** *Bp* **R** R DODD

HEADLEY (St Peter) Ashford Hill w Headley *Win*

HEADON (St Peter) E Markham w Askham, Headon w Upton and Grove *S'well*

HEADSTONE (St George) *Lon 23* **P** *Bp* **V** P HEMINGWAY, **C** S R KEEBLE

HEAGE (St Luke) *Derby 11* **P** *V Duffield* **P-in-c** D J T RYMER

HEALAUGH (St John the Baptist) w Wighill, Bilbrough and Askham Richard *York 1* **P** *Abp (3 turns), A G Wailes Fairburn Esq (1 turn)* **V** K BAILES

HEALD GREEN (St Catherine) *Ches 17* **P** *Bp* **V** R A KING, **C** G L JOYCE

HEALEY (Christ Church) *Man 19* **P** *Bp* **V** R BUTTERWORTH

HEALEY (St John) *Newc 3* **P** *V Bywell St Pet* **C** J R KELLY

HEALEY (St Paul) Masham and Healey *Ripon*

HEALEY (War Memorial Mission) S Ossett *Wakef*

HEALING (St Peter and St Paul) and Stallingborough *Linc 10* **P** *Bp* **Dn-in-c** D E KING

HEAMOOR (St Thomas) Madron *Truro*

HEANOR (St Laurence) *Derby 12* **P** *Wright Trustees* **V** C L BLAKEY, **C** M M MOOKERJI, **Par Dn** E S K HAWKINS

HEANTON PUNCHARDON (St Augustine) w Marwood *Ex 15* **P** *CPAS (3 turns), St Jo Coll Cam (1 turn)* **R** J E DYKES, **Hon C** R W CRANSTON

HEAP BRIDGE (St Thomas and St George) Bury Ch King w H Trin *Man*

HEAPEY (St Barnabas) *Blackb 4* **P** *V Leyland* **V** *Vacant* Chorley (02572) 63427

HEAPHAM (All Saints) Corringham *Linc*

HEARTSEASE (St Francis) Nor Heartsease St Fran *Nor*

HEATH (All Saints) *Derby 5* **P** *Duke of Devonshire and Simeon's Trustees (jt)* **V** B M SPROSTON

HEATH (Mission Church) Uttoxeter w Bramshall *Lich*

HEATH, LITTLE (Christ Church) *St Alb 2* **P** *Ch Patr Trust* **V** I D BROWN

HEATH, THE (not known) Bitterley w Middleton, Stoke St Milborough etc *Heref*

HEATH AND REACH (St Leonard) *St Alb 18* **P** *V Leighton Buzzard* **V** G FELLOWS

HEATH HAYES (St John) Cannock *Lich*

HEATH TOWN (Holy Trinity) Wednesfield Heath *Lich*

HEATHER (St John the Baptist) Ibstock w Heather *Leic*

HEATHERLANDS (St John) *Sarum 8* **P** *MMCET* **V** G A G LOUGHLIN, **C** R P OAKLEY

HEATHERYCLEUGH (St Thomas) *Dur 15* **P** *Bp* **V** D M SKELTON

HEATHFIELD (All Saints) *Chich 15* **P** *Bp* **V** B JACKSON

HEATHFIELD (St Catherine) Bovey Tracey St John, Chudleigh Knighton etc *Ex*

HEATHFIELD (St John the Baptist) Bradf w Oake, Hillfarrance and Heathfield *B & W*

HEATHFIELD (St Richard) *Chich 15* **P** *Bp* **V** M J LEWIS

HEATON (Christ Church) *Man 9* **P** *R Deane St Mary* **V** R E H JOHNSON, **C** H W BEARN

HEATON (St Barnabas) *Bradf 1* **P** *Trustees* **V** A D PROCTER

HEATON (St Martin) *Bradf 1* **P** *Bp* **V** P G ROGERS

HEATON CHAPEL (St Thomas) Heaton Norris St Thos *Man*

HEATON MERSEY (St John the Baptist) *Man 3* **P** *Bp* **R** R I McCALLA

HEATON MOOR (St Paul) *Man 3* **P** *Trustees* **R** S E W GUY

HEATON NORRIS (Christ w All Saints) *Man 3* **P** *Bp* **R** M K BOOTH

HEATON NORRIS (St Thomas) *Man 3* **P** *D&C* **R** R CROFT

HEATON REDDISH (St Mary) *Man 3* **P** *Trustees* **R** *Vacant* 061-477 6702

HEAVITREE (St Michael and All Angels) (St Lawrence) (St Loye) w Exeter (St Paul) *Ex 3* **P** *Patr Bd* **TR** M S HART, **TV** J C HALL, **C** J D A WILLIAMS

HEBBURN (St Cuthbert) *Dur 7* **P** *TR Jarrow* **P-in-c** J B HUNT

HEBBURN (St John) *Dur 7* **P** *Bp* **P-in-c** C S ROGERSON

HEBBURN (St Oswald) *Dur 7* **P** *The Crown* **V** R H BEATTY

HEBDEN (St Peter) Linton in Craven *Bradf*

HEBDEN BRIDGE (St James) *Wakef 3* **P** *V Halifax* **V** R C GODSALL

HEBRON (St Cuthbert) Longhirst *Newc*

HECK (St John the Baptist) Gt Snaith *Sheff*

HECKFIELD (St Michael) w Mattingley and Rotherwick *Win 5* **P** *New Coll Ox (2 turns), Bp (1 turn)* **V** A E BENNETT

HECKINGHAM (St Gregory) Raveningham *Nor*

HECKINGTON (St Andrew) *Linc 22* **P** *Bp (2 turns), Ven A C Foottit (1 turn)* **V** G SPENCER

HECKMONDWIKE (All Souls) (St James) *Wakef 8* **P** *V Birstall* **C** C F RAVEN

HEDDINGTON (St Andrew) Oldbury *Sarum*

HEDDON-ON-THE-WALL (St Andrew) *Newc 3* **P** *Ld Chan* **V** J R LITTLE

HEDENHAM (St Peter) Ditchingham, Hedenham and Broome *Nor*

HEDGE END North Coventional District *Win 9* **Min** D S FARLEY

HEDGE END (St John the Evangelist) *Win 9* **P** *Bp* **V** M SPENSER UNDERHILL

HEDGEFIELD (St Hilda) Ryton w Hedgefield *Dur*

HEDGERLEY (St Mary the Virgin) Farnham Royal w Hedgerley *Ox*

HEDNESFORD (St Peter) *Lich 4* **P** *Bp* **V** J M WATERS, **C** V C AGGETT, D K B HAWKINS

HEDON (St Augustine) w Paull *York 13* **P** *Abp* **V** W H McLAREN

HEDSOR (St Nicholas) and Bourne End *Ox 29* **P** *Bp* **R** H HARTLEY, **Hon C** B BRITTON

HEDWORTH (St Nicholas) *Dur 7* **P** *The Crown* **V** R C WARDALE

HEELEY (Christ Church) *Sheff 1* **P** *The Crown* **V** C HORSEMAN, **C** A M COLEBY

HEENE (St Botolph) *Chich 5* **P** *D&C* **R** P R ROBERTS, **NSM** C MACRAE

HEIGHAM (Holy Trinity) *Nor 5* **P** *Ch Trust Fund Trust* **R** K WHITE, **C** M R BAILEY

HEIGHAM (St Barnabas) (St Bartholomew) *Nor 5*   **P** *Bp*
  V H R CRESSWELL, **Hon C** C SIMMONDS
HEIGHAM (St Thomas) *Nor 5*   **P** *Bp*   **V** A C H LATHE
HEIGHINGTON (not known) Washingborough w
  Heighington and Canwick *Linc*
HEIGHINGTON (St Michael) *Dur 12*   **P** *D&C*
  V P H E THOMAS
HEIGHTINGTON (St Giles) Mamble w Bayton, Rock
  w Heightington etc *Worc*
HELFORD (St Paul's Mission Church) Manaccan w St
  Anthony-in-Meneage and St Martin *Truro*
HELHOUGHTON (All Saints) S, E w W Raynham,
  Helhoughton, etc *Nor*
HELIDON (St John the Baptist) Staverton w Helidon
  and Catesby *Pet*
HELIONS BUMPSTEAD (St Andrew) Steeple
  Bumpstead and Helions Bumpstead *Chelmsf*
HELLAND (St Helena) *Truro 10*   **P** *MMCET*
  P-in-c R D C WHITEMAN, **NSM** J L BRENDON-COOK
HELLESDON (St Mary) (St Paul and St Michael) *Nor 4*
  P *Bp*   **V** D M HOARE, **Hon C** G M BRIDGES
HELLIFIELD (St Aidan) *Bradf 5*   **P** *Ch Ch Ox*
  V G WALKER
HELLINGLY (St Peter and St Paul) and Upper Dicker
  Chich 15   **P** *Abp and Bp (jt)*   **V** *Vacant*   Hailsham
  (0323) 844236
HELLINGTON (St John the Baptist) Rockland St Mary
  w Hellington, Bramerton etc *Nor*
HELMDON (St Mary Magdalene) w Stuchbury and
  Radstone and Syresham w Whitfield *Pet 1*   **P** *Ox Univ,*
  Mert Coll Ox, and Worc Coll Ox (3 turns), Bp (1 turn),
  and DBP (1 turn)   **R** *Vacant*   Syresham (02805) 638
HELME (Christ Church) *Wakef 1*   **P** *Bp*
  P-in-c M C RUSSELL, **NSM** R T TUCK
HELMINGHAM (St Mary) w Framsden and Pettaugh w
  Winston *St E 18*   **P** *Ld Chan, MMCET, and Lord*
  Tollemache (by turn)   **P-in-c** K J SPOKES
HELMSLEY (All Saints) *York 18*   **P** *Lord Feversham*
  V D G C M SENIOR
HELMSLEY, UPPER (St Peter) Sand Hutton *York*
HELPERTHORPE (St Peter) Weaverthorpe w
  Helperthorpe, Luttons Ambo etc *York*
HELPRINGHAM (St Andrew) w Hale *Linc 22*
  P *Ld Chan (2 turns), D&C (1 turn), and DBP (1 turn)*
  R P R MASTERTON
HELPSTON (St Botolph) Etton w Helpston *Pet*
HELSBY (St Paul) and Dunham-on-the-Hill *Ches 3*   **P** *Bp*
  V J K BALL, **Par Dn** J E PEARCE
HELSINGTON (St John the Baptist) *Carl 9*   **P** *V Kendal*
  H Trin   **V** A F J LOFTHOUSE
HELSTON (St Michael) and Wendron *Truro 4*   **P** *Patr Bd*
  TR H PENTREATH, **TV** R J WEBBER, **C** G LAKER,
  NSM J P BULLOCK
HEMBLINGTON (All Saints) Blofield w Hemblington
  Nor
HEMEL HEMPSTEAD Apsley End (St Mary)
  Chambersbury (Hemel Hempstead) *St Alb*
HEMEL HEMPSTEAD Bennetts End (St Benedict) as
  above
HEMEL HEMPSTEAD Leverstock Green (Holy Trinity)
  as above
HEMEL HEMPSTEAD (St Mary) *St Alb 3*   **P** *Ld Chan*
  TR N D B ABBOTT, **TV** N W MARTIN, R E MERRY,
  I C COOPER, R A SCRIVENER, D J BEVINGTON,
  TM F A JACKSON, **Hon C** H J SMITH,
  NSM T J BARTON, M F T CLASBY
HEMINGBROUGH (St Mary the Virgin) *York 4*   **P** *Abp*
  V *Vacant*   Selby (0757) 638528
HEMINGBY (St Margaret) *Linc 11*   **P** *Bp (2 turns),*
  Ld Chan (2 turns), and DBP (1 turn)   **R** D J LAWRENCE
HEMINGFORD ABBOTS (St Margaret of Antioch) *Ely 9*
  P *Lord Hemingford*   **P-in-c** S R TALBOT
HEMINGFORD GREY (St James) *Ely 9*   **P** *Mrs G A Scott*
  P-in-c S R TALBOT
HEMINGSTONE (St Gregory) Coddenham w Gosbeck
  and Hemingstone w Henley *St E*
HEMINGTON (St Peter and St Paul) Polebrook and
  Lutton w Hemington and Luddington *Pet*
HEMINGTON (The Blessed Virgin Mary) Norton St
  Philip w Hemington, Hardington etc *B & W*
HEMLEY (All Saints) Waldringfield w Hemley and
  Newbourn *St E*
HEMLINGTON (St Timothy) Stainton-in-Cleveland
  York
HEMPNALL (St Margaret) *Nor 11*   **P** *Ld Chan (1 turn),*
  Patr Bd (5 turns)   **TR** E J GREEN, **C** K E A JAMES,
  Hon C D M GREEN
HEMPSTEAD (All Saints) Barningham w Matlaske w
  Baconsthorpe etc *Nor*

HEMPSTEAD (All Saints) S Gillingham *Roch*
HEMPSTEAD (St Andrew) Radwinter w Hempstead
  Chelmsf
HEMPSTEAD (St Andrew) Happisburgh w Walcot,
  Hempstead, Lessingham etc *Nor*
HEMPSTED (St Swithun) *Glouc 5*   **P** *Bp*
  P-in-c M J D IRVING, **NSM** J E NEWELL
HEMPTON (Holy Trinity) and Pudding Norton *Nor 20*
  P *The Crown*   **V** *Vacant*   Fakenham (0328) 2914
HEMPTON (St John the Evangelist) Deddington w
  Barford, Clifton and Hempton *Ox*
HEMSBY (St Mary) *Nor 2*   **P** *Major R A Ferrier*
  V W D B WILLIAMS, **Hon C** C A POWLES
HEMSWELL (All Saints) w Harpswell *Linc 2*   **P** *Ch Soc*
  Trust (2 turns), MMCET (1 turn)   **P-in-c** N BRUNNING
HEMSWORTH (St Helen) *Wakef 11*   **P** *Bp*
  R A P J MATTHEWS
HEMYOCK (St Mary) w Culm Davy and Clayhidon *Ex 4*
  P *DBP and SMF (jt)*   **R** A C B GROSSE
HENBURY (St Mary the Virgin) *Bris 8*   **P** *Lord*
  Middleton (1 turn), Bp (3 turns)   **V** H B TROTTER
HENBURY (St Thomas) *Ches 13*   **P** *Bp*   **V** J B PEEL
HENDFORD (St Mary the Virgin and All Saints) Yeovil
  H Trin *B & W*
HENDON (All Saints) Childs Hill *Lon 15*   **P** *Bp*
  V J P WAINWRIGHT
HENDON (Christ Church) *Lon 15*   **P** *Bp*
  V R E PARSONS
HENDON (St Alphage) *Lon 15*   **P** *Bp*   **V** H D MOORE
HENDON (St Ignatius) *Dur 9*   **P** *Bp*   **R** L G BARRON
HENDON (St Mary) (St Mary Magdalene) *Lon 15*   **P** *Bp*
  V R E PARSONS, **C** J S CLARKE, **Hon C** A H COOKE
HENDON (St Paul) Mill Hill *Lon 15*   **P** *Bp*
  V M D KETTLE, **C** J D CAMPBELL
HENDON, WEST (St John) *Lon 15*   **P** *Bp*
  V J M WARNER
HENDRED, EAST (St Augustine of Canterbury)
  Wantage Downs *Ox*
HENDRED, WEST (Holy Trinity) as above
HENFIELD (St Peter) w Shermanbury and Woodmancote
  Chich 9   **P** *Bp*   **P-in-c** A D McKEMEY,
  NSM D M WHITTOME, A McNEIL
HENGOED w Gobowen *Lich 25*   **P** *R Selattyn*
  V M J WITHEY
HENGROVE (Christ Church) *Bris 3*   **P** *Bp and Simeon's*
  Trustees (alt)   **V** P S FREAR
HENHAM (St Mary the Virgin) and Elsenham w Ugley
  Chelmsf 24   **P** *Ch Hosp, Ch Soc Trust, and Bp (jt)*
  P-in-c R W FARR
HENLEAZE (St Peter) *Bris 5*   **P** *Bp*   **V** F SMITH,
  NSM B J PULLAN, **Hon Par Dn** S M TYLER (nee WAITE)
HENLEY (St Peter) Coddenham w Gosbeck and
  Hemingstone w Henley *St E*
HENLEY IN ARDEN (St John the Baptist) Beaudesert
  and Henley-in-Arden w Ullenhall *Cov*
HENLEY-ON-THAMES (Holy Trinity) Rotherfield
  Greys H Trin *Ox*
HENLEY-ON-THAMES (St Mary the Virgin) *Ox 6*   **P** *Bp*
  R A PYBURN
HENLOW (St Mary the Virgin) *St Alb 22*   **P** *Ld Chan*
  V C G MATTOCK
HENNOCK (St Mary) *Ex 11*   **P** *MMCET*   **V** *Vacant*
  Bovey Tracey (0626) 833211
HENNY, GREAT (St Mary) and Little Henny w
  Middleton and Wickam St Paul w Twinstead *Chelmsf 17*
  P *Earl of Verulam, Bp, D&C St Paul's, and Ld Chan*
  (by turn)   **R** B A CAREW
HENSALL (St Paul) Gt Snaith *Sheff*
HENSHAW (All Hallows) Beltingham w Henshaw *Newc*
HENSINGHAM (St John) (Keekle Mission) *Carl 5*
  P *Trustees*   **V** I G MAINEY
HENSTEAD (St Mary) Hundred River Gp of Par *St E*
HENSTRIDGE (St Nicholas) and Charlton Horethorne w
  Stowell *B & W 8*   **P** *Bp (2 turns), K S D*
  Wingfield Digby Esq (1 turn)   **R** P HALLETT
HENTLAND (St Dubricius) How Caple w Sollarshope,
  Sellack etc *Heref*
HENTON (Christ Church) Coxley, Henton and Wookey
  B & W
HEPPLE (Christ Church) Rothbury *Newc*
HEPTONSTALL (St Thomas a Becket and St Thomas the
  Apostle) *Wakef 3*   **P** *V Halifax*   **P-in-c** D B BARTLETT
HEPWORTH (Holy Trinity) Upper Holme Valley
  Wakef
HEPWORTH (St Peter) w Hinderclay, Wattisfield and
  Thelnetham *St E 9*   **P** *Bp, K Coll Cam, MMCET, and*
  P J Holt-Wilson Esq (jt)   **R** J W FULTON

HEREFORD (All Saints) (St Barnabas Church Centre) *Heref 3* **P** *D&C Windsor* **V** *Vacant* Hereford (0432) 266588

HEREFORD (Holy Trinity) *Heref 3* **P** *Bp* **V** R V HEADING, **C** W ELLIOT

HEREFORD (St John the Baptist) *Heref 3* **P** *D&C* **V** P HAYNES, **C** M J GILL

HEREFORD (St Martin w St Francis) (South Wye Team Ministry) *Heref 3* **P** *Bp, D&C and Provost Worc Coll Ox (jt)* **TR** T P JONES, **TV** R C GREEN, A N JEVONS, R NORTH, P G HADDLETON, **C** E LLOYD

HEREFORD (St Nicholas) *Heref 3* **P** *Ld Chan* **R** W R KING

HEREFORD (St Paul) Tupsley *Heref*

HEREFORD (St Peter w St Owen) (St James) *Heref 3* **P** *Simeon's Trustees* **V** P T WOOD, **C** P A WILLIAMS, C HANSON

HEREFORD, LITTLE (St Mary Magdalene) Burford III w Lt Heref *Heref*

HERMITAGE (Holy Trinity) and Hampstead Norreys, Cold Ash andYattendon w Frilsham *Ox 14* **P** *Patr Bd* **TR** P R ALLIN, **TM** J WILBY, **C** M J WARREN

HERMITAGE (St Mary) Yetminster w Ryme Intrinseca and High Stoy *Sarum*

HERNE (St Martin) *Cant 7* **P** *Abp* **V** P D SALES, **C** G J SMITH, **Par Dn** J M BRADSHAW

HERNE BAY (Christ Church) (St Andrew's Church and Centre) *Cant 7* **P** *Simeon's Trustees* **Par Dn** H C DONSON

HERNE BAY (St Bartholomew) Reculver and Herne Bay St Bart *Cant*

HERNE HILL (St John) (St Paul) *S'wark 7* **P** *Bp and Trustees (jt)* **V** A O LADIPO, **Hon C** R A FARAH

HERNER (Chapel) Newport, Bishops Tawton and Tawstock *Ex*

HERNHILL (St Michael) Boughton under Blean w Dunkirk and Hernhill *Cant*

HERODSFOOT (All Saints) Duloe w Herodsfoot *Truro*

HERONSGATE (St John the Evangelist) Mill End and Heronsgate w W Hyde *St Alb*

HERRIARD (St Mary) w Winslade and Long Sutton and South Warnborough and Tunworth and Upton Grey and Weston Patrick *Win 5* **P** *Bp, Qu Coll Ox, St Jo Coll Ox, Viscount Camrose, and J L Jervoise Esq (jt)* **V** T J B JENKYNS

HERRINGFLEET (St Margaret) Somerleyton w Ashby, Fritton and Herringfleet *Nor*

HERRINGSWELL (St Ethelbert) Mildenhall *St E*

HERRINGTHORPE (St Cuthbert) *Sheff 6* **P** *Bp* **V** B H COOPER

HERRINGTON *Dur 6* **P** *Bp* **V** J S BAIN

HERSHAM (St Peter) *Guildf 8* **P** *Bp* **V** P J BOULTON-LEA, **C** N J ASH

HERSTMONCEUX (All Saints) and Wartling *Chich 15* **P** *Bp and Very Rev J H S Wild (jt)* **R** P G WARD

HERSTON (St Mark) Swanage and Studland *Sarum*

HERTFORD (All Saints) *St Alb 8* **P** *Ld Chan and Marquess Townshend (alt)* **V** D MOWBRAY, **NSM** M CAPEL-EDWARDS

HERTFORD (St Andrew) *St Alb 8* **P** *Duchy of Lanc* **R** G C EDWARDS, **Par Dn** M HARDING

HERTFORD HEATH (Holy Trinity) Lt Amwell *St Alb*

HERTINGFORDBURY (St Mary) *St Alb 8* **P** *The Crown* **P-in-c** J BIRTWISTLE, **Par Dn** R A CARUANA

HESKET-IN-THE-FOREST (St Mary the Virgin) and Armathwaite *Carl 4* **P** *D&C and E P Ecroyd Esq (jt)* **V** D C CROOK

HESKETH (All Saints) w Becconsall *Blackb 6* **P** *Trustees* **R** K POWELL

HESLERTON, EAST (St Andrew) Sherburn and W and E Heslerton w Yedingham *York*

HESLERTON, WEST (All Saints) as above

HESLINGTON (St Paul) *York 4* **P** *Abp* **V** F G HUNTER

HESSAY (St John the Baptist) Rufforth w Moor Monkton and Hessay *York*

HESSENFORD (St Anne) St Germans *Truro*

HESSETT (St Ethelbert) Rougham, Beyton w Hessett and Rushbrooke *St E*

HESSLE (All Saints) *York 15* **P** *Ld Chan* **V** R A H GREANY, **C** D G MOORE, J C FINNEMORE, **NSM** K FORSTER, A CRAVEN

HESTER WAY LANE (St Silas) Cheltenham St Mark *Glouc*

HESTON (All Saints) (St Leonard) *Lon 11* **P** *Bp* **V** T J L MAIDMENT, **C** M J HUGHES, K L W SYLVIA

HESWALL (Church of the Good Shepherd) (St Peter) *Ches 8* **P** *Exors Lt-Col Sir Walter Bromley-Davenport* **R** R E MORRIS, **Par Dn** J M HUNT

HETHE (St Edmund and St George) Stratton Audley and Godington, Fringford etc *Ox*

HETHEL (All Saints) Wreningham *Nor*

HETHERSETT (St Remigius) w Canteloff w Little Melton and Great Melton *Nor 13* **P** *G&C Coll Cam, E C Evans-Lombe Esq, and Em Coll Cam (by turn)* **R** B M LLEWELLYN, **NSM** J M TALBOT, D SHAKESPEARE

HETHERSGILL (St Mary) Bewcastle, Stapleton and Kirklinton etc *Carl*

HETTON, SOUTH (Holy Trinity) w Haswell *Dur 3* **P** *Bp* **V** K H DUNNE

HETTON-LE-HOLE (St Nicholas) *Dur 6* **P** *Bp* **R** R O DICK

HEVENINGHAM (St Margaret) Cratfield w Heveningham and Ubbeston etc *St E*

HEVER (St Peter) w Mark Beech *Roch 10* **P** *Bp and T G Talbot Esq (jt)* **R** B D SIMMONS

HEVERSHAM (St Peter) *Carl 9* **P** *Trin Coll Cam* **V** J C HANCOCK

HEVINGHAM (St Mary and St Botolph) w Hainford and Stratton Strawless *Nor 3* **P** *Bp and Sir T A Beevor, Bt (jt)* **R** P B FOREMAN

HEWELSFIELD (St Mary Magdalene) St Briavels w Hewelsfield *Glouc*

HEWISH (Good Shepherd) Crewkerne w Wayford *B & W*

HEWORTH (Holy Trinity) (Christ Church) (St Wulstan) *York 8* **P** *Patr Bd* **TR** D ANDREW, **TV** W C HEDLEY, J M FROST, **C** M HARRISON

HEWORTH (St Alban) *Dur 4* **P** *V Heworth St Mary* **V** M L MALLESON

HEWORTH (St Mary) *Dur 4* **P** *Bp* **V** R J KNELL, **C** W S JACKSON

HEXHAM (St Andrew) *Newc 4* **P** *Mercers' Co and Viscount Allendale (alt)* **R** M J MIDDLETON, **C** G A R MILNE, **NSM** E M NICHOLAS

HEXTABLE (St Peter) Swanley St Paul *Roch*

HEXTHORPE (St Jude) Doncaster St Jude *Sheff*

HEXTON (St Faith) Barton-le-Cley w Higham Gobion and Hexton *St Alb*

HEY (St John the Baptist) *Man 18* **P** *R Aston-under-Lyne St Mich* **V** P K HARRISON

HEYBRIDGE (St Andrew) (St George) w Langford *Chelmsf 13* **P** *D&C St Paul's and Lord Byron (alt)* **V** O F TRELLIS

HEYBROOK BAY (Holy Nativity) Wembury *Ex*

HEYDON (Holy Trinity), Great Chishill and Little Chishill, Chrishall, Elmdon w Wenden Lofts and Strethall *Chelmsf 25* **P** *Patr Bd* **R** D W PARROTT, **C** R D SIMPSON, **Hon C** J L BRENNAN, **Dss** E A SIMPSON

HEYDON (St Peter and St Paul) Saxthorpe w Corpusty, Blickling, Oulton etc *Nor*

HEYDOUR (St Michael and All Angels) Ancaster Wilsford Gp *Linc*

HEYFORD (St Peter and St Paul) w Stowe Nine Churches *Pet 3* **P** *J L R Crawley Esq and DBP (alt)* **R** D EVANS

HEYFORD, LOWER (St Mary) The Heyfords w Rousham and Somerton *Ox*

HEYFORD, UPPER (St Mary) as above

HEYFORDS w Rousham and Somerton, The *Ox 2* **P** *New Coll Ox, CCC Ox, C Cottrell-Dormer Esq, and P W G Barnes Esq (by turn)* **R** J H WILSON

HEYHOUSES (St Nicholas) Sabden and Pendleton *Blackb*

HEYHOUSES ON SEA (St Anne) *Blackb 11* **P** *J C Hilton Esq* **V** D WELCH

HEYSHAM (St Peter) (St Andrew) *Blackb 12* **P** *C E C Royds Esq* **R** E LACEY, **C** L H HOW

HEYSHAM, HIGHER (St James) Heysham *Blackb*

HEYSHOTT (St James) *Chich 10* **P** *Bp* **P-in-c** C BOXLEY

HEYSIDE (St Mark) *Man 18* **P** *Trustees* **V** *Vacant* Shaw (0706) 847177

HEYTESBURY (St Peter and St Paul) and Sutton Veny *Sarum 14* **P** *Bp* **R** *Vacant* Warminster (0985) 40713

HEYTHROP (St Nicholas) Enstone and Heythrop *Ox*

HEYWOOD (St James) *Man 19* **P** *Bp* **V** M J ROBINSON

HEYWOOD (St Luke) (All Souls) *Man 19* **P** *Bp and R Bury St Mary (jt)* **V** C KNOWLES

HEYWOOD (St Margaret) *Man 19* **P** *Bp* **V** I J STAMP

HIBALDSTOW (St Hibald) Scawby, Redbourne and Hibaldstow *Linc*

HICKLETON (St Wilfrid) Goldthorpe w Hickleton *Sheff*

HICKLING (St Luke) w Kinoulton and Broughton Sulney (Upper Broughton) *S'well 9* **P** *Prime Min, Qu Coll Cam, and Bp (by turn)* **R** P J BRAMELD

HICKLING (St Mary) and Waxham w Sea Palling *Nor 10*
  P *Bp and Major J M Mills (jt)* **V** W J CAMERON
HIGH: *see also under substantive place names*
HIGH CROSS (St John the Evangelist) *St Alb 8* **P** *DBP*
  V H J SHARMAN
HIGH HOYLAND (All Saints), Scissett and Clayton West
  Wakef 6 **P** *Bp* **R** M F CLEVERLEY
HIGH LANE (St Thomas) *Ches 16* **P** *R Stockport*
  V R D CLARKE
HIGH SPEN (St Patrick) and Rowlands Gill *Dur 5* **P** *Bp*
  V M JACKSON
HIGHAM (St John the Evangelist) Padiham *Blackb*
HIGHAM (St John the Evangelist) and Merston *Roch 6*
  P *St Jo Coll Cam* **V** A P PINCHIN
HIGHAM (St Mary) *St E 3* **P** *Bp* **V** *Vacant*
HIGHAM FERRERS (St Mary the Virgin) w Chelveston
  Pet 10 **P** *Sir Stephen Hastings and Bp (alt)*
  V E BUCHANAN
HIGHAM GOBION (St Margaret) Barton-le-Cley w
  Higham Gobion and Hexton *St Alb*
HIGHAM GREEN (St Stephen) Barrow w Denham St
  Mary and Higham Green *St E*
HIGHAM HILL (St Andrew) Walthamstow St Andr
  Chelmsf
HIGHAM-ON-THE-HILL (St Peter) w Fenny Drayton and
  Witherley *Leic 13* **P** *D&C, and Lord O'Neill (jt)*
  P-in-c M CHARLES
HIGHAMPTON (Holy Cross) Black Torrington, Bradf
  w Cookbury etc *Ex*
HIGHAMS PARK (All Saints) Hale End *Chelmsf 8* **P** *Bp*
  V M OAKES
HIGHBRIDGE (St John the Evangelist) *B & W 1* **P** *Bp*
  V C G CHIPLIN
HIGHBROOK (All Saints) and West Hoathly *Chich 6*
  P *Ld Chan* **V** *Vacant* Sharpthorne (0342) 810494
HIGHBURY (Christ Church) (St John) (St Saviour) *Lon 6*
  P *Ch Trust Fund Trust and Islington Ch Trust (jt)*
  V J R LITTLEWOOD
HIGHBURY NEW PARK (St Augustine) *Lon 6*
  P *Trustees* **V** P M ALLCOCK
HIGHCLERE (St Michael and All Angels) and
  Ashmansworth w Crux Easton *Win 6* **P** *Earl of*
  Carnarvon **R** T F HORSINGTON
HIGHCLIFFE (St Mark) w Hinton Admiral *Win 8*
  P *Sir George Tapps-Gervis-Meyrick, Bt, and Bp (alt)*
  V J N SEAFORD, **C** B L PICKETT, **Hon C** K G DAVIS
HIGHER: *see also under substantive place names*
HIGHER FOLD Leigh (St Matthew) Bedf Leigh *Man*
HIGHERTOWN (All Saints) and Baldhu *Truro 6* **P** *Bp*
  and Viscount Falmouth (alt) **V** W A D BERRYMAN
HIGHFIELD (All Saints) *Ox 4* **P** *Bp* **V** J E COCKE,
  C J T LAW
HIGHFIELD (St Catherine) New Bury *Man*
HIGHFIELD (St Matthew) *Liv 15* **P** *Trustees*
  V W H HARRINGTON
HIGHFIELD (St Paul) Hemel Hempstead *St Alb*
HIGHGATE (All Saints) *Lon 20* **P** *Bp*
  V D H HUBBARD, **Hon C** J S BOWDEN
HIGHGATE (St Augustine) *Lon 20* **P** *Bp* **V** T BUGBY
HIGHGATE (St Michael) *Lon 20* **P** *Bp* **V** J J FIELDING,
  C R A HAMILTON, **Par Dn** M SHERWIN
HIGHGATE CENTRE (not known) Bredbury St Barn
  Ches
HIGHGATE RISE (St Anne) Brookfield *Lon 20* **P** *Bp*
  P-in-c C G POPE
HIGHLEY (St Mary) *Heref 9* **P** *MMCET*
  V C G WILLIAMS, **C** T C WILSON
HIGHMORE (St Paul) Nettlebed w Bix and Highmore
  Ox
HIGHNAM (Holy Innocents), Lassington, Rudford,
  Tibberton and Taynton *Glouc 3* **P** *D&C,*
  T J Fenton Esq, and A E Woolley (jt) **R** P J GREEN,
  Hon C G N CRAGO, **NSM** D R EADY
HIGHTERS HEATH (Immanuel) *Birm 8* **P** *Bp*
  V N C M SALTER
HIGHTOWN (St Barnabas) Hartshead and Hightown
  Wakef
HIGHTOWN (St Stephen) *Liv 5* **P** *Bp* **V** *Vacant*
  051-929 2469
HIGHWEEK (All Saints) (St Mary) and Teigngrace *Ex 11*
  P *Bp* **R** C R KNOTT
HIGHWORTH (St Michael) w Sevenhampton and
  Inglesham and Hannington *Bris 12* **P** *Bp (4 turns),*
  Mrs M G Hussey-Freke (1 turn) **V** A N GRAHAM,
  C M J LODGE, **NSM** T S MAGSON
HILBOROUGH (All Saints) w Bodney *Nor 18* **P** *DBP*
  P-in-c C W T CHALCRAFT, **C** G H WHEATLEY
HILDENBOROUGH (St John the Evangelist) *Roch 10*
  P *V Tonbridge* **V** R J BAWTREE, **C** S JONES,
  NSM E M TOY

HILDERSHAM (Holy Trinity) *Ely 4* **P** *Trustees*
  P-in-c G E TURNER
HILDERSTONE (Christ Church) Fulford w Hilderstone
  Lich
HILFIELD (St Nicholas) Yetminster w Ryme Intrinseca
  and High Stoy *Sarum*
HILGAY (All Saints) *Ely 16* **P** *Hertf Coll Ox*
  R A G COCHRANE
HILL (St James) *Birm 9* **P** *Bp* **V** R D HINDLEY,
  C D R PATTERSON, **Hon C** R A ROGERS
HILL (St Michael) Stone w Woodford and Hill *Glouc*
HILL CROOME (St Mary) Ripple, Earls Croome w Hill
  Croome and Strensham *Worc*
HILL TOP (Mission Room) Greasley *S'well*
HILLESDEN (All Saints) Lenborough *Ox*
HILLESLEY (St Giles) Kingswood w Alderley and
  Hillesley *Glouc*
HILLFARRANCE (Holy Cross) Bradf w Oake,
  Hillfarrance and Heathfield *B & W*
HILLINGDON (All Saints) *Lon 24* **P** *Bp*
  V R A PHILLIPS, **Hon C** R H M FLETCHER
HILLINGDON (St John the Baptist) *Lon 24* **P** *Bp*
  V L D MACKENZIE, **C** J M KNIGHT
HILLINGTON (St Mary the Virgin) *Nor 21* **P** *Major the*
  Hon G Dawnay **C** G R HALL
HILLMORTON (St John the Baptist) *Cov 6* **P** *Bp and*
  TR Rugby **V** A P HAINES
HILLOCK (St Andrew) *Man 14* **P** *Bp and R Stand All SS*
  V J McGRATH
HILLSBOROUGH and Wadsley Bridge (Christ Church)
  Sheff 4 **P** *Ch Patr Trust* **V** A NEWMAN,
  C P A WILLIAMS
HILLTOP (Mission Room) Endon w Stanley *Lich*
HILMARTON (St Lawrence) Bremhill w Foxham and
  Hilmarton *Sarum*
HILPERTON (St Michael and All Angels) w Whaddon and
  Staverton w Hilperton Marsh *Sarum 17*
  P *R Trowbridge St Jas and Viscount Long (alt)*
  R R B HICKS, **Par Dn** S S WILKINS
HILPERTON MARSH (St Mary) Hilperton w Whaddon
  and Staverton etc *Sarum*
HILSTON (St Margaret) Roos and Garton in
  Holderness w Tunstall etc *York*
HILTON (All Saints) Milton Abbas, Hilton w
  Cheselbourne etc *Sarum*
HILTON (St Mary Magdalene) *Ely 9* **P** *Bp*
  V N E GREEN
HILTON IN CLEVELAND (St Peter) *York 22* **P** *DBP*
  P-in-c M D A DYKES
HIMBLETON (St Mary Magdalen) Bowbrook S *Worc*
HIMLEY (St Michael and All Angels) *Lich 6* **P** *Bp*
  P-in-c S E ABLEWHITE
HINCASTER (Mission Room) Heversham *Carl*
HINCHLEY WOOD (St Christopher) *Guildf 8* **P** *Bp*
  V R D ROBINSON
HINCKLEY (Assumption of St Mary the Virgin)
  (St Francis) (St Paul) *Leic 13* **P** *Bp* **Dss** M PLATT
HINCKLEY (Holy Trinity) (St John the Evangelist) *Leic 13*
  P *DBP* **TR** G D HAYLES
HINDERCLAY (St Mary) Hepworth, Hinderclay,
  Wattisfield and Thelnetham *St E*
HINDERWELL (St Hilda) w Roxby *York 23* **P** *Abp*
  R D J DERMOTT
HINDHEAD (St Alban) *Guildf 3* **P** *Adn Surrey*
  V J N E BUNDOCK
HINDLEY (All Saints) *Liv 14* **P** *R Wigan*
  V P H BURMAN, **AV** D C MAYLOR
HINDLEY (St Peter) *Liv 14* **P** *St Pet Coll Ox*
  V C D S WOODHOUSE, **AV** M D TETLEY
HINDLEY GREEN (St John) *Liv 14* **P** *Bp* **V** *Vacant*
  Wigan (0942) 55833
HINDLIP (St James) Salwarpe and Hindlip w Martin
  Hussingtree *Worc*
HINDOLVESTON (St George) Foulsham w
  Hindolveston and Guestwick *Nor*
HINDON (St John the Baptist) Tisbury *Sarum*
HINDRINGHAM (St Martin) Barney, Fulmodeston w
  Croxton, Hindringham etc *Nor*
HINDSFORD (St Anne) *Man 13* **P** *Bp* **V** A S WELLS
HINGHAM (St Andrew) w Woodrising w Scoulton *Nor 12*
  P *Earl of Verulam and Trustees (alt)* **R** D J BOURNE
HINKSEY, NEW (St John the Evangelist) S Hinksey *Ox*
HINKSEY, NORTH (St Lawrence) and Wytham *Ox 7*
  P *Bp* **R** P H RYE, **Hon C** R T BECKWITH
HINKSEY, SOUTH (St Lawrence) *Ox 7* **P** *Bp*
  V E J C DAVIS, **Hon C** B SINGH
HINSTOCK (St Oswald) and Sambrook *Lich 22* **P** *Bp*
  and R Edgmond (jt) **R** G A H ATKINS

HINTLESHAM (St Nicholas) w Chattisham *St E 3*
P *St Chad's Coll Dur (3 turns)*, *Bp (1 turn)*
P-in-c N J HARTLEY

HINTON ADMIRAL (St Michael and All Angels)
Highcliffe w Hinton Admiral *Win*

**HINTON AMPNER (All Saints) w Bramdean and
Kilmeston** *Win 1*　**P** *D&C and The Crown (alt)*
R *Vacant*　Bramdean (096279) 223

HINTON BLEWETT (St Margaret)　E w W Harptree
and Hinton Blewett *B & W*

HINTON CHARTERHOUSE (St John the Baptist)
Freshford, Limpley Stoke and Hinton Charterhouse
B & W

HINTON-IN-THE-HEDGES (Holy Trinity)
Farthinghoe w Hinton-in-the-Hedges w Steane *Pet*

HINTON MARTEL (St John the Evangelist) *Sarum 10*
P *Earl of Shaftesbury*　**R** W H BARNARD

HINTON-ON-THE-GREEN (St Peter)　Sedgeberrow w
Hinton-on-the-Green *Worc*

HINTON PARVA (St Swithun)　Lyddington and
Wanborough and Bishopstone etc *Bris*

HINTON ST GEORGE (St George)　Merriott w Hinton,
Dinnington and Lopen *B & W*

HINTON ST MARY (St Mary)　Sturminster Newton and
Hinton St Mary *Sarum*

HINTON WALDRIST (St Margaret)　Cherbury *Ox*

HINTS (St Bartholomew) *Lich 5*　**P** *Personal Reps
A E Jones Esq*　**V** *Vacant*

HINXHILL (St Mary)　Mersham w Hinxhill *Cant*

HINXTON (St Mary and St John) *Ely 7*　**P** *Jes Coll Cam*
V A L WAY,　**Hon Par Dn** B E WAY

HINXWORTH (St Nicholas) w Newnham and Radwell
St Alb 5　**P** *Bp (3 turns)*, *R Smyth Esq (1 turn)*, *and
N J A Farr Esq (1 turn)*　**Hon C** J LAING

HIPSWELL (St John the Evangelist) *Ripon 2*　**P** *Bp*
V G K TIBBO

HISTON (St Andrew) *Ely 5*　**P** *MMCET*
V H K McCURDY,　**Par Dn** J M PRATT

HITCHAM (All Saints) w Little Finborough *St E 10*　**P** *Bp
and Pemb Coll Ox (alt)*　**R** C E WETHERALL

HITCHAM (St Mary)　Burnham w Dropmore, Hitcham
and Taplow *Ox*

HITCHIN (Holy Saviour) (St Faith) (St Mark) (St Mary)
St Alb 9　**P** *Patr Bd*　**TR** C J OFFER,
TV W T A MATTHEWS,　D A HALL,　L D HARMAN,
C T F PYKE,　**Hon Par Dn** M ETHERIDGE

HITTISLEIGH (St Andrew) *Ex 12*　**P** *Bp*　**V** C J L NAPIER

HIXON (St Peter) w Stowe-by-Chartley *Lich 21*　**P** *DBP*
NSM J M OAKES

HOAR CROSS (Holy Angels) w Newchurch *Lich 20*　**P** *Bp
and Meynell Ch Trustees*　**P-in-c** H HUGHES,
NSM G E TOWLSON

HOARWITHY (St Catherine)　How Caple w
Sollarshope, Sellack etc *Heref*

HOATH (Holy Cross)　St Nicholas at Wade w Sarre and
Chislet w Hoath *Cant*

HOATHLY, EAST (not known)　Chiddingly w E
Hoathly *Chich*

HOATHLY, WEST (St Margaret)　Highbrook and W
Hoathly *Chich*

HOBS MOAT (St Mary) *Birm 13*　**P** *Bp*　**V** D A LEAHY

**HOBY (All Saints) cum Rotherby w Brooksby, Ragdale and
Thrussington** *Leic 6*　**P** *Bp and DBP (jt)*
NSM S T W GEARY

HOCKERILL (All Saints) *St Alb 4*　**P** *Bp Lon*
V A J ALLSOP,　**C** N F A REYNOLDS,
NSM A I JOHNSTON

**HOCKERING (St Michael), Honingham, East Tuddenham
and North Tuddenham** *Nor 12*　**P** *J V Berney Esq
(1 turn)*, *DBP (2 turns)*　**R** *Vacant*　Norwich (0603)
880121

HOCKERTON (St Nicholas)　Kirklington w Hockerton
S'well

**HOCKHAM w Shropham Group of Parishes (Great w
Little Hockham w Larling w Illington w Shropham,
Snetterton and Wretham)** *Nor 17*　**P** *Bp, Major
E H C Garnier, DBP, and Charterhouse (jt)*
V D F BUTTON

HOCKHAM, GREAT (Holy Trinity)　see above

HOCKLEY (St Matthew)　Wilnecote *Lich*

HOCKLEY (St Peter and St Paul) *Chelmsf 14*
P *Wadh Coll Ox*　**V** P H T LYNESS

HOCKLIFFE (St Nicholas)　Leighton Buzzard w
Eggington, Hockliffe etc *St Alb*

HOCKWOLD (St James) w Wilton *Ely 15*　**P** *G&C Coll
Cam*　**R** A J ROWE

HOCKWORTHY (St Simon and St Jude)　Sampford
Peverell, Uplowman, Holcombe Rogus etc *Ex*

HODDESDON (St Catherine and St Paul) *St Alb 6*
P *Peache Trustees*　**V** J H SPRINGBETT,　**C** W J YATES

HODDLESDEN (St Paul)　Darwen St Pet w Hoddlesden
Blackb

HODGE HILL (St Philip and St James) *Birm 11*　**P** *Bp*
TR R J TAYLOR,　**TV** H L M SOWDON,
Par Dn W E DUDLEY

HODNET (St Luke) w Weston under Redcastle *Lich 24*
P *A E H Heber-Percy Esq*　**R** J H GREEN

HODTHORPE (St Martin)　Whitwell *Derby*

HOE (St Andrew)　Swanton Morley w Beetley w E
Bilney and Hoe *Nor*

HOE, WEST (St Michael)　Plymouth St Andr w St Paul
and St Geo *Ex*

HOE BENHAM (not known)　Welford w Wickham and
Gt Shefford, Boxford etc *Ox*

HOGGESTON (Holy Cross)　Schorne *Ox*

HOGHTON (Holy Trinity) *Blackb 6*　**P** *V Leyland*
V *Vacant*　Hoghton (025485) 2529

HOGNASTON (St Bartholomew)　Hulland, Atlow,
Bradley and Hognaston *Derby*

HOGSTHORPE (St Mary)　Chapel St Leonards w
Hogsthorpe *Linc*

HOLBEACH (All Saints) *Linc 16*　**P** *Bp*　**V** P HILL

HOLBEACH FEN (St John) *Linc 16*　**P** *Bp*　**V** *Vacant*

**HOLBEACH MARSH (St Luke) (St Mark) (St Martin)
(St Matthew)** *Linc 16*　**P** *V Holbeach*　**V** W A S PARKER

HOLBECK (St Luke the Evangelist) *Ripon 6*　**P** *Bp,
V Leeds St Pet, and Meynell Ch Trust (jt)*
P-in-c C P JOHNSON,　**C** P B STOODLEY

HOLBETON (All Saints) *Ex 21*　**P** *The Crown*
V K W KNIGHT

HOLBORN (St Alban the Martyr) w Saffron Hill (St Peter)
Lon 1　**P** *D&C St Paul's*　**V** J B GASKELL

**HOLBORN (St George the Martyr) Queen Square (Holy
Trinity) (St Bartholomew) Grays Inn Road** *Lon 1*
P *Ch Soc Trust*　**R** D K WERNER

HOLBORN (St-Giles-in-the-Fields)　St Giles-in-the-
Fields *Lon*

HOLBROOK (All Saints) w Freston and Woolverstone
St E 5　**P** *Bp*　**P-in-c** A B LEIGHTON

HOLBROOK (St Michael) and Little Eaton *Derby 11*
P *DBP*　**NSM** P J OWEN-JONES

HOLBROOK ROAD (St Swithin)　Belper *Derby*

HOLBROOKS (St Luke) *Cov 2*　**P** *Bp*　**V** J F TWISLETON,
NSM W H POULTNEY

HOLBURY (Good Shepherd)　Fawley *Win*

HOLCOMBE (Emmanuel) (Canon Lewis Hall) *Man 10*
P *R Bury St Mary*　**R** F BOWYER

HOLCOMBE (St Andrew)　Coleford w Holcombe
B & W

HOLCOMBE (St George)　Dawlish *Ex*

HOLCOMBE BURNELL (St John the Baptist) *Ex 6*　**P** *Bp*
P-in-c A J STONE

HOLCOMBE ROGUS (All Saints)　Sampford Peverell,
Uplowman, Holcombe Rogus etc *Ex*

HOLCOT (St Mary and All Saints)　Brixworth w Holcot
Pet

HOLDENHURST (St John the Evangelist) *Win 7*　**P** *Bp*
V P H RENYARD

HOLDGATE (Holy Trinity)　Diddlebury w Munslow,
Holdgate and Tugford *Heref*

HOLFORD (St Mary the Virgin)　Quantoxhead *B & W*

**HOLKHAM (St Withiburga) w Egmere w Warham, Wells-
next-the-Sea and Wighton** *Nor 20*　**P** *Viscount Coke
(2 turns), M J Beddard Esq (2 turns), and D&C (1 turn)*
R W A J SAYER

HOLLACOMBE (St Petroc)　Holsworthy w Hollacombe
and Milton Damerel *Ex*

HOLLAND, GREAT (All Saints)　Kirby-le-Soken w Gt
Holland *Chelmsf*

HOLLAND, NEW (Christ Church)　Barrow and Goxhill
Linc

HOLLAND FEN (All Saints)　Brothertoft Gp *Linc*

HOLLAND-ON-SEA (St Bartholomew) *Chelmsf 26*
P *Ch Patr Trust*　**V** A I PAGET

HOLLESLEY (All Saints)　Boyton w Capel St Andrew
and Hollesley *St E*

HOLLINFARE (St Helen) *Liv 12*　**P** *R Warrington*
V A J BOOTH

**HOLLINGBOURNE (All Saints) and Hucking w Leeds and
Broomfield** *Cant 15*　**P** *Abp*　**V** C M DENT

HOLLINGDEAN (St Richard)　Brighton St Matthias
Chich

HOLLINGTON (St John the Evangelist)　Croxden *Lich*

**HOLLINGTON (St John the Evangelist) (St Peter and
St Paul)** *Chich 17*　**P** *Ch Patr Trust*　**NSM** K E PIERCE

HOLLINGTON (St Leonard) (St Anne) *Chich 17*
P *E G Brabazon Esq* **R** E F P BRYANT,
C K A MEPHAM
HOLLINGWOOD (St Francis) Staveley and Barrow
Hill *Derby*
HOLLINGWORTH (St Hilda) Milnrow *Man*
HOLLINGWORTH (St Mary) *Ches 14* **P** *Trustees*
V E PRATT
HOLLINSWOOD (not known) Cen Telford *Lich*
HOLLINWOOD (St Margaret) *Man 18* **P** *R Prestwich
St Mary* **V** A GEORGE, **C** P R LOMAS
HOLLOWAY (St Francis of Assisi) W Holl St Luke *Lon*
HOLLOWAY (St Mark) (Emmanuel) *Lon 6* **P** *CPAS*
V R S CAMPBELL, **C** S D BESSANT, D E SMITH
HOLLOWAY (St Mary Magdalene) *Lon 6* **P** *Bp and
V Islington St Mary (jt)* **V** S J W COX, **C** R A LEWIS
HOLLOWAY, UPPER (St Peter) (St John) *Lon 6*
P *CPAS and Islington Ch Trust (jt)* **V** M R WHITE,
Par Dn E E BALL
HOLLOWAY, WEST (St Luke) *Lon 6* **P** *Lon Coll Div
Trustees* **V** T J PIGREM, **Par Dn** V A DICK
HOLLOWELL (St James) Guilsborough w Hollowell
and Cold Ashby *Pet*
HOLLY HILL (Church Centre) Frankley *Birm*
HOLLYBUSH (All Saints) Berrow w Pendock,
Eldersfield, Hollybush etc *Worc*
HOLLYM (St Nicholas) Patrington w Hollym, Welwick
and Winestead *York*
HOLMBRIDGE (St David) Upper Holme Valley *Wakef*
HOLMBURY ST MARY (St Mary the Virgin) Wotton
and Holmbury St Mary *Guildf*
HOLMCROFT (St Bertelin) Stafford *Lich*
HOLME (Holy Trinity) Burton and Holme *Carl*
HOLME (St Giles) Langford w Holme *S'well*
HOLME (St Giles) w Conington *Ely 13* **P** *Ld Chan and
J H B Heathcote Esq (alt)* **V** G J SHARPE
HOLME, EAST (St John the Evangelist) Wareham
Sarum
HOLME CULTRAM (St Cuthbert) *Carl 3* **P** *V Holme
Cultram St Mary* **V** A D WHIPP
HOLME CULTRAM (St Mary) *Carl 3* **P** *Ox Univ*
V A D WHIPP
HOLME EDEN (St Paul) *Carl 2* **P** *DBP* **V** J S CASSON
HOLME HALE (St Andrew) Necton w Holme Hale *Nor*
HOLME-IN-CLIVIGER (St John the Divine) *Blackb 3*
P *Mrs C P Creed* **P-in-c** A R FREARSON
HOLME LACY (St Cuthbert) w Dinedor *Heref 4*
P *Patr Bd* **V** T P JONES, **TV** R NORTH
HOLME-NEXT-THE-SEA (St Mary) Hunstanton St
Mary w Ringstead Parva, Holme etc *Nor*
**HOLME-ON-SPALDING MOOR (All Saints) (Old School
Mission Room)** *York 7* **P** *St Jo Coll Cam* **V** D S COOK
HOLME PIERREPONT (St Edmund) Radcliffe-on-
Trent and Shelford etc *S'well*
**HOLME RUNCTON (St James) w South Runcton and
Wallington** *Ely 16* **P** *Bp* **R** J C W NOLAN
HOLME WOOD (St Christopher) Tong *Bradf*
HOLMER (St Bartholomew) (St Mary) w Huntington
Heref 3 **P** *D&C* **V** G FLEMING
HOLMER GREEN (Christ Church) Penn Street *Ox*
HOLMES CHAPEL (St Luke) Church Hulme *Ches*
HOLMESDALE (St Philip) Dronfield w Holmesfield
Derby
HOLMESFIELD (St Swithin) as above
HOLMEWOOD (St Alban Mission) Heath *Derby*
HOLMFIELD (St Andrew) *Wakef 4* **P** *Bp* **V** G A BANKS
HOLMFIRTH (Holy Trinity) Upper Holme Valley
Wakef
HOLMPTON (St Nicholas) Easington w Skeffling,
Kilnsea and Holmpton *York*
HOLMSIDE (St John) *Dur 8* **P** *The Crown* **V** *Vacant*
Lanchester (0207) 521910
HOLMWOOD (St Mary Magdalene) *Guildf 7* **P** *Bp*
V W D LANG
HOLMWOOD, NORTH (St John the Evangelist) *Guildf 12*
P *Bp* **V** W C FREDERICK
HOLNE (St Mary the Virgin) Widecombe-in-the-Moor,
Leusdon, Princetown etc *Ex*
HOLNEST (Church of the Assumption) Dungeon Hill
Sarum
**HOLSWORTHY (St Peter and St Paul) w Hollacombe and
Milton Damerel** *Ex 9* **P** *DBP and Mrs F M Palmer (jt)*
R R M REYNOLDS
HOLT (St Andrew) *Nor 22* **P** *St Jo Coll Cam*
R S S GREGORY
HOLT (St James) Wimborne Minster and Holt *Sarum*
HOLT (St Katharine) Broughton Gifford, Gt Chalfield
and Holt *Sarum*
HOLT (St Martin) Grimley w Holt *Worc*

HOLTBY (Holy Trinity) Stockton-on-the-Forest w
Holtby and Warthill *York*
**HOLTON (St Bartholomew) and Waterperry w Albury and
Waterstock** *Ox 1* **P** *DBP* **R** D M W ROBINSON
HOLTON (St Nicholas) Camelot Par *B & W*
HOLTON (St Peter) Halesworth w Linstead, Chediston,
Holton etc *St E*
HOLTON-CUM-BECKERING (All Saints) Wickenby
Gp *Linc*
HOLTON-LE-CLAY (St Peter) *Linc 10* **P** *Ld Chan*
V J M THOMPSON, **Hon C** L F FIELD
HOLTON-LE-MOOR (St Luke) S Kelsey Gp *Linc*
HOLTON ST MARY (St Mary) w Great Wenham *St E 3*
P *Bp and Sir Joshua Rowley, Bt (alt)*
P-in-c B A TOLL, M B ETTLINGER
HOLTS (St Hugh) Conventional District *Man 18*
C-in-c M JONES
HOLTSPUR (St Thomas) Beaconsfield *Ox*
HOLTYE (St Peter) Cowden w Hammerwood *Chich*
HOLWELL (St Laurence) The Caundles w Folke and
Holwell *Sarum*
HOLWELL (St Leonard) Ab Kettleby Gp *Leic*
HOLWELL (St Mary the Virgin) Alvescot w Black
Bourton, Shilton, Holwell etc *Ox*
HOLWELL (St Peter) Ickleford w Holwell *St Alb*
HOLWORTH (St Catherine by the Sea) Broadmayne,
W Knighton, Owermoigne etc *Sarum*
HOLY ISLAND (St Mary the Virgin) *Newc 12* **P** *Bp*
V D ADAM, **Hon C** C E TRISTRAM
HOLYBOURNE (Holy Rood) Froyle and Holybourne
Win
HOLYMOORSIDE (St Peter) Brampton St Thos *Derby*
HOLYSTONE (St Mary the Virgin) Alwinton w
Holystone and Alnham *Newc*
HOLYWELL (St John the Baptist) w Needingworth *Ely 11*
P *Bp* **R** O SWAN
HOLYWELL (St Mary) Seghill *Newc*
HOMERSFIELD (St Mary) Flixton w Homersfield and
S Elmham *St E*
HOMERTON (Christ Church on the Mead) Hackney
Marsh *Lon*
HOMERTON (St Barnabas w St Paul) as above
HOMERTON (St Luke) *Lon 5* **P** *St Olave Hart Street
Trustees* **V** C D HEWITT,
Hon C C J M MAXWELL, G S KENDALL
HOMINGTON (St Mary the Virgin) Chalke Valley E
Sarum
HONEYCHURCH (St Mary) N Tawton, Bondleigh,
Sampford Courtenay etc *Ex*
HONICKNOWLE (St Francis) *Ex 23* **P** *Ld Chan*
V *Vacant* Plymouth (0752) 773874
HONILEY (St John the Baptist) Hatton w Haseley,
Rowington w Lowsonford etc *Cov*
HONING (St Peter and St Paul) Smallburgh w Dilham w
Honing and Crostwight *Nor*
HONINGHAM (St Andrew) Hockering, Honingham, E
and N Tuddenham *Nor*
HONINGTON (All Saints) Shipston-on-Stour w
Honington and Idlicote *Cov*
HONINGTON (All Saints) w Sapiston and Troston *St E 9*
P *Ld Chan (2 turns), Duke of Grafton (1 turn)*
P-in-c P M OLIVER, **Par Dn** E S FOGDEN
HONINGTON (St Wilfred) Barkston and Hough Gp
Linc
**HONITON (St Michael) (St Paul), Gittisham, Combe
Raleigh, Monkton and Awliscombe** *Ex 5* **P** *DBP*
TR J W I TREVELYAN, **TV** A J WADSWORTH,
C P F HUTCHINSON, **Hon C** R C H SAUNDERS
HONLEY (St Mary) *Wakef 1* **P** *R Almondbury*
V W J GIBSON
HOO (All Hallows) High Halstow w All Hallows and
Hoo St Mary *Roch*
HOO (St Andrew and St Eustachius) Charsfield w
Debach, Monewden, Hoo etc *St E*
HOO (St Werburgh) *Roch 6* **P** *D&C* **V** D A LOW
HOOBROOK (St Cecilia) Kidderminster St Geo *Worc*
HOOE (St John the Evangelist) *Ex 24* **P** *Keble Coll Ox*
V A B ROBINSON
HOOE (St Oswald) *Chich 14* **P** *Bp* **V** P C CLEMENTS
HOOK (St John the Evangelist) *Win 5* **P** *Bp*
R S J FOSTER
HOOK (St Mary the Virgin) w Airmyn *Sheff 11* **P** *Bp and
Ch Soc Trust (Jt)* **V** H BAGNALL
HOOK (St Mary) w Warsash *Portsm 2* **P** *Bp*
P-in-c T A J READER, **NSM** P A BOGGUST
HOOK (St Paul) *S'wark 14* **P** *The Crown* **V** D C WARD
HOOK COMMON (Good Shepherd) Upton-upon-
Severn *Worc*

HOOK NORTON (St Peter) w Great Rollright, Swerford and Wigginton Ox 3　P Bp, DBP, BNC Ox, and Jes Coll Ox (jt)　R M R C PRICE
HOOKE (St Giles)　Beaminster Area Sarum
HOOLE (All Saints) Ches 2　P Simeon's Trustees
　V B C REEVE,　C R J KITELEY, T A MAPSTONE
HOOLE (St Michael) Blackb 6　P Reps of Mrs E A Dunne and Mrs D Downes (jt)　R A R LINTON
HOOLEY (Mission Hall)　Redhill St Jo S'wark
HOOTON (St Paul) Ches 9　P Trustees
　V R W CAMPBELL
HOOTON PAGNELL (All Saints)　Bilham Sheff
HOOTON ROBERTS (St John)　Thrybergh w Hooton Roberts Sheff
HOPE (Holy Trinity) w Shelve Heref 13　P New Coll Ox (3 turns), Lady More (1 turn)　R N D MINSHALL
HOPE (St James) Man 6　P Trustees　V D SHARPLES
HOPE (St Peter) and Castleton Derby 2　P Bp and D&C Lich (jt)　V M F COLLIER
HOPE BAGOT (St John the Baptist)　Burford II w Greete and Hope Bagot Heref
HOPE BOWDLER (St Andrew) w Eaton-under-Heywood Heref 11　P DBP, Bp Birm, and Mrs R Bell (jt)　R M BROMFIELD
HOPE COVE (St Clement)　Malborough w S Huish, W Alvington and Churchstow Ex
HOPE MANSEL (St Michael)　Weston-under-Penyard w Hope Mansel and the Lea Heref
HOPE-UNDER-DINMORE (St Mary the Virgin)　Bodenham w Hope-under-Dinmore, Felton etc Heref
HOPESAY (St Mary the Virgin)　Lydbury N w Hopesay and Edgton Heref
HOPTON (All Saints), Market Weston, Barningham and Coney Weston St E 9　P Ld Chan and Bp (alt)　R C P GANE
HOPTON (St Margaret) w Corton Nor 15　P Ld Chan and D&C (alt)　V C R CHAPMAN
HOPTON (St Peter)　Salt and Sandon w Burston Lich
HOPTON, UPPER (St John the Evangelist) Wakef 10　P V Mirfield　P-in-c P W LEITCH
HOPTON CASTLE (St Edward)　Clungunford w Clunbury and Clunton, Bedstone etc Heref
HOPTON WAFERS (St Michael and All Angels)　Cleobury Mortimer w Hopton Wafers Heref
HOPWAS (St Chad)　Tamworth Lich
HOPWOOD (St John) Man 19　P R Bury St Mary
　V J R BROCKLEHURST
HORAM (Christ Church) (St James) Chich 15　P Bp
　V J LASHBROOKE
HORBLING (St Andrew) Linc 13　P Bp
　V H J THEODOSIUS
HORBURY (St Peter and St Leonard) w Horbury Bridge (St John) Wakef 12　P Provost　V O J AISBITT
HORBURY JUNCTION (St Mary) Wakef 12　P DBP
　V R A CLEMENTS,　NSM M C ALDCROFT
HORDEN (St Mary) Dur 3　P Bp　V A BOWSER
HORDLE (All Saints) Win 10　P Bp　V M G ANDERSON, **Hon C** R S HALSE, F G WELCH,　NSM J G SMITH
HORDLEY (St Mary the Virgin)　Baschurch and Weston Lullingfield w Hordley Lich
HORFIELD (Holy Trinity) Bris 6　P Bp　R J H WILSON, **C** J J HASLER
HORFIELD (St Gregory) Bris 6　P Bp　V J A MORLEY-BUNKER,　NSM A R GOOD
HORHAM (St Mary)　Stradbroke, Horham, Athelington and Redlingfield St E
HORKESLEY, GREAT (All Saints) (St John) Chelmsf 20　P Ball Coll Ox　R C G A WOODS
HORKESLEY, LITTLE (St Peter and St Paul)　Wormingford, Mt Bures and Lt Horkesley Chelmsf
HORKSTOW (St Maurice) Linc 6　P DBP
　V A J DRAPER
HORLEY (St Bartholomew) (St Francis) (St Wilfrid) S'wark 24　P Patr Bd　TR S H MASLEN, TV J J LEPINE, K B ROBINSON,　**Par Dn** C E DAKIN (nee HOLLETT)
HORLEY (St Etheldreda) w Hornton and Hanwell, Shenington and Alkerton Ox 5　P Ld Chan, Lord De La Warr, and DBP (by turn)　R A LANCASHIRE
HORLEY ROW (St Wilfrid)　Horley S'wark
HORMEAD (St Mary), Wyddial, Anstey, Brent Pelham and Meesden St Alb 5　P St Jo Coll Cam, Ch Coll Cam, and Bp (by turn)　**P-in-c** G A DREW
HORMEAD (St Nicholas)　Hormead, Wyddial, Anstey, Brent Pelham etc St Alb
HORN HILL (St Paul)　Chalfont St Peter Ox
HORN PARK (St Francis)　Eltham St Jo S'wark
HORNBLOTTON (St Peter)　Six Pilgrims B & W

HORNBY (St Margaret) w Claughton Blackb 15　P D R Battersby Esq and DBF (alt)　V C P G WODEMAN
HORNBY (St Mary) Ripon 4　P D&C York
　V R J PEARSON
HORNCASTLE (St Mary the Virgin) w Low Toynton Linc 11　P Bp (2 turns), Baroness Wiloughby de Eresby (1 turn)　V N A THORNLEY,　C G S DARLISON
HORNCHURCH Elm Park (St Nicholas)　Elm Park St Nic Hornchurch Chelmsf
HORNCHURCH (Holy Cross) Chelmsf 4　P Bp and New Coll Ox (alt)　V R B N HAYCRAFT, **Par Dn** S M PAPWORTH
HORNCHURCH (St Andrew) (St George) (St Matthew) Chelmsf 4　P New Coll Ox　V A C H PEATFIELD, **C** A V WATSON,　**Par Dn** B A BAKER
HORNCHURCH, SOUTH (St John and St Matthew)　Rainham Chelmsf
HORNDALE (St Francis)　Newton Aycliffe Dur
HORNDON, EAST (St Francis) and West Horndon w Little Warley Chelmsf 10　P Bp and Brentwood Sch **P-in-c** C F WELLS
HORNDON ON THE HILL (St Peter and St Paul) Chelmsf 16　P D&C St Paul's　V D J WILLIAMS
HORNE (St Mary) S'wark 23　P Bp　R W G WOOD
HORNING (St Benedict) w Beeston St Laurence and Ashmanhaugh Nor 9　P Bp and Sir Ronald Preston, Bt (jt)　R H A R EDGELL
HORNINGHOLD (St Peter)　Hallaton w Horninghold, Allexton, Tugby etc Leic
HORNINGLOW (St John the Divine) Lich 20　P Trustees　V P J JEFFERIES,　NSM P N BARNES
HORNINGSEA (St Peter) Ely 6　P St Jo Coll Cam **P-in-c** L A MARSH
HORNINGSHAM (St John the Baptist)　Warminster St Denys, Upton Scudamore etc Sarum
HORNINGTOFT (St Edmund)　Colkirk w Oxwick w Pattesley, Whissonsett etc Nor
HORNSEA (St Nicholas) w Atwick York 12　P Ld Chan
　V B H WILCOX
HORNSEY (Christ Church) Lon 20　P Bp
　V J E TOWNSEND
HORNSEY (Holy Innocents) Lon 20　P Bp
P-in-c G B SEABROOK
HORNSEY (St Mary) (St George) Lon 20　P Bp
　R G B SEABROOK, **C** S M MASTERS, M PERRY, C W W BARBER
HORNSEY RISE Whitehall Park Team, The (St Mary) (St Andrew) Lon 6　P Patr Bd　TR M J COLMER, TV S P SAYERS,　C C W W BARBER
HORNTON (St John the Baptist)　Horley w Hornton and Hanwell, Shenington etc Ox
HORRABRIDGE (St John the Baptist)　Sampford Spiney w Horrabridge Ex
HORRINGER (St Leonard) cum Ickworth St E 13　P DBP　R H G HARRISON
HORSEHEATH (All Saints) Ely 4　P Charterhouse **P-in-c** W N C GIRARD
HORSELL (St Mary the Virgin) Guildf 12　P Bp
　V C J FOWLES,　C C R BRIGGS,　NSM B ASHLEY
HORSENDON (St Michael and All Angels)　Bledlow w Saunderton and Horsenden Ox
HORSEY (All Saints)　Winterton w E and W Somerton and Horsey Nor
HORSFORD (All Saints) and Horsham St Faith Nor 4　P Bp　V J B BOSTON
HORSFORTH (St Margaret) Ripon 7　P Bp
　V M E SIDDLE,　C D G CANTRELL
HORSHAM (Holy Trinity) (St Leonard) (St Mary the Virgin) (St Peter in the Causeway) Chich 8　P Patr Bd TR D E E TANSILL, TV D J PROUD, N E D MILMINE, G T MELVIN, C G PIPER,　NSM B SINTON
HORSHAM ST FAITH (St Mary and Andrew)　Horsford and Horsham St Faith Nor
HORSINGTON (All Saints) w Stixwould Linc 11　P DBP **P-in-c** R I McMASTER
HORSINGTON (St John the Baptist)　Abbas and Templecombe w Horsington B & W
HORSLEY (Holy Trinity)　Bellingham/Otterburn Gp Newc
HORSLEY (St Clement) Derby 12　P Bp
P-in-c P S WALES
HORSLEY (St Martin) and Newington Bagpath w Kingscote Glouc 16　P Bp (2 turns), DBP (1 turn)　V G DEWHURST
HORSLEY, EAST (St Martin) Guildf 10　P D&C Cant
　R E B HUBAND
HORSLEY, WEST (St Mary) Guildf 10
　P Col A R N Weston　R P E B ROBINSON

HORSLEY HILL S Shields (St Lawrence the Martyr)
Dur 7 **P** *D&C* **V** D C COULING
HORSLEY WOODHOUSE (St Susanna) *Derby 12* **P** *Bp*
P-in-c D J PHYPERS
HORSMONDEN (St Margaret) *Roch 11* **P** *Bp*
R *Vacant* Brenchley (089272) 2521
HORSPATH (St Giles) Garsington and Horspath *Ox*
HORSTEAD (All Saints) Coltishall w Gt Hautbois and
Horstead *Nor*
HORSTED, LITTLE (St Michael and All Angels) *Chich 21*
P *Rt Rev P J Ball* **R** C J PETERS
HORSTED KEYNES (St Giles) *Chich 6* **P** *Bp*
R D A STONEBANKS
HORTON (All Saints) *Bradf 2* **P** *J F Bardsley Esq*
P-in-c W HOLLIDAY, **C** P C HACKWOOD
HORTON (St James the Elder) and Little Sodbury *Glouc 7*
P *Duke of Beaufort (1 turn), CPAS (2 turns)*
R K V ENSOR
HORTON (St Mary Magdalene) Hardingstone and
Horton and Piddington *Pet*
HORTON (St Mary the Virgin) *Newc 1* **P** *V Woodhorn w*
Newbiggin **V** I C YOUNG, **C** A STOKER
HORTON (St Michael) *Lich 14* **P** *Bp* **P-in-c** B H PEEL
HORTON (St Michael and All Angels) Riverside *Ox*
HORTON (St Peter) Donyatt w Horton, Broadway and
Ashill *B & W*
HORTON (St Wolfrida) and Chalbury *Sarum 10* **P** *Earl*
of Shaftesbury **V** *Vacant*
HORTON, GREAT (St John the Evangelist) *Bradf 2*
P *V Bradf* **V** S ALLEN, **C** A G KAYE, **NSM** L J SLOW
HORTON-CUM-STUDLEY (St Barnabas) *Ox 1*
P *V Beckley* **V** A G A de VERE
HORTON-IN-RIBBLESDALE (St Oswald) Langcliffe
w Stainforth and Horton *Bradf*
HORTON KIRBY (St Mary) *Roch 2* **P** *Bp* **V** L E LAKER
HORWICH (Holy Trinity) (St Catherine) (St Elizabeth)
Man 11 **P** *Patr Bd* **TR** D W GATENBY,
TV D B GRIFFITHS, W P BREW, **C** R J CARMYLLIE
HORWOOD (St Michael) Newton Tracey, Alverdiscott,
Huntshaw etc *Ex*
HORWOOD, GREAT (St James) Winslow w Gt
Horwood and Addington *Ox*
HORWOOD, LITTLE (St Nicholas) Mursley w
Swanbourne and Lt Horwood *Ox*
HOSE (St Michael) Harby, Long Clawson and Hose *Leic*
HOTHAM (St Oswald) *York 14* **P** *Ld Chan*
R P N HAYWARD
HOTHFIELD (St Margaret) Westwell, Hothfield,
Eastwell and Boughton Aluph *Cant*
HOUGH GREEN (All Saints) Ditton St Mich *Liv*
HOUGH-ON-THE-HILL (All Saints) Barkston and
Hough Gp *Linc*
HOUGHAM (All Saints) as above
HOUGHAM (St Laurence) Alkham w Capel le Ferne
and Hougham *Cant*
HOUGHTON (All Saints) Broughton, Bossington,
Houghton and Mottisfont *Win*
HOUGHTON (St Giles) Walsingham and Houghton
Nor
HOUGHTON (St John the Evangelist) (St Peter) *Carl 3*
P *Trustees* **V** J McALLEN, **C** S D N VIBERT
HOUGHTON (St Martin) Coxford Gp *Nor*
HOUGHTON (St Mary) w Wyton *Ely 9* **P** *Bp*
R D D BILLINGS
HOUGHTON (St Nicholas) Bury and Houghton *Chich*
**HOUGHTON, GREAT (St Mary) and LITTLE (St Mary
the Blessed Virgin) w Brafield on the Green** *Pet 7*
P *Magd Coll Ox, Mrs A C Usher, and*
C G V Davidge Esq (jt) **R** A J BEHRENS
HOUGHTON, GREAT (St Michael and All Angels)
Darfield *Sheff*
HOUGHTON, NEW (Christ Church) Pleasley *Derby*
HOUGHTON CONQUEST (All Saints) Wilshamstead
and Houghton Conquest *St Alb*
HOUGHTON LE SPRING (St Michael and All Angels)
Dur 6 **P** *Bp* **R** P T FISHER, **C** I H JORYSZ,
Par Dn C A DICK
HOUGHTON-ON-THE-HILL (St Catharine) Keyham and
Hungarton *Leic 5* **P** *Bp* **R** O S BENNETT,
NSM J S HOPEWELL
HOUGHTON REGIS (All Saints) (St Thomas) *St Alb 18*
P *DBP* **V** G M NEAL, **C** C W WOOD
HOUND (St Edward the Confessor) (St Mary the Virgin)
Win 9 **P** *St Mary's Coll Win* **V** J R WILLIAMS
HOUNSLOW (Holy Trinity) (St Paul) *Lon 11* **P** *Bp*
V J H BARTER, **C** P B DENTON, **Hon C** J W GARRATT,
NSM N LAWRENCE
HOUNSLOW (St Mary the Virgin) Isleworth St Mary
Lon

HOUNSLOW (St Stephen) *Lon 11* **P** *Bp*
V R L RAMSDEN
HOUNSLOW WEST (Good Shepherd) *Lon 11* **P** *Bp*
V A A COSLETT
HOVE (All Saints) *Chich 4* **P** *Bp*
C J S G COTMAN, M K DAVIS
**HOVE (Bishop Hannington Memorial Church) (Holy
Cross)** *Chich 4* **P** *Trustees* **V** D A ROSS,
C G L WINCHESTER, C G SPINKS, **NSM** E G DORE
HOVE (Holy Trinity) Conventional District *Chich 4*
C-in-c D A COTT
HOVE (St Andrew Old Church) *Chich 4* **P** *V Hove*
V G R WALKER
HOVE (St Barnabas) and St Agnes *Chich 4* **P** *Bp and*
V Hove (alt) **V** F J ARROWSMITH
HOVE (St John the Baptist) *Chich 4* **P** *V Hove*
V *Vacant*
HOVE (St Patrick) *Chich 4* **P** *Bp, V Hove, and*
V Brighton (jt) **V** A B SHARPE
HOVE (St Philip) Aldrington *Chich*
HOVE (St Thomas the Apostle) *Chich 4* **P** *Bp*
V M J GUDGEON
HOVERINGHAM (St Michael) Thurgarton w
Hoveringham and Bleasby etc *S'well*
HOVETON (St John) Wroxham w Hoveton and
Belaugh *Nor*
HOVETON (St Peter) as above
HOVINGHAM (All Saints) Street Team Min *York*
**HOW CAPLE (St Andrew and St Mary) w Sollarshope,
Sellack, Kings Caple, Foy, Hentland and Hoarwithy**
Heref 8 **P** *Bp, D&C, and Brig A F L Clive (jt)*
R M G WOODWARD
HOWDEN Team Ministry, The (St Peter) *York 14* **P** *Abp*
(4 turns), Ld Chan (1 turn)
TV S A EVASON, C I COATES, **C** R W DAVILL
HOWE (St Mary the Virgin) Gt w Lt Poringland and
Howe *Nor*
HOWE BRIDGE (St Michael and All Angels) *Man 13*
P *Trustees* **V** D H BRACEY, **C** A T FLAHERTY
HOWELL (St Oswald) Heckington *Linc*
HOWELL HILL (St Paul) *Guildf 9* **P** *Bp*
V A H R THOMAS, **C** S M OAKLEY
HOWGILL (Holy Trinity) Firbank, Howgill and
Killington *Bradf*
HOWICK (St Michael and All Angels) Longhoughton w
Howick *Newc*
HOWLE HILL (St John the Evangelist) Walford and
Saint John, w Bishopswood etc *Heref*
HOWSHAM (St John) Sand Hutton *York*
**HOXNE (St Peter and St Paul) w Denham, Syleham and
Wingfield** *St E 17* **P** *Bp and DBP (jt)* **R** A R LOWE
HOXTON (Holy Trinity) (St Mary) *Lon 5* **P** *Bp*
V S M WILSON, **C** R J READER
HOXTON (St Anne) (St Columba) *Lon 5* **P** *The Crown*
V A J WYNNE, **Hon C** T J RUSS
HOXTON (St John the Baptist) Shoreditch St Leon and
Hoxton St Jo *Lon*
HOYLAKE (Holy Trinity and St Hildeburgh) *Ches 8*
P *Bp* **V** P L WILLIAMS
HOYLAND, NETHER (St Andrew) *Sheff 7* **P** *Bp*
V G HURST
HOYLAND, NETHER (St Peter) *Sheff 7* **P** *Sir Stephen
Hastings* **V** K M WRAY
**HOYLANDSWAINE (St John the Evangelist) and Silkstone
w Stainborough** *Wakef 7* **P** *Bp* **V** D BIRCH
HUBBERHOLME (St Michael and All Angels)
Kettlewell w Conistone, Hubberholme etc *Bradf*
HUCCABY (St Raphael) Widecombe-in-the-Moor,
Leusdon, Princetown etc *Ex*
HUCCLECOTE (St Philip and St James) *Glouc 5* **P** *Bp*
V P H KENCHINGTON, **C** J D BURN
HUCKING (St Margaret) Hollingbourne and Hucking w
Leeds and Broomfield *Cant*
HUCKLOW, GREAT (Mission Room) Bradwell *Derby*
**HUCKNALL TORKARD (St Mary Magdalene) (St Peter
and St Paul) (St John's Mission Church)** *S'well 4* **P** *Bp*
TR F G GREEN, **TV** T R HAGGIS, **C** M H F BEACH,
NSM R HALLETT
HUDDERSFIELD (Holy Trinity) *Wakef 5* **P** *Simeon's
Trustees* **V** E O ROBERTS, **Par Dn** J WESTON
HUDDERSFIELD (St John the Evangelist)
N Huddersfield *Wakef*
HUDDERSFIELD (St Peter and All Saints) *Wakef 5*
P *DBP* **V** B W MAGUIRE, **C** D A EARL,
NSM D KENT
HUDDERSFIELD (St Thomas) *Wakef 5* **P** *DBP*
P-in-c R S GILES

HUDDERSFIELD, NORTH (St Cuthbert) *Wakef 5*
P *DBP* TR B DAGNALL, TV E D ALLISON,
C J SYKES
HUDDINGTON (St James) Bowbrook S *Worc*
HUDSWELL (St Michael and All Angels) Richmond w
Hudswell *Ripon*
HUGGATE (St Mary) Pocklington and Owsthorpe and
Kilnwick Percy etc *York*
HUGGLESCOTE (St John the Baptist) w Donington,
Ellistown and Snibston *Leic 8* P *Bp*
TR J RICHARDSON, TV R G DAVIS
HUGHENDEN (St Michael) *Ox 29* P *DBP*
V J EASTGATE, NSM F J FRIEND
HUGHLEY (St John the Baptist) Wenlock *Heref*
HUGILL (St Anne) *Carl 9* P *V Kendal H Trin*
P-in-c K B ELLWOOD
HUISH (St James the Less) Shebbear, Buckland
Filleigh, Sheepwash etc *Ex*
HUISH (St Nicholas) Swanborough *Sarum*
HUISH, NORTH (St Mary) Diptford, N Huish,
Harberton and Harbertonford *Ex*
HUISH, SOUTH (Holy Trinity) Malborough w S Huish,
W Alvington and Churchstow *Ex*
HUISH CHAMPFLOWER (St Peter) Chipstable w
Huish Champflower and Clatworthy *B & W*
HUISH EPISCOPI (Blessed Virgin Mary) Langport
Area Chs *B & W*
HULCOTE (St Nicholas) Cranfield and Hulcote w
Salford *St Alb*
HULCOTT (All Saints) Aylesbury w Bierton and
Hulcott *Ox*
HULL (Holy Apostles) Kingston upon Hull H Trin *York*
HULL Lowgate (St Mary the Virgin) Kingston upon
Hull St Mary *York*
HULL Newington (St John the Baptist) Newington w
Dairycoates *York*
HULL Newland (St John) *York 15* P *Abp*
V M H VERNON, C S P WALKER, J C WEETMAN
HULL Sculcoates (St Mary) *York 15* P *V Sculcoates*
NSM J G LEEMAN
HULL Sculcoates (St Stephen) *York 15* P *Ld Chan*
(2 turns), V Hull H Trin (1 turn), and Abp (1 turn)
V F A C S BOWN
HULL (St Cuthbert) *York 15* P *Abp* V J D DAGLISH
HULL (St George) Marfleet *York*
HULL (St Giles) as above
HULL (St Hilda) as above
HULL (St Martin) (Transfiguration) *York 15* P *Abp*
V E WILSON, C M A FRYER
HULL (St Philip) Marfleet *York*
HULL (St Thomas) Derringham Bank *York*
HULL, NORTH (St Michael and All Angels) *York 15*
P *Abp* V D A WALKER, C J L CAMPBELL,
Hon C R HUNTER
HULLAND (Christ Church), Atlow, Bradley and
Hognaston *Derby 8* P *Bp, D&C Lich, Trustees, and*
Exors Col I P A M Walker-Okeover (by turn)
R R K SMITH
HULLAVINGTON (St Mary Magdalene) Stanton St
Quintin, Hullavington, Grittleton etc *Bris*
HULLBRIDGE (St Thomas of Canterbury) Hockley
Chelmsf
HULLBRIDGE (St Thomas of Canterbury) *Chelmsf 14*
P *Bp* V D J SHERWOOD
HULME (Ascension) *Man 4* P *Trustees*
R J A R METHUEN, C P S INMAN, Hon C H C WEST
HULME WALFIELD (St Michael) Eaton and Hulme
Walfield *Ches*
HULTON, LITTLE (St John the Baptist) *Man 12* P *Bp*
V *Vacant* 061-790 2338
HULTON, OVER (St Andrew) Deane *Man*
HUMBER (St Mary the Virgin) Leominster *Heref*
HUMBERSTON (St Peter) *Linc 10* P *Bp* V I H TINKLER
HUMBERSTONE (St Mary) *Leic 1* P *DBP*
V C R OXLEY, C M E LAMBERT
HUMBERSTONE, NEW (St Barnabas) *Leic 1* P *Bp*
P-in-c N H JIGNASU
HUMBLE, WEST (St Michael) Mickleham *Guildf*
HUMBLETON (St Peter) Burton Pidsea and
Humbleton w Elsternwick *York*
HUMPHREY PARK (St Clement) Urmston *Man*
HUMSHAUGH (St Peter) w Simonburn and Wark *Newc 2*
P *Bp*, R S V PRINS
HUNCOAT (St Augustine) Accrington St Jo w Huncoat
Blackb
HUNCOTE (St James the Greater) Narborough and
Huncote *Leic*
HUNDERTON ST MARTIN (St Francis) *Heref*
St Martin w St Fran (S Wye Team Min) *Heref*

HUNDLEBY (St Mary) Spilsby w Hundleby *Linc*
HUNDON (All Saints) w Barnardiston *St E 8* P *Jes Coll*
Cam (2 turns), Miss A Hallam (1 turn) R J J COOPER
HUNDRED RIVER Group of Parishes, The *St E 14*
P *DBP, Shadingfield Properties Ltd, Bp, Miss to*
Seamen, and F D L Barnes Esq (by turn)
P-in-c C J ATKINSON
HUNGARTON (St John the Baptist) Houghton-on-the-
Hill, Keyham and Hungarton *Leic*
HUNGERFORD (St Lawrence) and Denford *Ox 14*
P *D&C Windsor* V A W SAWYER
HUNMANBY (All Saints) w Muston *York 16* P *MMCET*
V C M F WHITEHEAD
HUNNINGHAM (St Margaret) *Cov 10* P *Ld Chan*
P-in-c D C JESSETT
HUNSDON (St Dunstan) (St Francis) w Widford and
Wareside *St Alb 8* P *DBP* R J RISBY
HUNSINGORE (St John the Baptist) Lower Nidderdale
Ripon
HUNSLET (St Mary) *Ripon 6* P *Bp (2 turns) and*
V Leeds St Pet (1 turn) V J W PARKER
HUNSLET MOOR (St Peter) and St Cuthbert *Ripon 6*
P *Bp* V R BROOKE
HUNSLEY (St Peter) Rowley w Skidby *York*
HUNSTANTON (St Edmund) w Ringstead *Nor 21*
P *H Le Strange Esq* V *Vacant* Hunstanton (04853)
2157
HUNSTANTON (St Mary) w Ringstead Parva, Holme-
next-the-Sea and Thornham *Nor 21* P *Bp and*
H Le Strange Esq (alt) V M B SEXTON, C R J BOWETT
HUNSTANWORTH (St James) Blanchland w
Hunstanworth and Edmundbyers etc *Newc*
HUNSTON (St Leodegar) N Mundham w Hunston and
Merston *Chich*
HUNSTON (St Michael) Badwell Ash w Gt Ashfield,
Stowlangtoft etc *St E*
HUNTINGDON (All Saints w St John the Baptist)
(St Barnabas) (St Mary) *Ely 9* P *Bp*
TR M L GRUNDY, TV T MASLEN, J R SANSOM
HUNTINGFIELD (St Mary) Cratfield w Heveningham
and Ubbeston etc *St E*
HUNTINGTON (All Saints) *York 8* P *Patr Bd*
TR H N MACKAY, TV C J CULLWICK,
Par Dn O J LAMBERT
HUNTINGTON (St Luke) *Ches 2* P *Bp* V D M WILSON
HUNTINGTON (St Mary Magdalene) Holmer w
Huntington *Heref*
HUNTINGTON (St Thomas) Cannock *Lich*
HUNTINGTON (St Thomas a Becket) Kington w
Huntington, Old Radnor, Kinnerton etc *Heref*
HUNTLEY (St John the Baptist) and Longhope *Glouc 3*
P *Bp* R J G WHEELDON
HUNTON (St James) Wonston and Stoke Charity w
Hunton *Win*
HUNTON (St Mary) Coxheath w E Farleigh, Hunton
and Linton *Roch*
HUNTS CROSS (St Hilda) *Liv 4* P *Bp*
V G E GREENWOOD, NSM J C LYNN
HUNTSHAM (All Saints) Sampford Peverell,
Uplowman, Holcombe Rogus etc *Ex*
HUNTSHAW (St Mary Magdalene) Newton Tracey,
Alverdiscott, Huntshaw etc *Ex*
HUNTSPILL (St Peter and All Hallows) *B & W 1* P *Ball*
Coll Ox R *Vacant* Burnham-on-Sea (0278) 788102
HUNWICK (St Paul) *Dur 10* P *V Auckland*
P-in-c P F BLANCH
HUNWORTH (St Lawrence) Thornage w Brinton w
Hunworth and Stody *Nor*
HURDSFIELD (Holy Trinity) *Ches 13* P *Hyndman*
Trustees V J G TSIPOURAS
HURLEY (St Mary the Virgin) *Ox 13* P *DBP*
P-in-c P W D IND
HURLEY (Resurrection) Baxterley w Hurley and Wood
End and Merevale etc *Birm*
HURSLEY (All Saints) and Ampfield *Win 11*
P *T H Faber Esq and Lord Lifford (jt)* V A L MOORE
HURST Fawkenhurst *Cant*
HURST (St John the Evangelist) *Man 17* P *The Crown*
V *Vacant* 061-330 1935
HURST (St Nicholas) *Ox 16* P *Bp* V D H LOVERIDGE
HURST GREEN (Holy Trinity) *Chich 15* P *Bp*
V F W BUTLER
HURST GREEN (St John the Evangelist) *S'wark 23* P *Bp*
V G F R RUSSELL, NSM M J SELLER
HURST GREEN (St John the Evangelist) and Mitton
Bradf 5 P *Bp and J E R Aspinall Esq (jt)* V B M CAVE
HURSTBOURNE PRIORS (St Andrew) Barton Stacey
and Bullington etc *Win*

HURSTBOURNE TARRANT (St Peter) and Faccombe and Vernham Dean and Linkenholt *Win 3*   **P** *Bp*
   V M HARLEY

HURSTPIERPOINT (Holy Trinity) (St George) *Chich 9*
   P *Woodard Schs*   **R** D M REEVE

HURSTWOOD, HIGH (Holy Trinity) *Chich 21*   **P** *Abp*
   V I GIBSON

HURWORTH (All Saints) *Dur 12*   **P** *Ch Soc Trust*
   R R R A GRAHAM

HUSBANDS BOSWORTH (All Saints) w Mowsley and Knaptoft and Theddingworth *Leic 4*   **P** *DBP (2 turns),*
Bp (1 turn)   **R** R W WIDDOWSON

HUSBORNE CRAWLEY (St Mary Magdalene or St James)   Aspley Guise w Husborne Crawley and Ridgmont *St Alb*

HUSTHWAITE (St Nicholas)   Coxwold and Husthwaite *York*

HUTHWAITE (All Saints) *S'well 4*   **P** *V Sutton-in-Ashfield*   **R** I OAKLEY

HUTTOFT (St Margaret)   Sutton, Huttoft and Anderby *Linc*

HUTTON (All Saints) (St Peter) *Chelmsf 10*
   P *D&C St Paul's*   **R** W H REED

HUTTON (Blessed Virgin Mary) *B & W 12*   **P** *DBP*
   R T A THOMAS

HUTTON, NEW (St Stephen)   Grayrigg, Old Hutton and New Hutton *Carl*

HUTTON, OLD (St John the Evangelist)   as above

HUTTON BONVILLE (St Laurence)   Gt Smeaton w Appleton Wiske and Birkby etc *Ripon*

HUTTON BUSCEL (St Matthew)   Wykeham and Hutton Buscel *York*

HUTTON CRANSWICK (St Peter) w Skerne, Watton and Beswick *York 11*   **P** *Abp*   **V** R I JONES

HUTTON HENRY (St Francis)   Wingate Grange *Dur*

HUTTON-IN-THE-FOREST (St James)   Skelton and Hutton-in-the-Forest w Ivegill *Carl*

HUTTON-LE-HOLE (St Chad)   Lastingham w Appleton-le-Moors, Rosedale etc *York*

HUTTON MAGNA (St Mary)   Barningham w Hutton Magna and Wycliffe *Ripon*

HUTTON ROOF (St John the Divine)   Kirkby Lonsdale *Carl*

HUTTON RUDBY (All Saints)   Rudby in Cleveland w Middleton *York*

HUTTONS AMBO (St Margaret)   Whitwell w Crambe, Flaxton, Foston etc *York*

HUXHAM (St Mary the Virgin)   Stoke Canon, Poltimore w Huxham and Rewe etc *Ex*

HUXLEY (St Andrew)   Hargrave *Ches*

HUYTON (St George) *Liv 2*   **P** *Bp*   **V** D G TOWLER,
   C P HRYZIUK

HUYTON (St Michael) *Liv 2*   **P** *Lord Derby*
   V J A STANLEY,   **AV** J R SKINNER   **C** E COLLISON,
   Par Dn J L ROBERTS

HUYTON QUARRY (St Gabriel) *Liv 2*   **P** *V Huyton St Mich*   **V** J KIDDLE

HYDE (St George) *Ches 14*   **P** *R Stockport St Mary*
   V J H DARCH,   **C** P T CHANTRY,   **NSM** H F CHANTRY

HYDE (St Thomas) *Ches 14*   **P** *Bp*   **P-in-c** J MARTIN

HYDE, EAST (Holy Trinity)   Woodside w E Hyde *St Alb*

HYDE, WEST (St Thomas)   Mill End and Heronsgate w W Hyde *St Alb*

HYDE COMMON (Holy Ascension) *Win 8*   **P** *Keble Coll Ox*   **V** J A DAVIES

HYDE HEATH (Mission Church)   Lt Missenden *Ox*

HYDE PARK CRESCENT (St John)   Paddington St Jo w St Mich *Lon*

HYDNEYE (St Peter) Conventional District *Chich 16*
   C-in-c M G ONIONS,   **Min** N S READE

HYKEHAM (All Saints) (St Hugh) (St Michael and All Angels) *Linc 18*   **P** *Ld Chan and Bp (alt)*
   TR E L RENNARD,   **TV** P D GODDEN,   **C** M R RENNARD,
   NSM J T ROOKE

HYLTON, NORTH (St Margaret) Castletown *Dur 9*
   P *Bp*   **P-in-c** K M TRIVASSE

HYLTON, SOUTH (St Mary) *Dur 9*   **P** *Bp*
   V J E RUSCOE

HYSON GREEN (St Paul)   Basford w Hyson Green *S'well*

HYSSINGTON (St Etheldreda)   Churchstoke w Hyssington and Sarn *Heref*

HYTHE Butts Ash (St Anne)   Hythe *Win*

HYTHE (St John the Baptist) *Win 10*   **P** *Bp*
   V P F MURPHY,   **Hon C** J M WEBSTER,
   NSM W F WEARN

HYTHE (St Leonard) (St Michael and All Angels) *Cant 5*
   P *R Saltwood*   **V** N H WOODS,   **C** D J WHEELER

HYTHE, WEST (St Mary)   Sellindge w Monks Horton and Stowting etc *Cant*

IBBERTON (St Eustace)   Okeford Fitzpaine, Ibberton, Belchalwell etc *Sarum*

IBSLEY (St Martin)   Ellingham and Harbridge and Ibsley *Win*

IBSTOCK (St Denys) w Heather *Leic 8*   **P** *Bp and MMCET (jt)*   **R** R N EVERETT

IBSTONE (St Nicholas)   Stokenchurch and Ibstone *Ox*

ICKBURGH (St Peter) w Langford *Nor 18*   **P** *Bp*
   P-in-c R O DAVIES

ICKENHAM (St Giles) *Lon 24*   **P** *Eton Coll*
   R P M H KELLY,   **NSM** P ROBINSON

ICKFORD (St Nicholas)   Worminghall w Ickford, Oakley and Shabbington *Ox*

ICKHAM (St John the Evangelist)   Littlebourne and Ickham w Wickhambreaux etc *Cant*

ICKLEFORD (St Katherine) w Holwell *St Alb 9*   **P** *DBP*
   R R I OAKLEY

ICKLESHAM (St Nicolas) *Chich 20*   **P** *Ld Chan*
   V *Vacant*   Hastings (0424) 814207

ICKLETON (St Mary Magdalene) *Ely 7*   **P** *Ld Chan*
   V A L WAY,   **Hon Par Dn** B E WAY

ICKLINGHAM (All Saints w St James)   Mildenhall *St E*

ICOMB (St Mary)   Westcote w Icomb and Bledington *Glouc*

IDBURY (St Nicholas)   Shipton-under-Wychwood w Milton-under-Wychwood *Ox*

IDDESLEIGH (St James) w Dowland *Ex 20*   **P** *Bp*
   R *Vacant*

IDE (St Ida)   Dunchideock and Shillingford St George w Ide *Ex*

IDE HILL (St Mary the Virgin)   Sundridge w Ide Hill *Roch*

IDEFORD (St Mary the Virgin)   Teignmouth, Ideford w Luton, Ashcombe etc *Ex*

IDEN (All Saints)   Rye *Chich*

IDLE (Holy Trinity) *Bradf 3*   **P** *V Calverley*
   V D A JOHNSON

IDLICOTE (St James the Great)   Shipston-on-Stour w Honington and Idlicote *Cov*

IDRIDGEHAY (St James)   Wirksworth w Alderwasley, Carsington etc *Derby*

IDSWORTH (St Hubert)   Blendworth w Chalton w Idsworth *Portsm*

IFFLEY (St Mary the Virgin) *Ox 4*   **P** *Ch Ch Ox*
   R P S M JUDD,   **C** I C HUTCHINSON-CERVANTES

IFIELD (St Margaret) *Chich 7*   **P** *Bp*   **TR** D L PARKER,
   TV C R BEARD,
   C S C PARRETT, J C WALL,
   NSM K A McRAE

IFIELD (St Margaret)   Gravesend H Family w Ifield *Roch*

IFORD (St Nicholas) w Kingston and Rodmell *Chich 18*
   P *Bp*   **V** G M DAW

IFORD (St Saviour) *Win 7*   **P** *Bp*   **V** I M SCOTT-THOMPSON,   **Hon C** N M BENCE

IGHTFIELD (St John the Baptist) w Calverhall *Lich 29*
   P *T C Heywood-Lonsdale Esq*   **P-in-c** J H TYERS

IGHTHAM (St Peter) *Roch 9*   **P** *Sir John Winnifrith*
   R J H B TALBOT

IKEN (St Botolph)   Orford w Sudbourne, Chillesford, Butley and Iken *St E*

ILAM (Holy Cross) w Blore Ray and Okeover *Lich 11*
   P *Personal Reps Sir Peter Walker-Okeover*
   P-in-c P E R HALL

ILCHESTER (St Mary Major) w Northover, Limington, Yeovilton and Podimore *B & W 6*   **P** *Bp (1 turn),*
Bp Lon (7 turns), and Wadh Coll Ox (1 turn)   **R** *Vacant*
   Ilchester (0935) 840296

ILDERTON (St Michael)   Glendale Gp *Newc*

ILFORD, GREAT (St Alban) *Chelmsf 7*   **P** *Bp*
   V D I MILNES,   **Hon C** M R GRIFFIN

ILFORD, GREAT (St Andrew) *Chelmsf 7*   **P** *Bp*
   V P L DEEMING,   **Par Dn** J E EATON

ILFORD, GREAT (St Clement) (St Margaret of Antioch)
Chelmsf 7   **P** *Patr Bd*   **TR** T H SHANNON,   **TV** J E IVES

ILFORD, GREAT (St John the Evangelist) *Chelmsf 7*
   P *Bp*   **V** S J TYLER,
   NSM R A D ENEVER, C W KARUNARATNA

ILFORD, GREAT (St Luke) *Chelmsf 7*   **P** *Bp*
   V K A L HINDS

ILFORD, GREAT (St Mary) *Chelmsf 7*   **P** *V Ilford*
   V J B BARNES,   **C** S G BATES

ILFORD, LITTLE (St Barnabas) *Chelmsf 5*   **P** *Bp*
   R B J ARSCOTT

ILFORD, LITTLE (St Michael and All Angels) *Chelmsf 5*
   P *Hertf Coll Ox*   **R** J P WHITWELL,   **C** J BROWN

ILFRACOMBE (Holy Trinity) (St Peter), Lee, Woolacombe, Bittadon and Mortehoe *Ex 15* **P** *Patr Bd* **TR** N JACKSON-STEVENS, **TV** R G PECKHAM, **C** D J DETTMER

ILFRACOMBE (St Philip and St James) w West Down *Ex 15* **P** *Bp and Ch Trust Fund Trust (jt)* **V** C E G TENNANT

ILKESTON (Holy Trinity) *Derby 13* **P** *Bp* **P-in-c** W F P ENOCH

ILKESTON (St John the Evangelist) *Derby 13* **P** *V Ilkeston St Mary* **V** K S W RICHARDS

ILKESTON (St Mary the Virgin) *Derby 13* **P** *Bp* **C** M SMITH

ILKETSHALL ST ANDREW (St Andrew) Rumburgh w S Elmham w the Ilketshalls *St E*

ILKETSHALL ST JOHN (St John the Baptist) as above

ILKETSHALL ST LAWRENCE (St Lawrence) as above

ILKETSHALL ST MARGARET (St Margaret) as above

ILKLEY (All Saints) *Bradf 4* **P** *Hyndman Trustees* **V** P J C MARSHALL, **C** A J E KIDD

ILKLEY (St Margaret) *Bradf 4* **P** *CR* **V** R D HOYAL

ILLINGWORTH (St Mary) *Wakef 4* **P** *V Halifax* **V** C D E CLARKE

ILLOGAN (not known) *Truro 2* **P** *Ch Soc Trust* **R** D J STEVENS, **C** I D THACKER, **NSM** D L HOLLINGDALE

ILMER (St Peter) Princes Risborough w Ilmer *Ox*

ILMINGTON (St Mary) and Stretton-on-Fosse and Ditchford w Preston-on-Stour w Whitchurch and Atherstone-on-Stour *Cov 9* **P** *Bp, MMCET, and Ms C A Alston-Roberts-West (jt)* **P-in-c** V L STORY

ILMINSTER (Blessed Virgin Mary) Whitelackington *B & W 18* **P** *Bp* **V** W D JONES

ILSINGTON (St Michael) *Ex 11* **P** *D&C Windsor* **V** M F GLARE

ILSLEY, EAST (St Mary) Compton w E Ilsley *Ox*

ILSLEY, WEST (All Saints) Beedon and Peasemore w W Ilsley and Farnborough *Ox*

ILSTON (St Michael and All Angels) Gaulby *Leic*

ILTON (St Peter) w Hambridge, Earnshill, Isle Brewers and Isle Abbotts *B & W 18* **P** *Bp (4 turns), D&C Bris (1 turn)* **R** C D R BOOTS

IMMINGHAM (St Andrew) *Linc 10* **P** *DBP* **V** H W P HALL, **C** J R SIMPSON, B A HARRISON, **Hon C** W E H COSENS

IMPINGTON (St Andrew) *Ely 5* **P** *Adn Ely* **Par Dn** J M PRATT

INCE (St James) Thornton le Moors w Ince and Elton *Ches*

INCE IN MAKERFIELD (Christ Church) (St Christopher) *Liv 14* **P** *Simeon's Trustees* **V** M I STOCKLEY

INCE IN MAKERFIELD (St Mary) *Liv 14* **P** *Simeon's Trustees* **V** G B KEEGAN

INDIAN QUEEN (St Francis) St Enoder *Truro*

INGATESTONE (St Edmund and St Mary) w Buttsbury *Chelmsf 10* **P** *Bp* **P-in-c** P E COULTON

INGESTRE (St Mary the Virgin) Stafford St Jo and Tixall w Ingestre *Lich*

INGHAM (All Saints) w Cammeringham w Fillingham *Linc 3* **P** *Bp and Ball Coll Ox (jt)* **V** M J SILLEY

INGHAM (Holy Trinity) w Sutton *Nor 10* **P** *Bp* **R** *Vacant*

INGHAM (St Bartholomew) w Ampton and Great and Little Livermere *St E 13* **P** *Bp (3 turns), D J Turner Esq (1 turn)* **R** R H NORBURN

INGLEBY ARNCLIFFE (All Saints) Osmotherley w E Harlsey and Ingleby Arncliffe *York*

INGLEBY BARWICK (St Francis) Stainton-in-Cleveland *York*

INGLEBY GREENHOW (St Andrew) w Bilsdale Priory, Kildale and Westerdale *York 22* **P** *Abp, Adn Cleveland, Bp Whitby, Viscount de l'Isle, R G Beckett Esq, and Mrs C M Sutcliffe (jt)* **V** M K TIMBRELL

INGLETON (St John the Evangelist) Denton and Ingleton *Dur*

INGLETON (St Mary the Virgin) w Chapel le Dale *Bradf 6* **P** *Bp* **V** R J H FRY

INGOL (St Margaret) *Blackb 14* **P** *Bp* **V** A N WIBBERLEY, **NSM** T DE LACEY

INGOLDISTHORPE (St Michael) Snettisham w Ingoldisthorpe and Fring *Nor*

INGOLDMELLS (St Peter and St Paul) w Addlethorpe *Linc 8* **P** *Ld Chan and Wadh Coll Ox (alt)* **R** S G RIDLEY

INGOLDSBY (St Bartholomew) *Linc 14* **P** *Ch Coll Cam, Sir Lyonel Tollemache, Bt, D&C, Bp, and DBP*

(by turn) **R** R BURGESS, **NSM** K A C BROWN, I R WALTERS

INGRAM (St Michael) Glendale Gp *Newc*

INGRAVE (St Nicholas) Gt Warley w Childerditch and Ingrave *Chelmsf*

INGRAVE (St Stephen) Conventional District *Chelmsf 10* **C-in-c** J RYELAND

INGROW (St John the Evangelist) cum Hainworth *Bradf 8* **P** *Bp* **Par Dn** C B POLLARD, **NSM** G A BRIGHOUSE

INGS (St Anne) Hugill *Carl*

INGWORTH (St Lawrence) Erpingham w Calthorpe, Ingworth, Aldborough etc *Nor*

INHAM NOOK (St Barnabas) Chilwell *S'well*

INKBERROW (St Peter) w Cookhill and Kington w Dormston *Worc 1* **P** *Bp* **R** G S CROSS

INKERSALL (St Columba) Staveley and Barrow Hill *Derby*

INKPEN (St Michael) W Woodhay w Enborne, Hampstead Marshall etc *Ox*

INSKIP (St Peter) *Blackb 10* **P** *V St Michael's-on-Wyre* **V** G M HILTON-TURVEY

INSTOW (All Saints Chapel) (St John the Baptist) *Ex 17* **P** *Christie Trustees* **R** G A SATTERLY

INTWOOD (All Saints) Swardeston w E Carleton, Intwood, Keswick etc *Nor*

INWARDLEIGH (St Petroc) Okehampton w Inwardleigh *Ex*

INWORTH (All Saints) Messing w Inworth *Chelmsf*

IPING (St Mary) Stedham w Iping, Elsted and Treyford-cum-Didling *Chich*

IPPLEPEN (St Andrew) w Torbryan *Ex 10* **P** *D&C Windsor* **V** P W DARBY

IPSDEN (St Mary the Virgin) N Stoke w Mongewell and Ipsden *Ox*

IPSLEY (St Peter) *Worc 7* **P** *Patr Bd* **TR** R M ADAMS, **TV** A J KELSO, A E J TOSTEVIN, **NSM** J W DAVEY

IPSTONES (St Leonard) w Berkhamsytch and Onecote w Bradnop *Lich 12* **P** *Bp and R Leek and Meerbrook (jt)* **V** S G PRICE

IPSWICH (All Hallows) *St E 4* **P** *Bp* **V** P F HOCKING, **C** P J CARTER, **NSM** R F ALLARD

IPSWICH (All Saints) *St E 4* **P** *Bp* **V** A G WILCOX

IPSWICH (St Andrew) *St E 4* **P** *Bp* **V** G I HOUSE, **C** P E GRIFFITHS

IPSWICH (St Augustine of Hippo) *St E 4* **P** *Bp* **V** J E N ELLISTON, **C** K M KING, R L C KING

IPSWICH (St Bartholomew) *St E 4* **P** *Bp* **V** J E BURROWS

IPSWICH (St Clement w St Luke) (Holy Trinity) *St E 4* **P** *Ch Patr Trust* **P-in-c** R G WARREN

IPSWICH (St Francis) (St Clare's Church Centre) *St E 4* **P** *Bp* **TR** M G S WHITCOMBE, **Par Dn** A E DAVIE (nee JONES)

IPSWICH (St Helen) (St James) *St E 4* **P** *Ch Patr Trust* **R** D P HAZLEWOOD

IPSWICH (St John the Baptist) *St E 4* **P** *Simeon's Trustees* **V** J C CASSELTON, **C** M D ROGERS

IPSWICH (St Margaret) *St E 4* **P** *Simeon's Trustees* **V** J F MOCKFORD, **C** T D GILES

IPSWICH (St Mary at Stoke) w St Peter and St Mary Quay *St E 4* **P** *Bp* **TR** J D YATES, **TV** J D HAYDEN, **C** P BOURNER

IPSWICH (St Mary at the Elms) *St E 4* **P** *PCC* **P-in-c** M K ORME

IPSWICH (St Mary-le-Tower) (St Nicholas) *St E 4* **P** *Bp (3 turns), Ch Patr Trust (1 turn)* **V** K B JONES

IPSWICH (St Matthew) *St E 4* **P** *Ld Chan* **C** G K BENNETT, D B HENNESSEY

IPSWICH (St Michael) *St E 4* **P** *Simeon's Trustees* **V** *Vacant*

IPSWICH (St Thomas) *St E 4* **P** *Bp* **V** M F WEST

IRBY (St Chad's Mission Church) Thurstaston *Ches*

IRBY-IN-THE-MARSH (All Saints) Bratoft w Irby-in-the-Marsh *Linc*

IRBY ON HUMBER (St Andrew) Laceby *Linc*

IRCHESTER (St Katharine) *Pet 10* **P** *Bp* **V** *Vacant* Rushden (0933) 312674

IRCHESTER, LITTLE (St John) Irchester *Pet*

IREBY (St James) Bolton w Ireby and Uldale *Carl*

IRELAND WOOD (St Paul) *Ripon 7* **P** *R Adel* **V** W D JONES, **C** M S FOY, C C GARRUD

IRELETH w Askam (St Peter) *Carl 8* **P** *V Dalton-in-Furness* **V** D SANDERSON

IRLAM (St John the Baptist) *Man 2* **P** *Trustees* **V** P J P WETZ, **Par Dn** M E DICKER

IRNHAM (St Andrew) Corby Glen *Linc*

IRON ACTON (St James the Less) *Bris 7* **P** *Ch Ch Ox* **R** A F WAKER

IRON-BRIDGE (St Luke)   Coalbrookdale, Iron-Bridge and Lt Wenlock *Heref*

IRONVILLE (Christ Church)   Riddings and Ironville *Derby*

IRSTEAD (St Michael)   Neatishead, Barton Turf and Irstead *Nor*

IRTHINGTON (St Kentigern), Crosby-on-Eden and Scaleby *Carl 2*   **P** *Bp*   **V** D RIDGWAY

IRTHLINGBOROUGH (St Peter) *Pet 10*   **P** *Sir Stephen Hastings*   **R** R G KNIGHT

IRTON (St Paul)   Eskdale, Irton, Muncaster and Waberthwaite *Carl*

ISEL (St Michael)   Bassenthwaite, Isel and Setmurthy *Carl*

ISFIELD (St Margaret) *Chich 21*   **P** *Abp*   **R** C J PETERS

ISHAM (St Peter) w Pytchley *Pet 11*   **P** *Bp*   **R** P R GATENBY

ISLE ABBOTTS (Blessed Virgin Mary)   Ilton w Hambridge, Earnshill, Isle Brewers etc *B & W*

ISLE BREWERS (All Saints)   as above

ISLE OF DOGS (Christ Church) (St John) (St Luke) *Lon 7*   **P** *Bp*   **V** N R HOLTAM,   **TV** N J ORCHARD,   **Par Dn** F C CLARINGBULL (nee DAVID)

ISLEHAM (St Andrew) *Ely 3*   **P** *Ld Chan*   **P-in-c** D J KIGHTLEY

ISLEWORTH (All Saints) *Lon 11*   **P** *D&C Windsor*   **V** J D R HAYWARD,   **C** N C FINCHAM

ISLEWORTH (St Francis of Assisi) *Lon 11*   **P** *Bp*   **P-in-c** K D MOULE

ISLEWORTH (St John the Baptist) *Lon 11*   **P** *V Isleworth All SS*   **P-in-c** R F BLACKBURN

ISLEWORTH (St Luke)   Spring Grove St Mary *Lon*

ISLEWORTH (St Mary the Virgin) *Lon 11*   **P** *Bp*   **P-in-c** P R WRAGG

ISLEY WALTON (All Saints)   Breedon cum Isley Walton and Worthington *Leic*

ISLINGTON (St James the Apostle) (St Peter) *Lon 6*   **P** *Bp*   **V** W G MARLOW

ISLINGTON (St Mary) *Lon 6*   **P** *CPAS*   **V** G L CLAYDON,   **C** P KELLEM,   **Par Dn** E V LAKE

ISLIP (St Nicholas) *Pet 10*   **P** *L G Stopford-Sackville Esq*   **R** *Vacant*   Thrapston (08012) 3053

ISLIP (St Nicholas) w Charlton on Otmoor, Oddington, Noke and Woodeaton *Ox 2*   **P** *D&C Westmr, Rev E H W Crusha, and Qu Coll Ox (jt)*   **R** R L STURCH,   **Par Dn** J M MOUNT

ISTEAD RISE (St Barnabas) *Roch 4*   **P** *Bp*   **V** R SMITH

ITCHEN ABBAS (St John the Baptist) cum Avington *Win 1*   **P** *Bp*   **R** *Vacant*   Itchen Abbas (096278) 244

ITCHENOR, WEST (St Nicholas)   W Wittering and Birdham w Itchenor *Chich*

ITCHINGFIELD (St Nicholas) w Slinfold *Chich 7*   **P** *Bp*   **R** P J J KNIGHT,   **NSM** J P HURD, J P GRAVES

ITTERINGHAM (St Mary)   Wickmere w Lt Barningham, Itteringham etc *Nor*

IVEGILL (Christ Church)   Skelton and Hutton-in-the-Forest w Ivegill *Carl*

IVER (St Peter) *Ox 23*   **P** *Trustees*   **V** A D ROSE,   **C** J ACREMAN

IVER HEATH (St Margaret) *Ox 23*   **P** *Trustees*   **R** D S REYNISH

IVINGHOE (St Mary the Virgin) w Pitstone and Slapton *Ox 26*   **P** *Bp and Ch Ch Ox (jt)*   **V** *Vacant*   Cheddington (0296) 668260

IVINGTON (St John)   Leominster *Heref*

IVY HATCH (not known)   Ightham *Roch*

IVY ROW (Mission Room)   Roos and Garton in Holderness w Tunstall etc *York*

IVYBRIDGE (St John the Evangelist) w Harford *Ex 21*   **P** *Bp*   **V** F H COLES,   **C** A D WILLIS,   **Par Dn** P FIVE (nee KNOTT)

IVYCHURCH (St George)   St Mary's Bay w St Mary-in-the-Marsh etc *Cant*

IWADE (All Saints) *Cant 14*   **NSM** D W WEBB

IWERNE COURTNEY (St Mary)   see below

IWERNE MINSTER (St Mary)   see below

IWERNE STEPLETON (St Mary)   see below

IWERNES, Sutton Waldron and Fontmell Magna, The *Sarum 7*   **P** *Bp, D&C Windsor, DBP, and G A L F Pitt-Rivers Esq (jt)*   **V** E A SELLGREN,   **NSM** J H SIMMONS

IXWORTH (St Mary) and Bardwell *St E 9*   **P** *St Jo Coll Ox, DBP, and Bp (by turn)*   **V** P M OLIVER,   **C** D W FINCH

IXWORTH THORPE (All Saints)   Ixworth and Bardwell *St E*

JACKFIELD (St Mary) *Heref 14*   **P** *Bp*   **P-in-c** W W LUCAS

JACOBSTOW (St James)   St Gennys, Jacobstow w Warbstow and Treneglos *Truro*

JACOBSTOWE (St James)   Hatherleigh, Meeth, Exbourne and Jacobstowe *Ex*

JARROW (St John the Baptist) (St Mark) (St Paul) (St Peter) *Dur 7*   **P** *Bp*   **TR** R CORKER,   **TV** I D HUNTER SMART, A OATES, B R TURNBULL

JARROW GRANGE (Christ Church) *Dur 7*   **P** *Lord Northbourne*   **R** N SWAINSON

JARVIS BROOK (St Michael and All Angels) *Chich 19*   **P** *Bp*   **V** I E MORRISON

JERSEY (All Saints) *Win 15*   **P** *R St Helier, Bp, and The Crown (by turn)*   **V** *Vacant*   Jersey (0534) 24885

JERSEY Gouray (St Martin) *Win 15*   **P** *Bp and The Crown (alt)*   **P-in-c** J D DODD

JERSEY Greve d'Azette (St Nicholas)   Jersey St Clem *Win*

JERSEY (Holy Trinity) *Win 15*   **P** *The Crown*   **R** A KEOGH

JERSEY Millbrook (St Matthew) *Win 15*   **P** *The Crown*   **V** N D BEAMER

JERSEY (St Andrew) *Win 15*   **P** *Dean of Jersey*   **V** D J SPRINGHAM

JERSEY (St Brelade) (Communicare Chapel) (St Aubin) *Win 15*   **P** *The Crown*   **R** M A HALLIWELL,   **C** C I BUCKLEY,   **Hon Par Dn** J M GURDON

JERSEY (St Clement) *Win 15*   **P** *The Crown*   **R** M BEAL

JERSEY (St Helier) *Win 15*   **P** *The Crown*   **R** B A O'FERRALL

JERSEY (St James) *Win 15*   **P** *Bp*   **P-in-c** D V WASTIE

JERSEY (St John) *Win 15*   **P** *The Crown*   **R** M G ST JOHN NICOLLE

JERSEY (St Lawrence) *Win 15*   **P** *The Crown*   **R** N D BEAMER

JERSEY (St Luke) *Win 15*   **P** *Bp and The Crown (alt)*   **V** D V WASTIE

JERSEY (St Mark) *Win 15*   **P** *Bp*   **V** W N HALL

JERSEY (St Martin) *Win 15*   **P** *The Crown*   **R** L J TURNER

JERSEY (St Mary) *Win 15*   **P** *The Crown*   **R** A HART

JERSEY (St Ouen) (St George) *Win 15*   **P** *The Crown*   **R** R G SPECK

JERSEY (St Paul) Proprietary Chapel *Win 15*   **Min** M P H STEAR

JERSEY (St Peter) *Win 15*   **P** *The Crown*   **R** B J GILES,   **Hon C** A D WILLIAMS

JERSEY (St Saviour) *Win 15*   **P** *The Crown*   **R** *Vacant*

JERSEY (St Simon) *Win 15*   **P** *R St Helier, Bp, and The Crown (by turn)*   **V** *Vacant*   Jersey (0534) 24885

JERSEY DE GROUVILLE (St Martin) (St Peter la Roque) *Win 15*   **P** *The Crown*   **R** T A G M HAMPTON

JESMOND (Clayton Memorial Church) *Newc 5*   **P** *Trustees*   **V** D R J HOLLOWAY,   **C** J J S PRYKE, R J A TULLOCH

JESMOND (Holy Trinity) *Newc 5*   **P** *Trustees*   **V** M C LIPPIATT

JEVINGTON (St Andrew)   E Dean w Friston and Jevington *Chich*

JOYDENS WOOD St Barnabas Conventional District *Roch 16*   **Min** D H HORTON

JURBY (St Patrick) *S & M 4*   **P** *Bp*   **V** F S WHITE

KEA (All Hallows) (Old Church) *Truro 6*   **P** *V St Clement*   **V** R J REDRUP

KEAL, EAST (St Helen)   Marden Hill Gp *Linc*

KEAL, WEST (St Helen)   as above

KEARSLEY MOOR (St Stephen) *Man 6*   **P** *R E Farnworth and Kearsley*   **V** K F WAINWRIGHT

KEASDEN (St Matthew)   Clapham-with-Keasden and Austwick *Bradf*

KEDDINGTON (St Margaret)   Louth *Linc*

KEDINGTON (St Peter and St Paul) *St E 8*   **P** *Walsingham Coll Trust*   **R** P J EDWARDS

KEEDWELL HILL (Ascension)   Long Ashton *B & W*

KEELBY (St Bartholomew) w Riby and Aylesby *Linc 10*   **P** *DBP (2 turns), J E Spillman Esq (1 turn)*   **V** A S CAVE

KEELE (St John the Baptist)   Betley and Keele *Lich*

KEEVIL (St Leonard)   Steeple Ashton w Semington and Keevil *Sarum*

KEGWORTH (St Andrew) *Leic 7*   **P** *Ch Coll Cam*   **R** R L NASH

KEIGHLEY (All Saints) *Bradf 8*   **P** *Bp and R Keighley St Andr*   **V** *Vacant*   Keighley (0535) 607002

KEIGHLEY (St Andrew) *Bradf 8*   **P** *Bp*   **TR** C P HUTCHINSON

KEINTON MANDEVILLE (St Mary Magdalene) w Lydford on Fosse *B & W 3*   **P** *Ch Soc Trust, J H Cordle Esq and Dr O W Holmes (1 turn), A J Whitehead Esq (2 turns), and Bp (1 turn)*   **R** A H L BOWHILL

KELBROOK (St Mary) *Bradf 7* **P** *Bp*
P-in-c E J TOWNSON
KELBY (St Andrew) Ancaster Wilsford Gp *Linc*
KELHAM (St Wilfrid) Averham w Kelham *S'well*
KELLET, NETHER (St Mark) Bolton le Sands *Blackb*
KELLET, OVER (St Cuthbert) *Blackb 15* **P** *Reformation Ch Trust* K CLAPHAM
KELLING (St Mary) Weybourne Gp *Nor*
KELLINGTON (St Edmund) w Whitley *Wakef 11*
P *DBP* **Dn-in-c** B LYDON, **NSM** E BROWN
KELLOE (St Helen) *Dur 14* **P** *Bp* **P-in-c** R A CHAPMAN
KELLS (St Peter) *Carl 5* **P** *Bp* **V** T J HYSLOP,
C B ROWE
KELLY (St Mary the Virgin) w Bradstone *Ex 25*
P *W F Kelly Esq* **R** J A C WILSON
KELMARSH (St Denys) Clipston w Naseby and Haselbech w Kelmarsh *Pet*
KELMSCOTT (St George) Broughton Poggs w Filkins, Broadwell etc *Ox*
KELSALE (St Peter) Kelsale-cum-Carlton, Middleton-cum-Fordley etc *St E*
KELSALE-CUM-CARLTON, Middleton-cum-Fordley and Theberton w Eastbridge *St E 19* **P** *DBP, Prime Min, and Ch Patr Trust (by turn)* **R** R S SMITH
KELSALL (St Philip) *Ches 2* **P** *V Tarvin* **V** F C CONANT
KELSEY Group, The SOUTH (St Mary) *Linc 5* **P** *Bp (3 turns), M F Young Esq (1 turn)* **R** M P GRANTHAM
KELSEY, NORTH (All Hallows) *Linc 6* **P** *Bp*
V R J G PARKER
KELSHALL (St Faith) Therfield w Kelshall *St Alb*
KELSTON (St Nicholas) Bath Weston St Jo w Kelston *B & W*
KELVEDON (St Mary the Virgin) *Chelmsf 27* **P** *Bp*
V D J D THORNTON, **NSM** B J MAPLEY
KELVEDON HATCH (St Nicholas) *Chelmsf 10* **P** *Bp*
P-in-c J D BROWN
KEMBERTON (St Andrew), Sutton Maddock and Stockton *Lich 26* **P** *MMCET and J L Hamilton Esq (jt)*
NSM P H J THORNEYCROFT
KEMBLE (All Saints), Poole Keynes, Somerford Keynes and Sharncote *Glouc 12* **P** *DBP, Duchy of Lanc, and Mrs M J Peachey (by turn)* **V** G R MARTIN
KEMERTON (St Nicholas) Woolstone w Gotherington and Oxenton etc *Glouc*
KEMP TOWN (St Mary) *Chich 2* **P** *Bp, Mrs R A Hinton, A C R Elliott Esq, and Canon D Walker (jt)* **V** D C PAIN
KEMPSEY (St Mary the Virgin) and Severn Stoke w Croome d'Abitot *Worc 5* **P** *D&C and Earl of Cov (alt)*
R R C TOOGOOD
KEMPSFORD (St Mary) w Welford *Glouc 13* **P** *Bp*
P-in-c J F GREGORY
KEMPSHOTT (St Mark) *Win 4* **P** *Bp* **V** K V BATT,
Hon C D E APPLIN
KEMPSTON (All Saints) *St Alb 16* **P** *Bp* **V** R N CARTER
KEMPSTON (Transfiguration) *St Alb 16* **P** *Bp*
V J R BROWN, **C** D J MUSKETT, **Hon Par Dn** G A WEBB
KEMSING (St Mary the Virgin) w Woodlands *Roch 9*
P *DBP* **V** C C HORN, **NSM** J G GOULDING, J M CORBY
KENARDINGTON (St Mary) Appledore w Brookland, Fairfield, Brenzett etc *Cant*
KENCHESTER (St Michael) and Bridge Sollers *Heref 4*
P *Ld Chan* **R** *Vacant*
KENCOT (St George) Broughton Poggs w Filkins, Broadwell etc *Ox*
KENDAL (Holy Trinity) (All Hallows Chapel) *Carl 9*
P *Trin Coll Cam* **V** G A HOWE, **C** R J A MITCHELL,
NSM P SMITH
KENDAL (St George) *Carl 9* **P** **V** *Kendal H Trin*
V D R JACKSON
KENDAL (St Thomas) *Carl 9* **P** *CPAS* **V** R A MACHIN,
C D C WOOD
KENDERCHURCH (St Mary) Ewyas Harold w Dulas, Kenderchurch etc *Heref*
KENDRAY (St Andrew) Ardsley *Sheff*
KENILWORTH (St John the Evangelist) *Cov 4*
P *Simeon's Trustees* **V** R D TURNER,
C J C ROBERTSON
KENILWORTH (St Nicholas) (St Barnabas) *Cov 4*
P *Ld Chan* **V** D J RAKE, **C** K J MOBBERLEY
KENLEY (All Saints) *S'wark 21* **P** *Abp* **V** M VONBERG
KENLEY (St John the Baptist) Wenlock *Heref*
KENN (St Andrew) Exminster and Kenn *Ex*
KENN (St John the Evangelist) Yatton Moor *B & W*
KENNERLEIGH (St John the Baptist) N Creedy *Ex*
KENNET, EAST (Christ Church) Upper Kennett *Sarum*
KENNETT (St Nicholas) *Ely 3* **P** *Mrs M F de Packh*
P-in-c A F NICHOLAS
KENNETT, UPPER *Sarum 20* **P** *Bp* **TR** G R J FORCE-JONES, **TV** D C FROST, **Hon Par Dn** H N STACEY

KENNINGHALL (St Mary) Quidenham *Nor*
KENNINGTON (St John the Divine w St James the Apostle) *S'wark 9* **P** *Ripon Coll Cuddesdon and Bp (jt)*
V L DENNEN, **NSM** W C BEAVER, P ANSDELL-EVANS
KENNINGTON (St Mark) *S'wark 10* **P** *Abp*
V J M STARR, **C** R P GRAFTON, **Hon C** M K BARLING
KENNINGTON (St Mary) *Cant 10* **P** *Abp*
V C G PREECE, **C** M W HAYTON
KENNINGTON (St Swithun) *Ox 10* **P** *Bp*
V H BLOOMFIELD
KENNINGTON CROSS (St Anselm) N Lambeth *S'wark*
KENNINGTON PARK (St Agnes) *S'wark 8* **P** *Trustees*
P-in-c S C EVERSON, **Hon C** A H A V BROWN
KENNY HILL (St James) Mildenhall *St E*
KENSAL GREEN (St John) *Lon 2* **P** *Bp* **V** R D BEAL
KENSAL RISE (St Mark) (St Martin) *Lon 21* **P** *St Olave Hart Street Trustees and Bp (jt)* **V** N L JACKSON,
C P A SMITH
KENSAL TOWN (St Thomas) (St Andrew) (St Philip) *Lon 12* **P** *Hyndman Trustees* **P-in-c** D FLETCHER,
Hon C P J MATHIE
KENSINGTON (St Barnabas) *Lon 12* **P** *V Kensington St Mary Abbots w St Geo and Ch Ch* **P-in-c** J D IRVINE,
C M L CLARKSON
KENSINGTON (St Helen) (Holy Trinity) *Lon 12* **P** *Bp*
V A SIMPSON
KENSINGTON (St James) Notting Dale St Clem w St Mark and St Jas *Lon*
KENSINGTON (St John the Baptist) *Lon 12* **P** *Trustees*
P-in-c G F BRIGHT, **Hon C** A T PHYALL
KENSINGTON (St Mary Abbots) (St George) (Christ Church) *Lon 12* **P** *Bp* **V** I L ROBSON,
C F J GELLI, P R MYLES, **Hon C** H D SOX,
NSM T C H CURL
KENSINGTON (St Philip) Earl's Court *Lon 12* **P** *Bp*
V M B E FORREST
KENSINGTON, SOUTH (Holy Trinity w All Saints) *Lon 3*
P *D&C Westmr* **P-in-c** M S ISRAEL
KENSINGTON, SOUTH (St Augustine) *Lon 3* **P** *Keble Coll Ox* **V** K V HEWITT, **Hon C** G JOHNSON
KENSINGTON, SOUTH (St Jude) *Lon 3* **P** *Dame Jewell Magnus-Allcroft* **P-in-c** D PRICE
KENSINGTON, SOUTH (St Luke) *Lon 8* **P** *Ch Patr Trust* **V** D PRICE, **C** D A STONE
KENSINGTON, SOUTH (St Stephen) *Lon 12* **P** *Guild of All So* **V** C G COLVEN, **C** J W TOWERS
KENSINGTON, WEST (St Mary) Fulham St Mary N End *Lon*
KENSINGTON, WEST The Boltons (St Mary) W Brompton St Mary w St Pet *Lon*
KENSWORTH (St Edward the Confessor) (St Mary the Virgin), Studham and Whipsnade *St Alb 18* **P** *Ld Chan and D&C St Paul's (alt)* **V** P M PALMER
KENT TOWN E Molesey St Paul *Guildf*
KENTCHURCH (St Mary) Ewyas Harold w Dulas, Kenderchurch etc *Heref*
KENTFORD (St Mary) Gazeley w Dalham, Moulton and Kentford *St E*
KENTISBEARE (St Mary) w Blackborough *Ex 4*
P *Exors G C Wyndham Esq* **R** S A SAUNDERS
KENTISBURY (St Thomas) Shirwell, Loxhore, Kentisbury, Arlington, etc *Ex*
KENTISH TOWN (St Benet and All Saints) *Lon 17*
P *D&C St Paul's* **P-in-c** R N ARNOLD
KENTISH TOWN (St John the Baptist) *Lon 17*
P *V St Pancras* **P-in-c** R N ARNOLD, **C** S FRY
KENTISH TOWN (St Martin) (St Andrew) *Lon 17*
P *Dame Jewell Magnus-Allcroft* **V** P D CONRAD
KENTISH TOWN (St Silas the Martyr) *Lon 17* **P** *Bp*
P-in-c G C ROWLANDS
KENTMERE (St Cuthbert) Staveley w Kentmere *Carl*
KENTON (All Saints) Debenham w Aspall and Kenton *St E*
KENTON (All Saints), Mamhead, Powderham, Cofton and Starcross *Ex 6* **P** *Earl of Devon, D&C, D&C Sarum, and SMF (jt)* **R** H M KITCHEN
KENTON (Ascension) *Newc 5* **P** *Bp* **V** V T DICKINSON
KENTON (St Mary the Virgin) *Lon 23* **P** *Bp*
V R BROWN, **C** P C B ALLEN, C R HARDY
KENTON, SOUTH (Annunciation) Wembley Park St Aug *Lon*
KENWYN (St George) *Truro 6* **P** *The Crown*
P-in-c D S R WILLS, **Hon C** P A ROBSON,
NSM W C H STRIBLEY
KENWYN (St John) *Truro 6* **P** *V Kenwyn St Cuby*
P-in-c B W BUNT
KENWYN (St Keyne) w St Allen *Truro 6* **P** *Bp*
R M S BYROM

KERESLEY (St Thomas) and Coundon *Cov 2*   **P** *Bp*
  V J PANTING, **C** E A DONALDSON
KERESLEY END (Church of the Ascension)   Keresley
  and Coundon *Cov*
KERRIDGE (Holy Trinity)   Bollington St Jo *Ches*
KERSAL, LOWER (St Aidan) *Man 6*   **P** *Bp*
  V G D MORRIS
KERSAL MOOR (St Paul) *Man 6*   **P** *Trustees*
  R S FLETCHER, **C** M R S SMITH
KERSEY (St Mary) w Lindsey *St E 3*   **P** *Bp*
  P-in-c W J SANDS
KERSWELL GREEN (St John the Baptist)   Kempsey
  and Severn Stoke w Croome d'Abitot *Worc*
KESGRAVE (All Saints) *St E 4*   **P** *Bp*   **V** D R W HARES,
  Par Dn C A GARRARD
KESSINGLAND (St Edmund) w Gisleham *Nor 15*
  P *Ld Chan (1 turn)*, *Bp (2 turns)*   **R** L O HARRIS
KESTON (not known) (St Audrey) *Roch 13*   **P** *D&C*
  R A J COX
KESWICK (All Saints)   Swardeston w E Carleton,
  Intwood, Keswick etc *Nor*
KESWICK (St John) *Carl 6*   **P** *Trustees*   **V** N P HOLMES
KESWICK, EAST (St Mary Magdalene)   Bardsey *Ripon*
KETLEY (St Mary the Virgin) and Oakengates *Lich 28*
  P *Bp*   **V** A S GOUGH
KETTERING (All Saints) *Pet 11*   **P** *SMF*
  V D J T MILLER, **Par Dn** J A ROSE
KETTERING (St Andrew) *Pet 11*   **P** *Bp*   **V** P A JEPPS
KETTERING (St Mary the Virgin) (St John the Evangelist)
  Pet 11   **P** *SMF*   **V** H S HODGETTS
KETTERING (St Peter and St Paul) (St Michael and All
  Angels) *Pet 11*   **P** *Comdr L M M Saunders Watson*
  R F PEARCE, **C** R A STACKPOLE
KETTERINGHAM (St Peter)   Swardeston w E
  Carleton, Intwood, Keswick etc *Nor*
KETTLEBASTON (St Mary) *St E 10*   **P** *Guild of All So*
  P-in-c C E WETHERALL
KETTLEBROOK (St Andrew)   Tamworth *Lich*
KETTLEBURGH (St Andrew)   Brandeston w
  Kettleburgh *St E*
KETTLENESS (St John the Baptist)   Lythe w Ugthorpe
  York
KETTLESTONE AND PENSTHORPE (All Saints)   Gt
  w Lt Snoring w Kettlestone and Pensthorpe *Nor*
KETTLETHORPE (St Peter and St Paul) *Linc 2*   **P** *DBP*
  R L SALT
KETTLEWELL (St Mary) w Conistone, Hubberholme and
  Arncliff w Halton Gill *Bradf 7*   **P** *Bp*, *Mrs A M Harries*
  and W R G Bell Esq (jt)   **V** E D BLANCHARD,
  C B W LEVICK
KETTON (St Mary the Virgin) *Pet 8*   **P** *Bp*
  V M W M SAUNDERS
KEW (St Anne) *S'wark 15*   **P** *The Crown*   **V** P McCRORY
KEW St Francis of Assisi Conventional District *Liv 9*
  P *Bp*   **C-in-c** R MIDDLETON
KEW (St Philip and All Saints) (St Luke) *S'wark 15*   **P** *Bp*
  V N DARBY
KEWSTOKE (St Paul) w Wick St Lawrence *B & W 12*
  P *Ld Chan*   **V** C R VINCENT
KEXBY (St Paul) w Wilberfoss *York 7*   **P** *Viscount*
  de Vesci and Lord Egremont (alt)   **P-in-c** S P IREDALE
KEYHAM (All Saints)   Houghton-on-the-Hill, Keyham
  and Hungarton *Leic*
KEYHAM, NORTH (St Thomas) *Ex 22*   **P** *Bp*
  V J M B SMETHURST
KEYINGHAM (St Nicholas) w Ottringham, Halsham and
  Sunk Island *York 13*   **P** *Abp (3 turns)*, *DBP (1 turn)*
  R I R S WALKER, **Hon Par Dn** S J WALKER
KEYMER (St Cosmas and St Damian)   Clayton w
  Keymer *Chich*
KEYMER (St Francis of Assisi)   as above
KEYNSHAM (St Francis) (St John the Baptist) *B & W 11*
  P *Patr Bd*   **TR** R M C FRITH, **TV** S W COOK,
  C P M HOLLINGSWORTH, S M STEVENETTE,
  NSM A A J CLARIDGE
KEYSOE (St Mary the Virgin) w Bolnhurst and Little
  Staughton *St Alb 21*   **P** *CCC Ox (1 turn)*, *Bp (2 turns)*
  V J C LAIRD
KEYSTON (St John the Baptist) and Bythorn *Ely 10*
  P *Sir Stephen Hastings (2 turns)*, *Bp (1 turn)*
  P-in-c J HINDLEY, **NSM** B A BEARCROFT
KEYWORTH (St Mary Magdalene) *S'well 9*   **P** *Bp*
  R J L D HARDY
KIBWORTH (St Wilfrid) and Smeeton Westerby and
  Saddington *Leic 5*   **P** *Mert Coll Ox and Bp (jt)*
  R F W DAWSON, **NSM** R H HUTCHINGS
KIDBROOKE (St James) (St Nicholas) (Holy Spirit)
  S'wark 1   **P** *Patr Bd*   **TR** K W HITCH,

TV P B D CRICK, J G HESKINS,
  NSM L T E EDEN, K F SITCH
KIDDERMINSTER (St George) (St Chad) (St John the
  Baptist Church Hall) *Worc 10*   **P** *Patr Bd*
  TR N J W BARKER, **TV** A J PIGGOTT,
  Par Dn A M JONES, **Hon C** T STOUT
KIDDERMINSTER (St John the Baptist) (Holy Innocents)
  Worc 10   **P** *Patr Bd*   **C** M S BRIDGEN,
  Par Dn L M GIBSON
KIDDERMINSTER (St Mary and All Saints) w Trimpley,
  Franche, Broadwaters and Upper Arley *Worc 10*   **P** *Bp*
  TR A J POSTLETHWAITE, **TV** G S BAKER, P VICKERS,
  C A J WRIGHT
KIDDINGTON (St Nicholas)   Wootton w Glympton and
  Kiddington *Ox*
KIDLINGTON (St Mary the Virgin) w Hampton Poyle
  Ox 7   **P** *Patr Bd*   **TR** G C M SMITH, **TV** R G COPPEN,
  Par Dn S E IRWIN
KIDLINGTON, SOUTH (St John the Baptist)
  Kidlington w Hampton Poyle *Ox*
KIDMORE END (St John the Baptist) *Ox 6*   **P** *Bp*
  V G D FOULIS BROWN
KIDSGROVE (St Thomas) *Lich 15*   **P** *MMCET*
  V *Vacant*   Stoke-on-Trent (0782) 771367
KILBURN (Mission Room)   Horsley *Derby*
KILBURN Priory Road (St Mary w All Souls) *Lon 16*
  P *Bp and Ch Patr Trust (jt)*   **P-in-c** P W WHEATLEY
KILBURN (St Augustine) (St John) *Lon 2*   **P** *SMF*
  V P T RIVERS
KILBURN (St Mary)   Thirkleby w Kilburn and Bagby
  York
KILBURN, WEST (St Luke) (St Simon) (St Jude) *Lon 2*
  P *CPAS*   **V** R D de BERRY, **Par Dn** E J BARRATT
KILBY (St Mary Magdalene)   Fleckney and Kilby *Leic*
KILDALE (St Cuthbert)   Ingleby Greenhow w Bilsdale
  Priory, Kildale etc *York*
KILDWICK (St Andrew) *Bradf 8*   **P** *Ch Ch Ox*
  V I F N BUSBY
KILHAM (All Saints)   Rudston w Boynton and Kilham
  York
KILKHAMPTON (St James the Great) w Morwenstow
  Truro 8   **P** *DBP and Bp (jt)*   **R** B G DORRINGTON
KILLAMARSH (St Giles) *Derby 3*   **P** *The Crown*
  R J F STATHAM
KILLINGHALL (St Thomas the Apostle) *Ripon 1*
  P *Sir Thomas Ingilby, Bt*   **P-in-c** A G HUDSON
KILLINGHOLME, NORTH AND SOUTH (St Denys)
  Habrough Gp *Linc*
KILLINGTON (All Saints)   Firbank, Howgill and
  Killington *Bradf*
KILLINGWORTH (St John) *Newc 1*   **P** *V Longbenton*
  St Bart   **P-in-c** M S JONES
KILMERSDON (St Peter and St Paul) w Babington
  B & W 13   **P** *Lord Hylton*   **R** C P J TURNER
KILMESTON (St Andrew)   Hinton Ampner w
  Bramdean and Kilmeston *Win*
KILMINGTON (St Giles) w Shute *Ex 5*   **P** *Bp and D&C*
  (alt)   **V** D J R MOSELEY
KILMINGTON (St Mary the Virgin)   Upper Stour
  Sarum
KILNDOWN (Christ Church)   Goudhurst w Kilndown
  Cant
KILNGREEN (Diggle Mission Church)   Saddleworth
  Man
KILNHURST (St Thomas) *Sheff 12*   **P** *Ld Chan*
  V P S LINDECK
KILNSEA (St Helen)   Easington w Skeffling, Kilnsea and
  Holmpton *York*
KILNWICK (All Saints)   Bainton w N Dalton,
  Middleton-on-the-Wolds etc *York*
KILNWICK PERCY (St Helen)   Pocklington and
  Owsthorpe and Kilnwick Percy etc *York*
KILPECK (St Mary and St David)   Ewyas Harold w
  Dulas, Kenderchurch etc *Heref*
KILSBY (St Faith)   Barby w Kilsby *Pet*
KILTON (St Nicholas)   Quantoxhead *B & W*
KILVERSTONE (St Andrew)   Thetford *Nor*
KILVINGTON (St Mary) *S'well 3*   **P** *E G Staunton Esq*
  P-in-c S F RISING
KILVINGTON, SOUTH (St Wilfrid)   Thirsk *York*
KILWORTH, NORTH (St Andrew) w SOUTH (St
  Nicholas) and Misterton *Leic 11*   **P** *Ld Chan,*
  R R D Belgrave Esq, and Rev C E N Richards (by turn)
  R *Vacant*   Market Harborough (0858) 880436
KIMBERLEY (Holy Trinity) *S'well 7*   **P** *Bp*
  R D W WILDE
KIMBERLEY (St Peter)   Barnham Broom *Nor*
KIMBERWORTH (St Thomas) (St Mark) *Sheff 6*   **P** *Bp*
  V N J BUCK, **Par Dn** J TRICKETT

KIMBERWORTH PARK (St John) *Sheff 6*　P *Bp*
　V M G R D SMITH
KIMBLE, GREAT (St Nicholas)　Ellesborough, The
　Kimbles and Stoke Mandeville *Ox*
KIMBLE, LITTLE (All Saints)　as above
KIMBLESWORTH (St Philip and St James)　Sacriston
　and Kimblesworth *Dur*
KIMBOLTON (St Andrew) *Ely 10*　P *Trustees of Duke of
　Man*　V R A FROST
KIMBOLTON (St James the Great) w Hamnish and
　Middleton-on-the-Hill *Heref 7*　P *Bp*　V A TALBOT-
　PONSONBY
KIMCOTE (All Saints)　Gilmorton w Peatling Parva and
　Kimcote etc *Leic*
KIMMERIDGE (St Nicholas of Myra)　Corfe Castle,
　Church Knowle, Kimmeridge etc *Sarum*
KIMPTON (St Peter and St Paul)　Appleshaw, Kimpton,
　Thruxton and Fyfield *Win*
KIMPTON (St Peter and St Paul) w Ayot (St Lawrence)
　St Alb 14　P *Bp*　R D R GRAEBE
KINETON (St Peter) *Cov 8*　P *Lady Willoughby de Broke*
　V R MIGHALL
KING CROSS (St Paul) *Wakef 4*　P *Bp*　V G OAKES
KING STERNDALE (Christ Church)　Buxton w
　Burbage and King Sterndale *Derby*
KINGHAM (St Andrew) w Churchill, Daylesford and
　Sarsden *Ox 3*　P *Ch Soc Trust*　R D A STREATER
KINGS BROMLEY (All Saints)　The Ridwares and
　Kings Bromley *Lich*
KING'S CAPLE (St John the Baptist)　How Caple w
　Sollarshope, Sellack etc *Heref*
KING'S CLIFFE (All Saints) w Apethorpe *Pet 8*　P *Lord
　Brassey and Bp (alt)*　R J HUMPHRIES
KINGS HEATH (All Saints) *Birm 8*　P *V Moseley St Mary*
　V J DE WIT,　C A W N S CANE
KINGS HEATH (St Augustine) *Pet 7*　P *Bp*
　V S G C SMITH
KING'S HILL (St Andrew)　Wednesbury St Bart *Lich*
KINGS LANGLEY (All Saints) *St Alb 3*　P *Abp*
　V P R STEARN
KINGS LYNN (All Saints)　S Lynn *Nor*
KING'S LYNN (St Edmund)　N Lynn w St Marg and St
　Nic *Nor*
KING'S LYNN (St Margaret)　as above
KING'S LYNN (St Nicholas)　as above
KING'S LYNN (St Peter)　W Lynn *Nor*
KINGS NORTON (St John the Baptist)　Gaulby *Leic*
KINGS NORTON (St Nicholas) *Birm 4*　P *Patr Bd*
　TV S P HUGHES, D P BYRNE, R BRISTOW,
　Hon Par Dn M G HUDSON
KING'S PYON (St Mary the Virgin)　Canon Pyon w
　Kings Pyon and Birley *Heref*
KINGS RIPTON (St Peter) *Ely 9*　P *Lord de Ramsey*
　P-in-c B J HYDER-SMITH
KING'S STANLEY (St George)　The Stanleys *Glouc*
KING'S SUTTON (St Peter and St Paul) w Newbottle and
　Charlton *Pet 1*　P *SMF and Lady Townsend (jt)*
　V J D CORBETT
KINGS WALDEN (St Mary) *St Alb 9*　P *Sir Thomas
　Pilkington*　P-in-c I NICKLIN
KING'S WORTHY (St Mary) (St Mary's Chapel) *Win 13*
　P *Univ Coll Ox and Exors Lord Northbrook (alt)*
　R H CHALL
KINGSBRIDGE (St Edmund the King and Martyr) and
　Dodbrooke *Ex 14*　P *Bp*　R C C ROBINS
KINGSBURY (Holy Innocents) *Lon 21*　P *D&C St Paul's*
　V A W PORTER
KINGSBURY (St Andrew) *Lon 21*　P *The Crown*
　V Vacant　081-205 7447
KINGSBURY (St Peter and St Paul) *Birm 12*　P *Bp*
　V Vacant　Tamworth (0827) 873500
KINGSBURY EPISCOPI (St Martin) w East Lambrook
　B & W 18　P *Bp (2 turns), D&C (1 turn)*
　V D A BURTON
KINGSCLERE (St Mary) *Win 6*　P *Bp*　V H B LEATHLEY
KINGSCLERE WOODLANDS (St Paul)　Ashford Hill
　w Headley *Win*
KINGSCOTE (St John the Baptist)　Horsley and
　Newington Bagpath w Kingscote *Glouc*
KINGSDON (All Saints)　Somerton w Compton
　Dundon, the Charltons etc *B & W*
KINGSDOWN (St Edmund the King and Martyr) *Roch 9*
　P *D&C*　R B E S GODFREY
KINGSDOWN (St John the Evangelist)　Ringwould w
　Kingsdown *Cant*
KINGSDOWN (St Matthew)　Bris St Matt and St Nath
　Bris
KINGSEY (St Nicholas)　Haddenham w Cuddington,
　Kingsey etc *Ox*

KINGSHURST (St Barnabas) *Birm 11*　P *Bp*
　V C S JONES
KINGSKERSWELL (St Mary) w Coffinswell *Ex 10*
　P *V St Marychurch*　V J F LEONARD
KINGSLAND (St Michael and All Angels) *Heref 7*
　P *DBP*　R S B THOMAS,　NSM G N PRIDAY
KINGSLEY (All Saints)　E and W Worldham, Hartley
　Mauditt w Kingsley etc *Win*
KINGSLEY (St John the Evangelist) *Ches 3*
　P *V Frodsham*　V R C PULLEN
KINGSLEY (St Werburgh) *Lich 12*
　P *Mrs G I A Dalrymple-Hamilton*　R Vacant　Cheadle
　(0538) 754754
KINGSLEY MOOR (St John the Baptist)　Kingsley *Lich*
KINGSNORTH (St Michael and All Angels) w Shadoxhurst
　Cant 10　P *Abp*　R W E M LENNOX
KINGSNYMPTON (St James)　S Molton w Nymet St
　George, High Bray etc *Ex*
KINGSTAG (not known)　Stock and Lydlinch *Sarum*
KINGSTANDING (St Luke) *Birm 3*　P *Bp*
　P-in-c B H PARRY,　C D J A SMITH
KINGSTANDING (St Mark) *Birm 3*　P *Bp*
　V A D MAYES,　Hon C A BARTLETT
KINGSTEIGNTON (St Michael) *Ex 11*　P *Bp*
　V C H BENSON
KINGSTHORPE (St John the Baptist) w Northampton
　(St David) *Pet 4*　P *Patr Bd*　TR M R H BAKER,
　TV R D PRATT, D M FAREY,　C B B C PROWSE
KINGSTON (All Saints and St Andrew)　Bourn and
　Kingston w Caxton and Longstowe *Ely*
KINGSTON (St Giles)　Barham w Bishopsbourne and
　Kingston *Cant*
KINGSTON (St James)　Bigbury, Ringmore and
　Kingston *Ex*
KINGSTON (St James)　Shorwell w Kingston *Portsm*
KINGSTON (St James), Langton Matravers and Worth
　Matravers *Sarum 9*　P *Bp, Lt-Col H E Scott, and
　R Swanage and Studland (jt)*　R R N K WATTON,
　NSM P M CHADWICK
KINGSTON (St Pancras)　Iford w Kingston and Rodmell
　Chich
KINGSTON BAGPUIZE (St John the Baptist)　Fyfield
　w Tubney and Kingston Bagpuize *Ox*
KINGSTON BUCI (St Julian) *Chich 4*　P *Lord Egremont*
　R S C KERSLEY,　C M H GABRIEL
KINGSTON DEVERILL (St Mary)　The Deverills
　Sarum
KINGSTON HILL (St Paul) *S'wark 14*　P *DBP*
　V H L WHYTE
KINGSTON LACY (St Stephen)　Sturminster Marshall,
　Kingston Lacy and Shapwick *Sarum*
KINGSTON LISLE (St John the Baptist)　Ridgeway *Ox*
KINGSTON-ON-SOAR (St Winifred)　W Leake w
　Kingston-on-Soar etc *S'well*
KINGSTON PARK (not known)　Newc Epiphany *Newc*
KINGSTON SEYMOUR (All Saints)　Yatton Moor
　B & W
KINGSTON ST MARY (Blessed Virgin Mary)　Broomfield
　and Cheddon Fitzpaine *B & W 20*　P *D&C Bris and Bp
　(alt)*　R G C H WATSON
KINGSTON UPON HULL (Holy Trinity) *York 15*
　P *Patr Soc*　V J W WALLER,　Par Dn J A WRIGHT,
　Hon C M BATES
KINGSTON UPON HULL Southcoates (St Aidan) *York 15*
　P *Simeon's Trustees*　V M C GREEN,
　Par Dn S WORRALL
KINGSTON UPON HULL (St Alban) *York 15*　P *Abp*
　V W CHARLTON,　C K C NORTHOVER
KINGSTON UPON HULL (St Mary) *York 15*　P *Abp*
　V Vacant
KINGSTON UPON HULL (St Matthew w St Barnabas)
　York 15　P *V Hull H Trin*　V J A BAGSHAWE
KINGSTON UPON HULL (St Nicholas) *York 15*　P *Abp*
　V S I TYRRELL,　C D A ROGERS,
　Par Dn V P HEWETSON
KINGSTON UPON THAMES (All Saints) (St John the
　Evangelist) *S'wark 14*　P *K Coll Cam*
　V R W MACKENNA,　C A O ROLAND
KINGSTON UPON THAMES (St Luke) *S'wark 14*　P *Bp*
　V C W B VICKERY,　Hon C M J F MANNALL
KINGSTON VALE (St John the Baptist) *S'wark 14*　P *Bp*
　V M C FREEMAN
KINGSTONE (St John and All Saints)　Dowlishwake w
　Kingstone, Chillington etc *B & W*
KINGSTONE (St John the Baptist) w Gratwich *Lich 21*
　P *Bp*　P-in-c A G SADLER,　C R M VIDAL-HALL
KINGSTONE (St Michael and All Angels) w Clehonger,
　Eaton Bishop, Allensmore and Thruxton *Heref 1*　P *Bp*

(2 turns), *Prime Min (1 turn)*   **R** B A M GILLETT,
C D J BOWEN
KINGSWEAR (St Thomas of Canterbury) Brixham w
Churston Ferrers and Kingswear *Ex*
KINGSWINFORD (St Mary) *Lich 1*   **P** *DBP*
V J S LUNGLEY,   **C** R H WAKERELL, D M HARTLEY
KINGSWOOD (Church of the Ascension) (Holy Trinity)
Bris 2   **P** *Patr Bd*   **TR** C H HUTCHINS,
TV M R COCKING,   **C** R D M MARTIN
KINGSWOOD (St Andrew) *S'wark 24*   **P** *Bp and*
R&S Ch Trust (jt)   **V** H MORGAN,   **Hon C** R F SHAW
KINGSWOOD (St Mary the Virgin) w Alderley and
Hillesley *Glouc 7*   **P** *Bp, DBP and*
R M G S Hale Esq (jt)   **R** D L PARKINSON
KINGSWOOD, LOWER (Wisdom of God) Kingswood
S'wark
KINGTON (St James) Inkberrow w Cookhill and
Kington w Dormston *Worc*
KINGTON (St Mary) w Huntington, Old Radnor,
Kinnerton and Knill *Heref 5*   **P** *Bp, D&C, and*
D&C Worc (jt)   **R** H D G JENKYNS
KINGTON (St Michael) *Bris 9*   **P** *Patr Bd*
NSM G H BOLT
KINGTON, WEST (St Mary the Virgin) *Bris 9*   **P** *Bp*
P-in-c J N A BRADBURY,   **NSM** J E B MARSH
KINGTON LANGLEY (St Peter) Langley Fitzurse *Bris*
KINGTON MAGNA (All Saints) Gillingham *Sarum*
KINGWESTON (All Saints) Barton St David w
Kingweston *B & W*
KINLET (St John the Baptist) Neen Savage w Kinlet
Heref
KINNERLEY (St Mary) w Melverley and Knockin w
Maesbrook *Lich 25*   **R** D N AUSTERBERRY,
NSM A B STRATFORD
KINNERSLEY (St James) Lyonshall w Titley, Almeley
and Kinnersley *Heref*
KINNERTON (St Mary the Virgin) Kington w
Huntington, Old Radnor, Kinnerton etc *Heref*
KINNERTON, HIGHER (All Saints) Dodleston *Ches*
KINNINVIE (Mission Room) Barnard Castle w
Whorlton *Dur*
KINOULTON (St Luke) Hickling w Kinoulton and
Broughton Sulney *S'well*
KINSBOURNE GREEN (St Mary) Harpenden St Nic
St Alb
KINSHAM (All Saints) Presteigne w Discoed, Kinsham
and Lingen *Heref*
KINSLEY (Ascension) w Wragby *Wakef 11*   **P** *Bp and*
Lord St Oswald (jt)   **V** H GALLAGHER
KINSON (St Andrew) (St Philip) *Sarum 8*   **P** *Patr Bd*
TR V R BARRON,   **TV** R C HARRISON,
C R M GOLDENBERG,   **NSM** R J HARRISON
KINTBURY (St Mary the Virgin) w Avington *Ox 14*
P *DBP (2 turns), Bp (1 turn)*   **V** M J GILLHAM
KINVER (St Peter) and Enville *Lich 6*   **P** *Bp, Mrs*
E Bissill, and DBP (jt)   **C** D I HAYNES,
Hon Par Dn M MORRIS
KINWARTON (St Mary the Virgin) w Great Alne and
Haselor *Cov 7*   **P** *Bp*   **P-in-c** S R BURCH
KIPPAX (St Mary the Virgin) w Allerton Bywater *Ripon 8*
P *Bp*   **TR** T KEDDIE,   **TV** R HUMPHRIS,
Par Dn E M JONES
KIPPINGTON (St Mary) *Roch 8*   **P** *DBP*   **V** J B LOWE
KIRBY, WEST (St Andrew) *Ches 8*   **P** *D&C*
R D C KELLY
KIRBY, WEST (St Bridget) *Ches 8*   **P** *D&C*
R D M FERRIDAY,   **C** I C WATTS,   **NSM** J M BEAZLEY
KIRBY BEDON (St Andrew) w Bixley and Whitlingham
Nor 14   **P** *BNC Ox (2 turns), Bp (1 turn)*
P-in-c I J BAILEY
KIRBY BELLARS (St Peter) Melton Gt Framland *Leic*
KIRBY CANE (All Saints) Gillingham w Geldeston,
Stockton, Ellingham etc *Nor*
KIRBY GRINDALYTHE (St Andrew) Weaverthorpe
w Helperthorpe, Luttons Ambo etc *York*
KIRBY KNOWLE (St Wilfrid) *York 20*   **P** *Abp*
P-in-c P R A R HOARE
KIRBY-LE-SOKEN (St Michael) w Great Holland
Chelmsf 26   **P** *Bp and CPAS (jt)*   **R** J F PRICE
KIRBY MISPERTON (St Laurence) w Normanby, Edston
and Salton *York 21*   **P** *Countess Feversham, Abp, and*
St Jo Coll Cam (by turn)   **R** G F SHERWOOD
KIRBY MUXLOE (St Bartholomew) *Leic 12*   **P** *Bp*
TR G H SUART,   **TV** J A COUTTS,   **Hon C** J M GREEN
KIRBY-ON-THE-MOOR (All Saints), Cundall w Norton-
le-Clay and Skelton-cum-Newby *Ripon 3*   **P** *Bp,*
Sir Arthur Collins, and R E J Compton Esq (jt)
P-in-c J FOSTER

KIRBY SIGSTON (St Lawrence) Northallerton w Kirby
Sigston *York*
KIRBY UNDERDALE (All Saints) Bishop Wilton w
Full Sutton, Kirby Underdale etc *York*
KIRBY WISKE (St John the Baptist) Ainderby Steeple
w Yafforth and Kirby Wiske etc *Ripon*
KIRDFORD (St John the Baptist) *Chich 11*   **P** *Lord*
Egremont   **V** E A D VARGAS
KIRK BRAMWITH (St Mary) Fishlake w Sykehouse,
Kirk Bramwith, Fenwick etc *Sheff*
KIRK DEIGHTON (All Saints) Spofforth w Kirk
Deighton *Ripon*
KIRK ELLA (St Andrew) *York 15*   **P** *D&C*
V J A G SCOTT,   **C** W D NICHOL
KIRK FENTON (St Mary) w Kirkby Wharfe and Ulleskelfe
York 1   **P** *Abp and Trustees of Capt J Fielden*
V R A CLEGG
KIRK HALLAM (All Saints) *Derby 13*   **P** *Bp*
V D E PEET
KIRK HAMMERTON (St John the Baptist) Lower
Nidderdale *Ripon*
KIRK IRETON (Holy Trinity) Wirksworth w
Alderwasley, Carsington etc *Derby*
KIRK LANGLEY (St Michael) *Derby 11*
P *G Meynell Esq and J M Clark-Maxwell (alt)*
P-in-c D HUGHES,   **NSM** E DIXON, H M MEYNELL
KIRK SANDALL and Edenthorpe (Good Shepherd) *Sheff 9*
P *Ld Chan*   **R** G TAYLOR
KIRK SMEATON (St Peter) Womersley and Kirk
Smeaton *Wakef*
KIRKANDREWS ON EDEN (St Mary) Burgh-by-
Sands and Kirkbampton w Kirkandrews etc *Carl*
KIRKANDREWS ON ESK (St Andrew) Nicholforest
and Kirkandrews on Esk *Carl*
KIRKBAMPTON (St Peter) Burgh-by-Sands and
Kirkbampton w Kirkandrews etc *Carl*
KIRKBRIDE (St Bridget or St Bride) w Newton Arlosh
Carl 3   **P** *Earl of Lonsdale and V Holme Cultram (alt)*
P-in-c R P H FRANK,   **Par Dn** G M DYER,
NSM T N DYER
KIRKBURN (St Mary) Wetwang and Garton-on-the-
Wolds w Kirkburn *York*
KIRKBURTON (All Hallows) *Wakef 6*   **P** *Bp*
V D BARRACLOUGH
KIRKBY (St Andrew) S Kelsey Gp *Linc*
KIRKBY (St Chad) (St Mark) (St Martin) (not known)
Liv 7   **P** *Patr Bd*   **TR** A B HAWLEY,
TV J H CATLIN, A J E GREEN,
C B G SCHUNEMANN, M W FOLLAND, J P HERBERT,
K R M BRISTOW
KIRKBY, SOUTH (All Saints) *Wakef 11*   **P** *Guild of*
All So   **V** P WRIGHT
KIRKBY FLEETHAM (St Mary) w Langton on Swale and
Scruton *Ripon 4*   **P** *Bp Ripon and D&C York (jt)*
R K McLEOD
KIRKBY GREEN (Holy Cross) Scopwick Gp *Linc*
KIRKBY IN ASHFIELD (St Thomas) *S'well 4*   **P** *Bp*
R D R L WHITE
KIRKBY IN ASHFIELD (St Wilfrid) *S'well 4*   **P** *Bp*
R A BUTT
KIRKBY-IN-CLEVELAND (St Augustine) *York 22*
P *Abp*   **V** D J BOASE
KIRKBY-IN-MALHAMDALE (St Michael the Archangel)
w Coniston Cold *Bradf 5*   **P** *Bp and D&C (jt)*
V B W NEWTH
KIRKBY IRELETH (St Cuthbert) *Carl 8*   **P** *D&C York*
V G MURFET
KIRKBY LAYTHORPE (St Denys) *Linc 22*   **P** *Bp and*
DBP (alt)   **R** R J ABRAHAM
KIRKBY LONSDALE (St Mary the Virgin) *Carl 9*
P *Patr Bd*   **TR** G W BETTRIDGE,   **TM** J EASTWOOD,
NSM P FINLINSON
KIRKBY MALHAM (St Michael the Archangel)
Kirkby-in-Malhamdale w Coniston Cold *Bradf*
KIRKBY MALLORY (All Saints) Newbold de Verdun
and Kirkby Mallory *Leic*
KIRKBY MALZEARD (St Andrew) Fountains Gp
Ripon
KIRKBY-ON-BAIN (St Mary) *Linc 11*   **P** *Ld Chan*
P-in-c S W PEARCE
KIRKBY OVERBLOW (All Saints) *Ripon 1*   **P** *Bp*
R B A TUNSTALL
KIRKBY RAVENSWORTH (St Peter and St Felix)
Gilling and Kirkby Ravensworth *Ripon*
KIRKBY STEPHEN (not known) w Mallerstang and
Crosby Garrett w Soulby *Carl 1*   **P** *Bp,*
Earl of Lonsdale, and Lord Hothfield (jt)
R W F GREETHAM

**KIRKBY THORE (St Michael) w Temple Sowerby and w
Newbiggin** *Carl 1* **P** *Lord Hothfield (3 turns)*,
Major and Mrs Sawrey-Cookson (1 turn)
R I L MCLOUGHLIN
KIRKBY UNDERWOOD (St Mary and All Saints)
Rippingale Gp *Linc*
KIRKBY WHARFE (St John the Baptist) Kirk Fenton
w Kirkby Wharfe and Ulleskelfe *York*
KIRKBY WOODHOUSE (St John the Evangelist) *S'well 4*
P *Bp* **V** M J MACDONALD
**KIRKBYMOORSIDE (All Saints) w Gillamoor, Farndale
and Bransdale** *York 18* **P** *Countess Feversham*
V A HUGHES
KIRKCAMBECK (St Kentigern) Lanercost w
Kirkcambeck and Walton *Carl*
KIRKDALE (St Gregory) *York 18* **P** *Ox Univ*
V J M WARDEN
KIRKDALE (St Lawrence) *Liv 3* **P** *CPAS* **V** N F BOON
KIRKDALE (St Mary and St Athanasius) *Liv 3*
P *Simeon's Trustees* **V** *Vacant* 051-933 6860
KIRKDALE (St Paul) Bóotle St Mary w St Paul *Liv*
KIRKHAM (St Michael) *Blackb 11* **P** *Ch Ch Ox*
V R A NELSON
KIRKHAUGH (Holy Paraclete) Alston Team *Newc*
KIRKHEATON (St Bartholomew) Kirkwhelpington,
Kirkharle, Kirkheaton and Cambo *Newc*
KIRKHEATON (St John the Baptist) *Wakef 1* **P** *Ch Trust
Fund Trust* **R** W L HALLING, **C** J F DUNNETT
KIRKHOLT (St Thomas) *Man 19* **P** *Bp* **V** B H LOCKE
KIRKLAND (Mission Church) Lamplugh w Ennerdale
Carl
KIRKLAND (St Lawrence) Skirwith, Ousby and
Melmerby w Kirkland *Carl*
KIRKLEATHAM (St Cuthbert) (St Hilda) *York 17*
P *Abp* **V** J D PURDY, **C** C J SIMMONS
KIRKLEVINGTON (St Martin) *York 22* **P** *Abp*
V D MOORE
KIRKLEY (St Peter and St John) Lowestoft and Kirkley
Nor
**KIRKLINGTON (St Michael) w Burneston and Wath and
Pickhill** *Ripon 4* **P** *Ch Soc Trust, Mrs M St B Anderson,
G W Prior-Wandesforde Esq, and DBP (jt)*
R C N R MANSELL
KIRKLINGTON (St Swithin) w Hockerton *S'well 15*
P *Bp* **P-in-c** D J BARTLETT
KIRKLINTON (St Cuthbert) Bewcastle, Stapleton and
Kirklinton etc *Carl*
KIRKNEWTON (St Gregory) Glendale Gp *Newc*
KIRKOSWALD (St Oswald), Renwick and Ainstable *Carl 4*
P *Bp and E P Ecroyd Esq (jt)* **V** D M FOWLER
KIRKSTALL (St Stephen) *Ripon 7* **P** *Patrons Leeds
St Pet* **V** P J BRINDLE
KIRKSTEAD (St Leonard) Woodhall Spa and
Kirkstead *Linc*
KIRKTHORPE (St Peter) Warmfield *Wakef*
**KIRKWHELPINGTON (St Bartholomew) w Kirkharle,
Kirkheaton and Cambo** *Newc 11* **P** *Ld Chan (2 turns),
J P P Anderson Esq (1 turn), and Bp (1 turn)*
V F B RODRIGUEZ-VEGLIO
KIRMINGTON (St Helen) *Linc 6* **P** *Earl of Yarborough*
V S PHILLIPS
KIRMOND-LE-MIRE (St Martin) Walesby *Linc*
KIRSTEAD (St Margaret) Brooke, Kirstead, Mundham
w Seething and Thwaite *Nor*
KIRTLING (All Saints) *Ely 4* **P** *Mrs D A Bowlby and
Countess Ellesmere (alt)* **V** A F HOMER
**KIRTLINGTON (St Mary the Virgin) w Bletchingdon,
Weston-on-The Green and Hampton Gay** *Ox 2*
P *Qu Coll Ox, St Jo Coll Ox, and C G R Buxton (jt)*
R D WILCOX, **NSM** G M SUMNER
KIRTON (Holy Trinity) *S'well 3* **P** *SMF* **R** I CLARK
KIRTON (St Mary and St Martin) w Falkenham *St E 2*
P *Ld Chan* **P-in-c** J E SWAIN
KIRTON IN HOLLAND (St Peter and St Paul) *Linc 21*
P *Mercers' Co* **V** J D TRINDER, **NSM** J FUNDY
KIRTON IN LINDSEY (St Andrew) *Linc 6* **P** *Bp*
V D I WALKER
KISLINGBURY (St Luke) w Rothersthorpe *Pet 3* **P** *Bp
(2 turns), DBP (1 turn)* **R** C T DAVIES
KITTISFORD (St Nicholas) Wellington and Distr
B & W
KLIVE (The Blessed Virgin Mary) Quantoxhead *B & W*
KNAITH (St Mary) *Linc 2* **P** *Exors Lt-Col
J E W G Sandars* **V** J S CROFT
KNAPHILL (Holy Trinity) *Guildf 12* **P** *V Woking St Jo*
V R B WATSON
KNAPTON (St Peter) Trunch *Nor*
KNAPWELL (All Saints) Elsworth w Knapwell *Ely*

KNARESBOROUGH (Holy Trinity) (St John the Baptist)
Ripon 1 **P** *Bp and Earl of Harewood (jt)*
R A C BETTS, **C** A J PEARSON, J SAXTON,
NSM J P CAPERON
KNARESDALE (St Jude) Alston Team *Newc*
**KNEBWORTH (St Martin) (St Mary the Virgin and
St Thomas of Canterbury)** *St Alb 12* **P** *Hon
D A Fromanteel* **R** R M JAMES
KNEESALL (St Bartholomew) w Laxton and Wellow
S'well 3 **P** *DBP and Bp (jt)* **V** M W TIPPER
KNEETON (St Helen) E Bridgford and Kneeton *S'well*
KNIGHTLEY (Christ Church) High Offley and Norbury
Lich
KNIGHTON (St John the Baptist) Clarendon Park St Jo
w Knighton St Mich *Leic*
KNIGHTON (St Mary Magdalene) (St Guthlac) *Leic 2*
P *Bp* **V** C D ALLEN, **C** T S G VALE, **NSM** M R SEDEN
KNIGHTON (St Michael and All Angels) Clarendon
Park St Jo w Knighton St Mich *Leic*
KNIGHTON (Village Hall) Mucklestone *Lich*
KNIGHTON, WEST (St Peter) Broadmayne, W
Knighton, Owermoigne etc *Sarum*
KNIGHTON-ON-TEME (St Michael and All Angels)
Teme Valley N *Worc*
**KNIGHTS ENHAM (St Michael and All Angels) (St Paul's
Church Centre)** *Win 3* **P** *Bp* **R** A EDMEADS
KNIGHTWICK (St Mary) Martley and Wichenford,
Knightwick etc *Worc*
KNILL (St Michael and All Angels) Kington w
Huntington, Old Radnor, Kinnerton etc *Heref*
KNIPTON (All Saints) Croxton Kerrial, Knipton,
Harston, Branston etc *Leic*
KNIVETON (St Michael and All Angels) Fenny
Bentley, Kniveton, Thorpe and Tissington *Derby*
KNOCKHOLT (St Katharine) w Halstead *Roch 8*
P *D&C* **R** H J M BURY
KNOCKIN (St Mary) Kinnerley w Melverley and
Knockin w Maesbrook *Lich*
KNODISHALL (St Lawrence) Aldringham w Thorpe,
Knodishall w Buxlow etc *St E*
KNOOK (St Margaret) Heytesbury and Sutton Veny
Sarum
KNOSSINGTON (St Peter) Whatborough Gp of Par
Leic
KNOTTING (St Margaret) Sharnbrook and Knotting w
Souldrop *St Alb*
KNOTTINGLEY (St Botolph) *Wakef 11* **P** *Bp and
V Pontefract (alt)* **V** W T HICKS, **C** G MANN,
NSM E BROWN
KNOTTY ASH (St John) *Liv 2* **P** *R W Derby*
V J G M ROOKE
KNOWBURY Clee Hill (St Peter Mission Room)
Wigmore Abbey *Heref*
KNOWBURY (St Paul) *Heref 12* **P** *Bp*
P-in-c J V ROBERTS
KNOWL HILL (St Peter) w Littlewick *Ox 13* **P** *Bp and
Trustees (alt)* **V** P NEWTON
KNOWLE (Mission Room) Coreley w Doddington
Heref
KNOWLE (St Barnabas) *Bris 3* **P** *Bp* **V** H FARLIE
KNOWLE (St Boniface) Crediton and Shobrooke *Ex*
KNOWLE (St John) E Budleigh and Bicton *Ex*
KNOWLE (St John the Baptist) (St Lawrence and St Anne)
Birm 13 **P** *Bp* **V** A J M DOW, **C** J J N SYKES
KNOWLE (St Martin) (Holy Nativity) *Bris 3* **P** *Bp*
TV R G MINSON, **C** C J SEVILLE
KNOWLTON (St Clement) Nonington w Wymynswold
and Goodnestone etc *Cant*
KNOWSLEY (St Mary) *Liv 2* **P** *Lord Derby*
Hon C J T LEIGHTON
KNOWSTONE (St Peter) Bishopsnympton, Rose Ash,
Mariansleigh etc *Ex*
**KNOYLE, EAST (St Mary the Virgin), Semley and
Sedgehill** *Sarum 13* **P** *Bp and Ch Ch Ox*
R A T JOHNSON
KNOYLE, WEST (St Mary the Virgin) Mere w W
Knoyle and Maiden Bradley *Sarum*
KNUTSFORD (St Cross) Cross Town *Ches 12*
P *Mrs J Singer* **V** P O MOULTON
KNUTSFORD (St John the Baptist) and Toft *Ches 12*
P *Bp (3 turns), Mrs L M Anderson (1 turn)*
V M W WALTERS, **C** P H BRECKWOLDT
KNUTTON (St Mary) *Lich 15* **P** *Brig Sir Alex Gibbons
and T H G Howard-Sneyd Esq (alt)* **V** P G HOUGH
KNUZDEN (St Oswald) *Blackb 2* **P** *Bp* **V** J G REEVES
KNYPERSLEY (St John the Evangelist) *Lich 14* **P** *CPAS*
V S ORME
KYME, NORTH (St Luke) Kirkby Laythorpe *Linc*
KYME, SOUTH (St Mary and All Saints) as above

KYNNERSLEY (St Chad)   Edgmond w Kynnersley and Preston Wealdmoors *Lich*

KYRE WYARD (St Mary)   Teme Valley S *Worc*

LACEBY (St Margaret) *Linc 10*   P *Earl of Yarborough and Ridley Hall Cam (jt)*   R A J ADAMSON

LACEY GREEN (Church Hall)   Wilmslow *Ches*

LACEY GREEN (St John the Evangelist) *Ox 21*   P *R Princes Risborough*   V P R L HALE

LACH DENNIS (All Saints)   Lostock Gralam *Ches*

LACHE cum SALTNEY (St Mark) *Ches 2*   P *Bp*   V S A WILCOCKSON,   C T J HAYES

LACKFORD (St Lawrence)   Culford, W Stow and Wordwell w Flempton etc *St E*

LACOCK (St Cyriac) w Bowden Hill *Bris 9*   P *A M Burnett-Brown Esq (2 turns), Ms Z M Dunlop (1 turn)*   P-in-c M H ROSS

LADBROKE (All Saints)   Harbury and Ladbroke *Cov*

LADDINGFORD (St Mary)   Yalding w Collier Street *Roch*

LADOCK (St Ladoca)   Probus, Ladock and Grampound w Creed *Truro*

LADY BAY (All Hallows) *S'well 10*   P *Bp*   V R W BRECKLES

LADYBARN (St Chad) *Man 8*   P *Bp*   R D K PRYCE

LADYBROOK (St Mary the Virgin) *S'well 2*   P *Bp*   V W STOCKTON

LADYWOOD (St John the Evangelist)   Birm St Jo Ladywood *Birm*

LAFFORD, SOUTH *Linc 22*   P *G Heathcote Esq, Bp, J Wilson Esq, D&C, DBP, N Playne Esq, Sir Bruno Welby, Bt, Baroness Willoughby de Eresby (by turn)*   R S H SPEERS,   C C H WILSON,   Hon C R S CUTTS

LAINDON (St Nicholas) w Dunton *Chelmsf 9*   P *Bp*   R N C PAUL

LAIRA (St Mary) *Ex 24*   P *Bp*   P-in-c T J NOTTAGE

LAISTERDYKE (St Mary) *Bradf 3*   P *Simeon's Trustees*   V A F POPPLEWELL

LAITHKIRK (not known)   Romaldkirk w Laithkirk *Ripon*

LAKE (Good Shepherd) *Portsm 7*   P *Bp*   P-in-c C E WALL

LAKENHAM (St Alban) *Nor 5*   P *D&C*   P-in-c K W REEVES

LAKENHAM (St John the Baptist and All Saints) *Nor 5*   P *D&C*   V A L BEWLEY,   NSM V E C BURCH

LAKENHAM (St Mark) *Nor 6*   P *D&C*   V J L WILSON,   R E S ANANA

LAKENHEATH (St Mary) *St E 11*   P *D&C Ely*   V R G DAVIES

LALEHAM (All Saints) *Lon 13*   V P R BROWN

LAMARSH (Holy Innocents)   Alphamstone w Lamarsh and Pebmarsh *Chelmsf*

LAMBERHURST (St Mary) and Matfield *Roch 11*   P *D&C and V Brenchley (jt)*   V R J MIDDLEWICK

LAMBETH, NORTH (St Anselm) (St Mary's Mission) (St Peter) *S'wark 10*   P *The Crown (1 turn), Patr Bd (2 turns)*   TR A R GRANT,   TV R M DAVIES, R H CRAIG,   C H B BROWNE

LAMBETH, SOUTH (St Anne and All Saints) *S'wark 10*   P *Abp and Bp*   V C J E MOODY,   C M R HARRISON

LAMBETH, SOUTH (St Stephen) *S'wark 10*   P *CPAS*   V C P GUINNESS

LAMBLEY (Holy Trinity) *S'well 11*   P *Rev W J Gull*   R *Vacant*   Burton Joyce (060231) 3531

LAMBLEY (St Mary and St Patrick)   Alston Team *Newc*

LAMBOURN (St Michael and All Angels) *Ox 14*   P *Bp*   V W J STEWART

LAMBOURNE (St Mary and All Saints) w Abridge and Stapleford Abbotts *Chelmsf 2*   P *CCC Cam and Ld Chan (alt)*   R G R LOCK

LAMBROOK, EAST (St James)   Kingsbury Episcopi w E Lambrook *B & W*

LAMERTON (St Peter)   Milton Abbot, Dunterton, Lamerton etc *Ex*

LAMESLEY (St Andrew) *Dur 4*   P *Bp*   V *Vacant*   091-487 6490

LAMMAS (St Andrew)   Buxton w Oxnead, Lammas and Brampton *Nor*

LAMORBEY (Holy Redeemer) *Roch 16*   P *Bp*   V N I KERR

LAMORBEY (Holy Trinity) *Roch 16*   P *D Malcolm Esq*   V D V COSSAR

LAMORRAN (Holy Trinity) and Merther *Truro 6*   P *Viscount Falmouth*   R *Vacant*   Tresillian (087252) 272

LAMORRAN Tresillian (Holy Trinity)   Lamorran and Merther *Truro*

LAMPLUGH (St Michael) w Ennerdale *Carl 5*   P *Trustees*   R J P SIMPSON

LAMPORT (All Saints)   Maidwell w Draughton, Lamport w Faxton *Pet*

LAMYATT (St Mary and St John)   Bruton and Distr *B & W*

LANCASTER (Christ Church) (Christ Church Worship Centre) (St John) *Blackb 12*   P *V Lanc and Trustees (alt)*   V P J BALLARD

LANCASTER (St Mary) *Blackb 12*   P *Trustees*   V M E BARTLETT,   C P R F CLEMENCE, M P KEIGHLEY,   Hon C S P MEWS

LANCASTER (St Thomas) *Blackb 12*   P *CPAS*   C J D GRUNDY

LANCHESTER (All Saints) *Dur 8*   P *Ld Chan*   V P WATERHOUSE

LANCING (St James the Less) w Coombes *Chich 5*   P *Bp Lon*   R R G RUSSELL,   C F R SEARLE

LANCING (St Michael and All Angels) *Chich 5*   P *Bp*   V D GODDARD

LANDBEACH (All Saints) *Ely 6*   P *CCC Cam*   R D P E REINDORP

LANDCROSS (Holy Trinity), Littleham, Monkleigh and Weare Giffard *Ex 17*   P *Bp*   R G J HANSFORD

LANDEWEDNACK (St Wynwallow)   St Ruan w St Grade and Landewednack *Truro*

LANDFORD (St Andrew)   Bramshaw and Landford w Plaitford *Sarum*

LANDKEY (St Paul)   Barnstaple *Ex*

LANDRAKE (St Michael) w St Erney and Botus Fleming *Truro 11*   P *Bp and MMCET (jt)*   V G W SMYTH

LANDSCOVE (St Matthew)   Broadhempston, Woodland, Staverton etc *Ex*

LANDULPH (St Leonard and St Dilpe)   St Dominic, Landulph and St Mellion w Pillaton *Truro*

LANDYWOOD (St Andrew)   Gt Wyrley *Lich*

LANE END (Holy Trinity) w Cadmore End *Ox 29*   P *Bp*   V R H JENNINGS

LANEAST (St Sidwell and St Gulvat)   Bolventor *Truro*

LANEHAM (St Peter)   Rampton w Laneham, Treswell, Cottam and Stokeham *S'well*

LANERCOST (St Mary Magdalene) w Kirkcambeck and Walton *Carl 2*   P *Bp, Adn, Earl of Carlisle, and PCC Lanercost (jt)*   P-in-c C J MORRIS

LANESIDE (St Peter) *Blackb 1*   P *V Haslingden St Jas*   V J EATOCK,   C A FISHWICK

LANGAR (St Andrew)   Cropwell Bishop w Colston Bassett, Granby etc *S'well*

LANGCLIFFE (St John the Evangelist) w Stainforth and Horton-in-Ribblesdale *Bradf 5*   P *Bp, Adn Craven, W R G Bell Esq, N Caton Esq, and Churchwarden of Horton-in-Ribblesdale (jt)*   V N S COULTON-TORDOFF

LANGDALE (Holy Trinity) (Mission Chapel) *Carl 10*   P *R Grasmere*   P-in-c W WADE

LANGDALE END (St Peter)   Wykeham and Hutton Buscel *York*

LANGDON, EAST (St Augustine)   St Margarets-at-Cliffe w Westcliffe etc *Cant*

LANGDON, WEST (St Mary the Virgin)   as above

LANGDON HILLS (St Mary and All Saints) *Chelmsf 9*   P *D&C St Paul's*   R A BARRETT,   C R A L ROSE

LANGFORD (St Andrew) *St Alb 22*   P *Ld Chan*   V G BRADSHAW

LANGFORD (St Bartholomew) w Holme *S'well 3*   P *Bp*   P-in-c J L SMITH

LANGFORD (St Giles)   Heybridge w Langford *Chelmsf*

LANGFORD (St Matthew)   Broughton Poggs w Filkins, Broadwell etc *Ox*

LANGFORD (Blessed Virgin Mary)   Burrington and Churchill *B & W*

LANGFORD, LITTLE (St Nicholas of Mira)   Yarnbury *Sarum*

LANGFORD BUDVILLE (St Peter)   Wellington and Distr *B & W*

LANGHAM (not known)   Gillingham *Sarum*

LANGHAM (St Mary the Virgin)   Boxted w Langham *Chelmsf*

LANGHAM (St Mary the Virgin)   Badwell Ash w Gt Ashfield, Stowlangtoft etc *St E*

LANGHAM (St Peter and St Paul) *Pet 14*   P *Bp*   V A J F DULLEY

LANGHAM EPISCOPI (St Andrew and St Mary)   Stiffkey and Cockthorpe w Morston, Langham etc *Nor*

LANGHAM PLACE (All Souls) *Lon 4*   P *The Crown*   R R T BEWES,   C I R BENTLEY, S F F PARKE,   S M WOOKEY,   Hon C O K de la T de BERRY, J R W STOTT,   NSM C M HOBDEN

LANGHO BILLINGTON (St Leonard) *Blackb 8*   P *V Blackb*   V Q H WILSON

LANGLEY (All Saints and Martyrs) and Parkfield *Man 19*
P *Patr Bd* **TR** I L JOHNSON,
TV R J SMITH, R C N HARGER
LANGLEY (St Francis) Fawley *Win*
LANGLEY (St John) *Birm 5* **P** *Bp* **V** R T ETHERIDGE
LANGLEY (St John the Evangelist) Clavering w
Langley and Arkesden *Chelmsf*
LANGLEY (St Mary) Otham w Langley *Cant*
LANGLEY (St Mary the Virgin) Wolverton w Norton
Lindsey and Langley *Cov*
LANGLEY (St Michael) Chedgrave w Hardley and
Langley *Nor*
LANGLEY (St Michael and All Angels) *Birm 5* **P** *The
Crown* **V** C M BEAVER
LANGLEY, NORTH St Luke Conventional District
Chich 16 **C-in-c** J M GRAVES
LANGLEY BURRELL (St Peter) Chippenham St Paul
w Hardenhuish etc *Bris*
LANGLEY FITZURSE (St Peter) *Bris 9* **P** *Bp*
P-in-c J C POARCH
LANGLEY GREEN (St Leonard) Ifield *Chich*
LANGLEY MARISH (St Mary the Virgin) *Ox 23*
P *Patr Bd* **TR** J R HURST,
TV A W CLEEVE, J N DAY, A P BROWN
LANGLEY MARSH (St Luke Mission Church)
Wiveliscombe *B & W*
LANGLEY MILL (St Andrew) *Derby 12* **P** *V Heanor*
V I R JONAS
LANGLEY PARK (All Saints) Esh *Dur*
LANGLEY PARK (St Peter's Church Hall) Beckenham
St Barn *Roch*
LANGLEY STREET (Mission Room) Derby St Barn
Derby
LANGLEYBURY (St Paul) *St Alb 13* **P** *D W A Loyd Esq*
V F H GIMSON
LANGNEY (St Richard of Chichester) *Chich 16* **P** *Bp*
V R E BUTLER
LANGOLD (St Luke) *S'well 6* **P** *Bp*
P-in-c R E WHEATON, **C** I R LILLEY
LANGPORT Area Churches, The (All Saints) *B & W 6*
P *Patr Bd* **TR** T V COOK,
TV S J CONNOR, W G BURMAN
LANGRICK (St Margaret of Scotland) Brothertoft Gp
Linc
LANGRIDGE (St Mary Magdalene) Swainswick w
Langridge *B & W*
LANGRISH (St John the Evangelist) *Portsm 5* **P** *Bp*
V P R WADSWORTH, **C** A RICHARDS
LANGSTONE (St Nicholas) Havant *Portsm*
LANGTOFT Group, The (St Michael) *Linc 13* **P** *DBP,
D&C, and Ld Chan (by turn)* **V** R E CHESTERTON
LANGTOFT (St Peter) w Foxholes, Butterwick, Cottam
and Thwing *York 11* **P** *Abp and Keble Coll Ox
(2 turns), Ld Chan (1 turn)* **V** R E CARLILL
LANGTON (St Andrew) Birdsall w Langton *York*
LANGTON (St Margaret) w Woodhall *Linc 11* **P** *Bp*
P-in-c R I McMASTER
LANGTON (St Peter) Woodhall Spa and Kirkstead *Linc*
LANGTON, GREAT (St Wilfrid) Kirkby Fleetham w
Langton on Swale and Scruton *Ripon*
LANGTON, GREAT (The Good Shepherd) as above
LANGTON BY PARTNEY (St Peter and St Paul) w
Sutterby *Linc 7* **P** *J C P Langton Esq* **R** G ROBSON
LANGTON-BY-WRAGBY (St Giles) Wragby *Linc*
LANGTON GREEN (All Saints) *Roch 11* **P** *R Speldhurst*
V C K CHANNER
LANGTON HERRING (St Peter) Abbotsbury,
Portesham and Langton Herring *Sarum*
LANGTON LONG (All Saints) Blandford Forum and
Langton Long *Sarum*
LANGTON MATRAVERS (St George) Kingston,
Langton Matravers and Worth Matravers *Sarum*
LANGTON ON SWALE (St Wilfrid) Kirkby Fleetham
w Langton on Swale and Scruton *Ripon*
LANGTREE *Ox 6* **P** *Patr Bd* **TR** J D SHEPHERD,
TV C D ROGERS
LANGTREE (not known) Shebbear, Buckland Filleigh,
Sheepwash etc *Ex*
LANGWATHBY (St Peter) Addingham, Edenhall,
Langwathby and Culgaith *Carl*
LANGWITH, UPPER (Holy Cross) w Langwith Bassett
and Whaley Thorns and Scarcliffe *Derby 3* **P** *Bp
(2 turns), Duke of Devonshire (1 turn)* **R** G R BEVAN
LANGWORTH (St Hugh) Barlings *Linc*
LANHYDROCK (St Hydrock) Bodmin w Lanhydrock
and Lanivet *Truro*
LANIVET (St Ia) as above

LANLIVERY (St Brevita) w Luxulyan *Truro 10* **P** *Bp
(1 turn), Adn Bodmin (1 turn), and DBP (2 turns)*
V D J KEIGHLEY
LANNER (Christ Church) Redruth w Lanner and
Treleigh *Truro*
LANREATH (St Marnarck) *Truro 12* **P** *J B Kitson Esq
and Mrs S R Parker (alt)* **R** A R INGLEBY
LANSALLOS (St Ildierna) *Truro 12* **P** *DBP and
W Grundy-Mills Esq (alt)* **R** J K P S ROBERTSHAW
LANSDOWN (St Stephen) Charlcombe w Bath St Steph
B & W
LANTEGLOS BY CAMELFORD (St Julitta) w Advent
Truro 10 **P** *Duchy of Cornwall* **R** I H MORRIS
LANTEGLOS BY FOWEY (St Wyllow) *Truro 12*
P *D&C* **V** R W THOMAS
LAPAL (St Peter) Halesowen *Worc*
**LAPFORD (St Thomas of Canterbury), Nymet Rowland
and Coldridge** *Ex 16* **P** *Bp* **R** D J WHITE
LAPLEY (All Saints) w Wheaton Aston *Lich 3* **P** *Keble
Coll Ox* **V** R F DABORN, **Hon C** R C W DAMPIER
LAPWORTH (St Mary the Virgin) *Birm 13* **P** *Mert Coll
Ox* **R** A V WILLMONT
LARCHFIELD (St George) Boyne Hill *Ox*
LARKFIELD (Holy Trinity) *Roch 7* **P** *DBP*
V J T GUNN, **C** R N McCONACHIE
LARLING (St Ethelbert) Hockham w Shropham Gp of
Par *Nor*
LASBOROUGH (St Mary) Shipton Moyne w
Westonbirt and Lasborough *Glouc*
LASHAM (St Mary) Bentworth and Shalden and
Lasham *Win*
LASHBROOK (Mission Room) Shiplake w Dunsden *Ox*
LASTINGHAM (St Mary) w Appleton-le-Moors, Rosedale
and Cropton *York 18* **P** *Abp (2 turns), Ld Chan
(1 turn)* **V** F J A HEWITT, **Par Dn** C M STREETER
LATCHFORD (Christ Church) *Ches 4* **P** *R Grappenhall*
V A SHAW
LATCHFORD (St James) (St Hilda) *Ches 4*
P *R Grappenhall* **V** J E NICE, **NSM** G J HARDMAN
LATCHINGDON (Christ Church) Creeksea w
Althorne, Latchingdon and N Fambridge *Chelmsf*
LATHBURY (All Saints) Newport Pagnell w Lathbury
and Moulsoe *Ox*
LATHOM PARK (St John) Ormskirk *Liv*
LATIMER (St Mary Magdalene) Chenies and Lt
Chalfont, Latimer and Flaunden *Ox*
LATTON (St John the Baptist) Cricklade w Latton *Bris*
LAUGHTON (All Saints) w Ripe and Chalvington *Chich 18*
P *Earl of Chich, Hertf Coll Ox, and BNC Ox (by turn)*
R R N KENWARD
LAUGHTON (All Saints) w Wildsworth *Linc 22*
P *Meynell Ch Trustees* **V** *Vacant*
LAUGHTON (St Luke) Foxton w Gumley and
Laughton and Lubenham *Leic*
LAUGHTON-EN-LE-MORTHEN (All Saints) w
Throapham *Sheff 5* **P** *Bp* **V** R W IVELL
LAUNCELLS (St Andrew and St Swithin) Stratton and
Launcells *Truro*
LAUNCESTON (St Mary Magdalene) *Truro 9* **P** *Bp*
P-in-c T J G NEWCOMBE
LAUNCESTON (St Stephen) (St Thomas the Apostle)
Truro 9 **P** *D&C and PCC (jt)* **V** M L UREN
LAUNTON (Assumption of the Blessed Virgin Mary)
Bicester w Bucknell, Caversfield and Launton *Ox*
LAVANT (St Mary) (St Nicholas) *Chich 3* **P** *Earl of
March and Kinrara* **R** C DAVIES
LAVENDER HILL (Ascension) *S'wark 13* **P** *Keble Coll
Ox* **V** J H CUTHBERT
LAVENDON (St Michael) w Cold Brayfield, Clifton Reynes
and Newton Blossomville *Ox 27* **P** *T V Sutthery Esq,
Rev S F Hamill-Stewart, Exors of M E Farrer Esq, and
Bp (jt)* **R** D P CIANCHI
LAVENHAM (St Peter and St Paul) *St E 10* **P** *G & C Coll
Cam* **R** D W W PEARCE
LAVER, HIGH (All Saints) w Magdalen Laver and Little
Laver and Matching *Chelmsf 6* **P** *Bp*
P-in-c P T C MASHEDER
LAVER, LITTLE (St Mary the Virgin) see above
LAVERSTOCK (St Andrew) *Sarum 15* **P** *D&C*
V W G BULL
LAVERSTOKE (St Mary) Overton w Laverstoke and
Freefolk *Win*
LAVERTON (The Blessed Virgin Mary) Norton St
Philip w Hemington, Hardington etc *B & W*
LAVINGTON, WEST and the Cheverells *Sarum 19* **P** *Bp*
R H G HOSKINS
LAVINGTON, WEST (St Mary Magdalene) Cocking,
Bepton and W Lavington *Chich*

LAWFORD (St Mary) *Chelmsf 23*   **P** *St Jo Coll Cam*
   R P E BALL,   **NSM** P C M PRESTNEY
LAWHITTON (St Michael)   Lezant w Lawhitton and S
   Petherwin w Trewen *Truro*
LAWLEY (St John the Evangelist)   Cen Telford *Lich*
LAWRENCE WESTON (St Peter) *Bris 8*   **P** *Bp*
   V S R P SPILSBURY,   **Par Dn** P S SHIPP
LAWSHALL (All Saints) w Shimplingthorne and Alpheton
   St E 12   **P** *DBP and Lord de Saumarez (alt)*
   R D F FOSBUARY
LAWTON (All Saints)   Church Lawton *Ches*
LAWTON MOOR (St Michael) *Man 8*   **P** *Bp*
   V K BUTTERWORTH
LAXEY (Christ Church) *S & M 2*   **P** *Bp*
   V W H SCATTERGOOD
LAXFIELD (All Saints) *St E 17*   **P** *Simeon's Trustees*
   V R A MARCHANT
LAXTON (All Saints)   Bulwick, Blatherwycke w
   Harringworth and Laxton *Pet*
LAXTON (St Michael)   Kneesall w Laxton and Wellow
   S'well
LAXTON (St Peter)   Howden Team Min *York*
LAYER BRETON (St Mary the Virgin)   Birch w Layer
   Breton and Layer Marney *Chelmsf*
LAYER-DE-LA-HAYE (St John the Baptist) *Chelmsf 19*
   P *Bp*   **V** M H CLARKE
LAYER MARNEY (St Mary the Virgin)   Birch w Layer
   Breton and Layer Marney *Chelmsf*
LAYHAM (St Andrew)   Hadleigh w Layham and Shelley
   St E
LAYSTON W BUNTINGFORD (St Peter)   Aspenden
   and Layston w Buntingford *St Alb*
LAYTON, EAST (Christ Church)   Forcett and
   Aldbrough and Melsonby *Ripon*
LAZONBY (St Nicholas)   Gt Salkeld w Lazonby *Carl*
LEA (St Christopher) (St Barnabas) *Blackb 14*   **P** *Bp*
   V A PARKINSON
LEA (St Giles)   Garsdon, Lea and Cleverton and
   Charlton *Bris*
LEA (St Helen) *Linc 2*   **P** *DBP*   **R** J S CROFT
LEA, THE (St John the Baptist)   Weston-under-Penyard
   w Hope Mansel and the Lea *Heref*
LEA AND HOLLOWAY (Christ Church)   Tansley,
   Dethick, Lea and Holloway *Derby*
LEA CROSS (St Anne)   Pontesbury I and II *Heref*
LEA HALL (St Richard) *Birm 10*   **P** *Bp*   **V** M A YATES
LEA MARSTON (St John the Baptist)   The Whitacres
   and Shustoke *Birm*
LEADEN RODING (St Michael)   Aythorpe w High and
   Leaden Roding *Chelmsf*
LEADENHAM (St Swithin) *Linc 23*   **P** *P R Reeve Esq*
   R B J BENNETT
LEADGATE (St Ives) *Dur 8*   **P** *Bp*   **V** D HALL
LEAFIELD (St Michael and All Angels)   Ramsden,
   Finstock and Fawler, Leafield etc *Ox*
LEAGRAVE (St Luke) *St Alb 20*   **P** *Bp*   **V** M L BANKS,
   C M J FLOWERDEW,   **Hon Par Dn** J H HARRIS
LEAHOLM (St James' Chapel)   Glaisdale *York*
LEAKE (St Mary) w Over and Nether Silton and Kepwick
   York 20   **P** *Abp*   **P-in-c** P R A R HOARE
LEAKE, EAST (St Mary) *S'well 8*   **P** *Bp*   **R** S J SMITH,
   Hon C D J DAVIES
LEAKE, NEW (St Jude)   Stickney Gp *Linc*
LEAKE, OLD (St Mary) w Wrangle *Linc 20*   **P** *Bp and*
   DBP (alt)   **V** K TARGETT
LEAKE, WEST (St Helena) w Kingston-on-Soar and
   Ratcliffe-on-Soar *S'well 10*   **P** *Lord Belper*   **R** *Vacant*
LEAM LANE (St Andrew) *Dur 4*   **P** *Bp*
   Par Dn J M PERKINS
LEAMINGTON, SOUTH (St John the Baptist) *Cov 11*
   P *Bp*   **V** T L F MANDER
LEAMINGTON HASTINGS (All Saints) and Birdingbury
   Cov 6   **P** *Bp and Mrs H M O Lodder (alt)*
   P-in-c H J H STEVINSON
LEAMINGTON PRIORS (All Saints) *Cov 11*   **P** *Bp*
   NSM R JONES
LEAMINGTON PRIORS (St Mary) *Cov 11*   **P** *Ch Patr*
   Trust   **C** M WARNES
LEAMINGTON PRIORS (St Paul) *Cov 11*   **P** *Ch Patr*
   Trust   **V** B MERRINGTON,   **C** N G SHAW
LEAMINGTON SPA (Holy Trinity) and Old Milverton
   Cov 11   **P** *Bp and M Heber-Percy Esq (jt)*
   V K J COOKE
LEAMINGTON SPA (St Mark New Milverton)   New
   Milverton *Cov*
LEAMORE (St Aidan)   Blakenall Heath *Lich*
LEASINGHAM (St Andrew) *Linc 22*   **P** *DBP*
   R F RODGERS
LEASOWE (St Chad) *Ches 7*   **P** *Bp*   **Par Dn** P M CLARK

LEATHERHEAD (All Saints) (St Mary and St Nicholas)
   Guildf 10   **P** *D&C Roch*   **V** D J EATON,
   C P W MICKLETHWAITE
LEATHLEY (St Oswald) w Farnley, Fewston and
   Blubberhouses *Bradf 4*   **P** *Bp and G N le G Horton-*
   Fawkes Esq   **R** P J WINSTONE
LEATON (Holy Trinity) and Albrighton w Battlefield
   Lich 27   **P** *Col H Lloyd and J F Sparrow Esq (jt)*
   V M W TURNER
LEAVELAND (St Laurence)   Selling w Throwley,
   Sheldwich w Badlesmere etc *Cant*
LEAVENHEATH (St Matthew)   Stoke by Nayland w
   Leavenheath *St E*
LEAVENING (not known)   Burythorpe, Acklam and
   Leavening w Westow *York*
LEAVESDEN (All Saints) *St Alb 13*   **P** *Bp*
   V C P HUITSON,   **C** P J WILKIN,   **Par Dn** R J BASS
LECHLADE (St Lawrence) *Glouc 13*   **P** *Em Coll Cam*
   V S C PARSONS,   **NSM** A M McFARLAND
LECK (St Peter)   Tunstall w Melling and Leck *Blackb*
LECKFORD (St Nicholas)   Stockbridge and Longstock
   and Leckford *Win*
LECKHAMPSTEAD (Assumption of the Blessed Virgin
   Mary) N Buckm *Ox*
LECKHAMPSTEAD (St James)   Brightwalton w
   Catmore, Leckhampstead etc *Ox*
LECKHAMPTON (St Christopher)   Leckhampton SS
   Phil and Jas w Cheltenham St Jas *Glouc*
LECKHAMPTON (St Peter) *Glouc 11*   **P** *Bp*
   R G R H SMITH
LECKHAMPTON (St Philip and St James) w Cheltenham
   (St James) *Glouc 10*   **P** *Bp*   **V** D C NYE,
   C P A JOHNSON, C M R PEMBERTON,   **NSM** J KNIGHT
LECONFIELD (St Catherine)   Lockington and Lund and
   Scorborough w Leconfield *York*
LEDBURY (St Michael and All Angels) (St Katherine's
   Chapel) w Eastnor *Heref 6*   **P** *Bp and J F S Hervey-*
   Bathurst Esq (jt)   **R** C M OLDROYD,   **C** C L BEEVERS
LEDGEMOOR (Mission Room)   Canon Pyon w Kings
   Pyon and Birley *Heref*
LEDSHAM (All Saints) w Fairburn *York 6*   **P** *G H H*
   Wheler Esq   **V** P WARREN
LEDSTON LUCK (not known)   Ledsham w Fairburn
   York
LEE (Good Shepherd) (St Peter) *S'wark 3*   **P** *R Lee*
   St Marg   **V** L S C HARVEY,   **Par Dn** S G SPEAR,
   NSM M MONK
LEE (St Augustine) Grove Park *S'wark 3*   **P** *Bp*
   V J P HAYES
LEE (St John the Baptist) *Ox 28*   **P** *Bp*   **V** G A de BURGH-
   THOMAS
LEE (St Margaret) *S'wark 3*   **P** *Ld Chan*
   R R C B BUTLER
LEE (St Matthew)   Ilfracombe, Lee, Woolacombe,
   Bittadon etc *Ex*
LEE (St Mildred) Burnt Ash Hill *S'wark 3*   **P** *Bp*
   V M C HILL,   **Hon C** R C HENSON
LEE BROCKHURST (St Peter) *Lich 29*   **P** *Lord Barnard*
   V N MacGREGOR
LEE MOOR (Mission Church)   Shaugh Prior *Ex*
LEE-ON-THE-SOLENT (St Faith) *Portsm 3*   **P** *Bp*
   V M S KENNING,   **C** K B GREEN
LEEBOTWOOD (St Mary) w Longnor *Heref 11*   **P** *DBP*
   P-in-c J D M FALL
LEEDS (All Souls) *Ripon 7*   **P** *V Leeds St Pet, Simeon's*
   Trustees, and DBP (jt)   **C** P F ROBERTS
LEEDS Belle Isle (St John and St Barnabas) *Ripon 6*
   P *Bp*   **V** E CHEETHAM
LEEDS (Emmanuel) *Ripon 7*   **P** *Trustees*   **V** *Vacant*
LEEDS Gipton (Church of the Epiphany) *Ripon 5*   **P** *Bp*
   V B J MENEY,   **Hon C** J L SUTCLIFFE
LEEDS Halton (St Wilfrid) *Ripon 5*   **P** *Bp*
   V G B ATHERTON,   **C** P F HUNT
LEEDS (Parish Church)   Leeds City *Ripon*
LEEDS Richmond Hill (All Saints) (St Hilda) (St Saviour)
   Ripon 8   **P** *Bp and Keble Coll Ox (jt)*   **V** N A TURNER,
   C A P NUNN
LEEDS (St Aidan) *Ripon 5*   **P** *V Leeds St Pet*
   V A L TAYLOR,   **C** N P GEORGE
LEEDS (St Cyprian and St James) Harehills *Ripon 5*
   P *Bp*   **V** H A THOMPSON
LEEDS (St George) *Ripon 7*   **P** *Simeon's Trustees*
   V D J L HAWKINS,   **C** D MANN, J H GOODING,
   NSM M B HANSON
LEEDS (St Margaret of Antioch) (All Hallows) *Ripon 7*
   P *Bp and DBP (jt)*   **P-in-c** S R BAXTER,
   Par Dn E M BAXTER
LEEDS (St Nicholas)   Hollingbourne and Hucking w
   Leeds and Broomfield *Cant*

LEEDS (St Wilfrid) *Ripon 5*   **P** *Bp*   **V** D BOOTH
LEEDS CITY (St Peter) (Holy Trinity) *Ripon 5*   **P** *DBP*
P-in-c E D MURFET,   **Par Dn** H BEGLEY,
Hon C E H SMITHIES
LEEDSTOWN (St James's Mission Church)   Crowan w
Godolphin *Truro*
LEEK (All Saints) (St Edward the Confessor) (St John the
Evangelist) (St Luke) (St Paul) and Meerbrook *Lich 14*
P *Patr Bd*   **TR** K E JONES,
TV J P EADES, K R HAYWOOD,   **NSM** B R WILSON
LEEK WOOTTON (All Saints) *Cov 4*   **P** *Lord Leigh*
V *Vacant*   Kenilworth (0926) 54832
LEEMING (St John the Baptist) *Ripon 4*
P *R Kirklington w Burneston etc*   **V** *Vacant*   Bedale
(0677) 23498
LEEMING BAR (St Augustine)   Bedale *Ripon*
LEES HILL (Mission Hall)   Lanercost w Kirkcambeck
and Walton *Carl*
LEESFIELD Knoll's Lane (St Agnes)   Leesfield *Man*
LEESFIELD (St Thomas) *Man 18*   **P** *Bp*
V A T P HARRISON,   **NSM** A KERR
LEFTWICH (Farm of the Good Shepherd)   Davenham
Ches
LEGBOURNE (All Saints) *Linc 12*   **P** *Ch Trust Fund*
Trust and Bp (jt)   **V** J F DOWMAN
LEGBURTHWAITE (Mission Church)   St Johns-in-the-
Vale w Wythburn *Carl*
LEGH, HIGH (St John)   Over Tabley and High Legh
Ches
LEGSBY (St Thomas) *Linc 5*   **P** *Bp*   **V** *Vacant*
LEICESTER Ascension (St Aidan) (St Anne) (St Augustine)
Leic 2   **P** *Bp*   **TV** C DUNKLEY,   **P-in-c** I W HARRISON,
C C W ROGERS
LEICESTER Christ the Saviour (St Hilda) (St Peter)
(St Saviour) *Leic 1*   **P** *Bp*   **V** S F BOULD,   **C** S R KIRBY,
NSM A D BREAR
LEICESTER (Holy Apostles) (St Oswald) *Leic 2*   **P** *DBP*
and Ridley Hall Cam (jt)   **V** R J TONKIN,
Par Dn R E EDGE
LEICESTER (Holy Spirit) (St Andrew) (St Nicholas) *Leic 2*
P *Bp*   **TR** M V ROBERTS,   **TV** J W PACKWOOD,
Par Dn M J MUMFORD, J M A SEMEONOFF,
Hon C R SEMEONOFF
LEICESTER (Holy Trinity w St John the Divine) *Leic 2*
P *Peache Trustees*   **V** R W MORGAN,   **AP** M G IPGRAVE,
C A WARD, N BAINES,   **Hon C** F R ENTWISTLE
LEICESTER (Martyrs) *Leic 2*   **P** *Bp*   **V** R J FREEMAN,
C R G BIRCHALL
LEICESTER Resurrection (St Alban) *Leic 1*   **P** *Bp*
TR A W ROBINSON,   **TV** M C WARNER, R C BUSH
LEICESTER (St Aidan)   Leic Ascension *Leic*
LEICESTER (St Alban)   Leic Resurr *Leic*
LEICESTER (St Anne)   Leic Ascension *Leic*
LEICESTER (St Augustine)   as above
LEICESTER (St Barnabas)   New Humberstone *Leic*
LEICESTER (St Chad) *Leic 1*   **P** *Bp*
V K F CULVERWELL,   **C** D N J-M BAYLISS
LEICESTER (St Christopher) *Leic 2*   **P** *MMCET*
V I W Y GEMMELL,   **C** D E MALE
LEICESTER (St Elizabeth) Nether Hall *Leic 1*   **P** *DBP*
P-in-c M E C DREW,   **C** P ROYSTON-BALL
LEICESTER (St Hilda)   Leic Ch Sav *Leic*
LEICESTER (St James the Greater) *Leic 2*   **P** *Bp*
V D N HOLE,   **Hon C** A S IRESON,   **NSM** A T HELM
LEICESTER (St Margaret and All Saints) *Leic 2*   **P** *Bp*
V *Vacant*   Leicester (0533) 27362
LEICESTER (St Mary de Castro) *Leic 2*   **P** *Bp*
V M P WALLS,   **Hon C** M N G STEWART
LEICESTER (St Paul) *Leic 2*   **P** *Bp*   **V** G W H SEALY
LEICESTER (St Peter)   Leic Ch Sav *Leic*
LEICESTER (St Philip) *Leic 1*   **P** *Adn Leic, V Evington,*
V Leic H Trin, G A Cooling Esq, and A S Price Esq (jt)
V T S BYRON,   **C** R A WHITE
LEICESTER (St Saviour)   Leic Ch Sav *Leic*
LEICESTER (St Theodore of Canterbury) *Leic 1*   **P** *Bp*
V J J LEONARD
LEICESTER FOREST EAST (St Andrew)   Kirby
Muxloe *Leic*
LEIGH (All Saints)   Ashton Keynes, Leigh and Minety
Bris
LEIGH (All Saints) *Lich 21*   **P** *Bp*   **R** K R THACKER
LEIGH (St Andrew)   Yetminster w Ryme Intrinseca and
High Stoy *Sarum*
LEIGH (St Bartholomew) *S'wark 24*   **P** *N J Charrington*
Esq   **V** *Vacant*   Dawes Green (030678) 224
LEIGH (St Catherine)   Twigworth, Down Hatherley,
Norton, The Leigh etc *Glouc*
LEIGH (St Clement) *Chelmsf 12*   **P** *Bp*   **R** S F JONES

LEIGH (St Edburga)   Alfrick, Lulsley, Suckley, Leigh
and Bransford *Worc*
LEIGH (St John the Evangelist) *Man 13*   **P** *Bp*
V R R USHER,   **Hon C** J M DRUMMOND
LEIGH (St Mary) *Roch 10*   **P** *Ch Trust Fund Trust*
V T V E OVERTON
LEIGH (St Mary the Virgin) *Man 13*   **P** *Bp*
V J T FINNEY,   **Par Dn** B A JENNER
LEIGH, LITTLE (St Michael and All Angels) and Lower
Whitley *Ches 4*   **P** *P G Greenall Esq and*
V Gt Budworth (alt)   **NSM** R BIGGIN
LEIGH, NORTH (St Mary) *Ox 9*   **P** *Ld Chan*
V J R MORGAN,   **NSM** S A BAREHAM
LEIGH, SOUTH (St James the Great) *Ox 8*   **P** *Bp*
P-in-c S L BESSENT
LEIGH, WEST (St Alban) *Portsm 4*   **P** *Bp*   **V** S EVANS
LEIGH DELAMERE (St Margaret)   Stanton St Quintin,
Hullavington, Grittleton etc *Bris*
LEIGH-ON-SEA (St Aidan) the Fairway *Chelmsf 12*
P *Bp*   **V** D F A SUTHERLAND,   **Hon Par Dn** F M PRYER
LEIGH-ON-SEA (St James) *Chelmsf 12*   **P** *Bp*
V B J SCHOOLING,   **NSM** C R BEECHAM,
Hon Par Dn E J A INGRAM
LEIGH-ON-SEA (St Margaret) *Chelmsf 12*   **P** *Bp*
V R L LAW,   **C** W NEWTON
LEIGH PARK (St Francis) *Portsm 4*   **P** *Bp*
V G P KNOWLES,   **C** M D BAILEY, J HENNING
LEIGH UPON MENDIP (St Giles) w Stoke St Michael
B & W 4   **P** *DBP and V Doulting (jt)*   **V** P D WINKS
LEIGH WOODS (St Mary the Virgin)   Abbots Leigh w
Leigh Woods *Bris*
LEIGHLAND (St Giles)   Old Cleeve, Leighland and
Treborough *B & W*
LEIGHS, GREAT (St Mary the Virgin) *Chelmsf 11*
P *Linc Coll Ox*   **R** S J BRYANT
LEIGHS, LITTLE (St John) *Chelmsf 11*   **P** *Reformation*
Ch Trust   **R** *Vacant*
LEIGHTERTON (St Andrew)   Boxwell, Leighterton,
Didmarton, Oldbury etc *Glouc*
LEIGHTON (Holy Trinity)   Trelystan *Heref*
LEIGHTON (St Mary)   Buildwas and Leighton w Eaton
Constantine etc *Lich*
LEIGHTON BROMSWOLD (St Mary) *Ely 10*   **P** *Bp*
V G L NORTH
LEIGHTON BUZZARD (All Saints) w Eggington,
Hockliffe and Billington *St Alb 18*   **P** *Bp*
V P H WHITTAKER,   **Par Dn** E M CONSTANTINE,
Hon C P J MOSS,   **NSM** V H SMITH
LEIGHTON-CUM-MINSHULL VERNON (St Peter)
Ches 15   **P** *Bp*   **V** *Vacant*   Church Minshull (027071)
213
LEINTHALL EARLES (St Andrew)   Aymestrey and
Leinthall Earles w Wigmore etc *Heref*
LEINTHALL STARKES (St Mary Magdalene)   as above
LEINTWARDINE Adforton (St Andrew)   Wigmore
Abbey *Heref*
LEINTWARDINE (St Mary Magdalene)   as above
LEIRE (St Peter) w Ashby Parva and Dunton Bassett
Leic 11   **P** *Ball Coll Ox, Exors Major T G F Paget, and*
Adn Loughb (by turn)   **R** *Vacant*   Leire (0455) 209421
LEISTON (St Margaret) *St E 19*   **P** *Haberdashers' Co*
V D C LOWE,   **Par Dn** M I BLACKALL
LELANT (St Uny)   Carbis Bay w Lelant *Truro*
LEMINGTON, LOWER (St Leonard)   Moreton-in-
Marsh w Batsford, Todenham etc *Glouc*
LEMSFORD (St John the Evangelist) *St Alb 7*   **P** *Lord*
Brocket   **P-in-c** R S INGAMELLS
LENBOROUGH *Ox 22*   **P** *Ch Ch Ox, Ld Chan, and Cam*
Univ (by turn)   **P-in-c** J HUDSON
LENHAM (St Mary) w Boughton Malherbe *Cant 15*
P *Viscount Chilston and Lord Cornwallis (jt)*
R D E C WRIGHT
LENTON (Holy Trinity) (Priory Church of St Anthony)
S'well 14   **P** *CPAS*   **V** D L T SCOTT,   **C** I D BUNTING
LENTON (St Peter)   Ingoldsby *Linc*
LENTON ABBEY (St Barnabas) *S'well 14*   **P** *CPAS*
V G GREGORY
LENWADE (All Saints)   Weston Longville w Morton
and the Witchinghams *Nor*
LEOMINSTER (St Peter and St Paul) *Heref 7*   **P** *Patr Bd*
TR M W HOOPER,
TV N G WETHERALL, J E LEWIS, P J PRIVETT,
C J TALBOT-PONSONBY, C B BULL
LEONARD STANLEY (St Swithun)   The Stanleys
Glouc
LEPTON (St John) *Wakef 6*   **P** *R Kirkheaton*
V G F WHITCROFT
LESBURY (St Mary) w Alnmouth *Newc 9*   **P** *Dioc Soc*
V B COWEN

LESNEWTH (St Michael and All Angels)   Boscastle w Davidstow *Truro*

LESSINGHAM (All Saints)   Happisburgh w Walcot, Hempstead, Lessingham etc *Nor*

LETCHWORTH (St Mary the Virgin) (St Michael) *St Alb 9*   **P** *Guild of All So*   **R** R R ROBINSON

LETCHWORTH (St Paul) w Willian *St Alb 9*   **P** *Bp*   **V** J B PARSONS,   **C** P F TIZZARD,   **Hon C** M J BREBNER

LETCOMBE BASSETT (St Michael and All Angels) Ridgeway *Ox*

LETCOMBE REGIS (St Andrew)   as above

LETHERINGHAM (St Mary)   Charsfield w Debach, Monewden, Hoo etc *St E*

LETHERINGSETT (St Andrew)   Blakeney w Cley, Wiveton, Glandford etc *Nor*

LETTON w (St John the Baptist) Staunton, Byford, Mansel Gamage and Monnington *Heref 5*   **P** *Sir John Cotterell, Bt (2 turns), Exors Mrs Dew (1 turn), Ch Ch Ox (3 turns), and DBP (1 turn)*   **P-in-c** R A BIRT,   **NSM** L C RHODES

LETTY GREEN (St John)   Hertingfordbury *St Alb*

LETWELL (St Peter)   Firbeck w Letwell *Sheff*

LEUSDON (St John the Baptist)   Widecombe-in-the-Moor, Leusdon, Princetown etc *Ex*

LEVEDALE (Mission Church)   Penkridge Team *Lich*

LEVEN (Holy Trinity) w Catwick *York 12*   **P** *Exors Sir Henry Strickland-Constable, Bt and Simeon's Trustees (alt)*   **R** P M DAVIES

LEVEN VALLEY *Carl 10*   **P** *Mrs C M Chaplin, V Colton, and Bp (jt)*   **V** *Vacant*   Newby Bridge (05395) 31476

LEVENS (St John the Evangelist) *Carl 9*   **P** *Trustees*   **V** A F J LOFTHOUSE

LEVENSHULME (St Mark) *Man 3*   **P** *Bp*   **R** N P TAYLOR

LEVENSHULME (St Peter) *Man 3*   **P** *Trustees*   **R** R A J AXTELL,   **Par Dn** A-M C BAKER

LEVENSHULME, SOUTH (St Andrew) *Man 3*   **P** *Bp*   **R** J L CLEGG

LEVER, GREAT (St Michael w St Bartholomew) Dixon Green *Man*

LEVER, GREAT (St Michael w St Bartholomew) *Man 12*   **P** *Bp*   **R** E J HALLIDAY

LEVER, LITTLE (St Matthew) *Man 12*   **P** *V Bolton-le-Moors St Pet*   **V** C H TELFORD,   **NSM** I C ANTHONY

LEVER BRIDGE (St Stephen and All Martyrs) *Man 9*   **P** *The Crown*   **V** *Vacant*   Bolton (0204) 28300

LEVERINGTON (St Leonard) *Ely 19*   **P** *Bp*   **R** P H N COLLINS,   **C** J A COOMBS

LEVERTON (St Helen)   Benington w Leverton *Linc*

LEVERTON, NORTH and SOUTH (St Martin) *S'well 5*   **P** *Bp*   **V** R AKERMAN

LEVERTON, SOUTH (All Saints)   N and S Leverton *S'well*

LEVINGTON (St Peter)   Nacton and Levington w Bucklesham and Foxhall *St E*

LEVISHAM (St John the Baptist)   Middleton w Newton, Levisham and Lockton *York*

LEWANNICK (St Martin)   Bolventor *Truro*

LEWES All Saints (St Mary) (St Anne) (St Michael) (St Thomas at Cliffe) *Chich 18*   **P** *Ld Chan (3 turns), Patr Bd (1 turn)*   **TR** B KEETON,   **TV** A PIPER,   **C** G L LINNEGAR,   **NSM** R V C HEBBORN, D L I PERKS, P D YATES

LEWES (St John sub Castro) *Chich 18*   **P** *Bp*   **R** R M BELL

LEWES (St John the Baptist)   Southover *Chich*

LEWISHAM (St Mary) *S'wark 3*   **P** *Earl of Dartmouth*   **V** D GARLICK,   **C** S M NYAHWA

LEWISHAM (St Stephen) and St Mark *S'wark 3*   **P** *Keble Coll Ox*   **V** G KIRK,   **Hon C** F D GARDOM

LEWISHAM (St Swithun) Hither Green *S'wark 3*   **P** *V Lewisham St Mary*   **V** D J SPICER,   **Par Dn** M GODDARD,   **Hon Par Dn** E BAKER

LEWKNOR (St Margaret)   Tetsworth, Adwell w S Weston, Lewknor etc *Ox*

LEWSEY (St Hugh)   Luton Lewsey St Hugh *St Alb*

LEWTRENCHARD (St Peter)   Marystowe, Coryton, Stowford, Lewtrenchard etc *Ex*

LEXDEN (St Leonard) *Chelmsf 19*   **P** *Bp*   **R** P A MARSHALL,   **Hon C** H HEATH

LEXHAM, EAST (St Andrew)   Litcham, Kempston, Lexham, Mileham, Beeston etc *Nor*

LEXHAM, WEST (St Nicholas)   as above

LEYBOURNE (St Peter and St Paul) *Roch 7*   **P** *Major Sir David Hawley, Bt*   **P-in-c** J T GUNN

LEYBURN (St Matthew) w Bellerby *Ripon 4*   **P** *Lord Bolton and Mrs M E Scragg (alt)*   **V** J MELLORS

LEYFIELDS (St Francis)   Tamworth *Lich*

LEYLAND (St Ambrose) *Blackb 6*   **P** *V Leyland*   **V** A F RANSON,   **C** P D HALLETT

LEYLAND (St Andrew) *Blackb 6*   **P** *CPAS*   **V** K HORSFALL,   **C** R M REITH, A V WEST

LEYLAND (St James the Apostle) *Blackb 6*   **P** *Sir Henry Farington, Bt*   **V** R A MOORE

LEYSTERS (St Andrew)   Bockleton w Leysters *Heref*

LEYTON (All Saints) *Chelmsf 8*   **P** *V St Mary's Leyton*   **V** D S LOCK

LEYTON (Christ Church) *Chelmsf 8*   **P** *Ch Trust Fund Trust*   **V** M E BURKILL

LEYTON (Emmanuel) *Chelmsf 8*   **P** *Bp*   **V** *Vacant*   081-539 2200

LEYTON (St Catherine) *Chelmsf 8*   **P** *V St Mary's Leyton*   **V** A J HOWARD

LEYTON St Luke *Chelmsf 8*   **P** *Bp*   **V** *Vacant*   081-539 7882

LEYTON (St Mary w St Edward) *Chelmsf 8*   **P** *Simeon's Trustees*   **C** T D HULL,   **Dss** A BUTLER

LEYTON (St Paul) *Chelmsf 8*   **P** *V St Mary's Leyton*   **V** *Vacant*   081-539 2250

LEYTONSTONE (Holy Trinity) Harrow Green *Chelmsf 8*   **P** *Bp*   **V** J A SWAINE,   **C** C SILVER

LEYTONSTONE (St Andrew) *Chelmsf 8*   **P** *Bp*   **V** D MOTTERSHEAD,   **NSM** R N MULKERN

LEYTONSTONE (St John the Baptist) *Chelmsf 8*   **P** *Bp*   **V** R C FIELD,   **C** A E MELANIPHY

LEYTONSTONE (St Margaret w St Columba) *Chelmsf 8*   **P** *Bp*   **V** J P SHEEHY,   **C** P A KNIGHTS

LEZANT (St Briochus) w Lawhitton and South Petherwin w Trewen *Truro 9*   **P** *Bp and Ox Univ (jt)*   **R** P MUNN

LEZAYRE (Holy Trinity) *S & M 4*   **P** *The Crown*   **V** B E SHEPHARD

LEZAYRE (St Olave) Ramsey *S & M 4*   **P** *The Crown and Bp (alt)*   **V** J H SHEEN,   **Hon C** J C WALNE

LICHBOROUGH (St Martin)   Greens Norton w Bradden and Lichborough *Pet*

LICHFIELD (Christ Church) *Lich 2*   **P** *Bp*   **V** I W WILLIAMS

LICHFIELD (St Chad) *Lich 2*   **P** *D&C*   **R** E G H TOWNSHEND,   **C** N S HOWE,   **NSM** B WILLIAMS

LICHFIELD St John's Hospital *Lich 2*   **P** *Bp*   **Master** H I CLUTTERBUCK

LICHFIELD (St Mary) (St Michael) *Lich 2*   **P** *D&C*   **R** D A SMITH,   **C** T J LEYLAND,   **NSM** J PATTEN, J ANKETELL,   **Dss** H SAMPSON

LICKEY, THE (Holy Trinity) *Birm 4*   **P** *V Bromsgrove*   **V** P D CHIPPENDALE

LIDEN (St Timothy)   Swindon Dorcan *Bris*

LIDGET GREEN (St Wilfrid)   Bradf St Wilfrid Lidget Green *Bradf*

LIDLINGTON (St Margaret)   Marston Morteyne w Lidlington *St Alb*

LIFTON (St Mary) *Ex 25*   **P** *Countess de Wolovey*   **R** J A C WILSON

LIGHT HALL (St Luke)   Shirley *Birm*

LIGHTBOWNE (St Luke) *Man 5*   **P** *D&C*   **R** A J LLEWIS

LIGHTCLIFFE (St Matthew) *Wakef 2*   **P** *V Halifax*   **V** D WILDING

LIGHTHORNE (St Laurence) *Cov 8*   **P** *Lady Willoughby de Broke*   **P-in-c** E J A BRAZIER

LIGHTWATER (All Saints) *Guildf 6*   **P** *Ld Chan and Bp (alt)*   **V** A W BRANT

LILBOURNE (All Saints)   Crick and Yelvertoft w Clay Coton and Lilbourne *Pet*

LILLESHALL (St John the Evangelist) (St Michael and All Angels) and Sheriffhales *Lich 22*   **P** *Bp*   **V** *Vacant*   Telford (0952) 604281

LILLEY (St Peter)   Offley w Lilley *St Alb*

LILLINGSTONE DAYRELL (St Nicholas)   N Buckm *Ox*

LILLINGSTONE LOVELL (Assumption of The Blessed Virgin Mary)   as above

LILLINGTON (St Martin)   Sherborne w Castleton and Lillington *Sarum*

LILLINGTON (St Mary Magdalene) *Cov 11*   **P** *Bp*   **V** D J PHILLPOT,   **C** G HOWELLS,   **NSM** R JONES

LILLIPUT (Holy Angels) *Sarum 8*   **P** *Bp*   **V** C HODGE

LIMBER MAGNA (St Peter) w Brocklesby *Linc 6*   **P** *Earl of Yarborough*   **V** S PHILLIPS,   **C** C MACDONALD

LIMEHOUSE (St Anne) (St Peter) *Lon 7*   **P** *BNC Ox*   **R** J F D PEARCE,   **Hon Par Dn** A E PEARCE

LIMESIDE (St Chad)   Oldham St Chad Limeside *Man*

LIMINGTON (The Blessed Virgin Mary)   Ilchester w Northover, Limington, Yeovilton etc *B & W*

LIMPENHOE (St Botolph)   Reedham w Cantley w Limpenhoe and Southwood *Nor*

LIMPLEY STOKE (St Mary)   Freshford, Limpley Stoke and Hinton Charterhouse *B & W*
LIMPSFIELD (St Andrew) (St Peter) and Titsey *S'wark 23*   **P** *Bp*   **R** D J PARSONS,   **Par Dn** S E LEESON, **Hon C** B C C COMPTON, M J NAZIR-ALI
LINBY (St Michael) w Papplewick *S'well 4*   **P** T W A Cundy Esq   **R** K H TURNER
LINCHMERE (St Peter) *Chich 10*   **P** *DBP*   **V** A H WAY
LINCOLN (All Saints) *Linc 15*   **P** *Bp*   **V** J B APPLETON
LINCOLN Minster Group, The (St Mary Magdalene) (St Michael on the Mount) (St Peter in Eastgate) *Linc 15*   **P** *Adn Linc, D&C, and Bp (by turn)*   **R** J B BAYLEY, **Hon C** W M JACOB
LINCOLN (St Botolph by Bargate) *Linc 15*   **P** *Bp*   **P-in-c** K R OWEN
LINCOLN (St Faith) (St Martin) (St Peter-at-Arches) *Linc 15*   **P** *Bp*   **V** R T SHAW,   **Hon Par Dn** P WINTON
LINCOLN (St George) Swallowbeck *Linc 15*   **P** *Bp and V Skellingthorpe (jt)*   **V** J R TAYLOR
LINCOLN (St Giles) *Linc 15*   **P** *Bp*   **V** E B BARLOW, **C** I G SILK
LINCOLN (St John the Baptist) (St John the Evangelist) *Linc 15*   **P** *Bp*   **V** Vacant   Lincoln (0522) 25621
LINCOLN (St Mary-le-Wigford) (St Benedict) (St Mark) *Linc 15*   **P** *Bp*   **V** K R COOK
LINCOLN (St Nicholas) (St John) Newport *Linc 15*   **P** *Bp and D&C (alt)*   **V** B L WISKEN,   **NSM** S GOLDSMITH
LINCOLN (St Peter-at-Gowts) (St Andrew) *Linc 15*   **P** *Bp*   **V** D J BAKER
LINCOLN (St Swithin) *Linc 15*   **P** *Bp*   **P-in-c** D G KERRIDGE
LINDAL IN MARTON (St Peter)   Pennington w Lindal and Marton *Carl*
LINDALE (St Paul) w Field Broughton *Carl 10*   **P** *Bp*   **P-in-c** J R WRAIGHT
LINDFIELD (All Saints) *Chich 6*   **P** *Ch Soc Trust*   **V** J G McKECHNIE,   **C** A G THOM,   **Par Dn** N LAYTON
LINDLEY (St Stephen) *Wakef 5*   **P** *V Huddersfield*   **V** M T A HAYNES
LINDOW (St John) *Ches 12*   **P** *Bp*   **V** R D PETERS
LINDRIDGE (St Lawrence)   Teme Valley N *Worc*
LINDSELL (St Mary the Virgin)   Stebbing w Lindsell *Chelmsf*
LINDSEY (St Peter)   Kersey w Lindsey *St E*
LINFORD (St Francis)   E and W Tilbury and Linford *Chelmsf*
LINFORD, GREAT (St Andrew)   Stantonbury and Willen *Ox*
LINFORD, LITTLE (St Leonard)   Haversham w Lt Linford, Tyringham w Filgrave *Ox*
LINGDALE (Mission Room)   Boosbeck w Moorsholm *York*
LINGEN (St Michael and All Angels)   Presteigne w Discoed, Kinsham and Lingen *Heref*
LINGFIELD (St Peter and St Paul) and Crowhurst *S'wark 23*   **P** *Bp*   **V** A B RAMSAY, **Par Dn** D C EDWARDS,   **NSM** D J ABEL
LINGWOOD (St Peter)   Burlingham St Edmund w Lingwood, Strumpshaw etc *Nor*
LINKENHOLT (St Peter)   Hurstbourne Tarrant, Faccombe, Vernham Dean etc *Win*
LINKINHORNE (St Mellor) *Truro 12*   **P** *DBP*   **V** P R MEDLEY
LINLEY (St Leonard) w Willey and Barrow *Heref 14*   **P** *Lord Forester*   **P-in-c** W W LUCAS
LINLEY GREEN (not known)   Acton Beauchamp and Evesbatch w Stanford Bishop *Heref*
LINSLADE (St Barnabas) (St Mary) *Ox 26*   **P** *Bp*   **V** M J PEEL,   **C** J E SCLATER
LINSTEAD PARVA (St Margaret)   Halesworth w Linstead, Chediston, Holton etc *St E*
LINTHORPE (St Barnabas) *York 19*   **P** *Abp*   **V** I D REID,   **C** T McDONOUGH, I R PARKINSON, **NSM** R A MORRIS
LINTHWAITE (Christ Church) *Wakef 5*   **P** *R Almondbury*   **V** C H COON
LINTON (Christ Church) and Castle Gresley *Derby 16*   **P** *Bp*   **P-in-c** W C E ROSE
LINTON (St Aidan)   Ashington *Newc*
LINTON (St Mary) *Ely 4*   **P** *Bp*   **V** J H THOMSON, **NSM** M W B O'LOUGHLIN, A C ARMSTRONG
LINTON (St Mary the Virgin) w Upton Bishop and Aston Ingham *Heref 8*   **P** *St Jo Coll Ox, D&C, and Preb H L Whatley (jt)*   **R** A F RICKETTS
LINTON (St Nicholas)   Coxheath w E Farleigh, Hunton and Linton *Roch*
LINTON IN CRAVEN (St Michael and All Angels) *Bradf 7*   **P** *D&C*   **V** Vacant   Skipton (0756) 752575

LINWOOD (St Cornelius) *Linc 5*   **P** *MMCET*   **R** Vacant
LIPHOOK (Church Centre)   Bramshott *Portsm*
LISCARD (St John)   Egremont St Jo *Ches*
LISCARD (St Mary w St Columba) *Ches 7*   **P** *Bp*   **V** T GRIFFITHS
LISCARD (St Thomas) *Ches 7*   **P** *Bp*   **P-in-c** R T NELSON,   **NSM** B D HARRY
LISKEARD (St Martin), St Keyne, St Pinnock, Morval and Bradoc *Truro 12*   **P** *Patr Bd (2 turns), Ld Chan (1 turn)*   **TR** D H P DAVEY,   **TV** J C COLLARD, M GRIFFITHS, **NSM** P C BELLENES
LISS (St Mary) (St Peter) *Portsm 5*   **P** *Bp*   **R** B E COOK, **C** D H HEATLEY, B T WILLIAMS,   **Hon C** D J VARNEY
LISS FOREST (St Saviour)   Liss *Portsm*
LISSET (St James of Compostella)   Beeford w Frodingham and Foston *York*
LISSINGTON (St John the Baptist)   Wickenby Gp *Linc*
LISTON (not known)   Pentlow, Foxearth, Liston and Borley *Chelmsf*
LITCHAM (All Saints), Kempston, East and West Lexham, Mileham, Beeston next Mileham and Stanfield *Nor 19*   **P** *Bp, W R B Foster Esq, Mrs E M Olesen, Ch Soc Trust, and DBP(jt)*   **R** P W RUSHTON
LITCHFIELD (St James the Less)   Whitchurch w Tufton and Litchfield *Win*
LITHERLAND (St Andrew) *Liv 1*   **P** *Bp*   **P-in-c** C H KIRKE
LITHERLAND (St John and St James) *Liv 1*   **P** *CPAS*   **V** D V ROUCH
LITHERLAND (St Paul) Hatton Hill *Liv 1*   **P** *Bp*   **V** R H CLARK
LITHERLAND (St Philip) *Liv 1*   **P** *Trustees*   **V** A SCAIFE,   **C** P J SAVAGE,   **Hon C** J T LEIGHTON
LITLINGTON (St Catherine)   Shingay Gp of Par *Ely*
LITLINGTON (St Michael the Archangel)   Alfriston w Lullington, Litlington and W Dean *Chich*
LITTLE: *see also under substantive place name*
LITTLE BIRCH (St Mary)   Much Birch w Lt Birch, Much Dewchurch etc *Heref*
LITTLEBOROUGH (Holy Trinity) *Man 19*   **P** *TR Rochdale*   **V** J B PETTIFER
LITTLEBOROUGH (St Nicholas)   N Wheatley, W Burton, Bole, Saundby, Sturton etc *S'well*
LITTLEBOURNE (St Vincent) and Ickham w Wickhambreaux and Stodmarsh *Cant 1*   **P** *Abp, D&C, Ch Trust Fund Trust, and Adn Cant (jt)*   **R** A J ALLAN
LITTLEBURY (Holy Trinity)   Saffron Walden w Wendens Ambo and Littlebury *Chelmsf*
LITTLEBURY GREEN (St Peter)   as above
LITTLEDEAN (St Ethelbert)   Cinderford St Steph w Littledean *Glouc*
LITTLEHAM (St Margaret) w Exmouth *Ex 1*   **P** *Patr Bd*   **TR** K F MIDDLETON,   **TV** J G DAVIES, **Hon C** M VINCER,   **Hon Par Dn** E M MORRIS
LITTLEHAM (St Swithin)   Landcross, Littleham, Monkleigh etc *Ex*
LITTLEHAMPTON (St James) (St Mary) and Wick *Chich 1*   **P** *Bp*   **TR** R J CASWELL, **TV** J S A HUDSON, J S BLOOMFIELD,   **Par Dn** E J DAVIES
LITTLEHEMPSTON (St John the Baptist)   Broadhempston, Woodland, Staverton etc *Ex*
LITTLEMOOR (St Francis of Assisi)   Preston w Sutton Poyntz and Osmington w Poxwell *Sarum*
LITTLEMORE (St Mary the Virgin and St Nicholas) *Ox 4*   **P** *Or Coll Ox*   **V** D G NICHOLLS
LITTLEOVER (St Peter) *Derby 10*   **P** *PCC*   **V** W B G MATHER,   **C** J V WHITFIELD, A P L SMITH
LITTLEPORT (St George) (St Matthew) *Ely 14*   **P** *Bp*   **V** I H FIRMSTONE
LITTLETON (St Catherine of Alexandria)   Crawley and Littleton and Sparsholt w Lainston *Win*
LITTLETON (St Mary Magdalene) *Lon 13*   **P** *C W L Barratt Esq*   **R** R J B DAKIN
LITTLETON, HIGH (Holy Trinity) *B & W 13*   **P** *Hyndman Trustees*   **V** P M HAND
LITTLETON, NORTH (St Nicholas)   Cleeve Prior and The Littletons *Worc*
LITTLETON, SOUTH (St Michael)   as above
LITTLETON DREW (All Saints)   Nettleton w Littleton Drew *Bris*
LITTLETON ON SEVERN (St Mary of Malmesbury) w Elberton *Bris 8*   **P** *Bp*   **P-in-c** B G CARNE
LITTLEWICK (St John the Evangelist)   Knowl Hill w Littlewick *Ox*
LITTLEWICK (St Thomas)   Horsell *Guildf*
LITTLEWORTH (Holy Ascension) *Ox 17*   **P** *Or Coll Ox*   **V** Vacant
LITTON (Christ Church)   Tideswell *Derby*

LITTON (St Mary the Virgin)   Chewton Mendip w Ston
  Easton, Litton etc *B & W*
LITTON CHENEY (St Mary)   Bride Valley *Sarum*
LIVERMERE, GREAT (St Peter)   Ingham w Ampton
  and Gt and Lt Livermere *St E*
LIVERPOOL (All Souls) Springwood *Liv 4*   P *The Crown*
  V G G AMEY,   Par Dn E M STOREY
LIVERPOOL (Christ Church) Norris Green *Liv 8*   P *Bp*
  V C D HENDRICKSE
LIVERPOOL (Our Lady and St Nicholas w St Anne) *Liv 3*
  P *Patr Bd*   TR N A FRAYLING,
  TV I B TEESDALE, J BARKER
LIVERPOOL (St Christopher) Norris Green *Liv 8*   P *Bp*
  V W M TODD,   C A G PHILLIPS
LIVERPOOL (St Luke in the City) (St Bride w St Saviour)
  (St Michael in the City) (St Stephen w St Catherine) *Liv 6*
  P *Patr Bd*   TR N BLACK,   TV C A MARSH, M J FRY
LIVERPOOL (St Paul) Stoneycroft *Liv 8*   P *St Chad's
  Coll Dur*   NSM D BENSON
LIVERPOOL (St Philip w St David) *Liv 3*   P *Bp*
  P-in-c J A GARNETT
LIVERSEDGE (Christ Church) *Wakef 8*   P *V Birstall*
  V L H WOOD
LIVERTON (St Martin)   Easington w Liverton *York*
LIVERTON MINES (St Hilda)   as above
LIVESEY (St Andrew) *Blackb 5*   P *Trustees*
  V D GASKELL
LLANCILLO (St Peter)   Ewyas Harold w Dulas,
  Kenderchurch etc *Heref*
LLANDINABO (St Junabius)   Much Birch w Lt Birch,
  Much Dewchurch etc *Heref*
LLANFAIR WATERDINE (St Mary)   Bucknell w
  Chapel Lawn, Llanfair Waterdine etc *Heref*
LLANGARRON (St Deinst) w Llangrove, Whitchurch and
  Ganarew *Heref 8*   P *Bp, DBP, and D&C (jt)*
  R W C MASSEY
LLANGROVE (Christ Church)   Llangarron w
  Llangrove, Whitchurch and Ganarew *Heref*
LLANGUA (St James)   Ewyas Harold w Dulas,
  Kenderchurch etc *Heref*
LLANVEYNOE (St Beuno and St Peter)   Clodock and
  Longtown w Craswall, Llanveynoe etc *Heref*
LLANWARNE (Christ Church)   Much Birch w Lt Birch,
  Much Dewchurch etc *Heref*
LLANYBLODWEL (St Michael) and Trefonen *Lich 25*
  P *Bp and Earl of Powis (jt)*   R C R BALL
LLANYMYNECH (St Agatha) *Lich 25*   P *Bp*
  R T VILLIERS
LOBLEY HILL (All Saints) *Dur 5*   P *Bp*   V R K HOPPER,
  C P W JUDSON
LOCKERLEY (St John) and East Dean w East and West
  Tytherley *Win 11*   P *DBP (1 turn), H B G Dalgety Esq
  (2 turns)*   V M E BURSON-THOMAS
LOCKING (St Augustine) *B & W 12*   P *MMCET*
  V M C COTTERELL
LOCKINGE (All Saints)   Wantage Downs *Ox*
LOCKINGE, WEST (All Souls)   as above
LOCKINGTON (St Mary) and Lund and Scorborough w
  Leconfield *York 9*   P *Abp*   R L N JANICKER
LOCKINGTON (St Nicholas)   Castle Donington and
  Lockington cum Hemington *Leic*
LOCKS HEATH (St John the Baptist) *Portsm 2*   P *Bp*
  V R J S EVENS,   C J R G WATSON,   NSM J V RICHARDS
LOCKTON (St Giles)   Middleton w Newton, Levisham
  and Lockton *York*
LODDINGTON (St Leonard)   Broughton w Loddington
  and Cransley etc *Pet*
LODDINGTON (St Michael and All Angels) *Leic 3*   P *Bp*
  P-in-c H T P EVANS
LODDISWELL (St Michael and All Angels)   Woodleigh
  and Loddiswell *Ex*
LODDON (Holy Trinity) w Sisland *Nor 14*   P *Bp*
  (3 turns), E G Gilbert Esq (1 turn)*   V P E GREEN
LODE (St James)   Bottisham and Lode w Long Meadow
  Ely
LODERS (St Mary Magdalene)   Askerswell, Loders and
  Powerstock *Sarum*
LODGE, THE (St John)   Weston Rhyn *Lich*
LODGE MOOR (St Luke) *Sheff 4*   P *CPAS*
  V J J WITCOMBE,   Par Dn M D WITCOMBE
LODSWORTH (St Peter)   Lurgashall, Lodsworth and
  Selham *Chich*
LOFTHOUSE (Christ Church) *Ripon 8*   P *DBP*
  V N G BURTON
LOFTUS-IN-CLEVELAND (St Leonard) and Carlin How
  w Skinningrove *York 17*   P *Ld Chan (2 turns), Abp
  (1 turn)*   R D G HODGSON
LOLWORTH (All Saints) *Ely 5*   P *SMF*   R *Vacant*
  Crafts Hill (0954) 81001

LONAN (All Saints) *S & M 2*   P *The Crown*
  V W H SCATTERGOOD
LONDESBOROUGH (All Saints) *York 7*
  P *R F Ashwin Esq*   R K G SKIPPER
LONDON Foster Lane (St Vedast)   St Vedast w St Mich-
  le-Querne etc *Lon*
LONDON Holborn (St Sepulchre)   St Sepulchre w Ch Ch
  Greyfriars etc *Lon*
LONDON Roscoe Street (St Luke's Church Centre)
  St Giles Cripplegate w St Bart Moor Lane etc *Lon*
LONDON (St Mary Woolnoth)   St Edm the King and St
  Mary Woolnoth etc *Lon*
LONDON, LITTLE (St Stephen)   Bramley *Win*
LONDON CITY CHURCHES:
All Hallows Berkynchirche-by-the-Tower w St Dunstan-in-
  the-East, *Lon 1*   P *Abp*   V P A DELANEY,
  C I C THURSTON,   Hon C G R de MELLO, M D C FORRER,
  NSM J DAGLEISH
St Andrew-by-the-Wardrobe w St Ann Blackfriars
  Lon 1   P *PCC and Mercers' Co (jt)*   R J W PAUL
St Bartholomew the Great, Smithfield *Lon 1*
  P *D&C Westmr*   Hon C A C WINTER
St Bartholomew the Less, Smithfield Gate *Lon 1*
  P *St Bart's Hosp*   V A M WHAWELL
St Botolph Aldgate w H Trin Minories *Lon 1*   P *Bp*
  V M A JOHNSON,   Par Dn M N A JONES,
  Hon C J W HOLDEN, F P COLEMAN,
  Hon Par Dn A GURNEY, K LEECH
St Botolph without Bishopgate *Lon 1*   P *D&C St Paul's*
  R A J TANNER,   Hon C H J M TURNER
St Bride Fleet Street w Bridewell and Trinity Gough Square
  Lon 1   P *D&C Westmr*   R J OATES
St Clement Eastcheap w St Martin Orgar *Lon 1*
  P *D&C St Paul's*   P-in-c M J WOODGATE,
  Hon C M B KIDDLE
St Edmund the King, St Mary Woolnoth St w Nicholas
  Acons, All Hallows Lombard Street, St Benet
  Gracechurch, St Leonard Eastcheap, St Dionis
  Backchurch, St Mary Woolchurch, Haw *Lon 1*   P *The
  Crown (3 turns), D&C Cant (1 turn), Bp (1 turn), and
  Abp Cant (1 turn)*   R R HAYES
St Giles Cripplegate w St Bartholomew Moor Lane, St
  Alphage London Wall, St Luke Old Street, St Mary
  Charterhouse St Paul Clerkenwell *Lon 1*
  P *D&C St Paul's*   R D RHODES,   AP D E VINCE,
  Par Dn M ROBINSON,   Hon C W H FOX-ROBINSON
St Helen Bishopsgate w St Andrew Undershaft, St Martin
  Outwich, St Mary Axe *Lon 1*   R R C LUCAS,
  C H PALMER, G J MOTE
St James Garlickhythe w St Michael Queenhithe and Holy
  Trinity-the-Less *Lon 1*   P *D&C St Paul's*   R J W PAUL,
  Hon C W D BAKER
St Magnus the Martyr w St Margaret New Fish Street and
  St Michael Crooked Lane *Lon 1*   P *DBP*
  R M J WOODGATE
St Margaret Lothbury and St Stephen Coleman Street w St
  Christopher-le-Stocks, St Bartholomew-by-the-
  Exchange, St Olave Old Jewry, St Martin Pomeroy,
  St Mildred Poultry and St Mary Colechurch *Lon 1*
  P *Simeon's Trustees*   R T S FARRELL
St Mary at Hill w St Andrew Hubbard, St George Botolph
  Lane and St Botolph by Billingsgate *Lon 1*   P *Ball Coll
  Ox (2 turns), PCC (1 turn), and Abp (1 turn)*
  R B A C KIRK-DUNCAN
St Mary le Bow w St Pancras Soper Lane, All Hallows
  Honey Lane, All Hallows Bread Street, St John the
  Evangelist Watling Street, St Augustine w St Faith under
  St Paul's and St Mildred Bread Street w St Margaret
  Moyses *Lon 1*   P *Grocers' Co (1 turn), Abp (2 turns)*
  R V A STOCK,   C S D DEWEY
St Michael Cornhill w St Peter le Poer and St Benet Fink
  Lon 1   P *Drapers' Co*   R D B EVANS
St Olave Hart Street w All Hallows Staining and St
  Catherine Coleman *Lon 1*   P *Trustees*   R J F COWLING
St Peter Cornhill *Lon 1*   P *City Corp*   P-in-c J H L CROSS
St Sepulchre w Christ Church Greyfriars and St Leonard
  Foster Lane *Lon 1*   P *St Jo Coll Ox*
  R *Vacant*
St Stephen Walbrook and St Swithun London Stone w
  St Benet Sherehog and St Mary Bothaw w St Laurence
  Pountney *Lon 1*   P *Grocers' Co and Magd Coll Cam
  (alt)*   R E C VARAH
St Vedast w St Michael-le-Querne, St Matthew Friday
  Street, St Peter Cheap, St Alban Wood Street, St Olave
  Silver Street, St Michael Wood Street, St Mary Staining,
  St Anne and St Agnes, St John Zachary Gresham Street
  Lon 1   P *D&C St Paul's*   R R J AVENT
LONDON DOCKS (St Peter) w Wapping (St John) *Lon 7*
  P *Bp*   R D PEEL

LONDON GUILD CHURCHES:
All Hallows London Wall *Lon 1* **P** *Ld Chan*
　P-in-c A J TANNER
St Andrew Holborn *Lon 1* **P** *Bp* **V** R E D SHARPLEY
St Benet Paul's Wharf *Lon 1* **P** *Bp* **V** A P HAWKINS
St Botolph without Aldersgate *Lon 1* **P** *Bp*
　V T S FARRELL
St Dunstan in the West *Lon 1* **P** *Abp* **P-in-c** A T J SALTER
St Katharine Cree *Lon 1* **P** *Bp* **P-in-c** H ROM
St Lawrence Jewry *Lon 1* **P** *City Corp* **V** D J BURGESS
St Margaret Pattens *Lon 1* **P** *Ld Chan* **V** *Vacant*
St Martin Ludgate *Lon 1* **P** *D&C St Paul's*
　P-in-c T E EVANS
St Mary Abchurch *Lon 1* **P** *CCC Cam*
　P-in-c O R CLARKE
St Mary Aldermary *Lon 1* **P** *The Crown and*
　Ld Chan (alt) **P-in-c** V A STOCK
St Michael Paternoster Royal *Lon 1* **P** *Bp* **V** *Vacant*
LONDONDERRY (St Mark) (Holy Trinity) *Birm 5* **P** *Bp*
　V R LEIGH
LONDONTHORPE (St John the Baptist) Grantham
　Linc
LONG ASHTON (All Saints) *B & W 14* **P** *Bp*
　V H B TASKER
LONG BENNINGTON (St Swithin) w Foston *Linc 19*
　P *Duchy of Cornwall* **V** R AMIS, **NSM** C C MUNN
LONG BENTON (St Bartholomew) *Newc 6* **P** *Ball Coll*
　Ox **V** R W GOUNDRY
LONG BENTON (St Mary Magdalene) *Newc 6* **P** *Ball*
　Coll Ox **V** A J SHIPTON
LONG BREDY (St Peter) Bride Valley *Sarum*
LONG BUCKBY (St Lawrence) w Watford *Pet 2* **P** *Bp*
　and Ld Chan (alt) **V** M P TANNER
LONG BURTON (St James) Dungeon Hill *Sarum*
LONG CLAWSON (St Remigius) Harby, Long Clawson
　and Hose *Leic*
LONG COMPTON (St Peter and St Paul), Whichford and
　Barton-on-the-Heath *Cov 9* **P** *Bp*, *Trin Coll Ox, and*
　Ch Ch Ox (by turn) **V** E J RAINSBERRY
LONG CRENDON (St Mary the Virgin) w Chearsley and
　Nether Winchendon *Ox 21* **P** *Bp and R V Spencer-*
　Bernard Esq (jt) **V** S YOUNG
LONG CRICHEL (St Mary) Witchampton and Hinton
　Parva, Long Crichel etc *Sarum*
LONG CROSS (Christ Church) *Guildf 11*
　P *J D Tringham Esq* **P-in-c** A B OLSEN
LONG DITTON (St Mary) *S'wark 14* **P** *Bp*
　R C W PRITCHARD
LONG EATON (St John) *Derby 13* **P** *Bp* **V** G R PERCY,
　C P J BROOKS
LONG EATON (St Laurence) *Derby 13* **P** *Bp*
　V G M KNOX
LONG HANBOROUGH (Christ Church) Hanborough
　and Freeland *Ox*
LONG ITCHINGTON (Holy Trinity) and Marton *Cov 10*
　P *Bp* **V** F L MARRIOTT
LONG LANE (Christ Church) Longford, Long Lane,
　Dalbury and Radbourne *Derby*
LONG LAWFORD (St John) Newbold on Avon *Cov*
LONG LOAD (Christ Church) Langport Area Chs
　B & W
LONG MARSTON (All Saints) Tring *St Alb*
LONG MARSTON (All Saints) *York 1* **P** *C York Esq*
　R J A RENDALL
LONG MARTON (St Margaret and St James) w Dufton
　and w Milburn *Carl 1* **P** *Lord Hothfield*
　R A HERBERT
LONG MELFORD (Holy Trinity) (St Catherine) *St E 12*
　P *Bp* **R** C J SANSBURY
LONG NEWNTON (Holy Trinity) Ashley, Crudwell,
　Hankerton, Long Newnton etc *Bris*
LONG PRESTON (St Mary the Virgin) w Tosside *Bradf 5*
　P *D&C Ch Ch Ox and V Gisburn (alt)* **V** L E AUSTIN
LONG RISTON (St Margaret) Skirlaugh w Long Riston
　York
LONG STANTON (All Saints) w St Michael *Ely 5*
　P *Magd Coll Cam and Bp (alt)* **R** E BATY
LONG STANTON (St Michael and All Angels)
　Wenlock *Heref*
LONG SUTTON (All Saints) Herriard w Winslade and
　Long Sutton etc *Win*
LONG SUTTON (Holy Trinity) Langport Area Chs
　B & W
LONG SUTTON (St Mary) Sutton St Mary *Linc*
LONG WHATTON (All Saints) Hathern, Long
　Whatton and Diseworth w Belton etc *Leic*
LONG WITTENHAM (St Mary the Virgin) Dorchester
　Ox

LONGBOROUGH (St James), Sezincote, Condicote and
　the Swells *Glouc 15* **P** *Lord Leigh, Mrs S Peake, DBP,*
　and Ch Ch Ox (by turn) **R** E B HYDE
LONGBRIDGE (St John the Baptist) *Birm 4* **P** *Bp*
　V L J OAKES
LONGBRIDGE DEVERILL (St Peter and St Paul) The
　Deverills *Sarum*
LONGCOT (St Mary the Virgin) Ashbury, Compton
　Beauchamp and Longcot w Fernham *Ox*
LONGDEN (St Ruthen) and Annscroft w Pulverbatch
　Heref 13 **P** *Bp and MMCET (jt)* **R** G L JONES,
　Hon C J J WADDINGTON-FEATHER, J F JONES (nee
　HUBBARD)
LONGDON (St James) *Lich 2* **P** *Bp*
　P-in-c P L HOLLIDAY
LONGDON (St Mary), Castlemorton, Bushley, Queenhill w
　Holdfast *Worc 5* **P** *Bp, D&C Westmrs, and Ch Union*
　Trustees (jt) **V** R M HARDING
LONGDON-UPON-TERN (St Bartholomew), Rodington,
　Uppington and Wrockwardine *Lich 30* **P** *Lord*
　Barnard, V M E Holt Esq, MMCET, and Bp (jt)
　R D R OSBORNE, **C** A T BARTLAM
LONGFIELD (Mission Room) (St Mary Magdalene) *Roch 1*
　P *Ld Chan* **R** J R CHALLICE
LONGFLEET (St Mary) *Sarum 8* **P** *MMCET*
　V D B HUTCHINSON, **Hon C** R G W FARDON
LONGFORD (St Chad), Long Lane, Dalbury and
　Radbourne *Derby 14* **P** *Bp, R Church Broughton, and*
　Major J W Chandos-Pole (jt) **P-in-c** M W CLARK
LONGFORD (St Thomas) *Cov 2* **P** *Bp* **V** D I BRUCE
LONGFRAMLINGTON (St Mary the Virgin) w Brinkburn
　Newc 9 **P** *Bp* **V** J P H CLARK
LONGHAM (St Andrew and St Peter) Gressenhall w
　Longham w Wendling etc *Nor*
LONGHILL (St Margaret) Sutton St Mich *York*
LONGHIRST (St John the Evangelist) *Newc 11* **P** *Bp*
　V *Vacant* Morpeth (0670) 790253
LONGHOPE (All Saints) Huntley and Longhope *Glouc*
LONGHORSLEY (St Helen) *Newc 11* **P** *Ld Chan*
　V *Vacant* Longhorsley (067088) 218
LONGHOUGHTON (St Peter and St Paul) w Howick
　Newc 9 **P** *Duke of Northd and Bp (alt)* **V** C SCOTT
LONGLEVENS (Holy Trinity) Wotton St Mary *Glouc*
LONGNEWTON (St Mary) w Elton *Dur 16* **P** *Bp and*
　St Chad's Coll Dur (alt) **P-in-c** N C JONES
LONGNEY (St Lawrence) Hardwicke, Quedgeley and
　Elmore w Longney *Glouc*
LONGNOR (St Bartholomew), Quarnford and Sheen
　Lich 11 **P** *Bp, V Alstonfield, and H F Harpur-*
　Crewe Esq (jt) **V** A C F NICOLL
LONGNOR (St Mary) Leebotwood w Longnor *Heref*
LONGPARISH (St Nicholas) Barton Stacey and
　Bullington etc *Win*
LONGRIDGE (St Lawrence) (St Paul) *Blackb 14*
　P *Trustees* **V** R W E AWRE
LONGSDON (St Chad) *Lich 14* **P** *Bp* **V** B H PEEL
LONGSIGHT (St John w St Cyprian) *Man 3*
　P *Prime Min and Bp (alt)* **R** S F BRANDES
LONGSIGHT (St Luke) *Man 1* **P** *D&C and Trustees (jt)*
　R P N CLARK, **Par Dn** S M EVANS
LONGSLEDDALE (St Mary) Skelsmergh w Selside and
　Longsleddale *Carl*
LONGSOLE (Mission Room) Barming *Roch*
LONGSTOCK (St Mary) Stockbridge and Longstock
　and Leckford *Win*
LONGSTONE (St Giles) *Derby 2* **P** *V Bakewell*
　V *Vacant* Great Longstone (062987) 257
LONGSTOWE (St Mary) Bourn and Kingston w Caxton
　and Longstowe *Ely*
LONGTHORPE (St Botolph) *Pet 13* **P** *Sir Stephen*
　Hastings **V** *VACANT* Peterborough (0733) 263016
LONGTON (St Andrew) *Blackb 6* **P** *J M G Rawstorne,*
　J R Rawstorne and A F Rawstorne (jt)
　V T M THOMPSON, **C** C J SWIFT, **NSM** M SAWLE
LONGTON (St James and St John) *Lich 18* **P** *Bp*
　R *Vacant* Stoke-on-Trent (0782) 313470
LONGTON (St Mark) Edensor *Lich*
LONGTON (St Mary and St Chad) *Lich 18* **P** *Bp*
　V C LANTSBERY
LONGTON, NEW (All Saints) *Blackb 6* **P** *Bp*
　V D M ROGERS
LONGWELL GREEN (All Saints) *Bris 2* **P** *Bp*
　V R W DENT
LONGWOOD (St Mark) *Wakef 5* **P** *V Huddersfield*
　V D ROBINSON, **AP** N T B STRAFFORD
LONGWORTH (St Mary) Cherbury *Ox*
LOOE, EAST (St Mary) St Martin w E and W Looe
　Truro
LOOE, WEST (St Nicholas) as above

LOOSE (All Saints) *Cant 15* **P** *Abp* **V** R C COATES
LOPEN (All Saints) Merriott w Hinton, Dinnington and Lopen *B & W*
LOPHAM NORTH (St Nicholas) Bressingham w N and S Lopham and Fersfield *Nor*
LOPHAM SOUTH (St Andrew) as above
LOPPINGTON (St Michael and All Angels) w Newtown *Lich 29* **P** *Bp and R Wem (jt)* **P-in-c** P J RICHMOND
LORD'S HILL (Local Ecumenical Project) *Win 12* **P** *Bp* **V** J L H PAGE
LORTON (St Cuthbert) and Loweswater w Buttermere *Carl 6* **P** *Bp and Earl of Lonsdale (alt)* **V** M R BRAITHWAITE
LOSCOE (St Luke) *Derby 12* **P** *Bp* **V** M T FERMER
LOSTOCK (St Thomas and St John) Conventional District *Man 11* **C-in-c** I E BUTTERWORTH
LOSTOCK GRALAM (St John the Evangelist) *Ches 6* **P** *V Witton* **V** K W DAVEY
LOSTOCK HALL (St James) *Blackb 6* **P** *Bp* **V** W G BOWNESS
LOSTWITHIEL (St Bartholomew), St Winnow w St Nectan's Chapel, St Veep and Boconnoc *Truro 10* **P** *D&C and A D G Fortescue Esq (jt)* **R** A E ALLARDICE
LOTHERSDALE (Christ Church) Carleton and Lothersdale *Bradf*
LOTHERTON (St James) Aberford w Saxton *York*
LOTTISHAM (The Blessed Virgin Mary) Baltonsborough w Butleigh and W Bradley *B & W*
LOUDWATER (St Peter) *Ox 21* **P** *MMCET* **V** T G BUTLIN, **NSM** G B McGUINNESS
LOUGHBOROUGH (All Saints) (Holy Trinity) *Leic 7* **P** *Bp and Em Coll Cam (jt)* **R** L G E HANCOCK
LOUGHBOROUGH (Emmanuel) *Leic 7* **P** *Em Coll Cam* **R** M N PHILLIPS, **C** P WIMSETT, **NSM** R BOOKLESS
LOUGHBOROUGH (Good Shepherd) *Leic 7* **P** *Bp* **V** P H CLAY, **NSM** R J STRETTON
LOUGHBOROUGH (St Peter) *Leic 7* **P** *Bp* **V** D PATERSON
LOUGHTON (All Saints) Watling Valley *Ox*
LOUGHTON (not known) Ditton Priors w Neenton, Burwarton etc *Heref*
LOUGHTON (St John the Baptist) (St Gabriel) (St Nicholas) *Chelmsf 2* **P** *W W Maitland Esq* **R** G R HOLLEY, **C** G K WELCH, M J TAYLOR, **Hon C** O B WELLS, **NSM** F C W MELLOR, J DELFGOU
LOUGHTON (St Mary the Virgin) (St Michael and All Angels) *Chelmsf 2* **P** *Patr Bd* **TV** K G GARRETT, **P-in-c** D J BROOMFIELD
LOUND (St Anne) Babworth w Sutton-cum-Lound *S'well*
LOUND (St John the Baptist) Blundeston w Flixton and Lound *Nor*
LOUNDSLEY GREEN (Church of the Ascension) Old Brampton and Loundsley Green *Derby*
LOUTH (Holy Trinity) (St James) (St Michael) *Linc 12* **P** *Patr Bd* **TR** D W OWEN, **TV** R R LETALL, **TM** B A HILL, **C** D B WOODS, **NSM** R W MANSFIELD
LOVERSALL (St Katherine) Wadworth w Loversall *Sheff*
LOVINGTON (St Thomas a Becket) Six Pilgrims *B & W*
LOW: *see also under substantive place names*
LOW FELL (St Helen) Gateshead St Helen *Dur*
LOW HILL (Good Shepherd) Bushbury *Lich*
LOW MOOR (Holy Trinity) *Bradf 2* **P** *V Bradf* **V** D F BROWN
LOW MOOR (St Mark) *Bradf 2* **P** *Bp* **P-in-c** M A TAYLOR
LOW VALLEY (St Matthew) Darfield *Sheff*
LOWDHAM (St Mary the Virgin) *S'well 11* **P** *Bp* **V** E ASHBY
LOWER: *see also under substantive place names*
LOWER MANOR (St Andrew) Sheff Manor *Sheff*
LOWER WINDRUSH *Ox 8* **P** *Bp, DBP, St Jo Coll Ox, D&C Ex, and B Babington-Smith Esq (jt)* **R** P A CADOGAN
LOWESBY (All Saints) Whatborough Gp of Par *Leic*
LOWESTOFT (Christ Church) *Nor 15* **P** *CPAS* **V** P R PAYN
LOWESTOFT (St Margaret) (Good Shepherd) (St Andrew) and Kirkley *Nor 15* **P** *Patr Bd* **TR** P I ALLTON, **TV** P M FARROW, P J MEADER, M D THAYER, T W RIESS, **C** E J SMITH
LOWESWATER (St Bartholomew) Lorton and Loweswater w Buttermere *Carl*
LOWFIELD HEATH (St Michael) Crawley *Chich*
LOWGATE (St Mary) Hexham *Newc*

LOWICK (St John the Baptist) and Kyloe w Ancroft *Newc 12* **P** *D&C Dur (2 turns), Bp (1 turn)* **P-in-c** W P HEWITT
LOWICK (St Luke) Egton-cum-Newland and Lowick *Carl*
LOWICK (St Peter) w Sudborough and Slipton *Pet 10* **P** *L G Stopford-Sackville Esq and Bp (alt)* **R** *Vacant* Thrapston (08012) 3216
LOWSONFORD (St Luke) Hatton w Haseley, Rowington w Lowsonford etc *Cov*
LOWTHER (St Michael) and Askham *Carl 1* **P** *Earl of Lonsdale* **R** D J RADCLIFFE
LOWTHORPE (St Martin) Burton Agnes w Harpham and Lowthorpe etc *York*
LOWTON (St Luke) *Liv 16* **P** *Bp* **R** K ALLDRED
LOWTON (St Mary) *Liv 16* **P** *Bp* **V** R BRITTON
LOXBEARE (St Michael and All Angels) Washfield, Stoodleigh, Withleigh etc *Ex*
LOXHORE (St Michael and All Angels) Shirwell, Loxhore, Kentisbury, Arlington, etc *Ex*
LOXLEY (St Nicholas) Hampton Lucy w Charlecote and Loxley *Cov*
LOXTON (St Andrew) Crook Peak *B & W*
LOXWOOD (St John the Baptist) Alfold and Loxwood *Guildf*
LOZELLS (St Paul and St Silas) *Birm 6* **P** *Aston Patr Trust* **V** E W RUSSELL, **NSM** E B WATSON
LUBENHAM (All Saints) Foxton w Gumley and Laughton and Lubenham *Leic*
LUCCOMBE (Blessed Virgin Mary) *B & W 17* **P** *Bp* **R** E J MILLER, **Hon C** M J DUVALL
LUCKER (St Hilda) Bamburgh and Lucker *Newc*
LUCKINGTON (St Mary and St Ethelbert) Sherston Magna, Easton Grey, Luckington etc *Bris*
LUDBOROUGH (St Mary) Fotherby *Linc*
LUDDENDEN (St Mary) w Luddenden Foot *Wakef 3* **P** *Bp and V Halifax (alt)* **V** M J MORPHY
LUDDESDOWN (St Peter and St Paul) Cobham w Luddesdowne and Dode *Roch*
LUDDINGTON (All Saints) Stratford w Bishopton *Cov*
LUDDINGTON (St Margaret) Polebrook and Lutton w Hemington and Luddington *Pet*
LUDDINGTON (St Oswald) N Axholme Gp *Linc*
LUDFORD (St Giles) *Heref 12* **P** *Exors H E Whitaker* **P-in-c** J F BAULCH
LUDFORD MAGNA (St Mary) Binbrook Gp *Linc*
LUDGERSHALL (St James) Tidworth, Ludgershall and Faberstown *Sarum*
LUDGERSHALL (St Mary the Virgin) w Wotton Underwood and Ashendon *Ox 24* **P** *CPAS and Bp (jt)* **R** C S JEE
LUDGVAN (St Ludgvan and St Paul) *Truro 5* **P** *Lord St Levan* **R** A PARSONS
LUDHAM (St Catherine) w Potter Heigham *Nor 10* **P** *Bp* **V** B S T MORGAN
LUDLOW (St John) (St Laurence) *Heref 12* **P** *Earl of Plymouth* **R** J F BAULCH, **C** R K NEWTON, A N TOOP, **NSM** F R LOVETT, C V HUTT
LUFFENHAM, NORTH (St John the Baptist) Edith Weston w N Luffenham and Lyndon w Manton *Pet*
LUFFENHAM, SOUTH (St Mary the Virgin) Barrowden and Wakerley w S Luffenham *Pet*
LUFTON (St Peter and St Paul) *B & W 7* **P** *Bp* **R** *Vacant*
LUGWARDINE (St Peter) w Bartestree and Weston Beggard *Heref 4* **P** *D&C* **P-in-c** J O MORRIS
LULLINGSTONE (St Botolph) Eynsford w Farningham and Lullingstone *Roch*
LULLINGTON (All Saints) Beckington w Standerwick, Berkley, Rodden etc *B & W*
LULLINGTON (All Saints) *Derby 16* **P** *Bp* **V** W F BATES
LULLINGTON (not known) Alfriston w Lullington, Litlington and W Dean *Chich*
LULWORTHS (St Andrew) (Holy Trinity), Winfrith Newburgh and Chaldon, The *Sarum 9* **P** *Bp (3 turns), Col Sir Joseph Weld (1 turn)* **R** S GILL
LUMB (St Michael) Newchurch *Man*
LUMLEY (Christ Church) *Dur 1* **P** *Bp* **V** J R STRINGER
LUND (All Saints) Lockington and Lund and Scorborough w Leconfield *York*
LUND (St John the Evangelist) *Blackb 11* **P** *Ch Ch Ox* **V** M S MALKINSON
LUNDWOOD (St Mary Magdalene) *Wakef 7* **P** *Bp* **V** M C E BOOTES
LUNDY ISLAND St Helen Extra Parochial Place *Ex 15* *Vacant*
LUPPITT (St Mary) Dunkeswell, Sheldon and Luppitt *Ex*

LUPSET (St George) *Wakef 12*   **P** *Bp*   **V** G CLAY,
Par Dn E J CLAY
LUPTON (All Saints)   Kirkby Lonsdale *Carl*
LURGASHALL (St Laurence), Lodsworth and Selham
Chich 11   **P** Cowdray Trust and Lord Egremont (alt)
R D H R CORNISH
LUSBY (St Peter)   Marden Hill Gp *Linc*
LUSTLEIGH (St John the Baptist) *Ex 11*   **P** *Bp*
P-in-c K E JACKSON
LUTON (All Saints) (St Peter) *St Alb 20*   **P** *Bp*
V G S N PRASADAM,   **Par Dn** J PRASADAM
LUTON (Christ Church) *Roch 5*   **P** *R Chatham*
R B R FROCHE,   **C** A RIDER, S R DYER,
Hon Par Dn A C DYER
LUTON Lewsey (St Hugh) *St Alb 20*   **P** *Bp*
V A G FORMAN,   **C** G R KEGG
LUTON Limbury (St Augustine of Canterbury) *St Alb 20*
P *Bp*   **V** R I CHEETHAM,   **Hon C** J Y ABSLEY
LUTON (St Andrew) *St Alb 20*   **P** *Bp*   **V** P STOKES
LUTON (St Anne) *St Alb 20*   **P** *Peache Trustees, Bp, and
V Luton (jt)*   **V** P C BUDGELL,
Hon Par Dn R A BUDGELL
LUTON (St Christopher) Round Green *St Alb 20*   **P** *Bp*
V R B ETHERINGTON,   **NSM** S M HUDSPITH
LUTON (St Francis) *St Alb 20*   **P** *Peache Trustees, Bp,
and V Luton (jt)*   **V** A T SHARP,   **Par Dn** J DANIEL
LUTON (St John)   Teignmouth, Ideford w Luton,
Ashcombe etc *Ex*
LUTON (St Mary) *St Alb 20*   **P** *Peache Trustees*
V N P J BELL,   **C** C F PETTET, R D S SANDERS,
Par Dn S R SANDERS
LUTON (St Matthew) High Town *St Alb 20*   **P** *Ch Patr
Trust*   **V** W G SEAL
LUTON (St Paul) *St Alb 20*   **P** *Peache Trustees*
V A SELLERS
LUTON (St Saviour) *St Alb 20*   **P** *Bp*   **V** P F SWINGLER,
NSM D C ANDERSON
LUTTERWORTH (St Mary) w Cotesbach *Leic 11*
P *The Crown (3 turns), Ld Chan (1 turn)*
R M H W COUSSENS,   **C** A W JOHNSON
LUTTON (St Nicholas) w Gedney Drove End, Dawsmere
Linc 16   **P** *The Crown, Ld Chan, and V Long Sutton
(by turn)*   **V** A R KENNEDY
LUTTON (St Peter)   Polebrook and Lutton w
Hemington and Luddington *Pet*
LUTTONS AMBO (St Mary)   Weaverthorpe w
Helperthorpe, Luttons Ambo etc *York*
LUXBOROUGH (Blessed Virgin Mary)   Exton and
Winsford and Cutcombe w Luxborough *B & W*
LUXULYAN (St Cyrus and St Julietta)   Lanlivery w
Luxulyan *Truro*
LYDBROOK (Holy Jesus) *Glouc 4*   **P** *Bp*
V M J FOSTER
**LYDBURY NORTH (St Michael and All Angels) w Hopesay
and Edgton** *Heref 10*   **P** *Earl of Powis (3 turns),
Mrs R E Bell (1 turn)*   **R** A F DENYER,
Hon C M P THOMPSON-McCAUSLAND
LYDD (All Saints) *Cant 13*   **P** *Abp*   **R** J HEWES
LYDDEN (St Mary the Virgin)   Temple Ewell w Lydden
Cant
**LYDDINGTON (All Saints) and Wanborough and
Bishopstone w Hinton Parva** *Bris 11*   **P** *Bp and
Ld Chan (alt)*   **R** A D FENSOME,   **NSM** L H COLTON
LYDDINGTON (St Andrew) w Stoke Dry and Seaton
Pet 14   **P** *Bp, Burghley Ho Preservation Trust, and
R E M Elborne Esq (by turn)*   **NSM** B R H TAYLOR
**LYDEARD ST LAWRENCE (St Lawrence) w Brompton
Ralph, Combe Florey, Ash Priors and Tolland** *B & W 21*
P *Ld Chan (2 turns), W H J Hancock Esq (2 turns), and
MMCET (1 turn)*   **R** J C F HAWNT
**LYDFORD (St Petrock), Brent Tor, Bridestowe and
Sourton** *Ex 25*   **P** *Bp (3 turns), Duchy of Cornwall
(1 turn)*   **TR** M H BATEMAN,
Hon C R D ORMSBY, D C ORMSBY
LYDFORD ON FOSSE (St Peter)   Keinton Mandeville
w Lydford on Fosse *B & W*
LYDGATE (St Anne) *Man 18*   **P** *Bp*   **NSM** E OGDEN
LYDGATE (St Mary) w Ousden and Cowlinge *St E 11*
P *DBP*   **P-in-c** E R CROUCHMAN
LYDHAM (Holy Trinity)   Wentnor w Ratlinghope,
Myndtown, Norbury etc *Heref*
LYDIARD MILLICENT (All Saints)   see below
LYDIARD TREGOZE (St Mary)   see below
LYDIARDS, The *Bris 13*   **P** *Patr Bd*   **TR** J R FLORY,
TV K M BOXALL,   **C** R J BURLES,
Par Dn E A H THOMAS,   **Hon C** W H ANDREW
LYDIATE (St Thomas) *Liv 11*   **P** *R Halsall*
V A A DAVIES

LYDLINCH (St Thomas a Beckett)   Stock and Lydlinch
Sarum
LYDNEY (St Mary the Virgin) w Aylburton *Glouc 4*
P *Ld Chan*   **V** D F F EVANS,   **C** D A CHAPLIN,
NSM M D MILLER, I F CALDER
LYE, THE (Christchurch) and Stambermill *Worc 11*
P *Bp and CPAS (alt)*   **V** D M WOODHOUSE
LYFORD (St Mary)   Cherbury *Ox*
LYME REGIS (St Michael the Archangel) *Sarum 3*   **P** *Bp*
V M J DELL
**LYMINGE (St Mary and St Ethelburga) w Paddlesworth
and Stanford w Postling and Radegund** *Cant 5*   **P** *Abp*
R F KENT
LYMINGTON (St Thomas the Apostle) *Win 10*   **P** *Bp*
V M J JOINT,   **C** J H McCORMACK,   **NSM** A BLEASE
LYMINGTON Woodside (All Saints)   Lymington *Win*
LYMINSTER (St Mary Magdalene) *Chich 1*   **P** *Eton Coll
and BNC Ox*   **V** J E SLEGG
LYMM (St Mary the Virgin) *Ches 4*   **P** *Bp*
R G L DAVIES
LYMPNE (St Stephen)   Sellindge w Monks Horton and
Stowting etc *Cant*
LYMPSHAM (St Christopher)   Brent Knoll, E Brent and
Lympsham *B & W*
LYMPSTONE (Nativity of the Blessed Virgin Mary) *Ex 1*
P *SMF*   **P-in-c** J CLAPHAM
LYNCH (St Luke) w Iping Marsh and Milland *Chich 10*
P *Cowdray Trust and Bp (jt)*   **V** H I GORDON-CUMMING
LYNCHMERE   Linchmere *Chich*
LYNCOMBE (St Bartholomew)   Bath St Bart *B & W*
LYNDHURST (St Michael) and Emery Down *Win 10*
P *Bp and P J P Green Esq (alt)*   **V** A R GRAHAM
LYNDON (St Martin)   Edith Weston w N Luffenham
and Lyndon w Manton *Pet*
LYNEAL (St John the Evangelist)   Petton w Cockshutt,
Welshampton and Lyneal etc *Lich*
LYNEHAM (St Michael) w Bradenstoke *Sarum 18*
P *Ld Chan*   **V** *Vacant*
LYNEMOUTH (St Aidan)   Cresswell and Lynemouth
Newc
LYNESACK (St John the Evangelist) *Dur 11*   **P** *Bp*
V N B P KING
LYNG (St Bartholomew)   Stoke St Gregory w
Burrowbridge and Lyng *B & W*
LYNG (St Margaret), Sparham, Elsing and Bylaugh *Nor 8*
P *DPB and E C Evans-Lombe Esq*   **R** M F C TAYLOR
LYNGFORD (St Peter)   Taunton Lyngford *B & W*
LYNMOUTH (St John the Baptist)   Lynton, Brendon,
Countisbury, Lynmouth etc *Ex*
LYNN (St John the Evangelist) *Nor 23*   **P** *Bp*
V P M RYLEY
**LYNN, NORTH (St Edmund) (St Margaret and
St Nicholas)** *Nor 23*   **P** *D&C*   **P-in-c** M L YORKE,
C R H G BRAND
LYNN, SOUTH (All Saints) *Nor 23*   **P** *Bp*
P-in-c J L C ABLEWHITE
LYNN, WEST (St Peter) *Nor 23*   **P** *DBP*
P-in-c A J CLEMENTS
LYNSTED (St Peter and St Paul) w Kingsdown *Cant 6*
P *Adn Cant*   **V** *Vacant*   Teynham (0795) 521371
**LYNTON (St Mary the Virgin), Brendon, Countisbury,
Lynmouth, Barbrook, Parracombe and Martinhoe**
Ex 18   **P** *DBP*   **TR** P J FOX,   **TV** W G HOWELLS
LYONS (St Michael and All Angels) *Dur 6*   **P** *The Crown*
R R L BURR
LYONSDOWN (Holy Trinity) *St Alb 2*   **P** *Ch Patr Trust*
V G R HUDDLESTON,   **Hon Par Dn** N J LEVERIDGE
**LYONSHALL (St Michael and All Angels) w Titley,
Almeley and Kinnersley** *Heref 5*   **P** *Bp, D&C, and
Ch Patr Trust (jt)*   **V** D R LOWE
LYSTON (not known)   Pentlow, Foxearth, Liston and
Borley *Chelmsf*
LYTCHETT MATRAVERS (St Mary the Virgin) *Sarum 8*
P *DBP*   **R** N J C LLOYD,   **Hon Par Dn** E J L LLOYD
LYTCHETT MINSTER (not known) *Sarum 8*   **P** *Bp*
V E C CARDALE,   **C** A M DOYLE
LYTHAM (St Cuthbert) *Blackb 11*   **P** *DBP*
V L A CRAGG,   **C** C A BELL,   **Hon Par Dn** S HEYS
LYTHAM (St John the Divine) *Blackb 11*
P *J C Hilton Esq*   **V** C J CARLISLE
LYTHE (St Oswald) w Ugthorpe *York 23*   **P** *Abp*
V W SMITH
MABE (St Laudus) *Truro 3*   **P** *Bp*   **V** C J K FIRTH
MABLETHORPE (St Mary) w Trusthorpe *Linc 8*   **P** *Bp
Lon (2 turns), Bp Linc (1 turn)*   **NSM** B WRIGHTSON
MACCLESFIELD (St John the Evangelist) *Ches 13*   **P** *Bp*
V R M SALENIUS
MACCLESFIELD (St Paul) *Ches 13*   **P** *Bp*
V S R MARSH

MACCLESFIELD Team Parish, The (All Saints) (Christ Church) (St Michael and All Angels) (St Peter) *Ches 13* **P** *Patr Bd* **TR** J BRIGGS, **TV** J C G STALEY, **C** J S BISHOP, **NSM** J A MYNETT

MACKWORTH (All Saints) *Derby 11* **P** *J M Clark-Maxwell* **P-in-c** D HUGHES, **NSM** E DIXON

MACKWORTH (St Francis) *Derby 9* **P** *Bp* **V** B W G HACKNEY, **C** R J VALENTINE

MADEHURST (St Mary Magdalene) Slindon, Eartham and Madehurst *Chich*

MADELEY (All Saints) *Lich 15* **P** *J C Crewe Esq* **V** M N GRIFFIN

MADELEY (St Michael) *Heref 14* **P** *CPAS* **P-in-c** R L PAMPLIN, **C** H A SCRIVEN

MADINGLEY (St Mary Magdalene) *Ely 5* **P** *Bp* **V** *Vacant*

MADLEY (Nativity of the Blessed Virgin Mary) w Tyberton, Preston-on-Wye and Blakemere *Heref 1* **P** *D&C* **NSM** R S JONES

MADRESFIELD (St Mary) Newland, Guarlford and Madresfield *Worc*

MADRON (St Maddern) *Truro 5* **P** *Bp* **V** N H TOOGOOD, **Hon C** F R HARWOOD

MAER (St Peter) Chapel Chorlton, Maer and Whitmore *Lich*

MAESBROOK (St John) Kinnerley w Melverley and Knockin w Maesbrook *Lich*

MAESBURY (St John the Baptist) Oswestry H Trin *Lich*

MAGDALEN LAVER (St Mary Magdalen) High Laver w Magdalen Laver and Lt Laver etc *Chelmsf*

MAGHAM DOWN (St Mark) Hailsham *Chich*

MAGHULL (St Andrew) (St James) (St Peter) *Liv 11* **P** *Patr Bd* **TR** J M GOODCHILD, **TV** B A MUSK, G A PERERA, C D P LUND, **Hon C** W H TULLOCH

MAIDA VALE (St Peter) Paddington St Pet *Lon*

MAIDA VALE (St Saviour) Paddington St Sav *Lon*

MAIDEN BRADLEY (All Saints) Mere w W Knoyle and Maiden Bradley *Sarum*

MAIDEN NEWTON (St Mary) Melbury *Sarum*

MAIDENHEAD (All Saints) Boyne Hill *Ox*

MAIDENHEAD (St Andrew and St Mary Magdalene) *Ox 13* **P** *Peache Trustees* **V** T K PARKIN

MAIDENHEAD (St Luke) *Ox 13* **P** *Bp* **V** D M WEST, **NSM** R A CHEEK

MAIDFORD (St Peter and St Paul) Blakesley w Adstone and Maidford etc *Pet*

MAIDS MORETON (St Edmund) N Buckm *Ox*

MAIDSTONE (All Saints) (St Philip) w St Stephen Tovil *Cant 15* **P** *Abp* **C** B BARNES, D R HANCOCK

MAIDSTONE Barming Heath (St Andrew) Barming Heath *Cant*

MAIDSTONE (St Faith) *Cant 15* **P** *Abp* **V** I H CROFTS

MAIDSTONE (St Luke the Evangelist) *Cant 15* **P** *Trustees* **V** C SAMPSON, **C** E M WRIGHT

MAIDSTONE (St Martin) *Cant 15* **P** *Abp* **V** P M RAMPTON, **C** I L GARRETT

MAIDSTONE (St Michael and All Angels) *Cant 15* **P** *Abp* **V** P J GIBBONS

MAIDSTONE (St Paul) *Cant 15* **P** *Abp* **V** N H TAYLOR

MAIDWELL (St Mary) w Draughton and Lamport w Faxton *Pet 2* **P** *Bp (3 turns), Sir Ian Isham (1 turn)* **P-in-c** W G GIBBS, B LEE

MAINSTONE (St John the Baptist) Bishop's Castle w Mainstone *Heref*

MAISEMORE (St Giles) *Glouc 6* **P** *Bp* **NSM** F A EVANS

MAKER (St Mary and St Julian) w Rame *Truro 11* **P** *The Crown and Earl of Mount Edgcumbe* **V** R A DOYLE

MALBOROUGH (All Saints) w South Huish, West Alvington and Churchstow *Ex 14* **P** *Bp and D&C (jt)* **V** D J NEWPORT, **NSM** H G R PILL, **Hon Par Dn** M A FREEMAN (nee ADAMS)

MALDEN (St James) *S'wark 14* **P** *Bp* **V** C J DAVIES, **Hon C** A HARDY

MALDEN (St John) *S'wark 14* **P** *Mert Coll Ox* **V** R D G WEYMAN, **Par Dn** D A NICHOLSON

MALDEN, NEW (St John the Divine) and Coombe (Christ Church) *S'wark 14* **P** *CPAS* **V** J S DOWNEY, **C** G WINTLE, **NSM** I R L PRIOR, N M E PUTMAN

MALDON (All Saints w St Peter) *Chelmsf 13* **P** *Bp* **V** A J DUNLOP, **Par Dn** P C COTTON

MALDON (St Mary) w Mundon *Chelmsf 13* **P** *D&C Westmr* **R** A M A McINTOSH

MALEW Ballasalla (St Mary the Virgin) Malew *S & M*

MALEW (St Mark) (St Moluag or St Lupus) *S & M 1* **P** *The Crown* **V** E W FISHER

MALIN BRIDGE (St Polycarp) *Sheff 4* **P** *Bp* **V** A WHITELEY

MALINS LEE (St Leonard) Cen Telford *Lich*

MALLERSTANG (St Mary) Kirkby Stephen w Mallerstang etc *Carl*

MALLING, EAST (St James) *Roch 7* **P** *D&C* **V** D A RUDDLE

MALLING, SOUTH (St Michael) *Chich 18* **P** *MMCET* **V** A T HINDLEY

MALLING, WEST (St Mary) w Offham *Roch 7* **P** *Ld Chan and DBP (alt)* **V** R B STEVENSON

MALMESBURY (St Peter and St Paul) w Westport and Brokenborough *Bris 12* **P** *Ch Trust Fund Trust* **V** J C P BARTON

MALPAS (St Andrew) Truro St Paul and St Clem *Truro*

MALPAS (St Oswald) and Threapwood *Ches 5* **P** *DBF* **R** T ETHERIDGE

MALTBY (All Saints) *Linc 8* **P** *DBP* **R** G I GEORGE-JONES

MALTBY (St Bartholomew) (Ascension) (Venerable Bede) *Sheff 5* **P** *Bp* **TR** V J FILER, **TV** D S WALKER, **C** C DRAPER

MALTON, NEW (St Michael) *York 3* **P** *Sir Stephen Hastings* **V** R ROGERS

MALTON, OLD (St Mary the Virgin) *York 3* **P** *Sir Stephen Hastings* **V** J C MANCHESTER

MALVERN (Holy Trinity) (St James) *Worc 2* **P** *Bp and D&C Westmr (jt)* **V** P C G BILLINGHAM, **C** C A MOSS, **NSM** J B P WILLIAMSON

MALVERN (St Andrew) *Worc 2* **P** *Bp* **P-in-c** R NEWTON

MALVERN, GREAT (Christchurch) *Worc 2* **P** *Bp* **P-in-c** P M J GINEVER, **Par Dn** J D HAYWARD

MALVERN, GREAT (St Mary and St Michael) *Worc 2* **P** *Bp* **P-in-c** J W CHARLEY, **C** D M STEVENSON

MALVERN, LITTLE (St Giles), Malvern Wells and Wyche *Worc 2* **P** *Bp, V Malvern, and T M Berington Esq (jt)* **P-in-c** M H J DUNN, **NSM** E G KNOWLES

MALVERN, WEST (St James) Malvern H Trin and St Jas *Worc*

MALVERN LINK (Church of the Ascension) (St Matthias) w Cowleigh *Worc 2* **P** *Patr Bd* **TR** J H DAVIES, **TV** D S M SMITH, C E J ROTHWELL, **NSM** J H SADLER, **Hon Par Dn** R HERBERT

MALVERN WELLS (St Peter) Lt Malvern, Malvern Wells and Wyche *Worc*

MAMBLE (St John the Baptist) w Bayton, Rock w Heightington w Far Forest *Worc 4* **P** *Ld Chan and R Ribbesford w Bewdley etc (alt)* **V** R MANN

MAMHEAD (St Thomas the Apostle) Kenton, Mamhead, Powderham, Cofton and Starcross *Ex*

MANACCAN (St Manaccus and St Dunstan) w St Anthony-in-Meneage and St Martin-in-Meneage *Truro 4* **P** *Ld Chan* **V** J T McCABE

MANATON (St Winifred) Moretonhampstead, N Bovey and Manaton *Ex*

MANBY (St Mary) Mid Marsh Gp *Linc*

MANCETTER (St Peter) *Cov 5* **P** *Ch Patr Trust* **V** A S MAIRS

MANCHESTER (Apostles) w Miles Platting (St Cuthbert) *Man 1* **P** *DBP* **R** A DURRANS, **C** D McCOULOUGH

MANCHESTER Cheetwood (St Alban) Cheetwood St Alb *Man*

MANCHESTER Clayton (St Cross w St Paul) *Man 1* **P** *Bp* **R** N J PRIOR, **C** I J FILES

MANCHESTER (Good Shepherd) (Church of the Resurrection) *Man 1* **P** *Prime Min* **R** M G PRICE

MANCHESTER (St Ann) *Man 4* **P** *Bp* **R** *Vacant* 061-881 1229

MANCHESTER (St John Chrysostom) Victoria Park *Man 4* **P** *Bp* **R** M J G MELROSE

MANCHESTER Whitworth (not known) *Man 4* **P** *Bp* **TR** J A ARMES, **TV** A P JOHNSON, **C** K S E OKEKE, **Par Dn** A J SERVANT

MANEA (St Nicholas) *Ely 18* **P** *Bp* **V** J DAVIS

MANEY (St Peter) *Birm 9* **P** *Bp* **V** J C W ROSE, **NSM** J E GREGORY

MANFIELD (All Saints) Barton and Manfield w Cleasby *Ripon*

MANGOTSFIELD (St James) *Bris 7* **P** *Peache Trustees* **V** J W WEDGBURY

MANLEY (St John the Evangelist) Alvanley *Ches*

MANNINGFORD BRUCE (St Peter) Swanborough *Sarum*

MANNINGHAM (St Chad) *Bradf 1* **P** *Keble Coll Ox* **V** S R CROWE

MANNINGHAM (St Mary Magdalene and St Michael and All Angels) (St Paul and St Jude) *Bradf 1* **P** *Patr Bd* **TR** A KITCHEN, **TV** G H COLES, **TM** P A TURNER (nee SYMINGTON), **NSM** J C HALSALL

MANNINGS HEATH (Church of the Good Shepherd) Nuthurst *Chich*
MANOR PARK (St Barnabas) Lt Ilford St Barn *Chelmsf*
MANOR PARK (St John the Baptist) W Slough *Ox*
MANOR PARK (St John the Evangelist) Lt Ilford St Mich *Chelmsf*
MANOR PARK (St Mary the Virgin) as above
MANOR PARK (St Michael and All Angels) as above
MANOR PARK (William Temple) Sheff Manor *Sheff*
MANSEL LACY (St Michael) Credenhill w Brinsop, Mansel Lacey, Yazor etc *Heref*
MANSERGH (St Peter) Kirkby Lonsdale *Carl*
MANSFIELD (St Augustine) *S'well 2* **P** *Bp*
  V J M BURGESS
MANSFIELD (St John the Evangelist) *S'well 2* **P** *Bp*
  V K L SHILL, **C** S LEES
MANSFIELD (St Lawrence) *S'well 2* **P** *Bp*
  V A CHAPPELL
MANSFIELD (St Mark) *S'well 2* **P** *Bp*
  P-in-c M J DOBBS
MANSFIELD (St Peter and St Paul) *S'well 2* **P** *Bp*
  V R T WARBURTON, **C** J SANKEY
MANSFIELD WOODHOUSE (St Edmund King and Martyr) *S'well 2* **P** *Bp* **V** D B STEVEN,
  C I N PALLETT, D J HULL
MANSTON (St Catherine) St Laurence in Thanet *Cant*
MANSTON (St James) *Ripon 8* **P** *R Barwick in Elmet*
  V J R HOLMES, **C** D BURROWS, R L A PATERSON
MANSTON (St Nicholas) Childe Okeford, Manston, Hammoon and Hanford *Sarum*
MANTHORPE (St John the Evangelist) Grantham *Linc*
MANTON (St Hibald) *Linc 6* **P** *Bp* **R** D I WALKER
MANTON (St Mary the Virgin) Edith Weston w N Luffenham and Lyndon w Manton *Pet*
MANUDEN (St Mary the Virgin) w Berden *Chelmsf 24*
  P *Patr Bd and Ch Hosp (alt)* **P-in-c** C BISHOP
MAPERTON (St Peter and St Paul) Camelot Par *B & W*
MAPLEBECK (St Radegund) *S'well 15* **P** *Sir Stephen Hastings* **V** H H WILCOX
MAPLEDURHAM (St Margaret) Caversham and Mapledurham *Ox*
MAPLEDURWELL (St Mary) Newnham w Nately Scures w Mapledurwell etc *Win*
MAPLESTEAD, GREAT (St Giles) and LITTLE (St John) w Gestingthorpe *Chelmsf 17* **P** *Bp* **V** K F BELBEN
MAPPERLEY (Holy Trinity) W Hallam and Mapperley *Derby*
MAPPLEBOROUGH GREEN (Holy Ascension) Studley *Cov*
MAPPLETON (All Saints) Aldbrough, Mappleton w Goxhill and Withernwick *York*
MAPPLETON (St Mary) Ashbourne w Mapleton *Derby*
MAPPOWDER (St Peter and St Paul) Hazelbury Bryan w Stoke Wake etc *Sarum*
MARAZION (All Saints) *Truro 5* **P** *V St Hilary*
  V A K TORRY
MARBURY (St Michael) *Ches 5* **P** *Bp* **V** G H SANSOME
MARCH (St John) *Ely 18* **P** *Bp* **R** T AMBROSE
MARCH (St Mary) *Ely 18* **P** *Bp* **R** D W SPENCER
MARCH (St Peter) *Ely 18* **P** *Bp* **R** D W SPENCER
MARCH (St Wendreda) *Ely 18* **P** *MMCET*
  R P BAXANDALL, **NSM** S TOOKE,
  Hon Par Dn S M BARCLAY
MARCHAM (All Saints) w Garford *Ox 10* **P** *Ch Ch Ox*
  V D P PRITCHARD
MARCHINGTON (St Peter) w Marchington Woodlands *Lich 21* **P** *V Hanbury w Newborough*
  P-in-c A G SADLER, **C** R M VIDAL-HALL
MARCHINGTON WOODLANDS (St John) Marchington w Marchington Woodlands *Lich*
MARCHWOOD (St John) *Win 10* **P** *Bp* **R** J D CURTIS
MARCLE, LITTLE (St Michael and All Angels) *Heref 6*
  P *Bp* **P-in-c** C M OLDROYD, **C** C L BEEVERS
MARCLE, MUCH (St Bartholomew) *Heref 6*
  P *E Money-Kyrle Esq* **V** G F HOLLEY
MARDEN (All Saints) Redhorn *Sarum*
MARDEN (St Hilda) Cullercoats St Geo *Newc*
MARDEN (St Mary the Virgin) w Amberley and Wisteston *Heref 4* **P** *D&C* **V** D B HEWLETT, **C** U J SUMMERS
MARDEN (St Michael and All Angels) *Cant 11* **P** *Abp*
  V J H WAITE
MARDEN, EAST (St Peter) Compton, the Mardens, Stoughton and Racton *Chich*
MARDEN, NORTH (St Mary) as above
MARDEN ASH (St James) High Ongar w Norton Mandeville *Chelmsf*
MARDEN HILL Group, The *Linc 7* **P** *Bp (2 turns)*,
  B Eley Esq & DBP (jt), *Baroness Willoughby, Duchy of*

Lanc, J Pain Esq & M Dudley Hewitt Esq (jt), *A Lee Esq (by turn)* **P-in-c** A M SULLIVAN
MAREHAM-LE-FEN (St Helen) and Revesby *Linc 11*
  P *Bp and Mrs A D Lee (alt)* **R** S CRABTREE
MAREHAM ON THE HILL (All Saints) *Linc 11* **P** *Bp*
  V *Vacant*
MARESFIELD (St Bartholomew) *Chich 21* **P** *Ch Trust Fund Trust* **R** K J BOULLIER
MARFLEET (St Giles) (St George) (St Hilda) (St Philip) *York 15* **P** *Patr Bd* **TR** W J G HEALE,
  TV A F RABLEN, D J SENIOR, M A DONALDSON
MARGARET MARSH (St Margaret) Shaston *Sarum*
MARGARET RODING (St Margaret) High and Gd Easter w Margaret Roding *Chelmsf*
MARGARETTING (St Margaret) Fryerning w Margaretting *Chelmsf*
MARGATE (All Saints) *Cant 9* **P** *Abp*
  V M J A ANDERSON
MARGATE Cliftonville (St Paul) Cliftonville *Cant*
MARGATE (Holy Trinity) *Cant 9* **P** *Ch Patr Trust*
  V C W FLETCHER
MARGATE (St John the Baptist in Thanet) *Cant 9* **P** *Abp*
  V N BALDOCK, **C** C M GREGORY
MARHAM (Holy Trinity) *Ely 16* **P** *St Jo Coll Cam*
  V J D A LINN
MARHAMCHURCH (St Marwenne) Bude Haven and Marhamchurch *Truro*
MARHOLM (St Mary the Virgin) *Pet 13* **P** *Sir Stephen Hastings* **P-in-c** P M HAWKINS
MARIANSLEIGH (St Mary) Bishopsnympton, Rose Ash, Mariansleigh etc *Ex*
MARISHES, THE (Chapel) Pickering *York*
MARK (Holy Cross) w Allerton *B & W 1* **P** *Bp and D&C (jt)* **R** M T PAVEY
MARK BEECH (Holy Trinity) Hever w Mark Beech *Roch*
MARK CROSS (St Mark) Rotherfield w Mark Cross *Chich*
MARKBY (St Peter) Hannah cum Hagnaby w Markby *Linc*
MARKET BOSWORTH (St Peter), Cadeby w Sutton Cheney and Congerstone *Leic 13* **P** *DBP*
  TR J C SEYMOUR, **Par Dn** M M FOWLER
MARKET DEEPING (St Guthlac) *Linc 13* **P** *Ld Chan*
  R S D EARIS
MARKET DRAYTON (St Mary) Drayton in Hales *Lich*
MARKET HARBOROUGH (St Dionysius) *Leic 4* **P** *Bp*
  V B M B ADDISON, **C** J G GIBBINS
MARKET HARBOROUGH (Transfiguration) and Little Bowden (St Hugh) (St Nicholas) *Leic 4* **P** *Bp*
  R J B SEATON
MARKET LAVINGTON (St Mary of the Assumption) and Easterton *Sarum 19* **P** *Bp and Ch Ch Ox (alt)*
  V *Vacant* Lavington (038081) 3309
MARKET OVERTON (St Peter and St Paul) Teigh w Whissendine and Market Overton *Pet*
MARKET RASEN (St Thomas the Apostle) *Linc 5*
  P *Ld Chan* **V** M J CARTWRIGHT, **NSM** D L INKPIN
MARKET STAINTON (St Michael and All Angels) Asterby Gp *Linc*
MARKET WEIGHTON (All Saints) *York 7* **P** *Abp*
  V *Vacant* Market Weighton (0430) 873230
MARKET WESTON (St Mary) Hopton, Market Weston, Barningham etc *St E*
MARKFIELD (St Michael) *Leic 12* **P** *MMCET*
  R G T WILLETT
MARKHAM, EAST (St John the Baptist) w Askham, Headon w Upton and Grove *S'well 5* **P** *Grove Settled Estate Trustees and SMF (jt)* **R** G J WICKSTEAD
MARKHAM CLINTON (All Saints) Tuxford w Weston and Markham Clinton *S'well*
MARKINGTON (St Michael) w South Stainley and Bishop Thornton *Ripon 3* **P** *Bp (1 turn), D&C (1 turn), Sir Thomas Ingilby, Bt and N A Hudleston Esq (1 turn)*
  V S D ASKEW
MARKS GATE (St Mark) Chadwell Heath *Chelmsf 1*
  P *Bp* **V** R K GAYLER
MARKS TEY (St Andrew) w Aldham and Little Tey *Chelmsf 20* **P** *CPAS, Ch Patr Trust and MMCET (jt)*
  R B SNELLING, **Hon C** S G HUCKLE
MARKSBURY (St Peter) Farmborough, Marksbury and Stanton Prior *B & W*
MARKYATE STREET (St John the Baptist) *St Alb 14*
  P *Bp* **V** M J CROW, **NSM** P J C McGRANAGHAN
MARLBOROUGH (St Mary the Virgin) *Sarum 20*
  P *Patr Bd* **TV** J R SARGANT, **C** M F D CRIPPS
MARLBROOK (St Luke) Catshill and Dodford *Worc*
MARLDON (St John the Baptist) *Ex 10* **P** *Bp*
  V G L BROCKHOUSE

MARLESFORD (St Andrew) Campsea Ashe w Marlesford, Parham and Hacheston *St E*
MARLEY HILL (St Cuthbert) *Dur 5* **P** *The Crown*
V A GALES
MARLINGFORD (Assumption of the Blessed Virgin Mary) Easton w Colton and Marlingford *Nor*
MARLOW, GREAT (All Saints) *Ox 29* **P** *Bp*
P-in-c N J MOLONY, **C** A A EAGLES, C J P CHADWICK
MARLOW, LITTLE (St John the Baptist) *Ox 29* **P** *DBP*
V *Vacant* Bourne End (06285) 22795
MARLOW BOTTOM (St Mary the Virgin) Gt Marlow *Ox*
MARLPIT HILL (St Paulinus) Edenbridge *Roch*
MARLPOOL (All Saints) *Derby 12* **P** *V Heanor*
V D PERKINS
MARLSTON (St Mary) Bucklebury w Marlston *Ox*
MARNHULL (St Gregory) *Sarum 6* **P** *DBF* **R** *Vacant* Marnhull (0258) 820247
MAROWN (Old Parish Church) (St Runius) *S & M 3*
P *The Crown* **V** A M CONVERY
MARPLE (All Saints) *Ches 16* **P** *R Stockport St Mary*
C R M CLARK
MARPLE, LOW (St Martin) St Martin *Ches 16* **P** *Keble Coll Ox* **V** J H CAM
MARR (St Helen) Bilham *Sheff*
MARSDEN (St Bartholomew) *Wakef 5* **P** *R Almondbury*
V D M RIPPINGALE
MARSDEN, GREAT (St John the Evangelist) *Blackb 7*
P *The Crown* **V** M J HOY
MARSDEN, LITTLE (St Paul) *Blackb 7* **P** *Bp*
V J W LEE
MARSH (St George) Lanc St Mary *Blackb*
MARSH (St James chapel) Huddersfield H Trin *Wakef*
MARSH BALDON (St Peter) Dorchester *Ox*
MARSH FARM (Holy Cross) *St Alb 20* **P** *Bp* **V** *Vacant* Luton (0582) 575757
MARSH GIBBON (St Mary the Virgin) Swan *Ox*
MARSHAM (All Saints) *Nor 3* **P** *Bp*
P-in-c R J HEWETSON
MARSHCHAPEL (St Mary the Virgin) Tetney, Marshchapel and N Coates *Linc*
MARSHFIELD (St Mary the Virgin) w Cold Ashton and Tormarton w West Littleton *Bris 2* **P** *New Coll Ox and Bp (alt)* **C** M P WESTLAKE
MARSHLAND, The *Sheff 11* **P** *Ld Chan and Bp (alt)*
V P IRESON, **NSM** K W SARGEANTSON
MARSHLAND ST JAMES (St James) *Ely 17* **P** *Bp*
P-in-c C N BALES
MARSHWOOD VALE Team Ministry, The (St Mary) *Sarum 3* **P** *Patr Bd* **C** D D PAIRMAN, **NSM** R L HOLLANDS
MARSKE (St Edmund) Downholme and Marske *Ripon*
MARSKE, NEW (St Thomas) *York 17* **P** *Abp*
V R F ROWLING
MARSKE IN CLEVELAND (St Mark) *York 17*
P *Trustees* **V** D H LAMBERT, **Par Dn** M A PASKETT
MARSTON (St Alban) Stafford *Lich*
MARSTON (St Lawrence) Greatworth and Marston St Lawrence etc *Pet*
MARSTON (St Leonard) Stafford *Lich*
MARSTON (St Mary) Barkston and Hough Gp *Linc*
MARSTON (St Nicholas) *Ox 4* **P** *Bp* **V** A R PRICE
MARSTON, NEW (St Michael and All Angels) *Ox 4*
P *Bp* **P-in-c** E C MILLER
MARSTON, NORTH (Assumption of the Blessed Virgin Mary) Schorne *Ox*
MARSTON, SOUTH (St Mary Magdalene) Stratton St Margaret w S Marston etc *Bris*
MARSTON BIGOT (St Leonard) Nunney and Witham Friary, Marston Bigot etc *B & W*
MARSTON GREEN (St Leonard) *Birm 11* **P** *Birm Dioc Trustees* **V** R V ALLEN, **Hon Par Dn** D M WHITMORE
MARSTON MAGNA (Blessed Virgin Mary) Chilton Cantelo, Ashington, Mudford, Rimpton etc *B & W*
MARSTON MEYSEY (St James) Meysey Hampton w Marston Meysey and Castle Eaton *Glouc*
MARSTON MONTGOMERY (St Giles) Alkmonton, Cubley, Marston, Montgomery etc *Derby*
MARSTON MORTEYNE (St Mary the Virgin) w Lidlington *St Alb 19 ·* **P** *Bp and St Jo Coll Cam (alt)* **R** J GREENWAY
MARSTON SICCA (St James the Great) Quinton w Marston Sicca *Glouc*
MARSTON TRUSSELL (St Nicholas) Welford w Sibbertoft and Marston Trussell *Pet*
MARSTON UPON DOVE (St Mary) w Scropton *Derby 14*
P N J M Spurrier *Esq* **V** B FREER
MARSTOW (St Matthew) Walford and Saint John, w Bishopswood etc *Heref*

MARSWORTH (All Saints) Cheddington w Mentmore and Marsworth *Ox*
MARTHALL (All Saints) w Over Peover *Ches 12* **P** *DBP*
V J F SPEAKMAN
MARTHAM (St Mary) w Repps w Bastwick *Nor 2*
P *K Edw VI Gr Sch and D&C (jt)* **V** P S PAINE
MARTIN (All Saints) W Downland *Sarum*
MARTIN (Holy Trinity) Scopwick Gp *Linc*
MARTIN (St Michael) w Thornton *Linc 11* **P** *Bp and SMF (alt)* **P-in-c** S W PEARCE
MARTIN HUSSINGTREE (St Michael) Salwarpe and Hindlip w Martin Hussingtree *Worc*
MARTINDALE (Old Church) Barton, Pooley Bridge and Martindale *Carl*
MARTINDALE (St Peter) as above
MARTINHOE (St Martin) Lynton, Brendon, Countisbury, Lynmouth etc *Ex*
MARTLESHAM (St Mary the Virgin) w Brightwell *St E 2*
P *Bp* **R** B D LILLISTONE, **C** I HOOPER
MARTLEY (St Peter) and Wichenford, Knightwick and Doddenham, Broadwas and Cotheridge *Worc 3*
P *D&C (2 turns), Bp (1 turn)* **R** W N RICHARDS
MARTOCK (All Saints) w Ash *B & W 7* **P** *Bp*
V P N H CONEY, **Hon C** V M WRIGHT
MARTON (Room) Sinnington *York*
MARTON (St Esprit) Long Itchington and Marton *Cov*
MARTON (St James) Capesthorne w Siddington and Marton *Ches*
MARTON (St Margaret of Antioch) *Linc 2* **P** *Bp*
V L SALT
MARTON (St Mark) *Heref 13* **P** *V Chirbury* **V** *Vacant*
MARTON (St Mary) Stillington and Marton w Moxby *York*
MARTON (St Paul) *Blackb 9* **P** *V Poulton-le-Fylde*
V M PICKERING, **C** D M BEAL, P W ALLSOP
MARTON-CUM-GRAFTON (Christ Church) Gt and Lt Ouseburn w Marton-cum-Grafton *Ripon*
MARTON-IN-CHIRBURY (St Mark) Marton *Heref*
MARTON-IN-CLEVELAND (St Cuthbert) *York 19*
P *Abp* **V** G FISHER, **C** W J FORD
MARTON IN CRAVEN (St Peter) Broughton, Marton and Thornton *Bradf*
MARTON MOSS (St Nicholas) *Blackb 9* **P** *Bp*
V P RICHARDSON
MARTYR WORTHY (St Swithun) Easton and Martyr Worthy *Win*
MARWOOD (St Michael and All Angels) Heanton Punchardon w Marwood *Ex*
MARYFIELD (St Philip and St James) Antony w Sheviock *Truro*
MARYPORT (St Mary) (Christ Church) *Carl 7*
P *Trustees* **V** *Vacant* Maryport (0900) 813077
MARYSTOWE (St Mary the Virgin), Coryton, Stowford, Lewtrenchard and Thrushelton *Ex 25*
P P T L Newman *Esq*, Mrs A M Baring-Gould Almond, Air Cdre P L Donkin, *and* R H Wollocombe *Esq (by turn)* **V** G W BALL
MARYTAVY (St Mary) *Ex 25* **P** *Guild of All So*
R P M COMERFORD
MASBROUGH (St Paul) *Sheff 6* **P** *Bp and Ld Chan (alt)*
V M OCJOY
MASHAM (St Mary the Virgin) and Healey *Ripon 3*
P *Trin Coll Cam* **V** B ABELL
MASSINGHAM, GREAT (St Mary) and LITTLE (St Andrew) and Harple *Nor 19* **P** *Bp, J H Brereton Esq, and DBP (jt)* **R** *Vacant* Great Massingham (048524) 211
MASTIN MOOR (St Paul) Staveley and Barrow Hill *Derby*
MATCHBOROUGH (Christ Church) Ipsley *Worc*
MATCHING (St Mary) High Laver w Magdalen Laver and Lt Laver etc *Chelmsf*
MATCHING GREEN (St Edmund) as above
MATFEN (Holy Trinity) Stamfordham w Matfen *Newc*
MATFIELD (St Luke) Lamberhurst and Matfield *Roch*
MATHON (St John the Baptist) Cradley w Mathon and Storridge *Heref*
MATLASKE (St Peter) Barningham w Matlaske w Baconsthorpe etc *Nor*
MATLOCK (St Giles) (St John the Baptist) *Derby 7* **P** *Bp*
R P D PETERKEN
MATLOCK BANK (All Saints) *Derby 7* **P** *Bp*
V J O GOLDSMITH, **NSM** K J ORFORD
MATLOCK BATH (Holy Trinity) *Derby 7* **P** *Ch Trust Fund Trust* **V** H COLLARD, **NSM** C J BAKER
MATSON (St Katherine) *Glouc 5* **P** *D&C*
R H D BROAD, **C** J C CORNELL
MATTERDALE (not known) Greystoke, Matterdale, Mungrisdale & W'millock *Carl*

MATTERSEY (All Saints) Everton and Mattersey w Clayworth *S'well*

MATTINGLEY (not known) Heckfield w Mattingley and Rotherwick *Win*

MATTISHALL (All Saints) w Mattishall Burgh, Welborne and Yaxham *Nor 12* **P** *G&C Coll Cam and Bp (alt)* **R** *Vacant* Dereham (0362) 850243

MATTISHALL BURGH (St Peter) Mattishall w Mattishall Burgh, Welborne etc *Nor*

MAUGHOLD (St Maughold) *S & M 4* **P** *The Crown* **V** D J GREEN, **NSM** B L HUMPHREYS, E C B CORLETT

MAULDEN (St Mary) *St Alb 15* **P** *Bp* **R** D LEWTHWAITE

MAUNBY (St Michael) Ainderby Steeple w Yafforth and Kirby Wiske etc *Ripon*

MAUTBY (St Peter and St Paul) Filby w Thrigby, Mautby, Stokesby, Herringby etc *Nor*

MAVESYN RIDWARE (St Nicholas) The Ridwares and Kings Bromley *Lich*

MAVIS ENDERBY (St Michael) Marden Hill Gp *Linc*

MAWDESLEY (St Peter) *Blackb 4* **P** *R Croston* **R** D J REYNOLDS

MAWGAN (St Mawgan) Cury and Gunwalloe w Mawgan *Truro*

MAWNAN (St Mawnan) (St Michael) *Truro 3* **P** *Bp* **R** N J EVA

MAXEY (St Peter) w Northborough *Pet 13* **P** *D&C* **V** A SHEASBY

MAXSTOKE (St Michael and All Angels) *Birm 11* **P** *Lord Leigh* **V** R G BOLLARD, **NSM** L LEWIS

MAYBRIDGE (St Richard) *Chich 5* **P** *Bp* **V** R T E B WOODS

MAYBUSH Redbridge (All Saints) Southn Maybush St Pet *Win*

MAYFAIR (Christ Church) *Lon 3* **P** *Bp* **Hon C** A M ANSELL

MAYFIELD (St Dunstan) *Chich 15* **P** *Keble Coll Ox* **V** G W HOLMES, **C** W J L STRONG

MAYFIELD (St John the Baptist) *Lich 21* **P** *Ch Soc Trust* **P-in-c** P E R HALL

MAYFORD (Emmanuel) Woking St Jo *Guildf*

MAYHILL (All Saints) Huntley and Longhope *Glouc*

MAYLAND (St Barnabas) (St Barnabas Family Centre) *Chelmsf 13* **P** *Lord Fitzwalter and Bp (alt)* **V** *Vacant* Maldon (0621) 740943

MEANWOOD (Holy Trinity) *Ripon 7* **P** *Bp* **V** R M WIGGEN

MEARE (Blessed Virgin Mary and All Saints) Glastonbury w Meare, W Pennard and Godney *B & W*

MEARS ASHBY (All Saints) and Hardwick and Sywell w Overstone *Pet 6* **P** *Duchy of Cornwall (2 turns), Bracegirdle Trustees (1 turn), and Mrs C E Edmiston (1 turn)* **R** *Vacant* Northampton (0604) 810298

MEASHAM (St Lawrence) *Leic 9* **P** *CPAS* **V** J N PEARSON

MEAVY (St Peter) Yelverton, Meavy, Sheepstor and Walkhampton *Ex*

MEDBOURNE (St Giles) Six Saints circa Holt *Leic*

MEDMENHAM (St Peter and St Paul) Hambleden Valley *Ox*

MEDOMSLEY (St Mary Magdalene) *Dur 8* **P** *Bp* **V** K A WYLD

MEDSTEAD (St Andrew) cum Wield *Win 2* **P** *The Crown* **R** T SMITH, **NSM** T J RIVIERE

MEERBROOK (St Matthew) Leek and Meerbrook *Lich*

MEESDEN (St Mary) Hormead, Wyddial, Anstey, Brent Pelham etc *St Alb*

MEETH (St Michael and All Angels) Hatherleigh, Meeth, Exbourne and Jacobstowe *Ex*

MEIR (Holy Trinity) *Lich 12* **P** *Bp* **C** K L ROUND

MEIR HEATH (St Francis of Assisi) *Lich 18* **P** *Bp* **V** J W PAWSON

MEIR PARK (St Clare) Meir Heath *Lich*

MELBECKS (Holy Trinity) Swaledale *Ripon*

MELBOURN (All Saints) *Ely 8* **P** *D&C* **V** J K GREASLEY

MELBOURNE (St Michael) *Derby 15* **P** *Bp* **V** F ROSS

MELBOURNE (St Monica) Seaton Ross Gp of Par *York*

MELBURY (St Mary the Virgin) (St Oswald) *Sarum 1* **P** *Patr Bd* **TR** J G MILLER, **TV** D LOWE, T R WEST, **NSM** N E de CHAZAL

MELBURY ABBAS (St Thomas) Shaston *Sarum*

MELBURY BUBB (St Mary the Virgin) Melbury *Sarum*

MELBURY OSMUND (St Osmund) as above

MELCHBOURNE (St Mary Magdalene) The Stodden Churches *St Alb*

MELCOMBE HORSEY (St Andrew) Milton Abbas, Hilton w Cheselbourne etc *Sarum*

MELDON (St John the Baptist) Bolam w Whalton and Hartburn w Meldon *Newc*

MELDRETH (Holy Trinity) *Ely 8* **P** *D&C* **V** J K GREASLEY

MELKSHAM (St Barnabas) (St Michael and All Angels) *Sarum 17* **P** *DBP* **TR** M B G PAIN, **TV** F J BALLINGER

MELKSHAM FOREST (St Andrew) Melksham *Sarum*

MELLING (St Thomas) *Liv 11* **P** *R Halsall* **V** M E PLUNKETT

MELLING (St Wilfrid) Tunstall w Melling and Leck *Blackb*

MELLIS (St Mary the Virgin) Thornhams Magna and Parva, Gislingham and Mellis *St E*

MELLOR (St Mary) *Blackb 2* **P** *V Blackb* **V** J P HUDSON

MELLOR (St Thomas) *Derby 6* **P** *Bp* **V** R M PHILLIPS

MELLS (St Andrew) w Buckland Dinham, Elm, Whatley, Vobster and Chantry *B & W 4* **P** *DBP (2 turns), Bp (1 turns)* **R** D OLIVE

MELMERBY (St John the Baptist) Skirwith, Ousby and Melmerby w Kirkland *Carl*

MELPLASH (Christ Church) Beaminster Area *Sarum*

MELSONBY (St James the Great) Forcett and Aldbrough and Melsonby *Ripon*

MELTHAM Christ the King (St Bartholomew) (St James) *Wakef 5* **P** *R Almondbury w Farnley Tyas, and Simeon's Trustees (jt)* **V** A R VIGARS, **Par Dn** C LITTLE, **NSM** P ROLLS

MELTON Great Framland *Leic 3* **P** *Bp, Peaches Trustees, Major F R D Burdett Fisher (jt)* **TR** D H THORPE, **TV** G L SPENCER, D B ROY, **C** A C DEEGAN

MELTON (St Andrew) *St E 7* **P** *D&C Ely* **P-in-c** M SANDERS, **Hon Par Dn** H C SANDERS

MELTON, GREAT (All Saints) Hethersett w Canteloff w Lt and Gt Melton *Nor*

MELTON, HIGH (St James) Barnburgh w Melton on the Hill *Sheff*

MELTON, LITTLE (All Saints) Hethersett w Canteloff w Lt and Gt Melton *Nor*

MELTON, WEST (St Cuthbert) Brampton Bierlow *Sheff*

MELTON CONSTABLE (St Peter) w Swanton Novers *Nor 22* **P** *Lord Hastings* **P-in-c** H J BLACKER, K G TAYLOR

MELTON MOWBRAY (St Mary) Melton Gt Framland *Leic*

MELTON ROSS (Ascension) w New Barnetby *Linc 6* **P** *Earl of Yarborough* **V** P J WHITE

MELVERLEY (St Peter) Kinnerley w Melverley and Knockin w Maesbrook *Lich*

MEMBURY (St John the Baptist) Yarcombe w Membury and Upottery *Ex*

MENDHAM (All Saints) Fressingfield, Mendham, Metfield, Weybread etc *St E*

MENDLESHAM (St Mary) *St E 6* **P** *SMF* **V** P T GRAY

MENHENIOT (not known) *Truro 12* **P** *Ex Coll Ox* **V** K P MELLOR

MENITH WOOD (Chapel) Teme Valley N *Worc*

MENSTON (St John the Divine) w Woodhead *Bradf 4* **P** *Bp* **V** J S WARD, **Par Dn** D MAWBEY

MENTMORE (St Mary the Virgin) Cheddington w Mentmore and Marsworth *Ox*

MEOLE BRACE (Holy Trinity) *Lich 27* **P** *Mrs D M Bather* **V** K T ROBERTS

MEOLS, GREAT (St John the Baptist) *Ches 8* **P** *Bp* **V** K J PRITCHARD

MEOLS, NORTH (St Cuthbert) *Liv 9* **P** *Personal Reps R F Hesketh* **P-in-c** B J GERRARD, **Hon C** L EYRES

MEON, EAST (All Saints) *Portsm 5* **P** *Ld Chan* **V** P R WADSWORTH, **C** A RICHARDS

MEON, WEST (St John the Evangelist) and Warnford *Portsm 5* **P** *Bp and DBP (alt)* **R** K C A WILLS

MEONSTOKE (St Andrew) w Corhampton cum Exton *Portsm 1* **P** *Bp* **R** D E HENLEY, **NSM** J R BARNETT

MEOPHAM (St John the Baptist) w Nurstead *Roch 1* **P** *D&C and Lt-Col F B Edmeades (jt)* **R** D L WILLIAMS

MEPAL (St Mary) Witcham w Mepal *Ely*

MEPPERSHALL (St Mary the Virgin) w Campton and Stondon *St Alb 22* **P** *St Jo Coll Cam (1 turn), Bp (2 turns)* **R** J H BARRALL

MERE (St Michael the Archangel) w West Knoyle and Maiden Bradley *Sarum 14* **P** *Bp* **V** W H VELLIOTT, **Hon Par Dn** P A RUNDLE

MERESIDE (St Wilfrid) Blackpool St Wilfrid *Blackb*

MEREVALE (St Mary the Virgin) Baxterley w Hurley and Wood End and Merevale etc *Birm*

MEREWORTH (St Lawrence) w West Peckham *Roch 7*
  P *Viscount Falmouth and D&C (alt)* **R** K G F HOLDING
MERIDEN (St Laurence) and Packington *Cov 4*
  P *Provost & Chapter and Earl of Aylesford (jt)*
  R M H DAWKINS
MERRINGTON (St John the Evangelist) *Dur 10* **P** *D&C*
  V *Vacant* Spennymoor (0388) 816101
MERRIOTT (All Saints) w Hinton, Dinnington and Lopen
  B & W 16 **P** *D&C Bris (2 turns), Bp (1 turn)*
  R J C KING
MERROW (St John the Evangelist) *Guildf 5* **P** *Earl of*
  Onslow **R** M D B LEWIS
MERRY HILL (St Joseph) Penn Fields *Lich*
MERRYMEET (St Mary) Menheniot *Truro*
MERSEA, EAST (St Edmund) W w E Mersea *Chelmsf*
MERSEA, WEST (St Peter and St Paul) w East Mersea
  Chelmsf 19 **P** *Bp and The Crown (alt)*
  R J A G SWALLOW
MERSHAM (St John the Baptist) w Hinxhill *Cant 12*
  P *Abp* **R** W R KILFORD
MERSTHAM (St Katharine) (Epiphany) and Gatton
  S'wark 24 **P** *Abp* **R** R J M GROSVENOR,
  Par Dn C MILLAR
MERSTHAM, SOUTH (All Saints) *S'wark 24* **P** *Bp*
  V E C LAST
MERSTON (St Giles) N Mundham w Hunston and
  Merston *Chich*
MERTON (All Saints) Shebbear, Buckland Filleigh,
  Sheepwash etc *Ex*
MERTON (St James) *S'wark 11* **P** *Bp and V Merton*
  St Mary (jt) **V** I C DAVIES, **Par Dn** J E DICKER
MERTON (St John the Divine) *S'wark 11* **P** *Bp and*
  V Merton St Mary (jt) **V** K I UPHILL
MERTON (St Mary) *S'wark 11* **P** *Bp*
  V R St L BROADBERRY
MERTON (St Peter) Caston w Griston, Merton,
  Thompson etc *Nor*
MERTON (St Swithun) Ambrosden w Mert and
  Piddington *Ox*
MESHAW (St John) Witheridge, Thelbridge,
  Creacombe, Meshaw etc *Ex*
MESSING (All Saints) w Inworth *Chelmsf 27* **P** *DBP*
  V *Vacant* Tiptree (0621) 815434
MESSINGHAM (Holy Trinity) *Linc 4* **P** *Bp*
  V G PARROTT
MESTY CROFT (St Luke) Wednesbury St Paul Wood
  Green *Lich*
METFIELD (St John the Baptist) Fressingfield,
  Mendham, Metfield, Weybread etc *St E*
METHERINGHAM (St Wilfred) w Blankney *Linc 18*
  P *Bp* **V** *Vacant* Metheringham (0526) 20204
METHLEY (St Oswald) w Mickletown *Ripon 8*
  P *Bp (3 turns), Duchy of Lanc (1 turn)*
  R M G WHITTOCK
METHWOLD (St George) *Ely 15* **P** *Ld Chan*
  V J B ROWSELL
METTINGHAM (All Saints) Ringsfield w Redisham,
  Barsham, Shipmeadow etc *St E*
METTON (St Andrew) Roughton and Felbrigg, Metton,
  Sustead etc *Nor*
MEVAGISSEY (St Peter) and St Ewe *Truro 1* **P** *Bp and*
  Penrice Ho (St Austell) Ltd **R** A WAKEFIELD
MEXBOROUGH (St John the Baptist) *Sheff 12* **P** *Adn*
  York **V** K HUTCHINSON, **C** J WHEATLEY
MEYSEY HAMPTON (St Mary) w Marston Meysey and
  Castle Eaton *Glouc 13* **P** *Ch Soc Trust* **P-in-c** H BUSK
MICHAEL (St Michael and All Angels) *S & M 3*
  P *The Crown* **V** J D GELLING
MICHAELCHURCH ESCLEY (St Michael) Clodock
  and Longtown w Craswall, Llanveynoe etc *Heref*
MICHAELSTOW (St Michael) St Tudy w St Mabyn and
  Michaelstow *Truro*
MICHELDEVER (St Mary) and East Stratton,
  Woodmancote and Popham *Win 13* **P** *Exors Lord*
  Northbrook (3 turns), Bp (2 turns) **V** *Vacant*
  Micheldever (096289) 233
MICHELMERSH (Our Lady) and Timsbury and Farley
  Chamberlayne and Braishfield *Win 11* **P** *Bp*
  R D B KINGTON
MICKLEFIELD (St Mary the Virgin) *York 6* **P** *Abp*
  P-in-c P S RAMSDEN
MICKLEGATE (Holy Trinity) and Bishophill Junior
  (St Mary) *York 8* **P** *D&C* **R** G S HIGGINSON
MICKLEHAM (St Michael) *Guildf 7* **P** *St Jo Foundn Sch*
  R P R INCE
MICKLEHURST (All Saints) *Ches 14* **P** *Bp*
  V D BOOTH
MICKLEOVER (All Saints) *Derby 10* **P** *MMCET*
  V A E HAVARD, **Par Dn** S STAFF

MICKLEOVER (St John) *Derby 10* **P** *Bp*
  V A B McCABE
MICKLETON (St Lawrence) *Glouc 11* **P** *Ld Chan*
  V J C HUNTRISS
MICKLEY (St George) *Newc 3* **P** *Bp* **V** J E SYMONS
MICKLEY (St John the Evangelist) Fountains Gp *Ripon*
MID MARSH Group, The *Linc 12* **P** *Rear Admiral*
  G P D Hall, Bp, D&C, and Lord Deramore (by turn)
  R P G FAULKNER
MIDDLE: *see also under substantive place names*
MIDDLE RASEN Group, The *Linc 5* **P** *Bp and DBP (jt)*
  R J W COTTON
MIDDLEHAM (St Mary and St Alkelda) w Coverdale and
  East Witton *Ripon 4* **P** *Bp, R Craven-Smith-*
  Milnes Esq, and W R Burdon Esq (jt)
  R M T BROADBENT, **NSM** A S BROWN
MIDDLESBROUGH (All Saints) *York 19* **P** *Abp*
  V C D E WHEAT, **C** G S ASKEY,
  NSM G E HOLROYD, D P R MARTIN
MIDDLESBROUGH (Ascension) *York 19* **P** *Abp*
  V M SPENCELEY
MIDDLESBROUGH (Holy Trinity) N Ormesby *York*
MIDDLESBROUGH (St Agnes) *York 19* **P** *Abp*
  V P J CARRINGTON
MIDDLESBROUGH (St Barnabas) Linthorpe *York*
MIDDLESBROUGH (St Chad) *York 19* **P** *Abp*
  V P F LANGFORD
MIDDLESBROUGH (St Columba w St Paul) *York 19*
  P *Abp* **P-in-c** R W A GUIVER
MIDDLESBROUGH (St Cuthbert) *York 19* **P** *Abp*
  P-in-c J B WILCOX, **NSM** S C CHALLENGER
MIDDLESBROUGH (St John the Evangelist) *York 19*
  P *Abp* **P-in-c** A CAMPBELL-WILSON
MIDDLESBROUGH (St Martin of Tours) *York 19*
  P *Abp* **V** P H PEVERELL, **C** S M EAST
MIDDLESBROUGH (St Oswald) *York 19* **P** *Abp*
  V S N FISHER
MIDDLESBROUGH (St Thomas) *York 19* **P** *Abp*
  V W A J WELLS
MIDDLESMOOR (St Chad) Upper Nidderdale *Ripon*
MIDDLESTOWN (St Luke) *Wakef 12* **P** *R Thornhill*
  V L J SHUTT
MIDDLETON (All Saints) Gt and Lt Henny w
  Middleton, Wickham St Paul etc *Chelmsf*
MIDDLETON (Holy Ghost) Kirkby Lonsdale *Carl*
MIDDLETON (Holy Trinity) Bitterley w Middleton,
  Stoke St Milborough etc *Heref*
MIDDLETON (Holy Trinity) *Heref 13* **P** *V Chirbury*
  V N D MINSHALL
MIDDLETON (Holy Trinity) Kelsale-cum-Carlton,
  Middleton-cum-Fordley etc *St E*
MIDDLETON (St Andrew) w Newton, Levisham and
  Lockton *York 21* **P** *Abp* **R** D W GOODWIN
MIDDLETON (St Cross) *Ripon 6* **P** *DBP*
  V M S HATTON, **Par Dn** P J SWIFT
MIDDLETON (St George) (St Laurence) *Dur 12* **P** *Bp*
  R *Vacant* Dinsdale (0325) 332410
MIDDLETON (St John the Baptist) *Birm 9* **P** *Bp*
  V *Vacant*
MIDDLETON (St Leonard) (St Margaret) *Man 19* **P** *Bp*
  R N J FEIST, **C** S J RICHARDSON
MIDDLETON (St Mary the Virgin) *Ripon 6*
  P *V Rothwell* **V** A L GLASBY, **Par Dn** C A JAMES
MIDDLETON (St Mary) w East Winch *Nor 23* **P** *Bp and*
  W O Lancaster Esq (alt) **V** P J BELL
MIDDLETON (St Michael and All Angels) Youlgreave,
  Middleton, Stanton-in-Peak etc *Derby*
MIDDLETON (St Nicholas) Felpham w Middleton
  Chich
MIDDLETON-BY-WIRKSWORTH (Holy Trinity)
  Wirksworth w Alderwasley, Carsington etc *Derby*
MIDDLETON CHENEY (All Saints) w Chacombe *Pet 1*
  P *BNC Ox (2 turns), Bp (1 turn)* **R** G C THOMAS
MIDDLETON-IN-CHIRBY (Holy Trinity) Middleton
  Heref
MIDDLETON-IN-TEESDALE (St Mary the Virgin) w
  Forest and Frith *Dur 11* **P** *Lord Barnard and The*
  Crown (alt) **R** G LINDEN
MIDDLETON JUNCTION (St Gabriel) *Man 19* **P** *Bp*
  V I B COOK
MIDDLETON ON LEVEN (St Cuthbert) Rudby in
  Cleveland w Middleton *York*
MIDDLETON-ON-SEA Conventional District *Chich 1*
  C-in-c P W NEWSAM
MIDDLETON-ON-THE-HILL (St Mary the Virgin)
  Kimbolton w Hamnish and Middleton-on-the-Hill *Heref*
MIDDLETON-ON-THE-WOLDS (St Andrew) Bainton
  w N Dalton, Middleton-on-the-Wolds etc *York*

MIDDLETON SCRIVEN (St John the Baptist)
Billingsley w Sidbury, Middleton Scriven etc *Heref*
MIDDLETON STONEY (All Saints) Chesterton w
Middleton Stoney and Wendlebury *Ox*
**MIDDLETON TYAS (St Michael and All Angels) w Croft
and Eryholme** *Ripon 2* **P** *Prime Min and V Gilling (alt)*
R *D J HOPKINSON*
MIDDLETOWN (St John the Baptist) Gt Wollaston
Heref
MIDDLEWICH (St Michael and All Angels) w Byley *Ches 6*
P *Bp* **V** *E W COX*
MIDDLEZOY (Holy Cross) and Othery and Moorlinch
B & W 5 **P** *Bp Worc (1 turn), Bp (2 turns)*
V *D A EVANS*
MIDGHAM (St Matthew) Woolhampton w Midgham
and Beenham Valance *Ox*
MIDHOPE (St James) Penistone and Thurlstone *Wakef*
MIDHURST (St Mary Magdalene and St Denis) *Chich 10*
P *Cowdray Trust* **V** *D CHANING-PEARCE*
MIDSOMER NORTON (St John the Baptist) w Clandown
B & W 13 **P** *Ch Ch Ox* **V** *M K SPARROW,*
Hon C *J C COPUS*
MIDVILLE (St Peter) Stickney Gp *Linc*
MILBER (St Luke) *Ex 11* **P** *Bp* **V** *J F BOARDMAN*
MILBORNE PORT (St John the Evangelist) w Goathill
B & W 8 **P** *Mrs J E Smith (2 turns), Trustees (1 turn)*
V *B C B WHITWORTH*
MILBORNE ST ANDREW (St Andrew) w Dewlish *Sarum 2*
P *Rev J L Baillie* **P-in-c** *P J GREWCOCK,*
NSM *N L BEGGS*
MILBORNE WICK (Mission Church) Milborne Port w
Goathill *B & W*
MILBOURNE (Holy Saviour) Ponteland *Newc*
MILBURN (St Cuthbert) Long Marton w Dufton and w
Milburn *Carl*
MILCOMBE (St Laurence) Bloxham w Milcombe and S
Newington *Ox*
MILDEN (St Peter) Monks Eleigh w Chelsworth and
Brent Eleigh etc *St E*
MILDENHALL (St John the Baptist) Marlborough
Sarum
MILDENHALL (St Mary) *St E 11* **P** *Patr Bd (2 turns),
Bp (1 turn)* **TR** *D S MEIKLE,*
TV *K W HOLDER, G S ANDERSON, D GARDNER,*
C *C E HALLIWELL,* **NSM** *P W TAMS*
MILDMAY GROVE (St Jude and St Paul) *Lon 6*
P *Islington Ch Trust* **V** *R S WILLIAMS,* **C** *P G DAY*
MILE CROSS (St Catherine) Horsford and Horsham St
Faith *Nor*
MILE CROSS (St Catherine) *Nor 4* **P** *Dr J P English,
Canon G F Bridger, Rev K W Habershon, and Rev
H Palmer (jt)* **V** *D M SALWAY,* **C** *P L COLEY*
MILE END Old Town (Holy Trinity) Bow H Trin and
All Hallows *Lon*
MILE END Old Town (St Paul) Bow Common *Lon*
MILEHAM (St John the Baptist) Litcham, Kempston,
Lexham, Mileham, Beeston etc *Nor*
MILES PLATTING (St Cuthbert) Man Apostles w
Miles Platting *Man*
MILFORD (Holy Trinity) Belper Ch Ch and Milford
Derby
MILFORD (St John the Evangelist) *Guildf 4* **P** *V Witley*
V *R J WELLS,* **NSM** *D C G BROWN*
MILFORD, SOUTH (St Mary the Virgin) Monk Fryston
and S Milford *York*
MILFORD-ON-SEA (All Saints) *Win 10* **P** *Bp*
V *A M C DUNN*
MILKWALL (St Luke) Coleford w Staunton *Glouc*
MILL END (St Peter) and Heronsgate w West Hyde
St Alb 10 **P** *Bp and V Rickmansworth* **C** *P M FLYNN,*
Hon Par Dn *J A BLANCHARD*
MILL HILL (John Keble Church) *Lon 15* **P** *Bp*
V *O R OSMOND,* **Par Dn** *A M BURDEN,*
Hon C *R M HILLS*
MILL HILL (St Michael and All Angels) *Lon 15* **P** *Bp*
V *D F SHARPE,* **NSM** *R M HILLS*
MILL LODGE (St Mary Magdalene) Shirley *Birm*
MILLAND (St Luke) Lynch w Iping Marsh and Milland
Chich
MILLBROOK (All Saints) St John w Millbrook *Truro*
MILLBROOK (Christ the King) Barton Seagrave w
Warkton *Pet*
MILLBROOK (Holy Trinity) *Win 12* **P** *Bp*
R *R N H HOLYHEAD*
MILLBROOK Regents Park (St Clement) Millbrook
Win
MILLBROOK (St James) *Ches 14* **P** *Bp, V Stalybridge
St Paul, and Mrs E Bissill (jt)* **P-in-c** *A P GOODCHILD*

MILLBROOK (St Michael and All Angels) Ampthill w
Millbrook and Steppingley *St Alb*
MILLERS DALE (St Anne) Tideswell *Derby*
MILLFIELD (St Mark) *Dur 9* **P** *Bp* **V** *M J JACKSON,*
C *C M HOOPER*
MILLFIELD (St Mary) *Dur 9* **P** *The Crown*
P-in-c *B SKELTON*
MILLHOUSES (Holy Trinity) *Sheff 2* **P** *Bp*
V *R W F HOWELL,* **NSM** *I W DRAFFAN*
MILLHOUSES (St Oswald) Sheff St Oswald *Sheff*
MILLINGTON (St Margaret) Pocklington and
Owsthorpe and Kilnwick Percy etc *York*
MILLOM Holburn Hill (Mission) Millom *Carl*
MILLOM (Holy Trinity) (St George) *Carl 8* **P** *Bp and
Trustees (jt)* **V** *S R BURROWS,* **Par Dn** *M E HODGE*
MILNROW (St James) *Man 19* **P** *TR Rochdale*
V *M R EDWARDS,* **NSM** *R WHYBORN*
MILNTHORPE (St Thomas) Beetham and Milnthorpe
Carl
MILSON (St George) Neen Sollars w Milson *Heref*
MILSTEAD (St Mary and the Holy Cross) Bredgar w
Bicknor and Frinsted w Wormshill etc *Cant*
MILSTON (St Mary) Bulford, Figheldean and Milston
Sarum
MILTON (All Saints) *Ely 6* **P** *K Coll Cam* **R** *F J KILNER*
MILTON (St Blaise) Steventon w Milton *Ox*
**MILTON (St James) (St Andrew's Church Centre)
(St Patrick)** *Portsm 6* **P** *V Portsea St Mary*
V *J R HUMPHREYS,* **C** *D F G BUTLIN, B G HIGGINS,*
NSM *L C DENNESS*
MILTON (St John the Evangelist) Adderbury w Milton
Ox
MILTON (St Mary Magdalene) *Win 8* **P** *V Milford*
R *S A OUTHWAITE,* **C** *N A CARTER*
MILTON (St Peter) w St Jude *B & W 12* **P** *Ld Chan*
V *C D TAYLOR,* **C** *M J WYNES*
MILTON (St Philip and St James) *Lich 14* **P** *Bp*
V *P H MYERS*
MILTON (St Simon and St Jude) Gillingham *Sarum*
**MILTON, GREAT (St Mary the Virgin) w LITTLE (St
James) and Great Haseley** *Ox 1* **P** *Bp and
D&C Windsor (jt)* **R** *C R ABBOTT*
MILTON, SOUTH (All Saints) Thurlestone w S Milton
Ex
**MILTON ABBAS (St James the Great), Hilton w
Cheselbourne and Melcombe Horsey** *Sarum 7* **P** *Bp
(3 turns) and G A L F Pitt-Rivers Esq (1 turn)*
R *R S FERGUSON*
**MILTON ABBOT (St Constantine), Dunterton, Lamerton
and Sydenham Demerel** *Ex 25* **P** *Bp,
J W Tremayne Esq and Bedf Estates (jt)* **V** *Vacant
Milton Abbot (082287) 471*
MILTON BRYAN (St Peter) Woburn w Eversholt,
Milton Bryan, Battlesden etc *St Alb*
MILTON CLEVEDON (St James) Evercreech w
Chesterblade and Milton Clevedon *B & W*
MILTON COMBE (Holy Spirit) Buckland Monachorum
Ex
MILTON DAMEREL (Holy Trinity) Holsworthy w
Hollacombe and Milton Damerel *Ex*
MILTON ERNEST (All Saints) *St Alb 21* **P** *Bp*
V *A P MOTTRAM*
MILTON KEYNES (Christ the Cornerstone) *Ox 25* **P** *Bp*
V *D GOLDIE*
MILTON KEYNES VILLAGE (All Saints) Walton
Milton Keynes *Ox*
MILTON LILBOURNE (St Peter) Pewsey Team Min
Sarum
MILTON MALSOR (Holy Cross) Collingtree w
Courteenhall and Milton Malsor *Pet*
MILTON NEXT GRAVESEND (Christ Church) *Roch 4*
P *Bp* **V** *J S KING,* **NSM** *D HITCHCOCK*
**MILTON NEXT GRAVESEND (St Peter and St Paul) w
Denton** *Roch 4* **P** *Bp* **R** *V J LAWRENCE*
MILTON NEXT SITTINGBOURNE (Holy Trinity) *Cant 14*
P *D&C* **V** *W DRURY*
MILTON REGIS (St Mary) Sittingbourne St Mary *Cant*
MILTON-UNDER-WYCHWOOD (St Simon and St
Jude) Shipton-under-Wychwood w Milton-under-
Wychwood *Ox*
MILVERTON (St Michael) w Halse and Fitzhead *B & W 21*
P *Adn Taunton (4 turns), Bp and V Wiveliscombe
(1 turn)* **R** *J G PESCOD*
MILVERTON, NEW (St Mark) *Cov 11* **P** *CPAS*
V *A MORT*
MILVERTON, OLD (St James) Leamington Spa and
Old Milverton *Cov*
MILWICH (All Saints) Fradswell, Gayton, Milwich and
Weston *Lich*

MIMMS, NORTH N Mymms *St Alb*

MIMMS, SOUTH (Christ Church) *Lon 14* P *Ch Patr Trust* C M H McGOWAN, C D J BURGESS, C J P HOBBS, NSM P W LIDDELOW

MINCHINHAMPTON (Holy Trinity) *Glouc 8* P *Bp* R D S YERBURGH, Hon C G P KNOTT, NSM P GRAHAM

MINEHEAD (St Andrew) (St Michael) (St Peter) *B & W 17* P *Lt-Col W Luttrell* V C H SARALIS, C T W HARFORD

MINETY (St Leonard) Ashton Keynes, Leigh and Minety *Bris*

MININGSBY WITH EAST KIRKBY (St Nicholas) Marden Hill Gp *Linc*

MINLEY (St Andrew) *Guildf 1* P *Bp* V I M HANCOCK

MINNIS BAY (St Thomas) Birchington w Acol and Minnis Bay *Cant*

MINSKIP (Mission Room) Aldborough w Boroughbridge and Roecliffe *Ripon*

MINSTEAD (All Saints) Copythorne and Minstead *Win*

MINSTER (St Mary the Virgin) w Monkton *Cant 9* P *Abp* V R C HOULDSWORTH

MINSTER (St Merteriana) Boscastle w Davidstow *Truro*

MINSTER IN SHEPPEY (St Mary and St Sexburga) *Cant 14* P *Ch Patr Trust* V G H SPENCER, C D J BARNES, NSM J G KNELL

MINSTER LOVELL (St Kenelm) and Brize Norton *Ox 8* P *Eton Coll and Ch Ch Ox (jt)* V A W D GABB-JONES

MINSTERLEY (Holy Trinity) *Heref 13* P *DBP and Bp (alt)* V T O MENDEL

MINSTERWORTH (St Peter) Churcham w Bulley and Minsterworth *Glouc*

MINTERNE MAGNA (St Andrew) Cerne Abbas w Godmanstone and Minterne Magna *Sarum*

MINTING (St Andrew) Bardney *Linc*

MIREHOUSE (St Andrew) *Carl 5* P *Bp* V E F H GRIMSHAW

MIRFIELD Eastthorpe (St Paul) *Wakef 10* P *V Mirfield* P-in-c P W LEITCH

MIRFIELD (St Mary) *Wakef 10* P *Bp* V M SQUIRES, C N H S BERSWEDEN

MISERDEN (St Andrew) Bisley, Oakridge, Miserden and Edgeworth *Glouc*

MISSENDEN, GREAT (St Peter and St Paul) w Ballinger and Little Hampden *Ox 28* P *Bp* P-in-c D RYDINGS, NSM J H PIERCE

MISSENDEN, LITTLE (St John the Baptist) *Ox 28* P *Earl Howe* P-in-c D R HEMSLEY

MISSION (St John the Baptist) Bawtry w Austerfield and Misson *S'well*

MISTERTON (All Saints) and West Stockwith *S'well 1* P *D&C York and Bp (alt)* V M F B HARDY

MISTERTON (St Leonard) Haselbury Plucknett, Misterton and N Perrott *B & W*

MISTERTON (St Leonard) N w S Kilworth and Misterton *Leic*

MISTLEY (St Mary and St Michael) w Manningtree and Bradfield *Chelmsf 23* P *DBP and Bp (jt)* R P E PARKER

MITCHAM (Ascension) Pollards Hill *S'wark 11* P *Bp* V Vacant 081-764 1258

MITCHAM (Christ Church) *S'wark 11* P *Bp* V A WHITTLE

MITCHAM (St Barnabas) *S'wark 11* P *Bp* V Vacant 081-648 2571

MITCHAM (St Mark) *S'wark 11* P *Bp* V P R TILLEY, C J G PRYSOR-JONES, Hon C N SUSTINS

MITCHAM (St Olave) *S'wark 11* P *The Crown* V G G THOMPSON

MITCHAM (St Peter and St Paul) *S'wark 11* P *Keble Coll Ox* P-in-c J M SHEPHERD, C M A BUTCHERS, Par Dn J E COUPER

MITCHELDEAN (St Michael and All Angels) Abenhall w Mitcheldean *Glouc*

MITFORD (St Mary Magdalene) *Newc 11* P *Brig E C Mitford* V D A WOOD

MITHIAN (St Peter) w Mount Hawke *Truro 6* P *Bp* V P WOODHALL

MITTON (All Hallows) Hurst Green and Mitton *Bradf*

MITTON, LOWER (St Michael and All Angels) *Worc 12* P *V Kidderminster* V B GILBERT, C A J SMITH

MIXBURY (All Saints) Finmere w Mixbury, Cottisford, Hardwick etc *Ox*

MIXENDEN (Holy Nativity) *Wakef 4* P *Bp* V R J BRADNUM

MOBBERLEY (St Wilfrid) *Ches 12* P *Bp* R M GRAHAM

MOCCAS (St Michael and All Angels) Cusop w Clifford, Hardwicke, Bredwardine etc *Heref*

MODBURY (St George) *Ex 14* P *DBP* V J S COLE

MODDERSHALL (All Saints) Stone Ch Ch and Oulton *Lich*

MOGGERHANGER (St John the Evangelist) Northill w Moggerhanger *St Alb*

MOIRA (St Hilda) Donisthorpe and Moira w Stretton-en-le-Field *Leic*

MOLASH (St Peter) Challock w Molash *Cant*

MOLDGREEN (Christ Church) *Wakef 1* P *R Kirkheaton* V J HARRIS

MOLESCROFT (St Leonard) Beverley Minster *York*

MOLESEY, EAST (St Mary) *Guildf 8* P *Bp* P-in-c D A WOTTON

MOLESEY, EAST (St Paul) *Guildf 8* P *Bp* P-in-c R L COTTON

MOLESEY, WEST (St Peter) *Guildf 8* P *Rev W K Perry-Gore* V W A J YEEND

MOLESWORTH (St Peter) Brington w Molesworth and Old Weston *Ely*

MOLLAND (St Mary) Bishopsnympton, Rose Ash, Mariansleigh etc *Ex*

MOLLINGTON (All Saints) Claydon w Mollington *Ox*

MOLTON, NORTH (All Saints) see below

MOLTON, SOUTH (St Mary Magdalene) w Nymet St George, High Bray, Charles, Filleigh, East Buckland, Warkleigh, Satterleigh, Chittlehamholt, Kingsnympton, Romansleigh, North Molton, Twitchen and Chittlehampton *Ex 19* P *DBP* TR M J HOMEWOOD, TV G COWDRY, J S WHITE, J H BELL, C W H N WATTS

MONEWDEN (St Mary) Charsfield w Debach, Monewden, Hoo etc *St E*

MONGEHAM, GREAT (St Martin) w Ripple and Sutton by Dover *Cant 8* P *Abp* R A C STRATTA

MONK BRETTON (St Paul) *Wakef 7* P *V Royston* V C IRVING, C R C MACKINNON

MONK FRYSTON (St Wilfrid of Ripon) and South Milford *York 6* P *Ld Chan and Abp (alt)* R Vacant South Milford (0977) 682357

MONK SHERBORNE (All Saints) The Sherbornes w Pamber *Win*

MONK SOHAM (St Peter) Worlingworth, Southolt, Tannington, Bedfield etc *St E*

MONKEN HADLEY (St Mary the Virgin) *Lon 14* P *N A Dove Esq* R J A M JENKINS

MONKHESLEDEN (St Mary w St John) Castle Eden w Monkhesleden *Dur*

MONKHOPTON (St Peter) Upton Cressett w Monk Hopton *Heref*

MONKLAND (All Saints) Leominster *Heref*

MONKLEIGH (St George) Landcross, Littleham, Monkleigh etc *Ex*

MONKOKEHAMPTON (All Saints) *Ex 20* P *Bp* R Vacant

MONKS COPPENHALL (Christ Church) Crewe Ch Ch and St Pet *Ches*

MONKS ELEIGH (St Peter) w Chelsworth and Brent Eleigh w Milden *St E 10* P *Ld Chan (2 turns), M J Hawkins Esq (1 turn), and Bp (1 turn)* R R A BIRD

MONKS HORTON (St Peter) Sellindge w Monks Horton and Stowting etc *Cant*

MONKS KIRBY (St Editha) w Pailton and Stretton-under-Fosse *Cov 6* P *Trin Coll Cam* V P S RUSSELL, NSM D J BAYFORD

MONKS RISBOROUGH (St Dunstan) *Ox 26* P *Bp* R P D C AMOR, NSM A A TAYLOR

MONKSEATON (St Mary) *Newc 8* P *Bp* V J L HALLATT, C A J HALE, Hon C C G BELLAMY

MONKSEATON (St Peter) *Newc 8* P *Bp* V P J DUNLOP, C N WILSON

MONKSILVER (All Saints) Stogumber w Nettlecombe and Monksilver *B & W*

MONKTON (St Mary Magdalene) Minster w Monkton *Cant*

MONKTON (St Mary Magdalene) Honiton, Gittisham, Combe Raleigh, Monkton etc *Ex*

MONKTON, WEST (St Augustine) *B & W 20* P *Bp* R R SCHOFIELD

MONKTON COMBE (St Michael) Combe Down w Monkton Combe and S Stoke *B & W*

MONKTON FARLEIGH (St Peter), South Wraxall and Winsley *Sarum 17* P *D&C Bris (2 turns), Bp (1 turn)* R D G SMITH, NSM M A CLARK

MONKTON WYLD (St Andrew) Marshwood Vale Team Min *Sarum*

MONKWEARMOUTH (All Saints) *Dur 9* P *Bp* V M BARBER

MONKWEARMOUTH (St Andrew) *Dur 9* P *Bp* V M L BECK, C A J GREADY, Par Dn G M BECK

MONKWEARMOUTH (St Peter) *Dur 9* P *Bp* C E G LLOYD

MONKWOOD (Mission Church)   Bishop's Sutton and Ropley and W Tisted *Win*

MONNINGTON-ON-WYE (St Mary)   Letton w Staunton, Byford, Mansel Gamage etc *Heref*

MONTACUTE (St Catherine) *B & W* 7   **P** *Bp*   **V** *Vacant*

MONTFORD (St Chad)   Bicton, Montford w Shrawardine and Fitz *Lich*

MONTON (St Paul) *Man* 2   **P** *TR Eccles* **V** V H MARKLAND

MONXTON (St Mary)   Amport, Grateley, Monxton and Quarley *Win*

MONYASH (St Leonard)   Taddington, Chelmorton and Flagg, and Monyash *Derby*

MOOR (St Thomas)   Fladbury, Wyre Piddle and Moor *Worc*

MOOR ALLERTON (St John the Evangelist) (St Stephen) *Ripon* 5   **P** *Patr Bd*   **TR** J D W KING, **TV** P JACKSON, W I BARBOUR,   **Par Dn** P A RIDING

MOOR GRANGE (St Andrew)   Hawksworth Wood *Ripon*

MOOR MILNER (Church Institute)   Daresbury *Ches*

MOOR MONKTON (All Saints)   Rufforth w Moor Monkton and Hessay *York*

MOORBRIDGE LANE (St Luke)   Stapleford *S'well*

MOORCOURT (St Mary)   Pembridge w Moorcourt, Shobdon, Staunton etc *Heref*

MOORDOWN (St John the Baptist) *Win* 7   **P** *Bp* **P-in-c** W A SWAIN

MOORENDS (St Wilfrith) *Sheff* 11   **P** *Bp* **V** N D SENNITT

MOORHOUSE (Chantry Chapel)   Kneesall w Laxton and Wellow *S'well*

MOORHOUSES (St Lawrence)   Mareham-le-Fen and Revesby *Linc*

MOORLINCH (Blessed Virgin Mary)   Middlezoy and Othery and Moorlinch *B & W*

MOORSHOLM (St Mary)   Boosbeck w Moorsholm *York*

MORBORNE (All Saints)   Stilton w Denton and Caldecote etc *Ely*

MORCHARD BISHOP (St Mary)   N Creedy *Ex*

MORCOTT (St Mary the Virgin) w Glaston and Bisbrooke *Pet* 14   **P** *Coutts & Co and Peterho Cam (alt)* **R** K P LINGARD

MORDEN (Emmanuel Church Hall) (St George) (St Lawrence) (St Martin) *S'wark* 11   **P** *Patr Bd* **TR** R F SKINNER,   **TV** W J N DURANT, R M de VIAL, W MUNCEY,   **C** P J DYKES

MORDEN (St Mary)   Red Post *Sarum*

MORDIFORD (Holy Rood)   Hampton Bishop and Mordiford w Dormington *Heref*

MORE (St Peter)   Wentnor w Ratlinghope, Myndtown, Norbury etc *Heref*

MOREBATH (St George)   Bampton, Morebath, Clayhanger and Petton *Ex*

MORECAMBE (St Barnabas) *Blackb* 12   **P** *R Poulton-le-Sands*   **V** *Vacant* Morecambe (0524) 411283

MORELEIGH (All Saints)   Halwell w Moreleigh *Ex*

MORESBY (St Bridget) *Carl* 5   **P** *Earl of Lonsdale* **R** G D A THORBURN

MORESBY PARKS (Mission Church)   Moresby *Carl*

MORESTEAD (not known)   Twyford and Owslebury and Morestead *Win*

MORETON (Christ Church) *Ches* 8   **P** *Simeon's Trustees* **R** R A WALTON,   **C** P H DAVIES

MORETON Hall Estate St Edmund Conventional District *St E* 13   **Min** J L ALDERTON-FORD

MORETON (St Mary)   Fyfield and Moreton w Bobbingworth *Chelmsf*

MORETON (St Mary) and Church Eaton *Lich* 16   **P** *Bp and V Gnosall (alt)*   **R** *Vacant* Stafford (0785) 823091

MORETON (St Nicholas) and Woodsford w Tincleton *Sarum* 2   **P** *Hon Mrs M A Bartenk and Miss M B F Frampton (alt)*   **R** P D STEVENS

MORETON, SOUTH (St John the Baptist) w NORTH (All Saints), Aston Tirrold and Aston Upthorpe *Ox* 18   **P** *Adn Berks, Hertf Coll Ox, and Magd Coll Ox (jt)* **R** A FOTTER

MORETON CORBET (St Bartholomew) *Lich* 29   **P** *Sir John Corbet, Bt*   **R** *Vacant*

MORETON-IN-MARSH (St David) w Batsford, Todenham and Lower Lemington *Glouc* 15   **P** *Bp and Lord Dulverton (jt)*   **R** T C EKIN,   **NSM** J B HILLS

MORETON MORRELL (Holy Cross)   Newbold Pacey w Moreton Morrell *Cov*

MORETON-ON-LUGG (St Andrew)   Wellington w Pipe-cum-Lyde and Moreton-on-Lugg *Heref*

MORETON PINKNEY (St Mary the Virgin)   Weedon Lois w Plumpton and Moreton Pinkney etc *Pet*

MORETON SAY (St Margaret of Antioch) *Lich* 24   **P** *A E H Heber-Percy Esq*   **P-in-c** P A LEONARD-JOHNSON,   **C** J H GRAHAM

MORETON VALENCE (St Stephen)   Standish w Haresfield and Moreton Valence etc *Glouc*

MORETONHAMPSTEAD (St Andrew), North Bovey and Manaton *Ex* 11   **P** *Bp (3 turns), DBP (1 turn)* **R** J H HEATH

MORGAN'S VALE (St Birinus)   Redlynch and Morgan's Vale *Sarum*

MORLAND (St Lawrence), Thrimby and Great Strickland *Carl* 1   **P** *D&C*   **V** M H CROSS

MORLEY (St Botolph) (St Peter) w Deopham, Hackford, Wicklewood and Crownthorpe *Nor* 13   **P** *Bp, D&C Cant, Earl of Kimberley, A E H Heber-Percy Esq, and D&C Nor (jt)*   **R** J HALL

MORLEY (St Matthew) *Derby* 12   **P** *Bp* **P-in-c** M A ROYLE,   **Hon C** A C ROBERTSON

MORLEY (St Paul) Townend *Wakef* 8   **P** *V Batley and V Morley St Peter (alt)*   **V** I D JOHNSTONE

MORLEY (St Peter) w Churwell *Wakef* 8   **P** *Bp* **V** J H CATLEY

MORNINGTHORPE (St John the Baptist)   Hempnall *Nor*

MORPETH (St Aidan) (St James) (St Mary the Virgin) *Newc* 11   **P** *Bp*   **R** A S CRAIG,   **C** S J LIDDLE, W RIGBY

MORSTON (All Saints)   Stiffkey and Cockthorpe w Morston, Langham etc *Nor*

MORTEHOE (St Mary Magdalene)   Ilfracombe, Lee, Woolacombe, Bittadon etc *Ex*

MORTIMER COMMON (St John)   Stratfield Mortimer *Ox*

MORTIMER WEST END (St Saviour) w Padworth *Ox* 12   **P** *Englefield Est Trust and Ld Chan (alt)* **P-in-c** J A ELLIS

MORTLAKE (St Mary) w East Sheen *S'wark* 15   **P** *Patr Bd*   **TR** B A SAUNDERS,   **TV** J C ANSELL, M A JOHNSON,   **C** P R WELLS,   **Hon C** P D KING

MORTOMLEY (St Saviour) *Sheff* 7   **P** *Bp* **V** D G RHODES,   **C** N A DAWSON

MORTON (Holy Cross) and Stonebroom *Derby* 1   **P** *Bp (2 turns), St Jo Coll Cam (1 turn)*   **R** *Vacant* Ripley (0773) 872470

MORTON (St Denis)   Rolleston w Fiskerton, Morton and Upton *S'well*

MORTON (St John the Baptist) w Hacconby *Linc* 13   **P** *Bp*   **V** F C YOUNG

MORTON (St Luke) *Bradf* 8   **P** *Bp*   **V** A M E BROWN

MORTON (St Paul) *Linc* 2   **P** *Bp*   **V** D F BOUTLE

MORTON (St Philip and St James) *Lich* 25   **P** *Ld Chan* **V** T VILLIERS,   **C** D PEARSON

MORTON BAGOT (Holy Trinity)   Spernall, Morton Bagot and Oldberrow *Cov*

MORVAH (St Bridget of Sweden)   Pendeen w Morvah *Truro*

MORVAL (St Wenna)   Liskeard, St Keyne, St Pinnock, Morval etc *Truro*

MORVILLE (St Gregory) w Aston Eyre *Heref* 9   **P** *DBP* **Hon C** H J PATTERSON

MORWENSTOW (St John the Baptist)   Kilkhampton w Morwenstow *Truro*

MOSBOROUGH (St Mark) *Sheff* 1   **P** *Bp* **V** R F NEWMAN,   **C** P J MOTT

MOSELEY (St Agnes) *Birm* 8   **P** *V Moseley St Mary* **V** D J NEW

MOSELEY (St Anne) *Birm* 8   **P** *V Moseley St Mary* **V** L C BROTHERTON

MOSELEY (St Mary) *Birm* 8   **P** *Bp*   **V** H J OSBORNE, **C** D S McDONOUGH,   **Hon C** J G HASLAM,   **Dss** J A GRIFFIN

MOSLEY COMMON (St John) *Man* 13   **P** *Bp* **V** A J LINDOP

MOSS BANK (Mission Church)   Carr Mill *Liv*

MOSS SIDE (Christ Church) *Man* 4   **P** *Trustees* **R** H OGDEN

MOSS SIDE (St James w St Clement) *Man* 4   **P** *Bp* **R** G A WHEALE,   **Hon C** D M SEBER

MOSSER (St Philip) (Michael's Chapel) *Carl* 6   **P** *Bp* **V** C GODDARD

MOSSLEY HILL (St Barnabas) *Liv* 4   **P** *Bp* **V** D POSTLES

MOSSLEY (Holy Trinity) *Ches* 11   **P** *R Astbury* **V** G C W MATTHEWS

MOSSLEY (St George) *Man* 17   **P** *R Ashton-under-Lyne St Mich*   **V** R J LINDSAY

MOSSLEY ESTATE (St Thomas Church)   Bloxwich *Lich*

MOSSLEY HILL (St Matthew and St James) *Liv 4*
 P *Trustees* **V** D E WILLS, **C** C G HOUGHTON
MOSSWOOD (St Barnabas) Cannock *Lich*
MOSTERTON (St Mary) Beaminster Area *Sarum*
MOSTON (St Chad) *Man 5* **P** *Bp* **R** G O'NEILL
MOSTON (St John) Ashley Lane *Man 5* **P** *Bp*
 R N D HAWLEY
MOSTON (St Luke) Lightbowne *Man*
MOSTON (St Mary) *Man 5* **P** *D&C* **R** D J LOW
MOTCOMBE (St Mary) Shaston *Sarum*
MOTSPUR PARK (Holy Cross) *S'wark 11* **P** *Bp*
 V D G MIHILL
MOTTINGHAM (St Andrew) (St Alban Mission Church)
 S'wark 1 **P** *Bp* **P-in-c** M R KEMP,
 Par Dn Y V CLARKE, **Hon C** J R W ACKLAND,
 NSM D WARREN
MOTTINGHAM (St Edward the Confessor) *S'wark 1*
 P *Bp* **P-in-c** W G CAMPEN
MOTTISFONT (St Andrew) Broughton, Bossington,
 Houghton and Mottisfont *Win*
MOTTISTONE (St Peter and St Paul) Brighstone and
 Brooke w Mottistone *Portsm*
MOTTRAM IN LONGDENDALE (St Michael) w
 Woodhead *Ches 14* **P** *Bp* **V** A J REES,
 NSM R L HILLS
MOULSECOOMB (St Andrew) *Chich 2* **P** *Bp*
 TR C R LANSDALE, **TV** P R SEAMAN, D J BIGGS,
 C J A LUSTED
MOULSFORD (St John the Baptist) Streatley w
 Moulsford *Ox*
MOULSHAM (St John the Evangelist) *Chelmsf 11*
 P *Provost Chelmsf* **V** J C HASSELL
MOULSHAM (St Luke) *Chelmsf 11* **P** *Bp*
 V R E FARRELL, **C** B BROWN
MOULSOE (Assumption of the Blessed Virgin Mary)
 Streatley w Moulsford *Ox*
MOULTON (All Saints) (Mission Room) *Linc 17* **P** *DBP*
 V *Vacant* Holbeach (0406) 370791
MOULTON (Mission Church) Middleton Tyas w Croft
 and Eryholme *Ripon*
MOULTON (St James) Cowbit *Linc*
MOULTON (St Peter) Gazeley w Dalham, Moulton and
 Kentford *St E*
MOULTON (St Peter and St Paul) *Pet 4* **P** *Ch Soc Trust*
 V V H J GILLETT
MOULTON (St Stephen the Martyr) *Ches 6*
 P *R Davenham* **V** J CORRADINE
MOULTON, GREAT (St Michael) Bunwell, Carleton
 Rode, Tibenham, Gt Moulton etc *Nor*
MOUNT BURES (St John) Wormingford, Mt Bures and
 Lt Horkesley *Chelmsf*
MOUNT HAWKE (St John the Baptist) Mithian w Mt
 Hawke *Truro*
MOUNT PELLON (Christ Church) *Wakef 4* **P** *Bp*
 V A J FOSTER, **Hon C** H MAKIN
MOUNTFIELD (All Saints) Brightling, Dallington,
 Mountfield & Netherfield *Chich*
MOUNTNESSING (St Giles) Doddinghurst and
 Mountnessing *Chelmsf*
MOUNTSORREL (Christ Church) (St Peter) *Leic 7*
 P *CPAS and Bp* **V** G F J CRATE
MOW COP (St Luke's Mission Church) Odd Rode *Ches*
MOW COP (St Thomas) *Lich 17* **P** *Prime Min*
 V A NORKETT
MOWSLEY (St Nicholas) Husbands Bosworth w
 Mowsley and Knaptoft etc *Leic*
MOXLEY (All Saints) *Lich 8* **P** *Prime Min* **V** *Vacant*
 Bilston (0902) 491807
MUCH: *see also under substantive place names*
MUCH BIRCH (St Mary and St Thomas a Becket) w
 Little Birch, Much Dewchurch, Llanwarne and
 Llandinabo *Heref 4* **P** *A W Twiston-Davies Esq*
 (1 turn), Bp (3 turns), and Ld Chan (1 turn)
 R C G HOLLOWOOD, **C** P H WILSON,
 Hon C K B GARLICK, **NSM** D J ENOCH
MUCHELNEY (St Peter and St Paul) Langport Area
 Chs *B & W*
MUCKLESTONE (St Mary) *Lich 13* **P** *Mrs F F Friend*
 R *Vacant* Ashley (063087) 2210
MUDEFORD (All Saints) Christchurch *Win*
MUDFORD (Blessed Virgin Mary) Chilton Cantelo,
 Ashington, Mudford, Rimpton etc *B & W*
MUGGINTON (All Saints) and Kedleston *Derby 11*
 P *Major J W Chandos-Pole* **P-in-c** D HUGHES,
 NSM P SIMPKIN, **Hon Par Dn** D L SIMPKIN
MUGGLESWICK (All Saints) Blanchland w
 Hunstanworth and Edmundbyers etc *Newc*
MUKER (St Mary) Swaledale *Ripon*

MULBARTON (St Mary Magdalene) w Kenningham
 Nor 13 **P** *Mrs R M Watkinson* **R** R A JAMES
MULLION (St Mellanus) *Truro 4* **P** *Bp*
 V B F THOMPSON
MUMBY (St Thomas of Canterbury) Willoughby *Linc*
MUNCASTER (St Michael) Eskdale, Irton, Muncaster
 and Waberthwaite *Carl*
MUNDEN, LITTLE (All Saints) The Mundens w
 Sacombe *St Alb*
MUNDENS, THE w Sacombe *St Alb 8* **P** *Ch Trust Fund*
 Trust, K Coll Cam, and R M A Smith Esq (jt)
 R A G MORTON
MUNDESLEY (All Saints) Trunch *Nor*
MUNDFORD (St Leonard) w Lynford *Nor 18* **P** *Ch Patr*
 Trust **P-in-c** R O DAVIES
MUNDHAM (St Peter) Brooke, Kirstead, Mundham w
 Seething and Thwaite *Nor*
MUNDHAM, NORTH (St Stephen) w Hunston and
 Merston *Chich 3* **P** *St Jo Coll Cam* **R** V C de R MALAN
MUNGRISDALE (St Kentigern) Greystoke,
 Matterdale, Mungrisdale & W'millock *Carl*
MUNSLEY (St Bartholomew) Tarrington w Stoke
 Edith, Aylton, Pixley etc *Heref*
MUNSLOW (St Michael) Diddlebury w Munslow,
 Holdgate and Tugford *Heref*
MUNSTER SQUARE (Christ Church) (St Mary
 Magdalene) *Lon 17* **P** *Bp* **V** M J MARKEY
MUNSTONE (Church Room) Holmer w Huntington
 Heref
MURCOTT (Mission Room) Islip w Charlton on
 Otmoor, Oddington, Noke etc *Ox*
MURROW (Corpus Christi) Southea w Murrow and
 Parson Drove *Ely*
MURSLEY (St Mary the Virgin) w Swanbourne and Little
 Horwood *Ox 26* **P** *Ch Soc Trust, Ch Patr Soc, and Hon*
 J T Fremantle (by turn) **R** S L WILMOT
MURSTON (All Saints) w Bapchild and Tonge *Cant 14*
 P *Abp and St Jo Coll Cam (jt)* **R** *Vacant*
 Sittingbourne (0795) 72929
MURTON (St James) Osbaldwick w Murton *York*
MURTON (St John the Baptist) Appleby *Carl*
MUSBURY (St Michael) Colyton, Southleigh, Offwell,
 Widworthy etc *Ex*
MUSBURY (St Thomas) *Blackb 1* **P** *The Crown*
 V A SOWERBUTTS
MUSGRAVE (St Theobald) Brough w Stainmore,
 Musgrave and Warcop *Carl*
MUSKHAM, NORTH (St Wilfrid) and South Muskham
 S'well 3 **P** *Ld Chan* **V** R B FEARN
MUSKHAM, SOUTH (St Wilfrid) N and S Muskham
 S'well
MUSTON (All Saints) Hunmanby w Muston *York*
MUSTON (St John the Baptist) Bottesford and Muston
 Leic
MUSWELL HILL (St James) (St Matthew) *Lon 20* **P** *Bp*
 and CPAS (jt) **V** M BUNKER,
 C J M WOOD, G J WILLIAMS, **Hon C** P F WATSON
MUTFORD (St Andrew) Carlton Colville w Mutford
 and Rushmere *Nor*
MYDDLE (St Peter) *Lich 29* **P** *Bp* **R** C P COLLIS SMITH
MYDDLETON SQUARE (St Mark) *Lon 6* **P** *City Corp*
 P-in-c B A BOUCHER
MYLAND (St Michael) Colchester St Mich Myland
 Chelmsf
MYLOR (St Mylor) w Flushing *Truro 3* **P** *Bp* **V** *Vacant*
 Falmouth (0326) 74408
MYLOR BRIDGE (All Saints) Mylor w Flushing *Truro*
MYMMS, NORTH (St Mary) (St Michael) *St Alb 7* **P** *Bp*
 V T W J RANSON, **Hon Par Dn** M K ROBINS
MYMMS, SOUTH (King Charles the Martyr) *St Alb 2*
 P *Bp Lon* **V** R H WILLIAMS, **NSM** D M WILLIAMS
MYMMS, SOUTH (St Giles) and Ridge *St Alb 2* **P** *DBP*
 V R E GAGE
MYNDTOWN (St John the Baptist) Wentnor w
 Ratlinghope, Myndtown, Norbury etc *Heref*
MYTHOLMROYD (St Michael) *Wakef 3* **P** *Bp*
 V D C HODGSON
MYTON ON SWALE (St Mary) Brafferton w Pilmoor,
 Myton on Swale etc *York*
NABB (Mission Church) Wrockwardine Wood *Lich*
NACKINGTON (St Mary) Petham and Waltham w
 Lower Hardres etc *Cant*
NACTON (St Martin) and Levington w Bucklesham and
 Foxhall *St E 2* **P** *DBP* **R** G L GRANT
NAFFERTON (All Saints) w Wansford *York 11* **P** *Abp*
 V J R BOOTH
NAILSEA (Christ Church) *B & W 14* **P** *R Nailsea*
 V A Q H WHEELER, **C** S D PAYNTER

NAILSEA (Holy Trinity) *B & W 14*   **P** *MMCET*
  R J T SIMONS, **C** R LANDALL
NAILSTONE (All Saints) and Carlton w Shackerstone
  Leic 13   **P** *The Crown and DBP (alt)*   **R** W E QUINNEY
NAILSWORTH (St George) *Glouc 16*   **P** *Bp*
  V J D STRONG
NANPANTAN (St Mary in Charnwood) Loughb Em
  Leic
NANPEAN (St George) St Stephen in Brannel *Truro*
NANSTALLION (St Stephen's Mission Room) Bodmin
  w Lanhydrock and Lanivet *Truro*
NANTWICH (St Mary) *Ches 15*   **P** *Q H Crewe Esq and*
  J C Crewe Esq (jt)   **R** J R PRICE, **C** W J MUSSON,
  NSM C I WELLS
NAPTON-ON-THE-HILL (St Lawrence), Lower
  Shuckburgh and Stockton *Cov 10*   **P** *Ld Chan (2 turns),*
  Sir Rupert Shuckburgh, Bt (1 turn), and New Coll Ox
  (2 turns)   **R** P L JACKSON
NARBOROUGH (All Saints) and Huncote *Leic 10*
  P *SMF*   **R** N J BURTON
NARBOROUGH (All Saints) w Narford *Nor 23*   **P** *Bp*
  V S R NAIRN
NARFORD (St Mary) Narborough w Narford *Nor*
NASEBY (All Saints) Clipston w Naseby and Haselbech
  w Kelmarsh *Pet*
NASH (All Saints) w Thornton, Beachampton and
  Thornborough *Ox 22*   **P** *Mrs S Doulton (2 turns),*
  Sir Ralph Verney, Bt (2 turns), and G & C Coll Cam
  (1 turn)   **P-in-c** A K PRING
NASH (St John the Baptist) Burford I *Heref*
NASSINGTON (St Mary the Virgin and All Saints) w
  Yarwell and Woodnewton *Pet 12*   **P** *Lord Brassey and*
  Bp (alt)   **V** C J PEARSON
NATELY SCURES (St Swithun) Newnham w Nately
  Scures w Mapledurwell etc *Win*
NATLAND (St Mark) *Carl 9*   **P** *V Kendal H Trin*
  V T PARK, **NSM** M P JAYNE
NAUGHTON (St Mary) Whatfield w Semer, Nedging
  and Naughton *St E*
NAUNTON (St Andrew) Upper and Lower Slaughter w
  Eyford and Naunton *Glouc*
NAUNTON BEAUCHAMP (St Bartholomew)
  Abberton, Naunton Beauchamp and Bishampton etc
  Worc
NAVENBY (St Peter) Graffoe *Linc*
NAVESTOCK (St Thomas) *Chelmsf 10*   **P** *Bp*
  P-in-c J D BROWN
NAWTON (St Hilda) Kirkdale *York*
NAYLAND (St James) w Wiston *St E 3*   **P** *Ld Chan*
  (2 turns) and DBP (1 turn)   **V** D A C STRANACK,
  Hon C D B WATLING
NAYLAND DRIVE (Church Centre) Clacton St Jas
  Chelmsf
NAZEING (All Saints) (St Giles) *Chelmsf 3*   **P** *Ld Chan*
  V M D WEBSTER, **NSM** P A VOSS
NEASDEN (St Catherine w St Paul) *Lon 21*   **P** *Bp and*
  D&C St Paul's (jt)   **V** E E GAUNT
NEATISHEAD (St Peter), Barton Turf and Irstead *Nor 9*
  P *Bp*   **R** A E GREEN
NECHELLS (St Clement) Duddeston w Nechells *Birm*
NECTON (All Saints) w Holme Hale *Nor 18*   **P** *Major-*
  Gen Robin Broke and MMCET (alt)   **R** P J TAYLOR,
  C R K EAST
NEDGING (St Mary) Whatfield w Semer, Nedging and
  Naughton *St E*
NEEDHAM (St Peter) Redenhall, Harleston, Wortwell
  and Needham *Nor*
NEEDHAM MARKET (St John the Baptist) w Badley
  St E 1   **P** *PCC*   **V** R S STRINGER
NEEN SAVAGE (St Mary) w Kinlet *Heref 12*   **P** *Ld Chan*
  and R E B Childe Esq (alt)   **V** *Vacant*
NEEN SOLLARS (All Saints) w Milson *Heref 12*   **P** *Worc*
  Coll Ox   **P-in-c** R A HORSFIELD
NEENTON (All Saints) Ditton Priors w Neenton,
  Burwarton etc *Heref*
NEITHROP (St Paul) Banbury *Ox*
NELSON (St Bede) *Blackb 7*   **P** *Bp*   **V** G L CROOK
NELSON St Mary Nelson in Lt Marsden *Blackb*
NELSON (St Philip) *Blackb 7*   **P** *Bp*   **V** S J R HARTLEY,
  NSM E J BOOTH
NELSON IN LITTLE MARSDEN St Mary *Blackb 7*
  P *Trustees*   **V** S BAXTER
NEMPNETT THRUBWELL (The Blessed Virgin Mary)
  Chew Stoke w Nempnett Thrubwell *B & W*
NENTHEAD (St John) Alston Team *Newc*
NESS, GREAT (St Andrew) Ruyton XI Towns w Gt
  and Lt Ness *Lich*
NESS, LITTLE (St Martin) as above

NESTON (St Mary and St Helen) *Ches 9*   **P** *D&C*
  V A V SHUFFLEBOTHAM, **C** P. BOYLES,
  Par Dn D V COOKSON
NESTON (St Philip and St James) Gtr Corsham *Bris*
NESTON, LITTLE (St Michael and All Angels) Neston
  Ches
NETHER: *see under substantive place name*
NETHERAVON (All Saints) w Fittleton and Enford
  Sarum 12   **P** *Ch Hosp (1 turn), Bp (2 turns)*
  V P R L POWNE
NETHERBURY (St Mary) Beaminster Area *Sarum*
NETHEREXE (St John the Baptist) Stoke Canon,
  Poltimore w Huxham and Rewe etc *Ex*
NETHERFIELD (St George) w Colwick *S'well 11*   **P** *DBP*
  R R W H MILLER, **Hon C** K D WILLIAMS
NETHERFIELD (St John the Baptist) Brightling,
  Dallington, Mountfield & Netherfield *Chich*
NETHERHAMPTON (St Katherine) Wilton w
  Netherhampton and Fugglestone *Sarum*
NETHERLEY (Christ Church) Gateacre *Liv*
NETHERNE (St Luke) Merstham and Gatton *S'wark*
NETHERSEAL (St Peter) Nether and Over Seale *Derby*
NETHERTHONG (All Saints) Upper Holme Valley
  Wakef
NETHERTHORPE (St Bartholomew) (St Stephen) *Sheff 4*
  P *Patr Bd*   **TM** J L BROWN,
  TV W F BAZELY, N A CLEMAS
NETHERTON (All Souls) *Carl 7*   **P** *Bp*   **V** N W CARTER
NETHERTON (St Andrew) Middlestown *Wakef*
NETHERTON (St Andrew) *Worc 9*   **P** *V Dudley*
  V F J WILLCOX
NETHERTON (St Oswald) *Liv 1*   **P** *Bp*   **V** A A ROSS,
  C T RICH, C WARRILOW
NETHERWITTON (St Giles) *Newc 11*   **P** *Ld Chan*
  P-in-c W A GOFTON
NETLEY ABBEY Hound *Win*
NETLEY MARSH (St Matthew) Totton *Win*
NETTLEBED (St Bartholomew) w Bix and Highmore *Ox 6*
  P *Ch Patr Trust, Earl of Macclesfield, DBP, and*
  R Rotherfield Greys (jt)   **R** B J WEAVER
NETTLECOMBE (Blessed Virgin Mary) Stogumber w
  Nettlecombe and Monksilver *B & W*
NETTLEDEN (Ashridge Chapel) Potten End w
  Nettleden *St Alb*
NETTLEDEN (St Lawrence) as above
NETTLEHAM (All Saints) *Linc 3*   **P** *Bp*
  V A W J BURTON
NETTLESTEAD (St Mary) Gt and Lt Blakenham w
  Baylham and Nettlestead *St E*
NETTLESTEAD (St Mary the Virgin) E Peckham and
  Nettlestead *Roch*
NETTLETON (St John the Baptist) Swallow *Linc*
NETTLETON (St Mary) w Littleton Drew *Bris 9*   **P** *Bp*
  and Adn Swindon (alt)   **P-in-c** J N A BRADBURY
NEVENDON (St Peter) Basildon, St Martin of Tours w
  Nevendon *Chelmsf*
NEVILLE'S CROSS (St John) Conventional District *Dur 2*
  P *Bp*   **C-in-c** M F RUSK
NEW: *see also under substantive names*
NEW BOROUGH and Leigh (St John) *Sarum 10*
  P *Ch Soc Trust*   **V** B W J LOMAX, **C** P W HUNTER
NEW BUILDINGS (Beacon Church) Sandford w Upton
  Hellions *Ex*
NEW FERRY (St Mark) *Ches 8*   **P** *R Bebington*
  V D F WALKER, **C** E W McLEOD
NEW HAW (All Saints) *Guildf 11*   **P** *Bp*   **V** G J TICKNER,
  NSM J S RICHARDS, R A MILLER
NEW MILL (Christ Church) Upper Holme Valley
  Wakef
NEW MILLS (St George) (St James the Less) *Derby 6*
  P *V Glossop*   **V** J H K NORTON, **C** J MORTON
NEW SPRINGS (St John) *Liv 14*   **P** *Bp*
  P-in-c J C SHARPLES
NEWALL GREEN (St Francis of Assisi) *Man 8*   **P** *Bp*
  V A ATHERTON
NEWARK-UPON-TRENT (St Mary Magdalene) (St
  Augustine's Mission Church) (Christ Church) (St
  Leonard) *S'well 3*   **P** *The Crown*   **TR** R A J HILL,
  TV G K KNOTT, A HOWES,
  C J M FOLLETT, S R MEPHAM, H M WALKER
NEWBALD (St Nicholas) *York 14*   **P** *Abp*   **V** J WALKER
NEWBARNS (St Paul) w Hawcoat *Carl 8*   **P** *DBP*
  R C C JENKIN, **C** S W OSMAN
NEWBIGGIN (St Edmund) Kirkby Thore w Temple
  Sowerby and w Newbiggin *Carl*
NEWBIGGIN-BY-THE-SEA (St Bartholomew)
  Woodhorn w Newbiggin *Newc*
NEWBIGGIN HALL (St Wilfrid) Whorlton *Newc*

NEWBOLD (St John the Evangelist) and Dunston *Derby 5*
  P *V Chesterfield* **R** R J ROSS,
  C A C BEDELL, A H HART,
  NSM P S RHODES, J E HUNT, S I MITCHELL
NEWBOLD (St Peter)   Rochdale *Man*
NEWBOLD DE VERDUN (St James) and Kirkby Mallory
 Leic 13 **P** *Bp and Trin Coll Ox (jt)* **R** C E FOX
NEWBOLD ON AVON (St Botolph) *Cov 6*
  P *H A F W Boughton Leigh Esq* **V** P M WILKINSON
NEWBOLD ON STOUR (St David)   Tredington and
 Darlingscott w Newbold on Stour *Cov*
NEWBOLD PACEY (St George) w Moreton Morrell *Cov 8*
  P *Qu Coll Ox and Lt-Col J E Little (alt)*
  P-in-c E J A BRAZIER
NEWBOROUGH (All Saints)   Hanbury w Newborough
 Lich
NEWBOROUGH (St Bartholomew) *Pet 13* **P** *The Crown*
  V K P FITZGIBBON
NEWBOTTLE (St James)   King's Sutton and Newbottle
 and Charlton *Pet*
NEWBOTTLE (St Matthew) *Dur 6* **P** *Bp* **V** S R TAYLOR
NEWBOURN (St Mary)   Waldringfield w Hemley and
 Newbourn *St E*
NEWBROUGH (St Peter)   Warden w Newbrough *Newc*
NEWBURGH (Christ Church) *Liv 11* **P** *Bp*
  P-in-c N T B DEANE, **NSM** D M BURROWS
NEWBURN (St Michael and All Angels) *Newc 7*
  P M M CET **V** R G BATEMAN,
  C S J T GATENBY, D E CANT
NEWBURY (St John the Evangelist) (St Nicholas and
 St Mary) *Ox 14* **P** *Bp* **TR** D C M COOK,
  TV G E BENNETT, J W D CARTWRIGHT,
  C S A WHITMORE, **NSM** J H G LEWIS
NEWBY (St Mark) *York 16* **P** *Abp* **V** S FOX
NEWCASTLE (Christ Church) (St Ann) *Newc 5* **P** *Bp*
  V G J WILLIAMS
NEWCASTLE (Epiphany) *Newc 5* **P** *Bp*
  TR D J ELKINGTON, **TV** M THOMPSON,
  TM J I COLLINSON, **C** E F WOOD
NEWCASTLE (St Andrew) (St Luke) *Newc 5* **P** *Bp and*
 V Gosforth St Nic (jt) **V** A W J MAGNESS
NEWCASTLE (St John the Evangelist)   Clun w Bettws-
 y-Crwyn and Newc *Heref*
NEWCASTLE (St Philip) and (St Augustine) *Newc 7*
  P *Bp* **V** J E SADLER, **C** A J PATTERSON
NEWCASTLE UNDER LYME (St George) *Lich 15*
  P *R Newc w Butterton* **V** D C MARSHALL,
  Hon Par Dn A MARSHALL
NEWCASTLE UNDER LYME (St Giles) w Butterton
 (St Thomas) *Lich 15* **P** *Simeon's Trustees*
  R J G RIDYARD
NEWCASTLE UNDER LYME (St Paul) *Lich 15*
  P *Trustees* **V** M D HARDING
NEWCASTLE UPON TYNE Byker (St Anthony)
 Byker St Ant *Newc*
NEWCASTLE UPON TYNE Byker (St Martin)   Byker
 St Martin *Newc*
NEWCASTLE UPON TYNE Byker (St Michael w
 St Lawrence)   Byker St Mich w St Lawr *Newc*
NEWCASTLE UPON TYNE Byker (St Silas)   Byker St
 Silas *Newc*
NEWCASTLE UPON TYNE Fenham (St James and
 St Basil)   Fenham St Jas and St Basil *Newc*
NEWCASTLE UPON TYNE Heaton (St Gabriel) *Newc 6*
  P *Bp* **V** C M F UNWIN, **C** J M DOTCHIN,
  Hon C M E CHAPMAN
NEWCASTLE UPON TYNE High Elswick (St Paul)
 High Elswick St Paul *Newc*
NEWCASTLE UPON TYNE High Heaton (St Francis)
 Newc 6 **P** *Bp* **V** W J HATCHLEY, **C** J D HOPKINS
NEWCASTLE UPON TYNE (Holy Cross) *Newc 7* **P** *Bp*
  V M J WEBB, **C** A B BARTLETT, **Hon C** P E DAVIES
NEWCASTLE UPON TYNE Jesmond   Jesmond
 Clayton Memorial *Newc*
NEWCASTLE UPON TYNE Jesmond (Holy Trinity)
 Jesmond H Trin *Newc*
NEWCASTLE UPON TYNE Low Elswick (St Stephen)
 Low Elswick *Newc*
NEWCASTLE UPON TYNE Scotswood (St Margaret)
 Scotswood *Newc*
NEWCASTLE UPON TYNE (St Barnabas and St Jude)
 Newc 5 **V** *Jesmond Clayton Memorial and*
 CPAS (alt) **V** R W BURROWS
NEWCASTLE UPON TYNE (St George) *Newc 5* **P** *Bp*
  V F R DEXTER, **C** C J CLINCH
NEWCASTLE UPON TYNE (St Hilda) *Newc 5* **P** *Bp*
  P-in-c G G KEYES
NEWCASTLE UPON TYNE (St John the Baptist) *Newc 5*
  P *V Newc* **V** J R DUDLEY

NEWCASTLE UPON TYNE (St Matthew w St Mary)
 Newc 7 **P** *Bp* **V** H W WALKER
NEWCASTLE UPON TYNE (St Thomas) Proprietary
 Chapel *Newc 5* **P** *Trustees of St Thos Chpl Charity*
  Master I D HOUGHTON
NEWCASTLE UPON TYNE Walker (Christ Church)
 Walker *Newc*
NEWCASTLE UPON TYNE Walkergate (St Oswald)
 Walkergate *Newc*
NEWCASTLE UPON TYNE, WEST Benwell   Benwell
 Team *Newc*
NEWCHAPEL (St James the Apostle) *Lich 17* **P** *CPAS*
  V P D HOWARD
NEWCHURCH (All Saints) *Portsm 7* **P** *Bp* **V** *Vacant*
 Isle of Wight (0983) 865504
NEWCHURCH (Christ Church)   Hoar Cross w
 Newchurch *Lich*
NEWCHURCH (not known) and Glazebury All Saints
 Liv 16 **P** *Bp* **R** R G LEWIS
NEWCHURCH (St Nicholas w St John) *Man 15* **P** *Bp*
  R A T TOOMBS
NEWCHURCH (St Peter and St Paul)   Dymchurch w
 Burmarsh and Newchurch *Cant*
NEWCHURCH-IN-PENDLE (St Mary)   Fence and
 Newchurch-in-Pendle *Blackb*
NEWDIGATE (St Peter) *Guildf 7* **P** *Ld Chan*
  R C MANCHESTER
NEWENDEN (St Peter)   Sandhurst w Newenden *Cant*
NEWENT (St Mary the Virgin) and Gorsley w Cliffords
 Mesne *Glouc 3* **P** *Bp* **R** I W MARCHANT,
  C P PHILLIPS, **NSM** R G CHIVERS
NEWHALL (St John) *Derby 16* **P** *Bp* **V** K W FRYER
NEWHAVEN (St Michael) *Chich 18* **P** *Ch Patr Trust*
  R N WESTON
NEWHEY (St Thomas) *Man 19* **P** *Bp* **V** S H TOMLINE
NEWICK (St Mary) *Chich 21* **P** *Ch Soc Trust and*
 J H Cordle Esq (jt) **R** P P FRANCIS,
  Hon Par Dn J D GRAY
NEWINGTON (St Christopher)   St Laurence in Thanet
 Cant
NEWINGTON (St Giles)   Dorchester *Ox*
NEWINGTON St John the Baptist w Dairycoates St Mary
 and St Peter *York 15* **P** *Abp* **P-in-c** D A B SMITH
NEWINGTON (St Mary) *S'wark 8* **P** *Bp* **R** M A HART,
  C S M CAPLE, **Hon C** J WASH
NEWINGTON (St Mary the Virgin) w Hartlip and
 Stockbury *Cant 14* **P** *Abp* **V** R A E KENT
NEWINGTON (St Nicholas)   Cheriton All So w
 Newington *Cant*
NEWINGTON (St Paul) *S'wark 8* **P** *Bp* **V** G D SHAW
NEWINGTON, SOUTH (St Peter ad Vincula)   Bloxham
 w Milcombe and S Newington *Ox*
NEWLAND (All Saints) and Redbrook w Clearwell *Glouc 4*
  P *Bp* **V** D J F ADDISON
NEWLAND (St Leonard), Guarlford and Madresfield
 Worc 2 **P** *Exors Countess Beauchamp and Beauchamp*
 Trustees (alt) **R** D H MARTIN
NEWLANDS (not known)   Thornthwaite cum
 Braithwaite and Newlands *Carl*
NEWLAY LANE (St Margaret's Church Hall)   Bramley
 Ripon
NEWLYN (St Newlyn) *Truro 5* **P** *Bp* **P-in-c** W FISH
NEWLYN (St Peter) *Truro 5* **P** *Bp* **V** R L STRANGE,
  Hon C W C COLLINS
NEWMARKET (All Saints) *St E 11* **P** *Bp*
  V R M RIMMER
NEWMARKET (St Mary the Virgin) w Exning (St Agnes)
 St E 11 **P** *Bp and DBP (alt)* **R** G C SMITH,
  C S V COPE
NEWNHAM (St Michael and All Angels)   Badby w
 Newnham *Pet*
NEWNHAM (St Nicholas) w Nately Scures w Mapledurwell
 w Up Nately w Greywell *Win 5* **P** *Bp, Qu Coll Ox,*
 and Exors Lady Malmesbury (jt) **R** M R HAWES
NEWNHAM (St Peter and St Paul)   Doddington,
 Newnham and Wychling *Cant*
NEWNHAM (St Peter) w Awre and Blakeney *Glouc 3*
  P *Haberdashers' Co and Bp (alt)* **V** G A J HUTTON
NEWNHAM (St Vincent)   Hinxworth w Newnham and
 Radwell *St Alb*
NEWTON, NORTH (St James)   Swanborough *Sarum*
NEWPORT (St John the Baptist) *Portsm 8* **P** *Ch Patr*
 Trust **V** A BROWN, **C** A P MARSDEN
NEWPORT (St John the Baptist), Bishops Tawton and
 Tawstock *Ex 15* **P** *Patr Bd* **TR** W G BENSON,
  TV J C CARVOSSO, **NSM** D F GIBSON
NEWPORT (St Mary the Virgin) w Widdington *Chelmsf 24*
  P *Bp* **P-in-c** S SANDERSON,
  Hon Par Dn E W CHAPMAN

NEWPORT (St Nicholas) w Longford and Chetwynd
Lich 22 **P** Bp **R** R T HIBBERT, **C** J W ALLAN
NEWPORT (St Stephen) Howden Team Min York
NEWPORT (St Thomas) Portsm 8 **P** Bp **V** J F BUCKETT
NEWPORT PAGNELL (St Luke) w Lathbury and Moulsoe
Ox 27 **P** Bp, Ch Ch Ox, and Lord Carrington (jt)
R J H LEWIS, **C** J PEARCE, **Hon C** R C A LESLIE
NEWQUAY (St Michael) Truro 7 **P** Bp
V H M WILLIAMS, **C** M M ENNIS
NEWSHAM (St Bede) Newc 1 **P** Bp **V** J R PRINGLE
NEWSHOLME (St John) Oakworth Bradf
NEWSOME (St John the Evangelist) and Armitage Bridge
Wakef 1 **P** DBP, V Rashcliffe and Lockwood, and
R Almondbury (jt) **V** I JACKSON, **C** P J HIBBERT
NEWSTEAD (St Mary the Virgin) Annesley Our Lady
and All SS S'well
NEWTIMBER (St John the Evangelist) Poynings w
Edburton, Newtimber and Pyecombe Chich
NEWTON and TOFT (St Michael) Middle Rasen Gp
Linc
NEWTON (Church Hall) Blackwell Derby
NEWTON (Mission Church) Embleton w Rennington
and Rock Newc
NEWTON (St Botolph) S Lafford Linc
NEWTON (St James) Ely 7 **P** Bp **R** J TOFTS
NEWTON (St John the Baptist) Clodock and Longtown
w Craswall, Llanveynoe etc Heref
NEWTON (St Luke) Hatf St Alb
NEWTON (St Margaret) Lt Shelford w Newton Ely
NEWTON (St Michael) Plas Newton Ches
NEWTON (St Michael and All Angels) Ches 8
P R W Kirby St Bridget **V** Vacant
NEWTON (St Oswald) Gt Ayton w Easby and Newton
in Cleveland York
NEWTON (St Petrock) Shebbear, Buckland Filleigh,
Sheepwash etc Ex
NEWTON (St Stephen) Flowery Field Ches 14 **P** Bp
V Vacant 061-368 3333
NEWTON (Good Shepherd) Clifton upon Dunsmore
and Newton Cov
NEWTON, NORTH (St Peter) w St Michaelchurch,
Thurloxton and Durston B & W 15 **P** Bp (3 turns),
Sir Benjamin Slade, Bt (1 turn) **R** S W DAVIES
NEWTON, OLD (St Mary) w Stowupland St E 6
P Ch Patr Trust and DBP (alt) **V** Vacant
Stowmarket (0449) 673121
NEWTON, SOUTH (St Andrew) Sarum 16 **P** DBP
P-in-c K G BEAKE
NEWTON, WEST (St Matthew) Carl 7 **P** Bp **V** Vacant
NEWTON, WEST (St Peter and St Paul) Sandringham w
W Newton Nor
NEWTON ABBOT Highweek and Teigngrace Ex
NEWTON ABBOT (St Leonard) Wolborough w
Newton Abbot Ex
NEWTON ABBOT (St Michael) as above
NEWTON ABBOT (St Paul) as above
NEWTON ARLOSH (St John the Evangelist) Kirkbride
w Newton Arlosh Carl
NEWTON AYCLIFFE (St Clare) Dur 14 **P** Bp
TR P A BALDWIN, **C** D G PATON-WILLIAMS,
P J WILSON, S M WRIST-KNUDSEN
NEWTON BLOSSOMVILLE (St Nicolas) Lavendon w
Cold Brayfield, Clifton Reynes etc Ox
NEWTON BROMSWOLD (St Peter) Rushden w
Newton Bromswold Pet
NEWTON-BY-CASTLE-ACRE (All Saints) Castle
Acre w Newton, Rougham and Southacre Nor
NEWTON CAP (St Paul) Auckland St Andr and St
Anne Dur
NEWTON FERRERS (Holy Cross) w Revelstoke Ex 21
P Bp and Comdr P E Yonge **P-in-c** T R DEACON
NEWTON FLOTMAN (St Mary the Virgin)
Swainsthorpe w Newton Flotman Nor
NEWTON GREEN (All Saints) Assington w Newton
Green and Lt Cornard St E
NEWTON HALL (All Saints) Dur 2 **P** D&C
P-in-c M J HARDY
NEWTON HALL (St James) Corbridge w Halton and
Newton Hall Newc
NEWTON HARCOURT (St Luke) Gt Glen, Stretton
Magna and Wistow etc Leic
NEWTON HEATH (All Saints) Man 5 **P** D&C
R D G ATTFIELD, **Par Dn** B McNIVEN
NEWTON HEATH (St Wilfrid and St Anne) Man 5
P The Crown **R** S R ASHTON
NEWTON IN MAKERFIELD (Emmanuel) Liv 16 **P** Bp
R R BUSHELL
NEWTON IN MAKERFIELD (St Peter) Liv 16 **P** Lord
Newton **V** W BYNON

NEWTON IN MOTTRAM (St Mary) Ches 14
P V Mottram **V** D SIMPSON
NEWTON KYME (St Andrew) Tadcaster w Newton
Kyme York
NEWTON-LE-WILLOWS (All Saints) Liv 16 **P** Bp
V D HALL
NEWTON LONGVILLE (St Faith) w Stoke Hammond and
Whaddon Ox 26 **P** Exors R J Dalziel Smith Esq, New
Coll Ox, and Cam Univ (by turn) **R** A A WHALLEY
NEWTON ON OUSE (All Saints) Skelton w Shipton
and Newton on Ouse York
NEWTON-ON-RAWCLIFFE (St John) Middleton w
Newton, Levisham and Lockton York
NEWTON-ON-TRENT (St Peter) Linc 2 **P** DBP
V L SALT
NEWTON POPPLEFORD (St Luke) w Harpford Ex 7
P DBP and V Aylesbeare (alt) **V** R G MERWOOD
NEWTON PURCELL (St Michael) Finmere w Mixbury,
Cottisford, Hardwick etc Ox
NEWTON REGIS (St Mary) w Seckington and Shuttington
Birm 12 **P** Birm Dioc Trustees and Mrs E V G Inge-
Innes-Lillingston (alt) **R** S R MARRIOTT
NEWTON REIGNY (St John) Penrith w Newton
Reigny and Plumpton Wall Carl
NEWTON SOLNEY (St Mary the Virgin) Bretby w
Newton Solney Derby
NEWTON ST CYRES (St Cyres and St Julitta)
Thorverton, Cadbury, Upton Pyne etc Ex
NEWTON ST LOE (Holy Trinity) Saltford w Corston
and Newton St Loe B & W
NEWTON TONY (St Andrew) Bourne Valley Sarum
NEWTON TRACEY (St Thomas a Becket), Alverdiscott,
Huntshaw, Yarnscombe and Horwood Ex 20 **P** Bp,
Ld Chan and Lord Clinton (by turn)
P-in-c R J P ACWORTH
NEWTON VALENCE (St Mary) and Selborne and East
Tisted w Colemore Win 2 **P** Bp, Earl of Selborne, and
Sir James Scott (jt) **R** J F W ANDERSON
NEWTOWN (Holy Spirit) Calbourne w Newtown
Portsm
NEWTOWN (Holy Trinity) Soberton w Newtown
Portsm
NEWTOWN (King Charles the Martyr) Loppington w
Newtown Lich
NEWTOWN (St Mary the Virgin) Hungerford and
Denford Ox
NEWTOWN (St Mary the Virgin and St John the Baptist)
Burghclere w Newtown and Ecchinswell w Sydmonton
Win
NEWTOWN (St Paul) Longnor, Quarnford and Sheen
Lich
NEWTOWN LINFORD (All Saints) Leic 12
P Lord Deramore **V** Vacant Markfield (0530)
242955
NIBLEY, NORTH (St Martin) Wotton-under-Edge w
Ozleworth and N Nibley Glouc
NICHOLFOREST (St Nicholas) and Kirkandrews on Esk
Carl 2 **P** Bp, Sir Charles Graham, Bt, and PCC (jt)
V P J RIDLEY
NIDD (St Paul and St Margaret) Ripon 1 **P** Viscount
Mountgarret and R Knaresborough (alt) **P-in-c** R KENT
NIDDERDALE, LOWER Ripon 8 **P** Trustees K Bell,
DBP, and C J Dent Esq (jt) **P-in-c** P F C SMITH
NIDDERDALE, UPPER Ripon 3 **P** D&C and V Masham
and Healey (jt) **V** A P KAUNHOVEN
NINEBANKS (St Mark) Allendale w Whitfield Newc
NINEFIELDS (St Lawrence School Worship Centre)
Waltham H Cross Chelmsf
NINFIELD (St Mary the Virgin) Chich 14 **P** D&C Cant
R P C CLEMENTS
NITON (St John the Baptist) Portsm 7 **P** Qu Coll Ox
P-in-c H W COOPER, **C** S LLOYD
NOAK HILL (St Thomas) Harold Hill St Geo Chelmsf
NOCTON (All Saints) w Dunston and Potterhanworth
Linc 18 **P** Ld Chan and Br Field Products Ltd (alt)
V R RODGER
NOEL PARK (St Mark) Lon 19 **P** Bp **V** C G BACK,
Hon C J R KIRKPATRICK
NOKE (St Giles) Islip w Charlton on Otmoor,
Oddington, Noke etc Ox
NOMANS HEATH (St Mary the Virgin) Lich 5 **P** Bp
V Vacant
NONINGTON (St Mary the Virgin) w Wymynswold and
Goodnestone w Chillenden and Knowlton Cant 1
P Abp and Lord Fitzwalter (jt) **V** I C HAWKINS
NORBITON (St Peter) S'wark 14 **P** V Kingston All SS
V S P LYON, **C** J M A LEE,
Hon Par Dn H M JESTY, C E HUMPHRIES

NORBURY (All Saints)   Wentnor w Ratlinghope,
Myndtown, Norbury etc *Heref*
NORBURY (St Mary and St Barlok) w Snelston *Derby 8*
P *J R G Stanton Esq, L A Clowes Esq and V Ashbourne*
(by turn)   **R** J R J READ
NORBURY (St Oswald) *S'wark 22*   **P** *Bp*
V P A THOMPSON
NORBURY (St Peter)   High Offley and Norbury *Lich*
NORBURY (St Philip) *S'wark 22*   **P** *Bp*
V P L WASHINGTON
NORBURY (St Stephen) and Thornton Heath *S'wark 22*
P *Bp*   **V** F J M POLE
NORBURY (St Thomas) *Ches 16*   **P** *Lord Newton*
V W F M COLLINS,   **C** R H GREEN,   **Par Dn** K MARTIN
NORDELPH (Holy Trinity)   Wimbotsham w Stow
Bardolph and Stow Bridge etc *Ely*
NORDEN (St Paul) w Ashworth *Man 19*   **P** *Bp*
V K N PROCTOR
NORFOLK PARK (St Leonard)   Heeley *Sheff*
NORHAM (St Cuthbert) and Duddo *Newc 12*   **P** *D&C*
(1 turn), D&C Dur (2 turns)   **V** R THOMPSON
NORK (St Paul) *Guildf 9*   **P** *The Crown*   **V** P J BROOKS
NORLAND (St Luke)   Sowerby Bridge w Norland
Wakef
NORLANDS (St James)   Notting Dale St Clem w St
Mark and St Jas *Lon*
NORLEY (St John the Evangelist) and Crowton *Ches 3*
P *Bp and V Weaverham (jt)*   **V** R H N ROBB
NORMACOT (Holy Evangelists) *Lich 18*   **P** *DBP*
V S CARTER
NORMANBY (St Andrew)   Kirby Misperton w
Normanby, Edston and Salton *York*
NORMANBY (St George)   Eston w Normanby *York*
NORMANBY-LE-WOLD (St Peter)   Walesby *Linc*
NORMANTON (All Saints) *Wakef 9*   **P** *Trin Coll Cam*
V J C CUTTELL,   **C** T C DAVIS
NORMANTON (St Giles) *Derby 10*   **P** *CPAS*
V R B BLOWERS,   **C** J T PYE
NORMANTON, SOUTH (St Michael and All Angels)
Derby 1   **P** *MMCET*   **R** E E CHAMBERLAIN
NORMANTON-LE-HEATH (Holy Trinity)   Packington
w Normanton-le-Heath *Leic*
NORMANTON-ON-SOAR (St James)   Sutton
Bonington w Normanton-on-Soar *S'well*
NORMANTON-ON-TRENT (St Matthew)   Sutton w
Carlton and Normanton upon Trent *S'well*
NORRIS BANK (St Martin) *Man 3*   **R** B LIPSCOMBE
NORRISTHORPE (All Souls)   Heckmondwike *Wakef*
NORTH: *see under substantive place names*
NORTH AXHOLME Group, The *Linc 1*   **P** *The Crown*
V J GIBBONS
NORTH CAVE (All Saints) w Cliffe *York 14*
P *P W J Carver Esq*   **V** P N HAYWARD
NORTH CHAPEL (St Michael) w Ebernoe *Chich 11*
P *Lord Egremont*   **R** C G F KIRKHAM
NORTH COVE (St Botolph)   Worlingham w Barnby and
N Cove *St E*
NORTH END (Chapel of Ease)   Burton Dassett *Cov*
NORTH END (St Francis)   Portsea N End St Mark
Portsm
NORTH END (St Nicholas)   as above
NORTH HILL (St Torney)   Bolventor *Truro*
NORTH SHIELDS (Christ Church)   N Shields *Newc*
NORTH SHIELDS (St Augustine) (Christ Church) *Newc 5*
P *Patr Bd*   **TR** W N STOCK,   **TV** M GOLIGHTLY,
C P S McCONNELL
NORTHALLERTON (All Saints) w Kirby Sigston *York 20*
P *D&C Dur*   **V** I J FOX,   **C** T A SMITH, M J HORTON
NORTHAM (St Margaret) w Westward Ho! and Appledore
Ex 17   **P** *DBP*   **TR** D N CHANCE,   **TV** R VARTY
NORTHAMPTON (All Saints w St Katherine) *Pet 4*   **P** *Bp*
V S H M GODFREY,   **C** K E MACNAB
NORTHAMPTON (Christ Church) *Pet 4*   **P** *Bp*
V S B H DELVES-BROUGHTON
NORTHAMPTON (Emmanuel) *Pet 4*   **P** *DBP*
TR J F A M KNIGHT,   **TV** M W EDEN,   **C** A R B JOWITT
**NORTHAMPTON (Holy Sepulchre w St Andrew and
St Lawrence)** *Pet 4*   **P** *Bp*   **V** K E ANDERSON
NORTHAMPTON (Holy Trinity) *Pet 4*   **P** *Bp*
V H N ANNIS
**NORTHAMPTON (St Alban the Martyr) (Glorious
Ascension)** *Pet 4*   **P** *Bp*   **V** R W GREENLAND,
C C M UPTON
NORTHAMPTON (St Benedict) *Pet 7*   **P** *Bp*   **V** *Vacant*
Northampton (0604) 768624
NORTHAMPTON (St David)   Kingsthorpe w Northn St
Dav *Pet*
NORTHAMPTON (St Giles) *Pet 4*   **P** *Simeon's Trustees*
V P A M GOMPERTZ,   **C** M A SLATER

NORTHAMPTON (St James) *Pet 4*   **P** *Bp*   **V** J T SHORT,
Par Dn M M CLARKE
NORTHAMPTON (St Mary the Virgin) *Pet 4*   **P** *Bp*
V G I BURGON,   **C** A W WILLSON
NORTHAMPTON (St Matthew) *Pet 4*   **P** *DBP*
V J I MORTON,   **Hon C** M M CLARKE,
NSM S A TEBBUTT
**NORTHAMPTON (St Michael and All Angels w
St Edmund)** *Pet 4*   **P** *Bp*   **V** W P K KENTIGERN-FOX
NORTHAMPTON (St Paul) *Pet 4*   **P** *Bp*   **V** *Vacant*
Northampton (0604) 712688
NORTHAMPTON (St Peter) w Upton *Pet 4*   **P** *R Foundn
of St Kath*   **C** J A FAVELL
NORTHAW (St Thomas of Canterbury) *St Alb 6*
P *Mrs K R Dore*   **V** J N BATEMAN-CHAMPAIN,
Hon Par Dn B L COOKE
NORTHBOROUGH (St Andrew)   Maxey w
Northborough *Pet*
NORTHBOURNE (St Augustine)   Eastry and
Northbourne w Tilmanstone etc *Cant*
NORTHCHURCH (St Mary)   Berkhamsted St Mary
St Alb
NORTHCOURT (Christ Church)   Abingdon *Ox*
NORTHENDEN (St Wilfrid) *Man 8*   **P** *Bp*
R G S FORSTER
NORTHFIELD (St Laurence) *Birm 4*   **P** *Keble Coll Ox*
R R I WARREN,   **C** N C A VON MALAISE,
Hon C D C MERCHANT,   P B CLIFF
NORTHFLEET (St Botolph) *Roch 4*   **P** *The Crown*
V M M CAMP
NORTHGATE (St Elizabeth)   Crawley *Chich*
NORTHIAM (St Mary) *Chich 20*   **P** *MMCET*
R P A O'GORMAN
NORTHILL (St Mary the Virgin) w Moggerhanger
St Alb 17   **P** *Grocers' Co and Bp (alt)*   **R** T D DESERT
NORTHINGTON (St John the Evangelist)   The
Candover Valley *Win*
**NORTHLEACH (St Peter and St Paul) w Hampnett and
Farmington** *Glouc 14*   **P** *Bp*   **P-in-c** J P BROWN,
C J W S FIELDGATE,   **NSM** D W HUTCHIN
NORTHLEIGH (St Giles)   Colyton, Southleigh, Offwell,
Widworthy etc *Ex*
NORTHLEW (St Thomas of Canterbury) w Ashbury *Ex 12*
P *The Crown*   **R** J REASON
NORTHMOOR (St Denys)   Lower Windrush *Ox*
NORTHMOOR GREEN (St Peter and St John)   N
Petherton w Northmoor Green *B & W*
NORTHOLT (St Joseph) W End *Lon 22*   **P** *DBP*
V D M BRADSHAW,   **C** J W KNILL-JONES
NORTHOLT (St Mary) (St Hugh) (St Richard) *Lon 22*
P *BNC Ox*   **R** J H BELL,   **C** J HIBBERD,   D A PLUMMER
NORTHOLT PARK (St Barnabas) *Lon 22*   **P** *Bp*
V J RHODES-WRIGLEY,   **C** S W POWELL
NORTHORPE (St John the Baptist)   Scotton w
Northorpe *Linc*
NORTHOWRAM (St Matthew) *Wakef 2*   **P** *Bp*
V J L MARSHALL,   **C** P WHITTINGHAM,
Par Dn J M HOGGARD
NORTHREPPS (St Mary) *Nor 7*   **P** *Duchy of Lanc*
R D L AINSWORTH
NORTHWICH (St Helen)   Witton *Ches*
NORTHWICH (St Luke) (Holy Trinity) *Ches 6*   **P** *Bp*
V R W CROOK
NORTHWOLD (St Andrew) *Ely 15*   **P** *Bp*
R J B ROWSELL
NORTHWOOD (Emmanuel) *Lon 23*   **P** *Ch Trust Fund
Trust*   **V** D J OSBORNE,   **C** G C ROWLANDSON,
Par Dn J J WILSON
NORTHWOOD (Holy Trinity)   Hanley H Ev *Lich*
NORTHWOOD (Holy Trinity) *Lon 23*   **P** *Trustees*
V P T HANCOCK,   **C** J F SPINKS,   **Par Dn** O J FIELD
NORTHWOOD Pinner Road (St Edmund the King)
Northwood Hills St Edm *Lon*
NORTHWOOD (St John the Baptist) *Portsm 8*   **P** *Bp*
P-in-c R J SALTER
NORTHWOOD (St Mark)   Kirkby *Liv*
NORTHWOOD GREEN (Mission Church)   Westbury-
on-Severn w Flaxley and Blaisdon *Glouc*
NORTHWOOD HILLS (St Edmund the King) *Lon 23*
P *Bp*   **V** R J AMES,   **NSM** K E LIMBERT
NORTON (All Saints)   Stanton St Quintin, Hullavington,
Grittleton etc *Bris*
NORTON (All Saints)   Brington w Whilton and Norton
Pet
NORTON (St Andrew)   Pakenham w Norton and
Tostock *St E*
NORTON (St Berteline and St Christopher) *Ches 3*
P *DBP*   **V** R J GATES,   **C** T P EDGE

NORTON (St Egwin) Harvington, Norton and Lenchwick *Worc*
NORTON (St George) (St Nicholas) *St Alb 9* **P** *Bp*
V C F LILEY, **C** C D C THORPE
NORTON (St James) *Sheff 2* **P** *CCC Cam*
R M J MORGAN
NORTON (St James) Stoulton w Drake's Broughton and Pirton etc *Worc*
NORTON (St Mary) *Cant 6* **P** *Ld Chan* **R** *Vacant*
NORTON (St Mary) Twigworth, Down Hatherley, Norton, The Leigh etc *Glouc*
NORTON (St Mary the Virgin) *Dur 16* **P** *Bp*
V M S SIMMONS, **C** P R C HAMILTON-MANON, C J G HELLIWELL
NORTON (St Michael and All Angels) *Dur 16*
P *V Norton St Mary* **V** I C R CALDWELL
NORTON (St Peter) Norton *York*
NORTON, EAST (All Saints) Hallaton w Horninghold, Allexton, Tugby etc *Leic*
NORTON, OVER (St James) Chipping Norton *Ox*
NORTON BAVANT (All Saints) Heytesbury and Sutton Veny *Sarum*
NORTON BRIDGE (St Luke) Chebsey *Lich*
NORTON CANES (St James) *Lich 4* **P** *Bp*
R P LOCKETT
NORTON CANON (St Nicholas) Weobley w Sarnesfield and Norton Canon *Heref*
NORTON CUCKNEY (St Mary) *S'well 6* **P** *Lady Alexandra Cavendish Bentinck* **P-in-c** J R WILLIAMS
NORTON DISNEY (St Peter) Thurlby w Norton Disney *Linc*
NORTON FITZWARREN (All Saints) *B & W 20*
P *MMCET* **R** D N STEVENSON
NORTON IN HALES (St Chad) Woore and Norton in Hales *Lich*
NORTON IN THE MOORS (St Bartholomew) *Lich 14*
P *Lord Norton* **R** W K ROWELL
NORTON JUXTA MALTON (St Peter) *York 2* **P** *Abp*
V D B COOPER
NORTON JUXTA TWYCROSS (Holy Trinity) Orton-on-the-Hill w Twycross etc *Leic*
NORTON-LE-CLAY (St John the Evangelist) Kirby-on-the-Moor, Cundall w Norton-le-Clay etc *Ripon*
NORTON LEES (St Paul) Norton Woodseats St Paul *Sheff*
NORTON LINDSEY (Holy Trinity) Wolverton w Norton Lindsey and Langley *Cov*
NORTON MALREWARD (Holy Trinity) *B & W 11* **P** *Bp*
R T K VIVIAN
NORTON MANDEVILLE (All Saints) High Ongar w Norton Mandeville *Chelmsf*
NORTON ST PHILIP (St Philip and St James) w Hemington, Hardington and Laverton *B & W 4* **P** *Bp and J B Owen-Jones Esq* (alt) **R** T J FARMILOE
NORTON SUB HAMDON (Blessed Virgin Mary) w West Chinnock, Chiselborough and Middle Chinnock *B & W 7*
P *Bp* **R** B J DALTON
NORTON SUBCOURSE (St Mary) Raveningham *Nor*
NORTON WOODSEATS (St Chad) *Sheff 2* **P** *Bp*
V E HUME, **Par Dn** P NEEDHAM
NORTON WOODSEATS (St Paul) *Sheff 2* **P** *R Norton*
V M P HIRONS
NORWELL (St Laurence), w Ossington, Cromwell and Caunton *S'well 3* **P** *Bp, SMF, and Mrs P Goedhuis* (jt)
V R A WHITTAKER
NORWICH Heartsease (St Francis) *Nor 6* **P** *Bp*
V B R BAXTER
NORWICH (St Andrew) *Nor 6* **P** *DBF*
P-in-c R ALLINGTON-SMITH
NORWICH (St Augustine) Nor Over-the-Water *Nor*
NORWICH (St George) as above
NORWICH (St George) Tombland *Nor 6* **P** *Bp*
NSM J C MINNS
NORWICH (St Giles) *Nor 6* **P** *Ld Chan and Bp* (alt)
P-in-c D A ABRAHAM
NORWICH (St Helen) *Nor 6* **P** *Gt Hosp Nor*
P-in-c K M HARRE
NORWICH (St Julian) Nor St Pet Parmentergate w St Jo *Nor*
NORWICH (St Mary in the Marsh) *Nor 6* **P** *D&C*
P-in-c M S McLEAN, **Hon C** P W E CURRIE
NORWICH (St Mary Magdalene) Nor Over-the-Water *Nor*
NORWICH (St Peter Mancroft) (St John Maddermarket)
Nor 6 **P** *DBF* **R** D M SHARP, **C** A C BILLETT, **NSM** R J M COLLIER
NORWICH St Peter Parmentergate w St John de Sepulchre (St Julian) *Nor 6* **P** *Patr Bd* **R** J M MOUNTNEY, **TV** H R G COOKE, **C** M J HALL

NORWICH (St Stephen) *Nor 6* **P** *D&C*
P-in-c K A A WESTON,
NSM P G RUTHERFORD, P A ATKINSON
NORWICH Timberhill (St John) Nor St Pet Parmentergate w St Jo *Nor*
NORWICH OVER-THE-WATER *Nor 6* **P** *Patr Bd*
TR R M S WOODHAM, **TV** A P WARD,
TM H M WAKEMAN
NORWOOD (St Luke) *S'wark 12* **P** *Abp*
V P H RONAYNE, **C** G J JENKINS
NORWOOD (St Margaret) Upper Norwood All SS *S'wark*
NORWOOD (St Mary the Virgin) *Lon 23* **P** *SMF*
R M F GODDARD
NORWOOD, SOUTH (Holy Innocents) *S'wark 22* **P** *Bp*
V R D NEWMAN
NORWOOD, SOUTH (St Alban the Martyr) *S'wark 22*
P *Bp* **V** G H J DUNNING
NORWOOD, SOUTH (St Mark) *S'wark 22* **P** *Bp*
V P E THROWER
NORWOOD, UPPER (All Saints) *S'wark 22*
P *V Croydon* **V** A D MIDDLETON, **C** P F TURNBULL,
Hon C V PARSONS
NORWOOD, UPPER (St John) *S'wark 22* **P** *Bp*
V D G MARTIN, **NSM** J HILL
NOTGROVE (St Bartholomew) Cold Aston w Notgrove and Turkdean *Glouc*
NOTTING DALE (St Clement) (St Mark) and Norlands (St James) *Lon 12* **P** *Bp* **V** E A BURTON,
C D B PERKINS
NOTTING HILL (All Saints) (St Columb) *Lon 12* **P** *SMF*
V J K BROWNSELL, **C** D C CLUES, **NSM** R E DUGUID
NOTTING HILL (St John) (St Peter) *Lon 12* **P** *Bp*
V H J STRINGER, **C** A J WATSON,
Hon Par Dn D O ONSLOW
NOTTING HILL (St Michael and All Angels) (Christ Church) (Saint Francis) *Lon 12* **P** *Trustees*
V A B ANDREWS
NOTTINGHAM (All Saints) *S'well 12* **P** *Trustees*
V N PEYTON, **Par Dn** E MATTHEWS-LOYDALL
NOTTINGHAM (St Andrew) *S'well 12* **P** *Peache Trustees*
V *Vacant* Nottingham (0602) 604961
NOTTINGHAM (St Ann w Emmanuel) *S'well 12*
P *Trustees* **V** J P NEILL, **NSM** E A CARRINGTON
NOTTINGHAM (St George w St John the Baptist) *S'well 12*
P *Bp* **V** A R WAGSTAFF
NOTTINGHAM (St Jude) *S'well 12* **P** *CPAS*
V S E DYAS, **C** S D SILVESTER
NOTTINGHAM (St Mary the Virgin) and St Catharine
S'well 12 **P** *Bp* **V** J E M NEALE, **C** J K PENNINGTON
NOTTINGHAM (St Nicholas) *S'well 12* **P** *CPAS*
R D J HUGGETT, **C** J J FLETCHER, **NSM** J D BEALES
NOTTINGHAM (St Peter and St James) *S'well 12* **P** *Bp*
R L J MORLEY, J W HUCKLE, **Assoc Min** E P FORSHAW
NOTTINGHAM (St Saviour) *S'well 12* **P** *CPAS*
P-in-c J W BENTHAM
NOTTINGHAM (St Stephen) Basford w Hyson Green *S'well*
NOWTON (St Peter) Hawstead and Nowton w Stanningfield etc *St E*
NUFFIELD (Holy Trinity) *Ox 6* **P** *MMCET*
R J F SHEARER
NUN MONKTON (St Mary) Lower Nidderdale *Ripon*
NUNBURNHOLME (St James) and Warter *York 7*
P *Abp and Marquis of Normanby* (jt) **R** K G SKIPPER
NUNEATON (St Mary the Virgin) *Cov 5* **P** *V Nuneaton*
V J T GRATY, **C** D J P ISIORHO
NUNEATON (St Nicolas) *Cov 5* **P** *The Crown*
V G J HARDWICK, **C** V E W RUSHTON
NUNHEAD (St Antony) (St Silas) *S'wark 6* **P** *Bp*
V A R C BROWNE, **NSM** R O SMITH, P VOWLES
NUNNEY (All Saints) and Witham Friary, Marston Bigot, Wanstrow and Cloford *B & W 4* **P** *Bp, SMF and C N Clarke Esq, and Exors of Duke of Somerset* (jt)
R J K HODDER
NUNNINGTON (All Saints) Harome w Stonegrave, Nunnington and Pockley *York*
NUNTHORPE (St Mary's Church Hall) (St Mary the Virgin) *York 22* **P** *Abp* **V** K R GOOD, **C** I R COLSON,
NSM P M HARRISON
NUNTON (St Andrew) Odstock w Nunton and Bodenham *Sarum*
NURSLING (St Boniface) (St John the Evangelist) and Rownhams *Win 11* **P** *Bp* **R** I D GARDNER
NURSTEAD (St Mildred) Meopham w Nurstead *Roch*
NUTBOURNE (St Wilfrid) Chidham *Chich*
NUTFIELD (St Peter and St Paul) *S'wark 24* **P** *Jes Coll Ox* **R** G I WILLIAMS

NUTFIELD, LOWER (Christ Church) *S'wark 24*
  P *Ch Patr Trust* **P-in-c** A E THOMPSON
NUTHALL (St Patrick) *S'well 7* **P** *Bp* **R** R PALIN
NUTHURST (St Andrew) *Chich 8* **P** *Bp Lon* **R** *Vacant*
  Lower Beeding (040376) 279
NUTHURST (St Thomas) Packwood w Hockley Heath
  Birm
NUTLEY (St James the Less) *Chich 21* **P** *R Maresfield*
  V K J BOULLIER
NYMET (St George) S Molton w Nymet St George,
  High Bray etc *Ex*
NYMET ROWLAND (St Bartholomew) Lapford,
  Nymet Rowland and Coldridge *Ex*
NYMET TRACEY (St Bartholomew) Bow w Broad
  Nymet *Ex*
NYMPSFIELD (St Bartholomew) Uley w Owlpen and
  Nympsfield *Glouc*
NYNEHEAD (All Saints) Wellington and Distr *B & W*
OADBY (St Paul) (St Peter) *Leic 5* **P** **R** D H CLARK,
  Par Dn W M THOMSON, **Hon C** M J NOTLEY,
  NSM G TURNOCK
OAKAMOOR (Holy Trinity) Alton w Bradley-le-Moors
  and Oakamoor w Cotton *Lich*
OAKDALE (St George) *Sarum 8* **P** *Bp*
  TR M F PERHAM, **TV** C G ROBINSON, J C OAKES,
  Par Dn L A WALKER, **NSM** D G BELLAIRS-COX
OAKE (St Bartholomew) Bradf w Oake, Hillfarrance
  and Heathfield *B & W*
OAKENGATES (Holy Trinity) Ketley and Oakengates
  Lich
OAKENSHAW (Church of the Good Shepherd)
  Willington and Sunnybrow *Dur*
OAKENSHAW cum Woodlands (St Andrew) *Bradf 2*
  P *Bp* **P-in-c** P G WALKER
OAKFIELD (St John) *Portsm 7* **P** *V St Helens* **V** L FOX
OAKFORD (St Peter) Washfield, Stoodleigh, Withleigh
  etc *Ex*
OAKHAM (All Saints) w Hambleton and Egleton and
  Braunston w Brooke *Pet 14* **P** *Dr E R Hanbury*
  (1 turn), D&C Linc (2 turns) **V** C MAYHEW,
  C N A KERR, D H LEWIS
OAKHANGER (St Luke's Mission Church) Alsager Ch
  Ch *Ches*
OAKHANGER (St Mary Magdalene) E and W
  Worldham, Hartley Mauditt w Kingsley etc *Win*
OAKHILL (All Saints) Ashwick w Oakhill and Binegar
  B & W
OAKHILL Eastwood View (shared church) Clifton St
  Jas *Sheff*
OAKINGTON (St Andrew) *Ely 5* **P** *Qu Coll Cam*
  V J C ALEXANDER
OAKLEY (St Mary) Worminghall w Ickford, Oakley
  and Shabbington *Ox*
OAKLEY (St Mary) Bromham w Oakley and Stagsden
  St Alb
OAKLEY (St Nicholas) N Hartismere *St E*
OAKLEY, EAST (St John) Church Oakley and
  Wootton St Lawrence *Win*
OAKLEY, GREAT (All Saints) w Wix *Chelmsf 23*
  P *Ch Patr Trust and St Jo Coll Cam (jt)*
  R L J DE GROOSE, **NSM** P E H PALMER
OAKLEY, GREAT (St Michael) Corby SS Pet and
  Andr w Gt and Lt Oakley *Pet*
OAKLEY, LITTLE (St Peter) as above
OAKMOOR Bishopsnympton, Rose Ash, Mariansleigh
  etc *Ex*
OAKRIDGE (St Bartholomew) Bisley, Oakridge,
  Miserden and Edgeworth *Glouc*
OAKS IN CHARNWOOD (St James the Greater) and Copt
  Oak *Leic 8* **P** *DBP* **V** G A PADDOCK
OAKSEY (All Saints) Ashley, Crudwell, Hankerton,
  Long Newnton etc *Bris*
OAKWOOD (St Thomas) *Lon 18* **P** *Bp* **V** J D TRIGG,
  C N T ATKINSON
OAKWORTH (Christ Church) *Bradf 8* **P** *Bp* **V** *Vacant*
  Haworth (0535) 43386
OARE (Blessed Virgin Mary) w Culbone *B & W 17* **P** *Bp*
  P-in-c R BEEVERS
OARE (Holy Trinity) Swanborough *Sarum*
OARE (St Bartholomew) Chieveley w Winterbourne
  and Oare *Ox*
OARE (St Peter) The Brents and Davington w Oare and
  Luddenham *Cant*
OATLANDS (St Mary) *Guildf 8* **P** *Bp* **V** *Vacant*
  Weybridge (0932) 47963
OBORNE (St Cuthbert) Queen Thorne *Sarum*
OCCOLD (St Michael) *St E 16* **P** *Lt-Comdr G C Marshall*
  P-in-c R H SMITH

OCKBROOK (All Saints) *Derby 13* **P** *Lt-Col T H Pares*
  V D M F NEWMAN, **Par Dn** R J SHIRRAS,
  Hon C J W DAINES, **NSM** J D BISHOP
OCKENDON, NORTH (St Mary Magdalene) *Chelmsf 4*
  P *Bp* **P-in-c** F J HACKETT
OCKENDON, SOUTH (St Nicholas) *Chelmsf 16* **P** *Guild*
  of All So **R** H BLACK
OCKER HILL (St Mark) *Lich 8* **P** *Bp* **V** S R MELLOR
OCKFORD RIDGE (St Mark) Godalming *Guildf*
OCKHAM (All Saints) w Hatchford *Guildf 10* **P** *Bp*
  P-in-c G A WILKINSON
OCKLEY (St Margaret) w Okewood and Forest Green
  Guildf 7 **P** *Bp and J P M H Evelyn Esq (alt)*
  R C de F TICKNER
OCLE PYCHARD (St James the Great) Stoke Lacy,
  Moreton Jeffries w Much Cowarne etc *Heref*
ODCOMBE (St Peter and St Paul) *B & W 7* **P** *Ch Ch Ox*
  R *Vacant* West Coker (093586) 2224
ODD RODE (All Saints) *Ches 11* **P** *R Astbury*
  R R N WELBOURNE, **C** H W STRATTON
ODDINGLEY (St James) Bowbrook S *Worc*
ODDINGTON (St Andrew) Islip w Charlton on
  Otmoor, Oddington, Noke etc *Ox*
ODDINGTON (St Nicholas) Broadwell, Evenlode,
  Oddington and Adlestrop *Glouc*
ODDINGTON (The Holy Ascension) as above
ODELL (All Saints) and Pavenham *St Alb 21* **P** *Lord*
  Luke of Pavenham **R** J T LIGHTOWLER,
  NSM D R BANNARD-SMITH
ODIHAM (All Saints) *Win 5* **P** *Bp* **V** R C HUBBLE
ODSTOCK (St Mary) w Nunton and Bodenham *Sarum 11*
  P *Earl of Radnor* **P-in-c** R P HOLLINGSHURST
OFFCHURCH (St Gregory) *Cov 10* **P** *Bp*
  P-in-c D BEARDSHAW
OFFENHAM (St Mary and St Melburgh) and Bretforton
  Worc 1 **P** *Bp and D&C (alt)* **V** *Vacant* Evesham
  (0386) 442096
OFFERTON (St Alban) Stockport St Alb Hall Street
  Ches
OFFERTON (St John) as above
OFFHAM (Old St Peter) Hamsey *Chich*
OFFHAM (St Michael) W Malling w Offham *Roch*
OFFLEY (St Mary Magdalene) w Lilley *St Alb 9* **P** *St Jo*
  Coll Cam **P-in-c** I NICKLIN
OFFLEY, HIGH (St Mary the Virgin) and Norbury *Lich 13*
  P *Bp* **R** *Vacant* Woodseaves (0785) 284392
OFFLEY HAY (Mission Church) Eccleshall *Lich*
OFFORD D'ARCY (All Saints) w Offord Cluny *Ely 12*
  P *Ld Chan* **R** P J TAYLOR
OFFTON (St Mary) Somersham w Flowton and Offton
  w Willisham *St E*
OFFWELL (St Mary the Virgin) Colyton, Southleigh,
  Offwell, Widworthy etc *Ex*
OGBOURNE (St Andrew) Ridgeway *Sarum*
OGBOURNE (St George) as above
OGLEY HAY (St James) *Lich 2* **P** *Bp* **V** C N THOMAS,
  C S P GIRLING
OGWELL (St Bartholomew) and Denbury *Ex 11* **P** *Bp*
  and SMF (jt) **R** G F WATTS, **Hon Par Dn** I RUSSELL
OKEFORD FITZPAINE (St Andrew), Ibberton,
  Belchalwell and Wooland *Sarum 6* **P** *F A L F Pitt-*
  Rivers Esq (3 turns), M J Scott-Williams Esq (1 turn)
  R *Vacant* Hazelbury Bryan (02586) 260
OKEHAMPTON (All Saints) (St James) w Inwardleigh
  Ex 12 **P** *Lt-Col V W Calmady-Hamlyn (2 turns),*
  Simeon's Trustees (1 turn) **V** R C CHAMBERLAIN,
  C R M PRIEST
OKEWOOD (St John the Baptist) Ockley w Okewood
  and Forest Green *Guildf*
OLD: *see also under substantive place names*
OLD FORD (St Paul w St Stephen) (St Mark) Victoria Park
  Lon 7 **P** *Hyndman Trustees and CPAS (jt)*
  V C YOUNG, **C** N HELM, **Par Dn** J OSBORNE,
  Hon C D F WAXHAM
OLD HILL (Holy Trinity) *Worc 9* **P** *Ch Soc Trust*
  C P D J SWANN
OLD LANE (Mission Church) Bloxwich *Lich*
OLD WIVES LEES (Mission Church) Chilham *Cant*
OLDBERROW (St Mary) Spernall, Morton Bagot and
  Oldberrow *Cov*
OLDBROOK (Community Church) Woughton *Ox*
OLDBURY *Birm 5* **P** *Bp* **P-in-c** R T ETHERIDGE
OLDBURY *Sarum 18* **P** *Bp, CPAS, Earl of Shelborne,*
  and E Money-Kyrle Esq (jt) **R** R C BUTLER,
  NSM E LEWIS
OLDBURY (St Nicholas) Bridgnorth, Tasley, Astley
  Abbotts, Oldbury etc *Heref*
OLDBURY-ON-SEVERN (St Arilda) *Glouc 7* **P** *Ch Ch*
  Ox **P-in-c** R W MARTIN

OLDBURY-ON-THE-HILL (St Arild) Boxwell,
Leighterton, Didmarton, Oldbury etc *Glouc*
OLDCOTES (St Mark's Mission Church) Langold *S'well*
OLDHAM Moorside (St Thomas) *Man 18* **P** *Trustees*
V J H GRAY
OLDHAM (St Ambrose) *Man 18* **P** *Bp* **V** B P H JAMES
OLDHAM (St Andrew) (St Mary w St Peter) *Man 18*
P *Patr Bd* **TR** J SYKES, **TV** L W CARSON-
FEATHAM, C H RAZZALL
OLDHAM (St Barnabas) *Man 18* **P** *The Crown*
V F A CORBIN
OLDHAM (St Chad) Limeside *Man 18* **P** *Bp* **V** *Vacant*
061-624 0970
OLDHAM (St James) *Man 18* **P** *R Prestwich St Mary*
V P PLUMPTON
OLDHAM (St Paul) *Man 18* **P** *Bp* **V** H G SUTCLIFFE,
C D J QUARMBY
OLDHAM (St Stephen and All Martyrs) Lower Moor
Man 18 **P** *Bp* **V** K LIVESEY
OLDHURST (St Peter) Somersham w Pidley and
Oldhurst *Ely*
OLDLAND (St Anne) *Bris 2* **P** *Bp* **V** M H PERRY
OLDRIDGE (St Thomas) *Ex 6* **P** *Em Coll Cam*
P-in-c A J STONE
OLDSWINFORD (St Mary) Old Swinford Stourbridge
Worc
OLIVER'S BATTERY (St Mark) Stanmore *Win*
OLLERTON (St Giles) (St Paulinus) w Boughton *S'well 6*
P *Ld Chan and Bp (alt)* **V** D T PERRETT, **C** J J VAN
DEN BERG
OLNEY (St Peter and St Paul) w Emberton *Ox 27* **P** *Bp*
R C J BURDON, **Par Dn** A S BURROW,
Hon C C M LOOKER
OLTON (St Margaret) *Birm 13* **P** *Bp and*
V Bickenhill (jt) **V** N S DODDS, **C** G H SAUNDERS
OLVESTON (St Mary of Malmesbury) *Bris 8* **P** *D&C*
P-in-c B G CARNE, **Par Dn** A D THORNE
OMBERSLEY (St Andrew) w Doverdale *Worc 8* **P** *Bp*
and Lord Sandys (alt) **P-in-c** S P KERR
ONCHAN (St Peter) *S & M 2* **P** *The Crown*
V D BAGGALEY, **NSM** R HARPER
ONECOTE (St Luke) Ipstones w Berkhamsytch and
Onecote w Bradnop *Lich*
ONEHOUSE (St John the Baptist) Gt Finborough w
Onehouse and Harleston *St E*
ONGAR, HIGH (St Mary the Virgin) w Norton Mandeville
Chelmsf 6 **P** *Ch Soc Trust* **R** R J GRIFFITHS
ONIBURY (St Michael and All Angels) Culmington w
Onibury, Bromfield etc *Heref*
OPENSHAW (St Barnabas) *Man 1* **P** *Trustees*
R J WALLER
OPENSHAW, HIGHER (St Clement) *Man 1* **P** *Trustees*
R W NELSON
OPENWOODGATE (St Mark) Belper *Derby*
ORBY (All Saints) *Linc 8* **P** *Bp* **V** *Vacant*
ORCHARD (Community Centre) Egglescliffe *Dur*
ORCHARD PORTMAN (St Michael) Staple Fitzpaine,
Orchard Portman, Thurlbear etc *B & W*
ORCHARD WAY (St Barnabas) Cheltenham St Mark
Glouc
ORCHARDLEIGH (Blessed Virgin Mary) Beckington
w Standerwick, Berkley, Rodden etc *B & W*
ORCHESTON (St Mary) Tilshead, Orcheston and
Chitterne *Sarum*
ORCOP (St John the Baptist) St Weonards w Orcop,
Garway, Tretire etc *Heref*
ORDSALL (All Hallows) (St Alban) *S'well 5* **P** *Bp*
R A N EVANS, **C** P WATSON
ORE (Christ Church) *Chich 17* **P** *Simeon's Trustees*
V J G PANGBOURNE, **NSM** F ROWSON
ORE (St Barnabas) *Chich 17* **P** *Simeon's Trustees*
R F J GREED, **NSM** D K MOYNAGH
ORESTON (Church of the Good Shepherd) Plymstock
Ex
ORFORD (St Andrew) *Liv 12* **P** *Bp* **V** J HILTON
**ORFORD (St Bartholomew) w Sudbourne, Chillesford,
Butley and Iken** *St E 7* **P** *Bp* **R** D B GRAY
ORFORD (St Margaret) *Liv 12* **P** *Bp* **V** M S FINLAY
**ORLESTONE (St Mary) w Snave and Ruckinge w
Warehorne** *Cant 12* **P** *Abp and Ld Chan (alt)*
R S E WEST-LINDELL
ORLETON (St George) w Brimfield *Heref 7* **P** *Bp*
R P J WALTER
ORLINGBURY (St Mary) Gt w Lt Harrowden and
Orlingbury *Pet*
ORMESBY (St Cuthbert) *York 19* **P** *Abp*
Par Dn J E VAUGHAN-WILSON
ORMESBY (St Margaret) (St Michael) w Scratby *Nor 2*
P *D&C* **V** J W WILSON

ORMESBY, NORTH (Holy Trinity) *York 19* **P** *Abp*
V D M TROTTER
ORMSBY Group, The SOUTH (St Leonard) *Linc 7*
P *A J Massingberd-Mundy Esq, Sir Thomas Ingilby, Bt,*
Mert Coll Ox, Bp, and DBP (jt)
R R W B MASSINGBERD-MUNDY
ORMSGILL (St Francis) Barrow St Matt *Carl*
ORMSIDE (St James) *Carl 1* **P** *Bp and D&C (jt)*
R P E P NORTON
ORMSKIRK (St Peter and St Paul) *Liv 11* **P** *Lord Derby*
V K THORNTON, **C** G BOLAND
ORPINGTON (All Saints) *Roch 15* **P** *D&C*
V R R LUNNON, **C** K M PARRY, **Par Dn** H W TURNER,
NSM M T SKINNER
ORPINGTON (Christ Church) *Roch 15* **P** *Ch Trust Fund*
Trust, Bp, and V Orpington (jt) **V** A C EAVES,
C M R KEIRLE
ORPINGTON (St Andrew) *Roch 15* **P** *Bp*
V J A GROVES
ORRELL (St Luke) *Liv 15* **P** *Bp* **V** C POPE
ORSETT (St Giles and All Saints) and Bulphan *Chelmsf 16*
P *Bp* **R** V R HARROD, **NSM** J M WHITEHORN
ORSTON (St Mary) Whatton w Aslockton,
Hawksworth, Scarrington etc *S'well*
**ORTON (All Saints) and Tebay w Ravenstonedale and
Newbiggin-on-Lune** *Carl 1* **P** *Bp and Ravenstonedale*
Trustees (1 turn), Resident Landowners (1 turn)
R *Vacant* Orton (05874) 532
ORTON (St Giles) *Carl 1* **P** *MMCET* **R** I F BLACK
ORTON LONGUEVILLE (Holy Trinity) *Ely 13* **P** *Bp*
P-in-c M SOULSBY
**ORTON-ON-THE-HILL (St Edith of Polesworth) w
Twycross and Norton juxta Twycross** *Leic 13*
P *The Crown (2 turns), Bp (1 turn)* **V** K W BASTOCK
ORTON WATERVILLE (St Mary) *Ely 13* **P** *Pemb Coll*
Cam **P-in-c** G GOSWELL, **C** F E G BRAMPTON
ORWELL (St Andrew) *Ely 8* **P** *Bp and DBP (alt)*
R *Vacant*
OSBALDWICK (St Thomas) w Murton *York 4* **P** *Abp*
V R A STONE, **NSM** P TAIT
OSBOURNBY (St Peter and St Paul) S Lafford *Linc*
OSCOTT (All Saints) Kingstanding St Mark *Birm*
OSENEY CRESCENT (St Luke) *Lon 17* **P** *The Crown*
P-in-c R N ARNOLD, **C** R P P MARTIN
OSGATHORPE (St Mary the Virgin) Hathern, Long
Whatton and Diseworth w Belton etc *Leic*
OSMASTON (St Martin) Brailsford w Shirley and
Osmaston w Edlaston *Derby*
OSMINGTON (St Osmond) Preston w Sutton Poyntz
and Osmington w Poxwell *Sarum*
OSMONDTHORPE (St Philip) *Ripon 8* **P** *Bp*
V G R GREEN
**OSMOTHERLEY (St Peter) w East Harlsey and Ingleby
Arncliffe** *York 20* **P** *J B Barnard (1 turn), Ld Chan*
(2 turns) **V** A H DODD
OSMOTHERLY (St John) Ulverston St Mary w H Trin
Carl
OSPRINGE (St Peter and St Paul) Eastling w Ospringe
and Stalisfield w Otterden *Cant*
**OSSETT (St Oswald's Mission Room) (Holy and Undivided
Trinity) cum Gawthorpe** *Wakef 10* **P** *R Dewsbury*
V M GREEN
OSSETT, SOUTH (Christ Church) *Wakef 10* **P** *Bp*
V F J MARSH, **NSM** R PHILPOTT, R E RICHARDSON
OSSINGTON (Holy Rood) Norwell w Ossington,
Cromwell and Caunton *S'well*
OSWALDKIRK (St Oswald) Ampleforth and
Oswaldkirk and Gilling E *York*
OSWALDTWISTLE (Immanuel) (All Saints) *Blackb 1*
P *Trustees* **V** F PARR, **C** S J LOCKE
OSWALDTWISTLE (St Paul) *Blackb 1* **P** *Trustees*
V M D RATCLIFFE
OSWESTRY (Holy Trinity) *Lich 25* **P** *V Oswestry*
St Oswald **V** J M R A REAKES-WILLIAMS
OSWESTRY (St Oswald) *Lich 25* **P** *Earl of Powis*
V D B CROWHURST, **C** A R BAILEY
OTFORD (St Bartholomew) *Roch 9* **P** *D&C Westmr*
V D W TOWNE
OTFORD LANE (Mission Hall) Knockholt w Halstead
Roch
OTHAM (St Nicholas) w Langley *Cant 15* **P** *Abp and*
CPAS (jt) **R** D A MUSTON, **NSM** D W BOND
OTHERY (St Michael) Middlezoy and Othery and
Moorlinch *B & W*
OTLEY (All Saints) *Bradf 4* **P** *Bp* **V** I T RODLEY,
C S J LORD
OTLEY (St Mary) Clopton w Otley, Swilland and
Ashbocking *St E*

OTTER VALE Ottery St Mary, Alfington, W Hill, Tipton etc *Ex*

OTTERBOURNE (St Matthew) Compton and Otterbourne *Win*

OTTERBURN (St John the Evangelist) Bellingham/Otterburn Gp *Newc*

OTTERFORD (St Leonard) Churchstanton, Buckland St Mary and Otterford *B & W*

OTTERHAM (St Denis) Boscastle w Davidstow *Truro*

OTTERINGTON, NORTH (St Michael and All Angels) The Thorntons and The Otteringtons *York*

OTTERINGTON, SOUTH (St Andrew) as above

OTTERSHAW (Christ Church) *Guildf 11* **P** *Bp*
V J W BATT

OTTERTON (St Michael) and Colaton Raleigh *Ex 1*
P *Lord Clinton and Bp (jt)* **P-in-c** T A DAVISON

OTTERY ST MARY (St Mary the Virgin), Alfington, West Hill and Tipton St John w Venn Ottery *Ex 7* **P** *Patr Bd*
TR P J McGEE, **Par Dn** A M JORDAN

OTTRINGHAM (St Wilfrid) Keyingham w Ottringham, Halsham and Sunk Is *York*

OUGHTIBRIDGE (Ascension) *Sheff 7* **P** *V Wadsley*
V L E G BONIFACE

OUGHTRINGTON (St Peter) *Ches 10* **P** *Bp* **R** *Vacant*
Lymm (092 575) 2388

OULTON (St John the Evangelist) Stone Ch Ch and Oulton *Lich*

OULTON (St John) w Woodlesford *Ripon 8* **P** *Bp*
V J F HAMILTON

OULTON (St Michael) *Nor 15* **P** *Ch Soc Trust*
R *Vacant* Lowestoft (0502) 65722

OULTON (St Peter and St Paul) Saxthorpe w Corpusty, Blickling, Oulton etc *Nor*

OULTON BROAD (St Mark) (St Luke the Evangelist)
Nor 15 **P** *Simeon's Trustees* **V** W A STEWART,
C J C WILKINSON, V M ELPHICK,
Hon Par Dn J M STEWART

OUNDLE (St Peter) *Pet 12* **P** *Bp* **V** L R CADDICK,
NSM D M JARMY

OUSBY (St Luke) Skirwith, Ousby and Melmerby w Kirkland *Carl*

OUSDEN (St Peter) Lydgate w Ousden and Cowlinge *St E*

OUSEBURN, GREAT (St Mary) and LITTLE (Holy Trinity) w Marton-cum-Grafton *Ripon 3* **P** *Bp and St Jo Coll Cam (alt)* **V** S J TALBOTT

OUT RAWCLIFFE (St John the Evangelist) Hambleton w Out Rawcliffe *Blackb*

OUTLANE (St Mary Magdalene) Stainland *Wakef*

OUTWELL (St Clement) *Ely 19* **P** *Bp* **R** T J HEGGS

OUTWOOD (St John) *S'wark 23* **P** *Bp*
P-in-c W G WOOD

OUTWOOD (St Mary Magdalene) *Wakef 12* **P** *V Stanley*
V J W BUTTERWORTH

OUTWOOD COMMON (St John) Gt Burstead *Chelmsf*

OVAL WAY (All Saints) Chalfont St Peter *Ox*

OVENDEN (St George) *Wakef 4* **P** *V Halifax*
V S J L CROFT, **C** T J E MAYFIELD

OVENDEN (St John the Evangelist) Bradshaw *Wakef*

OVER: *see also under substantive place names*

OVER (St Chad) *Ches 6* **P** *Bp* **V** I H BLYDE

OVER (St John the Evangelist) *Ches 6* **P** *Lord Delamere and W R Cullimore Esq (jt)* **V** S F HAMILL-STEWART

OVER (St Mary) *Ely 5* **P** *Trin Coll Cam* **V** M WARRICK

OVERBURY (St Faith) w Teddington, Alstone and Little Washbourne w Beckford and Ashton under Hill *Worc 4*
P *D&C and MMCET (jt)* **V** J T W B JENKYNS,
NSM H M HUMPHREY

OVERCHURCH (St Mary) Upton *Ches*

OVERPOOL (St Francis) Ellesmere Port *Ches*

OVERSEAL (St Matthew) Nether and Over Seale *Derby*

OVERSTONE (St Nicholas) Mears Ashby and Hardwick and Sywell etc *Pet*

OVERSTRAND (St Martin) *Nor 7* **P** *DBP*
R R H CHATHAM

OVERTON (St Helen) *Blackb 12* **P** *V Lanc* **V** C BIRKET

OVERTON (St Mary) w Laverstoke and Freefolk *Win 6*
P *Bp* **R** N P CUMMING

OVERTON (St Michael and All Angels) Upper Kennett *Sarum*

OVING (All Saints) Schorne *Ox*

OVING (St Andrew) *Chich 3* **P** *Bp* **V** *Vacant*

OVINGDEAN (St Wulfran) *Chich 2* **P** *SMF*
P-in-c T S STRATFORD

OVINGHAM (St Mary the Virgin) *Newc 3* **P** *Bp*
V D L GOODACRE

OVINGTON (St John the Evangelist) Watton w Carbrooke and Ovington *Nor*

OVINGTON (St Mary) w Tilbury *Chelmsf 17*
P *M H Granger Esq* **R** *Vacant*

OVINGTON (St Peter) New Alresford w Ovington and Itchen Stoke *Win*

OWERMOIGNE (St Michael) Broadmayne, W Knighton, Owermoigne etc *Sarum*

OWERSBY, NORTH (St Martin) S Kelsey Gp *Linc*

OWLERTON (St John the Baptist) *Sheff 4* **P** *Ch Patr Trust* **V** D T BOTTLEY

OWLPEN (Holy Cross) Uley w Owlpen and Nympsfield *Glouc*

OWLSMOOR (St George) *Ox 16* **P** *Bp* **V** M R DUDLEY

OWLSWICK (Chapel) Monks Risborough *Ox*

OWMBY (St Peter and St Paul) and Normanby w Glentham *Linc 3* **P** *Duchy of Lanc (2 turns), D&C (2 turns), and Bp (1 turn)* **R** I R HOWITT

OWSLEBURY (St Andrew) Twyford and Owslebury and Morestead *Win*

OWSTON (All Saints) *Sheff 8* **P** *DBP* **V** R A C GRIEVE

OWSTON (St Andrew) Whatborough Gp of Par *Leic*

OWSTON (St Martin) *Linc 1* **P** *The Crown*
V A J RHODES

OWTHORNE (St Matthew) and Rimswell w Withernsea *York 13* **P** *Ld Chan and Abp (alt)* **V** P I ADDISON

OWTHORPE (St Margaret) *S'well 9* **P** *Trustees of Sir Rupert Bromley* **P-in-c** G B BARRODALE

OWTON MANOR (St James) *Dur 13* **P** *Bp*
V P ANDERTON, **AP** R A CHAPMAN

OXBOROUGH (St John the Evangelist) w Foulden and Caldecote *Nor 18* **P** *G&C Coll Cam*
P-in-c C W T CHALCRAFT, **C** G H WHEATLEY

OXCLOSE (not known) *Dur 1* **P** *R Washington, TR Usworth and V Fatfield (jt)* **V** D A ROBERTS

OXENDEN (St Helen) Arthingworth, Harrington w Oxendon and E Farndon *Pet*

OXENHALL (St Anne) Redmarley D'Abitot, Bromesberrow w Pauntley etc *Glouc*

OXENHOPE (St Mary the Virgin) *Bradf 8* **P** *Bp*
V B GRAINGER

OXENTON Woolstone w Gotherington and Oxenton etc *Glouc*

OXFORD Canning Crescent (St Luke) Ox St Aldate w St Matt *Ox*

OXFORD (St Aldate) (St Matthew) *Ox 7* **P** *Simeon's Trustees and Ox Ch Trust (jt)* **R** D R MACINNES,
C J F SAMWAYS, R A CHARKHAM,
Hon C A R WINGFIELD-DIGBY,
NSM E JOHNSON, J C H M LEE, T R W GEDYE, J EDMONDS-SEAL

OXFORD (St Andrew) *Ox 7* **P** *Trustees* **V** R F KEY,
C P MOORE, **Hon C** E G H SAUNDERS

OXFORD (St Barnabas and St Paul) *Ox 7* **P** *Keble Coll Ox* **V** E M WRIGHT, **NSM** D W MASON

OXFORD (St Clement) *Ox 4* **P** *Ox Ch Trust*
C L K ROSE, **NSM** A BEETHAM, N F HALLAM

OXFORD (St Ebbe w Holy Trinity and St Peter-le-Bailey)
Ox 7 **P** *Ox Ch Trust* **R** D C M FLETCHER,
C V E ROBERTS, **Par Dn** P J WHELAN

OXFORD (St Giles) (St Philip) (St James) (St Margaret)
Ox 7 **P** *St Jo Coll Ox* **V** J GAWNE-CAIN,
C K G HORSWELL, H CLEGG, **NSM** D R HOLMES

OXFORD (St Mary Magdalene) *Ox 7* **P** *Ch Ch Ox*
V H M WYBREW

OXFORD (St Mary the Virgin) (St Cross or Holywell) (St Peter in the East) *Ox 7* **P** *Or Coll Ox and Mert Coll Ox (jt)* **V** B W MOUNTFORD, **C** M A H RODEN

OXFORD (St Michael at the North Gate w St Martin and All Saints) *Ox 7* **P** *Linc Coll Ox* **V** S J PIX,
NSM E A SIMMONDS

OXFORD (St Thomas the Martyr) (St Frideswide) and Binsey *Ox 7* **P** *Ch Ch Ox* **V** R M SWEENEY,
NSM R C de V MARTIN

OXHEY (All Saints) *St Alb 13* **P** *Bp* **V** P J RIVETT,
Hon Par Dn P I LEECH

OXHEY (St Matthew) *St Alb 13* **P** *DBP* **V** J ORME,
C L J MILLER

OXHILL (St Lawrence) Tysoe w Oxhill and Whatcote *Cov*

OXLEY (Epiphany) *Lich 10* **P** *Bp* **V** G C FOWELL

OXNEAD (St Michael & all Angels) Buxton w Oxnead, Lammas and Brampton *Nor*

OXON and Shelton *Lich 27* **P** *V Shrewsbury SS Chad & Mary* **V** P F T FISHER,
Par Dn P M FREEMAN

OXSHOTT (St Andrew) *Guildf 10* **P** *Bp*
V J P CRESSWELL

OXTED (St Mary) *S'wark 23* **P** *Bp* **R** G BENNETT,
NSM F A HARDING

OXTON (St Peter and St Paul) *S'well 15*   **P** *Ld Chan, Bp,
and Comdr M B P Francklin (by turn)*
   V M J BROCK, **Dn-in-c pt** M A KEENE
OXTON (St Saviour) *Ches 1*   **P** *J B C Robin Esq*
   V A J POULTER, **C** W J HOGG, S E MOURANT
PACKINGTON (Holy Rood) w Normanton-le-Heath *Leic 9*
   P *MMCET and The Crown (alt)*   **P-in-c** H A BURTON
PACKINGTON (St James)   Meriden and Packington
   Cov
PACKWOOD (St Giles) w Hockley Heath *Birm 13*
   P *DBP and Bp (alt)*   **V** P H ROE
PADBURY (St Mary the Virgin)   Lenborough *Ox*
PADDINGTON (Emmanuel) Harrow Road *Lon 2*
   P *Hyndman Trustees*   **V** M M H JONES
PADDINGTON St David's Welsh Church (Extra-Parochial)
   Lon 2   **P-in-c** A P HAWKINS
PADDINGTON (St James) *Lon 2*   **P** *Bp*   **V** D A PERKIN,
   C G M BUCKLE
**PADDINGTON (St John the Evangelist) (St Michael and
   All Angels)** *Lon 2*   **P** *DBP*   **V** T J BIRCHARD,
   C O C M ROSS, **Hon C** C D V RICHARDS
PADDINGTON (St Luke the Evangelist)   W Kilburn
   St Luke w St Simon and St Jude *Lon*
PADDINGTON (St Mary) *Lon 2*   **P** *Bp*   **V** A E J FOSTER,
   C D L LAWRENCE-MARCH
PADDINGTON (St Mary Magdalene) *Lon 2*   **P** *Keble
   Coll Ox*   **V** R F BUSHAU
PADDINGTON (St Peter) *Lon 2*   **P** *Ch Patr Trust*
   P-in-c S J HOBBS
PADDINGTON (St Saviour) *Lon 2*   **P** *Bp*
   V G S BRADLEY, **C** W H BAYNES, **Hon C** M GIBSON,
   NSM F E BLACKMORE
PADDINGTON (St Stephen w St Luke) *Lon 2*   **P** *Bp*
   V T J KNIGHTS
PADDINGTON GREEN (St Mary)   Paddington St Mary
   Lon
PADDLESWORTH (St Oswald)   Lyminge w
   Paddlesworth, Stanford w Postling etc *Cant*
PADDOCK WOOD (St Andrew) *Roch 10*   **P** *D&C Cant*
   V D G StL WINTER, **C** A KEELER
PADGATE (Christ Church) *Liv 12*   **P** *Patr Bd*
   TR N T MOFFATT,
   TV J E GILBERT, M H MILLS, P W ORMROD,
   Par Dn J M MORRELL
PADIHAM (St Leonard) (St Anne and St Elizabeth)
   Blackb 3   **P** *Bp*   **V** J C DUXBURY, **C** R M SPURIN
PADSTOW (St Petrock) *Truro 7*
   P *C R Prideaux Brune Esq*   **V** M A BOXALL
PADWORTH (St John the Baptist)   Mortimer W End w
   Padworth *Ox*
PAGANHILL (The Holy Spirit)   Whiteshill *Glouc*
PAGHAM (St Thomas a Becket) *Chich 1*   **P** *Abp*
   V J W MAYNARD
PAGLESHAM (St Peter)   Canewdon w Paglesham
   Chelmsf
PAIGNTON (Christ Church) (School Room) *Ex 10*
   P *Peache Trustees*   **V** R C ADAMS
PAIGNTON (St John the Baptist) (St Andrew) (St Boniface)
   Ex 10   **P** *DBP*   **V** S L LEACH, **C** G K MAYER,
   Par Dn P D MAYER, **Hon Par Dn** C M BISHOP
PAIGNTON (St Paul) Preston *Ex 10*   **P** *Bp*
   V D G BELING
PAILTON (St Denys)   Monks Kirby w Pailton and
   Stretton-under-Fosse *Cov*
PAINSWICK (St Mary the Virgin) w Sheepscombe *Glouc 1*
   P *Ld Chan*   **V** M R MILES
PAKEFIELD (All Saints and St Margaret) *Nor 15*
   P *Ch Patr Trust*   **R** F DYSON
PAKENHAM (St Mary) w Norton and Tostock *St E 9*
   P *Bp and Peterho Cam (jt)*   **V** *Vacant* Pakenham
   (0359) 30287
PALGRAVE (St Peter)   N Hartismere *St E*
PALLION (St Luke) *Dur 9*   **P** *Bp*   **V** W G EAST
PALMARSH (Holy Cross)   Hythe *Cant*
PALMERS GREEN (St John the Evangelist) *Lon 18*
   P *V Southgate Ch Ch*   **V** R C KNOWLING
PALTERTON (St Luke's Mission Room)   Upper
   Langwith w Langwith Bassett etc *Derby*
PAMBER (St Mary and St John the Baptist)   The
   Sherbornes w Pamber *Win*
PAMBER HEATH (St Luke)   Tadley St Pet *Win*
PAMPISFORD (St John the Baptist) *Ely 7*
   P *Mrs B A Killander*   **V** *Vacant*
PANCRASWEEK (St Pancras)   Pyworthy, Pancrasweek
   and Bridgerule *Ex*
PANFIELD (St Mary the Virgin) *Chelmsf 18*   **P** *Bp*
   P-in-c G BARTLETT

**PANGBOURNE (St James the Less) w Tidmarsh and
   Sulham** *Ox 12*   **P** *Bp, Ch Soc Trust, and
   Mrs I E Moon (jt)*   **R** J C HUTCHINSON
PANNAL (St Robert of Knaresborough) w Beckwithshaw
   Ripon 1   **P** *Bp and Peache Trustees (jt)*
   V M de la P BERESFORD-PEIRSE
PANSHANGER (United Church)   Digswell and
   Panshanger *St Alb*
PAPCASTLE (Mission Church)   Bridekirk *Carl*
PAPPLEWICK (St James)   Linby w Papplewick *S'well*
PAPWORTH EVERARD (St Peter) *Ely 1*   **P** *DBP*
   R P S DUFFETT
PAR (St Mary the Virgin) (Good Shepherd) *Truro 1*
   P *The Crown*   **V** R N STRANACK
PARHAM (St Mary the Virgin)   Campsea Ashe w
   Marlesford, Parham and Hacheston *St E*
PARHAM (St Peter)   Amberley w N Stoke and Parham,
   Wiggonholt etc *Chich*
PARKEND (St Paul)   Dean Forest St Paul *Glouc*
PARKESTON (St Paul)   Dovercourt and Parkeston
   Chelmsf
PARKFIELD (Holy Trinity)   Langley and Parkfield *Man*
PARKGATE (St Thomas)   Neston *Ches*
**PARKHAM (St James), Alwington, Buckland Brewer and
   Abbotsham** *Ex 17*   **P** *The Crown (1 turn),
   Mrs M E Shallis (1 turn), Adn Barnstaple and Lt-Col
   T J Pine-Coffin (2 turns)*   **R** W G BLAKEY, **C** D YATES,
   Hon C J A WHEELER
PARKLANDS St Wilfrid Conventional District *Chich 3*
   C-in-c S G COTTRELL, **NSM** D A MORLING, M A JEWELL
PARKSTONE (Good Shepherd)   Heatherlands St Jo
   Sarum
PARKSTONE (St Luke) *Sarum 8*   **P** *Ch Trust Fund Trust*
   P-in-c J W DAVIES
PARKSTONE (St Peter) w Branksea and (St Osmund)
   Sarum 8   **P** *Patr Bd*   **TR** P R HUXHAM, **C** A P JEANS,
   Hon Par Dn D J NEWMAN
PARKWOOD (Christ Church)   Maidstone St Martin
   Cant
PARLAUNT ROAD (Christ the Worker)   Langley
   Marish *Ox*
PARLEY, WEST (All Saints) (St Mark) *Sarum 10*
   P *P E E Prideaux-Brune Esq*   **R** F G RASON
PARNDON, GREAT (St Mary) *Chelmsf 3*   **P** *Bp*
   R C P BURTON, **C** R LLOYD, **Par Dn** J M RAGAN,
   NSM A B WODEHOUSE
PARNDON, LITTLE (St Mary)   Harlow New Town w
   Lt Parndon *Chelmsf*
PARR Blackbrook (St Paul)   see below
PARR Derbyshire Hill (St Philip)   see below
PARR (St Peter) *Liv 10*   **P** *Patr Bd*   **TR** D A THOMPSON,
   TV P C CATON, P J THOMAS, **C** D G GAVIN
PARR MOUNT (Holy Trinity) *Liv 10*   **P** *V St Helens*
   V C S WOODS, **NSM** R J G HOPKINS
PARRACOMBE (Christ Church)   Lynton, Brendon,
   Countisbury, Lynmouth etc *Ex*
PARTINGTON (St Mary) and Carrington *Ches 10*   **P** *Bp
   and V Bowdon (alt)*   **V** I J HUTCHINGS, **C** J R WATTS,
   NSM E H J R BIRD
PARTNEY (St Nicholas) *Linc 7*   **P** *DBP, Bp, Baroness
   Willoughby de Eresby, and Mrs E M V Drake (by turn)*
   R G C MARTIN
PARTRIDGE GREEN (St Michael and All Angels)   W
   Grinstead *Chich*
PARWICH (St Peter) w Alsop en le Dale *Derby 8*
   P *D A G Shields Esq*   **P-in-c** J COOPER
PASSENHAM (St Guthlac) *Pet 5*   **P** *MMCET*
   R C J MURRAY, **Par Dn** G ORPIN
PASTON (All Saints) *Pet 13*   **P** *Bp*   **R** R A LOVELESS
PASTON (St Margaret)   Trunch *Nor*
PATCHAM (All Saints) *Chich 2*   **P** *MMCET*
   V D L N GUTSELL, **C** L L ABBOTT, M R YOUNG,
   Par Dn H E PATTEN
PATCHAM, SOUTH (Christ the King) *Chich 2*   **P** *Bp*
   V D H HUMPHREY, **NSM** J H LYON
PATCHING (St John the Divine)   Findon w Clapham
   and Patching *Chich*
PATCHWAY (St Chad) *Bris 6*   **P** *Trustees*   **C** C D BLAKE
PATELEY BRIDGE (St Cuthbert)   Upper Nidderdale
   Ripon
PATHFINDER (St John the Evangelist)   Whitestone *Ex*
PATNEY (St Swithin)   Redhorn *Sarum*
PATRICK (Holy Trinity) *S & M 3*   **P** *Bp*
   V B H PARTINGTON, **NSM** H G R SLADE
PATRICK BROMPTON (St Patrick) and Hunton *Ripon 4*
   P *Bp*   **V** R J PEARSON
PATRICROFT (Christ Church) *Man 2*   **P** *Bp*
   V D E BUTLER

PATRINGTON (St Patrick) w Hollym, Welwick and Winestead *York 13* **P** *DBP, Ld Chan, and CPAS (by turn)* **R** I M WELLERY

PATRIXBOURNE (St Mary) w Bridge and Bekesbourne *Cant 1* **P** *Abp* **V** R GILBERT

PATSHULL (St Mary) Pattingham w Patshull *Lich*

PATTERDALE (St Patrick) *Carl 4* **P** *Trustees* **P-in-c** G SCOTT

PATTINGHAM (St Chad) w Patshull *Lich 6* **P** *Bp and Lady Kwiatkowska (jt)* **V** R A BRADBURY

PATTISHALL (Holy Cross) w Cold Higham and Gayton w Tiffield *Pet 5* **P** *Bp, SS Coll Cam, and SMF (jt)* **R** *Vacant* Pattishall (0327) 830243

PAUL (St Pol de Lion) *Truro 5* **P** *Ld Chan* **V** G HARPER, **Hon C** P A ROBSON

PAULERSPURY (St James the Apostle) Whittlebury w Paulerspury *Pet*

PAULL (St Andrew and St Mary) Hedon w Paull *York*

PAULSGROVE (St Michael and All Angels) *Portsm 6* **P** *Bp* **V** B R BARNES, **C** G J GILES, E E MANNS

PAULTON (Holy Trinity) *B & W 13* **P** *Bp and R Chewton Mendip (alt)* **V** J E INGHAM

PAUNTLEY (St John the Evangelist) Redmarley D'Abitot, Bromesberrow w Pauntley etc *Glouc*

PAVENHAM (St Peter) Odell and Pavenham *St Alb*

PAWLETT (St John the Baptist) Puriton and Pawlett *B & W*

PAXFORD (Mission Church) Blockley w Aston Magna and Bourton on the Hill *Glouc*

PAXTON, GREAT (Holy Trinity) *Ely 12* **P** *D&C Linc* **V** P J TAYLOR

PAXTON, LITTLE (St James) *Ely 12* **P** *D&C Linc* **V** P G LEWIS

PAYHEMBURY (St Mary the Virgin) Broadhembury, Payhembury and Plymtree *Ex*

PEACEHAVEN (Ascension) *Chich 18* **P** *Bp* **V** I R PHELPS, **Par Dn** A V BOWMAN

PEAK DALE (Holy Trinity) Wormhill, Peak Forest w Peak Dale and Dove Holes *Derby*

PEAK FOREST (St Charles the King and Martyr) as above

PEAKIRK (St Pega) w Glinton *Pet 13* **P** *D&C* **R** J C OULD

PEAR TREE (Jesus Chapel) Southn St Mary Extra *Win*

PEASE POTTAGE (Ascension) Slaugham *Chich*

PEASEDOWN ST JOHN (St John the Baptist) w Wellow *B & W 13* **P** *Bp and R H Horton-Fawkes Esq (jt)* **V** H R L BONSEY

PEASEMORE (St Barnabas) Beedon and Peasemore w W Ilsley and Farnborough *Ox*

PEASENHALL (St Michael) w Sibton *St E 19* **P** *CPAS and Personal Reps Lt Comdr J A Brooke (jt)* **V** *Vacant* Peasenhall (072879) 256

PEASE'S WEST (St George) Crook *Dur*

PEASLAKE (St Mark) Shere *Guildf*

PEASLEY CROSS (Mission Hall) Parr Mt *Liv*

PEASMARSH (St Michael) Shalford *Guildf*

PEASMARSH (St Peter and St Paul) Beckley and Peasmarsh *Chich*

PEATLING MAGNA (All Saints) Willoughby Waterleys, Peatling Magna etc *Leic*

PEATLING PARVA (St Andrew) Gilmorton w Peatling Parva and Kimcote etc *Leic*

PEBMARSH (St John the Baptist) Alphamstone w Lamarsh and Pebmarsh *Chelmsf*

PEBWORTH (St Peter) w Dorsington and Honeybourne *Glouc 10* **P** *Bp* **R** T R C OVERTHROW

PECKHAM (St John w St Andrew) *S'wark 6* **P** *Bp* **P-in-c** M S JOHNSON, **Hon C** J E LANE

PECKHAM (St Mary Magdalene) (St Paul) *S'wark 6* **P** *Ch Patr Soc* **V** M F PAYNE, **C** M J PRITCHARD

PECKHAM (St Saviour) *S'wark 7* **P** *Bp* **V** W C HEATLEY

PECKHAM, EAST (Holy Trinity) and Nettlestead *Roch 7* **P** *St Pet Coll Ox and D&C Cant (jt)* **P-in-c** P N S HAYNES

PECKHAM, WEST (St Dunstan) Mereworth w W Peckham *Roch*

PECKLETON (St Mary Magdalene) Desford and Peckleton w Tooley *Leic*

PEDLINGE (Estate Chapel) Saltwood *Cant*

PEDMORE (St Peter) *Worc 11* **P** *Oldswinford Hosp* **R** A L HAZLEWOOD

PEEL (St Paul) *Man 12* **P** *Patr Bd* **C** P BRODY, **Par Dn** H BRUNYEE, **NSM** J KERR

PEEL GREEN (St Michael and All Angels and St Catherine) Barton w Peel Green *Man*

PEGSWOOD (St Margaret) Bothal *Newc*

PELDON (St Mary) w Great and Little Wigborough *Chelmsf 19* **P** *Ch Soc Trust and Mr T Wheatley-Hubbard* **P-in-c** J S SHORT, **NSM** J NEWHAM

PELSALL (St Michael and All Angels) *Lich 7* **P** *Bp* **V** D F MAWSON, **C** D J TURNER

PELTON (Holy Trinity) *Dur 9* **P** *R Chester le Street* **V** W A TAYLOR

PELTON, WEST (St Paul) *Dur 1* **P** *Bp* **P-in-c** R F BIANCHI, **NSM** M R BIANCHI

PELYNT (St Nun) *Truro 12* **P** *J B Kitson and Mrs S R Parker (alt)* **V** A R INGLEBY

PEMBERTON (St Francis of Assisi) Kitt Green *Liv 15* **P** *R Wigan and Bp (jt)* **V** R C HARDCASTLE

PEMBERTON (St John) *Liv 15* **P** *R Wigan* **R** J A SOUTHERN

PEMBERTON (St Mark) Newtown *Liv 15* **P** *Duke of Sutherland, Bp, and R Pemberton St Jo (jt)* **V** M E GREENWOOD, **C** D J P MOORE

PEMBRIDGE (St Mary the Virgin) w Moorcourt, Shobdon, Staunton-on-Arrow and Byton *Heref 5* **P** *Ld Chan (1 turn), J R Whitehead Esq and Miss R Whitehead (1 turn), and DBP (2 turns)* **R** S HOLLINGHURST

PEMBURY (St Peter) *Roch 11* **P** *Ch Ch Ox* **V** R H BRASIER

PEN SELWOOD (St Michael) *B & W 2* **P** *Bp* **R** R J CLOETE

PENCOMBE (St John) Bredenbury w Grendon Bishop and Wacton etc *Heref*

PENCOYD (St Denys) St Weonards w Orcop, Garway, Tretire etc *Heref*

PENCOYS (St Andrew) Redruth w Lanner and Treleigh *Truro*

PENDEEN (St John the Baptist) w Morvah *Truro 5* **P** *R A H Aitken and C W M Aitken (jt)* **V** A ROWELL, **NSM** J HARPER

PENDEFORD (St Paul) Tettenhall Regis *Lich*

PENDLEBURY (St Augustine) Swinton and Pendlebury *Man*

PENDLEBURY (St John) *Man 6* **P** *Trustees* **V** C JONES, **C** A N BATEMAN

PENDLETON (All Saints) Sabden and Pendleton *Blackb*

PENDLETON (St Ambrose) *Man 6* **P** *Bp* **V** *Vacant* 061-745 7608

PENDLETON (St Thomas) w Charlestown *Man 6* **P** *Patr Bd* **TR** G HOWARD, **TV** D A KNIGHT, T W BROADBENT, **Hon C** D J H KEYTE

PENDOCK CROSS (Holy Redeemer) Berrow w Pendock, Eldersfield, Hollybush etc *Worc*

PENDOMER (St Roch) W Coker w Hardington Mandeville, E Chinnock etc *B & W*

PENGE (Christ Church w Holy Trinity) Anerley *Roch*

PENGE (St John the Evangelist) *Roch 12* **P** *Simeon's Trustees* **V** J D KILFORD, **Par Dn** J A HUGHMAN

PENGE (St Paul) *Roch 12* **P** *Ch Patr Trust* **V** D I CHARNOCK

PENGE LANE (Holy Trinity) *Roch 12* **P** *CPAS* **V** J A WHEELER

PENHILL (St Peter) *Bris 10* **P** *Bp* **V** *Vacant* Swindon (0793) 721921

PENHURST (St Michael the Archangel) Ashburnham w Penhurst *Chich*

PENISTONE (St John the Baptist) and Thurlstone *Wakef 7* **P** *Bp* **TR** D C TURNBULL, **TV** G W MIDGLEY, **C** S R S SWALES

PENKETH (St Paul) *Liv 13* **P** *Bp* **V** P W HOCKLEY

PENKHULL (St Thomas) *Lich 18* **P** *R Stoke-on-Trent* **V** I MAITIN

PENKRIDGE Team, The (St Michael and All Angels) *Lich 3* **P** *Patr Bd* **TR** G STATON, **TV** D P SMITH, **Res Min** M A HARRIS, **C** P R CARTER, **NSM** C L CARTER (nee SMITH)

PENN (Holy Trinity) *Ox 20* **P** *Earl Howe* **P-in-c** P J WIDDICOMBE

PENN (St Bartholomew) (St Anne) *Lich 6* **P** *Bp* **V** G M F WILLIAMS, **C** M H HAWKSWORTH

PENN FIELDS St Philip (St Aidan) *Lich 6* **P** *Ch Trust Fund Trust* **V** W H NASH, **C** M J HUNTER, B E CROSBY

PENN STREET (Holy Trinity) *Ox 20* **P** *Earl Howe* **V** N J STOWE

PENNARD, EAST (All Saints) Ditcheat w E Pennard and Pylle *B & W*

PENNARD, WEST (St Nicholas) Glastonbury w Meare, W Pennard and Godney *B & W*

PENNINGTON (Christ Church) *Man 13* **P** *Trustees* **V** P W LEAKEY, **C** A W HARDY, **Hon C** W G SPEDDING

PENNINGTON (St Mark) *Win 10* **P** *V Milford* **V** J D PIBWORTH

PENNINGTON (St Michael and the Holy Angels) w Lindal and Marton *Carl 8*   **P** *Bp*   **P-in-c** S D RUDKIN
PENNYCROSS (St Pancras) *Ex 22*   **P** *CPAS*
  V L E DENNY, **C** W O PANG
PENNYWELL (St Thomas)   Sunderland Pennywell St Thos *Dur*
PENPONDS (Holy Trinity) *Truro 2*   **P** *The Crown*
  V *Vacant*   Camborne (0209) 712329
PENRITH (Christ Church) (St Andrew) w Newton Reigny and Plumpton Wall *Carl 4*   **P** *Bp*
  TV M A HESLOP, R W HOWE
PENRUDDOCK (All Saints)   Greystoke, Matterdale, Mungrisdale & W'millock *Carl*
PENSAX (St James the Great)   Teme Valley N *Worc*
PENSBY (St Michael and All Angels)   Barnston *Ches*
PENSHAW (All Saints) *Dur 6*   **P** *Bp*   **R** K WALKER
PENSHURST (St John the Baptist) and Fordcombe
  Roch 11   **P** *Viscount De L'Isle*   **R** M STYLER-WHITTLE
PENSILVA (St John)   St Ive w Quethiock *Truro*
PENSNETT (St Mark) *Lich 1*   **P** *Bp*   **V** N S FOX
PENTEWAN (All Saints)   St Austell *Truro*
PENTLOW (St George and St Gregory), Foxearth, Liston and Borley *Chelmsf 17*   **P** *Mr K Foster and Bp, and DBP (by turn)*   **R** J T DAVIES
PENTNEY (St Mary Magdalene) w West Bilney *Nor 23*
  P *Bp*   **V** S R NAIRN
PENTON MEWSEY (Holy Trinity)   Hatherden w Tangley, Weyhill and Penton Mewsey *Win*
PENTONVILLE (St Silas w All Saints) (St James) *Lon 6*
  P *Bp*   **V** A T J SALTER, **Hon C** D F PAULEY
PENTRICH (St Matthew)   Swanwick and Pentrich *Derby*
PENTRIDGE (St Rumbold)   Handley w Gussage St Andrew and Pentridge *Sarum*
PENWERRIS (St Michael and All Angels) (Holy Spirit)
  Truro 3   **P** *V St Gluvias*   **C** G CHAPMAN
PENWORTHAM (St Leonard) *Blackb 6*   **P** *Bp*
  V R TOWNLEY
PENWORTHAM (St Mary) *Blackb 6*
  P *J M G Rawstorne, J R Rawstorne and A F Rawstorne (jt)*   **C** P E M HOLLANDS
PENZANCE (St John the Baptist) *Truro 5*   **P** *Bp*
  V M R JUPE
PENZANCE (St Mary the Virgin) (St Paul) *Truro 5*   **P** *Bp*
  V D BOUNDY
PEOPLETON (St Nicholas) and White Ladies Aston w Churchill and Spetchley *Worc 4*   **P** *Bp and Major R J G Berkeley (alt)*   **P-in-c** H G PHILLIPS
PEOVER, NETHER (St Oswald) *Ches 12*   **P** *Man Univ*
  V K M BURGHALL
PEOVER, OVER (St Lawrence)   Marthall w Over Peover *Ches*
PEPER HAROW (St Nicholas)   Compton w Shackleford and Peper Harow *Guildf*
PEPLOW (The Epiphany)   Hodnet w Weston under Redcastle *Lich*
PERIVALE (St Mary w St Nicholas) *Lon 22*   **P** *Trustees*
  R *Vacant*   081-997 1948
PERLETHORPE (St John the Evangelist) *S'well 6*
  P *Earl Manvers' Trustees*   **P-in-c** J R WILLIAMS
PERRANARWORTHAL (St Piran)   St Stythians w Perranarworthal and Gwennap *Truro*
PERRANPORTH (St Michael's Mission Church)
  Perranzabuloe *Truro*
PERRANUTHNOE (St Michael and St Piran)   St Hilary w Perranuthnoe *Truro*
PERRANZABULOE (St Piran) *Truro 6*   **P** *D&C*
  V A J WRIGHT
PERROTT, NORTH (St Martin)   Haselbury Plucknett, Misterton and N Perrott *B & W*
PERROTT, SOUTH (St Mary)   Beaminster Area *Sarum*
PERRY BARR (St John the Evangelist) *Birm 3*   **P** *Lord Calthorpe*   **V** B H PARRY, **C** P D ANDREWS
PERRY BEECHES (St Matthew) *Birm 3*   **P** *St Martin's Trustees*   **V** S P M MACKENZIE
PERRY COMMON (St Martin) *Birm 6*   **P** *Bp*
  V J E M BARBER
PERRY GREEN (St Thomas)   Much Hadham *St Alb*
PERRY HILL (St George) *S'wark 4*   **P** *Bp and D&C (alt)*
  V W G GOLBOURNE
PERRY STREET (All Saints) *Roch 4*   **P** *Bp*
  V J G K BATSON, **C** D V GOWER
PERSHORE (Holy Cross) w Pinvin, Wick and Birlingham
  Worc 4   **P** *Patr Bd*   **V** W J M COOMBS,
  Hon C D CHATWIN, **NSM** R M NICHOLLS
PERTENHALL (St Peter)   The Stodden Churches *St Alb*
PETER TAVY (St Peter) *Ex 25*   **P** *Guild of All Souls*
  R P M COMERFORD
PETERBOROUGH (All Saints) *Pet 13*   **P** *Bp*
  V E G ORLAND

PETERBOROUGH (Christ the Carpenter) *Pet 13*   **P** *Bp*
  V C J SMITH
PETERBOROUGH (Holy Spirit) Bretton *Pet 13*   **P** *Bp*
  V P M HAWKINS, **C** B M SMITH
PETERBOROUGH (St Barnabas) *Pet 13*   **P** *Bp*
  P-in-c M D DAVIES
PETERBOROUGH (St John the Baptist) (Mission Church)
  Pet 13   **P** *Bp*   **V** A J HOWITT
PETERBOROUGH (St Jude) *Pet 13*   **P** *Bp*   **V** D G BOND,
  C M G CROOK
PETERBOROUGH (St Mark) *Pet 13*   **P** *Bp*   **V** *Vacant*
  Peterborough (0733) 54516
PETERBOROUGH (St Mary) Boongate (St Michael)
  Pet 13   **P** *D&C*   **V** J BATES, **C** J L EVANS
PETERBOROUGH (St Paul) *Pet 13*   **P** *Bp*   **V** B SECKER
PETERCHURCH (St Peter) w Vowchurch, Turnastone and Dorstone *Heref 1*   **P** *Bp (2 turns), Bp Birm (1 turn)*
  R J C de la T DAVIES, **NSM** J J HILLMAN
PETERLEE (St Cuthbert) *Dur 3*   **P** *Bp*
  V K I WOODHOUSE, **C** P T ALLINSON, P DOUGLASS
PETERSFIELD (St Peter) *Portsm 5*   **P** *Bp*   **V** C LOWSON,
  NSM J C GRACE
PETERSHAM (All Saints) (St Peter) *S'wark 15*   **P** *Bp*
  P-in-c D L GAMBLE
PETERSMARLAND (St Peter)   Shebbear, Buckland Filleigh, Sheepwash etc *Ex*
PETERSTOW (St Peter)   Ross w Brampton Abbotts, Bridstow and Peterstow *Heref*
PETHAM (All Saints) and Waltham w Lower Hardres and Nackington w Upper Hardres and Stelling *Cant 2*
  P *Abp, St Jo Coll Ox, and Trustees Lord Tomlin (jt)*
  P-in-c R W BATEMAN, **C** P G COX
PETHERTON, NORTH (St Mary the Virgin) w Northmoor Green *B & W 15*   **P** *Dr R Addy*   **V** B C CASTLE,
  Hon C N A F TOWNEND
PETHERTON, SOUTH (St Peter and St Paul) w the Seavingtons *B & W 16*   **P** *D&C*   **R** C G MOORE,
  C I C WHITTLE
PETHERWIN, NORTH (St Paternus)   Bolventor *Truro*
PETHERWIN, SOUTH (St Paternus)   Lezant w Lawhitton and S Petherwin w Trewen *Truro*
PETROCKSTOWE (St Petrock)   Shebbear, Buckland Filleigh, Sheepwash etc *Ex*
PETT (St Mary and St Peter)   Guestling and Pett *Chich*
PETT LEVEL (St Nicholas)   as above
PETTAUGH (St Catherine)   Helmingham w Framsden and Pettaugh w Winston *St E*
PETTISTREE (St Peter and St Paul)   Wickham Market w Pettistree and Easton *St E*
PETTON (not known) w Cockshutt, Welshampton and Lyneal w Colemere *Lich 23*   **P** *Bp,
  R K Mainwaring Esq, and Personal Reps Lord Brownlow (jt)*   **R** J DURNELL
PETTON (St Petrock)   Bampton, Morebath, Clayhanger and Petton *Ex*
PETTS WOOD (St Francis) *Roch 15*   **P** *Bp*
  V R E THOMPSON
PETWORTH (St Mary) *Chich 11*   **P** *Lord Egremont*
  R D F GRANT
PEVENSEY (St Nicholas) (St Wilfred) *Chich 16*   **P** *Bp*
  V A C H CHRISTIAN
PEWSEY Team Ministry, The (St John the Baptist)
  Sarum 21   **P** *Patr Bd*   **TR** C G FOX, **TM** D E TWISS
PHEASEY (St Chad) *Lich 7*   **P** *DBP*   **V** M J G BINNEY,
  Par Dn M P STOKES
PHILBEACH GARDENS (St Cuthbert)   Earl's Court St Cuth w St Matthias *Lon*
PHILLACK (St Felicitas) w Gwithian and Gwinear *Truro 5*
  P *Wg Comdr T P D la Touche and Bp (alt)*
  R P J BROOKS, **NSM** A J HANCOCK
PHILLEIGH (St Philleigh)   St Just in Roseland w Philleigh *Truro*
PICKENHAM, NORTH (St Andrew) w SOUTH (All Saints) and Houghton on the Hill *Nor 18*   **P** *Ch Soc Trust*   **R** D G W GREEN
PICKERING (St Peter and St Paul) *York 21*   **P** *Abp*
  V G LAWN
PICKHILL (All Saints)   Kirklington w Burneston and Wath and Pickhill *Ripon*
PICKWELL (All Saints)   Burrough Hill Pars *Leic*
PICKWORTH (All Saints)   Gt and Lt Casterton w Pickworth and Tickencote *Pet*
PICKWORTH (St Andrew)   S Lafford *Linc*
PICTON (St Hilary)   Kirklevington *York*
PIDDINGHOE (St John)   Telscombe w Piddinghoe and Southease *Chich*
PIDDINGTON (St John the Baptist)   Hardingstone and Horton and Piddington *Pet*

PIDDINGTON (St Nicholas) Ambrosden w Mert and Piddington *Ox*

PIDDLE, NORTH (St Michael) Upton Snodsbury and Broughton Hackett etc *Worc*

PIDDLEHINTON (St Mary the Virgin) see below

PIDDLETRENTHIDE (All Saints) w Plush, Alton Pancras and Piddlehinton *Sarum 2* **P** Eton Coll, D&C Sarum, and D&C Win (by turn) **P-in-c** D N G PARRY

PIDLEY CUM FENTON (All Saints) Somersham w Pidley and Oldhurst *Ely*

PIERCEBRIDGE (St Mary) Coniscliffe *Dur*

PILHAM (All Saints) Blyton w Pilham *Linc*

PILL (Christ Church) w Easton in Gordano and Portbury *B & W 14* **P** Bp **V** R F D KINSEY, **NSM** I M TUCKER

PILLATON (St Modwen) Penkridge Team *Lich*

PILLATON (St Odolph) St Dominic, Landulph and St Mellion w Pillaton *Truro*

PILLERTON HERSEY (St Mary) Butlers Marston and the Pillertons w Ettington *Cov*

PILLEY (Mission Church) Tankersley *Sheff*

PILLEY (St Nicholas) Boldre w S Baddesley *Win*

PILLING (St John the Baptist) *Blackb 10* **P** A F Mason-Hornby Esq and H D H Elletson Esq (alt) **V** G S RANSON, **Hon C** K W BATEMAN

PILNING (St Peter) w Compton Greenfield *Bris 8* **P** Bp **V** J R BARFF

PILSLEY (St Mary the Virgin) N Wingfield, Clay Cross and Pilsley *Derby*

PILTON (All Saints) Aldwincle w Thorpe Achurch, Pilton, Wadenhoe etc *Pet*

PILTON (St John the Baptist) w Croscombe, North Wootton and Dinder *B & W 9* **P** Bp and Peache Trustees (jt) **R** G MILLIER

PILTON (St Mary the Virgin) w Ashford *Ex 15* **P** Ld Chan **V** J C SPEAR

PILTON (St Nicholas) Preston and Ridlington w Wing and Pilton *Pet*

PIMLICO Bourne Street (St Mary) Pimlico St Mary Graham Terrace *Lon*

PIMLICO (St Barnabas) *Lon 3* **P** Bp **P-in-c** O J HOLTH

PIMLICO (St Gabriel) *Lon 3* **P** Bp **V** D W SKEOCH, **NSM** Sir W D PATTINSON

PIMLICO (St James the Less) Westmr St Sav and St Jas Less *Lon*

PIMLICO (St Mary) Graham Terrace *Lon 3* **P** Trustees **V** W S SCOTT, **C** N J M KAVANAGH, **Hon C** D PRIEST

PIMLICO (St Peter) w Westminster (Christ Church) *Lon 3* **P** Bp **V** D B TILLYER, **NSM** A R CHIDWICK

PIMLICO (St Saviour) Westmr St Sav and St Jas Less *Lon*

PIMPERNE (St Peter), Stourpaine, Durweston and Bryanston *Sarum 7* **P** DBP (2 turns), D&C (1 turn) **R** G S M SQUAREY

PINCHBECK (St Mary) *Linc 17* **P** Mrs B S Corley **V** D R HILL

PINCHBECK, WEST (St Bartholomew) Surfleet *Linc*

PINHOE (St Michael and All Angels) (Hall) and Broadclyst *Ex 1* **P** Patr Bd **TR** A J MORTIMER, **TV** J T THOMPSON, **NSM** M GENT

PINNER (St John the Baptist) *Lon 23* **P** V Harrow **V** D J TUCK, **Hon C** M S NATTRASS, **NSM** I W MURRAY

PINVIN (St Nicholas) Pershore w Pinvin, Wick and Birlingham *Worc*

PINXTON (St Helen) (Church Hall) *Derby 1* **P** Bp **R** R J I PAGET

PIPE-CUM-LYDE (St Peter) Wellington w Pipe-cum-Lyde and Moreton-on-Lugg *Heref*

PIPEWELL (St Mary) Rothwell w Orton, Rushton w Glendon and Pipewell *Pet*

PIRBRIGHT (St Michael) *Guildf 12* **P** Ld Chan **V** R E N STREVENS

PIRNOUGH (All Hallows) Ditchingham, Hedenham and Broome *Nor*

PIRTON (St Mary) *St Alb 9* **P** D&C Ely **V** D A CLENDON

PIRTON (St Peter) Stoulton w Drake's Broughton and Pirton etc *Worc*

PISHILL (not known) Nettlebed w Bix and Highmore *Ox*

PITCHCOMBE (St John the Baptist) The Edge, Pitchcombe, Harescombe and Brookthorpe *Glouc*

PITCHFORD (St Michael and All Angels) Condover w Frodesley, Acton Burnell etc *Heref*

PITCOMBE (St Leonard) Bruton and Distr *B & W*

PITMINSTER (St Mary and St Andrew) w Corfe *B & W 20* **P** DBP and Personal Reps of Mrs J H Spurway (alt) **V** R L RAIKES, **Hon C** C CANTI

PITNEY (St John the Baptist) Langport Area Chs *B & W*

PITSEA (St Gabriel) *Chelmsf 9* **P** Bp **R** L B LANEY, **C** H L LEE

PITSFORD (All Saints) w Boughton *Pet 2* **P** Bp **R** S J TROTT

PITSMOOR (Christ Church) *Sheff 3* **P** Ch Patr Trust and DBP (Alt) **V** D J H SPARKES

PITTINGTON (St Laurence) Sherburn w Pittington *Dur*

PITTON (St Peter) Alderbury Team *Sarum*

PITTVILLE Cheltenham (All Saints) *Glouc 11* **P** Bp **V** W J JENNINGS, **NSM** M E THAME

PIXHAM (not known) Dorking w Ranmore *Guildf*

PIXLEY (St Andrew) Tarrington w Stoke Edith, Aylton, Pixley etc *Heref*

PLAISTOW (Holy Trinity) Kirdford *Chich*

PLAISTOW (St Martin) (St Mary) (St Philip and St James) *Chelmsf 5* **P** Patr Bd **TV** C F TURNER, A B KING, **P-in-c** P S ANDERSON, **C** R H WILLIAMS

PLAISTOW (St Mary) *Roch 13* **P** Bp **V** P R HENWOOD

PLAITFORD (St Peter) Bramshaw and Landford w Plaitford *Sarum*

PLALTS HEATH (St Edmund) Lenham w Boughton Malherbe *Cant*

PLAS NEWTON (St Michael) *Ches 2* **P** Simeon's Trustees **V** Vacant

PLATT (St Mary the Virgin) *Roch 9* **P** Bp **V** R V DOUGLAS

PLATT BRIDGE (St Nathaniel) *Liv 14* **P** Bp **V** B GREGORY, **Par Dn** P A BARNETT

PLAXTOL (not known) *Roch 9* **P** Bp **R** M B HOBBS

PLAYDEN (St Michael) Rye *Chich*

PLAYFORD (St Mary) Gt and Lt Bealings w Playford and Culpho *St E*

PLEASLEY (St Michael) *Derby 3* **P** Capt H B C Davie-Thornhill **R** I E WINTERBOTTOM

PLEASLEY HILL (St Barnabas) *S'well 2* **P** Bp **Dn-in-c** A M SMYTHE

PLEASLEY VALE (St Chad) Mansf Woodhouse *S'well*

PLEMSTALL (St Peter) w Guilden Sutton *Ches 2* **P** Capt P Egerton Warburton **V** J A MALBON

PLESHEY (Holy Trinity) *Chelmsf 11* **P** Bp **C** W C MILLS

PLUCKLEY (St Mary) Egerton w Pluckley *Cant*

PLUCKLEY (St Nicholas) as above

PLUMBLAND (St Cuthbert) and Gilcrux *Carl 7* **P** Bp and Exors E S C Curwen (jt) **R** F L PRICE

PLUMPTON (All Saints) (St Michael and All Angels) *Chich 18* **P** Bp **R** G D BROSTER

PLUMPTON (St John the Baptist) Weedon Lois w Plumpton and Moreton Pinkney etc *Pet*

PLUMPTON WALL (St John the Evangelist) Penrith w Newton Reigny and Plumpton Wall *Carl*

PLUMSTEAD (Ascension) *S'wark 1* **P** Bp **V** M J KINGSTON

PLUMSTEAD Shooters Hill (All Saints) *S'wark 1* **P** CPAS **V** H D OWEN, **Hon C** A L AYRES

PLUMSTEAD (St John the Baptist) w St James and St Paul *S'wark 1* **P** Simeon's Trustees and CPAS (alt) **V** P J ROGERS, **C** N J ANSTEY

PLUMSTEAD (St Mark) and St Margaret *S'wark 1* **P** DBP **V** N E DAVIES

PLUMSTEAD (St Michael) Barningham w Matlaske w Baconsthorpe etc *Nor*

PLUMSTEAD (St Nicholas) *S'wark 1* **P** V Plumstead St Mark w St Marg **V** M J P DYMOCK

PLUMSTEAD, GREAT (St Mary) w LITTLE (St Gervase and Protase) and Witton *Nor 1* **P** Bp and D&C (jt) **R** B W TOMLINSON

PLUMTREE (St Mary) *S'well 9* **P** DBP **R** J J STAFFORD

PLUNGAR (St Helen) Barkestone w Plungar, Redmile and Stathern *Leic*

PLYMOUTH Crownhill (Ascension) *Ex 23* **P** Bp **V** L M MALSOM

PLYMOUTH (Emmanuel) (St Augustine), Efford (St Paul) *Ex 24* **P** Patr Bd **TR** T J NOTTAGE, **TV** I J LOVETT, **C** S J CONEYS

PLYMOUTH (St Andrew) (St George and St Paul) *Ex 24* **P** Ch Patr Trust **V** J F W WATSON, **C** M CHESTER, K F FREEMAN

PLYMOUTH (St Gabriel) Peverell *Ex 24* **P** Bp **V** J J STARK, **NSM** L J HOWARTH

PLYMOUTH (St James the Less) Ham *Ex 22* **P** Keble Coll Ox **V** A J HAWKER

PLYMOUTH (St John the Evangelist) Sutton on Plym *Ex*

PLYMOUTH (St Jude) *Ex 24* **P** Trustees **V** B F SWABEY, **C** N COOPER

PLYMOUTH (St Mary the Virgin) Laira *Ex*

PLYMOUTH (St Matthias)   Charles w St Matthias
Plymouth *Ex*
PLYMOUTH (St Peter) (All Saints) *Ex 22*   P *Keble Coll
Ox*   V S PHILPOTT,   C D J NIXON
PLYMOUTH (St Simon) *Ex 24*   P *St Simon Trustees*
V J C STYLER
PLYMPTON (St Mary the Blessed Virgin) *Ex 23*   P *Bp*
V J F RICHARDS,   C G J STANTON,
NSM M BRIMICOMBE
PLYMPTON (St Maurice) *Ex 23*   P *D&C Windsor*
R T E THOMAS
PLYMSTOCK (St Mary and All Saints) *Ex 24*   P *D&C
Windsor*   V P H W HAWKINS,   C A P G FRAMPTON-
MORGAN, N J CHARRINGTON,   **Par Dn** J J SPEAR
PLYMTREE (St John the Baptist)   Broadhembury,
Payhembury and Plymtree *Ex*
POCKLEY (St John the Baptist)   Harome w Stonegrave,
Nunnington and Pockley *York*
POCKLINGTON (All Saints) and Owsthorpe and Kilnwick
Percy w Great Givendale, Huggate and Millington *York 7*
P *Abp*   R R H K PROSSER
PODIMORE (St Peter)   Ilchester w Northover,
Limington, Yeovilton etc *B & W*
PODINGTON (St Mary the Virgin)   Wymington w
Podington *St Alb*
POINT CLEAR (Mission)   St Osyth *Chelmsf*
POINTON (Christ Church)   Sempringham w Pointon and
Birthorpe *Linc*
POKESDOWN (All Saints) *Win 7*   P *V Christchurch*
V B G APPS,   **Hon C** W R NESBITT
POKESDOWN (St James) *Win 7*   P *Bp*
V A F J CHAMBERS
POLDENS, WEST *B & W 5*   P *Bp*   V A E D MURDOCH
POLEBROOK (All Saints) and Lutton w Hemington and
Luddington *Pet 12*   P *Bp, Sir Stephen Hastings, and
R K Measures Esq (by turn)*   R *Vacant*   Oundle (0832)
72500
POLEGATE (St John) (St Wilfred) *Chich 16*   P *Bp*
V P R THOMPSON,   C K HODSON
POLESWORTH (St Editha) *Birm 12*   P *Ld Chan*
V D C BYFORD
POLING (St Nicholas) *Chich 1*   P *Bp*   V J E SLEGG
POLLINGTON (St John the Baptist)   Gt Snaith *Sheff*
POLPERRO (St John the Baptist)   Talland *Truro*
POLRUAN (St Saviour)   Lanteglos by Fowey *Truro*
POLSTEAD (St Mary) *St E 3*   P *St Jo Coll Ox*
P-in-c G MARSDEN
POLTIMORE (St Mary the Virgin)   Stoke Canon,
Poltimore w Huxham and Rewe etc *Ex*
PONDERS END (St Matthew) *Lon 18*   P *V Enfield*
V J D SCOTT
PONDERSBRIDGE (St Thomas)   Whittlesey and
Pondersbridge *Ely*
PONSANOOTH (St Michael and All Angels)   Mabe
Truro
PONSBOURNE (St Mary)   Lt Berkhamsted and
Bayford, Essendon etc *St Alb*
PONSONBY (not known)   Beckermet St Jo and St
Bridget w Ponsonby *Carl*
PONTEFRACT (All Saints) *Wakef 11*   P *Bp*
V E FOWKES
PONTEFRACT (St Giles w St Mary) *Wakef 11*   P *Bp*
V G HIGGINS
PONTELAND (St Mary the Virgin) *Newc 7*   P *Mert Coll
Ox*   V J M LOWEN,
Hon C P G WOLFENDEN, C G THORNE, **Dss** A A ELKINGTON
PONTESBURY 1st and 2nd Portions (St George) *Heref 13*
P *St Chad's Coll Dur*   R D H ROBERTS
PONTON, GREAT (Holy Cross)   Colsterworth Gp *Linc*
PONTON, LITTLE (St Guthlac)   as above
POOL (St Wilfrid) w Arthington *Ripon 1*
P *C E W Sheepshanks Esq and V Otley (jt)*
V D R H de la HOYDE
POOLE (St James w St Paul) *Sarum 8*   P *Ch Soc Trust
and J H Cordle Esq (jt)*   R S C HOLBROOKE-JONES
POOLE KEYNES (St Michael and All Angels)   Kemble,
Poole Keynes, Somerford Keynes etc *Glouc*
POOLEY BRIDGE (St Paul)   Barton, Pooley Bridge
and Martindale *Carl*
POOLSBROOK (St Alban)   Staveley and Barrow Hill
Derby
POORTON, NORTH (St Mary Magdalene)   Askerswell,
Loders and Powerstock *Sarum*
POPLAR (All Saints) *Lon 7*   P *Patr Bd*   **TR** L A GREEN,
TV W D N WEIR,   C P BRISTOW,   **Par Dn** V W HYDON,
Hon C W F SHERGOLD
POPPLETON, NETHER (St Everilda) w UPPER (All
Saints) *York 1*   P *Abp*   V L J GREEN,
Hon C M C S FOSSETT

POPPLETON ROAD (Mission Room)   York St Paul
York
PORCHESTER (St James) *S'well 11*   P *Bp*
V R D A MORE,   C C A K MAIDEN
PORINGLAND, GREAT (All Saints) w Little Poringland
and Howe *Nor 14*   P *G H H Wheler Esq and DBP (alt)*
R R B HEMS
PORLOCK (St Dubricius) w Stoke Pero *B & W 17*
P *Ld Chan*   R C MUNT
PORLOCK WEIR (St Nicholas)   Porlock w Stoke Pero
B & W
PORT ERIN (St Catherine)   Rushen *S & M*
PORT ISAAC (St Peter)   St Endellion w Port Isaac and
St Kew *Truro*
PORT ST MARY (St Mary)   Rushen *S & M*
PORTBURY (Blessed Virgin Mary)   Pill w Easton in
Gordano and Portbury *B & W*
PORTCHESTER (St Mary) *Portsm 2*   P *Personal Reps
Mrs E S Borthwick Norton*   V M L S THOMAS,
C T W EADY,   **Hon C** G S VARNHAM
PORTESHAM (St Peter)   Abbotsbury, Portesham and
Langton Herring *Sarum*
PORTHILL (St Andrew)   Wolstanton *Lich*
PORTHLEVEN (St Bartholomew) w Sithney *Truro 4*
P *Bp*   V S W JONES
PORTHPEAN (St Levan)   St Austell *Truro*
PORTINSCALE (Mission)   Crosthwaite Keswick *Carl*
PORTISHEAD (St Peter) *B & W 14*   P *Mrs E Haigh*
R A C TAYLOR,   **Sen AP** W L ROBERTS,   C P A M WEST
PORTKELLIS (St Christopher)   Helston and Wendron
Truro
PORTLAND (All Saints w St Peter) *Sarum 5*   P *Bp*
R D V GERRISH,   C E S MITCHELL
PORTLAND (St John) *Sarum 5*   P *Hyndman Trustees*
V F F HICKS
PORTLEMOUTH, EAST (St Winwaloe Onocaus)
Charleton w Buckland Tout Saints etc *Ex*
PORTLOE (All Saints)   Veryan w Ruan Lanihorne
Truro
PORTMAN SQUARE (St Paul)   Langham Place All So
Lon
PORTON (St Nicholas)   Bourne Valley *Sarum*
PORTREATH (St Mary)   Illogan *Truro*
PORTSDOWN (Christ Church) *Portsm 4*   P *Simeon's
Trustees*   V J K HEWITT,   NSM M MORGAN
PORTSEA (All Saints) *Portsm 6*   P *V Portsea St Mary and
Bp (jt)*   V *Vacant*   Portsmouth (0705) 820983
PORTSEA (Ascension) *Portsm 6*   P *Bp*   V M P MORGAN
PORTSEA North End (St Mark) *Portsm 6*   P *V Portsea
St Mary*   V R F ROBINSON,   C R C WHITE
PORTSEA (St Alban) *Portsm 6*   P *Bp*   V G K TAYLOR
PORTSEA (St Cuthbert) *Portsm 6*   P *Bp*
V K M L H BANTING,   C P CLARK,   NSM J L FELLOWS
PORTSEA (St George) *Portsm 6*   P *Bp*   V C M HILL
PORTSEA (St Luke) *Portsm 6*   P *Ch Patr Trust*
V M J SMITHSON,   NSM D H GIBSON
PORTSEA (St Mary) (St Faith and St Barnabas)
(St Wilfrid) *Portsm 6*   P *Win Coll*
V J M BROTHERTON,
C R N S LEECE, A J McCULLOCH, M C DOE, A C DE SMET
PORTSEA (St Saviour) *Portsm 6*   P *Bp*   V T KNIGHT,
Hon C M CHALAHAN,   NSM J R DIAPER
PORTSLADE Mile End (Good Shepherd) Conventional
District *Chich 4*   **C-in-c** P D CLEGG
PORTSLADE (St Nicholas) (St Andrew) *Chich 4*   P *Bp*
V R H RUSHFORTH,   C E D JENKINS
PORTSWOOD (Christ Church) *Win 12*   P *Bp*
V D C JAMES,   AV J F A WILLIAMS
PORTSWOOD (St Denys) *Win 12*   P *Bp*   V D J TIZZARD,
NSM R G CLARKE
POSLINGFORD (St Mary)   Clare w Poslingford,
Cavendish etc *St E*
POSTBRIDGE (St Gabriel)   Widecombe-in-the-Moor,
Leusdon, Princetown etc *Ex*
POSTLING (St Mary and St Radegund)   Lyminge w
Paddlesworth, Stanford w Postling etc *Cant*
POSTWICK (All Saints)   Brundall w Braydeston and
Postwick *Nor*
POTT SHRIGLEY (St Christopher) *Ches 13*   P *MMCET*
V G H GREENHOUGH
POTTEN END (Holy Trinity) w Nettleden *St Alb 3*   P *Bp*
V D J ELLIOTT
POTTER HEIGHAM (St Nicholas)   Ludham w Potter
Heigham *Nor*
POTTERHANWORTH (St Andrew)   Nocton w
Dunston and Potterhanworth *Linc*
POTTERNE (St Mary the Virgin) w Worton and Marston
Sarum 19   P *Bp*   V P WILKINSON

POTTERNEWTON (St Martin) *Ripon 5*   **P** *Trustees*
  V R W SHAW,   **C** S C COWLING,   **Par Dn** D LEPPINGTON,
  NSM V I MORGAN

POTTERS BAR (St Mary and All Saints) *St Alb 2*   **P** *Bp*
  Lon   **V** J J STRATTON,   **C** P M REECE

POTTERS GREEN (St Philip Deacon) *Cov 1*   **P** *Ld Chan*
  V D J ISON

POTTERS MARSTON (St Mary)   Barwell w Potters
  Marston and Stapleton *Leic*

POTTERSPURY (St Nicholas) w Furtho and Yardley
  Gobion and Cosgrove *Pet 5*   **P** *D&C (2 turns), Jes Coll*
  Ox (1 turn)   **V** E H LURKINGS

POTTO (St Mary)   Whorlton w Carlton and Faceby *York*

POTTON (St Mary the Virgin) w Sutton and Cockayne
  Hatley *St Alb 17*   **P** *The Crown (3 turns), St Jo Coll Ox*
  (1 turn)   **R** I W ARTHUR,   **NSM** D L SMITH

POUGHILL (St Michael and All Angels)   N Creedy *Ex*

POUGHILL (St Olaf King and Martyr) *Truro 8*   **P** *Ch Soc*
  Trust   **V** L H KEENAN

POULNER (St John)   Ringwood *Win*

POULSHOT (St Peter)   Rowde and Poulshot *Sarum*

POULTON (St Luke) *Ches 7*   **P** *Bp*   **V** J P EDWARDSON

POULTON (St Michael and All Angels)   The Ampneys
  w Driffield and Poulton *Glouc*

POULTON LANCELYN (Holy Trinity) *Ches 8*
  P *R Bebington*   **V** R J KIRKLAND

POULTON-LE-FYLDE (St Chad) *Blackb 13*   **P** *DBP*
  V C BERRYMAN,   **C** W R PLIMMER,   P H HUDSON

POULTON-LE-SANDS (Holy Trinity) w Morecambe
  (St Laurence) *Blackb 12*   **P** *V Lanc*   **R** J A H CLEGG,
  C I H RENNIE

POUND HILL (St Barnabas)   Worth *Chich*

POUNDSBRIDGE (Chapel)   Penshurst and Fordcombe
  Roch

POUNDSTOCK (St Winwaloe)   Week St Mary w
  Poundstock and Whitstone *Truro*

POWDERHAM (St Clement Bishop and Martyr)
  Kenton, Mamhead, Powderham, Cofton and Starcross
  Ex

POWERSTOCK (St Mary the Virgin)   Askerswell,
  Loders and Powerstock *Sarum*

POWICK (St Peter)   Powyke *Worc*

POWYKE (St Peter) *Worc 2*   **P** *Croome Estate Trustees*
  P-in-c J R ILSON

POYNINGS (Holy Trinity) w Edburton, Newtimber and
  Pyecombe *Chich 9*   **P** *Ld Chan (1 turn), Bp and Abp*
  (1 turn)   **R** G JEFFERY

POYNTINGTON (All Saints)   Queen Thorne *Sarum*

POYNTON (St George) *Ches 17*   **P** *Bp*
  C S M MANSFIELD,   **NSM** R J BROOKE

POYNTON, HIGHER (St Martin)   Poynton *Ches*

PRATTS BOTTOM (All Souls)   Green Street Green
  Roch

PREES (St Chad) *Lich 29*   **P** *Bp*   **V** W J WEBB

PREESALL (St Oswald) *Blackb 10*   **P** *Bp*   **V** E ANGUS

PRENTON (St Stephen) *Ches 1*   **P** *Bp*
  V L R LAWRENCE,   **C** G M BREFFITT,   D J SWALES,
  NSM W H HEAPS

PRENTON DELL (St Alban)   Prenton *Ches*

PRESCOT (St Mary) (St Paul) *Liv 10*   **P** *K Coll Cam*
  V T M STEEL,   **C** S B SMITH,   **NSM** T FAGAN

PRESHUTE (St George)   Marlborough *Sarum*

PRESTBURY (St Mary) (St Nicholas) *Glouc 11*
  P *Mrs F L Baghot de la Bere Aldendifer*
  V G I HAZLEWOOD,   **C** L A C MACLEAN, N GOSNELL,
  NSM N G LOWTON

PRESTBURY (St Peter) *Ches 13*   **P** *C F Legh Esq*
  V D W MOIR,   **Par Dn** J N CLARKE,   **Hon C** R OTTLEY

PRESTEIGNE (St Andrew) w Discoed, Kinsham and
  Lingen *Heref 5*   **P** *Bp*   **R** B A GILL

PRESTLEIGH (St James Mission Church)   Shepton
  Mallet w Doulting *B & W*

PRESTOLEE (Holy Trinity)   E Farnworth and Kearsley
  Man

PRESTON Acregate Lane (Mission)   Preston St Matt
  Blackb

PRESTON (All Saints) *Blackb 14*   **P** *Trustees*
  P-in-c F COOPER

PRESTON (All Saints)   Siddington w Preston *Glouc*

PRESTON (All Saints) and Sproatley in Holderness
  York 13   **P** *Abp*   **P-in-c** S ROBINSON

PRESTON (Church of the Ascension) *Lon 21*   **P** *Bp*
  V F C HUMPHRIES

PRESTON (Emmanuel) *Blackb 14*   **P** *R Preston*
  V J WIXON,   **Par Dn** J M TURNER

PRESTON (Good Shepherd)   Brighton Gd Shep Preston
  Chich

PRESTON (St Alban)   Brighton Resurr *Chich*

PRESTON (St Andrew) w Sutton Poyntz and Osmington w
  Poxwell *Sarum 5*   **P** *Patr Bd*   **TR** J K COOMBS,
  TV J S HOLLAND,   **Par Dn** P S THOMAS

PRESTON (St Augustine and St Saviour)   Brighton St
  Aug and St Sav *Chich*

PRESTON (St Cuthbert) *Blackb 14*   **P** *Bp*
  V M C R CRIPPS,   **C** D P BANBURY

PRESTON (St John) (Christ the King Chapel) (St George)
  (St Saviour w St James) (St Stephen) *Blackb 14*
  P *Patr Bd*   **TV** D BARTON,   B E PENN,   H D McKEE

PRESTON (St John the Baptist) *Glouc 12*   **P** *Bp*
  P-in-c R J LEGG

PRESTON (St John the Evangelist) *Chich 2*   **P** *Bp*
  V F MITCHINSON

PRESTON (St Jude w St Paul) *Blackb 14*   **P** *Bp and*
  V Preston St John   **V** B J W ROBINSON

PRESTON (St Luke) (St Oswald) *Blackb 14*   **P** *Bp and*
  Simeon's Trustees (jt)   **V** M A MANLEY

PRESTON (St Mark's Worship Centre) *Blackb 14*
  P *Patr Bd*   **V** *Vacant*

PRESTON (St Martin)   Kings Walden *St Alb*

PRESTON (St Mary) *Blackb 14*   **P** *Trustees*
  P-in-c B ROTHWELL

PRESTON (St Mary the Virgin) *St E 10*   **P** *Em Coll Cam*
  P-in-c C E WETHERALL

PRESTON (St Matthew) (St Hilda) *Blackb 14*   **P** *Bp*
  V M A BURGESS

PRESTON (St Matthias)   Brighton St Matthias *Chich*

PRESTON (St Mildred)   Wingham w Elmstone and
  Preston w Stourmouth *Cant*

PRESTON (St Paul)   Paignton St Paul Preston *Ex*

PRESTON (St Peter and St Paul) and Ridlington w Wing
  and Pilton *Pet 14*   **P** *Bp, Baroness Willoughby de*
  Eresby and DBP (jt)   **R** A M S WILSON

PRESTON, EAST (St Mary) w Kingston *Chich 1*   **P** *D&C*
  V J H KIMBERLEY

PRESTON, GREAT (St Aidan)   Kippax w Allerton
  Bywater *Ripon*

PRESTON BAGOT (All Saints)   Claverdon w Preston
  Bagot *Cov*

PRESTON BISSET (St John the Baptist)   Swan *Ox*

PRESTON BROOK (St Faith)   Daresbury *Ches*

PRESTON CAPES (St Peter and St Paul)   Charwelton w
  Fawsley and Preston Capes *Pet*

PRESTON NEXT FAVERSHAM (St Catherine) w
  Goodnestone and Graveney *Cant 6*   **P** *Abp*
  V G B HUNT,   **C** A A GOLD

PRESTON ON STOUR (St Mary)   Ilmington w Stretton-
  on-Fosse etc *Cov*

PRESTON ON TEES (All Saints) *Dur 16*   **P** *Bp*
  V D T OSMAN,   **C** S A K ALLABY

PRESTON-ON-WYE (St Lawrence)   Madley w
  Tyberton, Preston-on-Wye and Blakemere *Heref*

PRESTON PATRICK (St Patrick) *Carl 9*   **P** *Bp*
  V P M SMITH

PRESTON PLUCKNETT (St James the Great) (St Peter)
  B & W 8   **P** *Bp (2 turns), Mrs S W Rawlins (1 turn)*
  V A PERRIS,   **C** R J SNOW

PRESTON UNDER SCARR (St Margaret)   Wensley
  Ripon

PRESTON WEALDMOORS (St Lawrence)   Edgmond
  w Kynnersley and Preston Wealdmoors *Lich*

PRESTON WYNNE (Holy Trinity)   Bodenham w Hope-
  under-Dinmore, Felton etc *Heref*

PRESTONVILLE (St Luke) *Chich 2*   **P** *Trustees*
  V C A M MARCH,   **NSM** G B ROBERTS

PRESTWICH (St Gabriel) *Man 14*   **P** *Bp*
  V R M POWLEY

PRESTWICH (St Hilda) *Man 14*   **P** *Trustees*
  V D T McCANN

PRESTWICH (St Margaret) (St George) *Man 14*
  P *R Prestwich St Mary*   **V** M ASHWORTH

PRESTWICH (St Mary the Virgin) *Man 14*   **P** *Trustees*
  R F BIBBY

PRESTWOLD (St Andrew)   Wymeswold and Prestwold
  w Hoton *Leic*

PRESTWOOD (Holy Trinity) and Great Hampden *Ox 28*
  P *Bp and Hon I H Hope-Morley (jt)*   **P-in-c** J R WHITE,
  Par Dn C NICHOLSON

PRICKWILLOW (St Peter) *Ely 14*   **P** *Bp*   **V** A BARTLE,
  Hon Par Dn M A GUITE

PRIDDY (St Lawrence) *B & W 1*   **P** *Bp*
  V E A MACPHERSON

PRIESTWOOD (St Andrew)   Bracknell *Ox*

PRIMROSE HILL (Holy Trinity)   Lydney w Aylburton
  Glouc

PRIMROSE HILL (St Mary the Virgin) w Avenue Road
  (St Paul) *Lon 16*   **P** *Trustees*   **V** J A OVENDEN,

C F W STEPHENS, **NSM** C L VAN DER PUMP,
S V WEBSTER
PRINCE ALBERT ROAD (St Mark) Regents Park St
Mark *Lon*
PRINCE CONSORT ROAD (Holy Trinity) S
Kensington H Trin w All SS *Lon*
PRINCE'S PARK (St Paul) *Liv 4* **V** *Vacant*
PRINCES RISBOROUGH (St Mary) w Ilmer *Ox 21*
P *Ld Chan* **R** J E A SMITH
PRINCETOWN (St Michael and All Angels)
Widecombe-in-the-Moor, Leusdon, Princetown etc *Ex*
PRIORS DEAN (not known) Hawkley w Priors Dean
Portsm
**PRIORS HARDWICK (St Mary the Virgin) w Priors
Marston and Wormleighton** *Cov 10* **P** *Earl Spencer*
P-in-c K J PHILLIPS
PRIORS LEE (St Peter) (St Georges) *Lich 28* **P** *Bp and
V Shifnal (jt)* **V** G L HANCOX
PRIORS MARSTON (St Leonard) Priors Hardwick,
Priors Marston and Wormleighton *Cov*
PRIORS PARK (Mission Hall) Tewkesbury w Walton
Cardiff *Glouc*
PRISTON (St Luke) Timsbury and Priston *B & W*
PRITTLEWELL (All Saints) Southend *Chelmsf*
PRITTLEWELL (St Luke) *Chelmsf 15* **P** *Bp*
V D F C GIRLING
PRITTLEWELL (St Mary the Virgin) *Chelmsf 15* **P** *Bp*
V R A MASON, **NSM** J L BARKER
PRITTLEWELL (St Peter) *Chelmsf 15* **P** *Bp*
P-in-c R C WELLS
PRITTLEWELL (St Stephen) *Chelmsf 15* **P** *Bp*
V R J STANLEY
**PROBUS (St Probus and St Grace), Ladock and
Grampound w Creed** *Truro 6* **P** *DBP*
TR J F WHITLOCK, **TV** A J WADE, **C** J M PILGRIM
PRUDHOE (St Mary Magdalene) *Newc 3* **P** *Dioc Soc*
V P ADAMSON, **C** J M BREARLEY
**PUBLOW (All Saints) w Pensford, Compton Dando and
Chelwood** *B & W 11* **P** *Bp* **R** J N COE
PUCKINGTON (St Andrew) Shepton Beauchamp w
Barrington, Stocklinch etc *B & W*
PUCKLECHURCH (St Thomas a Becket) and Abson *Bris 7*
P *D&C* **V** I L HANCOCK
PUDDINGTON (St Thomas a Becket) N Creedy *Ex*
PUDDLETOWN (St Mary the Virgin) and Tolpuddle
Sarum 2 **P** *Trustees, Ch Ch Ox, and Viscount
Rothermere (by turn)* **P-in-c** R H WILKINS
PUDLESTON (St Peter) Leominster *Heref*
PUDSEY (St Lawrence and St Paul) *Bradf 3* **P** *Bp and
V Calverley (jt)* **V** H M WIGLEY, **C** M L JEFFERIES,
Par Dn S M ROSSETER
PULBOROUGH (St Mary) *Chich 12* **P** *Lord Egremont*
R K W DENFORD
PULFORD (St Mary the Virgin) Eccleston and Pulford
Ches
PULHAM (St Mary Magdalene) (St Mary the Virgin)
Nor 16 **P** *The Crown* **R** G R EPPS
PULHAM (St Thomas a Beckett) Dungeon Hill *Sarum*
PULHAM MARKET (St Mary Magdalene) Pulham *Nor*
PULHAM ST MARY (St Mary the Virgin) as above
PULLOXHILL (St James the Apostle) Silsoe, Pulloxhill
and Flitton *St Alb*
PULVERBATCH (St Edith) Longden and Annscroft w
Pulverbatch *Heref*
PUNCKNOWLE (St Mary the Blessed Virgin) Bride
Valley *Sarum*
PUNNETS TOWN (St Peter) Heathfield *Chich*
PURBROOK (St John the Baptist) *Portsm 4* **P** *Bp*
V R I P COUTTS
PUREWELL (St John) Christchurch *Win*
PURFLEET (St Stephen) Aveley and Purfleet *Chelmsf*
PURITON (St Michael and All Angels) and Pawlett
B & W 15 **P** *Ld Chan (1 turn), D&C Windsor (2 turns)*
V C C E MEREDITH
PURLEIGH (All Saints), Cold Norton and Stow Maries
Chelmsf 13 **P** *Suttons Hosp, Or Coll Ox, and Bp (jt)*
R L S TILLETT
PURLEY (Christ Church) *S'wark 21* **P** *Bp*
V J H CARROLL, **C** I G BISHOP,
NSM J N EMBERTON, J R K FENWICK
PURLEY (St Barnabas) *S'wark 21* **P** *Bp* **V** A C WAIT
PURLEY (St Mark) Woodcote *S'wark 21* **P** *Bp*
V R H GIBBS, **Par Dn** H RHODES
PURLEY (St Mary the Virgin) *Ox 12* **P** *Ld Chan*
R R B HOWELL
PURLEY (St Swithun) *S'wark 21* **P** *Bp* **V** J K GREIG,
Hon C D BROAD
PURLWELL (St Andrew) *Wakef 10* **P** *Bp* **Dn-in-c**
S GOLDTHORPE, **Hon C** B A GEESON

PURSE CAUNDLE (St Peter) The Caundles w Folke
and Holwell *Sarum*
PURSTON (St Thomas) cum South Featherstone *Wakef 11*
P *Bp* **V** A S RAMSDEN, **Hon C** S P DICKINSON
PURTON (St John) Sharpness w Purton and Brookend
Glouc
PURTON (St Mary) *Bris 13* **P** *Bp* **V** R H D BLAKE,
NSM E G HALL
PUSEY (All Saints) *Ox 17* **P** *Bp* **R** *Vacant*
PUTFORD (St Stephen) *Ex 9* **P** *Bp* **V** H J ROCHE
PUTLEY (not known) Tarrington w Stoke Edith,
Aylton, Pixley etc *Heref*
PUTNEY (St Margaret) *S'wark 17* **P** *Bp*
V D M H REECE, **NSM** R C BENSON
PUTNEY (St Mary) (All Saints) *S'wark 17* **P** *D&C Worc*
V J S FRASER, **C** S A EVANS
PUTTENHAM (St John the Baptist) and Wanborough
Guildf 5 **P** *T I Perkins Esq and Ld Chan (alt)*
P-in-c W R FILLERY
PUTTENHAM (St Mary) Tring *St Alb*
PUXTON (St Saviour) Congresbury w Puxton and
Hewish St Ann *B & W*
PYE NEST (St James) King Cross *Wakef*
PYECOMBE (Transfiguration) Poynings w Edburton,
Newtimber and Pyecombe *Chich*
PYLLE (St Thomas a Becket) Ditcheat w E Pennard and
Pylle *B & W*
PYPE HAYES (St Mary the Virgin) *Birm 6* **P** *Trustees*
V J F RYAN, **C** G W NELSON
PYRFORD (Church of the Good Shepherd) Wisley w
Pyrford *Guildf*
PYRFORD (St Nicolas) as above
PYRTON (St Mary) Watlington w Pyrton and Shirburn
Ox
PYTCHLEY (All Saints) Isham w Pytchley *Pet*
PYWORTHY (St Swithun), Pancrasweek and Bridgerule
Ex 9 **P** *DBP* **P-in-c** R BURROW
QUADRING (St Margaret) Gosberton Clough and
Quadring *Linc*
QUAINTON (Holy Cross and St Mary) Schorne *Ox*
QUANTOXHEAD (Blessed Virgin Mary) (St Ethelreda)
B & W 19 **P** *Bp, Lady Gass, and Lt-Col W Luttrell (jt)*
R R L HANCOCK
QUANTOXHEAD, EAST (Blessed Virgin Mary)
Quantoxhead *B & W*
QUANTOXHEAD, WEST (St Ethelreda) as above
QUARLEY (St Michael and All Angels) Amport,
Grateley, Monxton and Quarley *Win*
QUARNDON (St Paul) *Derby 11* **P** *Exors Viscount
Scarsdale* **V** J D MORISON
QUARNFORD (St Paul) Longnor, Quarnford and
Sheen *Lich*
QUARRENDON ESTATE (St Peter) Aylesbury w
Bierton and Hulcott *Ox*
QUARRINGTON (St Botolph) w Old Sleaford *Linc 22*
P *Bp* **R** D J MUSSON
QUARRY BANK (Christ Church) *Lich 1* **P** *Prime Min*
V T G CHAPMAN
QUARRY HILL (St Mary) Leeds City *Ripon*
QUATFORD (St Mary Magdalene) Bridgnorth, Tasley,
Astley Abbotts, Oldbury etc *Heref*
QUATT (St Andrew) Alveley and Quatt *Heref*
QUEDGELEY (St James) Hardwicke, Quedgeley and
Elmore w Longney *Glouc*
**QUEEN CAMEL (St Barnabas) w West Camel, Corton
Denham, Sparkford, Weston Bampfylde and Sutton
Montis** *B & W 3* **P** *Bp and DBP (2 turns), Ch Patr
Trust, MMCET and Rev G Bennett (1 turn)*
R B L MORRIS
QUEEN CHARLTON (St Margaret) Keynsham *B & W*
QUEEN THORNE *Sarum 4* **P** *Bp, Rev J M P Goodden,
Major K S D Wingfield Digby, and MMCET (jt)*
P-in-c A E H RUTTER
QUEENBOROUGH (Holy Trinity) *Cant 14* **P** *Abp*
V R N MURCH
QUEENHILL (St Nicholas) Longdon, Castlemorton,
Bushley, Queenhill etc *Worc*
QUEENSBURY (All Saints) *Lon 23* **P** *The Crown*
V J N LUSCOMBE, **Par Dn** N A McINTOSH
QUEENSBURY (Holy Trinity) *Bradf 2* **P** *Bp*
V R G WOOD
QUENDON (not known) w Rickling and Wicken Bonhunt
Chelmsf 24 **P** *Bp and Keble Coll Ox (jt)*
P-in-c R J S BURN
QUENIBOROUGH (St Mary) Barkby and
Queniborough *Leic*
QUENINGTON (St Swithun) Coln St Aldwyn,
Hatherop, Quenington etc *Glouc*

QUERNMORE (St Peter) Dolphinholme w Quernmore *Blackb*

QUETHIOCK (St Hugh) St Ive w Quethiock *Truro*

QUIDENHAM (St Andrew) *Nor 17* **P** *Ld Chan (1 turn)*, *Patr Bd (3 turns)* **TV** J B V RIVIERE, **C** C B WRAY

QUINTON and PRESTON DEANERY (St John the Baptist) Wootton w Quinton and Preston Deanery *Pet*

QUINTON (St Swithun) w Marston Sicca *Glouc 10* **P** *D&C Worc and Bp (jt)* **V** P WAKEFIELD

QUINTON, THE (Christ Church) *Birm 2* **P** *Bp* **C** C J CROOKS

QUINTON ROAD WEST (St Boniface) *Birm 2* **P** *Bp* **V** W BROWN

QUORN (St Bartholomew) see below

QUORNDON (St Bartholomew) *Leic 7* **P** *Bp* **V** D H BOWLER, **NSM** M J MORRIS

QUY (St Mary) Stow w Quy *Ely*

RACKENFORD (All Saints) Washfield, Stoodleigh, Withleigh etc *Ex*

RACKHEATH (Holy Trinity) and Salhouse *Nor 1* **P** *Bp* **R** B V ROGERS, **Hon C** P A ROGERS

RACTON (St Peter) Compton, the Mardens, Stoughton and Racton *Chich*

RADBOURNE (St Andrew) Longford, Long Lane, Dalbury and Radbourne *Derby*

RADCLIFFE (St Andrew) Black Lane *Man 14* **P** *R Radcliffe St Mary* **V** P N W GRAYSHON

RADCLIFFE (St Mary) *Man 14* **P** *Trustees* **P-in-c** C H ELLIS

RADCLIFFE (St Thomas and St John) (St Philip Mission Church) *Man 14* **P** *Trustees* **P-in-c** C H ELLIS

RADCLIFFE-ON-TRENT (St Mary) and Shelford w Holme Pierrepont and Adbolton *S'well 8* **P** *DBP (2 turns)*, *Ld Chan (1 turn)* **R** K H NEWCOMBE, **Hon C** D E BENNETT

RADCLIVE (St John the Evangelist) Tingewick w Water Stratford, Radclive etc *Ox*

RADDINGTON (St Michael) Chipstable w Huish Champflower and Clatworthy *B & W*

RADFORD (All Souls) w Christ Church and St Michael *S'well 12* **P** *Bp* **V** *Vacant* Nottingham (0602) 785364

RADFORD (St Nicholas) *Cov 2* **P** *Bp* **V** G HANDS, **Dss** M M OBEE

RADFORD (St Peter) *S'well 12* **P** *Bp* **V** J WALKER

RADFORD, NORTH (St Francis of Assisi) Cov St Fran N Radford *Cov*

RADFORD SEMELE (St Nicholas) and Ufton *Cov 10* **P** *Bp* **V** J S HAYNES

RADIPOLE (Emmanuel) (St Adhelm) (St Ann) and Melcombe Regis *Sarum 5* **P** *Patr Bd* **TR** R HOPE, **TV** D N H MAKEPEACE, P W FINCH, **C** R W S SUFFERN, J M MEADOWS, **NSM** J E TURNER

RADLETT (Christ Church) (St John) *St Alb 1* **P** *V Aldenham* **V** M L LESITER, **C** D RIDGEWAY, **Par Dn** S M HALMSHAW, **NSM** J F MILLER

RADLEY (St James the Great) and Sunningwell *Ox 10* **P** *Radley Coll and DBP (by turn)* **R** K KINNAIRD, **C** W J F FLETCHER-CAMPBELL

RADNAGE (St Mary) W Wycombe w Bledlow Ridge, Bradenham and Radnage *Ox*

RADNOR, OLD (St Stephen) Kington w Huntington, Old Radnor, Kinnerton etc *Heref*

RADSTOCK (St Nicholas) w Writhlington *B & W 13* **P** *Bp* **R** C P J TURNER, **C** J P ROWE

RADWAY (St Peter) Warmington w Shotteswell and Radway w Ratley *Cov*

RADWELL (All Saints) Hinxworth w Newnham and Radwell *St Alb*

RADWINTER (St Mary the Virgin) w Hempstead *Chelmsf 25* **P** *Keble Coll Ox* **R** B J MACDONALD-MILNE

RAGDALE (All Saints) Hoby cum Rotherby w Brooksby, Ragdale & Thru'ton *Leic*

RAGNALL (St Leonard) Dunham-on-Trent w Darlton, Ragnall etc *S'well*

RAINFORD (All Saints) *Liv 11* **P** *V Prescot* **V** F R N MICHELL, **Par Dn** P MAKIN

RAINHAM (St Helen and St Giles) *Chelmsf 4* **P** *MMCET* **TV** M E PORTER, **P-in-c** T G LYNDS, **C** G M TARRY, G J VENABLES

RAINHAM (St Margaret) *Roch 3* **P** *Bp* **V** B M M O'CONNOR

RAINHILL (St Ann) *Liv 13* **P** *Trustees* **V** W R D ALEXANDER, **C** K DAGGER

RAINOW (Holy Trinity) w Saltersford and Forest *Ches 13* **P** *Bp* **V** L LEWIS

RAINTON (not known) Baldersby w Dalton, Dishforth etc *York*

RAINTON, EAST (St Cuthbert) *Dur 6* **P** *D&C* **V** D GUEST

RAINTON, WEST (St Mary) *Dur 6* **P** *Bp* **R** D GUEST

RAINWORTH (St Simon and St Jude) *S'well 2* **P** *DBP* **V** J FERN, **Par Dn** P A CHAPMAN

RAITHBY (Holy Trinity) *Linc 7* **P** *Baroness Willoughby de Eresby* **R** G ROBSON

RAITHBY (St Peter) *Linc 12* **P** *Bp and Viscount Chaplain (alt)* **R** J F DOWMAN

RAME (St Germanus) Maker w Rame *Truro*

RAMPISHAM (St Michael and All Angels) Melbury Sarum

RAMPSIDE (St Michael) Aldingham and Dendron and Rampside *Carl*

RAMPTON (All Saints) *Ely 5* **R** *Vacant* Willingham (0954) 60379

RAMPTON (All Saints) w Laneham, Treswell, Cottam and Stokeham *S'well 5* **P** *D&C York and The Crown (alt)* **R** D DUCKWORTH

RAMSBOTTOM (St Andrew) *Man 10* **P** *Bp* **V** I M ROGERSON

RAMSBOTTOM (St John) (St Paul) *Man 10* **P** *Prime Min and Bp (alt)* **V** D P VALE, **NSM** D ALTHAM

RAMSBURY (Holy Cross) Whitton *Sarum*

RAMSDALE (Christ Church) Baughurst, Ramsdell, Wolverton w Ewhurst etc *Win*

RAMSDEN (Church of Unity) Orpington All SS *Roch*

RAMSDEN (St James), Finstock and Fawler, Leafield w Wychwood and Wilcote *Ox 3* **P** *Bp, V Charlbury, and Sir Mark Norman, Bt (jt)* **V** E A JOHNSON

RAMSDEN CRAYS (St Mary the Virgin) w Ramsden Bellhouse (St Mary the Virgin) *Chelmsf 9* **P** *Reformation Ch Trust* **P-in-c** D P SHAW

RAMSDEN HEATH (St John) Downham w S Hanningfield *Chelmsf*

RAMSEY (St Michael) w Little Oakley and Wrabness *Chelmsf 23* **P** *Ld Chan* **R** S R NORTHFIELD

RAMSEY (St Olave) Lezayre St Olave Ramsey *S & M*

RAMSEY, SOUTH (St Paul) *S & M 4* **P** *Bp* **V** D B FOSTER

RAMSEY ST MARY'S (St Mary) see below

RAMSEYS (St Thomas a Becket) (St Mary) and Upwood, The *Ely 11* **P** *Patr Bd* **TR** E DUCKETT, **TV** I M G FRIARS

RAMSGATE (Christ Church) *Cant 9* **P** *Ch Patr Trust* **V** S YOUNG

RAMSGATE (Holy Trinity) (St George) *Cant 9* **P** *Abp* **R** P A ADAMS

RAMSGATE (St Luke) *Cant 9* **P** *CPAS* **V** G C PEARSON

RAMSGATE (St Mark) *Cant 9* **P** *CPAS* **V** R K BAKER

RAMSGILL (St Mary) Upper Nidderdale *Ripon*

RAMSHOLT (All Saints) Alderton w Ramsholt and Bawdsey *St E*

RANBY (St German) Asterby Gp *Linc*

RANBY (St Martin) Babworth w Sutton-cum-Lound *S'well*

RAND (St Oswald) Wragby *Linc*

RANDWICK (St John the Baptist) *Glouc 1* **P** *V Standish* **V** *Vacant* Stroud (0453) 764727

RANGEMORE (All Saints) Dunstall w Rangemore and Tatenhill *Lich*

RANGEWORTHY (Holy Trinity) Wickwar w Rangeworthy *Glouc*

RANMOOR (St John the Evangelist) *Sheff 4* **P** *Trustees* **V** R M JARRATT, **C** J M THOMPSON, **Hon Par Dn** B C BROOKE

RANMORE (St Barnabas) Dorking w Ranmore *Guildf*

RANSKILL (St Barnabas) Scrooby *S'well*

RANTON (All Saints) Ellenhall w Ranton *Lich*

RANWORTH (St Helen) w Panxworth and Woodbastwick *Nor 1* **P** *Bp and J Cator Esq (jt)* **V** P McFADYEN

RASHCLIFFE (St Stephen) and Lockwood *Wakef 5* **P** *R Almondbury and R Kirkheaton (jt)* **P-in-c** M J ARCHER

RASKELF (St Mary) Easingwold w Raskelfe *York*

RASTRICK (St John the Divine) *Wakef 2* **P** *Bp* **V** D G MILLER

RASTRICK (St Matthew) *Wakef 2* **P** *V Halifax* **V** B FIRTH, **C** H J R FEREDAY

RATBY (St Philip and St James) w Groby *Leic 12* **P** *Patr Bd* **TR** P R BLACKMAN

RATCLIFFE CULEY (All Saints) Sibson w Sheepy and Ratcliffe Culey *Leic*

RATCLIFFE-ON-SOAR (Holy Trinity) W Leake w Kingston-on-Soar etc *S'well*

RATCLIFFE ON THE WREAKE (St Botolph) E Goscote w Ratcliffe and Rearsby *Leic*

RATHMELL (Holy Trinity) Giggleswick and Rathmell w Wigglesworth *Bradf*

RATLEY (St Peter ad Vincula)   Warmington w
Shotteswell and Radway w Ratley *Cov*
RATLINGHOPE (St Margaret)   Wentnor w
Ratlinghope, Myndtown, Norbury etc *Heref*
RATTERY (Blessed Virgin Mary) *Ex 13*   P *Sir Rivers
Carew, Bt*   V *Vacant*
RATTLESDEN (St Nicholas) w Thorpe Morieux and
Brettenham *St E 10*   P *Bp (2 turns), Ld Chan (1 turn)*
R S HABGOOD
RAUCEBY, NORTH (St Peter)   Ancaster Wilsford Gp
Linc
RAUGHTON HEAD (All Saints) w Gatesgill *Carl 3*
P *DBP*   P-in-c W KELLY
RAUNDS (St Peter) *Pet 10*   P *Bp*   V B LEATHERLAND
RAVENDALE Group, The *Linc 10*   P *Ld Chan, Trustees
of D Parkinson Settled Estates, and Bp (by turn)*
R D J HAWKSBEE
RAVENDALE, EAST (St Martin)   Ravendale Gp *Linc*
RAVENFIELD (St James)   Bramley and Ravenfield
Sheff
RAVENGLASS (Mission Room)   Kells *Carl*
RAVENHEAD (St John)   Parr Mt *Liv*
RAVENHEAD (St John the Evangelist) *Liv 10*
P *V St Helens*   V E R DORAN
RAVENINGHAM (St Andrew) *Nor 14*   P *Patr Bd*
TR W F R BATSON,   TV C POULARD
RAVENSCAR (St Hilda)   Scalby w Ravenscar and
Staintondale *York*
RAVENSDEN (All Saints)   Wilden w Colmworth and
Ravensden *St Alb*
RAVENSHEAD (St Peter) *S'well 4*   P *Bp*   V A A CONN
RAVENSTHORPE (St Denys)   W Haddon w Winwick
and Ravensthorpe *Pet*
RAVENSTHORPE (St Saviour) *Wakef 10*   P *V Mirfield*
V I E WILDEY
RAVENSTONE (All Saints)   Gayhurst w Ravenstone,
Stoke Goldington etc *Ox*
RAVENSTONE (St Michael and All Angels) and
Swannington *Leic 8*   P *Ld Chan and V Whitwick (alt)*
R K C EMMETT
RAVENSTONEDALE (St Oswald)   Orton and Tebay w
Ravenstonedale etc *Carl*
RAWCLIFFE (St James) *Sheff 11*   P *V Gt Snaith*
V G HOLLINGSWORTH
RAWCLIFFE (St Mark)   Clifton *York*
RAWCLIFFE BRIDGE (St Philip)   Rawcliffe *Sheff*
RAWDON (St Peter) *Bradf 4*   P *Bp and Trustees (jt)*
V J C BARNES,   C J P SMITH
RAWMARSH (St Mary the Virgin) w Parkgate *Sheff 6*
P *Ld Chan*   R A WATSON,   C A J COOPER
RAWNSLEY (St Michael)   Hednesford *Lich*
RAWRETH (St Nicholas) w Rettendon *Chelmsf 14*
P *Ld Chan and Pemb Coll Cam (alt)*   R A CORNISH
RAWTENSTALL (St Mary) *Man 15*   P *CPAS*
V *Vacant*   Rossendale (0706) 215585
RAWTHORPE (St James) *Wakef 1*   P *DBP*
V R D BALDOCK
RAYDON (St Mary) *St E 3*   P *Reformation Ch Trust*
P-in-c M B ETTLINGER
RAYLEIGH (Holy Trinity) (St Michael) *Chelmsf 14*
P *MMCET*   R P F TAYLOR,
C J E NOBBS, B R PENFOLD,   NSM J M HILL,
Hon Par Dn I E L LAWRENCE
RAYNE (All Saints) *Chelmsf 18*   P *DBP*   R *Vacant*
Braintree (0376) 21938
RAYNES PARK (St Saviour) *S'wark 11*   P *Bp*
V G J BENTLEY
RAYNHAM, EAST (St Mary)   S, E w W Raynham,
Helhoughton, etc *Nor*
RAYNHAM, SOUTH (St Martin), East w West Raynham,
Helhoughton, Weasenham and Wellingham *Nor 19*
P *Bp, Marquess Townshend, and Viscount Coke
(by turn)*   R A J JACOBS
READ IN WHALLEY (St John the Evangelist) *Blackb 8*
P *V Whalley*   V H A REID
READING (All Saints) *Ox 15*   P *Bp*   V P T H JONES,
C J W MORTIBOYS
READING Castle Street (St Mary) Proprietary Chapel
Ox 15   Min D N SAMUEL
READING Greyfriars (St James) *Ox 15*   P *Ch Trust Fund
Trust*   V P N DOWNHAM,   C L J BROWNE
READING (Holy Trinity) *Ox 15*   P *SMF*
V F T BONHAM,   NSM R H LUSTY
READING (St Agnes w St Paul) *Ox 15*   P *Bp*
V D I A BRAZELL,   C J G S MORGAN,
Par Dn E J BRAZELL
READING (St Barnabas) *Ox 15*   P *Bp*   R C F BOND,
NSM G L FRENCH

READING (St Giles w St Saviour) *Ox 15*   P *Bp*
R B M DUTSON,   C R K HARRISON
READING (St John the Evangelist and St Stephen) *Ox 15*
P *Simeon's Trustees*   V A J BURDON,   C H W ELLIS,
Par Dn P M BURDON,   NSM K P WIGGINS
READING (St Luke) (St Bartholomew) *Ox 15*   P *Bp and
V Reading St Giles (alt)*   V R J PREECE,   C M L HEIDT,
NSM B D E BLACKMAN
READING (St Mark) *Ox 15*   P *Bp*   V R G HAYNE
READING (St Mary the Virgin) (St Laurence) *Ox 15*
P *Bp*   R B SHENTON,   Hon C N W S CRANFIELD
READING (St Matthew) *Ox 15*   P *Bp*   V R R D SPEARS,
NSM K R COOPER
REAPSMOOR (St John)   Longnor, Quarnford and
Sheen *Lich*
REARSBY (St Michael and All Angels)   E Goscote w
Ratcliffe and Rearsby *Leic*
RECULVER (St Mary the Virgin) and Herne Bay
(St Bartholomew) *Cant 7*   P *Abp*   V S J WELCH,
Par Dn N M WANSTALL
RED HOUSE (St Cuthbert)   Sunderland Red Ho *Dur*
RED POST *Sarum 7*   P *Mrs V M Chattey, H W Plunkett-
Ernle-Erle-Drax Esq, and Bp (by turn)*
V H I M MADDOX
REDBOURN (St Mary) *St Alb 14*   P *Earl of Verulam*
V J G PEDLAR,   NSM A D OSBORNE
REDBROOK (St Saviour)   Newland and Redbrook w
Clearwell *Glouc*
REDCAR (St Peter) *York 17*   P *Trustees*
V J A ROBERTSON,   C S SMITH
REDCLIFFE BAY (St Nicholas)   Portishead *B & W*
REDDAL HILL (St Luke) *Worc 9*   P *The Crown*
V J M BRIERLEY
REDDISH (St Elisabeth) *Man 3*   P *Bp*   R R TOVEY,
C R E A ADAMSON
REDDISH, NORTH (St Agnes) *Man 3*   P *The Crown*
R S DOUBTFIRE
REDDITCH (St Stephen) *Worc 7*   P *Bp*   V D C SALT,
NSM H M HOTCHIN
REDDITCH, The Ridge: Redditch (St George), Headless
Cross, Webheath and Crabbs Cross *Worc 7*   P *Bp*
TV P E JONES, M HERBERT, M F BARTLETT,
NSM I J MERRY
REDE (All Saints)   Chedburgh w Depden, Rede and
Hawkedon *St E*
REDENHALL (Assumption of the Blessed Virgin Mary),
Harleston, Wortwell and Needham *Nor 16*   P *Bp and
Sir Allan Adair (jt)*   R *Vacant*   Harleston (0379)
852068
REDFIELD (St Leonard)   E Bris *Bris*
REDGRAVE cum Botesdale (St Mary) w Rickinghall
St E 16   P *P J H Wilson Esq*   R R G BILLINGHURST
REDHILL (Christ Church)   Wrington w Butcombe
B & W
REDHILL (Holy Trinity) *S'wark 24*   P *Simeon's Trustees*
V D P R SHACKLOCK,   C S J BAILEY
REDHILL (St John the Evangelist) (Meadvale Hall)
S'wark 24   P *Bp*   V T G A WOODERSON,
C P M DOWLING
REDHILL (St Matthew) *S'wark 24*   P *Bp*
V R D W HAWKINS,   NSM D T BRYANT
REDHORN *Sarum 19*   P *Patr Bd*   TR I G HUGHES,
TV B J SMITH
REDISHAM (St Peter)   Ringsfield w Redisham,
Barsham, Shipmeadow etc *St E*
REDLAND (not known)   Bris 6   P *Ch Trust Fund Trust*
V J M PERRIS,   NSM J G CAINE, B E KELLY
REDLINGFIELD (St Andrew)   Stradbroke, Horham,
Athelington and Redlingfield *St E*
REDLYNCH (St Mary) and Morgan's Vale *Sarum 11*
P *DBF and V Downton (alt)*   V R C LOWRIE
REDLYNCH (St Peter)   Bruton and Distr *B & W*
REDMARLEY D'ABITOT (St Bartholomew) and
Bromesberrow w Pauntley, Upleadon and Oxenhall
Glouc 3   P *Bp and Rev D J M Niblett (jt)*
Hon C W E W BARBER
REDMARSHALL (St Cuthbert) *Dur 16*   P *The Crown*
R P S ATKINSON
REDMILE (St Peter)   Barkestone w Plungar, Redmile
and Stathern *Leic*
REDMIRE (St Mary)   Aysgarth and Bolton cum
Redmire *Ripon*
REDNAL (St Stephen the Martyr) *Birm 4*   P *Bp*
V P W THOMAS
REDRUTH (St Andrew) (St Euny) w Lanner and Treleigh
Truro 2   P *DBP*   TR M P SIMCOCK,   TV J W L COBB,
C G PENGELLY, R W ASPDEN
REED (St Mary)   Barkway, Reed and Buckland w Barley
St Alb

REEDHAM (St John the Baptist) w Cantley w Limpenhoe and Southwood *Nor 1* **P** *Lt-Col E R F Gilbert (1 turn)*, *Ch Soc Trust (2 turns)* **R** J HANDLEY

REEPHAM (St Mary) and Hackford w Whitwell and Kerdiston, Thurning w Wood Dalling and Salle *Nor 8* **P** *Bp, CCC Cam, Pemb Coll Cam, Trin Coll Cam, and Ch Soc Trust (jt)* **R** G DODSON

REEPHAM (St Peter and St Paul) Fiskerton w Reepham *Linc*

REGENT'S PARK (Christchurch) Munster Square Ch Ch and St Mary Magd *Lon*

REGENT'S PARK (St Mark) *Lon 16* **P** *D&C St Paul's* **V** T P N D JONES, **Hon C** J F HUMBLE, **NSM** J M YATES

REGIL (St James Mission Church) Winford w Felton Common Hill *B & W*

REIGATE South Park (St Luke) Reigate St Luke S Park *S'wark*

REIGATE (St Luke) South Park *S'wark 24* **P** *Bp* **V** A J MAYER, **C** D G WAKEFIELD, **NSM** G TYLER

REIGATE (St Mark) *S'wark 24* **P** *Bp* **V** I H ROBERTSON

REIGATE (St Mary Magdalene) *S'wark 24* **P** *Trustees* **V** R I THOMSON, **C** S G HOLLAND, A J SMITH, **Par Dn** S M BROWN, **Hon C** M J H FOX, **NSM** D A HAGGAN

REIGATE (St Philip) Conventional District *S'wark 24* **Min** J P SCOTT

REIGATE HEATH (not known) Reigate St Mary *S'wark*

REIGHTON (St Peter) w Speeton *York 10* **P** *Exors Sir Henry Strickland-Constable, Bt (3 turns), Abp (1 turn)* **V** *Vacant*

REKENDYKE *Dur 7* **P** *The Crown and D&C* **V** A J BEALING, **Par Dn** P R BEALING

REMENHAM (St Nicholas) *Ox 6* **P** *Jes Coll Ox* **P-in-c** A PYBURN

REMPSTONE (All Saints) *S'well 10* **P** *SS Coll Cam* **P-in-c** S J SMITH

RENDCOMB (St Peter) *Glouc 12* **P** *Major M T N H Wills* **P-in-c** P J SUDBURY

RENDHAM (St Michael) w Sweffling *St E 19* **P** *CPAS* **R** C D R STEVENS

RENDLESHAM (St Gregory the Great) Eyke w Bromeswell, Rendlesham, Tunstall etc *St E*

RENHOLD (All Saints) *St Alb 16* **P** *MMCET* **P-in-c** P E WILSON

RENISHAW (St Matthew) Eckington w Handley and Ridgeway *Derby*

RENNINGTON (All Saints) Embleton w Rennington and Rock *Newc*

RENWICK (All Saints) Kirkoswald, Renwick and Ainstable *Carl*

REPPS (St Peter) Martham w Repps w Bastwick *Nor*

REPTON (St Wystan) *Derby 16* **P** *Major F R D Burdett Fisher (1 turn), H F Harpur-Crewe Esq (2 turns)* **V** J R P BARKER

RESTON, NORTH (St Edith) *Linc 8* **P** *D&C* **V** *Vacant*

RETFORD (St Saviour) *S'well 5* **P** *Simeon's Trustees* **V** A C StJ WALKER

RETFORD, EAST (St Swithin) *S'well 5* **P** *Bp* **V** J L OTTEY, **C** D B BAMBER

RETFORD, WEST (St Michael) *S'well 5* **P** *Meynell Ch Trust* **R** J L OTTEY

RETTENDON (All Saints) Rawreth w Rettendon *Chelmsf*

REVELSTOKE (St Peter) Newton Ferrers w Revelstoke *Ex*

REVESBY (St Lawrence) Mareham-le-Fen and Revesby *Linc*

REWE (St Mary the Virgin) Stoke Canon, Poltimore w Huxham and Rewe etc *Ex*

REYDON (St Margaret) *St E 15* **P** *Personal Reps Earl of Stradbroke* **V** H V EDWARDS, **Hon Par Dn** A K E SORENSEN

REYMERSTON (St Peter) w Cranworth, Letton, Southburgh, Whinburgh and Westfield *Nor 12* **P** *Ch Soc Trust and MMCET (jt)* **P-in-c** D R RYE

RHODES (All Saints) (St Thomas) *Man 19* **P** *R Middleton* **V** G D GARRETT

RHYDYCROESAU (Christ Church) *Lich 25* **P** *Bp* **P-in-c** D B CROWHURST

RIBBESFORD (St Leonard) w Bewdley and Dowles *Worc 10* **P** *E J Winnington-Ingram Esq* **R** R J GIBBS, **NSM** G D MORPHY

RIBBLETON (St Mary) (St Anne's Church Centre) (Ascension) *Blackb 14* **P** *Patr Bd* **TR** B H PITHERS, **TV** M F WOOD, **C** R K HENSHALL

RIBBY w Wrea (St Nicholas) *Blackb 11* **P** *V Kirkham* **V** R C WELLS

RIBCHESTER (St Wilfred) w Stidd *Blackb 14* **P** *Bp* **R** A D HINDLEY

RIBSTON, LITTLE (St Helen) Spofforth w Kirk Deighton *Ripon*

RIBY (St Edmund) Keelby w Riby and Aylesby *Linc*

RICCALL (St Mary) *York 4* **P** *Abp* **V** P P WOOD

RICHARD'S CASTLE (All Saints) *Heref 12* **P** *Bp Worc* **P-in-c** J F BAULCH

RICHINGS PARK (St Leonard) Ivor *Ox*

RICHMOND (Holy Trinity) and Christ Church *S'wark 15* **P** *CPAS* **V** D C CASSON, **Par Dn** R H JAMIESON

RICHMOND (St Luke) Kew St Phil and All SS w St Luke *S'wark*

RICHMOND (St Mary Magdalene) (St Matthias) (St John the Divine) *S'wark 15* **P** *K Coll Cam* **V** B L H CARPENTER, **C** W F WARREN, P J H DUNN

RICHMOND (St Mary w Holy Trinity) w Hudswell *Ripon 2* **P** *Bp* **R** C N H WHITE, **C** W M SIMMS

RICKERSCOTE (St Peter) *Lich 16* **P** *Bp and V Stafford St Paul (jt)* **V** K L WASSALL

RICKINGHALL (St Mary) Redgrave cum Botesdale w Rickinghall *St E*

RICKLING (All Saints) Quendon w Rickling and Wicken Bonhunt *Chelmsf*

RICKMANSWORTH (St Mary the Virgin) *St Alb 10* **P** *Bp* **V** B L DRIVER, **NSM** G L BLACKTOP, **Hon Par Dn** A P L SHAW

RIDDINGS (Holy Spirit) Bottesford w Ashby *Linc*

RIDDINGS (St James) and Ironville *Derby 1* **P** *Wright Trustees and V Alfreton (jt)* **V** M R KNIGHT

RIDDLESDEN (St Mary the Virgin) *Bradf 8* **P** *Bp* **V** G D N SMITH

RIDDLESDOWN (St James) *S'wark 21* **P** *Bp* **Par Dn** D J ROWLAND, **NSM** J DAGLEISH

RIDDLESWORTH (St Peter) Garboldisham w Blo' Norton, Riddlesworth etc *Nor*

RIDGE (St Margaret) S Mymms and Ridge *St Alb*

RIDGEWAY *Ox 19* **P** *DBP, CCC Ox, and Qu Coll Ox (jt)* **R** A WADGE

RIDGEWAY *Sarum 20* **P** *Patr Bd* **TR** N T POLLOCK, **TV** M STRANGE

RIDGEWAY (St John the Evangelist) Eckington w Handley and Ridgeway *Derby*

RIDGEWELL (St Laurence) w Ashen, Birdbrook and Sturmer *Chelmsf 17* **P** *Duchy of Lanc, Bp, and DBP (by turn)* **R** M D HEWITT

RIDGMONT (All Saints) Aspley Guise w Husborne Crawley and Ridgmont *St Alb*

RIDING MILL (St James) *Newc 3* **P** *Viscount Allendale* **V** *Vacant* Riding Mill (043482) 240

RIDLEY (St Peter) *Roch 1* **P** *J R A B Scott Esq* **R** *Vacant*

RIDLINGTON (St Mary Magdalene and St Andrew) Preston and Ridlington w Wing and Pilton *Pet*

RIDLINGTON (St Peter) Bacton w Edingthorpe w Witton and Ridlington *Nor*

RIDWARES and Kings Bromley, The *Lich 2* **P** *Bp, Lord Leigh, and D&C (jt)* **R** F FINCH, **Par Dn** S FINN, **NSM** I C CONWAY

RIEVAULX (St Mary) Helmsley *York*

RIGSBY (St James) Alford w Rigsby *Linc*

RIGTON, NORTH (St John) Kirkby Overblow *Ripon*

RILLINGTON (St Andrew) w Scampston, Wintringham and Thorpe Bassett *York 2* **P** *Major G R H Cholmley* **V** F B WILLIAMS

RIMPTON (Blessed Virgin Mary) Chilton Cantelo, Ashington, Mudford, Rimpton etc *B & W*

RIMSWELL (St Mary) Owthorne and Rimswell w Withernsea *York*

RINGLAND (St Peter) Taverham w Ringland *Nor*

RINGLEY Outwood (St Aidan) see below

RINGLEY (St Saviour) *Man 14* **P** *R Prestwich St Mary* **P-in-c** P F DAVEY

RINGMER (St Mary the Virgin) *Chich 18* **P** *Abp* **V** H M MOSELEY, **NSM** J R LOWERSON

RINGMORE (All Hallows) Bigbury, Ringmore and Kingston *Ex*

RINGSFIELD (All Saints) w Redisham, Barsham, Shipmeadow and Mettingham *St E 14* **P** *Magd Coll Cam and Ch Soc Trust (1 turn), Mrs B I T Suckling (1 turn), and CPAS (1 turn)* **P-in-c** F GEORGE

RINGSHALL (St Catherine) w Battisford, Barking w Darmsden and Great Bricett *St E 1* **P** *Bp, Ch Patr Trust, and J C W de la Bere Esq (jt)* **R** H D CHAPMAN

RINGSTEAD (Nativity of the Blessed Virgin Mary) Denford w Ringstead *Pet*

RINGSTEAD (St Andrew) Hunstanton St Edm w Ringstead *Nor*

RINGWAY (All Saints) and St Mary *Ches 10* **P** *Bp*
V B B GRIBBIN
RINGWOOD (St Peter and St Paul) *Win 8* **P** *K Coll Cam*
V J R TURPIN, **C** A E BARTON
RINGWOULD (St Nicholas) w Kingsdown *Cant 8*
P *R S C Monins Esq and Ch Patr Trust (jt)* **R** J A SILK
RIPE (St John the Baptist) Laughton w Ripe and
Chalvington *Chich*
RIPLEY (All Saints) *Derby 12* **P** *Wright Trustees*
V R P FULLER, **C** G F SMALL
RIPLEY (All Saints) *Ripon 3* **P** *Sir Thomas Ingilby, Bt*
R *Vacant* Harrogate (0423) 770147
RIPLEY (St Mary) *Guildf 12* **P** *Bp* **V** C J ELSON
RIPON (Holy Trinity) *Ripon 3* **P** *Simeon's Trustees*
V R B B WILD
RIPPINGALE Group, The (St Andrew) *Linc 13*
P *Baroness Willoughby de Eresby, Charterhouse, Bp,*
and St Jo Coll Dur (jt) **R** R HARRIS
RIPPLE (St Mary the Virgin) Gt Mongeham w Ripple
and Sutton by Dover *Cant*
**RIPPLE (St Mary), Earls Croome w Hill Croome and
Strensham** *Worc 5* **P** *Bp and Trustees of late Rev
G Le S Amphlett (alt)* **R** F R HIGGINS
RIPPONDEN (St Bartholomew) *Wakef 4* **P** *Bp and
V Halifax (jt)* **V** C W DIXON, **C** H N LAWRANCE,
NSM M JAMES
**RISBY (St Giles) w Great Saxham, Little Saxham and
Westley** *St E 13* **P** *Ld Chan, Trustees of Sir William
Stirling, and DBP (by turn)* **P-in-c** C J ROGERS
RISE (All Saints) Sigglesthorne and Rise w Nunkeeling
and Bewholme *York*
RISE PARK (not known) Bestwood *S'well*
RISEHOLME (St Mary) Nettleham *Linc*
RISELEY (All Saints) w Bletsoe *St Alb 21* **P** *MMCET*
V D J BOURNE
RISHTON (St Peter and St Paul) *Blackb 8* **P** *Trustees*
V P A SMITH
RISHWORTH (St John) Ripponden *Wakef*
RISLEY (All Saints) *Derby 13* **P** *Bp* **P-in-c** D HOWES
RISSINGTONS, The (St John the Baptist) (St Peter)
Glouc 15 **P** *C T R Wingfield Esq, Ld Chan, and DBP
(by turn)* **R** D BUSH
RITCHINGS PARK (St Leonard) Iver *Ox*
RIVENHALL (St Mary the Virgin and All Saints)
Chelmsf 27 **P** *DBP* **R** N S COOPER
RIVER (St Peter and St Paul) *Cant 4* **P** *Abp*
R P W A BOWERS, **NSM** L R CRUTTENDEN
RIVERHEAD (St Mary) w Dunton Green *Roch 8*
P *R Sevenoaks and Bp (jt)* **V** G T CUNLIFFE
**RIVERSIDE: Colnbrook, Datchet, Dorney, Eton, Eton
Wick, Horton, Wraysbury** *Ox 23* **P** *Patr Bd*
TR W L KNIGHT,
TV C H PONTIN, S J NEWELL, P W ABRAHAMS,
C P SWART-RUSSELL
RIVINGTON (not known) *Man 11* **P** *PCC*
P-in-c J JERMY
ROADE (St Mary the Virgin) and Ashton w Hartwell *Pet 5*
P *Ld Chan and Bp (alt)* **V** C H DAVIDSON
ROADHEAD Kinkry Hill (Mission Room) Bewcastle,
Stapleton and Kirklinton etc *Carl*
ROADWATER (St Luke) Old Cleeve, Leighland and
Treborough *B & W*
ROBERTSBRIDGE (Mission Room) Salehurst *Chich*
ROBERTTOWN (All Saints) *Wakef 8* **P** *V Birstall*
V D G RHODES
ROBOROUGH (St Peter) Beaford, Roborough and St
Giles in the Wood *Ex*
ROBY (St Bartholomew) *Liv 2* **P** *Bp* **V** G S PEARSON,
C P D BASKERVILLE
ROCESTER (St Michael) *Lich 21* **P** *Trustees*
V J B HALL
ROCHDALE Deeplish (St Luke) *Man 19* **P** *Bp*
V D C R WIDDOWS
**ROCHDALE (St Chad) (Good Shepherd) (St John the
Divine)** *Man 19* **P** *Bp* **TV** G C DOBBS,
J HARGREAVES, C A POWELL, A SHACKLETON,
R J STILLMAN, **C** C FALLONE, **NSM** I G KAY
ROCHDALE (St George w St Alban) *Man 19* **P** *Bp*
V R COWARD
ROCHE (St Gomonda of the Rock) and Withiel *Truro 1*
P *Bp and DBP (jt)* **R** D J A POLLARD
ROCHESTER (St Justus) *Roch 5* **P** *Bp*
V J G C LAWRENCE
ROCHESTER (St Margaret) (St Peter's Parish Centre)
Roch 5 **P** *Bp and D&C (jt)* **R** H THOMSON,
Par Dn E P I WESTBROOK, **NSM** H DAUBNEY
ROCHESTER ROW (St Stephen) Westmr St Steph w St
Jo *Lon*

ROCHFORD (St Andrew) *Chelmsf 14* **P** *Bp*
R A N GODSELL
ROCHFORD (St Michael) Teme Valley S *Worc*
ROCK (St Peter and St Paul) Mamble w Bayton, Rock w
Heightington etc *Worc*
ROCK (St Philip and St James) Embleton w Rennington
and Rock *Newc*
ROCK FERRY (St Peter) *Ches 1* **P** *Bp* **V** R C TOAN,
C P A BROWN
ROCKBEARE (St Mary w St Andrew) Aylesbeare,
Rockbeare, Farringdon etc *Ex*
ROCKBOURNE (St Andrew) W Downland *Sarum*
ROCKCLIFFE (St Mary the Virgin) and Blackford *Carl 2*
P *D&C* **V** R D A TANKARD
ROCKHAMPTON (St Oswald) Falfield w
Rockhampton *Glouc*
ROCKINGHAM (St Leonard) Gretton w Rockingham
and Caldecote *Pet*
ROCKLAND (All Saints) Lt w Gt Ellingham w
Rockland *Nor*
ROCKLAND (St Peter) as above
**ROCKLAND ST MARY (St Mary) w Hellington,
Bramerton with Surlingham, Claxton and Carleton
St Peter** *Nor 14* **P** *Bp and Adn Norfolk (1 turn),
MMCET (1 turn)* **R** J A LEDWARD,
C C H R WHITEMAN
RODBOROUGH (St Mary Magdalene) *Glouc 8* **P** *Bp*
R *Vacant* Stroud (0453) 764399
RODBOURNE (Holy Rood) Gt Somerford, Lt
Somerford, Seagry, Corston etc *Bris*
RODBOURNE CHENEY (St Mary) *Bris 10* **P** *Patr Bd*
TR G W CREES, **TV** R W ADAMS, **C** N A HECTOR,
Par Dn M J GUILLEBAUD
RODDEN (All Saints) Beckington w Standerwick,
Berkley, Rodden etc *B & W*
RODE (St Lawrence) Rode Major *B & W*
RODE, NORTH (St Michael) Bosley and N Rode w
Wincle and Wildboarclough *Ches*
RODE HEATH (Good Shepherd) Odd Rode *Ches*
RODE HILL (Christ Church) see below
RODE MAJOR (St Lawrence) (Christ Church) *B & W 4*
P *Bp* **R** *Vacant* Frome (0373) 830251
RODHUISH (St Bartholomew) Dunster, Carhampton
and Withycombe w Rodhuish *B & W*
RODING, HIGH (All Saints) Aythorpe w High and
Leaden Roding *Chelmsf*
RODING, HIGH (Mission Hall) as above
RODINGTON (St George) Longdon-upon-Tern,
Rodington, Uppington etc *Lich*
RODLEY (Ecumenical Centre) Bramley *Ripon*
RODLEY (Mission Church) Westbury-on-Severn w
Flaxley and Blaisdon *Glouc*
RODMARTON (St Peter) Coates, Rodmarton and
Sapperton etc *Glouc*
RODMELL (St Peter) Iford w Kingston and Rodmell
Chich
RODMERSHAM (St Nicholas) Tunstall w Rodmersham
Cant
RODNEY STOKE (St Leonard) w Draycott *B & W 1*
P *Bp* **P-in-c** J C HALL
ROEHAMPTON (Holy Trinity) *S'wark 17* **P** *Bp*
V J S COX, **Hon C** D PEACOCK
ROFFEY (All Saints) Roughey (or Roffey) *Chich*
**ROGATE (St Bartholomew) w Terwick and Trotton w
Chithurst** *Chich 10* **P** *Ld Chan* **NSM** S J CHAPMAN
ROGERS LANE (St Andrew's Chapel) Stoke Poges *Ox*
ROKEBY (St Mary) w Brignall *Ripon 2* **P** *Ld Chan and
Bp (alt)* **R** *Vacant*
ROKER (St Aidan) Monkwearmouth All SS *Dur*
**ROLLESBY (St George) w Burgh w Billockby w Ashby w
Oby, Thurne and Clippesby** *Nor 2* **P** *Bp,
R J H Tacon Esq, and DBP (jt)* **R** C W COUSINS
**ROLLESTON (Holy Trinity) w Fiskerton, Morton and
Upton** *S'well 15* **P** *Ld Chan* **C** A I TUCKER
ROLLESTON (St John the Baptist) Billesdon and
Skeffington *Leic*
ROLLESTON (St Mary) *Lich 20* **P** *MMCET*
R M D BIRT
ROLLESTONE (St Andrew) Shrewton *Sarum*
ROLLRIGHT, GREAT (St Andrew) Hook Norton w
Gt Rollright, Swerford etc *Ox*
ROLLRIGHT, LITTLE (St Phillip) Lt Compton w
Chastleton, Cornwell etc *Ox*
ROLVENDEN (St Mary the Virgin) *Cant 11* **P** *Abp*
Dn-in-c A E WILLIAMS
ROMALDKIRK (St Romald) w Laithkirk *Ripon 2* **P** *Bp
and Earl of Strathmore's Trustees (alt)* **R** C R BOFF
ROMANBY (St James) Northallerton w Kirby Sigston
York

ROMANSLEIGH (St Rumon)   S Molton w Nymet St George, High Bray etc *Ex*
ROMFORD (Ascension) Collier Row *Chelmsf 4*   **P** *Trustees*   **V** G P LAUT
ROMFORD (Good Shepherd) Collier Row *Chelmsf 4*   **P** *CPAS*   **V** J B BATTMAN,   **C** A M RIMMER
ROMFORD (St Alban) *Chelmsf 4*   **P** *Bp*   **NSM** P A EVANS
ROMFORD (St Andrew) (St Agnes) *Chelmsf 4*   **P** *New Coll Ox*   **R** B J LEWIS,   **C** R WARD
ROMFORD (St Edward the Confessor) *Chelmsf 4*   **P** *New Coll Ox*   **V** D W M JENNINGS,   **C** A J CARLILL, **Par Dn** V E PERRY,   **NSM** G K ARBER
ROMFORD (St John the Divine) *Chelmsf 4*   **P** *Bp*   **V** G P LAW
ROMILEY (St Chad)   Chadkirk *Ches*
ROMNEY, NEW (St Nicholas) w OLD (St Clement) and Midley *Cant 13*   **P** *Abp*   **V** L P FORD
ROMSEY (St Mary and St Ethelflaeda) *Win 11*   **P** *Bp*   **V** N C JONES,   **C** J S MARTIN,   **Hon C** S F LUTHER
ROMSLEY (St Kenelm) *Worc 9*   **P** *R Halesowen*   **R** M G CLARKE
ROOKERY, THE (St Saviour)   Mow Cop *Lich*
ROOKHOPE (St John the Evangelist)   Eastgate w Rookhope *Dur*
ROOS (All Saints) and Garton in Holderness w Tunstall, Grimston and Hilston *York 13*   **P** *Abp (1 turn)*, *SMF (2 turns)*   **R** J D ADEY
ROOSE (St Perran)   Barrow St Geo w St Luke *Carl*
ROPLEY (St Peter)   Bishop's Sutton and Ropley and W Tisted *Win*
ROPSLEY (St Peter) *Linc 14*   **P** *Bp*   **R** W B FOSTER
ROSE ASH (St Peter)   Bishopsnympton, Rose Ash, Mariansleigh etc *Ex*
ROSEDALE (St Lawrence)   Lastingham w Appleton-le-Moors, Rosedale etc *York*
ROSHERVILLE (St Mark) *Roch 4*   **P** *DBP*   **V** *Vacant*   Gravesend (0474) 534430
ROSLEY (Holy Trinity)   Westward, Rosley-w-Woodside and Welton *Carl*
ROSLISTON (St Mary)   Walton on Trent w Croxall etc *Derby*
ROSS (St Mary the Virgin) w Brampton Abbotts, Bridstow and Peterstow *Heref 8*   **P** *DBP*   **TV** P J BROADBENT, **TM** F M HANCOCK,   **C** B R CONAWAY
ROSSINGTON (St Michael) *Sheff 10*   **P** *Bp*   **R** M J SECCOMBE
ROSSINGTON, NEW (St Luke) *Sheff 10*   **P** *Bp*   **V** N A BARR
ROSTHERNE (St Mary) w Bollington *Ches 12*   **P** *C L S Cornwall-Legh Esq*   **V** N D ROGERS
ROTHBURY (All Saints) *Newc 9*   **P** *Duchy of Lanc*   **R** L F TEDDERSHAW,   **C** G SOUTH
ROTHERBY (All Saints)   Hoby cum Rotherby w Brooksby, Ragdale & Thru'ton *Leic*
ROTHERFIELD (St Denys) w Mark Cross *Chich 19*   **P** *Bp, Adn Lewes and Hastings, and Ch Patr Trust (jt)*   **R** J F HALE
ROTHERFIELD GREYS (Holy Trinity) *Ox 6*   **P** *R Rotherfield Greys St Nich*   **V** D R B CARTER
ROTHERFIELD GREYS (St Nicholas) *Ox 6*   **P** *Trin Coll Ox*   **R** B G BUTLER-SMITH
ROTHERFIELD PEPPARD (All Saints) *Ox 6*   **P** *Jes Coll Ox*   **R** B G BUTLER-SMITH
ROTHERHAM (All Saints) *Sheff 6*   **P** *Bp*   **V** S G N BRINDLEY,   **C** N M WRIGHT
ROTHERHAM Ferham Park (St Paul)   Masbrough *Sheff*
ROTHERHITHE (Holy Trinity) *S'wark 5*   **P** *R Rotherhithe St Mary*   **V** P D MAURICE, **Par Dn** J FORTUNE-WOOD,   **Hon C** I M KENWAY
ROTHERHITHE (St Katharine) w St Barnabas *S'wark 5*   **P** *Bp and R Rotherhithe St Mary (alt)*   **P-in-c** T HOPPERTON,   **C** R P H BUCK
ROTHERHITHE (St Mary) w All Saints *S'wark 5*   **P** *Clare Coll Cam*   **R** C E N RICHARDS
ROTHERSTHORPE (St Peter and St Paul)   Kislingbury w Rothersthorpe *Pet*
ROTHERWICK (not known)   Heckfield w Mattingley and Rotherwick *Win*
ROTHLEY (St Mary the Virgin and St John the Baptist) *Leic 6*   **P** *MMCET*   **V** D C KIRKWOOD
ROTHWELL (Holy Trinity) *Ripon 8*   **P** *Bp*   **V** F E REDHEAD,   **C** D F HANDLEY,   **NSM** G W SELLERS
ROTHWELL (Holy Trinity) w Orton and Rushton w Glendon and Pipwell *Pet 11*   **P** *Hosp of Jes (1 turn), Bp (2 turns), J Hipwell Esq (1 turn), and Mert Coll Ox (1 turn)*   **R** P R ROSE,   **NSM** P G LAMBERT
ROTHWELL (St Mary the Virgin)   Swallow *Linc*

ROTTINGDEAN (St Margaret) *Chich 2*   **P** *Bp*   **V** K D RICHARDS,   **NSM** J M APPLEBY
ROUGH CLOSE (St Matthew)   Meir Heath *Lich*
ROUGH COMMON (St Gabriel)   Harbledown *Cant*
ROUGH HAY (St Christopher)   Darlaston St Lawr *Lich*
ROUGH HILLS (St Martin) *Lich 10*   **P** *Bp*   **V** J C OAKES
ROUGHAM (St Mary)   Castle Acre w Newton, Rougham and Southacre *Nor*
ROUGHAM (St Mary), Beyton w Hessett and Rushbrooke *St E 10*   **P** *MMCET, Ld Chan, Mrs V J Clarke, and Bp (by turn)*   **R** R F WEBB
ROUGHEY All Saints *Chich 8*   **P** *Bp*   **V** A R REED, **NSM** P GRAVES
ROUGHTON (St Margaret) w Haltham *Linc 11*   **P** *R H Spurrier Esq*   **P-in-c** S W PEARCE
ROUGHTON (St Mary) and Felbrigg, Metton, Sustead, Bessingham and Gunton w Hanworth *Nor 7*   **P** *Bp and Exors G Whately (jt)*   **R** *Vacant*   Cromer (0263) 768075
ROUGHTOWN (St John the Baptist) *Man 17*   **P** *Bp*   **V** H J HUGHES
ROUNDHAY (St Edmund) *Ripon 5*   **P** *Bp*   **V** J R SWAIN, **C** J TREETOPS,   D E MARSHALL
ROUNDHAY (St John the Evangelist) *Ripon 5*   **P** *DBF*   **V** *Vacant*   Leeds (0532) 658583
ROUNDS GREEN (St James) *Birm 5*   **P** *V Langley*   **V** R A SLATER
ROUNDSHAW Local Ecumenical Project *S'wark 25*   **Min** W J BLAKEMAN
ROUNDTHORN (St Matthew and St Aidan) *Man 18*   **P** *Bp*   **V** D M ALLEN
ROUNTON, EAST (St Laurence)   Rounton w Welbury *York*
ROUNTON, WEST (St Oswald) and East Routon w Welbury *York 20*   **P** *Ld Chan*   **P-in-c** B J MAYNE
ROUS LENCH (St Peter)   Church Lench w Rous Lench and Abbots Morton *Worc*
ROUSHAM (St Leonard and St James)   The Heyfords w Rousham and Somerton *Ox*
ROUTH (All Saints) *York 9*   **P** *Ch Soc Trust and Reformation Ch Trust (jt)*   **R** *Vacant*
ROWANFIELD (Emmanuel)   Cheltenham St Mark *Glouc*
ROWBERROW (St Michael and All Angels)   Axbridge w Shipham and Rowberrow *B & W*
ROWDE (St Matthew) and Poulshot *Sarum 19*   **P** *Bp and DBP (alt)*   **R** R H BASTEN
ROWINGTON (St Lawrence)   Hatton w Haseley, Rowington w Lowsonford etc *Cov*
ROWLAND LUBBOCK (Memorial Hall)   E Horsley *Guildf*
ROWLANDS CASTLE (St John the Baptist) *Portsm 4*   **P** *Bp*   **R** N STUART-LEE
ROWLANDS GILL (St Barnabas)   High Spen and Rowlands Gill *Dur*
ROWLEDGE (St James) *Guildf 3*   **P** *Adn Surrey*   **V** C J RICHARDSON
ROWLESTONE (St Peter)   Ewyas Harold w Dulas, Kenderchurch etc *Heref*
ROWLEY (St Peter) w Skidby *York 9*   **P** *Abp and Sir David Hildyard (jt)*   **R** J M TRIGG
ROWLEY REGIS (St Giles) *Birm 5*   **P** *Ld Chan*   **V** D C L EVE,   **Par Dn** J BIRKETT
ROWNER (St Mary the Virgin) *Portsm 3*   **P** *R J F Prideaux-Brune Esq*   **R** C R GEORGE, **C** B D GOLDSMITH
ROWNEY GREEN (Mission Chapel)   Alvechurch *Worc*
ROWSLEY (St Katherine) *Derby 2*   **P** *Duke of Rutland*   **Dn-in-c** A WELCH
ROWSTON (St Clement)   Digby *Linc*
ROWTON (All Hallows) *Lich 30*   **P** *Lord Barnard*   **V** K D MINTY
ROXBOURNE (St Andrew) *Lon 23*   **P** *Bp*   **P-in-c** D J COCKBILL,   **Hon Par Dn** C J PRICE
ROXBY (St Mary)   Winterton Gp *Linc*
ROXBY (St Nicholas)   Hinderwell w Roxby *York*
ROXETH (Christ Church) and Harrow (St Peter) *Lon 23*   **P** *Bp and Ch Patr Trust (jt)*   **V** B C COLLINS, **C** P J SOURBUT
ROXHOLME   Leasingham *Linc*
ROXTON (St Mary Magdalene) w Great Barford *St Alb 17*   **P** *Trin Coll Cam*   **V** G N DOBSON
ROXWELL (St Michael and All Angels) *Chelmsf 11*   **P** *New Coll Ox*   **P-in-c** D C BARTLE
ROYDON (All Saints)   Grimston, Congham and Roydon *Nor*
ROYDON (St Peter) *Chelmsf 3*   **P** *Earl Cowley*   **V** P J COLLINS

ROYDON (St Remigius) *Nor 16* **P** *DBP*
P-in-c W M C BESTELINK
ROYSTON (St John the Baptist) *St Alb 5* **P** *Bp*
V K W T W JOHNSON, **C** P L OXBORROW,
NSM J H FIDLER
ROYSTON (St John the Baptist) *Wakef 7* **P** *Bp*
V J L HUDSON, **C** J A BOOTH
ROYTON (St Anne) Longsight *Man 18* **P** *Bp*
V D SHARPLES
ROYTON (St Paul) *Man 18* **P** *R Prestwich St Mary*
V P R S BOLTON, **NSM** B HARTLEY
RUAN LANIHORNE (St Rumon) Veryan w Ruan
Lanihorne *Truro*
RUAN MINOR (St Rumon) St Ruan w St Grade and
Landewednack *Truro*
RUARDEAN (St John the Baptist) *Glouc 4* **P** *Bp*
R C T DAVIES
RUBERY (St Chad) *Birm 4* **P** *The Crown*
V J J J BARRETT
RUCKINGE (St Mary Magdalene) Orlestone w Snave
and Ruckinge w Warehorne *Cant*
RUCKLAND (St Olave) S Ormsby Gp *Linc*
RUDBY IN CLEVELAND (All Saints) w Middleton
York 22 **P** *Abp* **V** D F LICKESS
RUDDINGTON (St Peter) *S'well 10* **P** *Simeon's Trustees*
V F G HARRISON
RUDFORD (St Mary the Virgin) Highnam, Lassington,
Rudford, Tibberton etc *Glouc*
RUDGWICK (Holy Trinity) *Chich 8* **P** *Ld Chan*
V J D MORRIS
RUDHAM, EAST (St Mary) Coxford Gp *Nor*
RUDHEATH (Licensed Room) Witton *Ches*
RUDSTON (All Saints) Boynton and Kilham *York 10*
P *Abp (2 turns). Ld Chan (1 turn)* **V** M S FARGUS
RUFFORD (St Mary the Virgin) *Blackb 6* **P** *Bp*
R R E SWANN
RUFFORTH (All Saints) w Moor Monkton and Hessay
York 1 **P** *MMCET and Abp (alt)* **R** J A RENDALL
RUGBY (St Andrew) (St George) (St John) (St Peter)
(St Philip) *Cov 6* **P** *Bp* **TR** M L LANGRISH,
TV P J WILSON, A J BURNISTON, P M de la P BERESFORD,
C D R GOULD, H M ISON, **Hon Par Dn** P A MARTINDALE
RUGBY (St Matthew) *Cov 6* **P** *Ch Trust Fund Trust*
V M P SAXBY, **C** R J COOKE
RUGELEY (St Augustine) (Good Shepherd) *Lich 4*
P *Patr Bd* **TR** M J NEWMAN,
TV P N SUCH, R CHARLES
RUISHTON (St George) w Thornfalcon *B & W 20* **P** *Bp*
and Dr W R Chisholm-Batten (alt) **V** D F GOODFIELD
RUISLIP (St Martin) *Lon 24* **P** *D&C Windsor*
C P A EAGLES, V R K SACKEY
RUISLIP (St Mary) *Lon 24* **P** *Bp* **V** B G COPUS
RUISLIP MANOR (St Paul) *Lon 24* **P** *Bp* **V** A C BALL,
Par Dn M WHEELER
RUMBOLDSWYKE (St Mary) Whyke w
Rumboldswhyke and Portfield *Chich*
RUMBURGH (St Michael and All Angels and St Felix) w
South Elham (All Saints) (St James) (St Michael) w the
Ilketshalls *St E 14* **P** *Ld Chan (1 turn), Bp (2 turns),*
and Duke of Norfolk (1 turn) **P-in-c** J M S FALKNER,
C I S MORGAN
RUNCORN (All Saints) *Ches 3* **P** *Ch Ch Ox*
V T R BARKER
RUNCORN (Holy Trinity) *Ches 3* **P** *Bp* **V** *Vacant*
Runcorn (09285) 72299
RUNCORN (St John the Evangelist) Weston *Ches 3*
P *Bp* **V** J BRONNERT
RUNCORN (St Michael and All Angels) *Ches 3* **P** *Bp*
V A R RIDLEY
RUNCTON, NORTH (All Saints) w Hardwick and Setchey
Nor 23 **P** *H N D Gurney Esq* **R** *Vacant*
King's Lynn (0553) 840271
RUNCTON, SOUTH (St Andrew) Holme Runcton w
S Runcton and Wallington *Ely*
RUNCTON HOLME (St James) as above
RUNHALL (All Saints) Barnham Broom *Nor*
RUNHAM (St Peter and St Paul) Filby w Thrigby,
Mautby, Stokesby, Herringby etc *Nor*
RUNNINGTON (St Peter and St Paul) Wellington and
Distr *B & W*
RUNTON (Holy Trinity) Aylmerton w Runton *Nor*
RUNTON, EAST (St Andrew) as above
RUNWELL (St Mary) Wickford and Runwell *Chelmsf*
RUSCOMBE (St James the Great) and Twyford *Ox 16*
P *Bp* **V** G R HAMBORG
RUSH GREEN (St Augustine) Romford *Chelmsf 4* **P** *Bp*
NSM D HENDERSON
RUSHALL (Christ the King) (St Michael the Archangel)
Lich 7 **P** *Sir Andrew Buchanan, Bt and*

H C S Buchanan Esq (jt) **V** M J LEADBEATER,
C C I DYTOR
RUSHALL (St Mary) Dickleburgh, Langmere,
Shimpling, Thelveton etc *Nor*
RUSHALL (St Matthew) Uphavon w Rushall and
Charlton *Sarum*
RUSHBROOKE (St Nicholas) Rougham, Beyton w
Hessett and Rushbrooke *St E*
RUSHBURY (St Peter) *Heref 11* **P** *Bp Birm*
R M BROMFIELD
RUSHDEN (St Mary) Sandon, Wallington and Rushden
w Clothall *St Alb*
RUSHDEN (St Mary) (St Peter) (St Mark) w Newton
Bromswold *Pet 10* **P** *CPAS* **R** A SMITH,
C A R PRITCHARD, R J LEE, **Par Dn** D E KERR,
NSM E J TYE
RUSHEN Christ Church (Holy Trinity) *S & M 1*
P *The Crown* **V** F H BIRD,
NSM W H MARTIN, S M WATTERSON
RUSHFORD (St John the Evangelist) Garboldisham w
Blo' Norton, Riddlesworth etc *Nor*
RUSHLAKE GREEN (Little St Mary) Warbleton and
Bodle Street Green *Chich*
RUSHMERE (St Andrew) *St E 4* **P** *Bp*
Par Dn C A GRAY
RUSHMERE (St Michael) Carlton Colville w Mutford
and Rushmere *Nor*
RUSHMOOR (St Francis) Churt *Guildf*
RUSHOCK (St Michael) Elmley Lovett w Hampton
Lovett and Elmbridge etc *Worc*
RUSHOLME (Holy Trinity) *Man 4* **P** *CPAS*
R A PORTER, **C** A M MacLEAY
RUSHTON (All Saints) Rothwell w Orton, Rushton w
Glendon and Pipewell *Pet*
RUSHTON (St Lawrence) *Lich 14* **P** *R Leek and*
Meerbrook **P-in-c** B H PEEL
RUSHTON SPENCER Rushton *Lich*
RUSKIN PARK (St Saviour) Herne Hill *S'wark*
RUSKINGTON (All Saints) *Linc 22* **P** *DBP*
R D ASKEW
RUSLAND (St Paul) Colton w Satterthwaite and
Rusland *Carl*
RUSPER (St Mary Magdalene) *Chich 8* **P** *Bp*
P-in-c E A PASSINGHAM
RUSTHALL (St Paul) (St Paul's Mission Church) *Roch 11*
P *R Speldhurst* **V** R E WHYTE, **Par Dn** J M J BAILEY
RUSTINGTON (St Peter and St Paul) *Chich 1* **P** *Bp*
V K L MASTERS, **C** A C CARR
RUSTON, SOUTH Tunstead w Sco' Ruston *Nor*
RUSTON PARVA (St Nicholas) Burton Agnes w
Harpham and Lowthorpe etc *York*
RUSWARP (St Bartholomew) Aislaby and Ruswarp
York
RUYTON XI TOWNS (St John the Baptist) w Great Ness
and Little Ness *Lich 23* **P** *Bp and Guild of All So (jt)*
and Ld Chan (alt) **V** R D BRADBURY
RYAL (All Saints) Stamfordham w Matfen *Newc*
RYARSH (St Martin) Birling, Addington, Ryarsh and
Trottiscliffe *Roch*
RYBURGH, GREAT (St Andrew) and LITTLE w Gateley
and Testerton *Nor 20* **P** *Ch Coll Cam* **R** F A HILL
RYDAL (St Mary) *Carl 10* **P** *Bp* **P-in-c** P A A WALKER
RYDE (All Saints) *Portsm 7* **P** *Bp* **V** *Vacant* Isle of
Wight (0983) 63516
RYDE (Holy Trinity) *Portsm 7* **P** *Bp*
P-in-c M J SHEFFIELD, **C** M A J EXELL, **NSM** T F SEAR
RYDE (St James) Proprietary Chapel *Portsm 7* **P** *Ch Soc*
Trust **C-in-c** B G C BAKER
RYE (St Mary the Virgin) *Chich 20* **P** *Patr Bd*
TR W A G BUXTON, **TV** D R FROST, E M HAVELL,
Hon C J BANNISTER
RYE HARBOUR (Holy Spirit) see above
RYE PARK (St Cuthbert) *St Alb 6* **P** *DBP*
V H J SPANNER
RYECROFT (St Nicholas) Rawmarsh w Parkgate *Sheff*
RYEDALE, UPPER *York 18* **P** *Abp, Adn Cleveland,*
R G Beckett Esq, and Exors Capt V M Wombwell (jt)
R A G ALDERSON
RYHALL (St John the Evangelist) w Essendine *Pet 8*
P *Burghley Ho Preservation Trust* **P-in-c**
M J THOMPSON
RYHILL (St James) *Wakef 9* **P** *Bp* **V** M E ROGERS
RYHOPE (St Paul) *Dur 9* **P** *Bp* **V** G W FLETCHER,
NSM R N TEMPERLEY
RYLSTONE (St Peter) Burnsall w Rylstone *Bradf*
RYME INTRINSECA (St Hypolytus) Yetminster w
Ryme Intrinseca and High Stoy *Sarum*
RYPE (St John the Baptist) Laughton w Ripe and
Chalvington *Chich*

RYSTON (St Michael) w Roxham *Ely 16* **P** *Bp*
V R JEFFREE
RYTHER (All Saints) *York 6* **P** *Ld Chan*
P-in-c R E MESSER
RYTON (Holy Cross) w Hedgefield *Dur 5* **P** *Bp*
R S TOWARD, **NSM** K B POTTER
RYTON (Mission Chapel) Condover w Frodesley, Acton
Burnell etc *Heref*
RYTON (St Andrew) *Lich 26* **P** *Oriel Coll Ox*
NSM P H J THORNEYCROFT
RYTON ON DUNSMORE (St Leonard) w Bubbenhall
Cov 6 **P** *Bp (1 turn), Provost & Chapter (2 turns)*
V J T SYKES
SABDEN (Heyhouses) St Nicholas and Pendleton-in-
Whalley All Saints *Blackb 8* **P** *Bp and Trustees (jt)*
V R NICHOLSON
SACKLETON (St George the Martyr) Street Team Min
York
SACOMBE (St Catherine) The Mundens w Sacombe
St Alb
SACRISTON (St Peter) and Kimblesworth *Dur 2* **P** *The*
Crown **V** P R MURRAY
SADBERGE (St Andrew) *Dur 12* **P** *Bp*
P-in-c R J COOPER
SADDINGTON (St Helen) Kibworth and Smeeton
Westerby and Saddington *Leic*
SADDLEWORTH (St Chad) (Parochial Hall) *Man 18*
P *Bp* **V** P T STEVENS, **NSM** C MARSDEN
SAFFRON WALDEN (St Mary) w Wendens Ambo and
Littlebury *Chelmsf 25* **P** *Patr Bd* **TR** D P HARLOW,
TV S F C WILLIAMS, **C** J E BURDITT,
NSM J D RUSSELL-SMITH
SAHAM TONEY (St George) Ashill w Saham Toney
Nor
ST AGNES (St Agnes) *Truro 6* **P** *D&C* **V** M J ADAMS
ST AGNES (St Agnes) Scilly Is *Truro*
ST ALBANS (Christ Church) *St Alb 11* **P** *Trustees*
V B T LYONS
ST ALBANS (St Luke) *St Alb 11* **P** *DBP* **V** P G RICH
ST ALBANS (St Mary) Marshalswick *St Alb 11* **P** *Bp*
V R E PYKE, **Hon Par Dn** C POLHILL
ST ALBANS (St Michael) *St Alb 11* **P** *Earl of Verulam*
V T M BEAUMONT
ST ALBANS (St Paul) *St Alb 11* **P** *V St Alb St Pet*
V R W GILL, **C** A R T CLODE, **Hon Par Dn** G M ABBOTT
ST ALBANS (St Peter) *St Alb 11* **P** *The Crown*
V A H MEDFORTH, **C** D M B WILMOT,
Hon Par Dn J A M FARDON
ST ALBANS (St Saviour) *St Alb 11* **P** *Bp* **V** D D HART
ST ALBANS (St Stephen) *St Alb 11* **P** *J N W Dudley Esq*
V J W PRAGNELL, **C** L M WANJIE
ST ALLEN (St Alleyne) Kenwyn w St Allen *Truro*
ST ANNES-ON-THE-SEA (St Anne) Heyhouses on Sea
Blackb
ST ANNES-ON-THE-SEA (St Margaret) *Blackb 11* **P** *Bp*
V I D H ROBINS
ST ANNES-ON-THE-SEA (St Thomas) *Blackb 11*
P *J C Hilton Esq* **V** W FIELDING,
Hon C R M CLARKSON
ST ANTHONY-IN-MENEAGE (St Anthony)
Manaccan w St Anthony-in-Meneage and St Martin
Truro
ST AUSTELL (Holy Trinity) *Truro 1* **P** *The Crown*
V A F MATTHEW, **C** S FOULKES, **Hon C** A SYKES,
NSM R P MacRAE
ST BEES (St Mary and St Bega) *Carl 5* **P** *Trustees*
V P R BRYAN
ST BLAZEY (St Blaise) *Truro 1* **P** *Bp* **V** F M BOWERS,
P-in-c R N STRANACK
ST BREOKE (St Breoke) and Egloshayle *Truro 10* **P** *Bp*
and DBP (jt) **R** P TWISLETON, **C** D S SMITH
ST BREWARD (St Breward) Blisland w St Breward
Truro
ST BRIAVELS (St Mary the Virgin) w Hewelsfield *Glouc 4*
P *D&C Heref* **V** *Vacant* Dean (0594) 530345
ST BURYAN (St Buriana), St Levan and Sennen *Truro 5*
P *Duchy of Cornwall* **R** R LEGG, **NSM** J S HALKES
ST CLEER (St Clarus) *Truro 12* **P** *Ld Chan*
V M A FRIGGENS, **NSM** L S B BURTON
ST CLEMENT (St Clement) Truro St Paul and St Clem
Truro
ST CLETHER (St Clederus) Bolventor *Truro*
ST COLAN (not known) St Columb Minor and St Colan
Truro
ST COLUMB MAJOR (St Columba) w St Wenn *Truro 7*
P *Bp* **R** *Vacant* St Columb (0637) 880252
ST COLUMB MINOR (St Columba) and St Colan *Truro 7*
P *Bp* **V** J F EDWARDS, **C** S L BRYAN

ST DAY (Holy Trinity) *Truro 2* **P** *D&C* **V** *Vacant*
St Day (0209) 820275
ST DECUMANS (St Decuman) *B & W 19* **P** *Bp*
V R M BARNETT
ST DENNIS (St Denys) *Truro 1* **P** *Bp* **R** G PERRY
ST DEVEREUX (St Dubricius) Ewyas Harold w Dulas,
Kenderchurch etc *Heref*
ST DOMINIC (St Dominica), Landulph and St Mellion w
Pillaton *Truro 11* **P** *D&C and Trustees Major*
J Coryton, Duchy of Cornwall, and SMF (by turn)
R R H EVERETT
ST EDMUNDS Anchorage Lane Conventional District
Sheff 8 **C-in-c** P G HARBORD
ST ENODER (St Enoder) *Truro 7* **P** *Bp*
P-in-c J C PARSONS
ST ENODOC (not known) St Minver *Truro*
ST ERME (St Hermes) Probus, Ladock and Grampound
w Creed *Truro*
ST ERNEY (St Erney) Landrake w St Erney and Botus
Fleming *Truro*
ST ERTH (St Erth) *Truro 5* **P** *D&C* **V** A T NEAL
ST ERVAN (St Ervan) St Mawgan w St Ervan and St
Eval *Truro*
ST EVAL (St Uvelas) as above
ST EWE (All Saints) Mevagissey and St Ewe *Truro*
ST GENNYS (St Gennys), Jacobstow w Warbstow and
Treneglos *Truro 8* **P** *Bp and Earl of St Germans (jt)*
R P J RANDELL
ST GEORGES (St George) Priors Lee and St Georges
Lich
ST GERMANS (St Germans of Auxerre) *Truro 11*
P *D&C Windsor* **V** S COFFIN
ST GILES-IN-THE-FIELDS *Lon 3* **P** *Bp*
R G C TAYLOR
ST GILES IN THE HEATH (not known) Werrington,
St Giles in the Heath and Virginstow *Truro*
ST GILES IN THE WOOD (St Giles) Beaford,
Roborough and St Giles in the Wood *Ex*
ST GLUVIAS (St Gluvias) *Truro 3* **P** *Bp* **V** J HARRIS
ST GORAN (St Goranus) w St Michael Caerhays *Truro 1*
P *Bp* **V** G GOULD
ST HELENS (St Helen) (Barton Street Mission)
(St Andrew) *Liv 10* **P** *Trustees*
P-in-c C H B BYWORTH,
C D WILBRAHAM, T R STRATFORD
ST HELENS (St Helen) (St Catherine by the Green)
Portsm 7 **P** *Bp* **V** M L HILL-TOUT
ST HELENS (St Mark) *Liv 10* **P** *Trustees*
P-in-c J LABDON
ST HELENS (St Matthew) Thatto Heath *Liv 10* **P** *Bp*
V C L BRAY
ST HELIER (St Peter) (Bishop Andrewes Church)
S'wark 25 **P** *Bp* **V** B M BRANCHE,
C R CHAGON, G PADDICK
ST HILARY (St Hilary) w Perranuthnoe *Truro 5* **P** *D&C*
and Mrs S R Parker (jt) **R** J D CURSON
ST IPPOLYTS (St Ippolyts) *St Alb 9* **P** *Bp* **V** *Vacant*
Hitchin (0462) 57552
ST ISSEY (St Issey) w St Petroc Minor *Truro 7* **P** *Keble*
Coll Ox **R** B W KINSMEN
ST IVE (St Ive) w Quethiock *Truro 12* **P** *Bp (1 turn), The*
Crown (2 turns) **R** R J LUCAS
ST IVES (All Saints) *Ely 11* **P** *Guild of All So*
V J D MOORE
ST IVES (St Ia the Virgin) *Truro 5* **P** *V Lelant*
V W A LEAH
ST JOHN (St John the Baptist) w Millbrook *Truro 11*
P *Bp and Col Sir John Carew-Pole, Bt (alt)*
R T W PILKINGTON
ST JOHN IN BEDWARDINE (St John the Baptist) *Worc 3*
P *D&C* **V** J H GREEN, **C** D SHARPLES, R E WINTLE
ST JOHN IN WEARDALE (St John the Baptist) *Dur 15*
P *Bp* **V** D M SKELTON
ST JOHN LEE (St John of Beverley) *Newc 4* **P** *Viscount*
Allendale **R** N B WARNER
ST JOHN ON BETHNAL GREEN *Lon 7* **P** *Patr Bd*
TV E J BRACK, **NSM** R A VAUGHAN
ST JOHNS-IN-THE-VALE (St John) w Wythburn *Carl 6*
P *Bp and V Crosthwaite (alt)* **V** C G DARRALL
ST JOHN'S WOOD (St John) *Lon 4* **P** *Bp* **V** J SLATER,
C A S WALKER, D W FRITH
ST JULIOT (St Julitta) Boscastle w Davidstow *Truro*
ST JUST IN PENWITH (St Just) *Truro 5* **P** *Ld Chan*
V S W LEACH
ST JUST IN ROSELAND (St Just) w Philleigh *Truro 6*
P *A M J Galsworthy Esq and MMCET (jt)*
R E R ANDREWS
ST KEVERNE (St Keverne) *Truro 4* **P** *CPAS*
V T M GOULDSTONE, **C** G M JARVIS

ST KEW (St James the Great) St Endellion w Port Isaac and St Kew *Truro*
ST KEYNE (St Keyna) Liskeard, St Keyne, St Pinnock, Morval etc *Truro*
ST LAURENCE IN THANET (St Laurence) *Cant 9*
P *Abp* V PJ COTTON, C R R COLES
ST LAWRENCE (Old Church) (St Lawrence) *Portsm 7*
P *Bp* R H W COOPER
ST LAWRENCE (St Peter's Chapel) *Chelmsf 12* P *Bp*
R *Vacant*
ST LEONARD (St Leonard) Hawridge w Cholesbury and St Leonard *Ox*
ST LEONARDS and St Ives (All Saints) *Win 8* P *Bp*
V J E OWEN
ST LEONARDS (Christ Church and St Mary Magdalen)
Chich 17 P *Bp and Trustees (jt)* R D G CARTER,
Sen AP S J A GROVES, C S McKENNA,
NSM M N HARPER, R G RALPH
ST LEONARDS, UPPER (St John the Evangelist) *Chich 17*
P *Trustees* R R G CARTER
ST LEONARDS-ON-SEA (St Ethelburga) *Chich 17*
P *Hyndman Trustees* V A I SMYTH
ST LEONARDS-ON-SEA (St Leonard) *Chich 17*
P *Hyndman Trustees* R J B CROSS
ST LEONARDS-ON-SEA (St Matthew) Silverhill St Matt *Chich*
ST LEONARDS-ON-SEA (St Peter and St Paul) *Chich 17*
P *Bp* V A P-A BROWN
ST LEVAN (St Levan) St Buryan, St Levan and Sennen *Truro*
ST MABYN (St Mabena) St Tudy w St Mabyn and Michaelstow *Truro*
ST MARGARET'S (St Margaret) Clodock and Longtown w Craswall, Llanveynoe etc *Heref*
ST MARGARETS-AT-CLIFFE (St Margaret of Antioch) w Westcliffe and East Langdon w West Langdon *Cant 4*
P *Abp* V C J WAYTE, NSM B E LANGMAN
ST MARGARETS ON THAMES (All Souls) *Lon 11* P *Bp*
P-in-c R J HAMMOND
ST MARTHA-ON-THE-HILL (St Martha) Albury w St Martha *Guildf*
ST MARTIN (St Martin) w East and West Looe *Truro 12*
P *Bp and Rev W M M Picken (jt)* R N S FOX
ST MARTIN-IN-MENEAGE (St Martin) Manaccan w St Anthony-in-Meneage and St Martin *Truro*
ST MARTIN-IN-THE-FIELDS *Lon 3* P *Bp*
V G H BROWN, C M J HENWOOD, J S PRIDMORE,
NSM J M BENNETT
ST MARTIN'S (St Martin) *Lich 25* P *Lord Trevor*
V J A CARR
ST MARTIN'S (St Martin) Scilly Is *Truro*
ST MARY ABBOTS Kensington St Mary Abbots w St Geo *Lon*
ST MARY-AT-LATTON Harlow *Chelmsf 3*
P *J L H Arkwright Esq* V P J BEECH,
C D M NEWMAN, Hon C G R NEAVE
ST MARY BOURNE (St Peter) and Woodcott *Win 6*
P *Bp* V M A COPPEN
ST MARY CRAY and St Paul's (St Paulinus) Cray *Roch 15*
P *Bp* V B H STEVENS
ST MARYCHURCH (St Mary the Virgin) *Ex 10* P *D&C*
V K C MOSS, C A K DANGERFIELD,
Hon C R GREGORY
ST MARYLEBONE (All Saints) *Lon 4* P *Bp*
V D H HUTT, C P McGEARY,
Hon C J A YOUNGER, C A JONES
ST MARYLEBONE (Annunciation) Bryanston Street
Lon 4 P *Bp* V M W BURGESS
ST MARYLEBONE (Holy Trinity) (St Marylebone) *Lon 4*
R J L CHATER, C I B BROWN, Hon C R F McLAREN
ST MARYLEBONE (St Cyprian) *Lon 4* P *Bp*
V P R HARDING, C D WHITE
ST MARYLEBONE (St Mark) Hamilton Terrace *Lon 4*
P *The Crown* V D A R AIRD, Hon C J PAPWORTH
ST MARYLEBONE (St Mark w St Luke) Bryanston Square St Mary w St Marylebone St Mark *Lon*
ST MARYLEBONE (St Peter and St John) Langham Place All So *Lon*
ST MARYLEBONE, St Paul *Lon 4* P *Prime Min*
R J P MAPLE, Par Dn A R HACK
ST MARY'S (St Mary) Scilly Is *Truro*
ST MARY'S BAY (All Saints) w St Mary-in-the-Marsh (St Mary the Virgin) and Ivychurch *Cant 13* P *Abp*
V J M A ROBERTS
ST MAWES (not known) St Just in Roseland w Philleigh *Truro*
ST MAWGAN (St Mawgan) w St Ervan and St Eval
Truro 7 P *D&C and Bp (alt)* R J G SLEE

ST MELLION (St Melanus) St Dominic, Landulph and St Mellion w Pillaton *Truro*
ST MERRYN (St Merryn) *Truro 7* P *Bp*
Hon C D POWELL, NSM J D PHILLIPS
ST MEWAN (St Mewan) *Truro 1*
P *A J M Galsworthy Esq (2 turns)*, *Penrice Ho (St Austell) Ltd (1 turn)*, and *DBP (1 turn)*
P-in-c B H R CLENCH
ST MEWAN Sticker (St Mark's Mission Church) St Mewan *Truro*
ST MICHAEL PENKEVIL (St Michael) *Truro 6*
P *Viscount Falmouth* P-in-c A J L BARNETT
ST MICHAEL ROCK (not known) St Minver *Truro*
ST MICHAELCHURCH (St Michael) N Newton w St Michaelchurch, Thurloxton etc *B & W*
ST MICHAELS ON WYRE (St Michael) *Blackb 10*
P *R P Hornby Esq* V K H GIBBONS
ST MINVER (St Menefreda) *Truro 10* P *DBP*
V A L GENT
ST NECTAN (not known) Lostwithiel, St Winnow w St Nectan's Chpl etc *Truro*
ST NEOT (St Neot) and Warleggan *Truro 12*
P *R G Grylls Esq (2 turns)*, *DBP (1 turn)*
R H C T OLIVEY
ST NEOTS (St Mary) *Ely 12* P *P W Rowley Esq*
V B CURRY, Par Dn R C BENDING,
Hon C T R HENTHORNE
ST NEWLYN EAST (St Newlina) Newlyn St Newlyn *Truro*
ST NICHOLAS AT WADE (St Nicholas) w Sarre and Chislet w Hoath *Cant 7* P *Abp* V O D WILLIAMS,
NSM R D PLANT, I J BROWN
ST OSWALD IN LEE w Bingfield (St Mary) *Newc 2*
P *Bp* P-in-c C S PRICE
ST OSYTH (St Peter and St Paul) *Chelmsf 26* P *Bp*
V J A ALLARD
ST PANCRAS (Holy Cross) (St Jude) (St Peter) *Lon 17*
P *Bp* V T C RICHARDSON, NSM R G RALPH
ST PANCRAS (Holy Trinity w St Barnabas) Haverstock Hill H Trin w Kentish Town St Barn *Lon*
ST PANCRAS (Old Church) w Bedford New Town (St Matthew) *Lon 17* P *D&C St Paul's* V P DYSON
ST PANCRAS (St Pancras) (St James) (Christ Church)
Lon 17 P *D&C St Paul's* V D J L BEAN,
Hon C D M LAWSON
ST PAUL'S CRAY (St Barnabas) *Roch 15* P *CPAS*
V G C DAY, C J E RAWLING
ST PAUL'S WALDEN (All Saints) *St Alb 9* P *D&C St Paul's* V D C FRENCH
ST PETER IN THE ISLE OF THANET (St Peter the Apostle) (St Andrew) *Cant 9* P *Abp* V N A S BURY,
C M C BOWERS, J A SAGE
ST PETER-UPON-CORNHILL St Pet Cornhill *Lon*
ST PETROC MINOR (not known) St Issey w St Petroc Minor *Truro*
ST PINNOCK (St Pinnock) Liskeard, St Keyne, St Pinnock, Morval etc *Truro*
ST RUAN w St Grade and Landewednack *Truro 4*
P *CPAS and A F Vyvyan-Robinson (jt)* R D KNIGHT
ST SAMPSON (St Sampson) *Truro 1* P *Bp*
R M J OATEY
ST STEPHEN IN BRANNEL (not known) *Truro 1*
P *Capt J D G Fortescue* R P L EUSTICE,
Hon C C P B BLACKWELL-SMYTH
ST STEPHENS (St Stephen) Saltash *Truro*
ST STYTHIANS w Perranarworthal and Gwennap *Truro 2*
P *Viscount Falmouth (2 turns)*, *D&C (1 turn)*
V M J W WARNER, NSM I D T LITTLE
ST TEATH (St Teatha) *Truro 10* P *Bp* V M H PEARCE
ST TUDY (St Tudy) w St Mabyn and Michaelstow *Truro 10*
P *D&C Ox*, *Viscount Falmouth*, and *Duchy of Cornwall (by turn)* R R J L WOOD
ST VEEP (St Cyricius) Lostwithiel, St Winnow w St Nectan's Chpl etc *Truro*
ST WENN (St Wenna) St Columb Major w St Wenn *Truro*
ST WEONARDS (St Weonard) w Orcop, Garway, Tretire, Michaelchurch, Pencoyd, Welsh Newton and Llanrothal
Heref 8 P *Bp, D&C, and MMCET (jt)* R S R ASHTON
ST WINNOW (St Winnow) Lostwithiel, St Winnow w St Nectan's Chpl etc *Truro*
SAINTBURY (St Nicholas) Willersey, Saintbury, Weston-sub-Edge etc *Glouc*
SALCOMBE (Holy Trinity) *Ex 7* P *Keble Coll Ox*
V P R C ABRAM
SALCOMBE REGIS (St Mary and St Peter) Sidmouth, Woolbrook, Salcombe Regis, Sidbury etc *Ex*
SALCOT VIRLEY (St Mary the Virgin) Tollesbury w Salcot Virley *Chelmsf*

SALE (St Anne) (St Francis's Church Hall) *Ches 10*
  P *DBP* **V** J SUTTON, **C** W J BAKER
SALE (St Paul) *Ches 10* **P** *Trustees* **V** R SELWOOD
SALEBY (St Margaret) w Beesby *Linc 8* **P** *Bp*
  R G I GEORGE-JONES
SALEHURST (St Mary) *Chich 15* **P** *Bp*
  V J B LAMBOURNE
SALESBURY (St Peter) *Blackb 2* **P** *V Blackb*
  V J W HARTLEY
SALFORD Ordsall (St Clement) *Man 6* **P** *Bp* **R** *Vacant*
  061-872 0948
SALFORD (Sacred Trinity) *Man 6* **P** *Exors Sir Josslyn*
  Gore-Booth, Bt **P-in-c** G BABB
SALFORD (St Ignatius and Stowell Memorial) *Man 6*
  P *Bp* **R** R K S BRACEGIRDLE
SALFORD (St Mary) Lt Compton w Chastleton,
  Cornwell etc *Ox*
SALFORD (St Mary) Cranfield and Hulcote w Salford
  St Alb
SALFORD (St Paul w Christ Church) *Man 6*
  P *The Crown and Trustees (alt)* **R** D S C WYATT,
  Hon C B F BUCKLEY
SALFORD (St Philip w St Stephen) *Man 6* **P** *D&C*
  R P D FOSTER
SALFORD PRIORS (St Matthew) *Cov 7* **P** *Peache*
  Trustees **V** G L MAUDSLEY
SALFORDS (Christ the King) *S'wark 24* **P** *Bp*
  V P C EDWARDS, **NSM** P M HARTLEY
SALHOUSE (All Saints) Rackheath and Salhouse *Nor*
**SALING, GREAT (St James) w LITTLE (St Peter and St
  Paul)** *Chelmsf 18* **P** *Bp* **P-in-c** G BARTLETT
SALISBURY (St Francis) *Sarum 15* **P** *Bp*
  V R E DUNNINGS
SALISBURY (St Mark) *Sarum 15* **P** *Bp* **V** J E JACKSON
SALISBURY (St Martin) *Sarum 15* **P** *Bp* **R** J L G LEVER
SALISBURY (St Thomas and St Edmund) *Sarum 15*
  P *Bp and D&C (alt)* **R** M A WHATMOUGH
SALKELD, GREAT (St Cuthbert) w Lazonby *Carl 4*
  P *Bp* **Dn-in-c** K REALE
SALLE (St Peter and St Paul) Reepham, Hackford w
  Whitwell, Kerdiston etc *Nor*
SALT (St James the Great) and Sandon w Burston *Lich 16*
  P *Keble Coll Ox and Personal Reps Earl of
  Harrowby (jt)* **V** R M GRACE
SALTASH (St Nicholas and St Faith) *Truro 11* **P** *Patr Bd*
  TR R E B MAYNARD, **TV** B A ANDERSON, **C** A J LING,
  NSM N C ASHTON, W JONES
SALTBURN-BY-THE-SEA (Emmanuel) *York 17* **P** *Abp,
  Adn Cleveland, Marquis of Zetland, and
  M Jarratt Esq (jt)* **V** R A SMAILES
SALTBY (St Peter) Croxton Kerrial, Knipton, Harston,
  Branston etc *Leic*
SALTDEAN (St Nicholas) *Chich 2* **P** *Bp*
  V R E CHATWIN
SALTER STREET (St Patrick) Tanworth St Patr Salter
  Street *Birm*
SALTERHEBBLE (All Saints) *Wakef 4* **P** *Ch Trust Fund
  Trust* **V** T J WILSON
SALTERSFORD (St John the Baptist) Rainow w
  Saltersford and Forest *Ches*
SALTFLEETBY (St Peter) *Linc 12* **P** *Or Coll Ox, Bp,
  and MMCET (jt)* **P-in-c** D LUMB
**SALTFORD (Blessed Virgin Mary) w Corston and Newton
  St Loe** *B & W 11* **P** *DBP (2 turns), Duchy of Cornwall
  (1 turn)* **R** G R W HALL, **C** S P PHILLIPSON-MASTERS
SALTHOUSE (St Nicholas) Weybourne Gp *Nor*
SALTLEY (St Saviour) *Birm 10* **P** *Trustees*
  P-in-c T E JONES
SALTNEY FERRY (St Matthew) Lache cum Saltney
  Ches
SALTON (St John of Beverley) Kirby Misperton w
  Normanby, Edston and Salton *York*
SALTWOOD (St Peter and St Paul) *Cant 5* **P** *Abp*
  R R G HUMPHRISS
SALVINGTON (St Peter) Durrington *Chich*
**SALWARPE (St Michael) and Hindlip w Martin
  Hussingtree** *Worc 8* **P** *Bp, D&C, and Exors Lady
  Hindlip (by turn)* **R** A J WILLIS
SALWAY ASH (Holy Trinity) Beaminster Area *Sarum*
SAMBOURNE (Mission Church) Coughton *Cov*
SAMBROOK (St Luke) Hinstock and Sambrook *Lich*
SAMLESBURY (St Leonard the Less) *Blackb 6*
  P *V Blackb* **V** *Vacant* Samlesbury (077477) 229
SAMPFORD, GREAT (St Michael) The Sampfords
  Chelmsf
SAMPFORD, LITTLE (St Mary) as above
SAMPFORD ARUNDEL (Holy Cross) Wellington and
  Distr *B & W*
SAMPFORD BRETT (St George) Bicknoller w
  Crowcombe and Sampford Brett *B & W*

SAMPFORD COURTENAY (St Andrew) N Tawton,
  Bondleigh, Sampford Courtenay etc *Ex*
**SAMPFORD PEVERELL (St John the Baptist),
  Uplowman, Holcombe Rogus, Hockworthy,
  Burlescombe, Huntsham and Halberton w Ash Thomas**
  Ex 4 **P** *Patr Bd* **TR** M C BOYES, **TV** R J PERRY
SAMPFORD SPINEY (St Mary) w Horrabridge *Ex 25*
  P *D&C Windsor* **R** C FURNESS
SAMPFORDS, The *Chelmsf 25* **P** *New Coll Ox (1 turn),
  Guild of All So (2 turns)* **R** M E GLASSWELL
SANCREED (St Creden) *Truro 5* **P** *D&C* **V** S W LEACH
SANCTON (All Saints) *York 7* **P** *Abp* **V** J WALKER
SAND HILL (Church of the Good Shepherd)
  Farnborough *Guildf*
SAND HUTTON (St Leonard) Thirsk *York*
SAND HUTTON (St Mary) *York 3* **P** *Abp (2 turns),
  D&C Dur (1 turn)* **V** J W VALENTINE
SANDAL (St Catherine) *Wakef 9* **V** *Sandal Magna*
  P-in-c M P CROFT
SANDAL MAGNA (St Helen) *Wakef 9* **P** *Peache Trustees*
  V R D STRAPPS
SANDBACH (St Mary) *Ches 11* **P** *DBP*
  V D W G STOCKER, **Hon C** A E CORBETT
SANDBACH HEATH (St John the Evangelist) *Ches 11*
  P *V Sandwich* **V** E J GORDON
SANDBANKS (St Nicolas) Canford Cliffs and
  Sandbanks *Sarum*
**SANDERSTEAD (All Saints) (St Anthony) (St Edmund the
  King and Martyr)** *S'wark 21* **P** *DBP* **TR** T A SMAIL,
  TV D S HEYWOOD, P C GULVIN, **C** P A CORNISH,
  Hon C V H PAYNE, **NSM** K L BULFIELD
SANDERSTEAD (St Mary) *S'wark 21* **P** *Bp*
  V M W ELFRED
SANDFORD (All Saints) Burrington and Churchill
  B & W
SANDFORD (St Martin) Westcote Barton w Steeple
  Barton, Duns Tew etc *Ox*
SANDFORD (St Martin) Wareham *Sarum*
SANDFORD (St Swithin) w Upton Hellions *Ex 2*
  P *12 Govs of Crediton Ch* **R** C G EDWARDS
SANDFORD-ON-THAMES (St Andrew) *Ox 4* **P** *DBP*
  P-in-c R C MORGAN
SANDFORD ORCAS (St Nicholas) Queen Thorne
  Sarum
SANDGATE (St Paul) *Cant 5* **P** *Ld Chan* **V** C E N DAVIS
SANDHURST (St Lawrence) Twigworth, Down
  Hatherley, Norton, The Leigh etc *Glouc*
SANDHURST (St Michael and All Angels) *Ox 16* **P** *Bp*
  R *Vacant* Yateley (0252) 872168
SANDHURST (St Nicholas) (Mission Church) w Newenden
  Cant 11 **P** *Abp* **R** H DENGATE
SANDHURST, LOWER (St Mary) Sandhurst *Ox*
SANDIACRE (St Giles) *Derby 13* **P** *Ld Chan*
  R W B COONEY
SANDIWAY (St John the Evangelist) *Ches 6* **P** *Bp*
  V J V GRIFFITH
SANDLEHEATH (St Aldhelm) Fordingbridge *Win*
SANDON (All Saints) Salt and Sandon w Burston *Lich*
SANDON (All Saints), Wallington and Rushden w Clothall
  St Alb 5 **P** *Duchy of Lanc (1 turn), Marquess of
  Salisbury (1 turn), and Bp (2 turns)* **R** J H LISTER
SANDON (St Andrew) *Chelmsf 11* **P** *Qu Coll Cam*
  R S F FOSTER
SANDOWN (Christ Church) *Portsm 7* **P** *Ch Patr Trust*
  V D M LOW, **C** S MARTIN
SANDOWN, LOWER (St John the Evangelist) *Portsm 7*
  P *Bp* **V** *Vacant*
SANDRIDGE (St Leonard) *St Alb 14* **P** *Earl Spencer*
  V P J NELSON
SANDRINGHAM (St Mary Magdalene) w West Newton
  Nor 21 **P** *The Crown* **R** G R HALL, **C** M P ADAMS
SANDS (St Mary and St George) High Wycombe *Ox*
SANDS (Church of the Good Shepherd) Seale *Guildf*
SANDSEND (St Mary) Lythe w Ugthorpe *York*
SANDWICH (St Clement) *Cant 8* **P** *Adn Cant*
  NSM R A GARDEN
SANDY (St Swithun) *St Alb 17* **P** *Lord Pym*
  R E E J ROWLAND, **Par Dn** L KLIMAS
SANDY LANE (St Mary and St Nicholas) Bromham,
  Chittoe and Sandy Lane *Sarum*
SANDYLANDS (St John) *Blackb 12* **P** *Bp* **V** R H SMART
SANKEY, GREAT (St Mary) *Liv 13* **P** *Lord Lilford*
  V G McKIBBIN
SANTAN (St Sanctain) *S & M 1* **P** *The Crown*
  V G B CLAYTON
SANTON (All Saints) Brandon and Santon Downham
  St E
SANTON DOWNHAM (St Mary the Virgin) as above

SAPCOTE (All Saints) and Sharnford w Wigston Parva
Leic 13 **P** *Ld Chan and DBP (alt)* **R** D W TYLDESLEY
SAPEY, LOWER (St Bartholomew) Clifton-on-Teme,
Lower Sapey and the Shelsleys *Worc*
SAPEY, UPPER (St Michael) Edvin Loach w Tedstone
Delamere etc *Heref*
SAPPERTON (St Kenelm) Coates, Rodmarton and
Sapperton etc *Glouc*
SAPPERTON (St Nicholas) w Braceby *Linc 14* **P** *Bp*
(1 turn), Sir Richard Welby, Bt (3 turns) **R** W B FOSTER
SARISBURY (St Paul) *Portsm 2* **P** *V Titchfield*
V R H MOSELEY
SARK (St Peter) *Win 14* **P** *Le Seigneur de Sercq*
V *Vacant* Sark (048183) 2040
SARN (Holy Trinity) Churchstoke w Hyssington and
Sarn *Heref*
SARNESFIELD (St Mary) Weobley w Sarnesfield and
Norton Canon *Heref*
SARRATT (Holy Cross) *St Alb 10* **P** *Bp*
P-in-c D J DREDGE
SARSDEN (St James) Kingham w Churchill, Daylesford
and Sarsden *Ox*
SATLEY (St Cuthbert) *Dur 15* **P** *Ld Chan* **V** *Vacant*
Bishop Auckland (0388) 730091
SATTERLEIGH (St Peter) S Molton w Nymet St
George, High Bray etc *Ex*
SATTERTHWAITE (All Saints) Colton w Satterthwaite
and Rusland *Carl*
SAUGHALL, GREAT (All Saints) *Ches 9* **P** *Bp*
V G ROBINSON, **NSM** A DILWORTH
SAUL (St James the Great) Frampton on Severn,
Arlingham, Saul etc *Glouc*
SAUNDERTON (St Mary and St Nicholas) Bledlow w
Saunderton and Horsenden *Ox*
SAUNTON (St Anne) Braunton *Ex*
SAUSTHORPE (St Andrew) Aswardby w Sausthorpe
Linc
SAVERNAKE FOREST (St Katharine) Gt and Lt
Bedwyn and Savernake Forest *Sarum*
SAW MILLS (St Mary) Ambergate *Derby*
SAWBRIDGEWORTH (Great St Mary) *St Alb 4* **P** *Bp*
V R H CHILD
SAWLEY (All Saints) (St Mary) *Derby 13* **P** *D&C Lich*
R J R WARMAN, **C** M G HUGGETT
SAWLEY (St Michael) Fountains Gp *Ripon*
SAWREY (St Peter) Hawkshead and Low Wray w
Sawrey *Carl*
SAWSTON (St Mary) *Ely 7* **P** *SMF* **V** R L POWELL,
C R D TOMKINSON
SAWTRY (All Saints) *Ely 13* **P** *Duke of Devonshire*
R *Vacant* Ramsey (0487) 830215
SAXBY (St Helen) Spridlington w Saxby and Firsby
Linc
SAXBY (St Peter) Waltham on the Wolds, Stonesby,
Saxby etc *Leic*
SAXBY ALL SAINTS (All Saints) *Linc 6*
P R H H Barton Esq **R** A J DRAPER
SAXELBYE (St Peter) Ab Kettleby Gp *Leic*
SAXHAM, GREAT (St Andrew) Risby w Gt and Lt
Saxham and Westley *St E*
SAXHAM, LITTLE (St Nicholas) as above
SAXILBY (St Botolph) w Ingleby and Broxholme *Linc 2*
P *Bp and DBP (jt)* **R** E R COOK
SAXLINGHAM (St Margaret) Gunthorpe w Bale w
Field Dalling, Saxlingham etc *Nor*
SAXLINGHAM NETHERGATE (St Mary) and Shotesham
Nor 11 **P** *Adn and Mrs M E Hicks (jt)* **R** J H DOBSON
SAXMUNDHAM (St John the Baptist) *St E 19*
P *Mrs A H V Aldous* **R** A M R PLATT
SAXTEAD (All Saints) Framlingham w Saxtead *St E*
SAXTHORPE (St Andrew) w Corpusty, Blickling, Oulton
and Heydon w Irmingland *Nor 3* **P** *Pemb Coll Cam*
(1 turn), MMCET and Bp (1 turn) **R** J W STUBENBORD
SAXTON (All Saints) Aberford w Saxton *York*
SAYERS COMMON (Christ Church) Albourne w
Sayers Common and Twineham *Chich*
SCALBY (St Laurence) w Ravenscar and Staintondale
York 16 **P** *Abp (1 turn), D&C Nor (2 turns)*
V C N TUBBS
SCALDWELL (St Peter and St Paul) Walgrave w
Hannington and Wold and Scaldwell *Pet*
SCALEBY (All Saints) Irthington, Crosby-on-Eden and
Scaleby *Carl*
SCALFORD (St Egelwin) w Goadby Marwood and
Wycombe and Chadwell, Eastwell and Eaton *Leic 3*
P *Ld Chan and Bp (alt)* **R** L N KING
SCAMMONDEN, WEST (St Bartholomew) Barkisland
w W Scammonden *Wakef*

SCAMPSTON (St Martin) Rillington w Scampston,
Wintringham etc *York*
SCAMPTON (St John the Baptist) Aisthorpe w
Scampton w Thorpe le Fallows etc *Linc*
SCARBOROUGH (St Columba) *York 16* **P** *Abp*
P-in-c G R SOUTHEY
SCARBOROUGH (St James w Holy Trinity) *York 16*
P *Abp and CPAS (jt)* **V** R H MARTIN
SCARBOROUGH (St Luke) *York 16* **P** *Abp*
V M P CHAPPELL, **NSM** D M B SHARPE
SCARBOROUGH (St Mark) Newby *York*
SCARBOROUGH (St Martin) *York 16* **P** *Trustees*
Par Dn M B HUMPHRIES, **NSM** M SHIPLEY
SCARBOROUGH (St Mary) w Christ Church and (Holy
Apostles) *York 16* **P** *Abp* **V** E A CROFTON,
C M BURLEY
SCARBOROUGH (St Saviour w All Saints) *York 16*
P *Abp* **V** J TALLANT
SCARCLIFFE (St Leonard) Upper Langwith w
Langwith Bassett etc *Derby*
SCARISBRICK (St Mark) (Good Shepherd) *Liv 11*
P *V Ormskirk* **V** *Vacant* Scarisbrick (0704) 880317
SCARLE, NORTH (All Saints) Swinderby *Linc*
SCARLE, SOUTH (St Helena) Collingham w S Scarle
and Besthorpe and Girton *S'well*
SCARNING (St Peter and St Paul) E Dereham and
Scarning *Nor*
SCARRINGTON (St John of Beverley) Whatton w
Aslockton, Hawksworth, Scarrington etc *S'well*
SCARTHO (St Giles) *Linc 9* **P** *Jes Coll Ox*
R B A J PEARMAIN, **C** T W THOMPSON
SCAWBY (St Hibald), Redbourne and Hibaldstow *Linc 6*
P *Lt-Col R Sutton-Nelthorpe (2 turns), Bp (1 turn), and*
Duke of St Alb (1 turn) **V** P E COPPEN
SCAWTHORPE (St Luke) Doncaster St Leon and St
Jude *Sheff*
SCAWTON (St Mary) Upper Ryedale *York*
SCAYNES HILL (St Augustine) *Chich 6* **P** *Bp*
P-in-c G B MITCHELL
SCHOLES (St Philip) Barwick in Elmet *Ripon*
SCHOLES (St Philip and St James) *Wakef 8* **P** *Bp*
V P J BEVAN
SCHORNE *Ox 24* **P** *Patr Bd (2 turns), Ld Chan (1 turn)*
TR P A LAWRENCE, **TV** I T WHITE, T M THORP
SCILLY ISLANDS: St Mary's, St Agnes, St Martin's,
Bryher and Tresco *Truro 6* **P** *Duchy of Cornwall*
TR M J PHILLIPS, **NSM** K D CAMPION
SCISSETT (St Augustine) High Hoyland, Scissett and
Clayton W *Wakef*
SCOFTON (St John the Evangelist) w Osberton *S'well 6*
P *G M T Foljambe Esq* **V** R E WHEATON
SCOLE (St Andrew) w Brockdish, Billingford, Thorpe
Abbots and Thorpe Parva *Nor 16* **P** *Bp, Ex Coll Ox,*
MMCET, Adn Norfolk, and Exors Lady Mann (jt)
R M D W PADDISON, **C** J M CAMPBELL
SCOPWICK Group, The (Holy Cross) *Linc 18*
P *Ld Chan* **V** G SMITH
SCORBOROUGH (St Leonard) Lockington and Lund
and Scorborough w Leconfield *York*
SCORTON (St Peter) *Blackb 10* **P** *V Lanc*
P-in-c R H BAKER
SCOT HAY (St Paul) Silverdale and Alsagers Bank *Lich*
SCOT WILLOUGHBY (St Andrew) S Lafford *Linc*
SCOTBY (All Saints) *Carl 2* **P** *Trustees* **V** F W BOVILL
SCOTFORTH (St Paul) *Blackb 12* **P** *Trustees*
V D G BELLINGER
SCOTHERNE (St Germain) Dunholme *Linc*
SCOTSWOOD (St Margaret) *Newc 7* **P** *Bp* **V** H SCOTT
SCOTTER (St Peter) w East Ferry *Linc 4* **P** *Bp*
R D W R BIRD, **NSM** L RADFORD, R I WATTS
SCOTTON (St Genewys) w Northorpe *Linc 4*
P *Ld Chan* **Dn-in-c** K A WINDSLOW,
NSM W KEAST, D L LANGFORD
SCOTTON (St Thomas) Farnham w Scotton, Staveley,
Copgrove etc *Ripon*
SCOTTOW (All Saints) *Nor 9* **P** *Bp* **V** *Vacant*
SCOULTON (Holy Trinity) Hingham w Woodrising w
Scoulton *Nor*
SCOUTHEAD (St Paul) Dobcross w Scouthead *Man*
SCRAMBLESBY (St Martin) Asterby Gp *Linc*
SCRAPTOFT (All Saints) *Leic 1* **P** *Dr M J A Sharp and*
Bp (jt) **V** M E C DREW
SCRAYINGHAM (St Peter and St Paul) Stamford
Bridge Gp of Par *York*
SCREDINGTON (St Andrew) Helpringham w Hale
Linc
SCREMBY (St Peter and St Paul) Partney *Linc*
SCREMERSTON (St Peter) *Newc 12* **P** *Bp*
V J W SHEWAN

SCREVETON (St Wilfrid) Car Colston w Screveton *S'well*

SCRIVELSBY (St Benedict) w Dalderby *Linc 11* **P** *Lt-Col J L M Dymoke* **P-in-c** S W PEARCE

SCROOBY (St Wilfrid) *S'well 5* **P** *Bp* **V** J N GREEN

SCROPTON (St Paul) Marston on Dove w Scropton *Derby*

SCRUTON (St Radegund) Kirkby Fleetham w Langton on Swale and Scruton *Ripon*

SCULCOATES (St Paul) w Christ Church and St Silas *York 15* **P** *Abp* **P-in-c** R G GARNER

SCULTHORPE (St Mary and All Saints) w Dunton and Doughton *Nor 20* **P** *Ld Chan (1 turn)*, *J Labouchere Esq (3 turns)* **R** *Vacant*

SCUNTHORPE (All Saints) *Linc 4* **P** *Bp* **V** M A BATTY

SCUNTHORPE (Resurrection) Berkeley *Linc 4* **P** *Bp* **V** D F REAGON

SEA MILLS (St Edyth) *Bris 8* **P** *Bp* **V** P R BAILEY, **NSM** D J A ADAMS

SEA PALLING (St Margaret) Hickling and Waxham w Sea Palling *Nor*

SEA VIEW (St Peter) *Portsm 7* **P** *Bp* **V** M L HILL-TOUT

SEABOROUGH (St John) Beaminster Area *Sarum*

SEABROOK (Mission Hall) Cheriton *Cant*

SEACOMBE (St Paul) *Ches 7* **P** *Trustees* **V** S F WALKER

SEACROFT (St James) (Church of the Ascension) (St Richard) *Ripon 8* **P** *DBF* **TR** D R GRICE, **TV** P J LANGFORD, D E P WILKINSON

SEAFORD (St Leonard) w Sutton *Chich 18* **P** *Ld Chan* **V** M R THOMPSON, **C** J A HAYWARD, G J WHITING

SEAFORTH (St Thomas) *Liv 1* **P** *Sir William Gladstone, Bt* **V** P A WINN

SEAGRAVE (All Saints) Sileby, Cossington and Seagrave *Leic*

SEAGRY (St Mary the Virgin) Gt Somerford, Lt Somerford, Seagry, Corston etc *Bris*

SEAHAM (St Mary the Virgin) w Seaham Harbour *Dur 3* **P** *Bp* **V** P JOBSON, **C** M J WRAY, **NSM** L HOOD

SEAHAM, NEW (Christ Church) *Dur 3* **P** *Bp* **V** D G KENNEDY

SEAHAM HARBOUR (St John) Seaham w Seaham Harbour *Dur*

SEAL (St Lawrence) *Roch 8* **P** *Bp* **P-in-c** B P SIMMONS

SEAL (St Peter and St Paul) *Roch 8* **P** *DBP* **V** A R O MORRIS

SEALE (St Lawrence) *Guildf 3* **P** *Adn Surrey* **P-in-c** W R FILLERY

SEALE, NETHER AND OVER (St Matthew) (St Peter) *Derby 16* **P** *Bp and C W Worthington (alt)* **R** W F BATES

SEAMER (St Martin) w East Ayton *York 16* **P** *Abp* **V** J C MELLING

SEAMER IN CLEVELAND (St Martin) *York 22* **P** *Lord Egremont* **P-in-c** M D A DYKES

SEARBY (St Nicholas) w Owmby *Linc 5* **P** *D&C* **P-in-c** D SAUNDERS

SEASALTER (St Alphege Old Church) Whitstable *Cant*

SEASCALE (St Cuthbert) and Drigg *Carl 5* **P** *DBP* **V** W J P GRIME

SEATHWAITE (Holy Trinity) Broughton and Duddon *Carl*

SEATON (All Hallows) Lyddington w Stoke Dry and Seaton *Pet*

SEATON (St Gregory) *Ex 5* **P** *DBP* **V** S E O CROFT

SEATON (St Paul) Camerton, Seaton and W Seaton *Carl*

SEATON, WEST (Holy Trinity) as above

SEATON CAREW (Holy Trinity) *Dur 13* **P** *Bp* **V** W WORLEY

SEATON HIRST (St John) (St Andrew) *Newc 11* **P** *Bp* **TR** P A GETTERLEY, **TV** A J A ROMANIS

SEATON ROSS Group of Parishes, The (St Edmund) *York 7* **P** *Ld Chan (1 turn)*, *Abp and Schroder Exor & Trustee Co (2 turns)* **R** J V ANDREWS

SEATON SLUICE (St Paul) Delaval *Newc*

SEAVINGTON (St Michael and St Mary) S Petherton w the Seavingtons *B & W*

SEBERGHAM (St Mary) Caldbeck, Castle Sowerby and Sebergham *Carl*

SECKINGTON (All Saints) Newton Regis w Seckington and Shuttington *Birm*

SEDBERGH (St Andrew), Cautley and Garsdale *Bradf 6* **P** *Trin Coll Cam* **V** A W FELL, **Hon C** R A C GREENLAND

SEDGEBERROW (St Mary the Virgin) w Hinton-on-the-Green *Worc 1* **P** *D&C and Lasletts Charity (alt)* **R** C J JOHNSTON-HUBBOLD

SEDGEBROOK (St Lawrence) W w E Allington and Sedgebrook *Linc*

SEDGEFIELD (St Edmund) *Dur 14* **P** *Bp* **R** M Q KING, **C** R M A CLARKE

SEDGEHILL (St Katherine) E Knoyle, Semley and Sedgehill *Sarum*

SEDGEFORD (St Mary) Heacham and Sedgeford *Nor*

SEDGLEY (All Saints) *Lich 1* **P** *DBP* **V** B M HARRIS, **C** P G J HUGHES, E H MYATT

SEDGLEY (St Mary the Virgin) *Lich 1* **P** *V Sedgley All SS* **V** J D POINTS, J S WATTS

SEDLESCOMBE (St John the Baptist) w Whatlington *Chich 14* **P** *Ld Chan and Bp (alt)* **R** C I PRITCHARD

SEEND (Holy Cross) and Bulkington *Sarum 19* **P** *D&C (3 turns)*, *Bp (1 turn)* **V** A R WEBB

SEER GREEN (Holy Trinity) and Jordans *Ox 20* **P** *Bp* **P-in-c** W T WHIFFEN

SEETHING (St Margaret) Brooke, Kirstead, Mundham w Seething and Thwaite *Nor*

SEFTON (St Helen) *Liv 5* **P** *Bp* **R** O J YANDELL

SEGHILL (Holy Trinity) *Newc 1* **P** *The Crown* **V** A MURRAY

SEIGHFORD (St Chad), Derrington and Cresswell *Lich 16* **P** *Personal Reps Major C Eld, Personal Reps E T Fletcher-Twemlow, and Qu Eliz Grant Trustees (jt)* **P-in-c** G G HODSON

SELATTYN (St Mary) *Lich 25* **P** *Mrs P Hamilton Hill* **P-in-c** N G COATSWORTH

SELBORNE (St Mary) Newton Valence, Selborne and E Tisted w Colemore *Win*

SELBY (St James the Apostle) *York 6* **P** *Simeon's Trustees* **V** D BOND, **Par Dn** M J CUNDIFF

SELBY ABBEY (St Mary and St Germain) (St Richard) *York 6* **P** *Abp* **V** P L DODD, **C** D J SIMPSON

SELHAM (St James) Lurgashall, Lodsworth and Selham *Chich*

SELLACK (St Tysilio) How Caple w Sollarshope, Sellack etc *Heref*

SELLINDGE (St Mary the Virgin) w Monks Horton and Stowting and Lympne w West Hythe *Cant 12* **P** *Abp* **V** P GOODSELL, **Hon C** P M THACKRAY

SELLING (St Mary the Virgin) w Throwley and Sheldwich w Badlesmere and Leaveland *Cant 6* **P** *Abp and D&C (jt)* **R** J V H RUSSELL, **Hon C** M JOHNSON

SELLY OAK (St Mary) *Birm 2* **P** *Bp* **V** C J ALDRIDGE

SELLY PARK (St Stephen) (St Wulstan) (St Stephen's Centre) *Birm 8* **P** *Trustees* **V** C J S TURNER, **C** J P H CLARKE, R E CHAMBERLAIN, **Hon C** K J R GODSELL, C L ALLEN

SELMESTON (St Mary) Berwick w Selmeston and Alciston *Chich*

SELSDON (St John) (St Francis) *S'wark 19* **P** *Bp* **TR** L A D WATSON, **TV** B A WELLS, **C** I S BROTHWOOD, **Par Dn** S MARTIN, **NSM** K HOLT

SELSEY (St Peter) *Chich 3* **P** *Bp* **R** V R CASSAM

SELSIDE (St Thomas) Skelsmergh w Selside and Longsleddale *Carl*

SELSLEY (All Saints) Cainscross w Selsley *Glouc*

SELSTON (St Helen) *S'well 4* **P** *Wright Trustees* **V** J F JACKLIN, **NSM** G E HILL

SELWORTHY (All Saints) (Lynch Chapel) and Timberscombe and Wootton Courtenay *B & W 17* **P** *Bp (2 turns)*, *Sir Richard Acland, Bt (1 turn)* **R** E J MILLER, **Hon C** M J DUVALL

SEMER (All Saints) Whatfield w Semer, Nedging and Naughton *St E*

SEMINGTON (St George) Steeple Ashton w Semington and Keevil *Sarum*

SEMLEY (St Leonard) E Knoyle, Semley and Sedgehill *Sarum*

SEMPRINGHAM (St Andrew) w Pointon and Birthorpe *Linc 21* **P** *The Crown* **V** H J THEODOSIUS

SEND (St Mary the Virgin) *Guildf 12* **P** *Bp* **V** T W KING

SENNEN (St Sennen) St Buryan, St Levan and Sennen *Truro*

SENNICOTTS (St Mary) Funtington and Sennicotts *Chich*

SESSAY (St Cuthbert) *York 20* **P** *Viscount Downe* **P-in-c** D H BRYANT

SETCHEY (St Mary) N Runcton w Hardwick and Setchey *Nor*

SETMURTHY (St Barnabas) Bassenthwaite, Isel and Setmurthy *Carl*

SETTLE (Holy Ascension) *Bradf 5* **P** *Trustees* **V** T VAUGHAN

SETTRINGTON (All Saints) w North Grimston and Wharram *York 2* **P** *Abp and Lord Middleton (jt)* **P-in-c** J T M DAWSON

SEVENHAMPTON (St Andrew) w Charlton Abbotts and Hawling w Whittington *Glouc 14* **P** *Bp, Exors*

E W W Bailey, MMCET, and Mrs E V J Charleston (jt)
V P B HOBBS
SEVENHAMPTON (St James) Highworth w
Sevenhampton and Inglesham etc *Bris*
SEVENOAKS (St John the Baptist) *Roch 8* **P** *Guild of
All So* **V** M P SHIELDS, **C** S J HAYLETT,
NSM C J R DAWSON
SEVENOAKS (St Luke) Conventional District *Roch 8*
C-in-c R J MASON
SEVENOAKS (St Nicholas) *Roch 8* **P** *Trustees*
R O M THOMSON, **C** J S JUCKES,
Hon C N N HENSHAW, D G MILTON-THOMPSON
SEVENOAKS WEALD (St George) *Roch 8*
P *R Sevenoaks* **P-in-c** D J CROWTHER, L DRYDEN
SEVERN BEACH (St Nicholas) Pilning w Compton
Greenfield *Bris*
SEVERN STOKE (St Dennis) Kempsey and Severn
Stoke w Croome d'Abitot *Worc*
SEVINGTON (St Mary) *Cant 10* **P** *Ch Soc Trust*
P-in-c W R KILFORD
SEWARDS END (not known) Saffron Walden w
Wendens Ambo and Littlebury *Chelmsf*
SEWERBY (St John) Bridlington H Trin and Sewerby w
Marton *York*
SEWSTERN (Holy Trinity) Wymondham w
Edmondthorpe, Buckminster etc *Leic*
SHABBINGTON (St Mary Magdalene) Worminghall w
Ickford, Oakley and Shabbington *Ox*
SHACKERSTONE (St Peter) Nailstone and Carlton w
Shackerstone *Leic*
SHACKLEFORD (St Mary the Virgin) Compton w
Shackleford and Peper Harow *Guildf*
SHADFORTH (St Cuthbert) *Dur 2* **P** *D&C*
P-in-c G WATSON, **NSM** A H PAGE
SHADINGFIELD (St John the Baptist) Hundred River
Gp of Par *St E*
SHADOXHURST (St Peter and St Paul) Kingsnorth w
Shadoxhurst *Cant*
SHADWELL (St Paul) *Ripon 5* **P** *V Thorner*
V W J HULSE
SHADWELL (St Paul) w Ratcliffe (St James) *Lon 7* **P** *Bp*
R *Vacant* 071-488 4633
SHAFTESBURY (St James) Shaston *Sarum*
SHAFTESBURY (St Peter) as above
SHAFTON (St Hugh) Felkirk w Brierley *Wakef*
SHALBOURNE (St Michael and All Angels)
Wexcombe *Sarum*
SHALDEN (St Peter and St Paul) Bentworth and
Shalden and Lasham *Win*
SHALDON (St Nicholas) (St Peter) *Ex 10* **P** *SMF*
V A L MANHIRE
SHALFLEET (St Michael the Archangel) *Portsm 8*
P *Ld Chan* **V** J F R RYALL
SHALFORD (St Andrew) Wethersfield w Shalford
Chelmsf
SHALFORD (St Mary the Virgin) *Guildf 5* **P** *Ld Chan*
V D N HOBDEN
SHALSTONE (St Edward the Confessor) Westbury w
Turweston, Shalstone and Biddlesden *Ox*
SHAMLEY GREEN (Christ Church) *Guildf 2* **P** *Bp*
V M C HUGHES, **Hon AP** E S WILLIAMS
SHANGTON (St Nicholas) Gaulby *Leic*
SHANKLIN (St Blasius) *Portsm 7* **P** *Bp*
NSM A W SWANBOROUGH
SHANKLIN (St Saviour) *Portsm 7* **P** *Bp* **V** *Vacant*
SHAP (St Michael) w Swindale *Carl 1* **P** *Earl of Lonsdale*
V J T SPENCE
SHAPWICK (Blessed Virgin Mary) w Ashcott and Burtle
B & W 5 **P** *Lord Vestey (2 turns), Bp (1 turn)*
V H L BAXTER
SHAPWICK (St Bartholomew) Sturminster Marshall,
Kingston Lacy and Shapwick *Sarum*
SHARD END (All Saints) *Birm 11* **P** *Keble Coll Ox*
V P J NICHOLAS
SHARDLOW (St James) Elvaston and Shardlow *Derby*
SHARESHILL (St Luke and St Mary the Virgin) *Lich 3*
P *Bp* **V** G F SMITH
SHARLSTON (St Luke) *Wakef 9* **P** *Bp* **V** J J GILL
SHARNBROOK (St Peter) and Knotting w Souldrop
St Alb 21 **P** *Bp* **R** R O HUBBARD
SHARNFORD (St Helen) Sapcote and Sharnford w
Wigston Parva *Leic*
SHARPNESS (St Andrew) w Purton and Brookend *Glouc 2*
P *Bp* **V** D P MINCHEW
SHARRINGTON (All Saints) Gunthorpe w Bale w
Field Dalling, Saxlingham etc *Nor*
SHASTON *Sarum 6* **P** *Patr Bd* **TR** D DICKER,
TV D D BOTTERILL, T TAYLOR, **NSM** D A LAWES

SHAUGH PRIOR (St Edward the King and Martyr) *Ex 21*
P *D&C Windsor* **V** F G DENMAN
SHAVINGTON (St Mark) Weston *Ches*
SHAW (Christchurch) Atworth w Shaw and Whitley
Sarum
SHAW cum DONNINGTON (St Mary) *Ox 14* **P** *DBP*
R B TAYLOR
SHAW (Holy Trinity) *Man 19* **P** *R Prestwich St Mary*
V A N WILSON
SHAW HILL (St Mary and St John) *Birm 10* **P** *Bp*
P-in-c T E JONES
SHAWBURY (St Mary the Virgin) *Lich 29* **P** *Sir John
Corbet, Bt* **C** D PEARSON
SHAWELL (All Saints) Swinford w Catthorpe, Shawell
and Stanford *Leic*
SHEARSBY (St Mary Magdalene) Arnesby w Shearsby
and Bruntingthorpe *Leic*
**SHEBBEAR (St Michael), Buckland Filleigh, Sheepwash,
Langtree, Newton St Petrock, Petrockstowe,
Petersmarland, Merton and Huish** *Ex 20* **P** *Ld Chan
(1 turn), Patr Bd (2 turns)* **TR** N G MEAD,
TV J P BENSON
SHEDFIELD (St John the Baptist) *Portsm 1* **P** *DBP*
V G B MORRELL, **Hon C** W T S MOORE,
NSM B R McHUGH
SHEEN (St Luke) Longnor, Quarnford and Sheen *Lich*
SHEEN, EAST (All Saints) Mortlake w E Sheen *S'wark*
SHEEN, EAST (Christ Church) as above
SHEEPSCOMBE (St John the Evangelist) Painswick w
Sheepscombe *Glouc*
SHEEPSTOR (St Leonard) Yelverton, Meavy,
Sheepstor and Walkhampton *Ex*
SHEEPWASH (St Lawrence) Shebbear, Buckland
Filleigh, Sheepwash etc *Ex*
SHEEPY (All Saints) Sibson w Sheepy and Ratcliffe
Culey *Leic*
SHEERING (St Mary the Virgin) Hatf Heath and
Sheering *Chelmsf*
SHEERNESS (Holy Trinity w St Paul) *Cant 14*
P *V Minster-in-Sheppey* **V** D WALKER
SHEERWATER (St Michael and All Angels) Woodham
Guildf
SHEET (St Mary Magdalene) *Portsm 5* **P** *Bp*
V P D INGRAMS, **NSM** C M PEEL
SHEFFIELD Abbeydale *Sheff 2* **P** *Ch Burgesses*
V M E ALFLATT, **Hon Par Dn** O M PRICE
SHEFFIELD Broomhall (St Mark) *Sheff 4*
P *Ch Burgesses* **V** A ALKER, **Par Dn** J Y TILLIER
SHEFFIELD Gillcar (St Silas) *Sheff 2* **P** *Ch Burgesses*
V M F HOLLAND
SHEFFIELD Norwood (St Leonard) *Sheff 3* **P** *Bp*
V T W ELLIS, **C** R E WHITEHOUSE
SHEFFIELD Parson Cross (St Cecilia) *Sheff 3* **P** *Bp*
V G K BOSTOCK, **C** T H WOOD, G J MARCER
SHEFFIELD Sharrow (St Andrew) *Sheff 2* **P** *Trustees*
V N P A JOWETT, **Par Dn** E A CARNELLEY,
Hon Par Dn H A JOWETT
SHEFFIELD (St Aidan w St Luke) *Sheff Manor Sheff*
SHEFFIELD St Barnabas and (St Mary) *Sheff 2*
P *Ch Burgesses and Provost Sheff (alt)* **V** J C SULLIVAN
SHEFFIELD (St Catherine of Siena) Richmond Road
Sheff 1 **P** *The Crown* **V** H LOXLEY
SHEFFIELD (St Cuthbert) *Sheff 3* **P** *Ch Burgesses*
V G V LETTS
SHEFFIELD (St John the Evangelist) *Sheff 1*
P *Ch Burgesses* **V** C W KEMP, **C** A G KENDALL,
Par Dn B HICKS
SHEFFIELD (St Matthew) Carver Street *Sheff 2* **P** *Bp*
V E W FISHER
SHEFFIELD (St Oswald) *Sheff 2* **P** *Ch Burgesses*
V *Vacant* Sheffield (0742) 550793
SHEFFIELD (St Paul) Wordsworth Avenue *Sheff 3*
P *DBP* **V** L M ATKINSON, **Par Dn** J F HARDY
SHEFFIELD MANOR (St Swithun) *Sheff 1* **P** *Patr Bd*
TV J M WRAW, **TM** B A HARRISON,
TV R W B ATKINSON, **C** R J H BEARD
SHEFFIELD PARK (St John the Evangelist) Sheff St Jo
Sheff
SHEFFORD (St Michael) *St Alb 22* **P** *Adn Bedford,
R Clifton, and R Campton (jt)* **V** D R SMITH
SHEFFORD, GREAT (St Mary) Welford w Wickham
and Gt Shefford, Boxford etc *Ox*
SHEINTON (St Peter and St Paul) Wenlock *Heref*
SHELDON (St Giles) *Birm 11* **P** *K S D Wingfield
Digby Esq* **R** G W HERBERT, **C** D T SHAW,
Hon Par Dn A BOULT
SHELDON (St James the Greater) Dunkeswell, Sheldon
and Luppitt *Ex*

SHELDON (St Michael and All Angels) Ashford w
Sheldon *Derby*
SHELDWICH (St James) Selling w Throwley, Sheldwich
w Badlesmere etc *Cant*
SHELF (St Michael and All Angels) *Bradf 2* **P** *Bp*
V D PEEL, **C** M GARSIDE, J Y W RITCHIE
SHELFANGER (All Saints) Winfarthing w Shelfanger w
Burston w Gissing etc *Nor*
SHELFORD (St Peter and St Paul) Radcliffe-on-Trent
and Shelford etc *S'well*
SHELFORD, GREAT (St Mary) *Ely 7* **P** *Bp*
V C J HERBERT
SHELFORD, LITTLE (All Saints) w Newton *Ely 7* **P** *Bp*
R S G TAYLOR
SHELLAND (King Charles the Martyr) Buxhall w
Shelland *St E*
SHELLEY (All Saints) Hadleigh w Layham and Shelley
St E
SHELLEY (Emmanuel) and Shepley *Wakef 6*
P *V Kirkburton* **V** A HEZEL
SHELLEY (St Peter) Chipping Ongar w Shelley *Chelmsf*
SHELLINGFORD (St Faith) *Ox 17* **P** *J J Twynam Esq*
NSM C A SPARKES
SHELSLEY BEAUCHAMP (All Saints) Clifton-on-
Teme, Lower Sapey and the Shelsleys *Worc*
SHELSLEY WALSH (St Andrew) as above
SHELTON (Christ Church) Oxon and Shelton *Lich*
SHELTON (St Mark) Hanley H Ev *Lich*
SHELTON (St Mary) Hempnall *Nor*
SHELTON (St Mary) The Stodden Churches *St Alb*
SHELTON (St Mary and All Saints) *S'well 3* **P** *Bp*
R *Vacant*
SHELVE (All Saints) Hope w Shelve *Heref*
SHENFIELD (St Mary the Virgin) *Chelmsf 10*
P R H *Courage Esq* **R** P J MASON, **C** R D WITHNELL
SHENINGTON (Holy Trinity) Horley w Hornton and
Hanwell, Shenington etc *Ox*
SHENLEY (St Martin) *St Alb 1* **P** *DBP*
P-in-c C J TWYCROSS
SHENLEY (St Mary) Watling Valley *Ox*
SHENLEY GREEN (St David) *Birm 4* **P** *Bp*
V C J W JACKSON
SHENSTONE (St John the Baptist) *Lich 2* **P** *MMCET*
V B ANDREW, **NSM** J B ASTON
SHENTON (St John the Evangelist) Market Bosworth,
Cadeby w Sutton Cheney etc *Leic*
SHEPHERD'S BUSH (St Stephen) (St Thomas) *Lon 9*
P *Bp* **V** J H ASBRIDGE
SHEPLEY (St Paul) Shelley and Shepley *Wakef*
SHEPPERDINE (Chapel) Oldbury-on-Severn *Glouc*
SHEPPERTON (St Nicholas) *Lon 13* **P** *Bp*
R C R TRUSS, **C** J L VINCENT
SHEPRETH (All Saints) *Ely 8* **P** *Bp* **V** M W BAKER
SHEPSHED (St Botolph) *Leic 7* **P** *Lord Crawshaw*
V M C BRANDON, **C** C D BRADLEY
**SHEPTON BEAUCHAMP (St Michael) w Barrington,
Stocklinch, Puckington and Bradon** *B & W 18* **P** *CR*
R E WILKES
SHEPTON MALLET (St Peter and St Paul) w Doulting
B & W 9 **P** *Duchy of Cornwall and Bp (alt)*
R J S T WOOLMER, **C** B W J MITFORD, **NSM** M J SMITH
SHEPTON MONTAGUE (St Peter) Bruton and Distr
B & W
SHEPWELL GREEN (St Matthias) Willenhall St Giles
Lich
**SHERBORNE (Abbey Church of St Mary) (All Souls)
(St Paul) w Castleton and Lillington** *Sarum 4*
P *Major K S D Wingfield Digby* **V** R A WILLIS,
C J P TOWNEND, J D LAKE
**SHERBORNE (St Mary Magdalene), Windrush, The
Barringtons and Aldsworth** *Glouc 14*
P C T R *Wingfield Esq, Ch Ch Ox, and DBP (by turn)*
P-in-c M T GEE
SHERBORNES (St Andrew) (Vyne Chapel) w Pamber, The
Win 4 **P** *Bp and Qu Coll Ox (jt)* **R** J N HAMILTON
SHERBOURNE (All Saints) Barford w Wasperton and
Sherbourne *Cov*
**SHERBURN (St Hilda) and West and East Heslerton w
Yedingham** *York 2* **P** *D&C (2 turns), The Crown
(2 turns), and Sir Stephen Hastings (3 turns)*
R P POCKFORD
SHERBURN (St Mary) w Pittington *Dur 2* **P** *D&C*
V D J BELL, **C** G E GLOVER
SHERBURN IN ELMET (All Saints) *York 1* **P** *Abp*
V *Vacant* South Milford (0977) 682122
SHERE (St James) *Guildf 2* **P** *Mrs H Bray*
R N B FARBRIDGE, **NSM** G EGERTON
SHEREFORD (St Nicholas) Toftrees w Shereford *Nor*

SHERFIELD ENGLISH (St Leonard) Awbridge w
Sherfield English *Win*
**SHERFIELD-ON-LODDON and Stratfield Saye w Hartley
Wespall w Stratfield Turgis** *Win 4* **P** *Bp, Duke of
Wellington, and D&C Windsor (jt)* **R** J N THOMAS
SHERFIELD-ON LODDON (St Leonard) Sherfield-on-
Loddon and Stratfield Saye etc *Win*
SHERFORD (St Martin) Stokenham w Sherford *Ex*
**SHERIFF HUTTON (St Helen and the Holy Cross) and
Farlington** *York 5* **P** *Abp (2 turns), DBP (1 turn)*
P-in-c D W D LEE
SHERIFFHALES (St Mary) Lilleshall and Sheriffhales
Lich
SHERINGHAM (St Peter) *Nor 7* **P** *Bp* **V** M C GRAY,
NSM J A HENDERSON
SHERINGHAM, UPPER (All Saints) Weybourne Gp
Nor
**SHERINGTON (St Laud) w Chicheley, North Crawley,
Astwood and Hardmead** *Ox 27* **P** *Bp (2 turns),
MMCET (1 turn), and Maj J G B Chester (1 turn)*
R M C STANTON-SARINGER
SHERMANBURY (St Giles) Henfield w Shermanbury
and Woodmancote *Chich*
SHERNBOURNE (St Peter and St Paul) Dersingham w
Anmer and Shernborne *Nor*
SHERRARDS GREEN (St Mary the Virgin) Gt
Malvern Ch Ch *Worc*
SHERRINGTON (St Cosmo and St Damian) Ashton
Gifford *Sarum*
**SHERSTON MAGNA (Holy Cross), Easton Grey,
Luckington, Alderton and Foxley w Bremilham** *Bris 12*
P *D&C, Bp, Adn Swindon and Lord Lilford (jt)*
V W H THOMSON-GLOVER, **Hon C** G H EDWARDS
SHERWOOD (St Martin) *S'well 13* **P** *Bp* **V** C GALE,
Par Dn P HUTCHINSON
SHERWOOD PARK (St Philip) Tunbridge Wells St Jas
Roch
SHEVINGTON (St Anne) *Blackb 4* **P** *R Standish*
V F A O D DAWSON
SHEVIOCK (Blessed Virgin Mary) Antony w Sheviock
Truro
SHIELDS, SOUTH (St Aidan) w (St Stephen) *Dur 7* **P** *Bp
and D&C* **R** *Vacant* 091-456 1831
SHIELDS, SOUTH (St Hilda w St Thomas) *Dur 7*
P *D&C* **V** M T PEACH
SHIELDS, SOUTH (St Jude) Rekendyke *Dur*
SHIELDS, SOUTH (St Oswin) *Dur 7* **P** *The Crown*
V G F FINN
SHIELDS, SOUTH (St Simon) *Dur 7* **P** *The Crown*
V R F TOBIN
SHIFFORD (St Mary) Bampton w Clanfield *Ox*
SHIFNAL (St Andrew) *Lich 26* **P** *J Brook Esq*
V R H PRENTIS
SHILBOTEL (St James) Shilbottle *Newc*
SHILBOTTLE (St James) *Newc 9* **P** *Dioc Soc*
V R J GLOVER
SHILDON (St John) w Eldon *Dur 10* **P** *Bp (2 turns), The
Crown (1 turn)* **V** R CUTHBERTSON,
Par Dn A MELTON
SHILDON, NEW (All Saints) *Dur 10* **P** *Bp*
V R V STAPLETON
SHILLING OKEFORD (Holy Rood) *Sarum 6* **P** *DBP*
P-in-c A G WATTS
SHILLINGFORD (St George) Dunchideock and
Shillingford St George w Ide *Ex*
SHILLINGSTONE (Holy Rood) Shilling Okeford
Sarum
SHILLINGTON (All Saints) *St Alb 22* **P** *Bp*
V D MORGAN
SHILTON (St Andrew) Bulkington w Shilton and Ansty
Cov
SHILTON (Holy Rood) Alvescot w Black Bourton,
Shilton, Holwell etc *Ox*
SHIMPLINGTHORNE (St George) Lawshall w
Shimplingthorne and Alpheton *St E*
SHINCLIFFE (St Mary the Virgin) *Dur 2* **P** *D&C*
R S M SANDHAM, **NSM** R D THOMSON
SHINEY ROW (St Oswald) *Dur 6* **P** *The Crown*
V J S BAIN
SHINFIELD (St Mary) *Ox 15* **P** *D&C Heref*
V S N H BAKER, **NSM** A S HOLMES
SHINGAY Group of Parishes, The *Ely 8* **P** *Bp,
Mrs E E Sclater, Ch Patr Trust, Down Coll Cam,
New Coll Ox, and Jes Coll Cam (jt)* **V** J W TRAVERS
SHIPBOURNE (St Giles) *Roch 10* **P** *E Cazalet Esq*
P-in-c J H B TALBOT, **Hon C** P I RUDLAND
SHIPDHAM (All Saints) w East and West Bradenham
Nor 12 **P** *Bp* **R** F W IRWIN

SHIPHAM (St Leonard)   Axbridge w Shipham and
Rowberrow *B & W*
SHIPHAY COLLATON (St John the Baptist) *Ex 10*   P *Bp*
V D A PINCHES
SHIPLAKE (St Peter and St Paul) w Dunsden *Ox 6*
P *D&C Windsor and DBP (jt)*   V *Vacant*   Wargrave
(073522) 2967
SHIPLEY (St Mary the Virgin) *Chich 8*
P *C R Burrell Esq*   V R M GILES
SHIPLEY (St Paul) and Frizinghall St Margaret *Bradf 1*
P *Patr Bd*   TR J R HENSON,   TV P H BOOTH,
C A J ATKINS,   NSM K N MEDHURST
SHIPLEY (St Peter) *Bradf 1*   P *TR Shipley St Paul and
Frizinghall*   V J D THOMPSTONE,   C D M ROBINSON
SHIPPON (St Mary Magdalene) *Ox 10*   P *Bp*   V *Vacant*
SHIPSTON-ON-STOUR (St Edmund) w Honington and
Idlicote *Cov 9*   P *Jes Coll Ox, D&C Worc, Bp (jt)*
R J R WILLIAMS
SHIPTON (Holy Evangelist)   Skelton w Shipton and
Newton on Ouse *York*
SHIPTON (St James)   Wenlock *Heref*
SHIPTON BELLINGER (St Peter) *Win 3*   P *Bp*
V A R H MACLEOD
SHIPTON GORGE (St Martin)   Bride Valley *Sarum*
SHIPTON MOYNE (St John the Baptist) w Westonbirt and
Lasborough *Glouc 16*   P *Westonbirt Sch and DBP (jt)*
P-in-c S C WOOD
SHIPTON OLIFFE (St Oswald)   Dowdeswell and
Andoversford w the Shiptons etc *Glouc*
SHIPTON ON CHERWELL (Holy Cross)   Yarnton w
Begbroke and Shipton on Cherwell *Ox*
SHIPTON SOLLARS (St Mary)   Dowdeswell and
Andoversford w the Shiptons etc *Glouc*
SHIPTON-UNDER-WYCHWOOD (St Mary) w Milton-
under-Wychwood, Fifield and Idbury *Ox 3*   P *Bp*
V G G B CANNING
SHIPTONTHORPE (All Saints) w Hayton *York 7*   P *Abp*
V K G SKIPPER
SHIRBURN (All Saints)   Watlington w Pyrton and
Shirburn *Ox*
SHIREBROOK (Holy Trinity) *Derby 3*   P *Bp*
V T J MARSHALL
SHIREGREEN (St Hilda) *Sheff 3*   P *Bp*
V M R H BELLAMY
SHIREGREEN (St James and St Christopher) *Sheff 3*
P *Provost Sheff*   V B G KYRIACOU
SHIREHAMPTON (St Mary) *Bris 8*   P *Bp*
V F R SYMONS,   NSM A W WHEELER
SHIREMOOR (St Mark) *Newc 8*   P *Bp*   V M C VINE,
C P J BENFIELD
SHIREOAKS (St Luke) *S'well 6*   P *Bp*
P-in-c J ROBINSON
SHIRESHEAD (St James) *Blackb 12*   P *V Cockerham*
P-in-c J K BROCKBANK
SHIRLAND (St Leonard) *Derby 1*   P *Adn Chesterfield
and Trustees*   R D J MURDOCH,   NSM R SMITH
SHIRLEY (St George) *S'wark 19*   P *Bp*   V B J LEE,
Par Dn G P REEVES,   Hon C N N KIRKUP
SHIRLEY (St James) (St John) *Win 12*   P *Ch Patr Trust*
V P E IRWIN-CLARK,   C A M PETIT
SHIRLEY (St James the Great) *Birm 13*   P *Patr Bd*
TR M G B C CADDY,   TV W K McMASTER,
C C M LANGSTON
SHIRLEY (St John) *S'wark 19*   P *Bp*   V A H R QUINN,
Hon C H G LEWIS,   A C COLLIER
SHIRLEY (St Michael)   Brailsford w Shirley and
Osmaston w Edlaston *Derby*
SHIRLEY WARREN (St Jude)   Southn St Jude *Win*
SHIRWELL (St Peter), Loxhore, Kentisbury, Arlington,
East Down, Bratton Fleming, Challacombe and Stoke
Rivers *Ex 18*   P *Patr Bd*   TR C J HUDSON,
TV J B H RICHARDS,   NSM F J MACARTNEY
SHOBDON (St John the Evangelist)   Pembridge w
Moorcourt, Shobdon, Staunton etc *Heref*
SHOBNALL (St Aidan) *Lich 20*   P *Bp*   V J L HOWITT
SHOBROOKE (St Swithin)   Crediton and Shobrooke *Ex*
SHOCKLACH (St Edith)   Tilston and Shocklach *Ches*
SHOEBURY, NORTH (St Mary the Virgin) *Chelmsf 15*
P *Ld Chan*   V S CARTER,   C T M CODLING
SHOEBURY, SOUTH (St Andrew) (St Peter) *Chelmsf 15*
P *Hyndman Trustees*   R P A RAYNER,
C M B WOODMANSEY,   Hon C R A CARTWRIGHT
SHOLDEN (St Nicholas)   Deal St Leon and St Rich and
Sholden *Cant*
SHOLING (St Francis of Assisi) (St Mary) *Win 12*   P *Bp*
V B J HARTNELL,   C R W HARRISON,   G J HOUGHTON,
Hon C F STOTT
SHOOTERS HILL (Christ Church) *S'wark 1*   P *Bp*
P-in-c R W JAMES

SHORE (St Barnabas) *Man 19*   P *D&C*   V P ROBINSON
SHOREDITCH (St Leonard) and Hoxton (St John the
Baptist) *Lon 5*   P *Patr Bd*   TR P R TURP,
TV W M MACNAUGHTON
SHOREHAM (St Giles)   Kingston Buci *Chich*
SHOREHAM (St Peter and St Paul) *Roch 9*   P *D&C*
Westmr   V B J SIMMONS
SHOREHAM, NEW (St Mary de Haura) *Chich 4*   P *Bp*
V M SHEPPARD,   NSM E K HOWARD
SHOREHAM, OLD (St Nicholas) *Chich 4*   P *Bp*
V M SHEPPARD,   NSM E K HOWARD
SHOREHAM BEACH (Good Shepherd) *Chich 4*   P *Bp*
V C BLAGG,   NSM D P WEBBER
SHORNE (St Peter and St Paul) *Roch 4*   P *D&C*
V B C H FORTNUM
SHORT HEATH (Holy Trinity)   Willenhall H Trin *Lich*
SHORT HEATH (St Margaret) *Birm 6*   P *Bp*
V A E POWER
SHORTHAMPTON (All Saints)   Charlbury w
Shorthampton *Ox*
SHORTLANDS (All Saints' Community Church)
Bromley SS Pet and Paul *Roch*
SHORTLANDS (St Mary) *Roch 12*   P *Bp*
V D S R REDMAN,   Hon C P LEUNG,
NSM J G MEDCALF
SHORTWOOD (All Saints)   Nailsworth *Glouc*
SHORWELL (St Peter) w Kingston *Portsm 8*   P *Bp*
P-in-c J W RUSSELL,   NSM C A B MARKE,   M K NICHOLAS
SHOSCOMBE (St Julian)   Camerton w Dunkerton,
Foxcote and Shoscombe *B & W*
SHOTESHAM (All Saints w St Mary)   Saxlingham
Nethergate and Shotesham *Nor*
SHOTLEY (St John) *Newc 3*   P *Lord Crewe's Trustees*
P-in-c T J ATKINS,   NSM R VICKERS
SHOTLEY (St Mary) Conventional District *St E 5*
Min R SPITTLE
SHOTTERMILL (St Stephen) *Guildf 4*   P *Adn Surrey*
C I CREER
SHOTTERY (St Andrew) *Cov 8*   P *Bp*   V S A BEAKE,
C S W FLETCHER
SHOTTESBROOKE (St John the Baptist)   White
Waltham w Shottesbrooke *Ox*
SHOTTESWELL (St Lawrence)   Warmington w
Shotteswell and Radway w Ratley *Cov*
SHOTTISHAM (St Margaret) w Sutton *St E 7*   P *Bp*
P-in-c J M GATES
SHOTTLE (St Lawrence)   Hazelwood *Derby*
SHOTTON (St Saviour) *Dur 3*   P *Bp*   V J F MASSHEDAR
SHOTWICK (St Michael)   Burton and Shotwick *Ches*
SHOULDHAM (All Saints) *Ely 16*   P *Bp*   V J D A LINN
SHOULDHAM THORPE (St Mary) *Ely 16*   P *Bp*
V J D A LINN
SHRAWARDINE (St Mary)   Bicton, Montford w
Shrawardine and Fitz *Lich*
SHRAWLEY (St Mary) and Witley w Astley *Worc 12*
P *Bp and Guild of All So (jt)*   P-in-c R P HEAPS
SHRED (Mission Church)   Slaithwaite w E Scammonden
Wakef
SHREWSBURY (All Saints and St Michael) (St Mary the
Virgin) *Lich 27*   P *Bp*   V B T MADDOX
SHREWSBURY (Holy Cross) (St Peter) *Lich 27*   P *Bp*
V F I ROSS,   C P J MYERS
SHREWSBURY (Holy Trinity) (St Julian) *Lich 27*   P *Bp
and Ch Patr Trust (jt)*   V P G FIRMIN
SHREWSBURY (St Alkmund) *Lich 27*   P *Bp*
P-in-c M POLLIT
SHREWSBURY (St Chad) (St Mary) *Lich 27*   P *Bp*
V M POLLIT,   Res Min A J PRICE
SHREWSBURY (St George of Cappadocia) *Lich 27*
P *V Shrewsbury St Chad*   V R W D BIDDLE
SHREWSBURY (St Giles) w Sutton and Atcham *Lich 27*
P *Bp and R L Burton Esq (jt)*   R P J WILLIAMS
SHREWTON (St Mary) *Sarum 16*   P *Ld Chan*
V S M W TRICKETT
SHRIVENHAM (St Andrew) w Watchfield and Bourton
Ox 17   P *Ld Chan*   V T D RAWDON-MOGG
SHROPHAM (St Peter)   Hockham w Shropham Gp of
Par *Nor*
SHRUB END (All Saints) (St Cedd) *Chelmsf 19*   P *Bp*
V D E COWIE
SHUCKBURGH, LOWER (St John the Baptist)
Napton-on-the-Hill, Lower Shuckburgh etc *Cov*
SHUDY CAMPS (St Mary) *Ely 4*   P *Bp*
NSM M W B O'LOUGHLIN
SHURDINGTON (St Paul)   Badgeworth w Shurdington
Glouc
SHURLOCK ROW (All Saints)   Waltham *Ox*
SHUSTOKE (St Cuthbert)   The Whitacres and Shustoke
Birm

SHUTE (St Michael)   Kilmington w Shute *Ex*
SHUTFORD (St Martin)   Broughton w N Newington and Shutford etc *Ox*
SHUTTINGTON (St Matthew)   Newton Regis w Seckington and Shuttington *Birm*
SHUTTLEWOOD (St Laurence Mission Church) Bolsover *Derby*
SHUTTLEWORTH (St John)   Ramsbottom St Jo and St Paul *Man*
SIBBERTOFT (St Helen)   Welford w Sibbertoft and Marston Trussell *Pet*
SIBDON CARWOOD (St Michael) w Halford *Heref 11*   **P** *Bp and R Holden (alt)*   **V** *Vacant* Craven Arms (05882) 3307
SIBERTSWOLD (St Andrew)   Eythorne and Elvington w Waldershare etc *Cant*
SIBFORD (Holy Trinity)   Epwell w Sibford, Swalcliffe and Tadmarton *Ox*
SIBLE HEDINGHAM (St Peter) *Chelmsf 22*   **P** *Bp and Most Rev G D Hand (jt)*   **R** C J ELLIOTT
SIBSEY (St Margaret) w Frithville *Linc 20*   **P** Ld Chan   **V** W G PAGE
SIBSON (St Botolph) w Sheepy and Ratcliffe Culey *Leic 13*   **P** *Pemb Coll Ox and MMCET (alt)*   **R** *Vacant* Tamworth (0827) 880301
SIBTHORPE (St Peter) *S'well 3*   **P** *Bp*   **V** G A FIRTH
SIBTON (St Peter)   Peasenhall w Sibton *St E*
SICKLINGHALL (St Peter's Mission Church)   Kirkby Overblow *Ripon*
SIDBURY (Holy Trinity)   Billingsley w Sidbury, Middleton Scriven etc *Heref*
SIDBURY (St Giles and St Peter)   Sidmouth, Woolbrook, Salcombe Regis, Sidbury etc *Ex*
SIDCUP (Christ Church) Longland *Roch 16*   **P** *Ch Trust Fund Trust*   **V** R A SUTTON,   **Hon C** J M BALL, H D YALL
SIDCUP (St Andrew) *Roch 16*   **P** *Bp*   **V** W ROBBINS, **Hon C** B W SHARPE
SIDCUP (St John the Evangelist) *Roch 16*   **P** *D&C*   **V** S L S ALLEN,   **Hon C** B M VINCENT
SIDDAL (St Mark) *Wakef 4*   **P** *Ch Trust Fund Trust*   **V** A THORP,   **NSM** H M THORP
SIDDINGTON (All Saints)   Capesthorne w Siddington and Marton *Ches*
SIDDINGTON (St Peter) w Preston *Glouc 12*   **P** *Ld Chan and R T G Chester-Master Esq (alt)*   **R** H J MORRIS
SIDESTRAND (St Michael) *Nor 7*   **P** *Bp*   **R** D L AINSWORTH
SIDFORD (St Peter)   Sidmouth, Woolbrook, Salcombe Regis, Sidbury etc *Ex*
SIDLESHAM (St Mary the Virgin) *Chich 3*   **P** *Bp*   **P-in-c** D S POLLARD
SIDLEY (All Saints) *Chich 14*   **P** *R Bexhill*   **V** N A TAYLOR,   **NSM** S M TAYLOR
SIDLOW BRIDGE (Emmanuel) *S'wark 24*   **P** *DBP*   **R** *Vacant*
SIDMOUTH (All Saints) *Ex 7*   **P** *CPAS*   **P-in-c** J V MAPSON
SIDMOUTH (St Nicholas w St Giles), Woolbrook, Salcombe Regis, Sidbury w Sidford *Ex 7*   **P** *Patr Bd*   **TR** R M SIGRIST,   **TV** I C MORTER, D L D ROBOTTOM, J S LEE
SIGGLESTHORNE (St Lawrence) and Rise w Nunkeeling and Bewholme *York 12*   **P** *Prime Min and Ld Chan (alt)*   **R** *Vacant* Hornsea (0964) 533033
SILCHESTER (St Mary) *Win 4*   **P** *Duke of Wellington*   **R** D C McKEEMAN
SILCHESTER COMMON (Mission Church)   Silchester *Win*
SILEBY (St Mary), Cossington and Seagrave *Leic 6*   **P** *Patr Bd*   **TR** A J TURNER,   **TV** P A E SPRINGATE
SILK WILLOUGHBY (St Denis) *Linc 22*   **P** *Sir Lyonel Tollemache, Bt*   **P-in-c** D J MUSSON
SILKSTONE (All Saints)   Hoylandswaine and Silkstone w Stainborough *Wakef*
SILKSTONE COMMON (Mission Room)   as above
SILKSWORTH (St Matthew) *Dur 9*   **P** *Bp*   **V** S RYCROFT
SILLOTH (Christ Church) w Silloth St Paul *Carl 7*   **P** *Simeon's Trustees (2 turns), V Holme Cultram St Mary (1 turn)*   **V** *Vacant* Silloth (06973) 31413
SILSDEN (St James) *Bradf 8*   **P** *Bp, Adn Craven, and Trustees (jt)*   **V** J D NOWELL
SILSOE (St James), Pulloxhill and Flitton *St Alb 15*   **P** *Ball Coll Ox and Bp (alt)*   **V** B L NIXON
SILTON (St Nicholas) *Sarum 6*   **P** *DBP*   **R** *Vacant*
SILTON, NETHER (All Saints)   Leake w Over and Nether Silton and Kepwick *York*
SILTON, OVER (St Mary)   as above
SILVER END (St Francis)   Rivenhall *Chelmsf*

SILVERDALE (St John) *Blackb 15*   **P** *V Warton*   **V** R MASHEDER
SILVERDALE (St Luke) and Alsagers Bank *Lich 15*   **P** *Bp and T H G Howard-Sneyd (jt)*   **V** R N WHITTINGHAM
SILVERHILL (St Matthew) *Chich 17*   **P** *Simeon's Trustees*   **R** R M COMBES
SILVERSTONE (St Michael) and Abthorpe w Slapton *Pet 5*   **P** *The Crown, Leeson's Trustees, and T L Langton-Lockton Esq (by turn)*   **R** J D SMITH
SILVERTON (St Mary) *Ex 4*   **P** *Bp*   **R** M G SMITH
SILVINGTON (St Michael)   Stottesdon w Farlow, Cleeton and Silvington *Heref*
SIMONBURN (St Mungo)   Humshaugh w Simonburn and Wark *Newc*
SIMONSTONE (St Peter)   Padiham *Blackb*
SIMPSON (St Thomas)   Woughton *Ox*
SINFIN (St Stephen) *Derby 10*   **P** *CPAS*   **V** *Vacant* Derby (0332) 760186
SINFIN MOOR (not known) *Derby 10*   **P** *Bp*   **P-in-c** D S SHRISUNDER
SINGLETON (St Anne) w Weeton (St Michael) *Blackb 13*   **P** *R Dumbreck and V Kirkham (jt)*   **V** D WILLIAMS
SINGLETON (St Mary the Virgin) *Chich 13*   **P** *Bp*   **R** P M JENKINS
SINGLETON, GREAT (St Anne)   Singleton w Weeton *Blackb*
SINNINGTON (All Saints) *York 21*   **P** *Simeon's Trustees*   **V** R W J INDER
SISLAND (St Mary)   Loddon w Sisland *Nor*
SISSINGHURST (Holy Trinity) w Frittenden *Cant 11*   **P** *CPAS*   **V** I M BUTLER
SITHNEY (St Sithney)   Porthleven w Sithney *Truro*
SITTINGBOURNE (Holy Trinity) w Bobbing *Cant 14*   **P** *Abp*   **V** R A LOVE,   **NSM** B D FOULGER, E J WILLIAMS
SITTINGBOURNE (St Mary) *Cant 14*   **P** *Abp*   **V** J W TIPPING,   **NSM** D W WEBB
SITTINGBOURNE (St Michael) *Cant 14*   **P** *Abp*   **V** F E TURNER,   **C** S BETSON
SIX HILLS (Mission)   Old Dalby and Nether Broughton *Leic*
SIX MILE BOTTOM (St George)   Lt Wilbraham *Ely*
SIX PILGRIMS, The *B & W 3*   **P** *Ch Soc Trust, D&C, DBF, and Bp (by turn)*   **R** R A C SIMMONS
SIX SAINTS circa Holt: Bringhurst, Great Easton, Medbourne cum Holt, Stockerston and Blaston *Leic 4*   **P** *D&C Pet and Adn Leic (2 turns), St Jo Coll Cam (1 turn)*   **R** S R LONG
SIXHILLS (All Saints)   Barkwith Gp *Linc*
SKEEBY (St Agatha's District Church)   Easby w Brompton on Swale and Bolton on Swale *Ripon*
SKEFFINGTON (St Thomas a Beckett)   Billesdon and Skeffington *Leic*
SKEFFLING (St Helen)   Easington w Skeffling, Kilnsea and Holmpton *York*
SKEGBY (St Andrew) *S'well 4*   **P** *Ld Chan*   **V** J OGLEY
SKEGNESS and Winthorpe (St Clement) (St Matthew) *Linc 8*   **P** *Earl of Scarborough and Bp (alt)*   **R** E G ADLEY,   **C** S J HOLMES,   **NSM** C H LILLEY
SKELBROOKE (St Michael and All Angels)   Burghwallis w Skelbrooke *Sheff*
SKELLINGTHORPE (St Lawrence) w Doddington *Linc 18*   **P** *MMCET*   **V** R W KAY
SKELLOW (St Michael and All Angels)   Owston *Sheff*
SKELMANTHORPE (St Aidan) *Wakef 6*   **P** *Bp*   **P-in-c** P D REYNOLDS
SKELMERSDALE (Church at the Centre) *Liv 11*   **P** *Bp*   **V** A J EDWARDS
SKELMERSDALE (St Paul) *Liv 11*   **P** *V Ormskirk*   **V** G R RICHENS,   **C** R PLANT
SKELSMERGH (St John the Baptist) w Selside and Longsleddale *Carl 9*   **P** *V Kendal H Trin and DBP (alt)*   **R** R D J DEW
SKELTON (All Saints) w Upleatham *York 17*   **P** *Abp*   **R** T N EVANS,   **NSM** I T GUY
SKELTON (Christ the Consoler)   Kirby-on-the-Moor, Cundall w Norton-le-Clay etc *Ripon*
SKELTON (St Giles) w Shipton and Newton on Ouse *York 5*   **P** *Abp*   **R** J RICHARDSON
SKELTON (St Michael) and Hutton-in-the-Forest w Ivegill *Carl 4*   **P** *Bp, D&C, and CCC Ox (jt)*   **R** B DAWSON
SKENDLEBY (St Peter and St Paul)   Partney *Linc*
SKERNE (St Leonard)   Hutton Cranswick w Skerne, Watton and Beswick *York*
SKERTON (St Chad) *Blackb 12*   **P** *Bp*   **V** T A G BILL
SKERTON (St Luke) *Blackb 12*   **P** *Trustees*   **V** J F FAIRCLOUGH,   **C** A J G WILLIM
SKEYTON (All Saints)   Swanton Abbott w Skeyton *Nor*

SKIDBY (St Michael) Rowley w Skidby *York*

SKILGATE (St John the Baptist) Brompton Regis w Upton and Skilgate *B & W*

SKILLINGTON (St James) Colsterworth Gp *Linc*

SKIPSEA (All Saints) w Ulrome and Barmston w Fraisthorpe *York 10* **P** *Abp, Hon Susan Cunliffe-Lister and Exors Dr W Kane (jt)* **R** *Vacant* Skipsea (026286) 284

SKIPTON (Christ Church) *Bradf 7* **P** *R Skipton H Trin* **V** J E PEERS, **C** D W MEWIS

SKIPTON (Holy Trinity) *Bradf 7* **P** *Ch Ch Ox* **R** D B ALDRED, **C** R M WIGRAM

SKIPTON ON SWALE (St John) Baldersby w Dalton, Dishforth etc *York*

SKIPWITH (St Helen) Bubwith w Skipwith *York*

SKIRBECK (Holy Trinity) *Linc 20* **P** *Trustees* **V** B C OSBORNE, **C** S M SAMUELS, **NSM** J C COLE

SKIRBECK (St Nicholas) *Linc 20* **P** *DBP* **R** A F WAKELIN

SKIRBECK QUARTER (St Thomas) *Linc 20* **P** *DBP* **V** J R MOORE, **NSM** M A BARSLEY

SKIRLAUGH (St Augustine) w Long Riston *York 12* **P** *Abp* **V** D W PERRY

SKIRPENBECK (St Mary) Stamford Bridge Gp of Par *York*

SKIRWITH (St John the Evangelist), Ousby and Melmerby w Kirkland *Carl 4* **P** *DBP and D&C (jt)* **V** A G R WILSON

SLAD (Holy Trinity) Stroud and Uplands w Slad *Glouc*

SLADE GREEN (St Augustine) *Roch 14* **P** *Bp* **V** R A FREEMAN

SLAIDBURN (St Andrew) *Bradf 5* **P** *Ch Soc Trust* **R** B DARBYSHIRE

SLAITHWAITE (St James) w East Scammonden *Wakef 5* **P** *V Huddersfield* **V** C R TOWNSEND

SLALEY (St Mary the Virgin) *Newc 3* **P** *Bp* **C** J R KELLY

SLAPTON (Holy Cross) Ivinghoe w Pitstone and Slapton *Ox*

SLAPTON (St Botolph) Silverstone and Abthorpe w Slapton *Pet*

SLAPTON (St James of Compostella) E Allington, Slapton and Strete *Ex*

SLAUGHAM (St Mary) *Chich 6* **P** *M R Warren Esq* **R** J E POSTILL, **Hon C** K W HABERSHON, F V PYM

SLAUGHTER, UPPER (St Peter) and LOWER (St Mary) w Eyford and Naunton *Glouc 15* **P** *F E B Witts Esq and Bp (alt)* **P-in-c** T WILLIAMS

SLAUGHTERFORD (St Nicholas) Biddestone w Slaughterford *Bris*

SLAWSTON (All Saints) Hallaton w Horninghold, Allexton, Tugby etc *Leic*

SLEAFORD (St Denys) New Sleaford *Linc*

SLEAFORD, NEW (St Denys) *Linc 22* **P** *Bp* **V** J S THOROLD, **C** F C THORNETT, **NSM** P G HARDING

SLEDMERE (St Mary) and Cowlam w Fridaythorpe, Fimber and Thixendale *York 11* **P** *Abp and Sir Tatton Sykes (jt)* **P-in-c** D PICK

SLEEKBURN (St John) *Newc 1* **P** *D&C* **P-in-c** P DAWSON

SLEIGHTS (St John) Eskdaleside w Ugglebarnby and Sneaton *York*

SLIMBRIDGE (St John the Evangelist) *Glouc 2* **P** *Magd Coll Ox* **R** E C CHARLESWORTH

SLINDON (St Chad) Eccleshall *Lich*

SLINDON (St Mary), Eartham and Madehurst *Chich 1* **P** *Bp, D&C, and Exors Miss L J Izard (jt)* **R** J R M COSSAR, **NSM** H J M COSSAR

SLINFOLD (St Peter) Itchingfield w Slinfold *Chich*

SLINGSBY (All Saints) Street Team Min *York*

SLIPTON (St John the Baptist) Lowick w Sudborough and Slipton *Pet*

SLITTING MILL (St John the Baptist) Rugeley *Lich*

SLOANE STREET (Holy Trinity) Upper Chelsea H Trin w St Jude *Lon*

SLOLEY (St Bartholomew) Worstead w Westwick and Sloley *Nor*

SLOUGH (St Paul) (Christ Church) *Ox 23* **P** *Trustees* **V** G T KAYE, **C** A G RIVETT, **NSM** A R CULLINGWORTH

SLOUGH, WEST *Ox 23* **P** *Patr Bd* **TR** M E W WESTNEY, **TV** F A WRIGHT, P C FAULKNER, W M HETLING

SLYNE (St Luke) w Hest *Blackb 15* **P** *Bp* **V** J B SELVEY

SMALL HEATH (St Aidan) Birm St Aid Small Heath *Birm*

SMALL HEATH (St Gregory the Great) *Birm 7* **P** *Bp* **P-in-c** J F P MORRISON-WELLS, **C** D K CHANDA

SMALLBRIDGE (St John the Baptist) *Man 19* **P** *Bp* **P-in-c** R S JONES

SMALLBURGH (St Peter) w Dilham w Honing and Crostwight *Nor 9* **P** *Bp, T R Cubitt Esq, and J C Wickman Esq (jt)* **P-in-c** G D CORDY

SMALLEY (St John the Baptist) *Derby 12* **P** *Bp* **P-in-c** M A ROYLE

SMALLFIELD (Church Room) Burstow *S'wark*

SMALLHYTHE (St John the Baptist) Tenterden St Mildred w Smallhythe *Cant*

SMALLTHORNE (St Saviour) *Lich 17* **P** *R Norton in the Moors* **V** R J COSSLETT

SMALLWOOD (St John the Baptist) Astbury and Smallwood *Ches*

SMANNELL (Christ Church) w Enham Alamein *Win 3* **P** *Bp* **R** D E C JARDINE

SMARDEN (St Michael) Biddenden and Smarden *Cant*

SMAWTHORPE St Michael *Wakef 11* **P** *Bp* **V** E I CHETWYND

SMEATON, GREAT (St Eloy) w Appleton Wiske and Birkby and Danby Wiske w Hutton Bonville *Ripon 2* **P** *MMCET (2 turns), Abp York (1 turn)* **R** F SNOW

SMEETH (St Mary) Brabourne w Smeeth *Cant*

SMEETON WESTERBY (Christ Church) Kibworth and Smeeton Westerby and Saddington *Leic*

SMETHCOTT (St Michael) w Woolstaston *Heref 11* **P** *DBP* **P-in-c** J D M FALL

SMETHWICK (Holy Trinity) (St Alban) *Birm 5* **P** *Bp* **V** D RAYNER

SMETHWICK (Old Church) *Birm 5* **P** *Dorothy Parkes Trustees* **V** B A HALL

SMETHWICK (St Matthew w St Chad) *Birm 5* **P** *Bp and V Smethwick (alt)* **V** J R A STROYAN

SMETHWICK (St Stephen and St Michael) *Birm 5* **P** *Bp* **V** K J SKIPPON

SMETHWICK, WEST (St Paul) *Birm 5* **P** *Bp* **P-in-c** D RAYNER, **C** J A READ

SMISBY (St James) Ticknall, Smisby and Stanton by Bridge *Derby*

SMITHILLS HALL (Chapel) Halliwell St Pet *Man*

SMORRALL LANE (St Andrew) Bedworth *Cov*

SNAILBEACH (St Luke) Minsterley *Heref*

SNAILWELL (St Peter) *Ely 3* **P** *Mrs A Crawley* **P-in-c** D J KIGHTLEY

SNAINTON (St Stephen) Brompton-by-Sawdon w Snainton, Ebberston etc *York*

SNAITH (St Laurence Priory) Gt Snaith *Sheff*

SNAITH, GREAT (Holy Trinity) (St John the Baptist) (St Paul) *Sheff 11* **P** *Bp* **TR** C ROBERTS, **TV** P A INGRAM

SNAPE (St John the Baptist) Sternfield w Benhall and Snape *St E*

SNAPE CASTLE (Chapel of St Mary) W Tanfield and Well w Snape and N Stainley *Ripon*

SNARESTONE (St Bartholomew) Appleby Magna and Swepstone w Snarestone *Leic*

SNARFORD (St Lawrence) Wickenby Gp *Linc*

SNARGATE (St Dunstan) Appledore w Brookland, Fairfield, Brenzett etc *Cant*

SNEAD (St Mary the Virgin) Wentnor w Ratlinghope, Myndtown, Norbury etc *Heref*

SNEATON (St Hilda) Eskdaleside w Ugglebarnby and Sneaton *York*

SNEINTON (St Christopher) w St Philip *S'well 12* **P** *CPAS and Trustees (alt)* **V** I M BLAKE

SNEINTON (St Cyprian) *S'well 12* **P** *Bp* **V** W J GULL, **C** R F B SMITH

SNEINTON (St Matthias) *S'well 12* **P** *Bp* **P-in-c** W A PORTER

SNEINTON (St Stephen) (St Alban) *S'well 12* **P** *SMF and Bp (alt)* **V** D A HAILES

SNELLAND (All Saints) Wickenby Gp *Linc*

SNELSTON (St Peter) Norbury w Snelston *Derby*

SNETTISHAM (St Mary) w Ingoldisthorpe and Fring *Nor 21* **P** *Bp, CPAS, and D&C (jt)* **R** S T LANE, **Hon C** H A KARRACH

SNEYD (Holy Trinity) *Lich 17* **P** *Bp* **V** B L WILLIAMS

SNEYD GREEN (St Andrew) *Lich 17* **P** *Bp* **V** B THOMPSON

SNIBSTON (St Mary) Hugglescote w Donington, Ellistown and Snibston *Leic*

SNITTERBY (St Nicholas) Bishop Norton, Wadingham and Snitterby *Linc*

SNITTERFIELD (St James the Great) w Bearley *Cov 7* **P** *Bp and V Wootton Wawen* **V** M M WATKINS

SNODLAND (All Saints) (Christ Church) *Roch 1* **P** *Bp and CPAS (jt)* **R** J E TIPP

SNORING, GREAT (St Mary) w LITTLE (St Andrew) w Kettlestone and Pensthorpe *Nor 20*   **P** *DBP (1 turn), St Jo Coll Cam (2 turns)*   **R** R C ASHLING,   **C** J K JONES

SNOWDEN HILL Chapel Farm (not known) Penistone and Thurlstone *Wakef*

SNOWSHILL (St Barnabas) Childswyckham w Aston Somerville, Buckland etc *Glouc*

SOBERTON (St Peter) w Newtown *Portsm 1*   **P** *Bp*   **V** P J GARRATT

SOCKBURN (All Saints) Dinsdale w Sockburn *Dur*

SODBURY, LITTLE (St Adeline) Horton and Lt Sodbury *Glouc*

SODBURY, OLD (St John the Baptist) Chipping Sodbury and Old Sodbury *Glouc*

SOHAM (St Andrew) *Ely 3*   **P** *Pemb Coll Cam*   **V** M G F SHEARS,   **Par Dn** A F PLEDGER

SOHO (St Anne) (St Thomas) (St Peter) *Lon 3*   **P** *R Westmr St Jas*   **C** F C STEVENS

SOLIHULL (Catherine de Barnes) (St Alphege) (St Helen) (St Michael) *Birm 13*   **P** *Patr Bd*   **TR** P E HAWKINS,   **TV** A S MONTGOMERIE, T M H BOYNS, G L HODKINSON,   **C** S J P LOONE,   **Hon C** W H ROBERTS,   **NSM** G M PEARSON

SOLLARS HOPE (St Michael) How Caple w Sollarshope, Sellack etc *Heref*

SOMBORNE w Ashley *Win 11*   **P** *Bp*   **V** J L PHILLIPS

SOMERBY (All Saints) Burrough Hill Pars *Leic*

SOMERBY (St Margaret) Barnetby le Wold Gp *Linc*

SOMERBY, OLD (St Mary Magdalene) *Linc 14*   **P** *Baroness Willoughby de Eresby*   **R** W B FOSTER

SOMERCOTES and Grainthorpe w Conisholme *Linc 12*   **P** *Duchy of Lanc (2 turns), Magd Coll Cam and Bp (1 turn)*   **R** J PATTERSON

SOMERCOTES (St Thomas) *Derby 1*   **P** *Bp*   **V** P DAWKES

SOMERCOTES, NORTH (St Mary) Somercotes and Grainthorpe w Conisholme *Linc*

SOMERFORD (All Saints) Astbury and Smallwood *Ches*

SOMERFORD (St Mary) Christchurch *Win*

SOMERFORD, GREAT (St Peter and St Paul), Little Somerford, Seagry and Corston w Rodbourne *Bris 12*   **P** *Bp, MMCET, and Ex Coll Ox (3 turns), Ld Chan (2 turns)*   **R** J E G OSWALD

SOMERFORD, LITTLE (St John the Baptist) Gt Somerford, Lt Somerford, Seagry, Corston etc *Bris*

SOMERFORD KEYNES (All Saints) Kemble, Poole Keynes, Somerford Keynes etc *Glouc*

SOMERLEYTON (St Mary) w Ashby, Fritton and Herringfleet *Nor 15*   **P** *Lord Somerleyton and A Y Aylett Esq (jt)*   **R** D B DOUGALL

SOMERS TOWN (St Mary the Virgin) *Lon 17*   **P** *D&C St Paul's*   **V** P DYSON,   **C** P J WALLIS, D R EVANS

SOMERSAL HERBERT (St Peter) Sudbury and Somersal Herbert *Derby*

SOMERSBY (St Margaret) S Ormsby Gp *Linc*

SOMERSHAM (St John the Baptist) w Pidley and Oldhurst *Ely 11*   **P** *Bp*   **P-in-c** D J EVANS

SOMERSHAM (St Mary) w Flowton and Offton w Willisham *St E 1*   **P** *Bp and MMCET (jt)*   **R** J M POTTER

SOMERTON (St James) The Heyfords w Rousham and Somerton *Ox*

SOMERTON (St Margaret) Glem Valley United Benefice *St E*

SOMERTON (St Michael and All Angels) w Compton Dundon, the Charltons and Kingsdon *B & W 6*   **P** *Bp Lon (1 turn), Bp (2 turns), and DBP (1 turn)*   **R** R E TOSTEVIN,   **C** B E PRIORY

SOMERTON, WEST (St Mary) Winterton w E and W Somerton and Horsey *Nor*

SOMPTING (St Mary the Virgin) (St Peter) *Chich 5*   **P** *OStJ*   **V** R J FRIARS

SONNING (St Andrew) (St Patrick) *Ox 16*   **P** *Bp*   **V** C H MORGAN,   **Hon C** A C E SANDERS

SONNING COMMON (Christ the King) Kidmore End *Ox*

SOOKHOLME (St Augustine) Warsop *S'well*

SOOTHILL (St Luke) Hanging Heaton *Wakef*

SOPLEY (St Michael and All Angels) Burton and Sopley *Win*

SOPWORTH (St Mary the Virgin) Boxwell, Leighterton, Didmarton, Oldbury etc *Glouc*

SOTHERTON (St Andrew) Uggeshall w Sotherton, Wangford and Henham *St E*

SOTTERLEY (St Margaret) Hundred River Gp of Par *St E*

SOTWELL (St James) Brightwell w Sotwell *Ox*

SOUDLEY (St Michael) Cinderford St Jo *Glouc*

SOULBURY (All Saints) Stewkley w Soulbury and Drayton Parslow *Ox*

SOULBY (St Luke) Kirkby Stephen w Mallerstang etc *Carl*

SOULDERN (Annunciation of the Blessed Virgin Mary) Fritwell w Souldern and Ardley w Fewcott *Ox*

SOULDROP (All Saints) Sharnbrook and Knotting w Souldrop *St Alb*

SOUNDWELL (St Stephen) *Bris 2*   **P** *Bp*   **V** W R HARRISON

SOURTON (St Thomas of Canterbury) Lydford, Brent Tor, Bridestowe and Sourton *Ex*

SOUTH: *see also under substantive place names*

SOUTH BANK (St John) *York 19*   **P** *Abp*   **V** M AISBITT,   **C** D A COOK

SOUTH CAVE (All Saints) and Ellerker w Broomfleet *York 14*   **P** *CPAS and D&C Dur (jt)*   **V** D C BAILEY,   **Par Dn** E A CULLING

SOUTH COVE (St Lawrence) Wrentham w Benacre, Covehithe, Frostenden etc *St E*

SOUTH HILL (St Sampson) w Callington *Truro 11*   **P** *PCC*   **R** R OAKES

SOUTH MOOR (St George) *Dur 8*   **P** *Bp*   **V** D PERCY

SOUTH POOL (St Nicholas and St Cyriac) Charleton w Buckland Tout Saints etc *Ex*

SOUTH SHIELDS (All Saints) *Dur 7*   **P** *Patr Bd*   **TR** J D MILLER,   **TV** R A SEARLE,   **C** S GALLAGHER

SOUTH SHORE (Holy Trinity) *Blackb 9*   **P** *J C Hilton Esq*   **V** B DUNN

SOUTH SHORE (St Peter) *Blackb 9*   **P** *Trustees*   **V** C HOOLE

SOUTH WYE Team Ministry Heref St Martin w St Fran (S Wye Team Min) *Heref*

SOUTHACRE (St George) Castle Acre w Newton, Rougham and Southacre *Nor*

SOUTHACRE (St George) as above

SOUTHALL (Christ the Redeemer) *Lon 22*   **P** *Bp*   **P-in-c** J T SMITH

SOUTHALL (Holy Trinity) *Lon 22*   **P** *Ch Patr Trust*   **P-in-c** D I BARNES

SOUTHALL (St George) *Lon 22*   **P** *D&C St Paul's*   **P-in-c** D I BARNES,   **C** J KOTHARE

SOUTHALL GREEN (St John) *Lon 22*   **P** *Ch Patr Trust*   **V** D L E BRONNERT,   **C** S P GATES

SOUTHAM (St James) *Cov 10*   **P** *The Crown*   **R** R S WERRELL

SOUTHAM (Ascension) Bishop's Cleeve *Glouc*

SOUTHAMPTON City Centre (St Mary) (St Michael) *Win 12*   **P** *Bp*   **TR** R R WHEELER,   **TV** M J WALKER, D B CONSTABLE,   **Par Dn** S A ROBERTS, P S WALKER

SOUTHAMPTON Maybush (St Peter) *Win 12*   **P** *Bp*   **V** N BOAKES,   **C** R W GOODHEW, C A LE PREVOST

SOUTHAMPTON (St Alban) *Win 12*   **P** *Bp*   **P-in-c** J M MOORE,   **Hon C** J H DAVIES

SOUTHAMPTON (St Barnabas) *Win 12*   **P** *Bp*   **V** B J FRY

SOUTHAMPTON (St Mark) *Win 12*   **P** *Ch Patr Trust*   **V** P D COOPER

SOUTHAMPTON (St Mary Extra) *Win 12*   **P** *Bp*   **V** B P JAMES

SOUTHAMPTON Thornhill (St Christopher) *Win 12*   **P** *Bp*   **V** R P DAVIES,   **Par Dn** C BASTON

SOUTHAMPTON Warren Avenue (St Jude) *Win 12*   **P** *Bp*   **V** *Vacant* Southampton (0703) 774603

SOUTHAMPTON Winkle Street (St Julian) Southn (City Cen) *Win*

SOUTHBERGH (St Andrew) Reymerston w Cranworth, Letton, Southburgh etc *Nor*

SOUTHBOROUGH (St Peter) (Christ Church) (St Matthew) *Roch 11*   **P** *CPAS*   **V** J C PORTHOUSE,   **C** J A WHITING, G P LANHAM

SOUTHBOROUGH (St Thomas) *Roch 11*   **P** *Bp*   **V** R M SMITH

SOUTHBOURNE (All Saints) Pokesdown All SS *Win*

SOUTHBOURNE (St Christopher) *Win 7*   **P** *Bp*   **V** J G BARKER,   **Hon C** W R NESBITT

SOUTHBOURNE (St John the Evangelist) w West Thorney *Chich 13*   **P** *Bp*   **V** R W POIL,   **NSM** D A HIDER, B MOSSE

SOUTHBOURNE (St Katharine) (St Nicholas) *Win 7*   **P** *Bp*   **V** R B JONES,   **Hon C** W R NESBITT, R G A BRITTON

SOUTHBROOM (St James) *Sarum 19*   **P** *D&C*   **V** M A WARD,   **Hon C** T V F PAPE

SOUTHCHURCH (Christ Church) *Chelmsf 15*   **P** *Bp*   **V** M J HARRIS

SOUTHCHURCH (Holy Trinity) *Chelmsf 15* **P** *Abp*
R M A BALLARD
SOUTHCOATES (St Aidan)   Kingston upon Hull
Southcoates St Aid *York*
SOUTHCOURT (Good Shepherd)   Walton H Trin *Ox*
SOUTHDENE (St Martin)   Kirkby *Liv*
SOUTHEA (Emmanuel) w Murrow and Parson Drove *Ely*
19 **P** *Bp* **V** R J SEAMAN
SOUTHEASE (St Peter)   Telscombe w Piddinghoe and
Southease *Chich*
SOUTHEND (St John the Baptist) (St Mark) *Chelmsf 15*
P *Bp and Patr Bd* **TR** R J A HAMER,
TV M G BLYTH, K R DALLY, D J ELLA
SOUTHEND (St John the Baptist)   Catford (Southend)
and Downham *S'wark*
SOUTHEND (St Peter)   Bradfield and Stanford Dingley
Ox
SOUTHEND-ON-SEA (St Saviour) Westcliff *Chelmsf 15*
P *Bp, Adn S'end, and Churchwardens (jt)*
V J EWINGTON, **C** L J BUFFEE
SOUTHERY (St Mary) *Ely 16* **P** *Guild of All So*
R A G COCHRANE
SOUTHFIELDS (St Barnabas) *S'wark 17* **P** *Bp*
V D E EMMOTT
SOUTHFLEET (St Nicholas) *Roch 4* **P** *CPAS*
R C D GOBLE
SOUTHGATE (Christ Church) *Lon 18*
P *V Edmonton All SS* **V** C R J FOSTER,
C A P WINTON, P C BROWNE
SOUTHGATE (Shared Church)   Grange St Andr *Ches*
SOUTHGATE (St Andrew) *Lon 18* **P** *Bp*
V P STAYLOR, **C** R J WILLIAMSON
SOUTHGATE (St Mary) *Chich 7* **P** *Patr Bd*
TR A F HAWKER, **TV** D J LEE, I G PRIOR, J R J BURLEY,
C T L RINGLAND, **NSM** P D DAKIN
SOUTHGATE, NEW (St Paul) *Lon 14*
P *V Southgate Ch Ch* **V** R M TAYLOR
SOUTHILL (All Saints) *St Alb 22* **P** *S C Whitbread Esq*
V M REDFEARN
SOUTHLAKE (St James's Church Centre)   Woodley *Ox*
SOUTHLEIGH (St Lawrence)   Colyton, Southleigh,
Offwell, Widworthy etc *Ex*
SOUTHMEAD (St Stephen) *Bris 8* **P** *Bp*
V G S PARFITT, **Par Dn** A E MEERE
SOUTHMINSTER (St Leonard) *Chelmsf 13* **P** *Govs*
Charterhouse **V** D L LUMB
SOUTHOE (St Leonard) *Ely 12* **P** *Mert Coll Ox*
R P G LEWIS
SOUTHOVER (St John the Baptist) *Chich 18* **P** *CPAS*
R P J J MARKBY, **NSM** S L PANTER MARSHALL
SOUTHPORT (All Saints) *Liv 9* **P** *Trustees*
P-in-c J E BASSETT
SOUTHPORT (All Souls) *Liv 9* **P** *V Southport All SS*
P-in-c J E BASSETT
SOUTHPORT (Christ Church) *Liv 9* **P** *Trustees*
V G C GRINHAM, **C** D G KIRBY
SOUTHPORT (Emmanuel) *Liv 9* **P** *PCC*
V M D WHYTE, **C** A P J GALBRAITH,
SOUTHPORT (Holy Trinity) *Liv 9* **P** *Trustees*
V *Vacant*   Southport (0704) 38560
SOUTHPORT (St Luke) *Liv 9* **P** *V Southport H Trin*
V J K BRIGHAM
SOUTHPORT (St Philip) (St Paul) *Liv 9* **P** *V Southport*
Ch Ch and Trustees (jt) **V** B C LAW
SOUTHPORT (St Simon and St Jude) *Liv 9* **P** *Trustees*
NSM I D DAWSON
SOUTHREPPS (St James)   Trunch *Nor*
SOUTHREY (St John the Divine)   Bardney *Linc*
SOUTHROP (St Peter)   Coln St Aldwyn, Hatherop,
Quenington etc *Glouc*
SOUTHSEA (Holy Spirit) *Portsm 6* **P** *Bp* **V** R L EVANS,
C A G SAGE
SOUTHSEA (St Jude) *Portsm 6* **P** *Trustees*
V J V BYRNE, **C** J D GILPIN, **Par Dn** C A BELL,
NSM G B HILL
SOUTHSEA (St Luke)   Portsea St Luke *Portsm*
SOUTHSEA (St Peter) *Portsm 6* **P** *Bp* **V** R J DICKSON
SOUTHSEA (St Simon) *Portsm 6* **P** *Ch Patr Trust*
V E A PRATT, **Hon C** P A LEWIS
SOUTHTOWN (St Mary) *Nor 2* **P** *Bp* **V** M A MORGAN
SOUTHWARK (Christ Church) *S'wark 8* **P** *Marshall's*
Charity **R** P B CHALLEN, **C** N B HARRIS,
NSM A HURST
SOUTHWARK (Holy Trinity w St Matthew) *S'wark 8*
P *Bp* **V** J A F GALBRAITH, **C** J D F GREENER
SOUTHWARK (St Alphege) *S'wark 8* **P** *Walsingham*
Coll Trust Assn **V** E MATHIESON

SOUTHWARK (St George the Martyr) *S'wark 8*
P *Ld Chan (3 turns), Lon Corp (1 turn)*
P-in-c A S LUCAS
SOUTHWARK (St Hugh)   Bermondsey St Hugh CD
S'wark
SOUTHWARK (St Jude) *S'wark 8* **P** *Ch Patr Soc*
V *Vacant*
SOUTHWATER (Holy Innocents) *Chich 8* **P** *V Horsham*
V P MESSENGER
SOUTHWAY (Holy Spirit) *Ex 23* **P** *Ld Chan*
V D M WOOD, **C** J C WHITE, **Par Dn** P A WHITE,
NSM M J FAIRALL
SOUTHWELL (Holy Trinity) *S'well 15* **P** *CPAS*
V E A C CARDWELL
SOUTHWELL (St Andrew)   Portland All SS w St Pet
Sarum
SOUTHWICK (Holy Trinity) *Dur 9* **P** *D&C*
P-in-c R DIXON
SOUTHWICK (St Columba) *Dur 9* **P** *Bp*
V M P SAUNDERS
SOUTHWICK (St Cuthbert)   Sunderland Red Ho *Dur*
SOUTHWICK (St James) w Boarhunt *Portsm 1*
P-in-c A R MOORE
SOUTHWICK (St Mary the Virgin)   Benefield and
Southwick w Glapthorn *Pet*
SOUTHWICK (St Michael and All Angels) *Chich 4*
P *Ld Chan* **R** C EVERETT-ALLEN, **C** B F ASHDOWN,
Hon C H F McNEIGHT, **NSM** M A ALLCHIN
SOUTHWICK (St Peter) *Chich 4* **P** *Bp*
P-in-c G C CAREY
SOUTHWICK (St Thomas)   N Bradley, Southwick and
Heywood *Sarum*
SOUTHWOLD (St Edmund King and Martyr) *St E 15*
P *Simeon's Trustees* **V** P E BUSTIN
SOUTHWOOD (Mission Church)   Evercreech w
Chesterblade and Milton Clevedon *B & W*
SOWERBY (St Mary) *Wakef 4* **P** *DBP*
V J W MUIR, **Par Dn** B PEDLEY,
Hon C J C K FREEBORN
SOWERBY (St Oswald) *York 20* **P** *Abp* **V** D H BRYANT
SOWERBY BRIDGE (Christ Church) w Norland *Wakef 4*
P *V Halifax* **V** P J JEFFERY
SOWTON (St Michael and All Angels)   Aylesbeare,
Rockbeare, Farringdon etc *Ex*
SPALDING (St John the Baptist) w Deeping St Nicholas
Linc 17 **P** *Bp* **V** K A ALMOND, **C** P D STELL
SPALDING (St Mary and St Nicholas) *Linc 17* **P** *Feoffees*
V P G F NORWOOD, **C** H P JANSMA, C M DAVIES
SPALDING (St Paul) *Linc 17* **P** *Bp and V Spalding (jt)*
V L C ACKLAM, **NSM** P W J WINN
SPALDWICK (St James) w Barham and Woolley *Ely 10*
P *Bp* **P-in-c** A T SCHOFIELD
SPARHAM (St Mary) Lyng, Sparham, Elsing and
Bylaugh *Nor*
SPARKBROOK (Christ Church) *Birm 7* **P** *Aston Patr*
Trust **P-in-c** S A HOLLOWAY
SPARKBROOK (Emmanuel)   Sparkhill w Greet and
Sparkbrook *Birm*
SPARKBROOK (St Agatha) w Balsall Heath St Barnabas
Birm 7 **P** *Bp* **V** J A HERVE, **Hon C** A E BOND
SPARKFORD (St Mary Magdalene)   Queen Camel w W
Camel, Corton Denham etc *B & W*
SPARKHILL (St John the Evangelist) w Greet St Bede and
Sparkbrook Emmanuel *Birm 7* **P** *Dioc Trustees and*
Aston Trustees (alt) **V** M R F MACLACHLAN,
C P M BRACHER
SPARKWELL (All Saints) *Ex 21* **P** *D&C Windsor*
V F G DENMAN
SPARSHOLT (Holy Cross)   Ridgeway *Ox*
SPARSHOLT (St Stephen)   Crawley and Littleton and
Sparsholt w Lainston *Win*
SPAXTON (St Margaret) w Goathurst, Enmore and
Charlynch *B & W 15* **P** *Bp, MMCET and Ch Trust*
Fund Trust (jt) **R** J S BARKS
SPEEN (St Mary the Virgin)   Newbury *Ox*
SPEETON (St Leonard)   Reighton w Speeton *York*
SPEKE (St Aidan) (All Saints) *Liv 4* **P** *Bp*
TV J P NICHOLSON
SPELDHURST (St Mary the Virgin) w Groombridge and
Ashurst *Roch 11* **P** *DBP* **R** G F HYDER,
Hon C B E E MARSHALL
SPELSBURY (All Saints)   Chadlington and Spelsbury,
Ascott under Wychwood *Ox*
SPENCERS WOOD (St Michael and All Angels)   Beech
Hill, Grazeley and Spencers Wood *Ox*
SPENNITHORNE (St Michael) w Finghall and Hauxwell
Ripon 4 **P** *R J Dalton Esq and M C A Wyvill Esq (alt)*
R W H PRUDOM

SPENNYMOOR (St Paul)   Whitworth w Spennymoor *Dur*

SPERNALL, Morton Bagot and Oldberrow *Cov 7*   P *Mrs J M Pinney and Bp (alt)*   R K L STOCK

SPETISBURY (St John the Baptist) w Charlton Marshall and Blandford St Mary *Sarum 7*   P *Worc Coll Ox (1 turn), Bp (2 turns)*   R D B PENNAL

SPEXHALL (St Peter)   Halesworth w Linstead, Chediston, Holton etc *St E*

SPILSBY (St James) w Hundleby *Linc 7*   P *Baroness Willoughby de Eresby*   V G ROBSON,   C H ROTHWELL

SPITAL (St Agnes)   Clewer St Andr *Ox*

SPITAL (St Leonard's Mission Room)   Chesterfield All SS *Derby*

SPITALFIELDS (Christ Church w All Saints) *Lon 7*   P MMCET   R P W BOWTELL

SPITALGATE (St John the Evangelist)   Grantham *Linc*

SPITTAL (St John) *Newc 12*   P *Bp and Mercers' Co (alt)*   V J W SHEWAN

SPIXWORTH (St Peter) w Crostwick *Nor 4*   P *Bp and DBP (alt)*   R *Vacant* Norwich (0603) 898258

SPOFFORTH (All Saints) w Kirk Deighton *Ripon 1*   P *Bp*   R G JONES

SPONDON (St Werburgh) *Derby 9*   P *Capt P J B Drury-Lowe*   V G O MARSHALL,   Par Dn P A GOWER

SPORLE (St Mary)   Gt and Lt Dunham w Gt and Lt Fransham and Sporle *Nor*

SPOTLAND (St Clement) *Man 19*   P *Bp*   V A LITTON

SPRATTON (St Andrew) *Pet 2*   P *Bp*   V B LEE

SPREYTON (St Michael) *Ex 12*   P *Bp*   V C J L NAPIER

SPRIDLINGTON (All Saints) w Saxby and Firsby *Linc 3*   P *Major-Gen Walter Hutton (3 turns), Earl of Scarbrough (1 turn)*   P-in-c I R HOWITT

SPRIGG'S ALLEY (Mission Room)   Chinnor w Emmington and Sydenham etc *Ox*

SPRING GROVE (St Mary) *Lon 11*   P *Ch Patr Trust*   V D G WILSON,   C M SAVILLE-DEANE, L P D ESSER,   Hon Par Dn M A WARMAN

SPRING PARK (All Saints) *S'wark 19*   P *Bp*   V B L HAMMOND,   Hon Par Dn J M TOMLINSON

SPRINGFIELD (All Saints) *Chelmsf 11*   P *Air Cdre N S Paynter*   R R J BROWN

SPRINGFIELD (Holy Trinity) *Chelmsf 11*   P *Simeon's Trustees*   V J K HAYWARD,   C A K WILSON

SPRINGFIELD (St Christopher) *Birm 8*   P *Trustees*   V H KOPSCH

SPRINGFIELD, EAST (Church of Our Saviour) (not known) *Chelmsf 11*   P *Bp*   P-in-c C E HOPKINSON

SPRINGFIELD, NORTH (St Augustine of Canterbury) *Chelmsf 11*   P *Bp*   P-in-c J D HAYWARD,   Hon Par Dn P M A PEELING

SPRINGFIELDS (St Stephen)   Wolv St Steph *Lich*

SPRINGTHORPE (St George and St Laurence)   Corringham *Linc*

SPRINGWELL (St Mary w St Peter)   Sunderland Springwell w Thorney Close *Dur*

SPROATLEY (St Swithin)   Preston and Sproatley in Holderness *York*

SPROTBROUGH (St Mary the Virgin) *Sheff 8*   P *Bp*   R S J MATTHEWS

SPROUGHTON (All Saints) w Burstall *St E 5*   P *D&C Cant (1 turn), Bp (2 turns)*   P-in-c R F PALLANT

SPROXTON (St Bartholomew)   Croxton Kerrial, Knipton, Harston, Branston etc *Leic*

SPROXTON (St Chad)   Helmsley *York*

SQUIRRELS HEATH (All Saints) *Chelmsf 4*   P *Bp*   V A D C EVANS

SROWSTON (St Cuthbert) (St Mary and St Margaret) w Beeston *Nor 4*   P *D&C*   R C W M AITKEN,   C P BROWN,   Hon C L WOOD

ST ENDELLION (St Endelienta) w Port Isaac and St Kew *Truro 10*   P *Bp*   R *Vacant* Port Isaac (020888) 442

ST-GEORGE-IN-THE-EAST (St Mary) *Lon 7*   P *Bp*   V J D M PATON

ST-GEORGE-IN-THE-EAST w St Paul *Lon 7*   P *Bp*   R G W CRAIG,   Hon C M J W COOK

ST-MARY-LE-STRAND w St Clement Danes *Lon 3*   P *Ld Chan and Burley Ho Preservation Trust (alt)*   R E R C THOMPSON,   NSM D J DERRICK

STADHAMPTON (St John the Baptist)   Dorchester *Ox*

STAFFHURST WOOD (St Silvan)   Limpsfield and Titsey *S'wark*

STAFFORD (Christ Church) (St Chad) (St Mary) *Lich 16*   P *Patr Bd*   TV T D HAWKINGS, R H W ARGUILE,   C P N ASHMAN,   NSM M J FISHER

STAFFORD (St John the Baptist) and Tixall w Ingestre *Lich 16*   P *Bp and Earl of Shrewsbury and Talbot (jt)*   V J A GEAR,   C N C PEDLEY

STAFFORD (St Paul) Forebridge *Lich 16*   P *V Castle Ch*   V T A HANDLEY

STAFFORD, WEST (St Andrew) w Frome Billet *Sarum 2*   P *Brig S Floyer-Acland*   P-in-c P C WHEATLEY

STAGSDEN (St Leonard)   Bromham w Oakley and Stagsden *St Alb*

STAGSHAW CHAPEL (St Aidan)   St Jo Lee *Newc*

STAINBY (St Peter)   Witham Gp *Linc*

STAINCLIFFE (Christ Church) *Wakef 10*   P *V Batley*   V B E H BAKER

STAINCROSS (St John the Divine) *Wakef 7*   P *Bp*   V D A CATON

STAINDROP (St Mary) *Dur 11*   P *Lord Barnard*   V *Vacant* Staindrop (0833) 60237

STAINES (Christ Church) *Lon 13*   P *Bp*   V L O LINDO

STAINES (St Mary) (St Peter) *Lon 13*   P *Ld Chan*   V D S RICHARDSON,   C D R WITTS

STAINFIELD (St Andrew)   Bardney *Linc*

STAINFORTH (St Mary) *Sheff 11*   P *Bp*   V C SMITH

STAINFORTH (St Peter)   Langcliffe w Stainforth and Horton *Bradf*

STAINING (St Luke Mission Church)   Blackpool St Mich *Blackb*

STAINLAND (St Andrew) *Wakef 2*   P *V Halifax*   V S DANDO,   C D M ROWLEY

STAINLEY, NORTH (St Mary the Virgin)   W Tanfield and Well w Snape and N Stainley *Ripon*

STAINLEY, SOUTH (St Wilfrid)   Markington w S Stainley and Bishop Thornton *Ripon*

STAINMORE (St Stephen)   Brough w Stainmore, Musgrave and Warcop *Carl*

STAINTON (St Winifred)   Tickhill w Stainton *Sheff*

STAINTON, GREAT (All Saints)   Bishopton w Gt Stainton *Dur*

STAINTON BY LANGWORTH (St John the Baptist)   Barlings *Linc*

STAINTON DALE (St John the Baptist)   Scalby w Ravenscar and Staintondale *York*

STAINTON-IN-CLEVELAND (St Peter and St Paul) *York 22*   P *Abp*   V M K BROADHEAD,   C G J WOOD, L T J HILLARY, I M GRAHAM

STAINTON LE VALE (St Andrew)   Walesby *Linc*

STAITHES (St Peter)   Hinderwell w Roxby *York*

STAKEFORD (Holy Family)   Choppington *Newc*

STALBRIDGE (St Mary) *Sarum 6*   P *CCC Cam*   P-in-c R H FRANKLIN

STALHAM (St Mary) and East Ruston w Brunstead *Nor 10*   P *Exors R Ives and DBP (alt)*   V *Vacant* Stalham (0692) 80250

STALISFIELD (St Mary)   Eastling w Ospringe and Stalisfield w Otterden *Cant*

STALLING BUSK (St Matthew)   Askrigg w Stallingbusk *Ripon*

STALLINGBOROUGH (St Peter and St Paul)   Healing and Stallingborough *Linc*

STALMINE (St James) *Blackb 10*   P *V Lanc*   V T G MIDDLEDITCH

STALYBRIDGE (Holy Trinity and Christ Church) *Ches 14*   P *Trustees*   V T G N GREEN,   C J R GIBBS

STALYBRIDGE (St George) *Man 17*   P *Lord Deramore and R Ashton-under-Lyne St Mich (jt)*   V M J R TINKER,   NSM R FOX

STALYBRIDGE (St Paul) *Ches 14*   P *Trustees*   V P L ROBINSON,   C S J HUNT

STAMBOURNE (St Peter and St Thomas)   Toppesfield and Stambourne *Chelmsf*

STAMBRIDGE (St Mary and All Saints) *Chelmsf 14*   P *Ld Chan (1 turn), Govs Charterhouse (3 turns)*   P-in-c F W B KENNY

STAMFORD (All Saints) (St John the Baptist) *Linc 13*   P *Ld Chan and Burghley Ho Preservation Trust (alt)*   V J H RICHARDSON,   C E J REAST,   Hon C D M BOND

STAMFORD (Christ Church) Conventional District *Linc 13*   C-in-c D J SPICER

STAMFORD (St George) (St Paul) *Linc 13*   P *Burghley Ho Preservation Trust*   R K S SWITHINBANK

STAMFORD (St Mary the Virgin) (St Michael) *Linc 13*   P *Burghley Ho Preservation Trust*   R *Vacant* Stamford (0780) 63142

STAMFORD BARON (St Martin) *Linc 13*   P *Burghley Ho Preservation Trust*   V *Vacant* Stamford (0780) 51424

STAMFORD BRIDGE Group of Parishes, The (St John the Baptist) *York 7*   P *Lord Egremont (2 turns), The Crown (1 turn), and Ld Chan (1 turn)*   R J HARRISON

STAMFORD HILL (St Bartholomew) *Lon 19*   P *The Crown*   V *Vacant* 081-800 1554

STAMFORD HILL (St Thomas) *Lon 19* **P** *R Hackney*
  V E S MORROW
STAMFORDHAM (St Mary the Virgin) w Matfen *Newc 3*
  P *Ld Chan* **V** R CAVAGAN
STANBRIDGE (St John the Baptist) Totternhoe,
  Stanbridge and Tilsworth *St Alb*
STANBURY (Mission Church) Haworth *Bradf*
STAND (All Saints) *Man 14* **P** *Earl of Wilton*
  R R W WARNER
**STANDISH (St Nicholas) w Haresfield and Moreton
  Valence w Whitminster** *Glouc 8* **P** *Bp and Col Sir Piers
  Bengough (jt)* **V** J A L B CATERER
STANDISH (St Wilfred) *Blackb 4* **P** *Bp*
  R P K WARREN, **C** M L HARTLEY
STANDLAKE (St Giles) Lower Windrush *Ox*
STANDON (All Saints) and Cotes Heath *Lich 13* **P** *Bp
  and V Eccleshall (jt)* **R** J H DEAKIN
STANDON (St Mary) *St Alb 4* **P** *Ch Fund Trust Fund*
  V J L PELLEY
STANFIELD (St Margaret) Litcham, Kempston,
  Lexham, Mileham, Beeston etc *Nor*
STANFORD (All Saints) Lyminge w Paddlesworth,
  Stanford w Postling etc *Cant*
STANFORD (All Saints) *Nor 18* **P** *Bp* **V** *Vacant*
STANFORD (St Nicholas) Swinford w Catthorpe,
  Shawell and Stanford *Leic*
STANFORD BISHOP (St James) Acton Beauchamp
  and Evesbatch w Stanford Bishop *Heref*
STANFORD DINGLEY (St Denys) Bradfield and
  Stanford Dingley *Ox*
**STANFORD IN THE VALE (St Denys) w Goosey and
  Hatford** *Ox 17* **P** *D&C Westmr (3 turns), Simeon's
  Trustees (2 turns)* **V** M T WENHAM
STANFORD-LE-HOPE (St Margaret) w Mucking
  Chelmsf 16 **P** *MMCET* **R** P H WILLIAMS,
  C P D PEARSON
STANFORD ON SOAR (St John the Baptist) *S'well 10*
  P *DBP* **P-in-c** S J SMITH
STANFORD-ON-TEME (St Mary) Teme Valley N
  Worc
STANFORD RIVERS (St Margaret) Greensted-juxta-
  Ongar w Stanford Rivers *Chelmsf*
**STANGROUND (St John the Baptist) (St Michael and All
  Angels) and Farcet** *Ely 13* **P** *Em Coll Cam*
  TR D E S DE SILVA
STANHOE (All Saints) Docking w The Birchams and
  Stanhoe w Barwick *Nor*
STANHOPE (St Thomas) w Frosterley *Dur 15* **P** *Bp and
  The Crown (alt)* **R** C N LOVELL, **NSM** D W WOOD
STANION (St Peter) Brigstock w Stanion *Pet*
STANLEY (All Saints) (St Andrew) *Derby 13* **P** *Bp*
  V B A H KILLICK
STANLEY (St Agnes) Endon w Stanley *Lich*
STANLEY (St Anne) *Liv 8* **P** *R W Derby*
  V M C DAVIES, **C** J A TAYLOR
STANLEY (St Peter) *Wakef 12* **P** *Provost*
  V P L HOWARD
STANLEY (St Stephen) *Dur 8* **P** *Bp (2 turns), The Crown
  (1 turn)* **TR** J P RICHARDSON,
  TV D M BEATER, S T ROBSON
STANLEY (St Thomas) *Dur 15* **P** *R Brancepeth*
  V A FEATHERSTONE
STANLEY PONTLARGE (Chapel) Winchcombe,
  Gretton, Sudeley Manor etc *Glouc*
STANLEYS, The *Glouc 8* **P** *Mrs M J Hollings and Jes
  Coll Cam (jt)* **V** P L CHICKEN
STANMER (not known) w Falmer *Chich 2* **P** *Bp*
  P-in-c A N ROBINSON
STANMORE (St Luke) *Win 13* **P** *Bp* **V** N P SEAL,
  C M G DOUGLAS
STANMORE, GREAT (St John the Evangelist) *Lon 23*
  P *R O Bernays Esq* **R** M H V BOWLES, **C** R A LEE,
  Hon C C J E SPENCER
STANMORE, LITTLE (St Lawrence) *Lon 23* **P** *Bp*
  C S J HOYLE
STANNEY (St Andrew) Ellesmere Port *Ches*
STANNINGFIELD (St Nicholas) Hawstead and Nowton
  w Stanningfield etc *St E*
STANNINGLEY (St Thomas) *Ripon 6* **P** *V Leeds St Pet*
  R K A PAYNE, **C** T W LIPSCOMB
STANNINGTON (Christ Church) *Sheff 4* **P** *Bp*
  V P W WEST, **C** M WOODHEAD
STANNINGTON (St Mary the Virgin) *Newc 1* **P** *Bp*
  V B G SULLIVAN
STANSFIELD (All Saints) *St E 8* **P** *Ld Chan*
  P-in-c T S WRIGHT
STANSTEAD (St James) Glem Valley United Benefice
  St E

STANSTEAD ABBOTS (St Andrew) *St Alb 8* **P** *Peache
  Trustees* **P-in-c** B F J GOODWIN, **Hon Par Dn** A C LONG
STANSTEAD ST MARGARET (St Mary the Virgin)
  Gt Amwell w St Marg *St Alb*
STANSTED (St Mary) w Fairseat and Vigo *Roch 9* **P** *Bp*
  R D G CLARK
STANSTED (St Paul) (Christ Church) *Chich 13* **P** *Earl of
  Bessborough* **V** J L W ROBINSON
STANSTED MOUNTFITCHET (St John) *Chelmsf 24*
  P *Bp*, **C** J A CARDELL-OLIVER,
  Hon Par Dn B C WALLACE, M K BOOKER
STANTON (All Saints) (St John the Baptist) *St E 9*
  P *The Crown* **R** F T HOWARD
STANTON (St Gabriel) Marshwood Vale Team Min
  Sarum
STANTON (St Mary) Denstone w Ellastone and Stanton
  Lich
STANTON (St Mary and All Saints) Markfield *Leic*
STANTON (St Michael and All Angels) Toddington,
  Stanton, Didbrook w Hailes etc *Glouc*
STANTON BY BRIDGE (St Michael) Ticknall, Smisby
  and Stanton by Bridge *Derby*
**STANTON-BY-DALE (St Michael and All Angels) w Dale
  Abbey** *Derby 15* **P** *Bp* **R** I E GOODING
STANTON DREW (Blessed Virgin Mary) Bishop
  Sutton and Stanton Drew and Stowey *B & W*
STANTON FITZWARREN (St Leonard) Stratton St
  Margaret w S Marston etc *Bris*
STANTON HARCOURT (St Michael) Lower Windrush
  Ox
STANTON HILL (All Saints) Skegby *S'well*
STANTON-IN-PEAK (Holy Trinity) Youlgreave,
  Middleton, Stanton-in-Peak etc *Derby*
STANTON LACY (Hayton Bent Hall) Culmington w
  Onibury, Bromfield etc *Heref*
STANTON LACY (St Peter) as above
STANTON ON HINE HEATH (St Andrew) *Lich 29*
  P *Sir Alex Stanier, Bt* **C** D PEARSON
STANTON-ON-THE-WOLDS (All Saints) *S'well 9*
  P *Trustees of Sir Rupert Bromley* **P-in-c** J L D HARDY
STANTON PRIOR (St Lawrence) Farmborough,
  Marksbury and Stanton Prior *B & W*
STANTON ST BERNARD (All Saints) Swanborough
  Sarum
STANTON ST JOHN (St John the Baptist) Wheatley w
  Forest Hill and Stanton St John *Ox*
**STANTON ST QUINTIN (St Giles), Hullavington and
  Grittleton wNorton and Leigh Delamere** *Bris 12* **P** *Bp*,
  Eton Coll, and R W Neeld Esq (by turn)
  P-in-c J W M MORGAN, **Par Dn** A MADDOCK
STANTONBURY (Christ Church) and Willen *Ox 25*
  P *Patr Bd* **TR** M C J REINDORP,
  TV D R BYRNE, I JAGGER, R WARD,
  Par Dn F J L WINFIELD, R V PARRETT,
  NSM D G EVERETT, D B MILLS, R V GREEN
STANWAY (St Albright) (St Andrew) *Chelmsf 20*
  P *Magd Coll Ox ·* **V** A F BELL
STANWAY (St Peter) Toddington, Stanton, Didbrook
  w Hailes etc *Glouc*
STANWELL (St Mary the Virgin) *Lon 13* **P** *Ld Chan*
  V D C PEMBERTON, **NSM** L LAWRENCE
STANWICK (St Laurence) w Hargrave *Pet 10*
  P *Ld Chan (2 turns), F S Wier Esq (1 turn)*
  R A R TWYFORD
STANWIX (St Michael) *Carl 3* **P** *Bp* **V** C S SIMS,
  C J D CLARK
STAPEHILL (All Saints) Hampreston *Sarum*
STAPENHILL (Immanuel) Conventional District *Derby 16*
  Min G D SIMMONS
STAPENHILL (St Peter) w Cauldwell *Derby 16* **P** *Ch Soc
  Trust* **C** P W GOODMAN
STAPLE (St James) Woodnesborough w Worth and
  Staple *Cant*
**STAPLE FITZPAINE (St Peter) w Orchard Portman,
  Thurlbear and Stoke St Mary** *B & W 20* **P** *Bp*
  R G COOKE
STAPLE TYE (St James) Gt Parndon *Chelmsf*
STAPLECROSS (St Mark) Ewhurst *Chich*
STAPLEFIELD COMMON (St Mark) *Chich 6*
  P *V Cuckfield* **P-in-c** A J C FREEMAN
STAPLEFORD (All Saints) Carlton-le-Moorland w
  Stapleford *Linc*
STAPLEFORD (St Andrew) *Ely 7* **P** *D&C*
  P-in-c K F M FISHER
**STAPLEFORD (St Andrew's Mission Church) (St Helen)
  (St Luke)** *S'well 7* **P** *CPAS* **V** C J HALL,
  C D G BANNOCKS, **Par Dn** V E RAMPTON
STAPLEFORD (St Mary) Bramfield w Stapleford and
  Waterford *St Alb*

STAPLEFORD (St Mary Magdalene)   Waltham on the Wolds, Stonesby, Saxby etc *Leic*

STAPLEFORD (St Mary) w Berwick (St James) *Sarum 16*   **P** *D&C Windsor*   **V** *Vacant* Stapleford (0708) 790261

STAPLEFORD ABBOTTS (St Mary)   Lambourne w Abridge and Stapleford Abbotts *Chelmsf*

STAPLEFORD TAWNEY (St Mary the Virgin) w Theydon Mount *Chelmsf 6*   **P** *DPB*   **P-in-c** P H W CHAPMAN

STAPLEGROVE (St John) *B & W 20*   **P** *Bp*   **R** N C VENNING

STAPLEHURST (All Saints) *Cant 11*   **P** *St Jo Coll Cam*   **R** T H VICKERY

STAPLETON (Holy Trinity) *Bris 7*   **P** *Bp*   **R** J A RISDON

STAPLETON (St John) *Heref 11*   **P** *DBP*   **P-in-c** J D M FALL

STAPLETON (St Martin)   Barwell w Potters Marston and Stapleton *Leic*

STAPLETON (St Mary)   Bewcastle, Stapleton and Kirklinton etc *Carl*

STARBECK (St Andrew) *Ripon 1*   **P** *V Harrogate Ch Ch*   **V** M B TAYLOR

STARCROSS (St Paul)   Kenton, Mamhead, Powderham, Cofton and Starcross *Ex*

STARSTON (St Margaret) *Nor 16*   **P** *Bp*   **P-in-c** M N FRANCE

STARTFORTH (Holy Trinity) w Bowes *Ripon 2*   **P** *Earl of Lonsdale and Lords of the Manor of Bowes (alt)*   **V** P J McCARTHY

STATFOLD (St Matthew)   Clifton Campville w Chilcote *Lich*

STATHERN (St Guthlac)   Barkestone w Plungar, Redmile and Stathern *Leic*

STAUGHTON, GREAT (St Andrew) *Ely 12*   **P** *St Jo Coll Ox*   **V** W N BROOK

STAUGHTON, LITTLE (All Saints)   Keysoe w Bolnhurst and Lt Staughton *St Alb*

STAUNTON (All Saints)   Coleford w Staunton *Glouc*

STAUNTON (St James)   Hartpury w Corse and Staunton *Glouc*

STAUNTON (St Mary) w Flawborough *S'well 3*   **P** *E G Staunton Esq*   **P-in-c** S F RISING

STAUNTON HAROLD (Holy Trinity)   Breedon cum Isley Walton and Worthington *Leic*

STAUNTON ON ARROW (St Peter)   Pembridge w Moorcourt, Shobdon, Staunton etc *Heref*

STAUNTON-ON-WYE (St Mary the Virgin)   Letton w Staunton, Byford, Mansel Gamage etc *Heref*

STAVELEY (All Saints)   Farnham w Scotton, Staveley, Copgrove etc *Ripon*

STAVELEY (St James) w Kentmere *Carl 9*   **P** *V Kendal H Trin*   **V** J WOOLCOCK

STAVELEY (St John the Baptist) and Barrow Hill *Derby 3*   **P** *Bp, Adn Chesterfield, and Duke of Devonshire (jt)*   **TR** W A BUTT,   **TV** P R SMITH, C W D VOGT

STAVELEY IN CARTMEL (St Mary)   Leven Valley *Carl*

STAVERTON (St Catherine) w Boddington and Tredington w Stoke Orchard and Hardwicke *Glouc 11*   **P** *Bp*   **V** J B THOMFRAY

STAVERTON (St Mary the Virgin) Helidon and Catesby *Pet 3*   **P** *Ch Ch Ox and Bp (alt)*   **V** *Vacant* Daventry (0327) 702466

STAVERTON (St Paul)   Hilperton w Whaddon and Staverton etc *Sarum*

STAVERTON (St Paul de Leon)   Broadhempston, Woodland, Staverton etc *Ex*

STAWELL (St Francis)   Middlezoy and Othery and Moorlinch *B & W*

STAWLEY (St Michael and All Angels)   Wellington and Distr *B & W*

STEANE (St Peter)   Farthinghoe w Hinton-in-the-Hedges w Steane *Pet*

STEART BAY (St Andrew)   Cannington, Otterhampton, Combwich and Stockland *B & W*

STEBBING (St Mary the Virgin) w Lindsell *Chelmsf 21*   **P** *Bp*   **V** J S SUTTON,   **NSM** S C BAZLINTON

STECHFORD (All Saints) (St Andrew) *Birm 10*   **P** *St Pet Coll Ox*   **V** J M GIBBS,   **NSM** E OWEN

STEDHAM (St James) w Iping, Elsted and Treyford-cum-Didling *Chich 10*   **P** *Bp*   **R** J G COLLINS

STEEP (All Saints) *Portsm 5*   **P** *Ld Chan*   **V** D J SNELGAR

STEEPING, GREAT (All Saints)   Firsby w Gt Steeping *Linc*

STEEPING, LITTLE (St Andrew) *Linc 7*   **P** *Baroness Willoughby de Eresby*   **R** G ROBSON

STEEPLE (St Lawrence and All Saints) *Chelmsf 13*   **V** *Vacant*

STEEPLE (St Michael and All Angels)   Corfe Castle, Church Knowle, Kimmeridge etc *Sarum*

STEEPLE ASHTON (St Mary the Virgin) w Semington and Keevil *Sarum 17*   **P** *D&C Win (1 turn), Magd Coll Cam (3 turns)*   **V** D M HART

STEEPLE ASTON (St Peter and St Paul) w North Aston and Tackley *Ox 9*   **P** *BNC Ox, St Jo Coll Ox, and Exors of Lt-Col A D Taylor (jt)*   **R** W M T HOLLAND,   **Dss** A M SHUKMAN

STEEPLE BARTON (St Mary)   Westcote Barton w Steeple Barton, Duns Tew etc *Ox*

STEEPLE BUMPSTEAD (St Mary) and Helions Bumpstead *Chelmsf 17*   **P** *Ld Chan*   **V** G R MANSFIELD

STEEPLE CLAYDON (St Michael)   The Claydons *Ox*

STEEPLE LANGFORD (All Saints)   Yarnbury *Sarum*

STEEPLE MORDEN (St Peter and St Paul)   Shingay Gp of Par *Ely*

STEETLY (All Saints)   Whitwell *Derby*

STEETON (St Stephen) *Bradf 8*   **P** *V Kildwick*   **V** J M BEARPARK,   **C** E NICOL

STELLA (St Cuthbert) *Dur 5*   **P** *Bp*   **R** C R MURRIE

STELLING (St Mary)   Petham and Waltham w Lower Hardres etc *Cant*

STENIGOT (St Nicholas)   Asterby Gp *Linc*

STEPNEY (St Dunstan and All Saints) *Lon 7*   **P** *Bp*   **R** M B SHREWSBURY,   **C** J W DRAPER,   **Par Dn** G D IRESON

STEPPINGLEY (St Lawrence)   Ampthill w Millbrook and Steppingley *St Alb*

STERNFIELD (St Mary Magdalene) w Benhall and Snape *St E 19*   **P** *Mrs A H V Aldous, Mrs A C V Wentworth, and Mrs M A Bertin (by turn)*   **R** N H BEVAN

STERT (St James)   Redhorn *Sarum*

STETCHWORTH (St Peter) *Ely 4*   **P** *Duke of Sutherland*   **P-in-c** G I ARNOLD

STEVENAGE (All Saints) Pin Green *St Alb 12*   **P** *Bp*   **V** C D FUTCHER,   **C** S G PUGH

STEVENAGE (Holy Trinity) *St Alb 12*   **P** *Bp*   **V** G H NEWTON,   **C** P R CRESSALL,   **Par Dn** H K DERHAM,   **NSM** A MARINER

STEVENAGE (St Andrew and St George) *St Alb 12*   **P** *Bp*   **R** M BARNSLEY,   **C** A C STEWART-SYKES,   **Par Dn** T M STEWART-SYKES

STEVENAGE (St Hugh Chells) *St Alb 12*   **P** *Bp*   **V** N J C PIGOTT

STEVENAGE (St Mary) Sheppall w Aston *St Alb 12*   **P** *Bp*   **V** G B WHITE,   **C** R D SEYMOUR-WHITELEY,   **NSM** A M GRIEVES

STEVENAGE (St Nicholas) *St Alb 12*   **P** *Bp*   **V** J R BAINBRIDGE

STEVENAGE (St Peter) Broadwater *St Alb 12*   **P** *Bp*   **V** D J BRENTNALL

STEVENTON (St Michael and All Angels) w Milton *Ox 10*   **P** *Ch Ch Ox and D&C Westmr (jt)*   **P-in-c** J DALY

STEVENTON (St Nicholas)   N Waltham and Steventon, Ashe and Deane *Win*

STEVINGTON (Church Room) (St Mary the Virgin) *St Alb 21*   **P** *Bp*   **P-in-c** P N JEFFERY

STEWARDS LANE (St Thomas)   Ditton St Mich *Liv*

STEWKLEY (St Michael and All Angels) w Soulbury and Drayton Parslow *Ox 26*   **P** *Bp, Earl of Rosebery, and MMCET (jt)*   **V** P A DALLAWAY

STEWTON (St Andrew)   Louth *Linc*

STEYNING (St Andrew) *Chich 12*   **P** *MMCET*   **V** P J BURCH,   **NSM** H M SEMPLE

STIBBARD (All Saints) *Nor 20*   **P** *Mrs H M Cook*   **R** F A HILL

STIBBINGTON (St John the Baptist) *Ely 13*   **P** *Sir Stephen Hastings*   **P-in-c** P O POOLEY

STICKFORD (St Helen)   Stickney Gp *Linc*

STICKLEPATH (St Mary)   S Tawton and Belstone *Ex*

STICKLEPATH (St Paul)   Barnstaple *Ex*

STICKNEY Group, The (St Luke) *Linc 7*   **P** *DBP, Ld Chan, and Bp (by turn)*   **V** J R WORSDALL

STIDD (St Saviour)   Ribchester w Stidd *Blackb*

STIFFKEY (St John and St Mary) and Cockthorpe w Morston, Langham and Binham *Nor 22*   **P** *Bp, Sir Euan Anstruther-Gough-Calthorpe, Bt, and DBP (by turn)*   **R** *Vacant* Binham (032875) 246

STIFFORD (St Cedd) (St Mary) *Chelmsf 16*   **P** *Bp*   **R** M A COHEN,   **C** G E COLDHAM

STIFFORD, SOUTH (St Mary the Virgin)   Grays Thurrock *Chelmsf*

STILLINGFLEET (St Helen)   Escrick and Stillingfleet w Naburn *York*

STILLINGTON (St John)   Grindon and Stillington *Dur*

STILLINGTON (St Nicholas) and Marton w Moxby *York 5*   **P** *Abp*   **P-in-c** W H BATES

STILTON (St Mary Magdalene) w Denton and Caldecote and Folkesworth w Morborne and Haddon *Ely 13*
P *Mrs H R Horne and Bp, Ld Chan (alt)*
R R LONGFOOT

STINCHCOMBE (St Cyr) Cam w Stinchcombe *Glouc*

STINSFORD (St Michael) Charminster and Stinsford *Sarum*

STIRCHLEY (All Saints) Cen Telford *Lich*

STIRCHLEY (Ascension) *Birm 4* P *R Kings Norton*
V D C BAKER, NSM M PRATT,
Hon Par Dn E E CLULEE

STISTED (All Saints) w Bradwell-juxta-Coggeshall and Pattiswick *Chelmsf 18* P *Mrs D E G Keen, and Abp (by turn)* P-in-c J MARVELL

STITHIANS (St Stythians) St Stythians w Perranarworthal and Gwennap *Truro*

STIXWOULD (St Peter) Horsington w Stixwould *Linc*

STOAK (St Lawrence) Ellesmere Port *Ches*

STOCK (St Barnabas) and Lydlinch *Sarum 6*
P *G A L F Pitt-Rivers Esq (2 turns), Col J L Yeatman (2 turns), and V Iwerne Minster (1 turn)* P-in-c J C DAY

STOCK HARVARD (All Saints) *Chelmsf 11*
P *Miss L C Harvard* R R A J BUCKINGHAM

STOCKBRIDGE (Old St Peter) (St Peter) and Longstock and Leckford *Win 11* P *Bp and St Jo Coll Ox (jt)*
R F A E CHADWICK

STOCKBURY (St Mary Magdalene) Newington w Hartlip and Stockbury *Cant*

STOCKCROSS (St John) Welford w Wickham and Gt Shefford, Boxford etc *Ox*

STOCKERSTON (St Peter) Six Saints circa Holt *Leic*

STOCKING FARM (St Luke) *Leic 1* P *Bp*
V J K HANCOCK, Hon C K F SHEPHERD

STOCKING PELHAM (St Mary) Braughing w Furneux Pelham and Stocking Pelham *St Alb*

STOCKINGFORD (St Paul) *Cov 5* P *V Nuneaton*
P-in-c M F VINCENT

STOCKLAND (St Mary Magdalene) Cannington, Otterhampton, Combwich and Stockland *B & W*

STOCKLAND (St Michael and All Angels) w Dalwood *Ex 5*
P *DBP* Hon C J N C GIDDINGS

STOCKLAND GREEN (St Mark) *Birm 6* P *The Crown*
V A T P NEWSUM

STOCKLEIGH ENGLISH (St Mary the Virgin) N Creedy *Ex*

STOCKLEIGH POMEROY (St Mary the Virgin) as above

STOCKLINCH (St Mary Magdalene) Shepton Beauchamp w Barrington, Stocklinch etc *B & W*

STOCKPORT (St Alban) Hall Street *Ches 18* P *Bp*
V M A WHETTER, C M ROWLANDS

STOCKPORT (St Augustine) Cheadle Heath *Ches*

STOCKPORT (St George) *Ches 18* P *Trustees*
V J M ROFF, C B HIGGINS, Par Dn M MALCOLM

STOCKPORT (St Mark) *Ches 18* P *Bp* V B K COOPER

STOCKPORT (St Mary) *Ches 18* P *G&C Coll Cam*
R A M FAIRHURST, NSM J BOWLES,
Hon Par Dn H C BRIDGE

STOCKPORT (St Matthew) *Ches 18* P *Bp*
V G HALLAM

STOCKPORT (St Saviour) *Ches 18* P *Trustees*
V D F HAY, Par Dn J A KENDALL

STOCKPORT (St Thomas) (St Peter) *Ches 18* P *Bp and Ch Union (jt)* R K D N KENRICK, C K R BROOKES

STOCKSBRIDGE (St Matthias) *Sheff 7* P *Bp*
V D P PALMER

STOCKSFIELD (St John) Bywell St Pet *Newc*

STOCKTON (St Andrew) Teme Valley N *Worc*

STOCKTON (St Chad) *Dur 16* P *Bp* V W P B CARLIN

STOCKTON (St Chad) Kemberton, Sutton Maddock and Stockton *Lich*

STOCKTON (St John the Baptist) Yarnbury *Sarum*

STOCKTON (St Mark) *Dur 16* P *Bp* V C B WESLEY,
Hon Par Dn J M THOMAS

STOCKTON (St Michael and All Angels) Napton-on-the-Hill, Lower Shuckburgh etc *Cov*

STOCKTON (St Michael and All Angels) Gillingham w Geldeston, Stockton, Ellingham etc *Nor*

STOCKTON HEATH (St Thomas) *Ches 4*
P *P G Greenall Esq* V T P F KENNY, C P M GILBERT,
NSM D L MELLOR

STOCKTON-ON-TEES Green Vale (Holy Trinity) Conventional District *Dur 16* C-in-c J D HARGREAVE

STOCKTON-ON-TEES (St Chad) Stockton St Chad *Dur*

STOCKTON ON TEES (St James) *Dur 16* P *Bp*
V W T G GRIFFITHS

STOCKTON-ON-TEES (St John the Baptist) *Dur 16*
P *Bp* V S IRWIN

STOCKTON-ON-TEES (St Mark) Stockton St Mark *Dur*

STOCKTON-ON-TEES (St Paul) *Dur 16* P *The Crown*
V P M HOOD

STOCKTON-ON-TEES (St Peter) *Dur 16* P *Bp*
V M A WHITEHEAD, C C H KNIGHTS, NSM M WATTS

STOCKTON-ON-TEES (St Thomas) *Dur 16* P *Bp*
V D J WHITTINGTON, C A E HARRISON,
NSM P A BLIGH

STOCKTON-ON-THE-FOREST (Holy Trinity) w Holtby and Warthill *York 4* P *Abp* R F H BLANCHARD

STOCKWELL (St Michael) *S'wark 10* P *V Kennington St Mark* V Vacant 071-274 6357

STOCKWELL GREEN (St Andrew) *S'wark 9* P *Abp, Bp, and TR N Lambeth (jt)* V P R SIMMONDS

STOCKWITH, EAST (St Peter) *Linc 2* P *Ld Chan*
V Vacant

STOCKWITH, WEST (St Mary the Virgin) Misterton and W Stockwith *S'well*

STOCKWOOD (Christ the Servant) Bris Ch the Servant Stockwood *Bris*

STODDEN Churches, The *St Alb 21* P *MMCET and DBP (alt)* R Vacant Bedford (0234) 708531

STODMARSH (St Mary) Littlebourne and Ickham w Wickhambreaux etc *Cant*

STODY (St Mary) Thornage w Brinton w Hunworth and Stody *Nor*

STOGUMBER (Blessed Virgin Mary) w Nettlecombe and Monksilver *B & W 19* P *D&C, and D&C Windsor (alt)* R R C SPURR

STOGURSEY (St Andrew) w Fiddington *B & W 19*
P *Eton Coll and DBP (alt)* R A E APPLEGARTH

STOKE (St Mary and St Andrew) Colsterworth Gp *Linc*

STOKE (St Michael) Cov Caludon *Cov*

STOKE (St Peter and St Paul) Grain w Stoke *Roch*

STOKE, EAST (St Oswald) w Syerston *S'well 3* P *Bp*
R G A FIRTH

STOKE, NORTH (not known) Amberley w N Stoke and Parham, Wiggonholt etc *Chich*

STOKE, NORTH (St Martin) Bath Weston All SS w N Stoke *B & W*

STOKE, NORTH (St Mary the Virgin) w Mongewell and Ipsden *Ox 6* P *St Jo Coll Cam (2 turns), DBP (1 turn)*
V A C P FISHER

STOKE, SOUTH (St Andrew) Goring w S Stoke *Ox*

STOKE, SOUTH (St James the Great) Combe Down w Monkton Combe and S Stoke *B & W*

STOKE, SOUTH (St Leonard) Arundel w Tortington and S Stoke *Chich*

STOKE, WEST (St Andrew) *Chich 13* P *Bp*
R D A JOHNSON

STOKE ABBOTT (St Mary) Beaminster Area *Sarum*

STOKE ALBANY (St Botolph) w Wilbarston *Pet 9*
P *Comdr L M M Saunders-Watson* R F L SCUFFHAM

STOKE ALDERMOOR (St Catherine) Cov Caludon *Cov*

STOKE ASH (All Saints) Thorndon w Rishangles, Stoke Ash, Thwaite etc *St E*

STOKE BARDOLPH (St Luke) Gedling *S'well*

STOKE BISHOP (St Mary Magdalene) *Bris 8* P *Bp*
V A R HENDERSON, C S W JONES,
NSM R L BELL, J M REX

STOKE BLISS (St Peter) Teme Valley S *Worc*

STOKE BRUERNE (St Mary the Virgin) w Grafton Regis and Alderton *Pet 5* P *BNC Ox and Ld Chan (alt)*
R H A M PICKARD

STOKE BY CLARE (St John the Baptist) Clare w Poslingford, Cavendish etc *St E*

STOKE BY NAYLAND (St Mary) w Leavenheath *St E 3*
P *Sir Joshua Rowley, Bt* V C M SEMPER

STOKE CANON (St Mary Magdalene), Poltimore w Huxham and Rewe w Netherexe *Ex 2* P *D&C, Lady Stucley, and Bp (by turn)* V P D LAVIS

STOKE CHARITY (St Mary and St Michael) Wonston and Stoke Charity w Hunton *Win*

STOKE CLIMSLAND (not known) *Truro 9* P *Duchy of Cornwall* R T J FULLER, Hon C J E LITTLEWOOD

STOKE D'ABERNON (St Mary the Virgin) *Guildf 10*
P *K Coll Cam* R D C VINCENT

STOKE DAMEREL (St Andrew w St Luke) *Ex 22*
P *Trustees of Lord St Levan* R G D CRYER,
Par Dn E A THOMAS (nee REEVES)

STOKE DOYLE (St Rumbold) Aldwincle w Thorpe Achurch, Pilton, Wadenhoe etc *Pet*

STOKE DRY (St Andrew) Lyddington w Stoke Dry and Seaton *Pet*

STOKE EDITH (St Mary) Tarrington w Stoke Edith, Aylton, Pixley etc *Heref*

STOKE FERRY (All Saints) w Wretton *Ely 15*
  P *Ld Chan* **V** A R BENNETT
STOKE FLEMING (St Peter) Blackawton and Stoke
  Fleming *Ex*
STOKE GABRIEL (St Gabriel) and Collaton (St Mary)
  Ex 13 **P** *Bp* **V** J SCHOLEFIELD
STOKE GIFFORD (St Michael) *Bris 6* **P** *Bp*
  TR D J POWELL, **TV** S J SMITH
STOKE GOLDING (St Margaret) w Dadlington *Leic 13*
  P *Bp* **P-in-c** C A R GASH
STOKE GOLDINGTON (St Peter) Gayhurst w
  Ravenstone, Stoke Goldington etc *Ox*
STOKE HAMMOND (St Luke) Newton Longville w
  Stoke Hammond and Whaddon *Ox*
STOKE HEATH (St Alban) Cov E *Cov*
STOKE HILL (St Peter) *Guildf 5* **P** *Bp* **V** D J FURNESS
STOKE HOLY CROSS (Holy Cross) w Dunston *Nor 14*
  P *D&C* **V** D C BROOME
STOKE-IN-TEIGNHEAD (St Andrew) w Combe-in-
  Teignhead and Haccombe *Ex 11* **P** *Sir Rivers Carew, Bt*
  R R A SOUTHWOOD
STOKE LACY (St Peter and St Paul) and Moreton Jeffries
  w Much Cowarne, Ocle Pychard and Ullingswick *Heref 2*
  P *D&C, Bp Birm, P H G Morgan Esq, and Bp (by turn)*
  R M TURTLE, **C** D PEARCE
STOKE LYNE (St Peter) Stratton Audley and
  Godington, Fringford etc *Ox*
STOKE MANDEVILLE (St Mary the Virgin)
  Ellesborough, The Kimbles and Stoke Mandeville *Ox*
STOKE NEWINGTON (St Andrew) *Lon 5* **P** *Bp*
  V R K BALLANTINE
STOKE NEWINGTON St Faith (St Matthias) and All
  Saints *Lon 5* **P** *City Corp* **V** C A ROWE,
  NSM R A FARLEY
STOKE NEWINGTON (St Mary) (Old Parish Church)
  Lon 5 **P** *Bp* **R** A G SCOTT, **C** D WOODSIDE
STOKE NEWINGTON (St Olave) *Lon 5* **P** *Ld Chan*
  V P JAMESON
STOKE NEWINGTON COMMON (St Michael and All
  Angels) *Lon 5* **P** *Bp* **P-in-c** N R EVANS,
  NSM H W J VALENTINE
STOKE-NEXT-GUILDFORD (St John the Evangelist)
  Guildf 5 **P** *Simeon's Trustees* **R** S R SIZER
STOKE ORCHARD (St James the Great) Staverton w
  Boddington and Tredington etc *Glouc*
STOKE PARK (St Peter) Ipswich St Mary at Stoke w St
  Pet & St Mary Quay *St E*
STOKE PERO (not known) Porlock w Stoke Pero
  B & W
STOKE POGES (St Giles) *Ox 23* **P** *Trustees Duke of*
  Leeds Trust **V** C E HARRIS
STOKE PRIOR (St Luke) Leominster *Heref*
STOKE PRIOR (St Michael), Wychbold and Upton
  Warren *Worc 8* **P** *Bp and D&C (alt)*
  R P B EMMERSON
STOKE RIVERS (St Bartholomew) Shirwell, Loxhore,
  Kentisbury, Arlington, etc *Ex*
STOKE ROW (St John the Evangelist) Langtree *Ox*
STOKE ST GREGORY (St Gregory) w Burrowbridge and
  Lyng *B & W 20* **P** *D&C (2 turns), R O Meade-*
  King Esq (1 turn) **V** C F E ROWLEY, **Hon C** J T TYLER
STOKE ST MARY (St Mary) Staple Fitzpaine, Orchard
  Portman, Thurlbear etc *B & W*
STOKE ST MICHAEL (St Michael) Leigh upon Mendip
  w Stoke St Michael *B & W*
STOKE ST MILBOROUGH (St Milburgha) Bitterley w
  Middleton, Stoke St Milborough etc *Heref*
STOKE SUB HAMDON (Blessed Virgin Mary) (All Saints
  Mission Church) *B & W 7* **P** *Ch Patr Trust*
  V H A HALLETT
STOKE TALMAGE (St Mary Magdalene) Tetsworth,
  Adwell w S Weston, Lewknor etc *Ox*
STOKE TRISTER (St Andrew) Charlton Musgrove,
  Cucklington and Stoke Trister *B & W*
STOKE UPON TERN (St Peter) *Lich 24* **P** *Lt-Col*
  Sir John Corbet, Bt **R** D W RENSHAW
STOKE-UPON-TRENT (St Peter-ad-Vincula) (St Paul)
  Lich 18 **P** *Bp* **TV** M J CHADWICK
STOKEHAM (St Peter) Rampton w Laneham, Treswell,
  Cottam and Stokeham *S'well*
STOKENCHURCH (St Peter and St Paul) and Ibstone
  Ox 29 **P** *Bp* **V** J A TRIGG
STOKENHAM (St Michael and All Angels) w Sherford
  Ex 14 **P** *The Crown* **V** T J JONES,
  Hon C C E TICQUET
STOKESAY (St Christopher) (St John the Baptist) *Heref 11*
  P *T P D La Touche Esq* **V** *Vacant* Craven Arms
  (05882) 2729

STOKESBY (St Andrew) Filby w Thrigby, Mautby,
  Stokesby, Herringby etc *Nor*
STOKESLEY (St Peter and St Paul) *York 22* **P** *Abp*
  R M D A DYKES, **Par Dn** S J GOULD
STOLFORD (St Peter) Stogursey w Fiddington *B & W*
STON EASTON (Blessed Virgin Mary) Chewton
  Mendip w Ston Easton, Litton etc *B & W*
STONDON (All Saints) Meppershall w Campton and
  Stondon *St Alb*
STONDON MASSEY (St Peter and St Paul) Blackmore
  and Stondon Massey *Chelmsf*
STONE (All Saints) w Woodford and Hill *Glouc 2*
  P *Major R Jenner-Fust and V Berkeley (alt)*
  V P C F WOOSTER
STONE (Christ Church) and Oulton-with-Moddershall
  Lich 19 **P** *Simeon's Trustees* **V** D J WILLIAMS
STONE near Dartford (St Mary) *Roch 2* **P** *Bp*
  R J A RANDALL
STONE (St John the Baptist) w Dinton and Hartwell *Ox 21*
  P *Bp and Grocers' Co (jt)* **R** D J COOKE
STONE (St Mary the Virgin) Chaddesley Corbett and
  Stone *Worc*
STONE (St Michael) w Aston (St Saviour) *Lich 19* **P** *Bp*
  R T H KAYE, **Par Dn** E A HADLEY
STONE CROSS (St Luke) N Langley CD *Chich*
STONE-IN-OXNEY (St Mary the Virgin) Wittersham w
  Stone-in-Oxney and Ebony *Cant*
STONE QUARRY (St Luke) E Grinstead St Swithun
  Chich
STONEBRIDGE (St Michael and All Angels) *Lon 21*
  P *Bp* **V** R L SMITH, **Par Dn** R J THOMPSON
STONEBROOM (St Peter) Morton and Stonebroom
  Derby
STONEFOLD (St John) Haslingden w Grane and
  Stonefold *Blackb*
STONEGATE (St Peter) *Chich 19* **P** *E J B Hardcastle and*
  M H Reid (jt) **P-in-c** W D MAUNDRELL
STONEGRAVE (Holy Trinity) Harome w Stonegrave,
  Nunnington and Pockley *York*
STONEHAM, NORTH (All Saints) *Win 9*
  P *R H W Fleming Esq* **R** C W TAYLOR,
  P-in-c R S GURR, **C** H J MAYELL
STONEHAM, NORTH (St Nicholas) Valley Park *Win*
STONEHAM, SOUTH (St Mary) *Win 12* **P** *TR Southn*
  City Cen **V** *Vacant* Southampton (0703) 555487
STONEHAM BASSETT, NORTH (St Michael) N
  Stoneham *Win*
STONEHAM BASSETT GREEN, NORTH (St
  Christopher) as above
STONEHOUSE (St Cyr) *Glouc 8* **P** *The Crown*
  V J N K HARRIS
STONEHOUSE (St Paul) Plymouth St Andr w St Paul
  and St Geo *Ex*
STONELEIGH (St John the Baptist) *Guildf 9* **P** *Bp*
  V *Vacant* 081-393 3738
STONELEIGH (St Mary the Virgin) w Ashow and
  Baginton *Cov 4* **P** *Lord Leigh and Bp (jt)*
  R D E WEBSTER, **NSM** E JOHNSON
STONESBY (St Peter) Waltham on the Wolds,
  Stonesby, Saxby etc *Leic*
STONESFIELD (St James the Great) w Combe *Ox 9*
  P *Duke of Marlborough* **R** *Vacant* Stonesfield
  (099389) 664
STONEY MIDDLETON (St Martin) Curbar and Stoney
  Middleton *Derby*
STONEY STANTON (St Michael) Croft and Stoney
  Stanton *Leic*
STONEYCROFT (All Saints) *Liv 8* **P** *Bp*
  V P D TAYLOR, **C** J R BROUGHTON
STONEYCROFT (St Paul) Liv St Paul Stoneycroft *Liv*
STONEYDELPH (St Martin in the Delph) Glascote and
  Stonydelph *Lich*
STONHAM ASPAL (St Mary and St Lambert)
  Crowfield w Stonham Aspal and Mickfield *St E*
STONHAM PARVA (St Mary) Creeting St Mary,
  Creeting St Peter etc *St E*
STONNALL (St Peter) *Lich 1* **P** *V Shenstone*
  P-in-c J R FAGAN
STONTON WYVILLE (St Denys) Church Langton w
  Tur Langton, Thorpe Langton etc *Leic*
STONY STRATFORD (St Mary and St Giles) *Ox 25*
  P *Bp* **V** C H J CAVELL-NORTHAM
STOODLEIGH (St Margaret) Washfield, Stoodleigh,
  Withleigh etc *Ex*
STOPHAM (St Mary the Virgin) and Fittleworth *Chich 11*
  P *D&C and Sir Brian Barttelot, Bt (jt)* **R** F H DOE
STOPSLEY (St Thomas) *St Alb 20* **P** *Bp*
  V F A ESTDALE

STORRIDGE (St John the Baptist) Cradley w Mathon and Storridge *Heref*
STORRINGTON (St Mary) *Chich 12* **P** *Keble Coll Ox* **R** M J HORE
STORTH (All Saints Mission) Arnside *Carl*
STOTFOLD (St Mary the Virgin) *St Alb 22* **P** *Bp* **V** V L NORTH
STOTTESDON (St Mary) w Farlow, Cleeton St Mary and Silvington *Heref 9* **P** *Bp* **R** W J BROMLEY
STOUGHTON (Emmanuel) *Guildf 5* **P** *Simeon's Trustees* **V** J F SALTER, **C** J R TERRANOVA
STOUGHTON (St Mary) Compton, the Mardens, Stoughton and Racton *Chich*
STOUGHTON (St Mary and All Saints) Thurnby w Stoughton *Leic*
STOULTON (St Edmund) w Drake's Broughton and Pirton and Norton *Worc 4* **P** *Earl of Cov, D&C, and Bp (jt)* **R** *Vacant* Worcester (0905) 840528
STOUR, EAST (Christ Church) Gillingham *Sarum*
STOUR, UPPER *Sarum 14* **P** *Exors H P R Hoare (1 turn), Bp (2 turns), and Bourton Chpl Trustees (1 turn)* **R** B C ATKINSON
STOUR, WEST (St Mary) Gillingham *Sarum*
STOUR PROVOST (St Michael and All Angels) as above
STOUR ROW (All Saints) as above
STOUR VALLEY GROUP, THE Clare w Poslingford, Cavendish etc *St E*
STOURBRIDGE Norton (St Michael and All Angels) *Worc 11* **P** *Bp* **V** M J BEASLEY
STOURBRIDGE (St John the Evangelist) Old Swinford Stourbridge *Worc*
STOURBRIDGE (St Mary) as above
STOURBRIDGE (St Thomas) *Worc 11* **P** *Bp* **V** S HUTCHINSON, **NSM** C S MOORHOUSE
STOURPAINE (Holy Trinity) Pimperne, Stourpaine, Durweston and Bryanston *Sarum*
STOURPORT (St Michael and All Angels) Lower Mitton *Worc*
STOURTON (St Peter) Kinver and Enville *Lich*
STOURTON (St Peter) Upper Stour *Sarum*
STOURTON CAUNDLE (St Peter) The Caundles w Folke and Holwell *Sarum*
STOVEN (St Margaret) Hundred River Gp of Par *St E*
STOW w Quy *Ely 6* **P** *Bp* **P-in-c** R A MINTER
STOW, WEST (St Mary) Culford, W Stow and Wordwell w Flempton etc *St E*
STOW BARDOLPH (Holy Trinity) Wimbotsham w Stow Bardolph and Stow Bridge etc *Ely*
STOW BEDON (St Botolph) Caston w Griston, Merton, Thompson etc *Nor*
STOW BRIDGE Mission (St Peter) Wimbotsham w Stow Bardolph and Stow Bridge etc *Ely*
STOW IN LINDSEY (St Mary the Virgin) *Linc 2* **P** *Bp* **R** G S RICHARDSON
STOW LONGA (St Botolph) *Ely 10* **P** *Bp* **V** R A FROST
STOW MARIES (St Mary and St Margaret) Purleigh, Cold Norton and Stow Maries *Chelmsf*
STOW ON THE WOLD (St Edward) *Glouc 15* **P** *DBP* **R** R F ROTHERY
STOWE (Assumption of St Mary the Virgin) *Ox 22* **P** *Stowe Sch* **P-in-c** M D DRURY
STOWE (St Michael and All Angels) Bucknell w Chapel Lawn, Llanfair Waterdine etc *Heref*
STOWE, UPPER (St James) Heyford w Stowe Nine Churches *Pet*
STOWE BY CHARTLEY (St John the Baptist) Hixon w Stowe-by-Chartley *Lich*
STOWE NINE CHURCHES (St Michael) Heyford w Stowe Nine Churches *Pet*
STOWELL (St Leonard) Chedworth, Yanworth and Stowell, Coln Rogers etc *Glouc*
STOWELL (St Mary Magdalene) Henstridge and Charlton Horethorne w Stowell *B & W*
STOWEY (St Nicholas and Blessed Virgin Mary) Bishop Sutton and Stanton Drew and Stowey *B & W*
STOWEY, NETHER (Blessed Virgin Mary) w Over Stowey *B & W 19* **P** *D&C Windsor and MMCET (alt)* **V** R L PARKER
STOWEY, OVER (St Peter and St Paul) Nether Stowey w Over Stowey *B & W*
STOWFORD (St John) Marystowe, Coryton, Stowford, Lewtrenchard etc *Ex*
STOWLANGTOFT (St George) Badwell Ash w Gt Ashfield, Stowlangtoft etc *St E*
STOWMARKET (St Peter and St Mary) *St E 6* **P** *Ch Patr Trust* **V** J R HARROLD
STOWTING (St Mary the Virgin) Sellindge w Monks Horton and Stowting etc *Cant*

STOWUPLAND (Holy Trinity) Old Newton w Stowupland *St E*
STRADBROKE (All Saints) w Horham, Athelington and Redlingfield *St E 17* **P** *Bp (3 turns), Lt-Comdr G C Marshall (1 turn), and Dr G I Soden (1 turn)* **R** D J STREETER
STRADISHALL (St Margaret) Wickhambrook w Stradishall and Denston *St E*
STRADSETT (St Mary) Crimplesham w Stradsett *Ely*
STRAITS, THE (St Andrew) Sedgley All SS *Lich*
STRAMSHALL (St Michael and All Angels) *Lich 21* **P** *V Uttoxeter* **P-in-c** A G SADLER, **C** A O L HODGSON
STRANTON (All Saints) *Dur 13* **P** *St Jo Coll Dur* **V** M A JENNETT
STRATFIELD MORTIMER (St Mary) *Ox 12* **P** *Eton Coll* **V** J A ELLIS, **C** D M MATHESON
STRATFIELD SAYE (St Mary) Sherfield-on-Loddon and Stratfield Saye etc *Win*
STRATFORD (St John the Evangelist) and Christ Church w Forest Gate St James *Chelmsf 5* **P** *V W Ham* **P-in-c** D A RICHARDS, **C** F W ATKINS, **Hon C** J P RICHARDSON
STRATFORD NEW TOWN (St Paul) *Chelmsf 5* **P** *Ch Patr Trust* **V** R E GROVE
STRATFORD ST MARY (St Mary) *St E 3* **P** *Duchy of Lanc* **P-in-c** M B ETTLINGER
STRATFORD SUB CASTLE (St Lawrence) *Sarum 15* **P** *D&C* **P-in-c** B J HOPKINSON
STRATFORD-UPON-AVON (Holy Trinity) w Bishopton *Cov 8* **P** *Bp* **TR** G D SPILLER
STRATTON (St Andrew) and Launcells *Truro 8* **P** *Duchy of Cornwall and CPAS (alt)* **R** T C MOORE
STRATTON (St Mary) (St Michael) and Wacton *Nor 11* **P** *G&C Coll Cam, DBP, and New Coll Ox (by turn)* **R** *Vacant* Long Stratton (0508) 30238
STRATTON (St Mary the Virgin) Bradf Peverell, Stratton, Frampton etc *Sarum*
STRATTON (St Peter) w Baunton *Glouc 12* **P** *R T G Chester-Master Esq* **P-in-c** H A S COCKS, **NSM** D H S LEESON
STRATTON, EAST (All Saints) Micheldever and E Stratton, Woodmancote etc *Win*
STRATTON, UPPER (St Philip) *Bris 12* **P** *Bp* **V** K J I GREENSLADE
STRATTON AUDLEY (St Mary and St Edburga) and Godington, Fringford w Hethe and Stoke Lyne *Ox 2* **P** *Ch Ch Ox, Ld Chan, and CCC Ox (by turn)* **R** A HICHENS
STRATTON ON THE FOSSE (St Vigor) Chilcompton w Downside and Stratton on the Fosse *B & W*
STRATTON ST MARGARET (St Margaret) w South Marston and Stanton Fitzwarren *Bris 12* **P** *Patr Bd* **TR** M J H HOWELL, **TV** A M R HOUSMAN, **C** D J DAY
STRATTON STRAWLESS (St Margaret) Hevingham w Hainford and Stratton Strawless *Nor*
STREAT (not known) w Westmeston *Chich 9* **P** *Woodard Schs* **NSM** A W VINEY
STREATHAM (Christ Church) *S'wark 12* **P** *R Streatham St Leon* **V** C J IVORY
STREATHAM Furzedown (St Paul) Streatham St Paul *S'wark*
STREATHAM (Immanuel) (St Andrew) *S'wark 12* **P** *Bp, Hyndman Trustees, and R Streatham St Leon (jt)* **V** D O ISHERWOOD
STREATHAM (St Leonard) *S'wark 12* **P** *Bp* **R** J R WILCOX, **C** X SOOSAINAYAGAM
STREATHAM (St Paul) (St Andrew's Church Hall) *S'wark 16* **P** *Bp* **V** N A PARISH
STREATHAM (St Peter) *S'wark 12* **P** *St Steph Ho Ox* **V** J R HALL, **C** R FARROW, **Hon C** C T CAVANAGH
STREATHAM, WEST (St James) *S'wark 16* **P** *CPAS* **V** *Vacant* 081-677 3947
STREATHAM HILL (St Margaret the Queen) *S'wark 12* **P** *Bp* **V** G T WILLIAMS, **NSM** L M WRIGHT
STREATHAM PARK (St Alban) *S'wark 16* **P** *Ch Soc Trust* **V** M D MARSHALL
STREATHAM VALE (Holy Redeemer) *S'wark 12* **P** *CPAS* **V** *Vacant* 081-764 5808
STREATLEY (St Margaret) *St Alb 20* **P** *Bp* **V** R W WOOD
STREATLEY (St Mary) w Moulsford *Ox 18* **P** *Bp* **V** R J DAVISON, **Hon C** J P MACKNEY
STREET (Holy Trinity) (Mission Church) w Walton *B & W 5* **P** *DBP* **R** D C EVANS, **C** R D GORDON, E W GRAY
STREET Team Ministry, The *York 3* **P** *Patr Bd* **TR** G S SIMPSON, **TV** J D WALKER
STREETLY (All Saints) *Lich 7* **P** *Bp* **V** P A R HAMMERSLEY, **C** C D MITCHELL

STRELLEY (All Saints)   Bilborough w Strelley *S'well*
STRENSALL (St Mary the Virgin) *York 5*   **P** *Abp*
   V G C GALLEY
STRENSHAM (St John the Baptist)   Ripple, Earls
   Croome w Hill Croome and Strensham *Worc*
STRETE (St Michael)   E Allington, Slapton and Strete
   Ex
STRETFORD (All Saints) *Man 7*   **P** *Bp*
   R P K TOWNLEY,   **C** N SALT
STRETFORD (St Bride) *Man 7*   **P** *Trustees*
   R A P HOBSON
STRETFORD (St Matthew) *Man 7*   **P** *D&C*
   R H R ENTWISTLE
STRETFORD (St Peter) *Man 7*   **P** *The Crown*   **R** *Vacant*
   061-865 1802
STRETHALL (St Mary the Virgin)   Heydon, Gt and Lt
   Chishill, Chrishall etc *Chelmsf*
STRETHAM (St James) w Thetford *Ely 14*   **P** *Bp*
   R J S ASKEY
STRETTON (St John)   Penkridge Team *Lich*
STRETTON (St Mary) w Claymills *Lich 20*   **P** *Baroness*
   Gretton   **V** A R WAYTE
STRETTON (St Matthew) and Appleton Thorn *Ches 4*
   P *Mrs P F du Bois Grantham and Dr S P L du Bois*
   Davidson (jt)   **V** R ROWLANDS
STRETTON (St Nicholas)   Greetham and Thistleton w
   Stretton and Clipsham *Pet*
STRETTON, LITTLE (All Saints)   Church Stretton
   Heref
STRETTON GRANDISON (St Laurence)   Bosbury w
   Wellington Heath etc *Heref*
STRETTON MAGNA (St Giles)   Gt Glen, Stretton
   Magna and Wistow etc *Leic*
STRETTON ON DUNSMORE (All Saints)   Bourton w
   Frankton and Stretton on Dunsmore etc *Cov*
STRETTON ON DUNSMORE (Mission Church)   as
   above
STRETTON ON FOSSE (St Peter)   Ilmington w
   Stretton-on-Fosse etc *Cov*
STRETTON PARVA (St John the Baptist)   Gaulby *Leic*
STRETTON SUGWAS (St Mary Magdalene) *Heref 4*
   P *DBP*   **P-in-c** M A KELK
STRAGGLETHORPE (St Michael)   Brant Broughton
   and Beckingham *Linc*
STRICKLAND, GREAT (St Barnabas)   Morland,
   Thrimby and Gt Strickland *Carl*
STRINES (St Paul)   Marple All SS *Ches*
STRINGSTON (not known)   Quantoxhead *B & W*
STRIXTON (St John)   Wollaston and Strixton *Pet*
STROOD (St Francis) *Roch 6*   **P** *Bp*   **V** B R INGRAM,
   C D J WALKER
STROOD (St Nicholas) (St Mary) *Roch 6*   **P** *Bp and*
   D&C (jt)   **V** A A MUSTOE
STROUD (Holy Trinity) (St Alban Mission Church)
   Glouc 1   **P** *Bp*   **P-in-c** D T MERRY,   **C** W H SMITH
STROUD (Mission Church)   Steep *Portsm*
STROUD (St Laurence) and Uplands w Slad *Glouc 1*
   P *Bp*   **V** B C E COKER,   **C** S W ELDRIDGE
STROUD GREEN (Holy Trinity) *Lon 20*   **P** *Bp*
   V B K LUNN,   **C** W P WATERS
STROXTON (All Saints)   Harlaxton *Linc*
STRUBBY (St Oswald)   Withern *Linc*
STRUMPSHAW (St Peter)   Burlingham St Edmund w
   Lingwood, Strumpshaw etc *Nor*
STUBBINGS (St James the Less) *Ox 13*   **P** *DBP*
   P-in-c P W D IND
STUBBINS (St Philip)   Edenfield and Stubbins *Man*
STUBBS CROSS (St Francis)   Kingsnorth w Shadoxhurst
   Cant
STUBSHAW CROSS (St Luke)   Ashton-in-Makerfield
   St Thos *Liv*
STUBTON (St Martin)   Claypole *Linc*
STUDHAM (St Mary the Virgin)   Kensworth, Studham
   and Whipsnade *St Alb*
STUDLAND (St Nicholas)   Swanage and Studland
   Sarum
STUDLEY (Nativity of the Blessed Virgin Mary) *Cov 7*
   P *DBP*   **P-in-c** R D BENNETT,   **C** S R TASH
STUDLEY (St John the Evangelist) *Sarum 17*
   P *R Trowbridge St Jas*   **V** P J STONE,   **C** S J COOMBS,
   NSM F J ATKINS
STUDLEY, HORTON-CUM (St Barnabas)   Horton-
   cum-Studley *Ox*
STUKELEY, GREAT (St Bartholomew) w LITTLE (St
   Martin) *Ely 9*   **P** *SMF and Bp*   **P-in-c** A P LUDLOW
STUNTNEY (Holy Cross) *Ely 14*   **P** *D&C*
   P-in-c S E B SHIPLEY
STURMER (St Mary)   Ridgewell w Ashen, Birdbrook
   and Sturmer *Chelmsf*

STURMINSTER MARSHALL (St Mary), Kingston Lacy
   and Shapwick *Sarum 10*   **P** *Eton Coll and Nat Trust*
   (alt)   **V** I J MAYO
STURMINSTER NEWTON (St Mary) and Hinton St Mary
   Sarum 5   **P** *G A L F Pitt-Rivers Esq (3 turns),*
   Col J L Yeatman (2 turns), and V Iwerne Minster (1 turn)
   P-in-c J C DAY
STURRY (St Nicholas) w Fordwich and Westbere w
   Hersden *Cant 3*   **P** *Abp, Ld Chan, and St Aug Foundn*
   Cant (by turn)   **R** P J GAUSDEN
STURTON (St Hugh)   Stow in Lindsey *Linc*
STURTON, GREAT (All Saints)   Hemingby *Linc*
STURTON-LE-STEEPLE (St Peter and St Paul)
   N Wheatley, W Burton, Bole, Saundby, Sturton etc
   S'well
STUSTON (All Saints)   N Hartismere *St E*
STUTTON (St Aidan)   Tadcaster w Newton Kyme *York*
STUTTON (St Peter)   Brantham w Stutton *St E*
STYVECHALE (St James) *Cov 3*   **P** *Col A M H Gregory-*
   Hood   **V** J LEACH
SUCKLEY (St John the Baptist)   Alfrick, Lulsley,
   Suckley, Leigh and Bransford *Worc*
SUDBOROUGH (All Saints)   Lowick w Sudborough
   and Slipton *Pet*
SUDBOURNE (All Saints)   Orford w Sudbourne,
   Chillesford, Butley and Iken *St E*
SUDBROOKE (St Edward)   Barlings *Linc*
SUDBURY (All Saints) and Somersal Herbert *Derby 14*
   P *Bp and DBP (alt)*   **P-in-c** K JARDIN
SUDBURY (All Saints) w Ballingdon and Brundon *St E 12*
   P *Simeon's Trustees*   **V** L F SIMPKINS
SUDBURY (St Andrew) *Lon 21*   **P** *Bp*   **V** R G DREYER,
   C M R SUTHERLAND
SUDBURY (St Gregory) St Peter and Chilton *St E 12*
   P *Bp (3 turns), Ch Soc Trust (1 turn)*   **R** D M STIFF
SUDDEN (St Aidan)   Rochdale *Man*
SUDLEY MANOR (St Mary)   Winchcombe, Gretton,
   Sudeley Manor etc *Glouc*
SUFFIELD (St Margaret) *Nor 9*   **P** *Personal Reps*
   G Whately   **R** *Vacant*
SUFFIELD PARK (St Martin)   Cromer *Nor*
SUGLEY (Holy Saviour) *Newc 7*   **P** *Bp*   **V** *Vacant*   091-
   267 4633
SULBY (St Stephen's Chapel)   Lezayre *S & M*
SULGRAVE (St James the Less)   Culworth w Sulgrave
   and Thorpe Mandeville *Pet*
SULHAM (St Nicholas)   Pangbourne w Tidmarsh and
   Sulham *Ox*
SULHAMSTEAD ABBOTS (St Mary) and Bannister w
   Ufton Nervet *Ox 12*   **P** *Qu Coll Ox and Or Coll Ox (alt)*
   R M WATTS
SULLINGTON (St Mary) and Thakeham w Warminghurst
   Chich 12   **P** *Bp and DBP (alt)*   **R** N E LEMPRIERE
SUMMERFIELD (Christ Church) (Cavendish Road Hall)
   Birm 2   **P** *R Birm St Martin w Bordesley*
   V J B KNIGHT,   **C** S H COULSON, H A C MORSE
SUMMERFIELD (St John's Chapel)   Hartlebury *Worc*
SUMMERSDALE (St Michael)   Chich St Paul and St Pet
   Chich
SUMMERSTOWN (St Mary) *S'wark 16*   **P** *Ch Soc Trust*
   V R J RYAN
SUMMERTOWN (St Michael and All Angels)
   Wolvercote w Summertown *Ox*
SUNBURY, UPPER (St Saviour) *Lon 13*   **P** *V Sunbury*
   V A F P BROWN
SUNBURY-ON-THAMES (St Mary) *Lon 13*
   P *D&C St Paul's*   **C** N A P EVANS
SUNDERLAND Pennywell (St Thomas) *Dur 9*   **P** *Bp*
   V M A MILLWARD
SUNDERLAND Red House (St Cuthbert) *Dur 9*   **P** *D&C*
   V M BEBBINGTON
SUNDERLAND Springwell (St Mary) w Thorney Close
   (St Peter) *Dur 9*   **P** *Bp*   **V** K HUNT,   **C** N A REED
SUNDERLAND (St Bede) Town End Farm *Dur 9*   **P** *Bp*
   V J W POULTER
SUNDERLAND (St Chad) *Dur 9*   **P** *Bp*   **V** J D CHADD,
   NSM J M M FRANCIS
SUNDERLAND (St Michael) *Dur 9*   **P** *Bp*
   TR G G GIBSON,   **TV** M D GARDNER,   **C** G BUTTERY
SUNDERLAND, NORTH (St Paul) *Newc 10*   **P** *Lord*
   Crewe's Trustees   **V** D G ROGERSON
SUNDERLAND POINT (Mission Church)   Overton
   Blackb
SUNDON (St Mary) *St Alb 20*   **P** *Bp*   **V** L S PULLAN
SUNDRIDGE (St Mary) w Ide Hill *Roch 8*   **P** *Abp*
   R D H BOZON
SUNNINGDALE (Holy Trinity) *Ox 11*   **P** *Bp*   **V** M HILL
SUNNINGHILL (St Michael and All Angels) *Ox 11*
   P *St Jo Coll Cam*   **V** T W GUNTER,   **NSM** G R PARISH

SUNNINGWELL (St Leonard)   Radley and Sunningwell *Ox*

SUNNYSIDE (St Barnabas)   E Grinstead St Swithun *Chich*

SUNNYSIDE (St Michael and All Angels) w Bourne End *St Alb 3*   **P** *CPAS*   **V** S P BREUKELMAN, **NSM** R CLARKSON

SURBITON (St Andrew) (St Mark) *S'wark 14*   **P** *Bp* **V** D JACKSON,   **C** G D SWINTON,   **NSM** B E NICHOLS

SURBITON (St Matthew) *S'wark 14*   **P** *R&S Ch Trust* **V** S A HONES,   **C** H D UFFINDELL

SURBITON HILL (Christ Church) *S'wark 14*   **P** *Ch Soc Trust and Trustees (jt)*   **V** D I FRASER,   **C** S TAYLOR, **NSM** D J BENDELL

SURFLEET (St Lawrence) *Linc 17*   **P** *Bp and V Pinchbeck (jt)*   **V** M P SKILLINGS

SURLINGHAM (St Mary)   Rockland St Mary w Hellington, Bramerton etc *Nor*

SUSSEX GARDENS (St James)   Paddington St Jas *Lon*

SUSTEAD (St Peter and St Paul)   Roughton and Felbrigg, Metton, Sustead etc *Nor*

SUTCOMBE (St Andrew) *Ex 9*   **P** *Bp*   **R** H J ROCHE

SUTTERBY (not known)   Langton w Sutterby *Linc*

SUTTERTON (St Mary) w Fosdyke and Algarkirk *Linc 21* **P** *Prime Min, Bp and DBP (alt)*   **R** J D DUCKETT, **NSM** J F UDY

SUTTON (All Saints)   Potton w Sutton and Cockayne Hatley *St Alb*

SUTTON (All Saints)   Shottisham w Sutton *St E*

SUTTON (All Saints) w Shopland *Chelmsf 14*   **P** *SMF* **P-in-c** G A BISHTON

SUTTON (Christ Church) *S'wark 25*   **P** *R Sutton St Nic* **V** A E MATHERS,   **Par Dn** M S RANDALL

SUTTON (Mission Room)   Felixkirk w Boltby *York*

SUTTON (St Andrew) *Ely 14*   **P** *D&C* **V** R E REYNOLDS,   **NSM** T R HOLLAND, M T COOPER

SUTTON (St Bartholomew)   Babworth w Sutton-cum-Lound *S'well*

SUTTON (St Clement), Huttoft and Anderby *Linc 8* **P** *Bp (2 turns), Magd Coll Cam (1 turn)*   **R** G J WILCOX, **NSM** W D W BAKER

SUTTON (St George) (St Barnabas's Mission Church) *Ches 13*   **P** *Trustees*   **V** D S HARRISON, **NSM** P MAYBURY

SUTTON (St James) *Ches 13*   **P** *Trustees* **V** C F EASTWOOD

SUTTON (St James) and Wawne (St Peter) *York 15* **P** *Patr Bd*   **TR** T W DOHERTY,   **C** J H M DUMULLA, **Par Dn** D R M DOHERTY

SUTTON (St John the Baptist)   Barlavington, Burton w Coates, Sutton and Bignor *Chich*

SUTTON (St Mary)   Calow and Sutton cum Duckmanton *Derby*

SUTTON (St Michael)   Ingham w Sutton *Nor*

SUTTON (St Michael and All Angels)   Castor w Sutton and Upton *Pet*

SUTTON (St Nicholas) *S'wark 25*   **P** *Hertf Coll Ox* **R** D HAZLEHURST,   **Par Dn** J A G POPP, **Hon Par Dn** R FARMAN

SUTTON (St Nicholas) (All Saints) (St Michael and All Angels) *Liv 10*   **P** *Patr Bd*   **TR** J L HIGHAM, **TV** A D J EWELL, J TATTERSALL, S A MATHER

SUTTON (St Thomas) *Bradf 8*   **P** *Ch Ch Ox* **V** C F TREVOR

SUTTON w Carlton and Normanton upon Trent and Marnham *S'well 3*   **P** *Bp*   **V** P M BISHOP

SUTTON, EAST (St Peter and St Paul)   Sutton Valence w E Sutton and Chart Sutton *Cant*

SUTTON, GREAT (St John the Evangelist) *Ches 9* **P** *V Eastham*   **V** T J VIRTUE

SUTTON AT HONE (St John the Baptist) *Roch 2*   **P** *D&C* **V** F E J WILLOUGHBY

SUTTON BASSETT (All Saints)   Ashley w Weston by Welland and Sutton Bassett *Pet*

SUTTON BENGER (All Saints)   Christian Malford w Sutton Benger etc *Bris*

SUTTON BONINGTON (St Michael) (St Anne) w Normanton-on-Soar *S'well 10*   **P** *Bp*   **R** A CLARKE

SUTTON BRIDGE (St Matthew) *Linc 16*   **P** *Bp* **V** G P WILLIAMS

SUTTON BY DOVER (St Peter and St Paul)   Gt Mongeham w Ripple and Sutton by Dover *Cant*

SUTTON CHENEY (St James)   Market Bosworth, Cadeby w Sutton Cheney etc *Leic*

SUTTON COLDFIELD (Holy Trinity) *Birm 9*   **P** *Bp* **R** E G LONGMAN,   **C** M J PARTRIDGE,   **NSM** W A WOOD

SUTTON COLDFIELD (St Chad) *Birm 9*   **P** *Bp* **P** A W WATTS

SUTTON COLDFIELD (St Columba) *Birm 9*   **P** *Bp* **V** R F JENKINS

SUTTON COURTENAY (All Saints) w Appleford *Ox 10* **P** *D&C Windsor*   **P-in-c** A L THOMAS

SUTTON GREEN (All Souls)   Woking St Pet *Guildf*

SUTTON HILL (Pastoral Centre)   Madeley *Heref*

SUTTON IN ASHFIELD (St Mary Magdalene) *S'well 4* **P** *Bp*   **V** D WALKER,   **C** B G DUCKWORTH, H R SMITH

SUTTON IN ASHFIELD (St Michael and All Angels) *S'well 4*   **P** *Bp*   **P-in-c** D WALKER, **C** B G DUCKWORTH

SUTTON IN HOLDERNESS (St Michael) *York 15* **P** *Abp*   **V** M P CHAFFEY

SUTTON LE MARSH (St Clement)   Sutton, Huttoft and Anderby *Linc*

SUTTON MADDOCK (St Mary)   Kemberton, Sutton Maddock and Stockton *Lich*

SUTTON MANDEVILLE (All Saints)   Fovant, Sutton Mandeville and Teffont Evias etc *Sarum*

SUTTON MONTIS (Holy Trinity)   Queen Camel w W Camel, Corton Denham etc *B & W*

SUTTON NEW TOWN (St Barnabas) *S'wark 25*   **P** *Bp* **V** T G LEARY,   **NSM** O WHYMAN

SUTTON ON DERWENT (St Michael)   Elvington w Sutton on Derwent and E Cottingwith *York*

SUTTON ON PLYM (St John the Evangelist) *Ex 24* **P** *Keble Coll Ox*   **V** B R LAY

SUTTON-ON-SEA (St Clement)   Sutton, Huttoft and Anderby *Linc*

SUTTON ON THE FOREST (All Hallows) *York 5* **P** *Ld Chan*   **P-in-c** T A McCOULOUGH

SUTTON ON THE HILL (St Michael)   Ch Broughton w Barton Blount, Boylestone etc *Derby*

SUTTON-ON-TRENT (All Saints)   Sutton w Carlton and Normanton upon Trent etc *S'well*

SUTTON PARK (St Andrew)   Sutton St Jas and Wawne *York*

SUTTON ST EDMUND (St Edmund)   The Suttons w Tydd *Linc*

SUTTON ST JAMES (St James)   as above

SUTTON ST MARY (otherwise known as Long Sutton) (St Mary) *Linc 16*   **P** *Lady McGeoch* **V** O G FOLKARD,   **NSM** R SPIVEY

SUTTON ST MICHAEL (St Michael)   Sutton St Nicholas w Sutton St Michael *Heref*

SUTTON ST NICHOLAS   Lutton w Gedney Drove End, Dawsmere *Linc*

SUTTON ST NICHOLAS (St Nicholas) w Sutton St Michael *Heref 4*   **P** *Bp*   **R** M A PAICE

SUTTON UNDER BRAILES (St Thomas a Becket) *Cov 9* **P** *Bp*   **R** N J MORGAN,   **NSM** J W ROLFE

SUTTON VALENCE (St Mary the Virgin) w East Sutton and Chart Sutton *Cant 15*   **P** *Abp York* **V** D R BARKER

SUTTON VENY (St John the Evangelist)   Heytesbury and Sutton Veny *Sarum*

SUTTON WALDRON (St Bartholomew)   The Iwernes, Sutton Waldron and Fontmell Magna *Sarum*

SUTTONS w Tydd, The *Linc 16*   **P** *Ld Chan (1 turn),* *V Long Sutton (2 turns)*   **V** P V NOBLE

SWABY (St Nicholas)   Withern *Linc*

SWADLINCOTE (Emmanuel) *Derby 16*   **P** *V Gresley* **V** R M PARSONS

SWAFFHAM (St Peter and St Paul) *Nor 18*   **P** *Bp* **V** M P GREEN

SWAFFHAM BULBECK (St Mary) *Ely 3*   **P** *Bp* **P-in-c** I R SECRETT

SWAFFHAM PRIOR (St Mary) *Ely 3*   **P** *D&C* **P-in-c** I R SECRETT

SWAFIELD (St Nicholas)   Trunch *Nor*

SWAINSTHORPE (St Peter) w Newton Flotman *Nor 13* **P** *Bp*   **R** G HEDGER

SWAINSWICK (Blessed Virgin Mary) w Langridge *B & W 10*   **P** *Or Coll Ox and Ld Chan (alt)* **R** V F E ROGERS

SWALCLIFFE (St Peter and St Paul)   Epwell w Sibford, Swalcliffe and Tadmarton *Ox*

SWALECLIFFE (St John the Baptist)   Whitstable *Cant*

SWALEDALE *Ripon 2*   **P** *Bp*   **V** P S MIDWOOD

SWALLOW (Holy Trinity) *Linc 5*   **P** *Rev J R H and H C Thorold, DBP, Bp, and Earl of Yarborough (by turn)*   **R** P S C WALKER

SWALLOWCLIFFE (St Peter)   Tisbury *Sarum*

SWALLOWFIELD (All Saints) *Ox 15*   **P** *D&C Heref* **V** J G SUMNER

SWALWELL (Holy Trinity) *Dur 5*   **P** *R Whickham* **V** J M H GIBSON

SWAN *Ox 24*   **P** *Patr Bd*   **TV** D A HISCOCK

SWANAGE (All Saints) (St Mary the Virgin) and Studland
Sarum 9 **P** *Patr Bd* **TR** D K CALLARD,
TV F SCAMMELL, A A ROBERTS, **NSM** C P MERRICK,
Hon Par Dn J A FRY
SWANBOROUGH *Sarum 9* **P** *Patr Bd*
TR J C WHETTEM, **TV** J D N GRAY, **C** E J CHITHAM
SWANBOURNE (St Swithun) Mursley w Swanbourne
and Lt Horwood *Ox*
SWANLAND (St Barnabas) N Ferriby *York*
SWANLEY (St Mary) *Roch 2* **P** *Guild of All So*
V P G EDWARDS, **C** M N R BOWIE, **NSM** R H COLLINS
SWANLEY (St Paul) *Roch 2* **P** *Merchant Taylors' Co*
V D J BETTS
SWANMORE (St Barnabas) *Portsm 1* **P** *DBP*
V M R WELCH
**SWANMORE (St Michael and All Angels) w Havenstreet
(St Peter)** *Portsm 7* **P** *SMF*
P-in-c S M CHALONER, M J SHEFFIELD, **C** M A J EXELL,
NSM T F SEAR, T I CARD
SWANNINGTON (St George) Ravenstone and
Swannington *Leic*
SWANNINGTON (St Margaret) Alderford w
Attlebridge and Swannington *Nor*
SWANSCOMBE (St Peter and St Paul) *Roch 4* **P** *DBP*
R T J MERCER
SWANTON ABBOTT (St Michael) w Skeyton *Nor 9*
P *J T D Shaw Esq* **R** *Vacant* Swanton Abbott
(069269) 212
**SWANTON MORLEY (All Saints) w Beetley w East
Bilney and Hoe** *Nor 19* **P** *G&C Coll Cam, Ld Chan,
and DBP (by turn)* **R** L A WILMAN
SWANTON NOVERS (St Edmund) Melton Constable
w Swanton Novers *Nor*
SWANWICK (St Andrew) and Pentrich *Derby 1*
P *Wright Trustees and Duke of Devonshire (alt)*
V P A B VESSEY, **NSM** C C WARNER
SWANWICK (St Barnabas) Sarisbury *Portsm*
SWARBY (St Mary and All Saints) S Lafford *Linc*
SWARCLIFFE (St Luke) Seacroft *Ripon*
**SWARDESTON (St Mary the Virgin) w East Carleton,
Intwood, Keswick and Ketteringham** *Nor 13* **P** *Bp,
DBP, and Miss M B Unthank (jt)* **R** G M C JONES
SWARKESTONE (St James) Barrow-on-Trent w
Twyford and Swarkestone *Derby*
SWARTHMORE (Mission Church) Pennington w
Lindal and Marton *Carl*
SWATON (St Michael) Helpringham w Hale *Linc*
SWAVESEY (St Andrew) *Ely 5* **P** *Jes Coll Cam*
V J D YULE, **NSM** A F JESSON
SWAY (St Luke) *Win 10* **P** *Bp* **V** N R MADDOCK
SWAYFIELD (St Nicholas) Corby Glen *Linc*
SWEFFLING (St Mary) Rendham w Sweffling *St E*
SWELL (St Catherine) Curry Rivel w Fivehead and
Swell *B & W*
SWELL, LOWER (St Mary) Longborough, Sezincote,
Condicote and the Swells *Glouc*
SWELL, UPPER (St Mary) as above
SWEPSTONE (St Peter) Appleby Magna and Swepstone
w Snarestone *Leic*
SWERFORD (St Mary) Hook Norton w Gt Rollright,
Swerford etc *Ox*
SWETTENHAM (St Peter) Brereton w Swettenham
Ches
SWILLAND (St Mary) Clopton w Otley, Swilland and
Ashbocking *St E*
SWILLINGTON (St Mary) *Ripon 8* **P** *Bp*
R K WILLIAMS
SWIMBRIDGE (St James the Apostle) and West Buckland
Ex 18 **P** *Bp and Trustees of Earl Fortescue (jt)*
V P BOWERS
SWINBROOK (St Mary) Asthall and Swinbrook w
Widford *Ox*
SWINDERBY (All Saints) *Linc 18* **P** *Bp, Ld Chan,
E M K Kirk Esq, and D&C (by turn)* **V** G C GOALBY
SWINDON (All Saints) *Bris 10* **P** *Bp*
P-in-c P J BENNETT
SWINDON (Christ Church) (St Mary) *Bris 13* **P** *Ld Chan*
V O C BARRACLOUGH, **C** J W F GOSLING, R W SANDAY
SWINDON Dorcan *Bris 12* **P** *Bp* **C** R N HUNGERFORD
**SWINDON New Town (St Mark) (St Adhelm) (St Luke)
(St Saviour)** *Bris 13* **P** *Patr Bd* **TR** L R HURRELL,
TV M J FOUNTAINE, J E POTTER, **Hon C** F W T FULLER,
NSM A S PAGETT
SWINDON (St Andrew) (St John the Baptist) *Bris 13*
P *Ld Chan* **TR** N J MONK
SWINDON (St Augustine) *Bris 10* **P** *Bp* **V** C DOBB
SWINDON (St John the Evangelist) *Lich 6*
P *H Cooke Esq, A T Jenks Esq, and S King Esq (jt)*
P-in-c S E ABLEWHITE

**SWINDON (St Lawrence) w Uckington and Elmstone
Hardwicke** *Glouc 11* **P** *Bp* **R** M E BENNETT
SWINDON, NEW (St Barnabas) Gorse Hill *Bris 10* **P** *Bp*
V R J HARRIS
SWINDON, WEST The Lydiards *Bris*
SWINE (St Mary) *York 12* **P** *W J A Wilberforce and
Baroness de Stempel (jt)* **V** *Vacant* Hull (0482)
815250
SWINEFLEET (St Margaret) The Marshland *Sheff*
SWINESHEAD (St Mary) *Linc 21* **P** *Bp*
V D J OSBOURNE
SWINESHEAD (St Nicholas) The Stodden Churches
St Alb
**SWINFORD (All Saints) w Catthorpe, Shawell and
Stanford** *Leic 11* **P** *DBP and Ld Chan (alt)*
P-in-c P J C CLEMENTS, **NSM** R H HUTCHINGS
SWINFORD, OLD Stourbridge (St Mary) *Worc 11* **P** *Bp*
R D O BELL, **C** D W BUSK,
Hon Par Dn L J WOOLHOUSE
SWINGFIELD (St Peter) Hawkinge w Acrise and
Swingfield *Cant*
SWINHOPE (St Helen) Binbrook Gp *Linc*
SWINNOW (Christ the Saviour) Stanningley St Thos
Ripon
SWINSTEAD (St Mary) Corby Glen *Linc*
SWINTON (Holy Rood) *Man 2* **P** *TR Swinton and
Pendlebury* **V** M W DAGGETT
SWINTON (St Margaret) *Sheff 12* **P** *Sir Stephen Hastings*
V M R JACKSON
SWINTON (St Peter) All Saints and Pendlebury *Man 2*
P *Patr Bd* **TR** M R GRIFFITHS, **TV** W N A BARDSLEY,
C J G HAIGH, D A DAVIES
SWITHLAND (St Leonard) *Leic 7* **P** *Ld Chan*
P-in-c F R WALTERS
SWYNCOMBE (St Botolph) w Britwell Salome *Ox 1*
P *Bp and Ld Chan (alt)* **R** J A FURNESS,
NSM E R M HENDERSON
SWYNNERTON (St Mary) and Tittensor *Lich 19* **P** *Bp
and Simeon's Trustees (jt)* **R** B J BREWER,
NSM N M RUSSELL
SWYRE (Holy Trinity) Bride Valley *Sarum*
SYDE (St Mary) Brimpsfield, Cranham, Elkstone and
Syde *Glouc*
SYDENHAM (All Saints) *S'wark 4* **P** *V Sydenham St Bart*
P-in-c J O ARDLEY, **C** H D SHILSON-THOMAS,
Par Dn S M BURNETT
SYDENHAM (Holy Trinity) *S'wark 4* **P** *Simeon's
Trustees* **V** N E D S SCHIBILD, **C** R P DORMANDY
SYDENHAM (St Bartholmew) *S'wark 4* **P** *Earl of
Dartmouth* **V** D R JACKSON, **Par Dn** A M SHILSON-
THOMAS
SYDENHAM (St Mary) Chinnor w Emmington and
Sydenham etc *Ox*
SYDENHAM (St Philip) *S'wark 4* **P** *V Sydenham St Bart*
V P W TIERNAN
**SYDENHAM, LOWER (St Michael and All Angels) Bell
Green** *S'wark 4* **P** *Bp* **P-in-c** J O ARDLEY,
C H D SHILSON-THOMAS, **Par Dn** S M BURNETT,
NSM R W POTTIER
SYDENHAM DAMEREL (St Mary) Milton Abbot,
Dunterton, Lamerton etc *Ex*
SYDERSTONE (St Mary) Coxford Gp *Nor*
SYDLING (St Nicholas) Bradf Peverell, Stratton,
Frampton etc *Sarum*
SYERSTON (All Saints) E Stoke w Syerston *S'well*
SYKEHOUSE (Holy Trinity) Fishlake w Sykehouse,
Kirk Bramwith, Fenwick etc *Sheff*
SYLEHAM (St Mary) Hoxne w Denham, Syleham and
Wingfield *St E*
SYMONDS GREEN (Christ the King) Stevenage H Trin
St Alb
SYMONDSBURY (St John the Baptist) and Chideock
Sarum 3 **P** *Bp* **R** A C JONES
SYRESHAM (St James) Helmdon w Stuchbury and
Radstone etc *Pet*
SYSTON (St Anne) *Bris 2* **P** *Bp* **R** D G MITCHELL
SYSTON (St Mary) Barkston and Hough Gp *Linc*
SYSTON (St Peter and St Paul) *Leic 6* **P** *Ox Univ*
V K R COURT, **C** C A FLATTERS
SYSTONBY (not known) Melton Gt Framland *Leic*
SYWELL (St Peter and St Paul) Mears Ashby and
Hardwick and Sywell etc *Pet*
TABLEY, OVER (St Paul) and High Legh *Ches 12* **P** *Bp
and Mrs P H Langford-Brooke (1 turn)*, C L S Cornwall-
Legh (1 turn)* **P-in-c** W WATKINS
TACKLEY (St Nicholas) Steeple Aston w N Aston and
Tackley *Ox*
TACOLNESTON (All Saints) Wreningham *Nor*

TADCASTER (St Mary) w Newton Kyme *York 1* **P** *Abp*
  V M ANKER
**TADDINGTON (St Michael and All Angels), Chelmorton
  and Flagg, and Monyash** *Derby 4* **P** *V Bakewell*
  V E J THOMPSON
TADDIPORT (St Mary Magdalene) Gt and Lt
  Torrington and Frithelstock *Ex*
TADLEY (St Peter) (St Paul) *Win 4* **P** *Bp*
  R J M NOCKELS
TADLEY, NORTH (St Mary) *Win 4* **P** *Bp* **V** B J NORRIS
TADLOW (St Giles) Shingay Gp of Par *Ely*
TADMARTON (St Nicholas) Epwell w Sibford,
  Swalcliffe and Tadmarton *Ox*
TADWORTH (Good Shepherd) *S'wark 24*
  P *V Kingswood St Andr* **V** R H McLEAN, **C** C A WOOD
TAKELEY (Holy Trinity) w Little Canfield *Chelmsf 21*
  P *Bp and Ch Coll Cam* **R** E S BRITT
TALATON (St James the Apostle) Whimple, Talaton
  and Clyst St Lawr *Ex*
TALBOT VILLAGE (St Mark) *Sarum 8* **P** *Trustees*
  V C J F RUTLEDGE, **Par Dn** M F PALMER,
  NSM C H MEAD
TALKE O' THE HILL (St Martin) *Lich 15* **P** *V Audley*
  R J D HOLT
TALKIN (not known) Hayton St Mary *Carl*
TALLAND (St Tallan) *Truro 12* **P** *DBP and W Grundy-
  Mills Esq (alt)* **V** J K P S ROBERTSHAW
TALLINGTON (St Laurence) Uffington *Linc*
TAMERTON, NORTH (St Denis) Bolventor *Truro*
TAMERTON FOLIOT (St Mary) *Ex 23* **P** *Ld Chan*
  V C W H GOODWINS
TAMWORTH (St Editha) *Lich 5* **P** *Bp* **V** J A WIDDAS,
  C R W JACKSON, P J MOCKFORD, S G MAY
TANDRIDGE (St Peter) *S'wark 23* **P** *DBP* **V** *Vacant*
  Oxted (0883) 712432
TANFIELD (St Margaret) *Dur 8* **P** *Bp* **V** R SHAW
**TANFIELD, WEST (St Nicholas) and Well w Snape and
  North Stainley** *Ripon 3* **P** *Bp and Mrs M E Bourne-
  Arton (alt)* **R** D W EYLES
TANGLEY (St Thomas of Canterbury) Hatherden w
  Tangley, Weyhill and Penton Mewsey *Win*
TANGMERE (St Andrew) *Chich 3* **P** *Earl of March and
  Kinrara* **Hon Par Dn** B R RUNDLE
TANKERSLEY (St Peter) *Sheff 7* **P** *Sir Stephen Hastings*
  R N M HARRISON
TANNINGTON (St Ethelbert) Worlingworth, Southolt,
  Tannington, Bedfield etc *St E*
TANSLEY (Holy Trinity), Dethick, Lea and Holloway
  Derby 7 **P** *Bp, V Crich, and DBF (jt)* **R** J B HURST
TANSOR (St Mary) Warmington, Tansor, Cotterstock
  and Fotheringhay *Pet*
TANWORTH (St Mary Magdalene) *Birm 13*
  P *F D Muntz Esq* **V** M W TUNNICLIFFE
TANWORTH (St Patrick) Salter Street *Birm 13*
  P *V Tanworth* **V** C K RACE
TAPLOW (St Nicholas) Burnham w Dropmore,
  Hitcham and Taplow *Ox*
TARDEBIGGE (St Bartholomew) *Worc 7* **P** *Earl of
  Plymouth* **V** *Vacant*
TARLETON (Holy Trinity) *Blackb 6* **P** *St Pet Coll Ox*
  R W RILEY
TARLTON (St Osmund) Coates, Rodmarton and
  Sapperton etc *Glouc*
TARPORLEY (St Helen) *Ches 5* **P** *Bp (4 turns), D&C
  (1 turn), and Sir John Grey Regerton, Bt (1 turn)*
  R G L COOKSON
TARRANT GUNVILLE (St Mary) see below
TARRANT HINTON (St Mary) see below
TARRANT KEYNSTON (All Saints) see below
TARRANT MONKTON (All Saints) see below
TARRANT RUSHTON (St Mary) see below
TARRANT VALLEY *Sarum 7* **P** *Pemb Coll Cam
  (1 turn), Bp (2 turns), and Univ Coll Ox (1 turn)*
  R D C STEVENS
TARRING, WEST (St Andrew) *Chich 5* **P** *Abp*
  R W E JERVIS, **C** W DOYLE
TARRING NEVILLE (St Mary) Denton w S Heighton
  and Tarring Neville *Chich*
**TARRINGTON (St Philip and St James) w Stoke Edith,
  Aylton, Pixley, Munsley, Putley and Yarkhill** *Heref 6*
  P *A T Foley Esq, D&C, Hopton Trustees,
  H W Wiggin Esq, and J Hervey-Bathurst Esq (jt)*
  R J R SCARTH
TARVIN (St Andrew) *Ches 2* **P** *Bp* **V** A E BACKHOUSE
TASBURGH (St Mary) w Tharston, Forncett and Flordon
  Nor 11 **P** *MMCET, Bp, St Jo Coll Cam, and
  DBP (by turn)* **R** D R HARRISON
TASLEY (St Peter and St Paul) Bridgnorth, Tasley,
  Astley Abbotts, Oldbury etc *Heref*

TATENHILL (St Michael and All Angels) Dunstall w
  Rangemore and Tatenhill *Lich*
TATHAM (St James the Less) Wray w Tatham and
  Tatham Fells *Blackb*
TATHAM FELLS (Good Shepherd) as above
TATHWELL (St Vedast) Raithby *Linc*
TATSFIELD (St Mary) *S'wark 23* **P** *Bp*
  P-in-c C J CORKE
TATTENHALL (St Alban) and Handley *Ches 5* **P** *Bp and
  D&C (jt)* **R** G G TURNER
TATTENHAM CORNER (St Mark) and Burgh Heath
  Guildf 9 **P** *Bp* **V** M J BURNS
TATTENHOE (St Giles) Watling Valley *Ox*
TATTERFORD (St Margaret) Coxford Gp *Nor*
TATTERSETT (All Saints and St Andrew) as above
TATTERSHALL (Holy Trinity) Coningsby w
  Tattershall *Linc*
TATTINGSTONE (St Mary) Bentley w Tattingstone
  St E
TATWORTH (St John the Evangelist) *B & W 16*
  P *V Chard* **V** R C P TERRELL
TAUNTON (All Saints) *B & W 20* **P** *Bp* **V** A J WRIGHT
TAUNTON (Holy Trinity) *B & W 20* **P** *Bp* **V** M D LEWIS
TAUNTON (St Andrew) *B & W 20* **P** *Bp*
  V R E FLOWER, **NSM** C F CRAGGS
TAUNTON (St James) *B & W 20* **P** *Simeon's Trustees*
  V A P BANNISTER
TAUNTON (St John the Evangelist) *B & W 20* **P** *Bp*
  P-in-c D ROBERTS
TAUNTON (St Mary Magdalene) *B & W 20* **P** *Ch Patr
  Trust* **V** R F ACWORTH, **C** C C BROWN
TAUNTON (St Peter) Lyngford *B & W 20* **P** *Bp*
  V R J RAY, **C** M F W BOND, **NSM** P A SELF
TAVERHAM (St Edmund) w Ringland *Nor 4* **P** *Bp and
  Major J M Mills (alt)* **R** J E G CLARK
TAVISTOCK (St Eustachius) and Gulworthy (St Paul)
  Ex 25 **P** *Bp* **V** R T GILPIN, **Par Dn** R WARING,
  NSM R WARING
TAW VALLEY Newport, Bishops Tawton and Tawstock
  Ex
TAWSTOCK (St Peter) as above
**TAWTON, NORTH (St Peter), Bondleigh, Sampford
  Courtenay and Honeychurch** *Ex 12* **P** *MMCET, K Coll
  Cam, and D&C (jt)* **R** A R GIBSON
TAWTON, SOUTH (St Andrew) and Belstone *Ex 12*
  P *D&C Windsor and Bp (jt)* **R** N H BLISS
TAYNTON (St John the Evangelist) Burford w
  Fulbrook and Taynton *Ox*
TAYNTON (St Laurence) Highnam, Lassington,
  Rudford, Tibberton etc *Glouc*
TEALBY (All Saints) Walesby *Linc*
TEAN, UPPER (Christ Church) *Lich 12* **P** *R Checkley*
  V J L ASTON
TEBAY (St James) Orton and Tebay w Ravenstonedale
  etc *Carl*
TEDBURN ST MARY (St Mary) *Ex 6* **P** *DBP*
  R D R E WERNER
**TEDDINGTON (St Mark) and Hampton Wick (St John the
  Baptist)** *Lon 11* **P** *Bp* **V** J P WARNER
TEDDINGTON (St Mary) (St Alban the Martyr) *Lon 10*
  P *Bp* **V** R T CARTER
TEDDINGTON (St Nicholas) Overbury w Teddington,
  Alstone etc *Worc*
**TEDDINGTON (St Peter and St Paul) and Fulwell
  (St Michael and St George)** *Lon 10* **P** *Bp*
  V D H PALMER, **Hon C** M L NICHOLAS
TEDSTONE DELAMERE (St James) Edvin Loach w
  Tedstone Delamere etc *Heref*
TEDSTONE WAFER (St Mary) as above
TEFFONT EVIAS (St Michael) Fovant, Sutton
  Mandeville and Teffont Evias etc *Sarum*
TEFFONT MAGNA (St Edward) as above
TEIGH (Holy Trinity) Whissendine and Market Overton
  Pet 14 **P** *Bp and Lady Gretton (alt)* **R** P A PAYNTON
TEIGNGRACE (St Peter and St Paul) Highweek and
  Teigngrace *Ex*
**TEIGNMOUTH (St James) (St Michael the Archangel),
  Ideford w Luton, Ashcombe and Bishopsteignton** *Ex 6*
  P *Patr Bd* **TR** P G LUFF, **TV** D H JAMES,
  C D B M GILL, **Par Dn** J W DEBENHAM, C M S LUFF
**TELFORD, CENTRAL: Dawley, Lawley, Malinslee,
  Stirchley, Brookside and Hollinswood** *Lich 28*
  P *Patr Bd (3 turns), The Crown (1 turn)*
  TR G M K MORGAN, **TV** D W YABBACOME,
  N J KELLY, P G FLAWLEY, **Par Dn** J E BLAND,
  NSM T E DAVIS
TELFORD PARK (St Thomas) *S'wark 12* **P** *Trustees*
  P-in-c R W H ALLEN
TELLISFORD (All Saints) Rode Major *B & W*

TELSCOMBE (St Laurence) w Piddinghoe and Southease *Chich 18* **P** *Gorham Trustees* **R** R J G HOLMES

TEME VALLEY NORTH: Knighton-on-Teme, Lindridge, Pensax, Menith Wood, Stanford-on-Teme and Stockton *Worc 12* **P** *Bp and D&C (alt)* **R** R G SMITH

TEME VALLEY SOUTH: Eastham, Rochford, Stoke Bliss, Hanley Child, Hanley William and Kyre Wyard *Worc 12* **P** *Ld Chan, Bp, and Mrs V D Miles (by turn)* **R** M P LACK

TEMPLE (St Catherine) Blisland w St Breward *Truro*

TEMPLE BALSALL (St Mary) *Birm 13* **P** *Lady Leveson Hosp* **V** R H P WATSON WILLIAMS

TEMPLE BRUER (St John the Baptist) Graffoe *Linc*

TEMPLE CLOUD (St Barnabas) Clutton w Cameley *B & W*

TEMPLE EWELL (St Peter and St Paul) w Lydden *Cant 4* **P** *Abp* **R** P CHRISTIAN

TEMPLE FORTUNE (St Barnabas) *Lon 15* **P** *Bp* **V** C C TAYLOR

TEMPLE GRAFTON (St Andrew) w Binton *Cov 7* **P** *Dioc Trustees* **V** E F WILLIAMS

TEMPLE GUITING (St Mary) The Guitings, Cutsdean and Farmcote *Glouc*

TEMPLE HIRST (St John the Baptist) Haddlesey w Hambleton and Birkin *York*

TEMPLE NORMANTON (St James the Apostle) *Derby 5* **P** *Bp* **V** H R O ANDERSON

TEMPLE SOWERBY (St James) Kirkby Thore w Temple Sowerby and w Newbiggin *Carl*

TEMPLECOMBE (Blessed Virgin Mary) Abbas and Templecombe w Horsington *B & W*

TEMPLETON (St Margaret) Washfield, Stoodleigh, Withleigh etc *Ex*

TEMPSFORD (St Peter) Blunham w Tempsford and Lt Barford *St Alb*

TEN MILE BANK (St Mark) Hilgay *Ely*

TENBURY (St Mary) *Heref 12* **P** *Rev F J Evans* **TR** D S DORMOR, **TV** G P HOWELL, **C** C I FLETCHER

TENBURY (St Michael and All Angels) *Heref 12* **P** *St Mich Coll* **NSM** J GRAY

TENDRING (St Edmund King and Martyr) and Little Bentley w Beaufort cum Moze *Chelmsf 26* **P** *Em Coll Cam, DBP, and Ball Coll Ox (by turn)* **R** D R TILSTON

TENTERDEN (St Michael and All Angels) *Cant 11* **P** *Abp* **V** A H NORMAN

TENTERDEN (St Mildred) w Smallhythe *Cant 11* **P** *D&C* **V** D G TRUSTRAM

TERLING (All Saints) Fairstead w Terling and White Notley etc *Chelmsf*

TERRIERS (St Francis) *Ox 29* **P** *V High Wycombe* **V** S PURNELL, **NSM** M J WILLIAMS

TERRINGTON (All Saints) Bulmer w Dalby, Terrington and Welburn *York*

TERRINGTON ST CLEMENT (St Clement) *Ely 17* **P** *The Crown* **V** J F WILSON

TERRINGTON ST JOHN (St John) *Ely 17* **P** *The Crown* **V** R C WRIGHT

TERWICK (St Peter) Rogate w Terwick and Trotton w Chithurst *Chich*

TESTON (St Peter and St Paul) Wateringbury w Teston and W Farleigh *Roch*

TESTWOOD (St Winfrid) Totton *Win*

TETBURY (St Mary the Virgin) w Beverston *Glouc 16* **P** *Lt-Col J J B Pope (5 turns), The Crown (1 turn)* **V** J W HAWTHORNE

TETCOTT (Holy Cross) Ashwater, Halwill, Beaworthy, Clawton etc *Ex*

TETFORD (St Mary) S Ormsby Gp *Linc*

TETNEY (St Peter and St Paul), Marshchapel and North Coates *Linc 10* **P** *Bp (2 turns), Trustees (1 turn), and Duchy of Lanc (1 turn)* **R** *Vacant* Marshchapel (047286) 599

TETSWORTH (St Giles), Adwell w South Weston, Lewknor and Stoke Talmage w Wheatfield *Ox 1* **P** *Bp, Peache Trustees, W R A Birch Reynardson Esq, Earl of Macclesfield, and Mrs D C H Mann (jt)* **R** H B L BRIERLY, **Dss** M A BRIERLY

TETTENHALL REGIS (St Michael and All Angels) *Lich 6* **P** *Patr Bd* **TR** J D MAKEPEACE, **TV** G R HARPER, J J N QUIN, **C** S M SICHEL, D J WALLER

TETTENHALL WOOD (Christ Church) *Lich 6* **P** *Patr Bd* **TR** G H SMITH, **TM** M A SMALLMAN, **TV** S H CARTER

TEVERSAL (St Katherine) *S'well 4* **P** *DBP* **R** D A JONES

TEVERSHAM (All Saints) *Ely 6* **P** *Bp* **P-in-c** C D BOULTON, **C** P K REED

TEW, GREAT (St Michael and All Angels) w Little Tew *Ox 3* **P** *Bp and J M Johnston Esq (jt)* **P-in-c** H S COLCHESTER

TEW, LITTLE (St John the Evangelist) Gt w Lt Tew *Ox*

TEWIN (St Peter) Datchworth w Tewin *St Alb*

TEWKESBURY (Holy Trinity) *Glouc 9* **P** *Ch Soc Trust* **V** J F HAUGHAN

TEWKESBURY (St Mary the Virgin) w Walton Cardiff *Glouc 9* **P** *Ld Chan* **V** M E TAVINOR, **C** S HOLMES

TEY, GREAT (St Barnabas) and Wakes Colne w Chappel *Chelmsf 20* **P** *DBP, PCC Chappel and Bp (jt)* **R** J RICHARDSON

TEY, LITTLE (St James the Less) Marks Tey w Aldham and Lt Tey *Chelmsf*

TEYNHAM (St Mary) (Primary School Worship Centre) *Cant 6* **P** *Adn Cant* **P-in-c** G H COLMAN

THAKEHAM (St Mary) Sullington and Thakeham w Warminghurst *Chich*

THAME (All Saints) (St Mary the Virgin) w Towersey *Ox 1* **P** *Peache Trustees* **V** C C NEAL, **C** I H GILMOUR, **Par Dn** C D STIRLING, **Hon C** B S W GREEN

THAMES DITTON (St Nicholas) *Guildf 8* **P** *K Coll Cam* **V** K J COVE

THAMES VIEW (Christ Church) Barking St Marg w St Patr *Chelmsf*

THAMESMEAD (Church of the Cross) (St Paul's Ecumenical Centre) *S'wark 1* **P** *Bp* **TR** C M BYERS, **TV** N A McKINNON, I HARPER, **Par Dn** J WADSWORTH

THANINGTON (St Nicholas) (St Faith's Mission Church) *Cant 3* **P** *Abp* **V** L J W COX

THARSTON (St Mary) Tasburgh w Tharston, Forncett and Flordon *Nor*

THATCHAM (St Mary) *Ox 14* **P** *Woodard Sch* **V** P L SEAR, **C** J M P HEDGES, **Par Dn** V J HICKS

THAXTED (St John the Baptist, Our Lady and St Laurence) *Chelmsf 25* **P** *Bp* **V** R N ROWE

THE: *see under substantive place names*

THEALE (Christ Church) Wedmore w Theale and Blackford *B & W*

THEALE (Holy Trinity) and Englefield *Ox 12* **P** *Magd Coll Ox and Englefield Est Trust (jt)* **R** D RICE, **Hon C** M A P WOOD

THEBERTON (St Peter) Kelsale-cum-Carlton, Middleton-cum-Fordley etc *St E*

THEDDINGWORTH (All Saints) Husbands Bosworth w Mowsley and Knaptoft etc *Leic*

THEDDLETHORPE (St Helen) *Linc 12* **P** *Baroness Willoughby de Eresby (2 turns), Bp (1 turn)* **P-in-c** D LUMB

THELBRIDGE (St David) Witheridge, Thelbridge, Creacombe, Meshaw etc *Ex*

THELNETHAM (St Nicholas) Hepworth, Hinderclay, Wattisfield and Thelnetham *St E*

THELVETON (St Andrew) Dickleburgh, Langmere, Shimpling, Thelveton etc *Nor*

THELWALL (All Saints) *Ches 4* **P** *Keble Coll Ox* **V** M L RIDLEY

THEMELTHORPE (St Andrew) Twyford w Guist w Bintry w Themelthorpe etc *Nor*

THENFORD (St Mary the Virgin) Greatworth and Marston St Lawrence etc *Pet*

THERFIELD (St Mary the Virgin) w Kelshall *St Alb 5* **P** *Ld Chan and D&C St Paul's (alt)* **R** E L R SMITH

THETFORD (St Cuthbert) (St Peter) *Nor 17* **P** *Patr Bd* **TR** A D McGREGOR, **TV** M J M HUGHES, K WILSON, **C** A V HEDGES, **NSM** B R HOGWOOD

THETFORD, LITTLE (St George) Stretham w Thetford *Ely*

THEYDON BOIS (St Mary) *Chelmsf 2* **P** *M G E N Buxton Esq* **V** D DRISCOLL, **NSM** K G PATTINSON

THEYDON GARNON (All Saints) *Chelmsf 2* **P** *Bp* **P-in-c** R A K LOXLEY

THEYDON MOUNT (St Michael) Stapleford Tawney w Theydon Mt *Chelmsf*

THIMBLEBY (St Margaret) *Linc 11* **P** *Bp* **P-in-c** S W PEARCE

THIRKLEBY (All Saints) w Kilburn and Bagby *York 20* **P** *Abp* **V** D G BILES

THIRSK (St Mary) *York 20* **P** *Abp* **TR** R LEWIS, **TV** R M KIRKMAN, **C** A J HARDING

THISTLETON (St Nicholas) Greetham and Thistleton w Stretton and Clipsham *Pet*

THIXENDALE (St Mary) Sledmere and Cowlam w Fridaythorpe, Fimer etc *York*

THOCKRINGTON (St Aidan) Chollerton w Birtley and Thockrington *Newc*

THOMPSON (St Martin) Caston w Griston, Merton, Thompson etc *Nor*

THONGSBRIDGE (St Andrew)   Upper Holme Valley
Wakef
THORESBY, NORTH (St Helen) Linc 10
   P Mrs W B Ashley   R R K EMM
THORESBY, SOUTH (St Andrew)   Withern Linc
THORESWAY (St Mary)   Swallow Linc
THORGANBY (All Saints)   Binbrook Gp Linc
THORGANBY (St Helen)   Wheldrake w Thorganby
York
THORINGTON (St Peter) w Wenhaston and Bramfield
St E 15   P Ch Patr Trust (1 turn), Ld Chan (3 turns)
   V J E MURRELL
THORLEY (St James the Great) St Alb 4   P Bp
   R C P SLAUGHTER,   Par Dn   A M LOVEGROVE,
   NSM   D HIRST
THORLEY (St Swithun) Portsm 8   P Bp
   V K R CHEESEMAN
THORMANBY (St Mary Magdalene)   Brafferton w
Pilmoor, Myton on Swale etc York
THORNABY ON TEES (St Luke) (St Mark) (St Paul)
(St Peter ad Vincula) York 19   P Abp
   TR D L TURNHAM,   TV C A MITCHELL,
   D L SPOKES, G WARD
THORNAGE (All Saints) w Brinton w Hunworth and Stody
Nor 22   P Lord Hastings and DBP (alt)
   P-in-c K G TAYLOR
THORNBOROUGH (St Mary)   Nash w Thornton,
Beachampton and Thornborough Ox
THORNBURY (St Anna)   Bredenbury w Grendon
Bishop and Wacton etc Heref
THORNBURY (St Margaret) Bradf 3   P Vs Bradf,
Calverley and Laisterdyke (jt)   V J K DAY,
   NSM A J CLARKE
THORNBURY (St Mary) (St Paul) Glouc 7   P Ch Ch Ox
   V M G P VOOGHT,   C R P HARLEY,   P M LYES-WILSDON
THORNBURY (St Peter)   Black Torrington, Bradf w
Cookbury etc Ex
THORNBY (St Helen)   Cottesbrooke w Gt Creaton and
Thornby Pet
THORNCOMBE (Blessed Virgin Mary) w Winsham and
Cricket St Thomas B & W 16   P Bp Worc and Exors
Comdr W J Eyre (jt)   V B R SUTTON
THORNDON (All Saints) w Rishangles, Stoke Ash, Thwaite
and Wetheringsett cum Brockford St E 16   P Bp,
Capt F P Brooke-Popham, MMCET, and Ch Soc
Trust (jt)   R D G WOODWARDS,   Par Dn C E BROOKS
THORNE (St Nicholas) Sheff 11   P Bp   V P M BROWN,
   C S M WRIGHT
THORNE COFFIN (St Andrew)   Tintinhull w
Chilthorne Domer, Yeovil Marsh etc B & W
THORNE ST MARGARET (St Margaret)   Wellington
and Distr B & W
THORNER (St Peter) Ripon 8   P Earl of Mexborough
   V S J BROWN,   NSM A B HAIGH
THORNES (St James) w Christ Church Wakef 12   P DBP
   V G GOOD
THORNEY CLOSE (St Peter)   Sunderland Springwell w
Thorney Close Dur
THORNEY, WEST (St Nicholas)   Southbourne w W
Thorney Chich
THORNEY ABBEY (St Mary and St Botolph) Ely 19
   P Bp   V R H ROLLETT
THORNEY HILL (All Saints)   Bransgore Win
THORNEY w WIGSLEY AND BROADHOLME (St
Helen)   Harby w Thorney and N and S Clifton S'well
THORNEYBURN (St Aidan)   Bellingham/Otterburn
Gp Newc
THORNFALCON (Holy Cross)   Ruishton w
Thornfalcon B & W
THORNFORD (St Mary Magdalene)   Bradf Abbas and
Thornford w Beer Hackett Sarum
THORNGUMBALD (St Mary)   Burstwick w
Thorngumbald York
THORNHAM (All Saints)   Hunstanton St Mary w
Ringstead Parva, Holme etc Nor
THORNHAM (St James) Man 18   P Bp   V G M IKIN
THORNHAM w Gravel Hole (St John) Man 19
   P R Middleton St Leon   V R MOUGHTIN
THORNHAM MAGNA (St Mary Magdalene) w Thornham
Parva, Gislingham and Mellis St E 16   P Bp, Lord
Henniker, and MMCET (jt)   R R W LEE
THORNHAM PARVA (St Mary)   Thornhams Magna
and Parva, Gislingham and Mellis St E
THORNHAUGH (St Andrew)   Wittering w Thornhaugh
and Wansford Pet
THORNHILL (Mission Church)   Beckermet St Jo and St
Bridget w Ponsonby Carl
THORNHILL (St Michael and All Angels) Wakef 10
   P Lord Savile   R N D J WEBB

THORNHILL LEES (Holy Innocents w St Mary) Wakef 10
   P Bp   V J R ASHWORTH
THORNLEY (St Bartholomew) Dur 1   P Bp
   P-in-c S WARD
THORNLEY (St Bartholomew)   Wolsingham and
Thornley Dur
THORNTHWAITE (St Mary the Virgin) cum Braithwaite
and Newlands Carl 6   P V Crosthwaite and V Keswick
St Jo (alt)   V D C W POST
THORNTHWAITE (St Saviour)   Dacre w Hartwith and
Darley w Thornthwaite Ripon
THORNTON (St Frideswyde) Liv 5   P R Sefton
   V C RENWICK
THORNTON (St James) Bradf 1   P V Bradf
   Hon C A HOLLIDAY
THORNTON (St Michael)   Seaton Ross Gp of Par York
THORNTON (St Michael and All Angels)   Nash w
Thornton, Beachampton and Thornborough Ox
THORNTON (St Peter), Bagworth and Stanton Leic 12
   P MMCET   V A S COSTERTON
THORNTON (St Wilfrid)   Martin w Thornton Linc
THORNTON, LITTLE (St John) Blackb 13   P Bp
   V A J CHENNELL
THORNTON CURTIS (St Laurence)   Ulceby Gp Linc
THORNTON DALE (All Saints) and Ellerburne w Wilton
York 21   P Mrs E M Morgan and Abp (alt)
   R J D S CLARK
THORNTON HEATH (St Jude w St Aidan) S'wark 22
   P Bp   V C H A GARRETT
THORNTON HEATH (St Paul) S'wark 22   P The Crown
   V Vacant   081-653 2762
THORNTON HOUGH (All Saints) Ches 9   P Simeon's
Trustees   V J C CLARKE
THORNTON IN CRAVEN (St Mary)   Broughton,
Marton and Thornton Bradf
THORNTON IN LONSDALE (St Oswald) w Burton in
Lonsdale Bradf 6   P Bp   V M J BAMFORTH
THORNTON LE BEANS (not known)   The Thorntons
and The Otteringtons York
THORNTON LE FEN (St Peter)   Brothertoft Gp Linc
THORNTON-LE-FYLDE (Christ Church) Blackb 13
   P Trustees   V D PRYTHERCH,   C A J FULLER
THORNTON-LE-MOOR (All Saints)   S Kelsey Gp Linc
THORNTON LE MOORS (St Mary) w Ince and Elton
Ches 3   P Bp   V J F HUDGHTON
THORNTON LE STREET (St Leonard)   The Thorntons
and The Otteringtons York
THORNTON RUST (Mission Room)   Aysgarth and
Bolton cum Redmire Ripon
THORNTON STEWARD (St Oswald)   Thornton
Watlass w Thornton Steward Ripon
THORNTON WATLASS (St Mary the Virgin) w Thornton
Steward Ripon 4   P Bp and D S Dodsworth Esq (jt)
   C-in-c R W GROSSE
THORNTONS and The Otteringtons, The York 20
   P Ch Ch Ox, Linc Coll Ox, and Abp (by turn)
   R E W SPILLER
THOROTON (St Helena)   Whatton w Aslockton,
Hawksworth, Scarrington etc S'well
THORP ARCH (All Saints) w Walton York 1
   P G H H Wheler Esq and G Lane Fox Esq (alt)
   P-in-c P W THOMAS
THORPE (St Andrew) (Good Shepherd) Nor 6   P Trustees
of W J Birkbeck Esq   R A J SNASDELL,   C A J TODD
Thorpe (St Laurence)   Farndon w Thorpe, Hawton and
Cotham S'well
THORPE (St Leonard)   Fenny Bentley, Kniveton,
Thorpe and Tissington Derby
THORPE (St Mary) Guildf 11   P Keble Coll Ox
   V M J H ROTHWELL
THORPE (St Matthew) Nor 6   P R Thorpe St Andr
   V C J BLACKMAN,   C D K ALEXANDER
THORPE ABBOTS (All Saints)   Scole, Brockdish,
Billingford, Thorpe Abbots etc Nor
THORPE ACHURCH (St John the Baptist)   Aldwincle
w Thorpe Achurch, Pilton, Wadenhoe etc Pet
THORPE ARNOLD (St Mary the Virgin)   Melton Gt
Framland Leic
THORPE AUDIN (Mission Room)   Badsworth Wakef
THORPE BASSETT (All Saints)   Rillington w
Scampston, Wintringham etc York
THORPE BAY (St Augustine) Chelmsf 15   P Bp
   V E H BEAVAN,   C R B THOMPSON
THORPE CONSTANTINE (St Constantine) Lich 5
   P Mrs E V G Inge-Innes   P-in-c A C SOLOMON
THORPE EDGE (St John the Divine) Bradf 3
   P Vs Bradf, Calverley, and Idle (jt)   V M W THOMPSON
THORPE END (St David)   Gt w Lt Plumstead and
Witton Nor

THORPE EPISCOPI (St Andrew)   Thorpe *Nor*
THORPE HAMLET (St Matthew)   Thorpe St Matt *Nor*
THORPE HESLEY (Holy Trinity) *Sheff 6*   **P** *Sir Stephen*
Hastings   **V** A G ANDERSON,   **Par Dn** L E POCOCK
THORPE LANGTON (St Leonard)   Church Langton w
Tur Langton, Thorpe Langton etc *Leic*
THORPE-LE-SOKEN (St Michael) *Chelmsf 26*   **P** *Bp*
V B J SHANNON
THORPE MALSOR (All Saints)   Broughton w
Loddington and Cransley etc *Pet*
THORPE MANDEVILLE (St John the Baptist)
Culworth w Sulgrave and Thorpe Mandeville *Pet*
THORPE MARKET (St Margaret)   Trunch *Nor*
THORPE MORIEUX (St Mary the Virgin)   Rattlesden
w Thorpe Morieux and Brettenham *St E*
THORPE-NEXT-HADDISCOE (St Matthias)
Raveningham *Nor*
THORPE-ON-THE-HILL (St Michael)   Swinderby *Linc*
THORPE SALVIN (St Peter)   Harthill and Thorpe
Salvin *Sheff*
THORPE SATCHVILLE (St Michael and All Angels)
S Croxton Gp *Leic*
THORPE ST PETER (St Peter) *Linc 8*   **P** *Bp*   **V** *Vacant*
THORPE WILLOUGHBY (St Francis of Assisi)
Brayton *York*
THORRINGTON (St Mary Magdalene)   Frating w
Thorrington *Chelmsf*
THORVERTON (St Thomas of Canterbury), Cadbury,
Upton Pyne, Brampford Speke and Newton St Cyres *Ex 2*
P *Ld Chan (1 turn), Patr Bd (3 turns)*   **TR** P E JEFFORD,
TV D WILLIAMS
THRANDESTON (St Margaret)   N Hartismere *St E*
THRAPSTON (St James) *Pet 10*   **P** *Ld Chan*   **R** D R BIRD
THREAPWOOD (St John)   Malpas and Threapwood
Ches
THRECKINGHAM (St Peter)   S Lafford *Linc*
THREE BRIDGES (St Richard)   Crawley *Chich*
THREE LEGGED CROSS (All Saints)   Verwood *Sarum*
THRELKELD (St Mary) *Carl 6*   **P** *Trustees*
P-in-c C G DARRALL
THREXTON (All Saints)   Gt and Lt Cressingham w
Threxton *Nor*
THRIGBY (St Mary)   Filby w Thrigby, Mautby,
Stokesby, Herringby etc *Nor*
THRIMBY (St Mary)   Morland, Thrimby and Gt
Strickland *Carl*
THRINGSTONE (St Andrew) *Leic 8*   **P** *Duchy of Lanc*
V B MATTHEWS
THRIPLOW (St George) *Ely 8*   **P** *Bp*   **P-in-c** J B MYNORS
THROCKING (Holy Trinity)   Cottered w Broadfield and
Throcking *St Alb*
THROCKLEY (St Mary the Virgin)   Newburn *Newc*
THROCKMORTON (Chapelry)   Abberton, Naunton
Beauchamp and Bishampton etc *Worc*
THROOP (St Paul) *Win 7*   **P** *Ch Soc Trust*
V G E WALLACE
THROPTON (St Andrew)   Rothbury *Newc*
THROWLEIGH (St Mary the Virgin)   Chagford w
Gidleigh and Throwleigh *Ex*
THROWLEY (St Michael and All Angels)   Selling w
Throwley, Sheldwich w Badlesmere etc *Cant*
THRUMPTON (All Saints) *S'well 10*   **P** *G F Seymour Esq*
V A C SUTHERLAND
THRUSCROSS (All Saints)   Dacre w Hartwith and
Darley w Thornthwaite *Ripon*
THRUSHELTON (St George)   Marystowe, Coryton,
Stowford, Lewtrenchard etc *Ex*
THRUSSINGTON (Holy Trinity)   Hoby cum Rotherby
w Brooksby, Ragdale & Thru'ton *Leic*
THRUXTON (St Bartholomew)   Kingstone w
Clehonger, Eaton Bishop etc *Heref*
THRUXTON (St Peter and St Paul)   Appleshaw,
Kimpton, Thruxton and Fyfield *Win*
THRYBERGH (St Leonard) w Hooton Roberts *Sheff 6*
P *Sir Stephen Hastings and J C M Fullerton Esq (jt)*
R D J FORD,   **C** C T GIBSON
THUNDERSLEY (St Michael and All Angels) (St Peter)
Chelmsf 12   **P** *Bp*   **R** P J SANDBERG,
C D L HUMPHREY
THUNDERSLEY, NEW (St George) *Chelmsf 12*   **P** *Bp*
V J R D KEMP,   **C** R I WILKINSON
THUNDRIDGE (St Mary) *St Alb 8*   **P** *Bp*
V H J SHARMAN
THURCASTON (All Saints) *Leic 12*   **P** *Em Coll Cam*
R D F BREWIN
THURCROFT (St Simon and St Jude) *Sheff 5*   **P** *Bp*
V J K BUTTERFIELD

THURGARTON (St Peter) w Hoveringham and Bleasby w
Halloughton *S'well 15*   **P** *Ld Chan and Trin Coll*
Cam (alt)   **V** R A KIRTON,   **NSM** S A DAVENPORT
THURGOLAND (Holy Trinity)   Wortley w Thurgoland
Sheff
THURLASTON (All Saints)   Enderby w Lubbesthorpe
and Thurlaston *Leic*
THURLASTON (St Edmund King and Martyr)
Dunchurch *Cov*
THURLBY (St Firmin) w Carlby *Linc 13*   **P** *Bp, Burghley*
Ho Preservation Trust, and DBP (by turn)
V M J N HOWES
THURLBY (St Germain) w Norton Disney *Linc 18*   **P** *Bp*
and W R S Brown Esq (alt)   **R** D T OSBORN
THURLEIGH (St Peter) *St Alb 21*   **P** *Bp*
V A P MOTTRAM
THURLESTONE (All Saints) w South Milton *Ex 14*
P *D&C*   **R** P S STEPHENS
THURLOW, GREAT (All Saints)   Haverhill w
Withersfield, the Wrattings etc *St E*
THURLOW, LITTLE (St Peter)   as above
THURLOXTON (St Giles)   N Newton w St
Michaelchurch, Thurloxton etc *B & W*
THURLSTONE (St Saviour)   Penistone and Thurlstone
Wakef
THURLTON (All Saints)   Raveningham *Nor*
THURMASTON (St Michael and All Angels) *Leic 6*   **P** *Bp*
V T R MARTIN,   **C** M J COURT
THURNBY (St Luke) w Stoughton *Leic 5*   **P** *MMCET*
V G W DUNSETH
THURNBY LODGE (Christ Church) *Leic 1*   **P** *Bp*
P-in-c P A TAILBY,   **Par Dn** E W I PLANT
THURNE (St Edmund)   Rollesby w Burgh w Billockby w
Ashby w Oby etc *Nor*
THURNHAM (St Mary the Virgin)   Bearsted w
Thurnham *Cant*
THURNING (St Andrew)   Reepham, Hackford w
Whitwell, Kerdiston etc *Nor*
THURNING (St James the Great)   Barnwell w
Tichmarsh, Thurning and Clapton *Pet*
THURNSCOE (St Helen) *Sheff 12*   **P** *Sir Stephen Hastings*
R P F GASCOIGNE
THURNSCOE (St Hilda) *Sheff 12*   **P** *Bp*
V A G HOUNSOME
THURROCK, LITTLE (St John) *Chelmsf 16*   **P** *Bp*
V E N P TUFNELL,   **C** R J TWITTY
THURROCK, LITTLE (St Mary the Virgin)   Grays
Thurrock *Chelmsf*
THURROCK, WEST (Church Centre)   as above
THURSBY (St Andrew) *Carl 3*   **P** *D&C*
P-in-c K SMALLDON,   **Par Dn** K REALE
THURSFORD (St Andrew)   Barney, Fulmodeston w
Croxton, Hindringham etc *Nor*
THURSLEY (St Michael and All Angels) *Guildf 4*
P *V Witley*   **V** J T McDOWALL
THURSTASTON (St Bartholomew) *Ches 8*   **P** *D&C*
R M B KELLY
THURSTON (St Peter) *St E 9*   **P** *Bp*   **V** D M B MATHERS
THURSTONLAND (St Thomas)   Upper Holme Valley
Wakef
THURTON (St Ethelbert) w Ashby Saint Mary, Bergh
Apton w Yelverton and Framingham Pigot *Nor 14*
P *Bp and Major J H Thursby, Bp and MMCET,*
Ld Chan (by turn)   **R** G E JESSUP
THUXTON (St Paul)   Barnham Broom *Nor*
THWAITE (All Saints)   Erpingham w Calthorpe,
Ingworth, Aldborough etc *Nor*
THWAITE (St George)   Thorndon w Rishangles, Stoke
Ash, Thwaite etc *St E*
THWAITE (St Mary)   Brooke, Kirstead, Mundham w
Seething and Thwaite *Nor*
THWAITES (St Anne)   Millom *Carl*
THWAITES BROW (St Barnabas) *Bradf 8*   **P** *DBP*
V P J ENDALL
THWING (All Saints)   Langtoft w Foxholes, Butterwick,
Cottam etc *York*
TIBBERTON (All Saints) w Bolas Magna and Waters
Upton *Lich 22*   **P** *R Edgmond, MMCET, and*
J B Davies Esq (jt)   **R** *Vacant*   Sambrook (095279) 409
TIBBERTON (Holy Trinity)   Highnam, Lassington,
Rudford, Tibberton etc *Glouc*
TIBBERTON (St Peter ad Vincula)   Bowbrook S *Worc*
TIBENHAM (All Saints)   Bunwell, Carleton Rode,
Tibenham, Gt Moulton etc *Nor*
TIBSHELF (St John the Baptist) *Derby 1*   **P** *MMCET*
V E J ABLETT
TICEHURST (St Mary) and Flimwell *Chich 19*   **P** *Bp,*
E J B Harcastle Esq, and A F Drewe Esq (jt)
V R J GOODCHILD

TICHBORNE (St Andrew) Cheriton w Tichborne and Beauworth *Win*

TICHMARSH (St Mary the Virgin) Barnwell w Tichmarsh, Thurning and Clapton *Pet*

TICKENCOTE (St Peter) Gt and Lt Casterton w Pickworth and Tickencote *Pet*

TICKENHAM (St Quiricus and St Julietta) *B & W 14* **P** Ld Chan **R** R W I GHEST

TICKHILL (St Mary) w Stainton *Sheff 10* **P** Bp **V** J A BOWERING

TICKNALL (St George), Smisby and Stanton by Bridge *Derby 15* **P** Bp and H F Harpur-Crewe (jt) **V** N R LIFTON

TICKTON (St Paul) Beverley Minster *York*

TIDBURY GREEN (St John the Divine) Shirley *Birm*

TIDCOMBE (St Michael) Wexcombe *Sarum*

TIDDINGTON (St Peter) Alveston *Cov*

TIDEBROOK (St John the Baptist) *Chich 19* **P** V Wadhurst and V Mayfield (alt) **V** M G P INSLEY

TIDEFORD (St Luke) St Germans *Truro*

TIDENHAM (St Mary) w Beachley and Lancaut *Glouc 4* **P** Bp **V** B R GREEN

TIDENHAM CHASE (St Michael and All Angels) Tidenham w Beachley and Lancaut *Glouc*

TIDESWELL (St John the Baptist) *Derby 4* **P** D&C Lich **V** J D SLYFIELD, **NSM** E D MILROY

TIDMARSH (St Laurence) Pangbourne w Tidmarsh and Sulham *Ox*

TIDMINGTON (not known) Shipston-on-Stour w Honington and Idlicote *Cov*

TIDWORTH (Holy Trinity), Ludgershall and Faberstown *Sarum 12* **P** Ld Chan and DBP (alt) **R** J ROSE-CASEMORE, **Par Dn** M A PARSONS

TIFFIELD (St John the Baptist) Pattishall w Cold Higham and Gayton w Tiffield *Pet*

TILBROOK (All Saints) *Ely 10* **P** SMF **P-in-c** J HINDLEY, **NSM** B A BEARCROFT

TILBURY, EAST (St Katherine) and West Tilbury and Linford *Chelmsf 16* **P** Ld Chan **R** D J LOEWENDAHL

TILBURY DOCKS (St John the Baptist) *Chelmsf 16* **P** Bp **V** I R MOODY, **C** A G D CLAPP

TILBURY JUXTA CLARE (St Margaret) Ovington w Tilbury *Chelmsf*

TILE CROSS (St Peter) *Birm 11* **P** Bp **V** N C FOSTER, **C** D T LEWIS

TILE HILL (St Oswald) *Cov 3* **P** Bp **V** B J DOOLAN

TILEHURST (St Catherine of Siena) *Ox 15* **P** Magd Coll Ox **V** S W M HARTLEY

TILEHURST (St George) *Ox 15* **P** Bp **C** N A LEIGH-HUNT

TILEHURST (St Mary Magdalene) *Ox 15* **P** Bp **V** R C W SMITH, **C** N J GANDY

TILEHURST (St Michael) *Ox 15* **P** Magd Coll Ox **R** C M P JONES

TILFORD (All Saints) *Guildf 3* **P** Bp **P-in-c** D J INNES

TILGATE (Holy Trinity) Southgate *Chich*

TILLINGHAM (St Nicholas) *Chelmsf 13* **P** D&C St Paul's **P-in-c** I M FINN

TILLINGTON (All Hallows) *Chich 11* **P** Lord Egremont **R** G A EVANS

TILMANSTONE (St Andrew) Eastry and Northbourne w Tilmanstone etc *Cant*

TILNEY ALL SAINTS (All Saints) *Ely 17* **P** Pemb Coll Cam **V** R C WRIGHT

TILNEY ST LAWRENCE (St Lawrence) *Ely 17* **P** Pemb Coll Cam **V** R C WRIGHT

TILSHEAD (St Thomas a Becket), Orcheston and Chitterne *Sarum 16* **P** Bp (3 turns), D&C (1 turn) **P-in-c** C E EASON

TILSTOCK (Christ Church) and Whixall *Lich 29* **P** R Whitchurch and V Prees (jt) **V** B E WARRILLOW

TILSTON (St Mary) and Shocklach *Ches 5* **P** Bp **R** C G DICKENSON

TILSTONE FEARNALL (St Jude) and Wettenhall *Ches 5* **P** Bp and V Over St Chad (alt) **V** Vacant Tarporley (08293) 2449

TILSWORTH (All Saints) Totternhoe, Stanbridge and Tilsworth *St Alb*

TILTON ON THE HILL (St Peter) Whatborough Gp of Par *Leic*

TILTY (St Mary the Virgin) Broxted w Chickney and Tilty etc *Chelmsf*

TIMBERLAND (St Andrew) Scopwick Gp *Linc*

TIMBERSCOMBE (St Petroc) Selworthy and Timberscombe and Wootton Courtenay *B & W*

TIMPERLEY (Christ Church) (St Andrew) (St Catherine) *Ches 10* **P** Trustees **V** D PROBETS, **C** R W HURLSTON, **Hon C** M E HEPWORTH, **NSM** G M GILL

TIMSBURY (Blessed Virgin Mary) and Priston *B & W 10* **P** Ball Coll Ox (3 turns), W V Jenkins Esq (1 turn) **R** J P C REED

TIMSBURY (St Andrew) Michelmersh, Timsbury, Farley Chamberlayne etc *Win*

TIMWORTH (St Andrew) Fornham All SS and St Martin w Timworth *St E*

TINCLETON (St John the Evangelist) Moreton and Woodsford w Tincleton *Sarum*

TINDALE (Mission Church) Gilsland *Carl*

TINGEWICK (St Mary Magdalen) w Water Stratford, Radclive and Chackmore *Ox 22* **P** New Coll Ox and DBP (jt) **P-in-c** J HUDSON

TINGRITH (St Nicholas) Westoning w Tingrith *St Alb*

TINSLEY (St Lawrence) *Sheff 1* **P** Sir Stephen Hastings **V** H W EVEREST

TINTAGEL (St Materiana) *Truro 10* **P** D&C Windsor **V** I H GREGORY

TINTINHULL (St Margaret) w Chilthorne Domer, Yeovil Marsh and Thorne Coffin *B & W 7* **P** Guild of All So **R** P G CLARKE

TINTWISTLE (Christ Church) *Ches 14* **P** Trustees **V** W HODSON

TINWELL (All Saints) *Pet 8* **P** Burghley Ho Preservation Trust **R** Vacant

TIPTOE (St Andrew) Hordle *Win*

TIPTON Great Bridge (St Luke) Tipton St Martin and St Paul *Lich*

TIPTON (St John) Ottery St Mary, Alfington, W Hill, Tipton etc *Ex*

TIPTON (St John the Evangelist) *Lich 8* **P** V W Bromwich St Jas **V** T J B WHATMORE, **C** G C GOWARD

TIPTON (St Mark) Ocker Hill *Lich*

TIPTON (St Martin) (St Paul) *Lich 8* **P** MMCET **V** J H ALGAR

TIPTON (St Matthew) *Lich 8* **P** Simeon's Trustees **V** M S PHILPS

TIPTREE (St Luke) Tolleshunt Knights w Tiptree and Gt Braxted *Chelmsf*

TIRLEY (St Michael) Hasfield w Tirley and Ashleworth *Glouc*

TISBURY (St John the Baptist) *Sarum 13* **P** Patr Bd (3 turns), Ld Chan (1 turn) **TR** C J MEYRICK, **TV** J M ACHESON, **NSM** M A SHALLCROSS, R WREN, **Hon Par Dn** J E TREASURE

TISMANS COMMON (St John the Baptist) Rudgwick *Chich*

TISSINGTON (St Mary) Fenny Bentley, Kniveton, Thorpe and Tissington *Derby*

TISTED, EAST w Colemore (St James) Newton Valence, Selborne and E Tisted w Colemore *Win*

TISTED, WEST (St Mary Magdalene) Bishop's Sutton and Ropley and W Tisted *Win*

TITCHFIELD (St Peter) *Portsm 2* **P** D&C Win **V** Vacant Titchfield (0329) 42324

TITCHWELL (St Mary) Brancaster w Burnham Deepdale and Titchwell *Nor*

TITLEY (St Peter) Lyonshall w Titley, Almeley and Kinnersley *Heref*

TITTENSOR (St Luke) Swynnerton and Tittensor *Lich*

TITTLESHALL (St Mary) w Godwick *Nor 19* **P** Viscount Coke **R** Vacant

TIVERTON (St Andrew) *Ex 8* **P** Bp **V** P G HARRISON, **Hon C** D A CLARK

TIVERTON (St George) *Ex 8* **P** MMCET **V** C G H DUNN

TIVERTON (St Paul) W Exe *Ex*

TIVERTON (St Peter) *Ex 8* **P** Peache Trustees **R** D A E WHITAKER

TIVETSHALL (St Mary and St Margaret) Winfarthing w Shelfanger w Burston w Gissing etc *Nor*

TIVIDALE (St Michael the Archangel) (Holy Cross) (St Augustine) *Lich 8* **P** Bp **V** L CROWE, **C** S P DAY

TIVINGTON (St Leonard) Selworthy and Timberscombe and Wootton Courtenay *B & W*

TIXALL (St John the Baptist) Stafford St Jo and Tixall w Ingestre *Lich*

TIXOVER (St Luke) Easton on the Hill, Collyweston w Duddington etc *Pet*

TOCKENHAM (St Giles) Broad Town, Clyffe Pypard and Tockenham *Sarum*

TOCKHOLES (St Stephen) Darwen St Cuth w Tockholes St Steph *Blackb*

TOCKWITH (Epiphany) and Bilton w Bickerton *York 1* **P** Abp and D&C (jt) **V** D J TOMPKINS

TODBER (St Andrew) Gillingham *Sarum*

TODDINGTON (St Andrew), Stanton, Didbrook w Hailes and Stanway *Glouc 17*   P   *DBP, Lord Neidpath, and Bp (by turn)*   **P-in-c** P L C RICHARDS

TODDINGTON (St George of England) *St Alb 18*   P   *Bp*   R   T A KNOX

TODENHAM (St Thomas of Canterbury)   Moreton-in-Marsh w Batsford, Todenham etc *Glouc*

TODMORDEN (Christ Church)   Todmorden *Wakef*

TODMORDEN (St Mary) (Christ Church) *Wakef 3*   P   *Bp*   V   P N CALVERT

TODWICK (St Peter and St Paul) *Sheff 5*   P   *Bp*   R   J R NEWTON

TOFT (St Andrew) w Caldecote and Childerley *Ely 1*   P   *Ch Coll Cam*   R   A R McKEARNEY,   **NSM**   A G WILMAN,   D A J WILMAN

TOFT (St John the Evangelist)   Knutsford St Jo and Toft *Ches*

TOFT MONKS (St Margaret)   Raveningham *Nor*

TOFT NEXT NEWTON (St Peter and St Paul)   Middle Rasen Gp *Linc*

TOFTREES (All Saints) w Shereford *Nor 20*   P   *Marquess Townshend*   V   *Vacant*

TOFTS, WEST and Buckenham Parva *Nor 18*   P   *Guild of All So*   R   *Vacant*

TOKYNGTON (St Michael) *Lon 21*   P   *Bp*   V   R J METIVIER,   **Par Dn**   P M WISE

TOLLADINE (Christ Church)   Worc St Barn w Ch Ch *Worc*

TOLLAND (St John the Baptist)   Lydeard St Lawrence w Brompton Ralph etc *B & W*

TOLLARD ROYAL (St Peter ad Vincula) w Farnham, Gussage St Michael and Gussage All Saints, Ashmore and Chettle *Sarum 7*   P   *Bp, Adn Dorset, Ch Soc Trust, A C L Sturge Esq, and J P C Bourke Esq (2 turns), Ld Chan (1 turn)*   R   G B BELL

TOLLER FRATRUM (St Basil)   Melbury *Sarum*

TOLLER PORCORUM (St Andrew)   Beaminster Area *Sarum*

TOLLER WHELME (St John)   Melbury *Sarum*

TOLLERTON (St Michael)   Alne *York*

TOLLERTON (St Peter) *S'well 9*   P   *Lady Shrigley-Ball*   R   *Vacant*   Plumtree (06077) 2349

TOLLESBURY (St Mary) w Salcot Virley *Chelmsf 27*   P   *Bp (1 turn), Ex Coll Ox (3 turns)*   V   K M B LOVELL

TOLLESHUNT D'ARCY (St Nicholas) w Tolleshunt Major (St Nicholas) *Chelmsf 27*   P   *Mrs E A Comerford and MMCET (jt)*   **P-in-c**   P R SOUTHERN

TOLLESHUNT KNIGHTS w Tiptree and Great Braxted *Chelmsf 27*   P   *Bp (2 turns), Ld Chan (2 turns), and CCC Cam (1 turn)*   R   J A PRATT

TOLLINGTON PARK (St Mark)   Holloway St Mark w Em *Lon*

TOLPUDDLE (St John the Evangelist)   Puddletown and Tolpuddle *Sarum*

TOLWORTH (Emmanuel)   Surbiton Hill Ch Ch *S'wark*

TOLWORTH (St George)   Surbiton St Matt *S'wark*

TONBRIDGE (St Peter and St Paul) (St Saviour) *Roch 10*   P   *Mabledon Trust*   V   M A PERRY,   C   P W L WALKER, C J L NOBLE,   **Par Dn**   G E TOVAR, J AUSTIN

TONBRIDGE (St Stephen) (St Eanswythe Mission Church) *Roch 10*   P   *CPAS*   V   W D MACDOUGALL, C   M J RAINSBURY,   P D BRYER

TONG (St Bartholomew) *Lich 26*   P   *Bp*   V   G FROST

TONG (St James) *Bradf 3*   P   *CR*   **TR**   C G N DEY,   C   J M GREEN

TONGE (St Giles)   Murston w Bapchild and Tonge *Cant*

TONGE (St Michael) w Alkrington *Man 19*   P   *R Middleton St Leon*   **Par Dn**   S M GAWTHROP

TONGE FOLD (St Chad) *Man 9*   P   *Bp and Wm Hulme Trustees (alt)*   V   A J BUTTERWORTH

TONGE MOOR (St Augustine) (St Aidan) *Man 16*   P   *Keble Coll Ox*   V   B J FINDLAY,   C   R H DAVIES

TONGHAM (St Paul) *Guildf 1*   P   *Adn Surrey*   V   C P AWLEY

TONWELL (St Mary the Virgin)   Bengeo *St Alb*

TOOT BALDON (St Lawrence)   Dorchester *Ox*

TOOTING (All Saints) *S'wark 16*   P   *Bp*   V   S J L KING

TOOTING (St Augustine) *S'wark 16*   P   *Bp*   V   S J LOPEZ FERREIRO

TOOTING Tooting Graveney (St Nicholas) *S'wark 16*   P   *MMCET*   R   J B HALL

TOOTING, UPPER (Holy Trinity) *S'wark 16*   P   *R Streatham St Leon*   V   J R BINNS,   **Par Dn**   P J ROSE-CASEMORE,   **Hon C**   A B RAFFINGTON

TOP VALLEY ESTATE (St Philip)   Bestwood *S'well*

TOPCLIFFE (St Columba) *York 20*   P   *D&C*   **P-in-c**   J THOM

TOPCROFT (St Margaret)   Hempnall *Nor*

TOPPESFIELD (St Margaret) and Stambourne *Chelmsf 22*   P   *The Crown and Duchy of Lanc (alt)*   R   W R JESSUP

TOPSHAM (St Margaret) *Ex 1*   P   *D&C*   V   R W C JEFFERY,   **NSM**   H A FULFORD

TORBRYAN (Holy Trinity)   Ipplepen w Torbryan *Ex*

TORKSEY (St Peter) *Linc 2*   P   *DBP*   V   L SALT

TORMARTON (St Mary Magdalene)   Marshfield w Cold Ashton and Tormarton etc *Bris*

TORPENHOW (St Michael and All Angels) *Carl 7*   P   *Bp*   V   *Vacant*   Low Ireby (09657) 295

TORPOINT (St James) *Truro 11*   P   *R Antony*   V   K W NOAKES,   C   G C BARRETT

TORQUAY (St John) and Ellacombe (Christ Church) *Ex 10*   P   *Ch Patr Trust and Bp (jt)*   V   R W BECK

TORQUAY (St Luke) *Ex 10*   P   *D&C*   **P-in-c**   A A DUKE

TORQUAY (St Martin) Barton *Ex 10*   P   *V St Marychurch*   V   D J PROTHERO,   C   M H JAMES

TORQUAY (St Mary Magdalene)   Upton *Ex*

TORQUAY (St Matthias) (St Mark) (Holy Trinity) *Ex 10*   P   *Ch Patr Trust, Bp and Torwood Trustees (jt)*   R   P J LARKIN,   C   A TREMLETT,   **Hon Par Dn**   P G H COOKE, J M PRINGLE

TORRE (All Saints) *Ex 10*   P   *Bp*   V   R I McDOWALL

TORRINGTON, EAST (St Michael)   Barkwith Gp *Linc*

TORRINGTON, GREAT (St Michael), Little Torrington and Frithelstock *Ex 20*   P   *Ch Ch Ox (8 turns), Lord Clinton (1 turn), and J de C Stevens-Guille Esq (1 turn)*   V   J D HUMMERSTONE

TORRINGTON, LITTLE (St Giles)   see above

TORRINGTON, WEST (St Michael)   Barkwith Gp *Linc*

TORRISHOLME (Ascension) *Blackb 12*   P   *Bp*   V   W B GORNALL,   C   R A PETTITT

TORTWORTH (St Leonard)   Cromhall w Tortworth and Tytherington *Glouc*

TORVER (St Luke) *Carl 8*   P   *Peache Trustees*   R   S J SKINNER,   **Hon Par Dn**   J M SKINNER

TOSELAND (St Michael)   Graveley w Papworth St Agnes w Yelling etc *Ely*

TOSSIDE (St Bartholomew)   Long Preston w Tosside *Bradf*

TOSTOCK (St Andrew)   Pakenham w Norton and Tostock *St E*

TOTHAM, GREAT (St Peter) *Chelmsf 27*   P   *Bp*   V   M J HATCHETT,   **NSM**   P W YOULE

TOTHAM, LITTLE (All Saints)   Goldhanger w Lt Totham *Chelmsf*

TOTLAND BAY (Christ Church) *Portsm 8*   P   *Ch Patr Trust*   V   *Vacant*   Isle of Wight (0983) 752031

TOTLEY (All Saints) *Sheff 2*   P   *Bp*   V   J D BENSON

TOTNES (St Mary) and Berry Pomeroy *Ex 13*   P   *Patr Bd*   **P-in-c**   T R SMITH,   **NSM**   C BERDINNER

TOTON (St Peter)   Attenborough *S'well*

TOTTENHAM (All Hallows) *Lon 19*   P   *D&C St Paul's*   V   R B PEARSON

TOTTENHAM (Holy Trinity) *Lon 19*   P   *Bp*   **Par Dn**   E J JONES

TOTTENHAM (St Ann) Hanger Lane *Lon 19*   P   *D&C St Paul's*   V   A E DADD

TOTTENHAM (St Benet Fink) *Lon 19*   P   *D&C St Paul's*   V   M A DAVENPORT

TOTTENHAM (St Mary) *Lon 19*   P   *Bp*   V   C H J TUCKWELL,   C   S J POTHEN

TOTTENHAM (St Paul) *Lon 19*   P   *V Tottenham All Hallows*   V   A S HOPES,   C   C D EYDEN,   **NSM**   J C VAUGHAN

TOTTENHAM (St Philip the Apostle) *Lon 19*   P   *Bp*   **P-in-c**   K EVANS

TOTTENHILL (St Botolph) w Wormegay *Ely 16*   P   *Bp*   V   J C W NOLAN

TOTTERIDGE (St Andrew) *St Alb 2*   P   *R Hatfield*   V   J H KNOWLES-BROWN

TOTTERNHOE (St Giles), Stanbridge and Tilsworth *St Alb 18*   P   *Bp*   V   P C HOLLAND

TOTTINGTON (St Anne) *Man 10*   P   *R Bury St Mary*   V   G A SUTCLIFFE

TOTTON *Win 10*   P   *Bp*   **TR**   W B METCALFE,   **TV**   J E HAIR, G R BIGGS, D W GRIMWOOD

TOW LAW (St Philip and St James) *Dur 15*   P   *Bp*   V   *Vacant*   Bishop Auckland (0388) 730335

TOWCESTER (St Lawrence) w Easton Neston *Pet 5*   P   *Bp and Lord Hesketh (alt)*   V   J E ATWELL,   **NSM**   P ADAMS

TOWEDNACK (St Tewinock) *Truro 5*   P   *Bp*   **P-in-c**   S W MIDDLETON-DANSKY

TOWER CHAPEL (St Nicholas)   Whitehaven *Carl*

TOWERSEY (St Catherine)   Thame w Towersey *Ox*

TOWN END FARM (St Bede)   Sunderland Town End Farm *Dur*

TOWNSTAL (St Clement)   Dartmouth *Ex*

TOXTETH (St Cyprian w Christ Church) *Liv 3*
　P *Simeon's Trustees*　　**V** *D A LEWIS*,
　C *G C BUTTANSHAW*
TOXTETH (St Margaret) *Liv 6*　**P** *St Chad's Coll Dur*
　V *R GALLAGHER*
TOXTETH (St Philemon) (St Gabriel) St Cleopas *Liv 6*
　P *Patr Bd*　　**TR** *C M BEDFORD*,
　TV *P H JANVIER, J W WHITLEY*,　**Par Dn** *A E S QUILLIAM*
TOXTETH PARK (Christ Church) *Liv 6*　**P** *Trustees*
　P-in-c *M T RANDALL*
TOXTETH PARK (St Agnes and St Pancras) *Liv 6*
　P *St Chad's Coll Dur*　　**V** *D H McKITTRICK*
TOXTETH PARK (St Bede) *Liv 6*　**P** *Simeon's Trustees*
　P-in-c *M T RANDALL*,　**Par Dn** *J C M BISSEX*
TOXTETH PARK (St Clement) *Liv 6*　**P** *Trustees*
　V *Vacant*　051-733 5410
TOXTETH PARK (St Michael-in-the-Hamlet) (St Andrew)
　Liv 6　**P** *Simeon's Trustees*　　**V** *S FORBES*
TOYNTON, HIGH (St John the Baptist) *Linc 11*　**P** *Bp*
　V *Vacant*
TOYNTON ALL SAINTS (All Saints)　Marden Hill Gp
　Linc
TOYNTON ST PETER (St Peter)　as above
TOYS HILL (Hall)　Four Elms *Roch*
TRAFALGAR SQUARE (St Martin-in-the-Fields)　St
　Martin-in-the-Fields *Lon*
TRAFFORD, OLD (St Hilda) *Man 7*　**P** *The Crown*
　R *D G BARNETT*
TRAFFORD, OLD (St John the Evangelist) *Man 7*
　P *The Crown*　**R** *C S FORD*,　**Par Dn** *M C HODSON*
TRANMERE (St Catherine) *Ches 1*　**P** *R Bebington*
　V *S R BECKLEY*,　**NSM** *W H HEAPS, K THOMPSON*
TRANMERE (St Paul w St Luke) *Ches 1*　**P** *Bp*
　V *D J JOHNSON*,　**C** *B WOOD*
TRANMERE PARK (St Peter's Hall)　Guiseley w Esholt
　Bradf
TRAWDEN (St Mary the Virgin) *Blackb 7*　**P** *Bp*
　NSM *R L ALLEN*
TREALES (Christ Church) *Blackb 11*　**P** *V Kirkham*
　P-in-c *P A L MADDOCK*
TREBOROUGH (St Peter)　Old Cleeve, Leighland and
　Treborough *B & W*
TREDINGTON (St Gregory) and Darlingscott w Newbold
　on Stour *Cov 9*　**P** *Jes Coll Ox*　**R** *J P ELLIOTT*
TREDINGTON (St John the Baptist)　Staverton w
　Boddington and Tredington etc *Glouc*
TREETON (St Helen) *Sheff 6*　**P** *Ch Trust Fund*
　R *A J LACEY*
TREFONEN (All Saints)　Llanyblodwel and Trefonen
　Lich
TREGADILLET (St Mary's Mission)　Launceston St
　Steph w St Thos *Truro*
TREGONY (not known) w St Cuby and Cornelly *Truro 6*
　P *Bp*　　**R** *C F P SHEPHERD*
TREKNOW (Holy Family)　Tintagel *Truro*
TRELEIGH (St Stephen)　Redruth w Lanner and
　Treleigh *Truro*
TRELYSTAN (St Mary the Virgin) *Heref 13*　**P** *Bp*
　V *P D HARRATT*
TREMAINE (St Winwalo)　Bolventor *Truro*
TRENEGLOS (St Gregory)　St Gennys, Jacobstow w
　Warbstow and Treneglos *Truro*
TRENT (St Andrew)　Queen Thorne *Sarum*
TRENT VALE (St John the Evangelist) *Lich 18*
　P *R Stoke-on-Trent*　**V** *B L AMB*
TRENTHAM (St Mary and All Saints) *Lich 19*
　P *Countess of Sutherland*　**V** *D MARSH*,　**C** *L P BEARD*
TRENTISHOE (St Peter) *Ex 18*　**P** *Bp*
　P-in-c *C J HUDSON*
TRESCO (St Nicholas)　Scilly Is *Truro*
TRESHAM (Chapel)　Kingswood w Alderley and
　Hillesley *Glouc*
TRESLOTHAN (St John the Evangelist) *Truro 2*
　P *Mrs W A Pendarves*　**V** *C F H SUTCLIFFE*
TRESMERE (St Nicholas)　Bolventor *Truro*
TRESWELL (St John the Baptist)　Rampton w
　Laneham, Treswell, Cottam and Stokeham *S'well*
TRETHEVY (St Piran)　Tintagel *Truro*
TRETIRE (St Mary)　St Weonards w Orcop, Garway,
　Tretire etc *Heref*
TREVALGA (St Petroc)　Boscastle w Davidstow *Truro*
TREVENSON (St Illogan)　Illogan *Truro*
TREVERBYN (St Peter) *Truro 1*　**P** *The Crown*
　V *J B SAUNDERS*
TREVONE (St Saviour)　Padstow *Truro*
TREWEN (St Michael)　Lezant w Lawhitton and S
　Petherwin w Trewen *Truro*
TREYFORD-CUM-DIDLING (St Andrew)　Stedham w
　Iping, Elsted and Treyford-cum-Didling *Chich*

TRIMDON (St Mary Magdalene) *Dur 14*　**P** *Miss S Moore*
　V *J WILLIAMSON*
TRIMDON GRANGE (St Alban)　Trimdon Station *Dur*
TRIMDON STATION (St Alban) (St Paul) *Dur 14*　**P** *Bp*
　V *Vacant*　Wellfield (0429) 880872
TRIMINGHAM (St John the Baptist)　Trunch *Nor*
TRIMLEY (St Martin) (St Mary the Virgin) *St E 2*　**P** *Bp*
　and Ld Chan (alt)　**R** *C LEFFLER*
TRIMPLEY (Holy Trinity)　Kidderminster St Mary and
　All SS w Trimpley etc *Worc*
TRING (St Martha) (St Peter and St Paul) (St Mary)
　St Alb 3　**P** *Bp*　　**TR** *J A S PAYNE COOK*,
　TV *G R WARREN, M M NATHANAEL*,
　Hon Par Dn *J E K RIDGWAY*
TROSTON (St Mary the Virgin)　Honington w Sapiston
　and Troston *St E*
TROTTISCLIFFE (St Peter and St Paul)　Birling,
　Addington, Ryarsh and Trottiscliffe *Roch*
TROTTON (St George)　Rogate w Terwick and Trotton
　w Chithurst *Chich*
TROUTBECK (Jesus Christ) *Carl 10*　**P** *Bp*
　P-in-c *W E BARKER*
TROWBRIDGE (Holy Trinity) *Sarum 17*　**P** *Patr Bd*
　TR *E W M KELLY*,　**TV** *D J COOPER*,
　Par Dn *B A BAYLEY*
TROWBRIDGE (St James) *Sarum 17*　**P** *Ch Patr Trust*
　R *C F BROWN*,　**Par Dn** *B A BAYLEY, M J RIDGEWELL*
TROWBRIDGE (St Thomas) and West Ashton *Sarum 17*
　P *CPAS*　**Hon C** *A S REYNOLDS*,　**NSM** *J DARLING*
TROWELL (St Helen) *S'well 7*　**P** *Lord Middleton*
　R *T HATTON*
TROWSE (St Andrew) *Nor 14*　**P** *D&C*　**V** *G F WALKER*
TRULL (All Saints) w Angersleigh *B & W 20*　**P** *DBP and*
　Personal Reps of the late Mrs J H Spurway (jt)
　R *J M PRIOR*
TRUMPINGTON (St Mary and St Michael) *Ely 2*　**P** *Trin*
　Coll Cam　**V** *N J THISTLETHWAITE*
TRUNCH (St Botolph) *Nor 7*　**P** *Duchy of Lanc (3 turns)*,
　Patr Bd (1 turn)　**TR** *J R RANDALL*,
　TV *A B NORTON, E A CUNNINGTON*,　**NSM** *R H MacPHEE*
TRURO (St George the Martyr)　Kenwyn St Geo *Truro*
TRURO (St John the Evangelist)　Kenwyn St Jo *Truro*
TRURO (St Mary's Cathedral and Parish Church) *Truro 6*
　P *The Crown*　**R** *D J SHEARLOCK*,　**C** *I F FRITH*
TRURO (St Paul) (St Clement) *Truro 6*　**P** *Bp*
　V *P B STAPLES*
TRUSHAM (St Michael and All Angels)　Christow,
　Ashton, Trusham and Bridford *Ex*
TRUSLEY (All Saints)　Ch Broughton w Barton Blount,
　Boylestone etc *Derby*
TRUSTHORPE (St Peter)　Mablethorpe w Trusthorpe
　Linc
TRYSULL (All Saints)　Wombourne w Trysull and
　Bobbington *Lich*
TRYTHALL (Mission Church)　Gulval *Truro*
TUBNEY (St Lawrence)　Fyfield w Tubney and Kingston
　Bagpuize *Ox*
TUCKHILL (Holy Innocents)　Claverley w Tuckhill
　Heref
TUCKINGMILL (All Saints) *Truro 2*　**P** *Bp*　**V** *B P LUCK*
TUCKSWOOD (St Paul) *Nor 5*　**P** *Bp*　**V** *J M STRIDE*
TUDDENHAM (St Martin)　Westerfield and
　Tuddenham St Martin w Witnesham *St E*
TUDDENHAM (St Mary)　Mildenhall *St E*
TUDDENHAM, EAST (All Saints)　Hockering,
　Honingham, E and N Tuddenham *Nor*
TUDDENHAM, NORTH (St Mary the Virgin)　as above
TUDELEY (All Saints) w Capel *Roch 10*　**P** *Bp*
　V *S D RILEY*
TUDHOE (St David) *Dur 10*　**P** *D&C*　**V** *P E B WELBY*
TUDHOE GRANGE (St Andrew) *Dur 10*　**P** *Bp*
　V *N D BAKER*
TUEBROOK (St John)　W Derby (or Tuebrook) St Jo
　Liv
TUFFLEY (St Barnabas) *Glouc 5*　**P** *Bp*　**V** *A J MINCHIN*,
　C *M S RILEY, J HEARN*
TUFNELL PARK (St George and All Saints) *Lon 6*
　P *Trustees and CPAS (jt)*　**V** *D I LISTER*
TUFTON (St Mary)　Whitchurch w Tufton and Litchfield
　Win
TUGBY (St Thomas a Becket)　Hallaton w Horninghold,
　Allexton, Tugby etc *Leic*
TUGFORD (St Catherine)　Diddlebury w Munslow,
　Holdgate and Tugford *Heref*
TULSE HILL (Holy Trinity and St Matthias) *S'wark 9*
　P *Simeon's Trustees and Peache Trustees (jt)*
　V *J M SENTAMU*,　**C** *T R J GODDEN*,
　NSM *M B POOLE, D J LUBBOCK*

TUNBRIDGE WELLS (Holy Trinity w Christ Church)
Roch 11   **P** *Mabledon Trust and CPAS (jt)*
V J W BANNER

TUNBRIDGE WELLS (King Charles the Martyr) *Roch 11*
P *Trustees*   **V** B L GANT, **Hon C** C J S GILL

TUNBRIDGE WELLS (St Barnabas) *Roch 11*   **P** *Guild of All So*   **V** M S NICHOLLS

TUNBRIDGE WELLS (St James) *Roch 11*   **P** *Ch Trust Fund Trust*   **V** N G NORGATE,
C D J ABBOTT, M J DUERDEN

TUNBRIDGE WELLS (St John) *Roch 11*   **P** *CPAS and V H Trin Tun Wells (jt)*   **V** C D COLLINS, **C** C COOPER

TUNBRIDGE WELLS (St Luke) *Roch 11*   **P** *Five Trustees*
V R A WHYTE

TUNBRIDGE WELLS (St Mark) Broadwater Down
Roch 11   **P** *Bp Chich*   **V** F R CUMBERLEGE

TUNBRIDGE WELLS (St Peter) Windmill Fields *Roch 11*
P *Trustees and CPAS (jt)*   **Hon Par Dn** V E BRANDON

TUNSTALL (All Saints)   Roos and Garton in Holderness w Tunstall etc *York*

TUNSTALL (Christ Church) *Lich 17*   **P** *Bp*   **V** *Vacant*
Stoke-on-Trent (0782) 88288

TUNSTALL (Holy Trinity)   Catterick *Ripon*

TUNSTALL (St John the Baptist) w Melling and Leck
Blackb 15   **P** *Bp, Lord Shuttleworth, Judge E S Temple, and Ripon Coll Cuddesdon (jt)*
V P A W COTTON

TUNSTALL (St John the Baptist) w Rodmersham *Cant 14*
P *D&C and G L Doubleday Esq (jt)*   **R** D MATTHIAE

TUNSTALL (St Michael and All Angels)   Eyke w Bromeshall, Rendlesham, Tunstall etc *St E*

TUNSTEAD (Holy Trinity) *Man 15*   **P** *Bp and Dioc Chan (jt)*   **V** E J ASHWORTH

TUNSTEAD (St Mary) w Sco' Ruston *Nor 9*   **P** *Bp*
P-in-c A R LONG

TUNWORTH (All Saints)   Herriard w Winslade and Long Sutton etc *Win*

TUPSLEY (St Paul) *Heref 3*   **P** *Bp*   **V** J D REESE,
C J D S DUNNILL, T M ALBAN-JONES, B WOOLLASTON

TUPTON, NEW (St John)   N Wingfield, Clay Cross and Pilsley *Derby*

TUR LANGTON (St Andrew)   Church Langton w Tur Langton, Thorpe Langton etc *Leic*

TURKDEAN (All Saints)   Cold Aston w Notgrove and Turkdean *Glouc*

TURNASTONE (St Mary Magdalene)   Peterchurch w Vowchurch, Turnastone and Dorstone *Heref*

TURNDITCH (All Saints) *Derby 11*   **P** *Bp*
V N DAUGHTRY

TURNERS HILL (St Leonard) *Chich 7*   **P** *Bp*
V J S LOXTON

TURNFORD (St Clement)   Cheshunt *St Alb*

TURNHAM GREEN (Christ Church) *Lon 11*   **P** *Bp*
V R E ADFIELD

TURNWORTH (St Mary)   Winterbourne Stickland and Turnworth etc *Sarum*

TURTON (St Anne) (St James) *Man 16*   **P** *Bp*
V J H DAULMAN, **Hon C** R LADDS

TURVEY (All Saints) *St Alb 21*   **P** *Mrs P K C Hanbury*
R P N JEFFERY

TURVILLE (St Mary)   Hambleden Valley *Ox*

TURWESTON (Assumption of the Blessed Virgin Mary)
Westbury w Turweston, Shalstone and Biddlesden *Ox*

TUSHINGHAM (St Chad) and Whitewell (St Mary) *Ches 5*
P *MMCET*   **R** P WINCHESTER

TUTBURY (St Mary the Virgin) *Lich 20*   **P** *Duchy of Lanc*   **V** T J GANZ

TUTSHILL (St Luke)   Tidenham w Beachley and Lancaut *Glouc*

TUTTINGTON (St Peter and St Paul)   Colby w Banningham and Tuttington *Nor*

TUXFORD (St Nicholas) w Weston and Markham Clinton
S'well 3   **P** *Ld Chan and Bp (alt)*   **V** J E MARTIN

TWEEDMOUTH (St Bartholomew) *Newc 12*   **P** *D&C Dur*   **V** G A ELCOAT, **NSM** T THOMPSON

TWERTON-ON-AVON   Bath Twerton-on-Avon *B & W*

TWICKENHAM (All Hallows) *Lon 10*   **P** *D&C St Paul's*
P-in-c G A BARBER

TWICKENHAM (All Saints) *Lon 10*   **P** *Bp*
P-in-c P L BUSTIN

TWICKENHAM (St Mary the Virgin) *Lon 10*
P *D&C Windsor*   **V** A GLYN-JONES, **C** M J PARKER,
Hon C A F B ROGERS

TWICKENHAM, EAST (St Stephen) (St Paul) *Lon 10* **P** *CPAS*   **V** M G PEPPIATT, **C** N S CRAWLEY

TWICKENHAM COMMON (Holy Trinity) *Lon 10*   **P** *Bp*
V D A WALTER

TWIGWORTH (St Matthew), Down Hatherley, Norton, The Leigh, Evington and Sandhurst *Glouc 6*   **P** *Bp*

(1 turn), Ld Chan (2 turns), and D&C Bris (1 turn)
V J O'BRIEN

TWINEHAM (St Peter)   Albourne w Sayers Common and Twineham *Chich*

TWINSTEAD (St John the Evangelist)   Gt and Lt Henny w Middleton, Wickham St Paul etc *Chelmsf*

TWITCHEN (St Peter)   S Molton w Nymet St George, High Bray etc *Ex*

TWO GATES (St Peter)   Wilnecote *Lich*

TWO MILE ASH (not known)   Watling Valley *Ox*

TWO MILE HILL (St Michael) *Bris 2*   **P** *Prime Min*
V S P BOWERS

TWYCROSS (St James)   Orton-on-the-Hill w Twycross etc *Leic*

TWYFORD (Assumption of the Blessed Virgin Mary)
Swan *Ox*

TWYFORD (St Andrew)   Barrow-on-Trent w Twyford and Swarkestone *Derby*

TWYFORD (St Andrew)   S Croxton Gp *Leic*

TWYFORD (St Mary) and Owslebury and Morestead
Win 13   **P** *Em Coll Cam and Bp (alt)*   **V** P V LIPPIETT

TWYFORD (St Mary the Virgin)   Ruscombe and Twyford *Ox*

TWYFORD (St Nicholas) w Guist w Bintry w Themelthorpe w Wood Norton *Nor 8*   **P** *Bp and DBP (alt)*
R A K GREENHOUGH

TWYNING (St Mary Magdalene) *Glouc 9*   **P** *Ch Ch Ox*
P-in-c A C BERRY

TWYWELL (St Nicholas)   Cranford w Grafton Underwood and Twywell *Pet*

TYBERTON (St Mary)   Madley w Tyberton, Preston-on-Wye and Blakemere *Heref*

TYDD (St Mary)   The Suttons w Tydd *Linc*

TYDD ST GILES (St Giles) *Ely 19*   **P** *Bp*   **R** J TOFTS

TYE GREEN (St Barnabas)   Fairstead w Terling and White Notley etc *Chelmsf*

TYE GREEN (St Stephen) w St Andrew Netteswell
Chelmsf 3   **P** *J L H Arkwright Esq*   **R** R BRAY

TYLDESLEY (St George) w Shakerley *Man 13*   **P** *Bp*
V K LANGTON

TYLER HILL (St Francis)   Hackington *Cant*

TYLERS GREEN (St Margaret) *Ox 29*   **P** *Earl Howe*
V M E HALL

TYLER'S HILL (St George)   Gt Chesham *Ox*

TYNEMOUTH Balkwell (St Peter)   Balkwell *Newc*

TYNEMOUTH Cullercoats (St Paul) *Newc 8*   **P** *Dioc Soc*
V N BANKS, **NSM** D F TITTLEY

TYNEMOUTH Shiremoor (St Mark)   Shiremoor *Newc*

TYNEMOUTH (St John Percy) *Newc 8*   **P** *Dioc Soc*
V J M PENNINGTON, **C** C H HOPE

TYNEMOUTH PRIORY (Holy Saviour) *Newc 8*   **P** *Dioc Soc*   **V** R D TAYLOR

TYNINGS LANE (St Mary's Mission Church)   Aldridge *Lich*

TYRINGHAM (St Peter)   Haversham w Lt Linford, Tyringham w Filgrave *Ox*

TYRLEY (Mission Room)   Drayton in Hales *Lich*

TYSELEY (St Edmund) *Birm 7*   **P** *The Crown*
V P A EVENS

TYSOE (Assumption of the Blessed Virgin Mary) w Oxhill and Whatcote *Cov 9*   **P** *Marquess of Northn and DBP (jt)*   **V** P R BROWN

TYTHBY (Holy Trinity)   Cropwell Bishop w Colston Bassett, Granby etc *S'well*

TYTHERINGTON (St James)   Cromhall w Tortworth and Tytherington *Glouc*

TYTHERINGTON (St James)   Heytesbury and Sutton Veny *Sarum*

TYTHERLEY, EAST (St Peter)   Lockerley and E Dean w E and W Tytherley *Win*

TYTHERLEY, WEST (St Peter)   as above

TYTHERTON KELLAWAYS (St Giles)   Christian Malford w Sutton Benger etc *Bris*

TYTHERTON LUCAS (St Nicholas)   Chippenham St Andr w Tytherton Lucas *Bris*

TYWARDREATH (St Andrew) w Tregaminion *Truro 1*
P *DBP*   **V** M J OATEY

UBLEY (St Bartholomew)   Blagdon w Compton Martin and Ubley *B & W*

UCKFIELD (Holy Cross) (St Saviour) *Chich 21*   **P** *Abp*
R C J PETERS, **C** A BAMFORD, **Hon C** C G STABLES,
NSM C HOWARTH, R C DALLING, G FRANCE

UDIMORE (St Mary)   Brede w Udimore *Chich*

UFFCULME (St Mary the Virgin) *Ex 4*   **P** *Bp*
V G M FRASER, **Hon Par Dn** D E SEALE

UFFINGTON (Holy Trinity), Upton Magna and Withington *Lich 30*   **P** *J R de Q Quincey*   **R** C S COOKE

UFFINGTON (St Mary) w Woolstone and Baulking *Ox 17*
P *Bp*   **V** *Vacant*   Uffington (036782) 633

UFFINGTON (St Michael and All Angels) *Linc 13*
P *Personal Reps of Lady Muriel Barclay-Harvey
(2 turns), Bp (1 turn), and Ld Chan (2 turns)*
R G C SMITH
UFFORD (St Andrew) Barnack w Ufford and Bainton
Pet
UFFORD (St Mary) w Bredfield and Hasketon *St E 7*
P *Bp, Ld Chan, and Exors T E Bloise-Brooke Esq
(by turn)* **R** J W DREW
UFTON (St Michael and All Angels) Radford Semele
and Ufton *Cov*
UFTON NERVET (St Peter) Sulhamstead Abbots and
Bannister w Ufton Nervet *Ox*
UGBOROUGH (St Peter) *Ex 21* **P** *Grocers' Co*
P-in-c P R LEVERTON
**UGGESHALL (St Mary) w Sotherton, Wangford and
Henham** *St E 15* **P** *Exors Earl of Stradbroke*
R E M COPLEY
UGGLEBARNBY (All Saints) Eskdaleside w
Ugglebarnby and Sneaton *York*
UGLEY (St Peter) Henham and Elsenham w Ugley
Chelmsf
UGTHORPE (Christ Church) Lythe w Ugthorpe *York*
ULCEBY (All Saints) Willoughby *Linc*
ULCEBY Group, The (St Nicholas) *Linc 6* **P** *Ld Chan*
V A R MARSDEN
ULCOMBE (All Saints) Harrietsham w Ulcombe *Cant*
ULDALE (St James) Bolton w Ireby and Uldale *Carl*
ULEY (St Giles) w Owlpen and Nympsfield *Glouc 2*
P *Ld Chan* **R** C R AWLINSON, **Hon C** M D PAISH,
NSM M O TUCKER
ULGHAM (St John the Baptist) *Newc 11* **P** *Bp*
V P R HESELTON
ULLENHALL (St Mary the Virgin) Beaudesert and
Henley-in-Arden w Ullenhall *Cov*
ULLESKELFE (St Saviour) Kirk Fenton w Kirkby
Wharfe and Ulleskelfe *York*
ULLEY (Holy Trinity) Aston cum Aughton and Ulley
Sheff
ULLINGSWICK (St Luke) Stoke Lacy, Moreton Jeffries
w Much Cowarne etc *Heref*
ULPHA (St John) Broughton and Duddon *Carl*
ULROME (St Andrew) Skipsea w Ulrome and
Barmston w Fraisthorpe *York*
ULTING (All Saints) Hatf Peverel w Ulting *Chelmsf*
ULVERSTON (St Mary w Holy Trinity) (St Jude) *Carl 8*
P *Peache Trustees* **R** J HOLDEN, **C** S FARMER
UMBERLEIGH (Church of the Good Shepherd)
S Molton w Nymet St George, High Bray etc *Ex*
UNDERBARROW (All Saints) *Carl 9* **P** *V Kendal H Trin*
V A F J LOFTHOUSE
UNDERRIVER (St Margaret) *Roch 8* **P** *Bp*
P-in-c B P SIMMONS
UNDERSKIDDAW (Parish Room) Crosthwaite
Keswick *Carl*
UNDERWOOD (St Michael and All Angels) Brinsley w
Underwood *S'well*
UNSTONE (St Mary) Dronfield w Holmesfield *Derby*
UNSWORTH (St George) *Man 10* **P** *R Prestwich St Mary*
V R M F HAIGH, **C** P R FRENCH
UP HATHERLEY (St Philip and St James) *Glouc 11*
P *Ch Union* **V** J H HEIDT, **C** C B THURSTON
UP MARDEN (St Michael) Compton, the Mardens,
Stoughton and Racton *Chich*
UP NATELY (St Stephen) Newnham w Nately Scures w
Mapledurwell etc *Win*
UP WALTHAM (St Mary the Virgin) *Chich 11* **P** *Lord
Egremont* **R** G A EVANS
UPCHURCH (St Mary the Virgin) w Lower Halstow
Cant 14 **P** *D&C* **V** J P LEFROY
UPHAM (All Saints) (Blessed Mary of Upham) *Portsm 1*
P *Ld Chan* **R** S E WILKINSON
UPHAVON (St Mary the Virgin) w Rushall and Charlton
Sarum 12 **P** *Mert Coll Ox, Ld Chan, and Ch Ch Ox
(by turn)* **R** D G SLOGGETT
UPHILL (St Nicholas) (St Barnabas Mission Church)
B & W 12 **P** *Ch Soc Trust* **R** D N MITCHELL,
C M J NORMAN, R A CADDELL
UPHOLLAND (St Thomas the Martyr) *Liv 11* **P** *Patr Bd*
TR P GOODRICH, **TV** S W ELSTOB,
C P A LOCK, T H ALLEN
UPLANDS (All Saints) Stroud and Uplands w Slad
Glouc
UPLEADON (St Mary the Virgin) Redmarley D'Abitot,
Bromesberrow w Pauntley etc *Glouc*
UPLOWMAN (St Peter) Sampford Peverell,
Uplowman, Holcombe Rogus etc *Ex*
UPLYME (St Peter and St Paul) w Axmouth *Ex 5*
P *CPAS and Hyndman Trustees (jt)* **R** F S WORTH

UPMINSTER (St Laurence) *Chelmsf 4*
P *Rev H R Holden* **R** S SWIFT, **C** D J MEAKIN,
Hon Par Dn J E SKIPPER
UPNOR (St Philip and St James) Frindsbury w Upnor
Roch
UPOTTERY (St Mary the Virgin) Yarcombe w
Membury and Upottery *Ex*
UPPER: *see also under substantive place names*
UPPER HOLME VALLEY, The *Wakef 6* **P** *Patr Bd*
TR J M SAUSBY, **TV** J N CAPSTICK, **Hon C** J M HILES,
NSM P MOATE
UPPERBY (St John the Baptist) *Carl 3* **P** *D&C*
V *Vacant* Carlisle (0228) 23380
UPPERTHONG (St John the Evangelist) Upper Holme
Valley *Wakef*
**UPPINGHAM (St Peter and St Paul) w Ayston and
Wardley w Belton** *Pet 14* **P** *Bp* **R** J I WILLETT,
C I A LOVETT, A J GILBERT
UPPINGTON (Holy Trinity) Longdon-upon-Tern,
Rodington, Uppington etc *Lich*
UPSHIRE (St Thomas) Waltham H Cross *Chelmsf*
UPTON (All Saints) *Linc 2* **P** *Bp* **V** J S CROFT
UPTON (Holy Ascension) *Ches 2* **P** *Duke of Westmr*
V G H CONWAY, **NSM** G J WELCH
UPTON (St Dunstan) Lytchett Minster *Sarum*
UPTON (St James) Brompton Regis w Upton and
Skilgate *B & W*
UPTON (St John the Baptist) Castor w Sutton and
Upton *Pet*
UPTON (St Laurence) Upton cum Chalvey *Ox*
UPTON (St Margaret) S Walsham and Upton *Nor*
UPTON (St Margaret) and Copmanford *Ely 10* **P** *Bp*
P-in-c R W B van de WEYER, **NSM** I D GIBSON
UPTON (St Mary) *Ches 8* **P** *Simeon's Trustees*
V N M WALKER, **C** G P BENSON, F S K WAINAINA
UPTON (St Mary Magdalene) *Ex 10* **P** *Simeon's Trustees
and Ch Patr Trust (alt)* **R** B J R GERRY
UPTON (St Mary the Virgin) Blewbury, Hagbourne and
Upton *Ox*
UPTON (St Peter and St Paul) Rolleston w Fiskerton,
Morton and Upton *S'well*
UPTON BISHOP (St John the Baptist) Linton w Upton
Bishop and Aston Ingham *Heref*
UPTON CRESSETT w Monk Hopton *Heref 9* **P** *DBP
and Miss E A Bird (alt)* **Hon C** H J PATTERSON
UPTON CROSS (St Paul) Linkinhorne *Truro*
UPTON CUM CHALVEY (St Mary) *Ox 23* **P** *Bp*
TR R A FERGUSON, **TV** A W DICKINSON,
Par Dn P M THOMAS
UPTON GREY (St Mary) Herriard w Winslade and
Long Sutton etc *Win*
UPTON HELLIONS (St Mary the Virgin) Sandford w
Upton Hellions *Ex*
UPTON LOVELL (St Augustine of Canterbury) Ashton
Gifford *Sarum*
UPTON MAGNA (St Lucia) Uffington, Upton Magna
and Withington *Lich*
UPTON NOBLE (St Mary Magdalene) Bruton and Distr
B & W
UPTON PARK (St Alban) E Ham w Upton Park
Chelmsf
UPTON PRIORY (Church of the Resurrection) *Ches 13*
P *Bp* **V** D J SAMBELL, **NSM** U B GAMBLES
UPTON PYNE (Our Lady) Thorverton, Cadbury,
Upton Pyne etc *Ex*
UPTON SCUDAMORE (St Mary the Virgin)
Warminster St Denys, Upton Scudamore etc *Sarum*
**UPTON SNODSBURY (St Kenelm) and Broughton Hackett
w the Flyfords and North Piddle** *Worc 4* **P** *Ld Chan,
Bp and Croome Estate Trustees (alt)* **Dn-in-c**
J WOOLLCOMBE
UPTON ST LEONARDS (St Leonard) *Glouc 6* **P** *Bp*
R T P JACKSON
UPTON-UPON-SEVERN (St Peter and Paul) *Worc 5*
P *Bp* **R** A R KING, **NSM** J A FRASER
UPTON WARREN (St Michael) Stoke Prior, Wychbold
and Upton Warren *Worc*
UPWELL (Christ Church) *Ely 18* **P** *R T Townley Esq*
R H G REID
UPWELL (St Peter) *Ely 19* **P** *R T Townley Esq*
R T J HEGGS
UPWEY (St Laurence) Bincombe w Broadwey, Upwey
and Buckland Ripers *Sarum*
UPWOOD (St Peter) The Ramseys and Upwood *Ely*
URCHFONT (St Michael and All Angels) Redhorn
Sarum
URMSTON (St Clement) *Man 7* **P** *Bp* **V** A M TILTMAN,
C C W READ

URSWICK (St Mary the Virgin and St Michael) *Carl 8*
P *Resident Landowners*   V D W WOODS
USHAW MOOR (St Luke) *Dur 2*   P *Bp*   V T J TOWERS
USSELBY (St Margaret)   S Kelsey Gp *Linc*
USWORTH (Holy Trinity) (St Michael and All Angels)
Dur 1   P *Patr Bd*   TR J W ELLIOTT,
TV N S GOSSWINN,   **Par Dn** C LOFGREN
UTKINTON (St Paul)   Tarporley *Ches*
UTLEY (St Mark) *Bradf 8*   P *Bp and R Keighley*
St Andr (jt)   V W D JAMIESON,   NSM W GREEN
UTTERBY (St Andrew)   Fotherby *Linc*
UTTOXETER (St Mary the Virgin) w Bramshall *Lich 21*
P *D&C Windsor*   P-in-c A G SADLER,
C V C SWEET,   A O L HODGSON
UXBRIDGE (St Andrew) (St John the Evangelist)
(St Margaret) (St Peter) *Lon 24*   P *Bp*
TR M J COLCLOUGH,   TV G J STEELE,
TM C J HEADLEY
VALLEY END (St Saviour)   Chobham w Valley End
Guildf
VALLEY PARK *Win 9*   P *Bp*   V T E DAYKIN
VANGE (All Saints) (St Chad) *Chelmsf 9*   P *MMCET*
R J E BATEMAN
VAUXHALL (St Peter)   N Lambeth *S'wark*
VENN OTTERY (St Gregory)   Ottery St Mary,
Alfington, W Hill, Tipton etc *Ex*
VENTNOR (Holy Trinity) *Portsm 7*   P *Bp*
P-in-c D H LAURIE
VENTNOR (St Catherine) *Portsm 7*   P *Ch Patr Trust*
P-in-c D H LAURIE,   C D J H POWE
VERNHAM DEAN (St Mary the Virgin)   Hurstbourne
Tarrant, Faccombe, Vernham Dean etc *Win*
VERWOOD (St Michael and All Angels) *Sarum 10*   P *Bp*
V A G GILL,   C T L PESKETT,   P J A HASTINGS
VERYAN (St Symphoriana) w Ruan Lanihorne *Truro 6*
P *D&C and DBP (jt)*   R M B GEACH
VICTORIA DOCKS (Ascension) *Chelmsf 5*   P *Bp*
P-in-c R F H HOWARTH
VICTORIA DOCKS St Luke *Chelmsf 5*   P *Ld Chan*
P-in-c K MELBOURNE
VIGO (Village Hall)   Stansted w Fairseat and Vigo *Roch*
VINEY HILL (All Saints) *Glouc 4*   P *Univ Coll Ox*
P-in-c G J HUTCHINSON
VIRGINIA WATER (Christ Church) *Guildf 11*
P *Simeon's Trustees*   V D W VAIL,   C J T PETERS
VIRGINSTOW (St Bridget)   Werrington, St Giles in the
Heath and Virginstow *Truro*
VOWCHURCH (St Bartholomew)   Peterchurch w
Vowchurch, Turnastone and Dorstone *Heref*
WABERTHWAITE (St John)   Eskdale, Irton,
Muncaster and Waberthwaite *Carl*
WACTON (All Saints)   Stratton St Mary w Stratton St
Michael etc *Nor*
WADDESDON (St Michael and All Angels) w Over
Winchendon and Fleet Marston *Ox 24*   P *Duke of*
Marlborough   R C M HUTCHINGS
WADDINGHAM (St Mary and St Peter)   Bishop
Norton, Wadingham and Snitterby *Linc*
WADDINGTON (St Helen) *Bradf 5*   P *E C Parker Esq*
V A G BAILEY
WADDINGTON (St Michael) *Linc 18*   P *Linc Coll Ox*
R J L A JACOB,   NSM S E KIDDLE
WADDON (St George)   Croydon St Jo *S'wark*
WADENHOE (St Michael and All Angels)   Aldwincle w
Thorpe Achurch, Pilton, Wadenhoe etc *Pet*
WADHURST (St Peter and St Paul) *Chich 19*
P *E J B Hardcastle Esq and M R Toynbee Esq (jt)*
V M G P INSLEY
WADINGHAM (St Mary and St Peter)   Bishop Norton,
Wadingham and Snitterby *Linc*
WADSHELF (Mission Room)   Old Brampton and
Loundsley Green *Derby*
WADSLEY (Christchurch) *Sheff 4*   P *Ch Patr Trust*
V D B JEANS,   C A M CUTTING
WADWORTH (St John the Baptist) w Loversall *Sheff 10*
P *V Doncaster and DBP (alt)*   V R M HARVEY
WAINCLIFFE (St David)   Beeston *Ripon*
WAINFLEETS (All Saints) (St Mary) (St Michael) and
Croft, The *Linc 8*   P *Ld Chan, Bp and*
T E P Barnard Esq (alt)   R P F COATES
WAITHE (St Martin) *Linc 10*   P *Personal Reps*
C L E Haigh   V R K EMM
WAKEFIELD Chantry Bridge (St Mary)   Wakef St Andr
and St Mary *Wakef*
WAKEFIELD (St Andrew and St Mary) (St Swithun)
Wakef 12   P *Peache Trustees*   V B S ELLIS
WAKEFIELD (St John the Baptist) *Wakef 12*   P *Provost*
V E V DAVEY

WAKERING, GREAT (St Nicholas) w Foulness *Chelmsf 15*
P *Bp*   V *Vacant*   Southend-on-Sea (0702) 219226
WAKERING, LITTLE (St Mary the Virgin)   Barling w
Lt Wakering *Chelmsf*
WAKERLEY (St John the Baptist)   Barrowden and
Wakerley w S Luffenham *Pet*
WAKES COLNE (All Saints)   Gt Tey and Wakes Colne
w Chappel *Chelmsf*
WALBERSWICK (St Andrew) w Blythburgh *St E 15*
P *Sir Charles Blois*   P-in-c H V EDWARDS,   J E MURRELL
WALBERTON (St Mary) w Binsted *Chich 21*   P *Bp*
V M J SULLY
WALCOT Bath Walcot *B & W*
WALCOT (All Saints)   Happisburgh w Walcot,
Hempstead, Lessingham etc *Nor*
WALCOT (St Nicholas)   S Lafford *Linc*
WALCOT (St Oswald)   Billinghay *Linc*
WALDEN, LITTLE (St John)   Saffron Walden w
Wendens Ambo and Littlebury *Chelmsf*
WALDERSLADE (St William)   Chatham St Wm *Roch*
WALDINGFIELD, GREAT (St Lawrence)   Acton w Gt
Waldingfield *St E*
WALDINGFIELD, LITTLE (St Lawrence)
Edwardstone w Groton and Lt Waldingfield *St E*
WALDITCH (St Mary)   Bridport *Sarum*
WALDRINGFIELD (All Saints) w Hemley and Newbourn
St E 2   P *Canon T Waller and Rev A H N Waller,*
Ld Chan, and Sir Joshua Rowley, Bt (by turn)
R J P WALLER
WALDRON (All Saints) *Chich 15*   P *Ex Coll Ox*
R D J PASKINS
WALES (St John the Baptist) *Sheff 5*   P *Bp*
V H J PATRICK
WALESBY (St Edmund) *S'well 3*   P *DBP*   V I CLARK
WALESBY (St Mary and All Saints) *Linc 5*   P *Bp, DBP,*
and W Drake Esq (jt)   R G H BABINGTON
WALFORD (St Michael and All Angels) and Saint John, w
Bishopswood, Goodrich, Marstow and Welsh Bicknor
Heref 8   P *Bp and Ld Chan (alt)*   R P TARLING
WALGRAVE (St Peter) w Hannington and Wold and
Scaldwell *Pet 2*   P *Bp (2 turns), BNC Ox (1 turn)*
R D G THOMAS
WALHAM GREEN (St John) (St James) *Lon 9*   P *Bp*
V M R WEBSTER,   C D M B BELL
WALKDEN (St Barnabas' Mission)   Walkden Moor *Man*
WALKDEN MOOR (St Paul) *Man 12*   P *Bp*
V A E BALLARD,   C J T ALLISON
WALKER (Christ Church) *Newc 6*   P *Bp*   V R BEST
WALKERGATE (St Oswald) *Newc 6*   P *Bp*
V K MOULDER,   C P V PARKER
WALKERINGHAM (St Mary Magdalene)   Beckingham
w Walkeringham *S'well*
WALKERN (St Mary the Virgin)   Benington w Walkern
St Alb
WALKHAMPTON (St Mary the Virgin)   Yelverton,
Meavy, Sheepstor and Walkhampton *Ex*
WALKINGTON (All Hallows)   Bishop Burton w
Walkington *York*
WALKLEY (St Mary) *Sheff 4*   P *Bp*   V I K DUFFIELD
WALL (St George)   St Oswald in Lee w Bingfield *Newc*
WALL (St John the Baptist) *Lich 2*   P *R Lich SS Mary*
and Mich   P-in-c D A SMITH
WALLASEY (St Hilary) *Ches 7*   P *Bp*   R R ORTON,
C M R G SMITH
WALLASEY (St Nicholas) *Ches 7*   P *Bp*   V E J BENTLEY
WALLINGFORD (St Mary le More w All Hallows)
(St Leonard) and St Peter w Crowmarsh Gifford
(St Mary Magdalene) and Newnham Murren *Ox 18*
P *Bp*   TR A E GOOD,   TV G B BRAUND,
C J A GORDON,   Hon C W P HEDGCOCK
WALLINGTON (Holy Trinity) (St Patrick) *S'wark 25*
P *Ch Soc Trust*   V D V LEWIS,   C M J RIGBY,
T M HUMPHREY,   NSM M B WHITE,   B E BROWN
WALLINGTON Roundshaw (St Paul)   Roundshaw CD
S'wark
WALLINGTON (St Mary)   Sandon, Wallington and
Rushden w Clothall *St Alb*
WALLISDOWN (St Saviour)   Talbot Village *Sarum*
WALLOP, NETHER (St Andrew)   Over Wallop w
Nether Wallop *Win*
WALLOP, OVER (St Peter) w Nether Wallop *Win 3*
P *D&C York and Earl of Portsm (alt)*
R G G CHAPMAN
WALLSEND (St John the Evangelist) *Newc 8*   P *Bp*
V F WILSON
WALLSEND (St Luke) *Newc 8*   P *Bp*   V J G INGE,
C S M WELLS
WALLSEND (St Peter) *Newc 8*   P *Bp*   R J DEWAR

WALMER (St Mary) (St Saviour) (Blessed Virgin Mary)
Cant 8   **P** Abp   **V** B A HAWKINS,   **Par Dn** M K DAVIES
WALMERSLEY (Christ Church) Man 10   **P** Trustees
V B STANNARD,   **Hon Par Dn** M E MAYOH
WALMLEY (St John the Evangelist) Birm 9   **P** Trustess
V M B HARPER,   **C** D A SLIM
WALMSLEY (Christ Church) Man 16   **P** V Bolton-le-
Moors St Pet   **V** J I McFIE,   **C** D BOWERS, C R HONOUR
WALNEY ISLAND (St Mary the Virgin) Carl 8
P V Dalton-in-Furness   **V** R J WILLIAMSON
WALPOLE (St Mary the Virgin) Halesworth w
Linstead, Chediston, Holton etc St E
WALPOLE ST PETER (St Peter and St Paul) w St Andrew
Ely 17   **P** The Crown and DBP (alt)   **R** A R TREEN
WALSALL (St Andrew) Lich 7   **P** Bp   **V** R A HANSON
WALSALL (St Gabriel) Fulbrook Lich 7   **P** Bp
V T R H COYNE
WALSALL (St Mary and All Saints) Palfrey Lich 7   **P** Bp
V Vacant   Walsall (0922) 21769
WALSALL (St Matthew) (St Luke) (St Martin) Lich 7
P Patr Bd   **TR** M B SANDERS,
TV M J BUTT, A G C SMITH, J E SHARPE,   **C** P TYSON
WALSALL (St Paul) Lich 7   **P** R Walsall   **V** J S DAVIS,
Par Dn E M BARNES
WALSALL (St Peter) Lich 7   **P** R Walsall   **V** J S ARTISS
WALSALL (Annunciation of Our Lady)   Walsall St
Gabr Fullbrook Lich
WALSALL THE PLECK (St John) and Bescot Lich 7
P V Walsall   **V** J H MARTIN,   **Par Dn** H J SMART
WALSALL WOOD (St John) Lich 7   **P** R Walsall
V M A RHODES,   **C** D S TURNER
WALSDEN (St Peter) Wakef 3   **P** Bp   **P-in-c** G FRYER
WALSGRAVE ON SOWE (St Mary) Cov 1   **P** Ld Chan
V M TYLER,   **NSM** F E TYLER
WALSHAM, NORTH (St Nicholas) w Antingham Nor 9
P Bp   **V** M W SMITH,   **C** T C DIAPER
WALSHAM, SOUTH (St Laurence w St Mary) and Upton
Nor 1   **P** Qu Coll Cam and Bp (jt)   **R** G A HENDY
WALSHAM LE WILLOWS (St Mary) and Finningham w
Westhorpe St E 9   **P** R M Martineau Esq, DBP, and
Ch Union (jt)   **R** J S WOOD
WALSHAW (Christ Church) Man 10   **P** Simeon's
Trustees   **V** I N FISHWICK,   **C** A J THEWLIS
WALSINGHAM (St Mary and All Saints) (St Peter) and
Houghton (St Giles) Nor 20   **P** J Gurney Esq
V M J REAR
WALSOKEN (All Saints) Ely 19   **P** DBP
R I E D FARROW
WALTERSTONE (St Mary)   Ewyas Harold w Dulas,
Kenderchurch etc Heref
WALTHAM (All Saints) Linc 10   **P** The Crown
R W J A NUNNERLEY
WALTHAM (Holy Cross) Chelmsf 2   **P** Patr Bd
TR P J B HOBSON,   **TV** P H AWORTH,
C J J CRUSE, D P RITCHIE
WALTHAM (St Bartholomew)   Petham and Waltham w
Lower Hardres etc Cant
WALTHAM (St Lawrence) Ox 13   **P** Lord Braybrooke
V P RADLEY
WALTHAM, GREAT (St Mary and St Lawrence) w Ford
End Chelmsf 11   **P** Trin Coll Ox   **V** L A A CARTER
WALTHAM, LITTLE (St Martin) Chelmsf 11
P Ex Coll Ox   **R** H ANSELL
WALTHAM, NEW (St Matthew) Linc 10   **P** The Crown
V R J BRADSHAW
WALTHAM, NORTH (St Michael) and Steventon, Ashe
and Deane Win 6   **P** DBP   **R** G R TURNER
WALTHAM ABBEY (Holy Cross)   Waltham H Cross
Chelmsf
WALTHAM CROSS (Christ Church) St Alb 6
P V Cheshunt   **V** M J BANISTER,   **C** A P HOLFORD
WALTHAM ON THE WOLDS (St Mary Magdalene),
Stonesby, Saxby w Stapleford and Wyfordby Leic 3
P Duke of Rutland, Lady Gretton, and Sir Lyonel
Tollemache, Bt (jt)   **R** J P STONE
WALTHAMSTOW (St Andrew) Chelmsf 8   **P** Bp
V M R J LAND
WALTHAMSTOW (St Barnabas and St James the Great)
Chelmsf 8   **P** Bp   **V** A D COUCHMAN
WALTHAMSTOW (St Gabriel) Chelmsf 8   **P** Simeon's
Trustees   **V** J GUTTERIDGE
WALTHAMSTOW (St John) Chelmsf 8
P TR Walthamstow   **V** A H MUST,
Hon Par Dn S A MUST
WALTHAMSTOW (St Luke) Chelmsf 8   **P** Simeon's
Trustees   **V** P J WOOD,   **C** A I KEECH
WALTHAMSTOW (St Mary) (St Stephen) Chelmsf 8
P Patr Bd   **TR** P J TRENDALL,   **TV** N S KAGGWA,
C R G V FOREMAN, P J BOARDMAN

WALTHAMSTOW (St Michael and All Angels) Chelmsf 8
P Bp   **P-in-c** J TETLOW
WALTHAMSTOW (St Peter-in-the-Forest) Chelmsf 8
P Bp   **C** K WILSON,   **Hon Par Dn** D E P PALK
WALTHAMSTOW (St Saviour) Chelmsf 8   **P** Bp
V P D D JAMES,   **C** C J DAVIES
WALTON (Holy Trinity)   Street w Walton B & W
WALTON (Holy Trinity) Ox 21   **P** Patr Bd and DBP (jt)
TR D S BREWIN,   **TV** N A HAND, R G HART,
C S J REED, P D F HORNER,   **Par Dn** A E COOKE
WALTON (not known)   Gilmorton w Peatling Parva and
Kimcote etc Leic
WALTON (St John)   Brampton St Thos Derby
WALTON (St John the Evangelist) Ches 4
P P G Greenall Esq   **V** W J HIGHTON
WALTON (St Mary)   Lanercost w Kirkcambeck and
Walton Carl
WALTON (St Mary) (St Philip) St E 2   **P** Ch Trust Fund
Trust   **V** J CULL,   **C** G J ARCHER, Y P IRVINE
WALTON (St Paul)   Sandal St Helen Wakef
WALTON (St Peter)   Thorp Arch w Walton York
WALTON (St Thomas)   Baswich (or Berkswich) Lich
WALTON, EAST (St Mary)   Gayton Gp of Par Nor
WALTON, HIGHER (All Saints) Blackb 6   **P** V Blackb
Par Dn B SHILLCOCK
WALTON (Milton Keynes) Ox 25   **P** Patr Bd
TR N J COTTON,   **TV** D K MIELL
WALTON, WEST (St Mary) Ely 17   **P** Ld Chan
C G HOWARD
WALTON BRECK (Christ Church) Liv 7   **P** Simeon's
Trustees   **V** S B PIERCE
WALTON BRECK (Holy Trinity) Liv 7   **P** Simeon's
Trustees   **V** G D PARKIN
WALTON D'EIVILLE (St James) Cov 8   **P** Sir Richard
Hamilton, Bt   **R** N V HOWES
WALTON IN GORDANO (St Mary)   E Clevedon and
Walton w Weston w Clapton B & W
WALTON IN GORDANO (St Paul)   as above
WALTON-LE-DALE (St Leonard) Blackb 6   **P** V Blackb
V Vacant   Preston (0772) 52962
WALTON LE SOKEN (All Saints) (St George) Chelmsf 26
P Bp   **V** G D A BENNET
WALTON LE WOLDS (St Mary)   Barrow upon Soar w
Walton le Wolds Leic
WALTON-ON-THAMES (St Mary) Guildf 8   **P** Bp
V T J SEDGLEY,   **C** D W GREEN, A E D CUFFE-FULLER,
NSM R C CUFFE-FULLER
WALTON ON THE HILL (St John) Liv 7   **P** Bp, Adn,
and R Walton (jt)   **V** S GROSSCURTH
WALTON ON THE HILL (St Luke) Liv 7   **P** Bp
V H E ROSS
WALTON ON THE HILL (St Mary) (St Aidan) Liv 5
P Bp   **TV** P C ATHERTON,
C G L DRIVER, H I J SOUTHERN
WALTON-ON-THE-HILL (St Peter) Guildf 9   **P** Bp
R J S HARRIS
WALTON ON TRENT (St Lawrence) w Croxall and Coton
in the Elms w Rosliston Derby 16   **P** Bp and
D W H Neilson Esq (jt)   **P-in-c** J W THORPE
WALWORTH (St Christopher) (St Peter) S'wark 8   **P** Bp
TV G P ANNAS,   **P-in-c** G S MURRAY,   **Par Dn** R A SHAW
WALWORTH (St John w the Lady Margaret) S'wark 8
P Bp   **V** V A DAVIES,   **C** A D CAIN,   **Hon C** E DAWSON
WAMBROOK (Blessed Virgin Mary)   Combe St
Nicholas w Wambrook B & W
WANBOROUGH (St Andrew)   Lyddington and
Wanborough and Bishopstone etc Bris
WANBOROUGH (St Bartholomew)   Puttenham and
Wanborough Guildf
WANDSWORTH (All Saints) (Holy Trinity) S'wark 17
P Ch Soc Trust   **V** A G SIRMAN,
C C J KING, W A WILSON
WANDSWORTH Southfields (St Michael and All Angels)
S'wark 17   **P** Ch Soc Trust   **V** D J CASIOT
WANDSWORTH (St Anne) S'wark 17   **P** Bp
V M H CLARK,   **C** K PARKES
WANDSWORTH (St Faith) S'wark 17   **P** Bp
V C C M COWARD
WANDSWORTH (St Stephen) S'wark 17   **P** CPAS
V G M VEVERS,   **Hon C** J H FREEMAN
WANDSWORTH Wimbledon Park (St Paul) S'wark 17
P Bp   **V** W A J ALLBERRY,   **NSM** G E D BONHAM-
CARTER, A J TOWNSEND
WANDSWORTH COMMON (St Mary Magdalene)
S'wark 16   **P** Bp   **V** I KITTERINGHAM
WANGFORD (St Peter)   Uggeshall w Sotherton,
Wangford and Henham St E
WANLIP (Our Lady and St Nicholas)   Birstall and
Wanlip Leic

WANSFORD (St Mary)   Nafferton w Wansford *York*

WANSFORD (St Mary the Virgin)   Wittering w Thornhaugh and Wansford *Pet*

WANSTEAD (Holy Trinity) Hermon Hill *Chelmsf 7*   P   *Bp*
  V   A H ASHDOWN,   Hon Par Dn   D E P PALK

WANSTEAD (St Mary) (Christ Church) *Chelmsf 7*   P   *Bp*
  C   R S P HINGLEY

WANSTROW (Blessed Virgin Mary)   Nunney and Witham Friary, Marston Bigot etc *B & W*

WANTAGE (St Peter and St Paul) *Ox 19*
  P   *D&C Windsor*   V   A R WRIGHT,   C   L T MCKENNA,
  NSM   P H JOHNS

WANTAGE DOWNS *Ox 19*   P   *Bp, CCC Ox, and*
  C L Loyd Esq (jt)
  NSM   C J KING,   M G D ENDEAN,   D J PAGE

WANTISDEN (St John the Baptist)   Eyke w Bromeswell, Rendlesham, Tunstall etc *St E*

WAPLEY (St Peter)   Yate New Town *Bris*

WAPPENBURY (St John the Baptist) w Weston under Wetherley *Cov 10*   P   *Bp*   P-in-c   D C JESSETT

WAPPENHAM (St Mary the Virgin)   Weedon Lois w Plumpton and Moreton Pinkney etc *Pet*

WARBLETON (St Mary) and Bodle Street Green *Chich 15*
  P   *Rev E S Haviland*   R   J R McGOWAN

WARBLINGTON (St Thomas a Becket) and Emsworth *Portsm 4*   P   *Bp and J H Norris Esq (alt)*
  R   D J F PARTRIDGE,   C   J I OYET,   Par Dn   R J BULLOCK

WARBOROUGH (St Lawrence) *Ox 1*   P   *CCC Ox*
  V   *Vacant*   Warborough (086732) 8381

WARBOYS (St Mary Magdalene) *Ely 11*   P   *Ch Soc Trust*
  P-in-c   S O LEEKE

WARBSTOW (St Werburgh)   St Gennys, Jacobstow w Warbstow and Treneglos *Truro*

WARBURTON (St Werburgh) *Ches 10*
  P   *Hon M L W Flower*   P-in-c   B HARRIS

WARCOP (St Columba)   Brough w Stainmore, Musgrave and Warcop *Carl*

WARD END (Christ Church)   Burney Lane *Birm*

WARD END (St Margaret) *Birm 10*   P   *Aston Patr Trust*
  V   R G LEWIS

WARDEN (St Michael and All Angels) w Newbrough *Newc 4*   P   *Bp*   V   J W GLEDHILL

WARDEN, OLD (St Leonard) *St Alb 17*
  P   *R O Shuttleworth Trustees*   V   *Vacant*

WARDINGTON (St Mary Magdalene)   Cropredy w Gt Bourton and Wardington *Ox*

WARDLE (St James the Apostle) *Man 19*
  P   *V Smallbridge St Jo*   V   K W PORTER

WARDLEWORTH (St Mary w St James)   Rochdale *Man*

WARDLEY (St Botolph)   Uppingham w Ayston and Wardley w Belton *Pet*

WARDLOW (Good Shepherd)   Longstone *Derby*

WARE (Christ Church) *St Alb 8*   P   *CPAS*
  V   D H WHEATON,   C   P A WILLIAMS

WARE (St Mary the Virgin) *St Alb 8*   P   *Trin Coll Cam*
  V   H E WILCOX,   Hon C   J H HORNER,
  NSM   M CAPEL-EDWARDS,   M S E M BEAZLEY

WAREHAM (Lady St Mary) (St Martin) *Sarum 9*
  P   *Patr Bd*   TR   P G HARDMAN,   TV   H E SQUIRE,
  C   B L M PHILLIPS,   Hon Par Dn   M H MULRAINE

WAREHORNE (St Matthew)   Orlestone w Snave and Ruckinge w Warehorne *Cant*

WARESIDE (Holy Trinity)   Hunsdon w Widford and Wareside *St Alb*

WARESLEY (St James) *Ely 12*   P   *Pemb Coll Cam*
  V   W J PATTERSON

WARFIELD (St Michael the Archangel) *Ox 11*   P   *DBP*
  V   B H MEARDON

WARGRAVE (St Mary the Virgin) *Ox 16*   P   *Lord Remnant*   V   J W RATINGS,   NSM   M D W PARTRIDGE

WARHAM (All Saints)   Holkham w Egmere w Warham, Wells and Wighton *Nor*

WARK (St Michael)   Humshaugh w Simonburn and Wark *Newc*

WARKLEIGH (St John)   S Molton w Nymet St George, High Bray etc *Ex*

WARKTON (St Edmund)   Barton Seagrave w Warkton *Pet*

WARKWORTH (St Lawrence) and Acklington *Newc 9*
  P   *Bp and Duke of Northd (alt)*   V   G A NEWMAN

WARKWORTH (St Mary the Virgin)   Greatworth and Marston St Lawrence etc *Pet*

WARLEGGAN (St Neot)   St Neot and Warleggan *Truro*

WARLEY (St John the Evangelist) *Wakef 4*   P   *V Halifax*
  V   T L SWINHOE,   NSM   J S BRADBERRY

WARLEY, GREAT (Christ Church) *Chelmsf 10*   P   *Bp*
  V   P W H GOODE

WARLEY, GREAT (St Mary the Virgin) w Childerditch and Ingrave *Chelmsf 10*   P   *Hon G C D Jeffreys, MMCET and Ch Patr Trust (jt)*   P-in-c   D A HART

WARLEY, LITTLE (St Peter)   E and W Horndon w Lt Warley *Chelmsf*

WARLEY WOODS (St Hilda) *Birm 5*   P   *Bp*
  V   M GRAHAM

WARLINGHAM (All Saints) w Chelsham and Farleigh *S'wark 18*   P   *Bp (3 turns), Mert Coll Ox (1 turn)*
  R   *Vacant*   Upper Warlingham (08832) 4125

WARMFIELD (St Peter) *Wakef 9*   P   *Oley Trustees Clare Coll Cam*   V   A C MARTLEW

WARMINGHAM (St Leonard)   Elworth and Warmingham *Ches*

WARMINGTON (St Mary the Blessed Virgin), Tansor w Cotterstock and Fotheringhay *Pet 12*   P   *Bp and D&C Linc (alt)*   P-in-c   M W R COVINGTON

WARMINGTON (St Michael) w Shotteswell and Radway w Ratley *Cov 8*   P   *Bp*   R   R P PAUL

WARMINSTER (Christ Church) *Sarum 14*
  P   *R Warminster St Denys etc*   V   F J WOODS

WARMINSTER (St Denys), Upton Scudamore and Horningsham *Sarum 14*   P   *Qu Coll Ox (1 turn), Bp (2 turns)*   R   R SHARPE,   C   P J D HAWKSWORTH

WARMLEY (St Barnabas) *Bris 2*   P   *Bp*
  V   D G MITCHELL,   Par Dn   M P SIMPSON

WARMSWORTH (St Peter) *Sheff 10*   P   *Bp*
  R   J A P BOOTH,   C   K E TONES

WARMWELL (Holy Trinity)   Broadmayne, W Knighton, Owermoigne etc *Sarum*

WARNBOROUGH, SOUTH (St Andrew)   Herriard w Winslade and Long Sutton etc *Win*

WARNDON (St Nicholas) *Worc 6*   P   *Bp*   V   *Vacant*

WARNDON (St Wulstan)   Worc St Wulstan *Worc*

WARNERS END (St Alban)   Hemel Hempstead *St Alb*

WARNFORD (Our Lady)   W Meon and Warnford *Portsm*

WARNHAM (St Margaret) *Chich 8*   P   *J C Lucas Esq*
  V   J R TAYLOR

WARNINGLID (St Andrew)   Slaugham *Chich*

WARREN PARK (St Clare) *Portsm 4*   P   *Bp*
  NSM   M S HARPER

WARREN ROW (St Paul)   Knowl Hill w Littlewick *Ox*

WARRINGTON (Holy Trinity) *Liv 12*   P   *R Warrington*
  V   *Vacant*   Warrington (0925) 30057

WARRINGTON (St Ann) *Liv 12*   P   *Simeon's Trustees*
  V   S R PARISH

WARRINGTON (St Barnabas) Bank Quay *Liv 12*
  P   *R Warrington and Bp (jt)*   V   M RAYNOR,
  NSM   J BROCKLEBANK

WARRINGTON (St Elphin) (St John) *Liv 12*   P   *Lord Lilford*   R   J O COLLING,
  C   M R NICHOLLS,   A H MANSON-BRAILSFORD

WARSLOW (St Lawrence)   Alstonfield, Butterton, Warslow w Elkstone etc *Lich*

WARSOP (St Peter and St Paul) *S'well 2*   P   *Trustees*
  R   C W BOWMAN,   C   A A TOOBY,
  Hon Par Dn   J V SHARPE

WARTER (St James)   Nunburnholme and Warter *York*

WARTHILL (St Mary)   Stockton-on-the-Forest w Holtby and Warthill *York*

WARTLING (St Mary Magdalene)   Herstmonceux and Wartling *Chich*

WARTNABY (St Michael)   Ab Kettleby Gp *Leic*

WARTON (Holy Trinity) *Birm 12*   P   *V Polesworth*
  V   *Vacant*

WARTON (St Oswald or Holy Trinity) w Yealand Conyers (St John) *Blackb 15*   P   *Bp*   V   F B ODDY,
  Hon C   C R P ANSTEY

WARTON (St Paul) *Blackb 11*   P   *Ch Ch Ox*
  V   G WORTHINGTON

WARWICK (St Leonard)   Wetheral w Warw *Carl*

WARWICK (St Mary) (St Nicholas) *Cov 11*   P   *Ld Chan and Patr Bd (alt)*   TR   S C LITTLE,
  TV   A A GORHAM,   P J SUTCLIFFE,   Par Dn   G SANDERSON

WARWICK (St Paul) *Cov 11*   P   *TR Warw*
  V   G L LYNCH-WATSON

WASDALE, NETHER (St Michael)   Gosforth w Nether Wasdale and Wasdale Head *Carl*

WASDALE HEAD (not known)   as above

WASH COMMON (St George)   Newbury *Ox*

WASHBOURNE, GREAT (St Mary)   Alderton w Gt Washbourne *Glouc*

WASHBROOK (St Mary)   Copdock w Washbrook and Belstead *St E*

WASHFIELD (St Mary the Virgin), Stoodleigh, Withleigh, Calverleigh, Oakford, Templeton, Loxbeare, Rackenford, Cruwys Morchard, Chevithorne, Cove,

Bickleigh and Cadeleigh *Ex 8* **P** *DBP*
  TR H G WHITTY, **TV** C H MEE, R C THORP
WASHFORD (St Mary) Old Cleeve, Leighland and
  Treborough *B & W*
WASHFORD PYNE (St Peter) N Creedy *Ex*
WASHINGBOROUGH (St John) w Heighington and
  Canwick *Linc 18* **P** *DBP and Mercers' Co (jt)*
  R A C BELL, **Hon C** W A CRANIDGE
WASHINGTON (Holy Trinity) *Dur 1* **P** *Bp*
  R C LINGARD, **C** W D TAYLOR
WASHINGTON (St Mary) Ashington w Buncton,
  Wiston and Washington *Chich*
WASHWOOD HEATH (St Mark) *Birm 10* **P** *V Saltley*
  P-in-c R E CRANE, **Hon C** A J PRESCOTT,
  NSM P M EATON
WASING (St Nicholas) Aldermaston w Wasing and
  Brimpton *Ox*
WASKERLEY (St Andrew) Blanchland w
  Hunstanworth and Edmundbyers etc *Newc*
WASPERTON (St John the Baptist) Barford w
  Wasperton and Sherbourne *Cov*
WASS (St Thomas) Coxwold and Husthwaite *York*
WATCHET (Holy Cross Chapel) St Decumans *B & W*
WATCHET (St Decuman) as above
WATCHFIELD (St Thomas's Chapel) Shrivenham w
  Watchfield and Bourton *Ox*
WATER EATON (St Frideswide) *Ox 25* **P** *Bp*
  V *Vacant*
WATER NEWTON (St Remigius) *Ely 13* **P** *Keble*
  Coll Ox **P-in-c** P O POOLEY
WATER ORTON (St Peter and St Paul) *Birm 11*
  P *Patr Bd* **P-in-c** S T MAYES
WATER STRATFORD (St Giles) Tingewick w Water
  Stratford, Radclive etc *Ox*
WATERBEACH (St John) *Ely 6* **P** *Bp*
  V D P E REINDORP
WATERDEN (All Saints) N and S Creake w Waterden
  Nor
WATERFALL (St James and St Bartholomew) Calton,
  Cauldon, Grindon and Waterfall *Lich*
WATERFOOT (St James the Great) *Man 15* **P** *Trustees*
  V R T RICHARDSON
WATERFORD (St Michael and All Angels) Bramfield
  w Stapleford and Waterford *St Alb*
WATERHEAD (Holy Trinity) *Man 18* **P** *The Crown*
  V C E SHAW
WATERHOUSES (St Paul) *Dur 2* **P** *R Brancepeth*
  V P J A KENNEDY
WATERINGBURY (St John the Baptist) w Teston and
  West Farleigh *Roch 7* **P** *Peache Trustees and D&C (jt)*
  R D BISH
WATERLOO (Christ Church) (St Mary) *Liv 1*
  P *Trustees* **V** R J HUTCHINSON
WATERLOO (St John) *Liv 1* **P** *Trustees*
  V P W DEARNLEY
WATERLOO (St John the Evangelist) (St Andrew) *S'wark*
  10 **P** *Abp and CPAS (jt)* **V** R J YEOMANS,
  Par Dn I M PAGE
WATERLOOVILLE (St George) *Portsm 4* **P** *Bp*
  V M FERRIER
WATERMILLOCK (All Saints) Greystoke, Matterdale,
  Mungrisdale & Watermillock *Carl*
WATERMOOR (Holy Trinity) Cirencester *Glouc*
WATERPERRY (St Mary the Virgin) Holton and
  Waterperry w Albury and Waterstock *Ox*
WATERS UPTON (St Michael) Tibberton w Bolas
  Magna and Waters Upton *Lich*
WATERSTOCK (St Leonard) Holton and Waterperry w
  Albury and Waterstock *Ox*
WATERTHORPE (Emmanuel) Mosborough *Sheff*
WATFORD (Christ Church) (St Mark) *St Alb 13* **P** *Bp,*
  V Watford, and Churchwardens (jt) **V** R C LEWIS,
  Par Dn A R BEEVER
WATFORD (St Andrew) *St Alb 13* **P** *Bp and*
  Churchwardens (jt) **V** N B MOORE
WATFORD (St John) *St Alb 13* **P** *Bp* **V** R SALTER
WATFORD (St Luke) *St Alb 13* **P** *Bp, Adn St Alb,*
  V Watford, and Ch Trust Fund Trust (jt) **V** *Vacant*
  Watford (0923) 31205
WATFORD (St Mary) *St Alb 13* **P** *Ch Trust Fund Trust*
  V J M WOODGER, **C** B S P LEATHERS,
  Par Dn D K DAWES, **NSM** A D MILTON
WATFORD (St Michael and All Angels) *St Alb 13* **P** *Bp*
  V J B BROWN, **C** G A FINLAYSON
WATFORD (St Peter) *St Alb 13* **P** *Bp* **V** C P COTTEE
WATFORD (St Peter and St Paul) Long Buckby w
  Watford *Pet*
WATH (St Mary) Kirklington w Burneston and Wath
  and Pickhill *Ripon*

WATH BROW (Mission Church) Cleator Moor w
  Cleator *Carl*
WATH-UPON-DEARNE (All Saints) w Adwick-upon-
  Dearne *Sheff 12* **P** *D&C of Ch Ch Ox* **V** M WRIGHT,
  C D C GLOVER
WATLING VALLEY, Milton Keynes (not known) *Ox 25*
  P *Patr Bd* **R** F G GODBER, **TV** S F MORRIS,
  R D TRUMPER
WATLINGTON (St Leonard) w Pyrton and Shirburn *Ox 1*
  P *Bp, Ch Ch Ox, and Earl of Macclesfield (by turn)*
  V C I EVANS
WATLINGTON (St Peter and St Paul) *Ely 16* **P** *Bp*
  R J C W NOLAN
WATTISFIELD (St Margaret) Hepworth, Hinderclay,
  Wattisfield and Thelnetham *St E*
WATTLESBOROUGH (St Margaret) Alberbury w
  Cardeston *Heref*
WATTON (St Mary) Hutton Cranswick w Skerne,
  Watton and Beswick *York*
WATTON (St Mary) w Carbrooke and Ovington *Nor 18*
  P *Ld Chan (3 turns), Cam Univ (1 turn), and SMF*
  (2 turns) **V** P H HARRISON, **C** J T EYRE
WATTON AT STONE (St Mary and St Andrew) *St Alb 12*
  P *R M A Smith Esq* **R** R A THOMSON
WAVENDON w WALTON Assumption (St Mary the
  Virgin) Walton Milton Keynes *Ox*
WAVERTON (Christ Church) Bromfield w Waverton
  Carl
WAVERTON (St Peter) *Ches 5* **P** *Bp* **R** J M G DAVIES
WAVERTREE (Holy Trinity) *Liv 6* **P** *Bp*
  R R L METCALF, **C** C HURST, **NSM** L B BRUCE
WAVERTREE (St Bridget) *Liv 6* **P** *R Wavertree Holy*
  Trin **P-in-c** W J SANDERS
WAVERTREE (St Mary) *Liv 6* **P** *Bp*
  R R H L WILLIAMS, **C** J A THOMAS
WAVERTREE (St Thomas) *Liv 6* **P** *Simeon's Trustees*
  V A H MASON
WAWNE (St Peter) Sutton St Jas and Wawne *York*
WAXHAM, GREAT (St John) Hickling and Waxham w
  Sea Palling *Nor*
WAYFORD (St Michael and All Angels) Crewkerne w
  Wayford *B & W*
WEALD, NORTH Bassett (St Andrew) *Chelmsf 6* **P** *Bp*
  V T C THORPE
WEALD, SOUTH (St Peter) *Chelmsf 10* **P** *Bp*
  V C J TRAVERS
WEAR (St Luke) *Ex 3* **P** *V Topsham* **V** P J S CROCKETT
WEARE (St Gregory) Crook Peak *B & W*
WEARE GIFFARD (Holy Trinity) Landcross,
  Littleham, Monkleigh etc *Ex*
WEASENHAM (All Saints) S, E w W Raynham,
  Helhoughton, etc *Nor*
WEASENHAM (St Peter) as above
WEASTE (St Luke w All Saints) *Man 6* **P** *Bp and*
  V Eccles (jt) **V** R F EFEMEY
WEAVERHAM (St Mary the Virgin) *Ches 6* **P** *Bp*
  V G F PARSONS, **C** C E LARSEN
WEAVERTHORPE (St Andrew) w Helperthorpe, Luttons
  Ambo and Kirby Grindalythe *York 2* **P** *D&C (1 turn),*
  Abp (2 turns) **V** *Vacant* West Lutton (09443) 213
WEBHEATH (St Philip) Redditch, The Ridge *Worc*
WEDDINGTON (St James) and Caldecote *Cov 5* **P** *Bp*
  R A J ADAMS
WEDMORE (St Mary) w Theale and Blackford *B & W 1*
  P *Bp* **V** D R MILLER
WEDNESBURY (St Bartholomew) *Lich 8* **P** *Bp*
  V P J RAINSFORD, **NSM** D MARSH
WEDNESBURY (St James and St John) *Lich 8*
  P *Trustees* **R** I B COOK, **NSM** R C GILBERT
WEDNESBURY (St Paul) Wood Green *Lich 8* **P** *Bp*
  V C R GOUGH, **C** A R TEAL, **Par Dn** C A MARSH
WEDNESFIELD (St Augustine and St Chad) *Lich 10*
  P *Patr Bd* **TR** J N CRAIG, **TM** P M MILLICHAMP,
  TV C R DUNCAN, **C** F R MILLER, **Par Dn** V E DUNCAN
WEDNESFIELD (St Gregory) *Lich 10* **P** *Bp*
  V E KEMBALL
WEDNESFIELD HEATH (Holy Trinity) *Lich 10*
  P *CPAS* **V** A G PALMER,
  C C A St A RAMSAY, D GHOSH
WEEDON (School Chapel) Schorne *Ox*
WEEDON BEC (St Peter and St Paul) w Everdon *Pet 3*
  P *Bp* **V** D JACKS
WEEDON LOIS (St Mary and St Peter) w Plumpton and
  Moreton Pinkney and Wappenham *Pet 1* **P** *Bp,*
  Jes Coll Ox, and Or Coll Ox (by turn) **V** J W B PHILLIPS
WEEFORD (St Mary the Virgin) Whittington w
  Weeford *Lich*

WEEK ST MARY (St Mary the Virgin) w Poundstock and Whitstone *Truro 8* **P** *SS Coll Cam, Walsingham Coll, and Guild of All So (jt)* **R** J G EDWARDS

WEEKE Win St Matt *Win*

WEEKLEY (St Mary the Virgin) Geddington w Weekley *Pet*

WEELEY (St Andrew) and Little Clacton *Chelmsf 26* **P** *Bp and BNC Ox (alt)* **R** E W NUGENT

WEETHLEY (St James) Alcester and Arrow w Oversley and Weethley *Cov*

WEETING (St Mary) *Ely 15* **P** *G&C Coll Cam* **R** A J ROWE

WEETON (St Barnabas) Kirkby Overblow *Ripon*

WEETON (St Michael) Singleton w Weeton *Blackb*

WEETSLADE (St Paul) *Newc 1* **P** *Bp* **V** I F DOWNS

WELBORNE (All Saints) Mattishall w Mattishall Burgh, Welborne etc *Nor*

WELBOURN (St Chad) *Linc 23* **P** *Hyndman Trustees* **R** B J BENNETT

WELBURN (St John the Evangelist) Bulmer w Dalby, Terrington and Welburn *York*

WELBURY (St Leonard) Rounton w Welbury *York*

WELBY (not known) Melton Gt Framland *Leic*

WELBY (St Bartholemew) Ancaster Wilsford Gp *Linc*

WELCOMBE (St Nectan) Hartland and Welcombe *Ex*

WELDON (St Mary the Virgin) w Deene *Pet 9* **P** *DBP and E Brudenell Esq (jt)* **R** T WITHERS GREEN

WELFORD (St Gregory) w Wickham and Great Shefford, Boxford and Stockcross *Ox 14* **P** *Bp and BNC Ox (jt)* **R** N C SANDS, **Hon C** S B APPLETON

WELFORD (St Mary the Virgin) w Sibbertoft and Marston Trussell *Pet 2* **P** *Bp* **V** *Vacant* Welford (0858) 575252

WELFORD (St Peter) w Weston and Clifford Chambers *Glouc 10* **P** *DBP* **R** P R BERROW

WELHAM (St Andrew) Gt Bowden w Welham, Glooston and Cranoe *Leic*

WELL (St Margaret) *Linc 8* **P** *J Reeve Esq* **R** G I GEORGE-JONES

WELL (St Michael) W Tanfield and Well w Snape and N Stainley *Ripon*

WELL HILL (Mission) Chelsfield *Roch*

WELLAND (St James) Hanley Castle, Hanley Swan and Welland *Worc*

WELLESBOURNE (St Peter) *Cov 8* **P** *Ld Chan* **V** N V HOWES, **C** R C ROGERS

WELLING (St John the Evangelist) *Roch 14* **P** *Bp* **V** P F WORTHEN, **C** A D WOODING JONES

WELLING (St Mary the Virgin) *S'wark 1* **P** *Bp* **C** G J SMITH

WELLINGBOROUGH (All Hallows) *Pet 6* **P** *Exors of Major E C S Byng-Maddick* **V** I C HUNT, **C** G N STARTIN

WELLINGBOROUGH (All Saints) *Pet 6* **P** *V Wellingborough* **V** H C SMART, **C** N G STARTIN

WELLINGBOROUGH (St Andrew) *Pet 6* **P** *Bp* **V** J R WESTWOOD

WELLINGBOROUGH (St Barnabas) *Pet 6* **P** *Bp* **V** D W WITCHELL

WELLINGBOROUGH (St Mark) *Pet 6* **P** *Bp* **V** I R LOWELL

WELLINGBOROUGH (St Mary the Virgin) *Pet 6* **P** *Guild of All So* **P-in-c** A I P ROBINSON

WELLINGHAM (St Andrew) S, E w W Raynham, Helhoughton, etc *Nor*

WELLINGORE (All Saints) Graffoe *Linc*

WELLINGTON (All Saints) (St John the Baptist) and District *B & W 21* **P** *Patr Bd* **R** T W STOKES, **TV** R E PITT, A G B ROWE, **C** R B EDWARDS, **Hon C** G R TODD

WELLINGTON (All Saints) w Eyton (St Catherine) *Lich 28* **P** *Ch Trust Fund Trust* **P-in-c** M E POTTER, **C** J A LAWSON

WELLINGTON (Christ Church) *Lich 28* **P** *V Wellington w Eyton* **P-in-c** P H BEARD

WELLINGTON (St Margaret of Antioch) w Pipe-cum-Lyde and Moreton-on-Lugg *Heref 4* **P** *Bp, Ch Union, and D&C (by turn)* **R** W P JOHNS

WELLINGTON HEATH (Christ Church) Bosbury w Wellington Heath etc *Heref*

WELLOW (St Julian the Hospitaller) Peasedown St John w Wellow *B & W*

WELLOW (St Margaret) *Win 11* **P** *Bp* **V** D BLAIR-BROWN

WELLOW (St Swithun) Kneesall w Laxton and Wellow *S'well*

WELLS (St Cuthbert) w Wookey Hole *B & W 9* **P** *D&C* **V** K W DAVIS

WELLS (St Thomas) w Horrington *B & W 9* **P** *D&C* **V** C T TOOKEY, **NSM** S M MUNNS

WELLS-NEXT-THE-SEA (St Nicholas) Holkham w Egmere w Warham, Wells and Wighton *Nor*

WELNEY (St Mary) *Ely 18* **P** *Bp* **R** H G REID

WELSH BICKNOR (St Margaret) Walford and Saint John, w Bishopswood etc *Heref*

WELSH FRANKTON (St Andrew) Ellesmere and Welsh Frankton *Lich*

WELSH NEWTON (St Mary the Virgin) St Weonards w Orcop, Garway, Tretire etc *Heref*

WELSH NEWTON COMMON (St Faith) as above

WELSHAMPTON (St Michael) Petton w Cockshutt, Welshampton and Lyneal etc *Lich*

WELTON (St Helen) w Melton *York 15* **P** *DBP* **V** F A GORDON-KERR

WELTON (St James) Westward, Rosley-w-Woodside and Welton *Carl*

WELTON (St Martin) w Ashby St Ledgers *Pet 3* **P** *Bp* **P-in-c** J W HARGREAVES

WELTON (St Mary) *Linc 3* **P** *Bp* **V** B J P PRITCHARD, **NSM** K A GUY

WELTON-LE-MARSH (St Martin) w Gunby *Linc 8* **P** *J M Montgomery-Massingberd Esq* **R** *Vacant*

WELTON-LE-WOLD (St Martin) Louth *Linc*

WELWICK (St Mary) Patrington w Hollym, Welwick and Winestead *York*

WELWYN (St Mary the Virgin) (St Michael) w Ayot St Peter *St Alb 7* **P** *All So Coll Ox* **V** J R ROGERS

WELWYN GARDEN CITY (St Francis of Assisi) *St Alb 7* **P** *Bp* **V** P A LOUIS, **Par Dn** J N RAPLEY

WEM (St Peter and St Paul) *Lich 29* **P** *Lord Barnard* **R** N MacGREGOR

WEMBDON (St George) *B & W 15* **P** *Ch Soc Trust* **V** *Vacant* Bridgwater (0278) 423468

WEMBLEY (St John the Evangelist) *Lon 21* **P** *Ch Patr Trust* **P-in-c** D C FRANCIS, **C** G J PETERS

WEMBLEY, NORTH (St Cuthbert) *Lon 21* **P** *Bp* **V** T H COMLEY

WEMBLEY PARK (St Augustine) *Lon 21* **P** *Bp* **V** J C GORE, **C** P DAY, **NSM** A C BAYLEY

WEMBURY (St Werburgh) *Ex 21* **P** *D&C Windsor* **V** T FREEMAN

WEMBWORTHY (St Michael) w Eggesford *Ex 16* **P** *Bp and G A L Cruwys Esq (jt)* **R** J N STOCKWELL

WENDENS AMBO (St Mary the Virgin) Saffron Walden w Wendens Ambo and Littlebury *Chelmsf*

WENDLEBURY (St Giles) Chesterton w Middleton Stoney and Wendlebury *Ox*

WENDLING (St Peter and St Paul) Gressenhall w Longham w Wendling etc *Nor*

WENDOVER (St Agnes's Chapel) (St Mary) *Ox 28* **P** *Ld Chan* **V** A F MEYNELL, **Par Dn** J R HICKS, **NSM** B J ROBERTS, H W HESLOP

WENDRON(St Wendron) Helston and Wendron *Truro*

WENDY (All Saints) Shingay Gp of Par *Ely*

WENHAM, GREAT (St John) Holton St Mary w Gt Wenham *St E*

WENHASTON (St Peter) Thorington w Wenhaston and Bramfield *St E*

WENLOCK *Heref 11* **P** *Patr Bd* **TR** R B DAVIES, **TV** M A KINNA, M C CLUETT, **NSM** C M HAYNES

WENLOCK, LITTLE (St Lawrence) Coalbrookdale, Iron-Bridge and Lt Wenlock *Heref*

WENLOCK, MUCH (Holy Trinity) Wenlock *Heref*

WENNINGTON (St Mary and St Peter) *Chelmsf 4* **P** *MMCET* **P-in-c** T G LYNDS

WENSLEY (Holy Trinity) *Ripon 4* **P** *Lord Bolton* **R** D DALTON

WENTBRIDGE (St John) Darrington w Wentbridge *Wakef*

WENTNOR (St Michael and All Angels) w Ratlinghope, Myndtown, Norbury, More, Lydham and Snead *Heref 10* **P** *Ch Ch Ox (2 turns),Col A P Sykes (2 turns), and Lady More (1 turn)* **R** F J CARLOS

WENTWORTH (Harley Mission Church) (Holy Trinity) *Sheff 12* **P** *Sir Stephen Hastings* **V** C H WHITEMAN

WENTWORTH (St Peter) Witchford w Wentworth *Ely*

WEOBLEY (St Peter and St Paul) w Sarnesfield and Norton Canon *Heref 5* **P** *Bp (2 turns), R A Marshall Esq (1 turn)* **V** R A BIRT, **C** B M REES, **NSM** L C RHODES

WEOLEY CASTLE (St Gabriel) *Birm 2* **P** *Bp* **V** M D CASTLE, **C** R J PRESTON

WEREHAM (St Margaret) *Ely 16* **P** *Bp* **V** *Vacant*

WERNETH (St Paul) *Ches 16* **P** *Trustees* **P-in-c** B S PERCIVAL

WERNETH (St Thomas) *Man 18* **P** *Bp* **V** *Vacant* 061-678 8926

WERRINGTON (St John the Baptist) *Pet 13* **P** *Bp*
C W N CRAFT
WERRINGTON (St Martin of Tours) w St Giles in the
Heath and Virginstow *Truro 9* **P** *R Williams Esq and
Ld Chan (alt)* **P-in-c** A J M BROWNRIDGE
WERRINGTON (St Philip) *Lich 12* **P** *V Caverswall*
V J L HUMPHREYS
WESHAM (Christ Church) *Blackb 11* **P** *V Kirkham*
V A J WHYTE
WESSINGTON (Christ Church) S Wingfield and
Wessington *Derby*
WEST: *see also under substantive place names*
WEST BAY (St John) Bridport *Sarum*
WEST DOWN (St Calixtus) Ilfracombe SS Phil and Jas
w W Down *Ex*
WEST END (Holy Trinity) Bisley and W End *Guildf*
WEST END (St George) Esher *Guildf*
WEST END (St James) *Win 9* **P** *Bp* **V** J M PRESTON,
C P G McAVOY
WEST END (St John the Evangelist) High Wycombe *Ox*
WEST GREEN (Christ Church w St Peter) *Lon 19* **P** *Bp*
V J T HAMBLIN
WEST GREEN (St Peter) Crawley *Chich*
WEST HEATH (St Anne) *Birm 4* **P** *Bp* **V** B GREEN,
C S P MAYOSS-HURD
WEST HILL (St Michael the Archangel) Ottery St
Mary, Alfington, W Hill, Tipton etc *Ex*
WEST MOORS (St Mary the Virgin) (St John the
Evangelist) *Sarum 10* **P** *Bp* **V** I K CHISHOLM
WEST ORCHARD (St Luke) Shaston *Sarum*
WEST RASEN (All Saints) Middle Rasen Gp *Linc*
WEST ROW (St Peter) Mildenhall *St E*
WESTACRE (All Saints) Gayton Gp of Par *Nor*
WESTBERE (All Saints) Sturry w Fordwich and
Westbere w Hersden *Cant*
WESTBOROUGH (All Saints) Claypole *Linc*
WESTBOROUGH (St Clare) (St Francis) *Guildf 5* **P** *Bp*
TR H G MEIRION-JONES, **TV** J P WHITTAKER,
C A M CLARKE
WESTBOURNE Christ Church Conventional District
Win 7 **Min** B C RUFF
WESTBOURNE (St John the Baptist) *Chich 13* **P** *Bp*
R B J MARSHALL
WESTBROOK (St James) Hood Manor *Liv 12* **P** *Bp,
R Warrington, and V Gt Sankey (jt)* **V** D W LONG
WESTBROOK (St Philip) Old Hall and Callands *Liv 12*
P *Bp and R Warrington (jt)* **V** P C O DAWSON
WESTBURY (All Saints) *Sarum 14* **P** *Bp* **V** M J FLIGHT,
Par Dn D K BELLAMY
WESTBURY (St Augustine) w Turweston, Shalstone and
Biddlesden *Ox 22* **P** *Bp, D&C Westmr,
Mrs M L G Purefoy, and Exors Mrs E M Gordon (jt)*
P-in-c M N FULLAGAR
WESTBURY (St Mary) *Heref 13* **P** *Bp* **R** R J PEARCE
WESTBURY-ON-SEVERN (St Peter and St Paul) w
Flaxley and Blaisdon *Glouc 3* **P** *Sir Thomas Crawley-
Boevey, Bt (1 turn), D&C Heref (2 turns), and Trustees
late T Place Esq (1 turn)* **V** D A COLBY,
NSM M WHITE
WESTBURY-ON-TRYM (Holy Trinity) *Bris 8* **P** *SMF*
V G M COLLINS, **C** N J K COURT
WESTBURY-ON-TRYM (St Alban) *Bris 8* **P** *Bp*
V J A H BOWES, **Hon Par Dn** S HARDING
WESTBURY PARK (St Alban) Westbury-on-Trym St
Alb *Bris*
WESTBURY SUB MENDIP (St Lawrence) w Easton
B & W 1 **P** *Bp* **V** E A MACPHERSON
WESTCLIFF (Church of Reconciliation) Old Brumby
Linc
WESTCLIFF (St Alban) Southend *Chelmsf*
WESTCLIFF (St Andrew) *Chelmsf 15* **P** *Bp*
V E R LITTLER, **Par Dn** A L COZENS
WESTCLIFF (St Cedd and the Saints of Essex) *Chelmsf 15*
P *Bp* **P-in-c** G R STEEL
WESTCLIFF (St Michael and All Angels) *Chelmsf 15*
P *Bp* **V** A O WIGRAM, **C** D HILDRED
WESTCLIFF (St Paul) Prittlewell *Chelmsf*
WESTCLIFF (St Saviour) Southend St Sav Westcliff
Chelmsf
WESTCLIFFE (St Peter) St Margarets-at-Cliffe w
Westcliffe etc *Cant*
WESTCOMBE PARK (St George) *S'wark 1* **P** *CPAS*
P-in-c I H OWERS
WESTCOTE (St Mary the Virgin) w Icomb and Bledington
Glouc 15 **P** *D&C Worc, Ch Ch Ox, and Bp (by turn)*
P-in-c G F JONES, **Hon C** P J VAN DE KASTEELE
WESTCOTE BARTON (St Edward the Confessor) w
Steeple Barton, Duns Tew and Sandford St Martin *Ox 9*

P *Duke of Marlborough, Exors Mrs Rittson-Thomas,
DBP, D C D Webb Esq, and Bp (jt)* **R** A W DAVIES
WESTCOTT (Holy Trinity) *Guildf 7* **P** *Mrs N A Barclay*
V J D H WEYMAN
WESTCOTT (St Mary) Waddesdon w Over Winchendon
and Fleet Marston *Ox*
WESTDENE (The Ascension) Patcham *Chich*
WESTERDALE (Christ Church) Ingleby Greenhow w
Bilsdale Priory, Kildale etc *York*
WESTERFIELD (St Mary Magdalene) and Tuddenham
(St Martin) w Witnesham *St E 4* **P** *Bp, Peterho Cam,
and DBP (alt)* **R** H LUNNEY, **NSM** M J STONE
WESTERHAM (St Mary the Virgin) *Roch 8*
P *J St A Warde Esq* **V** P A BIRD
WESTERLEIGH (St James the Great) Yate New Town
Bris
WESTERN DOWNLAND *Sarum 13* **P** *Hyndman
Trustees, Sir William van Straubenzee, and
W J Purvis Esq (jt)* **R** M E RIDLEY
WESTFIELD (St Andrew) Reymerston w Cranworth,
Letton, Southburgh etc *Nor*
WESTFIELD (St John the Baptist) *Chich 20* **P** *Bp*
V E N L FRANCE
WESTFIELD (St Mark) Woking St Pet *Guildf*
WESTFIELD (St Mary) *Carl 7* **P** *Bp* **V** A MITCHELL
WESTFIELD (St Peter) *B & W 13* **P** *Bp* **V** J B THICKE
WESTGATE (St Andrew) *Dur 15* **P** *Bp*
V D M SKELTON
WESTGATE (St James) *Cant 9* **P** *Abp*
V J A CHEESEMAN
WESTGATE (St Martin) Torrisholme *Blackb*
WESTGATE COMMON (St Michael) *Wakef 12*
P *V Alverthorpe* **V** R J HOWARD
WESTGATE-ON-SEA (St Saviour) *Cant 9* **P** *Abp*
V S M EVANS, **Hon Par Dn** E N HUGHES
WESTHALL (St Andrew) Hundred River Gp of Par
St E
WESTHAM (St Mary) *Chich 16* **P** *Duke of Devonshire*
V A C GINNO
WESTHAMPNETT (St Peter) W Hampnett *Chich*
WESTHEAD (St James) *Liv 11* **P** *V Ormskirk*
P-in-c N T B DEANE
WESTHIDE (St Bartholomew) Withington w Westhide
Heref
WESTHOPE (Mission Room) Canon Pyon w Kings
Pyon and Birley *Heref*
WESTHORPE (St Margaret) Walsham le Willows and
Finningham w Westhorpe *St E*
WESTHOUGHTON (St Bartholomew) *Man 11* **P** *Patr Bd*
TR S C ATTON-BROWN, **Par Dn** F E F WARD
WESTHOUSES (St Saviour) Blackwell *Derby*
WESTLANDS (St Andrew) *Lich 15* **P** *Simeon's Trustees*
V W G H GARDINER
WESTLEIGH (St Paul) *Man 13* **P** *V Leigh St Mary*
V T D HARGREAVES-STEAD
WESTLEIGH (St Peter) *Ex 17* **P** *D&C*
V G A SATTERLY
WESTLEIGH (St Peter) *Man 13* **P** *Bp, Dioc Chan, and
V Leigh St Mary (jt)* **V** R COOKE
WESTLETON (St Peter) w Dunwich *St E 19* **P** *Ch Patr
Trust (2 turns), Shadingfield Properties Ltd (1 turn)*
V R J GINN
WESTLEY (St Mary) Risby w Gt and Lt Saxham and
Westley *St E*
WESTLEY WATERLESS (St Mary the Less) *Ely 4*
P *Exors C L Thomas* **P-in-c** N E H HOLMES
WESTMEADS (St Michael and All Angels) Aldwick
Chich
WESTMESTON (St Martin) Streat w Westmeston *Chich*
WESTMILL (St Mary the Virgin) *St Alb 5* **P** *K Coll Lon*
P-in-c J H GROWNS
WESTMINSTER Hanover Square (St George) Hanover
Square St Geo w St Mark *Lon*
WESTMINSTER (St James) Piccadilly *Lon 3* **P** *Bp
(2 turns), Ld Chan (1 turn)* **R** D St J REEVES,
Par Dn U S MONBERG, **Hon C** D G S BARTON,
N E McCURRY, S B CATHIE
WESTMINSTER (St Matthew) *Lon 3* **P** *D&C Westmr*
V R B M HAYES, **Hon C** R CRAWFORD
WESTMINSTER (St Saviour) (St James the Less) *Lon 3*
P *D&C Westmr and Duke of Westmr (jt)*
P-in-c R J ROGERS, **C** P A BAGOTT
WESTMINSTER (St Stephen) (St John) *Lon 3*
P *The Crown* **V** R J C CHARTRES,
C N D R NICHOLLS, P W FELLOWS
WESTMINSTER (St-Mary-le-Strand) St-Mary-le-Strand
w St Clem Danes *Lon*
WESTOE, SOUTH (St Michael and All Angels) *Dur 7*
P *Bp* **V** J M HANCOCK, **C** H A CAMM

WESTON (All Saints)   Bath Weston All SS w N Stoke *B & W*

WESTON (All Saints) *Ches 15*   **P** *Bp*   **V** D A PARKER

WESTON (All Saints)   Welford w Weston and Clifford Chambers *Glouc*

WESTON (All Saints) *Guildf 8*   **P** *Bp*   **V** A P BOTWRIGHT

WESTON (All Saints)   Tuxford w Weston and Markham Clinton *S'well*

WESTON (All Saints) w Denton *Bradf 4*   **P** *Lt-Col H V Dawson and C Wyvill Esq (jt)*   **V** D E CREASER

WESTON (Holy Trinity) *St Alb 12*   **P** *Mrs A M Pryor*   **V** E J POOLE,   **NSM** B KNIGHT

WESTON (Holy Trinity) *Win 12*   **P** *Bp*   **V** *Vacant* Southampton (0703) 448421

WESTON (St Mary)   Cowbit *Linc*

WESTON (St Peter)   Hundred River Gp of Par *St E*

WESTON, OLD (St Swithun)   Brington w Molesworth and Old Weston *Ely*

WESTON, SOUTH (St Lawrence)   Tetsworth, Adwell w S Weston, Lewknor etc *Ox*

WESTON BAMPFYLDE (Holy Cross)   Queen Camel w W Camel, Corton Denham etc *B & W*

WESTON BEGGARD (St John the Baptist)   Lugwardine w Bartestree and Weston Beggard *Heref*

WESTON BY WELLAND (St Mary)   Ashley w Weston by Welland and Sutton Bassett *Pet*

WESTON COLVILLE (St Mary) *Ely 4*   **P** *D&C*   **R** *Vacant*

WESTON COYNEY (St Andrew)   Caverswall *Lich*

WESTON ESTATE CHURCH (not known)   Otley *Bradf*

WESTON FAVELL (St Peter) *Pet 4*   **P** *DBP*   **R** C W WAKE,   **NSM** O E KILLINGBACK

WESTON HILLS (St John)   Cowbit *Linc*

WESTON IN GORDANO (St Peter and St Paul)   E Clevedon and Walton w Weston w Clapton *B & W*

WESTON LONGVILLE (All Saints) w Morton on the Hill w Great and Little Witchingham *Nor 8*   **P** *J V Berney Esq (1 turn), New Coll Ox (3 turns)*   **R** J P PILLINGWORTH

WESTON LULLINGFIELD (Holy Trinity)   Baschurch and Weston Lullingfield w Hordley *Lich*

WESTON MILL (St Philip)   Devonport St Boniface and St Phil *Ex*

WESTON-ON-THE-GREEN (St Mary)   Kirtlington w Bletchingdon, Weston etc *Ox*

WESTON-ON-TRENT (St Mary the Virgin)   Aston-on-Trent and Weston-on-Trent *Derby*

WESTON PATRICK (St Lawrence)   Herriard w Winslade and Long Sutton etc *Win*

WESTON POINT (Christ Church)   Runcorn St Jo Weston *Ches*

WESTON RHYN (St John) *Lich 25*   **P** *Bp*   **P-in-c** N G COATSWORTH

WESTON-SUB-EDGE (St Lawrence)   Willersey, Saintbury, Weston-sub-Edge etc *Glouc*

WESTON-SUPER-MARE Central Parishes (All Saints) (Emmanuel) (St John the Baptist) *B & W 12*   **P** *Patr Bd*   **TR** J T HAYWARD,   **TV** I L J FROOM, J M LEWIS,   **C** C M HORSEMAN

WESTON-SUPER-MARE (Christ Church) *B & W 12*   **P** *Trustees*   **V** G W HOBDEN,   **C** C WAUDBY

WESTON-SUPER-MARE (St Andrew) Bournville *B & W 12*   **P** *Bp*   **V** R J ALLEN

WESTON-SUPER-MARE (St Paul) *B & W 12*   **P** *Bp*   **V** N T L McKITTRICK,   **NSM** A J NEVILLE

WESTON TURVILLE (St Mary the Virgin) *Ox 28*   **P** *All So Coll Ox*   **P-in-c** D N WALES

WESTON-UNDER-LIZARD (St Andrew)   Blymhill w Weston-under-Lizard *Lich*

WESTON-UNDER-PENYARD (St Lawrence) w Hope Mansel and the Lea *Heref 8*   **P** *Bp (3 turns), R Linton (1 turn)*   **R** R D HAMBLETON

WESTON UNDER REDCASTLE (St Luke)   Hodnet w Weston under Redcastle *Lich*

WESTON UNDER WETHERLEY (St Michael)   Wappenbury w Weston under Wetherley *Cov*

WESTON UNDERWOOD (St Laurence)   Gayhurst w Ravenstone, Stoke Goldington etc *Ox*

WESTON UPON TRENT (St Andrew)   Fradswell, Gayton, Milwich and Weston *Lich*

WESTON ZOYLAND (Blessed Virgin Mary) w Chedzoy *B & W 15*   **P** *Bp*   **V** R O FRY

WESTONBIRT (St Catherine)   Shipton Moyne w Westonbirt and Lasborough *Glouc*

WESTONING (St Mary Magdalene) w Tingrith *St Alb 15*   **P** *Ld Chan*   **V** M J HILL

WESTOW (St Mary)   Burythorpe, Acklam and Leavening w Westow *York*

WESTWARD (St Hilda), Rosley-with-Woodside and Welton *Carl 3*   **P** *D&C*   **P-in-c** N L ROBINSON,   **Par Dn** K REALE

WESTWARD HO! (Holy Trinity)   Northam w Westward Ho and Appledore *Ex*

WESTWELL (St Mary)   Alvescot w Black Bourton, Shilton, Holwell etc *Ox*

WESTWELL (St Mary) w Hothfield and Eastwell w Boughton Aluph *Cant 10*   **P** *Abp and Lord Hothfield (jt)*   **V** J F GLEADALL

WESTWICK (St Botolph)   Worstead w Westwick and Sloley *Nor*

WESTWOOD Jacksdale (St Mary)   Selston *S'well*

WESTWOOD (Mission Church)   Golcar *Wakef*

WESTWOOD (St John the Baptist) *Cov 3*   **P** *Bp*   **V** R D ALLON-SMITH,   **C** C A HOST

WESTWOOD (St Mary the Virgin) and Wingfield *Sarum 17*   **P** *D&C Bris, CPAS, and Bp (jt)*   **R** R M LOWRIE

WESTWOOD (St Paul)   Pinhoe and Broadclyst *Ex*

WESTWOOD, LOW (Christ Church)   Ebchester *Dur*

WETHERAL (Holy Trinity and St Constantine) w Warwick *Carl 2*   **P** *D&C*   **R** C T MATTHEWS,   **NSM** P TIPLADY

WETHERBY (St James) *Ripon 1*   **P** *Bp*   **V** A M BARTON,   **C** D J PEAT

WETHERDEN (St Mary the Virgin)   Haughley w Wetherden *St E*

WETHERINGSETT (All Saints)   Thorndon w Rishangles, Stoke Ash, Thwaite etc *St E*

WETHERSFIELD (St Mary Magdalene) w Shalford *Chelmsf 18*   **P** *Bp*   **P-in-c** J F H SHEAD

WETLEY ROCKS (St John the Baptist) *Lich 14*   **P** *Bp*   **V** D R WHITELEY

WETTENHALL (St David)   Tilstone Fearnall and Wettenhall *Ches*

WETTON (St Margaret)   Alstonfield, Butterton, Warslow w Elkstone etc *Lich*

WETWANG (St Nicholas) and Garton-on-the-Wolds w Kirkburn *York 11*   **P** *Ld Chan*   **V** G G HOLMAN

WEXCOMBE *Sarum 21*   **P** *DBP*   **TR** D M RYDER,   **TV** F Y-C HUNG, N A LEIGH-HUNT

WEXHAM (St Mary) *Ox 26*   **P** *Ld Chan*   **R** G W FARMER

WEYBOURNE (All Saints), Upper Sheringham, Kelling, Salthouse, Bodham and East and West Beckham (The Weybourne Group) *Nor 22*   **P** *Bp (2 turns), Sir Charles Mott-Radclyffe (1 turn), D&C (1 turn), and Lord Walpole (1 turn)*   **R** M H SELLORS

WEYBREAD (St Andrew)   Fressingfield, Mendham, Metfield, Weybread etc *St E*

WEYBRIDGE (St James) *Guildf 8*   **P** *Ld Chan*   **R** J D GREEN

WEYHILL (St Michael and All Angels)   Hatherden w Tangley, Weyhill and Penton Mewsey *Win*

WEYMOUTH (Holy Trinity) (St Nicholas) *Sarum 5*   **P** *Bp*   **V** S S VENNER,   **C** P HUNTER, T H ROBERTS,   **NSM** R A WEAVER,   **Hon Par Dn** R E MILVERTON

WEYMOUTH (St Edmund) *Sarum 5*   **P** *R Wyke Regis*   **V** J R ADAMS

WEYMOUTH (St John)   Radipole and Melcombe Regis *Sarum*

WEYMOUTH (St Mary)   as above

WEYMOUTH (St Paul) *Sarum 5*   **P** *Bp*   **V** D J GREEN

WHADDON (St Margaret)   Glouc St Geo w Whaddon *Glouc*

WHADDON (St Mary) *Ely 8*   **P** *D&C Windsor*   **V** J F AITCHISON

WHADDON (St Mary)   Newton Longville w Stoke Hammond and Whaddon *Ox*

WHADDON (St Mary)   Alderbury Team *Sarum*

WHADDON (St Mary the Virgin)   Hilperton w Whaddon and Staverton etc *Sarum*

WHALEY BRIDGE (St James) *Ches 16*   **P** *Bp and Bp Derby (alt)*   **R** D C SPEEDY

WHALEY THORNS (St Luke)   Upper Langwith w Langwith Bassett etc *Derby*

WHALLEY (St Mary and All Saints) *Blackb 8*   **P** *Hulme Trustees*   **V** J M ACKROYD

WHALLEY RANGE (St Edmund) *Man 4*   **P** *Simeon's Trustees*   **R** R J HORROCKS,   **Par Dn** J A HORROCKS

WHALLEY RANGE (St Margaret) *Man 4*   **P** *Trustees*   **R** R G BOULTER

WHALTON (St Mary Magdalene)   Bolam w Whalton and Hartburn w Meldon *Newc*

WHAPLODE (St Mary) *Linc 16*   **P** *Ld Chan*   **V** *Vacant* Holbeach (0406) 370318

WHAPLODE DROVE (St John the Baptist) *Linc 16*   **P** *Feoffees*   **V** *Vacant* Holbeach (0406) 330392

WHARNCLIFFE SIDE (not known)   Oughtibridge *Sheff*

WHARRAM (St Mary) Settrington w N Grimston and Wharram *York*
WHARTON (Christ Church) *Ches 6* **P** *R Davenham* **V** T D HERBERT, **C** M L EAMAN
WHATBOROUGH Group of Parishes, The *Leic 4* **P** *Bp* **V** H R BROAD
WHATCOTE (St Peter) Tysoe w Oxhill and Whatcote *Cov*
WHATFIELD (St Margaret) w Semer, Nedging and Naughton *St E 3* **P** *Bp, Jes Coll Cam,* and *Reformation Ch Trust (jt)* **P-in-c** H J CRELLIN
WHATLINGTON (St Mary Magdalene) Sedlescombe w Whatlington *Chich*
WHATSTANDWELL (Mission Room) Crich *Derby*
WHATTON (St John of Beverley) w Aslockton, Hawksworth, Scarrington, Orston and Thoroton *S'well 8* **P** *Trustees* **V** D H BRIDGE-COLLYNS
WHEATACRE (All Saints) Raveningham *Nor*
WHEATCROFT (St Michael and All Angels) Scarborough St Martin *York*
WHEATFIELD (St Andrew) Tetsworth, Adwell w S Weston, Lewknor etc *Ox*
WHEATHAMPSTEAD (St Helen) *St Alb 14* **P** *Bp* **R** T PURCHAS, **NSM** J HAZELWOOD, **Hon Par Dn** C P A PURCHAS
WHEATHILL (Holy Trinity) Ditton Priors w Neenton, Burwarton etc *Heref*
WHEATLEY (St Mary) Doncaster St Mary *Sheff*
WHEATLEY (St Mary the Virgin) w Forest Hill and Stanton St John *Ox 1* **P** *Bp, Linc Coll Ox,* and *New Coll Ox (by turn)* **V** M T FARTHING
WHEATLEY, NORTH (St Peter and St Paul) and West Burton w Bole and Saundby and Sturton w Littleborough *S'well 5* **P** *Lord Middleton and G M T Foljambe Esq (alt)* **R** A READER-MOORE, **C** J H LITTLE
WHEATLEY HILL (All Saints) *Dur 3* **P** *Bp* **P-in-c** M J SHEARING
WHEATLEY HILLS (St Aidan) *Sheff 9* **P** *Bp* **V** L C JENKINS
WHEATLEY PARK (St Paul) Conventional District *Sheff 9* **C-in-c** G CREASEY
WHEATON ASTON (St Mary) Lapley w Wheaton Aston *Lich*
WHEELOCK (Christ Church) *Ches 11* **P** *V Sandbach* **V** P D BRADBROOK
WHELDRAKE (St Helen) w Thorganby *York 4* **P** *Abp and Sir Mervyn Dunnington-Jefferson (jt)* **R** J C P COCKERTON
WHELFORD (St Anne) Kempsford w Welford *Glouc*
WHELNETHAM, GREAT (St Thomas a Becket) and LITTLE (St Mary) w Bradfield St George *St E 10* **P** *Bp* **R** J CROSS
WHELPLEY HILL (St Michael and All Angels) Ashley Green *Ox*
WHENBY (St Martin) Bulmer w Dalby, Terrington and Welburn *York*
WHEPSTEAD (St Petronilla) Chevington w Hargrave and Whepstead w Brockley *St E*
WHERSTEAD (St Mary) *St E 5* **P** *MMCET* **P-in-c** J D YATES
WHERWELL (St Peter and Holy Cross) Chilbolton cum Wherwell *Win*
WHETSTONE (St John the Apostle) *Lon 14* **P** *Bp* **V** P J HENDERSON
WHETSTONE (St Peter) *Leic 10* **P** *Bp* **V** P W J FOLKS
WHICHAM (St Mary) Bootle, Corney, Whicham and Whitbeck *Carl*
WHICHFORD (St Michael) Long Compton, Whichford and Barton-on-the-Heath *Cov*
WHICKHAM (St Mary the Virgin) *Dur 5* **P** *Ld Chan* **R** G S PEDLEY, **C** M H HARRISON
WHILTON (St Andrew) Brington w Whilton and Norton *Pet*
WHIMPLE (St Mary), Talaton and Clyst (St Lawrence) *Ex 7* **P** *DBP, D&C and MMCET (jt)* **R** A G WILLIAMS
WHINBURGH (St Mary) Reymerston w Cranworth, Letton, Southburgh etc *Nor*
WHINMOOR (St Paul) Seacroft *Ripon*
WHINNEY HILL (St Peter) Thrybergh w Hooton Roberts *Sheff*
WHIPPINGHAM (St Mildred) w East Cowes *Portsm 8* **P** *Ld Chan* **P-in-c** S D CLEAVER, **NSM** G L LONG
WHIPSNADE (St Mary Magdalene) Kensworth, Studham and Whipsnade *St Alb*
WHIPTON (St Boniface) *Ex 3* **P** *Bp* **V** C P BARRETT

WHISSENDINE (St Andrew) Teigh w Whissendine and Market Overton *Pet*
WHISSONSETT (St Mary) Colkirk w Oxwick w Pattesley, Whissonsett etc *Nor*
WHISTON (St Mary Magdalene) *Sheff 6* **P** *Bp* **R** G C M MILLS, **C** J G FAIRHURST
WHISTON (St Mary the Virgin) *Pet 7* **P** *Marquess of Northn* **R** *Vacant*
WHISTON (St Mildred) Foxt w Whiston *Lich*
WHISTON (St Nicholas) *Liv 2* **P** *V Prescot* **V** *Vacant* 051-426 6329
WHITACRE, NETHER (St Giles) The Whitacres and Shustoke *Birm*
WHITACRE, OVER (St Leonard) as above
WHITACRES and Shustoke, The *Birm 11* **P** *S W Digby Esq (1 turn), Bp (2 turns), and Ld Chan (1 turn)* **R** J D WATERSTREET
WHITBECK (St Mary) Bootle, Corney, Whicham and Whitbeck *Carl*
WHITBOURNE (Bringsty Iron Church) Edvin Loach w Tedstone Delamere etc *Heref*
WHITBOURNE (St John the Baptist) as above
WHITBURN (St Mary) *Dur 9* **P** *Bp* **R** K R SMITH, **Par Dn** N M JAY
WHITBY (St Hilda) (St John) (St Mary) *York 23* **P** *Abp* **R** B A HOPKINSON, **C** B HARRISON, **Par Dn** C M DURNFORD
WHITBY (St Thomas) Ellesmere Port *Ches*
WHITBY ROAD (St Michael) W Slough *Ox*
WHITCHURCH (All Hallows) w Tufton and Litchfield *Win 6* **P** *Bp* **V** M J GRYLLS
WHITCHURCH (St Alkmund) *Lich 29* **P** *Bp* **R** R D JENKINS
WHITCHURCH (St Andrew) *Ex 25* **P** *Bp* **V** *Vacant* Tavistock (0822) 612185
WHITCHURCH (St Augustine) (St Nicholas) *Bris 3* **P** *Bp* **V** I T HOLDCROFT, **C** P K HUGHES, **NSM** E A J CHIVERS
WHITCHURCH (St Dubricius) Llangarron w Llangrove, Whitchurch and Ganarew *Heref*
WHITCHURCH (St John the Evangelist) Schorne *Ox*
WHITCHURCH (St Lawrence) Lt Stanmore St Lawr *Lon*
WHITCHURCH (St Mary the Virgin) Ilmington w Stretton-on-Fosse etc *Cov*
WHITCHURCH (St Mary the Virgin) *Ox 6* **P** *Bp* **R** R M HUGHES
WHITCHURCH CANONICORUM (St Candida and Holy Cross) Marshwood Vale Team Min *Sarum*
WHITCHURCH HILL (St John the Baptist) Whitchurch St Mary *Ox*
WHITE COLNE (St Andrew) Earls Colne and White Colne *Chelmsf*
WHITE LADIES ASTON (St John) Peopleton and White Ladies Aston etc *Worc*
WHITE NOTLEY (St Etheldreda) Fairstead w Terling and White Notley etc *Chelmsf*
WHITE RODING (St Martin) Abbess Roding, Beauchamp Roding and White Roding *Chelmsf*
WHITE WALTHAM (St Mary the Virgin) w Shottesbrooke *Ox 13* **P** *Sir John Smith* **V** T E F COULSON
WHITE WELL (St Mary) St Paul's Walden *St Alb*
WHITECHAPEL (St James) w Admarsh-in-Bleasdale *Blackb 10* **P** *Bp and V Lanc (alt)* **V** G CONNOR
WHITEGATE (St Mary) w Little Budworth *Ches 6* **P** *Bp, Lord Delamere and W R Cullimore Esq (alt)* **V** D A D SMITH
WHITEHAVEN (St James) *Carl 5* **P** *Patr Bd* **V** J H BAKER, **TV** N A R REBERT, **C** R BOWLZER
WHITEHAWK (St Cuthman) *Chich 2* **P** *Bp* **P-in-c** J D WRIGHT
WHITEHILLS (St Mark) Kingsthorpe w Northn St Dav *Pet*
WHITELACKINGTON (The Blessed Virgin Mary) Ilminster w Whitelackington *B & W*
WHITEPARISH (All Saints) Alderbury Team *Sarum*
WHITESHILL (St Paul) *Glouc 1* **P** *Bp* **V** M F JEFFERY
WHITESTAUNTON (St Andrew) *B & W 16* **P** *Gp Capt N W D Marwood-Elton* **P-in-c** P REGAN
WHITESTONE (St Catherine) *Ex 6* **P** *Em Coll Cam* **P-in-c** A J STONE
WHITEWELL (St Mary) Tushingham and Whitewell *Ches*
WHITEWELL (St Michael) Chipping and Whitewell *Blackb*
WHITFIELD (Holy Trinity) Allendale w Whitfield *Newc*
WHITFIELD (St James) (St Luke) *Derby 6* **P** *Bp* **V** E E LOBB, **C** T G ANDERSON
WHITFIELD (St John) Allendale w Whitfield *Newc*

WHITFIELD (St John the Evangelist)   Helmdon w Stuchbury and Radstone etc *Pet*

WHITFIELD (St Peter) w Guston *Cant 4*   **P** *Abp and D&C (alt)*   **V** J W PHILPOTT

WHITFORD (St Mary at the Cross)   Kilmington w Shute *Ex*

WHITGIFT (St Mary Magdalene)   The Marshland *Sheff*

WHITGREAVE (St John the Evangelist)   Stafford *Lich*

WHITKIRK (St Mary) *Ripon 8*   **P** *Meynell Trustees*   **V** P A SUMMERS,   **C** S C BROWN

WHITLEIGH (St Chad) *Ex 23*   **P** *Bp*   **V** J M KIRKPATRICK,   **C** T J LEWIS

WHITLEY (Christ Church) *Ox 15*   **P** *Bp*   **V** E A ESSERY,   **C** T C PLATTS,   **NSM** G S UDALL

WHITLEY (St Helen) *Newc 4*   **P** *Bp*   **V** A D DUNCAN

WHITLEY (St James) *Cov 1*   **P** *Bp*   **P-in-c** D W LAWSON

WHITLEY, LOWER (St Mary and St Michael) (St Luke) *Wakef 10*   **P** *Lord Savile*   **V** N D J WEBB

WHITLEY BRIDGE (All Saints)   Kellington w Whitley *Wakef*

WHITMINSTER (St Andrew)   Standish w Haresfield and Moreton Valence etc *Glouc*

WHITMORE (St Mary and All Saints)   Chapel Chorlton, Maer and Whitmore *Lich*

WHITNASH (St Margaret) *Cov 11*   **P** *Lord Leigh*   **R** A B GARDNER,   **C** R J R AMYS

WHITNEY (St Peter and St Paul)   Eardisley w Bollingham, Willersley, Brilley etc *Heref*

WHITSBURY (St Leonard)   W Downland *Sarum*

WHITSTABLE (All Saints) *Cant 7*   **P** *DBP*   **TR** C G LEWIS,   **TV** D W FLEWKER, R P C PODGER, K I WITTWER, P G TAYLOR,   **Par Dn** S C BENBOW,   **Hon Par Dn** E M CAPPER

WHITSTONE (St Anne)   Week St Mary w Poundstock and Whitstone *Truro*

WHITTINGHAM (St Bartholomew) and Edlingham w Bolton Chapel *Newc 9*   **P** *D&C Carl and D&C Dur (alt)*   **V** J A FERGUSON

WHITTINGTON (Christ Church) *Ely 15*   **P** *Ch Patr Trust*   **V** *Vacant*

WHITTINGTON (St Bartholomew) *Derby 5*   **P** *Bp*   **R** D C PICKERING

WHITTINGTON (St Bartholomew)   Sevenhampton w Charlton Abbotts and Hawling etc *Glouc*

WHITTINGTON (St Giles) w Weeford *Lich 2*   **P** *Bp*   **V** P D BROTHWELL,   **Hon C** C M J IBALL

WHITTINGTON (St John the Baptist) *Lich 25*   **P** *Mrs P Hamilton Hill*   **R** D R NORTH

WHITTINGTON (St Michael the Archangel) w Arkholme and Gressingham *Blackb 15*   **P** *Ch Ch Ox, V Lanc, and V Melling (by turn)*   **V** *Vacant*   Hornby (05242) 21359

WHITTINGTON (St Philip and St James)   Worc SE *Worc*

WHITTINGTON, NEW (St Barnabas) *Derby 5*   **P** *Bp*   **V** J PINDER-PACKARD

WHITTLE-LE-WOODS (St John the Evangelist) *Blackb 4*   **P** *V Leyland*   **V** D M GILKES,   **C** T F DITCHFIELD

WHITTLEBURY (St Mary) w Paulerspury *Pet 5*   **P** *The Crown and New Coll Ox (alt)*   **V** E D HOUSTON

WHITTLESEY (St Andrew) (St Mary) and Pondersbridge *Ely 18*   **P** *Patr Bd*   **TR** J M STEVENETTE

WHITTLESFORD (St Mary and St Andrew) *Ely 7*   **P** *Jes Coll Cam*   **P-in-c** K C OVERTON

WHITTON *Sarum 20*   **P** *Patr Bd*   **TR** P BUNDAY,   **TV** J S KINGSLEY-SMITH, R K HYATT

WHITTON (St Augustine of Canterbury) *Lon 10*   **P** *Bp*   **V** R J COSH,   **Par Dn** V K LUCAS,   **Hon C** H JAMES

WHITTON (St John the Baptist)   Alkborough *Linc*

WHITTON (St Mary)   Burford II w Greete and Hope Bagot *Heref*

WHITTON (St Mary) (Ascension) and Thurleston w Akenham *St E 4*   **P** *Bp (2 turns), G K Drury Esq (1 turn)*   **R** G G BAULCOMB,   **C** I A WILSON

WHITTON (St Philip and St James) *Lon 10*   **P** *V Twickenham St Mary*   **V** C J SWIFT

WHITTONSTALL (St Philip and St James) *Newc 3*   **P** *D&C*   **V** *Vacant*

WHITWELL (St John the Evangelist) w Crambe, Flaxton, Foston and Huttons Ambo *York 3*   **P** *Abp and D&C Dur (jt)*   **R** P GREGORY

WHITWELL (St Lawrence) *Derby 3*   **P** *Bp*   **R** C A ROGERS

WHITWELL (St Mary)   St Paul's Walden *St Alb*

WHITWELL (St Mary and St Rhadegunde) *Portsm 7*   **P** *Bp*   **V** H W COOPER,   **C** S LLOYD

WHITWELL (St Michael and All Angels)   Reepham, Hackford w Whitwell, Kerdiston etc *Nor*

WHITWELL (St Michael and All Angels)   Empingham and Exton w Horn w Whitwell *Pet*

WHITWICK (St John the Baptist) *Leic 8*   **P** *Duchy of Lanc*   **V** P S LAWRIE

WHITWOOD (All Saints) *Wakef 11*   **P** *Bp*   **R** C S BARTER

WHITWORTH (not known)   Man Whitworth *Man*

WHITWORTH (not known) w Spennymoor *Dur 10*   **P** *D&C*   **V** N C GRIFFIN

WHITWORTH (St Bartholomew) *Man 19*   **P** *Keble Coll Ox*   **V** D H HUGHES

WHIXALL (St Mary)   Tilstock and Whixall *Lich*

WHIXLEY (Ascension) w Green Hammerton *Ripon 3*   **P** *DBP and R Knaresborough (alt)*   **V** R A NOAKES

WHORLTON (Holy Cross Old Church) w Carlton and Faceby *York 22*   **P** *Mrs H J F L Steel and Mrs K F L Davies (jt)*   **V** J A WILSON

WHORLTON (St John the Evangelist) *Newc 7*   **P** *Bp*   **TR** S H CONNOLLY,   **TV** J R ERRINGTON, D J TULLY,   **C** T P GIBBONS

WHORLTON (St Mary)   Barnard Castle w Whorlton *Dur*

WHYKE (St George) w Rumboldswhyke St Mary and Portfield All Saints *Chich 3*   **P** *Bp*   **R** D J BRECKNELL

WHYTELEAFE (St Luke) *S'wark 18*   **P** *Bp*   **P-in-c** J E SMITH

WIBTOFT (Assumption of Our Lady)   Claybrooke cum Wibtoft and Frolesworth *Leic*

WICHENFORD (St Lawrence)   Martley and Wichenford, Knightwick etc *Worc*

WICK (All Saints)   Littlehampton and Wick *Chich*

WICK (St Bartholomew) w Doynton and Dyrham *Bris 2*   **P** *Simeon's Trustees, Ld Chan, and M H W Blaythwayt Esq (by turn)*   **V** P F YACOMENI

WICK (St Mary)   Pershore w Pinvin, Wick and Birlingham *Worc*

WICK ST LAWRENCE (St Lawrence)   Kewstoke w Wick St Lawrence *B & W*

WICKEN (St John the Evangelist) *Pet 5*   **P** *Soc Merchant Venturers Bris*   **R** *Vacant*

WICKEN (St Laurence) *Ely 3*   **P** *Ch Patr Trust*   **V** R F BELOE

WICKEN BONHUNT (St Margaret)   Quendon w Rickling and Wicken Bonhunt *Chelmsf*

WICKENBY Group, The (St Peter and St Laurence) *Linc 5*   **P** *DBP, D&C York, Bp, and Charterhouse (by turn)*   **R** J H C DAVIES

WICKERSLEY (St Alban) *Sheff 6*   **P** *DBP*   **R** R J DRAPER,   **NSM** M J WHIPP

WICKFORD (St Andrew) (St Catherine) and Runwell *Chelmsf 9*   **P** *Patr Bd*   **TR** D W LOWMAN,   **TV** A E PAYNE, C R CHUDLEY,   **C** B J RUTT-FIELD,   **NSM** R V GOODWIN

WICKHAM (St Nicholas) *Portsm 1*   **P** *P S Rashleigh Trust*   **R** R A A HIRST

WICKHAM (St Paul and All Saints)   Gt and Lt Henny w Middleton, Wickham St Paul etc *Chelmsf*

WICKHAM (St Swithun)   Welford w Wickham and Gt Shefford, Boxford etc *Ox*

WICKHAM, EAST (St Michael) *S'wark 1*   **P** *Provost and Chapter*   **V** A P MITCHELL,   **Hon C** C HEARD

WICKHAM, WEST (St Francis) *S'wark 19*   **P** *Bp*   **V** O N EVERSON

WICKHAM, WEST (St John) *S'wark 19*   **P** *Bp*   **V** J D B POOLE

WICKHAM, WEST (St Mary) *Ely 4*   **P** *Bp*   **P-in-c** W N C GIRARD

WICKHAM, WEST (St Mary of Nazareth) *S'wark 19*   **P** *Bp*   **V** F S MADGE

WICKHAM BISHOPS (St Bartholomew) w Little Braxted *Chelmsf 27*   **P** *Bp (3 turns), CCC Cam (1 turn)*   **R** C J SLY

WICKHAM MARKET (All Saints) w Pettistree and Easton *St E 18*   **P** *Ch Trust Fund Trust, MMCET, and Ld Chan (by turn)*   **V** G D R BELL,   **NSM** J M HUTCHINSON

WICKHAM SKEITH (St Andrew) *St E 6*   **P** *Ch Patr Trust*   **P-in-c** P T GRAY

WICKHAMBREAUX (St Andrew)   Littlebourne and Ickham w Wickhambreaux etc *Cant*

WICKHAMBROOK (All Saints) w Stradishall and Denston *St E 8*   **P** *Ld Chan and Mrs G S M MacRae (alt)*   **V** W H DAVIS

WICKHAMFORD (St John the Baptist)   Badsey w Aldington and Wickhamford *Worc*

WICKHAMPTON (St Andrew)   Freethorpe w Wickhampton, Halvergate etc *Nor*

WICKLEWOOD (All Saints)   Morley w Deopham, Hackford, Wicklewood etc *Nor*

WICKMERE (St Andrew) w Little Barningham, Itteringham and Edgefield *Nor 3* **P** *Lord Walpole* **R** K A HAWKES

WICKWAR (Holy Trinity) w Rangeworthy *Glouc 7* **P** *Bp and Earl of Ducie (jt)* **R** *Vacant* Chipping Sodbury (0454) 294267

WIDCOMBE Bath Widcombe *B & W*

WIDDINGTON (St Mary) Newport w Widdington *Chelmsf*

WIDDRINGTON (Holy Trinity) *Newc 11* **P** *Bp* **V** P R HESELTON

WIDDRINGTON STATION (St Mary) Ulgham *Newc*

WIDECOMBE-IN-THE-MOOR (St Pancras), Leusdon, Princetown, Postbridge, Huccaby and Holne *Ex 11* **P** *Duchy of Cornwall (1 turn), Patr Bd (2 turns)* **TR** J P HELLIER, **TV** C J L CURD, **NSM** C V L CURD

WIDEMOUTH BAY (Our Lady and St Anne) Week St Mary w Poundstock and Whitstone *Truro*

WIDFORD (St John the Baptist) Hunsdon w Widford and Wareside *St Alb*

WIDFORD (St Mary) (Holy Spirit) *Chelmsf 11* **P** *CPAS* **R** R H CADMAN, **C** N L RANSOM

WIDFORD (St Oswald) Asthall and Swinbrook w Widford *Ox*

WIDLEY w Wymering *Portsm 6* **P** *E G Nugee Esq* **V** D C FREEMAN, **NSM** G C RUMBOLD

WIDMER END (Good Shepherd) Hazlemere *Ox*

WIDMERPOOL (St Peter) Willoughby-on-the-Wolds w Wysall and Widmerpool *S'well*

WIDNES (St Ambrose) *Liv 13* **P** *Trustees* **V** P T JONES

WIDNES (St John) *Liv 13* **P** *Bp and V Farnworth (jt)* **V** D J GAIT

WIDNES (St Mary) *Liv 13* **P** *Bp* **P-in-c** J MILLER

WIDNES (St Paul) *Liv 13* **P** *Bp* **P-in-c** A HODGE

WIDWORTHY (St Cuthbert) Colyton, Southleigh, Offwell, Widworthy etc *Ex*

WIELD (St James) Medstead cum Wield *Win*

WIGAN (All Saints) *Liv 14* **P** *Bp* **R** K M FORREST, **C** S STRICKLEBANK

WIGAN New Springs (St John) New Springs *Liv*

WIGAN (St Andrew) *Liv 15* **P** *R Wigan* **V** R N ARBERY

WIGAN (St Anne) *Liv 15* **P** *Bp* **V** R CRANKSHAW

WIGAN (St Barnabas) Marsh Green *Liv 15* **P** *V Pemberton St Mark Newtown and Bp (jt)* **V** J WINNARD

WIGAN (St Catherine) *Liv 14* **P** *R Wigan* **V** C R SMITH

WIGAN (St George) *Liv 14* **P** *R Wigan* **V** B C HARRISON

WIGAN (St James) (St Thomas) *Liv 15* **P** *R Wigan and Bp (jt)* **V** A D G WRIGHT

WIGAN (St Michael and All Angels) *Liv 15* **P** *R Wigan* **V** D G CLAWSON

WIGAN (St Stephen) *Liv 14* **P** *Bp* **P-in-c** E P TODD

WIGAN Whelley (St Stephen) Wigan St Steph *Liv*

WIGBOROUGH, GREAT (St Stephen) Peldon w Gt and Lt Wigborough *Chelmsf*

WIGBOROUGH, LITTLE (St Nicholas) as above

WIGGATON (St Edward the Confessor) Ottery St Mary, Alfington, W Hill, Tipton etc *Ex*

WIGGENHALL (St Mary Magdalen) *Ely 17* **P** *MMCET* **V** A D HARVEY

WIGGENHALL ST GERMANS (St Mary the Virgin) and Islington St Mary *Ely 17* **P** *Ld Chan (2 turns), Bp (1 turn)* **V** A D HARVEY

WIGGINTON (St Bartholomew) *St Alb 3* **P** *Bp* **V** B H JONES

WIGGINTON (St Giles) Hook Norton w Gt Rollright, Swerford etc *Ox*

WIGGINTON (St Leonard) (St James) *Lich 5* **P** *V Tamworth* **V** M G C NORTON

WIGGINTON (St Mary and St Nicholas) Haxby w Wigginton *York*

WIGGLESWORTH (School) Giggleswick and Rathmell w Wigglesworth *Bradf*

WIGGONHOLT (not known) Amberley w N Stoke and Parham, Wiggonholt etc *Chich*

WIGHILL (All Saints) Healaugh w Wighill, Bilbrough and Askham Richard *York*

WIGHTON (All Saints) Holkham w Egmere w Warham, Wells and Wighton *Nor*

WIGMORE (St James the Apostle) Aymestrey and Leinthall Earles w Wigmore etc *Heref*

WIGMORE ABBEY *Heref 12* **P** *Guild of All So, D P H Lennox Esq, J W Watkins Esq, C C Hartley Esq, and Bp (jt)* **P** P W WALTON

WIGSTON, SOUTH (St Thomas) Glen Parva and S Wigston *Leic*

WIGSTON MAGNA (All Saints) (St Wistan) *Leic 5* **P** *Haberdashers' Co* **V** E J GREEN, **C** J A LINES

WIGSTON PARVA (St Mary the Virgin) Sapcote and Sharnford w Wigston Parva *Leic*

WIGTOFT (St Peter and St Paul) Bicker and Wigtoft *Linc*

WIGTON (St Mary) *Carl 3* **P** *Bp* **P-in-c** G P RAVALDE

WIKE (School Room) Bardsey *Ripon*

WILBARSTON (All Saints) Stoke Albany w Wilbarston *Pet*

WILBERFOSS (St John the Baptist) Kexby w Wilberfoss *York*

WILBRAHAM, GREAT (St Nicholas) *Ely 6* **P** *DBP* **P-in-c** B E KERLEY, **C** N A BRICE

WILBRAHAM, LITTLE (St John) *Ely 6* **P** *CCC Cam* **P-in-c** B E KERLEY, **C** N A BRICE

WILBURTON (St Peter) *Ely 14* **P** *Adn Ely* **V** M P WADSWORTH

WILBURY (St Thomas) *St Alb 9* **P** *Bp* **V** D E DOWLING

WILBY (All Saints) Quidenham *Nor*

WILBY (St Mary the Virgin) Gt Doddington and Wilby *Pet*

WILBY (St Mary) w Brundish *St E 17* **P** *Dr F H C Marriott and Miss A W G Marriott (3 turns), Bp (1 turn)* **P-in-c** R A MARCHANT

WILCOT (Holy Cross) Swanborough *Sarum*

WILCOTE (St Peter) Ramsden, Finstock and Fawler, Leafield etc *Ox*

WILDBOARCLOUGH (St Saviour) Bosley and N Rode w Wincle and Wildboarclough *Ches*

WILDEN (All Saints) *Worc 12* **P** *Earl of Bewdley* **P-in-c** C R LEVEY, **Par Dn** M E STANTON-HYDE

WILDEN (St Nicholas) w Colmworth and Ravensden *St Alb 21* **P** *Ld Chan, Bp, and DBP* **R** W J G HEFFER

WILFORD (St Wilfrid) *S'well 10* **P** *Lt Col Peter Clifton* **R** P NEWTON

WILFORD HILL (St Paul) *S'well 10* **P** *DBP* **V** G J PIGOTT, **NSM** J H BATESON, **Hon Par Dn** B M GRIFFITHS

WILKSBY (All Saints) Mareham-le-Fen and Revesby *Linc*

WILLAND (St Mary the Virgin) *Ex 4* **P** *CPAS* **R** K D AGNEW

WILLASTON (Christ Church) *Ches 9* **P** *DBF* **V** K C TAYLOR

WILLASTON (St Luke) Wistaston *Ches*

WILLEN (St Mary Magdalen) Stantonbury and Willen *Ox*

WILLENHALL (Holy Trinity) *Lich 10* **P** *Patr Bd* **TR** E F BUXTON, **TV** I H MURRAY, **C** D MELVILLE, **Par Dn** B MORGAN

WILLENHALL (St Anne) *Lich 10* **P** *Mrs L Grant-Wilson* **V** C J P DRAYCOTT

WILLENHALL (St Giles) *Lich 10* **P** *Trustees* **V** C R MARSHALL

WILLENHALL (St John the Divine) *Cov 1* **P** *V Cov H Trin* **V** T J COLLING

WILLENHALL (St Stephen) *Lich 10* **P** *Bp* **V** D R HARTLAND

WILLERBY (St Luke) Kirk Ella *York*

WILLERBY (St Peter) w Ganton and Folkton *York 16* **P** *M H Wrigley Esq, MMCET, and Rev C G Day (by turn)* **R** A A MACKENZIE

WILLERSEY (St Peter), Saintbury, Weston-sub-Edge and Aston-sub-Edge *Glouc 10* **P** *Gen Sir John Gibbon and Major G B Gibbon, Earl of Harrowby, and Bp (by turn)* **P-in-c** J M MASON

WILLESBOROUGH (Christ Church) (St Mary the Virgin) *Cant 10* **P** *D&C* **R** M J MCENERY, **C** T D WATSON

WILLESDEN (St Mark) Kensal Rise St Mark and St Martin *Lon*

WILLESDEN (St Martin) as above

WILLESDEN (St Mary) *Lon 21* **P** *D&C St Paul's* **V** D J REES, **Hon C** J L McKENZIE

WILLESDEN (St Matthew) *Lon 21* **P** *Bp* **V** L J WHITING

WILLESDEN GREEN (St Andrew) (St Francis of Assisi) *Lon 21* **P** *Bp* **V** D J IRWIN, **C** A D WEBB, N SPICER, **NSM** N D BIRD

WILLESDEN GREEN (St Gabriel) *Lon 21* **P** *Bp* **P-in-c** D F LAMBERT, **Par Dn** A M RUMBLE

WILLEY (St Leonard) Churchover w Willey *Cov*

WILLIAN (All Saints) Letchworth St Paul w Willian *St Alb*

WILLINGALE (St Christopher) w Shellow and Berners Roding *Chelmsf 11* **P** *Ld Chan* **R** *Vacant*

WILLINGDON (St Mary the Virgin) *Chich 16* **P** *D&C* **V** J R P ASHBY, **C** C H LOVELESS, **NSM** G J GRIFFITHS

WILLINGHAM (St Mary and All Saints) *Ely 5* **P** *Bp* **R** G J ACKERLEY

WILLINGHAM, NORTH (St Thomas) Walesby *Linc*

WILLINGHAM, SOUTH (St Martin)   Barkwith Gp *Linc*
WILLINGHAM BY STOW (St Helen) *Linc 2*   **P** *Bp*
  P-in-c G S RICHARDSON
WILLINGTON (St Lawrence)   Cople w Willington
  St Alb
WILLINGTON (St Michael) *Derby 16*   **P** *CPAS*
  V C R WILSON
WILLINGTON (St Stephen) and Sunnybrow *Dur 10*
  P *R Brancepeth*   **R** D G HERON
**WILLINGTON Team, The (Good Shepherd) (St Mary the
  Virgin) (St Paul)** *Newc 8*   **P** *Prime Min*
  TR G E W BUCKLER,   **TV** B C HURST, J A PYLE,
  Par Dn F A ELTRINGHAM
WILLINGTON QUAY (St Paul)   Willington Team *Newc*
WILLISHAM (St Mary)   Somersham w Flowton and
  Offton w Willisham *St E*
WILLITON (St Peter) *B & W 19*   **P** *V Watchet*
  V J C ANDREWS
WILLOUGHBY (St Helen) *Linc 8*   **P** *Baroness
  Willoughby de Eresby, Ball Coll Ox, and Bp (jt)*
  R D C ROBINSON
WILLOUGHBY (St Nicholas)   Grandborough w
  Willoughby and Flecknoe *Cov*
**WILLOUGHBY-ON-THE-WOLDS (St Mary and All
  Saints) w Wysall and Widerpool** *S'well 9*   **P** *MMCET*
  V J M PROTHERO
**WILLOUGHBY WATERLEYS (St Mary), Peatling Magna
  and Ashby Magna** *Leic 10*   **P** *R* P ETCHELLS
WILLOUGHTON (St Andrew)   Corringham *Linc*
WILMCOTE (St Andrew)   Aston Cantlow and Wilmcote
  w Billesley *Cov*
WILMINGTON (St Mary and St Peter)   Arlington,
  Folkington and Wilmington *Chich*
WILMINGTON (St Michael) *Roch 2*   **P** *D&C*
  V C F JOHNSON,   **Hon Par Dn** P J IVESON
WILMSLOW (St Bartholomew) *Ches 12*   **P** *Bp*
  R P J HUNT,   **C** K E HINE,   **Par Dn** P M PULLAN,
  NSM F H BARKER, R A YATES
WILNE (St Chad) and Draycott w Breaston *Derby 13*
  P *Bp*   **R** W A PEMBERTON
WILNECOTE (Holy Trinity) *Lich 5*   **P** *V Tamworth*
  P-in-c A P HARPER,   **C** R J GORDON
WILSDEN (St Matthew)   Harden and Wilsden *Bradf*
WILSFORD (St Mary)   Ancaster Wilsford Gp *Linc*
WILSFORD (St Michael)   Woodford Valley *Sarum*
WILSFORD (St Nicholas)   Redhorn *Sarum*
WILSHAMSTEAD (All Saints) and Houghton Conquest
  St Alb 19   **P** *St Jo Coll Cam and Bp (alt)*
  V D R PALMER,   **NSM** R C WHITE
WILSHAW (St Mary)   Meltham *Wakef*
WILSILL (St Michael and All Angels)   Upper
  Nidderdale *Ripon*
WILSTHORPE (St Faith)   Langtoft Gp *Linc*
WILSTONE (St Cross)   Tring *St Alb*
WILTON (St Cuthbert) *York 17*   **P** *Abp*   **V** *Vacant*
WILTON (St George) *B & W 20*   **P** *Mrs E C Cutbush*
  TR M D MOYNAGH,   **TV** M D CLARK,
  C G P AYLETT, N J AYLETT,   **Hon C** R W COLWILL,
  NSM M J VENABLES
WILTON (St George)   Thornton Dale and Ellerburne w
  Wilton *York*
**WILTON (St Mary and St Nicholas) w Netherhampton and
  Fugglestone** *Sarum 16*   **P** *Earl of Pembroke*
  R B R COOPER,   **Hon Par Dn** S V COLLINS
WILTON PLACE (St Paul) *Lon 3*   **P** *Bp*
  V A C C COURTAULD
WIMBISH (All Saints)   Debden and Wimbish w
  Thunderley *Chelmsf*
WIMBLEDON (Emmanuel) Ridgway Proprietary Chapel
  S'wark 11   **Min** J J M FLETCHER,   **C** G FYLES,
  Hon C D L JOHNSON
WIMBLEDON (St Luke) *S'wark 11*   **P** *Simeon's Trustees*
  V *Vacant*   081-946 3396
**WIMBLEDON (St Mary) (St Matthew) (St Mark) (St John
  the Baptist)** *S'wark 11*   **P** *Patr Bd*   **TR** G A PARROTT,
  TV C E BLANKENSHIP, M J R FARR,   **C** A G STUDDERT-
  KENNEDY
WIMBLEDON, SOUTH (All Saints) *S'wark 11*   **P** *Bp*
  V K J BALE,   **Hon C** J FRANCIS
WIMBLEDON, SOUTH (Holy Trinity and St Peter)
  S'wark 11   **P** *Bp and TR Wimbledon St Mary (jt)*
  V D S GATLIFFE,   **C** J M FRANCIS
WIMBLEDON, SOUTH (St Andrew) *S'wark 11*   **P** *Bp*
  P-in-c A D WAKEFIELD
WIMBLEDON, WEST (Christ Church) *S'wark 11*
  P *TR Wimbledon*   **V** V READ,   **NSM** D LANKEY
WIMBLEDON PARK   Wimbledon St Luke *S'wark*
WIMBLINGTON (St Peter) *Ely 18*   **P** *St Jo Coll Dur*
  R J DAVIS

**WIMBORNE MINSTER (St Cuthberga) and Holt
  (St James)** *Sarum 10*   **P** *Patr Bd*   **TR** D R PRICE,
  TV M R GODSON,   **C** S R BATTY
WIMBORNE (St Giles)   Cranborne w Boveridge,
  Edmondsham etc *Sarum*
WIMBORNE (St John the Evangelist)   New Boro and
  Leigh *Sarum*
**WIMBOTSHAM (St Mary) w Stow Bardolph and Stow
  Bridge w Nordelph** *Ely 16*   **P** *Bp and
  R T Townley Esq (jt)*   **R** K W A ROBERTS
WIMPOLE (St Andrew) *Ely 8*   **P** *Bp*   **R** *Vacant*
WINCANTON (St Peter and St Paul) *B & W 2*   **P** *D&C*
  R R J CLOETE,   **C** G WEYMONT
WINCH, EAST (All Saints)   Middleton w E Winch *Nor*
WINCH, WEST (St Mary) *Nor 23*   **P** *Ld Chan*
  R J S K FRESTON
WINCHAM (St Andrew)   Lostock Gralam *Ches*
**WINCHCOMBE (St Peter), Gretton, Sudeley Manor and
  Stanley Pontlarge** *Glouc 17*   **P** *Lady Ashcombe*
  V M J PAGE,   **C** J E B KENCHINGTON
WINCHELSEA (St Richard) (St Thomas) *Chich 20*
  P *Guild of All So*   **R** C G SCOTT
WINCHENDON, NETHER (St Nicholas)   Long
  Crendon w Chearsley and Nether Winchendon *Ox*
WINCHENDON, OVER (St Mary Magdalene)
  Waddesdon w Over Winchendon and Fleet Marston *Ox*
**WINCHESTER (All Saints), Chilcomb (St Andrew), Chesil
  St Peter** *Win 13*   **P** *Bp and Ld Chan (alt)*
  R J C HATTON,   **Hon C** T E HEMMING
WINCHESTER (Christ Church) *Win 13*   **P** *Simeon's
  Trustees*   **V** J A MITCHELL-INNES,   **C** W E HENDERSON
WINCHESTER (Holy Trinity)   Winnall *Win*
WINCHESTER (St Barnabas) *Win 13*   **P** *Bp*
  V R C STONE,   **NSM** W J WILSON
WINCHESTER (St Cross Hospital w St Faith) *Win 13*
  P *Bp*   **Master** A C B DEEDES
WINCHESTER (St John the Baptist w St Martin Winnall)
  Winnall *Win*
**WINCHESTER (St Lawrence and St Maurice) (St Swithun-
  upon-Kingsgate)** *Win 13*   **P** *Ld Chan*   **R** D V SCOTT,
  Hon C J M KERR,   **NSM** N H de la MOUETTE
WINCHESTER St Matthew (St Paul's Mission Church)
  Win 13   **P** *Bp*   **R** *Sir* J O C ALLEYNE. Bt,
  NSM N W BIRKETT
WINCHESTER Stanmore (St Luke)   Stanmore *Win*
WINCHESTER HYDE (St Bartholomew) *Win 13*
  P *Ld Chan*   **V** N G SMITH,   **NSM** J A FOREMAN
WINCHFIELD (St Mary the Virgin)   Hartley Wintney,
  Elvetham, Winchfield etc *Win*
WINCHMORE HILL (Holy Trinity) *Lon 18*
  P *V Winchmore Hill St Paul*   **V** C M GRAY,
  Hon C B G RODFORD
WINCHMORE HILL (St Andrew)   Amersham *Ox*
WINCHMORE HILL (St Paul) *Lon 18*   **P** *V Edmonton*
  V D J NASH,   **C** J E HALL,   **Par Dn** C M MORTON
WINCLE (St Michael)   Bosley and N Rode w Wincle and
  Wildboarclough *Ches*
WINCOBANK (St Thomas)   Brightside w Wincobank
  Sheff
WINDERMERE (St Martin) (St John the Evangelist)
  Carl 10   **P** *Bp and Trustees (jt)*   **P-in-c** C M BUTT
WINDERMERE (St Mary)   Applethwaite *Carl*
WINDHILL (Christ Church) *Bradf 1*   **P** *Bp*
  V G PERCIVAL
WINDLESHAM (St John the Baptist) *Guildf 6*
  P *Ld Chan*   **R** J A R PIERSSENE,   **Hon C** J R HANDFORD
WINDRUSH (St Peter)   Sherborne, Windrush, the
  Barringtons etc *Glouc*
**WINDSOR, NEW (Holy Trinity) (St John the Baptist w All
  Saints)** *Ox 13*   **P** *Ld Chan*   **TR** J W G WHALE,
  TV J G CRUICKSHANK, B R TWOHIG,   **C** A W H BUNCH
**WINDSOR, OLD (St Luke's Mission Room) (St Peter and
  St Andrew)** *Ox 13*   **P** *Ld Chan*   **V** J W STAPLES
WINESTEAD (St German)   Patrington w Hollym,
  Welwick and Winestead *York*
**WINFARTHING (St Mary) w Shelfanger w Burston w
  Gissing and Tivetshall** *Nor 16*   **P** *Ld Chan, Bp and
  DBP (jt), Hertf Coll Ox (alt)*   **R** D V WHALE
**WINFORD (Blessed Virgin Mary and St Peter) w Felton
  Common Hill** *B & W 11*   **P** *Worc Coll Ox and
  Mrs H D Pullman (jt)*   **R** J BOLTON
WINFORTON (St Michael and All Angels)   Eardisley w
  Bollingham, Willersley, Brilley etc *Heref*
WINFRITH NEWBURGH (St Christopher)   The
  Lulworths, Winfrith Newburgh and Chaldon *Sarum*
WING (St Peter and St Paul)   Preston and Ridlington w
  Wing and Pilton *Pet*
WING w Grove (All Saints) *Ox 26*   **P** *Bp*   **V** M D SMITH

WINGATE GRANGE (Holy Trinity) *Dur 3* **P** *Bp*
  V P GRUNDY
WINGATES (St John the Evangelist) *Man 11* **P** *R Deane St Mary* **V** A J DOBB
WINGERWORTH (All Saints) *Derby 5* **P** *Bp*
  R S MILLINGTON, **Hon C** F H SHAW
WINGFIELD (St Andrew) Fressingfield, Mendham, Metfield, Weybread etc *St E*
WINGFIELD (St Mary) Westwood and Wingfield *Sarum*
WINGFIELD, NORTH (St Lawrence), Clay Cross and Pilsley *Derby 5* **P** *Bp* **TR** H L ORMEROD,
  TV P A LETFORD, A TELFORD, P G BYSOUTH,
  Par Dn B DALE
WINGFIELD, SOUTH (All Saints) and Wessington
  Derby 1 **P** *Duke of Devonshire and V Crich (jt)*
  V W M RUMBALL
WINGHAM (St Mary the Virgin) w Elmstone and Preston w Stourmouth *Cant 1* **P** *Lord Fitzwalter and D&C (alt)*
  V P J BROWNBRIDGE
WINGRAVE (St Peter and St Paul) w Rowsham, Aston Abbotts and Cublington *Ox 26* **P** *Bp and Linc Coll Ox (jt)* **R** R ON WILLMOTT, **NSM** P R BINNS
WINKBURN (St John of Jerusalem) *S'well 15* **P** *Bp*
  P-in-c H H WILCOX
WINKFIELD (St Mary the Virgin) and Cranbourne *Ox 11*
  P *Bp* **V** S H BAYNES
WINKLEBURY (Good Shepherd) *Win 4* **P** *MMCET*
  V E B PRUEN
WINKLEIGH (All Saints) *Ex 16* **P** *D&C* **V** P NIXSON,
  Hon C G A HAMEY
WINKSLEY (St Cuthbert and St Oswald) Fountains Gp *Ripon*
WINLATON (St Paul) *Dur 5* **P** *Bp* **R** E JONES
WINMARLEIGH (St Luke) Cockerham w Winmarleigh and Glasson *Blackb*
WINNALL (Holy Trinity) (St John the Baptist w St Martin) *Win 13* **P** *Bp* **R** R J H TEARE
WINNERSH (St Mary the Virgin) Hurst *Ox*
WINSCOMBE (St James) *B & W 12* **P** *D&C*
  V B B SALMON
WINSFORD (St Mary Magdalene) Exton and Winsford and Cutcombe w Luxborough *B & W*
WINSHAM (St Stephen) Thorncombe w Winsham and Cricket St Thomas *B & W*
WINSHILL (St Mark) *Derby 16* **P** *Lady H M Gretton and Baroness Gretton (jt)* **V** A J PATTERSON
WINSLEY (St Nicholas) Monkton Farleigh, S Wraxall and Winsley *Sarum*
WINSLOW (St Laurence) w Great Horwood and Addington *Ox 24* **P** *Ld Chan (3 turns), New Coll Ox (2 turns), and DBP (1 turn)* **R** W F JOHNSTON,
  Par Dn J M REES, **Hon Par Dn** B J HESELTINE
WINSON (St Michael) Bibury w Winson and Barnsley *Glouc*
WINSTER (Holy Trinity) *Carl 9* **P** *V Kendal H Trin*
  V K PARTINGTON
WINSTER (St John the Baptist) S Darley, Elton and Winster *Derby*
WINSTON (St Andrew) *Dur 11* **P** *Bp* **R** T J D OLLIER
WINSTON (St Andrew) Helmingham w Framsden and Pettaugh w Winston *St E*
WINSTONE (St Bartholomew) Daglingworth w the Duntisbournes and Winstone *Glouc*
WINTERBOURNE (St James) Chieveley w Winterbourne and Oare *Ox*
WINTERBOURNE (St Michael the Archangel) *Bris 7*
  P *St Jo Coll Ox* **R** E I BAILEY
WINTERBOURNE ABBAS (St Mary) The Winterbournes and Compton Valence *Sarum*
WINTERBOURNE BASSETT (St Katharine) Upper Kennett *Sarum*
WINTERBOURNE CLENSTON (St Nicholas) Winterbourne Stickland and Turnworth etc *Sarum*
WINTERBOURNE DOWN (All Saints) Frenchay and Winterbourne Down *Bris*
WINTERBOURNE EARLS (St Michael and All Angels) Bourne Valley *Sarum*
WINTERBOURNE GUNNER (St Mary) as above
WINTERBOURNE HOUGHTON (St Andrew) Winterbourne Stickland and Turnworth etc *Sarum*
WINTERBOURNE KINGSTON (St Nicholas) Red Post *Sarum*
WINTERBOURNE MONKTON (St Mary Magdalen) Upper Kennett *Sarum*
WINTERBOURNE MONKTON (St Simon and St Jude) Dorchester *Sarum*
WINTERBOURNE ST MARTIN (St Martin) The Winterbournes and Compton Valence *Sarum*

WINTERBOURNE STEEPLETON (St Michael) as above
WINTERBOURNE STICKLAND (St Mary) and Turnworth, Winterbourne Houghton, Winterbourne Whitechurch and Winterbourne Clenston *Sarum 7*
  P *Bp (3 turns), P D H Chichester Esq and Exors Mrs V P Railston (1 turn)* **R** R S GREEN,
  NSM A M F HALL
WINTERBOURNE STOKE (St Peter) *Sarum 16* **P** *Bp*
  P-in-c S M W TRICKETT
WINTERBOURNE WHITECHURCH (St Mary) Winterbourne Stickland and Turnworth etc *Sarum*
WINTERBOURNE ZELSTONE (St Mary) Red Post *Sarum*
WINTERBOURNES and Compton Valence, The *Sarum 2*
  P *Adn Sherborne, Linc Coll Ox, and Sir Robert Williams, Bt (by turn)* **P-in-c** J M DAVEY
WINTERBURN (Chapel of Ease) Gargrave *Bradf*
WINTERINGHAM (All Saints) Alkborough *Linc*
WINTERSLOW (All Saints) (St John) *Sarum 11* **P** *St Jo Coll Ox* **R** C R F COHEN
WINTERTON Group, The (All Saints) *Linc 4* **P** *Lord St Oswald, Bp, and Capt J G G P Elwes (jt)*
  V D EDGAR
WINTERTON (Holy Trinity and All Saints) w East and West Somerton and Horsey *Nor 2* **P** *Bp, SMF, and D&C (jt)* **R** P J G BARNES-CLAY
WINTHORPE (All Saints) *S'well 3* **P** *Keble Coll Ox*
  P-in-c J L SMITH
WINTHORPE (St Mary) Skegness and Winthorpe *Linc*
WINTON (St Mary Magdalene) *Man 2* **P** *Trustees*
  V D R SUTTON
WINTRINGHAM (St Peter) Rillington w Scampston, Wintringham etc *York*
WINWICK (All Saints) *Ely 10* **P** *Bp* **P-in-c** R W B van de WEYER, **NSM** I D GIBSON
WINWICK (St Michael and All Angels) W Haddon w Winwick and Ravensthorpe *Pet*
WINWICK (St Oswald) *Liv 16* **P** *Bp*
  R D A PANKHURST
WIRKSWORTH (St Mary) w Alderwasley, Carsington, Idridgehay, Kirk Ireton and Middleton *Derby 7* **P** *Bp*
  R R S CANEY, **C** C M WOADDEN, **Par Dn** P M HIGHAM
  (nee ANNS)
WISBECH (St Augustine) *Ely 19* **P** *Bp* **V** R D BULL
WISBECH (St Peter and St Paul) *Ely 19* **P** *Bp*
  V W A L ZWALF, **Par Dn** J E PHILLIPS
WISBECH ST MARY (St Mary) *Ely 19* **P** *Bp*
  P-in-c P H N COLLINS, **C** J A COOMBS
WISBOROUGH GREEN (St Peter ad Vincula) *Chich 11*
  P *Bp Lon* **V** E L B CIECHANOWICZ
WISHAW (St Chad) *Birm 9* **P** *Bp* **R** *Vacant* Curdworth (0675) 70331
WISHFORD, GREAT (St Giles) *Sarum 16* **P** *Earl of Pembroke* **P-in-c** K G BEAKE
WISLEY (not known) w Pyrford *Guildf 12* **P** *Bp*
  R F J ASHE, **C** J P HARKIN, **Hon C** P M BOND,
  NSM K R CROOKS
WISSETT (St Andrew) Halesworth w Linstead, Chediston, Holton etc *St E*
WISSINGTON (St Mary the Virgin) Nayland w Wiston *St E*
WISTANSTOW (Holy Trinity) *Heref 11* **P** *Bp*
  P-in-c R S PAYNE
WISTASTON (St Mary) *Ches 15* **P** *Trustees*
  R W J WHITE
WISTON (St Mary) Ashington w Buncton, Wiston and Washington *Chich*
WISTOW (All Saints) *York 6* **P** *Abp* **V** D BOND
WISTOW (St John the Baptist) *Ely 11* **P** *Bp*
  P-in-c S O LEEKE
WISTOW (St Wistan) Gt Glen, Stretton Magna and Wistow etc *Leic*
WITCHAM (St Martin) w Mepal *Ely 14* **P** *D&C*
  R R F REYNOLDS, **NSM** M T COOPER
WITCHAMPTON (St Mary and St Cuthberga and All Saints) and Hinton Parva, Long Crichel w Moor Crichel *Sarum 10* **P** *Hon Mrs M A Marten*
  P-in-c G E WALTON
WITCHFORD (St Andrew) w Wentworth *Ely 14* **P** *D&C*
  R *Vacant* Ely (0353) 2341
WITCHINGHAM GREAT (St Mary) Weston Longville w Morton and the Witchinghams *Nor*
WITCOMBE, GREAT (St Mary) *Glouc 6* **P** *M W Hicks Beach Esq* **P-in-c** P H NAYLOR, **NSM** W J BOON
WITHAM Group, The *Linc 14* **P** *Sir Lyonel Tollemache, Bt, Rev J R H and H C Thorold, and Bp (jt)*
  R N A STONE

WITHAM (St Nicholas) *Chelmsf 27* **P** *Bp*
V D SHERLOCK, **C** K R PLAISTER
WITHAM, NORTH (St Mary) Witham Gp *Linc*
WITHAM, SOUTH (St John the Baptist) as above
**WITHAM FRIARY (Blessed Virgin Mary and St John the
Baptist and All Saints)** Nunney and Witham Friary,
Marston Bigot etc *B & W*
WITHAM-ON-THE-HILL (St Andrew) Edenham w
Witham-on-the-Hill *Linc*
WITHCALL (St Martin) Raithby *Linc*
**WITHERIDGE (St John the Baptist), Thelbridge,
Creacombe, Meshaw, East and West Worlington** *Ex 19*
P *Bp, Exors Sir Denis Stucley, C M K Bruton Esq and
MMCET (jt)* **V** L P R MEERING
WITHERLEY (St Peter) Higham-on-the-Hill w Fenny
Drayton and Witherley *Leic*
WITHERN *Linc 8* **P** *Ld Chan (1 turn), D&C (1 turn),
Bp (2 turns), Duchy of Lanc(1 turn), and DBP (1 turn)*
R *Vacant*
WITHERNICK (St Alban) Aldbrough, Mappleton w
Goxhill and Withernwick *York*
WITHERNSEA (St Nicholas) Owthorne and Rimswell
w Withernsea *York*
WITHERSDALE (St Mary Magdalene) Fressingfield,
Mendham, Metfield, Weybread etc *St E*
WITHERSFIELD (St Mary the Virgin) Haverhill w
Withersfield, the Wrattings etc *St E*
WITHERSLACK (St Paul) *Carl 9* **P** *DBP*
V K PARTINGTON
WITHIEL (St Clement) Roche and Withiel *Truro*
WITHIEL FLOREY (St Mary Magdalene) Brompton
Regis w Upton and Skilgate *B & W*
WITHINGTON (St Christopher) *Man 8* **P** *The Crown*
R M R AINSWORTH
WITHINGTON (St Crispin) *Man 4* **P** *Bp*
R R E WILLIAMS
WITHINGTON (St John the Baptist) Uffington, Upton
Magna and Withington *Lich*
**WITHINGTON (St Michael and All Angels) and Compton
Abdale w Haselton** *Glouc 14* **P** *Bp (2 turns), Ld Chan
(1 turn)* **P-in-c** C D J G BURSLEM
WITHINGTON (St Paul) *Man 8* **P** *Trustees*
R N W DAWSON, **C** I BLAY
WITHINGTON (St Peter) w Westhide *Heref 4* **P** *Bp*
R M A PAICE
WITHINGTON, LOWER (St Peter) Chelford w Lower
Withington *Ches*
WITHLEIGH (St Catherine) Washfield, Stoodleigh,
Withleigh etc *Ex*
WITHNELL (St Paul) *Blackb 4* **P** *V Leyland*
P-in-c G R LOXHAM
WITHYBROOK (All Saints) Wolvey w Burton
Hastings, Copston Magna etc *Cov*
WITHYCOMBE (St Nicholas) Dunster, Carhampton
and Withycombe w Rodhuish *B & W*
WITHYCOMBE RALEIGH (All Saints) Withycombe
Raleigh *Ex*
**WITHYCOMBE RALEIGH (St John the Evangelist)
(St John in the Wilderness) (All Saints)** *Ex 1* **P** *Patr Bd*
TR J A BENTON, **TV** P K CRANCH, **C** A H MACDONALD
WITHYHAM (St John the Evangelist) *Chich 19* **P** *Guild
of All So* **V** R G DINNIS
WITHYHAM (St Michael and All Angels) *Chich 19*
P *Earl de la Warr* **P-in-c** A E D HARRIS
WITHYPOOL (St Andrew) Exford, Exmoor,
Hawkridge and Withypool *B & W*
WITHYWOOD (Shared Church) Conventional District
Bris 1 **C-in-c** B E PEARCE, **C** B A FESSEY
WITLEY (All Saints) *Guildf 4* **P** *Mrs C M Chandler and
R D Chandler Esq (jt)* **V** I C S FENTON
WITLEY, GREAT (St Michael) Shrawley and Witley w
Astley *Worc*
WITLEY, LITTLE (St Michael) as above
WITNESHAM (St Mary) Westerfield and Tuddenham
St Martin w Witnesham *St E*
WITNEY (St Mary the Virgin) *Ox 8* **P** *Patr Bd*
TR R E MEREDITH, **TV** A R HAWKEN, N J S PARRY,
C J T D GARDOM, **Hon C** J H COOK
WITTENHAM, LITTLE (St Peter) Dorchester *Ox*
WITTERING (All Saints) w Thornhaugh and Wansford
Pet 8 **P** *Burghley Ho Preservation Trust (2 turns), Bp
(1 turn)* **R** H R WATSON
WITTERING, EAST (St Anne) Earnley and E
Wittering *Chich*
**WITTERING, WEST (St Peter and St Paul) and Birdham
w Itchenor** *Chich 3* **P** *Bp* **R** T C SMYTH
**WITTERSHAM (St John the Baptist) w Stone-in-Oxney
and Ebony** *Cant 13* **P** *Abp* **R** S D HARRIS

WITTON (St Helen) *Ches 6* **P** *Bp* **V** A A LONG,
C J B HARRIS
WITTON (St Margaret) Bacton w Edingthorpe w Witton
and Ridlington *Nor*
WITTON (St Margaret) Gt w Lt Plumstead and Witton
Nor
WITTON (St Mark) *Blackb 2* **P** *V Blackb*
V D R THOMAS
WITTON, EAST (St John the Evangelist) Middleham w
Coverdale and E Witton *Ripon*
WITTON, NETHER (St Giles) Netherwitton *Newc*
WITTON, WEST (St Bartholomew) *Ripon 4* **P** *Lord
Bolton* **V** *Vacant*
WITTON GILBERT (St Michael and All Angels) *Dur 2*
P *D&C* **R** M J VAIZEY
WITTON LE WEAR (St Philip and St James) and Firtree
Dur 10 **P** *Bp and The Crown (alt)* **V** H TAYLOR
WITTON PARK (St Paul) *Dur 10* **P** *Bp* **V** N M J-
W BEDDOW
WIVELISCOMBE (St Andrew) *B & W 21* **P** *Bp*
V C J B MARSHALL, **C** J R J HISCOX
WIVELSFIELD (St Peter and St John the Baptist) *Chich 6*
P *DBP* **V** S A FALLOWS
WIVENHOE (St Mary) *Chelmsf 19* **P** *Bp* **R** S HARDIE
WIVETON (St Mary) Blakeney w Cley, Wiveton,
Glandford etc *Nor*
WIX (St Mary the Virgin) Gt Oakley w Wix *Chelmsf*
WIXFORD (St Milburga) Exhall w Wixford *Cov*
WIXOE (St Leonard) Clare w Poslingford, Cavendish
etc *St E*
**WOBURN (St Mary) w Eversholt, Milton Bryan,
Battlesden and Pottesgrove** *St Alb 15* **P** *Bedf Estates
Trustees* **V** P R MILLER
WOBURN SANDS (St Michael) *St Alb 15* **P** *Bp*
V N JEFFERY
WOBURN SQUARE (Christ Church) Bloomsbury St
Geo w Woburn Square Ch Ch *Lon*
WOKING (Christ Church) *Guildf 12* **P** *Ridley Hall Cam*
V M F HERBERT, **C** C J M VAUGHAN
WOKING (St John the Baptist) *Guildf 12* **P** *V Woking
St Pet* **V** J SONG, **C** D F PENNANT, **Hon C** G H REID
WOKING (St Mary of Bethany) *Guildf 12* **P** *V Woking
Ch Ch* **V** R DERBRIDGE, **Dss** A M HARRIS
WOKING (St Paul) *Guildf 12* **P** *Ridley Hall Cam*
V S C PITTIS
WOKING (St Peter) *Guildf 12* **P** *Ch Soc Trust*
V B J GRIMSTER, **C** I SMITH
WOKINGHAM (All Saints) *Ox 16* **P** *Bp* **R** B C BAILEY,
C C J DYER, **Hon C** E R FIDDAMAN
WOKINGHAM (St Paul) *Ox 16* **P** *DBP* **R** P N RAPSEY,
C P CHAPLIN, **NSM** R G HOLMES
WOKINGHAM (St Sebastian) *Ox 16* **P** *Bp*
V D R BURDEN
WOLBOROUGH (St Mary) w Newton Abbot *Ex 11*
P *Earl of Devon* **P-in-c** D L STEVENS,
NSM A K CLARKE
WOLD (St Andrew) Walgrave w Hannington and Wold
and Scaldwell *Pet*
WOLD NEWTON (All Saints) Binbrook Gp *Linc*
WOLD NEWTON (All Saints) Burton Fleming w
Fordon, Grindale etc *York*
WOLDINGHAM (St Agatha) (St Paul) *S'wark 18* **P** *Bp*
P-in-c E B WOOD, **NSM** M C JOHNSON
WOLFERLOW (St Andrew) Edvin Loach w Tedstone
Delamere etc *Heref*
WOLFERTON (St Peter) w Babingley *Nor 21* **P** *The
Crown* **P-in-c** G R HALL
WOLFORD (St Michael and All Angels) w Burmington
Cov 9 **P** *Mert Coll Ox* **V** D C BROWN
WOLLASTON (St James) *Worc 11* **P** *Bp*
V M J WILLOWS
WOLLASTON (St Mary) and Strixton *Pet 6* **P** *Bp*
V G S R COX
WOLLASTON, GREAT (All Saints) (St John the Baptist)
Heref 13 **P** *Bp* **V** R J PEARCE
WOLLATON (St Leonard) *S'well 14* **P** *Lord Middleton*
R D W S JAMES, **C** R GOODHAND, **NSM** P D C BROWN
WOLLATON PARK (St Mary) *S'well 14* **P** *CPAS*
V G GREGORY
WOLLESCOTE (St Andrew) *Worc 11* **P** *Bp*
V R C H FRANKLIN
WOLSINGHAM (St Mary and St Stephen) and Thornley
Dur 15 **P** *Bp* **R** R L WELSH
WOLSTANTON (St Margaret) *Lich 15* **P** *Bp*
TR K H MILLER, **TV** J A HILLMAN, G JOHNSON
WOLSTON (St Margaret) and Church Lawford *Cov 6*
P *DBP (2 turns), Bp (1 turn)* **V** P WATKINS,
Hon C P A H SIMMONDS

WOLVERCOTE (St Peter) w Summertown *Ox 7*
  P *Patr Bd* **TR** A M GANN, **TV** D A E MICHAELS,
  Hon C D S WIPPELL, **NSM** W L A PRYOR, G G WRIGHT
WOLVERHAMPTON Pond Lane (Mission Hall) *Wolv*
  St Luke *Lich*
WOLVERHAMPTON (St Andrew) *Lich 10* **P** *Bp*
  V J L SMITH
WOLVERHAMPTON (St Chad) (St Mark's Centre)
  (St Peter) *Lich 10* **P** *Patr Bd* **TR** J C B HALL-
  MATTHEWS, **TV** J F EDGE, M GODFREY, N POUNDE,
  C K WILKIN, **NSM** R A COMMANDER
WOLVERHAMPTON (St John) *Lich 10* **P** *Bp*
  P-in-c J R HOPCRAFT
WOLVERHAMPTON (St Jude) *Lich 10* **P** *CPAS*
  V H H DAVIES
WOLVERHAMPTON (St Luke) Blakenhall *Lich 10*
  P *Trustees* **V** E MALCOLM, **C** M A JONES
WOLVERHAMPTON (St Martin) Rough Hills *Lich*
WOLVERHAMPTON (St Matthew) *Lich 10* **P** *Baldwin*
  Pugh Trustees **V** J R McMANUS, **Par Dn** R J HUDSON-
  WILKIN
WOLVERHAMPTON (St Stephen) *Lich 10* **P** *Bp*
  V D I STANDEN
WOLVERLEY (St John the Baptist) and Cookley *Worc 10*
  P *D&C and Bp (jt)* **V** G SHILVOCK
WOLVERTON (Holy Trinity) (St George the Martyr)
  Ox 25 **P** *Bp* **R** R G RHODES, **TV** J R HOLROYD
WOLVERTON (St Katherine) Baughurst, Ramsdell,
  Wolverton w Ewhurst etc *Win*
WOLVERTON (St Mary the Virgin) w Norton Lindsey and
  Langley *Cov 7* **P** *Bp* **P-in-c** J B NIGHTINGALE
WOLVEY (St John the Baptist) w Burton Hastings,
  Copston Magna and Withybrook *Cov 5* **P** *Bp*
  V R J JAMES
WOLVISTON (St Peter) *Dur 16* **P** *D&C*
  R G W R HARPER
WOMBOURNE (St Benedict) w Trysull and Bobbington
  Lich 6 **P** *Patr Bd* **TR** S HUYTON,
  TV W S FROST, C HUGHES
WOMBRIDGE (St Mary and St Leonard) *Lich 28*
  V R W BAILEY
WOMBWELL (St Mary) *Sheff 12* **P** *Trin Coll Cam*
  R E MITCHELL, **C** B SWINDELL, **Par Dn** G S ROSE
WOMBWELL JUMP (St George) Wombwell *Sheff*
WOMERSLEY (St Martin) and Kirk Smeaton *Wakef 11*
  V S M HIND
WONERSH (St John the Baptist) *Guildf 2* **P** *Selw Coll*
  Cam **V** M K WILLIAMS, **C** P M C KETTLE
WONSTON (Holy Trinity) and Stoke Charity w Hunton
  Win 13 **P** *Bp and D&C (jt)* **R** A JARDINE,
  NSM R C CLARKSON
WONSTON, SOUTH (St Margaret) Wonston and Stoke
  Charity w Hunton *Win*
WOOBURN (St Paul) *Ox 29* **P** *Bp* **V** R D S CAINK
WOOD DALLING (St Andrew) Reepham, Hackford w
  Whitwell, Kerdiston etc *Nor*
WOOD DITTON (St Mary) w Saxon Street *Ely 4* **P** *Duke*
  of Sutherland **V** A F HOMER
WOOD END (St Chad) *Cov 1* **P** *Ld Chan*
  V D T PETTIFOR, **C** L B NORTHALL
WOOD END (St Michael and All Angels) Baxterley w
  Hurley and Wood End and Merevale etc *Birm*
WOOD GREEN (Holy Trinity) Witney *Ox*
WOOD GREEN (St Michael) w Bounds Green (St Gabriel)
  (St Michael-at-Bowes) *Lon 19* **P** *Patr Bd*
  TR J C BROADHURST, **TV** N G T WHEELER,
  C N P WHEELER, C J VIPERS, **Hon C** S J D'MORIAS
WOOD GREEN (St Paul) Wednesbury St Paul Wood
  Green *Lich*
WOOD NORTON (All Saints) Twyford w Guist w
  Bintry w Themelthorpe etc *Nor*
WOOD STREET (St Alban) Worplesdon *Guildf*
WOODBASTWICK (St Fabian and St Sebastian)
  Ranworth w Panxworth and Woodbastwick *Nor*
WOODBERRY DOWN (St Olave) Stoke Newington St
  Olave *Lon*
WOODBOROUGH (St Mary Magdalene)
  Swanborough *Sarum*
WOODBOROUGH (St Swithun) *S'well 11* **P** *Bp*
  V W G CALTHROP-OWEN
WOODBRIDGE (St John the Evangelist) *St E 7*
  P *Ch Patr Trust* **V** P H MILLER
WOODBRIDGE (St Mary the Virgin) *St E 7* **P** *Bp*
  Hon C J P B ASHTON
WOODBURY (Holy Cross) Axminster, Chardstock,
  Combe Pyne and Rousdon *Ex*
WOODBURY (St Swithun) *Ex 1* **P** *D&C* **V** D J SHARE
WOODBURY SALTERTON (Holy Trinity) Clyst St
  Mary, Clyst St George etc *Ex*

WOODCHESTER (St Mary) *Glouc 8* **P** *Simeon's*
  Trustees **P-in-c** D N GREEN
WOODCHURCH (All Saints) *Cant 10* **P** *Abp*
  R S G FRANKLIN
WOODCHURCH (Holy Cross) *Ches 1* **P** *DBP*
  R A D DEAN, **C** C J P CRISALL, **Hon C** A H B TAYLOR
WOODCOTE (St Leonard) Langtree *Ox*
WOODCOTE (St Peter) Lilleshall and Sheriffhales *Lich*
WOODCOTT (St James) St Mary Bourne and Woodcott
  Win
WOODDITTON (St Mary) Wood Ditton w Saxon Street
  Ely
WOODEATON (Holy Rood) Islip w Charlton on
  Otmoor, Oddington, Noke etc *Ox*
WOODFORD (Christ Church) *Ches 12* **P** *Exors Lt-*
  Col Sir Walter Bromley-Davenport **V** J H HALL
WOODFORD (St Barnabas) *Chelmsf 7* **P** *Bp*
  V A CROSS
WOODFORD (St Mary the Virgin) *Pet 10* **P** *DBP*
  R M C PRENTICE
WOODFORD (St Mary w St Philip and St James) *Chelmsf*
  7 **P** *Bp* **R** S R BIRCHNALL, **C** A E TURNER,
  NSM A BROWN, A D BROWNE
WOODFORD, SOUTH Hermon Hill (Holy Trinity)
  Wanstead H Trin Hermon Hill *Chelmsf*
WOODFORD BRIDGE (St Paul) *Chelmsf 7*
  P *R Woodford* **V** R C MATTHEWS
WOODFORD HALSE (St Mary the Virgin) w Eydon *Pet 1*
  P *Ld Chan (2 turns) and Bp (1 turn)* **V** J M COURTIE
WOODFORD VALLEY (All Saints) *Sarum 12* **P** *Bp*
  V J L REYNOLDS
WOODFORD WELLS (All Saints) (St Andrew) *Chelmsf 7*
  P *Trustees* **V** M J COLE,
  C G St G CATCHPOLE, C R LEES
WOODGREEN (St Boniface) Hale w S Charford *Win*
WOODHALL (St James the Great) *Bradf 3* **P** *Bp*
  V J A HOLFORD
WOODHALL SPA and Kirkstead *Linc 11* **P** *Bp*
  P-in-c R I McMASTER
WOODHAM (All Saints) *Guildf 12* **P** *Bp*
  V P G P FARRELL, **NSM** A J K MACKENZIE
WOODHAM (St Elizabeth of Hungary) Newton
  Aycliffe *Dur*
WOODHAM FERRERS (St Mary) and Bicknacre
  Chelmsf 11 **P** *Lord Fitzwalter* **R** P R DOWMAN
WOODHAM FERRERS, SOUTH (Holy Trinity) (St Mary)
  Chelmsf 11 **P** *Bp* **V** R W SIMMONDS, **C** N W STEEL
WOODHAM MORTIMER (St Margaret) w Hazeleigh
  Chelmsf 13 **P** *Bp* **P-in-c** J M HALL
WOODHAM WALTER (St Michael) *Chelmsf 13*
  P *Ch Soc Trust* **P-in-c** J M HALL
WOODHAY, EAST (St Martin) and Woolton Hill *Win 6*
  P *Bp* **R** D J CARTER, **NSM** T E DOREY
WOODHAY, WEST (St Laurence) w Enborne, Hampstead
  Marshall, Inkpen and Combe *Ox 14* **P** *Bp,*
  D&C Windsor, and J R Henderson Esq (jt)
  P-in-c C W PAKENHAM
WOODHEAD (St James) Mottram in Longdendale w
  Woodhead *Ches*
WOODHORN w Newbiggin *Newc 11* **P** *Bp* **V** J B HAY
WOODHOUSE (Christ Church) *Wakef 5* **P** *Bp*
  V S K M HENRY
WOODHOUSE (St Mark) and Wrangthorn *Ripon 7*
  P *DBP* **V** J B LANGDON
WOODHOUSE (St Mary in the Elms) *Leic 7* **P** *DBP*
  V *Vacant* Woodhouse Eaves (0509) 890226
WOODHOUSE CLOSE (not known) Bishop Auckland
  Woodhouse Close CD *Dur*
WOODHOUSE EAVES (St Paul) *Leic 7* **P** *DBP*
  P-in-c D M BUXTON
WOODHOUSE MILL (St James) Handsworth
  Woodhouse *Sheff*
WOODHOUSE PARK (Wm Temple Church)
  Wythenshawe Wm Temple Ch *Man*
WOODHOUSES (not known) Bardsley *Man*
WOODHOUSES (St John the Divine) Dunham Massey
  St Mark *Ches*
WOODHURST (St John the Baptist) Bluntisham cum
  Earith w Colne and Woodhurst *Ely*
WOODINGDEAN (Holy Cross) *Chich 2* **P** *Bp*
  TR B G CARTER
WOODKIRK (St Mary) W Ardsley *Wakef*
WOODLAND (St John the Baptist) Broadhempston,
  Woodland, Staverton etc *Ex*
WOODLAND (St John the Evangelist) Broughton and
  Duddon *Carl*
WOODLAND (St Mary) Lynesack *Dur*
WOODLANDS (All Saints) *Sheff 8* **P** *Bp*
  V M J GODFREY

WOODLANDS (Ascension)   Cranborne w Boveridge, Edmondsham etc *Sarum*

WOODLANDS (Mission Chapel)   W Meon and Warnford *Portsm*

WOODLANDS (St Katherine) *B & W 4*   **P** *DBP*
V G J WRAYFORD

WOODLANDS (St Mary)   Kemsing w Woodlands *Roch*

WOODLANDS (St Stephen)   Welford w Wickham and Gt Shefford, Boxford etc *Ox*

WOODLEIGH (St Mary the Virgin) and Loddiswell *Ex 14*
P *D&C and MMCET (jt)*   **R** R J LAW

WOODLESFORD (All Saints)   Oulton w Woodlesford *Ripon*

WOODLEY (St John the Evangelist) *Ox 15*   **P** *DBP*
V I L S WATSON,   **C** R J FISHER,   **Par Dn** L M BROWN

WOODMANCOTE (Mission Church)   Westbourne *Chich*

WOODMANCOTE (St James)   Micheldever and E Stratton, Woodmancote etc *Win*

WOODMANCOTE (St Mark)   Dursley *Glouc*

WOODMANCOTE (St Peter)   Henfield w Shermanbury and Woodmancote *Chich*

WOODMANSEY (St Peter)   Beverley Minster *York*

WOODMANSTERNE (St Peter) *S'wark 25*   **P** *Ld Chan*
R C C COOPER

WOODNESBOROUGH (St Mary the Blessed Virgin) w Worth and Staple *Cant 8*   **P** *Abp*   **Dn-in-c** E R ROUTH,
NSM K I HAGGAR

WOODNEWTON (St Mary)   Nassington w Yarwell and Woodnewton *Pet*

WOODPLUMPTON (St Anne) *Blackb 10*
P *V St Michael's-on-Wyre*   **V** P J PIKE

WOODRISING (St Nicholas)   Hingham w Woodrising w Scoulton *Nor*

WOODSETTS (St George) *Sheff 5*   **P** *Bp*   **V** H LIDDLE

WOODSFORD (St John the Baptist)   Moreton and Woodsford w Tincleton *Sarum*

WOODSIDE (St Andrew) w East Hyde *St Alb 20*   **P** *D&C St Paul's*   **V** D R BOLSTER

WOODSIDE (St James) *Ripon 7*   **P** *Bp*   **V** P Q TUDGE

WOODSIDE GREEN (St Andrew)   Gt Hallingbury and Lt Hallingbury *Chelmsf*

WOODSIDE PARK (St Barnabas) *Lon 14*   **P** *Ch Patr Trust*   **V** J S H COLES,   **C** M R ALDRIDGE,
NSM J R GULLAND

WOODSTOCK (St Mary Magdalene)   Bladon w Woodstock *Ox*

WOODSTON (St Augustine of Canterbury) (Mission Church) *Ely 13*   **P** *Bp*   **R** D G STEVENS

WOODTHORPE (St Mark) *S'well 11*   **P** *Bp*
V F W BRIDGER,   **C** G R BOOTH,
Assoc Min R W BRIDGER

WOODTHORPE (St Peter)   Staveley and Barrow Hill *Derby*

WOODTON (All Saints)   Hempnall *Nor*

WOODVILLE (St Stephen) *Derby 16*   **P** *Bp*
V R E MORTIMER-ANDERSON

WOOKEY (St Matthew)   Coxley, Henton and Wookey *B & W*

WOOKEY HOLE (St Mary Magdalene)   Wells St Cuth w Wookey Hole *B & W*

WOOL (Holy Rood) and East Stoke *Sarum 9*   **P** *Bp (3 turns), Keble Coll Ox (1 turn)*   **R** T N STUBBS

WOOLACOMBE (St Sabinus)   Ilfracombe, Lee, Woolacombe, Bittadon etc *Ex*

WOOLASTON (St Andrew) w Alvington *Glouc 4*   **P** *DBP*
P-in-c L NEUDEGG,   **Hon C** J M NEUDEGG

WOOLAVINGTON (Blessed Virgin Mary) w Cossington and Bawdrip *B & W 15*   **P** *D&C Windsor and J A Church Esq (alt)*   **V** *Vacant*   Puriton (0278) 683408

WOOLBEDING (All Hallows) *Chich 10*   **P** *Cowdray Trust*   **R** D CHANING-PEARCE

WOOLBROOK (St Francis of Assisi)   Sidmouth, Woolbrook, Salcombe Regis, Sidbury etc *Ex*

WOOLER (St Mary)   Glendale Gp *Newc*

WOOLFARDISWORTHY (Holy Trinity) and Buck Mills *Ex 17*   **P** *SMF and Bp (alt)*   **V** D A BATES

WOOLFARDISWORTHY EAST (St Mary)   N Creedy *Ex*

WOOLFOLD (St James) *Man 10*   **P** *R Bury St Mary*
V G P MITCHELL

WOOLHAMPTON (St Peter) w Midgham and Beenham Valance *Ox 12*   **P** *Bp, Keble Coll Ox, and CPAS (jt)*
R J L WATSON

WOOLHOPE (St George) *Heref 4*   **P** *D&C*
P-in-c E R I CHURCHUS

WOOLLAND (not known)   Okeford Fitzpaine, Ibberton, Belchalwell etc *Sarum*

WOOLLEY (All Saints)   Swainswick w Langridge *B & W*

WOOLLEY (St Peter) *Wakef 9*   **P** *Bp*   **V** J S PEARSON

WOOLMER GREEN (St Michael)   Welwyn w Ayot St Peter *St Alb*

WOOLPIT (Blessed Virgin Mary) w Drinkstone *St E 10*
P *Bp and A Harvie-Clark Esq (alt)*   **R** A G TAYLOR,
NSM K C BROMAGE

WOOLSTASTON (St Michael and All Angels)   Smethcott w Woolstaston *Heref*

WOOLSTHORPE (St James) *Linc 19*   **P** *Duke of Rutland*
R J M ASHLEY,   **NSM** S J HADLEY

WOOLSTON (Church of the Ascension)   Padgate *Liv*

WOOLSTON (St Mark) *Win 12*   **P** *Bp*
V F P MATTHEWS,   **NSM** R G CLARKE

WOOLSTONE (All Saints)   Uffington w Woolstone and Baulking *Ox*

WOOLSTONE (not known)   Woughton *Ox*

WOOLSTONE (St Martin) w Gotherington and Oxenton, and Kemerton *Glouc 9*   **P** *DBP and Croome Estate*
R *Vacant*   Bishops Cleeve (024267) 2921

WOOLTON, MUCH (St Peter) *Liv 4*   **P** *Bp*
R J V ROBERTS,   **C** R J DRIVER,   **Par Dn** J MARSDEN

WOOLTON HILL (St Thomas)   E Woodhay and Woolton Hill *Win*

WOOLVERSTONE (St Michael)   Holbrook w Freston and Woolverstone *St E*

WOOLVERTON (St Lawrence)   Rode Major *B & W*

WOOLWICH (St Mary Magdalene) (St Michael and All Angels) *S'wark 1*   **P** *Bp and Keble Coll Ox (jt)*
R D E RHYS

WOOLWICH (St Thomas) *S'wark 1*   **P** *Bp*
R M A HORSEY

WOOLWICH, NORTH (St John) w Silvertown *Chelmsf 5*
P *Bp and Lon Corp (alt)*   **P-in-c** P H F DUNCAN

WOONTON (Mission Room)   Lyonshall w Titley, Almeley and Kinnersley *Heref*

WOORE (St Leonard) and Norton in Hales *Lich 24*   **P** *Bp and CPAS (jt)*   **P-in-c** P M JAMES

WOOSEHILL (Community Church)   Bearwood *Ox*

WOOTTON Boars Hill (St Peter) *Ox 10*   **P** *Bp*
V P N CHALLENGER

WOOTTON (St Andrew)   Ulceby Gp *Linc*

WOOTTON (St Edmund) *Portsm 8*   **P** *DBP*
P-in-c R J EMBLIN

WOOTTON (St George the Martyr) w Quinton and Preston Deanery *Pet 7*   **P** *Ex Coll Ox and Bp (alt)*
R D SCHOLEY

WOOTTON (St Martin)   Elham w Denton and Wootton *Cant*

WOOTTON (St Mary the Virgin) *St Alb 19*   **P** *MMCET*
V C P STRONG

WOOTTON (St Mary) w Glympton and Kiddington *Ox 9*
P *New Coll Ox (2 turns), Bp(1 turn), and Exors of E W Towler Esq (1 turn)*   **R** L W DOOLAN

WOOTTON, NORTH (All Saints) w SOUTH (St Mary) *Nor 23*   **P** *Ld Chan and G Howard Esq (alt)*
R B R OAKE

WOOTTON, NORTH (St Peter)   Pilton w Croscombe, N Wootton and Dinder *B & W*

WOOTTON BASSETT (St Bartholomew and All Saints) *Sarum 18*   **P** *DBP*   **V** B J GARRATT,
Hon C P M O GILES

WOOTTON BRIDGE (St Mark)   Wootton *Portsm*

WOOTTON COURTENAY (All Saints)   Selworthy and Timberscombe and Wootton Courtenay *B & W*

WOOTTON FITZPAINE (not known)   Marshwood Vale Team Min *Sarum*

WOOTTON RIVERS (St Andrew)   Pewsey Team Min *Sarum*

WOOTTON ST LAWRENCE (St Lawrence)   Church Oakley and Wootton St Lawrence *Win*

WOOTTON WAWEN (St Peter) *Cov 7*   **P** *K Coll Cam*
P-in-c J ALFORD

WORCESTER (St Andrew and All Saints w St Helen)   Worc City St Paul and Old St Martin etc *Worc*

WORCESTER (St Barnabas) (Christ Church) *Worc 6*
P *Bp*   **TR** P J A LEVERTON,   **C** M J STRANGE,
P J RAHILLY

WORCESTER (St Clement) *Worc 6*   **P** *D&C*
R F T HOLT

WORCESTER (St George w St Mary Magdalene) *Worc 6*
P *Bp and V Claines (jt)*   **V** S LOWE

WORCESTER (St John in Bedwardine)   St Jo in Bedwardine *Worc*

WORCESTER (St Martin in the Cornmarket)   Worc City St Paul and Old St Martin etc *Worc*

WORCESTER (St Michael) *Worc 3*   **P** *Bp*
V P R HOLZAPFEL

WORCESTER (St Stephen)   Barbourne *Worc*

WORCESTER (St Wulstan) *Worc 6*   **P** *Bp*   **V** I READ

WORCESTER (St Wulstan) Warndon St Nic *Worc*
WORCESTER CITY (St Paul) (Old St Martin w
  St Swithun) (St Nicholas and All Saints) *Worc 6* P *Bp
  and D&C (jt)* R J C EVEREST, Par Dn B MORDECAI,
  NSM A M WHERRY
WORCESTER SOUTH EAST (St Martin w St Peter)
  (St Mark in the Cherry Orchard) (Holy Trinity w
  St Matthew) *Worc 6* P *Patr Bd* TR M A O LEWIS,
  TV C FOWLER, W J C HOPLEY, NSM D E HASSELL
WORDSLEY (Holy Trinity) *Lich 1* P *Patr Bd*
  TR W M SMITH, TV R N LATHAM, R A BROADBENT,
  NSM G HODGSON
WORFIELD (St Peter) *Heref 9* P *J R S Greenshields Esq*
  V B N STEVENSON
WORKINGTON (St John) *Carl 7* P *R Workington*
  V J M COOK
WORKINGTON (St Michael) *Carl 7* P *Exors
  E S C Curwen* R T H M SAMPSON, C H BROWN
WORKSOP (St Anne) *S'well 6* P *Bp* V F T BEECH,
  C P C ROBINSON
WORKSOP (St John the Evangelist) *S'well 6* P *CPAS*
  V B A HUNT, C J YALLOP
WORKSOP (St Paul) *S'well 6* P *Bp* V I C McCARTHY
WORKSOP PRIORY (St Mary and St Cuthbert) *S'well 6*
  P *St Steph Ho Ox* V B L HOLDRIDGE,
  C M WAKELY, M WAGSTAFF
WORLABY (St Clement) *Linc 6* P *DBP*
  V S W ANDREW
WORLDHAM, EAST (St Mary the Virgin) and West
  Worldham, Hartley Mauditt w Kingsley and Oakhanger
  Win 2 P *D&C and Bp (alt)* V P G L COLE
WORLDHAM, WEST (St Nicholas) E and W
  Worldham, Hartley Mauditt w Kingsley etc *Win*
WORLE (St Martin) (St Mark's Church Centre) *B & W 12*
  P *Ld Chan* V N KENT, C A D NORRIS, H M WILLIAMS,
  Hon C T M TOMLINSON, Hon Par Dn A NORRIS
WORLESTON (St Oswald) Acton and Worleston *Ches*
WORLINGHAM (All Saints) w Barnby and North Cove
  St E 14 P *Ld Chan* R A A B JONES
WORLINGTON (All Saints) Mildenhall *St E*
WORLINGTON, EAST (St Mary) Witheridge,
  Thelbridge, Creacombe, Meshaw etc *Ex*
WORLINGTON, WEST (St Mary) as above
WORLINGWORTH (St Mary) w Southolt, Tannington,
  Bedfield and Monk Soham *St E 17* P *Lord Henniker,
  R C Rous Esq and Bp, and DBP (by turn)*
  P-in-c J D B MINCHER
WORMBRIDGE (St Peter) Ewyas Harold w Dulas,
  Kenderchurch etc *Heref*
WORMEGAY (St Michael and All Angels and Holy
  Cross) Tottenhill w Wormegay *Ely*
WORMHILL (St Margaret) and Peak Forest w Peak Dale
  and Dove Holes *Derby 4* P *Bp and Duke of
  Devonshire (jt)* V O J POST
WORMINGFORD (St Andrew), Mount Bures and Little
  Horkesley *Chelmsf 20* P *J J Tufnell Esq, Major-Gen
  P H de Havilland, and Keble Coll Ox (jt)*
  V J W LARTER
WORMINGHALL (St Peter and St Paul) w Ickford, Oakley
  and Shabbington *Ox 21* P *Bp and Guild of All So (jt)*
  R A R DE PURY
WORMINGTON (St Katharine) Dumbleton w
  Wormington *Glouc*
WORMLEIGHTON (St Peter) Priors Hardwick, Priors
  Marston and Wormleighton *Cov*
WORMLEY (Church Room) Broxbourne w Wormley
  St Alb
WORMLEY (St Laurence) as above
WORMSHILL (St Giles) Bredgar w Bicknor and
  Frinsted w Wormshill etc *Cant*
WORPLESDON (St Mary the Virgin) *Guildf 5* P *Eton
  Coll* R R P ROBINS, C B M SHAND
WORSALL, HIGH AND LOW (All Saints) *York 22*
  P *Abp (3 turns), V Northallerton (1 turn)* V D MOORE
WORSBROUGH (St Mary) *Sheff 7* P *DBP*
  V T HUDSON
WORSBROUGH (St Thomas) (St James) *Sheff 7* P *Bp
  and The Crown (alt)* V D C GAY
WORSBROUGH COMMON (St Luke) *Sheff 7* P *Bp*
  V P MORLEY
WORSLEY (St Mark) *Man 2* P *Bp* TV S D A KILLWICK,
  C S B GREY
WORSLEY MESNES (not known) Wigan St Jas w St
  Thos *Liv*
WORSTEAD (St Mary) w Westwick and Sloley *Nor 9*
  P *D&C (1 turn), DBP (2 turns)* P-in-c A R LONG
WORSTHORNE (St John the Evangelist) *Blackb 3*
  P *Trustees* V E P A FURNESS

WORTH (St Nicholas) *Chich 7* P *DBP*
  TR P C KEFFORD, TV S W BARNES, B R COOK,
  C D A PICKEN
WORTH (St Peter and St Paul) Woodnesborough w
  Worth and Staple *Cant*
WORTH MATRAVERS (St Aldhelm) Kingston,
  Langton Matravers and Worth Matravers *Sarum*
WORTH MATRAVERS (St Nicholas) as above
WORTHAM (St Mary the Virgin) N Hartismere *St E*
WORTHEN (All Saints) *Heref 13* P *New Coll Ox
  (8 turns), Lady More (1 turn), I Chirbury (1 turn)*
  R N D MINSHALL
WORTHING Christ the King (Christ Church) (Holy
  Trinity) (St Matthew) (St Paul) *Chich 5* P *Patr Bd*
  TR G G GUINNESS, TV J A WILKINSON
WORTHING (St Andrew) *Chich 5* P *Keble Coll Ox*
  V E J R CHOWN, Hon C E G OGDEN
WORTHING (St George) (Emmanuel) *Chich 5* P *Ch Soc
  Trust* V D E A MARROW
WORTHING (St Margaret) N Elmham w Billingford
  and Worthing *Nor*
WORTHING, WEST (St John the Divine) *Chich 5* P *Bp*
  V K WOOD, NSM K SMITH
WORTHINGTON (St Matthew) Breedon cum Isley
  Walton and Worthington *Leic*
WORTING (St Thomas of Canterbury) *Win 4*
  P *MMCET* R S H TRAPNELL
WORTLEY (St Leonard) w Thurgoland *Sheff 7*
  P *Dowager Countess of Wharncliffe and V Silkstone (jt)*
  V D WARNER
WORTLEY, NEW (St Mary's Parish Centre) St Bart
  Armley w St Mary New Wortley *Ripon*
WORTLEY DE LEEDS (St John the Evangelist) *Ripon 6*
  P *Trustees* V J N O HORTON
WORTON (Christ Church) Potterne w Worton and
  Marston *Sarum*
WORTON, NETHER (St James) Over w Nether
  Worton *Ox*
WORTON, OVER (Holy Trinity) w Nether Worton *Ox 5*
  P *Exors of J B Schuster Esq* R *Vacant*
WOTTON (St John the Evangelist) and Holmbury St Mary
  Guildf 7 P *Bp and J P M H Evelyn Esq (jt)*
  R V P WHITE
WOTTON ST MARY WITHOUT (Holy Trinity) *Glouc 5*
  P *Bp* V P M NUNN, C A T FRASER, S E RUSHTON
WOTTON-UNDER-EDGE (St Mary the Virgin) w
  Ozleworth and North Nibley *Glouc 2* P *Ch Ch Ox*
  V J A C MAY, NSM E M CHAPPELL
WOTTON UNDERWOOD (All Saints) Ludgershall w
  Wotton Underwood and Ashendon *Ox*
WOUGHTON *Ox 25* P *Patr Bd* TR N P H POND,
  TV S FOSTER, C M A HOUSTON,
  Par Dn F J BEVERIDGE
WOUGHTON-ON-THE-GREEN (St Mary) Woughton
  Ox
WOULDHAM (All Saints) Burham and Wouldham
  Roch
WRABNESS (All Saints) Ramsey w Lt Oakley and
  Wrabness *Chelmsf*
WRAGBY (All Saints) *Linc 11* V A R RUTHERFORD
WRAGBY (St Michael and Our Lady) Kinsley w
  Wragby *Wakef*
WRAMPLINGHAM (St Peter and St Paul) Barnham
  Broom *Nor*
WRANGBROOK (St Michael) Badsworth *Wakef*
WRANGLE (St Mary and St Nicholas) Old Leake w
  Wrangle *Linc*
WRANGTHORN (St Augustine of Hippo) Woodhouse
  and Wrangthorn *Ripon*
WRATTING, GREAT (St Mary) Haverhill w
  Withersfield, the Wrattings etc *St E*
WRATTING, LITTLE (St Mary) as above
WRATTING, WEST (St Andrew) *Ely 4* P *D&C*
  NSM L R WICKHAM
WRAWBY (St Mary the Virgin) *Linc 6* P *Bp*
  V P J WHITE
WRAXALL (All Saints) *B & W 14* P *Trustees*
  R D J PAYNE
WRAXALL (St Mary) Melbury *Sarum*
WRAXALL, NORTH (St James) Colerne w N Wraxall
  Bris
WRAXALL, SOUTH (St James) Monkton Farleigh, S
  Wraxall and Winsley *Sarum*
WRAY (Holy Trinity) w Tatham and Tatham Fells
  Blackb 15 P *Bp, Trustees and PCCs (jt)*
  V R F JACKSON
WRAY, LOW (St Margaret) Hawkshead and Low Wray
  w Sawrey *Carl*
WRAYSBURY (St Andrew) Riverside *Ox*

WREAY (St Mary) *Carl 3*   **P** *D&C*   **P-in-c** P KYBIRD
WRECCLESHAM (St Peter) *Guildf 3*   **P** *Bp*
  V P H C DICKENS,   **Hon C** B J SMITH
WRENBURY (St Margaret)   Baddiley and Wrenbury w
  Burleydam *Ches*
WRENINGHAM (All Saints) *Nor 13*   **P** *Ld Chan (1 turn)*,
  Patr Bd (4 turns)   **TR** K G CROCKER,
  TV S G STEPHENSON
**WRENTHAM (St Nicholas) w Benacre, Covehithe,
  Frostenden and South Cove** *St E 15*   **P** *Sir John
  Gooch, Bt*   **R** C J H PARSONS
WRENTHORPE (St Anne) *Wakef 12*   **P** *Bp*
  V J K BUTTERWORTH
WRESSLE (St John of Beverly)   Howden Team Min
  York
WRESTLINGWORTH (St Peter)   Dunton w
  Wrestlingworth and Eyeworth *St Alb*
WRETHAM (St Ethelbert)   Hockham w Shropham Gp
  of Par *Nor*
WRETTON (All Saints)   Stoke Ferry w Wretton *Ely*
WRIBBENHALL (All Saints) *Worc 10*
  P *V Kidderminster* **Dn-in-c** H HUGHES
WRIGHTINGTON (St James the Great) *Blackb 4*   **P** *Bp*
  V *Vacant*   Eccleston (0257) 451332
WRINGTON (All Saints) w Butcombe *B & W 12*   **P** *SMF*
  R D R HOOPER,   **Hon C** B C E FRENCH
WRITTLE (All Saints) w Highwood *Chelmsf 11*
  P *New Coll Ox*   **P-in-c** P W NOKES,   **C** J M PAUL,
  Par Dn C A McCAFFERTY
WROCKWARDINE (St Peter)   Longdon-upon-Tern,
  Rodington, Uppington etc *Lich*
WROCKWARDINE WOOD (Holy Trinity) *Lich 28*   **P** *Bp*
  R A T MILLER
WROOT (St Pancras)   Epworth and Wroot *Linc*
WROSE (St Cuthbert) *Bradf 3*   **P** *The Crown*
  V P N AYERS
WROTHAM (St George) *Roch 9*   **P** *D&C*
  R G A ROBSON
WROUGHTON (St John the Baptist) *Bris 13*   **P** *Bp*
  R E J WOODS,   **C** S F EVERETT
WROXALL (St John) *Portsm 7*   **P** *Bp*   **V** A TEDMAN
WROXALL (St John the Evangelist)   Wroxall *Portsm*
WROXALL (St Leonard)   Hatton w Haseley, Rowington
  w Lowsonford etc *Cov*
WROXETER (St Mary)   Buildwas and Leighton w Eaton
  Constantine etc *Lich*
**WROXHAM (St Mary) w Hoveton St John w Hoveton
  St Peter and Belaugh** *Nor 9*   **P** *Bp*   **R** H C BRADBURY
WROXTON (All Saints)   Broughton w N Newington and
  Shutford etc *Ox*
WYBERTON (St Leodegar) *Linc 21*   **P** *DBP*
  R R H IRESON
WYBUNBURY (St Chad) w Doddington (St John) *Ches 15*
  P *Bp and Sir Evelyn Broughton, Bt (jt)*   **V** *Vacant*
  Bridgemere (09365) 327
WYCH, HIGH (St James) and Gilston w Eastwick *St Alb 4*
  P *V Sawbridgeworth (2 turns), P T S Bowlby Esq
  (1 turn)*   **R** D C CLARKE
WYCHBOLD (St Mary de Wyche)   Stoke Prior,
  Wychbold and Upton Warren *Worc*
WYCHE (All Saints)   Lt Malvern, Malvern Wells and
  Wyche *Worc*
WYCHLING (St Margaret)   Doddington, Newnham and
  Wychling *Cant*
WYCHNOR (St Leonard) *Lich 2*   **P** *Personal Reps
  W H Harrison*   **V** *Vacant*
WYCK RISSINGTON (St Laurence)   The Rissingtons
  Glouc
WYCLIFFE (St Mary)   Barningham w Hutton Magna
  and Wycliffe *Ripon*
WYCOMBE, HIGH (All Saints) (St Peter) *Ox 29*
  P *Patr Bd*   **TR** P BAYES,   **TV** D J ROBERTSON,
  F D HILLEBRAND, G HOLDSTOCK, T D HONEY,
  J P HUGHES,   **C** D R McDOUGALL, D HONOUR,
  Par Dn J HONOUR,   **NSM** P VINEY, M J PRAGNELL,
  C J WILLIAMS
**WYCOMBE, WEST (St Laurence) (St Paul) w Bledlow
  Ridge, Bradenham and Radnage** *Ox 29*   **P** *Bp, DBP,
  Peache Trustees, and Sir Francis Dashwood (jt)*
  R M J STAINES,   **NSM** A C WOODS
WYCOMBE AND CHADWELL (St Mary)   Scalford w
  Goadby Marwood and Wycombe etc *Leic*
WYCOMBE LANE (St Mary)   Wooburn *Ox*
WYCOMBE MARSH (St Anne)   High Wycombe *Ox*
WYDDIAL (St Giles)   Hormead, Wyddial, Anstey,
  Brent Pelham etc *St Alb*
WYE (St Gregory and St Martin) w Brook *Cant 2*   **P** *Abp*
  V D J MARRIOTT,   **NSM** D J VENABLES
WYESHAM (St James)   Dixton *Heref*

WYFORDBY (St Mary)   Waltham on the Wolds,
  Stonesby, Saxby etc *Leic*
WYKE   Win St Matt *Win*
WYKE (Holy Trinity)   Bruton and Distr *B & W*
WYKE (St Mark) *Guildf 5*   **P** *Bp*   **V** N C TURTON
WYKE (St Mary the Virgin) *Bradf 2*   **P** *Bp*
  V R C DOWSON,   **Par Dn** P M HOLLINGS
WYKE REGIS (All Saints) *Sarum 5*   **P** *D&C*
  R K A HUGO
WYKEHAM (All Saints) and Hutton Buscel *York 21*
  P *Viscount Downe and Sir Stephen Hastings (alt)*
  V E RICHARDS
WYKEHAM (St Nicholas)   Wickham *Portsm*
WYKEN (Church of Risen Christ)   Cov Caludon *Cov*
WYKEN (Holy Cross)   as above
WYKEN (St Mary Magdalene)   as above
WYLAM (St Oswin) *Newc 3*   **P** *Bp*   **V** S S HUXLEY
WYLDE GREEN (Emmanuel) *Birm 9*   **P** *Bp*
  V H J PITCHFORD
WYLYE (St Mary the Virgin)   Yarnbury *Sarum*
WYMERING (St Peter and St Paul)   Widley w
  Wymering *Portsm*
WYMESWOLD (St Mary) and Prestwold w Hoton *Leic 7*
  P *S J Packe-Drury-Lowe and Bp (by turn)*
  V L ROBINSON
WYMINGTON (St Lawrence) w Podington *St Alb 21*
  P *R M Orlebar Esq (1 turn)*, *DBP (3 turns)*
  R A R H WOODWARD
WYMONDHAM (St Mary and St Thomas) *Nor 13*   **P** *Bp*
  V J E BARNES,   **C** T S LAWES, P T S KERLEY
**WYMONDHAM (St Peter) w Edmondthorpe, Buckminster
  w Sewstern, Coston and Garthorpe** *Leic 3*   **P** *Ld Chan
  and Sir Lyonel Tollemache, Bt (alt)*
  R A R THREADGILL
**WYMONDLEY, GREAT (St Mary the Virgin) and Little
  Wymondley w Graveley and Chivesfield** *St Alb 9*   **P** *Bp
  and MMCET (jt)*   **R** P J MADDEX
WYMONDLEY, LITTLE (St Mary the Virgin)   Gt and
  Lt Wymondley w Graveley and Chivesfield *St Alb*
WYMYNSWOLD (St Margaret)   Nonington w
  Wymynswold and Goodnestone etc *Cant*
WYNFORD EAGLE (St Laurence)   Melbury *Sarum*
WYNYARD PARK (Chapel)   Grindon and Stillington
  Dur
WYRE PIDDLE (not known)   Fladbury, Wyre Piddle
  and Moor *Worc*
WYRESDALE, OVER (Christ Church) *Blackb 12*   **P** *Bp*
  P-in-c J A HEMMINGS
WYRLEY, GREAT (St Mark) *Lich 4*   **P** *R Cannock*
  V A F CREBER,   **Par Dn** R BIDDLE
WYSALL (Holy Trinity)   Willoughby-on-the-Wolds w
  Wysall and Widmerpool *S'well*
WYTHALL (St Mary) *Birm 4*   **P** *R Kings Norton*
  V P M THOMSON
WYTHAM (All Saints)   N Hinksey and Wytham *Ox*
WYTHBURN (not known)   St Johns-in-the-Vale w
  Wythburn *Carl*
WYTHENSHAWE   Lawton Moor (St Michael and All
  Angels)   Lawton Moor *Man*
WYTHENSHAWE (St Martin) *Man 8*   **P** *Bp*
  V P J DINES,   **Par Dn** O E SIBBALD
WYTHENSHAWE (St Richard of Chichester) *Man 8*
  P *Bp*   **V** G A LAWSON
WYTHENSHAWE (William Temple Church) *Man 8*
  P *Bp*   **V** H B EALES,   **C** I C J GORTON
WYTHER (Venerable Bede) *Ripon 6*   **P** *Bp*
  V R G PLACE,   **Par Dn** D ESCOLME
WYTHOP (St Margaret)   Cockermouth w Embleton and
  Wythop *Carl*
WYVERSTONE (St George)   Bacton w Wyverstone and
  Cotton *St E*
WYVILL (St Catherine)   Harlaxton *Linc*
YAFFORTH (All Saints)   Ainderby Steeple w Yafforth
  and Kirby Wiske etc *Ripon*
YALDING (St Peter and St Paul) w Collier Street *Roch 7*
  P *Ld Chan*   **V** *Vacant*   Maidstone (0622) 814182
YANWORTH (St Michael)   Chedworth, Yanworth and
  Stowell, Coln Rogers etc *Glouc*
YAPHAM (St Martin)   Barmby Moor w Allerthorpe,
  Fangfoss and Yapham *York*
YAPTON (St Mary)   Clymping and Yapton w Ford *Chich*
**YARCOMBE (St John the Baptist) w Membury and
  Upottery** *Ex 5*   **P** *The Crown (2 turns), Bp (1 turn)*
  V P D GOTELEE,   **Hon C** A METCALFE
YARDLEY (St Cyprian)   Hay Mill *Birm 10*   **P** *Bp*
  V R C SIMPSON
YARDLEY (St Edburgha) *Birm 10*   **P** *St Pet Coll Ox*
  V F S COLLINS,   **C** R P BILLINGSLEY,
  Par Dn J E DOUGLAS

YARDLEY (St Lawrence)   Ardeley *St Alb*
YARDLEY, SOUTH (St Michael and All Angels) *Birm 10*
   P *Bp*   **V** K PUNSHON,   **NSM** G R PIKE
YARDLEY GOBION (St Leonard)   Potterspury,
   Furtho, Yardley Gobion and Cosgrove *Pet*
YARDLEY HASTINGS (St Andrew), Denton and Grendon
   w Castle Ashby *Pet 7*   **P** *Bp and Marquess of*
   Northn (alt)   **R** M R RYALL
YARDLEY WOOD (Christ Church) *Birm 8*   **P** *Bp*
   V D W JAMES
YARKHILL (St John the Baptist)   Tarrington w Stoke
   Edith, Aylton, Pixley etc *Heref*
YARLINGTON (Blessed Virgin Mary)   Camelot Par
   B & W
YARM (St Mary Magdalene) *York 22*   **P** *Abp*
   R D W SMITH,   **NSM** P W ELLIOTT, M LOCKEY
YARMOUTH (St James) *Portsm 8*   **P** *Keble Coll Ox*
   R K R CHEESEMAN
YARMOUTH, GREAT (St James) (St John) (St Nicholas)
   (St Paul) *Nor 2*   **P** *Patr Bd*   **TV** M MAKOWER,
   C M J KINGHAM,   **Hon C** T F DRURY
YARMOUTH, GREAT (St Luke)   Southtown *Nor*
YARNBURY *Sarum 16*   **P** *Bp, CCC Ox, and D&C (by*
   turn)   **R** B THOMAS
YARNFIELD (Mission Room St Barnabas)   Swynnerton
   and Tittensor *Lich*
YARNSCOMBE (St Andrew)   Newton Tracey,
   Alverdiscott, Huntshaw etc *Ex*
YARNTON (St Bartholomew) w Begbroke and Shipton on
   Cherwell *Ox 9*   **P** *BNC Ox, Duke of Marlborough,*
   Trustees C Wolfson Trust (jt)   **R** E CRAIG
YARPOLE (St Leonard)   Eye, Croft w Yarpole and
   Lucton *Heref*
YARWELL (St Mary Magdalene)   Nassington w Yarwell
   and Woodnewton *Pet*
YATE New Town (St Mary) *Bris 7*   **P** *Bp*
   TR C D SUTCH,   **TM** S R RESTALL,
   TV D G BAINBRIDGE, K B JONES
YATELEY (St Peter) *Win 5*   **P** *Bp*   **V** H WILSON,
   C T G WARR, E J COOK, P A VARGESON, R G MARTIN,
   NSM B R LILLINGTON
YATESBURY (All Saints)   Oldbury *Sarum*
YATTENDON (St Peter and St Paul)   Hermitage and
   Hampstead Norreys, Cold Ash etc *Ox*
YATTON (All Saints)   Much Marcle *Heref*
YATTON KEYNELL (St Margaret) *Bris 9*   **P** *Bp*
   P-in-c J N A BRADBURY,   **NSM** J E B MARSH
YATTON MOOR (Blessed Virgin Mary) *B & W 14*
   P *DBF*   **TR** J L RUFFLE
YAVERLAND (St John the Baptist)   Brading w
   Yaverland *Portsm*
YAXHAM (St Peter)   Mattishall w Mattishall Burgh,
   Welborne etc *Nor*
YAXLEY (St Mary the Virgin)   Eye w Braiseworth and
   Yaxley *St E*
YAXLEY (St Peter) *Ely 13*   **P** *Ld Chan*
   V P J SHEPHERD,   **NSM** G LIMBRICK
YEADON (St Andrew) *Bradf 4*   **P** *Bp*   **V** K C POTTER
YEADON (St John the Evangelist) *Bradf 4*   **P** *R Guiseley*
   w Esholt   **V** J F N ROBINSON
YEALAND CONYERS (St John the Evangelist)
   Warton St Oswald w Yealand Conyers *Blackb*
YEALMPTON (St Bartholomew) *Ex 21*   **P** *Bp*
   P-in-c M A WILKINSON
YEARSLEY (Holy Trinity)   Crayke w Brandsby and
   Yearsley *York*
YEAVELEY (Holy Trinity)   Alkmonton, Cubley,
   Marston, Montgomery etc *Derby*
YEDINGHAM (St John the Baptist)   Sherburn and W
   and E Heslerton w Yedingham *York*
YELDEN (St Mary)   The Stodden Churches *St Alb*
YELDHAM, GREAT (St Andrew) w LITTLE (St John the
   Baptist) *Chelmsf 17*   **P** *Bp and Ld Chan (alt)*
   R P J STREET
YELFORD (St Nicholas and St Swithin)   Lower
   Windrush *Ox*
YELLING (Holy Cross)   Graveley w Papworth St Agnes
   w Yelling etc *Ely*

YELVERTOFT (All Saints)   Crick and Yelvertoft w Clay
   Coton and Lilbourne *Pet*
YELVERTON (St Mary)   Thurton *Nor*
YELVERTON (St Paul), Meavy, Sheepstor and
   Walkhampton *Ex 25*   **P** *Patr Bd*   **TR** G R WITTS,
   NSM J W M WEIR, M SALMON
YEOFORD CHAPEL (Holy Trinity)   Crediton and
   Shobrooke *Ex*
YEOVIL (Holy Trinity) *B & W 8*   **P** *The Crown*
   V J D BENNETT
YEOVIL (St Andrew) (St John the Baptist) w Kingston
   Pitney *B & W 8*   **P** *Mrs S W Rawlins (3 turns), DBP*
   (1 turn)   **R** R N INWOOD,   **C** S J TYNDALL,
   NSM A J YOUNG
YEOVIL (St Michael and All Angels) *B & W 8*   **P** *Bp*
   V M D ELLIS,   **C** R C REDDING, J B V LAURENCE
YEOVIL (St Peter)   Preston Plucknett *B & W*
YEOVIL MARSH (All Saints)   Tintinhull w Chilthorne
   Domer, Yeovil Marsh etc *B & W*
YETMINSTER (St Andrew) w Ryme Intrinseca and High
   Stoy *Sarum 4*   **P** *Duchy of Cornwall (1 turn), Bp*
   (3 turns)   **R** P G HOOPER,   **C** R S GLEN
YIEWSLEY (St Matthew) *Lon 24*   **P** *V Hillingdon*
   P-in-c C R GOWER
YOCKLETON (Holy Trinity) *Heref 13*   **P** *Bp*
   R R J PEARCE
YORK Acomb (St Aidan)   Acomb St Steph *York*
YORK (All Saints)   Huntington *York*
YORK (All Saints) North Street *York 8*   **P** *D&C*
   P-in-c E E S JONES
YORK (All Saints) Pavement w St Crux (St Martin)
   (St Helen) (St Denys) *York 8*   **P** *Abp*
   TV T L PRESTON, J A CORKER
YORK (Christ Church)   Heworth *York*
YORK (Holy Trinity)   as above
YORK (St Barnabas) *York 8*   **P** *CPAS*
   P-in-c J G F GRAHAM-BROWN
YORK (St Chad) *York 8*   **P** *Abp*   **V** D B EMMOTT
YORK (St Clement w St Mary) Bishophill Senior *York 8*
   P *Abp*   **R** E E S JONES
YORK (St Edward the Confessor)   Dringhouses *York*
YORK (St Hilda) *York 8*   **P** *Abp*   **V** J W WILMER
YORK (St Lawrence w St Nicholas) *York 8*   **P** *D&C*
   V P S THORNTON
YORK (St Luke) *York 8*   **P** *Abp*   **V** G H WEBSTER,
   C D J WOOLLARD
YORK (St Martin-cum-Gregory)   Micklegate H Trin and
   Bishophill Junior St Mary *York*
YORK (St Mary)   as above
YORK (St Michael-le-Belfrey) (St Cuthbert) *York 8*
   P *Abp*   **V** G A CRAY,   **C** C PUCKRIN,   **Par Dn** J H FIFE
YORK (St Olave w St Giles) *York 8*   **P** *Abp*
   V A C HODGE
YORK (St Oswald)   Fulford *York*
YORK (St Paul) Holgate Road *York 8*   **P** *CPAS*
   R D R WOOLDRIDGE,   **C** B EVES
YORK (St Philip and St James)   Clifton *York*
YORK (St Thomas w St Maurice) *York 8*   **P** *Abp*
   V P WORDSWORTH
YORK (St Wulstan)   Heworth *York*
YORK TOWN (St Michael) *Guildf 6*   **P** *Bp*
   V J P B WYNBURNE,   **C** M N CORNELL
YORKLEY, LOWER (St Luke's Church Centre)   Dean
   Forest St Paul *Glouc*
YOULGREAVE (All Saints), Middleton, Stanton-in-Peak
   and Birchover *Derby 2*   **P** *Duke of Devonshire and*
   Capt H B C Davie-Thornhill (jt)   **V** R TAYLOR
YOXALL (St Peter) *Lich 2*   **P** *Bp*   **R** *Vacant* Yoxall
   (0543) 472528
YOXFORD (St Peter) *St E 19*   **P** *Bp*   **P-in-c** C WRAY,
   Hon C J W DRAPER
ZEAL, SOUTH (St Mary)   S Tawton and Belstone *Ex*
ZEAL MONACHORUM (St Peter) *Ex 2*   **P** *DBP*
   R B H GALES
ZEALS (St Martin)   Upper Stour *Sarum*
ZENNOR (St Senera) *Truro 5*   **P** *Bp*
   P-in-c S W MIDDLETON-DANSKY

INDEX OF WELSH BENEFICES

An index of the benefices of the Church in Wales. In each case the full name of the benefice is given, together with the diocese and the names and appointments of the clergy serving there. The following are the main abbreviations used; for others see the full list of abbreviations:—

C	Curate	**P-in-c**	Priest-in-charge
C-in-c	Curate-in-charge	**R**	Rector
Dn-in-c	Deacon-in-charge	**TM**	Team Minister
Hon C	Honorary curate	**TV**	Team Vicar
NSM	Non-stipendiary Minister	**V**	Vicar

ABER-PORTH w Tre-main and Blaen-porth *St D*
  R A F HERRICK
ABERAMAN and Abercwmboi *Llan* **V** R DONKIN
ABERAVON *Llan* **V** S BARNES, **NSM** J S DUNN
ABERAVON Holy Trinity (Sandfields) *Llan*
  V E T WILSON
ABERCANAID *Llan* **P-in-c** G G FOSTER
ABERCARN *Mon* **V** R J SUMMERS
ABERCRAVE and Callwen *S & B* **V** D EVANS
ABERCYNON *Llan* **V** N P JONES
ABERDARE *Llan* **V** D G JAMES, **C** C B W SMITH
ABERDARE St Fagan *Llan* **V** S J RYAN
ABERDARON w Rhiw and Llanfaelrhys w Llangwnadl
  and Penllech w Bryncroes *Ban* **R** *Vacant*
ABEREDW w Llandilo Graban and Llanbadarn-y-Garreg
  w Crickadarn and Gwenddwr *S & B* **V** J R HAMBIDGE
ABERFFRAW and Llangwyfan w Llangadwaladr *Ban*
  V *Vacant*
ABERGAVENNY Holy Trinity *Mon* **V** R P MATTHEWS
ABERGAVENNY St Mary w Llanwenarth Citra *Mon*
  V C G SYKES, **C** C WATKINS, **NSM** D W F ROSSITER
ABERGELE *St As* **V** D J ROBERTS, **NSM** D WILLIAMS
ABERGWILI w Llanfihangel-uwch-Gwili and Capel-y-
  Groes *St D* **V** J K DAVIES
ABERPERGWM and Blaengwrach *Llan*
  V R A GORDON
ABERSYCHEN and Garndiffaith *Mon* **V** D E STANDISH
ABERTILLERY *Mon* **V** R D WILLIAMS
ABERYSTRUTH (Blaina) and Nantyglo *Mon*
  R *Vacant* Blaina (0495) 290079
ABERYSTWYTH *St D* **R** S R BELL,
  TV W A STRANGE, H M WILLIAMS, **C** A T G JOHN,
  NSM C V JOHN
AMLWCH *Ban* **R** H E GRIFFITH
ARTHOG w Fairbourne w Llangelynin (Llwyngwril) w
  Rhoslefain *Ban* **V** A M HIRST, **NSM** C A LLEWELLYN
BAGILLT *St As* **V** B TAYLOR, **NSM** M M GRAHAM
BAGLAN *Llan* **V** D W LEWIS
BANGOR Cathedral *Ban* **R** T E P EDWARDS,
  TV R M KEATING, G W HEWITT, **C** D H JAMES
BANGOR MONACHORUM and Worthenbury *St As*
  R P R OWENS
BANGOR TEIFI w Henllan and Llanfairorllwyn w
  Llangynllo *St D* **R** D PUGH
BARGOED and Deri w Brithdir *Llan* **V** P A COX,
  C R E HIGGINS
BARRY All Saints *Llan* **R** J G D OEPPEN,
  NSM B J EVANS
BASSALEG *Mon* **V** J T LEWIS,
  C M N PREVETT, J F GRAY
BEAUMARIS *Ban* **R** G M HUGHES
BEDDGELERT *Ban* **V** K M KENT
BEDWAS and Rudry *Mon* **R** J D E DAVIES
BEDWELLTY *Mon* **V** D J CARPENTER
BEGELLY w Ludchurch and Crunwere *St D*
  R D G WILLIAMS
BEGUILDY and Heyope *S & B* **V** G L J WARRINGTON
BERRIEW and Manafon *St As* **V** T W PRITCHARD
BERSE and Southsea *St As* **V** R N PARRY
BETTWS *Mon* **V** D W COOLING, **NSM** M D COOLING
  (nee YOUNG)
BETTWS St David *St D* **V** A J R THOMAS,
  C H M JENKINS, **NSM** R P JONES
BETTWS BLEDRWS *St D* **P-in-c** D T W PRICE
BETTWS CEDEWAIN and Tregynon and Llanwyddelan
  St As **V** R H FAIRBROTHER
BETTWS NEWYDD w Trostrey and Kemeys
  Commander and Llanfihangel Gobion w Llanfair
  Kilgeddin *Mon* **R** J R STACEY
BETTWS-Y-COED and Capel Curig w Penmachno w
  Dolwyddelan *Ban* **V** J B DAVIES
BISHOPSTON *S & B* **R** A B EVASON
BISTRE *St As* **V** J R KENNETT-ORPWOOD
BLACKWOOD *Mon* **V** B HARONSKI

BLAENAVON w Capel Newydd *Mon* **V** B J LLOYD
BODEDERN w Llechcynfarwy and Llechylched w
  Ceirchiog w Llanfihangel-yn-Nhowyn w Caergeiliog *Ban*
  Dn-in-c C M EVANS
BODELYWDDAN *St As* **V** R V BYLES
BORTH and Eglwysfach w Llangynfelin *St D*
  V G ARMSTEAD
BRECHFA w Abergorlech and Llanfihangel Rhos-y-corn
  St D **R** P H B THOMAS
BRECON St David (Llanfaes) w Llanspyddid and
  Llanilltyd *S & B* **V** D E THOMAS
BRECON St Mary and Battle w Llanddew *S & B*
  V D H JONES, **C** H M LERVY
BRONLLYS and Llanvillo w Llandefaelog Tregraig *S & B*
  V P DIXON
BROUGHTON *St As* **V** R A SUTER
BRYMBO *St As* **V** G R MATTHIAS
BRYNAMAN w Cwmllynfell *St D* **V** A TEALE
BRYNEGLWYS *St As* **Dn-in-c** M C HARVEY
BRYNGWYN and Newchurch and Llanbedr Painscastle
  and Llanddewi Fach *S & B* **P-in-c** M P RALPH-
  BOWMAN, **NSM** H J FISHER
BRYNMAWR *S & B* **V** N JONES
BRYNYMAEN w Trofarth *St As* **V** L PARRY JONES
BUCKLEY *St As* **V** *Vacant* Buckley (0244) 2645
BUILTH and Llanddewi'r Cwm w Llangynog and
  Maesmynis and Llanynys and Alltmawr *S & B*
  V E C JOHN
BURRY PORT and Pwll *St D* **V** G D HARRIES,
  NSM E J W ROBERTS
BURTON and Rosemarket *St D* **R** J HALE
BUTTINGTON and Pool Quay *St As* **V** D H WILLIAMS
BWLCHGWYN *St As* **V** E B WILLIAMS
CADOXTON-JUXTA-BARRY *Llan* **R** G R STEELE
CADOXTON-JUXTA-NEATH *Llan* **V** N M COOPER
CAER Rhun w Llangelynin w Llanbedr-y-Cennin *Ban*
  V D C ROBERTS
CAERAU St Cynfelin *Llan* **V** E G JONES
CAERAU w Ely *Llan* **V** J C BUTTIMORE, **C** B H SHARP
CAEREITHIN *S & B* **V** T G MORRIS
CAERLEON *Mon* **V** P R S MORGAN, **C** M G HADDOCK
CAERPHILLY *Llan* **R** M J SHORT,
  C I A JONES, V C HODGSON
CAERWENT w Dinham and Llanfair Discoed and
  Shirenewton w Newchurch *Mon* **V** P W WOODMAN
CAERWYS and Bodfari *St As* **R** J V WARING
CALDICOT *Mon* **V** P J S EDWARDS, **C** S J STEPHENS
CAMROSE and St Lawrence w Ford and Haycastle *St D*
  V B JONES
CANTON St Catherine *Llan* **V** A D HUNTER
CANTON St John *Llan* **R** D A V FRAYNE
CANTON St Luke *Llan* **V** G F HORWOOD
CAPEL COELBREN *S & B* **P-in-c** B H JONES
CARDIFF Dewi Sant *Llan* **V** F J S DAVIES
CARDIFF St Andrew and St Teilo *Llan* **V** *Vacant*
  Cardiff (0222) 32407
CARDIFF St John *Llan* **V** M R ELLIS,
  C S M GRIFFITHS, N R SANDFORD, **NSM** E J BURKE
CARDIFF St Mary and St Stephen w Cardiff St Dyfrig and
  St Samson *Llan* **V** K J JORDAN, **C** E C R COUNSELL
CARDIGAN and Mount and Verwick *St D*
  V W H RICHARDS
CARMARTHEN St David *St D* **V** I D JOHN,
  C D R REES
CARMARTHEN St Peter *St D* **V** T R K GOULSTONE,
  C N JOHN
CASTLEMARTIN w Warren and Angle and
  Rhoscrowther and Pwllcrochan *St D* **R** R B WEBLEY
CEFN *St As* **R** R H GRIFFITHS
CEFN COED and Capel Nantddu w Vaynor and Capel
  Taffechan *S & B* **V** B H JOHN
CERRIG-Y-DRUDION w Llanfihangel Glyn Myfyr and
  Llangwm w Yspytty Ifan and Pentrevoelas and Bettws
  Gwerfil Goch and Dinmael *St As* **Dn-in-c** S BRUSH

CHEPSTOW *Mon*   **V** J P HARRIS
CHIRK *St As*   **V** M B ROBERTS
CHRIST CHURCH *Mon*   **V** R G HACKETT
CILCEN and Nannerch and Rhydymwyn *St As*
   R R H WILLIAMS
CILFYNYDD *Llan*   **P-in-c** M J MARSDEN
CILGERRAN w Bridell and Llantwyd *St D*
   R E L THOMAS
CILYBEBYLL *Llan*   **R** E L HOUGH
CILYCWM and Ystradffin w St Barnabus Rhandirmwyn
   and Llanfair-ar-y-Bryn *St D*   **P-in-c** A M KETTLE
CLYDACH *S & B*   **V** D H E MOSFORD, **C** P J GWYNN
COITY w Nolton *Llan*   **R** D RICHARDS,
   C S J BARNES, A J TURNER
COLWINSTON w Llandow and Llysworney *Llan*
   R R W A JONES
COLWYN *St As*   **V** D V GRIFFITH
COLWYN BAY *St As*   **V** T G DAVIES
CONNAH'S QUAY *St As*   **V** D P MORRIS, **C** P KINSEY
CONWIL CAIO w Llansawel and Talley *St D*
   V C E JONES
CONWY w Gyffin *Ban*   **V** P R JONES
CORWEN and Llangar w Gwyddelwern and Llawr-y-
   Bettws *St As*   **R** E M EVANS, **C** H FENTON
COSHESTON w Nash and Upton *St D*
   P-in-c A THOMAS, **Dn-in-c** L A F C WATKINS
COYCHURCH w Llangan and St Mary Hill *Llan*
   R K ANDREWS
CRICCIETH w Treflys *Ban*   **R** B C MORGAN,
   C T BONNET
CRICKHOWELL w Cwmdu and Tretower *S & B*
   NSM W J MORRIS
CRYNANT *Llan*   **V** S F MINTY
CWMAMAN *St D*   **V** D R OLIVER, **NSM** D J THOMAS
CWMAMAN *Llan*   **V** G H BOWEN
CWMAVON (Michaelston-super-Avon) *Llan*
   V K W CHANT
CWMBACH *Llan*   **V** R LLOYD
CWMBRAN *Mon*   **R** A J EDWARDS,
   TV P C TITCOMBE, J S WILLIAMS, M R AINSCOUGH,
   NSM J M JENKINS, E J MARTIN
CWMCARN *Mon*   **V** P M WINCHESTER
CWMDDAUDDWR w St Harmon's and Llanwrthwl
   S & B   **V** D T HURLEY
CWMPARC *Llan*   **V** R E DAVIES
CWMTILLERY *Mon*   **V** R E PAIN
CYMMER and Porth *Llan*   **V** P M LEONARD
CYNCOED *Mon*   **R** J C WOODWARD,
   TV H TRENCHARD
CYNWIL ELFED and Newchurch *St D*   **V** *Vacant*
   Cynwyl Elfed (026787) 350
DAFEN and Llwynhendy *St D*   **V** D M C DAVIES,
   Dn-in-c A M GRAY
DALE and St Brides w Marloes *St D*   **V** P R DAVIES,
   NSM R D REED
DENBIGH and Nantglyn *St As*   **R** R J WILLIAMS,
   C N PURVEY-TYRER
DENEIO (Pwllheli) w Abererch *Ban*   **V** R F DONALDSON
DEVYNOCK w Rhydybriw and Llandilo'r-fan *S & B*
   V M P WILDING
DINAS and Penygraig w Williamstown *Llan*
   V S J BODYCOMBE
DINGESTOW and Llangovan w Penyclawdd and Tregaer
   and Cwmcarvan *Mon*   **V** G LEACH
DOLBENMAEN w Llanystymdwy w Llangybi and
   Llanarmon *Ban*   **R** W JONES
DOLFOR *St As*   **V** *Vacant*
DOLGELLY w Llanfachreth and Brithdir and
   Bryncoedifor and Llanelltyd *Ban*   **R** A JONES
DOWLAIS *Llan*   **R** *Vacant*   Merthyr Tydfil (0685)
   722118
DWYGYFYLCHI (Penmaenmawr) *Ban*
   V G B HUGHES, **C** J C HARVEY, **NSM** D J DREDGE
DYFFRYN *Llan*   **V** T G SMITH
DYSERTH and Trelawnyd and Cwm *St As*
   V R W ROWLAND, **NSM** S T GRIFFITHS
EBBW VALE *Mon*   **R** J ROGERS,
   TV C J NICKLESS, N J HODGE, **C** R JEFFORD
EGLWYSBREWIS w St Athan and Flemingston and
   Gileston *Llan*   **R** J W BINNY
EGLWYSILAN *Llan*   **R** J E PARKIN
ESCLUSHAM *St As*   **V** P H VARAH
EWENNY w St Bride's Major *Llan*   **R** J C BALDWIN
FAIRWATER *Llan*   **V** M M DAVIES, **NSM** R L FORD
FELINFOEL *St D*   **V** A J MEATS
FERNDALE w Maerdy *Llan*   **V** P J BENNETT
FESTINIOG w Blaenau Festiniog *Ban*   **V** *Vacant*
   Blaenau Ffestiniog (0766) 830382
FFYNNONGROEW *St As*   **V** S D GREEN

FISHGUARD w Llanychaer and Pontfaen w Morvil and
   Llanychllwydog *St D*   **V** W C G MORGAN
FLEUR-DE-LIS *Mon*   **V** B M W STARES
FLINT *St As*   **R** G R JONES
GABALFA *Llan*   **V** R M E PATERSON,
   C M W SSERUNKUMA
GARTHBEIBIO and Llanerfyl and Llangadfan *St As*
   R *Vacant*
GELLYGAER *Llan*   **R** H N SOBEY, **C** S J MORGAN
GLAN ELY *Llan*   **V** R H MORGAN, **C** S LISK
GLANOGWEN *Ban*   **V** A WILLIAMS
GLANTAWE *S & B*   **V** D ROBERTS
GLASBURY St Peter w Glasbury All Saints and Llowes w
   Clyro and Bettws *S & B*   **V** G M REED
GLYNCORRWG w Afan Vale and Cymmer Afan *Llan*
   R G J WAGGETT, **TV** J A P WALKER
GLYNDYFRDWY and Llansantffraid Glyn Dyfrdwy
   (Carrog) *St As*   **V** R S THOMAS
GLYNTAFF *Llan*   **V** K D LERRY
GOLDCLIFFE and Whiston and Nash *Mon*   **V** *Vacant*
   Newport (0633) 278106
GORSEDD w Brynford and Ysceifiog *St As*
   V J W K SOMERVILLE
GORSEINON *S & B*   **V** J I HOLDSWORTH,
   C D A WALKER, **NSM** W G G JAMES
GORSLAS *St D*   **V** R I PROTHEROE
GOWERTON *S & B*   **V** C J COLEBROOK
GOYTREY w Llanover *Mon*   **R** C R F CALE
GRAIG St Jo *Llan*   **V** M J MARSDEN
GRANGETOWN (Canton) *Llan*   **V** L V DAVIES
GRESFORD *St As*   **V** D GRIFFITHS
GRIFFITHSTOWN *Mon*   **V** R BAYLEY
GROSMONT and Skenfrith and Llangattock Lingoed w
   Llanfair Chapel *Mon*   **R** D K POPE
GUILSFIELD *St As*   **R** J L TODD
GWAUN-CAE-GURWEN *St D*   **V** N G EVANS
GWERNAFFIELD and Llanferres *St As*
   V J B THELWELL, **NSM** J STEPHENS
GWERSYLLT *St As*   **V** W T CLACKEY
HALKYN and Caerfallwch *St As*   **R** L EDWARDS
HANMER and Bronington and Bettisfield and Tallarn
   Green *St As*   **V** A G M DAVIES
HARLECH and Llanfair-juxta-Harlech w Llanfihangel-y-
   Traethau and Llandecwyn *Ban*   **V** P D JAMES
HAVERFORDWEST St Martin w Lambston *St D*
   V D J R LEAN, **NSM** M N H GRAINGER
HAVERFORDWEST St Mary and St Thomas w
   Haroldston St Issells *St D*   **R** D EVANS,
   NSM A CLARK
HAWARDEN *St As*   **R** T P DAVIES,
   TV H G A JALLAND, S CAWLEY,
   P-in-c P J BILLINGHURST
HAY w Llanigon and Capel-y-Ffin *S & B*   **V** D E REES
HENFYNYW w Aberaeron and Llanddewi Aber-arth
   St D   **V** M L REES, **C** M W SOAR, **NSM** D W HEAL
HENLLAN and Llannefydd and Bylchau *St As*
   R J P P WILLIAMS
HERBRANDSTON and Hasguard w St Ishmael's *St D*
   R D PARRY
HIRWAUN *Llan*   **V** R J CHISWELL, **C** M J STRONG
HOLT *St As*   **V** J T HUGHES
HOLYHEAD w Rhoscolyn w Llanfair-yn-Neubwll *Ban*
   R J ASHLEY-ROBERTS
HOLYWELL *St As*   **V** J T EVANS, **Hon C** J K MUSSON
HOPE *St As*   **R** K H WILLIAMS
HUBBERTSON *St D*   **R** P BROWN, **C** P H SMITH
ILSTON w Pennard *S & B*   **V** D B JAMES
ITTON and St Arvans w Penterry and Kilgwrrwg w
   Devauden *Mon*   **V** J H WINSTON
JEFFREYSTON w Reynoldston and E Williamston and
   Loveston *St D*   **R** N P DAVIES
JOHNSTON w Steynton *St D*   **R** R M JENKINS,
   C P H MORGANS
KENFIG HILL *Llan*   **V** G W JAMES
KERRY and Llanmerewig *St As*   **V** *Vacant*   Kerry
   (068688) 466
KIDWELLY and Llandefaelog *St D*   **V** G J DAVIES
KILLAY *S & B*   **V** D J WILKINSON, **C** D M SWYER
KNIGHTON and Norton *S & B*   **V** A J HAWKINS
LALESTON w Tythegston and Merthyr Mawr *Llan*
   V E J EVANS, **NSM** G W RIMELL
LAMPETER Pont Steffan w Silian *St D*
   V W S T MORGAN, **NSM** D B THOMAS
LAMPETER VELFREY and Llanddewi Velfrey *St D*
   R M G R MORRIS
LAMPHEY w Hodgeston and Carew *St D*
   V G A DAVIES
LANDORE *S & B*   **V** *Vacant*

LAUGHARNE w Llansadurnen and Llandawke *St D*
  V D B G DAVIES
LETTERSTON w Llanfair Nant-y-Gof and Puncheston w
  Little Newcastle and Castle Bythe *St D*   **R** R GRIFFITHS
LLAN-NON *St D*   **V** J H GRAVELL,   **NSM** W R HUGHES
LLANABER (Barmouth) w Caerdeon *Ban*
  R P W D FLAVELL
LLANAELHAEARN w Clynnog Fawr *Ban*
  R I THOMAS
LLANARTH and Capel Cynon w Talgarreg and St Mark
  St D   **V** C L BOLTON
LLANARTHNEY and Llanddarog *St D*   **V** *Vacant*
  Llanddarog (026786) 268
LLANASA *St As*   **V** J G GRIFFITHS
LLANBADARN FAWR and Llandegley and Llanfihangel
  Rhydithon w Abbey Cwmhir *S & B*   **R** N D HALL
LLANBADARN FAWR w Capel Bangor *St D*
  V B J H JONES,   **C** D K HEARNE,
  NSM B V GRIFFITH, G WATKINS
LLANBADOC *Mon*   **NSM** P A BRYANT
LLANBEBLIG w Caernarfon and Betws Garmon w
  Waunfawr *Ban*   **R** B W THOMAS,
  C I W JONES, J N GILLIBRAND
LLANBEDROG w Llannor w Llanfihangel Bachellaeth w
  Bodfuan *Ban*   **R** C H F PARRY
LLANBERIS w Llanrug *Ban*   **R** P H PRITCHARD
LLANBEULAN w Llanfaelog and Talyllyn *Ban*
  R T WYNNE
LLANBISTER and Llanbadarn Fynydd w Llananno *S & B*
  V R HART
LLANBLETHIAN w Cowbridge and Llandough w
  St Mary Church *Llan*   **V** G E WILLIAMS,
  C N HADFIELD,   **NSM** N E WILLIAMS
LLANCARFAN w Llantrithyd *Llan*   **V** W J FIELD
LLANDAFF Cathedral w Capel Llanilterne *Llan*
  V A R DAVIES,   **NSM** B-H KHOO
LLANDAFF North *Llan*   **V** C D FRY
LLANDDEWI RHYDDERCH and Llangattock-juxta-
  Usk and Llanarth w Clytha and Llansantffraed *Mon*
  V M S SADLER
LLANDDEWI YSTRADENNY *S & B*
  P-in-c N J DAVIS-JONES
LLANDDEWIBREFI w Llanbadarn Odwyn and Cellan w
  Llanfair Clydogau and Llangybi *St D*   **V** A W WILLIAMS
LLANDDULAS and Llysfaen *St As*   **R** J W M ROBERTS
LLANDEFALLE and Llyswen w Boughrood and
  Llanstephen w Talachddu *S & B*   **V** R M H JONES
LLANDEGAI and Llandegai St Ann w Tregarth *Ban*
  V M PRICE-ROBERTS
LLANDEGFAN w Llandysilio (Menai Bridge) *Ban*
  V R JONES,   **Hon C** P A G WESTLAKE
LLANDEGLA and Llanarmon yn Ial *St As*   **R** C B HALL
LLANDILO FAWR and Taliaris *St D*   **V** *Vacant*
  Llandeilo (0558) 822421
LLANDILO TALYBONT (Pontardulais) *S & B*
  V J P H WALTERS
LLANDINAM w Trefeglwys w Penstrowed *Ban*
  V M G H B TUDOR
LLANDINGAT (Llandovery) w Myddfai *St D*
  V B T RICE
LLANDINORWIG w Penisa'r-waen *Ban*   **V** *Vacant*
  Llanberis (0286) 870867
LLANDOGO and Tintern *Mon*   **R** J E L WHITE
LLANDOUGH w Leckwith *Llan*   **R** K H P EVANS
LLANDRILLO and Llandderfel *St As*   **V** G W JONES
LLANDRILLO-YN-RHOS *St As*   **V** E G PRICE
LLANDRINDOD w Cefnllys and Disserth *S & B*
  R G M H HUGHES,   **NSM** A TWEED
LLANDRYGARN w Bodwrog and Heneglwys and
  Trewalchmai *Ban*   **V** J F W JONES,   **NSM** E D JERMAN
LLANDUDNO *Ban*   **R** D G RICHARDS,   **C** A C BUCKLEY
LLANDWROG ST THOMAS w Llandwrog *Ban*
  V *Vacant*   Llanwnda (0286) 831103
LLANDYBIE *St D*   **V** W J L EVANS,   **C** D BOWEN
LLANDYFODWG *Llan*   **V** *Vacant*
LLANDYGWYDD and Cenarth w Cilrhedyn and
  Llangoedmore w Llechryd *St D*   **V** D M MORRIS
LLANDYRNOG and Llangwyfan *St As*   **R** *Vacant*
LLANDYSILIO and Penrhos and Llandrinio w Criggion
  St As   **R** R A BIRD
LLANDYSSILIO w Egremont and Llanglydwen w
  Cilymaenllwyd and Llanfyrnach *St D*   **V** *Vacant*
  Clynderwen (0437) 563203
LLANDYSSUL *St D*   **V** J H ROWLANDS
LLANEDY w Tycroes and Saron *St D*   **V** T J WILLIAMS
LLANEGRYN and Llanfihangel-y-Pennant
  (Abergynolwyn) w Talyllyn *Ban*   **V** D C BRYANT
LLANEGWAD w Llanfynydd *St D*   **V** G H THOMAS

LLANELIAN and Bettws-yn-Rhos *St As*
  R R H KENDRICK
LLANELLY *S & B*   **V** J R ELLIS
LLANELLY Christchurch *St D*   **V** T G JONES
LLANELLY St Elli *St D*   **V** A R WILLIAMS,   **C** R J LEWIS
LLANELLY St Paul *St D*   **V** J A HOPKINS
LLANELWEDD w Llanfaredd w Llansantffraed-in-Elwell
  w Bettws Disserth and Cregrina w Glascombe and
  Rhulen *S & B*   **V** P A C PEARCEY
LLANENDDWYN (Dyffryn) w Llanddwywe and
  Llanbedr w Llandanwg *Ban*   **R** R A BEACON
LLANENGAN and Llangian *Ban*   **R** W L JONES
LLANERCHAERON w Ciliau Aeron and Dihewyd and
  Mydroilyn *St D*   **R** C N COOPER
LLANERCHYMEDD *Ban*   **V** D PRYS
LLANEUGRAD w Llanallgo and Penrhosligwy w
  Llanfihangel Tre'r Beirdd *Ban*   **R** P HUGHES,
  Hon C G D LOVELUCK
LLANFABON *Llan*   **NSM** J H POWELL
LLANFACHRAETH *Ban*   **R** R J HUGHES
LLANFAETHLU w Llanfwrog and Llanrhyddlad w
  Llanfair-yng-Nghornwy w Llanrhwydrus *Ban*
  R W H DAVIES
LLANFAIR CAEREINION w Llanllugan *St As*
  V P K D EVANS
LLANFAIR DYFFRYN CLWYD and Derwen and
  Llanelidan and Efenechtyd *St As*   **V** G H TRIMBY
LLANFAIR-IS-GAER and Llanddeiniolen *Ban*
  V G C OWEN
LLANFAIR MATHAFARNEITHAF w Llanbedrgoch
  Ban   **R** C S WILLIAMS,   **NSM** L J PERRY
LLANFAIR TALHAIARN and Llansannan w
  Llangerniew and Gwytherin *St As*   **R** C A BILLINGTON
LLANFAIRFECHAN w Aber *Ban*   **R** E T JONES
LLANFAIRPWLL w Penmynydd *Ban*   **R** T O EVANS
LLANFALLTEG w Clunderwen and Castell Dwyran *St D*
  P-in-c G R RENOWDEN
LLANFECHELL w Bodewryd w Rhosbeirio w
  Llanfflewin and Llanbadrig *Ban*   **R** G W EDWARDS
LLANFIHANGEL-AR-ARTH *St D*   **V** G M L EVANS
LLANFIHANGEL CRUCORNEY w Old Castle and
  Cwmyoy and Llanthony *Mon*   **V** D W T DUNN
LLANFIHANGEL GENAU'R-GLYN and Llangorwen
  St D   **V** M H JOHN
LLANFIHANGEL TALYLLYN w Llanywern and
  Llangasty Talyllyn *S & B*   **P-in-c** R A F PARSONS
LLANFIHANGEL-Y-CREUDDYN w Llanafan-y-
  Trawscoed and Llanwnnws and Yspytty Ystwyth *St D*
  Dn-in-c E M R MORGAN
LLANFIHANGEL YSCEIFOG (Gaerwen) and
  Llanffinan w Llanidan and Llanddanielfab and
  Llanedwen *Ban*   **NSM** I JONES
LLANFIHANGEL YSTRAD and Cilcennin w Trefilan
  and Nantcwnlle *St D*   **V** D P DAVIES
LLANFOIST and Llanellen *Mon*   **R** T A FOSTER
LLANFOR w Rhosygwalia *St As*   **R** *Vacant*
LLANFRECHFA and Llanddewi Fach w Llandegveth
  Mon   **V** A SILVERTHORN,   **NSM** C H PEAD
LLANFRECHFA UPPER (Pontnewydd) *Mon*
  V L W WAY
LLANFRYNACH and Cantref w Llanhamlach *S & B*
  V P G R SIMS
LLANFWROG and Clocaenog and Gyffylliog *St As*
  R G C JONES
LLANFYLLIN and Bwlchycibau *St As*   **R** *Vacant*
LLANFYNYDD *St As*   **R** A J POOLMAN
LLANGADOG and Gwynfe w Llanddeusant *St D*
  V R E JONES
LLANGANTEN and Llangammarch and Llanfechan and
  Llanlleonfel *S & B*   **V** J P SMITH
LLANGATHEN w Llanfihangel Cilfargen and
  Llanfihangel Aberbythych *St D*   **V** *Vacant*   Dryslwyn
  (05584) 455
LLANGATTOCK and Llangyndir *S & B*
  V K RICHARDS
LLANGEFNI w Tregaian and Llangristiolus w
  Cerrigceinwen *Ban*   **R** G T JONES,   **C** A C JONES
LLANGEINOR *Llan*   **V** C J SANDERSON
LLANGEITHO and Blaenpennal w Bettws Leiki and
  Gartheli *St D*   **C** B E MORRIS
LLANGELER *St D*   **V** L J L WOODLIFFE
LLANGENNECH and Hendy *St D*   **V** *Vacant*
  Llangennech (0554) 324
LLANGENNY and Llanbedr Ystradyw w Patricio *S & B*
  V C J BLANCHARD
LLANGOLLEN w Trevor and Llantysilio *St As*
  V M J WALKER,   **C** D T B LEWIS,   **NSM** M R WILLIAMS
LLANGORSE w Cathedine *S & B*   **V** *Vacant*
  Llangorse (087484) 298

LLANGRANNOG and Llandysiliogogo *St D*
P-in-c D J ROWLANDS

LLANGUICKE (Pontardawe) *S & B* **P-in-c** D T JENKINS

LLANGUNNOR and Cwmffrwd *St D* **V** N R GRIFFIN,
C M S TAYLOR

LLANGWM and Freystrop *St D* **R** W G HOOPER

LLANGWM UCHAF w Llangwm Isaf w Gwernesney and
Llangeview and Wolvesnewton *Mon* **V** G ASTON

LLANGYBI *Mon* **R** *Vacant* Tredunnock (063349) 214

LLANGYFELACH *S & B* **V** L HOPKINS

LLANGYNHAFAL and Llanbedr Duffryn Clwyd *St As*
R P R OWEN

LLANGYNOG *St As* **P-in-c** W P S DAVIES

LLANGYNWYD w Maesteg *Llan* **V** E B THOMAS,
C R G AUSTIN, R E MOVERLEY, **NSM** G H J BALL

LLANGYSTENYN *St As* **R** T E MART

LLANHARAN w Peterston-super-Montem *Llan*
V P N THOMPSON

LLANHARRY *Llan* **P-in-c** J G WILLIAMS

LLANHILLETH *Mon* **V** A J WAY

LLANIDLOES w Llangurig *Ban* **V** D J PARRY,
NSM K FERGUSON

LLANILAR w Rhostie and Llangwyryfon w Llanfihangel
Lledrod *St D* **V** E G JONES

LLANILID w Pencoed *Llan* **R** E D EVANS

LLANISHEN and Lisvane *Llan* **V** N G JONES,
C M A STARK, P S WEEDING

LLANISHEN w Trellech Grange and Llanfihangel Tor-y-
Mynydd w Llangunnog and Llansoy *Mon* **V** P C PRICE

LLANLLECHID *Ban* **V** *Vacant* Bangor (0248)
601859

LLANLLWCH w Llangain and Llangynog *St D*
V D L B EVANS, **C** S E JONES

LLANLLWCHAEARN and Llanina *St D* **R** R C JONES

LLANLLWNI *St D* **V** B D WITT

LLANLLYFNI *Ban* **R** D N JONES

LLANMARTIN *Mon* **R** K A E TYTE, **TV** C J WILCOX

LLANPUMSAINT w Llanllawddog *St D* **V** T J R JONES

LLANRHAIADR YN CINMERCH and Prion *St As*
V C W EVANS

LLANRHAIADR-YN-MOCHNANT and Llanarmon
Mynydd Mawr w Pennant and Hirnant *St As*
Dn-in-c V E LEWIS

LLANRHIAN w Llanhowel and Carnhedryn w
Llanrheithan *St D* **V** *Vacant* Croesgoch (0348)
831354

LLANRHIDIAN w Llanmadoc and Cheriton *S & B*
V J W GRIFFIN

LLANRHOS (Eglwysrhos) *St As* **V** W D JENKINS,
C M R BALKWILL, **NSM** J M WILLIAMS

LLANRUMNEY *Mon* **V** P VANN

LLANSADWRN w Llanddona and Llaniestyn w
Pentraeth w Llanddyfnan *Ban* **R** E ROBERTS

LLANSADWRN w Llanwrda and Manordeilo *St D*
V W D A GRIFFITHS

LLANSAMLET *S & B* **V** S K PRIOR, **C** A G LOAT,
NSM T J WILLIAMS

LLANSANNOR and Llanfrynach w Penllyn and
Ystradowen *Llan* **R** B M LODWICK

LLANSANTFFRAED and Llanbadarn Trefeglwys w
Llanrhystyd *St D* **V** *Vacant* Llanon (0974) 202394

LLANSANTFFRAID GLAN CONWAY and Eglwysfach
St As **R** K HOWARD

LLANSANTFFRAID GLYN CEIRIOG and Llanarmon
Dyffryn Ceiriog and Pontfadog *St As*
Dn-in-c M V JONES

LLANSANTFFRAID-YN-MECHAIN and Llanfechain
St As **V** L ROGERS

LLANSAWEL w Briton Ferry *Llan* **V** I D HAMER

LLANSILIN w Llangadwaladr and Llangedwyn *St As*
V C F CARTER

LLANSTADWELL *St D* **V** M K LIKEMAN

LLANSTEFFAN and Llan-y-bri and Llandeilo Abercywyn
St D **V** H G ROBERTS

LLANTILIO CROSSENNY and Penrhos w Llanvetherine
and Llanvapley *Mon* **V** *Vacant*

LLANTILLIO PERTHOLEY w Bettws Chapel and
Llanddewi Skirrid *Mon* **V** D FRANCIS,
NSM J M DRAPER

LLANTRISANT *Llan* **V** E HUGHES

LLANTWIT FADRE *Llan* **V** M K JONES

LLANTWIT MAJOR *Llan* **R** D M JENKINS,
TV P G MORRIS, M KOMOR, **C** D Y L HELLARD,
NSM D V GINN

LLANVEIGAN and Llanthetty and Glyncollwng w
Llansantffraed-juxta-Usk *S & B* **V** W S P JACKSON

LLANWDDYN and Llanfihangel-yng-Nghwynfa and
Llwydiarth *St As* **V** A J LEGG, **NSM** J S P LEGG

LLANWENARTH ULTRA *Mon* **R** R T GREY

LLANWNDA and Goodwick St Peter w Manorowen and
Llanstinan *St D* **V** S B THATCHER

LLANWNDA w Llanfaglan *Ban* **V** *Vacant* Llanwnda
(0286) 830543

LLANWNNOG and Caersws w Carno *Ban*
V D J CHAPMAN

LLANWRST and Llanddoget and Capel Garmon *St As*
R W R MORTIMER

LLANWRTYD w Llanddulas in Tir Abad and Eglwys Oen
Duw and Llanfihangel Abergwessin and Llanddewi
S & B **V** I B BESSANT

LLANWYNNO *Llan* **V** J M HUGHES

LLANYBYTHER and Llanwenog w Llanwnnen *St D*
V E D GRIFFITHS

LLANYCHAIARN w Llanddeiniol *St D* **V** J R JENKINS

LLANYCIL w Bala and Frongoch and Llangower w
Llanuwchllyn *St As* **R** G THOMAS

LLANYNYS w Llanychan *St As* **P-in-c** D J WILLIAMS

LLANYRE w Llanfihangel Helygen *S & B* **V** J W J REES

LLAWHADEN w Bletherston and Llan-y-cefn *St D*
V W P NASH

LLAY *St As* **V** K J BRAY

LLWYNDERW *S & B* **V** A E PIERCE, **C** T J WILLIAMS

LLYWEL and Traianglas w Llanulid (Cray) *S & B*
V G O MADDOX

LOUGHER *S & B* **V** M T DAVIES,
NSM N L WILLIAMS, K MORGAN

MACHEN *Mon* **R** C F WARREN, **NSM** P A STEPHENS-
WILKINSON

MACHYNLLETH and Llanwrin *Ban* **R** E W ROWLANDS

MAENCLOCHOG w Henry's Moat and Mynachlogddu
and Llangolman w Llandeilo *St D* **V** A BAILEY

MAENTWROG w Trawsfynydd *Ban* **R** B EVANS

MAESGLAS Newport (Conventional District) *Mon*
C-in-c A B WATERS

MAGOR w Redwick and Undy *Mon* **V** P G COBB,
C D J DUNN

MALLWYD w Cemaes and Llanymawddwy *Ban*
R G J VAUGHAN-JONES

MALPAS *Mon* **V** R M CAPPER

MAMHILAD and Pontymoile *Mon* **P-in-c** J D EVANS

MANOBIER and St Florence w Redberth *St D*
V V F MILLGATE

MANORDEIFI and Capel Colman w Llanfihangel
Penbedw and Clydey w Penrieth and Castellan *St D*
R J O DAVIES

MANSELTON *S & B* **V** T H JONES

MARCHWIEL and Isycoed *St As* **R** T O JONES

MARGAM *Llan* **V** D G BELCHER

MARSHFIELD and Peterstone Wentloog and
Coedkernew w St Bride's Wentloog *Mon*
V T J GREEDY

MARTLETWY w Lawrenny and Minwear and Yerbeston
w Templeton *St D* **V** *Vacant*

MATHERN and Mounton w St Pierre *Mon*
V A R WILLIE

MATHRY w St Edren's and Grandston w St Nicholas and
Jordanston *St D* **V** G O ASSON

MEIDRIM and Llanboidy and Merthyr *St D*
V P L FELTON

MEIFOD and Llangynyw *St As* **V** G MORGAN

MELIDEN and Gwaenysgor *St As* **V** D P D H REES

MERTHYR CYNOG and Dyffryn Honddu w
Garthbrengy w Llandefaelog-Fach and Llanfihangel
Fechan *S & B* **V** T C JOHNS, **NSM** J E PHILLIPS

MERTHYR DYFAN *Llan* **R** T A DOHERTY,
C S M JOHN

MERTHYR TYDFIL and Cyfarthfa *Llan* **R** D S LEE,
TV S S MORGAN

MEYLLTEYRN w Botwnnog and Llandygwnnin w
Llaniestyn *Ban* **R** A EDWARDS, **C** J E TYENDALL

MILFORD HAVEN *St D* **V** J H M DAVIES,
C T J HEWITT

MINERA *St As* **V** C I DAY

MISKIN *Llan* **V** N C H BROWN

MOCHDRE *St As* **V** *Vacant*

MOLD *St As* **V** J S DAVIES, **C** G W WILLIAMS

MONKTON *St D* **V** R G LLOYD

MONMOUTH St Mary *Mon* **V** J W C COUTTS,
Par Dn U M P KROLL

MONTGOMERY and Forden and Llandyssil *St As*
R B LETSON

MORRISTON *S & B* **V** A J KNIGHT,
C R T EDWARDS, S S ARAPUK

MOSTYN *St As* **V** S D GREEN

MOUNTAIN ASH *Llan* **V** D YEOMAN

MYNYDDISLWYN *Mon* **V** *Vacant* Blackwood
(0495) 224240

NANTYMOEL w Wyndham *Llan* **V** *Vacant*
Bridgend (0656) 840248
NARBERTH w Mounton w Robeston Wathen and
Crinow *St D* **R** T H THOMAS
NEATH w Llantwit *Llan* **R** W P THOMAS,
C D G MORRIS, J A GRIFFITHS
NEVERN and Y Beifil w Eglwyswrw and Meline and
Eglwyswen and Llanfair Nantgwyn *St D*
V A C SALMON, **NSM** J G M LADD
NEVIN w Pistyll w Tudweiliog w Llandudwen w Edern
Ban **V** E W THOMAS
NEW Moat w Llysyfran *St D* **R** *Vacant*
NEW RADNOR and Llanfihangel Nantmelan and
Evancoyd w Gladestry and Colva *S & B* **V** G TURNER
NEW TREDEGAR *Mon* **V** D J YOUNG
NEWBOROUGH w Llangeinwen *Ban* **R** R L NEWALL
NEWBRIDGE *Mon* **V** L S DEAS
NEWBRIDGE-ON-WYE and Llanfihangel Brynpabuan w
Cwmbach Llechryd and Llanafan Fawr *S & B*
V *Vacant*
NEWCASTLE *Llan* **V** M D WITCOMBE
NEWCASTLE EMLYN w Llandyfriog and Troedyraur
St D **V** D P D GRIFFITHS
NEWPORT (Crindau) All Saints *Mon* **P-in-c** I S DOULL
NEWPORT (Maindee) St John the Evangelist *Mon*
V J HARRIS, **C** P K WALKER, **NSM** J K BEARDMORE
NEWPORT St Andrew *Mon* **V** H J DAVIES,
C S G WILLSON
NEWPORT St John Baptist *Mon* **V** C D WESTBROOK
NEWPORT St Julian *Mon* **V** D R WILLIAMS,
C C J CANN, **NSM** I R GALT, H W G CLABON
NEWPORT St Mark *Mon* **V** K W SHARPE
NEWPORT St Matthew *Mon* **V** J P HARRIS
NEWPORT St Paul *Mon* **V** W E KELLY
NEWPORT St Stephen and Holy Trinity *Mon*
V D NICHOLSON, **C** J C DOWDING
NEWPORT St Teilo *Mon* **V** P B MARTIN,
NSM I R GALT
NEWPORT St Woolos Cathedral *Mon* **V** D G LEWIS,
C C H A GRIFFITHS, A C EDWARDS
NEWPORT w Cilgwyn and Dinas w Llanllawer *St D*
R H M THOMAS, **NSM** P L DAVIES
NEWTON St Peter *S & B* **V** D THOMAS, **C** D W DAVIES
NEWTON NOTTAGE *Llan* **R** D M JOHN,
C J F SEWARD
NEWTOWN w Llanllwchaiarn w Aberhafesp *St As*
R P B JONES, **NSM** A R MARSHALL, G K MARSHALL,
J WOOD
NOLTON w Roch *St D* **R** A CRAVEN
NORTHOP *St As* **V** G L JONES
OVERTON and Erbistock and Penley *St As*
R W H HUGHES
OXWICH w Penmaen and Nicholaston *S & B*
V K EVANS
OYSTERMOUTH *S & B* **V** G H THOMAS,
C D R PAYNE, **NSM** D J H WATKINS
PANTEG *Mon* **R** D G BRUNNING
PEMBREY *St D* **V** V P ROBERTS
PEMBROKE St Mary and St Michael *St D*
V C W BOWEN, **C** D J MORTIMORE
PEMBROKE DOCK *St D* **V** A THOMAS
PENALLT and Trellech *Mon* **V** J K C DENERLEY
PENARTH All Saints *Llan* **V** F A G MUDGE,
C M H ROWLANDS
PENARTH w Lavernock *Llan* **R** N H COLLINS,
C M R PREECE
PENBOYR *St D* **V** R M GRIFFITHS
PENBRYN and Betws Ifan w Bryngwyn *St D*
P-in-c W J G VARNEY
PENCARREG and Llanycrwys *St D* **V** T J W RICHARDS
PENCLAWDD *S & B* **V** T EVANS
PENDERIN w Ystradfellte and Pontneathvaughan *S & B*
R J H SCOTT
PENDINE w Llanmiloe and Eglwys Gymyn w Marros *St D*
R C L LAWS
PENDOYLAN and Welsh St Donats *Llan*
V D G P WILLIAMS
PENEGOES and Darowen w Llanbrynmair *Ban*
R G ap GWILYM
PENHOW and St Brides Netherwent w Llandevenny and
Llanvaches and Llandevaud *Mon* **V** J HEALES
PENLLERGAER *S & B* **V** D E MORRIS
PENMAEN and Crumlin *Mon* **V** T N COLEMAN
PENMARK w Porthkerry *Llan* **V** S C PARE
PENNAL w Corris and Esgaergeiliog *Ban*
R G ap IORWERTH
PENRHIWCEIBER w Matthewstown and Ynysboeth
Llan **V** G J FRANCIS
PENRHYNCOCH and Elerch *St D* **V** D E B FRANCIS

PENRHYNDEUDRAETH and Llanfrothen *Ban*
V *Vacant* Penrhyndeudraeth (0766) 770324
PENTIR *Ban* **V** P O BUTLER
PENTRE St Peter *Llan* **C** M DAVIES
PENTYRCH *Llan* **V** G W A HOLCOMBE
PENYCAE *St As* **V** C H GIBBS
PENYDARREN *Llan* **V** W B MORGAN
PENYFAI w Tondu *Llan* **V** P R MASSON
PETERSTON-SUPER-ELY w St Brides-super-Ely *Llan*
R E YOUNG
PONT ROBERT w Pont Dolanog *St As* **Cl-in-c** J ROCK
PONTBLYDDYN *St As* **V** C O BENNETT
PONTLOTTYN w Fochriw *Llan* **V** A D H DAVIS
PONTYATES and Llangyndeyrn *St D* **V** *Vacant*
Pontyates (0269) 860451
PONTYBEREM *St D* **V** S R THOMAS
PONTYCLUN w Talygarn *Llan* **V** A M REYNOLDS
PONTYCYMMER and Blaengarw *Llan* **V** M H BOIT
PONTYPOOL *Mon* **R** B R PIPPEN,
TV N L HIBBINS, M L COX
PONTYPRIDD St Catherine w Pontypridd St Matthew
Llan **V** J H S THOMAS, **C** E E DAVIES,
NSM S I DAVIES
PORT EYNON w Rhosili and Llanddewi and Knelston
S & B **V** D J MOSFORD
PORT TALBOT St Agnes w Oakwood *Llan*
V T I GRIFFITHS
PORT TALBOT St Theodore *Llan* **V** N LEA,
C M J GOUGH
PORTH St Paul w Trealaw *Llan* **V** M J DAVIES
PORTSKEWETT and Roggiett w Llanfihangel Rogiet
Mon **R** T H J PALMER
PRENDERGAST w Rudbaxton *St D* **R** G D GWYTHER
PRESTATYN *St As* **V** P C SOUTHERTON
PWLLGWAUN w Llanddewi Rhondda *Llan*
V M L CHIPLIN
PYLE w Kenfig *Llan* **V** P G WHITE, **NSM** P G L JONES
RADYR *Llan* **R** W G BARLOW, **C** B JOHN
RAGLAN w Llandenny and Bryngwyn *Mon*
V S L GUEST
RESOLVEN w Tonna *Llan* **V** P RAIKES
REYNOLDSTON w Penrice and Llangennith *S & B*
R P J WILLIAMS
RHAYADER and Nantmel *S & B* **V** L A MARSHALL
RHESYCAE *St As* **P-in-c** L EDWARDS
RHOSLLANERCHRUGOG *St As* **V** D J HART
RHOSYMEDRE *St As* **V** M J SCARTH
RHUDDLAN *St As* **V** R G MORGAN
RHYDYFELIN *Llan* **V** C P SUTTON
RHYL w Rhyl St Ann *St As* **V** H J LLOYD,
C D Q BELLAMY
RHYMNEY *Mon* **V** D J JONES
RISCA *Mon* **V** K M DENISON, **NSM** J A WELSH
ROATH St German *Llan* **V** M I WILLIAMS,
C R O LLOWNDES, **NSM** R L FANTHORPE
ROATH St Margaret *Llan* **V** P I REID,
C K J MORRIS, P A HINDS
ROATH St Martin *Llan* **V** H G CLARKE
ROATH St Saviour *Llan* **V** A RABJOHNS,
Hon C K A BRADSHAW
ROCKFIELD and St Maughen's w Llangattock-vibon-
Avel and Llanfihangel-ystern-Llewern *Mon*
V G E LOVITT
ROSSETT *St As* **V** T PIERCE
RUABON *St As* **V** D M R WILLIAMS
RUMNEY *Mon* **V** D A G HATHAWAY,
NSM M I R DOWSETT
RUTHIN w Llanrhydd *St As* **R** D J WILLIAMS
ST ANDREW'S MAJOR and Michaelston-le-Pit *Llan*
R J G KEANE
ST ASAPH Cathedral and Tremeirchion *St As*
V C R RENOWDEN, R H GRIFFITHS
ST BRIDE'S MINOR w Bettws *Llan* **R** J F WARD
ST CLEARS w Llangynin and Llanddowror and
Llanfihangel Abercywyn *St D* **V** G A EDWARDS
ST DAVIDS Cathedral *St D* **V** B LEWIS
ST DOGMAEL'S w Moylgrove and Monington *St D*
V E R WILLIAMS
ST FAGANS w Michaelston-super-Ely *Llan*
R A R WINTLE
ST HILARY *Llan* **V** D J ADLINGTON
ST HILARY Greenway *Mon* **V** M J GOLLOP
ST ISHMAEL'S w Llansaint and Ferryside *St D*
V R THOMAS
ST ISSELL'S and Amroth *St D* **V** M BUTLER
ST MELLONS and Michaelston-y-Fedw *Mon*
V D KELLEN, **C** A W TYLER, **NSM** G R DAVIES
ST NICHOLAS w Bonvilston and St George-super-Ely
Llan **R** F W PRICE

ST PETROX w Stackpole Elidor (Cheriton) and
Bosherston w St Twynnells *St D*   **R** J H RICHARDS
ST THOMAS-OVER-MONNOW w Wonastow and
Michel Troy *Mon*   **V** N H PRICE,   **NSM** G EVANS
SEVEN SISTERS *Llan*   **V** R I BLACKMORE
SHOTTON *St As*   **V** A C ROBERTS
SIX BELLS *Mon*   **V** R E PAIN
SKETTY *S & B*   **V** S BROOKS,   **C** P W HART, R J SWYER
(nee HARRIS)
SKEWEN *Llan*   **V** S J DUNSTAN,   **C** I E DAVIES
SLEBECH and Uzmaston w Boulston *St D*
V W H WATKINS
SPITTAL w Treffgarne and Ambleston w St Dogwells *St D*
V R D WHITE
SULLY *Llan*   **R** E B DOWDING
SWANSEA Christchurch *S & B*   **V** E T HUNT
SWANSEA (Cockett) St Peter *S & B*   **V** A G LEE,
C R H MORGAN
SWANSEA St Barnabas *S & B*   **V** D H JONES
SWANSEA St Gabriel *S & B*   **V** E M WASTELL
SWANSEA St James *S & B*   **V** A G HOWELLS,
C J WIGLEY
SWANSEA St Jude *S & B*   **V** D W WHITE
SWANSEA St Luke (Cwmbwrla) *S & B*
V J L WORKMAN
SWANSEA St Mark and St John *S & B*   **V** M C JOHN,
C S J COLEMAN
SWANSEA St Mary w Holy Trinity *S & B*   **V** D E LEWIS,
C A T R LEWIS,   **NSM** P WARD
SWANSEA St Matthew w Greenhill *S & B*
P-in-c L O WARD
SWANSEA St Nicholas *S & B*   **V** D M GRIFFITHS
SWANSEA St Thomas and Kilvey *S & B*   **V** W M DAVIES
TALGARTH and Llanelieu *S & B*   **V** D T WALTERS
TENBY *St D*   **R** C J HARVEY,   **TV** N F GILLMAN,
C S LEYSHON
TONGWYNLAIS *Llan*   **V** R L BROWN
TONYPANDY w Clydach Vale *Llan*   **V** N CAHILL
TONYREFAIL w Gilfach Goch *Llan*   **V** E HASTEY,
C G MILLAR
TOWYN and St George *St As*   **P-in-c** J W JAUNDRILL
TOWYN w Aberdovey *Ban*   **V** J M RILEY,
NSM R H BARBER
TRALLWNG and Bettws Penpont w Aberyskir and
Llanfihangel Nantbran *S & B*   **V** B M JONES
TREBOETH *S & B*   **V** N J SHEARD
TREDEGAR St George *Mon*   **V** L J HARRIES
TREDEGAR St James *Mon*   **V** R R WEST
TREDUNNOC and Llantrissent w Llanhennoc and
Llanllowel *Mon*   **V** J KNOWLES

TREFDRAETH *Ban*   **R** *Vacant*   Bodorgan (0407)
840280
TREFNANT *St As*   **R** T A STILLINGS
TREGARON w Ystrad Meurig and Strata Florida *St D*
V C J D PROBERT
TREHARRIS w Bedlinog *Llan*   **V** A R BOYD-WILLIAMS
TREHERBERT w Treorchy *Llan*   **V** C T REANEY
TRELECH-A'R-BETTWS w Abernant and Llanwinio
St D   **V** D E EVANS
TREUDDYN and Nercwys and Erryrys *St As*
P-in-c J B JONES
TROEDRHIWGARTH *Llan*   **NSM** C E LASKEY
TROEDYRHIW w Merthyr Vale *Llan*
V I P MAINWARING
TYCOCH All Souls *S & B*   **V** R BRITTON
TYLORSTOWN w Ynyshir *Llan*   **V** A E MORTON
USK and Monkswood w Glascoed Chapel and Gwehelog
Mon   **V** R L DAVIES
WALTON WEST w Talbenny and Haroldston West *St D*
R B D B O'MALLEY
WALWYN'S CASTLE w Robeston West *St D*
P-in-c D J LOWEN
WAUNARLLWYDD *S & B*   **V** P C FRENCH
WELSHPOOL w Castle Caereinion *St As*
R G SWINDLEY,   **NSM** B T JOHNS
WENVOE and St Lythans *Llan*   **R** B T JOHNS
WHITCHURCH *Llan*   **V** F G TURNER,   **C** E M LE
GRICE, R A ANGEL, C D CLARKE
WHITCHURCH w Solva and St Elvis w Brawdy and
Llandeloy *St D*   **V** R J E W REES
WHITFORD *St As*   **V** R E KILGOUR
WHITLAND (Eglwys Fair Glan-taf) w Kiffig and Henllan
Amgoed and Llangan *St D*   **V** D E FAULKNER
WHITTON and Pilleth and Cascob w Llangynllo and
Bleddfa *S & B*   **V** J L VICKERY
WISTON w Walton East and Clarbeston *St D*   **V** R JONES
WREXHAM *St As*   **R** B SMITH,
TV J J PAGE, R EVANS,   **TM** S M HUYTON,
C G L GRIFFITHS, D J BLACK
YNYSCYHAIARN w Penmorfa and Portmadoc *Ban*
V W ROBERTS
YNYSDDU *Mon*   **V** D JONES
YSBYTY Cynfyn w Llantrisant and Eglwys Newydd *St D*
V H A CHIPLIN
YSTALYFERA *S & B*   **V** L T G EVANS
YSTRAD MYNACH w Llanbradach *Llan*
V M D BROOKS
YSTRAD RHONDDA w Ynyscynon *Llan*
V D H RHYDDERCH
YSTRADGYNLAIS *S & B*   **R** D G EVANS
YSTRADYFODWG *Llan*   **V** P N COLEMAN

INDEX OF SCOTTISH INCUMBENCIES

An index of the incumbencies of the Scottish Episcopal Church. In each case the the full name of the benefice is given, together with the diocese and the names and appointments of the clergy serving there. The following are the main abbreviations used; for others see the full list of abbreviations:—

C	Curate	**NSM**	Non-stipendiary Minister
C-in-c	Curate-in-charge	**P-in-c**	Priest-in-charge
Dn-in-c	Deacon-in-charge	**R**	Rector
Dss	Deaconess	**TM**	Team Minister
Hon C	Honorary Curate		

ABERCHIRDER St Marnan *Mor*   **R** H M LOPDELL-
BRADSHAW, **Hon C** J C S ARNAUD, **NSM** A S DUNCAN
ABERDEEN St Andrew's Cathedral *Ab*
R W D WIGHTMAN, **NSM** R FINNIE
ABERDEEN St Clement *Ab*   **R** *Vacant* Aberdeen
(0224) 691055
ABERDEEN St James *Ab*   **R** M C PATERNOSTER
ABERDEEN St John the Evangelist *Ab*   **R** A B ALLAN,
NSM R B EDWARDS
ABERDEEN St Margaret of Scotland *Ab*   **R** A E NIMMO
ABERDEEN St Mary *Ab*   **R** J D ALEXANDER
ABERDEEN St Ninian *Ab*   **P-in-c** W D WIGHTMAN,
NSM R FINNIE
ABERDEEN St Peter *Ab*   **R** F J L PHELAN
ABERDOUR St Columba (West Fife Team Ministry)
St And   **NSM** R A DENNISTON
ABERFOYLE St Mary *St And*   **P-in-c** J R BETTELEY
ABERLOUR St Margaret of Scotland *Mor*
R J M DUNCAN
ABOYNE St Peter *Ab*   **R** P G D JONES,
NSM A F R FENNELL
AIRDRIE St Paul *Glas*   **R** *Vacant* Airdrie (0236)
63402
ALEXANDRIA St Mungo *Glas*   **R** M F HICKFORD
ALFORD St Andrew *Ab*   **R** D P BOVEY,
NSM J BURCHILL
ALLOA St John the Evangelist *St And*
P-in-c A H D KNOCK, **C** S J HARRISON,
NSM E FORGAN
ALYTH St Ninian *St And*   **R** H M D PETZSCH,
NSM P S FERNANDO
ANNAN St John the Evangelist *Glas*   **R** A NEAL
ARBROATH St Mary *Bre*   **R** W F WARD
ARDBRECKNISH St James *Arg*   **R** A M MACLEAN
ARDCHATTAN Holy Spirit *Arg*   **R** A M MACLEAN
ARDROSSAN St Andrew *Glas*   **R** S B SYMONS,
NSM J JENKINS
ARPAFEELIE St John the Evangelist *Mor*
R J A HOWARD, **NSM** D McALISTER
ARRAN, ISLE OF *Arg*   **NSM** T A PRINGLE
AUCHINDOIR St Mary *Ab*   **R** D P BOVEY,
NSM J BURCHILL
AUCHMITHIE St Peter *Bre*   **R** M J BUNCE
AUCHTERARDER St Kessog *St And*
R E M ROBERTSON, **NSM** W B ROOTES
AYR Holy Trinity *Glas*   **R** P B FRANCIS,
C M A F BYRNE, **NSM** H ANSON
BAILLIESTON St John *Glas*   **C** D REID,
NSM J FREEBAIRN-SMITH
BALERNO St Mungo *Edin*   **R** M J H ROUND,
NSM J PELHAM, J DYER
BALLACHULISH St John *Arg*   **R** K E WIGSTON
BALLATER St Kentigern *Ab*   **R** P G D JONES,
NSM A F R FENNELL
BANCHORY St Ternan *Ab*   **R** G C MUNGAVIN
BANFF St Andrew *Ab*   **R** R M HAINES
BARROWFIELD St John the Baptist *Glas*   **R** *Vacant*
BATHGATE St Columba *Edin*
Hon C J A MONTGOMERY, **NSM** C CHAPLIN
BEARSDEN All Saints *Glas*   **R** K T ROACH
BIELDSIDE St Devenick *Ab*   **R** K D GORDON,
NSM T A HART, **Dss** J E MACCORMACK
BISHOPBRIGGS St James-the-Less *Glas*
R S D N BARRETT
BLAIRGOWRIE St Catherine *St And*
R H M D PETZSCH, **NSM** P S FERNANDO, D A CAMERON
BO'NESS St Catharine *Edin*   **P-in-c** N D MacCALLUM
BRAEMAR St Margaret *Ab*   **P-in-c** P G D JONES,
NSM A F R FENNELL
BRECHIN St Andrew *Bre*   **R** M J BUNCE,
NSM S G LETTON
BRIDGE OF ALLAN St Saviour *St And*   **R** J M CROOK,
NSM D FINLAYSON
BRIDGE OF WEIR St Mary *Glas*   **R** E G LINDSAY
BRORA St Columba *Mor*   **P-in-c** A R GORDON

BROUGHTY FERRY St Mary *Bre*   **R** R W BREADEN,
C E M FAULKES, **Hon C** A R TREW
BUCKIE All Saints *Ab*   **R** J THOMPSON
BUCKSBURN St Machar *Ab*   **P-in-c** D HEDDLE
BURNTISLAND St Serf (West Fife Team Ministry)
St And   **C** K S NICHOLSON, **NSM** R A DENNISTON
BURRAVOE St Colman *Ab*   **R** L S SMITH,
NSM E H LUMMIS
CALLANDER St Andrew *St And*   **R** J R BETTELEY
CAMBUSLANG St Cuthbert *Glas*   **R** A M BURN-
MURDOCH, **NSM** M A DANSON
CAMPBELTOWN St Kiaran *Arg*   **R** K V PAGAN
CARNOUSTIE Holy Rood *Bre*   **R** D B MACKAY,
Hon C J B HARDIE
CASTLE DOUGLAS St Ninian *Glas*   **R** P P DANCE
CATTERLINE St Philip *Bre*   **NSM** G H J PAISEY
CHALLOCH w Newton Stewart *Glas*   **R** W C DANSKIN
CLARKSTON St Aidan *Glas*   **R** B P OWEN,
Hon Par Dn K R BREWIN
CLYDEBANK St Columba *Glas*   **R** R J A HASLAM,
NSM G L NICOLL
COATBRIDGE St John the Evangelist *Glas*
R T M S MORLEY
COLDSTREAM St Mary and All Souls *Edin*
P-in-c R M GILL, **NSM** M D G C RYAN
COMRIE St Serf *St And*   **R** H G C LEE,
NSM R F PATERSON
COUPAR ANGUS St Anne *St And*   **R** H M D PETZSCH,
NSM P S FERNANDO
COVE BAY St Mary *Ab*   **P-in-c** F J L PHELAN
CRIEFF St Columba *St And*   **R** H G C LEE,
NSM R F PATERSON
CROMARTY St Regulus *Mor*   **R** J A HOWARD,
NSM D McALISTER
CRUDEN St James the Less *Ab*   **R** G H STRANRAER-
MULL, **NSM** M A EATON, J F F SHEPHERD,
G P WHALLEY, D E F FIRMIN, A L JAMES
CULLODEN St Mary-in-the-Fields *Mor*
P-in-c A A HORSLEY
CUMBERNAULD Holy Name *Glas*
P-in-c J F C WOODLEY
CUMBRAE (Millport) Cathedral of The Isles and
Collegiate Church of the Holy Spirit *Arg*
R D McCUBBIN
CUMINESTOWN St Luke *Ab*   **R** R M HAINES
CUPAR St James the Great *St And*   **R** P J E CREAN
DALBEATTIE Christ Church *Glas*   **R** G W A BACON,
Hon Par Dn J W BACON
DALKEITH St Mary *Edin*   **R** D M CAMERON,
Hon C W M WATT, **NSM** W B ELLIOT
DALMAHOY St Mary *Edin*   **R** W L F MOUNSEY
DALRY *Glas*   **Hon C** I BOFFEY
DINGWALL St James the Great *Mor*   **R** S J HOTCHEN
DOLLAR St James the Great *St And*   **R** C P SHERLOCK,
NSM F A M LAWRY, H I SOGA
DORNOCH St Finnbarr *Mor*   **P-in-c** A R GORDON
DOUGLAS Sancta Sophia *Glas*   **R** B H C GORDON
DOUNE St Modoc *St And*   **P-in-c** J R BETTELEY,
NSM S M COATES
DRUMLITHIE St John the Baptist *Bre*   **R** M J R TURNER
DRUMTOCHTY St Palladius *Bre*   **R** M J R TURNER,
NSM D P STEEL
DUFFTOWN St Michael and All Angels *Ab*
R D P BOVEY
DUMBARTON St Augustine *Glas*   **R** A M MACPHERSON
DUMFRIES St John the Evangelist *Glas*   **C** D W BAYNE
DUNBAR St Anne *Edin*   **R** A S BLACK,
C K R WHITEFIELD, **Hon C** F R STEVENSON,
NSM J WOOD
DUNBLANE St Mary *St And*   **R** G TELLINI,
NSM J W ALLAN
DUNDEE St John the Baptist *Bre*   **P-in-c** J J MORROW,
C I G STEWART, **NSM** J P FORBES
DUNDEE St Luke *Bre*   **R** J WALKER,
NSM L STEVENSON

DUNDEE St Margaret Lochee *Bre*   **R** W J McAUSLAND,
C P M BALFOUR
DUNDEE St Martin *Bre*   **C** I G STEWART,
Hon C J MORRISON
DUNDEE St Mary Magdalene *Bre*   **R** D SHEPHERD,
Hon C M T BONE
DUNDEE St Ninian *Bre*   **P-in-c** A W CUMMINS
DUNDEE St Paul's Cathedral *Bre*
R P O SANDERSON, P J HARVIE,
NSM G J H PONT, G M GREIG
DUNDEE St Salvador *Bre*   **R** H P DUFF,   **NSM** D ELDER
DUNFERMLINE Holy Trinity (West Fife Team Ministry)
St And   **R** D L REDWOOD,   **C** R G W NOCK,
NSM M KESTON
DUNKELD (with Birnam) St Mary *St And*
R D H WRIGHT,   **NSM** I ATKINSON
DUNOON Holy Trinity *Arg*   **R** G A GUINNESS
DUNS Christ Church *Edin*   **R** C J MARTIN,
Hon C A J TABRAHAM, M E JONES, G R W BURTON,
NSM E S JONES, J MORSON
DUROR St Adamnan *Arg*   **R** D W DAY
EAST KILBRIDE St Mark *Glas*   **R** K G G GIBSON
EASTRIGGS St John the Evangelist *Glas*
NSM S J CHISHOLM
EDINBURGH Cathedral Church of St Mary *Edin*
R I J PATON, G J T FORBES,   **C** A J BAIN,
Hon C J P ROSS,
NSM E G MALLOCH, R B HOGG, I RYRIE
EDINBURGH Christ Church *Edin*   **R** J A MEIN,
Par Dn A M LOWE
EDINBURGH Clermiston Emmanuel *Edin*
P-in-c P J WARREN
EDINBURGH Good Shepherd *Edin*   **R** D H RIMMER
EDINBURGH Holy Cross *Edin*   **R** W D KORNAHRENS,
C A J FULLER,   **NSM** M F HARRISON
EDINBURGH Old St Paul *Edin*   **R** L A MOSES,
TV A J M SINCLAIR,   **C** D A HUGHES,
Hon C D A B JOWITT,   **NSM** R G W STRONG, C NAISMITH
EDINBURGH St Andrew and St Aidan *Edin*
R T G ENGH,   **TV** A C MURPHY,   **NSM** J G C BARR
EDINBURGH St Barnabas *Edin*   **NSM** P D DIXON
EDINBURGH St Columba *Edin*   **R** B A HARDY,
TV R O GOULD, J S RICHARDSON,   **NSM** A B SHEWAN
EDINBURGH St Cuthbert *Edin*   **R** D R COLE
EDINBURGH St David of Scotland *Edin*
P-in-c J N WYNN-EVANS,   **C** S C LISTON
EDINBURGH St Fillan *Edin*   **R** F W TOMLINSON,
Hon C J W DUFFY,   **NSM** D EMERSON
EDINBURGH St Hilda *Edin*   **R** F W TOMLINSON,
NSM D EMERSON
EDINBURGH St James the Less *Edin*
R S L ROBERTSON
EDINBURGH St John the Evangelist *Edin*
R N CHAMBERLAIN,   **C** D R H EDWARDSON,
NSM P J BRAND, D B G FORMAN
EDINBURGH St Luke *Edin*   **TV** G MACGREGOR
EDINBURGH St Margaret of Scotland *Edin*
P-in-c L A MOSES
EDINBURGH St Mark *Edin*   **R** T G ENGH,
TV A C MURPHY,   **NSM** J G C BARR
EDINBURGH St Martin of Tours *Edin*
R W J T BROCKIE,   **NSM** D YEOMAN
EDINBURGH St Michael and All Saints *Edin*
R T A R COLE,   **NSM** J E ROULSTON
EDINBURGH St Ninian *Edin*   **P-in-c** G SPENCER
EDINBURGH St Paul and St George *Edin*
R R W SIMPSON,   **TV** M P MAUDSLEY
EDINBURGH St Peter *Edin*   **R** I D ZASS-OGILVIE,
C P A RENNIE,   **NSM** D I LLOCKER
EDINBURGH St Philip and St James *Edin*
R R A GRANT,   **NSM** K W RATHBAND
EDINBURGH St Salvador *Edin*   **R** K PEARSON
EDINBURGH St Thomas (Private Chapel) *Edin*
I M J PARKER,   **C** P F D TAYLOR
EDINBURGH St Vincent (Private Chapel) *Edin*
I M A CLARK
ELGIN Holy Trinity w Lossiemouth St Margaret *Mor*
R J D PAUL
ELIE AND EARLSFERRY St Michael and All Angels
St And   **P-in-c** S G HALL,   **NSM** T SHARPUS-JONES
ELLON St Mary on the Rock *Ab*   **R** G H STRANRAER-
MULL,   **NSM** M A EATON, J F F SHEPHERD,
G P WHALLEY, D E F FIRMIN, A L JAMES
EORRAPAIDH St Moluag *Arg*   **R** *Vacant*
EYEMOUTH St Ebba *Edin*   **NSM** J MORSON
FALKIRK Christ Church *Edin*   **R** A D BRUNO
FASQUE St Andrew *Bre*   **R** M J R TURNER
FOCHABERS Gordon Chapel *Mor*   **R** J M DUNCAN

FORFAR St John the Evangelist *St And*
R R G L McALISTER,   **NSM** J M PRIOR
FORRES St John the Evangelist *Mor*   **R** R W FORREST
FORT WILLIAM St Andrew *Arg*   **R** J H J MACLEAY
FORTROSE St Andrew *Mor*   **R** J A HOWARD,
NSM D McALISTER
FRASERBURGH St Pet w New Pitsligo St Jo *Ab*
R R F BURKITT
FYVIE All Saints *Ab*   **R** A B MacGILLIVRAY
GALASHIELS St Peter *Edin*   **R** T D MORRIS
GARTCOSH St Andrew *Glas*   **R** *Vacant*
GATEHOUSE OF FLEET St Mary *Glas*   **R** C M BROUN
GIRVAN St John *Glas*   **R** F G LEE,   **NSM** B H G COLLIE
GLASGOW All Saints *Glas*   **R** D HUNTER
GLASGOW Cathedral Church of St Mary the Virgin *Glas*
R M E GRANT,   **Min** K L MACAULAY
GLASGOW Good Shepherd w Ascension *Glas*
R R J BURNS,   **C** S ROBERTSON,   **Hon C** S A MARSH
GLASGOW Holy Cross *Glas*   **C-in-c** P G M FLETCHER,
NSM D D KEEBLE
GLASGOW St Bride *Glas*   **R** G M M THOMSON,
NSM I T DRAPER
GLASGOW St Gabriel Govan *Glas*   **NSM** A G BOYD
GLASGOW St George *Glas*   **Hon C** S M P MAITLAND
GLASGOW St Kentigern *Glas*   **Hon C** J GRAHAM
GLASGOW St Margaret *Glas*   **R** N J PARKES,
C D S MUNGAVIN,   **Hon C** G D WHITE
GLASGOW St Matthew *Glas*   **R** S P HOLLAND
GLASGOW St Ninian *Glas*   **R** D W J REID,
Hon C R F GRAHAM
GLASGOW St Oswald *Glas*   **R** P J D S SCOTT,
C D H PEYTON JONES,   **Hon C** A R LOBANOV-ROSTOVSKY
GLASGOW St Serf *Glas*   **C** D REID
GLASGOW St Silas (Private Chapel) *Glas*
R R J SHIMWELL,   **Hon C** M CLANCY,
Asst Team Chapl G E W SCOBIE
GLENCARSE All Saints *Bre*   **P-in-c** K J CAVANAGH
GLENCOE St Mary *Arg*   **R** K E WIGSTON
GLENROTHES St Luke the Evangelist *St And*
R H B FARQUHARSON,   **NSM** G N BENSON
GLENURQUHART St Ninian *Mor*   **NSM** J A HUTTON
GOUROCK St Bartholomew *Glas*   **R** M R M WILSON
GRANGEMOUTH St Mary *Edin*   **R** N D MacCALLUM
GRANTOWN-ON-SPEY St Columba *Mor*
P-in-c A WHEATLEY
GREENOCK St John the Evangelist *Glas*   **R** C D LYON
GRETNA All Saints *Glas*   **R** *Vacant* Gretna (0461)
38268
GRULINE St Columba *Arg*   **R** *Vacant*
GULLANE St Adrian *Edin*   **R** J C LINDSAY
HADDINGTON Holy Trinity *Edin*   **R** A S BLACK,
C K R WHITEFIELD,   **NSM** J WOOD
HAMILTON St Mary the Virgin *Glas*
R T C O MONTGOMERY
HAWICK St Cuthbert *Edin*   **R** J M A WILLANS,
NSM D K MAYBURY,   **Dss** D L MAYBURY
HELENSBURGH St Michael and All Angels *Glas*
R A B LAING,   **NSM** B M THATCHER
HUNTLY Christ Church *Mor*   **R** H M LOPDELL-
BRADSHAW
INNERLEITHEN St Andrew *Edin*   **P-in-c** A H HURT
INSCH St Drostan *Ab*   **R** A B MacGILLIVRAY
INVERARAY All Saints *Arg*   **R** *Vacant*
INVERBERVIE St David *Bre*   **P-in-c** S J EVANS
INVERGORDON St Ninian *Mor*   **R** C H CLAPSON
INVERGORDON St Ninian (Independent Mission) *Mor*
I C H CLAPSON
INVERGOWRIE All Souls *Bre*   **P-in-c** I JONES
INVERKEITHING St Peter (West Fife Team Ministry)
St And   **NSM** V A NELLIST
INVERNESS St Andrew's Cathedral *Mor*
R A A HORSLEY,   **Hon C** J W L TAYLOR, A A SINCLAIR
INVERNESS St John the Evangelist *Mor*
P-in-c W J BULLEY,   **Hon C** E S STRANGE
INVERNESS St Michael and All Angels *Mor*
R L A BLACK
INVERURIE St Mary *Ab*   **R** D P BOVEY,
NSM J BURCHILL
IRVINE St Andrew (Local Ecumenical Experiment) *Glas*
C-in-c S B SYMONS,   **NSM** J JENKINS
ISLAY St Columba *Arg*   **R** K V PAGAN
JEDBURGH St John the Evangelist *Edin*   **R** A C RYRIE
JOHNSTONE St John *Glas*   **R** J T MURRAY
KEITH Holy Trinity *Mor*   **R** H M LOPDELL-BRADSHAW,
Hon C J C S ARNAUD,   **NSM** A S DUNCAN
KELSO St Andrew *Edin*   **R** J S DAVIDSON,
NSM G T C TAMS
KEMNAY St Anne *Ab*   **P-in-c** D P BOVEY,
NSM J BURCHILL

KENTALLEN St Moluag *Arg* **R** *Vacant*
KILLIN St Fillan *St And* **R** C E J FRYER
KILMACOLM St Fillan *Glas* **R** E G LINDSAY
KILMARNOCK Holy Trinity *Glas* **R** D M MAIN,
  NSM J JENKINS
KILMARTIN St Columba *Arg* **R** R F F FLATT
KILMAVEONAIG St Adamnan *St And*
  R C B R PRESTON-THOMAS
KINCARDINE O'NEIL Christ Church *Ab*
  R G C MUNGAVIN
KINGHORN St Mary and St Leonard *St And*
  R J R LEIGH, **NSM** G N BENSON, M R FREEMAN
KINLOCH RANNOCH All Saints *St And*
  P-in-c J L L FAGERSON
KINLOCHLEVEN St Paul *Arg* **R** *Vacant*
KINLOCHMOIDART St Finian *Arg*
  NSM D N CLIFFORD
KINROSS St Paul *St And* **R** A I WATT
KIRCUDBRIGHT St Francis of Assisi (Greyfriars) *Glas*
  R C M BROUN
KIRKCALDY St Peter *St And* **R** J R LEIGH,
  NSM G N BENSON, M R FREEMAN
KIRKWALL St Olaf *Ab* **R** *Vacant* Kirkwall (0856)
  2024
KIRRIEMUIR St Mary *St And* **P-in-c** R W B THOMSON,
  NSM D MACLEAN, J M PRIOR
KISHORN Courthill Chapel *Mor* **R** *Vacant*
LADYBANK St Mary *St And* **R** P J E CREAN
LANARK Christ Church *Glas* **R** B H C GORDON
LANGHOLM All Saints *Glas* **R** *Vacant* Gretna
  (0461) 268
LARGS St Columba *Glas* **R** G D DUNCAN,
  Hon C E M LOGUE, N E H NEWTON, **Hon Par Dn** J POW
LASSWADE St Leonard *Edin* **R** D M CAMERON,
  Hon C W M WATT, **NSM** W B ELLIOT
LAURENCEKIRK St Laurence *Bre* **R** M J R TURNER,
  NSM D P STEEL
LENZIE St Cyprian *Glas* **R** K J SHAW,
  Hon C D HADFIELD
LERWICK St Magnus *Ab* **R** L S SMITH,
  NSM E H LUMMIS
LEVEN St Margaret *St And* **NSM** R T EVANS
LEVERBURGH *Arg* **Hon C** W D COLES
LINLITHGOW St Peter *Edin* **P-in-c** M C REED,
  Hon C J A MONTGOMERY
LIVINGSTON (Local Ecumenical Project) *Edin*
  TV P C J BURGESS, **NSM** S S COX
LOCHALSH St Donnan *Mor* **R** *Vacant*
LOCHBUIE St Kilda *Arg* **R** *Vacant*
LOCHEARNHEAD St Angus *St And* **P-in-c** H G C LEE
LOCHGELLY St Finnian (West Fife Team Ministry)
  St And **NSM** A M H ROBERTSON
LOCHGILPHEAD Christ Church *Arg* **R** R F F FLATT
LOCKERBIE All Saints *Glas* **R** A NEAL
LONGSIDE St John *Ab* **C** J H BOOKER,
  NSM J M S FORSYTH
LUNAN HEAD St Margaret *St And* **R** R G L McALISTER
MAYBOLE St Oswald *Glas* **R** F G LEE,
  NSM B H G COLLIE
MELROSE Holy Trinity *Edin* **R** P A BURT
MILNGAVIE St Andrew *Glas* **R** K T ROACH
MOFFAT St John the Evangelist *Glas*
  NSM J STEVENSON
MONIFIETH Holy Trinity *Bre* **R** R JONES
MONTROSE St Mary and St Peter *Bre* **R** S J EVANS
MOTHERWELL Holy Trinity *Glas* **R** K G STEPHEN
MUCHALLS St Ternan *Bre* **Dn-in-c** K R A DALL
MUSSELBURGH St Peter *Edin* **R** K F SCOTT,
  C J M JONES
MUTHILL St James *St And* **R** E M ROBERTSON
NAIRN St Columba *Mor* **R** R W FORREST,
  C C MACDONALD
NETHER LOCHABER St Bride *Arg* **R** *Vacant*
NEW GALLOWAY St Margaret of Scotland *Glas*
  NSM J BANKS
NEWBURGH St Katherine *St And* **NSM** A P PEEBLES
NEWPORT-ON-TAY St Mary *St And*
  R J M RICHARDSON
NORTH BERWICK St Baldred *Edin* **R** J C LINDSAY

OBAN St John's Cathedral *Arg* **R** A M MACLEAN,
  C F J KING
OLD DEER St Drostan *Ab* **C** J H BOOKER,
  NSM J M S FORSYTH
OLDMELDRUM St Matthew *Ab* **R** A B MacGILLIVRAY
ONICH St Bride *Arg* **R** K E WIGSTON
PAISLEY Holy Trinity *Glas* **R** B A HUTTON
PAISLEY St Barnabas *Glas* **R** B A HUTTON
PEEBLES St Peter *Edin* **R** G J SCOTT
PENICUIK St James the Less *Edin* **R** J F A FARRANT,
  C H B T HOLLAND, **NSM** N F SUTTLE, F E McLEAN
PERTH St John the Baptist *St And* **R** A B CAMERON,
  Hon C H L YOUNG, R H DARROCH, W F HARRIS
PERTH St Ninian's Cathedral *St And* **R** K G FRANZ,
  Min I D BARCROFT, **C** J M McLUCKIE,
  NSM R F SAUNDERS
PETERHEAD St Peter *Ab* **C** J H BOOKER
PINMORE *Glas* **P-in-c** F G LEE, **NSM** B H G COLLIE
PITLOCHRY Holy Trinity *St And* **R** C B R PRESTON-
  THOMAS
PITTENWEEM St John the Evangelist *St And*
  P-in-c S G HALL, **NSM** T SHARPUS-JONES
POOLEWE St Maelrubha *Mor* **R** *Vacant*
PORT GLASGOW St Mary the Virgin *Glas*
  R D G WALLACE
PORTNACROIS Holy Cross *Arg* **R** *Vacant*
PORTPATRICK St Ninian *Glas* **R** *Vacant*
PORTREE St Columba *Arg* **R** *Vacant*
PORTSOY St John the Baptist *Ab* **R** J THOMPSON
PRESTONPANS St Andrew *Edin* **P-in-c** K F SCOTT,
  C J M JONES
PRESTWICK St Ninian *Glas* **R** P D NOBLE
RENFREW (with Erskine) St Margaret *Glas*
  R D G E St J CHADWICK
ROSLYN Rosslyn Chapel *Edin* **P-in-c** E N DOWNING
ROTHESAY St Paul *Arg* **P-in-c** E P PACEY
ROTHIEMURCHUS St John the Baptist *Mor*
  P-in-c A WHEATLEY
ST ANDREWS All Saints *St And* **R** R E INGHAM
ST ANDREWS St Andrew *St And* **R** R A GILLIES,
  C P B ROBERTSON, **Hon C** W H BROOME,
  NSM T SHARPUS-JONES, D A BEADLE, J D MARTIN
ST FILLANS Church of the Holy Spirit *St And*
  R *Vacant*
SELKIRK St John the Evangelist *Edin* **NSM** E S JONES
SOUTH QUEENSFERRY Priory Church St Mary of
  Mount Carmel *Edin* **P-in-c** D W McCARTHY
STANLEY St Columba *St And* **NSM** R F SAUNDERS
STIRLING Holy Trinity *Edin* **R** J W McINTYRE
STONEHAVEN St James *Bre* **NSM** G H J PAISEY
STORNOWAY St Peter *Arg* **R** S J G BENNIE
STRANRAER St John the Evangelist *Glas* **R** *Vacant*
STRATHNAIRN St Paul *Mor* **P-in-c** A A HORSLEY,
  Hon C S A T MALLIN
STRATHPEFFER St Anne *Mor* **R** S J HOTCHEN
STRATHTAY St Andrew *St And* **R** D H WRIGHT
STRICHEN All Saints *Ab* **C** J H BOOKER,
  NSM J M S FORSYTH
STROMNESS St Mary *Ab* **R** G J SIMMONS
STRONTIAN *Arg* **NSM** D N CLIFFORD
TAIN St Andrew *Mor* **R** D J PAXMAN
TARFSIDE St Drostan *Bre* **R** M J BUNCE
TAYPORT St Margaret of Scotland *St And*
  R J M RICHARDSON
THURSO St Peter and Holy Rood *Mor*
  P-in-c J C HADFIELD
TIGHNABRUAICH *Arg* **R** E P PACEY
TROON St Ninian *Glas* **R** J A TRIMBLE,
  NSM J A MASON
TURRIFF St Congan *Ab* **R** R M HAINES
UDDINGSTON St Andrew *Glas* **R** A M BURN-
  MURDOCH, **NSM** M A DANSON
ULLAPOOL St Mary the Virgin *Mor* **R** C R DORMER
WEST LINTON St Mungo *Edin* **R** J F A FARRANT,
  C H B T HOLLAND, **NSM** F F McLEAN
WESTHILL Trinity *Ab* **P-in-c** I J FERGUSON
WHITERASHES All Saints *Ab* **R** A B MacGILLIVRAY
WICK St John the Evangelist *Mor* **R** J C HADFIELD
WISHAW St Andrew *Glas* **R** K G STEPHEN

INDEX OF IRISH BENEFICES

An index of the benefices of the Church of Ireland. In each case the full name of the benefice is given, together with the diocese and the names and appointments of the clergy serving there. The following are the main abbreviations used; for others see the full list of abbreviations:—

Bp's C	Bishop's Curate	**I**	Incumbent (includes Rector or Vicar)
C	Curate	**NSM**	Auxiliary Minister
C-in-c	Curate-in-charge	**P-in-c**	Priest-in-charge
Hon C	Honorary Curate		

ABBEYLEIX w The Old Church, Ballyroan, Ballinakill, Killermogh, Aughmacart, Durrow and Attanagh *C & O*
  I P A HARVEY
ABBEYSTREWRY (Skibbereen) w Creagh, Tullagh (Baltimore), Castlehaven (Castletownshend) and Caheragh *C, C & R*   **I** R C A HENDERSON
ACHONRY St Crumnathy's Cathedral w Tubbercurry and Killoran (Rathbarron) *T, K & A*   **I** S I McGEE
ACTON w Drumbanagher *Arm*   **Bp's C** J CLYDE
ADARE w Kilpeacon and Croom *L & K*
  I M J B NUTTALL, **NSM** R G GRAHAM
AGHADERG (Loughbrickland) w Donaghmore and Scarva *D & D*   **I** G N LITTLE
AGHADOWEY w Kilrea *D & R*   **I** S D BARTON
AGHADRUMSEE w Clogh and Drumsnatt *Clogh*
  I V E KILLE
AGHALEE *D & D*   **I** J A HARRON
AGHALURCHER (Colebrook) w Tattykeeran, Cooneen and Mullaghfad *Clogh*   **I** W T LONG
AGHAVEA (Brookeborough) *Clogh*   **I** J McCLOUGHLIN
AGHERTON (Portstewart) *Conn*   **I** T F CALLAN
AHOGHILL w Portglenone *Conn*   **I** W K M BREW
ANNAGH (Belturbet) w Drumaloor, Cloverhill, Drumgoon (Cootehill), Dernakesh, Ashfield and Killesherdoney *K, E & A*   **I** W D JOHNSTON,
  C I GALLAGHER
ANNAGHMORE *Arm*   **I** R J N PORTEUS
ANNAHILT w Magherahamlet *D & D*   **I** E KINGSTON
ANNALONG *D & D*   **I** B T BLACOE
ANTRIM All Saints *Conn*   **I** J L FORSYTHE
ARDAGH w Tashinny, Shrule (Ballymahon) and Kilcommick (Kenagh) *K, E & A*
  Bp's C A W KINGSTON
ARDAMINE w Kiltennel, Glascarrig, Kilnamanagh and Kilmuckridge *C & O*   **I** J JACOB
ARDARA w Glencolumbkille, Inniskeel, Glenties and Lettermacaward *D & R*   **I** M S HARTE,
  NSM M C CLASSON, **Hon Par Dn** P M FLEURY
ARDCLINIS (Carnlough) and Tickmacrevan (Glenarm) w Layde and Cushendun *Conn*   **I** K B de S SCOTT
ARDEE w Charlestown and Collon *Arm*   **I** *Vacant* Ardee (41) 53320
ARDMORE (Moyntaghs) w Craigavon *D & D*
  I D COLLINS
ARDSTRAW w Baronscourt, Badoney Lower and Badoney Upper (Gortin) and Greenan *D & R*   **I** J PIKE
ARDTREA w Desertcreat *Arm*   **I** J C WILSON
ARKLOW w Inch and Kilbride *D & G*   **I** D G MOYNAN
ARMAGH St Mark w Aghavilly *Arm*   **I** J W McKEGNEY,
  C I W ELLIS
ARMAGH St Patrick's Cathedral *Arm*   **I** H CASSIDY
ARMOY St Patrick w Loughguile and Drumtullagh *Conn*
  I W E McCRORY
ARVAGH w Carrigallen, Gowna and Columbkille (Aughnacliffe) *K, E & A*   **I** J R T WATSON
ATHBOY w Ballivor and Killallon (Clonmellon) *M & K*
  I *Vacant*
ATHLONE w Benown (Kilkenny West), Kiltoom and Forgney *M & K*   **I** I J POWER
ATHY w Kilberry, Fontstown and Kilkea *D & G*
  I J L CRAMPTON
AUGHAVAL (Westport) w Achill, Knappagh, Dugort, Castlebar and Turlough *T, K & A*   **I** W J HEASLIP
AUGHER w Newtownsaville and Eskrahoole *Clogh*
  I D BURNS
AUGHRIM w Ballinasloe (Creagh), Clontuskert, Ahascragh and Woodlawn (Kilconnell) *L & K*
  I T A SULLIVAN
BAILIEBOROUGH w Knockbride, Shercock and Mullagh *K, E & A*   **I** *Vacant* Cavan (49) 65436
BALLIBAY w Mucknoe (Castleblayney) and Clontibret *Clogh*   **NSM** G A KNOWD
BALLINDERRY *Conn*   **I** E J HARRIS
BALLINDERRY w Tamlaght and Arboe *Arm*
  I H J W MOORE

BALLINTOY w Rathlin and Dunseverick *Conn*
  I J N PATTERSON
BALLISODARE w Collooney and Emlaghfad (Ballymote) *T, K & A*   **I** R M STRATFORD
BALLYBEEN *D & D*   **I** W E McGIRR
BALLYDEHOB w Aghadown *C, C & R*   **I** J J PERROTT
BALLYHALBERT w Ardkeen *D & D*   **I** F W A BELL
BALLYHOLME *D & D*   **I** A F ABERNETHY, **C** D J BELL
BALLYMACARRETT St Martin (Southern Mission) *D & D*   **Bp's C** I R BETTS
BALLYMACARRETT St Patrick *D & D*   **I** D COE
BALLYMACASH *Conn*   **I** W G IRWIN
BALLYMASCANLAN w Creggan and Rathcor *Arm*
  I G M KINGSTON
BALLYMENA (Kirconriola) w Ballyclug *Conn*
  I S G E LLOYD, **C** G J O DUNSTAN
BALLYMONEY w Finvoy and Rasharkin *Conn*
  I E R LAVERY, **C** C J POLLOCK
BALLYMORE St Mark *Arm*   **I** P W ROOKE
BALLYNAFEIGH St Jude *D & D*   **I** W M MOORE,
  C S GILCHRIST
BALLYNURE and Ballyeaston (Ballyclare) *Conn*
  I J F A BOND
BALLYPHILIP w Ardquin (Portaferry) *D & D*
  I *Vacant*
BALLYRASHANE w Kildollagh *Conn*   **I** N C SHORTT
BALLYSCULLION (Bellaghy) *D & R*   **I** F J REILLY
BALLYWALTER w Inishargie *D & D*   **I** J R L BOWLEY
BALLYWILLAN (Portrush) *Conn*   **I** H HOPKINS,
  C B STEWART
BALTEAGH w Carrick *D & R*   **I** J J HEMPHILL
BALTINGLASS w Ballynure, Stratford-upon-Slaney and Rathvilly *C & O*   **I** M A McCULLAGH
BANDON w Rathclaren, Innishannon, Ballinadee and Brinny *C, C & R*   **I** R L CLARKE, **C** D L SANDES
BANGOR St Comgall *D & D*   **I** W R D McCREERY,
  C K M POULTON
BANGOR, The Primacy *D & D*   **C** J I H STAFFORD
BANGOR ABBEY *D & D*   **I** H LECKEY,
  C J C T SKILLEN, A S DELAMERE
BEARA (Castletownbere) *C, C & R*   **I** *Vacant* Cork (21) 63036
BELFAST All SS *Conn*   **I** C WEST, **NSM** R MOORE
BELFAST Christ Church *Conn*   **I** S N M BAYLY
BELFAST Holy Trinity (Joanmount) and Ardoyne *Conn*
  I J N T CAMPBELL, **C** P R CAMPION
BELFAST Malone St John *Conn*   **I** A E T HARPER
BELFAST St Aidan *Conn*   **I** W R KELLY, **C** J MOULD
BELFAST St Andrew (Glencairn) *Conn*
  NSM S K HOUSTON
BELFAST St Anne's Cathedral *Conn*   **I** J SHEARER,
  C W D HUMPHRIES
BELFAST St Barnabas *Conn*   **I** H D HEATLEY
BELFAST St Bartholomew *Conn*   **I** G B MOLLER
BELFAST St Brendan (Sydenham) *D & D*
  I J R P FERGUSON
BELFAST St Christopher *D & D*   **I** S A CROWTHER
BELFAST St Clement *D & D*   **I** J STEWART
BELFAST St Donard *D & D*   **I** H N PEDLOW,
  C D P KERR
BELFAST St George *Conn*   **I** P F BARRETT,
  NSM G W ODLING-SMEE
BELFAST St James w St Silas *Conn*   **I** J O ROLSTON,
  NSM R MAXWELL
BELFAST St Katharine *Conn*   **I** W J TAGGART
BELFAST St Mark (Ballysillan) *Conn*   **I** L J MEDHURST
BELFAST St Mary (Crumlin Road) w Holy Redeemer *Conn*   **I** J P WALKER, **C** A MALLON
BELFAST St Mary Magdalene *Conn*   **I** *Vacant*
BELFAST St Matthew *Conn*   **I** R HENDERSON
BELFAST St Michael *Conn*   **I** N B DODDS,
  C D W GAMBLE
BELFAST St Nicholas *Conn*   **I** F J RUSK
BELFAST St Ninian *Conn*   **I** J R HOWARD
BELFAST St Paul *Conn*   **I** J W K TAYLOR
BELFAST St Peter *Conn*   **I** S R McBRIDE

BELFAST St Simon w St Philip (Drew Memorial) *Conn*
  I W T HOEY
BELFAST St Stephen w St Luke *Conn*
  Bp's C R H MOORE
BELFAST St Thomas *Conn*   **I** W A LEWIS,
  NSM G W C McCARTNEY
BELFAST Upper Falls (St John the Baptist) *Conn*
  C J NOLAN
BELFAST Upper Malone (Epiphany) *Conn*   **I** S J BLACK
BELFAST Whiterock (St Columba) *Conn*
  Bp's C C J McCOLLUM
BELVOIR *D & D*   **I** T KEIGHTLEY
BILLY w Derrykeighan (Dervock) *Conn*   **I** A A JOHNS
BIRR w Eglish, Lorrha, Dorrha and Lockeen *L & K*
  I D L KEEGAN
BLESSINGTON w Kilbride, Ballymore Eustace and
  Hollywood *D & G*   **I** R S STOKES
BOYLE and Elphin w Aghanagh (Ballinafad), Kilbryan,
  Ardcarne and Croghan *K, E & A*   **I** W E R GARRETT
BRACKAVILLE (Coalisland) w Donaghendry and
  Ballyclog *Arm*   **I** J T P TWOMEY
BRAY *D & G*   **I** D S G GODFREY,   **NSM** K V KENNERLEY
BRIGHT w Ballee and Killough *D & D*   **I** I P POULTON
BROOMHEDGE *Conn*   **I** P J GALBRAITH
BUNCLODY (Newtownbarry) w Kildavin and Clonegal
  C & O   **I** N J W WAUGH
CALEDON w Brantry *Arm*   **I** F E BEAMISH
CALRY *K, E & A*   **I** T P S WOOD
CAMLOUGH w Mullaglass *Arm*   **I** R G HOEY
CAMUS-JUXTA-BANN (Macosquin) *D & R*
  I P S WILSON
CAMUS-JUXTA-MOURNE (Strabane) *D & R*
  I F W FAWCETT
CAPPAGH w Lislimnaghan *D & R*   **I** D J QUINN
CARLOW w Urglin (Rutland Church) and Staplestown
  C & O   **I** G G DOWD
CARNALEA St Gall *D & D*   **I** W P HOUSTON
CARNEW w Kilrush *C & O*   **I** *Vacant*
CARNMONEY *Conn*   **I** N B JACKSON
CARNTEEL and Crilly *Arm*   **I** G P BRIDLE
CARRICKFERGUS *Conn*   **I** B J COURTNEY,
  C K M YOUNG, W L BENNETT
CARRICKMACROSS w Magheracloone *Clogh*
  I H H BOYLAND
CARRIGALINE w Killanully and Monkstown *C, C & R*
  I A J HOUSTON
CARRIGROHANE w Garrycloyne (Blarney), Inniscarra
  and Magourney (Coachford) *C, C & R*   **I** H C MILLER
CARROWDORE w Millisle *D & D*   **I** T R WEST
CASHEL St John the Baptist Cathedral w Magorban,
  Tipperary, Clonbeg and Ballintemple *C & O*
  I G M D WOODWORTH
CASTLECOMER w the Colliery Church, Mothel and
  Bilbo *C & O*   **I** R B MacCARTHY
CASTLEDAWSON *D & R*   **I** R J STEWART
CASTLEKNOCK and Mulhuddart w Clonsilla *D & G*
  I W P COLTON, **C** S C WALLS
CASTLEMACADAM w Ballinaclash, Aughrim and
  Macreddin *D & G*   **I** J HARTIN
CASTLEPOLLARD and Oldcastle w Loughcrew, Mount
  Nugent, Mayne and Drumcree *M & K*   **I** N T RUDDOCK
CASTLEROCK w Dunboe and Fermoyle *D & R*
  I W B JOHNSTON
CASTLEWELLAN w Kilcoo (Bryansford) *D & D*
  I R F GREER
CELBRIDGE w Straffan and Newcastle-Lyons *D & G*
  I P R THOMAS
CLANE w Donadea and Coolcarrigan *M & K*
  I D FRAZER
CLARA w Liss, Ardnurcher (Horseleap), Moate and
  Clonmacnoise *M & K*   **I** C W FINNEY
CLEENISH w Mullaghdun *Clogh*   **I** W S WRIGHT
CLOGHER St Macartan's Cathedral w Errigal Portclare
  Clogh   **I** J S FRAZER
CLOGHERNEY w Seskinore and Drumnakilly *Arm*
  I D B WILSON
CLONALLON w Warrenpoint *D & D*
  I M D J McCREADY
CLONDALKIN w Rathcoole *D & G*   **I** J E McCULLAGH
CLONDEHORKEY (Ballymore) w Cashel *D & R*
  I D GRISCOME
CLONDEVADDOCK w Portsalon and Leatbeg *D & R*
  I *Vacant* Tamney (74) 59020
CLONENAGH (Mountrath) w Offerlane, Borris-in-
  Ossory and Seirkieran *C & O*   **I** H H J GRAY
CLONES w Killeevan *Clogh*   **I** R W MARSDEN
CLONFEACLE w Derrygortreavy *Arm*   **I** A J PARKHILL

CLONFERT (St Brendan's Cathedral) w Donanaughta
  (Eyrecourt), Banagher (Rynagh) and Lickmolassy
  (Portumna) *L & K*   **I** M COMBER
CLONMEL Union (Rushbrooke) *C, C & R*   **I** *Vacant*
  Cork (21) 811790
CLONMEL w Innislounagh, Tullaghmelan, Fethard,
  Kilvemnon and Cahir *C & O*   **I** I J E KNOX
CLONSAST w Rathangan, Thomastown (Clonbullogue),
  Monasteroris (Edenderry), Carbury and Rahan *M & K*
  I R W DEANE
CLOONCLARE (Manorhamilton) w Rossinver
  (Kinlough), Killasnett (Glencar), Drumlease and Finner
  (Bundoran) *K, E & A*   **I** *Vacant*
CLOONEY w Strathfoyle *D & R*   **I** J C D MAYES,
  C J R D SLATER
CLOUGHFERN *Conn*   **I** J ROONEY
CLOUGHJORDAN w Borrisokane, Ballingary,
  Borrisnafarney and Modreeny *L & K*
  I S C D ATKINSON
CLOYNE St Colman's Cathedral w Inch, Corkbeg
  (Whitegate), Midleton and Gurranekennefeake (East
  Ferry) *C, C & R*   **I** G P St J HILLIARD
COLERAINE *Conn*   **I** K H CLARKE,
  C G J WHITEHEAD, T J CADDEN
COMBER *D & D*   **I** J P O BARRY
CONNOR w Antrim St Patrick *Conn*   **I** S JONES
CONVOY w Monellan and Donaghmore *D & R*
  I R C HANNA
CONWAL (Letterkenny) w Aughanunshin and Gartan
  D & R   **I** W W MORTON
CORK St Fin Barre's Cathedral w St Nicholas *C, C & R*
  I J M G CAREY,   **NSM** P T HANNA
CORK (St Luke) w Shandon (St Ann) (St Mary) *C, C & R*
  I G A SALTER
CRAIGS w Dunaghy and Killagan *Conn*   **I** J C BUDD
CREGAGH St Finnian *D & D*   **I** J N BATTYE
CRINKEN *D & G*   **I** W E C STOREY
CROSSPATRICK Group w Kilcommon, Kilpipe and
  Preban *C & O*   **I** C CHALLENDER
CULMORE w Muff and Belmont *D & R*
  I C L MACONACHIE
CUMBER LOWER w Banagher *D & R*
  I G F ANDERSON
CUMBER UPPER w Learmount *D & R*   **I** J A MARTIN
CURRIN w Drum and Newbliss *Clogh*   **I** T B GOLDING
DALKEY St Patrick *D & G*   **I** R B ROUNTREE,
  C T F BLENNERHASSETT
DELGANY *D & G*   **I** C J PRICE,   **NSM** C E BAKER
DERG (Castlederg) w Termonamongan *D & R*
  I W P QUILL
DERRIAGHY w Colin *Conn*   **I** G E GRAHAM
DERRYLORAN (Cookstown) *Arm*   **I** J M BARTON,
  NSM S R T BOYD
DERRYVOLGIE *Conn*   **I** J N B WILKINSON
DERRYVULLEN NORTH (Irvinestown) w
  Castlearchdale *Clogh*   **I** V E S McKEON
DERRYVULLEN SOUTH w Garvary *Clogh*
  I J W STEWART
DESERTLYN (Moneymore) w Ballyeglish *Arm*
  I B LIVINGSTON
DESERTMARTIN w Termoneeny *D & R*
  I K R KINGSTON
DEVENISH w Boho *Clogh*   **I** J I CARSON
DINGLE w Killiney and Kilgobbin *L & K*
  NSM H A P STEPHENS
DIOC Curate *C & O*   **I** *Vacant*
DONACAVEY (Fintona) w Barr *Clogh*   **I** J HAY
DONAGH w Tyholland and Errigal Truagh *Clogh*
  I *Vacant*
DONAGHADEE *D & D*   **I** R S HEWITT
DONAGHCLONEY w Waringstown *D & D*
  I J C MOORE,   **C** A J RUFLI
DONAGHEADY (Donemana) *D & R*   **I** *Vacant*
  Strabane (0504) 8017
DONAGHMORE w Upper Donaghmore *Arm*
  I F K LIVINGSTONE
DONEGAL w Killymard, Lough Eske and Laghey *D & R*
  I T H TRIMBLE
DONOUGHMORE and Donard w Dunlavin *D & G*
  I S P SEMPLE
DOUGLAS w St Michael (Blackrock), Frankfield and
  Marmullane (Passage) *C, C & R*   **I** R E B WHITE,
  C S F GLENFIELD,   **NSM** T R LESTER
DOWN Holy and Undivided Trinity Cathedral *D & D*
  I H LECKEY
DOWN Holy Trinity w Hollymount *D & D*
  I S M J DICKSON
DROGHEDA St Peter w Ballymakenny, Beaulieu,
  Mellifont and Termonfeckin *Arm*   **I** C J G BEVAN

DROMARA w Garvaghy *D & D*   I *Vacant*
DROMORE *Clogh*   I D H HANNA
DROMORE Cathedral of Christ the Redeemer *D & D*
   I W B NEILL,   C R P KELLY
DRUMACHOSE (Limavady) *D & R*   I S McVEIGH
DRUMBEG *D & D*   I C W M COOPER
DRUMBO *D & D*   I J C BELL
DRUMCLAMPH w Lower Langfield (Drumquin) and
   Upper Langfield *D & R*   I F D CREIGHTON
DRUMCLIFFE (Ennis) w Kilrush, Kilfenora, Kilfarboy
   (Milltown Malbay), Kilnasoolagh, Shannon and
   Kilferagh (Kilkee) *L & K*   I R W P DOHERTY
DRUMCLIFFE w Lissadell and Munninane *K, E & A*
   I R F HAYMAN
DRUMCREE *Arm*   I J A PICKERING
DRUMGATH (Rathfriland) w Drumgooland (Ballyward)
   and Clonduff (Hilltown) *D & D*   I W A SEALE
DRUMGLASS (Dungannon) w Moygashel *Arm*
   I F D SWANN,   C C G WYLIE
DRUMKEERAN (Tubrid) w Templecarne (Pettigo) and
   Muckross *Clogh*   I *Vacant*   Kesh (03656) 31210
DRUMMAUL (Randalstown) w Duneane and
   Ballyscullion *Conn*   I J R WILSON
DRUMRAGH (Omagh) w Mountfield *D & R*
   I B McCARTHY,   C P R DRAPER
DRUNG w Castleterra (Ballyhaise), Larah and Lavey and
   Killoughter (Redhills) *K, E & A*   C G W BUTLER
DUBLIN Booterstown *D & G*   I D J O BARR
DUBLIN Christ Church Cathedral Group: (St Andrew)
   (St Werburgh) (St Michan) (St Paul) and Grangegorman
   D & G   I D P R CARMODY, J T F PATERSON,
   C D W OXLEY
DUBLIN Clontarf *D & G*   I T HASKINS
DUBLIN Crumlin w Chapelizod *D & G*   NSM D BURNS
DUBLIN Drumcondra w North Strand *D & G*
   I R K BROOKES
DUBLIN Irish Church Missions and St Thomas *D & G*
   I W J BRIDCUT
DUBLIN Irishtown w Donnybrook *D & G*
   I R H BERTRAM,   NSM J M GORDON
DUBLIN Mount Merrion *D & G*   I T S HIPWELL
DUBLIN Rathfarnham *D & G*   I A WILSON
DUBLIN Rathmines w Harold's Cross *D & G*
   I N G McENDOO
DUBLIN Sandford w Milltown *D & G*   I R D HARMAN,
   NSM J TEGGIN
DUBLIN Sandymount St John the Evangelist *D & G*
   P-in-c W J LOWRY,   C G P IRVINE
DUBLIN Santry w Glasnevin *D & G*   I V G STACEY
DUBLIN St Ann w St Mark and St Stephen *D & G*
   I C A EMPEY,   C A L HARRISON,   NSM W BLACK
DUBLIN St Bartholomew w Christ Church Leeson Park
   D & G   I J A McKAY,   C N K DUNNE
DUBLIN St George and St Thomas *D & G*
   Bp's C G E DYKE
DUBLIN St George w St Thomas, Finglas and Free
   Church *D & G*   C M W SEARIGHT
DUBLIN St Patrick's Cathedral Group: St Catherine and
   St James w St Audoen *D & G*   I J W R CRAWFORD,
   C J T CARROLL
DUBLIN Whitechurch *D & G*   I A H N McKINLEY,
   C J D M CLARKE
DUBLIN Zion Church *D & G*   I W R J GOURLEY,
   NSM E A H WILKINSON
DUN LAOGHAIRE *D & G*   I R C ARMSTRONG
DUNBOYNE UNION w Kilcock, Maynooth, Moyglare,
   Dunshaughlin, Ballymaglasson *M & K*
   I G L WILLIAMSON
DUNDALK w Heynestown *Arm*   I R R WILSON,
   C D A WORKMAN
DUNDELA St Mark *D & D*   I J E MOORE,
   C M F TAYLOR
DUNDONALD St Elizabeth *D & D*   I E CROOKS,
   C F McCREA
DUNFANAGHY, Raymunterdoney and Tullaghbegley
   D & R   I F N WARREN
DUNGANSTOWN w Redcross and Conary *D & G*
   I J R HEANEY
DUNGIVEN w Bovevagh *D & R*   I T R CONWAY
DUNLECKNEY (Bagenalstown) w Nurney, Lorum and
   Kiltennel (Killedmond) *C & O*   I C A FAULL
DUNLUCE (Bushmills) *Conn*   I W J F MOORE
DUNMURRY *Conn*   I J T R RODGERS
EDENDERRY w Clanabogan *D & R*   I R W CLARKE
EGLANTINE *Conn*   I C W BELL
EGLISH w Killylea *Arm*   I J M BATCHELOR
EMATRIS St John the Evangelist w Rockcorry, Aghabog
   and Aughnamullan *Clogh*   I J T A MERRY

ENNISCORTHY w Clone, Clonmore, Monart and
   Templescobin *C & O*   I K S WILKINSON,
   NSM J DEACON
ENNISKILLEN St Macartan's Cathedral *Clogh*
   I J F McCARTHY
ERRIGAl w Garvagh *D & R*   I S SIMPSON
ERRIGLE KEEROGUE w Ballygawley and Killeshil
   Arm   I B J HARPER
FAHAN LOWER (Buncrana) and Fahan Upper *D & R*
   Bp's C F L GRAHAM
FANLOBBUS w Drimoleague, Drinagh and Coolkellure
   C, C & R   I D A CATTERALL
FAUGHANVALE (Eglinton) *D & R*   I C B LEEKE
FENAGH w Myshall, Aghade and Ardoyne *C & O*
   I C C RUDDOCK
FERMOY w Ballyhooley, Knockmourne, Ardnageehy
   (Glenville) and Brigown (Mitchelstown) *C, C & R*
   I *Vacant*   Fermoy (25) 31772
FERNS St Edan's Cathedral w Kilbride, Toombe,
   Kilcormack and Ballycarney *C & O*   I D K L EARL
FIDDOWN (Piltown) w Clonegam (Portlaw), Guilcagh
   and Kilmeaden *C & O*   I A L DAVIES
FINAGHY (St Polycarp) *Conn*   I R W JONES
FIVEMILETOWN *Clogh*   I R J RIDDEL
GALLOON (Newtownbutler) w Drummully *Clogh*
   I N P BAYLOR
GALWAY w Kilcummin (Oughterard) *T, K & A*
   I L D A FORREST,   C C H THOMSON
GARRISON w Slavin and Belleek *Clogh*   I V IRWIN
GEASHILL w Killeigh and Ballycommon *M & K*
   I *Vacant*
GILFORD *D & D*   C A P PATTERSON
GILNAHIRK St Dorothea *D & D*   I T C KINAHAN
GLENAGEARY *D & G*   I G C S LINNEY,
   C P M WILLOUGHBY
GLENAVY w Tunny and Crumlin *Conn*
   I T O THOMPSON
GLENCRAIG *D & D*   I P S P HEWITT
GLENDERMOTT *D & R*   I R N MOORE,
   NSM H J K McLAUGHLIN
GLYNN w Raloo *Conn*   Bp's C J A FAIR
GOREY w Kilnahue *C & O*   I P J KNOWLES,
   NSM J F FORBES
GREENISLAND *Conn*   I S H LOWRY
GREY ABBEY w Kircubbin *D & D*   I W A McMONAGLE
GREYSTONES *D & G*   I E J SWANN
GROOMSPORT *D & D*   I J D TYNEY
GWEEDORE (Bunbeg), Carrickfin and Templecrone
   D & R   P-in-c S R WHITE
HELEN'S BAY *D & D*   I R NESBITT
HILLSBOROUGH *D & D*   I J F DINNEN
HOLMPATRICK (Skerries) w Balbriggan and Kenure
   D & G   I J F HAMMOND
HOLYWOOD *D & D*   I J A MONROE,   C D HILLIARD
HOWTH *D & G*   I C G HYLAND
INISHMACSAINT (Derrygonnelly) *Clogh*
   I C R A EASTON
INVER w Mountcharles, Killaghtee and Killybegs *D & R*
   I B M BOWER
JORDANSTOWN *Conn*   I E J MOORE
JULIANSTOWN and Colpe w Drogheda and Duleek
   M & K   I A J NELSON
KEADY w Armaghbreague and Derrynoose *Arm*
   I W G NEELY
KELLS w Ballaghtobin, Kilmoganny, Ennisnag, Inistioge
   and Kilfane *C & O*   I *Vacant*   Kilkenny (56) 28115
KELLS w Balrathboyne, Moynalty, Donaghpatrick and
   Castletown *M & K*   I A R COLDEN
KENMARE w Sneem (Kilcrohane), Dromod (Waterville)
   and Valentia *L & K*   P-in-c R M CALDWELL
KILBARRON (Ballyshannon) w Rossnowlagh and
   Drumholm *D & R*   I W B PAINE
KILBRIDE *Conn*   I C HALL-THOMPSON
KILBRONEY (Rostrevor) *D & D*   I D C L JAMESON
KILCOLMAN w Kiltallagh, Killorglin, Knockane and
   Glenbeigh *L & K*   I M J D SHANNON,
   C M J McCANN, J C STEPHENS
KILCOOLEY w Littleton (Borris), Crohane and Fertagh
   C & O   I E C ARGYLE
KILCRONAGHAN (Tobermore) w Draperstown and
   Sixtowns *D & R*   I J M WHITE
KILDARE St Brigid's Cathedral w Kilmeague and
   Curragh Garrison Church *M & K*   I M BYRNE
KILDRESS w Altedesert *Arm*   I W M ADAIR
KILGARIFFE (Clonakilty) w Kilmalooda, Kilnagross,
   Timoleague and Courtmacsherry *C, C & R*
   I D O N SEALY
KILKEEL *D & D*   I D A McCLAY

KILKENNY St Canice Cathedral w St John, Aghour and Kilmanagh *C & O*   **C** H E FINLAY

KILL (Kill o' the Grange) *D & G*   **I** W S GIBBONS

KILLALA St Patrick's Cathedral w Dunfeeny, Crossmolina and Kilcommon Erris *T, K & A*   **I** E G ARDIS

KILLALOE St Flannan's Cathedral w Stradbally, Clonlara, Mountshannon, Abingdon and Tuomgraney *L & K*   **I** E C T PERDUE,   **NSM** A M O FERGUSON

KILLANEY w Carryduff St Ignatius *D & D*   **I** R FOX

KILLANNE w Killegney, Rossdroit and Templeshanbo *C & O*   **I** A M JACKSON

KILLARNEY w Aghadoe and Muckross *L & K*   **I** B F B LOUGHEED

KILLEAD w Gartree *Conn*   **Bp's C** J R L MUSGRAVE

KILLESHANDRA w Killegar and Derrylane *K, E & A*   **I** *Vacant*

KILLESHER *K, E & A*   **I** J R SIDES

KILLESHIN w Cloydagh and Killabban (Castletown) *C & O*   **I** G W CHAMBERS

KILLINAGH (Blacklion) w Kiltyclogher and Innismagrath (Drumkeeran) *K, E & A*   **I** R S P RICHEY

KILLINCHY w Kilmood and Tullynakill *D & D*   **I** R R W DEVENNEY

KILLINEY (Ballybrack) *D & G*   **I** E C J WOODS

KILLINEY Holy Trinity *D & G*   **I** H C MILLS

KILLOWEN *D & R*   **I** I H McDONALD,   **NSM** V E HANSON

KILLUCAN w Clonard and Castlelost (Rochfort Bridge) *M & K*   **I** *Vacant*   Mullingar (44) 74128

KILLYLEAGH *D & D*   **I** C R MITCHELL

KILLYMAN *Arm*   **I** M HARVEY

KILMACDUAGH w Ardrahan *L & K*   **I** *Vacant*

KILMAKEE (Seymour Hill) *Conn*   **I** F G RUTLEDGE,   **C** I TEMPLETON (nee McCUTCHEON)

KILMALLOCK w Kilflynn, Kilfinane, Knockaney, Bruff and Caherconlish *L & K*   **I** E B SNOW,   **NSM** T A SHERLOCK

KILMEGAN (Dundrum) w Maghera *D & D*   **I** B R RUSSELL

KILMOCOMOGUE UNION *C, C & R*   **I** C L PETERS

KILMOE (Goleen) w Teampol-na-mbocht (The Altar), Schull and Crookhaven *C, C & R*   **I** N M CUMMINS

KILMORE St Aidan w St Saviour *Arm*   **I** E T DUNDAS

KILMORE St Fethlimidh's Cathedral w Ballintemple, Kildallon, Newtowngore and Corrawallen *K, E & A*   **I** J C COMBE,   **C** S JOHNSON

KILMORE w Inch *D & D*   **I** L T C STEVENSON

KILMOREMOY (Ballina) w Castleconnor, Easkey, Kilglass and Straid (Foxford) *T, K & A*   **I** S IRVINE

KILROOT and Templecorran *Conn*   **I** I F R PATTERSON

KILSARAN w Drumcar, Dunleer and Dunany *Arm*   **C** A V G FLYNN

KILSCORAN w Killinick and Mulrankin *C & O*   **I** H J KEOGH

KILSKEERY w Trillick *Clogh*   **I** W J JOHNSTON

KILTEGAN w Hacketstown, Clonmore and Moyne *C & O*   **I** J L HAWORTH

KILTERNAN *D & G*   **I** D T MUIR

KILTOGHART (Carrick-on-Shannon) w Drumshambo, Annaduff and Kilronan *K, E & A*   **I** *Vacant*

KILWARLIN UPPER (St John) w Kilwarlin Lower (St James) *D & D*   **I** T D ALLEN

KILWAUGHTER w Cairncastle and Craigy Hill *Conn*   **I** W C McNEE

KINAWLEY (Derrylin) w Drumany and Crom *K, E & A*   **I** *Vacant*

KINGSCOURT (Enniskeen) w Drumconrath, Syddan and Moybologue *M & K*   **I** T G CORRIGAN

KINNEIGH (Ballineen) w Ballymoney, Kilmeen, Desertserges, Killowen and Murragh (Newcestown) *C, C & R*   **I** R P B MATHEWS

KINSALE w Runcurran (Summer Cove), Ballymartle and Templetrine *C, C & R*   **I** D WILLIAMS

KNOCK St Columba *D & D*   **I** G A McCAMLEY,   **C** I MOORE

KNOCKBREDA *D & D*   **I** P F PATTERSON,   **C** E J COULTER

KNOCKNAGONEY Annunciation *D & D*   **Bp's C** D BROWN

KNOCKNAMUCKLEY *D & D*   **I** J A McMASTER

LACK (Colaghty) *Clogh*   **I** R J JOHNSTON

LAMBEG *Conn*   **I** K A McREYNOLDS

LARNE and Inver *Conn*   **I** J A FAIR

LECALE Group w Saul, Loughinisland, Ardglass, Dunsford, Ballyculter and Kilclief *D & D*   **I** J A B MAYNE,   **C** B S CADDEN

LECKPATRICK w Dunnalong *D & R*   **I** D H J FERRY

LEIGHLIN St Laserian's Cathedral w Grange Sylvae, Shankill, Clonagoose (Borris) and Gowran *C & O*   **I** *Vacant*

LESKINFERE w Ballycanew and Monamolin *C & O*   **I** *Vacant*   Gorey (55) 27120

LIMERICK CITY St Mary's Cathedral w St Michael *L & K*   **I** J M G SIRR,   **C** C J YOUNG,   **NSM** M M GRAYSTACK

LISBELLAW *Clogh*   **I** R J ST LEGER

LISBURN Christ Church *Conn*   **I** S McCOMB,   **C** W A CAPPER, S J CAMPBELL

LISBURN Christ Church Cathedral *Conn*   **I** J T McCAMMON

LISBURN St Paul *Conn*   **I** K W COCHRANE,   **C** I A WILLIAMSON

LISMORE St Carthage's Cathedral w Cappoquin, Kilwatermoy (Fountains), Dungarvan, Kilrossanty (Comeragh), Stradbally and Rossmire (Kilmacthomas) *C & O*   **I** C W WEEKES

LISNADILL w Kildarton *Arm*   **I** M C KENNEDY

LISNASKEA *Clogh*   **I** *Vacant*   Lisnaskea (03657) 21237

LISSAN *Arm*   **I** R H BOYD

LONDONDERRY Christ Church *D & R*   **I** D S McLEAN

LONDONDERRY St Augustine *D & R*   **I** C HOWE

LOUGHGALL w Grange *Arm*   **I** *Vacant*

LOUGHGILLY w Clare *Arm*   **I** J L WILSON

LUCAN w Leixlip *D & G*   **I** E H DESPARD

LURGAN Shankill (Christ the Redeemer) (St Andrew) *D & D*   **I** K R GOOD,   **C** B J A CRUISE

LURGAN St John the Evangelist *D & D*   **I** S G BOURKE,   **C** I C BALLENTINE

LURGAN (Virginia) w Billis, Killinkere, Munterconnaught, Ballymachugh, Kildrumferton (Kilnaleck), and Ballyjamesduff *K, E & A*   **I** R G KINGSTON,   **C** R A CHALMERS

MAGHERA w Killelagh *D & R*   **I** *Vacant*

MAGHERACROSS (Ballinamallard) *Clogh*   **I** D P HOEY

MAGHERACULMONEY (Kesh) *Clogh*   **I** N N CROSSEY

MAGHERADROLL (Ballynahinch) *D & D*   **I** W W RUSSELL

MAGHERAFELT *Arm*   **I** T SCOTT

MAGHERAGALL *Conn*   **I** G A CHEEVERS

MAGHERALIN w Dollingstown *D & D*   **I** R L HUTCHINSON,   **C** T D STEVENSON

MAGHERALLY w Annaclone *D & D*   **I** G N SPROULE

MAGUIRESBRIDGE w Derrybrusk *Clogh*   **I** *Vacant*   Lisnaskea (03657) 250

MALAHIDE w Balgriffin *D & G*   **I** N E C GAMBLE

MALLOW w Doneraile St Mary and Castletownroche *C, C & R*   **I** *Vacant*   Mallow (22) 21473

MALLUSK *Conn*   **I** J S MARTIN

MARYBOROUGH w Dysart Enos and Ballyfin *C & O*   **I** P M DAY

MEVAGH (Carrigart) w Glenalla *D & R*   **I** D GRISCOME

MILLTOWN *Arm*   **I** M E G MOORE

MOHILL w Farnaught, Aughavas, Outeragh (Ballinamore), Kiltubride and Drumreilly *K, E & A*   **I** C L B H MEISSNER

MOIRA *D & D*   **I** C R J RUDD

MONAGHAN w Tydavnet and Kilmore *Clogh*   **I** *Vacant*

MONASTEREVAN w Nurney and Rathdaire *M & K*   **I** *Vacant*   Monasterevan (45) 25411

MONKSTOWN *Conn*   **Bp's C** A A McCARTNEY

MONKSTOWN *D & G*   **I** K DALTON

MOSSLEY *Conn*   **I** N R CUTCLIFFE,   **C** J J MOULD

MOSTRIM (Edgeworthstown) w Granard, Clonbroney (Ballinalea), Killoe, Rathaspeck (Rathowen) and Streete *K, E & A*   **I** T G HUDSON

MOUNT MERRION Pentecost *D & D*   **I** R C NEILL

MOUNTMELLICK w Coolbanagher, Rosenallis and Clonaslee *M & K*   **I** R S J BOURKE

MOVIDDY (Aherla), Kilbonane, Kilmurry, Templemartin and Macroom *C, C & R*   **NSM** J E FENNING

MOVILLA *D & D*   **I** M WITHERS

MOVILLE w Greencastle, Donagh, Cloncha and Culdaff *D & R*   **I** H GILMORE

MOY w Charlemont *Arm*   **I** C W M ROLSTON

MUCKAMORE *Conn*   **I** E W HASSEN

MULLABRACK w Markethill and Kilcluney *Arm*   **I** W R FERGUSON,   **NSM** N J HUGHES

MULLAVILLY *Arm*   **I** I M ELLIS,   **NSM** D W ROBINSON

MULLINGAR w Portnashangan, Moyliscar, Kilbixy (Ballinacargy) and Almoritia *M & K*   **I** S F GILLMOR,   **C** S ZIETSMAN

NAAS w Kill and Rathmore *M & K*   **I** W J STEWART

NARRAGHMORE w Timolin, Castledermot and
  Kinneagh *D & G*   I   J C HEALEY,   **NSM**   D PIERPOINT
NAVAN w Kentstown, Tara, Slane, Painestown and
  Stackallen *M & K*   I   A J GRIMASON
NENAGH w Ballymackey, Templederry and Killodiernan
  L & K   I   P L TOWERS
NEW ROSS w Old Ross, Whitechurch, Fethard St Mogue,
  Killesk and Tintern *C & O*   I   *Vacant*
NEWBRIDGE w Carnalway and Kilcullen *M & K*
  I   W B HENEY
NEWCASTLE *D & D*   I   T R WILLIAMS
NEWCASTLE w Newtownmountkennedy and Calary
  D & G   I   T R JENNINGS
NEWRY St Mary *D & D*   I   T G D ANDREWS
NEWRY St Patrick *D & D*   I   M R WILSON
NEWTOWNARDS *D & D*   I   K J SMYTH,
  C A J TOTTEN,   **Hon C** N L WHITE
NEWTOWNHAMILTON w Ballymoyer and Pomeroy
  and Belleek *Arm*   I   C F MOORE,   **NSM** W J A DAWSON
OMEY w Ballynakill, Errislannan and Roundstone
  (Moyrus) *T, K & A*   I   A M A PREVITE
ORANGEFIELD St John w Moneyreagh *D & D*
  I   W J R LAVERTY,   **C** P THOMPSON
PORTADOWN St Columba *Arm*   I   N N LYNAS,
  C N McCAUSLAND
PORTADOWN St Mark *Arm*   I   W R TWADDELL,
  C D MORROW, E P DUNDAS
PORTARLINGTON (French Church) w Cloneyhurke and
  Lea *M & K*   I   J S PEOPLES
POWERSCOURT (Enniskerry) w Kilbride and
  Annacrevy *D & G*   I   R D SMITH
RAHENY w Coolock *D & G*   I   C M WILSON,
  C B A PIERCE
RAMOAN w Ballycastle and Culfeightrin *Conn*
  I   W A DUNCAN,   **NSM** C SINCLAIR
RAPHOE St Eunan's Cathedral w Raymochy and
  Clonleigh (Lifford) *D & R*   I   S W REEDE
RATHCOOLE *Conn*   I   S D HAZLETT
RATHCOONEY (Glanmire) w Little Island and
  Carrigtwohill *C, C & R*   I   M H G MAYES
RATHDOWNEY w Castlefleming, Donaghmore,
  Rathsaran and Aghavoe *C & O*   I   J G MURRAY
RATHDRUM w Glenealy, Derralossary and Laragh
  D & G   I   C N R HALLIDAY
RATHKEALE w Askeaton, Foynes and Kilcornan *L & K*
  I   K S DUNN
RATHMICHAEL *D & G*   I   W J MARSHALL
RATHMOLYON w Castlerickard, Rathcore and Agher
  M & K   I   R G McCOLLUM
RATHMULLAN w Tyrella *D & D*   I   *Vacant*
  Ballykinler (039685) 237
RICHHILL *Arm*   I   R W R COLTHURST
ROSCOMMON w Donamon, Rathcline (Lanesborough),
  Kilkeevin (Castlerea), Kiltullagh (Ballinlough) and
  Tybohine (Frenchpark) *K, E & A*   I   *Vacant*
  Roscommon (903) 26230
ROSCREA w Kyle, Bourney and Corbally *L & K*
  I   J A A CONDELL
ROSS St Fachtna's Cathedral (Rosscarbery) w Kilmacabea
  (Leap), Myross, Kilfaughnabeg (Glandore) and
  Castleventry *C, C & R*   I   R K TOWNLEY
ROSSORY *Clogh*   I   C T PRINGLE
SAINTFIELD *D & D*   I   N W WOODROW
SALLAGHY *Clogh*   **Bp's C** W FENTON
SEAGOE *D & D*   I   D R CHILLINGWORTH
SEAPATRICK (Banbridge) *D & D*   I   W J SCOTT,
  C D H BOYLAND
SHINRONE w Aghancon, Dunkerrin and Kinnitty *L & K*
  I   R B HAYTHORNTHWAITE
SIXMILECROSS w Termonmaguirke *Arm*
  I   M A ARMSTRONG
SKERRY (Broughshane) w Rathcavan and
  Newtowncrommelin *Conn*   I   T V STONEY
SKREEN w Kilmacshalgan and Dromard *T, K & A*
  Bp's C A G MITCHELL

SLIGO St Mary and St John the Baptist Cathedral w
  Knocknarea and Rosses Point *K, E & A*   I   *Vacant*
STILLORGAN w Blackrock *D & G*   I   M A GRAHAM
STONEYFORD *Conn*   **Bp's C** C J WILCOCK
STORMONT St Molua *D & D*   I   E R HAMILTON
STRADBALLY w Ballintubbert, Coraclone, Timogue
  and Luggacurren *C & O*   I   W BEARE
STRANORLAR w Meenglas and Kilteevogue *D & R*
  I   J E HENDERSON
SWANLINBAR w Tomregan (Ballyconnell), Kinawley,
  Drumlane and Templeport *K, E & A*   I   R G KEOGH
SWORDS w Donabate and Kilsallaghan *D & G*
  I   W S BAIRD
TAGHMON w Horetown and Bannow *C & O*
  I   E A BRANDON
TALLAGHT *D & G*   I   W S LAING,   **NSM** A W YOUNG
TAMLAGHT O'CRILLY, Upper w Lower *D & R*
  I   H R GIVEN
TAMLAGHTARD w Aghanloo *D & R*   I   *Vacant*
  Bellarena (05047) 239
TAMLAGHTFINLAGAN (Limavady) w Myroe *D & R*
  I   R D MOORE
TANEY w St Nahi *D & G*   I   W D SINNAMON,
  C F C APPELBE,   **NSM** R C REED
TARTARAGHAN w Diamond *Arm*   I   W E C FLEMING
TAUGHBOYNE St Baithan w Craigadooish,
  Newtowncunningham and Killea (Carrigans) *D & R*
  I   D W T CROOKS
TAUNAGH (Riverstown) w Kilmactranny,
  Ballysumaghan and Killery (Ballintogher) *K, E & A*
  I   *Vacant*   Sligo (71) 65368
TEMPLEBREEDY (Crosshaven) w Tracton and Nohoval
  C, C & R   I   P H A LAWRENCE
TEMPLEMICHAEL (Longford) w Clongish
  (Newtownforbes), Clooncumber, Killashee and
  Ballymacormack *K, E & A*   I   R S JACKSON
TEMPLEMORE St Columb's Cathedral Londonderry
  D & R   I   D C ORR,   **C** D SKUCE
TEMPLEMORE w Thurles, Kilfithmone, Holycross and
  Mealiffe *C & O*   I   N YOUNG
TEMPLEPATRICK w Donegore *Conn*   I   E H GOUGH
TEMPO and Clabby *Clogh*   I   D R JUPE
TRALEE w Kilmoyley, Ballymacelligott, Ballyseedy,
  Kilnaughtin (Tarbert), Listowel and Ballybunnion
  L & K   I   R WARREN
TRIM St Patrick's Cathedral w Bective and Galtrim
  M & K   I   J A G BARRETT
TRORY w Killadeas *Clogh*   I   T R MOORE
TUAM St Mary's Cathedral w Cong and Aasleagh
  T, K & A   I   W J GRANT
TULLAMORE w Durrow, Newtownfertullagh, Rahan,
  Tyrellspass and Killoughy *M & K*   I   *Vacant*
  Tullamore (506) 21367
TULLANISKIN w Clonoe *Arm*   I   G R SHAW
TULLOW *D & G*   I   K A KEARON
TULLOW w Shillelagh, Aghold and Mullinacuff *C & O*
  I   N J W SHERWOOD
TULLYAUGHNISH (Ramelton) w Kilmacrennan and
  Killygarvan *D & R*   I   W B A SMEATON
TULLYLISH *D & D*   I   D WILSON
TYNAN w Middletown *Arm*   **Bp's C** R D LAWRENSON
URNEY (Cavan) w Denn and Derryheen *K, E & A*
  I   M R LIDWILL
URNEY w Sion Mills *D & R*   I   R C THOMPSON
WATERFORD Christ Church Cathedral w Killea
  (Dunmore East), Drumcannon (Tramore) and Dunhill
  (Annestown) *C & O*   I   W B A NEILL
WEXFORD w Ardcolm and Killurin *C & O*
  I   T H W DUNWOODY,   **NSM** I T EASTWOOD
WHITEHEAD w Islandmagee *Conn*   I   K E RUDDOCK
WHITEHOUSE *Conn*   I   E J H SHEPHERD
WICKLOW w Killiskey *D & G*   I   S PETTIGREW
WILLOWFIELD *D & D*   I   N JARDINE
WOODSCHAPEL w Gracefield *Arm*   I   T S COULSON
YOUGHAL w Ardmore, Castlemartyr and Ballycotton
  C, C & R   I   SIR H M D M S G DURAND, Bt

CATHEDRALS
Church of England

(BATH AND) WELLS (St Andrew)   DEAN R LEWIS
CANS RES S R CUTT, G O FARRAN, P de N LUCAS,
VEN C E THOMAS   EDUCN OFFICER C M BONNEYWELL
BIRMINGHAM (St Philip)   PROVOST P A BERRY
CANS RES VEN C J G BARTON, L M DAVIES
SUCC M PALMER
BLACKBURN (St Mary)   PROVOST L JACKSON
CANS RES B M BEAUMONT, G I HIRST, M A KITCHENER,
J M TAYLOR
BRADFORD (St Peter)   PROVOST J S RICHARDSON
CANS RES K H COOK, C J HAYWARD
CHAPLS P A WALKER, R E WALKER
BRISTOL (Holy Trinity)   DEAN A W CARR
CANS RES P F JOHNSON, A LL J REDFERN, J L SIMPSON
SUCC R H CHUBB   CHAPL S A N DARLEY
CANTERBURY (Christ)   DEAN J A SIMPSON
CANS RES P G C BRETT, C A LEWIS, J DE SAUSMAREZ,
VEN M S TILL   PREC S SEALY
CARLISLE (Holy Trinity)   DEAN H E C STAPLETON
CAN RES R A CHAPMAN, R C JOHNS, VEN C P STANNARD
CATHL DN M A MARSH
CHELMSFORD (St Mary, St Peter and St Cedd)
PROVOST J H MOSES   CANS RES P G BRETT, D C KNIGHT,
P G SOUTHWELL-SANDER, B P THOMPSON, T THOMPSON
CHAPL J D JONES
CHESTER (Christ and Blessed Virgin Mary)
DEAN S S SMALLEY   CANS RES O A CONWAY,
C D BIDDELL
CHICHESTER (Holy Trinity)   DEAN J D TREADGOLD
CANS RES R T GREENACRE, F J HAWKINS, J F HESTER
PRIEST VICAR D NASON
COVENTRY (St Michael)   PROVOST J F PETTY
CANS RES G T HUGHES, M SADGROVE, P OESTREICHER
SUCC J F BLACKMAN
DERBY (All Saints)   PROVOST B H LEWERS
CANS RES G A CHESTERMAN, VEN R S DELL, I GATFORD,
G R ORCHARD
DURHAM (Christ and Blessed Virgin Mary)
DEAN J R ARNOLD   CANS RES R L COPPIN, T HART,
VEN J D HODGSON, VEN M C PERRY
PREC C W NEWLANDS
ELY (Holy Trinity)   DEAN M J HIGGINS
CANS RES D J GREEN, J RONE   MIN CANS F J KILNER,
S E B SHIPLEY
EXETER (St Peter)   DEAN R M S EYRE
CANS RES A C MAWSON, K C PARRY, VEN J RICHARDS
PRIEST VICAR G DAXTER
GLOUCESTER (St Peter and Holy Trinity)
DEAN K N JENNINGS   CANS RES A L DUNSTAN,
R P GREENWOOD, R D M GREY   CHAPL V F FAULL
GUILDFORD (Holy Spirit)   DEAN A G WEDDERSPOON
CANS RES P G CROFT, R D FENWICK, F S TELFER
HEREFORD (Blessed Virgin Mary and St Ethelbert)
DEAN P HAYNES   CANS RES P R ILES, R A MASTERS,
J TILLER, VEN A H WOODHOUSE   SUCC M J GILL
LEICESTER (St Martin)   PROVOST A C WARREN
CAN RES M T H BANKS   PREC A CLEMENTS
LICHFIELD (Blessed Virgin Mary and St Chad)
DEAN J H LANG   CANS RES A N BARNARD, J HOWE,
VEN R B NINIS, W J TURNER
PRIEST VICAR P L HOLLIDAY
LINCOLN (Blessed Virgin Mary)   DEAN B D JACKSON
CANS RES B R DAVIS, VEN J H C LAURENCE, J S NURSER
CHAPL J MONTAGUE
LIVERPOOL (Christ)   DEAN R D C WALTERS
CANS RES D J HUTTON, K J RILEY, H G THOMAS,
M M WOLFE   CHAPL J C LYNN
LONDON (St Paul)   DEAN T E EVANS
CANS RES VEN G H CASSIDY, R J HALLIBURTON, C J HILL,
M J SAWARD   MIN CANS C J MANN, S J WAINE
CHAPL C T J CHESSUN
MANCHESTER (St Mary, St Denys and St George)
DEAN R M WADDINGTON   CANS RES J R ATHERTON,
B DUNCAN, VEN R B HARRIS, A E RADCLIFFE
NEWCASTLE (St Nicholas)   PROVOST N G COULTON
CANS RES I F BENNETT, R LANGLEY, P R STRANGE,
VEN W J THOMAS
NORWICH (Holy Trinity)   DEAN J P BURBRIDGE
CANS RES C E BESWICK, D H BISHOP, M S McLEAN

OXFORD (Christ Church)   DEAN E W HEATON
CANS RES O M T O'DONOVAN, J M PEIRCE,
VEN F V WESTON, M F WILES, R D WILLIAMS
PREC J R N J BOMYER
PETERBOROUGH (St Peter, St Paul and St Andrew)
DEAN R G WISE   CANS RES T R CHRISTIE, J HIGHAM,
T WILMOTT
PORTSMOUTH (St Thomas of Canterbury)
PROVOST D S STANCLIFFE   CANS RES C J BRADLEY,
M D DOE, R H ECKERSLEY, D T ISAAC   PREC B FENTON
RIPON (St Peter and St Wilfrid)   DEAN C R CAMPLING
CANS RES D G FORD, M R GLANVILLE-SMITH,
P J MARSHALL   MIN CANS P GREENWELL, M P SPURGEON
ROCHESTER (Christ and Blessed Virgin Mary)
DEAN E F SHOTTER   CANS RES J M ARMSON, R J R LEA,
E R TURNER, VEN N L WARREN   SUCC G J KIRK
ST ALBANS (St Alban)   DEAN P C MOORE   CANS RES
C GARNER, B G E PETTIFER, G R S RITSON, M C SANSOM,
C B SLEE   PREC M P J BONNEY   CHAPL A M STEAD
ST EDMUNDSBURY (St James)   PROVOST R FURNELL
CANS RES R GARRARD, A M SHAW, G J TARRIS
CHAPL M E MINGINS
SALISBURY (Blessed Virgin Mary)
DEAN H G DICKINSON   CANS RES D J C DAVIES,
I G D DUNLOP, J R STEWART
CATHL DN C M FARRINGTON
SHEFFIELD (St Peter and St Paul)
PROVOST J W GLADWIN   CANS RES J R GILES,
VEN S R LOWE, T M PAGE, C M SMITH
SODOR AND MAN (St German)   DEAN THE BISHOP
CAN PREC B H KELLY
SOUTHWARK (St Saviour and St Mary Overie)
PROVOST D L EDWARDS   CANS RES M KITCHEN,
D S PAINTER, P H PENWARDEN, P B PRICE,
I G SMITH-CAMERON   SUCC N J WORN
SOUTHWELL (Blessed Virgin Mary)
PROVOST D LEANING   CANS RES M R AUSTIN,
P H BOULTON, I G COLLINS, D P KEENE
VICAR CHORAL J A WARDLE
TRURO (St Mary)   DEAN D J SHEARLOCK
CANS RES W J P BOYD, R O OSBORNE,
VEN R L RAVENSCROFT
WAKEFIELD (All Saints)   PROVOST J E ALLEN
CANS RES R D BAXTER, C DAWSON, I C KNOX
CATHL DN A JENNINGS
WINCHESTER (Holy Trinity, St Peter, St Paul and St
Swithun)   DEAN T R BEESON   CANS RES P A BRITTON,
E R G JOB, A F KNIGHT, RT REV M R J MANKTELOW,
A K WALKER
WORCESTER (Christ and Blessed Virgin Mary)
DEAN R M C JEFFERY   CANS RES VEN F H W BENTLEY,
I M MacKENZIE, D G THOMAS   PREC T E HOLME
YORK (St Peter)   DEAN J E SOUTHGATE
CANS RES R A HOCKLEY, R MAYLAND, R METCALFE,
J TOY   VICAR CHORAL L C CARBERRY

Collegiate Churches

COLLEGIATE CHURCH OF ST PETER, Westminster
(Westminster Abbey)   DEAN M C O MAYNE
CANS P S BATES, D C GRAY, A E HARVEY, C D SEMPER
PREC A H F LUFF   CHAPL P J FERGUSON
QUEEN'S FREE CHAPEL OF ST GEORGE
Windsor Castle (St George's Chapel)
DEAN P R MITCHELL   CANS A A COLDWELLS,
M A MOXON, D M STANESBY, J A WHITE
MIN CANS T HARVEY, S F JONES

Diocese in Europe

GIBRALTAR (Holy Trinity)   DEAN B W HORLOCK
MALTA Valletta (St Paul)   PRO-CATHEDRAL
CHAN P COUSINS
BRUSSELS (Holy Trinity)   PRO-CATHEDRAL
CHAN VEN J LEWIS

Church in Wales

The name of the Dean is given, together with other clergy holding full-time appointments.

BANGOR (St Deiniol)　DEAN T E P EDWARDS
　CAN RES R LL OWEN　MIN CAN D H JAMES
LLANDAFF (St Peter and St Paul)　DEAN A R DAVIES
　SUCC S P KIRK
MONMOUTH Newport (St Woolos)　DEAN D G LEWIS
　MIN CAN A C EDWARDS
ST ASAPH (St Asaph)　DEAN C R RENOWDEN
　PRIEST VICAR R H GRIFFITHS
ST DAVIDS (St David and St Andrew)　DEAN B LEWIS
　MIN CAN J T WILLIAMS　SUCC A F HERRICK
(SWANSEA AND) BRECON (St John the Evangelist)
　DEAN D H JONES　CAN RES B H JONES
　MIN CAN H M LERVY

Scottish Episcopal Church

For the members of the chapter the *Year Book and Directory of the Scottish Episcopal Church* should be consulted.

Aberdeen and Orkney

ABERDEEN (St Andrew)　PROVOST D HOWARD

Argyll and The Isles

OBAN (St John)　PROVOST A M MACLEAN
　CHAPL F J KING
CUMBRAE (Holy Spirit) Cathedral of The Isles
　PROVOST D McCUBBIN

Brechin

DUNDEE (St Paul)　PROVOST P O SANDERSON

Edinburgh

EDINBURGH (St Mary)　PROVOST G J T FORBES
　VICE-PROVOST I J PATON　CHAPL A J BAIN

Glasgow and Galloway

GLASGOW (St Mary)　PROVOST M E GRANT
　CHAPL K L MACAULAY　DN S R PAISLEY

Moray, Ross and Caithness

INVERNESS (St Andrew)　PROVOST A A HORSLEY

St Andrews, Dunkeld and Dunblane

PERTH (St Ninian)　PROVOST K G FRANZ
　PREC I D BARCROFT

Church of Ireland

Most Cathedrals are parish churches and the Dean is usually, but not always, the incumbent. For the members of the chapter the *Church of Ireland Directory* should be consulted. The name of the Dean is given, together with other clergy holding full-time appointments.

NATIONAL CATHEDRAL OF ST PATRICK, Dublin
　Vacant　DEAN'S VICAR C R J BRADLEY
CATHEDRAL OF ST ANNE, Belfast　J SHEARER
　VICAR CHORAL W D HUMPHRIES
(St Anne's is a cathedral of the dioceses of Down and Dromore and of Connor)

PROVINCE OF ARMAGH

Armagh

ARMAGH (St Patrick)　H CASSIDY

Clogher

CLOGHER (St Macartan)　J F McCARTHY
ENNISKILLEN (St Macartan) *Dean of Clogher*

Derry and Raphoe

DERRY (St Columb)　D C ORR
RAPHOE (St Eunan)　S W REEDE

Down and Dromore

DOWN (Holy and Undivided Trinity)　H LECKEY
DROMORE (Christ the Redeemer)　M R WILSON

Connor

LISBURN (Christ)　J A FAIR *Dean of Connor*

Kilmore, Elphin and Ardagh

KILMORE (St Fethlimidh)　J C COMBE
SLIGO (St Mary and St John the Baptist)　*Vacant*
　(Dean of Elphin and Ardagh)

Tuam, Killala and Achonry

TUAM (St Mary)　W J GRANT
KILLALA (St Patrick)　E G ARDIS
ACHONRY (St Crumnathy)　THE BISHOP

PROVINCE OF DUBLIN

Dublin and Glendalough

DUBLIN (Holy Trinity) Christ Church　J T F PATERSON
　PREC J R BARTLETT

Meath and Kildare

TRIM (St Patrick)
　J A G BARRETT *Dean of Clonmacnoise*
KILDARE (St Brigid)　M BYRNE

Cashel and Ossory

CASHEL (St John the Baptist)　G M D WOODWORTH
WATERFORD (Blessed Trinity) Christ Church
　W B A NEILL
LISMORE (St Carthage)　C W WEEKES
KILKENNY (St Canice)　*Vacant (Dean of Ossory)*
　BISHOP'S VICAR H E FINLAY
LEIGHLIN (St Laserian)　*Vacant*
FERNS (St Edan)　D K L EARL

Cork, Cloyne and Ross

CORK (St Fin Barre)　J M G CAREY
CLOYNE (St Colman)　G P ST J HILLIARD
ROSS (St Fachtna)　R K TOWNLEY

Limerick and Killaloe

LIMERICK (St Mary)　J M G SIRR
KILLALOE (St Flannan)　E C T PERDUE

THEOLOGICAL COLLEGES AND COURSES

This index includes the name of the Principal or Warden and the names of staff members who are Anglican clergy and whose appointments are at least half-time.

Theological Colleges

Chichester Theological College   Chichester, W Sussex PO19 1SG (Chichester (0243) 783369)
PRIN P G ATKINSON   VICE-PRIN W S CROFT
DIR STUDIES P M COLLINS   TUTORS/LECTS G DOWNS.
BRO REGINALD SSF

Church of Ireland Theological College   Braemor Park, Dublin 14, Republic of Ireland (010-353-1-975506)
PRIN J R BARTLETT   VICE-PRIN M E STEWART
TUTORS/LECTS K V KENNERLY. J J MARSDEN.
T W GORDON

Coates Hall Theological College   Rosebery Crescent, Edinburgh EH12 5JT (031-337 3838)
PRIN K S MASON   VICE-PRIN/DIR STUDIES J W GODDARD
TUTOR D L COLLINGWOOD

College of the Resurrection   Mirfield, W Yorks WF14 0BW (Mirfield (0924) 490441)
PRIN D J LANE   VICE-PRIN G GUIVER CR
DIR STUDIES P ALLAN CR   TUTORS/LECTS T E EDGAR.
J GRIBBEN CR

Cranmer Hall   St John's College, Durham DH1 3RJ (091-374 3579)
PRIN *St John's* A C THISELTON
WARDEN *Cranmer Hall* I P M CUNDY
DIR PAST STUDIES J L PRITCHARD
TUTORS/LECTS C M JONES. M PARKER. M R VASEY

Lincoln Theological College   Wordsworth Street, Lincoln LN1 3BP (Lincoln (0522) 538885)
WARDEN W M JACOB   SUB-WARDEN N S F ALLDRIT
DIR STUDIES N BURGESS

Oak Hill Theological College   Chase Side, Southgate, London N14 4PS (081-449 0467)
PRIN G F BRIDGER   VICE-PRIN D H FIELD
ACADEMIC REGISTRAR R W HEINZE
TUTORS/LECTS G L BRAY. G M BUTTERWORTH.
R A HINES. P D A WESTON

The Queen's College at Birmingham   Somerset Road, Edgbaston, Birmingham B15 2QH (Birmingham (021) 454 1527)
PRIN J B WALKER[1]   VICE-PRIN D C PARKER
TUTORS D J KENNEDY. J L WILKINSON, B M WOODWARD

Ridley Hall   Cambridge CB3 9HG (Cambridge (0223) 353040)
PRIN H F DE WAAL   VICE-PRIN N S POLLARD
DIR STUDIES J S BEGBIE
TUTORS/LECTS A M E OSMASTON. J PARR

Ripon College Cuddesdon   Cuddesdon, Oxford OX9 9EX (Wheatley (08677) 4427 or 4595 or 4404)
PRIN J H GARTON   VICE-PRIN A R BILLINGS
DIR STUDIES J L DRAPER   TUTORS/LECTS A A LE GRYS

St Deiniol's Library   Hawarden, Deeside, Clwyd CH5 3DF (Chester (0244) 532350)
WARDEN P J JAGGER   SUB-WARDEN E M BURGESS

St John's College   Bramcote, Nottingham NG9 3DS (Nottingham (0602) 251114)
PRIN J E GOLDINGAY   DIR STUDIES M B THOMPSON
TUTORS/LECTS J R BOWEN. A F CHATFIELD. G A COOPER.
C E HART. D M MUIR. T G OLIVER. J E M SINCLAIR

St Michael and All Angels' College   54 Cardiff Road, Llandaff, Cardiff CF5 2YF (Cardiff (0222) 563379)
WARDEN J H L ROWLANDS   SUB-WARDEN R M HARPER
DIR PAST STUDIES J GAINER

St Stephen's House   16 Marston Street, Oxford OX4 1JX (Oxford (0865) 247874)
PRIN E R BARNES   VICE-PRIN C P IRVINE
DIR STUDIES F F J FRANKLIN   TUTORS R HANNAFORD.
E B BARDWELL

Salisbury and Wells Theological College   19 The Close, Salisbury, Wilts SP1 2EE (Salisbury (0722) 332235)
PRIN P A CROWE   VICE-PRIN T J DENNIS
DIR STUDIES D V WAY

Trinity College   Stoke Hill, Bristol, Avon BS59 1JP (Bristol (0272) 682803)
PRIN D K GILLETT   VICE-PRIN J NOLLAND
DIR STUDIES D J E ATTWOOD
TUTORS/LECTS C J D GREENE, P P JENSON, R H PESKETT.
P J ROBERTS, S M ROSE

Westcott House   Jesus Lane, Cambridge CB5 8BP (Cambridge (0223) 350074)
PRIN R W N HOARE   VICE-PRIN M G V ROBERTS
DIR STUDIES A K BERGQUIST

Wycliffe Hall   54 Banbury Road, Oxford OX2 6PW (Oxford (0865) 274000)
PRIN R T FRANCE   SEN TUTOR P J M SOUTHWELL
TUTORS/LECTS G HEGARTY, A E McGRATH, V M SINTON,
G O STONE, G S TOMLIN, D WENHAM

Part-Time Courses

Canterbury School of Ministry   1 Lady Wootton's Green, Canterbury CT1 1TL (Canterbury (0227) 459401)
PRIN A J AMOS   VICE-PRIN J A C MANTLE

Carlisle Diocesan Training Institute   Church House, West Walls, Carlisle, Cumbria CA3 8UE (0228-22573)
PRIN M S LANGLEY

East Anglian Ministerial Training Course   E A M T C Office, Westcott House, Jesus Lane, Cambridge CB5 8BP (Cambridge (0223) 322633)
PRIN J G E KEMP   VICE-PRIN J B MYNORS
DIR PAST STUDIES B E WAY

East Midlands Ministry Training Course   Department of Adult Education, The University, Nottingham NG7 2RD (Nottingham (0602) 484848)
PRIN S F PARSONS[2]   VICE-PRIN M J TAYLOR

Gloucester and Hereford School for Ministry   College Green, Gloucester GL1 2LX (Gloucester (0452) 410022)
PRIN D C BRINDLEY   VICE-PRIN J F JONES

North East Ordination Course   Carter House, Pelaw Leazes Lane, Durham DH1 1TB (091-384 8317)
PRIN T PITT

Northern Ordination Course   Luther King House, Brighton Grove, Rusholme, Manchester M14 5JP (051-225 6668)
PRIN M J WILLIAMS   DIR STUDIES M M PARRY
TUTORS/LECTS W H HOPKINSON, C STERRY

Oak Hill Ministerial Training Course   Oak Hill College, Chase Side, Southgate, London N14 4PS (081-449 0467)
PRIN G F BRIDGER   DEAN D H FIELD
TUTORS/LECTS M ABBOTT, G L BRAY.
G M BUTTERWORTH. R W HEINZE. R A HINES

Oxford Ministry Course   Church House, North Hinksey, Oxford OX2 0NB (Oxford (0865) 244566)
PRIN V N H STRUDWICK   ASSOC PRIN G M SUMNER

St Albans Diocese Ministerial Training Scheme   Holywell Lodge, 41 Holywell Hill, St Albans, Herts AL1 1HE (St Albans (0727) 55530)
PRIN B G E PETTIFER   DIR STUDIES G V GILLARD
COURSE DIRS C HARDMAN, M REDFEARN

Southern Dioceses Ministerial Training Scheme   19 The Close, Salisbury SP1 2EE (0722-412996)
PRIN J J FULLER   VICE-PRIN R D HACKING
TUTOR T M W PINNER

Southwark Ordination Course   28 Blackfriars Road, London SE1 8NY (071-928 4793)
PRIN M J BADDELEY   DIR STUDIES A RACE

South West Ministry Training Course   32 Barnfield Road, Exeter, Devon EX1 1RX (0392 72091)
JOINT-PRINS J C SAXBEE. D J P HEWLETT

West Midlands Ministerial Training Course   The Queen's College, Somerset Road, Edgbaston, Birmingham B15 2QH (021-454 8597)
PRIN P R WHALE   VICE-PRIN P G FULLJAMES
TUTOR A JOYCE

Pre-Theological Training Courses

Aston Training Scheme   148 Court Oak Road, Harborne, Birmingham B17 9AB (021-427 5225)
PRIN D R SPILLER   VICE-PRIN P HAMMERSLEY
DIR STUDIES J PARSONS

The Simon of Cyrene Theological Insitute   2 St Anne's Crescent, Wandsworth, London SW18 2LR (081-874 1353)
PRIN S GOODRIDGE   TUTOR T SIMPSON

---

[1] Dr Walker is a Church of Scotland minister

[2] Dr Parsons is a layperson

CHAPLAINS TO HER MAJESTY'S SERVICES

ROYAL NAVY

Chaplain of the Fleet and Archdeacon for the Royal Navy
Ven M H G HENLEY CB, QHC
Ministry of Defence, Lacon House, Theobald's Road, London WC1X 8RY
071-430 6847

Chaplains RN

J P AMES	P S GALE	P NEEDHAM
D BARLOW	S J GOLDING	R NURTON
G J BATTEN	D H GOODBURN	S P PICKERING
R D BAXENDALE	J GREEN	M G POLL
S D BROOKES	H S GRIFFITHS	R L PYNE
M BROTHERTON	M J HARMAN	J E F RAWLINGS
R F BUCKLEY	J A HEMPENSTALL	E D J-B RENFREY
M W BUCKS	R G HILLIARD	A M ROSS
I J BUTLER	C W W HOWARD	I W RUTHERFORD
A M CALLON	M H JACKSON	S P SPRINGETT
B R CLARKE	P W JACKSON	S E STEPHENS
R C CUTLER	C JARMAN	R C SWEET
T DEVAMANIKKAM	N E JOHNSON	B H TALBOTT
R G DEVONSHIRE	E W JONES	D W W THOMAS
I EGLIN	T J LEWIS	G M WALSH
G M ELMORE	C J LUCKRAFT	B WALTON
B D S FAIRBANK	B G G MARSHALL	P W WARLAND
W H FRANKLIN	A J F METTERS	W E WELDON
C A FRENCH	I F NAYLOR	M L WISHART

ARMY

Chaplain-General to the Forces   Rev J HARKNESS OBE, QHC
(The present Chaplain-General is a Church of Scotland Minister)

Deputy Chaplain-General and Archdeacon of the Army   Ven G H ROBLIN OBE, QHC
Ministry of Defence (Army), Bagshot Park, Bagshot, Surrey GU19 5PL
Bagshot (0276) 71717

Chaplains to the Forces

J G W ANDREWS	R L GREEN	D J PEACHELL
A R N APPLEBY	S E GRIFFITH	D PEARSON-MILES
W G ASHTON	G F HADFIELD	K J PILLAR
K P ATHERLEY	R J HALL	J A H POLLARD
D G BAILEY	R W HAYTER	D J M POLLOCK
J A BARRIE	A J HEAGERTY	B D PRATT
G M BASS	D C HEAVER	A H PRICE
K D BELL	R A HEMMINGS	J R PRICE
J BLACKBURN	J J HOLLIMAN	S P RANDALL
J W BLAIR	J P HOOLEY	S ROBBINS
A J BOYD	D R JONES	W ROBSON
K M BRETEL	H L JONES	A J ROSE
C S T BRODDLE	M F JONES	L S ROSE
A J BROWN	R T JONES	P M RUTHERFORD
L H BRYAN	K R JOYCE	D B SMALL
M A G BRYCE	R L S KEAT	M J SMITH
A BUNNELL	N A KNIGHTS JOHNSON	P F A SPRINGFORD
R M BURT	R G LAIRD	R W STEVENS
A K BURTT	J M LOVEDAY	M R N STEVENSON
P J CABLE	R McALLEN	A P S SYNNOTT
R P CALDER	R C McCARTNEY	J TEE
A C CARRUTHERS	R A McDOWALL	P THOMPSON
P M CARTER	T R McKNIGHT	D A TICKNER
R F CLAYTON-JONES	R M MITCHELL	J C VERNON
J D S COATES	J W R MORRISON	C J A WALKER
J C D COOK	E P MOSLEY	D M T WALTERS
A W CUMBERLIDGE	J M NEVILL	G S S WATTS
A DEAN	R A OWEN	J C R WEBB
B ELLIOTT	D J PALMER	C P WELLS
C W GIBBS	F W PARKINSON	R E WILLIAMS
S G GOLDEN	S P PARSELLE	C M WILSON
J R B GOUGH	V J PAYNE	M A J WILSON
		K WRAY

ROYAL AIR FORCE

Chaplain-in-Chief   Ven B H LUCAS QHC
Assistant Chaplains-in-Chief   J E DAIMOND QHC, A P BISHOP,
A T R GOODE, G B McAVOY, P R TURNER
Ministry of Defence, Adastral House, Theobald's Road, London WC1X 8RU
071-430 7268

Chaplains RAF

P J ABELL	R D HESKETH	R NOBLE
J F AMBROSE	A D HEWETT	S J ORAM
R W BAILEY	C E HEWITT	G C OWEN
N B P BARRY	S H HOLT	C PARNELL-HOPKINSON
G S BROWN	J W G HUGHES	R J PENTLAND
K R BROWN	N B W JAMES	J C ROBERTS
N A BRYAN	A C E KNIGHT	M P ROEMMELE
J P M CHAFFEY	I A LAMBERT	B J RUMBOLD
L E D CLARK	A H J LANE	P SLADEN
S T COLLIS	T R LEE	B SMITH
E CORE	P R LEWIS	L E SPICER
J E COYNE	C W LONG	B R STEVENS
A J DAVIES	M F LOVELESS	A H THOMAS
C W K DAVIES	D J McKAVANAGH	I M THOMAS
M J ELLIOTT	D S MACKENZIE	A J TURNER
A P R FLETCHER	A B McMULLON	I S WARD
A C GATRILL	K MADDY	R A P WARD
A J D GILBERT	J M MASKELL	S J WARE
I F GREENHALGH	J MORLEY	I J WESTON
S GREENHALGH	C P MORTIMER	A L WILLIS
N P HERON	P J NICKOLS-RAWLE	J K WILSON
		D WYNNE-JONES

HOME OFFICE PRISON SERVICE
(England and Wales)

Chaplain General of Prisons   Ven K S POUND
Assistant Chaplain General (HQ)   G B K DODSWORTH
Prison Service Chaplaincy, Home Office, Cleland House, Page Street, London SW1P 4LN
071-217 6662

Assistant Chaplains General
J R HARGREAVES, R C PAYNE, P J TAYLOR
Home Office, Calthorpe House, Hagley Road, Birmingham B16 8QR
021-455 9855

At institutions with more than one chaplain the names are listed in order of seniority.

PRISONS

Acklington   T A McCARTHY
Albany   J H FLOWERS
Aldington   L WILLIAMS
Ashwell   J RIDLEY
Askham Grange   D H WATTS
Bedford   P E WILSON
Belmarsh   G HERRETT, P GREEN
Birmingham   B J GRACIE
Blantyre House   J H WAITE
Blundeston   R T COOK
Brinsford   G J SEWELL
Bristol   M PETERS
Brixton   P WESTWOOD
Bullwood Hall   J R D KEMP
Camp Hill   R A RUDD
Canterbury   H J CROWIE
Cardiff   M J KIDDLE
Channings Wood   I G HALLIWELL
Chelmsford   J K HAYWARD
Coldingley   G CLARKSON
Cookham Wood   J KING
Dartmoor   J D BIRD
Dorchester   D H SIM
Downview   A R BODDY
Drake Hall   J S COOKE
Durham   E M DIXON, J W GEEN
Eastwood Park   R W MARTIN
Elmley   G WILLIAMS
Everthorpe   R G RATHBONE
Exeter   W H BIRDWOOD
Featherstone   G A F GRIFFIN
Ford   B BARNES-CEENEY
Frankland   R ATTLEY
Full Sutton   I D GOMERSALL
Garth   P D AINSLEY
Gartree   S BINDOFF
Gloucester   A M LYNETT
Grendon   J F JAMES
Haslar   P A SUTTON
Haverigg   B G FLUX
Highpoint   E C GODFREY
Holloway   C BURGESS, M L KEARNS
Hull   C B DICK
Kingston   E H O'CONNOR
Kirkham   J LYNN
Lancaster   P R F CLEMENCE
Latchmere House   D L GAMBLE
Leeds   J M DIXON, D O CASSWELL

Leicester   M STARK
Lewes   D L I PERKS
Leyhill   A K SWANN
Lincoln   A R DUCE
Lindholme   P TARLETON
Littlehey   L MASTERS
Liverpool   A M BALL, A HIRST
Long Lartin   R F LODGE
Maidstone   E G HINN
Manchester   N PROCTOR
Moorland   S C BONNEY
Morton Hall   M R RENNARD
Mount, The   J K CRICHTON
New Hall   M E SMITH
North Sea Camp   B R GRELLIER
Northeye   G C NICHOLSON
Norwich   P C ROBSON
Nottingham   J E FITZGERALD
Oxford   H D DUPREE
Parkhurst   B G ANDERSON
Pentonville   W St C COLLINS
Preston   R P SPRATT
Ranby   G E S LARNER
Reading   D K HASTINGS
Rochester   R HIGGINBOTTOM
Rudgate   J W THEOBALD
Send   A R BODDY
Shepton Mallet   B W J MITFORD
Shrewsbury   R W D BIDDLE
Spring Hill   J F JAMES
Stafford   S BRACE
Standford Hill   R T GREEN
Stocken   M C CRADDUCK
Styal   P J JENNINGS
Sudbury   C COPLEY
Swaleside   D J BURTON
Swansea   E T HUNT
Thorp Arch   J W THEOBALD
Verne, The   J M BLOOMFIELD
Wakefield   W A NOBLETT
Wandsworth   P G W MEADEN, E SUTHERLAND
Wayland   G T DOCKRELL, J FELLINGHAM
Whatton   J PULMAN
Whitemoor   W J SALMON
Winchester   M J M NORTON
Wormwood Scrubs   R J GUYMER, P A NEWMAN,
   G E STEVENSON
Wymott   S RITCHIE

YOUNG OFFENDER INSTITUTIONS

Aylesbury   H D POTTER
Campsfield House   R G COPPEN
Castington   J M TRUMAN
Deerbolt   A P HARVEY
Dover   M W ROBERTS
Erlestoke   J P R SAUNT
Finnamore Wood   R R EARNSHAW
Foston Hall   C COPLEY
Gaynes Hall   P J TAYLOR
Glen Parva   J H J TEARNAN, H K DODHIA
Gringley   I R BAKER
Guys Marsh   D D BOTTERILL
Hatfield   P IRESON
Hewell Grange   M L PALMER

Hindley   R GIBBARD
Hollesley Bay Colony   E A GILES
Huntercombe   R R EARNSHAW
Kirklevington Grange   D MOORE
Lowdham Grange   W G CALTHROP-OWEN
Northallerton   B J MAYNE
Onley   G DARVILL
Portland   M L STEER
Stoke Heath   J M LUCAS
Swinfen Hall   J B ASTON, J R FAGAN
Usk   R L DAVIES
Wellingborough   N C DENT
Werrington   J L HUMPHREYS
Wetherby   D LAWRANCE

REMAND CENTRES

Brockhill   M L PALMER
Low Newton   E CUMMINGS

Pucklechurch   I L WILLS
Risley   D J WOODLEY

WHOLE-TIME HOSPITAL CHAPLAINS
(England and Wales)

An index of whole-time hospital chaplains (at their base hospital as defined by the Hospital Chaplaincies Council).
At institutions with more than one chaplain the names are listed in order of seniority.

Hospital Chaplaincies Council: Secretary Rev M BOURNE
Church House, Great Smith Street, London SW1P 3NZ
071-222 9011

ADDENBROOKE'S Cambridge   I J P MORRIS
ALEXANDRA Redditch   B M JONES
ALL SAINTS Birmingham   D L HART
ARROWE PARK Birkenhead   D E FATHERS
ASHWORTH   J C COSSINS
BARNSLEY DISTRICT GENERAL   M P YATES
BASINGSTOKE DISTRICT   P J GOOLD. J HEARN
BASSETLAW DISTRICT GENERAL   A J COOPER
BEDFORD GENERAL   J A TIBBS
BEXLEY   H A HATCHMAN
BOLTON GENERAL   N K GRAY
BRADFORD ROYAL INFIRMARY   O A OLUMIDE
BRIGHTON HEALTH AUTHORITY   G S JOHNSON
BRISTOL CHILDREN'S   C A M MANN
BRISTOL ROYAL INFIRMARY   A M M JARVIE
BROADGREEN Liverpool   A H P BAILLIE
BROADMOOR Crowthorne   T WALT
BROOK GENERAL London   J H SMITH
BROOKWOOD Woking   J R H PALMER
CARLTON HAYES   P F GREEN
CENTRAL Warwick   J E BAILEY
CHARING CROSS London   C W CAWRSE
CHELTENHAM GENERAL AND DELANCEY
   W B IRVINE
CHERRY KNOWLE Sunderland   C J WORSFOLD
CHESTERFIELD AND NORTH DERBY ROYAL
   J F SERJEANT
CHURCHILL Oxford   M E PARSONS
CLAYBURY Woodford Bridge   M O PRITCHARD
COALVILLE COMMUNITY   C F PATEY
COLCHESTER GENERAL   R SMITH
COUNTESS OF CHESTER   J A ROBERTS
DARLINGTON MEMORIAL   B SELMES
DERBY CITY   S TURNBULL
DERBY ROYAL INFIRMARY   T J PEARCE
DERRIFORD Plymouth   P S MACPHERSON
DONCASTER ROYAL INFIRMARY   J S B CROSSLEY
DRYBURN Durham   J READ
DUDLEY ROAD Birmingham   B A WIGLEY
DULWICH   J M ALLFORD
EALING GENERAL   P ROWNTREE
EAST BIRMINGHAM   A M BOYD
EAST SURREY Redhill   N WALTER
EASTBOURNE GROUP   W J R MORRISON
EPSOM DISTRICT   C VALLINS
EXETER GROUP   D J WALFORD
FAIRFIELD Hitchin   C H BROWNLIE
FARNBOROUGH Orpington   N J BUNKER
FREEMAN Newcastle upon Tyne   M MASTERMAN.
   C A ASHLEY
FRENCHAY Bristol   R H TORRENS
FRIMLEY PARK   A W WARNER
FULBOURN Cambridge   J M LAW
FURNESS GENERAL   G GARBUTT
GEORGE ELIOT Nuneaton   E C POGMORE
GLENFIELD AND GLENFRITH Leicester
   T H GIRLING
GLENSIDE Bristol   R MEREDITH-JONES
GLOUCESTERSHIRE ROYAL   D H GODWIN
GOOD HOPE Sutton Coldfield   A T BALL
GREAT ORMOND STREET London   D R A BACON.
   R M PARTRIDGE
GREENWICH DISTRICT London   S W BRAND
GRIMSBY DISTRICT GENERAL   H D TER BLANCHE.
   H D CONNOLL
GUY'S London   C H N SMITH

HAMMERSMITH London   E MORRIS
HARPERBURY Radlett   N HULME
HARROGATE DISTRICT   R R WATSON
HEREFORD COUNTY   P A ROBERTS
HERRISON Dorchester   N D TOOTH
HIGH ROYDS Menston   W RUCK
HIGHCROFT Birmingham   F LONGBOTTOM
HILL END St Albans   J A WOOLLEY
HOMERTON London   D W HIZA. G S KENDALL
HOPE Salford   F N HOLMAN, A R MIR, W J McKAE
HORTON Epsom   A J LYNN
HULL ROYAL INFIRMARY   M P PICKERING
IPSWICH   J BROOKS. R WILKINSON
JAMES PAGET Gorleston   W C SNOOK
JERSEY GROUP   M INMAN
JOHN RADCLIFFE Oxford   N P FENNEMORE
KENT AND CANTERBURY Canterbury
   P R HEARTFIELD
KING'S COLLEGE London   S T MEYER
KINGSTON   A GRIFFITHS
KINGSWAY   S L RAYNER
KNOWLE Fareham   J L SHARPE
LANCASTER MOOR Lancaster   D V A BROWN
LEAVESDEN Abbots Langley   C L SMITH
LEEDS GENERAL INFIRMARY   D J RIVERS
LEICESTER GENERAL   R B HUNT
LEICESTER ROYAL INFIRMARY   C S RUSHFORTH.
   L J BUTLER
LEICESTERSHIRE HOSPICE   K G T COOK
LEWISHAM   A L SHAW
LINCOLN COUNTY   M W THORPE
LITTLEMORE Oxford   F B STEVENSON
LIVERPOOL ROYAL   S C PRATT
LONG GROVE Epsom   G D KING
LUTON AND DUNSTABLE   G MORGAN
MAIDSTONE   D A PORTER
MANCHESTER ROYAL INFIRMARY   A M RHODES.
   R J HURLOCK, V R SLATER
MANOR Epsom   R N T MOORE
MANOR Walsall   E J LEWIS
MAPPERLEY AND COMMUNITY Nottingham
   G A BUCKLER
MAUDSLEY London   J H FOSKETT
MAYDAY Thornton Heath   I G WOODROFFE
MEDWAY HEALTH AUTHORITY   H J CONNELL
MIDDLESEX London   D J MASON, P M G P G de FORTIS
MIDDLEWOOD Sheffield   J W BROWNING
MONYHULL Birmingham   B J B EASTER
MOSELEY HALL Birmingham   R G GLEESON
MUSGROVE PARK Taunton   G D EVANS
NAPSBURY St Albans   J D JOHNSON
NATIONAL HOSPITAL FOR NEUROLOGY AND
   NEUROSURGERY London   P W LEWIS
NETHERNE Coulsdon   N J COPSEY
NEW CROSS Wolverhampton   D J JOHNSON
NEWCASTLE UPON TYNE GENERAL   M J WILSON
NEWHAM GENERAL   L C STEWARD
NORFOLK AND NORWICH   L A J WARD
NORTH MANCHESTER GENERAL   M R MORGAN
NORTH STAFFORDSHIRE ROYAL INFIRMARY
   Stoke-on-Trent   C J STONE, K M BOND
NORTH TEES Stockton-on-Tees   W D HEADS
NORTHAMPTON GENERAL   L TURNER
NORTHERN GENERAL Sheffield   D E R EQUEALL.
   L A SHIPTON
NORTHWICK PARK Harrow   A J ANDREWS

NOTTINGHAM CITY   M J KERRY, D C F TUDOR,
M C GARDNER
ODSTOCK AND DISTRICT Salisbury   G M EVANS
OLDCHURCH Romford   C J CAREY
OLDHAM ROYAL   F D STUART
PASTURES Derby   G MARTIN
PEMBURY Tunbridge Wells   A P AYLING
PETERBOROUGH DISTRICT HOSPITALS
J N CHUBB
PILGRIM Boston   M G JOHNSON
PINDERFIELDS Wakefield   R W CRESSEY
POOLE GENERAL   E J LLOYD
PRESTON ROYAL   R T FLEMING
PRESTWICH Manchester   N BARNES
PRINCESS MARGARET Swindon   B M RICHARDS,
A BUCKNALL
PRINCESS ROYAL Telford   G A CROSSLEY
PRUDHOE Northumberland   M H WHEELWRIGHT
QUEEN ALEXANDRA Portsmouth   N H GERRANS
QUEEN ELIZABETH Birmingham   J W WOODWARD
QUEEN ELIZABETH Gateshead   J R PERRY
QUEEN ELIZABETH II Welwyn Garden City
G N BUSTARD
QUEEN ELIZABETH King's Lynn   A L HAIG
QUEEN MARY'S HOSPITAL FOR CHILDREN
Carshalton   H A SMITH
RAMPTON Retford   R A SIMMONS
ROTHERHAM DISTRICT HEALTH AUTHORITY
R E N WESTON
ROUNDWAY Devizes   G BARTON
ROYAL ALBERT Lancaster   R C DOBSON
ROYAL BERKSHIRE Reading   V MULLER
ROYAL CORNWALL Truro   C C R MERIVALE
ROYAL DEVON AND EXETER Exeter
M K WEATHERLEY
ROYAL EAST SUSSEX Hastings   R W DRAY
ROYAL FREE London   P W SPECK, P J B HINDLE
ROYAL HALLAMSHIRE Sheffield   W WATSON,
M J KELLAM
ROYAL HAMPSHIRE COUNTY Winchester
B K WENSLEY, R S CLARKE
ROYAL LONDON Whitechapel   P J COWELL,
C D NEWELL
ROYAL MARSDEN London and Surrey   D F BROWN,
J W SMITH
ROYAL SHREWSBURY   D W JOHNSON
ROYAL SOUTH HAMPSHIRE   D F KING
ROYAL SURREY AND DISTRICT Guildford
R R WYNNE-GREEN
ROYAL SUSSEX COUNTY Brighton   E G N HOLNESS
ROYAL UNITED Bath   C M ROBERTS
ROYAL VICTORIA INFIRMARY Newcastle upon
Tyne   A MAUDE, T WHITFIELD
RUBERY HILL Birmingham   V J F COX
ST ANDREW'S Northampton   J E CAMP
ST AUGUSTINE'S Canterbury   G W P WILTON
ST BARTHOLOMEW'S London   A M WHAWELL,
V H GOSHAI
ST CHARLES'S London   N J ROBERTS
ST CRISPIN Northampton   C R GOODLEY
ST FRANCIS'S Haywards Heath   L D POODHUN

ST GEORGE'S GROUP London   H A JOHNSON,
I M AINSWORTH-SMITH
ST GEORGE'S Lincoln   J A GREEN
ST GEORGE'S Stafford   G E O'BRIEN
ST HELIER'S Carshalton   C J MARSHALL
ST JAMES'S UNIVERSITY Leeds   H H HUXHAM,
P L BENSON
ST JOHN'S Aylesbury   M R SAUNDERS
ST LAWRENCE'S Bodmin   R S MITCHELL
ST LAWRENCE'S Caterham   R LAMONT
ST MARGARET'S Birmingham   P W JENNINGS
ST MARY'S (PRAED STREET) London   B A NEWTON
ST MARY'S GENERAL Portsmouth   H C THEOBALD,
P R ELLMORE
ST NICHOLAS'S Newcastle-upon-Tyne   F B ALLEN
ST PETER'S Chertsey   M A MORRIS
ST THOMAS'S London   M J STEVENS, A M HARLEY
SCUNTHORPE DISTRICT HEALTH AUTHORITY
D LOMAS
SEACROFT AND KILLINGBECK HOSPITALS Leeds
J E DAINTY
SELLY OAK Birmingham   D WRAPSON
SHOTLEY BRIDGE   K ALLISON
SOUTH WARWICKSHIRE HOSPITALS   P S KNIGHT
SOUTHAMPTON GENERAL   J P H SARGENT
SOUTHMEAD Bristol   D C DAVIES,
J V THOMPSON (nee LILLIE)
SPRINGFIELD London   A P R KYRIAKIDES-YELDHAM
STAFFORD DISTRICT GENERAL   I S VAUGHAN
STANLEY ROYD Wakefield   C M GARTLAND
STOKE MANDEVILLE Aylesbury   D CRAWLEY
STOKE-ON-TRENT CITY   D J HAWKINS
SUNDERLAND DISTRICT HOSPITALS   P H WEBB
TOOTING BEC London   A H BORTHWICK
TORBAY Torquay   J E HETHERINGTON
TOWERS Humberstone   N L COOK
UNIVERSITY COLLEGE London   T MORLEY,
D M LAWSON
UNIVERSITY HOSPITAL OF WALES Cardiff
D R LLOYD-RICHARDS
UNIVERSITY Nottingham   D J STOTER, J R HEATON,
J E SHEPHERD
WALSGRAVE Coventry   D H ROBINSON, D A HUNTLEY
WARLINGHAM PARK Croydon   A A WILSON
WARRINGTON DISTRICT GENERAL   P D MEARS
WATFORD GENERAL   M J CARTER
WEST MIDDLESEX Isleworth   J J CONGDON
WEST PARK Epsom   D B A JOHNSON
WEST SUFFOLK Bury St Edmunds   D G HOLLANDS
WESTMINSTER London   A RICHARDSON, B P HUGHES
WEXHAM PARK Slough   P J HARBORD
WHIPPS CROSS London   E J PORTEOUS
WHISTON   M THOMAS
WHITTINGTON London   P W A WHELAN
WHITTINGTON Preston   K S TIMBRELL
WINTERTON Sedgefield   I C SMITH
WINWICK Warrington   P G HOUGHTON
WITHAM COURT ESMI UNIT   D YOUNG
WITHINGTON (UNIVERSITY) Manchester
J F C PERRYMAN, J M AUSTERBERRY
WORCESTER ROYAL INFIRMARY   L R D RYDER,
J M HUGHES
WYTHENSHAWE Manchester   J R L CLARK

DIOCESAN OFFICES

CHURCH OF ENGLAND

BATH AND WELLS The Old Deanery, Wells, Somerset BA5 2UG
Tel: Wells (0749) 73308/73747

BIRMINGHAM 175 Harborne Park Road, Harborne, Birmingham B17 0BH
Tel: Birmingham 021-427 5141

BLACKBURN Diocesan Offices, Cathedral Close, Blackburn, Lancs BB1 5AA
Tel: Blackburn (0254) 54421

BRADFORD Cathedral Hall, Stott Hill, Bradford, W Yorks BD1 4ET
Tel: Bradford (0274) 725958

BRISTOL Diocesan Church House, 23 Great George Street, Bristol, Avon BS1 5QZ
Tel: Bristol (0272) 214411

CANTERBURY Diocesan House, Lady Wootton's Green, Canterbury, Kent CT1 1NQ
Tel: Canterbury (0227) 459401

CARLISLE Church House, West Walls, Carlisle, Cumbria CA3 8UE
Tel: Carlisle (0228) 22573

CHELMSFORD Guy Harlings, 53 New Street, Chelmsford, Essex CM1 1NG
Tel: Chelmsford (0245) 266731

CHESTER Diocesan House, Raymond Street, Chester CH1 4PN
Tel: Chester (0244) 379222

CHICHESTER Diocesan Church House, 9 Brunswick Square, Hove, E Sussex BN3 1EN
Tel: Brighton (0273) 29023

COVENTRY Church House, Palmerston Road, Coventry CV5 6FJ
Tel: Coventry (0203) 74328

DERBY Derby Church House, Full Street, Derby DE1 3DR
Tel: Derby (0332) 382233

DURHAM Auckland Castle, Market Place, Bishop Auckland, Co. Durham DL14 7QJ
Tel: Bishop Auckland (0388) 604515

ELY Bishop Woodford House, Barton Road, Ely, Cambs CB7 4DX
Tel: Ely (0353) 663579

EUROPE Diocesan Office, 5A Gregory Place, Kensington, London W8 4NG
Tel: 071-937 2796/7

EXETER Diocesan House, Palace Gate, Exeter, Devon EX1 1HX
Tel: Exeter (0392) 72686

GLOUCESTER Church House, College Green, Gloucester GL1 2LY
Tel: Gloucester (0452) 410022

GUILDFORD Diocesan House, Quarry St, Guildford, Surrey GU1 3XG
Tel: Guildford (0483) 571826

HEREFORD The Palace, Hereford HR4 9BL
Tel: Hereford (0432) 353863/4

LEICESTER Church House, 3/5 St Martin's East, Leicester LE1 5FX
Tel: Leicester (0353) 27445/6

LICHFIELD St Mary's House, Lichfield, Staffs WS13 7LD
Tel: Lichfield (0543) 414551

LINCOLN The Old Palace, Lincoln LN2 1PU
Tel: Lincoln (0522) 29241

LIVERPOOL Church House, 1 Hanover Street, Liverpool L1 3DW
Tel: 051-709 9722

LONDON London Diocesan House, 30 Causton Street, London SW1P 4AU
Tel: 071-821 9351

MANCHESTER Diocesan Church House, 90 Deansgate, Manchester M3 2GH
Tel: Manchester 061-833 9521

NEWCASTLE	Church House, Grainger Park Road, Newcastle upon Tyne NE4 8SX *Tel:* Newcastle 091-226 0622
NORWICH	Holland Court, Cathedral Close, Norwich, Norfolk NR1 4DU *Tel:* Norwich (0603) 628491
OXFORD	Diocesan Church House, North Hinksey, Oxford OX2 0NB *Tel:* Oxford (0865) 244566
PETERBOROUGH	The Palace, Peterborough, Cambs PE1 1YB *Tel:* Peterborough (0733) 64448/9
PORTSMOUTH	Cathedral House, St Thomas's Street, Portsmouth, Hants PO1 2HA *Tel:* Portsmouth (0705) 825731
RIPON	Ripon Diocesan Office, St Mary's Street, Leeds LS9 7DP *Tel:* Leeds (0532) 487487
ROCHESTER	St Nicholas Church, Boley Hill, Rochester, Kent ME1 1SL *Tel:* Medway (0634) 830333
ST ALBANS	Holywell Lodge, 41 Holywell Hill, St Albans, Herts AL1 1HE *Tel:* St Albans (0727) 54532
ST EDMUNDSBURY AND IPSWICH	Diocesan House, 13/15 Tower Street, Ipswich, Suffolk IP1 3BG *Tel:* Ipswich (0473) 211028
SALISBURY	Church House, Crane Street, Salisbury, Wilts SP1 2QB *Tel:* Salisbury (0722) 333074/335876
SHEFFIELD	St Matthew's House, 45 Carver Street, Sheffield S1 4FT *Tel:* Sheffield (0742) 726528
SODOR AND MAN	24 Athol Street, Douglas, Isle of Man *Tel:* Douglas (0624) 75367
SOUTHWARK	94 Lambeth Road, London SE1 7PS *Tel:* 071-928 6637
SOUTHWELL	Dunham House, Westgate, Southwell, Notts NG25 0JL *Tel:* Southwell (0636) 814331
TRURO	Diocesan House, Kenwyn, Truro, Cornwall TR1 3DU *Tel:* Truro (0872) 74351
WAKEFIELD	Church House, 1 South Parade, Wakefield WF1 1LP *Tel:* Wakefield (0924) 371802
WINCHESTER	Church House, 9 The Close, Winchester, Hants SO23 9LS *Tel:* Winchester (0962) 844644
WORCESTER	The Old Palace, Deansway, Worcester WR1 2JE *Tel:* Worcester (0905) 20537/8 and 28764
YORK	Church House, Ogleforth, York, N Yorks YO1 2JE *Tel:* York (0904) 611696

ASSISTANT BISHOPS OF THE CHURCH OF ENGLAND

Bath & Wells	A K HAMILTON
	A M STOCKWOOD
	J S WALLER
	R P WILSON
Birmingham	M H D WHINNEY
Blackburn	G K GIGGALL
Bradford	D R J EVANS
Bristol	J GIBBS
	F S TEMPLE
Canterbury	W A FRANKLIN
	R S HOOK
	R D SAY
Chichester	M GREEN
	W W HUNT
	E G KNAPP-FISHER
	M H St J MADDOCKS
	J H L MORRELL
	S W PHIPPS
Coventry	J C S DALY
	V S NICHOLLS
Derby	K J F SKELTON
Durham	H W MOORE
Ely	R L FISHER
Exeter	R F CARTWRIGHT
	I C DOCKER
	R C O GOODCHILD
	P J PASTERFIELD
Gloucester	F T HORAN
	J GIBBS
	W S LLEWELLYN
	D B PORTER
	A P TREMLETT
	R W WOODS
Leicester	G W E C ASHBY
	J E L MORT
Lichfield	R O BOWLBY
	K C ORAM
Lincoln	G F COLIN
	R S CUTTS
	H R DARBY
Liverpool	G C CHADWICK
	J W ROXBURGH
London	M E MARSHALL
	J R G NEALE
	A F B ROGERS
	M A P WOOD
(Willesden)	D S ARDEN

Manchester	E R WICKHAM
Newcastle	K E GILL
Oxford	L J ASHTON
	A K CRAGG
	P K WALKER
	R C C WATSON
	M A P WOOD
Portsmouth	E E CURTIS
	W W HUNT
	E J K ROBERTS
Ripon	R EMMERSON,
	J W A HOWE
	D A RAWCLIFFE
Rochester	C O BUCHANAN,
	J W H FLAGG
St Albans	Lord RUNCIE
Salisbury	J K CAVELL
	F S TEMPLE
Sheffield	K H PILLAR
	K J F SKELTON
Southwark	C O BUCHANAN
	E M H CAPPER
	A R M GORDON
	J T HUGHES
	H W MONTEFIORE
	M J NAZIR-ALI
	J R G NEALE
	S W PHIPPS
Truro	R F CARTWRIGHT
	C J E MEYER
Wakefield	R A M GENDERS
Winchester	H B DEHQANI-TAFTI
	L L REES
Worcester	D H N ALLENBY
	J A A MAUND
	K J WOOLLCOMBE
York	G E I COCKIN
	R K WIMBUSH
	R J WOOD

Europe (Auxiliary Bishops)

E H M CAPPER
D P dos S de PINA CABRAL
A W M WEEKES

DEANERIES AND RURAL DEANS
OF THE CHURCH OF ENGLAND

The number given to each deanery below corresponds to that given in the benefice entries in the combined English benefice and church index on pages 819ff. Where archdeaconries come within the jurisdiction of suffragan or area bishops under established schemes, the respective bishop is indicated.

The dioceses of Liverpool, London and Manchester and the three Nottingham deaneries in the diocese of Southwell use the title Area Dean.

BATH AND WELLS
ARCHDEACONRY OF WELLS

1. AXBRIDGE   R C DEAN
2. BRUTON   P W M REVELL
3. CARY   P W M REVELL
4. FROME   T J FARMILOE
5. GLASTONBURY   B H ADAMS
6. ILCHESTER   H A HALLETT
7. MARTOCK   D J RICHARDS
8. MERSTON   D J HUNT
9. SHEPTON MALLET   C T TOOKEY

ARCHDEACONRY OF BATH

10. BATH   A R WALLACE
11. CHEW MAGNA   C A HADLEY
12. LOCKING   C D TAYLOR
13. MIDSOMER NORTON   J E INGHAM
14. PORTISHEAD   H B TASKER

ARCHDEACONRY OF TAUNTON

15. BRIDGWATER   J S BARKS
16. CREWKERNE   C G MOORE
17. EXMOOR   J A ATKIN
18. ILMINSTER   E WILKES
19. QUANTOCK   R L PARKER
20. TAUNTON   R E FLOWER
21. TONE   T W STOKES

BIRMINGHAM
ARCHDEACONRY OF BIRMINGHAM

1. BIRMINGHAM CITY   J G WESSON
2. EDGBASTON   I M MICHAEL
3. HANDSWORTH   B H PARRY
4. KINGS NORTON   B GREEN
5. WARLEY   M GRAHAM

ARCHDEACONRY OF ASTON

6. ASTON   E W RUSSELL
7. BORDESLEY   M R F MACLACHLAN
8. MOSELEY   J DE WIT
9. SUTTON COLDFIELD   J D PIGOTT
10. YARDLEY   F S COLLINS

ARCHDEACONRY OF COLESHILL

11. COLESHILL   R G BOLLARD
12. POLESWORTH   D C BYFORD
13. SOLIHULL   M W TUNNICLIFFE

BLACKBURN
ARCHDEACONRY OF BLACKBURN

1. ACCRINGTON   J EATOCK
2. BLACKBURN   P S GRIERSON
3. BURNLEY   R McCULLOUGH
4. CHORLEY   B G MOORE
5. DARWEN   R P CARTMELL
6. LEYLAND   T M THOMPSON
7. PENDLE   J C PRIESTLEY
8. WHALLEY   Q H WILSON

ARCHDEACONRY OF LANCASTER

9. BLACKPOOL   D J N MADDOCK
10. GARSTANG   R G GREENALL
11. KIRKHAM   W FIELDING
12. LANCASTER   J A H CLEGG
13. POULTON   D PRYTHERCH
14. PRESTON   S J FINCH
15. TUNSTALL   R P PRICE

BRADFORD
ARCHDEACONRY OF BRADFORD

1. AIREDALE   R S ANDERSON
2. BOWLING AND HORTON   D F BROWN
3. CALVERLEY   D SUTCLIFFE
4. OTLEY   M A SAVAGE

ARCHDEACONRY OF CRAVEN

5. BOWLAND   G WALKER
6. EWECROSS   N J A KINSELLA
7. SKIPTON   D B ALDRED
8. SOUTH CRAVEN   C F TREVOR

BRISTOL
ARCHDEACONRY OF BRISTOL

1. BEDMINSTER   D FRAYNE
2. BITTON   D G MITCHELL
3. BRISLINGTON   J N HARRISON
4. BRISTOL CITY   E A MORRIS
5. CLIFTON   P M BERG
6. HORFIELD   J M PERRIS
7. STAPLETON   R J BURBRIDGE
8. WESTBURY AND SEVERNSIDE   P R BAILEY

ARCHDEACONRY OF SWINDON

9. CHIPPENHAM   R G CLIFTON
10. CRICKLADE   J L WARE
11. HIGHWORTH   M J H HOWELL
12. MALMESBURY   W H THOMSON-GLOVER
13. WROUGHTON   E J WOODS

CANTERBURY
ARCHDEACONRY OF CANTERBURY

1. BRIDGE, EAST   C C BARLOW
2. BRIDGE, WEST   D J MARRIOTT
3. CANTERBURY   J M GLEDHILL
4. DOVER   A F SIMPER
5. ELHAM   R O STROUD
6. OSPRINGE   J V H RUSSELL
7. RECULVER   P D SALES
8. SANDWICH   J M A ROBERTS
9. THANET   C W FLETCHER

ARCHDEACONRY OF MAIDSTONE

10. CHARING, EAST   R G E GAZZARD
11. CHARING, WEST   J RECORD
12. LYMPNE NORTH   J M STEPHENS
13. LYMPNE SOUTH   J HEWES
14. SITTINGBOURNE   D MATTHIAE
15. SUTTON   A WATSON

CARLISLE
ARCHDEACONRY OF CARLISLE

1. APPLEBY   W F GREETHAM
2. BRAMPTON   C T MATTHEWS
3. CARLISLE   C S SIMS
4. PENRITH   D C ELLIS

ARCHDEACONRY OF WEST CUMBERLAND

5. CALDER   P R BRYAN
6. DERWENT   S H WILLCOX
7. SOLWAY   T H M SAMPSON

ARCHDEACONRY OF WESTMORLAND AND FURNESS

8. FURNESS   J HOLDEN
9. KENDAL   T PARK
10. WINDERMERE   K E WOOD

CHELMSFORD
ARCHDEACONRY OF WEST HAM
(BISHOP OF BARKING)

1. BARKING AND DAGENHAM   D S AINGE
2. EPPING FOREST   G R HOLLEY
3. HARLOW   M D WEBSTER
4. HAVERING   D W M JENNINGS
5. NEWHAM   J P WHITWELL
6. ONGAR   M G SELLIX
7. REDBRIDGE   T H SHANNON
8. WALTHAM FOREST   P J WOOD

ARCHDEACONRY OF SOUTHEND
(BISHOP OF BRADWELL)

9. BASILDON   P D ASHTON
10. BRENTWOOD   P W H GOODE
11. CHELMSFORD   J K HAYWARD
12. HADLEIGH   P J SANDBERG
13. MALDON AND DENGIE   A J DUNLOP
14. ROCHFORD   P F TAYLOR
15. SOUTHEND-ON-SEA   A O WIGRAM
16. THURROCK   D J WILLIAMS

ARCHDEACONRY OF COLCHESTER
(BISHOP OF COLCHESTER)

17. BELCHAMP   P J STREET
18. BRAINTREE   B DAVIES
19. COLCHESTER   P A MARSHALL
20. DEDHAM AND TEY   C G A WOODS
21. DUNMOW   A R JACK
22. HALSTEAD AND COGGESHALL   B E ROSE
23. HARWICH   P E BALL
24. NEWPORT AND STANSTED   C BISHOP
25. SAFFRON WALDEN   B J MACDONALD-MILNE
26. ST OSYTH   M R C SWINDLEHURST
27. WITHAM   C J SLY

CHESTER
ARCHDEACONRY OF CHESTER

1. BIRKENHEAD   R J GILLINGS
2. CHESTER   R S LUNT
3. FRODSHAM   J K BALL
4. GREAT BUDWORTH   G L DAVIES
5. MALPAS   J M G DAVIES
6. MIDDLEWICH   E W COX
7. WALLASEY   B E LEE
8. WIRRAL NORTH   G M TURNER
9. WIRRAL SOUTH   N P CHRISTENSEN

ARCHDEACONRY OF MACCLESFIELD

10. BOWDON   D ASHWORTH
11. CONGLETON   R SUTTON
12. KNUTSFORD   N D ROGERS
13. MACCLESFIELD   D W MOIR
14. MOTTRAM   J E W BOWERS
15. NANTWICH   D ROSTRON
16. CHADKIRK   D C SPEEDY
17. CHEADLE   R H HACK
18. STOCKPORT   A M FAIRHURST

CHICHESTER
ARCHDEACONRY OF CHICHESTER

1. ARUNDEL AND BOGNOR   M H WEAVER
2. BRIGHTON   E W M WALKER
3. CHICHESTER   K W CATCHPOLE
4. HOVE   F J ARROWSMITH
5. WORTHING   P R ROBERTS

ARCHDEACONRY OF HORSHAM

6. CUCKFIELD   I J BRACKLEY
7. EAST GRINSTEAD   J R BROWN
8. HORSHAM   D E E TANSILL
9. HURST   R L CLARKE
10. MIDHURST   M C JUDGE

11. PETWORTH   F H DOE
12. STORRINGTON   M J HORE
13. WESTBOURNE   R W POIL

ARCHDEACONRY OF LEWES AND HASTINGS

14. BATTLE AND BEXHILL   D RANKIN
15. DALLINGTON   D D FRICKER
16. EASTBOURNE   N S READE
17. HASTINGS   D G CARTER
18. LEWES AND SEAFORD   M R THOMPSON
19. ROTHERFIELD   C H ATHERSTONE
20. RYE   A M P SMITH
21. UCKFIELD   C J PETERS

COVENTRY
ARCHDEACONRY OF COVENTRY

1. COVENTRY EAST   G F WARNER
2. COVENTRY NORTH   G HANDS
3. COVENTRY SOUTH   A E DARBY
4. KENILWORTH   R D TURNER
5. NUNEATON   J F LAW
6. RUGBY   J T RANDALL

ARCHDEACONRY OF WARWICK

7. ALCESTER   G L MAUDSLEY
8. FOSSE   N V HOWES
9. SHIPSTON   N J MORGAN
10. SOUTHAM   K J PHILLIPS
11. WARWICK AND LEAMINGTON   K LINDOP

DERBY
ARCHDEACONRY OF CHESTERFIELD

1. ALFRETON   J M C COLBOURN
2. BAKEWELL AND EYAM   M F COLLIER
3. BOLSOVER AND STAVELEY   I E WINTERBOTTOM
4. BUXTON   J C TOMLINSON
5. CHESTERFIELD   S MILLINGTON
6. GLOSSOP   R M PHILLIPS
7. WIRKSWORTH   H COLLARD

ARCHDEACONRY OF DERBY

8. ASHBOURNE   D H SANSUM
9. DERBY NORTH   G O MARSHALL
10. DERBY SOUTH   D C MACDONALD
11. DUFFIELD   A T REDMAN
12. HEANOR   M A ROYLE
13. ILKESTON   J R WARMAN
14. LONGFORD   D MILNER
15. MELBOURNE   F ROSS
16. REPTON   J R P BARKER

DURHAM
ARCHDEACONRY OF DURHAM

1. CHESTER LE STREET   P G WALKER
2. DURHAM   J N GREAVES
3. EASINGTON   K I WOODHOUSE
4. GATESHEAD   K HUXLEY
5. GATESHEAD WEST   J G HAMMERSLEY
6. HOUGHTON LE SPRING   P T FISHER
7. JARROW   J M HANCOCK
8. LANCHESTER   P WATERHOUSE
9. WEARMOUTH   G G GIBSON

ARCHDEACONRY OF AUCKLAND

10. AUCKLAND   N D BAKER
11. BARNARD CASTLE   T J D OLLIER
12. DARLINGTON   L GREADY
13. HARTLEPOOL   M H WHITEHEAD
14. SEDGEFIELD   M Q KING
15. STANHOPE   C N LOVELL
16. STOCKTON   M S SIMMONS

ELY
ARCHDEACONRY OF ELY

1. BOURN   H D SEARLE
2. CAMBRIDGE   D J CONNER
3. FORDHAM   M G F SHEARS
4. LINTON   E J COTGROVE
5. NORTH STOWE   C A BARBER

6. QUY   B E KERLEY
7. SHELFORD   R L POWELL
8. SHINGAY   J K GREASLEY

ARCHDEACONRY OF HUNTINGDON

9. HUNTINGDON   W M DEBNEY
10. LEIGHTONSTONE   J HINDLEY
11. ST IVES   E DUCKETT
12. ST NEOTS   B CURRY
13. YAXLEY   P J SHEPHERD

ARCHDEACONRY OF WISBECH

14. ELY   R J MACKLIN
15. FELTWELL   J B ROWSELL
16. FINCHAM   P F KEELING
17. LYNN MARSHLAND   I W SMITH
18. MARCH   T AMBROSE
19. WISBECH   P H N COLLINS

EXETER
ARCHDEACONRY OF EXETER

1. AYLESBEARE   D O'L MARKHAM
2. CADBURY   B H GALES
3. CHRISTIANITY   B R TUBBS
4. CULLOMPTON   K D AGNEW
5. HONITON   D A GUNN-JOHNSON
6. KENN   J H GOOD
7. OTTERY   R M SIGRIST
8. TIVERTON   C G H DUNN

ARCHDEACONRY OF TOTNES

9. HOLSWORTHY   H J ROCHE
10. IPPLEPEN   K C MOSS
11. MORETON   J P HELLIER
12. OKEHAMPTON   W F CURTIS
13. TOTNES   I J BUTLER
14. WOODLEIGH   P HANCOCK

ARCHDEACONRY OF BARNSTAPLE

15. BARNSTAPLE   R P REEVE
16. CHULMLEIGH   P NIXSON
17. HARTLAND   W G BLAKEY
18. SHIRWELL   C J HUDSON
19. SOUTH MOLTON   G COWDRY
20. TORRINGTON   N G MEAD

ARCHDEACONRY OF PLYMOUTH

21. IVYBRIDGE   A K F MACEY
22. PLYMOUTH DEVONPORT   S PHILPOTT
23. PLYMOUTH MOORSIDE   J F RICHARDS
24. PLYMOUTH SUTTON   P H W HAWKINS
25. TAVISTOCK   M H BATEMAN

GLOUCESTER
ARCHDEACONRY OF GLOUCESTER

1. BISLEY   M R MILES
2. DURSLEY   C RAWLINSON
3. FOREST NORTH   G P JENKINS
4. FOREST SOUTH   D F F EVANS
5. GLOUCESTER CITY   P M NUNN
6. GLOUCESTER NORTH   T P JACKSON
7. HAWKESBURY   *Vacant*
8. STONEHOUSE   N E L BAKER
9. TEWKESBURY   J H MEAD

ARCHDEACONRY OF CHELTENHAM

10. CHELTENHAM   D C NYE
11. CAMPDEN   T R C OVERTHROW
12. CIRENCESTER   H S RINGROSE
13. FAIRFORD   P G C JEFFRIES
14. NORTHLEACH   J P BROWN
15. STOW   R F ROTHERY
16. TETBURY   J D STRONG
17. WINCHCOMBE   A M LEE

GUILDFORD
ARCHDEACONRY OF SURREY

1. ALDERSHOT   A C P BODDINGTON
2. CRANLEIGH   M C HUGHES
3. FARNHAM   J N E BUNDOCK

4. GODALMING   R C D MACKENNA
5. GUILDFORD   J F SALTER
6. SURREY HEATH   C EDMONDS

ARCHDEACONRY OF DORKING

7. DORKING   M J FARRANT
8. EMLY   C M SCOTT
9. EPSOM   M J C WILSON
10. LEATHERHEAD   A C WARNER
11. RUNNYMEDE   D L H HEAD
12. WOKING   J SONG

HEREFORD
ARCHDEACONRY OF HEREFORD

1. ABBEYDORE   F E RODGERS
2. BROMYARD   D W GOULD
3. HEREFORD CITY   P T WOOD
4. HEREFORD RURAL   D C MILLER
5. KINGTON AND WEOBLEY   K NEWBON
6. LEDBURY   C N H ATTWOOD
7. LEOMINSTER   M W HOOPER
8. ROSS AND ARCHENFIELD   S R ASHTON

ARCHDEACONRY OF LUDLOW

9. BRIDGNORTH   R SHARP
10. CLUN FOREST   D R P HAYES
11. CONDOVER   M S STEDMAN
12. LUDLOW   R A HORSFIELD
13. PONTESBURY   D H ROBERTS
14. TELFORD SEVERN GORGE   C HILL

LEICESTER
ARCHDEACONRY OF LEICESTER

1. CHRISTIANITY (LEICESTER) NORTH   T S BYRON
2. CHRISTIANITY (LEICESTER) SOUTH   D N HOLE
3. FRAMLAND (Melton)   A E H CLAYTON
4. GARTREE FIRST DEANERY (Harborough)   D V TREANOR
5. GARTREE SECOND DEANERY (Wigston)   B R GLOVER
6. GOSCOTE   K R COURT

ARCHDEACONRY OF LOUGHBOROUGH

7. AKELEY EAST (Loughborough)   G F J CRATE
8. AKELEY SOUTH (Coalville)   J RICHARDSON
9. AKELEY WEST (Ashby)   M J PENNY
10. GUTHLAXTON FIRST DEANERY (Blaby)   B DAVIS
11. GUTHLAXTON SECOND DEANERY (Lutterworth)   J BACKHOUSE
12. SPARKENHOE EAST   M S WOODS
13. SPARKENHOE WEST (Hinckley and Bosworth)   J C SEYMOUR

LICHFIELD
ARCHDEACONRY OF LICHFIELD

1. HIMLEY   W M SMITH
2. LICHFIELD   M G WOODERSON
3. PENKRIDGE   A E WILLIAMS
4. RUGELEY   D R H THOMAS
5. TAMWORTH   K M JUKES
6. TRYSULL   J D MAKEPEACE
7. WALSALL   P A R HAMMERSLEY
8. WEDNESBURY   I B COOK
9. WEST BROMWICH   D J BELCHER
10. WOLVERHAMPTON   P J CHAPMAN

ARCHDEACONRY OF STOKE-ON-TRENT

11. ALSTONFIELD   D M TINSLEY
12. CHEADLE   N JEFFERYES
13. ECCLESHALL   J H DEAKIN
14. LEEK   E A FARLEY
15. NEWCASTLE   M D HARDING
16. STAFFORD   J POTTS
17. STOKE NORTH   T THAKE
18. STOKE   J W PAWSON
19. TRENTHAM   G L SIMPSON
20. TUTBURY   D M MORRIS
21. UTTOXETER   J B HALL

ARCHDEACONRY OF SALOP

22. EDGMOND   R T HIBBERT
23. ELLESMERE   D R D JONES
24. HODNET   J H GREEN
25. OSWESTRY   J A CARR
26. SHIFNAL   R B BALKWILL
27. SHREWSBURY   B T MADDOX
28. TELFORD   C HILL
29. WEM AND WHITCHURCH   R D JENKINS
30. WROCKWARDINE   T W B FOX

LINCOLN

ARCHDEACONRY OF STOW

1. AXHOLME, ISLE OF   J GIBBONS
2. CORRINGHAM   E R COOK
3. LAWRES   B J P PRITCHARD
4. MANLAKE   P B HEARN
5. WEST WOLD   M J CARTWRIGHT
6. YARBOROUGH   E J P HEPWORTH

ARCHDEACONRY OF LINDSEY

7. BOLINGBROKE   R W B MASSINGBERD-MUNDY
8. CALCEWAITHE AND CANDLESHOE
      S G RIDLEY
9. GRIMSBY AND CLEETHORPES   B A J PEARMAIN
10. HAVERSTOE   H W P HALL
11. HORNCASTLE   S W PEARCE
12. LOUTHESK   J W M VYSE

ARCHDEACONRY OF LINCOLN

13. AVELAND AND NESS w STAMFORD
      H J THEODOSIUS
14. BELTISLOE   N A STONE
15. CHRISTIANITY   J D BROWN
16. ELLOE EAST   O G FOLKARD
17. ELLOE WEST   K A ALMOND
18. GRAFFOE   R RODGER
19. GRANTHAM   R AMIS
20. HOLLAND EAST   B C OSBORNE
21. HOLLAND WEST   D J OSBOURNE
22. LAFFORD   J S THOROLD
23. LOVEDEN   R CLARK

LIVERPOOL

ARCHDEACONRY OF LIVERPOOL

1. BOOTLE   R CAPPER
2. HUYTON   J A STANLEY
3. LIVERPOOL NORTH   G J BUTLAND
4. LIVERPOOL SOUTH   J V ROBERTS
5. SEFTON   F A BRISCOE
6. TOXTETH AND WAVERTREE   M M WOLFE
7. WALTON   J H CATLIN
8. WEST DERBY   J R I WIKELEY

ARCHDEACONRY OF WARRINGTON

9. NORTH MEOLS   M D WHYTE
10. ST HELENS   C H B BYWORTH
11. ORMSKIRK   M J SMOUT
12. WARRINGTON   J O COLLING
13. WIDNES   J MILLER
14. WIGAN EAST   K M FORREST
15. WIGAN WEST   D LYON
16. WINWICK   R BRITTON

LONDON

ARCHDEACONRY OF LONDON

1. THE CITY   A J TANNER

ARCHDEACONRY OF CHARING CROSS
(BISHOP OF FULHAM)

2. WESTMINSTER PADDINGTON   A E J FOSTER
3. WESTMINSTER ST MARGARET   D B TILLYER
4. WESTMINSTER ST MARYLEBONE   P R HARDING

ARCHDEACONRY OF HACKNEY
(BISHOP OF STEPNEY)

5. HACKNEY   A WINDROSS
6. ISLINGTON   M J COLMER
7. TOWER HAMLETS   C YOUNG

ARCHDEACONRY OF MIDDLESEX
(BISHOP OF KENSINGTON)

8. CHELSEA   J A K MILLAR
9. HAMMERSMITH   G Q D PIPER
10. HAMPTON   D H PALMER
11. HOUNSLOW   P A TUFT
12. KENSINGTON   J K BROWNSELL
13. SPELTHORNE   D S RICHARDSON

ARCHDEACONRY OF HAMPSTEAD
(BISHOP OF EDMONTON)

14. BARNET, CENTRAL   M H McGOWAN
15. BARNET, WEST   M D KETTLE
16. CAMDEN, NORTH (Hampstead)   P W WHEATLEY
17. CAMDEN, SOUTH (Holborn and St Pancras)
      P DYSON
18. ENFIELD   D J NASH
19. HARINGEY, EAST   J C BROADHURST
20. HARINGEY, WEST   B K LUNN

ARCHDEACONRY OF NORTHOLT
(BISHOP OF WILLESDEN)

21. BRENT   J C GORE
22. EALING   R JONES
23. HARROW   R F SWAN
24. HILLINGDON   M J COLCLOUGH

MANCHESTER

ARCHDEACONRY OF MANCHESTER

1. ARDWICK   A DURRANS
2. ECCLES   *Vacant*
3. HEATON   A PUGMIRE
4. HULME   G A WHEALE
5. MANCHESTER, NORTH   D I ERRIDGE
6. SALFORD   G HOWARD
7. STRETFORD   W J TWIDELL
8. WITHINGTON   N W DAWSON

ARCHDEACONRY OF BOLTON

9. BOLTON   R C CRASTON
10. BURY   G G ROXBY
11. DEANE   D W GATENBY
12. FARNWORTH   A E BALLARD
13. LEIGH   J T FINNEY
14. RADCLIFFE AND PRESTWICH   R W WARNER
15. ROSSENDALE   R E MALLINSON
16. WALMSLEY   J I McFIE

ARCHDEACONRY OF ROCHDALE

17. ASHTON-UNDER-LYNE   C A E LAWRENCE
18. OLDHAM   L R TOONE
19. ROCHDALE   A SHACKLETON

NEWCASTLE

ARCHDEACONRY OF NORTHUMBERLAND

1. BEDLINGTON   M NELSON
2. BELLINGHAM   S V PRINS
3. CORBRIDGE   J E DURNFORD
4. HEXHAM   R B COOK
5. NEWCASTLE CENTRAL   P G H HISCOCK
6. NEWCASTLE EAST   W J HATCHLEY
7. NEWCASTLE WEST   V G ASHWIN
8. TYNEMOUTH   G F REVETT

ARCHDEACONRY OF LINDISFARNE

9. ALNWICK   P ELLIOTT
10. BAMBURGH AND GLENDALE   W WADDLE
11. MORPETH   A S CRAIG
12. NORHAM   G A ELCOAT

NORWICH

ARCHDEACONRY OF NORWICH

1. BLOFIELD   R M BAKER
2. FLEGG   J W WILSON
3. INGWORTH   G R DRAKE
4. NORWICH NORTH   D M SALWAY
5. NORWICH SOUTH   A C H LATHE
6. NORWICH EAST   W D MORTON
7. REPPS   P H ATKINS

8. SPARHAM   A J HAWES
9. TUNSTEAD   H C BRADBURY
10. WAXHAM   B S T MORGAN

ARCHDEACONRY OF NORFOLK

11. DEPWADE   P E HALLS
12. HINGHAM AND MITFORD   D J BOURNE
13. HUMBLEYARD   W D M STURDY
14. LODDON   G F WALKER
15. LOTHINGLAND   L O HARRIS
16. REDENHALL   M D W PADDISON
17. THETFORD AND ROCKLAND   A D McGREGOR

ARCHDEACONRY OF LYNN

18. BRECKLAND   P J TAYLOR
19. BRISLEY AND ELMHAM   L A WILMAN
20. BURNHAM AND WALSINGHAM   W A J SAYER
21. HEACHAM AND RISING   G R HALL
22. HOLT   K W FARMER
23. LYNN   S R NAIRN

OXFORD

ARCHDEACONRY OF OXFORD
(BISHOP OF DORCHESTER)

1. ASTON AND CUDDESDON   D M W ROBINSON
2. BICESTER AND ISLIP   R B JENNISON
3. CHIPPING NORTON   M J CHADWICK
4. COWLEY   J BARTON
5. DEDDINGTON   T WIMBUSH
6. HENLEY   A PYBURN
7. OXFORD   G C M SMITH
8. WITNEY   R E MEREDITH
9. WOODSTOCK   J R MORGAN

ARCHDEACONRY OF BERKSHIRE
(BISHOP OF READING)

10. ABINGDON   D P PRITCHARD
11. BRACKNELL   C G CLARKE
12. BRADFIELD   D G MEARA
13. MAIDENHEAD   J F W V COPPING
14. NEWBURY   C T SCOTT-DEMPSTER
15. READING   E A ESSERY
16. SONNING   J W RATINGS
17. VALE OF WHITE HORSE   D J HOWSON
18. WALLINGFORD   C J STOTT
19. WANTAGE   A R WRIGHT

ARCHDEACONRY OF BUCKINGHAM
(BISHOP OF BUCKINGHAM)

20. AMERSHAM   M A HILL
21. AYLESBURY   D S BREWIN
22. BUCKINGHAM   N A THORP
23. BURNHAM   S N D BROWN
24. CLAYDON   W F JOHNSTON
25. MILTON KEYNES   N P H POND
26. MURSLEY   H R M HARRIES
27. NEWPORT   D LUNN
28. WENDOVER   J R WHITE
29. WYCOMBE   D J ROBERTSON

PETERBOROUGH

ARCHDEACONRY OF NORTHAMPTON

1. BRACKLEY   S E CRAWLEY
2. BRIXWORTH   T H ROPER
3. DAVENTRY   G J JOHNSON
4. NORTHAMPTON   J F A M KNIGHT
5. TOWCESTER   J E ATWELL
6. WELLINGBOROUGH   H C SMART
7. WOOTTON   J T SHORT

ARCHDEACONRY OF OAKHAM

8. BARNACK   G H RICHMOND
9. CORBY   M A CRAGGS
10. HIGHAM   R G KNIGHT
11. KETTERING   D J T MILLER
12. OUNDLE   M W R COVINGTON
13. PETERBOROUGH   T R CHRISTIE
14. RUTLAND   A M S WILSON

PORTSMOUTH

ARCHDEACONRY OF PORTSMOUTH

1. BISHOPS WALTHAM   M R WELCH
2. FAREHAM   R W H KINGSTON
3. GOSPORT   D G JAMES
4. HAVANT   G P KNOWLES
5. PETERSFIELD   B E COOK
6. PORTSMOUTH   T KNIGHT

ARCHDEACONRY OF ISLE OF WIGHT

7. WIGHT, EAST   S M CHALONER
8. WIGHT, WEST   A BROWN

RIPON

ARCHDEACONRY OF RICHMOND

1. HARROGATE   A M BARTON
2. RICHMOND   C R BOFF
3. RIPON   R B B WILD
4. WENSLEY   M T BROADBENT

ARCHDEACONRY OF LEEDS

5. ALLERTON   J R SWAIN
6. ARMLEY   J M OLIVER
7. HEADINGLEY   G C DARVILL
8. WHITKIRK   M G WHITTOCK

ROCHESTER

ARCHDEACONRY OF ROCHESTER

1. COBHAM   D L WILLIAMS
2. DARTFORD   A T WATERMAN
3. GILLINGHAM   S H DUNN
4. GRAVESEND   S F SIDEBOTHAM
5. ROCHESTER   K A GARDINER
6. STROOD   D J SILCOCK

ARCHDEACONRY OF TONBRIDGE

7. MALLING   D A RUDDLE
8. SEVENOAKS   M P SHIELDS
9. SHOREHAM   J H B TALBOT
10. TONBRIDGE   D G St L WINTER
11. TUNBRIDGE WELLS   R E WHYTE

ARCHDEACONRY OF BROMLEY

12. BECKENHAM   D S R REDMAN
13. BROMLEY   P R HENWOOD
14. ERITH   J R BALCH
15. ORPINGTON   R R LUNNON
16. SIDCUP   S L S ALLEN

ST ALBANS

ARCHDEACONRY OF ST ALBANS

1. ALDENHAM   P B MORGAN
2. BARNET   A G K ESDAILE
3. BERKHAMSTED   A J S FREEMAN
4. BISHOP'S STORTFORD   J L PELLEY
5. BUNTINGFORD   P J M BRIGHT
6. CHESHUNT   T D L LLOYD
7. HATFIELD   D R VENESS
8. HERTFORD   D H WHEATON
9. HITCHIN   C F LILEY
10. RICKMANSWORTH   B L DRIVER
11. ST ALBANS   J W PRAGNELL
12. STEVENAGE   M BARNSLEY
13. WATFORD   B K ANDREWS
14. WHEATHAMPSTEAD   D R GRAEBE

ARCHDEACONRY OF BEDFORD

15. AMPTHILL   D LEWTHWAITE
16. BEDFORD   J A L HULBERT
17. BIGGLESWADE   E E J ROWLAND
18. DUNSTABLE   D C SELF
19. ELSTOW   J K DIXON
20. LUTON   N P MORRELL
21. SHARNBROOK   A R H WOODWARD
22. SHEFFORD   T MAINES

ST EDMUNDSBURY AND IPSWICH
ARCHDEACONRY OF IPSWICH

1. BOSMERE   H D CHAPMAN
2. COLNEYS   G L GRANT
3. HADLEIGH   G W ARRAND
4. IPSWICH   J C CASSELTON
5. SAMFORD   A B LEIGHTON
6. STOWMARKET   J R HARROLD
7. WOODBRIDGE   N DAVIS

ARCHDEACONRY OF SUDBURY

8. CLARE   E J BETTS
9. IXWORTH   P M OLIVER
10. LAVENHAM   D W W PEARCE
11. MILDENHALL   G C SMITH
12. SUDBURY   L F SIMPKINS
13. THINGOE   S PETTITT

ARCHDEACONRY OF SUFFOLK

14. BECCLES AND SOUTH ELMHAM   S C MORRIS
15. HALESWORTH   P E BUSTIN
16. HARTISMERE   D G WOODWARDS
17. HOXNE   D J STREETER
18. LOES   H G PEARSON
19. SAXMUNDHAM   D C LOWE

SALISBURY
ARCHDEACONRY OF SHERBORNE

1. BEAMINSTER   J LILLEY
2. DORCHESTER   D J LETCHER
3. LYME BAY   J W GANN
4. SHERBORNE   R A WILLIS
5. WEYMOUTH   S S VENNER

ARCHDEACONRY OF DORSET

6. BLACKMORE VALE   D DICKER
7. MILTON AND BLANDFORD   G S M SQUAREY
8. POOLE   P R HUXHAM
9. PURBECK   P G HARDMAN
10. WIMBORNE   D R PRICE

ARCHDEACONRY OF SARUM

11. ALDERBURY   C R F COHEN
12. AVON   P D SLATER
13. CHALKE   T C CURRY
14. HEYTESBURY   R SHARPE
15. SALISBURY   M A WHATMOUGH
16. WYLYE AND WILTON   S V COLLINS

ARCHDEACONRY OF WILTS

17. BRADFORD   W A MATTHEWS
18. CALNE   A G WOODS
19. DEVIZES   C BRYANT
20. MARLBOROUGH   G R J FORCE-JONES
21. PEWSEY   D M RYDER

SHEFFIELD
ARCHDEACONRY OF SHEFFIELD

1. ATTERCLIFFE   *Vacant*
2. ECCLESALL   G G MacINTOSH
3. ECCLESFIELD   L M ATKINSON
4. HALLAM   R M JARRATT
5. LAUGHTON   P WRIGHT
6. ROTHERHAM   M O C JOY
7. TANKERSLEY   D WARNER

ARCHDEACONRY OF DONCASTER

8. ADWICK-LE-STREET   A N ATTWOOD
9. DONCASTER   D N GIBBS
10. DONCASTER, WEST   J A BOWERING
11. SNAITH AND HATFIELD   J W SWEED
12. WATH   J W A WOODS

SODOR AND MAN

1. CASTLETOWN   G B CLAYTON
2. DOUGLAS   D WHITWORTH
3. PEEL   B H PARTINGTON
4. RAMSEY   J H SHEEN

SOUTHWARK
ARCHDEACONRY OF LEWISHAM
(BISHOP OF WOOLWICH)

1. GREENWICH   D H F SHIRESS
2. DEPTFORD   W G CORNECK
3. LEWISHAM, EAST   L S C HARVEY
4. LEWISHAM, WEST   J O ARDLEY

ARCHDEACONRY OF SOUTHWARK
(BISHOP OF WOOLWICH)

5. BERMONDSEY   P D MAURICE
6. CAMBERWELL   R W G BOMFORD
7. DULWICH   J B NAYLOR
8. SOUTHWARK AND NEWINGTON   V A DAVIES

ARCHDEACONRY OF LAMBETH
(BISHOP OF KINGSTON)

9. CLAPHAM AND BRIXTON   J HACKETT
10. LAMBETH   C J E MOODY
11. MERTON   P R TILLEY
12. STREATHAM   P H RONAYNE

ARCHDEACONRY OF WANDSWORTH
(BISHOP OF KINGSTON)

13. BATTERSEA   P CLARK
14. KINGSTON   S P LYON
15. RICHMOND AND BARNES   B A SAUNDERS
16. TOOTING   I KITTERINGHAM
17. WANDSWORTH   M H CLARK

ARCHDEACONRY OF CROYDON
(BISHOP OF CROYDON)

18. CATERHAM   C J L BOSWELL
19. CROYDON ADDINGTON   L A D WATSON
20. CROYDON CENTRAL   N GODWIN
21. CROYDON SOUTH   M VONBERG
22. CROYDON NORTH   P L WASHINGTON

ARCHDEACONRY OF REIGATE
(BISHOP OF CROYDON)

23. GODSTONE   A B RAMSAY
24. REIGATE   S H MASLEN
25. SUTTON   M R GOODLAD

SOUTHWELL
ARCHDEACONRY OF NEWARK

1. BAWTRY   W H THACKRAY
2. MANSFIELD   R T WARBURTON
3. NEWARK   R A J HILL
4. NEWSTEAD   A A CONN
5. RETFORD   G E HOLLOWAY
6. WORKSOP   R E WHEATON

ARCHDEACONRY OF NOTTINGHAM

7. BEESTON   C J HALL
8. BINGHAM   A HAYDOCK
9. BINGHAM SOUTH   J L D HARDY
10. BINGHAM WEST   A C SUTHERLAND
11. GEDLING   R D A MORE
12. NOTTINGHAM CENTRAL   L J MORLEY
13. NOTTINGHAM NORTH   C GALE
14. NOTTINGHAM WEST   C H KNOWLES
15. SOUTHWELL   D J BARTLETT

TRURO
ARCHDEACONRY OF CORNWALL

1. ST AUSTELL   J B SAUNDERS
2. CARNMARTH NORTH   N J POCOCK
3. CARNMARTH SOUTH   C J K FIRTH
4. KERRIER   R F LAW
5. PENWITH   M H FISHER
6. POWDER   M J ADAMS
7. PYDAR   J F EDWARDS

ARCHDEACONRY OF BODMIN

8. STRATTON   A J VINCENT
9. TRIGG MAJOR   J D FERGUSON
10. TRIGG MINOR AND BODMIN   K ROGERS
11. WIVELSHIRE, EAST   B A ANDERSON
12. WIVELSHIRE, WEST   K P MELLOR

WAKEFIELD
ARCHDEACONRY OF HALIFAX

1. ALMONDBURY   R L WHITELEY
2. BRIGHOUSE AND ELLAND   J R FLACK
3. CALDER VALLEY   P N CALVERT
4. HALIFAX   R S GIBSON
5. HUDDERSFIELD   E O ROBERTS
6. KIRKBURTON   J A A LODGE

ARCHDEACONRY OF PONTEFRACT

7. BARNSLEY   D C TURNBULL
8. BIRSTALL   B F WOOD
9. CHEVET   R D STRAPPS
10. DEWSBURY   R M WILSON
11. PONTEFRACT   R H TAYLOR
12. WAKEFIELD   B S ELLIS

WINCHESTER
ARCHDEACONRY OF BASINGSTOKE

1. ALRESFORD   C R SMITH
2. ALTON   P G L COLE
3. ANDOVER   A R WILDS
4. BASINGSTOKE   C N WRIGHT
5. ODIHAM   R C HUBBLE
6. WHITCHURCH   N P CUMMING

ARCHDEACONRY OF WINCHESTER

7. BOURNEMOUTH   D H R JONES
8. CHRISTCHURCH   J N SEAFORD
9. EASTLEIGH   B N HARLEY
10. LYNDHURST   M G ANDERSON
11. ROMSEY   N C JONES
12. SOUTHAMPTON   J J S WATSON
13. WINCHESTER   R J H TEARE

CHANNEL ISLANDS

14. GUERNSEY   Very Rev J R FENWICK
15. JERSEY   Very Rev B A O'FERRALL

WORCESTER
ARCHDEACONRY OF WORCESTER

1. EVESHAM   J W HAMPTON
2. MALVERN   J H DAVIES

3. MARTLEY AND WORCESTER WEST
   J W HERBERT
4. PERSHORE   C J RIDOUT
5. UPTON   A R KING
6. WORCESTER EAST   J C EVEREST

ARCHDEACONRY OF DUDLEY

7. BROMSGROVE   D C SALT
8. DROITWICH   W D S WELLS
9. DUDLEY   J L SAMUEL
10. KIDDERMINSTER   A J POSTLETHWAITE
11. STOURBRIDGE   D O BELL
12. STOURPORT   G E COOKE

YORK
ARCHDEACONRY OF YORK
(BISHOP OF SELBY)

1. AINSTY, NEW   J A RENDALL
2. BUCKROSE   F B WILLIAMS
3. BULMER AND MALTON   E T CHAPMAN
4. DERWENT   F G HUNTER
5. EASINGWOLD   G C GALLEY
6. SELBY   D BOND
7. SOUTH WOLD   J V ANDREWS
8. YORK, CITY OF   R G FLETCHER

ARCHDEACONRY OF EAST RIDING
(BISHOP OF HULL)

9. BEVERLEY   W E R WILKINSON
10. BRIDLINGTON   J C MEEK
11. HARTHILL   G G HOLMAN
12. HOLDERNESS, NORTH   P M DAVIES
13. HOLDERNESS, SOUTH   W H McLAREN
14. HOWDEN   D C BAILEY
15. HULL   F A GORDON-KERR
16. SCARBOROUGH   C M F WHITEHEAD

ARCHDEACONRY OF CLEVELAND
(BISHOP OF WHITBY)

17. GUISBOROUGH   D H LAMBERT
18. HELMSLEY   F J A HEWITT
19. MIDDLESBROUGH   S C WRIGHT
20. MOWBRAY   *Vacant*
21. PICKERING   E RICHARDS
22. STOKESLEY   K R GOOD
23. WHITBY   E NEWLYN

CHAPLAINS OF THE DIOCESE OF GIBRALTAR IN EUROPE

Vicar-General   Canon P O Deacon
5A Gregory Place, London W8 4NG
071-937 2796

Austria

Vienna   S J B PEAKE

Belgium

Antwerp St Boniface   C R C COUSSMAKER
Antwerp Seafarers' Centre   C T BABB
Brussels w Charleroi   J LEWIS, A M STRANGE
Ghent w Ypres   J C WALKER
Ostend w Knokke and Brugge   G M HART
Tervuren w Liege   S J G SEAMER

Bulgaria

Sofia   D A S BROWN

Canary Islands

Las Palmas w Lanzarote   E C FORD
Playa de Las Americas   C R BOND
Puerto de la Cruz Tenerife   T J SPONG

Denmark

Copenhagen w Aarhus   D R CAPES

Finland

Helsinki   T A STRAND

France

Beaulieu-sur-Mer   B B MATTHEWS
Bordeaux w Monteton, Tocane, Petite Cotes and Limeuil
   D J WARDROP
Boulogne-sur-Mer w Calais and Lille   W SCOTT
Cannes w Grasse   K B ANDERSON
Chantilly   J G V FOSTER
Dunkerque Missions to Seamen   A R W RIMMER
Lyon w Grenoble   P R MAY
Maison-Laffitte   O B EATON
Marseille w Aix-en-Provence   P N CASSIDY
Nice   J M LIVINGSTONE
Paris St Michael   M B LEA, W R LOVATT
Paris St George   M P DRAPER
Sophia Antipolis   D W ASHTON
St Raphael   T F UNSWORTH
Strasbourg   W J MILLIGAN, J L MURRAY
Toulouse w Biarritz, Cahors and Pau   P R TOPHAM
Versailles w Grandchamp and Gif-sur-Yvette
   R M D ORAM

Germany

Bonn w Cologne   J K NEWSOME
Dusseldorf   J I BATTY
Hamburg w Kiel   D G PROSSER
Stuttgart   M S NAIDU

Gibraltar

Gibraltar   B W HORLOCK

Greece

Athens w Kyfissia, Patras, Thessaloniki and Voula
   W H CHIVERS

Hungary

Budapest   S J B PEAKE

Italy

Florence w Siena and Assisi   G L C WESTWELL
Milan w Genoa and Verese   I L PHILLIPS
Naples w Sorrento, Capri and Bari   M BULLOCK
Palermo w Taormina (Sicily)   T A WATSON
Rome   P S MARCHANT

San Remo   B WARDROBE
Venice w Trieste   W H BAAR

Luxembourg

Luxembourg   C G POOLE

Malta

Gozo   A V ALBUTT
Valletta w Sliema   P J COUSINS, J B WHELAN

Monaco

Monte Carlo   C W DANES

Morocco

Casablanca   A W K BROWN

Netherlands

Amsterdam   J WHEATLEY PRICE
Eindhoven   R A LENS VAN RIJN
Netherlands, East (Nijmegen and Twente)
   G W WOODWARD
Rotterdam (and Missions to Seamen)
   M W FULLJAMES, (Dss) W G van DONGEN
Schiedam Missions to Seamen   D I DAVIES
The Hague   J A WALLIS, G G ALLEN, R W G DE MURALT
Utrecht w Amersfoort, Harderwijk and Zwolle
   S J TWYCROSS
Vlissingen Missions to Seamen   B THOMPSON
Voorschoten   G G ALLEN

Norway

**Oslo w Bergen, Drammen, Stavanger, Trondheim and
   Tonsberg**   G A C BROWN, R P LANE

Portugal

Algarve   P J W BLACKBURN, W G CHESHAM
Lisbon, Greater   J K ROBINSON
Madeira   A W S BROWN
Porto (or Oporto)   D WARD-BODDINGTON

Romania

Bucharest   D A S BROWN

Spain

Barcelona   R W SEWELL
Costa Blanca   R E HICKES, J ap L DAVIES
Costa del Sol East   R S MATHESON
Costa del Sol West   S L ELKINGTON
Ibiza w San Antonio and Santa Eulalia   R H D SMITH
Madrid w Bilbao   H W SCRIVEN
Malaga w Almunecar and Nerja   P H GOODERICK
Mojacar   D H CORDELL
Palma de Mallorca and Balearic Isles   W J HAWTHORNE,
   R D GREENWOOD, A RUBIO

Sweden

Gothenburg w Halmstad, Jonkoping and Uddevalla
   G HANCOCKS
Stockholm w Gavle and Vasteras   W G REID

Switzerland

Bern w Neuchatel   D C WOTHERSPOON
Geneva   M P PULESTON
Lausanne   L F STEEL
Lugano   L V WRIGHT
Montreux w Gstaad   A W M WEEKES
Vevey w Chateau d'Oex and Villars   D J R RITCHIE,
   G B CROOK
Zurich w St Gallen and Winterthur   P J HAWKER,
   J P ADAMS

Turkey

Istanbul w Moda   I W L SHERWOOD
Izmir w Bornova   G B EVANS

USSR

Moscow   T A STRAND

Yugoslavia

Belgrade w Zagreb   G T DOYLE

BISHOPS OF ANGLICAN DIOCESES OVERSEAS

AUSTRALIA

PROVINCE OF NEW SOUTH WALES

Armidale — Peter Chiswell
Bishopscourt, PO Box 198,
Armidale, NSW 2350, Australia

Bathurst — Bruce W Wilson
Bishopscourt, PO Box 23,
Bathurst, NSW 2795, Australia

Canberra and Goulburn — Owen D Dowling
The Anglican Registry, GPO Box
1981, Canberra, ACT 2601
Australia

Grafton — Bruce A Schultz
Bishopsholme, 35 Victoria Street,
Grafton, NSW 2460, Australia

Newcastle — Alfred C Holland
Bishopscourt, Brown Street,
Newcastle, NSW 2300, Australia

(Auxiliary Bishop) — Richard F Appleby
Diocesan Registry, 250 Darby
Street, Newcastle, NSW 2300,
Australia

Riverina — Barry R Hunter
Bishop's Lodge, Box 10, PO,
Narrandera, NSW 2700, Australia

Sydney (Archbishop) — Donald W B Robinson
Box Q190, Queen Victoria PO,
Sydney NSW 2000, Australia

(Assistants)
(Bishop of North Sydney) — Paul W Barnett
address as above

John R Reid
address as above

E Donald Cameron
address as above

R Harry Goodhew
Woollongong Church Centre, Market
Street, Woollongong 2500, Australia

Peter R Watson
Anglican Church Centre,
45 Hunter Street, Parramatta,
NSW 2150, Australia

PROVINCE OF QUEENSLAND

Brisbane (Archbishop) — Peter J Hollingworth
Bishopsbourne, Box 421,
GPO, Brisbane 4001,
Queensland, Australia

(Assistants)
(Bishop of Western Region) — Adrian O Charles
Box 421, GPO, Brisbane 4001,
Australia

G V Browning
(address as above)

Carpentaria — Anthony F B Hall-Matthews
PO Box 180, Earlville,
Queensland 4871, Australia

(Assistant) — Kiwami Dai
Bishop's House, PO Box 79
Thursday Island, Queensland 4875,
Australia

North Queensland — H John Lewis
Diocesan Registry, Box 1244,
Townsville, North Queensland 4810,
Australia

(Assistants) — George Tung Yep
PO Box 600, Earlville,
Queensland 4870, Australia

Arthur A Malcolm
Bishop's House, 177 Smith Street,
Yarrabah, North Queensland 4871,
Australia

Northern Territory — Clyde M Wood
Bishop's House, PO Box 39352,
Winnellie, NT 0820, Australia

Rockhampton — George A Hearn
Lis Escop, PO Box 116,
Rockhampton, Queensland 4700
Australia

PROVINCE OF SOUTH AUSTRALIA

Adelaide (Archbishop) — Ian G C George
Church Office, 44 Currie Street,
Adelaide, S Australia 5000

The Murray — Graham H Walden
PO Box 269, Murray Bridge,
South Australia 5253

Willochra — David H McCall
Bishop's House, PO Box 68,
Gladstone, South Australia 5473

PROVINCE OF VICTORIA

Ballarat — John Hazlewood
Bishopscourt, 454 Wendouree Parade,
Ballarat, Victoria 3350, Australia

Bendigo — Oliver S Heyward
PO Box 144, Bendigo,
Victoria 3550, Australia

Gippsland — Colin D Sheumack
Bishopscourt, PO Box 383, Sale,
Victoria 3850, Australia

Melbourne (Archbishop and Acting Primate) — Keith Rayner
St Paul's Cathedral Buildings,
209 Flinders Lane, Melbourne 3000,
Australia

(Assistants) — James A Grant
(address as above)

Robert L Butterss
(address as above)

John C Stewart
(address as above)

John W Wilson
(address as above)

J Bayton
(Bishop in Geelong)
The Bishop's House
364 Shannon Avenue, Newtown
Victoria 3220, Australia

Wangaratta — Robert Beal
Bishop's Lodge, Wangaratta, Victoria
3677, Australia

PROVINCE OF WESTERN AUSTRALIA

Bunbury — Hamish T Jamieson
Bishopscourt, PO Box 15, Bunbury,
W Australia 6230

North West Australia — Vacant
Bishop's House, 11 Mark Way,
Mt Tarcoola, (Box 140 PO), Geraldton,
W Australia 6530

(Assistant) — Bernard R Buckland
(Bishop for Kimberleys)
PO Box 158, Broome 6725,
W Australia

Perth (Archbishop) — Peter F Carnley
GPO Box W2607, Perth 6001
W Australia

(Assistants) — Brian R Kyme
(address as above)

Goldfields Region — Benjamin Wright
PO Box 439, Kalgoorlie 6430,
W Australia

DIOCESE OF TASMANIA

Tasmania — Phillip K Newell
Bishopscourt, 26 Fitzroy Place,
Sandy Bay 7005, Tasmania, Australia

(Assistant) — Mervyn Stanton
65 Sirius Street, Howrah 7018,
Tasmania, Australia

BRAZIL

Brasilia
Almir dos Santos
HIGS 706 Bloco L/c 28, Caixa Postal
07-0515, 70359 Brasilia, DF Brazil

Central Brazil
Sydney A Ruiz
Rue Fonseca Guimaraes, 12 – Sta
Tereza, 20240, Rio de Janeiro
RJ Brazil

Northern Brazil
Clovis E Rodrigues
Av Conselheiro Aguiar, 2178/602-boa
Viagem, Caixa Postal 04904, 51020
Recife PE Brazil

Pelotas
Luiz O Prado
Rua Santa Cruz, 997-Centro, 96015
Pelotas RS Brazil

South Central Brazil
Glauco Soares de Lima
Rua Borges Lagoa CEP 172, 04038,
Sao Paulo, SP Brazil

Southern Brazil
Claudio V S Gastal
Av Ludelfo Boehl, 320 –
Teresopolis, Caixa Postal 11504,
91700 Porto Alegre, RS Brazil

South Western Brazil (Primate)
Olavo V Luiz
Rua Cel. Niederauer 1222,
Caixa Postal 98, 97001,
Santa Maria RS Brazil

BURMA *see* MYANMAR

BURUNDI, RWANDA AND ZAIRE

Boga Zaire
Njojo Byanka
EAZ Boga-Zaire, c/o PO 2185,
Nairobi, Kenya

Bujumbura
Pie Ntukamazina
c/o BP 1300, Bujumbura,
Burundi

Bukavu
Jean Balufuga Dirokpa
BP 2876, Bukavu, Zaire

(Assistant)
Kolini Mbona
BP 2699, Lubumbashi, Zaire

Butare
A Nshamihigo
BP 225, Butare, Rwanda

(Assistant)
Daniel Nduhura
(address as above)

Buye
Samuel Ndayisenga
EEB Buye, BP 94, Ngozi, Burundi

Gitega
Jean Nduwayo
BP 23, Gitega, Burundi

Kigali
Adoniya Sebununguri
EER, BP 61, Kigali, Rwanda

Kisangani
S Tibefa Mugera
BP 861, Kisangani, Zaire

Matena (Primate)
Samuel Sindamuka
BP 2098 Matena, Burundi

Shaba
E M Kolini
c/o United Methodist Church,
PO Box 22037, Kitwe, Zambia

Shyira
Augustin Nshamihigo
BP 1, Vunga, via Ruhengeri, Rwanda
(please forward)

CANADA

Primate of Canada
Michael G Peers
600 Jarvis Street, Toronto,
ON M4Y 2J6 Canada

PROVINCE OF BRITISH COLUMBIA

British Columbia
Ronald F Shepherd
Bishop's Close, 912 Vancouver Street,
Victoria BC V8V 3V7 Canada

Caledonia
John E Hannen
PO Box 278, Prince Rupert,
BC V8J 3P6 Canada

Cariboo
Vacant
1244 Victoria Street,
Kamloops BC V2C 2A9 Canada

Kootenay
David P Crawley
Box 549, Kelowna BC V1Y 7P2
Canada

New Westminster (Archbishop)
Douglas W Hambidge
Suite 302, 814 Richards Street,
Vancouver BC V6B 3A7 Canada

Yukon
Ronald C Ferris
PO Box 4247, Whitehorse,
Yukon Y1A 3T3 Canada

PROVINCE OF CANADA

Central Newfoundland
Edward Marsh
34 Fraser Road, Gander,
NF A1V 1K7 Canada

Eastern Newfoundland and Labrador
Martin Mate
19 King's Bridge Rd, St John's
NF A1C 3K4 Canada

Fredericton
George C Lemmon
Bishop's Court, 115 Church Street,
Fredericton NB E3B 1HB
Canada

Montreal
Andrew Hutchinson
Synod Office, 1444 Union Avenue,
Montreal PQ H3A 2B8 Canada

(Suffragan)
James A MacLean
(address as above)

Nova Scotia
Arthur G Peters
5732 College Street, Halifax,
NS B3H 1X3 Canada

(Assistant)
Hugh P Allan
(address as above)

Quebec
Bruce Stavert
36 rue Desjardins, Quebec,
PQ G1R 4L5 Canada

Western Newfoundland (Archbishop)
S Stewart Payne
83 West Street,
Corner Brook NF A2H 2Y6 Canada

PROVINCE OF ONTARIO

Algoma
Leslie E Peterson
Box 1168, Sault Ste Marie,
ON P6A 5N7 Canada

Huron
Percy O'Driscoll
4-220 Dundas Street, London,
ON N6A 1H3 Canada

(Suffragans)
Charles R Townshend
(address as above)
J Peck
(address as above)

Moosonee
Caleb J Lawrence
Bishopstope Box 841,
Schumacher ON P0N 1G0 Canada

Niagara (Archbishop)
John C Bothwell
Niagara Church House,
67 Victoria Avenue,
South Hamilton ON L8N 2S8 Canada

(Co-adjutor)
Walter G Asbil
(address as above)

Ontario
Allan A Read
The Diocesan Centre,
90 Johnson Street, Kingston
ON K7L 1XL Canada

Ottawa
Edwin K Lackey
Bishop's Office, 71 Bronson Avenue,
Ottawa ON K1R 6G6 Canada

(Suffragan)
John A Baycroft
(address as above)

Toronto
Terence Finlay
Synod House, 135 Adelaide Street East,
Toronto ON M5C 1L8 Canada

(Suffragans)
Douglas Blackwell
300 Dundas Street West, Whitby,
ON L1N 2M5, Canada

Arthur D Brown
Bishop's Room, St Paul's L'Amoureaux,
333 Finch Ave E, Scarborough
ON M1W 2R9, Canada

Joachim Fricker
2052 Mississauga Road,
Mississauga ON L5H 2KO Canada

J Taylor Pryce
8 Pinehurst Court, Aurora,
ON L4G 3Z3 Canada

PROVINCE OF RUPERT'S LAND

The Arctic	Christopher Williams Box 164, Iqaluit, NWT, X0A 0H0 Canada
Athabasca	Gary F Woolsey Box 6868 Peace River AB T8S 1S6 Canada
Brandon	John F S Conlin 341 13th Street, Brandon, MB R7A 4P8 Canada
Calgary	J B Curtis Synod Office, Olga House, 3015 Glencoe Road SW, Calgary AB T2S 2L9 Canada
Edmonton	Kenneth L Genge 10033 84th Avenue, Edmonton, AB T6E 2G6 Canada
Keewatin	T W R Collings Bishopstowe, Box 118, Kenora, ON P9N 3X1 Canada
Qu'Appelle	Eric Bays Bishop's Court, 1501 College Ave, Regina SK S4P 1B8 Canada
Rupert's Land (Archbishop)	Walter Jones 935 Nesbitt Bay, Winnipeg, Manitoba MB R3T 1W6 Canada
Saskatchewan	Thomas O Morgan Box 1088, 2030 Second Ave W, Prince Albert, SK S6V 5S6 Canada
(Suffragan)	C J Arthurson Box 96, La Ronge, Saskatchewan, S0J 1L0 Canada
Saskatoon	Roland A Wood PO Box 1965, Saskatoon, SK S7K 3S5 Canada

CENTRAL AFRICA

Botswana (Archbishop)	W P Khotso Makhulu PO Box 769, Gaborone, Botswana
Central Zambia	Clement W Hlanya-Shaba PO Box 70172, Ndola, Zambia
Harare	Peter R Hatendi Bishopsmount Close, PO U A7, Harare, Zimbabwe
Lake Malawi	Peter N Nyanja PO Box 30349, Lilongwe 3, Malawi
The Lundi	Jonathan Siyachitema PO Box 25, Gweru, Zimbabwe
Lusaka	Stephen Mumba Bishop's Lodge, PO Box 30183 Lusaka, Zambia
Manicaland	Elijah M Masuko 115 Main St, Mutare, Zimbabwe
Matabeleland	Theophilus T Naledi PO Box 2422, Bulawayo, Zimbabwe
Northern Zambia	Bernard Malango PO Box 20173, Kitwe, Zambia
Southern Malawi	Nathaniel B Aipa PO Box Chilema, Zomba, Malawi

CEYLON – SRI LANKA

Colombo	J J Gnanapragasam Bishop's House, 368/1 Baudhaloka Mawatha, Colombo 7, Sri Lanka
Kurunagala	Andrew O Kumarage Bishop's House, Kandy Road, Kurunagala, Sri Lanka

INDIAN OCEAN

Antananarivo	Remi Rabenirina Évêché Anglican, Ambohimanoro, 101 Antananarivo, Malagasy Republic
Antsiranana	Keith J Benzies Évêché Anglican, BP 278, Antsiranana, Malagasy Republic
Mauritius	Rex Donat Bishop's House, Phoenix, Mauritius

Seychelles (Archbishop)	French Chang-Him PO Box 44, Victoria, Mahé, Seychelles
Toamasina	Donald Westwood Smith La Mission Anglicane, rue de la Fraternité, Toamasina, Malagasy Republic

JAPAN

Chubu	Samuel W Hoyo 47-1 Yamawaki-cho, Showa-ku Nagoya 466, Japan
Hokkaido	Augustine H Amagi Kita 15jo, 20 Nishi 5-chome, Kita-ku, Sapporo 001, Japan
Kita Kanto	James T Yashiro 2-172 Sakuragi-cho, Omiya 330, Japan
Kobe	Vacant 5-11-1 Shimoyamate Dori, Chuo-ku, Kobe 650, Japan
Kyoto	John Toshiharu Okano Shimotachiuri-agaru, Karasumadori, Kamikyo-ku, Kyoto 602, Japan
Kyushu	Joseph N Iida 2-9-22 Kusagae, Chuo-ku, Fukuoka 810, Japan
Okinawa	Paul S Nakamura 7-7 Makiminato 5-chome, Urasoe-shi, Okinawa 901-21, Japan
Osaka (Archbishop)	Christopher I Kikawada 8-30 Tojo-cho, Tennoji-ku, Osaka 543, Japan
Tohoku	Cornelius Y Tazaki 2-13-15 Kokubu-cho, Aoba-hu, Sendai 980, Japan
Tokyo	John Makoto Takeda 3-6-18 Shiba-koen, Minato-ku, Tokyo 105, Japan
Yokohama	Raphael S Kajiwara 14-57 Mitsusawa Shimo-cho, Kanagawa-ku, Yokohama 221, Japan

JERUSALEM & THE MIDDLE EAST

Cyprus & the Gulf	John E Brown 2 Grigori Afxentiou Street, PO Box 2075, Nicosia, Cyprus
Egypt	Ghais A Malik Diocesan Office, PO Box 87, Zamalek Distribution, Cairo, Egypt
Iran (Bishop in)	Iraj Mottahedeh PO Box 135, Postal Code 81465, Isfahan, Iran
Jerusalem (Primate)	Samir Kafity St George's Close, PO Box 1248, Jerusalem 91019
(Assistant)	Elia Khoury PO Box 598, Amman, Jordan

KENYA

Eldoret	Vacant PO Box 3404, Eldoret, Kenya
Embu	Moses Njue PO Box 189, Embu, Kenya
(Assistant)	Robert M Beak (address as above)
Katakwa	Eliud O Okiring PO Box 60, Malakisi, Kenya
Kirinyaga	David M. Gitari Diocese of Kirinyaga, PO Box 95, Kutus, Kenya
Machakos	Benjamin M P Nzimbi PO Box 282, Machakos, Kenya
Maseno North	James I Mundia PO Box 416, Kakamega, Kenya
Maseno South	J Henry Okullu PO Box 114, Kisumu, Kenya
(Assistant)	Haggai Nyang PO Box 380, Kisumu, Kenya

Maseno West	Joseph O Wesonga PO Box 793, Siaya, Kenya
Mombasa	Crispus D Nzano PO Box 80072, Mombasa, Kenya
Mt Kenya Central	John Mahiani PO Box 121, Murang'a, Kenya
Mt Kenya South	George M Njuguna PO Box 23031, Lower Kabete, Kenya
Nairobi (Archbishop)	Manasses Kuria PO Box 40502, Nairobi, Kenya
Nakuru	Stephen M Njihia PO Box 56, Nakuru, Kenya
Nambale	Isaac Namango PO Box 4, Nambale, Kenya

MELANESIA

Central Melanesia (Archbishop)	Amos Waiaru Bishop's House, Tandai Highway PO Box 19, Honiara, Solomon Islands
Hanuato'o	James Mason Bishop's House, Kirakira, Makira/Ulawa Province, Solomon Islands
Malaita	Raymond Aumae Bishop's House, PO Box 7, Auki, Malaita, Solomon Islands
Temotu	Lazarus S Munamua Bishop's House, Luesalo, Lata, Santa Cruz, Temotu Province, Solomon Islands
Vanuatu	Harry Tevi Bishop's House, PO Box 238, Luganville, Santo, Vanuatu
Ysabel	Ellison Pogo Bishop's House, Jejevo, Buala, Ysabel, Solomon Islands

MYANMAR (formerly BURMA)

Mandalay	Timothy Mya Wah Bishopscourt, 22nd Street, ('C' Road), Mandalay, Myanmar
(Assistant)	J Kumsawng Tu Emmanuel Church, Mohnyin, Myitkyina, Myanmar
Myitkyina	A Hla Aung Cathedral Church of Christ the King, Thida Ya, Myitkyina, Kachin State, Myanmar
Pa'an	George Kyaw Mya Diocesan Office, Nat-shin-Naung Road, Toungoo, Myanmar
Sittwe	Barnabas Theung Hawi St John's Church, Paletwa, Akyab, Southern Chin State, Via Sittwe, Myanmar
Yangon (Archbishop)	Andrew Mya Han Bishopscourt, 140 Pyidaungsu Yeiktha Road, Dagon PO, Yangon, Myanmar
(Assistant)	Samuel San Si Htay (address as above)

NEW ZEALAND
(AOTEAROA, NEW ZEALAND
AND POLYNESIA)

Aotearoa	Whakahuihui Vercoe (Bishop to the Maoris) 2 Maclean Street, PO Box 146, Rotorua, New Zealand
Auckland	Bruce C Gilberd PO Box 37-023, Parnell, Auckland, New Zealand
(Assistants)	Godfrey E Wilson 50 Clark Road, Papakura, Auckland, New Zealand
	Edward G Buckle 14 Kiwi Avenue, Maunu, (Box 10043, Te Mai PO) Whangarei, New Zealand

Christchurch	David J Coles PO Box 8471, Riccarton, Christchurch, New Zealand
Dunedin	Penelope A Jamieson PO Box 5445, 164 Moray Place, Dunedin, New Zealand
Nelson	Derek L Eaton PO Box 100, 218 Trafalgar Street, Nelson, New Zealand
Polynesia (Bishop in)	Jabez L Bryce Bishop's House, Box 35 GPO, Suva, Fiji Islands
Waiapu	Murray J Mills 8 Cameron Terrace, PO Box 227, Napier, Hawkes Bay, New Zealand
(Assistant)	George H Conner Bishop's House, 60 Judea Road, Tauranga, Aotearoa, New Zealand
Waikato	Roger A Herft PO Box 21, Hamilton, Waikato, New Zealand
Wellington (Archbishop)	Brian N Davis PO Box 12-046, Wellington 1, New Zealand
(Assistants)	Thomas J Brown PO Box 12-046, Wellington, New Zealand
	Brian R Carrell PO Box 422, Palmerston North, New Zealand

NIGERIA

Aba	Augustine Onyeyiriehukwu Iwuagwu Bishop's House, PO Box 212, Aba, Nigeria
Abuja	Peter J Akinola Bishopscourt, Doula Street, Wuse, PO Box 212, Abuja, Nigeria
Akoko	J O K Olowokure Bishopscourt, Lennon Hill, PO Box 572, Ikare-Akoko, Ondo State, Nigeria
Akure	Emmanuel B Gbonigi Bishopscourt, Alagbaka GRA, PO Box 1622, Akure, Nigeria
Asaba	Roland N C Nwosu Bishopscourt, Cable Point, PO Box 216, Asaba, Bendel State, Nigeria
Awka	Maxwell S Anikwenwa Bishopscourt, Ifite, Awka Road, PO Box 130, Awka, Anambra State, Nigeria
Bauchi	E O Chukwuma Bishop's House, Bununu Road, New GRA, PO Box 2450, Bauchi, Nigeria
Benin	John K George Bishopscourt, PO Box 82, Benin City, Bendel State, Nigeria
Calabar	W G Ekprikpo Bishopscourt, PO Box 74, Calabar, Cross River State, Nigeria
Egba Abeokuta (formerly Egba-Egbado)	Titus I Akintayo Bishopscourt, Onikolobo, PO Box 267, Ibara, Abeokuta, Nigeria
Egbado	Timothy I O Bolaji Bishopscourt, PO Box 8, Ilaro, Nigeria
Ekiti	Charles A Akinbola Bishopscourt, PO Box 12, Ado-Ekiti, Nigeria
Enugu	Gideon N Otubelu Bishop's House, Uwani, PO Box 418, Enugu, Nigeria
Ibadan	Gideon N Olajide Bishopscourt, (Arigid Street, Bodija), PO Box 3075, Ibadan, Nigeria
Ife	Gabriel B Oloniyo Bishopscourt, Parakin Layout, Ile-Ife, Nigeria

Ijebu	Abraham O Olowoyo Bishopscourt Ejirin Road, PO Box 112, Ijebu-Ode, Nigeria
Ijebu Remo	E O I Ogundana Bishopscourt, Ewusi Street, PO Box 522, Sagamu, Nigeria
Ilesa	E A Ademowo Bishopscourt, Oke-Oye, PO Box 237, Ilesa, Nigeria
Jos	Timothy E I Adesola Bishopscourt, PO Box 6283, Jos, Nigeria
Kaduna	Titus Ogbonyomi Bishopscourt, 4 Kanta Road, PO Box 72, Kaduna, Northern Nigeria
Kafanchan	William W Diya Bishopscourt, 5b Jemma's Street PO Box 29, Kafanchan-Kaduna State, Nigeria
Kano	Benjamin O Omosebi Bishopscourt, 1B Stadium Road, PO Box 362, Kano, Nigeria
Katsina	James S Kwasu Bishopscourt, (New GRA, opposite WTC Road, behind Sabon Gari Police Station), PO Box 905, Katsina, Nigeria
Kwara	Herbert Haruna Bishopscourt, Fate Road, PO Box 1884, Ilorin, Kwara State, Nigeria
Lagos (Archbishop)	Joseph A Adetiloye PO Box 13, (Bishopscourt, 29 Marina), Lagos, Nigeria
Maiduguri	Emmanuel K Mani Bishopscourt, 1 Lake Chad Club Road, GRA, PO Box 1693, Maiduguri, Borno State, Nigeria
Makurdi	Vacant Bishopscourt, PO Box 1, Makurdi, Nigeria
Minna	Vacant Bishopscourt, Dutsen Kura, PO Box 64, Minna, Nigeria
The Niger (Bishop on)	Jonathan Onyemelukwe Bishopscourt, PO Box 42, Onitsha, Nigeria
Niger Delta	Samuel O Elenwa Bishop's Lodge, PO Box 115, Port Harcourt, Nigeria
Okigwe-Orlu	Samuel C N Ebo Bishopscourt, PO Box 260, Nkwerre, Imo State, Nigeria
Ondo	Samuel O Aderin Bishopscourt, College Road, PO Box 265, Ondo, Nigeria
Osun	Seth Oni Fagbemi Bishopscourt, Isale-Aro, PO Box 285, Osogbo, Nigeria
Owerri	Benjamin Nwankiti Bishopscourt, Egbu, PO Box 31, Owerri, Imo State, Nigeria
Owo	Abraham Awosan Bishopscourt, PO Box 472, Owo, Ondo State, Nigeria
Sokoto	Josiah Idowu-Fearon Bishop's Lodge, Dendo Road, PO Box 3489, Sokoto, Nigeria
Uyo	Ebenezar E Nglass Bishopscourt, Uyo, Akwa Ibom State, Nigeria
Warri	John Dafiewhare Bishopscourt, PO Box 18, Ughelli, Nigeria
Yola	Christian O Efobi 10 Hong Road, PO Box 601, Yola-Gongola State, Nigeria

PAPUA NEW GUINEA

Aipo Rongo	Paul Richardson PO Box 893, Mount Hagan, Western Highlands Province, Papua New Guinea

Dogura	Blake Kerina PO Box 19, Dogura, via Alotau, MBP Papua New Guinea
New Guinea Islands (Primate)	Bevan Meredith Bishop's House, PO Box 159, Rabaul, ENBP, Papua New Guinea
Popondota	Walter Siba PO Box 26, Popondetta, Oro Province, Papua New Guinea
Port Moresby	Isaac Gadebo PO Box 6491, Boroko, Papua New Guinea

THE PHILIPPINES

The Philippines (Primate of the Philippines)	Richard Abellon PO Box 3167, Manila, Philippines
Central Philippines	Manuel C Lumpias 281 E Rodrigues Sr Blvd, Quezon City, PO Box 655, Manila 2800, Philippines
North Central Philippines	Artemio Masweng Zabala c/o PO Box 655, Manila 2801, Philippines
Northern Luzon	Ignacio C Soliba Episcopal Diocese of Northern Luzon, Bulanao, Tabuk, Kalinga-Apayao 1401, Philippines
Northern Philippines	Robert L O Longid Diocesan Office, Bontoc, Mt Province 0601, Philippines
Southern Philippines	Narcisco V Ticobay Diocesan Office, Sinsuat Ave, PO Box 113, Cotabato City 9301, Philippines

SOUTHERN AFRICA

Bloemfontein	Thomas S Stanage Bishop's House, 16 York Road, Bloemfontein 9301, South Africa
Cape Town (Primate)	Desmond M Tutu Bishopscourt, Claremont, Cape Province 7700, South Africa
(Suffragans)	Charles H Albertyn Bishopsholme, 18 Rue Ursula, Glenhaven, Bellville 7530, South Africa
	Edward Mackenzie 39 Paradise Road, Newlands 7700, South Africa
	Alan G Quinlan 77 Kildare Road, Newlands 7700, South Africa
Christ the King	Peter J Lee PO Box 37, Kliptown 1812, South Africa
George	Derek C Damant Bishop's Lea, PO Box 227, George 6530, Cape Province, South Africa
Grahamstown	David P Russell Bishopsbourne, PO Box 162, Grahamstown, Cape Province 6140, South Africa
(Suffragan)	Eric Pike PO Box 493, Queenstown (2 Villagers Road, Balmoral, Queenstown 5320) South Africa
Johannesburg	Duncan Buchanan Diocesan Office, PO Box 1131, Johannesburg 2000, South Africa
Kimberley & Kuruman	Winston N Ndungane PO Box 45, Kimberley 8300, Cape Province, South Africa
Klerksdorp	David C T Nkwe PO Box 11417, Klerksdorp 2570, South Africa
Lebombo	Dinis Sengulane Caixa Postale 120, Maputo, Moçambique
Lesotho	Philip S Mokuku Bishop's House, PO Box MS 87, Maseru, Lesotho, Southern Africa

(Suffragan)	Donald P Nestor PO Box 87, Maseru, Lesotho, Southern Africa		

SUDAN

Bor	Nathaniel Garang c/o PO Box 44838, Nairobi, Kenya
Juba (Archbishop)	Benjamin W Yugusuk c/o Dr John Atkins, ECS Liaison Officer, PO Box 47429, Nairobi, Kenya
(Assistant)	Michael S Lugor (address as above)
*Kadugli	Mubarek Khamis PO Box 65, Omdurman, Dem Rep of Sudan
Kajo Keji	Manasse B Dawidi c/o PO Box 44838, Nairobi, Kenya
Khartoum	Bulus Idris Tia PO Box 65, Omdurman, Dem Rep of Sudan
(Assistant)	Butrus Kowo Kori (address as above)
Maridi	Joseph Marona c/o PO Box 44838, Nairobi, Kenya
Mundri	Eluzai Munda c/o PO Box 44838, Nairobi, Kenya
Rumbek	Gabriel Roric Jur St Barnabas' Pro Cathedral, Rumbek, Lakes' Province, Dem Rep of Sudan
Wau (Acting Bishop)	Gabriel Roric Jur The Episcopal Church of the Sudan, PO Box 65, Omdurman, Dem Rep of Sudan
Yambio	Daniel Zindo Western Equatoria Province, Southern Region, Yambio, Dem Rep of Sudan
*Yei	Seme L Solomona c/o PO Box 44838, Nairobi, Kenya

Dioceses still to be inaugurated

Namibia	James Kauluma PO Box 57, Windhoek, Namibia, South West Africa
Natal	Michael Nuttall Bishop's House, 5 Chaceley Place, Morningside, Durban 4001, South Africa
(Suffragans)	Ross Cuthbertson PO Box 899, Pietermaritzburg, Natal 3200, South Africa
	Matthew M Makhay PO Box 463, Ladysmith 3370, South Africa
Niassa	Paulino T Manhique Missao Anglicana de Messumba, CP 264, Lichinga, Niassa, Moçambique
Order of Ethiopia (Bishop of the)	Sigqibo Dwane, PO Box 629, Grahamstown 6140, South Africa
Port Elizabeth	Bruce R Evans 75 River Road, Walmer, PE 6065, South Africa
Pretoria	Richard A Kraft Bishop's House, 264 Celliers St. PO Box 1032, Pretoria 0001 South Africa
St Helena	John H Ruston PO Box 62, Bishopsholme, St Helena Island, South Atlantic
St John's	Jacob Z Dlamini PO Box 163, Umtata, Transkei, Southern Africa
(Suffragan)	Geoff Davies PO Box 644, Kokstad 4700, South Africa
St Mark the Evangelist	Philip John Le Feuvre PO Box 643, Pietermaritzburg 0070, South Africa
South Eastern Transvaal	David A Beetge PO Box 114, Springs 1560, South Africa
Swaziland	Bernard L Mkhabela PO Box 118, Mbabane, Swaziland
Zululand	Lawrence B Zulu PO Box 147, Eshowe 3815, Zululand, Southern Africa

SOUTHERN CONE OF AMERICA

Argentina	David Leake Calle 25 de Mayo 282, CP 1002, Buenos Aires, Argentina
Chile (Obispo Primado)	Colin F Bazley Casilla de Correo 50675, Santiago, Chile
(Assistant)	Ian A Morrison Casilla de Correo 1973, Concepcion, Chile
Northern Argentina	Maurice Sinclair Casilla de Correo 187, 4400 Salta. Argentina
(Assistant)	Mario L Marino Iglesia Anglicana, Casilla 19, CP 3636 Ingeniero Juarez, FCNGB, Formosa, Argentina
Paraguay	John Ellison Iglesia Anglicana Paraguya, Casilla de Correo 1124, Asuncion, Paraguay
Peru & Bolivia	Alan Winstanley Apartado 18-1032, Miraflores, Lima 18, Peru
Uruguay	Harold William Godfrey Reconquista 522, Casilla 6108, 11000, Montevideo, Uruguay

TANZANIA

Central Tanganyika	Godfrey Mdimi Mhogolo Makay House, PO Box 15, Dodoma, Tanzania
Dar-es-Salaam (Retires 31.12.91)	Christopher Mlangwa PO Box 25016, Ilala, Dar-es-Salaam, Tanzania
(Suffragan)	John Watanabe (address as above)
Kagera	Christopher Ruhuza PO Box 18, Ngara, Tanzania
Mara	Gershom O Nyaronga PO Box 131, Musoma, Tanzania
Masasi	Richard Norgate Mtandi, Private Bag, PO Masasi, Tanzania
Morogoro	Dudley Mageni PO Box 320, Morogoro, Tanzania
Mount Kilimanjaro	Simon Makundi PO Box 1057, Arusha, Tanzania
Mpwapwa	Simon Chiwanga PO Box 2, Mpwapwa, Tanzania
Rift Valley	Alpha Mohamed c/o PO Box 899, Dodoma, Tanzania
Ruaha	Donald Mtetemela Box 1028, Iringa, Tanzania
Ruvuma	Stanford S Shauri PO Box 1, Liuli, Mbinga District, Tanzania
South-West Tanganyika	Charles J Mwaigoga PO Box 32, Njombe, Tanzania
Tabora	Francis Ntiruka, Diocese of Tabora, PO Box 1408, Tabora, Tanzania
Victoria Nyanza	John Changae PO Box 278, Mwanza, Tanzania

Western Tanganyika	Gerald Mpango PO Box 13, Kasulu, Tanzania
Zanzibar and Tanga (Archbishop)	John A Ramadhani PO Box 35, Korogwe, Tanzania

UGANDA

Bukedi	Nicodemus Okille PO Box 170, Tororo, Uganda
Bunyoro-Kitara	Wilson N Turumanya PO Box 20, Hoima, Uganda
Busoga	Cyprian Bamwoze PO Box 1658, Jinja, Uganda
East Ankole	Amos Betungura PO Box 14, Mbarara, Ankole, Uganda
Kampala (Archbishop)	Yona Okoth PO Box 14123, Kampala, Uganda
(Assistant)	A Gonahasa PO Box 335, Kampala, Uganda
Karamoja	Peter Lomongin Karamoja Diocese, Private Bag, PO Kapenguria, via Kitale, Kenya
Kigezi	William Rukirande PO Box 65, Kabale, Kigezi, Uganda
Lango	Melchizedek Otim PO Box 6, Lira, Uganda
(Assistant)	William M Okodi (address as above)
Luwero	Mesusera Bujimbi PO Box 125, Luwero, Uganda
Madi & West Nile	Vacant PO Box 370, Arua, Uganda
Mbale	Akisoferi M Wesonga Bishop's House, PO Box 473, Mbale, Uganda
Mityana	Nelson Mutebi PO Box 102, Mityana, Uganda
Muhabura	Ernest Shalita Church of Uganda, PO Box 22, Kisoro, Uganda
Mukono	Livingstone M Nkoyoyo PO Box 39, Mukono, Uganda
Namirembe	Misaeri Kauma PO Box 14297, Kampala, Uganda
North Kigezi	Yustasi Ruhindi PO Box 23, Rukungiri, Uganda
Northern Uganda	Gideon Oboma PO Box 232, Gulu, Uganda
Ruwenzori	Eustace Kamanyire Bishop's House, PO Box 37, Fort Portal, Uganda
Soroti	Geresom Ilukor PO Box 107, Soroti, Uganda
South Ruwenzori	Zebedee K Masereka PO Box 142, Kasese, Uganda
West Ankole	Yoramu Bamunoba PO Box 140, Bushenyi, Uganda
West Buganda	Christopher D Senyonjo PO Box 242, Masaka, Uganda
(Assistant)	George Sinabulya (address as above)

UNITED STATES OF AMERICA

The roman numerals indicate to which of the nine provinces of ECUSA the diocese belongs.

Presiding Bishop	Edmond L Browning Episcopal Church Center, 815 Second Ave, New York, NY 10017 USA
Alabama (IV)	Robert O Miller Carpenter House, 521 N 20th St. Birmingham AL 35203 USA
Alaska (VIII)	Steven Charleston Box 70441, Fairbanks AK 99707-0441, USA

Albany (II)	David S Ball 62 South Swan St, Albany, NY 12210 USA
Arizona (VIII)	Joseph T Heistand PO Box 13647, Phoenix, AZ 85002 USA
Arkansas (VII)	Herbert A Donovan Jr Cathedral House, PO Box 164668, 300 West 17th St, Little Rock, AR 72216 USA
Atlanta (IV)	Frank Kellogg Allan 2744 Peachtree Road NW, Atlanta, GA 30363, USA
Bethlehem (III)	J Mark Dyer 333 Wyandotte St, Bethlehem, PA 18015 USA
California (VIII)	William E Swing 1055 Taylor St, San Francisco, CA 94108 USA
(Assistants)	G R Millard 501 Fanita Way, Menlo Park, CA 94025, USA
	J R Wyatt 1204 Chelsea Way, Redwood City, CA 94061, USA
Central Florida (IV)	John W Howe 1017E Robinson Street, Orlando, FL 32801, USA
(Assistant)	Herbert D Edmondson 1404 Ruthdern Road, Daytona Beach, FL 32014 USA
Central Gulf Coast (IV)	Charles F Duvall 201 N Baylen Street, Penacola, FL 32591-3330, USA
Central New York (II)	O'Kelly Whitaker 310 Montgomery St, Suite 200, Syracuse, NY 13202-2093 USA
(Coadjutor)	David B Joslin (address as above)
Central Pennsylvania (III)	Charlie F McNutt 221 N Front St, Box 11937, Harrisburg PA 17101-1937 USA
Chicago (V)	Frank T Griswold 65 East Huron St, Chicago, IL 60611 USA
(Suffragan)	William Wiedrich (address as above)
Colombia (IX)	Bernardo Merino-Botero Apartado Aereo 52964, Bogota 2, Colombia, South America
Colorado (VI)	William J Winterrowd Box 18 M, Capitol Hill Station, Denver CO 80218 USA
(Suffragan)	William H Wolfrum (address as above)
Connecticut (I)	Arthur E Walmsley 1335 Asylum Ave, Hartford, CT 06105 USA
(Suffragans)	Clarence N Coleridge 29 Indian Road, Trumbull CT 06611 USA
	Jeffery W Rowthorn 337 Main Street, Portland, CT 06480 USA
Cuernavaca (IX)	Jose G Saucedo Apartado Postal 192, Admon 4, CP 62431, Cuernavaca, Morelos, Mexico
Dallas (VII)	Donis D Patterson 1630 Garrett Street, Dallas, Texas 75206 USA
Delaware (III)	C Cabell Tennis 2020 Tatnall St, Wilmington, DE 19802 USA
Dominican Republic (IX)	Julio César Holguin Apartado 764, Santo Domingo, Dominican Republic
East Carolina (IV)	Brice S Sanders PO Box 1336, Kinston NC 28503 USA
East Tennessee (IV)	W E Saunders PO Box 3807, Knoxville TN 37927-3850 USA

(Co-adjutor)	Robert G Tharp	(address as above)
Eastern Oregon (VIII)	Rustin R Kimsey	PO Box 620, The Dalles, Oregon 97058, USA
Easton (III)	Elliott L Sorge	Box 1027, Easton MD 21601 USA
Eau Claire (V)	William C Wantland	510 South Farwell St, Eau Claire, WI 54701 USA
Ecuador, Central Diocese (IX)	Jose Neptali Larrea-Moreno	Apartado 353-A, Quito, Ecuador, South America
Ecuador, Litoral Diocese (IX)	Vacant	Apartado Box 5250, Calle Bogota, 1010, Bario Centenario, Guayaquil, Ecuador, South America
El Camino Real (VIII)	Richard L Shimpfy	PO Box 1903, Monterey, CA 93940 USA
El Salvador (IX)	Vacant	Apartado (01) 6, San Salvador, El Salvador
(Bishop in Charge)	James H Ottley	Box R, Balboa, Republic of Panama
Europe, Convocation of American Churches in	Matthew P Bigliardi	23 Avenue George V, 75008 Paris, France
Florida (IV)	Frank S Cerveny	325 Market St, Jacksonville, FL 32202 USA
(Assistant)	Robert P Varley	(address as above)
Fond du Lac (V)	William L Stevens	PO Box 149, Grafton Hall, 39 North Sophia St, Fond du Lac, WI 54936-0149, USA
Fort Worth (VII)	Clarence C Pope	Suite 110, 6300 Ridglea Place, Fort Worth TX 76116 USA
Georgia (IV)	Harry W Shipps	611 E Bay St. Savannah GA 31401 USA
Guatemala (IX)	Armando R Guerra	Apartado 58a, Guatemala City, Guatemala, Central America
Haiti (II)	Luc A J Garnier	Eglise Episcopale d'Haiti, BP 1309, Port-au-Prince, Haiti
Hawaii (VII)	Donald P Hart	Diocesan Office, 229 Queen Emma Sq, Honolulu HI 96813 USA
Honduras (IX)	Leopold Frade	Apartado 586, San Pedro Sula, Honduras, Central America
Idaho (VIII)	John S Thornton	PO Box 936, Boise, ID 83701 USA
Indianapolis (V)	Edward W Jones	1100 West 42nd St, Indianapolis, IN 46208 USA
Iowa (VI)	C Christopher Epting	225 37th St, Des Moines IA 50312 USA
Kansas (VII)	William E Smalley	Bethany Place, 833-35 Polk St, Topeka KS 66612 USA
Kentucky (IV)	David B Reed	600 East Main St, Louisville, KY 40202 USA
Lexington (IV)	Don A Wimberley	PO Box 610, Lexington KY 40586 USA
Long Island (II)	Orris G Walker Jr	36 Cathedral Ave, Garden City, NY 11530 USA
Los Angeles (VIII)	Fred H Borsch	1220 West 4th St, Los Angeles CA 90017 USA
(Suffragan)	Chester L Talton	(address as above)

Louisiana (IV)	James B Brown	1623 Seventh St, New Orleans, LA 70115-4111 USA
Maine (I)	Edward C Chalfont	Loring House, 143 State St, Portland ME 04101 USA
Maryland (III)	A Theodore Eastman	4 East St, University Parkway, Baltimore, MD 21208, USA
(Suffragan)	Charles L Longest	(address as above)
Massachusetts (I)	David E Johnson	138 Tremont Street, Boston, MA 02111 USA
(Suffragan)	Barbara Harris	(address as above)
(Assistant)	David Birney	(address as above)
Mexico (IX)	Sergio Carranza-Gómez	Ave San Jeronimo 117, Col S Angel, Deleg A Obregon, 01000 Mexico DF
	Martiniano Garcia-Montiel	(address as above)
Michigan (V)	R Stewart Wood	4800 Woodward Ave, Detroit, MI 48201 USA
(Suffragan)	H Irving Mayson	(address as above)
Milwaukee (V)	Roger J White	804 East Juneau Ave, Milwaukee, WI 53202 USA
Minnesota (VI)	Robert M Anderson	430 Oak Grove, Box 306, Minneapolis, MN 55403, USA
(Suffragan)	Sanford Z K Hampton	(address as above)
Mississippi (IV)	Duncan M Gray Jr	PO Box 23107, Jackson MS 39225-3107 USA
(Coadjutor)	A C Marble	(address as above)
Missouri (V)	William A Jones Jr	1210 Locust St, St Louis, MO 63103 USA
(Coadjutor)	Hays H Rockwell	(address as above)
Montana (VI)	Charles I Jones	515 North Park Ave, Helena, MT 59601 USA
Navajoland (VIII)	Steven Tsosie Plummer	Navajoland Area Mission, Box 720, Farmington, NM 87499, USA
Nebraska (VI)	James E Krotz	200 North 62nd St, Omaha NE 68132-6357 USA
Nevada (VIII)	Stewart C Zabriskie	PO Box 6357, 2390 West 7th St, Reno NV 89513 USA
New Hampshire (I)	Douglas E Theuner	63 Green St, Concord NH 03301 USA
New Jersey (II)	G P Mellick Belshaw	808 West State St, Trenton, NJ 08618 USA
(Suffragan)	Vincent K Pettit	(address as above)
New York (II)	Richard F Grein	Synod House, 1047 Amsterdam Ave, Cathedral Heights, New York, NY 10025 USA
(Suffragan)	Walter D Dennis	(address as above)
Newark (II)	John S Spong	24 Rector St, Newark NJ 07102 USA
(Suffragan)	Jack McKelvey	(address as above)
(Assistant)	Walter C Righter	(address as above)

Nicaragua (IX)	Sturdie Downs Apartado 1207, Managua, Nicaragua	South Dakota (VI)	Craig B Anderson Box 517, 200 West 18th Street, Sioux Falls, South Dakota 57104 USA
North Carolina (VI)	Robert W Estill PO Box 17025, 210 St Alban's Dr Raleigh NC 27619-7025 USA	Southeast Florida (IV)	Calvin O Schofield Jr 525 NE 15 St, Miami FL 33132 USA
North Dakota (VI)	Andrew H Fairfield 2315 N University Dr., Fargo ND 58109-8340 USA	Southeastern Mexico (IX)	Claro Huerta-Ramos Avenida de las Americas #73, Col Aguacatal, 91130 Jalapa, Veracruz, Mexico
Northern California (VIII)	John L Thompson Box 161268, 1318 27th Street, Sacramento CA 95816 USA	Southern Ohio (V)	William G Black 412 Sycamore St, Cincinnati OH 45202 USA
(Coadjutor)	Jerry Lamb (address as above)	(Coadjutor)	Herbert Thompson (address as above)
Northern Indiana (V)	Francis C Gray Cathedral House, 117 N Lafayette Blvd, South Bend, IN 46601 USA	Southern Virginia (III)	C Charles Vaché 600 Talbot Hall Rd, Norfolk VA 23505 USA
Northern Mexico (IX)	German Martinez-Marquez Acatlán Simon Bolivar 2005 Norte, Colonia Mitras Centro, 64460 Monterrey NL, Mexico	(Coadjutor)	Frank H Vest (address as above)
Northern Michigan (V)	Thomas K Ray 131 E. Ridge St, Marquette MI 49855 USA	Southwest Florida (IV)	Roger Harris PO Drawer 491, St Petersburg FL 33731 USA
Northwest Texas (VII)	Sam B Hulsey PO Box 1067, Lubbock TX 79408 USA	Southwestern Virginia (III)	Arthur Heath Light 100 First St SW, PO Box 2279, Roanoke, VA 24009 USA
Northwestern Pennsylvania (III)	Donald J Davis 145 West 6th St, Erie PA 16501 USA	Spokane (VIII)	Frank J Terry 245 E 13th Ave, Spokane WA 99202 USA
(Coadjutor)	Robert D Rowley Jr (address as above)	Springfield (V)	Donald M Hultstrand 821 Sth 2nd St, Springfield IL 62704 USA
Ohio (V)	James R Moodey 2230 Euclid Ave, Cleveland, OH 44115-2499 USA		
(Suffragan)	Arthur B Williams (address as above)	Taiwan (VIII)	John Chieh-Tsung Chien 1-105-7 Hangchow South Rd, Taipei Taiwan 10044, Republic of China
Oklahoma	Robert M Moody 924 North Robinson Street, Oklahoma City, OK 73102 USA	Tennessee (IV)	George L Reynolds 42 Rutledge Hill, Nashville, TN 37210 USA
Olympia (VIII)	Vincent W Warner Jr PO Box 12126, 1551 10th Ave E, Seattle WA 98102 USA	Texas (VII)	Maurice M Benitez 3203 West Alabama St, Houston TX 77098 USA
Oregon (VIII)	Robert L Ladehoff PO Box 467, Lake Oswego, OR 97034-0467 USA	(Suffragan)	William E Stirling (address as above)
Panama (IX)	James H Ottley Box R, Balboa, Republic of Panama	(Assistant)	Anselmo Carral Box 2247, Austin, TX 78768, USA
(Suffragan)	Victor Scantlebury (address as above)	Upper South Carolina (IV)	William A Beckham Box 1789, Columbia SC 29202 USA
Pennsylvania (III)	Allen L Bartlett 240 South Fourth Street, Philadelphia PA 19106 USA	(Assistant)	William F Carr (address as above)
(Suffragan)	Franklin D Turner (address as above)	Utah (VIII)	George E Bates 231 East First South St, Salt Lake City UT 84110-3090 USA
Pittsburgh (III)	Alden M Hathaway 325 Oliver Ave, Pittsburgh PA 15222-2467 USA	Vermont (I)	Daniel L Swenson The Bishop's House, Rock Point, Burlington VT 05401 USA
Quincy (V)	Edward H MacBurney 3601 N North St, Peoria IL 61604 USA	Virgin Islands (II)	Egbert D Taylor PO Box 7488, St Thomas, Virgin Islands VI 00801 USA
(Assistant Bishop)	Brother John Charles FODC (address as above)	Virginia (III)	Peter Lee 110 W Franklin St, Richmond VA 23220 USA
Rhode Island (I)	George N Hunt 275 Main St, Providence RI 02903 USA	(Assistant)	Robert P Atkinson (address as above)
Rio Grande (VII)	Terrence Kelshaw 4304 Carlisle NE, Albuquerque NM 87107 USA	Washington (III)	Ronald H Haines Episcopal Church House, Mount St, Alban, Washington DC 20016 USA
Rochester (II)	William G Burrill 935 East Ave, Rochester NY 14607 USA	West Missouri (VII)	John C Buchanan PO Box 413227, Kansas City, MO 64141-3227 USA
San Diego (VIII)	C Brinkley Morton 2728 Sixth Ave, San Diego CA 92103-6397 USA	West Tennessee (IV)	Alex D Dickson 692 Poplar Ave, Memphis TN 38105 USA
San Joaquin (VIII)	John David Schofield 4159 E Dakota Ave, Fresno CA 93726 USA	West Texas (VII)	John H MacNaughton PO Box 6885, San Antonio TX 78209 USA
South Carolina (IV)	Edward L Salmon Box 20127, 126 Coming Street Charleston SC 29413-0127 USA	(Suffragan)	Earl N McArthur (address as above)

West Virginia (III)	John H Smith PO Box 5400, Charlestown WV 25361-0400 USA
Western Kansas (VII)	John F Ashby Box 2507, Salina, Kansas 67402-2507 USA
Western Louisiana (IV)	Robert J Hargrove Jr PO Box 2031, Alexandria, LA 71309 USA
Western Massachusetts (I)	Andrew F Wissemann 37 Chestnut St, Springfield MA 01103 USA
Western Mexico (IX)	Samuel Espinoza Apartado 2-1220, 44100, Guadalajara, Jalisco, Mexico
Western Michigan (V)	Edward L Lee Jr The Cathedral, 2600 Vincent Ave, Kalamazoo MI 49008 USA
Western New York (II)	David C Bowman 114 Delaware Ave, Buffalo NY 14209 USA
Western North Carolina (IV)	Robert H Johnson Box 368, Vance Avenue, Black Mountain, NC 28711 USA
Wyoming (VI)	Bob G Jones 104 South Fourth St, Laramie WY 82070 USA

WEST AFRICA

Accra	Francis W Thompson PO Box 8, Accra, Ghana
Bo	Michael Keili MacRobert St, PO Box 21, Bo, Southern Province, Sierra Leone
Cape Coast	Vacant Bishopscourt, PO Box 38, Cape Coast, Ghana
Freetown	Prince E Thompson Bishopscourt, PO Box 128, Freetown, Sierra Leone
Gambia	Solomon T Johnson Bishopscourt, PO Box 51, Banjul, Gambia
Guinea	Vacant PO Box 105, Conakry, Guinea Bissau
Koforidua	Robert Okine PO Box 980, Koforidua, Ghana
Kumasi	Edmund Yeboah St Cyprian's Church House, PO Box 144, Kumasi, Ghana
Liberia (Archbishop)	George D Browne PO Box 277, Monrovia, Liberia
(Suffragan)	Edward de Neufville (address as above)
Sekondi	Theophilus Annobil PO Box 85, Sekondi, Ghana
Sunyani/ Tamale	Joseph K Dadson Bishop's House, PO Box 110, Tamale NR. Ghana

WEST INDIES

Barbados	Drexel Gomez Bishop's Court, St Michael, Barbados
Belize	Brother Desmond SSF Bishopsthorpe, PO Box 535, Southern Foreshore, Belize City, Belize
Guyana	Randolph O George Austin House, Georgetown 1, Guyana
Jamaica	Neville W de Souza Church House, 2 Caledonia Ave, Kingston 5, Jamaica
(Suffragans)	Herman Spence (Bishop of Kingston) (address as above)
	Alfred C Reid (Bishop of Montego Bay) PO Box 346, Montego Bay, St James, Jamaica

	William A Murray (Bishop of Mandeville) PO Box 41, Mandeville, Jamaica
Nassau & the Bahamas	Michael Eldon Addington House, PO Box N-7107, Nassau, Bahamas
North Eastern Caribbean and Aruba (Archbishop)	Orland U Lindsay Bishop's Lodge, PO Box 23, St John's, Antigua
(Suffragan)	Alfred E Jeffery All Saints' Rectory, PO Box 1023, St John's, Antigua
Trinidad & Tobago	Clive O Abdulah Hayes Court, 21 Maraval Rd, Port of Spain, Trinidad
Windward Islands	Philip E R Elder PO Box 128, Bishop's House, Kingstown, St Vincent, West Indies

EXTRA-PROVINCIAL DIOCESES

Bermuda (Canterbury)	W J Down Bishop's Lodge, Box 769, Hamilton HM CX, Bermuda
China	K H Ting 378 Mo Chou Road, Nanjing, China
Costa Rica (Extra-Provincial to IX)	Cornelius J Wilson Apartado 2773, 1000 San José, Costa Rica
Cuba	Emilio J Hernandez Calle 13, No 874, Vedado Habana 4, Cuba
Hong Kong (China)	Peter Kwong Bishop's House, 1 Lower Albert Road Hong Kong
§Kuching (Canterbury)	John Leong Chee Yun Bishop's House, PO Box 347, Kuching, Sarawak, East Malaysia
Lusitanian Church (Canterbury)	Fernando Soares Rua Elias Garcia 107 - 1° Dto, 4400 VN de Gaia, Portugal
Puerto Rico (Extra Provin- cial to IX)	David Alvarez Centro Diocesano San Justo, PO Box C, Saint Just, Puerto Rico 00750
†§Pusan (Canterbury)	Bunso Chae Hon Kim PO Box 43, Hae-un-Dae, Pusan, 607-04, Korea
§Sabah (Canterbury)	Yong Ping Chung PO Box 10811, 88809 Kota Kinabalu, Sabah, E Malaysia
†§Seoul (Canterbury)	Simon S Kim 3 Chong Dong, Chung Ku, Seoul 100-120, Republic of Korea
§Singapore (Canterbury)	Moses Tay Bishopsbourne, 4 Bishopsgate, Singapore 1024
Spanish Reformed Episcopal Church (Canterbury)	Arturo S Galan Calle Beneficencia 18, 28004, Madrid, Spain
†§Taejon (Canterbury)	Paul Hwan Yoon PO Box 22, Taejon 300, Republic of Korea
Venezuela (Extra-Provincial to IX)	Onell Soto Apartado 60008, Chacao del Este, Caracas 1060, Venezuela
§West Malaysia (Canterbury)	John G Savarimuthu Rumah Bishop, 14 Pesiaran Stonor, Kuala Lumpur 50450, West Malaysia

† Anglican Church in Korea
§ Also members of the Council of the Churches of East Asia

BISHOPS OF CHURCHES WHERE ANGLICANS HAVE UNITED WITH CHRISTIANS OF OTHER TRADITIONS

NORTH INDIA

Agra	W O Simon Bishop's House, Stewart Ward School Compound, Sikandra, Agra 282007, UP, India
Amritsar	Anand Chandu Lal 40 Rose Ave, Opposite Customs House, Amritsar 143001, India
Andaman and Nicobar Islands	Edmund Matthew Cathedral Compound, Mus, Car Nicobar 744301, India Bishop's House, Port Blair, Andaman Islands 744101, India
Assam	E W Talibuddin Bishop's Kuti, Shillong 1, 793001 Assam, India
Barrackpore	Samar Bairagi Bishop's Lodge, 86 Middle Road, Barrackpore 743101, W Bengal, India
Bhopal	M B Singh 7 Old Sehore Rd, Indore 452001, MP, India
Bombay	Samuel B Joshua St John's House, Duxbury Lane, Colaba, Bombay 400005, India
Calcutta	Dinesh C Gorai Bishop's House, 51 Chowringhee, Calcutta 700071, India
Chandigarh	Joel Vidyasagal Mal Bishop's House, Mission Compound, Brown Rd, Ludhiana 141008, Punjab, India
Chota Nagpur	Z J Terom Bishop's Lodge, PO Box 1, Ranchi, 834001 Bihar, India
Cuttack	J K Mohanty Bishop's House, Madhusudan Rd, Cuttack 753001, Orissa, India
Darjeeling (Moderator)	John E Ghose Bishop's House, Darjeeling 734101, W Bengal, India
Delhi	Pritam Santram Bishop's House, 1 Church Lane, New Delhi 110001, India
Durgapur (Acting Bishop)	John E Ghose (also Bishop of Darjeeling) Bishop's House, Darjeeling 734101, W Bengal, India
Gujarat	Paul Chauhan Bishop's House, Ellis Bridge, Ahmedabad 380006, Gujarat State, India
Jabalpur (Deputy Moderator)	F C Jonathan 1033 Napier Town, Jabalpur, MP 482001, India
Kolhapur	I P Andrews Bishop's House, EP School Compound, Kolhapur 416003, Maharashtra, India
Lucknow	Arthur Raja Yusuf Bishop's House, 25 Mahatma Gandhi Marg, Allahabad 211001, UP, India
Nagpur	Vinod Peter Cathedral House, Nagpur 440001, Maharashtra, India
Nasik	Dinkar J Vairagar Bishop's House, 1 Outram Rd, Tarakpur, Ahmednagar 414001, Maharashtra, India
Patna	N M Bagh Bishop's House, Christ Church Compound, Bhagalpur 812001, Bihar, India
Rajasthan	E C Anthony 62/X Savitri Girls' College Road, Civil Lines, Ajmer 305006, India
Sambalpur	Lingaram Tandy Mission Compound, Bolangir 767001, Orissa, India

SOUTH INDIA

Coimbatore (Bishop in)	William Joseph Bishop's House, Coimbatore 641018, South India
Dornakal (Bishop in)	D Noah Samuel Bishop's House, Dornakal SC Rly, Andhra Pradesh 506381, South India
East Kerala (Bishop in)	K J Samuel Bishop's House, Melukavumattom 686652, South India
Jaffna (Bishop in)	David Jeyaratnam Ambalavanar Bishop's House, Vaddukoddai, Sri Lanka
Kanyakumari (Bishop in)	G Christdhas CSA Bishop's House, opp. Collectorate, Ramavarapuram, Nagercoil 629001, South India
Karimnagar (Bishop in)	K E Swamidas Bishop's House, Mukarampura PO, Karim Nagar 505002, Andhra Pradesh, South India
Karnataka Central (Bishop in)	C D Jathanna Bishop's House, Trinity Church, Bangalore 560027, South India
Karnataka North (Moderator's Commissary)	V P Dandin Bishop's House, Haliyal Rd, Dharwar 508008, Mysore State, South India
Karnataka South (Moderator's Commissary)	D P Shettian Bishop's House, Balmatta, Bangalore 575001 SK South India
Krishna-Godavari (Bishop in)	T B D Prakasa Rao Bishop Azariah High School Campus, Vijayawada 520010, AP South India
Madhya Kerala (Bishop in)	M C Mani Bishop's House, Chetty St, Kottayam 686001, Kerala State, South India
Madras (Bishop in)	Mazilimani Azariah Bishop's House, Cathedral Road, Madras 600086, South India
(Assistant)	Henry Thanaraj Diocesan Office, Post Box 4914 Madras 600086, South India
Madurai-Ramnad (Deputy Moderator)	D Pothirajulu Bishop's House, P B No 233, CMH Compound, East Gate, Madurai 625001, Tamil Nadu, South India
Medak (Moderator)	Victor Premasagar Bishop's House, Cathedral Compound, Medak 502110 AP South India
Nandyal (Bishop in)	B Ryder Devapriyam Bishop's House, Nandyal, RS Kurnool District, Andhra Pradesh, South India
North Kerala (Bishop in)	Dr P G Kruvilla Diocesan Office, Shoranpur 679121, Kerala State, South India
Rayalaseema (Bishop in)	L V Azariah Bishop's House, Cuddapah 516001, Cuddapah District 518502, South India
South Kerala (Bishop in)	Dr Samuel Amirtham Bishop's House, LMS Compound, Trivandrum 695033, South India
Tiruchirapalli-Thanjavur (Bishop in)	R Paulraj PO Box 31, 8 Racquet Court Lane, Tiruchirapalli 620001, South India
Tirunelveli (Bishop in)	Jason S Dharmaraj Bishopstowe, Box 18, Palayamkottai-627002, Tirunelveli T Nadu, South India

Vellore (Bishop *in*)	R Trinity Bhaskeran Ashram Bungalow, Filterbed Rd, Vellore, N Arcot Dt. 632001, South India

BANGLADESH

Dhaka (Moderator)	Barnabas Dwijen Mondal St Thomas's Church, 54 Johnson Road, Dhaka 1, Bangladesh
Kushtia	Michael S Baroi 94 N S Road, Thanapara, Kushtia, Bangladesh

PAKISTAN

Faisalabad (Moderator)	Zahir-ud-din Mirza Bishop's House, PO Box 27, Mission Rd, Gojra, Faisalabad, Pakistan
Hyderabad	Bashir Jiwan St Thomas Cathedral, 27 Liaquat Road, Civil Lines, Hyderabad, Sind, Pakistan

Karachi	Arne Rudvin Bishop's House, Trinity Close, Abdullah Haroon Road, Karachi 0405, Pakistan
Lahore	Alexander J Malik Bishopsbourne, Cathedral Close, The Mall, Lahore 3, Pakistan
Multan	Samuel D Chand 113 Qasim Rd, Multan Cantt, Pakistan
Peshawar	S L Alexander St John's Church, 1 Sir-Seyed Rd, Peshawar Cantonment, North West Frontier Province, Pakistan
Rawind	Samuel Azariah 15-A Warris Road Lahore 3, Pakistan
Sialkot	Samuel Parvaiz Lal Kothi, Barah Patthar, Sialkot 2, Pakistan

ADDRESSES OF PROVINCIAL OFFICES

From which further information may be sought.

Australia. PO Box Q190, Queen Victoria PO, Sydney 2000, NSW, Australia.

Brazil. Caixa Postal 11.510,90641 Porto Alegre, RS Brazil.

Burundi, Rwanda and Zaire. BP 1300, Bujumbura, Burundi.

Canada. 600 Jarvis St, Toronto, Ontario M4Y 2J6, Canada.

Central Africa. PO Box 769, Gaborone, Botswana.

Ceylon. 368/1 Bauddlaloka Mawatha, Colombo 7, Sri Lanka.

East Asia. (Council of the Churches of East Asia). PO Box 655, Manila, Philippines 2081.

England. Church House, Great Smith Street, London SW1P 3NZ, England.

Indian Ocean. Box 44, Victoria, Seychelles.

Ireland. Church of Ireland House, Church Avenue, Rathmines, Dublin 6, Irish Republic.

Japan. 4-21 Higashi l-chome, Shibuya-ku, Tokyo, Japan 150.

Jerusalem & the Middle East. PO Box 2075, Nicosia 118, Cyprus.

Kenya. PO Box 40502, Nairobi, Kenya.

Melanesia. PO Box 19, Honiara, Solomon Islands.

Myanmar (formerly Burma). PO Box 1412, 140 Pyidaungsu-Yeiktha Rd, Dagon PO, Yangon, Myanmar.

New Zealand. PO Box 2148, Rotorua, New Zealand.

Nigeria. PO Box 1666, Ibadan, Nigeria.

Papua New Guinea. Box 304 Lae, Papua New Guinea.

Philippines. c/o Prime Bishop of the Philippines, PO Box 3167, Manila, Philippines.

Scotland. 21 Grosvenor Crescent, Edinburgh EH12 5EE, Scotland.

Southern Africa. Bishopscourt, Claremont, CP 7700, Republic of South Africa.

South America. Casilla 561, Vina Del Mar, Chile.

Sudan. PO Box 44838, Nairobi, Kenya.

Tanzania. PO Box 899, Dodoma, Tanzania.

Uganda. PO Box 14123, Kampala, Uganda.

USA. 815 Second Ave, New York, NY 10017, USA.

Wales. 39 Cathedral Rd, Cardiff, S Glamorgan CF1 9XF, Wales.

West Africa. PO Box 8, Accra, Ghana.

West Indies. Bishopscourt, St Michael, Barbados, West Indies.

South India. Synod Office, Cathedral PO, Madras, India.

North India. CNI Bhavan, 16 Pandit Pant Marg, New Delhi 110001, India.

Pakistan. c/o Holy Trinity Cathedral, Cathedral Close, Fatima Jinnah Road, Karachi 3, Pakistan.

Bangladesh. St Thomas Church, 54 Johnson Road, Dhaka-1, Bangladesh.

DIRECTORIES OF THE ANGLICAN PROVINCES

The following Provinces of the Anglican Communion are known to publish directories of their clergy. These may be ordered through Church House Bookshop, 31 Great Smith Street, London SW1P 3BN, which has information of the cost and availability of current and future editions.

Australia. *The Sydney Diocesan Year Book* contains lists of clergy in the various dioceses of Australia as well as more complete details of its own clergy. Published annually.
Sydney Diocesan Registry, Anglican Church of Australia, PO Box 0190, Queen Victoria Buildings, Sydney 2000, Australia.

Canada. *The Anglican Year Book*. Published annually.
Anglican Book Centre, 600 Jarvis Street, Toronto, Ontario, M4Y 2J6, Canada.

Ireland. *Church of Ireland Directory*. Published annually.
Styletype Publishing Co. (Ireland) Ltd., Sheldon House, 60 Pembroke Road, Dublin 4.

Japan (in Japanese). *Seikokai Yearbook*. Published annually.
Nippon Sei Ko Kai Provincial Office, 4-21 Higashi 1-chome, Shibuya-Ku, Tokyo, Japan 150.

Jerusalem and the Middle East. *A Provincial Directory*. Published annually.
Provincial Office, Box 1248, 20 Nablus Road, Jerusalem.

New Zealand. *Clerical Directory*. Published annually.
Provincial Secretary, PO Box 2148, Rotorua, New Zealand.

Nigeria. *Nigeria Churchman's Year Book*.
Church House, 29 Marina, PO Box 78, Lagos, Nigeria.

Scotland. *Year Book and Directory of the Scottish Episcopal Church*. Published annually.
Secretary General and Treasurer, 21 Grosvenor Crescent, Edinburgh EH12 5EE.

Southern Africa. *Clerical Directory*. Published annually.
Provincial Office, Bishopscourt, Claremont, Cape Province 7700, South Africa.

Southern Cone of America. *Directorio Provincial*. Published every three years.
Casilla 50675, Santiago, Chile.

United States. *Episcopal Clerical Directory*. Published annually.
Church Hymnal Corporation, 800 Second Avenue, New York, NY 10017, USA.

West Africa. *West African Churchman's Calendar and Clerical Directory*. Published approximately every five years; latest 1985.
The Secretariat, Church of the Province of West Africa, Bishopscourt, PO Box 8, Accra, Ghana.

Diocesan lists are the source of information for the Churches of Brazil, Central Africa and Sri Lanka. In the West Indies, the Diocese of Jamaica publishes a Clerical Directory.

Close links with many overseas provinces are maintained by the United Society for the Propagation of the Gospel and by the Church Missionary Society, both at Partnership House, 157 Waterloo Road, London SE1 8XA (for USPG), and SE1 8UU (for CMS).

The Bible Churchmen's Missionary Society at 251 Lewisham Way, London SE4 1XF also has contacts with many provinces overseas.

The South American Missionary Society, serving not only that sub-continent but also the Iberian peninsula, is at Allen Gardiner House, Pembury Road, Tunbridge Wells, Kent TN2 3QU.

For the Provinces not listed above, information should be sought from the Provincial Secretary or from dioceses (for addresses see pp. 1048 and 1037ff). Details of other Anglican missionary societies may be found in the *Church of England Year Book*.

SUCCESSION OF ARCHBISHOPS AND BISHOPS

In a number of dioceses, especially for the medieval period, the dating of some episcopal appointments is not known for certain. For ease of reference, the date of consecration is given when known; or, in the case of more modern appointments, the date of confirmation of election. More information on the dates of individual bishops can be found in the Royal Historical Society's *Handbook of British Chronology.*

ENGLAND

PROVINCE OF CANTERBURY

Canterbury

597	Augustine
604	Laurentius
619	Mellitus
624	Justus
627	Honorius
655	Deusdedit
668	Theodorus
693	Berhtwald
731	Tatwine
735	Nothelm
740	Cuthbert
761	Bregowine
765	Jaenberht
793	Æthelheard
805	Wulfred
832	Feologild
833	Ceolnoth
870	Æthelred
890	Plegmund
914	Æthelhelm
923	Wulfhelm
942	Oda
959	Ælfsige
959	Byrhthelm
960	Dunstan
c988	Athelgar
990	Sigeric Serio
995	Ælfric
1005	Ælfheah
1013	Lyfing [Ælfstan]
1020	Æthelnoth
1038	Eadsige
1051	Robert of Jumièges
1052	Stigand
1070	Lanfranc
1093	Anselm
1114	Ralph d'Escures
1123	William de Corbeil
1139	Theobald of Bec
1162	Thomas Becket
1174	Richard [of Dover]
1184	Baldwin
1193	Hubert Walter
1207	Stephen Langton
1229	Richard le Grant
1234	Edmund Rich
1245	Boniface of Savoy
1273	Robert Kilwardby
1279	John Pecham
1294	Robert Winchelsey
1313	Walter Reynolds
1328	Simon Mepham
1333	John Stratford
1349	Thomas Bradwardine
1349	Simon Islip
1366	Simon Langham
1368	William Whittlesey
1375	Simon Sudbury

1381	William Courtenay
1396	Thomas Arundel[1]
1398	Roger Walden
1414	Henry Chichele
1443	John Stafford
1452	John Kempe
1454	Thomas Bourgchier
1486	John Morton
1501	Henry Deane
1503	William Warham
1533	Thomas Cranmer
1556	Reginald Pole
1559	Matthew Parker
1576	Edmund Grindal
1583	John Whitgift
1604	Richard Bancroft
1611	George Abbot
1633	William Laud
1660	William Juxon
1663	Gilbert Sheldon
1678	William Sancroft
1691	John Tillotson
1695	Thomas Tenison
1716	William Wake
1737	John Potter
1747	Thomas Herring
1757	Matthew Hutton
1758	Thomas Secker
1768	Frederick Cornwallis
1783	John Moore
1805	Charles Manners Sutton
1828	William Howley
1848	John Bird Sumner
1862	Charles Thomas Longley
1868	Archibald Campbell Tait
1883	Edward White Benson
1896	Frederick Temple
1903	Randall Thomas Davidson
1928	Cosmo Gordon Lang
1942	William Temple
1945	Geoffrey Francis Fisher
1961	Arthur Michael Ramsey
1974	Frederick Donald Coggan
1980	Robert Alexander Kennedy Runcie
1991	George Leonard Carey

London

	Theanus
	Eluanus
	Cadar
	Obinus
	Conanus
	Palladius
	Stephanus
	Iltutus
	Theodwinus
	Theodredus
	Hilarius

314	Restitutus
	Guitelinus
	Fastidius
	Vodinus
	Theonus
c604	Mellitus
664	Cedd[2]
666	Wini
675	Eorcenwald
693	Waldhere
716	Ingwald
745	Ecgwulf
772	Wigheah
782	Eadbeorht
789	Eadgar
793	Coenwalh
796	Eadbald
798	Heathoberht
803	Osmund
c811	Æthelnoth
824	Ceolberht
862	Deorwulf
898	Swithwulf
898	Heahstan
900	Wulfsige
926	Æthelweard
926	Leofstan
926	Theodred
—	Wulfstan I
953	Brihthelm
959	Dunstan
964	Ælfstan
996	Wulfstan II
1004	Ælfhun
1014	Ælfwig
1035	Ælfweard
1044	Robert of Jumièges
1051	William
1075	Hugh of Orival
1086	Maurice
1108	Richard de Belmeis
1128	Gilbert [the Universal]
1141	Robert de Sigillo
1152	Richard de Belmeis II
1163	Gilbert Foliot
1189	Richard Fitz Neal
1199	William of Ste-Mere-Eglise
1221	Eustace de Fauconberg
1229	Roger Niger
1244	Fulk Basset
1260	Henry Wingham
1263	Henry of Sandwich
1274	John Chishull
1280	Richard Gravesend
1306	Ralph Baldock
1313	Gilbert Segrave
1317	Richard Newport
1319	Stephen Gravesend
1338	Richard Bintworth

[1] On 19 October 1399 Boniface IX annulled Arundel's translation to St Andrews and confirmed him in the See of Canterbury.

[2] See vacant for a term of years.

London—continued

1355 Michael Northburgh
1362 Simon Sudbury
1375 William Courtenay
1382 Robert Braybrooke
1404 Roger Walden
1406 Nicholas Bubwith
1407 Richard Clifford
1421 John Kempe
1426 William Gray
1431 Robert Fitz-Hugh
1436 Robert Gilbert
1450 Thomas Kempe
1489 Richard Hill
1496 Thomas Savage
1502 William Warham
1504 William Barons [Barnes]
1506 Richard Fitz-James
1522 Cuthbert Tunstall [Tonstall]
1530 John Stokesley
1540 Edmund Bonner
1550 Nicholas Ridley
1553 Edmund Bonner (rest.)
1559 Edmund Grindal
1570 Edwin Sandys
1577 John Aylmer
1595 Richard Fletcher
1597 Richard Bancroft
1604 Richard Vaughan
1607 Thomas Ravis
1610 George Abbot
1611 John King
1621 George Montaigne [Mountain]
1628 William Laud
1633 William Juxon
1660 Gilbert Sheldon
1663 Humfrey Henchman
1676 Henry Compton
1714 John Robinson
1723 Edmund Gibson
1748 Thomas Sherlock
1761 Thomas Hayter
1762 Richard Osbaldeston
1764 Richard Terrick
1778 Robert Lowth
1787 Beilby Porteus
1809 John Randolph
1813 William Howley
1828 Charles James Blomfield
1856 Archibald Campbell Tait
1869 John Jackson
1885 Frederick Temple
1897 Mandell Creighton
1901 Arthur Foley Winnington-Ingram
1939 Geoffrey Francis Fisher
1945 John William Charles Wand
1956 Henry Colville Montgomery
      Campbell
1961 Robert Wright Stopford
1973 Gerald Alexander Ellison
1981 Graham Douglas Leonard
1991 David Michael Hope

†Westminster

1540 Thomas Thirlby

Winchester

BISHOPS OF THE WEST SAXONS
634 Birinus
650 Ægilberht

BISHOPS OF WINCHESTER
660 Wine
670 Leutherius

---

676 Haedde
705 Daniel
744 Hunfrith
756 Cyneheard
778 Æthelheard
778 Ecbald
785 Dudd
c785 Cyneberht
803 Eahlmund
814 Wigthegn
825 Herefrith[1]
838 Eadmund
c838 Eadhun
839 Helmstan
852 Swithhun
867 Ealhferth
877 Tunberht
879 Denewulf
909 Frithestan
931 Byrnstan
934 Ælfheah I
951 Ælfsige I
960 Brihthelm
963 Æthelwold I
984 Ælfheah II
1006 Cenwulf
1006 Æthelwold II
c1014 Ælfsige II
1032 Ælfwine
1043 Stigand
      Ælfsige III?
1070 Walkelin
1107 William Giffard
1129 Henry of Blois
1174 Richard of Ilchester [Toclyve]
1189 Godfrey de Lucy
1205 Peter des Roches
1244 Will. de Raleigh
1260 Aymer de Valance [of
      Lusignan]
1262 John Gervaise
1268 Nicholas of Ely
1282 John of Pontoise
1305 Henry Merewell [or Woodlock]
1316 John Sandale
1320 Rigaud of Assier
1323 John Stratford
1333 Adam Orleton
1346 William Edendon [Edington]
1367 William of Wykeham
1404 Henry Beaufort
1447 William of Waynflete
1487 Peter Courtenay
1493 Thomas Langton
1501 Richard Fox
1529 Thomas Wolsey
1531 Stephen Gardiner (dep.)
1551 John Ponet [Poynet]
1553 Stephen Gardiner (rese.)
1556 John White (dep.)
1561 Robert Horne
1580 John Watson
1584 Thomas Cowper [Cooper]
1595 William Wickham [Wykeham]
1596 William Day
1597 Thomas Bilson
1616 James Montague
1619 Lancelot Andrewes
1628 Richard Neile
1632 Walter Curll
1660 Brian Duppa
1662 George Morley
1684 Peter Mews
1707 Jonathan Trelawney
1721 Charles Trimnell
1723 Richard Willis

1734 Benjamin Hoadly
1761 John Thomas
1781 Brownlow North
1820 George Pretyman Tomline
1827 Charles Richard Sumner
1869 Samuel Wilberforce
1873 Edward Harold Browne
1891 Anthony Wilson Thorold
1895 Randall Thomas Davidson
1903 Herbert Edward Ryle
1911 Edward Stuart Talbot
1923 Frank Theodore Woods
1932 Cyril Forster Garbett
1942 Mervyn George Haigh
1952 Alwyn Terrell Petre Williams
1961 Sherard Falkner Allison
1975 John Vernon Taylor
1985 Colin Clement Walter James

Bath and Wells

BISHOPS OF WELLS
909 Athelm
925 Wulfhelm I
928 Ælfheah
938 Wulfhelm II
956 Byrhthelm
974 Cyneweard
979 Sigegar
997 Ælfwine
999 Lyfing
1018 Æthelwine (eject.)
1013 Brihtwine (dep.)
      Æthelwine (rest.)
      Beorhtwine (rest.)
1024 Brihtwig [also Merehwit]
1033 Duduc
1061 Gisa
1088 John of Tours [de Villula]

BISHOPS OF BATH
1090 John of Tours [de Villula]
1123 Godfrey
1136 Robert
1174 Reg. Fitz Jocelin
1192 Savaric FitzGeldewin

BATH AND GLASTONBURY
1206 Jocelin of Wells

BATH AND WELLS
1244 Roger of Salisbury
1248 William Bitton I
1265 Walter Giffard
1267 William Bitton II
1275 Robert Burnell
1293 William of March
1302 Walter Hasleshaw
1309 John Droxford
1329 Ralph of Shrewsbury
1364 John Barnet
1367 John Harewell
1386 Walter Skirlaw
1388 Ralph Erghum
1401 Henry Bowet
1407 Nicholas Bubwith
1425 John Stafford
1443 Thomas Beckington
1466 Robert Stillington
1492 Richard Fox
1495 Oliver King
1504 Adriano de Castello [di Corneto]
1518 Thomas Wolsey
1523 John Clerk

---

[1] Never signed without Wigthegn.

Bath and Wells—continued

1541 William Knight
1548 William Barlow
1554 Gilbert Bourne
1560 Gilbert Berkeley
1584 Thomas Godwin
1593 John Still
1608 James Montague
1616 Arthur Lake
1626 William Laud
1628 Leonard Mawe
1629 Walter Curll
1632 William Piers
1670 Robert Creighton
1673 Peter Mews
1685 Thomas Ken (dep.)
1691 Richard Kidder
1704 George Hooper
1727 John Wynne
1743 Edward Willes
1774 Charles Moss
1802 Richard Beadon
1824 George Henry Law
1845 Richard Bagot
1854 Robert John Eden, Lord
      Auckland
1869 Arthur Charles Hervey
1894 George Wyndham Kennion
1921 St. John Basil Wynne Wilson
1937 Francis Underhill
1943 John William Charles Wand
1946 Harold William Bradfield
1960 Edward Barry Henderson
1975 John Monier Bickersteth
1987 George Leonard Carey
1991 James Lawton Thompson

Birmingham

1905 Charles Gore
1911 Henry Russell Wakefield
1924 Ernest William Barnes
1953 John Leonard Wilson
1969 Laurence Ambrose Brown
1978 Hugh William Montefiore
1987 Mark Santer

Bristol

1542 Paul Bush
1554 John Holyman
1562 Richard Cheyney
1581 John Bullingham (held
      Gloucester and Bristol
      1586–9)
1589 Richard Fletcher
[See vacant for ten years]
1603 John Thornborough
1617 Nicholas Felton
1619 Rowland Searchfield
1623 Robert Wright
1633 George Coke
1637 Robert Skinner
1642 Thomas Westfield
1644 Thomas Howell
1661 Gilbert Ironside
1672 Guy Carleton
1679 William Gulston
1684 John Lake
1685 Jonathan Trelawney
1689 Gilbert Ironside
1691 John Hall
1710 John Robinson
1714 George Smalridge
1719 Hugh Boulter
1724 William Bradshaw

1733 Charles Cecil
1735 Thomas Secker
1737 Thomas Gooch
1738 Joseph Butler
1750 John Conybeare
1756 John Hume
1758 Philip Yonge
1761 Thomas Newton
1782 Lewis Bagot
1783 Christopher Wilson
1792 Spencer Madan
1794 Henry Reginald Courtenay
1797 Ffolliott Herbert Walker
      Cornewall
1803 George Pelham
1807 John Luxmoore
1808 William Lort Mansel
1820 John Kaye
1827 Robert Gray
1834 Joseph Allen
[1836 to 1897, united
      with **Gloucester**]
1897 George Forrest Browne
1914 George Nickson
1933 Clifford Salisbury Woodward
1946 Frederick Arthur Cockin
1959 Oliver Stratford Tomkins
1975 Ernest John Tinsley
1985 Barry Rogerson

Chelmsford

1914 John Edwin Watts-Ditchfield
1923 Frederic Sumpter Guy Warman
1929 Henry Albert Wilson
1951 Sherard Falkner Allison
1962 John Gerhard Tiarks
1971 Albert John Trillo
1986 John Waine

Chichester

BISHOPS OF SELSEY
681 Wilfrid
716 Eadberht
731 Eolla
733 Sigga [Sigeferth]
765 Aaluberht
c765 Oswald [Osa]
780 Gislhere
786 Tota
c789 Wihthun
c811 Æthelwulf
c824 Cynered
845 Guthheard
900 Wighelm
909 Beornheah
931 Wulfhun
943 Ælfred
955 Daniel
956 Brihthelm
963 Eadhelm
980 Æthelgar
990 Ordbriht
1009 Ælfmaer
1032 Æthelric I
1039 Grimketel
1047 Heca
1058 Æthelric II
1070 Stigand

BISHOPS OF CHICHESTER
1075 Stigand

1088 Godfrey
1091 Ralph Luffa
1125 Seffrid I [d'Escures Pelochin]
1147 Hilary
1174 John Greenford
1180 Seffrid II
1204 Simon FitzRobert
1215 Richard Poore
1218 Ranulf of Wareham
1224 Ralph Nevill
1245 Richard Wich
1254 John Climping
1262 Stephen Bersted [or Pagham]
1288 Gilbert de St. Leofard
1305 John Langton
1337 Robert Stratford
1362 William Lenn
1369 William Reade
1386 Thomas Rushock
1390 Richard Mitford
1396 Robert Waldby
1397 Robert Reade
1417 Stephen Patrington
1418 Henry de la Ware
1421 John Kempe
1421 Thomas Polton
1426 John Rickingale
1431 Simon Sydenham
1438 Richard Praty
1446 Adam de Moleyns
1450 Reginald Pecock
1459 John Arundel
1478 Edward Story
1504 Richard Fitz-James
1508 Robert Sherburne
1536 Richard Sampson
1543 George Day (dep.)
1552 John Scory
1553 George Day (rest.)
1557 John Christopherson
1559 William Barlow
1570 Richard Curtis
1586 Thomas Bickley
1596 Anthony Watson
1605 Lancelot Andrewes
1609 Samuel Harsnett
1619 George Carleton
1628 Richard Montague
1638 Brian Duppa
1642 Henry King
1670 Peter Gunning
1675 Ralph Brideoake
1679 Guy Carleton
1685 John Lake
1689 Simon Patrick
1691 Robert Grove
1696 John Williams
1709 Thomas Manningham
1722 Thomas Bowers
1724 Edward Waddington
1731 Francis Hare
1740 Matthias Mawson
1754 William Ashburnham
1798 John Buckner
1824 Robert James Carr
1831 Edward Maltby
1836 William Otter
1840 Philip Nicholas Shuttleworth
1842 Ashurst Turner Gilbert
1870 Richard Durnford
1896 Ernest Roland Wilberforce
1908 Charles John Ridgeway
1919 Winfrid Oldfield Burrows
1929 George Kennedy Allen Bell
1958 Roger Plumpton Wilson
1974 Eric Waldram Kemp

Coventry

1918 Huyshe Wolcott Yeatman-Biggs
1922 Charles Lisle Carr
1931 Mervyn George Haigh
1943 Neville Vincent Gorton
1956 Cuthbert Killick Norman
     Bardsley
1976 John Gibbs
1985 Simon Barrington-Ward

Derby

1927 Edmund Courtenay Pearce
1936 Alfred Edward John Rawlinson
1959 Geoffrey Francis Allen
1969 Cyril William Johnston Bowles
1988 Peter Spencer Dawes

Dorchester[1]

634 Birinus
650 Agilbert
c660 Ætla
c888 Ahlheard

Ely

1109 Hervey
1133 Nigel
1174 Geoffrey Ridel
1189 William Longchamp
1198 Eustace
1220 John of Fountains
1225 Geoffrey de Burgo
1229 Hugh of Northwold
1255 William of Kilkenny
1258 Hugh of Balsham
1286 John of Kirkby
1290 William of Louth
1299 Ralph Walpole
1303 Robert Orford
1310 John Ketton
1316 John Hotham
1337 Simon Montacute
1345 Thomas de Lisle
1362 Simon Langham
1367 John Barnet
1374 Thomas Arundel
1388 John Fordham
1426 Philip Morgan
1438 Lewis of Luxembourg
1444 Thomas Bourgchier
1454 William Grey
1479 John Morton
1486 John Alcock
1501 Richard Redman
1506 James Stanley
1515 Nicholas West
1534 Thomas Goodrich
1555 Thomas Thirlby
1559 Richard Cox
1600 Martin Heton
1609 Lancelot Andrewes
1619 Nicolas Felton
1628 John Buckeridge
1631 Francis White
1638 Matthew Wren
1667 Benjamin Laney
1675 Peter Gunning
1684 Francis Turner
1691 Simon Patrick
1707 John Moore
1714 William Fleetwood
1723 Thomas Greene
1738 Robert Butts

1748 Thomas Gooch
1754 Matthias Mawson
1771 Edmund Keene
1781 James Yorke
1808 Thomas Dampier
1812 Bowyer Edward Sparke
1836 Joseph Allen
1845 Thomas Turton
1864 Edward Harold Browne
1873 James Russell Woodford
1886 Alwyne Frederick Compton
1905 Frederick Henry Chase
1924 Leonard Jauncey White-
     Thomson
1934 Bernard Oliver Francis Heywood
1941 Harold Edward Wynn
1957 Noel Baring Hudson
1964 Edward James Keymer Roberts
1977 Peter Knight Walker
1990 Stephen Whitefield Sykes

Exeter

BISHOPS OF CORNWALL
870 Kenstec
893 Asser
931 Conan
950 Æthelge [ard]
c955 Daniel
963 Wulfsige Comoere
990 Ealdred
1009 Æthelsige
1018 Buruhwold
1027 Lyfing, Bp. of Crediton,
     Cornwall and Worcester
1046 Leofric, Bp. of Crediton and
     Cornwall
[See transferred to Exeter 1050]

BISHOPS OF CREDITON
909 Eadwulf
934 Æthelgar
953 Ælfwold I
973 Sideman
979 Ælfric
987 Ælfwold II
1008 Ælfwold III
1015 Eadnoth
1027 Lyfing
1046 Leofric[2]

BISHOPS OF EXETER
1050 Leofric
1072 Osbern Fitz-Osbern
1107 Will. Warelwast
1138 Robert Warelwast
1155 Robert II of Chichester
1161 Bartholomew
1186 John the Chanter
1194 Henry Marshall
1214 Simon of Apulia
1224 William Brewer
1245 Richard Blund
1258 Walter Bronescombe
1280 Peter Quinel [Wyvill]
1292 Thomas Bitton
1308 Walter Stapeldon
1327 James Berkeley
1328 John Grandisson
1370 Thomas Brantingham
1395 Edmund Stafford
1419 John Catterick
1420 Edmund Lacy
1458 George Nevill

1465 John Booth
1478 Peter Courtenay
1487 Richard Fox
1493 Oliver King
1496 Richard Redman
1502 John Arundel
1505 Hugh Oldham
1519 John Veysey (resig.)
1551 Miles Coverdale
1553 John Veysey (rest.)
1555 James Turberville
1560 William Alley [or Allei]
1571 William Bradbridge
1579 John Woolton
1595 Gervase Babington
1598 William Cotton
1621 Valentine Carey
1627 Joseph Hall
1642 Ralph Brownrigg
1660 John Gauden
1662 Seth Ward
1667 Anthony Sparrow
1676 Thomas Lamplugh
1689 Jonathan Trelawney
1708 Offspring Blackall
1717 Lancelot Blackburn
1724 Stephen Weston
1742 Nicholas Claget
1747 George Lavington
1762 Frederick Keppel
1778 John Ross
1792 William Buller
1797 Henry Reginald Courtenay
1803 John Fisher
1807 George Pelham
1820 William Carey
1830 Christopher Bethell
1831 Henry Phillpotts
1869 Frederick Temple
1885 Edward Henry Bickersteth
1901 Herbert Edward Ryle
1903 Archibald Robertson
1916 Rupert Ernest William
     Gascoyne Cecil
1936 Charles Edward Curzon
1949 Robert Cecil Mortimer
1973 Eric Arthur John Mercer
1985 Geoffrey Hewlett Thompson

Gloucester

1541 John Wakeman alias Wiche
1551 John Hooper
1554 James Brooks
1562 Richard Cheyney[3]
1581 John Bullingham[4]
1598 Godfrey Goldsborough
1605 Thomas Ravis
1607 Henry Parry
1611 Giles Thompson
1612 Miles Smith
1625 Godfrey Goodman
1661 William Nicolson
1672 John Pritchett
1681 Robert Frampton
1691 Edward Fowler
1715 Richard Willis
1721 Joseph Wilcocks
1731 Elias Sydall
1735 Martin Benson
1752 James Johnson
1760 William Warburton
1779 James Yorke
1781 Samuel Hallifax

---

[1] Originally a West Saxon, after Ahlheard's time a Mercian, bishopric. See transferred to Lincoln 1077.
[2] Removed See from Crediton.
[3] Also Bishop of Bristol.
[4] Held Gloucester and Bristol 1581-9.

Gloucester—continued

1789 Richard Beadon
1802 George Isaac Huntingford
1815 Henry Ryder
1824 Christopher Bethell
1830 James Henry Monk
[1836 to 1897, united with Bristol]
BISHOPS OF GLOUCESTER AND
BRISTOL
1836 James Henry Monk
1856 Charles Baring
1861 William Thomson
1863 Charles John Ellicott[1]
BISHOPS OF GLOUCESTER
1897 Charles John Ellicott
1905 Edgar Charles Sumner Gibson
1923 Arthur Cayley Headlam
1946 Clifford Salisbury Woodward
1954 Wilfred Marcus Askwith
1962 Basil Tudor Guy
1975 John Yates

Guildford

1927 John Harold Greig
1934 John Victor Macmillan
1949 Henry Colville Montgomery
        Campbell
1956 Ivor Stanley Watkins
1961 George Edmund Reindorp
1973 David Alan Brown
1983 Michael Edgar Adie

Hereford

676 Putta
688 Tyrhtel
710 Torhthere
c731 Wahlstod
736 Cuthberht
741 Podda
c758 Acca
c770 Headda
777 Aldberht
786 Esne
c788 Ceolmund
c798 Utel
801 Wulfheard
824 Beonna
c832 Eadwulf
c839 Cuthwulf
866 Mucel
c866 Deorlaf
888 Cynemund
890 Eadgar
c931 Tidhelm
940 Wulfhelm
c940 Ælfric
971 Æthelwulf
1016 Æthelstan
1056 Leofgar
1056 Ealdred, Bp of Hereford and
        Worcester
1060 Walter
1079 Robert Losinga
1096 Gerard
1107 Reinhelm
1115 Geoffrey de Clive
1121 Richard de Capella
1131 Robert de Bethune
1148 Gilbert Foliot

1163 Robert of Melun
1174 Robert Foliot
1186 William de Vere
1200 Giles de Braose
1216 Hugh of Mapenore
1219 Hugh Foliot
1234 Ralph Maidstone
1240 Peter d'Aigueblanche
1269 John Breton
1275 Thomas Cantilupe
1283 Richard Swinfeld
1317 Adam Orleton
1327 Thomas Charlton
1344 John Trilleck
1361 Lewis Charleton
1370 William Courtenay
1375 John Gilbert
1389 John Trefnant
1404 Robert Mascall
1417 Edmund Lacy
1420 Thomas Polton
1422 Thomas Spofford
1449 Richard Beauchamp
1451 Reginald Boulers
1453 John Stanbury
1474 Thomas Milling
1492 Edmund Audley
1502 Adriano de Castello [di Corneto]
1504 Richard Mayeu
1516 Charles Booth
1535 Edward Fox
1539 John Skip
1553 John Harley
1554 Robert Parfew or Wharton
1559 John Scory
1586 Herbert Westfaling
1603 Robert Bennett
1617 Francis Godwin
1634 Augustine Lindsell
1635 Matthew Wren
1635 Theophilus Field
1636 George Coke
1661 Nicolas Monk
1662 Herbert Croft
1691 Gilbert Ironside
1701 Humphrey Humphries
1713 Philip Bisse
1721 Benjamin Hoadly
1724 Henry Egerton
1746 James Beauclerk
1787 John Harley
1788 John Butler
1803 Ffolliott Herbert Walker
        Cornewall
1808 John Luxmoore
1815 George Isaac Huntingford
1832 Edward Grey
1837 Thomas Musgrave
1848 Renn Dickson Hampden
1868 James Atlay
1895 John Percival
1918 Herbert Hensley Henson
1920 Martin Linton Smith
1931 Charles Lisle Carr
1941 Richard Godfrey Parsons
1949 Tom Longworth
1961 Mark Allin Hodson
1974 John Richard Gordon Eastaugh
1990 John Keith Oliver

Leicester

Also see Lincoln.

NEW FOUNDATION

1927 Cyril Charles Bowman Bardsley
1940 Guy Vernon Smith
1953 Ronald Ralph Williams
1979 Cecil Richard Rutt
1991 Thomas Frederick Butler

Lichfield

BISHOPS OF MERCIA
656 Diuma[2]
658 Ceollach
659 Trumhere
662 Jaruman
BISHOPS OF LICHFIELD
669 Chad[3]
672 Winfrith
676 Seaxwulf
691 Headda[4]
731 Aldwine
737 Hwita
757 Hemele
765 Cuthfrith
769 Berhthun
779 Hygeberht[5]
801 Aldwulf
816 Herewine
818 Æthelwald
830 Hunberht
836 Cyneferth
845 Tunberht
869 Eadberht
883 Wulfred
900 Wigmund or Wilferth
915 Ælfwine
941 Wulfgar
949 Cynesige
964 Wynsige
975 Ælfheah
1004 Godwine
1020 Leofgar
1026 Brihtmær
1039 Wulfsige
1053 Leofwine
1072 Peter
BISHOPS OF LICHFIELD,
CHESTER, AND COVENTRY[6]
1075 Peter
1086 Robert de Limesey[6]
1121 Robert Peche
1129 Roger de Clinton
1149 Walter Durdent
1161 Richard Peche
1183 Gerard La Pucelle
1188 Hugh Nonant
1198 Geoffrey Muschamp
1215 William Cornhill
1224 Alex. Stavensby
1240 Hugh Pattishall
1246 Roger Weseham
1258 Roger Longespée
1296 Walter Langton
1322 Roger Northburgh
1360 Robert Stretton
1386 Walter Skirlaw
1386 Richard le Scrope
1398 John Burghill

[1] Gloucester only from 1897.
[2] Abp of the Mercians, the Lindisfari, and the Middle Angles.
[3] Bp of the Mercians and Lindisfari.
[4] Bp of Lichfield and Leicester.
[5] Abp of Lichfield after 787.
[6] 1102 Robert de Limesey, Bp of Lichfield, moved the See to Coventry. Succeeding Bishops are usually termed *of Coventry* until 1228. Then *Coventry and Lichfield* was the habitual title until the Reformation. *Chester* was used by some 12th-century Bishops, and popularly afterwards. After the Reformation *Lichfield and Coventry* was used until 1846.

Lichfield—continued

1415 John Catterick
1420 William Heyworth
1447 William Booth
1452 Nicholas Close
1453 Reginald Boulers
1459 John Hales
1493 William Smith
1496 John Arundel
1503 Geoffrey Blyth
1534 Rowland Lee
1541 [**Chester** formed
    as a bishopric]
1543 Richard Sampson
1554 Ralph Baynes
1560 Thomas Bentham
1580 William Overton
1609 George Abbot
1610 Richard Neile
1614 John Overall
1619 Thomas Morton
1632 Robert Wright
1644 Accepted Frewen
1661 John Hackett
1671 Thomas Wood
1692 William Lloyd
1699 John Hough
1717 Edward Chandler
1731 Richard Smalbroke
1750 Fred. Cornwallis
1768 John Egerton
1771 Brownlow North
1775 Richard Hurd
1781 James Cornwallis [4th Earl
    Cornwallis]
1824 Henry Ryder
1836 [Coventry transferred
    to Worcester diocese]
1836 Samuel Butler
1840 James Bowstead
1843 John Lonsdale
1868 George Augustus Selwyn
1878 William Dalrymple Maclagan
1891 Augustus Legge
1913 John Augustine Kempthorne
1937 Edward Sydney Woods
1953 Arthur Stretton Reeve
1975 Kenneth John Fraser Skelton
1984 Keith Norman Sutton

Lincoln

BISHOPS OF LINDSEY

634 Birinus
650 Agilbert
660 Aetlai
678 Eadhaed
680 Æthelwine
693 (?)Edgar
731 (?)Cyneberht
733 Alwig
750 Aldwulf
767 Ceolwulf
796 Eadwulf
839 Beorhtred
869 Burgheard
933 Ælfred
953 Leofwine
996 Sigefrith

BISHOPS OF LEICESTER

664 Wilfrid, tr. from York
679 Cuthwine
691 Headda[1] (founder of Lichfield
    Cathedral 705-37)
727 Aldwine

737 Torhthelm
764 Eadberht
785 Unwona
803 Wernberht
816 Ræthhun
840 Ealdred
844 Ceolred
874 [See of Leicester removed to
    Dorchester]

BISHOPS OF DORCHESTER
(after it became a Mercian See)

c888 Ahlheard
900 Wigmund or Wilferth
909 Cenwulf
925 Wynsige
c951 Osketel
953 Leofwine
975 Ælfnoth
979 Æscwig
1002 Ælfheln
1006 Eadnoth I
1016 Æthelric
1034 Eadnoth II
1049 Ulf
1053 Wulfwig
1067 Remigius

BISHOPS OF LINCOLN

1072 Remigius
1094 Robert Bloett
1123 Alexander
1148 Robert de Chesney
1183 Walter de Coutances
1186 Hugh of Avalon
1203 William of Blois
1209 Hugh of Wells
1235 Robert Grosseteste
1254 Henry Lexington [Sutton]
1258 Richard Gravesend
1280 Oliver Sutton [Lexington]
1300 John Dalderby
1320 Henry Burghersh
1342 Thomas Bek
1347 John Gynewell
1363 John Bokyngham [Buckingham]
1398 Henry Beaufort
1405 Philip Repingdon
1420 Richard Fleming
1431 William Gray
1436 William Alnwick
1450 Marmaduke Lumley
1452 John Chedworth
1472 Thomas Rotherham [Scott]
1480 John Russell
1495 William Smith
1514 Thomas Wolsey
1514 William Atwater
1521 John Longland
1547 Henry Holbeach [Rands]
1552 John Taylor
1554 John White
1557 Thomas Watson
1560 Nicholas Bullingham
1571 Thomas Cooper
1584 William Wickham
1595 William Chaderton
1608 William Barlow
1614 Richard Neile
1617 George Monteigne [Mountain]
1621 John Williams
1642 Thomas Winniffe
1660 Robt. Sanderson
1663 Benjamin Laney
1667 William Fuller
1675 Thomas Barlow

1692 Thomas Tenison
1695 James Gardiner
1705 William Wake
1716 Edmund Gibson
1723 Richard Reynolds
1744 John Thomas
1761 John Green
1779 Thomas Thurlow
1787 George Pretyman [Pretyman
    Tomline after June 1803]
1820 George Pelham
1827 John Kaye
1853 John Jackson
1869 Christopher Wordsworth
1885 Edward King
1910 Edward Lee Hicks
1920 William Shuckburgh Swayne
1933 Frederick Cyril Nugent Hicks
1942 Henry Aylmer Skelton
1946 Leslie Owen
1947 Maurice Henry Harland
1956 Kenneth Riches
1975 Simon Wilton Phipps
1987 Robert Maynard Hardy

Norwich

BISHOPS OF DUNWICH

631 Felix
648 Thomas
c653 Berhtgils [Boniface]
c670 Bisi
c673 Æcce
693 Alric (?)
716 Eardred
731 Aldbeorht I
747 Æscwulf
747 Eardwulf
775 Cuthwine
775 Aldbeorht II
781 Ecglaf
781 Heardred
793 Ælfhun
798 Tidferth
824 Waermund[2]
825 Wilred
836 Husa
870 Æthelwold

BISHOPS OF ELMHAM

673 Beaduwine
706 Nothberht
c731 Heathulac
736 Æthelfrith
758 Eanfrith
c781 Æthelwulf
c785 Alhheard
814 Sibba
824 Hunferth
824 Hunbeorht
836 Cunda[3]
c933 Ælfred[4]
c945 Æthelweald (?)
956 Eadwulf
970 Ælfric I
974 Theodred I
982 Theodred II
997 Æthelstan
1001 Ælfgar
1021 Ælfwine
1038 Ælfric II
1039 Ælfric III
1043 Stigand[5]
1043 Grimketel[6]
1044 Stigand (rest.)
1047 Æthelmaer

---

[1] Bp of Leicester and Lichfield.
[4] Bp of Elmham or Lindsey.

[2] Bp of Dunwich or Elmham.
[5] Dep. before consecration.

[3] Bp of Elmham or Dunwich.
[6] Bp of Selsey and Elmham.

Norwich—continued

BISHOPS OF THETFORD
1070 Herfast
1086 William de Beaufai
1091 Herbert Losinga

BISHOPS OF NORWICH
1091 Herbert Losinga
1121 Everard of Montgomery
1146 William de Turbe
1175 John of Oxford
1200 John de Gray
1222 Pandulf Masca
1226 Thomas Blundeville
1239 William Raleigh
1245 Walter Suffield or Calthorp
1258 Simon Walton
1266 Roger Skerning
1278 William Middleton
1289 Ralph Walpole
1299 John Salmon
1325 [Robert de Baldock]
1325 William Ayermine
1337 Anthony Bek
1344 William of Norwich [Bateman]
1356 Thomas Percy
1370 Henry Spencer [Dispenser]
1407 Alexander Tottington
1413 Richard Courtenay
1416 John Wakeryng
1426 William Ainwick
1436 Thomas Brown
1446 Walter Lyhert [le Hart]
1472 James Goldwell
1499 Thomas Jane
1501 Richard Nykke
1536 William Reppes [Rugge]
1550 Thomas Thirlby
1554 John Hopton
1560 John Parkhurst
1575 Edmund Freke
1585 Edmund Scambler
1595 William Redman
1603 John Jegon
1618 John Overall
1619 Samuel Harsnett
1629 Francis White
1632 Richard Corbet
1635 Matthew Wren
1638 Richard Montagu
1641 Joseph Hall
1661 Edward Reynolds
1676 Antony Sparrow
1685 William Lloyd
1691 John Moore
1708 Charles Trimnell
1721 Thomas Green
1723 John Leng
1727 William Baker
1733 Robert Butts
1738 Thomas Gooch
1748 Samuel Lisle
1749 Thomas Hayter
1761 Philip Yonge
1783 Lewis Bagot
1790 George Horne
1792 Charles Manners Sutton
1805 Henry Bathurst
1837 Edward Stanley
1849 Samuel Hinds
1857 John Thomas Pelham
1893 John Sheepshanks
1910 Bertram Pollock
1942 Percy Mark Herbert

1959 William Launcelot Scott
    Fleming
1971 Maurice Arthur Ponsonby
    Wood
1985 Peter John Nott

Oxford

1542 Robert King[1]
1558 [Thomas Goldwell]
1567 Hugh Curen [Curwen]
1589 John Underhill
1604 John Bridges
1619 John Howson
1628 Richard Corbet
1632 John Bancroft
1641 Robert Skinner
1663 William Paul
1665 Walter Blandford
1671 Nathaniel Crewe [Lord Crewe]
1674 Henry Compton
1676 John Fell
1686 Samuel Parker
1688 Timothy Hall
1690 John Hough
1699 William Talbot
1715 John Potter
1737 Thomas Secker
1758 John Hume
1766 Robert Lowth
1777 John Butler
1788 Edward Smallwell
1799 John Randolph
1807 Charles Moss
1812 William Jackson
1816 Edward Legge
1827 Charles Lloyd
1829 Richard Bagot
1845 Samuel Wilberforce
1870 John Fielder Mackarness
1889 William Stubbs
1901 Francis Paget
1911 Charles Gore
1919 Hubert Murray Burge
1925 Thomas Banks Strong
1937 Kenneth Escott Kirk
1955 Harry James Carpenter
1971 Kenneth John Woollcombe
1978 Patrick Campbell Rodger
1987 Richard Douglas Harries

Peterborough

1541 John Chamber
1557 David Pole
1561 Edmund Scambler
1585 Richard Howland
1601 Thomas Dove
1630 William Piers
1633 Augustine Lindsell
1634 Francis Dee
1639 John Towers
1660 Benjamin Laney
1663 Joseph Henshaw
1679 William Lloyd
1685 Thomas White
1691 Richard Cumberland
1718 White Kennett
1729 Robert Clavering
1747 John Thomas
1757 Richard Terrick
1764 Robert Lambe
1769 John Hinchliffe
1794 Spencer Madan
1813 John Parsons
1819 Herbert Marsh

1839 George Davys
1864 Francis Jeune
1868 William Connor Magee
1891 Mandell Creighton
1897 Edward Carr Glyn
1916 Frank Theodore Woods
1924 Cyril Charles Bowman Bardsley
1927 Claude Martin Blagden
1949 Spencer Stottisbury Gwatkin
    Leeson
1956 Robert Wright Stopford
1961 Cyril Eastaugh
1972 Douglas Russell Feaver
1984 William John Westwood

Portsmouth

1927 Ernest Neville Lovett
1936 Frank Partridge
1942 William Louis Anderson
1949 William Launcelot Scott
    Fleming
1960 John Henry Lawrence Phillips
1975 Archibald Ronald McDonald
    Gordon
1984 Timothy John Bavin

Rochester

604 Justus
624 Romanus
633 Paulinus
644 Ithamar
664 Damianus
669 Putta
676 Cwichelm
678 Gebmund
716 Tobias
727 Aldwulf
741 Dunn
747 Eardwulf
772 Diora
785 Waermund I
805 Beornmod
844 Tatnoth
868 Badenoth
868 Waermund II
868 Cuthwulf
880 Swithwulf
900 Ceolmund
c926 Cyneferth
c934 Burhric
949 Beorhtsige
955 [Daniel?] Rochester or Selsey
964 Ælfstan
995 Godwine I
1046 Godwine II
1058 Siward
1076 Arnost
1077 Gundulf
1108 Ralph d'Escures
1115 Ernulf
1125 John
1137 John II
1142 Ascelin
1148 Walter
1182 Waleran
1185 Gilbert Glanvill
1215 Benedict of Sausetun [Sawston]
1227 Henry Sandford
1238 Richard Wendene
1251 Lawrence of St. Martin
1274 Walter Merton
1278 John Bradfield
1283 Thomas Ingoldsthorpe
1292 Thomas of Wouldham

---

[1] Bp Pheon. *in partibus*. Of Oseney 1542–5. See transferred to Oxford 1545.

Rochester—continued

1319 Hamo Hethe
1353 John Sheppey
1362 William of Whittlesey
1364 Thomas Trilleck
1373 Thomas Brinton
1389 William Bottlesham [Bottisham]
1400 John Bottlesham
1404 Richard Young
1419 John Kempe
1422 John Langdon
1435 Thomas Brouns
1437 William Wells
1444 John Low
1468 Thomas Rotherham [otherwise
     Scott]
1472 John Alcock
1476 John Russell
1480 Edmund Audley
1493 Thomas Savage
1497 Richard Fitz-James
1504 John Fisher
1535 John Hilsey [Hildesleigh]
1540 Nicolas Heath
1544 Henry Holbeach
1547 Nicholas Ridley
1550 John Ponet [Poynet]
1551 John Scory
1554 Maurice Griffith
1560 Edmund Gheast [Guest]
1572 Edmund Freke
1576 John Piers
1578 John Young
1605 William Barlow
1608 Richard Neile
1611 John Buckeridge
1628 Walter Curll
1630 John Bowle
1638 John Warner
1666 John Dolben
1683 Francis Turner
1684 Thomas Sprat
1713 Francis Atterbury
1723 Samuel Bradford
1731 Joseph Wilcocks
1756 Zachary Pearce
1774 John Thomas
1793 Samuel Horsley
1802 Thomas Dampier
1809 Walker King
1827 Hugh Percy
1827 George Murray
1860 Joseph Cotton Wigram
1867 Thomas Legh Claughton
1877 Anthony Wilson Thorold
1891 Randall Thomas Davidson
1895 Edward Stuart Talbot
1905 John Reginald Harmer
1930 Martin Linton Smith
1940 Christopher Maude Chavasse
1961 Richard David Say
1988 Anthony Michael Arnold
     Turnbull

St Albans

1877 Thomas Legh Claughton
1890 John Wogan Festing
1903 Edgar Jacob
1920 Michael Bolton Furse
1944 Philip Henry Loyd
1950 Edward Michael Gresford Jones
1970 Robert Alexander Kennedy
     Runcie
1980 John Bernard Taylor

St Edmundsbury and Ipswich

1914 Henry Bernard Hodgson
1921 Albert Augustus David
1923 Walter Godfrey Whittingham
1940 Richard Brook
1954 Arthur Harold Morris
1966 Leslie Wilfrid Brown
1978 John Waine
1986 John Dennis

Salisbury

BISHOPS OF SHERBORNE

705 Ealdhelm
709 Forthhere
736 Hereweald
774 Æthelmod
793 Denefrith
801 Wigberht
825 Ealhstan
868 Heahmund
877 Æthelheah
889 Wulfsige I
900 Asser
c909 Æthelweard
c909 Waerstan
925 Æthelbald
925 Sigehelm
934 Ælfred
943 Wulfsige II
958 Ælfwold I
979 Æthelsige I
992 Wulfsige III
1002 Æthelric
1012 Æthelsige II
1017 Brihtwine I
1017 Ælfmaer
1023 Brihtwine II
1045 Ælfwold II
1058 Hereman, bp of Ramsbury

BISHOPS OF RAMSBURY

909 Æthelstan
927 Oda
949 Ælfric I
951 Osulf
970 Ælfstan
981 Wulfgar
986 Sigeric
993 Ælfric II
1005 Brihtwold
1045 Hereman[1]

BISHOPS OF SALISBURY

1078 Osmund
     Osmer
1107 Roger
1142 Jocelin de Bohun
1189 Hubert Walter
1194 Herbert Poore
1217 Richard Poore
1229 Robert Bingham
1247 William of York
1257 Giles of Bridport
1263 Walter de la Wyle
1274 Robert Wickhampton
1284 Walter Scammel
1287 Henry Brandeston
1289 William de la Corner
1292 Nicholas Longespée
1297 Simon of Ghent
1315 Roger de Mortival
1330 Robert Wyville
1375 Ralph Erghum
1388 John Waltham
1395 Richard Mitford

1407 Nicholas Bubwith
1407 Robert Hallum
1417 John Chaundler
1427 Robert Nevill
1438 William Aiscough
1450 Richard Beauchamp
1482 Lionel Woodville
1485 Thomas Langton
1494 John Blythe
1500 Henry Deane
1502 Edmund Audley
1525 Lorenzo Campeggio
1535 Nicholas Shaxton
1539 John Salcot [Capon]
1560 John Jewell
1571 Edmund Gheast [Guest]
1577 John Piers
1591 John Coldwell
1598 Henry Cotton
1615 Robert Abbot
1618 Martin Fotherby
1620 Robert Townson [Toulson]
1621 John Davenant
1641 Brian Duppa
1660 Humfrey Henchman
1663 John Earle
1665 Alexander Hyde
1667 Seth Ward
1689 Gilbert Burnet
1715 William Talbot
1721 Richard Wilis
1723 Benjamin Hoadly
1734 Thomas Sherlock
1748 John Gilbert
1757 John Thomas
1761 Robert Hay Drummond
1761 John Thomas
1766 John Hume
1782 Shute Barrington
1791 John Douglas
1807 John Fisher
1825 Thomas Burgess
1837 Edward Denison
1854 Walter Kerr Hamilton
1869 George Moberly
1885 John Wordsworth
1911 Frederic Edward Ridgeway
1921 St. Clair George Alfred
     Donaldson
1936 Ernest Neville Lovett
1946 Geoffrey Charles Lester Lunt
1949 William Louis Anderson
1963 Joseph Edward Fison
1973 George Edmund Reindorp
1982 John Austin Baker

Southwark

1905 Edward Stuart Talbot
1911 Hubert Murray Burge
1919 Cyril Forster Garbett
1932 Richard Godfrey Parsons
1942 Bertram Fitzgerald Simpson
1959 Arthur Mervyn Stockwood
1981 Ronald Oliver Bowlby

Truro

1877 Edward White Benson
1883 Geo. Howard Wilkinson
1891 John Gott
1906 Charles William Stubbs
1912 Winfrid Oldfield Burrows
1919 Frederic Sumpter Guy Warman
1923 Walter Howard Frere
1935 Joseph Wellington Hunkin
1951 Edmund Robert Morgan

[1] Ramsbury was added to Sherborne in 1058 when Hereman became Bishop of Sherborne. The See was moved to Salisbury in 1078.

Truro—continued

1960 John Maurice Key
1973 Graham Douglas Leonard
1981 Peter Mumford
1990 Michael Thomas Ball

Worcester

680 Bosel
691 Oftfor
693 Ecgwine
718 Wilfrid I
745 Milred
775 Waermund
777 Tilhere
781 Heathured
798 Deneberht
822 Heahberht
845 Alhhun
873 Waerferth
915 Æthelhun
922 Wilferth II
929 Cenwald
957 Dunstan
961 Oswald
992 Ealdwulf
1002 Wulfstan I
1016 Leofsige
1027 Lyfing
1033 Brihtheah
1040 Æltric Puttoc, Bp of York and
    Worcester
1041 Lyfing (restored)
1046 Ealdred, Bp of Hereford and
    Worcester 1056–60
1062 Wulfstan II
1096 Samson
1115 Theulf
1125 Simon
1151 John of Pagham
1158 Aldred

1164 Roger of Gloucester
1180 Baldwin
1186 William of Northolt
1191 Robert Fitz Ralph
1193 Henry de Sully
1196 John of Coutances
1200 Mauger
1214 Walter de Gray
1216 Silvester of Evesham
1218 William of Blois
1237 Walter Cantilupe
1266 Nicolas of Ely
1268 Godfrey Giffard
1302 Walter Gainsborough
1308 Walter Reynolds
1313 Walter Maidstone
1317 Thomas Cobham
1327 Adam Orleton
1334 Simon Montacute
1337 Thomas Hempnall
1339 Wulstan Bransford
1350 John Thoresby
1353 Reginald Brian
1362 John Barnet
1364 William of Whittlesey
1369 William Lenn
1375 Henry Wakefield
1396 Robert Tideman of Winchcomb
1401 Richard Clifford
1407 Thomas Peverel
1419 Philip Morgan
1426 Thomas Polton
1435 Thomas Bourgchier
1444 John Carpenter
1476 John Alcock
1487 Robert Morton
1497 Giovanni de' Gigli
1499 Silvestro de' Gigli
1521 Julius de Medici Guilio de
    Medici [admin.]
1523 Geronimo Ghinucci
1535 Hugh Latimer
1539 John Bell

1544 Nicholas Heath (dep.)
1552 John Hooper
1554 Nicholas Heath (rest.)
1555 Richard Pates
1559 Edwin Sandys
1571 Nicholas Bullingham
1577 John Whitgift
1584 Edmund Freke
1593 Richard Fletcher
1596 Thomas Bilson
1597 Gervase Babington
1610 Henry Parry
1617 John Thornborough
1641 John Prideaux
1660 George Morley
1662 John Gauden
1662 John Earle
1663 Robert Skinner
1671 Walter Blandford
1675 James Fleetwood
1683 William Thomas
1689 Edward Stillingfleet
1699 William Lloyd
1717 John Hough
1743 Isaac Maddox
1759 James Johnson
1774 Brownlow North
1781 Richard Hurd
1808 Ffoliott Herbert Walker
    Cornewall
1831 Robert James Carr
1841 Henry Pepys
1861 Henry Philpott
1891 John James Stewart Perowne
1902 Charles Gore
1905 Huyshe Wolcott Yeatman-Biggs
1919 Ernest Harold Pearce
1931 Arthur William Thomson
    Perowne
1941 William Wilson Cash
1956 Lewis Mervyn Charles-Edwards
1970 Robert Wylmer Woods
1982 Philip Harold Ernest Goodrich

PROVINCE OF YORK

York

BISHOPS

314 Eborius
625 Paulinus
[Vacancy 633–64]
664 Cedda
664 Wilfrid I
678 Bosa (ret.)
686 Bosa (rest.)
691 Wilfrith (rest.)
706 John of Beverley
718 Wilfrid II

ARCHBISHOPS

734 Egberht
767 Æthelberht
780 Eanbald I
796 Eanbald II
808 Wulfsige
837 Wigmund
854 Wulfherc
900 Æthelbald
c928 Hrothweard
931 Wulfstan I
956 Osketel
971 Oswald
971 Edwald
992 Ealdwulf [1]
1003 Wulfstan II

1023 Ælfric Puttoc
1041 Æthelric
1051 Cynesige
1061 Ealdred
1070 Thomas I of Bayeux
1100 Gerard
1109 Thomas II
1119 Thurstan
1143 William Fitzherbert
1147 Henry Murdac
1153 William Fitzherbert (rest.)
1154 Roger of Pont l'Eveque
1191 Geoffrey Plantagenet
1215 Walter de Gray
1256 Sewal de Bovill
1258 Godfrey Ludham [Kineton]
1266 Walter Giffard
1279 William Wickwane
1286 John Romanus [le Romeyn]
1298 Henry Newark
1300 Thomas Corbridge
1306 William Greenfield
1317 William Melton
1342 William de la Zouche
1352 John Thoresby
1374 Alexander Neville
1388 Thomas Arundel
1396 Robert Waldby

1398 Richard le Scrope
1407 Henry Bowet
1426 John Kempe
1452 William Booth
1464 George Nevill
1476 Lawrence Booth
1480 Thomas Rotherham [Scott]
1501 Thomas Savage
1508 Christopher Bainbridge
1514 Thomas Wolsey
1531 Edward Lee
1545 Robert Holgate
1555 Nicholas Heath
1561 Thomas Young
1570 Edmund Grindal
1577 Edwin Sandys
1589 John Piers
1595 Matthew Hutton
1606 Tobias Matthew
1628 George Montaigne [Mountain]
1629 Samuel Harsnett
1632 Richard Neile
1641 John Williams
1660 Accepted Frewen
1664 Richard Sterne
1683 John Dolben
1688 Thomas Lamplugh
1691 John Sharp

[1] Ealdwulf and Wulfstan II held the Sees of York and Worcester together. Ælfric Puttoc held both 1040–1 and Ealdred 1060–1.

York—continued

1714 William Dawes
1724 Lancelot Blackburn
1743 Thomas Herring
1747 Matthew Hutton
1757 John Gilbert
1761 Robert Hay Drummond
1777 William Markham
1808 Edward Venables Vernon
    Harcourt
1847 Thomas Musgrave
1860 Charles Thos. Longley
1863 William Thomson
1891 William Connor Magee
1891 William Dalrymple Maclagan
1909 Cosmo Gordon Lang
1929 William Temple
1942 Cyril Forster Garbett
1956 Arthur Michael Ramsey
1961 Frederick Donald Coggan
1975 Stuart Yarworth Blanch
1983 John Stapylton Habgood

Durham

BISHOPS OF LINDISFARNE[1]
635 Aidan
651 Finan
661 Colman
664 Tuda
[Complications involving Wilfrid
    and Chad]
681 Eata
685 Cuthberht
[Vacancy during which Wilfrid
    administered the see]
688 Eadberht
698 Eadferth
731 Æthelweald
740 Cynewulf
781 Higbald
803 Ecgberht
821 Heathwred
830 Ecgred
845 Eanberht
854 Eardwulf

BISHOPS OF HEXHAM
664 Wilfrith
678 Eata
681 Tunberht
684 Cuthbert
685 Eata (rest.)
687 John of Beverley
709 Acca
734 Frithoberht
767 Ahlmund
781 Tilberht
789 Æthelberht
797 Heardred
800 Eanberht
813 Tidferth

BISHOPS OF CHESTER-LE-STREET[2]
899 Eardwulf
899 Cutheard
915 Tilred
925 Wigred
944 Uhtred
944 Seaxhelm
944 Ealdred
968 Ælfsige
990 Aldhun

BISHOPS OF DURHAM
990 Aldhun d. 1018
[See vacant 1018–1020]
1020 Edmund
c1040 Eadred
1041 Æthelric
1056 Æthelwine
1071 Walcher
1081 William of Saint Calais
1099 Ralph [Ranulf] Flambard
1133 Geoffrey Rufus
1143 William of Sainte-Barbe
1153 Hugh of le Puiset
1197 Philip of Poitiers
1217 Richard Marsh
1228 Richard Poore
1241 Nicholas Farnham
1249 Walter Kirkham
1261 Robert Stichill
1274 Robert of Holy Island
1284 Anthony Bek
1311 Richard Kellaw
1318 Lewis de Beaumont
1333 Richard of Bury
1345 Thomas Hatfield
1382 John Fordham
1388 Walter Skirlaw
1406 Thomas Langley
1438 Robert Nevill
1457 Lawrence Booth
1476 William Dudley
1485 John Shirwood
1494 Richard Fox
1502 William Senhouse [Sever]
1507 Christopher Bainbridge
1509 Thomas Ruthall
1523 Thomas Wolsey
1530 Cuthbert Tunstall
1561 James Pilkington
1577 Richard Barnes
1589 Matthew Hutton
1595 Tobias Matthew
1606 William James
1617 Richard Neile
1628 George Montaigne [Mountain]
1628 John Howson
1632 Thomas Morton
1660 John Cosin
1674 Nathaniel Crew [Lord Crew]
1721 William Talbot
1730 Edward Chandler
1750 Joseph Butler
1752 Richard Trevor
1771 John Egerton
1787 Thomas Thurlow
1791 Shute Barrington
1826 William Van Mildert
1836 Edward Maltby
1856 Chaarles Thomas Longley
1860 Henry Montague Villiers
1861 Charles Baring
1879 Joseph Barber Lightfoot
1890 Brooke Foss Westcott
1901 Handley Carr Glyn Moule
1920 Herbert Hensley Henson
1939 Alwyn Terrell Petre Williams
1952 Arthur Michael Ramsey
1956 Maurice Henry Harland
1966 Ian Thomas Ramsey
1973 John Stapylton Habgood
1984 David Edward Jenkins

Blackburn

1927 Percy Mark Herbert
1942 Wilfred Marcus Askwith

1954 Walter Hubert Baddeley
1960 Charles Robert Claxton
1972 Robert Arnold Schürhoff
    Martineau
1982 David Stewart Cross
1989 Alan David Chesters

Bradford

1920 Arthur William Thomson
    Perowne
1931 Alfred Walter Frank Blunt
1956 Frederick Donald Coggan
1961 Clement George St. Michael
    Parker
1972 Ross Sydney Hook
1981 Geoffrey John Paul
1984 Robert Kerr Williamson

Carlisle

1133 Aethelwulf
1203 Bernard
1219 Hugh of Beaulieu
1224 Walter Mauclerc
1247 Silvester Everdon
1255 Thomas Vipont
1258 Robert de Chause
1280 Ralph Ireton
1292 John of Halton
1325 John Ross
1332 John Kirkby
1353 Gilbert Welton
1363 Thomas Appleby
1396 Robert Reade
1397 Thomas Merks
1400 William Strickland
1420 Roger Whelpdale
1424 William Barrow
1430 Marmaduke Lumley
1450 Nicholas Close
1452 William Percy
1462 John Kingscote
1464 Richard le Scrope
1468 Edward Story
1478 Richard Bell
1496 William Senhouse [Sever]
1504 Roger Layburne
1508 John Penny
1521 John Kite
1537 Robert Aldrich
1556 Owen Oglethorpe
1561 John Best
1570 Richard Barnes
1577 John May
1598 Henry Robinson
1616 Robert Snowden
1621 Richard Milbourne
1624 Richard Senhouse
1626 Francis White
1629 Barnabas Potter
1642 James Ussher
1660 Richard Sterne
1664 Edward Rainbowe
1684 Thomas Smith
1702 William Nicolson
1718 Samuel Bradford
1723 John Waugh
1735 George Fleming
1747 Richard Osbaldeston
1762 Charles Lyttleton
1769 Edmund Law
1787 John Douglas
1791 Edward Venables Vernon
    [Harcourt]
1808 Samuel Goodenough
1827 Hugh Percy

[1] See transferred to Chester-le-Street 883.
[2] See transferred to Durham 995.

Carlisle—continued

1856 Henry Montagu Villiers
1860 Samuel Waldegrave
1869 Harvey Goodwin
1892 John Wareing Bardsley
1905 John William Diggle
1920 Henry Herbert Williams
1946 Thomas Bloomer
1966 Sydney Cyril Bulley
1972 Henry David Halsey
1989 Ian Harland

Chester

1541 John Bird
1554 George Cotes
1556 Cuthbert Scott
1561 William Downham
1579 William Chaderton
1595 Hugh Bellott
1597 Richard Vaughan
1604 George Lloyd
1616 Thomas Morton
1619 John Bridgeman
1660 Brian Walton
1662 Henry Ferne
1662 George Hall
1668 John Wilkins
1673 John Pearson
1686 Thomas Cartwright
1689 Nicolas Stratford
1708 William Dawes
1714 Francis Gastrell
1726 Samuel Peploe
1752 Edmund Keene
1771 William Markham
1777 Beilby Porteus
1788 William Cleaver
1800 Henry William Majendie
1810 Bowyer Edward Sparke
1812 George Henry Law
1824 Charles James Blomfield
1828 John Bird Sumner
1848 John Graham
1865 William Jacobson
1884 William Stubbs
1889 Francis John Jayne
1919 Henry Luke Paget
1932 Geoffrey Francis Fisher
1939 Douglas Henry Crick
1955 Gerald Alexander Ellison
1974 Hubert Victor Whitsey
1982 Michael Alfred Baughen

Liverpool

1880 John Charles Ryle
1900 Francis James Chavasse
1923 Albert Augustus David
1944 Clifford Arthur Martin
1966 Stuart Yarworth Blanch
1975 David Stuart Sheppard

Manchester

1848 James Prince Lee
1870 James Fraser
1886 James Moorhouse
1903 Edmund Arbuthnott Knox
1921 William Temple
1929 Frederic Sumpter Guy Warman
1947 William Derrick Lindsay Greer
1970 Patrick Campbell Rodger
1978 Stanley Eric Francis Booth-
    Clibborn

Newcastle

1882 Ernest Roland Wilberforce

1896 Edgar Jacob
1903 Arthur Thomas Lloyd
1907 Norman Dumenil John Straton
1915 Herbert Louis Wild
1927 Harold Ernest Bilbrough
1941 Noel Baring Hudson
1957 Hugh Edward Ashdown
1973 Ronald Oliver Bowlby
1981 Andrew Alexander Kenny
    Graham

Ripon

*c*678 Eadheath

NEW FOUNDATION

1836 Charles Thomas Longley
1857 Robert Bickersteth
1884 William Boyd Carpenter
1912 Thomas Wortley Drury
1920 Thomas Banks Strong
1926 Edward Arthur Burroughs
1935 Geoffrey Charles Lester Lunt
1946 George Armitage Chase
1959 John Richard Humpidge
    Moorman
1975 Stuart Hetley Price
1977 David Nigel de Lorentz Young

Sheffield

1914 Leonard Hedley Burrows
1939 Leslie Stannard Hunter
1962 Francis John Taylor
1971 William Gordon Fallows
1980 David Ramsay Lunn

Sodor and Man[1]

447 Germanus
    Conindrius
    Romulus
    Machutus
    Conanus
    Contentus
    Baldus
    Malchus
    Torkinus
    Brendanus
[Before 1080 Roolwer]
    William
    Hamond
1113 Wimund
1151 John
1160 Gamaliel
    Ragnald
    Christian of Argyle
    Michael
1203 Nicholas de Meaux
    Nicholas II
1217 Reginald
1226 John
1229 Simon of Argyle
1252 Richard
1275 Mark of Galloway
1305 Alan
1321 Gilbert Maclelan
1329 Bernard de Linton
1334 Thomas
1348 William Russell
1387 John Donegan
1387 Michael
1392 John Sproten
1402 Conrad
1402 Theodore Bloc
1429 Richard Messing Andrew

1435 John Seyre
1455 Thomas Burton
1458 Thomas Kirklam
1472 Angus
1478 Richard Oldham
1487 Hugh Blackleach
1513 Hugh Hesketh
1523 John Howden
1546 Henry Man
1556 Thomas Stanley
1570 John Salisbury
1576 John Meyrick
1600 George Lloyd
1605 John Philips
1634 William Forster
1635 Richard Parr
1661 Samuel Rutter
1663 Isaac Barrow
1671 Henry Bridgman
1683 John Lake
1685 Baptist Levinz
1698 Thomas Wilson
1755 Mark Hildesley
1773 Richard Richmond
1780 George Mason
1784 Claudius Crigan
1814 George Murray
1828 William Ward
1838 James Bowstead
1840 Henry Pepys
1841 Thomas Vowler Short
1847 Walter Augustus Shirley
1847 Robert John Eden
1854 Horatio Powys
1877 Rowley Hill
1887 John Wareing Bardsley
1892 Norman Dumenil John Straton
1907 Thomas Wortley Drury
1912 James Denton Thompson
1925 Charles Leonard Thornton-
    Duesbery
1928 William Stanton Jones
1943 John Ralph Strickland Taylor
1954 Benjamin Pollard
1966 George Eric Gordon
1974 Vernon Sampson Nicholls
1983 Arthur Henry Attwell
1989 Noel Debroy Jones

Southwell

1884 George Ridding
1904 Edwyn Hoskyns
1926 Bernard Oliver Francis
    Heywood
1928 Henry Mosley
1941 Frank Russell Barry
1964 Gordon David Savage
1970 John Denis Wakeling
1985 Michael Humphrey Dickens
    Whinney
1988 Patrick Burnet Harris

Wakefield

1888 William Walsham How
1897 George Rodney Eden
1928 James Buchanan Seaton
1938 Campbell Richard Hone
1946 Henry McGowan
1949 Roger Plumpton Wilson
1958 John Alexander Ramsbotham
1968 Eric Treacy
1976 Colin Clement Walter James
1985 David Michael Hope

---

[1] Included in the province of York by Act of Parliament 1542. Prior to Richard Oldham there is some uncertainty as to several names and dates. From 1425 to 1553 there was an English and Scottish succession. It is not easy to say which claimant was Bishop either *je jure* or *de facto*.

BISHOPS SUFFRAGAN IN ENGLAND

Asterisks indicate a temporary lapse in appointment

1536 Thomas Manning *Ipswich*
      John Salisbury *Thetford*
      William More *Colchester*
1537 Thomas Sparke *Berwick*
      John Bird *Penrith*
      Lewis Thomas *Shrewsbury*
      Thomas Morley *Marlborough*
      Richard Yngworth *Dover*
      John Hodgkins *Bedford*
1538 Henry Holbeach *Bristol*
      William Finch *Taunton*
      Robert Sylvester [Pursglove]
      Hull
1539 Richard Thornden *Dover*
1539 John Bradley *Shaftesbury*
1567 Richard Barnes *Nottingham*
1569 Richard Rogers *Dover*
1592 John Sterne *Colchester*

Aston (Birmingham)

1954 Clement George St Michael
      Parker
1962 David Brownfield Porter
1972 Mark Green
1982 Michael Humphrey Dickens
      Whinney
1985 Colin Ogilvie Buchanan
1989 Vacant

Barking (Chelmsford)

1901 Thomas Stevens
1919 James Theodore Inskip
1948 Hugh Rowlands Gough
1959 William Frank Percival Chadwick
1975 Albert James Adams
1983 James William Roxburgh
1991 John Frederick Sainsbury

Barrow-in-Furness (Carlisle)

1889 Henry Ware
1909 Campbell West-Watson
1926 Herbert Sidney Pelham

Basingstoke (Winchester)

1973 Colin Clement Walter James
1977 Michael Richard John Manktelow

Bedford (St Albans)

1879 William Walsham How
1888 Robert Claudius Billing
      [In London Diocese to 1898]
      *   *
1935 James Lumsden Barkway
1939 Aylmer Skelton
1948 Claude Thomas Thellusson
      Wood
1953 Angus Campbell MacInnes
1957 Basil Tudor Guy
1963 Albert John Trillo
1968 John Tyrrell Holmes Hare
1977 Andrew Alexander Kenny
      Graham
1981 David John Farmbrough

Beverley (York)

1889 Robert Jarratt Crosthwaite

Birkenhead (Chester)

1965 Eric Arthur John Mercer
1974 Ronald Brown

Bolton (Manchester)

1984 David George Galliford
1991 David Bonser

Bradwell (Chelmsford)

1968 William Neville Welch
1973 John Gibbs
1976 Charles Derek Bond

Brixworth (Peterborough)

1989 Paul Everard Barber

Buckingham (Oxford)

1914 Edward Domett Shaw
1921 Philip Herbert Eliot
1944 Robert Milton Hay
1960 Gordon David Savage
1964 George Christopher Cutts Pepys
1974 Simon Hedley Burrows

Burnley (Blackburn)

1901 Edwyn Hoskyns
1905 Alfred Pearson
1909 Henry Henn
1931 Edgar Priestley Swain
1950 Charles Keith Kipling Prosser
1955 George Edward Holderness
1970 Richard Charles Challinor
      Watson
1988 Ronald James Milner

Colchester (Chelmsford)

1882 Alfred Blomfield
1894 Henry Frank Johnson
1909 Robert Henry Whitcombe
      [In St Albans Diocese to 1914]
1922 Thomas Alfred Chapman
1933 Charles Henry Ridsdale
1946 Frederick Dudley Vaughan
      Narborough
1966 Roderic Norman Coote
1988 Michael Edwin Vickers

Coventry (Worcester)

1891 Henry Bond Bowlby
1894 Edmund Arbuthnott Knox

Crediton (Exeter)

1897 Robert Edward Trefusis
1930 William Frederick Surtees
1954 Wilfrid Arthur Edmund Westall
1974 Philip John Pasterfield
1984 Peter Everard Coleman

Croydon (Southwark)

[In Canterbury Diocese till 1985]
1904 Henry Horace Pereira
      *   *
1930 Edward Sydney Woods
1937 William Louis Anderson
1942 Maurice Henry Harland
1947 Cuthbert Killick Norman
      Bardsley
1957 John Taylor Hughes
1977 Geoffrey Stuart Snell
1985 Wilfred Denniston Wood

Derby (Southwell)

1889 Edward Ash Were
1909 Charles Thomas Abraham

Doncaster (Sheffield)

1972 Stuart Hetley Price
1976 David Stewart Cross
1982 William Michael Dermot
      Persson

Dorchester (Oxford)

1939 Gerald Burton Allen
1952 Kenneth Riches
1957 David Goodwin Loveday
1972 Peter Knight Walker
1979 Conrad John Eustace Meyer
1988 Anthony John Russell

Dorking (Guildford)

1905 Cecil Henry Boutflower
      *   *
1968 Kenneth Dawson Evans
1986 David Peter Wilcox

Dover (Canterbury)

1870 Edward Parry
1890 George Rodney Eden
1898 William Walsh
1916 Harold Ernest Bilbrough
1927 John Victor Macmillan
1935 Alfred Careywollaston Rose
1957 Lewis Evan Meredith
1964 Anthony Paul Tremlett
1980 Richard Henry McPhail Third

Dudley (Worcester)

1974 Michael Ashley Mann
1977 Anthony Charles Dumper

Dunwich (St Edmundsbury and Ipswich)

1934 Maxwell Homfray Maxwell-
      Gumbleton
1945 Clement Mallory Ricketts
1955 Thomas Herbert Cashmore
1967 David Rokeby Maddock
1977 William Johnston
1980 Eric Nash Devenport

Edmonton (London)

1970 Alan Francis Bright Rogers
1975 William John Westwood
1985 Brian John Masters

Fulham (London)

1926 Basil Staunton Batty
1947 William Marshall Selwyn
1949 George Ernest Ingle
1955 Robert Wright Stopford
1957 Roderic Norman Coote
1966 Alan Francis Bright Rogers
1970 John Richard Satterthwaite
1982 Brian John Masters
1985 John Klyberg

Grantham (Lincoln)

1905 Welbore MacCarthy
1920 John Edward Hine
1930 Ernest Morell Blackie
1935 Arthur Ivan Greaves
1937 Algernon Augustus Markham
1949 Anthony Otter
1965 Ross Sydney Hook
1972 Dennis Gascoyne Hawker
1987 William Ind

Grimsby (Lincoln)

1935 Ernest Morell Blackie
1937 Arthur Ivan Greaves
1958 Kenneth Healey
1966 Gerald Fitzmaurice Colin
1979 David Tustin

Guildford (Winchester)

1874 John Sutton Utterton
1888 George Henry Sumner
1909 John Hugh Granville Randolph

Hertford (St Albans)

1968 Albert John Trillo
1971 Hubert Victor Whitsey
1974 Peter Mumford
1982 Kenneth Harold Pillar
1990 Robin Smith

Horsham (Chichester)

1968 Simon Wilton Phipps
1975 Ivor Colin Docker
1991 John William Hind

Hull (York)

1891 Richard Frederick Lefevre
　　　Blunt
1910 John Augustine Kempthorne
1913 Francis Gurdon
　　　　*　　　*
1931 Bernard Oliver Francis Heywood
1934 Henry Townsend Vodden
1957 George Frederick Townley
1965 Hubert Laurence Higgs
1977 Geoffrey John Paul
1981 Donald George Snelgrove

Hulme (Manchester)

1924 John Charles Hill
1930 Thomas Sherwood Jones
1945 Hugh Leycester Hornby
1953 Kenneth Venner Ramsey
1975 David George Galliford
1984 Colin John Fraser Scott

Huntingdon (Ely)

1966 Robert Arnold Schurhoff
　　　Martineau
1972 Eric St Quintin Wall
1980 William Gordon Roe

Ipswich (Norwich)

1899 George Carnac Fisher
1906 Henry Luke Paget

Islington (London)

1898 Charles Henry Turner

Jarrow (Durham)

1906 George Nickson
1914 John Nathaniel Quirk
1924 Samuel Kirshbaum Knight
1932 James Geoffrey Gordon
1939 Leslie Owen
1944 David Colin Dunlop
1950 John Alexander Ramsbotham
1958 Mervyn Armstrong
1965 Alexander Kenneth Hamilton
1980 Michael Thomas Ball
1990 Alan Smithson

Kensington (London)

1901 Frederic Edward Ridgeway
1911 John Primatt Maud
1932 Bertram Fitzgerald Simpson
1942 Henry Colville Montgomery
　　　Campbell
1949 Cyril Eastaugh
1962 Edward James Keymer Roberts
1964 Ronald Cedric Osbourne
　　　Goodchild
1981 Mark Santer
1987 John Hughes

Kingston upon Thames (Southwark)

1905 Cecil Hook
1915 Samuel Mumford Taylor
1922 Percy Mark Herbert
1927 Frederick Ochterlony Taylor
　　　Hawkes
1952 William Percy Gilpin
1970 Hugh William Montefiore
1978 Keith Norman Sutton
1984 Peter Stephen Maurice Selby

Knaresborough (Ripon)

1905 Lucius Frederick Moses
　　　Bottomley Smith
1934 Paul Fulcrand Dalacour de
　　　Labilliere
1938 John Norman Bateman-
　　　Champain
1948 Henry Handley Vully de
　　　Candole
1965 John Howard Cruse
1972 Ralph Emmerson
1979 John Dennis
1987 Malcolm James Menin

Lancaster (Blackburn)

1936 Benjamin Pollard
1955 Anthony Leigh Egerton
　　　Hoskyns-Abrahall
1975 Dennis Fountain Page
1985 Ian Harland
1989 John Nicholls

Leicester (Peterborough)

1888 Francis Henry Thicknesse
1903 Lewis Clayton
1913 Norman MacLeod Lang

Lewes (Chichester)

1909 Leonard Hedley Burrows
1914 Herbert Edward Jones
1920 Henry Kemble Southwell
1926 Thomas William Cook
1929 William Champion Streatfield
1929 Hugh Maudsley Hordern
1946 Geoffrey Hodgson Warde
1959 James Herbert Lloyd Morrell
1977 Peter John Ball

Ludlow (Hereford)

1981 Stanley Mark Wood
1987 Ian Macdonald Griggs

Lynn (Norwich)

1963 William Somers Llewellyn
1972 William Aubrey Aitken
1986 David Edward Bentley

Maidstone (Canterbury)

1944 Leslie Owen
1956 Stanley Woodley Betts
1969 Geoffrey Lewis Tiarks
1976 Richard Henry McPhail Third
1980 Robert Maynard Hardy
1987 David James Smith

Malmesbury (Bristol)

1927 Ronald Erskine Ramsay
1946 Ivor Stanley Watkins
1956 Edward James Keymer Roberts
1962 Clifford Leofric Purdy Bishop
1973 Frederick Stephen Temple
1983 Peter James Firth

Marlborough (London)

1888 Alfred Earle

Middleton (Manchester)

1927 Richard Godfrey Parsons
1932 Cecil Wilfred Wilson
1938 Arthur Fawssett Alston
1943 Edward Worsfold Mowll
1952 Frank Woods
1958 Robert Nelson
1959 Edward Ralph Wickham
1982 Donald Alexander Tytler

Nottingham

1870 Henry Mackenzie
1877 Edward Trollope

Penrith (Carlisle) [see also Richmond]

1939 Grandage Edwards Powell
1944 Herbert Victor Turner
1959 Sydney Cyril Bulley
1967 Reginald Foskett
1970 William Edward Augustus Pugh
1979 George Lanyon Hacker

Plymouth (Exeter)

1923 John Howard Bertram
　　　Masterman
1934 Francis Whitfield Daukes
1950 Norman Harry Clarke
1962 Wilfred Guy Sanderson
1972 Richard Fox Cartwright
1982 Kenneth Albert Newing
1988 Richard Stephen Hawkins

Pontefract (Wakefield)

1931 Campbell Richard Hone
1939 Tom Longworth
1949 Arthur Harold Morris
1954 George William Clarkson
1961 Eric Treacy
1968 William Gordon Fallows
1971 Thomas Richard Hare

Ramsbury (Salisbury)

1974 John Robert Geoffrey Neale
1989 Peter St George Vaughan

Reading (Oxford)

1889 James Leslie Randall
　　　　*　　　*
1942 Arthur Groom Parham
1954 Eric Henry Knell
1972 Eric Wild
1982 Ronald Graham Gregory Foley
1989 John Frank Ewan Bone

Repton (Derby)

1965 William Warren Hunt
1977 Stephen Edmund Verney
1986 Francis Henry Arthur
　　　Richmond

Richmond (Ripon) [Known as Penrith 1888-9]

1888 John James Pulleine
1913 Francis Charles Kilner

St Germans (Truro)

1905 John Rundle Cornish
　　　　*　　　*
1974 Cecil Richard Rutt
1979 [Michael] Reginald Lindsay
　　　Fisher
1985 John Richard Allan Llewellin

Selby (York)

1939 Harry St John Stirling
       Woollcombe
1941 Carey Frederick Knyvett
1962 Douglas Noel Sargent
1971 Morris Henry St John
       Maddocks
1983 Clifford Conder Barker
1991 Humphrey Vincent Taylor

Sheffield (York)

1901 John Nathaniel Quirk

Sherborne (Salisbury)

1925 Robert Crowther Abbott
1928 Gerald Burton Allen
1936 Harold Nickinson Rodgers
1947 John Maurice Key
1960 Victor Joseph Pike
1976 John Dudley Galtrey Kirkham

Sherwood (Southwell)

1965 Kenneth George Thompson
1975 Harold Richard Darby
1989 Alan Wyndham Morgan

Shrewsbury (Lichfield)

1888 Sir Lovelace Tomlinson Stamer
       *   *
1940 Eric Knightley Chetwode
       Hamilton
1944 Robert Leighton Hodson
1959 William Alonzo Parker
1969 Francis William Cocks
1980 Leslie Lloyd Rees
1987 John Dudley Davies

Southampton (Winchester)

1895 William Awdry
1896 George Carnac Fisher
1898 Hon. Arthur Temple Lyttleton
1903 James Macarthur
1921 Cecil Henry Boutflower
1933 Arthur Baillie Lumsdaine
       Karney
1943 Edmund Robert Morgan
1951 Kenneth Edward Norman
       Lamplugh
1972 John Kingsmill Cavell
1984 Edward David Cartwright
1988 John Freeman Perry

Southwark (Rochester)

1891 Huyshe Wolcott Yeatman-Biggs

Stafford (Lichfield)

1909 Edward Ash Were
1915 Lionel Payne Crawfurd
1934 Douglas Henry Crick

Stafford—continued

1938 Lempriere Durell Hammond
1958 Richard George Clitherow
1975 John Waine
1979 John Stevens Waller
1987 Michael Charles Scott-Joynt

Stepney (London)

1895 George Forres Browne
1897 Arthur Foley Winnington-
       Ingram
1901 Cosmo Gordon Lang
1909 Henry Luke Paget
1919 Henry Mosley
1928 Charles Edward Curzon
1936 Robert Hamilton Moberly
1952 Joost de Blank
1957 Francis Evered Lunt
1968 Ernest Urban Trevor
       Huddleston
1978 James Lawton Thompson

Stockport (Chester)

1949 Frank Jackson Okell
1951 David Henry Saunders
       Saunders-Davis
1965 Rupert Gordon Strutt
1984 Frank Pilkington Sargeant

Taunton (Bath and Wells)

1911 Charles Fane De Salis
1931 George Arthur Hollis
1945 Harry Thomas
1955 Mark Allin Hodson
1962 Francis Horner West
1977 Peter John Nott
1986 Nigel Simeon McCulloch

Tewkesbury (Gloucester)

1938 Augustine John Hodson
1955 Edward Barry Henderson
1960 Forbes Trevor Horan
1973 Thomas Carlyle Joseph Robert
       Hamish Deakin
1986 Geoffrey David Jeremy Walsh

Thetford (Norwich)

1894 Arthur Thomas Lloyd
1903 John Philips Alcott Bowers
       *   *
1945 John Walker Woodhouse
1953 Martin Patrick Grainge
       Leonard
1963 Eric William Bradley Cordingly
1977 Hugh Charles Blackburne
1981 Timothy Dudley-Smith

Tonbridge (Rochester)

1959 Russell Berridge White
1968 Henry David Halsey
1973 Philip Harold Ernest Goodrich
1982 David Henry Bartleet

Warrington (Liverpool)

1918 Martin Linton Smith
1920 Edwin Hone Kempson
1927 Herbert Gresford Jones
1946 Charles Robert Claxton
1960 Laurence Ambrose Brown
1970 John Monier Bickersteth
1976 Michael Henshall

Warwick(Coventry)

1980 Keith Appleby Arnold
1990 Clive Handford

Whalley (Blackburn)

1909 Atherton Gwillym Rawstorne

Whitby (York)

1923 Harry St John Stirling
       Woollcombe
1939 Harold Evelyn Hubbard
1947 Walter Hubert Baddeley
1954 Philip William Wheeldon
1961 George D'Oyly Snow
1972 John Yates
1976 Clifford Conder Barker
1983 Gordon Bates

Willesden (London)

1911 William Willcox Perrin
1929 Guy Vernon Smith
1940 Henry Colville Montgomery
       Campbell
1942 Edward Michael Gresford Jones
1950 Gerald Alexander Ellison
1955 George Ernest Ingle
1964 Graham Douglas Leonard
1974 Geoffrey Hewlett Thompson
1985 Thomas Frederick Butler

Wolverhampton (Lichfield)

1979 Barry Rogerson
1985 Christopher John Mayfield

Woolwich (Southwark)

1905 John Cox Leeke
1918 William Woodcock Hough
1932 Arthur Llewellyn Preston
1936 Leslie Hamilton Lang
1947 Robert William Stannard
1959 John Arthur Thomas Robinson
1969 David Stuart Sheppard
1975 Michael Eric Marshall
1984 Albert Peter Hall

WALES

Archbishops of Wales

1920 Alfred George Edwards
       (St Asaph, 1889–1934)
1934 Charles Alfred Howell Green
       (Bangor, 1928–44)
1944 David Lewis Prosser
       (St David's, 1927–50)
1949 John Morgan
       (Llandaff, 1939–57)

1957 Alfred Edwin Morris
       (Monmouth, 1945–67)
1968 William Glyn Hughes Simon
       (Llandaff, 1957–71)
1971 Gwilym Owen Williams
       (Bangor, 1957–82)
1983 Derrick Greenslade Childs
       (Monmouth, 1972–87)
1987 George Noakes
       (St David's, 1982–1991)

Bangor[1]

c550 Deiniol [Daniel]
c775 Elfod [Elbodugen]
1092 Hervé
[Vacancy 1109–20]
1120 David the Scot
1140 Maurice [Meurig]
[Vacancy 1161–77]
1177 Guy Rufus [Gwion Goch]

[1]Very few of the names of the Celtic bishops have been preserved.

Bangor—continued

[*Vacancy c* 1190–5]
1195 Alan [Alban]
1197 Robert of Shrewsbury
[*Vacancies* 1212–15]
1215 Cadwgan
1237 Richard
1267 Anian or Einion
1307 Gruflydd ab Iowerth
1309 Anian [*Einion*] Sais
1328 Matthew de Englefield
1357 Thomas de Ringstead
1366 Gervase de Castro
1371 Hywel ap Gronwy
1372 John Gilbert
1376 John Swaffham
1400 Richard Young
[*Vacancy c* 1404–8]
1408 Benedict Nicolls
1418 William Barrow
1425 John Cliderow
1436 Thomas Cheriton
1448 John Stanbury
1453 James Blakedon
1465 Richard Edenham
1495 Henry Dean
1500 Thomas Pigot
1505 Thomas Penny
1509 Thomas Skevington
1534 John Salcot or Capon
1539 John Bird
1542 Arthur Bulkeley
1555 William Glynn
1559 Rowland Meyrick
1566 Nicholas Robinson
1586 Hugh Bellot
1596 Richard Vaughan
1598 Henry Rowlands
1616 Lewis Bayly
1632 David Dolben
1634 Edmund Griffith
1637 William Roberts
1666 Robert Morgan
1673 Humphrey Lloyd
1689 Humphrey Humphreys
1702 John Evans
1716 Banjamin Hoadley
1721 Richard Reynolds
1723 William Baker
1728 Thomas Sherlock
1734 Charles Cecil
1738 Thomas Herring
1743 Matthew Hutton
1748 Zachary Pearce
1756 John Egerton
1769 John Ewer
1775 John Moore
1783 John Warren
1800 William Cleaver
1807 John Randolph
1809 Henry William Majendie
1830 Christopher Bethell
1859 James Colquhoun Campbell
1890 Daniel Lewis Lloyd
1899 Watkin Herbert Williams
1925 Daniel Davies
1928 Charles Alfred Howell Green
       (Archbishop of Wales 1934)
1944 David Edwardes Davies
1949 John Charles Jones
1957 Gwilym Owen Williams
       (Archbishop of Wales 1971)
1982 John Cledan Mears

Llandaff[1]

*c*550 Teiliau
*c*872 Cyfeiliag
*c*880 Libiau
*c*940 Marchlwys
   982 Gwyzan
*c*995 Bledri
1027 Joseph
1056 Herewald
1107 Urban
[*Vacancy of six years*]
1140 Uchtryd
1148 Nicolas ap Gwrgant
[*Vacancy of two years*]
1186 William Saltmarsh
1193 Henry of Abergavenny
1219 William of Goldcliff
1230 Elias of Radnor
1245 William de Burgh
1254 John de Ware
1257 William of Radnor
1266 Willam de Breuse or Brus
1297 John of Monmouth
1323 John of Eaglescliffe
1344 John Paschal
1361 Roger Cradock
1383 Thomas Rushook
1386 William Bottesham
1389 Edmund Bromfield
1393 Tideman de Winchcomb
1395 Andrew Barret
1396 John Burghill
1398 Thomas Peverel
1408 John de la Zouch [Fulford]
1425 John Wells
1441 Nicholas Ashby
1458 John Hunden
1476 John Smith
1478 John Marshall
1496 John Ingleby
1500 Miles Salley
1517 George de Athequa
1537 Robert Holdgate or Holgate
1545 Anthony Kitchin
1567 Hugh Jones
1575 William Blethin
1591 Gervase Babington
1595 William Morgan
1601 Francis Godwin
1618 George Carleton
1619 Theophilus Field
1627 William Murray
1640 Morgan Owen
1660 Hugh Lloyd
1667 Francis Davies
1675 William Lloyd
1679 William Beaw
1706 John Tyler
1725 Robert Clavering
1729 John Harris
1739 Matthias Mawson
1740 John Gilbert
1749 Edward Cressett
1755 Richard Newcome
1761 John Ewer
1769 Jonathan Shipley
1769 Shute Barrington
1782 Richard Watson
1816 Herbert Marsh
1819 William Van Mildert
1826 Charles Richard Sumner
1828 Edward Copleston
1849 Alfred Ollivant

1883 Richard Lewis
1905 Joshua Pritchard Hughes
1931 Timothy Rees
1939 John Morgan (Archbishop of
       Wales 1949)
1957 William Glyn Hughes Simon
       (Archbishop of Wales 1968)
1971 Eryl Stephen Thomas
1975 John Richard Worthington
       Poole-Hughes
1985 Roy Thomas Davies

Monmouth

1921 Charles Alfred Howell Green
1928 Gilbert Cunningham Joyce
1940 Alfred Edwin Monahan
1945 Alfred Edwin Morris
       (Archbishop of Wales 1957)
1968 Eryl Stephen Thomas
1972 Derrick Greenslade Childs
       (Archbishop of Wales 1983)
1986 Royston Clifford Wright

St Asaph[2]

*c*560 Kentigern
*c*573 Asaph
1143 Gilbert
1152 Geoffrey of Monmouth
1154 Richard
1160 Godfrey
1175 Adam
1183 John I
1186 Reiner
1225 Abraham
1235 Hugh
1242 Hywel Ab Ednyfed
1249 Anian I or Einion
1267 John II
1268 Anian II
1293 Llywelyn de Bromfield
1315 Dafydd ap Bleddyn
1346 John Trevor I
1357 Llywelyn ap Madoc ab Ellis
1377 William de Spridlington
1382 Lawrence Child
1390 Alexander Bache
1395 John Trevor II
1411 Robert de Lancaster
1433 John Lowe
1444 Reginald Pecock
1451 Thomas Bird *alias* Knight
1471 Richard Redman
1496 Michael Deacon
1500 Dafydd ab Iorwerth
1504 Dafydd ab Owain
1513 Edmund Birkhead
1518 Henry Standish
1536 Robert Warton or Parfew
1555 Thomas Goldwell
1560 Richard Davies
1561 Thomas Davies
1573 William Hughes
1601 William Morgan
1604 Richard Parry
1624 John Hanmer
1629 John Owen
1660 George Griffith
1667 Henry Glemham
1670 Isaac Barrow
1680 William Lloyd
1692 Edward Jones
1703 George Hooper
1704 William Beveridge

[1]The traditional list of bishops of the Celtic Church has little historical foundation. But the names of the following, prior to Urban, may be regarded as fairly trustworthy though the dates are very uncertain.
[2]Prior to the Norman period there is considerable uncertainty as to names and dates.

St Asaph—continued

1708 Will. Fleetwood
1715 John Wynne
1727 Francis Hare
1732 Thomas Tanner
1736 Isaac Maddox
1744 Samuel Lisle
1748 Robert Hay Drummond
1761 Richard Newcome
1769 Jonathan Shipley
1789 Samuel Hallifax
1790 Lewis Bagot
1802 Samuel Horsley
1806 William Cleaver
1815 John Luxmore
1830 William Carey
1846 Thomas Vowler Short
1870 Joshua Hughes
1889 Alfred George Edwards
    (Archbishop of Wales 1920)
1934 William Thomas Havard
1950 David Daniel Bartlett
1971 Harold John Charles
1982 Alwyn Rice Jones

St David's[1]

c601 David
c606 Cynog
 831 Sadyrnfyw
    Meurig
c840 Novis
   ?Idwal
c906 Asser
   Llunwerth
 944 Eneuris
c961 Rhydderch
c999 Morgeneu
1023 Morgeneu
1023 Erwyn
1039 Tramerin
1061 Joseph
1061 Bleddud
1072 Sulien
1078 Abraham
1080 Sulien (again)

1085 Wilfrid
1115 Bernard
1148 David Fitz-Gerald
1176 Peter de Leiâ
1203 Geoffrey de Henlaw
1215 Gervase [Iorwerth]
1231 Anselm le Gras
1248 Thomas le Waleys
1256 Richard de Carew
1280 Thomas Bek
1296 David Martin
1328 Henry Gower
1347 John Thoresby
1350 Reginald Brian
1352 Thomas Fastolf
1362 Adam Houghton
1389 John Gilbert
1397 Guy de Mohne
1408 Henry Chichele
1414 John Catterick
1415 Stephen Patrington
1418 Benedict Nichols
1434 Thomas Rodburn [Rudborne]
1442 William Lindwood
1447 John Langton
1447 John de la Bere
1460 Robert Tully
1482 Richard Martin
1483 Thomas Langton
1485 Hugh Pavy
1496 John Morgan [Young]
1505 Robert Sherborn
1509 Edward Vaughan
1523 Richard Rawlins
1536 William Barlow
1548 Robert Ferrar
1554 Henry Morgan
1560 Thomas Young
1561 Richard Davies
1582 Marmaduke Middleton
1594 Anthony Rudd
1615 Richard Milbourne
1621 William Laud
1627 Theophilus Field
1636 Roger Mainwaring
1660 William Lucy

1678 William Thomas
1683 Laurence Womock
1686 John Lloyd
1687 Thomas Watson
[Vacancy 1699–1705]
1705 George Bull
1710 Philip Bisse
1713 Adam Ottley
1724 Richard Smallbrooke
1731 Elias Sydall
1732 Nicholas Claggett
1743 Edward Willes
1744 Richard Trevor
1753 Anthony Ellis
1761 Samuel Squire
1766 Robert Lowth
1766 Charles Moss
1774 James Yorke
1779 John Warren
1783 Edward Smallwell
1788 Samuel Horsley
1794 William Stewart
1801 George Murray
1803 Thomas Burgess
1825 John Banks Jenkinson
1840 Connop Thirlwall
1874 William Basil Tickell Jones
1897 John Owen
1927 David Lewis Prosser
    (Archbishop of Wales 1944)
1950 William Thomas Havard
1956 John Richards Richards
1971 Eric Matthias Roberts
1982 George Noakes (Archbishop of
    Wales 1987)

Swansea and Brecon

1923 Edward Latham Bevan
1934 John Morgan
1939 Edward William Williamson
1953 William Glyn Hughes Simon
1957 John James Absalom Thomas
1976 Benjamin Noel Young Vaughan
1988 Dewi Morris Bridges

[1] The following names occur in early records though the dates given cannot always be reconciled.

SCOTLAND

Sources—Bp Dowden's *The Bishops of Scotland* (Glasgow 1912), for all the sees up to the Reformation, and for Aberdeen and Moray to the present time.

For bishops after the Reformation (and for a few of the earliest ones before Queen Margaret)—Grub, *Ecclesiastical History of Scotland* (Edinburgh 1861, 4 vols.) and Bp Keith and Bp Russel, *Scottish Bishops* (2nd ed. Edinburgh 1824).

Scottish episcopal elections became subject immediately to Roman confirmation in 1192. The subordination of the Scottish Church to York became less direct in 1165, and its independence was recognized in a bill of Celestine III in 1192. St. Andrews was raised to metropolitan rank on 17 August 1472 and the Archbishop became primate of all Scotland with the same legative rights as the archbishop of Canterbury on 27 March 1487.

The dates in the margin are those of the consecration or translation to the particular see of the bishops named; or in the case of bishops elect, who are not known to have been consecrated, they are those of the election; or in the case of titular bishops, of the date of their appointment.

The date of the death has been given where there was a long interregnum, or where there is dislocation (as at the Reformation and at the Revolution), or for some special reason to make the history intelligible.

The extra information in the list of College Bishops is given for the reason just stated.

St Andrews

St Andrews, Dunkeld and Dunblane

 906 Cellach I
 915(?) Fothad I
 955 Malisius I
 963 Maelbridge
 970 Cellach II
 996(?) Malasius II
  (?) Malmore

1025 Alwyn
1028 Maelduin
1055 Tuthald or Tuadal
1059 Fothad II
1077 {
to   Gregory (elect)
    Catharas (elect)
1107 {
    Edmarus (elect)
    Godricus (elect)
1109 Turgot
1120 Eadmer (elect)

1127 Robert
1159 Waldeve (elect)
1160 Ernald
1165 Richard
1178 Hugh
1180 John the Scot
1198 Roger de Beaumont
1202 William Malveisin
1238 Geoffrey (elect)
1240 David de Bernham

St Andrews—continued

1253 Robert de Stuteville (elect)
1254 Abel de Golin
1255 Gamelin
1273 William Wischard
1280 William Fraser
1298 William de Lamberton
1328 James Bennet
1342 William de Laundels
1385 Stephen de Pay (elect)
1386(?) Walter Trayl
1388 Alexander de Neville
1398 Thomas de Arundel
1401 Thomas Stewart (elect)
1402 Walter de Danielston (elect)
1403(?) Gilbert Greenlaw
1403 Henry Wardlaw
1408 John Trevor
1440 James Kennedy

ARCHBISHOPS

1465 Patrick Graham
1478 William Scheves
1497 James Stewart (elect)
1504 Alexander Stewart (elect)
1513 John Hepburn (elect)
1513 Innocenzo Cibò (elect)
1514 Andrew Forman
1522 James Betoun
1538 David Betoun [coadj.]
1547 John Hamilton
1551 Gavin Hamilton [coadj.] d. 1571
1572 John Douglas (titular)
1576 Patrick Adamson (titular)
         d. 1592
1611 George Gladstanes
1615 John Spottiswoode, d. 1639
1661 James Sharp
1679 Alexander Burnet
1684 Arthur Rose, d. 1704

BISHOPS OF FIFE

[1704 to 1726 See vacant]
1726 James Rose
1733 Robert Keith
1743 Robert White
1761 Henry Edgar

BISHOPS OF ST ANDREWS

1842 Patrick Torry
1853 Charles Wordsworth
1893 George Howard Wilkinson
1908 Charles Edward Plumb
1931 Edward Thomas Scott Reid
1938 James Lumsden Barkway
1949 Arnold Brian Burrowes
1955 John William Alexander Howe
1969 Michael Geoffrey Hare Duke

†Dunkeld

849(?) Tuathal
865(?) Flaithbertach
1114 Cormac
1147 Gregory
1170 Richard I
1178 Walter de Bidun (elect)
1183(?) John I, the Scot
1203 Richard II, de Prebenda
1212(?) John II, de Leycester
1214(?) Hugh de Sigillo
1229 Matthew Scot (elect)
1229 Gilbert
1236(?) Geoffrey de Liberatione
1252 Richard III, of Inverkeithing
1273(?) Robert de Stuteville

1283(?) Hugh de Strivelin [Stirling]
         (elect)
1283 William
1288 Matthew de Crambeth
1309 John de Leek (elect)
1312 William Sinclair
1337 Malcolm de Innerpeffray (elect)
1344 Richard de Pilmor
1347 Robert de Den (elect)
1347(?) Duncan de Strathearn
1355 John Luce
1370 John de Carrick (elect)
1371(?) Michael de Monymusk
1377(?) Andrew Umfray (elect)
1379 John de Peblys [? of Peebles]
1379 Robert de Derling
1390(?) Nicholas Duffield
1391 Robert Sinclair
1398(?) Robert de Cardeny
1430 William Gunwardby
1437 Donald MacNaughton (elect)
1438 James Kennedy
1440(?) Thomas Livingston
1440 Alexander de Lawedre [Lauder]
         (elect)
1442 James de Brois [Brewhous]
1447 William Turnbull (elect)
1448 John Ralston
1452(?) Thomas Lauder
1476 James Livingston
1483 Alexander Inglis (elect)
1484 George Brown
1515 Andrew Stewart (elect)
1516 Gavin Douglas
1524 Robert Cockburn
1526(?) George Crichton
1546 John Hamilton
1552 Robert Crichton
1572 James Paton (titular)
1585 Peter Rollock (titular)
1607 James Nicolson (titular)
1611(?) Alexander Lindsay dep. 1638
1662 George Haliburton
1665 Henry Guthrie
1677 William Lindsay
1679 Andrew Bruce
1686 John Hamilton
1717 Thomas Rattray
1743 John Alexander
1776(?) Charles Rose
1792 Jonathan Watson
1808 Patrick Torry
1842 Held with St Andrews

†Dunblane

1162 Laurence
c1180 Symon
1198 Johathan
c1196 W[illelmus]
1215 Abraham
1225 Ralph (elect)
c1227 Osbert
1233 Clement
1259 Robert de Prebenda
1284 William I
1296 Alpin
1301 Nicholas
1307 Nicholas de Balmyle
1318(?) Roger de Balnebrich (elect)
1322 Maurice
c1347 William II
c1361 Walter de Coventre
c1372 Andrew
c1380 Dougal
1403(?) Finlay or Dermoch

1419 William Stephen
1430 Michael Ochiltree
1447(?) Robert Lauder
1468 John Hepburn
1487 James Chisholm
1527 William Chisholm I
1561 William Chisholm II [coadj.]
1575 Andrew Graham (titular)
1611 George Graham
1616 Adam Bellenden
1636 James Wedderburn
1661 Robert Leighton
1673 James Ramsay
1684 Robert Douglas
[1716 to 1731 See vacant]
1731 John Gillan
1735 Robert White
1744 Thomas Ogilvie (elect)
1774 Charles Rose, d. 1791
1776 Held with **Dunkeld**

Edinburgh

1634 William Forbes
1634 David Lindsay
1662 George Wishart
1672 Alexander Young
1679 John Paterson
1687 Alexander Rose
1720 John Fullarton
1727 Arthur Millar
1727 Andrew Lumsden
1733 David Freebairn
[1739 to 1776 See vacant]
1776 William Falconer
1787 William Abernethy Drummond
1806 Daniel Sandford
1830 James Walker
1841 Charles Hughes Terrot
1872 Henry Cotterill
1886 John Dowden
1910 George Henry Somerset
         Walpole
1929 Harry Seymour Reid
1939 Ernest Denny Logie Danson
1947 Kenneth Charles Harman
         Warner
1961 Kenneth Moir Carey
1975 Alastair Iain Macdonald
         Haggart
1986 Richard Frederick Holloway

Aberdeen
Aberdeen and Orkney

BISHOPS AT MURTHLAC
       (?) Beyn [Beanus]
       (?) Donort
       (?) Cormac

BISHOPS AT ABERDEEN
1132 Nechtan
c1150 Edward
c1172 Matthew
c1201 John
c1208 Adam de Kalder
1228 Matthew Scot (elect)
1230 Gilbert de Strivelyn
1240 Radulf de Lamley
c1247 Peter de Ramsey
1258 Richard de Pottun
1272 Hugh de Bennum
1282 Henry le Chene
1329 Walter Herok (elect)
1329 Alexander I, de Kyninmund
1344 William de Deyn
1351 John de Rate

† Indicates a diocese no longer extant or united with another diocese.

Aberdeen—continued

1356 Alexander II, de Kyninmund
1380 Adam de Tynyngham
1391 Gilbert de Grenlaw
1422 Henry de Lychton [Leighton]
c1441 Ingram de Lindsay
1458 Thomas Spens
1480 Robert Blackadder (elect)
1488 William Elphinstone
1515 Robert Forman (elect)
1516 Alexander Gordon
1519 Gavin Dunbar
1529 George Learmonth [coadj.]
1533 William Stewart
1547 William Gordon
1577 David Cunningham (elect)
1611 Peter Blackburn
1616 Alexander Forbes
1618 Patrick Forbes of Corse
1635 Adam Bellenden [Bannatyne]
1662 David Mitchell
1663 Alexander Burnet
1664 Patrick Scougal
1682 George Halyburton
[1715 to 1721 See vacant]
1721 Archibald Campbell
1724 James Gadderar
1733 William Dunbar
1746 Andrew Gerard
1768 Robert Kilgour
1786 John Skinner
1816 William Skinner
1857 Thomas George Spink Suther
1883 Arthur Gascoigne Douglas
1906 Rowland Ellis
1912 Anthony Mitchell
1917 Frederic Llewellyn Deane
1943 Herbert William Hall
1956 Edward Frederick Easson
1973 Ian Forbes Begg
1978 Frederick Charles Darwent

†Orkney

1035   Henry
1050   Turolf
1072   John
1072   Adalbert
1073   Radulf
1108   Roger
1114   Radulf Novell
1102   William I, 'the Old'
1168(?) William II
1188(?) Bjarni
1224   Jofreyrr
1248   Henry I
1270   Peter
1286   Dolgfinn
1310   William III
c1369 William IV
c1384 Robert Sinclair
1384(?) John
1394   Henry II
1396(?) John Pak
1407   Alexander Vaus (elect)
1415   William Stephenson
1420   Thomas Tulloch
1461   William Tulloch
1477   Andrew Painter
1500   Edward Stewart
1524   John Benston [coadj.]
1526(?) Robert Maxwell
1541   Robert Reid
1559   Adam Bothwell
1611   James Law
1615   George Graham
1639   Robert Barron (elect)
1661   Thomas Sydserf

1664 Andrew Honeyman
1677 Murdo Mackenzie
1688 Andrew Bruce, See afterwards
     administered with **Caithness**
1857 Held with **Aberdeen**

Brechin

1153(?) Samson
1178 Turpin
1202 Radulf
1215 Hugh
1218 Gregory
1246 Albin
1269(?) William de Crachin (elect)
1275 William Comyn
1296 Nicholas
1298 John de Kyninmund
1328 Adam de Moravia
1350 Philip Wilde
1351 Patrick de Locrys [Leuchars]
1383 Stephen de Cellario
1411 Walter Forrester
1426 John de Crannach
1455 George Schoriswood
1464 Patrick Graham
1465 John Balfour
1489 William Meldrum
1523 John Hepburn
1557 Donald Campbell (elect)
1565(?) John Sinclair (elect)
1566 Alexander Campbell (titular)
1610 Andrew Lamb
1619 David Lindsay
1634 Thomas Sydserf
1635 Walter Whitford
1662 David Strachan
1672 Robert Laurie
1678 George Haliburton
1682 Robert Douglas
1684 Alexander Cairncross
1684 James Drummond
[1695 to 1709 Held with **Edinburgh**]
1709 John Falconar
1724 Robert Norrie
1726 John Ochterlonie
1742 James Rait
1778 George Innes
1787 William Abernethy Drummond
1788 John Strachan
1810 George Gleig
1840 David Moir
1847 Alexander Penrose Forbes
1876 Hugh Willoughby Jermyn
1904 Walter John Forbes Robberds
1935 Kenneth Donald Mackenzie
1944 Eric Graham
1959 John Chappell Sprott
1975 Lawrence Edward Luscombe
1990 Robert Halliday

Moray

Moray, Ross and Caithness

1114 Gregory
1153(?) William
1164 Felix
1172 Simon de Tonei
1187 Richard de Lincoln
1203 Brice de Douglas
1224(?) Andrew de Moravia
1244(?) Simon
1251 Radulf de Leycester (elect)
1253 Archibald
1299 David de Moravia
1326 John de Pilmor
1363 Alexander Bur
1397 William de Spyny
1407 John de Innes

1415   Henry Leighton
1422   Columba de Dunbar
1437   John de Winchester
1460(?) James Stewart
1463   David Stewart
1477   William de Tulloch
1487   Andrew Stewart
1501(?) Andrew Forman
1516(?) James Hepburn
1525   Robert Shaw
1532(?) Alexander Stewart
1538(?) Patrick Hepburn
1574   George Douglas
1611   Alexander Douglas
1623   John Guthrie
1662   Murdo Mackenzie
1677   James Aitken
1680   Colin Falconer
1687   Alexander Rose
1688   William Hay
1707   Held with **Edinburgh**
1725   Held with **Aberdeen**
1727   William Dunbar
1737   George Hay (elect)
1742   William Falconar
1777   Arthur Petrie
1787   Andrew Macfarlane
1798   Alexander Jolly
1838   Held with **Ross**
1851   Robert Eden
1886   James Butler Knill Kelly
1904   Arthur John Maclean
1943   Piers Holt Wilson
1953   Duncan MacInnes
1970   George Minshull Sessford

†Ross

1131(?) Macbeth
1150(?) Simon
1161   Gregory
1195   Reginald
1213   Andrew de Moravia (elect)
1215(?) Robert I
1250   Robert II
1272   Matthew
1275(?) Robert III de Fyvin
1295(?) Adam de Derlingtun (elect)
1297(?) Thomas de Dundee
1325   Roger
1351   Alexander Stewart
1372   Alexander de Kylwos
1398(?) Alexander de Waghorn
1418   Thomas Lyell (elect)
       Griffin Yonge (elect)
1420   John Bulloch
1441(?) Andrew de Munro (elect)
1441(?) Thomas Tulloch
1464(?) Henry Cockburn
1478   John Wodman
1481   William Elphinstone (elect)
1483   Thomas Hay
1492   John Guthrie
1498   John Frisel [Fraser]
c1507 Robert Cockburn
c1525 James Hay
c1539 Robert Cairncross
1552   David Painter
1561(?) Henry Sinclair
1566   John Lesley
1575   Alexander Hepburn
1611   David Lindsay
1613   Patrick Lindsay
1633   John Maxwell
1662   John Paterson
1679   Alexander Young
1684   James Ramsay
[1696 See vacant or held with **Caithness** until 1727]

Ross—continued

1727 Held with **Moray**
1742 Held with **Caithness**
1762 Robert Forbes
1777 Held with **Moray**
1819 David Low
1851 Held with **Moray**

†Caithness

c1146 Andrew
c1187 John
1214 Adam
1223(?) Gilbert de Moravia
1250(?) William
1263 Walter de Baltrodin
1273(?) Nicholas (elect)
1275 Archibald Herok
1278 Richard (elect)
1279(?) Hervey de Dundee (elect)
1282 Alan de St. Edmund
1295 John or James (elect)
1296 Adam de Derlingtun
1297 Andrew
1306 Fercard Belegaumbe
1328(?) David
1341 Alan de Moravia
1343 Thomas de Fingask
1370 Malcolm de Dumbrek
1381 Alexander Man
1414 Alexander Vaus
1425 John de Crannach
1428 Robert Strabrok
1446 John Innes
1448 William Mudy
1478(?) Prospero Camogli de Medici
1484(?) John Sinclair (elect)
1502 Andrew Stewart I
1517(?) Andrew Stewart II
1542 Robert Stewart (elect)
1600 George Gledstanes (elect)
1611 Alexander Forbes
1616 John Abernethy
1662 Patrick Forbes
1680 Andrew Wood
[1695 See vacant]
1731 Robert Keith
1741 Wm. Falconas
1762 Held with **Ross**
[1742 See Vacant]
1777 Held with **Moray**

Glasgow

Glasgow and Galloway

550(?) Kentigern or Mungo (No record of his successors)
1114(?) Michael
1118(?) John
1147 Herbert
1164 Ingram
1175 Jocelin
1199 Hugh de Roxburgh (elect)
1200 William Malveisin
1202 Florence (elect)
1208 Walter de St Albans
1233 William de Bondington
1259 Nicholas de Moffat (elect)
1259 John de Cheam
1268 Nicholas de Moffat (again elect)
1271 William Wischard (elect)
1273 Robert Wischard
1317 Stephen de Donydouer (elect)
1318 John de Eglescliffe
1323 John de Lindsay

1337 John Wischard
1339 William Rae
1367 Walter Wardlaw
1388 Matthew de Glendonwyn
1391 John Framisden (titular)
1408 William Lauder
1427 John Cameron
1447 James de Brois [Brewhouse]
1448 William Turnbull
1456 Andrew de Durrisdeer
1475 John Laing
1483 George Carmichael (elect)

ARCHBISHOPS

1483 Robert Blackadder (Archb. 9 Jan. 1492)
1509 James Betoun I
1525 Gavin Dunbar
1551 Alexander Gordon
1552 James Betoun II, restored 1587
1571 John Porterfield (titular)
1573 James Boyd (titular)
1581 Robert Montgomery (titular)
1585 William Erskine (titular)
1610 John Spottiswoode
1615 James Law
1633 Patrick Lindsay
1661 Andrew Fairfoul
1664 Alexander Burnet, restored 1674
1671 Robert Leighton, resigned 1674, d. 1684
1679 Arthur Rose
1684 Alexander Cairncross d. 1701
1687 John Paterson,[1] d. 1708
[1708 Vacant]

BISHOPS

1731 Alexander Duncan, d. 1733
[1733 Vacant]
1787 Held with **Edinburgh**
1805 William Abernethy Drummond
1809-37 Held with **Edinburgh**
1837 Michael Russell
1848 Walter John Trower
1859 William Scott Wilson
1888 William Thomas Harrison
1904 Archibald Ean Campbell
1921 Edward Thomas Scott Reid
1931 John Russell Darbyshire
1938 John Charles Halland How
1952 Francis Hamilton Moncreiff
1974 Frederick Goldie
1981 Derek Alec Rawcliffe
1991 John Mitchell Taylor

†Galloway or Candida Casa or Whithorn[2]

Ninian, d. 432(?)
(?) Octa
681 Trumwine
731 Penthelm, d. 735(?)
735 Frithowald, d. 764
763 Pehtwine, d. 776
777 Ethelbert
791 Beadwulf
1140 Gilla-Aldan
1154 Christian
1189 John
1214 Walter
1235 Odo Ydonc (elect)
1235 Gilbert
1255 Henry
1294 Thomas de Kircudbright [de Daltoun]
1327 Simon de Wedale

1355 Michael Malconhalgh
1359(?) Thomas Macdowell (elect)
1359 Thomas
1364 Adam de Lanark
(?) David Douglas, d. 1373
(?) James Carron, resigned 1373
1378 Ingram de Kethnis (elect)
1379 Oswald
1380 Thomas de Rossy
(?) Francis Ramsay, d. 1402
1406 Elisaeus Adougan
1414(?) Gilbert Cavan (elect)
1415 Thomas de Butil
1422 Alexander Vaus
1451 Thomas Spens
1457(?) Thomas Vaus (elect)
1459 Ninian Spot
1482(?) George Vaus
1508(?) James Betoun (elect)
1509(?) David Arnot
1526 Henry Wemyss
1541(?) Andrew Dury
1559(?) Alexander Gordon
1610 Gavin Hamilton
1612(?) William Couper
1619 Andrew Lamb
1635 Thomas Sydserf
1661 James Hamilton
1675 John Paterson
1679 Arthur Rose
1680 James Aitken
1688 John Gordon, d. 1726
1697 Held with **Edinburgh**
1837 Held with **Glasgow**

Argyll or Lismore

Argyll and The Isles

1193 Harald
1240 William
1253 Alan
1268 Laurence de Erganis
1300 Andrew
1342 Angusde Ergadia (elect)
1344 Martinde Ergaill
1387 John Dugaldi
1397(?) Bean Johannis
1420(?) Finlay de Albany
1428 George Lauder
1476 Robert Colquhoun
1504 David Hamilton
1532 Robert Montgomery
1539(?) William Cunningham (elect)
1553(?) James Hamilton (elect)
1580 Neil Campbell (titular)
1611 John Campbell (titular)
1613 Andrew Boyd
1637 James Fairlie
1662 David Fletcher
1665 John Young (elect)
1666 William Scroggie
1675 Arthur Rose
1679 Colin Falconer
1680 Hector Maclean
1688 Alexander Monro (elect)
Held with **Ross**
1847 Alexander Ewing
1874 George Mackarness
1883 James Robert Alexander Chinnery-Haldane
1907 Kenneth Mackenzie
1942 Thomas Hannay
1963 Richard Knyvet Wimbush
1977 George Kennedy Buchanan Henderson

---

[1] After the deposition of John Paterson at the Revolution the See ceased to be Archiepiscopal.
[2] The traditional founder of the See is St. Ninian. But nothing authentic is known of the bishops prior to the accession of Gilla-Aldan between 1133 and 1140.

†The Isles

900 Patrick
1080 Roolwer
1080 William
1095 Hamundr
1138 Wimund
1152 John I
1152(?) Ragnald
1154 Gamaliel
1170 Christian
1194 Michael
1210 Nicholas I
1219 Nicholas II of Meaux
1226(?) Reginald
1226 Simon
1249 Laurence (elect)
1253 Richard
1275 Gilbert (elect)
1275 Mark
1305 Alan
1324 Gilbert Maclelan
1328 Bernard de Linton
1331 Thomas de Rossy
1349 William Russell
1374 John Donkan
1387 Michael
1392 John Sproten (**Man**) (titular)
1402(?) Conrad (**Man**) (titular)
1402(?) Theodore Bloc (**Man**) (titular)
1410 Richard Messing (**Man**)
1422 Michael Anchire
1425(?) John Burgherlinus (**Man**)
1428 Angus I
1441(?) John Hectoris [McCachane] Macgilleon
1472 Angus II
1487 John Campbell
1511 George Hepburn
1514 John Campbell (elect)
1530(?) Ferchar MacEachan (elect)
1550(?) Roderick Maclean
1553(?) Alexander Gordon
1567 John Carswell (titular)
1573 John Campbell
1605 Andrew Knox
1619 Thomas Knox
1628 John Leslie
1634 Neil Campbell
1662 Robert Wallace
1677 Andrew Wood
1680 Archibald Graham [or McIlvernock]

Held with **Orkney** and **Caithness**
1819 Held with **Argyll**

College Bishops, Consecrated without Sees

1705 John Sage, d. 1711
1705 John Fullarton
(**Edinburgh** 1720), d. 1727
1709 Henry Christie, d. 1718
1709 John Falconar
(**Fife** 1720), d. 1723
1711 Archibald Campbell
(**Aberdeen** 1721), d. 1744
1712 James Gadderar
(**Aberdeen** 1725, **Moray** 1725), d. 1733
1718 Arthur Millar
(**Edinburgh** 1727), d. 1727
1718 William Irvine, d. 1725
1722 Andrew Cant, d. 1730
1722 David Freebairn
(**Edinburgh** 1733)
1726 John Ochterlonie
(**Brechin** 1731), d. 1742
1726 James Ross
(**Fife** 1731), d. 1733
1727 John Gillan
(**Dunblane** 1731), d. 1735
1727 David Ranken, d. 1728

Bishops who Have Held the Office of Primus

1704 Alexander Rose
(**Edinburgh**, 1704–20)
1720 John Fullarton
(**Edinburgh**, 1720–27)
1727 Arthur Millar
(**Edinburgh**, 1727)
1727 Andrew Lumsden
(**Edinburgh**, 1727–33)
1731 David Freebairn
(**Edinburgh**, 1733–39)
1738 Thomas Rattray
(**Dunkeld**, 1727–43)
1743 Robert Keith
(**Caithness**, 1731–41)
1757 Robert White
(**Dunblane**, 1735–43, **St. Andrews**, 1743–61)

1762 William Falconar
(**Orkney** and **Caithness**, 1741–62)
1782 Robert Kilgour
(**Aberdeen**, 1768–86)
1788 John Skinner
(**Aberdeen**, 1786–1816)
1816 George Gleig
(**Brechin**, 1810–40)
1837 James Walker
(**Edinburgh**, 1880–41)
1841 William Skinner
(**Aberdeen**, 1816–57)
1857 Charles H. Terrot
(**Edinburgh**, 1841–72)
1862 Robert Eden
(**Moray, Ross**, and **Caithness**, 1851–86)
1886 Hugh W. Jermyn
(**Brechin**, 1875–1903)
1901 James B. K. Kelly
(**Moray, Ross**, and **Caithness**, 1886–1904)
1904 George H. Wilkinson
(**St. Andrews, Dunkeld**, and **Dunblane**, 1893–1907)
1908 Walter J. F. Robberds
(**Brechin**, 1904–34)
1935 Arthur J. Maclean
(**Moray, Ross**, and **Caithness**, 1904–43)
1943 E. D. Logie Danson
(**Edinburgh**, 1939–46)
1946 John C. H. How
(**Glasgow** and **Galloway**, 1938–52)
1952 Thomas Hannay
(**Argyll** and **The Isles**, 1942–62)
1962 Francis Hamilton Moncreiff
(**Glasgow** and **Galloway**, 1952–74)
1974 Richard Knyvet Wimbush
(**Argyll** and **The Isles**, 1963–77)
1977 Alastair Iain Macdonald (Haggart
(**Edinburgh**, 1975–85)
1985 Lawrence Edward Luscombe
(**Brechin**, 1975–)
1990 George Kennedy Buchanan Henderson
(**Argyll** and **The Isles**, 1977–   )

IRELAND

PROVINCE OF ARMAGH

†Achonry

BISHOPS

c558 Cathfuidh
1152 Mael Ruanaid ua Ruadain
1159 Gille na Naehm O Ruadain [Gelasius]
1208 Clemens O Sniadaig
1220 Connmach O Torpaig [Carus]
1226 Gilla Isu O Cleirig [Gelasius]
1237 Tomas O Ruadhan
1238 Oengus O Clumain [Elias]
1251 Tomas O Maicin
1266 Tomas O Miadachain [Dionysus]
1286 Benedict O Bracain
1312 David of Kilheny
1348 David II

1348 Nicol Alias Muircheartach O hEadhra
1374 William Andrew
1385 Simon
c1390 Tomas mac Muirgheasa MacDonn-chadha
1401 Brian mac Seaain O h-Eadhra
1410 Maghnus O h-Eadhra
1424 Donatus
1424 Richard Belmer
1436 Tadhg O Dalaigh
1442 James Blakedon
1449 Cornelius O Mochain
1463 Brian O hEasdhra [Benedictus]
1470 Nicholas Forden
1475 Robert Wellys
1484 Thomas fitzRichard

1484 Tomas O Conghalain
1489 John Bustamente
1492 Thomas Ford
1508 Eugenius O Flannagain
1522 Cormac O Snighe
1547 Thomas O Fihilly
1562 Eugene O'Harte
1613 Miler Magrath (with **Cashel**)
United to **Killala** 1622

†Annadown

BISHOPS

1189 Conn ua Mellaig [Concors]
1202 Murchad ua Flaithbertaig
1242 Tomas O Mellaig

Annadown—continued

1251 Conchobar [Concors]
1283 John de Ufford
1308 Gilbert O Tigernaig
1323 Jacobus O Cethernaig
1326 Robert Petit
1328 Albertus
1329 Tomas O Mellaig
1359 Dionysius
1393 Johannes
1394 Henry Trillow
1402 John Bryt
1408 John Wynn
1421 John Boner [Camere]
1425 Seean Mac Braddaigh
1428 Seamus O Lonnghargain
1431 Donatus O Madagain
1446 Thomas Salscot
1450 Redmund Bermingham
1458 Thomas Barrett
1496 Francis Brunand
1540 John Moore
[United to **Tuam** c1555]

†Ardagh

454 Mel
c670 Erard
874 Faelghus
Cele 1048
1152 Mac Raith ua Morain
1172 Gilla Crist O hEothaig
[Christianus]
O'Tirlenain 1187
ua hEislinnen
Annud O Muiredaig 1216
1217 Robert
1224 M.
1228 Ioseph mac Teichthechain
1229 Mac Raith Mac Serraig
1232 Gilla Isu mac in Scelaige O
Tormaid [Gelasius]
1232 Iocelinus
1238 Brendan Mac Teichthechain
1256 Milo of Dunstable
1290 Matha O'h-Eothaig [Mattheus]
1323 Robert Wirsop (did not get
possession)
1324 Mac Eoaighseoan
1347 Eoghan O Ferghail [Audovenus]
1368 William Mac Carmaic
1373 Cairbre O'Ferghail [Charles]
1373 John Aubrey
1392 Henry Nony (did not get
possession)
1396 Comedinus Mac Bradaigh
[Gilbert]
1400 Adam Leyns
1419 Conchobar O'Ferghail
[Cornelius]
1425 Risdeard O'Ferghail
[1444 O'Murtry, not cons, res.]
1445 Cormac Mac Shamhradhain
1462 Seaan O'Ferghail
1467 Donatus O'Ferghail
1482 William O'Ferghail
1517 Ruaidri O'Maoileoin
1517 Rory O'Mallone [Roger
O'Melleine]
1541 Richard O'Ferrall
1553 Patrick MacMahon
[1572 John Garvey, not consecrated]
1583 Lysach O'Ferrall
1604 Robert Draper
1613 Thomas Moigne
1629 William Bedell

1633 John Richardson
1661 Robert Maxwell
1673 Francis Marsh
1682 William Sheridan
1692 Ulysses Burgh
1604–33 and 1661–92 and 1661–92 and
1692–1751 Held by the Bi-
shops of **Kilmore**
1751–1839 Held by the Archbishops of
Tuam
United to **Kilmore** 1839

Armagh

BISHOPS
444 Patrick
Benignus 467
Jarlath 481
Cormac 497
Dubthach 513
Ailill I 526
Ailill II 536
David O'Faranan 551
Carlaen 588
MacLaisre 623
-640 Thomian MacRonan
Segeni 688
Suibhne 730
-732 Congusa
Affinth 794
-811 Nundha
-818 Artri
835 Forannan
Mael Patraic I 862
Fethgna 875
Cathasach MacRobartach 883
Mochta 893
c900 Maelaithghin
Cellach
Mael Ciarain 915
Joseph 936
Mael Patraic II 936
Cathasach MacDolgen 966
Maelmiure 994
Airindach 100
Maeltuile 1032
1032 Hugh O'Ferris
Mael Patraic III 1096
1099 Caincomrac O'Boyle

ARCHBISHOPS
1105 Cellach mac Aeda meic Mael
Isu [Celsus]
1132 Mael maedoc Ua Morgair
[Malachais]
1137 Gilla Meic Liac mac Diarmata
meic Ruaidri [Gelasius]
1174 Conchobar O Conchaille
[Concors]
1175 Gille in Coimhedh O Caran
[Gilbertus]
1180 Tomaltach O Conchobair
[Thomas]
1184 Mael Isu Ua Cerbaill
[Malachias]
1202 Echdonn mac Gilla Uidir
[Eugenius]
1217 Lucas Netterville
1227 Donatus O Fidabra
1240 Albert Suebeer of Cologne
1247 Reginald
1258 Abraham O'Conallain
1261 Mael Patraic O Scannail
1270 Nicol Mac Mael Isu
1303 Michael MacLochlainn (not
confirmed)
1304 Dionysius (not confirmed)

1306 John Taaffe
1307 Walter Jorz
1311 Roland Jorz
1324 Stephen Segrave
1334 David Mag Oireachtaigh
1347 Richard FitzRalph
1362 Milo Sweetman
1383 John Colton
1404 Nicholas Fleming
1418 John Swayne
1439 John Prene
1444 John Mey
1457 John Bole [Bull]
1471 John Foxhalls or Foxholes
1475 Edmund Connesburgh
1480 Ottaviano Spinelli [de Palatio]
1513 John Kite
1521 George Cromer
1543 George Dowdall
1552 Hugh Goodacre
1553 George Dowdall (again)
[1560 Donat MacTeague, not recognized by the Crown, 1562]
1563 Adam Loftus
1568 Thomas Lancaster
1584 John Long
1589 John Garvey
1595 Henry Ussher
1613 Christopher Hampton
1625 James Ussher
[Interregnum 1656–61]
1661 John Bramhall
1663 James Margetson
1679 Michael Boyle
1703 Narcissus Marsh
1714 Thomas Lindsay
1724 Hugh Boulter
1742 John Hoadly
1747 George Stone
1765 Richard Robinson [afterwards
Baron Rokeby]
1795 William Newcome
1800 William Stuart
1822 John George Beresford
Clogher united to Armagh 1850–86
1862 Marcus Gervais Beresford
1886 Robert Bentknox
1893 Robert Samuel Gregg
1896 William Alexander
1911 John Baptist Crozier
1920 Charles Frederick D'Arcy
1938 John Godfrey FitzMaurice Day
1939 John Allen Fitzgerald Gregg
1959 James McCann
1969 George Otto Simms
1980 John Ward Armstrong
1986 Robert Henry Alexander Eames

Clogher

c493 MacCarthinn or Ferdachrioch
Ailill 869
1135 Cinaeth O Baigill
1135 Gilla Crist O Morgair
[Christianus]
(moved his see to Louth)

BISHOPS OF LOUTH
1135 Gilla Crist O Morgair
[Christianus]
1138 Aed O Ceallaide [Edanus]
1178 Mael Isu O Cerbaill [Malachias]
1187 Gilla Crist O Mucaran
[Christinus]
1194 Mael Isu Ua Mael Chiarain
1197 Gilla Tigernaig Mac Gilla
Ronain [Thomas]

† Indicates a diocese no longer extant or united with another diocese.

Clogher—continued

BISHOPS OF CLOGHER

1218 Donatus O Fidabra
1228 Nehemias
1245 David O Bracain
1268 Michael Mac an tSair
1287 Matthew Mac Cathasaigh I
-1310 Henricus
1316 Gelasius O Banain
1320 Nicholas Mac Cathasaigh
1356 Brian Mac Cathmaoil [Bernard]
1362 Matthew Mac Cathasaigh II
—   Aodh O hEothaigh [alias O
     Neill]
1373 John O Corcrain [Würzburg]
1390 Art Mac Cathmhail
1433 Piaras Mag Uidhir [Petrus]
1450 Rossa mac Tomais Oig Mag
     Uidhir [Rogerius]
1475 Florence Woolley
[1484 Niall mac Seamuis Mac
     Mathghamna]
1484 John Edmund de Courci
1494 Seamus Mac Pilip Mac
     Mathghamna
1500 Andreas
1502 Nehemias O Cluanain
1504 Giolla Padraig O Conalaigh
     [Patrick]
1505 Eoghan Mac Cathmhail
     [Eugenius]
1517 Padraig O Cuilin
1535 Aodh O Cearbhalain [Odo]
1517 Patrick O'Cullen
1535 Hugh O'Carolan
1570 Miler Magrath
1605 George Montgomery
1621 James Spottiswood
1645 Henry Jones
1661 John Leslie
1671 Robert Leslie
1672 Roger Boyle
1691 Richard Tennison
1697 St. George Ashe
1717 John Stearne
1745 Robert Clayton
1758 John Garnett
1782 John Hotham (bt. 1794)
1796 William Foster
1797 John Porter
1819 John George Beresford
1820 Percy Jocelyn
1822 Robert Ponsonby Tottenham
     Luftus
United to **Armagh** 1850–86
1886 Charles Maurice Stack
1903 Charles Frederick D'Arcy
1908 Maurice Day
1923 James MacManaway
1944 Richard Tyner
1958 Alan Alexander Buchanan
1970 Richard Patrick Crosland
     Hanson
1973 Robert William Heavener
1980 Gordon McMullan
1986 Brian Desmond Anthony
     Hannon

Connor

 506 Oengus MacNessa 514
     Lughadh 543
 640 Dïmma Dubh. [the Black]
     Duchonna the Pious 725
     Cunnen *or* Cuinden 1038
     Flann O'Sculu 1117
1124 Mael Maedoc Ua Morgair
     [Malachias]

-1152 MaelPatraic O'Banain
1172 Nehemias
1178 Reginaldus
1226 Eustacius
1242 Adam
1245 Isaac de Newcastle-on-Tyne
1258 William de Portroyal
1261 William de Hay [*or* la Haye]
1263 Robert de Flanders
1275 Peter de Dunach
1293 Johannes
1320 Richard
1321 James de Couplith
1323 John de Eglecliff
1323 Robert Wirsop
1324 Jacabus O Cethernaig
1353 William Mercier
1374 Paulus
1389 Johannes
[1420 Seaan O Luachrain not
     consecrated]
1423 Eoghan O'Domhnaill
1429 Domhnall O'Meraich 1431
1431 John Fossade [Festade]
1459 Patricius
1459 Simon Elvington
     United to **Down** 1441
1945 Charles King Irwin
1956 Robert Cyril Hamilton Glover
     Elliott
1969 Arthur Hamilton Butler
1981 William John McCappin
1987 Samuel Greenfield Poyntz

Derry

Derry and Raphoe

     Caencomhrac 927
-937 Finachta MacKellach
-949 Mael Finnen

BISHOPS OF MAGHERA
(Where the See was in the twelfth and
the thirteenth centuries)
1107 Mael Coluim O Brolchain
—   Mael Brigte O Brolchain
1152 O Gormgaile Muiredach O
     Cobthaig [Mauricius]
1173 Amhlaim O Muirethaig
1185 Fogartach O Cerballain
     [Florentius]
*c*1230 Gilla in Coimhded O Cerbal-
     lain [Germanus]
*c*1280 Fogartach O Cerballain II
     [Florentius]

BISHOPS OF DERRY
(Where the See was resettled)
1295 Enri Mac Airechtaig
     [O'Reghly] [of Ardagh]
1297 Gofraid MacLochlainn
     [Godfrey]
1316 Aed O Neill [Odo]
1319 Michael Mac Lochlainn
     [Maurice]
1349 Simon
1391 Johannes
1391 John Dongan
1394 Seoan O Mochain
1398 Aodh [Hugo]
1401 Seoan O Flannabhra
1415 Domhnall Mac Cathmhail
1419 Domhnall O Mearaich
1429 Eoghan O Domhnaill
     [Eugenius]
1433 John Oguguin
[1456 John Bole, appointment not
completed, trld. to Armagh]
1458 Bartholomew O Flannagain

*c*1464 Johannes
1467 Nicholas Weston
1485 Domhnall O Fallamhain
1501 Seamus mac Pilip Mac
     Mathghamna [MacMahon]
1520 Ruaidhri O Domhnaill
1520 Rory O'Donnell
1554 Eugene O'Doherty
-1568 F. [doubtful authority]
1569 Redmond O'Gallagher
[1603 Denis Campbell, not
     consecrated]
1605 George Montgomery
1610 Brutus Babington
[1611 Christopher Hampton, not
     consecrated]
1613 John Tanner
1617 George Downham
1634 John Bramhall
1661 George Wild
1666 Robert Mossom
1680 Michael Ward
1681 Ezekiel Hopkins
1691 William King
1703 Charles Hickman
1714 John Hartstonge
1717 St. George Ashe
1718 William Nicolson
1727 Henry Downes
1735 Thomas Rundle
1743 Carew Reynell
1745 George Stone
1747 William Barnard
1768 Frederick Augustus Hervey
     [afterwards Earl of Bristol]
1803 William Knox
1831 Richard Ponsonby
Raphoe united to Derry from 1834
1853 William Higgin
1867 William Alexander
1896 George Alexander Chadwick,
     res.
1916 Joseph Irvine Peacocke
1945 Robert M'Neil Boyd
1958 Charles John Tyndall
1970 Cuthbert Irvine Peacocke
1975 Robert Henry Alexander
     Eames
1980 James Mehaffey

Down

Down and Dromore

     Fergus 584
     Suibhne 825
     Graithene 956
     Finghin 964
     Flaithbertach 1043
     MaelKevin 1086
—   Mael Muire 1117
     Oengus Ua Gormain 1123
—   [Anonymous]
*c*1124 Mael Maedoc O Morgair
     [Malachias]
1152 Mael Isu mac in Chleirig
     Chuirr [Malachias]
1175 Gilla Domangairt Mac
     Cormaic
*c*1176 Echmilid [Malachias]
*c*1202 Radulfus
1224 Thomas
1251 Randulphus
1258 Reginaldus
1265 Thomas Lydel
1277 Nicholas le Blund
1305 Thomas Ketel
1314 Thomas Bright
1328 John of Baliconingham
1329 Ralph of Kilmessan

Down—continued

1353 Richard Calf I
1365 Robert of Aketon
1367 William White
1369 Richard Calf [II]
1386 John Ross
1394 John Dongan
1413 John Cely *or* Sely
1445 Ralph Alderle

BISHOPS OF DOWN AND CONNOR

1441 John Fossard
1447 Thomas Pollard
1451 Richard Wolsey
1456 Thomas Knight
1469 Tadhg O Muirgheasa [Thaddaeus]
1489 Tiberio Ugolino
1520 Robert Blyth
1542 Eugene Magennis
1565 James MacCawell
1569 John Merriman
1572 Hugh Allen
1593 Edward Edgeworth
1596 John Charden
1602 Robert Humpston
1607 John Todd, res.
1612 James Dundas
1613 Robert Echlin
1635 Henry Leslie
1661 Jeremy Taylor
1667 Roger Boyle
1672 Thomas Hacket
1694 Samuel Foley
1695 Edward Walkington
1699 Edward Smyth
1721 Francis Hutchinson
1739 Carew Reynell
1743 John Ryder
1752 John Whitcombe
1752 Robert Downes
1753 Arthur Smyth
1765 James Traill
1784 William Dickson
1804 Nathaniel Alexander
1823 Richard Mant

BISHOPS OF DOWN, CONNOR AND DROMORE

1849 Robert Bent Knox
1886 William Reeves
1892 Thomas James Welland
1907 John Baptist Crozier
1911 Charles Frederick D'Arcy
1919 Charles Thornton Primrose Grierson
1934 John Frederick McNeice
1942 Charles King Irwin

BISHOPS OF DOWN AND DROMORE

1945 William Shaw Kerr
1955 Frederick Julian Mitchell
1970 George Alderson Quin
1980 Robert Henry Alexander Eames
1986 Gordon McMullan

†Dromore

Mael Brighde 974
Riagan 1101
1197 Ua Ruanada
1227 Geraldus
1245 Andreas
1284 Tigernach I
1290 Gervasius
— Tigernach II
1309 Florentius Mac Donnocain
1351 Anonymous

1366 Milo
1369 Christophorus
— Cornelius 1382
1382 John O'Lannoy
1398 Thomas Orwell
1400 John Waltham
1402 Roger Appleby
1408 Richard Payl
1410 Marcus
1411 John Chourles
1414 Seaan O Ruanadha
1419 Nicholas Wartre
1429 Thomas Rackelf
1431 William
1431 David Chirbury
1450 Thomas Scrope [Bradley]
1450 Thomas Radcliff
1456 Donatus O h-Anluain [Ohendua]
1457 Richard Messing
1463 William Egremond
— Aonghus [Aeneas] 1476
1476 Robert Kirke
1480 Yvo Guillen
1483 George Braua
1511 Tadhg O Raghallaigh [Thaddeus]
1536 Quintin O Quigley [Cogley]
1539 Roger McHugh
1540 Arthur Magennis
1607 John Todd
[1613 John Tanner, not consecrated]
1613 Theophilus Buckworth
1661 Robert Leslie
1661 Jeremy Taylor (administered the diocese)
1667 George Rust
1671 Essex Digby
1683 Capel Wiseman
1695 Tobias Pullein
1713 John Stearne
1717 Ralph Lambert
1727 Charles Cobbe
1732 Henry Maule
1744 Thomas Fletcher
1745 Jemmett Browne
1745 George Marlay
1763 John Oswald
1763 Edward Young
1765 Henry Maxwell
1766 William Newcome
1775 James Hawkins
1780 William de la Poer Beresford
1782 Thomas Percy
1811 George Hall
1812 John Leslie
1819 James Saurin
United to **Down** since 1842

†Elphin

Domnall mac Flannacain Ua Dubhthaig 1136
Muiredach O Dubhthaig 1150
1152 Mael Isu O Connachtain
Flannacan O Dubhthaig 1168
c1177 Tomaltach mac Aeda Ua Conchobhair [Thomas]
c1180 Florint Ua Riacain Ui Maelrvanaid
1206 Ardgar O Conchobhair
1226 Dionysius O Mordha
c1230 Alanus
1231 Donnchad mac Fingein O Conchobhair [Dionysius Donatus]
1245 Eoin O Mugroin
1247 Tomaltach mac Toirrdelbaig O Conchobhair [Thomas]

1260 Mael Sechlainn O Conchobhair [Milo]
1262 Tomas mac Fergail mac Diarmata
1266 Muiris O Conchobhair
[1285 Amlaim O Tommaltaig, not consecrated]
1285 Gilla Isu mac in Liathanaig O Conchobhair
1297 Maelsechlainn mac Briain [Malachias]
1303 Donnchad O Flannacain, [Donatus]
1307 Cathal O Conchobhair
1310 Mael Sechlainn Mac Aedha
1313 Lurint O Lachtnain [Laurence]
1326 Sean O Finnachta
1355 Carolus
1357 Gregory O Mochain
1372 Thomas Barrett
1383 Seoan O Mochain
1407 Seaan O Grada
1405 Gerald Caneton
1412 Thomas Colby
1418 Robert Fosten
1421 Edmund Barrett
1427 Johannes
1429 Laurence O Beolain
1429 William O hEidighean
1448 Conchobhar O Maolalaidh
1458 Nicholas O Flanagan
1487 Hugo Arward
1492 Riocard mac Briain O gCuanach
1499 George Brana
1501 Cornelius O Flannagain
1508 Christopher Fisher
1525 John Maxey
1539 William Maginn 1541(?)
1539 Gabriel de Sancto Serio
1541 Conach *or* Con O'Negall *or* O'Shyagall
1552 Roland Burke [de Burgo]
1582 Thomas Chester
1583 John Lynch
1611 Edward King
1639 Henry Tilson
1661 John Parker
1667 John Hodson
1691 Simon Digby
1720 Henry Downes
1724 Theophilus Bolton
1730 Robert Howard
1740 Edward Synge
1762 William Gore
1772 Jemmett Browne
1775 Charles Dodgson
1795 John Law
1810 Power le Poer Trench
1819 John Leslie 1854
United to **Kilmore** and **Ardagh** on the death of Bp Beresford in 1841 when Bp Leslie became Bp of the united dioceses.

†Killala

Muiredach
Kellach
O Maolfogmair I 1137
O Maolfogmair II 1151
Imar O Ruaidhin 1176
1179 O Maolfogmair III
1199 Domnall Ua Becdha
1207 Cormac O'Tarpy
O'Kelly 1214
1226 Aengus O Maolfogmair [Elias]
Gille Cellaig O Ruaidhin 1253
1253 Seoan O Laidig

Killala—continued

1281 Donnchad O Flaithbertaig
    [Donatus]
1307 John Tankard
    Sean O Flaithim 1343
1344 James Bermingham
1347 William O Dubhda
1351 Robert Elyot
1381 Thomas Lodowys
1383 Conchobar O Coineoil
    [Cornelius]
1390 Thomas Horwell [Orwell]
1400 Thomas Barrett
1403 Muircheartach Cleirach mac
    Donnchadha O Dubhda
    Connor O'Connell 1423
1427 Fergal Mac Martain
1431 Thaddaeus Mac Creagh
1432 Brian O Coneoil
1447 Robert Barrett
1452 Ruaidhri Bairead [Barrett]
1453 Thomas
1459 Richard Viel
    Miler O'Connell 1461
1461 Donatus O Conchobhair
1470 Tomas Bairead [Barrett]
1487 John de Tuderto [Seaan O
    Caissin]
1500 Thomas Clerke
1508 Malachias O Clumhain
1513 Risdeard Bairead
1545 Redmond O'Gallagher
1570 Donat O'Gallagher
1580 John O'Casey
1592 Owen O'Conor
1613 Miler Magrath
Achonry united to Killala 1622
1623 Archibald Hamilton
1630 Archibald Adair, dep., but
    subsequently restored
164 John Maxwell
1661 Henry Hall
1664 Thomas Bayly
1671 Thomas Otway
1680 John Smith
1681 William Smyth
1682 Richard Tennison
1691 William Lloyd
1717 Henry Downes
1720 Charles Cobbe
1727 Robert Howard
1730 Robert Clayton
173 Mordecai Cary
175 Richard Robinson [afterwards
    Baron Rokeby]
1759 Samuel Hutchinson
1781 William Cecil Pery
1784 William Preston
1787 John Law
1795 John Porter
1798 Joseph Stock
1810 James Verschoyle
United to **Tuam** since 1834

Kilmore

Kilmore, Elphin and Ardagh

—   Aed Ua Finn 1136
—   Muirchertach Ua
    Maelmocherge 1149
1152 Tuathal Ua Connachtaig
    [Thadeus]
1202 Mi Ua Dobailen
—   Flann O Connachtaig
    [Florentius] 1231
1237 Congalach Mac Idneoil
1251 Simon O Ruairc

1286 Mauricius
—   Matha Mac Duibne 1314
1320 Padraig O Cridecain
—   Conchobhar Mac Conshnamha
    [Ford] 1355
1356 Richard O Raghilligh
1373 Johannes
1388 Thomas Rushook, O.P.
1392 Sean O Raghilligh I [John]
1398 Nicol Mac Bradaigh
1401 Sean O'Raghilligh II
1407 John Stokes
1409 David O'Fairchellaigh
1422 Domhnall O Gabhann
1445 Aindrias Mac Bradaigh
1455 Fear Sithe Mag Dhuibhne
1465 Sean O Raghilligh II
1476 Cormac Mag Shamhradhain
1480 Tomas MacBradaigh
1512 Diarmaid O Raghilligh
1530 Edmund Nugent
1540 Sean Mac Bradaigh
1585 John Garvey
1604 Robert Draper
1613 Thomas Moigne
1629 William Bedell
1643 Robert Maxwell
1673 Francis Marsh
1682 William Sheridan
1693 William Smyth
1699 Edward Wetenhall
1715 Timothy Godwin
1727 Josiah Hott
1742 Joseph Story
1757 John Cradock
1772 Denison Cumberland
1775 George Lewis Jones
1790 William Foster
1796 Charles Broderick
1802 George de la Poer Beresford
Ardagh united to Kilmore 1839
Elphin united to Kilmore 1841
1841 John Leslie
1854 Marcus Gervais Beresford
1862 Hamilton Verschoyle
1870 Charles Leslie
1870 Thomas Carson
1874 John Richard Darley
1884 Samuel Shone
1897 Alfred George Elliott
1915 William Richard Moore
1930 Arthur William Barton
1939 Albert Edward Hughes
1950 Frederick Julian Mitchell
1956 Charles John Tyndall
1959 Edward Francis Butler Moore
1981 William Gilbert Wilson

†Mayo

Gerald 732
Muiredach [*or* Murray]
    McInracht 732
Aidan 773
1172 Gilla Isu Ua Mailin
    Cele O Dubhthaig 1210
1210 ?Patricius
1428 William Prendergast
1430 Nicholas 'Wogmay'
1439 Odo O h-Uiginn
1432 Martin Campania
1457 Simon de Duren
1493 John Bel
1541 Eugenius Macan Brehon
United to **Tuam** 1559

†Raphoe

Sean O Gairedain
Donell O Garvan

Felemy O Syda
Oengus O'Lappin 959
1150 Muiredhach O'Cofley
1156 Gille in Coimhded Ua Carain
    [Gilbertus]
—   Anonymous
1204 Mael Isu Ua Doirig
—   Anonymous
1253 Mael Padraig O Scannail
    [Patricius]
1263 John de Alneto
1265 Cairpre O Scuapa
1275 Fergal O Firghil [Florentius]
1306 Enri Mac-in-Chrossain
    [Henricus]
1319 Tomas Mac Carmaic Ui
    Domhnaill
1363 Padraig Mac Maonghail
1367 Conchobar Mac Carmaic Ui
    Domhnaill [Cornelius]
1397 Seoan MacMenmain
1400 Eoin MacCarmaic [Johannes]
-1413 Anthony
-1414 Robert Rubire
1416 John McCormic
1420 Lochlainn O Gallchobhair I
    [Laurentius]
1440 Cornelius Mac Giolla Brighde
1443 Lochlainn O Gallchobhair II
    [Laurentius]
1479 John de Rogeriis
1482 Meanma Mac Carmail
    [Menclaus Mac Carmacain]
1514 Conn O Cathain [Cornelius]
1534 Eamonn O Gallchobhair
1547 Arthur o'Gallagher
1563 Donnell Magonigle [*or*
    McCongail]
[1603 Denis Campbell, not
    consecrated]
1605 George Montgomery
1611 Andrew Knox
1633 John Leslie
1661 Robert Leslie
1671 Ezekiel Hopkins
1682 William Smyth
1693 Alexander Cairncross
1701 Robert Huntington
1702 John Pooley
1713 Thomas Lindsay
1714 Edward Synge
1716 Nicholas Forster
1744 William Barnard
1747 Philip Twysden
1753 Robert Downes
1763 John Oswald
1780 James Hawkins
1807 John George Beresford
1819 William Magee
1822 William Bissett
United to **Derry** since 1834

Tuam

Tuam, Killala and Achonry

BISHOPS
Murrough O'Nioc 1032
Hugh O'Hessian 1085
Cathusach Ua Conaill 1117
O Clerig 1137
Muiredach Ua Dubhthaig 1150

ARCHBISHOPS
1152 Aed Ua h-Oisin [Edanus]
1167 Cadhla Ua Dubhthaig
    [Catholicus]
1202 Felix Ua Ruanada

Tuam—continued

1236 Mael Muire O Lachtain
[Marianus]
1250 Flann Mac Flainn [Florentius]
[1256 James O'Laghtnan, not confirmed or consecrated]
1257 Walter de Salerno
1258 Tomaltach O Conchobair
[Thomas]
1286 Stephen de Fulbourn
1289 William de Bermingham
1312 Mael Sechlainn Mac Aeda
1348 Tomas MacCerbhaill
[MacCarwill]
1364 Eoin O Grada
1372 Gregory O Mochain I
1384 Gregory O Mochain II
1387 William O Cormacain
1393 Muirchertach mac Pilb O
Cellaigh
1410 John Babingle
1411 Cornelius
1430 John Bermingham [Winfield]

†Ardfert

BISHOPS
Anmchad O h-Anmchada 1117
1152 Mael Brenain Ua Ronain
Gilla Mac Aiblen
O'Anmehadha 1166
Domnall O Connairche 1193
1200 David Ua Duibdithrib
Anonymous 1217
1218 John
1218 Gilbertus
1237 Brendan
1253 Christianus
1257 Philippus
1265 Johannes
1286 Nicolaus
1288 Nicol O Samradain
1336 Ailin O hEichthighirn
1331 Edmund of Caermaerthen
1348 John de Valle
1372 Cornelius O Tigernach
1380 William Bull
1411 Nicholas FitzMaurice
1404 Nicholas Ball
1405 Tomas O Ceallaigh
1409 John Attilburgh [Artilburch]
1450 Maurice Stack
1452 Maurice O Conchobhair
1461 John Stack
1461 John Pigge
1473 Philip Stack
1495 John FitzGerald
[see vacant in 1534]
1536 James FitzMaurice
1588 Nicholas Kenan
1600 John Crosbie
1622 John Steere
1628 William Steere
1641 Thomas Fulwar
United to **Limerick** 1661

†Ardmore

1153 Eugenius
Incorporated with **Lismore** 1192

Cashel

*Cashel, Waterford, Lismore, Ossory
Ferns and Leighlin*

BISHOPS
Cormac MacCuillenan 908
Donnell O'Heney 1096 *or* 1098

1438 Tomas mac Muirchearthaigh O
Cellaigh
1441 John de Burgo
1452 Donatus O Muiredaigh
1485 William Seoighe [Joyce]
1503 Philip Pinson
1506 Muiris O Fithcheallaigh
1514 Tomas O Maolalaidh
1537 Christopher Bodkin
1573 William O'Mullally *or* Lealy
Annadown united to Tuam *c*1555
Mayo united to Tuam 1559
1595 Nehemiah Donnellan
1609 William O'Donnell *or* Daniel
1629 Randolph *or* Ralph Barlow
1638 Richard Boyle
1645 John Maxwell
1661 Samuel Pullen
1667 John Parker
1679 John Vesey
1716 Edward Synge
1742 Josiah Hort
1752 John Ryder

PROVINCE OF DUBLIN

ARCHBISHOPS
*c*1111 Mael Ios Ua h-Ainmire
Mael Iosa Ua Fogludha
[Mauricius] 1131
Domnall Ua Conaing 1137
Gilla Naomh O'Marty 1149
–1152 Donat O'Lonergan I
–*c*1160 M.
1172 Domnall O h-Ualla-chain
[Donatus]
1186 Muirghes O h-Enna [Matheus]
*c*1208 Donnchad Ua Longargain I
[Donatus]
1216 Donnchad Ua Longargain II
[Donatus]
1224 Mairin O Briain [Marianus]
1238 David mac Ceallaig [O'Kelly]
1254 David Mac Cearbaill [Mac
Carwill]
1290 Stiamna O Bracain
1303 Maurice Mac Cearbaill
1317 William FitzJohn
1327 Seoan Mac Cerbaill
1329 Walter le Rede
1332 Eoin O Grada
1346 Radulphus O Cellaigh [Kelly]
1362 George Roche [de Rupe]
1365 Tomas Mac Cearbhaill
1374 Philip of Torrington
1382 Michael
1384 Peter Hackett
1406 Richard O Hedian
1442 John Cantwell I
1452 John Cantwell II
1484 David Creagh
1504 Maurice FitzGerald
1525 Edmund Butler
1553 Roland Baron *or* FitzGerald
1567 James MacCawell
Emly united to Cashel 1569
1571 Miler Magrath
1623 Malcolm Hamilton
1630 Archibald Hamilton
1661 Thomas Fulwar
1667 Thomas Price
[See vacant 1685–91]
1691 Narcissus Marsh
1694 William Palliser
[1727 William Nicolson, not
enthroned]
1727 Timothy Goodwin
1730 Theophilus Bolton

1775 Jemmett Browne
1782 Joseph Dean Bourke
[afterwards Earl of Mayo]
1794 William Beresford [afterwards
Baron Decies]
1819 Power le Poer Trench
Killala united to Tuam from 1834

BISHOPS
1839 Thomas Plunket [afterwards
Baron Plunket]
1867 Charles Brodrick Bernard
1890 James O'Sullivan
1913 Benjamin John Plunket
1920 Arthur Edwin Ross
1923 John Ort
1928 John Mason Harden
1932 William Hardy Holmes
1939 John Winthrop Crozier
1958 Arthur Hamilton Butler
1970 John Coote Duggan
1986 John Robert Winder Neill

1744 Arthur Price
1752 John Whitcombe
1754 Michael Cox
1779 Charles Agar
1801 Charles Brodrick
1822 Richard Laurence
Waterford and **Lismore** united to
Cashel from 1833: on the death of
Abp Laurence in 1838 the province
was united to Dublin and the see
ceased to be an Archbishopric
BISHOPS
1839 Stephen Creagh Sandes
1843 Robert Daly
1872 Maurice FitzGerald Day
1900 Henry Stewart O'Hara
1919 Robert Miller
1931 John Frederick McNeice
1935 Thomas Arnold Harvey
1958 William Cecil De Pauley
1968 John Ward Armstrong
Ossory united to Cashel 1977
1980 Noel Vincent Willoughby

†Clonfert

Moena, *or* Moynean, *or*
Moeinend 572
Cummin the Tall 662
Ceannfaeladh 807
Laithbheartach 822
Ruthnel *or* Ruthme 826
Cormac MacEdain 922
Ciaran O'Gabbla 953
Cathal 963
Eochu 1031
O'Corcoran 1095
Muiredach Ua h-Enlainge
1117
Gille Patraic Ua Ailcinned
1149
*c*1152 Petrus Ua Mordha
1172 Mail Isu mac in Baird
1179 Celechair Ua h-Armedaig
Muirchertach Ua'Maeluidir
1187
Domnall Ua Finn 1195
Muirchertach Ua Carmacain
1204
1205 Mael Brigte Ua hErurain
1224 Cormac O Luimlin [Carus]
1248 Thomas
1259 Tomas mac Domnaill Moire O
Cellaig

Clonfert—continued

1266 Johannes de Alatre
1296 Robert
c1302 John
1308 Gregorius O Brocaig
1320 Robert Le Petit
1322 Seoan O Leaain
1347 Tomas mac Gilbert O Cellaigh I
1378 Muircheartach mac Pilib O Cellaigh [Maurice]
1393 William O Cormacain
1398 David Corre
1398 Enri O Conmaigh
1405 Tomasi O Cellaigh II
1410 Cobhthach O Madagain
1438 Seaan O hEidin
1441 John White
1447 Conchobhar O Maolalaidh
1448 Cornelius O Cuinnlis
1463 Matthaeus Mag Raith
1508 David de Burgo
1509 Dionysius O'Mordha
1534 Roland de Burgo
1536 Richard Nangle
1580 Hugh
1582 Stephen Kirwan
1602 Roland Lynch
1627 Robert Dawson
1644 William Baily
1665 Edward Wolley
1691 William FitzGerald
1722 Theophilus Bolton
1724 Arthur Price
1730 Edward Synge
1732 Mordecai Cary
1736 John Whitcombe
1752 Arthur Smyth
1753 William Carmichael
1758 William Gote
1762 John Oswald
1763 Denison Cumberland
1772 Walter Cope
1782 John Law
1787 Richard Marlay
1795 Charles Broderick
1796 Hugh Hamilton
1798 Matthew Young
1801 George de la l'oer Beresford
1802 Nathaniel Alexander
1804 Christopher Butson
United to **Killaloe** since 1834

†Clonmacnoise

-663 Baitan O'Cormac
-839 Joseph [of Rossmore]
     Maclodhar 890
     Cairbre Crom 904
     Loingsech 919
-940 Donough I
-953 Donough II
-966 Cormae O'Cillin
     Maenach 971
     Conaing O'Cosgraigh 998
     Male Poil 1001
     Flaithbertach 1038
     Celechar 1067
     O'Mallaen 1093
     Christian Aherne 1104
?1111 Domnall mac Flannacain Ua Dubthaig
1152 Muirchertach Ua Maeluidir
     Cathal Ua Maeileoin 1207
c1207 Muirchertach Ua Muiricen
1214 Aed O Maeileoin I
1227 Aed O Maeileoin II [Elias]
1236 Thomas Fitzpatrick

1252 Tomas O Cuinn
1280 Anonymous
1282 Gilbert (not consecrated)
1290 William O Dubhthaigh
1298 William O Finnein
1303 Domnall O Braein
1324 Lughaid O Dalaigh
1337 Henricus
1349 Simon
1369 Richard [Braybroke]
1371 Hugo
1388 Philippus O Maoil
1389 Milo Corr
1397 O'Gallagher
1397 Philip Nangle
1423 David Prendergast
1426 Cormac Mac Cochlain [Cornelius]
1444 Sean O Dalaigh
1449 Thomas
1458 Robertus
1458 William
1459 John
1487 Walter Blake
1509 Tomas O Maolalaigh
1516 Quintin O h-Uiginn
1539 Richard O'Hogan
1539 Florence Kirwan
1556 Peter Wall [Wale]
United to **Meath** 1569

†Cloyne

     Reachtaidh 887
1148 Gilla na Naem O Muirchertaig [Nehemias]
     Ua Dubcroin 1159
     Ua Flannacain 1167
1177 Matthaeus Ua Mongaig
1201 Laurence Ua Suilleabain
1205 C.
1281 Luke
c1224 Florence
1226 Daniel
1237 David mac Cellaig [O'Kelly]
1240 Ailinn O Suilleabain
1247 Daniel
1265 Reginaldus
1275 Alan O Longain
1284 Nicholas of Effingham
1323 Maurice O Solchain
1333 John Brid
1351 John Whitekot
1363 John Swaffham
1376 Richard Wye
1394 Gerard Caneton
1413 Adam Payn
United to **Cork** 1418–1638
1638 George Synge
1661–1678 Held by the Bishops of Cork
1679 Patrick Sheridan
1683 Edward Jones
1693 William Palliser
1694 Tobias Pullein
1695 St. George Ashe
1697 John Pooley
1702 Charles Crow
1726 Henry Maule
1732 Edward Synge
1734 George Berkeley
1753 James Stopford
1759 Robert Johnson
1767 Frederick Augustus Hervery
1768 Charles Agar
1780 George Chinnery
1781 Richard Woodward
1794 William Bennett

1820 Charles Mongan Warburton
1826 John Brinkley
United to **Cork** on the death of Bp Brinkley in 1835

Cork

Cork, Cloyne and Ross
     Donnell 876
     Soer Bhreatach 892
     Dubhdhurn O'Stefam 959
     Cathmogh 969
     Mugron O'Mutan 1057
1138 Gregory
   ? Ua Menngorain 1147
1148 Gilla Aedha Ua Maigin
1174 [Gregorius] O h-Aedha [O Hea]
c1182 Reginaldus I
1187 Aicher
1192 Murchad Ua h-Aedha
     Anonymous 1214
1215 Mairin Ua Briain [Marianus]
1225 Gilbertus
1248 Laurentius
1265 William of Jerpoint
1267 Reginaldus
1277 Robert Mac Donnchada
1302 Seoan Mac Cearbaill [Mac Carwill]
1321 Philip of Slane
1327 Walter le Rede
1330 John of Ballyconingham
1347 John Roche
1359 Gerald de Barri
1396 Roger Ellesmere
1406 Richard Kynmoure
1409 Patrick Fox
1409 Milo fitzJohn
1425 John Paston
1418 Adam Payn
   429 Jordan Purcell
1472 William Roche (Coadjutor)
1463 Gerald FitzGerald
1490 Tadhg Mac Carthaigh
1499 John FitzEdmund FitzGerald
1499 Patrick Cant
1523 John Benet
1536 Dominic Tyrre [Tirrey]
1562 Roger Skiddy
1570 Richard Dyxon
1572 Matthew Sheyn
Ross united to Cork 1583
1583 William Lyon
1618 John Boyle
1620 Richard Boyle
1638 William Chappell
1661 Michael Boyle
1663 Edward Synge
1679 Edward Wetenhall
1699 Dive Downes
1710 Peter Browne
1735 Robert Clayton
1745 Jemmett Browne
1772 Isaac Mann
1789 Euseby Cleaver
1789 William Foster
1790 William Bennet
1794 Thomas Stopford
1805 John George Beresford
1807 Thomas St. Laurence
1831 Samuel Kyle
Cloyne united to Cork from 1835
1848 James Wilson
1857 William FitzGerald
1862 John Gregg
1878 Robert Samuel Gregg
1894 William Edward Meade
1912 Charles Benjamin Dowse
1933 William Edward Flewett

Cork—continued

1938 Robert Thomas Hearn
1952 George Otto Sims
1957 Richard Gordon Perdue
1978 Samuel Greenfield Poyntz
1988 Robert Alexander Warke

Dublin

Dublin and Glendalough
BISHOPS
Sinhail 790
c1028 Dunan [Donatus]
1074 Gilla Patraic
1085 Donngus
1096 Samuel Ua'h-Aingliu
ARCHBISHOPS
1121 Grene [Gregorius]
1162 Lorcan Ua'Tuathail
    [Laurentius]
1182 John Cumin
1213 Henry de Loundres
Glendalough united to Dublin
1230 Luke
125 Fulk de Sandford
1279 John de Derlington
1286 John de Sandford
1295 Thomas de Chadworth
1296 William de Hotham
1299 Richard de Ferings
[1307 Richard de Havering, not
consecrated]
1311 John de Leche
1317 Alexander de Bicknor
1349 John de St. Paul
1363 Thomas Minot
1376 Robert de Wikeford
1391 Robert Waldeby
1396 Richard Northalis
1397 Thomas Cranley
1418 Richard Talbot
1451 Michael Tregury
1472 John Walton
1484 Walter Fitzsimons
1512 William Rokeby
1521 Hugh Inge
1529 John Alan
1535 George Browne
1555 Hugh Curwin
1567 Adam Loftus
1605 Thomas Jones
1619 Lancelot Bulkeley
1661 James Margetson
1663 Michael Boyle
1679 John Parker
1682 Francis Marsh
1694 Narcissus Marsh
1703 William King
1730 John Hoadly
1743 Charles Cobbe
1765 William Carmichael
1766 Arthur Smyth
1772 John Cradock
1779 Robert Fowler
1801 Charles Agar [Earl of
    Normanton]
1809 Euseby Cleaver
1820 John George Beresford
1822 William Magee
1831 Richard Whately
Kildare united to Dublin 1846
1864 Richard Chenevix Trench, res.
1885 William Conyngham [Lord
    Plunket]
1897 Joseph Ferguson Peacocke
1915 John Henry Bernard
1919 Charles Frederick D'Arcy
1920 John Allen Fitzgerald Gregg

1939 Arthur William Barton
1956 George Otto Simms
1969 Alan Alexander Buchanan
1977 Henry Robert McAdoo
1985 Donald Arthur Richard Caird

†Emly

Raidghil 881
Ua Ruaich 953
Faelan 980
MaelFinan 1030
Diarmait Ua Flainnchua 1114
1152 Gilla in Choimhded Ua
    h-Ardmhail
Mael Isu Ua Laigenain 1163
1172 Ua Meic Stia
1177 Charles O'Buacalla
1177 Isaac O'Hamery
1192 Ragnall Ua Flainnchua
1205 M.
1209 William
1212 Henry
1227 John Collingham
1238 Daniel
1238 Christianus
1251 Gilbert O'Doverty
1266 Florence or Laurence O'hAirt
1272 Matthew MacGormain
1275 David O Cossaig
1286 William de Clifford
1306 Thomas Cantock [Quantock]
1309 William Roughead
1335 Richard le Walleys
1353 John Esmond
1363 David Penlyn [Foynlyn]
1363 William
1405 Nicholas Ball
1421 John Rishberry
1422 Robert Windell
1428 Thomas de Burgo
1428 Robert Portland
1445 Cornelius O Cuinnlis
1444 Robert
1448 Cornelius O Maolalaidh
1449 William O Hetigan
1476 Pilib O Cathail
1494 Donatus Mac Briain
1498 Cinneidigh Mac Briain
1507 Tomas O hUrthaille
1543 Angus O'Hernan
1551 Raymond de Burgo
United to **Cashel** 1569
Transferred to **Limerick** 1976

†Ferns

-598 Edar *or* Maedoc *or* Hugh
    Maeldogair 676
    Coman 678
    Diratus 693
    Cillenius 715
    Cairbre O'Kearney 1095
    Ceallach Ua Colmain 1117
    Mael Eoin Ua Dunacain 1125
    Ua Cattain 1135
1178 Ioseph Ua h-Aeda
1186 Ailbe Ua Maelmuaid [Albinus]
1224 John of St. John
1254 Geoffrey of St. John
1258 Hugh of Lamport
1283 Richard of Northampton
1304 Simon of Evesham
1305 Robert Walrand
1312 Adam of Northampton
1347 Hugh de Saltu [of Leixlip]
1347 Geoffrey Grandfeld
1349 John Esmond
1350 William Charnells

1363 Thomas Dene
1400 Patrick Barret
1418 Robert Whittey
1453 Tadhg O Beirn
1457 John Purcell I
1479 Laurence Nevill
1505 Edmund Comerford
1510 Nicholas Comyn
1519 John Purcell II
1539 Alexander Devereux
1566 John Devereux
1582 Hugh Allen
Leighlin united to Ferns 1597
1600 Robert Grave
1601 Nicholas Stafford
1605 Thomas Ram
1635 George Andrews
1661 Robert Price
1667 Richard Boyle
1683 Narcissus Marsh
1691 Bartholomew Vigors
1722 Josiah Hort
1727 John Hoadly
1730 Arthur Price
1734 Edward Synge
1740 George Stone
1743 William Cottrell
1744 Robert Downes
1752 John Garnet
1758 William Carmichael
1758 Thomas Salmon
1759 Richard Robinson
1761 Charles Jackson
1765 Edward Young
1772 Joseph Deane Bourke
1782 Walter Cope
1787 William Preston
1789 Euseby Cleaver
1809 Percy Jocelyn
1820 Robert Ponsonby Tottenham
    Loftus
1822 Thomas Elrington
United to **Ossory** 1835

†Glendalough

Dairchell 678
Eterscel 814
Dungal 904
Cormac 927
Nuadha 920 [*or* Neva]
Gilda Na Naomh *c.* 1080
Cormac O'Mail 1101
Aed Ua Modain 1126
1140 Anonymous
1152 Gilla na Naem
1157 Cinaed O Ronain [Celestinus]
1176 Maelcallann Ua Cleirchen
    [Malchus]
1186 Macrobius
1192 William Piro
1214 Robert de Bedford
United to **Dublin**
After the union with Dublin some
rival bishops appear
c1216 Bricheus
1468 John
1475 Michael
1481 Denis White
    John 1494
1494 Ivo Ruffi
1495 John
1500 Francis Fitzjohn of Corduba

†Iniscattery (Scattery Island)

861 Aidan
959 Cinaeda O'Chommind

Iniscattery—continued

973　Scandlam O'Lenz
　　　O'Bruil 1069
　　　O'Bruil II 1081
　　　Dermot O'Lennain 1119
　　　Aed Ua'Bechain 1188
　　　Cearbhal Ua'h-Enna [Carolus]
　　　1193
1360　Tomas Mac Mathghamhna
1392　John Donkan
1414　Richard Belmer
　　　Dionysius 1447
1447　John Grene
Incorporated with **Limerick**

†Kells

　　　Mael Finnen 968
c1152　Tuathal Ua Connachtarg
1185　Anonymous
1202　M. Ua Dobailen
Incorporated with **Meath**

†Kildare

　　　Conlaedh 520
　　　Hugh [or Hed] the Black 639
　　　Maeldoborcon 709
　　　Eutigern 762
　　　Lomthiull 787
　　　Snedbran 787
　　　Tuatchar 834
　　　Orthanach 840
　　　Aedgene Britt 864
　　　Maenghal 870
　　　Lachtnan 875
　　　Suibhne 881
　　　Scannal 885
　　　Lergus 888
　　　Mael Findan 950
　　　Annchadh 981
　　　Murrough McFlan 986
-1030　MaelMartain
　　　MaelBrighde 1042
　　　Finn 1085
　　　MaelBrighde O'Brolchan 1097
　　　Hugh [Heremon] 1100
　　　Ferdomnach 1101
　　　Cormac O Cathassaig 1146
　　　Ua Duibhin 1148
1152　Finn mac Mael Muire Mac
　　　Cianain
　　　Fin mac Gussain Ua Gormain
1161　Malachias Ua Brain
1177　Nehemias
1206　Cornelius Mac Fealain
1223　Ralph of Bristol
1233　John of Taunton
1258　Simon of Kilkenny
1280　Nicholas Cusack
1300　Walter Calf [de Veel]
1333　Richard Houlot
1352　Thomas Giffard
1366　Robert of Aketon [Acton]
1404　John Madock
1431　William fitzEdward
1449　Geoffrey Hereford
1456　John Bole [Bull]
1464　Richard Lang
1474　David Cone
1475　James Wall
　　　William Barret
1480　Edward Lane
1526　Thomas Dillon
1529　Walter Wellesley
1540　William Miagh
1550　Thomas Lancaster
1555　Thomas Leverous
1560　Alexander Craik

1564　Robert Daly
1583　Daniel Neylan
1604　William Pilsworth
1636　Robert Ussher
1644　William Golborne
1661　Thomas Price
1667　Ambrose Jones
1679　Anthony Dopping
1682　William Moreton
1705　Welbore Ellis
1731　Charles Cobbe
1743　George Stone
1745　Thomas Fletcher
1761　Richard Robinson
1765　Charles Jackson
1790　George Lewis Jones
1804　Charles Lindsay
United to **Dublin** after the death of Bp
Lindsay in 1846
1976　Separated from Dublin and
　　　united to **Meath**

†Kilfenora

1172　Anonymous
1205　F.
1224　Johannes
1254　Christianus
　　　Anonymous 1264
1266　Mauricius
1273　Florentius O Tigernaig
1281　Congalach [O Lochlainn]
1291　G.
1299　Simon O Cuirrin
1303　Maurice O Briain
1323　Risdeard O Lochlainn
c1355　Dionysius
1372　Henricus
　　　Cornelius
1390　Patricius
1421　Feidhlimidh mac
　　　Mathghamhna O Lochlainn
　　　[Florentius]
1433　Fearghal
1434　Dionysius O Connmhaigh
1447　John Greni
1476　[? Denis] O Tombaigh
1491　Muircheartach mac
　　　Murchadha O Briain
　　　[Mauricius]
1514　Maurice O'Kelly
1541　John O'Neylan
-1585　Daniel, bishop-elect
1606　Bernard Adams [with Limerick
　　　q.v.]
1617　John Steere
1622　William Murray
[1628　Richard Betts, not consecrated]
1630　James Heygate
1638　Robert Sibthorp
1661–1741　Held by the Archbishops
　　　of Tuam
1742–52　Held by the Bishop of
　　　Clonfert
United to **Killaloe** 1752

†Killaloe

BISHOPS
　　　O'Gerruidher 1054
　　　Domnall Ua hEnna 1098
　　　Mael Muire O Dunain 1117
　　　Domnall Ua Conaing 1131
　　　Domnall Ua Longargain 1137
　　　Tadg Ua Longargain 1161
　　　Donnchad mac Diarmata Ua
　　　Briain 1164
1179　Constantin mac Toirrdelbaig
　　　Ua Briain
1194　Diarmait Ua Conaing

1201　Conchobhar Ua h-Enna
　　　[Cornelius]
1217　Robert Travers
1221　Domnall Ua h-Enna [Donatus]
1231　Domnall O Cenneitig
　　　[Donatus]
1253　Isoc O Cormacain [Isaac]
1268　Mathgamain O h-Ocain [O
　　　Hogan]
1281　Maurice O h-Ocain
1299　David Mac Mathghamna [Mac
　　　Mahon]
1317　Tomas O Cormacain I
1323　Brian O Cosgraig
1326　David Mac Briain [David of
　　　Emly]
?1326　natus O Heime
1343　Tomas O h-Ogain
1355　Tomas O Cormacain II
1389　Mathghamain Mag Raith
1400　Donatus Mag Raith
1409　Robert Mulfield
1418　Eugenius O Faolain
1423　Thadeus Mag Raith I
1429　Seamus O Lonnghargain
1443　Donnchadh mac
　　　Toirdhealbhaigh O Briain
1460　Thadeus Mag Raith II
1463　Matthaeus O Griobhtha
1483　Toirdhealbhach mac
　　　Mathghamhna O Briain
　　　[Theodoricus]
1523　Thadeus
1526　Seamus O Cuirrin
1546　Cornelius O'Dea
1554　Turlough [or Terence] O'Brien
　　　II
1570　Maurice [or Murtagh] O'Brien-
　　　Arra
1613　John Rider
1633　Lewis Jones
1647　Edward Parry
1661　Edward Worth
1669　Daniel Wytter
1675　John Roan
1693　Henry Ryder
1696　Thomas Lindsay
1713　Thomas Vesey
1714　Nicholas Forster
1716　Charles Carr
1740　Joseph Story
1742　John Ryder
1743　Jemmet Browne
1745　Richard Chenevix
1746　Nicholas Synge
Kilfenora united to Killaloe 1752
1771　Robert Fowler
1779　George Chinnery
1780　Thomas Barnard
1794　William Knox
1803　Charles Dalrymple Lindsay
1804　Nathaniel Alexander
1804　Robert Ponsonby Tottenham
　　　Loftus
1820　Richard Mant
1823　Alexander Arbuthnot
-1828　Richard Ponsonby
1831　Edmund Knox [with Clonfert]
Clonfert united to Killaloe 1834
Kilmacduagh united to Killaloe 1834
1834　Christopher Butson
1836　Stephen Crengh Sandes
1839　Ludlow Tonson [afterwards
　　　Baron Riversdale]
1862　William FitzGerald
1884　William Bennet Chester
1893　Frederick Richards Wynne
1897　Mervyn Archdall

Killaloe—continued

1912 Charles Benjamin Dowse
1913 Thomas Sterling Berry, res.
1924 Henry Edmund Patton
1943 Robert M'Neil Boyd
1945 Hedley Webster
1953 Richard Gordon Perdue
1957 Henry Arthur Stanistreet
1972 Edwin Owen
1976 United to **Limerick**

†Kilmacduagh

? Ua Cleirig 1137
Imar Ua Ruaidin 1176
Rugnad O'Rowan 1178
1179 Mac Gilla Cellaig Ua Ruaidin
1206 Ua Cellaig
Mael Muire O Connmaig 1224
1227 Aed [Odo]
Conchobhar O Muiredaig 1247
1248 Gilla Cellaig O Ruaidin
[Gilbertus]
1249 David yFredrakern
1254 Mauricius O Leaain
1284 David O Setachain
1290 Luirint O Lachtnain
[Laurentius]
1307 Lucas
1326 Johannes
1360 Nicol O Leaain
1394 Gregory O Leaain
1405 Enri O Connmhaigh
1409 Dionysius
1409 Eugene O Faolain
1418 Diarmaid O Donnchadha
1419 Nicol O Duibhghiolla
1419 Seaan O Connmhaigh
1441 Dionysius O Donnchadha
1479 Cornelius O Mullony
1503 Matthaeus O Briain
1533 Christopher Bodkin
1573 Stephen O'Kirwan
[1584 Thomas Burke, not
consecrated]
1587 Roland Lynch
1627–1836 Held in commendam by
the Bishops of Clonfert
United to **Killaloe** since 1834

†Leighlin

-633 Laserian *or* Molaise
-865 Mainchin
-940 Conella McDonegan
Daniel 969
Cleitic O'Muinic 1050
c1096 Ferdomnac
Mael Eoin Ua Dunacain 1125
Sluaigedach Ua Cathain 1145
1152 Dungal O Caellaide
1192 Johannes
1197 Johannes
1202 Herlewin
1217 Richard [Fleming]
1228 William le Chauniver
1252 Thomas
1275 Nicholas Chever
1309 Maurice de Blanchville
1321 Meiler le Poer
1344 Radulphus O Ceallaigh
1349 Thomas of Brakenberg
1360 Johannes
1362 William (not consecrated)
1363 John Young
1371 Philip FitzPeter
1385 John Griffin
1398 Thomas Peverell
1400 Richard Bocomb
1419 John Mulgan

1432 Thomas Fleming
— Diarmaid 1464
1464 Milo Roche
1490 Nicholas Magwyr
1513 Thomas Halsey
1524 Mauricius O Deoradhain
1527 Matthew Sanders
1550 Robert Travers
1555 Thomas O'Fihelly
1567 Donnell *or* Daniel Cavanagh
1589 Richard Meredith
United to **Ferns** since 1597 on the
death of Bp Meredith

Limerick

*Limerick, Ardfert, Aghadoe, Killaloe,
Kilfenora, Clonfert, Kilmacduagh and
Emly*

-1106 Gilli alias Gilla Espaic
1140 Patricius
1150 Erolb [? = Harold]
1152 Torgesius
1179 Brictius
1203 Donnchad Ua'Briain
[Donatus]
1207 Geoffrey
-1215 Edmund
1223 Hubert de Burgo
1252 Robert de Emly *or* Neil
1273 Gerald [*or* Miles] de Mareshall
1302 Robert de Dundonald
1312 Eustace de Aqua *or* de l'Eau
1336 Maurice de Rochfort
1354 Stephen Lawless
1360 Stephen Wall [de Valle]
1369 Peter Curragh
1399 Bernardus O Conchobhair
1400 Conchobhar O Deadhaidh
1426 John Mothel res.
Iniscattery incorporated with
Limerick
1456 Thomas Leger
1458 William Russel, *alias* Creagh
1463 Thomas Arthur
[1486 Richard Stakpoll, not
consecrated]
1486 John Dunowe
1489 John O'Phelan [Folan]
1524 Sean O Cuinn
1551 William Casey
1557 Hugh de Lacey *or* Lees, dep.
1571 William Casey (again)
1594 John Thornburgh
1604 Bernard Adams
1626 Francis Gough
1634 George Webb
1643 Robert Sibthorp
Ardfert united to Limerick 1661
1661 Edward Synge
1664 William Fuller
1667 Francis Marsh
1673 John Vesey
1679 Simon Digby
1692 Nathaniel Wilson
1695 Thomas Smyth
1725 William Burscough
1755 James Leslie
1771 James Averill
1772 William Gore
1784 William Cecil Pery
1794 Thomas Barnard
1806 Charles Morgan Warburton
1820 Thomas Elrington
1823 John Jebb
1834 Edmund Knox
1849 William Higgin
1854 Henry Griffin
1866 Charles Graves

1899 Thomas Bunbury
1907 Raymond D'Audemra Orpen
1921 Harry Vere White
1934 Charles King Irwin
1942 Evelyn Charles Hodges
1961 Robert Wyse Jackson
1970 Donald Arthur Richard Caird
Killaloe united to Limerick 1976
Emily transferred to Limerick 1976
1976 Edwin Owen
1984 Walton Hewcombe Francis
Empey
1985 Edward Flewett Darling

†Lismore

Ronan 764
Cormac MacCuillenan 918
-999 Cinneda O'Chonmind
Niall mac Meic Aedacain 1113
Ua Daightig 1119
1121 Mael Isu Ua h-Ainmere
Mael Muire Ua Loingsig 1150
1151 Gilla Crist Ua Connairche
[Christianus]
1179 Felix
Ardmore incorporated with
Lismore 1192
1203 Malachias, O'Heda or O'Danus
1216 Thomas
1219 Robert of Bedford
1228 Griffin Christopher
1248 Ailinn O Suilleabain
1253 Thomas
1270 John Roche
1280 Richard Corre
1309 William Fleming
1310 R.
1322 John Leynagh
1356 Roger Cradock, provision
annulled
1358 Thomas le Reve
United to **Waterford** 1363

Meath

Meath and Kildare

BISHOPS OF THE SEE OF
CLONARD
Senach 588
-640 Colman 654
Dubhduin O'Phelan 718
Tole 738
-778 Fulartach 779
Clothcu 796
Clemens 826
Cormac MacSuibhne
Cumsuth 858
Suarlech 870
Ruman MacCathasaid 922
Colman MacAilild 1028
Tuathal O'Dubhamaigh 1028

BISHOPS OF MEATH
1096 Mael Muire Ua Dunain
1128 Eochaid O Cellaig
1151 Etru Ua Miadacain [Eleuzerius]
1177 Echtigern mac Mael Chiarain
[Eugenius]
1192 Simon Rochfort
(The See was transferred from Clonard
to Newtown near Trim, 1202)
Kells incorporated with Meath
1224 Donan De [Deodatus] (not
consecrated)
1227 Ralph Petit
1231 Richard de la Corner
1253 Geoffrey Cusack
1255 Hugo de Taghmon
1283 Walter de Fulburn
1287 Thomas St. Leger

Meath—continued

1322 Seoan Mac Cerbaill [John
      MacCarwill]
1327 William de Paul
1350 William St. Leger
1353 Nicholas [Allen]
1369 Stephen de Valle [Wall]
1380 William Andrew
1385 Alexander Petit or de Balscot
1401 Robert Montayne
1412 Edward Dant sey
[1430 Thomas Scurlog, apparently not
      consecrated]
1430 William Hadsor
1435 William Silk
1450 Edmund Ouldhall
1460 William Shirwood
1483 John Payne
1507 William Rokeby
1512 Hugh Inge
1523 Richard Wilson
1529 Edward Staples
1554 William Walsh
1563 Hugh Brady
Clonmacnoise united to Meath 1569
1584 Thomas Jones
1605 Roger Dod
1612 George Montgomery
1621 James Usher
1625 Anthony Martin
      [Interregnum 1650 61]
1661 Henry Leslie
1661 Henry Jones
1682 Anthony Dopping
1697 Richard Tennison
1705 William Moreton
1716 John Evans
1724 Henry Downes
1727 Ralph Lambert
1732 Welbore Ellis
1734 Arthur Price
1744 Henry Maule
1758 William Carmichael
1765 Richard Pococke
1765 Arthur Smyth
1766 Henry Maxwell
1798 Thomas Lewis O'Beirne
1823 Nathaniel Alexander
1840 Charles Dickinson
1842 Edward Stopford
1850 Thomas Stewart Townsend
1852 James Henderson Singer
1866 Samuel Butcher
1876 William Conyngham, Lord
      Plunket
1885 Charles Parsons Reichel
1894 Joseph Ferguson Peacocke
1897 James Bennett Keene
1919 Benjamin John Plunket
1926 Thomas Gibson George Collins
1927 John Orr
1938 William Hardy Holmes
1945 James McCann
1959 Robert Bonsall Pike
Kildare united to Meath 1976
1976 Donald Arthur Richard Caird
1985 Walton Newcombe Francis
      Empey

†Ossory

Dermot 973
1152 Domnall Ua Fogartaig
1180 Felix Ua Duib Slaine
1202 Hugo de Rous [Hugo Rufus]
1220 Peter Mauveisin
1231 William of Kilkenny
1233 Walter de Brackley

1245 Geoffrey de Turville
1251 Hugh de Mapilton
1260 Geoffrey St. Leger
1287 Roger of Wexford
1289 Michael d'Exeter
1303 William FitzJohn
1317 Richard Ledred
1361 John de Tatenhale
1366 William
    — John of Oxford
1371 Alexander Petit [de Balscot]
1387 Richard Northalis
1396 Thomas Peverell
1399 John Waltham
1400 John Griffin
1400 John
1401 Roger Appleby
1402 John Waltham (again)
1407 Thomas Snell
1417 Patrick Foxe
1421 Dionysius O Deadhaidh
1427 Thomas Barry
1460 David Hacket
1479 Seaan O hEidigheain
1487 Oliver Cantwell
1528 Milo Baron [or FitzGerald]
1553 John Bale
1554 John Tonory
1567 Christopher Gaffney
1577 Nicholas Walsh
1586 John Horsfall
1610 Richard Deane
1613 Jonas Wheeler
1641 Griffith Williams
1672 John Parry
1678 Benjamin Parry
1678 Michael Ward
1680 Thomas Otway
1693 John Hartstonge
1714 Thomas Vesey
1731 Edward Tennison
1736 Charles Este
1741 Anthony Dopping
1743 Michael Cox
1754 Edward Maurice
1755 Richard Pococke
1765 Charles Dodgson
1775 William Newcome
1779 John Hotham
1782 William Heresford
1795 Thomas Lewis O'Beirne
1799 Hugh Hamilton
1806 John Kearney
1813 Robert Fowler
Ferns united to **Ossory** 1835
1842 James Thomas O'Brien
1874 Robert Samuel Gregg
1878 William Fakenham Walsh
1897 John Baptist Crozier
1907 Charles Frederick D'Arcy
1911 John Henry Bernard
1915 John Allen Fitzgerald Gregg
1920 John Godfrey FitzMaurice Day
1938 Ford Tichbourne
1940 John Percy Phair
1962 Henry Robert McAdoo
1977 United to **Cashel**

†Ross

Nechtan MacNechtain 1160
Isaac O'Cowen 1161
O'Carroll 1168
1177 Benedictus
1192 Mauricius
1198 Daniel
1224 Fineen O Clothna [Florentius]
c1250 Malachy
1254 Mauricius

1269 Walter O Mithigein
1275 Peter O h-Uallachain,
      [? Patrick]
1291 Laurentius
1310 Matthaeus O Finn
1331 Laurentius O h-Uallachain
1336 Dionysius
1379 Bernard O Conchobhair
1399 Peter Curragh
1400 Thadeus O Ceallaigh
1401 Mac Raith O hEidirsgeoil
      [Macrobius]
1402 Stephen Brown
1403 Matthew
1418 Walter Formay
1424 John Bloxworth
1426 Conchobhar Mac Fhaolchadha
      [Cornelius]
      Maurice Brown 1431
1431 Walter of Leicester
1434 Richard Clerk
1448 Domhnall O Donnobhain
      John 1460
1460 Robert Colynson
-1464 Thomas
1464 John Hornse alias Skipton
1473 Aodh O hEidirsgeoil [Odo]
1482 Tadhg Mac Carthaigh
1494 John Edmund Courci
1517 Seaan O Muirthile
1519 Tadgh O Raghallaigh
      [Thaddeus]
1523 Bonaventura
1526 Diarmaid Mac Carthaigh
1544 Dermot McDonnell
1551 John
1554 Maurice O'Fihelly
1559 Maurice O'Hea
1561 Thomas O'Herlihy
1582 William Lyon [with Cork and
      Cloyne after 1581]
United to **Cork** 1583

†Waterford

1096 Mael Ius Ua h-Ainmere
1152 Toistius
1175 Augustinus Ua Selbaig
      Anonymous 1199
1200 Robert I
1204 David the Welshman
1210 Robert II [Breathnach]
1223 William Wace
1227 Walter
1232 Stephen
1250 Henry
1252 Philip
1255 Walter de Southwell
1274 Stephen de Fulbourn
1286 Walter de Fulbourn
1308 Matthew
1323 Nicholas Welifed
1338 Richard Francis
1349 Robert Elyot
1350 Roger Cradock
Lismore united to Waterford 1363
1363 Thomas le Reve
1394 Robert Read
1396 Thomas Sparkford
1397 John Deping
1400 Thomas Snell
1407 Roger of Appleby (see under
      Ossory)
1409 John Geese
1414 Thomas Colby
1421 John Geese (again)
1426 Richard Cantwell
1446 Robert Poer
1473 Richard Martin

Waterford—continued

1475 John Bulcomb
1480 Nicol O hAonghusa
1483 Thomas Purcell
1519 Nicholas Comyn
1551 Patrick Walsh
1579 Marmaduke Middleton
1582 Miler Magrath [in com. with
     Cashel, see below]

1589 Thomas Wetherhead *or*
     Walley
1592 Miler Magrath (again)
1608 John Lancaster
1619 Michael Boyle
1636 John Atherton
1641 Archibald Adair
1661 George Baker
1666 Hugh Gore
1691 Nathaniel Foy

1708 Thomas Mills
1740 Charles Este
1746 Richard Chenevix
1779 William Newcome
1795 Richard Marlay
1802 Power le Poer Trench
1810 Joseph Stock
1813 Richard Bourke
United to **Cashel** under Church
Temporalities Act 1833

CLERGY WHO HAVE DIED SINCE
THE LAST EDITION

A list of clergy who have died since 31 July 1989, when compilation of the 1989/90 edition was completed.

ABBOTT, John Williamson
ACKROYD, Christopher
ACTON, Thomas Leslie
ADAMS, Albert Leslie
ADAMS, Aldred Samuel
ADAMS, George Henry
ADAMSON, Frederick
ADENEY, Bernard Frederick
ALDER, Richard Aubrey
ALEXANDER, Kelsick Ernest
ALLEN, Derek William
ALLEN, Eric
ALLISON, William Osborne
ANDERSON, William Brace
ANDREWS, Ronald Sidney
ANGUS, Francis James Glendenning
ANTHONY, Hugh George Barnabas
APPLETON, Leonard George
ARCH, Peter Arthur John
ARKELL, Richard Gordon
ARMSTRONG, Geoffrey William Harry
ARMSTRONG, Henry Denis
ARMSTRONG, John Arthur Lloyd
ARTHUR, Charles Williams
ASHBY, Eric
✠ATTWELL, Arthur Henry
AYRE, George
BACON, Frederick John
BACON, Harold
BADGER, John Lee
BAILEY, Anthony Deans
BAILEY, Ernest
BAILEY, Reginald James
BAILEY, Victor Joseph
BAKER, Alfred Searcy Kendall
✠BAKER, William Scott
BALDWIN, Joan (Sister Joanna)
BANHAM, Harry Eustace Lorrane
BARBER, Frank Thomas
✠BARDSLEY, Cuthbert Killick Norman
BARHAM, William Allan Berridge
BARLOW, Montague Michael
BARTLETT, Archibald Thomas
BARTLETT, Douglas William Guest
BARTON, Thelma Vivienne Elsie
BATEMAN, John de Beverley
BATTY, William Alan
BAYES, Charles Sidney
BAZIRE, Reginald Victor
BEAR, Harold Gatehouse
BEATON, Alexander Thomas Alistair
BECK, Ernest Edward
BECKE, Justice
BEDDOW, Leslie Philip
BEECHEY, George Emyr
BEESLEY, Dennis Arthur
✠BEGG, Ian Forbes
BELL, Thomas Donald
BENNETT, Christopher Cayley Oliver
BENNETT, Geoffrey Samuel
BERESFORD, John Claudius William
BERRY, Richard
BERRY, Samuel John
BEVIS, William Albert
BILLINGTON, Eric
BIRCH, Leonard James
BIRCHAM, Ronald George
BIRCHETT, Ronald John
BISBROWN, Alan Kay
BISHOP, Edward Forbes
BISHOP, William Fletcher (Hugh)
BLAKE, Edward Cyril
BLAKE, Thomas Herbert
BLEWETT, Philip Richard Walton
BLUM, Fred Johannes
BOLTON, George Henry Denne
BOLTON, Robert
BOND, Alan Gilman
BOUNDS, Stanley Frederick
BOWEN, Sydney Meirion
BOX, Harry Charles Edmond

BOYD, Henry Johnston
BRACE, Thomas Harry
BRADFORD, David Millar
BRADFORD, Kenneth
BRADLEY, Charles John Andrew
BRAMLEY-MOORE, Michael
✠BRAZIER, Percy James
BRETHERTON, Mary
BREW, Robert Sidney
BRIGGS, William Sorby
BRITTAIN, William Denis
BROMHAM, Arthur
BROUGHAM, Frank
BROWN, Dennis Stanley Raymond
BROWNE, Clifford Jesse
BROWNE, Edwin Stafford
BROWNE, William Eric
BROWNING, Martin Charles
BROWNING, Michael Charles
BROWNING, William Frank
BROWNRIGG, Robert Graham
BRYANT, Wilfred Thomas
BUCKLEY, Geoffrey Lloyd
BUCKWELL, Charles Cecil Leighton
✠BULLEY, Sydney Cyril
BUNCH, Francis Christopher
BUNN, Peter William
BURFORD, Jack William
BURGE, Anthony Ernest Robert
BURMAN, Patrick Richard Breach
BURROWS, Walter Joseph Mayes
BURT, Eric John
BUSH, Percy Edward
✠BUTLER, Arthur Hamilton
BUTLER, John
BUTTOLPH, Robert Henry
BYARD, Henry Adeane
BYLES, Alfred Thomas Plested
BYROM, Thomas Jackson
CADE, Ronald William
CAPEY, Richard Cyril Neil
CAPRON, James Septimus
CARDALE, Arthur Mudge
CARDELL OLIVER, Ivan Alexander
CARR, James Anthony
CARTER, Gordon Albert
CARTWRIGHT, Hugh Benjamin Simons
CARTWRIGHT, John Mountfort
CARVER, Clifford Henry George
CATCHPOLE, Harry Ebenezer
CATLEY, Eric Denis
CATTERICK, Peter John
CAUWOOD, Phillip
CAWOOD, William
✠CHADWICK, William Frank Percival
CHALMERS, Reginald Paul
CHAMPNESS, George William Horace
CHANTLER, William Oliver
CHAPMAN, Kenneth George
CHARLES, John Bolton
CHARLES, Sebastian
CHARMAN, Frederick Ernest
CHAVASSE, Evelyn Henry
CHERRINGTON, Frank
CHETWYND, Sydney Arthur
CHICK, Arthur Bernard
CHIDGEY, Geoffrey Peter
CHISHOLM, Harold Venn
CHITTY, Ernest Hedley
CHRISTIAN, Robert Christopher Graham
  (Lawrence)
CHURCH, George Harold Christian
CHURCHILL, John Howard
CLARK, Sidney Harvie
CLARKE, Herbert Alan
CLARKSON, Ivon George Townley
CLIBBENS, Mervyn Arthur Roy
COATH, Richard Kenneth Routh
COBB, Anthony Bernard Joseph
COBB, Bruce Ian
COBBAN-LEA, Maurice William

COEY, David Stuart
COLEMAN, Alan
COLLINS, Arthur Lionel
COLLINS, Harold Victor Norman
COLLINS, Kenneth Marritt
COMBER, Thomas Graham
COOKE, Greville Vaughan Turner
COOPER, Dennis Howard
COOPER, William Gough Porter
COPE, Anthony William Groves
COPESTAKE, Victor Henry
CORFMAT, Percy Thomas Walter
CORNISH, Stanley James
COSTIN, Arthur John
COTTER, Bernard
COULTHARD, John Richard
COURT, Arthur Albert
COWGILL, John Wilfrid Alban
COX, Cyril Edwin
COX, Percy Campbell
COX, Robert Roland
COX, Ronald Thomas
CRABB, John Anthony
CRADDOCK, Sydney Thomas
CRAFT, Ernest Charles
CRAIG, James Alexander
CRAWFORD, Maurice Victor
CREW, Richard John
CRIBB, Nicholas Llanwarne
CRISP, John Edward
CROCKETT, Benjamin Stephen Walcott
CULLINGFORD, Cecil Howard Dunstan
CUTCHER, George Charles
da COSTA, John Robert
DAGLEY, Frederick
DAHL, Murdoch Edgcumbe
DAINTITH, Richard
DAKIN, James Benjamin
DALBY, Francis Bruce
DALE, John Clifford
DART, Thomas Henry
DAVIDSON, Stanley Guest
DAVIES, Geoffrey Colin
DAVIES, John Byron
DAVIES, John Edward
DAVIES, John Gordon
DAVIES, William John
DAVIES, William Thomas Henry Basil
DAVIS, Eustace Bowater
DAVIS, Vincent Paul
DAWE, Clement George
DEDMAN, Stanley Charles
DENNETT, Stephen Frederick James
DENNISON, Thomas
DESCH, Roland Cecil
DEVER, John Curzon
DEVLIN, Edward John
DEW, William Harold
DEWEY, William Robert
DICKIN, William Charles
DICKINSON, John Compton
DIGHT, Harri Jandrell
DILWORTH, Arthur
DIXON, John Henry Milward
DIXON, John Stanfield
DOBSON, Roger
DODD, John
DODSON, Robert George Everard
DOGGETT, Stanley William
DOHERTY, Philip John
DONALDSON, Walter Sloan
DONNAN, William Henry
DOOLEY, Roy Wilfred
DOUGLAS, Peter John McKechnie
DOWNS, Albert Victor
DRUETT, Albert Edward
DRUITT, Geoffrey Poulter
DRUITT, Kenneth Harwood
DUCKETT, Alfred George
DUDLEY, Ralph Edward Hughes
DUGMORE, Clifford William

CLERGY WHO HAVE DIED SINCE THE LAST EDITION

DUNN, Sidney Albert
DUNSBY, Cyril Frederick
DUROSE, Harry Vernon
DURSTON, Aubrey George
DYSON, Stanley Senior
EARLE, Joseph Edward
✝EASTAUGH, John Richard Gordon
EASTMAN, Derek Ian Tennent
EATON, Albert William
ECCLESTONE, Giles Stephen
EDWARDS, John Russell
ELDERKIN, Denys Frank
ELIOT, Harlovin Harwood ffolliott
ELIOTT, George Vivian Heyman
ELLARD-HANDLEY, Philip Ellard
ELLIOTT, Eric Patrick Moore
ELLIOTT-CANNON, Arthur Elliott
ELLIS, David Edward
EMERY, Graham
EMMOTT, Frederick William
ENTWISTLE, Ronald William Hurst
ETCHES, Richard Geoffrey Adderley
EVANS, Cadwaladr Gwilym Jones
EVANS, Daniel Trevor
EVANS, David Douglas Lloyd
EVANS, Edward Percy
EVANS, Frank Dennis
EVANS, Frederic John Everard
EVANS, James
EVANS, Robert Rowland
EVANS, Vernie Leslie Tudor
EVANS, William Penrhys
EYNON, Ettrick Harold
FARRINGTON, Harold Ernest
FAWCETT, John
FAWKES, Edward George Dalton
FFRENCH-BEYTAGH, Gonville Aubie
FINCHAM, Frank Goldworth
FISHER, Harry
FISHER, Joseph Reuben
FISHER, Robert St John
FISHLEY, George Reuben
✝FLEMING, William Launcelot Scott
FLINT, John Edgar Keith
FLOYD, Stephen Walter
FOLKARD, Laurence Goring
FOOT, William Verner
FORBES, Douglas Stewart
FORBES, Frank Agar
FORDHAM, Frank Henry Vernon
FORSTER, Leslie John
FOSTER, Charles George Peebles
FOX-DAVIES, Mortimer Edmond
FRANCIS, Graham Louis
FRANCIS, James Matthew
FRANKLAND, William
FRANKLIN, Henry Laurence
FREEMAN, Gerald Douglas Langston
FRITH, Algernon Jasper
FROGGATT, Geoffrey Samuel
FROST, William Joshua Theodore
FULLJAMES, Owen Ralph
FULTON, Jeffrey
GAGG, Percival Stanley
GAMON, John Stott
GARDNER, Douglas George
GARRETT, John Robert
GAUL, Reginald Clifford
GEIPEL, Henry Cecil
GEORGE, Hubert Edgar
GEORGE, Walter
GEORGE, William Ronald
GIBBIN, Robert William
GIFFORD, Douglas John
GILROY, Paul
GLEAVE, Charles Haughton
GODDARD, David Ivan
GOLDSMID, Peter Edward
GOOD, James
GOODCHILD, Charles Frank
GOODCHILD, James Brian
GORDON, Ernest Leopold Henry
GORDON, John Beauchamp
GOULD, Frank
GRAHAM, Douglas Leslie
GRANT, Douglas George
GRANT, William Ainslie Macintosh
GRAY, Viera
GREEN, Howard Vernon

GRIFFIN, Charles Whittaker
GRIFFITHS, John Handel Wood
GRIFFITHS, Rowland Powell
GRIFFITHS, William Reginald
GRIST, Robert Frederick
GRISWELL, Herbert Henry
GUNDRY, Dudley William
GWILYM-JONES, David Brinley
HADKINSON, Frank
HAIG-BROWN, William John
HALL, Francis James Thomas
HALL, George
HAMBLY, Richard Arthur William
HAMILTON, Noble Holton
HAMMERTON, Raymond Keith
HAMMOND, Edward Guy
HANNA, Charles Patrick
HANSON, Anthony Tyrrell
HARFORD, Christopher Edward Audley
HARKER, Hugh Alfred
HARLAND, Robert Peirson
HARPER, Alfred Geoffrey
HARRIES, Raymond John
HARRIS, Brian Ronald
HARRIS, Reginald Walter Norwood
HARRIS, Robert Austin Meire
HARRIS, Rupert Gustavus Musgrave
HARRISON, Roy
HART, Eric John
HART, Kendrick Hopwood
HARTLEY, Thomas
HARVEY, John Ray
HARWOOD, William George
HASLAM, James Alexander Gordon
HASSETT, Jack Richard
HAVENS, Charles
HAWKER, Gerald Wynne
HAWKINS, Emma Alison
HAWKINS, Robert Henry
HAYDOCK, Joseph William
HAYES, Cuthbert Rowland James
HAYLLAR, Sidney Philip
HAZELTON, Robert John
HEAD, Ronald Edwin
HEAL, Harold Francis
HEALEY, Charles William
HEATHCOTE, Arthur Edwin
HEATON, Thomas
HENDERSON, Robert McGregor
HENRY, Leslie Victor
HENSHALL, Edwin
HERBERT, Charles Robert Valentine
HERITAGE, Henry Rymer
HETHERINGTON, Richard Nevill
HEWITT, George William Henry
HICKINBOTHAM, James Peter
HICKS, Peter John
HILBORNE, Douglas Eric
HILL, Bernard
HILL, Eric Claude Combe
HILL, John Cyril
HILL, John Paul
HILLIARD, Stephen Patrick
HINTON, John Percy
HOBBS, Kenneth Brian
HOBSON, Stephen Newton
HODGINS, John Joseph Albert
HODGSON, Alfred
HODGSON, William Tempest
HOGG, Sydney George
HOLMES, Arthur William Seddon
HOOD, Norman Arthur
HOOKER, Kenneth Howard
HOOPER, Stanley Frederick
HOPE, Richard Earwaker
HOPKINS, William
HORROCKS, Joseph Barnes
HOSKINS, Hubert Henry
HOUGHTON, Ralph Edward Cunliffe
HOWELL, Charles Ernest
HUDSON, John Stuart
HUGHES, Evan Emrys
HUGHES, Gwilym Frank
HUGHES, Ieuan Delvin Powell
HUGHES, John Neville
HUGHES, Philip Edgcumbe
HUME, Cecil
HUNT, Martin Howard
HUNT, Philip Edgar

HURST, Alan Greaves
HUTCHEON, Harold
HUTCHINGS, Cecil Laurence Gifford
HUTCHISON, Alfred Powell
HYDE-LINAKER, John Etheridge
HYSLOP, Robert Henry
HYSLOP, Thomas
ILLINGWORTH, Jean
INCHLEY, John
INSULL, Francis
IVES, William
JACKSON, Kenneth Herbert
JACOB, William Ungoed
JAGGARD, Alan Lionel
JAMES, Garfield Hughes
JAMES, Raymond Victor
JASPER, Ronald Claud Dudley
JEACOCK, Roland Newport
JEFFERY, Peter Richard
JENKINS, Edward Morgan
JENNER, William Jack
JESSOP, Gilbert Laird Osborne
JOAD, Albert Howard
JOHNSON, Christopher Percival
JOHNSTON, Cecil Macaulay
JOLLIFFE, Stanley Frederick
JONES, Alfred Richard
JONES, Arthur Llewellyn
JONES, Charles Frederick
JONES, David Gwynfryn
JONES, David Rees
JONES, Edward Lanphier Brooke
JONES, Edward Wynn
JONES, Eynon Edryd Cyndeirne
JONES, Gwyn Sproule
JONES, John Clifford
JONES, John Dillwyn Llewellyn
JONES, Leslie Morgan
JONES, Raymond Morgan
JONES, Samuel Wynne Evans
JONES, Thomas Edward
JONES, Thomas Benjamin
JONES, Vincent Gower
JORDAN, William Geoffrey
KAYLL, Arthur Gregory
KEIR, Trevor David
KELLETT, Harold
KENT, John Aldwyn Pelham
KENWORHY, Jonathan Malcolm Athol
KING, Arthur
KING, Michael Christopher
KINGSTON, George
KISSACK, Albert Westby Grandin
KNIGHT, Herbert Frank
KNOWLES, John Arthur
LACY-JONES, Cledwyn
LAFFORD, Percival John
LAMB, George
LAMB, John William
LANCASTER, Charles William
LANCE, John du Boulay
LANCE, Raymond Sullivan Knox
LANHAM, Gordon Joicey
LAUGHTON, John Robert Carr
LAWRENCE, Lionel Frank
LAWS, Howard Stracey
LEAKE, William Alfred
LEATHERDALE, Vincent William Storey
LEE, William Dunsmore
LEECH, Frank
LEESON, Martin Lister
LEIGH-WOOD, Kenneth James
LEMON, Albert St John
LEWIS, Albert Edward
LEWIS, Charles William
LEWIS, Eric Desmond
LEWIS, Frank Stanley
LEWIS, Raymond John
LEYSHON, Thomas Evan
LILLIE, William Walter
LINDSAY, William Richard
LITTLEWOOD, Walter
LLEWELYN, John Humphrey Norman
LLOYD-JONES, William Richard
LONG, Edwin George
LONG, Frederick George Craigen
LOUGH, Arthur Geoffrey
LUCAS, Robert Holdsworth Tindall
LUMGAIR, David

LUND, Peter
LYNDON, Philip John
LYONS, Frank
McAVAN, Gordon William
McCARTER, Colin Heyes
McCULLOCH, Joseph
McDERMOTT, Robert Preston
MACFARLANE, Cyril St Martin Bloomfield
McGILL, James
McGLAUGHLIN, Basil Gordon Young
McKEW, John Porter
MACKLEY, Frederick Roy
MACLEHOSE, Alexander
MACLEOD, Donald Norman
McMURRAY, Brian Harold
MACNAUGHTON-JONES, Tilbury Cecil
McNICOL, Malcolm
McNUTT, Albert Thompson
MACONCHY, Richard Julian John
MACRORY, Robert Donald
MACROW, David James
MADDOCKS, Dennis Samuel
MAJOR, Charles Alan
MANDEVILLE, Maurice Valentine
MANLEY, Gordon Noel
MANN, Eric
MANTLE, Norman James
MAPLE, Harold Walter James
MARDON, John Hedley
MARSH, Denis Wilton (Brother Denis)
MARSH, Ivor Frank
MARTIN, Harvey Charlick
MASON, Lancelot
MASSEY, Richard Standring
MATHER, Bernard Edelston
MATHEWS, Laurence William
MATHIAS, William James
MATTHEWS, Thomas Ernest
MAUGHAN, Joseph
MAURICE, Lionel Selwyn
MAX, Alexander Llewhellin
MAYBURY, Henry Kilworth
MBWANA, Martin
MEAD, George Thomas
MEAR, Robert William
MEIGH, Simon John
MILES, Gilbert Henry
MILLAR, Lynn Hartley
MILLER, Charles Ernest
MILLER, Raymond Kenneth
MILLICAN, Anthony Gordon
MILLMAN, Geoffrey
MILLS, Stanley
MILNE, William
MILTON-SMITH, Charles Henry
MINSHULL, William Howell
MITCHELL, Victor Sidney William
MOLE, Eric Edward
MOLYNEUX, William
MONTGOMERIE, William Arthur
MOORE, Evelyn Garth
MORCOM-HARNEIS, Theophilus William
MORGAN, Hubert Charles Trevor
MORRIS, John
MORRIS, John Howes
MORRIS, Wilfred
MORRISON, Herbert Andrew
MORRISON, Nial Ranald
MORTON, Alexander Francis
MOTLEY, Edward William John
MOWATE, Arthur Jack
MOXON, William John
MOYLE, Frank William
MUIR, Ian Gordon
MUNSON, Arthur George
MUSKER, Francis Charles Bernard
MUTUKISNA, Christopher Wilmot
NASH, Harry Neville
NAYLOR, Henry Harrison
NEILL, Gerald Monro
NELSON, Arthur Basil
NESLING, Horace William
NEWELL, Charles John Cuthbert
NEWTON, Cecil
NICHOLS, Charles Philip
NOBLE, Alexander Eric Lionel Edward
NOBLE, Douglas

NOBLE, Douglas Oswald
NORMAN, Paul Gordon
NORRIS, Basil Charles
NORTHMORE, Solomon Roy
NORWOOD, Clarence William
NOTMAN, Eric
NUNNELEY, James Edward
OADE, John Leonard
ODDY, John Scotthorn
ODLING-SMEE, Charles William
OLIVER, Kenneth Cyril
ORBELL, John Heddle Ray
O'RYAN, John Whiteford
OSMOND, Alec Edward
OWEN, David Thomas
OWEN, Thomas Robert
PADDOCK, William Frank
PAGE, John Knott
PAGET, Arthur Gordon Westwood
PAINE, Douglas Leonard
PAINE, Humphrey John
PAINE, John Henry Fairman
PALIN, Reginald Culliford
PALMER, Basil Charles Donaldson
PALMER, Stephen Roundell
PARKER, Eric Clince
PARKER, Robert Vlieland
PARKES, Alfred David
PARKINSON, Kenneth Frank Armstrong
PARKS, Geoffrey Harper
PARSONS, Douglas Cyril
PARTRIDGE, Alfred Joseph
PASSANT, George Harry
PATERSON, Donald Alexander
PATERSON, William Lawrence
PATEY, Donald Weare
PATTISON, Edwin Gibson
PAYTON, Wilfrid Ernest Granville
PEARSON, Thomas Henry Edward
PEEK, John Brian
PEGLER, Albert Dahl
PENNY, Edwin Arthur
PERKINS, Claude Ambrose
PERRY, Eric Akers
PICKLES, Hugh John
PICKLES, Sydney George
PICTON, William James
PORTNALL, Ernest William George
POVEY, William Charles Alfred
POWELL, Kenneth John
POWNALL, Geoffrey Carr
PRATT, Kenneth Wilfred
PREWER, Felix Owen
PRICE, Dewi Emlyn
PRICE, Ernest Cyril Courtney
PRICE, Richard James
PRICHARD, Lewis David
PRINGLE, John
PROCKTER, Anthony John
PROCTER, Kenneth Stuart
PUGH, David Bligh
PULESTON, Derrick Carr
✠QUIN, George Alderson
RADICE, Anthony Alister Hutton
RAMAGE, John Eric
✠RAMSBOTHAM, John Alexander
✠RAMSEY, Kenneth Venner
RAWLINGS, David Ewart
RAWSTORNE, Robert Gwilym
READ, Francis Richard Waller
REES, Arthur Winnington
REES, Owain Peredur Dyfed
REID THOMAS, David Gwyn
✠REINDORP, George Edmund
RENDELL, Roy Richardson Neville
RHODES, Cecil
RICE, Leslie Frank
✠RICHARDS, John Richards
RICHARDS, Winfrid James Kirby
RICHARDSON, Alan Brickell
RICHARDSON, John Farquhar
RICHES, Claude Christopher
RICKARD, George Frederick
RIDLER, Gordon Harold
RIDLEY, Thomas George
RINTOUL, Keith Richard Scott
ROBERTS, Roger Lewis
ROBERTSON, Clement Gordon Cumpper
ROBINSON, Sydney Ernest Fisher

ROBSON, Reginald
ROGERS, Geoffrey John
ROGERS, Glyndwr
ROSE, Alfred Reginald Thomas
ROSS, Clifford Edwin
ROWSELL, Clifford Sanders
ROWTON-LEE, Edwin
ROYCROFT, John
ROYLE, George Herbert Watson
RUMSEY, Stephen Henry
RUNDLE, Donald Peter
RUSSELL, Harold Percy
RUSTON, Cuthbert Mark
RUTHERFORD, Thomas William Hardy
RUTTER, David Carter
SAGE, Colston William
SALMON, Thomas Frederick
SAUNDERS, Ernest John
SAUNDERS, George William
SAUNDERS, Roan George
SAVAGE, David
✠SAVAGE, Gordon David
SAYWELL, Sydney Wells
SCOONES, James Mansell
SCOTT, Edward Geoffrey Spencer
SCOTT, George
SCOTT, George
SCOTT, John
SCOTT, John Edward
SCOTT, John Nicolson
SCOTT, John Trevor
SEACOME, Michael Owen
SHARP, Thomas Crawford
SHARPE, Victor Clifford
SHELFORD, Gordon Hope McNeill
SHEPHERD, Charles Lawton
SHEPHERD, Maurice Alfred
SHEPHERD, Norman Edward
SHEPPARD, Patrick Ashton Gregg
SHERLOCK, George Henry Kenneth
SIBTHORP, Ronald Ellwood
SIMONSON, Werner Siegmund Moritz
SINCLAIR, John Malcolm
SINGER, Samuel Stanfield
SIRR, William James Douglas
SISLEY, Frederick Herbert
SKELHORN, Joseph Roy
SLATER, Ronald George
SMART, Edward Rogers
SMETHURST, John Brian
SMITH, Cecil Knowles
SMITH, David Gordon
SMITH, Harold George
SMITH, Percy George
SMYTH, John
SOUTHGATE, Norman Frederick
SOUTHWELL, Eric Medder Baden
SOWTER, Richard Francis
SPALDING, Hubert John
SPEED, Alfred Blenkarn
SPELLER, George
SPENCER, Robert John
SPURGIN, Basil Layton
STAMP, Ewen Campbell Morrell
STEEL, Frederick George
STEELE, Edward Harry
STEELE, John William Jackson
STEER, Herbert Philip
STEGGALL, John Alexander
STEPHENS, Frederick William
STEPHENS, Joseph Gwynfor
STEVENS, Rupert John
STEWARD, Robert Edward Alan
STILEMAN, John William Hampson
STRANACK, John Robert Shuckburgh
STRICKLAND, George Henry
STRINGER, Henry Richard
STURDY, John Brian
STYLER, Leslie Moreton
SUTCH, Douglas Reginald
SUTER, Martin Edward Hayles
SUTTON, Harry Chamberlain
SUTTON, John Parker
SWEETING, Philip James
TAGG, Kenneth
TALBOT, Jack
TALBOT, James Edward
TALBOT, Richard Henry
TAYLER, William Henry Stuart

CLERGY WHO HAVE DIED SINCE THE LAST EDITION

TAYLOR, Cyril Vincent
TAYLOR, George Downham Row
TAYLOR, Norman Wentworth
THICKITT, John Laurence
THIRKELL, Edward William Hylton
THOMAS, John Iorwerth
THOMAS, Lewis Madoc
THOMAS, Rosser Elwyn
THOMAS, William Byron
THOMPSON, Arthur
THOMPSON, Brian Theodore
THOMPSON, Frederick Arthur
THOMPSON, Kenneth Charles
THOMPSON, Lionel Arthur
THOMSON, Cyril
THORNHILL, Francis William Philip
THORNLEY, Harold
THORNTON, Kenneth William
THORNTON, Ronald Charleton
THURLOW, Alfred Gilbert Goddard
TINDALE, Robert
TINNISWOOD, William Robert
TISDALL, Charles Gordon St Clair
TODHUNTER, Frank
TOOLE-MACKSON, Kenneth Toole
TOWNSHEND, Horace Lyle Hume
TRAFFORD, Nelson
TREBBLE, William Henry
TREBY, Raymond Harold
TREGLOWN, Geoffrey Leonard
TREVIVIAN, Roy
TREVOR, Colin Stuart
TUFF, Harold
TULLOCH, William Joseph
TUNNADINE, Henry Christopher
TURKINGTON, Ivan
TURNBULL, Allen Chorlton
TURNBULL, John Desmond Stewart
TURNER, Donald Hugh
ULLMER, Derek Sefton
URQUHART, Edwin John
USHER, Thomas Gordon
VAUGHAN, George Ralph
VAUGHAN, Thomas Gareth
VIDLER, Alexander Roper

VIGAR, Charles Hatton
VINCENT, Ian Humphrey
VOLLER, Henry
VYVYAN JONES, Frederick Charles
WAIN, Frank Lonsdale
WAIN, Norman
WALDEN-ASPY, Frederick Charles
WALKER, Charles
WALKER, David Andrew
WALKER, James Robert
WALKER, Richard Bickersteth Roscoe
WALKER, William
WALLACE, Alistair
WALLER, Richard Charles Eisdell
WALLIS, Roger Charles Theodore
WALTER, John Allen
WALTER, William James
WALTERS, John Rufus
WALTERS, William Edward Felix
WANSEY, Peter Nottidge
WARD, Herbert
WARDLE, John Alan (Brother Jacob)
WARMAN, Francis Frederic Guy
WARNE, Donald Caleb
WARNER, Cyril Robert
WARNER, Henry Homan
WARREN, John Herbert Edwin
WATKINS, Thomas George
WATKINS, Thomas George David
WATSON, Ian Arthur
WATSON, Lionel George
WATSON, Richard John Sutton
WATSON, Vernon Owen
WATTS, James
WEBB, Eric Roland
WEBB, Ivo Frederick Fiennes
WEBB, Jack Raymond Conran
WELCHMAN, Roger de Beaufort
WELLMAN, Jack Dover
WENHAM, John Terence
WEST, Leonard Ernest
WESTRUP, George Allan
WETHERALL, Theodore Sumner
WHEELER, Eric William
WHITCOMBE, Guy Rowland

WHITE, Geoffrey Howard
WHITE, William Henry
WHITEFIELD, Geoffrey George
WHITEHEAD, Geoffrey Arnold
WHITEHOUSE, Isaac
WHITLOCK, George William
WHITTAKER, Peter John
WHITTER, Frank Cedric
WHYNTIE, Howard William
WIGRAM, Marcus Walter
WIGRAM, Oswald Thomas Edward
✠WILD, Eric
WILDE, Thomas Harold
WILKINS, Roderic John
WILKINSON, Charles Frederick
WILKINSON, William David George
WILLIAMS, Cyril Bertram
WILLIAMS, David John Mihangel
WILLIAMS, Everard
WILLIAMS, Frederick Joseph
WILLIAMS, Gordon
✠WILLIAMS, Gwilym Owen
WILLIAMS, Harold Claude Noel
WILLIAMS, Harry Craven
WILLIAMS, Kenneth Edward Chilton
WILLIAMS, William Alfred
WILMOT, Edward Franklin Slaney
WILSON, Charles Gordon
WILSON, Derek Hamilton Aitken
WINCOTT, Stanley Cyrus
WINDERBANK, Frank
WINTERS, Robert Hunter
WOLSEY, Ronald George
WOLTERS, Conrad Clifton
WOOD, Colin George William
WOOD, Reginald Kingsley
WOODHALL, Norman John
WOOLLER, Herbert
WORSLEY, Godfrey Stuart Harling
WRIGHT, Charles Piachaud
WRIGHT, Edward Denzil Chetwood
WRIGHT, Philip Arthur
YATES, Howard
YORK, Reginald Frank
YOUNG, John David
YOUNG, John Kenneth

ADDRESSES UNKNOWN

The following are clergy whose addresses are currently unknown. Fuller details are contained in the biographical section. We would be grateful for any information to help us complete our records.

ALLEN, David Newall. b 37. **d** 65. Hon C Man Victoria Park *Man* 76-83
ARMSTRONG, Colin John. b 32. **d** 61. Chapl and Tutor Middx Poly 78-85
ASH, Joseph Raymond. b 17. **d** 47. Chapl RAF 50-72
BACKHOUSE, Robert. b 45. **d** 70. Publicity Sec CPAS 74-78
BAGLEY, Richard Alexander. b 25. **d** 53. Malta from 58
BAKER, Thomas James William. b 35. **d** 61. V Thatcham *Ox* 79-84
BALLANTYNE, John Ivan Terence. b 32. **d** 57. S Africa from 64
BARBER, David. b 45. **d** 72. Chapl Brook Gen Hosp and Greenwich Distr Hosp Lon 77-80
BATSON, David Frederick. b 38. **d** 62. Lic to Offic *Worc* 68-83
BEAK, Richard John. b 34. **d** 62. Perm to Offic *Leic* 80-82
BENFORD, Brian. b 47. **d** 85. NSM Stocksbridge *Sheff* 85-91
BODYCOMB, Peter Lionel. b 28. **d** 67. V Egham Hythe *Guildf* 75-77
BOWEN, David Gregory. b 47. **d** 74. TV Stantonbury *Ox* 80-82
BOWLER, Roy Harold. b 27. **d** 53. Zimbabwe from 80
BRADBURY, Alan Harry. b 32. **d** 57. Lic to Offic *Win* 74-84
BRITTON, Neil Bryan. b 35. **d** 63. Asst Chapl Villars *Eur* 74-81
BROWN, Julian Keith. b 57. **d** 85. C Luton All SS w St Pet *St Alb* 88-91
BURCH, John Anthony. b 37. **d** 69. Perm to Offic *Ely* 82-90
BURROWS, Clifford Robert. b 37. **d** 76. Perm to Offic *Glas* 86-89
CALDWELL, Alan Alfred. b 48. **d** 73. R Baxterley w Hurley and Wood End and Merevale etc *Birm* 87-91
CARPENTER, Justin David William. b 43. **d** 67. Chapl St Wilfrid's Sch Ex 78-90
CLIFF, Maisie. b 87. Asst CF 87-90
COOMBE, Michael Thomas. b 31. **d** 75. Chapl Marseille *Eur* 86-89
COWEN, Peter Stewart. b 42. **d** 67. V Harringay St Paul *Lon* 78-80
EAVES, Brian Maxwell. b 40. **d** 69. Monaco from 91
EDWARDS, Richard Sinclair. b 46. **d** 71. TV Hitchin *St Alb* 77-81
FITZGERALD, Thomas Martin William. b 30. **d** 72. Kenya from 81
FLUCK, Paul John Martin. b 46. **d** 73. USA from 85
FLUDE, Maurice Haddon. b 41. **d** 69. Perm to Offic *S'wark* 76-81
FOSTER, Thomas Andrew Hayden. b 43. **d** 73. I New Ross w Old Ross, Whitechurch, Fethard etc *C & O* 89-91; Dioc Info Officer (Ferns) 90-91
FOX, Michael John Howard. b 32. **d** 58. Saudi Arabia from 66
FRASER-SMITH, Keith Montague. b 48. **d** 73. Egypt from 77
GAMBLE, Thomas Richard. b 42. **d** 65. Chapl Warminster Sch Wilts 77-80
GARDINER, Brian John. b 31. **d** 60. C Caversham *Ox* 73-77
GAUNTLETT, Gilbert Bernard. b 36. **d** 61. Asst Master Stourport High Sch 79-85
GILL, Frank Emmanuel. b 34. **d** 75. W Indies from 82
GINGELL, John Lawrence. b 27. **d** 55. Bp's Ind Adv *Derby* 75-80
GRAHAM, Alan. b 50. **d** 74. R Horsmonden *Roch* 86-90; Chapl HM Pris Blantyre Ho 88-90
GRAY, Paul Alfred. b 41. **d** 82. TV Lynton, Brendon, Countisbury, Lynmouth etc *Ex* 85-86
GRIFFITH, John Rodney. b 40. **d** 66. CF 71-85
HIBBERD, Brian Jeffery. b 35. **d** 60. Carisbrooke High Sch 73-91; Perm to Offic *Portsm* 82-91
HILL, Geoffrey Dennison. b 31. **d** 56. P-in-c Torver *Carl* 76-79
HILL, Trevor Walton. b 30. **d** 59. P-in-c Doddington w Wychling *Cant* 80-82; P-in-c Newnham 80-82
HINCHEY, Peter John. b 30. **d** 58. R Foots Cray *Roch* 78-81
HINTON, Michael Ernest. b 33. **d** 57. Bermuda from 87
HODGE, Dr Denis Ian. b 32. **d** 69. New Zealand from 76
HORSFIELD, Allan. b 48. **d** 72. P-in-c Rudston w Boynton *York* 77-82
INESON, David Antony. b 36. **d** 62. TV Langley and Parkfield *Man* 86-88
JAMES, Henry Glyn. b 26. **d** 52. rtd 91

JOBBER, Barry William. b 38. **d** 75. V Goldenhill *Lich* 79-80
JOHNSON, Beverley Charles. b 35. **d** 61. S Africa from 91
JOYCE, Martin Ernest Chancellor. b 50. **d** 73. V Blackpool St Mich *Blackb* 85-87
KAVANAGH, Graham George. b 47. **d** 74. USA from 77
KAYE, Peter Alan. b 47. **d** 72. Chapl Jo Conolly Hosp Birm 74-80; Rubery Hill and Jos Sheldon Hosps Birm 74-80
KING-SMITH, Philip Hugh (Brother Robert). b 28. **d** 54. SSF from 64; USA from 66
KNIGHT, David Charles. b 32. **d** 57. C Edmonton All SS w St Mich *Lon* 83; Chapl N Middx Hosp 83
LAMB, Nicholas Henry. b 52. **d** 79. Bethany Fellowship 84-87
LANG, William Peter. b 43. **d** 69. TR St Marylebone Ch Ch *Lon* 78-83
LEAK, David. b 42. **d** 79. R Castlemartin w Warren and Angle etc *St D* 83-90
LEAVER, Robin Alan. b 39. **d** 64. P-in-c Cogges *Ox* 77-84
LEAWORTHY, John Owen. b 40. **d** 82. Chapl HM Pris Full Sutton 89-91
LEVINGSTON, Peter Owen Wingfield. b 31. **d** 58. rtd 78
LITTLEJOHN, Theodore Harold. b 32. **d** 64. P-in-c Plymouth St Aug *Ex* 76-77
LIVERSUCH, Ian Martin. b 56. **d** 83. Canada from 91
McDERMOTT, John Alexander James. b 52. **d** 81. R Benington w Walkern *St Alb* 86-87
McMULLEN, Ronald Norman. b 36. **d** 63. USA from 88
McNEICE, Alan Denor. b 34. **d** 64. C Kensington St Barn *Lon* 78-79
MAGEE, Frederick Hugh. b 33. **d** 59. USA from 87
MEAD, Nicholas Charles. b 50. **d** 85. C Whittlesey *Ely* 88-89
MITCHELL, Leonard David. b 30. **d** 61. Canada from 67
MOLL, Randell Tabrum. b 41. **d** 66. rtd 81
MORGAN, Ian David John. b 57. **d** 83. C New Shoreham *Chich* 86-88
MORRISON, Frederick George. b 37. **d** 63. USA from 85
MUMFORD, John Alexander. b 52. **d** 77. USA from 85
NADKARNI, Edward Wasant. b 41. **d** 69. Chapl Lanc Univ *Blackb* 78-83
NICHOLAS, Patrick. b 37. **d** 62. C Portsea St Mary *Portsm* 75
NORTHCOTT, William Mark. b 36. **d** 64. R Glenrothes *St And* 90-91; Asst Dioc Supernumerary 90-91
NUNN, Miss Christina Mary. **d** 87. Par Dn Hilperton w Whaddon and Staverton etc *Sarum* 87-90
PADDOCK, John Allan Barnes. b 51. **d** 80. Chapl RAF 86-91
PEMBERTON, Arthur. b 48. **d** 79. R The Quinton *Birm* 84-91
RANKEN, John Peter. b 33. **d** 59. Zambia 68-75
RIDGEWELL, Kenneth William. b 29. **d** 59. rtd 86
RITCHIE, William James. b 62. **d** 86. Egypt from 89
ROBINSON, Arthur Robert Basil. b 32. **d** 58. V Golcar *Wakef* 77-83
ROSE, James Edward. b 50. **d** 75. Hon C Gipsy Hill Ch Ch *S'wark* 82-86
RUCK, John. b 47. **d** 80. Indonesia from 87
RUNDLE, Nicholas John. b 59. **d** 84. Australia from 91
SAUNDERS, Ronald. b 37. **d** 68. TV Wrexham *St As* 87-88
SMITH, Francis Christian Lynford. b 36. **d** 74. Chapl Dulwich Coll 81-91
SMITH, Stephen John Stanyon. b 49. **d** 85. USA from 89
SMYTHE, Peter John. b 32. **d** 58. V Billesdon w Goadby and Rolleston *Leic* 65-71
STANLEY, Arthur Patrick. b 32. **d** 55. Dep Asst Chapl Gen 74-83
STAVELEY-WADHAM, Robert Andrew. b 43. **d** 81. P-in-c Austrey *Birm* 84-87; P-in-c Warton 84-87
STEVENS, Martin Leonard. b 35. **d** 62. V Felling *Dur* 74-86
STOKES, Roger Sidney. b 47. **d** 72. Chapl HM Pris Full Sutton 87-89
SWINNEY, Fergus William. b 37. **d** 69. V Longhirst *Newc* 75-80
TANBURN, John Walter. b 30. **d** 56. R Morley *Nor* 72-82
TARRANT, John Michael. b 38. **d** 62. V Forest Row *Chich* 75-87
TINNISWOOD, Robin Jeffries. b 41. **d** 70. TV Ifield *Chich* 79-85
TOWLER, John Frederick. b 42. **d** 66. Prec Worc Cathl *Worc* 77-81
VAMPLEW, Peter Gordon. **d** 59. C Poole *Sarum* 70-76

VASEY, Arthur Stuart. b 37. **d** 71. C Middlesb St Thos *York* 85-86

WADE, Andrew James Bentinck. b 54. **d** 85. C Norbury St Steph and Thornton Heath *S'wark* 88-90

WAINWRIGHT, Peter Anthony. b 45. **d** 75. V Woking St Paul *Guildf* 79-84

WELLER, Ronald Howden. b 18. **d** 60. New Zealand from 74; rtd 83

WESTMUCKETT, John Spencer. b 30. **d** 55. R Brightling, Dallington, Mountfield & Netherfield *Chich* 85-87

WIDDESS, Peter Henry. b 53. **d** 77. Asst Chapl Wiesbaden *Eur* 82

WIGNALL, Paul Graham. b 49. **d** 74. C Shepherd's Bush St Steph w St Thos *Lon* 84

WILLS, John Trevethan. b 21. **d** 50. Torryburn Sch 60-61

WINSTANLEY, John Graham. b 47. **d** 71. R Kersal Moor *Man* 79-87

WINTERBOURNE, George. b 20. **d** 67. Perm to Offic *B & W* 79-80

WOOD, Philip Hervey. b 42. **d** 74. Asst Chapl HM Pris Wandsworth 88-89

WOODHALL, Michael Leslie. b 36. **d** 74. V Leeds St Cypr Harehills *Ripon* 80-83

SCOTLAND

| 0 | 10 | 20 | 30 | 40 | 50miles |
| 0 | 20 | 40 | 60 | 80km |

— Diocesan boundary

······· Regional boundary

● Location of Cathedral

ABERDEEN and ORKNEY

ABERDEEN and ORKNEY

SHETLAND ISLANDS

MORAY

ROSS and CAITHNESS

HIGHLAND

Inverness

GRAMPIAN

ABERDEEN and ORKNEY

Aberdeen

ARGYLL

and

THE ISLES

Oban

ST.ANDREWS

DUNKELD and DUNBLANE

TAYSIDE

BRECHIN

Perth

Dundee

CENTRAL

FIFE

STRATHCLYDE

Glasgow

GLASGOW and GALLOWAY

Edinburgh

LOTHIAN

EDINBURGH

BORDERS

GALLOWAY

DUMFRIES AND GALLOWAY

IRELAND

ENGLAND

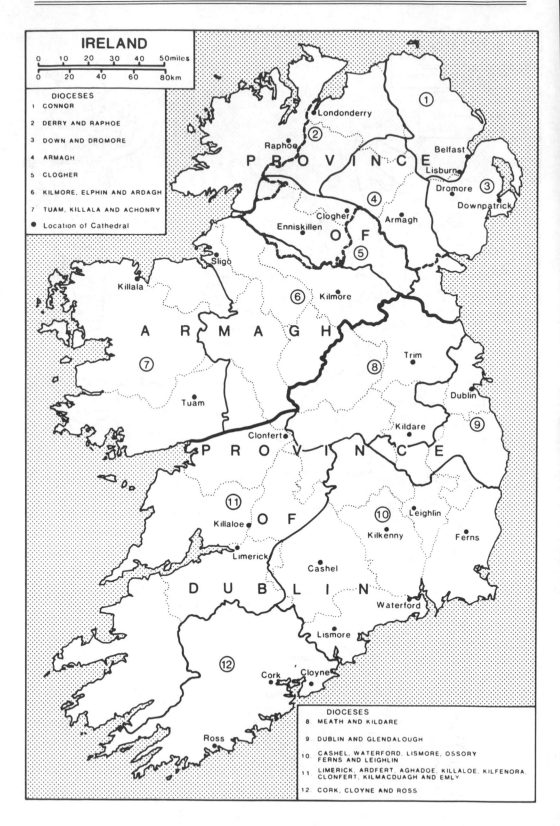

IRELAND

| 0 | 10 | 20 | 30 | 40 | 50 miles |
| 0 | 20 | 40 | 60 | 80 km |

DIOCESES

1 CONNOR

2 DERRY AND RAPHOE

3 DOWN AND DROMORE

4 ARMAGH

5 CLOGHER

6. KILMORE, ELPHIN AND ARDAGH

7 TUAM, KILLALA AND ACHONRY

● Location of Cathedral

P R O V I N C E

O F

A R M A G H

P R O V I N C E

O F

D U B L I N

Londonderry

Raphoe

Belfast

Lisburn

Dromore

Downpatrick

Clogher

Armagh

Enniskillen

Sligo

Killala

Kilmore

Trim

Dublin

Tuam

Kildare

Clonfert

Killaloe

Leighlin

Kilkenny

Ferns

Limerick

Cashel

Waterford

Lismore

Cork

Cloyne

Ross

DIOCESES

8. MEATH AND KILDARE

9. DUBLIN AND GLENDALOUGH

10. CASHEL, WATERFORD, LISMORE, OSSORY
FERNS AND LEIGHLIN

11. LIMERICK, ARDFERT, AGHADOE, KILLALOE, KILFENORA,
CLONFERT, KILMACDUAGH AND EMLY

12. CORK, CLOYNE AND ROSS